Statistics Sources

ISSN 0585-198X

Statistics Sources

Nineteenth Edition
1996

A Subject Guide to Data on Industrial, Business, Social, Educational, Financial, and Other Topics for the United States and Internationally

Volume 2
J-Z
Appendixes

Jacqueline Wasserman O'Brien
and **Steven R. Wasserman**
Editors

 Gale Research Inc.

An International Thomson Publishing Company

NEW YORK • LONDON • BONN • BOSTON • DETROIT • MADRID
MELBOURNE • MEXICO CITY • PARIS • SINGAPORE • TOKYO
TORONTO • WASHINGTON • ALBANY NY • BELMONT CA • CINCINNATI OH

Jacqueline Wasserman O'Brien and Steven R. Wasserman, *Editors*
Richard Rose, *Word Processing Consultant*

Gale Research Inc. Staff

Donna Wood, *Senior Editor and Project Coordinator*

Mary Beth Trimper, *Production Manager*
Shanna Heilveil, *Production Assistant*

Cynthia D. Baldwin,, *Product Design Manager*
Barbara J. Yarrow, *Graphic Services Supervisor*
Sherrell Hobbs, *Macintosh Artist*

∞™ The paper used in this publication meets the minimum requirements of American National Standard for Information Sciences--Permanence Paper for Printed Library Materials, ANSI Z39.48-1984.

♻ This book is printed on recycled paper that meets Environmental Protection Agency standards.

Library of Congress Catalog Card Number: 84-82356
ISBN 0-8103-9091-4 (set)
ISBN 0-8103-9092-2 (Volume 1)
ISBN 0-8103-9093-0 (Volume 2)
ISSN 0585-198X

Printed in the United States of America

I(T)P™ Gale Research Inc., an International Thomson Publishing Company.
ITP logo is a trademark under license.

CONTENTS

Volume 1

Volume 2

PREFACE

As *Statistics Sources* approaches its twentieth edition (the present volume is the nineteenth edition), the constant and painstaking effort to continue to bolster and add value to its content in the interest of its users continues unabated. The work continues to be an easy-to-use alphabetically arranged dictionary and guide to current sources of factual quantitative information on well over 20,000 specific subjects, incorporating almost 100,000 citations and more than 2,000 sources readily leading users to the widest possible range of print and non-print, published and unpublished, and electronic and other forms of U.S. and international statistical sources for economic, business, financial, industrial, cultural, social, educational, and other topics.

Revisions and Additions for the Nineteenth Edition

In an effort to consolidate and merge redundant material, countless entries have been fully revised. The nineteenth edition also marks the addition of innumerably more sources than ever before in order to further strengthen access to the widest possible range of pertinent approaches to locating data. While the number of pages in this edition is a small reduction from the previous edition, a far more extensive range of new sources is being included for the first time. For the user this means that many more citations are provided without sacrificing access to narrow specific topics. The result is to make the work easier to use and at the same time more comprehensive. The following examples illustrate this point: ITALY - Cocoa (Beans) Production - See ITALY - Crops; FRANCE - Tungsten Production and Consumption - See FRANCE - Mining and Mineral Products; INDIA - Egg Production - See INDIA - Dairy Products. The merging of naturally related topics permits the user to find sources under narrow and specific subjects. The exhaustive use of cross references refers the user to the broader term where an expanded range of sources is identified.

Preparation of This Edition

This nineteenth edition of *Statistics Sources* fully and thoroughly updates, revises, and extends the scope and content of the eighteenth edition. Complete revisions incorporate a wider range of current data sources from the "Selected Bibliography of Key Statistical Sources," "Federal Statistical Telephone Contacts," and "Federal Statistical Data Bases" sections, through the main body of the work, and throughout the two appendixes.

During the preparation of this edition, as in each earlier edition, the editors thoroughly analyzed and indexed hundreds of American information sources, several years of *Statistical Abstract of the United States*, numerous basic statistical publications from many organizations, and special statistical issues of professional, technical, and trade journals. Additional sources of international statistics are cited in this edition, increasing the range of access points within a user's reference shelves.

Arrangement and Content

The familiar and convenient arrangement of the basic work continues as a straight alphabetic list of subjects. Sources of statistical information are arranged alphabetically by issuing organization within each subject category. In addition to both print and machine-readable sources, a considerable number of organizations, government agencies, trade and professional groups, and international bodies are cited because they are important sources of statistical data, even if they do not ordinarily publish all of the statistics they compile. In such instances, specific inquiries may be addressed to the organization mentioned. As in earlier editions, the street address of the publisher of any work cited has been provided wherever possible, followed by the telephone number of the source.

Interfiled within the subject categories are geographic headings for states and individual countries. Listings for state data center agencies that make census information and data available to the public are included with the citations of sources for each state. These listings appear under the heading "State Data Center Agencies," which immediately follows the citation for "Primary Statistics Source" under each state subheading.

Individual citations for each country are subarranged by an alphabetic list of specific subjects, enabling the user to pinpoint sources of statistics on subjects such as agriculture, education, energy, imports, population, and consumer prices. Two types of key statistical sources are cited in listings for countries (as applicable and available) and precede the alphabetical listing of specific subjects for the country. The first citation is to the National Statistical Office, if the country has such an office. This is followed by a reference to the major printed sources for the country, termed the Primary Statistics Source or Sources. These sources should be consulted by users seeking more in-depth data, particularly for technical and commercial activities in countries other than the U. S. and Canada.

Introductory Materials Pinpoint
Key Sources and Individuals

The "Selected Bibliography of Key Statistical Sources," "Federal Statistical Telephone Contacts," and the "Federal Statistical Data Bases" sections precede the main section of *Statistics Sources*. The "Selected Bibliography" provides an annotated guide to a selected group of major, general statistical compendia and related works, and includes dictionaries of terms, almanacs, census publications, periodical sources, and guides to machine-readable and online data sources. Both governmental and non-governmental sources are cited. A source's availability in machine-readable form or as an online database is noted wherever possible. The "Telephone Contacts" section provides the names and telephone numbers of individuals and agencies within the U. S. federal government with expertise in identifying the most current sources of statistical data. "Federal Statistical Data Bases" identifies the most significant U. S. federal government statistical files available in machine-readable form, including magnetic tape, diskette, and, in some instances, CD-

ROM. This section, arranged by broad subject category, identifies the issuing agency of each file and provides details on how to obtain the file.

Appendixes Identify Published and Nonpublished Sources

Two appendixes identify the sources of information used to compile this directory. The "Source Publications" appendix provides an alphabetic listing of the specific publication titles of every printed source mentioned in *Statistics Sources*, along with the issuing or publishing bodies, their addresses and phone numbers. The "Sources of Nonpublished Statistical Data" appendix identifies the agencies, institutions, and other organizations which are cited as sources of nonpublished statistical information in this edition.

The Status of Eastern European Countries

Efforts have continued to revise and reorganize the arrangement of statistical data on and about the countries which comprised the former Eastern European Bloc. But even while some of the new jurisdictional entities have been in existence for some months, this has not translated itself into more than a limited and spotty selection of new statistical tools and sources reflecting the recently formed nations. Thus, the majority of statistical resources still arrange the data along the lines of the former nation states such as the Soviet Union, Yugoslavia, and Czechoslovakia, since so much data is still presented in many essential statistical tools issued by international governmental and non-governmental bodies. But we also include the names of the recently constituted nations and provide, where they have come into being, details of statistical sources covering the new states that have just appeared. We also link the two possibilities together through the use of "see also" references so that the user continues to have recourse to all the current options.

Editors' Note

Statistics Sources may best be described as a finding guide to statistics. It does not purport to cite sources of in depth statistics on technical and commercial activities in specific foreign countries. For such purposes, the reader is referred to the Primary Statistics Source, or the National Statistical Office mentioned at the head of the geographic listings, as well as to the particular works cited in the selected bibliography which forms the first component of the work.

The painstaking task of accurately inputting the manuscript for this edition has been the contribution of Carla Rose and Peggy Barrett. Particular thanks is due to Carla Rose for the composing and printing of the entire manuscript.

Jacqueline Wasserman O'Brien
and Steven R. Wasserman
Editors

STATISTICS SOURCES
J–Z
Appendixes

J

Jamaica - National Statistical Office

Statistical Institute of Jamaica, Nine Swallowfield Road, Kingston 5, Jamaica.

Jamaica - Primary Statistics Sources

Statistical Institute of Jamaica, Nine Swallowfield Road, Kingston 5, Jamaica; *Quarterly Abstract of Statistics, Statistical Abstract,* and *Statistical Yearbook of Jamaica.*

JAMAICA - AGRICULTURE

The Economist Intelligence Unit, 111 West 57th Street, New York, New York 10019 (800) 938-4685; *The New Latin America Market Atlas.*

Facts on File, 460 Park Avenue South, New York, New York 10016 (800) 443-8323; *The New Book of World Rankings.*

Food and Agricultural Organization of the United Nations (FAO), Via delle Terme di Caracalla, 00100 Rome, Italy (Telephone Number in U.S. (202) 653-2400); *The State of Food and Agriculture,* and *Trade Yearbook.*

G.K. Hall and Company, 70 Lincoln Street, Boston, Massachusetts 02111 (617) 423-3990; *The World in Figures.*

Gale Research Incorporated, 835 Penobscot Building, Detroit, Michigan 48226; *International Historical Statistics The Americas and Australasia.*

Inter-American Development Bank, 1300 New York Avenue, NW, Washington, D.C. 20577 (202) 623-1753; *Economic and Social Progress in Latin America.*

Statistical Office of the United Nations, Publishing Service, New York, New York 10017 (800) 253-9646; *Statistical Yearbook for Latin America and the Caribbean.*

Times Books, 201 East 50th Street, New York, New York 10022 (212) 751-2600; *The Economist Book of Vital World Statistics.*

JAMAICA - AIRLINE SERVICE

The Economist Intelligence Unit, 111 West 57th Street, New York, New York 10019 (800) 938-4685; *The New Latin America Market Atlas.*

Facts on File, 460 Park Avenue South, New York, New York 10016 (800) 443-8323; *The New Book of World Rankings.*

G.K. Hall and Company, 70 Lincoln Street, Boston, Massachusetts 02111 (617) 423-3990; *The World in Figures.*

International Civil Aviation Organization, 1000 Sherbrooke Street West, Suite 400, Montreal, Quebec, Canada H3A 2R2 (514) 285-8219; *Civil Aviation Statistics of the World.*

Statistical Office of the United Nations, Publishing Service, New York, New York 10017 (800) 253-9646; *Statistical Yearbook.*

Times Books, 201 East 50th Street, New York, New York 10022 (212) 751-2600; *The Economist Book of Vital World Statistics.*

JAMAICA - ALUMINUM PRODUCTION AND CONSUMPTION - See JAMAICA - MINING AND MINERAL PRODUCTS

JAMAICA - ANIMAL HEALTH

Food and Agricultural Organization of the United Nations (FAO), Via delle Terme di Caracalla, 00100, Rome, Italy (Telephone Number in U.S. (202) 653-2400); *Animal Health Yearbook.*

JAMAICA - AREA AND DENSITY OF POPULATION

Euromonitor Publications Limited, 87-88 Turnmill Street, London EC1M 5QU, England; *International Marketing Data and Statistics.*

Facts on File, 460 Park Avenue South, New York, New York 10016 (800) 443-8323; *The New Book of World Rankings.*

Food and Agricultural Organization of the United Nations (FAO), Via delle Terme di Caracalla, 00100 Rome, Italy (Telephone Number in U.S. (202) 653-2400); *The State of Food and Agriculture.*

G.K. Hall and Company, 70 Lincoln Street, Boston, Massachusetts 02111 (617) 423-3990; *The World in Figures.*

Inter-American Development Bank, 1300 New York Avenue, NW, Washington, D.C. 20577 (202) 623-1753; *Economic and Social Progress in Latin America.*

Statistical Office of the United Nations, Publishing Service, New York, New York 10017 (800) 253-9646; *Statistical Yearbook.*

Times Books, 201 East 50th Street, New York, New York 10022 (212) 751-2600; *The Economist Book of Vital World Statistics.*

United Nations Educational, Scientific and Cultural Organization (UNESCO), 7 Place de Fontenoy, F-75700 Paris, France (Telephone Number in U.S. (212) 963-5981; *Statistical Yearbook.*

JAMAICA - ARMS EXPORTS AND IMPORTS

U.S. Arms Control and Disarmament Agency, 320 Twenty-first Street, NW, Washington, D.C. 20451 (202) 647-8677; *World Military Expenditures and Arms Transfers.*

JAMAICA - BALANCE OF PAYMENTS

The Economist Intelligence Unit, 111 West 57th Street, New York, New York 10019 (800) 938-4685; *The New Latin America Market Atlas,* and *The World Market Atlas.*

G.K. Hall and Company, 70 Lincoln Street, Boston, Massachusetts 02111 (617) 423-3990; *The World in Figures.*

Inter-American Development Bank, 1300 New York Avenue, NW, Washington, D.C. 20577 (202) 623-1753; *Economic and Social Progress in Latin America.*

International Monetary Fund, 700 Nineteenth Street, NW, Washington, D.C. 20431 (202) 623-7000; *Balance of Payments Yearbook.*

Times Books, 201 East 50th Street, New York, New York 10022 (212) 751-2600; *The Economist Book of Vital World Statistics.*

JAMAICA - BANKING

Facts on File, 460 Park Avenue South, New York, New York 10016 (800) 443-8323; *The New Book of World Rankings.*

G.K. Hall and Company, 70 Lincoln Street, Boston, Massachusetts 02111 (617) 423-3990; *The World in Figures.*

Inter-American Development Bank, 1300 New York Avenue, NW, Washington, D.C. 20577 (202) 623-1753; *Economic and Social Progress in Latin America.*

International Monetary Fund, 700 Nineteenth Street, NW, Washington, D.C. 20431 (202) 623-7000; *International Financial Statistics.*

Statistical Office of the United Nations, Publishing Service, New York, New York 10017 (800) 253-9646; *Statistical Yearbook,* and *Statistical Yearbook for Latin America and the Caribbean.*

JAMAICA - BARLEY PRODUCTION - See JAMAICA - CROPS

JAMAICA - BAUXITE EXPORTS

International Monetary Fund, 700 Nineteenth Street, NW, Washington, D.C. 20431 (202) 623-7000; *International Financial Statistics.*

Organization of American States (OAS), General Secretariat, Washington, D.C. 20006 (202) 458-3533; *Statistical Bulletin of the OAS.*

JAMAICA - BAUXITE PRODUCTION AND CONSUMPTION - See JAMAICA - MINING AND MINERAL PRODUCTS

JAMAICA - BEER PRODUCTION

Facts on File, 460 Park Avenue South, New York, New York 10016 (800) 443-8323; *The New Book of World Rankings.*

Statistical Office of the United Nations, Publishing Service, New York, New York 10017 (800) 253-9646; *Statistical Yearbook.*

JAMAICA - BIRTH RATE

Facts on File, 460 Park Avenue South, New York, New York 10016 (800) 443-8323; *The New Book of World Rankings.*

Statistical Office of the United Nations, Publishing Service, New York, New York 10017 (800) 253-9646; *Demographic Yearbook, Statistical Yearbook,* and *Statistical Yearbook for Latin America and the Caribbean.*

Times Books, 201 East 50th Street, New York, New York 10022 (212) 751-2600; *The Economist Book of Vital World Statistics.*

World Health Organization, Office of Publications, Avenue Appia, CH-1211 Geneva 27, Switzerland (Telephone Number in U.S. (518) 436-9686); *World Health Statistics Annual.*

JAMAICA - BONDS

G.K. Hall and Company, 70 Lincoln Street, Boston, Massachusetts 02111 (617) 423-3990; *The World in Figures.*

Inter-American Development Bank, 1300 New York Avenue, NW, Washington, D.C. 20577 (202) 623-1753; *Economic and Social Progress in Latin America.*

Organization of American States (OAS), General Secretariat, Washington, D.C. 20006 (202) 458-3533; *Statistical Bulletin of the OAS.*

Statistical Office of the United Nations, Publishing Service, New York, New York 10017 (800) 253-9646; *Statistical Yearbook.*

JAMAICA - BOOK PRODUCTION

G.K. Hall and Company, 70 Lincoln Street, Boston, Massachusetts 02111 (617) 423-3990; *The World in Figures.*

United Nations Educational, Scientific and Cultural Organization (UNESCO), 7 Place de Fontenoy, F-75700 Paris, France (Telephone Number in U.S. (212) 963-5981); *Statistical Yearbook.*

JAMAICA - BROADCASTING

Billboard Limited, Post Office Box 9027, 1006 AA Amsterdam, The Netherlands (Telephone Number in U.S. (212) 764-7300); *World Radio TV Handbook.*

Facts on File, 460 Park Avenue South, New York, New York 10016 (800) 443-8323; *The New Book of World Rankings.*

G.K. Hall and Company, 70 Lincoln Street, Boston, Massachusetts 02111 (617) 423-3990; *The World in Figures.*

Times Books, 201 East 50th Street, New York, New York 10022 (212) 751-2600; *The Economist Book of Vital World Statistics.*

JAMAICA - BUSINESS

G.K. Hall and Company, 70 Lincoln Street, Boston, Massachusetts 02111 (617) 423-3990; *The World in Figures.*

Inter-American Development Bank, 1300 New York Avenue, NW, Washington, D.C. 20577 (202) 623-1517; *Economic and Social Progress in Latin America.*

JAMAICA - BUSINESS AND PROFESSIONAL LICENSES

International Monetary Fund, 700 Nineteenth Street, NW, Washington, D.C. 20431 (202) 623-7000; *Government Finance Statistics Yearbook.*

JAMAICA - CABBAGE PRODUCTION - See JAMAICA - CROPS

JAMAICA - CALORIE SUPPLY

Food and Agricultural Organization of the United Nations (FAO), Via delle Terme di Caracalla, 00100 Rome, Italy (Telephone Number in U.S. (202) 653-2400); *The State of Food and Agriculture.*

Statistical Office of the United Nations, Publishing Service, New York, New York 10017 (800) 253-9646; *Statistical Yearbook for Latin America and the Caribbean.*

JAMAICA - CAPITAL INVESTMENT

Inter-American Development Bank, 1300 New York Avenue, NW, Washington, D.C. 20577 (202) 623-1753; *Economic and Social Progress in Latin America.*

JAMAICA - CAPITAL REVENUE

Inter-American Development Bank, 1300 New York Avenue, NW, Washington, D.C. 20577 (202) 623-1753; *Economic and Social Progress in Latin America.*

International Monetary Fund, 700 Nineteenth Street, NW, Washington, D.C. 20431 (202) 623-7000; *Government Finance Statistics Yearbook.*

JAMAICA - CATTLE - See JAMAICA - LIVESTOCK AND POULTRY

JAMAICA - CEMENT PRODUCTION - See JAMAICA - MINING AND MINERAL PRODUCTS

JAMAICA - CHEMICAL (ORGANIC) PRODUCTION - See JAMAICA - MINING AND MINERAL PRODUCTS

JAMAICA - CHICKENS - See JAMAICA - LIVESTOCK AND POULTRY

JAMAICA - CIGAR AND CIGARETTE PRODUCTION - See JAMAICA - TOBACCO PRODUCTION

JAMAICA - CLASS STRUCTURE

G.K. Hall and Company, 70 Lincoln Street, Boston, Massachusetts 02111 (617) 423-3990; *The World in Figures.*

JAMAICA - CLIMATE

Facts on File, 460 Park Avenue South, New York, New York 10016 (800) 443-8323; *The New Book of World Rankings.*

G.K. Hall and Company, 70 Lincoln Street, Boston, Massachusetts 02111 (617) 423-3990; *The World in Figures.*

JAMAICA - COAL PRODUCTION - See JAMAICA - MINING AND MINERAL PRODUCTS

JAMAICA - COCOA (BEANS) PRODUCTION - See JAMAICA - CROPS

JAMAICA - COFFEE PRODUCTION AND CONSUMPTION - See JAMAICA - CROPS

JAMAICA - COMMUNICATIONS

Gale Research Incorporated, 835 Penobscot Building, Detroit, Michigan 48226 (800) 877-4253; *International Historical Statistics The Americas and Australasia.*

G.K. Hall and Company, 70 Lincoln Street, Boston, Massachusetts 02111 (617) 423-3990; *The World in Figures.*

Inter-American Development Bank, 1300 New York Avenue, NW, Washington, D.C. 20577 (202) 623-1753; *Economic and Social Progress in Latin America.*

JAMAICA - CONSTRUCTION INDUSTRY

The Economist Intelligence Unit, 111 West 57th Street, New York, New York 10019 (800) 938-4685; *The New Latin America Market Atlas.*

Facts on File, 460 Park Avenue South, New York, New York 10016 (800) 443-8323; *The New Book of World Rankings.*

Inter-American Development Bank, 1300 New York Avenue, NW, Washington, D.C. 20577 (202) 623-1753; *Economic and Social Progress in Latin America.*

Statistical Office of the United Nations, Publishing Service, New York, New York 10017 (800) 253-9646; *Construction Statistics Yearbook,* and *Statistical Yearbook.*

JAMAICA - CONSUMER PRICE INDEX

G.K. Hall and Company, 70 Lincoln Street, Boston, Massachusetts 02111 (617) 423-3990; *The World in Figures.*

International Labour Office, I.L.O. Publications, CH-1211, Geneva 22, Switzerland; *Yearbook of Labour Statistics.*

Statistical Office of the United Nations, Publishing Service, New York, New York 10017 (800) 253-9646; *Statistical Yearbook.*

JAMAICA - CONSUMER PRICES

The Economist Intelligence Unit, 111 West 57th Street, New York, New York 10019 (800) 938-4685; *The New Latin America Market Atlas.*

International Labour Office, I.L.O. Publications, CH-1211, Geneva 22, Switzerland; *Yearbook of Labour Statistics.*

International Monetary Fund, 700 Nineteenth Street, NW, Washington, D.C. 20431 (202) 623-7000; *International Financial Statistics.*

Organization of American States (OAS), General Secretariat, Washington, D.C. 20006 (202) 458-3533; *Statistical Bulletin of the OAS.*

Times Books, 201 East 50th Street, New York, New York 10022 (212) 751-2600; *The Economist Book of Vital World Statistics.*

JAMAICA - CONSUMPTION

The Economist Intelligence Unit, 111 West 57th Street, New York, New York 10019 (800) 938-4685; *The New Latin America Market Atlas.*

G.K. Hall and Company, 70 Lincoln Street, Boston, Massachusetts 02111 (617) 423-3990; *The World in Figures.*

Inter-American Development Bank, 1300 New York Avenue, NW, Washington, D.C. 20577 (202) 623-1753; *Economic and Social Progress in Latin America.*

Statistical Office of the United Nations, Publishing Service, New York, New York 10017 (800) 253-9646; *Statistical Yearbook for Latin America and the Caribbean.*

JAMAICA - CORN PRODUCTION - See JAMAICA - CROPS

JAMAICA - CORPORATE TAXES - See JAMAICA - TAXATION

JAMAICA - COTTON - See JAMAICA - CROPS

JAMAICA - CRIME

Yale University Press, Yale Station, New Haven, Connecticut 06520 (203) 432-0940; *Violence and Crime in Cross-National Perspective.*

JAMAICA - CROPS

The Economist Intelligence Unit, 111 West 57th Street, New York, New York 10019 (800) 938-4685; *The New Latin America Market Atlas.*

Facts on File, 460 Park Avenue South, New York, New York 10016 (800) 443-8323; *The New Book of World Rankings.*

Food and Agricultural Organization of the United Nations (FAO) Via delle Terme di Caracalla, 00100 Rome, Italy (Telephone Number in U.S. (202) 653-2400); *The State of Food and Agriculture,* and *Production Yearbook.*

International Monetary Fund, 700 Nineteenth Street, NW, Washington, D.C. 20431 (202) 623-7000; *International Financial Statistics.*

Organization of American States (OAS), General Secretariat, Washington, D.C. 20006 (202) 458-3533; *Statistical Bulletin of the OAS.*

G.K. Hall and Company, 70 Lincoln Street, Boston, Massachusetts 02111 (617) 423-3990; *The World in Figures.*

Statistical Office of the United Nations, Publishing Service, New York, New York 10017 (800) 253-9646; *Statistical Yearbook.*

JAMAICA - CUSTOMS DUTIES

G.K. Hall and Company, 70 Lincoln Street, Boston, Massachusetts 02111 (617) 423-3990; *The World in Figures.*

Inter-American Development Bank, 1300 New York Avenue, NW, Washington, D.C. 20577 (202) 623-1753; *Economic and Social Progress in Latin America.*

International Monetary Fund, 700 Nineteenth Street, NW, Washington, D.C. 20431 (202) 623-7000; *Government Finance Statistics Yearbook.*

JAMAICA - DAIRY PRODUCTS

Facts on File, 460 Park Avenue South, New York, New York 10016 (800) 443-8323; *The New Book of World Rankings.*

Food and Agricultural Organization of the United Nations (FAO), Via delle Terme di Caracalla, 00100 Rome, Italy (Telephone Number in U.S. (202) 653-2400); *Production Yearbook, The State of Food and Agriculture.*

Statistical Office of the United Nations, Publishing Service, New York, New York 10017 (800) 253-9646; *Statistical Yearbook.*

JAMAICA - DEATH RATE

G.K. Hall and Company, 70 Lincoln Street, Boston, Massachusetts 02111 (617) 423-3990; *The World in Figures.*

Statistical Office of the United Nations, Publishing Service, New York, New York 10017 (800) 253-9646; *Statistical Yearbook.*

Times Books, 201 East 50th Street, New York, New York 10022 (212) 751-2600; *The Economist Book of Vital World Statistics.*

World Health Organization, Office of Publications, Avenue Appia, CH-1211 Geneva 27, Switzerland; *World Health Statistics Annual.*

JAMAICA - DEBT

The Economist Intelligence Unit, 111 West 57th Street, New York, New York 10019 (800) 938-4685; *The New Latin America Market Atlas.*

JAMAICA - DEFENSE

The Economist Intelligence Unit, 111 West 57th Street, New York, New York 10019 (800) 938-4685; *The New Latin America Market Atlas.*

JAMAICA - DEFENSE EXPENDITURES

G.K. Hall and Company, 70 Lincoln Street, Boston, Massachusetts 02111 (617) 423-3990; *The World in Figures.*

International Monetary Fund, 700 Nineteenth Street, NW, Washington, D.C. 20431 (202) 623-7000; *Government Finance Statistics Yearbook.*

U.S. Arms Control and Disarmament Agency, 320 Twenty-first Street, NW, Washington, D.C. 20451 (202) 647-8677; *World Military Expenditures and Arms Transfers.*

JAMAICA - DEMOGRAPHY

The Economist Intelligence Unit, 111 West 57th Street, New York, New York 10019 (800) 938-4685; *The World Market Atlas.*

Facts on File, 460 Park Avenue South, New York, New York 10016 (800) 443-8323; *The New Book of World Rankings.*

G.K. Hall and Company, 70 Lincoln Street, Boston, Massachusetts 02111 (617) 423-3990; *The World in Figures.*

JAMAICA - DEVELOPMENT ASSISTANCE

G.K. Hall and Company, 70 Lincoln Street, Boston, Massachusetts 02111 (617) 423-3990; *The World in Figures.*

Inter-American Development Bank, 1300 New York Avenue, NW, Washington, D.C. 20577 (202) 623-1753; *Economic and Social Progress in Latin America.*

Statistical Office of the United Nations, Publishing Service, New York, New York 10017 (800) 253-9646; *Statistical Yearbook.*

JAMAICA - DIAMOND PRODUCTION - See JAMAICA - MINING AND MINERAL PRODUCTS

JAMAICA - DISCOUNT RATES

Inter-American Development Bank, 1300 New York Avenue, NW, Washington, D.C. 20577 (202) 623-1753; *Economic and Social Progress in Latin America*.

Organization of American States (OAS), General Secretariat, Washington, D.C. 20006 (202) 458-3533; *Statistical Bulletin of the OAS*.

Statistical Office of the United Nations, Publishing Service, New York, New York 10017 (800) 253-9646; *Statistical Yearbook*.

JAMAICA - DISEASES

G.K. Hall and Company, 70 Lincoln Street, Boston, Massachusetts 02111 (617) 423-3990; *The World in Figures*.

World Health Organization, Office of Publications, Avenue Appia, CH-1211 Geneva 27, Switzerland (Telephone Number in U.S. (518) 436-9686); *World Health Statistics Annual*.

JAMAICA - DIVORCE RATES

Facts on File, 460 Park Avenue South, New York, New York 10016 (800) 443-8323; *The New Book of World Rankings*.

Statistical Office of the United Nations, Publishing Service, New York, New York 10017 (800) 253-9646; *Demographic Yearbook*, and *Statistical Yearbook*.

JAMAICA - DOMESTIC PRODUCT

G.K. Hall and Company, 70 Lincoln Street, Boston, Massachusetts 02111 (617) 423-3990; *The World in Figures*.

JAMAICA - ECONOMY

Euromonitor Publications Limited, 87-88 Turnmill Street, London EC1M 5QU, England; *International Marketing Data and Statistics*.

Facts on File, 460 Park Avenue South, New York, New York 10016 (800) 443-8323; *The New Book of World Rankings*.

G.K. Hall and Company, 70 Lincoln Street, Boston, Massachusetts 02111 (617) 423-3990; *The World in Figures*.

Inter-American Development Bank, 1300 New York Avenue, NW, Washington, D.C. 20577 (202) 623-1753; *Economic and Social Progress in Latin America*.

Organization of American States (OAS), General Secretariat, Washington, D.C. 20006 (202) 458-3533; *Statistical Bulletin of the OAS*.

Statistical Office of the United Nations, Publishing Service, New York, New York 10017 (800) 253-9646; *Economic Survey of Latin America and the Caribbean*.

JAMAICA - EDUCATION

The Economist Intelligence Unit, 111 West 57th Street, New York, New York 10019 (800) 938-4685; *The New Latin America Market Atlas*, and *The World Market Atlas*.

Facts on File, 460 Park Avenue South, New York, New York 10016 (800) 443-8323; *The New Book of World Rankings*.

Gale Research Incorporated, 835 Penobscot Building, Detroit, Michigan 48226 (800) 877-4253; *International Historical Statistics The Americas and Australasia*.

G.K. Hall and Company, 70 Lincoln Street, Boston, Massachusetts 02111 (617) 423-3990; *The World in Figures*.

International Monetary Fund, 700 Nineteenth Street, NW, Washington, D.C. 20431 (202) 623-7000; *Government Finance Statistics Yearbook*.

Statistical Office of the United Nations, Publishing Service, New York, New York 10017 (800) 253-9646; *Statistical Yearbook for Latin America and the Caribbean*.

Times Books, 201 East 50th Street, New York, New York 10022 (212) 751-2600; *The Economist Book of Vital World Statistics*.

United Nations Educational, Scientific and Cultural Organization (UNESCO), 7 Place de Fontenoy, F-75700 Paris, France (Telephone Number in U.S. (212) 963-5981); *Statistical Yearbook*.

JAMAICA - EGG PRODUCTION AND CONSUMPTION - See JAMAICA - DAIRY PRODUCTS

JAMAICA - ELECTRICITY

The Economist Intelligence Unit, 111 West 57th Street, New York, New York 10019 (800) 938-4685; *The New Latin America Market Atlas*.

Facts on File, 460 Park Avenue South, New York, New York 10016 (800) 443-8323; *The New Book of World Rankings*.

Inter-American Development Bank, 1300 New York Avenue, NW, Washington, D.C. 20577 (202) 623-1753; *Economic and Social Progress in Latin America*.

Organization of American States (OAS), General Secretariat, Washington, D.C. 20006 (202) 458-3533; *Statistical Bulletin of the OAS*.

Statistical Office of the United Nations, Publishing Service, New York, New York 10017 (800) 253-9646; *Statistical Yearbook*.

JAMAICA - EMPLOYMENT

Euromonitor Publications Limited, 87-88 Turnmill Street, London EC1M 5QU, England; *International Marketing Data and Statistics*.

Facts on File, 460 Park Avenue South, New York, New York 10016 (800) 443-8323; *The New Book of World Rankings*.

International Labour Office, I.L.O. Publications, CH-1211, Geneva 22, Switzerland; *Yearbook of Labour Statistics*.

Statistical Office of the United Nations, Publishing Service, New York, New York 10017 (800) 253-9646; *Statistical Yearbook for Latin America and the Caribbean*.

JAMAICA - ENERGY

The Economist Intelligence Unit, 111 West 57th Street, New York, New York 10019 (800) 938-4685; *The New Latin America Market Atlas*.

Facts on File, 460 Park Avenue South, New York, New York 10016 (800) 443-8323; *The New Book of World Rankings*.

Food and Agricultural Organization of the United Nations (FAO), Via delle Terme di Caracalla, 00100 Rome, Italy (Telephone Number in U.S. (202) 653-2400); *The State of Food and Agriculture*.

G.K. Hall and Company, 70 Lincoln Street, Boston, Massachusetts 02111 (617) 423-3990; *The World in Figures*.

Statistical Office of the United Nations, Publishing Service, New York, New York 10017 (800) 253-9646; *Energy Statistics Yearbook*, *Statistical Yearbook*, and *Statistical Yearbook for Latin America and the Caribbean*.

Times Books, 201 East 50th Street, New York, New York 10022 (212) 751-2600; *The Economist Book of Vital World Statistics*.

JAMAICA - EXCHANGE RATES

Euromonitor Publications Limited, 87-88 Turnmill Street, London EC1M 5QU, England; *International Marketing Data and Statistics*.

Inter-American Development Bank, 1300 New York Avenue, NW, Washington, D.C. 20577 (202) 623-1753; *Economic and Social Progress in Latin America*.

International Civil Aviation Organization, 1000 Sherbrooke Street West, Suite 400, Montreal, Quebec, Canada H3A 2R2 (514) 285-8219; *Civil Aviation Statistics of the World*.

International Monetary Fund, 700 Nineteenth Street, NW, Washington, D.C. 20431 (202) 623-7000; *International Financial Statistics*.

Organization of American States (OAS), General Secretariat, Washington, D.C. 20006 (202) 458-3533; *Statistical Bulletin of the OAS*.

Statistical Office of the United Nations, Publishing Service, New York, New York 10017 (800) 253-9646; *Statistical Yearbook*.

JAMAICA - EXCISE TAXES - See JAMAICA - TAXATION

JAMAICA - EXPORTS

The Economist Intelligence Unit, 111 West 57th Street, New York, New York 10019 (800) 938-4685; *The New Latin America Market Atlas*, and *The World Market Atlas*.

Euromonitor Publications Limited, 87-88 Turnmill Street, London EC1M 5QU, England; *International Marketing Data and Statistics*.

Food and Agricultural Organization of the United Nations (FAO) Via delle Terme di Caracalla, 00100 Rome, Italy (Telephone Number in U.S. (202) 653-2400); *The State of Food and Agriculture*.

G.K. Hall and Company, 70 Lincoln Street, Boston, Massachusetts 02111 (617) 423-3990; *The World in Figures*.

Inter-American Development Bank, 1300 New York Avenue, NW, Washington, D.C. 20577 (202) 623-1753; *Economic and Social Progress in Latin America*.

International Monetary Fund, 700 Nineteenth Street, NW, Washington, D.C. 20431 (202) 623-7000; *Direction of Trade Statistics*, *Government Finance Statistics Yearbook*, and *International Financial Statistics*.

Organization of American States (OAS), General Secretariat, Washington, D.C. 20006 (202) 458-3533; *Statistical Bulletin of the OAS*.

Statistical Office of the United Nations, Publishing Service, New York, New York 10017 (800) 253-9646; *Statistical Yearbook for Latin America and the Caribbean*, and *Trade in Manufactures of Developing Countries*.

Times Books, 201 East 50th Street, New York, New York 10022 (212) 751-2600; *The Economist Book of Vital World Statistics*.

JAMAICA - EXTERNAL FINANCING

Inter-American Development Bank, 1300 New York Avenue, NW, Washington, D.C. 20577 (202) 623-1753; *Economic and Social Progress in Latin America*.

Statistical Office of the United Nations, Publishing Service, New York, New York 10017 (800) 253-9646; *Statistical Yearbook for Latin America and the Caribbean*.

JAMAICA - EXTERNAL INDEBTEDNESS

Inter-American Development Bank, 1300 New York Avenue, NW, Washington, D.C. 20577 (202) 623-1753; *Economic and Social Progress in Latin America*.

Statistical Office of the United Nations, Publishing Service, New York, New York 10017 (800) 253-9646; *Statistical Yearbook for Latin America and the Caribbean*.

JAMAICA - EXTERNAL TRADE

Food and Agricultural Organization of the United Nations (FAO), Via delle Terme di Caracalla, 00100 Rome, Italy (Telephone Number in U.S. (202) 653-2400); *The State of Food and Agriculture*, and *Trade Yearbook*.

Gale Research Incorporated, 835 Penobscot Building, Detroit, Michigan 48226 (800) 877-4253; *International Historical Statistics The Americas and Australasia*.

G.K. Hall and Company, 70 Lincoln Street, Boston, Massachusetts 02111 (617) 423-3990; *The World in Figures*.

Inter-American Development Bank, 1300 New York Avenue, NW, Washington, D.C. 20577 (202) 623-1753; *Economic and Social Progress in Latin America*.

Statistical Office of the United Nations, Publishing Service, New York, New York 10017 (800) 253-9646; *Statistical Yearbook*, and *Statistical Yearbook for Latin America and the Caribbean*.

JAMAICA - FABRIC PRODUCTION - See JAMAICA - TEXTILE INDUSTRY

JAMAICA - FARM CROPS - See JAMAICA - CROPS

JAMAICA - FEMALE WORKING POPULATION - See JAMAICA - EMPLOYMENT

JAMAICA - FERTILITY RATES

Facts on File, 460 Park Avenue South, New York, New York 10016 (800) 443-8323; *The New Book of World Rankings*.

Times Books, 201 East 50th Street, New York, New York 10022 (212) 751-2600; *The Economist Book of Vital World Statistics*.

JAMAICA - FERTILIZER

The Economist Intelligence Unit, 111 West 57th Street, New York, New York 10019 (800) 938-4685; *The New Latin America Market Atlas*.

Food and Agricultural Organization of the United Nations (FAO), Via delle Terme di Caracalla, 00100, Rome, Italy (Telephone Number in U.S. (202) 653-2400); *Fertilizer Yearbook*, and *The State of Food and Agriculture*.

Statistical Office of the United Nations, Publishing Service, New York, New York 10017 (800) 253-9646; *Statistical Yearbook*.

JAMAICA - FETAL MORTALITY

Statistical Office of the United Nations, Publishing Service, New York, New York 10017 (800) 253-9646; *Demographic Yearbook*.

World Health Organization, Office of Publications, Avenue Appia, CH-1211 Geneva 27, Switzerland (Telephone Number in U.S. (518) 436-9686); *World Health Statistics Annual*.

JAMAICA - FINANCE

Facts on File, 460 Park Avenue South, New York, New York 10016 (800) 443-8323; *The New Book of World Rankings*.

Gale Research Incorporated, 835 Penobscot Building, Detroit, Michigan 48226 (800) 877-4253; *International Historical Statistics The Americas and Australasia*.

G.K. Hall and Company, 70 Lincoln Street, Boston, Massachusetts 02111 (617) 423-3990; *The World in Figures*.

Inter-American Development Bank, 1300 New York Avenue, NW, Washington, D.C. 20577 (202) 623-1753; *Economic and Social Progress in Latin America*.

International Monetary Fund, 700 Nineteenth Street, NW, Washington, D.C. 20431 (202) 623-7000; *International Financial Statistics*.

Organization of American States (OAS), General Secretariat, Washington, D.C. 20006 (202) 458-3533; *Statistical Bulletin of the OAS*.

JAMAICA - FISHERIES

Facts on File, 460 Park Avenue South, New York, New York 10016 (800) 443-8323; *The New Book of World Rankings*.

Food and Agricultural Organization of the United Nations (FAO), Via delle Terme di Caracalla, 00100 Rome, Italy (Telephone Number in U.S. (202) 653-2400); *The State of Food and Agriculture*, and *Yearbook of Fishery Statistics*.

Inter-American Development Bank, 1300 New York Avenue, NW, Washington, D.C. 20577 (202) 623-1753; *Economic and Social Progress in Latin America*.

Statistical Office of the United Nations, Publishing Service, New York, New York 10017 (800) 253-9646; *Statistical Yearbook*.

JAMAICA - FLOUR PRODUCTION

Statistical Office of the United Nations, Publishing Service, New York, New York 10017 (800) 253-9646; *Statistical Yearbook*.

JAMAICA - FOOD

Food and Agricultural Organization of the United Nations (FAO), Via delle Terme di Caracalla, 00100, Rome, Italy (Telephone Number in U.S. (202) 653-2400); *Production Yearbook*, and *The State of Food and Agriculture*.

G.K. Hall and Company, 70 Lincoln Street, Boston, Massachusetts 02111 (617) 423-3990; *The World in Figures*.

JAMAICA - FOREIGN AID

G.K. Hall and Company, 70 Lincoln Street, Boston, Massachusetts 02111 (617) 423-3990; *The World in Figures*.

Inter-American Development Bank, 1300 New York Avenue, NW, Washington, D.C. 20577 (202) 623-1753; *Economic and Social Progress in Latin America*.

JAMAICA - FOREIGN DEBT

The Economist Intelligence Unit, 111 West 57th Street, New York, New York 10019 (800) 938-4685; *The New Latin America Market Atlas*.

Inter-American Development Bank, 1300 New York Avenue, NW, Washington, D.C. 20577 (202) 623-1753; *Economic and Social Progress in Latin America*.

JAMAICA - FOREIGN INDEBTEDNESS

Inter-American Development Bank, 1300 New York Avenue, NW, Washington, D.C. 20577 (202) 623-1753; *Economic and Social Progress in Latin America*.

Statistical Office of the United Nations, Publishing Service, New York, New York 10017 (800) 253-9646; *Economic Survey of Latin America and the Caribbean*.

JAMAICA - FOREIGN INVESTMENT

The Economist Intelligence Unit, 111 West 57th Street, New York, New York 10019 (800) 938-4685; *The New Latin America Market Atlas*.

JAMAICA - FOREIGN TRADE

The Economist Intelligence Unit, 111 West 57th Street, New York, New York 10019 (800) 938-4685; *The New Latin America Market Atlas*.

Euromonitor Publications Limited, 87-88 Turnmill Street, London EC1M 5QU, England; *International Marketing Data and Statistics*.

Facts on File, 460 Park Avenue South, New York, New York 10016 (800) 443-8323; *The New Book of World Rankings*.

Food and Agricultural Organization of the United Nations (FAO), Via delle Terme di Caracalla, 00100 Rome, Italy (Telephone Number in U.S. (202) 653-2400); *The State of Food and Agriculture*.

G.K. Hall and Company, 70 Lincoln Street, Boston, Massachusetts 02111 (617) 423-3990; *The World in Figures*.

Inter-American Development Bank, 1300 New York Avenue, NW, Washington, D.C. 20577 (202) 623-1753; *Economic and Social Progress in Latin America*.

International Monetary Fund, 700 Nineteenth Street, NW, Washington, D.C. 20431 (202) 623-7000; *International Financial Statistics*.

Statistical Office of the United Nations, Publishing Service, New York, New York 10017 (800) 253-9646; *Economic Survey of Latin America and the Caribbean, International Trade Statistics Yearbook*, and *Statistical Yearbook*.

JAMAICA - FORESTRY AND FOREST PRODUCTS

The Economist Intelligence Unit, 111 West 57th Street, New York, New York 10019 (800) 938-4685; *The New Latin America Market Atlas*.

Facts on File, 460 Park Avenue South, New York, New York 10016 (800) 443-8323; *The New Book of World Rankings*.

Food and Agricultural Organization of the United Nations (FAO), Via delle Terme di Caracalla, 00100 Rome, Italy (Telephone Number in U.S. (202) 653-2400); *The State of Food and Agriculture*, and *Yearbook of Forest Products*.

G.K. Hall and Company, 70 Lincoln Street, Boston, Massachusetts 02111 (617) 423-3990; *The World in Figures*.

Inter-American Development Bank, 1300 New York Avenue, NW, Washington, D.C. 20577 (202) 623-1753; *Economic and Social Progress in Latin America*.

Statistical Office of the United Nations, Publishing Service, New York, New York 10017 (800) 253-9646; *Statistical Yearbook*.

United Nations Educational, Scientific and Cultural Organization (UNESCO), 7 Place de Fontenoy, F-75700 Paris, France (Telephone Number in U.S. (212) 963-5981); *Statistical Yearbook*.

JAMAICA - GAS PRODUCTION - See JAMAICA - MINING AND MINERAL PRODUCTS

JAMAICA - GENERAL INDUSTRIAL STATISTICS

Statistical Office of the United Nations, Publishing Service, New York, New York 10017 (800) 253-9646; *Industrial Statistics Yearbook*.

JAMAICA - GENERAL MORTALITY

Statistical Office of the United Nations, Publishing Service, New York, New York 10017 (800) 253-9646; *Demographic Yearbook*.

World Health Organization, Office of Publications, Avenue Appia, CH-1211 Geneva 27, Switzerland (Telephone Number in U.S. (518) 436-9686); *World Health Statistics Annual*.

JAMAICA - GEOGRAPHIC DATA

Facts on File, 460 Park Avenue South, New York, New York 10016 (800) 443-8323; *The New Book of World Rankings*.

JAMAICA - GOATS - See JAMAICA - LIVESTOCK AND POULTRY

JAMAICA - GOLD HOLDINGS

International Monetary Fund, 700 Nineteenth Street, NW, Washington, D.C. 20431 (202) 623-7000; *International Financial Statistics*.

Statistical Office of the United Nations, Publishing Service, New York, New York 10017 (800) 253-9646; *Statistical Yearbook*.

JAMAICA - GOLD PRODUCTION AND CONSUMPTION - See JAMAICA - MINING AND MINERAL PRODUCTS

JAMAICA - GOLD RESERVES

The Economist Intelligence Unit, 111 West 57th Street, New York, New York 10019 (800) 938-4685; *The New Latin America Market Atlas*.

JAMAICA - GOVERNMENT

G.K. Hall and Company, 70 Lincoln Street, Boston, Massachusetts 02111 (617) 423-3990; *The World in Figures*.

Inter-American Development Bank, 1300 New York Avenue, NW, Washington, D.C. 20577 (202) 623-1753; *Economic and Social Progress in Latin America*.

JAMAICA - GOVERNMENT CONSUMPTION

Inter-American Development Bank, 1300 New York Avenue, NW, Washington, D.C. 20577 (202) 623-1753; *Economic and Social Progress in Latin America*.

JAMAICA - GOVERNMENT EXPENDITURES

Inter-American Development Bank, 1300 New York Avenue, NW, Washington, D.C. 20577 (202) 623-1753; *Economic and Social Progress in Latin America*.

International Monetary Fund, 700 Nineteenth Street, NW, Washington, D.C. 20431 (202) 623-7000; *Government Finance Statistics Yearbook*.

JAMAICA - GOVERNMENT FINANCES

Inter-American Development Bank, 1300 New York Avenue, NW, Washington, D.C. 20577 (202) 623-1753; *Economic and Social Progress in Latin America*.

International Monetary Fund, 700 Nineteenth Street, NW, Washington, D.C. 20431 (202) 623-7000; *International Financial Statistics*.

Statistical Office of the United Nations, Publishing Service, New York, New York 10017 (800) 253-9646; *Statistical Yearbook*.

JAMAICA - GOVERNMENT REVENUES

Inter-American Development Bank, 1300 New York Avenue, NW, Washington, D.C. 20577 (202) 623-1753; *Economic and Social Progress in Latin America*.

International Monetary Fund, 700 Nineteenth Street, NW, Washington, D.C. 20431 (202) 623-7000; *Government Finance Statistics Yearbook*.

Times Books, 201 East 50th Street, New York, New York 10022 (212) 751-2600; *The Economist Book of Vital World Statistics*.

JAMAICA - GRAIN PRODUCTION - See JAMAICA - CROPS

JAMAICA - GRANTS

International Monetary Fund, 700 Nineteenth Street, NW, Washington, D.C. 20431 (202) 623-7000; *Government Finance Statistics Yearbook*.

JAMAICA - GROSS DOMESTIC PRODUCT

The Economist Intelligence Unit, 111 West 57th Street, New York, New York 10019 (800) 938-4685; *The New Latin America Market Atlas*, and *The World Market Atlas*.

Euromonitor Publications Limited, 87-88 Turnmill Street, London EC1M 5QU, England; *International Marketing Data and Statistics*.

Facts on File, 460 Park Avenue South, New York, New York 10016 (800) 443-8323; *The New Book of World Rankings*.

G.K. Hall and Company, 70 Lincoln Street, Boston, Massachusetts 02111 (617) 423-3990; *The World in Figures*.

Inter-American Development Bank, 1300 New York Avenue, NW, Washington, D.C. 20577 (202) 623-1753; *Economic and Social Progress in Latin America*.

Organization of American States (OAS), General Secretariat, Washington, D.C. 20006 (202) 458-3533; *Statistical Bulletin of the OAS*.

Statistical Office of the United Nations, Publishing Service, New York, New York 10017 (800) 253-9646; *Statistical Yearbook*, and *Statistical Yearbook for Latin America and the Caribbean*.

Times Books, 201 East 50th Street, New York, New York 10022 (212) 751-2600; *The Economist Book of Vital World Statistics*.

JAMAICA - GROSS NATIONAL PRODUCT

Euromonitor Publications Limited, 87-88 Turnmill Street, London EC1M 5QU, England; *International Marketing Data and Statistics*.

Inter-American Development Bank, 1300 New York Avenue, NW, Washington, D.C. 20577 (202) 623-1753; *Economic and Social Progress in Latin America*.

U.S. Arms Control and Disarmament Agency, 320 Twenty-first Street, NW, Washington, D.C. 20451 (202) 647-8677; *World Military Expenditures and Arms Transfers*.

JAMAICA - GROUNDNUTS PRODUCTION - See JAMAICA - CROPS

JAMAICA - HEALTH

The Economist Intelligence Unit, 111 West 57th Street, New York, New York 10019 (800) 938-4685; *The New Latin America Market Atlas*.

Facts on File, 460 Park Avenue South, New York, New York 10016 (800) 443-8323; *The New Book of World Rankings*.

G.K. Hall and Company, 70 Lincoln Street, Boston, Massachusetts 02111 (617) 423-3990; *The World in Figures*.

Statistical Office of the United Nations, Publishing Service, New York, New York 10017 (800) 253-9646; *Statistical Yearbook*, and *Statistical Yearbook for Latin America and the Caribbean*.

Times Books, 201 East 50th Street, New York, New York 10022 (212) 751-2600; *The Economist Book of Vital World Statistics*.

World Health Organization, Office of Publications, Avenue Appia, CH-1211 Geneva 27, Switzerland (Telephone Number in U.S. (518) 436-9686); *World Health Statistics Annual*.

JAMAICA - HEALTH EXPENDITURES

International Monetary Fund, 700 Nineteenth Street, NW, Washington, D.C. 20431 (202) 623-7000; *Government Finance Statistics Yearbook*.

Statistical Office of the United Nations, Publishing Service, New York, New York 10017 (800) 253-9646; *Statistical Yearbook for Latin America and the Caribbean*.

JAMAICA - HIDE PRODUCTION

Food and Agricultural Organization of the United Nations (FAO), Via delle Terme di Caracalla, 00100 Rome, Italy (Telephone Number in U.S. (202) 653-2400); *Production Yearbook*.

JAMAICA - HIGHWAYS

The Economist Intelligence Unit, 111 West 57th Street, New York, New York 10019 (800) 938-4685; *The New Latin America Market Atlas*.

G.K. Hall and Company, 70 Lincoln Street, Boston, Massachusetts 02111 (617) 423-3990; *The World in Figures*.

JAMAICA - HORSES - See JAMAICA - LIVESTOCK AND POULTRY

JAMAICA - HOURS OF WORK - See JAMAICA - EMPLOYMENT

JAMAICA - HOUSING AND HOUSING UNITS

Facts on File, 460 Park Avenue South, New York, New York 10016 (800) 443-8323; *The New Book of World Rankings*.

Statistical Office of the United Nations, Publishing Service, New York, New York 10017 (800) 253-9646; *Statistical Yearbook for Latin America and the Caribbean*.

JAMAICA - HOUSING EXPENDITURES

International Monetary Fund, 700 Nineteenth Street, NW, Washington, D.C. 20431 (202) 623-7000; *Government Finance Statistics Yearbook*.

JAMAICA - ILLITERACY RATES

The Economist Intelligence Unit, 111 West 57th Street, New York, New York 10019 (800) 938-4685; *The New Latin America Market Atlas*.

JAMAICA - ILLITERATE POPULATION

The Economist Intelligence Unit, 111 West 57th Street, New York, New York 10019 (800) 938-4685; *The World Market Atlas*.

G.K. Hall and Company, 70 Lincoln Street, Boston, Massachusetts 02111 (617) 423-3990; *The World in Figures*.

Statistical Office of the United Nations, Publishing Service, New York, New York 10017 (800) 253-9646; *Statistical Yearbook for Latin America and the Caribbean*.

United Nations Educational, Scientific and Cultural Organization (UNESCO), 7 Place de Fontenoy, F-75700 Paris, France (Telephone Number in U.S. (313) 060-6001); *Statistical Yearbook*.

JAMAICA - IMPORTS

The Economist Intelligence Unit, 111 West 57th Street, New York, New York 10019 (800) 938-4685; *The New Latin America Market Atlas*, and *The World Market Atlas*.

Euromonitor Publications Limited, 87-88 Turnmill Street, London EC1M 5QU, England; *International Marketing Data and Statistics*.

Food and Agricultural Organization of the United Nations (FAO), Via delle Terme di Caracalla, 00100 Rome, Italy (Telephone Number in U.S. (202) 653-2400); *The State of Food and Agriculture*.

G.K. Hall and Company, 70 Lincoln Street, Boston, Massachusetts 02111 (617) 423-3990; *The World in Figures*.

Inter-American Development Bank, 1300 New York Avenue, NW, Washington, D.C. 20577 (202) 623-1753; *Economic and Social Progress in Latin America*.

International Monetary Fund, 700 Nineteenth Street, NW, Washington, D.C. 20431 (202) 623-7000; *Direction of Trade Statistics, Government Finance Statistics Yearbook*, and *International Financial Statistics*.

Organization of American States (OAS), General Secretariat, Washington, D.C. 20006 (202) 458-3533; *Statistical Bulletin of the OAS*.

Statistical Office of the United Nations, Publishing Service, New York, New York 10017 (800) 253-9646; *Statistical Yearbook for Latin America and the Caribbean*.

Times Books, 201 East 50th Street, New York, New York 10022 (212) 751-2600; *The Economist Book of Vital World Statistics*.

JAMAICA - INCOME DISTRIBUTION

Statistical Office of the United Nations, Publishing Service, New York, New York 10017 (800) 253-9646; *Statistical Yearbook for Latin America and the Caribbean*.

JAMAICA - INCOME TAXES - See JAMAICA - TAXATION

JAMAICA - INDUSTRY

Euromonitor Publications Limited, 87-88 Turnmill Street, London EC1M 5QU, England; *International Marketing Data and Statistics*.

Facts on File, 460 Park Avenue South, New York, New York 10016 (800) 443-8323; *The New Book of World Rankings*.

Gale Research Incorporated, 835 Penobscot Building, Detroit, Michigan 48226 (800) 877-4253; *International Historical Statistics The Americas and Australasia*.

G.K. Hall and Company, 70 Lincoln Street, Boston, Massachusetts 02111 (617) 423-3990; *The World in Figures*.

International Labour Office, I.L.O. Publications, CH-1211, Geneva 22, Switzerland; *Yearbook of Labour Statistics*.

Statistical Office of the United Nations, Publishing Service, New York, New York 10017 (800) 253-9646; *Statistical Yearbook*, and *Economic Survey of Latin America and the Caribbean*.

Times Books, 201 East 50th Street, New York, New York 10022 (212) 751-2600; *The Economist Book of Vital World Statistics*.

World Intellectual Property Organization, 34 Chemin des Colombettes, CH-1211 Geneva 20, Switzerland; *Industrial Property Statistics*.

JAMAICA - INFANT AND MATERNAL MORTALITY

The Economist Intelligence Unit, 111 West 57th Street, New York, New York 10019 (800) 938-4685; *The New Latin America Market Atlas*.

Statistical Office of the United Nations, Publishing Service, New York, New York 10017 (800) 253-9646; *Demographic Yearbook*, and *Statistical Yearbook*.

Times Books, 201 East 50th Street, New York, New York 10022 (212) 751-2600; *The Economist Book of Vital World Statistics*.

World Health Organization, Office of Publications, Avenue Appia, CH-1211 Geneva 27, Switzerland (Telephone Number in U.S. (518) 436-9686); *World Health Statistics Annual*.

JAMAICA - INFLATIONARY FACTORS

Statistical Office of the United Nations, Publishing Service, New York, New York 10017 (800) 253-9646; *Economic Survey of Latin America and the Caribbean*.

JAMAICA - INTEREST RATES

Inter-American Development Bank, 1300 New York Avenue, NW, Washington, D.C. 20577 (202) 623-1753; *Economic and Social Progress in Latin America*.

Organization of American States (OAS), General Secretariat, Washington, D.C. 20006 (202) 458-3533; *Statistical Bulletin of the OAS*.

JAMAICA - INTERNATIONAL FINANCE

Inter-American Development Bank, 1300 New York Avenue, NW, Washington, D.C. 20577 (202) 623-1753; *Economic and Social Progress in Latin America*.

JAMAICA - INTERNATIONAL LIQUIDITY

Inter-American Development Bank, 1300 New York Avenue, NW, Washington, D.C. 20577 (202) 623-1753; *Economic and Social Progress in Latin America*.

International Monetary Fund, 700 Nineteenth Street, NW, Washington, D.C. 20431 (202) 623-7000; *International Financial Statistics*.

JAMAICA - INTERNATIONAL RESERVES

Organization of American States (OAS), General Secretariat, Washington, D.C. 20006 (202) 458-3533; *Statistical Bulletin of the OAS*.

JAMAICA - INTERNATIONAL RESERVES EXCLUDING GOLD

Inter-American Development Bank, 1300 New York Avenue, NW, Washington, D.C. 20577 (202) 623-1753; *Economic and Social Progress in Latin America*.

Statistical Office of the United Nations, Publishing Service, New York, New York 10017 (800) 253-9646; *Statistical Yearbook*.

JAMAICA - INTERNATIONAL STATISTICS

Inter-American Development Bank, 1300 New York Avenue, NW, Washington, D.C. 20577 (202) 623-1753; *Economic and Social Progress in Latin America.*

JAMAICA - INVESTMENT

Inter-American Development Bank, 1300 New York Avenue, NW, Washington, D.C. 20577 (202) 623-1753; *Economic and Social Progress in Latin America.*

Statistical Office of the United Nations, Publishing Service, New York, New York 10017 (800) 253-9646; *Statistical Yearbook for Latin America and the Caribbean.*

JAMAICA - IRON ORE PRODUCTION AND CONSUMPTION - See JAMAICA - MINING AND MINERAL PRODUCTS

JAMAICA - IRRIGATION

Euromonitor Publications Limited, 87-88 Turnmill Street, London EC1M 5QU, England; *International Marketing Data and Statistics.*

Inter-American Development Bank, 1300 New York Avenue, NW, Washington, D.C. 20577 (202) 623-1753; *Economic and Social Progress in Latin America.*

JAMAICA - LABOR

The Economist Intelligence Unit, 111 West 57th Street, New York, New York 10019 (800) 938-4685; *The New Latin America Market Atlas.*

JAMAICA - LABOR FORCE

Euromonitor Publications Limited, 87-88 Turnmill Street, London EC1M 5QU, England; *International Marketing Data and Statistics.*

Facts on File, 460 Park Avenue South, New York, New York 10016 (800) 443-8323; *The New Book of World Rankings.*

Food and Agricultural Organization of the United Nations (FAO), Via delle Terme di Caracalla, 00100 Rome, Italy (Telephone Number in U.S. (202) 653-2400); *The State of Food and Agriculture.*

Gale Research Incorporated, 835 Penobscot Building, Detroit, Michigan 48226 (800) 877-4253; *International Historical Statistics The Americas and Australasia.*

G.K. Hall and Company, 70 Lincoln Street, Boston, Massachusetts 02111 (617) 423-3990; *The World in Figures.*

Times Books, 201 East 50th Street, New York, New York 10022 (212) 751-2600; *The Economist Book of Vital World Statistics.*

JAMAICA - LABOR PRODUCTIVITY

International Labour Office, I.L.O. Publications, CH-1211, Geneva 22, Switzerland; *Yearbook of Labour Statistics.*

JAMAICA - LAND AREA

The Economist Intelligence Unit, 111 West 57th Street, New York, New York 10019 (800) 938-4685; *The New Latin America Market Atlas.*

JAMAICA - LAND USE

Euromonitor Publications Limited, 87-88 Turnmill Street, London EC1M 5QU, England; *International Marketing Data and Statistics.*

Food and Agricultural Organization of the United Nations (FAO), Via delle Terme di Caracalla, 00100 Rome, Italy (Telephone Number in U.S. (202) 653-2400); *Production Yearbook.*

G.K. Hall and Company, 70 Lincoln Street, Boston, Massachusetts 02111 (617) 423-3990; *The World in Figures.*

Inter-American Development Bank, 1300 New York Avenue, NW, Washington, D.C. 20577 (202) 623-1753; *Economic and Social Progress in Latin America.*

JAMAICA - LIBRARIES

Facts on File, 460 Park Avenue South, New York, New York 10016 (800) 443-8323; *The New Book of World Rankings.*

United Nations Educational, Scientific and Cultural Organization (UNESCO), 7 Place de Fontenoy, F-75700 Paris, France (Telephone Number in U.S. (212) 963-5981); *Statistical Yearbook.*

JAMAICA - LIFE EXPECTANCY RATE

The Economist Intelligence Unit, 111 West 57th Street, New York, New York 10019 (800) 938-4685; *The New Latin America Market Atlas.*

JAMAICA - LIVESTOCK AND POULTRY

Euromonitor Publications Limited, 87-88 Turnmill Street, London EC1M 5QU, England; *International Marketing Data and Statistics.*

Facts on File, 460 Park Avenue South, New York, New York 10016 (800) 443-8323; *The New Book of World Rankings.*

Food and Agricultural Organization of the United Nations (FAO), Via delle Terme di Caracalla, 00100 Rome, Italy (Telephone Number in U.S. (202) 653-2400); *Production Yearbook,* and *The State of Food and Agriculture.*

G.K. Hall and Company, 70 Lincoln Street, Boston, Massachusetts 02111 (617) 423-3990; *The World in Figures.*

Statistical Office of the United Nations, Publishing Service, New York, New York 10017 (800) 253-9646; *Statistical Yearbook.*

JAMAICA - LIVING LEVELS

G.K. Hall and Company, 70 Lincoln Street, Boston, Massachusetts 02111 (617) 423-3990; *The World in Figures.*

Statistical Office of the United Nations, Publishing Service, New York, New York 10017 (800) 253-9646; *Statistical Yearbook for Latin America and the Caribbean.*

Times Books, 201 East 50th Street, New York, New York 10022 (212) 751-2600; *The Economist Book of Vital World Statistics.*

JAMAICA - MAIL - NUMBER OF PIECES SENT OR RECEIVED

Statistical Office of the United Nations, Publishing Service, New York, New York 10017 (800) 253-9646; *Statistical Yearbook.*

JAMAICA - MAIN ECONOMIC INDICATORS - See JAMAICA - ECONOMY

JAMAICA - MANUFACTURING

The Economist Intelligence Unit, 111 West 57th Street, New York, New York 10019 (800) 938-4685; *The New Latin America Market Atlas.*

Facts on File, 460 Park Avenue South, New York, New York 10016 (800) 443-8323; *The New Book of World Rankings.*

G.K. Hall and Company, 70 Lincoln Street, Boston, Massachusetts 02111 (617) 423-3990; *The World in Figures.*

Inter-American Development Bank, 1300 New York Avenue, NW, Washington, D.C. 20577 (202) 623-1753; *Economic and Social Progress in Latin America.*

Statistical Office of the United Nations, Publishing Service, New York, New York 10017 (800) 253-9646; *Statistical Yearbook for Latin America and the Caribbean,* and *Statistical Yearbook.*

Times Books, 201 East 50th Street, New York, New York 10022 (212) 751-2600; *The Economist Book of Vital World Statistics.*

JAMAICA - MARRIAGE RATES

Facts on File, 460 Park Avenue South, New York, New York 10016 (800) 443-8323; *The New Book of World Rankings.*

Statistical Office of the United Nations, Publishing Service, New York, New York 10017 (800) 253-9646; *Demographic Yearbook,* and *Statistical Yearbook.*

JAMAICA - MEAT PRODUCTION - See JAMAICA - LIVESTOCK AND POULTRY

JAMAICA - MERCHANT SHIPPING

G.K. Hall and Company, 70 Lincoln Street, Boston, Massachusetts 02111 (617) 423-3990; *The World in Figures.*

Statistical Office of the United Nations, Publishing Service, New York, New York 10017 (800) 253-9646; *Statistical Yearbook.*

Times Books, 201 East 50th Street, New York, New York 10022 (212) 751-2600; *The Economist Book of Vital World Statistics.*

U.S. Department of Transportation, Maritime Administration, 400 Seventh Street, SW, Washington, D.C. 20590 (202) 366-5807; *A Statistical Analysis of the World's Merchant Fleets.*

JAMAICA - MILITARY

The Economist Intelligence Unit, 111 West 57th Street, New York, New York 10019 (800) 938-4685; *The New Latin America Market Atlas.*

G.K. Hall and Company, 70 Lincoln Street, Boston, Massachusetts 02111 (617) 423-3990; *The World in Figures.*

The International Institute for Strategic Studies, 23 Tavistock Street, London WC2E 7NQ, England; *The Military Balance.*

U.S. Arms Control and Disarmament Agency, 320 Twenty-first Street, NW, Washington, D.C. 20451 (202) 647-8677; *World Military Expenditures and Arms Transfers.*

JAMAICA - MILK PRODUCTION - See JAMAICA - DAIRY PRODUCTS

JAMAICA - MINING AND MINERAL PRODUCTS

Commodity Research Bureau, Incorporated, 75 Wall Street, New York, New York 10005 (212) 504-7754; *Commodity Year Book.*

The Economist Intelligence Unit, 111 West 57th Street, New York, New York 10019 (800) 938-4685; *The New Latin America Market Atlas.*

Facts on File, 460 Park Avenue South, New York, New York 10016 (800) 443-8323; *The New Book of World Rankings.*

G.K. Hall and Company, 70 Lincoln Street, Boston, Massachusetts 02111 (617) 423-3990; *The World in Figures.*

Inter-American Development Bank, 1300 New York Avenue, NW, Washington, D.C. 20577 (202) 623-1753; *Economic and Social Progress in Latin America.*

Statistical Office of the United Nations, Publishing Service, New York, New York 10017 (800) 253-9646; *Statistical Yearbook,* and *Statistical Yearbook for Latin America and the Caribbean.*

JAMAICA - MONEY EXCHANGE RATE

Euromonitor Publications Limited, 87-88 Turnmill Street, London EC1M 5QU, England; *International Marketing Data and Statistics.*

Inter-American Development Bank, 1300 New York Avenue, NW, Washington, D.C. 20577 (202) 623-1753; *Economic and Social Progress in Latin America.*

International Monetary Fund, 700 Nineteenth Street, NW, Washington, D.C. 20431 (202) 623-7000; *International Financial Statistics.*

Statistical Office of the United Nations, Publishing Service, New York, New York 10017 (800) 253-9646; *Statistical Yearbook.*

JAMAICA - MONEY RATES - MARKET

Inter-American Development Bank, 1300 New York Avenue, NW, Washington, D.C. 20577 (202) 623-1753; *Economic and Social Progress in Latin America.*

Statistical Office of the United Nations, Publishing Service, New York, New York 10017 (800) 253-9646; *Statistical Yearbook.*

JAMAICA - MONEY RESERVES

Euromonitor Publications Limited, 87-88 Turnmill Street, London EC1M 5QU, England; *International Marketing Data and Statistics.*

Inter-American Development Bank, 1300 New York Avenue, NW, Washington, D.C. 20577 (202) 623-1753; *Economic and Social Progress in Latin America.*

JAMAICA - MONEY SUPPLY

Euromonitor Publications Limited, 87-88 Turnmill Street, London EC1M 5QU, England; *International Marketing Data and Statistics.*

G.K. Hall and Company, 70 Lincoln Street, Boston, Massachusetts 02111 (617) 423-3990; *The World in Figures.*

Inter-American Development Bank, 1300 New York Avenue, NW, Washington, D.C. 20577 (202) 623-1753; *Economic and Social*

Progress in Latin America.

International Monetary Fund, 700 Nineteenth Street, NW, Washington, D.C. 20431 (202) 623-7000; *International Financial Statistics.*

Statistical Office of the United Nations, Publishing Service, New York, New York 10017 (800) 253-9646; *Statistical Yearbook.*

JAMAICA - MOTION PICTURES

Statistical Office of the United Nations, Publishing Service, New York, New York 10017 (800) 253-9646; *Statistical Yearbook.*

JAMAICA - MOTOR VEHICLE TAXES - See JAMAICA - TAXATION

JAMAICA - MOTOR VEHICLES IN USE

The Economist Intelligence Unit, 111 West 57th Street, New York, New York 10019 (800) 938-4685; *The New Latin America Market Atlas.*

G.K. Hall and Company, 70 Lincoln Street, Boston, Massachusetts 02111 (617) 423-3990; *The World in Figures.*

Statistical Office of the United Nations, Publishing Service, New York, New York 10017 (800) 253-9646; *Statistical Yearbook.*

Times Books, 201 East 50th Street, New York, New York 10022 (212) 751-2600; *The Economist Book of Vital World Statistics.*

JAMAICA - MULES - See JAMAICA - LIVESTOCK AND POULTRY

JAMAICA - MUSEUMS

Facts on File, 460 Park Avenue South, New York, New York 10016 (800) 443-8323; *The New Book of World Rankings.*

United Nations Educational, Scientific and Cultural Organization (UNESCO), 7 Place de Fontenoy, F-75700 Paris, France (Telephone Number in U.S. (212) 963-5981); *Statistical Yearbook.*

JAMAICA - NATALITY - See JAMAICA - BIRTH RATE

JAMAICA - NATIONAL ACCOUNTS

Gale Research Incorporated, 835 Penobscot Building, Detroit, Michigan 48226 (800) 877-4253; *International Historical Statistics The Americas and Australasia.*

Inter-American Development Bank, 1300 New York Avenue, NW, Washington, D.C. 20577 (202) 623-1753; *Economic and Social Progress in Latin America.*

International Monetary Fund, 700 Nineteenth Street, NW, Washington, D.C. 20431 (202) 623-7000; *International Financial Statistics.*

Organization of American States (OAS), General Secretariat, Washington, D.C. 20006 (202) 458-3533; *Statistical Bulletin of the OAS.*

Statistical Office of the United Nations, Publishing Service, New York, New York 10017 (800) 253-9646; *Statistical Yearbook*, and *National Accounts Statistics.*

JAMAICA - NATIONAL INCOME

Facts on File, 460 Park Avenue South, New York, New York 10016 (800) 443-8323; *The New Book of World Rankings.*

G.K. Hall and Company, 70 Lincoln Street, Boston, Massachusetts 02111 (617) 423-3990; *The World in Figures.*

Inter-American Development Bank, 1300 New York Avenue, NW, Washington, D.C. 20577 (202) 623-1753; *Economic and Social Progress in Latin America.*

Statistical Office of the United Nations, Publishing Service, New York, New York 10017 (800) 253-9646; *Statistical Yearbook*, and *Statistical Yearbook for Latin America and the Caribbean.*

JAMAICA - NATIONAL PRODUCT

Facts on File, 460 Park Avenue South, New York, New York 10016 (800) 443-8323; *The New Book of World Rankings.*

Statistical Office of the United Nations, Publishing Service, New York, New York 10017 (800) 253-9646; *Statistical Yearbook.*

JAMAICA - NATURAL GAS PRODUCTION - See JAMAICA - MINING AND MINERALS PRODUCTS

JAMAICA - NEWSPAPER PRODUCTION - See JAMAICA - FORESTRY AND FOREST PRODUCTS

JAMAICA - NEWSPRINT - See JAMAICA - FORESTRY AND FOREST PRODUCTS

JAMAICA - NUTRITION

Statistical Office of the United Nations, Publishing Service, New York, New York 10017 (800) 253-9646; *Statistical Yearbook for Latin America and the Caribbean.*

JAMAICA - OCCUPATIONS - See JAMAICA - LABOR FORCE

JAMAICA - PAPER - See JAMAICA - FORESTRY AND FOREST PRODUCTS

JAMAICA - PATENTS

Statistical Office of the United Nations, Publishing Service, New York, New York 10017 (800) 253-9646; *Statistical Yearbook.*

JAMAICA - PEANUT PRODUCTION - See JAMAICA - CROPS

JAMAICA - PESTICIDE USE

Food and Agricultural Organization of the United Nations (FAO), Via delle Terme di Caracalla, 00100 Rome, Italy (Telephone Number in U.S. (202) 653-2400); *The State of Food and Agriculture.*

JAMAICA - PETROLEUM INDUSTRY

The Economist Intelligence Unit, 111 West 57th Street, New York, New York 10019 (800) 938-4685; *The New Latin America Market Atlas.*

Facts on File, 460 Park Avenue South, New York, New York 10016 (800) 443-8323; *The New Book of World Rankings.*

Food and Agricultural Organization of the United Nations (FAO), Via delle Terme di Caracalla, 00100 Rome, Italy (Telephone Number in U.S. (202) 653-2400); *The State of Food and Agriculture.*

G.K. Hall and Company, 70 Lincoln Street, Boston, Massachusetts 02111 (617) 423-3990; *The World in Figures.*

Inter-American Development Bank, 1300 New York Avenue, NW, Washington, D.C. 20577 (202) 623-1753; *Economic and Social Progress in Latin America.*

Statistical Office of the United Nations, Publishing Service, New York, New York 10017 (800) 253-9646; *Statistical Yearbook.*

JAMAICA - PIGS - See JAMAICA - LIVESTOCK AND POULTRY

JAMAICA - POPULATION

The Economist Intelligence Unit, 111 West 57th Street, New York, New York 10019 (800) 938-4685; *The New Latin America Market Atlas,* and *The World Market Atlas.*

Euromonitor Publications Limited, 87-88 Turnmill Street, London EC1M 5QU, England; *International Marketing Data and Statistics.*

Facts on File, 460 Park Avenue South, New York, New York 10016 (800) 443-8323; *The New Book of World Rankings.*

Food and Agricultural Organization of the United Nations (FAO), Via delle Terme di Caracalla, 00100 Rome, Italy (Telephone Number in U.S. (202) 653-2400); *Production Yearbook.*

Gale Research Incorporated, 835 Penobscot Building, Detroit, Michigan 48226 (800) 877-4253; *International Historical Statistics The Americas and Australasia.* ˙

G.K. Hall and Company, 70 Lincoln Street, Boston, Massachusetts 02111 (617) 423-3990; *The World in Figures.*

Inter-American Development Bank, 1300 New York Avenue, NW, Washington, D.C. 20577 (202) 623-1753; *Economic and Social Progress in Latin America.*

International Labour Office, I.L.O. Publications, CH-1211, Geneva 22, Switzerland; *Yearbook of Labour Statistics.*

Organization of American States (OAS), General Secretariat, Washington, D.C. 20006 (202) 458-3533; *Statistical Bulletin of the OAS.*

Statistical Office of the United Nations, Publishing Service, New York, New York 10017 (800) 253-9646; *Demographic Yearbook, Statistical Yearbook,* and *Statistical Yearbook for Latin America and the Caribbean.*

Times Books, 201 East 50th Street, New York, New York 10022 (212) 751-2600; *The Economist Book of Vital World Statistics.*

United Nations Educational, Scientific and Cultural Organization (UNESCO), 7 Place de Fontenoy, F-75700 Paris, France (Telephone Number in U.S. (212) 963-5981); *Statistical Yearbook.*

U.S. Arms Control and Disarmament Agency, 320 Twenty-first Street, NW, Washington, D.C. 20451 (202) 647-8677; *World Military Expenditures and Arms Transfers.*

World Health Organization, Office of Publications, Avenue Appia, CH-1211 Geneva 27, Switzerland (Telephone Number in U.S. (518) 436-9686); *World Health Statistics Annual.*

JAMAICA - POST OFFICES

Facts on File, 460 Park Avenue South, New York, New York 10016 (800) 443-8323; *The New Book of World Rankings.*

JAMAICA - POTATO PRODUCTION - See JAMAICA - CROPS

JAMAICA - POWER PRODUCTION INDUSTRY

Statistical Office of the United Nations, Publishing Service, New York, New York 10017 (800) 253-9646; *Statistical Yearbook.*

JAMAICA - PRICES

Facts on File, 460 Park Avenue South, New York, New York 10016 (800) 443-8323; *The New Book of World Rankings.*

Food and Agricultural Organization of the United Nations (FAO), Via delle Terme di Caracalla, 00100 Rome, Italy (Telephone Number in U.S. (202) 653-2400); *Production Yearbook,* and *The State of Food and Agriculture.*

Gale Research Incorporated, 835 Penobscot Building, Detroit, Michigan 48226 (800) 877-4253; *International Historical Statistics The Americas and Australasia.*

G.K. Hall and Company, 70 Lincoln Street, Boston, Massachusetts 02111 (617) 423-3990; *The World in Figures.*

International Labour Office, I.L.O. Publications, CH-1211, Geneva 22, Switzerland; *Yearbook of Labour Statistics.*

International Monetary Fund, 700 Nineteenth Street, NW, Washington, D.C. 20431 (202) 623-7000; *International Financial Statistics.*

Statistical Office of the United Nations, Publishing Service, New York, New York 10017 (800) 253-9646; *Economic Survey of Latin America and the Caribbean,* and *Statistical Yearbook for Latin America and the Caribbean.*

JAMAICA - PRINTING AND WRITING PAPER - See JAMAICA - FORESTRY AND FOREST PRODUCTS

JAMAICA - PRODUCTION

Facts on File, 460 Park Avenue South, New York, New York 10016 (800) 443-8323; *The New Book of World Rankings.*

G.K. Hall and Company, 70 Lincoln Street, Boston, Massachusetts 02111 (617) 423-3990; *The World in Figures.*

JAMAICA - PRODUCTIVITY

Euromonitor Publications Limited, 87-88 Turnmill Street, London EC1M 5QU, England; *International Marketing Data and Statistics.*

JAMAICA - PROPERTY TAXES

Inter-American Development Bank, 1300 New York Avenue, NW, Washington, D.C. 20577 (202) 623-1753; *Economic and Social Progress in Latin America.*

International Monetary Fund, 700 Nineteenth Street, NW, Washington, D.C. 20431 (202) 623-7000; *Government Finance Statistics Yearbook.*

JAMAICA - PUBLIC CONSUMPTION FUND

Inter-American Development Bank, 1300 New York Avenue, NW, Washington, D.C. 20577 (202) 623-1753; *Economic and Social Progress in Latin America.*

JAMAICA - PUBLIC EXPENDITURE

Inter-American Development Bank, 1300 New York Avenue, NW, Washington, D.C. 20577 (202) 623-1753; *Economic and Social Progress in Latin America.*

Organization of American States (OAS), General Secretariat, Washington, D.C. 20006 (202) 458-3533; *Statistical Bulletin of the OAS.*

Statistical Office of the United Nations, Publishing Service, New York, New York 10017 (800) 253-9646; *Statistical Yearbook for Latin America and the Caribbean.*

JAMAICA - PUBLIC FINANCE

Facts on File, 460 Park Avenue South, New York, New York 10016 (800) 443-8323; *The New Book of World Rankings.*

Inter-American Development Bank, 1300 New York Avenue, NW, Washington, D.C. 20577 (202) 623-1753; *Economic and Social Progress in Latin America.*

Organization of American States (OAS), General Secretariat, Washington, D.C. 20006 (202) 458-3533; *Statistical Bulletin of the OAS.*

JAMAICA - PUBLIC REVENUES

Inter-American Development Bank, 1300 New York Avenue, NW, Washington, D.C. 20577 (202) 623-1753; *Economic and Social Progress in Latin America.*

Organization of American States (OAS), General Secretariat, Washington, D.C. 20006 (202) 458-3533; *Statistical Bulletin of the OAS.*

JAMAICA - RADIO BROADCASTING - See JAMAICA - BROADCASTING

JAMAICA - RADIO RECEIVER PRODUCTION

Statistical Office of the United Nations, Publishing Service, New York, New York 10017 (800) 253-9646; *Statistical Yearbook.*

JAMAICA - RAILWAYS

The Economist Intelligence Unit, 111 West 57th Street, New York, New York 10019 (800) 938-4685; *The New Latin America Market Atlas.*

G.K. Hall and Company, 70 Lincoln Street, Boston, Massachusetts 02111 (617) 423-3990; *The World in Figures.*

Jane's Information Group, Sentinel House, 163 Brighton Road, Coulsdon, Surrey CR5 2NH, England (Telephone Number in U.S. (703) 683-3700); *Jane's World Railways.*

Statistical Office of the United Nations, Publishing Service, New York, New York 10017 (800) 253-9646; *Statistical Yearbook.*

JAMAICA - RELIGION

Facts on File, 460 Park Avenue South, New York, New York 10016 (800) 443-8323; *The New Book of World Rankings.*

JAMAICA - RENT PRICES

International Labour Office, I.L.O. Publications, CH-1211, Geneva 22, Switzerland; *Yearbook of Labour Statistics.*

JAMAICA - RESERVES EXCLUDING GOLD

The Economist Intelligence Unit, 111 West 57th Street, New York, New York 10019 (800) 938-4685; *The New Latin America Market Atlas.*

JAMAICA - RETAIL TRADE

G.K. Hall and Company, 70 Lincoln Street, Boston, Massachusetts 02111 (617) 423-3990; *The World in Figures.*

Inter-American Development Bank, 1300 New York Avenue, NW, Washington, D.C. 20577 (202) 623-1753; *Economic and Social Progress in Latin America.*

JAMAICA - RICE PRODUCTION - See JAMAICA - CROPS

JAMAICA - ROOT AND TUBER PRODUCTION - See JAMAICA CROPS

JAMAICA - ROUNDWOOD PRODUCTION - See JAMAICA - FORESTRY AND FOREST PRODUCTS

JAMAICA - RUBBER PRODUCTION

Facts on File, 460 Park Avenue South, New York, New York 10016 (800) 443-8323; *The New Book of World Rankings.*

JAMAICA - SAWNWOOD PRODUCTION - See JAMAICA - FORESTRY AND FOREST PRODUCTS

JAMAICA - SCIENCE AND TECHNOLOGY - EXPENDITURE FOR RESEARCH

Statistical Office of the United Nations, Publishing Service, New York, New York 10017 (800) 253-9646; *Statistical Yearbook.*

JAMAICA - SCIENTISTS AND TECHNICIANS

Statistical Office of the United Nations, Publishing Service, New York, New York 10017 (800) 253-9646; *Statistical Yearbook.*

JAMAICA - SENIOR CITIZENS

Facts on File, 460 Park Avenue South, New York, New York 10016 (800) 443-8323; *The New Book of World Rankings.*

JAMAICA - SHEEP - See JAMAICA - LIVESTOCK AND POULTRY

JAMAICA - SILVER PRODUCTION - See JAMAICA - MINING AND MINERAL PRODUCTS

JAMAICA - SOCIAL DATA

Facts on File, 460 Park Avenue South, New York, New York 10016 (800) 443-8323; *The New Book of World Rankings.*

G.K. Hall and Company, 70 Lincoln Street, Boston, Massachusetts 02111 (617) 423-3990; *The World in Figures.*

JAMAICA - SOCIAL SECURITY

Inter-American Development Bank, 1300 New York Avenue, NW, Washington, D.C. 20577 (202) 623-1753; *Economic and Social Progress in Latin America.*

International Monetary Fund, 700 Nineteenth Street, NW, Washington, D.C. 20431 (202) 623-7000; *Government Finance Statistics Yearbook.*

JAMAICA - SOCIOECONOMIC DATA

Inter-American Development Bank, 1300 New York Avenue, NW, Washington, D.C. 20577 (202) 623-1753; *Economic and Social Progress in Latin America.*

JAMAICA - SOYBEAN PRODUCTION - See JAMAICA - CROPS

JAMAICA - STAMP TAXES AND DUTIES - See JAMAICA - SEE TAXATION

JAMAICA - STATE BUDGET REVENUE AND EXPENDITURES

Euromonitor Publications Limited, 87-88 Turnmill Street, London EC1M 5QU, England; *International Marketing Data and Statistics.*

Inter-American Development Bank, 1300 New York Avenue, NW, Washington, D.C. 20577 (202) 623-1753; *Economic and Social Progress in Latin America.*

JAMAICA - STEEL - See JAMAICA - MINING AND MINERAL PRODUCTS

JAMAICA - STOCKS - COMMODITY - MARKET PRICE - INDEX

Food and Agricultural Organization of the United Nations (FAO), Via delle Terme di Caracalla, 00100 Rome, Italy (Telephone Number in U.S. (202) 653-2400); *The State of Food and Agriculture.*

JAMAICA - SUGAR - See JAMAICA - CROPS

JAMAICA - SULPHURIC ACID PRODUCTION - See JAMAICA - MINING AND MINERAL PRODUCTS

JAMAICA - TAXATION

G.K. Hall and Company, 70 Lincoln Street, Boston, Massachusetts 02111 (617) 423-3990; *The World in Figures.*

Inter-American Development Bank, 1300 New York Avenue, NW, Washington, D.C. 20577 (202) 623-1753; *Economic and Social Progress in Latin America.*

International Monetary Fund, 700 Nineteenth Street, NW, Washington, D.C. 20431 (202) 623-7000; *Government Finance Statistics Yearbook.*

Statistical Office of the United Nations, Publishing Service, New York, New York 10017 (800) 253-9646; *Statistical Yearbook for Latin America and the Caribbean.*

JAMAICA - TELEPHONES IN USE

American Telephone and Telegraph Company, 26 Parsippany Road, Whippany, New Jersey 07981 (800) 338-4038; *The World's Telephones.*

The Economist Intelligence Unit, 111 West 57th Street, New York, New York 10019 (800) 938-4685; *The New Latin America Market Atlas.*

G.K. Hall and Company, 70 Lincoln Street, Boston, Massachusetts 02111 (617) 423-3990; *The World in Figures.*

Statistical Office of the United Nations, Publishing Service, New York, New York 10017 (800) 253-9646; *Statistical Yearbook.*

JAMAICA - TELEVISION BROADCASTING - See JAMAICA - BROADCASTING

JAMAICA - TELEVISION RECEIVER PRODUCTION

Statistical Office of the United Nations, Publishing Service, New York, New York 10017 (800) 253-9646; *Statistical Yearbook.*

JAMAICA - TEXTILE INDUSTRY

G.K. Hall and Company, 70 Lincoln Street, Boston, Massachusetts 02111 (617) 423-3990; *The World in Figures.*

Statistical Office of the United Nations, Publishing Service, New York, New York 10017 (800) 253-9646; *Statistical Yearbook.*

JAMAICA - THEATRE

United Nations Educational, Scientific and Cultural Organization (UNESCO), 7 Place de Fontenoy, F-75700 Paris, France (Telephone Number in U.S. (212) 963-5981); *Statistical Yearbook.*

JAMAICA - TIRE (MOTOR VEHICLE) PRODUCTION

Statistical Office of the United Nations, Publishing Service, New York, New York 10017 (800) 253-9646; *Statistical Yearbook.*

JAMAICA - TOBACCO PRODUCTION

Facts on File, 460 Park Avenue South, New York, New York 10016 (800) 443-8323; *The New Book of World Rankings.*

Statistical Office of the United Nations, Publishing Service, New York, New York 10017 (800) 253-9646; *Statistical Yearbook.*

JAMAICA - TOURISM

The Economist Intelligence Unit, 111 West 57th Street, New York, New York 10019 (800) 938-4685; *The New Latin America Market Atlas.*

Facts on File, 460 Park Avenue South, New York, New York 10016 (800) 443-8323; *The New Book of World Rankings.*

G.K. Hall and Company, 70 Lincoln Street, Boston, Massachusetts 02111 (617) 423-3990; *The World in Figures.*

Organization of American States (OAS), General Secretariat, Washington, D.C. 20006 (202) 458-3533; *Statistical Bulletin of the OAS.*

Statistical Office of the United Nations, Publishing Service, New York, New York 10017 (800) 253-9646; *Statistical Yearbook,* and *Statistical Yearbook for Latin America and the Caribbean.*

Times Books, 201 East 50th Street, New York, New York 10022 (212) 751-2600; *The Economist Book of Vital World Statistics.*

World Tourism Organization, Calle Capitan Haya 42, E-28020 Madrid, Spain; *Yearbook of Tourism Statistics*.

JAMAICA - TRACTORS IN USE

The Economist Intelligence Unit, 111 West 57th Street, New York, New York 10019 (800) 938-4685; *The New Latin America Market Atlas*.

Statistical Office of the United Nations, Publishing Service, New York, New York 10017 (800) 253-9646; *Statistical Yearbook*.

JAMAICA - TRADE - See JAMAICA - FOREIGN TRADE

JAMAICA - TRADEMARKS AND SERVICE MARKS

Statistical Office of the United Nations, Publishing Service, New York, New York 10017 (800) 253-9646; *Statistical Yearbook*.

JAMAICA - TRANSPORTATION AND COMMUNICATIONS

The Economist Intelligence Unit, 111 West 57th Street, New York, New York 10019 (800) 938-4685; *The New Latin America Market Atlas*.

Facts on File, 460 Park Avenue South, New York, New York 10016 (800) 443-8323; *The New Book of World Rankings*.

Gale Research Incorporated, 835 Penobscot Building, Detroit, Michigan 48226 (800) 877-4253; *International Historical Statistics The Americas and Australasia*.

G.K. Hall and Company, 70 Lincoln Street, Boston, Massachusetts 02111 (617) 423-3990; *The World in Figures*.

Inter-American Development Bank, 1300 New York Avenue, NW, Washington, D.C. 20577 (202) 623-1753; *Economic and Social Progress in Latin America*.

Statistical Office of the United Nations, Publishing Service, New York, New York 10017 (800) 253-9646; *Statistical Yearbook for Latin America and the Caribbean*.

JAMAICA - TREASURY BILL RATES

Organization of American States (OAS), General Secretariat, Washington, D.C. 20006 (202) 458-3533; *Statistical Bulletin of the OAS*.

JAMAICA - UNEMPLOYMENT

The Economist Intelligence Unit, 111 West 57th Street, New York, New York 10019 (800) 938-4685; *The New Latin America Market Atlas*.

Euromonitor Publications Limited, 87-88 Turnmill Street, London EC1M 5QU, England; *International Marketing Data and Statistics*.

International Labour Office, I.L.O. Publications, CH-1211, Geneva 22, Switzerland; *Yearbook of Labour Statistics*.

Organization of American States (OAS), General Secretariat, Washington, D.C. 20006 (202) 458-3533; *Statistical Bulletin of the OAS*.

Statistical Office of the United Nations, Publishing Service, New York, New York 10017 (800) 253-9646; *Statistical Yearbook*.

JAMAICA - VITAL STATISTICS

Euromonitor Publications Limited, 87-88 Turnmill Street, London EC1M 5QU, England; *International Marketing Data and Statistics*.

Gale Research Incorporated, 835 Penobscot Building, Detroit, Michigan 48226 (800) 877-4253; *International Historical Statistics The Americas and Australasia*.

G.K. Hall and Company, 70 Lincoln Street, Boston, Massachusetts 02111 (617) 423-3990; *The World in Figures*.

Statistical Office of the United Nations, Publishing Service, New York, New York 10017 (800) 253-9646; *Statistical Yearbook*.

World Health Organization, Office of Publications, Avenue Appia, CH-1211 Geneva 27, Switzerland (Telephone Number in U.S. (518) 436-9686); *World Health Statistics Annual*.

JAMAICA - WAGES

G.K. Hall and Company, 70 Lincoln Street, Boston, Massachusetts 02111 (617) 423-3990; *The World in Figures*.

International Labour Office, I.L.O. Publications, CH-1211, Geneva 22, Switzerland; *Yearbook of Labour Statistics*.

Organization of American States (OAS), General Secretariat, Washington, D.C. 20006 (202) 458-3533; *Statistical Bulletin of the OAS*.

JAMAICA - WEATHER

Facts on File, 460 Park Avenue South, New York, New York 10016 (800) 443-8323; *The New Book of World Rankings*.

G.K. Hall and Company, 70 Lincoln Street, Boston, Massachusetts 02111 (617) 423-3990; *The World in Figures*.

JAMAICA - WELFARE

Inter-American Development Bank, 1300 New York Avenue, NW, Washington, D.C. 20577 (202) 623-1753; *Economic and Social Progress in Latin America*.

International Monetary Fund, 700 Nineteenth Street, NW, Washington, D.C. 20431 (202) 623-7000; *Government Finance Statistics Yearbook*.

JAMAICA - WHEAT PRODUCTION AND PRICES - See JAMAICA - CROPS

JAMAICA - WHOLESALE PRICES

Inter-American Development Bank, 1300 New York Avenue, NW, Washington, D.C. 20577 (202) 623-1753; *Economic and Social Progress in Latin America*.

JAMAICA - WHOLESALE TRADE

Inter-American Development Bank, 1300 New York Avenue, NW, Washington, D.C. 20577 (202) 623-1753; *Economic and Social Progress in Latin America*.

JAMAICA - WINE PRODUCTION

Facts on File, 460 Park Avenue South, New York, New York 10016 (800) 443-8323; *The New Book of World Rankings*.

JAMAICA - WOOL PRODUCTION

Facts on File, 460 Park Avenue South, New York, New York 10016 (800) 443-8323; *The New Book of World Rankings.*

Japan - National Statistical Office

Statistics Bureau, Management and Coordination Agency, 19-1 Wakamatsucho, Shinjuku, Tokyo 162, Japan.

Japan - Primary Statistics Sources

Management and Coordination Agency, Statistics Bureau, Tokyo, Japan; *Japan Statistical Yearbook, Monthly Statistics of Japan,* and *Statistical Indicators on Social Life.*

Japan - Databases

I.N. Industry Statistics Database, I.N. Information Corporation, Database Center Building, 6F, 1-7-18, Konan, Minato-ku, Tokyo 108, Japan. Subject coverage: Japanese industry statistics.

Japanese Economic Situation, Nikko Research Center, 1-1-3 Marunouchi, Chiyoda-ku, Tokyo 100, Japan. Subject coverage: Time series of macroeconomic Japanese data.

Nihon Keizai Shimbun, Inc. (NIKKEI), Databook Bureau, 1-9-5 Ohtemachi, Chiyoda-ku, Tokyo 100, Japan. Offers the following databases: (1) NEEDS-Economy - Data on major economic statistics for the Japanese economy; (2) NEEDS-Money - Data on money supply, interest rates, and money flow.

NRI/E Japan Economic and Business Database, Nomura Research Institute, Financial Engineering Department, Data Bank Section, Dai-Ni Yamaman Building, 6-7 Koami-Cho, Nihonbashi, Chuo-ku, Tokyo 103, Japan. Subject coverage: Japan economy and business.

Research/Report Reference Database, Mainichi Newspapers, Media Planning Division, 1-1-1 Hitotsubashi, Chiyoda-ku, Tokyo 100-51, Japan. Subject coverage: Statistical research and policy information.

JAPAN - ABORTIONS

Statistical Office of the United Nations, Publishing Service, New York, New York 10017 (800) 253-9646; *Demographic Yearbook.*

JAPAN - AGRICULTURE

Euromonitor Publications Limited, 87-88 Turnmill Street, London EC1M 5QU, England; *International Marketing Data and Statistics,* and *The Pacific Basin: An Economic Handbook.*

European Community Information Service, 2100 M Street, NW, Washington, D.C. 20037 (202) 862-9500; *Basic Statistics of the Community.*

Facts on File, 460 Park Avenue South, New York, New York 10016 (800) 443-8323; *The New Book of World Rankings.*

Food and Agricultural Organization of the United Nations (FAO), Via delle Terme di Caracalla, 00100 Rome, Italy (Telephone Number in U.S. (202) 653-2400); *Production Yearbook,* and *The State of Food and Agriculture.*

G.K. Hall and Company, 70 Lincoln Street, Boston, Massachusetts 02111 (617) 423-3990; *The World in Figures.*

National Technical Information Service, 5285 Port Royal Road, Springfield, Virginia 22161 (703) 487-4600; *Handbook of Economic Statistics.*

Organisation for Economic Co-operation and Development (OECD), 2 rue Andre-Pascal, 75 Paris 16, France (Telephone Number in U.S. (202) 785-6323); *Economic Accounts for Agriculture, Indicators of Industrial Activity,* and *OECD Economic Surveys: Japan.*

Statistical Office of the United Nations, Publishing Service, New York, New York 10017 (800) 253-9646; *Statistical Yearbook,* and *Statistical Yearbook for Asia and the Pacific.*

Statistics Bureau, Management and Coordination Agency, Japan; *Statistical Indicators on Social Life.*

Times Books, 201 East 50th Street, New York, New York 10022 (212) 751-2600; *The Economist Book of Vital World Statistics.*

JAPAN - AIRLINE SERVICE

The Economist Intelligence Unit (Asia) Limited, 10th Floor, Luk Kwok Centre, 72 Gloucester Road, Wanchai, Hong Kong (Phone Number in U.S. (800) 938-4685); *Asian Market Atlas.*

European Community Information Service, 2100 M Street, NW, Washington, D.C. 20037 (202) 862-9500; *Basic Statistics of the Community.*

Facts on File, 460 Park Avenue South, New York, New York 10016 (800) 443-8323; *The New Book of World Rankings.*

G.K. Hall and Company, 70 Lincoln Street, Boston, Massachusetts 02111 (617) 423-3990; *The World in Figures.*

International Civil Aviation Organization, 1000 Sherbrooke Street West, Suite 400, Montreal, Quebec H3A 2R2, Canada (514) 285-8219; *Civil Aviation Statistics of the World.*

National Technical Information Service, 5285 Port Royal Road, Springfield, Virginia 22161 (703) 487-4600; *Handbook of Economic Statistics.*

Organisation for Economic Co-operation and Development (OECD), 2 rue Andre-Pascal, 75 Paris 16, France (Telephone Number in U.S. (202) 785-6323); *Tourism Policy and International Tourism in OECD Member Countries.*

Statistical Office of the United Nations, Publishing Service, New York, New York 10017 (800) 253-9646; *Statistical Yearbook.*

Times Books, 201 East 50th Street, New York, New York 10022 (212) 751-2600; *The Economist Book of Vital World Statistics.*

JAPAN - ALMOND PRODUCTION - See JAPAN - CROPS

JAPAN - ALUMINUM PRODUCTION AND CONSUMPTION - See JAPAN - MINING AND MINERAL PRODUCTS

JAPAN - ANIMAL FEEDINGSTUFFS

Organisation for Economic Co-operation and Development (OECD), 2 rue Andre-Pascal, 75 Paris 16, France (Telephone Number in U.S. (202) 785-6323); *Foreign Trade by Commodities.*

Statistical Office of the United Nations, Publishing Service, New York, New York 10017 (800) 253-9646; *Statistical Yearbook.*

JAPAN - ANIMAL HEALTH

Food and Agricultural Organization of the United Nations (FAO), Via delle Terme di Caracalla, 00100, Rome, Italy (Telephone Number in U.S. (202) 653-2400); *Animal Health Yearbook*.

JAPAN - ANTIMONY AND ANTIMONY ORE - See JAPAN - MINING AND MINERAL PRODUCTS

JAPAN - APPLE PRODUCTION - See JAPAN - CROPS

JAPAN - AREA AND DENSITY OF POPULATION

Euromonitor Publications Limited, 87-88 Turnmill Street, London EC1M 5QU, England; *International Marketing Data and Statistics*, and *The Pacific Basin: An Economic Handbook*.

European Community Information Service, 2100 M Street, NW, Washington, D.C. 20037 (202) 862-9500; *Basic Statistics of the Community*.

Facts on File, 460 Park Avenue South, New York, New York 10016 (800) 443-8323; *The New Book of World Rankings*.

Food and Agricultural Organization of the United Nations (FAO), Via delle Terme di Caracalla, 00100 Rome, Italy (Telephone Number in U.S. (202) 653-2400); *The State of Food and Agriculture*.

G.K. Hall and Company, 70 Lincoln Street, Boston, Massachusetts 02111 (617) 423-3990; *The World in Figures*.

National Technical Information Service, 5285 Port Royal Road, Springfield, Virginia 22161 (703) 487-4600; *Handbook of Economic Statistics*.

Statistical Office of the United Nations, Publishing Service, New York, New York 10017 (800) 253-9646; *Statistical Yearbook*.

Statistics Bureau, Management and Coordination Agency, Japan; *Statistical Indicators on Social Life*.

Times Books, 201 East 50th Street, New York, New York 10022 (212) 751-2600; *The Economist Book of Vital World Statistics*.

United Nations Educational, Scientific and Cultural Organization (UNESCO), 7 Place de Fontenoy, F-75700 Paris, France (Telephone Number in U.S. (212) 963-5981); *Statistical Yearbook*.

JAPAN - ARMS EXPORTS AND IMPORTS

U.S. Arms Control and Disarmament Agency, 320 Twenty-first Street, NW, Washington, D.C. 20451 (202) 647-8677; *World Military Expenditures and Arms Transfers*.

JAPAN - ARSENIC PRODUCTION AND CONSUMPTION - See JAPAN - MINING AND MINERAL PRODUCTS

JAPAN - BALANCE OF PAYMENTS

The Economist Intelligence Unit, 111 West 57th Street, New York, New York 10019 (800) 938-4685; *The World Market Atlas*.

European Community Information Service, 2100 M Street, NW, Washington, D.C. 20037 (202) 862-9500; *Basic Statistics of the Community*.

G.K. Hall and Company, 70 Lincoln Street, Boston, Massachusetts 02111 (617) 423-3990; *The World in Figures*.

International Monetary Fund, 700 Nineteenth Street, NW, Washington, D.C. 20431 (202) 623-7000; *Balance of Payments Yearbook*, and *International Financial Statistics*.

National Technical Information Service, 5285 Port Royal Road, Springfield, Virginia 22161 (703) 487-4600; *Handbook of Economic Statistics*.

Organisation for Economic Co-operation and Development (OECD), 2 rue Andre-Pascal, 75 Paris 16, France (Telephone Number in U.S. (202) 785-6323); *Economic Outlook, Geographical Distribution of Financial Flows to Developing Countries, Main Economic Indicators - Historical Statistics*, and *OECD Economic Surveys: Japan*.

Times Books, 201 East 50th Street, New York, New York 10022 (212) 751-2600; *The Economist Book of Vital World Statistics*.

JAPAN - BANKING

Facts on File, 460 Park Avenue South, New York, New York 10016 (800) 443-8323; *The New Book of World Rankings*.

G.K. Hall and Company, 70 Lincoln Street, Boston, Massachusetts 02111 (617) 423-3990; *The World in Figures*.

International Monetary Fund, 700 Nineteenth Street, NW, Washington, D.C. 20431 (202) 623-7000; *Government Finance Statistics Yearbook*, and *International Financial Statistics*.

National Technical Information Service, 5285 Port Royal Road, Springfield, Virginia 22161 (703) 487-4600; *Handbook of Economic Statistics*.

Organisation for Economic Co-operation and Development (OECD), 2 rue Andre-Pascal, 75 Paris 16, France (Telephone Number in U.S. (202) 785-6323); *Economic Outlook, Financial Market Trends*, and *OECD Economic Surveys: Japan*.

Statistical Office of the United Nations, Publishing Service, New York, New York 10017 (800) 253-9646; *Statistical Yearbook*.

JAPAN - BARLEY PRODUCTION - See JAPAN - CROPS

JAPAN - BAUXITE PRODUCTION AND CONSUMPTION - See JAPAN - MINING AND MINERAL PRODUCTS

JAPAN - BEER PRODUCTION

Facts on File, 460 Park Avenue South, New York, New York 10016 (800) 443-8323; *The New Book of World Rankings*.

Statistical Office of the United Nations, Publishing Service, New York, New York 10017 (800) 253-9646; *Statistical Yearbook*.

JAPAN - BEVERAGES - PRODUCTION INDEX

Organisation for Economic Co-operation and Development (OECD), 2 rue Andre-Pascal, 75 Paris 16, France (Telephone Number in U.S. (202) 785-6323); *Indicators of Industrial Activity*.

JAPAN - BIRTH RATE

The Economist Intelligence Unit (Asia) Limited, 10th Floor, Luk Kwok Centre, 72 Gloucester Road, Wanchai, Hong Kong (Phone Number in U.S. (800) 938-4685); *Asian Market Atlas*.

Euromonitor Publications Limited, 87-88 Turnmill Street, London EC1M 5QU, England; *The Pacific Basin: An Economic Handbook*.

European Community Information Service, 2100 M Street, NW, Washington, D.C. 20037 (202) 862-9500; *Basic Statistics of the Community.*

Facts on File, 460 Park Avenue South, New York, New York 10016 (800) 443-8323; *The New Book of World Rankings.*

Organisation for Economic Co-operation and Development (OECD), 2 rue Andre-Pascal, 75 Paris 16, France (Telephone Number in U.S. (202) 785-6323); *Labour Force Statistics.*

Statistics Bureau, Management and Coordination Agency, Japan; *Statistical Indicators on Social Life.*

Statistical Office of the United Nations, Publishing Service, New York, New York 10017 (800) 253-9646; *Demographic Yearbook,* and *Statistical Yearbook.*

Times Books, 201 East 50th Street, New York, New York 10022 (212) 751-2600; *The Economist Book of Vital World Statistics.*

World Health Organization, Office of Publications, Avenue Appia, CH-1211 Geneva 27, Switzerland (Telephone Number in U.S. (518) 436-9686); *World Health Statistics Annual.*

JAPAN - BISMUTH PRODUCTION AND CONSUMPTION - See JAPAN - MINING AND MINERAL PRODUCTS

JAPAN - BONDS

European Community Information Service, 2100 M Street, NW, Washington, D.C. 20037 (202) 862-9500; *Basic Statistics of the Community.*

G.K. Hall and Company, 70 Lincoln Street, Boston, Massachusetts 02111 (617) 423-3990; *The World in Figures.*

Organisation for Economic Co-operation and Development (OECD), 2 rue Andre-Pascal, 75 Paris 16, France (Telephone Number in U.S. (202) 785-6323); *Financial Market Trends.*

Statistical Office of the United Nations, Publishing Service, New York, New York 10017 (800) 253-9646; *Statistical Yearbook.*

JAPAN - BOOK PRODUCTION

G.K. Hall and Company, 70 Lincoln Street, Boston, Massachusetts 02111 (617) 423-3990; *The World in Figures.*

Organisation for Economic Co-operation and Development (OECD), 2 rue Andre-Pascal, 75 Paris 16, France (Telephone Number in U.S. (202) 785-6323); *Indicators of Industrial Activity.*

United Nations Educational, Scientific and Cultural Organization (UNESCO), 7 Place de Fontenoy, F-75700 Paris, France (Telephone Number in U.S. (212) 963-5981); *Statistical Yearbook.*

JAPAN - BROADCASTING

Billboard Limited, Post Office Box 9027, 1006 AA Amsterdam, The Netherlands (Telephone Number in U.S. (212) 764-7300); *World Radio TV Handbook.*

The Economist Intelligence Unit (Asia) Limited, 10th Floor, Luk Kwok Centre, 72 Gloucester Road, Wanchai, Hong Kong (Phone Number in U.S. (800) 938-4685); *Asian Market Atlas.*

European Community Information Service, 2100 M Street, NW, Washington, D.C. 20037 (202) 862-9500; *Basic Statistics of the*

Community.

Facts on File, 460 Park Avenue South, New York, New York (800) 443-8323; *The New Book of World Rankings.*

G.K. Hall and Company, 70 Lincoln Street, Boston, Massachusetts 02111 (617) 423-3990; *The World in Figures.*

Times Books, 201 East 50th Street, New York, New York 10022 (212) 751-2600; *The Economist Book of Vital World Statistics.*

United Nations Educational, Scientific and Cultural Organization (UNESCO), 7 Place de Fontenoy, F-75700 Paris, France (Telephone Number in U.S. (212) 963-5981); *Statistical Yearbook.*

JAPAN - BUSINESS

European Community Information Service, 2100 M Street, NW, Washington, D.C. 20037 (202) 862-9500; *Basic Statistics of the Community.*

G.K. Hall and Company, 70 Lincoln Street, Boston, Massachusetts 02111 (617) 423-3990; *The World in Figures.*

JAPAN - BUTTER - See JAPAN - DAIRY PRODUCTS

JAPAN - CABBAGE PRODUCTION - See JAPAN - CROPS

JAPAN - CADMIUM PRODUCTION AND CONSUMPTION - See JAPAN - MINING AND MINERAL PRODUCTS

JAPAN - CALORIE SUPPLY

Food and Agricultural Organization of the United Nations (FAO), Via delle Terme di Caracalla, 00100 Rome, Italy (Telephone Number in U.S. (202) 653-2400); *The State of Food and Agriculture.*

JAPAN - CAPITAL INVESTMENT

National Technical Information Service, 5285 Port Royal Road, Springfield, Virginia 22161 (703) 487-4600; *Handbook of Economic Statistics.*

Organisation for Economic Co-operation and Development (OECD), 2 rue Andre-Pascal, 75 Paris 16, France (Telephone Number in U.S. (202) 785-6323); *Economic Outlook,* and *Financial Market Trends.*

JAPAN - CAPITAL REVENUE

International Monetary Fund, 700 Nineteenth Street, NW, Washington, D.C. 20431 (202) 623-7000; *Government Finance Statistics Yearbook.*

Organisation for Economic Co-operation and Development (OECD), 2 rue Andre-Pascal, 75 Paris 16, France (Telephone Number in U.S. (202) 785-6323); *Economic Outlook,* and *Financial Market Trends.*

JAPAN - CASHEW NUT PRODUCTION - See JAPAN - CROPS

JAPAN - CASTOR BEAN PRODUCTION - See JAPAN - CROPS

JAPAN - CATTLE - See JAPAN - LIVESTOCK AND POULTRY

JAPAN - CAULIFLOWER PRODUCTION - See JAPAN - CROPS

JAPAN - CAUSTIC SODA PRODUCTION

European Community Information Service, 2100 M Street, NW, Washington, D.C. 20037 (202) 862-9500; *Basic Statistics of the*

Community.

National Technical Information Service, 5285 Port Royal Road, Springfield, Virginia 22161 (703) 487-4600; *Handbook of Economic Statistics.*

Organisation for Economic Co-operation and Development (OECD), 2 rue Andre-Pascal, 75 Paris 16, France (Telephone Number in U.S. (202) 785-6323); *Indicators of Industrial Activity.*

Statistical Office of the United Nations, Publishing Service, New York, New York 10017 (800) 253-9646; *Statistical Yearbook.*

JAPAN - CEMENT PRODUCTION - See JAPAN - MINING AND MINERAL PRODUCTS

JAPAN - CEREAL PRODUCTION - See JAPAN - CROPS

JAPAN - CHEESE - See JAPAN - DAIRY PRODUCTS

JAPAN - CHEMICAL (ORGANIC) PRODUCTION - See JAPAN - MINING AND MINERAL PRODUCTS

JAPAN - CHESTNUT PRODUCTION - See JAPAN - CROPS

JAPAN - CHICKENS - See JAPAN - LIVESTOCK AND POULTRY

JAPAN - CHROMITE PRODUCTION AND CONSUMPTION - See JAPAN - MINING AND MINERAL PRODUCTS

JAPAN - CHROMIUM ORE PRODUCTION AND CONSUMPTION - See JAPAN - MINING AND MINERAL PRODUCTS

JAPAN - CIGAR AND CIGARETTE PRODUCTION - See JAPAN - TOBACCO PRODUCTION

JAPAN - CLASS STRUCTURE

European Community Information Service, 2100 M Street, NW, Washington, D.C. 20037 (202) 862-9500; *Basic Statistics of the Community.*

G.K. Hall and Company, 70 Lincoln Street, Boston, Massachusetts 02111 (617) 423-3990; *The World in Figures.*

JAPAN - CLIMATE

Facts on File, 460 Park Avenue South, New York, New York 10016 (800) 443-8323; *The New Book of World Rankings.*

G.K. Hall and Company, 70 Lincoln Street, Boston, Massachusetts 02111 (617) 423-3990; *The World in Figures.*

Statistics Bureau, Management and Coordination Agency, Japan; *Statistical Indicators on Social Life.*

JAPAN - CLOTHING - PRODUCTION INDEX

Organisation for Economic Co-operation and Development (OECD), 2 rue Andre-Pascal, 75 Paris 16, France (Telephone Number in U.S. (202) 785-6323); *Indicators of Industrial Activity.*

JAPAN - CLOTHING EXPORTS AND IMPORTS

European Community Information Service, 2100 M Street, NW, Washington, D.C. 20037 (202) 862-9500; *Basic Statistics of the Community.*

Organisation for Economic Co-operation and Development (OECD), 2 rue Andre-Pascal, 75 Paris 16, France (Telephone Number in U.S. (202) 785-6323); *Textile Industry in OECD Countries.*

Statistical Office of the United Nations, Publishing Service, New York, New York 10017 (800) 253-9646; *Trade in Manufactures of Developing Countries.*

JAPAN - COAL PRODUCTION - See JAPAN - MINING AND MINERAL PRODUCTS

JAPAN - COBALT PRODUCTION AND CONSUMPTION - See JAPAN - MINING AND MINERAL PRODUCTS

JAPAN - COCOA (BEANS) PRODUCTION - See JAPAN - CROPS

JAPAN - COFFEE - See JAPAN - CROPS

JAPAN - COKE OVEN COKE PRODUCTION - See JAPAN - MINING AND MINERAL PRODUCTS

JAPAN - COKE OVEN ORE PRODUCTION AND CONSUMPTION - See JAPAN - MINING AND MINERAL PRODUCTS

JAPAN - COKE PRODUCTION AND CONSUMPTION - See JAPAN - MINING AND MINERAL PRODUCTS

JAPAN - COMMUNICATIONS

European Community Information Service, 2100 M Street, NW, Washington, D.C. 20037 (202) 862-9500; *Basic Statistics of the Community.*

G.K. Hall and Company, 70 Lincoln Street, Boston, Massachusetts 02111 (617) 423-3000; *The World in Figures.*

Statistical Office of the United Nations, Publishing Service, New York, New York 10017 (800) 253-9646; *Statistical Yearbook for Asia and the Pacific.*

JAPAN - CONSTRUCTION INDUSTRY

European Community Information Service, 2100 M Street, NW, Washington, D.C. 20037 (202) 862-9500; *Basic Statistics of the Community.*

Facts on File, 460 Park Avenue South, New York, New York 10016 (800) 443-8323; *The New Book of World Rankings.*

Organisation for Economic Co-operation and Development (OECD), 2 rue Andre-Pascal, 75 Paris 16, France (Telephone Number in U.S. (202) 785-6323); *Industrial Structure Statistics, The Iron and Steel Industry, Main Economic Indicators - Historical Statistics,* and *OECD Economic Surveys: Japan.*

Statistical Office of the United Nations, Publishing Service, New York, New York 10017 (800) 253-9646; *Construction Statistics Yearbook,* and *Statistical Yearbook.*

JAPAN - CONSUMER PRICE INDEX

European Community Information Service, 2100 M Street, NW, Washington, D.C. 20037 (202) 862-9500; *Basic Statistics of the Community.*

G.K. Hall and Company, 70 Lincoln Street, Boston, Massachusetts 02111 (617) 423-3990; *The World in Figures.*

National Technical Information Service, 5285 Port Royal Road, Springfield, Virginia 22161 (703) 487-4600; *Handbook of Economic Statistics.*

Organisation for Economic Co-operation and Development (OECD), 2 rue Andre-Pascal, 75 Paris 16, France (Telephone Number in U.S. (202) 785-6323); *Economic Outlook.*

JAPAN - CONSUMER PRICE INDEX NUMBERS

Statistical Office of the United Nations, Publishing Service, New York, New York 10017 (800) 253-9646; *Statistical Yearbook.*

JAPAN - CONSUMER PRICES

European Community Information Service, 2100 M Street, NW, Washington, D.C. 20037 (202) 862-9500; *Basic Statistics of the Community.*

International Labour Office, I.L.O. Publications, CH-1211, Geneva 22, Switzerland; *Yearbook of Labour Statistics.*

International Monetary Fund, 700 Nineteenth Street, NW, Washington, D.C. 20431 (202) 623-7000; *International Financial Statistics.*

Organisation for Economic Co-operation and Development (OECD), 2 rue Andre-Pascal, 75 Paris 16, France (Telephone Number in U.S. (202) 785-6323); *Economic Outlook.*

Times Books, 201 East 50th Street, New York, New York 10022 (212) 751-2600; *The Economist Book of Vital World Statistics.*

JAPAN - CONSUMPTION

Euromonitor Publications Limited, 87-88 Turnmill Street, London EC1M 5QU, England; *The Pacific Basin: An Economic Handbook.*

European Community Information Service, 2100 M Street, NW, Washington, D.C. 20037 (202) 862-9500; *Basic Statistics of the Community.*

G.K. Hall and Company, 70 Lincoln Street, Boston, Massachusetts 02111 (617) 423-3990; *The World in Figures.*

International Monetary Fund, 700 Nineteenth Street, NW, Washington, D.C. 20431 (202) 623-7000; *International Financial Statistics.*

International Lead and Zinc Study Group, Metro House, 58 St. James's Street, London SW1A 1LD, England; *Lead and Zinc Statistics.*

International Rubber Study Group, York House, 8th Floor, Empire Way, Wembley, London HA9 0PA, England; *Rubber Statistical Bulletin.*

National Technical Information Service, 5285 Port Royal Road, Springfield, Virginia 22161 (703) 487-4600; *Handbook of Economic Statistics.*

Organisation for Economic Co-operation and Development (OECD), 2 rue Andre-Pascal, 75 Paris 16, France (Telephone Number in U.S. (202) 785-6323); *The Footwear, Raw Hides and Skins, and Leather Industry in OECD Countries, The Iron and Steel Industry, Meat Balances in OECD Member Countries, The Non-Ferrous Metals Industry, The Pulp and Paper Industry,* and *Textile Industry in OECD Countries.*

Statistics Bureau, Management and Coordination Agency, Japan; *Statistical Indicators on Social Life.*

JAPAN - COPPER AND COPPER ORE - See JAPAN -MINING AND MINERAL PRODUCTS

JAPAN - CORN PRODUCTION - See JAPAN - CROPS

JAPAN - CORPORATE INCOME TAXES - See JAPAN - TAXATION

JAPAN - CORPORATE TAXES - See JAPAN - TAXATION

JAPAN - COTTON - See JAPAN - CROPS

JAPAN - CRIME

International Criminal Police Organization (INTERPOL), 26 rue Armengaud, 92210 Saint Cloud, France; *International Crime Statistics.*

Statistics Bureau, Management and Coordination Agency, Japan; *Statistical Indicators on Social Life.*

Yale University Press, Yale Station, New Haven, Connecticut 06520; *Violence and Crime in Cross-National Perspective.*

JAPAN - CROPS

Commodity Research Bureau, Incorporated, 75 Wall Street, New York, New York 10005 (212) 504-7754; *Commodity Year Book.*

European Community Information Service, 2100 M Street, NW, Washington, D.C. 20037 (202) 862-9500; *Basic Statistics of the Community.*

Facts on File, 460 Park Avenue South, New York, New York 10016 (800) 443-8323; *The New Book of World Rankings.*

Food and Agricultural Organization of the United Nations (FAO), Via delle Terme di Caracalla, 00100 Rome, Italy (Telephone Number in U.S. (202) 653-2400); *Production Yearbook,* and *The State of Food and Agriculture.*

G.K. Hall and Company, 70 Lincoln Street, Boston, Massachusetts 02111 (617) 423-3990; *The World in Figures.*

National Technical Information Service, 5285 Port Royal Road, Springfield, Virginia 22161 (703) 487-4600; *Handbook of Economic Statistics.*

Organisation for Economic Co-operation and Development (OECD), 2 rue Andre-Pascal, 75 Paris 16, France (Telephone Number in U.S. (202) 785-6323); *Economic Accounts for Agriculture, Foreign Trade by Commodities, Indicators of Industrial Activity,* and *Textile Industry in OECD Countries.*

Statistical Office of the United Nations, Publishing Service, New York, New York 10017 (800) 253-9646; *Statistical Yearbook.*

Statistics Bureau, Management and Coordination Agency, Japan; *Statistical Indicators on Social Life.*

JAPAN - CUSTOMS DUTIES

European Community Information Service, 2100 M Street, NW, Washington, D.C. 20037 (202) 862-9500; *Basic Statistics of the Community.*

G.K. Hall and Company, 70 Lincoln Street, Boston, Massachusetts 02111 (617) 423-3990; *The World in Figures*.

International Monetary Fund, 700 Nineteenth Street, NW, Washington, D.C. 20431 (202) 623-7000; *Government Finance Statistics Yearbook*.

Organisation for Economic Co-operation and Development (OECD), 2 rue Andre-Pascal, 75 Paris 16, France (Telephone Number in U.S. (202) 785-6323); *Economic Accounts for Agriculture*, and *The Non-Ferrous Metals Industry*.

JAPAN - DAIRY PRODUCTS

Commodity Research Bureau, Incorporated, 75 Wall Street, New York, New York 10005 (212) 504-7754; *Commodity Year Book*.

European Community Information Service, 2100 M Street, NW, Washington, D.C. 20037 (202) 862-9500; *Basic Statistics of the Community*.

Facts on File, 460 Park Avenue South, New York, New York (800) 443-8323; *The New Book of World Rankings*.

Food and Agricultural Organization of the United Nations (FAO), Via delle Terme di Caracalla, 00100 Rome, Italy (Telephone Number in U.S. (202) 653-2400); *Production Yearbook*, and *The State of Food and Agriculture*.

National Technical Information Service, 5285 Port Royal Road, Springfield, Virginia 22161 (703) 487-4600; *Handbook of Economic Statistics*.

Organisation for Economic Co-operation and Development (OECD), 2 rue Andre-Pascal, 75 Paris 16, France (Telephone Number in U.S. (202) 785-6323); *Economic Accounts for Agriculture*, and *Milk, Milk Products, and Egg Balances in OECD Member Countries*.

Statistical Office of the United Nations, Publishing Service, New York, New York 10017 (800) 253-9646; *Statistical Yearbook*.

JAPAN - DEATH RATES

The Economist Intelligence Unit (Asia) Limited, 10th Floor, Luk Kwok Centre, 72 Gloucester Road, Wanchai, Hong Kong (Phone Number in U.S. (800) 938-4685); *Asian Market Atlas*.

Euromonitor Publications Limited, 87-88 Turnmill Street, London EC1M 5QU, England; *The Pacific Basin: An Economic Handbook*.

European Community Information Service, 2100 M Street, NW, Washington, D.C. 20037 (202) 862-9500; *Basic Statistics of the Community*.

G.K. Hall and Company, 70 Lincoln Street, Boston, Massachusetts 02111 (617) 423-3990; *The World in Figures*.

Statistical Office of the United Nations, Publishing Service, New York, New York 10017 (800) 253-9646; *Statistical Yearbook*.

Statistics Bureau, Management and Coordination Agency, Japan; *Statistical Indicators on Social Life*.

Times Books, 201 East 50th Street, New York, New York 10022 (212) 751-2600; *The Economist Book of Vital World Statistics*.

World Health Organization, Office of Publications, Avenue Appia, CH-1211 Geneva 27, Switzerland (Telephone Number in U.S. (518) 436-9686); *World Health Statistics Annual*.

JAPAN - DEFENSE EXPENDITURES

G.K. Hall and Company, 70 Lincoln Street, Boston, Massachusetts 02111 (617) 423-3990; *The World in Figures*.

National Technical Information Service, 5285 Port Royal Road, Springfield, Virginia 22161 (703) 487-4600; *Handbook of Economic Statistics*.

U.S. Arms Control and Disarmament Agency, 320 Twenty-first Street, NW, Washington, D.C. 20451 (202) 647-8677; *World Military Expenditures and Arms Transfers*.

JAPAN - DEMOGRAPHY

The Economist Intelligence Unit, 111 West 57th Street, New York, New York 10019 (800) 938-4685; *The World Market Atlas*.

The Economist Intelligence Unit (Asia) Limited, 10th Floor, Luk Kwok Centre, 72 Gloucester Road, Wanchai, Hong Kong (Phone Number in U.S. (800) 938-4685); *Asian Market Atlas*.

European Community Information Service, 2100 M Street, NW, Washington, D.C. 20037 (202) 862-9500; *Basic Statistics of the Community*.

Facts on File, 460 Park Avenue South, New York, New York 10016 (800) 443-8323; *The New Book of World Rankings*.

G.K. Hall and Company, 70 Lincoln Street, Boston, Massachusetts 02111 (617) 423-3990; *The World in Figures*.

JAPAN - DEVELOPMENT ASSISTANCE

European Community Information Service, 2100 M Street, NW, Washington, D.C. 20037 (202) 862-9500; *Basic Statistics of the Community*.

G.K. Hall and Company, 70 Lincoln Street, Boston, Massachusetts 02111 (617) 423-3990; *The World in Figures*.

Organisation for Economic Co-operation and Development (OECD), 2 rue Andre-Pascal, 75 Paris 16, France (Telephone Number in U.S. (202) 785-6323); *Geographical Distribution of Financial Flows to Developing Countries*.

Statistical Office of the United Nations, Publishing Service, New York, New York 10017 (800) 253-9646; *Statistical Yearbook*.

JAPAN - DIAMONDS - See JAPAN - MINING AND MINERAL PRODUCTS

JAPAN - DISCOUNT RATES

Organisation for Economic Co-operation and Development (OECD), 2 rue Andre-Pascal, 75 Paris 16, France (Telephone Number in U.S. (202) 785-6323); *Financial Market Trends*.

Statistical Office of the United Nations, Publishing Service, New York, New York 10017 (800) 253-9646; *Statistical Yearbook*.

JAPAN - DISEASES

G.K. Hall and Company, 70 Lincoln Street, Boston, Massachusetts 02111 (617) 423-3990; *The World in Figures*.

Statistics Bureau, Management and Coordination Agency, Japan; *Statistical Indicators on Social Life*.

World Health Organization, Office of Publications, Avenue Appia, CH-1211 Geneva 27, Switzerland (Telephone Number in U.S. (518) 436-9686); *World Health Statistics Annual*.

JAPAN - DIVORCE RATES

Facts on File, 460 Park Avenue South, New York, New York 10016 (800) 443-8323; *The New Book of World Rankings*.

Statistical Office of the United Nations, Publishing Service, New York, New York 10017 (800) 253-9646; *Demographic Yearbook*, and *Statistical Yearbook*.

Statistics Bureau, Management and Coordination Agency, Japan; *Statistical Indicators on Social Life*.

JAPAN - DOMESTIC PRODUCT

European Community Information Service, 2100 M Street, NW, Washington, D.C. 20037 (202) 862-9500; *Basic Statistics of the Community*.

G.K. Hall and Company, 70 Lincoln Street, Boston, Massachusetts 02111 (617) 423-3990; *The World in Figures*.

JAPAN - DUCKS - See JAPAN - LIVESTOCK AND POULTRY

JAPAN - ECONOMY

Euromonitor Publications Limited, 87-88 Turnmill Street, London EC1M 5QU, England; *International Marketing Data and Statistics*.

European Community Information Service, 2100 M Street, NW, Washington, D.C. 20037 (202) 862-9500; *Basic Statistics of the Community*.

Facts on File, 460 Park Avenue South, New York, New York 10016 (800) 443-8323; *The New Book of World Rankings*.

G.K. Hall and Company, 70 Lincoln Street, Boston, Massachusetts 02111 (617) 423-3990; *The World in Figures*.

National Technical Information Service, 5285 Port Royal Road, Springfield, Virginia 22161 (703) 487-4600; *Handbook of Economic Statistics*.

Organisation for Economic Co-operation and Development (OECD), 2 rue Andre-Pascal, 75 Paris 16, France (Telephone Number in U.S. (202) 785-6323); *Economic Outlook, Geographical Distribution of Financial Flows to Developing Countries, Main Economic Indicators - Historical Statistics, OECD Economic Surveys: Japan*, and *OECD Employment Outlook*.

Statistics Bureau, Management and Coordination Agency, Japan; *Statistical Indicators on Social Life*.

JAPAN - EDUCATION

The Economist Intelligence Unit, 111 West 57th Street, New York, New York 10019 (800) 938-4685; *The World Market Atlas*.

The Economist Intelligence Unit (Asia) Limited, 10th Floor, Luk Kwok Centre, 72 Gloucester Road, Wanchai, Hong Kong (Phone Number in U.S. (800) 938-4685); *Asian Market Atlas*.

Euromonitor Publications Limited, 87-88 Turnmill Street, London EC1M 5QU, England; *The Pacific Basin: An Economic Handbook*.

European Community Information Service, 2100 M Street, NW, Washington, D.C. 20037 (202) 862-9500; *Basic Statistics of the Community*.

Facts on File, 460 Park Avenue South, New York, New York 10016 (800) 443-8323; *The New Book of World Rankings*.

G.K. Hall and Company, 70 Lincoln Street, Boston, Massachusetts 02111 (617) 423-3990; *The World in Figures*.

Organisation for Economic Co-operation and Development (OECD), 2 rue Andre-Pascal, 75 Paris 16, France (Telephone Number in U.S. (202) 785-6323); *Education in OECD Countries*.

Statistical Office of the United Nations, Publishing Service, New York, New York 10017 (800) 253-9646; *Statistical Yearbook for Asia and the Pacific*.

Statistics Bureau, Management and Coordination Agency, Japan; *Statistical Indicators on Social Life*.

Times Books, 201 East 50th Street, New York, New York 10022 (212) 751-2600; *The Economist Book of Vital World Statistics*.

United Nations Educational, Scientific and Cultural Organization (UNESCO), 7 Place de Fontenoy, F-75700 Paris, France (Telephone Number in U.S. (212) 963-5981); *Statistical Yearbook*.

JAPAN - EGG PRODUCTION AND CONSUMPTION - See JAPAN - DAIRY PRODUCTS

JAPAN - EGGPLANT PRODUCTION - See JAPAN - CROPS

JAPAN - ELECTRICITY

Commodity Research Bureau, Incorporated, One Liberty Plaza, New York, New York 10006; *Commodity Year Book*.

European Community Information Service, 2100 M Street, NW, Washington, D.C. 20037 (202) 862-9500; *Basic Statistics of the Community*.

Facts on File, 460 Park Avenue South, New York, New York 10016 (800) 443-8323; *The New Book of World Rankings*.

National Technical Information Service, 5285 Port Royal Road, Springfield, Virginia 22161 (703) 487-4600; *Handbook of Economic Statistics*.

Organisation for Economic Co-operation and Development (OECD), 2 rue Andre-Pascal, 75 Paris 16, France (Telephone Number in U.S. (202) 785-6323); *Energy Statistics of OECD Countries, Indicators of Industrial Activity*, and *Industrial Structure Statistics*.

Penn Well Publishing Company, 1421 South Sheridan Road, Post Office Box 1260, Tulsa, Oklahoma 74101 (800) 752-9764; *International Energy Statistics Sourcebook*.

Statistical Office of the United Nations, Publishing Service, New York, New York 10017 (800) 253-9646; *Electric Power in Asia and the Pacific*, and *Statistical Yearbook*.

Times Books, 201 East 50th Street, New York, New York 10022 (212) 751-2600; *The Economist Book of Vital World Statistics*.

JAPAN - EMPLOYMENT

Euromonitor Publications Limited, 87-88 Turnmill Street, London EC1M 5QU, England; *International Marketing Data and Statistics*, and *The Pacific Basin: An Economic Handbook.*

European Community Information Service, 2100 M Street, NW, Washington, D.C. 20037 (202) 862-9500; *Basic Statistics of the Community.*

Facts on File, 460 Park Avenue South, New York, New York 10016 (800) 443-8323; *The New Book of World Rankings.*

International Labour Office, I.L.O. Publications, CH-1211, Geneva 22, Switzerland; *Yearbook of Labour Statistics.*

Organisation for Economic Co-operation and Development (OECD), 2 rue Andre-Pascal, 75 Paris 16, France (Telephone Number in U.S. (202) 785-6323); *The Iron and Steel Industry, OECD Employment Outlook, OECD Economic Surveys: Japan,* and *Textile Industry in OECD Countries.*

Statistical Office of the United Nations, Publishing Service, New York, New York 10017 (800) 253-9646; *Statistical Yearbook.*

Statistics Bureau, Management and Coordination Agency, Japan; *Statistical Indicators on Social Life.*

JAPAN - ENERGY

European Community Information Service, 2100 M Street, NW, Washington, D.C. 20037 (202) 862-9500; *Basic Statistics of the Community.*

Facts on File, 460 Park Avenue South, New York, New York 10016 (800) 443-8323; *The New Book of World Rankings.*

Food and Agricultural Organization of the United Nations (FAO), Via delle Terme di Caracalla, 00100 Rome, Italy (Telephone Number in U.S. (202) 653-2400); *The State of Food and Agriculture.*

G.K. Hall and Company, 70 Lincoln Street, Boston, Massachusetts 02111 (617) 423-3990; *The World in Figures.*

National Technical Information Service, 5285 Port Royal Road, Springfield, Virginia 22161 (703) 487-4600; *Handbook of Economic Statistics.*

Organisation for Economic Co-operation and Development (OECD), 2 rue Andre-Pascal, 75 Paris 16, France (Telephone Number in U.S. (202) 785-6323); *Coal Information, Energy Statistics of OECD Countries, OECD Environmental Data,* and *Oil and Gas Information.*

Penn Well Publishing Company, 1421 South Sheridan Road, Post Office Box 1260, Tulsa, Oklahoma 74101 (800) 752-9764; *International Energy Statistics Sourcebook.*

Statistical Office of the United Nations, Publishing Service, New York, New York 10017 (800) 253-9646; *Energy Statistics Yearbook, Statistical Yearbook,* and *World Energy Supplies.*

Times Books, 201 East 50th Street, New York, New York 10022 (212) 751-2600; *The Economist Book of Vital World Statistics.*

JAPAN - ENGINEERING AND METAL PRODUCTS - EXPORTS AND IMPORTS

European Community Information Service, 2100 M Street, NW, Washington, D.C. 20037 (202) 862-9500; *Basic Statistics of the Community.*

Statistical Office of the United Nations, Publishing Service, New York, New York 10017 (800) 253-9646; *Trade in Manufactures of*

Developing Countries.

JAPAN - ENVIRONMENT

Organization for Economic Co-operation and Development (OECD), 2 rue Andre-Pascal, 75 Paris 16, France (Telephone Number in U.S. (202) 785-6323): *OECD Environmental Data.*

JAPAN - EXCHANGE RATES

The Economist Intelligence Unit (Asia) Limited, 10th Floor, Luk Kwok Centre, 72 Gloucester Road, Wanchai, Hong Kong (Phone Number in U.S. (800) 938-4685); *Asian Market Atlas.*

Euromonitor Publications Limited, 87-88 Turnmill Street, London EC1M 5QU, England; *International Marketing Data and Statistics,* and *The Pacific Basin: An Economic Handbook.*

International Civil Aviation Organization, 1000 Sherbrooke Street West, Suite 400, Montreal, Quebec H3A 2R2, Canada (514) 285-8219; *Civil Aviation Statistics of the World.*

International Monetary Fund, 700 Nineteenth Street, NW, Washington, D.C. 20431 (202) 623-7000; *International Financial Statistics.*

National Technical Information Service, 5285 Port Royal Road, Springfield, Virginia 22161 (703) 487-4600; *Handbook of Economic Statistics.*

Organisation for Economic Co-operation and Development (OECD), 2 rue Andre-Pascal, 75 Paris 16, France (Telephone Number in U.S. (202) 785-6323); *Economic Outlook, Financial Market Trends, Revenue Statistics of OECD Member Countries,* and *Tourism Policy and International Tourism in OECD Member Countries.*

Statistical Office of the United Nations, Publishing Service, New York, New York 10017 (800) 253-9646; *Statistical Yearbook.*

JAPAN - EXCISE TAXES - See JAPAN - TAXATION

JAPAN - EXPORTS

American Automobile Manufacturers Association, 1401 H Street, NW, Suite 900, Washington, D.C. 20005 (202) 326-5500; *World Motor Vehicle Data.*

The Economist Intelligence Unit, 111 West 57th Street, New York, New York 10019 (800) 938-4685; *The World Market Atlas.*

The Economist Intelligence Unit (Asia) Limited, 10th Floor, Luk Kwok Centre, 72 Gloucester Road, Wanchai, Hong Kong (Phone Number in U.S. (800) 938-4685); *Asian Market Atlas.*

Euromonitor Publications Limited, 87-88 Turnmill Street, London EC1M 5QU, England; *International Marketing Data and Statistics,* and *The Pacific Basin: An Economic Handbook.*

European Community Information Service, 2100 M Street, NW, Washington, D.C. 20037 (202) 862-9500; *Basic Statistics of the Community.*

Food and Agricultural Organization of the United Nations (FAO), Via delle Terme di Caracalla, 00100 Rome, Italy (Telephone Number in U.S. (202) 653-2400); *The State of Food and Agriculture.*

G.K. Hall and Company, 70 Lincoln Street, Boston, Massachusetts 02111 (617) 423-3990; *The World in Figures.*

International Lead and Zinc Study Group, Metro House, 58 St. James's Street, London SW1A 1LD, England; *Lead and Zinc Statistics*.

International Monetary Fund, 700 Nineteenth Street, NW, Washington, D.C. 20431 (202) 623-7000; *Direction of Trade Statistics*, and *International Financial Statistics*.

International Rubber Study Group, York House, 8th Floor, Empire Way, Wembley, London HA9 0PA, England; *Rubber Statistical Bulletin*.

National Technical Information Service, 5285 Port Royal Road, Springfield, Virginia 22161 (703) 487-4600; *Handbook of Economic Statistics*.

Organisation for Economic Co-operation and Development (OECD), 2 rue Andre-Pascal, 75 Paris 16, France (Telephone Number in U.S. (202) 785-6323); *Economic Outlook, The Footwear, Raw Hides and Skins, and Leather Industry in OECD Countries, Foreign Trade by Commodities, Geographical Distribution of Financial Flows to Developing Countries, Industrial Structure Statistics, The Iron and Steel Industry, Milk, Milk Products, and Egg Balances in OECD Member Countries, OECD Economic Surveys: Japan, The Pulp and Paper Industry,* and *Review of Fisheries in OECD Member Countries*.

Statistical Office of the United Nations, Publishing Service, New York, New York 10017 (800) 253-9646; *Foreign Trade Statistics of Asia and the Pacific*.

Statistics Bureau, Management and Coordination Agency, Japan; *Statistical Indicators on Social Life*.

Times Books, 201 East 50th Street, New York, New York 10022 (212) 751-2600; *The Economist Book of Vital World Statistics*.

JAPAN - EXTERNAL FINANCING

Organisation for Economic Co-operation and Development (OECD), 2 rue Andre-Pascal, 75 Paris 16, France (Telephone Number in U.S. (202) 785-6323); *Economic Outlook,* and *Financial Market Trends*.

JAPAN - EXTERNAL INDEBTEDNESS

National Technical Information Service, 5285 Port Royal Road, Springfield, Virginia 22161 (703) 487-4600; *Handbook of Economic Statistics*.

Organisation for Economic Co-operation and Development (OECD), 2 rue Andre-Pascal, 75 Paris 16, France (Telephone Number in U.S. (202) 785-6323); *Financial Market Trends,* and *Geographical Distribution of Financial Flows to Developing Countries*.

JAPAN - EXTERNAL TRADE

European Community Information Service, 2100 M Street, NW, Washington, D.C. 20037 (202) 862-9500; *Basic Statistics of the Community*.

Food and Agricultural Organization of the United Nations (FAO), Via delle Terme di Caracalla, 00100 Rome, Italy (Telephone Number in U.S. (202) 653-2400); *The State of Food and Agriculture,* and *Trade Yearbook*.

G.K. Hall and Company, 70 Lincoln Street, Boston, Massachusetts 02111 (617) 423-3990; *The World in Figures*.

National Technical Information Service, 5285 Port Royal Road, Springfield, Virginia 22161 (703) 487-4600; *Handbook of Economic Statistics*.

Statistical Office of the United Nations, Publishing Service, New York, New York 10017 (800) 253-9646; *Statistical Yearbook,* and *Statistical Yearbook for Asia and the Pacific*.

JAPAN - FABRIC PRODUCTION - See JAPAN - TEXTILE INDUSTRY

JAPAN - FARM CROPS - See JAPAN - CROPS

JAPAN - FEMALE WORKING POPULATION - See JAPAN - EMPLOYMENT

JAPAN - FERTILITY RATES

The Economist Intelligence Unit (Asia) Limited, 10th Floor, Luk Kwok Centre, 72 Gloucester Road, Wanchai, Hong Kong (Phone Number in U.S. (800) 938-4685); *Asian Market Atlas*.

Facts on File, 460 Park Avenue South, New York, New York 10016 (800) 443-8323; *The New Book of World Rankings*.

Times Books, 201 East 50th Street, New York, New York 10022 (212) 751-2600; *The Economist Book of Vital World Statistics*.

JAPAN - FERTILIZER

European Community Information Service, 2100 M Street, NW, Washington, D.C. 20037 (202) 862-9500; *Basic Statistics of the Community*.

Food and Agricultural Organization of the United Nations (FAO), Via delle Terme di Caracalla, 00100, Rome, Italy (Telephone Number in U.S. (202) 653-2400); *Fertilizer Yearbook,* and *The State of Food and Agriculture*.

National Technical Information Service, 5285 Port Royal Road, Springfield, Virginia 22161 (703) 487-4600; *Handbook of Economic Statistics*.

Organisation for Economic Co-operation and Development (OECD), 2 rue Andre-Pascal, 75 Paris 16, France (Telephone Number in U.S. (202) 785-6323); *Economic Accounts for Agriculture,* and *Foreign Trade by Commodities*.

Statistical Office of the United Nations, Publishing Service, New York, New York 10017 (800) 253-9646; *Statistical Yearbook*.

JAPAN - FETAL MORTALITY

European Community Information Service, 2100 M Street, NW, Washington, D.C. 20037 (202) 862-9500; *Basic Statistics of the Community*.

Statistical Office of the United Nations, Publishing Service, New York, New York 10017 (800) 253-9646; *Demographic Yearbook*.

World Health Organization, Office of Publications, Avenue Appia, CH-1211 Geneva 27, Switzerland (Telephone Number in U.S. (518) 436-9686); *World Health Statistics Annual*.

JAPAN - FIBRE PRODUCTION - See JAPAN - TEXTILE INDUSTRY

JAPAN - FILAMENT PRODUCTION - See JAPAN - TEXTILE INDUSTRY

JAPAN - FILMS - See JAPAN - MOTION PICTURES

JAPAN - FINANCE

Euromonitor Publications Limited, 87-88 Turnmill Street, London EC1M 5QU, England; *The Pacific Basin: An Economic Handbook*.

European Community Information Service, 2100 M Street, NW, Washington, D.C. 20037 (202) 862-9500; *Basic Statistics of the Community*.

Facts on File, 460 Park Avenue South, New York, New York 10016 (800) 443-8323; *The New Book of World Rankings*.

G.K. Hall and Company, 70 Lincoln Street, Boston, Massachusetts 02111 (617) 423-3990; *The World in Figures*.

International Monetary Fund, 700 Nineteenth Street, NW, Washington, D.C. 20431 (202) 623-7000; *International Financial Statistics*.

Organisation for Economic Co-operation and Development (OECD), 2 rue Andre-Pascal, 75 Paris 16, France (Telephone Number in U.S. (202) 785-6323); *Economic Outlook, Financial Market Trends, Geographical Distribution of Financial Flows to Developing Countries, Main Economic Indicators - Historical Statistics*, and *OECD Financial Statistics*.

Statistical Office of the United Nations, Publishing Service, New York, New York 10017 (800) 253-9646; *Statistical Yearbook for Asia and the Pacific*.

Statistics Bureau, Management and Coordination Agency, Japan; *Statistical Indicators on Social Life*.

JAPAN - FISHERIES

Facts on File, 460 Park Avenue South, New York, New York 10016; *The New Book of World Rankings*.

Food and Agricultural Organization of the United Nations (FAO), Via delle Terme di Caracalla, 00100 Rome, Italy (Telephone Number in U.S. (202) 653-2400); *The State of Food and Agriculture*.

National Technical Information Service, 5285 Port Royal Road, Springfield, Virginia 22161 (703) 487-4600; *Handbook of Economic Statistics*.

Organisation for Economic Co-operation and Development (OECD), 2 rue Andre-Pascal, 75 Paris 16, France (Telephone Number in U.S. (202) 785-6323); *Foreign Trade by Commodities*, and *Review of Fisheries in OECD Member Countries*.

Statistical Office of the United Nations, Publishing Service, New York, New York 10017 (800) 253-9646; *Statistical Yearbook*.

JAPAN - FLAX AND FLAX FIBRE PRODUCTION - See JAPAN - TEXTILE INDUSTRY

JAPAN - FLOUR PRODUCTION

Commodity Research Bureau, Incorporated, 75 Wall Street, New York, New York 10005 (212) 504-7754; *Commodity Year Book*.

European Community Information Service, 2100 M Street, NW, Washington, D.C. 20037 (202) 862-9500; *Basic Statistics of the Community*.

Statistical Office of the United Nations, Publishing Service, New York, New York 10017 (800) 253-9646; *Statistical Yearbook*.

JAPAN - FOOD

European Community Information Service, 2100 M Street, NW, Washington, D.C. 20037 (202) 862-9500; *Basic Statistics of the Community*.

Food and Agricultural Organization of the United Nations (FAO), Via delle Terme di Caracalla, 00100 Rome, Italy (Telephone Number in U.S. (202) 653-2400); *Production Yearbook*, and *The State of Food and Agriculture*.

G.K. Hall and Company, 70 Lincoln Street, Boston, Massachusetts 02111 (617) 423-3990; *The World in Figures*.

Organisation for Economic Co-operation and Development (OECD), 2 rue Andre-Pascal, 75 Paris 16, France (Telephone Number in U.S. (202) 785-6323); *Food Consumption Statistics*, and *Foreign Trade by Commodities*.

Statistical Office of the United Nations, Publishing Service, New York, New York 10017 (800) 253-9646; *Statistical Yearbook for Asia and the Pacific*, and *Trade in Manufactures of Developing Countries*.

JAPAN - FOOTWEAR - PRODUCTION INDEX

Organisation for Economic Co-operation and Development (OECD), 2 rue Andre-Pascal, 75 Paris 16, France (Telephone Number in U.S. (202) 785-6323); *Indicators of Industrial Activity*.

JAPAN - FOREIGN AID

G.K. Hall and Company, 70 Lincoln Street, Boston, Massachusetts 02111 (617) 423-3990; *The World in Figures*.

National Technical Information Service, 5285 Port Royal Road, Springfield, Virginia 22161 (703) 487-4600; *Handbook of Economic Statistics*.

JAPAN - FOREIGN DEBT

International Monetary Fund, 700 Nineteenth Street, NW, Washington, D.C. 20431 (202) 623-7000; *Government Finance Statistics Yearbook*.

Organisation for Economic Co-operation and Development (OECD), 2 rue Andre-Pascal, 75 Paris 16, France (Telephone Number in U.S. (202) 785-6323); *Economic Outlook*.

JAPAN - FOREIGN INDEBTEDNESS

Euromonitor Publications Limited, 87-88 Turnmill Street, London EC1M 5QU, England; *The Pacific Basin: An Economic Handbook*.

Organisation for Economic Co-operation and Development (OECD), 2 rue Andre-Pascal, 75 Paris 16, France (Telephone Number in U.S. (202) 785-6323); *Economic Outlook*, and *Financial Market Trends*.

JAPAN - FOREIGN TRADE

The Economist Intelligence Unit (Asia) Limited, 10th Floor, Luk Kwok Centre, 72 Gloucester Road, Wanchai, Hong Kong (Phone Number in U.S. (800) 938-4685); *Asian Market Atlas*.

Euromonitor Publications Limited, 87-88 Turnmill Street, London EC1M 5QU, England; *International Marketing Data and Statistics*.

European Community Information Service, 2100 M Street, NW, Washington, D.C. 20037 (202) 862-9500; *Basic Statistics of the Community*.

Facts on File, 460 Park Avenue South, New York, New York 10016; *The New Book of World Rankings*.

Food and Agricultural Organization of the United Nations (FAO), Via delle Terme di Caracalla, 00100 Rome, Italy (Telephone Number in U.S. (202) 653-2400); *The State of Food and Agriculture*.

G.K. Hall and Company, 70 Lincoln Street, Boston, Massachusetts 02111 (617) 423-3990; *The World in Figures*.

International Monetary Fund, 700 Nineteenth Street, NW, Washington, D.C. 20431 (202) 623-7000; *International Financial Statistics*.

National Technical Information Service, 5285 Port Royal Road, Springfield, Virginia 22161 (703) 487-4600; *Handbook of Economic Statistics*.

Organisation for Economic Co-operation and Development (OECD), 2 rue Andre-Pascal, 75 Paris 16, France (Telephone Number in U.S. (202) 785-6323); *Economic Outlook, The Footwear, Raw Hides and Skins, and Leather Industry in OECD Countries, Foreign Trade by Commodities, Main Economic Indicators - Historical Statistics, Maritime Transport, Meat Balances in OECD Member Countries,* and *OECD Economic Surveys: Japan*.

Statistical Office of the United Nations, Publishing Service, New York, New York 10017 (800) 253-9646; *Statistical Yearbook, International Trade Statistics Yearbook,* and *Trade in Manufactures of Developing Countries*.

World Bureau of Metal Statistics, 27-A High Street, Ware, Herts. SG12 9BA, England; *World Metal Statistics*.

JAPAN - FORESTRY AND FOREST PRODUCTS

American Forest and Paper Association, 1250 Connecticut Avenue, NW, Washington, D.C. 20036 (202) 463-2455; *Wood Pulp and Fiber Statistics*.

The Economist Intelligence Unit (Asia) Limited, 10th Floor, Luk Kwok Centre, 72 Gloucester Road, Wanchai, Hong Kong (Phone Number in U.S. (800) 938-4685); *Asian Market Atlas*.

European Community Information Service, 2100 M Street, NW, Washington, D.C. 20037 (202) 862-9500; *Basic Statistics of the Community*.

Facts on File, 460 Park Avenue South, New York, New York 10016; *The New Book of World Rankings*.

Food and Agricultural Organization of the United Nations (FAO), Via delle Terme di Caracalla, 00100 Rome, Italy (Telephone Number in U.S. (202) 653-2400); *The State of Food and Agriculture,* and *Yearbook of Forest Products*.

G.K. Hall and Company, 70 Lincoln Street, Boston, Massachusetts 02111 (617) 423-3990; *The World in Figures*.

National Technical Information Service, 5285 Port Royal Road, Springfield, Virginia 22161 (703) 487-4600; *Handbook of Economic Statistics*.

Organisation for Economic Co-operation and Development (OECD), 2 rue Andre-Pascal, 75 Paris 16, France (Telephone Number in U.S. (202) 785-6323); *Foreign Trade by Commodities, Indicators of Industrial Activity, Industrial Structure Statistics,* and *The Pulp and Paper Industry*.

Statistical Office of the United Nations, Publishing Service, New York, New York 10017 (800) 253-9646; *Statistical Yearbook*.

United Nations Educational, Scientific and Cultural Organization (UNESCO), 7 Place de Fontenoy, F-75700 Paris, France (Telephone Number in U.S. (212) 963-5981); *Statistical Yearbook*.

JAPAN - FRUIT PRODUCTION

European Community Information Service, 2100 M Street, NW, Washington, D.C. 20037 (202) 862-9500; *Basic Statistics of the Community*.

Organisation for Economic Co-operation and Development (OECD), 2 rue Andre-Pascal, 75 Paris 16, France (Telephone Number in U.S. (202) 785-6323); *Economic Accounts for Agriculture,* and *Foreign Trade by Commodities*.

JAPAN - FURNITURE AND WOOD PRODUCTS EXPORTS AND IMPORTS

European Community Information Service, 2100 M Street, NW, Washington, D.C. 20037 (202) 862-9500; *Basic Statistics of the Community*.

Organisation for Economic Co-operation and Development (OECD), 2 rue Andre-Pascal, 75 Paris 16, France (Telephone Number in U.S. (202) 785-6323); *Foreign Trade by Commodities,* and *Industrial Structure Statistics*.

Statistical Office of the United Nations, Publishing Service, New York, New York 10017 (800) 253-9646; *Trade in Manufactures of Developing Countries*.

JAPAN - GARLIC PRODUCTION - See JAPAN - CROPS

JAPAN - GAS - See JAPAN - MINING AND MINERAL PRODUCTS

JAPAN - GENERAL INDUSTRIAL STATISTICS

European Community Information Service, 2100 M Street, NW, Washington, D.C. 20037 (202) 862-9500; *Basic Statistics of the Community*.

Statistical Office of the United Nations, Publishing Service, New York, New York 10017 (800) 253-9646; *Industrial Statistics Yearbook*.

JAPAN - GENERAL MORTALITY

European Community Information Service, 2100 M Street, NW, Washington, D.C. 20037 (202) 862-9500; *Basic Statistics of the Community*.

Statistical Office of the United Nations, Publishing Service, New York, New York 10017 (800) 253-9646; *Demographic Yearbook*.

World Health Organization, Office of Publications, Avenue Appia, CH-1211 Geneva 27, Switzerland (Telephone Number in U.S. (518) 436-9686); *World Health Statistics Annual*.

JAPAN - GEOGRAPHIC DATA

European Community Information Service, 2100 M Street, NW, Washington, D.C. 20037 (202) 862-9500; *Basic Statistics of the Community*.

Facts on File, 460 Park Avenue South, New York, New York 10016 (800) 443-8323; *The New Book of World Rankings*.

JAPAN - GLASS AND GLASS PRODUCTS - PRODUCTION INDEX

Organisation for Economic Co-operation and Development (OECD), 2 rue Andre-Pascal, 75 Paris 16, France (Telephone Number in U.S. (202) 785-6323); *Indicators of Industrial Activity.*

JAPAN - GOATS - See JAPAN - LIVESTOCK AND POULTRY

JAPAN - GOLD HOLDINGS

International Monetary Fund, 700 Nineteenth Street, NW, Washington, D.C. 20431 (202) 623-7000; *International Financial Statistics.*

Statistical Office of the United Nations, Publishing Service, New York, New York 10017 (800) 253-9646; *Statistical Yearbook.*

JAPAN - GOLD PRODUCTION AND CONSUMPTION - See JAPAN - MINING AND MINERAL PRODUCTS

JAPAN - GOVERNMENT

European Community Information Service, 2100 M Street, NW, Washington, D.C. 20037 (202) 862-9500; *Basic Statistics of the Community.*

G.K. Hall and Company, 70 Lincoln Street, Boston, Massachusetts 02111 (617) 423-3990; *The World in Figures.*

JAPAN - GOVERNMENT CONSUMPTION

European Community Information Service, 2100 M Street, NW, Washington, D.C. 20037 (202) 862-9500; *Basic Statistics of the Community.*

International Monetary Fund, 700 Nineteenth Street, NW, Washington, D.C. 20431 (202) 623-7000; *International Financial Statistics.*

JAPAN - GOVERNMENT EXPENDITURE

European Community Information Service, 2100 M Street, NW, Washington, D.C. 20037 (202) 862-9500; *Basic Statistics of the Community.*

Organisation for Economic Co-operation and Development (OECD), 2 rue Andre-Pascal, 75 Paris 16, France (Telephone Number in U.S. (202) 785-6323); *Economic Outlook.*

JAPAN - GOVERNMENT FINANCES

European Community Information Service, 2100 M Street, NW, Washington, D.C. 20037 (202) 862-9500; *Basic Statistics of the Community.*

International Monetary Fund, 700 Nineteenth Street, NW, Washington, D.C. 20431 (202) 623-7000; *International Financial Statistics.*

Organisation for Economic Co-operation and Development (OECD), 2 rue Andre-Pascal, 75 Paris 16, France (Telephone Number in U.S. (202) 785-6323); *Economic Outlook.*

Statistical Office of the United Nations, Publishing Service, New York, New York 10017 (800) 253-9646; *Statistical Yearbook.*

JAPAN - GOVERNMENT REVENUES

European Community Information Service, 2100 M Street, NW, Washington, D.C. 20037 (202) 862-9500; *Basic Statistics of the Community.*

International Monetary Fund, 700 Nineteenth Street, NW, Washington, D.C. 20431 (202) 623-7000; *Government Finance Statistics Yearbook.*

Organisation for Economic Co-operation and Development (OECD), 2 rue Andre-Pascal, 75 Paris 16, France (Telephone Number in U.S. (202) 785-6323); *Economic Outlook,* and *Revenue Statistics of OECD Member Countries.*

Times Books, 201 East 50th Street, New York, New York 10022 (212) 751-2600; *The Economist Book of Vital World Statistics.*

JAPAN - GRAIN PRODUCTION - See JAPAN - CROPS

JAPAN - GRANTS

International Monetary Fund, 700 Nineteenth Street, NW, Washington, D.C. 20431 (202) 623-7000; *Government Finance Statistics Yearbook.*

National Technical Information Service, 5285 Port Royal Road, Springfield, Virginia 22161 (703) 487-4600; *Handbook of Economic Statistics.*

Organisation for Economic Co-operation and Development (OECD), 2 rue Andre-Pascal, 75 Paris 16, France (Telephone Number in U.S. (202) 785-6323); *Geographical Distribution of Financial Flows to Developing Countries.*

JAPAN - GREEN PEPPER AND CHILIE PRODUCTION - See JAPAN - CROPS

JAPAN - GROSS DOMESTIC PRODUCT

The Economist Intelligence Unit, 111 West 57th Street, New York, New York 10019 (800) 938-4085; *The World Market Atlas.*

The Economist Intelligence Unit (Asia) Limited, 10th Floor, Luk Kwok Centre, 72 Gloucester Road, Wanchai, Hong Kong (Phone Number in U.S. (800) 938-4685); *Asian Market Atlas.*

Euromonitor Publications Limited, 87-88 Turnmill Street, London EC1M 5QU, England; *International Marketing Data and Statistics,* and *The Pacific Basin: An Economic Handbook.*

European Community Information Service, 2100 M Street, NW, Washington, D.C. 20037 (202) 862-9500; *Basic Statistics of the Community.*

Facts on File, 460 Park Avenue South, New York, New York (800) 443-8323; *The New Book of World Rankings.*

G.K. Hall and Company, 70 Lincoln Street, Boston, Massachusetts 02111 (617) 423-3990; *The World in Figures.*

International Monetary Fund, 700 Nineteenth Street, NW, Washington, D.C. 20431 (202) 623-7000; *International Financial Statistics.*

National Technical Information Service, 5285 Port Royal Road, Springfield, Virginia 22161 (703) 487-4600; *Handbook of Economic Statistics.*

Organisation for Economic Co-operation and Development (OECD), 2 rue Andre-Pascal, 75 Paris 16, France (Telephone Number in U.S. (202) 785-6323); *Economic Outlook, Geographical Distribution of Financial Flows to Developing Countries*, and *Revenue Statistics of OECD Member Countries*.

Statistical Office of the United Nations, Publishing Service, New York, New York 10017 (800) 253-9646; *Statistical Yearbook*.

Times Books, 201 East 50th Street, New York, New York 10022 (212) 751-2600; *The Economist Book of Vital World Statistics*.

JAPAN - GROSS NATIONAL PRODUCT

Euromonitor Publications Limited, 87-88 Turnmill Street, London EC1M 5QU, England; *International Marketing Data and Statistics*.

European Community Information Service, 2100 M Street, NW, Washington, D.C. 20037 (202) 862-9500; *Basic Statistics of the Community*.

National Technical Information Service, 5285 Port Royal Road, Springfield, Virginia 22161 (703) 487-4600; *Handbook of Economic Statistics*.

Organisation for Economic Co-operation and Development (OECD), 2 rue Andre-Pascal, 75 Paris 16, France (Telephone Number in U.S. (202) 785-6323); *Economic Outlook*, and *Geographical Distribution of Financial Flows to Developing Countries*.

U.S. Arms Control and Disarmament Agency, 320 Twenty-first Street, NW, Washington, D.C. 20451 (202) 647-8677; *World Military Expenditures and Arms Transfers*.

JAPAN - GROUNDNUTS PRODUCTION - See JAPAN - CROPS

JAPAN - HAY PRODUCTION - See JAPAN - CROPS

JAPAN - HAZELNUT PRODUCTION - See JAPAN - CROPS

JAPAN - HEALTH

The Economist Intelligence Unit (Asia) Limited, 10th Floor, Luk Kwok Centre, 72 Gloucester Road, Wanchai, Hong Kong (Phone Number in U.S. (800) 938-4685); *Asian Market Atlas*.

Euromonitor Publications Limited, 87-88 Turnmill Street, London EC1M 5QU, England; *The Pacific Basin: An Economic Handbook*.

European Community Information Service, 2100 M Street, NW, Washington, D.C. 20037 (202) 862-9500; *Basic Statistics of the Community*.

Facts on File, 460 Park Avenue South, New York, New York 10016; *The New Book of World Rankings*.

G.K. Hall and Company, 70 Lincoln Street, Boston, Massachusetts 02111 (617) 423-3990; *The World in Figures*.

Organisation for Economic Corporation and Development (OECD), 2 rue Andre-Pascal, 75 Paris 16, France (Telephone Number in U.S. (202) 785-6323); *OECD Health Systems: Facts and Trends*.

Statistical Office of the United Nations, Publishing Service, New York, New York 10017 (800) 253-9646; *Statistical Yearbook*.

Statistics Bureau, Management and Coordination Agency, Japan; *Statistical Indicators on Social Life*.

Times Books, 201 East 50th Street, New York, New York 10022 (212) 751-2600; *The Economist Book of Vital World Statistics*.

World Health Organization, Office of Publications, Avenue Appia, CH-1211 Geneva 27, Switzerland (Telephone Number in U.S. (518) 436-9686); *World Health Statistics Annual*.

JAPAN - HEMP FIBRE PRODUCTION - See JAPAN - TEXTILE INDUSTRY

JAPAN - HIDE PRODUCTION

Food and Agricultural Organization of the United Nations (FAO), Via delle Terme di Caracalla, 00100 Rome, Italy (Telephone Number in U.S. (202) 653-2400); *Production Yearbook*.

Organisation for Economic Co-operation and Development (OECD), 2 rue Andre-Pascal, 75 Paris 16, France (Telephone Number in U.S. (202) 785-6323); *The Footwear, Raw Hides and Skins, and Leather Industry in OECD Countries, Foreign Trade by Commodities*, and *Indicators of Industrial Activity*.

JAPAN - HIGHWAYS

The Economist Intelligence Unit (Asia) Limited, 10th Floor, Luk Kwok Centre, 72 Gloucester Road, Wanchai, Hong Kong (Phone Number in U.S. (800) 938-4685); *Asian Market Atlas*.

European Community Information Service, 2100 M Street, NW, Washington, D.C. 20037 (202) 862-9500; *Basic Statistics of the Community*.

G.K. Hall and Company, 70 Lincoln Street, Boston, Massachusetts 02111 (617) 423-3990; *The World in Figures*.

International Road Federation, 525 School Street, SW, Washington, D.C. 20024 (202) 554-2106; *World Road Statistics*.

JAPAN - HOME FINANCE

Organisation for Economic Co-operation and Development (OECD), 2 rue Andre-Pascal, 75 Paris 16, France (Telephone Number in U.S. (202) 785-6323); *Main Economic Indicators - Historical Statistics*.

JAPAN - HONEY PRODUCTION

Commodity Research Bureau, Incorporated, 75 Wall Street, New York, New York 10005 (212) 504-7754; *Commodity Year Book*.

JAPAN - HOPS PRODUCTION - See JAPAN - CROPS

JAPAN - HORSES - See JAPAN - LIVESTOCK AND POULTRY

JAPAN - HOURS OF WORK - See JAPAN - EMPLOYMENT

JAPAN - HOUSING AND HOUSING UNITS

European Community Information Service, 2100 M Street, NW, Washington, D.C. 20037 (202) 862-9500; *Basic Statistics of the Community*.

Facts on File, 460 Park Avenue South, New York, New York 10016; *The New Book of World Rankings*.

National Technical Information Service, 5285 Port Royal Road, Springfield, Virginia 22161 (703) 487-4600; *Handbook of Economic Statistics*.

Statistical Office of the United Nations, Publishing Service, New York, New York 10017 (800) 253-9646; *Statistical Yearbook.*

Statistics Bureau, Management and Coordination Agency, Japan; *Statistical Indicators on Social Life.*

JAPAN - HOUSING CONSTRUCTION - See JAPAN - CONSTRUCTION INDUSTRY

JAPAN - HOUSING EXPENDITURES

European Community Information Service, 2100 M Street, NW, Washington, D.C. 20037 (202) 862-9500; *Basic Statistics of the Community.*

JAPAN - HYDROCHLORIC ACID PRODUCTION

European Community Information Service, 2100 M Street, NW, Washington, D.C. 20037 (202) 862-9500; *Basic Statistics of the Community.*

Statistical Office of the United Nations, Publishing Service, New York, New York 10017 (800) 253-9646; *Statistical Yearbook.*

JAPAN - ILLITERATE POPULATION

The Economist Intelligence Unit, 111 West 57th Street, New York, New York 10019 (800) 938-4685; *The World Market Atlas.*

G.K. Hall and Company, 70 Lincoln Street, Boston, Massachusetts 02111 (617) 423-3990; *The World in Figures.*

United Nations Educational, Scientific and Cultural Organization (UNESCO), 7 Place de Fontenoy, F-76700 Paris, France (Telephone Number in U.S. (212) 963-5981); *Statistical Yearbook.*

JAPAN - IMPORTS

American Automobile Manufacturers Association, 1401 H Street, NW, Suite 900, Washington, D.C. 20005 (202) 326-5500; *World Motor Vehicle Data.*

The Economist Intelligence Unit, 111 West 57th Street, New York, New York 10019 (800) 938-4685; *The World Market Atlas.*

The Economist Intelligence Unit (Asia) Limited, 10th Floor, Luk Kwok Centre, 72 Gloucester Road, Wanchai, Hong Kong (Phone Number in U.S. (800) 938-4685); *Asian Market Atlas.*

Euromonitor Publications Limited, 87-88 Turnmill Street, London EC1M 5QU, England; *International Marketing Data and Statistics,* and *The Pacific Basin: An Economic Handbook.*

European Community Information Service, 2100 M Street, NW, Washington, D.C. 20037 (202) 862-9500; *Basic Statistics of the Community.*

Food and Agricultural Organization of the United Nations (FAO), Via delle Terme di Caracalla, 00100 Rome, Italy (Telephone Number in U.S. (202) 653-2400); *The State of Food and Agriculture.*

G.K. Hall and Company, 70 Lincoln Street, Boston, Massachusetts 02111 (617) 423-3990; *The World in Figures.*

International Lead and Zinc Study Group, Metro House, 58 St. James's Street, London SW1A 1LD England; *Lead and Zinc Statistics.*

International Monetary Fund, 700 Nineteenth Street, NW, Washington, D.C. 20431 (202) 623-7000; *Direction of Trade Statistics,* and *International Financial Statistics.*

International Rubber Study Group, York House, 8th Floor, Empire Way, Wembley, London HA9 0PA, England; *Rubber Statistical Bulletin.*

National Technical Information Service, 5285 Port Royal Road, Springfield, Virginia 22161 (703) 487-4600; *Handbook of Economic Statistics.*

Organisation for Economic Co-operation and Development (OECD), 2 rue Andre-Pascal, 75 Paris 16, France (Telephone Number in U.S. (202) 785-6323); *Economic Outlook, The Footwear, Raw Hides and Skins, and Leather Industry in OECD Countries, Industrial Structure Statistics, The Iron and Steel Industry, Milk, Milk Products, and Egg Balances in OECD Member Countries, OECD Economic Surveys: Japan, The Pulp and Paper Industry,* and *Review of Fisheries in OECD Member Countries.*

Statistical Office of the United Nations, Publishing Service, New York, New York 10017 (800) 253-9646; *Foreign Trade Statistics of Asia and the Pacific.*

Times Books, 201 East 50th Street, New York, New York 10022 (212) 751-2600; *The Economist Book of Vital World Statistics.*

JAPAN - INCOME TAXES - See JAPAN - TAXATION

JAPAN - INDUSTRIAL METALS PRODUCTION - See JAPAN - MINING AND MINERAL PRODUCTS

JAPAN - INDUSTRY

Euromonitor Publications Limited, 87-88 Turnmill Street, London EC1M 5QU, England; *International Marketing Data and Statistics.*

European Community Information Service, 2100 M Street, NW, Washington, D.C. 20037 (202) 862-9500; *Basic Statistics of the Community.*

Facts on File, 460 Park Avenue South, New York, New York (800) 443-8323; *The New Book of World Rankings.*

G.K. Hall and Company, 70 Lincoln Street, Boston, Massachusetts 02111 (617) 423-3990; *The World in Figures.*

International Labour Office, I.L.O. Publications, CH-1211, Geneva 22, Switzerland; *Yearbook of Labour Statistics.*

National Technical Information Service, 5285 Port Royal Road, Springfield, Virginia 22161 (703) 487-4600; *Handbook of Economic Statistics.*

Organisation for Economic Co-operation and Development (OECD), 2 rue Andre-Pascal, 75 Paris 16, France (Telephone Number in U.S. (202) 785-6323); *Economic Outlook, Industrial Structure Statistics, Main Economic Indicators - Historical Statistics,* and *OECD Environmental Data.*

Statistical Office of the United Nations, Publishing Service, New York, New York 10017 (800) 253-9646; *Statistical Yearbook,* and *Statistical Yearbook for Asia and the Pacific.*

Statistics Bureau, Management and Coordination Agency, Japan; *Statistical Indicators on Social Life.*

Times Books, 201 East 50th Street, New York, New York 10022 (212) 751-2600; *The Economist Book of Vital World Statistics.*

World Intellectual Property Organization, 34 Chemin des Colombettes, CH-1211 Geneva 20, Switzerland; *Industrial Property Statistics.*

JAPAN - INFANT MORTALITY RATE

The Economist Intelligence Unit (Asia) Limited, 10th Floor, Luk Kwok Centre, 72 Gloucester Road, Wanchai, Hong Kong (Phone Number in U.S. (800) 938-4685); *Asian Market Atlas.*

European Community Information Service, 2100 M Street, NW, Washington, D.C. 20037 (202) 862-9500; *Basic Statistics of the Community.*

Statistical Office of the United Nations, Publishing Service, New York, New York 10017 (800) 253-9646; *Demographic Yearbook,* and *Statistical Yearbook.*

Statistics Bureau, Management and Coordination Agency, Japan; *Statistical Indicators on Social Life.*

Times Books, 201 East 50th Street, New York, New York 10022 (212) 751-2600; *The Economist Book of Vital World Statistics.*

World Health Organization, Office of Publications, Avenue Appia, CH-1211 Geneva 27, Switzerland (Telephone Number in U.S. (518) 436-9686); *World Health Statistics Annual.*

JAPAN - INFLATIONARY FACTORS

National Technical Information Service, 5285 Port Royal Road, Springfield, Virginia 22161 (703) 487-4600; *Handbook of Economic Statistics.*

JAPAN - INTEREST RATES

Euromonitor Publications Limited, 87-88 Turnmill Street, London EC1M 5QU, England; *The Pacific Basin: An Economic Handbook.*

National Technical Information Service, 5285 Port Royal Road, Springfield, Virginia 22161 (703) 487-4600; *Handbook of Economic Statistics.*

Organisation for Economic Co-operation and Development (OECD), 2 rue Andre-Pascal, 75 Paris 16, France (Telephone Number in U.S. (202) 785-6323); *Economic Outlook, Financial Market Trends, Main Economic Indicators - Historical Statistics,* and *OECD Financial Statistics.*

JAPAN - INTERNAL TRADE

European Community Information Service, 2100 M Street, NW, Washington, D.C. 20037 (202) 862-9500; *Basic Statistics of the Community.*

Organisation for Economic Co-operation and Development (OECD), 2 rue Andre-Pascal, 75 Paris 16, France (Telephone Number in U.S. (202) 785-6323); *Main Economic Indicators - Historical Statistics.*

Statistical Office of the United Nations, Publishing Service, New York, New York 10017 (800) 253-9646; *Statistical Yearbook,* and *Statistical Yearbook for Asia and the Pacific.*

JAPAN - INTERNATIONAL FINANCE

European Community Information Service, 2100 M Street, NW, Washington, D.C. 20037 (202) 862-9500; *Basic Statistics of the Community.*

Organisation for Economic Co-operation and Development (OECD), 2 rue Andre-Pascal, 75 Paris 16, France (Telephone Number in U.S. (202) 785-6323); *Economic Outlook,* and *Financial Market Trends.*

JAPAN - INTERNATIONAL LIQUIDITY

International Monetary Fund, 700 Nineteenth Street, NW, Washington, D.C. 20431 (202) 623-7000; *International Financial Statistics.*

Organisation for Economic Co-operation and Development (OECD), 2 rue Andre-Pascal, 75 Paris 16, France (Telephone Number in U.S. (202) 785-6323); *Economic Outlook,* and *Financial Market Trends.*

JAPAN - INTERNATIONAL RESERVES EXCLUDING GOLD

National Technical Information Service, 5285 Port Royal Road, Springfield, Virginia 22161 (703) 487-4600; *Handbook of Economic Statistics.*

Statistical Office of the United Nations, Publishing Service, New York, New York 10017 (800) 253-9646; *Statistical Yearbook.*

JAPAN - INTERNATIONAL STATISTICS

Organisation for Economic Co-operation and Development (OECD), 2 rue Andre-Pascal, 75 Paris 16, France (Telephone Number in U.S. (202) 785-6323); *Financial Market Trends,* and *Tourism Policy and International Tourism in OECD Member Countries.*

JAPAN - INVESTMENTS

International Monetary Fund, 700 Nineteenth Street, NW, Washington, D.C. 20431 (202) 623-7000; *International Financial Statistics.*

Organisation for Economic Co-operation and Development (OECD), 2 rue Andre-Pascal, 75 Paris 16, France (Telephone Number in U.S. (202) 785-6323); *Economic Outlook, Financial Market Trends, Industrial Structure Statistics, The Iron and Steel Industry,* and *Textile Industry in OECD Countries.*

JAPAN - IRON ORE - See JAPAN - MINING AND MINERAL PRODUCTS

JAPAN - IRRIGATION

Euromonitor Publications Limited, 87-88 Turnmill Street, London EC1M 5QU, England; *International Marketing Data and Statistics.*

JAPAN - JUTE PRODUCTION - See JAPAN - CROPS

JAPAN - LABOR FORCE

The Economist Intelligence Unit (Asia) Limited, 10th Floor, Luk Kwok Centre, 72 Gloucester Road, Wanchai, Hong Kong (Phone Number in U.S. (800) 938-4685); *Asian Market Atlas.*

Euromonitor Publications Limited, 87-88 Turnmill Street, London EC1M 5QU, England; *International Marketing Data and Statistics,* and *The Pacific Basin: An Economic Handbook.*

European Community Information Service, 2100 M Street, NW, Washington, D.C. 20037 (202) 862-9500; *Basic Statistics of the Community.*

Facts on File, 460 Park Avenue South, New York, New York (800) 443-8323; *The New Book of World Rankings.*

Food and Agricultural Organization of the United Nations (FAO), Via delle Terme di Caracalla, 00100 Rome, Italy (Telephone Number in U.S. (202) 653-2400); *The State of Food and Agriculture.*

G.K. Hall and Company, 70 Lincoln Street, Boston, Massachusetts 02111 (617) 423-3990; *The World in Figures.*

National Technical Information Service, 5285 Port Royal Road, Springfield, Virginia 22161 (703) 487-4600; *Handbook of Economic Statistics.*

Organisation for Economic Co-operation and Development (OECD), 2 rue Andre-Pascal, 75 Paris 16, France (Telephone Number in U.S. (202) 785-6323); *Economic Outlook, The Iron and Steel Industry, Labour Force Statistics, Main Economic Indicators - Historical Statistics, Maritime Transport, OECD Economic Surveys: Japan, OECD Employment Outlook,* and *Textile Industry in OECD Countries.*

Statistics Bureau, Management and Coordination Agency, Japan; *Statistical Indicators on Social Life.*

Times Books, 201 East 50th Street, New York, New York 10022 (212) 751-2600; *The Economist Book of Vital World Statistics.*

JAPAN - LABOR PRODUCTIVITY

International Labour Office, I.L.O. Publications, CH-1211, Geneva 22, Switzerland; *Yearbook of Labour Statistics.*

Organisation for Economic Co-operation and Development (OECD), 2 rue Andre-Pascal, 75 Paris 16, France (Telephone Number in U.S. (202) 785-6323); *Economic Outlook,* and *OECD Employment Outlook.*

JAPAN - LAND USE

Euromonitor Publications Limited, 87-88 Turnmill Street, London EC1M 5QU, England; *International Marketing Data and Statistics.*

European Community Information Service, 2100 M Street, NW, Washington, D.C. 20037 (202) 862-9500; *Basic Statistics of the Community.*

Food and Agricultural Organization of the United Nations (FAO), Via delle Terme di Caracalla, 00100 Rome, Italy (Telephone Number in U.S. (202) 653-2400); *Production Yearbook.*

G.K. Hall and Company, 70 Lincoln Street, Boston, Massachusetts 02111 (617) 423-3990; *The World in Figures.*

JAPAN - LEAD AND LEAD ORE - See JAPAN - MINING AND MINERAL PRODUCTS

JAPAN - LEATHER - PRODUCTION INDEX

Organisation for Economic Co-operation and Development (OECD), 2 rue Andre-Pascal, 75 Paris 16, France (Telephone Number in U.S. (202) 785-6323); *Indicators of Industrial Activity.*

JAPAN - LEATHER AND FOOTWEAR EXPORTS AND IMPORTS

European Community Information Service, 2100 M Street, NW, Washington, D.C. 20037 (202) 862-9500; *Basic Statistics of the Community.*

Organisation for Economic Co-operation and Development (OECD), 2 rue Andre-Pascal, 75 Paris 16, France (Telephone Number in U.S. (202) 785-6323); *The Footwear, Raw Hides and Skins, and Leather Industry in OECD Countries.*

Statistical Office of the United Nations, Publishing Service, New York, New York 10017 (800) 253-9646; *Trade in Manufactures of Developing Countries.*

JAPAN - LIBRARIES

Facts on File, 460 Park Avenue South, New York, New York (800) 443-8323; *The New Book of World Rankings.*

United Nations Educational, Scientific and Cultural Organization (UNESCO), 7 Place de Fontenoy, F-75700 Paris, France (Telephone Number in U.S. (212) 963-5981); *Statistical Yearbook.*

JAPAN - LIFE EXPECTANCY

The Economist Intelligence Unit (Asia) Limited, 10th Floor, Luk Kwok Centre, 72 Gloucester Road, Wanchai, Hong Kong (Phone Number in U.S. (800) 938-4685); *Asian Market Atlas.*

JAPAN - LIGNITE PRODUCTION - See JAPAN - MINING AND MINERAL PRODUCTS

JAPAN - LIVESTOCK AND POULTRY

Commodity Research Bureau, Incorporated, 75 Wall Street, New York, New York 10005 (212) 504-7754; *Commodity Year Book.*

Euromonitor Publications Limited, 87-88 Turnmill Street, London EC1M 5QU, England; *International Marketing Data and Statistics.*

European Community Information Service, 2100 M Street, NW, Washington, D.C. 20037 (202) 862-9500; *Basic Statistics of the Community.*

Facts on File, 460 Park Avenue South, New York, New York 10016; *The New Book of World Rankings.*

Food and Agricultural Organization of the United Nations (FAO), Via delle Terme di Caracalla, 00100 Rome, Italy (Telephone Number in U.S. (202) 653-2400); *Production Yearbook,* and *The State of Food and Agriculture.*

G.K. Hall and Company, 70 Lincoln Street, Boston, Massachusetts 02111 (617) 423-3990; *The World in Figures.*

National Technical Information Service, 5285 Port Royal Road, Springfield, Virginia 22161 (703) 487-4600; *Handbook of Economic Statistics.*

Organisation for Economic Co-operation and Development (OECD), 2 rue Andre-Pascal, 75 Paris 16, France (Telephone Number in U.S. (202) 785-6323); *Economic Accounts for Agriculture, Indicators of Industrial Activity,* and *Meat Balances in OECD Member Countries.*

Statistical Office of the United Nations, Publishing Service, New York, New York 10017 (800) 253-9646; *Statistical Yearbook.*

JAPAN - LIVING LEVELS

G.K. Hall and Company, 70 Lincoln Street, Boston, Massachusetts 02111 (617) 423-3990; *The World in Figures*.

Organisation for Economic Co-operation and Development (OECD), 2 rue Andre-Pascal, 75 Paris 16, France (Telephone Number in U.S. (202) 785-6323); *Economic Outlook*.

Statistics Bureau, Management and Coordination Agency, Japan; *Statistical Indicators on Social Life*.

Times Books, 201 East 50th Street, New York, New York 10022 (212) 751-2600; *The Economist Book of Vital World Statistics*.

JAPAN - MACHINERY - PRODUCTION INDEX

Organisation for Economic Co-operation and Development (OECD), 2 rue Andre-Pascal, 75 Paris 16, France (Telephone Number in U.S. (202) 785-6323); *Indicators of Industrial Activity*.

JAPAN - MAGNESIUM PRODUCTION AND CONSUMPTION - See JAPAN - MINING AND MINERAL PRODUCTS

JAPAN - MAIL - NUMBER OF ITEMS SENT AND RECEIVED

Statistical Office of the United Nations, Publishing Service, New York, New York 10017 (800) 253-9646; *Statistical Yearbook*.

JAPAN - MAIN ECONOMIC INDICATORS - See JAPAN - ECONOMY

JAPAN - MANGANESE AND MANGANESE ORE - See JAPAN - MINING AND MINERAL PRODUCTS

JAPAN - MANPOWER

Statistical Office of the United Nations, Publishing Service, New York, New York 10017 (800) 253-9646; *Statistical Yearbook for Asia and the Pacific*.

JAPAN - MANUFACTURING

American Automobile Manufacturers Association, 1401 H Street, NW, Suite 900, Washington, D.C. 20005 (202) 326-5500; *World Motor Vehicle Data*.

European Community Information Service, 2100 M Street, NW, Washington, D.C. 20037 (202) 862-9500; *Basic Statistics of the Community*.

Facts on File, 460 Park Avenue South, New York, New York 10016; *The New Book of World Rankings*.

G.K. Hall and Company, 70 Lincoln Street, Boston, Massachusetts 02111 (617) 423-3990; *The World in Figures*.

National Technical Information Service, 5285 Port Royal Road, Springfield, Virginia 22161 (703) 487-4600; *Handbook of Economic Statistics*.

Organisation for Economic Co-operation and Development (OECD), 2 rue Andre-Pascal, 75 Paris 16, France (Telephone Number in U.S. (202) 785-6323); *Foreign Trade by Commodities, Indicators of Industrial Activity, Industrial Structure Statistics*, and *OECD Economic Surveys: Japan*.

Statistical Office of the United Nations, Publishing Service, New York, New York 10017 (800) 253-9646; *Statistical Yearbook*.

Statistics Bureau, Management and Coordination Agency, Japan; *Statistical Indicators on Social Life*, and *Statistical Yearbook*.

Times Books, 201 East 50th Street, New York, New York 10022 (212) 751-2600; *The Economist Book of Vital World Statistics*.

JAPAN - MARRIAGE RATES

European Community Information Service, 2100 M Street, NW, Washington, D.C. 20037 (202) 862-9500; *Basic Statistics of the Community*.

Facts on File, 460 Park Avenue South, New York, New York 10016; *The New Book of World Rankings*.

Statistical Office of the United Nations, Publishing Service, New York, New York 10017 (800) 253-9646; *Demographic Yearbook*, and *Statistical Yearbook*.

Statistics Bureau, Management and Coordination Agency, Japan; *Statistical Indicators on Social Life*.

JAPAN - MEAT PRODUCTION - See JAPAN - LIVESTOCK AND POULTRY

JAPAN - MERCHANT SHIPPING

European Community Information Service, 2100 M Street, NW, Washington, D.C. 20037 (202) 862-9500; *Basic Statistics of the Community*.

G.K. Hall and Company, 70 Lincoln Street, Boston, Massachusetts 02111 (617) 423-3990; *The World in Figures*.

Lloyd's Register of Shipping, 17 Battery Place, New York, New York 10004; *Register of Ships*.

National Technical Information Service, 5285 Port Royal Road, Springfield, Virginia 22161 (703) 487-4600; *Handbook of Economic Statistics*.

Organisation for Economic Co-operation and Development (OECD), 2 rue Andre-Pascal, 75 Paris 16, France (Telephone Number in U.S. (202) 785-6323); *Maritime Transport*.

Statistical Office of the United Nations, Publishing Service, New York, New York 10017 (800) 253-9646; *Statistical Yearbook*.

Times Books, 201 East 50th Street, New York, New York 10022 (212) 751-2600; *The Economist Book of Vital World Statistics*.

U.S. Department of Transportation, Maritime Administration, 400 Seventh Street, SW, Washington, D.C. 20590; *A Statistical Analysis of the World's Merchant Fleets*.

JAPAN - MERCURY PRODUCTION AND CONSUMPTION - See JAPAN - MINING AND MINERAL PRODUCTS

JAPAN - METAL PRODUCTS - See JAPAN - MINING AND MINERAL PRODUCTS

JAPAN - MILITARY

The Economist Intelligence Unit (Asia) Limited, 10th Floor, Luk Kwok Centre, 72 Gloucester Road, Wanchai, Hong Kong (Phone Number in U.S. (800) 938-4685); *Asian Market Atlas*.

G.K. Hall and Company, 70 Lincoln Street, Boston, Massachusetts 02111 (617) 423-3990; *The World in Figures*.

The International Institute for Strategic Studies, 23 Tavistock Street, London WC2E 7NQ, England; *The Military Balance.*

U.S. Arms Control and Disarmament Agency, 320 Twenty-first Street, NW, Washington, D.C. 20451 (202) 647-8677; *World Military Expenditures and Arms Transfers.*

JAPAN - MILK PRODUCTION - See JAPAN - DAIRY PRODUCTS

JAPAN - MILLET PRODUCTION - See JAPAN - CROPS

JAPAN - MINING AND MINERAL PRODUCTS

Commodity Research Bureau, Incorporated, 75 Wall Street, New York, New York 10005 (212) 504-7754; *Commodity Year Book.*

European Community Information Service, 2100 M Street, NW, Washington, D.C. 20037 (202) 862-9500; *Basic Statistics of the Community.*

Facts on File, 460 Park Avenue South, New York, New York 10016 (800) 443-8323; *The New Book of World Rankings.*

G.K. Hall and Company, 70 Lincoln Street, Boston, Massachusetts 02111 (617) 423-3990; *The World in Figures.*

International Lead and Zinc Study Group, Metro House, 58 St. James's Street, London SW1A 1LD England; *Lead and Zinc Statistics.*

National Technical Information Service, 5285 Port Royal Road, Springfield, Virginia 22161 (703) 487-4600; *Handbook of Economic Statistics.*

Organisation for Economic Co-operation and Development (OECD), 2 rue Andre-Pascal, 75 Paris 16, France (Telephone Number in U.S. (202) 785-6323); *Coal Information, Energy Statistics of OECD Countries, Foreign Trade by Commodities, Indicators of Industrial Activity, Industrial Structure Statistics, The Iron and Steel Industry, The Non-Ferrous Metals Industry,* and *OECD Economic Surveys: Japan.*

Penn Well Publishing Company, 1421 South Sheridan Road, Post Office Box 1260, Tulsa, Oklahoma 74101 (800) 752-9764; *International Energy Statistics Sourcebook.*

Statistical Office of the United Nations, Publishing Service, New York, New York 10017 (800) 253-9646; *Statistical Yearbook.*

World Bureau of Metal Statistics, 27-A High Street, Ware, Herts. SG12 9BA, England; *World Metal Statistics.*

JAPAN - MOLYBDENUM AND MOLYBDENUM ORE - See JAPAN - MINING AND MINERAL PRODUCTS

JAPAN - MONEY AND CREDIT

Organisation for Economic Co-operation and Development (OECD), 2 rue Andre-Pascal, 75 Paris 16, France (Telephone Number in U.S. (202) 785-6323); *OECD Economic Surveys: Japan.*

JAPAN - MONEY EXCHANGE RATE

Euromonitor Publications Limited, 87-88 Turnmill Street, London EC1M 5QU, England; *International Marketing Data and Statistics.*

European Community Information Service, 2100 M Street, NW, Washington, D.C. 20037 (202) 862-9500; *Basic Statistics of the Community.*

International Monetary Fund, 700 Nineteenth Street, NW, Washington, D.C. 20431 (202) 623 7000; *International Financial Statistics.*

Organisation for Economic Co-operation and Development (OECD), 2 rue Andre-Pascal, 75 Paris 16, France (Telephone Number in U.S. (202) 785-6323); *Economic Outlook, Financial Market Trends,* and *Tourism Policy and International Tourism in OECD Member Countries.*

Statistical Office of the United Nations, Publishing Service, New York, New York 10017 (800) 253-9646; *Statistical Yearbook.*

JAPAN - MONEY RATES - MARKET

European Community Information Service, 2100 M Street, NW, Washington, D.C. 20037 (202) 862-9500; *Basic Statistics of the Community.*

Organisation for Economic Co-operation and Development (OECD), 2 rue Andre-Pascal, 75 Paris 16, France (Telephone Number in U.S. (202) 785-6323); *Economic Outlook,* and *Financial Market Trends.*

Statistical Office of the United Nations, Publishing Service, New York, New York 10017 (800) 253-9646; *Statistical Yearbook.*

JAPAN - MONEY RESERVES

Euromonitor Publications Limited, 87-88 Turnmill Street, London EC1M 5QU, England; *International Marketing Data and Statistics.*

European Community Information Service, 2100 M Street, NW, Washington, D.C. 20037 (202) 862-9500; *Basic Statistics of the Community.*

Organisation for Economic Co-operation and Development (OECD), 2 rue Andre-Pascal, 75 Paris 16, France (Telephone Number in U.S. (202) 785-6323); *Economic Outlook,* and *Financial Market Trends.*

JAPAN - MONEY SUPPLY

Euromonitor Publications Limited, 87-88 Turnmill Street, London EC1M 5QU, England; *International Marketing Data and Statistics.*

European Community Information Service, 2100 M Street, NW, Washington, D.C. 20037 (202) 862-9500; *Basic Statistics of the Community.*

G.K. Hall and Company, 70 Lincoln Street, Boston, Massachusetts 02111 (617) 423-3990; *The World in Figures.*

International Monetary Fund, 700 Nineteenth Street, NW, Washington, D.C. 20431 (202) 623-7000; *International Financial Statistics.*

Organisation for Economic Co-operation and Development (OECD), 2 rue Andre-Pascal, 75 Paris 16, France (Telephone Number in U.S. (202) 785-6323); *Economic Outlook.*

Statistical Office of the United Nations, Publishing Service, New York, New York 10017 (800) 253-9646; *Statistical Yearbook.*

JAPAN - MOTION PICTURES

Statistical Office of the United Nations, Publishing Service, New York, New York 10017 (800) 253-9646; *Statistical Yearbook.*

United Nations Educational, Scientific and Cultural Organization (UNESCO), 7 Place de Fontenoy, F-75700 Paris, France (Telephone

Number in U.S. (212) 963-5981); *Statistical Yearbook.*

JAPAN - MOTOR VEHICLE PRODUCTION

American Automobile Manufacturers Association, 1401 H Street, NW, Suite 900, Washington, D.C. 20005 (202) 326-5500; *World Motor Vehicle Data.*

European Community Information Service, 2100 M Street, NW, Washington, D.C. 20037 (202) 862-9500; *Basic Statistics of the Community.*

National Technical Information Service, 5285 Port Royal Road, Springfield, Virginia 22161 (703) 487-4600; *Handbook of Economic Statistics.*

Organisation for Economic Co-operation and Development (OECD), 2 rue Andre-Pascal, 75 Paris 16, France (Telephone Number in U.S. (202) 785-6323); *Foreign Trade by Commodities,* and *Indicators of Industrial Activity.*

Statistical Office of the United Nations, Publishing Service, New York, New York 10017 (800) 253-9646; *Statistical Yearbook.*

JAPAN - MOTOR VEHICLE TAXES - See JAPAN - TAXATION

JAPAN - MOTOR VEHICLES IN USE

American Automobile Manufacturers Association, 1401 H Street, NW, Suite 900, Washington, D.C. 20005 (202) 326-5500; *World Motor Vehicle Data.*

European Community Information Service, 2100 M Street, NW, Washington, D.C. 20037 (202) 862-9500; *Basic Statistics of the Community.*

G.K. Hall and Company, 70 Lincoln Street, Boston, Massachusetts 02111 (617) 423-3990; *The World in Figures.*

International Road Federation, 525 School Street, SW, Washington, D.C. 20024 (202) 554-2106; *World Road Statistics.*

Statistical Office of the United Nations, Publishing Service, New York, New York 10017 (800) 253-9646; *Statistical Yearbook.*

Times Books, 201 East 50th Street, New York, New York 10022 (212) 751-2600; *The Economist Book of Vital World Statistics.*

JAPAN - MULES - See JAPAN - LIVESTOCK AND POULTRY

JAPAN - MUSEUMS

Facts on File, 460 Park Avenue South, New York, New York (800) 443-8323; *The New Book of World Rankings.*

Statistics Bureau, Management and Coordination Agency, Japan; *Statistical Indicators on Social Life.*

United Nations Educational, Scientific and Cultural Organization (UNESCO), 7 Place de Fontenoy, F-75700 Paris, France (Telephone Number in U.S. (212) 963-5981); *Statistical Yearbook.*

JAPAN - NATALITY - See JAPAN - BIRTH RATE

JAPAN - NATIONAL ACCOUNTS

European Community Information Service, 2100 M Street, NW, Washington, D.C. 20037 (202) 862-9500; *Basic Statistics of the Community.*

International Monetary Fund, 700 Nineteenth Street, NW, Washington, D.C. 20431 (202) 623-7000; *International Financial Statistics.*

Organisation for Economic Co-operation and Development (OECD), 2 rue Andre-Pascal, 75 Paris 16, France (Telephone Number in U.S. (202) 785-6323); *Economic Outlook.*

Statistical Office of the United Nations, Publishing Service, New York, New York 10017 (800) 253-9646; *National Accounts Statistics, Statistical Yearbook,* and *Statistical Yearbook for Asia and the Pacific.*

JAPAN - NATIONAL INCOME

Facts on File, 460 Park Avenue South, New York, New York (800) 443-8323; *The New Book of World Rankings.*

G.K. Hall and Company, 70 Lincoln Street, Boston, Massachusetts 02111 (617) 423-3990; *The World in Figures.*

Organisation for Economic Co-operation and Development (OECD), 2 rue Andre-Pascal, 75 Paris 16, France (Telephone Number in U.S. (202) 785-6323); *Economic Outlook.*

Statistical Office of the United Nations, Publishing Service, New York, New York 10017 (800) 253-9646; *Statistical Yearbook.*

JAPAN - NATIONAL PRODUCT

European Community Information Service, 2100 M Street, NW, Washington, D.C. 20037 (202) 862-9500; *Basic Statistics of the Community.*

Facts on File, 460 Park Avenue South, New York, New York (800) 443-8323; *The New Book of World Rankings.*

Organisation for Economic Co-operation and Development (OECD), 2 rue Andre-Pascal, 75 Paris 16, France (Telephone Number in U.S. (202) 785-6323); *Economic Outlook,* and *Main Economic Indicators - Historical Statistics.*

Statistical Office of the United Nations, Publishing Service, New York, New York 10017 (800) 253-9646; *Statistical Yearbook.*

JAPAN - NATURAL GAS PRODUCTION - See JAPAN - MINING AND MINERAL PRODUCTS

JAPAN - NATURAL RUBBER PRODUCTION

European Community Information Service, 2100 M Street, NW, Washington, D.C. 20037 (202) 862-9500; *Basic Statistics of the Community.*

International Rubber Study Group, York House, 8th Floor, Empire Way, Wembley, London HA9 0PA, England; *Rubber Statistical Bulletin.*

National Technical Information Service, 5285 Port Royal Road, Springfield, Virginia 22161 (703) 487-4600; *Handbook of Economic Statistics.*

JAPAN - NEWSPAPER PRODUCTION AND CONSUMPTION - See JAPAN - FORESTRY AND FOREST PRODUCTS

JAPAN - NEWSPRINT - See JAPAN - FORESTRY AND FOREST PRODUCTS

JAPAN - NICKEL AND NICKEL ORE - See JAPAN -MINING AND MINERAL PRODUCTS

JAPAN - NITRIC ACID PRODUCTION - See JAPAN - MINING AND MINERAL PRODUCTS

JAPAN - OATS PRODUCTION - See JAPAN - CROPS

JAPAN - OCCUPATIONS - See JAPAN - LABOR FORCE

JAPAN - OIL PRODUCING CROPS

European Community Information Service, 2100 M Street, NW, Washington, D.C. 20037 (202) 862-9500; *Basic Statistics of the Community.*

Organisation for Economic Co-operation and Development (OECD), 2 rue Andre-Pascal, 75 Paris 16, France (Telephone Number in U.S. (202) 785-6323); *Foreign Trade by Commodities.*

JAPAN - ONION PRODUCTION - See JAPAN - CROPS

JAPAN - ORANGE PRODUCTION - See JAPAN - CROPS

JAPAN - PALM KERNEL PRODUCTION - See JAPAN - CROPS

JAPAN - PAPER - See JAPAN - FORESTRY AND FOREST PRODUCTS

JAPAN - PATENTS

Statistical Office of the United Nations, Publishing Service, New York, New York 10017 (800) 253-9646; *Statistical Yearbook.*

World Intellectual Property Organization, 34 Chemin des Colombettes, CH-1211 Geneva 20, Switzerland; *Industrial Property Statistics.*

JAPAN - PEANUT PRODUCTION - See JAPAN - CROPS

JAPAN - PEPPER PRODUCTION - See JAPAN - CROPS

JAPAN - PERIODICALS

United Nations Educational, Scientific and Cultural Organization (UNESCO), 7 Place de Fontenoy, F-75700 Paris, France (Telephone Number in U.S. (212) 963-5981); *Statistical Yearbook.*

JAPAN - PESTICIDE USE

Food and Agricultural Organization of the United Nations (FAO), Via delle Terme di Caracalla, 00100 Rome, Italy (Telephone Number in U.S. (202) 653-2400); *The State of Food and Agriculture.*

JAPAN - PETROLEUM INDUSTRY

European Community Information Service, 2100 M Street, NW, Washington, D.C. 20037 (202) 862-9500; *Basic Statistics of the Community.*

Facts on File, 460 Park Avenue South, New York, New York (800) 443-8323; *The New Book of World Rankings.*

Food and Agricultural Organization of the United Nations (FAO), Via delle Terme di Caracalla, 00100 Rome, Italy (Telephone Number in U.S. (202) 653-2400); *The State of Food and Agriculture.*

G.K. Hall and Company, 70 Lincoln Street, Boston, Massachusetts 02111 (617) 423-3990; *The World in Figures.*

National Technical Information Service, 5285 Port Royal Road, Springfield, Virginia 22161 (703) 487-4600; *Handbook of Economic Statistics.*

Organisation for Economic Co-operation and Development (OECD), 2 rue Andre-Pascal, 75 Paris 16, France (Telephone Number in U.S. (202) 785-6323); *Energy Statistics of OECD Countries, Foreign Trade by Commodities, Indicators of Industrial Activity,* and *Oil and Gas Information.*

Penn Well Publishing Company, 1421 South Sheridan Road, Post Office Box 1260, Tulsa, Oklahoma 74101 (800) 752-9764; *International Energy Statistics Sourcebook.*

Statistical Office of the United Nations, Publishing Service, New York, New York 10017 (800) 253-9646; *Statistical Yearbook.*

JAPAN - PHOSPHATES AND PHOSPHATE ROCK PRODUCTION - See JAPAN - MINING AND MINERAL PRODUCTS

JAPAN - PIG-IRON AND FERRO-ALLOY PRODUCTION - See JAPAN - MINING AND MINERAL PRODUCTS

JAPAN - PIGS - See JAPAN - LIVESTOCK AND POULTRY

JAPAN - PIPELINES FOR OIL AND PETROLEUM PRODUCTS

National Technical Information Service, 5285 Port Royal Road, Springfield, Virginia 22161 (703) 487-4600; *Handbook of Economic Statistics.*

JAPAN - PLASTIC AND RESIN PRODUCTION

Commodity Research Bureau, Incorporated, 75 Wall Street, New York, New York 10005 (212) 504-7754; *Commodity Year Book.*

European Community Information Service, 2100 M Street, NW, Washington, D.C. 20037 (202) 862-9500; *Basic Statistics of the Community.*

Organisation for Economic Co-operation and Development (OECD), 2 rue Andre-Pascal, 75 Paris 16, France (Telephone Number in U.S. (202) 785-6323); *Foreign Trade by Commodities.*

Statistical Office of the United Nations, Publishing Service, New York, New York 10017 (800) 253-9646; *Statistical Yearbook.*

JAPAN - PLATINUM PRODUCTION - See JAPAN - MINING AND MINERAL PRODUCTS

JAPAN - POPULATION

The Economist Intelligence Unit, 111 West 57th Street, New York, New York 10019 (800) 938-4685; *The World Market Atlas.*

The Economist Intelligence Unit (Asia) Limited, 10th Floor, Luk Kwok Centre, 72 Gloucester Road, Wanchai, Hong Kong (Phone Number in U.S. (800) 938-4685); *Asian Market Atlas.*

Euromonitor Publications Limited, 87-88 Turnmill Street, London EC1M 5QU, England; *International Marketing Data and Statistics,* and *The Pacific Basin: An Economic Handbook.*

European Community Information Service, 2100 M Street, NW, Washington, D.C. 20037 (202) 862-9500; *Basic Statistics of the Community.*

Facts on File, 460 Park Avenue South, New York, New York (800) 443-8323; *The New Book of World Rankings.*

Food and Agricultural Organization of the United Nations (FAO), Via delle Terme di Caracalla, 00100 Rome, Italy (Telephone Number in U.S. (202) 653-2400); *Production Yearbook.*

G.K. Hall and Company, 70 Lincoln Street, Boston, Massachusetts 02111 (617) 423-3990; *The World in Figures.*

International Labour Office, I.L.O. Publications, CH-1211, Geneva 22, Switzerland; *Yearbook of Labour Statistics.*

National Technical Information Service, 5285 Port Royal Road, Springfield, Virginia 22161 (703) 487-4600; *Handbook of Economic Statistics.*

Statistical Office of the United Nations, Publishing Service, New York, New York 10017 (800) 253-9646; *Demographic Yearbook, Statistical Yearbook,* and *Statistical Yearbook for Asia and the Pacific.*

Statistics Bureau, Management and Coordination Agency, Japan; *Statistical Indicators on Social Life.*

Times Books, 201 East 50th Street, New York, New York 10022 (212) 751-2600; *The Economist Book of Vital World Statistics.*

United Nations Educational, Scientific and Cultural Organization (UNESCO), 7 Place de Fontenoy, F-75700 Paris, France (Telephone Number in U.S. (212) 963-5981); *Statistical Yearbook.*

U.S. Arms Control and Disarmament Agency, 320 Twenty-first Street, NW, Washington, D.C. 20451 (202) 647-8677; *World Military Expenditures and Arms Transfers.*

World Health Organization, Office of Publications, Avenue Appia, CH-1211 Geneva 27, Switzerland (Telephone Number in U.S. (518) 436-9686); *World Health Statistics Annual.*

JAPAN - POST OFFICES

Facts on File, 460 Park Avenue South, New York, New York (800) 443-8323; *The New Book of World Rankings.*

JAPAN - POTATO PRODUCTION - See JAPAN - CROPS

JAPAN - POWER PRODUCTION INDUSTRY

European Community Information Service, 2100 M Street, NW, Washington, D.C. 20037 (202) 862-9500; *Basic Statistics of the Community.*

Statistical Office of the United Nations, Publishing Service, New York, New York 10017 (800) 253-9646; *Electric Power in Asia and the Pacific,* and *Statistical Yearbook.*

JAPAN - PRICES

European Community Information Service, 2100 M Street, NW, Washington, D.C. 20037 (202) 862-9500; *Basic Statistics of the Community.*

Facts on File, 460 Park Avenue South, New York, New York (800) 443-8323; *The New Book of World Rankings.*

Food and Agricultural Organization of the United Nations (FAO), Via delle Terme di Caracalla, 00100 Rome, Italy (Telephone Number in U.S. (202) 653-2400); *Production Yearbook,* and *The State of Food and Agriculture.*

G.K. Hall and Company, 70 Lincoln Street, Boston, Massachusetts 02111 (617) 423-3990; *The World in Figures.*

International Labour Office, I.L.O. Publications, CH-1211, Geneva 22, Switzerland; *Yearbook of Labour Statistics.*

International Lead and Zinc Study Group, Metro House, 58 St. James's Street, London SW1A 1LD England; *Lead and Zinc Statistics.*

International Monetary Fund, 700 Nineteenth Street, NW, Washington, D.C. 20431 (202) 623-7000; *International Financial Statistics.*

International Rubber Study Group, York House, 8th Floor, Empire Way, Wembley, London HA9 0PA, England; *Rubber Statistical Bulletin.*

National Technical Information Service, 5285 Port Royal Road, Springfield, Virginia 22161 (703) 487-4600; *Handbook of Economic Statistics.*

Organisation for Economic Co-operation and Development (OECD), 2 rue Andre-Pascal, 75 Paris 16, France (Telephone Number in U.S. (202) 785-6323); *Economic Outlook, The Footwear, Raw Hides and Skins, and Leather Industry in OECD Countries, Indicators of Industrial Activity, The Iron and Steel Industry, Main Economic Indicators - Historical Statistics,* and *The Pulp and Paper Industry.*

World Bureau of Metal Statistics, 27-A High Street, Ware, Herts. SG12 9BA, England; *World Metal Statistics.*

JAPAN - PRINTING AND WRITING PAPER - See JAPAN - FORESTRY AND FOREST PRODUCTS

JAPAN - PRODUCTION

American Automobile Manufacturers Association, 1401 H Street, NW, Suite 900, Washington, D.C. 20005 (202) 326-5500; *World Motor Vehicle Data.*

European Community Information Service, 2100 M Street, NW, Washington, D.C. 20037 (202) 862-9500; *Basic Statistics of the Community.*

Facts on File, 460 Park Avenue South, New York, New York (800) 443-8323; *The New Book of World Rankings.*

G.K. Hall and Company, 70 Lincoln Street, Boston, Massachusetts 02111 (617) 423-3990; *The World in Figures.*

International Lead and Zinc Study Group, Metro House, 58 St. James's Street, London SW1A 1LD England; *Lead and Zinc Statistics.*

International Rubber Study Group, York House, 8th Floor, Empire Way, Wembley, London HA9 0PA, England; *Rubber Statistical Bulletin.*

National Technical Information Service, 5285 Port Royal Road, Springfield, Virginia 22161 (703) 487-4600; *Handbook of Economic Statistics.*

Organisation for Economic Co-operation and Development (OECD), 2 rue Andre-Pascal, 75 Paris 16, France (Telephone Number in U.S. (202) 785-6323); *Economic Outlook, The Footwear, Raw Hides and Skins, and Leather Industry in OECD Countries, Indicators of Industrial Activity, Industrial Structure Statistics, The Iron and Steel Industry, Meat Balances in OECD Member Countries, Milk, Milk*

Products, and Egg Balances in OECD Member Countries, The Non-Ferrous Metals Industry, The Pulp and Paper Industry, and *Textile Industry in OECD Countries.*

Statistics Bureau, Management and Coordination Agency, Japan; *Statistical Indicators on Social Life.*

JAPAN - PRODUCTIVITY

Euromonitor Publications Limited, 87-88 Turnmill Street, London EC1M 5QU, England; *International Marketing Data and Statistics.*

European Community Information Service, 2100 M Street, NW, Washington, D.C. 20037 (202) 862-9500; *Basic Statistics of the Community.*

Organisation for Economic Co-operation and Development (OECD), 2 rue Andre-Pascal, 75 Paris 16, France (Telephone Number in U.S. (202) 785-6323); *Economic Outlook.*

JAPAN - PROPERTY TAXES - See JAPAN - TAXATION

JAPAN - PUBLIC CONSUMPTION FUND

European Community Information Service, 2100 M Street, NW, Washington, D.C. 20037 (202) 862-9500; *Basic Statistics of the Community.*

Organisation for Economic Co-operation and Development (OECD), 2 rue Andre-Pascal, 75 Paris 16, France (Telephone Number in U.S. (202) 785-6323); *Revenue Statistics of OECD Member Countries.*

JAPAN - PUBLIC EXPENDITURES

European Community Information Service, 2100 M Street, NW, Washington, D.C. 20037 (202) 862-9500; *Basic Statistics of the Community.*

National Technical Information Service, 5285 Port Royal Road, Springfield, Virginia 22161 (703) 487-4600; *Handbook of Economic Statistics.*

Organisation for Economic Co-operation and Development (OECD), 2 rue Andre-Pascal, 75 Paris 16, France (Telephone Number in U.S. (202) 785-6323); *Revenue Statistics of OECD Member Countries.*

Statistics Bureau, Management and Coordination Agency, Japan; *Statistical Indicators on Social Life.*

JAPAN - PUBLIC FINANCE

Facts on File, 460 Park Avenue South, New York, New York (800) 443-8323; *The New Book of World Rankings.*

National Technical Information Service, 5285 Port Royal Road, Springfield, Virginia 22161 (703) 487-4600; *Handbook of Economic Statistics.*

Organisation for Economic Co-operation and Development (OECD), 2 rue Andre-Pascal, 75 Paris 16, France (Telephone Number in U.S. (202) 785-6323); *Revenue Statistics of OECD Member Countries.*

JAPAN - PUBLIC HEALTH

European Community Information Service, 2100 M Street, NW, Washington, D.C. 20037 (202) 862-9500; *Basic Statistics of the Community.*

JAPAN - PUBLIC REVENUES

National Technical Information Service, 5285 Port Royal Road, Springfield, Virginia 22161 (703) 487-4600; *Handbook of Economic Statistics.*

Organisation for Economic Co-operation and Development (OECD), 2 rue Andre-Pascal, 75 Paris 16, France (Telephone Number in U.S. (202) 785-6323); *Revenue Statistics of OECD Member Countries.*

JAPAN - RADIO BROADCASTING - See JAPAN - BROADCASTING

JAPAN - RADIO RECEIVER PRODUCTION

Statistical Office of the United Nations, Publishing Service, New York, New York 10017 (800) 253-9646; *Statistical Yearbook.*

JAPAN - RAILWAYS

European Community Information Service, 2100 M Street, NW, Washington, D.C. 20037 (202) 862-9500; *Basic Statistics of the Community.*

G.K. Hall and Company, 70 Lincoln Street, Boston, Massachusetts 02111 (617) 423-3990; *The World in Figures.*

Jane's Information Group, Sentinel House, 163 Brighton Road, Coulsdon, Surrey CR5 2NH, England (Telephone Number in U.S. (703) 683-3700); *Jane's World Railways.*

National Technical Information Service, 5285 Port Royal Road, Springfield, Virginia 22161 (703) 487-4600; *Handbook of Economic Statistics.*

Statistical Office of the United Nations, Publishing Service, New York, New York 10017 (800) 253-9646; *Statistical Yearbook.*

JAPAN - RANCHING

European Community Information Service, 2100 M Street, NW, Washington, D.C. 20037 (202) 862-9500; *Basic Statistics of the Community.*

JAPAN - RAPESEED PRODUCTION - See JAPAN - CROPS

JAPAN - RELIGION

Facts on File, 460 Park Avenue South, New York, New York (800) 443-8323; *The New Book of World Rankings.*

JAPAN - RENT PRICES

International Labour Office, I.L.O. Publications, CH-1211, Geneva 22, Switzerland; *Yearbook of Labour Statistics.*

JAPAN - RETAIL TRADE

European Community Information Service, 2100 M Street, NW, Washington, D.C. 20037 (202) 862-9500; *Basic Statistics of the Community.*

G.K. Hall and Company, 70 Lincoln Street, Boston, Massachusetts 02111 (617) 423-3990; *The World in Figures.*

Statistical Office of the United Nations, Publishing Service, New York, New York 10017 (800) 253-9646; *Statistical Yearbook.*

JAPAN - RICE PRODUCTION - See JAPAN - CROPS

JAPAN - ROOT AND TUBER PRODUCTION - See JAPAN - CROPS

JAPAN - ROUNDWOOD PRODUCTION - See JAPAN - FORESTRY AND FOREST PRODUCTS

JAPAN - RUBBER PRODUCTION AND CONSUMPTION

Commodity Research Bureau, Incorporated, 75 Wall Street, New York, New York 10005 (212) 504-7754; *Commodity Year Book.*

European Community Information Service, 2100 M Street, NW, Washington, D.C. 20037 (202) 862-9500; *Basic Statistics of the Community.*

Facts on File, 460 Park Avenue South, New York, New York (800) 443-8323; *The New Book of World Rankings.*

International Rubber Study Group, York House, 8th Floor, Empire Way, Wembley, London HA9 0PA, England; *Rubber Statistical Bulletin.*

National Technical Information Service, 5285 Port Royal Road, Springfield, Virginia 22161 (703) 487-4600; *Handbook of Economic Statistics.*

Organisation for Economic Co-operation and Development (OECD), 2 rue Andre-Pascal, 75 Paris 16, France (Telephone Number in U.S. (202) 785-6323); *Foreign Trade by Commodities.*

Statistical Office of the United Nations, Publishing Service, New York, New York 10017 (800) 253-9646; *Statistical Yearbook.*

JAPAN - RYE PRODUCTION - See JAPAN - CROPS

JAPAN - SAFFLOWER SEED PRODUCTION - See JAPAN - CROPS

JAPAN - SALT PRODUCTION - See JAPAN - MINING AND MINERAL PRODUCTS

JAPAN - SAWNWOOD PRODUCTION - See JAPAN - FORESTRY AND FOREST PRODUCTS

JAPAN - SCIENCE AND TECHNOLOGY - EXPENDITURE FOR RESEARCH

European Community Information Service, 2100 M Street, NW, Washington, D.C. 20037 (202) 862-9500; *Basic Statistics of the Community.*

Statistical Office of the United Nations, Publishing Service, New York, New York 10017 (800) 253-9646; *Statistical Yearbook.*

JAPAN - SCIENTISTS, ENGINEERS AND TECHNICIANS

European Community Information Service, 2100 M Street, NW, Washington, D.C. 20037 (202) 862-9500; *Basic Statistics of the Community.*

Statistical Office of the United Nations, Publishing Service, New York, New York 10017 (800) 253-9646; *Statistical Yearbook.*

United Nations Educational, Scientific and Cultural Organization (UNESCO), 7 Place de Fontenoy, F-75700 Paris, France (Telephone Number in U.S. (212) 963-5981); *Statistical Yearbook.*

JAPAN - SENIOR CITIZENS

Facts on File, 460 Park Avenue South, New York, New York (800) 443-8323; *The New Book of World Rankings.*

JAPAN - SESAME SEED PRODUCTION - See JAPAN - CROPS

JAPAN - SHEEP - See JAPAN - LIVESTOCK AND POULTRY

JAPAN - SHIPBUILDING - PRODUCTION INDEX

Organisation for Economic Co-operation and Development (OECD), 2 rue Andre-Pascal, 75 Paris 16, France (Telephone Number in U.S. (202) 785-6323); *Indicators of Industrial Activity.*

JAPAN - SILVER PRODUCTION AND CONSUMPTION - See JAPAN - MINING AND MINERAL PRODUCTS

JAPAN - SISAL PRODUCTION - See JAPAN - CROPS

JAPAN - SOCIAL DATA

European Community Information Service, 2100 M Street, NW, Washington, D.C. 20037 (202) 862-9500; *Basic Statistics of the Community.*

Facts on File, 460 Park Avenue South, New York, New York (800) 443-8323; *The New Book of World Rankings.*

G.K. Hall and Company, 70 Lincoln Street, Boston, Massachusetts 02111 (617) 423-3990; *The World in Figures.*

JAPAN - SOCIAL SECURITY

European Community Information Service, 2100 M Street, NW, Washington, D.C. 20037 (202) 862-9500; *Basic Statistics of the Community.*

Organisation for Economic Co-operation and Development (OECD), 2 rue Andre-Pascal, 75 Paris 16, France (Telephone Number in U.S. (202) 785-6323); *Revenue Statistics of OECD Member Countries.*

JAPAN - SOCIOECONOMIC DATA

European Community Information Service, 2100 M Street, NW, Washington, D.C. 20037 (202) 862-9500; *Basic Statistics of the Community.*

Organisation for Economic Co-operation and Development (OECD), 2 rue Andre-Pascal, 75 Paris 16, France (Telephone Number in U.S. (202) 785-6323); *Economic Outlook.*

JAPAN - SOYBEAN PRODUCTION - See JAPAN - CROPS

JAPAN - STAMP TAXES AND DUTIES - See JAPAN - TAXATION

JAPAN - STATE BUDGET REVENUE EXPENDITURES

Euromonitor Publications Limited, 87-88 Turnmill Street, London EC1M 5QU, England; *International Marketing Data and Statistics.*

JAPAN - STEEL - See JAPAN - MINING AND MINERAL PRODUCTS

JAPAN - STOCKS - COMMODITY - MARKET PRICE - INDEXES

Food and Agricultural Organization of the United Nations (FAO), Via delle Terme di Caracalla, 00100 Rome, Italy (Telephone Number in U.S. (202) 653-2400); *The State of Food and Agriculture.*

International Lead and Zinc Study Group, Metro House, 58 St. James's Street, London SW1A 1LD England; *Lead and Zinc Statistics.*

Statistical Office of the United Nations, Publishing Service, New York, New York 10017 (800) 253-9646; *Statistical Yearbook*.

World Bureau of Metal Statistics, 27-A High Street, Ware, Herts. SG12 9BA, England; *World Metal Statistics*.

JAPAN - STRAW PRODUCTION - See JAPAN - CROPS

JAPAN - SUGAR AND SUGARBEET PRODUCTION - See JAPAN - CROPS

JAPAN - SULPHUR AND SULPHURIC ACID PRODUCTION - See JAPAN - MINING AND MINERAL PRODUCTS

JAPAN - SUNFLOWER PRODUCTION - See JAPAN - CROPS

JAPAN - TAXATION

European Community Information Service, 2100 M Street, NW, Washington, D.C. 20037 (202) 862-9500; *Basic Statistics of the Community*.

G.K. Hall and Company, 70 Lincoln Street, Boston, Massachusetts 02111 (617) 423-3990; *The World in Figures*.

International Monetary Fund, 700 Nineteenth Street, NW, Washington, D.C. 20431 (202) 623-7000; *Government Finance Statistics Yearbook*.

International Road Federation, 525 School Street, SW, Washington, D.C. 20024 (202) 554-2106, *World Road Statistics*.

Organisation for Economic Co-operation and Development (OECD), 2 rue Andre-Pascal, 75 Paris 10, France (Telephone Number in U.S. (202) 785-6323); *Revenue Statistics of OECD Member Countries*.

JAPAN - TEA PRODUCTION AND CONSUMPTION - See JAPAN - CROPS

JAPAN - TELEGRAPH SERVICE

Statistical Office of the United Nations, Publishing Service, New York, New York 10017 (800) 253-9646; *Statistical Yearbook*.

JAPAN - TELEPHONES IN USE

American Telephone and Telegraph Company, 26 Parsippany Road, Whippany, New Jersey 07981 (800) 338-4038; *The World's Telephones*.

The Economist Intelligence Unit (Asia) Limited, 10th Floor, Luk Kwok Centre, 72 Gloucester Road, Wanchai, Hong Kong (Phone Number in U.S. (800) 938-4685); *Asian Market Atlas*.

Euromonitor Publications Limited, 87-88 Turnmill Street, London EC1M 5QU, England; *The Pacific Basin: An Economic Handbook*.

European Community Information Service, 2100 M Street, NW, Washington, D.C. 20037 (202) 862-9500; *Basic Statistics of the Community*.

G.K. Hall and Company, 70 Lincoln Street, Boston, Massachusetts 02111 (617) 423-3990; *The World in Figures*.

Statistical Office of the United Nations, Publishing Service, New York, New York 10017 (800) 253-9646; *Statistical Yearbook*.

JAPAN - TELEVISION BROADCASTING - See JAPAN - BROADCASTING

JAPAN - TELEVISION RECEIVER PRODUCTION

European Community Information Service, 2100 M Street, NW, Washington, D.C. 20037 (202) 862-9500; *Basic Statistics of the Community*.

National Technical Information Service, 5285 Port Royal Road, Springfield, Virginia 22161 (703) 487-4600; *Handbook of Economic Statistics*.

Statistical Office of the United Nations, Publishing Service, New York, New York 10017 (800) 253-9646; *Statistical Yearbook*.

JAPAN - TELEVISION RECEIVERS - IN USE

Statistical Office of the United Nations, Publishing Service, New York, New York 10017 (800) 253-9646; *Statistical Yearbook*.

JAPAN - TEXTILE INDUSTRY

American Forest and Paper Association, 1250 Connecticut Avenue, NW, Washington, D.C. 20036 (202) 463-2455; *Wood Pulp and Fiber Statistics*.

European Community Information Service, 2100 M Street, NW, Washington, D.C. 20037 (202) 862-9500; *Basic Statistics of the Community*.

Food and Agricultural Organization of the United Nations (FAO), Via delle Terme di Caracalla, 00100 Rome, Italy (Telephone Number in U.S. (202) 653-2400); *Production Yearbook*.

G.K. Hall and Company, 70 Lincoln Street, Boston, Massachusetts 02111 (617) 423-3990; *The World in Figures*.

National Technical Information Service, 5285 Port Royal Road, Springfield, Virginia 22161 (703) 487-4600; *Handbook of Economic Statistics*.

Organisation for Economic Co-operation and Development (OECD), 2 rue Andre-Pascal, 75 Paris 16, France (Telephone Number in U.S. (202) 785-6323); *Foreign Trade by Commodities*, *Indicators of Industrial Activity*, *Industrial Structure Statistics*, and *Textile Industry in OECD Countries*.

Statistical Office of the United Nations, Publishing Service, New York, New York 10017 (800) 253-9646; *Statistical Yearbook*, and *Trade in Manufactures of Developing Countries*.

JAPAN - THEATRE

United Nations Educational, Scientific and Cultural Organization (UNESCO), 7 Place de Fontenoy, F-75700 Paris, France (Telephone Number in U.S. (212) 963-5981); *Statistical Yearbook*.

JAPAN - TIMBER - See JAPAN - FORESTRY AND FOREST PRODUCTS

JAPAN - TIN - See JAPAN - MINING AND MINERAL PRODUCTS

JAPAN - TIRE (MOTOR VEHICLE) PRODUCTION

International Rubber Study Group, York House, 8th Floor, Empire Way, Wembley, London HA9 0PA, England; *Rubber Statistical Bulletin*.

National Technical Information Service, 5285 Port Royal Road, Springfield, Virginia 22161 (703) 487-4600; *Handbook of Economic Statistics*.

Statistical Office of the United Nations, Publishing Service, New York, New York 10017 (800) 253-9646; *Statistical Yearbook*.

JAPAN - TOBACCO PRODUCTION

Commodity Research Bureau, Incorporated, 75 Wall Street, New York, New York 10005 (212) 504-7754; *Commodity Year Book*.

European Community Information Service, 2100 M Street, NW, Washington, D.C. 20037 (202) 862-9500; *Basic Statistics of the Community*.

Facts on File, 460 Park Avenue South, New York, New York (800) 443-8323; *The New Book of World Rankings*.

Organisation for Economic Co-operation and Development (OECD), 2 rue Andre-Pascal, 75 Paris 16, France (Telephone Number in U.S. (202) 785-6323); *Foreign Trade by Commodities, Indicators of Industrial Activity*, and *Industrial Structure Statistics*.

Statistical Office of the United Nations, Publishing Service, New York, New York 10017 (800) 253-9646; *Statistical Yearbook*.

JAPAN - TOURISM

Euromonitor Publications Limited, 87-88 Turnmill Street, London EC1M 5QU, England; *The Pacific Basin: An Economic Handbook*.

Facts on File, 460 Park Avenue South, New York, New York (800) 443-8323; *The New Book of World Rankings*.

G.K. Hall and Company, 70 Lincoln Street, Boston, Massachusetts 02111 (617) 423-3990; *The World in Figures*.

Organisation for Economic Co-operation and Development (OECD), 2 rue Andre-Pascal, 75 Paris 16, France (Telephone Number in U.S. (202) 785-6323); *Tourism Policy and International Tourism in OECD Member Countries*.

Statistical Office of the United Nations, Publishing Service, New York, New York 10017 (800) 253-9646; *Statistical Yearbook*.

Times Books, 201 East 50th Street, New York, New York 10022 (212) 751-2600; *The Economist Book of Vital World Statistics*.

World Tourism Organization, Calle Capitan Haya 42, E-28020 Madrid, Spain; *Yearbook of Tourism Statistics*.

JAPAN - TRACTORS IN USE

Statistical Office of the United Nations, Publishing Service, New York, New York 10017 (800) 253-9646; *Statistical Yearbook*.

JAPAN - TRADE - See JAPAN - FOREIGN TRADE

JAPAN - TRADEMARKS AND SERVICE MARKS

Statistical Office of the United Nations, Publishing Service, New York, New York 10017 (800) 253-9646; *Statistical Yearbook*.

World Intellectual Property Organization, 34 Chemin des Colombettes, CH-1211 Geneva 20, Switzerland; *Industrial Property Statistics*.

JAPAN - TRANSPORTATION AND COMMUNICATIONS

The Economist Intelligence Unit (Asia) Limited, 10th Floor, Luk Kwok Centre, 72 Gloucester Road, Wanchai, Hong Kong (Phone Number in U.S. (800) 938-4685); *Asian Market Atlas*.

Euromonitor Publications Limited, 87-88 Turnmill Street, London EC1M 5QU, England; *The Pacific Basin: An Economic Handbook*.

European Community Information Service, 2100 M Street, NW, Washington, D.C. 20037 (202) 862-9500; *Basic Statistics of the Community*.

Facts on File, 460 Park Avenue South, New York, New York (800) 443-8323; *The New Book of World Rankings*.

G.K. Hall and Company, 70 Lincoln Street, Boston, Massachusetts 02111 (617) 423-3990; *The World in Figures*.

Statistical Office of the United Nations, Publishing Service, New York, New York 10017 (800) 253-9646; *Statistical Yearbook for Asia and the Pacific*.

JAPAN - TUNGSTEN PRODUCTION AND CONSUMPTION - See JAPAN - MINING AND MINERAL PRODUCTS

JAPAN - TURKEYS - See JAPAN - LIVESTOCK AND POULTRY

JAPAN - UNEMPLOYMENT

Euromonitor Publications Limited, 87-88 Turnmill Street, London EC1M 5QU, England; *International Marketing Data and Statistics*, and *The Pacific Basin: An Economic Handbook*.

European Community Information Service, 2100 M Street, NW, Washington, D.C. 20037 (202) 862-9500; *Basic Statistics of the Community*, and *Eurostat Review*.

International Labour Office, I.L.O. Publications, CH-1211, Geneva 22, Switzerland; *Yearbook of Labour Statistics*.

National Technical Information Service, 5285 Port Royal Road, Springfield, Virginia 22161 (703) 487-4600; *Handbook of Economic Statistics*.

Organisation for Economic Co-operation and Development (OECD), 2 rue Andre-Pascal, 75 Paris 16, France (Telephone Number in U.S. (202) 785-6323); *Economic Outlook, OECD Economic Surveys: Japan*, and *OECD Employment Outlook*.

Statistical Office of the United Nations, Publishing Service, New York, New York 10017 (800) 253-9646; *Statistical Yearbook*.

Statistics Bureau, Management and Coordination Agency, Japan; *Statistical Indicators on Social Life*.

JAPAN - URANIUM PRODUCTION AND CONSUMPTION - See JAPAN - MINING AND MINERAL PRODUCTS

JAPAN - UTILITIES

European Community Information Service, 2100 M Street, NW, Washington, D.C. 20037 (202) 862-9500; *Basic Statistics of the Community*.

Statistical Office of the United Nations, Publishing Service, New York, New York 10017 (800) 253-9646; *Electric Power in Asia and the Pacific*.

JAPAN - VANADIUM AND VANADIUM ORE - See JAPAN - MINING AND MINERAL PRODUCTS

JAPAN - VITAL STATISTICS

Euromonitor Publications Limited, 87-88 Turnmill Street, London EC1M 5QU, England; *International Marketing Data and Statistics*, and *The Pacific Basin: An Economic Handbook*.

European Community Information Service, 2100 M Street, NW, Washington, D.C. 20037 (202) 862-9500; *Basic Statistics of the Community*, and *Eurostat Review*.

JAPAN - WHOLESALE TRADE

European Community Information Service, 2100 M Street, NW, Washington, D.C. 20037 (202) 862-9500; *Basic Statistics of the Community*, and *Eurostat Review*.

Statistical Office of the United Nations, Publishing Service, New York, New York 10017 (800) 253-9646; *Statistical Yearbook*.

JAPAN - WINE PRODUCTION

European Community Information Service, 2100 M Street, NW, Washington, D.C. 20037 (202) 862-9500; *Basic Statistics of the Community*.

Facts on File, 460 Park Avenue South, New York, New York 10016 (800) 443-8323; *The New Book of World Rankings*.

Statistical Office of the United Nations, Publishing Service, New York, New York 10017 (800) 253-9646; *Statistical Yearbook*.

JAPAN - WOOD AND WOOD PULP - See JAPAN - FORESTRY AND FOREST PRODUCTS

JAPAN - WOOL - INDUSTRIAL CONSUMPTION

Organisation for Economic Co-operation and Development (OECD), 2 rue Andre-Pascal, 75 Paris 16, France (Telephone Number in U.S. (202) 785-6323); *Textile Industry in OECD Countries*.

Statistical Office of the United Nations, Publishing Service, New York, New York 10017 (800) 253-9646; *Statistical Yearbook*.

JAPAN - WOOL PRODUCTION

European Community Information Service, 2100 M Street, NW, Washington, D.C. 20037 (202) 862-9500; *Basic Statistics of the Community*.

Facts on File, 460 Park Avenue South, New York, New York 10016 (800) 443-8323; *The New Book of World Rankings*.

National Technical Information Service, 5285 Port Royal Road, Springfield, Virginia 22161 (703) 487-4600; *Handbook of Economic Statistics*.

Organisation for Economic Co-operation and Development (OECD), 2 rue Andre-Pascal, 75 Paris 16, France (Telephone Number in U.S. (202) 785-6323); *Economic Accounts for Agriculture*, and *Textile Industry in OECD Countries*.

JAPAN - YARN PRODUCTION

European Community Information Service, 2100 M Street, NW, Washington, D.C. 20037 (202) 862-9500; *Basic Statistics of the Community*.

Organisation for Economic Co-operation and Development (OECD), 2 rue Andre-Pascal, 75 Paris 16, France (Telephone Number in U.S.

(202) 785-6323); *Foreign Trade by Commodities*, and *Textile Industry in OECD Countries*.

Statistical Office of the United Nations, Publishing Service, New York, New York 10017 (800) 253-9646; *Statistical Yearbook*.

JAPAN - ZINC AND ZINC ORE - See JAPAN - MINING AND MINERAL PRODUCTS

JAPAN - ZOOS AND BOTANICAL GARDENS

United Nations Educational, Scientific and Cultural Organization (UNESCO), 7 Place de Fontenoy, F-75700 Paris, France (Telephone Number in U.S. (212) 963-5981); *Statistical Yearbook*.

JAPANESE POPULATION

U.S. Department of Commerce, Bureau of the Census, Suitland, Maryland 20233 (301) 763-4040; *Census of Population*, *General Population Characteristics, United States*.

JEWELRY, SILVERWARE, AND PLATED WARE - MANUFACTURING

U.S. Department of Commerce, Bureau of the Census, Suitland, Maryland 20233 (301) 763-4040; *Census of Manufactures*, *Annual Survey of Manufactures*.

JEWELRY STORES

U.S. Department of Commerce, Bureau of the Census, Suitland, Maryland 20233 (301) 763-4040; *County Business Patterns*, *Current Business Reports*, *Combined Annual and Revised Monthly Retail Trade*, and *Census of Retail Trade*.

JEWISH POPULATION - See RELIGION

JOB CORPS

U.S. Library of Congress, Congressional Research Service, 10 First Street, SE, Washington, D.C. 20540 (202) 707-5700; *Cash and Non-Cash Benefits for Persons With Limited Income: Eligibility Rules, Recipient and Expenditure Data*.

JOGGING

National Sporting Goods Association, 1699 Wall Street, Mount Prospect, Illinois 60056 (708) 439-4000; *Sports Participation in 1992*, and *The Sporting Goods Market in 1993*.

JOHNSTON ISLAND - AGRICULTURE

Food and Agricultural Organization of the United Nations (FAO), Via delle Terme di Caracalla, 00100 Rome, Italy (Telephone Number in U.S. (202) 653-2400); *Production Yearbook*, *The State of Food and Agriculture*, and *Trade Yearbook*.

G.K. Hall and Company, 70 Lincoln Street, Boston, Massachusetts 02111 (617) 423-3990; *The World in Figures*.

JOHNSTON ISLAND - AIRLINE SERVICE

G.K. Hall and Company, 70 Lincoln Street, Boston, Massachusetts 02111 (617) 423-3990; *The World in Figures*.

JOHNSTON ISLAND - ANIMAL HEALTH

Food and Agricultural Organization of the United Nations (FAO), Via delle Terme di Caracalla, 00100, Rome, Italy (Telephone Number in U.S. (202) 653-2400); *Animal Health Yearbook*.

JOHNSTON ISLAND - AREA AND DENSITY OF POPULATION

Food and Agricultural Organization of the United Nations (FAO), Via delle Terme di Caracalla, 00100 Rome, Italy (Telephone Number in U.S. (202) 653-2400); *The State of Food and Agriculture.*

G.K. Hall and Company, 70 Lincoln Street, Boston, Massachusetts 02111 (617) 423-3990; *The World in Figures.*

Statistical Office of the United Nations, Publishing Service, New York, New York 10017 (800) 253-9646; *Statistical Yearbook.*

JOHNSTON ISLAND - BALANCE OF PAYMENTS

G.K. Hall and Company, 70 Lincoln Street, Boston, Massachusetts 02111 (617) 423-3990; *The World in Figures.*

JOHNSTON ISLAND - BANKING

G.K. Hall and Company, 70 Lincoln Street, Boston, Massachusetts 02111 (617) 423-3990; *The World in Figures.*

JOHNSTON ISLAND - BIRTH RATES

Statistical Office of the United Nations, Publishing Service, New York, New York 10017 (800) 253-9646; *Demographic Yearbook.*

JOHNSTON ISLAND - BONDS

G.K. Hall and Company, 70 Lincoln Street, Boston, Massachusetts 02111 (617) 423-3990; *The World in Figures.*

JOHNSTON ISLAND - BOOK PRODUCTION

G.K. Hall and Company, 70 Lincoln Street, Boston, Massachusetts 02111 (617) 423-3990; *The World in Figures.*

JOHNSTON ISLAND - BROADCASTING

G.K. Hall and Company, 70 Lincoln Street, Boston, Massachusetts 02111 (617) 423-3990; *The World in Figures.*

JOHNSTON ISLAND - BUSINESS

G.K. Hall and Company, 70 Lincoln Street, Boston, Massachusetts 02111 (617) 423-3990; *The World in Figures.*

JOHNSTON ISLAND - CALORIE SUPPLY

Food and Agricultural Organization of the United Nations (FAO), Via delle Terme di Caracalla, 00100 Rome, Italy (Telephone Number in U.S. (202) 653-2400); *The State of Food and Agriculture.*

JOHNSTON ISLAND - CHEMICAL (ORGANIC) PRODUCTION - See JOHNSTON ISLAND - MINING AND MINERAL PRODUCTS

JOHNSTON ISLAND - CLASS STRUCTURE

G.K. Hall and Company, 70 Lincoln Street, Boston, Massachusetts 02111 (617) 423-3990; *The World in Figures.*

JOHNSTON ISLAND - CLIMATE

G.K. Hall and Company, 70 Lincoln Street, Boston, Massachusetts 02111 (617) 423-3990; *The World in Figures.*

JOHNSTON ISLAND - COAL PRODUCTION - See JOHNSTON ISLAND - MINING AND MINERAL PRODUCTS

JOHNSTON ISLAND - COMMUNICATIONS

G.K. Hall and Company, 70 Lincoln Street, Boston, Massachusetts 02111 (617) 423-3990; *The World in Figures.*

JOHNSTON ISLAND - CONSUMER PRICE INDEX

G.K. Hall and Company, 70 Lincoln Street, Boston, Massachusetts 02111 (617) 423-3990; *The World in Figures.*

JOHNSTON ISLAND - CONSUMPTION

G.K. Hall and Company, 70 Lincoln Street, Boston, Massachusetts 02111 (617) 423-3990; *The World in Figures.*

JOHNSTON ISLAND - CORN PRODUCTION - See JOHNSTON ISLAND - CROPS

JOHNSTON ISLAND - CORPORATE TAXES - See JOHNSTON ISLAND - TAXATION

JOHNSTON ISLAND - CROPS

Food and Agricultural Organization of the United Nations (FAO), Via delle Terme di Caracalla, 00100 Rome, Italy (Telephone Number in U.S. (202) 653-2400); *The State of Food and Agriculture.*

G.K. Hall and Company, 70 Lincoln Street, Boston, Massachusetts 02111 (617) 423-3990; *The World in Figures.*

JOHNSTON ISLAND - CUSTOMS DUTIES

G.K. Hall and Company, 70 Lincoln Street, Boston, Massachusetts 02111 (617) 423-3990; *The World in Figures.*

JOHNSTON ISLAND - DAIRY PRODUCTS

Food and Agricultural Organization of the United Nations (FAO), Via delle Terme di Caracalla, 00100 Rome, Italy (Telephone Number in U.S. (202) 653-2400); *The State of Food and Agriculture.*

JOHNSTON ISLAND - DEATH RATES

G.K. Hall and Company, 70 Lincoln Street, Boston, Massachusetts 02111 (617) 423-3990; *The World in Figures.*

JOHNSTON ISLAND - DEFENSE EXPENDITURES

G.K. Hall and Company, 70 Lincoln Street, Boston, Massachusetts 02111 (617) 423-3990; *The World in Figures.*

JOHNSTON ISLAND - DEMOGRAPHY

G.K. Hall and Company, 70 Lincoln Street, Boston, Massachusetts 02111 (617) 423-3990; *The World in Figures.*

JOHNSTON ISLAND - DEVELOPMENT ASSISTANCE

G.K. Hall and Company, 70 Lincoln Street, Boston, Massachusetts 02111 (617) 423-3990; *The World in Figures.*

JOHNSTON ISLAND - DISEASE

G.K. Hall and Company, 70 Lincoln Street, Boston, Massachusetts 02111 (617) 423-3990; *The World in Figures.*

JOHNSTON ISLAND - DIVORCE RATES

Statistical Office of the United Nations, Publishing Service, New York, New York 10017 (800) 253-9646; *Demographic Yearbook.*

JOHNSTON ISLAND - DOMESTIC PRODUCT

G.K. Hall and Company, 70 Lincoln Street, Boston, Massachusetts 02111 (617) 423-3990; *The World in Figures.*

JOHNSTON ISLAND - ECONOMY

G.K. Hall and Company, 70 Lincoln Street, Boston, Massachusetts 02111 (617) 423-3990; *The World in Figures.*

JOHNSTON ISLAND - EDUCATION

G.K. Hall and Company, 70 Lincoln Street, Boston, Massachusetts 02111 (617) 423-3990; *The World in Figures.*

JOHNSTON ISLAND - EGG PRODUCTION - See JOHNSTON ISLAND - DAIRY PRODUCTS

JOHNSTON ISLAND - ENERGY

Food and Agricultural Organization of the United Nations (FAO), Via delle Terme di Caracalla, 00100 Rome, Italy (Telephone Number in U.S. (202) 653-2400); *The State of Food and Agriculture.*

G.K. Hall and Company, 70 Lincoln Street, Boston, Massachusetts 02111 (617) 423-3990; *The World in Figures.*

JOHNSTON ISLAND - EXPORTS

Food and Agricultural Organization of the United Nations (FAO), Via delle Terme di Caracalla, 00100 Rome, Italy (Telephone Number in U.S. (202) 653-2400); *The State of Food and Agriculture.*

G.K. Hall and Company, 70 Lincoln Street, Boston, Massachusetts 02111 (617) 423-3990; *The World in Figures.*

JOHNSTON ISLAND - EXTERNAL TRADE

Food and Agricultural Organization of the United Nations (FAO) Via delle Terme di Caracalla, 00100 Rome, Italy (Telephone Number in U.S. (202) 653-2400); *The State of Food and Agriculture,* and *Trade Yearbook.*

G.K. Hall and Company, 70 Lincoln Street, Boston, Massachusetts 02111 (617) 423-3990; *The World in Figures.*

JOHNSTON ISLAND - FARM CROPS - See JOHNSTON ISLAND - CROPS

JOHNSTON ISLAND - FERTILIZER

Food and Agricultural Organization of the United Nations (FAO), Via delle Terme di Caracalla, 00100, Rome, Italy (Telephone Number in U.S. (202) 653-2400); *Fertilizer Yearbook,* and *The State of Food and Agriculture.*

JOHNSTON ISLAND - FETAL MORTALITY

Statistical Office of the United Nations, Publishing Service, New York, New York 10017 (800) 253-9646; *Demographic Yearbook.*

JOHNSTON ISLAND - FINANCE

G.K. Hall and Company, 70 Lincoln Street, Boston, Massachusetts 02111 (617) 423-3990; *The World in Figures.*

JOHNSTON ISLAND - FISHERIES

Food and Agricultural Organization of the United Nations (FAO), Via delle Terme di Caracalla, 00100 Rome, Italy (Telephone Number in U.S. (202) 653-2400); *The State of Food and Agriculture,* and *Yearbook of Fishery Statistics.*

JOHNSTON ISLAND - FOOD

G.K. Hall and Company, 70 Lincoln Street, Boston, Massachusetts 02111 (617) 423-3990; *The World in Figures.*

JOHNSTON ISLAND - FOREIGN AID

G.K. Hall and Company, 70 Lincoln Street, Boston, Massachusetts 02111 (617) 423-3990; *The World in Figures.*

JOHNSTON ISLAND - FOREIGN TRADE

Food and Agricultural Organization of the United Nations (FAO), Via delle Terme di Caracalla, 00100 Rome, Italy (Telephone Number in U.S. (202) 653-2400); *The State of Food and Agriculture.*

G.K. Hall and Company, 70 Lincoln Street, Boston, Massachusetts 02111 (617) 423-3990; *The World in Figures.*

JOHNSTON ISLAND - FORESTRY AND FOREST PRODUCTS

Food and Agricultural Organization of the United Nations (FAO), Via delle Terme di Caracalla, 00100 Rome, Italy (Telephone Number in U.S. (202) 653-2400); *The State of Food and Agriculture,* and *Yearbook of Forest Products.*

G.K. Hall and Company, 70 Lincoln Street, Boston, Massachusetts 02111 (617) 423-3990; *The World in Figures.*

JOHNSTON ISLAND - GENERAL MORTALITY

Statistical Office of the United Nations, Publishing Service, New York, New York 10017 (800) 253-9646; *Demographic Yearbook.*

JOHNSTON ISLAND - GOVERNMENT

G.K. Hall and Company, 70 Lincoln Street, Boston, Massachusetts 02111 (617) 423-3990; *The World in Figures.*

JOHNSTON ISLAND - GRAIN PRODUCTION - See JOHNSTON ISLAND - CROPS

JOHNSTON ISLAND - GROSS DOMESTIC PRODUCT

G.K. Hall and Company, 70 Lincoln Street, Boston, Massachusetts 02111 (617) 423-3990; *The World in Figures.*

JOHNSTON ISLAND - HEALTH

G.K. Hall and Company, 70 Lincoln Street, Boston, Massachusetts 02111 (617) 423-3990; *The World in Figures.*

JOHNSTON ISLAND - HIGHWAYS

G.K. Hall and Company, 70 Lincoln Street, Boston, Massachusetts 02111 (617) 423-3990; *The World in Figures.*

JOHNSTON ISLAND - ILLITERATE POPULATION

G.K. Hall and Company, 70 Lincoln Street, Boston, Massachusetts 02111 (617) 423-3990; *The World in Figures.*

JOHNSTON ISLAND - IMPORTS

Food and Agricultural Organization of the United Nations (FAO), Via delle Terme di Caracalla, 00100 Rome, Italy (Telephone Number in U.S. (202) 653-2400); *The State of Food and Agriculture.*

G.K. Hall and Company, 70 Lincoln Street, Boston, Massachusetts 02111 (617) 423-3990; *The World in Figures.*

JOHNSTON ISLAND - INDUSTRY

G.K. Hall and Company, 70 Lincoln Street, Boston, Massachusetts 02111 (617) 423-3990; *The World in Figures.*

JOHNSTON ISLAND - INFANT AND MATERNAL MORTALITY

Statistical Office of the United Nations, Publishing Service, New York, New York 10017 (800) 253-9646; *Demographic Yearbook.*

JOHNSTON ISLAND - LABOR FORCE

Food and Agricultural Organization of the United Nations (FAO), Via delle Terme di Caracalla, 00100 Rome, Italy (Telephone Number in U.S. (202) 653-2400); *The State of Food and Agriculture.*

G.K. Hall and Company, 70 Lincoln Street, Boston, Massachusetts 02111 (617) 423-3990; *The World in Figures.*

JOHNSTON ISLAND - LAND USE

Food and Agricultural Organization of the United Nations (FAO), Via delle Terme di Caracalla, 00100 Rome, Italy (Telephone Number in U.S. (202) 653-2400); *Production Yearbook.*

G.K. Hall and Company, 70 Lincoln Street, Boston, Massachusetts 02111 (617) 423-3990; *The World in Figures.*

JOHNSTON ISLAND - LIVESTOCK AND POULTRY

Food and Agricultural Organization of the United Nations (FAO), Via delle Terme di Caracalla, 00100 Rome, Italy (Telephone Number in U.S. (202) 653-2400); *Production Yearbook,* and *The State of Food and Agriculture.*

G.K. Hall and Company, 70 Lincoln Street, Boston, Massachusetts 02111 (617) 423-3990; *The World in Figures.*

JOHNSTON ISLAND - LIVING LEVELS

G.K. Hall and Company, 70 Lincoln Street, Boston, Massachusetts 02111 (617) 423-3990; *The World in Figures.*

JOHNSTON ISLAND - MANUFACTURING

G.K. Hall and Company, 70 Lincoln Street, Boston, Massachusetts 02111 (617) 423-3990; *The World in Figures.*

JOHNSTON ISLAND - MARRIAGE RATES

Statistical Office of the United Nations, Publishing Service, New York, New York 10017 (800) 253-9646; *Demographic Yearbook.*

JOHNSTON ISLAND - MEAT PRODUCTION - See JOHNSON ISLAND - LIVESTOCK AND POULTRY

JOHNSTON ISLAND - MERCHANT SHIPPING

G.K. Hall and Company, 70 Lincoln Street, Boston, Massachusetts 02111 (617) 423-3990; *The World in Figures.*

JOHNSTON ISLAND - MILITARY

G.K. Hall and Company, 70 Lincoln Street, Boston, Massachusetts 02111 (617) 423-3990; *The World in Figures.*

JOHNSTON ISLAND - MINING AND MINERAL PRODUCTS

G.K. Hall and Company, 70 Lincoln Street, Boston, Massachusetts 02111 (617) 423-3990; *The World in Figures.*

JOHNSTON ISLAND - MONEY SUPPLY

G.K. Hall and Company, 70 Lincoln Street, Boston, Massachusetts 02111 (617) 423-3990; *The World in Figures.*

JOHNSTON ISLAND - MOTOR VEHICLES IN USE

G.K. Hall and Company, 70 Lincoln Street, Boston, Massachusetts 02111 (617) 423-3990; *The World in Figures.*

JOHNSTON ISLAND - NATALITY - See JOHNSTON ISLAND - BIRTH RATES

JOHNSTON ISLAND - NATIONAL INCOME

G.K. Hall and Company, 70 Lincoln Street, Boston, Massachusetts 02111 (617) 423-3990; *The World in Figures.*

JOHNSTON ISLAND - NEWSPAPER PRODUCTION - See JOHNSTON ISLAND - FORESTRY AND FOREST PRODUCTS

JOHNSTON ISLAND - OCCUPATIONS - See JOHNSTON ISLAND - LABOR FORCE

JOHNSTON ISLAND - PESTICIDE USE

Food and Agricultural Organization of the United Nations (FAO), Via delle Terme di Caracalla, 00100 Rome, Italy (Telephone Number in U.S. (202) 653-2400); *The State of Food and Agriculture.*

JOHNSTON ISLAND - PETROLEUM INDUSTRY

Food and Agricultural Organization of the United Nations (FAO), Via delle Terme di Caracalla, 00100 Rome, Italy (Telephone Number in U.S. (202) 653-2400); *The State of Food and Agriculture.*

G.K. Hall and Company, 70 Lincoln Street, Boston, Massachusetts 02111 (617) 423-3990; *The World in Figures.*

JOHNSTON ISLAND - POPULATION

Food and Agricultural Organization of the United Nations (FAO), Via delle Terme di Caracalla, 00100 Rome, Italy (Telephone Number in U.S. (202) 653-2400); *Production Yearbook.*

G.K. Hall and Company, 70 Lincoln Street, Boston, Massachusetts 02111 (617) 423-3990; *The World in Figures.*

Statistical Office of the United Nations, Publishing Service, New York, New York 10017 (800) 253-9646; *Demographic Yearbook,* and *Statistical Yearbook.*

World Health Organization, Office of Publications, Avenue Appia, CH-1211 Geneva 27, Switzerland (Telephone Number in U.S. (518)

436-9686); *World Health Statistics Annual.*

JOHNSTON ISLAND - PRICES

Food and Agricultural Organization of the United Nations (FAO), Via delle Terme di Caracalla, 00100 Rome, Italy (Telephone Number in U.S. (202) 653-2400); *Production Yearbook*, and *The State of Food and Agriculture.*

G.K. Hall and Company, 70 Lincoln Street, Boston, Massachusetts 02111 (617) 423-3990; *The World in Figures.*

JOHNSTON ISLAND - PRODUCTION

G.K. Hall and Company, 70 Lincoln Street, Boston, Massachusetts 02111 (617) 423-3990; *The World in Figures.*

JOHNSTON ISLAND - RAILWAYS

G.K. Hall and Company, 70 Lincoln Street, Boston, Massachusetts 02111 (617) 423-3990; *The World in Figures.*

JOHNSTON ISLAND - RETAIL TRADE

G.K. Hall and Company, 70 Lincoln Street, Boston, Massachusetts 02111 (617) 423-3990; *The World in Figures.*

JOHNSTON ISLAND - SOCIAL DATA

G.K. Hall and Company, 70 Lincoln Street, Boston, Massachusetts 02111 (617) 423-3990; *The World in Figures.*

JOHNSTON ISLAND - STOCKS - COMMODITY - MARKET PRICE - INDEX

Food and Agricultural Organization of the United Nations (FAO); Via delle Terme di Caracalla, 00100 Rome, Italy (Telephone Number in U.S. (202) 653-2400); *The State of Food and Agriculture.*

JOHNSTON ISLAND - TAXATION

G.K. Hall and Company, 70 Lincoln Street, Boston, Massachusetts 02111 (617) 423-3990; *The World in Figures.*

JOHNSTON ISLAND - TELEPHONES IN USE

G.K. Hall and Company, 70 Lincoln Street, Boston, Massachusetts 02111 (617) 423-3990; *The World in Figures.*

JOHNSTON ISLAND - TEXTILE INDUSTRY

G.K. Hall and Company, 70 Lincoln Street, Boston, Massachusetts 02111 (617) 423-3990; *The World in Figures.*

JOHNSTON ISLAND - TOURISM

G.K. Hall and Company, 70 Lincoln Street, Boston, Massachusetts 02111 (617) 423-3990; *The World in Figures.*

JOHNSTON ISLAND - TRADE - See JOHNSTON ISLAND - FOREIGN TRADE

JOHNSTON ISLAND - TRANSPORTATION AND COMMUNICATIONS

G.K. Hall and Company, 70 Lincoln Street, Boston, Massachusetts 02111 (617) 423-3990; *The World in Figures.*

JOHNSTON ISLAND - VITAL STATISTICS

G.K. Hall and Company, 70 Lincoln Street, Boston, Massachusetts 02111 (617) 423-3990; *The World in Figures.*

World Health Organization, Office of Publications, Avenue Appia, CH-1211 Geneva 27, Switzerland (Telephone Number in U.S. (518) 436-9686); *World Health Statistics Annual.*

JOHNSTON ISLAND - WAGES

G.K. Hall and Company, 70 Lincoln Street, Boston, Massachusetts 02111 (617) 423-3990; *The World in Figures.*

JOHNSTON ISLAND - WEATHER

G.K. Hall and Company, 70 Lincoln Street, Boston, Massachusetts 02111 (617) 423-3990; *The World in Figures.*

Jordan - National Statistical Office

Department of Statistics, Post Office Box 2015, Amman, Jordan.

Jordan - Primary Statistics Source

Department of Statistics, Post Office Box 2015, Amman, Jordan; *Statistical Yearbook.*

JORDAN - AGRICULTURE

Economic Commission for Western Asia, Post Office Box 27, Baghdad, Iraq; *Statistical Abstract of Western Asia.*

Euromonitor Publications Limited, 87-88 Turnmill Street, London EC1M 5QU, England; *Middle East Economic Handbook.*

Facts on File, 460 Park Avenue South, New York, New York 10016 (800) 443-8323; *The New Book of World Rankings.*

Federal Statistical Office, Gustav - Stresemann - Ring 11, D-6200 Wiesbaden, Germany; *Jordan.*

Food and Agricultural Organization of the United Nations (FAO), Via delle Terme di Caracalla, 00100 Rome, Italy (Telephone Number in U.S. (202) 653-2400); *Production Yearbook*, *The State of Food and Agriculture*, and *Trade Yearbook.*

G.K. Hall and Company, 70 Lincoln Street, Boston, Massachusetts 02111 (617) 423-3990; *The World in Figures.*

Statistical Office of the United Nations, Publishing Service, New York, New York 10017 (800) 253-9646; *Statistical Yearbook.*

Times Books, 201 East 50th Street, New York, New York 10022; *The Economist Book of Vital World Statistics.*

JORDAN - AIRLINE SERVICE

Economic Commission for Western Asia, Post Office Box 27, Baghdad, Iraq; *Statistical Abstract of Western Asia.*

Facts on File, 460 Park Avenue South, New York, New York 10016 (800) 443-8323; *The New Book of World Rankings.*

G.K. Hall and Company, 70 Lincoln Street, Boston, Massachusetts 02111 (617) 423-3990; *The World in Figures.*

International Civil Aviation Organization, 1000 Sherbrooke Street West, Suite 400, Montreal, Quebec H3A 2R2, Canada (514) 285-8219; *Civil Aviation Statistics of the World*.

Statistical Office of the United Nations, Publishing Service, New York, New York 10017 (800) 253-9646; *Statistical Yearbook*.

Times Books, 201 East 50th Street, New York, New York 10022 (212) 751-2600; *The Economist Book of Vital World Statistics*.

JORDAN - ALUMINUM PRODUCTION - See JORDAN - MINING AND MINERAL PRODUCTS

JORDAN - ANIMAL HEALTH

Food and Agricultural Organization of the United Nations (FAO), Via delle Terme di Caracalla, 00100, Rome, Italy (Telephone Number in U.S. (202) 653-2400); *Animal Health Yearbook*.

JORDAN - AREA AND DENSITY OF POPULATION

Economic Commission for Western Asia, Post Office Box 27, Baghdad, Iraq; *Statistical Abstract of Western Asia*.

Euromonitor Publications Limited, 87-88 Turnmill Street, London EC1M 5QU, England; *International Marketing Data and Statistics*, and *Middle East Economic Handbook*.

Facts on File, 460 Park Avenue South, New York, New York 10016 (800) 443-8323; *The New Book of World Rankings*.

Federal Statistical Office, Gustav - Stresemann - Ring 11, D-6200 Wiesbaden, Germany; *Jordan*.

Food and Agricultural Organization of the United Nations (FAO), Via delle Terme di Caracalla, 00100 Rome, Italy (Telephone Number in U.S. (202) 653-2400); *The State of Food and Agriculture*.

G.K. Hall and Company, 70 Lincoln Street, Boston, Massachusetts 02111 (617) 423-3990; *The World in Figures*.

Statistical Office of the United Nations, Publishing Service, New York, New York 10017 (800) 253-9646; *Statistical Yearbook*.

Times Books, 201 East 50th Street, New York, New York 10022 (212) 751-2600; *The Economist Book of Vital World Statistics*.

United Nations Educational, Scientific and Cultural Organization (UNESCO), 7 Place de Fontenoy, F-75700 Paris, France (Telephone Number in U.S. (212) 963-5981); *Statistical Yearbook*.

JORDAN - ARMS EXPORTS AND IMPORTS

U.S. Arms Control and Disarmament Agency, 320 Twenty-first Street, NW, Washington, D.C. 20451 (202) 647-8677; *World Military Expenditures and Arms Transfers*.

JORDAN - BALANCE OF PAYMENTS

Economic Commission for Western Asia, Post Office Box 27, Baghdad, Iraq; *Statistical Abstract of Western Asia*.

The Economist Intelligence Unit, 111 West 57th Street, New York, New York 10019 (800) 938-4685; *The World Market Atlas*.

Federal Statistical Office, Gustav - Stresemann - Ring 11, D-6200 Wiesbaden, Germany; *Jordan*.

G.K. Hall and Company, 70 Lincoln Street, Boston, Massachusetts 02111 (617) 423-3990; *The World in Figures*.

International Monetary Fund, 700 Nineteenth Street, NW, Washington, D.C. 20431 (202) 623-7000; *Balance of Payments Yearbook*, and *International Financial Statistics*.

Times Books, 201 East 50th Street, New York, New York 10022 (212) 751-2600; *The Economist Book of Vital World Statistics*.

JORDAN - BALANCE OF TRADE

Economic Commission for Western Asia, Post Office Box 27, Baghdad, Iraq; *Statistical Abstract of Western Asia*.

JORDAN - BANKING

Economic Commission for Western Asia, Post Office Box 27, Baghdad, Iraq; *Statistical Abstract of Western Asia*.

Facts on File, 460 Park Avenue South, New York, New York 10016 (800) 443-8323; *The New Book of World Rankings*.

G.K. Hall and Company, 70 Lincoln Street, Boston, Massachusetts 02111 (617) 423-3990; *The World in Figures*.

International Monetary Fund, 700 Nineteenth Street, NW, Washington, D.C. 20431 (202) 623-7000; *Government Finance Statistics Yearbook*, and *International Financial Statistics*.

Statistical Office of the United Nations, Publishing Service, New York, New York 10017 (800) 253-9646; *Statistical Yearbook*.

JORDAN - BARLEY PRODUCTION - See JORDAN - CROPS

JORDAN - BEER PRODUCTION

Facts on File, 460 Park Avenue South, New York, New York 10016 (800) 443-8323; *The New Book of World Rankings*.

Statistical Office of the United Nations, Publishing Service, New York, New York 10017 (800) 253-9646; *Statistical Yearbook*.

JORDAN - BIRTH RATES

Euromonitor Publications Limited, 87-88 Turnmill Street, London EC1M 5QU, England; *Middle East Economic Handbook*.

Facts on File, 460 Park Avenue South, New York, New York 10016 (800) 443-8323; *The New Book of World Rankings*.

Statistical Office of the United Nations, Publishing Service, New York, New York 10017 (800) 253-9646; *Demographic Yearbook*, and *Statistical Yearbook*.

Times Books, 201 East 50th Street, New York, New York 10022 (212) 751-2600; *The Economist Book of Vital World Statistics*.

World Health Organization, Office of Publications, Avenue Appia, CH-1211 Geneva 27, Switzerland (Telephone Number in U.S. (518) 436-9686); *World Health Statistics Annual*.

JORDAN - BONDS

G.K. Hall and Company, 70 Lincoln Street, Boston, Massachusetts 02111 (617) 423-3990; *The World in Figures*.

International Monetary Fund, 700 Nineteenth Street, NW, Washington, D.C. 20431 (202) 623-7000; *Government Finance*

Statistics Yearbook.

JORDAN - BOOK PRODUCTION

G.K. Hall and Company, 70 Lincoln Street, Boston, Massachusetts 02111 (617) 423-3990; *The World in Figures.*

United Nations Educational, Scientific and Cultural Organization (UNESCO), 7 Place de Fontenoy, F-75700 Paris, France (Telephone Number in U.S. (212) 963-5981); *Statistical Yearbook.*

JORDAN - BROADCASTING

Billboard Limited, Post Office Box 9027, 1006 AA Amsterdam, The Netherlands (Telephone Number in U.S. (212) 764-7300); *World Radio TV Handbook.*

Facts on File, 460 Park Avenue South, New York, New York 10016 (800) 443-8323; *The New Book of World Rankings.*

G.K. Hall and Company, 70 Lincoln Street, Boston, Massachusetts 02111 (617) 423-3990; *The World in Figures.*

Times Books, 201 East 50th Street, New York, New York 10022 (212) 751-2600; *The Economist Book of Vital World Statistics.*

JORDAN - BUSINESS

G.K. Hall and Company, 70 Lincoln Street, Boston, Massachusetts 02111 (617) 423-3990; *The World in Figures.*

JORDAN - BUSINESS AND PROFESSIONAL LICENSES

International Monetary Fund, 700 Nineteenth Street, NW, Washington, D.C. 20431 (202) 623-7000; *Government Finance Statistics Yearbook.*

JORDAN - CABBAGE PRODUCTION - See JORDAN - CROPS

JORDAN - CALORIE SUPPLY

Food and Agricultural Organization of the United Nations (FAO), Via delle Terme di Caracalla, 00100 Rome, Italy (Telephone Number in U.S. (202) 653-2400); *The State of Food and Agriculture.*

JORDAN - CAPITAL REVENUES

International Monetary Fund, 700 Nineteenth Street, NW, Washington, D.C. 20431 (202) 623-7000; *Government Finance Statistics Yearbook.*

JORDAN - CATTLE - See JORDAN - LIVESTOCK AND POULTRY

JORDAN - CAULIFLOWER PRODUCTION - See JORDAN - CROPS

JORDAN - CEMENT PRODUCTION - See JORDAN - MINING AND MINERAL PRODUCTS

JORDAN - CHEESE PRODUCTION - See JORDAN - DAIRY PRODUCTS

JORDAN - CHEMICAL (ORGANIC) PRODUCTION - See JORDAN - MINING AND MINERAL PRODUCTS

JORDAN - CHICK PEA PRODUCTION - See JORDAN - CROPS

JORDAN - CHICKENS - See JORDAN - LIVESTOCK AND POULTRY

JORDAN - CIGARETTE PRODUCTION - See JORDAN - TOBACCO PRODUCTION

JORDAN - CLASS STRUCTURE

G.K. Hall and Company, 70 Lincoln Street, Boston, Massachusetts 02111 (617) 423-3990; *The World in Figures.*

JORDAN - CLIMATE

Facts on File, 460 Park Avenue South, New York, New York 10016 (800) 443-8323; *The New Book of World Rankings.*

G.K. Hall and Company, 70 Lincoln Street, Boston, Massachusetts 02111 (617) 423-3990; *The World in Figures.*

JORDAN - COAL PRODUCTION - See JORDAN - MINING AND MINERAL PRODUCTS

JORDAN - COFFEE PRODUCTION - See JORDAN - CROPS

JORDAN - COMMUNICATIONS

Economic Commission for Western Asia, Post Office Box 27, Baghdad, Iraq; *Statistical Abstract of Western Asia.*

Federal Statistical Office, Gustav - Stresemann - Ring 11, D-6200 Wiesbaden, Germany; *Jordan.*

G.K. Hall and Company, 70 Lincoln Street, Boston, Massachusetts 02111 (617) 423-3990; *The World in Figures.*

JORDAN - CONSTRUCTION INDUSTRY

Facts on File, 460 Park Avenue South, New York, New York 10016 (800) 443-8323; *The New Book of World Rankings.*

Statistical Office of the United Nations, Publishing Service, New York, New York 10017 (800) 253-9646; *Construction Statistics Yearbook,* and *Statistical Yearbook.*

JORDAN - CONSUMER PRICE INDEX

G.K. Hall and Company, 70 Lincoln Street, Boston, Massachusetts 02111 (617) 423-3990; *The World in Figures.*

Statistical Office of the United Nations, Publishing Service, New York, New York 10017 (800) 253-9646; *Statistical Yearbook.*

JORDAN - CONSUMER PRICES

International Labour Office, I.L.O. Publications, CH-1211, Geneva 22, Switzerland; *Yearbook of Labour Statistics.*

International Monetary Fund, 700 Nineteenth Street, NW, Washington, D.C. 20431 (202) 623-7000; *International Financial Statistics.*

Times Books, 201 East 50th Street, New York, New York 10022 (212) 751-2600; *The Economist Book of Vital World Statistics.*

JORDAN - CONSUMPTION

Euromonitor Publications Limited, 87-88 Turnmill Street, London EC1M 5QU, England; *Middle East Economic Handbook.*

G.K. Hall and Company, 70 Lincoln Street, Boston, Massachusetts 02111 (617) 423-3990; *The World in Figures.*

JORDAN - COPPER PRODUCTION - See JORDAN - MINING AND MINERAL PRODUCTS

JORDAN - CORN PRODUCTION - See JORDAN - CROPS

JORDAN - CORPORATE TAXES - See JORDAN - TAXATION

JORDAN - COTTON PRODUCTION - See JORDAN - CROPS

JORDAN - CRIME

International Criminal Police Organization (INTERPOL), 26 rue Armengaud, 92210 Saint Cloud, France; *International Crime Statistics.*

Yale University Press, Yale Station, New Haven, Connecticut 06520 (203) 432-0940; *Violence and Crime in Cross-National Perspective.*

JORDAN - CROPS

Facts on File, 460 Park Avenue South, New York, New York 10016 (800) 443-8323; *The New Book of World Rankings.*

Food and Agricultural Organization of the United Nations (FAO), Via delle Terme di Caracalla, 00100 Rome, Italy (Telephone Number in U.S. (202) 653-2400); *Production Yearbook,* and *The State of Food and Agriculture.*

G.K. Hall and Company, 70 Lincoln Street, Boston, Massachusetts 02111 (617) 423-3990; *The World in Figures.*

Statistical Office of the United Nations, Publishing Service, New York, New York 10017 (800) 253-9646; *Statistical Yearbook.*

JORDAN - CUSTOMS DUTIES

G.K. Hall and Company, 70 Lincoln Street, Boston, Massachusetts 02111 (617) 423-3990; *The World in Figures.*

International Monetary Fund, 700 Nineteenth Street, NW, Washington, D.C. 20431 (202) 623-7000; *Government Finance Statistics Yearbook.*

JORDAN - DAIRY PRODUCTS

Economic Commission for Western Asia, Post Office Box 27, Baghdad, Iraq; *Statistical Abstract of Western Asia.*

Facts on File, 460 Park Avenue South, New York, New York 10016 (800) 443-8323; *The New Book of World Rankings.*

Food and Agricultural Organization of the United Nations (FAO), Via delle Terme di Caracalla, 00100 Rome, Italy (Telephone Number in U.S. (202) 653-2400); *Production Yearbook,* and *The State of Food and Agriculture.*

Statistical Office of the United Nations, Publishing Service, New York, New York 10017 (800) 253-9646; *Statistical Yearbook.*

JORDAN - DEATH RATES

Euromonitor Publications Limited, 87-88 Turnmill Street, London EC1M 5QU, England; *Middle East Economic Handbook.*

G.K. Hall and Company, 70 Lincoln Street, Boston, Massachusetts 02111 (617) 423-3990; *The World in Figures.*

Statistical Office of the United Nations, Publishing Service, New York, New York 10017 (800) 253-9646; *Statistical Yearbook.*

Times Books, 201 East 50th Street, New York, New York 10022 (212) 751-2600; *The Economist Book of Vital World Statistics.*

World Health Organization, Office of Publications, Avenue Appia, CH-1211 Geneva 27, Switzerland (Telephone Number in U.S. (518) 436-9686); *World Health Statistics Annual.*

JORDAN - DEFENSE EXPENDITURES

G.K. Hall and Company, 70 Lincoln Street, Boston, Massachusetts 02111 (617) 423-3990; *The World in Figures.*

International Monetary Fund, 700 Nineteenth Street, NW, Washington, D.C. 20431 (202) 623-7000; *Government Finance Statistics Yearbook.*

U.S. Arms Control and Disarmament Agency, 320 Twenty-first Street, NW, Washington, D.C. 20451 (202) 647-8677; *World Military Expenditures and Arms Transfers.*

JORDAN - DEMOGRAPHY

The Economist Intelligence Unit, 111 West 57th Street, New York, New York 10019 (800) 938-4685; *The World Market Atlas.*

Facts on File, 460 Park Avenue South, New York, New York 10016 (800) 443-8323; *The New Book of World Rankings.*

G.K. Hall and Company, 70 Lincoln Street, Boston, Massachusetts 02111 (617) 423-3990; *The World in Figures.*

JORDAN - DEVELOPMENT ASSISTANCE

G.K. Hall and Company, 70 Lincoln Street, Boston, Massachusetts 02111 (617) 423-3990; *The World in Figures.*

Statistical Office of the United Nations, Publishing Service, New York, New York 10017 (800) 253-9646; *Statistical Yearbook.*

JORDAN - DIAMOND PRODUCTION - See JORDAN - MINING AND MINERAL PRODUCTS

JORDAN - DISCOUNT RATES

Statistical Office of the United Nations, Publishing Service, New York, New York 10017 (800) 253-9646; *Statistical Yearbook.*

JORDAN - DISEASES

G.K. Hall and Company, 70 Lincoln Street, Boston, Massachusetts 02111 (617) 423-3990; *The World in Figures.*

World Health Organization, Office of Publications, Avenue Appia, CH-1211 Geneva 27, Switzerland (Telephone Number in U.S. (518) 436-9686); *World Health Statistics Annual.*

JORDAN - DIVORCE RATES

Facts on File, 460 Park Avenue South, New York, New York 10016 (800) 443-8323; *The New Book of World Rankings.*

Statistical Office of the United Nations, Publishing Service, New York, New York 10017 (800) 253-9646; *Demographic Yearbook,* and *Statistical Yearbook.*

JORDAN - DOMESTIC PRODUCT

G.K. Hall and Company, 70 Lincoln Street, Boston, Massachusetts 02111 (617) 423-3990; *The World in Figures.*

JORDAN - ECONOMY

Euromonitor Publications Limited, 87-88 Turnmill Street, London EC1M 5QU, England; *International Marketing Data and Statistics*.

Facts on File, 460 Park Avenue South, New York, New York 10016 (800) 443-8323; *The New Book of World Rankings*.

G.K. Hall and Company, 70 Lincoln Street, Boston, Massachusetts 02111 (617) 423-3990; *The World in Figures*.

JORDAN - EDUCATION

Economic Commission for Western Asia, Post Office Box 27, Baghdad, Iraq; *Statistical Abstract of Western Asia*.

The Economist Intelligence Unit, 111 West 57th Street, New York, New York 10019 (800) 938-4685; *The World Market Atlas*.

Euromonitor Publications Limited, 87-88 Turnmill Street, London EC1M 5QU, England; *Middle East Economic Handbook*.

Facts on File, 460 Park Avenue South, New York, New York 10016 (800) 443-8323; *The New Book of World Rankings*.

Federal Statistical Office, Gustav - Stresemann - Ring 11, D-6200 Wiesbaden, Germany; *Jordan*.

G.K. Hall and Company, 70 Lincoln Street, Boston, Massachusetts 02111 (617) 423-3990; *The World in Figures*.

Times Books, 201 East 50th Street, New York, New York 10022 (212) 751-2600; *The Economist Book of Vital World Statistics*.

United Nations Educational, Scientific and Cultural Organization (UNESCO), 7 Place de Fontenoy, F-75700 Paris, France (Telephone Number in U.S. (212) 963-5981); *Statistical Yearbook*.

JORDAN - EGG PRODUCTION AND CONSUMPTION - See JORDAN - DAIRY PRODUCTS

JORDAN - EGGPLANT PRODUCTION - See JORDAN - CROPS

JORDAN - ELECTRICITY

Facts on File, 460 Park Avenue South, New York, New York 10016 (800) 443-8323; *The New Book of World Rankings*.

Penn Well Publishing Company, 1421 South Sheridan Road, Post Office Box 1260, Tulsa, Oklahoma 74101 (800) 752-9764; *International Energy Statistics Sourcebook*.

Statistical Office of the United Nations, Publishing Service, New York, New York 10017 (800) 253-9646; *Statistical Yearbook*.

Times Books, 201 East 50th Street, New York, New York 10022 (212) 751-2600; *The Economist Book of Vital World Statistics*.

JORDAN - EMPLOYMENT

Economic Commission for Western Asia, Post Office Box 27, Baghdad, Iraq; *Statistical Abstract of Western Asia*.

Euromonitor Publications Limited, 87-88 Turnmill Street, London EC1M 5QU, England; *International Marketing Data and Statistics*, and *Middle East Economic Handbook*.

Facts on File, 460 Park Avenue South, New York, New York 10016 (800) 443-8323; *The New Book of World Rankings*.

Federal Statistical Office, Gustav - Stresemann - Ring 11, D-6200 Wiesbaden, Germany; *Jordan*.

International Labour Office, I.L.O. Publications, CH-1211, Geneva 22, Switzerland; *Yearbook of Labour Statistics*.

Statistical Office of the United Nations, Publishing Service, New York, New York 10017 (800) 253-9646; *Statistical Yearbook*.

JORDAN - ENERGY

Economic Commission for Western Asia, Post Office Box 27, Baghdad, Iraq; *Statistical Abstract of Western Asia*.

Euromonitor Publications Limited, 87-88 Turnmill Street, London EC1M 5QU, England; *Middle East Economic Handbook*.

Facts on File, 460 Park Avenue South, New York, New York 10016 (800) 443-8323; *The New Book of World Rankings*.

Food and Agricultural Organization of the United Nations (FAO), Via delle Terme di Caracalla, 00100 Rome, Italy (Telephone Number in U.S. (202) 653-2400); *The State of Food and Agriculture*.

G.K. Hall and Company, 70 Lincoln Street, Boston, Massachusetts 02111 (617) 423-3990; *The World in Figures*.

Penn Well Publishing Company, 1421 South Sheridan Road, Post Office Box 1260, Tulsa, Oklahoma 74101 (800) 752-9764; *International Energy Statistics Sourcebook*.

Statistical Office of the United Nations, Publishing Service, New York, New York 10017 (800) 253-9646; *Energy Statistics Yearbook*, and *Statistical Yearbook*.

Times Books, 201 East 50th Street, New York, New York 10022 (212) 751-2600; *The Economist Book of Vital World Statistics*.

JORDAN - EXCHANGE RATES

Euromonitor Publications Limited, 87-88 Turnmill Street, London EC1M 5QU, England; *International Marketing Data and Statistics*, and *Middle East Economic Handbook*.

International Civil Aviation Organization, 1000 Sherbrooke Street West, Suite 400, Montreal, Quebec H3A 2R2, Canada (514) 285-8219; *Civil Aviation Statistics of the World*.

International Monetary Fund, 700 Nineteenth Street, NW, Washington, D.C. 20431 (202) 623-7000; *International Financial Statistics*.

Statistical Office of the United Nations, Publishing Service, New York, New York 10017 (800) 253-9646; *Statistical Yearbook*.

JORDAN - EXCISE TAXES - See JORDAN - TAXATION

JORDAN - EXPORTS

Economic Commission for Western Asia, Post Office Box 27, Baghdad, Iraq; *Statistical Abstract of Western Asia*.

The Economist Intelligence Unit, 111 West 57th Street, New York, New York 10019 (800) 938-4685; *The World Market Atlas*.

Euromonitor Publications Limited, 87-88 Turnmill Street, London EC1M 5QU, England; *International Marketing Data and Statistics*, and *Middle East Economic Handbook*.

Food and Agricultural Organization of the United Nations (FAO), Via delle Terme di Caracalla, 00100 Rome, Italy (Telephone Number in U.S. (202) 653-2400); *The State of Food and Agriculture*.

G.K. Hall and Company, 70 Lincoln Street, Boston, Massachusetts 02111 (617) 423-3990; *The World in Figures*.

International Monetary Fund, 700 Nineteenth Street, NW, Washington, D.C. 20431 (202) 623-7000; *Direction of Trade Statistics*, *Government Finance Statistics Yearbook*, and *International Financial Statistics*.

Times Books, 201 East 50th Street, New York, New York 10022 (212) 751-2600; *The Economist Book of Vital World Statistics*.

JORDAN - EXTERNAL TRADE

Food and Agricultural Organization of the United Nations (FAO), Via delle Terme di Caracalla, 00100 Rome, Italy (Telephone Number in U.S. (202) 653-2400); *The State of Food and Agriculture*, and *Trade Yearbook*.

G.K. Hall and Company, 70 Lincoln Street, Boston, Massachusetts 02111 (617) 423-3990; *The World in Figures*.

Statistical Office of the United Nations, Publishing Service, New York, New York 10017 (800) 253-9646; *Statistical Yearbook*.

JORDAN - FARM CROPS - See JORDAN - CROPS

JORDAN - FEMALE WORKING POPULATION - See JORDAN - EMPLOYMENT

JORDAN - FERTILITY RATES

Facts on File, 460 Park Avenue South, New York, New York 10016 (800) 443-8323; *The New Book of World Rankings*.

Times Books, 201 East 50th Street, New York, New York 10022 (212) 751-2600; *The Economist Book of Vital World Statistics*.

JORDAN - FERTILIZER

Food and Agricultural Organization of the United Nations (FAO), Via delle Terme di Caracalla, 00100, Rome, Italy (Telephone Number in U.S. (202) 653-2400); *Fertilizer Yearbook*, and *The State of Food and Agriculture*.

Statistical Office of the United Nations, Publishing Service, New York, New York 10017 (800) 253-9646; *Statistical Yearbook*.

JORDAN - FETAL MORTALITY

Statistical Office of the United Nations, Publishing Service, New York, New York 10017 (800) 253-9646; *Demographic Yearbook*.

JORDAN - FINANCE

Economic Commission for Western Asia, Post Office Box 27, Baghdad, Iraq; *Statistical Abstract of Western Asia*.

Euromonitor Publications Limited, 87-88 Turnmill Street, London EC1M 5QU, England; *Middle East Economic Handbook*.

Facts on File, 460 Park Avenue South, New York, New York 10016 (800) 443-8323; *The New Book of World Rankings*.

Federal Statistical Office, Gustav - Stresemann - Ring 11, D-6200 Wiesbaden, Germany; *Jordan*.

G.K. Hall and Company, 70 Lincoln Street, Boston, Massachusetts 02111 (617) 423-3990; *The World in Figures*.

International Monetary Fund, 700 Nineteenth Street, NW, Washington, D.C. 20431 (202) 623-7000; *Government Finance Statistics Yearbook*, and *International Financial Statistics*.

JORDAN - FISHERIES

Economic Commission for Western Asia, Post Office Box 27, Baghdad, Iraq; *Statistical Abstract of Western Asia*.

Facts on File, 460 Park Avenue South, New York, New York 10016 (800) 443-8323; *The New Book of World Rankings*.

Federal Statistical Office, Gustav - Stresemann - Ring 11, D-6200 Wiesbaden, Germany; *Jordan*.

Food and Agricultural Organization of the United Nations (FAO), Via delle Terme di Caracalla, 00100 Rome, Italy (Telephone Number in U.S. (202) 653-2400); *The State of Food and Agriculture*, and *Yearbook of Fishery Statistics*.

JORDAN - FLOUR PRODUCTION

Statistical Office of the United Nations, Publishing Service, New York, New York 10017 (800) 253-9646; *Statistical Yearbook*.

JORDAN - FOOD

Food and Agricultural Organization of the United Nations (FAO), Via delle Terme di Caracalla, 00100 Rome, Italy (Telephone Number in U.S. (202) 653-2400); *Production Yearbook*, and *The State of Food and Agriculture*.

G.K. Hall and Company, 70 Lincoln Street, Boston, Massachusetts 02111 (617) 423-3990; *The World in Figures*.

JORDAN - FOREIGN AID

G.K. Hall and Company, 70 Lincoln Street, Boston, Massachusetts 02111 (617) 423-3990; *The World in Figures*.

JORDAN - FOREIGN DEBT

International Monetary Fund, 700 Nineteenth Street, NW, Washington, D.C. 20431 (202) 623-7000; *Government Finance Statistics Yearbook*.

JORDAN - FOREIGN INDEBTEDNESS

Euromonitor Publications Limited, 87-88 Turnmill Street, London EC1M 5QU, England; *Middle East Economic Handbook*.

JORDAN - FOREIGN TRADE

Economic Commission for Western Asia, Post Office Box 27, Baghdad, Iraq; *Statistical Abstract of Western Asia*.

Euromonitor Publications Limited, 87-88 Turnmill Street, London EC1M 5QU, England; *International Marketing Data and Statistics*, and *Middle East Economic Handbook*.

Facts on File, 460 Park Avenue South, New York, New York 10016 (800) 443-8323; *The New Book of World Rankings*.

Federal Statistical Office, Gustav - Stresemann - Ring 11, D-6200 Wiesbaden, Germany; *Jordan*.

Food and Agricultural Organization of the United Nations (FAO), Via delle Terme di Caracalla, 00100 Rome, Italy (Telephone Number in U.S. (202) 653-2400); *The State of Food and Agriculture.*

G.K. Hall and Company, 70 Lincoln Street, Boston, Massachusetts 02111 (617) 423-3990; *The World in Figures.*

International Monetary Fund, 700 Nineteenth Street, NW, Washington, D.C. 20431 (202) 623-7000; *International Financial Statistics.*

Statistical Office of the United Nations, Publishing Service, New York, New York 10017 (800) 253-9646; *International Trade Statistics Yearbook,* and *Statistical Yearbook.*

JORDAN - FORESTRY AND FOREST PRODUCTS

Facts on File, 460 Park Avenue South, New York, New York 10016 (800) 443-8323; *The New Book of World Rankings.*

Federal Statistical Office, Gustav - Stresemann - Ring 11, D-6200 Wiesbaden, Germany; *Jordan.*

Food and Agricultural Organization of the United Nations (FAO), Via delle Terme di Caracalla, 00100 Rome, Italy (Telephone Number in U.S. (202) 653-2400); *The State of Food and Agriculture,* and *Yearbook of Forest Products.*

G.K. Hall and Company, 70 Lincoln Street, Boston, Massachusetts 02111 (617) 423-3990; *The World in Figures.*

Statistical Office of the United Nations, Publishing Service, New York, New York 10017 (800) 253-9646; *Statistical Yearbook.*

United Nations Educational, Scientific and Cultural Organization (UNESCO), 7 Place de Fontenoy, F-75700 Paris, France (Telephone Number in U.S. (212) 963-5981); *Statistical Yearbook.*

JORDAN - GAS PRODUCTION - See JORDAN - MINING AND MINERAL PRODUCTS

JORDAN - GENERAL INDUSTRIAL STATISTICS

Statistical Office of the United Nations, Publishing Service, New York, New York 10017 (800) 253-9646; *Industrial Statistics Yearbook.*

JORDAN - GENERAL MORTALITY

Statistical Office of the United Nations, Publishing Service, New York, New York 10017 (800) 253-9646; *Demographic Yearbook.*

World Health Organization, Office of Publications, Avenue Appia, CH-1211 Geneva 27, Switzerland (Telephone Number in U.S. (518) 436-9686); *World Health Statistics Annual.*

JORDAN - GEOGRAPHIC DATA

Facts on File, 460 Park Avenue South, New York, New York 10016 (800) 443-8323; *The New Book of World Rankings.*

JORDAN - GOATS - See JORDAN - LIVESTOCK AND POULTRY

JORDAN - GOLD HOLDINGS

International Monetary Fund, 700 Nineteenth Street, NW, Washington, D.C. 20431 (202) 623-7000; *International Financial Statistics.*

JORDAN - GOLD PRODUCTION AND CONSUMPTION - See JORDAN - MINING AND MINERAL PRODUCTS

JORDAN - GOVERNMENT

G.K. Hall and Company, 70 Lincoln Street, Boston, Massachusetts 02111 (617) 423-3990; *The World in Figures.*

JORDAN - GOVERNMENT EXPENDITURES

Economic Commission for Western Asia, Post Office Box 27, Baghdad, Iraq; *Statistical Abstract of Western Asia.*

International Monetary Fund, 700 Nineteenth Street, NW, Washington, D.C. 20431 (202) 623-7000; *Government Finance Statistics Yearbook.*

Times Books, 201 East 50th Street, New York, New York 10022 (212) 751-2600; *The Economist Book of Vital World Statistics.*

JORDAN - GOVERNMENT FINANCES

International Monetary Fund, 700 Nineteenth Street, NW, Washington, D.C. 20431 (202) 623-7000; *International Financial Statistics.*

Statistical Office of the United Nations, Publishing Service, New York, New York 10017 (800) 253-9646; *Statistical Yearbook.*

JORDAN - GOVERNMENT REVENUES

Economic Commission for Western Asia, Post Office Box 27, Baghdad, Iraq; *Statistical Abstract of Western Asia.*

International Monetary Fund, 700 Nineteenth Street, NW, Washington, D.C. 20431 (202) 623-7000; *Government Finance Statistics Yearbook.*

Times Books, 201 East 50th Street, New York, New York 10022 (212) 751-2600; *The Economist Book of Vital World Statistics.*

JORDAN - GRAIN PRODUCTION - See JORDAN - CROPS

JORDAN - GRANTS

International Monetary Fund, 700 Nineteenth Street, NW, Washington, D.C. 20431 (202) 623-7000; *Government Finance Statistics Yearbook.*

JORDAN - GREEN PEPPER AND CHILIE PRODUCTION - See JORDAN - CROPS

JORDAN - GROSS DOMESTIC PRODUCT

Economic Commission for Western Asia, Post Office Box 27, Baghdad, Iraq; *Statistical Abstract of Western Asia.*

The Economist Intelligence Unit, 111 West 57th Street, New York, New York 10019 (800) 938-4685; *The World Market Atlas.*

Euromonitor Publications Limited, 87-88 Turnmill Street, London EC1M 5QU, England; *International Marketing Data and Statistics,* and *Middle East Economic Handbook.*

Facts on File, 460 Park Avenue South, New York, New York 10016 (800) 443-8323; *The New Book of World Rankings.*

G.K. Hall and Company, 70 Lincoln Street, Boston, Massachusetts 02111 (617) 423-3990; *The World in Figures*.

Statistical Office of the United Nations, Publishing Service, New York, New York 10017 (800) 253-9646; *Statistical Yearbook*.

Times Books, 201 East 50th Street, New York, New York 10022 (212) 751-2600; *The Economist Book of Vital World Statistics*.

JORDAN - GROSS NATIONAL PRODUCT

Euromonitor Publications Limited, 87-88 Turnmill Street, London EC1M 5QU, England; *International Marketing Data and Statistics*.

U.S. Arms Control and Disarmament Agency, 320 Twenty-first Street, NW, Washington, D.C. 20451 (202) 647-8677; *World Military Expenditures and Arms Transfers*.

JORDAN - GROUNDNUT PRODUCTION - See JORDAN - CROPS

JORDAN - HEALTH

Economic Commission for Western Asia, Post Office Box 27, Baghdad, Iraq; *Statistical Abstract of Western Asia*.

Euromonitor Publications Limited, 87-88 Turnmill Street, London EC1M 5QU, England; *Middle East Economic Handbook*.

Facts on File, 460 Park Avenue South, New York, New York 10016 (800) 443-8323; *The New Book of World Rankings*.

Federal Statistical Office, Gustav - Stresemann - Ring 11, D-6200 Wiesbaden, Germany; *Jordan*.

G.K. Hall and Company, 70 Lincoln Street, Boston, Massachusetts 02111 (617) 423-3990; *The World in Figures*.

Statistical Office of the United Nations, Publishing Service, New York, New York 10017 (800) 253-9646; *Statistical Yearbook*.

Times Books, 201 East 50th Street, New York, New York 10022 (212) 751-2600; *The Economist Book of Vital World Statistics*.

World Health Organization, Office of Publications, Avenue Appia, CH-1211 Geneva 27, Switzerland (Telephone Number in U.S. (518) 436-9686); *World Health Statistics Annual*.

JORDAN - HEALTH EXPENDITURES

International Monetary Fund, 700 Nineteenth Street, NW, Washington, D.C. 20431 (202) 623-7000; *Government Finance Statistics Yearbook*.

JORDAN - HIDE PRODUCTION

Food and Agricultural Organization of the United Nations (FAO), Via delle Terme di Caracalla, 00100 Rome, Italy (Telephone Number in U.S. (202) 653-2400); *Production Yearbook*.

JORDAN - HIGHWAYS

Economic Commission for Western Asia, Post Office Box 27, Baghdad, Iraq; *Statistical Abstract of Western Asia*.

G.K. Hall and Company, 70 Lincoln Street, Boston, Massachusetts 02111 (617) 423-3990; *The World in Figures*.

International Road Federation, 525 School Street, SW, Washington, D.C. 20024 (202) 554-2106; *World Road Statistics*.

JORDAN - HORSES - See JORDAN - LIVESTOCK AND POULTRY

JORDAN - HOURS OF WORK - See JORDAN - EMPLOYMENT

JORDAN - HOUSING AND HOUSING UNITS

Facts on File, 460 Park Avenue South, New York, New York 10016 (800) 443-8323; *The New Book of World Rankings*.

JORDAN - HOUSING EXPENDITURES

International Monetary Fund, 700 Nineteenth Street, NW, Washington, D.C. 20431 (202) 623-7000; *Government Finance Statistics Yearbook*.

JORDAN - ILLITERATE POPULATION

The Economist Intelligence Unit, 111 West 57th Street, New York, New York 10019 (800) 938-4685; *The World Market Atlas*.

G.K. Hall and Company, 70 Lincoln Street, Boston, Massachusetts 02111 (617) 423-3990; *The World in Figures*.

United Nations Educational, Scientific and Cultural Organization (UNESCO), 7 Place de Fontenoy, F-75700 Paris, France (Telephone Number in U.S. (212) 963-5981); *Statistical Yearbook*.

JORDAN - IMPORTS

Economic Commission for Western Asia, Post Office Box 27, Baghdad, Iraq; *Statistical Abstract of Western Asia*.

The Economist Intelligence Unit, 111 West 57th Street, New York, New York 10019 (800) 938-4685; *The World Market Atlas*.

Euromonitor Publications Limited, 87-88 Turnmill Street, London EC1M 5QU, England; *International Marketing Data and Statistics*, and *Middle East Economic Handbook*.

Food and Agricultural Organization of the United Nations (FAO), Via delle Terme di Caracalla, 00100 Rome, Italy (Telephone Number in U.S. (202) 653-2400); *The State of Food and Agriculture*.

G.K. Hall and Company, 70 Lincoln Street, Boston, Massachusetts 02111 (617) 423-3990; *The World in Figures*.

International Monetary Fund, 700 Nineteenth Street, NW, Washington, D.C. 20431 (202) 623-7000; *Direction of Trade Statistics*, *Government Finance Statistics Yearbook*, and *International Financial Statistics*.

Statistical Office of the United Nations, Publishing Service, New York, New York 10017 (800) 253-9646; *Trade in Manufactures of Developing Countries*.

Times Books, 201 East 50th Street, New York, New York 10022 (212) 751-2600; *The Economist Book of Vital World Statistics*.

JORDAN - INCOME TAXES - See JORDAN - TAXATION

JORDAN - INDUSTRY

Euromonitor Publications Limited, 87-88 Turnmill Street, London EC1M 5QU, England; *International Marketing Data and Statistics*.

Facts on File, 460 Park Avenue South, New York, New York 10016 (800) 443-8323; *The New Book of World Rankings*.

Federal Statistical Office, Gustav - Stresemann - Ring 11, D-6200 Wiesbaden, Germany; *Jordan.*

G.K. Hall and Company, 70 Lincoln Street, Boston, Massachusetts 02111 (617) 423-3990; *The World in Figures.*

International Labour Office, I.L.O. Publications, CH-1211, Geneva 22, Switzerland; *Yearbook of Labour Statistics.*

Times Books, 201 East 50th Street, New York, New York 10022 (212) 751-2600; *The Economist Book of Vital World Statistics.*

JORDAN - INFANT AND MATERNAL MORTALITY

Statistical Office of the United Nations, Publishing Service, New York, New York 10017 (800) 253-9646; *Demographic Yearbook,* and *Statistical Yearbook.*

Times Books, 201 East 50th Street, New York, New York 10022 (212) 751-2600; *The Economist Book of Vital World Statistics.*

JORDAN - INTERNATIONAL LIQUIDITY

International Monetary Fund, 700 Nineteenth Street, NW, Washington, D.C. 20431 (202) 623-7000; *International Financial Statistics.*

JORDAN - INTERNATIONAL RESERVES EXCLUDING GOLD

Statistical Office of the United Nations, Publishing Service, New York, New York 10017 (800) 253-9646; *Statistical Yearbook.*

JORDAN - INVESTMENTS

International Monetary Fund, 700 Nineteenth Street, NW, Washington, D.C. 20431 (202) 623-7000; *International Financial Statistics.*

JORDAN - IRON ORE PRODUCTION AND CONSUMPTION - See JORDAN - MINING AND MINERAL PRODUCTS

JORDAN - IRRIGATION

Euromonitor Publications Limited, 87-88 Turnmill Street, London EC1M 5QU, England; *International Marketing Data and Statistics.*

JORDAN - LABOR FORCE

Economic Commission for Western Asia, Post Office Box 27, Baghdad, Iraq; *Statistical Abstract of Western Asia.*

Euromonitor Publications Limited, 87-88 Turnmill Street, London EC1M 5QU, England; *International Marketing Data and Statistics,* and *Middle East Economic Handbook.*

Facts on File, 460 Park Avenue South, New York, New York 10016 (800) 443-8323; *The New Book of World Rankings.*

Food and Agricultural Organization of the United Nations (FAO), Via delle Terme di Caracalla, 00100 Rome, Italy (Telephone Number in U.S. (202) 653-2400; *The State of Food and Agriculture.*

G.K. Hall and Company, 70 Lincoln Street, Boston, Massachusetts 02111 (617) 423-3990; *The World in Figures.*

JORDAN - LABOR PRODUCTIVITY

International Labour Office, I.L.O. Publications, CH-1211, Geneva 22, Switzerland; *Yearbook of Labour Statistics.*

JORDAN - LAND USE

Economic Commission for Western Asia, Post Office Box 27, Baghdad, Iraq; *Statistical Abstract of Western Asia.*

Euromonitor Publications Limited, 87-88 Turnmill Street, London EC1M 5QU, England; *International Marketing Data and Statistics.*

Food and Agricultural Organization of the United Nations (FAO), Via delle Terme di Caracalla, 00100 Rome, Italy (Telephone Number in U.S. (202) 653-2400); *Production Yearbook.*

G.K. Hall and Company, 70 Lincoln Street, Boston, Massachusetts 02111 (617) 423-3990; *The World in Figures.*

JORDAN - LIBRARIES

Facts on File, 460 Park Avenue South, New York, New York 10016 (800) 443-8323; *The New Book of World Rankings.*

United Nations Educational, Scientific and Cultural Organization (UNESCO), 7 Place de Fontenoy, F-75700 Paris, France (Telephone Number in U.S. (212) 963-5981); *Statistical Yearbook.*

JORDAN - LIVESTOCK AND POULTRY

Economic Commission for Western Asia, Post Office Box 27, Baghdad, Iraq; *Statistical Abstract of Western Asia.*

Euromonitor Publications Limited, 87-88 Turnmill Street, London EC1M 5QU, England; *International Marketing Data and Statistics.*

Facts on File, 460 Park Avenue South, New York, New York 10016 (800) 443-8323; *The New Book of World Rankings.*

Food and Agricultural Organization of the United Nations (FAO), Via delle Terme di Caracalla, 00100 Rome, Italy (Telephone Number in U.S. (202) 653-2400); *Production Yearbook,* and *The State of Food and Agriculture.*

G.K. Hall and Company, 70 Lincoln Street, Boston, Massachusetts 02111 (617) 423-3990; *The World in Figures.*

Statistical Office of the United Nations, Publishing Service, New York, New York 10017 (800) 253-9646; *Statistical Yearbook.*

JORDAN - LIVING LEVELS

G.K. Hall and Company, 70 Lincoln Street, Boston, Massachusetts 02111 (617) 423-3990; *The World in Figures.*

Times Books, 201 East 50th Street, New York, New York 10022 (212) 751-2600; *The Economist Book of Vital World Statistics.*

JORDAN - MAIL - NUMBER OF PIECES SENT OR RECEIVED

Statistical Office of the United Nations, Publishing Service, New York, New York 10017 (800) 253-9646; *Statistical Yearbook.*

JORDAN - MANUFACTURING

Facts on File, 460 Park Avenue South, New York, New York 10016 (800) 443-8323; *The New Book of World Rankings.*

G.K. Hall and Company, 70 Lincoln Street, Boston, Massachusetts 02111 (617) 423-3990; *The World in Figures.*

Statistical Office of the United Nations, Publishing Service, New York, New York 10017 (800) 253-9646; *Statistical Yearbook.*

Times Books, 201 East 50th Street, New York, New York 10022 (212) 751-2600; *The Economist Book of Vital World Statistics.*

JORDAN - MARRIAGE RATES

Facts on File, 460 Park Avenue South, New York, New York 10016 (800) 443-8323; *The New Book of World Rankings.*

Statistical Office of the United Nations, Publishing Service, New York, New York 10017 (800) 253-9646; *Demographic Yearbook,* and *Statistical Yearbook.*

JORDAN - MEAT PRODUCTION - See JORDAN - LIVESTOCK AND POULTRY

JORDAN - MERCHANT SHIPPING

Economic Commission for Western Asia, Post Office Box 27, Baghdad, Iraq; *Statistical Abstract of Western Asia.*

G.K. Hall and Company, 70 Lincoln Street, Boston, Massachusetts 02111 (617) 423-3990; *The World in Figures.*

Statistical Office of the United Nations, Publishing Service, New York, New York 10017 (800) 253-9646; *Statistical Yearbook.*

Times Books, 201 East 50th Street, New York, New York 10022 (212) 751-2600; *The Economist Book of Vital World Statistics.*

JORDAN - MILITARY

G.K. Hall and Company, 70 Lincoln Street, Boston, Massachusetts 02111 (617) 423-3990; *The World in Figures.*

The International Institute for Strategic Studies, 23 Tavistock Street, London WC2E 7NQ, England; *The Military Balance.*

U.S. Arms Control and Disarmament Agency, 320 Twenty-first Street, NW, Washington, D.C. 20451 (202) 647-8677; *World Military Expenditures and Arms Transfers.*

JORDAN - MILK PRODUCTION - See JORDAN - DAIRY PRODUCTS

JORDAN - MINING AND MINERAL PRODUCTS

Economic Commission for Western Asia, Post Office Box 27, Baghdad, Iraq; *Statistical Abstract of Western Asia.*

Facts on File, 460 Park Avenue South, New York, New York 10016 (800) 443-8323; *The New Book of World Rankings.*

G.K. Hall and Company, 70 Lincoln Street, Boston, Massachusetts 02111 (617) 423-3990; *The World in Figures.*

Penn Well Publishing Company, 1421 South Sheridan Road, Post Office Box 1260, Tulsa, Oklahoma 74101 (800) 752-9764; *International Energy Statistics Sourcebook.*

Statistical Office of the United Nations, Publishing Service, New York, New York 10017 (800) 253-9646; *Statistical Yearbook.*

JORDAN - MONEY EXCHANGE RATE

Euromonitor Publications Limited, 87-88 Turnmill Street, London EC1M 5QU, England; *International Marketing Data and Statistics.*

International Monetary Fund, 700 Nineteenth Street, NW, Washington, D.C. 20431 (202) 623-7000; *International Financial Statistics.*

Statistical Office of the United Nations, Publishing Service, New York, New York 10017 (800) 253-9646; *Statistical Yearbook.*

JORDAN - MONEY RESERVES

Euromonitor Publications Limited, 87-88 Turnmill Street, London EC1M 5QU, England; *International Marketing Data and Statistics.*

JORDAN - MONEY SUPPLY

Economic Commission for Western Asia, Post Office Box 27, Baghdad, Iraq; *Statistical Abstract of Western Asia.*

Euromonitor Publications Limited, 87-88 Turnmill Street, London EC1M 5QU, England; *International Marketing Data and Statistics.*

G.K. Hall and Company, 70 Lincoln Street, Boston, Massachusetts 02111 (617) 423-3990; *The World in Figures.*

International Monetary Fund, 700 Nineteenth Street, NW, Washington, D.C. 20431 (202) 623-7000; *International Financial Statistics.*

Statistical Office of the United Nations, Publishing Service, New York, New York 10017 (800) 253-9646; *Statistical Yearbook.*

JORDAN - MONUMENTS AND HISTORICAL SITES

United Nations Educational, Scientific and Cultural Organization (UNESCO), 7 Place de Fontenoy, F-75700 Paris, France (Telephone Number in U.S. (212) 963-5981); *Statistical Yearbook.*

JORDAN - MOTION PICTURES

Statistical Office of the United Nations, Publishing Service, New York, New York 10017 (800) 253-9646; *Statistical Yearbook.*

JORDAN - MOTOR VEHICLE TAXES - See JORDAN - TAXATION

JORDAN - MOTOR VEHICLES

Economic Commission for Western Asia, Post Office Box 27, Baghdad, Iraq; *Statistical Abstract of Western Asia.*

JORDAN - MOTOR VEHICLES IN USE

G.K. Hall and Company, 70 Lincoln Street, Boston, Massachusetts 02111 (617) 423-3990; *The World in Figures.*

International Road Federation, 525 School Street, SW, Washington, D.C. 20024 (202) 554-2106; *World Road Statistics.*

Statistical Office of the United Nations, Publishing Service, New York, New York 10017 (800) 253-9646; *Statistical Yearbook.*

Times Books, 201 East 50th Street, New York, New York 10022 (212) 751-2600; *The Economist Book of Vital World Statistics.*

JORDAN - MULES - See JORDAN - LIVESTOCK AND POULTRY

JORDAN - MUSEUMS

Facts on File, 460 Park Avenue South, New York, New York 10016 (800) 443-8323; *The New Book of World Rankings.*

United Nations Educational, Scientific and Cultural Organization (UNESCO), 7 Place de Fontenoy, F-75700 Paris, France (Telephone Number in U.S. (212) 963-5981); *Statistical Yearbook.*

JORDAN - NATALITY - See JORDAN - BIRTH RATE

JORDAN - NATIONAL ACCOUNTS

Economic Commission for Western Asia, Post Office Box 27, Baghdad, Iraq; *Statistical Abstract of Western Asia.*

Federal Statistical Office, Gustav - Stresemann - Ring 11, D-6200 Wiesbaden, Germany; *Jordan.*

International Monetary Fund, 700 Nineteenth Street, NW, Washington, D.C. 20431 (202) 623-7000; *International Financial Statistics.*

Statistical Office of the United Nations, Publishing Service, New York, New York 10017 (800) 253-9646; *National Accounts Statistics,* and *Statistical Yearbook.*

JORDAN - NATIONAL INCOME

Facts on File, 460 Park Avenue South, New York, New York 10016 (800) 443-8323; *The New Book of World Rankings.*

G.K. Hall and Company, 70 Lincoln Street, Boston, Massachusetts 02111 (617) 423-3990; *The World in Figures.*

Statistical Office of the United Nations, Publishing Service, New York, New York 10017 (800) 253-9646; *Statistical Yearbook.*

JORDAN - NATIONAL PRODUCT

Facts on File, 460 Park Avenue South, New York, New York 10016 (800) 443-8323; *The New Book of World Rankings.*

JORDAN - NATURAL GAS PRODUCTION - See JORDAN - MINING AND MINERAL PRODUCTS

JORDAN - NEWSPAPER PRODUCTION - See JORDAN - FORESTRY AND FOREST PRODUCTS

JORDAN - NEWSPRINT - See JORDAN - FORESTRY AND FOREST PRODUCTS

JORDAN - OCCUPATIONS - See JORDAN - LABOR FORCE

JORDAN - PAPER - See JORDAN - FORESTRY AND FOREST PRODUCTS

JORDAN - PATENTS

Statistical Office of the United Nations, Publishing Service, New York, New York 10017 (800) 253-9646; *Statistical Yearbook.*

JORDAN - PEANUT PRODUCTION - See JORDAN - CROPS

JORDAN - PERIODICALS

United Nations Educational, Scientific and Cultural Organization (UNESCO), 7 Place de Fontenoy, F-75700 Paris, France (Telephone Number in U.S. (212) 963-5981); *Statistical Yearbook.*

JORDAN - PESTICIDE USE

Food and Agricultural Organization of the United Nations (FAO), Via delle Terme di Caracalla, 00100 Rome, Italy (Telephone Number

in U.S. (202) 653-2400); *The State of Food and Agriculture.*

JORDAN - PETROLEUM INDUSTRY

Euromonitor Publications Limited, 87-88 Turnmill Street, London EC1M 5QU, England; *Middle East Economic Handbook.*

Facts on File, 460 Park Avenue South, New York, New York 10016 (800) 443-8323; *The New Book of World Rankings.*

Food and Agricultural Organization of the United Nations (FAO), Via delle Terme di Caracalla, 00100 Rome, Italy (Telephone Number in U.S. (202) 653-2400); *The State of Food and Agriculture.*

G.K. Hall and Company, 70 Lincoln Street, Boston, Massachusetts 02111 (617) 423-3990; *The World in Figures.*

Penn Well Publishing Company, 1421 South Sheridan Road, Post Office Box 1260, Tulsa, Oklahoma 74101 (800) 752-9764; *International Energy Statistics Sourcebook.*

Statistical Office of the United Nations, Publishing Service, New York, New York 10017 (800) 253-9646; *Statistical Yearbook.*

JORDAN - PHOSPHATE EXPORTS

International Monetary Fund, 700 Nineteenth Street, NW, Washington, D.C. 20431 (202) 623-7000; *International Financial Statistics.*

JORDAN - PHOSPHATE ROCK PRODUCTION - See JORDAN - MINING AND MINERAL PRODUCTS

JORDAN - PIGS - See JORDAN - LIVESTOCK AND POULTRY

JORDAN - POPULATION

The Economist Intelligence Unit, 111 West 57th Street, New York, New York 10019 (800) 938-4685; *The World Market Atlas.*

Euromonitor Publications Limited, 87-88 Turnmill Street, London EC1M 5QU, England; *International Marketing Data and Statistics,* and *Middle East Economic Handbook.*

Facts on File, 460 Park Avenue South, New York, New York 10016 (800) 443-8323; *The New Book of World Rankings.*

Federal Statistical Office, Gustav - Stresemann - Ring 11, D-6200 Wiesbaden, Germany; *Jordan.*

Food and Agricultural Organization of the United Nations (FAO), Via delle Terme di Caracalla, 00100 Rome, Italy (Telephone Number in U.S. (202) 653-2400); *Production Yearbook.*

G.K. Hall and Company, 70 Lincoln Street, Boston, Massachusetts 02111 (617) 423-3990; *The World in Figures.*

International Labour Office, I.L.O. Publications, CH-1211, Geneva 22, Switzerland; *Yearbook of Labour Statistics.*

Statistical Office of the United Nations, Publishing Service, New York, New York 10017 (800) 253-9646; *Demographic Yearbook,* and *Statistical Yearbook.*

Times Books, 201 East 50th Street, New York, New York 10022 (212) 751-2600; *The Economist Book of Vital World Statistics.*

United Nations Educational, Scientific and Cultural Organization (UNESCO), 7 Place de Fontenoy, F-75700 Paris, France (Telephone

Number in U.S. (212) 963-5981); *Statistical Yearbook*.

U.S. Arms Control and Disarmament Agency, 320 Twenty-first Street, NW, Washington, D.C. 20451 (202) 647-8677; *World Military Expenditures and Arms Transfers*.

World Health Organization, Office of Publications, Avenue Appia, CH-1211 Geneva 27, Switzerland (Telephone Number in U.S. (518) 436-9686); *World Health Statistics Annual*.

JORDAN - POST OFFICES

Facts on File, 460 Park Avenue South, New York, New York 10016 (800) 443-8323; *The New Book of World Rankings*.

JORDAN - POTATO PRODUCTION - See JORDAN - CROPS

JORDAN - POWER PRODUCTION INDUSTRY

Statistical Office of the United Nations, Publishing Service, New York, New York 10017 (800) 253-9646; *Statistical Yearbook*.

JORDAN - PRICES

Economic Commission for Western Asia, Post Office Box 27, Baghdad, Iraq; *Statistical Abstract of Western Asia*.

Facts on File, 460 Park Avenue South, New York, New York 10016 (800) 443-8323; *The New Book of World Rankings*.

Federal Statistical Office, Gustav - Stresemann - Ring 11, D-6200 Wiesbaden, Germany; *Jordan*.

Food and Agricultural Organization of the United Nations (FAO), Via delle Terme di Caracalla, 00100 Rome, Italy (Telephone Number in U.S. (202) 653-2400); *Production Yearbook*, and *The State of Food and Agriculture*.

G.K. Hall and Company, 70 Lincoln Street, Boston, Massachusetts 02111 (617) 423-3990; *The World in Figures*.

International Labour Office, I.L.O. Publications, CH-1211, Geneva 22, Switzerland; *Yearbook of Labour Statistics*.

International Monetary Fund, 700 Nineteenth Street, NW, Washington, D.C. 20431 (202) 623-7000; *International Financial Statistics*.

JORDAN - PRINTING AND WRITING PAPER - See JORDAN - FORESTRY AND FOREST PRODUCTS

JORDAN - PRODUCTION

Facts on File, 460 Park Avenue South, New York, New York 10016 (800) 443-8323; *The New Book of World Rankings*.

G.K. Hall and Company, 70 Lincoln Street, Boston, Massachusetts 02111 (617) 423-3990; *The World in Figures*.

JORDAN - PRODUCTIVITY

Euromonitor Publications Limited, 87-88 Turnmill Street, London EC1M 5QU, England; *International Marketing Data and Statistics*.

JORDAN - PROPERTY TAXES - See JORDAN - TAXATION

JORDAN - PUBLIC FINANCE

Facts on File, 460 Park Avenue South, New York, New York 10016 (800) 443-8323; *The New Book of World Rankings*.

International Monetary Fund, 700 Nineteenth Street, NW, Washington, D.C. 20431 (202) 623-7000; *International Financial Statistics*.

JORDAN - RADIO BROADCASTING - See JORDAN - BROADCASTING

JORDAN - RAILWAYS

G.K. Hall and Company, 70 Lincoln Street, Boston, Massachusetts 02111 (617) 423-3990; *The World in Figures*.

Jane's Information Group, Sentinel House, 163 Brighton Road, Coulsdon, Surrey CR5 2NH, England (Telephone Number in U.S. (703) 683-3700); *Jane's World Railways*.

JORDAN - RELIGION

Facts on File, 460 Park Avenue South, New York, New York 10016 (800) 443-8323; *The New Book of World Rankings*.

JORDAN - RENT PRICES

International Labour Office, I.L.O. Publications, CH-1211, Geneva 22, Switzerland; *Yearbook of Labour Statistics*.

JORDAN - RETAIL TRADE

G.K. Hall and Company, 70 Lincoln Street, Boston, Massachusetts 02111 (617) 423-3990; *The World in Figures*.

JORDAN - RICE PRODUCTION - See JORDAN - CROPS

JORDAN - ROOT AND TUBER PRODUCTION - See JORDAN - CROPS

JORDAN - ROUNDWOOD PRODUCTION - See JORDAN - FORESTRY AND FOREST PRODUCTS

JORDAN - RUBBER PRODUCTION AND CONSUMPTION

Facts on File, 460 Park Avenue South, New York, New York 10016 (800) 443-8323; *The New Book of World Rankings*.

JORDAN - SALT PRODUCTION - See JORDAN - MINING AND MINERAL PRODUCTS

JORDAN - SAWNWOOD PRODUCTION - See JORDAN - FORESTRY AND FOREST PRODUCTS

JORDAN - SCIENCE AND TECHNOLOGY - EXPENDITURE FOR RESEARCH

Statistical Office of the United Nations, Publishing Service, New York, New York 10017 (800) 253-9646; *Statistical Yearbook*.

JORDAN - SCIENTISTS AND TECHNICIANS

Statistical Office of the United Nations, Publishing Service, New York, New York 10017 (800) 253-9646; *Statistical Yearbook*.

JORDAN - SENIOR CITIZENS

Facts on File, 460 Park Avenue South, New York, New York 10016 (800) 443-8323; *The New Book of World Rankings*.

JORDAN - SESAME SEED PRODUCTION - See JORDAN - CROPS

JORDAN - SHEEP - See JORDAN - LIVESTOCK AND POULTRY

JORDAN - SILVER PRODUCTION AND CONSUMPTION - See JORDAN - MINING AND MINERAL PRODUCTS

JORDAN - SOCIAL DATA

Facts on File, 460 Park Avenue South, New York, New York 10016 (800) 443-8323; *The New Book of World Rankings.*

G.K. Hall and Company, 70 Lincoln Street, Boston, Massachusetts 02111 (617) 423-3990; *The World in Figures.*

JORDAN - SOCIAL SECURITY

International Monetary Fund, 700 Nineteenth Street, NW, Washington, D.C. 20431 (202) 623-7000; *Government Finance Statistics Yearbook.*

JORDAN - STAMP TAXES AND REVENUES - See JORDAN - TAXATION

JORDAN - STATE BUDGET REVENUE AND EXPENDITURES

Euromonitor Publications Limited, 87-88 Turnmill Street, London EC1M 5QU, England; *International Marketing Data and Statistics.*

JORDAN - STEEL - See JORDAN - MINING AND MINERAL PRODUCTS

JORDAN - STOCKS - COMMODITY - MARKET PRICE - INDEX

Food and Agricultural Organization of the United Nations (FAO), Via delle Terme di Caracalla, 00100 Rome, Italy (Telephone Number in U.S. (202) 653-2400); *The State of Food and Agriculture.*

JORDAN - SUGAR PRODUCTION AND CONSUMPTION - See JORDAN - CROPS

JORDAN - TAXATION

G.K. Hall and Company, 70 Lincoln Street, Boston, Massachusetts 02111 (617) 423-3990; *The World in Figures.*

International Monetary Fund, 700 Nineteenth Street, NW, Washington, D.C. 20431 (202) 623-7000; *Government Finance Statistics Yearbook.*

International Road Federation, 525 School Street, SW, Washington, D.C. 20024 (202) 554-2106; *World Road Statistics.*

JORDAN - TEA CONSUMPTION - See JORDAN - CROPS

JORDAN - TELEPHONES IN USE

American Telephone and Telegraph Company, 26 Parsippany Road, Whippany, New Jersey 07981 (800) 338-4038; *The World's Telephones.*

Euromonitor Publications Limited, 87-88 Turnmill Street, London EC1M 5QU, England; *Middle East Economic Handbook.*

G.K. Hall and Company, 70 Lincoln Street, Boston, Massachusetts 02111 (617) 423-3990; *The World in Figures.*

Statistical Office of the United Nations, Publishing Service, New York, New York 10017 (800) 253-9646; *Statistical Yearbook.*

JORDAN - TELEVISION BROADCASTING - See JORDAN - BROADCASTING

JORDAN - TEXTILE INDUSTRY

G.K. Hall and Company, 70 Lincoln Street, Boston, Massachusetts 02111 (617) 423-3990; *The World in Figures.*

JORDAN - THEATRE

United Nations Educational, Scientific and Cultural Organization (UNESCO), 7 Place de Fontenoy, F-75700 Paris, France (Telephone Number in U.S. (212) 963-5981); *Statistical Yearbook.*

JORDAN - TOBACCO PRODUCTION

Facts on File, 460 Park Avenue South, New York, New York 10016 (800) 443-8323; *The New Book of World Rankings.*

Statistical Office of the United Nations, Publishing Service, New York, New York 10017 (800) 253-9646; *Statistical Yearbook.*

JORDAN - TOURISM

Economic Commission for Western Asia, Post Office Box 27, Baghdad, Iraq; *Statistical Abstract of Western Asia.*

Euromonitor Publications Limited, 87-88 Turnmill Street, London EC1M 5QU, England; *Middle East Economic Handbook.*

Facts on File, 460 Park Avenue South, New York, New York 10016 (800) 443-8323; *The New Book of World Rankings.*

Federal Statistical Office, Gustav - Stresemann - Ring 11, D-6200 Wiesbaden, Germany, *Jordan.*

G.K. Hall and Company, 70 Lincoln Street, Boston, Massachusetts 02111 (617) 423-3990; *The World in Figures.*

Statistical Office of the United Nations, Publishing Service, New York, New York 10017 (800) 253-9646; *Statistical Yearbook.*

Times Books, 201 East 50th Street, New York, New York 10022 (212) 751-2600; *The Economist Book of Vital World Statistics.*

World Tourism Organization, Calle Capital Haya 42, E-28020 Madrid, Spain; *Yearbook of Tourism Statistics.*

JORDAN - TRACTORS IN USE

Statistical Office of the United Nations, Publishing Service, New York, New York 10017 (800) 253-9646; *Statistical Yearbook.*

JORDAN - TRADE - See JORDAN - FOREIGN TRADE

JORDAN - TRADEMARKS AND SERVICE MARKS

Statistical Office of the United Nations, Publishing Service, New York, New York 10017 (800) 253-9646; *Statistical Yearbook.*

JORDAN - TRANSPORTATION AND COMMUNICATIONS

Economic Commission for Western Asia, Post Office Box 27, Baghdad, Iraq; *Statistical Abstract of Western Asia.*

Euromonitor Publications Limited, 87-88 Turnmill Street, London EC1M 5QU, England; *Middle East Economic Handbook.*

Facts on File, 460 Park Avenue South, New York, New York 10016 (800) 443-8323; *The New Book of World Rankings.*

Federal Statistical Office, Gustav - Stresemann - Ring 11, D-6200 Wiesbaden, Germany; *Jordan.*

G.K. Hall and Company, 70 Lincoln Street, Boston, Massachusetts 02111 (617) 423-3990; *The World in Figures.*

JORDAN - TURKEYS - See JORDAN - LIVESTOCK AND POULTRY

JORDAN - UNEMPLOYMENT

Euromonitor Publications Limited, 87-88 Turnmill Street, London EC1M 5QU, England; *International Marketing Data and Statistics,* and *Middle East Economic Handbook.*

International Labour Office, I.L.O. Publications, CH-1211, Geneva 22, Switzerland; *Yearbook of Labour Statistics.*

JORDAN - VITAL STATISTICS

Euromonitor Publications Limited, 87-88 Turnmill Street, London EC1M 5QU, England; *International Marketing Data and Statistics,* and *Middle East Economic Handbook.*

G.K. Hall and Company, 70 Lincoln Street, Boston, Massachusetts 02111 (617) 423-3990; *The World in Figures.*

Statistical Office of the United Nations, Publishing Service, New York, New York 10017 (800) 253-9646; *Statistical Yearbook.*

World Health Organization, Office of Publications, Avenue Appia, CH-1211 Geneva 27, Switzerland (Telephone Number in U.S. (518) 436-9686); *World Health Statistics Annual.*

JORDAN - WAGES

Federal Statistical Office, Gustav - Stresemann - Ring 11, D-6200 Wiesbaden, Germany; *Jordan.*

G.K. Hall and Company, 70 Lincoln Street, Boston, Massachusetts 02111 (617) 423-3990; *The World in Figures.*

International Labour Office, I.L.O. Publications, CH-1211, Geneva 22, Switzerland; *Yearbook of Labour Statistics.*

Statistical Office of the United Nations, Publishing Service, New York, New York 10017 (800) 253-9646; *Statistical Yearbook.*

JORDAN - WALNUT PRODUCTION - See JORDAN - CROPS

JORDAN - WATERMELON PRODUCTION - See JORDAN - CROPS

JORDAN - WEATHER

Facts on File, 460 Park Avenue South, New York, New York 10016 (800) 443-8323; *The New Book of World Rankings.*

G.K. Hall and Company, 70 Lincoln Street, Boston, Massachusetts 02111 (617) 423-3990; *The World in Figures.*

JORDAN - WELFARE EXPENDITURES

International Monetary Fund, 700 Nineteenth Street, NW, Washington, D.C. 20431 (202) 623-7000; *Government Finance Statistics Yearbook.*

JORDAN - WHEAT PRODUCTION AND PRICES - See JORDAN - CROPS

JORDAN - WHOLESALE PRICES - INDEX NUMBERS

Statistical Office of the United Nations, Publishing Service, New York, New York 10017 (800) 253-9646; *Statistical Yearbook.*

JORDAN - WINE PRODUCTION

Facts on File, 460 Park Avenue South, New York, New York 10016 (800) 443-8323; *The New Book of World Rankings.*

JORDAN - WOOL PRODUCTION

Facts on File, 460 Park Avenue South, New York, New York 10016 (800) 443-8323; *The New Book of World Rankings.*

JUDICIAL SERVICE, FEDERAL - EMPLOYEES AND PAYROLLS

U.S. Office of Personnel Management, 1900 E Street, NW, Washington, D.C. 20415 (202) 606-1800; *Federal Civilian Workforce Statistics, Employment and Trends,* and unpublished data.

JUDICIAL SERVICE, FEDERAL - FEDERAL OUTLAYS

Executive Office of the President, Office of Management and Budget, Executive Office Building, Washington, D.C. 20503 (202) 395-3080; *Budget of the United States Government.*

JUICES

U.S. Department of Agriculture, Economic Research Service, Fourteenth Street and Independence Avenue, SW, Washington, D.C. 20005-4789 (202) 219-1504; *Food Consumption, Prices, and Expenditures,* and unpublished data.

JUVENILES - ARREST

U.S. Department of Justice, Federal Bureau of Investigation, Ninth Street and Pennsylvania Avenue, NW, Washington, D.C. 20535 (202) 732-3277; *Crime in the United States.*

JUVENILES - CORRECTION FACILITIES

U.S. Department of Commerce, Bureau of the Census, Suitland, Maryland 20233 (301) 763-4040; *Census of Population, General Population Characteristics.*

JUVENILES - COURT CASES

National Center for Juvenile Justice, 701 Forbes Avenue, Pittsburgh, Pennsylvania 15219 (412) 227-6950; *Juvenile Court Statistics.*

K

KANSAS - See also STATE DATA (FOR INDIVIDUAL STATES)

Kansas - Primary Statistics Source

University of Kansas, Institute for Public Policy and Business Research, 607 Blake Hall, Lawrence, Kansas 66045 (913) 864-3701; *Kansas Statistical Abstract*.

Kansas - State Data Centers

State Library, State Capitol Building, Room 343-N, Topeka, Kansas 66612, Mr. Marc Galbraith (913) 296-3296.

Division of the Budget, Room 152-E, State Capitol Building, Topeka, Kansas 66612 (913) 296-0025.

Institute for Public Policy and Business Research, 607 Blake Hall, The University of Kansas, Lawrence, Kansas 66045-2960, Ms. Thelma Helyar (913) 864 3123.

Center for Economic Development and Business Research, Box 48, Wichita State University, Wichita, Kansas 67208, Ms. Janet Nickel (316) 689-3225.

Population and Resources Laboratory, Department of Sociology, Kansas State University, Manhattan, Kansas 66506, Dr. Leonard Bloomquist (913) 532-5984.

KAZAKHSTAN - See also UNION OF SOVIET SOCIALIST REPUBLICS

KAZAKHSTAN - AGRICULTURE

Business International Moscow, 23 Profsoyuznaya Ulitsa 117859, Moscow (Telephone Number in U.S. (800) 938-4685); *The CIS Market Atlas*.

Encyclopedia Britannica, Incorporated, 310 South Michigan Avenue, Chicago, Illinois 60604 (312) 347-7000; *Britannica World Data*.

The World Bank, 1818 H Street, NW, Washington, D.C. 20433 (202) 477-1234; *Statistical Handbook: States of the Former USSR*.

KAZAKHSTAN - AIRLINE SERVICE

Business International Moscow, 23 Profsoyuznaya Ulitsa 117859, Moscow (Telephone Number in U.S. (800) 938-4685); *The CIS Market Atlas*.

Encyclopedia Britannica, Incorporated, 310 South Michigan Avenue, Chicago, Illinois 60604 (312) 347-7000; *Britannica World Data*.

KAZAKHSTAN - AREA AND DENSITY OF POPULATION

Business International Moscow, 23 Profsoyuznaya Ulitsa 117859, Moscow (Telephone Number in U.S. (800) 938-4685); *The CIS Market Atlas*.

KAZAKHSTAN - BANKING

Business International Moscow, 23 Profsoyuznaya Ulitsa 117859, Moscow (Telephone Number in U.S. (800) 938-4685); *The CIS Market Atlas*.

KAZAKHSTAN - BIRTH RATE

Business International Moscow, 23 Profsoyuznaya Ulitsa 117859, Moscow (Telephone Number in U.S. (800) 938-4685); *The CIS Market Atlas*.

Encyclopedia Britannica, Incorporated, 310 South Michigan Avenue, Chicago, Illinois 60604 (312) 347-7000; *Britannica World Data*.

KAZAKHSTAN - BUDGET

Business International Moscow, 23 Profsoyuznaya Ulitsa 117859, Moscow (Telephone Number in U.S. (800) 938-4685); *The CIS Market Atlas*.

KAZAKHSTAN - CAPITAL INVESTMENT

The World Bank, 1818 H Street, NW, Washington, D.C. 20433 (202) 477-1234; *Statistical Handbook: States of the Former USSR*.

KAZAKHSTAN - CATTLE - See KAZAKHSTAN - LIVESTOCK AND POULTRY

KAZAKHSTAN - CHEMICALS

Business International Moscow, 23 Profsoyuznaya Ulitsa, 117859, Moscow (Telephone Number in U.S. (800) 938-4685); *The CIS Market Atlas*.

KAZAKHSTAN - COAL PRODUCTION AND CONSUMPTION - See KAZAKHSTAN - MINING AND MINERAL PRODUCTS

KAZAKHSTAN - COMMUNICATIONS

Business International Moscow, 23 Profsoyuznaya Ulitsa, 117859, Moscow (Telephone Number in U.S. (800) 938-4685); *The CIS Market Atlas*.

KAZAKHSTAN - CONSTRUCTION INDUSTRY

Business International Moscow, 23 Profsoyuznaya Ulitsa, 117859, Moscow (Telephone Number in U.S. (800) 938-4685); *The CIS Market Atlas*.

Encyclopedia Britannica, Incorporated, 310 South Michigan Avenue, Chicago, Illinois 60604 (312) 347-7000; *Britannica World Data*.

KAZAKHSTAN - CONSUMER PRODUCTS

Business International Moscow, 23 Profsoyuznaya Ulitsa, 117859, Moscow (Telephone Number in U.S. (800) 938-4685); *The CIS Market Atlas*.

KAZAKHSTAN - CONSUMPTION

Business International Moscow, 23 Profsoyuznaya Ulitsa, 117859, Moscow (Telephone Number in U.S. (800) 938-4685); *The CIS Market Atlas*.

The World Bank, 1818 H Street, NW, Washington, D.C. 20433 (202) 477-1234; *Statistical Handbook: States of the Former USSR*.

KAZAKHSTAN - COTTON PRODUCTION AND CONSUMPTION - See KAZAKHSTAN - CROPS

KAZAKHSTAN - CROPS

The World Bank, 1818 H Street, NW, Washington, D.C. 20433 (202) 477-1234; *Statistical Handbook: States of the Former USSR*.

KAZAKHSTAN - DEATH RATES

Business International Moscow, 23 Profsoyuznaya Ulitsa, 117859, Moscow (Telephone Number in U.S. (800) 938-4685); *The CIS Market Atlas*.

KAZAKHSTAN - DEMOGRAPHY

Business International Moscow, 23 Profsoyuznaya Ulitsa, 117859, Moscow (Telephone Number in U.S. (800) 938-4685); *The CIS Market Atlas*.

Encyclopedia Britannica, Incorporated, 310 South Michigan Avenue, Chicago, Illinois 60604 (312) 347-7000; *Britannica World Data*.

The World Bank, 1818 H Street, NW, Washington, D.C. 20433 (202) 477-1234; *Statistical Handbook: States of the Former USSR*.

KAZAKHSTAN - DISEASES

Business International Moscow, 23 Profsoyuznaya Ulitsa, 117859, Moscow (Telephone Number in U.S. (800) 938-4685); *The CIS Market Atlas*.

KAZAKHSTAN - DIVORCE RATES

Encyclopedia Britannica, Incorporated, 310 South Michigan Avenue, Chicago, Illinois 60604 (312) 347-7000; *Britannica World Data*.

KAZAKHSTAN - DOMESTIC INVESTMENT

Business International Moscow, 23 Profsoyuznaya Ulitsa, 117859, Moscow (Telephone Number in U.S. (800) 938-4685); *The CIS Market Atlas*.

KAZAKHSTAN - ECONOMY

Business International Moscow, 23 Profsoyuznaya Ulitsa, 117859, Moscow (Telephone Number in U.S. (800) 938-4685); *The CIS Market Atlas*.

Encyclopedia Britannica, Incorporated, 310 South Michigan Avenue, Chicago, Illinois 60604 (312) 347-7000; *Britannica World Data*.

KAZAKHSTAN - EDUCATION

Business International Moscow, 23 Profsoyuznaya Ulitsa, 117859, Moscow (Telephone Number in U.S. (800) 938-4685); *The CIS Market Atlas*.

Encyclopedia Britannica, Incorporated, 310 South Michigan Avenue, Chicago, Illinois 60604 (312) 347-7000; *Britannica World Data*.

KAZAKHSTAN - ELECTRICITY

Business International Moscow, 23 Profsoyuznaya Ulitsa, 117859, Moscow (Telephone Number in U.S. (800) 938-4685); *The CIS Market Atlas*.

The World Bank, 1818 H Street, NW, Washington, D.C. 20433 (202) 477-1234; *Statistical Handbook: States of the Former USSR*.

KAZAKHSTAN - EMPLOYMENT

The World Bank, 1818 H Street, NW, Washington, D.C. 20433 (202) 477-1234; *Statistical Handbook: States of the Former USSR*.

KAZAKHSTAN - ENERGY

Business International Moscow, 23 Profsoyuznaya Ulitsa, 117859, Moscow (Telephone Number in U.S. (800) 938-4685); *The CIS Market Atlas*.

Encyclopedia Britannica, Incorporated, 310 South Michigan Avenue, Chicago, Illinois 60604 (312) 347-7000; *Britannica World Data*.

The World Bank, 1818 H Street, NW, Washington, D.C. 20433 (202) 477-1234; *Statistical Handbook: States of the Former USSR*.

KAZAKHSTAN - ENVIRONMENT

Business International Moscow, 23 Profsoyuznaya Ulitsa, 117859, Moscow (Telephone Number in U.S. (800) 938-4685); *The CIS Market Atlas*.

KAZAKHSTAN - EXPORTS

Business International Moscow, 23 Profsoyuznaya Ulitsa, 117859, Moscow (Telephone Number in U.S. (800) 938-4685); *The CIS Market Atlas*.

Encyclopedia Britannica, Incorporated, 310 South Michigan Avenue, Chicago, Illinois 60604 (312) 347-7000; *Britannica World Data*.

The World Bank, 1818 H Street, NW, Washington, D.C. 20433 (202) 477-1234; *Statistical Handbook: States of the Former USSR*.

KAZAKHSTAN - EXTERNAL TRADE

The World Bank, 1818 H Street, NW, Washington, D.C. 20433 (202) 477-1234; *Statistical Handbook: States of the Former USSR*.

KAZAKHSTAN - FABRIC PRODUCTION AND CONSUMPTION - See KAZAKHSTAN - TEXTILE INDUSTRY

KAZAKHSTAN - FERTILITY RATES

Encyclopedia Britannica, Incorporated, 310 South Michigan Avenue, Chicago, Illinois 60604 (312) 347-7000; *Britannica World Data.*

The World Bank, 1818 H Street, NW, Washington, D.C. 20433 (202) 477-1234; *Statistical Handbook: States of the Former USSR.*

KAZAKHSTAN - FISHERIES

Encyclopedia Britannica, Incorporated, 310 South Michigan Avenue, Chicago, Illinois 60604 (312) 347-7000; *Britannica World Data.*

KAZAKHSTAN - FOOTWEAR PRODUCTION AND CONSUMPTION - See KAZAKHSTAN - TEXTILE INDUSTRY

KAZAKHSTAN - FOREIGN INVESTMENT

Business International Moscow, 23 Profsoyuznaya Ulitsa, 117859, Moscow (Telephone Number in U.S. (800) 938-4685); *The CIS Market Atlas.*

KAZAKHSTAN - FOREIGN TRADE

Business International Moscow, 23 Profsoyuznaya Ulitsa, 117859, Moscow (Telephone Number in U.S. (800) 938-4685); *The CIS Market Atlas.*

Encyclopedia Britannica, Incorporated, 310 South Michigan Avenue, Chicago, Illinois 60604 (312) 347-7000; *Britannica World Data.*

The World Bank, 1818 H Street, NW, Washington, D.C. 20433 (202) 477-1234; *Statistical Handbook: States of the Former USSR.*

KAZAKHSTAN - FORESTRY AND FOREST PRODUCTS

Business International Moscow, 23 Profsoyuznaya Ulitsa, 117859, Moscow (Telephone Number in U.S. (800) 938-4685); *The CIS Market Atlas.*

Encyclopedia Britannica, Incorporated, 310 South Michigan Avenue, Chicago, Illinois 60604 (312) 347-7000; *Britannica World Data.*

KAZAKHSTAN - GOATS - See KAZAKHSTAN - LIVESTOCK AND POULTRY

KAZAKHSTAN - GOVERNMENT EXPENDITURE

The World Bank, 1818 H Street, NW, Washington, D.C. 20433 (202) 477-1234; *Statistical Handbook: States of the Former USSR.*

KAZAKHSTAN - GOVERNMENT REVENUE

The World Bank, 1818 H Street, NW, Washington, D.C. 20433 (202) 477-1234; *Statistical Handbook: States of the Former USSR.*

KAZAKHSTAN - GROSS DOMESTIC PRODUCT

The World Bank, 1818 H Street, NW, Washington, D.C. 20433 (202) 477-1234; *Statistical Handbook: States of the Former USSR.*

KAZAKHSTAN - HEALTH

Business International Moscow, 23 Profsoyuznaya Ulitsa, 117859, Moscow (Telephone Number in U.S. (800) 938-4685); *The CIS Market Atlas.*

Encyclopedia Britannica, Incorporated, 310 South Michigan Avenue, Chicago, Illinois 60604 (312) 347-7000; *Britannica World Data.*

KAZAKHSTAN - HIGHWAYS

Business International Moscow, 23 Profsoyuznaya Ulitsa, 117859, Moscow (Telephone Number in U.S. (800) 938-4685); *The CIS Market Atlas.*

Encyclopedia Britannica, Incorporated, 310 South Michigan Avenue, Chicago, Illinois 60604 (312) 347-7000; *Britannica World Data.*

KAZAKHSTAN - HOUSING AND HOUSING UNITS

Business International Moscow, 23 Profsoyuznaya Ulitsa, 117859, Moscow (Telephone Number in U.S. (800) 938-4685); *The CIS Market Atlas.*

KAZAKHSTAN - IMPORTS

Business International Moscow, 23 Profsoyuznaya Ulitsa, 117859, Moscow (Telephone Number in U.S. (800) 938-4685); *The CIS Market Atlas.*

Encyclopedia Britannica, Incorporated, 310 South Michigan Avenue, Chicago, Illinois 60604 (312) 347-7000; *Britannica World Data.*

The World Bank, 1818 H Street, NW, Washington, D.C. 20433 (202) 477-1234; *Statistical Handbook: States of the Former USSR*

KAZAKHSTAN - INDUSTRY

Business International Moscow, 23 Profsoyuznaya Ulitsa, 117859, Moscow (Telephone Number in U.S. (800) 938-4685); *The CIS Market Atlas.*

The World Bank, 1818 H Street, NW, Washington, D.C. 20433 (202) 477-1234; *Statistical Handbook: States of the Former USSR.*

KAZAKHSTAN - INFANT MORTALITY RATES

Business International Moscow, 23 Profsoyuznaya Ulitsa, 117859, Moscow (Telephone Number in U.S. (800) 938-4685); *The CIS Market Atlas.*

KAZAKHSTAN - LABOR FORCE

Business International Moscow, 23 Profsoyuznaya Ulitsa, 117859, Moscow (Telephone Number in U.S. (800) 938-4685); *The CIS Market Atlas.*

The World Bank, 1818 H Street, NW, Washington, D.C. 20433 (202) 477-1234; *Statistical Handbook: States of the Former USSR.*

KAZAKHSTAN - LAND USE

Encyclopedia Britannica, Incorporated, 310 South Michigan Avenue, Chicago, Illinois 60604 (312) 347-7000; *Britannica World Data.*

KAZAKHSTAN - LIFE EXPECTANCY

Business International Moscow, 23 Profsoyuznaya Ulitsa, 117859, Moscow (Telephone Number in U.S. (800) 938-4685); *The CIS Market Atlas.*

KAZAKHSTAN - LIVESTOCK AND POULTRY

Business International Moscow, 23 Profsoyuznaya Ulitsa, 117859, Moscow (Telephone Number in U.S. (800) 938-4685); *The CIS Market Atlas.*

Encyclopedia Britannica, Incorporated, 310 South Michigan Avenue, Chicago, Illinois 60604 (312) 347-7000; *Britannica World Data.*

KAZAKHSTAN - MANUFACTURING

Encyclopedia Britannica, Incorporated, 310 South Michigan Avenue, Chicago, Illinois 60604 (312) 347-7000; *Britannica World Data.*

KAZAKHSTAN - MARRIAGE RATES

Encyclopedia Britannica, Incorporated, 310 South Michigan Avenue, Chicago, Illinois 60604 (312) 347-7000; *Britannica World Data.*

KAZAKHSTAN - MEAT PRODUCTION - See KAZAKHSTAN - LIVESTOCK AND POULTRY

KAZAKHSTAN - MILITARY

The International Institute for Strategic Studies, 23 Tavistock Street, London WC2E 7NQ, England; *The Military Balance.*

KAZAKHSTAN - MINING AND MINERAL PRODUCTS

Business International Moscow, 23 Profsoyuznaya Ulitsa, 117859, Moscow (Telephone Number in U.S. (800) 938-4685); *The CIS Market Atlas.*

Encyclopedia Britannica, Incorporated, 310 South Michigan Avenue, Chicago, Illinois 60604 (312) 347-7000; *Britannica World Data.*

KAZAKHSTAN - MOTOR VEHICLES

Business International Moscow, 23 Profsoyuznaya Ulitsa, 117859, Moscow (Telephone Number in U.S. (800) 938-4685); *The CIS Market Atlas.*

KAZAKHSTAN - NATIONAL ACCOUNTS

The World Bank, 1818 H Street, NW, Washington, D.C. 20433 (202) 477-1234; *Statistical Handbook: States of the Former USSR.*

KAZAKHSTAN - NATIONAL INCOME

Business International Moscow, 23 Profsoyuznaya Ulitsa, 117859, Moscow (Telephone Number in U.S. (800) 938-4685); *The CIS Market Atlas.*

KAZAKHSTAN - PIGS - See KAZAKHSTAN - LIVESTOCK AND POULTRY

KAZAKHSTAN - POPULATION

Business International Moscow, 23 Profsoyuznaya Ulitsa, 117859, Moscow (Telephone Number in U.S. (800) 938-4685); *The CIS Market Atlas.*

Encyclopedia Britannica, Incorporated, 310 South Michigan Avenue, Chicago, Illinois 60604 (312) 347-7000; *Britannica World Data.*

The World Bank, 1818 H Street, NW, Washington, D.C. 20433 (202) 477-1234; *Statistical Handbook: States of the Former USSR.*

KAZAKHSTAN - POULTRY - See KAZAKHSTAN - LIVESTOCK AND POULTRY

KAZAKHSTAN - PRICES

The World Bank, 1818 H Street, NW, Washington, D.C. 20433 (202) 477-1234; *Statistical Handbook: States of the Former USSR.*

KAZAKHSTAN - PRODUCTION

The World Bank, 1818 H Street, NW, Washington, D.C. 20433 (202) 477-1234; *Statistical Handbook: States of the Former USSR.*

KAZAKHSTAN - PUBLIC FINANCE

The World Bank, 1818 H Street, NW, Washington, D.C. 20433 (202) 477-1234; *Statistical Handbook: States of the Former USSR.*

KAZAKHSTAN - RADIO RECEIVERS

Encyclopedia Britannica, Incorporated, 310 South Michigan Avenue, Chicago, Illinois 60604 (312) 347-7000; *Britannica World Data.*

KAZAKHSTAN - RAILWAYS

Business International Moscow, 23 Profsoyuznaya Ulitsa, 117859, Moscow (Telephone Number in U.S. (800) 938-4685); *The CIS Market Atlas.*

Encyclopedia Britannica, Incorporated, 310 South Michigan Avenue, Chicago, Illinois 60604 (312) 347-7000; *Britannica World Data.*

KAZAKHSTAN - RETAIL TRADE

Business International Moscow, 23 Profsoyuznaya Ulitsa, 117859, Moscow (Telephone Number in U.S. (800) 938-4685); *The CIS Market Atlas.*

KAZAKHSTAN - ROADS - See KAZAKHSTAN - HIGHWAYS

KAZAKHSTAN - ROUNDWOOD PRODUCTION AND CONSUMPTION - See KAZAKHSTAN - FORESTRY AND FOREST PRODUCTS

KAZAKHSTAN - SHEEP - See KAZAKHSTAN - LIVESTOCK AND POULTRY

KAZAKHSTAN - STEEL PRODUCTION AND CONSUMPTION - See KAZAKHSTAN - MINING AND MINERAL PRODUCTS

KAZAKHSTAN - TELEPHONES IN USE

Encyclopedia Britannica, Incorporated, 310 South Michigan Avenue, Chicago, Illinois 60604 (312) 347-7000; *Britannica World Data.*

KAZAKHSTAN - TELEVISION RECEIVERS

Encyclopedia Britannica, Incorporated, 310 South Michigan Avenue, Chicago, Illinois 60604 (312) 347-7000; *Britannica World Data.*

KAZAKHSTAN - TEXTILE INDUSTRY

Business International Moscow, 23 Profsoyuznaya Ulitsa, 117859, Moscow (Telephone Number in U.S. (800) 938-4685); *The CIS Market Atlas.*

KAZAKHSTAN - TOURISM

Business International Moscow, 23 Profsoyuznaya Ulitsa, 117859, Moscow (Telephone Number in U.S. (800) 938-4685); *The CIS Market Atlas.*

KAZAKHSTAN - TRANSPORTATION AND COMMUNICATION

Business International Moscow, 23 Profsoyuznaya Ulitsa, 117859, Moscow (Telephone Number in U.S. (800) 938-4685); *The CIS Market Atlas.*

Encyclopedia Britannica, Incorporated, 310 South Michigan Avenue, Chicago, Illinois 60604 (312) 347-7000; *Britannica World Data.*

KAZAKHSTAN - VITAL STATISTICS

Encyclopedia Britannica, Incorporated, 310 South Michigan Avenue, Chicago, Illinois 60604 (312) 347-7000; *Britannica World Data.*

KAZAKHSTAN - WAGES

Business International Moscow, 23 Profsoyuznaya Ulitsa, 117859, Moscow (Telephone Number in U.S. (800) 938-4685); *The CIS Market Atlas.*

The World Bank, 1818 H Street, NW, Washington, D.C. 20433 (202) 477-1234; *Statistical Handbook: States of the Former USSR.*

KAZAKHSTAN - WOOL PRODUCTION AND CONSUMPTION - See KAZAKHSTAN - TEXTILE INDUSTRY

KENTUCKY - See also STATE DATA (FOR INDIVIDUAL STATES)

Kentucky - Primary Statistics Source

Department of Existing Business and Industry, State Government of Kentucky, Capital Plaza Office Tower, Frankfort, Kentucky 40601 (502) 564-4886; *Kentucky Deskbook of Economic Statistics.*

Kentucky - State Data Centers

Center for Urban and Economic Research, College of Business and Public Administration, University of Louisville, Louisville, Kentucky 40292, Mr. Ron Crouch (502) 588-7990.

Office of Policy and Management, State of Kentucky, Capitol Annex, Frankfort, Kentucky 40601, Mr. Mike Mollins (502) 564-7300.

State Library Division, Department for Libraries and Archives, 300 Coffeetree Road, Post Office Box 537, Frankfort, Kentucky 40601, Ms. Brenda Fuller, (502) 875-7000.

Kenya - National Statistical Offices

Kenya Customs and Excise Department, Ministry of Finance, Post Office Box 40160, Nairobi, Kenya.

Ministry of Planning and National Development, Post Office Box 30266, Nairobi, Kenya.

Kenya - Primary Statistics Sources

Central Bureau of Statistics, Ministry of Planning and National Development, Post Office Box 30266, Nairobi, Kenya; *Statistical Abstract* and *Kenya Statistical Digest.*

KENYA - AGRICULTURE

Central Bureau of Statistics, Ministry of Economic Planning and Development, Post Office Box 30266, Nairobi, Kenya; *Republic of Kenya Statistical Abstract.*

Euromonitor Publications Limited, 87-88 Turnmill Street, London EC1M 5QU, England; *International Marketing Data and Statistics.*

Facts on File, 460 Park Avenue South, New York, New York 10016 (800) 443-8323; *The New Book of World Rankings.*

Food and Agricultural Organization of the United Nations (FAO), Via delle Terme di Caracalla, 00100 Rome, Italy (Telephone Number in U.S. (202) 653-2400); *Production Yearbook, The State of Food and Agriculture, Trade Yearbook,* and *Production Yearbook.*

G.K. Hall and Company, 70 Lincoln Street, Boston, Massachusetts 02111 (617) 423-3990; *The World in Figures.*

Statistical Office of the United Nations, Publishing Service, New York, New York 10017 (800) 253-9646; *Statistical Yearbook,* and *Survey of Economic and Social Conditions in Africa.*

Times Books, 201 East 50th Street, New York, New York 10022 (212) 751-2600; *The Economist Book of Vital World Statistics.*

The World Bank, 1818 H Street, NW, Washington, D.C. 20433 (202) 477-1234; *World Tables.*

United Nations Economic Commission for Africa, Africa Hall, Post Office Box 3001, Addis Ababa, Ethiopia (Telephone Number in U.S. (800) 253-9646); *African Statistical Yearbook.*

KENYA - AIRLINE SERVICE

Facts on File, 460 Park Avenue South, New York, New York 10016 (000) 443-8323; *The New Book of World Rankings.*

G.K. Hall and Company, 70 Lincoln Street, Boston, Massachusetts 02111 (617) 423-3990; *The World in Figures.*

Statistical Office of the United Nations, Publishing Service, New York, New York 10017 (800) 253-9646; *Statistical Yearbook.*

Times Books, 201 East 50th Street, New York, New York 10022 (212) 751-2600, *The Economist Book of Vital World Statistics.*

United Nations Economic Commission for Africa, Africa Hall, Post Office Box 3001, Addis Ababa, Ethiopia (Telephone Number in U.S. (800) 253-9646); *African Statistical Yearbook.*

KENYA - ALUMINUM PRODUCTION - See KENYA - MINING AND MINERAL PRODUCTS

KENYA - ANIMAL HEALTH

Food and Agricultural Organization of the United Nations (FAO), Via delle Terme di Caracalla, 00100 Rome, Italy (Telephone Number in U.S. (202) 653-2400); *Animal Health Yearbook.*

KENYA - AREA AND DENSITY OF POPULATION

African Development Bank, 01 BP 1387, Abidjan 01, Cote d'Ivoire; *Selected Statistics on Regional Member Countries.*

Euromonitor Publications Limited, 87-88 Turnmill Street, London EC1M 5QU, England; *International Marketing Data and Statistics.*

Facts on File, 460 Park Avenue South, New York, New York 10016 (800) 443-8323; *The New Book of World Rankings.*

Food and Agricultural Organization of the United Nations (FAO), Via delle Terme di Caracalla, 00100 Rome, Italy (Telephone Number in U.S. (202) 653-2400); *The State of Food and Agriculture.*

G.K. Hall and Company, 70 Lincoln Street, Boston, Massachusetts 02111 (617) 423-3990; *The World in Figures.*

Statistical Office of the United Nations, Publishing Service, New York, New York 10017 (800) 253-9646; *Statistical Yearbook,* and

Survey of Economic and Social Conditions in Africa.

Times Books, 201 East 50th Street, New York, New York 10022 (212) 751-2600; *The Economist Book of Vital World Statistics.*

United Nations Educational, Scientific and Cultural Organization (UNESCO), 7 Place de Fontenoy, F-75700 Paris, France (Telephone Number in U.S. (212) 963-5981); *Statistical Yearbook.*

KENYA - BALANCE OF PAYMENTS

African Development Bank, 01 BP 1387, Abidjan 01, Cote d'Ivoire; *Selected Statistics on Regional Member Countries.*

The Economist Intelligence Unit, 111 West 57th Street, New York, New York 10019 (800) 938-4685; *The World Market Atlas.*

G.K. Hall and Company, 70 Lincoln Street, Boston, Massachusetts 02111 (617) 423-3990; *The World in Figures.*

International Monetary Fund, 700 Nineteenth Street, NW, Washington, D.C. 20431 (202) 623-7000; *Balance of Payments Yearbook.*

Times Books, 201 East 50th Street, New York, New York 10022 (212) 751-2600; *The Economist Book of Vital World Statistics.*

The World Bank, 1818 H Street, NW, Washington, D.C. 20433 (202) 477-1234; *World Tables.*

United Nations Economic Commission for Africa, Africa Hall, Post Office Box 3001, Addis Ababa, Ethiopia (Telephone Number in U.S. (800) 253-9646); *African Statistical Yearbook.*

KENYA - BANKING

Facts on File, 460 Park Avenue South, New York, New York 10016 (800) 443-8323; *The New Book of World Rankings.*

G.K. Hall and Company, 70 Lincoln Street, Boston, Massachusetts 02111 (617) 423-3990; *The World in Figures.*

International Monetary Fund, 700 Nineteenth Street, NW, Washington, D.C. 20431 (202) 623-7000; *Government Finance Statistics Yearbook,* and *International Financial Statistics.*

United Nations Economic Commission for Africa, Africa Hall, Post Office Box 3001, Addis Ababa, Ethiopia (Telephone Number in U.S. (800) 253-9646); *African Statistical Yearbook.*

KENYA - BARLEY PRODUCTION - See KENYA - CROPS

KENYA - BEER PRODUCTION

Facts on File, 460 Park Avenue South, New York, New York 10016 (800) 443-8323; *The New Book of World Rankings.*

Statistical Office of the United Nations, Publishing Service, New York, New York 10017 (800) 253-9646; *Statistical Yearbook.*

KENYA - BIRTH RATE

Facts on File, 460 Park Avenue South, New York, New York 10016 (800) 443-8323; *The New Book of World Rankings.*

Statistical Office of the United Nations, Publishing Service, New York, New York 10017 (800) 253-9646; *Demographic Yearbook, Statistical Yearbook,* and *Survey of Economic and Social Conditions in Africa.*

Times Books, 201 East 50th Street, New York, New York 10022 (212) 751-2600; *The Economist Book of Vital World Statistics.*

The World Bank, 1818 H Street, NW, Washington, D.C. 20433 (202) 477-1234; *World Tables.*

KENYA - BONDS

G.K. Hall and Company, 70 Lincoln Street, Boston, Massachusetts 02111 (617) 423-3990; *The World in Figures.*

International Monetary Fund, 700 Nineteenth Street, NW, Washington, D.C. 20431 (202) 623-7000; *Government Finance Statistics Yearbook.*

KENYA - BOOK PRODUCTION

G.K. Hall and Company, 70 Lincoln Street, Boston, Massachusetts 02111 (617) 423-3990; *The World in Figures.*

KENYA - BROADCASTING

Billboard Limited, Post Office Box 9027, 1006 AA Amsterdam, The Netherlands (Telephone Number in U.S. (212) 764-7300); *World Radio TV Handbook.*

Facts on File, 460 Park Avenue South, New York, New York 10016 (800) 443-8323; *The New Book of World Rankings.*

G.K. Hall and Company, 70 Lincoln Street, Boston, Massachusetts 02111 (617) 423-3990; *The World in Figures.*

Times Books, 201 East 50th Street, New York, New York 10022 (212) 751-2600; *The Economist Book of Vital World Statistics.*

KENYA - BUSINESS

G.K. Hall and Company, 70 Lincoln Street, Boston, Massachusetts 02111 (617) 423-3990; *The World in Figures.*

KENYA - BUSINESS AND PROFESSIONAL LICENSES

International Monetary Fund, 700 Nineteenth Street, NW, Washington, D.C. 20431 (202) 623-7000; *Government Finance Statistics Yearbook.*

KENYA - BUTTER PRODUCTION - See KENYA - DAIRY PRODUCTS

KENYA - CALORIE SUPPLY

African Development Bank, 01 BP 1387, Abidjan 01, Cote d'Ivoire; *Selected Statistics on Regional Member Countries.*

Food and Agricultural Organization of the United Nations (FAO), Via delle Terme di Caracalla, 00100 Rome, Italy (Telephone Number in U.S. (202) 653-2400); *The State of Food and Agriculture.*

KENYA - CAPITAL REVENUE

International Monetary Fund, 700 Nineteenth Street, NW, Washington, D.C. 20431 (202) 623-7000; *Government Finance Statistics Yearbook.*

KENYA - CASHEW NUT PRODUCTION - See KENYA - CROPS

KENYA - CASTOR BEAN PRODUCTION - See KENYA - CROPS

KENYA - CATTLE - See KENYA - LIVESTOCK AND POULTRY

KENYA - CEMENT PRODUCTION - See KENYA - MINING AND MINERAL PRODUCTS

KENYA - CHEESE PRODUCTION AND CONSUMPTION - See KENYA - DAIRY PRODUCTS

KENYA - CHEMICAL (ORGANIC) PRODUCTION - See KENYA - MINING AND MINERAL PRODUCTS

KENYA - CHICKENS - See KENYA - LIVESTOCK AND POULTRY

KENYA - CIGARETTE PRODUCTION - See KENYA - TOBACCO PRODUCTION

KENYA - CLASS STRUCTURE

G.K. Hall and Company, 70 Lincoln Street, Boston, Massachusetts 02111 (617) 423-3990; *The World in Figures*.

KENYA - CLIMATE

Central Bureau of Statistics, Ministry of Economic Planning and Development, Post Office Box 30266, Nairobi, Kenya; *Republic of Kenya Statistical Abstract*.

Facts on File, 460 Park Avenue South, New York, New York 10016 (800) 443-8323; *The New Book of World Rankings*.

G.K. Hall and Company, 70 Lincoln Street, Boston, Massachusetts 02111 (617) 423-3990; *The World in Figures*.

KENYA - COAL PRODUCTION - See KENYA - MINING AND MINERAL PRODUCTS

KENYA - COFFEE - See KENYA - CROPS

KENYA - COMMUNICATIONS

Central Bureau of Statistics, Ministry of Economic Planning and Development, Post Office Box 30266, Nairobi, Kenya; *Republic of Kenya Statistical Abstract*.

G.K. Hall and Company, 70 Lincoln Street, Boston, Massachusetts 02111 (617) 423-3990; *The World in Figures*.

United Nations Economic Commission for Africa, Africa Hall, Post Office Box 3001, Addis Ababa, Ethiopia (Telephone Number in U.S. (800) 253-9646); *African Statistical Yearbook*.

KENYA - CONSTRUCTION INDUSTRY

Facts on File, 460 Park Avenue South, New York, New York 10016 (800) 443-8323; *The New Book of World Rankings*.

Statistical Office of the United Nations, Publishing Service, New York, New York 10017 (800) 253-9646; *Construction Statistics Yearbook*, and *Statistical Yearbook*.

United Nations Economic Commission for Africa, Africa Hall, Post Office Box 3001, Addis Ababa, Ethiopia (Telephone Number in U.S. (800) 253-9646); *African Statistical Yearbook*.

KENYA - CONSUMER PRICE INDEX

African Development Bank, 01 BP 1387, Abidjan 01, Cote d'Ivoire; *Selected Statistics on Regional Member Countries*.

G.K. Hall and Company, 70 Lincoln Street, Boston, Massachusetts 02111 (617) 423-3990; *The World in Figures*.

Statistical Office of the United Nations, Publishing Service, New York, New York 10017 (800) 253-9646; *Statistical Yearbook*, and *Survey of Economic and Social Conditions in Africa*.

United Nations Economic Commission for Africa, Africa Hall, Post Office Box 3001, Addis Ababa, Ethiopia (Telephone Number in U.S. (800) 253-9646); *African Statistical Yearbook*.

KENYA - CONSUMER PRICES

International Labour Office, I.L.O. Publications, CH-1211, Geneva 22, Switzerland; *Yearbook of Labour Statistics*.

International Monetary Fund, 700 Nineteenth Street, NW, Washington, D.C. 20431 (202) 623-7000; *International Financial Statistics*.

Times Books, 201 East 50th Street, New York, New York 10022 (212) 751-2600; *The Economist Book of Vital World Statistics*.

KENYA - CONSUMPTION

African Development Bank, 01 BP 1387, Abidjan 01, Cote d'Ivoire; *Selected Statistics on Regional Member Countries*.

G.K. Hall and Company, 70 Lincoln Street, Boston, Massachusetts 02111 (617) 423-3990; *The World in Figures*.

Statistical Office of the United Nations, Publishing Service, New York, New York 10017 (800) 253-9646; *Survey of Economic and Social Conditions in Africa*.

KENYA - COPPER AND COPPER ORE PRODUCTION AND CONSUMPTION - See KENYA - MINING AND MINERAL PRODUCTS

KENYA - CORN PRODUCTION - See KENYA - CROPS

KENYA - CORPORATE TAXES - See KENYA - TAXATION

KENYA - COTTON - See KENYA - CROPS

KENYA - CRIME

Yale University Press, Yale Station, New Haven, Connecticut 06520 (203) 432-0940; *Violence and Crime in Cross-National Perspective*.

KENYA - CROPS

Facts on File, 460 Park Avenue South, New York, New York 10016 (800) 443-8323; *The New Book of World Rankings*.

Food and Agricultural Organization of the United Nations (FAO), Via delle Terme di Caracalla, 00100 Rome, Italy (Telephone Number in U.S. (202) 653-2400); *Production Yearbook*, and *The State of Food and Agriculture*.

G.K. Hall and Company, 70 Lincoln Street, Boston, Massachusetts 02111 (617) 423-3990; *The World in Figures*.

International Monetary Fund, 700 Nineteenth Street, NW, Washington, D.C. 20431 (202) 623-7000; *International Financial Statistics*.

Statistical Office of the United Nations, Publishing Service, New York, New York 10017 (800) 253-9646; *Statistical Yearbook*.

United Nations Economic Commission for Africa, Africa Hall, Post Office Box 3001, Addis Ababa, Ethiopia (Telephone Number in U.S. (800) 253-9646); *African Statistical Yearbook*.

KENYA - CUSTOMS DUTIES

G.K. Hall and Company, 70 Lincoln Street, Boston, Massachusetts 02111 (617) 423-3990; *The World in Figures*.

International Monetary Fund, 700 Nineteenth Street, NW, Washington, D.C. 20431 (202) 623-7000; *Government Finance Statistics Yearbook*.

KENYA - DAIRY PRODUCTS

Facts on File, 460 Park Avenue South, New York, New York 10016 (800) 443-8323; *The New Book of World Rankings*.

Food and Agricultural Organization of the United Nations (FAO), Via delle Terme di Caracalla, 00100 Rome, Italy (Telephone Number in U.S. (202) 653-2400); *Production Yearbook*, and *The State of Food and Agriculture*.

Statistical Office of the United Nations, Publishing Service, New York, New York 10017 (800) 253-9646; *Statistical Yearbook*.

KENYA - DEATH RATES

G.K. Hall and Company, 70 Lincoln Street, Boston, Massachusetts 02111 (617) 423-3990; *The World in Figures*.

Statistical Office of the United Nations, Publishing Service, New York, New York 10017 (800) 253-9646; *Statistical Yearbook*, and *Survey of Economic and Social Conditions in Africa*.

Times Books, 201 East 50th Street, New York, New York 10022 (212) 751-2600; *The Economist Book of Vital World Statistics*.

KENYA - DEFENSE EXPENDITURES

G.K. Hall and Company, 70 Lincoln Street, Boston, Massachusetts 02111 (617) 423-3990; *The World in Figures*.

International Monetary Fund, 700 Nineteenth Street, NW, Washington, D.C. 20431 (202) 623-7000; *Government Finance Statistics Yearbook*.

KENYA - DEMOGRAPHY

The Economist Intelligence Unit, 111 West 57th Street, New York, New York 10019 (800) 938-4685; *The World Market Atlas*.

Facts on File, 460 Park Avenue South, New York, New York 10016 (800) 443-8323; *The New Book of World Rankings*.

G.K. Hall and Company, 70 Lincoln Street, Boston, Massachusetts 02111 (617) 423-3990; *The World in Figures*.

Statistical Office of the United Nations, Publishing Service, New York, New York 10017 (800) 253-9646; *Survey of Economic and Social Conditions in Africa*.

KENYA - DEVELOPMENT ASSISTANCE

G.K. Hall and Company, 70 Lincoln Street, Boston, Massachusetts 02111 (617) 423-3990; *The World in Figures*.

Statistical Office of the United Nations, Publishing Service, New York, New York 10017 (800) 253-9646; *Statistical Yearbook*.

KENYA - DIAMOND PRODUCTION - See KENYA - MINING AND MINERAL PRODUCTS

KENYA - DISEASE

G.K. Hall and Company, 70 Lincoln Street, Boston, Massachusetts 02111 (617) 423-3990; *The World in Figures*.

KENYA - DIVORCE RATES

Facts on File, 460 Park Avenue South, New York, New York 10016 (800) 443-8323; *The New Book of World Rankings*.

Statistical Office of the United Nations, Publishing Service, New York, New York 10017 (800) 253-9646; *Demographic Yearbook*.

KENYA - DOMESTIC PRODUCT

G.K. Hall and Company, 70 Lincoln Street, Boston, Massachusetts 02111 (617) 423-3990; *The World in Figures*.

KENYA - ECONOMY

African Development Bank, 01 BP 1387, Abidjan 01, Cote d'Ivoire; *Selected Statistics on Regional Member Countries*.

Euromonitor Publications Limited, 87-88 Turnmill Street, London EC1M 5QU, England; *International Marketing Data and Statistics*.

Facts on File, 460 Park Avenue South, New York, New York 10016 (800) 443-8323; *The New Book of World Rankings*.

G.K. Hall and Company, 70 Lincoln Street, Boston, Massachusetts 02111 (617) 423-3990; *The World in Figures*.

Statistical Office of the United Nations, Publishing Service, New York, New York 10017 (800) 253-9646; *Foreign Trade Statistics for Africa*.

KENYA - EDUCATION

African Development Bank, 01 BP 1387, Abidjan 01, Cote d'Ivoire; *Selected Statistics on Regional Member Countries*.

Central Bureau of Statistics, Ministry of Economic Planning and Development, Post Office Box 30266, Nairobi, Kenya; *Republic of Kenya Statistical Abstract*.

The Economist Intelligence Unit, 111 West 57th Street, New York, New York 10019 (800) 938-4685; *The World Market Atlas*.

Facts on File, 460 Park Avenue South, New York, New York 10016 (800) 443-8323; *The New Book of World Rankings*.

G.K. Hall and Company, 70 Lincoln Street, Boston, Massachusetts 02111 (617) 423-3990; *The World in Figures*.

International Monetary Fund, 700 Nineteenth Street, NW, Washington, D.C. 20431 (202) 623-7000; *Government Finance Statistics Yearbook*.

Statistical Office of the United Nations, Publishing Service, New York, New York 10017 (800) 253-9646; *Survey of Economic and Social Conditions in Africa*.

Times Books, 201 East 50th Street, New York, New York 10022 (212) 751-2600; *The Economist Book of Vital World Statistics*.

United Nations Economic Commission for Africa, Africa Hall, Post Office Box 3001, Addis Ababa, Ethiopia (Telephone Number in U.S. (800) 253-9646); *African Statistical Yearbook*.

United Nations Educational, Scientific and Cultural Organization (UNESCO), 7 Place de Fontenoy, F-75700 Paris, France (Telephone Number in U.S. (212) 963-5981); *Statistical Yearbook.*

The World Bank, 1818 H Street, NW, Washington, D.C. 20433 (202) 477-1234; *World Tables.*

KENYA - EGG PRODUCTION AND CONSUMPTION - See KENYA - DAIRY PRODUCTS

KENYA - ELECTRICITY

Facts on File, 460 Park Avenue South, New York, New York 10016 (800) 443-8323; *The New Book of World Rankings.*

Statistical Office of the United Nations, Publishing Service, New York, New York 10017 (800) 253-9646; *Statistical Yearbook,* and *Survey of Economic and Social Conditions in Africa.*

Times Books, 201 East 50th Street, New York, New York 10022 (212) 751-2600; *The Economist Book of Vital World Statistics.*

United Nations Economic Commission for Africa, Africa Hall, Post Office Box 3001, Addis Ababa, Ethiopia (Telephone Number in U.S. (800) 253-9646); *African Statistical Yearbook.*

KENYA - EMPLOYMENT

Euromonitor Publications Limited, 87-88 Turnmill Street, London EC1M 5QU, England; *International Marketing Data and Statistics.*

Facts on File, 460 Park Avenue South, New York, New York 10016 (800) 443-8323; *The New Book of World Rankings.*

International Labour Office, I.L.O. Publications, CH-1211, Geneva 22, Switzerland; *Yearbook of Labour Statistics.*

Statistical Office of the United Nations, Publishing Service, New York, New York 10017 (800) 253-9646; *Statistical Yearbook,* and *Survey of Economic and Social Conditions in Africa.*

United Nations Economic Commission for Africa, Africa Hall, Post Office Box 3001, Addis Ababa, Ethiopia (Telephone Number in U.S. (800) 253-9646); *African Statistical Yearbook.*

KENYA - ENERGY

Facts on File, 460 Park Avenue South, New York, New York 10016 (800) 443-8323; *The New Book of World Rankings.*

Food and Agricultural Organization of the United Nations (FAO), Via delle Terme di Caracalla, 00100 Rome, Italy (Telephone Number in U.S. (202) 653-2400); *The State of Food and Agriculture.*

G.K. Hall and Company, 70 Lincoln Street, Boston, Massachusetts 02111 (617) 423-3990; *The World in Figures.*

Statistical Office of the United Nations, Publishing Service, New York, New York 10017 (800) 253-9646; *Energy Statistics Yearbook,* and *Statistical Yearbook.*

Times Books, 201 East 50th Street, New York, New York 10022 (212) 751-2600; *The Economist Book of Vital World Statistics.*

United Nations Economic Commission for Africa, Africa Hall, Post Office Box 3001, Addis Ababa, Ethiopia (Telephone Number in U.S. (800) 253-9646); *African Statistical Yearbook.*

KENYA - EXCHANGE RATES

African Development Bank, 01 BP 1387, Abidjan 01, Cote d'Ivoire; *Selected Statistics on Regional Member Countries.*

Euromonitor Publications Limited, 87-88 Turnmill Street, London EC1M 5QU, England; *International Marketing Data and Statistics.*

International Monetary Fund, 700 Nineteenth Street, NW, Washington, D.C. 20431 (202) 623-7000; *International Financial Statistics.*

Statistical Office of the United Nations, Publishing Service, New York, New York 10017 (800) 253-9646; *Foreign Trade Statistics for Africa,* and *Statistical Yearbook.*

KENYA - EXCISE TAXES - See KENYA - TAXATION

KENYA - EXPORTS

African Development Bank, 01 BP 1387, Abidjan 01, Cote d'Ivoire; *Selected Statistics on Regional Member Countries.*

The Economist Intelligence Unit, 111 West 57th Street, New York, New York 10019 (800) 938-4685; *The World Market Atlas.*

Euromonitor Publications Limited, 87-88 Turnmill Street, London EC1M 5QU, England; *International Marketing Data and Statistics.*

Food and Agricultural Organization of the United Nations (FAO), Via delle Terme di Caracalla, 00100 Rome, Italy (Telephone Number in U.S. (202) 653-2400); *The State of Food and Agriculture.*

G.K. Hall and Company, 70 Lincoln Street, Boston, Massachusetts 02111 (617) 423-3990; *The World in Figures.*

International Monetary Fund, 700 Nineteenth Street, NW, Washington, D.C. 20431 (202) 623-7000; *Direction of Trade Statistics, Government Finance Statistics Yearbook,* and *International Financial Statistics.*

Statistical Office of the United Nations, Publishing Service, New York, New York 10017 (800) 253-9646; *Foreign Trade Statistics for Africa, Trade in Manufactures of Developing Countries,* and *Survey of Economic and Social Conditions in Africa.*

Times Books, 201 East 50th Street, New York, New York 10022 (212) 751-2600; *The Economist Book of Vital World Statistics.*

United Nations Economic Commission for Africa, Africa Hall, Post Office Box 3001, Addis Ababa, Ethiopia (Telephone Number in U.S. (800) 253-9646); *African Statistical Yearbook.*

The World Bank, 1818 H Street, NW, Washington, D.C. 20433 (202) 477-1234; *World Tables.*

KENYA - EXTERNAL INDEBTEDNESS

African Development Bank, 01 BP 1387, Abidjan 01, Cote d'Ivoire; *Selected Statistics on Regional Member Countries.*

Statistical Office of the United Nations, Publishing Service, New York, New York 10017 (800) 253-9646; *Survey of Economic and Social Conditions in Africa.*

KENYA - EXTERNAL TRADE

African Development Bank, 01 BP 1387, Abidjan 01, Cote d'Ivoire; *Selected Statistics on Regional Member Countries.*

Food and Agricultural Organization of the United Nations (FAO), Via delle Terme di Caracalla, 00100 Rome, Italy (Telephone Number in U.S. (202) 653-2400); *The State of Food and Agriculture*, and *Trade Yearbook*.

G.K. Hall and Company, 70 Lincoln Street, Boston, Massachusetts 02111 (617) 423-3990; *The World in Figures*.

Statistical Office of the United Nations, Publishing Service, New York, New York 10017 (800) 253-9646; *Statistical Yearbook*.

The World Bank, 1818 H Street, NW, Washington, D.C. 20433 (202) 477-1234; *World Tables*.

KENYA - FARM CROPS - See KENYA - CROPS

KENYA - FEMALE WORKING POPULATION - See KENYA - EMPLOYMENT

KENYA - FERTILITY RATES

Facts on File, 460 Park Avenue South, New York, New York 10016 (800) 443-8323; *The New Book of World Rankings*.

Statistical Office of the United Nations, Publishing Service, New York, New York 10017 (800) 253-9646; *Survey of Economic and Social Conditions in Africa*.

Times Books, 201 East 50th Street, New York, New York 10022 (212) 751-2600; *The Economist Book of Vital World Statistics*.

The World Bank, 1818 H Street, NW, Washington, D.C. 20433 (202) 477-1234; *World Tables*.

KENYA - FERTILIZER

Food and Agricultural Organization of the United Nations (FAO), Via delle Terme di Caracalla, 00100 Rome, Italy (Telephone Number in U.S. (202) 653-2400); *Fertilizer Yearbook*, and *The State of Food and Agriculture*.

Statistical Office of the United Nations, Publishing Service, New York, New York 10017 (800) 253-9646; *Statistical Yearbook*.

KENYA - FETAL MORTALITY

Statistical Office of the United Nations, Publishing Service, New York, New York 10017 (800) 253-9646; *Demographic Yearbook*.

KENYA - FINANCE

African Development Bank, 01 BP 1387, Abidjan 01, Cote d'Ivoire; *Selected Statistics on Regional Member Countries*.

Central Bureau of Statistics, Ministry of Economic Planning and Development, Post Office Box 30266, Nairobi, Kenya; *Republic of Kenya Statistical Abstract*.

Facts on File, 460 Park Avenue South, New York, New York 10016 (800) 443-8323; *The New Book of World Rankings*.

G.K. Hall and Company, 70 Lincoln Street, Boston, Massachusetts 02111 (617) 423-3990; *The World in Figures*.

International Monetary Fund, 700 Nineteenth Street, NW, Washington, D.C. 20431 (202) 623-7000; *International Financial Statistics*.

United Nations Economic Commission for Africa, Africa Hall, Post Office Box 3001, Addis Ababa, Ethiopia (Telephone Number in U.S. (800) 253-9646); *African Statistical Yearbook*.

KENYA - FISHERIES

Central Bureau of Statistics, Ministry of Economic Planning and Development, Post Office Box 30266, Nairobi, Kenya; *Republic of Kenya Statistical Abstract*.

Facts on File, 460 Park Avenue South, New York, New York 10016 (800) 443-8323; *The New Book of World Rankings*.

Food and Agricultural Organization of the United Nations (FAO), Via delle Terme di Caracalla, 00100 Rome, Italy (Telephone Number in U.S. (202) 653-2400); *The State of Food and Agriculture*.

Statistical Office of the United Nations, Publishing Service, New York, New York 10017 (800) 253-9646; *Statistical Yearbook*, and *Survey of Economic and Social Conditions in Africa*.

United Nations Economic Commission for Africa, Africa Hall, Post Office Box 3001, Addis Ababa, Ethiopia (Telephone Number in U.S. (800) 253-9646); *African Statistical Yearbook*.

KENYA - FLOUR PRODUCTION

Statistical Office of the United Nations, Publishing Service, New York, New York 10017 (800) 253-9646; *Statistical Yearbook*.

KENYA - FOOD

African Development Bank, 01 BP 1387, Abidjan 01, Cote d'Ivoire; *Selected Statistics on Regional Member Countries*.

Food and Agricultural Organization of the United Nations (FAO), Via delle Terme di Caracalla, 00100 Rome, Italy (Telephone Number in U.S. (202) 653-2400); *Production Yearbook*, and *The State of Food and Agriculture*.

G.K. Hall and Company, 70 Lincoln Street, Boston, Massachusetts 02111 (617) 423-3990; *The World in Figures*.

Statistical Office of the United Nations, Publishing Service, New York, New York 10017 (800) 253-9646; *Trade in Manufacturers of Developing Countries*.

KENYA - FOREIGN AID

G.K. Hall and Company, 70 Lincoln Street, Boston, Massachusetts 02111 (617) 423-3990; *The World in Figures*.

KENYA - FOREIGN DEBT

International Monetary Fund, 700 Nineteenth Street, NW, Washington, D.C. 20431 (202) 623-7000; *Government Finance Statistics Yearbook*.

KENYA - FOREIGN TRADE

Euromonitor Publications Limited, 87-88 Turnmill Street, London EC1M 5QU, England; *International Marketing Data and Statistics*.

Facts on File, 460 Park Avenue South, New York, New York 10016 (800) 443-8323; *The New Book of World Rankings*.

Food and Agricultural Organization of the United Nations (FAO), Via delle Terme di Caracalla, 00100 Rome, Italy (Telephone Number in U.S. (202) 653-2400); *The State of Food and Agriculture*.

G.K. Hall and Company, 70 Lincoln Street, Boston, Massachusetts 02111 (617) 423-3990; *The World in Figures.*

International Monetary Fund, 700 Nineteenth Street, NW, Washington, D.C. 20431 (202) 623-7000; *International Financial Statistics.*

Statistical Office of the United Nations, Publishing Service, New York, New York 10017 (800) 253-9646; *Foreign Trade Statistics for Africa, International Trade Statistics Yearbook,* and *Statistical Yearbook.*

United Nations Economic Commission for Africa, Africa Hall, Post Office Box 3001, Addis Ababa, Ethiopia (Telephone Number in U.S. (800) 253-9646); *African Statistical Yearbook.*

The World Bank, 1818 H Street, NW, Washington, D.C. 20433 (202) 477-1234; *World Tables.*

KENYA - FORESTRY AND FOREST PRODUCTS

Central Bureau of Statistics, Ministry of Economic Planning and Development, Post Office Box 30266, Nairobi, Kenya; *Republic of Kenya Statistical Abstract.*

Facts on File, 460 Park Avenue South, New York, New York 10016 (800) 443-8323; *The New Book of World Rankings.*

Food and Agricultural Organization of the United Nations (FAO), Via delle Terme di Caracalla, 00100 Rome, Italy (Telephone Number in U.S. (202) 653-2400); *The State of Food and Agriculture,* and *Yearbook of Forest Products.*

G.K. Hall and Company, 70 Lincoln Street, Boston, Massachusetts 02111 (617) 423-3990; *The World in Figures.*

Statistical Office of the United Nations, Publishing Service, New York, New York 10017 (800) 253-9646; *Statistical Yearbook.*

United Nations Economic Commission for Africa, Africa Hall, Post Office Box 3001, Addis Ababa, Ethiopia (Telephone Number in U.S. (800) 253-9646); *African Statistical Yearbook.*

United Nations Educational, Scientific and Cultural Organization (UNESCO), 7 Place de Fontenoy, F-75700 Paris, France (Telephone Number in U.S. (212) 963-5981); *Statistical Yearbook.*

KENYA - GAS PRODUCTION - See KENYA - MINING AND MINERAL PRODUCTS

KENYA - GENERAL INDUSTRIAL STATISTICS

Statistical Office of the United Nations, Publishing Service, New York, New York 10017 (800) 253-9646; *Industrial Statistics Yearbook.*

KENYA - GENERAL MORTALITY

Statistical Office of the United Nations, Publishing Service, New York, New York 10017 (800) 253-9646; *Demographic Yearbook.*

KENYA - GEOGRAPHIC DATA

Facts on File, 460 Park Avenue South, New York, New York 10016 (800) 443-8323; *The New Book of World Rankings.*

KENYA - GOATS - See KENYA - LIVESTOCK AND POULTRY

KENYA - GOLD HOLDINGS

International Monetary Fund, 700 Nineteenth Street, NW, Washington, D.C. 20431 (202) 623-7000; *International Financial Statistics.*

Statistical Office of the United Nations, Publishing Service, New York, New York 10017 (800) 253-9646; *Statistical Yearbook.*

The World Bank, 1818 H Street, NW, Washington, D.C. 20433 (202) 477-1234; *World Tables.*

KENYA - GOLD PRODUCTION AND CONSUMPTION - See KENYA - MINING AND MINERAL PRODUCTS

KENYA - GOVERNMENT

G.K. Hall and Company, 70 Lincoln Street, Boston, Massachusetts 02111 (617) 423-3990; *The World in Figures.*

KENYA - GOVERNMENT EXPENDITURES

International Monetary Fund, 700 Nineteenth Street, NW, Washington, D.C. 20431 (202) 623-7000; *Government Finance Statistics Yearbook.*

Times Books, 201 East 50th Street, New York, New York 10022 (212) 751-2600; *The Economist Book of Vital World Statistics.*

The World Bank, 1818 H Street, NW, Washington, D.C. 20433 (202) 477-1234; *World Tables.*

KENYA - GOVERNMENT FINANCES

International Monetary Fund, 700 Nineteenth Street, NW, Washington, D.C. 20431 (202) 623-7000; *International Financial Statistics.*

Statistical Office of the United Nations, Publishing Service, New York, New York 10017 (800) 253-9646; *Statistical Yearbook.*

KENYA - GOVERNMENT REVENUES

International Monetary Fund, 700 Nineteenth Street, NW, Washington, D.C. 20431 (202) 623-7000; *Government Finance Statistics Yearbook.*

Statistical Office of the United Nations, Publishing Service, New York, New York 10017 (800) 253-9646; *Survey of Economic and Social Conditions in Africa.*

Times Books, 201 East 50th Street, New York, New York 10022 (212) 751-2600; *The Economist Book of Vital World Statistics.*

The World Bank, 1818 H Street, NW, Washington, D.C. 20433 (202) 477-1234; *World Tables.*

KENYA - GRAIN PRODUCTION - See KENYA - CROPS

KENYA - GRANTS

International Monetary Fund, 700 Nineteenth Street, NW, Washington, D.C. 20431 (202) 623-7000; *Government Finance Statistics Yearbook.*

KENYA - GROSS DOMESTIC PRODUCT

African Development Bank, 01 BP 1387, Abidjan 01, Cote d'Ivoire; *Selected Statistics on Regional Member Countries.*

The Economist Intelligence Unit, 111 West 57th Street, New York, New York 10019 (800) 938-4685; *The World Market Atlas*.

Euromonitor Publications Limited, 87-88 Turnmill Street, London EC1M 5QU, England; *International Marketing Data and Statistics*.

Facts on File, 460 Park Avenue South, New York, New York 10016 (800) 443-8323; *The New Book of World Rankings*.

G.K. Hall and Company, 70 Lincoln Street, Boston, Massachusetts 02111 (617) 423-3990; *The World in Figures*.

Statistical Office of the United Nations, Publishing Service, New York, New York 10017 (800) 253-9646; *Statistical Yearbook*, and *Survey of Economic and Social Conditions in Africa*.

Times Books, 201 East 50th Street, New York, New York 10022 (212) 751-2600; *The Economist Book of Vital World Statistics*.

United Nations Economic Commission for Africa, Africa Hall, Post Office Box 3001, Addis Ababa, Ethiopia (Telephone Number in U.S. (800) 253-9646); *African Statistical Yearbook*.

The World Bank, 1818 H Street, NW, Washington, D.C. 20433 (202) 477-1234; *World Tables*.

KENYA - GROSS NATIONAL PRODUCT

Euromonitor Publications Limited, 87-88 Turnmill Street, London EC1M 5QU, England; *International Marketing Data and Statistics*.

The World Bank, 1818 H Street, NW, Washington, D.C. 20433 (202) 477-1234; *World Tables*.

KENYA - GROUNDNUT PRODUCTION - See KENYA - CROPS

KENYA - HEALTH

African Development Bank, 01 BP 1387, Abidjan 01, Cote d'Ivoire; *Selected Statistics on Regional Member Countries*.

Facts on File, 460 Park Avenue South, New York, New York 10016 (800) 443-8323; *The New Book of World Rankings*.

G.K. Hall and Company, 70 Lincoln Street, Boston, Massachusetts 02111 (617) 423-3990; *The World in Figures*.

Statistical Office of the United Nations, Publishing Service, New York, New York 10017 (800) 253-9646; *Statistical Yearbook*.

Times Books, 201 East 50th Street, New York, New York 10022 (212) 751-2600; *The Economist Book of Vital World Statistics*.

United Nations Economic Commission for Africa, Africa Hall, Post Office Box 3001, Addis Ababa, Ethiopia (Telephone Number in U.S. (800) 253-9646); *African Statistical Yearbook*.

KENYA - HEALTH EXPENDITURES

International Monetary Fund, 700 Nineteenth Street, NW, Washington, D.C. 20431 (202) 623-7000; *Government Finance Statistics Yearbook*.

KENYA - HIDE PRODUCTION

Food and Agricultural Organization of the United Nations (FAO), Via delle Terme di Caracalla, 00100 Rome, Italy (Telephone Number in U.S. (202) 653-2400); *Production Yearbook*.

KENYA - HIGHWAYS

G.K. Hall and Company, 70 Lincoln Street, Boston, Massachusetts 02111 (617) 423-3990; *The World in Figures*.

International Road Federation, 525 School Street, SW, Washington, D.C. 20024 (202) 554-2106; *World Road Statistics*.

Statistical Office of the United Nations, Publishing Service, New York, New York 10017 (800) 253-9646; *Survey of Economic and Social Conditions in Africa*.

United Nations Economic Commission for Africa, Africa Hall, Post Office Box 3001, Addis Ababa, Ethiopia (Telephone Number in U.S. (800) 253-9646); *African Statistical Yearbook*.

KENYA - HORSES - See KENYA - LIVESTOCK AND POULTRY

KENYA - HOURS OF WORK - See KENYA - EMPLOYMENT

KENYA - HOUSING AND HOUSING UNITS

Facts on File, 460 Park Avenue South, New York, New York 10016 (800) 443-8323; *The New Book of World Rankings*.

KENYA - HOUSING EXPENDITURES

International Monetary Fund, 700 Nineteenth Street, NW, Washington, D.C. 20431 (202) 623-7000; *Government Finance Statistics Yearbook*.

KENYA - ILLITERATE POPULATION

The Economist Intelligence Unit, 111 West 57th Street, New York, New York 10019 (800) 938-4685; *The World Market Atlas*.

G.K. Hall and Company, 70 Lincoln Street, Boston, Massachusetts 02111 (617) 423-3990; *The World in Figures*.

United Nations Educational, Scientific and Cultural Organization (UNESCO), 7 Place de Fontenoy, F-75700 Paris, France (Telephone Number in U.S. (212) 963-5981); *Statistical Yearbook*.

KENYA - IMPORTS

African Development Bank, 01 BP 1387, Abidjan 01, Cote d'Ivoire; *Selected Statistics on Regional Member Countries*.

The Economist Intelligence Unit, 111 West 57th Street, New York, New York 10019 (800) 938-4685; *The World Market Atlas*.

Euromonitor Publications Limited, 87-88 Turnmill Street, London EC1M 5QU, England; *International Marketing Data and Statistics*.

Food and Agricultural Organization of the United Nations (FAO), Via delle Terme di Caracalla, 00100 Rome, Italy (Telephone Number in U.S. (202) 653-2400); *The State of Food and Agriculture*.

G.K. Hall and Company, 70 Lincoln Street, Boston, Massachusetts 02111 (617) 423-3990; *The World in Figures*.

International Monetary Fund, 700 Nineteenth Street, NW, Washington, D.C. 20431 (202) 623-7000; *Direction of Trade Statistics*, *Government Finance Statistics Yearbook*, and *International Financial Statistics*.

Statistical Office of the United Nations, Publishing Service, New York, New York 10017 (800) 253-9646; *Foreign Trade Statistics for Africa*.

Times Books, 201 East 50th Street, New York, New York 10022 (212) 751-2600; *The Economist Book of Vital World Statistics,* and *Survey of Economic and Social Conditions in Africa.*

United Nations Economic Commission for Africa, Africa Hall, Post Office Box 3001, Addis Ababa, Ethiopia (Telephone Number in U.S. (800) 253-9646); *African Statistical Yearbook.*

The World Bank, 1818 H Street, NW, Washington, D.C. 20433 (202) 477-1234; *World Tables.*

KENYA - INCOME TAXES - See KENYA - TAXATION

KENYA - INDUSTRY

Central Bureau of Statistics, Ministry of Economic Planning and Development, Post Office Box 30266, Nairobi, Kenya; *Republic of Kenya Statistical Abstract.*

Euromonitor Publications Limited, 87-88 Turnmill Street, London EC1M 5QU, England; *International Marketing Data and Statistics.*

Facts on File, 460 Park Avenue South, New York, New York 10016 (800) 443-8323; *The New Book of World Rankings.*

G.K. Hall and Company, 70 Lincoln Street, Boston, Massachusetts 02111 (617) 423-3990; *The World in Figures.*

International Labour Office, I.L.O. Publications, CH-1211, Geneva 33, Switzerland; *Yearbook of Labour Statistics.*

Statistical Office of the United Nations, Publishing Service, New York, New York 10017 (800) 253-9646; *Statistical Yearbook,* and *Survey of Economic and Social Conditions in Africa.*

Times Books, 201 East 50th Street, New York, New York 10022 (212) 751-2600; *The Economist Book of Vital World Statistics.*

United Nations Economic Commission for Africa, Africa Hall, Post Office Box 3001, Addis Ababa, Ethiopia (Telephone Number in U.S. (800) 253-9646); *African Statistical Yearbook.*

The World Bank, 1818 H Street, NW, Washington, D.C. 20433 (202) 477-1234; *Statistical Handbook: States of the Former USSR,* and *World Tables.*

World Intellectual Property Organization, 34 Chemin des Colombettes, CH-1211 Geneva 20, Switzerland; *Industrial Property Statistics.*

KENYA - INFANT AND MATERNAL MORTALITY

Statistical Office of the United Nations, Publishing Service, New York, New York 10017 (800) 253-9646; *Demographic Yearbook, Statistical Yearbook,* and *Survey of Economic and Social Conditions in Africa.*

Times Books, 201 East 50th Street, New York, New York 10022 (212) 751-2600; *The Economist Book of Vital World Statistics.*

The World Bank, 1818 H Street, NW, Washington, D.C. 20433 (202) 477-1234; *World Tables.*

KENYA - INTERNAL TRADE

Statistical Office of the United Nations, Publishing Service, New York, New York 10017 (800) 253-9646; *Statistical Yearbook.*

KENYA - INTERNATIONAL LIQUIDITY

International Monetary Fund, 700 Nineteenth Street, NW, Washington, D.C. 20431 (202) 623-7000; *International Financial Statistics.*

KENYA - INTERNATIONAL RESERVES EXCLUDING GOLD

African Development Bank, 01 BP 1387, Abidjan 01, Cote d'Ivoire; *Selected Statistics on Regional Member Countries.*

Statistical Office of the United Nations, Publishing Service, New York, New York 10017 (800) 253-9646; *Statistical Yearbook.*

The World Bank, 1818 H Street, NW, Washington, D.C. 20433 (202) 477-1234; *World Tables.*

KENYA - IRON ORE PRODUCTION AND CONSUMPTION - See KENYA - MINING AND MINERAL PRODUCTS

KENYA - IRRIGATION

Euromonitor Publications Limited, 87-88 Turnmill Street, London EC1M 5QU, England; *International Marketing Data and Statistics.*

KENYA - LABOR FORCE

African Development Bank, 01 BP 1387, Abidjan 01, Cote d'Ivoire; *Selected Statistics on Regional Member Countries.*

Central Bureau of Statistics, Ministry of Economic Planning and Development, Post Office Box 30266, Nairobi, Kenya; *Republic of Kenya Statistical Abstract.*

Euromonitor Publications Limited, 87-88 Turnmill Street, London EC1M 5QU, England; *International Marketing Data and Statistics.*

Facts on File, 460 Park Avenue South, New York, New York 10016 (800) 443-8323; *The New Book of World Rankings.*

Food and Agricultural Organization of the United Nations (FAO), Via delle Terme di Caracalla, 00100 Rome, Italy (Telephone Number in U.S. (202) 653-2400); *The State of Food and Agriculture.*

G.K. Hall and Company, 70 Lincoln Street, Boston, Massachusetts 02111 (617) 423-3990; *The World in Figures.*

The World Bank, 1818 H Street, NW, Washington, D.C. 20433 (202) 477-1234; *World Tables.*

KENYA - LABOR PRODUCTIVITY

International Labour Office, I.L.O. Publications, CH-1211, Geneva 22, Switzerland; *Yearbook of Labour Statistics.*

KENYA - LAND USE

Euromonitor Publications Limited, 87-88 Turnmill Street, London EC1M 5QU, England; *International Marketing Data and Statistics.*

Food and Agricultural Organization of the United Nations (FAO), Via delle Terme di Caracalla, 00100 Rome, Italy (Telephone Number in U.S. (202) 653-2400); *Production Yearbook.*

G.K. Hall and Company, 70 Lincoln Street, Boston, Massachusetts 02111 (617) 423-3990; *The World in Figures.*

KENYA - LIBRARIES

Facts on File, 460 Park Avenue South, New York, New York 10016 (800) 443-8323; *The New Book of World Rankings*.

United Nations Educational, Scientific and Cultural Organization (UNESCO), 7 Place de Fontenoy, F-75700 Paris, France (Telephone Number in U.S. (212) 963-5981); *Statistical Yearbook*.

KENYA - LIFE EXPECTANCY

African Development Bank, 01 BP 1387, Abidjan 01, Cote d'Ivoire; *Selected Statistics on Regional Member Countries*.

KENYA - LITERACY RATE

Statistical Office of the United Nations, Publishing Service, New York, New York 10017 (800) 253-9646; *Survey of Economic and Social Conditions in Africa*.

KENYA - LIVESTOCK AND POULTRY

Euromonitor Publications Limited, 87-88 Turnmill Street, London EC1M 5QU, England; *International Marketing Data and Statistics*.

Facts on File, 460 Park Avenue South, New York, New York 10016 (800) 443-8323; *The New Book of World Rankings*.

Food and Agricultural Organization of the United Nations (FAO), Via delle Terme di Caracalla, 00100 Rome, Italy (Telephone Number in U.S. (202) 653-2400); *Production Yearbook*, and *The State of Food and Agriculture*.

G.K. Hall and Company, 70 Lincoln Street, Boston, Massachusetts 02111 (617) 423-3990; *The World in Figures*.

Statistical Office of the United Nations, Publishing Service, New York, New York 10017 (800) 253-9646; *Statistical Yearbook*, and *Survey of Economic and Social Conditions in Africa*.

United Nations Economic Commission for Africa, Africa Hall, Post Office Box 3001, Addis Ababa, Ethiopia (Telephone Number in U.S. (800) 253-9646); *African Statistical Yearbook*.

KENYA - LIVING LEVELS

G.K. Hall and Company, 70 Lincoln Street, Boston, Massachusetts 02111 (617) 423-3990; *The World in Figures*.

Times Books, 201 East 50th Street, New York, New York 10022 (212) 751-2600; *The Economist Book of Vital World Statistics*.

KENYA - MAIL - NUMBER OF ITEMS SENT AND RECEIVED

Statistical Office of the United Nations, Publishing Service, New York, New York 10017 (800) 253-9646; *Statistical Yearbook*.

KENYA - MANUFACTURING

Facts on File, 460 Park Avenue South, New York, New York 10016 (800) 443-8323; *The New Book of World Rankings*.

G.K. Hall and Company, 70 Lincoln Street, Boston, Massachusetts 02111 (617) 423-3990; *The World in Figures*.

Statistical Office of the United Nations, Publishing Service, New York, New York 10017 (800) 253-9646; *Statistical Yearbook*, and *Survey of Economic and Social Conditions in Africa*.

Times Books, 201 East 50th Street, New York, New York 10022 (212) 751-2600; *The Economist Book of Vital World Statistics*.

United Nations Economic Commission for Africa, Africa Hall, Post Office Box 3001, Addis Ababa, Ethiopia (Telephone Number in U.S. (800) 253-9646); *African Statistical Yearbook*.

The World Bank, 1818 H Street, NW, Washington, D.C. 20433 (202) 477-1234; *World Tables*.

KENYA - MARRIAGE RATES

Facts on File, 460 Park Avenue South, New York, New York 10016 (800) 443-8323; *The New Book of World Rankings*.

Statistical Office of the United Nations, Publishing Service, New York, New York 10017 (800) 253-9646; *Demographic Yearbook*.

KENYA - MEAT PRODUCTION - See KENYA - LIVESTOCK AND POULTRY

KENYA - MERCHANT SHIPPING

G.K. Hall and Company, 70 Lincoln Street, Boston, Massachusetts 02111 (617) 423-3990; *The World in Figures*.

Statistical Office of the United Nations, Publishing Service, New York, New York 10017 (800) 253-9646; *Statistical Yearbook*.

Times Books, 201 East 50th Street, New York, New York 10022 (212) 751-2600; *The Economist Book of Vital World Statistics*.

United Nations Economic Commission for Africa, Africa Hall, Post Office Box 3001, Addis Ababa, Ethiopia (Telephone Number in U.S. (800) 253-9646); *African Statistical Yearbook*.

U.S. Department of Transportation, Maritime Administration, 400 Seventh Street, SW, Washington, D.C. 20590 (202) 366-5807; *A Statistical Analysis of the World's Merchant Fleets*.

KENYA - MILITARY

G.K. Hall and Company, 70 Lincoln Street, Boston, Massachusetts 02111 (617) 423-3990; *The World in Figures*.

The International Institute for Strategic Studies, 23 Tavistock Street, London WC2E 7NQ, England; *The Military Balance*.

KENYA - MILK PRODUCTION - See KENYA - DAIRY PRODUCTS

KENYA - MILLET PRODUCTION - See KENYA - CROPS

KENYA - MINING AND MINERAL PRODUCTS

Facts on File, 460 Park Avenue South, New York, New York 10016 (800) 443-8323; *The New Book of World Rankings*.

G.K. Hall and Company, 70 Lincoln Street, Boston, Massachusetts 02111 (617) 423-3990; *The World in Figures*.

Statistical Office of the United Nations, Publishing Service, New York, New York 10017 (800) 253-9646; *Statistical Yearbook*.

United Nations Economic Commission for Africa, Africa Hall, Post Office Box 3001, Addis Ababa, Ethiopia (Telephone Number in U.S. (800) 253-9646); *African Statistical Yearbook*.

KENYA - MONEY EXCHANGE RATE

Euromonitor Publications Limited, 87-88 Turnmill Street, London EC1M 5QU, England; *International Marketing Data and Statistics*.

International Monetary Fund, 700 Nineteenth Street, NW, Washington, D.C. 20431 (202) 623-7000; *International Financial Statistics*.

Statistical Office of the United Nations, Publishing Service, New York, New York 10017 (800) 253-9646; *Statistical Yearbook*.

KENYA - MONEY RESERVES

Euromonitor Publications Limited, 87-88 Turnmill Street, London EC1M 5QU, England; *International Marketing Data and Statistics*.

KENYA - MONEY SUPPLY

African Development Bank, 01 BP 1387, Abidjan 01, Cote d'Ivoire; *Selected Statistics on Regional Member Countries*.

Euromonitor Publications Limited, 87-88 Turnmill Street, London EC1M 5QU, England; *International Marketing Data and Statistics*.

G.K. Hall and Company, 70 Lincoln Street, Boston, Massachusetts 02111 (617) 423-3990; *The World in Figures*.

International Monetary Fund, 700 Nineteenth Street, NW, Washington, D.C. 20431 (202) 623-7000; *International Financial Statistics*.

Statistical Office of the United Nations, Publishing Service, New York, New York 10017 (800) 253-9646; *Statistical Yearbook*.

The World Bank, 1818 H Street, NW, Washington, D.C. 20433 (202) 477-1234; *World Tables*.

KENYA - MONUMENTS AND HISTORICAL SITES

United Nations Educational, Scientific and Cultural Organization (UNESCO), 7 Place de Fontenoy, F-75700 Paris, France (Telephone Number in U.S. (212) 963-5981); *Statistical Yearbook*.

KENYA - MOTION PICTURES

Statistical Office of the United Nations, Publishing Service, New York, New York 10017 (800) 253-9646; *Statistical Yearbook*.

KENYA - MOTOR VEHICLES IN USE

G.K. Hall and Company, 70 Lincoln Street, Boston, Massachusetts 02111 (617) 423-3990; *The World in Figures*.

International Road Federation, 525 School Street, SW, Washington, D.C. 20024 (202) 554-2106; *World Road Statistics*.

Statistical Office of the United Nations, Publishing Service, New York, New York 10017 (800) 253-9646; *Statistical Yearbook*, and *Survey of Economic and Social Conditions in Africa*.

Times Books, 201 East 50th Street, New York, New York 10022 (212) 751-2600; *The Economist Book of Vital World Statistics*.

KENYA - MOTOR VEHICLE TAXES - See KENYA - TAXATION

KENYA - MUSEUMS

Facts on File, 460 Park Avenue South, New York, New York 10016 (800) 443-8323; *The New Book of World Rankings*.

United Nations Educational, Scientific and Cultural Organization (UNESCO), 7 Place de Fontenoy, F-75700 Paris, France (Telephone Number in U.S. (212) 963-5981); *Statistical Yearbook*.

KENYA - NATALITY - See KENYA - BIRTH RATE

KENYA - NATIONAL ACCOUNTS

African Development Bank, 01 BP 1387, Abidjan 01, Cote d'Ivoire; *Selected Statistics on Regional Member Countries*.

Central Bureau of Statistics, Ministry of Economic Planning and Development, Post Office Box 30266, Nairobi, Kenya; *Republic of Kenya Statistical Abstract*.

International Monetary Fund, 700 Nineteenth Street, NW, Washington, D.C. 20431 (202) 623-7000; *International Financial Statistics*.

Statistical Office of the United Nations, Publishing Service, New York, New York 10017 (800) 253-9646; *National Accounts Statistics*, and *Statistical Yearbook*.

United Nations Economic Commission for Africa, Africa Hall, Post Office Box 3001, Addis Ababa, Ethiopia (Telephone Number in U.S. (800) 253-9646); *African Statistical Yearbook*.

KENYA - NATIONAL INCOME

Facts on File, 460 Park Avenue South, New York, New York 10016 (800) 443-8323; *The New Book of World Rankings*.

G.K. Hall and Company, 70 Lincoln Street, Boston, Massachusetts 02111 (617) 423-3990; *The World in Figures*.

Statistical Office of the United Nations, Publishing Service, New York, New York 10017 (800) 253-9646; *Statistical Yearbook*.

KENYA - NATIONAL PRODUCT

Facts on File, 460 Park Avenue South, New York, New York 10016 (800) 443-8323; *The New Book of World Rankings*.

Statistical Office of the United Nations, Publishing Service, New York, New York 10017 (800) 253-9646; *Statistical Yearbook*.

KENYA - NATURAL GAS PRODUCTION - See KENYA - MINING AND MINERAL PRODUCTS

KENYA - NEWSPAPER PRODUCTION - See KENYA - FORESTRY AND FOREST PRODUCTS

KENYA - NEWSPRINT - See KENYA - FORESTRY AND FOREST PRODUCTS

KENYA - OATS PRODUCTION - See KENYA - CROPS

KENYA - OCCUPATIONS - See KENYA - LABOR FORCE

KENYA - PAPER - See KENYA - FORESTRY AND FOREST PRODUCTS

KENYA - PATENTS

Statistical Office of the United Nations, Publishing Service, New York, New York 10017 (800) 253-9646; *Statistical Yearbook.*

World Intellectual Property Organization, 34 Chemin des Colombettes, CH-1211 Geneva 20, Switzerland; *Industrial Property Statistics.*

KENYA - PEANUT PRODUCTION - See KENYA - CROPS

KENYA - PESTICIDE USE

Food and Agricultural Organization of the United Nations (FAO), Via delle Terme di Caracalla, 00100 Rome, Italy (Telephone Number in U.S. (202) 653-2400); *The State of Food and Agriculture.*

KENYA - PETROLEUM INDUSTRY

Facts on File, 460 Park Avenue South, New York, New York 10016 (800) 443-8323; *The New Book of World Rankings.*

Food and Agricultural Organization of the United Nations (FAO), Via delle Terme di Caracalla, 00100 Rome, Italy (Telephone Number in U.S. (202) 653-2400); *The State of Food and Agriculture.*

G.K. Hall and Company, 70 Lincoln Street, Boston, Massachusetts 02111 (617) 423-3990; *The World in Figures.*

International Monetary Fund, 700 Nineteenth Street, NW, Washington, D.C. 20431 (202) 623-7000; *International Financial Statistics.*

Statistical Office of the United Nations, Publishing Service, New York, New York 10017 (800) 253-9646; *Statistical Yearbook.*

KENYA - PIGS - See KENYA - LIVESTOCK AND POULTRY

KENYA - POPULATION

African Development Bank, 01 BP 1387, Abidjan 01, Cote d'Ivoire; *Selected Statistics on Regional Member Countries.*

Central Bureau of Statistics, Ministry of Economic Planning and Development, Post Office Box 30266, Nairobi, Kenya; *Republic of Kenya Statistical Abstract.*

The Economist Intelligence Unit, 111 West 57th Street, New York, New York 10019 (800) 938-4685; *The World Market Atlas.*

Euromonitor Publications Limited, 87-88 Turnmill Street, London EC1M 5QU, England; *International Marketing Data and Statistics.*

Facts on File, 460 Park Avenue South, New York, New York 10016 (800) 443-8323; *The New Book of World Rankings.*

Food and Agricultural Organization of the United Nations (FAO), Via delle Terme di Caracalla, 00100 Rome, Italy (Telephone Number in U.S. (202) 653-2400); *Production Yearbook.*

G.K. Hall and Company, 70 Lincoln Street, Boston, Massachusetts 02111 (617) 423-3990; *The World in Figures.*

International Labour Office, I.L.O. Publications, CH-1211, Geneva 22, Switzerland; *Yearbook of Labour Statistics.*

Statistical Office of the United Nations, Publishing Service, New York, New York 10017 (800) 253-9646; *Demographic Yearbook, Statistical Yearbook,* and *Survey of Economic and Social Conditions*

in Africa.

Times Books, 201 East 50th Street, New York, New York 10022 (212) 751-2600; *The Economist Book of Vital World Statistics.*

United Nations Educational, Scientific and Cultural Organization (UNESCO), 7 Place de Fontenoy, F-75700 Paris, France (Telephone Number in U.S. (212) 963-5981); *Statistical Yearbook.*

World Health Organization, Office of Publications, Avenue Appia, CH-1211 Geneva 27, Switzerland (Telephone Number in U.S. (518) 436-9686); *World Health Statistics Annual.*

KENYA - POST OFFICES

Facts on File, 460 Park Avenue South, New York, New York 10016 (800) 443-8323; *The New Book of World Rankings.*

KENYA - POTATO PRODUCTION - See KENYA - CROPS

KENYA - PRICES

Facts on File, 460 Park Avenue South, New York, New York 10016 (800) 443-8323; *The New Book of World Rankings.*

Food and Agricultural Organization of the United Nations (FAO), Via delle Terme di Caracalla, 00100 Rome, Italy (Telephone Number in U.S. (202) 653-2400); *Production Yearbook,* and *The State of Food and Agriculture.*

G.K. Hall and Company, 70 Lincoln Street, Boston, Massachusetts 02111 (617) 423-3990; *The World in Figures.*

International Labour Office, I.L.O. Publications, CH-1211, Geneva 22, Switzerland; *Yearbook of Labour Statistics.*

International Monetary Fund, 700 Nineteenth Street, NW, Washington, D.C. 20431 (202) 623-7000; *International Financial Statistics.*

United Nations Economic Commission for Africa, Africa Hall, Post Office Box 3001, Addis Ababa, Ethiopia (Telephone Number in U.S. (800) 253-9646); *African Statistical Yearbook.*

KENYA - PRINTING AND WRITING PAPER - See KENYA - FORESTRY AND FOREST PRODUCTS

KENYA - PRODUCTION

Facts on File, 460 Park Avenue South, New York, New York 10016 (800) 443-8323; *The New Book of World Rankings.*

G.K. Hall and Company, 70 Lincoln Street, Boston, Massachusetts 02111 (617) 423-3990; *The World in Figures.*

KENYA - PRODUCTIVITY

Euromonitor Publications Limited, 87-88 Turnmill Street, London EC1M 5QU, England; *International Marketing Data and Statistics.*

KENYA - PROPERTY TAXES - See KENYA - TAXATION

KENYA - PUBLIC FINANCE

Facts on File, 460 Park Avenue South, New York, New York 10016 (800) 443-8323; *The New Book of World Rankings.*

International Monetary Fund, 700 Nineteenth Street, NW, Washington, D.C. 20431 (202) 623-7000; *International Financial*

Statistics.

KENYA - RADIO BROADCASTING - See KENYA - BROADCASTING

KENYA - RAILWAYS

G.K. Hall and Company, 70 Lincoln Street, Boston, Massachusetts 02111 (617) 423-3990; *The World in Figures.*

Jane's Information Group, Sentinel House, 163 Brighton Road, Coulsdon, Surrey CR5 2NH, England (Telephone Number in U.S. (703) 683-3700); *Jane's World Railways.*

Statistical Office of the United Nations, Publishing Service, New York, New York 10017 (800) 253-9646; *Survey of Economic and Social Conditions in Africa.*

United Nations Economic Commission for Africa, Africa Hall, Post Office Box 3001, Addis Ababa, Ethiopia (Telephone Number in U.S. (800) 253-9646); *African Statistical Yearbook.*

KENYA - RELIGION

Facts on File, 460 Park Avenue South, New York, New York 10016 (800) 443-8323; *The New Book of World Rankings.*

KENYA - RENT PRICES

International Labour Office, I.L.O. Publications, CH-1211, Geneva 22, Switzerland; *Yearbook of Labour Statistics.*

KENYA - RETAIL TRADE

G.K. Hall and Company, 70 Lincoln Street, Boston, Massachusetts 02111 (617) 423-3990; *The World in Figures.*

Statistical Office of the United Nations, Publishing Service, New York, New York 10017 (800) 253-9646; *Statistical Yearbook.*

KENYA - RICE PRODUCTION - See KENYA - CROPS

KENYA - ROOT AND TUBER PRODUCTION - See KENYA - CROPS

KENYA - ROUNDWOOD PRODUCTION - See KENYA - FORESTRY AND FOREST PRODUCTS

KENYA - RUBBER PRODUCTION

Facts on File, 460 Park Avenue South, New York, New York 10016 (800) 443-8323; *The New Book of World Rankings.*

KENYA - SALT PRODUCTION

Statistical Office of the United Nations, Publishing Service, New York, New York 10017 (800) 253-9646; *Statistical Yearbook.*

KENYA - SAWNWOOD PRODUCTION - See KENYA - FORESTRY AND FOREST PRODUCTS

KENYA - SCIENCE AND TECHNOLOGY - EXPENDITURE FOR RESEARCH

Statistical Office of the United Nations, Publishing Service, New York, New York 10017 (800) 253-9646; *Statistical Yearbook.*

KENYA - SCIENTISTS AND TECHNICIANS

Statistical Office of the United Nations, Publishing Service, New York, New York 10017 (800) 253-9646; *Statistical Yearbook.*

United Nations Educational, Scientific and Cultural Organization (UNESCO), 7 Place de Fontenoy, F-75700 Paris, France (Telephone Number in U.S. (212) 963-5981); *Statistical Yearbook.*

KENYA - SENIOR CITIZENS

Facts on File, 460 Park Avenue South, New York, New York 10016 (800) 443-8323; *The New Book of World Rankings.*

KENYA - SESAME SEED PRODUCTION - See KENYA - CROPS

KENYA - SHEEP - See KENYA - LIVESTOCK AND POULTRY

KENYA - SILVER PRODUCTION AND CONSUMPTION - See KENYA - MINING AND MINERAL PRODUCTS

KENYA - SISAL PRODUCTION - See KENYA - CROPS

KENYA - SOCIAL DATA

African Development Bank, 01 BP 1387, Abidjan 01, Cote d'Ivoire; *Selected Statistics on Regional Member Countries.*

Facts on File, 460 Park Avenue South, New York, New York 10016 (800) 443-8323; *The New Book of World Rankings.*

G.K. Hall and Company, 70 Lincoln Street, Boston, Massachusetts 02111 (617) 423-3990; *The World in Figures.*

KENYA - STAMP TAXES AND DUTIES - See KENYA - TAXATION

KENYA - STATE BUDGET REVENUE AND EXPENDITURES

Euromonitor Publications Limited, 87-88 Turnmill Street, London EC1M 5QU, England; *International Marketing Data and Statistics.*

KENYA - STEEL PRODUCTION AND CONSUMPTION - See KENYA - MINING AND MINERAL PRODUCTS

KENYA - STOCKS - COMMODITY - MARKET PRICE - INDEX

Food and Agricultural Organization of the United Nations (FAO), Via delle Terme di Caracalla, 00100 Rome, Italy (Telephone Number in U.S. (202) 653-2400); *The State of Food and Agriculture.*

KENYA - SUGAR PRODUCTION AND CONSUMPTION - See KENYA - CROPS

KENYA - TAXATION

G.K. Hall and Company, 70 Lincoln Street, Boston, Massachusetts 02111 (617) 423-3990; *The World in Figures.*

International Monetary Fund, 700 Nineteenth Street, NW, Washington, D.C. 20431 (202) 623-7000; *Government Finance Statistics Yearbook.*

International Road Federation, 525 School Street, SW, Washington, D.C. 20024 (202) 554-2106; *World Road Statistics.*

The World Bank, 1818 H Street, NW, Washington, D.C. 20433 (202) 477-1234; *World Tables.*

KENYA - TEA - See KENYA - CROPS

KENYA - TELEGRAPH SERVICE

Statistical Office of the United Nations, Publishing Service, New York, New York 10017 (800) 253-9646; *Statistical Yearbook.*

KENYA - TELEPHONES IN USE

American Telephone and Telegraph Company, 26 Parsippany Road, Whippany, New Jersey 07981 (800) 338-4038; *The World's Telephones*.

G.K. Hall and Company, 70 Lincoln Street, Boston, Massachusetts 02111 (617) 423-3990; *The World in Figures*.

Statistical Office of the United Nations, Publishing Service, New York, New York 10017 (800) 253-9646; *Statistical Yearbook*.

KENYA - TELEVISION BROADCASTING - See KENYA - BROADCASTING

KENYA - TEXTILE INDUSTRY

G.K. Hall and Company, 70 Lincoln Street, Boston, Massachusetts 02111 (617) 423-3990; *The World in Figures*.

KENYA - TOBACCO PRODUCTION

Facts on File, 460 Park Avenue South, New York, New York 10016 (800) 443-8323; *The New Book of World Rankings*.

Statistical Office of the United Nations, Publishing Service, New York, New York 10017 (800) 253-9646; *Statistical Yearbook*.

KENYA - TOURISM

Central Bureau of Statistics, Ministry of Economic Planning and Development, Post Office Box 30266, Nairobi, Kenya; *Republic of Kenya Statistical Abstract*.

Facts on File, 460 Park Avenue South, New York, New York 10016 (800) 443-8323; *The New Book of World Rankings*.

G.K. Hall and Company, 70 Lincoln Street, Boston, Massachusetts 02111 (617) 423-3990; *The World in Figures*.

Statistical Office of the United Nations, Publishing Service, New York, New York 10017 (800) 253-9646; *Statistical Yearbook*.

Times Books, 201 East 50th Street, New York, New York 10022 (212) 751-2600; *The Economist Book of Vital World Statistics*.

United Nations Economic Commission for Africa, Africa Hall, Post Office Box 3001, Addis Ababa, Ethiopia (Telephone Number in U.S. (800) 253-9646); *African Statistical Yearbook*.

World Tourism Organization, Calle Capitan Haya 42, E-28020 Madrid, Spain; *Yearbook of Tourism Statistics*.

KENYA - TRACTORS IN USE

Statistical Office of the United Nations, Publishing Service, New York, New York 10017 (800) 253-9646; *Statistical Yearbook*.

KENYA - TRADE - See KENYA - FOREIGN TRADE

KENYA - TRADEMARKS AND SERVICE MARKS

Statistical Office of the United Nations, Publishing Service, New York, New York 10017 (800) 253-9646; *Statistical Yearbook*.

World Intellectual Property Organization, 34 Chemin des Colombettes, CH-1211 Geneva 20, Switzerland; *Industrial Property Statistics*.

KENYA - TRANSPORTATION AND COMMUNICATIONS

Central Bureau of Statistics, Ministry of Economic Planning and Development, Post Office Box 30266, Nairobi, Kenya; *Republic of Kenya Statistical Abstract*.

Facts on File, 460 Park Avenue South, New York, New York 10016 (800) 443-8323; *The New Book of World Rankings*.

G.K. Hall and Company, 70 Lincoln Street, Boston, Massachusetts 02111 (617) 423-3990; *The World in Figures*.

United Nations Economic Commission for Africa, Africa Hall, Post Office Box 3001, Addis Ababa, Ethiopia (Telephone Number in U.S. (800) 253-9646); *African Statistical Yearbook*.

KENYA - UNEMPLOYMENT

Euromonitor Publications Limited, 87-88 Turnmill Street, London EC1M 5QU, England; *International Marketing Data and Statistics*.

International Labour Office, I.L.O. Publications, CH-1211, Geneva 22, Switzerland; *Yearbook of Labour Statistics*.

KENYA - VITAL STATISTICS

Central Bureau of Statistics, Ministry of Economic Planning and Development, Post Office Box 30266, Nairobi, Kenya; *Republic of Kenya Statistical Abstract*.

Euromonitor Publications Limited, 87-88 Turnmill Street, London EC1M 5QU, England; *International Marketing Data and Statistics*.

G.K. Hall and Company, 70 Lincoln Street, Boston, Massachusetts 02111 (617) 423-3990; *The World in Figures*.

Statistical Office of the United Nations, Publishing Service, New York, New York 10017 (800) 253-9646; *Statistical Yearbook*.

World Health Organization, Office of Publications, Avenue Appia, CH-1211 Geneva 27, Switzerland (Telephone Number in U.S. (518) 436-9686); *World Health Statistics Annual*.

KENYA - WAGES

G.K. Hall and Company, 70 Lincoln Street, Boston, Massachusetts 02111 (617) 423-3990; *The World in Figures*.

International Labour Office, I.L.O. Publications, CH-1211, Geneva 22, Switzerland; *Yearbook of Labour Statistics*.

Statistical Office of the United Nations, Publishing Service, New York, New York 10017 (800) 253-9646; *Statistical Yearbook*.

KENYA - WEATHER

Facts on File, 460 Park Avenue South, New York, New York 10016 (800) 443-8323; *The New Book of World Rankings*.

G.K. Hall and Company, 70 Lincoln Street, Boston, Massachusetts 02111 (617) 423-3990; *The World in Figures*.

KENYA - WHEAT PRODUCTION AND PRICES - See KENYA - CROPS

KENYA - WHOLESALE TRADE

Statistical Office of the United Nations, Publishing Service, New York, New York 10017 (800) 253-9646; *Statistical Yearbook*.

KENYA - WINE PRODUCTION

Facts on File, 460 Park Avenue South, New York, New York 10016 (800) 443-8323; *The New Book of World Rankings.*

KENYA - WOOL PRODUCTION

Facts on File, 460 Park Avenue South, New York, New York 10016 (800) 443-8323; *The New Book of World Rankings.*

KENYA - YARN PRODUCTION

Statistical Office of the United Nations, Publishing Service, New York, New York 10017 (800) 253-9646; *Statistical Yearbook.*

KEOGH PLANS - PAYMENTS TO

U.S. Department of Commerce, Bureau of the Census, Suitland, Maryland 20233 (301) 763-4040; *Current Population Reports.*

U.S. Department of the Treasury, Internal Revenue Service, 1111 Constitution Avenue, NW, Washington, D.C. 20224 (202) 566-5000; *Statistics of Income, Individual Income Tax Returns.*

KIDNEY DISEASE AND INFECTIONS - DEATHS

U.S Department of Health and Human Services, National Center for Health Statistics, 3700 East-West Highway, Hyattsville, Maryland 20782 (301) 436-8500; *Vital Statistics of the United States, Monthly Vital Statistics Report,* and unpublished data.

Kiribati - National Statistical Office

Statistics Office, Ministry of Finance and Economic Planning, Post Office Box 67, Bariki, Tarawa, Kiribati.

Kiribati - Primary Statistics Source

Statistics Office, Ministry of Finance, P.O. Box 67, Bariki, Tarawa, Kiribati; *National Development Plan, 1983 - 1986.*

KIRIBATI - AGRICULTURE

Asian Development Bank, Post Office Box 789, Manila, 1099 Manila, Philippines; *Key Indicators of Developing Asian and Pacific Countries.*

Food and Agricultural Organization of the United Nations (FAO), Via delle Terme di Caracalla, 00100 Rome, Italy (Telephone Number in U.S. (202) 653-2400; *Production Yearbook, The State of Food and Agriculture,* and *Trade Yearbook.*

G.K. Hall and Company, 70 Lincoln Street, Boston, Massachusetts 02111 (617) 423-3990; *The World in Figures.*

KIRIBATI - AIRLINE SERVICE

G.K. Hall and Company, 70 Lincoln Street, Boston, Massachusetts 02111 (617) 423-3990; *The World in Figures.*

KIRIBATI - AREA AND DENSITY OF POPULATION

Food and Agricultural Organization of the United Nations (FAO), Via delle Terme di Caracalla, 00100 Rome, Italy (Telephone Number in U.S. (202) 653-2400; *The State of Food and Agriculture.*

G.K. Hall and Company, 70 Lincoln Street, Boston, Massachusetts 02111 (617) 423-3990; *The World in Figures.*

KIRIBATI - BALANCE OF PAYMENTS

G.K. Hall and Company, 70 Lincoln Street, Boston, Massachusetts 02111 (617) 423-3990; *The World in Figures.*

KIRIBATI - BANKING

Asian Development Bank, Post Office Box 789, 1099 Manila, Philippines; *Key Indicators of Developing Asian and Pacific Countries.*

G.K. Hall and Company, 70 Lincoln Street, Boston, Massachusetts 02111 (617) 423-3990; *The World in Figures.*

KIRIBATI - BONDS

Asian Development Bank, Post Office Box 789, 1099 Manila, Philippines; *Key Indicators of Developing Asian and Pacific Countries.*

G.K. Hall and Company, 70 Lincoln Street, Boston, Massachusetts 02111 (617) 423-3990; *The World in Figures.*

KIRIBATI - BOOK PRODUCTION

G.K. Hall and Company, 70 Lincoln Street, Boston, Massachusetts 02111 (617) 423-3990; *The World in Figures.*

KIRIBATI - BROADCASTING

Billboard Limited, Post Office Box 9027, 1006 AA Amsterdam, The Netherlands (Telephone Number in U.S. (212) 764-7300); *World Radio TV Handbook.*

G.K. Hall and Company, 70 Lincoln Street, Boston, Massachusetts 02111 (617) 423-3990; *The World in Figures.*

KIRIBATI - BUSINESS

G.K. Hall and Company, 70 Lincoln Street, Boston, Massachusetts 02111 (617) 423-3990; *The World in Figures.*

KIRIBATI - CALORIE SUPPLY

Asian Development Bank, Post Office Box 789, Manila, 1099 Manila, Philippines; *Key Indicators of Developing Asian and Pacific Countries.*

Food and Agricultural Organization of the United Nations (FAO), Via delle Terme di Caracalla, 00100 Rome, Italy (Telephone Number in U.S. (202) 653-2400); *The State of Food and Agriculture.*

KIRIBATI - CAPITAL INVESTMENT

Asian Development Bank, Post Office Box 789, 1099 Manila, Philippines; *Key Indicators of Developing Asian and Pacific Countries.*

KIRIBATI - CAPITAL REVENUE

Asian Development Bank, Post Office Box 789, 1099 Manila, Philippines; *Key Indicators of Developing Asian and Pacific Countries.*

KIRIBATI - CHEMICAL (ORGANIC) PRODUCTION - See KIRIBATI - MINING AND MINERAL PRODUCTS

KIRIBATI - CLASS STRUCTURE

G.K. Hall and Company, 70 Lincoln Street, Boston, Massachusetts 02111 (617) 423-3990; *The World in Figures*.

KIRIBATI - CLIMATE

G.K. Hall and Company, 70 Lincoln Street, Boston, Massachusetts 02111 (617) 423-3990; *The World in Figures*.

KIRIBATI - CLOTHING EXPORTS AND IMPORTS

South Pacific Commission, Post Box D5, Noumea Cedex, New Caledonia; *Statistical Bulletin of the South Pacific: Retail Price Indexes*.

KIRIBATI - COAL PRODUCTION - See KIRIBATI - MINING AND MINERAL PRODUCTS

KIRIBATI - COMMUNICATIONS

G.K. Hall and Company, 70 Lincoln Street, Boston, Massachusetts 02111 (617) 423-3990; *The World in Figures*.

KIRIBATI - CONSUMER PRICE INDEX

Asian Development Bank, Post Office Box 789, 1099 Manila, Philippines; *Key Indicators of Developing Asian and Pacific Countries*.

G.K. Hall and Company, 70 Lincoln Street, Boston, Massachusetts 02111 (617) 423-3990; *The World in Figures*.

KIRIBATI - CONSUMER PRICES

International Labour Office, I.L.O. Publications, CH-1211, Geneva 22, Switzerland; *Yearbook of Labour Statistics*.

KIRIBATI - CONSUMPTION

G.K. Hall and Company, 70 Lincoln Street, Boston, Massachusetts 02111 (617) 423-3990; *The World in Figures*.

South Pacific Commission, Post Box D5, Noumea Cedex, New Caledonia; *Statistical Bulletin of the South Pacific: Retail Price Indexes*.

KIRIBATI - CORN PRODUCTION - See KIRIBATI - CROPS

KIRIBATI - CORPORATE TAXES - See KIRIBATI - TAXATION

KIRIBATI - CROPS

Asian Development Bank, Post Office Box 789, 1099 Manila, Philippines; *Key Indicators of Developing Asian and Pacific Countries*.

Food and Agricultural Organization of the United Nations (FAO), Via delle Terme di Caracalla, 00100 Rome, Italy (Telephone Number in U.S. (202) 653-2400); *The State of Food and Agriculture*.

G.K. Hall and Company, 70 Lincoln Street, Boston, Massachusetts 02111 (617) 423-3990; *The World in Figures*.

KIRIBATI - CUSTOMS DUTIES

G.K. Hall and Company, 70 Lincoln Street, Boston, Massachusetts 02111 (617) 423-3990; *The World in Figures*.

KIRIBATI - DAIRY PRODUCTS

Food and Agricultural Organization of the United Nations (FAO), Via delle Terme di Caracalla, 00100 Rome, Italy (Telephone Number in U.S. (202) 653-2400); *The State of Food and Agriculture*.

KIRIBATI - DEATH RATES

G.K. Hall and Company, 70 Lincoln Street, Boston, Massachusetts 02111 (617) 423-3990; *The World in Figures*.

World Health Organization, Office of Publications, Avenue Appia, CH-1211 Geneva 27, Switzerland (Telephone Number in U.S. (518) 436-9686); *World Health Statistics Annual*.

KIRIBATI - DEFENSE EXPENDITURES

G.K. Hall and Company, 70 Lincoln Street, Boston, Massachusetts 02111 (617) 423-3990; *The World in Figures*.

KIRIBATI - DEMOGRAPHY

G.K. Hall and Company, 70 Lincoln Street, Boston, Massachusetts 02111 (617) 423-3990; *The World in Figures*.

KIRIBATI - DEVELOPMENT ASSISTANCE

Asian Development Bank, Post Office Box 789, 1099 Manila, Philippines; *Key Indicators of Developing Asian and Pacific Countries*.

G.K. Hall and Company, 70 Lincoln Street, Boston, Massachusetts 02111 (617) 423-3990; *The World in Figures*.

KIRIBATI - DISEASE

Asian Development Bank, Post Office Box 789, 1099 Manila, Philippines; *Key Indicators of Developing Asian and Pacific Countries*.

G.K. Hall and Company, 70 Lincoln Street, Boston, Massachusetts 02111 (617) 423-3990; *The World in Figures*.

World Health Organization, Office of Publications, Avenue Appia, CH-1211 Geneva 27, Switzerland (Telephone Number in U.S. (518) 436-9686); *World Health Statistics Annual*.

KIRIBATI - DOMESTIC PRODUCT

G.K. Hall and Company, 70 Lincoln Street, Boston, Massachusetts 02111 (617) 423-3990; *The World in Figures*.

KIRIBATI - ECONOMY

Asian Development Bank, Post Office Box 789, 1099 Manila, Philippines; *Key Indicators of Developing Asian and Pacific Countries*.

G.K. Hall and Company, 70 Lincoln Street, Boston, Massachusetts 02111 (617) 423-3990; *The World in Figures*.

KIRIBATI - EDUCATION

G.K. Hall and Company, 70 Lincoln Street, Boston, Massachusetts 02111 (617) 423-3990; *The World in Figures*.

United Nations Educational, Scientific and Cultural Organization (UNESCO), 7 Place de Fontenoy, F-75700 Paris, France (Telephone Number in U.S. (212) 963-5981); *Statistical Yearbook*.

KIRIBATI - EGG PRODUCTION AND CONSUMPTION - See KIRIBATI - DAIRY PRODUCTS

KIRIBATI - ELECTRICITY

Asian Development Bank, Post Office Box 789, 1099 Manila, Philippines; *Key Indicators of Developing Asian and Pacific Countries.*

Statistical Office of the United Nations, Publishing Service, New York, New York 10017 (800) 253-9646; *Electric Power in Asia and the Pacific.*

KIRIBATI - EMPLOYMENT

International Labour Office, I.L.O. Publications, CH-1211, Geneva 22, Switzerland; *Yearbook of Labour Statistics.*

KIRIBATI - ENERGY

Food and Agricultural Organization of the United Nations (FAO), Via delle Terme di Caracalla, 00100 Rome, Italy (Telephone Number in U.S. (202) 653-2400); *The State of Food and Agriculture.*

G.K. Hall and Company, 70 Lincoln Street, Boston, Massachusetts 02111 (617) 423-3990; *The World in Figures.*

Statistical Office of the United Nations, Publishing Service, New York, New York 10017 (800) 253-9646; *Statistical Yearbook.*

KIRIBATI - EXCHANGE RATES

Asian Development Bank, Post Office Box 789, 1099 Manila, Philippines; *Key Indicators of Developing Asian and Pacific Countries.*

KIRIBATI - EXPORTS

Asian Development Bank, Post Office Box 789, 1099 Manila, Philippines; *Key Indicators of Developing Asian and Pacific Countries.*

Food and Agricultural Organization of the United Nations (FAO), Via delle Terme di Caracalla, 00100 Rome, Italy (Telephone Number in U.S. (202) 653-2400); *The State of Food and Agriculture.*

G.K. Hall and Company, 70 Lincoln Street, Boston, Massachusetts 02111 (617) 423-3990; *The World in Figures.*

South Pacific Commission, Post Box D5, Noumea Cedex, New Caledonia; *Statistical Bulletin of the South Pacific: Overseas Trade.*

KIRIBATI - EXTERNAL FINANCING

Asian Development Bank, Post Office Box 789, 1099 Manila, Philippines; *Key Indicators of Developing Asian and Pacific Countries.*

KIRIBATI - EXTERNAL INDEBTEDNESS

Asian Development Bank, Post Office Box 789, 1099 Manila, Philippines; *Key Indicators of Developing Asian and Pacific Countries.*

KIRIBATI - EXTERNAL TRADE

Asian Development Bank, Post Office Box 789, 1099 Manila, Philippines; *Key Indicators of Developing Asian and Pacific Countries.*

Food and Agricultural Organization of the United Nations (FAO), Via delle Terme di Caracalla, 00100 Rome, Italy (Telephone Number in U.S. (202) 653-2400); *The State of Food and Agriculture,* and *Trade Yearbook.*

G.K. Hall and Company, 70 Lincoln Street, Boston, Massachusetts 02111 (617) 423-3990; *The World in Figures.*

KIRIBATI - FARM CROPS - See KIRIBATI - CROPS

KIRIBATI - FERTILIZER

Food and Agricultural Organization of the United Nations (FAO), Via delle Terme di Caracalla, 00100 Rome, Italy (Telephone Number in U.S. (202) 653-2400); *The State of Food and Agriculture.*

KIRIBATI - FINANCE

Asian Development Bank, Post Office Box 789, 1099 Manila, Philippines; *Key Indicators of Developing Asian and Pacific Countries.*

G.K. Hall and Company, 70 Lincoln Street, Boston, Massachusetts 02111 (617) 423-3990; *The World in Figures.*

KIRIBATI - FISHERIES

Food and Agricultural Organization of the United Nations (FAO), Via delle Terme di Caracalla, 00100 Rome, Italy (Telephone Number in U.S. (202) 653-2400); *The State of Food and Agriculture,* and *Yearbook of Fishery Statistics.*

KIRIBATI - FOOD

Food and Agricultural Organization of the United Nations (FAO), Via delle Terme di Caracalla, 00100 Rome, Italy (Telephone Number in U.S. (202) 653-2400); *Production Yearbook,* and *The State of Food and Agriculture.*

G.K. Hall and Company, 70 Lincoln Street, Boston, Massachusetts 02111 (617) 423-3990; *The World in Figures.*

South Pacific Commission, Post Box D5, Noumea Cedex, New Caledonia; *Statistical Bulletin of the South Pacific: Retail Price Indexes.*

KIRIBATI - FOREIGN AID

G.K. Hall and Company, 70 Lincoln Street, Boston, Massachusetts 02111 (617) 423-3990; *The World in Figures.*

KIRIBATI - FOREIGN TRADE

Asian Development Bank, Post Office Box 789, 1099 Manila, Philippines; *Key Indicators of Developing Asian and Pacific Countries.*

Food and Agricultural Organization of the United Nations (FAO), Via delle Terme di Caracalla, 00100 Rome, Italy (Telephone Number in U.S. (202) 653-2400); *The State of Food and Agriculture.*

G.K. Hall and Company, 70 Lincoln Street, Boston, Massachusetts 02111 (617) 423-3990; *The World in Figures.*

South Pacific Commission, Post Box D5, Noumea Cedex, New Caledonia; *Statistical Bulletin of the South Pacific: Overseas Trade.*

KIRIBATI - FORESTRY AND FOREST PRODUCTS

Food and Agricultural Organization of the United Nations (FAO), Via delle Terme di Caracalla, 00100 Rome, Italy (Telephone Number in U.S. (202) 653-2400); *The State of Food and Agriculture*.

G.K. Hall and Company, 70 Lincoln Street, Boston, Massachusetts 02111 (617) 423-3990; *The World in Figures*.

Statistical Office of the United Nations, Publishing Service, New York, New York 10017 (800) 253-9646; *Statistical Yearbook*.

KIRIBATI - GOVERNMENT

Asian Development Bank, Post Office Box 789, 1099 Manila, Philippines; *Key Indicators of Developing Asian and Pacific Countries*.

G.K. Hall and Company, 70 Lincoln Street, Boston, Massachusetts 02111 (617) 423-3990; *The World in Figures*.

KIRIBATI - GOVERNMENT EXPENDITURE

Asian Development Bank, Post Office Box 789, 1099 Manila, Philippines; *Key Indicators of Developing Asian and Pacific Countries*.

KIRIBATI - GOVERNMENT FINANCES

Asian Development Bank, Post Office Box 789, 1099 Manila, Philippines; *Key Indicators of Developing Asian and Pacific Countries*.

KIRIBATI - GOVERNMENT REVENUE

Asian Development Bank, Post Office Box 789, 1099 Manila, Philippines; *Key Indicators of Developing Asian and Pacific Countries*.

KIRIBATI - GRAIN PRODUCTION - See KIRIBATI - CROPS

KIRIBATI - GROSS DOMESTIC PRODUCT

Asian Development Bank, Post Office Box 789, 1099 Manila, Philippines; *Key Indicators of Developing Asian and Pacific Countries*.

G.K. Hall and Company, 70 Lincoln Street, Boston, Massachusetts 02111 (617) 423-3990; *The World in Figures*.

KIRIBATI - GROSS NATIONAL PRODUCT

Asian Development Bank, Post Office Box 789, 1099 Manila, Philippines; *Key Indicators of Developing Asian and Pacific Countries*.

KIRIBATI - HEALTH

G.K. Hall and Company, 70 Lincoln Street, Boston, Massachusetts 02111 (617) 423-3990; *The World in Figures*.

South Pacific Commission, Post Box D5, Noumea Cedex, New Caledonia; *Statistical Bulletin of the South Pacific: Retail Price Indexes*.

Statistical Office of the United Nations, Publishing Service, New York, New York 10017 (800) 253-9646; *Statistical Yearbook*.

World Health Organization, Office of Publications, Avenue Appia, CH-1211 Geneva 27, Switzerland (Telephone Number in U.S. (518) 436-9686); *World Health Statistics Annual*.

KIRIBATI - HIGHWAYS

G.K. Hall and Company, 70 Lincoln Street, Boston, Massachusetts 02111 (617) 423-3990; *The World in Figures*.

KIRIBATI - HOURS OF WORK - See KIRIBATI - EMPLOYMENT

KIRIBATI - HOUSING AND HOUSING UNITS

South Pacific Commission, Post Box D5, Noumea Cedex, New Caledonia; *Statistical Bulletin of the South Pacific: Retail Price Indexes*.

KIRIBATI - ILLITERATE POPULATION

G.K. Hall and Company, 70 Lincoln Street, Boston, Massachusetts 02111 (617) 423-3990; *The World in Figures*.

United Nations Educational, Scientific and Cultural Organization (UNESCO), 7 Place de Fontenoy, F-75700 Paris, France (Telephone Number in U.S. (212) 963-5981); *Statistical Yearbook*.

KIRIBATI - IMPORTS

Asian Development Bank, Post Office Box 789, 1099 Manila, Philippines; *Key Indicators of Developing Asian and Pacific Countries*.

Food and Agricultural Organization of the United Nations (FAO), Via delle Terme di Caracalla, 00100 Rome, Italy (Telephone Number in U.S. (202) 653-2400); *The State of Food and Agriculture*.

G.K. Hall and Company, 70 Lincoln Street, Boston, Massachusetts 02111 (617) 423-3990; *The World in Figures*.

South Pacific Commission, Post Box D5, Noumea Cedex, New Caledonia; *Statistical Bulletin of the South Pacific: Overseas Trade*.

KIRIBATI - INDUSTRY

G.K. Hall and Company, 70 Lincoln Street, Boston, Massachusetts 02111 (617) 423-3990; *The World in Figures*.

International Labour Office, I.L.O. Publications, CH-1211, Geneva 22, Switzerland; *Yearbook of Labour Statistics*.

KIRIBATI - INTERNATIONAL RESERVES EXCLUDING GOLD

Asian Development Bank, Post Office Box 789, 1099 Manila, Philippines; *Key Indicators of Developing Asian and Pacific Countries*.

KIRIBATI - INTERNATIONAL STATISTICS

Asian Development Bank, Post Office Box 789, 1099 Manila, Philippines; *Key Indicators of Developing Asian and Pacific Countries*.

KIRIBATI - LABOR FORCE

Food and Agricultural Organization of the United Nations (FAO), Via delle Terme di Caracalla, 00100 Rome, Italy (Telephone Number in U.S. (202) 653-2400); *The State of Food and Agriculture*.

G.K. Hall and Company, 70 Lincoln Street, Boston, Massachusetts 02111 (617) 423-3990; *The World in Figures*.

KIRIBATI - LABOR PRODUCTIVITY

International Labour Office, I.L.O. Publications, CH-1211, Geneva 22, Switzerland; *Yearbook of Labour Statistics*.

KIRIBATI - LAND USE

Food and Agricultural Organization of the United Nations (FAO), Via delle Terme di Caracalla, 00100 Rome, Italy (Telephone Number in U.S. (202) 653-2400); *Production Yearbook*.

G.K. Hall and Company, 70 Lincoln Street, Boston, Massachusetts 02111 (617) 423-3990; *The World in Figures*.

KIRIBATI - LIBRARIES

United Nations Educational, Scientific and Cultural Organization (UNESCO), 7 Place de Fontenoy, F-75700 Paris, France (Telephone Number in U.S. (212) 963-5981); *Statistical Yearbook*.

KIRIBATI - LIVESTOCK AND POULTRY

Food and Agricultural Organization of the United Nations (FAO), Via delle Terme di Caracalla, 00100 Rome, Italy (Telephone Number in U.S. (202) 653-2400); *Production Yearbook*, and *The State of Food and Agriculture*.

G.K. Hall and Company, 70 Lincoln Street, Boston, Massachusetts 02111 (617) 423-3990; *The World in Figures*.

KIRIBATI - LIVING LEVELS

G.K. Hall and Company, 70 Lincoln Street, Boston, Massachusetts 02111 (617) 423-3990; *The World in Figures*.

KIRIBATI - MANUFACTURING

Asian Development Bank, Post Office Box 789, 1099 Manila, Philippines; *Key Indicators of Developing Asian and Pacific Countries*.

G.K. Hall and Company, 70 Lincoln Street, Boston, Massachusetts 02111 (617) 423-3990; *The World in Figures*.

KIRIBATI - MEAT PRODUCTION - See KIRIBATI - LIVESTOCK AND POULTRY

KIRIBATI - MERCHANT SHIPPING

G.K. Hall and Company, 70 Lincoln Street, Boston, Massachusetts 02111 (617) 423-3990; *The World in Figures*.

KIRIBATI - MILITARY

G.K. Hall and Company, 70 Lincoln Street, Boston, Massachusetts 02111 (617) 423-3990; *The World in Figures*.

KIRIBATI - MINING AND MINERAL PRODUCTS

Asian Development Bank, Post Office Box 789, 1099 Manila, Philippines; *Key Indicators of Developing Asian and Pacific Countries*.

G.K. Hall and Company, 70 Lincoln Street, Boston, Massachusetts 02111 (617) 423-3990; *The World in Figures*.

KIRIBATI - MONEY SUPPLY

Asian Development Bank, Post Office Box 789, 1099 Manila, Philippines; *Key Indicators of Developing Asian and Pacific Countries*.

G.K. Hall and Company, 70 Lincoln Street, Boston, Massachusetts 02111 (617) 423-3990; *The World in Figures*.

KIRIBATI - MOTOR VEHICLES IN USE

G.K. Hall and Company, 70 Lincoln Street, Boston, Massachusetts 02111 (617) 423-3990; *The World in Figures*.

KIRIBATI - NATIONAL ACCOUNTS

Statistical Office of the United Nations, Publishing Service, New York, New York 10017 (800) 253-9646; *National Accounts Statistics*.

KIRIBATI - NATIONAL INCOME

G.K. Hall and Company, 70 Lincoln Street, Boston, Massachusetts 02111 (617) 423-3990; *The World in Figures*.

KIRIBATI - NEWSPAPER PRODUCTION - See KIRIBATI - FORESTRY AND FOREST PRODUCTS

KIRIBATI - OCCUPATIONS - See KIRIBATI - LABOR FORCE

KIRIBATI - PESTICIDE USE

Food and Agricultural Organization of the United Nations (FAO), Via delle Terme di Caracalla, 00100 Rome, Italy (Telephone Number in U.S. (202) 653-2400); *The State of Food and Agriculture*.

KIRIBATI - PETROLEUM INDUSTRY

Asian Development Bank, Post Office Box 789, 1099 Manila, Philippines; *Key Indicators of Developing Asian and Pacific Countries*.

Food and Agricultural Organization of the United Nations (FAO), Via delle Terme di Caracalla, 00100 Rome, Italy (Telephone Number in U.S. (202) 653-2400); *The State of Food and Agriculture*.

G.K. Hall and Company, 70 Lincoln Street, Boston, Massachusetts 02111 (617) 423-3990; *The World in Figures*.

KIRIBATI - POPULATION

Asian Development Bank, Post Office Box 789, 1099 Manila, Philippines; *Key Indicators of Developing Asian and Pacific Countries*.

Food and Agricultural Organization of the United Nations (FAO), Via delle Terme di Caracalla, 00100 Rome, Italy (Telephone Number in U.S. (202) 653-2400); *Production Yearbook*.

G.K. Hall and Company, 70 Lincoln Street, Boston, Massachusetts 02111 (617) 423-3990; *The World in Figures*.

International Labour Office, I.L.O. Publications, CH-1211, Geneva 22, Switzerland; *Yearbook of Labour Statistics*.

World Health Organization, Office of Publications, Avenue Appia, CH-1211 Geneva 27, Switzerland (Telephone Number in U.S. (518) 436-9686); *World Health Statistics Annual*.

KIRIBATI - POWER PRODUCTION INDUSTRY

Statistical Office of the United Nations, Publishing Service, New York, New York 10017 (800) 253-9646; *Electric Power in Asia and the Pacific.*

KIRIBATI - PRICES

Asian Development Bank, Post Office Box 789, 1099 Manila, Philippines; *Key Indicators of Developing Asian and Pacific Countries.*

Food and Agricultural Organization of the United Nations (FAO), Via delle Terme di Caracalla, 00100 Rome, Italy (Telephone Number in U.S. (202) 653-2400); *Production Yearbook,* and *The State of Food and Agriculture.*

G.K. Hall and Company, 70 Lincoln Street, Boston, Massachusetts 02111 (617) 423-3990; *The World in Figures.*

International Labour Office, I.L.O. Publications, CH-1211, Geneva 22, Switzerland; *Yearbook of Labour Statistics.*

South Pacific Commission, Post Box D5, Noumea Cedex, New Caledonia; *Statistical Bulletin of the South Pacific: Overseas Trade,* and *Statistical Bulletin of the South Pacific: Retail Price Indexes.*

KIRIBATI - PRODUCTION

G.K. Hall and Company, 70 Lincoln Street, Boston, Massachusetts 02111 (617) 423-3990; *The World in Figures.*

KIRIBATI - RAILWAYS

G.K. Hall and Company, 70 Lincoln Street, Boston, Massachusetts 02111 (617) 423-3990; *The World in Figures.*

KIRIBATI - RETAIL TRADE

G.K. Hall and Company, 70 Lincoln Street, Boston, Massachusetts 02111 (617) 423-3990; *The World in Figures.*

KIRIBATI - RICE PRODUCTION - See KIRIBATI - CROPS

KIRIBATI - SOCIAL DATA

Asian Development Bank, Post Office Box 789, 1099 Manila, Philippines; *Key Indicators of Developing Asian and Pacific Countries.*

G.K. Hall and Company, 70 Lincoln Street, Boston, Massachusetts 02111 (617) 423-3990; *The World in Figures.*

KIRIBATI - STOCKS - COMMODITY - MARKET PRICE - INDEX

Food and Agricultural Organization of the United Nations (FAO), Via delle Terme di Caracalla, 00100 Rome, Italy (Telephone Number in U.S. (202) 653-2400); *The State of Food and Agriculture.*

KIRIBATI - TAXATION

G.K. Hall and Company, 70 Lincoln Street, Boston, Massachusetts 02111 (617) 423-3990; *The World in Figures.*

KIRIBATI - TELEPHONES IN USE

American Telephone and Telegraph Company, 26 Parsippany Road, Whippany, New Jersey 07981 (800) 338-4038; *The World's Telephones.*

G.K. Hall and Company, 70 Lincoln Street, Boston, Massachusetts 02111 (617) 423-3990; *The World in Figures.*

KIRIBATI - TEXTILE INDUSTRY

G.K. Hall and Company, 70 Lincoln Street, Boston, Massachusetts 02111 (617) 423-3990; *The World in Figures.*

KIRIBATI - THEATRE

United Nations Educational, Scientific and Cultural Organization (UNESCO), 7 Place de Fontenoy, F-75700 Paris, France (Telephone Number in U.S. (212) 963-5981); *Statistical Yearbook.*

KIRIBATI - TOBACCO PRODUCTION

South Pacific Commission, Post Box D5, Noumea Cedex, New Caledonia; *Statistical Bulletin of the South Pacific: Retail Price Indexes.*

KIRIBATI - TOURISM

G.K. Hall and Company, 70 Lincoln Street, Boston, Massachusetts 02111 (617) 423-3990; *The World in Figures.*

World Tourism Organization, Calle Capitan Haya 42, E-28020 Madrid, Spain; *Yearbook of Tourism Statistics.*

KIRIBATI - TRADE - See KIRIBATI - FOREIGN TRADE

KIRIBATI - TRANSPORTATION AND COMMUNICATIONS

G.K. Hall and Company, 70 Lincoln Street, Boston, Massachusetts 02111 (617) 423-3990; *The World in Figures.*

South Pacific Commission, Post Box D5, Noumea Cedex, New Caledonia; *Statistical Bulletin of the South Pacific: Retail Price Indexes.*

KIRIBATI - UNEMPLOYMENT

International Labour Office, I.L.O. Publications, CH-1211, Geneva 22, Switzerland; *Yearbook of Labour Statistics.*

KIRIBATI - UTILITIES

Statistical Office of the United Nations, Publishing Service, New York, New York 10017 (800) 253-9646; *Electric Power in Asia and the Pacific.*

KIRIBATI - VITAL STATISTICS

G.K. Hall and Company, 70 Lincoln Street, Boston, Massachusetts 02111 (617) 423-3990; *The World in Figures.*

KIRIBATI - WAGES

G.K. Hall and Company, 70 Lincoln Street, Boston, Massachusetts 02111 (617) 423-3990; *The World in Figures.*

International Labour Office, I.L.O. Publications, CH-1211, Geneva 22, Switzerland; *Yearbook of Labour Statistics.*

KIRIBATI - WEATHER

G.K. Hall and Company, 70 Lincoln Street, Boston, Massachusetts 02111 (617) 423-3990; *The World in Figures*.

KIRIBATI - WHOLESALE PRICES - INDEX NUMBERS

Asian Development Bank, Post Office Box 789, 1099 Manila, Philippines; *Key Indicators of Developing Asian and Pacific Countries*.

KIWI FRUIT

U.S. Department of Agriculture, Economic Research Service, Fourteenth Street and Independence Avenue, SW, Washington, D.C. 20005-4789 (202) 219-1504; unpublished data.

U.S. Department of Agriculture, National Agricultural Statistics Service, Fourteenth Street and Independence Avenue, S.W. Washington, D.C. 20250 (202) 219-1504; *Noncitrus Fruits and Nuts*.

Korea (Democratic People's Republic Of) - National Statistical Office

Central Bureau of Statistics, Pyongyang, Democratic People's Republic of Korea.

Korea (Democratic People's Republic Of) - Primary Statistics Source

Superintendent of Documents, U.S. Government Printing Office, Washington, D.C. 20402; *Area Handbook for North Korea*.

KOREA (DEMOCRATIC PEOPLE'S REPUBLIC OF) - AGRICULTURE

Asian Development Bank, Post Office Box 789, 1099 Manila, Philippines; *Key Indicators of Developing Asian and Pacific Countries*.

Facts on File, 460 Park Avenue South, New York, New York 10016 (800) 443-8323; *The New Book of World Rankings*.

Food and Agricultural Organization of the United Nations (FAO), Via delle Terme di Caracalla, 00100 Rome, Italy (Telephone Number in U.S. (202) 653-2400); *The State of Food and Agriculture*, and *Trade Yearbook*.

G.K. Hall and Company, 70 Lincoln Street, Boston, Massachusetts 02111 (617) 423-3990; *The World in Figures*.

Statistical Office of the United Nations, Publishing Service, New York, New York 10017 (800) 253-9646; *Statistical Yearbook*.

Times Books, 201 East 50th Street, New York, New York 10022 (212) 751-2600; *The Economist Book of Vital World Statistics*.

KOREA (DEMOCRATIC PEOPLE'S REPUBLIC OF) - AIRLINE SERVICE

The Economist Intelligence Unit (Asia) Limited, 10th Floor, Luk Kwok Centre, 72 Gloucester Road, Wanchai, Hong Kong (Phone Number in U.S. (800) 938-4685); *Asian Market Atlas*.

Facts on File, 460 Park Avenue South, New York, New York 10016 (800) 443-8323; *The New Book of World Rankings*.

G.K. Hall and Company, 70 Lincoln Street, Boston, Massachusetts 02111 (617) 423-3990; *The World in Figures*.

Times Books, 201 East 50th Street, New York, New York 10022 (212) 751-2600; *The Economist Book of Vital World Statistics*.

KOREA (DEMOCRATIC PEOPLE'S REPUBLIC OF) - ALUMINUM PRODUCTION AND CONSUMPTION - See KOREA (DEMOCRATIC PEOPLE'S REPUBLIC OF) - MINING AND MINERAL PRODUCTS

KOREA (DEMOCRATIC PEOPLE'S REPUBLIC OF) - ANIMAL HEALTH

Food and Agricultural Organization of the United Nations (FAO), Via delle Terme di Caracalla, 00100 Rome, Italy (Telephone Number in U.S. (202) 653-2400); *Animal Health Yearbook*.

KOREA (DEMOCRATIC PEOPLE'S REPUBLIC OF) - AREA AND DENSITY OF POPULATION

Euromonitor Publications Limited, 87-88 Turnmill Street, London EC1M 5QU, England; *International Marketing Data and Statistics*.

Facts on File, 460 Park Avenue South, New York, New York 10016 (800) 443-8323; *The New Book of World Rankings*.

Food and Agricultural Organization of the United Nations (FAO), Via delle Terme di Caracalla, 00100 Rome, Italy (Telephone Number in U.S. (202) 653-2400); *The State of Food and Agriculture*.

G.K. Hall and Company, 70 Lincoln Street, Boston, Massachusetts 02111 (617) 423-3990; *The World in Figures*.

Statistical Office of the United Nations, Publishing Service, New York, New York 10017 (800) 253-9646; *Statistical Yearbook*.

Times Books, 201 East 50th Street, New York, New York 10022 (212) 751-2600; *The Economist Book of Vital World Statistics*.

KOREA (DEMOCRATIC PEOPLE'S REPUBLIC OF) - ARMS EXPORTS AND IMPORTS

U.S. Arms Control and Disarmament Agency, 320 Twenty-first Street, NW, Washington, D.C. 20451 (202) 647-8677; *World Military Expenditures and Arms Transfers*.

KOREA (DEMOCRATIC PEOPLE'S REPUBLIC OF) - BALANCE OF PAYMENTS

The Economist Intelligence Unit, 111 West 57th Street, New York, New York 10019 (800) 938-4685; *The World Market Atlas*.

G.K. Hall and Company, 70 Lincoln Street, Boston, Massachusetts 02111 (617) 423-3990; *The World in Figures*.

Times Books, 201 East 50th Street, New York, New York 10022 (212) 751-2600; *The Economist Book of Vital World Statistics*.

KOREA (DEMOCRATIC PEOPLE'S REPUBLIC OF) - BANKING

Asian Development Bank, Post Office Box 789, 1099 Manila, Philippines; *Key Indicators of Developing Asian and Pacific Countries*.

Facts on File, 460 Park Avenue South, New York, New York 10016 (800) 443-8323; *The New Book of World Rankings*.

G.K. Hall and Company, 70 Lincoln Street, Boston, Massachusetts 02111 (617) 423-3990; *The World in Figures*.

KOREA (DEMOCRATIC PEOPLE'S REPUBLIC OF) - BARLEY PRODUCTION - See KOREA (DEMOCRATIC PEOPLE'S REPUBLIC OF) - CROPS

KOREA (DEMOCRATIC PEOPLE'S REPUBLIC OF) - BEER PRODUCTION

Facts on File, 460 Park Avenue South, New York, New York 10016 (800) 443-8323; *The New Book of World Rankings*.

KOREA (DEMOCRATIC PEOPLE'S REPUBLIC OF) - BIRTH RATE

The Economist Intelligence Unit (Asia) Limited, 10th Floor, Luk Kwok Centre, 72 Gloucester Road, Wanchai, Hong Kong (Phone Number in U.S. (800) 938-4685); *Asian Market Atlas*.

Facts on File, 460 Park Avenue South, New York, New York 10016 (800) 443-8323; *The New Book of World Rankings*.

Statistical Office of the United Nations, Publishing Service, New York, New York 10017 (800) 253-9646; *Demographic Yearbook*, and *Statistical Yearbook*.

Times Books, 201 East 50th Street, New York, New York 10022 (212) 751-2600; *The Economist Book of Vital World Statistics*.

KOREA (DEMOCRATIC PEOPLE'S REPUBLIC OF) - BONDS

Asian Development Bank, Post Office Box 789, 1099 Manila, Philippines; *Key Indicators of Developing Asian and Pacific Countries*.

G.K. Hall and Company, 70 Lincoln Street, Boston, Massachusetts 02111 (617) 423-3990; *The World in Figures*.

KOREA (DEMOCRATIC PEOPLE'S REPUBLIC OF) - BOOK PRODUCTION

G.K. Hall and Company, 70 Lincoln Street, Boston, Massachusetts 02111 (617) 423-3990; *The World in Figures*.

KOREA (DEMOCRATIC PEOPLE'S REPUBLIC OF) - BROADCASTING

Billboard Limited, Post Office Box 9027, 1006 AA Amsterdam, The Netherlands (Telephone Number in U.S. (212) 764-7300); *World Radio TV Handbook*.

The Economist Intelligence Unit (Asia) Limited, 10th Floor, Luk Kwok Centre, 72 Gloucester Road, Wanchai, Hong Kong (Phone Number in U.S. (800) 938-4685); *Asian Market Atlas*.

Facts on File, 460 Park Avenue South, New York, New York 10016 (800) 443-8323; *The New Book of World Rankings*.

G.K. Hall and Company, 70 Lincoln Street, Boston, Massachusetts 02111 (617) 423-3990; *The World in Figures*.

Times Books, 201 East 50th Street, New York, New York 10022 (212) 751-2600; *The Economist Book of Vital World Statistics*.

KOREA (DEMOCRATIC PEOPLE'S REPUBLIC OF) - BUSINESS

G.K. Hall and Company, 70 Lincoln Street, Boston, Massachusetts 02111 (617) 423-3990; *The World in Figures*.

KOREA (DEMOCRATIC PEOPLE'S REPUBLIC OF) - CABBAGE PRODUCTION - See KOREA (DEMOCRATIC PEOPLE'S REPUBLIC OF) - CROPS

KOREA (DEMOCRATIC PEOPLE'S REPUBLIC OF) - CALORIE SUPPLY

Asian Development Bank, Post Office Box 789, 1099 Manila, Philippines; *Key Indicators of Developing Asian and Pacific Countries*.

Food and Agricultural Organization of the United Nations (FAO), Via delle Terme di Caracalla, 00100 Rome, Italy (Telephone Number in U.S. (202) 653-2400); *The State of Food and Agriculture*.

KOREA (DEMOCRATIC PEOPLE'S REPUBLIC OF) - CAPITAL INVESTMENT

Asian Development Bank, Post Office Box 789, 1099 Manila, Philippines; *Key Indicators of Developing Asian and Pacific Countries*.

KOREA (DEMOCRATIC PEOPLE'S REPUBLIC OF) - CATTLE - See KOREA (DEMOCRATIC PEOPLE'S REPUBLIC OF) - LIVESTOCK AND POULTRY

KOREA (DEMOCRATIC PEOPLE'S REPUBLIC OF) - CEMENT PRODUCTION - See KOREA (DEMOCRATIC PEOPLE'S REPUBLIC OF) - MINING AND MINERAL PRODUCTS

KOREA (DEMOCRATIC PEOPLE'S REPUBLIC OF) - CHEMICAL (ORGANIC) PRODUCTION - See KOREA (DEMOCRATIC PEOPLE'S REPUBLIC OF) - MINING AND MINERAL PRODUCTS

KOREA (DEMOCRATIC PEOPLE'S REPUBLIC OF) - CHESTNUT PRODUCTION - See KOREA (DEMOCRATIC PEOPLE'S REPUBLIC OF) - CROPS

KOREA (DEMOCRATIC PEOPLE'S REPUBLIC OF) - CHICKENS - See KOREA (DEMOCRATIC PEOPLE'S REPUBLIC OF) - LIVESTOCK AND POULTRY

KOREA (DEMOCRATIC PEOPLE'S REPUBLIC OF) - CIGARETTE PRODUCTION - See KOREA (DEMOCRATIC PEOPLE'S REPUBLIC OF) - TOBACCO PRODUCTION

KOREA (DEMOCRATIC PEOPLE'S REPUBLIC OF) - CLASS STRUCTURE

G.K. Hall and Company, 70 Lincoln Street, Boston, Massachusetts 02111 (617) 423-3990; *The World in Figures*.

KOREA (DEMOCRATIC PEOPLE'S REPUBLIC OF) - CLIMATE

Facts on File, 460 Park Avenue South, New York, New York 10016 (800) 443-8323; *The New Book of World Rankings*.

G.K. Hall and Company, 70 Lincoln Street, Boston, Massachusetts 02111 (617) 423-3990; *The World in Figures*.

KOREA (DEMOCRATIC PEOPLE'S REPUBLIC OF) - COAL PRODUCTION - See KOREA (DEMOCRATIC PEOPLE'S REPUBLIC OF) - MINING AND MINERAL PRODUCTS

KOREA (DEMOCRATIC PEOPLE'S REPUBLIC OF) - COFFEE PRODUCTION AND CONSUMPTION - See KOREA (DEMOCRATIC PEOPLE'S REPUBLIC OF) - CROPS

KOREA (DEMOCRATIC PEOPLE'S REPUBLIC OF) - COKE OVEN COKE PRODUCTION AND CONSUMPTION - See KOREA (DEMOCRATIC PEOPLE'S REPUBLIC OF) - MINING AND MINERAL PRODUCTS

KOREA (DEMOCRATIC PEOPLE'S REPUBLIC OF) - COMMUNICATIONS

G.K. Hall and Company, 70 Lincoln Street, Boston, Massachusetts 02111 (617) 423-3990; *The World in Figures*.

KOREA (DEMOCRATIC PEOPLE'S REPUBLIC OF) - CONSTRUCTION INDUSTRY

Facts on File, 460 Park Avenue South, New York, New York 10016 (800) 443-8323; *The New Book of World Rankings*.

KOREA (DEMOCRATIC PEOPLE'S REPUBLIC OF) - CONSUMER PRICE INDEX

Asian Development Bank, Post Office Box 789, 1099 Manila, Philippines; *Key Indicators of Developing Asian and Pacific Countries*.

G.K. Hall and Company, 70 Lincoln Street, Boston, Massachusetts 02111 (617) 423-3990; *The World in Figures*.

KOREA (DEMOCRATIC PEOPLE'S REPUBLIC OF) - CONSUMPTION

G.K. Hall and Company, 70 Lincoln Street, Boston, Massachusetts 02111 (617) 423-3990; *The World in Figures*.

KOREA (DEMOCRATIC PEOPLE'S REPUBLIC OF) - COPPER AND COPPER ORE - See KOREA (DEMOCRATIC PEOPLE'S REPUBLIC OF) - MINING AND MINERAL PRODUCTS

KOREA (DEMOCRATIC PEOPLE'S REPUBLIC OF) - CORN PRODUCTION - See KOREA (DEMOCRATIC PEOPLE'S REPUBLIC OF) - CROPS

KOREA (DEMOCRATIC PEOPLE'S REPUBLIC OF) - CORPORATE TAXES - See (KOREAN - DEMOCRATIC PEOPLE'S REPUBLIC OF) - TAXATION

KOREA (DEMOCRATIC PEOPLE'S REPUBLIC OF) - COTTON - See KOREA (DEMOCRATIC PEOPLE'S REPUBLIC OF) - CROPS

KOREA (DEMOCRATIC PEOPLE'S REPUBLIC OF) - CRIME

International Criminal Police Organization (INTERPOL), 26 rue Armengaud, 92210 Saint Cloud, France; *International Crime Statistics*.

Yale University Press, Yale Station, New Haven, Connecticut 06520 (203) 432-0940; *Violence and Crime in Cross-National Perspective*.

KOREA (DEMOCRATIC PEOPLE'S REPUBLIC OF) - CROPS

Asian Development Bank, Post Office Box 789, 1099 Manila, Philippines; *Key Indicators of Developing Asian and Pacific Countries*.

Facts on File, 460 Park Avenue South, New York, New York 10016 (800) 443-8323; *The New Book of World Rankings*.

Food and Agricultural Organization of the United Nations (FAO), Via delle Terme di Caracalla, 00100 Rome, Italy (Telephone Number in U.S. (202) 653-2400); *Production Yearbook*, and *The State of Food and Agriculture*.

Statistical Office of the United Nations, Publishing Service, New York, New York 10017 (800) 253-9646; *Statistical Yearbook*.

KOREA (DEMOCRATIC PEOPLE'S REPUBLIC OF) - CUSTOMS DUTIES

G.K. Hall and Company, 70 Lincoln Street, Boston, Massachusetts 02111 (617) 423-3990; *The World in Figures*.

KOREA (DEMOCRATIC PEOPLE'S REPUBLIC OF) - DAIRY PRODUCTS

Facts on File, 460 Park Avenue South, New York, New York 10016 (800) 443-8323; *The New Book of World Rankings*.

Food and Agricultural Organization of the United Nations (FAO), Via delle Terme di Caracalla, 00100 Rome, Italy (Telephone Number in U.S. (202) 653-2400); *The State of Food and Agriculture*.

Statistical Office of the United Nations, Publishing Service, New York, New York 10017 (800) 253-9646; *Statistical Yearbook*.

KOREA (DEMOCRATIC PEOPLE'S REPUBLIC OF) - DEATH RATES

The Economist Intelligence Unit (Asia) Limited, 10th Floor, Luk Kwok Centre, 72 Gloucester Road, Wanchai, Hong Kong (Phone Number in U.S. (800) 938-4685); *Asian Market Atlas*.

G.K. Hall and Company, 70 Lincoln Street, Boston, Massachusetts 02111 (617) 423-3990; *The World in Figures*.

Statistical Office of the United Nations, Publishing Service, New York, New York 10017 (800) 253-9646; *Statistical Yearbook*.

Times Books, 201 East 50th Street, New York, New York 10022 (212) 751-2600; *The Economist Book of Vital World Statistics*.

KOREA (DEMOCRATIC PEOPLE'S REPUBLIC OF) - DEFENSE EXPENDITURES

G.K. Hall and Company, 70 Lincoln Street, Boston, Massachusetts 02111 (617) 423-3990; *The World in Figures*.

U.S. Arms Control and Disarmament Agency, 320 Twenty-first Street, NW, Washington, D.C. 20451 (202) 647-8677; *World Military Expenditures and Arms Transfers*.

KOREA (DEMOCRATIC PEOPLE'S REPUBLIC OF) - DEMOGRAPHY

The Economist Intelligence Unit, 111 West 57th Street, New York, New York 10019 (800) 938-4685; *The World Market Atlas*.

The Economist Intelligence Unit (Asia) Limited, 10th Floor, Luk Kwok Centre, 72 Gloucester Road, Wanchai, Hong Kong (Phone Number in U.S. (800) 938-4685); *Asian Market Atlas*.

Facts on File, 460 Park Avenue South, New York, New York 10016 (800) 443-8323; *The New Book of World Rankings*.

G.K. Hall and Company, 70 Lincoln Street, Boston, Massachusetts 02111 (617) 423-3990; *The World in Figures*.

KOREA (DEMOCRATIC PEOPLE'S REPUBLIC OF) - DEVELOPMENT ASSISTANCE

Asian Development Bank, Post Office Box 789, 1099 Manila, Philippines; *Key Indicators of Developing Asian and Pacific Countries*.

G.K. Hall and Company, 70 Lincoln Street, Boston, Massachusetts 02111 (617) 423-3990; *The World in Figures*.

KOREA (DEMOCRATIC PEOPLE'S REPUBLIC OF) - DIAMOND PRODUCTION - See KOREA (DEMOCRATIC PEOPLE'S REPUBLIC OF) - MINING AND MINERAL PRODUCTS

KOREA (DEMOCRATIC PEOPLE'S REPUBLIC OF) - DISEASE

G.K. Hall and Company, 70 Lincoln Street, Boston, Massachusetts 02111 (617) 423-3990; *The World in Figures*.

KOREA (DEMOCRATIC PEOPLE'S REPUBLIC OF) - DIVORCE RATES

Facts on File, 460 Park Avenue South, New York, New York 10016 (800) 443-8323; *The New Book of World Rankings*.

Statistical Office of the United Nations, Publishing Service, New York, New York 10017 (800) 253-9646; *Demographic Yearbook*.

KOREA (DEMOCRATIC PEOPLE'S REPUBLIC OF) - DOMESTIC PRODUCT

G.K. Hall and Company, 70 Lincoln Street, Boston, Massachusetts 02111 (617) 423-3990; *The World in Figures*.

KOREA (DEMOCRATIC PEOPLE'S REPUBLIC OF) - ECONOMY

Asian Development Bank, Post Office Box 789, 1099 Manila, Philippines; *Key Indicators of Developing Asian and Pacific Countries*.

Euromonitor Publications Limited, 87-88 Turnmill Street, London EC1M 5QU, England; *International Marketing Data and Statistics*.

Facts on File, 460 Park Avenue South, New York, New York 10016 (800) 443-8323; *The New Book of World Rankings*.

G.K. Hall and Company, 70 Lincoln Street, Boston, Massachusetts 02111 (617) 423-3990; *The World in Figures*.

KOREA (DEMOCRATIC PEOPLE'S REPUBLIC OF) - EDUCATION

The Economist Intelligence Unit, 111 West 57th Street, New York, New York 10019 (800) 938-4685; *The World Market Atlas*.

The Economist Intelligence Unit (Asia) Limited, 10th Floor, Luk Kwok Centre, 72 Gloucester Road, Wanchai, Hong Kong (Phone Number in U.S. (800) 938-4685); *Asian Market Atlas*.

Facts on File, 460 Park Avenue South, New York, New York 10016 (800) 443-8323; *The New Book of World Rankings*.

G.K. Hall and Company, 70 Lincoln Street, Boston, Massachusetts 02111 (617) 423-3990; *The World in Figures*.

Times Books, 201 East 50th Street, New York, New York 10022 (212) 751-2600; *The Economist Book of Vital World Statistics*.

KOREA (DEMOCRATIC PEOPLE'S REPUBLIC OF) - EGG PRODUCTION AND CONSUMPTION - See JAPAN - DAIRY PRODUCTS

KOREA (DEMOCRATIC PEOPLE'S REPUBLIC OF) - EGGPLANT PRODUCTION - See KOREA (DEMOCRATIC PEOPLE'S REPUBLIC OF) - CROPS

KOREA (DEMOCRATIC PEOPLE'S REPUBLIC OF) - ELECTRICITY

Asian Development Bank, Post Office Box 789, 1099 Manila, Philippines; *Key Indicators of Developing Asian and Pacific Countries*.

Facts on File, 460 Park Avenue South, New York, New York 10016 (800) 443-8323; *The New Book of World Rankings*.

Statistical Office of the United Nations, Publishing Service, New York, New York 10017 (800) 253-9646; *Electric Power in Asia and the Pacific*, and *Statistical Yearbook*.

Times Books, 201 East 50th Street, New York, New York 10022 (212) 751-2600; *The Economist Book of Vital World Statistics*.

KOREA (DEMOCRATIC PEOPLE'S REPUBLIC OF) - EMPLOYMENT

Euromonitor Publications Limited, 87-88 Turnmill Street, London EC1M 5QU, England; *International Marketing Data and Statistics*.

Facts on File, 460 Park Avenue South, New York, New York 10016 (800) 443-8323; *The New Book of World Rankings*.

KOREA (DEMOCRATIC PEOPLE'S REPUBLIC OF) - ENERGY

Facts on File, 460 Park Avenue South, New York, New York 10016 (800) 443-8323; *The New Book of World Rankings*.

Food and Agricultural Organization of the United Nations (FAO), Via delle Terme di Caracalla, 00100 Rome, Italy (Telephone Number in U.S. (202) 653-2400); *The State of Food and Agriculture*.

G.K. Hall and Company, 70 Lincoln Street, Boston, Massachusetts 02111 (617) 423-3990; *The World in Figures*.

Statistical Office of the United Nations, Publishing Service, New York, New York 10017 (800) 253-9646; *Statistical Yearbook*, and *World Energy Supplies*.

Times Books, 201 East 50th Street, New York, New York 10022 (212) 751-2600; *The Economist Book of Vital World Statistics*.

KOREA (DEMOCRATIC PEOPLE'S REPUBLIC OF) - EXCHANGE RATES

Asian Development Bank, Post Office Box 789, 1099 Manila, Philippines; *Key Indicators of Developing Asian and Pacific Countries*.

The Economist Intelligence Unit (Asia) Limited, 10th Floor, Luk Kwok Centre, 72 Gloucester Road, Wanchai, Hong Kong (Phone Number in U.S. (800) 938-4685); *Asian Market Atlas*.

Euromonitor Publications Limited, 87-88 Turnmill Street, London EC1M 5QU, England; *International Marketing Data and Statistics*.

KOREA (DEMOCRATIC PEOPLE'S REPUBLIC OF) - EXPORTS

American Automobile Manufacturers Association, 1401 H Street, NW, Suite 900, Washington, D.C. 20005 (202) 326-5500; *World Motor Vehicle Data*.

Asian Development Bank, Post Office Box 789, 1099 Manila, Philippines; *Key Indicators of Developing Asian and Pacific Countries*.

The Economist Intelligence Unit, 111 West 57th Street, New York, New York 10019 (800) 938-4685; *The World Market Atlas*.

The Economist Intelligence Unit (Asia) Limited, 10th Floor, Luk Kwok Centre, 72 Gloucester Road, Wanchai, Hong Kong (Phone Number in U.S. (800) 938-4685); *Asian Market Atlas*.

Euromonitor Publications Limited, 87-88 Turnmill Street, London EC1M 5QU, England; *International Marketing Data and Statistics.*

Food and Agricultural Organization of the United Nations (FAO), Via delle Terme di Caracalla, 00100 Rome, Italy (Telephone Number in U.S. (202) 653-2400); *The State of Food and Agriculture.*

G.K. Hall and Company, 70 Lincoln Street, Boston, Massachusetts 02111 (617) 423-3990; *The World in Figures.*

International Monetary Fund, 700 Nineteenth Street, NW, Washington, D.C. 20431 (202) 623-7000; *Direction of Trade Statistics.*

Times Books, 201 East 50th Street, New York, New York 10022 (212) 751-2600; *The Economist Book of Vital World Statistics.*

KOREA (DEMOCRATIC PEOPLE'S REPUBLIC OF) - EXTERNAL FINANCING

Asian Development Bank, Post Office Box 789, 1099 Manila, Philippines; *Key Indicators of Developing Asian and Pacific Countries.*

KOREA (DEMOCRATIC PEOPLE'S REPUBLIC OF) - EXTERNAL INDEBTEDNESS

Asian Development Bank, Post Office Box 789, 1099 Manila, Philippines; *Key Indicators of Developing Asian and Pacific Countries.*

KOREA (DEMOCRATIC PEOPLE'S REPUBLIC OF) - EXTERNAL TRADE

Asian Development Bank, Post Office Box 789, 1099 Manila, Philippines; *Key Indicators of Developing Asian and Pacific Countries.*

Food and Agricultural Organization of the United Nations (FAO), Via delle Terme di Caracalla, 00100 Rome, Italy (Telephone Number in U.S. (202) 653-2400); *The State of Food and Agriculture,* and *Trade Yearbook.*

G.K. Hall and Company, 70 Lincoln Street, Boston, Massachusetts 02111 (617) 423-3990; *The World in Figures.*

KOREA (DEMOCRATIC PEOPLE'S REPUBLIC OF) - FARM CROPS - See KOREA (DEMOCRATIC PEOPLE'S REPUBLIC OF) - CROPS

KOREA (DEMOCRATIC PEOPLE'S REPUBLIC OF) - FEMALE WORKING POPULATION - See KOREA (DEMOCRATIC PEOPLE'S REPUBLIC OF) - EMPLOYMENT

KOREA (DEMOCRATIC PEOPLE'S REPUBLIC OF) - FERTILITY RATES

The Economist Intelligence Unit (Asia) Limited, 10th Floor, Luk Kwok Centre, 72 Gloucester Road, Wanchai, Hong Kong (Phone Number in U.S. (800) 938-4685); *Asian Market Atlas.*

Facts on File, 460 Park Avenue South, New York, New York 10016 (800) 443-8323; *The New Book of World Rankings.*

Times Books, 201 East 50th Street, New York, New York 10022 (212) 751-2600; *The Economist Book of Vital World Statistics.*

KOREA (DEMOCRATIC PEOPLE'S REPUBLIC OF) - FERTILIZER

Food and Agricultural Organization of the United Nations (FAO), Via delle Terme di Caracalla, 00100 Rome, Italy (Telephone Number in U.S. (202) 653-2400); *The State of Food and Agriculture.*

Statistical Office of the United Nations, Publishing Service, New York, New York 10017 (800) 253-9646; *Statistical Yearbook.*

KOREA (DEMOCRATIC PEOPLE'S REPUBLIC OF) - FETAL MORTALITY

Statistical Office of the United Nations, Publishing Service, New York, New York 10017 (800) 253-9646; *Demographic Yearbook.*

KOREA (DEMOCRATIC PEOPLE'S REPUBLIC OF) - FIBRE PRODUCTION - See KOREA (DEMOCRATIC PEOPLE'S REPUBLIC OF) - TEXTILE INDUSTRY

KOREA (DEMOCRATIC PEOPLE'S REPUBLIC OF) - FINANCE

Asian Development Bank, Post Office Box 789, 1099 Manila, Philippines; *Key Indicators of Developing Asian and Pacific Countries.*

Facts on File, 460 Park Avenue South, New York, New York 10016 (800) 443-8323; *The New Book of World Rankings.*

Food and Agricultural Organization of the United Nations (FAO), Via delle Terme di Caracalla, 00100 Rome, Italy (Telephone Number in U.S. (202) 653-2400); *The State of Food and Agriculture.*

G.K. Hall and Company, 70 Lincoln Street, Boston, Massachusetts 02111 (617) 423-3990; *The World in Figures.*

Statistical Office of the United Nations, Publishing Service, New York, New York 10017 (800) 253-9646; *Statistical Yearbook.*

KOREA (DEMOCRATIC PEOPLE'S REPUBLIC OF) - FISHERIES

Facts on File, 460 Park Avenue South, New York, New York 10016 (800) 443-8323; *The New Book of World Rankings.*

Food and Agricultural Organization of the United Nations (FAO), Via delle Terme di Caracalla, 00100 Rome, Italy (Telephone Number in U.S. (202) 653-2400); *The State of Food and Agriculture,* and *Yearbook of Fishery Statistics.*

KOREA (DEMOCRATIC PEOPLE'S REPUBLIC OF) - FOOD

Food and Agricultural Organization of the United Nations (FAO), Via delle Terme di Caracalla, 00100 Rome, Italy (Telephone Number in U.S. (202) 653-2400); *Production Yearbook,* and *The State of Food and Agriculture.*

G.K. Hall and Company, 70 Lincoln Street, Boston, Massachusetts 02111 (617) 423-3990; *The World in Figures.*

KOREA (DEMOCRATIC PEOPLE'S REPUBLIC OF) - FOREIGN AID

G.K. Hall and Company, 70 Lincoln Street, Boston, Massachusetts 02111 (617) 423-3990; *The World in Figures.*

KOREA (DEMOCRATIC PEOPLE'S REPUBLIC OF) - FOREIGN INDEBTEDNESS

Euromonitor Publications Limited, 87-88 Turnmill Street, London EC1M 5QU, England; *The Pacific Basin: An Economic Handbook.*

KOREA (DEMOCRATIC PEOPLE'S REPUBLIC OF) - FOREIGN TRADE

Asian Development Bank, Post Office Box 789, 1099 Manila, Philippines; *Key Indicators of Developing Asian and Pacific Countries.*

The Economist Intelligence Unit (Asia) Limited, 10th Floor, Luk Kwok Centre, 72 Gloucester Road, Wanchai, Hong Kong (Phone Number in U.S. (800) 938-4685); *Asian Market Atlas.*

Euromonitor Publications Limited, 87-88 Turnmill Street, London EC1M 5QU, England; *International Marketing Data and Statistics.*

Facts on File, 460 Park Avenue South, New York, New York 10016 (800) 443-8323; *The New Book of World Rankings.*

Food and Agricultural Organization of the United Nations (FAO), Via delle Terme di Caracalla, 00100 Rome, Italy (Telephone Number in U.S. (202) 653-2400); *The State of Food and Agriculture.*

G.K. Hall and Company, 70 Lincoln Street, Boston, Massachusetts 02111 (617) 423-3990; *The World in Figures.*

KOREA (DEMOCRATIC PEOPLE'S REPUBLIC OF) - FORESTRY AND FOREST PRODUCTS

American Forest and Paper Association, 1250 Connecticut Avenue, NW, Washington, D.C. 20036 (202) 463-2455; *Wood Pulp and Fiber Statistics.*

The Economist Intelligence Unit (Asia) Limited, 10th Floor, Luk Kwok Centre, 72 Gloucester Road, Wanchai, Hong Kong (Phone Number in U.S. (800) 938-4685); *Asian Market Atlas.*

Facts on File, 460 Park Avenue South, New York, New York 10016 (800) 443-8323; *The New Book of World Rankings.*

Food and Agricultural Organization of the United Nations (FAO), Via delle Terme di Caracalla, 00100 Rome, Italy (Telephone Number in U.S. (202) 653-2400); *The State of Food and Agriculture,* and *Yearbook of Forest Products.*

G.K. Hall and Company, 70 Lincoln Street, Boston, Massachusetts 02111 (617) 423-3990; *The World in Figures.*

Statistical Office of the United Nations, Publishing Service, New York, New York 10017 (800) 253-9646; *Statistical Yearbook.*

United Nations Educational, Scientific and Cultural Organization (UNESCO), 7 Place de Fontenoy, F-75700 Paris, France (Telephone Number in U.S. (212) 963-5981); *Statistical Yearbook.*

KOREA (DEMOCRATIC PEOPLE'S REPUBLIC OF) - GARLIC PRODUCTION - See KOREA (DEMOCRATIC PEOPLE'S REPUBLIC OF) - CROPS

KOREA (DEMOCRATIC PEOPLE'S REPUBLIC OF) - GAS PRODUCTION - See KOREA (DEMOCRATIC PEOPLE'S REPUBLIC OF) - MINING AND MINERAL PRODUCTS

KOREA (DEMOCRATIC PEOPLE'S REPUBLIC OF) - GENERAL MORTALITY

Statistical Office of the United Nations, Publishing Service, New York, New York 10017 (800) 253-9646; *Demographic Yearbook.*

KOREA (DEMOCRATIC PEOPLE'S REPUBLIC OF) - GEOGRAPHIC DATA

Facts on File, 460 Park Avenue South, New York, New York 10016 (800) 443-8323; *The New Book of World Rankings.*

KOREA (DEMOCRATIC PEOPLE'S REPUBLIC OF) - GOATS - See KOREA (DEMOCRATIC PEOPLE'S REPUBLIC OF) - LIVESTOCK AND POULTRY

KOREA (DEMOCRATIC PEOPLE'S REPUBLIC OF) - GOLD PRODUCTION AND CONSUMPTION - See KOREA (DEMOCRATIC PEOPLE'S REPUBLIC OF) - MINING AND MINERAL PRODUCTS

KOREA (DEMOCRATIC PEOPLE'S REPUBLIC OF) - GOVERNMENT

Asian Development Bank, Post Office Box 789, 1099 Manila, Philippines; *Key Indicators of Developing Asian and Pacific Countries.*

G.K. Hall and Company, 70 Lincoln Street, Boston, Massachusetts 02111 (617) 423-3990; *The World in Figures.*

KOREA (DEMOCRATIC PEOPLE'S REPUBLIC OF) - GOVERNMENT EXPENDITURE

Asian Development Bank, Post Office Box 789, 1099 Manila, Philippines; *Key Indicators of Developing Asian and Pacific Countries.*

KOREA (DEMOCRATIC PEOPLE'S REPUBLIC OF) - GOVERNMENT FINANCES

Asian Development Bank, Post Office Box 789, 1099 Manila, Philippines; *Key Indicators of Developing Asian and Pacific Countries.*

KOREA (DEMOCRATIC PEOPLE'S REPUBLIC OF) - GOVERNMENT REVENUE

Asian Development Bank, Post Office Box 789, 1099 Manila, Philippines; *Key Indicators of Developing Asian and Pacific Countries.*

KOREA (DEMOCRATIC PEOPLE'S REPUBLIC OF) - GRAIN PRODUCTION - See KOREA (DEMOCRATIC PEOPLE'S REPUBLIC OF) - CROPS

KOREA (DEMOCRATIC PEOPLE'S REPUBLIC OF) - GREEN PEPPER AND CHILIE PRODUCTION - See KOREA (DEMOCRATIC PEOPLE'S REPUBLIC OF) - CROPS

KOREA (DEMOCRATIC PEOPLE'S REPUBLIC OF) - GROSS DOMESTIC PRODUCT

Asian Development Bank, Post Office Box 789, 1099 Manila, Philippines; *Key Indicators of Developing Asian and Pacific Countries.*

The Economist Intelligence Unit, 111 West 57th Street, New York, New York 10019 (800) 938-4685; *The World Market Atlas.*

The Economist Intelligence Unit (Asia) Limited, 10th Floor, Luk Kwok Centre, 72 Gloucester Road, Wanchai, Hong Kong (Phone Number in U.S. (800) 938-4685); *Asian Market Atlas.*

Euromonitor Publications Limited, 87-88 Turnmill Street, London EC1M 5QU, England; *International Marketing Data and Statistics.*

Facts on File, 460 Park Avenue South, New York, New York 10016 (800) 443-8323; *The New Book of World Rankings.*

G.K. Hall and Company, 70 Lincoln Street, Boston, Massachusetts 02111 (617) 423-3990; *The World in Figures.*

Times Books, 201 East 50th Street, New York, New York 10022 (212) 751-2600; *The Economist Book of Vital World Statistics.*

KOREA (DEMOCRATIC PEOPLE'S REPUBLIC OF) - GROSS NATIONAL PRODUCT

Asian Development Bank, Post Office Box 789, 1099 Manila, Philippines; *Key Indicators of Developing Asian and Pacific Countries.*

Euromonitor Publications Limited, 87-88 Turnmill Street, London EC1M 5QU, England; *International Marketing Data and Statistics.*

U.S. Arms Control and Disarmament Agency, 320 Twenty-first Street, NW, Washington, D.C. 20451 (202) 647-8677; *World Military Expenditures and Arms Transfers.*

KOREA (DEMOCRATIC PEOPLE'S REPUBLIC OF) - HEALTH

The Economist Intelligence Unit (Asia) Limited, 10th Floor, Luk Kwok Centre, 72 Gloucester Road, Wanchai, Hong Kong (Phone Number in U.S. (800) 938-4685); *Asian Market Atlas.*

Facts on File, 460 Park Avenue South, New York, New York 10016 (800) 443-8323; *The New Book of World Rankings.*

G.K. Hall and Company, 70 Lincoln Street, Boston, Massachusetts 02111 (017) 423-3990; *The World in Figures.*

Times Books, 201 East 50th Street, New York, New York 10022 (212) 751-2600; *The Economist Book of Vital World Statistics.*

KOREA (DEMOCRATIC PEOPLE'S REPUBLIC OF) - HEMP FIBRE PRODUCTION - See KOREA (DEMOCRATIC PEOPLE'S REPUBLIC OF) - TEXTILE INDUSTRY

KOREA (DEMOCRATIC PEOPLE'S REPUBLIC OF) - HIDE PRODUCTION

Food and Agricultural Organization of the United Nations (FAO), Via delle Terme di Caracalla, 00100 Rome, Italy (Telephone Number in U.S. (202) 653-2400); *Production Yearbook.*

KOREA (DEMOCRATIC PEOPLE'S REPUBLIC OF) - HIGHWAYS

The Economist Intelligence Unit (Asia) Limited, 10th Floor, Luk Kwok Centre, 72 Gloucester Road, Wanchai, Hong Kong (Phone Number in U.S. (800) 938-4685); *Asian Market Atlas.*

G.K. Hall and Company, 70 Lincoln Street, Boston, Massachusetts 02111 (617) 423-3990; *The World in Figures.*

International Road Federation, 525 School Street, SW, Washington, D.C. 20024 (202) 554-2106; *World Road Statistics.*

KOREA (DEMOCRATIC PEOPLE'S REPUBLIC OF) - HORSES - See KOREA (DEMOCRATIC PEOPLE'S REPUBLIC OF) - LIVESTOCK AND POULTRY

KOREA (DEMOCRATIC PEOPLE'S REPUBLIC OF) - HOURS OF WORK - See KOREA (DEMOCRATIC PEOPLE'S REPUBLIC OF) - EMPLOYMENT

KOREA (DEMOCRATIC PEOPLE'S REPUBLIC OF) - HOUSING AND HOUSING UNITS

Facts on File, 460 Park Avenue South, New York, New York 10016 (800) 443-8323; *The New Book of World Rankings.*

KOREA (DEMOCRATIC PEOPLE'S REPUBLIC OF) - ILLITERATE POPULATION

The Economist Intelligence Unit, 111 West 57th Street, New York, New York 10019 (800) 938-4685; *The World Market Atlas.*

G.K. Hall and Company, 70 Lincoln Street, Boston, Massachusetts 02111 (617) 423-3990; *The World in Figures.*

KOREA (DEMOCRATIC PEOPLE'S REPUBLIC OF) - IMPORTS

American Automobile Manufacturers Association, 1401 H Street, NW, Suite 900, Washington, D.C. 20005 (202) 326-5500; *World Motor Vehicle Data.*

Asian Development Bank, Post Office Box 789, 1099 Manila, Philippines; *Key Indicators of Developing Asian and Pacific Countries.*

The Economist Intelligence Unit, 111 West 57th Street, New York, New York 10019 (800) 938-4685; *The World Market Atlas.*

The Economist Intelligence Unit (Asia) Limited, 10th Floor, Luk Kwok Centre, 72 Gloucester Road, Wanchai, Hong Kong (Phone Number in U.S. (800) 938-4685); *Asian Market Atlas.*

Euromonitor Publications Limited, 87-88 Turnmill Street, London EC1M 5QU, England; *International Marketing Data and Statistics.*

Food and Agricultural Organization of the United Nations (FAO), Via delle Terme di Caracalla, 00100 Rome, Italy (Telephone Number in U.S. (202) 653-2400); *The State of Food and Agriculture.*

G.K. Hall and Company, 70 Lincoln Street, Boston, Massachusetts 02111 (617) 423-3990; *The World in Figures.*

International Monetary Fund, 700 Nineteenth Street, NW, Washington, D.C. 20431 (202) 623-7000; *Direction of Trade Statistics.*

KOREA (DEMOCRATIC PEOPLE'S REPUBLIC OF) - INDUSTRIAL METALS PRODUCTION - See KOREA (DEMOCRATIC PEOPLE'S REPUBLIC OF) - MINING AND MINERAL PRODUCTS

KOREA (DEMOCRATIC PEOPLE'S REPUBLIC OF) - INDUSTRY

Euromonitor Publications Limited, 87-88 Turnmill Street, London EC1M 5QU, England; *International Marketing Data and Statistics.*

Facts on File, 460 Park Avenue South, New York, New York 10016 (800) 443-8323; *The New Book of World Rankings.*

G.K. Hall and Company, 70 Lincoln Street, Boston, Massachusetts 02111 (617) 423-3990; *The World in Figures.*

World Intellectual Property Organization, 34 Chemin des Colombettes, CH-1211 Geneva 20, Switzerland; *Industrial Property Statistics.*

KOREA (DEMOCRATIC PEOPLE'S REPUBLIC OF) - INFANT
AND MATERNAL MORTALITY RATE

The Economist Intelligence Unit (Asia) Limited, 10th Floor, Luk
Kwok Centre, 72 Gloucester Road, Wanchai, Hong Kong (Phone
Number in U.S. (800) 938-4685); *Asian Market Atlas*.

Statistical Office of the United Nations, Publishing Service, New
York, New York 10017 (800) 253-9646; *Demographic Yearbook*.

Times Books, 201 East 50th Street, New York, New York 10022 (212)
751-2600; *The Economist Book of Vital World Statistics*.

KOREA (DEMOCRATIC PEOPLE'S REPUBLIC OF) -
INTERNATIONAL RESERVES EXCLUDING GOLD

Asian Development Bank, Post Office Box 789, 1099 Manila,
Philippines; *Key Indicators of Developing Asian and Pacific
Countries*.

KOREA (DEMOCRATIC PEOPLE'S REPUBLIC OF) -
INTERNATIONAL STATISTICS

Asian Development Bank, Post Office Box 789, 1099 Manila,
Philippines; *Key Indicators of Developing Asian and Pacific
Countries*.

KOREA (DEMOCRATIC PEOPLE'S REPUBLIC OF) - IRON
ORE - See KOREA (DEMOCRATIC PEOPLE'S REPUBLIC OF) - MINING
AND MINERAL PRODUCTS

KOREA (DEMOCRATIC PEOPLE'S REPUBLIC OF) -
IRRIGATION

Euromonitor Publications Limited, 87-88 Turnmill Street, London
EC1M 5QU, England; *International Marketing Data and Statistics*.

KOREA (DEMOCRATIC PEOPLE'S REPUBLIC OF) - LABOR FORCE

The Economist Intelligence Unit (Asia) Limited, 10th Floor, Luk
Kwok Centre, 72 Gloucester Road, Wanchai, Hong Kong (Phone
Number in U.S. (800) 938-4685); *Asian Market Atlas*.

Euromonitor Publications Limited, 87-88 Turnmill Street, London
EC1M 5QU, England; *International Marketing Data and Statistics*.

Facts on File, 460 Park Avenue South, New York, New York 10016
(800) 443-8323; *The New Book of World Rankings*.

Food and Agricultural Organization of the United Nations (FAO),
Via delle Terme di Caracalla, 00100 Rome, Italy (Telephone Number
in U.S. (202) 653-2400); *The State of Food and Agriculture*.

G.K. Hall and Company, 70 Lincoln Street, Boston, Massachusetts
02111 (617) 423-3990; *The World in Figures*.

KOREA (DEMOCRATIC PEOPLE'S REPUBLIC OF) - LAND USE

Euromonitor Publications Limited, 87-88 Turnmill Street, London
EC1M 5QU, England; *International Marketing Data and Statistics*.

Food and Agricultural Organization of the United Nations (FAO),
Via delle Terme di Caracalla, 00100 Rome, Italy (Telephone Number
in U.S. (202) 653-2400); *Production Yearbook*.

G.K. Hall and Company, 70 Lincoln Street, Boston, Massachusetts
02111 (617) 423-3990; *The World in Figures*.

KOREA (DEMOCRATIC PEOPLE'S REPUBLIC OF) - LEAD AND LEAD
ORE PRODUCTION AND CONSUMPTION - See KOREA (DEMOCRATIC
PEOPLE'S REPUBLIC OF) - MINING AND MINERAL PRODUCTS

KOREA (DEMOCRATIC PEOPLE'S REPUBLIC OF) - LIBRARIES

Facts on File, 460 Park Avenue South, New York, New York 10016
(800) 443-8323; *The New Book of World Rankings*.

KOREA (DEMOCRATIC PEOPLE'S REPUBLIC OF) - LIFE
EXPECTANCY

The Economist Intelligence Unit (Asia) Limited, 10th Floor, Luk
Kwok Centre, 72 Gloucester Road, Wanchai, Hong Kong (Phone
Number in U.S. (800) 938-4685); *Asian Market Atlas*.

KOREA (DEMOCRATIC PEOPLE'S REPUBLIC OF) -
LIGNITE PRODUCTION - See KOREA (DEMOCRATIC PEOPLE'S
REPUBLIC OF) - MINING AND MINERAL PRODUCTS

KOREA (DEMOCRATIC PEOPLE'S REPUBLIC OF) -
LIVESTOCK AND POULTRY

Euromonitor Publications Limited, 87-88 Turnmill Street, London
EC1M 5QU, England; *International Marketing Data and Statistics*.

Facts on File, 460 Park Avenue South, New York, New York 10016
(800) 443-8323; *The New Book of World Rankings*.

Food and Agricultural Organization of the United Nations (FAO), Via
delle Terme di Caracalla, 00100 Rome, Italy (Telephone Number in
U.S. (202) 653-2400); *Production Yearbook*, and *The State of Food
and Agriculture*.

G.K. Hall and Company, 70 Lincoln Street, Boston, Massachusetts
02111 (617) 423-3990; *The World in Figures*.

Statistical Office of the United Nations, Publishing Service, New
York, New York 10017 (800) 253-9646; *Statistical Yearbook*.

KOREA (DEMOCRATIC PEOPLE'S REPUBLIC OF) - LIVING LEVELS

G.K. Hall and Company, 70 Lincoln Street, Boston, Massachusetts
02111 (617) 423-3990; *The World in Figures*.

Times Books, 201 East 50th Street, New York, New York 10022 (212)
751-2600; *The Economist Book of Vital World Statistics*.

KOREA (DEMOCRATIC PEOPLE'S REPUBLIC OF) - MANUFACTURING

American Automobile Manufacturers Association, 1401 H Street,
NW, Suite 900, Washington, D.C. 20005 (202) 326-5500; *World
Motor Vehicle Data*.

Asian Development Bank, Post Office Box 789, 1099 Manila,
Philippines; *Key Indicators of Developing Asian and Pacific
Countries*.

Facts on File, 460 Park Avenue South, New York, New York 10016
(800) 443-8323; *The New Book of World Rankings*.

G.K. Hall and Company, 70 Lincoln Street, Boston, Massachusetts
02111 (617) 423-3990; *The World in Figures*.

KOREA (DEMOCRATIC PEOPLE'S REPUBLIC OF) - MARRIAGE RATES

Facts on File, 460 Park Avenue South, New York, New York 10016
(800) 443-8323; *The New Book of World Rankings*.

Statistical Office of the United Nations, Publishing Service, New York, New York 10017 (800) 253-9646; *Demographic Yearbook.*

KOREA (DEMOCRATIC PEOPLE'S REPUBLIC OF) - MEAT PRODUCTION - See KOREA (DEMOCRATIC PEOPLE'S REPUBLIC OF) - LIVESTOCK AND POULTRY

KOREA (DEMOCRATIC PEOPLE'S REPUBLIC OF) - MERCHANT SHIPPING

G.K. Hall and Company, 70 Lincoln Street, Boston, Massachusetts 02111 (617) 423-3990; *The World in Figures.*

Lloyd's Register of Shipping, 17 Battery Place, New York, New York 10004; *Register of Ships.*

Statistical Office of the United Nations, Publishing Service, New York, New York 10017 (800) 253-9646; *Statistical Yearbook.*

Times Books, 201 East 50th Street, New York, New York 10022 (212) 751-2600; *The Economist Book of Vital World Statistics.*

U.S. Department of Transportation, Maritime Administration, 400 Seventh Street, SW, Washington, D.C. 20590 (202) 366-5807; *A Statistical Analysis of the World's Merchant Fleets.*

KOREA (DEMOCRATIC PEOPLE'S REPUBLIC OF) - MERCHANT VESSELS - TONNAGE LAUNCHED - See KOREA (DEMOCRATIC PEOPLE'S REPUBLIC OF) - MERCHANT SHIPPING

KOREA (DEMOCRATIC PEOPLE'S REPUBLIC OF) - MILITARY

The Economist Intelligence Unit (Asia) Limited, 10th Floor, Luk Kwok Centre, 72 Gloucester Road, Wanchai, Hong Kong (Phone Number in U.S. (800) 938-4685); *Asian Market Atlas.*

G.K. Hall and Company, 70 Lincoln Street, Boston, Massachusetts 02111 (617) 423-3990; *The World in Figures.*

The International Institute for Strategic Studies, 23 Tavistock Street, London WC2E 7NQ, England; *The Military Balance.*

U.S. Arms Control and Disarmament Agency, 320 Twenty-first Street, NW, Washington, D.C. 20451 (202) 647-8677; *World Military Expenditures and Arms Transfers.*

KOREA (DEMOCRATIC PEOPLE'S REPUBLIC OF) - MILK PRODUCTION - See KOREA (DEMOCRATIC PEOPLE'S REPUBLIC OF) - DAIRY PRODUCTS

KOREA (DEMOCRATIC PEOPLE'S REPUBLIC OF) - MILLET PRODUCTION - See KOREA (DEMOCRATIC PEOPLE'S REPUBLIC OF) - CROPS

KOREA (DEMOCRATIC PEOPLE'S REPUBLIC OF) - MINING AND MINERAL PRODUCTS

Asian Development Bank, Post Office Box 789, 1099 Manila, Philippines; *Key Indicators of Developing Asian and Pacific Countries.*

Facts on File, 460 Park Avenue South, New York, New York 10016 (800) 443-8323; *The New Book of World Rankings.*

G.K. Hall and Company, 70 Lincoln Street, Boston, Massachusetts 02111 (617) 423-3990; *The World in Figures.*

Statistical Office of the United Nations, Publishing Service, New York, New York 10017 (800) 253-9646; *Statistical Yearbook.*

KOREA (DEMOCRATIC PEOPLE'S REPUBLIC OF) - MONEY EXCHANGE RATES

Euromonitor Publications Limited, 87-88 Turnmill Street, London EC1M 5QU, England; *International Marketing Data and Statistics.*

KOREA (DEMOCRATIC PEOPLE'S REPUBLIC OF) - MONEY RESERVES

Euromonitor Publications Limited, 87-88 Turnmill Street, London EC1M 5QU, England; *International Marketing Data and Statistics.*

KOREA (DEMOCRATIC PEOPLE'S REPUBLIC OF) - MONEY SUPPLY

Asian Development Bank, Post Office Box 789, 1099 Manila, Philippines; *Key Indicators of Developing Asian and Pacific Countries.*

Euromonitor Publications Limited, 87-88 Turnmill Street, London EC1M 5QU, England; *International Marketing Data and Statistics.*

G.K. Hall and Company, 70 Lincoln Street, Boston, Massachusetts 02111 (617) 423-3990; *The World in Figures.*

KOREA (DEMOCRATIC PEOPLE'S REPUBLIC OF) - MOTOR VEHICLE PRODUCTION

American Automobile Manufacturers Association, 1401 H Street, NW, Suite 900, Washington, D.C. 20005 (202) 326-5500; *World Motor Vehicle Data.*

KOREA (DEMOCRATIC PEOPLE'S REPUBLIC OF) - MOTOR VEHICLES IN USE

American Automobile Manufacturers Association, 1401 H Street, NW, Suite 900, Washington, D.C. 20005 (202) 326-5500; *World Motor Vehicle Data.*

G.K. Hall and Company, 70 Lincoln Street, Boston, Massachusetts 02111 (617) 423-3990; *The World in Figures.*

International Road Federation, 525 School Street, SW, Washington, D.C. 20024 (202) 554-2106; *World Road Statistics.*

KOREA (DEMOCRATIC PEOPLE'S REPUBLIC OF) - MULES - See KOREA (DEMOCRATIC PEOPLE'S REPUBLIC OF) - LIVESTOCK AND POULTRY

KOREA (DEMOCRATIC PEOPLE'S REPUBLIC OF) - MUSEUMS

Facts on File, 460 Park Avenue South, New York, New York 10016 (800) 443-8323; *The New Book of World Rankings.*

KOREA (DEMOCRATIC PEOPLE'S REPUBLIC OF) - NATALITY - See KOREA (DEMOCRATIC PEOPLE'S REPUBLIC OF) - BIRTH RATES

KOREA (DEMOCRATIC PEOPLE'S REPUBLIC OF) - NATIONAL INCOME

Facts on File, 460 Park Avenue South, New York, New York 10016 (800) 443-8323; *The New Book of World Rankings.*

G.K. Hall and Company, 70 Lincoln Street, Boston, Massachusetts 02111 (617) 423-3990; *The World in Figures.*

KOREA (DEMOCRATIC PEOPLE'S REPUBLIC OF) - NATIONAL PRODUCT

Facts on File, 460 Park Avenue South, New York, New York 10016 (800) 443-8323; *The New Book of World Rankings*.

KOREA (DEMOCRATIC PEOPLE'S REPUBLIC OF) - NATURAL GAS PRODUCTION - See KOREA (DEMOCRATIC PEOPLE'S REPUBLIC OF) - MINING AND MINERAL PRODUCTS

KOREA (DEMOCRATIC PEOPLE'S REPUBLIC OF) - NEWSPAPER PRODUCTION AND CONSUMPTION - See KOREA (DEMOCRATIC PEOPLE'S REPUBLIC OF) - FORESTRY AND FOREST PRODUCTS

KOREA (DEMOCRATIC PEOPLE'S REPUBLIC OF) - NEWSPRINT - See KOREA (DEMOCRATIC PEOPLE'S REPUBLIC OF) - FORESTRY AND FOREST PRODUCTS

KOREA (DEMOCRATIC PEOPLE'S REPUBLIC OF) - OATS PRODUCTION - See KOREA (DEMOCRATIC PEOPLE'S REPUBLIC OF) - CROPS

KOREA (DEMOCRATIC PEOPLE'S REPUBLIC OF) - OCCUPATIONS - See KOREA (DEMOCRATIC PEOPLE'S REPUBLIC OF) - LABOR FORCE

KOREA (DEMOCRATIC PEOPLE'S REPUBLIC OF) - PAPER - See KOREA (DEMOCRATIC PEOPLE'S REPUBLIC OF) - FORESTRY AND FOREST PRODUCTS

KOREA (DEMOCRATIC PEOPLE'S REPUBLIC OF) - PATENTS

Statistical Office of the United Nations, Publishing Service, New York, New York 10017 (800) 253-9646; *Statistical Yearbook*.

World Intellectual Property Organization, 34 Chemin des Colombettes, CH-1211 Geneva 20, Switzerland; *Industrial Property Statistics*.

KOREA (DEMOCRATIC PEOPLE'S REPUBLIC OF) - PEANUT PRODUCTION - See KOREA (DEMOCRATIC PEOPLE'S REPUBLIC OF) - CROPS

KOREA (DEMOCRATIC PEOPLE'S REPUBLIC OF) - PESTICIDE USE

Food and Agricultural Organization of the United Nations (FAO), Via delle Terme di Caracalla, 00100 Rome, Italy (Telephone Number in U.S. (202) 653-2400); *The State of Food and Agriculture*.

KOREA (DEMOCRATIC PEOPLE'S REPUBLIC OF) - PETROLEUM INDUSTRY

Asian Development Bank, Post Office Box 789, 1099 Manila, Philippines; *Key Indicators of Developing Asian and Pacific Countries*.

Facts on File, 460 Park Avenue South, New York, New York 10016 (800) 443-8323; *The New Book of World Rankings*.

Food and Agricultural Organization of the United Nations (FAO), Via delle Terme di Caracalla, 00100 Rome, Italy (Telephone Number in U.S. (202) 653-2400); *The State of Food and Agriculture*.

G.K. Hall and Company, 70 Lincoln Street, Boston, Massachusetts 02111 (617) 423-3990; *The World in Figures*.

KOREA (DEMOCRATIC PEOPLE'S REPUBLIC OF) - PHOSPHATE ROCK PRODUCTION - See (KOREA - DEMOCRATIC PEOPLE'S REPUBLIC OF JORDAN) - MINING AND MINERAL PRODUCTS

KOREA (DEMOCRATIC PEOPLE'S REPUBLIC OF) - PIG-IRON AND FERRO-ALLOY PRODUCTION - See KOREA (DEMOCRATIC PEOPLE'S REPUBLIC OF) - MINING AND MINERAL PRODUCTS

KOREA (DEMOCRATIC PEOPLE'S REPUBLIC OF) - PIGS - See KOREA (DEMOCRATIC PEOPLE'S REPUBLIC OF) - LIVESTOCK AND POULTRY

KOREA (DEMOCRATIC PEOPLE'S REPUBLIC OF) - POPULATION

Asian Development Bank, Post Office Box 789, 1099 Manila, Philippines; *Key Indicators of Developing Asian and Pacific Countries*.

The Economist Intelligence Unit, 111 West 57th Street, New York, New York 10019 (800) 938-4685; *The World Market Atlas*.

The Economist Intelligence Unit (Asia) Limited, 10th Floor, Luk Kwok Centre, 72 Gloucester Road, Wanchai, Hong Kong (Phone Number in U.S. (800) 938-4685); *Asian Market Atlas*.

Euromonitor Publications Limited, 87-88 Turnmill Street, London EC1M 5QU, England; *International Marketing Data and Statistics*.

Facts on File, 460 Park Avenue South, New York, New York 10016 (800) 443-8323; *The New Book of World Rankings*.

Food and Agricultural Organization of the United Nations (FAO), Via delle Terme di Caracalla, 00100 Rome, Italy (Telephone Number in U.S. (202) 653-2400); *Production Yearbook*.

G.K. Hall and Company, 70 Lincoln Street, Boston, Massachusetts 02111 (617) 423-3990; *The World in Figures*.

Statistical Office of the United Nations, Publishing Service, New York, New York 10017 (800) 253-9646; *Demographic Yearbook*, and *Statistical Yearbook*.

Times Books, 201 East 50th Street, New York, New York 10022 (212) 751-2600; *The Economist Book of Vital World Statistics*.

U.S. Arms Control and Disarmament Agency, 320 Twenty-first Street, NW, Washington, D.C. 20451 (202) 647-8677; *World Military Expenditures and Arms Transfers*.

KOREA (DEMOCRATIC PEOPLE'S REPUBLIC OF) - POST OFFICES

Facts on File, 460 Park Avenue South, New York, New York 10016 (800) 443-8323; *The New Book of World Rankings*.

KOREA (DEMOCRATIC PEOPLE'S REPUBLIC OF) - POTATO PRODUCTION - See KOREA (DEMOCRATIC PEOPLE'S REPUBLIC OF) - CROPS

KOREA (DEMOCRATIC PEOPLE'S REPUBLIC OF) - POWER PRODUCTION INDUSTRY - ESTABLISHMENTS, PAYROLLS, VALUE ADDED, ETC.

Statistical Office of the United Nations, Publishing Service, New York, New York 10017 (800) 253-9646; *Electric Power in Asia and the Pacific*.

KOREA (DEMOCRATIC PEOPLE'S REPUBLIC OF) - PRICES

Asian Development Bank, Post Office Box 789, 1099 Manila, Philippines; *Key Indicators of Developing Asian and Pacific Countries*.

Facts on File, 460 Park Avenue South, New York, New York 10016 (800) 443-8323; *The New Book of World Rankings.*

Food and Agricultural Organization of the United Nations (FAO), Via delle Terme di Caracalla, 00100 Rome, Italy (Telephone Number in U.S. (202) 653-2400); *Production Yearbook,* and *The State of Food and Agriculture.*

G.K. Hall and Company, 70 Lincoln Street, Boston, Massachusetts 02111 (617) 423-3990; *The World in Figures.*

KOREA (DEMOCRATIC PEOPLE'S REPUBLIC OF) - PRINTING AND WRITING PAPER - See KOREA (DEMOCRATIC PEOPLE'S REPUBLIC OF) - FORESTRY AND FOREST PRODUCTS

KOREA (DEMOCRATIC PEOPLE'S REPUBLIC OF) - PRODUCTION

American Automobile Manufacturers Association, 1401 H Street, NW, Suite 900, Washington, D.C. 20005 (202) 326-5500; *World Motor Vehicle Data.*

Facts on File, 460 Park Avenue South, New York, New York 10016 (800) 443-8323; *The New Book of World Rankings.*

G.K. Hall and Company, 70 Lincoln Street, Boston, Massachusetts 02111 (617) 423-3990; *The World in Figures.*

KOREA (DEMOCRATIC PEOPLE'S REPUBLIC OF) - PRODUCTIVITY

Euromonitor Publications Limited, 87-88 Turnmill Street, London EC1M 5QU, England; *International Marketing Data and Statistics.*

KOREA (DEMOCRATIC PEOPLE'S REPUBLIC OF) - PUBLIC FINANCE

Facts on File, 460 Park Avenue South, New York, New York 10016 (800) 443-8323; *The New Book of World Rankings.*

KOREA (DEMOCRATIC PEOPLE'S REPUBLIC OF) - RADIO BROADCASTING - See KOREA (DEMOCRATIC PEOPLE'S REPUBLIC OF) - BROADCASTING

KOREA (DEMOCRATIC PEOPLE'S REPUBLIC OF) - RAILWAYS

G.K. Hall and Company, 70 Lincoln Street, Boston, Massachusetts 02111 (617) 423-3990; *The World in Figures.*

Jane's Information Group, Sentinel House, 163 Brighton Road, Coulsdon, Surrey CR5 2NH, England (Telephone Number in U.S. (703) 683-3700); *Jane's World Railways.*

KOREA (DEMOCRATIC PEOPLE'S REPUBLIC OF) - RELIGION

Facts on File, 460 Park Avenue South, New York, New York 10016 (800) 443-8323; *The New Book of World Rankings.*

KOREA (DEMOCRATIC PEOPLE'S REPUBLIC OF) - RETAIL TRADE

G.K. Hall and Company, 70 Lincoln Street, Boston, Massachusetts 02111 (617) 423-3990; *The World in Figures.*

KOREA (DEMOCRATIC PEOPLE'S REPUBLIC OF) - RICE PRODUCTION - See KOREA (DEMOCRATIC PEOPLE'S REPUBLIC OF) - CROPS

KOREA (DEMOCRATIC PEOPLE'S REPUBLIC OF) - ROOT AND TUBER PRODUCTION - See KOREA (DEMOCRATIC PEOPLE'S REPUBLIC OF) - CROPS

KOREA (DEMOCRATIC PEOPLE'S REPUBLIC OF) - ROUNDWOOD PRODUCTION - See KOREA (DEMOCRATIC PEOPLE'S REPUBLIC OF) - FORESTRY AND FOREST PRODUCTS

KOREA (DEMOCRATIC PEOPLE'S REPUBLIC OF) - RUBBER PRODUCTION AND CONSUMPTION

Facts on File, 460 Park Avenue South, New York, New York 10016 (800) 443-8323; *The New Book of World Rankings.*

KOREA (DEMOCRATIC PEOPLE'S REPUBLIC OF) - SALT PRODUCTION

Statistical Office of the United Nations, Publishing Service, New York, New York 10017 (800) 253-9646; *Statistical Yearbook.*

KOREA (DEMOCRATIC PEOPLE'S REPUBLIC OF) - SAWNWOOD PRODUCTION - See KOREA (DEMOCRATIC PEOPLE'S REPUBLIC OF) - FORESTRY AND FOREST PRODUCTS

KOREA (DEMOCRATIC PEOPLE'S REPUBLIC OF) - SENIOR CITIZENS

Facts on File, 460 Park Avenue South, New York, New York 10016 (800) 443-8323; *The New Book of World Rankings.*

KOREA (DEMOCRATIC PEOPLE'S REPUBLIC OF) - SHEEP - See KOREA (DEMOCRATIC PEOPLE'S REPUBLIC OF) - LIVESTOCK AND POULTRY

KOREA (DEMOCRATIC PEOPLE'S REPUBLIC OF) - SILVER PRODUCTION AND CONSUMPTION - See KOREA (DEMOCRATIC PEOPLE'S REPUBLIC OF) - MINING AND MINERAL PRODUCTS

KOREA (DEMOCRATIC PEOPLE'S REPUBLIC OF) - SOCIAL DATA

Asian Development Bank, Post Office Box 789, 1099 Manila, Philippines; *Key Indicators of Developing Asian and Pacific Countries.*

Facts on File, 460 Park Avenue South, New York, New York 10016 (800) 443-8323; *The New Book of World Rankings.*

G.K. Hall and Company, 70 Lincoln Street, Boston, Massachusetts 02111 (617) 423-3990; *The World in Figures.*

KOREA (DEMOCRATIC PEOPLE'S REPUBLIC OF) - SOYBEANS PRODUCTION - See KOREA (DEMOCRATIC PEOPLE'S REPUBLIC OF) - CROPS

KOREA (DEMOCRATIC PEOPLE'S REPUBLIC OF) - STATE BUDGET REVENUE AND EXPENDITURES

Euromonitor Publications Limited, 87-88 Turnmill Street, London EC1M 5QU, England; *International Marketing Data and Statistics.*

KOREA (DEMOCRATIC PEOPLE'S REPUBLIC OF) - STEEL PRODUCTION AND CONSUMPTION - See KOREA (DEMOCRATIC PEOPLE'S REPUBLIC OF) - MINING AND MINERAL PRODUCTS

KOREA (DEMOCRATIC PEOPLE'S REPUBLIC OF) - STOCKS - COMMODITY - MARKET PRICE - INDEX

Food and Agricultural Organization of the United Nations (FAO), Via delle Terme di Caracalla, 00100 Rome, Italy (Telephone Number in U.S. (202) 653-2400); *The State of Food and Agriculture.*

KOREA (DEMOCRATIC PEOPLE'S REPUBLIC OF) - SUGAR PRODUCTION AND CONSUMPTION - See KOREA (DEMOCRATIC PEOPLE'S REPUBLIC OF) - CROPS

KOREA (DEMOCRATIC PEOPLE'S REPUBLIC OF) - TAXATION

G.K. Hall and Company, 70 Lincoln Street, Boston, Massachusetts 02111 (617) 423-3990; *The World in Figures*.

International Road Federation, 525 School Street, SW, Washington, D.C. 20024 (202) 554-2106; *World Road Statistics*.

KOREA (DEMOCRATIC PEOPLE'S REPUBLIC OF) - TELEPHONES IN USE

American Telephone and Telegraph Company, 26 Parsippany Road, Whippany, New Jersey 07981 (800) 338-4038; *The World's Telephones*.

The Economist Intelligence Unit (Asia) Limited, 10th Floor, Luk Kwok Centre, 72 Gloucester Road, Wanchai, Hong Kong (Phone Number in U.S. (800) 938-4685); *Asian Market Atlas*.

G.K. Hall and Company, 70 Lincoln Street, Boston, Massachusetts 02111 (617) 423-3990; *The World in Figures*.

KOREA (DEMOCRATIC PEOPLE'S REPUBLIC OF) - TELEVISION BROADCASTING - See KOREA (DEMOCRATIC PEOPLE'S REPUBLIC OF) - BROADCASTING

KOREA (DEMOCRATIC PEOPLE'S REPUBLIC OF) - TEXTILE INDUSTRY

American Forest and Paper Association, 1250 Connecticut Avenue, NW, Washington, D.C. 20036 (202) 463-2455; *Wood Pulp and Fiber Statistics*.

Food and Agricultural Organization of the United Nations (FAO), Via delle Terme di Caracalla, 00100 Rome, Italy (Telephone Number in U.S. (202) 653-2400); *Production Yearbook*.

G.K. Hall and Company, 70 Lincoln Street, Boston, Massachusetts 02111 (617) 423-3990; *The World in Figures*.

KOREA (DEMOCRATIC PEOPLE'S REPUBLIC OF) - TOBACCO PRODUCTION

Facts on File, 460 Park Avenue South, New York, New York 10016 (800) 443-8323; *The New Book of World Rankings*.

Statistical Office of the United Nations, Publishing Service, New York, New York 10017 (800) 253-9646; *Statistical Yearbook*.

KOREA (DEMOCRATIC PEOPLE'S REPUBLIC OF) - TOURISM

Facts on File, 460 Park Avenue South, New York, New York 10016 (800) 443-8323; *The New Book of World Rankings*.

G.K. Hall and Company, 70 Lincoln Street, Boston, Massachusetts 02111 (617) 423-3990; *The World in Figures*.

KOREA (DEMOCRATIC PEOPLE'S REPUBLIC OF) - TRACTORS IN USE

Statistical Office of the United Nations, Publishing Service, New York, New York 10017 (800) 253-9646; *Statistical Yearbook*.

KOREA (DEMOCRATIC PEOPLE'S REPUBLIC OF) - TRADE - See KOREA (DEMOCRATIC PEOPLE'S REPUBLIC OF) - FOREIGN TRADE

KOREA (DEMOCRATIC PEOPLE'S REPUBLIC OF) - TRADEMARKS AND SERVICE MARKS

World Intellectual Property Organization, 34 Chemin des Colombettes, CH-1211 Geneva 20, Switzerland; *Industrial Property Statistics*.

KOREA (DEMOCRATIC PEOPLE'S REPUBLIC OF) - TRANSPORTATION AND COMMUNICATIONS

The Economist Intelligence Unit (Asia) Limited, 10th Floor, Luk Kwok Centre, 72 Gloucester Road, Wanchai, Hong Kong (Phone Number in U.S. (800) 938-4685); *Asian Market Atlas*.

Facts on File, 460 Park Avenue South, New York, New York 10016 (800) 443-8323; *The New Book of World Rankings*.

G.K. Hall and Company, 70 Lincoln Street, Boston, Massachusetts 02111 (617) 423-3990; *The World in Figures*.

KOREA (DEMOCRATIC PEOPLE'S REPUBLIC OF) - TUNGSTEN PRODUCTION AND CONSUMPTION - See KOREA (DEMOCRATIC PEOPLE'S REPUBLIC OF) - MINING AND MINERAL PRODUCTS

KOREA (DEMOCRATIC PEOPLE'S REPUBLIC OF) - UNEMPLOYMENT

Euromonitor Publications Limited, 87-88 Turnmill Street, London EC1M 5QU, England; *International Marketing Data and Statistics*.

KOREA (DEMOCRATIC PEOPLE'S REPUBLIC OF) - UTILITIES

Statistical Office of the United Nations, Publishing Service, New York, New York 10017 (800) 253-9646; *Electric Power in Asia and the Pacific*.

KOREA (DEMOCRATIC PEOPLE'S REPUBLIC OF) - VITAL STATISTICS

Euromonitor Publications Limited, 87-88 Turnmill Street, London EC1M 5QU, England; *International Marketing Data and Statistics*.

G.K. Hall and Company, 70 Lincoln Street, Boston, Massachusetts 02111 (617) 423-3990; *The World in Figures*.

Statistical Office of the United Nations, Publishing Service, New York, New York 10017 (800) 253-9646; *Statistical Yearbook*.

KOREA (DEMOCRATIC PEOPLE'S REPUBLIC OF) - WAGES

G.K. Hall and Company, 70 Lincoln Street, Boston, Massachusetts 02111 (617) 423-3990; *The World in Figures*.

KOREA (DEMOCRATIC PEOPLE'S REPUBLIC OF) - WALNUT PRODUCTION - See KOREA (DEMOCRATIC PEOPLE'S REPUBLIC OF) - CROPS

KOREA (DEMOCRATIC PEOPLE'S REPUBLIC OF) - WATERMELON PRODUCTION - See KOREA (DEMOCRATIC PEOPLE'S REPUBLIC OF) - CROPS

KOREA (DEMOCRATIC PEOPLE'S REPUBLIC OF) - WEATHER

Facts on File, 460 Park Avenue South, New York, New York 10016 (800) 443-8323; *The New Book of World Rankings*.

G.K. Hall and Company, 70 Lincoln Street, Boston, Massachusetts 02111 (617) 423-3990; *The World in Figures.*

KOREA (DEMOCRATIC PEOPLE'S REPUBLIC OF) - WHEAT PRODUCTION AND PRICES - See KOREA (DEMOCRATIC PEOPLE'S REPUBLIC OF) - CROPS

KOREA (DEMOCRATIC PEOPLE'S REPUBLIC OF) - WHOLESALE PRICES - INDEX NUMBERS

Asian Development Bank, Post Office Box 789, 1099 Manila, Philippines; *Key Indicators of Developing Asian and Pacific Countries.*

KOREA (DEMOCRATIC PEOPLE'S REPUBLIC OF) - WINE PRODUCTION

Facts on File, 460 Park Avenue South, New York, New York 10016 (800) 443-8323; *The New Book of World Rankings.*

KOREA (DEMOCRATIC PEOPLE'S REPUBLIC OF) - WOOD - See KOREA (DEMOCRATIC PEOPLE'S REPUBLIC OF) - FORESTRY AND FOREST PRODUCTS

KOREA (DEMOCRATIC PEOPLE'S REPUBLIC OF) - WOOL PRODUCTION

Facts on File, 460 Park Avenue South, New York, New York 10016 (800) 443-8323; *The New Book of World Rankings.*

KOREA (DEMOCRATIC PEOPLE'S REPUBLIC OF) - ZINC ORE PRODUCTION - See KOREA (DEMOCRATIC PEOPLE'S REPUBLIC OF) - MINING AND MINERAL PRODUCTS

Korea (Republic Of) - National Statistical Office

National Statistical Office, 90 Kyongun-dong, Chongno-gu, Seoul, Korea.

Korea (Republic Of) - Primary Statistics Sources

National Statistical Office, Seoul, Korea; *Korea Statistical Yearbook,* and *Monthly Statistics of Korea.*

KOREA (REPUBLIC OF) - ADMINISTRATIVE DISTRICTS

Korean Overseas Information Service, Ministry of Culture and Information, Seoul 110, Republic of Korea; *Statistical Data on Korea.*

KOREA (REPUBLIC OF) - AGRICULTURE

Euromonitor Publications Limited, 87-88 Turnmill Street, London EC1M 5QU, England; *International Marketing Data and Statistics,* and *The Pacific Basin: An Economic Handbook.*

Food and Agricultural Organization of the United Nations (FAO), Via delle Terme di Caracalla, 00100 Rome, Italy (Telephone Number in U.S. (202) 653-2400); *Production Yearbook, The State of Food and Agriculture,* and *Trade Yearbook.*

Statistical Office of the United Nations, Publishing Service, New York, New York 10017 (800) 253-9646; *Statistical Yearbook,* and *Statistical Yearbook for Asia and the Pacific.*

Times Books, 201 East 50th Street, New York, New York 10022 (212) 751-2600; *The Economist Book of Vital World Statistics.*

The World Bank, 1818 H Street, NW, Washington, D.C. 20433 (202) 477-1234; *World Tables.*

KOREA (REPUBLIC OF) - AIRLINE SERVICE

The Economist Intelligence Unit (Asia) Limited, 10th Floor, Luk Kwok Centre, 72 Gloucester Road, Wanchai, Hong Kong (Phone Number in U.S. (800) 938-4685); *Asian Market Atlas.*

Facts on File, 460 Park Avenue South, New York, New York 10016 (800) 443-8323; *The New Book of World Rankings.*

G.K. Hall and Company, 70 Lincoln Street, Boston, Massachusetts 02111 (617) 423-3990; *The World in Figures.*

International Civil Aviation Organization, 1000 Sherbrooke Street West, Suite 400, Montreal, Quebec H3A 2R2, Canada (514) 285-8219; *Civil Aviation Statistics of the World.*

Statistical Office of the United Nations, Publishing Service, New York, New York 10017 (800) 253-9646; *Statistical Yearbook.*

Times Books, 201 East 50th Street, New York, New York 10022 (212) 751-2600; *The Economist Book of Vital World Statistics.*

KOREA (REPUBLIC OF) - ALUMINIUM PRODUCTION AND CONSUMPTION - See KOREA (REPUBLIC OF) - MINING AND MINERAL PRODUCTS

KOREA (REPUBLIC OF) - ANIMAL HEALTH

Food and Agricultural Organization of the United Nations (FAO), Via delle Terme di Caracalla, 00100 Rome, Italy (Telephone Number in U.S. (202) 653-2400); *Animal Health Yearbook.*

KOREA (REPUBLIC OF) - ANTHRACITE PRODUCTION - See KOREA (REPUBLIC OF) - MINING AND MINERAL PRODUCTS

KOREA (REPUBLIC OF) - ANTIMONY ORE PRODUCTION AND CONSUMPTION - See KOREA (REPUBLIC OF) - MINING AND MINERAL PRODUCTS

KOREA (REPUBLIC OF) - AREA AND DENSITY OF POPULATION

Euromonitor Publications Limited, 87-88 Turnmill Street, London EC1M 5QU, England; *The Pacific Basin: An Economic Handbook,* and *International Marketing Data and Statistics.*

Facts on File, 460 Park Avenue South, New York, New York 10016 (800) 443-8323; *The New Book of World Rankings.*

Food and Agricultural Organization of the United Nations (FAO), Via delle Terme di Caracalla, 00100 Rome, Italy (Telephone Number in U.S. (202) 653-2400); *The State of Food and Agriculture.*

G.K. Hall and Company, 70 Lincoln Street, Boston, Massachusetts 02111 (617) 423-3990; *The World in Figures.*

Statistical Office of the United Nations, Publishing Service, New York, New York 10017 (800) 253-9646; *Statistical Yearbook.*

Times Books, 201 East 50th Street, New York, New York 10022 (212) 751-2600; *The Economist Book of Vital World Statistics.*

United Nations Educational, Scientific and Cultural Organization (UNESCO), 7 Place de Fontenoy, F-75700 Paris, France (Telephone in U.S. (212) 963-5981); *Statistical Yearbook.*

KOREA (REPUBLIC OF) - ARMS EXPORTS AND IMPORTS

U.S. Arms Control and Disarmament Agency, 320 Twenty-first Street, NW, Washington, D.C. 20451 (202) 647-8677; *World Military Expenditures and Arms Transfers.*

KOREA (REPUBLIC OF) - BALANCE OF PAYMENTS

The Economist Intelligence Unit, 111 West 57th Street, New York, New York 10019 (800) 938-4685; *The World Market Atlas.*

Euromonitor Publications Limited, 87-88 Turnmill Street, London EC1M 5QU, England; *Third World Economic Handbook.*

G.K. Hall and Company, 70 Lincoln Street, Boston, Massachusetts 02111 (617) 423-3990; *The World in Figures.*

International Monetary Fund, 700 Nineteenth Street, NW, Washington, D.C. 20431 (202) 623-7000; *Balance of Payments Yearbook.*

Korean Overseas Information Service, Ministry of Culture and Information, Seoul 110, Republic of Korea; *Statistical Data on Korea.*

Times Books, 201 East 50th Street, New York, New York 10022 (212) 751-2600; *The Economist Book of Vital World Statistics.*

The World Bank, 1818 H Street, NW, Washington, D.C. 20433 (202) 477-1234; *World Tables.*

KOREA (REPUBLIC OF) - BANKING

Facts on File, 460 Park Avenue South, New York, New York 10016 (800) 443-8323; *The New Book of World Rankings.*

G.K. Hall and Company, 70 Lincoln Street, Boston, Massachusetts 02111 (617) 423-3990; *The World in Figures.*

International Monetary Fund, 700 Nineteenth Street, NW, Washington, D.C. 20431 (202) 623-7000; *International Financial Statistics.*

Korean Overseas Information Service, Ministry of Culture and Information, Seoul 110, Republic of Korea; *Statistical Data on Korea.*

Statistical Office of the United Nations, Publishing Service, New York, New York 10017 (800) 253-9646; *Statistical Yearbook.*

KOREA (REPUBLIC OF) - BARLEY PRODUCTION - See KOREA (REPUBLIC OF) - CROPS

KOREA (REPUBLIC OF) - BEER PRODUCTION

Facts on File, 460 Park Avenue South, New York, New York 10016 (800) 443-8323; *The New Book of World Rankings.*

Statistical Office of the United Nations, Publishing Service, New York, New York 10017 (800) 253-9646; *Statistical Yearbook.*

KOREA (REPUBLIC OF) - BEES

Korean Overseas Information Service, Ministry of Culture and Information, Seoul 110, Republic of Korea; *Statistical Data on Korea.*

KOREA (REPUBLIC OF) - BIRTH RATES

The Economist Intelligence Unit (Asia) Limited, 10th Floor, Luk Kwok Centre, 72 Gloucester Road, Wanchai, Hong Kong (Phone Number in U.S. (800) 938-4685); *Asian Market Atlas.*

Euromonitor Publications Limited, 87-88 Turnmill Street, London EC1M 5QU, England; *The Pacific Basin: An Economic Handbook,* and *Third World Economic Handbook.*

Facts on File, 460 Park Avenue South, New York, New York 10016 (800) 443-8323; *The New Book of World Rankings.*

Statistical Office of the United Nations, Publishing Service, New York, New York 10017 (800) 253-9646; *Demographic Yearbook,* and *Statistical Yearbook.*

Times Books, 201 East 50th Street, New York, New York 10022 (212) 751-2600; *The Economist Book of Vital World Statistics.*

The World Bank, 1818 H Street, NW, Washington, D.C. 20433 (202) 477-1234; *World Tables.*

KOREA (REPUBLIC OF) - BONDS

G.K. Hall and Company, 70 Lincoln Street, Boston, Massachusetts 02111 (617) 423-3990; *The World in Figures.*

KOREA (REPUBLIC OF) - BOOK PRODUCTION

G.K. Hall and Company, 70 Lincoln Street, Boston, Massachusetts 02111 (617) 423-3990; *The World in Figures.*

United Nations Educational, Scientific and Cultural Organization (UNESCO), 7 Place de Fontenoy, F-75700 Paris, France (Telephone in U.S. (212) 963-5981); *Statistical Yearbook.*

KOREA (REPUBLIC OF) - BROADCASTING

Billboard Limited, Post Office Box 9027, 1006 AA Amsterdam, The Netherlands (Telephone Number in U.S. (212) 764-7300); *World Radio TV Handbook.*

The Economist Intelligence Unit (Asia) Limited, 10th Floor, Luk Kwok Centre, 72 Gloucester Road, Wanchai, Hong Kong (Phone Number in U.S. (800) 938-4685); *Asian Market Atlas.*

Facts on File, 460 Park Avenue South, New York, New York 10016 (800) 443-8323; *The New Book of World Rankings.*

G.K. Hall and Company, 70 Lincoln Street, Boston, Massachusetts 02111 (617) 423-3990; *The World in Figures.*

Times Books, 201 East 50th Street, New York, New York 10022 (212) 751-2600; *The Economist Book of Vital World Statistics.*

United Nations Educational, Scientific and Cultural Organization (UNESCO), 7 Place de Fontenoy, F-75700 Paris, France (Telephone in U.S. (212) 963-5981); *Statistical Yearbook.*

KOREA (REPUBLIC OF) - BUSINESS

G.K. Hall and Company, 70 Lincoln Street, Boston, Massachusetts 02111 (617) 423-3990; *The World in Figures.*

KOREA (REPUBLIC OF) - CABBAGE PRODUCTION - See KOREA (REPUBLIC OF) - CROPS

KOREA (REPUBLIC OF) - CALORIE INTAKE

Korean Overseas Information Service, Ministry of Culture and Information, Seoul 110, Republic of Korea; *Statistical Data on Korea.*

KOREA (REPUBLIC OF) - CALORIE SUPPLY

Food and Agricultural Organization of the United Nations (FAO), Via delle Terme di Caracalla, 00100 Rome, Italy (Telephone Number in U.S. (202) 653-2400); *The State of Food and Agriculture.*

KOREA (REPUBLIC OF) - CASTOR BEAN PRODUCTION - See KOREA (REPUBLIC OF) - CROPS

KOREA (REPUBLIC OF) - CATTLE - See KOREA (REPUBLIC OF) - LIVESTOCK AND POULTRY

KOREA (REPUBLIC OF) - CAUSTIC SODA PRODUCTION

Statistical Office of the United Nations, Publishing Service, New York, New York 10017 (800) 253-9646; *Statistical Yearbook.*

KOREA (REPUBLIC OF) - CEMENT PRODUCTION - See KOREA (REPUBLIC OF) - MINING AND MINERAL PRODUCTS

KOREA (REPUBLIC OF) - CHEMICAL (ORGANIC) PRODUCTION - See KOREA (REPUBLIC OF) - MINING AND MINERAL PRODUCTS

KOREA (REPUBLIC OF) - CHESTNUT PRODUCTION - See KOREA (REPUBLIC OF) - CROPS

KOREA (REPUBLIC OF) - CHICKENS - See KOREA (REPUBLIC OF) LIVESTOCK AND POULTRY

KOREA (REPUBLIC OF) - CIGARETTE PRODUCTION - See KOREA (REPUBLIC OF) - TOBACCO PRODUCTION

KOREA (REPUBLIC OF) - CLASS STRUCTURE

G.K. Hall and Company, 70 Lincoln Street, Boston, Massachusetts 02111 (617) 423-3990; *The World in Figures.*

KOREA (REPUBLIC OF) - CLIMATE

Facts on File, 460 Park Avenue South, New York, New York 10016 (800) 443-8323; *The New Book of World Rankings.*

G.K. Hall and Company, 70 Lincoln Street, Boston, Massachusetts 02111 (617) 423-3990; *The World in Figures.*

Korean Overseas Information Service, Ministry of Culture and Information, Seoul 110, Republic of Korea; *Statistical Data on Korea.*

KOREA (REPUBLIC OF) - CLOTHING EXPENDITURES

Korean Overseas Information Service, Ministry of Culture and Information, Seoul 110, Republic of Korea; *Statistical Data on Korea.*

KOREA (REPUBLIC OF) - CLOTHING EXPORTS AND IMPORTS

Euromonitor Publications Limited, 87-88 Turnmill Street, London EC1M 5QU, England; *Third World Economic Handbook.*

Statistical Office of the United Nations, Publishing Service, New York, New York 10017 (800) 253-9646; *Trade in Manufactures of Developing Countries.*

KOREA (REPUBLIC OF) - COAL PRODUCTION - See KOREA (REPUBLIC OF) - MINING AND MINERAL PRODUCTS

KOREA (REPUBLIC OF) - COFFEE PRODUCTION AND CONSUMPTION - See KOREA (REPUBLIC OF) - CROPS

KOREA (REPUBLIC OF) - COKE OVEN COKE PRODUCTION AND CONSUMPTION - See KOREA (REPUBLIC OF) - MINING AND MINERAL PRODUCTS

KOREA (REPUBLIC OF) - COMMUNICATION EXPENDITURES

Korean Overseas Information Service, Ministry of Culture and Information, Seoul 110, Republic of Korea; *Statistical Data on Korea.*

KOREA (REPUBLIC OF) - COMMUNICATIONS

Euromonitor Publications Limited, 87-88 Turnmill Street, London EC1M 5QU, England; *Third World Economic Handbook.*

G.K. Hall and Company, 70 Lincoln Street, Boston, Massachusetts 02111 (617) 423-3990; *The World in Figures.*

Statistical Office of the United Nations, Publishing Service, New York, New York 10017 (800) 253-9646; *Statistical Yearbook for Asia and the Pacific.*

KOREA (REPUBLIC OF) - CONSTRUCTION INDUSTRY

Facts on File, 460 Park Avenue South, New York, New York 10016 (800) 443-8323; *The New Book of World Rankings.*

Statistical Office of the United Nations, Publishing Service, New York, New York 10017 (800) 253-9646; *Construction Statistics Yearbook,* and *Statistical Yearbook.*

KOREA (REPUBLIC OF) - CONSUMER PRICE INDEX

G.K. Hall and Company, 70 Lincoln Street, Boston, Massachusetts 02111 (617) 423-3990; *The World in Figures.*

Statistical Office of the United Nations, Publishing Service, New York, New York 10017 (800) 253-9646; *Statistical Yearbook.*

KOREA (REPUBLIC OF) - CONSUMER PRICES

International Labour Office, I.L.O. Publications, CH-1211, Geneva 22, Switzerland; *Yearbook of Labour Statistics.*

Times Books, 201 East 50th Street, New York, New York 10022 (212) 751-2600; *The Economist Book of Vital World Statistics.*

KOREA (REPUBLIC OF) - CONSUMPTION

Euromonitor Publications Limited, 87-88 Turnmill Street, London EC1M 5QU, England; *The Pacific Basin: An Economic Handbook.*

G.K. Hall and Company, 70 Lincoln Street, Boston, Massachusetts 02111 (617) 423-3990; *The World in Figures.*

KOREA (REPUBLIC OF) - CONSUMPTION EXPENDITURES

Korean Overseas Information Service, Ministry of Culture and Information, Seoul 110, Republic of Korea; *Statistical Data on Korea.*

KOREA (REPUBLIC OF) - COPPER - See (KOREA -REPUBLIC OF) - MINING AND MINERAL PRODUCTS

KOREA (REPUBLIC OF) - CORN PRODUCTION - See KOREA
(REPUBLIC OF) - CROPS

KOREA (REPUBLIC OF) - CORPORATE TAXES - See KOREA
(REPUBLIC OF) - TAXATION

KOREA (REPUBLIC OF) - COTTON - See KOREA (REPUBLIC OF) -
CROPS

KOREA (REPUBLIC OF) - CROPS

Facts on File, 460 Park Avenue South, New York, New York 10016
(800) 443-8323; *The New Book of World Rankings*.

Food and Agricultural Organization of the United Nations (FAO),
Via delle Terme di Caracalla, 00100 Rome, Italy (Telephone Number
in U.S. (202) 653-2400); *The State of Food and Agriculture*, and
Production Yearbook.

G.K. Hall and Company, 70 Lincoln Street, Boston, Massachusetts
02111 (617) 423-3990; *The World in Figures*.

Statistical Office of the United Nations, Publishing Service, New
York, New York 10017 (800) 253-9646; *Statistical Yearbook*.

KOREA (REPUBLIC OF) - CULTURAL ASSETS

Korean Overseas Information Service, Ministry of Culture and
Information, Seoul 110, Republic of Korea; *Statistical Data on
Korea*.

KOREA (REPUBLIC OF) - CUSTOMS DUTIES

G.K. Hall and Company, 70 Lincoln Street, Boston, Massachusetts
02111 (617) 423-3990; *The World in Figures*.

KOREA (REPUBLIC OF) - DAIRY PRODUCTS

Facts on File, 460 Park Avenue South, New York, New York 10016
(800) 443-8323; *The New Book of World Rankings*.

Food and Agricultural Organization of the United Nations (FAO),
Via delle Terme di Caracalla, 00100 Rome, Italy (Telephone Number
in U.S. (202) 653-2400); *Production Yearbook*, and *The State of Food
and Agriculture*.

Statistical Office of the United Nations, Publishing Service, New
York, New York 10017 (800) 253-9646; *Statistical Yearbook*.

KOREA (REPUBLIC OF) - DEATH RATES

The Economist Intelligence Unit (Asia) Limited, 10th Floor, Luk
Kwok Centre, 72 Gloucester Road, Wanchai, Hong Kong (Phone
Number in U.S. (800) 938-4685); *Asian Market Atlas*.

Euromonitor Publications Limited, 87-88 Turnmill Street, London
EC1M 5QU, England; *The Pacific Basin: An Economic Handbook*,
and *Third World Economic Handbook*.

G.K. Hall and Company, 70 Lincoln Street, Boston, Massachusetts
02111 (617) 423-3990; *The World in Figures*.

Statistical Office of the United Nations, Publishing Service, New
York, New York 10017 (800) 253-9646; *Statistical Yearbook*.

Times Books, 201 East 50th Street, New York, New York 10022 (212)
751-2600; *The Economist Book of Vital World Statistics*.

KOREA (REPUBLIC OF) - DEFENSE EXPENDITURES

G.K. Hall and Company, 70 Lincoln Street, Boston, Massachusetts
02111 (617) 423-3990; *The World in Figures*.

U.S. Arms Control and Disarmament Agency, 320 Twenty-first
Street, NW, Washington, D.C. 20451 (202) 647-8677; *World Military
Expenditures and Arms Transfers*.

KOREA (REPUBLIC OF) - DEMOGRAPHY

The Economist Intelligence Unit, 111 West 57th Street, New York,
New York 10019 (800) 938-4685; *The World Market Atlas*.

The Economist Intelligence Unit (Asia) Limited, 10th Floor, Luk
Kwok Centre, 72 Gloucester Road, Wanchai, Hong Kong (Phone
Number in U.S. (800) 938-4685); *Asian Market Atlas*.

Facts on File, 460 Park Avenue South, New York, New York 10016
(800) 443-8323; *The New Book of World Rankings*.

G.K. Hall and Company, 70 Lincoln Street, Boston, Massachusetts
02111 (617) 423-3990; *The World in Figures*.

KOREA (REPUBLIC OF) - DEVELOPMENT ASSISTANCE

G.K. Hall and Company, 70 Lincoln Street, Boston, Massachusetts
02111 (617) 423-3990; *The World in Figures*.

Statistical Office of the United Nations, Publishing Service, New
York, New York 10017 (800) 253-9646; *Statistical Yearbook*.

KOREA (REPUBLIC OF) - DIAMOND PRODUCTION - See KOREA
(REPUBLIC OF) - MINING AND MINERAL PRODUCTS

KOREA (REPUBLIC OF) - DISCOUNT RATES

Statistical Office of the United Nations, Publishing Service, New
York, New York 10017 (800) 253-9646; *Statistical Yearbook*.

KOREA (REPUBLIC OF) - DISEASES

G.K. Hall and Company, 70 Lincoln Street, Boston, Massachusetts
02111 (617) 423-3990; *The World in Figures*.

Korean Overseas Information Service, Ministry of Culture and
Information, Seoul 110, Republic of Korea; *Statistical Data on Korea*.

KOREA (REPUBLIC OF) - DIVORCE RATES

Facts on File, 460 Park Avenue South, New York, New York 10016
(800) 443-8323; *The New Book of World Rankings*.

Statistical Office of the United Nations, Publishing Service, New
York, New York 10017 (800) 253-9646; *Demographic Yearbook*, and
Statistical Yearbook.

KOREA (REPUBLIC OF) - DOGS

Korean Overseas Information Service, Ministry of Culture and
Information, Seoul 110, Republic of Korea; *Statistical Data on Korea*.

KOREA (REPUBLIC OF) - DOMESTIC PRODUCT

G.K. Hall and Company, 70 Lincoln Street, Boston, Massachusetts
02111 (617) 423-3990; *The World in Figures*.

KOREA (REPUBLIC OF) - DUCKS - See KOREA (REPUBLIC OF) -
LIVESTOCK AND POULTRY

KOREA (REPUBLIC OF) - ECONOMY

Euromonitor Publications Limited, 87-88 Turnmill Street, London EC1M 5QU, England; *International Marketing Data and Statistics*, and *Third World Economic Handbook*.

Facts on File, 460 Park Avenue South, New York, New York 10016 (800) 443-8323; *The New Book of World Rankings*.

G.K. Hall and Company, 70 Lincoln Street, Boston, Massachusetts 02111 (617) 423-3990; *The World in Figures*.

KOREA (REPUBLIC OF) - EDUCATION

The Economist Intelligence Unit, 111 West 57th Street, New York, New York 10019 (800) 938-4685; *The World Market Atlas*.

The Economist Intelligence Unit (Asia) Limited, 10th Floor, Luk Kwok Centre, 72 Gloucester Road, Wanchai, Hong Kong (Phone Number in U.S. (800) 938-4685); *Asian Market Atlas*.

Euromonitor Publications Limited, 87-88 Turnmill Street, London EC1M 5QU, England; *The Pacific Basin: An Economic Handbook*.

Facts on File, 460 Park Avenue South, New York, New York 10016 (800) 443-8323; *The New Book of World Rankings*.

G.K. Hall and Company, 70 Lincoln Street, Boston, Massachusetts 02111 (617) 423-3990; *The World in Figures*.

Korean Overseas Information Service, Ministry of Culture and Information, Seoul 110, Republic of Korea; *Statistical Data on Korea*.

Statistical Office of the United Nations, Publishing Service, New York, New York 10017 (800) 253-9646; *Statistical Yearbook For Asia and the Pacific*.

Times Books, 201 East 50th Street, New York, New York 10022 (212) 751-2600; *The Economist Book of Vital World Statistics*.

United Nations Educational, Scientific and Cultural Organization (UNESCO), 7 Place de Fontenoy, F-75700 Paris, France (Telephone in U.S. (212) 963-5981); *Statistical Yearbook*.

The World Bank, 1818 H Street, NW, Washington, D.C. 20433 (202) 477-1234; *World Tables*.

KOREA (REPUBLIC OF) - EGG PRODUCTION - See KOREA (REPUBLIC OF) - DAIRY PRODUCTS

KOREA (REPUBLIC OF) - EGGPLANT PRODUCTION - See KOREA (REPUBLIC OF) - CROPS

KOREA (REPUBLIC OF) - ELECTRICITY

Facts on File, 460 Park Avenue South, New York, New York 10016 (800) 443-8323; *The New Book of World Rankings*.

Korean Overseas Information Service, Ministry of Culture and Information, Seoul 110, Republic of Korea; *Statistical Data on Korea*.

Statistical Office of the United Nations, Publishing Service, New York, New York 10017 (800) 253-9646; *Statistical Yearbook*.

Times Books, 201 East 50th Street, New York, New York 10022 (212) 751-2600; *The Economist Book of Vital World Statistics*.

KOREA (REPUBLIC OF) - EMPLOYMENT

Euromonitor Publications Limited, 87-88 Turnmill Street, London EC1M 5QU, England; *International Marketing Data and Statistics*, and *The Pacific Basin: An Economic Handbook*.

Facts on File, 460 Park Avenue South, New York, New York 10016 (800) 443-8323; *The New Book of World Rankings*.

International Labour Office, I.L.O. Publications, CH-1211, Geneva 22, Switzerland; *Yearbook of Labour Statistics*.

Korean Overseas Information Service, Ministry of Culture and Information, Seoul 110, Republic of Korea; *Statistical Data on Korea*.

Statistical Office of the United Nations, Publishing Service, New York, New York 10017 (800) 253-9646; *Statistical Yearbook*.

KOREA (REPUBLIC OF) - ENERGY

Business Information Display, Incorporated, 4202 Sorrento Valley Boulevard, San Diego, California 92121; *World Energy Industry*.

Facts on File, 460 Park Avenue South, New York, New York 10016 (800) 443-8323; *The New Book of World Rankings*.

Food and Agricultural Organization of the United Nations (FAO), Via delle Terme di Caracalla, 00100 Rome, Italy (Telephone Number in U.S. (202) 653-2400); *The State of Food and Agriculture*.

G.K. Hall and Company, 70 Lincoln Street, Boston, Massachusetts 02111 (617) 423-3990; *The World in Figures*.

Statistical Office of the United Nations, Publishing Service, New York, New York 10017 (800) 253-9646; *Energy Statistics Yearbook*, *Statistical Yearbook for Asia and the Pacific*, *Statistical Yearbook*, and *World Energy Supplies*.

Times Books, 201 East 50th Street, New York, New York 10022 (212) 751-2600; *The Economist Book of Vital World Statistics*.

KOREA (REPUBLIC OF) - ENGINEERING AND METAL PRODUCTS - EXPORTS AND IMPORTS

Statistical Office of the United Nations, Publishing Service, New York, New York 10017 (800) 253-9646; *Trade in Manufactures of Developing Countries*.

KOREA (REPUBLIC OF) - EXCHANGE RATES

The Economist Intelligence Unit (Asia) Limited, 10th Floor, Luk Kwok Centre, 72 Gloucester Road, Wanchai, Hong Kong (Phone Number in U.S. (800) 938-4685); *Asian Market Atlas*.

Euromonitor Publications Limited, 87-88 Turnmill Street, London EC1M 5QU, England; *The Pacific Basin: An Economic Handbook*.

International Civil Aviation Organization, 1000 Sherbrooke Street West, Suite 400, Montreal, Quebec H3A 2R2, Canada (514) 285-8219; *Civil Aviation Statistics of the World*.

KOREA (REPUBLIC OF) - EXPENDITURES PER HOUSEHOLD

Korean Overseas Information Service, Ministry of Culture and Information, Seoul 110, Republic of Korea; *Statistical Data on Korea*.

KOREA (REPUBLIC OF) - EXPORTS

The Economist Intelligence Unit, 111 West 57th Street, New York, New York 10019 (800) 938-4685; *The World Market Atlas.*

The Economist Intelligence Unit (Asia) Limited, 10th Floor, Luk Kwok Centre, 72 Gloucester Road, Wanchai, Hong Kong (Phone Number in U.S. (800) 938-4685); *Asian Market Atlas.*

Euromonitor Publications Limited, 87-88 Turnmill Street, London EC1M 5QU, England; *The Pacific Basin: An Economic Handbook,* and *International Marketing Data and Statistics,* and *Third World Economic Handbook.*

Food and Agricultural Organization of the United Nations (FAO), Via delle Terme di Caracalla, 00100 Rome, Italy (Telephone Number in U.S. (202) 653-2400); *The State of Food and Agriculture.*

G.K. Hall and Company, 70 Lincoln Street, Boston, Massachusetts 02111 (617) 423-3990; *The World in Figures.*

International Monetary Fund, 700 Nineteenth Street, NW, Washington, D.C. 20431 (202) 623-7000; *Direction of Trade Statistics.*

Korean Overseas Information Service, Ministry of Culture and Information, Seoul 110, Republic of Korea; *Statistical Data on Korea.*

Statistical Office of the United Nations, Publishing Service, New York, New York 10017 (800) 253-9646; *Trade in Manufactures of Developing Countries.*

Times Books, 201 East 50th Street, New York, New York 10022 (212) 751-2600; *The Economist Book of Vital World Statistics.*

The World Bank, 1818 H Street, NW, Washington, D.C. 20433 (202) 477-1234; *World Tables.*

KOREA (REPUBLIC OF) - EXTERNAL INDEBTEDNESS

Euromonitor Publications Limited, 87-88 Turnmill Street, London EC1M 5QU, England; *Third World Economic Handbook.*

The World Bank, 1818 H Street, NW, Washington, D.C. 20433 (202) 477-1234; *World Tables.*

KOREA (REPUBLIC OF) - EXTERNAL TRADE

Food and Agricultural Organization of the United Nations (FAO), Via delle Terme di Caracalla, 00100 Rome, Italy (Telephone Number in U.S. (202) 653-2400); *The State of Food and Agriculture,* and *Trade Yearbook.*

G.K. Hall and Company, 70 Lincoln Street, Boston, Massachusetts 02111 (617) 423-3990; *The World in Figures.*

Statistical Office of the United Nations, Publishing Service, New York, New York 10017 (800) 253-9646; *Statistical Yearbook,* and *Statistical Yearbook for Asia and the Pacific.*

KOREA (REPUBLIC OF) - FABRIC PRODUCTION - See KOREA (REPUBLIC OF) - TEXTILE INDUSTRY

KOREA (REPUBLIC OF) - FARM CROPS - See KOREA (REPUBLIC OF) - CROPS

KOREA (REPUBLIC OF) - FARM POPULATION

Korean Overseas Information Service, Ministry of Culture and Information, Seoul 110, Republic of Korea; *Statistical Data on Korea.*

KOREA (REPUBLIC OF) - FEMALE WORKING POPULATION - See KOREA (REPUBLIC OF) - EMPLOYMENT

KOREA (REPUBLIC OF) - FERTILITY RATES

The Economist Intelligence Unit (Asia) Limited, 10th Floor, Luk Kwok Centre, 72 Gloucester Road, Wanchai, Hong Kong (Phone Number in U.S. (800) 938-4685); *Asian Market Atlas.*

Facts on File, 460 Park Avenue South, New York, New York 10016 (800) 443-8323; *The New Book of World Rankings.*

Times Books, 201 East 50th Street, New York, New York 10022 (212) 751-2600; *The Economist Book of Vital World Statistics.*

The World Bank, 1818 H Street, NW, Washington, D.C. 20433 (202) 477-1234; *World Tables.*

KOREA (REPUBLIC OF) - FERTILIZER

Food and Agricultural Organization of the United Nations (FAO), Via delle Terme di Caracalla, 00100 Rome, Italy (Telephone Number in U.S. (202) 653-2400); *Fertilizer Yearbook,* and *The State of Food and Agriculture.*

Korean Overseas Information Service, Ministry of Culture and Information, Seoul 110, Republic of Korea; *Statistical Data on Korea.*

Statistical Office of the United Nations, Publishing Service, New York, New York 10017 (800) 253-9646; *Statistical Yearbook.*

KOREA (REPUBLIC OF) - FETAL MORTALITY

Statistical Office of the United Nations, Publishing Service, New York, New York 10017 (800) 253-9646; *Demographic Yearbook.*

KOREA (REPUBLIC OF) - FIBRE PRODUCTION - See KOREA (REPUBLIC OF) - TEXTILE INDUSTRY

KOREA (REPUBLIC OF) - FILAMENT PRODUCTION - See KOREA (REPUBLIC OF) - TEXTILE INDUSTRY

KOREA (REPUBLIC OF) - FILM - See KOREA (REPUBLIC OF) - MOTION PICTURES

KOREA (REPUBLIC OF) - FINANCE

Euromonitor Publications Limited, 87-88 Turnmill Street, London EC1M 5QU, England; *The Pacific Basin: An Economic Handbook.*

Facts on File, 460 Park Avenue South, New York, New York 10016 (800) 443-8323; *The New Book of World Rankings.*

G.K. Hall and Company, 70 Lincoln Street, Boston, Massachusetts 02111 (617) 423-3990; *The World in Figures.*

International Monetary Fund, 700 Nineteenth Street, NW, Washington, D.C. 20431 (202) 623-7000; *International Financial Statistics.*

Statistical Office of the United Nations, Publishing Service, New York, New York 10017 (800) 253-9646; *Statistical Yearbook for Asia and the Pacific.*

KOREA (REPUBLIC OF) - FISHERIES

Facts on File, 460 Park Avenue South, New York, New York 10016 (800) 443-8323; *The New Book of World Rankings.*

Food and Agricultural Organization of the United Nations (FAO), Via delle Terme di Caracalla, 00100 Rome, Italy (Telephone Number in U.S. (202) 653-2400); *The State of Food and Agriculture,* and *Yearbook of Fishery Statistics.*

Korean Overseas Information Service, Ministry of Culture and Information, Seoul 110, Republic of Korea; *Statistical Data on Korea.*

Statistical Office of the United Nations, Publishing Service, New York, New York 10017 (800) 253-9646; *Statistical Yearbook.*

KOREA (REPUBLIC OF) - FLAX FIBRE PRODUCTION - See KOREA (REPUBLIC OF) - TEXTILE INDUSTRY

KOREA (REPUBLIC OF) - FLOUR PRODUCTION

Statistical Office of the United Nations, Publishing Service, New York, New York 10017 (800) 253-9646; *Statistical Yearbook.*

KOREA (REPUBLIC OF) - FOOD

Food and Agricultural Organization of the United Nations (FAO), Via delle Terme di Caracalla, 00100 Rome, Italy (Telephone Number in U.S. (202) 653-2400); *The State of Food and Agriculture,* and *Production Yearbook.*

G.K. Hall and Company, 70 Lincoln Street, Boston, Massachusetts 02111 (617) 423-3990; *The World in Figures.*

Korean Overseas Information Service, Ministry of Culture and Information, Seoul 110, Republic of Korea; *Statistical Data on Korea.*

Statistical Office of the United Nations, Publishing Service, New York, New York 10017 (800) 253-9646; *Statistical Yearbook for Asia and the Pacific,* and *Trade in Manufactures of Developing Countries.*

KOREA (REPUBLIC OF) - FOOTWEAR EXPENDITURES

Korean Overseas Information Service, Ministry of Culture and Information, Seoul 110, Republic of Korea; *Statistical Data on Korea.*

KOREA (REPUBLIC OF) - FOREIGN AID

G.K. Hall and Company, 70 Lincoln Street, Boston, Massachusetts 02111 (617) 423-3990; *The World in Figures.*

KOREA (REPUBLIC OF) - FOREIGN HOUSEHOLDS

Korean Overseas Information Service, Ministry of Culture and Information, Seoul 110, Republic of Korea; *Statistical Data on Korea.*

KOREA (REPUBLIC OF) - FOREIGN INDEBTEDNESS

Euromonitor Publications Limited, 87-88 Turnmill Street, London EC1M 5QU, England; *The Pacific Basin: An Economic Handbook.*

KOREA (REPUBLIC OF) - FOREIGN INVESTMENTS

Korean Overseas Information Service, Ministry of Culture and Information, Seoul 110, Republic of Korea; *Statistical Data on Korea.*

KOREA (REPUBLIC OF) - FOREIGN TRADE

The Economist Intelligence Unit (Asia) Limited, 10th Floor, Luk Kwok Centre, 72 Gloucester Road, Wanchai, Hong Kong (Phone Number in U.S. (800) 938-4685); *Asian Market Atlas.*

Euromonitor Publications Limited, 87-88 Turnmill Street, London EC1M 5QU, England; *The Pacific Basin: An Economic Handbook,* and *Third World Economic Handbook.*

Facts on File, 460 Park Avenue South, New York, New York 10016 (800) 443-8323; *The New Book of World Rankings.*

Food and Agricultural Organization of the United Nations (FAO), Via delle Terme di Caracalla, 00100 Rome, Italy (Telephone Number in U.S. (202) 653-2400); *The State of Food and Agriculture.*

G.K. Hall and Company, 70 Lincoln Street, Boston, Massachusetts 02111 (617) 423-3990; *The World in Figures.*

Statistical Office of the United Nations, Publishing Service, New York, New York 10017 (800) 253-9646; *International Trade Statistics Yearbook,* and *Statistical Yearbook.*

KOREA (REPUBLIC OF) - FORESTRY AND FOREST PRODUCTS

The Economist Intelligence Unit (Asia) Limited, 10th Floor, Luk Kwok Centre, 72 Gloucester Road, Wanchai, Hong Kong (Phone Number in U.S. (800) 938-4685); *Asian Market Atlas.*

Euromonitor Publications Limited, 87-88 Turnmill Street, London EC1M 5QU, England; *Third World Economic Handbook.*

Facts on File, 460 Park Avenue South, New York, New York 10016 (800) 443-8323; *The New Book of World Rankings.*

Food and Agricultural Organization of the United Nations (FAO), Via delle Terme di Caracalla, 00100 Rome, Italy (Telephone Number in U.S. (202) 653-2400); *The State of Food and Agriculture,* and *Yearbook of Forest Products.*

G.K. Hall and Company, 70 Lincoln Street, Boston, Massachusetts 02111 (617) 423-3990; *The World in Figures.*

Korean Overseas Information Service, Ministry of Culture and Information, Seoul 110, Republic of Korea; *Statistical Data on Korea.*

Statistical Office of the United Nations, Publishing Service, New York, New York 10017 (800) 253-9646; *Statistical Yearbook.*

United Nations Educational, Scientific and Cultural Organization (UNESCO), 7 Place de Fontenoy, F-75700 Paris, France (Telephone in U.S. (212) 963-5981); *Statistical Yearbook.*

KOREA (REPUBLIC OF) - FURNITURE AND WOOD PRODUCTS EXPORTS AND IMPORTS

Statistical Office of the United Nations, Publishing Service, New York, New York 10017 (800) 253-9646; *International Trade Statistics Yearbook.*

KOREA (REPUBLIC OF) - FURNITURE EXPENDITURES

Korean Overseas Information Service, Ministry of Culture and Information, Seoul 110, Republic of Korea; *Statistical Data on Korea.*

KOREA (REPUBLIC OF) - GARLIC PRODUCTION - See KOREA (REPUBLIC OF) - CROPS

KOREA (REPUBLIC OF) - GAS PRODUCTION - See KOREA (REPUBLIC OF) - MINING AND MINERAL PRODUCTS

KOREA (REPUBLIC OF) - GENERAL INDUSTRIAL STATISTICS

Statistical Office of the United Nations, Publishing Service, New York, New York 10017 (800) 253-9646; *Industrial Statistics Yearbook.*

KOREA (REPUBLIC OF) - GENERAL MORTALITY

Statistical Office of the United Nations, Publishing Service, New York, New York 10017 (800) 253-9646; *Demographic Yearbook.*

KOREA (REPUBLIC OF) - GEOGRAPHIC DATA

Facts on File, 460 Park Avenue South, New York, New York 10016 (800) 443-8323; *The New Book of World Rankings.*

KOREA (REPUBLIC OF) - GOATS - See KOREA (REPUBLIC OF) - LIVESTOCK AND POULTRY

KOREA (REPUBLIC OF) - GOLD HOLDINGS

Statistical Office of the United Nations, Publishing Service, New York, New York 10017 (800) 253-9646; *Statistical Yearbook.*

The World Bank, 1818 H Street, NW, Washington, D.C. 20433 (202) 477-1234; *World Tables.*

KOREA (REPUBLIC OF) - GOLD PRODUCTION AND CONSUMPTION - See (JORDAN) - MINING AND MINERAL PRODUCTS

KOREA (REPUBLIC OF) - GOVERNMENT

G.K. Hall and Company, 70 Lincoln Street, Boston, Massachusetts 02111 (617) 423-3990; *The World in Figures.*

KOREA (REPUBLIC OF) - GOVERNMENT EXPENDITURE

Euromonitor Publications Limited, 87-88 Turnmill Street, London EC1M 5QU, England; *Third World Economic Handbook.*

The World Bank, 1818 H Street, NW, Washington, D.C. 20433 (202) 477-1234; *World Tables.*

KOREA (REPUBLIC OF) - GOVERNMENT FINANCES

Statistical Office of the United Nations, Publishing Service, New York, New York 10017 (800) 253-9646; *Statistical Yearbook.*

KOREA (REPUBLIC OF) - GOVERNMENT REVENUE

Times Books, 201 East 50th Street, New York, New York 10022 (212) 751-2600; *The Economist Book of Vital World Statistics.*

The World Bank, 1818 H Street, NW, Washington, D.C. 20433 (202) 477-1234; *World Tables.*

KOREA (REPUBLIC OF) - GRAIN PRODUCTION - See KOREA (REPUBLIC OF) - CROPS

KOREA (REPUBLIC OF) - GREEN PEPPER AND CHILIE PRODUCTION - See KOREA (REPUBLIC OF) - CROPS

KOREA (REPUBLIC OF) - GROSS DOMESTIC PRODUCT

The Economist Intelligence Unit, 111 West 57th Street, New York, New York 10019 (800) 938-4685; *The World Market Atlas.*

The Economist Intelligence Unit (Asia) Limited, 10th Floor, Luk Kwok Centre, 72 Gloucester Road, Wanchai, Hong Kong (Phone Number in U.S. (800) 938-4685); *Asian Market Atlas.*

Euromonitor Publications Limited, 87-88 Turnmill Street, London EC1M 5QU, England; *International Marketing Data and Statistics, The Pacific Basin: An Economic Handbook,* and *Third World Economic Handbook.*

Facts on File, 460 Park Avenue South, New York, New York 10016 (800) 443-8323; *The New Book of World Rankings.*

G.K. Hall and Company, 70 Lincoln Street, Boston, Massachusetts 02111 (617) 423-3990; *The World in Figures.*

Statistical Office of the United Nations, Publishing Service, New York, New York 10017 (800) 253-9646; *Statistical Yearbook.*

Times Books, 201 East 50th Street, New York, New York 10022 (212) 751-2600; *The Economist Book of Vital World Statistics.*

The World Bank, 1818 H Street, NW, Washington, D.C. 20433 (202) 477-1234; *World Tables.*

KOREA (REPUBLIC OF) - GROSS INDUSTRIAL PRODUCT - BY CATEGORIES OF GOODS

Euromonitor Publications Limited, 87-88 Turnmill Street, London EC1M 5QU, England; *Third World Economic Handbook.*

KOREA (REPUBLIC OF) - GROSS NATIONAL PRODUCT

Euromonitor Publications Limited, 87-88 Turnmill Street, London EC1M 5QU, England; *International Marketing Data and Statistics,* and *Third World Economic Handbook.*

Korean Overseas Information Service, Ministry of Culture and Information, Seoul 110, Republic of Korea; *Statistical Data on Korea.*

U.S. Arms Control and Disarmament Agency, 320 Twenty-first Street, NW, Washington, D.C. 20451 (202) 647-8677; *World Military Expenditures and Arms Transfers.*

The World Bank, 1818 H Street, NW, Washington, D.C. 20433 (202) 477-1234; *World Tables.*

KOREA (REPUBLIC OF) - GROUNDNUT PRODUCTION - See KOREA (REPUBLIC OF) - CROPS

KOREA (REPUBLIC OF) - HEALTH

The Economist Intelligence Unit (Asia) Limited, 10th Floor, Luk Kwok Centre, 72 Gloucester Road, Wanchai, Hong Kong (Phone Number in U.S. (800) 938-4685); *Asian Market Atlas.*

Euromonitor Publications Limited, 87-88 Turnmill Street, London EC1M 5QU, England; *The Pacific Basin: An Economic Handbook.*

Facts on File, 460 Park Avenue South, New York, New York 10016 (800) 443-8323; *The New Book of World Rankings.*

G.K. Hall and Company, 70 Lincoln Street, Boston, Massachusetts 02111 (617) 423-3990; *The World in Figures.*

Korean Overseas Information Service, Ministry of Culture and Information, Seoul 110, Republic of Korea; *Statistical Data on Korea.*

Statistical Office of the United Nations, Publishing Service, New York, New York 10017 (800) 253-9646; *Statistical Yearbook.*

Times Books, 201 East 50th Street, New York, New York 10022 (212) 751-2600; *The Economist Book of Vital World Statistics.*

KOREA (REPUBLIC OF) - HEMP FIBRE PRODUCTION - See KOREA (REPUBLIC OF) - TEXTILE INDUSTRY

KOREA (REPUBLIC OF) - HIDE PRODUCTION - ALL TYPES

Food and Agricultural Organization of the United Nations (FAO), Via delle Terme di Caracalla, 00100 Rome, Italy (Telephone Number in U.S. (202) 653-2400); *Production Yearbook.*

KOREA (REPUBLIC OF) - HIGHWAYS

The Economist Intelligence Unit (Asia) Limited, 10th Floor, Luk Kwok Centre, 72 Gloucester Road, Wanchai, Hong Kong (Phone Number in U.S. (800) 938-4685); *Asian Market Atlas.*

G.K. Hall and Company, 70 Lincoln Street, Boston, Massachusetts 02111 (617) 423-3990; *The World in Figures.*

International Road Federation, 525 School Street, SW, Washington, D.C. 20024 (202) 554-2106; *World Road Statistics.*

Korean Overseas Information Service, Ministry of Culture and Information, Seoul 110, Republic of Korea; *Statistical Data on Korea.*

KOREA (REPUBLIC OF) - HORSES - See KOREA (REPUBLIC OF) - LIVESTOCK AND POULTRY

KOREA (REPUBLIC OF) - HOURS OF WORK - See KOREA (REPUBLIC OF) - EMPLOYMENT

KOREA (REPUBLIC OF) - HOUSING AND HOUSING UNITS

Euromonitor Publications Limited, 87-88 Turnmill Street, London EC1M 5QU, England; *Third World Economic Handbook.*

Facts on File, 460 Park Avenue South, New York, New York 10016 (800) 443-8323; *The New Book of World Rankings.*

Korean Overseas Information Service, Ministry of Culture and Information, Seoul 110, Republic of Korea; *Statistical Data on Korea.*

KOREA (REPUBLIC OF) - HYDROCHLORIC ACID PRODUCTION

Statistical Office of the United Nations, Publishing Service, New York, New York 10017 (800) 253-9646; *Statistical Yearbook.*

KOREA (REPUBLIC OF) - ILLITERATE POPULATION

The Economist Intelligence Unit (Asia) Limited, 10th Floor, Luk Kwok Centre, 72 Gloucester Road, Wanchai, Hong Kong (800) 938-

4685; *The World Market Atlas.*

G.K. Hall and Company, 70 Lincoln Street, Boston, Massachusetts 02111 (617) 423-3990; *The World in Figures.*

United Nations Educational, Scientific and Cultural Organization (UNESCO), 7 Place de Fontenoy, F-75700 Paris, France (Telephone in U.S. (212) 963-5981); *Statistical Yearbook.*

KOREA (REPUBLIC OF) - IMPORT MARKETS

Korean Overseas Information Service, Ministry of Culture and Information, Seoul 110, Republic of Korea; *Statistical Data on Korea.*

KOREA (REPUBLIC OF) - IMPORTS

The Economist Intelligence Unit, 111 West 57th Street, New York, New York 10019 (800) 938-4685; *The World Market Atlas.*

The Economist Intelligence Unit (Asia) Limited, 10th Floor, Luk Kwok Centre, 72 Gloucester Road, Wanchai, Hong Kong (Phone Number in U.S. (800) 938-4685); *Asian Market Atlas.*

Euromonitor Publications Limited, 87-88 Turnmill Street, London EC1M 5QU, England; *International Marketing Data and Statistics, The Pacific Basin: An Economic Handbook, and Third World Economic Handbook.*

Food and Agricultural Organization of the United Nations (FAO), Via delle Terme di Caracalla, 00100 Rome, Italy (Telephone Number in U.S. (303) 653-2400); *The State of Food and Agriculture.*

G.K. Hall and Company, 70 Lincoln Street, Boston, Massachusetts 02111 (617) 423-3990; *The World in Figures.*

International Monetary Fund, 700 Nineteenth Street, NW, Washington, D.C. 20431 (202) 623-7000; *Direction of Trade Statistics.*

Korean Overseas Information Service, Ministry of Culture and Information, Seoul 110, Republic of Korea; *Statistical Data on Korea.*

Statistical Office of the United Nations, Publishing Service, New York, New York 10017 (800) 253-9646; *Trade in Manufactures of Developing Countries.*

Times Books, 201 East 50th Street, New York, New York 10022 (212) 751-2600; *The Economist Book of Vital World Statistics.*

The World Bank, 1818 H Street, NW, Washington, D.C. 20433 (202) 477-1234; *World Tables.*

KOREA (REPUBLIC OF) - INDUSTRIAL METALS PRODUCTION - See KOREA (REPUBLIC OF) - MINING AND MINERAL PRODUCTS

KOREA (REPUBLIC OF) - INDUSTRY

Euromonitor Publications Limited, 87-88 Turnmill Street, London EC1M 5QU, England; *International Marketing Data and Statistics, and Third World Economic Handbook.*

Facts on File, 460 Park Avenue South, New York, New York 10016 (800) 443-8323; *The New Book of World Rankings.*

G.K. Hall and Company, 70 Lincoln Street, Boston, Massachusetts 02111 (617) 423-3990; *The World in Figures.*

International Labour Office, I.L.O. Publications, CH-1211, Geneva 22, Switzerland; *Yearbook of Labour Statistics.*

Statistical Office of the United Nations, Publishing Service, New York, New York 10017 (800) 253-9646; *Statistical Yearbook*, and *Statistical Yearbook for Asia and the Pacific*.

Times Books, 201 East 50th Street, New York, New York 10022 (212) 751-2600; *The Economist Book of Vital World Statistics*.

The World Bank, 1818 H Street, NW, Washington, D.C. 20433 (202) 477-1234; *World Tables*.

KOREA (REPUBLIC OF) - INFANT AND MATERNAL MORTALITY

The Economist Intelligence Unit (Asia) Limited, 10th Floor, Luk Kwok Centre, 72 Gloucester Road, Wanchai, Hong Kong (Phone Number in U.S. (800) 938-4685); *Asian Market Atlas*.

Statistical Office of the United Nations, Publishing Service, New York, New York 10017 (800) 253-9646; *Demographic Yearbook*.

Times Books, 201 East 50th Street, New York, New York 10022 (212) 751-2600; *The Economist Book of Vital World Statistics*.

The World Bank, 1818 H Street, NW, Washington, D.C. 20433 (202) 477-1234; *World Tables*.

KOREA (REPUBLIC OF) - INTEREST RATES

Euromonitor Publications Limited, 87-88 Turnmill Street, London EC1M 5QU, England; *The Pacific Basin: An Economic Handbook*.

KOREA (REPUBLIC OF) - INTERNAL TRADE

Statistical Office of the United Nations, Publishing Service, New York, New York 10017 (800) 253-9646; *Statistical Yearbook*, and *Statistical Yearbook for Asia and the Pacific*.

KOREA (REPUBLIC OF) - INTERNATIONAL RESERVES EXCLUDING GOLD

Statistical Office of the United Nations, Publishing Service, New York, New York 10017 (800) 253-9646; *Statistical Yearbook*.

The World Bank, 1818 H Street, NW, Washington, D.C. 20433 (202) 477-1234; *World Tables*.

KOREA (REPUBLIC OF) - INVESTMENT

Korean Overseas Information Service, Ministry of Culture and Information, Seoul 110, Republic of Korea; *Statistical Data on Korea*.

KOREA (REPUBLIC OF) - IRON AND IRON ORE PRODUCTION - See KOREA (REPUBLIC OF) - MINING AND MINERAL PRODUCTS

KOREA (REPUBLIC OF) - IRRIGATION

Euromonitor Publications Limited, 87-88 Turnmill Street, London EC1M 5QU, England; *International Marketing Data and Statistics*.

KOREA (REPUBLIC OF) - LABOR FORCE

The Economist Intelligence Unit (Asia) Limited, 10th Floor, Luk Kwok Centre, 72 Gloucester Road, Wanchai, Hong Kong (Phone Number in U.S. (800) 938-4685); *Asian Market Atlas*.

Euromonitor Publications Limited, 87-88 Turnmill Street, London EC1M 5QU, England; *The Pacific Basin: An Economic Handbook*, and *International Marketing Data and Statistics*.

Facts on File, 460 Park Avenue South, New York, New York 10016 (800) 443-8323; *The New Book of World Rankings*.

Food and Agricultural Organization of the United Nations (FAO), Via delle Terme di Caracalla, 00100 Rome, Italy (Telephone Number in U.S. (202) 653-2400); *The State of Food and Agriculture*.

G.K. Hall and Company, 70 Lincoln Street, Boston, Massachusetts 02111 (617) 423-3990; *The World in Figures*.

Times Books, 201 East 50th Street, New York, New York 10022 (212) 751-2600; *The Economist Book of Vital World Statistics*.

The World Bank, 1818 H Street, NW, Washington, D.C. 20433 (202) 477-1234; *World Tables*.

KOREA (REPUBLIC OF) - LABOR PRODUCTIVITY

International Labour Office, I.L.O. Publications, CH-1211, Geneva 22, Switzerland; *Yearbook of Labour Statistics*.

KOREA (REPUBLIC OF) - LAND AREA

Korean Overseas Information Service, Ministry of Culture and Information, Seoul 110, Republic of Korea; *Statistical Data on Korea*.

KOREA (REPUBLIC OF) - LAND USE

Euromonitor Publications Limited, 87-88 Turnmill Street, London EC1M 5QU, England; *International Marketing Data and Statistics*.

Food and Agricultural Organization of the United Nations (FAO), Via delle Terme di Caracalla, 00100 Rome, Italy (Telephone Number in U.S. (202) 653-2400); *Production Yearbook*.

G.K. Hall and Company, 70 Lincoln Street, Boston, Massachusetts 02111 (617) 423-3990; *The World in Figures*.

KOREA (REPUBLIC OF) - LEAD AND LEAD ORE PRODUCTION - See KOREA (REPUBLIC OF) - MINING AND MINERAL PRODUCTS

KOREA (REPUBLIC OF) - LEATHER AND FOOTWEAR EXPORTS AND IMPORTS

Statistical Office of the United Nations, Publishing Service, New York, New York 10017 (800) 253-9646; *Trade in Manufactures of Developing Countries*.

KOREA (REPUBLIC OF) - LIBRARIES

Facts on File, 460 Park Avenue South, New York, New York 10016 (800) 443-8323; *The New Book of World Rankings*.

United Nations Educational, Scientific and Cultural Organization (UNESCO), 7 Place de Fontenoy, F-75700 Paris, France (Telephone in U.S. (212) 963-5981); *Statistical Yearbook*.

KOREA (REPUBLIC OF) - LIFE EXPECTANCY

The Economist Intelligence Unit (Asia) Limited, 10th Floor, Luk Kwok Centre, 72 Gloucester Road, Wanchai, Hong Kong (Phone Number in U.S. (800) 938-4685); *Asian Market Atlas*.

Korean Overseas Information Service, Ministry of Culture and Information, Seoul 110, Republic of Korea; *Statistical Data on Korea*.

KOREA (REPUBLIC OF) - LIVESTOCK AND POULTRY

Euromonitor Publications Limited, 87-88 Turnmill Street, London EC1M 5QU, England; *International Marketing Data and Statistics*.

Facts on File, 460 Park Avenue South, New York, New York 10016 (800) 443-8323; *The New Book of World Rankings*.

Food and Agricultural Organization of the United Nations (FAO), Via delle Terme di Caracalla, 00100 Rome, Italy (Telephone Number in U.S. (202) 653-2400); *Production Yearbook*, and *The State of Food and Agriculture*.

G.K. Hall and Company, 70 Lincoln Street, Boston, Massachusetts 02111 (617) 423-3990; *The World in Figures*.

Korean Overseas Information Service, Ministry of Culture and Information, Seoul 110, Republic of Korea; *Statistical Data on Korea*.

Statistical Office of the United Nations, Publishing Service, New York, New York 10017 (800) 253-9646; *Statistical Yearbook*.

KOREA (REPUBLIC OF) - LIVING LEVELS

G.K. Hall and Company, 70 Lincoln Street, Boston, Massachusetts 02111 (617) 423-3990; *The World in Figures*.

Times Books, 201 East 50th Street, New York, New York 10022 (212) 751-2600; *The Economist Book of Vital World Statistics*.

KOREA (REPUBLIC OF) - MAIL - NUMBER OF PIECES SENT OR RECEIVED

Statistical Office of the United Nations, Publishing Service, New York, New York 10017 (800) 253-9646; *Statistical Yearbook*.

KOREA (REPUBLIC OF) - MANGANESE ORE PRODUCTION - See KOREA (REPUBLIC OF) - MINING AND MINERAL PRODUCTS

KOREA (REPUBLIC OF) - MANPOWER

Statistical Office of the United Nations, Publishing Service, New York, New York 10017 (800) 253-9646; *Statistical Yearbook for Asia and the Pacific*.

KOREA (REPUBLIC OF) - MANUFACTURING

Euromonitor Publications Limited, 87-88 Turnmill Street, London EC1M 5QU, England; *Third World Economic Handbook*.

Facts on File, 460 Park Avenue South, New York, New York 10016 (800) 443-8323; *The New Book of World Rankings*.

G.K. Hall and Company, 70 Lincoln Street, Boston, Massachusetts 02111 (617) 423-3990; *The World in Figures*.

Statistical Office of the United Nations, Publishing Service, New York, New York 10017 (800) 253-9646; *Statistical Yearbook*.

Times Books, 201 East 50th Street, New York, New York 10022 (212) 751-2600; *The Economist Book of Vital World Statistics*.

The World Bank, 1818 H Street, NW, Washington, D.C. 20433 (202) 477-1234; *World Tables*.

KOREA (REPUBLIC OF) - MARRIAGE RATES

Facts on File, 460 Park Avenue South, New York, New York 10016 (800) 443-8323; *The New Book of World Rankings*.

Statistical Office of the United Nations, Publishing Service, New York, New York 10017 (800) 253-9646; *Demographic Yearbook*, and *Statistical Yearbook*.

KOREA (REPUBLIC OF) - MEAT PRODUCTION - See KOREA (REPUBLIC OF) - LIVESTOCK AND POULTRY

KOREA (REPUBLIC OF) - MEDICAL CARE EXPENDITURES

Korean Overseas Information Service, Ministry of Culture and Information, Seoul 110, Republic of Korea; *Statistical Data on Korea*.

KOREA (REPUBLIC OF) - MEDICAL FACILITIES

Korean Overseas Information Service, Ministry of Culture and Information, Seoul 110, Republic of Korea; *Statistical Data on Korea*.

KOREA (REPUBLIC OF) - MERCHANT SHIPPING

G.K. Hall and Company, 70 Lincoln Street, Boston, Massachusetts 02111 (617) 423-3990; *The World in Figures*.

Statistical Office of the United Nations, Publishing Service, New York, New York 10017 (800) 253-9646; *Statistical Yearbook*.

Times Books, 201 East 50th Street, New York, New York 10022 (212) 751-2600; *The Economist Book of Vital World Statistics*.

KOREA (REPUBLIC OF) - MILITARY

The Economist Intelligence Unit (Asia) Limited, 10th Floor, Luk Kwok Centre, 72 Gloucester Road, Wanchai, Hong Kong (Phone Number in U.S. (800) 938-4685); *Asian Market Atlas*.

G.K. Hall and Company, 70 Lincoln Street, Boston, Massachusetts 02111 (617) 423-3990; *The World in Figures*.

The International Institute for Strategic Studies, 23 Tavistock Street, London WC2E 7NQ, England; *The Military Balance*.

U.S. Arms Control and Disarmament Agency, 320 Twenty-first Street, NW, Washington, D.C. 20451 (202) 647-8677; *World Military Expenditures and Arms Transfers*.

KOREA (REPUBLIC OF) - MILK PRODUCTION - See KOREA (REPUBLIC OF) - DAIRY PRODUCTS

KOREA (REPUBLIC OF) - MILLET PRODUCTION - See KOREA (REPUBLIC OF) - CROPS

KOREA (REPUBLIC OF) - MINING AND MINERAL PRODUCTS

Euromonitor Publications Limited, 87-88 Turnmill Street, London EC1M 5QU, England; *Third World Economic Handbook*.

Facts on File, 460 Park Avenue South, New York, New York 10016 (800) 443-8323; *The New Book of World Rankings*.

G.K. Hall and Company, 70 Lincoln Street, Boston, Massachusetts 02111 (617) 423-3990; *The World in Figures*.

Korean Overseas Information Service, Ministry of Culture and Information, Seoul 110, Republic of Korea; *Statistical Data on Korea*.

Statistical Office of the United Nations, Publishing Service, New York, New York 10017 (800) 253-9646; *Statistical Yearbook*.

KOREA (REPUBLIC OF) - MOLYBDENUM ORE PRODUCTION - See KOREA (REPUBLIC OF) - MINING AND MINERAL PRODUCTS

KOREA (REPUBLIC OF) - MONEY EXCHANGE RATE

Euromonitor Publications Limited, 87-88 Turnmill Street, London EC1M 5QU, England; *International Marketing Data and Statistics*.

Statistical Office of the United Nations, Publishing Service, New York, New York 10017 (800) 253-9646; *Statistical Yearbook*.

KOREA (REPUBLIC OF) - MONEY RESERVES

Euromonitor Publications Limited, 87-88 Turnmill Street, London EC1M 5QU, England; *International Marketing Data and Statistics*.

KOREA (REPUBLIC OF) - MONEY SUPPLY

Euromonitor Publications Limited, 87-88 Turnmill Street, London EC1M 5QU, England; *International Marketing Data and Statistics*.

G.K. Hall and Company, 70 Lincoln Street, Boston, Massachusetts 02111 (617) 423-3990; *The World in Figures*.

International Monetary Fund, 700 Nineteenth Street, NW, Washington, D.C. 20431 (202) 623-7000; *International Financial Statistics*.

Statistical Office of the United Nations, Publishing Service, New York, New York 10017; *Statistical Yearbook*.

The World Bank, 1818 H Street, NW, Washington, D.C. 20433 (202) 477-1234; *World Tables*.

KOREA (REPUBLIC OF) - MOTION PICTURES

Korean Overseas Information Service, Ministry of Culture and Information, Seoul 110, Republic of Korea; *Statistical Data on Korea*.

Statistical Office of the United Nations, Publishing Service, New York, New York 10017 (800) 253-9646; *Statistical Yearbook*.

United Nations Educational, Scientific and Cultural Organization (UNESCO), 7 Place de Fontenoy, F-75700 Paris, France (Telephone in U.S. (212) 963-5981); *Statistical Yearbook*.

KOREA (REPUBLIC OF) - MOTOR VEHICLE ASSEMBLY

Korean Overseas Information Service, Ministry of Culture and Information, Seoul 110, Republic of Korea; *Statistical Data on Korea*.

Statistical Office of the United Nations, Publishing Service, New York, New York 10017 (800) 253-9646; *Statistical Yearbook*.

KOREA (REPUBLIC OF) - MOTOR VEHICLES IN USE

G.K. Hall and Company, 70 Lincoln Street, Boston, Massachusetts 02111 (617) 423-3990; *The World in Figures*.

International Road Federation, 525 School Street, SW, Washington, D.C. 20024 (202) 554-2106; *World Road Statistics*.

Korean Overseas Information Service, Ministry of Culture and Information, Seoul 110, Republic of Korea; *Statistical Data on Korea*.

Statistical Office of the United Nations, Publishing Service, New York, New York 10017 (800) 253-9646; *Statistical Yearbook*.

Times Books, 201 East 50th Street, New York, New York 10022 (212) 751-2600; *The Economist Book of Vital World Statistics*.

KOREA (REPUBLIC OF) - MUSEUMS

Facts on File, 460 Park Avenue South, New York, New York 10016 (800) 443-8323; *The New Book of World Rankings*.

United Nations Educational, Scientific and Cultural Organization (UNESCO), 7 Place de Fontenoy, F-75700 Paris, France (Telephone in U.S. (212) 963-5981); *Statistical Yearbook*.

KOREA (REPUBLIC OF) - NATALITY - See KOREA (REPUBLIC OF) - BIRTH RATES

KOREA (REPUBLIC OF) - NATIONAL ACCOUNTS

International Monetary Fund, 700 Nineteenth Street, NW, Washington, D.C. 20431 (202) 623-7000; *International Financial Statistics*.

Statistical Office of the United Nations, Publishing Service, New York, New York 10017 (800) 253-9646; *National Accounts Statistics, Statistical Yearbook*, and *Statistical Yearbook for Asia and the Pacific*.

KOREA (REPUBLIC OF) - NATIONAL INCOME

Facts on File, 460 Park Avenue South, New York, New York 10016 (800) 443-8323; *The New Book of World Rankings*.

G.K. Hall and Company, 70 Lincoln Street, Boston, Massachusetts 02111 (617) 423-3990; *The World in Figures*.

Korean Overseas Information Service, Ministry of Culture and Information, Seoul 110, Republic of Korea; *Statistical Data on Korea*.

Statistical Office of the United Nations, Publishing Service, New York, New York 10017 (800) 253-9646; *Statistical Yearbook*.

KOREA (REPUBLIC OF) - NATIONAL PRODUCT

Facts on File, 460 Park Avenue South, New York, New York 10016 (800) 443-8323; *The New Book of World Rankings*.

Statistical Office of the United Nations, Publishing Service, New York, New York 10017 (800) 253-9646; *Statistical Yearbook*.

KOREA (REPUBLIC OF) - NATURAL GAS PRODUCTION - See KOREA (REPUBLIC OF) - MINING AND MINERAL PRODUCTS

KOREA (REPUBLIC OF) - NEWS AGENCIES

Korean Overseas Information Service, Ministry of Culture and Information, Seoul 110, Republic of Korea; *Statistical Data on Korea*.

KOREA (REPUBLIC OF) - NEWSPAPER PRODUCTION AND CONSUMPTION - See KOREA (REPUBLIC OF) - FORESTRY AND FOREST PRODUCTS

KOREA (REPUBLIC OF) - NEWSPRINT - See KOREA (REPUBLIC OF) - FORESTRY AND FOREST PRODUCTS

KOREA (REPUBLIC OF) - NICKEL ORE PRODUCTION AND CONSUMPTION - See KOREA (REPUBLIC OF) - MINING AND MINERAL PRODUCTS

KOREA (REPUBLIC OF) - OCCUPATIONS - See KOREA (REPUBLIC OF) - LABOR FORCE

KOREA (REPUBLIC OF) - PAPER - See KOREA (REPUBLIC OF) - FORESTRY AND FOREST PRODUCTS

KOREA (REPUBLIC OF) - PATENTS

Statistical Office of the United Nations, Publishing Service, New York, New York 10017 (800) 253-9646; *Statistical Yearbook*.

KOREA (REPUBLIC OF) - PEANUT PRODUCTION - See KOREA (REPUBLIC OF) - CROPS

KOREA (REPUBLIC OF) - PERIODICALS

Korean Overseas Information Service, Ministry of Culture and Information, Seoul 110, Republic of Korea; *Statistical Data on Korea*.

United Nations Educational, Scientific and Cultural Organization (UNESCO), 7 Place de Fontenoy, F-75700 Paris, France (Telephone in U.S. (212) 963-5981); *Statistical Yearbook*.

KOREA (REPUBLIC OF) - PESTICIDE USE

Food and Agricultural Organization of the United Nations (FAO), Via delle Terme di Caracalla, 00100 Rome, Italy (Telephone Number in U.S. (202) 653-2400); *The State of Food and Agriculture*.

KOREA (REPUBLIC OF) - PETROLEUM INDUSTRY

Facts on File, 460 Park Avenue South, New York, New York 10016 (800) 443-8323; *The New Book of World Rankings*.

Food and Agricultural Organization of the United Nations (FAO), Via delle Terme di Caracalla, 00100 Rome, Italy (Telephone Number in U.S. (202) 653-2400); *The State of Food and Agriculture*.

G.K. Hall and Company, 70 Lincoln Street, Boston, Massachusetts 02111 (617) 423-3990; *The World in Figures*.

Statistical Office of the United Nations, Publishing Service, New York, New York 10017 (800) 253-9646; *Statistical Yearbook*.

KOREA (REPUBLIC OF) - PIG-IRON AND FERRO-ALLOY PRODUCTION - See KOREA (REPUBLIC OF) - MINING AND MINERAL PRODUCTS

KOREA (REPUBLIC OF) - PIGS - See KOREA (REPUBLIC OF) - LIVESTOCK AND POULTRY

KOREA (REPUBLIC OF) - PLASTICS AND RESIN PRODUCTION

Euromonitor Publications Limited, 87-88 Turnmill Street, London EC1M 5QU, England; *Third World Economic Handbook*.

Statistical Office of the United Nations, Publishing Service, New York, New York 10017 (800) 253-9646; *Statistical Yearbook*.

KOREA (REPUBLIC OF) - POPULATION

The Economist Intelligence Unit, 111 West 57th Street, New York, New York 10019 (800) 938-4685; *The World Market Atlas*.

The Economist Intelligence Unit (Asia) Limited, 10th Floor, Luk Kwok Centre, 72 Gloucester Road, Wanchai, Hong Kong (Phone Number in U.S. (800) 938-4685); *Asian Market Atlas*.

Euromonitor Publications Limited, 87-88 Turnmill Street, London EC1M 5QU, England; *International Marketing Data and Statistics*, *The Pacific Basin: An Economic Handbook*, and *Third World Economic Handbook*.

Facts on File, 460 Park Avenue South, New York, New York 10016 (800) 443-8323; *The New Book of World Rankings*.

Food and Agricultural Organization of the United Nations (FAO), Via delle Terme di Caracalla, 00100 Rome, Italy (Telephone Number in U.S. (202) 653-2400); *Production Yearbook*.

G.K. Hall and Company, 70 Lincoln Street, Boston, Massachusetts 02111 (617) 423-3990; *The World in Figures*.

International Labour Office, I.L.O. Publications, CH-1211, Geneva 22, Switzerland; *Yearbook of Labour Statistics*.

Korean Overseas Information Service, Ministry of Culture and Information, Seoul 110, Republic of Korea; *Statistical Data on Korea*.

Statistical Office of the United Nations, Publishing Service, New York, New York 10017 (800) 253-9646; *Demographic Yearbook*, *Statistical Yearbook*, and *Statistical Yearbook for Asia and the Pacific*.

Times Books, 201 East 50th Street, New York, New York 10022 (212) 751-2600; *The Economist Book of Vital World Statistics*.

United Nations Educational, Scientific and Cultural Organization (UNESCO), 7 Place de Fontenoy, F-75700 Paris, France (Telephone in U.S. (212) 963-5981); *Statistical Yearbook*.

U.S. Arms Control and Disarmament Agency, 320 Twenty-first Street, NW, Washington, D.C. 20451 (202) 647-8677; *World Military Expenditures and Arms Transfers*.

KOREA (REPUBLIC OF) - POST OFFICES

Facts on File, 460 Park Avenue South, New York, New York 10016 (800) 443-8323; *The New Book of World Rankings*.

Korean Overseas Information Service, Ministry of Culture and Information, Seoul 110, Republic of Korea; *Statistical Data on Korea*.

KOREA (REPUBLIC OF) - POTATO PRODUCTION - See KOREA (REPUBLIC OF) - CROPS

KOREA (REPUBLIC OF) - PRECIPITATION

Korean Overseas Information Service, Ministry of Culture and Information, Seoul 110, Republic of Korea; *Statistical Data on Korea*.

KOREA (REPUBLIC OF) - PRICES

Facts on File, 460 Park Avenue South, New York, New York 10016 (800) 443-8323; *The New Book of World Rankings*.

Food and Agricultural Organization of the United Nations (FAO), Via delle Terme di Caracalla, 00100 Rome, Italy (Telephone Number in U.S. (202) 653-2400); *Production Yearbook*, and *The State of Food and Agriculture*.

G.K. Hall and Company, 70 Lincoln Street, Boston, Massachusetts 02111 (617) 423-3990; *The World in Figures*.

International Labour Office, I.L.O. Publications, CH-1211, Geneva 22, Switzerland; *Yearbook of Labour Statistics*.

KOREA (REPUBLIC OF) - PRINTING AND WRITING PAPER - See KOREA (REPUBLIC OF) - FORESTRY AND FOREST PRODUCTS

KOREA (REPUBLIC OF) - PRODUCTION

Facts on File, 460 Park Avenue South, New York, New York 10016 (800) 443-8323; *The New Book of World Rankings*.

G.K. Hall and Company, 70 Lincoln Street, Boston, Massachusetts 02111 (617) 423-3990; *The World in Figures*.

KOREA (REPUBLIC OF) - PRODUCTIVITY

Euromonitor Publications Limited, 87-88 Turnmill Street, London EC1M 5QU, England; *International Marketing Data and Statistics*.

KOREA (REPUBLIC OF) - PUBLIC FINANCE

Facts on File, 460 Park Avenue South, New York, New York 10016 (800) 443-8323; *The New Book of World Rankings*.

KOREA (REPUBLIC OF) - RADIO BROADCASTING - See KOREA (REPUBLIC OF) - BROADCASTING

KOREA (REPUBLIC OF) - RADIO RECEIVERS - IN USE

Statistical Office of the United Nations, Publishing Service, New York, New York 10017 (800) 253-9646; *Statistical Yearbook*.

KOREA (REPUBLIC OF) - RAILWAYS

G.K. Hall and Company, 70 Lincoln Street, Boston, Massachusetts 02111 (617) 423-3990; *The World in Figures*.

Jane's Information Group, Sentinel House, 163 Brighton Road, Coulsdon, Surrey CR5 2NH, England (Telephone Number in U.S. (703) 683-3700); *Jane's World Railways*.

Korean Overseas Information Service, Ministry of Culture and Information, Seoul 110, Republic of Korea; *Statistical Data on Korea*.

Statistical Office of the United Nations, Publishing Service, New York, New York 10017 (800) 253-9646; *Statistical Yearbook*.

KOREA (REPUBLIC OF) - RAPESEED PRODUCTION - See KOREA (REPUBLIC OF) - CROPS

KOREA (REPUBLIC OF) - READING EXPENDITURES - EDUCATIONAL AND RECREATIONAL

Korean Overseas Information Service, Ministry of Culture and Information, Seoul 110, Republic of Korea; *Statistical Data on Korea*.

KOREA (REPUBLIC OF) - RELIGIONS

Facts on File, 460 Park Avenue South, New York, New York 10016 (800) 443-8323; *The New Book of World Rankings*.

Korean Overseas Information Service, Ministry of Culture and Information, Seoul 110, Republic of Korea; *Statistical Data on Korea*.

KOREA (REPUBLIC OF) - RENT PRICES

International Labour Office, I.L.O. Publications, CH-1211, Geneva 22, Switzerland; *Yearbook of Labour Statistics*.

KOREA (REPUBLIC OF) - RETAIL TRADE

Euromonitor Publications Limited, 87-88 Turnmill Street, London EC1M 5QU, England; *Third World Economic Handbook*.

G.K. Hall and Company, 70 Lincoln Street, Boston, Massachusetts 02111 (617) 423-3990; *The World in Figures*.

Statistical Office of the United Nations, Publishing Service, New York, New York 10017 (800) 253-9646; *Statistical Yearbook*.

KOREA (REPUBLIC OF) - RICE PRODUCTION - See KOREA (REPUBLIC OF) - CROPS

KOREA (REPUBLIC OF) - ROADS - See KOREA (REPUBLIC OF) - HIGHWAYS

KOREA (REPUBLIC OF) - ROOT AND TUBER PRODUCTION - See KOREA (REPUBLIC OF) - CROPS

KOREA (REPUBLIC OF) - ROUNDWOOD PRODUCTION - See KOREA (REPUBLIC OF) - FORESTRY AND FOREST PRODUCTS

KOREA (REPUBLIC OF) - RUBBER PRODUCTION AND CONSUMPTION

Euromonitor Publications Limited, 87-88 Turnmill Street, London EC1M 5QU, England; *Third World Economic Handbook*.

Facts on File, 460 Park Avenue South, New York, New York 10016 (800) 443-8323; *The New Book of World Rankings*.

Statistical Office of the United Nations, Publishing Service, New York, New York 10017 (800) 253-9646; *Statistical Yearbook*.

KOREA (REPUBLIC OF) - SALT PRODUCTION - See KOREA (REPUBLIC OF) - MINING AND MINERAL PRODUCTS

KOREA (REPUBLIC OF) - SAWNWOOD PRODUCTION - See KOREA (REPUBLIC OF) - FORESTRY AND FOREST PRODUCTS

KOREA (REPUBLIC OF) - SCIENCE AND TECHNOLOGY - EXPENDITURE FOR RESEARCH

Statistical Office of the United Nations, Publishing Service, New York, New York 10017 (800) 253-9646; *Statistical Yearbook*.

KOREA (REPUBLIC OF) - SCIENTISTS AND TECHNICIANS

Statistical Office of the United Nations, Publishing Service, New York, New York 10017 (800) 253-9646; *Statistical Yearbook*.

United Nations Educational, Scientific and Cultural Organization (UNESCO), 7 Place de Fontenoy, F-75700 Paris, France (Telephone in U.S. (212) 963-5981); *Statistical Yearbook*.

KOREA (REPUBLIC OF) - SENIOR CITIZENS

Facts on File, 460 Park Avenue South, New York, New York 10016 (800) 443-8323; *The New Book of World Rankings*.

KOREA (REPUBLIC OF) - SESAME SEED PRODUCTION - See KOREA (REPUBLIC OF) - CROPS

KOREA (REPUBLIC OF) - SHEEP - See KOREA (REPUBLIC OF) - LIVESTOCK AND POULTRY

KOREA (REPUBLIC OF) - SHIPBUILDING CAPACITY

Korean Overseas Information Service, Ministry of Culture and Information, Seoul 110, Republic of Korea; *Statistical Data on Korea.*

KOREA (REPUBLIC OF) - SILVER PRODUCTION AND CONSUMPTION - See KOREA (REPUBLIC OF) - MINING AND MINERAL PRODUCTS

KOREA (REPUBLIC OF) - SOCIAL DATA

Facts on File, 460 Park Avenue South, New York, New York 10016 (800) 443-8323; *The New Book of World Rankings.*

G.K. Hall and Company, 70 Lincoln Street, Boston, Massachusetts 02111 (617) 423-3990; *The World in Figures.*

KOREA (REPUBLIC OF) - SOYBEAN PRODUCTION - See KOREA (REPUBLIC OF) - CROPS

KOREA (REPUBLIC OF) - STATE BUDGET REVENUE AND EXPENDITURES

Euromonitor Publications Limited, 87-88 Turnmill Street, London EC1M 5QU, England; *International Marketing Data and Statistics.*

KOREA (REPUBLIC OF) - STEEL - See KOREA (REPUBLIC OF) - MINING AND MINERAL PRODUCTS

KOREA (REPUBLIC OF) STOCKS - COMMODITY - MARKET PRICE - INDEX

Food and Agricultural Organization of the United Nations (FAO), Via delle Terme di Caracalla, 00100 Rome, Italy (Telephone Number in U.S. (202) 653-2400); *The State of Food and Agriculture.*

KOREA (REPUBLIC OF) - SUGAR PRODUCTION AND CONSUMPTION - See KOREA (REPUBLIC OF) - CROPS

KOREA (REPUBLIC OF) - SULPHURIC ACID PRODUCTION - See (KOREA REPUBLIC OF) - MINING AND MINERAL PRODUCTS

KOREA (REPUBLIC OF) - TAXATION

G.K. Hall and Company, 70 Lincoln Street, Boston, Massachusetts 02111 (617) 423-3990; *The World in Figures.*

International Road Federation, 525 School Street, SW, Washington, D.C. 20024 (202) 554-2106; *World Road Statistics.*

The World Bank, 1818 H Street, NW, Washington, D.C. 20433 (202) 477-1234; *World Tables.*

KOREA (REPUBLIC OF) - TELEGRAPH SERVICE

Korean Overseas Information Service, Ministry of Culture and Information, Seoul 110, Republic of Korea; *Statistical Data on Korea.*

KOREA (REPUBLIC OF) - TELEPHONES IN USE

American Telephone and Telegraph Company, 26 Parsippany Road, Whippany, New Jersey 07981 (800) 338-4038; *The World's Telephones.*

The Economist Intelligence Unit (Asia) Limited, 10th Floor, Luk Kwok Centre, 72 Gloucester Road, Wanchai, Hong Kong (Phone Number in U.S. (800) 938-4685); *Asian Market Atlas.*

Euromonitor Publications Limited, 87-88 Turnmill Street, London EC1M 5QU, England; *The Pacific Basin: An Economic Handbook,* and *Third World Economic Handbook.*

G.K. Hall and Company, 70 Lincoln Street, Boston, Massachusetts 02111 (617) 423-3990; *The World in Figures.*

Korean Overseas Information Service, Ministry of Culture and Information, Seoul 110, Republic of Korea; *Statistical Data on Korea.*

Statistical Office of the United Nations, Publishing Service, New York, New York 10017 (800) 253-9646; *Statistical Yearbook.*

KOREA (REPUBLIC OF) - TELEVISION BROADCASTING - See KOREA (REPUBLIC OF) - BROADCASTING

KOREA (REPUBLIC OF) - TELEVISIONS IN USE

The Economist Intelligence Unit (Asia) Limited, 10th Floor, Luk Kwok Centre, 72 Gloucester Road, Wanchai, Hong Kong (Phone Number in U.S. (800) 938-4685); *Asian Market Atlas.*

Korean Overseas Information Service, Ministry of Culture and Information, Seoul 110, Republic of Korea; *Statistical Data on Korea.*

KOREA (REPUBLIC OF) - TEMPERATURE

Korean Overseas Information Service, Ministry of Culture and Information, Seoul 110, Republic of Korea; *Statistical Data on Korea.*

KOREA (REPUBLIC OF) - TEXTILE INDUSTRY

Euromonitor Publications Limited, 87-88 Turnmill Street, London EC1M 5QU, England; *Third World Economic Handbook.*

Food and Agricultural Organization of the United Nations (FAO), Via delle Terme di Caracalla, 00100 Rome, Italy (Telephone Number in U.S. (202) 653-2400); *Production Yearbook.*

G.K. Hall and Company, 70 Lincoln Street, Boston, Massachusetts 02111 (617) 423-3990; *The World in Figures.*

Statistical Office of the United Nations, Publishing Service, New York, New York 10017 (800) 253-9646; *Statistical Yearbook,* and *Trade in Manufactures of Developing Countries.*

KOREA (REPUBLIC OF) - THEATRE

United Nations Educational, Scientific and Cultural Organization (UNESCO), 7 Place de Fontenoy, F-75700 Paris, France (Telephone in U.S. (212) 963-5981); *Statistical Yearbook.*

KOREA (REPUBLIC OF) - TIN - See KOREA (REPUBLIC OF) - MINING AND MINERAL PRODUCTS

KOREA (REPUBLIC OF) - TIRE (MOTOR VEHICLE) PRODUCTION

Statistical Office of the United Nations, Publishing Service, New York, New York 10017 (800) 253-9646; *Statistical Yearbook.*

KOREA (REPUBLIC OF) - TOBACCO PRODUCTION

Euromonitor Publications Limited, 87-88 Turnmill Street, London EC1M 5QU, England; *Third World Economic Handbook.*

Facts on File, 460 Park Avenue South, New York, New York 10016 (800) 443-8323; *The New Book of World Rankings*.

Statistical Office of the United Nations, Publishing Service, New York, New York 10017 (800) 253-9646; *Statistical Yearbook*.

KOREA (REPUBLIC OF) - TOURISM

Euromonitor Publications Limited, 87-88 Turnmill Street, London EC1M 5QU, England; *The Pacific Basin: An Economic Handbook*, and *Third World Economic Handbook*.

Facts on File, 460 Park Avenue South, New York, New York 10016 (800) 443-8323; *The New Book of World Rankings*.

G.K. Hall and Company, 70 Lincoln Street, Boston, Massachusetts 02111 (617) 423-3990; *The World in Figures*.

Korean Overseas Information Service, Ministry of Culture and Information, Seoul 110, Republic of Korea; *Statistical Data on Korea*.

Statistical Office of the United Nations, Publishing Service, New York, New York 10017 (800) 253-9646; *Statistical Yearbook*.

Times Books, 201 East 50th Street, New York, New York 10022 (212) 751-2600; *The Economist Book of Vital World Statistics*.

World Tourism Organization, Calle Capitan Haya 42, E-28020 Madrid, Spain; *Yearbook of Tourism Statistics*.

KOREA (REPUBLIC OF) - TRACTORS IN USE

Statistical Office of the United Nations, Publishing Service, New York, New York 10017 (800) 253-9646; *Statistical Yearbook*.

KOREA (REPUBLIC OF) - TRADE - See KOREA (REPUBLIC OF) - FOREIGN TRADE

KOREA (REPUBLIC OF) - TRADEMARKS AND SERVICE MARKS

Statistical Office of the United Nations, Publishing Service, New York, New York 10017 (800) 253-9646; *Statistical Yearbook*.

KOREA (REPUBLIC OF) - TRANSPORTATION AND COMMUNICATIONS

The Economist Intelligence Unit (Asia) Limited, 10th Floor, Luk Kwok Centre, 72 Gloucester Road, Wanchai, Hong Kong (Phone Number in U.S. (800) 938-4685); *Asian Market Atlas*.

Euromonitor Publications Limited, 87-88 Turnmill Street, London EC1M 5QU, England; *The Pacific Basin: An Economic Handbook*, and *Third World Economic Handbook*.

Facts on File, 460 Park Avenue South, New York, New York 10016 (800) 443-8323; *The New Book of World Rankings*.

G.K. Hall and Company, 70 Lincoln Street, Boston, Massachusetts 02111 (617) 423-3990; *The World in Figures*.

Korean Overseas Information Service, Ministry of Culture and Information, Seoul 110, Republic of Korea; *Statistical Data on Korea*.

Statistical Office of the United Nations, Publishing Service, New York, New York 10017 (800) 253-9646; *Statistical Yearbook for Asia and the Pacific*.

KOREA (REPUBLIC OF) - TUNGSTEN PRODUCTION AND CONSUMPTION - See KOREA (REPUBLIC OF) - MINING AND MINERAL PRODUCTS

KOREA (REPUBLIC OF) - UNEMPLOYMENT

Euromonitor Publications Limited, 87-88 Turnmill Street, London EC1M 5QU, England; *International Marketing Data and Statistics*, and *The Pacific Basin: An Economic Handbook*.

International Labour Office, I.L.O. Publications, CH-1211, Geneva 22, Switzerland; *Yearbook of Labour Statistics*.

Korean Overseas Information Service, Ministry of Culture and Information, Seoul 110, Republic of Korea; *Statistical Data on Korea*.

Statistical Office of the United Nations, Publishing Service, New York, New York 10017 (800) 253-9646; *Statistical Yearbook*.

KOREA (REPUBLIC OF) - UTILITY EXPENDITURES

Korean Overseas Information Service, Ministry of Culture and Information, Seoul 110, Republic of Korea; *Statistical Data on Korea*.

KOREA (REPUBLIC OF) - VITAL STATISTICS

Euromonitor Publications Limited, 87-88 Turnmill Street, London EC1M 5QU, England; *International Marketing Data and Statistics*, *The Pacific Basin: An Economic Handbook*, and *Third World Economic Handbook*.

G.K. Hall and Company, 70 Lincoln Street, Boston, Massachusetts 02111 (617) 423-3990; *The World in Figures*.

KOREA (REPUBLIC OF) - WAGES

G.K. Hall and Company, 70 Lincoln Street, Boston, Massachusetts 02111 (617) 423-3990; *The World in Figures*.

International Labour Office, I.L.O. Publications, CH-1211, Geneva 22, Switzerland; *Yearbook of Labour Statistics*.

Statistical Office of the United Nations, Publishing Service, New York, New York 10017 (800) 253-9646; *Statistical Yearbook*.

KOREA (REPUBLIC OF) - WAGES AND PRICES

Statistical Office of the United Nations, Publishing Service, New York, New York 10017 (800) 253-9646; *Statistical Yearbook for Asia and the Pacific*.

KOREA (REPUBLIC OF) - WALNUT PRODUCTION - See KOREA (REPUBLIC OF) - CROPS

KOREA (REPUBLIC OF) - WATERMELON PRODUCTION - See KOREA (REPUBLIC OF) - CROPS

KOREA (REPUBLIC OF) - WEATHER

Facts on File, 460 Park Avenue South, New York, New York 10016 (800) 443-8323; *The New Book of World Rankings*.

G.K. Hall and Company, 70 Lincoln Street, Boston, Massachusetts 02111 (617) 423-3990; *The World in Figures*.

KOREA (REPUBLIC OF) - WHALING - See KOREA (REPUBLIC OF) - FISHERIES

KOREA (REPUBLIC OF) - WHEAT PRODUCTION AND PRICES - See KOREA (REPUBLIC OF) - CROPS

KOREA (REPUBLIC OF) - WHOLESALE PRICES - INDEX NUMBERS

Korean Overseas Information Service, Ministry of Culture and Information, Seoul 110, Republic of Korea; *Statistical Data on Korea.*

Statistical Office of the United Nations, Publishing Service, New York, New York 10017 (800) 253-9646; *Statistical Yearbook.*

KOREA (REPUBLIC OF) - WHOLESALE TRADE

Euromonitor Publications Limited, 87-88 Turnmill Street, London EC1M 5QU, England; *Third World Economic Handbook.*

Statistical Office of the United Nations, Publishing Service, New York, New York 10017 (800) 253-9646; *Statistical Yearbook.*

KOREA (REPUBLIC OF) - WINE PRODUCTION

Facts on File, 460 Park Avenue South, New York, New York 10016 (800) 443-8323; *The New Book of World Rankings.*

KOREA (REPUBLIC OF) - WOOD PULP PRODUCTION - See KOREA (REPUBLIC OF) - FORESTRY AND FOREST PRODUCTS

KOREA (REPUBLIC OF) - WOOL PRODUCTION AND CONSUMPTION

Facts on File, 460 Park Avenue South, New York, New York 10016 (800) 443-8323; *The New Book of World Rankings.*

Statistical Office of the United Nations, Publishing Service, New York, New York 10017 (800) 253-9646; *Statistical Yearbook.*

KOREA (REPUBLIC OF) - YARN PRODUCTION

Statistical Office of the United Nations, Publishing Service, New York, New York 10017 (800) 253-9646; *Statistical Yearbook.*

KOREA (REPUBLIC OF) - ZINC AND ZINC ORE PRODUCTION AND CONSUMPTION - See KOREA (REPUBLIC OF) - MINING AND MINERAL PRODUCTS

KOREA (REPUBLIC OF) - ZOOS AND BOTANICAL GARDENS

United Nations Educational, Scientific and Cultural Organization (UNESCO), 7 Place de Fontenoy, F-75700 Paris, France (Telephone in U.S. (212) 963-5981); *Statistical Yearbook.*

KOREAN CONFLICT

U.S. Congress, Joint Economic Committee, The Capitol, Washington, D.C. 20510, revised and updated by James L. Clayton, University of Utah, Salt Lake City, Utah 84112; *The Military Budget and National Economic Priorities*, Part 1, 91st Congress, 1st Session.

KOREAN POPULATION

U.S. Department of Commerce, Bureau of the Census, Suitland, Maryland 20233; *Census of Population, General Population Characteristics, United States*, and press release.

Kuwait - National Statistical Office

Central Statistical Office, The Ministry of Planning, Post Office Box 26188, Safat, Kuwait 13123.

Kuwait - Primary Statistics Sources

Central Statistical Office, Post Office Box 26188, Safat, Kuwait; *Annual Statistical Abstract*, and *Monthly Digest of Statistics.*

KUWAIT - AGRICULTURE

Central Statistical Office, Ministry of Planning, Post Office Box 26188, Safat, Kuwait; *Annual Statistical Abstract - State of Kuwait.*

Economic Commission for Western Asia, Post Office Box 27, Baghdad, Iraq; *Statistical Abstract of Western Asia.*

Euromonitor Publications Limited, 87-88 Turnmill Street, London EC1M 5QU, England; *International Marketing Data and Statistics*, and *Middle East Economic Handbook.*

Facts on File, 460 Park Avenue South, New York, New York 10016 (800) 443-8323; *The New Book of World Rankings.*

Food and Agricultural Organization of the United Nations (FAO), Via delle Terme di Caracalla, 00100 Rome, Italy (Telephone Number in U.S. (202) 653-2400); *Production Yearbook, The State of Food and Agriculture,* and *Trade Yearbook.*

G.K. Hall and Company, 70 Lincoln Street, Boston, Massachusetts 02111 (617) 423-3990; *The World in Figures.*

Statistical Office of the United Nations, Publishing Service, New York, New York 10017 (800) 253-9646; *Statistical Yearbook.*

Times Books, 201 East 50th Street, New York, New York 10022 (212) 751-2600; *The Economist Book of Vital World Statistics.*

The World Bank, 1818 H Street, NW, Washington, D.C. 20433 (202) 477 1234; *World Tables.*

KUWAIT - AIRLINE SERVICE

Economic Commission for Western Asia, Post Office Box 27, Baghdad, Iraq; *Statistical Abstract of Western Asia.*

Facts on File, 460 Park Avenue South, New York, New York 10016 (800) 443-8323; *The New Book of World Rankings.*

G.K. Hall and Company, 70 Lincoln Street, Boston, Massachusetts 02111 (617) 423-3990; *The World in Figures.*

International Civil Aviation Organization, 1000 Sherbrooke Street West, Suite 400, Montreal, Quebec H3A 2R2, Canada (514) 285-8219; *Civil Aviation Statistics of the World.*

Statistical Office of the United Nations, Publishing Service, New York, New York 10017 (800) 253-9646; *Statistical Yearbook.*

Times Books, 201 East 50th Street, New York, New York 10022 (212) 751-2600; *The Economist Book of Vital World Statistics.*

KUWAIT - ALUMINUM PRODUCTION AND CONSUMPTION - See KUWAIT - MINING AND MINERAL PRODUCTS

KUWAIT - ANIMAL HEALTH

Food and Agricultural Organization of the United Nations (FAO), Via delle Terme di Caracalla, 00100 Rome, Italy (Telephone Number in U.S. (202) 653-2400); *Animal Health Yearbook.*

KUWAIT - AREA AND DENSITY OF POPULATION

Economic Commission for Western Asia, Post Office Box 27, Baghdad, Iraq; *Statistical Abstract of Western Asia.*

Euromonitor Publications Limited, 87-88 Turnmill Street, London EC1M 5QU, England; *International Marketing Data and Statistics, and Middle East Economic Handbook.*

Facts on File, 460 Park Avenue South, New York, New York 10016 (800) 443-8323; *The New Book of World Rankings.*

Food and Agricultural Organization of the United Nations (FAO), Via delle Terme di Caracalla, 00100 Rome, Italy (Telephone Number in U.S. (202) 653-2400); *The State of Food and Agriculture.*

G.K. Hall and Company, 70 Lincoln Street, Boston, Massachusetts 02111 (617) 423-3990; *The World in Figures.*

Statistical Office of the United Nations, Publishing Service, New York, New York 10017 (800) 253-9646; *Statistical Yearbook.*

Times Books, 201 East 50th Street, New York, New York 10022 (212) 751-2600; *The Economist Book of Vital World Statistics.*

United Nations Educational, Scientific and Cultural Organization (UNESCO), 7 Place de Fontenoy, F-75700 Paris, France (Telephone in U.S. (212) 963-5981); *Statistical Yearbook.*

KUWAIT - ARMS EXPORTS AND IMPORTS

U.S. Arms Control and Disarmament Agency, 320 Twenty-first Street, NW, Washington, D.C. 20451 (202) 647-8677; *World Military Expenditures and Arms Transfers.*

KUWAIT - BALANCE OF PAYMENTS

Economic Commission for Western Asia, Post Office Box 27, Baghdad, Iraq; *Statistical Abstract of Western Asia.*

The Economist Intelligence Unit, 111 West 57th Street, New York, New York 10019 (800) 938-4685; *The World Market Atlas.*

G.K. Hall and Company, 70 Lincoln Street, Boston, Massachusetts 02111 (617) 423-3990; *The World in Figures.*

International Monetary Fund, 700 Nineteenth Street, NW, Washington, D.C. 20431 (202) 623-7000; *Balance of Payments Yearbook.*

Times Books, 201 East 50th Street, New York, New York 10022 (212) 751-2600; *The Economist Book of Vital World Statistics.*

The World Bank, 1818 H Street, NW, Washington, D.C. 20433 (202) 477-1234; *World Tables.*

KUWAIT - BALANCE OF TRADE

Economic Commission for Western Asia, Post Office Box 27, Baghdad, Iraq; *Statistical Abstract of Western Asia.*

KUWAIT - BANKING

Central Statistical Office, Ministry of Planning, Post Office Box 26188, Safat, Kuwait; *Annual Statistical Abstract - State of Kuwait.*

Economic Commission for Western Asia, Post Office Box 27, Baghdad, Iraq; *Statistical Abstract of Western Asia.*

Facts on File, 460 Park Avenue South, New York, New York 10016 (800) 443-8323; *The New Book of World Rankings.*

G.K. Hall and Company, 70 Lincoln Street, Boston, Massachusetts 02111 (617) 423-3990; *The World in Figures.*

International Monetary Fund, 700 Nineteenth Street, NW, Washington, D.C. 20431 (202) 623-7000; *International Financial Statistics.*

KUWAIT - BARLEY PRODUCTION - See KUWAIT - CROPS

KUWAIT - BEER PRODUCTION

Facts on File, 460 Park Avenue South, New York, New York 10016 (800) 443-8323; *The New Book of World Rankings.*

KUWAIT - BIRTH RATES

Euromonitor Publications Limited, 87-88 Turnmill Street, London EC1M 5QU, England; *Middle East Economic Handbook.*

Facts on File, 460 Park Avenue South, New York, New York 10016 (800) 443-8323; *The New Book of World Rankings.*

Statistical Office of the United Nations, Publishing Service, New York, New York 10017 (800) 253-9646; *Demographic Yearbook,* and *Statistical Yearbook.*

Times Books, 201 East 50th Street, New York, New York 10022 (212) 751-2600; *The Economist Book of Vital World Statistics.*

The World Bank, 1818 H Street, NW, Washington, D.C. 20433 (202) 477-1234; *World Tables.*

World Health Organization, Office of Publications, Avenue Appia, CH-1211 Geneva 27, Switzerland (Telephone Number in U.S. (518) 436-9686); *World Health Statistics Annual.*

KUWAIT - BONDS

G.K. Hall and Company, 70 Lincoln Street, Boston, Massachusetts 02111 (617) 423-3990; *The World in Figures.*

KUWAIT - BOOK PRODUCTION

G.K. Hall and Company, 70 Lincoln Street, Boston, Massachusetts 02111 (617) 423-3990; *The World in Figures.*

United Nations Educational, Scientific and Cultural Organization (UNESCO), 7 Place de Fontenoy, F-75700 Paris, France (Telephone in U.S. (212) 963-5981); *Statistical Yearbook.*

KUWAIT - BROADCASTING

Billboard Limited, Post Office Box 9027, 1006 AA Amsterdam, The Netherlands (Telephone Number in U.S. (212) 764-7300); *World Radio TV Handbook.*

Facts on File, 460 Park Avenue South, New York, New York 10016 (800) 443-8323; *The New Book of World Rankings.*

G.K. Hall and Company, 70 Lincoln Street, Boston, Massachusetts 02111 (617) 423-3990; *The World in Figures*.

Times Books, 201 East 50th Street, New York, New York 10022 (212) 751-2600; *The Economist Book of Vital World Statistics*.

KUWAIT - BUSINESS

G.K. Hall and Company, 70 Lincoln Street, Boston, Massachusetts 02111 (617) 423-3990; *The World in Figures*.

KUWAIT - CALORIE SUPPLY

Food and Agricultural Organization of the United Nations (FAO), Via delle Terme di Caracalla, 00100 Rome, Italy (Telephone Number in U.S. (202) 653-2400); *The State of Food and Agriculture*.

KUWAIT - CAPITAL REVENUE

International Monetary Fund, 700 Nineteenth Street, NW, Washington, D.C. 20431 (202) 623-7000; *Government Finance Statistics Yearbook*.

KUWAIT - CATTLE - See KUWAIT - LIVESTOCK AND POULTRY

KUWAIT - CAUSTIC SODA PRODUCTION

Statistical Office of the United Nations, Publishing Service, New York, New York 10017 (800) 253-9646; *Statistical Yearbook*.

KUWAIT - CEMENT PRODUCTION - See KUWAIT - MINING AND MINERAL PRODUCTS

KUWAIT - CHEMICAL (ORGANIC) PRODUCTION - See KUWAIT - MINING AND MINERAL PRODUCTS

KUWAIT - CHICKENS - See KUWAIT - LIVESTOCK AND POULTRY

KUWAIT - CIGARETTE PRODUCTION - See KUWAIT - TOBACCO PRODUCTION

KUWAIT - CLASS STRUCTURE

G.K. Hall and Company, 70 Lincoln Street, Boston, Massachusetts 02111 (617) 423-3990; *The World in Figures*.

KUWAIT - CLIMATE

Central Statistical Office, Ministry of Planning, Post Office Box 26188, Safat, Kuwait; *Annual Statistical Abstract - State of Kuwait*.

Facts on File, 460 Park Avenue South, New York, New York 10016 (800) 443-8323; *The New Book of World Rankings*.

G.K. Hall and Company, 70 Lincoln Street, Boston, Massachusetts 02111 (617) 423-3990; *The World in Figures*.

KUWAIT - COAL PRODUCTION - See KUWAIT - MINING AND MINERAL PRODUCTS

KUWAIT - COFFEE PRODUCTION AND CONSUMPTION - See KUWAIT - CROPS

KUWAIT - COMMUNICATIONS

Central Statistical Office, Ministry of Planning, Post Office Box 26188, Safat, Kuwait; *Annual Statistical Abstract - State of Kuwait*.

Economic Commission for Western Asia, Post Office Box 27, Baghdad, Iraq; *Statistical Abstract of Western Asia*.

G.K. Hall and Company, 70 Lincoln Street, Boston, Massachusetts 02111 (617) 423-3990; *The World in Figures*.

KUWAIT - CONSTRUCTION INDUSTRY

Facts on File, 460 Park Avenue South, New York, New York 10016 (800) 443-8323; *The New Book of World Rankings*.

Statistical Office of the United Nations, Publishing Service, New York, New York 10017 (800) 253-9646; *Construction Statistics Yearbook*, and *Statistical Yearbook*.

KUWAIT - CONSUMER PRICE INDEX

G.K. Hall and Company, 70 Lincoln Street, Boston, Massachusetts 02111 (617) 423-3990; *The World in Figures*.

Statistical Office of the United Nations, Publishing Service, New York, New York 10017 (800) 253-9646; *Statistical Yearbook*.

KUWAIT - CONSUMER PRICES

International Labour Office, I.L.O. Publications, CH-1211, Geneva 22, Switzerland; *Yearbook of Labour Statistics*.

International Monetary Fund, 700 Nineteenth Street, NW, Washington, D.C. 20431 (202) 623-7000; *International Financial Statistics*.

Times Books, 201 East 50th Street, New York, New York 10022 (212) 751-2600; *The Economist Book of Vital World Statistics*.

KUWAIT - CONSUMPTION

Euromonitor Publications Limited, 87-88 Turnmill Street, London EC1M 5QU, England; *Middle East Economic Handbook*.

G.K. Hall and Company, 70 Lincoln Street, Boston, Massachusetts 02111 (617) 423-3990; *The World in Figures*.

KUWAIT - COPPER PRODUCTION AND CONSUMPTION - See KUWAIT - MINING AND MINERAL PRODUCTS

KUWAIT - CORN PRODUCTION - See KUWAIT - CROPS

KUWAIT - CORPORATE TAXES - See KUWAIT - TAXATION

KUWAIT - COTTON PRODUCTION - See KUWAIT - CROPS

KUWAIT - CRIME

International Criminal Police Organization (INTERPOL), 26 rue Armengaud, 92210 Saint Cloud, France; *International Crime Statistics*.

Yale University Press, Yale Station, New Haven, Connecticut 06520; *Violence and Crime in Cross-National Perspective*.

KUWAIT - CROPS

Facts on File, 460 Park Avenue South, New York, New York 10016 (800) 443-8323; *The New Book of World Rankings*.

Food and Agricultural Organization of the United Nations (FAO), Via delle Terme di Caracalla, 00100 Rome, Italy (Telephone Number in U.S. (202) 653-2400); *The State of Food and Agriculture*.

G.K. Hall and Company, 70 Lincoln Street, Boston, Massachusetts 02111 (617) 423-3990; *The World in Figures.*

KUWAIT - CUSTOMS DUTIES

G.K. Hall and Company, 70 Lincoln Street, Boston, Massachusetts 02111 (617) 423-3990; *The World in Figures.*

International Monetary Fund, 700 Nineteenth Street, NW, Washington, D.C. 20431 (202) 623-7000; *Government Finance Statistics Yearbook.*

KUWAIT - DAIRY PRODUCTS

Economic Commission for Western Asia, Post Office Box 27, Baghdad, Iraq; *Statistical Abstract of Western Asia.*

Facts on File, 460 Park Avenue South, New York, New York 10016 (800) 443-8323; *The New Book of World Rankings.*

Food and Agricultural Organization of the United Nations (FAO), Via delle Terme di Caracalla, 00100 Rome, Italy (Telephone Number in U.S. (202) 653-2400); *The State of Food and Agriculture,* and *Production Yearbook.*

KUWAIT - DEATH RATES

Euromonitor Publications Limited, 87-88 Turnmill Street, London EC1M 5QU, England; *Middle East Economic Handbook.*

G.K. Hall and Company, 70 Lincoln Street, Boston, Massachusetts 02111 (617) 423-3990; *The World in Figures.*

Statistical Office of the United Nations, Publishing Service, New York, New York 10017 (800) 253-9646; *Statistical Yearbook.*

Times Books, 201 East 50th Street, New York, New York 10022 (212) 751-2600; *The Economist Book of Vital World Statistics.*

KUWAIT - DEFENSE EXPENDITURES

G.K. Hall and Company, 70 Lincoln Street, Boston, Massachusetts 02111 (617) 423-3990; *The World in Figures.*

International Monetary Fund, 700 Nineteenth Street, NW, Washington, D.C. 20431 (202) 623-7000; *Government Finance Statistics Yearbook.*

U.S. Arms Control and Disarmament Agency, 320 Twenty-first Street, NW, Washington, D.C. 20451 (202) 647-8677; *World Military Expenditures and Arms Transfers.*

KUWAIT - DEMOGRAPHY

The Economist Intelligence Unit, 111 West 57th Street, New York, New York 10019 (800) 938-4685; *The World Market Atlas.*

Facts on File, 460 Park Avenue South, New York, New York 10016 (800) 443-8323; *The New Book of World Rankings.*

G.K. Hall and Company, 70 Lincoln Street, Boston, Massachusetts 02111 (617) 423-3990; *The World in Figures.*

KUWAIT - DEVELOPMENT ASSISTANCE

G.K. Hall and Company, 70 Lincoln Street, Boston, Massachusetts 02111 (617) 423-3990; *The World in Figures.*

Statistical Office of the United Nations, Publishing Service, New York, New York 10017 (800) 253-9646; *Statistical Yearbook.*

KUWAIT - DIAMOND PRODUCTION - See KUWAIT - MINING AND MINERAL PRODUCTS

KUWAIT - DISEASE

G.K. Hall and Company, 70 Lincoln Street, Boston, Massachusetts 02111 (617) 423-3990; *The World in Figures.*

KUWAIT - DIVORCE RATES

Facts on File, 460 Park Avenue South, New York, New York 10016 (800) 443-8323; *The New Book of World Rankings.*

Statistical Office of the United Nations, Publishing Service, New York, New York 10017 (800) 253-9646; *Demographic Yearbook,* and *Statistical Yearbook.*

KUWAIT - DOMESTIC PRODUCT

G.K. Hall and Company, 70 Lincoln Street, Boston, Massachusetts 02111 (617) 423-3990; *The World in Figures.*

KUWAIT - ECONOMY

Euromonitor Publications Limited, 87-88 Turnmill Street, London EC1M 5QU, England; *International Marketing Data and Statistics.*

Facts on File, 460 Park Avenue South, New York, New York 10016 (800) 443-8323; *The New Book of World Rankings.*

G.K. Hall and Company, 70 Lincoln Street, Boston, Massachusetts 02111 (617) 423-3990; *The World in Figures.*

KUWAIT - EDUCATION

Central Statistical Office, Ministry of Planning, Post Office Box 26188, Safat, Kuwait; *Annual Statistical Abstract - State of Kuwait.*

Economic Commission for Western Asia, Post Office Box 27, Baghdad, Iraq; *Statistical Abstract of Western Asia.*

The Economist Intelligence Unit, 111 West 57th Street, New York, New York 10019 (800) 938-4685; *The World Market Atlas.*

Euromonitor Publications Limited, 87-88 Turnmill Street, London EC1M 5QU, England; *Middle East Economic Handbook.*

Facts on File, 460 Park Avenue South, New York, New York 10016 (800) 443-8323; *The New Book of World Rankings.*

G.K. Hall and Company, 70 Lincoln Street, Boston, Massachusetts 02111 (617) 423-3990; *The World in Figures.*

International Monetary Fund, 700 Nineteenth Street, NW, Washington, D.C. 20431 (202) 623-7000; *Government Finance Statistics Yearbook.*

Times Books, 201 East 50th Street, New York, New York 10022 (212) 751-2600; *The Economist Book of Vital World Statistics.*

United Nations Educational, Scientific and Cultural Organization (UNESCO), 7 Place de Fontenoy, F-75700 Paris, France (Telephone in U.S. (212) 963-5981); *Statistical Yearbook.*

The World Bank, 1818 H Street, NW, Washington, D.C. 20433 (202) 477-1234; *World Tables.*

KUWAIT - EGG PRODUCTION - See KUWAIT - DAIRY PRODUCTS

KUWAIT - ELECTRICITY

Facts on File, 460 Park Avenue South, New York, New York 10016 (800) 443-8323; *The New Book of World Rankings*.

Penn Well Publishing Company, 1421 South Sheridan Road, Post Office Box 1260, Tulsa, Oklahoma 74101 (800) 752-9764; *International Energy Statistics Sourcebook*.

Statistical Office of the United Nations, Publishing Service, New York, New York 10017 (800) 253-9646; *Statistical Yearbook*.

Times Books, 201 East 50th Street, New York, New York 10022 (212) 751-2600; *The Economist Book of Vital World Statistics*.

KUWAIT - EMPLOYMENT

Economic Commission for Western Asia, Post Office Box 27, Baghdad, Iraq; *Statistical Abstract of Western Asia*.

Euromonitor Publications Limited, 87-88 Turnmill Street, London EC1M 5QU, England; *International Marketing Data and Statistics*, and *Middle East Economic Handbook*.

Facts on File, 460 Park Avenue South, New York, New York 10016 (800) 443-8323; *The New Book of World Rankings*.

International Labour Office, I.L.O. Publications, CH 1211, Geneva 22, Switzerland; *Yearbook of Labour Statistics*.

Statistical Office of the United Nations, Publishing Service, New York, New York 10017 (800) 253-9646; *Statistical Yearbook*.

KUWAIT - ENERGY

Business Information Display, Incorporated, 4202 Sorrento Valley Boulevard, San Diego, California 92121; *World Energy Industry*.

Economic Commission for Western Asia, Post Office Box 27, Baghdad, Iraq; *Statistical Abstract of Western Asia*.

Euromonitor Publications Limited, 87-88 Turnmill Street, London EC1M 5QU, England; *Middle East Economic Handbook*.

Facts on File, 460 Park Avenue South, New York, New York 10016 (800) 443-8323; *The New Book of World Rankings*.

Food and Agricultural Organization of the United Nations (FAO), Via delle Terme di Caracalla, 00100 Rome, Italy (Telephone Number in U.S. (202) 653-2400); *The State of Food and Agriculture*.

G.K. Hall and Company, 70 Lincoln Street, Boston, Massachusetts 02111 (617) 423-3990; *The World in Figures*.

Penn Well Publishing Company, 1421 South Sheridan Road, Post Office Box 1260, Tulsa, Oklahoma 74101 (800) 752-9764; *International Energy Statistics Sourcebook*.

Statistical Office of the United Nations, Publishing Service, New York, New York 10017 (800) 253-9646; *Energy Statistics Yearbook*, and *Statistical Yearbook*.

Times Books, 201 East 50th Street, New York, New York 10022 (212) 751-2600; *The Economist Book of Vital World Statistics*.

KUWAIT - EXCHANGE RATE

Euromonitor Publications Limited, 87-88 Turnmill Street, London EC1M 5QU, England; *International Marketing Data and Statistics*, and *Middle East Economic Handbook*.

International Civil Aviation Organization, 1000 Sherbrooke Street West, Suite 400, Montreal, Quebec H3A 2R2, Canada (514) 285-8219; *Civil Aviation Statistics of the World*.

International Monetary Fund, 700 Nineteenth Street, NW, Washington, D.C. 20431 (202) 623-7000; *International Financial Statistics*.

Organization of Petroleum Exporting Countries, Obere Donaustrasse 93, 1020 Vienna 2, Austria; *OPEC Annual Statistical Bulletin*.

Statistical Office of the United Nations, Publishing Service, New York, New York 10017 (800) 253-9646; *Statistical Yearbook*.

KUWAIT - EXPORTS

American Automobile Manufacturers Association, 1401 H Eye Street, NW, Suite 900, Washington, D.C. 20005 (202) 326-5500; *World Motor Vehicle Data*.

Economic Commission for Western Asia, Post Office Box 27, Baghdad, Iraq; *Statistical Abstract of Western Asia*.

The Economist Intelligence Unit, 111 West 57th Street, New York, New York 10019 (800) 938-4685; *The World Market Atlas*.

Euromonitor Publications Limited, 87-88 Turnmill Street, London EC1M 5QU, England; *International Marketing Data and Statistics*, and *Middle East Economic Handbook*.

Food and Agricultural Organization of the United Nations (FAO), Via delle Terme di Caracalla, 00100 Rome, Italy (Telephone Number in U.S. (202) 653-2400); *The State of Food and Agriculture*.

G.K. Hall and Company, 70 Lincoln Street, Boston, Massachusetts 02111 (617) 423-3990; *The World in Figures*.

International Monetary Fund, 700 Nineteenth Street, NW, Washington, D.C. 20431 (202) 623-7000; *Direction of Trade Statistics*, and *International Financial Statistics*.

Organization of Petroleum Exporting Countries, Obere Donaustrasse 93, 1020 Vienna 2, Austria; *OPEC Annual Statistical Bulletin*.

Statistical Office of the United Nations, Publishing Service, New York, New York 10017 (800) 253-9646; *Trade in Manufactures of Developing Countries*.

Times Books, 201 East 50th Street, New York, New York 10022 (212) 751-2600; *The Economist Book of Vital World Statistics*.

The World Bank, 1818 H Street, NW, Washington, D.C. 20433 (202) 477-1234; *World Tables*.

KUWAIT - EXTERNAL INDEBTEDNESS

The World Bank, 1818 H Street, NW, Washington, D.C. 20433 (202) 477-1234; *World Tables*.

KUWAIT - EXTERNAL TRADE

Food and Agricultural Organization of the United Nations (FAO), Via delle Terme di Caracalla, 00100 Rome, Italy (Telephone Number in

U.S. (202) 653-2400); *The State of Food and Agriculture*, and *Trade Yearbook*.

G.K. Hall and Company, 70 Lincoln Street, Boston, Massachusetts 02111 (617) 423-3990; *The World in Figures*.

Statistical Office of the United Nations, Publishing Service, New York, New York 10017 (800) 253-9646; *Statistical Yearbook*.

KUWAIT - FARM CROPS - See KUWAIT - CROPS

KUWAIT - FEMALE WORKING POPULATION - See KUWAIT - EMPLOYMENT

KUWAIT - FERTILITY RATES

Facts on File, 460 Park Avenue South, New York, New York 10016 (800) 443-8323; *The New Book of World Rankings*.

Times Books, 201 East 50th Street, New York, New York 10022 (212) 751-2600; *The Economist Book of Vital World Statistics*.

The World Bank, 1818 H Street, NW, Washington, D.C. 20433 (202) 477-1234; *World Tables*.

KUWAIT - FERTILIZER

Food and Agricultural Organization of the United Nations (FAO), Via delle Terme di Caracalla, 00100 Rome, Italy (Telephone Number in U.S. (202) 653-2400); *Fertilizer Yearbook*, and *The State of Food and Agriculture*.

Statistical Office of the United Nations, Publishing Service, New York, New York 10017 (800) 253-9646; *Statistical Yearbook*.

KUWAIT - FETAL MORTALITY

Statistical Office of the United Nations, Publishing Service, New York, New York 10017 (800) 253-9646; *Demographic Yearbook*.

World Health Organization, Office of Publications, Avenue Appia, CH-1211 Geneva 27, Switzerland (Telephone Number in U.S. (518) 436-9686); *World Health Statistics Annual*.

KUWAIT - FINANCE

Central Statistical Office, Ministry of Planning, Post Office Box 26188, Safat, Kuwait; *Annual Statistical Abstract - State of Kuwait*.

Economic Commission for Western Asia, Post Office Box 27, Baghdad, Iraq; *Statistical Abstract of Western Asia*.

Euromonitor Publications Limited, 87-88 Turnmill Street, London EC1M 5QU, England; *Middle East Economic Handbook*.

Facts on File, 460 Park Avenue South, New York, New York 10016 (800) 443-8323; *The New Book of World Rankings*.

G.K. Hall and Company, 70 Lincoln Street, Boston, Massachusetts 02111 (617) 423-3990; *The World in Figures*.

International Monetary Fund, 700 Nineteenth Street, NW, Washington, D.C. 20431 (202) 623-7000; *International Financial Statistics*.

KUWAIT - FISHERIES

Central Statistical Office, Ministry of Planning, Post Office Box 26188, Safat, Kuwait; *Annual Statistical Abstract - State of Kuwait*.

Economic Commission for Western Asia, Post Office Box 27, Baghdad, Iraq; *Statistical Abstract of Western Asia*.

Facts on File, 460 Park Avenue South, New York, New York 10016 (800) 443-8323; *The New Book of World Rankings*.

Food and Agricultural Organization of the United Nations (FAO), Via delle Terme di Caracalla, 00100 Rome, Italy (Telephone Number in U.S. (202) 653-2400); *The State of Food and Agriculture*, and *Yearbook of Fishery Statistics*.

Statistical Office of the United Nations, Publishing Service, New York, New York 10017 (800) 253-9646; *Statistical Yearbook*.

KUWAIT - FLOUR PRODUCTION

Statistical Office of the United Nations, Publishing Service, New York, New York 10017 (800) 253-9646; *Statistical Yearbook*.

KUWAIT - FOOD

Food and Agricultural Organization of the United Nations (FAO), Via delle Terme di Caracalla, 00100 Rome, Italy (Telephone Number in U.S. (202) 653-2400); *Production Yearbook*, and *The State of Food and Agriculture*.

G.K. Hall and Company, 70 Lincoln Street, Boston, Massachusetts 02111 (617) 423-3990; *The World in Figures*.

KUWAIT - FOREIGN AID

G.K. Hall and Company, 70 Lincoln Street, Boston, Massachusetts 02111 (617) 423-3990; *The World in Figures*.

KUWAIT - FOREIGN INDEBTEDNESS

Euromonitor Publications Limited, 87-88 Turnmill Street, London EC1M 5QU, England; *Middle East Economic Handbook*.

KUWAIT - FOREIGN TRADE

Central Statistical Office, Ministry of Planning, Post Office Box 26188, Safat, Kuwait; *Annual Statistical Abstract - State of Kuwait*.

Economic Commission for Western Asia, Post Office Box 27, Baghdad, Iraq; *Statistical Abstract of Western Asia*.

Euromonitor Publications Limited, 87-88 Turnmill Street, London EC1M 5QU, England; *Middle East Economic Handbook*.

Facts on File, 460 Park Avenue South, New York, New York 10016 (800) 443-8323; *The New Book of World Rankings*.

Food and Agricultural Organization of the United Nations (FAO), Via delle Terme di Caracalla, 00100 Rome, Italy (Telephone Number in U.S. (202) 653-2400); *The State of Food and Agriculture*.

G.K. Hall and Company, 70 Lincoln Street, Boston, Massachusetts 02111 (617) 423-3990; *The World in Figures*.

International Monetary Fund, 700 Nineteenth Street, NW, Washington, D.C. 20431 (202) 623-7000; *International Financial Statistics*.

Statistical Office of the United Nations, Publishing Service, New York, New York 10017 (800) 253-9646; *International Trade Statistics Yearbook*, and *Statistical Yearbook*.

The World Bank, 1818 H Street, NW, Washington, D.C. 20433 (202) 477-1234; *World Tables*.

KUWAIT - FORESTRY AND FOREST PRODUCTS

Facts on File, 460 Park Avenue South, New York, New York 10016 (800) 443-8323; *The New Book of World Rankings*.

Food and Agricultural Organization of the United Nations (FAO), Via delle Terme di Caracalla, 00100 Rome, Italy (Telephone Number in U.S. (202) 653-2400); *The State of Food and Agriculture*, and *Yearbook of Forest Products*.

G.K. Hall and Company, 70 Lincoln Street, Boston, Massachusetts 02111 (617) 423-3990; *The World in Figures*.

Statistical Office of the United Nations, Publishing Service, New York, New York 10017 (800) 253-9646; *Statistical Yearbook*.

United Nations Educational, Scientific and Cultural Organization (UNESCO), 7 Place de Fontenoy, F-75700 Paris, France (Telephone in U.S. (212) 963-5981); *Statistical Yearbook*.

KUWAIT - GAS PRODUCTION - See KUWAIT -MINING AND MINERAL PRODUCTS

KUWAIT - GENERAL INDUSTRIAL STATISTICS

Statistical Office of the United Nations, Publishing Service, New York, New York 10017 (800) 253-9646; *Industrial Statistics Yearbook*.

KUWAIT - GENERAL MORTALITY

Statistical Office of the United Nations, Publishing Service, New York, New York 10017 (800) 253-9646; *Demographic Yearbook*.

World Health Organization, Office of Publications, Avenue Appia, CH-1211 Geneva 27, Switzerland (Telephone Number in U.S. (518) 436-9686); *World Health Statistics Annual*.

KUWAIT - GEOGRAPHIC DATA

Facts on File, 460 Park Avenue South, New York, New York 10016 (800) 443-8323; *The New Book of World Rankings*.

KUWAIT - GOATS - See (KUWAIT - REPUBLIC OF) - LIVESTOCK AND POULTRY

KUWAIT - GOLD HOLDINGS

International Monetary Fund, 700 Nineteenth Street, NW, Washington, D.C. 20431 (202) 623-7000; *International Financial Statistics*.

Statistical Office of the United Nations, Publishing Service, New York, New York 10017 (800) 253-9646; *Statistical Yearbook*.

The World Bank, 1818 H Street, NW, Washington, D.C. 20433 (202) 477-1234; *World Tables*.

KUWAIT - GOLD PRODUCTION - See KUWAIT - MINING AND MINERAL PRODUCTS

KUWAIT - GOVERNMENT

G.K. Hall and Company, 70 Lincoln Street, Boston, Massachusetts 02111 (617) 423-3990; *The World in Figures*.

KUWAIT - GOVERNMENT EXPENDITURES

Economic Commission for Western Asia, Post Office Box 27, Baghdad, Iraq; *Statistical Abstract of Western Asia*.

International Monetary Fund, 700 Nineteenth Street, NW, Washington, D.C. 20431 (202) 623-7000; *Government Finance Statistics Yearbook*.

Times Books, 201 East 50th Street, New York, New York 10022 (212) 751-2600; *The Economist Book of Vital World Statistics*.

The World Bank, 1818 H Street, NW, Washington, D.C. 20433 (202) 477-1234; *World Tables*.

KUWAIT - GOVERNMENT FINANCE

International Monetary Fund, 700 Nineteenth Street, NW, Washington, D.C. 20431 (202) 623-7000; *International Financial Statistics*.

KUWAIT - GOVERNMENT REVENUES

Economic Commission for Western Asia, Post Office Box 27, Baghdad, Iraq; *Statistical Abstract of Western Asia*.

International Monetary Fund, 700 Nineteenth Street, NW, Washington, D.C. 20431 (202) 623-7000; *Government Finance Statistics Yearbook*.

Times Books, 201 East 50th Street, New York, New York 10022 (212) 751-2600; *The Economist Book of Vital World Statistics*.

The World Bank, 1818 H Street, NW, Washington, D.C. 20433 (202) 477-1234; *World Tables*.

KUWAIT - GRAIN PRODUCTION - See KUWAIT - CROPS

KUWAIT - GRANTS

International Monetary Fund, 700 Nineteenth Street, NW, Washington, D.C. 20431 (202) 623-7000; *Government Finance Statistics Yearbook*.

KUWAIT - GROSS DOMESTIC PRODUCT

Economic Commission for Western Asia, Post Office Box 27, Baghdad, Iraq; *Statistical Abstract of Western Asia*.

The Economist Intelligence Unit, 111 West 57th Street, New York, New York 10019 (800) 938-4685; *The World Market Atlas*.

Euromonitor Publications Limited, 87-88 Turnmill Street, London EC1M 5QU, England; *International Marketing Data and Statistics*, and *Middle East Economic Handbook*.

Facts on File, 460 Park Avenue South, New York, New York 10016 (800) 443-8323; *The New Book of World Rankings*.

G.K. Hall and Company, 70 Lincoln Street, Boston, Massachusetts 02111 (617) 423-3990; *The World in Figures*.

Statistical Office of the United Nations, Publishing Service, New York, New York 10017 (800) 253-9646; *Statistical Yearbook*.

Times Books, 201 East 50th Street, New York, New York 10022 (212) 751-2600; *The Economist Book of Vital World Statistics*.

The World Bank, 1818 H Street, NW, Washington, D.C. 20433 (202) 477-1234; *World Tables*.

KUWAIT - GROSS NATIONAL PRODUCT

Euromonitor Publications Limited, 87-88 Turnmill Street, London EC1M 5QU, England; *International Marketing Data and Statistics*.

Organization of Petroleum Exporting Countries, Obere Donaustrasse 93, 1020 Vienna 2, Austria; *OPEC Annual Statistical Bulletin*.

U.S. Arms Control and Disarmament Agency, 320 Twenty-first Street, NW, Washington, D.C. 20451 (202) 647-8677; *World Military Expenditures and Arms Transfers*.

The World Bank, 1818 H Street, NW, Washington, D.C. 20433 (202) 477-1234; *World Tables*.

KUWAIT - HEALTH

Central Statistical Office, Ministry of Planning, Post Office Box 26188, Safat, Kuwait; *Annual Statistical Abstract - State of Kuwait*.

Economic Commission for Western Asia, Post Office Box 27, Baghdad, Iraq; *Statistical Abstract of Western Asia*.

Euromonitor Publications Limited, 87-88 Turnmill Street, London EC1M 5QU, England; *Middle East Economic Handbook*.

Facts on File, 460 Park Avenue South, New York, New York 10016 (800) 443-8323; *The New Book of World Rankings*.

G.K. Hall and Company, 70 Lincoln Street, Boston, Massachusetts 02111 (617) 423-3990; *The World in Figures*.

Statistical Office of the United Nations, Publishing Service, New York, New York 10017 (800) 253-9646; *Statistical Yearbook*.

Times Books, 201 East 50th Street, New York, New York 10022 (212) 751-2600; *The Economist Book of Vital World Statistics*.

KUWAIT - HEALTH EXPENDITURES

International Monetary Fund, 700 Nineteenth Street, NW, Washington, D.C. 20431 (202) 623-7000; *Government Finance Statistics Yearbook*.

KUWAIT - HIDE PRODUCTION

Food and Agricultural Organization of the United Nations (FAO), Via delle Terme di Caracalla, 00100 Rome, Italy (Telephone Number in U.S. (202) 653-2400); *Production Yearbook*.

KUWAIT - HIGHWAYS

Economic Commission for Western Asia, Post Office Box 27, Baghdad, Iraq; *Statistical Abstract of Western Asia*.

G.K. Hall and Company, 70 Lincoln Street, Boston, Massachusetts 02111 (617) 423-3990; *The World in Figures*.

International Road Federation, 525 School Street, SW, Washington, D.C. 20024 (202) 554-2106; *World Road Statistics*.

KUWAIT - HORSES - See KUWAIT - LIVESTOCK AND POULTRY

KUWAIT - HOURS OF WORK - See KUWAIT - EMPLOYMENT

KUWAIT - HOUSING AND HOUSING UNITS

Central Statistical Office, Ministry of Planning, Post Office Box 26188, Safat, Kuwait; *Annual Statistical Abstract - State of Kuwait*.

Facts on File, 460 Park Avenue South, New York, New York 10016 (800) 443-8323; *The New Book of World Rankings*.

KUWAIT - HOUSING EXPENDITURES

International Monetary Fund, 700 Nineteenth Street, NW, Washington, D.C. 20431 (202) 623-7000; *Government Finance Statistics Yearbook*.

KUWAIT - ILLITERATE POPULATION

The Economist Intelligence Unit, 111 West 57th Street, New York, New York 10019 (800) 938-4685; *The World Market Atlas*.

G.K. Hall and Company, 70 Lincoln Street, Boston, Massachusetts 02111 (617) 423-3990; *The World in Figures*.

United Nations Educational, Scientific and Cultural Organization (UNESCO), 7 Place de Fontenoy, F-75700 Paris, France (Telephone in U.S. (212) 963-5981); *Statistical Yearbook*.

KUWAIT - IMPORTS

American Automobile Manufacturers Association, 1401 H Street, NW, Suite 900, Washington, D.C. 20005 (202) 326-5500; *World Motor Vehicle Data*.

Economic Commission for Western Asia, Post Office Box 27, Baghdad, Iraq; *Statistical Abstract of Western Asia*.

The Economist Intelligence Unit, 111 West 57th Street, New York, New York 10019 (800) 938-4685; *The World Market Atlas*.

Euromonitor Publications Limited, 87-88 Turnmill Street, London EC1M 5QU, England; *International Marketing Data and Statistics*, and *Middle East Economic Handbook*.

Food and Agricultural Organization of the United Nations (FAO), Via delle Terme di Caracalla, 00100 Rome, Italy (Telephone Number in U.S. (202) 653-2400); *The State of Food and Agriculture*.

G.K. Hall and Company, 70 Lincoln Street, Boston, Massachusetts 02111 (617) 423-3990; *The World in Figures*.

International Monetary Fund, 700 Nineteenth Street, NW, Washington, D.C. 20431 (202) 623-7000; *Direction of Trade Statistics*, *International Financial Statistics*, and *Government Finance Statistics Yearbook*.

Statistical Office of the United Nations, Publishing Service, New York, New York 10017 (800) 253-9646; *Trade in Manufactures of Developing Countries*.

Times Books, 201 East 50th Street, New York, New York 10022 (212) 751-2600; *The Economist Book of Vital World Statistics*.

The World Bank, 1818 H Street, NW, Washington, D.C. 20433 (202) 477-1234; *World Tables*.

KUWAIT - INCOME TAXES - See KUWAIT - TAXATION

KUWAIT - INDUSTRY

Central Statistical Office, Ministry of Planning, Post Office Box 26188, Safat, Kuwait; *Annual Statistical Abstract - State of Kuwait*.

Euromonitor Publications Limited, 87-88 Turnmill Street, London EC1M 5QU, England; *International Marketing Data and Statistics*.

Facts on File, 460 Park Avenue South, New York, New York 10016 (800) 443-8323; *The New Book of World Rankings*.

G.K. Hall and Company, 70 Lincoln Street, Boston, Massachusetts 02111 (617) 423-3990; *The World in Figures*.

International Labour Office, I.L.O. Publications, CH-1211, Geneva 22, Switzerland; *Yearbook of Labour Statistics*.

Times Books, 201 East 50th Street, New York, New York 10022 (212) 751-2600; *The Economist Book of Vital World Statistics*.

The World Bank, 1818 H Street, NW, Washington, D.C. 20433 (202) 477-1234; *World Tables*.

KUWAIT - INFANT AND MATERNAL MORTALITY

Statistical Office of the United Nations, Publishing Service, New York, New York 10017 (800) 253-9646; *Demographic Yearbook*, and *Statistical Yearbook*.

Times Books, 201 East 50th Street, New York, New York 10022 (212) 751-2600; *The Economist Book of Vital World Statistics*.

The World Bank, 1818 H Street, NW, Washington, D.C. 20433 (202) 477-1234; *World Tables*.

World Health Organization, Office of Publications, Avenue Appia, CH-1211 Geneva 27, Switzerland (Telephone Number in U.S. (518) 436-9686); *World Health Statistics Annual*.

KUWAIT - INTERNATIONAL LIQUIDITY

International Monetary Fund, 700 Nineteenth Street, NW, Washington, D.C. 20431 (202) 623-7000; *International Financial Statistics*.

KUWAIT - INTERNATIONAL RESERVES EXCLUDING GOLD

Statistical Office of the United Nations, Publishing Service, New York, New York 10017 (800) 253-9646; *Statistical Yearbook*.

The World Bank, 1818 H Street, NW, Washington, D.C. 20433 (202) 477-1234; *World Tables*.

KUWAIT - IRON ORE PRODUCTION AND CONSUMPTION - See KUWAIT - MINING AND MINERAL PRODUCTS

KUWAIT - IRRIGATION

Euromonitor Publications Limited, 87-88 Turnmill Street, London EC1M 5QU, England; *International Marketing Data and Statistics*.

KUWAIT - LABOR FORCE

Central Statistical Office, Ministry of Planning, Post Office Box 26188, Safat, Kuwait; *Annual Statistical Abstract - State of Kuwait*.

Economic Commission for Western Asia, Post Office Box 27, Baghdad, Iraq; *Statistical Abstract of Western Asia*.

Euromonitor Publications Limited, 87-88 Turnmill Street, London EC1M 5QU, England; *International Marketing Data and Statistics*, and *Middle East Economic Handbook*.

Facts on File, 460 Park Avenue South, New York, New York 10016 (800) 443-8323; *The New Book of World Rankings*.

Food and Agricultural Organization of the United Nations (FAO), Via delle Terme di Caracalla, 00100 Rome, Italy (Telephone Number in U.S. (202) 653-2400); *The State of Food and Agriculture*.

G.K. Hall and Company, 70 Lincoln Street, Boston, Massachusetts 02111 (617) 423-3990; *The World in Figures*.

Times Books, 201 East 50th Street, New York, New York 10022 (212) 751-2600; *The Economist Book of Vital World Statistics*.

The World Bank, 1818 H Street, NW, Washington, D.C. 20433 (202) 477-1234; *World Tables*.

KUWAIT - LABOR PRODUCTIVITY

International Labour Office, I.L.O. Publications, CH-1211, Geneva 22, Switzerland; *Yearbook of Labour Statistics*.

KUWAIT LAND USE

Economic Commission for Western Asia, Post Office Box 27, Baghdad, Iraq; *Statistical Abstract of Western Asia*.

Euromonitor Publications Limited, 87-88 Turnmill Street, London EC1M 5QU, England; *International Marketing Data and Statistics*.

Food and Agricultural Organization of the United Nations (FAO), Via delle Terme di Caracalla, 00100 Rome, Italy (Telephone Number in U.S. (202) 653-2400); *Production Yearbook*.

G.K. Hall and Company, 70 Lincoln Street, Boston, Massachusetts 02111 (617) 423-3990; *The World in Figures*.

KUWAIT - LIBRARIES

Facts on File, 460 Park Avenue South, New York, New York 10016 (800) 443-8323; *The New Book of World Rankings*.

United Nations Educational, Scientific and Cultural Organization (UNESCO), 7 Place de Fontenoy, F-75700 Paris, France (Telephone in U.S. (212) 963-5981); *Statistical Yearbook*.

KUWAIT - LIVESTOCK AND POULTRY

Central Statistical Office, Ministry of Planning, Post Office Box 26188, Safat, Kuwait; *Annual Statistical Abstract - State of Kuwait*.

Economic Commission for Western Asia, Post Office Box 27, Baghdad, Iraq; *Statistical Abstract of Western Asia*.

Euromonitor Publications Limited, 87-88 Turnmill Street, London EC1M 5QU, England; *International Marketing Data and Statistics*.

Facts on File, 460 Park Avenue South, New York, New York 10016 (800) 443-8323; *The New Book of World Rankings*.

Food and Agricultural Organization of the United Nations (FAO), Via delle Terme di Caracalla, 00100 Rome, Italy (Telephone Number in U.S. (202) 653-2400); *Production Yearbook*, and *The State of Food and Agriculture*.

G.K. Hall and Company, 70 Lincoln Street, Boston, Massachusetts 02111 (617) 423-3990; *The World in Figures*.

Statistical Office of the United Nations, Publishing Service, New York, New York 10017 (800) 253-9646; *Statistical Yearbook*.

KUWAIT - LIVING LEVELS

G.K. Hall and Company, 70 Lincoln Street, Boston, Massachusetts 02111 (617) 423-3990; *The World in Figures*.

Times Books, 201 East 50th Street, New York, New York 10022 (212) 751-2600; *The Economist Book of Vital World Statistics*.

KUWAIT - MAIL - NUMBER OF PIECES SENT OR RECEIVED

Statistical Office of the United Nations, Publishing Service, New York, New York 10017 (800) 253-9646; *Statistical Yearbook*.

KUWAIT - MANUFACTURING

American Automobile Manufacturers Association, 1401 H Street, NW, Suite 900, Washington, D.C. 20005 (202) 326-5500; *World Motor Vehicle Data*.

Facts on File, 460 Park Avenue South, New York, New York 10016 (800) 443-8323; *The New Book of World Rankings*.

G.K. Hall and Company, 70 Lincoln Street, Boston, Massachusetts 02111 (617) 423-3990; *The World in Figures*.

Statistical Office of the United Nations, Publishing Service, New York, New York 10017 (800) 253-9646; *Statistical Yearbook*.

Times Books, 201 East 50th Street, New York, New York 10022 (212) 751-2600; *The Economist Book of Vital World Statistics*.

The World Bank, 1818 H Street, NW, Washington, D.C. 20433 (202) 477-1234; *World Tables*.

KUWAIT - MARRIAGE RATES

Facts on File, 460 Park Avenue South, New York, New York 10016 (800) 443-8323; *The New Book of World Rankings*.

Statistical Office of the United Nations, Publishing Service, New York, New York 10017 (800) 253-9646; *Demographic Yearbook*, and *Statistical Yearbook*.

KUWAIT - MEAT PRODUCTION - See KUWAIT - LIVESTOCK AND POULTRY

KUWAIT - MERCHANT SHIPPING

Economic Commission for Western Asia, Post Office Box 27, Baghdad, Iraq; *Statistical Abstract of Western Asia*.

G.K. Hall and Company, 70 Lincoln Street, Boston, Massachusetts 02111 (617) 423-3990; *The World in Figures*.

Lloyd's Register of Shipping, 17 Battery Place, New York, New York 10004; *Register of Ships*.

Organization of Petroleum Exporting Countries, Obere Donaustrasse 93, 1020 Vienna 2, Austria; *OPEC Annual Statistical Bulletin*.

Statistical Office of the United Nations, Publishing Service, New York, New York 10017 (800) 253-9646; *Statistical Yearbook*.

Times Books, 201 East 50th Street, New York, New York 10022 (212) 751-2600; *The Economist Book of Vital World Statistics*.

U.S. Department of Transportation, Maritime Administration, 400 Seventh Street, SW, Washington, D.C. 20590 (202) 366-5807; *A Statistical Analysis of the World's Merchant Fleets*.

KUWAIT - MILITARY

G.K. Hall and Company, 70 Lincoln Street, Boston, Massachusetts 02111 (617) 423-3990; *The World in Figures*.

The International Institute for Strategic Studies, 23 Tavistock Street, London WC2E 7NQ, England; *The Military Balance*.

U.S. Arms Control and Disarmament Agency, 320 Twenty-first Street, NW, Washington, D.C. 20451 (202) 647-8677; *World Military Expenditures and Arms Transfers*.

KUWAIT - MILK PRODUCTION - See KUWAIT - DAIRY PRODUCTS

KUWAIT - MINING AND MINERAL PRODUCTS

Economic Commission for Western Asia, Post Office Box 27, Baghdad, Iraq; *Statistical Abstract of Western Asia*.

Facts on File, 460 Park Avenue South, New York, New York 10016 (800) 443-8323; *The New Book of World Rankings*.

G.K. Hall and Company, 70 Lincoln Street, Boston, Massachusetts 02111 (617) 423-3990; *The World in Figures*.

Organization of Petroleum Exporting Countries, Obere Donaustrasse 93, 1020 Vienna 2, Austria; *OPEC Annual Statistical Bulletin*.

Penn Well Publishing Company, 1421 South Sheridan Road, Post Office Box 1260, Tulsa, Oklahoma 74101 (800) 752-9764; *International Energy Statistics Sourcebook*.

Statistical Office of the United Nations, Publishing Service, New York, New York 10017 (800) 253-9646; *Statistical Yearbook*.

United Nations Educational, Scientific and Cultural Organization (UNESCO), 7 Place de Fontenoy, F-75700 Paris, France (Telephone in U.S. (212) 963-5981); *Statistical Yearbook*.

KUWAIT - MONEY EXCHANGE RATE

Euromonitor Publications Limited, 87-88 Turnmill Street, London EC1M 5QU, England; *International Marketing Data and Statistics*.

International Monetary Fund, 700 Nineteenth Street, NW, Washington, D.C. 20431 (202) 623-7000; *International Financial Statistics*.

Statistical Office of the United Nations, Publishing Service, New York, New York 10017 (800) 253-9646; *Statistical Yearbook*.

KUWAIT - MONEY RESERVES

Euromonitor Publications Limited, 87-88 Turnmill Street, London EC1M 5QU, England; *International Marketing Data and Statistics*.

KUWAIT - MONEY SUPPLY

Economic Commission for Western Asia, Post Office Box 27, Baghdad, Iraq; *Statistical Abstract of Western Asia*.

Euromonitor Publications Limited, 87-88 Turnmill Street, London EC1M 5QU, England; *International Marketing Data and Statistics*.

G.K. Hall and Company, 70 Lincoln Street, Boston, Massachusetts 02111 (617) 423-3990; *The World in Figures*.

International Monetary Fund, 700 Nineteenth Street, NW, Washington, D.C. 20431 (202) 623-7000; *International Financial Statistics*.

Statistical Office of the United Nations, Publishing Service, New York, New York 10017 (800) 253-9646; *Statistical Yearbook*.

The World Bank, 1818 H Street, NW, Washington, D.C. 20433 (202) 477-1234; *World Tables*.

KUWAIT - MOTION PICTURES

Statistical Office of the United Nations, Publishing Service, New York, New York 10017 (800) 253-9646; *Statistical Yearbook*.

KUWAIT - MOTOR VEHICLE PRODUCTION

American Automobile Manufacturers Association, 1401 H Street, NW, Suite 900, Washington, D.C. 20005 (202) 326-5500; *World Motor Vehicle Data*.

KUWAIT - MOTOR VEHICLE TAXES - See KUWAIT - TAXATION

KUWAIT - MOTOR VEHICLES IN USE

American Automobile Manufacturers Association, 1401 H Street, NW, Suite 900, Washington, D.C. 20005 (202) 326-5500; *World Motor Vehicle Data*.

Economic Commission for Western Asia, Post Office Box 27, Baghdad, Iraq; *Statistical Abstract of Western Asia*.

G.K. Hall and Company, 70 Lincoln Street, Boston, Massachusetts 02111 (617) 423-3990; *The World in Figures*.

International Road Federation, 525 School Street, SW, Washington, D.C. 20024 (202) 554-2106; *World Road Statistics*.

Statistical Office of the United Nations, Publishing Service, New York, New York 10017 (800) 253-9646; *Statistical Yearbook*.

Times Books, 201 East 50th Street, New York, New York 10022 (212) 751-2600; *The Economist Book of Vital World Statistics*.

KUWAIT - MUSEUMS

Facts on File, 460 Park Avenue South, New York, New York 10016 (800) 443-8323; *The New Book of World Rankings*.

United Nations Educational, Scientific and Cultural Organization (UNESCO), 7 Place de Fontenoy, F-75700 Paris, France (Telephone in U.S. (212) 963-5981); *Statistical Yearbook*.

KUWAIT - NATALITY - See KUWAIT - BIRTH RATES

KUWAIT - NATIONAL ACCOUNTS

Economic Commission for Western Asia, Post Office Box 27, Baghdad, Iraq; *Statistical Abstract of Western Asia*.

International Monetary Fund, 700 Nineteenth Street, NW, Washington, D.C. 20431 (202) 623-7000; *International Financial Statistics*.

Statistical Office of the United Nations, Publishing Service, New York, New York 10017 (800) 253-9646; *National Accounts Statistics, and Statistical Yearbook*.

KUWAIT - NATIONAL INCOME

Central Statistical Office, Ministry of Planning, Post Office Box 26188, Safat, Kuwait; *Annual Statistical Abstract - State of Kuwait*.

Facts on File, 460 Park Avenue South, New York, New York 10016 (800) 443-8323; *The New Book of World Rankings*.

G.K. Hall and Company, 70 Lincoln Street, Boston, Massachusetts 02111 (617) 423-3990; *The World in Figures*.

Statistical Office of the United Nations, Publishing Service, New York, New York 10017 (800) 253-9646; *Statistical Yearbook*.

KUWAIT - NATIONAL PRODUCT

Facts on File, 460 Park Avenue South, New York, New York 10016 (800) 443-8323; *The New Book of World Rankings*.

KUWAIT - NATURAL GAS PRODUCTION - See KUWAIT - MINING AND MINERAL PRODUCTS

KUWAIT - NEWSPAPER PRODUCTION - See KUWAIT - FORESTRY AND FOREST PRODUCTS

KUWAIT - NEWSPRINT - See KUWAIT - FORESTRY AND FOREST PRODUCTS

KUWAIT - OCCUPATIONS - See KUWAIT - LABOR FORCE

KUWAIT - PAPER - See KUWAIT - FORESTRY AND FOREST PRODUCTS

KUWAIT - PEANUT PRODUCTION - See KUWAIT - CROPS

KUWAIT - PERIODICALS

United Nations Educational, Scientific and Cultural Organization (UNESCO), 7 Place de Fontenoy, F-75700 Paris, France (Telephone in U.S. (212) 963-5981); *Statistical Yearbook*.

KUWAIT - PESTICIDE USE

Food and Agricultural Organization of the United Nations (FAO), Via delle Terme di Caracalla, 00100 Rome, Italy (Telephone Number in U.S. (202) 653-2400); *The State of Food and Agriculture*.

KUWAIT - PETROLEUM INDUSTRY

Central Statistical Office, Ministry of Planning, Post Office Box 26188, Safat, Kuwait; *Annual Statistical Abstract - State of Kuwait*.

Euromonitor Publications Limited, 87-88 Turnmill Street, London EC1M 5QU, England; *Middle East Economic Handbook*.

Facts on File, 460 Park Avenue South, New York, New York 10016 (800) 443-8323; *The New Book of World Rankings*.

Food and Agricultural Organization of the United Nations (FAO), Via delle Terme di Caracalla, 00100 Rome, Italy (Telephone Number in U.S. (202) 653-2400); *The State of Food and Agriculture*

G.K. Hall and Company, 70 Lincoln Street, Boston, Massachusetts 02111 (617) 423-3990; *The World in Figures*.

International Monetary Fund, 700 Nineteenth Street, NW, Washington, D.C. 20431 (202) 623-7000; *International Financial Statistics*.

Organization of Petroleum Exporting Countries, Obere Donaustrasse 93, 1020 Vienna 2, Austria; *OPEC Annual Statistical Bulletin*.

Penn Well Publishing Company, 1421 South Sheridan Road, Post Office Box 1260, Tulsa, Oklahoma 74101 (800) 752-9764; *International Energy Statistics Sourcebook*.

Statistical Office of the United Nations, Publishing Service, New York, New York 10017 (800) 253-9646; *Statistical Yearbook*.

KUWAIT - PIGS - See KUWAIT - LIVESTOCK AND POULTRY

KUWAIT - PIPELINES FOR OIL AND PETROLEUM PRODUCTS

Organization of Petroleum Exporting Countries, Obere Donaustrasse 93, 1020 Vienna 2, Austria; *OPEC Annual Statistical Bulletin*.

KUWAIT - POPULATION

Central Statistical Office, Ministry of Planning, Post Office Box 26188, Safat, Kuwait; *Annual Statistical Abstract - State of Kuwait*.

Economic Commission for Western Asia, Post Office Box 27, Baghdad, Iraq; *Statistical Abstract of Western Asia*.

The Economist Intelligence Unit, 111 West 57th Street, New York, New York 10019 (800) 938-4685; *The World Market Atlas*.

Euromonitor Publications Limited, 87-88 Turnmill Street, London EC1M 5QU, England; *International Marketing Data and Statistics*, and *Middle East Economic Handbook*.

Facts on File, 460 Park Avenue South, New York, New York 10016 (800) 443-8323; *The New Book of World Rankings*.

Food and Agricultural Organization of the United Nations (FAO), Via delle Terme di Caracalla, 00100 Rome, Italy (Telephone Number in U.S. (202) 653-2400); *Production Yearbook*.

G.K. Hall and Company, 70 Lincoln Street, Boston, Massachusetts 02111 (617) 423-3990; *The World in Figures*.

International Labour Office, I.L.O. Publications, CH-1211, Geneva 22, Switzerland; *Yearbook of Labour Statistics*.

Statistical Office of the United Nations, Publishing Service, New York, New York 10017 (800) 253-9646; *Demographic Yearbook*, and *Statistical Yearbook*.

Times Books, 201 East 50th Street, New York, New York 10022 (212) 751-2600; *The Economist Book of Vital World Statistics*.

United Nations Educational, Scientific and Cultural Organization (UNESCO), 7 Place de Fontenoy, F-75700 Paris, France (Telephone in U.S. (212) 963-5981); *Statistical Yearbook*.

U.S. Arms Control and Disarmament Agency, 320 Twenty-first Street, NW, Washington, D.C. 20451 (202) 647-8677; *World Military Expenditures and Arms Transfers*.

World Health Organization, Office of Publications, Avenue Appia, CH-1211 Geneva 27, Switzerland (Telephone Number in U.S. (518)

436-9686); *World Health Statistics Annual*.

KUWAIT - POST OFFICES

Facts on File, 460 Park Avenue South, New York, New York 10016 (800) 443-8323; *The New Book of World Rankings*.

KUWAIT - POTATO PRODUCTION - See KUWAIT - CROPS

KUWAIT - PRICES

Economic Commission for Western Asia, Post Office Box 27, Baghdad, Iraq; *Statistical Abstract of Western Asia*.

Facts on File, 460 Park Avenue South, New York, New York 10016 (800) 443-8323; *The New Book of World Rankings*.

Food and Agricultural Organization of the United Nations (FAO), Via delle Terme di Caracalla, 00100 Rome, Italy (Telephone Number in U.S. (202) 653-2400); *Production Yearbook*, and *The State of Food and Agriculture*.

G.K. Hall and Company, 70 Lincoln Street, Boston, Massachusetts 02111 (617) 423-3990; *The World in Figures*.

International Labour Office, I.L.O. Publications, CH-1211, Geneva 22, Switzerland; *Yearbook of Labour Statistics*.

International Monetary Fund, 700 Nineteenth Street, NW, Washington, D.C. 20431 (202) 623-7000; *International Financial Statistics*.

KUWAIT - PRINTING AND WRITING PAPER - See KUWAIT - FORESTRY AND FOREST PRODUCTS

KUWAIT - PRODUCTION

American Automobile Manufacturers Association, 1401 H Street, NW, Suite 900, Washington, D.C. 20005 (202) 326-5500; *World Motor Vehicle Data*.

Facts on File, 460 Park Avenue South, New York, New York 10016 (800) 443-8323; *The New Book of World Rankings*.

G.K. Hall and Company, 70 Lincoln Street, Boston, Massachusetts 02111 (617) 423-3990; *The World in Figures*.

KUWAIT - PRODUCTIVITY

Euromonitor Publications Limited, 87-88 Turnmill Street, London EC1M 5QU, England; *International Marketing Data and Statistics*.

KUWAIT - PROPERTY TAXES - See KUWAIT - TAXATION

KUWAIT - PUBLIC FINANCE

Facts on File, 460 Park Avenue South, New York, New York 10016 (800) 443-8323; *The New Book of World Rankings*.

KUWAIT - RADIO BROADCASTING - See KUWAIT - BROADCASTING

KUWAIT - RAILWAYS

G.K. Hall and Company, 70 Lincoln Street, Boston, Massachusetts 02111 (617) 423-3990; *The World in Figures*.

KUWAIT - RELIGION

Facts on File, 460 Park Avenue South, New York, New York 10016 (800) 443-8323; *The New Book of World Rankings.*

KUWAIT - RENT PRICES

International Labour Office, I.L.O. Publications, CH-1211, Geneva 22, Switzerland; *Yearbook of Labour Statistics.*

KUWAIT - RETAIL TRADE

G.K. Hall and Company, 70 Lincoln Street, Boston, Massachusetts 02111 (617) 423-3990; *The World in Figures.*

KUWAIT - RICE PRODUCTION - See KUWAIT - CROPS

KUWAIT - ROUNDWOOD PRODUCTION - See KUWAIT - FORESTRY AND FOREST PRODUCTS

KUWAIT - RUBBER PRODUCTION AND CONSUMPTION

Facts on File, 460 Park Avenue South, New York, New York 10016 (800) 443-8323; *The New Book of World Rankings.*

KUWAIT - SALT PRODUCTION

Statistical Office of the United Nations, Publishing Service, New York, New York 10017 (800) 253-9646; *Statistical Yearbook.*

KUWAIT - SAWNWOOD PRODUCTION - See KUWAIT - FORESTRY AND FOREST PRODUCTS

KUWAIT - SCIENCE AND TECHNOLOGY - EXPENDITURE FOR RESEARCH

Statistical Office of the United Nations, Publishing Service, New York, New York 10017 (800) 253-9646; *Statistical Yearbook.*

KUWAIT - SCIENTISTS AND TECHNICIANS

Statistical Office of the United Nations, Publishing Service, New York, New York 10017 (800) 253-9646; *Statistical Yearbook.*

United Nations Educational, Scientific and Cultural Organization (UNESCO), 7 Place de Fontenoy, F-75700 Paris, France (Telephone in U.S. (212) 963-5981); *Statistical Yearbook.*

KUWAIT - SENIOR CITIZENS

Facts on File, 460 Park Avenue South, New York, New York 10016 (800) 443-8323; *The New Book of World Rankings.*

KUWAIT - SHEEP - See KUWAIT - LIVESTOCK AND POULTRY

KUWAIT - SILVER PRODUCTION AND CONSUMPTION - See KUWAIT - MINING AND MINERAL PRODUCTS

KUWAIT - SOCIAL DATA

Facts on File, 460 Park Avenue South, New York, New York 10016 (800) 443-8323; *The New Book of World Rankings.*

G.K. Hall and Company, 70 Lincoln Street, Boston, Massachusetts 02111 (617) 423-3990; *The World in Figures.*

KUWAIT - SOCIAL SECURITY

International Monetary Fund, 700 Nineteenth Street, NW, Washington, D.C. 20431 (202) 623-7000; *Government Finance Statistics Yearbook.*

KUWAIT - STATE BUDGET REVENUE AND EXPENDITURES

Euromonitor Publications Limited, 87-88 Turnmill Street, London EC1M 5QU, England; *International Marketing Data and Statistics.*

KUWAIT - STEEL - See KUWAIT - MINING AND MINERAL PRODUCTS

KUWAIT - STOCKS - COMMODITY - MARKET PRICE - INDEX

Food and Agricultural Organization of the United Nations (FAO), Via delle Terme di Caracalla, 00100 Rome, Italy (Telephone Number in U.S. (202) 653-2400); *The State of Food and Agriculture.*

KUWAIT - SUGAR PRODUCTION AND CONSUMPTION - See KUWAIT - CROPS

KUWAIT - TAXATION

G.K. Hall and Company, 70 Lincoln Street, Boston, Massachusetts 02111 (617) 423-3990; *The World in Figures.*

International Monetary Fund, 700 Nineteenth Street, NW, Washington, D.C. 20431 (202) 623-7000; *Government Finance Statistics Yearbook.*

International Road Federation, 525 School Street, SW, Washington, D.C. 20024 (202) 554-2106; *World Road Statistics.*

The World Bank, 1818 H Street, NW, Washington, D.C. 20433 (202) 477-1234; *World Tables.*

KUWAIT - TELEGRAPH SERVICE

Statistical Office of the United Nations, Publishing Service, New York, New York 10017 (800) 253-9646; *Statistical Yearbook.*

KUWAIT - TELEPHONES IN USE

American Telephone and Telegraph Company, 26 Parsippany Road, Whippany, New Jersey 07981 (800) 338-4038; *The World's Telephones.*

Euromonitor Publications Limited, 87-88 Turnmill Street, London EC1M 5QU, England; *Middle East Economic Handbook.*

G.K. Hall and Company, 70 Lincoln Street, Boston, Massachusetts 02111 (617) 423-3990; *The World in Figures.*

Statistical Office of the United Nations, Publishing Service, New York, New York 10017 (800) 253-9646; *Statistical Yearbook.*

KUWAIT - TELEVISION BROADCASTING - See KUWAIT - BROADCASTING

KUWAIT - TEXTILE INDUSTRY

G.K. Hall and Company, 70 Lincoln Street, Boston, Massachusetts 02111 (617) 423-3990; *The World in Figures.*

KUWAIT - THEATRE

United Nations Educational, Scientific and Cultural Organization (UNESCO), 7 Place de Fontenoy, F-75700 Paris, France (Telephone

in U.S. (212) 963-5981); *Statistical Yearbook.*

KUWAIT - TOBACCO PRODUCTION

Facts on File, 460 Park Avenue South, New York, New York 10016 (800) 443-8323; *The New Book of World Rankings.*

KUWAIT - TOURISM

Central Statistical Office, Ministry of Planning, Post Office Box 26188, Safat, Kuwait; *Annual Statistical Abstract - State of Kuwait.*

Economic Commission for Western Asia, Post Office Box 27, Baghdad, Iraq; *Statistical Abstract of Western Asia.*

Euromonitor Publications Limited, 87-88 Turnmill Street, London EC1M 5QU, England; *Middle East Economic Handbook.*

Facts on File, 460 Park Avenue South, New York, New York 10016 (800) 443-8323; *The New Book of World Rankings.*

G.K. Hall and Company, 70 Lincoln Street, Boston, Massachusetts 02111 (617) 423-3990; *The World in Figures.*

Statistical Office of the United Nations, Publishing Service, New York, New York 10017 (800) 253-9646; *Statistical Yearbook.*

Times Books, 201 East 50th Street, New York, New York 10022 (212) 751-2600; *The Economist Book of Vital World Statistics.*

KUWAIT - TRACTORS IN USE

Statistical Office of the United Nations, Publishing Service, New York, New York 10017 (800) 253-9646; *Statistical Yearbook.*

KUWAIT - TRADE - See KUWAIT - FOREIGN TRADE

KUWAIT - TRANSPORTATION AND COMMUNICATIONS

Economic Commission for Western Asia, Post Office Box 27, Baghdad, Iraq; *Statistical Abstract of Western Asia.*

Euromonitor Publications Limited, 87-88 Turnmill Street, London EC1M 5QU, England; *Middle East Economic Handbook.*

Facts on File, 460 Park Avenue South, New York, New York 10016 (800) 443-8323; *The New Book of World Rankings.*

G.K. Hall and Company, 70 Lincoln Street, Boston, Massachusetts 02111 (617) 423-3990; *The World in Figures.*

KUWAIT - UNEMPLOYMENT

Euromonitor Publications Limited, 87-88 Turnmill Street, London EC1M 5QU, England; *International Marketing Data and Statistics,* and *Middle East Economic Handbook.*

International Labour Office, I.L.O. Publications, CH-1211, Geneva 22, Switzerland; *Yearbook of Labour Statistics.*

KUWAIT - VITAL STATISTICS

Central Statistical Office, Ministry of Planning, Post Office Box 26188, Safat, Kuwait; *Annual Statistical Abstract - State of Kuwait.*

Euromonitor Publications Limited, 87-88 Turnmill Street, London EC1M 5QU, England; *International Marketing Data and Statistics,* and *Middle East Economic Handbook.*

G.K. Hall and Company, 70 Lincoln Street, Boston, Massachusetts 02111 (617) 423-3990; *The World in Figures.*

Statistical Office of the United Nations, Publishing Service, New York, New York 10017 (800) 253-9646; *Statistical Yearbook.*

World Health Organization, Office of Publications, Avenue Appia, CH-1211 Geneva 27, Switzerland (Telephone Number in U.S. (518) 436-9686); *World Health Statistics Annual.*

KUWAIT - WAGES

G.K. Hall and Company, 70 Lincoln Street, Boston, Massachusetts 02111 (617) 423-3990; *The World in Figures.*

International Labour Office, I.L.O. Publications, CH-1211, Geneva 22, Switzerland; *Yearbook of Labour Statistics.*

KUWAIT - WEATHER

Facts on File, 460 Park Avenue South, New York, New York 10016 (800) 443-8323; *The New Book of World Rankings.*

G. K. Hall and Company, 70 Lincoln Street, Boston, Massachusetts 02111 (617) 423-3990; *The World in Figures.*

KUWAIT - WELFARE EXPENDITURES

International Monetary Fund, 700 Nineteenth Street, NW, Washington, D.C. 20431 (202) 623-7000; *Government Finance Statistics Yearbook.*

KUWAIT - WHEAT PRODUCTION AND PRICES - See KUWAIT - CROPS

KUWAIT - WHOLESALE PRICES

International Monetary Fund, 700 Nineteenth Street, NW, Washington, D.C. 20431 (202) 623-7000; *International Financial Statistics.*

Statistical Office of the United Nations, Publishing Service, New York, New York 10017 (800) 253-9646; *Statistical Yearbook.*

KUWAIT - WINE PRODUCTION

Facts on File, 460 Park Avenue South, New York, New York 10016 (800) 443-8323; *The New Book of World Rankings.*

KUWAIT - WOOL PRODUCTION

Facts on File, 460 Park Avenue South, New York, New York 10016 (800) 443-8323; *The New Book of World Rankings.*

KYRGYZSTAN - See also UNION OF SOVIET SOCIALIST REPUBLICS

Kyrgyzstan - National Statistical Office

State Committee of Republic of Kyrgyzstan on Statistics, 374 Frunze Street, Bishkek 720884, Kyrgyzstan.

KYRGYZSTAN - AGRICULTURE

Business International Moscow, 23 Profsoyuznaya Ulitsa, 117859, Moscow (Telephone Number in U.S. (800) 938-4685); *The CIS Market Atlas.*

Encyclopedia Britannica, Incorporated, 310 South Michigan Avenue, Chicago, Illinois 60604 (312) 347-7000; *Britannica World Data.*

The World Bank, 1818 H Street, NW, Washington, D.C. 20433 (202) 477-1234; *Statistical Handbook: States of the Former USSR.*

KYRGYZSTAN - AIRLINE SERVICE

Business International Moscow, 23 Profsoyuznaya Ulitsa, 117859, Moscow (Telephone Number in U.S. (800) 938-4685); *The CIS Market Atlas.*

Encyclopedia Britannica, Incorporated, 310 South Michigan Avenue, Chicago, Illinois 60604 (312) 347-7000; *Britannica World Data.*

KYRGYZSTAN - AREA AND DENSITY OF POPULATION

Business International Moscow, 23 Profsoyuznaya Ulitsa, 117859, Moscow (Telephone Number in U.S. (800) 938-4685); *The CIS Market Atlas.*

KYRGYZSTAN - BANKING

Business International Moscow, 23 Profsoyuznaya Ulitsa, 117859, Moscow (Telephone Number in U.S. (800) 938-4685); *The CIS Market Atlas.*

KYRGYZSTAN - BIRTH RATES

Business International Moscow, 23 Profsoyuznaya Ulitsa, 117859, Moscow (Telephone Number in U.S. (800) 938-4685); *The CIS Market Atlas.*

Encyclopedia Britannica, Incorporated, 310 South Michigan Avenue, Chicago, Illinois 60604 (312) 347-7000; *Britannica World Data.*

KYRGYZSTAN - BUDGET

Business International Moscow, 23 Profsoyuznaya Ulitsa, 117859, Moscow (Telephone Number in U.S. (800) 938-4685); *The CIS Market Atlas.*

KYRGYZSTAN - CAPITAL INVESTMENT

The World Bank, 1818 H Street, NW, Washington, D.C. 20433 (202) 477-1234; *Statistical Handbook: States of the Former USSR.*

KYRGYZSTAN - CATTLE - See KYRGYZSTAN - LIVESTOCK AND POULTRY

KYRGYZSTAN - CHEMICALS

Business International Moscow, 23 Profsoyuznaya Ulitsa, 117859, Moscow (Telephone Number in U.S. (800) 938-4685); *The CIS Market Atlas.*

KYRGYZSTAN - COAL PRODUCTION AND CONSUMPTION - See KYRGYZSTAN - MINING AND MINERAL PRODUCTS

KYRGYZSTAN - COMMUNICATIONS

Business International Moscow, 23 Profsoyuznaya Ulitsa, 117859, Moscow (Telephone Number in U.S. (800) 938-4685); *The CIS Market Atlas.*

KYRGYZSTAN - CONSTRUCTION INDUSTRY

Business International Moscow, 23 Profsoyuznaya Ulitsa, 117859, Moscow (Telephone Number in U.S. (800) 938-4685); *The CIS Market Atlas.*

Encyclopedia Britannica, Incorporated, 310 South Michigan Avenue, Chicago, Illinois 60604 (312) 347-7000; *Britannica World Data.*

KYRGYZSTAN - CONSUMER PRODUCTS

Business International Moscow, 23 Profsoyuznaya Ulitsa, 117859, Moscow (Telephone Number in U.S. (800) 938-4685); *The CIS Market Atlas.*

KYRGYZSTAN - CONSUMPTION

Business International Moscow, 23 Profsoyuznaya Ulitsa, 117859, Moscow (Telephone Number in U.S. (800) 938-4685); *The CIS Market Atlas.*

The World Bank, 1818 H Street, NW, Washington, D.C. 20433 (202) 477-1234; *Statistical Handbook: States of the Former USSR.*

KYRGYZSTAN - COTTON PRODUCTION AND CONSUMPTION - See KYRGYZSTAN - CROPS

KYRGYZSTAN - CROPS

The World Bank, 1818 H Street, NW, Washington, D.C. 20433 (202) 477-1234; *Statistical Handbook: States of the Former USSR.*

KYRGYZSTAN - DEATH RATES

Business International Moscow, 23 Profsoyuznaya Ulitsa, 117859, Moscow (Telephone Number in U.S. (800) 938-4685); *The CIS Market Atlas.*

KYRGYZSTAN - DEMOGRAPHY

Business International Moscow, 23 Profsoyuznaya Ulitsa, 117859, Moscow (Telephone Number in U.S. (800) 938-4685); *The CIS Market Atlas.*

Encyclopedia Britannica, Incorporated, 310 South Michigan Avenue, Chicago, Illinois 60604 (312) 347-7000; *Britannica World Data.*

The World Bank, 1818 H Street, NW, Washington, D.C. 20433 (202) 477-1234; *Statistical Handbook: States of the Former USSR.*

KYRGYZSTAN - DISEASES

Business International Moscow, 23 Profsoyuznaya Ulitsa, 117859, Moscow (Telephone Number in U.S. (800) 938-4685); *The CIS Market Atlas.*

KYRGYZSTAN - DIVORCE RATES

Encyclopedia Britannica, Incorporated, 310 South Michigan Avenue, Chicago, Illinois 60604 (312) 347-7000; *Britannica World Data.*

KYRGYZSTAN - DOMESTIC INVESTMENT

Business International Moscow, 23 Profsoyuznaya Ulitsa, 117859, Moscow (Telephone Number in U.S. (800) 938-4685); *The CIS Market Atlas.*

KYRGYZSTAN - ECONOMY

Business International Moscow, 23 Profsoyuznaya Ulitsa, 117859, Moscow (Telephone Number in U.S. (800) 938-4685); *The CIS Market Atlas.*

Encyclopedia Britannica, Incorporated, 310 South Michigan Avenue, Chicago, Illinois 60604 (312) 347-7000; *Britannica World Data.*

KYRGYZSTAN - EDUCATION

Business International Moscow, 23 Profsoyuznaya Ulitsa, 117859, Moscow (Telephone Number in U.S. (800) 938-4685); *The CIS Market Atlas.*

Encyclopedia Britannica, Incorporated, 310 South Michigan Avenue, Chicago, Illinois 60604 (312) 347-7000; *Britannica World Data.*

KYRGYZSTAN - ELECTRICITY

Business International Moscow, 23 Profsoyuznaya Ulitsa, 117859, Moscow (Telephone Number in U.S. (800) 938-4685); *The CIS Market Atlas.*

The World Bank, 1818 H Street, NW, Washington, D.C. 20433 (202) 477-1234; *Statistical Handbook: States of the Former USSR.*

KYRGYZSTAN - EMPLOYMENT

The World Bank, 1818 H Street, NW, Washington, D.C. 20433 (202) 477-1234; *Statistical Handbook: States of the Former USSR.*

KYRGYZSTAN - ENERGY

Business International Moscow, 23 Profsoyuznaya Ulitsa, 117859, Moscow (Telephone Number in U.S. (800) 938-4685); *The CIS Market Atlas.*

Encyclopedia Britannica, Incorporated, 310 South Michigan Avenue, Chicago, Illinois 60604 (312) 347-7000; *Britannica World Data.*

The World Bank, 1818 H Street, NW, Washington, D.C. 20433 (202) 477-1234; *Statistical Handbook: States of the Former USSR.*

KYRGYZSTAN - ENVIRONMENT

Business International Moscow, 23 Profsoyuznaya Ulitsa, 117859, Moscow (Telephone Number in U.S. (800) 938-4685); *The CIS Market Atlas.*

KYRGYZSTAN - EXPORTS

Business International Moscow, 23 Profsoyuznaya Ulitsa, 117859, Moscow (Telephone Number in U.S. (800) 938-4685); *The CIS Market Atlas.*

Encyclopedia Britannica, Incorporated, 310 South Michigan Avenue, Chicago, Illinois 60604 (312) 347-7000; *Britannica World Data.*

The World Bank, 1818 H Street, NW, Washington, D.C. 20433 (202) 477-1234; *Statistical Handbook: States of the Former USSR.*

KYRGYZSTAN - EXTERNAL TRADE

The World Bank, 1818 H Street, NW, Washington, D.C. 20433 (202) 477-1234; *Statistical Handbook: States of the Former USSR.*

KYRGYZSTAN - FABRIC PRODUCTION AND CONSUMPTION - See KYRGYZSTAN - TEXTILE INDUSTRY

KYRGYZSTAN - FERTILITY RATES

Encyclopedia Britannica, Incorporated, 310 South Michigan Avenue, Chicago, Illinois 60604 (312) 347-7000; *Britannica World Data.*

The World Bank, 1818 H Street, NW, Washington, D.C. 20433 (202) 477-1234; *Statistical Handbook: States of the Former USSR.*

KYRGYZSTAN - FISHERIES

Encyclopedia Britannica, Incorporated, 310 South Michigan Avenue, Chicago, Illinois 60604 (312) 347-7000; *Britannica World Data.*

KYRGYZSTAN - FOOTWEAR PRODUCTION AND CONSUMPTION - See KYRGYZSTAN - TEXTILE INDUSTRY

KYRGYZSTAN - FOREIGN INVESTMENT

Business International Moscow, 23 Profsoyuznaya Ulitsa, 117859, Moscow (Telephone Number in U.S. (800) 938-4685); *The CIS Market Atlas.*

KYRGYZSTAN - FOREIGN TRADE

Business International Moscow, 23 Profsoyuznaya Ulitsa, 117859, Moscow (Telephone Number in U.S. (800) 938-4685); *The CIS Market Atlas.*

Encyclopedia Britannica, Incorporated, 310 South Michigan Avenue, Chicago, Illinois 60604 (312) 347-7000; *Britannica World Data.*

The World Bank, 1818 H Street, NW, Washington, D.C. 20433 (202) 477-1234; *Statistical Handbook: States of the Former USSR.*

KYRGYZSTAN - FORESTRY AND FOREST PRODUCTS

Business International Moscow, 23 Profsoyuznaya Ulitsa, 117859, Moscow (Telephone Number in U.S. (800) 938-4685); *The CIS Market Atlas.*

Encyclopedia Britannica, Incorporated, 310 South Michigan Avenue, Chicago, Illinois 60604 (312) 347-7000; *Britannica World Data.*

KYRGYZSTAN - GOATS - See KYRGYZSTAN - LIVESTOCK AND POULTRY

KYRGYZSTAN - GOVERNMENT EXPENDITURE

The World Bank, 1818 H Street, NW, Washington, D.C. 20433 (202) 477-1234; *Statistical Handbook: States of the Former USSR.*

KYRGYZSTAN - GOVERNMENT REVENUE

The World Bank, 1818 H Street, NW, Washington, D.C. 20433 (202) 477-1234; *Statistical Handbook: States of the Former USSR.*

KYRGYZSTAN - GROSS DOMESTIC PRODUCT

The World Bank, 1818 H Street, NW, Washington, D.C. 20433 (202) 477-1234; *Statistical Handbook: States of the Former USSR.*

KYRGYZSTAN - HEALTH

Business International Moscow, 23 Profsoyuznaya Ulitsa, 117859, Moscow (Telephone Number in U.S. (800) 938-4685); *The CIS Market Atlas.*

Encyclopedia Britannica, Incorporated, 310 South Michigan Avenue, Chicago, Illinois 60604 (312) 347-7000; *Britannica World Data.*

KYRGYZSTAN - HIGHWAYS

Business International Moscow, 23 Profsoyuznaya Ulitsa, 117859, Moscow (Telephone Number in U.S. (800) 938-4685); *The CIS Market Atlas.*

Encyclopedia Britannica, Incorporated, 310 South Michigan Avenue, Chicago, Illinois 60604 (312) 347-7000; *Britannica World Data.*

KYRGYZSTAN - HOUSING AND HOUSING UNITS

Business International Moscow, 23 Profsoyuznaya Ulitsa, 117859, Moscow (Telephone Number in U.S. (800) 938-4685); *The CIS Market Atlas.*

KYRGYZSTAN - IMPORTS

Business International Moscow, 23 Profsoyuznaya Ulitsa, 117859, Moscow (Telephone Number in U.S. (800) 938-4685); *The CIS Market Atlas.*

Encyclopedia Britannica, Incorporated, 310 South Michigan Avenue, Chicago, Illinois 60604 (312) 347-7000; *Britannica World Data.*

The World Bank, 1818 H Street, NW, Washington, D.C. 20433 (202) 477-1234; *Statistical Handbook: States of the Former USSR.*

KYRGYZSTAN - INDUSTRY

Business International Moscow, 23 Profsoyuznaya Ulitsa, 117859, Moscow (Telephone Number in U.S. (800) 938-4685); *The CIS Market Atlas.*

The World Bank, 1818 H Street, NW, Washington, D.C. 20433 (202) 477-1234; *Statistical Handbook: States of the Former USSR.*

KYRGYZSTAN - INFANT MORTALITY RATES

Business International Moscow, 23 Profsoyuznaya Ulitsa, 117859, Moscow (Telephone Number in U.S. (800) 938-4685); *The CIS Market Atlas.*

KYRGYZSTAN - LABOR FORCE

Business International Moscow, 23 Profsoyuznaya Ulitsa, 117859, Moscow (Telephone Number in U.S. (800) 938-4685); *The CIS Market Atlas.*

The World Bank, 1818 H Street, NW, Washington, D.C. 20433 (202) 477-1234; *Statistical Handbook: States of the Former USSR.*

KYRGYZSTAN - LAND USE

Encyclopedia Britannica, Incorporated, 310 South Michigan Avenue, Chicago, Illinois 60604 (312) 347-7000; *Britannica World Data.*

KYRGYZSTAN - LIFE EXPECTANCY

Business International Moscow, 23 Profsoyuznaya Ulitsa, 117859, Moscow (Telephone Number in U.S. (800) 938-4685); *The CIS Market Atlas.*

KYRGYZSTAN - LIVESTOCK AND POULTRY

Business International Moscow, 23 Profsoyuznaya Ulitsa, 117859, Moscow (Telephone Number in U.S. (800) 938-4685); *The CIS Market Atlas.*

Encyclopedia Britannica, Incorporated, 310 South Michigan Avenue, Chicago, Illinois 60604 (312) 047-7000; *Britannica World Data.*

KYRGYZSTAN - MANUFACTURING

Encyclopedia Britannica, Incorporated, 310 South Michigan Avenue, Chicago, Illinois 60604 (312) 347-7000; *Britannica World Data.*

KYRGYZSTAN - MARRIAGE RATES

Encyclopedia Britannica, Incorporated, 310 South Michigan Avenue, Chicago, Illinois 60604 (312) 347-7000; *Britannica World Data.*

KYRGYZSTAN - MEAT PRODUCTION - See KYRGYZSTAN - LIVESTOCK AND POULTRY

KYRGYZSTAN - MILITARY

The International Institute for Strategic Studies, 23 Tavistock Street, London WC2E 7NQ, England; *The Military Balance.*

KYRGYZSTAN - MINING AND MINERAL PRODUCTS

Business International Moscow, 23 Profsoyuznaya Ulitsa, 117859, Moscow (Telephone Number in U.S. (800) 938-4685); *The CIS Market Atlas.*

Encyclopedia Britannica, Incorporated, 310 South Michigan Avenue, Chicago, Illinois 60604 (312) 347-7000; *Britannica World Data.*

KYRGYZSTAN - MOTOR VEHICLES

Business International Moscow, 23 Profsoyuznaya Ulitsa, 117859, Moscow (Telephone Number in U.S. (800) 938-4685); *The CIS Market Atlas.*

KYRGYZSTAN - NATIONAL ACCOUNTS

The World Bank, 1818 H Street, NW, Washington, D.C. 20433 (202) 477 1234; *Statistical Handbook: States of the Former USSR.*

KYRGYZSTAN - NATIONAL INCOME

Business International Moscow, 23 Profsoyuznaya Ulitsa, 117859, Moscow (Telephone Number in U.S. (800) 938-4685); *The CIS Market Atlas.*

KYRGYZSTAN - PIGS - See KYRGYZSTAN - LIVESTOCK AND POULTRY

KYRGYZSTAN - POPULATION

Business International Moscow, 23 Profsoyuznaya Ulitsa, 117859, Moscow (Telephone Number in U.S. (800) 938-4685); *The CIS Market Atlas.*

Encyclopedia Britannica, Incorporated, 310 South Michigan Avenue, Chicago, Illinois 60604 (312) 347-7000; *Britannica World Data.*

The World Bank, 1818 H Street, NW, Washington, D.C. 20433 (202) 477-1234; *Statistical Handbook: States of the Former USSR.*

KYRGYZSTAN - POULTRY - See KYRGYZSTAN - LIVESTOCK AND POULTRY

KYRGYZSTAN - PRICES

The World Bank, 1818 H Street, NW, Washington, D.C. 20433 (202) 477-1234; *Statistical Handbook: States of the Former USSR.*

KYRGYZSTAN - PRODUCTION

The World Bank, 1818 H Street, NW, Washington, D.C. 20433 (202) 477-1234; *Statistical Handbook: States of the Former USSR.*

KYRGYZSTAN - PUBLIC FINANCE

The World Bank, 1818 H Street, NW, Washington, D.C. 20433 (202) 477-1234; *Statistical Handbook: States of the Former USSR.*

KYRGYZSTAN - RADIO RECEIVERS

Encyclopedia Britannica, Incorporated, 310 South Michigan Avenue, Chicago, Illinois 60604 (312) 347-7000; *Britannica World Data.*

KYRGYZSTAN - RAILWAYS

Business International Moscow, 23 Profsoyuznaya Ulitsa, 117859, Moscow (Telephone Number in U.S. (800) 938-4685); *The CIS Market Atlas.*

Encyclopedia Britannica, Incorporated, 310 South Michigan Avenue, Chicago, Illinois 60604 (312) 347-7000; *Britannica World Data.*

KYRGYZSTAN - RETAIL TRADE

Business International Moscow, 23 Profsoyuznaya Ulitsa, 117859, Moscow (Telephone Number in U.S. (800) 938-4685); *The CIS Market Atlas.*

KYRGYZSTAN - ROADS - See KYRGYZSTAN - HIGHWAYS

KYRGYZSTAN - ROUNDWOOD PRODUCTION AND CONSUMPTION - See KYRGYZSTAN - FORESTRY AND FOREST PRODUCTS

KYRGYZSTAN - SHEEP - See KYRGYZSTAN - LIVESTOCK AND POULTRY

KYRGYZSTAN - STEEL - See KYRGYZSTAN - MINING AND MINERAL PRODUCTS

KYRGYZSTAN - TELEPHONES IN USE

Encyclopedia Britannica, Incorporated, 310 South Michigan Avenue, Chicago, Illinois 60604 (312) 347-7000; *Britannica World Data.*

KYRGYZSTAN - TELEVISION RECEIVERS

Encyclopedia Britannica, Incorporated, 310 South Michigan Avenue, Chicago, Illinois 60604 (312) 347-7000; *Britannica World Data.*

KYRGYZSTAN - TEXTILE INDUSTRY

Business International Moscow, 23 Profsoyuznaya Ulitsa, 117859, Moscow (Telephone Number in U.S. (800) 938-4685); *The CIS Market Atlas.*

KYRGYZSTAN - TOURISM

Business International Moscow, 23 Profsoyuznaya Ulitsa, 117859, Moscow (Telephone Number in U.S. (800) 938-4685); *The CIS Market Atlas.*

KYRGYZSTAN - TRANSPORTATION AND COMMUNICATIONS

Business International Moscow, 23 Profsoyuznaya Ulitsa, 117859, Moscow (Telephone Number in U.S. (800) 938-4685); *The CIS Market Atlas.*

Encyclopedia Britannica, Incorporated, 310 South Michigan Avenue, Chicago, Illinois 60604 (312) 347-7000; *Britannica World Data.*

KYRGYZSTAN - VITAL STATISTICS

Encyclopedia Britannica, Incorporated, 310 South Michigan Avenue, Chicago, Illinois 60604 (312) 347-7000; *Britannica World Data.*

KYRGYZSTAN - WAGES

Business International Moscow, 23 Profsoyuznaya Ulitsa, 117859, Moscow (Telephone Number in U.S. (800) 938-4685); *The CIS Market Atlas.*

The World Bank, 1818 H Street, NW, Washington, D.C. 20433 (202) 477-1234; *Statistical Handbook: States of the Former USSR.*

KYRGYZSTAN - WOOL PRODUCTION AND CONSUMPTION - See KYRGYZSTAN - TEXTILE INDUSTRY

L

LABOR FORCE EMPLOYMENT AND EARNINGS - See also individual industries or occupations

LABOR FORCE EMPLOYMENT AND EARNINGS - AVERAGE PAY - STATES

U.S. Department of Labor, Bureau of Labor Statistics, Two Massachusetts Avenue, NE, Washington, D.C. 20212 (202) 606-7828; news release, *Employment and Wages, Annual Averages,* and *Average Annual Pay by State and Industry.*

LABOR FORCE EMPLOYMENT AND EARNINGS - AVERAGE PAY - STATES - METRO AREAS

U.S. Department of Labor, Bureau of Labor Statistics, Two Massachusetts Avenue, NE, Washington, D.C. 20212 (202) 606-7828; *Average Annual Pay Levels in Metropolitan Areas.*

LABOR FORCE EMPLOYMENT AND EARNINGS - CITY GOVERNMENT

U.S. Department of Commerce, Bureau of the Census, Suitland, Maryland 20233 (301) 763-4040; *City Employment,* and *Compendium of Public Employment.*

LABOR FORCE EMPLOYMENT AND EARNINGS - CIVILIAN LABOR FORCE - AMERICAN INDIAN, ESKIMO, ALEUT POPULATION

U.S. Department of Commerce, Bureau of the Census, Suitland, Maryland 20233 (301) 763-4040; *Current Population Reports,* and unpublished data.

LABOR FORCE EMPLOYMENT AND EARNINGS - CIVILIAN LABOR FORCE - ASIAN AND PACIFIC ISLANDER POPULATION

U.S. Department of Commerce, Bureau of the Census, Suitland, Maryland 20233 (301) 763-4040; *Current Population Reports,* and unpublished data.

LABOR FORCE EMPLOYMENT AND EARNINGS - CIVILIAN LABOR FORCE - BLACK POPULATION

U.S. Department of Commerce, Bureau of the Census, Suitland, Maryland 20233 (301) 763-4040; *Current Population Reports.*

U.S. Department of Labor, Bureau of Labor Statistics, Two Massachusetts Avenue, NE, Washington, D.C. 20212 (202) 606-7828; *Employment and Earnings, News, Monthly Labor Review,* Bulletin 2307, and unpublished data.

LABOR FORCE EMPLOYMENT AND EARNINGS - CIVILIAN LABOR FORCE - EDUCATIONAL ATTAINMENT

U.S. Department of Labor, Bureau of Labor Statistics, Two Massachusetts Avenue, NE, Washington, D.C. 20212 (202) 606-7828; Bulletin 2307 and unpublished data.

LABOR FORCE EMPLOYMENT AND EARNINGS - CIVILIAN LABOR FORCE - EMPLOYED

U.S. Department of Labor, Bureau of Labor Statistics, Two Massachusetts Avenue, NE, Washington, D.C. 20212 (202) 606-7828; *Employment and Earnings, Employment and Wages, Annual Averages, Monthly Labor Review, Geographic Profile of Employment and Unemployment,* Bulletin 2307, *News,* and unpublished data.

LABOR FORCE EMPLOYMENT AND EARNINGS - CIVILIAN LABOR FORCE - FEMALE

U.S. Department of Labor, Bureau of Labor Statistics, Two Massachusetts Avenue, NE, Washington, D.C. 20212 (202) 606-7828; *Employment and Earnings, Geographic Profile of Employment and Unemployment, Monthly Labor Review,* Bulletins 2217, 2340, 2307, and unpublished data.

LABOR FORCE EMPLOYMENT AND EARNINGS - CIVILIAN LABOR FORCE - FEMALE - AGE OF CHILDREN

U.S. Department of Labor, Bureau of Labor Statistics, Two Massachusetts Avenue, NE, Washington, D.C. 20212 (202) 606-7828; Bulletin 2307, and unpublished data.

LABOR FORCE EMPLOYMENT EARNINGS - CIVILIAN LABOR FORCE - FEMALE - CHILDREN IN PREPRIMARY SCHOOLS

U.S. Department of Commerce, Bureau of the Census, Suitland, Maryland 20233 (301) 763-4040; *Current Population Reports.*

LABOR FORCE EMPLOYMENT AND EARNINGS - CIVILIAN LABOR FORCE - FEMALE - MARITAL STATUS

U.S. Department of Labor, Bureau of Labor Statistics, Two Massachusetts Avenue, NE, Washington, D.C. 20212 (202) 606-7828; Bulletins 2217, 2340 and 2307, and unpublished data.

LABOR FORCE EMPLOYMENT AND EARNINGS - CIVILIAN LABOR FORCE - FULL TIME - PART TIME

U.S. Department of Labor, Bureau of Labor Statistics, Two Massachusetts Avenue, NE, Washington, D.C. 20212 (202) 606-7828; *Employment and Earnings,* and Bulletin 2307.

LABOR FORCE EMPLOYMENT AND EARNINGS - CIVILIAN LABOR FORCE - HIGH SCHOOL GRADUATES - DROPOUTS

U.S. Department of Labor, Bureau of Labor Statistics, Two Massachusetts Avenue, NE, Washington, D.C. 20212 (202) 606-7828, *News*, Bulletin 2307, and unpublished data.

LABOR FORCE EMPLOYMENT AND EARNINGS - CIVILIAN LABOR FORCE - HISPANIC ORIGIN POPULATION

U.S. Department of Commerce, Bureau of the Census, Suitland, Maryland 20233 (301) 763-4040; *Current Population Reports*.

U.S. Department of Labor, Bureau of Labor Statistics, Two Massachusetts Avenue, NE, Washington, D.C. 20212 (202) 606-7828; *Employment and Earnings, Monthly Labor Review*, Bulletin 2307, and unpublished data.

LABOR FORCE EMPLOYMENT AND EARNINGS - CIVILIAN LABOR FORCE - METROPOLITAN AREAS

U.S. Department of Labor, Bureau of Labor Statistics, Two Massachusetts Avenue, NE, Washington, D.C. 20212 (202) 606-7828; *Employment and Earnings*.

LABOR FORCE EMPLOYMENT AND EARNINGS - CIVILIAN LABOR FORCE - MINIMUM WAGE WORKERS

U.S. Department of Labor, Bureau of Labor Statistics, Two Massachusetts Avenue, NE, Washington, D.C. 20212 (202) 606-7828; unpublished data.

U.S. Department of Labor, Employment Standards Administration, Two Massachusetts Avenue, NE, Washington, D.C. 20212 (202) 606-7828; *Minimum Wage and Maximum Hours Standards Under the Fair Labor Standards Act*, and unpublished data.

LABOR FORCE EMPLOYMENT AND EARNINGS - CIVILIAN LABOR FORCE - NOT AT WORK

U.S. Department of Labor, Bureau of Labor Statistics, Two Massachusetts Avenue, NE, Washington, D.C. 20212 (202) 606-7828; *Employment and Earnings*, and unpublished data.

LABOR FORCE EMPLOYMENT AND EARNINGS - CIVILIAN LABOR FORCE - PARTICIPATION RATES

U.S. Department of Labor, Bureau of Labor Statistics, Two Massachusetts Avenue, NE, Washington, D.C. 20212 (202) 606-7828; *Employment and Earnings, Geographic Profile of Employment and Unemployment, Monthly Labor Review*, Bulletins 2307 2217, 2340, and unpublished data.

LABOR FORCE EMPLOYMENT AND EARNINGS - CIVILIAN LABOR FORCE - PARTICIPATION RATES - SELECTED COUNTRIES

Organization for Economic Cooperation and Development, 2 rue Andre-Pascal, 75 Paris 16, France (202) 785-6323; *Labour Force Statistics*.

U.S. Department of Labor, Bureau of Labor Statistics, Two Massachusetts Avenue, NE, Washington, D.C. 20212 (202) 606-7828; *Monthly Labor Review*, and *Comparative Labor Force Statistics for Ten Countries*.

LABOR FORCE EMPLOYMENT AND EARNINGS - CIVILIAN LABOR FORCE - PARTICIPATION RATES - WIVES, BY AGE OF YOUNGEST CHILD

U.S. Department of Labor, Bureau of Labor Statistics, Two Massachusetts Avenue, NE, Washington, D.C. 20212 (202) 606-7828; Bulletin 2340 and unpublished data.

LABOR FORCE EMPLOYMENT AND EARNINGS - CIVILIAN LABOR FORCE - PROJECTIONS

U.S. Department of Labor, Bureau of Labor Statistics, Two Massachusetts Avenue, NE, Washington, D.C. 20212 (202) 606-7828; *Employment and Earnings, Monthly Labor Review*, and unpublished data.

LABOR FORCE EMPLOYMENT AND EARNINGS - CIVILIAN LABOR FORCE - RACE

U.S. Department of Commerce, Bureau of the Census, Suitland, Maryland 20233 (301) 763-4040; *Current Population Reports*, and *Census of Population*.

U.S. Department of Labor, Bureau of Labor Statistics, Two Massachusetts Avenue, NE, Washington, D.C. 20212 (202) 606-7828; *Monthly Labor Review*, Bulletin 2307, *Employment and Earnings, News*, and unpublished data.

LABOR FORCE EMPLOYMENT AND EARNINGS - CIVILIAN LABOR FORCE - SCHOOL ENROLLMENT - PERSONS 16 TO 24 YEARS OLD

U.S. Department of Labor, Bureau of Labor Statistics, Two Massachusetts Avenue, NE, Washington, D.C. 20212 (202) 606-7828; Bulletin 2307, *News*, and unpublished data.

LABOR FORCE EMPLOYMENT AND EARNINGS - CIVILIAN LABOR FORCE - SELF-EMPLOYED WORKERS

U.S. Department of Labor, Bureau of Labor Statistics, Two Massachusetts Avenue, NE, Washington, D.C. 20212 (202) 606-7828; Bulletin 2307, *Employment and Earnings*, and unpublished data.

LABOR FORCE EMPLOYMENT AND EARNINGS - CIVILIAN LABOR FORCE - STATES

U.S. Department of Labor, Bureau of Labor Statistics, Two Massachusetts Avenue, NE, Washington, D.C. 20212 (202) 606-7828; *Geographic Profile of Employment and Unemployment*.

LABOR FORCE EMPLOYMENT AND EARNINGS - CIVILIAN LABOR FORCE - UNEMPLOYED

U.S. Department of Labor, Bureau of Labor Statistics, Two Massachusetts Avenue, NE, Washington, D.C. 20212 (202) 606-7828; *Employment and Earnings, Geographic Profile of Employment and Unemployment, News*, Bulletin 2307, and unpublished data.

LABOR FORCE EMPLOYMENT AND EARNINGS - CIVILIAN LABOR FORCE - WOMEN WHO GAVE BIRTH IN PREVIOUS YEAR

U.S. Department of Commerce, Bureau of the Census, Suitland, Maryland 20233 (301) 763-4040; *Current Population Reports*.

LABOR FORCE EMPLOYMENT AND EARNINGS - COLLECTIVE BARGAINING SETTLEMENTS

U.S. Department of Labor, Bureau of Labor Statistics, Two Massachusetts Avenue, NE, Washington, D.C. 20212 (202) 606-7828; *Current Wage Developments*, and *Compensation and Working*

Conditions.

LABOR FORCE EMPLOYMENT AND EARNINGS - DISABLED PERSONS

U.S. Department of Commerce, Bureau of the Census, Suitland, Maryland 20233 (301) 763-4040; unpublished data.

LABOR FORCE EMPLOYMENT AND EARNINGS - EARNINGS

U.S. Department of Commerce, Bureau of Economic Analysis, Fourteenth Street between Constitution Avenue and E Street, NW, Washington, D.C. 20230 (202) 606-9900; *The National Income and Product Accounts of the United States,* and *Survey of Current Business.*

U.S. Department of Commerce, Bureau of the Census, Suitland, Maryland 20233 (301) 763-4040; *Current Population Reports.*

U.S. Department of Labor, Bureau of Labor Statistics, Two Massachusetts Avenue, NE, Washington, D.C. 20212 (202) 606-7828; *Employment and Earnings,* Bulletins 2370 and 2429, *Employment and Wages, Annual Averages, Average Annual Pay by State and Industry, Average Annual Pay Levels in Metropolitan Areas, Monthly Labor Review, Productivity Measures for Selected Industries and Government Services,* and unpublished data.

LABOR FORCE EMPLOYMENT AND EARNINGS - ELDERLY

U.S. Department of Labor, Bureau of Labor Statistics, Two Massachusetts Avenue, NE, Washington, D.C. 20212 (202) 606-7828; *Employment and Earnings, Monthly Labor Review, News,* Bulletins 2217, 2307, and 2340 and unpublished data.

LABOR FORCE EMPLOYMENT AND EARNINGS - EMPLOYEE BENEFITS

U.S. Department of Labor, Bureau of Labor Statistics, Two Massachusetts Avenue, NE, Washington, D.C. 20212 (202) 606-7828; *Employee Benefits in Medium and Large Establishments, Employer Costs for Employee Compensation,* and *Employee Benefits in Small Private Establishments.*

U.S. Department of Labor, Pension and Welfare Benefits Administration, Two Massachusetts Avenue, NE, Washington, D.C. 20212 (202) 219-8921; *Private Pension Plan Bulletin.*

LABOR FORCE EMPLOYMENT AND EARNINGS - EMPLOYEE BENEFITS - GOVERNMENT EMPLOYEES

U.S. Department of Labor, Bureau of Labor Statistics, Two Massachusetts Avenue, NE, Washington, D.C. 20212 (202) 606-7828; *Employee Benefits in State and Local Governments.*

LABOR FORCE EMPLOYMENT AND EARNINGS - EMPLOYEES - STATES

U.S. Department of Labor, Bureau of Labor Statistics, Two Massachusetts Avenue, NE, Washington, D.C. 20212 (202) 606-7828; *Employment and Earnings,* and Bulletins 2370 and 2429.

LABOR FORCE EMPLOYMENT AND EARNINGS - EMPLOYMENT COST INDEX

U.S. Department of Labor, Bureau of Labor Statistics, Two Massachusetts Avenue, NE, Washington, D.C. 20212 (202) 606-7828; *Employment Cost Index.*

LABOR FORCE EMPLOYMENT AND EARNINGS - EMPLOYMENT PROJECTIONS

U.S. Department of Labor, Bureau of Labor Statistics, Two Massachusetts Avenue, NE, Washington, D.C. 20212 (202) 606-7828; *Monthly Labor Review.*

LABOR FORCE EMPLOYMENT AND EARNINGS - EMPLOYMENT TAXES AND CONTRIBUTIONS

Executive Office of the President, Office of Management and Budget, Executive Office Building, Washington, D.C. 20503 (202) 395-3080; *Budget of the United States Government.*

LABOR FORCE EMPLOYMENT AND EARNINGS - FEMALE

U.S. Department of Commerce, Bureau of the Census, Suitland, Maryland 20233 (301) 763-4040; *Current Population Reports.*

U.S. Department of Labor, Bureau of Labor Statistics, Two Massachusetts Avenue, NE, Washington, D.C. 20212 (202) 606-7828; *Employment and Earnings, Geographic Profile of Employment and Unemployment, Monthly Labor Review, News,* Bulletins 2217, 2307, and 2340, and unpublished data.

LABOR FORCE EMPLOYMENT AND EARNINGS - FOREIGN - OWNED FIRMS

Time Warner, 1675 Broadway, Rockefeller Center, New York, New York 10019 (212) 522-1212; *The Fortune Directories.*

U.S. Department of Commerce, Bureau of Economic Analysis, Fourteenth Street between Constitution Avenue and E Street, NW, Washington, D.C. 20230 (202) 606-9900; *Survey of Current Business.*

LABOR FORCE EMPLOYMENT AND EARNINGS - GOVERNMENT - See GOVERNMENT

LABOR FORCE EMPLOYMENT AND EARNINGS - HELP WANTED ADVERTISING

The Conference Board, 845 Third Avenue, New York, New York 10022 (212) 759-0900; *The Statistical Bulletin.*

U.S. Department of Labor, Employment and Training Administration, 200 Constitution Avenue, NW, Washington, D.C. 20210 (202) 219-0600; unpublished data.

LABOR FORCE EMPLOYMENT AND EARNINGS - HIGH SCHOOL GRADUATES AND DROPOUTS

U.S. Department of Labor, Bureau of Labor Statistics, Two Massachusetts Avenue, NE, Washington, D.C. 20212 (202) 606-7828; Bulletin 2307, and unpublished data.

LABOR FORCE EMPLOYMENT AND EARNINGS - HISPANIC ORIGIN POPULATION

U.S. Department of Commerce, Bureau of the Census, Suitland, Maryland 20233 (301) 763-4040; *Current Population Reports.*

U.S. Department of Labor, Bureau of Labor Statistics, Two Massachusetts Avenue, NE, Washington, D.C. 20212 (202) 606-7828; *Employment and Earnings, Monthly Labor Review,* and unpublished data.

LABOR FORCE EMPLOYMENT AND EARNINGS - HOURS

U.S. Department of Labor, Bureau of Labor Statistics, Two Massachusetts Avenue, NE, Washington, D.C. 20212 (202) 606-7828; *Employment and Earnings,* and Bulletins 2370 and 2429.

LABOR FORCE EMPLOYMENT AND EARNINGS - INDEXES OF COMPENSATION

U.S. Department of Labor, Bureau of Labor Statistics, Two Massachusetts Avenue, NE, Washington, D.C. 20212 (202) 606-7828; *Employment and Earnings,* and unpublished data.

LABOR FORCE EMPLOYMENT AND EARNINGS - JOB OPENINGS AND PLACEMENTS

U.S. Department of Labor, Employment and Training Administration, 200 Constitution Avenue, NW, Washington, D.C. 20210 (202) 219-7320; unpublished data.

LABOR FORCE EMPLOYMENT AND EARNINGS - METROPOLITAN AREAS

U.S. Department of Labor, Bureau of Labor Statistics, Two Massachusetts Avenue, NE, Washington, D.C. 20212 (202) 606-7828; *Average Annual Pay Levels in Metropolitan Areas,* and *Employment and Earnings.*

LABOR FORCE EMPLOYMENT AND EARNINGS - MINIMUM WAGE WORKERS

U.S. Department of Labor, Bureau of Labor Statistics, 200 Constitution Avenue, NW, Washington, D.C. 20210 (202) 219-7320; unpublished data.

U.S. Department of Labor, Employment Standards Administration, Two Massachusetts Avenue, NE, Washington, D.C. 20212 (202) 606-7828; *Minimum Wage and Maximum Hours Standards Under the Fair Labor Standards Act,* and unpublished data.

LABOR FORCE EMPLOYMENT AND EARNINGS - MULTIMEDIA USERS

Mediamark Research, Inc., 708 Third Avenue, New York, New York 10017 (212) 599-0444; *Multimedia Audiences.*

LABOR FORCE EMPLOYMENT AND EARNINGS - OCCUPATIONAL GROUPS - See OCCUPATIONS and individual occupations

LABOR FORCE EMPLOYMENT AND EARNINGS - OCCUPATIONAL SAFETY

National Safety Council, 1121 Spring Lake Drive, Itasca, Illinois 60143-3201 (708) 285-1121; *Accident Facts.*

U.S. Department of Labor, Bureau of Labor Statistics, Two Massachusetts Avenue, NE, Washington, D.C. 20212 (202) 606-7828; *Occupational Injuries and Illnesses in the United States by Industry.*

LABOR FORCE EMPLOYMENT AND EARNINGS - PRODUCTION WORKERS

U.S. Department of Commerce, Bureau of the Census, Suitland, Maryland 20233 (301) 763-4040; *Census of Manufactures,* and *Annual Survey of Manufactures.*

U.S. Department of Labor, Bureau of Labor Statistics, Two Massachusetts Avenue, NE, Washington, D.C. 20212 (202) 606-7828; *Employment and Earnings,* and Bulletins 2370 and 2429.

LABOR FORCE EMPLOYMENT AND EARNINGS - PRODUCTIVITY

U.S. Department of Labor, Bureau of Labor Statistics, Two Massachusetts Avenue, NE, Washington, D.C. 20212 (202) 606-7828; *Productivity Measures for Selected Industries and Government Services, Employment and Earnings.* and unpublished data.

LABOR FORCE EMPLOYMENT AND EARNINGS - SOCIAL INSURANCE COVERAGE

U.S. Department of Health and Human Services, Social Security Administration, 6401 Security Boulevard, Baltimore, Maryland 21235 (410) 965-1234; *Social Security Bulletin, Annual Statistical Supplement to the Social Security Bulletin,* and unpublished data.

LABOR FORCE EMPLOYMENT AND EARNINGS - STATE DATA

U.S. Department of Labor, Bureau of Labor Statistics, Two Massachusetts Avenue, NE, Washington, D.C. 20212 (202) 606-7828; Bulletin 2320, *Geographic Profile of Employment and Unemployment, Employment and Earnings. Employment and Wages, Annual Averages,* and *Average Annual Pay By State and Industry.*

LABOR FORCE EMPLOYMENT AND EARNINGS - UNEMPLOYED WORKERS - See also UNEMPLOYMENT

LABOR FORCE EMPLOYMENT AND EARNINGS - UNEMPLOYED WORKERS - AGE

U.S. Department of Labor, Bureau of Labor Statistics, Two Massachusetts Avenue, NE, Washington, D.C. 20212 (202) 606-7828; *Employment and Earnings, News,* Bulletin 2307, and unpublished data.

LABOR FORCE EMPLOYMENT AND EARNINGS - UNEMPLOYED WORKERS - AMERICAN INDIAN, ESKIMO, ALEUT POPULATION

U.S. Department of Commerce, Bureau of the Census, Suitland, Maryland 20233 (301) 763-4040; *Current Population Reports,* and unpublished data.

LABOR FORCE EMPLOYMENT AND EARNINGS - UNEMPLOYED WORKERS - ASIAN AND PACIFIC ISLANDER POPULATION

U.S. Department of Labor, Bureau of Labor Statistics, Two Massachusetts Avenue, NE, Washington, D.C. 20212 (202) 606-7828; *Current Population Reports,* and unpublished data.

LABOR FORCE EMPLOYMENT AND EARNINGS - UNEMPLOYED WORKERS - BLACK POPULATION

U.S. Department of Commerce, Bureau of the Census, Suitland, Maryland 20233 (301) 763-4040; *Current Population Reports.*

U.S. Department of Labor, Bureau of Labor Statistics, Two Massachusetts Avenue, NE, Washington, D.C. 20212 (202) 606-7828; *Employment and Earnings, News,* Bulletin 2307, and unpublished data.

LABOR FORCE EMPLOYMENT AND EARNINGS - UNEMPLOYED WORKERS - EDUCATIONAL ATTAINMENT

U.S. Department of Labor, Bureau of Labor Statistics, Two Massachusetts Avenue, NE, Washington, D.C. 20212 (202) 606-7828; Bulletin 2307, and unpublished data.

LABOR FORCE EMPLOYMENT AND EARNINGS - UNEMPLOYED WORKERS - HIGH SCHOOL GRADUATES AND DROPOUTS

U.S. Department of Labor, Bureau of Labor Statistics, Two Massachusetts Avenue, NE, Washington, D.C. 20212 (202) 606-7828; News, Bulletin 2307, and unpublished data.

LABOR FORCE EMPLOYMENT AND EARNINGS - UNEMPLOYED WORKERS - HISPANIC ORIGIN POPULATION

U.S. Department of Commerce, Bureau of the Census, Suitland, Maryland 20233 (301) 763-4040; Current Population Reports, and unpublished data.

U.S. Department of Labor, Bureau of Labor Statistics, Two Massachusetts Avenue, NE, Washington, D.C. 20212 (202) 606-7828; Employment and Earnings, Monthly Labor Review, and unpublished data.

LABOR FORCE EMPLOYMENT AND EARNINGS - UNEMPLOYED WORKERS - INDUSTRY

U.S. Department of Labor, Bureau of Labor Statistics, Two Massachusetts Avenue, NE, Washington, D.C. 20212 (202) 606-7828; Employment and Earnings.

LABOR FORCE EMPLOYMENT AND EARNINGS - UNEMPLOYED WORKERS - INTERNATIONAL COMPARISONS

U.S. Department of Labor, Bureau of Labor Statistics, Two Massachusetts Avenue, NE, Washington, D.C. 20212 (202) 606-7828; Comparative Labor Force Statistics for Ten Countries, and Monthly Labor Review.

LABOR FORCE EMPLOYMENT AND EARNINGS - UNEMPLOYED WORKERS - OCCUPATION

U.S. Department of Labor, Bureau of Labor Statistics, Two Massachusetts Avenue, NE, Washington, D.C. 20212 (202) 606-7828; Employment and Earnings.

LABOR FORCE EMPLOYMENT AND EARNINGS - UNEMPLOYED WORKERS - RACE

U.S. Department of Commerce, Bureau of the Census, Suitland, Maryland 20233 (301) 763-4040; Current Population Reports, and unpublished data.

U.S. Department of Labor, Bureau of Labor Statistics, Two Massachusetts Avenue, NE, Washington, D.C. 20212 (202) 606-7828; Employment and Earnings, Bulletin 2307 and unpublished data.

LABOR FORCE EMPLOYMENT AND EARNINGS - UNEMPLOYED WORKERS - REASON

U.S. Department of Labor, Bureau of Labor Statistics, Two Massachusetts Avenue, NE, Washington, D.C. 20212 (202) 606-7828; Employment and Earnings, and Bulletin 2307.

LABOR FORCE EMPLOYMENT AND EARNINGS - UNEMPLOYED WORKERS - SEX

U.S. Department of Labor, Bureau of Labor Statistics, Two Massachusetts Avenue, NE, Washington, D.C. 20212 (202) 606-7828; Employment and Earnings, Geographic Profile of Employment and Unemployment, Monthly Labor Review, Bulletin 2307, News, and unpublished data.

LABOR FORCE EMPLOYMENT AND EARNINGS - UNEMPLOYED WORKERS - STATES

U.S. Department of Labor, Bureau of Labor Statistics, Two Massachusetts Avenue, NE, Washington, D.C. 20212 (202) 606-7828; Geographic Profile of Employment and Unemployment.

U.S. Department of Labor, Employment and Training Administration, 200 Constitution Avenue, NW, Washington, D.C. 20210 (202) 219-7320; Unemployment Insurance, Financial Data.

LABOR FORCE EMPLOYMENT AND EARNINGS - UNEMPLOYED WORKERS - UNION MEMBERSHIP

American Federation of Labor and Congress of Industrial Organizations, 815 Sixteenth Street, NW, Washington, D.C. 20006 (202) 637-5000; Report of the AFL-CIO Executive Council.

U.S. Department of Labor, Bureau of Labor Statistics, Two Massachusetts Avenue, NE, Washington, D.C. 20212 (202) 606-7828; Employment and Earnings.

LABOR FORCE EMPLOYMENT AND EARNINGS - WORK STOPPAGES

U.S. Department of Labor, Bureau of Labor Statistics, Two Massachusetts Avenue, NE, Washington, D.C. 20212 (202) 606-7828; Compensation and Working Conditions.

LABOR FORCE EMPLOYMENT AND EARNINGS - WORKDAYS LOST

U.S. Department of Health and Human Services, National Center for Health Statistics, 3700 East-West Highway, Hyattsville, Maryland 20782 (301) 436-8500; Vital and Health Statistics, and unpublished data.

LABOR FORCE EMPLOYMENT AND EARNINGS - YOUTH EMPLOYMENT PROGRAMS

U.S. Library of Congress, 101 Independence Avenue, SE, Washington, D.C. 20540 (202) 707-5000; Cash and Noncash Benefits for Persons with Limited Income Eligibility Rules, Recipient and Expenditure Data.

LABOR MANAGEMENT RELATIONS

U.S. Department of Labor, Bureau of Labor Statistics, Two Massachusetts Avenue, NE, Washington, D.C. 20212 (202) 606-7828; Current Wage Developments, and Compensation and Working Conditions.

LABOR ORGANIZATIONS OR UNIONS

American Federation of Labor and Congress of Industrial Organizations, 815 Sixteenth Street, NW, Washington, D.C. 20006 (202) 637-5000; Report of the AFL-CIO Executive Council.

Gale Research Incorporated, 835 Penobscot Building, Detroit, Michigan 48226 (800) 877-4253; Encyclopedia of Associations.

LABOR ORGANIZATIONS OR UNIONS - COLLECTIVE BARGAINING SETTLEMENTS

U.S. Department of Labor, Bureau of Labor Statistics, Two Massachusetts Avenue, NE, Washington, D.C. 20212 (202) 606-7828; *Compensation and Working Conditions.*

LABOR ORGANIZATIONS OR UNIONS - EARNINGS

U.S. Department of Commerce, Bureau of the Census, Suitland, Maryland 20233 (301) 763-4040; *County Business Patterns.*

LABOR ORGANIZATIONS OR UNIONS - EMPLOYEES

U.S. Department of Commerce, Bureau of the Census, Suitland, Maryland 20233 (301) 763-4040; *County Business Patterns.*

LABOR ORGANIZATIONS OR UNIONS - ESTABLISHMENTS

U.S. Department of Commerce, Bureau of the Census, Suitland, Maryland 20233 (301) 763-4040; *County Business Patterns.*

LABOR ORGANIZATIONS OR UNIONS - MEMBERSHIP

American Federation of Labor and Congress of Industrial Organizations, 815 Sixteenth Street, NW, Washington, D.C. 20006 (202) 637-5000; *Report of the AFL-CIO Executive Council.*

U.S. Department of Labor, Bureau of Labor Statistics, Two Massachusetts Avenue, NE, Washington, D.C. 20212 (202) 606-7828; *Employment and Earnings.*

LABOR ORGANIZATIONS OR UNIONS - POLITICAL ACTION COMMITTEES (PAC)

Federal Election Commission, 999 E Street, NW, Washington, D.C. 20463 (800) 424-9530; *FEC Reports on Financial Activity, Final Report, Party and Non-Party Political Committees,* and press releases.

LABOR STRIKES

U.S. Department of Labor, Bureau of Labor Statistics, Two Massachusetts Avenue, NE, Washington, D.C. 20212 (202) 606-7828; *Compensation and Working Conditions.*

LABORATORIES - MEDICAL AND DENTAL

U.S. Department of Commerce, Bureau of the Census, Suitland, Maryland 20233 (301) 763-4040; *County Business Patterns,* and *Census of Service Industries.*

LAMB AND MUTTON - See also MEAT and MEAT PRODUCTS

U.S. Department of Agriculture, Economic Research Service, Fourteenth Street and Independence Avenue, SW, Washington, D.C. 20005-4789 (202) 219-1504; *Food Consumption, Prices, and Expenditures, Livestock and Meat Statistics, Agricultural Outlook,* and unpublished data.

LAMBS - See SHEEP AND LAMBS

LAND - See also FARMS and PUBLIC LANDS

LAND - AREA - CITIES

U.S. Department of Commerce, Bureau of the Census, Suitland, Maryland 20233 (301) 763-4040; *Census of Population,* and press releases.

LAND - AREA - COASTAL

U.S. Department of Commerce, Bureau of the Census, Suitland, Maryland 20233 (301) 763-4040; *Census of Population and Housing,* and unpublished data.

LAND - AREA - NATIONAL PARKS

U.S. Department of the Interior, National Park Service, C Street between Eighteenth and Nineteenth Streets, NW, Washington, D.C. 20240 (202) 208-6843; *National Park Statistical Abstract,* and unpublished data.

LAND - AREA - OUTLYING AREAS

U.S. Department of Commerce, Bureau of the Census, Suitland, Maryland 20233 (301) 763-4040; *Census of Population and Housing,* and unpublished data.

LAND - AREA - UNITED STATES

U.S. Department of Commerce, Bureau of the Census, Suitland, Maryland 20233 (301) 763-4040; *Census of Population and Housing, Areas of the United States, Area Measurement Reports,* and unpublished data.

LAND - FARMLAND

U.S. Department of Agriculture, Economic Research Service, Fourteenth Street and Independence Avenue, SW, Washington, D.C. 20005-4789 (202) 219-1504; *Farm Numbers and Land in Farms.*

U.S. Department of Agriculture, Soil Conservation Service, Fourteenth Street and Independence Avenue, SW, Washington, D.C. 20250 (202) 205-0027; *National Resources Inventory.*

U.S. Department of Commerce, Bureau of the Census, Suitland, Maryland 20233 (301) 763-4040; *Census of Agriculture.*

LAND - FEDERAL LAND

U.S. Department of the Interior, Bureau of Land Management, C Street between Eighteenth and Nineteenth Streets, NW, Washington, D.C. 20240 (202) 208-3435; *Public Land Statistics.*

U.S. General Services Administration, General Services Building, Eighteenth and F Streets, NW, Washington, D.C. 20405 (202) 708-5082; *Inventory Report on Real Property Owned by the United States Throughout the World.*

LAND - FOREIGN INVESTORS

U.S. Department of Commerce, Bureau of Economic Analysis, Fourteenth Street between Constitution Avenue and E Street, NW, Washington, D.C. 20230 (202) 606-9900; *Survey of Current Business,* and *Foreign Direct Investment in the United States, Operations of United States Affiliates of Foreign Companies.*

LAND - FOREST - AREA AND OWNERSHIP

U.S. Department of Agriculture, Forest Service, Fourteenth Street and Independence Avenue, SW, Washington, D.C. 20250 (202) 720-3760; *Forest Statistics of the United States,* and *Land Areas of the National Forest System.*

U.S. Department of Agriculture, Soil Conservation Service, Fourteenth Street and Independence Avenue, SW, Washington, D.C. 20250 (202) 205-0027; *National Resources Inventory.*

LAND - PARKS

National Association of State Park Directors, 126 Mill Branch Road, Tallahassee, Florida 32312 (904) 893-4959; *Annual Information Exchange.*

U.S. Department of the Interior, National Park Service, C Street between Eighteenth and Nineteenth Streets, NW, Washington, D.C. 20240 (202) 208-6843; *National Park Service Abstract*, and unpublished data.

LAND - URBAN LAND AND AREA - STATES

U.S. Department of Agriculture, Soil Conservation Service, Fourteenth Street and Independence Avenue, SW, Washington, D.C. 20250 (202) 205-0027; *National Resources Inventory.*

LAND - UTILIZATION

U.S. Department of Agriculture, Soil Conservation Service, Fourteenth Street and Independence Avenue, SW, Washington, D.C. 20250 (202) 205-0027; *National Resources Inventory.*

Laos (People's Democratic Republic)--National Statistical Office

Ministry of Economy, Planning and Finance, Post Office Box 46, Vientiane, Laos.

Laos (People's Democratic Republic)--Primary Statistics Sources

Service National de la Statistique, Ministere du Plan et de la Cooperation, Post Office Box 46, Vientiane, Laos; *Bulletin de Statistiques* (Statistical Bulletin); and *Annuaire Statistique* (Statistical Yearbook).

LAOS (PEOPLE'S DEMOCRATIC REPUBLIC) - AGRICULTURE

Asian Development Bank, Post Office Box 789, 1099 Manila, Philippines; *Key Indicators of Developing Asian and Pacific Countries.*

Facts on File, 460 Park Avenue South, New York, New York 10016 (800) 443-8323; *The New Book of World Rankings.*

Food and Agricultural Organization of the United Nations (FAO), Via delle Terme di Caracalla, 00100 Rome, Italy (Telephone Number in U.S. (202) 653-2400); *Production Yearbook, The State of Food and Agriculture*, and *Trade Yearbook.*

G.K. Hall and Company, 70 Lincoln Street, Boston, Massachusetts 02111 (617) 423-3990; *The World in Figures.*

Statistical Office of the United Nations, Publishing Service, New York, New York 10017 (800) 253-9646; *Statistical Yearbook*, and *Statistical Yearbook for Asia and the Pacific.*

Times Books, 201 East 50th Street, New York, New York 10022 (212) 751-2600; *The Economist Book of Vital World Statistics.*

LAOS (PEOPLE'S DEMOCRATIC REPUBLIC) - AIRLINE SERVICE

The Economist Intelligence Unit (Asia) Limited, 10th Floor, Luk Kwok Centre, 72 Gloucester Road, Wanchai, Hong Kong (Phone Number in U.S. (800) 938-4685); *Asian Market Atlas.*

Facts on File, 460 Park Avenue South, New York, New York 10016 (800) 443-8323; *The New Book of World Rankings.*

G.K. Hall and Company, 70 Lincoln Street, Boston, Massachusetts 02111 (617) 423-3990; *The World in Figures.*

Statistical Office of the United Nations, Publishing Service, New York, New York 10017 (800) 253-9646; *Statistical Yearbook.*

Times Books, 201 East 50th Street, New York, New York 10022 (212) 751-2600; *The Economist Book of Vital World Statistics.*

LAOS (PEOPLE'S DEMOCRATIC REPUBLIC) - ALUMINUM PRODUCTION AND CONSUMPTION - See LAOS (PEOPLE'S DEMOCRATIC REPUBLIC) - MINING AND MINERAL PRODUCTS

LAOS (PEOPLE'S DEMOCRATIC REPUBLIC) - ANIMAL HEALTH

Food and Agricultural Organization of the United Nations (FAO), Via delle Terme di Caracalla, 00100 Rome, Italy (Telephone Number in U.S. (202) 653-2400); *Animal Health Yearbook.*

LAOS (PEOPLE'S DEMOCRATIC REPUBLIC) - AREA AND DENSITY OF POPULATION

Euromonitor Publications Limited, 87-88 Turnmill Street, London EC1M 5QU, England; *International Marketing Data and Statistics.*

Facts on File, 460 Park Avenue South, New York, New York 10016 (800) 443-8323; *The New Book of World Rankings.*

Food and Agricultural Organization of the United Nations (FAO), Via delle Terme di Caracalla, 00100 Rome, Italy (Telephone Number in U.S. (202) 653-2400); *The State of Food and Agriculture.*

G.K. Hall and Company, 70 Lincoln Street, Boston, Massachusetts 02111 (617) 423-3990; *The World in Figures.*

Statistical Office of the United Nations, Publishing Service, New York, New York 10017 (800) 253-9646; *Statistical Yearbook.*

Times Books, 201 East 50th Street, New York, New York 10022 (212) 751-2600; *The Economist Book of Vital World Statistics.*

United Nations Educational, Scientific and Cultural Organization (UNESCO), 7 Place de Fontenoy, F-75700 Paris, France (Telephone Number in U.S. (212) 963-5981); *Statistical Yearbook.*

LAOS (PEOPLE'S DEMOCRATIC REPUBLIC) - ARMS EXPORTS AND IMPORTS

U.S. Arms Control and Disarmament Agency, 320 Twenty-first Street, NW, Washington, D.C. 20451 (202) 647-8677; *World Military Expenditures and Arms Transfers.*

LAOS (PEOPLE'S DEMOCRATIC REPUBLIC) - BALANCE OF PAYMENTS

The Economist Intelligence Unit, 111 West 57th Street, New York, New York 10019 (800) 938-4685; *The World Market Atlas.*

G.K. Hall and Company, 70 Lincoln Street, Boston, Massachusetts 02111 (617) 423-3990; *The World in Figures.*

LAOS (PEOPLE'S DEMOCRATIC REPUBLIC) - BANKING

Asian Development Bank, Post Office Box 789, 1099 Manila, Philippines; *Key Indicators of Developing Asian and Pacific*

Countries.

Facts on File, 460 Park Avenue South, New York, New York 10016 (800) 443-8323; *The New Book of World Rankings.*

G.K. Hall and Company, 70 Lincoln Street, Boston, Massachusetts 02111 (617) 423-3990; *The World in Figures.*

LAOS (PEOPLE'S DEMOCRATIC REPUBLIC) - BARLEY PRODUCTION - See LAOS (PEOPLE'S DEMOCRATIC REPUBLIC) - CROPS

LAOS (PEOPLE'S DEMOCRATIC REPUBLIC) - BEER PRODUCTION

Facts on File, 460 Park Avenue South, New York, New York 10016 (800) 443-8323; *The New Book of World Rankings.*

LAOS (PEOPLE'S DEMOCRATIC REPUBLIC) - BIRTH RATES

The Economist Intelligence Unit (Asia) Limited, 10th Floor, Luk Kwok Centre, 72 Gloucester Road, Wanchai, Hong Kong (Phone Number in U.S. (800) 938-4685); *Asian Market Atlas.*

Facts on File, 460 Park Avenue South, New York, New York 10016 (800) 443-8323; *The New Book of World Rankings.*

Statistical Office of the United Nations, Publishing Service, New York, New York 10017 (800) 253-9646; *Demographic Yearbook,* and *Statistical Yearbook.*

Times Books, 201 East 50th Street, New York, New York 10022 (212) 751-2600; *The Economist Book of Vital World Statistics.*

LAOS (PEOPLE'S DEMOCRATIC REPUBLIC) - BONDS

Asian Development Bank, Post Office Box 789, 1099 Manila, Philippines; *Key Indicators of Developing Asian and Pacific Countries.*

G.K. Hall and Company, 70 Lincoln Street, Boston, Massachusetts 02111 (617) 423-3990; *The World in Figures.*

LAOS (PEOPLE'S DEMOCRATIC REPUBLIC) - BOOK PRODUCTION

G.K. Hall and Company, 70 Lincoln Street, Boston, Massachusetts 02111 (617) 423-3990; *The World in Figures.*

LAOS (PEOPLE'S DEMOCRATIC REPUBLIC) - BROADCASTING

Billboard Limited, Post Office Box 9027, 1006 AA Amsterdam, The Netherlands (Telephone Number in U.S. (212) 764-7300); *World Radio TV Handbook.*

The Economist Intelligence Unit (Asia) Limited, 10th Floor, Luk Kwok Centre, 72 Gloucester Road, Wanchai, Hong Kong (Phone Number in U.S. (800) 938-4685); *Asian Market Atlas.*

Facts on File, 460 Park Avenue South, New York, New York 10016 (800) 443-8323; *The New Book of World Rankings.*

G.K. Hall and Company, 70 Lincoln Street, Boston, Massachusetts 02111 (617) 423-3990; *The World in Figures.*

Times Books, 201 East 50th Street, New York, New York 10022 (212) 751-2600; *The Economist Book of Vital World Statistics.*

LAOS (PEOPLE'S DEMOCRATIC REPUBLIC) - BUSINESS

G.K. Hall and Company, 70 Lincoln Street, Boston, Massachusetts 02111 (617) 423-3990; *The World in Figures.*

LAOS (PEOPLE'S DEMOCRATIC REPUBLIC) - CALORIE SUPPLY

Asian Development Bank, Post Office Box 789, 1099 Manila, Philippines; *Key Indicators of Developing Asian and Pacific Countries.*

Food and Agricultural Organization of the United Nations (FAO), Via delle Terme di Caracalla, 00100 Rome, Italy (Telephone Number in U.S. (202) 653-2400); *The State of Food and Agriculture.*

LAOS (PEOPLE'S DEMOCRATIC REPUBLIC) - CAPITAL INVESTMENT

Asian Development Bank, Post Office Box 789, 1099 Manila, Philippines; *Key Indicators of Developing Asian and Pacific Countries.*

LAOS (PEOPLE'S DEMOCRATIC REPUBLIC) - CAPITAL REVENUE

Asian Development Bank, Post Office Box 789, 1099 Manila, Philippines; *Key Indicators of Developing Asian and Pacific Countries.*

LAOS (PEOPLE'S DEMOCRATIC REPUBLIC) - CATTLE - See LAOS (PEOPLE'S DEMOCRATIC REPUBLIC) - LIVESTOCK AND POULTRY

LAOS (PEOPLE'S DEMOCRATIC REPUBLIC) - CEMENT PRODUCTION - See LAOS (PEOPLE'S DEMOCRATIC REPUBLIC) - MINING AND MINERAL PRODUCTS

LAOS (PEOPLE'S DEMOCRATIC REPUBLIC) - CHEMICAL (ORGANIC) PRODUCTION - See LAOS (PEOPLE'S DEMOCRATIC REPUBLIC) - MINING AND MINERAL PRODUCTS

LAOS (PEOPLE'S DEMOCRATIC REPUBLIC) - CHICKENS - See LAOS (PEOPLE'S DEMOCRATIC REPUBLIC) - LIVESTOCK AND POULTRY

LAOS (PEOPLE'S DEMOCRATIC REPUBLIC) - CIGARETTE PRODUCTION - See LAOS (PEOPLE'S DEMOCRATIC REPUBLIC) - TOBACCO PRODUCTION

LAOS (PEOPLE'S DEMOCRATIC REPUBLIC) - CLASS STRUCTURE

G.K. Hall and Company, 70 Lincoln Street, Boston, Massachusetts 02111 (617) 423-3990; *The World in Figures.*

LAOS (PEOPLE'S DEMOCRATIC REPUBLIC) - CLIMATE

Facts on File, 460 Park Avenue South, New York, New York 10016 (800) 443-8323; *The New Book of World Rankings.*

G.K. Hall and Company, 70 Lincoln Street, Boston, Massachusetts 02111 (617) 423-3990; *The World in Figures.*

LAOS (PEOPLE'S DEMOCRATIC REPUBLIC) - COAL PRODUCTION - See LAOS (PEOPLE'S DEMOCRATIC REPUBLIC) - MINING AND MINERAL PRODUCTS

LAOS (PEOPLE'S DEMOCRATIC REPUBLIC) - COFFEE PRODUCTION AND CONSUMPTION - See LAOS (PEOPLE'S DEMOCRATIC REPUBLIC) - CROPS

LAOS (PEOPLE'S DEMOCRATIC REPUBLIC) - COMMUNICATIONS

G.K. Hall and Company, 70 Lincoln Street, Boston, Massachusetts 02111 (617) 423-3990; *The World in Figures.*

Statistical Office of the United Nations, Publishing Service, New York, New York 10017 (800) 253-9646; *Statistical Yearbook for Asia and the Pacific.*

LAOS (PEOPLE'S DEMOCRATIC REPUBLIC) - CONSTRUCTION INDUSTRY

Facts on File, 460 Park Avenue South, New York, New York 10016 (800) 443-8323; *The New Book of World Rankings.*

LAOS (PEOPLE'S DEMOCRATIC REPUBLIC) - CONSUMER PRICE INDEX

Asian Development Bank, Post Office Box 789, 1099 Manila, Philippines; *Key Indicators of Developing Asian and Pacific Countries.*

G.K. Hall and Company, 70 Lincoln Street, Boston, Massachusetts 02111 (617) 423-3990; *The World in Figures.*

Statistical Office of the United Nations, Publishing Service, New York, New York 10017 (800) 253-9646; *Statistical Yearbook.*

LAOS (PEOPLE'S DEMOCRATIC REPUBLIC) - CONSUMER PRICES

International Labour Office, I.L.O. Publications, CH-1211, Geneva 22, Switzerland; *Yearbook of Labour Statistics.*

LAOS (PEOPLE'S DEMOCRATIC REPUBLIC) - CONSUMPTION

G.K. Hall and Company, 70 Lincoln Street, Boston, Massachusetts 02111 (617) 423-3990; *The World in Figures.*

LAOS (PEOPLE'S DEMOCRATIC REPUBLIC) - COPPER - See LAOS (PEOPLE'S DEMOCRATIC REPUBLIC) - MINING AND MINERAL PRODUCTS

LAOS (PEOPLE'S DEMOCRATIC REPUBLIC) - CORN PRODUCTION See LAOS (PEOPLE'S DEMOCRATIC REPUBLIC) - CROPS

LAOS (PEOPLE'S DEMOCRATIC REPUBLIC) - CORPORATE TAXES - See LAOS (PEOPLE'S DEMOCRATIC REPUBLIC) - TAXATION

LAOS (PEOPLE'S DEMOCRATIC REPUBLIC) - COTTON PRODUCTION - See LAOS (PEOPLE'S DEMOCRATIC REPUBLIC) - CROPS

LAOS (PEOPLE'S DEMOCRATIC REPUBLIC) - CRIME

Yale University Press, Yale Station, New Haven, Connecticut 06520 (203) 432-0940; *Violence and Crime in Cross-National Perspective.*

LAOS (PEOPLE'S DEMOCRATIC REPUBLIC) - CROPS

Asian Development Bank, Post Office Box 789, 1099 Manila, Philippines; *Key Indicators of Developing Asian and Pacific Countries.*

Facts on File, 460 Park Avenue South, New York, New York 10016 (800) 443-8323; *The New Book of World Rankings.*

Food and Agricultural Organization of the United Nations (FAO), Via delle Terme di Caracalla, 00100 Rome, Italy (Telephone Number

in U.S. (202) 653-2400); *The State of Food and Agriculture,* and *Production Yearbook.*

G.K. Hall and Company, 70 Lincoln Street, Boston, Massachusetts 02111 (617) 423-3990; *The World in Figures.*

Statistical Office of the United Nations, Publishing Service, New York, New York 10017 (800) 253-9646; *Statistical Yearbook.*

LAOS (PEOPLE'S DEMOCRATIC REPUBLIC) - CUSTOMS DUTIES

G.K. Hall and Company, 70 Lincoln Street, Boston, Massachusetts 02111 (617) 423-3990; *The World in Figures.*

LAOS (PEOPLE'S DEMOCRATIC REPUBLIC) - DAIRY PRODUCTS

Facts on File, 460 Park Avenue South, New York, New York 10016 (800) 443-8323; *The New Book of World Rankings.*

Food and Agricultural Organization of the United Nations (FAO), Via delle Terme di Caracalla, 00100 Rome, Italy (Telephone Number in U.S. (202) 653-2400); *Production Yearbook,* and *The State of Food and Agriculture.*

Statistical Office of the United Nations, Publishing Service, New York, New York 10017 (800) 253-9646; *Statistical Yearbook*

LAOS (PEOPLE'S DEMOCRATIC REPUBLIC) - DEATH RATES

The Economist Intelligence Unit (Asia) Limited, 10th Floor, Luk Kwok Centre, 72 Gloucester Road, Wanchai, Hong Kong (Phone Number in U.S. (800) 938-4685); *Asian Market Atlas.*

G.K. Hall and Company, 70 Lincoln Street, Boston, Massachusetts 02111 (617) 423-3990; *The World in Figures.*

Statistical Office of the United Nations, Publishing Service, New York, New York 10017 (800) 253-9646; *Statistical Yearbook.*

Times Books, 201 East 50th Street, New York, New York 10022 (212) 751-2600; *The Economist Book of Vital World Statistics.*

LAOS (PEOPLE'S DEMOCRATIC REPUBLIC) - DEFENSE EXPENDITURES

G.K. Hall and Company, 70 Lincoln Street, Boston, Massachusetts 02111 (617) 423-3990; *The World in Figures.*

U.S. Arms Control and Disarmament Agency, 320 Twenty-first Street, NW, Washington, D.C. 20451 (202) 647-8677; *World Military Expenditures and Arms Transfers.*

LAOS (PEOPLE'S DEMOCRATIC REPUBLIC) - DEMOGRAPHY

The Economist Intelligence Unit, 111 West 57th Street, New York, New York 10019 (800) 938-4685; *The World Market Atlas.*

The Economist Intelligence Unit (Asia) Limited, 10th Floor, Luk Kwok Centre, 72 Gloucester Road, Wanchai, Hong Kong (Phone Number in U.S. (800) 938-4685); *Asian Market Atlas.*

Facts on File, 460 Park Avenue South, New York, New York 10016 (800) 443-8323; *The New Book of World Rankings.*

G.K. Hall and Company, 70 Lincoln Street, Boston, Massachusetts 02111 (617) 423-3990; *The World in Figures.*

LAOS (PEOPLE'S DEMOCRATIC REPUBLIC) - DEVELOPMENT ASSISTANCE

Asian Development Bank, Post Office Box 789, 1099 Manila, Philippines; *Key Indicators of Developing Asian and Pacific Countries.*

G.K. Hall and Company, 70 Lincoln Street, Boston, Massachusetts 02111 (617) 423-3990; *The World in Figures.*

Statistical Office of the United Nations, Publishing Service, New York, New York 10017 (800) 253-9646; *Statistical Yearbook.*

LAOS (PEOPLE'S DEMOCRATIC REPUBLIC) - DIAMOND PRODUCTION - See LAOS (PEOPLE'S DEMOCRATIC REPUBLIC) - MINING AND MINERAL PRODUCTS

LAOS (PEOPLE'S DEMOCRATIC REPUBLIC) - DISEASE

G.K. Hall and Company, 70 Lincoln Street, Boston, Massachusetts 02111 (617) 423-3990; *The World in Figures.*

LAOS (PEOPLE'S DEMOCRATIC REPUBLIC) - DIVORCE

Facts on File, 460 Park Avenue South, New York, New York 10016 (800) 443-8323; *The New Book of World Rankings.*

Statistical Office of the United Nations, Publishing Service, New York, New York 10017 (800) 253-9646; *Demographic Yearbook.*

LAOS (PEOPLE'S DEMOCRATIC REPUBLIC) - DOMESTIC PRODUCT

G.K. Hall and Company, 70 Lincoln Street, Boston, Massachusetts 02111 (617) 423-3990; *The World in Figures.*

LAOS (PEOPLE'S DEMOCRATIC REPUBLIC) - DUCKS - See LAOS (PEOPLE'S DEMOCRATIC REPUBLIC) - LIVESTOCK AND POULTRY

LAOS (PEOPLE'S DEMOCRATIC REPUBLIC) - ECONOMY

Asian Development Bank, Post Office Box 789, 1099 Manila, Philippines; *Key Indicators of Developing Asian and Pacific Countries.*

Euromonitor Publications Limited, 87-88 Turnmill Street, London EC1M 5QU, England; *International Marketing Data and Statistics.*

Facts on File, 460 Park Avenue South, New York, New York 10016 (800) 443-8323; *The New Book of World Rankings.*

G.K. Hall and Company, 70 Lincoln Street, Boston, Massachusetts 02111 (617) 423-3990; *The World in Figures.*

LAOS (PEOPLE'S DEMOCRATIC REPUBLIC) - EDUCATION

The Economist Intelligence Unit, 111 West 57th Street, New York, New York 10019 (800) 938-4685; *The World Market Atlas.*

The Economist Intelligence Unit (Asia) Limited, 10th Floor, Luk Kwok Centre, 72 Gloucester Road, Wanchai, Hong Kong (Phone Number in U.S. (800) 938-4685; *Asian Market Atlas.*

Facts on File, 460 Park Avenue South, New York, New York 10016 (800) 443-8323; *The New Book of World Rankings.*

G.K. Hall and Company, 70 Lincoln Street, Boston, Massachusetts 02111 (617) 423-3990; *The World in Figures.*

Times Books, 201 East 50th Street, New York, New York 10022 (212) 751-2600; *The Economist Book of Vital World Statistics.*

United Nations Educational, Scientific and Cultural Organization (UNESCO), 7 Place de Fontenoy, F-75700 Paris, France (Telephone Number in U.S. (212) 963-5981); *Statistical Yearbook.*

LAOS (PEOPLE'S DEMOCRATIC REPUBLIC) - EGG PRODUCTION AND CONSUMPTION - See LAOS (PEOPLE'S DEMOCRATIC REPUBLIC) - DAIRY PRODUCTS

LAOS (PEOPLE'S DEMOCRATIC REPUBLIC) - ELECTRICITY

Asian Development Bank, Post Office Box 789, 1099 Manila, Philippines; *Key Indicators of Developing Asian and Pacific Countries.*

Facts on File, 460 Park Avenue South, New York, New York 10016 (800) 443-8323; *The New Book of World Rankings.*

Statistical Office of the United Nations, Publishing Service, New York, New York 10017 (800) 253-9646; *Statistical Yearbook.*

Times Books, 201 East 50th Street, New York, New York 10022 (212) 751-2600; *The Economist Book of Vital World Statistics.*

LAOS (PEOPLE'S DEMOCRATIC REPUBLIC) - EMPLOYMENT

Euromonitor Publications Limited, 87-88 Turnmill Street, London EC1M 5QU, England; *International Marketing Data and Statistics.*

Facts on File, 460 Park Avenue South, New York, New York 10016 (800) 443-8323; *The New Book of World Rankings.*

International Labour Office, I.L.O. Publications, CH-1211, Geneva 22, Switzerland; *Yearbook of Labour Statistics.*

LAOS (PEOPLE'S DEMOCRATIC REPUBLIC) - ENERGY

Facts on File, 460 Park Avenue South, New York, New York 10016 (800) 443-8323; *The New Book of World Rankings.*

Food and Agricultural Organization of the United Nations (FAO), Via delle Terme di Caracalla, 00100 Rome, Italy (Telephone Number in U.S. (202) 653-2400); *The State of Food and Agriculture.*

G.K. Hall and Company, 70 Lincoln Street, Boston, Massachusetts 02111 (617) 423-3990; *The World in Figures.*

Statistical Office of the United Nations, Publishing Service, New York, New York 10017 (800) 253-9646; *Energy Statistics Yearbook, Statistical Yearbook, Statistical Yearbook for Asia and the Pacific, and World Energy Supplies.*

Times Books, 201 East 50th Street, New York, New York 10022 (212) 751-2600; *The Economist Book of Vital World Statistics.*

LAOS (PEOPLE'S DEMOCRATIC REPUBLIC) - EXCHANGE RATES

Asian Development Bank, Post Office Box 789, 1099 Manila, Philippines; *Key Indicators of Developing Asian and Pacific Countries.*

The Economist Intelligence Unit (Asia) Limited, 10th Floor, Luk Kwok Centre, 72 Gloucester Road, Wanchai, Hong Kong (Phone Number in U.S. (800) 938-4685); *Asian Market Atlas.*

Euromonitor Publications Limited, 87-88 Turnmill Street, London EC1M 5QU, England; *International Marketing Data and Statistics.*

Statistical Office of the United Nations, Publishing Service, New York, New York 10017 (800) 253-9646; *Statistical Yearbook.*

LAOS (PEOPLE'S DEMOCRATIC REPUBLIC) - EXPORTS

Asian Development Bank, Post Office Box 789, 1099 Manila, Philippines; *Key Indicators of Developing Asian and Pacific Countries.*

The Economist Intelligence Unit, 111 West 57th Street, New York, New York 10019 (800) 938-4685; *The World Market Atlas.*

The Economist Intelligence Unit (Asia) Limited, 10th Floor, Luk Kwok Centre, 72 Gloucester Road, Wanchai, Hong Kong (Phone Number in U.S. (800) 938-4685); *Asian Market Atlas.*

Euromonitor Publications Limited, 87-88 Turnmill Street, London EC1M 5QU, England; *International Marketing Data and Statistics.*

Food and Agricultural Organization of the United Nations (FAO), Via delle Terme di Caracalla, 00100 Rome, Italy (Telephone Number in U.S. (202) 653-2400); *The State of Food and Agriculture.*

G.K. Hall and Company, 70 Lincoln Street, Boston, Massachusetts 02111 (617) 423-3990; *The World in Figures.*

International Monetary Fund, 700 Nineteenth Street, NW, Washington, D.C. 20431 (202) 623-7000; *Direction of Trade Statistics.*

Times Books, 201 East 50th Street, New York, New York 10022 (212) 751-2600; *The Economist Book of Vital World Statistics.*

LAOS (PEOPLE'S DEMOCRATIC REPUBLIC) - EXTERNAL INDEBTEDNESS

Asian Development Bank, Post Office Box 789, 1099 Manila, Philippines; *Key Indicators of Developing Asian and Pacific Countries.*

LAOS (PEOPLE'S DEMOCRATIC REPUBLIC) - EXTERNAL TRADE

Asian Development Bank, Post Office Box 789, 1099 Manila, Philippines; *Key Indicators of Developing Asian and Pacific Countries.*

Food and Agricultural Organization of the United Nations (FAO), Via delle Terme di Caracalla, 00100 Rome, Italy (Telephone Number in U.S. (202) 653-2400); *The State of Food and Agriculture,* and *Trade Yearbook.*

G.K. Hall and Company, 70 Lincoln Street, Boston, Massachusetts 02111 (617) 423-3990; *The World in Figures.*

Statistical Office of the United Nations, Publishing Service, New York, New York 10017 (800) 253-9646; *Statistical Yearbook.*

LAOS (PEOPLE'S DEMOCRATIC REPUBLIC) - FARM CROPS - See LAOS (PEOPLE'S DEMOCRATIC REPUBLIC) - CROPS

LAOS (PEOPLE'S DEMOCRATIC REPUBLIC) - FEMALE WORKING POPULATION - See LAOS (PEOPLE'S DEMOCRATIC REPUBLIC) - EMPLOYMENT

LAOS (PEOPLE'S DEMOCRATIC REPUBLIC) - FERTILITY RATES

The Economist Intelligence Unit (Asia) Limited, 10th Floor, Luk Kwok Centre, 72 Gloucester Road, Wanchai, Hong Kong (Phone Number in U.S. (800) 938-4685); *Asian Market Atlas.*

Facts on File, 460 Park Avenue South, New York, New York 10016 (800) 443-8323; *The New Book of World Rankings.*

Times Books, 201 East 50th Street, New York, New York 10022 (212) 751-2600; *The Economist Book of Vital World Statistics.*

LAOS (PEOPLE'S DEMOCRATIC REPUBLIC) - FERTILIZER

Food and Agricultural Organization of the United Nations (FAO), Via delle Terme di Caracalla, 00100 Rome, Italy (Telephone Number in U.S. (202) 653-2400); *Fertilizer Yearbook.*

Statistical Office of the United Nations, Publishing Service, New York, New York 10017 (800) 253-9646; *Statistical Yearbook.*

LAOS (PEOPLE'S DEMOCRATIC REPUBLIC) - FETAL MORTALITY

Statistical Office of the United Nations, Publishing Service, New York, New York 10017 (800) 253-9646; *Demographic Yearbook.*

LAOS (PEOPLE'S DEMOCRATIC REPUBLIC) - FINANCE

Asian Development Bank, Post Office Box 789, 1099 Manila, Philippines; *Key Indicators of Developing Asian and Pacific Countries.*

Facts on File, 460 Park Avenue South, New York, New York 10016 (800) 443-8323; *The New Book of World Rankings.*

G.K. Hall and Company, 70 Lincoln Street, Boston, Massachusetts 02111 (617) 423-3990; *The World in Figures.*

International Monetary Fund, 700 Nineteenth Street, NW, Washington, D.C. 20431 (202) 623-7000; *International Financial Statistics.*

Statistical Office of the United Nations, Publishing Service, New York, New York 10017 (800) 253-9646; *Statistical Yearbook for Asia and the Pacific.*

LAOS (PEOPLE'S DEMOCRATIC REPUBLIC) - FISHERIES

Facts on File, 460 Park Avenue South, New York, New York 10016 (800) 443-8323; *The New Book of World Rankings.*

Food and Agricultural Organization of the United Nations (FAO), Via delle Terme di Caracalla, 00100 Rome, Italy (Telephone Number in U.S. (202) 653-2400); *The State of Food and Agriculture,* and *Yearbook of Fishery Statistics.*

Statistical Office of the United Nations, Publishing Service, New York, New York 10017 (800) 253-9646; *Statistical Yearbook.*

LAOS (PEOPLE'S DEMOCRATIC REPUBLIC) - FOOD

Food and Agricultural Organization of the United Nations (FAO), Via delle Terme di Caracalla, 00100 Rome, Italy (Telephone Number in U.S. (202) 653-2400); *The State of Food and Agriculture,* and *Production Yearbook.*

G.K. Hall and Company, 70 Lincoln Street, Boston, Massachusetts 02111 (617) 423-3990; *The World in Figures.*

Statistical Office of the United Nations, Publishing Service, New York, New York 10017 (800) 253-9646; *Statistical Yearbook for Asia and the Pacific.*

LAOS (PEOPLE'S DEMOCRATIC REPUBLIC) - FOREIGN AID

G.K. Hall and Company, 70 Lincoln Street, Boston, Massachusetts 02111 (617) 423-3990; *The World in Figures.*

LAOS (PEOPLE'S DEMOCRATIC REPUBLIC) - FOREIGN TRADE

Asian Development Bank, Post Office Box 789, 1099 Manila, Philippines; *Key Indicators of Developing Asian and Pacific Countries.*

The Economist Intelligence Unit (Asia) Limited, 10th Floor, Luk Kwok Centre, 72 Gloucester Road, Wanchai, Hong Kong (Phone Number in U.S. (800) 938-4685); *Asian Market Atlas.*

Facts on File, 460 Park Avenue South, New York, New York 10016 (800) 443-8323; *The New Book of World Rankings.*

Food and Agricultural Organization of the United Nations (FAO), Via delle Terme di Caracalla, 00100 Rome, Italy (Telephone Number in U.S. (202) 653-2400); *The State of Food and Agriculture.*

G.K. Hall and Company, 70 Lincoln Street, Boston, Massachusetts 02111 (617) 423-3990; *The World in Figures.*

Statistical Office of the United Nations, Publishing Service, New York, New York 10017 (800) 253-9646; *International Trade Statistics, Statistical Yearbook*, and *Trade in Manufactures of Developing Countries.*

LAOS (PEOPLE'S DEMOCRATIC REPUBLIC) - FORESTRY AND FOREST PRODUCTS

The Economist Intelligence Unit (Asia) Limited, 10th Floor, Luk Kwok Centre, 72 Gloucester Road, Wanchai, Hong Kong (Phone Number in U.S. (800) 938-4685); *Asian Market Atlas.*

Facts on File, 460 Park Avenue South, New York, New York 10016 (800) 443-8323; *The New Book of World Rankings.*

Food and Agricultural Organization of the United Nations (FAO), Via delle Terme di Caracalla, 00100 Rome, Italy (Telephone Number in U.S. (202) 653-2400); *The State of Food and Agriculture*, and *Yearbook of Forest Products.*

G.K. Hall and Company, 70 Lincoln Street, Boston, Massachusetts 02111 (617) 423-3990; *The World in Figures.*

Statistical Office of the United Nations, Publishing Service, New York, New York 10017 (800) 253-9646; *Statistical Yearbook.*

United Nations Educational, Scientific and Cultural Organization (UNESCO), 7 Place de Fontenoy, F-75700 Paris, France (Telephone Number in U.S. (212) 963-5981); *Statistical Yearbook.*

LAOS (PEOPLE'S DEMOCRATIC REPUBLIC) - GAS PRODUCTION - See LAOS (PEOPLE'S DEMOCRATIC REPUBLIC) - MINING AND MINERAL PRODUCTS

LAOS (PEOPLE'S DEMOCRATIC REPUBLIC) - GENERAL MORTALITY

Statistical Office of the United Nations, Publishing Service, New York, New York 10017 (800) 253-9646; *Demographic Yearbook.*

LAOS (PEOPLE'S DEMOCRATIC REPUBLIC) - GEOGRAPHIC DATA

Facts on File, 460 Park Avenue South, New York, New York 10016 (800) 443-8323; *The New Book of World Rankings.*

LAOS (PEOPLE'S DEMOCRATIC REPUBLIC) - GOLD PRODUCTION AND CONSUMPTION

Facts on File, 460 Park Avenue South, New York, New York 10016 (800) 443-8323; *The New Book of World Rankings.*

LAOS (PEOPLE'S DEMOCRATIC REPUBLIC) - GOVERNMENT

Asian Development Bank, Post Office Box 789, 1099 Manila, Philippines; *Key Indicators of Developing Asian and Pacific Countries.*

G.K. Hall and Company, 70 Lincoln Street, Boston, Massachusetts 02111 (617) 423-3990; *The World in Figures.*

LAOS (PEOPLE'S DEMOCRATIC REPUBLIC) - GOVERNMENT FINANCES

Asian Development Bank, Post Office Box 789, 1099 Manila, Philippines; *Key Indicators of Developing Asian and Pacific Countries.*

Statistical Office of the United Nations, Publishing Service, New York, New York 10017 (800) 253-9646; *Statistical Yearbook.*

LAOS (PEOPLE'S DEMOCRATIC REPUBLIC) - GOVERNMENT REVENUE

Asian Development Bank, Post Office Box 789, 1099 Manila, Philippines; *Key Indicators of Developing Asian and Pacific Countries.*

LAOS (PEOPLE'S DEMOCRATIC REPUBLIC) - GRAIN PRODUCTION - See LAOS (PEOPLE'S DEMOCRATIC REPUBLIC) - CROPS

LAOS (PEOPLE'S DEMOCRATIC REPUBLIC) - GROSS DOMESTIC PRODUCT

Asian Development Bank, Post Office Box 789, 1099 Manila, Philippines; *Key Indicators of Developing Asian and Pacific Countries.*

The Economist Intelligence Unit, 111 West 57th Street, New York, New York 10019 (800) 938-4685; *The World Market Atlas.*

The Economist Intelligence Unit (Asia) Limited, 10th Floor, Luk Kwok Centre, 72 Gloucester Road, Wanchai, Hong Kong (Phone Number in U.S. (800) 938-4685); *Asian Market Atlas.*

Euromonitor Publications Limited, 87-88 Turnmill Street, London EC1M 5QU, England; *International Marketing Data and Statistics.*

Facts on File, 460 Park Avenue South, New York, New York 10016 (800) 443-8323; *The New Book of World Rankings.*

G.K. Hall and Company, 70 Lincoln Street, Boston, Massachusetts 02111 (617) 423-3990; *The World in Figures.*

Statistical Office of the United Nations, Publishing Service, New York, New York 10017 (800) 253-9646; *Statistical Yearbook.*

Times Books, 201 East 50th Street, New York, New York 10022 (212) 751-2600; *The Economist Book of Vital World Statistics.*

LAOS (PEOPLE'S DEMOCRATIC REPUBLIC) - GROSS
NATIONAL PRODUCT

Asian Development Bank, Post Office Box 789, 1099 Manila,
Philippines; *Key Indicators of Developing Asian and Pacific
Countries.*

Euromonitor Publications Limited, 87-88 Turnmill Street, London
EC1M 5QU, England; *International Marketing Data and Statistics.*

U.S. Arms Control and Disarmament Agency, 320 Twenty-first
Street, NW, Washington, D.C. 20451 (202) 647-8677; *World Military
Expenditures and Arms Transfers.*

LAOS (PEOPLE'S DEMOCRATIC REPUBLIC) - GROUNDNUT
PRODUCTION - See LAOS (PEOPLE'S DEMOCRATIC REPUBLIC) -
CROPS

LAOS (PEOPLE'S DEMOCRATIC REPUBLIC) - HEALTH

The Economist Intelligence Unit (Asia) Limited, 10th Floor, Luk
Kwok Centre, 72 Gloucester Road, Wanchai, Hong Kong (Phone
Number in U.S. (800) 938-4685); *Asian Market Atlas.*

Facts on File, 460 Park Avenue South, New York, New York 10016
(800) 443-8323; *The New Book of World Rankings.*

G.K. Hall and Company, 70 Lincoln Street, Boston, Massachusetts
02111 (617) 423-3990; *The World in Figures.*

Statistical Office of the United Nations, Publishing Service, New
York, New York 10017 (800) 253-9646; *Statistical Yearbook.*

Times Books, 201 East 50th Street, New York, New York 10022 (212)
751-2600; *The Economist Book of Vital World Statistics.*

LAOS (PEOPLE'S DEMOCRATIC REPUBLIC) - HIDE
PRODUCTION

Food and Agricultural Organization of the United Nations (FAO),
Via delle Terme di Caracalla, 00100 Rome, Italy (Telephone Number
in U.S. (202) 653-2400); *Production Yearbook.*

LAOS (PEOPLE'S DEMOCRATIC REPUBLIC) - HIGHWAYS

The Economist Intelligence Unit (Asia) Limited, 10th Floor, Luk
Kwok Centre, 72 Gloucester Road, Wanchai, Hong Kong (Phone
Number in U.S. (800) 938-4685); *Asian Market Atlas.*

G.K. Hall and Company, 70 Lincoln Street, Boston, Massachusetts
02111 (617) 423-3990; *The World in Figures.*

LAOS (PEOPLE'S DEMOCRATIC REPUBLIC) - HORSES - See LAOS
(PEOPLE'S DEMOCRATIC REPUBLIC) - LIVESTOCK AND POULTRY

LAOS (PEOPLE'S DEMOCRATIC REPUBLIC) - HOURS OF
WORK - See LAOS (PEOPLE'S DEMOCRATIC REPUBLIC) -
EMPLOYMENT

LAOS (PEOPLE'S DEMOCRATIC REPUBLIC) - HOUSING

Facts on File, 460 Park Avenue South, New York, New York 10016
(800) 443-8323; *The New Book of World Rankings.*

LAOS (PEOPLE'S DEMOCRATIC REPUBLIC) - ILLITERATE
POPULATION

The Economist Intelligence Unit, 111 West 57th Street, New York,
New York 10019 (800) 938-4685; *The World Market Atlas.*

G.K. Hall and Company, 70 Lincoln Street, Boston, Massachusetts
02111 (617) 423-3990; *The World in Figures.*

United Nations Educational, Scientific and Cultural Organization
(UNESCO), 7 Place de Fontenoy, F-75700 Paris, France (Telephone
Number in U.S. (212) 963-5981); *Statistical Yearbook.*

LAOS (PEOPLE'S DEMOCRATIC REPUBLIC) - IMPORTS

Asian Development Bank, Post Office Box 789, 1099 Manila,
Philippines; *Key Indicators of Developing Asian and Pacific
Countries.*

The Economist Intelligence Unit, 111 West 57th Street, New York,
New York 10019 (800) 938-4685; *The World Market Atlas.*

The Economist Intelligence Unit (Asia) Limited, 10th Floor, Luk
Kwok Centre, 72 Gloucester Road, Wanchai, Hong Kong (Phone
Number in U.S. (800) 938-4685); *Asian Market Atlas.*

Euromonitor Publications Limited, 87-88 Turnmill Street, London
EC1M 5QU, England; *International Marketing Data and Statistics.*

Food and Agricultural Organization of the United Nations (FAO), Via
delle Terme di Caracalla, 00100 Rome, Italy (Telephone Number in
U.S. (202) 653-2400); *The State of Food and Agriculture.*

G.K. Hall and Company, 70 Lincoln Street, Boston, Massachusetts
02111 (617) 423-3990; *The World in Figures.*

International Monetary Fund, 700 Nineteenth Street, NW,
Washington, D.C. 20431 (202) 623-7000; *Direction of Trade Statistics.*

LAOS (PEOPLE'S DEMOCRATIC REPUBLIC) - INDUSTRY

Euromonitor Publications Limited, 87-88 Turnmill Street, London
EC1M 5QU, England; *International Marketing Data and Statistics.*

Facts on File, 460 Park Avenue South, New York, New York 10016
(800) 443-8323; *The New Book of World Rankings.*

G.K. Hall and Company, 70 Lincoln Street, Boston, Massachusetts
02111 (617) 423-3990; *The World in Figures.*

International Labour Office, I.L.O. Publications, CH-1211, Geneva
22, Switzerland; *Yearbook of Labour Statistics.*

Statistical Office of the United Nations, Publishing Service, New
York, New York 10017 (800) 253-9646; *Statistical Yearbook for Asia
and the Pacific.*

Times Books, 201 East 50th Street, New York, New York 10022 (212)
751-2600; *The Economist Book of Vital World Statistics.*

LAOS (PEOPLE'S DEMOCRATIC REPUBLIC) - INFANT AND
MATERNAL MORTALITY

The Economist Intelligence Unit (Asia) Limited, 10th Floor, Luk
Kwok Centre, 72 Gloucester Road, Wanchai, Hong Kong (Phone
Number in U.S. (800) 938-4685); *Asian Market Atlas.*

Statistical Office of the United Nations, Publishing Service, New
York, New York 10017 (800) 253-9646; *Demographic Yearbook.*

Times Books, 201 East 50th Street, New York, New York 10022 (212)
751-2600; *The Economist Book of Vital World Statistics.*

LAOS (PEOPLE'S DEMOCRATIC REPUBLIC) - INTERNAL TRADE

Statistical Office of the United Nations, Publishing Service, New York, New York 10017 (800) 253-9646; *Statistical Yearbook for Asia and the Pacific.*

LAOS (PEOPLE'S DEMOCRATIC REPUBLIC) - INTERNATIONAL RESERVES EXCLUDING GOLD

Asian Development Bank, Post Office Box 789, 1099 Manila, Philippines; *Key Indicators of Developing Asian and Pacific Countries.*

LAOS (PEOPLE'S DEMOCRATIC REPUBLIC) - INTERNATIONAL STATISTICS

Asian Development Bank, Post Office Box 789, 1099 Manila, Philippines; *Key Indicators of Developing Asian and Pacific Countries.*

LAOS (PEOPLE'S DEMOCRATIC REPUBLIC) - IRON ORE PRODUCTION AND CONSUMPTION - See LAOS (PEOPLE'S DEMOCRATIC REPUBLIC) - MINING AND MINERAL PRODUCTS

LAOS (PEOPLE'S DEMOCRATIC REPUBLIC) - IRRIGATION

Euromonitor Publications Limited, 87-88 Turnmill Street, London EC1M 5QU, England; *International Marketing Data and Statistics.*

LAOS (PEOPLE'S DEMOCRATIC REPUBLIC) - LABOR FORCE

The Economist Intelligence Unit (Asia) Limited, 10th Floor, Luk Kwok Centre, 72 Gloucester Road, Wanchai, Hong Kong (Phone Number in U.S. (800) 938-4685); *Asian Market Atlas.*

Euromonitor Publications Limited, 87-88 Turnmill Street, London EC1M 5QU, England; *International Marketing Data and Statistics.*

Facts on File, 460 Park Avenue South, New York, New York 10016 (800) 443-8323; *The New Book of World Rankings.*

Food and Agricultural Organization of the United Nations (FAO), Via delle Terme di Caracalla, 00100 Rome, Italy (Telephone Number in U.S. (202) 653-2400); *The State of Food and Agriculture.*

G.K. Hall and Company, 70 Lincoln Street, Boston, Massachusetts 02111 (617) 423-3990; *The World in Figures.*

LAOS (PEOPLE'S DEMOCRATIC REPUBLIC) - LABOR PRODUCTIVITY

International Labour Office, I.L.O. Publications, CH-1211, Geneva 22, Switzerland; *Yearbook of Labour Statistics.*

LAOS (PEOPLE'S DEMOCRATIC REPUBLIC) - LAND USE

Euromonitor Publications Limited, 87-88 Turnmill Street, London EC1M 5QU, England; *International Marketing Data and Statistics.*

Food and Agricultural Organization of the United Nations (FAO), Via delle Terme di Caracalla, 00100 Rome, Italy (Telephone Number in U.S. (202) 653-2400); *Production Yearbook.*

G.K. Hall and Company, 70 Lincoln Street, Boston, Massachusetts 02111 (617) 423-3990; *The World in Figures.*

LAOS (PEOPLE'S DEMOCRATIC REPUBLIC) - LIBRARIES

Facts on File, 460 Park Avenue South, New York, New York 10016 (800) 443-8323; *The New Book of World Rankings.*

LAOS (PEOPLE'S DEMOCRATIC REPUBLIC) - LIFE EXPECTANCY

The Economist Intelligence Unit (Asia) Limited, 10th Floor, Luk Kwok Centre, 72 Gloucester Road, Wanchai, Hong Kong (Phone Number in U.S. (800) 938-4685); *Asian Market Atlas.*

LAOS (PEOPLE'S DEMOCRATIC REPUBLIC) - LIVESTOCK AND POULTRY

Euromonitor Publications Limited, 87-88 Turnmill Street, London EC1M 5QU, England; *International Marketing Data and Statistics.*

Facts on File, 460 Park Avenue South, New York, New York 10016 (800) 443-8323; *The New Book of World Rankings.*

Food and Agricultural Organization of the United Nations (FAO), Via delle Terme di Caracalla, 00100 Rome, Italy (Telephone Number in U.S. (202) 653-2400); *Production Yearbook,* and *The State of Food and Agriculture.*

G.K. Hall and Company, 70 Lincoln Street, Boston, Massachusetts 02111 (617) 423-3990; *The World in Figures.*

Statistical Office of the United Nations, Publishing Service, New York, New York 10017 (800) 253-9646; *Statistical Yearbook.*

LAOS (PEOPLE'S DEMOCRATIC REPUBLIC) - LIVING LEVELS

G.K. Hall and Company, 70 Lincoln Street, Boston, Massachusetts 02111 (617) 423-3990; *The World in Figures.*

Times Books, 201 East 50th Street, New York, New York 10022 (212) 751-2600; *The Economist Book of Vital World Statistics.*

LAOS (PEOPLE'S DEMOCRATIC REPUBLIC) - MAIL - NUMBER OF ITEMS SENT AND RECEIVED

Statistical Office of the United Nations, Publishing Service, New York, New York 10017 (800) 253-9646; *Statistical Yearbook.*

LAOS (PEOPLE'S DEMOCRATIC REPUBLIC) - MANPOWER

Statistical Office of the United Nations, Publishing Service, New York, New York 10017 (800) 253-9646; *Statistical Yearbook for Asia and the Pacific.*

LAOS (PEOPLE'S DEMOCRATIC REPUBLIC) - MANUFACTURING

Asian Development Bank, Post Office Box 789, 1099 Manila, Philippines; *Key Indicators of Developing Asian and Pacific Countries.*

Facts on File, 460 Park Avenue South, New York, New York 10016 (800) 443-8323; *The New Book of World Rankings.*

G.K. Hall and Company, 70 Lincoln Street, Boston, Massachusetts 02111 (617) 423-3990; *The World in Figures.*

LAOS (PEOPLE'S DEMOCRATIC REPUBLIC) - MARRIAGE RATES

Facts on File, 460 Park Avenue South, New York, New York 10016 (800) 443-8323; *The New Book of World Rankings.*

Statistical Office of the United Nations, Publishing Service, New York, New York 10017 (800) 253-9646; *Demographic Yearbook.*

LAOS (PEOPLE'S DEMOCRATIC REPUBLIC) - MEAT PRODUCTION - See LAOS (PEOPLE'S DEMOCRATIC REPUBLIC) - LIVESTOCK AND POULTRY

LAOS (PEOPLE'S DEMOCRATIC REPUBLIC) - MERCHANT SHIPPING

G.K. Hall and Company, 70 Lincoln Street, Boston, Massachusetts 02111 (617) 423-3990; *The World in Figures.*

LAOS (PEOPLE'S DEMOCRATIC REPUBLIC) - MILITARY

The Economist Intelligence Unit (Asia) Limited, 10th Floor, Luk Kwok Centre, 72 Gloucester Road, Wanchai, Hong Kong (Phone Number in U.S. (800) 938-4685); *Asian Market Atlas.*

G.K. Hall and Company, 70 Lincoln Street, Boston, Massachusetts 02111 (617) 423-3990; *The World in Figures.*

The International Institute for Strategic Studies, 23 Tavistock Street, London WC2E 7NQ, England; *The Military Balance.*

U.S. Arms Control and Disarmament Agency, 320 Twenty-first Street, NW, Washington, D.C. 20451 (202) 647-0077; *World Military Expenditures and Arms Transfers.*

LAOS (PEOPLE'S DEMOCRATIC REPUBLIC) - MINING AND MINERAL PRODUCTS

Asian Development Bank, Post Office Box 789, 1099 Manila, Philippines; *Key Indicators of Developing Asian and Pacific Countries.*

Facts on File, 460 Park Avenue South, New York, New York 10016 (800) 443-8323; *The New Book of World Rankings.*

G.K. Hall and Company, 70 Lincoln Street, Boston, Massachusetts 02111 (617) 423-3990; *The World in Figures.*

Statistical Office of the United Nations, Publishing Service, New York, New York 10017 (800) 253-9646; *Statistical Yearbook.*

LAOS (PEOPLE'S DEMOCRATIC REPUBLIC) - MONEY EXCHANGE RATE

Euromonitor Publications Limited, 87-88 Turnmill Street, London EC1M 5QU, England; *International Marketing Data and Statistics.*

Statistical Office of the United Nations, Publishing Service, New York, New York 10017 (800) 253-9646; *Statistical Yearbook.*

LAOS (PEOPLE'S DEMOCRATIC REPUBLIC) - MONEY RESERVES

Euromonitor Publications Limited, 87-88 Turnmill Street, London EC1M 5QU, England; *International Marketing Data and Statistics.*

LAOS (PEOPLE'S DEMOCRATIC REPUBLIC) - MONEY SUPPLY

Asian Development Bank, Post Office Box 789, 1099 Manila, Philippines; *Key Indicators of Developing Asian and Pacific Countries.*

Euromonitor Publications Limited, 87-88 Turnmill Street, London EC1M 5QU, England; *International Marketing Data and Statistics.*

G.K. Hall and Company, 70 Lincoln Street, Boston, Massachusetts 02111 (617) 423-3990; *The World in Figures.*

LAOS (PEOPLE'S DEMOCRATIC REPUBLIC) - MOTOR VEHICLES IN USE

G.K. Hall and Company, 70 Lincoln Street, Boston, Massachusetts 02111 (617) 423-3990; *The World in Figures.*

Statistical Office of the United Nations, Publishing Service, New York, New York 10017 (800) 253-9646; *Statistical Yearbook.*

Times Books, 201 East 50th Street, New York, New York 10022 (212) 751-2600; *The Economist Book of Vital World Statistics.*

LAOS (PEOPLE'S DEMOCRATIC REPUBLIC) - MUSEUMS

Facts on File, 460 Park Avenue South, New York, New York 10016 (800) 443-8323; *The New Book of World Rankings.*

LAOS (PEOPLE'S DEMOCRATIC REPUBLIC) - NATALITY - See LAOS (PEOPLE'S DEMOCRATIC REPUBLIC) - BIRTH RATES

LAOS (PEOPLE'S DEMOCRATIC REPUBLIC) - NATIONAL ACCOUNTS

Statistical Office of the United Nations, Publishing Service, New York, New York 10017 (800) 253-9646; *Statistical Yearbook.*

LAOS (PEOPLE'S DEMOCRATIC REPUBLIC) - NATIONAL INCOME

Facts on File, 460 Park Avenue South, New York, New York 10016 (800) 443-8323; *The New Book of World Rankings.*

G.K. Hall and Company, 70 Lincoln Street, Boston, Massachusetts 02111 (617) 423-3990; *The World in Figures.*

Statistical Office of the United Nations, Publishing Service, New York, New York 10017 (800) 253-9646; *Statistical Yearbook.*

LAOS (PEOPLE'S DEMOCRATIC REPUBLIC) - NATIONAL PRODUCT

Facts on File, 460 Park Avenue South, New York, New York 10016 (800) 443-8323; *The New Book of World Rankings.*

LAOS (PEOPLE'S DEMOCRATIC REPUBLIC) - NATURAL GAS - PRODUCTION - See LAOS (PEOPLE'S DEMOCRATIC REPUBLIC) - MINING AND MINERAL PRODUCTS

LAOS (PEOPLE'S DEMOCRATIC REPUBLIC) - NEWSPAPER CONSUMPTION AND PRODUCTION - See LAOS (PEOPLE'S DEMOCRATIC REPUBLIC) - FORESTRY AND FOREST PRODUCTS

LAOS (PEOPLE'S DEMOCRATIC REPUBLIC) - NEWSPRINT PRODUCTION AND CONSUMPTION - See LAOS (PEOPLE'S DEMOCRATIC REPUBLIC) - FORESTRY AND FOREST PRODUCTS

LAOS (PEOPLE'S DEMOCRATIC REPUBLIC) - OCCUPATIONS - See LAOS (PEOPLE'S DEMOCRATIC REPUBLIC) - LABOR FORCE

LAOS (PEOPLE'S DEMOCRATIC REPUBLIC) - PAPER - See LAOS (PEOPLE'S DEMOCRATIC REPUBLIC) - FORESTRY AND FOREST PRODUCTS

LAOS (PEOPLE'S DEMOCRATIC REPUBLIC) - PATENTS

Statistical Office of the United Nations, Publishing Service, New York, New York 10017 (800) 253-9646; *Statistical Yearbook.*

LAOS (PEOPLE'S DEMOCRATIC REPUBLIC) - PEANUT PRODUCTION - See LAOS (PEOPLE'S DEMOCRATIC REPUBLIC) - CROPS

LAOS (PEOPLE'S DEMOCRATIC REPUBLIC) - PESTICIDE USE

Food and Agricultural Organization of the United Nations (FAO), Via delle Terme di Caracalla, 00100 Rome, Italy (Telephone Number in U.S. (202) 653-2400); *The State of Food and Agriculture*.

LAOS (PEOPLE'S DEMOCRATIC REPUBLIC) - PETROLEUM INDUSTRY

Asian Development Bank, Post Office Box 789, 1099 Manila, Philippines; *Key Indicators of Developing Asian and Pacific Countries*.

Facts on File, 460 Park Avenue South, New York, New York 10016 (800) 443-8323; *The New Book of World Rankings*.

Food and Agricultural Organization of the United Nations (FAO), Via delle Terme di Caracalla, 00100 Rome, Italy (Telephone Number in U.S. (202) 653-2400); *The State of Food and Agriculture*.

G.K. Hall and Company, 70 Lincoln Street, Boston, Massachusetts 02111 (617) 423-3990; *The World in Figures*.

LAOS (PEOPLE'S DEMOCRATIC REPUBLIC) - PIGS - See LAOS (PEOPLE'S DEMOCRATIC REPUBLIC) - LIVESTOCK AND POULTRY

LAOS (PEOPLE'S DEMOCRATIC REPUBLIC) - POPULATION

Asian Development Bank, Post Office Box 789, 1099 Manila, Philippines; *Key Indicators of Developing Asian and Pacific Countries*.

The Economist Intelligence Unit, 111 West 57th Street, New York, New York 10019 (800) 938-4685; *The World Market Atlas*.

The Economist Intelligence Unit (Asia) Limited, 10th Floor, Luk Kwok Centre, 72 Gloucester Road, Wanchai, Hong Kong (Phone Number in U.S. (800) 938-4685); *Asian Market Atlas*.

Euromonitor Publications Limited, 87-88 Turnmill Street, London EC1M 5QU, England; *International Marketing Data and Statistics*.

Facts on File, 460 Park Avenue South, New York, New York 10016 (800) 443-8323; *The New Book of World Rankings*.

Food and Agricultural Organization of the United Nations (FAO), Via delle Terme di Caracalla, 00100 Rome, Italy (Telephone Number in U.S. (202) 653-2400); *Production Yearbook*.

G.K. Hall and Company, 70 Lincoln Street, Boston, Massachusetts 02111 (617) 423-3990; *The World in Figures*.

International Labour Office, I.L.O. Publications, CH-1211, Geneva 22, Switzerland; *Yearbook of Labour Statistics*.

Statistical Office of the United Nations, Publishing Service, New York, New York 10017 (800) 253-9646; *Demographic Yearbook*, *Statistical Yearbook*, and *Statistical Yearbook for Asia and the Pacific*.

Times Books, 201 East 50th Street, New York, New York 10022 (212) 751-2600; *The Economist Book of Vital World Statistics*.

United Nations Educational, Scientific and Cultural Organization (UNESCO), 7 Place de Fontenoy, F-75700 Paris, France (Telephone Number in U.S. (212) 963-5981); *Statistical Yearbook*.

U.S. Arms Control and Disarmament Agency, 320 Twenty-first Street, NW, Washington, D.C. 20451 (202) 647-8677; *World Military Expenditures and Arms Transfers*.

World Health Organization, Office of Publications, Avenue Appia, CH-1211 Geneva 27, Switzerland (Telephone Number in U.S. (518) 436-9686); *World Health Statistics Annual*.

LAOS (PEOPLE'S DEMOCRATIC REPUBLIC) - POST OFFICES

Facts on File, 460 Park Avenue South, New York, New York 10016 (800) 443-8323; *The New Book of World Rankings*.

LAOS (PEOPLE'S DEMOCRATIC REPUBLIC) - POTATO PRODUCTION - See LAOS (PEOPLE'S DEMOCRATIC REPUBLIC) - CROPS

LAOS (PEOPLE'S DEMOCRATIC REPUBLIC) - POULTRY MEAT - See LAOS (PEOPLE'S DEMOCRATIC REPUBLIC) - LIVESTOCK AND POULTRY

LAOS (PEOPLE'S DEMOCRATIC REPUBLIC) - PRICES

Asian Development Bank, Post Office Box 789, 1099 Manila, Philippines; *Key Indicators of Developing Asian and Pacific Countries*.

Facts on File, 460 Park Avenue South, New York, New York 10016 (800) 443-8323; *The New Book of World Rankings*.

Food and Agricultural Organization of the United Nations (FAO), Via delle Terme di Caracalla, 00100 Rome, Italy (Telephone Number in U.S. (202) 653-2400); *Production Yearbook*, and *The State of Food and Agriculture*.

G.K. Hall and Company, 70 Lincoln Street, Boston, Massachusetts 02111 (617) 423-3990; *The World in Figures*.

LAOS (PEOPLE'S DEMOCRATIC REPUBLIC) - PRINTING AND WRITING PAPER - See LAOS (PEOPLE'S DEMOCRATIC REPUBLIC) - FORESTRY AND FOREST PRODUCTS

LAOS (PEOPLE'S DEMOCRATIC REPUBLIC) - PRODUCTION

Facts on File, 460 Park Avenue South, New York, New York 10016 (800) 443-8323; *The New Book of World Rankings*.

G.K. Hall and Company, 70 Lincoln Street, Boston, Massachusetts 02111 (617) 423-3990; *The World in Figures*.

LAOS (PEOPLE'S DEMOCRATIC REPUBLIC) - PRODUCTIVITY

Euromonitor Publications Limited, 87-88 Turnmill Street, London EC1M 5QU, England; *International Marketing Data and Statistics*.

LAOS (PEOPLE'S DEMOCRATIC REPUBLIC) - PUBLIC FINANCE

Facts on File, 460 Park Avenue South, New York, New York 10016 (800) 443-8323; *The New Book of World Rankings*.

LAOS (PEOPLE'S DEMOCRATIC REPUBLIC) - RADIO BROADCASTING - See LAOS (PEOPLE'S DEMOCRATIC REPUBLIC) - BROADCASTING

LAOS (PEOPLE'S DEMOCRATIC REPUBLIC) - RAILWAY USE

G.K. Hall and Company, 70 Lincoln Street, Boston, Massachusetts 02111 (617) 423-3990; *The World in Figures*.

LAOS (PEOPLE'S DEMOCRATIC REPUBLIC) - RELIGION

Facts on File, 460 Park Avenue South, New York, New York 10016 (800) 443-8323; *The New Book of World Rankings.*

LAOS (PEOPLE'S DEMOCRATIC REPUBLIC) - RETAIL TRADE

G.K. Hall and Company, 70 Lincoln Street, Boston, Massachusetts 02111 (617) 423-3990; *The World in Figures.*

LAOS (PEOPLE'S DEMOCRATIC REPUBLIC) - RICE PRODUCTION - See LAOS (PEOPLE'S DEMOCRATIC REPUBLIC) - CROPS

LAOS (PEOPLE'S DEMOCRATIC REPUBLIC) - ROOT AND TUBER PRODUCTION - See LAOS (PEOPLE'S DEMOCRATIC REPUBLIC) - CROPS

LAOS (PEOPLE'S DEMOCRATIC REPUBLIC) - ROUNDWOOD PRODUCTION - See LAOS (PEOPLE'S DEMOCRATIC REPUBLIC) - FORESTRY AND FOREST PRODUCTS

LAOS (PEOPLE'S DEMOCRATIC REPUBLIC) - RUBBER PRODUCTION AND CONSUMPTION

Facts on File, 460 Park Avenue South, New York, New York 10016 (800) 443-8323; *The New Book of World Rankings.*

LAOS (PEOPLE'S DEMOCRATIC REPUBLIC) - SAWNWOOD PRODUCTION - See LAOS (PEOPLE'S DEMOCRATIC REPUBLIC) - FORESTRY AND FOREST PRODUCTS

LAOS (PEOPLE'S DEMOCRATIC REPUBLIC) - SCIENTISTS AND TECHNICIANS

Statistical Office of the United Nations, Publishing Service, New York, New York 10017 (800) 253-9646; *Statistical Yearbook.*

United Nations Educational, Scientific and Cultural Organization (UNESCO), 7 Place de Fontenoy, F-75700 Paris, France (Telephone Number in U.S. (212) 963-5981); *Statistical Yearbook.*

LAOS (PEOPLE'S DEMOCRATIC REPUBLIC) - SENIOR CITIZENS

Facts on File, 460 Park Avenue South, New York, New York 10016 (800) 443-8323; *The New Book of World Rankings.*

LAOS (PEOPLE'S DEMOCRATIC REPUBLIC) - SHEEP - See LAOS (PEOPLE'S DEMOCRATIC REPUBLIC) - LIVESTOCK AND POULTRY

LAOS (PEOPLE'S DEMOCRATIC REPUBLIC) - SILVER PRODUCTION AND CONSUMPTION - See LAOS (PEOPLE'S DEMOCRATIC REPUBLIC) - MINING AND MINERAL PRODUCTS

LAOS (PEOPLE'S DEMOCRATIC REPUBLIC) - SOCIAL DATA

Asian Development Bank, Post Office Box 789, 1099 Manila, Philippines; *Key Indicators of Developing Asian and Pacific Countries.*

Facts on File, 460 Park Avenue South, New York, New York 10016 (800) 443-8323; *The New Book of World Rankings.*

G.K. Hall and Company, 70 Lincoln Street, Boston, Massachusetts 02111 (617) 423-3990; *The World in Figures.*

LAOS (PEOPLE'S DEMOCRATIC REPUBLIC) - SOYBEAN PRODUCTION - See LAOS (PEOPLE'S DEMOCRATIC REPUBLIC) - CROPS

LAOS (PEOPLE'S DEMOCRATIC REPUBLIC) - STATE BUDGET

Euromonitor Publications Limited, 87-88 Turnmill Street, London EC1M 5QU, England; *International Marketing Data and Statistics.*

LAOS (PEOPLE'S DEMOCRATIC REPUBLIC) - STEEL - See LAOS (PEOPLE'S DEMOCRATIC REPUBLIC) - MINING AND MINERAL PRODUCTS

LAOS (PEOPLE'S DEMOCRATIC REPUBLIC) - STOCKS - COMMODITY - MARKET PRICE - INDEX

Food and Agricultural Organization of the United Nations (FAO), Via delle Terme di Caracalla, 00100 Rome, Italy (Telephone Number in U.S. (202) 653-2400); *The State of Food and Agriculture.*

LAOS (PEOPLE'S DEMOCRATIC REPUBLIC) - SUGAR PRODUCTION - See LAOS (PEOPLE'S DEMOCRATIC REPUBLIC) - CROPS

LAOS (PEOPLE'S DEMOCRATIC REPUBLIC) - TAXATION

G.K. Hall and Company, 70 Lincoln Street, Boston, Massachusetts 02111 (617) 423-3990; *The World in Figures.*

LAOS (PEOPLE'S DEMOCRATIC REPUBLIC) - TELEGRAPH SERVICE

American Telephone and Telegraph Company, 26 Parsippany Road, Whippany, New Jersey 07981 (800) 338-4038; *The World's Telephones.*

Statistical Office of the United Nations, Publishing Service, New York, New York 10017 (800) 253-9646; *Statistical Yearbook.*

LAOS (PEOPLE'S DEMOCRATIC REPUBLIC) - TELEPHONES IN USE

American Telephone and Telegraph Company, 26 Parsippany Road, Whippany, New Jersey 07981 (800) 338-4038; *The World's Telephones.*

The Economist Intelligence Unit (Asia) Limited, 10th Floor, Luk Kwok Centre, 72 Gloucester Road, Wanchai, Hong Kong (Phone Number in U.S. (800) 938-4685); *Asian Market Atlas.*

G.K. Hall and Company, 70 Lincoln Street, Boston, Massachusetts 02111 (617) 423-3990; *The World in Figures.*

Statistical Office of the United Nations, Publishing Service, New York, New York 10017 (800) 253-9646; *Statistical Yearbook.*

LAOS (PEOPLE'S DEMOCRATIC REPUBLIC) - TELEVISION

The Economist Intelligence Unit (Asia) Limited, 10th Floor, Luk Kwok Centre, 72 Gloucester Road, Wanchai, Hong Kong (Phone Number in U.S. (800) 938-4685); *Asian Market Atlas.*

LAOS (PEOPLE'S DEMOCRATIC REPUBLIC) - TELEVISION BROADCASTING - See LAOS (PEOPLE'S DEMOCRATIC REPUBLIC) - BROADCASTING

LAOS (PEOPLE'S DEMOCRATIC REPUBLIC) - TEXTILE INDUSTRY

G.K. Hall and Company, 70 Lincoln Street, Boston, Massachusetts 02111 (617) 423-3990; *The World in Figures.*

LAOS (PEOPLE'S DEMOCRATIC REPUBLIC) - TIN PRODUCTION - See LAOS (PEOPLE'S DEMOCRATIC REPUBLIC) - MINING AND MINERAL PRODUCTS

LAOS (PEOPLE'S DEMOCRATIC REPUBLIC) - TOBACCO PRODUCTION

Facts on File, 460 Park Avenue South, New York, New York 10016 (800) 443-8323; *The New Book of World Rankings*.

Statistical Office of the United Nations, Publishing Service, New York, New York 10017 (800) 253-9646; *Statistical Yearbook*.

LAOS (PEOPLE'S DEMOCRATIC REPUBLIC) - TOURISM

Facts on File, 460 Park Avenue South, New York, New York 10016 (800) 443-8323; *The New Book of World Rankings*.

G.K. Hall and Company, 70 Lincoln Street, Boston, Massachusetts 02111 (617) 423-3990; *The World in Figures*.

Times Books, 201 East 50th Street, New York, New York 10022 (212) 751-2600; *The Economist Book of Vital World Statistics*.

LAOS (PEOPLE'S DEMOCRATIC REPUBLIC) - TRACTORS IN USE

Statistical Office of the United Nations, Publishing Service, New York, New York 10017 (800) 253-9646; *Statistical Yearbook*.

LAOS (PEOPLE'S DEMOCRATIC REPUBLIC) - TRADE - See LAOS (PEOPLE'S DEMOCRATIC REPUBLIC) - FOREIGN TRADE

LAOS (PEOPLE'S DEMOCRATIC REPUBLIC) - TRADEMARKS AND SERVICE MARKS

Statistical Office of the United Nations, Publishing Service, New York, New York 10017 (800) 253-9646; *Statistical Yearbook*.

LAOS (PEOPLE'S DEMOCRATIC REPUBLIC) - TRANSPORTATION AND COMMUNICATIONS

The Economist Intelligence Unit (Asia) Limited, 10th Floor, Luk Kwok Centre, 72 Gloucester Road, Wanchai, Hong Kong (Phone Number in U.S. (800) 938-4685); *Asian Market Atlas*.

Facts on File, 460 Park Avenue South, New York, New York 10016 (800) 443-8323; *The New Book of World Rankings*.

G.K. Hall and Company, 70 Lincoln Street, Boston, Massachusetts 02111 (617) 423-3990; *The World in Figures*.

Statistical Office of the United Nations, Publishing Service, New York, New York 10017 (800) 253-9646; *Statistical Yearbook for Asia and the Pacific*.

LAOS (PEOPLE'S DEMOCRATIC REPUBLIC) - UNEMPLOYMENT

Euromonitor Publications Limited, 87-88 Turnmill Street, London EC1M 5QU, England; *International Marketing Data and Statistics*.

International Labour Office, I.L.O. Publications, CH-1211, Geneva 22, Switzerland; *Yearbook of Labour Statistics*.

LAOS (PEOPLE'S DEMOCRATIC REPUBLIC) - VITAL STATISTICS

Euromonitor Publications Limited, 87-88 Turnmill Street, London EC1M 5QU, England; *International Marketing Data and Statistics*.

G.K. Hall and Company, 70 Lincoln Street, Boston, Massachusetts 02111 (617) 423-3990; *The World in Figures*.

Statistical Office of the United Nations, Publishing Service, New York, New York 10017 (800) 253-9646; *Statistical Yearbook*.

World Health Organization, Office of Publications, Avenue Appia, CH-1211 Geneva 27, Switzerland (Telephone Number in U.S. (518) 436-9686); *World Health Statistics Annual*.

LAOS (PEOPLE'S DEMOCRATIC REPUBLIC) - WAGES

G.K. Hall and Company, 70 Lincoln Street, Boston, Massachusetts 02111 (617) 423-3990; *The World in Figures*.

International Labour Office, I.L.O. Publications, CH-1211, Geneva 22, Switzerland; *Yearbook of Labour Statistics*.

Statistical Office of the United Nations, Publishing Service, New York, New York 10017 (800) 253-9646; *Statistical Yearbook for Asia and the Pacific*.

LAOS (PEOPLE'S DEMOCRATIC REPUBLIC) - WEATHER

Facts on File, 460 Park Avenue South, New York, New York 10016 (800) 443-8323; *The New Book of World Rankings*.

G.K. Hall and Company, 70 Lincoln Street, Boston, Massachusetts 02111 (617) 423-3990; *The World in Figures*.

LAOS (PEOPLE'S DEMOCRATIC REPUBLIC) - WHEAT PRODUCTION - See LAOS (PEOPLE'S DEMOCRATIC REPUBLIC) - CROPS

LAOS (PEOPLE'S DEMOCRATIC REPUBLIC) - WHOLESALE PRICES - INDEX NUMBERS

Asian Development Bank, Post Office Box 789, 1099 Manila, Philippines; *Key Indicators of Developing Asian and Pacific Countries*.

LAOS (PEOPLE'S DEMOCRATIC REPUBLIC) - WINE PRODUCTION

Facts on File, 460 Park Avenue South, New York, New York 10016 (800) 443-8323; *The New Book of World Rankings*.

LAOS (PEOPLE'S DEMOCRATIC REPUBLIC) - WOOL PRODUCTION

Facts on File, 460 Park Avenue South, New York, New York 10016 (800) 443-8323; *The New Book of World Rankings*.

LARCENY - THEFT

U.S. Department of Justice, Bureau of Justice Statistics, 633 Indiana Avenue, NW, Washington, D.C. 20531 (202) 307-0781; *Criminal Victimization in the United States*.

U.S. Department of Justice, Federal Bureau of Investigation, Ninth Street and Pennsylvania Avenue, NW, Washington, D.C. 20535 (202) 324-3000; *Crime in the United States*, and *Population-at-Risk Rates and Selected Crime Indicators*.

LARD

U.S. Department of Agriculture, Economic Research Service, Fourteenth Street and Independence Avenue, SW, Washington, D.C. 20005-4789 (202) 219-1504; *Food Consumption, Prices and Expenditures*, and unpublished data.

LATEX - See RUBBER AND MISCELLANEOUS PLASTICS

LATVIA - See also UNION OF SOVIET SOCIALIST REPUBLICS

Latvia--Primary Statistics Sources

Latvijas Republikas Valsts Statistikas Komiteja, Riga, Latvia; *Latvijas Statistikas Gadagramata*.

LATVIA - AGRICULTURE

Business International Moscow, 23 Profsoyuznaya Ulitsa, 117859, Moscow (Telephone Number in U.S. (800) 938-4685); *The CIS Market Atlas*.

Encyclopedia Britannica, Incorporated, 310 South Michigan Avenue, Chicago, Illinois 60604 (312) 437-7000; *Britannica World Data*.

The World Bank, 1818 H Street, NW, Washington, D.C. 20433 (202) 477-1234; *Statistical Handbook: States of the Former USSR*.

LATVIA - AIRLINE SERVICE

Business International Moscow, 23 Profsoyuznaya Ulitsa, 117859, Moscow (Telephone Number in U.S. (800) 938-4685); *The CIS Market Atlas*.

Encyclopedia Britannica, Incorporated, 310 South Michigan Avenue, Chicago, Illinois 60604 (312) 437-7000; *Britannica World Data*.

LATVIA - AREA AND DENSITY OF POPULATION

Business International Moscow, 23 Profsoyuznaya Ulitsa, 117859, Moscow (Telephone Number in U.S. (800) 938-4685); *Tho CIS Market Atlas*.

LATVIA - BANKING

Business International Moscow, 23 Profsoyuznaya Ulitsa, 117859, Moscow (Telephone Number in U.S. (800) 938-4685); *The CIS Market Atlas*.

LATVIA - BIRTH RATES

Business International Moscow, 23 Profsoyuznaya Ulitsa, 117859, Moscow (Telephone Number in U.S. (800) 938-4685); *The CIS Market Atlas*.

Encyclopedia Britannica, Incorporated, 310 South Michigan Avenue, Chicago, Illinois 60604 (312) 437-7000; *Britannica World Data*.

LATVIA - BUDGET

Business International Moscow, 23 Profsoyuznaya Ulitsa, 117859, Moscow (Telephone Number in U.S. (800) 938-4685); *The CIS Market Atlas*.

LATVIA - CAPITAL INVESTMENT

The World Bank, 1818 H Street, NW, Washington, D.C. 20433 (202) 477-1234; *Statistical Handbook: States of the Former USSR*.

LATVIA - CATTLE - See LATVIA - LIVESTOCK AND POULTRY

LATVIA - CHEMICALS

Business International Moscow, 23 Profsoyuznaya Ulitsa, 117859, Moscow (Telephone Number in U.S. (800) 938-4685); *The CIS Market Atlas*.

LATVIA - COAL PRODUCTION AND CONSUMPTION - See LATVIA - MINING AND MINERAL PRODUCTS

LATVIA - COMMUNICATIONS

Business International Moscow, 23 Profsoyuznaya Ulitsa, 117859, Moscow (Telephone Number in U.S. (800) 938-4685); *The CIS Market Atlas*.

LATVIA - CONSTRUCTION INDUSTRY

Business International Moscow, 23 Profsoyuznaya Ulitsa, 117859, Moscow (Telephone Number in U.S. (800) 938-4685); *The CIS Market Atlas*.

Encyclopedia Britannica, Incorporated, 310 South Michigan Avenue, Chicago, Illinois 60604 (312) 437-7000; *Britannica World Data*.

LATVIA - CONSUMER PRODUCTS

Business International Moscow, 23 Profsoyuznaya Ulitsa, 117859, Moscow (Telephone Number in U.S. (800) 938-4685); *The CIS Market Atlas*.

LATVIA - CONSUMPTION

Business International Moscow, 23 Profsoyuznaya Ulitsa, 117859, Moscow (Telephone Number in U.S. (800) 938-4685); *The CIS Market Atlas*.

The World Bank, 1818 H Street, NW, Washington, D.C. 20433 (202) 477-1234; *Statistical Handbook: States of the Former USSR*.

LATVIA - COTTON PRODUCTION AND CONSUMPTION - See LATVIA - TEXTILE INDUSTRY

LATVIA - CROPS

The World Bank, 1818 H Street, NW, Washington, D.C. 20433 (202) 477-1234; *Statistical Handbook: States of the Former USSR*.

LATVIA - DEATH RATES

Business International Moscow, 23 Profsoyuznaya Ulitsa, 117859, Moscow (Telephone Number in U.S. (800) 938-4685); *The CIS Market Atlas*.

LATVIA - DEMOGRAPHY

Business International Moscow, 23 Profsoyuznaya Ulitsa, 117859, Moscow (Telephone Number in U.S. (800) 938-4685); *The CIS Market Atlas*.

The Economist Intelligence Unit, 111 West 57th Street, New York, New York 10019 (800) 938-4685; *The World Market Atlas*.

Encyclopedia Britannica, Incorporated, 310 South Michigan Avenue, Chicago, Illinois 60604 (312) 437-7000; *Britannica World Data*.

The World Bank, 1818 H Street, NW, Washington, D.C. 20433 (202) 477-1234; *Statistical Handbook: States of the Former USSR*.

LATVIA - DISEASES

Business International Moscow, 23 Profsoyuznaya Ulitsa, 117859, Moscow (Telephone Number in U.S. (800) 938-4685); *The CIS Market Atlas*.

LATVIA - DIVORCE RATES

Encyclopedia Britannica, Incorporated, 310 South Michigan Avenue, Chicago, Illinois 60604 (312) 437-7000; *Britannica World Data.*

LATVIA - DOMESTIC INVESTMENT

Business International Moscow, 23 Profsoyuznaya Ulitsa, 117859, Moscow (Telephone Number in U.S. (800) 938-4685); *The CIS Market Atlas.*

LATVIA - ECONOMY

Business International Moscow, 23 Profsoyuznaya Ulitsa, 117859, Moscow (Telephone Number in U.S. (800) 938-4685); *The CIS Market Atlas.*

Encyclopedia Britannica, Incorporated, 310 South Michigan Avenue, Chicago, Illinois 60604 (312) 437-7000; *Britannica World Data.*

LATVIA - EDUCATION

Business International Moscow, 23 Profsoyuznaya Ulitsa, 117859, Moscow (Telephone Number in U.S. (800) 938-4685); *The CIS Market Atlas.*

The Economist Intelligence Unit, 111 West 57th Street, New York, New York 10019 (800) 938-4685; *The World Market Atlas.*

Encyclopedia Britannica, Incorporated, 310 South Michigan Avenue, Chicago, Illinois 60604 (312) 437-7000; *Britannica World Data.*

LATVIA - ELECTRICITY

Business International Moscow, 23 Profsoyuznaya Ulitsa, 117859, Moscow (Telephone Number in U.S. (800) 938-4685); *The CIS Market Atlas.*

The World Bank, 1818 H Street, NW, Washington, D.C. 20433 (202) 477-1234; *Statistical Handbook: States of the Former USSR.*

LATVIA - EMPLOYMENT

The World Bank, 1818 H Street, NW, Washington, D.C. 20433 (202) 477-1234; *Statistical Handbook: States of the Former USSR.*

LATVIA - ENERGY

Business International Moscow, 23 Profsoyuznaya Ulitsa, 117859, Moscow (Telephone Number in U.S. (800) 938-4685); *The CIS Market Atlas.*

Encyclopedia Britannica, Incorporated, 310 South Michigan Avenue, Chicago, Illinois 60604 (312) 437-7000; *Britannica World Data.*

The World Bank, 1818 H Street, NW, Washington, D.C. 20433 (202) 477-1234; *Statistical Handbook: States of the Former USSR.*

LATVIA - ENVIRONMENT

Business International Moscow, 23 Profsoyuznaya Ulitsa, 117859, Moscow (Telephone Number in U.S. (800) 938-4685); *The CIS Market Atlas.*

LATVIA - EXPORTS

Business International Moscow, 23 Profsoyuznaya Ulitsa, 117859, Moscow (Telephone Number in U.S. (800) 938-4685); *The CIS Market Atlas.*

The Economist Intelligence Unit, 111 West 57th Street, New York, New York 10019 (800) 938-4685; *The World Market Atlas.*

LATVIA - EXTERNAL TRADE

The World Bank, 1818 H Street, NW, Washington, D.C. 20433 (202) 477-1234; *Statistical Handbook: States of the Former USSR.*

LATVIA - FABRIC PRODUCTION AND CONSUMPTION - See LATVIA - TEXTILE INDUSTRY

LATVIA - FERTILITY RATES

Encyclopedia Britannica, Incorporated, 310 South Michigan Avenue, Chicago, Illinois 60604 (312) 437-7000; *Britannica World Data.*

The World Bank, 1818 H Street, NW, Washington, D.C. 20433 (202) 477-1234; *Statistical Handbook: States of the Former USSR.*

LATVIA - FISHERIES

Encyclopedia Britannica, Incorporated, 310 South Michigan Avenue, Chicago, Illinois 60604 (312) 437-7000; *Britannica World Data.*

LATVIA - FOOTWEAR PRODUCTION AND CONSUMPTION - See LATVIA - TEXTILE INDUSTRY

LATVIA - FOREIGN INVESTMENT

Business International Moscow, 23 Profsoyuznaya Ulitsa, 117859, Moscow (Telephone Number in U.S. (800) 938-4685); *The CIS Market Atlas.*

LATVIA - FOREIGN TRADE

Business International Moscow, 23 Profsoyuznaya Ulitsa, 117859, Moscow (Telephone Number in U.S. (800) 938-4685); *The CIS Market Atlas.*

Encyclopedia Britannica, Incorporated, 310 South Michigan Avenue, Chicago, Illinois 60604 (312) 437-7000; *Britannica World Data.*

The World Bank, 1818 H Street, NW, Washington, D.C. 20433 (202) 477-1234; *Statistical Handbook: States of the Former USSR.*

LATVIA - FORESTRY AND FOREST PRODUCTS

Business International Moscow, 23 Profsoyuznaya Ulitsa, 117859, Moscow (Telephone Number in U.S. (800) 938-4685); *The CIS Market Atlas.*

Encyclopedia Britannica, Incorporated, 310 South Michigan Avenue, Chicago, Illinois 60604 (312) 437-7000; *Britannica World Data.*

LATVIA - GOATS - See LATVIA - LIVESTOCK AND POULTRY

LATVIA - GOVERNMENT EXPENDITURE

The World Bank, 1818 H Street, NW, Washington, D.C. 20433 (202) 477-1234; *Statistical Handbook: States of the Former USSR.*

LATVIA - GOVERNMENT REVENUE

The World Bank, 1818 H Street, NW, Washington, D.C. 20433 (202) 477-1234; *Statistical Handbook: States of the Former USSR.*

LATVIA - GROSS DOMESTIC PRODUCT

The Economist Intelligence Unit, 111 West 57th Street, New York, New York 10019 (800) 938-4685; *The World Market Atlas.*

The World Bank, 1818 H Street, NW, Washington, D.C. 20433 (202) 477-1234; *Statistical Handbook: States of the Former USSR.*

LATVIA - HEALTH

Business International Moscow, 23 Profsoyuznaya Ulitsa, 117859, Moscow (Telephone Number in U.S. (800) 938-4685); *The CIS Market Atlas.*

Encyclopedia Britannica, Incorporated, 310 South Michigan Avenue, Chicago, Illinois 60604 (312) 437-7000; *Britannica World Data.*

LATVIA - HIGHWAYS

Business International Moscow, 23 Profsoyuznaya Ulitsa, 117859, Moscow (Telephone Number in U.S. (800) 938-4685); *The CIS Market Atlas.*

Encyclopedia Britannica, Incorporated, 310 South Michigan Avenue, Chicago, Illinois 60604 (312) 437-7000; *Britannica World Data.*

LATVIA - HOUSING AND HOUSING UNITS

Business International Moscow, 23 Profsoyuznaya Ulitsa, 117859, Moscow (Telephone Number in U.S. (800) 938-4685); *The CIS Market Atlas.*

LATVIA - ILLITERATE POPULATION

The Economist Intelligence Unit, 111 West 57th Street, New York, New York 10019 (800) 938-4685; *The World Market Atlas.*

LATVIA - IMPORTS

Business International Moscow, 23 Profsoyuznaya Ulitsa, 117859, Moscow (Telephone Number in U.S. (800) 938-4685); *The CIS Market Atlas.*

The Economist Intelligence Unit, 111 West 57th Street, New York, New York 10019 (800) 938-4685; *The World Market Atlas.*

Encyclopedia Britannica, Incorporated, 310 South Michigan Avenue, Chicago, Illinois 60604 (312) 437-7000; *Britannica World Data.*

The World Bank, 1818 H Street, NW, Washington, D.C. 20433 (202) 477-1234; *Statistical Handbook: States of the Former USSR.*

LATVIA - INDUSTRY

Business International Moscow, 23 Profsoyuznaya Ulitsa, 117859, Moscow (Telephone Number in U.S. (800) 938-4685); *The CIS Market Atlas.*

The World Bank, 1818 H Street, NW, Washington, D.C. 20433 (202) 477-1234; *Statistical Handbook: States of the Former USSR.*

LATVIA - INFANT MORTALITY RATES

Business International Moscow, 23 Profsoyuznaya Ulitsa, 117859, Moscow (Telephone Number in U.S. (800) 938-4685); *The CIS Market Atlas.*

LATVIA - LABOR FORCE

Business International Moscow, 23 Profsoyuznaya Ulitsa, 117859, Moscow (Telephone Number in U.S. (800) 938-4685); *The CIS Market Atlas.*

The World Bank, 1818 H Street, NW, Washington, D.C. 20433 (202) 477-1234; *Statistical Handbook: States of the Former USSR.*

LATVIA - LAND USE

Encyclopedia Britannica, Incorporated, 310 South Michigan Avenue, Chicago, Illinois 60604 (312) 437-7000; *Britannica World Data.*

LATVIA - LIFE EXPECTANCY

Business International Moscow, 23 Profsoyuznaya Ulitsa, 117859, Moscow (Telephone Number in U.S. (800) 938-4685); *The CIS Market Atlas.*

LATVIA - LIVESTOCK AND POULTRY

Business International Moscow, 23 Profsoyuznaya Ulitsa, 117859, Moscow (Telephone Number in U.S. (800) 938-4685); *The CIS Market Atlas.*

Encyclopedia Britannica, Incorporated, 310 South Michigan Avenue, Chicago, Illinois 60604 (312) 437-7000; *Britannica World Data.*

LATVIA - MANUFACTURING

Encyclopedia Britannica, Incorporated, 310 South Michigan Avenue, Chicago, Illinois 60604 (312) 437-7000; *Britannica World Data.*

LATVIA - MARRIAGE RATES

Encyclopedia Britannica, Incorporated, 310 South Michigan Avenue, Chicago, Illinois 60604 (312) 437-7000; *Britannica World Data.*

LATVIA - MEAT PRODUCTION - See LATVIA - LIVESTOCK AND POULTRY

LATVIA - MILITARY

The International Institute for Strategic Studies, 23 Tavistock Street, London WC2E 7NQ, England; *The Military Balance.*

LATVIA - MINING AND MINERAL PRODUCTS

Business International Moscow, 23 Profsoyuznaya Ulitsa, 117859, Moscow (Telephone Number in U.S. (800) 938-4685); *The CIS Market Atlas.*

Encyclopedia Britannica, Incorporated, 310 South Michigan Avenue, Chicago, Illinois 60604 (312) 437-7000; *Britannica World Data.*

LATVIA - MOTOR VEHICLES

Business International Moscow, 23 Profsoyuznaya Ulitsa, 117859, Moscow (Telephone Number in U.S. (800) 938-4685); *The CIS Market Atlas.*

LATVIA - NATIONAL ACCOUNTS

The World Bank, 1818 H Street, NW, Washington, D.C. 20433 (202) 477-1234; *Statistical Handbook: States of the Former USSR.*

LATVIA - NATIONAL INCOME

Business International Moscow, 23 Profsoyuznaya Ulitsa, 117859, Moscow (Telephone Number in U.S. (800) 938-4685); *The CIS Market Atlas.*

LATVIA - PIGS - See LATVIA - LIVESTOCK AND POULTRY

LATVIA - POPULATION

Business International Moscow, 23 Profsoyuznaya Ulitsa, 117859, Moscow (Telephone Number in U.S. (800) 938-4685); *The CIS Market Atlas.*

The Economist Intelligence Unit, 111 West 57th Street, New York, New York 10019 (800) 938-4685; *The World Market Atlas.*

Encyclopedia Britannica, Incorporated, 310 South Michigan Avenue, Chicago, Illinois 60604 (312) 437-7000; *Britannica World Data.*

The World Bank, 1818 H Street, NW, Washington, D.C. 20433 (202) 477-1234; *Statistical Handbook: States of the Former USSR.*

LATVIA - POULTRY - See LATVIA - LIVESTOCK AND POULTRY

LATVIA - PRICES

The World Bank, 1818 H Street, NW, Washington, D.C. 20433 (202) 477-1234; *Statistical Handbook: States of the Former USSR.*

LATVIA - PRODUCTION

The World Bank, 1818 H Street, NW, Washington, D.C. 20433 (202) 477-1234; *Statistical Handbook: States of the Former USSR.*

LATVIA - PUBLIC FINANCE

The World Bank, 1818 H Street, NW, Washington, D.C. 20433 (202) 477-1234; *Statistical Handbook: States of the Former USSR.*

LATVIA - RADIO RECEIVERS

Encyclopedia Britannica, Incorporated, 310 South Michigan Avenue, Chicago, Illinois 60604 (312) 437-7000; *Britannica World Data.*

LATVIA - RAILWAYS

Business International Moscow, 23 Profsoyuznaya Ulitsa, 117859, Moscow (Telephone Number in U.S. (800) 938-4685); *The CIS Market Atlas.*

Encyclopedia Britannica, Incorporated, 310 South Michigan Avenue, Chicago, Illinois 60604 (312) 437-7000; *Britannica World Data.*

LATVIA - RETAIL TRADE

Business International Moscow, 23 Profsoyuznaya Ulitsa, 117859, Moscow (Telephone Number in U.S. (800) 938-4685); *The CIS Market Atlas.*

LATVIA - ROADS - See LATVIA - HIGHWAYS

LATVIA - ROUNDWOOD PRODUCTION AND CONSUMPTION - See LATVIA - FORESTRY AND FOREST PRODUCTS

LATVIA - SHEEP - See LATVIA - LIVESTOCK AND POULTRY

LATVIA - STEEL PRODUCTION AND CONSUMPTION - See LATVIA - MINING AND MINERAL PRODUCTS

LATVIA - TELEPHONES IN USE

Encyclopedia Britannica, Incorporated, 310 South Michigan Avenue, Chicago, Illinois 60604 (312) 437-7000; *Britannica World Data.*

LATVIA - TELEVISION RECEIVERS

Encyclopedia Britannica, Incorporated, 310 South Michigan Avenue, Chicago, Illinois 60604 (312) 437-7000; *Britannica World Data.*

LATVIA - TEXTILE INDUSTRY

Business International Moscow, 23 Profsoyuznaya Ulitsa, 117859, Moscow (Telephone Number in U.S. (800) 938-4685); *The CIS Market Atlas.*

LATVIA - TOURISM

Business International Moscow, 23 Profsoyuznaya Ulitsa, 117859, Moscow (Telephone Number in U.S. (800) 938-4685); *The CIS Market Atlas.*

LATVIA - TRANSPORTATION AND COMMUNICATIONS

Business International Moscow, 23 Profsoyuznaya Ulitsa, 117859, Moscow (Telephone Number in U.S. (800) 938-4685); *The CIS Market Atlas.*

Encyclopedia Britannica, Incorporated, 310 South Michigan Avenue, Chicago, Illinois 60604 (312) 437-7000; *Britannica World Data.*

LATVIA - VITAL STATISTICS

Encyclopedia Britannica, Incorporated, 310 South Michigan Avenue, Chicago, Illinois 60604 (312) 437-7000; *Britannica World Data.*

LATVIA - WAGES

Business International Moscow, 23 Profsoyuznaya Ulitsa, 117859, Moscow (Telephone Number in U.S. (800) 938-4685); *The CIS Market Atlas.*

The World Bank, 1818 H Street, NW, Washington, D.C. 20433 (202) 477-1234; *Statistical Handbook: States of the Former USSR.*

LATVIA - WOOL PRODUCTION AND CONSUMPTION - See LATVIA - TEXTILE INDUSTRY

LAUNDRY - CLEANING AND GARMENT SERVICES - EARNINGS

U.S. Department of Commerce, Bureau of the Census, Suitland, Maryland 20233 (301) 763-4040; *County Business Patterns*, and *Census of Service Industries.*

U.S. Department of Labor, Bureau of Labor Statistics, Two Massachusetts Avenue, NE, Washington, D.C. 20212 (202) 606-7828; *Employment and Earnings*, and Bulletins 2370 and 2429.

LAUNDRY - CLEANING AND GARMENT SERVICES - EMPLOYEES

U.S. Department of Commerce, Bureau of the Census, Suitland, Maryland 20233 (301) 763-4040; *County Business Patterns*, and *Census of Service Industries.*

U.S. Department of Labor, Bureau of Labor Statistics, Two Massachusetts Avenue, NE, Washington, D.C. 20212 (202) 606-7828; *Employment and Earnings*, and Bulletins 2370 and 2429.

LAUNDRY - CLEANING AND GARMENT SERVICES - ESTABLISHMENTS

International Franchise Association, 1350 New York Avenue, Suite 900, Washington, D.C. 20005; *Franchising in the Economy*.

U.S. Department of Commerce, Bureau of the Census, Suitland, Maryland 20233 (301) 763-4040; *Census of Service Industries*, and *County Business Patterns*.

LAUNDRY - CLEANING AND GARMENT SERVICES - PRODUCTIVITY

U.S. Department of Labor, Bureau of Labor Statistics, Two Massachusetts Avenue, NE, Washington, D.C. 20212 (202) 606-7828; *Productivity Measures for Selected Industries and Government Services*, and unpublished data.

LAUNDRY - CLEANING AND GARMENT SERVICES - RECEIPTS

International Franchise Association, 1350 New York Avenue, Suite 900, Washington, D.C. 20005 (202) 628-8000; *Franchising in the Economy*.

U.S. Department of Commerce, Bureau of the Census, Suitland, Maryland 20233 (301) 763-4040; *Current Business Reports*, and *Service Annual Survey, Census of Service Industries*.

LAW - DEGREES CONFERRED

U.S. Department of Education, 400 Maryland Avenue, SW, Washington, D.C. 20202 (202) 708-5366; *Digest of Education Statistics*.

LAW ENFORCEMENT - See also COURTS, CRIME and CORRECTIONAL INSTITUTIONS

LAW ENFORCEMENT - ARRESTS

U.S. Department of Justice, Federal Bureau of Investigation, Ninth Street and Pennsylvania Avenue, NW, Washington, D.C. 20535 (202) 324-3000; *Crime in the United States*.

U.S. Department of Justice, National Institute of Justice, 633 Indiana Avenue, NW, Washington, D.C. 20531 (202) 307-0781; *Drug Use Forecasting*.

LAW ENFORCEMENT - DRUG ENFORCEMENT

U.S. Department of Justice, Drug Enforcement Administration, 600-700 Army Navy Drive, Arlington, Virginia 22202 (202) 307-1000; *Annual Report*.

U.S. Department of Justice, Federal Bureau of Investigation, Ninth Street and Pennsylvania Avenue, NW, Washington, D.C. 20535 (202) 324-3000; *Crime in the United States*.

LAW ENFORCEMENT - EMPLOYEES

U.S. Department of Commerce, Bureau of the Census, Suitland, Maryland 20233 (301) 763-4040; *Public Employment, Government Finances*, and *City Employment*.

U.S. Department of Justice, Bureau of Justice Statistics, 633 Indiana Avenue, NW, Washington, D.C. 20531 (202) 307-0781; *Justice Expenditure and Employment in the U.S.*

U.S. Department of Labor, Bureau of Labor Statistics, Two Massachusetts Avenue, NE, Washington, D.C. 20212 (202) 606-7828; *Employment and Earnings*.

LAW ENFORCEMENT - EXPENDITURES

U.S. Department of Commerce, Bureau of the Census, Suitland, Maryland 20233 (301) 763-4040; *Historical Statistics on Governmental Finances and Employment*, and *Public Employment, State Government Finances, Government Finances*.

LAW ENFORCEMENT - POLICE OFFICERS

U.S. Department of Commerce, Bureau of the Census, Suitland, Maryland 20233 (301) 763-4040; *Public Employment, City Employment*, and *Government Finances*.

U.S. Department of Justice, Bureau of Justice Statistics, 633 Indiana Avenue, NW, Washington, D.C. 20531 (202) 307-0781; *Justice Expenditure and Employment in the U.S.* and *Profile of State and Local law Enforcement Agencies*.

U.S. Department of Justice, Federal Bureau of Investigation, Ninth Street and Pennsylvania Avenue, NW, Washington, D.C. 20535 (202) 307-3000; *Law Enforcement Officers Killed and Assaulted*.

U.S. Department of Labor, Bureau of Labor Statistics, Two Massachusetts Avenue, NE, Washington, D.C. 20212 (202) 606-7828; *Employment and Earnings*.

LAW ENFORCEMENT - WIRETAPS

Administrative Office of the United States Courts, United States Supreme Court Building, 1 Columbus Circle, NE, Washington, D.C. 20544 (202) 273-1120; *Report on Applications for Orders Authorizing or Approving the Interception of Wire, Oral or Electronic Communications*.

LAWN CARE

The National Gardening Association, 180 Flynn Avenue, Burlington, Vermont 05401 (802) 863-1308; *National Gardening Survey*.

U.S. Department of Commerce, Bureau of the Census, Suitland, Maryland 20233 (301) 763-4040; *Census of Retail Trade*.

LAWYERS - See also LEGAL SERVICES

American Bar Foundation, 750 North Lake Shore Drive, Chicago, Illinois 60611 (312) 988-5000; *Lawyer Statistical Report: The U.S. Legal Profession in the 1990s*.

LAWYERS - EMPLOYMENT

U.S. Department of Labor, Bureau of Labor Statistics, Two Massachusetts Avenue, NE, Washington, D.C. 20212 (202) 606-7828; *Employment and Earnings*.

LAWYERS - EMPLOYMENT - PROJECTIONS

U.S. Department of Labor, Bureau of Labor Statistics, Two Massachusetts Avenue, NE, Washington, D.C. 20212 (202) 606-7828; *Monthly Labor Review*.

LEAD

U.S. Department of the Interior, Bureau of Mines, 810 Seventh Street, NW, Washington, D.C. 20241 (202) 501-9649; *Mineral Commodity Summaries*.

LEAD - AIR QUALITY

Environmental Protection Agency, 401 M Street, SW, Washington, D.C. 20460 (202) 382-2090; *National Air Pollutant Emission Trends*, and *National Air Quality and Emissions Trends Report*.

LEAD - CONSUMPTION

U.S. Department of the Interior, Bureau of Mines, 810 Seventh Street, NW, Washington, D.C. 20241 (202) 501-9649; *Mineral Commodity Summaries*.

LEAD - EMPLOYMENT

U.S. Department of the Interior, Bureau of Mines, 810 Seventh Street, NW, Washington, D.C. 20241 (202) 501-9649; *Mineral Commodity Summaries*.

LEAD - FOREIGN TRADE

U.S. Department of the Interior, Bureau of Mines, 810 Seventh Street, NW, Washington, D.C. 20241 (202) 501-9649; *Annual Reports*, and *Mineral Commodity Summaries*.

LEAD - PRICES

U.S. Department of the Interior, Bureau of Mines, 810 Seventh Street, NW, Washington, D.C. 20241 (202) 501-9649; *Mineral Facts and Problems*, and *Mineral Commodity Summaries*.

LEAD - PRODUCTION AND VALUE

U.S. Department of the Interior, Bureau of Mines, 810 Seventh Street, NW, Washington, D.C. 20241 (202) 501-9649; *Annual Reports*, and *Mineral Commodity Summaries*.

LEAD - WATER QUALITY

U.S. Department of the Interior, Geological Survey, National Center, 12201 Sunrise Valley Drive, Reston, Virginia 22092 (703) 648-4460; *Water-Data Report*, and unpublished data.

LEAD - WORLD PRODUCTION

U.S. Department of the Interior, Bureau of Mines, 810 Seventh Street, NW, Washington, D.C. 20241 (202) 501-9649; *Annual Reports*, and *Mineral Commodity Summaries*.

LEATHER AND LEATHER PRODUCTS - MANUFACTURING - See also HIDES AND LEATHER PRODUCTS and FOOTWEAR

LEATHER AND LEATHER PRODUCTS - MANUFACTURING - CAPITAL

U.S. Department of Commerce, Bureau of the Census, Suitland, Maryland 20233 (301) 763-4040; *Census of Manufactures*, and *Annual Survey of Manufactures*.

LEATHER AND LEATHER PRODUCTS - MANUFACTURING - EARNINGS

U.S. Department of Commerce, Bureau of the Census, Suitland, Maryland 20233 (301) 763-4040; *Census of Manufacturers*, and *Annual Survey of Manufactures*.

U.S. Department of Labor, Bureau of Labor Statistics, Two Massachusetts Avenue, NE, Washington, D.C. 20212 (202) 606-7828; *Employment and Earnings*, and Bulletins 2307 and 2429.

LEATHER AND LEATHER PRODUCTS - MANUFACTURING - EMPLOYEES

U.S. Department of Commerce, Bureau of the Census, Suitland, Maryland 20233 (301) 763-4040; *Census of Manufactures*, and *Annual Survey of Manufactures*.

U.S. Department of Labor, Bureau of Labor Statistics, Two Massachusetts Avenue, NE, Washington, D.C. 20212 (202) 606-7828; *Employment and Earnings, Monthly Labor Review*, and Bulletins 2307 and 2429.

LEATHER AND LEATHER PRODUCTS - MANUFACTURING - ESTABLISHMENTS

U.S. Department of Commerce, Bureau of the Census, Suitland, Maryland 20233 (301) 763-4040; *Census of Manufactures*, and *Annual Survey of Manufactures*.

LEATHER AND LEATHER PRODUCTS - MANUFACTURING - GROSS DOMESTIC PRODUCT

U.S. Department of Commerce, Bureau of Economic Analysis, Fourteenth Street between Constitution Avenue and E Street, NW, Washington, D.C. 20230 (202) 606-9900; *The National Income and Product Accounts of the United States*, and *Survey of Current Business*.

LEATHER AND LEATHER PRODUCTS - MANUFACTURING - OCCUPATIONAL SAFETY

U.S. Department of Labor, Bureau of Labor Statistics, Two Massachusetts Avenue, NE, Washington, D.C. 20212 (202) 606-7828; *Occupational Injuries and Illnesses in the United States by Industry*.

LEATHER AND LEATHER PRODUCTS - MANUFACTURING - PRODUCTIVITY

Board of Governors of the Federal Reserve System, Twentieth Street and Constitution Avenue, NW, Washington, D.C. 20551 (202) 452-3000; *Federal Reserve Bulletin*.

LEATHER AND LEATHER PRODUCTS - MANUFACTURING - SHIPMENTS

U.S. Department of Commerce, Bureau of the Census, Suitland, Maryland 20233 (301) 763-4040; *Annual Survey of Manufactures*, and *Census of Manufactures*.

LEATHER AND LEATHER PRODUCTS - MANUFACTURING - VALUE ADDED

U.S. Department of Commerce, Bureau of the Census, Suitland, Maryland 20233 (301) 763-4040; *Census of Manufactures*, and *Annual Survey of Manufactures*.

Lebanon - National Statistical Office

Direction Central de la Statistique, Bir Hasan, Beirut, Lebanon.

Lebanon - Primary Statistics Sources

Direction Centrale de la Statistique, Ministere du Plan, Bir Hassan, Beirut, Lebanon; *Bulletin statistique mensuel* (Monthly Statistical Bulletin).

LEBANON - AGRICULTURE

Economic Commission for Western Asia, Post Office Box 27, Baghdad, Iraq; *Statistical Abstract of Western Asia*.

Euromonitor Publications Limited, 87-88 Turnmill Street, London EC1M 5QU, England; *International Marketing Data and Statistics*.

Facts on File, 460 Park Avenue South, New York, New York 10016 (800) 443-8323; *The New Book of World Rankings*.

Food and Agricultural Organization of the United Nations (FAO), Via delle Terme di Caracalla, 00100 Rome, Italy (Telephone Number in U.S. (202) 653-2400); *Production Yearbook*, *The State of Food and Agriculture*, and *Trade Yearbook*.

G.K. Hall and Company, 70 Lincoln Street, Boston, Massachusetts 02111 (617) 423-3990; *The World in Figures*.

Statistical Office of the United Nations, Publishing Service, New York, New York 10017 (800) 253-9646; *Statistical Yearbook*.

Times Books, 201 East 50th Street, New York, New York 10022 (212) 751-2600; *The Economist Book of Vital World Statistics*.

LEBANON - AIRLINE SERVICE

Economic Commission for Western Asia, Post Office Box 27, Baghdad, Iraq; *Statistical Abstract of Western Asia*.

Facts on File, 460 Park Avenue South, New York, New York 10016 (800) 443-8323; *The New Book of World Rankings*.

G.K. Hall and Company, 70 Lincoln Street, Boston, Massachusetts 02111 (617) 423-3990; *The World in Figures*.

International Civil Aviation Organization, 1000 Sherbrooke Street West, Suite 400, Montreal, Quebec H3A 2R2, Canada (514) 285-8219; *Civil Aviation Statistics of the World*.

Statistical Office of the United Nations, Publishing Service, New York, New York 10017 (800) 253-9646; *Statistical Yearbook*.

Times Books, 201 East 50th Street, New York, New York 10022 (212) 751-2600; *The Economist Book of Vital World Statistics*.

LEBANON - ALMOND PRODUCTION - See LEBANON - CROPS

LEBANON - ALUMINUM PRODUCTION AND CONSUMPTION - See (LEBANON) - MINING AND MINERAL PRODUCTS

LEBANON - ANIMAL HEALTH

Food and Agricultural Organization of the United Nations (FAO), Via delle Terme di Caracalla, 00100 Rome, Italy (Telephone Number in U.S. (202) 653-2400); *Animal Health Yearbook*.

LEBANON - AREA AND DENSITY OF POPULATION

Economic Commission for Western Asia, Post Office Box 27, Baghdad, Iraq; *Statistical Abstract of Western Asia*.

Euromonitor Publications Limited, 87-88 Turnmill Street, London EC1M 5QU, England; *International Marketing Data and Statistics*.

Facts on File, 460 Park Avenue South, New York, New York 10016 (800) 443-8323; *The New Book of World Rankings*.

Food and Agricultural Organization of the United Nations (FAO), Via delle Terme di Caracalla, 00100 Rome, Italy (Telephone Number in U.S. (202) 653-2400); *The State of Food and Agriculture*.

G.K. Hall and Company, 70 Lincoln Street, Boston, Massachusetts 02111 (617) 423-3990; *The World in Figures*.

Statistical Office of the United Nations, Publishing Service, New York, New York 10017 (800) 253-9646; *Statistical Yearbook*.

Times Books, 201 East 50th Street, New York, New York 10022 (212) 751-2600; *The Economist Book of Vital World Statistics*.

United Nations Educational, Scientific and Cultural Organization (UNESCO), 7 Place de Fontenoy, F-75700 Paris, France (Telephone Number in U.S. (212) 963-5981); *Statistical Yearbook*.

LEBANON - ARMS EXPORTS AND IMPORTS

U.S. Arms Control and Disarmament Agency, 320 Twenty-first Street, NW, Washington, D.C. 20451 (202) 647-8677; *World Military Expenditures and Arms Transfers*.

LEBANON - BALANCE OF PAYMENTS

Economic Commission for Western Asia, Post Office Box 27, Baghdad, Iraq; *Statistical Abstract of Western Asia*.

The Economist Intelligence Unit, 111 West 57th Street, New York, New York 10019 (800) 938-4685; *The World Market Atlas*.

G.K. Hall and Company, 70 Lincoln Street, Boston, Massachusetts 02111 (617) 423-3990; *The World in Figures*.

International Monetary Fund, 700 Nineteenth Street, NW, Washington, D.C. 20431 (202) 623-7000; *Balance of Payments Yearbook*.

LEBANON - BALANCE OF TRADE

Economic Commission for Western Asia, Post Office Box 27, Baghdad, Iraq; *Statistical Abstract of Western Asia*.

LEBANON - BANKING

Economic Commission for Western Asia, Post Office Box 27, Baghdad, Iraq; *Statistical Abstract of Western Asia*.

Facts on File, 460 Park Avenue South, New York, New York 10016 (800) 443-8323; *The New Book of World Rankings*.

G.K. Hall and Company, 70 Lincoln Street, Boston, Massachusetts 02111 (617) 423-3990; *The World in Figures*.

International Monetary Fund, 700 Nineteenth Street, NW, Washington, D.C. 20431 (202) 623-7000; *International Financial Statistics*.

LEBANON - BARLEY PRODUCTION - See LEBANON - CROPS

LEBANON - BEER PRODUCTION

Facts on File, 460 Park Avenue South, New York, New York 10016 (800) 443-8323; *The New Book of World Rankings*.

Statistical Office of the United Nations, Publishing Service, New York, New York 10017 (800) 253-9646; *Statistical Yearbook*.

LEBANON - BIRTH RATES

Facts on File, 460 Park Avenue South, New York, New York 10016 (800) 443-8323; *The New Book of World Rankings*.

Statistical Office of the United Nations, Publishing Service, New York, New York 10017 (800) 253-9646; *Demographic Yearbook*, and *Statistical Yearbook*.

Times Books, 201 East 50th Street, New York, New York 10022 (212) 751-2600; *The Economist Book of Vital World Statistics*.

LEBANON - BONDS

G.K. Hall and Company, 70 Lincoln Street, Boston, Massachusetts 02111 (617) 423-3990; *The World in Figures*.

LEBANON - BOOK PRODUCTION

G.K. Hall and Company, 70 Lincoln Street, Boston, Massachusetts 02111 (617) 423-3990; *The World in Figures*.

LEBANON - BROADCASTING

Billboard Limited, Post Office Box 9027, 1006 AA Amsterdam, The Netherlands (Telephone Number in U.S. (212) 764-7300); *World Radio TV Handbook*.

Facts on File, 460 Park Avenue South, New York, New York 10016 (800) 443-8323; *The New Book of World Rankings*.

G.K. Hall and Company, 70 Lincoln Street, Boston, Massachusetts 02111 (617) 423-3990; *The World in Figures*.

Times Books, 201 East 50th Street, New York, New York 10022 (212) 751-2600; *The Economist Book of Vital World Statistics*.

LEBANON - BUSINESS

G.K. Hall and Company, 70 Lincoln Street, Boston, Massachusetts 02111 (617) 423-3990; *The World in Figures*.

LEBANON - CABBAGE PRODUCTION - See LEBANON - CROPS

LEBANON - CALORIE SUPPLY

Food and Agricultural Organization of the United Nations (FAO), Via delle Terme di Caracalla, 00100 Rome, Italy (Telephone Number in U.S. (202) 653-2400); *The State of Food and Agriculture*.

LEBANON - CATTLE - See LEBANON - LIVESTOCK AND POULTRY

LEBANON - CAULIFLOWER PRODUCTION - See LEBANON - CROPS

LEBANON - CEMENT PRODUCTION - See LEBANON - MINING AND MINERAL PRODUCTS

LEBANON - CHEESE PRODUCTION AND CONSUMPTION - See LEBANON - DAIRY PRODUCTS

LEBANON - CHEMICAL (ORGANIC) PRODUCTION - See LEBANON - MINING AND MINERAL PRODUCTS

LEBANON - CHICK PEA PRODUCTION - See LEBANON - CROPS

LEBANON - CHICKENS - See LEBANON - LIVESTOCK AND POULTRY

LEBANON - CIGARETTE PRODUCTION - See LEBANON - TOBACCO PRODUCTION

LEBANON - CLASS STRUCTURE

G.K. Hall and Company, 70 Lincoln Street, Boston, Massachusetts 02111 (617) 423-3990; *The World in Figures*.

LEBANON - CLIMATE

Facts on File, 460 Park Avenue South, New York, New York 10016 (800) 443-8323; *The New Book of World Rankings*.

G.K. Hall and Company, 70 Lincoln Street, Boston, Massachusetts 02111 (617) 423-3990; *The World in Figures*.

LEBANON - COAL PRODUCTION - See LEBANON - MINING AND MINERAL PRODUCTS

LEBANON - COFFEE PRODUCTION AND CONSUMPTION - See LEBANON - CROPS

LEBANON - COMMUNICATIONS

Economic Commission for Western Asia, Post Office Box 27, Baghdad, Iraq; *Statistical Abstract of Western Asia*.

G.K. Hall and Company, 70 Lincoln Street, Boston, Massachusetts 02111 (617) 423-3990; *The World in Figures*.

LEBANON - CONSTRUCTION INDUSTRY

Facts on File, 460 Park Avenue South, New York, New York 10016 (800) 443-8323; *The New Book of World Rankings*.

Statistical Office of the United Nations, Publishing Service, New York, New York 10017 (800) 253-9646; *Construction Statistics Yearbook*.

LEBANON - CONSUMER PRICE INDEX

G.K. Hall and Company, 70 Lincoln Street, Boston, Massachusetts 02111 (617) 423-3990; *The World in Figures*.

Statistical Office of the United Nations, Publishing Service, New York, New York 10017 (800) 253-9646; *Statistical Yearbook*.

LEBANON - CONSUMER PRICES

International Labour Office, I.L.O. Publications, CH-1211, Geneva 22, Switzerland; *Yearbook of Labour Statistics*.

LEBANON - CONSUMPTION

G.K. Hall and Company, 70 Lincoln Street, Boston, Massachusetts 02111 (617) 423-3990; *The World in Figures*.

LEBANON - COPPER PRODUCTION AND CONSUMPTION - See LEBANON - MINING AND MINERAL PRODUCTS

LEBANON - CORN PRODUCTION - See LEBANON - CROPS

LEBANON - CORPORATE TAXES - See LEBANON - TAXATION

LEBANON - COTTON PRODUCTION - See LEBANON - CROPS

LEBANON - CRIME

International Criminal Police Organization (INTERPOL), 26 rue Armengaud, 92210 Saint Cloud, France; *International Crime Statistics*.

Yale University Press, Yale Station, New Haven, Connecticut 06520 (203) 432-0940; *Violence and Crime in Cross-National Perspective.*

LEBANON - CROPS

Facts on File, 460 Park Avenue South, New York, New York 10016 (800) 443-8323; *The New Book of World Rankings.*

Food and Agricultural Organization of the United Nations (FAO), Via delle Terme di Caracalla, 00100 Rome, Italy (Telephone Number in U.S. (202) 653-2400); *Production Yearbook,* and *The State of Food and Agriculture.*

G.K. Hall and Company, 70 Lincoln Street, Boston, Massachusetts 02111 (617) 423-3990; *The World in Figures.*

International Wheat Statistics, 23 Haymarket, London SW1Y 4SS, England; *World Wheat Statistics.*

Statistical Office of the United Nations, Publishing Service, New York, New York 10017 (800) 253-9646; *Statistical Yearbook.*

LEBANON - CUSTOMS DUTIES

G.K. Hall and Company, 70 Lincoln Street, Boston, Massachusetts 02111 (617) 423-3990; *The World in Figures.*

LEBANON - DAIRY PRODUCTS

Economic Commission for Western Asia, Post Office Box 27, Baghdad, Iraq; *Statistical Abstract of Western Asia.*

Facts on File, 460 Park Avenue South, New York, New York 10016 (800) 443-8323; *The New Book of World Rankings.*

Food and Agricultural Organization of the United Nations (FAO), Via delle Terme di Caracalla, 00100 Rome, Italy (Telephone Number in U.S. (202) 653-2400); *The State of Food and Agriculture,* and *Production Yearbook.*

Statistical Office of the United Nations, Publishing Service, New York, New York 10017 (800) 253-9646; *Statistical Yearbook.*

LEBANON - DEATH RATES

G.K. Hall and Company, 70 Lincoln Street, Boston, Massachusetts 02111 (617) 423-3990; *The World in Figures.*

Statistical Office of the United Nations, Publishing Service, New York, New York 10017 (800) 253-9646; *Statistical Yearbook.*

Times Books, 201 East 50th Street, New York, New York 10022 (212) 751-2600; *The Economist Book of Vital World Statistics.*

LEBANON - DEFENSE EXPENDITURES

G.K. Hall and Company, 70 Lincoln Street, Boston, Massachusetts 02111 (617) 423-3990; *The World in Figures.*

U.S. Arms Control and Disarmament Agency, 320 Twenty-first Street, NW, Washington, D.C. 20451 (202) 647-8677; *World Military Expenditures and Arms Transfers.*

LEBANON - DEMOGRAPHY

The Economist Intelligence Unit, 111 West 57th Street, New York, New York 10019 (800) 938-4685; *The World Market Atlas.*

Facts on File, 460 Park Avenue South, New York, New York 10016 (800) 443-8323; *The New Book of World Rankings.*

G.K. Hall and Company, 70 Lincoln Street, Boston, Massachusetts 02111 (617) 423-3990; *The World in Figures.*

LEBANON - DEVELOPMENT ASSISTANCE

G.K. Hall and Company, 70 Lincoln Street, Boston, Massachusetts 02111 (617) 423-3990; *The World in Figures.*

Statistical Office of the United Nations, Publishing Service, New York, New York 10017 (800) 253-9646; *Statistical Yearbook.*

LEBANON - DIAMOND PRODUCTION - See LEBANON - MINING AND MINERAL PRODUCTS

LEBANON - DISEASE

G.K. Hall and Company, 70 Lincoln Street, Boston, Massachusetts 02111 (617) 423-3990; *The World in Figures.*

LEBANON - DIVORCE

Facts on File, 460 Park Avenue South, New York, New York 10016 (800) 443-8323; *The New Book of World Rankings.*

Statistical Office of the United Nations, Publishing Service, New York, New York 10017 (800) 253-9646; *Demographic Yearbook,* and *Statistical Yearbook.*

LEBANON - DOMESTIC PRODUCT

G.K. Hall and Company, 70 Lincoln Street, Boston, Massachusetts 02111 (617) 423-3990; *The World in Figures.*

LEBANON - ECONOMY

Euromonitor Publications Limited, 87-88 Turnmill Street, London EC1M 5QU, England; *International Marketing Data and Statistics.*

Facts on File, 460 Park Avenue South, New York, New York 10016 (800) 443-8323; *The New Book of World Rankings.*

G.K. Hall and Company, 70 Lincoln Street, Boston, Massachusetts 02111 (617) 423-3990; *The World in Figures.*

LEBANON - EDUCATION

Economic Commission for Western Asia, Post Office Box 27, Baghdad, Iraq; *Statistical Abstract of Western Asia.*

The Economist Intelligence Unit, 111 West 57th Street, New York, New York 10019 (800) 938-4685; *The World Market Atlas.*

Facts on File, 460 Park Avenue South, New York, New York 10016 (800) 443-8323; *The New Book of World Rankings.*

G.K. Hall and Company, 70 Lincoln Street, Boston, Massachusetts 02111 (617) 423-3990; *The World in Figures.*

Times Books, 201 East 50th Street, New York, New York 10022 (212) 751-2600; *The Economist Book of Vital World Statistics.*

United Nations Educational, Scientific and Cultural Organization (UNESCO), 7 Place de Fontenoy, F-75700 Paris, France (Telephone Number in U.S. (212) 963-5981); *Statistical Yearbook.*

LEBANON - EGG PRODUCTION AND CONSUMPTION - See LEBANON - DAIRY PRODUCTS

LEBANON - EGGPLANT PRODUCTION - See LEBANON - CROPS

LEBANON - ELECTRICITY

Facts on File, 460 Park Avenue South, New York, New York 10016 (800) 443-8323; *The New Book of World Rankings*.

Statistical Office of the United Nations, Publishing Service, New York, New York 10017 (800) 253-9646; *Statistical Yearbook*.

Times Books, 201 East 50th Street, New York, New York 10022 (212) 751-2600; *The Economist Book of Vital World Statistics*.

LEBANON - EMPLOYMENT

Economic Commission for Western Asia, Post Office Box 27, Baghdad, Iraq; *Statistical Abstract of Western Asia*.

Euromonitor Publications Limited, 87-88 Turnmill Street, London EC1M 5QU, England; *International Marketing Data and Statistics*.

Facts on File, 460 Park Avenue South, New York, New York 10016 (800) 443-8323; *The New Book of World Rankings*.

International Labour Office, I.L.O. Publications, CH-1211, Geneva 22, Switzerland; *Yearbook of Labour Statistics*.

LEBANON - ENERGY

Economic Commission for Western Asia, Post Office Box 27, Baghdad, Iraq; *Statistical Abstract of Western Asia*.

Facts on File, 460 Park Avenue South, New York, New York 10016 (800) 443-8323; *The New Book of World Rankings*.

Food and Agricultural Organization of the United Nations (FAO), Via delle Terme di Caracalla, 00100 Rome, Italy (Telephone Number in U.S. (202) 653-2400); *The State of Food and Agriculture*.

G.K. Hall and Company, 70 Lincoln Street, Boston, Massachusetts 02111 (617) 423-3990; *The World in Figures*.

Statistical Office of the United Nations, Publishing Service, New York, New York 10017 (800) 253-9646; *Energy Statistics Yearbook*, and *Statistical Yearbook*.

Times Books, 201 East 50th Street, New York, New York 10022 (212) 751-2600; *The Economist Book of Vital World Statistics*.

LEBANON - EXCHANGE RATES

Euromonitor Publications Limited, 87-88 Turnmill Street, London EC1M 5QU, England; *International Marketing Data and Statistics*.

International Civil Aviation Organization, 1000 Sherbrooke Street West, Suite 400, Montreal, Quebec H3A 2R2, Canada (514) 285-8219; *Civil Aviation Statistics of the World*.

International Monetary Fund, 700 Nineteenth Street, NW, Washington, D.C. 20431 (202) 623-7000; *International Financial Statistics*.

Statistical Office of the United Nations, Publishing Service, New York, New York 10017 (800) 253-9646; *Statistical Yearbook*.

LEBANON - EXPORTS

Economic Commission for Western Asia, Post Office Box 27, Baghdad, Iraq; *Statistical Abstract of Western Asia*.

The Economist Intelligence Unit, 111 West 57th Street, New York, New York 10019 (800) 938-4685; *The World Market Atlas*.

Euromonitor Publications Limited, 87-88 Turnmill Street, London EC1M 5QU, England; *International Marketing Data and Statistics*.

Food and Agricultural Organization of the United Nations (FAO), Via delle Terme di Caracalla, 00100 Rome, Italy (Telephone Number in U.S. (202) 653-2400); *The State of Food and Agriculture*.

G.K. Hall and Company, 70 Lincoln Street, Boston, Massachusetts 02111 (617) 423-3990; *The World in Figures*.

International Monetary Fund, 700 Nineteenth Street, NW, Washington, D.C. 20431 (202) 623-7000; *Direction of Trade Statistics*.

Times Books, 201 East 50th Street, New York, New York 10022 (212) 751-2600; *The Economist Book of Vital World Statistics*.

LEBANON - EXTERNAL TRADE

Food and Agricultural Organization of the United Nations (FAO), Via delle Terme di Caracalla, 00100 Rome, Italy (Telephone Number in U.S. (202) 653-2400); *The State of Food and Agriculture*, and *Trade Yearbook*.

G.K. Hall and Company, 70 Lincoln Street, Boston, Massachusetts 02111 (617) 423-3990; *The World in Figures*.

Statistical Office of the United Nations, Publishing Service, New York, New York 10017 (800) 253-9646; *Statistical Yearbook*.

LEBANON - FARM CROPS - See LEBANON - CROPS

LEBANON - FEMALE WORKING POPULATION - See LEBANON - EMPLOYMENT

LEBANON - FERTILITY RATE

Facts on File, 460 Park Avenue South, New York, New York 10016 (800) 443-8323; *The New Book of World Rankings*.

Times Books, 201 East 50th Street, New York, New York 10022 (212) 751-2600; *The Economist Book of Vital World Statistics*.

LEBANON - FERTILIZER

Food and Agricultural Organization of the United Nations (FAO), Via delle Terme di Caracalla, 00100 Rome, Italy (Telephone Number in U.S. (202) 653-2400); *Fertilizer Yearbook*, and *The State of Food and Agriculture*.

Statistical Office of the United Nations, Publishing Service, New York, New York 10017 (800) 253-9646; *Statistical Yearbook*.

LEBANON - FETAL MORTALITY

Statistical Office of the United Nations, Publishing Service, New York, New York 10017 (800) 253-9646; *Demographic Yearbook*.

LEBANON - FILM - See LEBANON - MOTION PICTURES

LEBANON - FINANCE

Economic Commission for Western Asia, Post Office Box 27, Baghdad, Iraq; *Statistical Abstract of Western Asia*.

Facts on File, 460 Park Avenue South, New York, New York 10016 (800) 443-8323; *The New Book of World Rankings*.

G.K. Hall and Company, 70 Lincoln Street, Boston, Massachusetts 02111 (617) 423-3990; *The World in Figures*.

International Monetary Fund, 700 Nineteenth Street, NW, Washington, D.C. 20431 (202) 623-7000; *International Financial Statistics*.

LEBANON - FISHERIES

Economic Commission for Western Asia, Post Office Box 27, Baghdad, Iraq; *Statistical Abstract of Western Asia*.

Facts on File, 460 Park Avenue South, New York, New York 10016 (800) 443-8323; *The New Book of World Rankings*.

Food and Agricultural Organization of the United Nations (FAO), Via delle Terme di Caracalla, 00100 Rome, Italy (Telephone Number in U.S. (202) 653-2400); *The State of Food and Agriculture*, and *Yearbook of Fishery Statistics*.

Statistical Office of the United Nations, Publishing Service, New York, New York 10017 (800) 253-9646; *Statistical Yearbook*.

LEBANON - FLOUR PRODUCTION

Statistical Office of the United Nations, Publishing Service, New York, New York 10017 (800) 253-9646; *Statistical Yearbook*.

LEBANON - FOOD

Food and Agricultural Organization of the United Nations (FAO), Via delle Terme di Caracalla, 00100 Rome, Italy (Telephone Number in U.S. (202) 653-2400); *The State of Food and Agriculture*, and *Production Yearbook*.

G.K. Hall and Company, 70 Lincoln Street, Boston, Massachusetts 02111 (617) 423-3990; *The World in Figures*.

LEBANON - FOREIGN AID

G.K. Hall and Company, 70 Lincoln Street, Boston, Massachusetts 02111 (617) 423-3990; *The World in Figures*.

LEBANON - FOREIGN TRADE

Economic Commission for Western Asia, Post Office Box 27, Baghdad, Iraq; *Statistical Abstract of Western Asia*.

Facts on File, 460 Park Avenue South, New York, New York 10016 (800) 443-8323; *The New Book of World Rankings*.

Food and Agricultural Organization of the United Nations (FAO), Via delle Terme di Caracalla, 00100 Rome, Italy (Telephone Number in U.S. (202) 653-2400); *The State of Food and Agriculture*.

G.K. Hall and Company, 70 Lincoln Street, Boston, Massachusetts 02111 (617) 423-3990; *The World in Figures*.

International Monetary Fund, 700 Nineteenth Street, NW, Washington, D.C. 20431 (202) 623-7000; *International Financial Statistics*.

Statistical Office of the United Nations, Publishing Service, New York, New York 10017 (800) 253-9646; *International Trade Statistics Yearbook*, and *Statistical Yearbook*.

LEBANON - FORESTRY AND FOREST PRODUCTS

Facts on File, 460 Park Avenue South, New York, New York 10016 (800) 443-8323; *The New Book of World Rankings*.

Food and Agricultural Organization of the United Nations (FAO), Via delle Terme di Caracalla, 00100 Rome, Italy (Telephone Number in U.S. (202) 653-2400); *The State of Food and Agriculture*, and *Yearbook of Forest Products*.

G.K. Hall and Company, 70 Lincoln Street, Boston, Massachusetts 02111 (617) 423-3990; *The World in Figures*.

Statistical Office of the United Nations, Publishing Service, New York, New York 10017 (800) 253-9646; *Statistical Yearbook*.

United Nations Educational, Scientific and Cultural Organization (UNESCO), 7 Place de Fontenoy, F-75700 Paris, France (Telephone Number in U.S. (212) 963-5981); *Statistical Yearbook*.

LEBANON - GARLIC PRODUCTION - See LEBANON - CROPS

LEBANON - GAS PRODUCTION - See LEBANON - MINING AND MINERAL PRODUCTS

LEBANON - GENERAL MORTALITY

Statistical Office of the United Nations, Publishing Service, New York, New York 10017 (800) 253-9646; *Demographic Yearbook*.

LEBANON - GEOGRAPHIC DATA

Facts on File, 460 Park Avenue South, New York, New York 10016 (800) 443-8323; *The New Book of World Rankings*.

LEBANON - GOATS - See LEBANON - LIVESTOCK AND POULTRY

LEBANON - GOLD HOLDINGS

International Monetary Fund, 700 Nineteenth Street, NW, Washington, D.C. 20431 (202) 623-7000; *International Financial Statistics*.

Statistical Office of the United Nations, Publishing Service, New York, New York 10017 (800) 253-9646; *Statistical Yearbook*.

LEBANON - GOLD PRODUCTION AND CONSUMPTION - See LEBANON - MINING AND MINERAL PRODUCTS

LEBANON - GOVERNMENT

G.K. Hall and Company, 70 Lincoln Street, Boston, Massachusetts 02111 (617) 423-3990; *The World in Figures*.

LEBANON - GOVERNMENT EXPENDITURE

Economic Commission for Western Asia, Post Office Box 27, Baghdad, Iraq; *Statistical Abstract of Western Asia*.

LEBANON - GOVERNMENT FINANCES

International Monetary Fund, 700 Nineteenth Street, NW, Washington, D.C. 20431 (202) 623-7000; *International Financial Statistics*.

Statistical Office of the United Nations, Publishing Service, New York, New York 10017 (800) 253-9646; *Statistical Yearbook.*

LEBANON - GOVERNMENT REVENUE

Economic Commission for Western Asia, Post Office Box 27, Baghdad, Iraq; *Statistical Abstract of Western Asia.*

LEBANON - GRAIN PRODUCTION - See LEBANON - CROPS

LEBANON - GROSS DOMESTIC PRODUCT

Economic Commission for Western Asia, Post Office Box 27, Baghdad, Iraq; *Statistical Abstract of Western Asia.*

The Economist Intelligence Unit, 111 West 57th Street, New York, New York 10019 (800) 938-4685; *The World Market Atlas.*

Euromonitor Publications Limited, 87-88 Turnmill Street, London EC1M 5QU, England; *International Marketing Data and Statistics.*

Facts on File, 460 Park Avenue South, New York, New York 10016 (800) 443-8323; *The New Book of World Rankings.*

G.K. Hall and Company, 70 Lincoln Street, Boston, Massachusetts 02111 (617) 423-3990; *The World in Figures.*

Statistical Office of the United Nations, Publishing Service, New York, New York 10017 (800) 253-9646; *Statistical Yearbook.*

Times Books, 201 East 50th Street, New York, New York 10022 (212) 751-2600; *The Economist Book of Vital World Statistics.*

LEBANON - GROSS NATIONAL PRODUCT

Euromonitor Publications Limited, 87-88 Turnmill Street, London EC1M 5QU, England; *International Marketing Data and Statistics.*

U.S. Arms Control and Disarmament Agency, 320 Twenty-first Street, NW, Washington, D.C. 20451 (202) 647-8677; *World Military Expenditures and Arms Transfers.*

LEBANON - GROUNDNUT PRODUCTION - See LEBANON - CROPS

LEBANON - HEALTH

Economic Commission for Western Asia, Post Office Box 27, Baghdad, Iraq; *Statistical Abstract of Western Asia.*

Facts on File, 460 Park Avenue South, New York, New York 10016 (800) 443-8323; *The New Book of World Rankings.*

G.K. Hall and Company, 70 Lincoln Street, Boston, Massachusetts 02111 (617) 423-3990; *The World in Figures.*

Statistical Office of the United Nations, Publishing Service, New York, New York 10017 (800) 253-9646; *Statistical Yearbook.*

Times Books, 201 East 50th Street, New York, New York 10022 (212) 751-2600; *The Economist Book of Vital World Statistics.*

LEBANON - HIDE PRODUCTION

Food and Agricultural Organization of the United Nations (FAO), Via delle Terme di Caracalla, 00100 Rome, Italy (Telephone Number in U.S. (202) 653-2400); *Production Yearbook.*

LEBANON - HIGHWAYS

Economic Commission for Western Asia, Post Office Box 27, Baghdad, Iraq; *Statistical Abstract of Western Asia.*

G.K. Hall and Company, 70 Lincoln Street, Boston, Massachusetts 02111 (617) 423-3990; *The World in Figures.*

International Road Federation, 525 School Street, SW, Washington, D.C. 20024 (202) 554-2106; *World Road Statistics.*

LEBANON - HORSES - See LEBANON - LIVESTOCK AND POULTRY

LEBANON - HOURS OF WORK - See LEBANON - EMPLOYMENT

LEBANON - HOUSING

Facts on File, 460 Park Avenue South, New York, New York 10016 (800) 443-8323; *The New Book of World Rankings.*

LEBANON - ILLITERATE POPULATION

The Economist Intelligence Unit, 111 West 57th Street, New York, New York 10019 (800) 938-4685; *The World Market Atlas.*

G.K. Hall and Company, 70 Lincoln Street, Boston, Massachusetts 02111 (617) 423-3990; *The World in Figures.*

United Nations Educational, Scientific and Cultural Organization (UNESCO), 7 Place de Fontenoy, F-75700 Paris, France (Telephone Number in U.S. (212) 963-5981); *Statistical Yearbook.*

LEBANON - IMPORTS

Economic Commission for Western Asia, Post Office Box 27, Baghdad, Iraq; *Statistical Abstract of Western Asia.*

The Economist Intelligence Unit, 111 West 57th Street, New York, New York 10019 (800) 938-4685; *The World Market Atlas.*

Euromonitor Publications Limited, 87-88 Turnmill Street, London EC1M 5QU, England; *International Marketing Data and Statistics.*

Food and Agricultural Organization of the United Nations (FAO), Via delle Terme di Caracalla, 00100 Rome, Italy (Telephone Number in U.S. (202) 653-2400); *The State of Food and Agriculture.*

G.K. Hall and Company, 70 Lincoln Street, Boston, Massachusetts 02111 (617) 423-3990; *The World in Figures.*

International Monetary Fund, 700 Nineteenth Street, NW, Washington, D.C. 20431 (202) 623-7000; *Direction of Trade Statistics.*

LEBANON - INDUSTRY

Euromonitor Publications Limited, 87-88 Turnmill Street, London EC1M 5QU, England; *International Marketing Data and Statistics.*

Facts on File, 460 Park Avenue South, New York, New York 10016 (800) 443-8323; *The New Book of World Rankings.*

G.K. Hall and Company, 70 Lincoln Street, Boston, Massachusetts 02111 (617) 423-3990; *The World in Figures.*

International Labour Office, I.L.O. Publications, CH-1211, Geneva 22, Switzerland; *Yearbook of Labour Statistics.*

Statistical Office of the United Nations, Publishing Service, New York, New York 10017 (800) 253-9646; *Statistical Yearbook.*

LEBANON - INFANT AND MATERNAL MORTALITY

Statistical Office of the United Nations, Publishing Service, New York, New York 10017 (800) 253-9646; *Demographic Yearbook*, and *Statistical Yearbook*.

Times Books, 201 East 50th Street, New York, New York 10022 (212) 751-2600; *The Economist Book of Vital World Statistics*.

LEBANON - INTERNATIONAL LIQUIDITY

International Monetary Fund, 700 Nineteenth Street, NW, Washington, D.C. 20431 (202) 623-7000; *International Financial Statistics*.

LEBANON - INTERNATIONAL RESERVES EXCLUDING GOLD

Statistical Office of the United Nations, Publishing Service, New York, New York 10017 (800) 253-9646; *Statistical Yearbook*.

LEBANON - IRON ORE PRODUCTION AND CONSUMPTION - See LEBANON - MINING AND MINERAL PRODUCTS

LEBANON - IRRIGATION

Euromonitor Publications Limited, 87-88 Turnmill Street, London EC1M 5QU, England; *International Marketing Data and Statistics*.

LEBANON - LABOR FORCE

Economic Commission for Western Asia, Post Office Box 27, Baghdad, Iraq; *Statistical Abstract of Western Asia*.

Euromonitor Publications Limited, 87-88 Turnmill Street, London EC1M 5QU, England; *International Marketing Data and Statistics*.

Facts on File, 460 Park Avenue South, New York, New York 10016 (800) 443-8323; *The New Book of World Rankings*.

Food and Agricultural Organization of the United Nations (FAO), Via delle Terme di Caracalla, 00100 Rome, Italy (Telephone Number in U.S. (202) 653-2400); *The State of Food and Agriculture*.

G.K. Hall and Company, 70 Lincoln Street, Boston, Massachusetts 02111 (617) 423-3990; *The World in Figures*.

LEBANON - LABOR PRODUCTIVITY

International Labour Office, I.L.O. Publications, CH-1211, Geneva 22, Switzerland; *Yearbook of Labour Statistics*.

LEBANON - LAND USE

Economic Commission for Western Asia, Post Office Box 27, Baghdad, Iraq; *Statistical Abstract of Western Asia*.

Euromonitor Publications Limited, 87-88 Turnmill Street, London EC1M 5QU, England; *International Marketing Data and Statistics*.

Food and Agricultural Organization of the United Nations (FAO), Via delle Terme di Caracalla, 00100 Rome, Italy (Telephone Number in U.S. (202) 653-2400); *Production Yearbook*.

G.K. Hall and Company, 70 Lincoln Street, Boston, Massachusetts 02111 (617) 423-3990; *The World in Figures*.

LEBANON - LIBRARIES

Facts on File, 460 Park Avenue South, New York, New York 10016 (800) 443-8323; *The New Book of World Rankings*.

LEBANON - LIVESTOCK AND POULTRY

Economic Commission for Western Asia, Post Office Box 27, Baghdad, Iraq; *Statistical Abstract of Western Asia*.

Euromonitor Publications Limited, 87-88 Turnmill Street, London EC1M 5QU, England; *International Marketing Data and Statistics*.

Facts on File, 460 Park Avenue South, New York, New York 10016 (800) 443-8323; *The New Book of World Rankings*.

Food and Agricultural Organization of the United Nations (FAO), Via delle Terme di Caracalla, 00100 Rome, Italy (Telephone Number in U.S. (202) 653-2400); *Production Yearbook*, and *The State of Food and Agriculture*.

G.K. Hall and Company, 70 Lincoln Street, Boston, Massachusetts 02111 (617) 423-3990; *The World in Figures*.

Statistical Office of the United Nations, Publishing Service, New York, New York 10017 (800) 253-9646; *Statistical Yearbook*.

LEBANON - LIVING LEVELS

G.K. Hall and Company, 70 Lincoln Street, Boston, Massachusetts 02111 (617) 423-3990; *The World in Figures*.

Times Books, 201 East 50th Street, New York, New York 10022 (212) 751-2600; *The Economist Book of Vital World Statistics*.

LEBANON - MANUFACTURING

Facts on File, 460 Park Avenue South, New York, New York 10016 (800) 443-8323; *The New Book of World Rankings*.

G.K. Hall and Company, 70 Lincoln Street, Boston, Massachusetts 02111 (617) 423-3990; *The World in Figures*.

LEBANON - MARRIAGE RATES

Facts on File, 460 Park Avenue South, New York, New York 10016 (800) 443-8323; *The New Book of World Rankings*.

Statistical Office of the United Nations, Publishing Service, New York, New York 10017 (800) 253-9646; *Demographic Yearbook*, and *Statistical Yearbook*.

LEBANON - MEAT PRODUCTION - See LEBANON - LIVESTOCK AND POULTRY

LEBANON - MERCHANT SHIPPING

Economic Commission for Western Asia, Post Office Box 27, Baghdad, Iraq; *Statistical Abstract of Western Asia*.

G.K. Hall and Company, 70 Lincoln Street, Boston, Massachusetts 02111 (617) 423-3990; *The World in Figures*.

Lloyd's Register of Shipping, 17 Battery Place, New York, New York 10004 (212) 425-8050; *Register of Ships*.

Statistical Office of the United Nations, Publishing Service, New York, New York 10017 (800) 253-9646; *Statistical Yearbook*.

U.S. Department of Transportation, Maritime Administration, 400 Seventh Street, SW, Washington, D.C. 20590 (202) 366-5807; *A Statistical Analysis of the World's Merchant Fleets.*

LEBANON - MILITARY

G.K. Hall and Company, 70 Lincoln Street, Boston, Massachusetts 02111 (617) 423-3990; *The World in Figures.*

The International Institute for Strategic Studies, 23 Tavistock Street, London WC2E 7NQ, England; *The Military Balance.*

U.S. Arms Control and Disarmament Agency, 320 Twenty-first Street, NW, Washington, D.C. 20451 (202) 647-8677; *World Military Expenditures and Arms Transfers.*

LEBANON - MILK PRODUCTION - See LEBANON - DAIRY PRODUCTS

LEBANON - MINING AND MINERAL PRODUCTS

Economic Commission for Western Asia, Post Office Box 27, Baghdad, Iraq; *Statistical Abstract of Western Asia.*

Facts on File, 460 Park Avenue South, New York, New York 10016 (800) 443-8323; *The New Book of World Rankings.*

G.K. Hall and Company, 70 Lincoln Street, Boston, Massachusetts 02111 (617) 423-3990; *The World in Figures.*

Statistical Office of the United Nations, Publishing Service, New York, New York 10017 (800) 253-9646; *Statistical Yearbook.*

LEBANON - MONEY EXCHANGE RATE

Euromonitor Publications Limited, 87-88 Turnmill Street, London EC1M 5QU, England; *International Marketing Data and Statistics.*

International Monetary Fund, 700 Nineteenth Street, NW, Washington, D.C. 20431 (202) 623-7000; *International Financial Statistics.*

Statistical Office of the United Nations, Publishing Service, New York, New York 10017 (800) 253-9646; *Statistical Yearbook.*

LEBANON - MONEY RESERVES

Euromonitor Publications Limited, 87-88 Turnmill Street, London EC1M 5QU, England; *International Marketing Data and Statistics.*

LEBANON - MONEY SUPPLY

Economic Commission for Western Asia, Post Office Box 27, Baghdad, Iraq; *Statistical Abstract of Western Asia.*

Euromonitor Publications Limited, 87-88 Turnmill Street, London EC1M 5QU, England; *International Marketing Data and Statistics.*

G.K. Hall and Company, 70 Lincoln Street, Boston, Massachusetts 02111 (617) 423-3990; *The World in Figures.*

International Monetary Fund, 700 Nineteenth Street, NW, Washington, D.C. 20431 (202) 623-7000; *International Financial Statistics.*

Statistical Office of the United Nations, Publishing Service, New York, New York 10017 (800) 253-9646; *Statistical Yearbook.*

LEBANON - MOTION PICTURES

United Nations Educational, Scientific and Cultural Organization (UNESCO), 7 Place de Fontenoy, F-75700 Paris, France (Telephone Number in U.S. (212) 963-5981); *Statistical Yearbook.*

LEBANON - MOTOR VEHICLE TAXES - See LEBANON - TAXATION

LEBANON - MOTOR VEHICLES

Economic Commission for Western Asia, Post Office Box 27, Baghdad, Iraq; *Statistical Abstract of Western Asia.*

LEBANON - MOTOR VEHICLES IN USE

G.K. Hall and Company, 70 Lincoln Street, Boston, Massachusetts 02111 (617) 423-3990; *The World in Figures.*

International Road Federation, 525 School Street, SW, Washington, D.C. 20024 (202) 554-2106; *World Road Statistics.*

Statistical Office of the United Nations, Publishing Service, New York, New York 10017 (800) 253-9646; *Statistical Yearbook.*

Times Books, 201 East 50th Street, New York, New York 10022 (212) 751-2600; *The Economist Book of Vital World Statistics.*

LEBANON - MULES - See LEBANON - LIVESTOCK AND POULTRY

LEBANON - MUSEUMS

Facts on File, 460 Park Avenue South, New York, New York 10016 (800) 443-8323; *The New Book of World Rankings.*

United Nations Educational, Scientific and Cultural Organization (UNESCO), 7 Place de Fontenoy, F-75700 Paris, France (Telephone Number in U.S. (212) 963-5981); *Statistical Yearbook.*

LEBANON - NATALITY - See LEBANON - BIRTH RATES

LEBANON - NATIONAL ACCOUNTS

Economic Commission for Western Asia, Post Office Box 27, Baghdad, Iraq; *Statistical Abstract of Western Asia.*

Statistical Office of the United Nations, Publishing Service, New York, New York 10017 (800) 253-9646; *National Accounts Statistics,* and *Statistical Yearbook.*

LEBANON - NATIONAL INCOME

Facts on File, 460 Park Avenue South, New York, New York 10016 (800) 443-8323; *The New Book of World Rankings.*

G.K. Hall and Company, 70 Lincoln Street, Boston, Massachusetts 02111 (617) 423-3990; *The World in Figures.*

Statistical Office of the United Nations, Publishing Service, New York, New York 10017 (800) 253-9646; *Statistical Yearbook.*

LEBANON - NATIONAL PRODUCT

Facts on File, 460 Park Avenue South, New York, New York 10016 (800) 443-8323; *The New Book of World Rankings.*

LEBANON - NATURAL GAS - PRODUCTION - See LEBANON - MINING AND MINERAL PRODUCTS

LEBANON - NEWSPAPER PRODUCTION - See LEBANON - FORESTRY AND FORESTRY PRODUCTS

LEBANON - NEWSPRINT - See LEBANON - FORESTRY AND FOREST PRODUCTS

LEBANON - OATS PRODUCTION - See LEBANON - CROPS

LEBANON - OCCUPATIONS - See LEBANON - LABOR FORCE

LEBANON - PAPER - See LEBANON - FORESTRY AND FOREST PRODUCTS

LEBANON - PATENTS

Statistical Office of the United Nations, Publishing Service, New York, New York 10017 (800) 253-9646; *Statistical Yearbook.*

LEBANON - PEANUT PRODUCTION - See LEBANON - CROPS

LEBANON - PESTICIDE USE

Food and Agricultural Organization of the United Nations (FAO), Via delle Terme di Caracalla, 00100 Rome, Italy (Telephone Number in U.S. (202) 653 3400); *The State of Food and Agriculture.*

LEBANON - PETROLEUM INDUSTRY

Facts on File, 460 Park Avenue South, New York, New York 10016 (800) 443-8323; *The New Book of World Rankings.*

Food and Agricultural Organization of the United Nations (FAO), Via delle Terme di Caracalla, 00100 Rome, Italy (Telephone Number in U.S. (202) 653-2400); *The State of Food and Agriculture.*

G.K. Hall and Company, 70 Lincoln Street, Boston, Massachusetts 02111 (617) 423-3990; *The World in Figures.*

Statistical Office of the United Nations, Publishing Service, New York, New York 10017 (800) 253-9646; *Statistical Yearbook.*

LEBANON - PIGS - See LEBANON - LIVESTOCK AND POULTRY

LEBANON - POPULATION

Economic Commission for Western Asia, Post Office Box 27, Baghdad, Iraq; *Statistical Abstract of Western Asia.*

The Economist Intelligence Unit, 111 West 57th Street, New York, New York 10019 (800) 938-4685; *The World Market Atlas.*

Euromonitor Publications Limited, 87-88 Turnmill Street, London EC1M 5QU, England; *International Marketing Data and Statistics.*

Facts on File, 460 Park Avenue South, New York, New York 10016 (800) 443-8323; *The New Book of World Rankings.*

Food and Agricultural Organization of the United Nations (FAO), Via delle Terme di Caracalla, 00100 Rome, Italy (Telephone Number in U.S. (202) 653-2400); *Production Yearbook.*

G.K. Hall and Company, 70 Lincoln Street, Boston, Massachusetts 02111 (617) 423-3990; *The World in Figures.*

International Labour Office, I.L.O. Publications, CH-1211, Geneva 22, Switzerland; *Yearbook of Labour Statistics.*

Statistical Office of the United Nations, Publishing Service, New York, New York 10017 (800) 253-9646; *Demographic Yearbook,* and *Statistical Yearbook.*

Times Books, 201 East 50th Street, New York, New York 10022 (212) 751-2600; *The Economist Book of Vital World Statistics.*

United Nations Educational, Scientific and Cultural Organization (UNESCO), 7 Place de Fontenoy, F-75700 Paris, France (Telephone Number in U.S. (212) 963-5981); *Statistical Yearbook.*

U.S. Arms Control and Disarmament Agency, 320 Twenty-first Street, NW, Washington, D.C. 20451 (202) 647-8677; *World Military Expenditures and Arms Transfers.*

World Health Organization, Office of Publications, Avenue Appia, CH-1211 Geneva 27, Switzerland (Telephone Number in U.S. (518) 436-9686); *World Health Statistics Annual.*

LEBANON - POST OFFICES

Facts on File, 460 Park Avenue South, New York, New York 10016 (800) 443-8323; *The New Book of World Rankings.*

LEBANON - POTATO PRODUCTION - See LEBANON - CROPS

LEBANON - PRICES

Economic Commission for Western Asia, Post Office Box 27, Baghdad, Iraq; *Statistical Abstract of Western Asia.*

Facts on File, 460 Park Avenue South, New York, New York 10016 (800) 443-8323; *The New Book of World Rankings.*

Food and Agricultural Organization of the United Nations (FAO), Via delle Terme di Caracalla, 00100 Rome, Italy (Telephone Number in U.S. (202) 653-2400); *Production Yearbook,* and *The State of Food and Agriculture.*

G.K. Hall and Company, 70 Lincoln Street, Boston, Massachusetts 02111 (617) 423-3990; *The World in Figures.*

LEBANON - PRINTING AND WRITING PAPER - See LEBANON - FORESTRY AND FOREST PRODUCTS

LEBANON - PRODUCTION

Facts on File, 460 Park Avenue South, New York, New York 10016 (800) 443-8323; *The New Book of World Rankings.*

G.K. Hall and Company, 70 Lincoln Street, Boston, Massachusetts 02111 (617) 423-3990; *The World in Figures.*

LEBANON - PRODUCTIVITY

Euromonitor Publications Limited, 87-88 Turnmill Street, London EC1M 5QU, England; *International Marketing Data and Statistics.*

LEBANON - PUBLIC FINANCE

Facts on File, 460 Park Avenue South, New York, New York 10016 (800) 443-8323; *The New Book of World Rankings.*

LEBANON - RADIO BROADCASTING - See LEBANON - BROADCASTING

LEBANON - RAILWAYS

G.K. Hall and Company, 70 Lincoln Street, Boston, Massachusetts 02111 (617) 423-3990; *The World in Figures.*

Jane's Information Group, Sentinel House, 163 Brighton Road, Coulsdon, Surrey CR5 2NH, England (Telephone Number in U.S. (703) 683-3700); *Jane's World Railways.*

Statistical Office of the United Nations, Publishing Service, New York, New York 10017 (800) 253-9646; *Statistical Yearbook.*

LEBANON - RELIGION

Facts on File, 460 Park Avenue South, New York, New York 10016 (800) 443-8323; *The New Book of World Rankings.*

LEBANON - RETAIL TRADE

G.K. Hall and Company, 70 Lincoln Street, Boston, Massachusetts 02111 (617) 423-3990; *The World in Figures.*

LEBANON - RICE PRODUCTION - See LEBANON - CROPS

LEBANON - ROOT AND TUBER PRODUCTION - See LEBANON - CROPS

LEBANON - ROUNDWOOD PRODUCTION - See LEBANON- FORESTRY AND FOREST PRODUCTS

LEBANON - RUBBER PRODUCTION AND CONSUMPTION

Facts on File, 460 Park Avenue South, New York, New York 10016 (800) 443-8323; *The New Book of World Rankings.*

LEBANON - SALT PRODUCTION

Statistical Office of the United Nations, Publishing Service, New York, New York 10017 (800) 253-9646; *Statistical Yearbook.*

LEBANON - SAWNWOOD PRODUCTION - See LEBANON - FORESTRY AND FOREST PRODUCTS

LEBANON - SCIENTISTS AND TECHNICIANS

Statistical Office of the United Nations, Publishing Service, New York, New York 10017 (800) 253-9646; *Statistical Yearbook.*

United Nations Educational, Scientific and Cultural Organization (UNESCO), 7 Place de Fontenoy, F-75700 Paris, France (Telephone Number in U.S. (212) 963-5981); *Statistical Yearbook.*

LEBANON - SENIOR CITIZENS

Facts on File, 460 Park Avenue South, New York, New York 10016 (800) 443-8323; *The New Book of World Rankings.*

LEBANON - SHEEP - See LEBANON - LIVESTOCK AND POULTRY

LEBANON - SILVER PRODUCTION AND CONSUMPTION - See LEBANON - MINING AND MINERAL PRODUCTS

LEBANON - SOCIAL DATA

Facts on File, 460 Park Avenue South, New York, New York 10016 (800) 443-8323; *The New Book of World Rankings.*

G.K. Hall and Company, 70 Lincoln Street, Boston, Massachusetts 02111 (617) 423-3990; *The World in Figures.*

LEBANON - STATE BUDGET

Euromonitor Publications Limited, 87-88 Turnmill Street, London EC1M 5QU, England; *International Marketing Data and Statistics.*

LEBANON - STEEL - See LEBANON - MINING AND MINERAL PRODUCTS

LEBANON - STOCKS - COMMODITY - MARKET PRICE - INDEX

Food and Agricultural Organization of the United Nations (FAO), Via delle Terme di Caracalla, 00100 Rome, Italy (Telephone Number in U.S. (202) 653-2400); *The State of Food and Agriculture.*

LEBANON - SUGAR PRODUCTION AND CONSUMPTION - See LEBANON - CROPS

LEBANON - TAXATION

G.K. Hall and Company, 70 Lincoln Street, Boston, Massachusetts 02111 (617) 423-3990; *The World in Figures.*

International Road Federation, 525 School Street, SW, Washington, D.C. 20024 (202) 554-2106; *World Road Statistics.*

LEBANON - TELEPHONES IN USE

American Telephone and Telegraph Company, 26 Parsippany Road, Whippany, New Jersey 07981 (800) 338-4038; *The World's Telephones.*

G.K. Hall and Company, 70 Lincoln Street, Boston, Massachusetts 02111 (617) 423-3990; *The World in Figures.*

Statistical Office of the United Nations, Publishing Service, New York, New York 10017 (800) 253-9646; *Statistical Yearbook.*

LEBANON - TELEVISION BROADCASTING - See LEBANON - BROADCASTING

LEBANON - TEXTILE INDUSTRY

G.K. Hall and Company, 70 Lincoln Street, Boston, Massachusetts 02111 (617) 423-3990; *The World in Figures.*

LEBANON - TOBACCO PRODUCTION

Facts on File, 460 Park Avenue South, New York, New York 10016 (800) 443-8323; *The New Book of World Rankings.*

Statistical Office of the United Nations, Publishing Service, New York, New York 10017 (800) 253-9646; *Statistical Yearbook.*

LEBANON - TOURISM

Economic Commission for Western Asia, Post Office Box 27, Baghdad, Iraq; *Statistical Abstract of Western Asia.*

Facts on File, 460 Park Avenue South, New York, New York 10016; *The New Book of World Rankings.*

G.K. Hall and Company, 70 Lincoln Street, Boston, Massachusetts 02111 (617) 423-3990; *The World in Figures.*

Statistical Office of the United Nations, Publishing Service, New York, New York 10017 (800) 253-9646; *Statistical Yearbook.*

LEBANON - TRACTORS IN USE

Statistical Office of the United Nations, Publishing Service, New York, New York 10017 (800) 253-9646; *Statistical Yearbook.*

LEBANON - TRADE - See LEBANON - FOREIGN TRADE

LEBANON - TRADEMARKS AND SERVICE MARKS

Statistical Office of the United Nations, Publishing Service, New York, New York 10017 (800) 253-9646; *Statistical Yearbook.*

LEBANON - TRANSPORTATION AND COMMUNICATIONS

Economic Commission for Western Asia, Post Office Box 27, Baghdad, Iraq; *Statistical Abstract of Western Asia.*

Facts on File, 460 Park Avenue South, New York, New York 10016 (800) 443-8323; *The New Book of World Rankings.*

G.K. Hall and Company, 70 Lincoln Street, Boston, Massachusetts 02111 (617) 423-3990; *The World in Figures.*

LEBANON - UNEMPLOYMENT

Euromonitor Publications Limited, 87-88 Turnmill Street, London EC1M 5QU, England; *International Marketing Data and Statistics.*

International Labour Office, I.L.O. Publications, CH-1211, Geneva 22, Switzerland; *Yearbook of Labour Statistics.*

LEBANON - VITAL STATISTICS

Euromonitor Publications Limited, 87-88 Turnmill Street, London EC1M 5QU, England; *International Marketing Data and Statistics.*

G.K. Hall and Company, 70 Lincoln Street, Boston, Massachusetts 02111 (617) 423-3990; *The World in Figures.*

Statistical Office of the United Nations, Publishing Service, New York, New York 10017 (800) 253-9646; *Statistical Yearbook.*

World Health Organization, Office of Publications, Avenue Appia, CH-1211 Geneva 27, Switzerland (Telephone Number in U.S. (518) 436-9686); *World Health Statistics Annual.*

LEBANON - WAGES

G.K. Hall and Company, 70 Lincoln Street, Boston, Massachusetts 02111 (617) 423-3990; *The World in Figures.*

International Labour Office, I.L.O. Publications, CH-1211, Geneva 22, Switzerland; *Yearbook of Labour Statistics.*

LEBANON - WALNUT PRODUCTION - See LEBANON - CROPS

LEBANON - WATERMELON PRODUCTION - See LEBANON - CROPS

LEBANON - WEATHER

Facts on File, 460 Park Avenue South, New York, New York 10016 (800) 443-8323; *The New Book of World Rankings.*

G.K. Hall and Company, 70 Lincoln Street, Boston, Massachusetts 02111 (617) 423-3990; *The World in Figures.*

LEBANON - WHEAT PRODUCTION AND PRICES - See LEBANON - CROPS

LEBANON - WINE PRODUCTION

Facts on File, 460 Park Avenue South, New York, New York 10016 (800) 443-8323; *The New Book of World Rankings.*

Statistical Office of the United Nations, Publishing Service, New York, New York 10017 (800) 253-9646; *Statistical Yearbook.*

LEBANON - WOOL PRODUCTION

Facts on File, 460 Park Avenue South, New York, New York 10016 (800) 443-8323; *The New Book of World Rankings.*

LEBANON - YARN PRODUCTION

Statistical Office of the United Nations, Publishing Service, New York, New York 10017 (800) 253-9646; *Statistical Yearbook.*

LEEWARD ISLANDS - EXPORTS

International Monetary Fund, 700 Nineteenth Street, NW, Washington, D.C. 20431 (202) 623-7000; *Direction of Trade Statistics.*

LEEWARD ISLANDS - IMPORTS

International Monetary Fund, 700 Nineteenth Street, NW, Washington, D.C. 20431 (202) 623-7000; *Direction of Trade Statistics.*

LEEWARD ISLANDS - POPULATION

Statistical Office of the United Nations, Publishing Service, New York, New York 10017 (800) 253-9646; *Statistical Yearbook.*

LEGAL ASSISTANTS

U.S. Department of Labor, Bureau of Labor Statistics, Two Massachusetts Avenue, NE, Washington, D.C. 20212 (202) 606-7828; *Employment and Earnings.*

LEGAL SERVICES - EARNINGS

U.S. Department of Commerce, Bureau of the Census, Suitland, Maryland 20233 (301) 763-4040; *County Business Patterns,* and *Census of Service Industries.*

U.S. Department of Labor, Bureau of Labor Statistics, Two Massachusetts Avenue, NE, Washington, D.C. 20212 (202) 606-7828; *Employment and Earnings,* and Bulletins 2370 and 2429.

LEGAL SERVICES - EMPLOYEES

U.S. Department of Commerce, Bureau of Economic Analysis, Fourteenth Street between Constitution Avenue and E Street, NW, Washington, D.C. 20230 (202) 606-9900; *The National Income and Product Accounts of the United States,* and *Survey of Current Business.*

U.S. Department of Commerce, Bureau of the Census, Suitland, Maryland 20233 (301) 763-4040; *County Business Patterns,* and *Census of Service Industries.*

U.S. Department of Labor, Bureau of Labor Statistics, Two Massachusetts Avenue, NE, Washington, D.C. 20212 (202) 606-7828; *Employment and Earnings, Monthly Labor Review,* and Bulletins 2370 and 2429.

LEGAL SERVICES - ESTABLISHMENTS

U.S. Department of Commerce, Bureau of the Census, Suitland, Maryland 20233 (301) 763-4040; *County Business Patterns.*

LEGAL SERVICES - FINANCES

U.S. Department of Commerce, Bureau of the Census, Suitland, Maryland 20233 (301) 763-4040; *Census of Service Industries*, *Current Business Reports*, and *Service Annual Survey*.

LEGAL SERVICES - GROSS DOMESTIC PRODUCT

U.S. Department of Commerce, Bureau of Economic Analysis, Fourteenth Street between Constitution Avenue and E Street, NW, Washington, D.C. 20230 (202) 606-9900; *The National Income and Product Accounts of the United States*, and *Survey of Current Business*.

LEGAL SERVICES - OCCUPATIONAL SAFETY

U.S. Department of Labor, Bureau of Labor Statistics, Two Massachusetts Avenue, NE, Washington, D.C. 20212 (202) 606-7828; *Occupational Injuries and Illnesses in the United States by Industry*.

LEGAL SERVICES - RECEIPTS

U.S. Department of Commerce, Bureau of the Census, Suitland, Maryland 20233 (301) 763-4040; *Current Business Reports, Service Annual Survey*, and *Census of Service Industries*.

LEGISLATURES - STATE PARTY COMPOSITION

Council of State Governments, Post Office Box 11910, Iron Works Pike, Lexington, Kentucky 40578 (606) 231-1939 ; *State Elective Officials and the Legislatures*.

National Conference of State Legislatures, 1050 Seventeenth Street, Suite 2100, Denver, Colorado 80265 (303) 623-7800; *State Legislatures*.

LEISURE ACTIVITIES - See RECREATION

LEMONS

U.S. Department of Agriculture, National Agricultural Statistics Service, Fourteenth Street and Independence Avenue, SW, Washington, D.C. 20250 (202) 219-1504; *Citrus Fruits*, and *Economic Indicators of the Farm Sector: National Financial Summary*.

LEND-LEASE - GRANTS AND CREDITS

U.S. Department of Commerce, Bureau of Economic Analysis, Fourteenth Street between Constitution Avenue and E Street, NW, Washington, D.C. 20230 (202) 606-9900; press releases and unpublished data.

LEPROSY

U.S. Department of Health and Human Services, Center for Disease Control, 1600 Clifton Road, NE, Atlanta, Georgia 30333 (404) 639-3311; *Summary of Notifiable Diseases, United States*, and *Morbidity and Mortality Weekly Report*.

Lesotho - National Statistical Office

Bureau of Statistics, Post Office Box 455, Maseru 100, Lesotho.

Lesotho - Primary Statistics Sources

Bureau of Statistics, Post Office Box 455, Maseru 100, Lesotho; *Quarterly Statistical Bulletin*, and *Lesotho Statistical Yearbook*.

LESOTHO - AGRICULTURE

Facts on File, 460 Park Avenue South, New York, New York 10016 (800) 443-8323; *The New Book of World Rankings*.

Food and Agricultural Organization of the United Nations (FAO), Via delle Terme di Caracalla, 00100 Rome, Italy (Telephone Number in U.S. (202) 653-2400); *Production Yearbook, The State of Food and Agriculture*, and *Trade Yearbook*.

G.K. Hall and Company, 70 Lincoln Street, Boston, Massachusetts 02111 (617) 423-3990; *The World in Figures*.

Statistical Office of the United Nations, Publishing Service, New York, New York 10017 (800) 253-9646; *Statistical Yearbook*, and *Survey of Economic and Social Conditions in Africa*.

Times Books, 201 East 50th Street, New York, New York 10022 (212) 751-2600; *The Economist Book of Vital World Statistics*.

United Nations Economic Commission for Africa, Africa Hall, Post Office Box 3001, Addis Ababa, Ethiopia (Telephone Number in U.S. (800) 253-9646); *African Statistical Yearbook*.

The World Bank, 1818 H Street, NW, Washington, D.C. 20433 (202) 477-1234; *World Tables*.

LESOTHO - AIRLINE SERVICE

Facts on File, 460 Park Avenue South, New York, New York 10016 (800) 443-8323; *The New Book of World Rankings*.

G.K. Hall and Company, 70 Lincoln Street, Boston, Massachusetts 02111 (617) 423-3990; *The World in Figures*.

International Civil Aviation Organization, 1000 Sherbrooke Street West, Suite 400, Montreal, Quebec H3A 2R2, Canada (514) 285-8219; *Civil Aviation Statistics of the World*.

Times Books, 201 East 50th Street, New York, New York 10022 (212) 751-2600; *The Economist Book of Vital World Statistics*.

United Nations Economic Commission for Africa, Africa Hall, Post Office Box 3001, Addis Ababa, Ethiopia (Telephone Number in U.S. (800) 253-9646); *African Statistical Yearbook*.

LESOTHO - ALUMINUM PRODUCTION AND CONSUMPTION - See LESOTHO - MINING AND MINERAL PRODUCTS

LESOTHO - ANIMAL HEALTH

Food and Agricultural Organization of the United Nations (FAO), Via delle Terme di Caracalla, 00100 Rome, Italy (Telephone Number in U.S. (202) 653-2400); *Animal Health Yearbook*.

LESOTHO - AREA AND DENSITY OF POPULATION

African Development Bank, 01 BP 1387, Abidjan 01, Cote d'Ivoire; *Selected Statistics on Regional Member Countries*.

Facts on File, 460 Park Avenue South, New York, New York 10016 (800) 443-8323; *The New Book of World Rankings*.

Food and Agricultural Organization of the United Nations (FAO), Via delle Terme di Caracalla, 00100 Rome, Italy (Telephone Number in U.S. (202) 653-2400); *The State of Food and Agriculture*.

G.K. Hall and Company, 70 Lincoln Street, Boston, Massachusetts 02111 (617) 423-3990; *The World in Figures*.

Statistical Office of the United Nations, Publishing Service, New York, New York 10017 (800) 253-9646; *Statistical Yearbook*, and *Survey of Economic and Social Conditions in Africa*.

Times Books, 201 East 50th Street, New York, New York 10022 (212) 751-2600; *The Economist Book of Vital World Statistics*.

LESOTHO - ARMS EXPORTS AND IMPORTS

U.S. Arms Control and Disarmament Agency, 320 Twenty-first Street, NW, Washington, D.C. 20451 (202) 647-8677; *World Military Expenditures and Arms Transfers*.

LESOTHO - BALANCE OF PAYMENTS

African Development Bank, 01 BP 1387, Abidjan 01, Cote d'Ivoire; *Selected Statistics on Regional Member Countries*.

The Economist Intelligence Unit, 111 West 57th Street, New York, New York 10019 (800) 938-4685; *The World Market Atlas*.

G.K. Hall and Company, 70 Lincoln Street, Boston, Massachusetts 02111 (617) 423-3990; *The World in Figures*.

International Monetary Fund, 700 Nineteenth Street, NW, Washington, D.C. 20431 (202) 623-7000; *Balance of Payments Yearbook*.

Times Books, 201 East 50th Street, New York, New York 10022 (212) 751-2600; *The Economist Book of Vital World Statistics*.

United Nations Economic Commission for Africa, Africa Hall, Post Office Box 3001, Addis Ababa, Ethiopia (Telephone Number in U.S. (800) 253-9646); *African Statistical Yearbook*.

The World Bank, 1818 H Street, NW, Washington, D.C. 20433 (202) 477-1234; *World Tables*.

LESOTHO - BANKING

Facts on File, 460 Park Avenue South, New York, New York 10016 (800) 443-8323; *The New Book of World Rankings*.

G.K. Hall and Company, 70 Lincoln Street, Boston, Massachusetts 02111 (617) 423-3990; *The World in Figures*.

International Monetary Fund, 700 Nineteenth Street, NW, Washington, D.C. 20431 (202) 623-7000; *International Financial Statistics*.

United Nations Economic Commission for Africa, Africa Hall, Post Office Box 3001, Addis Ababa, Ethiopia (Telephone Number in U.S. (800) 253-9646); *African Statistical Yearbook*.

LESOTHO - BARLEY PRODUCTION - See LESOTHO - CROPS

LESOTHO - BEER PRODUCTION

Facts on File, 460 Park Avenue South, New York, New York 10016 (800) 443-8323; *The New Book of World Rankings*.

LESOTHO - BIRTH RATES

Facts on File, 460 Park Avenue South, New York, New York 10016 (800) 443-8323; *The New Book of World Rankings*.

Statistical Office of the United Nations, Publishing Service, New York, New York 10017 (800) 253-9646; *Demographic Yearbook, Statistical Yearbook*, and *Survey of Economic and Social Conditions in Africa*.

Times Books, 201 East 50th Street, New York, New York 10022 (212) 751-2600; *The Economist Book of Vital World Statistics*.

The World Bank, 1818 H Street, NW, Washington, D.C. 20433 (202) 477-1234; *World Tables*.

LESOTHO - BONDS

G.K. Hall and Company, 70 Lincoln Street, Boston, Massachusetts 02111 (617) 423-3990; *The World in Figures*.

LESOTHO - BOOK PRODUCTION

G.K. Hall and Company, 70 Lincoln Street, Boston, Massachusetts 02111 (617) 423-3990; *The World in Figures*.

LESOTHO - BROADCASTING

Billboard Limited, Post Office Box 9027, 1006 AA Amsterdam, The Netherlands (Telephone Number in U.S. (212) 704-7000); *World Radio TV Handbook*.

Facts on File, 460 Park Avenue South, New York, New York 10016 (800) 443-8323; *The New Book of World Rankings*.

G.K. Hall and Company, 70 Lincoln Street, Boston, Massachusetts 02111 (617) 423-3990; *The World in Figures*.

Times Books, 201 East 50th Street, New York, New York 10022 (212) 751-2600; *The Economist Book of Vital World Statistics*.

LESOTHO - BUSINESS

G.K. Hall and Company, 70 Lincoln Street, Boston, Massachusetts 02111 (617) 423-3990; *The World in Figures*.

LESOTHO - BUSINESS AND PROFESSIONAL LICENSES

International Monetary Fund, 700 Nineteenth Street, NW, Washington, D.C. 20431 (202) 623-7000; *Government Finance Statistics Yearbook*.

LESOTHO - CALORIE SUPPLY

African Development Bank, 01 BP 1387, Abidjan 01, Cote d'Ivoire; *Selected Statistics on Regional Member Countries*.

Food and Agricultural Organization of the United Nations (FAO), Via delle Terme di Caracalla, 00100 Rome, Italy (Telephone Number in U.S. (202) 653-2400); *The State of Food and Agriculture*.

LESOTHO - CAPITAL REVENUE

International Monetary Fund, 700 Nineteenth Street, NW, Washington, D.C. 20431 (202) 623-7000; *Government Finance Statistics Yearbook*.

LESOTHO - CATTLE - See LESOTHO - LIVESTOCK AND POULTRY

LESOTHO - CEMENT PRODUCTION - See LESOTHO - MINING AND MINERAL PRODUCTS

LESOTHO - CHEMICAL (ORGANIC) PRODUCTION - See LESOTHO - MINING AND MINERAL PRODUCTS

LESOTHO - CHICKENS - See LESOTHO - LIVESTOCK AND POULTRY

LESOTHO - CIGARETTE PRODUCTION - See LESOTHO - TOBACCO PRODUCTION

LESOTHO - CLASS STRUCTURE

G.K. Hall and Company, 70 Lincoln Street, Boston, Massachusetts 02111 (617) 423-3990; *The World in Figures.*

LESOTHO - CLIMATE

Facts on File, 460 Park Avenue South, New York, New York 10016 (800) 443-8323; *The New Book of World Rankings.*

G.K. Hall and Company, 70 Lincoln Street, Boston, Massachusetts 02111 (617) 423-3990; *The World in Figures.*

LESOTHO - COAL PRODUCTION - See LESOTHO - MINING AND MINERAL PRODUCTS

LESOTHO - COFFEE PRODUCTION AND CONSUMPTION - See LESOTHO - CROPS

LESOTHO - COMMUNICATIONS

G.K. Hall and Company, 70 Lincoln Street, Boston, Massachusetts 02111 (617) 423-3990; *The World in Figures.*

United Nations Economic Commission for Africa, Africa Hall, Post Office Box 3001, Addis Ababa, Ethiopia (Telephone Number in U.S. (800) 253-9646); *African Statistical Yearbook.*

LESOTHO - CONSTRUCTION INDUSTRY

Facts on File, 460 Park Avenue South, New York, New York 10016 (800) 443-8323; *The New Book of World Rankings.*

United Nations Economic Commission for Africa, Africa Hall, Post Office Box 3001, Addis Ababa, Ethiopia (Telephone Number in U.S. (800) 253-9646); *African Statistical Yearbook.*

World Intellectual Property Organization, 34 Chemin des Colombettes, CH-1211 Geneva 20, Switzerland; *Industrial Property Statistics.*

LESOTHO - CONSUMER PRICE INDEX

African Development Bank, 01 BP 1387, Abidjan 01, Cote d'Ivoire; *Selected Statistics on Regional Member Countries.*

G.K. Hall and Company, 70 Lincoln Street, Boston, Massachusetts 02111 (617) 423-3990; *The World in Figures.*

Statistical Office of the United Nations, Publishing Service, New York, New York 10017 (800) 253-9646; *Statistical Yearbook,* and *Survey of Economic and Social Conditions in Africa.*

United Nations Economic Commission for Africa, Africa Hall, Post Office Box 3001, Addis Ababa, Ethiopia (Telephone Number in U.S. (800) 253-9646); *African Statistical Yearbook.*

LESOTHO - CONSUMER PRICES

International Labour Office, I.L.O. Publications, CH-1211, Geneva 22, Switzerland; *Yearbook of Labour Statistics.*

International Monetary Fund, 700 Nineteenth Street, NW, Washington, D.C. 20431 (202) 623-7000; *International Financial Statistics.*

Times Books, 201 East 50th Street, New York, New York 10022 (212) 751-2600; *The Economist Book of Vital World Statistics.*

LESOTHO - CONSUMPTION

African Development Bank, 01 BP 1387, Abidjan 01, Cote d'Ivoire; *Selected Statistics on Regional Member Countries.*

G.K. Hall and Company, 70 Lincoln Street, Boston, Massachusetts 02111 (617) 423-3990; *The World in Figures.*

Statistical Office of the United Nations, Publishing Service, New York, New York 10017 (800) 253-9646; *Survey of Economic and Social Conditions in Africa.*

LESOTHO - COPPER PRODUCTION AND CONSUMPTION - See LESOTHO - MINING AND MINERAL PRODUCTS

LESOTHO - CORN PRODUCTION - See LESOTHO - CROPS

LESOTHO - CORPORATE TAXES - See LESOTHO - TAXATION

LESOTHO - COTTON PRODUCTION - See LESOTHO - CROPS

LESOTHO - CRIME

International Criminal Police Organization (INTERPOL), 26 rue Armengaud, 92210 Saint Cloud, France; *International Crime Statistics.*

LESOTHO - CROPS

Facts on File, 460 Park Avenue South, New York, New York 10016 (800) 443-8323; *The New Book of World Rankings.*

Food and Agricultural Organization of the United Nations (FAO), Via delle Terme di Caracalla, 00100 Rome, Italy (Telephone Number in U.S. (202) 653-2400); *The State of Food and Agriculture.*

G.K. Hall and Company, 70 Lincoln Street, Boston, Massachusetts 02111 (617) 423-3990; *The World in Figures.*

Statistical Office of the United Nations, Publishing Service, New York, New York 10017 (800) 253-9646; *Statistical Yearbook.*

United Nations Economic Commission for Africa, Africa Hall, Post Office Box 3001, Addis Ababa, Ethiopia (Telephone Number in U.S. (800) 253-9646); *African Statistical Yearbook.*

LESOTHO - CUSTOMS DUTIES

G.K. Hall and Company, 70 Lincoln Street, Boston, Massachusetts 02111 (617) 423-3990; *The World in Figures.*

International Monetary Fund, 700 Nineteenth Street, NW, Washington, D.C. 20431 (202) 623-7000; *Government Finance Statistics Yearbook.*

LESOTHO - DAIRY PRODUCTS

Facts on File, 460 Park Avenue South, New York, New York 10016 (800) 443-8323; *The New Book of World Rankings*.

Food and Agricultural Organization of the United Nations (FAO), Via delle Terme di Caracalla, 00100 Rome, Italy (Telephone Number in U.S. (202) 653-2400); *The State of Food and Agriculture*.

LESOTHO - DEATH RATES

G.K. Hall and Company, 70 Lincoln Street, Boston, Massachusetts 02111 (617) 423-3990; *The World in Figures*.

Statistical Office of the United Nations, Publishing Service, New York, New York 10017 (800) 253-9646; *Statistical Yearbook*, and *Survey of Economic and Social Conditions in Africa*.

Times Books, 201 East 50th Street, New York, New York 10022 (212) 751-2600; *The Economist Book of Vital World Statistics*.

LESOTHO - DEFENSE EXPENDITURES

G.K. Hall and Company, 70 Lincoln Street, Boston, Massachusetts 02111 (617) 423-3990; *The World in Figures*.

U.S. Arms Control and Disarmament Agency, 320 Twenty-first Street, NW, Washington, D.C. 20451 (202) 647-8677; *World Military Expenditures and Arms Transfers*.

LESOTHO - DEMOGRAPHY

The Economist Intelligence Unit, 111 West 57th Street, New York, New York 10019 (800) 938-4685; *The World Market Atlas*.

Facts on File, 460 Park Avenue South, New York, New York 10016 (800) 443-8323; *The New Book of World Rankings*.

G.K. Hall and Company, 70 Lincoln Street, Boston, Massachusetts 02111 (617) 423-3990; *The World in Figures*.

Statistical Office of the United Nations, Publishing Service, New York, New York 10017 (800) 253-9646; *Survey of Economic and Social Conditions in Africa*.

LESOTHO - DEVELOPMENT ASSISTANCE

G.K. Hall and Company, 70 Lincoln Street, Boston, Massachusetts 02111 (617) 423-3990; *The World in Figures*.

Statistical Office of the United Nations, Publishing Service, New York, New York 10017 (800) 253-9646; *Statistical Yearbook*.

LESOTHO - DIAMOND PRODUCTION - See LESOTHO - MINING AND MINERAL PRODUCTS

LESOTHO - DISEASE

G.K. Hall and Company, 70 Lincoln Street, Boston, Massachusetts 02111 (617) 423-3990; *The World in Figures*.

LESOTHO - DIVORCE

Facts on File, 460 Park Avenue South, New York, New York 10016 (800) 443-8323; *The New Book of World Rankings*.

Statistical Office of the United Nations, Publishing Service, New York, New York 10017 (800) 253-9646; *Demographic Yearbook*.

LESOTHO - DOMESTIC PRODUCT

G.K. Hall and Company, 70 Lincoln Street, Boston, Massachusetts 02111 (617) 423-3990; *The World in Figures*.

LESOTHO - ECONOMY

African Development Bank, 01 BP 1387, Abidjan 01, Cote d'Ivoire; *Selected Statistics on Regional Member Countries*.

Facts on File, 460 Park Avenue South, New York, New York 10016 (800) 443-8323; *The New Book of World Rankings*.

G.K. Hall and Company, 70 Lincoln Street, Boston, Massachusetts 02111 (617) 423-3990; *The World in Figures*.

LESOTHO - EDUCATION

African Development Bank, 01 BP 1387, Abidjan 01, Cote d'Ivoire; *Selected Statistics on Regional Member Countries*.

The Economist Intelligence Unit, 111 West 57th Street, New York, New York 10019 (800) 938-4685; *The World Market Atlas*.

Facts on File, 460 Park Avenue South, New York, New York 10016 (800) 443-8323; *The New Book of World Rankings*.

G.K. Hall and Company, 70 Lincoln Street, Boston, Massachusetts 02111 (617) 423-3990; *The World in Figures*.

International Monetary Fund, 700 Nineteenth Street, NW, Washington, D.C. 20431 (202) 623-7000; *Government Finance Statistics Yearbook*.

Statistical Office of the United Nations, Publishing Service, New York, New York 10017 (800) 253-9646; *Survey of Economic and Social Conditions in Africa*.

Times Books, 201 East 50th Street, New York, New York 10022 (212) 751-2600; *The Economist Book of Vital World Statistics*.

United Nations Economic Commission for Africa, Africa Hall, Post Office Box 3001, Addis Ababa, Ethiopia (Telephone Number in U.S. (800) 253-9646); *African Statistical Yearbook*.

United Nations Educational, Scientific and Cultural Organization (UNESCO), 7 Place de Fontenoy, F-75700 Paris, France (Telephone Number in U.S. (212) 963-5981); *Statistical Yearbook*.

The World Bank, 1818 H Street, NW, Washington, D.C. 20433 (202) 477-1234; *World Tables*.

LESOTHO - EGG PRODUCTION AND CONSUMPTION - See LESOTHO - DAIRY PRODUCTS

LESOTHO - ELECTRICITY

Statistical Office of the United Nations, Publishing Service, New York, New York 10017 (800) 253-9646; *Survey of Economic and Social Conditions in Africa*.

United Nations Economic Commission for Africa, Africa Hall, Post Office Box 3001, Addis Ababa, Ethiopia (Telephone Number in U.S. (800) 253-9646); *African Statistical Yearbook*.

LESOTHO - EMPLOYMENT

Facts on File, 460 Park Avenue South, New York, New York 10016 (800) 443-8323; *The New Book of World Rankings*.

International Labour Office, I.L.O. Publications, CH-1211, Geneva 22, Switzerland; *Yearbook of Labour Statistics.*

Statistical Office of the United Nations, Publishing Service, New York, New York 10017 (800) 253-9646; *Survey of Economic and Social Conditions in Africa.*

United Nations Economic Commission for Africa, Africa Hall, Post Office Box 3001, Addis Ababa, Ethiopia (Telephone Number in U.S. (800) 253-9646); *African Statistical Yearbook.*

LESOTHO - ENERGY

Facts on File, 460 Park Avenue South, New York, New York 10016 (800) 443-8323; *The New Book of World Rankings.*

Food and Agricultural Organization of the United Nations (FAO), Via delle Terme di Caracalla, 00100 Rome, Italy (Telephone Number in U.S. (202) 653-2400); *The State of Food and Agriculture.*

G.K. Hall and Company, 70 Lincoln Street, Boston, Massachusetts 02111 (617) 423-3990; *The World in Figures.*

Statistical Office of the United Nations, Publishing Service, New York, New York 10017 (800) 253-9646; *Energy Statistics Yearbook.*

United Nations Economic Commission for Africa, Africa Hall, Post Office Box 3001, Addis Ababa, Ethiopia (Telephone Number in U.S. (800) 253-9646); *African Statistical Yearbook.*

LESOTHO - EXCHANGE RATES

African Development Bank, 01 BP 1387, Abidjan 01, Cote d'Ivoire; *Selected Statistics on Regional Member Countries.*

International Civil Aviation Organization, 1000 Sherbrooke Street West, Suite 400, Montreal, Quebec H3A 2R2, Canada (514) 285-8219; *Civil Aviation Statistics of the World.*

International Monetary Fund, 700 Nineteenth Street, NW, Washington, D.C. 20431 (202) 623-7000; *International Financial Statistics.*

Statistical Office of the United Nations, Publishing Service, New York, New York 10017 (800) 253-9646; *Statistical Yearbook.*

LESOTHO - EXPORTS

African Development Bank, 01 BP 1387, Abidjan 01, Cote d'Ivoire; *Selected Statistics on Regional Member Countries.*

The Economist Intelligence Unit, 111 West 57th Street, New York, New York 10019 (800) 938-4685; *The World Market Atlas.*

Food and Agricultural Organization of the United Nations (FAO), Via delle Terme di Caracalla, 00100 Rome, Italy (Telephone Number in U.S. (202) 653-2400); *The State of Food and Agriculture.*

G.K. Hall and Company, 70 Lincoln Street, Boston, Massachusetts 02111 (617) 423-3990; *The World in Figures.*

International Monetary Fund, 700 Nineteenth Street, NW, Washington, D.C. 20431 (202) 623-7000; *Direction of Trade Statistics,* and *Government Finance Statistics Yearbook.*

Statistical Office of the United Nations, Publishing Service, New York, New York 10017 (800) 253-9646; *Survey of Economic and Social Conditions in Africa.*

Times Books, 201 East 50th Street, New York, New York 10022 (212) 751-2600; *The Economist Book of Vital World Statistics.*

United Nations Economic Commission for Africa, Africa Hall, Post Office Box 3001, Addis Ababa, Ethiopia (Telephone Number in U.S. (800) 253-9646); *African Statistical Yearbook.*

The World Bank, 1818 H Street, NW, Washington, D.C. 20433 (202) 477-1234; *World Tables.*

LESOTHO - EXTERNAL INDEBTEDNESS

African Development Bank, 01 BP 1387, Abidjan 01, Cote d'Ivoire; *Selected Statistics on Regional Member Countries.*

Statistical Office of the United Nations, Publishing Service, New York, New York 10017 (800) 253-9646; *Survey of Economic and Social Conditions in Africa.*

The World Bank, 1818 H Street, NW, Washington, D.C. 20433 (202) 477-1234; *World Tables.*

LESOTHO - EXTERNAL TRADE

African Development Bank, 01 BP 1387, Abidjan 01, Cote d'Ivoire; *Selected Statistics on Regional Member Countries.*

Food and Agricultural Organization of the United Nations (FAO), Via delle Terme di Caracalla, 00100 Rome, Italy (Telephone Number in U.S. (202) 653-2400); *The State of Food and Agriculture,* and *Trade Yearbook.*

G.K. Hall and Company, 70 Lincoln Street, Boston, Massachusetts 02111 (617) 423-3990; *The World in Figures.*

LESOTHO - FARM CROPS - See LESOTHO - CROPS

LESOTHO - FERTILITY RATE

Facts on File, 460 Park Avenue South, New York, New York 10016 (800) 443-8323; *The New Book of World Rankings.*

Statistical Office of the United Nations, Publishing Service, New York, New York 10017 (800) 253-9646; *Survey of Economic and Social Conditions in Africa.*

Times Books, 201 East 50th Street, New York, New York 10022 (212) 751-2600; *The Economist Book of Vital World Statistics.*

The World Bank, 1818 H Street, NW, Washington, D.C. 20433 (202) 477-1234; *World Tables.*

LESOTHO - FERTILIZER

Food and Agricultural Organization of the United Nations (FAO), Via delle Terme di Caracalla, 00100 Rome, Italy (Telephone Number in U.S. (202) 653-2400); *Fertilizer Yearbook,* and *The State of Food and Agriculture.*

Statistical Office of the United Nations, Publishing Service, New York, New York 10017 (800) 253-9646; *Statistical Yearbook.*

LESOTHO - FETAL MORTALITY

Statistical Office of the United Nations, Publishing Service, New York, New York 10017 (800) 253-9646; *Demographic Yearbook.*

LESOTHO - FINANCE

African Development Bank, 01 BP 1387, Abidjan 01, Cote d'Ivoire; *Selected Statistics on Regional Member Countries*.

Facts on File, 460 Park Avenue South, New York, New York 10016 (800) 443-8323; *The New Book of World Rankings*.

G.K. Hall and Company, 70 Lincoln Street, Boston, Massachusetts 02111 (617) 423-3990; *The World in Figures*.

International Monetary Fund, 700 Nineteenth Street, NW, Washington, D.C. 20431 (202) 623-7000; *Government Finance Statistics Yearbook*.

United Nations Economic Commission for Africa, Africa Hall, Post Office Box 3001, Addis Ababa, Ethiopia (Telephone Number in U.S. (800) 253-9646); *African Statistical Yearbook*.

LESOTHO - FISHERIES

Facts on File, 460 Park Avenue South, New York, New York 10016 (800) 443-8323; *The New Book of World Rankings*.

Food and Agricultural Organization of the United Nations (FAO), Via delle Terme di Caracalla, 00100 Rome, Italy (Telephone Number in U.S. (202) 653-2400); *The State of Food and Agriculture*, and *Yearbook of Fishery Statistics*.

Statistical Office of the United Nations, Publishing Service, New York, New York 10017 (800) 253-9646; *Survey of Economic and Social Conditions in Africa*.

United Nations Economic Commission for Africa, Africa Hall, Post Office Box 3001, Addis Ababa, Ethiopia (Telephone Number in U.S. (800) 253-9646); *African Statistical Yearbook*.

LESOTHO - FOOD

African Development Bank, 01 BP 1387, Abidjan 01, Cote d'Ivoire; *Selected Statistics on Regional Member Countries*.

Food and Agricultural Organization of the United Nations (FAO), Via delle Terme di Caracalla, 00100 Rome, Italy (Telephone Number in U.S. (202) 653-2400); *The State of Food and Agriculture*, and *Production Yearbook*.

G.K. Hall and Company, 70 Lincoln Street, Boston, Massachusetts 02111 (617) 423-3990; *The World in Figures*.

LESOTHO - FOREIGN AID

G.K. Hall and Company, 70 Lincoln Street, Boston, Massachusetts 02111 (617) 423-3990; *The World in Figures*.

LESOTHO - FOREIGN TRADE

Facts on File, 460 Park Avenue South, New York, New York 10016 (800) 443-8323; *The New Book of World Rankings*.

Food and Agricultural Organization of the United Nations (FAO), Via delle Terme di Caracalla, 00100 Rome, Italy (Telephone Number in U.S. (202) 653-2400); *The State of Food and Agriculture*.

G.K. Hall and Company, 70 Lincoln Street, Boston, Massachusetts 02111 (617) 423-3990; *The World in Figures*.

United Nations Economic Commission for Africa, Africa Hall, Post Office Box 3001, Addis Ababa, Ethiopia (Telephone Number in U.S.

(800) 253-9646); *African Statistical Yearbook*.

The World Bank, 1818 H Street, NW, Washington, D.C. 20433 (202) 477-1234; *World Tables*.

LESOTHO - FORESTRY AND FOREST PRODUCTS

Facts on File, 460 Park Avenue South, New York, New York 10016 (800) 443-8323; *The New Book of World Rankings*.

Food and Agricultural Organization of the United Nations (FAO), Via delle Terme di Caracalla, 00100 Rome, Italy (Telephone Number in U.S. (202) 653-2400); *The State of Food and Agriculture*, and *Yearbook of Forest Products*.

G.K. Hall and Company, 70 Lincoln Street, Boston, Massachusetts 02111 (617) 423-3990; *The World in Figures*.

Statistical Office of the United Nations, Publishing Service, New York, New York 10017 (800) 253-9646; *Statistical Yearbook*.

United Nations Economic Commission for Africa, Africa Hall, Post Office Box 3001, Addis Ababa, Ethiopia (Telephone Number in U.S. (800) 253-9646); *African Statistical Yearbook*.

United Nations Educational, Scientific and Cultural Organization (UNESCO), 7 Place de Fontenoy, F-75700 Paris, France (Telephone Number in U.S. (212) 963-5981); *Statistical Yearbook*.

LESOTHO - GAS PRODUCTION See LESOTHO - MINING AND MINERAL PRODUCTS

LESOTHO - GENERAL MORTALITY

Statistical Office of the United Nations, Publishing Service, New York, New York 10017 (800) 253-9646; *Demographic Yearbook*.

LESOTHO - GEOGRAPHIC DATA

Facts on File, 460 Park Avenue South, New York, New York 10016 (800) 443-8323; *The New Book of World Rankings*.

LESOTHO - GOATS - See LESOTHO - LIVESTOCK AND POULTRY

LESOTHO - GOLD HOLDINGS

The World Bank, 1818 H Street, NW, Washington, D.C. 20433 (202) 477-1234; *World Tables*.

LESOTHO - GOLD PRODUCTION AND CONSUMPTION - See LESOTHO - MINING AND MINERAL PRODUCTS

LESOTHO - GOVERNMENT

G.K. Hall and Company, 70 Lincoln Street, Boston, Massachusetts 02111 (617) 423-3990; *The World in Figures*.

LESOTHO - GOVERNMENT EXPENDITURE

The World Bank, 1818 H Street, NW, Washington, D.C. 20433 (202) 477-1234; *World Tables*.

LESOTHO - GOVERNMENT REVENUES

International Monetary Fund, 700 Nineteenth Street, NW, Washington, D.C. 20431 (202) 623-7000; *Government Finance Statistics Yearbook*.

Statistical Office of the United Nations, Publishing Service, New York, New York 10017 (800) 253-9646; *Survey of Economic and Social Conditions in Africa*.

Times Books, 201 East 50th Street, New York, New York 10022 (212) 751-2600; *The Economist Book of Vital World Statistics*.

The World Bank, 1818 H Street, NW, Washington, D.C. 20433 (202) 477-1234; *World Tables*.

LESOTHO - GRAIN PRODUCTION - See LESOTHO - CROPS

LESOTHO - GRANTS

International Monetary Fund, 700 Nineteenth Street, NW, Washington, D.C. 20431 (202) 623-7000; *Government Finance Statistics Yearbook*.

LESOTHO - GROSS DOMESTIC PRODUCT

African Development Bank, 01 BP 1387, Abidjan 01, Cote d'Ivoire; *Selected Statistics on Regional Member Countries*.

The Economist Intelligence Unit, 111 West 57th Street, New York, New York 10019 (800) 938-4685; *The World Market Atlas*.

Facts on File, 460 Park Avenue South, New York, New York 10016 (800) 443-8323; *The New Book of World Rankings*.

G.K. Hall and Company, 70 Lincoln Street, Boston, Massachusetts 02111 (617) 423-3990; *The World in Figures*.

Statistical Office of the United Nations, Publishing Service, New York, New York 10017 (800) 253-9646; *Statistical Yearbook*, and *Survey of Economic and Social Conditions in Africa*.

Times Books, 201 East 50th Street, New York, New York 10022 (212) 751-2600; *The Economist Book of Vital World Statistics*.

United Nations Economic Commission for Africa, Africa Hall, Post Office Box 3001, Addis Ababa, Ethiopia (Telephone Number in U.S. (800) 253-9646); *African Statistical Yearbook*.

The World Bank, 1818 H Street, NW, Washington, D.C. 20433 (202) 477-1234; *World Tables*.

LESOTHO - GROSS NATIONAL PRODUCT

U.S. Arms Control and Disarmament Agency, 320 Twenty-first Street, NW, Washington, D.C. 20451 (202) 647-8677; *World Military Expenditures and Arms Transfers*.

The World Bank, 1818 H Street, NW, Washington, D.C. 20433 (202) 477-1234; *World Tables*.

LESOTHO - HEALTH

African Development Bank, 01 BP 1387, Abidjan 01, Cote d'Ivoire; *Selected Statistics on Regional Member Countries*.

Facts on File, 460 Park Avenue South, New York, New York 10016 (800) 443-8323; *The New Book of World Rankings*.

G.K. Hall and Company, 70 Lincoln Street, Boston, Massachusetts 02111 (617) 423-3990; *The World in Figures*.

Statistical Office of the United Nations, Publishing Service, New York, New York 10017 (800) 253-9646; *Statistical Yearbook*.

Times Books, 201 East 50th Street, New York, New York 10022 (212) 751-2600; *The Economist Book of Vital World Statistics*.

United Nations Economic Commission for Africa, Africa Hall, Post Office Box 3001, Addis Ababa, Ethiopia (Telephone Number in U.S. (800) 253-9646); *African Statistical Yearbook*.

LESOTHO - HEALTH EXPENDITURES

International Monetary Fund, 700 Nineteenth Street, NW, Washington, D.C. 20431 (202) 623-7000; *Government Finance Statistics Yearbook*.

LESOTHO - HIDE PRODUCTION

Food and Agricultural Organization of the United Nations (FAO), Via delle Terme di Caracalla, 00100 Rome, Italy (Telephone Number in U.S. (202) 653-2400); *Production Yearbook*.

LESOTHO - HIGHWAYS

G.K. Hall and Company, 70 Lincoln Street, Boston, Massachusetts 02111 (617) 423-3990; *The World in Figures*.

International Road Federation, 525 School Street, SW, Washington, D.C. 20024 (202) 554-2106; *World Road Statistics*.

Statistical Office of the United Nations, Publishing Service, New York, New York 10017 (800) 253-9646; *Survey of Economic and Social Conditions in Africa*.

United Nations Economic Commission for Africa, Africa Hall, Post Office Box 3001, Addis Ababa, Ethiopia (Telephone Number in U.S. (800) 253-9646); *African Statistical Yearbook*.

LESOTHO - HORSES - See LESOTHO - LIVESTOCK AND POULTRY

LESOTHO - HOURS OF WORK - See LESOTHO - EMPLOYMENT

LESOTHO - HOUSING

Facts on File, 460 Park Avenue South, New York, New York 10016 (800) 443-8323; *The New Book of World Rankings*.

International Monetary Fund, 700 Nineteenth Street, NW, Washington, D.C. 20431 (202) 623-7000; *Government Finance Statistics Yearbook*.

LESOTHO - ILLITERATE POPULATION

The Economist Intelligence Unit, 111 West 57th Street, New York, New York 10019 (800) 938-4685; *The World Market Atlas*.

G.K. Hall and Company, 70 Lincoln Street, Boston, Massachusetts 02111 (617) 423-3990; *The World in Figures*.

United Nations Educational, Scientific and Cultural Organization (UNESCO), 7 Place de Fontenoy, F-75700 Paris, France (Telephone Number in U.S. (212) 963-5981); *Statistical Yearbook*.

LESOTHO - IMPORTS

African Development Bank, 01 BP 1387, Abidjan 01, Cote d'Ivoire; *Selected Statistics on Regional Member Countries*.

The Economist Intelligence Unit, 111 West 57th Street, New York, New York 10019 (800) 938-4685; *The World Market Atlas*.

Food and Agricultural Organization of the United Nations (FAO), Via delle Terme di Caracalla, 00100 Rome, Italy (Telephone Number in U.S. (202) 653-2400); *The State of Food and Agriculture*.

G.K. Hall and Company, 70 Lincoln Street, Boston, Massachusetts 02111 (617) 423-3990; *The World in Figures*.

International Monetary Fund, 700 Nineteenth Street, NW, Washington, D.C. 20431 (202) 623-7000; *Direction of Trade Statistics*, and *Government Finance Statistics Yearbook*.

Statistical Office of the United Nations, Publishing Service, New York, New York 10017 (800) 253-9646; *Survey of Economic and Social Conditions in Africa*.

United Nations Economic Commission for Africa, Africa Hall, Post Office Box 3001, Addis Ababa, Ethiopia (Telephone Number in U.S. (800) 253-9646); *African Statistical Yearbook*.

The World Bank, 1818 H Street, NW, Washington, D.C. 20433 (202) 477-1234; *World Tables*.

LESOTHO - INCOME TAXES - See LESOTHO - TAXATION

LESOTHO - INDUSTRY

Facts on File, 460 Park Avenue South, New York, New York 10016 (800) 443-8323; *The New Book of World Rankings*.

G.K. Hall and Company, 70 Lincoln Street, Boston, Massachusetts 02111 (617) 423-3990; *The World in Figures*.

International Labour Office, I.L.O. Publications, CH-1211, Geneva 22, Switzerland; *Yearbook of Labour Statistics*.

Times Books, 201 East 50th Street, New York, New York 10022 (212) 751-2600; *The Economist Book of Vital World Statistics*.

Statistical Office of the United Nations, Publishing Service, New York, New York 10017 (800) 253-9646; *Survey of Economic and Social Conditions in Africa*.

United Nations Economic Commission for Africa, Africa Hall, Post Office Box 3001, Addis Ababa, Ethiopia (Telephone Number in U.S. (800) 253-9646); *African Statistical Yearbook*.

The World Bank, 1818 H Street, NW, Washington, D.C. 20433 (202) 477-1234; *World Tables*.

LESOTHO - INFANT AND MATERNAL MORTALITY

Statistical Office of the United Nations, Publishing Service, New York, New York 10017 (800) 253-9646; *Demographic Yearbook*, *Statistical Yearbook*, and *Survey of Economic and Social Conditions in Africa*.

Times Books, 201 East 50th Street, New York, New York 10022 (212) 751-2600; *The Economist Book of Vital World Statistics*.

The World Bank, 1818 H Street, NW, Washington, D.C. 20433 (202) 477-1234; *World Tables*.

LESOTHO - INTERNATIONAL LIQUIDITY

International Monetary Fund, 700 Nineteenth Street, NW, Washington, D.C. 20431 (202) 623-7000; *International Financial Statistics*.

LESOTHO - INTERNATIONAL RESERVES EXCLUDING GOLD

African Development Bank, 01 BP 1387, Abidjan 01, Cote d'Ivoire; *Selected Statistics on Regional Member Countries*.

Statistical Office of the United Nations, Publishing Service, New York, New York 10017 (800) 253-9646; *Statistical Yearbook*.

The World Bank, 1818 H Street, NW, Washington, D.C. 20433 (202) 477-1234; *World Tables*.

LESOTHO - IRON ORE PRODUCTION AND CONSUMPTION - See LESOTHO - MINING AND MINERAL PRODUCTS

LESOTHO - LABOR FORCE

African Development Bank, 01 BP 1387, Abidjan 01, Cote d'Ivoire; *Selected Statistics on Regional Member Countries*.

Facts on File, 460 Park Avenue South, New York, New York 10016 (800) 443-8323; *The New Book of World Rankings*.

Food and Agricultural Organization of the United Nations (FAO), Via delle Terme di Caracalla, 00100 Rome, Italy (Telephone Number in U.S. (202) 653-2400); *The State of Food and Agriculture*.

G.K. Hall and Company, 70 Lincoln Street, Boston, Massachusetts 02111 (617) 423-3990; *The World in Figures*.

Times Books, 201 East 50th Street, New York, New York 10022 (212) 751-2600; *The Economist Book of Vital World Statistics*.

The World Bank, 1818 H Street, NW, Washington, D.C. 20433 (202) 477-1234; *World Tables*.

LESOTHO - LABOR PRODUCTIVITY

International Labour Office, I.L.O. Publications, CH-1211, Geneva 22, Switzerland; *Yearbook of Labour Statistics*.

LESOTHO - LAND USE

Food and Agricultural Organization of the United Nations (FAO), Via delle Terme di Caracalla, 00100 Rome, Italy (Telephone Number in U.S. (202) 653-2400); *Production Yearbook*.

G.K. Hall and Company, 70 Lincoln Street, Boston, Massachusetts 02111 (617) 423-3990; *The World in Figures*.

LESOTHO - LIBRARIES

Facts on File, 460 Park Avenue South, New York, New York 10016 (800) 443-8323; *The New Book of World Rankings*.

LESOTHO - LIFE EXPECTANCY

African Development Bank, 01 BP 1387, Abidjan 01, Cote d'Ivoire; *Selected Statistics on Regional Member Countries*.

LESOTHO - LITERACY RATE

Statistical Office of the United Nations, Publishing Service, New York, New York 10017 (800) 253-9646; *Survey of Economic and Social Conditions in Africa*.

LESOTHO - LIVESTOCK AND POULTRY

Facts on File, 460 Park Avenue South, New York, New York 10016 (800) 443-8323; *The New Book of World Rankings*.

Food and Agricultural Organization of the United Nations (FAO), Via delle Terme di Caracalla, 00100 Rome, Italy (Telephone Number in U.S. (202) 653-2400); *Production Yearbook*, and *The State of Food and Agriculture*.

G.K. Hall and Company, 70 Lincoln Street, Boston, Massachusetts 02111 (617) 423-3990; *The World in Figures*.

Statistical Office of the United Nations, Publishing Service, New York, New York 10017 (800) 253-9646; *Statistical Yearbook*, and *Survey of Economic and Social Conditions in Africa*.

United Nations Economic Commission for Africa, Africa Hall, Post Office Box 3001, Addis Ababa, Ethiopia (Telephone Number in U.S. (800) 253-9646); *African Statistical Yearbook*.

LESOTHO - LIVING LEVELS

G.K. Hall and Company, 70 Lincoln Street, Boston, Massachusetts 02111 (617) 423-3990; *The World in Figures*.

Times Books, 201 East 50th Street, New York, New York 10022 (212) 751-2600; *The Economist Book of Vital World Statistics*.

LESOTHO - MAIL - NUMBER OF ITEMS SENT AND RECEIVED

Statistical Office of the United Nations, Publishing Service, New York, New York 10017 (800) 253-9646; *Statistical Yearbook*.

LESOTHO - MANUFACTURING

Facts on File, 460 Park Avenue South, New York, New York 10016 (800) 443-8323; *The New Book of World Rankings*.

G.K. Hall and Company, 70 Lincoln Street, Boston, Massachusetts 02111 (617) 423-3990; *The World in Figures*.

Statistical Office of the United Nations, Publishing Service, New York, New York 10017 (800) 253-9646; *Survey of Economic and Social Conditions in Africa*.

United Nations Economic Commission for Africa, Africa Hall, Post Office Box 3001, Addis Ababa, Ethiopia (Telephone Number in U.S. (800) 253-9646); *African Statistical Yearbook*.

The World Bank, 1818 H Street, NW, Washington, D.C. 20433 (202) 477-1234; *World Tables*.

LESOTHO - MARRIAGE RATES

Facts on File, 460 Park Avenue South, New York, New York 10016 (800) 443-8323; *The New Book of World Rankings*.

Statistical Office of the United Nations, Publishing Service, New York, New York 10017 (800) 253-9646; *Demographic Yearbook*, and *Statistical Yearbook*.

LESOTHO - MEAT PRODUCTION - See LESOTHO - LIVESTOCK AND POULTRY

LESOTHO - MERCHANT SHIPPING

G.K. Hall and Company, 70 Lincoln Street, Boston, Massachusetts 02111 (617) 423-3990; *The World in Figures*.

United Nations Economic Commission for Africa, Africa Hall, Post Office Box 3001, Addis Ababa, Ethiopia (Telephone Number in U.S. (800) 253-9646); *African Statistical Yearbook*.

LESOTHO - MILITARY

G.K. Hall and Company, 70 Lincoln Street, Boston, Massachusetts 02111 (617) 423-3990; *The World in Figures*.

The International Institute for Strategic Studies, 23 Tavistock Street, London WC2E 7NQ, England; *The Military Balance*.

U.S. Arms Control and Disarmament Agency, 320 Twenty-first Street, NW, Washington, D.C. 20451 (202) 647-8677; *World Military Expenditures and Arms Transfers*.

LESOTHO - MILK PRODUCTION - See LESOTHO - DAIRY PRODUCTS

LESOTHO - MINING AND MINERAL PRODUCTS

Facts on File, 460 Park Avenue South, New York, New York 10016 (800) 443-8323; *The New Book of World Rankings*.

G.K. Hall and Company, 70 Lincoln Street, Boston, Massachusetts 02111 (617) 423-3990; *The World in Figures*.

Statistical Office of the United Nations, Publishing Service, New York, New York 10017 (800) 253-9646; *Statistical Yearbook*.

United Nations Economic Commission for Africa, Africa Hall, Post Office Box 3001, Addis Ababa, Ethiopia (Telephone Number in U.S. (800) 253-9646); *African Statistical Yearbook*.

LESOTHO - MONEY EXCHANGE RATE

International Monetary Fund, 700 Nineteenth Street, NW, Washington, D.C. 20431 (202) 623-7000; *International Financial Statistics*.

Statistical Office of the United Nations, Publishing Service, New York, New York 10017 (800) 253-9646; *Statistical Yearbook*.

LESOTHO - MONEY SUPPLY

African Development Bank, 01 BP 1387, Abidjan 01, Cote d'Ivoire; *Selected Statistics on Regional Member Countries*.

G.K. Hall and Company, 70 Lincoln Street, Boston, Massachusetts 02111 (617) 423-3990; *The World in Figures*.

International Monetary Fund, 700 Nineteenth Street, NW, Washington, D.C. 20431 (202) 623-7000; *International Financial Statistics*.

LESOTHO - MOTOR VEHICLE TAXES - See LESOTHO - TAXATION

LESOTHO - MOTOR VEHICLES IN USE

G.K. Hall and Company, 70 Lincoln Street, Boston, Massachusetts 02111 (617) 423-3990; *The World in Figures*.

International Road Federation, 525 School Street, SW, Washington, D.C. 20024 (202) 554-2106; *World Road Statistics*.

Statistical Office of the United Nations, Publishing Service, New York, New York 10017 (800) 253-9646; *Statistical Yearbook*, and *Survey of Economic and Social Conditions in Africa*.

LESOTHO - MULES - See LESOTHO - LIVESTOCK AND POULTRY

LESOTHO - MUSEUMS

Facts on File, 460 Park Avenue South, New York, New York 10016 (800) 443-8323; *The New Book of World Rankings.*

United Nations Educational, Scientific and Cultural Organization (UNESCO), 7 Place de Fontenoy, F-75700 Paris, France (Telephone Number in U.S. (212) 963-5981); *Statistical Yearbook.*

LESOTHO - NATALITY - See LESOTHO - BIRTH RATES

LESOTHO - NATIONAL ACCOUNTS

African Development Bank, 01 BP 1387, Abidjan 01, Cote d'Ivoire; *Selected Statistics on Regional Member Countries.*

Statistical Office of the United Nations, Publishing Service, New York, New York 10017 (800) 253-9646; *National Accounts Statistics,* and *Statistical Yearbook.*

United Nations Economic Commission for Africa, Africa Hall, Post Office Box 3001, Addis Ababa, Ethiopia (Telephone Number in U.S. (800) 253-9646); *African Statistical Yearbook.*

LESOTHO - NATIONAL INCOME

Facts on File, 460 Park Avenue South, New York, New York 10016 (800) 443-8323; *The New Book of World Rankings.*

G.K. Hall and Company, 70 Lincoln Street, Boston, Massachusetts 02111 (617) 423-3990; *The World in Figures.*

Statistical Office of the United Nations, Publishing Service, New York, New York 10017 (800) 253-9646; *Statistical Yearbook.*

LESOTHO - NATIONAL PRODUCT

Facts on File, 460 Park Avenue South, New York, New York 10016 (800) 443-8323; *The New Book of World Rankings.*

LESOTHO - NATURAL GAS - PRODUCTION - See LESOTHO - MINING AND MINERAL PRODUCTS

LESOTHO - NEWSPAPER PRODUCTION - See LESOTHO - FORESTRY AND FOREST PRODUCTS

LESOTHO - OCCUPATIONS - See LESOTHO - LABOR FORCE

LESOTHO - PATENTS

World Intellectual Property Organization, 34 Chemin des Colombettes, CH-1211 Geneva 20, Switzerland; *Industrial Property Statistics.*

LESOTHO - PEANUT PRODUCTION - See LESOTHO - CROPS

LESOTHO - PESTICIDE USE

Food and Agricultural Organization of the United Nations (FAO), Via delle Terme di Caracalla, 00100 Rome, Italy (Telephone Number in U.S. (202) 653-2400); *The State of Food and Agriculture.*

LESOTHO - PETROLEUM INDUSTRY

Facts on File, 460 Park Avenue South, New York, New York 10016 (800) 443-8323; *The New Book of World Rankings.*

Food and Agricultural Organization of the United Nations (FAO), Via delle Terme di Caracalla, 00100 Rome, Italy (Telephone Number in U.S. (202) 653-2400); *The State of Food and Agriculture.*

G.K. Hall and Company, 70 Lincoln Street, Boston, Massachusetts 02111 (617) 423-3990; *The World in Figures.*

LESOTHO - PIGS - See LESOTHO - LIVESTOCK AND POULTRY

LESOTHO - POPULATION

African Development Bank, 01 BP 1387, Abidjan 01, Cote d'Ivoire; *Selected Statistics on Regional Member Countries.*

The Economist Intelligence Unit, 111 West 57th Street, New York, New York 10019 (800) 938-4685; *The World Market Atlas.*

Facts on File, 460 Park Avenue South, New York, New York 10016 (800) 443-8323; *The New Book of World Rankings.*

Food and Agricultural Organization of the United Nations (FAO), Via delle Terme di Caracalla, 00100 Rome, Italy (Telephone Number in U.S. (202) 653-2400); *Production Yearbook.*

G.K. Hall and Company, 70 Lincoln Street, Boston, Massachusetts 02111 (617) 423-3990; *The World in Figures.*

International Labour Office, I.L.O. Publications, CH-1211, Geneva 22, Switzerland; *Yearbook of Labour Statistics.*

Statistical Office of the United Nations, Publishing Service, New York, New York 10017 (800) 253-9646; *Demographic Yearbook, Statistical Yearbook,* and *Survey of Economic and Social Conditions in Africa.*

Times Books, 201 East 50th Street, New York, New York 10022 (212) 751-2600; *The Economist Book of Vital World Statistics.*

United Nations Educational, Scientific and Cultural Organization (UNESCO), 7 Place de Fontenoy, F-75700 Paris, France (Telephone Number in U.S. (212) 963-5981); *Statistical Yearbook.*

U.S. Arms Control and Disarmament Agency, 320 Twenty-first Street, NW, Washington, D.C. 20451 (202) 647-8677; *World Military Expenditures and Arms Transfers.*

World Health Organization, Office of Publications, Avenue Appia, CH-1211 Geneva 27, Switzerland (Telephone Number in U.S. (518) 436-9686); *World Health Statistics Annual.*

LESOTHO - POST OFFICES

Facts on File, 460 Park Avenue South, New York, New York 10016 (800) 443-8323; *The New Book of World Rankings.*

LESOTHO - POTATO PRODUCTION - See LESOTHO - CROPS

LESOTHO - PRICES

Facts on File, 460 Park Avenue South, New York, New York 10016 (800) 443-8323; *The New Book of World Rankings.*

Food and Agricultural Organization of the United Nations (FAO), Via delle Terme di Caracalla, 00100 Rome, Italy (Telephone Number in U.S. (202) 653-2400); *Production Yearbook,* and *The State of Food and Agriculture.*

G.K. Hall and Company, 70 Lincoln Street, Boston, Massachusetts 02111 (617) 423-3990; *The World in Figures.*

International Labour Office, I.L.O. Publications, CH-1211, Geneva 22, Switzerland; *Yearbook of Labour Statistics*.

International Monetary Fund, 700 Nineteenth Street, NW, Washington, D.C. 20431 (202) 623-7000; *International Financial Statistics*.

United Nations Economic Commission for Africa, Africa Hall, Post Office Box 3001, Addis Ababa, Ethiopia (Telephone Number in U.S. (800) 253-9646); *African Statistical Yearbook*.

LESOTHO - PRODUCTION

Facts on File, 460 Park Avenue South, New York, New York 10016 (800) 443-8323; *The New Book of World Rankings*.

G.K. Hall and Company, 70 Lincoln Street, Boston, Massachusetts 02111 (617) 423-3990; *The World in Figures*.

LESOTHO - PROPERTY TAXES - See LESOTHO - TAXATION

LESOTHO - PUBLIC FINANCE

Facts on File, 460 Park Avenue South, New York, New York 10016 (800) 443-8323; *The New Book of World Rankings*.

LESOTHO - RADIO BROADCASTING - See LESOTHO - BROADCASTING

LESOTHO - RAILWAYS

G.K. Hall and Company, 70 Lincoln Street, Boston, Massachusetts 02111 (617) 423-3990; *The World in Figures*.

Statistical Office of the United Nations, Publishing Service, New York, New York 10017 (800) 253-9646; *Survey of Economic and Social Conditions in Africa*.

United Nations Economic Commission for Africa, Africa Hall, Post Office Box 3001, Addis Ababa, Ethiopia (Telephone Number in U.S. (800) 253-9646); *African Statistical Yearbook*.

LESOTHO - RELIGION

Facts on File, 460 Park Avenue South, New York, New York 10016 (800) 443-8323; *The New Book of World Rankings*.

LESOTHO - RENT PRICES

International Labour Office, I.L.O. Publications, CH-1211, Geneva 22, Switzerland; *Yearbook of Labour Statistics*.

LESOTHO - RETAIL TRADE

G.K. Hall and Company, 70 Lincoln Street, Boston, Massachusetts 02111 (617) 423-3990; *The World in Figures*.

LESOTHO - RICE PRODUCTION - See LESOTHO - CROPS

LESOTHO - RUBBER PRODUCTION AND CONSUMPTION

Facts on File, 460 Park Avenue South, New York, New York 10016 (800) 443-8323; *The New Book of World Rankings*.

LESOTHO - SCIENTISTS AND TECHNICIANS

United Nations Educational, Scientific and Cultural Organization (UNESCO), 7 Place de Fontenoy, F-75700 Paris, France (Telephone Number in U.S. (212) 963-5981); *Statistical Yearbook*.

LESOTHO - SENIOR CITIZENS

Facts on File, 460 Park Avenue South, New York, New York 10016 (800) 443-8323; *The New Book of World Rankings*.

LESOTHO - SHEEP - See LESOTHO - LIVESTOCK AND POULTRY

LESOTHO - SILVER PRODUCTION AND CONSUMPTION - See LESOTHO - MINING AND MINERAL PRODUCTS

LESOTHO - SOCIAL DATA

African Development Bank, 01 BP 1387, Abidjan 01, Cote d'Ivoire; *Selected Statistics on Regional Member Countries*.

Facts on File, 460 Park Avenue South, New York, New York 10016 (800) 443-8323; *The New Book of World Rankings*.

G.K. Hall and Company, 70 Lincoln Street, Boston, Massachusetts 02111 (617) 423-3990; *The World in Figures*.

LESOTHO - SOCIAL SECURITY EXPENDITURES

International Monetary Fund, 700 Nineteenth Street, NW, Washington, D.C. 20431 (202) 623-7000; *Government Finance Statistics Yearbook*.

LESOTHO - STAMP TAXES AND DUTIES - See LESOTHO - TAXATION

LESOTHO - STEEL PRODUCTION - See LESOTHO - MINING AND MINERAL PRODUCTS

LESOTHO - STOCKS - COMMODITY - MARKET PRICE - INDEX

Food and Agricultural Organization of the United Nations (FAO), Via delle Terme di Caracalla, 00100 Rome, Italy (Telephone Number in U.S. (202) 653-2400); *The State of Food and Agriculture*.

LESOTHO - SUGAR PRODUCTION AND CONSUMPTION - See LESOTHO - CROPS

LESOTHO - TAXATION

G.K. Hall and Company, 70 Lincoln Street, Boston, Massachusetts 02111 (617) 423-3990; *The World in Figures*.

International Monetary Fund, 700 Nineteenth Street, NW, Washington, D.C. 20431 (202) 623-7000; *Government Finance Statistics Yearbook*.

International Road Federation, 525 School Street, SW, Washington, D.C. 20024 (202) 554-2106; *World Road Statistics*.

The World Bank, 1818 H Street, NW, Washington, D.C. 20433 (202) 477-1234; *World Tables*.

LESOTHO - TELEPHONES IN USE

American Telephone and Telegraph Company, 26 Parsippany Road, Whippany, New Jersey 07981 (800) 338-4038; *The World's Telephones*.

G.K. Hall and Company, 70 Lincoln Street, Boston, Massachusetts 02111 (617) 423-3990; *The World in Figures*.

Statistical Office of the United Nations, Publishing Service, New York, New York 10017 (800) 253-9646; *Statistical Yearbook*.

LESOTHO - TELEVISION BROADCASTING - See LESOTHO - BROADCASTING

LESOTHO - TEXTILE INDUSTRY

G.K. Hall and Company, 70 Lincoln Street, Boston, Massachusetts 02111 (617) 423-3990; *The World in Figures*.

LESOTHO - TOBACCO PRODUCTION

Facts on File, 460 Park Avenue South, New York, New York 10016 (800) 443-8323; *The New Book of World Rankings*.

LESOTHO - TOURISM

Facts on File, 460 Park Avenue South, New York, New York 10016 (800) 443-8323; *The New Book of World Rankings*.

G.K. Hall and Company, 70 Lincoln Street, Boston, Massachusetts 02111 (617) 423-3990; *The World in Figures*.

Times Books, 201 East 50th Street, New York, New York 10022 (212) 751-2600; *The Economist Book of Vital World Statistics*.

United Nations Economic Commission for Africa, Africa Hall, Post Office Box 3001, Addis Ababa, Ethiopia (Telephone Number in U.S. (800) 253-9646); *African Statistical Yearbook*.

World Tourism Organization, Calle Capitan Haya 42, E-28020 Madrid, Spain; *Yearbook of Tourism Statistics*.

LESOTHO - TRACTORS IN USE

Statistical Office of the United Nations, Publishing Service, New York, New York 10017 (800) 253-9646; *Statistical Yearbook*.

LESOTHO - TRADE - See LESOTHO - FOREIGN TRADE

LESOTHO - TRADEMARKS AND SERVICE MARKS

World Intellectual Property Organization, 34 Chemin des Colombettes, CH-1211 Geneva 20, Switzerland, *Industrial Property Statistics*.

LESOTHO - TRANSPORTATION AND COMMUNICATIONS

Facts on File, 460 Park Avenue South, New York, New York 10016 (800) 443-8323; *The New Book of World Rankings*.

G.K. Hall and Company, 70 Lincoln Street, Boston, Massachusetts 02111 (617) 423-3990; *The World in Figures*.

United Nations Economic Commission for Africa, Africa Hall, Post Office Box 3001, Addis Ababa, Ethiopia (Telephone Number in U.S. (800) 253-9646); *African Statistical Yearbook*.

LESOTHO - UNEMPLOYMENT

International Labour Office, I.L.O. Publications, CH-1211, Geneva 22, Switzerland; *Yearbook of Labour Statistics*.

LESOTHO - VITAL STATISTICS

G.K. Hall and Company, 70 Lincoln Street, Boston, Massachusetts 02111 (617) 423-3990; *The World in Figures*.

Statistical Office of the United Nations, Publishing Service, New York, New York 10017 (800) 253-9646; *Statistical Yearbook*.

World Health Organization, Office of Publications, Avenue Appia, CH-1211 Geneva 27, Switzerland (Telephone Number in U.S. (518) 436-9686); *World Health Statistics Annual*.

LESOTHO - WAGES

G.K. Hall and Company, 70 Lincoln Street, Boston, Massachusetts 02111 (617) 423-3990; *The World in Figures*.

International Labour Office, I.L.O. Publications, CH-1211, Geneva 22, Switzerland; *Yearbook of Labour Statistics*.

LESOTHO - WEATHER

Facts on File, 460 Park Avenue South, New York, New York 10016 (800) 443-8323; *The New Book of World Rankings*.

G.K. Hall and Company, 70 Lincoln Street, Boston, Massachusetts 02111 (617) 423-3990; *The World in Figures*.

LESOTHO - WELFARE EXPENDITURES

International Monetary Fund, 700 Nineteenth Street, NW, Washington, D.C. 20431 (202) 623-7000; *Government Finance Statistics Yearbook*.

LESOTHO - WHEAT PRODUCTION - See LESOTHO - CROPS

LESOTHO - WINE PRODUCTION

Facts on File, 460 Park Avenue South, New York, New York 10016 (800) 443-8323; *The New Book of World Rankings*.

LESOTHO - WOOL PRODUCTION

Facts on File, 460 Park Avenue South, New York, New York 10016 (800) 443-8323; *The New Book of World Rankings*.

Statistical Office of the United Nations, Publishing Service, New York, New York 10017 (800) 253-9646; *Statistical Yearbook*.

LETTERS (POSTAL)

U.S. Postal Service, 475 L'Enfant Plaza West, SW, Washington, D.C. 20260 (202) 268-2000; *United States Domestic Postage Rates: Recent History*, and unpublished data.

LETTUCE

U.S. Department of Agriculture, Economic Research Service, Fourteenth Street and Independence Avenue, SW, Washington, D.C. 20005-4789 (202) 219-1504; *Economic Indicators of the Farm Sector: National Financial Summary, Food Cost Review*, and *Food Consumption, Prices, and Expenditures*, and unpublished data.

U.S. Department of Agriculture, National Agricultural Statistics Service, Fourteenth Street and Independence Avenue, SW, Washington, D.C. 20250 (202) 219-1504; *Agricultural Statistics*, and *Vegetables*.

LEVERAGED BUY-OUTS

Securities Data Company, 1180 Raymond Boulevard, Newark, New Jersey 07102 (201) 622-3100; *Merger and Corporate Transactions Database*.

Liberia - National Statistical Office

Bureau of Statistics, Ministry of Planning and Economic Affairs, Post Office Box 9016, Monrovia, Liberia.

Liberia - Primary Statistics Source

Ministry of Planning and Economic Affairs, P.O. Box 9016, Monrovia, Liberia; *Economic Survey of Liberia*, and *Quarterly Statistical Bulletin of Liberia*.

LIBERIA - AGRICULTURE

Euromonitor Publications Limited, 87-88 Turnmill Street, London EC1M 5QU, England; *International Marketing Data and Statistics*.

Facts on File, 460 Park Avenue South, New York, New York 10016 (800) 443-8323; *The New Book of World Rankings*.

Food and Agricultural Organization of the United Nations (FAO), Via delle Terme di Caracalla, 00100 Rome, Italy (Telephone Number in U.S. (202) 653-2400); *Production Yearbook, The State of Food and Agriculture*, and *Trade Yearbook*.

G.K. Hall and Company, 70 Lincoln Street, Boston, Massachusetts 02111 (617) 423-3990; *The World in Figures*.

Statistical Office of the United Nations, Publishing Service, New York, New York 10017 (800) 253-9646; *Survey of Economic and Social Conditions in Africa*, and *Statistical Yearbook*.

Times Books, 201 East 50th Street, New York, New York 10022 (212) 751-2600; *The Economist Book of Vital World Statistics*.

United Nations Economic Commission for Africa, Africa Hall, Post Office Box 3001, Addis Ababa, Ethiopia (Telephone Number in U.S. (800) 253-9646); *African Statistical Yearbook*.

The World Bank, 1818 H Street, NW, Washington, D.C. 20433 (202) 477-1234; *World Tables*.

LIBERIA - AIRLINE SERVICE

Facts on File, 460 Park Avenue South, New York, New York 10016 (800) 443-8323; *The New Book of World Rankings*.

G.K. Hall and Company, 70 Lincoln Street, Boston, Massachusetts 02111 (617) 423-3990; *The World in Figures*.

Times Books, 201 East 50th Street, New York, New York 10022 (212) 751-2600; *The Economist Book of Vital World Statistics*.

United Nations Economic Commission for Africa, Africa Hall, Post Office Box 3001, Addis Ababa, Ethiopia (Telephone Number in U.S. (800) 253-9646); *African Statistical Yearbook*.

LIBERIA - ALUMINUM PRODUCTION AND CONSUMPTION - See LIBERIA - MINING AND MINERAL PRODUCTS

LIBERIA - ANIMAL HEALTH

Food and Agricultural Organization of the United Nations (FAO), Via delle Terme di Caracalla, 00100 Rome, Italy (Telephone Number in U.S. (202) 653-2400); *Animal Health Yearbook*.

LIBERIA - AREA AND DENSITY OF POPULATION

African Development Bank, 01 BP 1387, Abidjan 01, Cote d'Ivoire; *Selected Statistics on Regional Member Countries*.

Euromonitor Publications Limited, 87-88 Turnmill Street, London EC1M 5QU, England; *International Marketing Data and Statistics*.

Facts on File, 460 Park Avenue South, New York, New York 10016 (800) 443-8323; *The New Book of World Rankings*.

Food and Agricultural Organization of the United Nations (FAO), Via delle Terme di Caracalla, 00100 Rome, Italy (Telephone Number in U.S. (202) 653-2400); *The State of Food and Agriculture*.

G.K. Hall and Company, 70 Lincoln Street, Boston, Massachusetts 02111 (617) 423-3990; *The World in Figures*.

Statistical Office of the United Nations, Publishing Service, New York, New York 10017 (800) 253-9646; *Statistical Yearbook*, and *Survey of Economic and Social Conditions in Africa*.

Times Books, 201 East 50th Street, New York, New York 10022 (212) 751-2600; *The Economist Book of Vital World Statistics*.

LIBERIA - ARMS EXPORTS AND IMPORTS

U.S. Arms Control and Disarmament Agency, 320 Twenty-first Street, NW, Washington, D.C. 20451 (202) 647-8677; *World Military Expenditures and Arms Transfers*.

LIBERIA - BALANCE OF PAYMENTS

African Development Bank, 01 BP 1387, Abidjan 01, Cote d'Ivoire; *Selected Statistics on Regional Member Countries*.

The Economist Intelligence Unit, 111 West 57th Street, New York, New York 10019 (800) 938-4685; *The World Market Atlas*.

G.K. Hall and Company, 70 Lincoln Street, Boston, Massachusetts 02111 (617) 423-3990; *The World in Figures*.

International Monetary Fund, 700 Nineteenth Street, NW, Washington, D.C. 20431 (202) 623-7000; *Balance of Payments Yearbook*.

Times Books, 201 East 50th Street, New York, New York 10022 (212) 751-2600; *The Economist Book of Vital World Statistics*.

United Nations Economic Commission for Africa, Africa Hall, Post Office Box 3001, Addis Ababa, Ethiopia (Telephone Number in U.S. (800) 253-9646); *African Statistical Yearbook*.

The World Bank, 1818 H Street, NW, Washington, D.C. 20433 (202) 477-1234; *World Tables*.

LIBERIA - BANKING

Facts on File, 460 Park Avenue South, New York, New York 10016 (800) 443-8323; *The New Book of World Rankings*.

G.K. Hall and Company, 70 Lincoln Street, Boston, Massachusetts 02111 (617) 423-3990; *The World in Figures*.

International Monetary Fund, 700 Nineteenth Street, NW, Washington, D.C. 20431 (202) 623-7000; *Government Finance Statistics Yearbook*, and *International Financial Statistics*.

United Nations Economic Commission for Africa, Africa Hall, Post Office Box 3001, Addis Ababa, Ethiopia (Telephone Number in U.S. (800) 253-9646); *African Statistical Yearbook.*

LIBERIA - BARLEY PRODUCTION - See LIBERIA - CROPS

LIBERIA - BEER PRODUCTION

Facts on File, 460 Park Avenue South, New York, New York 10016 (800) 443-8323; *The New Book of World Rankings.*

Statistical Office of the United Nations, Publishing Service, New York, New York 10017 (800) 253-9646; *Statistical Yearbook.*

LIBERIA - BIRTH RATES

Facts on File, 460 Park Avenue South, New York, New York 10016 (800) 443-8323; *The New Book of World Rankings.*

Statistical Office of the United Nations, Publishing Service, New York, New York 10017 (800) 253-9646; *Demographic Yearbook, Statistical Yearbook,* and *Survey of Economic and Social Conditions in Africa.*

Times Books, 201 East 50th Street, New York, New York 10022 (212) 751-2600; *The Economist Book of Vital World Statistics.*

The World Bank, 1818 H Street, NW, Washington, D.C. 20433 (202) 477-1234; *World Tables.*

LIBERIA - BONDS

G.K. Hall and Company, 70 Lincoln Street, Boston, Massachusetts 02111 (617) 423-3990; *The World in Figures.*

International Monetary Fund, 700 Nineteenth Street, NW, Washington, D.C. 20431 (202) 623-7000; *Government Finance Statistics Yearbook.*

LIBERIA - BOOK PRODUCTION

G.K. Hall and Company, 70 Lincoln Street, Boston, Massachusetts 02111 (617) 423-3990; *The World in Figures.*

LIBERIA - BROADCASTING

Billboard Limited, Post Office Box 9027, 1006 AA Amsterdam, The Netherlands (Telephone Number in U.S. (212) 764-7300); *World Radio TV Handbook.*

Facts on File, 460 Park Avenue South, New York, New York 10016 (800) 443-8323; *The New Book of World Rankings.*

G.K. Hall and Company, 70 Lincoln Street, Boston, Massachusetts 02111 (617) 423-3990; *The World in Figures.*

Times Books, 201 East 50th Street, New York, New York 10022 (212) 751-2600; *The Economist Book of Vital World Statistics.*

United Nations Educational, Scientific and Cultural Organization (UNESCO), 7 Place de Fontenoy, F-75700 Paris, France (Telephone Number in U.S. (212) 963-5981); *Statistical Yearbook.*

LIBERIA - BUSINESS

G.K. Hall and Company, 70 Lincoln Street, Boston, Massachusetts 02111 (617) 423-3990; *The World in Figures.*

LIBERIA - BUSINESS AND PROFESSIONAL LICENSES

International Monetary Fund, 700 Nineteenth Street, NW, Washington, D.C. 20431 (202) 623-7000; *Government Finance Statistics Yearbook.*

LIBERIA - CALORIE SUPPLY

African Development Bank, 01 BP 1387, Abidjan 01, Cote d'Ivoire; *Selected Statistics on Regional Member Countries.*

Food and Agricultural Organization of the United Nations (FAO), Via delle Terme di Caracalla, 00100 Rome, Italy (Telephone Number in U.S. (202) 653-2400); *The State of Food and Agriculture.*

LIBERIA - CAPITAL REVENUE

International Monetary Fund, 700 Nineteenth Street, NW, Washington, D.C. 20431 (202) 623-7000; *Government Finance Statistics Yearbook.*

LIBERIA - CATTLE - See LIBERIA - LIVESTOCK AND POULTRY

LIBERIA - CEMENT PRODUCTION - See LIBERIA - MINING AND MINERAL PRODUCTS

LIBERIA - CHEMICAL (ORGANIC) PRODUCTION - See LIBERIA - MINING AND MINERAL PRODUCTS

LIBERIA - CHICKENS - See LIBERIA - LIVESTOCK AND POULTRY

LIBERIA - CIGARETTE PRODUCTION - See LIBERIA - TOBACCO PRODUCTION

LIBERIA - CLASS STRUCTURE

G.K. Hall and Company, 70 Lincoln Street, Boston, Massachusetts 02111 (617) 423-3990; *The World in Figures.*

LIBERIA - CLIMATE

Facts on File, 460 Park Avenue South, New York, New York 10016 (800) 443-8323; *The New Book of World Rankings.*

G.K. Hall and Company, 70 Lincoln Street, Boston, Massachusetts 02111 (617) 423-3990; *The World in Figures.*

LIBERIA - COAL PRODUCTION - See LIBERIA - MINING AND MINERAL PRODUCTS

LIBERIA - COCOA (BEANS) PRODUCTION - See LIBERIA - CROPS

LIBERIA - COFFEE PRODUCTION AND CONSUMPTION - See LIBERIA - CROPS

LIBERIA - COMMUNICATIONS

G.K. Hall and Company, 70 Lincoln Street, Boston, Massachusetts 02111 (617) 423-3990; *The World in Figures.*

United Nations Economic Commission for Africa, Africa Hall, Post Office Box 3001, Addis Ababa, Ethiopia (Telephone Number in U.S. (800) 253-9646); *African Statistical Yearbook.*

LIBERIA - CONSTRUCTION INDUSTRY

Facts on File, 460 Park Avenue South, New York, New York 10016 (800) 443-8323; *The New Book of World Rankings.*

Statistical Office of the United Nations, Publishing Service, New York, New York 10017 (800) 253-9646; *Statistical Yearbook.*

United Nations Economic Commission for Africa, Africa Hall, Post Office Box 3001, Addis Ababa, Ethiopia (Telephone Number in U.S. (800) 253-9646); *African Statistical Yearbook.*

LIBERIA - CONSUMER PRICE INDEX

African Development Bank, 01 BP 1387, Abidjan 01, Cote d'Ivoire; *Selected Statistics on Regional Member Countries.*

G.K. Hall and Company, 70 Lincoln Street, Boston, Massachusetts 02111 (617) 423-3990; *The World in Figures.*

Statistical Office of the United Nations, Publishing Service, New York, New York 10017 (800) 253-9646; *Statistical Yearbook,* and *Survey of Economic and Social Conditions in Africa.*

Times Books, 201 East 50th Street, New York, New York 10022 (212) 751-2600; *The Economist Book of Vital World Statistics.*

United Nations Economic Commission for Africa, Africa Hall, Post Office Box 3001, Addis Ababa, Ethiopia (Telephone Number in U.S. (800) 253-9646); *African Statistical Yearbook.*

LIBERIA - CONSUMER PRICES

International Labour Office, I.L.O. Publications, CH-1211, Geneva 22, Switzerland; *Yearbook of Labour Statistics.*

International Monetary Fund, 700 Nineteenth Street, NW, Washington, D.C. 20431 (202) 623-7000; *International Financial Statistics.*

LIBERIA - CONSUMPTION

African Development Bank, 01 BP 1387, Abidjan 01, Cote d'Ivoire; *Selected Statistics on Regional Member Countries.*

G.K. Hall and Company, 70 Lincoln Street, Boston, Massachusetts 02111 (617) 423-3990; *The World in Figures.*

International Rubber Study Group, York House, Eighth Floor, Empire Way, Wembley, London HA9 0PA, England; *Rubber Statistical Bulletin.*

Statistical Office of the United Nations, Publishing Service, New York, New York 10017 (800) 253-9646; *Survey of Economic and Social Conditions in Africa.*

LIBERIA - COPPER PRODUCTION AND CONSUMPTION - See LIBERIA - MINING AND MINERAL PRODUCTS

LIBERIA - CORN PRODUCTION - See LIBERIA - CROPS

LIBERIA - CORPORATE INCOME TAXES - See LIBERIA - TAXATION

LIBERIA - CORPORATE TAXES - See LIBERIA - TAXATION

LIBERIA - COTTON PRODUCTION - See LIBERIA - CROPS

LIBERIA - CROPS

Facts on File, 460 Park Avenue South, New York, New York 10016 (800) 443-8323; *The New Book of World Rankings.*

Food and Agricultural Organization of the United Nations (FAO), Via delle Terme di Caracalla, 00100 Rome, Italy (Telephone Number

in U.S. (202) 653-2400); *The State of Food and Agriculture.*

G.K. Hall and Company, 70 Lincoln Street, Boston, Massachusetts 02111 (617) 423-3990; *The World in Figures.*

Statistical Office of the United Nations, Publishing Service, New York, New York 10017 (800) 253-9646; *Statistical Yearbook.*

United Nations Economic Commission for Africa, Africa Hall, Post Office Box 3001, Addis Ababa, Ethiopia (Telephone Number in U.S. (800) 253-9646); *African Statistical Yearbook.*

LIBERIA - CUSTOMS DUTIES

G.K. Hall and Company, 70 Lincoln Street, Boston, Massachusetts 02111 (617) 423-3990; *The World in Figures.*

International Monetary Fund, 700 Nineteenth Street, NW, Washington, D.C. 20431 (202) 623-7000; *Government Finance Statistics Yearbook.*

LIBERIA - DAIRY PRODUCTS

Facts on File, 460 Park Avenue South, New York, New York 10016 (800) 443-8323; *The New Book of World Rankings.*

Food and Agricultural Organization of the United Nations (FAO), Via delle Terme di Caracalla, 00100 Rome, Italy (Telephone Number in U.S. (202) 653-2400); *Production Yearbook,* and *The State of Food and Agriculture.*

LIBERIA - DEATH RATES

G.K. Hall and Company, 70 Lincoln Street, Boston, Massachusetts 02111 (617) 423-3990; *The World in Figures.*

Statistical Office of the United Nations, Publishing Service, New York, New York 10017 (800) 253-9646; *Statistical Yearbook,* and *Survey of Economic and Social Conditions in Africa.*

Times Books, 201 East 50th Street, New York, New York 10022 (212) 751-2600; *The Economist Book of Vital World Statistics.*

LIBERIA - DEFENSE EXPENDITURES

G.K. Hall and Company, 70 Lincoln Street, Boston, Massachusetts 02111 (617) 423-3990; *The World in Figures.*

International Monetary Fund, 700 Nineteenth Street, NW, Washington, D.C. 20431 (202) 623-7000; *Government Finance Statistics Yearbook.*

U.S. Arms Control and Disarmament Agency, 320 Twenty-first Street, NW, Washington, D.C. 20451 (202) 647-8677; *World Military Expenditures and Arms Transfers.*

LIBERIA - DEMOGRAPHY

The Economist Intelligence Unit, 111 West 57th Street, New York, New York 10019 (800) 938-4685; *The World Market Atlas.*

Facts on File, 460 Park Avenue South, New York, New York 10016 (800) 443-8323; *The New Book of World Rankings.*

G.K. Hall and Company, 70 Lincoln Street, Boston, Massachusetts 02111 (617) 423-3990; *The World in Figures.*

Statistical Office of the United Nations, Publishing Service, New York, New York 10017 (800) 253-9646; *Survey of Economic and*

Social Conditions in Africa.

LIBERIA - DEVELOPMENT ASSISTANCE

G.K. Hall and Company, 70 Lincoln Street, Boston, Massachusetts 02111 (617) 423-3990; *The World in Figures.*

Statistical Office of the United Nations, Publishing Service, New York, New York 10017 (800) 253-9646; *Statistical Yearbook.*

LIBERIA - DIAMONDS - See LIBERIA - MINING AND MINERAL PRODUCTS

LIBERIA - DISEASE

G.K. Hall and Company, 70 Lincoln Street, Boston, Massachusetts 02111 (617) 423-3990; *The World in Figures.*

LIBERIA - DIVORCE RATES

Facts on File, 460 Park Avenue South, New York, New York 10016 (800) 443-8323; *The New Book of World Rankings.*

Statistical Office of the United Nations, Publishing Service, New York, New York 10017 (800) 253-9646; *Demographic Yearbook,* and *Statistical Yearbook.*

LIBERIA - DOMESTIC PRODUCT

G.K. Hall and Company, 70 Lincoln Street, Boston, Massachusetts 02111 (617) 423-3990; *The World in Figures.*

LIBERIA - DUCKS - See LIBERIA - LIVESTOCK AND POULTRY

LIBERIA - ECONOMY

African Development Bank, 01 BP 1387, Abidjan 01, Cote d'Ivoire; *Selected Statistics on Regional Member Countries.*

Euromonitor Publications Limited, 87-88 Turnmill Street, London EC1M 5QU, England; *International Marketing Data and Statistics.*

Facts on File, 460 Park Avenue South, New York, New York 10016 (800) 443-8323; *The New Book of World Rankings.*

G.K. Hall and Company, 70 Lincoln Street, Boston, Massachusetts 02111 (617) 423-3990; *The World in Figures.*

Statistical Office of the United Nations, Publishing Service, New York, New York 10017 (800) 253-9646; *Foreign Trade Statistics for Africa.*

LIBERIA - EDUCATION

African Development Bank, 01 BP 1387, Abidjan 01, Cote d'Ivoire; *Selected Statistics on Regional Member Countries.*

The Economist Intelligence Unit, 111 West 57th Street, New York, New York 10019 (800) 938-4685; *The World Market Atlas.*

Facts on File, 460 Park Avenue South, New York, New York 10016 (800) 443-8323; *The New Book of World Rankings.*

G.K. Hall and Company, 70 Lincoln Street, Boston, Massachusetts 02111 (617) 423-3990; *The World in Figures.*

International Monetary Fund, 700 Nineteenth Street, NW, Washington, D.C. 20431 (202) 623-7000; *Government Finance Statistics Yearbook.*

Statistical Office of the United Nations, Publishing Service, New York, New York 10017 (800) 253-9646; *Survey of Economic and Social Conditions in Africa.*

Times Books, 201 East 50th Street, New York, New York 10022 (212) 751-2600; *The Economist Book of Vital World Statistics.*

United Nations Economic Commission for Africa, Africa Hall, Post Office Box 3001, Addis Ababa, Ethiopia (Telephone Number in U.S. (800) 253-9646; *African Statistical Yearbook.*

United Nations Educational, Scientific and Cultural Organization (UNESCO), 7 Place de Fontenoy, F-75700 Paris, France (Telephone Number in U.S. (212) 963-5981); *Statistical Yearbook.*

The World Bank, 1818 H Street, NW, Washington, D.C. 20433 (202) 477-1234; *World Tables.*

LIBERIA - EGG PRODUCTION AND CONSUMPTION - See LIBERIA - DAIRY PRODUCTS

LIBERIA - ELECTRICITY

Facts on File, 460 Park Avenue South, New York, New York 10016 (800) 443-8323; *The New Book of World Rankings.*

Statistical Office of the United Nations, Publishing Service, New York, New York 10017 (800) 253-9646; *Statistical Yearbook,* and *Survey of Economic and Social Conditions in Africa.*

Times Books, 201 East 50th Street, New York, New York 10022 (212) 751-2600; *The Economist Book of Vital World Statistics.*

United Nations Economic Commission for Africa, Africa Hall, Post Office Box 3001, Addis Ababa, Ethiopia (Telephone Number in U.S. (800) 253-9646); *African Statistical Yearbook.*

LIBERIA - EMPLOYMENT

Euromonitor Publications Limited, 87-88 Turnmill Street, London EC1M 5QU, England; *International Marketing Data and Statistics.*

Facts on File, 460 Park Avenue South, New York, New York 10016 (800) 443-8323; *The New Book of World Rankings.*

International Labour Office, I.L.O. Publications, CH-1211, Geneva 22, Switzerland; *Yearbook of Labour Statistics.*

Statistical Office of the United Nations, Publishing Service, New York, New York 10017 (800) 253-9646; *Survey of Economic and Social Conditions in Africa.*

United Nations Economic Commission for Africa, Africa Hall, Post Office Box 3001, Addis Ababa, Ethiopia (Telephone Number in U.S. (800) 253-9646); *African Statistical Yearbook.*

LIBERIA - ENERGY

Facts on File, 460 Park Avenue South, New York, New York 10016 (800) 443-8323; *The New Book of World Rankings.*

Food and Agricultural Organization of the United Nations (FAO), Via delle Terme di Caracalla, 00100 Rome, Italy (Telephone Number in U.S. (202) 653-2400); *The State of Food and Agriculture.*

G.K. Hall and Company, 70 Lincoln Street, Boston, Massachusetts 02111 (617) 423-3990; *The World in Figures.*

Statistical Office of the United Nations, Publishing Service, New York, New York 10017 (800) 253-9646; *Energy Statistics Yearbook*, and *Statistical Yearbook*.

Times Books, 201 East 50th Street, New York, New York 10022 (212) 751-2600; *The Economist Book of Vital World Statistics*.

United Nations Economic Commission for Africa, Africa Hall, Post Office Box 3001, Addis Ababa, Ethiopia (Telephone Number in U.S. (800) 253-9646); *African Statistical Yearbook*.

LIBERIA - EXCHANGE RATES

African Development Bank, 01 BP 1387, Abidjan 01, Cote d'Ivoire; *Selected Statistics on Regional Member Countries*.

Euromonitor Publications Limited, 87-88 Turnmill Street, London EC1M 5QU, England; *International Marketing Data and Statistics*.

International Monetary Fund, 700 Nineteenth Street, NW, Washington, D.C. 20431 (202) 623-7000; *International Financial Statistics*.

Statistical Office of the United Nations, Publishing Service, New York, New York 10017 (800) 253-9646; *Foreign Trade Statistics for Africa*, and *Statistical Yearbook*.

LIBERIA - EXCISE TAXES - See LIBERIA - TAXATION

LIBERIA - EXPORTS

African Development Bank, 01 BP 1387, Abidjan 01, Cote d'Ivoire; *Selected Statistics on Regional Member Countries*.

The Economist Intelligence Unit, 111 West 57th Street, New York, New York 10019 (800) 938-4685; *The World Market Atlas*.

Euromonitor Publications Limited, 87-88 Turnmill Street, London EC1M 5QU, England; *International Marketing Data and Statistics*.

Food and Agricultural Organization of the United Nations (FAO), Via delle Terme di Caracalla, 00100 Rome, Italy (Telephone Number in U.S. (202) 653-2400); *The State of Food and Agriculture*.

G.K. Hall and Company, 70 Lincoln Street, Boston, Massachusetts 02111 (617) 423-3990; *The World in Figures*.

International Monetary Fund, 700 Nineteenth Street, NW, Washington, D.C. 20431 (202) 623-7000; *Direction of Trade Statistics*, *Government Finance Statistics Yearbook*, and *International Financial Statistics*.

International Rubber Study Group, York House, Eighth Floor, Empire Way, Wembley, London HA 9 0PA, England; *Rubber Statistical Bulletin*.

Statistical Office of the United Nations, Publishing Service, New York, New York 10017 (800) 253-9646; *Foreign Trade Statistics for Africa*, and *Survey of Economic and Social Conditions in Africa*.

Times Books, 201 East 50th Street, New York, New York 10022 (212) 751-2600; *The Economist Book of Vital World Statistics*.

United Nations Economic Commission for Africa, Africa Hall, Post Office Box 3001, Addis Ababa, Ethiopia (Telephone Number in U.S. (800) 253-9646); *African Statistical Yearbook*.

The World Bank, 1818 H Street, NW, Washington, D.C. 20433 (202) 477-1234; *World Tables*.

LIBERIA - EXTERNAL INDEBTEDNESS

African Development Bank, 01 BP 1387, Abidjan 01, Cote d'Ivoire; *Selected Statistics on Regional Member Countries*.

Statistical Office of the United Nations, Publishing Service, New York, New York 10017 (800) 253-9646; *Survey of Economic and Social Conditions in Africa*.

The World Bank, 1818 H Street, NW, Washington, D.C. 20433 (202) 477-1234; *World Tables*.

LIBERIA - EXTERNAL TRADE

African Development Bank, 01 BP 1387, Abidjan 01, Cote d'Ivoire; *Selected Statistics on Regional Member Countries*.

Food and Agricultural Organization of the United Nations (FAO), Via delle Terme di Caracalla, 00100 Rome, Italy (Telephone Number in U.S. (202) 653-2400); *The State of Food and Agriculture*, and *Trade Yearbook*.

G.K. Hall and Company, 70 Lincoln Street, Boston, Massachusetts 02111 (617) 423-3990; *The World in Figures*.

Statistical Office of the United Nations, Publishing Service, New York, New York 10017 (800) 253-9646; *Statistical Yearbook*.

LIBERIA - FARM CROPS - See LIBERIA - CROPS

LIBERIA - FEMALE WORKING POPULATION - See LIBERIA - EMPLOYMENT

LIBERIA - FERTILITY RATES

Facts on File, 460 Park Avenue South, New York, New York 10016 (800) 443-8323; *The New Book of World Rankings*.

Statistical Office of the United Nations, Publishing Service, New York, New York 10017 (800) 253-9646; *Survey of Economic and Social Conditions in Africa*.

Times Books, 201 East 50th Street, New York, New York 10022 (212) 751-2600; *The Economist Book of Vital World Statistics*.

The World Bank, 1818 H Street, NW, Washington, D.C. 20433 (202) 477-1234; *World Tables*.

LIBERIA - FERTILIZER

Food and Agricultural Organization of the United Nations (FAO), Via delle Terme di Caracalla, 00100 Rome, Italy (Telephone Number in U.S. (202) 653-2400); *Fertilizer Yearbook*, and *The State of Food and Agriculture*.

Statistical Office of the United Nations, Publishing Service, New York, New York 10017 (800) 253-9646; *Statistical Yearbook*.

LIBERIA - FETAL MORTALITY

Statistical Office of the United Nations, Publishing Service, New York, New York 10017 (800) 253-9646; *Demographic Yearbook*.

LIBERIA - FINANCE

African Development Bank, 01 BP 1387, Abidjan 01, Cote d'Ivoire; *Selected Statistics on Regional Member Countries*.

Facts on File, 460 Park Avenue South, New York, New York 10016 (800) 443-8323; *The New Book of World Rankings.*

G.K. Hall and Company, 70 Lincoln Street, Boston, Massachusetts 02111 (617) 423-3990; *The World in Figures.*

International Monetary Fund, 700 Nineteenth Street, NW, Washington, D.C. 20431 (202) 623-7000; *Government Finance Statistics Yearbook,* and *International Financial Statistics.*

United Nations Economic Commission for Africa, Africa Hall, Post Office Box 3001, Addis Ababa, Ethiopia (Telephone Number in U.S. (800) 253-9646); *African Statistical Yearbook.*

LIBERIA - FISHERIES

Facts on File, 460 Park Avenue South, New York, New York 10016 (800) 443-8323; *The New Book of World Rankings.*

Food and Agricultural Organization of the United Nations (FAO), Via delle Terme di Caracalla, 00100 Rome, Italy (Telephone Number in U.S. (202) 653-2400); *The State of Food and Agriculture.*

Statistical Office of the United Nations, Publishing Service, New York, New York 10017 (800) 253-9646; *Statistical Yearbook,* and *Survey of Economic and Social Conditions in Africa.*

United Nations Economic Commission for Africa, Africa Hall, Post Office Box 3001, Addis Ababa, Ethiopia (Telephone Number in U.S. (800) 253-9646); *African Statistical Yearbook.*

LIBERIA - FOOD

African Development Bank, 01 BP 1387, Abidjan 01, Cote d'Ivoire; *Selected Statistics on Regional Member Countries.*

Food and Agricultural Organization of the United Nations (FAO), Via delle Terme di Caracalla, 00100 Rome, Italy (Telephone Number in U.S. (202) 653-2400); *The State of Food and Agriculture,* and *Production Yearbook.*

G.K. Hall and Company, 70 Lincoln Street, Boston, Massachusetts 02111 (617) 423-3990; *The World in Figures.*

LIBERIA - FOREIGN AID

G.K. Hall and Company, 70 Lincoln Street, Boston, Massachusetts 02111 (617) 423-3990; *The World in Figures.*

LIBERIA - FOREIGN DEBT

International Monetary Fund, 700 Nineteenth Street, NW, Washington, D.C. 20431 (202) 623-7000; *Government Finance Statistics Yearbook.*

LIBERIA - FOREIGN TRADE

Euromonitor Publications Limited, 87-88 Turnmill Street, London EC1M 5QU, England; *International Marketing Data and Statistics.*

Facts on File, 460 Park Avenue South, New York, New York 10016 (800) 443-8323; *The New Book of World Rankings.*

G.K. Hall and Company, 70 Lincoln Street, Boston, Massachusetts 02111 (617) 423-3990; *The World in Figures.*

Statistical Office of the United Nations, Publishing Service, New York, New York 10017 (800) 253-9646; *Foreign Trade Statistics for Africa, International Trade Statistics Yearbook,* and *Statistical*

Yearbook.

United Nations Economic Commission for Africa, Africa Hall, Post Office Box 3001, Addis Ababa, Ethiopia (Telephone Number in U.S. (800) 253-9646); *African Statistical Yearbook.*

The World Bank, 1818 H Street, NW, Washington, D.C. 20433 (202) 477-1234; *World Tables.*

LIBERIA - FORESTRY AND FOREST PRODUCTS

Facts on File, 460 Park Avenue South, New York, New York 10016 (800) 443-8323; *The New Book of World Rankings.*

Food and Agricultural Organization of the United Nations (FAO), Via delle Terme di Caracalla, 00100 Rome, Italy (Telephone Number in U.S. (202) 653-2400); *The State of Food and Agriculture,* and *Yearbook of Forest Products.*

G.K. Hall and Company, 70 Lincoln Street, Boston, Massachusetts 02111 (617) 423-3990; *The World in Figures.*

Statistical Office of the United Nations, Publishing Service, New York, New York 10017 (800) 253-9646; *Statistical Yearbook.*

United Nations Economic Commission for Africa, Africa Hall, Post Office Box 3001, Addis Ababa, Ethiopia (Telephone Number in U.S. (800) 253-9646); *African Statistical Yearbook.*

United Nations Educational, Scientific and Cultural Organization (UNESCO), 7 Place de Fontenoy, F-75700 Paris, France (Telephone Number in U.S. (212) 963-5901); *Statistical Yearbook.*

LIBERIA - GAS PRODUCTION - See LIBERIA - MINING AND MINERAL PRODUCTS

LIBERIA - GENERAL MORTALITY

Statistical Office of the United Nations, Publishing Service, New York, New York 10017 (800) 253-9646; *Demographic Yearbook.*

LIBERIA - GEOGRAPHIC DATA

Facts on File, 460 Park Avenue South, New York, New York 10016 (800) 443-8323; *The New Book of World Rankings.*

LIBERIA - GOATS - See LIBERIA - LIVESTOCK AND POULTRY

LIBERIA - GOLD HOLDINGS

Statistical Office of the United Nations, Publishing Service, New York, New York 10017 (800) 253-9646; *Statistical Yearbook.*

The World Bank, 1818 H Street, NW, Washington, D.C. 20433 (202) 477-1234; *World Tables.*

LIBERIA - GOLD PRODUCTION AND CONSUMPTION - See LIBERIA - MINING AND MINERAL PRODUCTS

LIBERIA - GOVERNMENT

G.K. Hall and Company, 70 Lincoln Street, Boston, Massachusetts 02111 (617) 423-3990; *The World in Figures.*

LIBERIA - GOVERNMENT EXPENDITURES

International Monetary Fund, 700 Nineteenth Street, NW, Washington, D.C. 20431 (202) 623-7000; *Government Finance Statistics Yearbook.*

Times Books, 201 East 50th Street, New York, New York 10022 (212) 751-2600; *The Economist Book of Vital World Statistics.*

The World Bank, 1818 H Street, NW, Washington, D.C. 20433 (202) 477-1234; *World Tables.*

LIBERIA - GOVERNMENT FINANCES

International Monetary Fund, 700 Nineteenth Street, NW, Washington, D.C. 20431 (202) 623-7000; *International Financial Statistics.*

Statistical Office of the United Nations, Publishing Service, New York, New York 10017 (800) 253-9646; *Statistical Yearbook.*

LIBERIA - GOVERNMENT REVENUES

International Monetary Fund, 700 Nineteenth Street, NW, Washington, D.C. 20431 (202) 623-7000; *Government Finance Statistics Yearbook.*

Statistical Office of the United Nations, Publishing Service, New York, New York 10017 (800) 253-9646; *Survey of Economic and Social Conditions in Africa.*

Times Books, 201 East 50th Street, New York, New York 10022 (212) 751-2600; *The Economist Book of Vital World Statistics.*

The World Bank, 1818 H Street, NW, Washington, D.C. 20433 (202) 477-1234; *World Tables.*

LIBERIA - GRAIN PRODUCTION - See LIBERIA - CROPS

LIBERIA - GRANTS

International Monetary Fund, 700 Nineteenth Street, NW, Washington, D.C. 20431 (202) 623-7000; *Government Finance Statistics Yearbook.*

LIBERIA - GROSS DOMESTIC PRODUCT

African Development Bank, 01 BP 1387, Abidjan 01, Cote d'Ivoire; *Selected Statistics on Regional Member Countries.*

The Economist Intelligence Unit, 111 West 57th Street, New York, New York 10019 (800) 938-4685; *The World Market Atlas.*

Euromonitor Publications Limited, 87-88 Turnmill Street, London EC1M 5QU, England; *International Marketing Data and Statistics.*

Facts on File, 460 Park Avenue South, New York, New York 10016 (800) 443-8323; *The New Book of World Rankings.*

G.K. Hall and Company, 70 Lincoln Street, Boston, Massachusetts 02111 (617) 423-3990; *The World in Figures.*

Statistical Office of the United Nations, Publishing Service, New York, New York 10017 (800) 253-9646; *Statistical Yearbook,* and *Survey of Economic and Social Conditions in Africa.*

Times Books, 201 East 50th Street, New York, New York 10022 (212) 751-2600; *The Economist Book of Vital World Statistics.*

United Nations Economic Commission for Africa, Africa Hall, Post Office Box 3001, Addis Ababa, Ethiopia (Telephone Number in U.S. (800) 253-9646; *African Statistical Yearbook.*

The World Bank, 1818 H Street, NW, Washington, D.C. 20433 (202) 477-1234; *World Tables.*

LIBERIA - GROSS NATIONAL PRODUCT

Euromonitor Publications Limited, 87-88 Turnmill Street, London EC1M 5QU, England; *International Marketing Data and Statistics.*

U.S. Arms Control and Disarmament Agency, 320 Twenty-first Street, NW, Washington, D.C. 20451 (202) 647-8677; *World Military Expenditures and Arms Transfers.*

The World Bank, 1818 H Street, NW, Washington, D.C. 20433 (202) 477-1234; *World Tables.*

LIBERIA - GROUNDNUT PRODUCTION - See LIBERIA - CROPS

LIBERIA - HEALTH

African Development Bank, 01 BP 1387, Abidjan 01, Cote d'Ivoire; *Selected Statistics on Regional Member Countries.*

Facts on File, 460 Park Avenue South, New York, New York 10016 (800) 443-8323; *The New Book of World Rankings.*

G.K. Hall and Company, 70 Lincoln Street, Boston, Massachusetts 02111 (617) 423-3990; *The World in Figures.*

Statistical Office of the United Nations, Publishing Service, New York, New York 10017 (800) 253-9646; *Statistical Yearbook.*

Times Books, 201 East 50th Street, New York, New York 10022 (212) 751-2600; *The Economist Book of Vital World Statistics.*

United Nations Economic Commission for Africa, Africa Hall, Post Office Box 3001, Addis Ababa, Ethiopia (Telephone Number in U.S. (800) 253-9646); *African Statistical Yearbook.*

LIBERIA - HEALTH EXPENDITURES

International Monetary Fund, 700 Nineteenth Street, NW, Washington, D.C. 20431 (202) 623-7000; *Government Finance Statistics Yearbook.*

LIBERIA - HIDE PRODUCTION

Food and Agricultural Organization of the United Nations (FAO), Via delle Terme di Caracalla, 00100 Rome, Italy (Telephone Number in U.S. (202) 653-2400); *Production Yearbook.*

LIBERIA - HIGHWAYS

G.K. Hall and Company, 70 Lincoln Street, Boston, Massachusetts 02111 (617) 423-3990; *The World in Figures.*

International Road Federation, 525 School Street, SW, Washington, D.C. 20024 (202) 554-2106; *World Road Statistics.*

Statistical Office of the United Nations, Publishing Service, New York, New York 10017 (800) 253-9646; *Survey of Economic and Social Conditions in Africa.*

United Nations Economic Commission for Africa, Africa Hall, Post Office Box 3001, Addis Ababa, Ethiopia (Telephone Number in U.S. (800) 253-9646); *African Statistical Yearbook.*

LIBERIA - HORSES - See LIBERIA - LIVESTOCK AND POULTRY

LIBERIA - HOURS OF WORK - See LIBERIA - EMPLOYMENT

LIBERIA - HOUSING

Facts on File, 460 Park Avenue South, New York, New York 10016 (800) 443-8323; *The New Book of World Rankings.*

LIBERIA - HOUSING EXPENDITURES

International Monetary Fund, 700 Nineteenth Street, NW, Washington, D.C. 20431 (202) 623-7000; *Government Finance Statistics Yearbook.*

LIBERIA - ILLITERATE POPULATION

The Economist Intelligence Unit, 111 West 57th Street, New York, New York 10019 (800) 938-4685; *The World Market Atlas.*

G.K. Hall and Company, 70 Lincoln Street, Boston, Massachusetts 02111 (617) 423-3990; *The World in Figures.*

United Nations Educational, Scientific and Cultural Organization (UNESCO), 7 Place de Fontenoy, F-75700 Paris, France (Telephone Number in U.S. (212) 963-5981); *Statistical Yearbook.*

LIBERIA - IMPORTS

African Development Bank, 01 BP 1387, Abidjan 01, Cote d'Ivoire; *Selected Statistics on Regional Member Countries.*

The Economist Intelligence Unit, 111 West 57th Street, New York, New York 10019 (800) 938-4685; *The World Market Atlas.*

Euromonitor Publications Limited, 87-88 Turnmill Street, London EC1M 5QU, England; *International Marketing Data and Statistics.*

Food and Agricultural Organization of the United Nations (FAO), Via delle Terme di Caracalla, 00100 Rome, Italy (Telephone Number in U.S. (202) 653-2400), *The State of Food and Agriculture.*

G.K. Hall and Company, 70 Lincoln Street, Boston, Massachusetts 02111 (617) 423-3990; *The World in Figures.*

International Monetary Fund, 700 Nineteenth Street, NW, Washington, D.C. 20431 (202) 623-7000; *Direction of Trade Statistics, Government Finance Statistics Yearbook,* and *International Financial Statistics.*

International Rubber Study Group, York House, Eighth Floor, Empire Way, Wembley, London HA9 0PA, England; *Rubber Statistical Bulletin.*

Statistical Office of the United Nations, Publishing Service, New York, New York 10017 (800) 253-9646; *Foreign Trade Statistics for Africa,* and *Survey of Economic and Social Conditions in Africa.*

Times Books, 201 East 50th Street, New York, New York 10022 (212) 751-2600; *The Economist Book of Vital World Statistics.*

United Nations Economic Commission for Africa, Africa Hall, Post Office Box 3001, Addis Ababa, Ethiopia (Telephone Number in U.S. (800) 253-9646); *African Statistical Yearbook.*

The World Bank, 1818 H Street, NW, Washington, D.C. 20433 (202) 477-1234; *World Tables.*

LIBERIA - INCOME TAXES - See LIBERIA - TAXATION

LIBERIA - INDUSTRY

Euromonitor Publications Limited, 87-88 Turnmill Street, London EC1M 5QU, England; *International Marketing Data and Statistics.*

Facts on File, 460 Park Avenue South, New York, New York 10016 (800) 443-8323; *The New Book of World Rankings.*

G.K. Hall and Company, 70 Lincoln Street, Boston, Massachusetts 02111 (617) 423-3990; *The World in Figures.*

International Labour Office, I.L.O. Publications, CH-1211, Geneva 22, Switzerland; *Yearbook of Labour Statistics.*

Statistical Office of the United Nations, Publishing Service, New York, New York 10017 (800) 253-9646; *Survey of Economic and Social Conditions in Africa.*

Times Books, 201 East 50th Street, New York, New York 10022 (212) 751-2600; *The Economist Book of Vital World Statistics.*

United Nations Economic Commission for Africa, Africa Hall, Post Office Box 3001, Addis Ababa, Ethiopia (Telephone Number in U.S. (800) 253-9646); *African Statistical Yearbook.*

The World Bank, 1818 H Street, NW, Washington, D.C. 20433 (202) 477-1234; *World Tables.*

World Intellectual Property Organization, 34 Chemin des Colombettes, CH 1211 Geneva 20, Switzerland; *Industrial Property Statistics.*

LIBERIA - INFANT AND MATERNAL MORTALITY

Statistical Office of the United Nations, Publishing Service, New York, New York 10017 (800) 253-9646; *Demographic Yearbook, Statistical Yearbook,* and *Survey of Economic and Social Conditions in Africa.*

Times Books, 201 East 50th Street, New York, New York 10022 (212) 751-2600; *The Economist Book of Vital World Statistics.*

The World Bank, 1818 H Street, NW, Washington, D.C. 20433 (202) 477-1234; *World Tables.*

LIBERIA - INTERNATIONAL LIQUIDITY

International Monetary Fund, 700 Nineteenth Street, NW, Washington, D.C. 20431 (202) 623-7000; *International Financial Statistics.*

LIBERIA - INTERNATIONAL RESERVES EXCLUDING GOLD

African Development Bank, 01 BP 1387, Abidjan 01, Cote d'Ivoire; *Selected Statistics on Regional Member Countries.*

Statistical Office of the United Nations, Publishing Service, New York, New York 10017 (800) 253-9646; *Statistical Yearbook.*

The World Bank, 1818 H Street, NW, Washington, D.C. 20433 (202) 477-1234; *World Tables.*

LIBERIA - IRON ORE - See LIBERIA - MINING AND MINERAL PRODUCTS

LIBERIA - IRRIGATION

Euromonitor Publications Limited, 87-88 Turnmill Street, London EC1M 5QU, England; *International Marketing Data and Statistics.*

LIBERIA - LABOR FORCE

African Development Bank, 01 BP 1387, Abidjan 01, Cote d'Ivoire; *Selected Statistics on Regional Member Countries*.

Euromonitor Publications Limited, 87-88 Turnmill Street, London EC1M 5QU, England; *International Marketing Data and Statistics*.

Facts on File, 460 Park Avenue South, New York, New York 10016 (800) 443-8323; *The New Book of World Rankings*.

Food and Agricultural Organization of the United Nations (FAO), Via delle Terme di Caracalla, 00100 Rome, Italy (Telephone Number in U.S. (202) 653-2400); *The State of Food and Agriculture*.

G.K. Hall and Company, 70 Lincoln Street, Boston, Massachusetts 02111 (617) 423-3990; *The World in Figures*.

The World Bank, 1818 H Street, NW, Washington, D.C. 20433 (202) 477-1234; *World Tables*.

LIBERIA - LABOR PRODUCTIVITY

International Labour Office, I.L.O. Publications, CH-1211, Geneva 22, Switzerland; *Yearbook of Labour Statistics*.

LIBERIA - LAND USE

Euromonitor Publications Limited, 87-88 Turnmill Street, London EC1M 5QU, England; *International Marketing Data and Statistics*.

Food and Agricultural Organization of the United Nations (FAO), Via delle Terme di Caracalla, 00100 Rome, Italy (Telephone Number in U.S. (202) 653-2400); *Production Yearbook*.

G.K. Hall and Company, 70 Lincoln Street, Boston, Massachusetts 02111 (617) 423-3990; *The World in Figures*.

LIBERIA - LIBRARIES

Facts on File, 460 Park Avenue South, New York, New York 10016 (800) 443-8323; *The New Book of World Rankings*.

LIBERIA - LIFE EXPECTANCY

African Development Bank, 01 BP 1387, Abidjan 01, Cote d'Ivoire; *Selected Statistics on Regional Member Countries*.

LIBERIA - LITERACY RATE

Statistical Office of the United Nations, Publishing Service, New York, New York 10017 (800) 253-9646; *Survey of Economic and Social Conditions in Africa*.

LIBERIA - LIVESTOCK AND POULTRY

Euromonitor Publications Limited, 87-88 Turnmill Street, London EC1M 5QU, England; *International Marketing Data and Statistics*.

Facts on File, 460 Park Avenue South, New York, New York 10016 (800) 443-8323; *The New Book of World Rankings*.

Food and Agricultural Organization of the United Nations (FAO), Via delle Terme di Caracalla, 00100 Rome, Italy (Telephone Number in U.S. (202) 653-2400); *Production Yearbook*, and *The State of Food and Agriculture*.

G.K. Hall and Company, 70 Lincoln Street, Boston, Massachusetts 02111 (617) 423-3990; *The World in Figures*.

Statistical Office of the United Nations, Publishing Service, New York, New York 10017 (800) 253-9646; *Statistical Yearbook*, and *Survey of Economic and Social Conditions in Africa*.

United Nations Economic Commission for Africa, Africa Hall, Post Office Box 3001, Addis Ababa, Ethiopia (Telephone Number in U.S. (800) 253-9646); *African Statistical Yearbook*.

LIBERIA - LIVING LEVELS

G.K. Hall and Company, 70 Lincoln Street, Boston, Massachusetts 02111 (617) 423-3990; *The World in Figures*.

Times Books, 201 East 50th Street, New York, New York 10022 (212) 751-2600; *The Economist Book of Vital World Statistics*.

LIBERIA - MAIL - NUMBER OF PIECES SENT OR RECEIVED

Statistical Office of the United Nations, Publishing Service, New York, New York 10017 (800) 253-9646; *Statistical Yearbook*.

LIBERIA - MANUFACTURING

Facts on File, 460 Park Avenue South, New York, New York 10016 (800) 443-8323; *The New Book of World Rankings*.

G.K. Hall and Company, 70 Lincoln Street, Boston, Massachusetts 02111 (617) 423-3990; *The World in Figures*.

Statistical Office of the United Nations, Publishing Service, New York, New York 10017 (800) 253-9646; *Survey of Economic and Social Conditions in Africa*.

United Nations Economic Commission for Africa, Africa Hall, Post Office Box 3001, Addis Ababa, Ethiopia (Telephone Number in U.S. (800) 253-9646); *African Statistical Yearbook*.

The World Bank, 1818 H Street, NW, Washington, D.C. 20433 (202) 477-1234; *World Tables*.

LIBERIA - MARRIAGE RATES

Facts on File, 460 Park Avenue South, New York, New York 10016 (800) 443-8323; *The New Book of World Rankings*.

Statistical Office of the United Nations, Publishing Service, New York, New York 10017 (800) 253-9646; *Demographic Yearbook*, and *Statistical Yearbook*.

LIBERIA - MEAT PRODUCTION - See LIBERIA - LIVESTOCK AND POULTRY

LIBERIA - MERCHANT SHIPPING

G.K. Hall and Company, 70 Lincoln Street, Boston, Massachusetts 02111 (617) 423-3990; *The World in Figures*.

Lloyd's Register of Shipping, 17 Battery Place, New York, New York 10004 (212) 425-8050; *Register of Ships*.

Statistical Office of the United Nations, Publishing Service, New York, New York 10017 (800) 253-9646; *Statistical Yearbook*.

Times Books, 201 East 50th Street, New York, New York 10022 (212) 751-2600; *The Economist Book of Vital World Statistics*.

United Nations Economic Commission for Africa, Africa Hall, Post Office Box 3001, Addis Ababa, Ethiopia (Telephone Number in U.S. (800) 253-9646); *African Statistical Yearbook*.

U.S. Department of Transportation, Maritime Administration, 400 Seventh Street, SW, Washington, D.C. 20590; *A Statistical Analysis of the World's Merchant Fleets*.

LIBERIA - MILITARY

G.K. Hall and Company, 70 Lincoln Street, Boston, Massachusetts 02111 (617) 423-3990; *The World in Figures*.

The International Institute for Strategic Studies, 23 Tavistock Street, London WC2E 7NQ, England; *The Military Balance*.

U.S. Arms Control and Disarmament Agency, 320 Twenty-first Street, NW, Washington, D.C. 20451 (202) 647-8677; *World Military Expenditures and Arms Transfers*.

LIBERIA - MILK PRODUCTION - See LIBERIA - DAIRY PRODUCTS

LIBERIA - MINING AND MINERAL PRODUCTS

Facts on File, 460 Park Avenue South, New York, New York 10016 (800) 443-8323; *The New Book of World Rankings*.

G.K. Hall and Company, 70 Lincoln Street, Boston, Massachusetts 02111 (617) 423-3990; *The World in Figures*.

International Monetary Fund, 700 Nineteenth Street, NW, Washington, D.C. 20431 (202) 623-7000; *International Financial Statistics*.

Statistical Office of the United Nations, Publishing Service, New York, New York 10017 (800) 253-9646; *Statistical Yearbook*.

United Nations Economic Commission for Africa, Africa Hall, Post Office Box 3001, Addis Ababa, Ethiopia (Telephone Number in U.S. (800) 253-9646); *African Statistical Yearbook*.

LIBERIA - MONEY EXCHANGE RATE

Euromonitor Publications Limited, 87-88 Turnmill Street, London EC1M 5QU, England; *International Marketing Data and Statistics*.

International Monetary Fund, 700 Nineteenth Street, NW, Washington, D.C. 20431 (202) 623-7000; *International Financial Statistics*.

Statistical Office of the United Nations, Publishing Service, New York, New York 10017 (800) 253-9646; *Statistical Yearbook*.

LIBERIA - MONEY RESERVES

Euromonitor Publications Limited, 87-88 Turnmill Street, London EC1M 5QU, England; *International Marketing Data and Statistics*.

LIBERIA - MONEY SUPPLY

African Development Bank, 01 BP 1387, Abidjan 01, Cote d'Ivoire; *Selected Statistics on Regional Member Countries*.

Euromonitor Publications Limited, 87-88 Turnmill Street, London EC1M 5QU, England; *International Marketing Data and Statistics*.

G.K. Hall and Company, 70 Lincoln Street, Boston, Massachusetts 02111 (617) 423-3990; *The World in Figures*.

International Monetary Fund, 700 Nineteenth Street, NW, Washington, D.C. 20431 (202) 623-7000; *International Financial Statistics*.

The World Bank, 1818 H Street, NW, Washington, D.C. 20433 (202) 477-1234; *World Tables*.

LIBERIA - MOTOR VEHICLE TAXES - See LIBERIA - TAXATION

LIBERIA - MOTOR VEHICLES IN USE

G.K. Hall and Company, 70 Lincoln Street, Boston, Massachusetts 02111 (617) 423-3990; *The World in Figures*.

International Road Federation, 525 School Street, SW, Washington, D.C. 20024 (202) 554-2106; *World Road Statistics*.

Statistical Office of the United Nations, Publishing Service, New York, New York 10017 (800) 253-9646; *Statistical Yearbook*, and *Survey of Economic and Social Conditions in Africa*.

Times Books, 201 East 50th Street, New York, New York 10022 (212) 751-2600; *The Economist Book of Vital World Statistics*.

LIBERIA - MUSEUMS

Facts on File, 460 Park Avenue South, New York, New York 10016 (800) 443-8323; *The New Book of World Rankings*.

LIBERIA - NATALITY - See LIBERIA - BIRTH RATES

LIBERIA - NATIONAL ACCOUNTS

African Development Bank, 01 BP 1387, Abidjan 01, Cote d'Ivoire; *Selected Statistics on Regional Member Countries*.

Statistical Office of the United Nations, Publishing Service, New York, New York 10017 (800) 253-9646; *National Accounts Statistics*, and *Statistical Yearbook*.

United Nations Economic Commission for Africa, Africa Hall, Post Office Box 3001, Addis Ababa, Ethiopia (Telephone Number in U.S. (800) 253-9646); *African Statistical Yearbook*.

LIBERIA - NATIONAL INCOME

Facts on File, 460 Park Avenue South, New York, New York 10016 (800) 443-8323; *The New Book of World Rankings*.

G.K. Hall and Company, 70 Lincoln Street, Boston, Massachusetts 02111 (617) 423-3990; *The World in Figures*.

Statistical Office of the United Nations, Publishing Service, New York, New York 10017 (800) 253-9646; *Statistical Yearbook*.

LIBERIA - NATIONAL PRODUCT

Facts on File, 460 Park Avenue South, New York, New York 10016 (800) 443-8323; *The New Book of World Rankings*.

Statistical Office of the United Nations, Publishing Service, New York, New York 10017 (800) 253-9646; *Statistical Yearbook*.

LIBERIA - NATURAL GAS - PRODUCTION - See LIBERIA - MINING AND MINERAL PRODUCTS

LIBERIA - NATURAL RUBBER PRODUCTION

International Rubber Study Group, York House, Eighth Floor, Empire Way, Wembley, London HA9 0PA, England; *Rubber Statistical Bulletin*.

Statistical Office of the United Nations, Publishing Service, New York, New York 10017 (800) 253-9646; *Statistical Yearbook.*

LIBERIA - NEWSPAPER PRODUCTION - See LIBERIA - FORESTRY AND FOREST PRODUCTS

LIBERIA - NEWSPRINT - See LIBERIA - FORESTRY AND FOREST PRODUCTS

LIBERIA - OCCUPATIONS - See LIBERIA - LABOR FORCE

LIBERIA - PALM KERNEL PRODUCTION - See LIBERIA - CROPS

LIBERIA - PAPER - See LIBERIA - FORESTRY AND FOREST PRODUCTS

LIBERIA - PATENTS

World Intellectual Property Organization, 34 Chemin des Colombettes, CH-1211 Geneva 20, Switzerland; *Industrial Property Statistics.*

LIBERIA - PEANUT PRODUCTION - See LIBERIA - CROPS

LIBERIA - PESTICIDE USE

Food and Agricultural Organization of the United Nations (FAO), Via delle Terme di Caracalla, 00100 Rome, Italy (Telephone Number in U.S. (202) 653-2400); *The State of Food and Agriculture.*

LIBERIA - PETROLEUM INDUSTRY

Facts on File, 460 Park Avenue South, New York, New York 10016 (800) 443-8323; *The New Book of World Rankings.*

Food and Agricultural Organization of the United Nations (FAO), Via delle Terme di Caracalla, 00100 Rome, Italy (Telephone Number in U.S. (202) 653-2400); *The State of Food and Agriculture.*

G.K. Hall and Company, 70 Lincoln Street, Boston, Massachusetts 02111 (617) 423-3990; *The World in Figures.*

Statistical Office of the United Nations, Publishing Service, New York, New York 10017 (800) 253-9646; *Statistical Yearbook.*

LIBERIA - PIGS - See LIBERIA - LIVESTOCK AND POULTRY

LIBERIA - POPULATION

African Development Bank, 01 BP 1387, Abidjan 01, Cote d'Ivoire; *Selected Statistics on Regional Member Countries.*

The Economist Intelligence Unit, 111 West 57th Street, New York, New York 10019 (800) 938-4685; *The World Market Atlas.*

Euromonitor Publications Limited, 87-88 Turnmill Street, London EC1M 5QU, England; *International Marketing Data and Statistics.*

Facts on File, 460 Park Avenue South, New York, New York 10016 (800) 443-8323; *The New Book of World Rankings.*

Food and Agricultural Organization of the United Nations (FAO), Via delle Terme di Caracalla, 00100 Rome, Italy (Telephone Number in U.S. (202) 653-2400); *Production Yearbook.*

G.K. Hall and Company, 70 Lincoln Street, Boston, Massachusetts 02111 (617) 423-3990; *The World in Figures.*

International Labour Office, I.L.O. Publications, CH-1211, Geneva 22, Switzerland; *Yearbook of Labour Statistics.*

Statistical Office of the United Nations, Publishing Service, New York, New York 10017 (800) 253-9646; *Demographic Yearbook, Statistical Yearbook,* and *Survey of Economic and Social Conditions in Africa.*

Times Books, 201 East 50th Street, New York, New York 10022 (212) 751-2600; *The Economist Book of Vital World Statistics.*

United Nations Educational, Scientific and Cultural Organization (UNESCO), 7 Place de Fontenoy, F-75700 Paris, France (Telephone Number in U.S. (212) 963-5981); *Statistical Yearbook.*

U.S. Arms Control and Disarmament Agency, 320 Twenty-first Street, NW, Washington, D.C. 20451 (202) 647-8677; *World Military Expenditures and Arms Transfers.*

World Health Organization, Office of Publications, Avenue Appia, CH-1211 Geneva 27, Switzerland (Telephone Number in U.S. (518) 436-9686); *World Health Statistics Annual.*

LIBERIA - POST OFFICES

Facts on File, 460 Park Avenue South, New York, New York 10016 (800) 443-8323; *The New Book of World Rankings.*

LIBERIA - POTATO PRODUCTION - See LIBERIA - CROPS

LIBERIA - PRICES

Facts on File, 460 Park Avenue South, New York, New York 10016 (800) 443-8323; *The New Book of World Rankings.*

Food and Agricultural Organization of the United Nations (FAO), Via delle Terme di Caracalla, 00100 Rome, Italy (Telephone Number in U.S. (202) 653-2400); *Production Yearbook,* and *The State of Food and Agriculture.*

G.K. Hall and Company, 70 Lincoln Street, Boston, Massachusetts 02111 (617) 423-3990; *The World in Figures.*

International Labour Office, I.L.O. Publications, CH-1211, Geneva 22, Switzerland; *Yearbook of Labour Statistics.*

International Monetary Fund, 700 Nineteenth Street, NW, Washington, D.C. 20431 (202) 623-7000; *International Financial Statistics.*

International Rubber Study Group, York House, Eighth Floor, Empire Way, Wembley, London HA9 0PA, England; *Rubber Statistical Bulletin.*

United Nations Economic Commission for Africa, Africa Hall, Post Office Box 3001, Addis Ababa, Ethiopia (Telephone Number in U.S. (800) 253-9646); *African Statistical Yearbook.*

LIBERIA - PRINTING AND WRITING PAPER - See LIBERIA - FORESTRY AND FOREST PRODUCTS

LIBERIA - PRODUCTION

Facts on File, 460 Park Avenue South, New York, New York 10016 (800) 443-8323; *The New Book of World Rankings.*

G.K. Hall and Company, 70 Lincoln Street, Boston, Massachusetts 02111 (617) 423-3990; *The World in Figures.*

International Rubber Study Group, York House, Eighth Floor, Empire Way, Wembley, London HA9 0PA, England; *Rubber Statistical Bulletin.*

LIBERIA - PRODUCTIVITY

Euromonitor Publications Limited, 87-88 Turnmill Street, London EC1M 5QU, England; *International Marketing Data and Statistics.*

LIBERIA - PROPERTY TAXES - See LIBERIA - TAXATION

LIBERIA - PUBLIC FINANCE

Facts on File, 460 Park Avenue South, New York, New York 10016 (800) 443-8323; *The New Book of World Rankings.*

LIBERIA - RADIO BROADCASTING - See LIBERIA - BROADCASTING

LIBERIA - RAILWAYS

G.K. Hall and Company, 70 Lincoln Street, Boston, Massachusetts 02111 (617) 423-3990; *The World in Figures.*

Jane's Information Group, Sentinel House, 163 Brighton Road, Coulsdon, Surrey CR5 2NH, England (Telephone Number in U.S. (703) 683-3700); *Jane's World Railways.*

Statistical Office of the United Nations, Publishing Service, New York, New York 10017 (800) 253-9646; *Survey of Economic and Social Conditions in Africa*

United Nations Economic Commission for Africa, Africa Hall, Post Office Box 3001, Addis Ababa, Ethiopia (Telephone Number in U.S. (800) 253-9646); *African Statistical Yearbook.*

LIBERIA - RELIGION

Facts on File, 460 Park Avenue South, New York, New York 10016 (800) 443-8323; *The New Book of World Rankings.*

LIBERIA - RENT PRICES

International Labour Office, I.L.O. Publications, CH-1211, Geneva 22, Switzerland; *Yearbook of Labour Statistics.*

LIBERIA - RETAIL TRADE

G.K. Hall and Company, 70 Lincoln Street, Boston, Massachusetts 02111 (617) 423-3990; *The World in Figures.*

LIBERIA - RICE PRODUCTION - See LIBERIA - CROPS

LIBERIA - ROOT AND TUBER PRODUCTION - See LIBERIA - CROPS

LIBERIA - ROUNDWOOD PRODUCTION - See LIBERIA - FORESTRY AND FOREST PRODUCTS

LIBERIA - RUBBER EXPORTS

International Monetary Fund, 700 Nineteenth Street, NW, Washington, D.C. 20431 (202) 623-7000; *International Financial Statistics.*

LIBERIA - RUBBER PRODUCTION AND CONSUMPTION

Facts on File, 460 Park Avenue South, New York, New York 10016 (800) 443-8323; *The New Book of World Rankings.*

International Rubber Study Group, York House, Eighth Floor, Empire Way, Wembley, London HA9 0PA, England; *Rubber Statistical Bulletin.*

Statistical Office of the United Nations, Publishing Service, New York, New York 10017 (800) 253-9646; *Statistical Yearbook.*

LIBERIA - SAWNWOOD PRODUCTION - See LIBERIA - FORESTRY AND FOREST PRODUCTS

LIBERIA - SCIENTISTS AND TECHNICIANS

United Nations Educational, Scientific and Cultural Organization (UNESCO), 7 Place de Fontenoy, F-75700 Paris, France (Telephone Number in U.S. (212) 963-5981); *Statistical Yearbook.*

LIBERIA - SENIOR CITIZENS

Facts on File, 460 Park Avenue South, New York, New York 10016 (800) 443-8323; *The New Book of World Rankings.*

LIBERIA - SHEEP - See LIBERIA - LIVESTOCK AND POULTRY

LIBERIA - SILVER PRODUCTION AND CONSUMPTION - See LIBERIA - MINING AND MINERAL PRODUCTS

LIBERIA - SOCIAL DATA

African Development Bank, 01 BP 1387, Abidjan 01, Cote d'Ivoire; *Selected Statistics on Regional Member Countries*

Facts on File, 460 Park Avenue South, New York, New York 10016 (800) 443-8323; *The New Book of World Rankings.*

G.K. Hall and Company, 70 Lincoln Street, Boston, Massachusetts 02111 (617) 423-3990; *The World in Figures.*

LIBERIA - SOCIAL SECURITY EXPENDITURES

International Monetary Fund, 700 Nineteenth Street, NW, Washington, D.C. 20431 (202) 623-7000; *Government Finance Statistics Yearbook.*

LIBERIA - STAMP TAXES AND DUTIES - See LIBERIA - TAXATION

LIBERIA - STATE BUDGET

Euromonitor Publications Limited, 87-88 Turnmill Street, London EC1M 5QU, England; *International Marketing Data and Statistics.*

LIBERIA - STEEL - See LIBERIA - MINING AND MINERAL PRODUCTS

LIBERIA - STOCKS - COMMODITY - MARKET PRICE - INDEX

Food and Agricultural Organization of the United Nations (FAO), Via delle Terme di Caracalla, 00100 Rome, Italy (Telephone Number in U.S. (202) 653-2400); *The State of Food and Agriculture.*

LIBERIA - SUGAR PRODUCTION AND CONSUMPTION - See LIBERIA - CROPS

LIBERIA - TAXATION

G.K. Hall and Company, 70 Lincoln Street, Boston, Massachusetts 02111 (617) 423-3990; *The World in Figures.*

International Monetary Fund, 700 Nineteenth Street, NW, Washington, D.C. 20431 (202) 623-7000; *Government Finance Statistics Yearbook.*

International Road Federation, 525 School Street, SW, Washington, D.C. 20024 (202) 554-2106; *World Road Statistics*.

The World Bank, 1818 H Street, NW, Washington, D.C. 20433 (202) 477-1234; *World Tables*.

LIBERIA - TELEPHONES IN USE

American Telephone and Telegraph Company, 26 Parsippany Road, Whippany, New Jersey 07981 (800) 338-4038; *The World's Telephones*.

G.K. Hall and Company, 70 Lincoln Street, Boston, Massachusetts 02111 (617) 423-3990; *The World in Figures*.

Statistical Office of the United Nations, Publishing Service, New York, New York 10017 (800) 253-9646; *Statistical Yearbook*.

LIBERIA - TELEVISION BROADCASTING - See LIBERIA - BROADCASTING

LIBERIA - TEXTILE INDUSTRY

G.K. Hall and Company, 70 Lincoln Street, Boston, Massachusetts 02111 (617) 423-3990; *The World in Figures*.

LIBERIA - TIRE (MOTOR VEHICLE) PRODUCTION

International Rubber Study Group, York House, Eighth Floor, Empire Way, Wembley, London HA9 0PA, England; *Rubber Statistical Bulletin*.

LIBERIA - TOBACCO PRODUCTION

Facts on File, 460 Park Avenue South, New York, New York 10016 (800) 443-8323; *The New Book of World Rankings*.

Statistical Office of the United Nations, Publishing Service, New York, New York 10017 (800) 253-9646; *Statistical Yearbook*.

LIBERIA - TOURISM

Facts on File, 460 Park Avenue South, New York, New York 10016 (800) 443-8323; *The New Book of World Rankings*.

G.K. Hall and Company, 70 Lincoln Street, Boston, Massachusetts 02111 (617) 423-3990; *The World in Figures*.

United Nations Economic Commission for Africa, Africa Hall, Post Office Box 3001, Addis Ababa, Ethiopia (Telephone Number in U.S. (800) 253-9646); *African Statistical Yearbook*.

LIBERIA - TRACTORS IN USE

Statistical Office of the United Nations, Publishing Service, New York, New York 10017 (800) 253-9646; *Statistical Yearbook*.

LIBERIA - TRADE - See LIBERIA - FOREIGN TRADE

LIBERIA - TRADEMARKS AND SERVICE MARKS

World Intellectual Property Organization, 34 Chemin des Colombettes, CH-1211 Geneva 20, Switzerland; *Industrial Property Statistics*.

LIBERIA - TRANSPORTATION AND COMMUNICATIONS

Euromonitor Publications Limited, 87-88 Turnmill Street, London EC1M 5QU, England; *International Marketing Data and Statistics*.

Facts on File, 460 Park Avenue South, New York, New York 10016 (800) 443-8323; *The New Book of World Rankings*.

G.K. Hall and Company, 70 Lincoln Street, Boston, Massachusetts 02111 (617) 423-3990; *The World in Figures*.

United Nations Economic Commission for Africa, Africa Hall, Post Office Box 3001, Addis Ababa, Ethiopia (Telephone Number in U.S. (800) 253-9646); *African Statistical Yearbook*.

LIBERIA - UNEMPLOYMENT

International Labour Office, I.L.O. Publications, CH-1211, Geneva 22, Switzerland; *Yearbook of Labour Statistics*.

Statistical Office of the United Nations, Publishing Service, New York, New York 10017 (800) 253-9646; *Statistical Yearbook*.

LIBERIA - VITAL STATISTICS

Euromonitor Publications Limited, 87-88 Turnmill Street, London EC1M 5QU, England; *International Marketing Data and Statistics*.

G.K. Hall and Company, 70 Lincoln Street, Boston, Massachusetts 02111 (617) 423-3990; *The World in Figures*.

Statistical Office of the United Nations, Publishing Service, New York, New York 10017 (800) 253-9646; *Statistical Yearbook*.

World Health Organization, Office of Publications, Avenue Appia, CH-1211 Geneva 27, Switzerland (Telephone Number in U.S. (518) 436-9686); *World Health Statistics Annual*.

LIBERIA - WAGES

G.K. Hall and Company, 70 Lincoln Street, Boston, Massachusetts 02111 (617) 423-3990; *The World in Figures*.

International Labour Office, I.L.O. Publications, CH-1211, Geneva 22, Switzerland; *Yearbook of Labour Statistics*.

LIBERIA - WEATHER

Facts on File, 460 Park Avenue South, New York, New York 10016 (800) 443-8323; *The New Book of World Rankings*.

G.K. Hall and Company, 70 Lincoln Street, Boston, Massachusetts 02111 (617) 423-3990; *The World in Figures*.

LIBERIA - WELFARE EXPENDITURES

International Monetary Fund, 700 Nineteenth Street, NW, Washington, D.C. 20431 (202) 623-7000; *Government Finance Statistics Yearbook*.

LIBERIA - WHEAT PRODUCTION

Facts on File, 460 Park Avenue South, New York, New York 10016 (800) 443-8323; *The New Book of World Rankings*.

LIBERIA - WINE PRODUCTION

Facts on File, 460 Park Avenue South, New York, New York 10016 (800) 443-8323; *The New Book of World Rankings*.

LIBERIA - WOOL PRODUCTION

Facts on File, 460 Park Avenue South, New York, New York 10016 (800) 443-8323; *The New Book of World Rankings*.

LIBRARIES AND LIBRARIANS

R.R. Bowker Company, 245 West Seventeenth Street, New York, New York 10011 (212) 645-9700; *The Bowker Annual: Library and Book Trade Almanac*, and *American Library Directory*.

U.S. Department of Education, 400 Maryland Avenue, SW, Washington, D.C. 20202 (202) 708-5366; *Digest of Education Statistics, Public Libraries in the United States*, and *Academic Libraries*.

LIBRARIES AND LIBRARIANS - CITY GOVERNMENTS

U.S. Department of Commerce, Bureau of the Census, Suitland, Maryland 20233 (301) 763-4040; *City Government Finances*.

LIBRARIES AND LIBRARIANS - DEGREES CONFERRED

U.S. Department of Education, National Center for Education Statistics, 400 Maryland Avenue, NW, Washington, D.C. 20202 (202) 708-5366; *Digest of Education Statistics*.

LIBRARIES AND LIBRARIANS - EMPLOYEES

U.S. Department of Commerce, Bureau of the Census, Suitland, Maryland 20233 (301) 763-4040; *City Employment*.

U.S. Department of Labor, Bureau of Labor Statistics, Two Massachusetts Avenue, NE, Washington, D.C. 20212 (202) 606-7828; *Employment and Earnings*.

LIBRARIES AND LIBRARIANS - GRANTS, FOUNDATIONS

The Foundation Center, 79 Fifth Avenue, New York, New York 10003; *Foundation Grants Index*.

Libya - National Statistical Office

Central Statistical Office, Ministry of Development and Planning, Tripoli, Libya.

Libya - Primary Statistics Sources

Census and Statistical Department, Secretariat of Planning, 40 Sharia Damascus, Tripoli, Libya; *Statistical Abstract of Libya*, and *Quarterly Bulletin of Statistics*.

LIBYA - AGRICULTURE

Euromonitor Publications Limited, 87-88 Turnmill Street, London EC1M 5QU, England; *International Marketing Data and Statistics*, and *Third World Economic Handbook*.

Facts on File, 460 Park Avenue South, New York, New York 10016 (800) 443-8323; *The New Book of World Rankings*.

Food and Agricultural Organization of the United Nations (FAO), Via delle Terme di Caracalla, 00100 Rome, Italy (Telephone Number in U.S. (202) 653-2400); *Production Yearbook, The State of Food and Agriculture*, and *Trade Yearbook*.

G.K. Hall and Company, 70 Lincoln Street, Boston, Massachusetts 02111 (617) 423-3990; *The World in Figures*.

Statistical Office of the United Nations, Publishing Service, New York, New York 10017 (800) 253-9646; *Statistical Yearbook*, and *Survey of Economic and Social Conditions in Africa*.

Times Books, 201 East 50th Street, New York, New York 10022 (212) 751-2600; *The Economist Book of Vital World Statistics*.

United Nations Economic Commission for Africa, Africa Hall, Post Office Box 3001, Addis Ababa, Ethiopia (Telephone Number in U.S. (800) 253-9646); *African Statistical Yearbook*.

The World Bank, 1818 H Street, NW, Washington, D.C. 20433 (202) 477-1234; *World Tables*.

LIBYA - AIRLINE SERVICE

Facts on File, 460 Park Avenue South, New York, New York 10016 (800) 443-8323; *The New Book of World Rankings*.

G.K. Hall and Company, 70 Lincoln Street, Boston, Massachusetts 02111 (617) 423-3990; *The World in Figures*.

Statistical Office of the United Nations, Publishing Service, New York, New York 10017 (800) 253-9646; *Statistical Yearbook*.

Times Books, 201 East 50th Street, New York, New York 10022 (212) 751-2600; *The Economist Book of Vital World Statistics*.

United Nations Economic Commission for Africa, Africa Hall, Post Office Box 3001, Addis Ababa, Ethiopia (Telephone Number in U.S. (800) 253-9646); *African Statistical Yearbook*.

LIBYA - ALMOND PRODUCTION - See LIBYA - CROPS

LIBYA - ALUMINUM PRODUCTION AND CONSUMPTION - See LIBYA - MINING AND MINERAL PRODUCTS

LIBYA - ANIMAL HEALTH

Food and Agricultural Organization of the United Nations (FAO), Via delle Terme di Caracalla, 00100 Rome, Italy (Telephone Number in U.S. (202) 653-2400); *Animal Health Yearbook*.

LIBYA - AREA AND DENSITY OF POPULATION

African Development Bank, 01 BP 1387, Abidjan 01, Cote d'Ivoire; *Selected Statistics on Regional Member Countries*.

Euromonitor Publications Limited, 87-88 Turnmill Street, London EC1M 5QU, England; *International Marketing Data and Statistics*, and *Middle East Economic Handbook*.

Facts on File, 460 Park Avenue South, New York, New York 10016 (800) 443-8323; *The New Book of World Rankings*.

Food and Agricultural Organization of the United Nations (FAO), Via delle Terme di Caracalla, 00100 Rome, Italy (Telephone Number in U.S. (202) 653-2400); *The State of Food and Agriculture*.

G.K. Hall and Company, 70 Lincoln Street, Boston, Massachusetts 02111 (617) 423-3990; *The World in Figures*.

Statistical Office of the United Nations, Publishing Service, New York, New York 10017 (800) 253-9646; *Statistical Yearbook*, and *Survey of Economic and Social Conditions in Africa*.

Times Books, 201 East 50th Street, New York, New York 10022 (212) 751-2600; *The Economist Book of Vital World Statistics*.

United Nations Educational, Scientific and Cultural Organization (UNESCO), 7 Place de Fontenoy, F-75700 Paris, France (Telephone Number in U.S. (212) 963-5981); *Statistical Yearbook*.

LIBYA - ARMS EXPORTS AND IMPORTS

U.S. Arms Control and Disarmament Agency, 320 Twenty-first Street, NW, Washington, D.C. 20451 (202) 647-8677; *World Military Expenditures and Arms Transfers*.

LIBYA - BALANCE OF PAYMENTS

African Development Bank, 01 BP 1387, Abidjan 01, Cote d'Ivoire; *Selected Statistics on Regional Member Countries*.

The Economist Intelligence Unit, 111 West 57th Street, New York, New York 10019 (800) 938-4685; *The World Market Atlas*.

Euromonitor Publications Limited, 87-88 Turnmill Street, London EC1M 5QU, England; *Third World Economic Handbook*.

G.K. Hall and Company, 70 Lincoln Street, Boston, Massachusetts 02111 (617) 423-3990; *The World in Figures*.

International Monetary Fund, 700 Nineteenth Street, NW, Washington, D.C. 20431 (202) 623-7000; *Balance of Payments Yearbook*, and *Balance of Payments Yearbook*.

Times Books, 201 East 50th Street, New York, New York 10022 (212) 751-2600; *The Economist Book of Vital World Statistics*.

United Nations Economic Commission for Africa, Africa Hall, Post Office Box 3001, Addis Ababa, Ethiopia (Telephone Number in U.S. (800) 253-9646); *African Statistical Yearbook*.

The World Bank, 1818 H Street, NW, Washington, D.C. 20433 (202) 477-1234; *World Tables*.

LIBYA - BANKING

Facts on File, 460 Park Avenue South, New York, New York 10016 (800) 443-8323; *The New Book of World Rankings*.

G.K. Hall and Company, 70 Lincoln Street, Boston, Massachusetts 02111 (617) 423-3990; *The World in Figures*.

International Monetary Fund, 700 Nineteenth Street, NW, Washington, D.C. 20431 (202) 623-7000; *International Financial Statistics*.

Statistical Office of the United Nations, Publishing Service, New York, New York 10017 (800) 253-9646; *Statistical Yearbook*.

United Nations Economic Commission for Africa, Africa Hall, Post Office Box 3001, Addis Ababa, Ethiopia (Telephone Number in U.S. (800) 253-9646); *African Statistical Yearbook*.

LIBYA - BARLEY PRODUCTION - See LIBYA - CROPS

LIBYA - BEER PRODUCTION

Facts on File, 460 Park Avenue South, New York, New York 10016 (800) 443-8323; *The New Book of World Rankings*.

Statistical Office of the United Nations, Publishing Service, New York, New York 10017 (800) 253-9646; *Statistical Yearbook*.

LIBYA - BIRTH RATES

Euromonitor Publications Limited, 87-88 Turnmill Street, London EC1M 5QU, England; *Middle East Economic Handbook*, and *Third World Economic Handbook*.

Facts on File, 460 Park Avenue South, New York, New York 10016 (800) 443-8323; *The New Book of World Rankings*.

Statistical Office of the United Nations, Publishing Service, New York, New York 10017 (800) 253-9646; *Demographic Yearbook, Statistical Yearbook*, and *Survey of Economic and Social Conditions in Africa*.

Times Books, 201 East 50th Street, New York, New York 10022 (212) 751-2600; *The Economist Book of Vital World Statistics*.

The World Bank, 1818 H Street, NW, Washington, D.C. 20433 (202) 477-1234; *World Tables*.

World Health Organization, Office of Publications, Avenue Appia, CH-1211 Geneva 27, Switzerland (Telephone Number in U.S. (518) 436-9686); *World Health Statistics Annual*.

LIBYA - BONDS

G.K. Hall and Company, 70 Lincoln Street, Boston, Massachusetts 02111 (617) 423-3990; *The World in Figures*.

LIBYA - BOOK PRODUCTION

G.K. Hall and Company, 70 Lincoln Street, Boston, Massachusetts 02111 (617) 423-3990; *The World in Figures*.

United Nations Educational, Scientific and Cultural Organization (UNESCO), 7 Place de Fontenoy, F-75700 Paris, France (Telephone Number in U.S. (212) 963-5981); *Statistical Yearbook*.

LIBYA - BROADCASTING

Billboard Limited, Post Office Box 9027, 1006 AA Amsterdam, The Netherlands (Telephone Number in U.S. (212) 764-7300); *World Radio TV Handbook*.

Facts on File, 460 Park Avenue South, New York, New York 10016 (800) 443-8323; *The New Book of World Rankings*.

G.K. Hall and Company, 70 Lincoln Street, Boston, Massachusetts 02111 (617) 423-3990; *The World in Figures*.

Times Books, 201 East 50th Street, New York, New York 10022 (212) 751-2600; *The Economist Book of Vital World Statistics*.

LIBYA - BUSINESS

G.K. Hall and Company, 70 Lincoln Street, Boston, Massachusetts 02111 (617) 423-3990; *The World in Figures*.

LIBYA - CALORIE SUPPLY

African Development Bank, 01 BP 1387, Abidjan 01, Cote d'Ivoire; *Selected Statistics on Regional Member Countries*.

Food and Agricultural Organization of the United Nations (FAO), Via delle Terme di Caracalla, 00100 Rome, Italy (Telephone Number in U.S. (202) 653-2400); *The State of Food and Agriculture*.

LIBYA - CATTLE - See LIBYA - LIVESTOCK AND POULTRY

LIBYA - CEMENT PRODUCTION - See LIBYA - MINING AND MINERAL PRODUCTS

LIBYA - CHEMICAL (ORGANIC) PRODUCTION - See LIBYA - MINING AND MINERAL PRODUCTS

LIBYA - CHICKENS - See LIBYA - LIVESTOCK AND POULTRY

LIBYA - CIGAR AND CIGARETTE PRODUCTION - See LIBYA - TOBACCO PRODUCTION

LIBYA - CLASS STRUCTURE

G.K. Hall and Company, 70 Lincoln Street, Boston, Massachusetts 02111 (617) 423-3990; *The World in Figures.*

LIBYA - CLIMATE

Facts on File, 460 Park Avenue South, New York, New York 10016 (800) 443-8323; *The New Book of World Rankings.*

G.K. Hall and Company, 70 Lincoln Street, Boston, Massachusetts 02111 (617) 423-3990; *The World in Figures.*

LIBYA - CLOTHING EXPORTS AND IMPORTS - See LIBYA - TEXTILE INDUSTRY

LIBYA - COAL PRODUCTION See LIBYA - MINING AND MINERAL PRODUCTS

LIBYA - COFFEE PRODUCTION AND CONSUMPTION - See LIBYA - CROPS

LIBYA - COMMUNICATIONS

Euromonitor Publications Limited, 87-88 Turnmill Street, London EC1M 5QU, England; *Third World Economic Handbook.*

G.K. Hall and Company, 70 Lincoln Street, Boston, Massachusetts 02111 (617) 423-3990; *The World in Figures.*

United Nations Economic Commission for Africa, Africa Hall, Post Office Box 3001, Addis Ababa, Ethiopia (Telephone Number in U.S. (800) 253-9646); *African Statistical Yearbook.*

LIBYA - CONSTRUCTION INDUSTRY

Facts on File, 460 Park Avenue South, New York, New York 10016 (800) 443-8323; *The New Book of World Rankings.*

Statistical Office of the United Nations, Publishing Service, New York, New York 10017 (800) 253-9646; *Statistical Yearbook.*

United Nations Economic Commission for Africa, Africa Hall, Post Office Box 3001, Addis Ababa, Ethiopia (Telephone Number in U.S. (800) 253-9646); *African Statistical Yearbook.*

LIBYA - CONSUMER PRICE INDEX

African Development Bank, 01 BP 1387, Abidjan 01, Cote d'Ivoire; *Selected Statistics on Regional Member Countries.*

G.K. Hall and Company, 70 Lincoln Street, Boston, Massachusetts 02111 (617) 423-3990; *The World in Figures.*

Statistical Office of the United Nations, Publishing Service, New York, New York 10017 (800) 253-9646; *Statistical Yearbook*, and *Survey of Economic and Social Conditions in Africa.*

United Nations Economic Commission for Africa, Africa Hall, Post Office Box 3001, Addis Ababa, Ethiopia (Telephone Number in U.S. (800) 253-9646); *African Statistical Yearbook.*

LIBYA - CONSUMER PRICES

International Labour Office, I.L.O. Publications, CH-1211, Geneva 22, Switzerland; *Yearbook of Labour Statistics.*

International Monetary Fund, 700 Nineteenth Street, NW, Washington, D.C. 20431 (202) 623-7000; *International Financial Statistics.*

Times Books, 201 East 50th Street, New York, New York 10022 (212) 751-2600; *The Economist Book of Vital World Statistics.*

LIBYA - CONSUMPTION

African Development Bank, 01 BP 1387, Abidjan 01, Cote d'Ivoire; *Selected Statistics on Regional Member Countries.*

Euromonitor Publications Limited, 87-88 Turnmill Street, London EC1M 5QU, England; *Middle East Economic Handbook.*

G.K. Hall and Company, 70 Lincoln Street, Boston, Massachusetts 02111 (617) 423-3990; *The World in Figures.*

Statistical Office of the United Nations, Publishing Service, New York, New York 10017 (800) 253-9646; *Survey of Economic and Social Conditions in Africa.*

LIBYA - COPPER PRODUCTION AND CONSUMPTION - See LIBYA - MINING AND MINERAL PRODUCTS

LIBYA - CORN PRODUCTION See LIBYA - CROPS

LIBYA - CORPORATE TAXES - See LIBYA - TAXATION

LIBYA - COTTON PRODUCTION - See LIBYA - CROPS

LIBYA - CRIME

International Criminal Police Organization (INTERPOL), 26 rue Armengaud, 92210 Saint Cloud, France; *International Crime Statistics.*

Yale University Press, Yale Station, New Haven, Connecticut 06520 (203) 432-0940; *Violence and Crime in Cross-National Perspective.*

LIBYA - CROPS

Facts on File, 460 Park Avenue South, New York, New York 10016 (800) 443-8323; *The New Book of World Rankings.*

Food and Agricultural Organization of the United Nations (FAO), Via delle Terme di Caracalla, 00100 Rome, Italy (Telephone Number in U.S. (202) 653-2400; *Production Yearbook*, and *The State of Food and Agriculture.*

G.K. Hall and Company, 70 Lincoln Street, Boston, Massachusetts 02111 (617) 423-3990; *The World in Figures.*

Statistical Office of the United Nations, Publishing Service, New York, New York 10017 (800) 253-9646; *Statistical Yearbook.*

United Nations Economic Commission for Africa, Africa Hall, Post Office Box 3001, Addis Ababa, Ethiopia (Telephone Number in U.S. (800) 253-9646); *African Statistical Yearbook.*

LIBYA - CUSTOMS DUTIES

G.K. Hall and Company, 70 Lincoln Street, Boston, Massachusetts 02111 (617) 423-3990; *The World in Figures.*

LIBYA - DAIRY PRODUCTS

Facts on File, 460 Park Avenue South, New York, New York 10016 (800) 443-8323; *The New Book of World Rankings*.

Food and Agricultural Organization of the United Nations (FAO), Via delle Terme di Caracalla, 00100 Rome, Italy (Telephone Number in U.S. (202) 653-2400); *The State of Food and Agriculture*, and *Production Yearbook*.

Statistical Office of the United Nations, Publishing Service, New York, New York 10017 (800) 253-9646; *Statistical Yearbook*.

LIBYA - DEATH RATES

Euromonitor Publications Limited, 87-88 Turnmill Street, London EC1M 5QU, England; *Middle East Economic Handbook*, and *Third World Economic Handbook*.

G.K. Hall and Company, 70 Lincoln Street, Boston, Massachusetts 02111 (617) 423-3990; *The World in Figures*.

Statistical Office of the United Nations, Publishing Service, New York, New York 10017 (800) 253-9646; *Statistical Yearbook*, and *Survey of Economic and Social Conditions in Africa*.

Times Books, 201 East 50th Street, New York, New York 10022 (212) 751-2600; *The Economist Book of Vital World Statistics*.

World Health Organization, Office of Publications, Avenue Appia, CH-1211 Geneva 27, Switzerland (Telephone Number in U.S. (518) 436-9686); *World Health Statistics Annual*.

LIBYA - DEFENSE EXPENDITURES

G.K. Hall and Company, 70 Lincoln Street, Boston, Massachusetts 02111 (617) 423-3990; *The World in Figures*.

U.S. Arms Control and Disarmament Agency, 320 Twenty-first Street, NW, Washington, D.C. 20451 (202) 647-8677; *World Military Expenditures and Arms Transfers*.

LIBYA - DEMOGRAPHY

The Economist Intelligence Unit, 111 West 57th Street, New York, New York 10019 (800) 938-4685; *The World Market Atlas*.

Facts on File, 460 Park Avenue South, New York, New York 10016 (800) 443-8323; *The New Book of World Rankings*.

G.K. Hall and Company, 70 Lincoln Street, Boston, Massachusetts 02111 (617) 423-3990; *The World in Figures*.

Statistical Office of the United Nations, Publishing Service, New York, New York 10017 (800) 253-9646; *Survey of Economic and Social Conditions in Africa*.

LIBYA - DEVELOPMENT ASSISTANCE

G.K. Hall and Company, 70 Lincoln Street, Boston, Massachusetts 02111 (617) 423-3990; *The World in Figures*.

Statistical Office of the United Nations, Publishing Service, New York, New York 10017 (800) 253-9646; *Statistical Yearbook*.

LIBYA - DIAMOND PRODUCTION - See LIBYA - MINING AND MINERAL PRODUCTS

LIBYA - DISCOUNT RATES

Statistical Office of the United Nations, Publishing Service, New York, New York 10017 (800) 253-9646; *Statistical Yearbook*.

LIBYA - DISEASE

G.K. Hall and Company, 70 Lincoln Street, Boston, Massachusetts 02111 (617) 423-3990; *The World in Figures*.

World Health Organization, Office of Publications, Avenue Appia, CH-1211 Geneva 27, Switzerland (Telephone Number in U.S. (518) 436-9686); *World Health Statistics Annual*.

LIBYA - DIVORCE

Facts on File, 460 Park Avenue South, New York, New York 10016 (800) 443-8323; *The New Book of World Rankings*.

Statistical Office of the United Nations, Publishing Service, New York, New York 10017 (800) 253-9646; *Demographic Yearbook*, and *Statistical Yearbook*.

LIBYA - DOMESTIC PRODUCT

G.K. Hall and Company, 70 Lincoln Street, Boston, Massachusetts 02111 (617) 423-3990; *The World in Figures*.

LIBYA - ECONOMY

African Development Bank, 01 BP 1387, Abidjan 01, Cote d'Ivoire; *Selected Statistics on Regional Member Countries*.

Euromonitor Publications Limited, 87-88 Turnmill Street, London EC1M 5QU, England; *International Marketing Data and Statistics*, and *Third World Economic Handbook*.

Facts on File, 460 Park Avenue South, New York, New York 10016 (800) 443-8323; *The New Book of World Rankings*.

G.K. Hall and Company, 70 Lincoln Street, Boston, Massachusetts 02111 (617) 423-3990; *The World in Figures*.

Statistical Office of the United Nations, Publishing Service, New York, New York 10017 (800) 253-9646; *Foreign Trade Statistics for Africa*.

LIBYA - EDUCATION

African Development Bank, 01 BP 1387, Abidjan 01, Cote d'Ivoire; *Selected Statistics on Regional Member Countries*.

The Economist Intelligence Unit, 111 West 57th Street, New York, New York 10019 (800) 938-4685; *The World Market Atlas*.

Euromonitor Publications Limited, 87-88 Turnmill Street, London EC1M 5QU, England; *Middle East Economic Handbook*.

Facts on File, 460 Park Avenue South, New York, New York 10016 (800) 443-8323; *The New Book of World Rankings*.

G.K. Hall and Company, 70 Lincoln Street, Boston, Massachusetts 02111 (617) 423-3990; *The World in Figures*.

Statistical Office of the United Nations, Publishing Service, New York, New York 10017 (800) 253-9646; *Survey of Economic and Social Conditions in Africa*.

Times Books, 201 East 50th Street, New York, New York 10022 (212) 751-2600; *The Economist Book of Vital World Statistics*.

United Nations Economic Commission for Africa, Africa Hall, Post Office Box 3001, Addis Ababa, Ethiopia (Telephone Number in U.S. (800) 253-9646); *African Statistical Yearbook*.

United Nations Educational, Scientific and Cultural Organization (UNESCO), 7 Place de Fontenoy, F-75700 Paris, France (Telephone Number in U.S. (212) 963-5981); *Statistical Yearbook*.

The World Bank, 1818 H Street, NW, Washington, D.C. 20433 (202) 477-1234; *World Tables*.

LIBYA - EGG PRODUCTION AND CONSUMPTION - See LIBYA - DAIRY PRODUCTS

LIBYA - ELECTRICITY

Facts on File, 460 Park Avenue South, New York, New York 10016 (800) 443-8323; *The New Book of World Rankings*.

Penn Well Publishing Company, 1421 South Sheridan Road, Post Office Box 1260, Tulsa, Oklahoma 74101 (800) 752-9764; *International Energy Statistics Sourcebook*.

Statistical Office of the United Nations, Publishing Service, New York, New York 10017 (800) 253-9646; *Statistical Yearbook*, and *Survey of Economic and Social Conditions in Africa*.

Times Books, 201 East 50th Street, New York, New York 10022 (212) 751-2600; *The Economist Book of Vital World Statistics*.

United Nations Economic Commission for Africa, Africa Hall, Post Office Box 3001, Addis Ababa, Ethiopia (Telephone Number in U.S. (800) 253-9646); *African Statistical Yearbook*.

LIBYA - EMPLOYMENT

Euromonitor Publications Limited, 87-88 Turnmill Street, London EC1M 5QU, England; *International Marketing Data and Statistics*, and *Middle East Economic Handbook*.

Facts on File, 460 Park Avenue South, New York, New York 10016 (800) 443-8323; *The New Book of World Rankings*.

International Labour Office, I.L.O. Publications, CH-1211, Geneva 22, Switzerland; *Yearbook of Labour Statistics*.

Statistical Office of the United Nations, Publishing Service, New York, New York 10017 (800) 253-9646; *Statistical Yearbook*, and *Survey of Economic and Social Conditions in Africa*.

United Nations Economic Commission for Africa, Africa Hall, Post Office Box 3001, Addis Ababa, Ethiopia (Telephone Number in U.S. (800) 253-9646); *African Statistical Yearbook*.

LIBYA - ENERGY

Facts on File, 460 Park Avenue South, New York, New York 10016 (800) 443-8323; *The New Book of World Rankings*.

Food and Agricultural Organization of the United Nations (FAO), Via delle Terme di Caracalla, 00100 Rome, Italy (Telephone Number in U.S. (202) 653-2400); *The State of Food and Agriculture*.

G.K. Hall and Company, 70 Lincoln Street, Boston, Massachusetts 02111 (617) 423-3990; *The World in Figures*.

Penn Well Publishing Company, 1421 South Sheridan Road, Post Office Box 1260, Tulsa, Oklahoma 74101 (800) 752-9764; *International Energy Statistics Sourcebook*.

Statistical Office of the United Nations, Publishing Service, New York, New York 10017 (800) 253-9646; *Energy Statistics Yearbook*, and *Statistical Yearbook*.

Times Books, 201 East 50th Street, New York, New York 10022 (212) 751-2600; *The Economist Book of Vital World Statistics*.

United Nations Economic Commission for Africa, Africa Hall, Post Office Box 3001, Addis Ababa, Ethiopia (Telephone Number in U.S. (800) 253-9646); *African Statistical Yearbook*.

LIBYA - EXCHANGE RATE

African Development Bank, 01 BP 1387, Abidjan 01, Cote d'Ivoire; *Selected Statistics on Regional Member Countries*.

Euromonitor Publications Limited, 87-88 Turnmill Street, London EC1M 5QU, England; *International Marketing Data and Statistics*, and *Middle East Economic Handbook*.

International Monetary Fund, 700 Nineteenth Street, NW, Washington, D.C. 20431 (202) 623-7000; *International Financial Statistics*.

Organization of Petroleum Exporting Countries, Obere Donaustrasse 93, 1020 Vienna 2, Austria; *OPEC Annual Statistical Bulletin*.

Statistical Office of the United Nations, Publishing Service, New York, New York 10017 (800) 253-9646; *Foreign Trade Statistics for Africa*, and *Statistical Yearbook*.

LIBYA - EXPORTS

African Development Bank, 01 BP 1387, Abidjan 01, Cote d'Ivoire; *Selected Statistics on Regional Member Countries*.

The Economist Intelligence Unit, 111 West 57th Street, New York, New York 10019 (800) 938-4685; *The World Market Atlas*.

Euromonitor Publications Limited, 87-88 Turnmill Street, London EC1M 5QU, England; *International Marketing Data and Statistics*, *Middle East Economic Handbook*, and *Third World Economic Handbook*.

Food and Agricultural Organization of the United Nations (FAO), Via delle Terme di Caracalla, 00100 Rome, Italy (Telephone Number in U.S. (202) 653-2400); *The State of Food and Agriculture*.

G.K. Hall and Company, 70 Lincoln Street, Boston, Massachusetts 02111 (617) 423-3990; *The World in Figures*.

International Monetary Fund, 700 Nineteenth Street, NW, Washington, D.C. 20431 (202) 623-7000; *Direction of Trade Statistics*, and *International Financial Statistics*.

Organization of Petroleum Exporting Countries, Obere Donaustrasse 93, 1020 Vienna 2, Austria; *OPEC Annual Statistical Bulletin*.

Statistical Office of the United Nations, Publishing Service, New York, New York 10017 (800) 253-9646; *Foreign Trade Statistics for Africa*, *Trade in Manufactures of Developing Countries*, and *Survey of Economic and Social Conditions in Africa*.

Times Books, 201 East 50th Street, New York, New York 10022 (212) 751-2600; *The Economist Book of Vital World Statistics*.

United Nations Economic Commission for Africa, Africa Hall, Post Office Box 3001, Addis Ababa, Ethiopia (Telephone Number in U.S. (800) 253-9646); *African Statistical Yearbook*.

The World Bank, 1818 H Street, NW, Washington, D.C. 20433 (202) 477-1234; *World Tables*.

LIBYA - EXTERNAL INDEBTEDNESS

African Development Bank, 01 BP 1387, Abidjan 01, Cote d'Ivoire; *Selected Statistics on Regional Member Countries*.

Euromonitor Publications Limited, 87-88 Turnmill Street, London EC1M 5QU, England; *Third World Economic Handbook*.

Statistical Office of the United Nations, Publishing Service, New York, New York 10017 (800) 253-9646; *Survey of Economic and Social Conditions in Africa*.

The World Bank, 1818 H Street, NW, Washington, D.C. 20433 (202) 477-1234; *World Tables*.

LIBYA - EXTERNAL TRADE

African Development Bank, 01 BP 1387, Abidjan 01, Cote d'Ivoire; *Selected Statistics on Regional Member Countries*.

Food and Agricultural Organization of the United Nations (FAO), Via delle Terme di Caracalla, 00100 Rome, Italy (Telephone Number in U.S. (202) 653-2400); *The State of Food and Agriculture*, and *Trade Yearbook*.

G.K. Hall and Company, 70 Lincoln Street, Boston, Massachusetts 02111 (617) 423-3990; *The World in Figures*.

Statistical Office of the United Nations, Publishing Service, New York, New York 10017 (800) 253-9646; *Statistical Yearbook*.

LIBYA - FARM CROPS - See LIBYA - CROPS

LIBYA - FEMALE WORKING POPULATION - See LIBYA - EMPLOYMENT

LIBYA - FERTILITY RATES

Facts on File, 460 Park Avenue South, New York, New York 10016 (800) 443-8323; *The New Book of World Rankings*.

Statistical Office of the United Nations, Publishing Service, New York, New York 10017 (800) 253-9646; *Survey of Economic and Social Conditions in Africa*.

Times Books, 201 East 50th Street, New York, New York 10022 (212) 751-2600; *The Economist Book of Vital World Statistics*.

The World Bank, 1818 H Street, NW, Washington, D.C. 20433 (202) 477-1234; *World Tables*.

LIBYA - FERTILIZER

Food and Agricultural Organization of the United Nations (FAO), Via delle Terme di Caracalla, 00100 Rome, Italy (Telephone Number in U.S. (202) 653-2400); *Fertilizer Yearbook*, and *The State of Food and Agriculture*.

Statistical Office of the United Nations, Publishing Service, New York, New York 10017 (800) 253-9646; *Statistical Yearbook*.

LIBYA - FETAL MORTALITY

Statistical Office of the United Nations, Publishing Service, New York, New York 10017 (800) 253-9646; *Demographic Yearbook*.

World Health Organization, Office of Publications, Avenue Appia, CH-1211 Geneva 27, Switzerland (Telephone Number in U.S. (518) 436-9686); *World Health Statistics Annual*.

LIBYA - FILM - See LIBYA - MOTION PICTURES

LIBYA - FINANCE

African Development Bank, 01 BP 1387, Abidjan 01, Cote d'Ivoire; *Selected Statistics on Regional Member Countries*.

Euromonitor Publications Limited, 87-88 Turnmill Street, London EC1M 5QU, England; *Middle East Economic Handbook*.

Facts on File, 460 Park Avenue South, New York, New York 10016 (800) 443-8323; *The New Book of World Rankings*.

G.K. Hall and Company, 70 Lincoln Street, Boston, Massachusetts 02111 (617) 423-3990; *The World in Figures*.

International Monetary Fund, 700 Nineteenth Street, NW, Washington, D.C. 20431 (202) 623-7000; *International Financial Statistics*.

United Nations Economic Commission for Africa, Africa Hall, Post Office Box 3001, Addis Ababa, Ethiopia (Telephone Number in U.S. (800) 253-9646); *African Statistical Yearbook*.

LIBYA - FISHERIES

Facts on File, 460 Park Avenue South, New York, New York 10016 (800) 443-8323; *The New Book of World Rankings*.

Food and Agricultural Organization of the United Nations (FAO), Via delle Terme di Caracalla, 00100 Rome, Italy (Telephone Number in U.S. (202) 653-2400); *The State of Food and Agriculture*, and *Yearbook of Fishery Statistics*.

Statistical Office of the United Nations, Publishing Service, New York, New York 10017 (800) 253-9646; *Statistical Yearbook*, and *Survey of Economic and Social Conditions in Africa*.

United Nations Economic Commission for Africa, Africa Hall, Post Office Box 3001, Addis Ababa, Ethiopia (Telephone Number in U.S. (800) 253-9646); *African Statistical Yearbook*.

LIBYA - FLOUR PRODUCTION

Statistical Office of the United Nations, Publishing Service, New York, New York 10017 (800) 253-9646; *Statistical Yearbook*.

LIBYA - FOOD

African Development Bank, 01 BP 1387, Abidjan 01, Cote d'Ivoire; *Selected Statistics on Regional Member Countries*.

Food and Agricultural Organization of the United Nations (FAO), Via delle Terme di Caracalla, 00100 Rome, Italy (Telephone Number in U.S. (202) 653-2400); *The State of Food and Agriculture*, and *Production Yearbook*.

G.K. Hall and Company, 70 Lincoln Street, Boston, Massachusetts 02111 (617) 423-3990; *The World in Figures*.

LIBYA - FOREIGN AID

G.K. Hall and Company, 70 Lincoln Street, Boston, Massachusetts 02111 (617) 423-3990; *The World in Figures*.

LIBYA - FOREIGN INDEBTEDNESS

Euromonitor Publications Limited, 87-88 Turnmill Street, London EC1M 5QU, England; *Middle East Economic Handbook*.

LIBYA - FOREIGN TRADE

Euromonitor Publications Limited, 87-88 Turnmill Street, London EC1M 5QU, England; *International Marketing Data and Statistics*, *Middle East Economic Handbook*, and *Third World Economic Handbook*.

Facts on File, 460 Park Avenue South, New York, New York 10016 (800) 443-8323; *The New Book of World Rankings*.

Food and Agricultural Organization of the United Nations (FAO), Via delle Terme di Caracalla, 00100 Rome, Italy (Telephone Number in U.S. (202) 653-2400); *The State of Food and Agriculture*.

G.K. Hall and Company, 70 Lincoln Street, Boston, Massachusetts 02111 (617) 423-3990; *The World in Figures*.

International Monetary Fund, 700 Nineteenth Street, NW, Washington, D.C. 20431 (202) 623-7000; *International Financial Statistics*.

Statistical Office of the United Nations, Publishing Service, New York, New York 10017 (800) 253-9646; *Foreign Trade Statistics for Africa*, *International Trade Statistics Yearbook*, and *Statistical Yearbook*.

United Nations Economic Commission for Africa, Africa Hall, Post Office Box 3001, Addis Ababa, Ethiopia (Telephone Number in U.S. (800) 253-9646); *African Statistical Yearbook*.

The World Bank, 1818 H Street, NW, Washington, D.C. 20433 (202) 477-1234; *World Tables*.

LIBYA - FORESTRY AND FOREST PRODUCTS

Euromonitor Publications Limited, 87-88 Turnmill Street, London EC1M 5QU, England; *Third World Economic Handbook*.

Facts on File, 460 Park Avenue South, New York, New York 10016 (800) 443-8323; *The New Book of World Rankings*.

Food and Agricultural Organization of the United Nations (FAO), Via delle Terme di Caracalla, 00100 Rome, Italy (Telephone Number in U.S. (202) 653-2400); *The State of Food and Agriculture*, and *Yearbook of Forest Products*.

G.K. Hall and Company, 70 Lincoln Street, Boston, Massachusetts 02111 (617) 423-3990; *The World in Figures*.

Statistical Office of the United Nations, Publishing Service, New York, New York 10017 (800) 253-9646; *Statistical Yearbook*.

United Nations Economic Commission for Africa, Africa Hall, Post Office Box 3001, Addis Ababa, Ethiopia (Telephone Number in U.S. (800) 253-9646); *African Statistical Yearbook*.

United Nations Educational, Scientific and Cultural Organization (UNESCO), 7 Place de Fontenoy, F-75700 Paris, France (Telephone Number in U.S. (212) 963-5981); *Statistical Yearbook*.

LIBYA - GAS - See LIBYA - MINING AND MINERAL PRODUCTS

LIBYA - GENERAL INDUSTRIAL STATISTICS

Statistical Office of the United Nations, Publishing Service, New York, New York 10017 (800) 253-9646; *Industrial Statistics Yearbook*.

LIBYA - GENERAL MORTALITY

Statistical Office of the United Nations, Publishing Service, New York, New York 10017 (800) 253-9646; *Demographic Yearbook*.

World Health Organization, Office of Publications, Avenue Appia, CH-1211 Geneva 27, Switzerland (Telephone Number in U.S. (518) 436-9686); *World Health Statistics Annual*.

LIBYA - GEOGRAPHIC DATA

Facts on File, 460 Park Avenue South, New York, New York 10016 (800) 443-8323; *The New Book of World Rankings*.

LIBYA - GOATS - See LIBYA - LIVESTOCK AND POULTRY

LIBYA - GOLD HOLDINGS

International Monetary Fund, 700 Nineteenth Street, NW, Washington, D.C. 20431 (202) 623-7000; *International Financial Statistics*.

Statistical Office of the United Nations, Publishing Service, New York, New York 10017 (800) 253-9646; *Statistical Yearbook*.

The World Bank, 1818 H Street, NW, Washington, D.C. 20433 (202) 477-1234; *World Tables*.

LIBYA - GOLD PRODUCTION - See LIBYA - MINING AND MINERAL PRODUCTS

LIBYA - GOVERNMENT

G.K. Hall and Company, 70 Lincoln Street, Boston, Massachusetts 02111 (617) 423-3990; *The World in Figures*.

LIBYA - GOVERNMENT EXPENDITURE

Euromonitor Publications Limited, 87-88 Turnmill Street, London EC1M 5QU, England; *Third World Economic Handbook*.

The World Bank, 1818 H Street, NW, Washington, D.C. 20433 (202) 477-1234; *World Tables*.

LIBYA - GOVERNMENT FINANCES

International Monetary Fund, 700 Nineteenth Street, NW, Washington, D.C. 20431 (202) 623-7000; *International Financial Statistics*.

Statistical Office of the United Nations, Publishing Service, New York, New York 10017 (800) 253-9646; *Statistical Yearbook*.

LIBYA - GOVERNMENT REVENUE

Statistical Office of the United Nations, Publishing Service, New York, New York 10017 (800) 253-9646; *Survey of Economic and Social Conditions in Africa*.

The World Bank, 1818 H Street, NW, Washington, D.C. 20433 (202) 477-1234; *World Tables*.

LIBYA - GRAIN PRODUCTION - See LIBYA - CROPS

LIBYA - GREEN PEPPER AND CHILIE PRODUCTION - See LIBYA - CROPS

LIBYA - GROSS DOMESTIC PRODUCT

African Development Bank, 01 BP 1387, Abidjan 01, Cote d'Ivoire; *Selected Statistics on Regional Member Countries.*

The Economist Intelligence Unit, 111 West 57th Street, New York, New York 10019 (800) 938-4685; *The World Market Atlas.*

Euromonitor Publications Limited, 87-88 Turnmill Street, London EC1M 5QU, England; *International Marketing Data and Statistics, Middle East Economic Handbook,* and *Third World Economic Handbook.*

Facts on File, 460 Park Avenue South, New York, New York 10016 (800) 443-8323; *The New Book of World Rankings.*

G.K. Hall and Company, 70 Lincoln Street, Boston, Massachusetts 02111 (617) 423-3990; *The World in Figures.*

Statistical Office of the United Nations, Publishing Service, New York, New York 10017 (800) 253-9646; *Statistical Yearbook,* and *Survey of Economic and Social Conditions in Africa.*

Times Books, 201 East 50th Street, New York, New York 10022 (212) 751-2600; *The Economist Book of Vital World Statistics.*

The World Bank, 1818 H Street, NW, Washington, D.C. 20433 (202) 477-1234; *World Tables.*

LIBYA - GROSS INDUSTRIAL PRODUCT - BY CATEGORIES OF GOODS

Euromonitor Publications Limited, 87-88 Turnmill Street, London EC1M 5QU, England; *Third World Economic Handbook.*

LIBYA - GROSS NATIONAL PRODUCT

Euromonitor Publications Limited, 87-88 Turnmill Street, London EC1M 5QU, England; *International Marketing Data and Statistics,* and *Third World Economic Handbook.*

Organization of Petroleum Exporting Countries, Obere Donaustrasse 93, 1020 Vienna 2, Austria; *OPEC Annual Statistical Bulletin.*

United Nations Economic Commission for Africa, Africa Hall, Post Office Box 3001, Addis Ababa, Ethiopia (Telephone Number in U.S. (800) 253-9646); *African Statistical Yearbook.*

U.S. Arms Control and Disarmament Agency, 320 Twenty-first Street, NW, Washington, D.C. 20451 (202) 647-8677; *World Military Expenditures and Arms Transfers.*

The World Bank, 1818 H Street, NW, Washington, D.C. 20433 (202) 477-1234; *World Tables.*

LIBYA - GROUNDNUTS PRODUCTION - See LIBYA - CROPS

LIBYA - HEALTH

African Development Bank, 01 BP 1387, Abidjan 01, Cote d'Ivoire; *Selected Statistics on Regional Member Countries.*

Euromonitor Publications Limited, 87-88 Turnmill Street, London EC1M 5QU, England; *Middle East Economic Handbook.*

Facts on File, 460 Park Avenue South, New York, New York 10016 (800) 443-8323; *The New Book of World Rankings.*

G.K. Hall and Company, 70 Lincoln Street, Boston, Massachusetts 02111 (617) 423-3990; *The World in Figures.*

Statistical Office of the United Nations, Publishing Service, New York, New York 10017 (800) 253-9646; *Statistical Yearbook.*

Times Books, 201 East 50th Street, New York, New York 10022 (212) 751-2600; *The Economist Book of Vital World Statistics.*

United Nations Economic Commission for Africa, Africa Hall, Post Office Box 3001, Addis Ababa, Ethiopia (Telephone Number in U.S. (800) 253-9646); *African Statistical Yearbook.*

World Health Organization, Office of Publications, Avenue Appia, CH-1211 Geneva 27, Switzerland (Telephone Number in U.S. (518) 436-9686); *World Health Statistics Annual.*

LIBYA - HIDE PRODUCTION

Food and Agricultural Organization of the United Nations (FAO), Via delle Terme di Caracalla, 00100 Rome, Italy (Telephone Number in U.S. (202) 653-2400); *Production Yearbook.*

LIBYA - HIGHWAYS

G.K. Hall and Company, 70 Lincoln Street, Boston, Massachusetts 02111 (617) 423-3990; *The World in Figures.*

International Road Federation, 525 School Street, SW, Washington, D.C. 20024 (202) 554-2106; *World Road Statistics.*

Statistical Office of the United Nations, Publishing Service, New York, New York 10017 (800) 253-9646; *Survey of Economic and Social Conditions in Africa.*

United Nations Economic Commission for Africa, Africa Hall, Post Office Box 3001, Addis Ababa, Ethiopia (Telephone Number in U.S. (800) 253-9646); *African Statistical Yearbook.*

LIBYA - HORSES - See LIBYA - LIVESTOCK AND POULTRY

LIBYA - HOURS OF WORK - See LIBYA - EMPLOYMENT

LIBYA - HOUSING AND HOUSING UNITS

Euromonitor Publications Limited, 87-88 Turnmill Street, London EC1M 5QU, England; *Third World Economic Handbook.*

Facts on File, 460 Park Avenue South, New York, New York 10016 (800) 443-8323; *The New Book of World Rankings.*

LIBYA - ILLITERATE POPULATION

The Economist Intelligence Unit, 111 West 57th Street, New York, New York 10019 (800) 938-4685; *The World Market Atlas.*

G.K. Hall and Company, 70 Lincoln Street, Boston, Massachusetts 02111 (617) 423-3990; *The World in Figures.*

United Nations Educational, Scientific and Cultural Organization (UNESCO), 7 Place de Fontenoy, F-75700 Paris, France (Telephone Number in U.S. (212) 963-5981); *Statistical Yearbook.*

LIBYA - IMPORTS

African Development Bank, 01 BP 1387, Abidjan 01, Cote d'Ivoire; *Selected Statistics on Regional Member Countries.*

The Economist Intelligence Unit, 111 West 57th Street, New York, New York 10019 (800) 938-4685; *The World Market Atlas.*

Euromonitor Publications Limited, 87-88 Turnmill Street, London EC1M 5QU, England; *International Marketing Data and Statistics, Middle East Economic Handbook,* and *Third World Economic Handbook.*

Food and Agricultural Organization of the United Nations (FAO), Via delle Terme di Caracalla, 00100 Rome, Italy (Telephone Number in U.S. (202) 653-2400); *The State of Food and Agriculture.*

G.K. Hall and Company, 70 Lincoln Street, Boston, Massachusetts 02111 (617) 423-3990; *The World in Figures.*

International Monetary Fund, 700 Nineteenth Street, NW, Washington, D.C. 20431 (202) 623-7000; *Direction of Trade Statistics,* and *International Financial Statistics.*

Statistical Office of the United Nations, Publishing Service, New York, New York 10017 (800) 253-9646; *Foreign Trade Statistics for Africa, Trade in Manufactures of Developing Countries,* and *Survey of Economic and Social Conditions in Africa.*

Times Books, 201 East 50th Street, New York, New York 10022 (212) 751-2600; *The Economist Book of Vital World Statistics.*

United Nations Economic Commission for Africa, Africa Hall, Post Office Box 3001, Addis Ababa, Ethiopia (Telephone Number in U.S. (800) 253-9646); *African Statistical Yearbook.*

The World Bank, 1818 H Street, NW, Washington, D.C. 20433 (202) 477-1234; *World Tables.*

LIBYA - INDUSTRY

Euromonitor Publications Limited, 87-88 Turnmill Street, London EC1M 5QU, England; *International Marketing Data and Statistics,* and *Third World Economic Handbook.*

Facts on File, 460 Park Avenue South, New York, New York 10016 (800) 443-8323; *The New Book of World Rankings.*

G.K. Hall and Company, 70 Lincoln Street, Boston, Massachusetts 02111 (617) 423-3990; *The World in Figures.*

International Labour Office, I.L.O. Publications, CH-1211, Geneva 22, Switzerland; *Yearbook of Labour Statistics.*

Times Books, 201 East 50th Street, New York, New York 10022 (212) 751-2600; *The Economist Book of Vital World Statistics.*

Statistical Office of the United Nations, Publishing Service, New York, New York 10017 (800) 253-9646; *Survey of Economic and Social Conditions in Africa.*

United Nations Economic Commission for Africa, Africa Hall, Post Office Box 3001, Addis Ababa, Ethiopia (Telephone Number in U.S. (800) 253-9646); *African Statistical Yearbook.*

The World Bank, 1818 H Street, NW, Washington, D.C. 20433 (202) 477-1234; *World Tables.*

LIBYA - INFANT AND MATERNAL MORTALITY

Statistical Office of the United Nations, Publishing Service, New York, New York 10017 (800) 253-9646; *Demographic Yearbook,* and *Survey of Economic and Social Conditions in Africa.*

Times Books, 201 East 50th Street, New York, New York 10022 (212) 751-2600; *The Economist Book of Vital World Statistics.*

The World Bank, 1818 H Street, NW, Washington, D.C. 20433 (202) 477-1234; *World Tables.*

World Health Organization, Office of Publications, Avenue Appia, CH-1211 Geneva 27, Switzerland (Telephone Number in U.S. (518) 436-9686); *World Health Statistics Annual.*

LIBYA - INTERNATIONAL RESERVES

International Monetary Fund, 700 Nineteenth Street, NW, Washington, D.C. 20431 (202) 623-7000; *International Financial Statistics.*

Statistical Office of the United Nations, Publishing Service, New York, New York 10017 (800) 253-9646; *Statistical Yearbook.*

LIBYA - INTERNATIONAL RESERVES EXCLUDING GOLD

African Development Bank, 01 BP 1387, Abidjan 01, Cote d'Ivoire; *Selected Statistics on Regional Member Countries.*

LIBYA - IRON ORE PRODUCTION - See LIBYA - MINING AND MINERAL PRODUCTS

LIBYA - IRRIGATION

Euromonitor Publications Limited, 87-88 Turnmill Street, London EC1M 5QU, England; *International Marketing Data and Statistics.*

LIBYA - LABOR FORCE

African Development Bank, 01 BP 1387, Abidjan 01, Cote d'Ivoire; *Selected Statistics on Regional Member Countries.*

Euromonitor Publications Limited, 87-88 Turnmill Street, London EC1M 5QU, England; *International Marketing Data and Statistics,* and *Middle East Economic Handbook.*

Facts on File, 460 Park Avenue South, New York, New York 10016 (800) 443-8323; *The New Book of World Rankings.*

Food and Agricultural Organization of the United Nations (FAO), Via delle Terme di Caracalla, 00100 Rome, Italy (Telephone Number in U.S. (202) 653-2400); *The State of Food and Agriculture.*

G.K. Hall and Company, 70 Lincoln Street, Boston, Massachusetts 02111 (617) 423-3990; *The World in Figures.*

The World Bank, 1818 H Street, NW, Washington, D.C. 20433 (202) 477-1234; *World Tables.*

LIBYA - LABOR PRODUCTIVITY

International Labour Office, I.L.O. Publications, CH-1211, Geneva 22, Switzerland; *Yearbook of Labour Statistics.*

LIBYA - LAND USE

Euromonitor Publications Limited, 87-88 Turnmill Street, London EC1M 5QU, England; *International Marketing Data and Statistics.*

Food and Agricultural Organization of the United Nations (FAO), Via delle Terme di Caracalla, 00100 Rome, Italy (Telephone Number in U.S. (202) 653-2400); *Production Yearbook*.

G.K. Hall and Company, 70 Lincoln Street, Boston, Massachusetts 02111 (617) 423-3990; *The World in Figures*.

LIBYA - LIBRARIES

Facts on File, 460 Park Avenue South, New York, New York 10016 (800) 443-8323; *The New Book of World Rankings*.

LIBYA - LIFE EXPECTANCY

African Development Bank, 01 BP 1387, Abidjan 01, Cote d'Ivoire; *Selected Statistics on Regional Member Countries*.

LIBYA - LITERACY RATE

Statistical Office of the United Nations, Publishing Service, New York, New York 10017 (800) 253-9646; *Survey of Economic and Social Conditions in Africa*.

LIBYA - LIVESTOCK AND POULTRY

Euromonitor Publications Limited, 87-88 Turnmill Street, London EC1M 5QU, England; *International Marketing Data and Statistics*.

Facts on File, 460 Park Avenue South, New York, New York 10016 (800) 443-8323; *The New Book of World Rankings*.

Food and Agricultural Organization of the United Nations (FAO), Via delle Terme di Caracalla, 00100 Rome, Italy (Telephone Number in U.S. (202) 653-2400); *Production Yearbook*, and *The State of Food and Agriculture*.

G.K. Hall and Company, 70 Lincoln Street, Boston, Massachusetts 02111 (617) 423-3990; *The World in Figures*.

Statistical Office of the United Nations, Publishing Service, New York, New York 10017 (800) 253-9646; *Statistical Yearbook*, and *Survey of Economic and Social Conditions in Africa*.

United Nations Economic Commission for Africa, Africa Hall, Post Office Box 3001, Addis Ababa, Ethiopia (Telephone Number in U.S. (800) 253-9646); *African Statistical Yearbook*.

LIBYA - LIVING LEVELS

G.K. Hall and Company, 70 Lincoln Street, Boston, Massachusetts 02111 (617) 423-3990; *The World in Figures*.

Times Books, 201 East 50th Street, New York, New York 10022 (212) 751-2600; *The Economist Book of Vital World Statistics*.

LIBYA - MAIL - NUMBER OF PIECES SENT OR RECEIVED

Statistical Office of the United Nations, Publishing Service, New York, New York 10017 (800) 253-9646; *Statistical Yearbook*.

LIBYA - MANUFACTURING

Euromonitor Publications Limited, 87-88 Turnmill Street, London EC1M 5QU, England; *Third World Economic Handbook*.

Facts on File, 460 Park Avenue South, New York, New York 10016 (800) 443-8323; *The New Book of World Rankings*.

G.K. Hall and Company, 70 Lincoln Street, Boston, Massachusetts 02111 (617) 423-3990; *The World in Figures*.

Statistical Office of the United Nations, Publishing Service, New York, New York 10017 (800) 253-9646; *Statistical Yearbook*, and *Survey of Economic and Social Conditions in Africa*.

United Nations Economic Commission for Africa, Africa Hall, Post Office Box 3001, Addis Ababa, Ethiopia (Telephone Number in U.S. (800) 253-9646); *African Statistical Yearbook*.

The World Bank, 1818 H Street, NW, Washington, D.C. 20433 (202) 477-1234; *World Tables*.

LIBYA - MARRIAGE RATES

Facts on File, 460 Park Avenue South, New York, New York 10016 (800) 443-8323; *The New Book of World Rankings*.

Statistical Office of the United Nations, Publishing Service, New York, New York 10017 (800) 253-9646; *Demographic Yearbook*, and *Statistical Yearbook*.

LIBYA - MEAT PRODUCTION - See LIBYA - LIVESTOCK AND POULTRY

LIBYA - MERCHANT SHIPPING

G.K. Hall and Company, 70 Lincoln Street, Boston, Massachusetts 02111 (617) 423-3990; *The World in Figures*.

Organization of Petroleum Exporting Countries, Obere Donaustrasse 93, 1020 Vienna 2, Austria; *OPEC Annual Statistical Bulletin*.

Statistical Office of the United Nations, Publishing Service, New York, New York 10017 (800) 253-9646; *Statistical Yearbook*.

Times Books, 201 East 50th Street, New York, New York 10022 (212) 751-2600; *The Economist Book of Vital World Statistics*.

United Nations Economic Commission for Africa, Africa Hall, Post Office Box 3001, Addis Ababa, Ethiopia (Telephone Number in U.S. (800) 253-9646); *African Statistical Yearbook*.

U.S. Department of Transportation, Maritime Administration, 400 Seventh Street, SW, Washington, D.C. 20590; *A Statistical Analysis of the World's Merchant Fleets*.

LIBYA - MILITARY

G.K. Hall and Company, 70 Lincoln Street, Boston, Massachusetts 02111 (617) 423-3990; *The World in Figures*.

The International Institute for Strategic Studies, 23 Tavistock Street, London WC2E 7NQ, England; *The Military Balance*.

U.S. Arms Control and Disarmament Agency, 320 Twenty-first Street, NW, Washington, D.C. 20451 (202) 647-8677; *World Military Expenditures and Arms Transfers*.

LIBYA - MILK PRODUCTION - See LIBYA - DAIRY PRODUCTS

LIBYA - MILLET PRODUCTION - See LIBYA - CROPS

LIBYA - MINING AND MINERAL PRODUCTS

Euromonitor Publications Limited, 87-88 Turnmill Street, London EC1M 5QU, England; *Third World Economic Handbook*.

Facts on File, 460 Park Avenue South, New York, New York 10016 (800) 443-8323; *The New Book of World Rankings*.

G.K. Hall and Company, 70 Lincoln Street, Boston, Massachusetts 02111 (617) 423-3990; *The World in Figures*.

Organization of Petroleum Exporting Countries, Obere Donaustrasse 93, 1020 Vienna 2, Austria; *OPEC Annual Statistical Bulletin*.

Penn Well Publishing Company, 1421 South Sheridan Road, Post Office Box 1260, Tulsa, Oklahoma 74101 (800) 752-9764; *International Energy Statistics Sourcebook*.

Statistical Office of the United Nations, Publishing Service, New York, New York 10017 (800) 253-9646; *Statistical Yearbook*.

United Nations Economic Commission for Africa, Africa Hall, Post Office Box 3001, Addis Ababa, Ethiopia (Telephone Number in U.S. (800) 253-9646); *African Statistical Yearbook*.

LIBYA - MONEY EXCHANGE RATE

Euromonitor Publications Limited, 87-88 Turnmill Street, London EC1M 5QU, England; *International Marketing Data and Statistics*.

International Monetary Fund, 700 Nineteenth Street, NW, Washington, D.C. 20431 (202) 623-7000; *International Financial Statistics*.

LIBYA - MONEY RESERVES

Euromonitor Publications Limited, 87-88 Turnmill Street, London EC1M 5QU, England; *International Marketing Data and Statistics*.

LIBYA - MONEY SUPPLY

African Development Bank, 01 BP 1387, Abidjan 01, Cote d'Ivoire; *Selected Statistics on Regional Member Countries*.

Euromonitor Publications Limited, 87-88 Turnmill Street, London EC1M 5QU, England; *International Marketing Data and Statistics*.

G.K. Hall and Company, 70 Lincoln Street, Boston, Massachusetts 02111 (617) 423-3990; *The World in Figures*.

International Monetary Fund, 700 Nineteenth Street, NW, Washington, D.C. 20431 (202) 623-7000; *International Financial Statistics*.

Statistical Office of the United Nations, Publishing Service, New York, New York 10017 (800) 253-9646; *Statistical Yearbook*.

The World Bank, 1818 H Street, NW, Washington, D.C. 20433 (202) 477-1234; *World Tables*.

LIBYA - MUSEUMS

Facts on File, 460 Park Avenue South, New York, New York 10016 (800) 443-8323; *The New Book of World Rankings*.

LIBYA - MOTION PICTURES

Statistical Office of the United Nations, Publishing Service, New York, New York 10017 (800) 253-9646; *Statistical Yearbook*.

United Nations Educational, Scientific and Cultural Organization (UNESCO), 7 Place de Fontenoy, F-75700 Paris, France (Telephone Number in U.S. (212) 963-5981); *Statistical Yearbook*.

LIBYA - MOTOR VEHICLE TAXES - See LIBYA - TAXATION

LIBYA - MOTOR VEHICLES IN USE

G.K. Hall and Company, 70 Lincoln Street, Boston, Massachusetts 02111 (617) 423-3990; *The World in Figures*.

International Road Federation, 525 School Street, SW, Washington, D.C. 20024 (202) 554-2106; *World Road Statistics*.

Statistical Office of the United Nations, Publishing Service, New York, New York 10017 (800) 253-9646; *Statistical Yearbook*, and *Survey of Economic and Social Conditions in Africa*.

Times Books, 201 East 50th Street, New York, New York 10022 (212) 751-2600; *The Economist Book of Vital World Statistics*.

LIBYA - MULES - See LIBYA - LIVESTOCK AND POULTRY

LIBYA - MUSEUMS

United Nations Educational, Scientific and Cultural Organization (UNESCO), 7 Place de Fontenoy, F-75700 Paris, France (Telephone Number in U.S. (212) 963-5981); *Statistical Yearbook*.

LIBYA - NATALITY - See LIBYA - BIRTH RATES

LIBYA - NATIONAL ACCOUNTS

African Development Bank, 01 BP 1387, Abidjan 01, Cote d'Ivoire; *Selected Statistics on Regional Member Countries*.

Statistical Office of the United Nations, Publishing Service, New York, New York 10017 (800) 253-9646; *National Accounts Statistics*, and *Statistical Yearbook*.

United Nations Economic Commission for Africa, Africa Hall, Post Office Box 3001, Addis Ababa, Ethiopia (Telephone Number in U.S. (800) 253-9646); *African Statistical Yearbook*.

LIBYA - NATIONAL INCOME

Facts on File, 460 Park Avenue South, New York, New York 10016 (800) 443-8323; *The New Book of World Rankings*.

G.K. Hall and Company, 70 Lincoln Street, Boston, Massachusetts 02111 (617) 423-3990; *The World in Figures*.

Statistical Office of the United Nations, Publishing Service, New York, New York 10017 (800) 253-9646; *Statistical Yearbook*.

LIBYA - NATIONAL PRODUCT

Facts on File, 460 Park Avenue South, New York, New York 10016 (800) 443-8323; *The New Book of World Rankings*.

Statistical Office of the United Nations, Publishing Service, New York, New York 10017 (800) 253-9646; *Statistical Yearbook*.

LIBYA - NATURAL GAS - See LIBYA - MINING AND MINERAL PRODUCTS

LIBYA - NEWSPAPER PRODUCTION - See LIBYA - FORESTRY AND FOREST PRODUCTS

LIBYA - NEWSPRINT - See LIBYA - FORESTRY AND FOREST PRODUCTS

LIBYA - OCCUPATIONS - See LIBYA - LABOR FORCE

LIBYA - PAPER - See LIBYA - FORESTRY AND FOREST PRODUCTS

LIBYA - PATENTS

Statistical Office of the United Nations, Publishing Service, New York, New York 10017 (800) 253-9646; *Statistical Yearbook.*

LIBYA - PEANUT PRODUCTION - See LIBYA - CROPS

LIBYA - PERIODICALS

United Nations Educational, Scientific and Cultural Organization (UNESCO), 7 Place de Fontenoy, F-75700 Paris, France (Telephone Number in U.S. (212) 963-5981); *Statistical Yearbook.*

LIBYA - PESTICIDE USE

Food and Agricultural Organization of the United Nations (FAO), Via delle Terme di Caracalla, 00100 Rome, Italy (Telephone Number in U.S. (202) 653-2400); *The State of Food and Agriculture.*

LIBYA - PETROLEUM INDUSTRY

Euromonitor Publications Limited, 87-88 Turnmill Street, London EC1M 5QU, England; *Middle East Economic Handbook.*

Facts on File, 460 Park Avenue South, New York, New York 10016 (800) 443-8323; *The New Book of World Rankings.*

Food and Agricultural Organization of the United Nations (FAO), Via delle Terme di Caracalla, 00100 Rome, Italy (Telephone Number in U.S. (202) 653-2400); *The State of Food and Agriculture.*

G.K. Hall and Company, 70 Lincoln Street, Boston, Massachusetts 02111 (617) 423-3990; *The World in Figures.*

Organization of Petroleum Exporting Countries, Obere Donaustrasse 93, 1020 Vienna 2, Austria; *OPEC Annual Statistical Bulletin.*

Penn Well Publishing Company, 1421 South Sheridan Road, Post Office Box 1260, Tulsa, Oklahoma 74101 (800) 752-9764; *International Energy Statistics Sourcebook.*

Statistical Office of the United Nations, Publishing Service, New York, New York 10017 (800) 253-9646; *Statistical Yearbook.*

LIBYA - PIGS - See LIBYA - LIVESTOCK AND POULTRY

LIBYA - PIPELINES FOR OIL AND PETROLEUM PRODUCTS

Organization of Petroleum Exporting Countries, Obere Donaustrasse 93, 1020 Vienna 2, Austria; *OPEC Annual Statistical Bulletin.*

LIBYA - PLASTIC AND RESIN PRODUCTION

Euromonitor Publications Limited, 87-88 Turnmill Street, London EC1M 5QU, England; *Third World Economic Handbook.*

LIBYA - POPULATION

African Development Bank, 01 BP 1387, Abidjan 01, Cote d'Ivoire; *Selected Statistics on Regional Member Countries.*

The Economist Intelligence Unit, 111 West 57th Street, New York, New York 10019 (800) 938-4685; *The World Market Atlas.*

Euromonitor Publications Limited, 87-88 Turnmill Street, London EC1M 5QU, England; *International Marketing Data and Statistics, Middle East Economic Handbook,* and *Third World Economic Handbook.*

Facts on File, 460 Park Avenue South, New York, New York 10016 (800) 443-8323; *The New Book of World Rankings.*

Food and Agricultural Organization of the United Nations (FAO), Via delle Terme di Caracalla, 00100 Rome, Italy (Telephone Number in U.S. (202) 653-2400); *Production Yearbook.*

G.K. Hall and Company, 70 Lincoln Street, Boston, Massachusetts 02111 (617) 423-3990; *The World in Figures.*

International Labour Office, I.L.O. Publications, CH-1211, Geneva 22, Switzerland; *Yearbook of Labour Statistics.*

Statistical Office of the United Nations, Publishing Service, New York, New York 10017 (800) 253-9646; *Demographic Yearbook, Statistical Yearbook,* and *Survey of Economic and Social Conditions in Africa.*

Times Books, 201 East 50th Street, New York, New York 10022 (212) 751-2600; *The Economist Book of Vital World Statistics.*

United Nations Educational, Scientific and Cultural Organization (UNESCO), 7 Place de Fontenoy, F-75700 Paris, France (Telephone Number in U.S. (212) 963-5981); *Statistical Yearbook.*

U.S. Arms Control and Disarmament Agency, 320 Twenty-first Street, NW, Washington, D.C. 20451 (202) 647-8677; *World Military Expenditures and Arms Transfers.*

World Health Organization, Office of Publications, Avenue Appia, CH-1211 Geneva 27, Switzerland (Telephone Number in U.S. (518) 436-9686); *World Health Statistics Annual.*

LIBYA - POST OFFICES

Facts on File, 460 Park Avenue South, New York, New York 10016 (800) 443-8323; *The New Book of World Rankings.*

LIBYA - POTATO PRODUCTION - See LIBYA - CROPS

LIBYA - PRICES

Facts on File, 460 Park Avenue South, New York, New York 10016 (800) 443-8323; *The New Book of World Rankings.*

Food and Agricultural Organization of the United Nations (FAO), Via delle Terme di Caracalla, 00100 Rome, Italy (Telephone Number in U.S. (202) 653-2400); *Production Yearbook,* and *The State of Food and Agriculture.*

G.K. Hall and Company, 70 Lincoln Street, Boston, Massachusetts 02111 (617) 423-3990; *The World in Figures.*

International Labour Office, I.L.O. Publications, CH-1211, Geneva 22, Switzerland; *Yearbook of Labour Statistics.*

International Monetary Fund, 700 Nineteenth Street, NW, Washington, D.C. 20431 (202) 623-7000; *International Financial Statistics.*

United Nations Economic Commission for Africa, Africa Hall, Post Office Box 3001, Addis Ababa, Ethiopia (Telephone Number in U.S. (800) 253-9646); *African Statistical Yearbook.*

LIBYA - PRINTING AND WRITING PAPER - See LIBYA - FORESTRY AND FOREST PRODUCTS

LIBYA - PRODUCTION

Euromonitor Publications Limited, 87-88 Turnmill Street, London EC1M 5QU, England; *Third World Economic Handbook.*

Facts on File, 460 Park Avenue South, New York, New York 10016 (800) 443-8323; *The New Book of World Rankings.*

G.K. Hall and Company, 70 Lincoln Street, Boston, Massachusetts 02111 (617) 423-3990; *The World in Figures.*

LIBYA - PRODUCTIVITY

Euromonitor Publications Limited, 87-88 Turnmill Street, London EC1M 5QU, England; *International Marketing Data and Statistics.*

LIBYA - PUBLIC FINANCE

Facts on File, 460 Park Avenue South, New York, New York 10016 (800) 443-8323; *The New Book of World Rankings.*

LIBYA - RADIO BROADCASTING   See LIBYA - BROADCASTING

LIBYA - RAILWAYS

G.K. Hall and Company, 70 Lincoln Street, Boston, Massachusetts 02111 (617) 423-3990; *The World in Figures.*

Jane's Information Group, Sentinel House, 163 Brighton Road, Coulsdon, Surrey CR5 2NH, England (Telephone Number in U.S. (703) 683-3700); *Jane's World Railways.*

United Nations Economic Commission for Africa, Africa Hall, Post Office Box 3001, Addis Ababa, Ethiopia (Telephone Number in U.S. (800) 253-9646); *African Statistical Yearbook.*

LIBYA - RELIGION

Facts on File, 460 Park Avenue South, New York, New York 10016 (800) 443-8323; *The New Book of World Rankings.*

LIBYA - RENT PRICES

International Labour Office, I.L.O. Publications, CH-1211, Geneva 22, Switzerland; *Yearbook of Labour Statistics.*

LIBYA - RETAIL TRADE

Euromonitor Publications Limited, 87-88 Turnmill Street, London EC1M 5QU, England; *Third World Economic Handbook.*

G.K. Hall and Company, 70 Lincoln Street, Boston, Massachusetts 02111 (617) 423-3990; *The World in Figures.*

LIBYA - RICE PRODUCTION - See LIBYA - CROPS

LIBYA - ROOT AND TUBER PRODUCTION - See LIBYA - CROPS

LIBYA - ROUNDWOOD PRODUCTION - See LIBYA - FORESTRY AND FOREST PRODUCTS

LIBYA - RUBBER PRODUCTION AND CONSUMPTION

Euromonitor Publications Limited, 87-88 Turnmill Street, London EC1M 5QU, England; *Third World Economic Handbook.*

Facts on File, 460 Park Avenue South, New York, New York 10016 (800) 443-8323; *The New Book of World Rankings.*

LIBYA - SALT PRODUCTION

Statistical Office of the United Nations, Publishing Service, New York, New York 10017 (800) 253-9646; *Statistical Yearbook.*

LIBYA - SAWNWOOD PRODUCTION - See LIBYA - FORESTRY AND FOREST PRODUCTS

LIBYA - SCIENTISTS AND TECHNICIANS

Statistical Office of the United Nations, Publishing Service, New York, New York 10017 (800) 253-9646; *Statistical Yearbook.*

United Nations Educational, Scientific and Cultural Organization (UNESCO), 7 Place de Fontenoy, F-75700 Paris, France (Telephone Number in U.S. (212) 963-5981); *Statistical Yearbook.*

LIBYA - SENIOR CITIZENS

Facts on File, 460 Park Avenue South, New York, New York 10016 (800) 443-8323; *The New Book of World Rankings.*

LIBYA - SHEEP - See LIBYA - LIVESTOCK AND POULTRY

LIBYA - SILVER PRODUCTION - See LIBYA - MINING AND MINERAL PRODUCTS

LIBYA - SOCIAL DATA

African Development Bank, 01 BP 1387, Abidjan 01, Cote d'Ivoire; *Selected Statistics on Regional Member Countries.*

Facts on File, 460 Park Avenue South, New York, New York 10016 (800) 443-8323; *The New Book of World Rankings.*

G.K. Hall and Company, 70 Lincoln Street, Boston, Massachusetts 02111 (617) 423-3990; *The World in Figures.*

LIBYA - STATE BUDGET

Euromonitor Publications Limited, 87-88 Turnmill Street, London EC1M 5QU, England; *International Marketing Data and Statistics.*

LIBYA - STEEL - See LIBYA - MINING AND MINERAL PRODUCTS

LIBYA - STOCKS - COMMODITY - MARKET PRICE - INDEX

Food and Agricultural Organization of the United Nations (FAO), Via delle Terme di Caracalla, 00100 Rome, Italy (Telephone Number in U.S. (202) 653-2400); *The State of Food and Agriculture.*

LIBYA - SUGAR PRODUCTION AND CONSUMPTION - See LIBYA - CROPS

LIBYA - TAXATION

G.K. Hall and Company, 70 Lincoln Street, Boston, Massachusetts 02111 (617) 423-3990; *The World in Figures.*

International Road Federation, 525 School Street, SW, Washington, D.C. 20024 (202) 554-2106; *World Road Statistics.*

The World Bank, 1818 H Street, NW, Washington, D.C. 20433 (202) 477-1234; *World Tables.*

LIBYA - TELEPHONES IN USE

American Telephone and Telegraph Company, 26 Parsippany Road, Whippany, New Jersey 07981 (800) 338-4038; *The World's Telephones*.

Euromonitor Publications Limited, 87-88 Turnmill Street, London EC1M 5QU, England; *Middle East Economic Handbook*, and *Third World Economic Handbook*.

G.K. Hall and Company, 70 Lincoln Street, Boston, Massachusetts 02111 (617) 423-3990; *The World in Figures*.

Statistical Office of the United Nations, Publishing Service, New York, New York 10017 (800) 253-9646; *Statistical Yearbook*.

LIBYA - TELEVISION BROADCASTING - See LIBYA - BROADCASTING

LIBYA - TEXTILE INDUSTRY

Euromonitor Publications Limited, 87-88 Turnmill Street, London EC1M 5QU, England; *Third World Economic Handbook*.

G.K. Hall and Company, 70 Lincoln Street, Boston, Massachusetts 02111 (617) 423-3990; *The World in Figures*.

LIBYA - THEATRE

United Nations Educational, Scientific and Cultural Organization (UNESCO), 7 Place de Fontenoy, F-75700 Paris, France (Telephone Number in U.S. (212) 963-5981); *Statistical Yearbook*.

LIBYA - TOBACCO PRODUCTION

Euromonitor Publications Limited, 87-88 Turnmill Street, London EC1M 5QU, England; *Third World Economic Handbook*.

Facts on File, 460 Park Avenue South, New York, New York 10016 (800) 443-8323; *The New Book of World Rankings*.

Statistical Office of the United Nations, Publishing Service, New York, New York 10017 (800) 253-9646; *Statistical Yearbook*.

LIBYA - TOURISM

Euromonitor Publications Limited, 87-88 Turnmill Street, London EC1M 5QU, England; *Middle East Economic Handbook*, and *Third World Economic Handbook*.

Facts on File, 460 Park Avenue South, New York, New York 10016 (800) 443-8323; *The New Book of World Rankings*.

G.K. Hall and Company, 70 Lincoln Street, Boston, Massachusetts 02111 (617) 423-3990; *The World in Figures*.

Statistical Office of the United Nations, Publishing Service, New York, New York 10017 (800) 253-9646; *Statistical Yearbook*.

Times Books, 201 East 50th Street, New York, New York 10022 (212) 751-2600; *The Economist Book of Vital World Statistics*.

LIBYA - TRACTORS IN USE

Statistical Office of the United Nations, Publishing Service, New York, New York 10017 (800) 253-9646; *Statistical Yearbook*.

LIBYA - TRADE - See LIBYA - FOREIGN TRADE

LIBYA - TRADEMARKS AND SERVICE MARKS

Statistical Office of the United Nations, Publishing Service, New York, New York 10017 (800) 253-9646; *Statistical Yearbook*.

LIBYA - TRANSPORTATION AND COMMUNICATIONS

Euromonitor Publications Limited, 87-88 Turnmill Street, London EC1M 5QU, England; *Middle East Economic Handbook*, and *Third World Economic Handbook*.

Facts on File, 460 Park Avenue South, New York, New York 10016 (800) 443-8323; *The New Book of World Rankings*.

G.K. Hall and Company, 70 Lincoln Street, Boston, Massachusetts 02111 (617) 423-3990; *The World in Figures*.

United Nations Economic Commission for Africa, Africa Hall, Post Office Box 3001, Addis Ababa, Ethiopia (Telephone Number in U.S. (800) 253-9646); *African Statistical Yearbook*.

LIBYA - UNEMPLOYMENT

Euromonitor Publications Limited, 87-88 Turnmill Street, London EC1M 5QU, England; *International Marketing Data and Statistics*, and *Middle East Economic Handbook*.

International Labour Office, I.L.O. Publications, CH-1211, Geneva 22, Switzerland; *Yearbook of Labour Statistics*.

Statistical Office of the United Nations, Publishing Service, New York, New York 10017 (800) 253-9646; *Statistical Yearbook*.

LIBYA - VITAL STATISTICS

Euromonitor Publications Limited, 87-88 Turnmill Street, London EC1M 5QU, England; *International Marketing Data and Statistics*, *Middle East Economic Handbook*, and *Third World Economic Handbook*.

G.K. Hall and Company, 70 Lincoln Street, Boston, Massachusetts 02111 (617) 423-3990; *The World in Figures*.

Statistical Office of the United Nations, Publishing Service, New York, New York 10017 (800) 253-9646; *Statistical Yearbook*.

World Health Organization, Office of Publications, Avenue Appia, CH-1211 Geneva 27, Switzerland (Telephone Number in U.S. (518) 436-9686); *World Health Statistics Annual*.

LIBYA - WAGES

G.K. Hall and Company, 70 Lincoln Street, Boston, Massachusetts 02111 (617) 423-3990; *The World in Figures*.

International Labour Office, I.L.O. Publications, CH-1211, Geneva 22, Switzerland; *Yearbook of Labour Statistics*.

LIBYA - WATERMELON PRODUCTION - See LIBYA - CROPS

LIBYA - WEATHER

Facts on File, 460 Park Avenue South, New York, New York 10016 (800) 443-8323; *The New Book of World Rankings*.

G.K. Hall and Company, 70 Lincoln Street, Boston, Massachusetts 02111 (617) 423-3990; *The World in Figures*.

LIBYA - WHEAT PRODUCTION - See LIBYA - CROPS

LIBYA - WHOLESALE TRADE

Euromonitor Publications Limited, 87-88 Turnmill Street, London EC1M 5QU, England; *Third World Economic Handbook.*

LIBYA - WINE PRODUCTION

Facts on File, 460 Park Avenue South, New York, New York 10016 (800) 443-8323; *The New Book of World Rankings.*

LIBYA - WOOD PULP PRODUCTION - See LIBYA - FORESTRY AND FOREST PRODUCTS

LIBYA - WOOL PRODUCTION

Facts on File, 460 Park Avenue South, New York, New York 10016 (800) 443-8323; *The New Book of World Rankings.*

LICENSED DRIVERS - BY AGE GROUPS

U.S. Department of Justice, Bureau of Justice Statistics, 633 Indiana Avenue, NW, Washington, D.C. 20531 (000) 700 3377; *Drunk Driving, Special Report.*

U.S. Department of Transportation, National Highway Traffic Safety Administration, 400 Seventh Street, SW, Washington, D.C. 20590 (202) 366-9550; *Selected Highway Statistics and Charts.*

LICENSES, PERMITS, ETC. - FISHING AND HUNTING

U.S. Department of the Interior, Fish and Wildlife Service, C Street between Eighteenth and Nineteenth Streets, NW, Washington, D.C. 20240 (202) 208-5634; *Federal Aid in Fish and Wildlife Restoration.*

LICENSES, PERMITS, ETC. - PUBLIC LANDS

U.S. Department of the Interior, Bureau of Land Management, C Street between Eighteenth and Nineteenth Streets, NW, Washington, D.C. 20240 (202) 208-3435; *Public Land Statistics.*

LICENSES, PERMITS, ETC. - TAXES

U.S. Department of Commerce, Bureau of the Census, Suitland, Maryland 20233 (301) 763-4040; *Historical Statistics on Governmental Finances and Employment, State Government Finances, State Government Tax Collections,* and *City Government Finances.*

Liechtenstein - National Statistical Office

Amt fur Volkswirtschaft des furstlichen Regierung, FL-9490 Vaduz, Liechtenstein.

Liechtenstein - Primary Statistics Source

Amt fur Volkswirtschaft des furstlichen Regierung, FL-9490 Vaduz, Liechtenstein *Statistisches Jahrbuch* (Statistical Yearbook).

LIECHTENSTEIN - AGRICULTURE

Food and Agricultural Organization of the United Nations (FAO), Via delle Terme di Caracalla, 00100 Rome, Italy (Telephone Number in U.S. (202) 653-2400); *Production Yearbook, The State of Food and Agriculture,* and *Trade Yearbook.*

G.K. Hall and Company, 70 Lincoln Street, Boston, Massachusetts 02111 (617) 423-3990; *The World in Figures.*

Statistical Office of the United Nations, Publishing Service, New York, New York 10017 (800) 253-9646; *Statistical Yearbook.*

LIECHTENSTEIN - AIRLINE SERVICE

G.K. Hall and Company, 70 Lincoln Street, Boston, Massachusetts 02111 (617) 423-3990; *The World in Figures.*

LIECHTENSTEIN - AREA AND DENSITY OF POPULATION

Food and Agricultural Organization of the United Nations (FAO), Via delle Terme di Caracalla, 00100 Rome, Italy (Telephone Number in U.S. (202) 653-2400); *The State of Food and Agriculture.*

G.K. Hall and Company, 70 Lincoln Street, Boston, Massachusetts 02111 (617) 423-3990; *The World in Figures.*

Statistical Office of the United Nations, Publishing Service, New York, New York 10017 (800) 253-9646; *Statistical Yearbook.*

United Nations Educational, Scientific and Cultural Organization (UNESCO), 7 Place de Fontenoy, F-75700 Paris, France (Telephone Number in U.S. (212) 963 6981); *Statistical Yearbook.*

LIECHTENSTEIN - BALANCE OF PAYMENTS

G.K. Hall and Company, 70 Lincoln Street, Boston, Massachusetts 02111 (617) 423-3990; *The World in Figures.*

LIECHTENSTEIN - BANKING

G.K. Hall and Company, 70 Lincoln Street, Boston, Massachusetts 02111 (617) 423-3990; *The World in Figures.*

LIECHTENSTEIN - BIRTH RATES

Statistical Office of the United Nations, Publishing Service, New York, New York 10017 (800) 253-9646; *Demographic Yearbook,* and *Statistical Yearbook.*

World Health Organization, Office of Publications, Avenue Appia, CH-1211 Geneva 27, Switzerland (Telephone Number in U.S. (518) 436-9686); *World Health Statistics Annual.*

LIECHTENSTEIN - BONDS

G.K. Hall and Company, 70 Lincoln Street, Boston, Massachusetts 02111 (617) 423-3990; *The World in Figures.*

LIECHTENSTEIN - BOOK PRODUCTION

G.K. Hall and Company, 70 Lincoln Street, Boston, Massachusetts 02111 (617) 423-3990; *The World in Figures.*

LIECHTENSTEIN - BROADCASTING

G.K. Hall and Company, 70 Lincoln Street, Boston, Massachusetts 02111 (617) 423-3990; *The World in Figures.*

LIECHTENSTEIN - BUSINESS

G.K. Hall and Company, 70 Lincoln Street, Boston, Massachusetts 02111 (617) 423-3990; *The World in Figures.*

LIECHTENSTEIN - CALORIE SUPPLY

Food and Agricultural Organization of the United Nations (FAO), Via delle Terme di Caracalla, 00100 Rome, Italy (Telephone Number in U.S. (202) 653-2400); *The State of Food and Agriculture*.

LIECHTENSTEIN - CATTLE - See LIECHTENSTEIN - LIVESTOCK AND POULTRY

LIECHTENSTEIN - CHEMICAL (ORGANIC) PRODUCTION - See LIECHTENSTEIN - MINING AND MINERAL PRODUCTS

LIECHTENSTEIN - CLASS STRUCTURE

G.K. Hall and Company, 70 Lincoln Street, Boston, Massachusetts 02111 (617) 423-3990; *The World in Figures*.

LIECHTENSTEIN - CLIMATE

G.K. Hall and Company, 70 Lincoln Street, Boston, Massachusetts 02111 (617) 423-3990; *The World in Figures*.

LIECHTENSTEIN - COAL PRODUCTION - See LIECHTENSTEIN - MINING AND MINERAL PRODUCTS

LIECHTENSTEIN - COMMUNICATIONS

G.K. Hall and Company, 70 Lincoln Street, Boston, Massachusetts 02111 (617) 423-3990; *The World in Figures*.

LIECHTENSTEIN - CONSUMER PRICE INDEX

G.K. Hall and Company, 70 Lincoln Street, Boston, Massachusetts 02111 (617) 423-3990; *The World in Figures*.

LIECHTENSTEIN - CONSUMPTION

G.K. Hall and Company, 70 Lincoln Street, Boston, Massachusetts 02111 (617) 423-3990; *The World in Figures*.

LIECHTENSTEIN - CORN PRODUCTION - See LIECHTENSTEIN - CROPS

LIECHTENSTEIN - CORPORATE TAXES - See LIECHTENSTEIN - TAXATION

LIECHTENSTEIN - CROPS

Food and Agricultural Organization of the United Nations (FAO), Via delle Terme di Caracalla, 00100 Rome, Italy (Telephone Number in U.S. (202) 653-2400); *The State of Food and Agriculture*.

G.K. Hall and Company, 70 Lincoln Street, Boston, Massachusetts 02111 (617) 423-3990; *The World in Figures*.

Statistical Office of the United Nations, Publishing Service, New York, New York 10017 (800) 253-9646; *Statistical Yearbook*.

LIECHTENSTEIN - CUSTOMS DUTIES

G.K. Hall and Company, 70 Lincoln Street, Boston, Massachusetts 02111 (617) 423-3990; *The World in Figures*.

LIECHTENSTEIN - DAIRY PRODUCTS

Food and Agricultural Organization of the United Nations (FAO), Via delle Terme di Caracalla, 00100 Rome, Italy (Telephone Number in U.S. (202) 653-2400); *The State of Food and Agriculture*.

LIECHTENSTEIN - DEATH RATES

G.K. Hall and Company, 70 Lincoln Street, Boston, Massachusetts 02111 (617) 423-3990; *The World in Figures*.

Statistical Office of the United Nations, Publishing Service, New York, New York 10017 (800) 253-9646; *Statistical Yearbook*.

LIECHTENSTEIN - DEFENSE EXPENDITURES

G.K. Hall and Company, 70 Lincoln Street, Boston, Massachusetts 02111 (617) 423-3990; *The World in Figures*.

LIECHTENSTEIN - DEMOGRAPHY

G.K. Hall and Company, 70 Lincoln Street, Boston, Massachusetts 02111 (617) 423-3990; *The World in Figures*.

LIECHTENSTEIN - DEVELOPMENT ASSISTANCE

G.K. Hall and Company, 70 Lincoln Street, Boston, Massachusetts 02111 (617) 423-3990; *The World in Figures*.

LIECHTENSTEIN - DISEASE

G.K. Hall and Company, 70 Lincoln Street, Boston, Massachusetts 02111 (617) 423-3990; *The World in Figures*.

LIECHTENSTEIN - DIVORCE RATES

Statistical Office of the United Nations, Publishing Service, New York, New York 10017 (800) 253-9646; *Demographic Yearbook*, and *Statistical Yearbook*.

LIECHTENSTEIN - DOMESTIC PRODUCT

G.K. Hall and Company, 70 Lincoln Street, Boston, Massachusetts 02111 (617) 423-3990; *The World in Figures*.

LIECHTENSTEIN - ECONOMY

G.K. Hall and Company, 70 Lincoln Street, Boston, Massachusetts 02111 (617) 423-3990; *The World in Figures*.

LIECHTENSTEIN - EDUCATION

G.K. Hall and Company, 70 Lincoln Street, Boston, Massachusetts 02111 (617) 423-3990; *The World in Figures*.

United Nations Educational, Scientific and Cultural Organization (UNESCO), 7 Place de Fontenoy, F-75700 Paris, France (Telephone Number in U.S. (212) 963-5981); *Statistical Yearbook*.

LIECHTENSTEIN - EGG PRODUCTION AND CONSUMPTION - See LIECHTENSTEIN - DAIRY PRODUCTS

LIECHTENSTEIN - ENERGY

Food and Agricultural Organization of the United Nations (FAO), Via delle Terme di Caracalla, 00100 Rome, Italy (Telephone Number in U.S. (202) 653-2400); *The State of Food and Agriculture*.

G.K. Hall and Company, 70 Lincoln Street, Boston, Massachusetts 02111 (617) 423-3990; *The World in Figures*.

LIECHTENSTEIN - EXPORTS

Food and Agricultural Organization of the United Nations (FAO), Via delle Terme di Caracalla, 00100 Rome, Italy (Telephone Number in

U.S. (202) 653-2400); *The State of Food and Agriculture.*

G.K. Hall and Company, 70 Lincoln Street, Boston, Massachusetts 02111 (617) 423-3990; *The World in Figures.*

LIECHTENSTEIN - EXTERNAL TRADE

Food and Agricultural Organization of the United Nations (FAO), Via delle Terme di Caracalla, 00100 Rome, Italy (Telephone Number in U.S. (202) 653-2400); *The State of Food and Agriculture,* and *Trade Yearbook.*

G.K. Hall and Company, 70 Lincoln Street, Boston, Massachusetts 02111 (617) 423-3990; *The World in Figures.*

LIECHTENSTEIN - FARM CROPS - See LIECHTENSTEIN - CROPS

LIECHTENSTEIN - FERTILIZER

Food and Agricultural Organization of the United Nations (FAO), Via delle Terme di Caracalla, 00100 Rome, Italy (Telephone Number in U.S. (202) 653-2400); *The State of Food and Agriculture.*

LIECHTENSTEIN - FETAL MORTALITY

Statistical Office of the United Nations, Publishing Service, New York, New York 10017 (800) 253-9646; *Demographic Yearbook.*

World Health Organization, Office of Publications, Avenue Appia, CH-1211 Geneva 27, Switzerland (Telephone Number in U.S. (518) 436-9686); *World Health Statistics Annual.*

LIECHTENSTEIN - FINANCE

G.K. Hall and Company, 70 Lincoln Street, Boston, Massachusetts 02111 (617) 423-3990; *The World in Figures.*

LIECHTENSTEIN - FISHERIES

Food and Agricultural Organization of the United Nations (FAO), Via delle Terme di Caracalla, 00100 Rome, Italy (Telephone Number in U.S. (202) 653-2400); *The State of Food and Agriculture,* and *Yearbook of Fishery Statistics.*

LIECHTENSTEIN - FOOD

Food and Agricultural Organization of the United Nations (FAO), Via delle Terme di Caracalla, 00100 Rome, Italy (Telephone Number in U.S. (202) 653-2400); *The State of Food and Agriculture,* and *Production Yearbook.*

G.K. Hall and Company, 70 Lincoln Street, Boston, Massachusetts 02111 (617) 423-3990; *The World in Figures.*

LIECHTENSTEIN - FOREIGN AID

G.K. Hall and Company, 70 Lincoln Street, Boston, Massachusetts 02111 (617) 423-3990; *The World in Figures.*

LIECHTENSTEIN - FOREIGN TRADE

Food and Agricultural Organization of the United Nations (FAO), Via delle Terme di Caracalla, 00100 Rome, Italy (Telephone Number in U.S. (202) 653-2400); *The State of Food and Agriculture.*

G.K. Hall and Company, 70 Lincoln Street, Boston, Massachusetts 02111 (617) 423-3990; *The World in Figures.*

LIECHTENSTEIN - FORESTRY AND FOREST PRODUCTS

Food and Agricultural Organization of the United Nations (FAO), Via delle Terme di Caracalla, 00100 Rome, Italy (Telephone Number in U.S. (202) 653-2400); *The State of Food and Agriculture.*

G.K. Hall and Company, 70 Lincoln Street, Boston, Massachusetts 02111 (617) 423-3990; *The World in Figures.*

Statistical Office of the United Nations, Publishing Service, New York, New York 10017 (800) 253-9646; *Statistical Yearbook.*

United Nations Educational, Scientific and Cultural Organization (UNESCO), 7 Place de Fontenoy, F-75700 Paris, France (Telephone Number in U.S. (212) 963-5981); *Statistical Yearbook.*

LIECHTENSTEIN - GENERAL MORTALITY

Statistical Office of the United Nations, Publishing Service, New York, New York 10017 (800) 253-9646; *Demographic Yearbook.*

World Health Organization, Office of Publications, Avenue Appia, CH-1211 Geneva 27, Switzerland (Telephone Number in U.S. (518) 436-9686); *World Health Statistics Annual.*

LIECHTENSTEIN - GOVERNMENT

G.K. Hall and Company, 70 Lincoln Street, Boston, Massachusetts 02111 (617) 423-3990; *The World in Figures.*

LIECHTENSTEIN - GRAIN PRODUCTION - See LIECHTENSTEIN - CROPS

LIECHTENSTEIN - GROSS DOMESTIC PRODUCT

G.K. Hall and Company, 70 Lincoln Street, Boston, Massachusetts 02111 (617) 423-3990; *The World in Figures.*

LIECHTENSTEIN - HEALTH

G.K. Hall and Company, 70 Lincoln Street, Boston, Massachusetts 02111 (617) 423-3990; *The World in Figures.*

LIECHTENSTEIN - HIGHWAYS

G.K. Hall and Company, 70 Lincoln Street, Boston, Massachusetts 02111 (617) 423-3990; *The World in Figures.*

LIECHTENSTEIN - HOUSING

Statistical Office of the United Nations, Publishing Service, New York, New York 10017 (800) 253-9646; *Statistical Yearbook.*

LIECHTENSTEIN - ILLITERATE POPULATION

G.K. Hall and Company, 70 Lincoln Street, Boston, Massachusetts 02111 (617) 423-3990; *The World in Figures.*

LIECHTENSTEIN - IMPORTS

Food and Agricultural Organization of the United Nations (FAO), Via delle Terme di Caracalla, 00100 Rome, Italy (Telephone Number in U.S. (202) 653-2400); *The State of Food and Agriculture.*

G.K. Hall and Company, 70 Lincoln Street, Boston, Massachusetts 02111 (617) 423-3990; *The World in Figures.*

LIECHTENSTEIN - INDUSTRY

G.K. Hall and Company, 70 Lincoln Street, Boston, Massachusetts 02111 (617) 423-3990; *The World in Figures*.

Statistical Office of the United Nations, Publishing Service, New York, New York 10017 (800) 253-9646; *Statistical Yearbook*.

LIECHTENSTEIN - INFANT AND MATERNAL MORTALITY

Statistical Office of the United Nations, Publishing Service, New York, New York 10017 (800) 253-9646; *Demographic Yearbook*, and *Statistical Yearbook*.

World Health Organization, Office of Publications, Avenue Appia, CH-1211 Geneva 27, Switzerland (Telephone Number in U.S. (518) 436-9686); *World Health Statistics Annual*.

LIECHTENSTEIN - LABOR FORCE

Food and Agricultural Organization of the United Nations (FAO), Via delle Terme di Caracalla, 00100 Rome, Italy (Telephone Number in U.S. (202) 653-2400); *The State of Food and Agriculture*.

G.K. Hall and Company, 70 Lincoln Street, Boston, Massachusetts 02111 (617) 423-3990; *The World in Figures*.

LIECHTENSTEIN - LAND USE

Food and Agricultural Organization of the United Nations (FAO), Via delle Terme di Caracalla, 00100 Rome, Italy (Telephone Number in U.S. (202) 653-2400); *Production Yearbook*.

G.K. Hall and Company, 70 Lincoln Street, Boston, Massachusetts 02111 (617) 423-3990; *The World in Figures*.

LIECHTENSTEIN - LIBRARIES

United Nations Educational, Scientific and Cultural Organization (UNESCO), 7 Place de Fontenoy, F-75700 Paris, France (Telephone Number in U.S. (212) 963-5981); *Statistical Yearbook*.

LIECHTENSTEIN - LIVESTOCK AND POULTRY

Food and Agricultural Organization of the United Nations (FAO), Via delle Terme di Caracalla, 00100 Rome, Italy (Telephone Number in U.S. (202) 653-2400); *Production Yearbook*, and *The State of Food and Agriculture*.

G.K. Hall and Company, 70 Lincoln Street, Boston, Massachusetts 02111 (617) 423-3990; *The World in Figures*.

Statistical Office of the United Nations, Publishing Service, New York, New York 10017 (800) 253-9646; *Statistical Yearbook*.

LIECHTENSTEIN - LIVING LEVELS

G.K. Hall and Company, 70 Lincoln Street, Boston, Massachusetts 02111 (617) 423-3990; *The World in Figures*.

LIECHTENSTEIN - MAIL - PIECES SENT OR RECEIVED

Statistical Office of the United Nations, Publishing Service, New York, New York 10017 (800) 253-9646; *Statistical Yearbook*.

LIECHTENSTEIN - MANUFACTURING

G.K. Hall and Company, 70 Lincoln Street, Boston, Massachusetts 02111 (617) 423-3990; *The World in Figures*.

LIECHTENSTEIN - MARRIAGE RATES

Statistical Office of the United Nations, Publishing Service, New York, New York 10017 (800) 253-9646; *Demographic Yearbook*, and *Statistical Yearbook*.

LIECHTENSTEIN - MEAT PRODUCTION - See LIECHTENSTEIN - LIVESTOCK AND POULTRY

LIECHTENSTEIN - MERCHANT SHIPPING

G.K. Hall and Company, 70 Lincoln Street, Boston, Massachusetts 02111 (617) 423-3990; *The World in Figures*.

LIECHTENSTEIN - MILITARY

G.K. Hall and Company, 70 Lincoln Street, Boston, Massachusetts 02111 (617) 423-3990; *The World in Figures*.

LIECHTENSTEIN - MINING AND MINERAL PRODUCTS

G.K. Hall and Company, 70 Lincoln Street, Boston, Massachusetts 02111 (617) 423-3990; *The World in Figures*.

LIECHTENSTEIN - MONEY SUPPLY

G.K. Hall and Company, 70 Lincoln Street, Boston, Massachusetts 02111 (617) 423-3990; *The World in Figures*.

LIECHTENSTEIN - MOTOR VEHICLES IN USE

G.K. Hall and Company, 70 Lincoln Street, Boston, Massachusetts 02111 (617) 423-3990; *The World in Figures*.

LIECHTENSTEIN - NATALITY - See LIECHTENSTEIN - BIRTH RATES

LIECHTENSTEIN - NATIONAL INCOME

G.K. Hall and Company, 70 Lincoln Street, Boston, Massachusetts 02111 (617) 423-3990; *The World in Figures*.

LIECHTENSTEIN - NEWSPAPER PRODUCTION - See LIECHTENSTEIN - FORESTRY AND FOREST PRODUCTS

LIECHTENSTEIN - OCCUPATIONS - See LIECHTENSTEIN - LABOR FORCE

LIECHTENSTEIN - PESTICIDE USE

Food and Agricultural Organization of the United Nations (FAO), Via delle Terme di Caracalla, 00100 Rome, Italy (Telephone Number in U.S. (202) 653-2400); *The State of Food and Agriculture*.

LIECHTENSTEIN - PETROLEUM INDUSTRY

Food and Agricultural Organization of the United Nations (FAO), Via delle Terme di Caracalla, 00100 Rome, Italy (Telephone Number in U.S. (202) 653-2400); *The State of Food and Agriculture*.

G.K. Hall and Company, 70 Lincoln Street, Boston, Massachusetts 02111 (617) 423-3990; *The World in Figures*.

LIECHTENSTEIN - PIGS - See LIECHTENSTEIN - LIVESTOCK AND POULTRY

LIECHTENSTEIN - POPULATION

Food and Agricultural Organization of the United Nations (FAO), Via delle Terme di Caracalla, 00100 Rome, Italy (Telephone Number in

U.S. (202) 653-2400); *Production Yearbook.*

G.K. Hall and Company, 70 Lincoln Street, Boston, Massachusetts 02111 (617) 423-3990; *The World in Figures.*

Statistical Office of the United Nations, Publishing Service, New York, New York 10017 (800) 253-9646; *Demographic Yearbook,* and *Statistical Yearbook.*

United Nations Educational, Scientific and Cultural Organization (UNESCO), 7 Place de Fontenoy, F-75700 Paris, France (Telephone Number in U.S. (212) 963-5981); *Statistical Yearbook.*

World Health Organization, Office of Publications, Avenue Appia, CH-1211 Geneva 27, Switzerland (Telephone Number in U.S. (518) 436-9686); *World Health Statistics Annual.*

LIECHTENSTEIN - POTATO PRODUCTION - See LIECHTENSTEIN - CROPS

LIECHTENSTEIN - PRICES

Food and Agricultural Organization of the United Nations (FAO), Via delle Terme di Caracalla, 00100 Rome, Italy (Telephone Number in U.S. (202) 653-2400); *Production Yearbook,* and *The State of Food and Agriculture.*

G.K. Hall and Company, 70 Lincoln Street, Boston, Massachusetts 02111 (617) 423-3990; *The World in Figures.*

LIECHTENSTEIN - PRODUCTION

G.K. Hall and Company, 70 Lincoln Street, Boston, Massachusetts 02111 (617) 423-3990; *The World in Figures.*

LIECHTENSTEIN - RAILWAY USE

G.K. Hall and Company, 70 Lincoln Street, Boston, Massachusetts 02111 (617) 423-3990; *The World in Figures.*

LIECHTENSTEIN - RETAIL TRADE

G.K. Hall and Company, 70 Lincoln Street, Boston, Massachusetts 02111 (617) 423-3990; *The World in Figures.*

LIECHTENSTEIN - ROOT AND TUBER PRODUCTION

Food and Agricultural Organization of the United Nations (FAO), Via delle Terme di Caracalla, 00100 Rome, Italy (Telephone Number in U.S. (202) 653-2400); *Production Yearbook.*

LIECHTENSTEIN - SCIENTISTS AND TECHNICIANS

United Nations Educational, Scientific and Cultural Organization (UNESCO), 7 Place de Fontenoy, F-75700 Paris, France (Telephone Number in U.S. (212) 963-5981); *Statistical Yearbook.*

LIECHTENSTEIN - SHEEP - See LIECHTENSTEIN - LIVESTOCK AND POULTRY

LIECHTENSTEIN - SOCIAL DATA

G.K. Hall and Company, 70 Lincoln Street, Boston, Massachusetts 02111 (617) 423-3990; *The World in Figures.*

LIECHTENSTEIN - STOCKS - COMMODITY - MARKET PRICE - INDEX

Food and Agricultural Organization of the United Nations (FAO), Via delle Terme di Caracalla, 00100 Rome, Italy (Telephone Number

in U.S. (202) 653-2400); *The State of Food and Agriculture.*

LIECHTENSTEIN - TAXATION

G.K. Hall and Company, 70 Lincoln Street, Boston, Massachusetts 02111 (617) 423-3990; *The World in Figures.*

LIECHTENSTEIN - TELEPHONES IN USE

American Telephone and Telegraph Company, 26 Parsippany Road, Whippany, New Jersey 07981 (800) 338-4038; *The World's Telephones.*

G.K. Hall and Company, 70 Lincoln Street, Boston, Massachusetts 02111 (617) 423-3990; *The World in Figures.*

Statistical Office of the United Nations, Publishing Service, New York, New York 10017 (800) 253-9646; *Statistical Yearbook.*

LIECHTENSTEIN - TEXTILE INDUSTRY

G.K. Hall and Company, 70 Lincoln Street, Boston, Massachusetts 02111 (617) 423-3990; *The World in Figures.*

LIECHTENSTEIN - TOURISM

G.K. Hall and Company, 70 Lincoln Street, Boston, Massachusetts 02111 (617) 423-3990; *The World in Figures.*

World Tourism Organization, Calle Capitan Haya 42, E-28020 Madrid, Spain; *Yearbook of Tourism Statistics.*

LIECHTENSTEIN - TRACTORS IN USE

Statistical Office of the United Nations, Publishing Service, New York, New York 10017 (800) 253-9646; *Statistical Yearbook.*

LIECHTENSTEIN - TRADE - See LIECHTENSTEIN - FOREIGN TRADE

LIECHTENSTEIN - TRADEMARKS AND SERVICE MARKS

Statistical Office of the United Nations, Publishing Service, New York, New York 10017 (800) 253-9646; *Statistical Yearbook.*

LIECHTENSTEIN - TRANSPORTATION AND COMMUNICATIONS

G.K. Hall and Company, 70 Lincoln Street, Boston, Massachusetts 02111 (617) 423-3990; *The World in Figures.*

LIECHTENSTEIN - VITAL STATISTICS

G.K. Hall and Company, 70 Lincoln Street, Boston, Massachusetts 02111 (617) 423-3990; *The World in Figures.*

Statistical Office of the United Nations, Publishing Service, New York, New York 10017 (800) 253-9646; *Statistical Yearbook.*

World Health Organization, Office of Publications, Avenue Appia, CH-1211 Geneva 27, Switzerland (Telephone Number in U.S. (518) 436-9686); *World Health Statistics Annual.*

LIECHTENSTEIN - WAGES

G.K. Hall and Company, 70 Lincoln Street, Boston, Massachusetts 02111 (617) 423-3990; *The World in Figures.*

LIECHTENSTEIN - WEATHER

G.K. Hall and Company, 70 Lincoln Street, Boston, Massachusetts 02111 (617) 423-3990; *The World in Figures.*

LIFE EXPECTANCY

U.S. Department of Health and Human Services, National Center for Health Statistics, 3700 East-West Highway, Hyattsville, Maryland 20782 (301) 436-8500; *Vital Statistics of the United States, Monthly Vital Statistics Reports, U.S. Life Tables and Actuarial Tables,* and unpublished data.

LIFE EXPECTANCY - FOREIGN COUNTRIES

U.S. Department of Commerce, Bureau of the Census, Suitland, Maryland 20233 (301) 763-4040; *International Data Base.*

LIFE EXPECTANCY - PROJECTIONS

U.S. Department of Commerce, Bureau of the Census, Suitland, Maryland 20233 (301) 763-4040; *Current Population Reports.*

LIFE INSURANCE

American Council of Life Insurance, 1001 Pennsylvania Avenue, NW, Washington, D.C. 20004 (202) 624-2000; *Life Insurance Fact Book,* and unpublished data.

LIFE INSURANCE - CAPITAL

American Council of Life Insurance, 1001 Pennsylvania Avenue, NW, Washington, D.C. 20004 (202) 624-2000; *Life Insurance Fact Book,* and unpublished data.

LIFE INSURANCE - CONSUMER EXPENDITURES

U.S. Department of Labor Statistics, Two Massachusetts Avenue, NE, Washington, D.C. 20212 (202) 606-7828; *Consumer Expenditure in 1992.*

LIFE INSURANCE - ESTABLISHMENTS

American Council of Life Insurance, 1001 Pennsylvania Avenue, NW, Washington, D.C. 20004 (202) 624-2000; *Life Insurance Fact Book,* and unpublished data.

U.S. Department of Commerce, Bureau of the Census, Suitland, Maryland 20233 (301) 763-4040; *County Business Patterns.*

LIFE INSURANCE - FINANCES

American Council of Life Insurance, 1001 Pennsylvania Avenue, NW, Washington, D.C. 20004 (202) 624-2000; *Life Insurance Fact Book,* and unpublished data.

Board of Governors of the Federal Reserve System, Twentieth Street and Constitution Avenue, NW, Washington, D.C. 20551 (202) 452-3000; *Annual Statistical Digest,* and *Federal Reserve Bulletin.*

U.S. Department of Health and Human Services, Social Security Administration, 6401 Security Boulevard, Baltimore, Maryland 21235 (410) 619-1296; *Annual Statistical Supplement to the Social Security Bulletin.*

LIFE INSURANCE - FLOW OF FUNDS

Board of Governors of the Federal Reserve System, Twentieth Street and Constitution Avenue, NW, Washington, D.C. 20551 (202)

452-3000; *Annual Statistical Digest.*

LIFE INSURANCE - IN FORCE

American Council of Life Insurance, 1001 Pennsylvania Avenue, NW, Washington, D.C. 20004 (202) 624-2000; *Life Insurance Fact Book.*

LIFE INSURANCE - INDIVIDUAL RETIREMENT ACCOUNTS

Investment Company Institute, 1400 H Street, Suite 600, Washington, D.C. 20005 (202) 326-5800; *Mutual Fund Fact Book.*

LIFE INSURANCE - MORTGAGE LOANS OUTSTANDING

Board of Governors of the Federal Reserve System, Twentieth Street and Constitution Avenue, NW, Washington, D.C. 20551 (202) 452-3000; *Federal Reserve Bulletin.*

LIFE INSURANCE - PURCHASES, POLICIES

American Council of Life Insurance, 1001 Pennsylvania Avenue, NW, Washington, D.C. 20004 (202) 624-2000; *Life Insurance Fact Book.*

LIFE INSURANCE - RESERVES

American Council of Life Insurance, 1001 Pennsylvania Avenue, NW, Washington, D.C. 20004 (202) 624-2000; *Life Insurance Fact Book,* and unpublished data.

Board of Governors of the Federal Reserve System, Twentieth Street and Constitution Avenue, NW, Washington, D.C. 20551 (202) 452-3000; *Annual Statistical Digest,* and *Federal Reserve Bulletin.*

LIFE INSURANCE - SALES

American Council of Life Insurance, 1001 Pennsylvania Avenue, NW, Washington, D.C. 20004 (202) 624-2000; *Life Insurance Fact Book.*

LIFE SCIENCES

U.S. National Science Foundation, 4201 Wilson Boulevard, Arlington, Virginia 22230 (703) 306-1234; *Characteristics of Recent Science and Engineering Graduates, Characteristics of Doctoral Scientists and Engineers in the U.S.,* and *Survey of Earned Doctorates, Selected Data on Science and Engineering Doctorate Awards.*

LIFE SCIENCES - DEGREES CONFERRED

U.S. Department of Education, 400 Maryland Avenue, SW, Washington, D.C. 20202 (202) 708-5366; *Digest of Education Statistics.*

U.S. National Science Foundation, 4201 Wilson Boulevard, Arlington, Virginia 22230 (703) 306-1234; *Characteristics of Recent Science and Engineering Graduates.*

LIFE SCIENCES - EMPLOYMENT

U.S. Department of Labor, Bureau of Labor Statistics, Two Massachusetts Avenue, NE, Washington, D.C. 20212 (202) 606-7828; *Monthly Labor Review.*

LIGHT AND POWER - See ELECTRIC LIGHT AND POWER INDUSTRY

LIME

U.S. Department of Agriculture, Economic Research Service, Fourteenth Street and Independence Avenue, SW, Washington, D.C. 20005-4789 (202) 219-1504; *Economic Indicators of the Farm Sector:*

National Financial Summary.

U.S. Department of the Interior, Bureau of Mines, 810 Seventh Street, NW, Washington, D.C. 20241 (202) 501-9649; *Annual Reports,* and *Mineral Commodity Summaries.*

LIMES

U.S. Department of Agriculture, National Agricultural Statistics Service, Fourteenth Street between Constitution Avenue and E Street, NW, Washington, D.C. 20230 (202) 219-1504; *Citrus Fruits,* and unpublished data.

LIQUEFIED PETROLEUM GASES - CONSUMPTION

U.S. Department of Energy, Energy Information Administration, Washington, D.C. 20585 (202) 586-8800; *Petroleum Supply Annual.*

LIQUOR STORES - RETAIL - EARNINGS

U.S. Department of Commerce, Bureau of the Census, Suitland, Maryland 20233 (301) 763-4040; *County Business Patterns,* and *Census of Retail Trade.*

LIQUOR STORES - RETAIL - EMPLOYEES

U.S. Department of Commerce, Bureau of the Census, Suitland, Maryland 20233 (301) 763-4040; *County Business Patterns,* and *Census of Retail Trade.*

LIQUOR STORES - RETAIL ESTABLISHMENTS

U.S. Department of Commerce, Bureau of the Census, Suitland, Maryland 20233 (301) 763-4040; *County Business Patterns,* and *Census of Retail Trade.*

LIQUOR STORES - RETAIL - PRODUCTIVITY

U.S. Department of Labor, Bureau of Labor Statistics, Two Massachusetts Avenue, NE, Washington, D.C. 20212 (202) 606-7828; *Productivity Measures for Selected Industries and Government Services,* and unpublished data.

LIQUOR STORES - RETAIL - SALES

U.S. Department of Commerce, Bureau of the Census, Suitland, Maryland 20233 (301) 763-4040; *Current Business Reports, Combined Annual and Revised Monthly Retail Trade, Census of Retail Trade,* and unpublished data.

LIQUORS AND BEVERAGES - ALCOHOLISM TREATMENT

U.S. Department of Health and Human Services, Substance Abuse and Mental Health Services Administration, 5600 Fishers Lane, Rockville, Maryland 20857 (301) 443-4797; *Highlights from the National Drug and Alcoholism Treatment Unit Survey.*

LIQUORS AND BEVERAGES - CONSUMPTION

U.S. Department of Agriculture, Economic Research Service, Fourteenth Street and Independence Avenue, SW, Washington, D.C. 20005-4789 (202) 219-1504; *Food Consumption, Prices, and Expenditures,* and unpublished data.

U.S. Department of Health and Human Services, National Center for Health Statistics, 3700 East-West Highway, Hyattsville, Maryland 20782 (301) 436-8500; *Health Promotion and Disease Prevention, United States, Vital and Health Statistics,* and unpublished data.

U.S. Department of Health and Human Services, Substance Abuse and Mental Health Services Administration, 5600 Fishers Lane, Rockville, Maryland 20857 (301) 443-4797; *National Household Survey on Drug Abuse.*

LIQUORS AND BEVERAGES - GOVERNMENT REVENUES

U.S. Department of Commerce, Bureau of the Census, Suitland, Maryland 20233 (301) 763-4040; *Historical Statistics on Governmental Finances and Employment, Government Finances, State Government Finances, State Government Tax Collections,* and *City Government Finances.*

LIQUORS AND BEVERAGES - STATE LEGISLATION

National Safety Council, 1121 Spring Lake Drive, Itasca, Illinois 60143-3201 (708) 285-1121; *Accident Facts.*

LITHUANIA - See also UNION OF SOVIET SOCIALIST REPUBLICS

Lithuania - Primary Statistics Source

Lithuanian Department of Statistics, Vilnius, Lithuania; *Lithuania's Statistics Yearbook.*

LITHUANIA - AGRICULTURE

Business International Moscow, 23 Profsoyuznaya Ulitsa, 117859, Moscow (Telephone Number in U.S. (800) 938-4685); *The CIS Market Atlas.*

Encyclopedia Britannica, Incorporated, 310 South Michigan Avenue, Chicago, Illinois 60604 (312) 437-7000; *Britannica World Data.*

The World Bank, 1818 H Street, NW, Washington, D.C. 20433 (202) 477-1234; *Statistical Handbook: States of the Former USSR.*

LITHUANIA - AIRLINE SERVICE

Business International Moscow, 23 Profsoyuznaya Ulitsa, 117859, Moscow (Telephone Number in U.S. (800) 938-4685); *The CIS Market Atlas.*

Encyclopedia Britannica, Incorporated, 310 South Michigan Avenue, Chicago, Illinois 60604 (312) 437-7000; *Britannica World Data.*

LITHUANIA - AREA AND DENSITY OF POPULATION

Business International Moscow, 23 Profsoyuznaya Ulitsa, 117859, Moscow (Telephone Number in U.S. (800) 938-4685); *The CIS Market Atlas.*

LITHUANIA - BANKING

Business International Moscow, 23 Profsoyuznaya Ulitsa, 117859, Moscow (Telephone Number in U.S. (800) 938-4685); *The CIS Market Atlas.*

LITHUANIA - BIRTH RATES

Business International Moscow, 23 Profsoyuznaya Ulitsa, 117859, Moscow (Telephone Number in U.S. (800) 938-4685); *The CIS Market Atlas.*

Encyclopedia Britannica, Incorporated, 310 South Michigan Avenue, Chicago, Illinois 60604 (312) 437-7000; *Britannica World Data.*

LITHUANIA - BUDGET

Business International Moscow, 23 Profsoyuznaya Ulitsa, 117859, Moscow (Telephone Number in U.S. (800) 938-4685); *The CIS Market Atlas.*

LITHUANIA - CAPITAL INVESTMENT

The World Bank, 1818 H Street, NW, Washington, D.C. 20433 (202) 477-1234; *Statistical Handbook: States of the Former USSR.*

LITHUANIA - CATTLE - See (LITHUANIA) - LIVESTOCK AND POULTRY

LITHUANIA - CHEMICALS

Business International Moscow, 23 Profsoyuznaya Ulitsa, 117859, Moscow (Telephone Number in U.S. (800) 938-4685); *The CIS Market Atlas.*

LITHUANIA - COAL PRODUCTION AND CONSUMPTION - See LITHUANIA - MINING AND MINERAL PRODUCTS

LITHUANIA - COMMUNICATIONS

Business International Moscow, 23 Profsoyuznaya Ulitsa, 117859, Moscow (Telephone Number in U.S. (800) 938-4685); *The CIS Market Atlas.*

LITHUANIA - CONSTRUCTION INDUSTRY

Business International Moscow, 23 Profsoyuznaya Ulitsa, 117859, Moscow (Telephone Number in U.S. (800) 938-4685); *The CIS Market Atlas.*

Encyclopedia Britannica, Incorporated, 310 South Michigan Avenue, Chicago, Illinois 60604 (312) 437-7000; *Britannica World Data.*

LITHUANIA - CONSUMER PRODUCTS

Business International Moscow, 23 Profsoyuznaya Ulitsa, 117859, Moscow (Telephone Number in U.S. (800) 938-4685); *The CIS Market Atlas.*

LITHUANIA - CONSUMPTION

Business International Moscow, 23 Profsoyuznaya Ulitsa, 117859, Moscow (Telephone Number in U.S. (800) 938-4685); *The CIS Market Atlas.*

The World Bank, 1818 H Street, NW, Washington, D.C. 20433 (202) 477-1234; *Statistical Handbook: States of the Former USSR.*

LITHUANIA - COTTON PRODUCTION AND CONSUMPTION - See LITHUANIA - CROPS

LITHUANIA - CROPS

The World Bank, 1818 H Street, NW, Washington, D.C. 20433 (202) 477-1234; *Statistical Handbook: States of the Former USSR.*

LITHUANIA - DEATH RATES

Business International Moscow, 23 Profsoyuznaya Ulitsa, 117859, Moscow (Telephone Number in U.S. (800) 938-4685); *The CIS Market Atlas.*

LITHUANIA - DEMOGRAPHY

Business International Moscow, 23 Profsoyuznaya Ulitsa, 117859, Moscow (Telephone Number in U.S. (800) 938-4685); *The CIS Market Atlas.*

The Economist Intelligence Unit, 111 West 57th Street, New York, New York 10019 (800) 938-4685; *The World Market Atlas.*

Encyclopedia Britannica, Incorporated, 310 South Michigan Avenue, Chicago, Illinois 60604 (312) 437-7000; *Britannica World Data.*

The World Bank, 1818 H Street, NW, Washington, D.C. 20433 (202) 477-1234; *Statistical Handbook: States of the Former USSR.*

LITHUANIA - DISEASES

Business International Moscow, 23 Profsoyuznaya Ulitsa, 117859, Moscow (Telephone Number in U.S. (800) 938-4685); *The CIS Market Atlas.*

LITHUANIA - DIVORCE RATES

Encyclopedia Britannica, Incorporated, 310 South Michigan Avenue, Chicago, Illinois 60604 (312) 437-7000; *Britannica World Data.*

LITHUANIA - DOMESTIC INVESTMENT

Business International Moscow, 23 Profsoyuznaya Ulitsa, 117859, Moscow (Telephone Number in U.S. (800) 938-4685); *The CIS Market Atlas.*

LITHUANIA - ECONOMY

Business International Moscow, 23 Profsoyuznaya Ulitsa, 117859, Moscow (Telephone Number in U.S. (800) 938-4685); *The CIS Market Atlas.*

Encyclopedia Britannica, Incorporated, 310 South Michigan Avenue, Chicago, Illinois 60604 (312) 437-7000; *Britannica World Data.*

LITHUANIA - EDUCATION

Business International Moscow, 23 Profsoyuznaya Ulitsa, 117859, Moscow (Telephone Number in U.S. (800) 938-4685); *The CIS Market Atlas.*

The Economist Intelligence Unit, 111 West 57th Street, New York, New York 10019 (800) 938-4685; *The World Market Atlas.*

Encyclopedia Britannica, Incorporated, 310 South Michigan Avenue, Chicago, Illinois 60604 (312) 437-7000; *Britannica World Data.*

LITHUANIA - ELECTRICITY

Business International Moscow, 23 Profsoyuznaya Ulitsa, 117859, Moscow (Telephone Number in U.S. (800) 938-4685); *The CIS Market Atlas.*

The World Bank, 1818 H Street, NW, Washington, D.C. 20433 (202) 477-1234; *Statistical Handbook: States of the Former USSR.*

LITHUANIA - EMPLOYMENT

The World Bank, 1818 H Street, NW, Washington, D.C. 20433 (202) 477-1234; *Statistical Handbook: States of the Former USSR.*

LITHUANIA - ENERGY

Business International Moscow, 23 Profsoyuznaya Ulitsa, 117859, Moscow (Telephone Number in U.S. (800) 938-4685); *The CIS Market Atlas.*

Encyclopedia Britannica, Incorporated, 310 South Michigan Avenue, Chicago, Illinois 60604 (312) 437-7000; *Britannica World Data.*

The World Bank, 1818 H Street, NW, Washington, D.C. 20433 (202) 477-1234; *Statistical Handbook: States of the Former USSR.*

LITHUANIA - ENVIRONMENT

Business International Moscow, 23 Profsoyuznaya Ulitsa, 117859, Moscow (Telephone Number in U.S. (800) 938-4685); *The CIS Market Atlas.*

LITHUANIA - EXPORTS

Business International Moscow, 23 Profsoyuznaya Ulitsa, 117859, Moscow (Telephone Number in U.S. (800) 938-4685); *The CIS Market Atlas.*

The Economist Intelligence Unit, 111 West 57th Street, New York, New York 10019 (800) 938-4685; *The World Market Atlas.*

Encyclopedia Britannica, Incorporated, 310 South Michigan Avenue, Chicago, Illinois 60604 (312) 437-7000; *Britannica World Data.*

The World Bank, 1818 H Street, NW, Washington, D.C. 20433 (202) 477-1234; *Statistical Handbook: States of the Former USSR.*

LITHUANIA - EXTERNAL TRADE

The World Bank, 1818 H Street, NW, Washington, D.C. 20433 (202) 477-1234; *Statistical Handbook: States of the Former USSR.*

LITHUANIA - FABRIC PRODUCTION AND CONSUMPTION - See LITHUANIA - TEXTILE INDUSTRY

LITHUANIA - FERTILITY RATES

Encyclopedia Britannica, Incorporated, 310 South Michigan Avenue, Chicago, Illinois 60604 (312) 437-7000; *Britannica World Data.*

The World Bank, 1818 H Street, NW, Washington, D.C. 20433 (202) 477-1234; *Statistical Handbook: States of the Former USSR.*

LITHUANIA - FISHERIES

Encyclopedia Britannica, Incorporated, 310 South Michigan Avenue, Chicago, Illinois 60604 (312) 437-7000; *Britannica World Data.*

LITHUANIA - FOOTWEAR PRODUCTION AND CONSUMPTION - See LITHUANIA - TEXTILE INDUSTRY

LITHUANIA - FOREIGN INVESTMENT

Business International Moscow, 23 Profsoyuznaya Ulitsa, 117859, Moscow (Telephone Number in U.S. (800) 938-4685); *The CIS Market Atlas.*

LITHUANIA - FOREIGN TRADE

Business International Moscow, 23 Profsoyuznaya Ulitsa, 117859, Moscow (Telephone Number in U.S. (800) 938-4685); *The CIS Market Atlas.*

Encyclopedia Britannica, Incorporated, 310 South Michigan Avenue, Chicago, Illinois 60604 (312) 437-7000; *Britannica World Data.*

The World Bank, 1818 H Street, NW, Washington, D.C. 20433 (202) 477-1234; *Statistical Handbook: States of the Former USSR.*

LITHUANIA - FORESTRY AND FOREST PRODUCTS

Business International Moscow, 23 Profsoyuznaya Ulitsa, 117859, Moscow (Telephone Number in U.S. (800) 938-4685); *The CIS Market Atlas.*

Encyclopedia Britannica, Incorporated, 310 South Michigan Avenue, Chicago, Illinois 60604 (312) 437-7000; *Britannica World Data.*

LITHUANIA - GOATS - See LITHUANIA - LIVESTOCK AND POULTRY

LITHUANIA - GOVERNMENT EXPENDITURE

The World Bank, 1818 H Street, NW, Washington, D.C. 20433 (202) 477-1234; *Statistical Handbook: States of the Former USSR.*

LITHUANIA - GOVERNMENT REVENUE

The World Bank, 1818 H Street, NW, Washington, D.C. 20433 (202) 477-1234; *Statistical Handbook: States of the Former USSR.*

LITHUANIA - GROSS DOMESTIC PRODUCT

The Economist Intelligence Unit, 111 West 57th Street, New York, New York 10019 (800) 938-4685; *The World Market Atlas.*

The World Bank, 1818 H Street, NW, Washington, D.C. 20433 (202) 477-1234; *Statistical Handbook: States of the Former USSR.*

LITHUANIA - HEALTH

Business International Moscow, 23 Profsoyuznaya Ulitsa, 117859, Moscow (Telephone Number in U.S. (800) 938-4685); *The CIS Market Atlas.*

Encyclopedia Britannica, Incorporated, 310 South Michigan Avenue, Chicago, Illinois 60604 (312) 437-7000; *Britannica World Data.*

LITHUANIA - HIGHWAYS

Business International Moscow, 23 Profsoyuznaya Ulitsa, 117859, Moscow (Telephone Number in U.S. (800) 938-4685); *The CIS Market Atlas.*

Encyclopedia Britannica, Incorporated, 310 South Michigan Avenue, Chicago, Illinois 60604 (312) 437-7000; *Britannica World Data.*

LITHUANIA - HOUSING AND HOUSING UNITS

Business International Moscow, 23 Profsoyuznaya Ulitsa, 117859, Moscow (Telephone Number in U.S. (800) 938-4685); *The CIS Market Atlas.*

LITHUANIA - ILLITERATE POPULATION

The Economist Intelligence Unit, 111 West 57th Street, New York, New York 10019 (800) 938-4685; *The World Market Atlas.*

LITHUANIA - IMPORTS

Business International Moscow, 23 Profsoyuznaya Ulitsa, 117859, Moscow (Telephone Number in U.S. (800) 938-4685); *The CIS Market Atlas.*

The Economist Intelligence Unit, 111 West 57th Street, New York, New York 10019 (800) 938-4685; *The World Market Atlas.*

Encyclopedia Britannica, Incorporated, 310 South Michigan Avenue, Chicago, Illinois 60604 (312) 437-7000; *Britannica World Data.*

The World Bank, 1818 H Street, NW, Washington, D.C. 20433 (202) 477-1234; *Statistical Handbook: States of the Former USSR.*

LITHUANIA - INDUSTRY

Business International Moscow, 23 Profsoyuznaya Ulitsa, 117859, Moscow (Telephone Number in U.S. (800) 938-4685); *The CIS Market Atlas.*

The World Bank, 1818 H Street, NW, Washington, D.C. 20433 (202) 477-1234; *Statistical Handbook: States of the Former USSR.*

World Intellectual Property Organization, 34 Chemin des Colombettes, CH-1211 Geneva 20, Switzerland; *Industrial Property Statistics.*

LITHUANIA - INFANT MORTALITY RATES

Business International Moscow, 23 Profsoyuznaya Ulitsa, 117859, Moscow (Telephone Number in U.S. (800) 938-4685); *The CIS Market Atlas.*

LITHUANIA - LABOR FORCE

Business International Moscow, 23 Profsoyuznaya Ulitsa, 117859, Moscow (Telephone Number in U.S. (800) 938-4685); *The CIS Market Atlas.*

The World Bank, 1818 H Street, NW, Washington, D.C. 20433 (202) 477-1234; *Statistical Handbook: States of the Former USSR.*

LITHUANIA - LAND USE

Encyclopedia Britannica, Incorporated, 310 South Michigan Avenue, Chicago, Illinois 60604 (312) 437-7000; *Britannica World Data.*

LITHUANIA - LIFE EXPECTANCY

Business International Moscow, 23 Profsoyuznaya Ulitsa, 117859, Moscow (Telephone Number in U.S. (800) 938-4685); *The CIS Market Atlas.*

LITHUANIA - LIVESTOCK AND POULTRY

Business International Moscow, 23 Profsoyuznaya Ulitsa, 117859, Moscow (Telephone Number in U.S. (800) 938-4685); *The CIS Market Atlas.*

Encyclopedia Britannica, Incorporated, 310 South Michigan Avenue, Chicago, Illinois 60604 (312) 437-7000; *Britannica World Data.*

LITHUANIA - MANUFACTURING

Encyclopedia Britannica, Incorporated, 310 South Michigan Avenue, Chicago, Illinois 60604 (312) 437-7000; *Britannica World Data.*

LITHUANIA - MARRIAGE RATES

Encyclopedia Britannica, Incorporated, 310 South Michigan Avenue, Chicago, Illinois 60604 (312) 437-7000; *Britannica World Data.*

LITHUANIA - MEAT PRODUCTION - See LITHUANIA - LIVESTOCK AND POULTRY

LITHUANIA - MILITARY

The International Institute for Strategic Studies, 23 Tavistock Street, London WC2E 7NQ, England; *The Military Balance.*

LITHUANIA - MINING AND MINERAL PRODUCTS

Business International Moscow, 23 Profsoyuznaya Ulitsa, 117859, Moscow (Telephone Number in U.S. (800) 938-4685); *The CIS Market Atlas.*

Encyclopedia Britannica, Incorporated, 310 South Michigan Avenue, Chicago, Illinois 60604 (312) 437-7000; *Britannica World Data.*

LITHUANIA - MOTOR VEHICLES

Business International Moscow, 23 Profsoyuznaya Ulitsa, 117859, Moscow (Telephone Number in U.S. (800) 938-4685); *The CIS Market Atlas.*

LITHUANIA - NATIONAL ACCOUNTS

The World Bank, 1818 H Street, NW, Washington, D.C. 20433 (202) 477-1234; *Statistical Handbook: States of the Former USSR.*

LITHUANIA - NATIONAL INCOME

Business International Moscow, 23 Profsoyuznaya Ulitsa, 117859, Moscow (Telephone Number in U.S. (800) 938-4685); *The CIS Market Atlas.*

LITHUANIA - PIGS - See LITHUANIA - LIVESTOCK AND POULTRY

LITHUANIA - PATENTS

World Intellectual Property Organization, 34 Chemin des Colombettes, CH-1211 Geneva 20, Switzerland; *Industrial Property Statistics.*

LITHUANIA - POPULATION

Business International Moscow, 23 Profsoyuznaya Ulitsa, 117859, Moscow (Telephone Number in U.S. (800) 938-4685); *The CIS Market Atlas.*

The Economist Intelligence Unit, 111 West 57th Street, New York, New York 10019 (800) 938-4685; *The World Market Atlas.*

Encyclopedia Britannica, Incorporated, 310 South Michigan Avenue, Chicago, Illinois 60604 (312) 437-7000; *Britannica World Data.*

The World Bank, 1818 H Street, NW, Washington, D.C. 20433 (202) 477-1234; *Statistical Handbook: States of the Former USSR.*

LITHUANIA - POULTRY - See LITHUANIA - LIVESTOCK AND POULTRY

LITHUANIA - PRICES

The World Bank, 1818 H Street, NW, Washington, D.C. 20433 (202) 477-1234; *Statistical Handbook: States of the Former USSR.*

LITHUANIA - PRODUCTION

The World Bank, 1818 H Street, NW, Washington, D.C. 20433 (202) 477-1234; *Statistical Handbook: States of the Former USSR.*

LITHUANIA - PUBLIC FINANCE

The World Bank, 1818 H Street, NW, Washington, D.C. 20433 (202) 477-1234; *Statistical Handbook: States of the Former USSR.*

LITHUANIA - RADIO RECEIVERS

Encyclopedia Britannica, Incorporated, 310 South Michigan Avenue, Chicago, Illinois 60604 (312) 437-7000; *Britannica World Data.*

LITHUANIA - RAILWAYS

Business International Moscow, 23 Profsoyuznaya Ulitsa, 117859, Moscow (Telephone Number in U.S. (800) 938-4685); *The CIS Market Atlas.*

Encyclopedia Britannica, Incorporated, 310 South Michigan Avenue, Chicago, Illinois 60604 (312) 437-7000; *Britannica World Data.*

LITHUANIA - RETAIL TRADE

Business International Moscow, 23 Profsoyuznaya Ulitsa, 117859, Moscow (Telephone Number in U.S. (800) 938-4685); *The CIS Market Atlas.*

LITHUANIA - ROADS   See LITHUANIA - HIGHWAYS

LITHUANIA - ROUNDWOOD PRODUCTION AND CONSUMPTION - See LITHUANIA - FORESTRY AND FOREST PRODUCTS

LITHUANIA - SHEEP   See LITHUANIA - LIVESTOCK AND POULTRY

LITHUANIA - STEEL PRODUCTION AND CONSUMPTION - See LITHUANIA - MINING AND MINERAL PRODUCTS

LITHUANIA - TELEPHONES IN USE

Encyclopedia Britannica, Incorporated, 310 South Michigan Avenue, Chicago, Illinois 60604 (312) 437-7000; *Britannica World Data.*

LITHUANIA - TELEVISION RECEIVERS

Encyclopedia Britannica, Incorporated, 310 South Michigan Avenue, Chicago, Illinois 60604 (312) 437-7000; *Britannica World Data.*

LITHUANIA - TEXTILE INDUSTRY

Business International Moscow, 23 Profsoyuznaya Ulitsa, 117859, Moscow (Telephone Number in U.S. (800) 938-4685); *The CIS Market Atlas.*

LITHUANIA - TOURISM

Business International Moscow, 23 Profsoyuznaya Ulitsa, 117859, Moscow (Telephone Number in U.S. (800) 938-4685); *The CIS Market Atlas.*

LITHUANIA - TRADEMARKS AND SERVICE MARKS

World Intellectual Property Organization, 34 Chemin des Colombettes, CH-1211 Geneva 20, Switzerland; *Industrial Property Statistics.*

LITHUANIA - TRANSPORTATION AND COMMUNICATIONS

Business International Moscow, 23 Profsoyuznaya Ulitsa, 117859, Moscow (Telephone Number in U.S. (800) 938-4685); *The CIS Market Atlas.*

Encyclopedia Britannica, Incorporated, 310 South Michigan Avenue, Chicago, Illinois 60604 (312) 437-7000; *Britannica World Data.*

LITHUANIA - VITAL STATISTICS

Encyclopedia Britannica, Incorporated, 310 South Michigan Avenue, Chicago, Illinois 60604 (312) 437-7000; *Britannica World Data.*

LITHUANIA - WAGES

Business International Moscow, 23 Profsoyuznaya Ulitsa, 117859, Moscow (Telephone Number in U.S. (800) 938-4685); *The CIS Market Atlas.*

The World Bank, 1818 H Street, NW, Washington, D.C. 20433 (202) 477-1234; *Statistical Handbook: States of the Former USSR.*

LITHUANIA - WOOL PRODUCTION AND CONSUMPTION - See LITHUANIA - TEXTILE INDUSTRY

LIVESTOCK AND LIVESTOCK PRODUCTS - See also ANIMALS - DOMESTIC, and Individual Classes

LIVESTOCK AND LIVESTOCK PRODUCTS - COMMODITY FUTURES TRADING

Commodity Research Bureau, 75 Wall Street, New York, New York 10005 (212) 504-7754; *CRB Commodity Index Report.*

U.S. Commodities Futures Trading Commission, 2033 K Street, NW, Washington, D.C. 20581 (202) 254-6387; *Annual Report.*

LIVESTOCK AND LIVESTOCK PRODUCTS - CONSUMPTION

U.S. Department of Agriculture, Economic Research Service, Fourteenth Street and Independence Avenue, SW, Washington, D.C. 20005-4789 (202) 219-1504; *Food Consumption, Prices, and Expenditures, Livestock and Meat Statistics,* and *Agricultural Outlook.*

LIVESTOCK AND LIVESTOCK PRODUCTS - FARM MARKETINGS - SALES

U.S. Department of Agriculture, Economic Research Service, Fourteenth Street and Independence Avenue, SW, Washington, D.C. 20005-4789 (202) 219-1504; *Economic Indicators of the Farm Sector: National Financial Summary,* and *Economic Indicators of the Farm Sector: State Financial Summary.*

U.S. Department of Commerce, Bureau of the Census, Suitland, Maryland 20233 (301) 763-4040; *Census of Agriculture.*

LIVESTOCK AND LIVESTOCK PRODUCTS - FARM OUTPUT AND MARKETING INDEXES

U.S. Department of Agriculture, Economic Research Service, Fourteenth Street and Independence Avenue, SW, Washington, D.C. 20005-4789 (202) 219-1504; *Agricultural Outlook.*

LIVESTOCK AND LIVESTOCK PRODUCTS - FOREIGN TRADE

U.S. Department of Agriculture, Economic Research Service, Fourteenth Street and Independence Avenue, SW, Washington, D.C. 20005-4789 (202) 219-1504; *Agricultural Statistics, Foreign Agricultural Trade of the United States, Livestock and Meat Statistics, Agricultural Outlook,* and *U.S. Merchandise Trade.*

LIVESTOCK AND LIVESTOCK PRODUCTS - NUMBER AND VALUE ON FARMS

U.S. Department of Agriculture, National Agricultural Statistics Service, Fourteenth Street and Independence Avenue, SW, Washington, D.C. 20250 (202) 219-1504; *Meat Animals - Production, Disposition, and Income, Agricultural Statistics,* and *Livestock and Meat Statistics.*

LIVESTOCK AND LIVESTOCK PRODUCTS - PRICES

U.S. Department of Agriculture, National Agricultural Statistics Service, Fourteenth Street and Independence Avenue, SW, Washington, D.C. 20250 (202) 219-1504; *Agricultural Prices: Annual Survey, Meat Animals - Production, Disposition, and Income,* and *Agricultural Statistics.*

LIVESTOCK AND LIVESTOCK PRODUCTS - PRODUCTION

U.S. Department of Agriculture, Economic Research Service, Fourteenth Street and Independence Avenue, SW, Washington, D.C. 20005-4789 (202) 219-1504; *Agricultural Statistics, Agricultural Outlook, Meat Animals - Production, Disposition and Income,* and *Livestock and Meat Statistics.*

LIVESTOCK AND LIVESTOCK PRODUCTS - PURCHASES

U.S. Department of Agriculture, Economic Research Service, Fourteenth Street and Independence Avenue, SW, Washington, D.C. 20005-4789 (202) 219-1504; *Economic Indicators of the Farm Sector: National Financial Summary.*

LIVESTOCK AND LIVESTOCK PRODUCTS - SUPPLY

U.S. Department of Agriculture, Economic Research Service, Fourteenth Street and Independence Avenue, SW, Washington, D.C. 20005-4789 (202) 219-1504; *Livestock and Meat Statistics,* and *Agricultural Outlook.*

LIVESTOCK AND LIVESTOCK PRODUCTS - VALUE ON FARMS

U.S. Department of Agriculture, National Agricultural Statistics Service, Fourteenth Street and Independence Avenue, SW, Washington, D.C. 20250 (202) 219-1504; *Agricultural Statistics,* and *Meat Animals - Production, Disposition, and Income.*

U.S. Department of Commerce, Bureau of the Census, Suitland, Maryland 20233 (301) 763-4040; *Census of Agriculture.*

LIVING COST - See CONSUMER PRICE INDEXES and PRICES

LOANS AND MORTGAGES - See also DEBT

LOANS AND MORTGAGES - AUTOMOBILE LOANS

American Bankers Association, 1120 Connecticut Avenue, NW, Washington, D.C. 20036 (202) 663-5000; *Consumer Credit Delinquency Bulletin.*

Board of Governors of the Federal Reserve System, Twentieth Street and Constitution Avenue, NW, Washington, D.C. 20551 (202) 452-3000; *Federal Reserve Bulletin, Annual Statistical Digest,* and unpublished data.

LOANS AND MORTGAGES - BANKS - COMMERCIAL

American Bankers Association, 1120 Connecticut Avenue, NW, Washington, D.C. 20036 (202) 663-5000; *Consumer Credit Delinquency Bulletin.*

U.S. Federal Deposit Insurance Corporation, 550 Seventeenth Street, NW, Washington, D.C. 20429 (202) 393-8400; *Annual Report, The FDIC Quarterly Banking Profile,* and *Statistics on Banking.*

LOANS AND MORTGAGES - CONSUMER CREDIT

Board of Governors of the Federal Reserve System, Twentieth Street and Constitution Avenue, NW, Washington, D.C. 20551 (202) 452-3000; *Federal Reserve Bulletin, Annual Statistical Digest,* and unpublished data.

LOANS AND MORTGAGES - CREDIT MARKET - FLOW OF FUNDS

Board of Governors of the Federal Reserve System, Twentieth Street and Constitution Avenue, NW, Washington, D.C. 20551 (202) 452-3000; *Annual Statistical Digest.*

LOANS AND MORTGAGES - CREDIT UNIONS

National Credit Union Administration, 1775 Duke Street, Alexandria, Virginia 22314 (703) 518-6300; *Annual Report of the National Credit Union Administration,* and unpublished data.

LOANS AND MORTGAGES - DELINQUENCY RATES

American Bankers Association, 1120 Connecticut Avenue, NW, Washington, D.C. 20036 (202) 663-5000; *Consumer Credit Delinquency Bulletin.*

Mortgage Bankers Association of America, 1125 Fifteenth Street, NW, Washington, D.C. 20005 (202) 861-6500; *National Delinquency Survey.*

U.S. Office of Thrift Supervision, 1700 G Street, NW, Washington, D.C. 20552 (202) 906-6000; *Surveillance and Analysis.*

LOANS AND MORTGAGES - FARM - See FARM MORTGAGE LOANS

LOANS AND MORTGAGES - FEDERAL GOVERNMENT LOANS

Executive Office of the President, Office of Management and Budget, Executive Office Building, Washington, D.C. 20503 (202) 395-3080; *Budget of the United States Government.*

LOANS AND MORTGAGES - FEDERAL HOUSING ADMINISTRATION

Mortgage Bankers Association of America, 1125 Fifteenth Street, NW, Washington, D.C. 20005 (202) 861-6500; *National Delinquency Survey.*

LOANS AND MORTGAGES - FORECLOSURE RATES

Mortgage Bankers Association of America, 1125 Fifteenth Street, NW, Washington, D.C. 20005 (202) 861-6500; *National Delinquency Survey.*

LOANS AND MORTGAGES - FOREIGN COUNTRIES

Board of Governors of the Federal Reserve System, Federal Financial Institutions Examination Council, Twentieth Street and Constitution Avenue, NW, Washington, D.C. 20551 (202) 452-3000; statistical release.

LOANS AND MORTGAGES - HOME MORTGAGE/EQUITY LOANS

American Bankers Association, 1120 Connecticut Avenue, NW, Washington, D.C. 20036 (202) 663-5000; *Consumer Credit Delinquency Bulletin.*

Board of Governors of the Federal Reserve System, Twentieth Street and Constitution Avenue, NW, Washington, D.C. 20551 (202) 452-3000; *Domestic Offices, Commercial Bank Assets and Liabilities,Consolidated Report of Condition*, and *Federal Reserve Bulletin*.

LOANS AND MORTGAGES - INSTALLMENT LOANS

American Bankers Association, 1120 Connecticut Avenue, NW, Washington, D.C. 20036 (202) 663-5000; *Consumer Credit Delinquency Bulletin*.

Board of Governors of the Federal Reserve System, Twentieth Street and Constitution Avenue, NW, Washington, D.C. 20551 (202) 452-3000; *Federal Reserve Bulletin, Annual Statistical Digest*, and unpublished data.

LOANS AND MORTGAGES - INTEREST RATES

Board of Governors of the Federal Reserve System, Twentieth Street and Constitution Avenue, NW, Washington, D.C. 20551 (202) 452-3000; *Federal Reserve Bulletin, Annual Statistical Digest*, and unpublished data.

Federal Housing Finance Board, 1777 F Street NW, Washington, D.C. 20006 (202) 408-2500; annual and monthly press releases.

LOANS AND MORTGAGES - LIFE INSURANCE

American Council of Life Insurance, 1001 Pennsylvania Avenue, NW, Washington, D.C. 20004 (202) 624-2000; *Life Insurance Fact Book*, and unpublished data.

LOANS AND MORTGAGES - MINORITY - OPERATED SMALL BUSINESSES

U.S. Small Business Administration, 409 Third Street, SW, Washington, D.C. 20416 (800) UASK-SBA; unpublished data.

LOANS AND MORTGAGES - MORTGAGE COMPANIES

U.S. Department of Housing and Urban Development, 451 Seventh Street, SW, Washington, D.C. 20410 (202) 708-1422; monthly and quarterly press releases based on the *Survey of Mortgage Lending Activity*.

LOANS AND MORTGAGES - MORTGAGES

Board of Governors of the Federal Reserve System, Twentieth Street and Constitution Avenue, NW, Washington, D.C. 20551 (202) 452-3000 (202) 452-3000; *Federal Reserve Bulletin, Annual Statistical Digest*, and *Domestic Offices, Commercial Bank Assets and Liabilities, Consolidated Report of Condition*.

U.S. Office of Thrift Supervision, 1700 G Street, NW, Washington, D.C. 20552 (202) 906-6000; *Surveillance and Analysis*.

LOANS AND MORTGAGES - PERSONAL LOANS

Board of Governors of the Federal Reserve System, Twentieth Street and Constitution Avenue, NW, Washington, D.C. 20551 (202) 452-3000; *Federal Reserve Bulletin, Annual Statistical Digest*, and unpublished data.

LOANS AND MORTGAGES - REFINANCINGS (MORTGAGES)

U.S. Department of Thrift Supervision, 1700 G Street, NW, Washington, D.C. 20552; *Surveillance and Analysis*.

LOANS AND MORTGAGES - REPOSSESSIONS - BANK LOANS

American Bankers Association, 1120 Connecticut Avenue, NW, Washington, D.C. 20036 (202) 663-5000; *Consumer Credit Delinquency Bulletin*.

LOANS AND MORTGAGES - SAVINGS INSTITUTIONS

National Credit Union Administration, 1775 Duke Street, Alexandria, Virginia 22314 (703) 518-6300; *Annual Report of the National Credit Union Administration*.

U.S. Office of Thrift Supervision, 1700 G Street, NW, Washington, D.C. 20552 (202) 906-6000; *Surveillance and Analysis*.

LOANS AND MORTGAGES - VETERANS ADMINISTRATION

Mortgage Bankers Association of America, 1125 Fifteenth Street, NW, Washington, D.C. 20005 (202) 861-6500; *National Delinquency Survey*.

U.S. Department of Veterans Affairs, 810 Vermont Avenue, NW, Washington, D.C. 20420 (202) 233-2300; *Annual Report of the Secretary of Veterans Affairs*.

LOBSTERS

U.S. Department of Commerce, National Oceanic and Atmospheric Administration, National Marine Fisheries Service, 1335 East-West Highway Silver Spring, Maryland 20910 (704) 259-2850; *Fishery Statistics of the United States*, and *Fisheries of the United States*.

LOCAL GOVERNMENT - See Individual Governmental Units and STATE AND LOCAL GOVERNMENT

LOCOMOTIVES (RAILROAD)

Association of American Railroads, American Railroads Building, 50 F Street, NW, Washington, D.C. 20001 (202) 639-2100; *Railroad Facts, Statistics of Railroads of Class I*, and *Analysis of Class I Railroads*.

U.S. Department of Transportation, Federal Railroad Administration, 400 Seventh Street, SW, Washington, D.C. 20590 (202) 366-4000; *Accident Bulletin*.

LODGING INDUSTRIES - See HOTELS AND OTHER LODGING PLACES

LOTTERIES

TLF Publications, Inc., Boyds, Maryland 20841 (301) 540-0123; *World Lottery Almanac, LaFleur's Fiscal 1993 Lottery Special Report*, and *LaFleur's Lottery World*.

U.S. Department of Commerce, Bureau of the Census, Suitland, Maryland 20233 (301) 763-4040; *State Government Finances*.

LOUISIANA - See STATE DATA (FOR INDIVIDUAL STATES)

Louisiana - Primary Statistics Source

Division of Business and Economic Research, University of New Orleans, New Orleans, Louisiana 70148 (504) 286-6248; *Statistical Abstract of Louisiana*.

Louisiana - State Data Centers

Office of Planning and Budget, Division of Administration, Post Office Box 94095, 1051 North Third Street, Baton Rouge, Louisiana 70804, Ms. Karen Paterson (504) 342-7410.

Division of Business and Economic Research, University of New Orleans, Lake Front, New Orleans, Louisiana 70148, Mr. Vincent Maruggi (504) 286-6980.

Division of Business Research, Louisiana Tech University, Post Office Box 10318, Ruston, Louisiana 71272, Dr. Edward O'Boyle (318) 257-3701.

Reference Department, Louisiana State Library, Post Office Box 131, Baton Rouge, Louisiana 70821, Mrs. Virginia Smith (504) 342-4920.

Center for Life Course and Population Studies, Department of Sociology, Room 126, Stubbs Hall, Louisiana State University, Baton Rouge, Louisiana 70803-5411, Mr. Charles Tolbert, Director (504) 388-5359.

Center for Business and Economic Research, Northeast Louisiana University, Monroe, Louisiana 71209, Dr. Jerry Wall (318) 342-1215.

LOUISIANA PURCHASE

U.S. Department of Commerce, Bureau of the Census, Suitland, Maryland 20233 (301) 763-4040; unpublished data.

U.S. Department of the Interior, Office of the Secretary, C Street between Eighteenth and Nineteenth Streets, NW, Washington, D.C. 20240 (202) 208-3171; *Areas of Acquisitions to the Territory of the United States.*

LUMBER - CONSUMPTION

U.S. Department of Agriculture, Forest Service, Fourteenth Street and Independence Avenue, SW, Washington, D.C. 20250 (202) 720-3760; *United States Timber Production, Trade, Consumption, and Price Statistics,* and *RPA Timber Assessment Update.*

U.S. Department of Commerce, Bureau of the Census, Suitland, Maryland 20233 (301) 763-4040; *Current Industrial Reports.*

LUMBER - FOREIGN TRADE

U.S. Department of Agriculture, Forest Service, Fourteenth Street and Independence Avenue, SW, Washington, D.C. 20250 (202) 720-3760; *U.S. Timber Production, Trade, Consumption, and Price Statistics.*

U.S. Department of Commerce, Bureau of the Census, Suitland, Maryland 20233 (301) 763-4040; *Current Industrial Reports,* and *U.S. Merchandise Trade: Exports, General Imports, and Imports for Consumption.*

LUMBER - PRICES

U.S. Department of Agriculture, Forest Service, Fourteenth Street and Independence Avenue, SW, Washington, D.C. 20250 (202) 720-3760; *United States Timber Production, Trade, Consumption, and Price Statistics.*

U.S. Department of Labor, Bureau of Labor Statistics, Two Massachusetts Avenue, NE, Washington, D.C. 20212 (202) 606-7828; *Producer Price Indexes.*

LUMBER - PRODUCTION

U.S. Department of Agriculture, Forest Service, Fourteenth Street and Independence Avenue, SW, Washington, D.C. 20250 (202) 720-3760; *United States Timber Production, Trade, Consumption, and Price Statistics.*

U.S. Department of Commerce, Bureau of the Census, Suitland, Maryland 20233 (301) 763-4040; *Current Industrial Reports.*

LUMBER - RAILROAD CAR LOADINGS

Association of American Railroads, American Railroads Building, 50 F Street, NW, Washington, D.C. 20001 (202) 639-2100; *Freight Commodity Statistics,* and *Weekly Railroad Traffic.*

LUMBER - WATERBORNE COMMERCE

U.S. Department of the Army, Corps of Engineers, The Pentagon, Washington, D.C. 20310 (202) 545-6700; *Waterborne Commerce of the United States.*

LUMBER AND WOOD PRODUCTS - MANUFACTURING - CAPITAL

U.S. Department of Commerce, Bureau of the Census, Suitland, Maryland 20233 (301) 763-4040; *Current Industrial Reports.*

LUMBER AND WOOD PRODUCTS - MANUFACTURING - EARNINGS

U.S. Department of Commerce, Bureau of the Census, Suitland, Maryland 20233 (301) 763-4040; *Census of Manufactures,* and *Annual Survey of Manufactures.*

U.S. Department of Labor, Bureau of Labor Statistics, Two Massachusetts Avenue, NE, Washington, D.C. 20212 (202) 606-7828; *Employment and Earnings,* and Bulletins 2370 and 2429.

LUMBER AND WOOD PRODUCTS - MANUFACTURING - EMPLOYEES

U.S. Department of Commerce, Bureau of Economic Analysis, Fourteenth Street between Constitution Avenue and E Street, NW, Washington, D.C. 20230 (202) 606-9900; *Survey of Current Business,* and *Foreign Direct Investment in the U.S., Operations of U.S. Affiliates of Foreign Companies.*

U.S. Department of Commerce, Bureau of the Census, Suitland, Maryland 20233 (301) 763-4040; *Census of Manufactures,* and *Annual Survey of Manufactures.*

U.S. Department of Commerce, International Trade Administration, Fourteenth Street between Constitution Avenue and E Street, NW, Washington, D.C. 20230 (202) 482-5487; *U.S. Industrial Outlook.*

U.S. Department of Labor, Bureau of Labor Statistics, Two Massachusetts Avenue, NE, Washington, D.C. 20212 (202) 606-7828; *Employment and Earnings, Monthly Labor Review,* and Bulletins 2370 and 2429.

LUMBER AND WOOD PRODUCTS - MANUFACTURING - ESTABLISHMENTS

U.S. Department of Commerce, Bureau of Economic Analysis, Fourteenth Street between Constitution Avenue and E Street, NW, Washington, D.C. 20230 (202) 606-9900; *Survey of Current Business,* and *Foreign Direct Investment in the U.S., Operations of U.S. Affiliates of Foreign Companies.*

U.S. Department of Commerce, Bureau of the Census, Suitland, Maryland 20233 (301) 763-4040; *United States Census of Manufactures*, and *Annual Survey of Manufactures*.

LUMBER AND WOOD PRODUCTS - MANUFACTURING - FOREIGN TRADE

U.S. Department of Agriculture, Forest Service, Fourteenth Street and Independence Avenue, SW, Washington, D.C. 20250 (202) 720-3760; *United States Timber Production, Trade, Consumption, and Price Statistics*.

U.S. Department of Commerce, Bureau of the Census, Suitland, Maryland 20233 (301) 763-4040; *U.S. Merchandise Trade*.

LUMBER AND WOOD PRODUCTS - MANUFACTURING - MERGERS AND ACQUISITIONS

Securities Data Company, 1180 Raymond Boulevard, Newark, New Jersey 07102 (201) 622-3100; *Merger and Corporate Transactions Database*.

LUMBER AND WOOD PRODUCTS - MANUFACTURING - OCCUPATIONAL SAFETY

U.S. Department of Labor, Bureau of Labor Statistics, Two Massachusetts Avenue, NE, Washington, D.C. 20212 (202) 606-7828; *Occupational Injuries and Illnesses in the United States by Industry*.

LUMBER AND WOOD PRODUCTS - MANUFACTURING - POLLUTION ABATEMENT

U.S. Department of Commerce, Bureau of the Census, Suitland, Maryland 20233 (301) 763-4040; *Current Industrial Reports*.

LUMBER AND WOOD PRODUCTS - MANUFACTURING - PRICES

U.S. Department of Labor, Bureau of Labor Statistics, Two Massachusetts Avenue, NE, Washington, D.C. 20212 (202) 606-7828; *Producer Price Indexes*.

LUMBER AND WOOD PRODUCTS - MANUFACTURING - PRODUCTIVITY

U.S. Department of Labor, Bureau of Labor Statistics, Two Massachusetts Avenue, NE, Washington, D.C. 20212 (202) 606-7828; *Productivity Measures for Selected Industries and Government Services*, and unpublished data.

LUMBER AND WOOD PRODUCTS - MANUFACTURING - RAILROAD CAR LOADINGS

Association of American Railroads, American Railroads Building, 50 F Street, NW, Washington, D.C. 20001 (202) 639-2333; *Freight Commodity Statistics*, and *Weekly Railroad Traffic*.

LUMBER AND WOOD PRODUCTS - MANUFACTURING - SHIPMENTS

U.S. Department of Commerce, Bureau of the Census, Suitland, Maryland 20233 (301) 763-4040; *Census of Manufactures*, and *Annual Survey of Manufactures*.

U.S. Department of Commerce, International Trade Administration, Fourteenth Street between Constitution Avenue and E Street, NW, Washington, D.C. 20230 (202) 482-5487; *U.S. Industrial Outlook*.

LUMBER AND WOOD PRODUCTS - MANUFACTURING - VALUE ADDED

U.S. Department of Commerce, Bureau of the Census, Suitland, Maryland 20233 (301) 763-4040; *Census of Manufactures*, and *Annual Survey of Manufactures*.

Luxembourg - National Statistical Office

Service Central de la Statistique et des Etudes Economiques, 19-21 Boulevard Royal, B.P. 304, L-2013, Luxembourg.

Luxembourg - Primary Statistics Sources

STATEC, 19-21 Boulevard Royal, B.P. 304, L-2013, Luxembourg; *Annuaire Statistique du Luxembourg* (Statistical Yearbook for Luxembourg), and *Bulletin du STATEC* (STATEC Bulletin).

LUXEMBOURG - ABORTIONS

European Community Information Service, 2100 M Street, NW, Washington, D.C. 20037 (202) 862-9500; *Demographic Statistics*.

LUXEMBOURG - AGRICULTURE

European Community Information Service, 2100 M Street, NW, Washington, D.C. 20037 (202) 862-9500; *Agriculture: Statistical Yearbook, Basic Statistics of the Community, Eurostatistics: Data for Short-Term Economic Analysis, Regions: Statistical Yearbook*.

Food and Agricultural Organization of the United Nations (FAO), Via delle Terme di Caracalla, 00100 Rome, Italy (Telephone Number in U.S. (202) 653-2400); *Production Yearbook, The State of Food and Agriculture*, and *Trade Yearbook*.

G.K. Hall and Company, 70 Lincoln Street, Boston, Massachusetts 02111 (617) 423-3990; *The World in Figures*.

Organisation for Economic Co-operation and Development (OECD), 2 rue Andre-Pascal, 75 Paris 16, France (Telephone in U.S. (202) 785-6323); *Economic Accounts for Agriculture, Indicators of Industrial Activity, Industrial Structure Statistics*, and *OECD Economic Surveys: Belgium - Luxembourg*.

Statistical Office of the United Nations, Publishing Service, New York, New York 10017 (800) 253-9646; *Statistical Yearbook*.

Times Books, 201 East 50th Street, New York, New York 10022 (212) 751-2600; *The Economist Book of Vital World Statistics*.

The World Bank, 1818 H Street, NW, Washington, D.C. 20433 (202) 477-1234; *World Tables*.

LUXEMBOURG - AIRLINE SERVICE

European Community Information Service, 2100 M Street, NW, Washington, D.C. 20037 (202) 862-9500; *Basic Statistics of the Community, Regions: Statistical Yearbook*, and *Transport Annual Statistics*.

G.K. Hall and Company, 70 Lincoln Street, Boston, Massachusetts 02111 (617) 423-3990; *The World in Figures*.

International Civil Aviation Organization, 1000 Sherbrooke Street West, Suite 400, Montreal, Quebec H3A 2R2, Canada (514) 285-8219; *Civil Aviation Statistics of the World*.

Organisation for Economic Co-operation and Development (OECD), 2 rue Andre-Pascal, 75 Paris 16, France (Telephone in U.S. (202) 785-6323); *Tourism Policy and International Tourism in OECD Member Countries.*

Statistical Office of the United Nations, Publishing Service, New York, New York 10017 (800) 253-9646; *Statistical Yearbook.*

Times Books, 201 East 50th Street, New York, New York 10022 (212) 751-2600; *The Economist Book of Vital World Statistics.*

LUXEMBOURG - ALMOND PRODUCTION - See LUXEMBOURG - CROPS

LUXEMBOURG - ALUMINUM PRODUCTION AND CONSUMPTION - See LUXEMBOURG - MINING AND MINERAL PRODUCTS

LUXEMBOURG - ANIMAL FEEDINGSTUFFS

Organisation for Economic Co-operation and Development (OECD), 2 rue Andre-Pascal, 75 Paris 16, France (Telephone in U.S. (202) 785-6323); *Foreign Trade by Commodities.*

LUXEMBOURG - ANIMAL HEALTH

Food and Agricultural Organization of the United Nations (FAO), Via delle Terme di Caracalla, 00100 Rome, Italy (Telephone Number in U.S. (202) 653-2400); *Animal Health Yearbook.*

LUXEMBOURG - ANTIMONY AND ANTIMONY ORE PRODUCTION AND CONSUMPTION - See LUXEMBOURG - MINING AND MINERAL PRODUCTS

LUXEMBOURG - APPLE PRODUCTION - See LUXEMBOURG - CROPS

LUXEMBOURG - AREA AND DENSITY OF POPULATION

European Community Information Service, 2100 M Street, NW, Washington, D.C. 20037 (202) 862-9500; *Basic Statistics of the Community,* and *Demographic Statistics.*

Food and Agricultural Organization of the United Nations (FAO), Via delle Terme di Caracalla, 00100 Rome, Italy (Telephone Number in U.S. (202) 653-2400); *The State of Food and Agriculture.*

G.K. Hall and Company, 70 Lincoln Street, Boston, Massachusetts 02111 (617) 423-3990; *The World in Figures.*

Statistical Office of the United Nations, Publishing Service, New York, New York 10017 (800) 253-9646; *Statistical Yearbook.*

Times Books, 201 East 50th Street, New York, New York 10022 (212) 751-2600; *The Economist Book of Vital World Statistics.*

LUXEMBOURG - ARMS EXPORTS AND IMPORTS

U.S. Arms Control and Disarmament Agency, 320 Twenty-first Street, NW, Washington, D.C. 20451 (202) 647-8677; *World Military Expenditures and Arms Transfers.*

LUXEMBOURG - ARSENIC PRODUCTION AND CONSUMPTION - See LUXEMBOURG - MINING AND MINERAL PRODUCTS

LUXEMBOURG - BALANCE OF PAYMENTS

European Community Information Service, 2100 M Street, NW, Washington, D.C. 20037 (202) 862-9500; *ACP: Basic Statistics, Basic Statistics of the Community, Energy Statistics Yearbook,* and *Eurostatistics: Data for Short-Term Economic Analysis.*

G.K. Hall and Company, 70 Lincoln Street, Boston, Massachusetts 02111 (617) 423-3990; *The World in Figures.*

Organisation for Economic Co-operation and Development (OECD), 2 rue Andre-Pascal, 75 Paris 16, France (Telephone in U.S. (202) 785-6323); *Economic Outlook, Geographical Distribution of Financial Flows to Developing Countries,* and *OECD Economic Surveys: Belgium -Luxembourg.*

Times Books, 201 East 50th Street, New York, New York 10022 (212) 751-2600; *The Economist Book of Vital World Statistics.*

The World Bank, 1818 H Street, NW, Washington, D.C. 20433 (202) 477-1234; *World Tables.*

LUXEMBOURG - BANANA PRODUCTION - See LUXEMBOURG - CROPS

LUXEMBOURG - BANKS AND BANKING

European Community Information Service, 2100 M Street, NW, Washington, D.C. 20037 (202) 862-9500; *ACP: Basic Statistics.*

G.K. Hall and Company, 70 Lincoln Street, Boston, Massachusetts 02111 (617) 423-3990; *The World in Figures.*

International Monetary Fund, 700 Nineteenth Street, NW, Washington, D.C. 20431 (202) 623-7000; *International Financial Statistics.*

Organisation for Economic Co-operation and Development (OECD), 2 rue Andre-Pascal, 75 Paris 16, France (Telephone in U.S. (202) 785-6323); *Economic Outlook, Financial Market Trends,* and *OECD Economic Surveys: Belgium - Luxembourg.*

LUXEMBOURG - BARLEY PRODUCTION - See LUXEMBOURG - CROPS

LUXEMBOURG - BAUXITE PRODUCTION AND CONSUMPTION - See LUXEMBOURG - MINING AND MINERAL PRODUCTS

LUXEMBOURG - BEER PRODUCTION

Statistical Office of the United Nations, Publishing Service, New York, New York 10017 (800) 253-9646; *Statistical Yearbook.*

LUXEMBOURG - BEVERAGES - PRODUCTION INDEX

Organisation for Economic Co-operation and Development (OECD), 2 rue Andre-Pascal, 75 Paris 16, France (Telephone in U.S. (202) 785-6323); *Indicators of Industrial Activity.*

LUXEMBOURG - BIRTH RATES

European Community Information Service, 2100 M Street, NW, Washington, D.C. 20037 (202) 862-9500; *Basic Statistics of the Community,* and *Demographic Statistics.*

Organisation for Economic Co-operation and Development (OECD), 2 rue Andre-Pascal, 75 Paris 16, France (Telephone in U.S. (202) 785-6323); *Labour Force Statistics.*

Statistical Office of the United Nations, Publishing Service, New York, New York 10017 (800) 253-9646; *Demographic Yearbook,* and *Statistical Yearbook.*

Times Books, 201 East 50th Street, New York, New York 10022 (212) 751-2600; *The Economist Book of Vital World Statistics.*

The World Bank, 1818 H Street, NW, Washington, D.C. 20433 (202) 477-1234; *World Tables*.

World Health Organization, Office of Publications, Avenue Appia, CH-1211 Geneva 27, Switzerland (Telephone Number in U.S. (518) 436-9686); *World Health Statistics Annual*.

LUXEMBOURG - BISMUTH PRODUCTION AND CONSUMPTION - See LUXEMBOURG - MINING AND MINERAL PRODUCTS

LUXEMBOURG - BONDS

European Community Information Service, 2100 M Street, NW, Washington, D.C. 20037 (202) 862-9500; *Basic Statistics of the Community*.

G.K. Hall and Company, 70 Lincoln Street, Boston, Massachusetts 02111 (617) 423-3990; *The World in Figures*.

Organisation for Economic Co-operation and Development (OECD), 2 rue Andre-Pascal, 75 Paris 16, France (Telephone in U.S. (202) 785-6323); *Financial Market Trends*.

Statistical Office of the United Nations, Publishing Service, New York, New York 10017 (800) 253-9646; *Statistical Yearbook*.

LUXEMBOURG - BOOK PRODUCTION

Euromonitor Publications Limited, 87-88 Turnmill Street, London EC1M 5QU, England; *European Marketing Data and Statistics*.

G.K. Hall and Company, 70 Lincoln Street, Boston, Massachusetts 02111 (617) 423-3990; *The World in Figures*.

Organisation for Economic Co-operation and Development (OECD), 2 rue Andre-Pascal, 75 Paris 16, France (Telephone in U.S. (202) 785-6323); *Indicators of Industrial Activity*.

United Nations Educational, Scientific and Cultural Organization (UNESCO), 7 Place de Fontenoy, F-75700 Paris, France (Telephone Number in U.S. (212) 963-5981); *Statistical Yearbook*.

LUXEMBOURG - BROADCASTING

Billboard Limited, Post Office Box 9027, 1006 AA Amsterdam, The Netherlands (Telephone Number in U.S. (212) 764-7300); *World Radio TV Handbook*.

European Community Information Service, 2100 M Street, NW, Washington, D.C. 20037 (202) 862-9500; *Basic Statistics of the Community*.

G.K. Hall and Company, 70 Lincoln Street, Boston, Massachusetts 02111 (617) 423-3990; *The World in Figures*.

Times Books, 201 East 50th Street, New York, New York 10022 (212) 751-2600; *The Economist Book of Vital World Statistics*.

United Nations Educational, Scientific and Cultural Organization (UNESCO), 7 Place de Fontenoy, F-75700 Paris, France (Telephone Number in U.S. (212) 963-5981); *Statistical Yearbook*.

LUXEMBOURG - BUSINESS

European Community Information Service, 2100 M Street, NW, Washington, D.C. 20037 (202) 862-9500; *Basic Statistics of the Community*.

G.K. Hall and Company, 70 Lincoln Street, Boston, Massachusetts 02111 (617) 423-3990; *The World in Figures*.

LUXEMBOURG - BUSINESS AND PROFESSIONAL LICENSES

International Monetary Fund, 700 Nineteenth Street, NW, Washington, D.C. 20431 (202) 623-7000; *Government Finance Statistics Yearbook*.

LUXEMBOURG - BUTTER - See LUXEMBOURG - DAIRY PRODUCTS

LUXEMBOURG - CABBAGE PRODUCTION - See LUXEMBOURG - CROPS

LUXEMBOURG - CADMIUM PRODUCTION AND CONSUMPTION - See LUXEMBOURG - MINING AND MINERAL PRODUCTS

LUXEMBOURG - CALORIE SUPPLY

Food and Agricultural Organization of the United Nations (FAO), Via delle Terme di Caracalla, 00100 Rome, Italy (Telephone Number in U.S. (202) 653-2400); *The State of Food and Agriculture*.

LUXEMBOURG - CAPITAL INVESTMENT

Organisation for Economic Co-operation and Development (OECD), 2 rue Andre-Pascal, 75 Paris 16, France (Telephone in U.S. (202) 785-6323); *Economic Outlook*, and *Financial Market Trends*.

LUXEMBOURG - CAPITAL REVENUE

International Monetary Fund, 700 Nineteenth Street, NW, Washington, D.C. 20431 (202) 623-7000; *Government Finance Statistics Yearbook*.

Organisation for Economic Co-operation and Development (OECD), 2 rue Andre-Pascal, 75 Paris 16, France (Telephone in U.S. (202) 785-6323); *Economic Outlook*, and *Financial Market Trends*.

LUXEMBOURG - CASHEW NUT PRODUCTION - See LUXEMBOURG - CROPS

LUXEMBOURG - CASTOR BEAN PRODUCTION - See LUXEMBOURG - CROPS

LUXEMBOURG - CATTLE - See LUXEMBOURG - LIVESTOCK AND POULTRY

LUXEMBOURG - CAULIFLOWER PRODUCTION - See LUXEMBOURG - CROPS

LUXEMBOURG - CAUSTIC SODA PRODUCTION

European Community Information Service, 2100 M Street, NW, Washington, D.C. 20037 (202) 862-9500; *Basic Statistics of the Community*.

Organisation for Economic Co-operation and Development (OECD), 2 rue Andre-Pascal, 75 Paris 16, France (Telephone in U.S. (202) 785-6323); *Indicators of Industrial Activity*.

LUXEMBOURG - CEMENT PRODUCTION - See LUXEMBOURG - MINING AND MINERAL PRODUCTS

LUXEMBOURG - CEREAL PRODUCTION - See LUXEMBOURG - CROPS

LUXEMBOURG - CHEESE - See LUXEMBOURG - DAIRY PRODUCTS

LUXEMBOURG - CHEMICAL INDUSTRY

European Community Information Service, 2100 M Street, NW, Washington, D.C. 20037 (202) 862-9500; *Industrial Production: Quarterly Statistics.*

LUXEMBOURG - CHEMICAL (ORGANIC) PRODUCTION - See LUXEMBOURG - MINING AND MINERAL PRODUCTS

LUXEMBOURG - CHESTNUT PRODUCTION - See LUXEMBOURG - CROPS

LUXEMBOURG - CHICKENS - See LUXEMBOURG - LIVESTOCK AND POULTRY

LUXEMBOURG - CHROMITE PRODUCTION AND CONSUMPTION - See LUXEMBOURG - MINING AND MINERAL PRODUCTS

LUXEMBOURG - CHROMIUM ORE PRODUCTION AND CONSUMPTION - See LUXEMBOURG - MINING AND MINERAL PRODUCTS

LUXEMBOURG - CLASS STRUCTURE

European Community Information Service, 2100 M Street, NW, Washington, D.C. 20037 (202) 862-9500; *Basic Statistics of the Community,* and *Labor Force Sample Survey.*

G.K. Hall and Company, 70 Lincoln Street, Boston, Massachusetts 02111 (617) 423-3990; *The World in Figures.*

LUXEMBOURG - CLIMATE

G.K. Hall and Company, 70 Lincoln Street, Boston, Massachusetts 02111 (617) 423-3990; *The World in Figures.*

LUXEMBOURG - CLOTHING - See LUXEMBOURG - TEXTILE INDUSTRY

LUXEMBOURG - COAL PRODUCTION - See LUXEMBOURG - MINING AND MINERAL PRODUCTS

LUXEMBOURG - COBALT PRODUCTION AND CONSUMPTION - See LUXEMBOURG - MINING AND MINERAL PRODUCTS

LUXEMBOURG - COCOA (BEANS) PRODUCTION - See LUXEMBOURG - CROPS

LUXEMBOURG - COFFEE - See LUXEMBOURG - CROPS

LUXEMBOURG - COKE AND COKE OVEN ORE PRODUCTION AND CONSUMPTION - See LUXEMBOURG - MINING AND MINERAL PRODUCTS

LUXEMBOURG - COMMUNICATIONS

European Community Information Service, 2100 M Street, NW, Washington, D.C. 20037 (202) 862-9500; *Basic Statistics of the Community,* and *Transport Annual Statistics.*

G.K. Hall and Company, 70 Lincoln Street, Boston, Massachusetts 02111 (617) 423-3990; *The World in Figures.*

LUXEMBOURG - CONSTRUCTION INDUSTRY

European Community Information Service, 2100 M Street, NW, Washington, D.C. 20037 (202) 862-9500; *Basic Statistics of the Community,* and *Labor Force Sample Survey.*

Organisation for Economic Co-operation and Development (OECD), 2 rue Andre-Pascal, 75 Paris 16, France (Telephone in U.S. (202) 785-6323); *Industrial Structure Statistics, The Iron and Steel Industry, Main Economic Indicators - Historical Statistics,* and *OECD Economic Surveys: Belgium - Luxembourg.*

Statistical Office of the United Nations, Publishing Service, New York, New York 10017 (800) 253-9646; *Statistical Yearbook.*

LUXEMBOURG - CONSUMER PRICE INDEX

European Community Information Service, 2100 M Street, NW, Washington, D.C. 20037 (202) 862-9500; *Basic Statistics of the Community,* and *Money and Finance.*

G.K. Hall and Company, 70 Lincoln Street, Boston, Massachusetts 02111 (617) 423-3990; *The World in Figures.*

Organisation for Economic Co-operation and Development (OECD), 2 rue Andre-Pascal, 75 Paris 16, France (Telephone in U.S. (202) 785-6323); *Economic Outlook.*

Statistical Office of the United Nations, Publishing Service, New York, New York 10017 (800) 253-9646; *Statistical Yearbook.*

LUXEMBOURG - CONSUMER PRICES

Euromonitor Publications Limited, 87-88 Turnmill Street, London EC1M 5QU, England; *European Marketing Data and Statistics, Basic Statistics of the Community,* and *Eurostatistics: Data for Short-Term Economic Analysis.*

International Labour Office, I.L.O. Publications, CH-1211, Geneva 22, Switzerland; *Yearbook of Labour Statistics.*

International Monetary Fund, 700 Nineteenth Street, NW, Washington, D.C. 20431 (202) 623-7000; *International Financial Statistics.*

Organisation for Economic Co-operation and Development (OECD), 2 rue Andre-Pascal, 75 Paris 16, France (Telephone in U.S. (202) 785-6323); *Economic Outlook,* and *Main Economic Indicators - Historical Statistics.*

Times Books, 201 East 50th Street, New York, New York 10022 (212) 751-2600; *The Economist Book of Vital World Statistics.*

LUXEMBOURG - CONSUMPTION

European Community Information Service, 2100 M Street, NW, Washington, D.C. 20037 (202) 862-9500; *Basic Statistics of the Community.*

G.K. Hall and Company, 70 Lincoln Street, Boston, Massachusetts 02111 (617) 423-3990; *The World in Figures.*

International Iron and Steel Institute, 120, rue Colonel Bourg, B-1140 Brussels, Belgium; *Steel Statistical Yearbook.*

Organisation for Economic Co-operation and Development (OECD), 2 rue Andre-Pascal, 75 Paris 16, France (Telephone in U.S. (202) 785-6323); *The Footwear, Raw Hides and Skins, and Leather Industry in OECD Countries, The Iron and Steel Industry, Meat Balances in OECD Member Countries, The Non-Ferrous Metals Industry, The Pulp and Paper Industry,* and *Textile Industry in OECD Countries.*

LUXEMBOURG - COPPER AND COPPER ORE PRODUCTION AND CONSUMPTION - See LUXEMBOURG - MINING AND MINERAL PRODUCTS

LUXEMBOURG - CORN PRODUCTION - See LUXEMBOURG - CROPS

LUXEMBOURG - CORPORATE TAXES - SEE LUXEMBOURG - TAXATION

LUXEMBOURG - COTTON - See LUXEMBOURG - CROPS

LUXEMBOURG - CRIME

International Criminal Police Organization (INTERPOL), 26 rue Armengaud, 92210 Saint Cloud, France; *International Crime Statistics*.

Yale University Press, Yale Station, New Haven, Connecticut 06520 (203) 432-0940; *Violence and Crime in Cross-National Perspective*.

LUXEMBOURG - CROPS

Commodity Research Bureau, Incorporated, 75 Wall Street, New York, New York 10005 (212) 504-7754; *Commodity Year Book*.

Euromonitor Publications Limited, 87-88 Turnmill Street, London EC1M 5QU, England; *European Marketing Data and Statistics*, and *Basic Statistics of the Community*.

European Community Information Service, 2100 M Street, NW, Washington, D.C. 20037 (202) 862-9500; *ACP: Basic Statistics, Agriculture: Statistical Yearbook, Basic Statistics of the Community, Crop Production: Quarterly Statistics, Eurostatistics: Data for Short Term Economic Analysis*, and *Regions: Statistical Yearbook*.

Food and Agricultural Organization of the United Nations (FAO), Via delle Terme di Caracalla, 00100 Rome, Italy (Telephone Number in U.S. (202) 653-2400); *Production Yearbook*, and *The State of Food and Agriculture*.

G.K. Hall and Company, 70 Lincoln Street, Boston, Massachusetts 02111 (617) 423-3990; *The World in Figures*.

International Wheat Statistics, 28 Haymarket, London SW1Y 4SS, England; *World Wheat Statistics*.

Organisation for Economic Co-operation and Development (OECD), 2 rue Andre-Pascal, 75 Paris 16, France (Telephone Number in U.S. (202) 785-6323); *Economic Accounts for Agriculture, Foreign Trade by Commodities*, and *Textile Industry in OECD Countries*.

Statistical Office of the United Nations, Publishing Service, New York, New York 10017 (800) 253-9646; *Statistical Yearbook*.

LUXEMBOURG - CUSTOMS DUTIES

European Community Information Service, 2100 M Street, NW, Washington, D.C. 20037 (202) 862-9500; *Basic Statistics of the Community*.

G.K. Hall and Company, 70 Lincoln Street, Boston, Massachusetts 02111 (617) 423-3990; *The World in Figures*.

Organisation for Economic Co-operation and Development (OECD), 2 rue Andre-Pascal, 75 Paris 16, France (Telephone in U.S. (202) 785-6323); *The Non-Ferrous Metals Industry*.

LUXEMBOURG - DAIRY PRODUCTS

Commodity Research Bureau, Incorporated, 75 Wall Street, New York, New York 10005 (212) 504-7754; *Commodity Year Book*.

European Community Information Service, 2100 M Street, NW, Washington, D.C. 20037 (202) 862-9500; *Basic Statistics of the Community*, and *Eurostatistics: Data for Short-Term Economic Analysis*.

Food and Agricultural Organization of the United Nations (FAO), Via delle Terme di Caracalla, 00100 Rome, Italy (Telephone Number in U.S. (202) 653-2400); *Production Yearbook*, and *The State of Food and Agriculture*.

Organisation for Economic Co-operation and Development (OECD), 2 rue Andre-Pascal, 75 Paris 16, France (Telephone in U.S. (202) 785-6323); *Economic Accounts for Agriculture*, and *Milk, Milk Products, and Egg Balances in OECD Member Countries*.

Statistical Office of the United Nations, Publishing Service, New York, New York 10017 (800) 253-9646; *Statistical Yearbook*.

LUXEMBOURG - DEATH RATES

European Community Information Service, 2100 M Street, NW, Washington, D.C. 20037 (202) 862-9500; *Basic Statistics of the Community*, and *Demographic Statistics*.

G.K. Hall and Company, 70 Lincoln Street, Boston, Massachusetts 02111 (617) 423-3990; *The World in Figures*.

Statistical Office of the United Nations, Publishing Service, New York, New York 10017 (800) 253-9646; *Statistical Yearbook*.

Times Books, 201 East 50th Street, New York, New York 10022 (212) 751-2600, *The Economist Book of Vital World Statistics*.

World Health Organization, Office of Publications, Avenue Appia, CH-1211 Geneva 27, Switzerland (Telephone Number in U.S. (518) 436-9686); *World Health Statistics Annual*.

LUXEMBOURG - DEFENSE EXPENDITURES

European Community Information Service, 2100 M Street, NW, Washington, D.C. 20037 (202) 862-9500; *Government Financing of Research and Development*.

G.K. Hall and Company, 70 Lincoln Street, Boston, Massachusetts 02111 (617) 423-3990; *The World in Figures*.

International Monetary Fund, 700 Nineteenth Street, NW, Washington, D.C. 20431 (202) 623-7000; *Government Finance Statistics Yearbook*.

U.S. Arms Control and Disarmament Agency, 320 Twenty-first Street, NW, Washington, D.C. 20451 (202) 647-8677; *World Military Expenditures and Arms Transfers*.

LUXEMBOURG - DEMOGRAPHY

The Economist Intelligence Unit, 111 West 57th Street, New York, New York 10019 (800) 938-4685; *The World Market Atlas*.

European Community Information Service, 2100 M Street, NW, Washington, D.C. 20037 (202) 862-9500; *Basic Statistics of the Community, Demographic Statistics, Employment and Unemployment*, and *Regions: Statistical Yearbook*.

G.K. Hall and Company, 70 Lincoln Street, Boston, Massachusetts 02111 (617) 423-3990; *The World in Figures*.

LUXEMBOURG - DEVELOPMENT ASSISTANCE

European Community Information Service, 2100 M Street, NW, Washington, D.C. 20037 (202) 862-9500; *ACP: Basic Statistics*, and *Basic Statistics of the Community*.

European Community Information Service, 2100 M Street, NW, Washington, D.C. 20037 (202) 862-9500; *Government Financing of Research and Development*.

G.K. Hall and Company, 70 Lincoln Street, Boston, Massachusetts 02111 (617) 423-3990; *The World in Figures*.

Organisation for Economic Co-operation and Development (OECD), 2 rue Andre-Pascal, 75 Paris 16, France (Telephone in U.S. (202) 785-6323); *Geographical Distribution of Financial Flows to Developing Countries*.

LUXEMBOURG - DIAMONDS - See LUXEMBOURG - MINING AND MINERAL PRODUCTS

LUXEMBOURG - DISCOUNT RATES

Organisation for Economic Co-operation and Development (OECD), 2 rue Andre-Pascal, 75 Paris 16, France (Telephone in U.S. (202) 785-6323); *Financial Market Trends*.

LUXEMBOURG - DISEASES

G.K. Hall and Company, 70 Lincoln Street, Boston, Massachusetts 02111 (617) 423-3990; *The World in Figures*.

World Health Organization, Office of Publications, Avenue Appia, CH-1211 Geneva 27, Switzerland (Telephone Number in U.S. (518) 436-9686); *World Health Statistics Annual*.

LUXEMBOURG - DIVORCE

European Community Information Service, 2100 M Street, NW, Washington, D.C. 20037 (202) 862-9500; *Demographic Statistics*.

Statistical Office of the United Nations, Publishing Service, New York, New York 10017 (800) 253-9646; *Demographic Yearbook*, and *Statistical Yearbook*.

LUXEMBOURG - DOMESTIC PRODUCT

European Community Information Service, 2100 M Street, NW, Washington, D.C. 20037 (202) 862-9500; *Basic Statistics of the Community*.

G.K. Hall and Company, 70 Lincoln Street, Boston, Massachusetts 02111 (617) 423-3990; *The World in Figures*.

LUXEMBOURG - DUCKS - See LUXEMBOURG - LIVESTOCK AND POULTRY

LUXEMBOURG - ECONOMY

Euromonitor Publications Limited, 87-88 Turnmill Street, London EC1M 5QU, England; *European Marketing Data and Statistics*.

European Community Information Service, 2100 M Street, NW, Washington, D.C. 20037 (202) 862-9500; *ACP: Basic Statistics, Basic Statistics of the Community, Energy Statistics Yearbook, Labor Force Sample Survey*, and *Money and Finance*.

G.K. Hall and Company, 70 Lincoln Street, Boston, Massachusetts 02111 (617) 423-3990; *The World in Figures*.

Organisation for Economic Co-operation and Development (OECD), 2 rue Andre-Pascal, 75 Paris 16, France (Telephone in U.S. (202) 785-6323); *Economic Outlook, Geographical Distribution of Financial Flows to Developing Countries, Main Economic Indicators - Historical Statistics, OECD Economic Surveys: Belgium - Luxembourg*, and *OECD Employment Outlook*,

LUXEMBOURG - EDUCATION

The Economist Intelligence Unit, 111 West 57th Street, New York, New York 10019 (800) 938-4685; *The World Market Atlas*.

Euromonitor Publications Limited, 87-88 Turnmill Street, London EC1M 5QU, England; *European Marketing Data and Statistics*.

European Community Information Service, 2100 M Street, NW, Washington, D.C. 20037 (202) 862-9500; *Basic Statistics of the Community*, and *Regions: Statistical Yearbook*.

G.K. Hall and Company, 70 Lincoln Street, Boston, Massachusetts 02111 (617) 423-3990; *The World in Figures*.

International Monetary Fund, 700 Nineteenth Street, NW, Washington, D.C. 20431 (202) 623-7000; *Government Finance Statistics Yearbook*.

Organisation for Economic Co-operation and Development (OECD), 2 rue Andre-Pascal, 75 Paris 16, France (Telephone Number in U.S. (202) 785-6323), *Education in OECD Countries*.

Times Books, 201 East 50th Street, New York, New York 10022 (212) 751-2600; *The Economist Book of Vital World Statistics*.

United Nations Educational, Scientific and Cultural Organization (UNESCO), 7 Place de Fontenoy, F-75700 Paris, France (Telephone Number in U.S. (212) 963-5981); *Statistical Yearbook*.

The World Bank, 1818 H Street, NW, Washington, D.C. 20433 (202) 477-1234; *World Tables*.

LUXEMBOURG - EGG PRODUCTION AND CONSUMPTION - See LUXEMBOURG - DAIRY PRODUCTS

LUXEMBOURG - ELECTRICITY

European Community Information Service, 2100 M Street, NW, Washington, D.C. 20037 (202) 862-9500; *Basic Statistics of the Community, Coal Information, Energy: Monthly Statistics, Energy Statistics Yearbook, Eurostatistics: Data for Short-Term Economic Analysis, Industrial Structure Statistics*, and *Regions: Statistical Yearbook*.

Organisation for Economic Co-operation and Development (OECD), 2 rue Andre-Pascal, 75 Paris 16, France (Telephone in U.S. (202) 785-6323); *Energy Statistics of OECD Countries*, and *Indicators of Industrial Activity*.

Statistical Office of the United Nations, Publishing Service, New York, New York 10017 (800) 253-9646; *Statistical Yearbook*.

Times Books, 201 East 50th Street, New York, New York 10022 (212) 751-2600; *The Economist Book of Vital World Statistics*.

LUXEMBOURG - EMPLOYMENT

Euromonitor Publications Limited, 87-88 Turnmill Street, London EC1M 5QU, England; *European Marketing Data and Statistics*.

European Community Information Service, 2100 M Street, NW, Washington, D.C. 20037 (202) 862-9500; *Earnings in Agriculture, Basic Statistics of the Community, Employment and Unemployment, Eurostatistics: Data for Short-Term Economic Analysis, Iron and Steel: Statistical Yearbook, Labor Force Sample Survey*, and *Transport Annual Statistics*.

International Labour Office, I.L.O. Publications, CH-1211, Geneva 22, Switzerland; *Yearbook of Labour Statistics*.

Organisation for Economic Co-operation and Development (OECD), 2 rue Andre-Pascal, 75 Paris 16, France (Telephone in U.S. (202) 785-6323); *Economic Outlook, The Iron and Steel Industry, OECD Economic Surveys: Belgium - Luxembourg, OECD Employment Outlook*, and *Textile Industry in OECD Countries*.

Statistical Office of the United Nations, Publishing Service, New York, New York 10017 (800) 253-9646; *Statistical Yearbook*.

LUXEMBOURG - ENERGY

Euromonitor Publications Limited, 87-88 Turnmill Street, London EC1M 5QU, England, *Basic Statistics of the Community, European Marketing Data and Statistics*, and *Labor Force Sample Survey*.

European Community Information Service, 2100 M Street, NW, Washington, D.C. 20037 (202) 862-9500; *Basic Statistics of the Community, Energy: Monthly Statistics, Energy Statistics Yearbook, Regions: Statistical Yearbook*, and *Transport Annual Statistics*.

Food and Agricultural Organization of the United Nations (FAO), Via delle Terme di Caracalla, 00100 Rome, Italy (Telephone Number in U.S. (202) 653-2400); *The State of Food and Agriculture*.

G.K. Hall and Company, 70 Lincoln Street, Boston, Massachusetts 02111 (617) 423-3990; *The World in Figures*.

Organisation for Economic Co-operation and Development (OECD), 2 rue Andre-Pascal, 75 Paris 16, France (Telephone in U.S. (202) 785-6323); *Coal Information, Energy Statistics of OECD Countries, OECD Environmental Data*, and *Oil and Gas Information*.

Statistical Office of the United Nations, Publishing Service, New York, New York 10017 (800) 253-9646; *Energy Statistics Yearbook, Statistical Yearbook*, and *World Energy Supplies*.

Times Books, 201 East 50th Street, New York, New York 10022 (212) 751-2600; *The Economist Book of Vital World Statistics*.

LUXEMBOURG - ENGINEERING AND METAL PRODUCTS

European Community Information Service, 2100 M Street, NW, Washington, D.C. 20037 (202) 862-9500; *Basic Statistics of the Community*, and *Industrial Production: Quarterly Statistics*.

Statistical Office of the United Nations, Publishing Service, New York, New York 10017 (800) 253-9646; *Trade in Manufactures of Developing Countries*.

LUXEMBOURG - EXCHANGE RATES

European Community Information Service, 2100 M Street, NW, Washington, D.C. 20037 (202) 862-9500; *Eurostatistics: Data for Short-Term Economic Analysis*, and *Money and Finance*.

International Civil Aviation Organization, 1000 Sherbrooke Street West, Suite 400, Montreal, Quebec H3A 2R2, Canada (514) 285-8219; *Civil Aviation Statistics of the World*.

International Monetary Fund, 700 Nineteenth Street, NW, Washington, D.C. 20431 (202) 623-7000; *International Financial Statistics*.

Organisation for Economic Co-operation and Development (OECD), 2 rue Andre-Pascal, 75 Paris 16, France (Telephone in U.S. (202) 785-6323); *Economic Outlook, Financial Market Trends, Revenue Statistics of OECD Member Countries*, and *Tourism Policy and International Tourism in OECD Member Countries*.

Statistical Office of the United Nations, Publishing Service, New York, New York 10017 (800) 253-9646; *Statistical Yearbook*.

LUXEMBOURG - EXCISE TAXES - See LUXEMBOURG - TAXATION

LUXEMBOURG - EXPORTS

American Automobile Manufacturers Association, 1401 H Street, NW, Suite 900, Washington, D.C. 20005 (202) 326-5500; *World Motor Vehicle Data*.

The Economist Intelligence Unit, 111 West 57th Street, New York, New York 10019 (800) 938-4685; *The World Market Atlas*.

European Community Information Service, 2100 M Street, NW, Washington, D.C. 20037 (202) 862-9500; *Basic Statistics of the Community, Energy: Monthly Statistics, Energy Statistics Yearbook, Eurostatistics: Data for Short-Term Economic Analysis, External Trade: Monthly Statistics, External Trade: Statistical Yearbook*, and *Fisheries: Yearly Statistics*.

Food and Agricultural Organization of the United Nations (FAO), Via delle Terme di Caracalla, 00100 Rome, Italy (Telephone Number in U.S. (202) 653-2400); *The State of Food and Agriculture*.

G.K. Hall and Company, 70 Lincoln Street, Boston, Massachusetts 02111 (617) 423-3990; *The World in Figures*.

International Iron and Steel Institute, 120, rue Colonel Bourg, B-1140 Brussels, Belgium; *Steel Statistical Yearbook*.

Organisation for Economic Co-operation and Development (OECD), 2 rue Andre-Pascal, 75 Paris 16, France (Telephone in U.S. (202) 785-6323); *Economic Outlook, The Footwear, Raw Hides and Skins, and Leather Industry in OECD Countries, Foreign Trade by Commodities, Geographical Distribution of Financial Flows to Developing Countries, Industrial Structure Statistics, The Iron and Steel Industry, Milk, Milk Products, and Egg Balances in OECD Member Countries, OECD Economic Surveys: Belgium - Luxembourg*, and *The Pulp and Paper Industry*.

Times Books, 201 East 50th Street, New York, New York 10022 (212) 751-2600; *The Economist Book of Vital World Statistics*.

The World Bank, 1818 H Street, NW, Washington, D.C. 20433 (202) 477-1234; *World Tables*.

LUXEMBOURG - EXTERNAL FINANCING

Organisation for Economic Co-operation and Development (OECD), 2 rue Andre-Pascal, 75 Paris 16, France (Telephone in U.S. (202) 785-6323); *Economic Outlook, Financial Market Trends*.

LUXEMBOURG - EXTERNAL INDEBTEDNESS

Organisation for Economic Co-operation and Development (OECD), 2 rue Andre-Pascal, 75 Paris 16, France (Telephone in U.S. (202) 785-6323); *Financial Market Trends*, and *Geographical Distribution of Financial Flows to Developing Countries*.

The World Bank, 1818 H Street, NW, Washington, D.C. 20433 (202) 477-1234; *World Tables.*

LUXEMBOURG - EXTERNAL TRADE

European Community Information Service, 2100 M Street, NW, Washington, D.C. 20037 (202) 862-9500; *ACP: Basic Statistics,* and *Basic Statistics of the Community, Eurostatistics: Data for Short-Term Economic Analysis, External Trade: Monthly Statistics,* and *External Trade: Statistical Yearbook.*

Food and Agricultural Organization of the United Nations (FAO), Via delle Terme di Caracalla, 00100 Rome, Italy (Telephone Number in U.S. (202) 653-2400); *The State of Food and Agriculture,* and *Trade Yearbook.*

G.K. Hall and Company, 70 Lincoln Street, Boston, Massachusetts 02111 (617) 423-3990; *The World in Figures.*

Statistical Office of the United Nations, Publishing Service, New York, New York 10017 (800) 253-9646; *Statistical Yearbook.*

LUXEMBOURG - FABRIC PRODUCTION - See LUXEMBOURG - TEXTILE INDUSTRY

LUXEMBOURG - FARM CROPS - See LUXEMBOURG - CROPS

LUXEMBOURG - FEMALE WORKING POPULATION - See LUXEMBOURG - EMPLOYMENT

LUXEMBOURG - FERTILITY RATES

European Community Information Service, 2100 M Street, NW, Washington, D.C. 20037 (202) 862-9500; *Demographic Statistics.*

Times Books, 201 East 50th Street, New York, New York 10022 (212) 751-2600; *The Economist Book of Vital World Statistics.*

The World Bank, 1818 H Street, NW, Washington, D.C. 20433 (202) 477-1234; *World Tables.*

LUXEMBOURG - FERTILIZER

European Community Information Service, 2100 M Street, NW, Washington, D.C. 20037 (202) 862-9500; *Basic Statistics of the Community.*

Food and Agricultural Organization of the United Nations (FAO), Via delle Terme di Caracalla, 00100 Rome, Italy (Telephone Number in U.S. (202) 653-2400); *Fertilizer Yearbook,* and *State of Food and Agriculture.*

Organisation for Economic Co-operation and Development (OECD), 2 rue Andre-Pascal, 75 Paris 16, France (Telephone in U.S. (202) 785-6323); *Economic Accounts for Agriculture,* and *Foreign Trade by Commodities.*

Statistical Office of the United Nations, Publishing Service, New York, New York 10017 (800) 253-9646; *Statistical Yearbook.*

LUXEMBOURG - FETAL MORTALITY

European Community Information Service, 2100 M Street, NW, Washington, D.C. 20037 (202) 862-9500; *Basic Statistics of the Community,* and *Demographic Statistics.*

Statistical Office of the United Nations, Publishing Service, New York, New York 10017 (800) 253-9646; *Demographic Yearbook.*

World Health Organization, Office of Publications, Avenue Appia, CH-1211 Geneva 27, Switzerland (Telephone Number in U.S. (518) 436-9686); *World Health Statistics Annual.*

LUXEMBOURG - FIBRE PRODUCTION - See LUXEMBOURG - TEXTILE INDUSTRY

LUXEMBOURG - FILAMENT PRODUCTION - See LUXEMBOURG - TEXTILE INDUSTRY

LUXEMBOURG - FINANCE

European Community Information Service, 2100 M Street, NW, Washington, D.C. 20037 (202) 862-9500; *ACP: Basic Statistics, Basic Statistics of the Community,* and *Eurostatistics: Data for Short-Term Economic Analysis.*

G.K. Hall and Company, 70 Lincoln Street, Boston, Massachusetts 02111 (617) 423-3990; *The World in Figures.*

International Monetary Fund, 700 Nineteenth Street, NW, Washington, D.C. 20431 (202) 623-7000; *International Financial Statistics.*

Organisation for Economic Co-operation and Development (OECD), 2 rue Andre-Pascal, 75 Paris 16, France (Telephone in U.S. (202) 785-6323); *Economic Outlook, Financial Market Trends, Geographical Distribution of Financial Flows to Developing Countries,* and *OECD Financial Statistics.*

LUXEMBOURG - FISHERIES

Euromonitor Publications Limited, 87-88 Turnmill Street, London EC1M 5QU, England; *European Marketing Data and Statistics.*

European Community Information Service, 2100 M Street, NW, Washington, D.C. 20037 (202) 862-9500; *Agriculture: Statistical Yearbook, Basic Statistics of the Community,* and *Fisheries: Yearly Statistics.*

Food and Agricultural Organization of the United Nations (FAO), Via delle Terme di Caracalla, 00100 Rome, Italy (Telephone Number in U.S. (202) 653-2400); *The State of Food and Agriculture,* and *Yearbook of Fishery Statistics.*

Organisation for Economic Co-operation and Development (OECD), 2 rue Andre-Pascal, 75 Paris 16, France (Telephone in U.S. (202) 785-6323); *Fisheries: Yearly Statistics, Foreign Trade by Commodities,* and *Industrial Structure Statistics.*

LUXEMBOURG - FLAX AND FLAX FIBRE PRODUCTION - See LUXEMBOURG - TEXTILE INDUSTRY

LUXEMBOURG - FLOUR PRODUCTION

European Community Information Service, 2100 M Street, NW, Washington, D.C. 20037 (202) 862-9500; *Basic Statistics of the Community.*

Statistical Office of the United Nations, Publishing Service, New York, New York 10017 (800) 253-9646; *Statistical Yearbook.*

LUXEMBOURG - FOOD

European Community Information Service, 2100 M Street, NW, Washington, D.C. 20037 (202) 862-9500; *Basic Statistics of the Community.*

Food and Agricultural Organization of the United Nations (FAO), Via delle Terme di Caracalla, 00100 Rome, Italy (Telephone Number in U.S. (202) 653-2400); *Production Yearbook*, and *The State of Food and Agriculture*.

G.K. Hall and Company, 70 Lincoln Street, Boston, Massachusetts 02111 (617) 423-3990; *The World in Figures*.

Organisation for Economic Co-operation and Development (OECD), 2 rue Andre-Pascal, 75 Paris 16, France (Telephone in U.S. (202) 785-6323); *Foreign Trade by Commodities*.

LUXEMBOURG - FOOTWEAR - PRODUCTION INDEX

Organisation for Economic Co-operation and Development (OECD), 2 rue Andre-Pascal, 75 Paris 16, France (Telephone in U.S. (202) 785-6323); *Indicators of Industrial Activity*.

LUXEMBOURG - FOREIGN AID

G.K. Hall and Company, 70 Lincoln Street, Boston, Massachusetts 02111 (617) 423-3990; *The World in Figures*.

LUXEMBOURG - FOREIGN DEBT

Organisation for Economic Co-operation and Development (OECD), 2 rue Andre-Pascal, 75 Paris 16, France (Telephone in U.S. (202) 785-6323); *Economic Outlook*.

LUXEMBOURG - FOREIGN INDEBTEDNESS

Organisation for Economic Co-operation and Development (OECD), 2 rue Andre-Pascal, 75 Paris 16, France (Telephone in U.S. (202) 785-6323); *Economic Outlook*, and *Financial Market Trends*.

LUXEMBOURG - FOREIGN OFFICIAL RESERVES

European Community Information Service, 2100 M Street, NW, Washington, D.C. 20037 (202) 862-9500; *Money and Finance*.

LUXEMBOURG - FOREIGN TRADE

Euromonitor Publications Limited, 87-88 Turnmill Street, London EC1M 5QU, England; *European Marketing Data and Statistics*.

European Community Information Service, 2100 M Street, NW, Washington, D.C. 20037 (202) 862-9500; *Basic Statistics of the Community, Energy Statistics Yearbook*, and *Iron and Steel: Statistical Yearbook*.

Food and Agricultural Organization of the United Nations (FAO), Via delle Terme di Caracalla, 00100 Rome, Italy (Telephone Number in U.S. (202) 653-2400); *The State of Food and Agriculture*.

G.K. Hall and Company, 70 Lincoln Street, Boston, Massachusetts 02111 (617) 423-3990; *The World in Figures*.

International Iron and Steel Institute, 120, rue Colonel Bourg, B-1140 Brussels, Belgium; *Steel Statistical Yearbook*.

Organisation for Economic Co-operation and Development (OECD), 2 rue Andre-Pascal, 75 Paris 16, France (Telephone in U.S. (202) 785-6323); *Economic Outlook, The Footwear, Raw Hides and Skins, and Leather Industry in OECD Countries, Foreign Trade by Commodities, Maritime Transport, Meat Balances in OECD Member Countries*, and *OECD Economic Surveys: Belgium - Luxembourg*.

Statistical Office of the United Nations, Publishing Service, New York, New York 10017 (800) 253-9646; *Trade in Manufactures of Developing Countries*, and *Statistical Yearbook*.

The World Bank, 1818 H Street, NW, Washington, D.C. 20433 (202) 477-1234; *World Tables*.

LUXEMBOURG - FORESTRY AND FOREST PRODUCTS

Euromonitor Publications Limited, 87-88 Turnmill Street, London EC1M 5QU, England; *European Marketing Data and Statistics*.

European Community Information Service, 2100 M Street, NW, Washington, D.C. 20037 (202) 862-9500; *Agriculture: Statistical Yearbook, Basic Statistics of the Community*, and *Industrial Production: Quarterly Statistics*.

Food and Agricultural Organization of the United Nations (FAO), Via delle Terme di Caracalla, 00100 Rome, Italy (Telephone Number in U.S. (202) 653-2400); *The State of Food and Agriculture*.

G.K. Hall and Company, 70 Lincoln Street, Boston, Massachusetts 02111 (617) 423-3990; *The World in Figures*.

Organisation for Economic Co-operation and Development (OECD), 2 rue Andre-Pascal, 75 Paris 16, France (Telephone in U.S. (202) 785-6323); *Foreign Trade by Commodities, Indicators of Industrial Activity, Industrial Structure Statistics*, and *The Pulp and Paper Industry*.

Statistical Office of the United Nations, Publishing Service, New York, New York 10017 (800) 253-9646; *Statistical Yearbook*.

United Nations Educational, Scientific and Cultural Organization (UNESCO), 7 Place de Fontenoy, F-75700 Paris, France (Telephone Number in U.S. (212) 963 5981); *Statistical Yearbook*.

LUXEMBOURG - FRUIT PRODUCTION - See LUXEMBOURG - CROPS

LUXEMBOURG - FURNITURE AND WOOD PRODUCTS - EXPORTS AND IMPORTS

European Community Information Service, 2100 M Street, NW, Washington, D.C. 20037 (202) 862-9500; *Basic Statistics of the Community*.

Organisation for Economic Co-operation and Development (OECD), 2 rue Andre-Pascal, 75 Paris 16, France (Telephone in U.S. (202) 785-6323); *Foreign Trade by Commodities*, and *Industrial Structure Statistics*.

Statistical Office of the United Nations, Publishing Service, New York, New York 10017 (800) 253-9646; *Trade in Manufactures of Developing Countries*.

LUXEMBOURG - GARLIC PRODUCTION - See LUXEMBOURG - CROPS

LUXEMBOURG - GAS - See LUXEMBOURG - MINING AND MINERAL PRODUCTS

LUXEMBOURG - GENERAL INDUSTRIAL STATISTICS

European Community Information Service, 2100 M Street, NW, Washington, D.C. 20037 (202) 862-9500; *Basic Statistics of the Community*.

Statistical Office of the United Nations, Publishing Service, New York, New York 10017 (800) 253-9646; *Industrial Statistics Yearbook*.

LUXEMBOURG - GENERAL MORTALITY

European Community Information Service, 2100 M Street, NW, Washington, D.C. 20037 (202) 862-9500; *Basic Statistics of the Community*, and *Demographic Statistics*.

Statistical Office of the United Nations, Publishing Service, New York, New York 10017 (800) 253-9646; *Demographic Yearbook*.

World Health Organization, Office of Publications, Avenue Appia, CH-1211 Geneva 27, Switzerland (Telephone Number in U.S. (518) 436-9686); *World Health Statistics Annual*.

LUXEMBOURG - GEOGRAPHIC DATA

European Community Information Service, 2100 M Street, NW, Washington, D.C. 20037 (202) 862-9500; *Basic Statistics of the Community*.

LUXEMBOURG - GLASS AND GLASS PRODUCTS - PRODUCTION INDEX - See LUXEMBOURG - MINING AND MINERAL PRODUCTS

LUXEMBOURG - GOATS - See LUXEMBOURG - LIVESTOCK AND POULTRY

LUXEMBOURG - GOLD HOLDINGS

The World Bank, 1818 H Street, NW, Washington, D.C. 20433 (202) 477-1234; *World Tables*.

LUXEMBOURG - GOLD PRODUCTION AND CONSUMPTION - See LUXEMBOURG - MINING AND MINERAL PRODUCTS

LUXEMBOURG - GOVERNMENT

European Community Information Service, 2100 M Street, NW, Washington, D.C. 20037 (202) 862-9500; *Basic Statistics of the Community*.

G.K. Hall and Company, 70 Lincoln Street, Boston, Massachusetts 02111 (617) 423-3990; *The World in Figures*.

LUXEMBOURG - GOVERNMENT CONSUMPTION

European Community Information Service, 2100 M Street, NW, Washington, D.C. 20037 (202) 862-9500; *Basic Statistics of the Community*.

LUXEMBOURG - GOVERNMENT EXPENDITURES

European Community Information Service, 2100 M Street, NW, Washington, D.C. 20037 (202) 862-9500; *Basic Statistics of the Community*, and *Government Financing of Research and Development*.

International Monetary Fund, 700 Nineteenth Street, NW, Washington, D.C. 20431 (202) 623-7000; *Government Finance Statistics Yearbook*.

Organisation for Economic Co-operation and Development (OECD), 2 rue Andre-Pascal, 75 Paris 16, France (Telephone in U.S. (202) 785-6323); *Economic Outlook*.

Times Books, 201 East 50th Street, New York, New York 10022 (212) 751-2600; *The Economist Book of Vital World Statistics*.

The World Bank, 1818 H Street, NW, Washington, D.C. 20433 (202) 477-1234; *World Tables*.

LUXEMBOURG - GOVERNMENT FINANCES

European Community Information Service, 2100 M Street, NW, Washington, D.C. 20037 (202) 862-9500; *Basic Statistics of the Community*, *Government Financing of Research and Development*, and *Money and Finances*.

Organisation for Economic Co-operation and Development (OECD), 2 rue Andre-Pascal, 75 Paris 16, France (Telephone in U.S. (202) 785-6323); *Economic Outlook*.

LUXEMBOURG - GOVERNMENT REVENUE

European Community Information Service, 2100 M Street, NW, Washington, D.C. 20037 (202) 862-9500; *Basic Statistics of the Community*, and *Government Financing of Research and Development*.

International Monetary Fund, 700 Nineteenth Street, NW, Washington, D.C. 20431 (202) 623-7000; *Government Finance Statistics Yearbook*.

Organisation for Economic Co-operation and Development (OECD), 2 rue Andre-Pascal, 75 Paris 16, France (Telephone in U.S. (202) 785-6323); *Economic Outlook*, and *Revenue Statistics of OECD Member Countries*.

Times Books, 201 East 50th Street, New York, New York 10022 (212) 751-2600; *The Economist Book of Vital World Statistics*.

The World Bank, 1818 H Street, NW, Washington, D.C. 20433 (202) 477-1234; *World Tables*.

LUXEMBOURG - GRAIN PRODUCTION - See LUXEMBOURG - CROPS

LUXEMBOURG - GRANTS

International Monetary Fund, 700 Nineteenth Street, NW, Washington, D.C. 20431 (202) 623-7000; *Government Finance Statistics Yearbook*.

Organisation for Economic Co-operation and Development (OECD), 2 rue Andre-Pascal, 75 Paris 16, France (Telephone in U.S. (202) 785-6323); *Geographical Distribution of Financial Flows to Developing Countries*.

LUXEMBOURG - GREEN PEPPER AND CHILIE PRODUCTION - See LUXEMBOURG - CROPS

LUXEMBOURG - GROSS DOMESTIC PRODUCT

The Economist Intelligence Unit, 111 West 57th Street, New York, New York 10019 (800) 938-4685; *The World Market Atlas*.

European Community Information Service, 2100 M Street, NW, Washington, D.C. 20037 (202) 862-9500; *Basic Statistics of the Community, Eurostatistics: Data for Short-Term Economic Analysis, Government Financing of Research and Development, Iron and Steel: Statistical Yearbook*, and *Money and Finance*.

G.K. Hall and Company, 70 Lincoln Street, Boston, Massachusetts 02111 (617) 423-3990; *The World in Figures*.

Organisation for Economic Co-operation and Development (OECD), 2 rue Andre-Pascal, 75 Paris 16, France (Telephone in U.S. (202) 785-6323); *Economic Outlook, Geographical Distribution of Financial Flows to Developing Countries*, and *Revenue Statistics of OECD Member Countries*.

Statistical Office of the United Nations, Publishing Service, New York, New York 10017 (800) 253-9646; *Statistical Yearbook*.

Times Books, 201 East 50th Street, New York, New York 10022 (212) 751-2600; *The Economist Book of Vital World Statistics*.

The World Bank, 1818 H Street, NW, Washington, D.C. 20433 (202) 477-1234; *World Tables*.

LUXEMBOURG - GROSS INDUSTRIAL PRODUCT - GROWTH RATES

European Community Information Service, 2100 M Street, NW, Washington, D.C. 20037 (202) 862-9500; *Government Financing of Research and Development*.

LUXEMBOURG - GROSS NATIONAL PRODUCT

European Community Information Service, 2100 M Street, NW, Washington, D.C. 20037 (202) 862-9500; *ACP: Basic Statistics*, and *Basic Statistics of the Community*.

Organisation for Economic Co-operation and Development (OECD), 2 rue Andre-Pascal, 75 Paris 16, France (Telephone in U.S. (202) 785-6323); *Economic Outlook*, and *Geographical Distribution of Financial Flows to Developing Countries*.

U.S. Arms Control and Disarmament Agency, 320 Twenty-first Street, NW, Washington, D.C. 20451 (202) 647-8677; *World Military Expenditures and Arms Transfers*.

The World Bank, 1818 H Street, NW, Washington, D.C. 20433 (202) 477-1234; *World Tables*.

LUXEMBOURG - GROUNDNUT PRODUCTION - See LUXEMBOURG - CROPS

LUXEMBOURG - HAY PRODUCTION - See LUXEMBOURG - CROPS

LUXEMBOURG - HAZELNUT PRODUCTION - See LUXEMBOURG - CROPS

LUXEMBOURG - HEALTH

European Community Information Service, 2100 M Street, NW, Washington, D.C. 20037 (202) 862-9500; *Basic Statistics of the Community*, and *Regions: Statistical Yearbook*.

G.K. Hall and Company, 70 Lincoln Street, Boston, Massachusetts 02111 (617) 423-3990; *The World in Figures*.

Organisation for Economic Co-operation and Development (OECD), 2 rue Andre-Pascal, 75 Paris 16, France (Telephone Number in U.S. (202) 785-6323); *OECD Health Systems: Facts and Trends*.

Statistical Office of the United Nations, Publishing Service, New York, New York 10017 (800) 253-9646; *Statistical Yearbook*.

Times Books, 201 East 50th Street, New York, New York 10022 (212) 751-2600; *The Economist Book of Vital World Statistics*.

World Health Organization, Office of Publications, Avenue Appia, CH-1211 Geneva 27, Switzerland (Telephone Number in U.S. (518) 436 0686); *World Health Statistics Annual*.

LUXEMBOURG - HEALTH EXPENDITURES

International Monetary Fund, 700 Nineteenth Street, NW, Washington, D.C. 20431 (202) 623-7000; *Government Finance*

Statistics Yearbook.

LUXEMBOURG - HEMP FIBRE PRODUCTION - See LUXEMBOURG - TEXTILE INDUSTRY

LUXEMBOURG - HIDE PRODUCTION

Food and Agricultural Organization of the United Nations (FAO), Via delle Terme di Caracalla, 00100 Rome, Italy (Telephone Number in U.S. (202) 653-2400); *Production Yearbook*.

Organisation for Economic Co-operation and Development (OECD), 2 rue Andre-Pascal, 75 Paris 16, France (Telephone in U.S. (202) 785-6323); *The Footwear, Raw Hides and Skins, and Leather Industry in OECD Countries*, *Foreign Trade by Commodities*, and *Indicators of Industrial Activity*.

LUXEMBOURG - HIGHWAYS

European Community Information Service, 2100 M Street, NW, Washington, D.C. 20037 (202) 862-9500; *Basic Statistics of the Community*, and *Transport Annual Statistics*.

G.K. Hall and Company, 70 Lincoln Street, Boston, Massachusetts 02111 (617) 423-3990; *The World in Figures*.

International Road Federation, 525 School Street, SW, Washington, D.C. 20024 (202) 554-2106; *World Road Statistics*.

Statistical Office of the United Nations, Publishing Service, New York, New York 10017 (800) 253-9646; *Annual Bulletin of Transport Statistics for Europe*.

LUXEMBOURG - HOPS PRODUCTION - See LUXEMBOURG - CROPS

LUXEMBOURG - HORSES - See LUXEMBOURG - LIVESTOCK AND POULTRY

LUXEMBOURG - HOURS OF WORK - See LUXEMBOURG - EMPLOYMENT

LUXEMBOURG - HOUSING AND HOUSING UNITS

European Community Information Service, 2100 M Street, NW, Washington, D.C. 20037 (202) 862-9500; *Basic Statistics of the Community*, *Labor Force Sample Survey*, and *Regions: Statistical Yearbook*.

LUXEMBOURG - HOUSING CONSTRUCTION - See LUXEMBOURG - CONSTRUCTION INDUSTRY

LUXEMBOURG - HOUSING EXPENDITURES

European Community Information Service, 2100 M Street, NW, Washington, D.C. 20037 (202) 862-9500; *Basic Statistics of the Community*.

International Monetary Fund, 700 Nineteenth Street, NW, Washington, D.C. 20431 (202) 623-7000; *Government Finance Statistics Yearbook*.

LUXEMBOURG - HYDROCHLORIC ACID PRODUCTION

European Community Information Service, 2100 M Street, NW, Washington, D.C. 20037 (202) 862-9500; *Basic Statistics of the Community*.

LUXEMBOURG - ILLITERATE POPULATION

The Economist Intelligence Unit, 111 West 57th Street, New York, New York 10019 (800) 938-4685; *The World Market Atlas*.

G.K. Hall and Company, 70 Lincoln Street, Boston, Massachusetts 02111 (617) 423-3990; *The World in Figures*.

LUXEMBOURG - IMPORTS

American Automobile Manufacturers Association, 1401 H Street, NW, Suite 900, Washington, D.C. 20005 (202) 326-5500; *World Motor Vehicle Data*.

The Economist Intelligence Unit, 111 West 57th Street, New York, New York 10019 (800) 938-4685; *The World Market Atlas*.

European Community Information Service, 2100 M Street, NW, Washington, D.C. 20037 (202) 862-9500; *Basic Statistics of the Community, Energy: Monthly Statistics, Energy Statistics Yearbook, Eurostatistics: Data for Short-Term Economic Analysis, External Trade: Monthly Statistics, External Trade: Statistical Yearbook*, and *Fisheries: Yearly Statistics*.

Food and Agricultural Organization of the United Nations (FAO), Via delle Terme di Caracalla, 00100 Rome, Italy (Telephone Number in U.S. (202) 653-2400); *The State of Food and Agriculture*.

G.K. Hall and Company, 70 Lincoln Street, Boston, Massachusetts 02111 (617) 423-3990; *The World in Figures*.

International Iron and Steel Institute, 120, rue Colonel Bourg, B-1140 Brussels, Belgium; *Steel Statistical Yearbook*.

Organisation for Economic Co-operation and Development (OECD), 2 rue Andre-Pascal, 75 Paris 16, France (Telephone in U.S. (202) 785-6323); *Economic Outlook, The Footwear, Raw Hides and Skins, and Leather Industry in OECD Countries, Industrial Structure Statistics, The Iron and Steel Industry, Milk, Milk Products, and Egg Balances in OECD Member Countries, OECD Economic Surveys: Belgium - Luxembourg*, and *The Pulp and Paper Industry*.

Times Books, 201 East 50th Street, New York, New York 10022 (212) 751-2600; *The Economist Book of Vital World Statistics*.

The World Bank, 1818 H Street, NW, Washington, D.C. 20433 (202) 477-1234; *World Tables*.

LUXEMBOURG - INCOME TAXES - See LUXEMBOURG - TAXATION

LUXEMBOURG - INDUSTRIAL METALS PRODUCTION - See LUXEMBOURG - MINING AND MINERAL PRODUCTS

LUXEMBOURG - INDUSTRY

European Community Information Service, 2100 M Street, NW, Washington, D.C. 20037 (202) 862-9500; *Basic Statistics of the Community, Employment and Unemployment, Eurostatistics: Data for Short-Term Economic Analysis*, and *Labor Force Sample Survey*.

G.K. Hall and Company, 70 Lincoln Street, Boston, Massachusetts 02111 (617) 423-3990; *The World in Figures*.

International Labour Office, I.L.O. Publications, CH-1211, Geneva 22, Switzerland; *Yearbook of Labour Statistics*.

Organisation for Economic Co-operation and Development (OECD), 2 rue Andre-Pascal, 75 Paris 16, France (Telephone in U.S. (202) 785-6323); *Economic Outlook, Industrial Structure Statistics*, and

Main Economic Indicators - Historical Statistics.

Statistical Office of the United Nations, Publishing Service, New York, New York 10017 (800) 253-9646; *Statistical Yearbook*.

Times Books, 201 East 50th Street, New York, New York 10022 (212) 751-2600; *The Economist Book of Vital World Statistics*.

The World Bank, 1818 H Street, NW, Washington, D.C. 20433 (202) 477-1234; *World Tables*.

World Intellectual Property Organization, 34 Chemin des Colombettes, CH-1211 Geneva 20, Switzerland; *Industrial Property Statistics*.

LUXEMBOURG - INFANT AND MATERNAL MORTALITY

European Community Information Service, 2100 M Street, NW, Washington, D.C. 20037 (202) 862-9500; *Basic Statistics of the Community*, and *Demographic Statistics*.

Statistical Office of the United Nations, Publishing Service, New York, New York 10017 (800) 253-9646; *Demographic Yearbook*, and *Statistical Yearbook*.

Times Books, 201 East 50th Street, New York, New York 10022 (212) 751-2600; *The Economist Book of Vital World Statistics*.

The World Bank, 1818 H Street, NW, Washington, D.C. 20433 (202) 477-1234; *World Tables*.

World Health Organization, Office of Publications, Avenue Appia, CH-1211 Geneva 27, Switzerland (Telephone Number in U.S. (518) 436-9686); *World Health Statistics Annual*.

LUXEMBOURG - INTEREST RATES

European Community Information Service, 2100 M Street, NW, Washington, D.C. 20037 (202) 862-9500; *Money and Finance*.

Organisation for Economic Co-operation and Development (OECD), 2 rue Andre-Pascal, 75 Paris 16, France (Telephone in U.S. (202) 785-6323); *Economic Outlook, Financial Market Trends*, and *OECD Financial Statistics*.

LUXEMBOURG - INTERNAL TRADE

European Community Information Service, 2100 M Street, NW, Washington, D.C. 20037 (202) 862-9500; *Basic Statistics of the Community*.

LUXEMBOURG - INTERNATIONAL FINANCE

European Community Information Service, 2100 M Street, NW, Washington, D.C. 20037 (202) 862-9500; *Basic Statistics of the Community*.

Organisation for Economic Co-operation and Development (OECD), 2 rue Andre-Pascal, 75 Paris 16, France (Telephone in U.S. (202) 785-6323); *Economic Outlook*, and *Financial Market Trends*.

LUXEMBOURG - INTERNATIONAL LIQUIDITY

International Monetary Fund, 700 Nineteenth Street, NW, Washington, D.C. 20431 (202) 623-7000; *International Financial Statistics*.

Organisation for Economic Co-operation and Development (OECD), 2 rue Andre-Pascal, 75 Paris 16, France (Telephone in U.S. (202) 785-

6323); *Economic Outlook*, and *Financial Market Trends*.

LUXEMBOURG - INTERNATIONAL RESERVES EXCLUDING GOLD

Statistical Office of the United Nations, Publishing Service, New York, New York 10017 (800) 253-9646; *Statistical Yearbook*.

The World Bank, 1818 H Street, NW, Washington, D.C. 20433 (202) 477-1234; *World Tables*.

LUXEMBOURG - INTERNATIONAL STATISTICS

Organisation for Economic Co-operation and Development (OECD), 2 rue Andre-Pascal, 75 Paris 16, France (Telephone in U.S. (202) 785-6323); *Financial Market Trends*, and *Tourism Policy and International Tourism in OECD Member Countries*.

LUXEMBOURG - INVESTMENTS

Organisation for Economic Co-operation and Development (OECD), 2 rue Andre-Pascal, 75 Paris 16, France (Telephone in U.S. (202) 785-6323); *Economic Outlook, Financial Market Trends, Industrial Structure Statistics, The Iron and Steel Industry*, and *Textile Industry in OECD Countries*.

LUXEMBOURG - IRON ORE - See LUXEMBOURG - MINING AND MINERAL PRODUCTS

LUXEMBOURG - JUTE PRODUCTION - See LUXEMBOURG - CROPS

LUXEMBOURG - LABOR FORCE

European Community Information Service, 2100 M Street, NW, Washington, D.C. 20037 (202) 862-9500; *Basic Statistics of the Community, Labor Force Sample Survey*, and *Regions. Statistical Yearbook*.

Food and Agricultural Organization of the United Nations (FAO), Via delle Terme di Caracalla, 00100 Rome, Italy (Telephone Number in U.S. (202) 653-2400); *The State of Food and Agriculture*.

G.K. Hall and Company, 70 Lincoln Street, Boston, Massachusetts 02111 (617) 423-3990; *The World in Figures*.

Organisation for Economic Co-operation and Development (OECD), 2 rue Andre-Pascal, 75 Paris 16, France (Telephone in U.S. (202) 785-6323); *Economic Outlook, The Iron and Steel Industry, Labour Force Statistics, Main Economic Indicators - Historical Statistics, Maritime Transport, OECD Economic Surveys: Belgium - Luxembourg, OECD Employment Outlook*, and *Textile Industry in OECD Countries*.

Times Books, 201 East 50th Street, New York, New York 10022 (212) 751-2600; *The Economist Book of Vital World Statistics*.

The World Bank, 1818 H Street, NW, Washington, D.C. 20433 (202) 477-1234; *World Tables*.

LUXEMBOURG - LABOR PRODUCTIVITY

International Labour Office, I.L.O. Publications, CH-1211, Geneva 22, Switzerland; *Yearbook of Labour Statistics*.

Organisation for Economic Co-operation and Development (OECD), 2 rue Andre-Pascal, 75 Paris 16, France (Telephone in U.S. (202) 785-6323); *Economic Outlook, Main Economic Indicators - Historical Statistics*, and *OECD Employment Outlook*.

LUXEMBOURG - LAND USE

Euromonitor Publications Limited, 87-88 Turnmill Street, London EC1M 5QU, England; *European Marketing Data and Statistics*.

European Community Information Service, 2100 M Street, NW, Washington, D.C. 20037 (202) 862-9500; *Agriculture: Statistical Yearbook, Basic Statistics of the Community, Crop Production: Quarterly Statistics*, and *Regions: Statistical Yearbook*.

Food and Agricultural Organization of the United Nations (FAO), Via delle Terme di Caracalla, 00100 Rome, Italy (Telephone Number in U.S. (202) 653-2400); *Production Yearbook*.

G.K. Hall and Company, 70 Lincoln Street, Boston, Massachusetts 02111 (617) 423-3990; *The World in Figures*.

LUXEMBOURG - LEAD AND LEAD ORE PRODUCTION AND CONSUMPTION - See LUXEMBOURG - MINING AND MINERAL PRODUCTS

LUXEMBOURG - LEATHER - PRODUCTION INDEX

Organisation for Economic Co-operation and Development (OECD), 2 rue Andre-Pascal, 75 Paris 16, France (Telephone in U.S. (202) 785-6323); *Indicators of Industrial Activity*.

LUXEMBOURG - LEATHER AND FOOTWEAR EXPORTS AND IMPORTS

European Community Information Service, 2100 M Street, NW, Washington, D.C. 20037 (202) 862-9500; *Basic Statistics of the Community*.

Organisation for Economic Co-operation and Development (OECD), 2 rue Andre-Pascal, 75 Paris 16, France (Telephone in U.S. (202) 785-6323); *The Footwear, Raw Hides and Skins, and Leather Industry in OECD Countries*.

LUXEMBOURG - LIBRARIES

Euromonitor Publications Limited, 87-88 Turnmill Street, London EC1M 5QU, England; *European Marketing Data and Statistics*.

LUXEMBOURG - LIGNITE PRODUCTION - See LUXEMBOURG - MINING AND MINERAL PRODUCTS

LUXEMBOURG - LIVESTOCK AND POULTRY

Commodity Research Bureau, Incorporated, 75 Wall Street, New York, New York 10005 (212) 504-7754; *Commodity Year Book*.

Euromonitor Publications Limited, 87-88 Turnmill Street, London EC1M 5QU, England; *European Marketing Data and Statistics*.

European Community Information Service, 2100 M Street, NW, Washington, D.C. 20037 (202) 862-9500; *Agriculture: Statistical Yearbook, Basic Statistics of the Community, Eurostatistics: Data for Short-Term Economic Analysis*, and *Regions: Statistical Yearbook*.

Food and Agricultural Organization of the United Nations (FAO), Via delle Terme di Caracalla, 00100 Rome, Italy (Telephone Number in U.S. (202) 653-2400); *Production Yearbook*, and *The State of Food and Agriculture*.

G.K. Hall and Company, 70 Lincoln Street, Boston, Massachusetts 02111 (617) 423-3990; *The World in Figures*.

Organisation for Economic Co-operation and Development (OECD), 2 rue Andre-Pascal, 75 Paris 16, France (Telephone in U.S. (202) 785-6323); *Economic Accounts for Agriculture*, and *Meat Balances in OECD Member Countries*.

LUXEMBOURG - LIVING LEVELS

G.K. Hall and Company, 70 Lincoln Street, Boston, Massachusetts 02111 (617) 423-3990; *The World in Figures*.

Organisation for Economic Co-operation and Development (OECD), 2 rue Andre-Pascal, 75 Paris 16, France (Telephone in U.S. (202) 785-6323); *Economic Outlook*.

Times Books, 201 East 50th Street, New York, New York 10022 (212) 751-2600; *The Economist Book of Vital World Statistics*.

LUXEMBOURG - MACHINERY - PRODUCTION INDEX

Organisation for Economic Co-operation and Development (OECD), 2 rue Andre-Pascal, 75 Paris 16, France (Telephone in U.S. (202) 785-6323); *Indicators of Industrial Activity*.

LUXEMBOURG - MAGNESIUM PRODUCTION AND CONSUMPTION - See LUXEMBOURG - MINING AND MINERAL PRODUCTS

LUXEMBOURG - MAIL - NUMBER OF PIECES SENT OR RECEIVED

European Community Information Service, 2100 M Street, NW, Washington, D.C. 20037 (202) 862-9500; *Transport Annual Statistics*.

Statistical Office of the United Nations, Publishing Service, New York, New York 10017 (800) 253-9646; *Statistical Yearbook*.

LUXEMBOURG - MAIN ECONOMIC INDICATORS - See LUXEMBOURG - ECONOMY

LUXEMBOURG - MANGANESE PRODUCTION AND CONSUMPTION - See LUXEMBOURG - MINING AND MINERAL PRODUCTS

LUXEMBOURG - MANUFACTURING

American Automobile Manufacturers Association, 1401 H Street, NW, Suite 900, Washington, D.C. 20005 (202) 326-5500; *World Motor Vehicle Data*.

European Community Information Service, 2100 M Street, NW, Washington, D.C. 20037 (202) 862-9500; *Basic Statistics of the Community, Eurostatistics: Data for Short-Term Economic Analysis, Industrial Production: Quarterly Statistics*, and *Labor Force Sample Survey*.

G.K. Hall and Company, 70 Lincoln Street, Boston, Massachusetts 02111 (617) 423-3990; *The World in Figures*.

Organisation for Economic Co-operation and Development (OECD), 2 rue Andre-Pascal, 75 Paris 16, France (Telephone in U.S. (202) 785-6323); *Indicators of Industrial Activity*, and *OECD Economic Surveys: Belgium - Luxembourg*.

Statistical Office of the United Nations, Publishing Service, New York, New York 10017 (800) 253-9646; *Statistical Yearbook*.

Times Books, 201 East 50th Street, New York, New York 10022 (212) 751-2600; *The Economist Book of Vital World Statistics*.

The World Bank, 1818 H Street, NW, Washington, D.C. 20433 (202) 477-1234; *World Tables*.

LUXEMBOURG - MARRIAGE RATES

European Community Information Service, 2100 M Street, NW, Washington, D.C. 20037 (202) 862-9500; *Basic Statistics of the Community*.

Statistical Office of the United Nations, Publishing Service, New York, New York 10017 (800) 253-9646; *Demographic Yearbook*, and *Statistical Yearbook*.

LUXEMBOURG - MEAT PRODUCTION - See LUXEMBOURG - LIVESTOCK AND POULTRY

LUXEMBOURG - MERCHANT SHIPPING

European Community Information Service, 2100 M Street, NW, Washington, D.C. 20037 (202) 862-9500; *Basic Statistics of the Community, Fisheries: Yearly Statistics, Transport Annual Statistics*, and *Regions: Statistical Yearbook*.

G.K. Hall and Company, 70 Lincoln Street, Boston, Massachusetts 02111 (617) 423-3990; *The World in Figures*.

Organisation for Economic Co-operation and Development (OECD), 2 rue Andre-Pascal, 75 Paris 16, France (Telephone in U.S. (202) 785-6323); *Maritime Transport*.

Statistical Office of the United Nations, Publishing Service, New York, New York 10017 (800) 253-9646; *Annual Bulletin of Transport Statistics for Europe*.

Times Books, 201 East 50th Street, New York, New York 10022 (212) 751-2600; *The Economist Book of Vital World Statistics*.

LUXEMBOURG - MERCURY PRODUCTION AND CONSUMPTION - See LUXEMBOURG - MINING AND MINERAL PRODUCTS

LUXEMBOURG - MILITARY

G.K. Hall and Company, 70 Lincoln Street, Boston, Massachusetts 02111 (617) 423-3990; *The World in Figures*.

The International Institute for Strategic Studies, 23 Tavistock Street, London WC2E 7NQ, England; *The Military Balance*.

LUXEMBOURG - MILK PRODUCTION - LUXEMBOURG - DAIRY PRODUCTS

LUXEMBOURG - MILLET PRODUCTION - See LUXEMBOURG - CROPS

LUXEMBOURG - MINING AND MINERAL PRODUCTS

Commodity Research Bureau, Incorporated, 75 Wall Street, New York, New York 10005 (212) 504-7754; *Commodity Year Book*.

European Community Information Service, 2100 M Street, NW, Washington, D.C. 20037 (202) 862-9500; *ACP: Basic Statistics, Basic Statistics of the Community, Energy: Monthly Statistics, Energy Statistics Yearbook, Eurostatistics: Data for Short-Term Economic Analysis, Industrial Production: Quarterly Statistics, Iron and Steel: Statistical Yearbook*, and *Regions: Statistical Yearbook*.

G.K. Hall and Company, 70 Lincoln Street, Boston, Massachusetts 02111 (617) 423-3990; *The World in Figures*.

International Iron and Steel Institute, 120, rue Colonel Bourg, B-1140 Brussels, Belgium; *Steel Statistical Yearbook.*

Organisation for Economic Co-operation and Development (OECD), 2 rue Andre-Pascal, 75 Paris 16, France (Telephone in U.S. (202) 785-6323); *Coal Information, Energy Statistics of OECD Countries, Foreign Trade by Commodities, Indicators of Industrial Activity, Industrial Structure Statistics, The Iron and Steel Industry, The Non-Ferrous Metals Industry,* and *OECD Economic Surveys: Belgium - Luxembourg.*

Statistical Office of the United Nations, Publishing Service, New York, New York 10017 (800) 253-9646; *Statistical Yearbook.*

LUXEMBOURG - MOLYBDENUM AND MOLYBDENUM ORE PRODUCTION AND CONSUMPTION - See LUXEMBOURG - MINING AND MINERAL PRODUCTS

LUXEMBOURG - MONEY AND CREDIT

Organisation for Economic Co-operation and Development (OECD), 2 rue Andre-Pascal, 75 Paris 16, France (Telephone in U.S. (202) 785-6323); *OECD Economic Surveys: Belgium - Luxembourg.*

LUXEMBOURG - MONEY EXCHANGE RATE

European Community Information Service, 2100 M Street, NW, Washington, D.C. 20037 (202) 862-9500; *Basic Statistics of the Community.*

International Monetary Fund, 700 Nineteenth Street, NW, Washington, D.C. 20431 (202) 623-7000; *International Financial Statistics.*

Organisation for Economic Co-operation and Development (OECD), 2 rue Andre-Pascal, 75 Paris 16, France (Telephone in U.S. (202) 785-6323); *Economic Outlook, Financial Market Trends,* and *Tourism Policy and International Tourism in OECD Member Countries.*

Statistical Office of the United Nations, Publishing Service, New York, New York 10017 (800) 253-9646; *Statistical Yearbook.*

LUXEMBOURG - MONEY RATES - MARKET

European Community Information Service, 2100 M Street, NW, Washington, D.C. 20037 (202) 862-9500; *Basic Statistics of the Community.*

Organisation for Economic Co-operation and Development (OECD), 2 rue Andre-Pascal, 75 Paris 16, France (Telephone in U.S. (202) 785-6323); *Economic Outlook,* and *Financial Market Trends.*

LUXEMBOURG - MONEY RESERVES

European Community Information Service, 2100 M Street, NW, Washington, D.C. 20037 (202) 862-9500; *Basic Statistics of the Community.*

Organisation for Economic Co-operation and Development (OECD), 2 rue Andre-Pascal, 75 Paris 16, France (Telephone in U.S. (202) 785-6323); *Economic Outlook,* and *Financial Market Trends.*

LUXEMBOURG - MONEY SUPPLY

European Community Information Service, 2100 M Street, NW, Washington, D.C. 20037 (202) 862-9500; *Basic Statistics of the Community, Eurostatistics: Data for Short-Term Economic Analysis,* and *Money and Finance.*

G.K. Hall and Company, 70 Lincoln Street, Boston, Massachusetts 02111 (617) 423-3990; *The World in Figures.*

Organisation for Economic Co-operation and Development (OECD), 2 rue Andre-Pascal, 75 Paris 16, France (Telephone in U.S. (202) 785-6323); *Economic Outlook.*

The World Bank, 1818 H Street, NW, Washington, D.C. 20433 (202) 477-1234; *World Tables.*

LUXEMBOURG - MOTION PICTURES

Statistical Office of the United Nations, Publishing Service, New York, New York 10017 (800) 253-9646; *Statistical Yearbook.*

LUXEMBOURG - MOTOR VEHICLE PRODUCTION

American Automobile Manufacturers Association, 1401 H Street, NW, Suite 900, Washington, D.C. 20005 (202) 326-5500; *World Motor Vehicle Data.*

European Community Information Service, 2100 M Street, NW, Washington, D.C. 20037 (202) 862-9500; *Basic Statistics of the Community,* and *Eurostatistics: Data for Short Term Economic Analysis.*

Organisation for Economic Co-operation and Development (OECD), 2 rue Andre-Pascal, 75 Paris 16, France (Telephone in U.S. (202) 785-6323); *Foreign Trade by Commodities,* and *Indicators of Industrial Activity.*

Times Books, 201 East 50th Street, New York, New York 10022 (212) 751-2600; *The Economist Book of Vital World Statistics.*

LUXEMBOURG - MOTOR VEHICLE TAXES - See LUXEMBOURG - TAXATION

LUXEMBOURG - MOTOR VEHICLES IN USE

American Automobile Manufacturers Association, 1401 H Street, NW, Suite 900, Washington, D.C. 20005 (202) 326-5500; *World Motor Vehicle Data.*

European Community Information Service, 2100 M Street, NW, Washington, D.C. 20037 (202) 862-9500; *Basic Statistics of the Community,* and *Transport Annual Statistics.*

G.K. Hall and Company, 70 Lincoln Street, Boston, Massachusetts 02111 (617) 423-3990; *The World in Figures.*

International Road Federation, 525 School Street, SW, Washington, D.C. 20024 (202) 554-2106; *World Road Statistics.*

Statistical Office of the United Nations, Publishing Service, New York, New York 10017 (800) 253-9646; *Statistical Yearbook.*

LUXEMBOURG - MULES - See LUXEMBOURG - LIVESTOCK AND POULTRY

LUXEMBOURG - MUSEUMS

Euromonitor Publications Limited, 87-88 Turnmill Street, London EC1M 5QU, England; *European Marketing Data and Statistics.*

United Nations Educational, Scientific and Cultural Organization (UNESCO), 7 Place de Fontenoy, F-75700 Paris, France (Telephone Number in U.S. (212) 963-5981); *Statistical Yearbook.*

LUXEMBOURG - NATALITY - See LUXEMBOURG - BIRTH RATES

LUXEMBOURG - NATIONAL ACCOUNTS

European Community Information Service, 2100 M Street, NW, Washington, D.C. 20037 (202) 862-9500; *Basic Statistics of the Community*, and *Eurostatistics: Data for Short-Term Economic Analysis*.

Organisation for Economic Co-operation and Development (OECD), 2 rue Andre-Pascal, 75 Paris 16, France (Telephone in U.S. (202) 785-6323); *Economic Outlook*.

Statistical Office of the United Nations, Publishing Service, New York, New York 10017 (800) 253-9646; *National Accounts Statistics*, and *Statistical Yearbook*.

LUXEMBOURG - NATIONAL INCOME

G.K. Hall and Company, 70 Lincoln Street, Boston, Massachusetts 02111 (617) 423-3990; *The World in Figures*.

Organisation for Economic Co-operation and Development (OECD), 2 rue Andre-Pascal, 75 Paris 16, France (Telephone in U.S. (202) 785-6323); *Economic Outlook*.

Statistical Office of the United Nations, Publishing Service, New York, New York 10017 (800) 253-9646; *Statistical Yearbook*.

LUXEMBOURG - NATIONAL PRODUCT

European Community Information Service, 2100 M Street, NW, Washington, D.C. 20037 (202) 862-9500; *Basic Statistics of the Community*.

Organisation for Economic Co-operation and Development (OECD), 2 rue Andre-Pascal, 75 Paris 16, France (Telephone in U.S. (202) 785-6323); *Economic Outlook*.

Statistical Office of the United Nations, Publishing Service, New York, New York 10017 (800) 253-9646; *Statistical Yearbook*.

LUXEMBOURG - NATURAL GAS PRODUCTION - See LUXEMBOURG - MINING AND MINERAL PRODUCTS

LUXEMBOURG - NATURAL RUBBER PRODUCTION

European Community Information Service, 2100 M Street, NW, Washington, D.C. 20037 (202) 862-9500; *Basic Statistics of the Community*.

LUXEMBOURG - NEWSPAPER PRODUCTION - See LUXEMBOURG - FORESTRY AND FOREST PRODUCTS

LUXEMBOURG - NEWSPRINT EXPORTS AND IMPORTS - See FORESTRY AND FOREST PRODUCTS

LUXEMBOURG - NICKEL AND NICKEL ORE PRODUCTION AND CONSUMPTION - See LUXEMBOURG - MINING AND MINERAL PRODUCTS

LUXEMBOURG - NITRIC ACID PRODUCTION - See LUXEMBOURG - MINING AND MINERAL PRODUCTS

LUXEMBOURG - OATS PRODUCTION - See LUXEMBOURG - CROPS

LUXEMBOURG - OCCUPATIONS - See LUXEMBOURG - LABOR FORCE

LUXEMBOURG - OIL PRODUCING CROPS

European Community Information Service, 2100 M Street, NW, Washington, D.C. 20037 (202) 862-9500; *Basic Statistics of the Community*.

Organisation for Economic Co-operation and Development (OECD), 2 rue Andre-Pascal, 75 Paris 16, France (Telephone in U.S. (202) 785-6323); *Foreign Trade by Commodities*.

LUXEMBOURG - ONION PRODUCTION - See LUXEMBOURG - CROPS

LUXEMBOURG - PALM KERNEL PRODUCTION - See LUXEMBOURG - CROPS

LUXEMBOURG - PAPER - See LUXEMBOURG - FORESTRY AND FOREST PRODUCTS

LUXEMBOURG - PATENTS

Statistical Office of the United Nations, Publishing Service, New York, New York 10017 (800) 253-9646; *Statistical Yearbook*.

World Intellectual Property Organization, 34 Chemin des Colombettes, CH-1211 Geneva 20, Switzerland; *Industrial Property Statistics*.

LUXEMBOURG - PEANUT PRODUCTION - See LUXEMBOURG - CROPS

LUXEMBOURG - PEPPER PRODUCTION - See LUXEMBOURG - CROPS

LUXEMBOURG - PERIODICALS

United Nations Educational, Scientific and Cultural Organization (UNESCO), 7 Place de Fontenoy, F-75700 Paris, France (Telephone Number in U.S. (212) 963-5981); *Statistical Yearbook*.

LUXEMBOURG - PESTICIDE USE

Food and Agricultural Organization of the United Nations (FAO), Via delle Terme di Caracalla, 00100 Rome, Italy (Telephone Number in U.S. (202) 653-2400); *The State of Food and Agriculture*.

LUXEMBOURG - PETROLEUM INDUSTRY

European Community Information Service, 2100 M Street, NW, Washington, D.C. 20037 (202) 862-9500; *ACP: Basic Statistics, Basic Statistics of the Community*, and *Energy Statistics Yearbook*.

Euromonitor Publications Limited, 87-88 Turnmill Street, London EC1M 5QU, England; *European Marketing Data and Statistics*.

Food and Agricultural Organization of the United Nations (FAO), Via delle Terme di Caracalla, 00100 Rome, Italy (Telephone Number in U.S. (202) 653-2400); *The State of Food and Agriculture*.

G.K. Hall and Company, 70 Lincoln Street, Boston, Massachusetts 02111 (617) 423-3990; *The World in Figures*.

Organisation for Economic Co-operation and Development (OECD), 2 rue Andre-Pascal, 75 Paris 16, France (Telephone in U.S. (202) 785-6323); *Energy Statistics of OECD Countries, Foreign Trade by Commodities, Indicators of Industrial Activity*, and *Oil and Gas Information*.

LUXEMBOURG - PHOSPHATE AND PHOSPHATE ROCK PRODUCTION - See LUXEMBOURG - MINING AND MINERAL PRODUCTS

LUXEMBOURG - PIG-IRON AND FERRO-ALLOY PRODUCTION - See LUXEMBOURG - MINING AND MINERAL PRODUCTS

LUXEMBOURG - PIGS - See LUXEMBOURG - LIVESTOCK AND POULTRY

LUXEMBOURG - PIPELINES FOR OIL AND PETROLEUM PRODUCTS

European Community Information Service, 2100 M Street, NW, Washington, D.C. 20037 (202) 862-9500; *Transport Annual Statistics*.

LUXEMBOURG - PLASTIC AND RESIN PRODUCTION

European Community Information Service, 2100 M Street, NW, Washington, D.C. 20037 (202) 862-9500; *Basic Statistics of the Community*.

Organisation for Economic Co-operation and Development (OECD), 2 rue Andre-Pascal, 75 Paris 16, France (Telephone in U.S. (202) 785-6323); *Foreign Trade by Commodities*.

LUXEMBOURG - PLATINUM PRODUCTION - See LUXEMBOURG - MINING AND MINERAL PRODUCTS

LUXEMBOURG - POPULATION

The Economist Intelligence Unit, 111 West 57th Street, New York, New York 10019 (800) 939-4695; *The World Market Atlas*.

Euromonitor Publications Limited, 87-88 Turnmill Street, London EC1M 5QU, England; *European Marketing Data and Statistics*.

European Community Information Service, 2100 M Street, NW, Washington, D.C. 20037 (202) 862-9500; *ACP: Basic Statistics, Basic Statistics of the Community, Demographic Statistics, Employment and Unemployment, Fisheries: Yearly Statistics, Iron and Steel: Statistical Yearbook, Labor Force Sample Survey*, and *Regions: Statistical Yearbook*.

Food and Agricultural Organization of the United Nations (FAO), Via delle Terme di Caracalla, 00100 Rome, Italy (Telephone Number in U.S. (202) 653-2400); *Production Yearbook*.

G.K. Hall and Company, 70 Lincoln Street, Boston, Massachusetts 02111 (617) 423-3990; *The World in Figures*.

International Labour Office, I.L.O. Publications, CH-1211, Geneva 22, Switzerland; *Yearbook of Labour Statistics*.

Statistical Office of the United Nations, Publishing Service, New York, New York 10017 (800) 253-9646; *Demographic Yearbook*, and *Statistical Yearbook*.

Times Books, 201 East 50th Street, New York, New York 10022 (212) 751-2600; *The Economist Book of Vital World Statistics*.

United Nations Educational, Scientific and Cultural Organization (UNESCO), 7 Place de Fontenoy, F-75700 Paris, France (Telephone Number in U.S. (212) 963-5981); *Statistical Yearbook*.

U.S. Arms Control and Disarmament Agency, 320 Twenty-first Street, NW, Washington, D.C. 20451 (202) 647-8677; *World Military Expenditures and Arms Transfers*.

World Health Organization, Office of Publications, Avenue Appia, CH-1211 Geneva 27, Switzerland (Telephone Number in U.S. (518) 436-9686); *World Health Statistics Annual*.

LUXEMBOURG - POTATO PRODUCTION - See LUXEMBOURG - CROPS

LUXEMBOURG - POULTRY - See LUXEMBOURG - LIVESTOCK AND POULTRY

LUXEMBOURG - POWER PRODUCTION INDUSTRY

European Community Information Service, 2100 M Street, NW, Washington, D.C. 20037 (202) 862-9500; *Basic Statistics of the Community*.

Statistical Office of the United Nations, Publishing Service, New York, New York 10017 (800) 253-9646; *Statistical Yearbook*.

LUXEMBOURG - PRICES

European Community Information Service, 2100 M Street, NW, Washington, D.C. 20037 (202) 862-9500; *Basic Statistics of the Community*, and *Eurostatistics: Data for Short-Term Economic Analysis*.

Food and Agricultural Organization of the United Nations (FAO), Via delle Terme di Caracalla, 00100 Rome, Italy (Telephone Number in U.S. (202) 653-2400); *Production Yearbook* and *The State of Food and Agriculture*.

G.K. Hall and Company, 70 Lincoln Street, Boston, Massachusetts 02111 (617) 423-3990; *The World in Figures*.

International Labour Office, I.L.O. Publications, CH-1211, Geneva 22, Switzerland; *Yearbook of Labour Statistics*.

International Monetary Fund, 700 Nineteenth Street, NW, Washington, D.C. 20431 (202) 623-7000; *International Financial Statistics*.

Organisation for Economic Co-operation and Development (OECD), 2 rue Andre-Pascal, 75 Paris 16, France (Telephone in U.S. (202) 785-6323); *Economic Outlook, The Footwear, Raw Hides and Skins, and Leather Industry in OECD Countries, Indicators of Industrial Activity, The Iron and Steel Industry*, and *The Pulp and Paper Industry*.

LUXEMBOURG - PRINTING AND WRITING PAPER - See LUXEMBOURG - FORESTRY AND FOREST PRODUCTS

LUXEMBOURG - PRODUCTION

American Automobile Manufacturers Association, 1401 H Street, NW, Suite 900, Washington, D.C. 20005 (202) 326-5500; *World Motor Vehicle Data*.

European Community Information Service, 2100 M Street, NW, Washington, D.C. 20037 (202) 862-9500; *Basic Statistics of the Community, Eurostatistics: Data for Short-Term Economic Analysis*, and *Fisheries: Yearly Statistics*.

G.K. Hall and Company, 70 Lincoln Street, Boston, Massachusetts 02111 (617) 423-3990; *The World in Figures*.

International Iron and Steel Institute, 120, rue Colonel Bourg, B-1140 Brussels, Belgium; *Steel Statistical Yearbook*.

Organisation for Economic Co-operation and Development (OECD), 2 rue Andre-Pascal, 75 Paris 16, France (Telephone in U.S. (202) 785-6323); *Economic Outlook, The Footwear, Raw Hides and Skins, and Leather Industry in OECD Countries, Indicators of Industrial Activity, Industrial Structure Statistics, The Iron and Steel Industry*,

Meat Balances in OECD Member Countries, The Non-Ferrous Metals Industry, The Pulp and Paper Industry, and *Textile Industry in OECD Countries.*

LUXEMBOURG - PRODUCTIVITY

European Community Information Service, 2100 M Street, NW, Washington, D.C. 20037 (202) 862-9500; *Basic Statistics of the Community.*

Organisation for Economic Co-operation and Development (OECD), 2 rue Andre-Pascal, 75 Paris 16, France (Telephone in U.S. (202) 785-6323); *Economic Outlook.*

LUXEMBOURG - PROPERTY TAXES - See LUXEMBOURG - TAXATION

LUXEMBOURG - PUBLIC CONSUMPTION FUND

European Community Information Service, 2100 M Street, NW, Washington, D.C. 20037 (202) 862-9500; *Basic Statistics of the Community.*

Organisation for Economic Co-operation and Development (OECD), 2 rue Andre-Pascal, 75 Paris 16, France (Telephone in U.S. (202) 785-6323); *Revenue Statistics of OECD Member Countries.*

LUXEMBOURG - PUBLIC EXPENDITURES

European Community Information Service, 2100 M Street, NW, Washington, D.C. 20037 (202) 862-9500; *Basic Statistics of the Community.*

Organisation for Economic Co-operation and Development (OECD), 2 rue Andre-Pascal, 75 Paris 16, France (Telephone in U.S. (202) 785-6323); *Revenue Statistics of OECD Member Countries.*

LUXEMBOURG - PUBLIC FINANCE

Organisation for Economic Co-operation and Development (OECD), 2 rue Andre-Pascal, 75 Paris 16, France (Telephone in U.S. (202) 785-6323); *Revenue Statistics of OECD Member Countries.*

LUXEMBOURG - PUBLIC HEALTH

European Community Information Service, 2100 M Street, NW, Washington, D.C. 20037 (202) 862-9500; *Basic Statistics of the Community.*

LUXEMBOURG - PUBLIC REVENUES

Organisation for Economic Co-operation and Development (OECD), 2 rue Andre-Pascal, 75 Paris 16, France (Telephone in U.S. (202) 785-6323); *Revenue Statistics of OECD Member Countries.*

LUXEMBOURG - RADIO BROADCASTING - See LUXEMBOURG - BROADCASTING

LUXEMBOURG - RAILWAYS

Euromonitor Publications Limited, 87-88 Turnmill Street, London EC1M 5QU, England; *European Marketing Data and Statistics.*

European Community Information Service, 2100 M Street, NW, Washington, D.C. 20037 (202) 862-9500; *Basic Statistics of the Community, Regions: Statistical Yearbook,* and *Transport Annual Statistics.*

G.K. Hall and Company, 70 Lincoln Street, Boston, Massachusetts 02111 (617) 423-3990; *The World in Figures.*

Jane's Information Group, Sentinel House, 163 Brighton Road, Coulsdon, Surrey CR5 2NH, England (Telephone Number in U.S. (703) 683-3700); *Jane's World Railways.*

Statistical Office of the United Nations, Publishing Service, New York, New York 10017 (800) 253-9646; *Annual Bulletin of Transport Statistics for Europe,* and *Statistical Yearbook.*

LUXEMBOURG - RANCHING

European Community Information Service, 2100 M Street, NW, Washington, D.C. 20037 (202) 862-9500; *Basic Statistics of the Community.*

LUXEMBOURG - RAPESEED PRODUCTION - See LUXEMBOURG-CROPS

LUXEMBOURG - RETAIL TRADE

European Community Information Service, 2100 M Street, NW, Washington, D.C. 20037 (202) 862-9500; *Basic Statistics of the Community,* and *Eurostatistics: Data for Short-Term Economic Analysis.*

G.K. Hall and Company, 70 Lincoln Street, Boston, Massachusetts 02111 (617) 423-3990; *The World in Figures.*

Statistical Office of the United Nations, Publishing Service, New York, New York 10017 (800) 253-9646; *Statistical Yearbook.*

LUXEMBOURG - RICE PRODUCTION - See LUXEMBOURG - CROPS

LUXEMBOURG - ROOT AND TUBER PRODUCTION - See LUXEMBOURG - CROPS

LUXEMBOURG - ROUNDWOOD PRODUCTION - See LUXEMBOURG - FORESTRY AND FOREST PRODUCTS

LUXEMBOURG - RUBBER PRODUCTION AND CONSUMPTION

European Community Information Service, 2100 M Street, NW, Washington, D.C. 20037 (202) 862-9500; *Basic Statistics of the Community.*

Organisation for Economic Co-operation and Development (OECD), 2 rue Andre-Pascal, 75 Paris 16, France (Telephone in U.S. (202) 785-6323); *Foreign Trade by Commodities.*

Statistical Office of the United Nations, Publishing Service, New York, New York 10017 (800) 253-9646; *Statistical Yearbook.*

LUXEMBOURG - RYE PRODUCTION - See LUXEMBOURG - CROPS

LUXEMBOURG - SAFFLOWER SEED PRODUCTION - See LUXEMBOURG - CROPS

LUXEMBOURG - SALT PRODUCTION

International Monetary Fund, 700 Nineteenth Street, NW, Washington, D.C. 20431 (202) 623-7000; *International Financial Statistics.*

Organisation for Economic Co-operation and Development (OECD), 2 rue Andre-Pascal, 75 Paris 16, France (Telephone in U.S. (202) 785-6323); *Indicators of Industrial Activity.*

LUXEMBOURG - SAVINGS ACCOUNT DEPOSITS

European Community Information Service, 2100 M Street, NW, Washington, D.C. 20037 (202) 862-9500; *Eurostatistics: Data for Short-Term Economic Analysis.*

LUXEMBOURG - SAWNWOOD PRODUCTION - See LUXEMBOURG - FORESTRY AND FOREST PRODUCTS

LUXEMBOURG - SCIENCE AND TECHNOLOGY - EXPENDITURE FOR RESEARCH

European Community Information Service, 2100 M Street, NW, Washington, D.C. 20037 (202) 862-9500; *Basic Statistics of the Community.*

LUXEMBOURG - SCIENTISTS, ENGINEERS AND TECHNICIANS

European Community Information Service, 2100 M Street, NW, Washington, D.C. 20037 (202) 862-9500; *Basic Statistics of the Community.*

LUXEMBOURG - SESAME SEED PRODUCTION - See LUXEMBOURG - CROPS

LUXEMBOURG - SHEEP - See LUXEMBOURG - LIVESTOCK AND POULTRY

LUXEMBOURG - SHIPBUILDING - PRODUCTION INDEX

Organisation for Economic Co-operation and Development (OECD), 2 rue Andre-Pascal, 75 Paris 16, France (Telephone in U.S. (202) 785-6323); *Indicators of Industrial Activity.*

LUXEMBOURG - SILVER PRODUCTION AND CONSUMPTION - See LUXEMBOURG - MINING AND MINERAL PRODUCTS

LUXEMBOURG - SISAL PRODUCTION - See LUXEMBOURG - CROPS

LUXEMBOURG - SOCIAL DATA

European Community Information Service, 2100 M Street, NW, Washington, D.C. 20037 (202) 862-9500; *ACP: Basic Statistics, Basic Statistics of the Community.*

G.K. Hall and Company, 70 Lincoln Street, Boston, Massachusetts 02111 (617) 423-3990; *The World in Figures.*

LUXEMBOURG - SOCIAL SECURITY

European Community Information Service, 2100 M Street, NW, Washington, D.C. 20037 (202) 862-9500; *Basic Statistics of the Community.*

Organisation for Economic Co-operation and Development (OECD), 2 rue Andre-Pascal, 75 Paris 16, France (Telephone in U.S. (202) 785-6323); *Revenue Statistics of OECD Member Countries.*

LUXEMBOURG - SOCIOECONOMIC DATA

European Community Information Service, 2100 M Street, NW, Washington, D.C. 20037 (202) 862-9500; *Basic Statistics of the Community.*

Organisation for Economic Co-operation and Development (OECD), 2 rue Andre-Pascal, 75 Paris 16, France (Telephone in U.S. (202) 785-6323); *Economic Outlook.*

LUXEMBOURG - SOYBEAN PRODUCTION - See LUXEMBOURG - CROPS

LUXEMBOURG - STAMP TAXES AND DUTIES - See LUXEMBOURG - TAXATION

LUXEMBOURG - STEEL - See LUXEMBOURG - MINING AND MINERAL PRODUCTS

LUXEMBOURG - STOCKS - COMMODITY - MARKET PRICE - INDEX

Food and Agricultural Organization of the United Nations (FAO), Via delle Terme di Caracalla, 00100 Rome, Italy (Telephone Number in U.S. (202) 653-2400); *The State of Food and Agriculture.*

LUXEMBOURG - STRAW PRODUCTION - See LUXEMBOURG - CROPS

LUXEMBOURG - SUGAR - See LUXEMBOURG - CROPS

LUXEMBOURG - SUGARBEET PRODUCTION - See LUXEMBOURG - CROPS

LUXEMBOURG - SULPHUR AND SULPHURIC ACID PRODUCTION - See LUXEMBOURG - MINING AND MINERAL PRODUCTS

LUXEMBOURG - SUNFLOWER PRODUCTION - See LUXEMBOURG - CROPS

LUXEMBOURG - TAXATION

European Community Information Service, 2100 M Street, NW, Washington, D.C. 20037 (202) 862-9500; *Basic Statistics of the Community.*

G.K. Hall and Company, 70 Lincoln Street, Boston, Massachusetts 02111 (617) 423-3990; *The World in Figures.*

International Monetary Fund, 700 Nineteenth Street, NW, Washington, D.C. 20431 (202) 623-7000; *Government Finance Statistics Yearbook.*

International Road Federation, 525 School Street, SW, Washington, D.C. 20024 (202) 554-2106; *World Road Statistics.*

Organisation for Economic Co-operation and Development (OECD), 2 rue Andre-Pascal, 75 Paris 16, France (Telephone in U.S. (202) 785-6323); *Revenue Statistics of OECD Member Countries.*

The World Bank, 1818 H Street, NW, Washington, D.C. 20433 (202) 477-1234; *World Tables.*

LUXEMBOURG - TEA PRODUCTION - See LUXEMBOURG - CROPS

LUXEMBOURG - TELEGRAPH SERVICE

European Community Information Service, 2100 M Street, NW, Washington, D.C. 20037 (202) 862-9500; *Transport Annual Statistics.*

Statistical Office of the United Nations, Publishing Service, New York, New York 10017 (800) 253-9646; *Statistical Yearbook.*

LUXEMBOURG - TELEPHONES IN USE

American Telephone and Telegraph Company, 26 Parsippany Road, Whippany, New Jersey 07981; *The World's Telephones.*

European Community Information Service, 2100 M Street, NW, Washington, D.C. 20037 (202) 862-9500; *Transport Annual Statistics.*

G.K. Hall and Company, 70 Lincoln Street, Boston, Massachusetts 02111 (617) 423-3990; *The World in Figures.*

Statistical Office of the United Nations, Publishing Service, New York, New York 10017 (800) 253-9646; *Statistical Yearbook.*

LUXEMBOURG - TELEVISION BROADCASTING - See LUXEMBOURG - BROADCASTING

LUXEMBOURG - TELEVISION RECEIVER PRODUCTION

European Community Information Service, 2100 M Street, NW, Washington, D.C. 20037 (202) 862-9500; *Basic Statistics of the Community.*

LUXEMBOURG - TEXTILE INDUSTRY

European Community Information Service, 2100 M Street, NW, Washington, D.C. 20037 (202) 862-9500; *Basic Statistics of the Community, Eurostatistics: Data for Short-Term Economic Analysis,* and *Industrial Production: Quarterly Statistics.*

Food and Agricultural Organization of the United Nations (FAO), Via delle Terme di Caracalla, 00100 Rome, Italy (Telephone Number in U.S. (202) 653-2400); *Production Yearbook.*

G.K. Hall and Company, 70 Lincoln Street, Boston, Massachusetts 02111 (617) 423-3990; *The World in Figures.*

Organisation for Economic Co-operation and Development (OECD), 2 rue Andre-Pascal, 75 Paris 16, France (Telephone in U.S. (202) 785-6323); *Indicators of Industrial Activity, Industrial Structure Statistics, Foreign Trade by Commodities,* and *Textile Industry in OECD Countries.*

Statistical Office of the United Nations, Publishing Service, New York, New York 10017 (800) 253-9646; *Trade in Manufactures of Developing Countries.*

LUXEMBOURG - THEATRE

United Nations Educational, Scientific and Cultural Organization (UNESCO), 7 Place de Fontenoy, F-75700 Paris, France (Telephone Number in U.S. (212) 963-5981); *Statistical Yearbook.*

LUXEMBOURG - TIMBER - RESOURCE FORESTS - See LUXEMBOURG - FORESTRY AND FOREST PRODUCTS

LUXEMBOURG - TIN - See LUXEMBOURG - MINING AND MINERAL PRODUCTS

LUXEMBOURG - TIRE (MOTOR VEHICLE) PRODUCTION

Statistical Office of the United Nations, Publishing Service, New York, New York 10017 (800) 253-9646; *Statistical Yearbook.*

LUXEMBOURG - TOBACCO PRODUCTION

Euromonitor Publications Limited, 87-88 Turnmill Street, London EC1M 5QU, England; *European Marketing Data and Statistics.*

European Community Information Service, 2100 M Street, NW, Washington, D.C. 20037 (202) 862-9500; *Basic Statistics of the Community,* and *Industrial Production: Quarterly Statistics.*

Organisation for Economic Co-operation and Development (OECD), 2 rue Andre-Pascal, 75 Paris 16, France (Telephone in U.S. (202) 785-6323); *Foreign Trade by Commodities, Indicators of Industrial Activity,* and *Industrial Structure Statistics.*

LUXEMBOURG - TOURISM

Euromonitor Publications Limited, 87-88 Turnmill Street, London EC1M 5QU, England; *European Marketing Data and Statistics.*

European Community Information Service, 2100 M Street, NW, Washington, D.C. 20037 (202) 862-9500; *Transport Annual Statistics.*

G.K. Hall and Company, 70 Lincoln Street, Boston, Massachusetts 02111 (617) 423-3990; *The World in Figures.*

Organisation for Economic Co-operation and Development (OECD), 2 rue Andre-Pascal, 75 Paris 16, France (Telephone in U.S. (202) 785-6323); *Tourism Policy and International Tourism in OECD Member Countries.*

Statistical Office of the United Nations, Publishing Service, New York, New York 10017 (800) 253-9646; *Statistical Yearbook.*

Times Books, 201 East 50th Street, New York, New York 10022 (212) 751-2600; *The Economist Book of Vital World Statistics.*

World Tourism Organization, Calle Capitan Haya 42, E-28020 Madrid, Spain; *Yearbook of Tourism Statistics.*

LUXEMBOURG - TRACTORS IN USE

European Community Information Service, 2100 M Street, NW, Washington, D.C. 20037 (202) 862-9500; *Transport Annual Statistics.*

Statistical Office of the United Nations, Publishing Service, New York, New York 10017 (800) 253-9646; *Statistical Yearbook.*

LUXEMBOURG - TRADE - See LUXEMBOURG - FOREIGN TRADE

LUXEMBOURG - TRADEMARKS AND SERVICE MARKS

Statistical Office of the United Nations, Publishing Service, New York, New York 10017 (800) 253-9646; *Statistical Yearbook.*

World Intellectual Property Organization, 34 Chemin des Colombettes, CH-1211 Geneva 20, Switzerland; *Industrial Property Statistics.*

LUXEMBOURG - TRANSPORTATION AND COMMUNICATIONS

European Community Information Service, 2100 M Street, NW, Washington, D.C. 20037 (202) 862-9500; *Basic Statistics of the Community, Energy Statistics Yearbook, Regions: Statistical Yearbook,* and *Transport Annual Statistics.*

G.K. Hall and Company, 70 Lincoln Street, Boston, Massachusetts 02111 (617) 423-3990; *The World in Figures.*

LUXEMBOURG - TUNGSTEN PRODUCTION AND CONSUMPTION - See LUXEMBOURG - MINING AND MINERAL PRODUCTS

LUXEMBOURG - TURKEYS - See LUXEMBOURG - LIVESTOCK AND POULTRY

LUXEMBOURG - UNEMPLOYMENT

Euromonitor Publications Limited, 87-88 Turnmill Street, London EC1M 5QU, England; *European Marketing Data and Statistics.*

European Community Information Service, 2100 M Street, NW, Washington, D.C. 20037 (202) 862-9500; *Basic Statistics of the Community, Employment and Unemployment, Eurostatistics: Data* for Short-Term Economic Analysis, Labor Force Sample Survey, and Regions: Statistical Yearbook.

International Labour Office, I.L.O. Publications, CH-1211, Geneva 22, Switzerland; Yearbook of Labour Statistics.

Organisation for Economic Co-operation and Development (OECD), 2 rue Andre-Pascal, 75 Paris 16, France (Telephone in U.S. (202) 785-6323); Economic Outlook, Labour Force Statistics, OECD Economic Surveys: Belgium - Luxembourg, and OECD Employment Outlook.

Statistical Office of the United Nations, Publishing Service, New York, New York 10017 (800) 253-9646; Statistical Yearbook.

LUXEMBOURG - URANIUM PRODUCTION AND CONSUMPTION - See LUXEMBOURG - MINING AND MINERAL PRODUCTS

LUXEMBOURG - VANADIUM AND VANADIUM ORE PRODUCTION AND CONSUMPTION - See LUXEMBOURG - MINING AND MINERAL PRODUCTS

LUXEMBOURG - VITAL STATISTICS

Euromonitor Publications Limited, 87-88 Turnmill Street, London EC1M 5QU, England; European Marketing Data and Statistics.

European Community Information Service, 2100 M Street, NW, Washington, D.C. 20037 (202) 862-9500; Basic Statistics of the Community.

G.K. Hall and Company, 70 Lincoln Street, Boston, Massachusetts 02111 (617) 423-3990; The World in Figures.

Statistical Office of the United Nations, Publishing Service, New York, New York 10017 (800) 253-9646; Statistical Yearbook.

World Health Organization, Office of Publications, Avenue Appia, CH-1211 Geneva 27, Switzerland (Telephone Number in U.S. (518) 436-9686); World Health Statistics Annual.

LUXEMBOURG - WAGES

Euromonitor Publications Limited, 87-88 Turnmill Street, London EC1M 5QU, England; European Marketing Data and Statistics.

European Community Information Service, 2100 M Street, NW, Washington, D.C. 20037 (202) 862-9500; Basic Statistics of the Community, Earnings in Agriculture, and Eurostatistics: Data for Short-Term Economic Analysis.

G.K. Hall and Company, 70 Lincoln Street, Boston, Massachusetts 02111 (617) 423-3990; The World in Figures.

International Labour Office, I.L.O. Publications, CH-1211, Geneva 22, Switzerland; Yearbook of Labour Statistics.

Organisation for Economic Co-operation and Development (OECD), 2 rue Andre-Pascal, 75 Paris 16, France (Telephone in U.S. (202) 785-6323); Economic Outlook, and Industrial Structure Statistics.

Statistical Office of the United Nations, Publishing Service, New York, New York 10017 (800) 253-9646; Statistical Yearbook.

LUXEMBOURG - WALNUT PRODUCTION - See LUXEMBOURG - CROPS

LUXEMBOURG - WATERWAYS IN USE

European Community Information Service, 2100 M Street, NW, Washington, D.C. 20037 (202) 862-9500; Basic Statistics of the Community, and Transport Annual Statistics.

Organisation for Economic Co-operation and Development (OECD), 2 rue Andre-Pascal, 75 Paris 16, France (Telephone in U.S. (202) 785-6323); Maritime Transport.

Statistical Office of the United Nations, Publishing Service, New York, New York 10017 (800) 253-9646; Annual Bulletin of Transport Statistics for Europe.

LUXEMBOURG - WEATHER

G.K. Hall and Company, 70 Lincoln Street, Boston, Massachusetts 02111 (617) 423-3990; The World in Figures.

LUXEMBOURG - WELFARE

European Community Information Service, 2100 M Street, NW, Washington, D.C. 20037 (202) 862-9500; Basic Statistics of the Community.

LUXEMBOURG - WELFARE EXPENDITURES

European Community Information Service, 2100 M Street, NW, Washington, D.C. 20037 (202) 862-9500; Basic Statistics of the Community.

International Monetary Fund, 700 Nineteenth Street, NW, Washington, D.C. 20431 (202) 623-7000; Government Finance Statistics Yearbook.

LUXEMBOURG - WHEAT PRODUCTION AND CONSUMPTION - See LUXEMBOURG - CROPS

LUXEMBOURG - WHOLESALE PRICES

European Community Information Service, 2100 M Street, NW, Washington, D.C. 20037 (202) 862-9500; Basic Statistics of the Community.

Statistical Office of the United Nations, Publishing Service, New York, New York 10017 (800) 253-9646; Statistical Yearbook.

LUXEMBOURG - WINE PRODUCTION

European Community Information Service, 2100 M Street, NW, Washington, D.C. 20037 (202) 862-9500; Basic Statistics of the Community.

LUXEMBOURG - WOOD AND WOOD PULP - See LUXEMBOURG - FORESTRY AND FOREST PRODUCTS

LUXEMBOURG - WOOL - INDUSTRIAL CONSUMPTION

Organisation for Economic Co-operation and Development (OECD), 2 rue Andre-Pascal, 75 Paris 16, France (Telephone in U.S. (202) 785-6323); Textile Industry in OECD Countries.

LUXEMBOURG - WOOL PRODUCTION

European Community Information Service, 2100 M Street, NW, Washington, D.C. 20037 (202) 862-9500; Basic Statistics of the Community.

Organisation for Economic Co-operation and Development (OECD), 2 rue Andre-Pascal, 75 Paris 16, France (Telephone in U.S. (202) 785-6323); *Economic Accounts for Agriculture*, and *Textile Industry in OECD Countries*.

LUXEMBOURG - YARN PRODUCTION

European Community Information Service, 2100 M Street, NW, Washington, D.C. 20037 (202) 862-9500; *Basic Statistics of the Community*.

Organisation for Economic Co-operation and Development (OECD), 2 rue Andre-Pascal, 75 Paris 16, France (Telephone in U.S. (202) 785-6323); *Foreign Trade by Commodities*, and *Textile Industry in OECD Countries*.

LUXEMBOURG - ZINC AND ZINC ORE PRODUCTION AND CONSUMPTION - See LUXEMBOURG - MINING AND MINERAL PRODUCTS

LYME DISEASE

U.S. Department of Health and Human Services, Centers for Disease Control and Prevention, 1600 Clifton Road, NE, Atlanta, Georgia 30333 (404) 639-3311; *Summary of Notifiable Diseases, U.S. Morbidity and Mortality Weekly Report*.

M

MACADAMIA NUTS

U.S. Department of Agriculture, National Agricultural Statistics Service, Fourteenth Street and Independence Avenue, SW, Washington, D.C. 20250 (202) 219-1504; *Noncitrus Fruits and Nuts*.

Macau - National Statistical Office

Direccao de Servicos de Estatistica e Lensos, Post Office Box 3022, Macau.

Macau - Primary Statistics Source

Reparticao Provincial dos Servicos de Estatistica, Macau, Macau, *Anuario Estatistico* (Statistical Yearbook), and *Boletim Mensal de Estatistica* (Monthly Bulletin of Statistics).

MACAU - AGRICULTURE

Food and Agricultural Organisation of the United Nations (FAO), Via delle Terme di Caracalla, 00100 Rome, Italy (Telephone Number in U.S. (202) 653-2400); *Production Yearbook, The State of Food and Agriculture*, and *Trade Yearbook*.

G.K. Hall and Company, 70 Lincoln Street, Boston, Massachusetts 02111 (617) 423-3990; *The World in Figures*.

Times Books, 201 East 50th Street, New York, New York 10022 (212) 751-2600; *The Economist Book of Vital World Statistics*.

MACAU - AIRLINE SERVICE

G.K. Hall and Company, 70 Lincoln Street, Boston, Massachusetts 02111 (617) 423-3990; *The World in Figures*.

MACAU - ANIMAL HEALTH

Food and Agricultural Organization of the United Nations (FAO), Via delle Terme di Caracalla, 00100 Rome, Italy (Telephone Number in U.S. (202) 653-2400); *Animal Health Yearbook*.

MACAU - AREA AND DENSITY OF POPULATION

Food and Agricultural Organization of the United Nations (FAO), Via delle Terme di Caracalla, 00100 Rome, Italy (Telephone Number in U.S. (202) 653-2400); *The State of Food and Agriculture*.

G.K. Hall and Company, 70 Lincoln Street, Boston, Massachusetts 02111 (617) 423-3990; *The World in Figures*.

Statistical Office of the United Nations, Publishing Service, New York, New York 10017 (800) 253-9646; *Statistical Yearbook*.

Times Books, 201 East 50th Street, New York, New York 10022 (212) 751-2600; *The Economist Book of Vital World Statistics*.

MACAU - BALANCE OF PAYMENTS

G.K. Hall and Company, 70 Lincoln Street, Boston, Massachusetts 02111 (617) 423-3990; *The World in Figures*.

MACAU - BANKING

G.K. Hall and Company, 70 Lincoln Street, Boston, Massachusetts 02111 (617) 423-3990; *The World in Figures*.

MACAU - BIRTH RATES

The Economist Intelligence Unit (Asia) Limited, 10th Floor, Luk Kwok Centre, 72 Gloucester Road, Wanchai, Hong Kong (Phone Number in U.S. (800) 938-4685); *Asian Market Atlas*

Statistical Office of the United Nations, Publishing Service, New York, New York 10017 (800) 253-9646; *Demographic Yearbook*, and *Statistical Yearbook*.

World Health Organization, Office of Publications, Avenue Appia, CH-1211 Geneva 27, Switzerland (Telephone Number in U.S. (518) 436-9686); *World Health Statistics Annual*.

MACAU - BONDS

G.K. Hall and Company, 70 Lincoln Street, Boston, Massachusetts 02111 (617) 423-3990; *The World in Figures*.

MACAU - BOOK PRODUCTION

G.K. Hall and Company, 70 Lincoln Street, Boston, Massachusetts 02111 (617) 423-3990; *The World in Figures*.

MACAU - BROADCASTING

Billboard Limited, Post Office Box 9027, 1006 AA Amsterdam, The Netherlands (Telephone Number in U.S. (212) 764-7300); *World Radio TV Handbook*.

The Economist Intelligence Unit (Asia) Limited, 10th Floor, Luk Kwok Centre, 72 Gloucester Road, Wanchai, Hong Kong (Phone Number in U.S. (800) 938-4685); *Asian Market Atlas*.

G.K. Hall and Company, 70 Lincoln Street, Boston, Massachusetts 02111 (617) 423-3990; *The World in Figures*.

Times Books, 201 East 50th Street, New York, New York 10022 (212) 751-2600; *The Economist Book of Vital World Statistics*.

MACAU - BUSINESS

G.K. Hall and Company, 70 Lincoln Street, Boston, Massachusetts 02111 (617) 423-3990; *The World in Figures*.

MACAU - CALORIE SUPPLY

Food and Agricultural Organization of the United Nations (FAO), Via delle Terme di Caracalla, 00100 Rome, Italy (Telephone Number in U.S. (202) 653-2400); *The State of Food and Agriculture*.

MACAU - CHEMICAL (ORGANIC) PRODUCTION - See MACAU - MINING AND MINERAL PRODUCTS

MACAU - CLASS STRUCTURE

G.K. Hall and Company, 70 Lincoln Street, Boston, Massachusetts 02111 (617) 423-3990; *The World in Figures*.

MACAU - CLIMATE

G.K. Hall and Company, 70 Lincoln Street, Boston, Massachusetts 02111 (617) 423-3990; *The World in Figures*.

MACAU - COAL PRODUCTION - See MACAU - MINING AND MINERAL PRODUCTS

MACAU - COMMUNICATIONS

G.K. Hall and Company, 70 Lincoln Street, Boston, Massachusetts 02111 (617) 423-3990; *The World in Figures*.

MACAU - CONSTRUCTION INDUSTRY

Statistical Office of the United Nations, Publishing Service, New York, New York 10017 (800) 253-9646; *Statistical Yearbook*.

MACAU - CONSTRUCTION STATISTICS BY CATEGORY OF BUILDINGS

Statistical Office of the United Nations, Publishing Service, New York, New York 10017 (800) 253-9646; *Construction Statistics Yearbook*.

MACAU - CONSUMER PRICE INDEX

G.K. Hall and Company, 70 Lincoln Street, Boston, Massachusetts 02111 (617) 423-3990; *The World in Figures*.

MACAU - CONSUMPTION

G.K. Hall and Company, 70 Lincoln Street, Boston, Massachusetts 02111 (617) 423-3990; *The World in Figures*.

MACAU - CORN PRODUCTION - See MACAU - CROPS

MACAU - CORPORATE TAXES - See MACAU - TAXATION

MACAU - CROPS

Food and Agricultural Organization of the United Nations (FAO), Via delle Terme di Caracalla, 00100 Rome, Italy (Telephone Number in U.S. (202) 653-2400); *The State of Food and Agriculture*.

G.K. Hall and Company, 70 Lincoln Street, Boston, Massachusetts 02111 (617) 423-3990; *The World in Figures*.

MACAU - CUSTOMS DUTIES

G.K. Hall and Company, 70 Lincoln Street, Boston, Massachusetts 02111 (617) 423-3990; *The World in Figures*.

MACAU - DAIRY PRODUCTS

Food and Agricultural Organization of the United Nations (FAO), Via delle Terme di Caracalla, 00100 Rome, Italy (Telephone Number in U.S. (202) 653-2400); *The State of Food and Agriculture*.

MACAU - DEATH RATES

The Economist Intelligence Unit (Asia) Limited, 10th Floor, Luk Kwok Centre, 72 Gloucester Road, Wanchai, Hong Kong (Phone Number in U.S. (800) 938-4685); *Asian Market Atlas*.

G.K. Hall and Company, 70 Lincoln Street, Boston, Massachusetts 02111 (617) 423-3990; *The World in Figures*.

MACAU - DEFENSE EXPENDITURES

G.K. Hall and Company, 70 Lincoln Street, Boston, Massachusetts 02111 (617) 423-3990; *The World in Figures*.

MACAU - DEMOGRAPHY

The Economist Intelligence Unit, 111 West 57th Street, New York, New York 10019 (800) 938-4685; *The World Market Atlas*.

The Economist Intelligence Unit (Asia) Limited, 10th Floor, Luk Kwok Centre, 72 Gloucester Road, Wanchai, Hong Kong (Phone Number in U.S. (800) 938-4685); *Asian Market Atlas*.

G.K. Hall and Company, 70 Lincoln Street, Boston, Massachusetts 02111 (617) 423-3990; *The World in Figures*.

MACAU - DEVELOPMENT ASSISTANCE

G.K. Hall and Company, 70 Lincoln Street, Boston, Massachusetts 02111 (617) 423-3990; *The World in Figures*.

Statistical Office of the United Nations, Publishing Service, New York, New York 10017 (800) 253-9646; *Statistical Yearbook*.

MACAU - DISEASE

G.K. Hall and Company, 70 Lincoln Street, Boston, Massachusetts 02111 (617) 423-3990; *The World in Figures*.

MACAU - DIVORCE

Statistical Office of the United Nations, Publishing Service, New York, New York 10017 (800) 253-9646; *Demographic Yearbook*.

MACAU - DOMESTIC PRODUCT

G.K. Hall and Company, 70 Lincoln Street, Boston, Massachusetts 02111 (617) 423-3990; *The World in Figures*.

MACAU - ECONOMY

G.K. Hall and Company, 70 Lincoln Street, Boston, Massachusetts 02111 (617) 423-3990; *The World in Figures*.

MACAU - EDUCATION

The Economist Intelligence Unit, 111 West 57th Street, New York, New York 10019 (800) 938-4685; *The World Market Atlas*.

The Economist Intelligence Unit (Asia) Limited, 10th Floor, Luk Kwok Centre, 72 Gloucester Road, Wanchai, Hong Kong (Phone Number in U.S. (800) 938-4685); *Asian Market Atlas*.

G.K. Hall and Company, 70 Lincoln Street, Boston, Massachusetts 02111 (617) 423-3990; *The World in Figures*.

United Nations Educational, Scientific and Cultural Organization (UNESCO), 7 Place de Fontenoy, F-75700 Paris, France (Telephone Number in U.S. (212) 963-5981); *Statistical Yearbook*.

MACAU - EGG PRODUCTION AND CONSUMPTION - See MACAU - DAIRY PRODUCTS

MACAU - ELECTRICITY

Statistical Office of the United Nations, Publishing Service, New York, New York 10017 (800) 253-9646; *Statistical Yearbook*.

Times Books, 201 East 50th Street, New York, New York 10022 (212) 751-2600; *The Economist Book of Vital World Statistics*.

United Nations Educational, Scientific and Cultural Organization (UNESCO), 7 Place de Fontenoy, F-75700 Paris, France (Telephone Number in U.S. (212) 963-5981); *Statistical Yearbook*.

MACAU - ENERGY

Food and Agricultural Organization of the United Nations (FAO), Via delle Terme di Caracalla, 00100 Rome, Italy (Telephone Number in U.S. (202) 653-2400); *The State of Food and Agriculture*.

G.K. Hall and Company, 70 Lincoln Street, Boston, Massachusetts 02111 (617) 423-3990; *The World in Figures*.

Statistical Office of the United Nations, Publishing Service, New York, New York 10017 (800) 253-9646; *Energy Statistics Yearbook, Statistical Yearbook*, and *World Energy Supplies*.

Times Books, 201 East 50th Street, New York, New York 10022 (212) 751-2600; *The Economist Book of Vital World Statistics*.

MACAU - EXCHANGE RATES

The Economist Intelligence Unit (Asia) Limited, 10th Floor, Luk Kwok Centre, 72 Gloucester Road, Wanchai, Hong Kong (Phone Number in U.S. (800) 938-4685); *Asian Market Atlas*.

MACAU - EXPORTS

The Economist Intelligence Unit, 111 West 57th Street, New York, New York 10019 (800) 938-4685; *The World Market Atlas*.

The Economist Intelligence Unit (Asia) Limited, 10th Floor, Luk Kwok Centre, 72 Gloucester Road, Wanchai, Hong Kong (Phone Number in U.S. (800) 938-4685); *Asian Market Atlas*.

Food and Agricultural Organization of the United Nations (FAO), Via delle Terme di Caracalla, 00100 Rome, Italy (Telephone Number in U.S. (202) 653-2400); *The State of Food and Agriculture*.

G.K. Hall and Company, 70 Lincoln Street, Boston, Massachusetts 02111 (617) 423-3990; *The World in Figures*.

International Monetary Fund, 700 Nineteenth Street, NW, Washington, D.C. 20431 (202) 623-7000; *Direction of Trade Statistics*.

Times Books, 201 East 50th Street, New York, New York 10022 (212) 751-2600; *The Economist Book of Vital World Statistics*.

MACAU - EXTERNAL TRADE

Food and Agricultural Organization of the United Nations (FAO), Via delle Terme di Caracalla, 00100 Rome, Italy (Telephone Number in U.S. (202) 653-2400); *The State of Food and Agriculture*, and *Trade Yearbook*.

G.K. Hall and Company, 70 Lincoln Street, Boston, Massachusetts 02111 (617) 423-3990; *The World in Figures*.

Statistical Office of the United Nations, Publishing Service, New York, New York 10017 (800) 253-9646; *Statistical Yearbook*.

MACAU - FARM CROPS - See MACAU - CROPS

MACAU - FERTILIZER

The Economist Intelligence Unit (Asia) Limited, 10th Floor, Luk Kwok Centre, 72 Gloucester Road, Wanchai, Hong Kong (Phone Number in U.S. (800) 938-4685); *Asian Market Atlas*.

Food and Agricultural Organization of the United Nations (FAO), Via delle Terme di Caracalla, 00100 Rome, Italy (Telephone Number in U.S. (202) 653-2400); *Fertilizer Yearbook*, and *The State of Food and Agriculture*.

Statistical Office of the United Nations, Publishing Service, New York, New York 10017 (800) 253-9646; *Statistical Yearbook*.

MACAU - FETAL MORTALITY

Statistical Office of the United Nations, Publishing Service, New York, New York 10017 (800) 253-9646; *Demographic Yearbook*.

World Health Organization, Office of Publications, Avenue Appia, CH-1211 Geneva 27, Switzerland (Telephone Number in U.S. (518) 436-9686); *World Health Statistics Annual*.

MACAU - FINANCE

G.K. Hall and Company, 70 Lincoln Street, Boston, Massachusetts 02111 (617) 423-3990; *The World in Figures*.

MACAU - FISHERIES

Food and Agricultural Organization of the United Nations (FAO), Via delle Terme di Caracalla, 00100 Rome, Italy (Telephone Number in U.S. (202) 653-2400); *The State of Food and Agriculture*, and *Yearbook of Fishery Statistics*.

Statistical Office of the United Nations, Publishing Service, New York, New York 10017 (800) 253-9646; *Statistical Yearbook*.

MACAU - FOOD

Food and Agricultural Organization of the United Nations (FAO), Via delle Terme di Caracalla, 00100 Rome, Italy (Telephone Number in U.S. (202) 653-2400); *Production Yearbook*, and *The State of Food and Agriculture*.

G.K. Hall and Company, 70 Lincoln Street, Boston, Massachusetts 02111 (617) 423-3990; *The World in Figures*.

MACAU - FOREIGN AID

G.K. Hall and Company, 70 Lincoln Street, Boston, Massachusetts 02111 (617) 423-3990; *The World in Figures*.

MACAU - FOREIGN TRADE

The Economist Intelligence Unit (Asia) Limited, 10th Floor, Luk Kwok Centre, 72 Gloucester Road, Wanchai, Hong Kong (Phone Number in U.S. (800) 938-4685); *Asian Market Atlas*.

Food and Agricultural Organization of the United Nations (FAO), Via delle Terme di Caracalla, 00100 Rome, Italy (Telephone Number in U.S. (202) 653-2400); *The State of Food and Agriculture*.

G.K. Hall and Company, 70 Lincoln Street, Boston, Massachusetts 02111 (617) 423-3990; *The World in Figures*.

Statistical Office of the United Nations, Publishing Service, New York, New York 10017 (800) 253-9646; *International Trade Statistics Yearbook*, and *Statistical Yearbook*.

MACAU - FORESTRY AND FOREST PRODUCTS

The Economist Intelligence Unit (Asia) Limited, 10th Floor, Luk Kwok Centre, 72 Gloucester Road, Wanchai, Hong Kong (Phone Number in U.S. (800) 938-4685); *Asian Market Atlas*.

Food and Agricultural Organization of the United Nations (FAO), Via delle Terme di Caracalla, 00100 Rome, Italy (Telephone Number in U.S. (202) 653-2400); *The State of Food and Agriculture*, and *Yearbook of Forest Products*.

G.K. Hall and Company, 70 Lincoln Street, Boston, Massachusetts 02111 (617) 423-3990; *The World in Figures*.

Statistical Office of the United Nations, Publishing Service, New York, New York 10017 (800) 253-9646; *Statistical Yearbook*.

United Nations Educational, Scientific and Cultural Organization (UNESCO), 7 Place de Fontenoy, F-75700 Paris, France (Telephone Number in U.S. (212) 963-5981); *Statistical Yearbook*.

MACAU - GENERAL INDUSTRIAL STATISTICS

Statistical Office of the United Nations, Publishing Service, New York, New York 10017 (800) 253-9646; *Industrial Statistics Yearbook*.

MACAU - GENERAL MORTALITY

Statistical Office of the United Nations, Publishing Service, New York, New York 10017 (800) 253-9646; *Statistical Yearbook*.

World Health Organization, Office of Publications, Avenue Appia, CH-1211 Geneva 27, Switzerland (Telephone Number in U.S. (518) 436-9686); *World Health Statistics Annual*.

MACAU - GOVERNMENT

G.K. Hall and Company, 70 Lincoln Street, Boston, Massachusetts 02111 (617) 423-3990; *The World in Figures*.

MACAU - GRAIN PRODUCTION - See MACAU - CROPS

MACAU - GROSS DOMESTIC PRODUCT

The Economist Intelligence Unit, 111 West 57th Street, New York, New York 10019 (800) 938-4685; *The World Market Atlas*.

The Economist Intelligence Unit (Asia) Limited, 10th Floor, Luk Kwok Centre, 72 Gloucester Road, Wanchai, Hong Kong (Phone Number in U.S. (800) 938-4685); *Asian Market Atlas*.

G.K. Hall and Company, 70 Lincoln Street, Boston, Massachusetts 02111 (617) 423-3990; *The World in Figures*.

Times Books, 201 East 50th Street, New York, New York 10022 (212) 751-2600; *The Economist Book of Vital World Statistics*.

MACAU - HEALTH

The Economist Intelligence Unit (Asia) Limited, 10th Floor, Luk Kwok Centre, 72 Gloucester Road, Wanchai, Hong Kong (Phone Number in U.S. (800) 938-4685); *Asian Market Atlas*.

G.K. Hall and Company, 70 Lincoln Street, Boston, Massachusetts 02111 (617) 423-3990; *The World in Figures*.

Statistical Office of the United Nations, Publishing Service, New York, New York 10017 (800) 253-9646; *Statistical Yearbook*.

Times Books, 201 East 50th Street, New York, New York 10022 (212) 751-2600; *The Economist Book of Vital World Statistics*.

MACAU - HIDE PRODUCTION

Food and Agricultural Organization of the United Nations (FAO), Via delle Terme di Caracalla, 00100 Rome, Italy (Telephone Number in U.S. (202) 653-2400); *Production Yearbook*.

MACAU - HIGHWAYS

The Economist Intelligence Unit (Asia) Limited, 10th Floor, Luk Kwok Centre, 72 Gloucester Road, Wanchai, Hong Kong (Phone Number in U.S. (800) 938-4685); *Asian Market Atlas*.

G.K. Hall and Company, 70 Lincoln Street, Boston, Massachusetts 02111 (617) 423-3990; *The World in Figures*.

MACAU - ILLITERATE POPULATION

The Economist Intelligence Unit, 111 West 57th Street, New York, New York 10019 (800) 938-4685; *The World Market Atlas*.

G.K. Hall and Company, 70 Lincoln Street, Boston, Massachusetts 02111 (617) 423-3990; *The World in Figures*.

United Nations Educational, Scientific and Cultural Organization (UNESCO), 7 Place de Fontenoy, F-75700 Paris, France (Telephone Number in U.S. (212) 963-5981); *Statistical Yearbook*.

MACAU - IMPORTS

The Economist Intelligence Unit, 111 West 57th Street, New York, New York 10019 (800) 938-4685; *The World Market Atlas*.

The Economist Intelligence Unit (Asia) Limited, 10th Floor, Luk Kwok Centre, 72 Gloucester Road, Wanchai, Hong Kong (Phone Number in U.S. (800) 938-4685); *Asian Market Atlas*.

Food and Agricultural Organization of the United Nations (FAO), Via delle Terme di Caracalla, 00100 Rome, Italy (Telephone Number in U.S. (202) 653-2400); *The State of Food and Agriculture*.

G.K. Hall and Company, 70 Lincoln Street, Boston, Massachusetts 02111 (617) 423-3990; *The World in Figures*.

International Monetary Fund, 700 Nineteenth Street, NW, Washington, D.C. 20431 (202) 623-7000; *Direction of Trade Statistics*.

Statistical Office of the United Nations, Publishing Service, New York, New York 10017 (800) 253-9646; *Trade in Manufactures of*

Developing Countries.

Times Books, 201 East 50th Street, New York, New York 10022 (212) 751-2600; *The Economist Book of Vital World Statistics.*

MACAU - INDUSTRY

G.K. Hall and Company, 70 Lincoln Street, Boston, Massachusetts 02111 (617) 423-3990; *The World in Figures.*

Times Books, 201 East 50th Street, New York, New York 10022 (212) 751-2600; *The Economist Book of Vital World Statistics.*

World Intellectual Property Organization, 34 Chemin des Colombettes, CH-1211 Geneva 20, Switzerland; *Industrial Property Statistics.*

MACAU - INFANT AND MATERNAL MORTALITY

The Economist Intelligence Unit (Asia) Limited, 10th Floor, Luk Kwok Centre, 72 Gloucester Road, Wanchai, Hong Kong (Phone Number in U.S. (800) 938-4685); *Asian Market Atlas.*

Statistical Office of the United Nations, Publishing Service, New York, New York 10017 (800) 253-9646; *Demographic Yearbook*, and *Statistical Yearbook.*

World Health Organization, Office of Publications, Avenue Appia, CH-1211 Geneva 27, Switzerland (Telephone Number in U.S. (518) 436-9686); *World Health Statistics Annual.*

MACAU - LABOR FORCE

The Economist Intelligence Unit (Asia) Limited, 10th Floor, Luk Kwok Centre, 72 Gloucester Road, Wanchai, Hong Kong (Phone Number in U.S. (800) 938-4685); *Asian Market Atlas.*

Food and Agricultural Organization of the United Nations (FAO), Via delle Terme di Caracalla, 00100 Rome, Italy (Telephone Number in U.S. (202) 653-2400); *The State of Food and Agriculture.*

G.K. Hall and Company, 70 Lincoln Street, Boston, Massachusetts 02111 (617) 423-3990; *The World in Figures.*

MACAU - LAND USE

Food and Agricultural Organization of the United Nations (FAO), Via delle Terme di Caracalla, 00100 Rome, Italy (Telephone Number in U.S. (202) 653-2400); *Production Yearbook.*

G.K. Hall and Company, 70 Lincoln Street, Boston, Massachusetts 02111 (617) 423-3990; *The World in Figures.*

MACAU - LIVESTOCK AND POULTRY

Food and Agricultural Organization of the United Nations (FAO), Via delle Terme di Caracalla, 00100 Rome, Italy (Telephone Number in U.S. (202) 653-2400); *Production Yearbook*, and *The State of Food and Agriculture.*

G.K. Hall and Company, 70 Lincoln Street, Boston, Massachusetts 02111 (617) 423-3990; *The World in Figures.*

MACAU - LIVING LEVELS

G.K. Hall and Company, 70 Lincoln Street, Boston, Massachusetts 02111 (617) 423-3990; *The World in Figures.*

MACAU - MAIL - PIECES SENT OR RECEIVED

Statistical Office of the United Nations, Publishing Service, New York, New York 10017 (800) 253-9646; *Statistical Yearbook.*

MACAU - MANUFACTURING

G.K. Hall and Company, 70 Lincoln Street, Boston, Massachusetts 02111 (617) 423-3990; *The World in Figures.*

Statistical Office of the United Nations, Publishing Service, New York, New York 10017 (800) 253-9646; *Statistical Yearbook.*

MACAU - MARRIAGE RATES

Statistical Office of the United Nations, Publishing Service, New York, New York 10017 (800) 253-9646; *Demographic Yearbook.*

MACAU - MEAT PRODUCTION - See MACAU - LIVESTOCK AND POULTRY

MACAU - MERCHANT SHIPPING

G.K. Hall and Company, 70 Lincoln Street, Boston, Massachusetts 02111 (617) 423-3990; *The World in Figures.*

Statistical Office of the United Nations, Publishing Service, New York, New York 10017 (800) 253-9646; *Statistical Yearbook.*

Times Books, 201 East 50th Street, New York, New York 10022 (212) 751-2600; *The Economist Book of Vital World Statistics.*

MACAU - MILITARY

The Economist Intelligence Unit (Asia) Limited, 10th Floor, Luk Kwok Centre, 72 Gloucester Road, Wanchai, Hong Kong (Phone Number in U.S. (800) 938-4685); *Asian Market Atlas.*

G.K. Hall and Company, 70 Lincoln Street, Boston, Massachusetts 02111 (617) 423-3990; *The World in Figures.*

MACAU - MINING AND MINERAL PRODUCTS

G.K. Hall and Company, 70 Lincoln Street, Boston, Massachusetts 02111 (617) 423-3990; *The World in Figures.*

MACAU - MONEY SUPPLY

G.K. Hall and Company, 70 Lincoln Street, Boston, Massachusetts 02111 (617) 423-3990; *The World in Figures.*

MACAU - MOTION PICTURES

Statistical Office of the United Nations, Publishing Service, New York, New York 10017 (800) 253-9646; *Statistical Yearbook.*

MACAU - MOTOR VEHICLES IN USE

G.K. Hall and Company, 70 Lincoln Street, Boston, Massachusetts 02111 (617) 423-3990; *The World in Figures.*

Statistical Office of the United Nations, Publishing Service, New York, New York 10017 (800) 253-9646; *Statistical Yearbook.*

MACAU - NATALITY - See MACAU - BIRTH RATES

MACAU - NATIONAL INCOME

G.K. Hall and Company, 70 Lincoln Street, Boston, Massachusetts 02111 (617) 423-3990; *The World in Figures.*

MACAU - NEWSPAPER PRODUCTION - See MACAU - FORESTRY AND FOREST PRODUCTS

MACAU - NEWSPRINT - See MACAU - FORESTRY AND FOREST PRODUCTS

MACAU - OCCUPATIONS - See MACAU - LABOR FORCE

MACAU - PAPER - See MACAU - FORESTRY AND FOREST PRODUCTS

MACAU - PATENTS

World Intellectual Property Organization, 34 Chemin des Colombettes, CH-1211 Geneva 20, Switzerland; *Industrial Property Statistics.*

MACAU - PESTICIDE USE

Food and Agricultural Organization of the United Nations (FAO), Via delle Terme di Caracalla, 00100 Rome, Italy (Telephone Number in U.S. (202) 653-2400); *The State of Food and Agriculture.*

MACAU - PETROLEUM INDUSTRY

Food and Agricultural Organization of the United Nations (FAO), Via delle Terme di Caracalla, 00100 Rome, Italy (Telephone Number in U.S. (202) 653-2400); *The State of Food and Agriculture.*

G.K. Hall and Company, 70 Lincoln Street, Boston, Massachusetts 02111 (617) 423-3990; *The World in Figures.*

MACAU - POPULATION

The Economist Intelligence Unit, 111 West 57th Street, New York, New York 10019 (800) 938-4685; *The World Market Atlas.*

The Economist Intelligence Unit (Asia) Limited, 10th Floor, Luk Kwok Centre, 72 Gloucester Road, Wanchai, Hong Kong (Phone Number in U.S. (800) 938-4685); *Asian Market Atlas.*

Food and Agricultural Organization of the United Nations (FAO), Via delle Terme di Caracalla, 00100 Rome, Italy (Telephone Number in U.S. (202) 653-2400); *Production Yearbook.*

G.K. Hall and Company, 70 Lincoln Street, Boston, Massachusetts 02111 (617) 423-3990; *The World in Figures.*

Statistical Office of the United Nations, Publishing Service, New York, New York 10017 (800) 253-9646; *Demographic Yearbook,* and *Statistical Yearbook.*

Times Books, 201 East 50th Street, New York, New York 10022 (212) 751-2600; *The Economist Book of Vital World Statistics.*

World Health Organization, Office of Publications, Avenue Appia, CH-1211 Geneva 27, Switzerland (Telephone Number in U.S. (518) 436-9686); *World Health Statistics Annual.*

MACAU - PRICES

Food and Agricultural Organization of the United Nations (FAO), Via delle Terme di Caracalla, 00100 Rome, Italy (Telephone Number in U.S. (202) 653-2400); *Production Yearbook,* and *The State of Food*

and Agriculture.

G.K. Hall and Company, 70 Lincoln Street, Boston, Massachusetts 02111 (617) 423-3990; *The World in Figures.*

MACAU - PRINTING AND WRITING PAPER - See MACAU - FORESTRY AND FOREST PRODUCTS

MACAU - PRODUCTION

G.K. Hall and Company, 70 Lincoln Street, Boston, Massachusetts 02111 (617) 423-3990; *The World in Figures.*

MACAU - RADIO BROADCASTING - See MACAU - BROADCASTING

MACAU - RAILWAY USE

G.K. Hall and Company, 70 Lincoln Street, Boston, Massachusetts 02111 (617) 423-3990; *The World in Figures.*

MACAU - RETAIL TRADE

G.K. Hall and Company, 70 Lincoln Street, Boston, Massachusetts 02111 (617) 423-3990; *The World in Figures.*

MACAU - ROUNDWOOD PRODUCTION - See MACAU - FORESTRY AND FOREST PRODUCTS

MACAU - SAWNWOOD PRODUCTION - See MACAU - FORESTRY AND FOREST PRODUCTS

MACAU - SOCIAL DATA

G.K. Hall and Company, 70 Lincoln Street, Boston, Massachusetts 02111 (617) 423-3990; *The World in Figures.*

MACAU - STOCKS - COMMODITY - MARKET PRICE - INDEX

Food and Agricultural Organization of the United Nations (FAO), Via delle Terme di Caracalla, 00100 Rome, Italy (Telephone Number in U.S. (202) 653-2400); *The State of Food and Agriculture.*

MACAU - TAXATION

G.K. Hall and Company, 70 Lincoln Street, Boston, Massachusetts 02111 (617) 423-3990; *The World in Figures.*

MACAU - TELEPHONES IN USE

American Telephone and Telegraph Company, 26 Parsippany Road, Whippany, New Jersey 07981 (800) 338-4038; *The World's Telephones.*

The Economist Intelligence Unit (Asia) Limited, 10th Floor, Luk Kwok Centre, 72 Gloucester Road, Wanchai, Hong Kong (Phone Number in U.S. (800) 938-4685); *Asian Market Atlas.*

G.K. Hall and Company, 70 Lincoln Street, Boston, Massachusetts 02111 (617) 423-3990; *The World in Figures.*

Statistical Office of the United Nations, Publishing Service, New York, New York 10017 (800) 253-9646; *Statistical Yearbook.*

MACAU - TELEVISION BROADCASTING - See MACAU - BROADCASTING

MACAU - TEXTILE INDUSTRY

G.K. Hall and Company, 70 Lincoln Street, Boston, Massachusetts 02111 (617) 423-3990; *The World in Figures.*

MACAU - TOURISM

G.K. Hall and Company, 70 Lincoln Street, Boston, Massachusetts 02111 (617) 423-3990; *The World in Figures.*

Statistical Office of the United Nations, Publishing Service, New York, New York 10017 (800) 253-9646; *Statistical Yearbook.*

Times Books, 201 East 50th Street, New York, New York 10022 (212) 751-2600; *The Economist Book of Vital World Statistics.*

World Tourism Organization, Calle Capitan Haya 42, E-28020 Madrid, Spain; *Yearbook of Tourism Statistics.*

MACAU - TRADE - See MACAU - FOREIGN TRADE

MACAU - TRADEMARKS AND SERVICE MARKS

World Intellectual Property Organization, 34 Chemin des Colombettes, CH-1211 Geneva 20, Switzerland; *Industrial Property Statistics.*

MACAU - TRANSPORTATION AND COMMUNICATIONS

The Economist Intelligence Unit (Asia) Limited, 10th Floor, Luk Kwok Centre, 72 Gloucester Road, Wanchai, Hong Kong (Phone Number in U.S. (800) 938-4685); *Asian Market Atlas.*

G.K. Hall and Company, 70 Lincoln Street, Boston, Massachusetts 02111 (617) 423-3990; *The World in Figures.*

MACAU - VITAL STATISTICS

G.K. Hall and Company, 70 Lincoln Street, Boston, Massachusetts 02111 (617) 423-3990; *The World in Figures.*

Statistical Office of the United Nations, Publishing Service, New York, New York 10017 (800) 253-9646; *Statistical Yearbook.*

World Health Organization, Office of Publications, Avenue Appia, CH-1211 Geneva 27, Switzerland (Telephone Number in U.S. (518) 436-9686); *World Health Statistics Annual.*

MACAU - WAGES

G.K. Hall and Company, 70 Lincoln Street, Boston, Massachusetts 02111 (617) 423-3990; *The World in Figures.*

MACAU - WEATHER

G.K. Hall and Company, 70 Lincoln Street, Boston, Massachusetts 02111 (617) 423-3990; *The World in Figures.*

MACAU - WINE PRODUCTION

Statistical Office of the United Nations, Publishing Service, New York, New York 10017 (800) 253-9646; *Statistical Yearbook.*

MACEDONIA - See also YUGOSLAVIA

MACEDONIA - AGRICULTURE

Encyclopedia Britannica, Incorporated, 310 South Michigan Avenue, Chicago, Illinois 60604 (312) 347-7000; *Britannica World Data.*

MACEDONIA - AIRLINE SERVICE

Encyclopedia Britannica, Incorporated, 310 South Michigan Avenue, Chicago, Illinois 60604 (312) 347-7000; *Britannica World Data.*

MACEDONIA - BIRTH RATES

Encyclopedia Britannica, Incorporated, 310 South Michigan Avenue, Chicago, Illinois 60604 (312) 347-7000; *Britannica World Data.*

MACEDONIA - CONSTRUCTION INDUSTRY

Encyclopedia Britannica, Incorporated, 310 South Michigan Avenue, Chicago, Illinois 60604 (312) 347-7000; *Britannica World Data.*

MACEDONIA - DEMOGRAPHY

Encyclopedia Britannica, Incorporated, 310 South Michigan Avenue, Chicago, Illinois 60604 (312) 347-7000; *Britannica World Data.*

MACEDONIA - DIVORCE RATES

Encyclopedia Britannica, Incorporated, 310 South Michigan Avenue, Chicago, Illinois 60604 (312) 347-7000; *Britannica World Data.*

MACEDONIA - ECONOMY

Encyclopedia Britannica, Incorporated, 310 South Michigan Avenue, Chicago, Illinois 60604 (312) 347-7000; *Britannica World Data.*

MACEDONIA - EDUCATION

Encyclopedia Britannica, Incorporated, 310 South Michigan Avenue, Chicago, Illinois 60604 (312) 347-7000; *Britannica World Data.*

MACEDONIA - ENERGY

Encyclopedia Britannica, Incorporated, 310 South Michigan Avenue, Chicago, Illinois 60604 (312) 347-7000; *Britannica World Data.*

MACEDONIA - EXPORTS

Encyclopedia Britannica, Incorporated, 310 South Michigan Avenue, Chicago, Illinois 60604 (312) 347-7000; *Britannica World Data.*

MACEDONIA - FERTILITY RATES

Encyclopedia Britannica, Incorporated, 310 South Michigan Avenue, Chicago, Illinois 60604 (312) 347-7000; *Britannica World Data.*

MACEDONIA - FISHERIES

Encyclopedia Britannica, Incorporated, 310 South Michigan Avenue, Chicago, Illinois 60604 (312) 347-7000; *Britannica World Data.*

MACEDONIA - FOREIGN TRADE

Encyclopedia Britannica, Incorporated, 310 South Michigan Avenue, Chicago, Illinois 60604 (312) 347-7000; *Britannica World Data.*

MACEDONIA - FORESTRY AND FOREST PRODUCTS

Encyclopedia Britannica, Incorporated, 310 South Michigan Avenue, Chicago, Illinois 60604 (312) 347-7000; *Britannica World Data.*

MACEDONIA - HEALTH

Encyclopedia Britannica, Incorporated, 310 South Michigan Avenue, Chicago, Illinois 60604 (312) 347-7000; *Britannica World Data.*

MACEDONIA - HIGHWAYS

Encyclopedia Britannica, Incorporated, 310 South Michigan Avenue, Chicago, Illinois 60604 (312) 347-7000; *Britannica World Data.*

MACEDONIA - IMPORTS

Encyclopedia Britannica, Incorporated, 310 South Michigan Avenue, Chicago, Illinois 60604 (312) 347-7000; *Britannica World Data.*

MACEDONIA - LAND USE

Encyclopedia Britannica, Incorporated, 310 South Michigan Avenue, Chicago, Illinois 60604 (312) 347-7000; *Britannica World Data.*

MACEDONIA - LIVESTOCK AND POULTRY

Encyclopedia Britannica, Incorporated, 310 South Michigan Avenue, Chicago, Illinois 60604 (312) 347-7000; *Britannica World Data.*

MACEDONIA - MANUFACTURING

Encyclopedia Britannica, Incorporated, 310 South Michigan Avenue, Chicago, Illinois 60604 (312) 347-7000; *Britannica World Data.*

MACEDONIA - MARRIAGE RATES

Encyclopedia Britannica, Incorporated, 310 South Michigan Avenue, Chicago, Illinois 60604 (312) 347-7000; *Britannica World Data.*

MACEDONIA - MILITARY

The International Institute for Strategic Studies, 23 Tavistock Street, London WC2E 7NQ, England; *The Military Balance.*

MACEDONIA - MINING AND MINERAL PRODUCTS

Encyclopedia Britannica, Incorporated, 310 South Michigan Avenue, Chicago, Illinois 60604 (312) 347-7000; *Britannica World Data.*

MACEDONIA - POPULATION

Encyclopedia Britannica, Incorporated, 310 South Michigan Avenue, Chicago, Illinois 60604 (312) 347-7000; *Britannica World Data.*

MACEDONIA - RADIO RECEIVERS

Encyclopedia Britannica, Incorporated, 310 South Michigan Avenue, Chicago, Illinois 60604 (312) 347-7000; *Britannica World Data.*

MACEDONIA - RAILWAYS

Encyclopedia Britannica, Incorporated, 310 South Michigan Avenue, Chicago, Illinois 60604 (312) 347-7000; *Britannica World Data.*

MACEDONIA - ROADS - See MACEDONIA - HIGHWAYS

MACEDONIA - TELEPHONES IN USE

Encyclopedia Britannica, Incorporated, 310 South Michigan Avenue, Chicago, Illinois 60604 (312) 347-7000; *Britannica World Data.*

MACEDONIA - TELEVISION RECEIVERS

Encyclopedia Britannica, Incorporated, 310 South Michigan Avenue, Chicago, Illinois 60604 (312) 347-7000; *Britannica World Data.*

MACEDONIA - TRANSPORTATION AND COMMUNICATIONS

Encyclopedia Britannica, Incorporated, 310 South Michigan Avenue, Chicago, Illinois 60604 (312) 347-7000; *Britannica World Data.*

MACEDONIA - VITAL STATISTICS

Encyclopedia Britannica, Incorporated, 310 South Michigan Avenue, Chicago, Illinois 60604 (312) 347-7000; *Britannica World Data.*

MACHINE TOOLS

U.S. Department of Commerce, Bureau of the Census, Suitland, Maryland 20233 (301) 763-4040; *Current Business Reports, Combined Annual and Revised Monthly Wholesale Trade,* and *Current Industrial Reports, Manufactures' Shipments, Inventories, and Orders.*

U.S. Department of Labor, Bureau of Labor Statistics, Two Massachusetts Avenue, NE, Washington, D.C. 20212 (202) 606-7828; *Productivity Measures for Selected Industries and Government Services,* and unpublished data.

MACHINERY - EXCEPT ELECTRICAL - MANUFACTURING - CAPITAL

U.S. Department of Commerce, Bureau of Economic Analysis, Fourteenth Street between Constitution Avenue and E Street, NW, Washington, D.C. 20230 (202) 606-9900; *Fixed Reproducible Tangible Wealth in the U.S.,* and *Survey of Current Business.*

U.S. Department of Commerce, Bureau of the Census, Suitland, Maryland 20233 (301) 763-4040; *Current Industrial Reports.*

MACHINERY - EXCEPT ELECTRICAL - MANUFACTURING - EARNINGS

U.S. Department of Commerce, Bureau of the Census, Suitland, Maryland 20233 (301) 763-4040; *Census of Manufactures,* and *Annual Survey of Manufactures.*

U.S. Department of Labor, Bureau of Labor Statistics, Two Massachusetts Avenue, NE, Washington, D.C. 20212 (202) 606-7828; *Employment and Earnings,* and Bulletins 2307 and 2429.

MACHINERY - EXCEPT ELECTRICAL - MANUFACTURING - EMPLOYEES

U.S. Department of Commerce, Bureau of the Census, Suitland, Maryland 20233 (301) 763-4040; *United States Census of Manufactures, Annual Survey of Manufactures,* and *County Business Patterns.*

Department of Labor, Bureau of Labor Statistics, Two Massachusetts Avenue, NE, Washington, D.C. 20212 (202) 606-7828; *Employment and Earnings,* and Bulletins 2307 and 2429.

MACHINERY - EXCEPT ELECTRICAL - MANUFACTURING - ESTABLISHMENTS

U.S. Department of Commerce, Bureau of the Census, Suitland, Maryland 20233 (301) 763-4040; *Census of Manufactures,* and *Annual Survey of Manufactures.*

MACHINERY - EXCEPT ELECTRICAL - MANUFACTURING - FOREIGN TRADE

U.S. Department of Commerce, Bureau of the Census, Suitland, Maryland 20233 (301) 763-4040; *U.S. Merchandise Trade.*

MACHINERY - EXCEPT ELECTRICAL - MANUFACTURING - GROSS DOMESTIC PRODUCT

U.S. Department of Commerce, Bureau of Economic Analysis, Fourteenth Street between Constitution Avenue and E Street, NW, Washington, D.C. 20230 (202) 606-9900; *The National Income and Product Accounts of the United States*, and *Survey of Current Business*.

MACHINERY - EXCEPT ELECTRICAL - MANUFACTURING - INVENTORIES

U.S. Department of Commerce, Bureau of the Census, Suitland, Maryland 20233 (301) 763-4040; *Current Industrial Reports, Manufactures' Shipments, Inventories, and Orders*.

MACHINERY - EXCEPT ELECTRICAL - MANUFACTURING - OCCUPATIONAL SAFETY

U.S. Department of Labor, Bureau of Labor Statistics, Two Massachusetts Avenue, NE, Washington, D.C. 20212 (202) 606-7828; *Occupational Injuries and Illnesses in the United States by Industry*.

MACHINERY - EXCEPT ELECTRICAL - MANUFACTURING - PATENT3

U.S. Department of Commerce, Patent and Trademark Office, 2011 Crystal Drive, Arlington, Virginia 22202 (703) 305-8341; *Patenting Trends in the United States, State Country Report*.

MACHINERY - EXCEPT ELECTRICAL - MANUFACTURING - PRODUCTIVITY

U.S. Department of Labor, Bureau of Labor Statistics, Two Massachusetts Avenue, NE, Washington, D.C. 20212 (202) 606-7828; *Productivity Measures for Selected Industries and Government Services*, and unpublished data.

MACHINERY - EXCEPT ELECTRICAL - MANUFACTURING - PROFITS

Forbes, Incorporated, 60 Fifth Avenue, New York, New York 10011 (212) 620-2200; *Forbes Annual Report on American Industry*.

U.S. Department of Commerce, Bureau of Economic Analysis, Fourteenth Street between Constitution Avenue and E Street, NW, washington, D.C. 20230 (202) 606-9900; *The National Income and Product Accounts of the U.S.*, and *Survey of Current Business*.

U.S. Department of Commerce, Bureau of the Census, Suitland, Maryland 20233 (301) 763-4040; *Quarterly Financial Report for Manufacturing, Mining and Trade Corporations*.

MACHINERY - EXCEPT ELECTRICAL - MANUFACTURING - RESEARCH AND DEVELOPMENT

U.S. National Science Foundation, 4201 Wilson Boulevard, Arlington, Virginia 22230 (703) 306-1234; *Research and Development in Industry*.

MACHINERY - EXCEPT ELECTRICAL - MANUFACTURING - SHIPMENTS

Forbes, Incorporated, 60 Fifth Avenue, New York, New York 10011 (212) 620-2200; *Forbes Annual Report on American Industry*.

U.S. Department of Commerce, Bureau of the Census, Suitland, Maryland 20233 (301) 763-4040; *Census of Manufactures, Annual Survey of Manufactures*, and *Current Industrial Reports, Manufactures Shipments, Inventories, and Orders*.

U.S. Department of Commerce, International Trade Administration, Fourteenth Street between Constitution Avenue and E Street, NW, Washington, D.C. 20230 (202) 482-3809; *Industrial Outlook*.

MACHINERY - EXCEPT ELECTRICAL - MANUFACTURING - VALUE ADDED

U.S. Department of Commerce, Bureau of the Census, Suitland, Maryland 20233 (301) 763-4040; *Census of Manufactures, Annual Survey of Manufactures*, and *County Business Patterns*.

MACKEREL - PACIFIC

U.S. Department of Commerce, National Oceanic and Atmospheric Administration, National Marine Fisheries Service, 1335 East-West Highway, Silver Spring, Maryland 20910 (301) 427-2239; *Fishery Statistics of the United States*, and *Fisheries of the United States*.

Madagascar - National Statistical Office

Direction Generale de la Banque des Donnes d L'Etat, BP 485, Antananarivo, Madagascar.

Madagascar - Primary Statistics Source

Institut National de la Statistique et de la Recherche Economique, BP 38, Antananarivo, Madagascar; *Bulletin mensuel de statistique*. (Monthly bulletin of statistics).

MADAGASCAR - AGRICULTURE

Euromonitor Publications Limited, 07-00 Turnmill Street, London EC1M 5QU, England; *International Marketing Data and Statistics*.

Facts on File, 460 Park Avenue South, New York, New York 10016 (800) 443-8323; *The New Book of World Rankings*.

Food and Agricultural Organization of the United Nations (FAO), Via delle Terme di Caracalla, 00100 Rome, Italy (Telephone Number in U.S. (202) 653-2400); *Production Yearbook, The State of Food and Agriculture*, and *Trade Yearbook*.

G.K. Hall and Company, 70 Lincoln Street, Boston, Massachusetts 02111 (617) 423-3990; *The World in Figures*.

Statistical Office of the United Nations, Publishing Service, New York, New York 10017 (800) 253-9646; *Statistical Yearbook*, and *Survey of Economic and Social Conditions in Africa*.

Times Books, 201 East 50th Street, New York, New York 10022 (212) 759-0900 (212) 751-2600; *The Economist Book of Vital World Statistics*.

United Nations Economic Commission for Africa, Africa Hall, Post Office Box 3001, Addis Ababa, Ethiopia (Telephone Number in U.S. (800) 253-9646); *African Statistical Yearbook*.

The World Bank, 1818 H Street, NW, Washington, D.C. 20433 (202) 477-1234; *World Tables*.

MADAGASCAR - AIRLINE SERVICE

Facts on File, 460 Park Avenue South, New York, New York 10016 (800) 443-8323; *The New Book of World Rankings*.

G.K. Hall and Company, 70 Lincoln Street, Boston, Massachusetts 02111 (617) 423-3990; *The World in Figures.*

International Civil Aviation Organization, 1000 Sherbrooke Street West, Suite 400, Montreal, Quebec H3A 2R2, Canada (514) 285-8219; *Civil Aviation Statistics of the World.*

Statistical Office of the United Nations, Publishing Service, New York, New York 10017 (800) 253-9646; *Statistical Yearbook.*

Times Books, 201 East 50th Street, New York, New York 10022 (212) 751-2600; *The Economist Book of Vital World Statistics.*

United Nations Economic Commission for Africa, Africa Hall, Post Office Box 3001, Addis Ababa, Ethiopia (Telephone Number in U.S. (800) 253-9646); *African Statistical Yearbook.*

MADAGASCAR - ALUMINUM PRODUCTION AND CONSUMPTION - See MADAGASCAR - MINING AND MINERAL PRODUCTS

MADAGASCAR - ANIMAL HEALTH

Food and Agricultural Organization of the United Nations (FAO), Via delle Terme di Caracalla, 00100 Rome, Italy (Telephone Number in U.S. (202) 653-2400); *Animal Health Yearbook.*

MADAGASCAR - AREA AND DENSITY OF POPULATION

African Development Bank, 01 BP 1387, Abidjan 01, Cote d'Ivoire; *Selected Statistics on Regional Member Countries.*

Euromonitor Publications Limited, 87-88 Turnmill Street, London EC1M 5QU, England; *International Marketing Data and Statistics.*

Facts on File, 460 Park Avenue South, New York, New York 10016 (800) 443-8323; *The New Book of World Rankings.*

Food and Agricultural Organization of the United Nations (FAO), Via delle Terme di Caracalla, 00100 Rome, Italy (Telephone Number in U.S. (202) 653-2400); *The State of Food and Agriculture.*

G.K. Hall and Company, 70 Lincoln Street, Boston, Massachusetts 02111 (617) 423-3990; *The World in Figures.*

Statistical Office of the United Nations, Publishing Service, New York, New York 10017 (800) 253-9646; *Statistical Yearbook,* and *Survey of Economic and Social Conditions in Africa.*

Times Books, 201 East 50th Street, New York, New York 10022 (212) 751-2600; *The Economist Book of Vital World Statistics.*

MADAGASCAR - ARMS EXPORTS AND IMPORTS

U.S. Arms Control and Disarmament Agency, 320 Twenty-first Street, NW, Washington, D.C. 20451 (202) 647-8677; *World Military Expenditures and Arms Transfers.*

MADAGASCAR - BALANCE OF PAYMENTS

African Development Bank, 01 BP 1387, Abidjan 01, Cote d'Ivoire; *Selected Statistics on Regional Member Countries.*

The Economist Intelligence Unit, 111 West 57th Street, New York, New York 10019 (800) 938-4685; *The World Market Atlas.*

G.K. Hall and Company, 70 Lincoln Street, Boston, Massachusetts 02111 (617) 423-3990; *The World in Figures.*

International Monetary Fund, 700 Nineteenth Street, NW, Washington, D.C. 20431 (202) 623-7000; *Balance of Payments Yearbook.*

Times Books, 201 East 50th Street, New York, New York 10022 (212) 751-2600; *The Economist Book of Vital World Statistics.*

United Nations Economic Commission for Africa, Africa Hall, Post Office Box 3001, Addis Ababa, Ethiopia (Telephone Number in U.S. (800) 253-9646); *African Statistical Yearbook.*

The World Bank, 1818 H Street, NW, Washington, D.C. 20433 (202) 477-1234; *World Tables.*

MADAGASCAR - BANKING

Facts on File, 460 Park Avenue South, New York, New York 10016 (800) 443-8323; *The New Book of World Rankings.*

G.K. Hall and Company, 70 Lincoln Street, Boston, Massachusetts 02111 (617) 423-3990; *The World in Figures.*

International Monetary Fund, 700 Nineteenth Street, NW, Washington, D.C. 20431 (202) 623-7000; *International Financial Statistics.*

United Nations Economic Commission for Africa, Africa Hall, Post Office Box 3001, Addis Ababa, Ethiopia (Telephone Number in U.S. (800) 253-9646); *African Statistical Yearbook.*

MADAGASCAR - BARLEY PRODUCTION - See MADAGASCAR - CROPS

MADAGASCAR - BEER PRODUCTION

Facts on File, 460 Park Avenue South, New York, New York 10016 (800) 443-8323; *The New Book of World Rankings.*

Statistical Office of the United Nations, Publishing Service, New York, New York 10017 (800) 253-9646; *Statistical Yearbook.*

MADAGASCAR - BIRTH RATES

Facts on File, 460 Park Avenue South, New York, New York 10016 (800) 443-8323; *The New Book of World Rankings.*

Statistical Office of the United Nations, Publishing Service, New York, New York 10017 (800) 253-9646; *Demographic Yearbook, Statistical Yearbook,* and *Survey of Economic and Social Conditions in Africa.*

Times Books, 201 East 50th Street, New York, New York 10022 (212) 751-2600; *The Economist Book of Vital World Statistics.*

The World Bank, 1818 H Street, NW, Washington, D.C. 20433 (202) 477-1234; *World Tables.*

MADAGASCAR - BONDS

G.K. Hall and Company, 70 Lincoln Street, Boston, Massachusetts 02111 (617) 423-3990; *The World in Figures.*

International Monetary Fund, 700 Nineteenth Street, NW, Washington, D.C. 20431 (202) 623-7000; *Government Finance Statistics Yearbook.*

MADAGASCAR - BOOK PRODUCTION

G.K. Hall and Company, 70 Lincoln Street, Boston, Massachusetts 02111 (617) 423-3990; *The World in Figures.*

United Nations Educational, Scientific and Cultural Organization (UNESCO), 7 Place de Fontenoy, F-75700 Paris, France (Telephone Number in U.S. (212) 963-5981); *Statistical Yearbook.*

MADAGASCAR - BROADCASTING

Billboard Limited, Post Office Box 9027, 1006 AA Amsterdam, The Netherlands (Telephone Number in U.S. (212) 764-7300); *World Radio TV Handbook.*

Facts on File, 460 Park Avenue South, New York, New York 10016 (800) 443-8323; *The New Book of World Rankings.*

G.K. Hall and Company, 70 Lincoln Street, Boston, Massachusetts 02111 (617) 423-3990; *The World in Figures.*

Times Books, 201 East 50th Street, New York, New York 10022 (212) 751-2600; *The Economist Book of Vital World Statistics.*

United Nations Educational, Scientific and Cultural Organization (UNESCO), 7 Place de Fontenoy, F-75700 Paris, France (Telephone Number in U.S. (212) 963-5981); *Statistical Yearbook.*

MADAGASCAR - BUSINESS

G.K. Hall and Company, 70 Lincoln Street, Boston, Massachusetts 02111 (617) 423-3990; *The World in Figures.*

MADAGASCAR - BUSINESS AND PROFESSIONAL LICENSES

International Monetary Fund, 700 Nineteenth Street, NW, Washington, D.C. 20431 (202) 623-7000; *Government Finance Statistics Yearbook.*

MADAGASCAR - CALORIE SUPPLY

African Development Bank, 01 BP 1387, Abidjan 01, Cote d'Ivoire; *Selected Statistics on Regional Member Countries.*

Food and Agricultural Organization of the United Nations (FAO), Via delle Terme di Caracalla, 00100 Rome, Italy (Telephone Number in U.S. (202) 653-2400); *The State of Food and Agriculture.*

MADAGASCAR - CAPITAL REVENUE

International Monetary Fund, 700 Nineteenth Street, NW, Washington, D.C. 20431 (202) 623-7000; *Government Finance Statistics Yearbook.*

MADAGASCAR - CASHEW NUT PRODUCTION - See MADAGASCAR - CROPS

MADAGASCAR - CASTOR BEAN PRODUCTION - See MADAGASCAR - CROPS

MADAGASCAR - CATTLE - See MADAGASCAR - LIVESTOCK AND POULTRY

MADAGASCAR - CEMENT PRODUCTION - See MADAGASCAR - MINING AND MINERAL PRODUCTS

MADAGASCAR - CHEMICAL (ORGANIC) PRODUCTION - See MADAGASCAR - MINING AND MINERAL PRODUCTS

MADAGASCAR - CHICKENS - See MADAGASCAR - LIVESTOCK AND POULTRY

MADAGASCAR - CHROMIUM ORE PRODUCTION - See MADAGASCAR - MINING AND MINERAL PRODUCTS

MADAGASCAR - CIGARETTE PRODUCTION - See MADAGASCAR - TOBACCO PRODUCTION

MADAGASCAR - CLASS STRUCTURE

G.K. Hall and Company, 70 Lincoln Street, Boston, Massachusetts 02111 (617) 423-3990; *The World in Figures.*

MADAGASCAR - CLIMATE

Facts on File, 460 Park Avenue South, New York, New York 10016 (800) 443-8323; *The New Book of World Rankings.*

G.K. Hall and Company, 70 Lincoln Street, Boston, Massachusetts 02111 (617) 423-3990; *The World in Figures.*

MADAGASCAR - CLOVES EXPORTS

International Monetary Fund, 700 Nineteenth Street, NW, Washington, D.C. 20431 (202) 623-7000; *International Financial Statistics.*

MADAGASCAR - COAL PRODUCTION - See MADAGASCAR - MINING AND MINERAL PRODUCTS

MADAGASCAR - COCOA PRODUCTION

Statistical Office of the United Nations, Publishing Service, New York, New York 10017 (800) 253-9040; *Statistical Yearbook.*

MADAGASCAR - COFFEE - See MADAGASCAR - CROPS

MADAGASCAR - COMMUNICATIONS

G.K. Hall and Company, 70 Lincoln Street, Boston, Massachusetts 02111 (617) 423-3990; *The World in Figures.*

United Nations Economic Commission for Africa, Africa Hall, Post Office Box 3001, Addis Ababa, Ethiopia (Telephone Number in U.S. (800) 253-9646); *African Statistical Yearbook.*

MADAGASCAR - CONSTRUCTION INDUSTRY

Facts on File, 460 Park Avenue South, New York, New York 10016 (800) 443-8323; *The New Book of World Rankings.*

Statistical Office of the United Nations, Publishing Service, New York, New York 10017 (800) 253-9646; *Construction Statistics Yearbook,* and *Statistical Yearbook.*

United Nations Economic Commission for Africa, Africa Hall, Post Office Box 3001, Addis Ababa, Ethiopia (Telephone Number in U.S. (800) 253-9646); *African Statistical Yearbook.*

MADAGASCAR - CONSUMER PRICE INDEX

African Development Bank, 01 BP 1387, Abidjan 01, Cote d'Ivoire; *Selected Statistics on Regional Member Countries.*

G.K. Hall and Company, 70 Lincoln Street, Boston, Massachusetts 02111 (617) 423-3990; *The World in Figures.*

Statistical Office of the United Nations, Publishing Service, New York, New York 10017 (800) 253-9646; *Statistical Yearbook*, and *Survey of Economic and Social Conditions in Africa*.

Times Books, 201 East 50th Street, New York, New York 10022 (212) 751-2600; *The Economist Book of Vital World Statistics*.

United Nations Economic Commission for Africa, Africa Hall, Post Office Box 3001, Addis Ababa, Ethiopia (Telephone Number in U.S. (800) 253-9646); *African Statistical Yearbook*.

MADAGASCAR - CONSUMER PRICES

International Labour Office, I.L.O. Publications, CH-1211, Geneva 22, Switzerland; *Yearbook of Labour Statistics*.

International Monetary Fund, 700 Nineteenth Street, NW, Washington, D.C. 20431 (202) 623-7000; *International Financial Statistics*.

MADAGASCAR - CONSUMPTION

African Development Bank, 01 BP 1387, Abidjan 01, Cote d'Ivoire; *Selected Statistics on Regional Member Countries*.

G.K. Hall and Company, 70 Lincoln Street, Boston, Massachusetts 02111 (617) 423-3990; *The World in Figures*.

Statistical Office of the United Nations, Publishing Service, New York, New York 10017 (800) 253-9646; *Survey of Economic and Social Conditions in Africa*.

MADAGASCAR - COPPER PRODUCTION - See MADAGASCAR - MINING AND MINERAL PRODUCTS

MADAGASCAR - CORN PRODUCTION - See MADAGASCAR - CROPS

MADAGASCAR - CORPORATE TAXES - See MADAGASCAR - TAXATION

MADAGASCAR - COTTON PRODUCTION AND CONSUMPTION - See MADAGASCAR - CROPS

MADAGASCAR - CRIME

Yale University Press, Yale Station, New Haven, Connecticut 06520 (203) 432-0940; *Violence and Crime in Cross-National Perspective*.

MADAGASCAR - CROPS

Facts on File, 460 Park Avenue South, New York, New York 10016 (800) 443-8323; *The New Book of World Rankings*.

Food and Agricultural Organization of the United Nations (FAO), Via delle Terme di Caracalla, 00100 Rome, Italy (Telephone Number in U.S. (202) 653-2400); *Production Yearbook*, and *The State of Food and Agriculture*.

G.K. Hall and Company, 70 Lincoln Street, Boston, Massachusetts 02111 (617) 423-3990; *The World in Figures*.

International Monetary Fund, 700 Nineteenth Street, NW, Washington, D.C. 20431 (202) 623-7000; *International Financial Statistics*.

Statistical Office of the United Nations, Publishing Service, New York, New York 10017 (800) 253-9646; *Statistical Yearbook*.

United Nations Economic Commission for Africa, Africa Hall, Post Office Box 3001, Addis Ababa, Ethiopia (Telephone Number in U.S. (800) 253-9646); *African Statistical Yearbook*.

MADAGASCAR - CUSTOMS DUTIES

G.K. Hall and Company, 70 Lincoln Street, Boston, Massachusetts 02111 (617) 423-3990; *The World in Figures*.

International Monetary Fund, 700 Nineteenth Street, NW, Washington, D.C. 20431 (202) 623-7000; *Government Finance Statistics Yearbook*.

MADAGASCAR - DAIRY PRODUCTS

Facts on File, 460 Park Avenue South, New York, New York 10016 (800) 443-8323; *The New Book of World Rankings*.

Food and Agricultural Organization of the United Nations (FAO), Via delle Terme di Caracalla, 00100 Rome, Italy (Telephone Number in U.S. (202) 653-2400); *Production Yearbook*, and *The State of Food and Agriculture*.

Statistical Office of the United Nations, Publishing Service, New York, New York 10017 (800) 253-9646; *Statistical Yearbook*.

MADAGASCAR - DEATH RATES

G.K. Hall and Company, 70 Lincoln Street, Boston, Massachusetts 02111 (617) 423-3990; *The World in Figures*.

Statistical Office of the United Nations, Publishing Service, New York, New York 10017 (800) 253-9646; *Statistical Yearbook*, and *Survey of Economic and Social Conditions in Africa*.

World Health Organization, Office of Publications, Avenue Appia, CH-1211 Geneva 27, Switzerland (Telephone Number in U.S. (518) 436-9686); *World Health Statistics Annual*.

MADAGASCAR - DEFENSE EXPENDITURES

G.K. Hall and Company, 70 Lincoln Street, Boston, Massachusetts 02111 (617) 423-3990; *The World in Figures*.

International Monetary Fund, 700 Nineteenth Street, NW, Washington, D.C. 20431 (202) 623-7000; *Government Finance Statistics Yearbook*.

U.S. Arms Control and Disarmament Agency, 320 Twenty-first Street, NW, Washington, D.C. 20451 (202) 647-8677; *World Military Expenditures and Arms Transfers*.

MADAGASCAR - DEMOGRAPHY

Facts on File, 460 Park Avenue South, New York, New York 10016 (800) 443-8323; *The New Book of World Rankings*.

G.K. Hall and Company, 70 Lincoln Street, Boston, Massachusetts 02111 (617) 423-3990; *The World in Figures*.

Statistical Office of the United Nations, Publishing Service, New York, New York 10017 (800) 253-9646; *Survey of Economic and Social Conditions in Africa*.

MADAGASCAR - DEVELOPMENT ASSISTANCE

G.K. Hall and Company, 70 Lincoln Street, Boston, Massachusetts 02111 (617) 423-3990; *The World in Figures*.

Statistical Office of the United Nations, Publishing Service, New York, New York 10017 (800) 253-9646; *Statistical Yearbook*.

MADAGASCAR - DIAMOND PRODUCTION - See MADAGASCAR - MINING AND MINERAL PRODUCTS

MADAGASCAR - DISEASE

G.K. Hall and Company, 70 Lincoln Street, Boston, Massachusetts 02111 (617) 423-3990; *The World in Figures*.

World Health Organization, Office of Publications, Avenue Appia, CH-1211 Geneva 27, Switzerland (Telephone Number in U.S. (518) 436-9686); *World Health Statistics Annual*.

MADAGASCAR - DIVORCE

Facts on File, 460 Park Avenue South, New York, New York 10016 (800) 443-8323; *The New Book of World Rankings*.

Statistical Office of the United Nations, Publishing Service, New York, New York 10017 (800) 253-9646; *Demographic Yearbook*.

MADAGASCAR - DOMESTIC PRODUCT

G.K. Hall and Company, 70 Lincoln Street, Boston, Massachusetts 02111 (617) 423-3990; *The World in Figures*.

MADAGASCAR - DUCKS

Food and Agricultural Organization of the United Nations (FAO), Via delle Terme di Caracalla, 00100 Rome, Italy (Telephone Number in U.S. (202) 653-2400); *Production Yearbook*.

MADAGASCAR - ECONOMY

African Development Bank, 01 BP 1387, Abidjan 01, Cote d'Ivoire; *Selected Statistics on Regional Member Countries*.

Euromonitor Publications Limited, 87-88 Turnmill Street, London EC1M 5QU, England; *International Marketing Data and Statistics*.

Facts on File, 460 Park Avenue South, New York, New York 10016 (800) 443-8323; *The New Book of World Rankings*.

G.K. Hall and Company, 70 Lincoln Street, Boston, Massachusetts 02111 (617) 423-3990; *The World in Figures*.

Statistical Office of the United Nations, Publishing Service, New York, New York 10017 (800) 253-9646; *Foreign Trade Statistics for Africa*.

MADAGASCAR - EDUCATION

African Development Bank, 01 BP 1387, Abidjan 01, Cote d'Ivoire; *Selected Statistics on Regional Member Countries*.

The Economist Intelligence Unit, 111 West 57th Street, New York, New York 10019 (800) 938-4685; *The World Market Atlas*.

Facts on File, 460 Park Avenue South, New York, New York 10016 (800) 443-8323; *The New Book of World Rankings*.

G.K. Hall and Company, 70 Lincoln Street, Boston, Massachusetts 02111 (617) 423-3990; *The World in Figures*.

International Monetary Fund, 700 Nineteenth Street, NW, Washington, D.C. 20431 (202) 623-7000; *Government Finance Statistics Yearbook*.

Statistical Office of the United Nations, Publishing Service, New York, New York 10017 (800) 253-9646; *Statistical Yearbook*, and *Survey of Economic and Social Conditions in Africa*.

Times Books, 201 East 50th Street, New York, New York 10022 (212) 751-2600; *The Economist Book of Vital World Statistics*.

United Nations Economic Commission for Africa, Africa Hall, Post Office Box 3001, Addis Ababa, Ethiopia (Telephone Number in U.S. (800) 253-9646); *African Statistical Yearbook*.

United Nations Educational, Scientific and Cultural Organization (UNESCO), 7 Place de Fontenoy, F-75700 Paris, France (Telephone Number in U.S. (212) 963-5981); *Statistical Yearbook*.

The World Bank, 1818 H Street, NW, Washington, D.C. 20433 (202) 477-1234; *World Tables*.

MADAGASCAR - EGG PRODUCTION AND CONSUMPTION - See MADAGASCAR - DAIRY PRODUCTS

MADAGASCAR - ELECTRICITY

Facts on File, 460 Park Avenue South, New York, New York 10016 (800) 443-8323; *The New Book of World Rankings*.

Statistical Office of the United Nations, Publishing Service, New York, New York 10017 (800) 253-9646; *Statistical Yearbook*, and *Survey of Economic and Social Conditions in Africa*.

Times Books, 201 East 50th Street, New York, New York 10022 (212) 751-2600; *The Economist Book of Vital World Statistics*.

United Nations Economic Commission for Africa, Africa Hall, Post Office Box 3001, Addis Ababa, Ethiopia (Telephone Number in U.S. (800) 253-9646); *African Statistical Yearbook*.

MADAGASCAR - EMPLOYMENT

Euromonitor Publications Limited, 87-88 Turnmill Street, London EC1M 5QU, England; *International Marketing Data and Statistics*.

Facts on File, 460 Park Avenue South, New York, New York 10016 (800) 443-8323; *The New Book of World Rankings*.

International Labour Office, I.L.O. Publications, CH-1211, Geneva 22, Switzerland; *Yearbook of Labour Statistics*.

Statistical Office of the United Nations, Publishing Service, New York, New York 10017 (800) 253-9646; *Statistical Yearbook*, and *Survey of Economic and Social Conditions in Africa*.

United Nations Economic Commission for Africa, Africa Hall, Post Office Box 3001, Addis Ababa, Ethiopia (Telephone Number in U.S. (800) 253-9646); *African Statistical Yearbook*.

MADAGASCAR - ENERGY

Facts on File, 460 Park Avenue South, New York, New York 10016 (800) 443-8323; *The New Book of World Rankings*.

Food and Agricultural Organization of the United Nations (FAO), Via delle Terme di Caracalla, 00100 Rome, Italy (Telephone Number in U.S. (202) 653-2400); *The State of Food and Agriculture*.

G.K. Hall and Company, 70 Lincoln Street, Boston, Massachusetts 02111 (617) 423-3990; *The World in Figures*.

Statistical Office of the United Nations, Publishing Service, New York, New York 10017 (800) 253-9646; *Energy Statistics Yearbook*, and *Statistical Yearbook*.

Times Books, 201 East 50th Street, New York, New York 10022 (212) 751-2600; *The Economist Book of Vital World Statistics*.

United Nations Economic Commission for Africa, Africa Hall, Post Office Box 3001, Addis Ababa, Ethiopia (Telephone Number in U.S. (800) 253-9646); *African Statistical Yearbook*.

MADAGASCAR - EXCHANGE RATES

African Development Bank, 01 BP 1387, Abidjan 01, Cote d'Ivoire; *Selected Statistics on Regional Member Countries*.

Euromonitor Publications Limited, 87-88 Turnmill Street, London EC1M 5QU, England; *International Marketing Data and Statistics*.

International Civil Aviation Organization, 1000 Sherbrooke Street West, Suite 400, Montreal, Quebec H3A 2R2, Canada (514) 285-8219; *Civil Aviation Statistics of the World*.

International Monetary Fund, 700 Nineteenth Street, NW, Washington, D.C. 20431 (202) 623-7000; *International Financial Statistics*.

Statistical Office of the United Nations, Publishing Service, New York, New York 10017 (800) 253-9646; *Foreign Trade Statistics for Africa*, and *Statistical Yearbook*.

MADAGASCAR - EXCISE TAXES - See MADAGASCAR - TAXATION

MADAGASCAR - EXPORTS

African Development Bank, 01 BP 1387, Abidjan 01, Cote d'Ivoire; *Selected Statistics on Regional Member Countries*.

The Economist Intelligence Unit, 111 West 57th Street, New York, New York 10019 (800) 938-4685; *The World Market Atlas*.

Euromonitor Publications Limited, 87-88 Turnmill Street, London EC1M 5QU, England; *International Marketing Data and Statistics*.

Food and Agricultural Organization of the United Nations (FAO), Via delle Terme di Caracalla, 00100 Rome, Italy (Telephone Number in U.S. (202) 653-2400); *The State of Food and Agriculture*.

G.K. Hall and Company, 70 Lincoln Street, Boston, Massachusetts 02111 (617) 423-3990; *The World in Figures*.

International Monetary Fund, 700 Nineteenth Street, NW, Washington, D.C. 20431 (202) 623-7000; *Direction of Trade Statistics, Government Finance Statistics Yearbook*, and *International Financial Statistics*.

Statistical Office of the United Nations, Publishing Service, New York, New York 10017 (800) 253-9646; *Foreign Trade Statistics for Africa*, and *Survey of Economic and Social Conditions in Africa*.

Times Books, 201 East 50th Street, New York, New York 10022 (212) 751-2600; *The Economist Book of Vital World Statistics*.

United Nations Economic Commission for Africa, Africa Hall, Post Office Box 3001, Addis Ababa, Ethiopia (Telephone Number in U.S. (800) 253-9646); *African Statistical Yearbook*.

The World Bank, 1818 H Street, NW, Washington, D.C. 20433 (202) 477-1234; *World Tables*.

MADAGASCAR - EXTERNAL INDEBTEDNESS

African Development Bank, 01 BP 1387, Abidjan 01, Cote d'Ivoire; *Selected Statistics on Regional Member Countries*.

Statistical Office of the United Nations, Publishing Service, New York, New York 10017 (800) 253-9646; *Survey of Economic and Social Conditions in Africa*.

The World Bank, 1818 H Street, NW, Washington, D.C. 20433 (202) 477-1234; *World Tables*.

MADAGASCAR - EXTERNAL TRADE

African Development Bank, 01 BP 1387, Abidjan 01, Cote d'Ivoire; *Selected Statistics on Regional Member Countries*.

Food and Agricultural Organization of the United Nations (FAO), Via delle Terme di Caracalla, 00100 Rome, Italy (Telephone Number in U.S. (202) 653-2400); *The State of Food and Agriculture*, and *Trade Yearbook*.

G.K. Hall and Company, 70 Lincoln Street, Boston, Massachusetts 02111 (617) 423-3990; *The World in Figures*.

Statistical Office of the United Nations, Publishing Service, New York, New York 10017 (800) 253-9646; *Statistical Yearbook*.

MADAGASCAR - FABRIC PRODUCTION - See MADAGASCAR - TEXTILE INDUSTRY

MADAGASCAR - FARM CROPS - See MADAGASCAR - CROPS

MADAGASCAR - FEMALE WORKING POPULATION - See MADAGASCAR - EMPLOYMENT

MADAGASCAR - FERTILITY RATES

Facts on File, 460 Park Avenue South, New York, New York 10016 (800) 443-8323; *The New Book of World Rankings*.

Statistical Office of the United Nations, Publishing Service, New York, New York 10017 (800) 253-9646; *Survey of Economic and Social Conditions in Africa*.

Times Books, 201 East 50th Street, New York, New York 10022 (212) 751-2600; *The Economist Book of Vital World Statistics*.

The World Bank, 1818 H Street, NW, Washington, D.C. 20433 (202) 477-1234; *World Tables*.

MADAGASCAR - FERTILIZER

Food and Agricultural Organization of the United Nations (FAO), Via delle Terme di Caracalla, 00100 Rome, Italy (Telephone Number in U.S. (202) 653-2400); *The State of Food and Agriculture*.

Statistical Office of the United Nations, Publishing Service, New York, New York 10017 (800) 253-9646; *Statistical Yearbook*.

MADAGASCAR - FETAL MORTALITY

Statistical Office of the United Nations, Publishing Service, New York, New York 10017 (800) 253-9646; *Demographic Yearbook*.

MADAGASCAR - FINANCE

African Development Bank, 01 BP 1387, Abidjan 01, Cote d'Ivoire; *Selected Statistics on Regional Member Countries*.

Facts on File, 460 Park Avenue South, New York, New York 10016 (800) 443-8323; *The New Book of World Rankings*.

G.K. Hall and Company, 70 Lincoln Street, Boston, Massachusetts 02111 (617) 423-3990; *The World in Figures*.

International Monetary Fund, 700 Nineteenth Street, NW, Washington, D.C. 20431 (202) 623-7000; *Government Finance Statistics Yearbook*.

United Nations Economic Commission for Africa, Africa Hall, Post Office Box 3001, Addis Ababa, Ethiopia (Telephone Number in U.S. (800) 253-9646); *African Statistical Yearbook*.

MADAGASCAR - FISHERIES

Facts on File, 460 Park Avenue South, New York, New York 10016 (800) 443-8323; *The New Book of World Rankings*.

Food and Agricultural Organization of the United Nations (FAO), Via delle Terme di Caracalla, 00100 Rome, Italy (Telephone Number in U.S. (202) 653-2400); *The State of Food and Agriculture*, and *Yearbook of Fishery Statistics*.

Statistical Office of the United Nations, Publishing Service, New York, New York 10017 (800) 253-9646; *Statistical Yearbook*, and *Survey of Economic and Social Conditions in Africa*.

United Nations Economic Commission for Africa, Africa Hall, Post Office Box 3001, Addis Ababa, Ethiopia (Telephone Number in U.S. (800) 253-9646); *African Statistical Yearbook*.

MADAGASCAR - FOOD

African Development Bank, 01 BP 1387, Abidjan 01, Cote d'Ivoire; *Selected Statistics on Regional Member Countries*.

Food and Agricultural Organization of the United Nations (FAO), Via delle Terme di Caracalla, 00100 Rome, Italy (Telephone Number in U.S. (202) 653-2400); *Production Yearbook*, and *The State of Food and Agriculture*.

G.K. Hall and Company, 70 Lincoln Street, Boston, Massachusetts 02111 (617) 423-3990; *The World in Figures*.

MADAGASCAR - FOREIGN AID

G.K. Hall and Company, 70 Lincoln Street, Boston, Massachusetts 02111 (617) 423-3990; *The World in Figures*.

MADAGASCAR - FOREIGN DEBT

International Monetary Fund, 700 Nineteenth Street, NW, Washington, D.C. 20431 (202) 623-7000; *Government Finance Statistics Yearbook*.

MADAGASCAR - FOREIGN TRADE

Euromonitor Publications Limited, 87-88 Turnmill Street, London EC1M 5QU, England; *International Marketing Data and Statistics*.

Facts on File, 460 Park Avenue South, New York, New York 10016 (800) 443-8323; *The New Book of World Rankings*.

Food and Agricultural Organization of the United Nations (FAO), Via delle Terme di Caracalla, 00100 Rome, Italy (Telephone Number in U.S. (202) 653-2400); *The State of Food and Agriculture*.

G.K. Hall and Company, 70 Lincoln Street, Boston, Massachusetts 02111 (617) 423-3990; *The World in Figures*.

Statistical Office of the United Nations, Publishing Service, New York, New York 10017 (800) 253-9646; *Foreign Trade Statistics for Africa*, *International Trade Statistics Yearbook*, and *Statistical Yearbook*.

United Nations Economic Commission for Africa, Africa Hall, Post Office Box 3001, Addis Ababa, Ethiopia (Telephone Number in U.S. (800) 253-9646); *African Statistical Yearbook*.

The World Bank, 1818 H Street, NW, Washington, D.C. 20433 (202) 477-1234; *World Tables*.

MADAGASCAR - FORESTRY AND FOREST PRODUCTS

Facts on File, 460 Park Avenue South, New York, New York 10016 (800) 443-8323; *The New Book of World Rankings*.

Food and Agricultural Organization of the United Nations (FAO), Via delle Terme di Caracalla, 00100 Rome, Italy (Telephone Number in U.S. (202) 653-2400); *The State of Food and Agriculture*, and *Yearbook of Forest Products*.

G.K. Hall and Company, 70 Lincoln Street, Boston, Massachusetts 02111 (617) 423-3990; *The World in Figures*.

Statistical Office of the United Nations, Publishing Service, New York, New York 10017 (800) 253-9646; *Statistical Yearbook*.

United Nations Economic Commission for Africa, Africa Hall, Post Office Box 3001, Addis Ababa, Ethiopia (Telephone Number in U.S. (800) 253-9646); *African Statistical Yearbook*.

United Nations Educational, Scientific and Cultural Organization (UNESCO), 7 Place de Fontenoy, F-75700 Paris, France (Telephone Number in U.S. (212) 963-5981); *Statistical Yearbook*.

MADAGASCAR - GAS PRODUCTION - See MADAGASCAR - MINING AND MINERAL PRODUCTS

MADAGASCAR - GENERAL INDUSTRIAL STATISTICS

Statistical Office of the United Nations, Publishing Service, New York, New York 10017 (800) 253-9646; *Industrial Statistics Yearbook*.

MADAGASCAR - GENERAL MORTALITY

Statistical Office of the United Nations, Publishing Service, New York, New York 10017 (800) 253-9646; *Demographic Yearbook*.

MADAGASCAR - GEOGRAPHIC DATA

Facts on File, 460 Park Avenue South, New York, New York 10016 (800) 443-8323; *The New Book of World Rankings*.

MADAGASCAR - GOATS - See MADAGASCAR - LIVESTOCK AND POULTRY

MADAGASCAR - GOLD HOLDINGS

Statistical Office of the United Nations, Publishing Service, New York, New York 10017 (800) 253-9646; *Statistical Yearbook*.

The World Bank, 1818 H Street, NW, Washington, D.C. 20433 (202) 477-1234; *World Tables*.

MADAGASCAR - GOLD PRODUCTION AND CONSUMPTION - See MADAGASCAR - MINING AND MINERAL PRODUCTS

MADAGASCAR - GOVERNMENT

G.K. Hall and Company, 70 Lincoln Street, Boston, Massachusetts 02111 (617) 423-3990; *The World in Figures.*

MADAGASCAR - GOVERNMENT EXPENDITURES

International Monetary Fund, 700 Nineteenth Street, NW, Washington, D.C. 20431 (202) 623-7000; *Government Finance Statistics Yearbook.*

The World Bank, 1818 H Street, NW, Washington, D.C. 20433 (202) 477-1234; *World Tables.*

MADAGASCAR - GOVERNMENT FINANCES

International Monetary Fund, 700 Nineteenth Street, NW, Washington, D.C. 20431 (202) 623-7000; *International Financial Statistics.*

MADAGASCAR - GOVERNMENT REVENUES

International Monetary Fund, 700 Nineteenth Street, NW, Washington, D.C. 20431 (202) 623-7000; *Government Finance Statistics Yearbook.*

Statistical Office of the United Nations, Publishing Service, New York, New York 10017 (800) 253-9646; *Survey of Economic and Social Conditions in Africa.*

The World Bank, 1818 H Street, NW, Washington, D.C. 20433 (202) 477-1234; *World Tables.*

MADAGASCAR - GRAIN PRODUCTION - See MADAGASCAR - CROPS

MADAGASCAR - GRANTS

International Monetary Fund, 700 Nineteenth Street, NW, Washington, D.C. 20431 (202) 623-7000; *Government Finance Statistics Yearbook.*

MADAGASCAR - GROSS DOMESTIC PRODUCT

African Development Bank, 01 BP 1387, Abidjan 01, Cote d'Ivoire; *Selected Statistics on Regional Member Countries.*

The Economist Intelligence Unit, 111 West 57th Street, New York, New York 10019 (800) 938-4685; *The World Market Atlas.*

Euromonitor Publications Limited, 87-88 Turnmill Street, London EC1M 5QU, England; *International Marketing Data and Statistics.*

Facts on File, 460 Park Avenue South, New York, New York 10016 (800) 443-8323; *The New Book of World Rankings.*

G.K. Hall and Company, 70 Lincoln Street, Boston, Massachusetts 02111 (617) 423-3990; *The World in Figures.*

Statistical Office of the United Nations, Publishing Service, New York, New York 10017 (800) 253-9646; *Statistical Yearbook,* and *Survey of Economic and Social Conditions in Africa.*

Times Books, 201 East 50th Street, New York, New York 10022 (212) 751-2600; *The Economist Book of Vital World Statistics.*

United Nations Economic Commission for Africa, Africa Hall, Post Office Box 3001, Addis Ababa, Ethiopia (Telephone Number in U.S. (800) 253-9646); *African Statistical Yearbook.*

The World Bank, 1818 H Street, NW, Washington, D.C. 20433 (202) 477-1234; *World Tables.*

MADAGASCAR - GROSS NATIONAL PRODUCT

Euromonitor Publications Limited, 87-88 Turnmill Street, London EC1M 5QU, England; *International Marketing Data and Statistics.*

U.S. Arms Control and Disarmament Agency, 320 Twenty-first Street, NW, Washington, D.C. 20451 (202) 647-8677; *World Military Expenditures and Arms Transfers.*

The World Bank, 1818 H Street, NW, Washington, D.C. 20433 (202) 477-1234; *World Tables.*

MADAGASCAR - GROUNDNUT PRODUCTION - See MADAGASCAR - CROPS

MADAGASCAR - HEALTH

African Development Bank, 01 BP 1387, Abidjan 01, Cote d'Ivoire; *Selected Statistics on Regional Member Countries.*

Facts on File, 460 Park Avenue South, New York, New York 10016 (800) 443-8323; *The New Book of World Rankings.*

G.K. Hall and Company, 70 Lincoln Street, Boston, Massachusetts 02111 (617) 423-3990; *The World in Figures.*

Statistical Office of the United Nations, Publishing Service, New York, New York 10017 (800) 253-9646; *Statistical Yearbook.*

Times Books, 201 East 50th Street, New York, New York 10022 (212) 751-2600; *The Economist Book of Vital World Statistics.*

United Nations Economic Commission for Africa, Africa Hall, Post Office Box 3001, Addis Ababa, Ethiopia (Telephone Number in U.S. (800) 253-9646); *African Statistical Yearbook.*

World Health Organization, Office of Publications, Avenue Appia, CH-1211 Geneva 27, Switzerland (Telephone Number in U.S. (518) 436-9686); *World Health Statistics Annual.*

MADAGASCAR - HEALTH EXPENDITURES

Food and Agricultural Organization of the United Nations (FAO), Via delle Terme di Caracalla, 00100 Rome, Italy (Telephone Number in U.S. (202) 653-2400); *Production Yearbook.*

MADAGASCAR - HIDE PRODUCTION

Food and Agricultural Organization of the United Nations (FAO), Via delle Terme di Caracalla, 00100 Rome, Italy (Telephone Number in U.S. (202) 653-2400); *Production Yearbook.*

MADAGASCAR - HIGHWAYS

G.K. Hall and Company, 70 Lincoln Street, Boston, Massachusetts 02111 (617) 423-3990; *The World in Figures.*

International Road Federation, 525 School Street, SW, Washington, D.C. 20024 (202) 554-2106; *World Road Statistics.*

Statistical Office of the United Nations, Publishing Service, New York, New York 10017 (800) 253-9646; *Survey of Economic and*

Social Conditions in Africa.

United Nations Economic Commission for Africa, Africa Hall, Post Office Box 3001, Addis Ababa, Ethiopia (Telephone Number in U.S. (800) 253-9646); *African Statistical Yearbook.*

MADAGASCAR - HORSES - See MADAGASCAR - LIVESTOCK AND POULTRY

MADAGASCAR - HOURS OF WORK - See MADAGASCAR - EMPLOYMENT

MADAGASCAR - HOUSING EXPENDITURES

Facts on File, 460 Park Avenue South, New York, New York 10016 (800) 443-8323; *The New Book of World Rankings.*

International Monetary Fund, 700 Nineteenth Street, NW, Washington, D.C. 20431 (202) 623-7000; *Government Finance Statistics Yearbook.*

MADAGASCAR - ILLITERATE POPULATION

The Economist Intelligence Unit, 111 West 57th Street, New York, New York 10019 (800) 938-4685; *The World Market Atlas.*

G.K. Hall and Company, 70 Lincoln Street, Boston, Massachusetts 02111 (617) 423-3990; *The World in Figures.*

United Nations Educational, Scientific and Cultural Organization (UNESCO), 7 Place de Fontenoy, F-75700 Paris, France (Telephone Number in U.S. (212) 963-5981); *Statistical Yearbook.*

MADAGASCAR - IMPORTS

African Development Bank, 01 BP 1387, Abidjan 01, Cote d'Ivoire; *Selected Statistics on Regional Member Countries.*

The Economist Intelligence Unit, 111 West 57th Street, New York, New York 10019 (800) 938-4685; *The World Market Atlas.*

Euromonitor Publications Limited, 87-88 Turnmill Street, London EC1M 5QU, England; *International Marketing Data and Statistics.*

Food and Agricultural Organization of the United Nations (FAO), Via delle Terme di Caracalla, 00100 Rome, Italy (Telephone Number in U.S. (202) 653-2400); *The State of Food and Agriculture.*

G.K. Hall and Company, 70 Lincoln Street, Boston, Massachusetts 02111 (617) 423-3990; *The World in Figures.*

International Monetary Fund, 700 Nineteenth Street, NW, Washington, D.C. 20431 (202) 623-7000; *Direction of Trade Statistics, Government Finance Statistics Yearbook,* and *International Financial Statistics.*

Statistical Office of the United Nations, Publishing Service, New York, New York 10017 (800) 253-9646; *Foreign Trade Statistics for Africa,* and *Survey of Economic and Social Conditions in Africa.*

Times Books, 201 East 50th Street, New York, New York 10022 (212) 751-2600; *The Economist Book of Vital World Statistics.*

United Nations Economic Commission for Africa, Africa Hall, Post Office Box 3001, Addis Ababa, Ethiopia (Telephone Number in U.S. (800) 253-9646); *African Statistical Yearbook.*

The World Bank, 1818 H Street, NW, Washington, D.C. 20433 (202) 477-1234; *World Tables.*

MADAGASCAR - INCOME TAXES - See MADAGASCAR - TAXATION

MADAGASCAR - INDUSTRY

Euromonitor Publications Limited, 87-88 Turnmill Street, London EC1M 5QU, England; *International Marketing Data and Statistics.*

Facts on File, 460 Park Avenue South, New York, New York 10016 (800) 443-8323; *The New Book of World Rankings.*

G.K. Hall and Company, 70 Lincoln Street, Boston, Massachusetts 02111 (617) 423-3990; *The World in Figures.*

International Labour Office, I.L.O. Publications, CH-1211, Geneva 22, Switzerland; *Yearbook of Labour Statistics.*

Statistical Office of the United Nations, Publishing Service, New York, New York 10017 (800) 253-9646; *Survey of Economic and Social Conditions in Africa.*

Times Books, 201 East 50th Street, New York, New York 10022 (212) 751-2600; *The Economist Book of Vital World Statistics.*

United Nations Economic Commission for Africa, Africa Hall, Post Office Box 3001, Addis Ababa, Ethiopia (Telephone Number in U.S. (000) 253-0646); *African Statistical Yearbook.*

The World Bank, 1818 H Street, NW, Washington, D.C. 20433 (202) 477-1234; *World Tables.*

MADAGASCAR - INFANT AND MATERNAL MORTALITY

Statistical Office of the United Nations, Publishing Service, New York, New York 10017 (800) 253-9646; *Demographic Yearbook, Statistical Yearbook,* and *Survey of Economic and Social Conditions in Africa.*

Times Books, 201 East 50th Street, New York, New York 10022 (212) 751-2600; *The Economist Book of Vital World Statistics.*

The World Bank, 1818 H Street, NW, Washington, D.C. 20433 (202) 477-1234; *World Tables.*

MADAGASCAR - INTERNATIONAL LIQUIDITY

International Monetary Fund, 700 Nineteenth Street, NW, Washington, D.C. 20431 (202) 623-7000; *International Financial Statistics.*

MADAGASCAR - INTERNATIONAL RESERVES EXCLUDING GOLD

African Development Bank, 01 BP 1387, Abidjan 01, Cote d'Ivoire; *Selected Statistics on Regional Member Countries.*

Statistical Office of the United Nations, Publishing Service, New York, New York 10017 (800) 253-9646; *Statistical Yearbook.*

The World Bank, 1818 H Street, NW, Washington, D.C. 20433 (202) 477-1234; *World Tables.*

MADAGASCAR - IRON ORE PRODUCTION AND CONSUMPTION - See MADAGASCAR - MINING AND MINERAL PRODUCTS

MADAGASCAR - IRRIGATION

Euromonitor Publications Limited, 87-88 Turnmill Street, London EC1M 5QU, England; *International Marketing Data and Statistics.*

MADAGASCAR - JUTE PRODUCTION - See MADAGASCAR - CROPS

MADAGASCAR - LABOR FORCE

African Development Bank, 01 BP 1387, Abidjan 01, Cote d'Ivoire; *Selected Statistics on Regional Member Countries.*

Euromonitor Publications Limited, 87-88 Turnmill Street, London EC1M 5QU, England; *International Marketing Data and Statistics.*

Facts on File, 460 Park Avenue South, New York, New York 10016 (800) 443-8323; *The New Book of World Rankings.*

Food and Agricultural Organization of the United Nations (FAO), Via delle Terme di Caracalla, 00100 Rome, Italy (Telephone Number in U.S. (202) 653-2400); *The State of Food and Agriculture.*

G.K. Hall and Company, 70 Lincoln Street, Boston, Massachusetts 02111 (617) 423-3990; *The World in Figures.*

Times Books, 201 East 50th Street, New York, New York 10022 (212) 751-2600; *The Economist Book of Vital World Statistics.*

The World Bank, 1818 H Street, NW, Washington, D.C. 20433 (202) 477-1234; *World Tables.*

MADAGASCAR - LABOR PRODUCTIVITY

International Labour Office, I.L.O. Publications, CH-1211, Geneva 22, Switzerland; *Yearbook of Labour Statistics.*

MADAGASCAR - LAND USE

Euromonitor Publications Limited, 87-88 Turnmill Street, London EC1M 5QU, England; *International Marketing Data and Statistics.*

Food and Agricultural Organization of the United Nations (FAO), Via delle Terme di Caracalla, 00100 Rome, Italy (Telephone Number in U.S. (202) 653-2400); *Production Yearbook.*

G.K. Hall and Company, 70 Lincoln Street, Boston, Massachusetts 02111 (617) 423-3990; *The World in Figures.*

MADAGASCAR - LIBRARIES

Facts on File, 460 Park Avenue South, New York, New York 10016 (800) 443-8323; *The New Book of World Rankings.*

United Nations Educational, Scientific and Cultural Organization (UNESCO), 7 Place de Fontenoy, F-75700 Paris, France (Telephone Number in U.S. (212) 963-5981); *Statistical Yearbook.*

MADAGASCAR - LIFE EXPECTANCY

African Development Bank, 01 BP 1387, Abidjan 01, Cote d'Ivoire; *Selected Statistics on Regional Member Countries.*

MADAGASCAR - LIGNITE PRODUCTION - See MADAGASCAR - MINING AND MINERAL PRODUCTS

MADAGASCAR - LITERACY RATE

Statistical Office of the United Nations, Publishing Service, New York, New York 10017 (800) 253-9646; *Survey of Economic and Social Conditions in Africa.*

MADAGASCAR - LIVESTOCK AND POULTRY

Euromonitor Publications Limited, 87-88 Turnmill Street, London EC1M 5QU, England; *International Marketing Data and Statistics.*

Facts on File, 460 Park Avenue South, New York, New York 10016 (800) 443-8323; *The New Book of World Rankings.*

Food and Agricultural Organization of the United Nations (FAO), Via delle Terme di Caracalla, 00100 Rome, Italy (Telephone Number in U.S. (202) 653-2400); *Production Yearbook,* and *The State of Food and Agriculture.*

G.K. Hall and Company, 70 Lincoln Street, Boston, Massachusetts 02111 (617) 423-3990; *The World in Figures.*

Statistical Office of the United Nations, Publishing Service, New York, New York 10017 (800) 253-9646; *Statistical Yearbook,* and *Survey of Economic and Social Conditions in Africa.*

United Nations Economic Commission for Africa, Africa Hall, Post Office Box 3001, Addis Ababa, Ethiopia (Telephone Number in U.S. (800) 253-9646); *African Statistical Yearbook.*

MADAGASCAR - LIVING LEVELS

G.K. Hall and Company, 70 Lincoln Street, Boston, Massachusetts 02111 (617) 423-3990; *The World in Figures.*

Times Books, 201 East 50th Street, New York, New York 10022 (212) 751-2600; *The Economist Book of Vital World Statistics.*

MADAGASCAR - MAIL TRAFFIC - NUMBER OF ITEMS SENT AND RECEIVED

Statistical Office of the United Nations, Publishing Service, New York, New York 10017 (800) 253-9646; *Statistical Yearbook.*

MADAGASCAR - MANUFACTURING

Facts on File, 460 Park Avenue South, New York, New York 10016 (800) 443-8323; *The New Book of World Rankings.*

G.K. Hall and Company, 70 Lincoln Street, Boston, Massachusetts 02111 (617) 423-3990; *The World in Figures.*

Statistical Office of the United Nations, Publishing Service, New York, New York 10017 (800) 253-9646; *Statistical Yearbook,* and *Survey of Economic and Social Conditions in Africa.*

Times Books, 201 East 50th Street, New York, New York 10022 (212) 751-2600; *The Economist Book of Vital World Statistics.*

United Nations Economic Commission for Africa, Africa Hall, Post Office Box 3001, Addis Ababa, Ethiopia (Telephone Number in U.S. (800) 253-9646); *African Statistical Yearbook.*

The World Bank, 1818 H Street, NW, Washington, D.C. 20433 (202) 477-1234; *World Tables.*

MADAGASCAR - MARRIAGE RATES

Facts on File, 460 Park Avenue South, New York, New York 10016 (800) 443-8323; *The New Book of World Rankings.*

Statistical Office of the United Nations, Publishing Service, New York, New York 10017 (800) 253-9646; *Demographic Yearbook.*

MADAGASCAR - MEAT PRODUCTION - See MADAGASCAR - LIVESTOCK AND POULTRY

MADAGASCAR - MERCHANT SHIPPING

G.K. Hall and Company, 70 Lincoln Street, Boston, Massachusetts 02111 (617) 423-3990; *The World in Figures*.

Statistical Office of the United Nations, Publishing Service, New York, New York 10017 (800) 253-9646; *Statistical Yearbook*.

Times Books, 201 East 50th Street, New York, New York 10022 (212) 751-2600; *The Economist Book of Vital World Statistics*.

United Nations Economic Commission for Africa, Africa Hall, Post Office Box 3001, Addis Ababa, Ethiopia (Telephone Number in U.S. (800) 253-9646); *African Statistical Yearbook*.

MADAGASCAR - MILITARY

G.K. Hall and Company, 70 Lincoln Street, Boston, Massachusetts 02111 (617) 423-3990; *The World in Figures*.

The International Institute for Strategic Studies, 23 Tavistock Street, London WC2E 7NQ, England; *The Military Balance*.

U.S. Arms Control and Disarmament Agency, 320 Twenty-first Street, NW, Washington, D.C. 20451 (202) 647-8677; *World Military Expenditures and Arms Transfers*.

MADAGASCAR - MILK PRODUCTION - See MADAGASCAR - DAIRY PRODUCTS

MADAGASCAR - MINING AND MINERAL PRODUCTS

Facts on File, 460 Park Avenue South, New York, New York 10016 (800) 443-8323; *The New Book of World Rankings*.

G.K. Hall and Company, 70 Lincoln Street, Boston, Massachusetts 02111 (617) 423-3990; *The World in Figures*.

Statistical Office of the United Nations, Publishing Service, New York, New York 10017 (800) 253-9646; *Statistical Yearbook*.

United Nations Economic Commission for Africa, Africa Hall, Post Office Box 3001, Addis Ababa, Ethiopia (Telephone Number in U.S. (800) 253-9646); *African Statistical Yearbook*.

MADAGASCAR - MONEY EXCHANGE RATES

Euromonitor Publications Limited, 87-88 Turnmill Street, London EC1M 5QU, England; *International Marketing Data and Statistics*.

International Monetary Fund, 700 Nineteenth Street, NW, Washington, D.C. 20431 (202) 623-7000; *International Financial Statistics*.

Statistical Office of the United Nations, Publishing Service, New York, New York 10017 (800) 253-9646; *Statistical Yearbook*.

MADAGASCAR - MONEY RESERVES

Euromonitor Publications Limited, 87-88 Turnmill Street, London EC1M 5QU, England; *International Marketing Data and Statistics*.

International Monetary Fund, 700 Nineteenth Street, NW, Washington, D.C. 20431 (202) 623-7000; *International Financial Statistics*.

Statistical Office of the United Nations, Publishing Service, New York, New York 10017 (800) 253-9646; *Statistical Yearbook*.

MADAGASCAR - MONEY SUPPLY

African Development Bank, 01 BP 1387, Abidjan 01, Cote d'Ivoire; *Selected Statistics on Regional Member Countries*.

G.K. Hall and Company, 70 Lincoln Street, Boston, Massachusetts 02111 (617) 423-3990; *The World in Figures*.

The World Bank, 1818 H Street, NW, Washington, D.C. 20433 (202) 477-1234; *World Tables*.

MADAGASCAR - MOTOR VEHICLE PRODUCTION

Statistical Office of the United Nations, Publishing Service, New York, New York 10017 (800) 253-9646; *Statistical Yearbook*.

MADAGASCAR - MOTOR VEHICLE TAXES - See MADAGASCAR - TAXATION

MADAGASCAR - MOTOR VEHICLES IN USE

G.K. Hall and Company, 70 Lincoln Street, Boston, Massachusetts 02111 (617) 423-3990; *The World in Figures*.

International Road Federation, 525 School Street, SW, Washington, D.C. 20024 (202) 554-2106; *World Road Statistics*.

Statistical Office of the United Nations, Publishing Service, New York, New York 10017 (800) 253-9646; *Statistical Yearbook*, and *Survey of Economic and Social Conditions in Africa*.

Times Books, 201 East 50th Street, New York, New York 10022 (212) 751-2600; *The Economist Book of Vital World Statistics*.

MADAGASCAR - MUSEUMS

Facts on File, 460 Park Avenue South, New York, New York 10016 (800) 443-8323; *The New Book of World Rankings*.

United Nations Educational, Scientific and Cultural Organization (UNESCO), 7 Place de Fontenoy, F 75700 Paris, France (Telephone Number in U.S. (212) 963-5981); *Statistical Yearbook*.

MADAGASCAR - NATALITY - See MADAGASCAR - BIRTH RATES

MADAGASCAR - NATIONAL ACCOUNTS

African Development Bank, 01 BP 1387, Abidjan 01, Cote d'Ivoire; *Selected Statistics on Regional Member Countries*.

Statistical Office of the United Nations, Publishing Service, New York, New York 10017 (800) 253-9646; *National Account Statistics*.

United Nations Economic Commission for Africa, Africa Hall, Post Office Box 3001, Addis Ababa, Ethiopia (Telephone Number in U.S. (800) 253-9646); *African Statistical Yearbook*.

MADAGASCAR - NATIONAL INCOME

Facts on File, 460 Park Avenue South, New York, New York 10016 (800) 443-8323; *The New Book of World Rankings*.

G.K. Hall and Company, 70 Lincoln Street, Boston, Massachusetts 02111 (617) 423-3990; *The World in Figures*.

Statistical Office of the United Nations, Publishing Service, New York, New York 10017 (800) 253-9646; *Statistical Yearbook.*

MADAGASCAR - NATIONAL PRODUCT

Facts on File, 460 Park Avenue South, New York, New York 10016 (800) 443-8323; *The New Book of World Rankings.*

MADAGASCAR - NATURAL GAS - PRODUCTION - See MADAGASCAR - MINING AND MINERAL PRODUCTS

MADAGASCAR - NEWSPAPER PRODUCTION - See MADAGASCAR - FORESTRY AND FOREST PRODUCTS

MADAGASCAR - NEWSPRINT PRODUCTION AND CONSUMPTION - See MADAGASCAR - FORESTRY AND FOREST PRODUCTS

MADAGASCAR - OCCUPATIONS - See MADAGASCAR - LABOR FORCE

MADAGASCAR - PALM OIL AND PALM KERNEL PRODUCTION - See MADAGASCAR - CROPS

MADAGASCAR - PAPER - See MADAGASCAR - FORESTRY AND FOREST PRODUCTS

MADAGASCAR - PEANUT PRODUCTION - See MADAGASCAR - CROPS

MADAGASCAR - PERIODICALS

United Nations Educational, Scientific and Cultural Organization (UNESCO), 7 Place de Fontenoy, F-75700 Paris, France (Telephone Number in U.S. (212) 963-5981); *Statistical Yearbook.*

MADAGASCAR - PESTICIDE USE

Food and Agricultural Organization of the United Nations (FAO), Via delle Terme di Caracalla, 00100 Rome, Italy (Telephone Number in U.S. (202) 653-2400); *The State of Food and Agriculture.*

MADAGASCAR - PETROLEUM INDUSTRY

Facts on File, 460 Park Avenue South, New York, New York 10016 (800) 443-8323; *The New Book of World Rankings.*

Food and Agricultural Organization of the United Nations (FAO), Via delle Terme di Caracalla, 00100 Rome, Italy (Telephone Number in U.S. (202) 653-2400); *The State of Food and Agriculture.*

G.K. Hall and Company, 70 Lincoln Street, Boston, Massachusetts 02111 (617) 423-3990; *The World in Figures.*

Statistical Office of the United Nations, Publishing Service, New York, New York 10017 (800) 253-9646; *Statistical Yearbook.*

MADAGASCAR - PIGS - See MADAGASCAR - LIVESTOCK AND POULTRY

MADAGASCAR - POPULATION

African Development Bank, 01 BP 1387, Abidjan 01, Cote d'Ivoire; *Selected Statistics on Regional Member Countries.*

The Economist Intelligence Unit, 111 West 57th Street, New York, New York 10019 (800) 938-4685; *The World Market Atlas.*

Euromonitor Publications Limited, 87-88 Turnmill Street, London EC1M 5QU, England; *International Marketing Data and Statistics.*

Facts on File, 460 Park Avenue South, New York, New York 10016 (800) 443-8323; *The New Book of World Rankings.*

Food and Agricultural Organization of the United Nations (FAO), Via delle Terme di Caracalla, 00100 Rome, Italy (Telephone Number in U.S. (202) 653-2400); *Production Yearbook.*

G.K. Hall and Company, 70 Lincoln Street, Boston, Massachusetts 02111 (617) 423-3990; *The World in Figures.*

International Labour Office, I.L.O. Publications, CH-1211, Geneva 22, Switzerland; *Yearbook of Labour Statistics.*

Statistical Office of the United Nations, Publishing Service, New York, New York 10017 (800) 253-9646; *Demographic Yearbook, Statistical Yearbook,* and *Survey of Economic and Social Conditions in Africa.*

Times Books, 201 East 50th Street, New York, New York 10022 (212) 751-2600; *The Economist Book of Vital World Statistics.*

U.S. Arms Control and Disarmament Agency, 320 Twenty-first Street, NW, Washington, D.C. 20451 (202) 647-8677; *World Military Expenditures and Arms Transfers.*

World Health Organization, Office of Publications, Avenue Appia, CH-1211 Geneva 27, Switzerland (Telephone Number in U.S. (518) 436-9686); *World Health Statistics Annual.*

MADAGASCAR - POTATO PRODUCTION - See MADAGASCAR - CROPS

MADAGASCAR - PRICES

Facts on File, 460 Park Avenue South, New York, New York 10016 (800) 443-8323; *The New Book of World Rankings.*

Food and Agricultural Organization of the United Nations (FAO), Via delle Terme di Caracalla, 00100 Rome, Italy (Telephone Number in U.S. (202) 653-2400); *Production Yearbook,* and *The State of Food and Agriculture.*

G.K. Hall and Company, 70 Lincoln Street, Boston, Massachusetts 02111 (617) 423-3990; *The World in Figures.*

International Labour Office, I.L.O. Publications, CH-1211, Geneva 22, Switzerland; *Yearbook of Labour Statistics.*

United Nations Economic Commission for Africa, Africa Hall, Post Office Box 3001, Addis Ababa, Ethiopia (Telephone Number in U.S. (800) 253-9646); *African Statistical Yearbook.*

MADAGASCAR - PRINTING AND WRITING PAPER - See MADAGASCAR - FORESTRY AND FOREST PRODUCTS

MADAGASCAR - PRODUCTION

Facts on File, 460 Park Avenue South, New York, New York 10016 (800) 443-8323; *The New Book of World Rankings.*

G.K. Hall and Company, 70 Lincoln Street, Boston, Massachusetts 02111 (617) 423-3990; *The World in Figures.*

MADAGASCAR - PRODUCTIVITY

Euromonitor Publications Limited, 87-88 Turnmill Street, London EC1M 5QU, England; *International Marketing Data and Statistics.*

MADAGASCAR - PROPERTY TAXES

International Monetary Fund, 700 Nineteenth Street, NW, Washington, D.C. 20431 (202) 623-7000; *Government Finance Statistics Yearbook.*

MADAGASCAR - PUBLIC FINANCE

Facts on File, 460 Park Avenue South, New York, New York 10016 (800) 443-8323; *The New Book of World Rankings.*

MADAGASCAR - RADIO BROADCASTING - See MADAGASCAR - BROADCASTING

MADAGASCAR - RAILWAY USE

G.K. Hall and Company, 70 Lincoln Street, Boston, Massachusetts 02111 (617) 423-3990; *The World in Figures.*

Statistical Office of the United Nations, Publishing Service, New York, New York 10017 (800) 253-9646; *Statistical Yearbook,* and *Survey of Economic and Social Conditions in Africa.*

MADAGASCAR - RAILWAYS

Jane's Information Group, Sentinel House, 163 Brighton Road, Coulsdon, Surrey CR5 2NH, England (Telephone Number in U.S. (703) 683-3700); *Jane's World Railways.*

United Nations Economic Commission for Africa, Africa Hall, Post Office Box 3001, Addis Ababa, Ethiopia (Telephone Number in U.S. (800) 253-9646); *African Statistical Yearbook.*

MADAGASCAR - RELIGION

Facts on File, 460 Park Avenue South, New York, New York 10016 (800) 443-8323; *The New Book of World Rankings.*

MADAGASCAR - RETAIL TRADE

G.K. Hall and Company, 70 Lincoln Street, Boston, Massachusetts 02111 (617) 423-3990; *The World in Figures.*

MADAGASCAR - RICE PRODUCTION - See MADAGASCAR - CROPS

MADAGASCAR - ROOT AND TUBER PRODUCTION - See MADAGASCAR - CROPS

MADAGASCAR - ROUNDWOOD PRODUCTION - See MADAGASCAR - FORESTRY AND FOREST PRODUCTS

MADAGASCAR - RUBBER PRODUCTION AND CONSUMPTION

Facts on File, 460 Park Avenue South, New York, New York 10016 (800) 443-8323; *The New Book of World Rankings.*

MADAGASCAR - SALT PRODUCTION

Statistical Office of the United Nations, Publishing Service, New York, New York 10017 (800) 253-9646; *Statistical Yearbook.*

MADAGASCAR - SAWNWOOD PRODUCTION - See MADAGASCAR - FORESTRY AND FOREST PRODUCTS

MADAGASCAR - SCIENCE AND TECHNOLOGY - EXPENDITURE FOR RESEARCH

Statistical Office of the United Nations, Publishing Service, New York, New York 10017 (800) 253-9646; *Statistical Yearbook.*

MADAGASCAR - SCIENTISTS AND TECHNICIANS

Statistical Office of the United Nations, Publishing Service, New York, New York 10017 (800) 253-9646; *Statistical Yearbook.*

MADAGASCAR - SENIOR CITIZENS

Facts on File, 460 Park Avenue South, New York, New York 10016 (800) 443-8323; *The New Book of World Rankings.*

MADAGASCAR - SHEEP - See MADAGASCAR - LIVESTOCK AND POULTRY

MADAGASCAR - SILVER PRODUCTION AND CONSUMPTION - See MADAGASCAR - MINING AND MINERAL PRODUCTS

MADAGASCAR - SISAL PRODUCTION - See MADAGASCAR - CROPS

MADAGASCAR - SOCIAL DATA

African Development Bank, 01 BP 1387, Abidjan 01, Cote d'Ivoire; *Selected Statistics on Regional Member Countries.*

Facts on File, 460 Park Avenue South, New York, New York 10016 (800) 443-8323; *The New Book of World Rankings.*

G.K. Hall and Company, 70 Lincoln Street, Boston, Massachusetts 02111 (617) 423-3990; *The World in Figures.*

MADAGASCAR - SOCIAL SECURITY EXPENDITURE

International Monetary Fund, 700 Nineteenth Street, NW, Washington, D.C. 20431 (202) 623-7000; *Government Finance Statistics Yearbook.*

MADAGASCAR - STAMP TAXES AND DUTIES - See MADAGASCAR - TAXATION

MADAGASCAR - STATE BUDGET

Euromonitor Publications Limited, 87-88 Turnmill Street, London EC1M 5QU, England; *International Marketing Data and Statistics.*

MADAGASCAR - STEEL - See MADAGASCAR - MINING AND MINERAL PRODUCTS

MADAGASCAR - STOCKS - COMMODITY - MARKET PRICE - INDEX

Food and Agricultural Organization of the United Nations (FAO), Via delle Terme di Caracalla, 00100 Rome, Italy (Telephone Number in U.S. (202) 653-2400); *The State of Food and Agriculture.*

MADAGASCAR - SUGAR PRODUCTION AND CONSUMPTION - See MADAGASCAR - CROPS

MADAGASCAR - TAXATION

G.K. Hall and Company, 70 Lincoln Street, Boston, Massachusetts 02111 (617) 423-3990; *The World in Figures.*

International Monetary Fund, 700 Nineteenth Street, NW, Washington, D.C. 20431 (202) 623-7000; *Government Finance Statistics Yearbook.*

International Road Federation, 525 School Street, SW, Washington, D.C. 20024 (202) 554-2106; *World Road Statistics.*

The World Bank, 1818 H Street, NW, Washington, D.C. 20433 (202) 477-1234; *World Tables.*

MADAGASCAR - TELEGRAPH SERVICE

Statistical Office of the United Nations, Publishing Service, New York, New York 10017 (800) 253-9646; *Statistical Yearbook.*

MADAGASCAR - TELEPHONES IN USE

American Telephone and Telegraph Company, 26 Parsippany Road, Whippany, New Jersey 07981 (800) 338-4038; *The World's Telephones.*

G.K. Hall and Company, 70 Lincoln Street, Boston, Massachusetts 02111 (617) 423-3990; *The World in Figures.*

Statistical Office of the United Nations, Publishing Service, New York, New York 10017 (800) 253-9646; *Statistical Yearbook.*

MADAGASCAR - TELEVISION BROADCASTING - See MADAGASCAR - BROADCASTING

MADAGASCAR - TEXTILE INDUSTRY

G.K. Hall and Company, 70 Lincoln Street, Boston, Massachusetts 02111 (617) 423-3990; *The World in Figures.*

Statistical Office of the United Nations, Publishing Service, New York, New York 10017 (800) 253-9646; *Statistical Yearbook.*

MADAGASCAR - THEATRE

United Nations Educational, Scientific and Cultural Organization (UNESCO), 7 Place de Fontenoy, F-75700 Paris, France (Telephone Number in U.S. (212) 963-5981); *Statistical Yearbook.*

MADAGASCAR - TOBACCO PRODUCTION

Facts on File, 460 Park Avenue South, New York, New York 10016 (800) 443-8323; *The New Book of World Rankings.*

Statistical Office of the United Nations, Publishing Service, New York, New York 10017 (800) 253-9646; *Statistical Yearbook.*

MADAGASCAR - TOURISM

Facts on File, 460 Park Avenue South, New York, New York 10016 (800) 443-8323; *The New Book of World Rankings.*

G.K. Hall and Company, 70 Lincoln Street, Boston, Massachusetts 02111 (617) 423-3990; *The World in Figures.*

Statistical Office of the United Nations, Publishing Service, New York, New York 10017 (800) 253-9646; *Statistical Yearbook.*

Times Books, 201 East 50th Street, New York, New York 10022 (212) 751-2600; *The Economist Book of Vital World Statistics.*

United Nations Economic Commission for Africa, Africa Hall, Post Office Box 3001, Addis Ababa, Ethiopia (Telephone Number in U.S. (800) 253-9646); *African Statistical Yearbook.*

World Tourism Organization, Calle Capitan Haya 42, E-28020 Madrid, Spain; *Yearbook of Tourism Statistics.*

MADAGASCAR - TRACTORS IN USE

Statistical Office of the United Nations, Publishing Service, New York, New York 10017 (800) 253-9646; *Statistical Yearbook.*

MADAGASCAR - TRADE - See MADAGASCAR - FOREIGN TRADE

MADAGASCAR - TRANSPORTATION AND COMMUNICATIONS

Facts on File, 460 Park Avenue South, New York, New York 10016 (800) 443-8323; *The New Book of World Rankings.*

G.K. Hall and Company, 70 Lincoln Street, Boston, Massachusetts 02111 (617) 423-3990; *The World in Figures.*

United Nations Economic Commission for Africa, Africa Hall, Post Office Box 3001, Addis Ababa, Ethiopia (Telephone Number in U.S. (800) 253-9646); *African Statistical Yearbook.*

MADAGASCAR - UNEMPLOYMENT

Euromonitor Publications Limited, 87-88 Turnmill Street, London EC1M 5QU, England; *International Marketing Data and Statistics.*

International Labour Office, I.L.O. Publications, CH-1211, Geneva 22, Switzerland; *Yearbook of Labour Statistics.*

Statistical Office of the United Nations, Publishing Service, New York, New York 10017 (800) 253-9646; *Statistical Yearbook.*

MADAGASCAR - VANILLA EXPORTS

International Monetary Fund, 700 Nineteenth Street, NW, Washington, D.C. 20431 (202) 623-7000; *International Financial Statistics.*

MADAGASCAR - VITAL STATISTICS

Euromonitor Publications Limited, 87-88 Turnmill Street, London EC1M 5QU, England; *International Marketing Data and Statistics.*

G.K. Hall and Company, 70 Lincoln Street, Boston, Massachusetts 02111 (617) 423-3990; *The World in Figures.*

Statistical Office of the United Nations, Publishing Service, New York, New York 10017 (800) 253-9646; *Statistical Yearbook.*

World Health Organization, Office of Publications, Avenue Appia, CH-1211 Geneva 27, Switzerland (Telephone Number in U.S. (518) 436-9686); *World Health Statistics Annual.*

MADAGASCAR - WAGES

G.K. Hall and Company, 70 Lincoln Street, Boston, Massachusetts 02111 (617) 423-3990; *The World in Figures.*

International Labour Office, I.L.O. Publications, CH-1211, Geneva 22, Switzerland; *Yearbook of Labour Statistics.*

MADAGASCAR - WEATHER

Facts on File, 460 Park Avenue South, New York, New York 10016 (800) 443-8323; *The New Book of World Rankings.*

G.K. Hall and Company, 70 Lincoln Street, Boston, Massachusetts 02111 (617) 423-3990; *The World in Figures.*

MADAGASCAR - WELFARE EXPENDITURES

International Monetary Fund, 700 Nineteenth Street, NW, Washington, D.C. 20431 (202) 623-7000; *Government Finance Statistics Yearbook.*

MADAGASCAR - WHEAT PRODUCTION

Facts on File, 460 Park Avenue South, New York, New York 10016 (800) 443-8323; *The New Book of World Rankings.*

MADAGASCAR - WINE PRODUCTION

Facts on File, 460 Park Avenue South, New York, New York 10016 (800) 443-8323; *The New Book of World Rankings.*

Statistical Office of the United Nations, Publishing Service, New York, New York 10017 (800) 253-9646; *Statistical Yearbook.*

MADAGASCAR - WOOL PRODUCTION

Facts on File, 460 Park Avenue South, New York, New York 10016 (800) 443-8323; *The New Book of World Rankings.*

MADAGASCAR - YARN PRODUCTION

Statistical Office of the United Nations, Publishing Service, New York, New York 10017 (800) 253-9646; *Statistical Yearbook.*

MAGAZINES - ADVERTISING EXPENDITURES

McCann-Erickson, Inc., 750 Third Avenue, New York, New York 10017; compiled for Crain Communications, Incorporated, 740 North Rush Street, Chicago, Illinois 60611 (212) 649-5200; in *Advertising Age.*

Publishers Information Bureau, 575 Lexington Avenue, New York, New York 10022 (212) 752-0055; as compiled by Leading National Advertisers, 11 West 42nd Street, New York, New York 10036 (212) 425-0050.

MAGAZINES - READING AND RECEIPTS

Veronis, Suhler and Associates, 350 Park Avenue, New York, New York 10022 (212) 935-4990; *Communications Industry Forecast Report.*

MAGNESIUM

U.S. Department of the Interior, Bureau of Mines, 810 Seventh Street, NW, Washington, D.C. 20241 (202) 501-9649; *Annual Reports,* and *Mineral Commodity Summaries.*

MAIL

U.S. Postal Service, 475 L'Enfant Plaza West, SW, Washington, D.C. 20260 (202) 268-2000; *Annual Report of the Postmaster General.*

MAINE - See also STATE DATA (FOR INDIVIDUAL STATES)

Maine - Primary Statistics Source

Maine Department of Economic and Community Development, State House Station 59, Augusta, Maine 04333 (207) 287-3153; *Maine: A Statistical Summary.*

Maine - State Data Centers

Division of Economic Analysis and Research, Maine Department of Labor, 20 Union Street, Augusta, Maine 04330, Ms. Jean Martin (207) 289-2271.

Maine State Library, State House, Station 64, Augusta, Maine 04333, Mr. Gary Nichols (207) 289-5600.

MALARIA

U.S. Department of Health and Human Services, Center for Disease Control, 1600 Clifton Road, NE, Atlanta, Georgia 30333 (404) 639-3311; *Summary of Notifiable Diseases,* and *U.S. Morbidity and Mortality Weekly Report.*

Malawi - National Statistical Office

National Statistical Office, Post Office Box 333, Zomba, Malawi.

Malawi - Primary Statistics Source

National Statistical Office, Post Office Box 333, Zomba, Malawi; *Malawi Statistical Yearbook,* and *Monthly Bulletin of Statistics.*

MALAWI - AGRICULTURE

Euromonitor Publications Limited, 87-88 Turnmill Street, London EC1M 5QU, England; *International Marketing Data and Statistics.*

Facts on File, 460 Park Avenue South, New York, New York 10016 (800) 443-8323; *The New Book of World Rankings.*

Food and Agricultural Organization of the United Nations (FAO), Via delle Terme di Caracalla, 00100 Rome, Italy (Telephone Number in U.S. (202) 653-2400); *Production Yearbook, The State of Food and Agriculture,* and *Trade Yearbook.*

G.K. Hall and Company, 70 Lincoln Street, Boston, Massachusetts 02111 (617) 423-3990; *The World in Figures.*

Statistical Office of the United Nations, Publishing Service, New York, New York 10017 (800) 253-9646; *Statistical Yearbook,* and *Survey of Economic and Social Conditions in Africa.*

Times Books, 201 East 50th Street, New York, New York 10022 (212) 751-2600; *The Economist Book of Vital World Statistics.*

United Nations Economic Commission for Africa, Africa Hall, Post Office Box 3001, Addis Ababa, Ethiopia (Telephone Number in U.S. (800) 253-9646); *African Statistical Yearbook.*

The World Bank, 1818 H Street, NW, Washington, D.C. 20433 (202) 477-1234; *World Tables.*

MALAWI - AIRLINE SERVICE

Facts on File, 460 Park Avenue South, New York, New York 10016 (800) 443-8323; *The New Book of World Rankings.*

G.K. Hall and Company, 70 Lincoln Street, Boston, Massachusetts 02111 (617) 423-3990; *The World in Figures.*

International Civil Aviation Organization, 1000 Sherbrooke Street West, Suite 400, Montreal, Quebec H3A 2R2, Canada (514) 285-8219; *Civil Aviation Statistics of the World.*

Statistical Office of the United Nations, Publishing Service, New York, New York 10017 (800) 253-9646; *Statistical Yearbook.*

Times Books, 201 East 50th Street, New York, New York 10022 (212) 751-2600; *The Economist Book of Vital World Statistics.*

United Nations Economic Commission for Africa, Africa Hall, Post Office Box 3001, Addis Ababa, Ethiopia (Telephone Number in U.S. (800) 253-9646); *African Statistical Yearbook.*

MALAWI - ALUMINUM PRODUCTION AND CONSUMPTION - See MALAWI - MINING AND MINERAL PRODUCTS

MALAWI - ANIMAL HEALTH

Food and Agricultural Organization of the United Nations (FAO), Via delle Terme di Caracalla, 00100 Rome, Italy (Telephone Number in U.S. (202) 653-2400); *Animal Health Yearbook.*

MALAWI - AREA AND DENSITY OF POPULATION

African Development Bank, 01 BP 1387, Abidjan 01, Cote d'Ivoire; *Selected Statistics on Regional Member Countries.*

Euromonitor Publications Limited, 87-88 Turnmill Street, London EC1M 5QU, England; *International Marketing Data and Statistics.*

Facts on File, 460 Park Avenue South, New York, New York 10016 (800) 443-8323; *The New Book of World Rankings.*

Food and Agricultural Organization of the United Nations (FAO), Via delle Terme di Caracalla, 00100 Rome, Italy (Telephone Number in U.S. (202) 653-2400); *The State of Food and Agriculture.*

G.K. Hall and Company, 70 Lincoln Street, Boston, Massachusetts 02111 (617) 423-3990; *The World in Figures.*

Statistical Office of the United Nations, Publishing Service, New York, New York 10017 (800) 253-9646; *Statistical Yearbook,* and *Survey of Economic and Social Conditions in Africa.*

Times Books, 201 East 50th Street, New York, New York 10022 (212) 751-2600; *The Economist Book of Vital World Statistics.*

MALAWI - ARMS EXPORTS AND IMPORTS

U.S. Arms Control and Disarmament Agency, 320 Twenty-first Street, NW, Washington, D.C. 20451 (202) 647-8677; *World Military Expenditures and Arms Transfers.*

MALAWI - BALANCE OF PAYMENTS

African Development Bank, 01 BP 1387, Abidjan 01, Cote d'Ivoire; *Selected Statistics on Regional Member Countries.*

The Economist Intelligence Unit, 111 West 57th Street, New York, New York 10019 (800) 938-4685; *The World Market Atlas.*

G.K. Hall and Company, 70 Lincoln Street, Boston, Massachusetts 02111 (617) 423-3990; *The World in Figures.*

International Monetary Fund, 700 Nineteenth Street, NW, Washington, D.C. 20431 (202) 623-7000; *Balance of Payments Yearbook,* and *International Financial Statistics.*

Times Books, 201 East 50th Street, New York, New York 10022 (212) 751-2600; *The Economist Book of Vital World Statistics.*

United Nations Economic Commission for Africa, Africa Hall, Post Office Box 3001, Addis Ababa, Ethiopia (Telephone Number in U.S. (800) 253-9646); *African Statistical Yearbook.*

The World Bank, 1818 H Street, NW, Washington, D.C. 20433 (202) 477-1234; *World Tables.*

MALAWI - BANKING

Asian Development Bank, Post Office Box 789, 1099 Manila, Philippines; *Key Indicators of Developing Asian and Pacific Countries.*

Facts on File, 460 Park Avenue South, New York, New York 10016 (800) 443-8323; *The New Book of World Rankings.*

G.K. Hall and Company, 70 Lincoln Street, Boston, Massachusetts 02111 (617) 423-3990; *The World in Figures.*

International Monetary Fund, 700 Nineteenth Street, NW, Washington, D.C. 20431 (202) 623-7000; *International Financial Statistics.*

United Nations Economic Commission for Africa, Africa Hall, Post Office Box 3001, Addis Ababa, Ethiopia (Telephone Number in U.S. (800) 253-9646); *African Statistical Yearbook.*

MALAWI - BARLEY PRODUCTION - See MALAWI - CROPS

MALAWI - BEER PRODUCTION

Facts on File, 460 Park Avenue South, New York, New York 10016 (800) 443-8323; *The New Book of World Rankings.*

Statistical Office of the United Nations, Publishing Service, New York, New York 10017 (800) 253-9646; *Statistical Yearbook.*

MALAWI - BIRTH RATES

Facts on File, 460 Park Avenue South, New York, New York 10016 (800) 443-8323; *The New Book of World Rankings.*

Statistical Office of the United Nations, Publishing Service, New York, New York 10017 (800) 253-9646; *Demographic Yearbook, Statistical Yearbook,* and *Survey of Economic and Social Conditions in Africa.*

Times Books, 201 East 50th Street, New York, New York 10022 (212) 751-2600; *The Economist Book of Vital World Statistics.*

The World Bank, 1818 H Street, NW, Washington, D.C. 20433 (202) 477-1234; *World Tables.*

MALAWI - BONDS

G.K. Hall and Company, 70 Lincoln Street, Boston, Massachusetts 02111 (617) 423-3990; *The World in Figures.*

MALAWI - BOOK PRODUCTION

G.K. Hall and Company, 70 Lincoln Street, Boston, Massachusetts 02111 (617) 423-3990; *The World in Figures.*

United Nations Educational, Scientific and Cultural Organization (UNESCO), 7 Place de Fontenoy, F-75700 Paris, France (Telephone Number in U.S. (212) 963-5981); *Statistical Yearbook.*

MALAWI - BROADCASTING

Billboard Limited, Post Office Box 9027, 1006 AA Amsterdam, The Netherlands (Telephone Number in U.S. (212) 764-7300); *World Radio TV Handbook.*

Facts on File, 460 Park Avenue South, New York, New York 10016 (800) 443-8323; *The New Book of World Rankings.*

G.K. Hall and Company, 70 Lincoln Street, Boston, Massachusetts 02111 (617) 423-3990; *The World in Figures.*

Times Books, 201 East 50th Street, New York, New York 10022 (212) 751-2600; *The Economist Book of Vital World Statistics*.

MALAWI - BUSINESS

G.K. Hall and Company, 70 Lincoln Street, Boston, Massachusetts 02111 (617) 423-3990; *The World in Figures*.

MALAWI - BUSINESS AND PROFESSIONAL LICENSES

International Monetary Fund, 700 Nineteenth Street, NW, Washington, D.C. 20431 (202) 623-7000; *Government Finance Statistics Yearbook*.

MALAWI - CABBAGE PRODUCTION - See MALAWI - CROPS

MALAWI - CALORIE SUPPLY

African Development Bank, 01 BP 1387, Abidjan 01, Cote d'Ivoire; *Selected Statistics on Regional Member Countries*.

Food and Agricultural Organization of the United Nations (FAO), Via delle Terme di Caracalla, 00100 Rome, Italy (Telephone Number in U.S. (202) 653-2400); *The State of Food and Agriculture*.

MALAWI - CAPITAL REVENUE

International Monetary Fund, 700 Nineteenth Street, NW, Washington, D.C. 20431 (202) 623-7000; *Government Finance Statistics Yearbook*.

MALAWI - CATTLE - See MALAWI - LIVESTOCK AND POULTRY

MALAWI - CEMENT PRODUCTION - See MALAWI - MINING AND MINERAL PRODUCTS

MALAWI - CHEMICAL (ORGANIC) PRODUCTION - See MALAWI - MINING AND MINERAL PRODUCTS

MALAWI - CHICKENS - See MALAWI - LIVESTOCK AND POULTRY

MALAWI - CIGARETTE PRODUCTION - See MALAWI - TOBACCO PRODUCTION

MALAWI - CLASS STRUCTURE

G.K. Hall and Company, 70 Lincoln Street, Boston, Massachusetts 02111 (617) 423-3990; *The World in Figures*.

MALAWI - CLIMATE

Facts on File, 460 Park Avenue South, New York, New York 10016 (800) 443-8323; *The New Book of World Rankings*.

G.K. Hall and Company, 70 Lincoln Street, Boston, Massachusetts 02111 (617) 423-3990; *The World in Figures*.

MALAWI - COAL PRODUCTION - See MALAWI - MINING AND MINERAL PRODUCTS

MALAWI - COFFEE PRODUCTION AND CONSUMPTION - See MALAWI - CROPS

MALAWI - COMMUNICATIONS

G.K. Hall and Company, 70 Lincoln Street, Boston, Massachusetts 02111 (617) 423-3990; *The World in Figures*.

United Nations Economic Commission for Africa, Africa Hall, Post Office Box 3001, Addis Ababa, Ethiopia (Telephone Number in U.S. (800) 253-9646); *African Statistical Yearbook*.

MALAWI - CONSTRUCTION INDUSTRY

Facts on File, 460 Park Avenue South, New York, New York 10016 (800) 443-8323; *The New Book of World Rankings*.

Statistical Office of the United Nations, Publishing Service, New York, New York 10017 (800) 253-9646; *Statistical Yearbook*.

United Nations Economic Commission for Africa, Africa Hall, Post Office Box 3001, Addis Ababa, Ethiopia (Telephone Number in U.S. (800) 253-9646); *African Statistical Yearbook*.

MALAWI - CONSUMER PRICE INDEX

African Development Bank, 01 BP 1387, Abidjan 01, Cote d'Ivoire; *Selected Statistics on Regional Member Countries*.

G.K. Hall and Company, 70 Lincoln Street, Boston, Massachusetts 02111 (617) 423-3990; *The World in Figures*.

Statistical Office of the United Nations, Publishing Service, New York, New York 10017 (800) 253-9646; *Statistical Yearbook*, and *Survey of Economic and Social Conditions in Africa*.

United Nations Economic Commission for Africa, Africa Hall, Post Office Box 3001, Addis Ababa, Ethiopia (Telephone Number in U.S. (800) 253-9646); *African Statistical Yearbook*.

MALAWI - CONSUMER PRICES

International Labour Office, I.L.O. Publications, CH-1211, Geneva 22, Switzerland; *Yearbook of Labour Statistics*.

International Monetary Fund, 700 Nineteenth Street, NW, Washington, D.C. 20431 (202) 623-7000; *International Financial Statistics*.

Times Books, 201 East 50th Street, New York, New York 10022 (212) 751-2600; *The Economist Book of Vital World Statistics*.

MALAWI - CONSUMPTION

African Development Bank, 01 BP 1387, Abidjan 01, Cote d'Ivoire; *Selected Statistics on Regional Member Countries*.

G.K. Hall and Company, 70 Lincoln Street, Boston, Massachusetts 02111 (617) 423-3990; *The World in Figures*.

Statistical Office of the United Nations, Publishing Service, New York, New York 10017 (800) 253-9646; *Survey of Economic and Social Conditions in Africa*.

MALAWI - COPPER PRODUCTION AND CONSUMPTION - See MALAWI - MINING AND MINERAL PRODUCTS

MALAWI - CORN PRODUCTION - See MALAWI - CROPS

MALAWI - CORPORATE TAXES - See MALAWI - TAXATION

MALAWI - COTTON PRODUCTION - See MALAWI - CROPS

MALAWI - CRIME

International Criminal Police Organization (INTERPOL), 26 rue Armengaud, 92210 Saint Cloud, France; *International Crime*

Statistics.

Yale University Press, Yale Station, New Haven, Connecticut 06520 (203) 432-0940; *Violence and Crime in Cross-National Perspective.*

MALAWI - CROPS

Commodity Research Bureau, Incorporated, 75 Wall Street, New York, New York 10005 (212) 504-7754; *Commodity Yearbook.*

Facts on File, 460 Park Avenue South, New York, New York 10016 (800) 443-8323; *The New Book of World Rankings.*

Food and Agricultural Organization of the United Nations (FAO), Via delle Terme di Caracalla, 00100 Rome, Italy (Telephone Number in U.S. (202) 653-2400); *Production Yearbook,* and *The State of Food and Agriculture.*

G.K. Hall and Company, 70 Lincoln Street, Boston, Massachusetts 02111 (617) 423-3990; *The World in Figures.*

International Monetary Fund, 700 Nineteenth Street, NW, Washington, D.C. 20431 (202) 623-7000; *International Financial Statistics.*

Statistical Office of the United Nations, Publishing Service, New York, New York 10017 (800) 253-9646; *Statistical Yearbook.*

United Nations Economic Commission for Africa, Africa Hall, Post Office Box 3001, Addis Ababa, Ethiopia (Telephone Number in U.S. (800) 253-9646); *African Statistical Yearbook.*

MALAWI - CUSTOMS DUTIES

G.K. Hall and Company, 70 Lincoln Street, Boston, Massachusetts 02111 (617) 423-3990; *The World in Figures.*

International Monetary Fund, 700 Nineteenth Street, NW, Washington, D.C. 20431 (202) 623-7000; *Government Finance Statistics Yearbook.*

MALAWI - DAIRY PRODUCTS

Facts on File, 460 Park Avenue South, New York, New York 10016 (800) 443-8323; *The New Book of World Rankings.*

Food and Agricultural Organization of the United Nations (FAO), Via delle Terme di Caracalla, 00100 Rome, Italy (Telephone Number in U.S. (202) 653-2400); *The State of Food and Agriculture.*

Statistical Office of the United Nations, Publishing Service, New York, New York 10017 (800) 253-9646; *Statistical Yearbook.*

MALAWI - DEATH RATES

G.K. Hall and Company, 70 Lincoln Street, Boston, Massachusetts 02111 (617) 423-3990; *The World in Figures.*

Statistical Office of the United Nations, Publishing Service, New York, New York 10017 (800) 253-9646; *Statistical Yearbook,* and *Survey of Economic and Social Conditions in Africa.*

Times Books, 201 East 50th Street, New York, New York 10022 (212) 751-2600; *The Economist Book of Vital World Statistics.*

World Health Organization, Office of Publications, Avenue Appia, CH-1211 Geneva 27, Switzerland (Telephone Number in U.S. (518) 436-9686); *World Health Statistics Annual.*

MALAWI - DEFENSE EXPENDITURES

G.K. Hall and Company, 70 Lincoln Street, Boston, Massachusetts 02111 (617) 423-3990; *The World in Figures.*

International Monetary Fund, 700 Nineteenth Street, NW, Washington, D.C. 20431 (202) 623-7000; *Government Finance Statistics Yearbook.*

U.S. Arms Control and Disarmament Agency, 320 Twenty-first Street, NW, Washington, D.C. 20451 (202) 647-8677; *World Military Expenditures and Arms Transfers.*

MALAWI - DEMOGRAPHY

The Economist Intelligence Unit, 111 West 57th Street, New York, New York 10019 (800) 938-4685; *The World Market Atlas.*

Facts on File, 460 Park Avenue South, New York, New York 10016 (800) 443-8323; *The New Book of World Rankings.*

G.K. Hall and Company, 70 Lincoln Street, Boston, Massachusetts 02111 (617) 423-3990; *The World in Figures.*

Statistical Office of the United Nations, Publishing Service, New York, New York 10017 (800) 253-9646; *Survey of Economic and Social Conditions in Africa.*

MALAWI - DEVELOPMENT ASSISTANCE

G.K. Hall and Company, 70 Lincoln Street, Boston, Massachusetts 02111 (617) 423-3990; *The World in Figures.*

Statistical Office of the United Nations, Publishing Service, New York, New York 10017 (800) 253-9646; *Statistical Yearbook.*

MALAWI - DIAMOND PRODUCTION - See MALAWI - MINING AND MINERAL PRODUCTS

MALAWI - DISEASE

G.K. Hall and Company, 70 Lincoln Street, Boston, Massachusetts 02111 (617) 423-3990; *The World in Figures.*

World Health Organization, Office of Publications, Avenue Appia, CH-1211 Geneva 27, Switzerland (Telephone Number in U.S. (518) 436-9686); *World Health Statistics Annual.*

MALAWI - DIVORCE

Facts on File, 460 Park Avenue South, New York, New York 10016 (800) 443-8323; *The New Book of World Rankings.*

Statistical Office of the United Nations, Publishing Service, New York, New York 10017 (800) 253-9646; *Demographic Yearbook.*

MALAWI - DOMESTIC PRODUCT

G.K. Hall and Company, 70 Lincoln Street, Boston, Massachusetts 02111 (617) 423-3990; *The World in Figures.*

MALAWI - ECONOMY

African Development Bank, 01 BP 1387, Abidjan 01, Cote d'Ivoire; *Selected Statistics on Regional Member Countries.*

Euromonitor Publications Limited, 87-88 Turnmill Street, London EC1M 5QU, England; *International Marketing Data and Statistics.*

Facts on File, 460 Park Avenue South, New York, New York 10016 (800) 443-8323; *The New Book of World Rankings*.

G.K. Hall and Company, 70 Lincoln Street, Boston, Massachusetts 02111 (617) 423-3990; *The World in Figures*.

MALAWI - EDUCATION

African Development Bank, 01 BP 1387, Abidjan 01, Cote d'Ivoire; *Selected Statistics on Regional Member Countries*.

The Economist Intelligence Unit, 111 West 57th Street, New York, New York 10019 (800) 938-4685; *The World Market Atlas*.

Facts on File, 460 Park Avenue South, New York, New York 10016 (800) 443-8323; *The New Book of World Rankings*.

G.K. Hall and Company, 70 Lincoln Street, Boston, Massachusetts 02111 (617) 423-3990; *The World in Figures*.

International Monetary Fund, 700 Nineteenth Street, NW, Washington, D.C. 20431 (202) 623-7000; *Government Finance Statistics Yearbook*.

Statistical Office of the United Nations, Publishing Service, New York, New York 10017 (800) 253-9646; *Survey of Economic and Social Conditions in Africa*.

Times Books, 201 East 50th Street, New York, New York 10022 (212) 751-2600; *The Economist Book of Vital World Statistics*.

United Nations Economic Commission for Africa, Africa Hall, Post Office Box 3001, Addis Ababa, Ethiopia (Telephone Number in U.S. (800) 253-9646); *African Statistical Yearbook*.

United Nations Educational, Scientific and Cultural Organization (UNESCO), 7 Place de Fontenoy, F-75700 Paris, France (Telephone Number in U.S. (212) 963-5981); *Statistical Yearbook*.

The World Bank, 1818 H Street, NW, Washington, D.C. 20433 (202) 477-1234; *World Tables*.

MALAWI - EGG PRODUCTION AND CONSUMPTION - See MALAWI - DAIRY PRODUCTS

MALAWI - ELECTRICITY

Facts on File, 460 Park Avenue South, New York, New York 10016 (800) 443-8323; *The New Book of World Rankings*.

Statistical Office of the United Nations, Publishing Service, New York, New York 10017 (800) 253-9646; *Statistical Yearbook*, and *Survey of Economic and Social Conditions in Africa*.

Times Books, 201 East 50th Street, New York, New York 10022 (212) 751-2600; *The Economist Book of Vital World Statistics*.

United Nations Economic Commission for Africa, Africa Hall, Post Office Box 3001, Addis Ababa, Ethiopia (Telephone Number in U.S. (800) 253-9646); *African Statistical Yearbook*.

MALAWI - EMPLOYMENT

Euromonitor Publications Limited, 87-88 Turnmill Street, London EC1M 5QU, England; *International Marketing Data and Statistics*.

Facts on File, 460 Park Avenue South, New York, New York 10016 (800) 443-8323; *The New Book of World Rankings*.

International Labour Office, I.L.O. Publications, CH-1211, Geneva 22, Switzerland; *Yearbook of Labour Statistics*.

Statistical Office of the United Nations, Publishing Service, New York, New York 10017 (800) 253-9646; *Statistical Yearbook*, and *Survey of Economic and Social Conditions in Africa*.

United Nations Economic Commission for Africa, Africa Hall, Post Office Box 3001, Addis Ababa, Ethiopia (Telephone Number in U.S. (800) 253-9646); *African Statistical Yearbook*.

MALAWI - ENERGY

Facts on File, 460 Park Avenue South, New York, New York 10016 (800) 443-8323; *The New Book of World Rankings*.

Food and Agricultural Organization of the United Nations (FAO), Via delle Terme di Caracalla, 00100 Rome, Italy (Telephone Number in U.S. (202) 653-2400); *The State of Food and Agriculture*.

G.K. Hall and Company, 70 Lincoln Street, Boston, Massachusetts 02111 (617) 423-3990; *The World in Figures*.

Statistical Office of the United Nations, Publishing Service, New York, New York 10017 (800) 253-9646; *Energy Statistics Yearbook*, and *Statistical Yearbook*.

Times Books, 201 East 50th Street, New York, New York 10022 (212) 751-2600; *The Economist Book of Vital World Statistics*.

United Nations Economic Commission for Africa, Africa Hall, Post Office Box 3001, Addis Ababa, Ethiopia (Telephone Number in U.S. (800) 253-9646); *African Statistical Yearbook*.

MALAWI - EXCHANGE RATES

African Development Bank, 01 BP 1387, Abidjan 01, Cote d'Ivoire; *Selected Statistics on Regional Member Countries*.

Euromonitor Publications Limited, 87-88 Turnmill Street, London EC1M 5QU, England; *International Marketing Data and Statistics*.

International Civil Aviation Organization, 1000 Sherbrooke Street West, Suite 400, Montreal, Quebec H3A 2R2, Canada (514) 285-8219; *Civil Aviation Statistics of the World*.

International Monetary Fund, 700 Nineteenth Street, NW, Washington, D.C. 20431 (202) 623-7000; *International Financial Statistics*.

Statistical Office of the United Nations, Publishing Service, New York, New York 10017 (800) 253-9646; *Statistical Yearbook*.

MALAWI - EXCISE TAXES - See MALAWI - TAXATION

MALAWI - EXPORTS

African Development Bank, 01 BP 1387, Abidjan 01, Cote d'Ivoire; *Selected Statistics on Regional Member Countries*.

The Economist Intelligence Unit, 111 West 57th Street, New York, New York 10019 (800) 938-4685; *The World Market Atlas*.

Euromonitor Publications Limited, 87-88 Turnmill Street, London EC1M 5QU, England; *International Marketing Data and Statistics*.

Food and Agricultural Organization of the United Nations (FAO), Via delle Terme di Caracalla, 00100 Rome, Italy (Telephone Number in U.S. (202) 653-2400); *The State of Food and Agriculture*.

G.K. Hall and Company, 70 Lincoln Street, Boston, Massachusetts 02111 (617) 423-3990; *The World in Figures.*

International Monetary Fund, 700 Nineteenth Street, NW, Washington, D.C. 20431 (202) 623-7000; *Direction of Trade Statistics,* and *International Financial Statistics.*

Statistical Office of the United Nations, Publishing Service, New York, New York 10017 (800) 253-9646; *Survey of Economic and Social Conditions in Africa.*

Times Books, 201 East 50th Street, New York, New York 10022 (212) 751-2600; *The Economist Book of Vital World Statistics.*

United Nations Economic Commission for Africa, Africa Hall, Post Office Box 3001, Addis Ababa, Ethiopia (Telephone Number in U.S. (800) 253-9646); *African Statistical Yearbook.*

The World Bank, 1818 H Street, NW, Washington, D.C. 20433 (202) 477-1234; *World Tables.*

MALAWI - EXTERNAL INDEBTEDNESS

African Development Bank, 01 BP 1387, Abidjan 01, Cote d'Ivoire; *Selected Statistics on Regional Member Countries.*

Statistical Office of the United Nations, Publishing Service, New York, New York 10017 (800) 253-9646; *Survey of Economic and Social Conditions in Africa.*

The World Bank, 1818 H Street, NW, Washington, D.C. 20433 (202) 477-1234; *World Tables.*

MALAWI - EXTERNAL TRADE

African Development Bank, 01 BP 1387, Abidjan 01, Cote d'Ivoire; *Selected Statistics on Regional Member Countries.*

Food and Agricultural Organization of the United Nations (FAO), Via delle Terme di Caracalla, 00100 Rome, Italy (Telephone Number in U.S. (202) 653-2400); *The State of Food and Agriculture,* and *Trade Yearbook.*

G.K. Hall and Company, 70 Lincoln Street, Boston, Massachusetts 02111 (617) 423-3990; *The World in Figures.*

Statistical Office of the United Nations, Publishing Service, New York, New York 10017 (800) 253-9646; *Statistical Yearbook.*

MALAWI - FARM CROPS - See MALAWI - CROPS

MALAWI - FEMALE WORKING POPULATION - See MALAWI - EMPLOYMENT

MALAWI - FERTILITY RATES

Facts on File, 460 Park Avenue South, New York, New York 10016 (800) 443-8323; *The New Book of World Rankings.*

Statistical Office of the United Nations, Publishing Service, New York, New York 10017 (800) 253-9646; *Survey of Economic and Social Conditions in Africa.*

Times Books, 201 East 50th Street, New York, New York 10022 (212) 751-2600; *The Economist Book of Vital World Statistics.*

The World Bank, 1818 H Street, NW, Washington, D.C. 20433 (202) 477-1234; *World Tables.*

MALAWI - FERTILIZER

Food and Agricultural Organization of the United Nations (FAO), Via delle Terme di Caracalla, 00100 Rome, Italy (Telephone Number in U.S. (202) 653-2400); *Fertilizer Yearbook,* and *The State of Food and Agriculture.*

Statistical Office of the United Nations, Publishing Service, New York, New York 10017 (800) 253-9646; *Statistical Yearbook.*

MALAWI - FETAL MORTALITY

Statistical Office of the United Nations, Publishing Service, New York, New York 10017 (800) 253-9646; *Demographic Yearbook.*

MALAWI - FINANCE

African Development Bank, 01 BP 1387, Abidjan 01, Cote d'Ivoire; *Selected Statistics on Regional Member Countries.*

Facts on File, 460 Park Avenue South, New York, New York 10016 (800) 443-8323; *The New Book of World Rankings.*

G.K. Hall and Company, 70 Lincoln Street, Boston, Massachusetts 02111 (617) 423-3990; *The World in Figures.*

International Monetary Fund, 700 Nineteenth Street, NW, Washington, D.C. 20431 (202) 623-7000; *International Financial Statistics.*

United Nations Economic Commission for Africa, Africa Hall, Post Office Box 3001, Addis Ababa, Ethiopia (Telephone Number in U.S. (800) 253-9646); *African Statistical Yearbook.*

MALAWI - FISHERIES

Facts on File, 460 Park Avenue South, New York, New York 10016 (800) 443-8323; *The New Book of World Rankings.*

Food and Agricultural Organization of the United Nations (FAO), Via delle Terme di Caracalla, 00100 Rome, Italy (Telephone Number in U.S. (202) 653-2400); *The State of Food and Agriculture,* and *Yearbook of Fishery Statistics.*

Statistical Office of the United Nations, Publishing Service, New York, New York 10017 (800) 253-9646; *Statistical Yearbook,* and *Survey of Economic and Social Conditions in Africa.*

United Nations Economic Commission for Africa, Africa Hall, Post Office Box 3001, Addis Ababa, Ethiopia (Telephone Number in U.S. (800) 253-9646); *African Statistical Yearbook.*

MALAWI - FOOD

African Development Bank, 01 BP 1387, Abidjan 01, Cote d'Ivoire; *Selected Statistics on Regional Member Countries.*

Food and Agricultural Organization of the United Nations (FAO), Via delle Terme di Caracalla, 00100 Rome, Italy (Telephone Number in U.S. (202) 653-2400); *Production Yearbook,* and *The State of Food and Agriculture.*

G.K. Hall and Company, 70 Lincoln Street, Boston, Massachusetts 02111 (617) 423-3990; *The World in Figures.*

MALAWI - FOREIGN AID

G.K. Hall and Company, 70 Lincoln Street, Boston, Massachusetts 02111 (617) 423-3990; *The World in Figures.*

MALAWI - FOREIGN DEBT

International Monetary Fund, 700 Nineteenth Street, NW, Washington, D.C. 20431 (202) 623-7000; *Government Finance Statistics Yearbook.*

MALAWI - FOREIGN TRADE

Euromonitor Publications Limited, 87-88 Turnmill Street, London EC1M 5QU, England; *International Marketing Data and Statistics.*

Facts on File, 460 Park Avenue South, New York, New York 10016 (800) 443-8323; *The New Book of World Rankings.*

Food and Agricultural Organization of the United Nations (FAO), Via delle Terme di Caracalla, 00100 Rome, Italy (Telephone Number in U.S. (202) 653-2400); *The State of Food and Agriculture.*

G.K. Hall and Company, 70 Lincoln Street, Boston, Massachusetts 02111 (617) 423-3990; *The World in Figures.*

Statistical Office of the United Nations, Publishing Service, New York, New York 10017 (800) 253-9646; *International Trade Statistics Yearbook, Statistical Yearbook,* and *Trade in Manufactures of Developing Countries.*

United Nations Economic Commission for Africa, Africa Hall, Post Office Box 3001, Addis Ababa, Ethiopia (Telephone Number in U.S. (800) 253-9646); *African Statistical Yearbook.*

The World Bank, 1818 H Street, NW, Washington, D.C. 20433 (202) 477-1234; *World Tables.*

MALAWI - FORESTRY AND FOREST PRODUCTS

Facts on File, 460 Park Avenue South, New York, New York 10016 (800) 443-8323; *The New Book of World Rankings.*

Food and Agricultural Organization of the United Nations (FAO), Via delle Terme di Caracalla, 00100 Rome, Italy (Telephone Number in U.S. (202) 653-2400); *The State of Food and Agriculture,* and *Yearbook of Forest Products.*

G.K. Hall and Company, 70 Lincoln Street, Boston, Massachusetts 02111 (617) 423-3990; *The World in Figures.*

Statistical Office of the United Nations, Publishing Service, New York, New York 10017 (800) 253-9646; *Statistical Yearbook.*

United Nations Economic Commission for Africa, Africa Hall, Post Office Box 3001, Addis Ababa, Ethiopia (Telephone Number in U.S. (800) 253-9646); *African Statistical Yearbook.*

United Nations Educational, Scientific and Cultural Organization (UNESCO), 7 Place de Fontenoy, F-75700 Paris, France (Telephone Number in U.S. (212) 963-5981); *Statistical Yearbook.*

MALAWI - GAS PRODUCTION - See MALAWI - MINING AND MINERAL PRODUCTS

MALAWI - GENERAL INDUSTRIAL STATISTICS

Statistical Office of the United Nations, Publishing Service, New York, New York 10017 (800) 253-9646; *Industrial Statistics Yearbook.*

MALAWI - GENERAL MORTALITY

Statistical Office of the United Nations, Publishing Service, New York, New York 10017 (800) 253-9646; *Demographic Yearbook.*

MALAWI - GEOGRAPHIC DATA

Facts on File, 460 Park Avenue South, New York, New York 10016 (800) 443-8323; *The New Book of World Rankings.*

MALAWI - GOATS - See MALAWI - LIVESTOCK AND POULTRY

MALAWI - GOLD HOLDINGS

International Monetary Fund, 700 Nineteenth Street, NW, Washington, D.C. 20431 (202) 623-7000; *International Financial Statistics.*

Statistical Office of the United Nations, Publishing Service, New York, New York 10017 (800) 253-9646; *Statistical Yearbook.*

The World Bank, 1818 H Street, NW, Washington, D.C. 20433 (202) 477-1234; *World Tables.*

MALAWI - GOLD PRODUCTION AND CONSUMPTION - See MALAWI - MINING AND MINERAL PRODUCTS

MALAWI - GOVERNMENT

G.K. Hall and Company, 70 Lincoln Street, Boston, Massachusetts 02111 (617) 423-3990; *The World in Figures.*

MALAWI - GOVERNMENT EXPENDITURES

International Monetary Fund, 700 Nineteenth Street, NW, Washington, D.C. 20431 (202) 623-7000; *Government Finance Statistics Yearbook.*

Times Books, 201 East 50th Street, New York, New York 10022 (212) 751-2600; *The Economist Book of Vital World Statistics.*

The World Bank, 1818 H Street, NW, Washington, D.C. 20433 (202) 477-1234; *World Tables.*

MALAWI - GOVERNMENT FINANCES

International Monetary Fund, 700 Nineteenth Street, NW, Washington, D.C. 20431 (202) 623-7000; *International Financial Statistics.*

Statistical Office of the United Nations, Publishing Service, New York, New York 10017 (800) 253-9646; *Statistical Yearbook.*

MALAWI - GOVERNMENT REVENUES

International Monetary Fund, 700 Nineteenth Street, NW, Washington, D.C. 20431 (202) 623-7000; *Government Finance Statistics Yearbook.*

Statistical Office of the United Nations, Publishing Service, New York, New York 10017 (800) 253-9646; *Survey of Economic and Social Conditions in Africa.*

Times Books, 201 East 50th Street, New York, New York 10022 (212) 751-2600; *The Economist Book of Vital World Statistics.*

The World Bank, 1818 H Street, NW, Washington, D.C. 20433 (202) 477-1234; *World Tables.*

MALAWI - GRAIN PRODUCTION - See MALAWI - CROPS

MALAWI - GRANTS

International Monetary Fund, 700 Nineteenth Street, NW, Washington, D.C. 20431 (202) 623-7000; *Government Finance Statistics Yearbook.*

MALAWI - GROSS DOMESTIC PRODUCT

African Development Bank, 01 BP 1387, Abidjan 01, Cote d'Ivoire; *Selected Statistics on Regional Member Countries.*

The Economist Intelligence Unit, 111 West 57th Street, New York, New York 10019 (800) 938-4685; *The World Market Atlas.*

Euromonitor Publications Limited, 87-88 Turnmill Street, London EC1M 5QU, England; *International Marketing Data and Statistics.*

Facts on File, 460 Park Avenue South, New York, New York 10016 (800) 443-8323; *The New Book of World Rankings.*

G.K. Hall and Company, 70 Lincoln Street, Boston, Massachusetts 02111 (617) 423-3990; *The World in Figures.*

Statistical Office of the United Nations, Publishing Service, New York, New York 10017 (800) 253-9646; *Statistical Yearbook,* and *Survey of Economic and Social Conditions in Africa.*

Times Books, 201 East 50th Street, New York, New York 10022 (212) 751-2600; *The Economist Book of Vital World Statistics.*

United Nations Economic Commission for Africa, Africa Hall, Post Office Box 3001, Addis Ababa, Ethiopia (Telephone Number in U.S. (800) 253-9646; *African Statistical Yearbook.*

The World Bank, 1818 H Street, NW, Washington, D.C. 20433 (202) 477-1234; *World Tables.*

MALAWI - GROSS NATIONAL PRODUCT

Euromonitor Publications Limited, 87-88 Turnmill Street, London EC1M 5QU, England; *International Marketing Data and Statistics.*

U.S. Arms Control and Disarmament Agency, 320 Twenty-first Street, NW, Washington, D.C. 20451 (202) 647-8677; *World Military Expenditures and Arms Transfers.*

The World Bank, 1818 H Street, NW, Washington, D.C. 20433 (202) 477-1234; *World Tables.*

MALAWI - GROUNDNUTS EXPORTS - See MALAWI - CROPS

MALAWI - HEALTH

African Development Bank, 01 BP 1387, Abidjan 01, Cote d'Ivoire; *Selected Statistics on Regional Member Countries.*

Facts on File, 460 Park Avenue South, New York, New York 10016 (800) 443-8323; *The New Book of World Rankings.*

G.K. Hall and Company, 70 Lincoln Street, Boston, Massachusetts 02111 (617) 423-3990; *The World in Figures.*

Statistical Office of the United Nations, Publishing Service, New York, New York 10017 (800) 253-9646; *Statistical Yearbook.*

Times Books, 201 East 50th Street, New York, New York 10022 (212) 751-2600; *The Economist Book of Vital World Statistics.*

United Nations Economic Commission for Africa, Africa Hall, Post Office Box 3001, Addis Ababa, Ethiopia (Telephone Number in U.S. (800) 253-9646); *African Statistical Yearbook.*

World Health Organization, Office of Publications, Avenue Appia, CH-1211 Geneva 27, Switzerland (Telephone Number in U.S. (518) 436-9686); *World Health Statistics Annual.*

MALAWI - HEALTH EXPENDITURES

International Monetary Fund, 700 Nineteenth Street, NW, Washington, D.C. 20431 (202) 623-7000; *Government Finance Statistics Yearbook.*

MALAWI - HIDE PRODUCTION

Food and Agricultural Organization of the United Nations (FAO), Via delle Terme di Caracalla, 00100 Rome, Italy (Telephone Number in U.S. (202) 653-2400); *Production Yearbook.*

MALAWI - HIGHWAYS

G.K. Hall and Company, 70 Lincoln Street, Boston, Massachusetts 02111 (617) 423-3990; *The World in Figures.*

International Road Federation, 525 School Street, SW, Washington, D.C. 20024 (202) 554-2106; *World Road Statistics.*

Statistical Office of the United Nations, Publishing Service, New York, New York 10017 (800) 253-9646; *Survey of Economic and Social Conditions in Africa.*

United Nations Economic Commission for Africa, Africa Hall, Post Office Box 3001, Addis Ababa, Ethiopia (Telephone Number in U.S. (800) 253-9646); *African Statistical Yearbook.*

MALAWI - HORSES - See MALAWI - LIVESTOCK AND POULTRY

MALAWI - HOURS OF WORK - See MALAWI - EMPLOYMENT

MALAWI - HOUSING

Facts on File, 460 Park Avenue South, New York, New York 10016 (800) 443-8323; *The New Book of World Rankings.*

MALAWI - HOUSING EXPENDITURES

International Monetary Fund, 700 Nineteenth Street, NW, Washington, D.C. 20431 (202) 623-7000; *Government Finance Statistics Yearbook.*

MALAWI - ILLITERATE POPULATION

The Economist Intelligence Unit, 111 West 57th Street, New York, New York 10019 (800) 938-4685; *The World Market Atlas.*

G.K. Hall and Company, 70 Lincoln Street, Boston, Massachusetts 02111 (617) 423-3990; *The World in Figures.*

United Nations Educational, Scientific and Cultural Organization (UNESCO), 7 Place de Fontenoy, F-75700 Paris, France (Telephone Number in U.S. (212) 963-5981); *Statistical Yearbook.*

MALAWI - IMPORTS

African Development Bank, 01 BP 1387, Abidjan 01, Cote d'Ivoire; *Selected Statistics on Regional Member Countries.*

The Economist Intelligence Unit, 111 West 57th Street, New York, New York 10019 (800) 938-4685; *The World Market Atlas*.

Euromonitor Publications Limited, 87-88 Turnmill Street, London EC1M 5QU, England; *International Marketing Data and Statistics*.

Food and Agricultural Organization of the United Nations (FAO), Via delle Terme di Caracalla, 00100 Rome, Italy (Telephone Number in U.S. (202) 653-2400); *The State of Food and Agriculture*.

G.K. Hall and Company, 70 Lincoln Street, Boston, Massachusetts 02111 (617) 423-3990; *The World in Figures*.

International Monetary Fund, 700 Nineteenth Street, NW, Washington, D.C. 20431 (202) 623-7000; *Direction of Trade Statistics, Government Finance Statistics Yearbook*, and *International Financial Statistics*.

Statistical Office of the United Nations, Publishing Service, New York, New York 10017 (800) 253-9646; *Trade in Manufactures of Developing Countries*, and *Survey of Economic and Social Conditions in Africa*.

Times Books, 201 East 50th Street, New York, New York 10022 (212) 751-2600; *The Economist Book of Vital World Statistics*.

United Nations Economic Commission for Africa, Africa Hall, Post Office Box 3001, Addis Ababa, Ethiopia (Telephone Number in U.S. (800) 253-9646); *African Statistical Yearbook*.

The World Bank, 1818 H Street, NW, Washington, D.C. 20433 (202) 477-1234; *World Tables*.

MALAWI - INCOME TAXES - See MALAWI - TAXATION

MALAWI - INDUSTRY

Euromonitor Publications Limited, 87-88 Turnmill Street, London EC1M 5QU, England; *International Marketing Data and Statistics*.

Facts on File, 460 Park Avenue South, New York, New York 10016 (800) 443-8323; *The New Book of World Rankings*.

G.K. Hall and Company, 70 Lincoln Street, Boston, Massachusetts 02111 (617) 423-3990; *The World in Figures*.

International Labour Office, I.L.O. Publications, CH-1211, Geneva 22, Switzerland; *Yearbook of Labour Statistics*.

Statistical Office of the United Nations, Publishing Service, New York, New York 10017 (800) 253-9646; *Statistical Yearbook*, and *Survey of Economic and Social Conditions in Africa*.

Times Books, 201 East 50th Street, New York, New York 10022 (212) 751-2600; *The Economist Book of Vital World Statistics*.

United Nations Economic Commission for Africa, Africa Hall, Post Office Box 3001, Addis Ababa, Ethiopia (Telephone Number in U.S. (800) 253-9646); *African Statistical Yearbook*.

The World Bank, 1818 H Street, NW, Washington, D.C. 20433 (202) 477-1234; *World Tables*.

World Intellectual Property Organization, 34 Chemin des Colombettes, CH-1211 Geneva 20, Switzerland; *Industrial Property Statistics*.

MALAWI - INFANT AND MATERNAL MORTALITY

Statistical Office of the United Nations, Publishing Service, New York, New York 10017 (800) 253-9646; *Demographic Yearbook, Statistical Yearbook*, and *Survey of Economic and Social Conditions in Africa*.

Times Books, 201 East 50th Street, New York, New York 10022 (212) 751-2600; *The Economist Book of Vital World Statistics*.

The World Bank, 1818 H Street, NW, Washington, D.C. 20433 (202) 477-1234; *World Tables*.

MALAWI - INTERNATIONAL LIQUIDITY

International Monetary Fund, 700 Nineteenth Street, NW, Washington, D.C. 20431 (202) 623-7000; *International Financial Statistics*.

MALAWI - INTERNATIONAL RESERVES EXCLUDING GOLD

African Development Bank, 01 BP 1387, Abidjan 01, Cote d'Ivoire; *Selected Statistics on Regional Member Countries*.

Statistical Office of the United Nations, Publishing Service, New York, New York 10017 (800) 253-9646; *Statistical Yearbook*.

The World Bank, 1818 H Street, NW, Washington, D.C. 20433 (202) 477-1234; *World Tables*.

MALAWI - IRON ORE PRODUCTION AND CONSUMPTION - See MALAWI - MINING AND MINERAL PRODUCTS

MALAWI - IRRIGATION

Euromonitor Publications Limited, 87-88 Turnmill Street, London EC1M 5QU, England; *International Marketing Data and Statistics*.

MALAWI - LABOR FORCE

African Development Bank, 01 BP 1387, Abidjan 01, Cote d'Ivoire; *Selected Statistics on Regional Member Countries*.

Euromonitor Publications Limited, 87-88 Turnmill Street, London EC1M 5QU, England; *International Marketing Data and Statistics*.

Facts on File, 460 Park Avenue South, New York, New York 10016 (800) 443-8323; *The New Book of World Rankings*.

Food and Agricultural Organization of the United Nations (FAO), Via delle Terme di Caracalla, 00100 Rome, Italy (Telephone Number in U.S. (202) 653-2400); *The State of Food and Agriculture*.

G.K. Hall and Company, 70 Lincoln Street, Boston, Massachusetts 02111 (617) 423-3990; *The World in Figures*.

The World Bank, 1818 H Street, NW, Washington, D.C. 20433 (202) 477-1234; *World Tables*.

MALAWI - LABOR PRODUCTIVITY

International Labour Office, I.L.O. Publications, CH-1211, Geneva 22, Switzerland; *Yearbook of Labour Statistics*.

MALAWI - LAND USE

Euromonitor Publications Limited, 87-88 Turnmill Street, London EC1M 5QU, England; *International Marketing Data and Statistics*.

Food and Agricultural Organization of the United Nations (FAO), Via delle Terme di Caracalla, 00100 Rome, Italy (Telephone Number in U.S. (202) 653-2400); *Production Yearbook.*

G.K. Hall and Company, 70 Lincoln Street, Boston, Massachusetts 02111 (617) 423-3990; *The World in Figures.*

MALAWI - LIBRARIES

Facts on File, 460 Park Avenue South, New York, New York 10016 (800) 443-8323; *The New Book of World Rankings.*

United Nations Educational, Scientific and Cultural Organization (UNESCO), 7 Place de Fontenoy, F-75700 Paris, France (Telephone Number in U.S. (212) 963-5981); *Statistical Yearbook.*

MALAWI - LIFE EXPECTANCY

African Development Bank, 01 BP 1387, Abidjan 01, Cote d'Ivoire; *Selected Statistics on Regional Member Countries.*

MALAWI - LITERACY RATE

Statistical Office of the United Nations, Publishing Service, New York, New York 10017 (800) 253-9646; *Survey of Economic and Social Conditions in Africa.*

MALAWI - LIVESTOCK AND POULTRY

Euromonitor Publications Limited, 87-88 Turnmill Street, London EC1M 5QU, England; *International Marketing Data and Statistics.*

Facts on File, 460 Park Avenue South, New York, New York 10016 (800) 443-8323; *The New Book of World Rankings.*

Food and Agricultural Organization of the United Nations (FAO), Via delle Terme di Caracalla, 00100 Rome, Italy (Telephone Number in U.S. (202) 653-2400); *Production Yearbook,* and *The State of Food and Agriculture.*

G.K. Hall and Company, 70 Lincoln Street, Boston, Massachusetts 02111 (617) 423-3990; *The World in Figures.*

Statistical Office of the United Nations, Publishing Service, New York, New York 10017 (800) 253-9646; *Survey of Economic and Social Conditions in Africa.*

United Nations Economic Commission for Africa, Africa Hall, Post Office Box 3001, Addis Ababa, Ethiopia (Telephone Number in U.S. (800) 253-9646); *African Statistical Yearbook.*

MALAWI - LIVING LEVELS

G.K. Hall and Company, 70 Lincoln Street, Boston, Massachusetts 02111 (617) 423-3990; *The World in Figures.*

Times Books, 201 East 50th Street, New York, New York 10022 (212) 751-2600; *The Economist Book of Vital World Statistics.*

MALAWI - MANUFACTURING

Facts on File, 460 Park Avenue South, New York, New York 10016 (800) 443-8323; *The New Book of World Rankings.*

G.K. Hall and Company, 70 Lincoln Street, Boston, Massachusetts 02111 (617) 423-3990; *The World in Figures.*

Statistical Office of the United Nations, Publishing Service, New York, New York 10017 (800) 253-9646; *Statistical Yearbook,* and

Survey of Economic and Social Conditions in Africa.

United Nations Economic Commission for Africa, Africa Hall, Post Office Box 3001, Addis Ababa, Ethiopia (Telephone Number in U.S. (800) 253-9646); *African Statistical Yearbook.*

The World Bank, 1818 H Street, NW, Washington, D.C. 20433 (202) 477-1234; *World Tables.*

MALAWI - MARRIAGE RATES

Facts on File, 460 Park Avenue South, New York, New York 10016 (800) 443-8323; *The New Book of World Rankings.*

Statistical Office of the United Nations, Publishing Service, New York, New York 10017 (800) 253-9646; *Demographic Yearbook.*

MALAWI - MEAT PRODUCTION - See MALAWI - LIVESTOCK AND POULTRY

MALAWI - MERCHANT SHIPPING

G.K. Hall and Company, 70 Lincoln Street, Boston, Massachusetts 02111 (617) 423-3990; *The World in Figures.*

Times Books, 201 East 50th Street, New York, New York 10022 (212) 751-2600; *The Economist Book of Vital World Statistics.*

United Nations Economic Commission for Africa, Africa Hall, Post Office Box 3001, Addis Ababa, Ethiopia (Telephone Number in U.S. (800) 253-9646); *African Statistical Yearbook.*

MALAWI - MILITARY

G.K. Hall and Company, 70 Lincoln Street, Boston, Massachusetts 02111 (617) 423-3990; *The World in Figures.*

The International Institute for Strategic Studies, 23 Tavistock Street, London WC2E 7NQ, England; *The Military Balance.*

U.S. Arms Control and Disarmament Agency, 320 Twenty-first Street, NW, Washington, D.C. 20451 (202) 647-8677; *World Military Expenditures and Arms Transfers.*

MALAWI - MILK PRODUCTION - See MALAWI - DAIRY PRODUCTS

MALAWI - MINING AND MINERAL PRODUCTS

Facts on File, 460 Park Avenue South, New York, New York 10016 (800) 443-8323; *The New Book of World Rankings.*

G.K. Hall and Company, 70 Lincoln Street, Boston, Massachusetts 02111 (617) 423-3990; *The World in Figures.*

Statistical Office of the United Nations, Publishing Service, New York, New York 10017 (800) 253-9646; *Statistical Yearbook.*

United Nations Economic Commission for Africa, Africa Hall, Post Office Box 3001, Addis Ababa, Ethiopia (Telephone Number in U.S. (800) 253-9646); *African Statistical Yearbook.*

MALAWI - MONEY EXCHANGE RATE

Euromonitor Publications Limited, 87-88 Turnmill Street, London EC1M 5QU, England; *International Marketing Data and Statistics.*

International Monetary Fund, 700 Nineteenth Street, NW, Washington, D.C. 20431 (202) 623-7000; *International Financial Statistics.*

Statistical Office of the United Nations, Publishing Service, New York, New York 10017 (800) 253-9646; *Statistical Yearbook.*

MALAWI - MONEY RESERVES

Euromonitor Publications Limited, 87-88 Turnmill Street, London EC1M 5QU, England; *International Marketing Data and Statistics.*

MALAWI - MONEY SUPPLY

African Development Bank, 01 BP 1387, Abidjan 01, Cote d'Ivoire; *Selected Statistics on Regional Member Countries.*

Euromonitor Publications Limited, 87-88 Turnmill Street, London EC1M 5QU, England; *International Marketing Data and Statistics.*

G.K. Hall and Company, 70 Lincoln Street, Boston, Massachusetts 02111 (617) 423-3990; *The World in Figures.*

International Monetary Fund, 700 Nineteenth Street, NW, Washington, D.C. 20431 (202) 623-7000; *International Financial Statistics.*

Statistical Office of the United Nations, Publishing Service, New York, New York 10017 (800) 253-9646; *Statistical Yearbook.*

The World Bank, 1818 H Street, NW, Washington, D.C. 20433 (202) 477-1234; *World Tables.*

MALAWI - MOTION PICTURES

Statistical Office of the United Nations, Publishing Service, New York, New York 10017 (800) 253-9646; *Statistical Yearbook.*

MALAWI - MOTOR VEHICLE TAXES - See MALAWI - TAXATION

MALAWI - MOTOR VEHICLES IN USE

G.K. Hall and Company, 70 Lincoln Street, Boston, Massachusetts 02111 (617) 423-3990; *The World in Figures.*

International Road Federation, 525 School Street, SW, Washington, D.C. 20024 (202) 554-2106; *World Road Statistics.*

Statistical Office of the United Nations, Publishing Service, New York, New York 10017 (800) 253-9646; *Statistical Yearbook,* and *Survey of Economic and Social Conditions in Africa.*

Times Books, 201 East 50th Street, New York, New York 10022 (212) 751-2600; *The Economist Book of Vital World Statistics.*

MALAWI - MUSEUMS

Facts on File, 460 Park Avenue South, New York, New York 10016 (800) 443-8323; *The New Book of World Rankings.*

United Nations Educational, Scientific and Cultural Organization (UNESCO), 7 Place de Fontenoy, F-75700 Paris, France (Telephone Number in U.S. (212) 963-5981); *Statistical Yearbook.*

MALAWI - NATALITY - See MALAWI - BIRTH RATES

MALAWI - NATIONAL ACCOUNTS

African Development Bank, 01 BP 1387, Abidjan 01, Cote d'Ivoire; *Selected Statistics on Regional Member Countries.*

International Monetary Fund, 700 Nineteenth Street, NW, Washington, D.C. 20431 (202) 623-7000; *International Financial Statistics.*

Statistical Office of the United Nations, Publishing Service, New York, New York 10017 (800) 253-9646; *National Account Statistics,* and *Statistical Yearbook.*

United Nations Economic Commission for Africa, Africa Hall, Post Office Box 3001, Addis Ababa, Ethiopia (Telephone Number in U.S. (800) 253-9646); *African Statistical Yearbook.*

MALAWI - NATIONAL INCOME

Facts on File, 460 Park Avenue South, New York, New York 10016 (800) 443-8323; *The New Book of World Rankings.*

G.K. Hall and Company, 70 Lincoln Street, Boston, Massachusetts 02111 (617) 423-3990; *The World in Figures.*

Statistical Office of the United Nations, Publishing Service, New York, New York 10017 (800) 253-9646; *Statistical Yearbook.*

MALAWI - NATIONAL PRODUCT

Facts on File, 460 Park Avenue South, New York, New York 10016 (800) 443-8323; *The New Book of World Rankings.*

Statistical Office of the United Nations, Publishing Service, New York, New York 10017 (800) 253-9646; *Statistical Yearbook.*

MALAWI - NATURAL GAS PRODUCTION - See MALAWI - MINING AND MINERAL PRODUCTS

MALAWI - NEWSPAPER PRODUCTION - See MALAWI - FORESTRY AND FORESTRY PRODUCTS

MALAWI - NEWSPRINT - See MALAWI - FORESTRY AND FOREST PRODUCTS

MALAWI - OCCUPATIONS - See MALAWI - LABOR FORCE

MALAWI - PAPER - See MALAWI - FORESTRY AND FOREST PRODUCTS

MALAWI - PATENTS

Statistical Office of the United Nations, Publishing Service, New York, New York 10017 (800) 253-9646; *Statistical Yearbook.*

World Intellectual Property Organization, 34 Chemin des Colombettes, CH-1211 Geneva 20, Switzerland; *Industrial Property Statistics.*

MALAWI - PEANUT PRODUCTION - See MALAWI - CROPS

MALAWI - PERIODICALS

United Nations Educational, Scientific and Cultural Organization (UNESCO), 7 Place de Fontenoy, F-75700 Paris, France (Telephone Number in U.S. (212) 963-5981); *Statistical Yearbook.*

MALAWI - PESTICIDE USE

Food and Agricultural Organization of the United Nations (FAO), Via delle Terme di Caracalla, 00100 Rome, Italy (Telephone Number in U.S. (202) 653-2400); *The State of Food and Agriculture.*

MALAWI - PETROLEUM INDUSTRY

Facts on File, 460 Park Avenue South, New York, New York 10016 (800) 443-8323; *The New Book of World Rankings*.

Food and Agricultural Organization of the United Nations (FAO), Via delle Terme di Caracalla, 00100 Rome, Italy (Telephone Number in U.S. (202) 653-2400); *The State of Food and Agriculture*.

G.K. Hall and Company, 70 Lincoln Street, Boston, Massachusetts 02111 (617) 423-3990; *The World in Figures*.

MALAWI - PIGS - See MALAWI - LIVESTOCK AND POULTRY

MALAWI - POPULATION

African Development Bank, 01 BP 1387, Abidjan 01, Cote d'Ivoire; *Selected Statistics on Regional Member Countries*.

The Economist Intelligence Unit, 111 West 57th Street, New York, New York 10019 (800) 938-4685; *The World Market Atlas*.

Euromonitor Publications Limited, 87-88 Turnmill Street, London EC1M 5QU, England; *International Marketing Data and Statistics*.

Facts on File, 460 Park Avenue South, New York, New York 10016 (800) 443-8323; *The New Book of World Rankings*.

Food and Agricultural Organization of the United Nations (FAO), Via delle Terme di Caracalla, 00100 Rome, Italy (Telephone Number in U.S. (202) 653-2400); *Production Yearbook*.

G.K. Hall and Company, 70 Lincoln Street, Boston, Massachusetts 02111 (617) 423-3990; *The World in Figures*.

International Labour Office, I.L.O. Publications, CH-1211, Geneva 22, Switzerland; *Yearbook of Labour Statistics*.

Statistical Office of the United Nations, Publishing Service, New York, New York 10017 (800) 253-9646; *Demographic Yearbook, Statistical Yearbook*, and *Survey of Economic and Social Conditions in Africa*.

Times Books, 201 East 50th Street, New York, New York 10022 (212) 751-2600; *The Economist Book of Vital World Statistics*.

U.S. Arms Control and Disarmament Agency, 320 Twenty-first Street, NW, Washington, D.C. 20451 (202) 647-8677; *World Military Expenditures and Arms Transfers*.

World Health Organization, Office of Publications, Avenue Appia, CH-1211 Geneva 27, Switzerland (Telephone Number in U.S. (518) 436-9686); *World Health Statistics Annual*.

MALAWI - POST OFFICES

Facts on File, 460 Park Avenue South, New York, New York 10016 (800) 443-8323; *The New Book of World Rankings*.

MALAWI - POTATO PRODUCTION - See MALAWI - CROPS

MALAWI - POWER PRODUCTION INDUSTRY - ESTABLISHMENTS, PAYROLLS, VALUE ADDED, ETC.

Statistical Office of the United Nations, Publishing Service, New York, New York 10017 (800) 253-9646; *Statistical Yearbook*.

MALAWI - PRICES

Facts on File, 460 Park Avenue South, New York, New York 10016 (800) 443-8323; *The New Book of World Rankings*.

Food and Agricultural Organization of the United Nations (FAO), Via delle Terme di Caracalla, 00100 Rome, Italy (Telephone Number in U.S. (202) 653-2400); *Production Yearbook*, and *The State of Food and Agriculture*.

G.K. Hall and Company, 70 Lincoln Street, Boston, Massachusetts 02111 (617) 423-3990; *The World in Figures*.

International Labour Office, I.L.O. Publications, CH-1211, Geneva 22, Switzerland; *Yearbook of Labour Statistics*.

United Nations Economic Commission for Africa, Africa Hall, Post Office Box 3001, Addis Ababa, Ethiopia (Telephone Number in U.S. (800) 253-9646); *African Statistical Yearbook*.

MALAWI - PRINTING AND WRITING PAPER CONSUMPTION - See MALAWI - FORESTRY AND FOREST PRODUCTS

MALAWI - PRODUCTION

Facts on File, 460 Park Avenue South, New York, New York 10016 (800) 443-8323; *The New Book of World Rankings*.

G.K. Hall and Company, 70 Lincoln Street, Boston, Massachusetts 02111 (617) 423-3990; *The World in Figures*.

MALAWI - PRODUCTIVITY

Euromonitor Publications Limited, 87-88 Turnmill Street, London EC1M 5QU, England; *International Marketing Data and Statistics*.

MALAWI - PROPERTY TAXES

International Monetary Fund, 700 Nineteenth Street, NW, Washington, D.C. 20431 (202) 623-7000; *Government Finance Statistics Yearbook*.

MALAWI - PUBLIC FINANCE

Facts on File, 460 Park Avenue South, New York, New York 10016 (800) 443-8323; *The New Book of World Rankings*.

MALAWI - RADIO BROADCASTING - See MALAWI - BROADCASTING

MALAWI - RADIO RECEIVER PRODUCTION

Statistical Office of the United Nations, Publishing Service, New York, New York 10017 (800) 253-9646; *Statistical Yearbook*.

MALAWI - RAILWAYS

G.K. Hall and Company, 70 Lincoln Street, Boston, Massachusetts 02111 (617) 423-3990; *The World in Figures*.

Jane's Information Group, Sentinel House, 163 Brighton Road, Coulsdon, Surrey CR5 2NH, England (Telephone Number in U.S. (703) 683-3700); *Jane's World Railways*.

Statistical Office of the United Nations, Publishing Service, New York, New York 10017 (800) 253-9646; *Statistical Yearbook*, and *Survey of Economic and Social Conditions in Africa*.

United Nations Economic Commission for Africa, Africa Hall, Post Office Box 3001, Addis Ababa, Ethiopia (Telephone Number in U.S.

(800) 253-9646); *African Statistical Yearbook*.

MALAWI - RELIGION

Facts on File, 460 Park Avenue South, New York, New York 10016 (800) 443-8323; *The New Book of World Rankings*.

MALAWI - RETAIL TRADE

G.K. Hall and Company, 70 Lincoln Street, Boston, Massachusetts 02111 (617) 423-3990; *The World in Figures*.

Statistical Office of the United Nations, Publishing Service, New York, New York 10017 (800) 253-9646; *Statistical Yearbook*.

MALAWI - RICE PRODUCTION - See MALAWI - CROPS

MALAWI - ROOT AND TUBER PRODUCTION - See MALAWI - CROPS

MALAWI - ROUNDWOOD PRODUCTION - See MALAWI - FORESTRY AND FOREST PRODUCTS

MALAWI - RUBBER PRODUCTION AND CONSUMPTION

Facts on File, 460 Park Avenue South, New York, New York 10016 (800) 443-8323; *The New Book of World Rankings*.

MALAWI - SAWNWOOD PRODUCTION - See FORESTRY AND FOREST PRODUCTS

MALAWI - SCIENTISTS AND TECHNOLOGISTS

United Nations Educational, Scientific and Cultural Organization (UNESCO), 7 Place de Fontenoy, F-75700 Paris, France (Telephone Number in U.S. (212) 963-5981); *Statistical Yearbook*.

MALAWI - SENIOR CITIZENS

Facts on File, 460 Park Avenue South, New York, New York 10016 (800) 443-8323; *The New Book of World Rankings*.

MALAWI - SHEEP - See MALAWI - LIVESTOCK AND POULTRY

MALAWI - SILVER PRODUCTION AND CONSUMPTION - See MALAWI - MINING AND MINERAL PRODUCTS

MALAWI - SISAL PRODUCTION - See MALAWI - CROPS

MALAWI - SOCIAL DATA

African Development Bank, 01 BP 1387, Abidjan 01, Cote d'Ivoire; *Selected Statistics on Regional Member Countries*.

Facts on File, 460 Park Avenue South, New York, New York 10016 (800) 443-8323; *The New Book of World Rankings*.

G.K. Hall and Company, 70 Lincoln Street, Boston, Massachusetts 02111 (617) 423-3990; *The World in Figures*.

MALAWI - SOCIAL SECURITY EXPENDITURES

International Monetary Fund, 700 Nineteenth Street, NW, Washington, D.C. 20431 (202) 623-7000; *Government Finance Statistics Yearbook*.

MALAWI - STAMP TAXES AND DUTIES - See MALAWI - TAXATION

MALAWI - STATE BUDGET

Euromonitor Publications Limited, 87-88 Turnmill Street, London EC1M 5QU, England; *International Marketing Data and Statistics*.

MALAWI - STEEL - See MALAWI - MINING AND MINERAL PRODUCTS

MALAWI - STOCKS - COMMODITY - MARKET PRICE - INDEX

Food and Agricultural Organization of the United Nations (FAO), Via delle Terme di Caracalla, 00100 Rome, Italy (Telephone Number in U.S. (202) 653-2400); *The State of Food and Agriculture*.

MALAWI - SUGAR - See MALAWI - CROPS

MALAWI - TAXATION

G.K. Hall and Company, 70 Lincoln Street, Boston, Massachusetts 02111 (617) 423-3990; *The World in Figures*.

International Monetary Fund, 700 Nineteenth Street, NW, Washington, D.C. 20431 (202) 623-7000; *Government Finance Statistics*.

International Road Federation, 525 School Street, SW, Washington, D.C. 20024 (202) 554-2106; *World Road Statistics*.

The World Bank, 1818 H Street, NW, Washington, D.C. 20433 (202) 477-1234; *World Tables*.

MALAWI - TEA - See MALAWI - CROPS

MALAWI - TELEPHONES IN USE

American Telephone and Telegraph Company, 26 Parsippany Road, Whippany, New Jersey 07981 (800) 338-4038; *The World's Telephones*.

G.K. Hall and Company, 70 Lincoln Street, Boston, Massachusetts 02111 (617) 423-3990; *The World in Figures*.

MALAWI - TELEVISION BROADCASTING - See MALAWI - BROADCASTING

MALAWI - TEXTILE INDUSTRY

G.K. Hall and Company, 70 Lincoln Street, Boston, Massachusetts 02111 (617) 423-3990; *The World in Figures*.

MALAWI - TOBACCO EXPORTS

Facts on File, 460 Park Avenue South, New York, New York 10016 (800) 443-8323; *The New Book of World Rankings*.

International Monetary Fund, 700 Nineteenth Street, NW, Washington, D.C. 20431 (202) 623-7000; *International Financial Statistics*.

Statistical Office of the United Nations, Publishing Service, New York, New York 10017 (800) 253-9646; *Statistical Yearbook*.

MALAWI - TOBACCO PRODUCTION

Facts on File, 460 Park Avenue South, New York, New York 10016 (800) 443-8323; *The New Book of World Rankings*.

Statistical Office of the United Nations, Publishing Service, New York, New York 10017 (800) 253-9646; *Statistical Yearbook*.

MALAWI - TOURISM

Facts on File, 460 Park Avenue South, New York, New York 10016 (800) 443-8323; *The New Book of World Rankings*.

G.K. Hall and Company, 70 Lincoln Street, Boston, Massachusetts 02111 (617) 423-3990; *The World in Figures*.

Statistical Office of the United Nations, Publishing Service, New York, New York 10017 (800) 253-9646; *Statistical Yearbook*.

Times Books, 201 East 50th Street, New York, New York 10022 (212) 751-2600; *The Economist Book of Vital World Statistics*.

United Nations Economic Commission for Africa, Africa Hall, Post Office Box 3001, Addis Ababa, Ethiopia (Telephone Number in U.S. (800) 253-9646); *African Statistical Yearbook*.

World Tourism Organization, Calle Capitan Haya 42, E-28020 Madrid, Spain; *Yearbook of Tourism Statistics*.

MALAWI - TRACTORS IN USE

Statistical Office of the United Nations, Publishing Service, New York, New York 10017 (800) 253-9646; *Statistical Yearbook*.

MALAWI - TRADE - See MALAWI - FOREIGN TRADE

MALAWI - TRADEMARKS AND SERVICE MARKS

Statistical Office of the United Nations, Publishing Service, New York, New York 10017 (800) 253-9646; *Statistical Yearbook*.

World Intellectual Property Organization, 34 Chemin des Colombettes, CH-1211 Geneva 20, Switzerland; *Industrial Property Statistics*.

MALAWI - TRANSPORTATION AND COMMUNICATIONS

Facts on File, 460 Park Avenue South, New York, New York 10016 (800) 443-8323; *The New Book of World Rankings*.

G.K. Hall and Company, 70 Lincoln Street, Boston, Massachusetts 02111 (617) 423-3990; *The World in Figures*.

United Nations Economic Commission for Africa, Africa Hall, Post Office Box 3001, Addis Ababa, Ethiopia (Telephone Number in U.S. (800) 253-9646); *African Statistical Yearbook*.

MALAWI - UNEMPLOYMENT

Euromonitor Publications Limited, 87-88 Turnmill Street, London EC1M 5QU, England; *International Marketing Data and Statistics*.

International Labour Office, I.L.O. Publications, CH-1211, Geneva 22, Switzerland; *Yearbook of Labour Statistics*.

MALAWI - VITAL STATISTICS

Euromonitor Publications Limited, 87-88 Turnmill Street, London EC1M 5QU, England; *International Marketing Data and Statistics*.

G.K. Hall and Company, 70 Lincoln Street, Boston, Massachusetts 02111 (617) 423-3990; *The World in Figures*.

Statistical Office of the United Nations, Publishing Service, New York, New York 10017 (800) 253-9646; *Statistical Yearbook*.

World Health Organization, Office of Publications, Avenue Appia, CH-1211 Geneva 27, Switzerland (Telephone Number in U.S. (518) 436-9686); *World Health Statistics Annual*.

MALAWI - WAGES

G.K. Hall and Company, 70 Lincoln Street, Boston, Massachusetts 02111 (617) 423-3990; *The World in Figures*.

International Labour Office, I.L.O. Publications, CH-1211, Geneva 22, Switzerland; *Yearbook of Labour Statistics*.

Statistical Office of the United Nations, Publishing Service, New York, New York 10017 (800) 253-9646; *Statistical Yearbook*.

MALAWI - WEATHER

Facts on File, 460 Park Avenue South, New York, New York 10016 (800) 443-8323; *The New Book of World Rankings*.

G.K. Hall and Company, 70 Lincoln Street, Boston, Massachusetts 02111 (617) 423-3990; *The World in Figures*.

MALAWI - WELFARE EXPENDITURES

International Monetary Fund, 700 Nineteenth Street, NW, Washington, D.C. 20431 (202) 623-7000; *Government Finance Statistics Yearbook*.

MALAWI - WHEAT PRODUCTION

Facts on File, 460 Park Avenue South, New York, New York 10016 (800) 443-8323; *The New Book of World Rankings*.

Statistical Office of the United Nations, Publishing Service, New York, New York 10017 (800) 253-9646; *Statistical Yearbook*.

MALAWI - WHOLESALE TRADE

Statistical Office of the United Nations, Publishing Service, New York, New York 10017 (800) 253-9646; *Statistical Yearbook*.

MALAWI - WINE PRODUCTION

Facts on File, 460 Park Avenue South, New York, New York 10016 (800) 443-8323; *The New Book of World Rankings*.

MALAWI - WOOL PRODUCTION

Facts on File, 460 Park Avenue South, New York, New York 10016 (800) 443-8323; *The New Book of World Rankings*.

Malaysia - National Statistical Office

Department of Statistics, Jalan Cenderasari, Kuala Lumpur, Malaysia.

Malaysia - Primary Statistics Source

Department of Statistics, Jalan Cenderasari, Kuala Lumpur, Malaysia; *Buku Tahunan Perangkaan* (Yearbook of Statistics).

MALAYSIA - AGRICULTURE

Asian Development Bank, Post Office Box 789, 1099 Manila, Philippines; *Key Indicators of Developing Asian and Pacific Countries*.

Euromonitor Publications Limited, 87-88 Turnmill Street, London EC1M 5QU, England; *The Pacific Basin: An Economic Handbook*.

Facts on File, 460 Park Avenue South, New York, New York 10016 (800) 443-8323; *The New Book of World Rankings*.

Food and Agricultural Organization of the United Nations (FAO), Via delle Terme di Caracalla, 00100 Rome, Italy (Telephone Number in U.S. (202) 653-2400); *Production Yearbook, The State of Food and Agriculture*, and *Trade Yearbook*.

Statistical Office of the United Nations, Publishing Service, New York, New York 10017 (800) 253-9646; *Statistical Yearbook*, and *Statistical Yearbook for Asia and the Pacific*.

Times Books, 201 East 50th Street, New York, New York 10022 (212) 751-2600; *The Economist Book of Vital World Statistics*.

The World Bank, 1818 H Street, NW, Washington, D.C. 20433 (202) 477-1234; *World Tables*.

MALAYSIA - AIRLINE SERVICE

The Economist Intelligence Unit (Asia) Limited, 10th Floor, Luk Kwok Centre, 72 Gloucester Road, Wanchai, Hong Kong (Phone Number in U.S. (800) 938-4685); *Asian Market Atlas*.

Facts on File, 460 Park Avenue South, New York, New York 10016 (800) 443-8323; *The New Book of World Rankings*.

International Civil Aviation Organization, 1000 Shorbrooke Street West, Suite 400, Montreal, Quebec H3A 2R2, Canada (514) 285-8219; *Civil Aviation Statistics of the World*.

Statistical Office of the United Nations, Publishing Service, New York, New York 10017 (800) 253-9646; *Statistical Yearbook*.

Times Books, 201 East 50th Street, New York, New York 10022 (212) 751-2600; *The Economist Book of Vital World Statistics*.

MALAYSIA - ALUMINUM PRODUCTION AND CONSUMPTION - See MALAYSIA - MINING AND MINERAL PRODUCTS

MALAYSIA - ANIMAL HEALTH

Food and Agricultural Organization of the United Nations (FAO), Via delle Terme di Caracalla, 00100 Rome, Italy (Telephone Number in U.S. (202) 653-2400); *Animal Health Yearbook*.

MALAYSIA - ANTIMONY AND ANTIMONY ORE CONSUMPTION AND PRODUCTION - See MALAYSIA - MINING AND MINERAL PRODUCTS

MALAYSIA - AREA AND DENSITY OF POPULATION

Euromonitor Publications Limited, 87-88 Turnmill Street, London EC1M 5QU, England; *International Marketing Data and Statistics*, and *The Pacific Basin: An Economic Handbook*.

Facts on File, 460 Park Avenue South, New York, New York 10016 (800) 443-8323; *The New Book of World Rankings*.

Food and Agricultural Organization of the United Nations (FAO), Via delle Terme di Caracalla, 00100 Rome, Italy (Telephone Number in U.S. (202) 653-2400); *The State of Food and Agriculture*.

Statistical Office of the United Nations, Publishing Service, New York, New York 10017 (800) 253-9646; *Statistical Yearbook*.

Times Books, 201 East 50th Street, New York, New York 10022 (212) 751-2600; *The Economist Book of Vital World Statistics*.

MALAYSIA - ARMS EXPORTS AND IMPORTS

U.S. Arms Control and Disarmament Agency, 320 Twenty-first Street, NW, Washington, D.C. 20451 (202) 647-8677; *World Military Expenditures and Arms Transfers*.

MALAYSIA - ARSENIC PRODUCTION AND CONSUMPTION - See MALAYSIA - MINING AND MINERAL PRODUCTS

MALAYSIA - BALANCE OF PAYMENTS

The Economist Intelligence Unit, 111 West 57th Street, New York, New York 10019 (800) 938-4685; *The World Market Atlas*.

International Monetary Fund, 700 Nineteenth Street, NW, Washington, D.C. 20431 (202) 623-7000; *Balance of Payments Yearbook*, and *International Financial Statistics*.

Times Books, 201 East 50th Street, New York, New York 10022 (212) 751-2600; *The Economist Book of Vital World Statistics*.

The World Bank, 1818 H Street, NW, Washington, D.C. 20433 (202) 477-1234; *World Tables*.

MALAYSIA - BANKING

Asian Development Bank, Post Office Box 789, 1099 Manila, Philippines, *Key Indicators of Developing Asian and Pacific Countries*.

Facts on File, 460 Park Avenue South, New York, New York 10016 (800) 443-8323; *The New Book of World Rankings*.

International Monetary Fund, 700 Nineteenth Street, NW, Washington, D.C. 20431 (202) 623-7000; *International Financial Statistics*.

MALAYSIA - BARLEY PRODUCTION - See MALAYSIA - CROPS

MALAYSIA - BAUXITE PRODUCTION AND CONSUMPTION - See MALAYSIA - MINING AND MINERAL PRODUCTS

MALAYSIA - BEER PRODUCTION

Facts on File, 460 Park Avenue South, New York, New York 10016 (800) 443-8323; *The New Book of World Rankings*.

MALAYSIA - BIRTH RATES

The Economist Intelligence Unit (Asia) Limited, 10th Floor, Luk Kwok Centre, 72 Gloucester Road, Wanchai, Hong Kong (Phone Number in U.S. (800) 938-4685); *Asian Market Atlas*.

Euromonitor Publications Limited, 87-88 Turnmill Street, London EC1M 5QU, England; *The Pacific Basin: An Economic Handbook*.

Facts on File, 460 Park Avenue South, New York, New York 10016 (800) 443-8323; *The New Book of World Rankings*.

Statistical Office of the United Nations, Publishing Service, New York, New York 10017 (800) 253-9646; *Demographic Yearbook*, and *Statistical Yearbook*.

Times Books, 201 East 50th Street, New York, New York 10022 (212) 751-2600; *The Economist Book of Vital World Statistics*.

The World Bank, 1818 H Street, NW, Washington, D.C. 20433 (202) 477-1234; *World Tables*.

World Health Organization, Office of Publications, Avenue Appia, CH-1211 Geneva 27, Switzerland (Telephone Number in U.S. (518) 436-9686); *World Health Statistics Annual*.

MALAYSIA - BISMUTH PRODUCTION AND CONSUMPTION - See MALAYSIA - MINING AND MINERAL PRODUCTS

MALAYSIA - BONDS

Asian Development Bank, Post Office Box 789, 1099 Manila, Philippines; *Key Indicators of Developing Asian and Pacific Countries*.

International Monetary Fund, 700 Nineteenth Street, NW, Washington, D.C. 20431 (202) 623-7000; *Government Finance Statistics Yearbook*.

MALAYSIA - BOOK PRODUCTION

United Nations Educational, Scientific and Cultural Organization (UNESCO), 7 Place de Fontenoy, F-75700 Paris, France (Telephone Number in U.S. (212) 963-5981); *Statistical Yearbook*.

MALAYSIA - BROADCASTING

Billboard Limited, Post Office Box 9027, 1006 AA Amsterdam, The Netherlands (Telephone Number in U.S. (212) 764-7300); *World Radio TV Handbook*.

The Economist Intelligence Unit (Asia) Limited, 10th Floor, Luk Kwok Centre, 72 Gloucester Road, Wanchai, Hong Kong (Phone Number in U.S. (800) 938-4685); *Asian Market Atlas*.

Facts on File, 460 Park Avenue South, New York, New York 10016 (800) 443-8323; *The New Book of World Rankings*.

Times Books, 201 East 50th Street, New York, New York 10022 (212) 751-2600; *The Economist Book of Vital World Statistics*.

United Nations Educational, Scientific and Cultural Organization (UNESCO), 7 Place de Fontenoy, F-75700 Paris, France (Telephone Number in U.S. (212) 963-5981); *Statistical Yearbook*.

MALAYSIA - BUSINESS AND PROFESSIONAL LICENSES

International Monetary Fund, 700 Nineteenth Street, NW, Washington, D.C. 20431 (202) 623-7000; *Government Finance Statistics Yearbook*.

MALAYSIA - CADMIUM PRODUCTION AND CONSUMPTION - See - MALAYSIA - MINING AND MINERAL PRODUCTS

MALAYSIA - CALORIE SUPPLY

Asian Development Bank, Post Office Box 789, 1099 Manila, Philippines; *Key Indicators of Developing Asian and Pacific Countries*.

Food and Agricultural Organization of the United Nations (FAO), Via delle Terme di Caracalla, 00100 Rome, Italy (Telephone Number in U.S. (202) 653-2400); *The State of Food and Agriculture*.

MALAYSIA - CAPITAL INVESTMENT

Asian Development Bank, Post Office Box 789, 1099 Manila, Philippines; *Key Indicators of Developing Asian and Pacific Countries*.

MALAYSIA - CAPITAL REVENUE

Asian Development Bank, Post Office Box 789, 1099 Manila, Philippines; *Key Indicators of Developing Asian and Pacific Countries*.

International Monetary Fund, 700 Nineteenth Street, NW, Washington, D.C. 20431 (202) 623-7000; *Government Finance Statistics Yearbook*.

MALAYSIA - CASHEW NUT PRODUCTION - See MALAYSIA - CROPS

MALAYSIA - CATTLE - See MALAYSIA - LIVESTOCK AND POULTRY

MALAYSIA - CEMENT PRODUCTION - See MALAYSIA - MINING AND MINERAL PRODUCTS

MALAYSIA - CHICKENS - See MALAYSIA - LIVESTOCK AND POULTRY

MALAYSIA - CHROMITE PRODUCTION AND CONSUMPTION - See MALAYSIA - MINING AND MINERAL PRODUCTS

MALAYSIA - CHROMIUM ORE PRODUCTION AND CONSUMPTION - See MALAYSIA - MINING AND MINERAL PRODUCTS

MALAYSIA - CIGAR AND CIGARETTE PRODUCTION - See MALAYSIA - TOBACCO PRODUCTION

MALAYSIA - CLIMATE

Facts on File, 460 Park Avenue South, New York, New York 10016 (800) 443-8323; *The New Book of World Rankings*.

MALAYSIA - CLOTHING EXPORTS

Statistical Office of the United Nations, Publishing Service, New York, New York 10017 (800) 253-9646; *Trade in Manufactures of Developing Countries*.

MALAYSIA - COAL PRODUCTION - See MALAYSIA - MINING AND MINERAL PRODUCTS

MALAYSIA - COBALT PRODUCTION AND CONSUMPTION - See MALAYSIA - MINING AND MINERAL PRODUCTS

MALAYSIA - COCOA PRODUCTION

Statistical Office of the United Nations, Publishing Service, New York, New York 10017 (800) 253-9646; *Statistical Yearbook*.

MALAYSIA - COFFEE PRODUCTION AND CONSUMPTION - See MALAYSIA - CROPS

MALAYSIA - COKE AND COKE OVEN ORE PRODUCTION AND CONSUMPTION - See MALAYSIA - MINING AND MINERAL PRODUCTS

MALAYSIA - COMMUNICATIONS

Statistical Office of the United Nations, Publishing Service, New York, New York 10017 (800) 253-9646; *Statistical Yearbook for Asia and the Pacific*.

MALAYSIA - CONSTRUCTION INDUSTRY

Facts on File, 460 Park Avenue South, New York, New York 10016 (800) 443-8323; *The New Book of World Rankings*.

Statistical Office of the United Nations, Publishing Service, New York, New York 10017 (800) 253-9646; *Construction Statistics Yearbook*, and *Statistical Yearbook*.

MALAYSIA - CONSUMER PRICE INDEX

Asian Development Bank, Post Office Box 789, 1099 Manila, Philippines; *Key Indicators of Developing Asian and Pacific Countries*.

Statistical Office of the United Nations, Publishing Service, New York, New York 10017 (800) 253-9646; *Statistical Yearbook*.

MALAYSIA - CONSUMER PRICES

International Labour Office, I.L.O. Publications, CH-1211, Geneva 22, Switzerland; *Yearbook of Labour Statistics*.

International Monetary Fund, 700 Nineteenth Street, NW, Washington, D.C. 20431 (202) 623-7000; *International Financial Statistics*.

Times Books, 201 East 50th Street, New York, New York 10022 (212) 751-2600; *The Economist Book of Vital World Statistics*.

MALAYSIA   CONSUMPTION

Euromonitor Publications Limited, 87-88 Turnmill Street, London EC1M 5QU, England; *The Pacific Basin: An Economic Handbook*.

International Rubber Study Group, York House, Eighth Floor, Empire Way, Wembley, London HA9 0PA, England; *Rubber Statistical Bulletin*.

MALAYSIA - COPPER AND COPPER ORE PRODUCTION AND CONSUMPTION - See MALAYSIA - MINING AND MINERAL PRODUCTS

MALAYSIA - CORN PRODUCTION - See MALAYSIA - CROPS

MALAYSIA - CORPORATE TAXES - See MALAYSIA - TAXATION

MALAYSIA - COTTON PRODUCTION - See MALAYSIA - CROPS

MALAYSIA - CRIME

International Criminal Police Organization (INTERPOL), 26 rue Armengaud, 92210 Saint Cloud, France; *International Crime Statistics*.

Yale University Press, Yale Station, New Haven, Connecticut 06520 (203) 432-0940; *Violence and Crime in Cross-National Perspective*.

MALAYSIA - CROPS

Asian Development Bank, Post Office Box 789, 1099 Manila, Philippines; *Key Indicators of Developing Asian and Pacific Countries*.

Facts on File, 460 Park Avenue South, New York, New York 10016 (800) 443-8323; *The New Book of World Rankings*.

Food and Agricultural Organization of the United Nations (FAO), Via delle Terme di Caracalla, 00100 Rome, Italy (Telephone Number in U.S. (202) 653-2400); *Production Yearbook*, and *The State of Food and Agriculture*.

International Monetary Fund, 700 Nineteenth Street, NW, Washington, D.C. 20431 (202) 623-7000; *International Financial Statistics*.

Statistical Office of the United Nations, Publishing Service, New York, New York 10017 (800) 253-9646; *Statistical Yearbook*.

MALAYSIA - CUSTOMS DUTIES

International Monetary Fund, 700 Nineteenth Street, NW, Washington, D.C. 20431 (202) 623-7000; *Government Finance Statistics Yearbook*.

MALAYSIA - DAIRY PRODUCTS

Facts on File, 460 Park Avenue South, New York, New York 10016 (800) 443-8323; *The New Book of World Rankings*.

Food and Agricultural Organization of the United Nations (FAO), Via delle Terme di Caracalla, 00100 Rome, Italy (Telephone Number in U.S. (202) 653-2400); *Production Yearbook*, and *The State of Food and Agriculture*.

Statistical Office of the United Nations, Publishing Service, New York, New York 10017 (800) 253-9646; *Statistical Yearbook*.

MALAYSIA - DEATH RATES

The Economist Intelligence Unit (Asia) Limited, 10th Floor, Luk Kwok Centre, 72 Gloucester Road, Wanchai, Hong Kong (Phone Number in U.S. (800) 938-4685); *Asian Market Atlas*.

Euromonitor Publications Limited, 87-88 Turnmill Street, London EC1M 5QU, England; *The Pacific Basin: An Economic Handbook*.

Statistical Office of the United Nations, Publishing Service, New York, New York 10017 (800) 253-9646; *Statistical Yearbook*.

Times Books, 201 East 50th Street, New York, New York 10022 (212) 751-2600; *The Economist Book of Vital World Statistics*.

World Health Organization, Office of Publications, Avenue Appia, CH-1211 Geneva 27, Switzerland (Telephone Number in U.S. (518) 436-9686); *World Health Statistics Annual*.

MALAYSIA - DEFENSE EXPENDITURES

U.S. Arms Control and Disarmament Agency, 320 Twenty-first Street, NW, Washington, D.C. 20451 (202) 647-8677; *World Military Expenditures and Arms Transfers*.

MALAYSIA - DEMOGRAPHY

The Economist Intelligence Unit, 111 West 57th Street, New York, New York 10019 (800) 938-4685; *The World Market Atlas*.

The Economist Intelligence Unit (Asia) Limited, 10th Floor, Luk Kwok Centre, 72 Gloucester Road, Wanchai, Hong Kong (Phone Number in U.S. (800) 938-4685); *Asian Market Atlas*.

Facts on File, 460 Park Avenue South, New York, New York 10016 (800) 443-8323; *The New Book of World Rankings*.

MALAYSIA - DEVELOPMENT ASSISTANCE

Asian Development Bank, Post Office Box 789, 1099 Manila, Philippines; *Key Indicators of Developing Asian and Pacific Countries*.

Statistical Office of the United Nations, Publishing Service, New York, New York 10017 (800) 253-9646; *Statistical Yearbook*.

MALAYSIA - DIAMOND PRODUCTION - See MALAYSIA - MINING AND MINERAL PRODUCTS

MALAYSIA - DISEASES

World Health Organization, Office of Publications, Avenue Appia, CH-1211 Geneva 27, Switzerland (Telephone Number in U.S. (518) 436-9686); *World Health Statistics Annual*.

MALAYSIA - DIVORCE

Facts on File, 460 Park Avenue South, New York, New York 10016 (800) 443-8323; *The New Book of World Rankings*.

Statistical Office of the United Nations, Publishing Service, New York, New York 10017 (800) 253-9646; *Demographic Yearbook*, and *Statistical Yearbook*.

MALAYSIA - DUCKS

Food and Agricultural Organization of the United Nations (FAO), Via delle Terme di Caracalla, 00100 Rome, Italy (Telephone Number in U.S. (202) 653-2400); *Production Yearbook*.

MALAYSIA - ECONOMY

Asian Development Bank, Post Office Box 789, 1099 Manila, Philippines; *Key Indicators of Developing Asian and Pacific Countries*.

Euromonitor Publications Limited, 87-88 Turnmill Street, London EC1M 5QU, England; *International Marketing Data and Statistics*.

Facts on File, 460 Park Avenue South, New York, New York 10016 (800) 443-8323; *The New Book of World Rankings*.

MALAYSIA - EDUCATION

The Economist Intelligence Unit, 111 West 57th Street, New York, New York 10019 (800) 938-4685; *The World Market Atlas*.

The Economist Intelligence Unit (Asia) Limited, 10th Floor, Luk Kwok Centre, 72 Gloucester Road, Wanchai, Hong Kong (Phone Number in U.S. (800) 938-4685); *Asian Market Atlas*.

Euromonitor Publications Limited, 87-88 Turnmill Street, London EC1M 5QU, England; *The Pacific Basin: An Economic Handbook*.

Facts on File, 460 Park Avenue South, New York, New York 10016 (800) 443-8323; *The New Book of World Rankings*.

Statistical Office of the United Nations, Publishing Service, New York, New York 10017 (800) 253-9646; *Statistical Yearbook for Asia and the Pacific*.

Times Books, 201 East 50th Street, New York, New York 10022 (212) 751-2600; *The Economist Book of Vital World Statistics*.

United Nations Educational, Scientific and Cultural Organization (UNESCO), 7 Place de Fontenoy, F-75700 Paris, France (Telephone Number in U.S. (212) 963-5981); *Statistical Yearbook*.

The World Bank, 1818 H Street, NW, Washington, D.C. 20433 (202) 477-1234; *World Tables*.

MALAYSIA - EGG PRODUCTION AND CONSUMPTION - See MALAYSIA - DAIRY PRODUCTS

MALAYSIA - ELECTRICITY

Asian Development Bank, Post Office Box 789, 1099 Manila, Philippines; *Key Indicators of Developing Asian and Pacific Countries*.

Facts on File, 460 Park Avenue South, New York, New York 10016 (800) 443-8323; *The New Book of World Rankings*.

Penn Well Publishing Company, 1421 South Sheridan Road, Post Office Box 1260, Tulsa, Oklahoma 74101 (800) 752-9764; *International Energy Statistics Sourcebook*.

Statistical Office of the United Nations, Publishing Service, New York, New York 10017 (800) 253-9646; *Electric Power in Asia and the Pacific*, and *Statistical Yearbook*.

MALAYSIA - EMPLOYMENT

Euromonitor Publications Limited, 87-88 Turnmill Street, London EC1M 5QU, England; *International Marketing Data and Statistics*, and *The Pacific Basin: An Economic Handbook*.

Facts on File, 460 Park Avenue South, New York, New York 10016 (800) 443-8323; *The New Book of World Rankings*.

International Labour Office, I.L.O. Publications, CH-1211, Geneva 22, Switzerland; *Yearbook of Labour Statistics*.

Statistical Office of the United Nations, Publishing Service, New York, New York 10017 (800) 253-9646; *Statistical Yearbook*.

MALAYSIA - ENERGY

Facts on File, 460 Park Avenue South, New York, New York 10016 (800) 443-8323; *The New Book of World Rankings*.

Food and Agricultural Organization of the United Nations (FAO), Via delle Terme di Caracalla, 00100 Rome, Italy (Telephone Number in U.S. (202) 653-2400); *The State of Food and Agriculture*.

Penn Well Publishing Company, 1421 South Sheridan Road, Post Office Box 1260, Tulsa, Oklahoma 74101 (800) 752-9764; *International Energy Statistics Sourcebook*.

Statistical Office of the United Nations, Publishing Service, New York, New York 10017 (800) 253-9646; *Energy Statistics Yearbook*, *Statistical Yearbook*, and *Statistical Yearbook for Asia and the Pacific*.

Times Books, 201 East 50th Street, New York, New York 10022 (212) 751-2600; *The Economist Book of Vital World Statistics*.

MALAYSIA - ENGINEERING AND METAL PRODUCTS EXPORTS AND IMPORTS

Statistical Office of the United Nations, Publishing Service, New York, New York 10017 (800) 253-9646; *Trade in Manufactures of Developing Countries*.

MALAYSIA - EXCHANGE RATES

Asian Development Bank, Post Office Box 789, 1099 Manila, Philippines; *Key Indicators of Developing Asian and Pacific Countries.*

The Economist Intelligence Unit (Asia) Limited, 10th Floor, Luk Kwok Centre, 72 Gloucester Road, Wanchai, Hong Kong (Phone Number in U.S. (800) 938-4685); *Asian Market Atlas.*

Euromonitor Publications Limited, 87-88 Turnmill Street, London EC1M 5QU, England; *International Marketing Data and Statistics,* and *The Pacific Basin: An Economic Handbook.*

International Civil Aviation Organization, 1000 Sherbrooke Street West, Suite 400, Montreal, Quebec H3A 2R2, Canada (514) 285-8219; *Civil Aviation Statistics of the World.*

International Monetary Fund, 700 Nineteenth Street, NW, Washington, D.C. 20431 (202) 623-7000; *International Financial Statistics.*

Statistical Office of the United Nations, Publishing Service, New York, New York 10017 (800) 253-9646; *Statistical Yearbook.*

MALAYSIA - EXCISE TAXES - See MALAYSIA - TAXATION

MALAYSIA - EXPORTS

American Automobile Manufacturers Association, 1401 H Street, NW, Suite 900, Washington, D.C. 20005 (202) 326-5500; *World Motor Vehicle Data.*

Asian Development Bank, Post Office Box 789, 1099 Manila, Philippines; *Key Indicators of Developing Asian and Pacific Countries.*

The Economist Intelligence Unit, 111 West 57th Street, New York, New York 10019 (800) 938-4685; *The World Market Atlas.*

The Economist Intelligence Unit, 111 West 57th Street, New York, New York 10019 (Phone Number in U.S. (800) 938-4685); *Asian Market Atlas.*

Euromonitor Publications Limited, 87-88 Turnmill Street, London EC1M 5QU, England; *International Marketing Data and Statistics,* and *The Pacific Basin: An Economic Handbook.*

Food and Agricultural Organization of the United Nations (FAO), Via delle Terme di Caracalla, 00100 Rome, Italy (Telephone Number in U.S. (202) 653-2400); *The State of Food and Agriculture.*

International Monetary Fund, 700 Nineteenth Street, NW, Washington, D.C. 20431 (202) 623-7000; *Direction of Trade Statistics, Government Finance Statistics Yearbook,* and *International Financial Statistics.*

International Rubber Study Group, York House, Eighth Floor, Empire Way, Wembley, London HA9 0PA, England; *Rubber Statistical Bulletin.*

Statistical Office of the United Nations, Publishing Service, New York, New York 10017 (800) 253-9646; *Foreign Trade Statistics of Asia and the Pacific,* and *Trade in Manufactures of Developing Countries.*

Times Books, 201 East 50th Street, New York, New York 10022 (212) 751-2600; *The Economist Book of Vital World Statistics.*

The World Bank, 1818 H Street, NW, Washington, D.C. 20433 (202) 477-1234; *World Tables.*

MALAYSIA - EXTERNAL FINANCING

Asian Development Bank, Post Office Box 789, 1099 Manila, Philippines; *Key Indicators of Developing Asian and Pacific Countries.*

MALAYSIA - EXTERNAL INDEBTEDNESS

Asian Development Bank, Post Office Box 789, 1099 Manila, Philippines; *Key Indicators of Developing Asian and Pacific Countries.*

The World Bank, 1818 H Street, NW, Washington, D.C. 20433 (202) 477-1234; *World Tables.*

MALAYSIA - EXTERNAL TRADE

Asian Development Bank, Post Office Box 789, 1099 Manila, Philippines; *Key Indicators of Developing Asian and Pacific Countries.*

Food and Agricultural Organization of the United Nations (FAO), Via delle Terme di Caracalla, 00100 Rome, Italy (Telephone Number in U.S. (202) 653-2400); *The State of Food and Agriculture,* and *Trade Yearbook.*

Statistical Office of the United Nations, Publishing Service, New York, New York 10017 (800) 253-9646; *Statistical Yearbook,* and *Statistical Yearbook for Asia and the Pacific.*

MALAYSIA - FABRIC PRODUCTION - See MALAYSIA - TEXTILE INDUSTRY

MALAYSIA - FARM CROPS - See MALAYSIA - CROPS

MALAYSIA - FEMALE WORKING POPULATION - See MALAYSIA - EMPLOYMENT

MALAYSIA - FERTILITY RATES

The Economist Intelligence Unit (Asia) Limited, 10th Floor, Luk Kwok Centre, 72 Gloucester Road, Wanchai, Hong Kong (Phone Number in U.S. (800) 938-4685); *Asian Market Atlas.*

Facts on File, 460 Park Avenue South, New York, New York 10016 (800) 443-8323; *The New Book of World Rankings.*

MALAYSIA - FERTILIZER

Food and Agricultural Organization of the United Nations (FAO), Via delle Terme di Caracalla, 00100 Rome, Italy (Telephone Number in U.S. (202) 653-2400); *The State of Food and Agriculture.*

Statistical Office of the United Nations, Publishing Service, New York, New York 10017 (800) 253-9646; *Statistical Yearbook.*

Times Books, 201 East 50th Street, New York, New York 10022 (212) 751-2600; *The Economist Book of Vital World Statistics.*

The World Bank, 1818 H Street, NW, Washington, D.C. 20433 (202) 477-1234; *World Tables.*

MALAYSIA - FETAL MORTALITY

Statistical Office of the United Nations, Publishing Service, New York, New York 10017 (800) 253-9646; *Demographic Yearbook.*

World Health Organization, Office of Publications, Avenue Appia, CH-1211 Geneva 27, Switzerland (Telephone Number in U.S. (518) 436-9686); *World Health Statistics Annual*.

MALAYSIA - FIBRE PRODUCTION - See MALAYSIA - TEXTILE INDUSTRY

MALAYSIA - FILMS - See MALAYSIA - MOTION PICTURES

MALAYSIA - FINANCE

Asian Development Bank, Post Office Box 789, 1099 Manila, Philippines; *Key Indicators of Developing Asian and Pacific Countries*.

Euromonitor Publications Limited, 87-88 Turnmill Street, London EC1M 5QU, England; *The Pacific Basin: An Economic Handbook*.

Facts on File, 460 Park Avenue South, New York, New York 10016 (800) 443-8323; *The New Book of World Rankings*.

International Monetary Fund, 700 Nineteenth Street, NW, Washington, D.C. 20431 (202) 623-7000; *International Financial Statistics*.

Statistical Office of the United Nations, Publishing Service, New York, New York 10017 (800) 253-9646; *Statistical Yearbook for Asia and the Pacific*.

MALAYSIA - FISHERIES

Facts on File, 460 Park Avenue South, New York, New York 10016 (800) 443-8323; *The New Book of World Rankings*.

Food and Agricultural Organization of the United Nations (FAO), Via delle Terme di Caracalla, 00100 Rome, Italy (Telephone Number in U.S. (202) 653-2400); *The State of Food and Agriculture*, and *Yearbook of Fishery Statistics*.

Statistical Office of the United Nations, Publishing Service, New York, New York 10017 (800) 253-9646; *Statistical Yearbook*.

MALAYSIA - FLOUR PRODUCTION

Statistical Office of the United Nations, Publishing Service, New York, New York 10017 (800) 253-9646; *Statistical Yearbook*.

MALAYSIA - FOOD

Food and Agricultural Organization of the United Nations (FAO), Via delle Terme di Caracalla, 00100 Rome, Italy (Telephone Number in U.S. (202) 653-2400); *Production Yearbook*, and *The State of Food and Agriculture*.

Statistical Office of the United Nations, Publishing Service, New York, New York 10017 (800) 253-9646; *Statistical Yearbook for Asia and the Pacific*, and *Trade in Manufactures of Developing Countries*.

MALAYSIA - FOREIGN DEBT

International Monetary Fund, 700 Nineteenth Street, NW, Washington, D.C. 20431 (202) 623-7000; *Government Finance Statistics Yearbook*.

MALAYSIA - FOREIGN INDEBTEDNESS

Euromonitor Publications Limited, 87-88 Turnmill Street, London EC1M 5QU, England; *The Pacific Basin: An Economic Handbook*.

MALAYSIA - FOREIGN TRADE

Asian Development Bank, Post Office Box 789, 1099 Manila, Philippines; *Key Indicators of Developing Asian and Pacific Countries*.

The Economist Intelligence Unit (Asia) Limited, 10th Floor, Luk Kwok Centre, 72 Gloucester Road, Wanchai, Hong Kong (Phone Number in U.S. (800) 938-4685); *Asian Market Atlas*.

Euromonitor Publications Limited, 87-88 Turnmill Street, London EC1M 5QU, England; *International Marketing Data and Statistics*, and *The Pacific Basin: An Economic Handbook*.

Facts on File, 460 Park Avenue South, New York, New York 10016 (800) 443-8323; *The New Book of World Rankings*.

Food and Agricultural Organization of the United Nations (FAO), Via delle Terme di Caracalla, 00100 Rome, Italy (Telephone Number in U.S. (202) 653-2400); *The State of Food and Agriculture*.

International Monetary Fund, 700 Nineteenth Street, NW, Washington, D.C. 20431 (202) 623-7000; *International Financial Statistics*.

Statistical Office of the United Nations, Publishing Service, New York, New York 10017 (800) 253-9646; *International Trade Statistics Yearbook*, and *Statistical Yearbook*.

The World Bank, 1818 H Street, NW, Washington, D.C. 20433 (202) 477-1234; *World Tables*.

MALAYSIA - FORESTRY AND FOREST PRODUCTS

American Forest and Paper Association, 1250 Connecticut Avenue, NW, Washington, D.C. 20036 (202) 463-2455; *Wood Pulp and Fiber Statistics*.

The Economist Intelligence Unit (Asia) Limited, 10th Floor, Luk Kwok Centre, 72 Gloucester Road, Wanchai, Hong Kong (Phone Number in U.S. (800) 938-4685); *Asian Market Atlas*.

Facts on File, 460 Park Avenue South, New York, New York 10016 (800) 443-8323; *The New Book of World Rankings*.

Food and Agricultural Organization of the United Nations (FAO), Via delle Terme di Caracalla, 00100 Rome, Italy (Telephone Number in U.S. (202) 653-2400); *The State of Food and Agriculture*, and *Yearbook of Forest Products*.

International Monetary Fund, 700 Nineteenth Street, NW, Washington, D.C. 20431 (202) 623-7000; *International Financial Statistics*.

Statistical Office of the United Nations, Publishing Service, New York, New York 10017 (800) 253-9646; *Statistical Yearbook*.

United Nations Educational, Scientific and Cultural Organization (UNESCO), 7 Place de Fontenoy, F-75700 Paris, France (Telephone Number in U.S. (212) 963-5981); *Statistical Yearbook*.

MALAYSIA - FURNITURE AND WOOD PRODUCTS EXPORTS AND IMPORTS

Statistical Office of the United Nations, Publishing Service, New York, New York 10017 (800) 253-9646; *Trade in Manufactures of Developing Countries*.

MALAYSIA - GAS PRODUCTION - See MALAYSIA - MINING AND MINERAL PRODUCTS

MALAYSIA - GENERAL INDUSTRIAL STATISTICS

Statistical Office of the United Nations, Publishing Service, New York, New York 10017 (800) 253-9646; *Industrial Statistics Yearbook.*

MALAYSIA - GENERAL MORTALITY

Statistical Office of the United Nations, Publishing Service, New York, New York 10017 (800) 253-9646; *Demographic Yearbook.*

World Health Organization, Office of Publications, Avenue Appia, CH-1211 Geneva 27, Switzerland (Telephone Number in U.S. (518) 436-9686); *World Health Statistics Annual.*

MALAYSIA - GEOGRAPHIC DATA

Facts on File, 460 Park Avenue South, New York, New York 10016 (800) 443-8323; *The New Book of World Rankings.*

MALAYSIA - GOATS - See MALAYSIA - LIVESTOCK AND POULTRY

MALAYSIA - GOLD HOLDINGS

Statistical Office of the United Nations, Publishing Service, New York, New York 10017 (800) 253-9646; *Statistical Yearbook.*

The World Bank, 1818 H Street, NW, Washington, D.C. 20433 (202) 477-1234; *World Tables.*

MALAYSIA - GOLD PRODUCTION AND CONSUMPTION - See MALAYSIA - MINING AND MINERAL PRODUCTS

MALAYSIA - GOVERNMENT

Asian Development Bank, Post Office Box 789, 1099 Manila, Philippines; *Key Indicators of Developing Asian and Pacific Countries.*

MALAYSIA - GOVERNMENT EXPENDITURES

Asian Development Bank, Post Office Box 789, 1099 Manila, Philippines; *Key Indicators of Developing Asian and Pacific Countries.*

International Monetary Fund, 700 Nineteenth Street, NW, Washington, D.C. 20431 (202) 623-7000; *Government Finance Statistics Yearbook.*

Times Books, 201 East 50th Street, New York, New York 10022 (212) 751-2600; *The Economist Book of Vital World Statistics.*

The World Bank, 1818 H Street, NW, Washington, D.C. 20433 (202) 477-1234; *World Tables.*

MALAYSIA - GOVERNMENT FINANCES

Asian Development Bank, Post Office Box 789, 1099 Manila, Philippines; *Key Indicators of Developing Asian and Pacific Countries.*

International Monetary Fund, 700 Nineteenth Street, NW, Washington, D.C. 20431 (202) 623-7000; *International Financial Statistics.*

Statistical Office of the United Nations, Publishing Service, New York, New York 10017 (800) 253-9646; *Statistical Yearbook.*

MALAYSIA - GOVERNMENT REVENUES

Asian Development Bank, Post Office Box 789, 1099 Manila, Philippines; *Key Indicators of Developing Asian and Pacific Countries.*

International Monetary Fund, 700 Nineteenth Street, NW, Washington, D.C. 20431 (202) 623-7000; *Government Finance Statistics Yearbook.*

Times Books, 201 East 50th Street, New York, New York 10022 (212) 751-2600; *The Economist Book of Vital World Statistics.*

The World Bank, 1818 H Street, NW, Washington, D.C. 20433 (202) 477-1234; *World Tables.*

MALAYSIA - GRAIN PRODUCTION - See MALAYSIA - CROPS

MALAYSIA - GRANTS

International Monetary Fund, 700 Nineteenth Street, NW, Washington, D.C. 20431 (202) 623-7000; *Government Finance Statistics Yearbook.*

MALAYSIA - GROSS DOMESTIC PRODUCT

Asian Development Bank, Post Office Box 789, 1099 Manila, Philippines; *Key Indicators of Developing Asian and Pacific Countries.*

The Economist Intelligence Unit, 111 West 57th Street, New York, New York 10019 (800) 938-4685; *The World Market Atlas.*

The Economist Intelligence Unit (Asia) Limited, 10th Floor, Luk Kwok Centre, 72 Gloucester Road, Wanchai, Hong Kong (Phone Number in U.S. (800) 938-4685); *Asian Market Atlas.*

Euromonitor Publications Limited, 87-88 Turnmill Street, London EC1M 5QU, England; *International Marketing Data and Statistics,* and *The Pacific Basin: An Economic Handbook.*

Facts on File, 460 Park Avenue South, New York, New York 10016 (800) 443-8323; *The New Book of World Rankings.*

Statistical Office of the United Nations, Publishing Service, New York, New York 10017 (800) 253-9646; *Statistical Yearbook.*

Times Books, 201 East 50th Street, New York, New York 10022 (212) 751-2600; *The Economist Book of Vital World Statistics.*

The World Bank, 1818 H Street, NW, Washington, D.C. 20433 (202) 477-1234; *World Tables.*

MALAYSIA - GROSS NATIONAL PRODUCT

Asian Development Bank, Post Office Box 789, 1099 Manila, Philippines; *Key Indicators of Developing Asian and Pacific Countries.*

Euromonitor Publications Limited, 87-88 Turnmill Street, London EC1M 5QU, England; *International Marketing Data and Statistics.*

U.S. Arms Control and Disarmament Agency, 320 Twenty-first Street, NW, Washington, D.C. 20451 (202) 647-8677; *World Military Expenditures and Arms Transfers.*

The World Bank, 1818 H Street, NW, Washington, D.C. 20433 (202) 477-1234; *World Tables*.

MALAYSIA - GROUNDNUT PRODUCTION - See MALAYSIA - CROPS

MALAYSIA - HEALTH

The Economist Intelligence Unit (Asia) Limited, 10th Floor, Luk Kwok Centre, 72 Gloucester Road, Wanchai, Hong Kong (Phone Number in U.S. (800) 938-4685); *Asian Market Atlas*.

Euromonitor Publications Limited, 87-88 Turnmill Street, London EC1M 5QU, England; *The Pacific Basin: An Economic Handbook*.

Facts on File, 460 Park Avenue South, New York, New York 10016 (800) 443-8323; *The New Book of World Rankings*.

Statistical Office of the United Nations, Publishing Service, New York, New York 10017 (800) 253-9646; *Statistical Yearbook*.

Times Books, 201 East 50th Street, New York, New York 10022 (212) 751-2600; *The Economist Book of Vital World Statistics*.

World Health Organization, Office of Publications, Avenue Appia, CH-1211 Geneva 27, Switzerland (Telephone Number in U.S. (518) 436-9686); *World Health Statistics Annual*.

MALAYSIA - HIDE PRODUCTION

Food and Agricultural Organization of the United Nations (FAO), Via delle Terme di Caracalla, 00100 Rome, Italy (Telephone Number in U.S. (202) 653-2400); *Production Yearbook*.

MALAYSIA - HIGHWAYS

The Economist Intelligence Unit (Asia) Limited, 10th Floor, Luk Kwok Centre, 72 Gloucester Road, Wanchai, Hong Kong (Phone Number in U.S. (800) 938-4685); *Asian Market Atlas*.

International Road Federation, 525 School Street, SW, Washington, D.C. 20024 (202) 554-2106; *World Road Statistics*.

MALAYSIA - HORSES - See MALAYSIA - LIVESTOCK AND POULTRY

MALAYSIA - HOURS OF WORK - See MALAYSIA - EMPLOYMENT

MALAYSIA - HOUSING EXPENDITURES

Facts on File, 460 Park Avenue South, New York, New York 10016 (800) 443-8323; *The New Book of World Rankings*.

International Monetary Fund, 700 Nineteenth Street, NW, Washington, D.C. 20431 (202) 623-7000; *Government Finance Statistics Yearbook*.

MALAYSIA - ILLITERATE POPULATION

The Economist Intelligence Unit, 111 West 57th Street, New York, New York 10019 (800) 938-4685; *The World Market Atlas*.

United Nations Educational, Scientific and Cultural Organization (UNESCO), 7 Place de Fontenoy, F-75700 Paris, France (Telephone Number in U.S. (212) 963-5981); *Statistical Yearbook*.

MALAYSIA - IMPORTS

American Automobile Manufacturers Association, 1401 H Street, NW, Suite 900, Washington, D.C. 20005 (202) 326-5500; *World Motor Vehicle Data*.

Asian Development Bank, Post Office Box 789, 1099 Manila, Philippines; *Key Indicators of Developing Asian and Pacific Countries*.

The Economist Intelligence Unit, 111 West 57th Street, New York, New York 10019 (800) 938-4685; *The World Market Atlas*.

The Economist Intelligence Unit (Asia) Limited, 10th Floor, Luk Kwok Centre, 72 Gloucester Road, Wanchai, Hong Kong (Phone Number in U.S. (800) 938-4685); *Asian Market Atlas*.

Euromonitor Publications Limited, 87-88 Turnmill Street, London EC1M 5QU, England; *International Marketing Data and Statistics*, and *The Pacific Basin: An Economic Handbook*.

Food and Agricultural Organization of the United Nations (FAO), Via delle Terme di Caracalla, 00100 Rome, Italy (Telephone Number in U.S. (202) 653-2400); *The State of Food and Agriculture*.

International Monetary Fund, 700 Nineteenth Street, NW, Washington, D.C. 20431 (202) 623-7000; *Direction of Trade Statistics, Government Finance Statistics Yearbook*, and *International Financial Statistics*.

International Rubber Study Group, York House, Eighth Floor, Empire Way, Wembley, London HA9 0PA, England; *Rubber Statistical Bulletin*.

Statistical Office of the United Nations, Publishing Service, New York, New York 10017 (800) 253-9646; *Foreign Trade Statistics of Asia and the Pacific*, and *Trade in Manufactures of Developing Countries*.

Times Books, 201 East 50th Street, New York, New York 10022 (212) 751-2600; *The Economist Book of Vital World Statistics*.

The World Bank, 1818 H Street, NW, Washington, D.C. 20433 (202) 477-1234; *World Tables*.

MALAYSIA - INCOME TAXES - See MALAYSIA - TAXATION

MALAYSIA - INDUSTRIAL METALS PRODUCTION - See MALAYSIA - MINING AND MINERAL PRODUCTS

MALAYSIA - INDUSTRY

Euromonitor Publications Limited, 87-88 Turnmill Street, London EC1M 5QU, England; *International Marketing Data and Statistics*.

Facts on File, 460 Park Avenue South, New York, New York 10016 (800) 443-8323; *The New Book of World Rankings*.

International Labour Office, I.L.O. Publications, CH-1211, Geneva 22, Switzerland; *Yearbook of Labour Statistics*.

Times Books, 201 East 50th Street, New York, New York 10022 (212) 751-2600; *The Economist Book of Vital World Statistics*.

Statistical Office of the United Nations, Publishing Service, New York, New York 10017 (800) 253-9646; *Statistical Yearbook for Asia and the Pacific*.

The World Bank, 1818 H Street, NW, Washington, D.C. 20433 (202) 477-1234; *World Tables*.

World Intellectual Property Organization, 34 Chemin des Colombettes, CH-1211 Geneva 20, Switzerland; *Industrial Property Statistics*.

MALAYSIA - INFANT AND MATERNAL MORTALITY

The Economist Intelligence Unit (Asia) Limited, 10th Floor, Luk Kwok Centre, 72 Gloucester Road, Wanchai, Hong Kong (Phone Number in U.S. (800) 938-4685); *Asian Market Atlas*.

Statistical Office of the United Nations, Publishing Service, New York, New York 10017 (800) 253-9646; *Demographic Yearbook*, and *Statistical Yearbook*.

Times Books, 201 East 50th Street, New York, New York 10022 (212) 751-2600; *The Economist Book of Vital World Statistics*.

The World Bank, 1818 H Street, NW, Washington, D.C. 20433 (202) 477-1234; *World Tables*.

World Health Organization, Office of Publications, Avenue Appia, CH-1211 Geneva 27, Switzerland (Telephone Number in U.S. (518) 436-9686); *World Health Statistics Annual*.

MALAYSIA - INTEREST RATES

Euromonitor Publications Limited, 87-88 Turnmill Street, London EC1M 5QU, England; *The Pacific Basin: An Economic Handbook*.

MALAYSIA - INTERNAL TRADE

Statistical Office of the United Nations, Publishing Service, New York, New York 10017 (800) 253-9646; *Statistical Yearbook for Asia and the Pacific*.

MALAYSIA - INTERNATIONAL LIQUIDITY

International Monetary Fund, 700 Nineteenth Street, NW, Washington, D.C. 20431 (202) 623-7000; *International Financial Statistics*.

MALAYSIA - INTERNATIONAL RESERVES EXCLUDING GOLD

Asian Development Bank, Post Office Box 789, 1099 Manila, Philippines; *Key Indicators of Developing Asian and Pacific Countries*.

Statistical Office of the United Nations, Publishing Service, New York, New York 10017 (800) 253-9646; *Statistical Yearbook*.

The World Bank, 1818 H Street, NW, Washington, D.C. 20433 (202) 477-1234; *World Tables*.

MALAYSIA - INTERNATIONAL STATISTICS

Asian Development Bank, Post Office Box 789, 1099 Manila, Philippines; *Key Indicators of Developing Asian and Pacific Countries*.

MALAYSIA - INVESTMENTS

International Monetary Fund, 700 Nineteenth Street, NW, Washington, D.C. 20431 (202) 623-7000; *International Financial Statistics*.

MALAYSIA - IRON ORE PRODUCTION AND CONSUMPTION - See MALAYSIA - MINING AND MINERAL PRODUCTS

MALAYSIA - IRRIGATION

Euromonitor Publications Limited, 87-88 Turnmill Street, London EC1M 5QU, England; *International Marketing Data and Statistics*.

MALAYSIA - LABOR FORCE

The Economist Intelligence Unit (Asia) Limited, 10th Floor, Luk Kwok Centre, 72 Gloucester Road, Wanchai, Hong Kong (Phone Number in U.S. (800) 938-4685); *Asian Market Atlas*.

Euromonitor Publications Limited, 87-88 Turnmill Street, London EC1M 5QU, England; *International Marketing Data and Statistics*, and *The Pacific Basin: An Economic Handbook*.

Facts on File, 460 Park Avenue South, New York, New York 10016 (800) 443-8323; *The New Book of World Rankings*.

Food and Agricultural Organization of the United Nations (FAO), Via delle Terme di Caracalla, 00100 Rome, Italy (Telephone Number in U.S. (202) 653-2400); *The State of Food and Agriculture*.

The World Bank, 1818 H Street, NW, Washington, D.C. 20433 (202) 477-1234; *World Tables*.

MALAYSIA - LABOR PRODUCTIVITY

International Labour Office, I.L.O. Publications, CH-1211, Geneva 22, Switzerland; *Yearbook of Labour Statistics*.

MALAYSIA - LAND USE

Euromonitor Publications Limited, 87-88 Turnmill Street, London EC1M 5QU, England; *International Marketing Data and Statistics*.

Food and Agricultural Organization of the United Nations (FAO), Via delle Terme di Caracalla, 00100 Rome, Italy (Telephone Number in U.S. (202) 653-2400); *Production Yearbook*.

MALAYSIA - LEAD AND LEAD ORE PRODUCTION AND CONSUMPTION - See MALAYSIA - MINING AND MINERAL PRODUCTS

MALAYSIA - LIBRARIES

Facts on File, 460 Park Avenue South, New York, New York 10016 (800) 443-8323; *The New Book of World Rankings*.

United Nations Educational, Scientific and Cultural Organization (UNESCO), 7 Place de Fontenoy, F-75700 Paris, France (Telephone Number in U.S. (212) 963-5981); *Statistical Yearbook*.

MALAYSIA - LIFE EXPECTANCY

The Economist Intelligence Unit (Asia) Limited, 10th Floor, Luk Kwok Centre, 72 Gloucester Road, Wanchai, Hong Kong (Phone Number in U.S. (800) 938-4685); *Asian Market Atlas*.

MALAYSIA - LIVESTOCK AND POULTRY

Euromonitor Publications Limited, 87-88 Turnmill Street, London EC1M 5QU, England; *International Marketing Data and Statistics*.

Facts on File, 460 Park Avenue South, New York, New York 10016 (800) 443-8323; *The New Book of World Rankings*.

Food and Agricultural Organization of the United Nations (FAO), Via delle Terme di Caracalla, 00100 Rome, Italy (Telephone Number in U.S. (202) 653-2400); *Production Yearbook*, and *The State of Food and Agriculture*.

Statistical Office of the United Nations, Publishing Service, New York, New York 10017 (800) 253-9646; *Statistical Yearbook*.

MALAYSIA - LIVING LEVELS

Times Books, 201 East 50th Street, New York, New York 10022 (212) 751-2600; *The Economist Book of Vital World Statistics.*

MALAYSIA - MAIL - NUMBER OF ITEMS SENT OR RECEIVED

Statistical Office of the United Nations, Publishing Service, New York, New York 10017 (800) 253-9646; *Statistical Yearbook.*

MALAYSIA - MAGNESIUM PRODUCTION AND CONSUMPTION - See MALAYSIA - MINING AND MINERAL PRODUCTS

MALAYSIA - MANGANESE PRODUCTION AND CONSUMPTION - See MALAYSIA - MINING AND MINERAL PRODUCTS

MALAYSIA - MANPOWER

Statistical Office of the United Nations, Publishing Service, New York, New York 10017 (800) 253-9646; *Statistical Yearbook for Asia and the Pacific.*

MALAYSIA - MANUFACTURING

American Automobile Manufacturers Association, 1401 H Street, NW, Suite 900, Washington, D.C. 20005 (202) 326-5500; *World Motor Vehicle Data.*

Asian Development Bank, Post Office Box 789, 1099 Manila, Philippines; *Key Indicators of Developing Asian and Pacific Countries.*

Facts on File, 460 Park Avenue South, New York, New York 10016 (800) 443-8323; *The New Book of World Rankings.*

Statistical Office of the United Nations, Publishing Service, New York, New York 10017 (800) 253-9646; *Statistical Yearbook.*

Times Books, 201 East 50th Street, New York, New York 10022 (212) 751-2600; *The Economist Book of Vital World Statistics.*

The World Bank, 1818 H Street, NW, Washington, D.C. 20433 (202) 477-1234; *World Tables.*

MALAYSIA - MARRIAGE RATES

Facts on File, 460 Park Avenue South, New York, New York 10016 (800) 443-8323; *The New Book of World Rankings.*

Statistical Office of the United Nations, Publishing Service, New York, New York 10017 (800) 253-9646; *Demographic Yearbook,* and *Statistical Yearbook.*

MALAYSIA - MEAT PRODUCTION - See MALAYSIA - LIVESTOCK AND POULTRY

MALAYSIA - MERCHANT SHIPPING

Lloyd's Register of Shipping, 17 Battery Place, New York, New York 10004 (212) 425-8050; *Register of Ships.*

Statistical Office of the United Nations, Publishing Service, New York, New York 10017 (800) 253-9646; *Statistical Yearbook.*

Times Books, 201 East 50th Street, New York, New York 10022 (212) 751-2600; *The Economist Book of Vital World Statistics.*

U.S. Department of Transportation, Maritime Administration, 400 Seventh Street, SW, Washington, D.C. 20590 (202) 366-5807; *A*

Statistical Analysis of the World's Merchant Fleets.

MALAYSIA - MERCURY PRODUCTION AND CONSUMPTION - See MALAYSIA - MINING AND MINERAL PRODUCTS

MALAYSIA - MILITARY

The Economist Intelligence Unit (Asia) Limited, 10th Floor, Luk Kwok Centre, 72 Gloucester Road, Wanchai, Hong Kong (Phone Number in U.S. (800) 938-4685); *Asian Market Atlas.*

The International Institute for Strategic Studies, 23 Tavistock Street, London WC2E 7NQ, England; *The Military Balance.*

U.S. Arms Control and Disarmament Agency, 320 Twenty-first Street, NW, Washington, D.C. 20451 (202) 647-8677; *World Military Expenditures and Arms Transfers.*

MALAYSIA - MILK PRODUCTION - See MALAYSIA - DAIRY PRODUCTS

MALAYSIA - MINING AND MINERAL PRODUCTS

Asian Development Bank, Post Office Box 789, 1099 Manila, Philippines; *Key Indicators of Developing Asian and Pacific Countries.*

Commodity Research Bureau, Incorporated, 75 Wall Street, New York, New York 10005 (212) 504-7754; *Commodity Yearbook.*

Facts on File, 460 Park Avenue South, New York, New York 10016 (800) 443-8323; *The New Book of World Rankings.*

International Monetary Fund, 700 Nineteenth Street, NW, Washington, D.C. 20431 (202) 623-7000; *International Financial Statistics.*

Penn Well Publishing Company, 1421 South Sheridan Road, Post Office Box 1260, Tulsa, Oklahoma 74101 (800) 752-9764; *International Energy Statistics Sourcebook.*

Statistical Office of the United Nations, Publishing Service, New York, New York 10017 (800) 253-9646; *Statistical Yearbook.*

MALAYSIA - MOLYBDENUM AND MOLYBDENUM ORE PRODUCTION AND CONSUMPTION - See MALAYSIA - MINING AND MINERAL PRODUCTS

MALAYSIA - MONEY EXCHANGE RATES

Euromonitor Publications Limited, 87-88 Turnmill Street, London EC1M 5QU, England; *International Marketing Data and Statistics.*

International Monetary Fund, 700 Nineteenth Street, NW, Washington, D.C. 20431 (202) 623-7000; *International Financial Statistics.*

Statistical Office of the United Nations, Publishing Service, New York, New York 10017 (800) 253-9646; *Statistical Yearbook.*

MALAYSIA - MONEY RESERVES

Euromonitor Publications Limited, 87-88 Turnmill Street, London EC1M 5QU, England; *International Marketing Data and Statistics.*

MALAYSIA - MONEY SUPPLY

Asian Development Bank, Post Office Box 789, 1099 Manila, Philippines; *Key Indicators of Developing Asian and Pacific*

Countries.

Euromonitor Publications Limited, 87-88 Turnmill Street, London EC1M 5QU, England; *International Marketing Data and Statistics*.

International Monetary Fund, 700 Nineteenth Street, NW, Washington, D.C. 20431 (202) 623-7000; *International Financial Statistics*.

Statistical Office of the United Nations, Publishing Service, New York, New York 10017 (800) 253-9646; *Statistical Yearbook*.

The World Bank, 1818 H Street, NW, Washington, D.C. 20433 (202) 477-1234; *World Tables*.

MALAYSIA - MONUMENTS AND HISTORICAL SITES

United Nations Educational, Scientific and Cultural Organization (UNESCO), 7 Place de Fontenoy, F-75700 Paris, France (Telephone Number in U.S. (212) 963-5981); *Statistical Yearbook*.

MALAYSIA - MOTION PICTURES

Statistical Office of the United Nations, Publishing Service, New York, New York 10017 (800) 253-9646; *Statistical Yearbook*.

United Nations Educational, Scientific and Cultural Organization (UNESCO), 7 Place de Fontenoy, F-75700 Paris, France (Telephone Number in U.S. (212) 963-5981); *Statistical Yearbook*.

MALAYSIA - MOTOR VEHICLE PRODUCTION

American Automobile Manufacturers Association, 1401 H Street, NW, Suite 900, Washington, D.C. 20005 (202) 326-5500; *World Motor Vehicle Data*.

Statistical Office of the United Nations, Publishing Service, New York, New York 10017 (800) 253-9646; *Statistical Yearbook*.

Times Books, 201 East 50th Street, New York, New York 10022 (212) 751-2600; *The Economist Book of Vital World Statistics*.

MALAYSIA - MOTOR VEHICLE TAXES - See MALAYSIA - TAXATION

MALAYSIA - MOTOR VEHICLES IN USE

American Automobile Manufacturers Association, 1401 H Street, NW, Suite 900, Washington, D.C. 20005 (202) 326-5500; *World Motor Vehicle Data*.

International Road Federation, 525 School Street, SW, Washington, D.C. 20024 (202) 554-2106; *World Road Statistics*.

Statistical Office of the United Nations, Publishing Service, New York, New York 10017 (800) 253-9646; *Statistical Yearbook*.

MALAYSIA - MUSEUMS

Facts on File, 460 Park Avenue South, New York, New York 10016 (800) 443-8323; *The New Book of World Rankings*.

United Nations Educational, Scientific and Cultural Organization (UNESCO), 7 Place de Fontenoy, F-75700 Paris, France (Telephone Number in U.S. (212) 963-5981); *Statistical Yearbook*.

MALAYSIA - NATALITY - See MALAYSIA - BIRTH RATES

MALAYSIA - NATIONAL ACCOUNTS

International Monetary Fund, 700 Nineteenth Street, NW, Washington, D.C. 20431 (202) 623-7000; *International Financial Statistics*.

Statistical Office of the United Nations, Publishing Service, New York, New York 10017 (800) 253-9646; *National Account Statistics*, *Statistical Yearbook*, and *Statistical Yearbook for Asia and the Pacific*.

MALAYSIA - NATIONAL INCOME

Facts on File, 460 Park Avenue South, New York, New York 10016 (800) 443-8323; *The New Book of World Rankings*.

Statistical Office of the United Nations, Publishing Service, New York, New York 10017 (800) 253-9646; *Statistical Yearbook*.

MALAYSIA - NATIONAL PRODUCT

Facts on File, 460 Park Avenue South, New York, New York 10016 (800) 443-8323; *The New Book of World Rankings*.

Statistical Office of the United Nations, Publishing Service, New York, New York 10017 (800) 253-9646; *Statistical Yearbook*.

MALAYSIA - NATURAL GAS PRODUCTION - See MALAYSIA - MINING AND MINERAL PRODUCTS

MALAYSIA - NATURAL RUBBER PRODUCTION

International Rubber Study Group, York House, Eighth Floor, Empire Way, Wembley, London HA9 0PA, England; *Rubber Statistical Bulletin*.

Statistical Office of the United Nations, Publishing Service, New York, New York 10017 (800) 253-9646; *Statistical Yearbook*.

MALAYSIA - NEWSPAPER PRODUCTION - See MALAYSIA - FORESTRY AND FOREST PRODUCTS

MALAYSIA - NEWSPRINT - See MALAYSIA - FORESTRY AND FOREST PRODUCTS

MALAYSIA - NICKEL AND NICKEL ORE PRODUCTION AND CONSUMPTION - See MALAYSIA - MINING AND MINERAL PRODUCTS

MALAYSIA - PALM OIL AND PALM KERNELS PRODUCTION - See MALAYSIA - CROPS

MALAYSIA - PAPER - See MALAYSIA - FORESTRY AND FOREST PRODUCTS

MALAYSIA - PATENTS

Statistical Office of the United Nations, Publishing Service, New York, New York 10017 (800) 253-9646; *Statistical Yearbook*.

World Intellectual Property Organization, 34 Chemin des Colombettes, CH-1211 Geneva 20, Switzerland; *Industrial Property Statistics*.

MALAYSIA - PEANUT PRODUCTION - See MALAYSIA - MALAYSIA - CROPS

MALAYSIA - PERIODICALS

United Nations Educational, Scientific and Cultural Organization (UNESCO), 7 Place de Fontenoy, F-75700 Paris, France (Telephone Number in U.S. (212) 963-5981); *Statistical Yearbook.*

MALAYSIA - PESTICIDE USE

Food and Agricultural Organization of the United Nations (FAO), Via delle Terme di Caracalla, 00100 Rome, Italy (Telephone Number in U.S. (202) 653-2400); *The State of Food and Agriculture.*

MALAYSIA - PETROLEUM INDUSTRY

Asian Development Bank, Post Office Box 789, 1099 Manila, Philippines; *Key Indicators of Developing Asian and Pacific Countries.*

Facts on File, 460 Park Avenue South, New York, New York 10016 (800) 443-8323; *The New Book of World Rankings.*

Food and Agricultural Organization of the United Nations (FAO), Via delle Terme di Caracalla, 00100 Rome, Italy (Telephone Number in U.S. (202) 653-2400); *The State of Food and Agriculture.*

International Monetary Fund, 700 Nineteenth Street, NW, Washington, D.C. 20431 (202) 623-7000; *International Financial Statistics.*

Penn Well Publishing Company, 1421 South Sheridan Road, Post Office Box 1260, Tulsa, Oklahoma 74101 (800) 752-9764; *International Energy Statistics Sourcebook.*

Statistical Office of the United Nations, Publishing Service, New York, New York 10017 (800) 253-9646; *Statistical Yearbook.*

MALAYSIA - PIGS - See MALAYSIA - LIVESTOCK AND POULTRY

MALAYSIA - PLATINUM PRODUCTION - See MALAYSIA - MINING AND MINERAL PRODUCTS .

MALAYSIA - POPULATION

Asian Development Bank, Post Office Box 789, 1099 Manila, Philippines; *Key Indicators of Developing Asian and Pacific Countries.*

The Economist Intelligence Unit, 111 West 57th Street, New York, New York 10019 (800) 938-4685; *The World Market Atlas.*

The Economist Intelligence Unit (Asia) Limited, 10th Floor, Luk Kwok Centre, 72 Gloucester Road, Wanchai, Hong Kong (Phone Number in U.S. (800) 938-4685); *Asian Market Atlas.*

Euromonitor Publications Limited, 87-88 Turnmill Street, London EC1M 5QU, England; *International Marketing Data and Statistics,* and *The Pacific Basin: An Economic Handbook.*

Facts on File, 460 Park Avenue South, New York, New York 10016 (800) 443-8323; *The New Book of World Rankings.*

Food and Agricultural Organization of the United Nations (FAO), Via delle Terme di Caracalla, 00100 Rome, Italy (Telephone Number in U.S. (202) 653-2400); *Production Yearbook.*

International Labour Office, I.L.O. Publications, CH-1211, Geneva 22, Switzerland; *Yearbook of Labour Statistics.*

Statistical Office of the United Nations, Publishing Service, New York, New York 10017 (800) 253-9646; *Demographic Yearbook, Statistical Yearbook,* and *Statistical Yearbook for Asia and the Pacific.*

Times Books, 201 East 50th Street, New York, New York 10022 (212) 751-2600; *The Economist Book of Vital World Statistics.*

U.S. Arms Control and Disarmament Agency, 320 Twenty-first Street, NW, Washington, D.C. 20451 (202) 647-8677; *World Military Expenditures and Arms Transfers.*

World Health Organization, Office of Publications, Avenue Appia, CH-1211 Geneva 27, Switzerland (Telephone Number in U.S. (518) 436-9686); *World Health Statistics Annual.*

MALAYSIA - POST OFFICES

Facts on File, 460 Park Avenue South, New York, New York 10016 (800) 443-8323; *The New Book of World Rankings.*

MALAYSIA - POTATO PRODUCTION - See MALAYSIA - CROPS

MALAYSIA - POWER PRODUCTION INDUSTRY - ESTABLISHMENTS, PAYROLLS, VALUE ADDED, ETC.

Statistical Office of the United Nations, Publishing Service, New York, New York 10017 (800) 253-9646; *Electric Power in Asia and the Pacific.*

MALAYSIA - PRICES

Asian Development Bank, Post Office Box 789, 1099 Manila, Philippines; *Key Indicators of Developing Asian and Pacific Countries.*

Facts on File, 460 Park Avenue South, New York, New York 10016 (800) 443-8323; *The New Book of World Rankings.*

Food and Agricultural Organization of the United Nations (FAO), Via delle Terme di Caracalla, 00100 Rome, Italy (Telephone Number in U.S. (202) 653-2400); *Production Yearbook,* and *The State of Food and Agriculture.*

International Labour Office, I.L.O. Publications, CH-1211, Geneva 22, Switzerland; *Yearbook of Labour Statistics.*

International Monetary Fund, 700 Nineteenth Street, NW, Washington, D.C. 20431 (202) 623-7000; *International Financial Statistics.*

International Rubber Study Group, York House, Eighth Floor, Empire Way, Wembley, London HA9 0PA, England; *Rubber Statistical Bulletin.*

MALAYSIA - PRINTING AND WRITING PAPER - See MALAYSIA - FORESTRY AND FOREST PRODUCTS

MALAYSIA - PRODUCTION

American Automobile Manufacturers Association, 1401 H Street, NW, Suite 900, Washington, D.C. 20005 (202) 326-5500; *World Motor Vehicle Data.*

Facts on File, 460 Park Avenue South, New York, New York 10016 (800) 443-8323; *The New Book of World Rankings.*

International Rubber Study Group, York House, Eighth Floor, Empire Way, Wembley, London HA9 0PA, England; *Rubber Statistical*

Bulletin.

MALAYSIA - PRODUCTIVITY

Euromonitor Publications Limited, 87-88 Turnmill Street, London EC1M 5QU, England; *International Marketing Data and Statistics.*

MALAYSIA - PROPERTY TAXES

International Monetary Fund, 700 Nineteenth Street, NW, Washington, D.C. 20431 (202) 623-7000; *Government Finance Statistics Yearbook.*

MALAYSIA - PUBLIC FINANCE

Facts on File, 460 Park Avenue South, New York, New York 10016 (800) 443-8323; *The New Book of World Rankings.*

MALAYSIA - RADIO BROADCASTING - See MALAYSIA - BROADCASTING

MALAYSIA - RAILWAY USE

Statistical Office of the United Nations, Publishing Service, New York, New York 10017 (800) 253-9646; *Statistical Yearbook.*

MALAYSIA - RAILWAYS

Jane's Information Group, Sentinel House, 163 Brighton Road, Coulsdon, Surrey CR5 2NH, England (Telephone Number in U.S. (703) 683 3700); *Jane's World Railways.*

MALAYSIA - RELIGION

Facts on File, 460 Park Avenue South, New York, New York 10016 (800) 443-8323; *The New Book of World Rankings.*

MALAYSIA - RETAIL TRADE

Statistical Office of the United Nations, Publishing Service, New York, New York 10017 (800) 253-9646; *Statistical Yearbook.*

MALAYSIA - RICE PRODUCTION - See MALAYSIA - CROPS

MALAYSIA - ROOT AND TUBER PRODUCTION - See MALAYSIA - CROPS

MALAYSIA - ROUNDWOOD PRODUCTION - See MALAYSIA - FORESTRY AND FOREST PRODUCTS

MALAYSIA - RUBBER PRODUCTION AND CONSUMPTION

Commodity Research Bureau, Incorporated, 75 Wall Street, New York, New York 10005 (212) 504-7754; *Commodity Yearbook.*

Facts on File, 460 Park Avenue South, New York, New York 10016 (800) 443-8323; *The New Book of World Rankings.*

International Rubber Study Group, York House, Eighth Floor, Empire Way, Wembley, London HA9 0PA, England; *International Financial Statistics,* and *Rubber Statistical Bulletin.*

MALAYSIA - SAWNWOOD PRODUCTION - See MALAYSIA - FORESTRY AND FOREST PRODUCTS

MALAYSIA - SCIENTISTS AND TECHNICIANS

Statistical Office of the United Nations, Publishing Service, New York, New York 10017 (800) 253-9646; *Statistical Yearbook.*

MALAYSIA - SENIOR CITIZENS

Facts on File, 460 Park Avenue South, New York, New York 10016 (800) 443-8323; *The New Book of World Rankings.*

MALAYSIA - SHEEP - See MALAYSIA - LIVESTOCK AND POULTRY

MALAYSIA - SILVER PRODUCTION AND CONSUMPTION - See MALAYSIA - MINING AND MINERAL PRODUCTS

MALAYSIA - SOCIAL DATA

Asian Development Bank, Post Office Box 789, 1099 Manila, Philippines; *Key Indicators of Developing Asian and Pacific Countries.*

Facts on File, 460 Park Avenue South, New York, New York 10016 (800) 443-8323; *The New Book of World Rankings.*

MALAYSIA - SOYBEAN PRODUCTION - See MALAYSIA - CROPS

MALAYSIA - STAMP TAXES AND DUTIES - See MALAYSIA - TAXATION

MALAYSIA - STATE BUDGET

Euromonitor Publications Limited, 87-88 Turnmill Street, London EC1M 5QU, England; *International Marketing Data and Statistics.*

MALAYSIA - STEEL - See MALAYSIA - MINING AND MINERAL PRODUCTS

MALAYSIA - STOCKS - COMMODITY - MARKET PRICE - INDEX

Food and Agricultural Organization of the United Nations (FAO), Via delle Terme di Caracalla, 00100 Rome, Italy (Telephone Number in U.S. (202) 653-2400); *The State of Food and Agriculture.*

MALAYSIA - SUGAR PRODUCTION AND CONSUMPTION - See MALAYSIA - CROPS

MALAYSIA - TAXATION

International Monetary Fund, 700 Nineteenth Street, NW, Washington, D.C. 20431 (202) 623-7000; *Government Finance Statistics.*

International Road Federation, 525 School Street, SW, Washington, D.C. 20024 (202) 554-2106; *World Road Statistics.*

The World Bank, 1818 H Street, NW, Washington, D.C. 20433 (202) 477-1234; *World Tables.*

MALAYSIA - TEA PRODUCTION - See MALAYSIA - CROPS

MALAYSIA - TELEGRAPH SERVICE

Statistical Office of the United Nations, Publishing Service, New York, New York 10017 (800) 253-9646; *Statistical Yearbook.*

MALAYSIA - TELEPHONES IN USE

American Telephone and Telegraph Company, 26 Parsippany Road, Whippany, New Jersey 07981 (800) 338-4038; *The World's Telephones.*

The Economist Intelligence Unit (Asia) Limited, 10th Floor, Luk Kwok Centre, 72 Gloucester Road, Wanchai, Hong Kong (Phone

Number in U.S. (800) 938-4685); *Asian Market Atlas*.

Statistical Office of the United Nations, Publishing Service, New York, New York 10017 (800) 253-9646; *Statistical Yearbook*.

MALAYSIA - TELEVISION BROADCASTING - See MALAYSIA - BROADCASTING

MALAYSIA - TELEVISION RECEIVER PRODUCTION

Statistical Office of the United Nations, Publishing Service, New York, New York 10017 (800) 253-9646; *Statistical Yearbook*.

MALAYSIA - TEXTILE INDUSTRY

American Forest and Paper Association, 1250 Connecticut Avenue, NW, Washington, D.C. 20036 (202) 463-2455; *Wood Pulp and Fiber Statistics*.

Statistical Office of the United Nations, Publishing Service, New York, New York 10017 (800) 253-9646; *Statistical Yearbook*, and *Trade in Manufactures of Developing Countries*.

MALAYSIA - THEATRE

United Nations Educational, Scientific and Cultural Organization (UNESCO), 7 Place de Fontenoy, F-75700 Paris, France (Telephone Number in U.S. (212) 963-5981); *Statistical Yearbook*.

MALAYSIA - TIN - See MALAYSIA - MINING AND MINERAL PRODUCTS

MALAYSIA - TIRE (MOTOR VEHICLE) PRODUCTION

International Rubber Study Group, York House, Eighth Floor, Empire Way, Wembley, London HA9 0PA, England; *Rubber Statistical Bulletin*.

Statistical Office of the United Nations, Publishing Service, New York, New York 10017 (800) 253-9646; *Statistical Yearbook*.

MALAYSIA - TOBACCO PRODUCTION

Facts on File, 460 Park Avenue South, New York, New York 10016 (800) 443-8323; *The New Book of World Rankings*.

Statistical Office of the United Nations, Publishing Service, New York, New York 10017 (800) 253-9646; *Statistical Yearbook*.

MALAYSIA - TOURISM

Euromonitor Publications Limited, 87-88 Turnmill Street, London EC1M 5QU, England; *The Pacific Basin: An Economic Handbook*.

Facts on File, 460 Park Avenue South, New York, New York 10016 (800) 443-8323; *The New Book of World Rankings*.

Statistical Office of the United Nations, Publishing Service, New York, New York 10017 (800) 253-9646; *Statistical Yearbook*.

Times Books, 201 East 50th Street, New York, New York 10022 (212) 751-2600; *The Economist Book of Vital World Statistics*.

World Tourism Organization, Calle Capitan Haya 42, E-28020 Madrid, Spain; *Yearbook of Tourism Statistics*.

MALAYSIA - TRACTORS IN USE

Statistical Office of the United Nations, Publishing Service, New York, New York 10017 (800) 253-9646; *Statistical Yearbook*.

MALAYSIA - TRADE - See MALAYSIA - FOREIGN TRADE

MALAYSIA - TRADEMARKS AND SERVICE MARKS

Statistical Office of the United Nations, Publishing Service, New York, New York 10017 (800) 253-9646; *Statistical Yearbook*.

World Intellectual Property Organization, 34 Chemin des Colombettes, CH-1211 Geneva 20, Switzerland; *Industrial Property Statistics*.

MALAYSIA - TRANSPORTATION AND COMMUNICATIONS

The Economist Intelligence Unit (Asia) Limited, 10th Floor, Luk Kwok Centre, 72 Gloucester Road, Wanchai, Hong Kong (Phone Number in U.S. (800) 938-4685); *Asian Market Atlas*.

Euromonitor Publications Limited, 87-88 Turnmill Street, London EC1M 5QU, England; *The Pacific Basin: An Economic Handbook*.

Facts on File, 460 Park Avenue South, New York, New York 10016 (800) 443-8323; *The New Book of World Rankings*.

Statistical Office of the United Nations, Publishing Service, New York, New York 10017 (800) 253-9646; *Statistical Yearbook for Asia and the Pacific*.

MALAYSIA - TUNGSTEN PRODUCTION AND CONSUMPTION - See MALAYSIA - MINING AND MINERAL PRODUCTS

MALAYSIA - UNEMPLOYMENT

Euromonitor Publications Limited, 87-88 Turnmill Street, London EC1M 5QU, England; *International Marketing Data and Statistics*, and *The Pacific Basin: An Economic Handbook*.

International Labour Office, I.L.O. Publications, CH-1211, Geneva 22, Switzerland; *Yearbook of Labour Statistics*.

Statistical Office of the United Nations, Publishing Service, New York, New York 10017 (800) 253-9646; *Statistical Yearbook*.

MALAYSIA - URANIUM PRODUCTION AND CONSUMPTION - See MALAYSIA - MINING AND MINERAL PRODUCTS

MALAYSIA - UTILITIES

Statistical Office of the United Nations, Publishing Service, New York, New York 10017 (800) 253-9646; *Electric Power in Asia and the Pacific*.

MALAYSIA - VANADIUM AND VANADIUM ORE PRODUCTION - See MALAYSIA - MINING AND MINERAL PRODUCTS

MALAYSIA - VITAL STATISTICS

Euromonitor Publications Limited, 87-88 Turnmill Street, London EC1M 5QU, England; *The Pacific Basin: An Economic Handbook*.

Statistical Office of the United Nations, Publishing Service, New York, New York 10017 (800) 253-9646; *Statistical Yearbook*.

World Health Organization, Office of Publications, Avenue Appia, CH-1211 Geneva 27, Switzerland (Telephone Number in U.S. (518)

436-9686); *World Health Statistics Annual.*

MALAYSIA - WAGES

International Labour Office, I.L.O. Publications, CH-1211, Geneva 22, Switzerland; *Yearbook of Labour Statistics.*

MALAYSIA - WAGES AND PRICES

Statistical Office of the United Nations, Publishing Service, New York, New York 10017 (800) 253-9646; *Statistical Yearbook for Asia and the Pacific.*

MALAYSIA - WATERMELON PRODUCTION - See MALAYSIA - CROPS

MALAYSIA - WEATHER

Facts on File, 460 Park Avenue South, New York, New York 10016 (800) 443-8323; *The New Book of World Rankings.*

MALAYSIA - WHEAT PRODUCTION - See MALAYSIA - CROPS

MALAYSIA - WHOLESALE PRICES - INDEX NUMBERS

Asian Development Bank, Post Office Box 789, 1099 Manila, Philippines; *Key Indicators of Developing Asian and Pacific Countries.*

MALAYSIA - WHOLESALE TRADE

Statistical Office of the United Nations, Publishing Service, New York, New York 10017 (800) 253-9646; *Statistical Yearbook.*

MALAYSIA - WINE PRODUCTION

Facts on File, 460 Park Avenue South, New York, New York 10016 (800) 443-8323; *The New Book of World Rankings.*

MALAYSIA - WOOD - See MALAYSIA - FORESTRY AND FOREST PRODUCTS

MALAYSIA - WOOL PRODUCTION

Facts on File, 460 Park Avenue South, New York, New York 10016 (800) 443-8323; *The New Book of World Rankings.*

MALAYSIA - YARN PRODUCTION

Statistical Office of the United Nations, Publishing Service, New York, New York 10017 (800) 253-9646; *Statistical Yearbook.*

MALAYSIA - ZINC AND ZINC ORE PRODUCTION AND CONSUMPTION - See MALAYSIA - MINING AND MINERAL PRODUCTS

MALAYSIA - ZOOS AND BOTANICAL GARDENS

United Nations Educational, Scientific and Cultural Organization (UNESCO), 7 Place de Fontenoy, F-75700 Paris, France (Telephone Number in U.S. (212) 963-5981); *Statistical Yearbook.*

Maldives - National Statistical Office

Ministry of Planning and Environment, Male 20-05, Republic of Maldives.

Maldives - Primary Statistics Source

Ministry of Planning and Development, Maldives; *Statistical Year Book of Maldives.*

MALDIVES - AGRICULTURE

Asian Development Bank, Post Office Box 789, 1099 Manila, Philippines; *Key Indicators of Developing Asian and Pacific Countries.*

Food and Agricultural Organization of the United Nations (FAO), Via delle Terme di Caracalla, 00100 Rome, Italy (Telephone Number in U.S. (202) 653-2400); *Production Yearbook, The State of Food and Agriculture,* and *Trade Yearbook.*

Statistical Office of the United Nations, Publishing Service, New York, New York 10017 (800) 253-9646; *Statistical Yearbook for Asia and the Pacific.*

MALDIVES - AREA AND DENSITY OF POPULATION

Food and Agricultural Organization of the United Nations (FAO), Via delle Terme di Caracalla, 00100 Rome, Italy (Telephone Number in U.S. (202) 653-2400); *The State of Food and Agriculture*

Statistical Office of the United Nations, Publishing Service, New York, New York 10017 (800) 253-9646; *Statistical Yearbook.*

MALDIVES - BANKING

Asian Development Bank, Post Office Box 789, 1099 Manila, Philippines; *Key Indicators of Developing Asian and Pacific Countries.*

MALDIVES - BIRTH RATES

Statistical Office of the United Nations, Publishing Service, New York, New York 10017 (800) 253-9646; *Demographic Yearbook,* and *Statistical Yearbook.*

World Health Organization, Office of Publications, Avenue Appia, CH-1211 Geneva 27, Switzerland (Telephone Number in U.S. (518) 436-9686); *World Health Statistics Annual.*

MALDIVES - BONDS

Asian Development Bank, Post Office Box 789, 1099 Manila, Philippines; *Key Indicators of Developing Asian and Pacific Countries.*

MALDIVES - BROADCASTING

Billboard Limited, Post Office Box 9027, 1006 AA Amsterdam, The Netherlands (Telephone Number in U.S. (212) 764-7300); *World Radio TV Handbook.*

United Nations Educational, Scientific and Cultural Organization (UNESCO), 7 Place de Fontenoy, F-75700 Paris, France (Telephone Number in U.S. (212) 963-5981); *Statistical Yearbook.*

MALDIVES - CALORIE SUPPLY

Asian Development Bank, Post Office Box 789, 1099 Manila, Philippines; *Key Indicators of Developing Asian and Pacific Countries.*

Food and Agricultural Organization of the United Nations (FAO), Via delle Terme di Caracalla, 00100 Rome, Italy (Telephone Number in

U.S. (202) 653-2400); *The State of Food and Agriculture.*

MALDIVES - CAPITAL INVESTMENT

Asian Development Bank, Post Office Box 789, 1099 Manila, Philippines; *Key Indicators of Developing Asian and Pacific Countries.*

MALDIVES - CAPITAL REVENUE

Asian Development Bank, Post Office Box 789, 1099 Manila, Philippines; *Key Indicators of Developing Asian and Pacific Countries.*

MALDIVES - COMMUNICATION

Statistical Office of the United Nations, Publishing Service, New York, New York 10017 (800) 253-9646; *Statistical Yearbook for Asia and the Pacific.*

MALDIVES - CONSUMER PRICE INDEX

Asian Development Bank, Post Office Box 789, 1099 Manila, Philippines; *Key Indicators of Developing Asian and Pacific Countries.*

MALDIVES - CORN PRODUCTION - See MALDIVES - CROPS

MALDIVES - CROPS

Asian Development Bank, Post Office Box 789, 1099 Manila, Philippines; *Key Indicators of Developing Asian and Pacific Countries.*

Food and Agricultural Organization of the United Nations (FAO), Via delle Terme di Caracalla, 00100 Rome, Italy (Telephone Number in U.S. (202) 653-2400); *Production Yearbook,* and *The State of Food and Agriculture.*

MALDIVES - DAIRY PRODUCTS

Food and Agricultural Organization of the United Nations (FAO), Via delle Terme di Caracalla, 00100 Rome, Italy (Telephone Number in U.S. (202) 653-2400); *The State of Food and Agriculture.*

MALDIVES - DEATH RATES

Statistical Office of the United Nations, Publishing Service, New York, New York 10017 (800) 253-9646; *Statistical Yearbook.*

MALDIVES - DEVELOPMENT ASSISTANCE

Asian Development Bank, Post Office Box 789, 1099 Manila, Philippines; *Key Indicators of Developing Asian and Pacific Countries.*

Statistical Office of the United Nations, Publishing Service, New York, New York 10017 (800) 253-9646; *Statistical Yearbook.*

MALDIVES - DIVORCE RATES

Statistical Office of the United Nations, Publishing Service, New York, New York 10017 (800) 253-9646; *Demographic Yearbook, Statistical Yearbook,* and *Statistical Yearbook for Asia and the Pacific.*

MALDIVES - ECONOMY

Asian Development Bank, Post Office Box 789, 1099 Manila, Philippines; *Key Indicators of Developing Asian and Pacific Countries.*

MALDIVES - EDUCATION

Statistical Office of the United Nations, Publishing Service, New York, New York 10017 (800) 253-9646; *Statistical Yearbook for Asia and the Pacific.*

United Nations Educational, Scientific and Cultural Organization (UNESCO), 7 Place de Fontenoy, F-75700 Paris, France (Telephone Number in U.S. (212) 963-5981); *Statistical Yearbook.*

MALDIVES - EGG PRODUCTION - See MALDIVES - DAIRY PRODUCTS

MALDIVES - ELECTRICITY

Asian Development Bank, Post Office Box 789, 1099 Manila, Philippines; *Key Indicators of Developing Asian and Pacific Countries.*

MALDIVES - ENERGY

Food and Agricultural Organization of the United Nations (FAO), Via delle Terme di Caracalla, 00100 Rome, Italy (Telephone Number in U.S. (202) 653-2400); *The State of Food and Agriculture.*

Statistical Office of the United Nations, Publishing Service, New York, New York 10017 (800) 253-9646; *Statistical Yearbook for Asia and the Pacific.*

MALDIVES - EXCHANGE RATES

Asian Development Bank, Post Office Box 789, 1099 Manila, Philippines; *Key Indicators of Developing Asian and Pacific Countries.*

Statistical Office of the United Nations, Publishing Service, New York, New York 10017 (800) 253-9646; *Statistical Yearbook.*

MALDIVES - EXPORTS

Asian Development Bank, Post Office Box 789, 1099 Manila, Philippines; *Key Indicators of Developing Asian and Pacific Countries.*

Food and Agricultural Organization of the United Nations (FAO), Via delle Terme di Caracalla, 00100 Rome, Italy (Telephone Number in U.S. (202) 653-2400); *The State of Food and Agriculture.*

International Monetary Fund, 700 Nineteenth Street, NW, Washington, D.C. 20431 (202) 623-7000; *Direction of Trade Statistics.*

MALDIVES - EXTERNAL FINANCING

Asian Development Bank, Post Office Box 789, 1099 Manila, Philippines; *Key Indicators of Developing Asian and Pacific Countries.*

MALDIVES - EXTERNAL INDEBTEDNESS

Asian Development Bank, Post Office Box 789, 1099 Manila, Philippines; *Key Indicators of Developing Asian and Pacific Countries.*

MALDIVES - EXTERNAL TRADE

Asian Development Bank, Post Office Box 789, 1099 Manila, Philippines; *Key Indicators of Developing Asian and Pacific Countries.*

Food and Agricultural Organization of the United Nations (FAO), Via delle Terme di Caracalla, 00100 Rome, Italy (Telephone Number in U.S. (202) 653-2400); *The State of Food and Agriculture,* and *Trade Yearbook.*

Statistical Office of the United Nations, Publishing Service, New York, New York 10017 (800) 253-9646; *Statistical Yearbook for Asia and the Pacific.*

MALDIVES - FARM CROPS - See MALDIVES - CROPS

MALDIVES - FERTILIZER

Food and Agricultural Organization of the United Nations (FAO), Via delle Terme di Caracalla, 00100 Rome, Italy (Telephone Number in U.S. (202) 653-2400); *The State of Food and Agriculture.*

MALDIVES - FETAL MORTALITY

Statistical Office of the United Nations, Publishing Service, New York, New York 10017 (800) 253-9646; *Demographic Yearbook.*

World Health Organization, Office of Publications, Avenue Appia, CH-1211 Geneva 27, Switzerland (Telephone Number in U.S. (518) 436-9686); *World Health Statistics Annual.*

MALDIVES - FINANCE

Asian Development Bank, Post Office Box 789, 1099 Manila, Philippines; *Key Indicators of Developing Asian and Pacific Countries.*

Statistical Office of the United Nations, Publishing Service, New York, New York 10017 (800) 253-9646; *Statistical Yearbook for Asia and the Pacific.*

MALDIVES - FISHERIES

Food and Agricultural Organization of the United Nations (FAO), Via delle Terme di Caracalla, 00100 Rome, Italy (Telephone Number in U.S. (202) 653-2400); *The State of Food and Agriculture,* and *Yearbook of Fishery Statistics.*

Statistical Office of the United Nations, Publishing Service, New York, New York 10017 (800) 253-9646; *Statistical Yearbook.*

MALDIVES - FOOD

Food and Agricultural Organization of the United Nations (FAO), Via delle Terme di Caracalla, 00100 Rome, Italy (Telephone Number in U.S. (202) 653-2400); *Production Yearbook,* and *The State of Food and Agriculture.*

Statistical Office of the United Nations, Publishing Service, New York, New York 10017 (800) 253-9646; *Statistical Yearbook for Asia and the Pacific.*

MALDIVES - FOREIGN TRADE

Asian Development Bank, Post Office Box 789, 1099 Manila, Philippines; *Key Indicators of Developing Asian and Pacific Countries.*

Food and Agricultural Organization of the United Nations (FAO), Via delle Terme di Caracalla, 00100 Rome, Italy (Telephone Number in U.S. (202) 653-2400); *The State of Food and Agriculture.*

MALDIVES - FORESTRY AND FOREST PRODUCTS

Food and Agricultural Organization of the United Nations (FAO), Via delle Terme di Caracalla, 00100 Rome, Italy (Telephone Number in U.S. (202) 653-2400); *The State of Food and Agriculture.*

Statistical Office of the United Nations, Publishing Service, New York, New York 10017 (800) 253-9646; *Statistical Yearbook.*

MALDIVES - GENERAL MORTALITY

Statistical Office of the United Nations, Publishing Service, New York, New York 10017 (800) 253-9646; *Demographic Yearbook.*

World Health Organization, Office of Publications, Avenue Appia, CH-1211 Geneva 27, Switzerland (Telephone Number in U.S. (518) 436-9686); *World Health Statistics Annual.*

MALDIVES - GOVERNMENT

Asian Development Bank, Post Office Box 789, 1099 Manila, Philippines; *Key Indicators of Developing Asian and Pacific Countries.*

MALDIVES - GOVERNMENT EXPENDITURE

Asian Development Bank, Post Office Box 789, 1099 Manila, Philippines; *Key Indicators of Developing Asian and Pacific Countries.*

MALDIVES - GOVERNMENT FINANCES

Asian Development Bank, Post Office Box 789, 1099 Manila, Philippines; *Key Indicators of Developing Asian and Pacific Countries.*

MALDIVES - GOVERNMENT REVENUE

Asian Development Bank, Post Office Box 789, 1099 Manila, Philippines; *Key Indicators of Developing Asian and Pacific Countries.*

MALDIVES - GRAIN PRODUCTION - See MALDIVES - CROPS

MALDIVES - GROSS DOMESTIC PRODUCT

Asian Development Bank, Post Office Box 789, 1099 Manila, Philippines; *Key Indicators of Developing Asian and Pacific Countries.*

Statistical Office of the United Nations, Publishing Service, New York, New York 10017 (800) 253-9646; *Statistical Yearbook.*

MALDIVES - GROSS NATIONAL PRODUCT

Asian Development Bank, Post Office Box 789, 1099 Manila, Philippines; *Key Indicators of Developing Asian and Pacific Countries.*

MALDIVES - HEALTH

Statistical Office of the United Nations, Publishing Service, New York, New York 10017 (800) 253-9646; *Statistical Yearbook.*

MALDIVES - ILLITERATE POPULATION

United Nations Educational, Scientific and Cultural Organization (UNESCO), 7 Place de Fontenoy, F-75700 Paris, France (Telephone Number in U.S. (212) 963-5981); *Statistical Yearbook.*

MALDIVES - IMPORTS

Asian Development Bank, Post Office Box 789, 1099 Manila, Philippines; *Key Indicators of Developing Asian and Pacific Countries.*

Food and Agricultural Organization of the United Nations (FAO), Via delle Terme di Caracalla, 00100 Rome, Italy (Telephone Number in U.S. (202) 653-2400); *The State of Food and Agriculture.*

International Monetary Fund, 700 Nineteenth Street, NW, Washington, D.C. 20431 (202) 623-7000; *Direction of Trade Statistics.*

MALDIVES - INDUSTRY

Statistical Office of the United Nations, Publishing Service, New York, New York 10017 (800) 253-9646; *Statistical Yearbook for Asia and the Pacific.*

MALDIVES - INFANT AND MATERNAL MORTALITY

Statistical Office of the United Nations, Publishing Service, New York, New York 10017 (800) 253-9646; *Demographic Yearbook,* and *Statistical Yearbook.*

World Health Organization, Office of Publications, Avenue Appia, CH-1211 Geneva 27, Switzerland (Telephone Number in U.S. (518) 436-9686); *World Health Statistics Annual.*

MALDIVES - INTERNAL TRADE

Statistical Office of the United Nations, Publishing Service, New York, New York 10017 (800) 253-9646; *Statistical Yearbook for Asia and the Pacific.*

MALDIVES - INTERNATIONAL RESERVES EXCLUDING GOLD

Asian Development Bank, Post Office Box 789, 1099 Manila, Philippines; *Key Indicators of Developing Asian and Pacific Countries.*

MALDIVES - INTERNATIONAL STATISTICS

Asian Development Bank, Post Office Box 789, 1099 Manila, Philippines; *Key Indicators of Developing Asian and Pacific Countries.*

MALDIVES - LABOR FORCE

Food and Agricultural Organization of the United Nations (FAO), Via delle Terme di Caracalla, 00100 Rome, Italy (Telephone Number in U.S. (202) 653-2400); *The State of Food and Agriculture.*

MALDIVES - LAND USE

Food and Agricultural Organization of the United Nations (FAO), Via delle Terme di Caracalla, 00100 Rome, Italy (Telephone Number in U.S. (202) 653-2400); *Production Yearbook.*

MALDIVES - LIVESTOCK AND POULTRY

Food and Agricultural Organization of the United Nations (FAO), Via delle Terme di Caracalla, 00100 Rome, Italy (Telephone Number in U.S. (202) 653-2400); *Production Yearbook,* and *The State of Food and Agriculture.*

MALDIVES - MAIL - NUMBER OF ITEMS SENT AND RECEIVED

Statistical Office of the United Nations, Publishing Service, New York, New York 10017 (800) 253-9646; *Statistical Yearbook.*

MALDIVES - MANPOWER

Statistical Office of the United Nations, Publishing Service, New York, New York 10017 (800) 253-9646; *Statistical Yearbook for Asia and the Pacific.*

MALDIVES - MANUFACTURING

Asian Development Bank, Post Office Box 789, 1099 Manila, Philippines; *Key Indicators of Developing Asian and Pacific Countries.*

MALDIVES - MARRIAGE RATES

Statistical Office of the United Nations, Publishing Service, New York, New York 10017 (800) 253-9646; *Demographic Yearbook,* and *Statistical Yearbook.*

MALDIVES - MEAT PRODUCTION - See MALDIVES - LIVESTOCK AND POULTRY

MALDIVES - MERCHANT SHIPPING

Statistical Office of the United Nations, Publishing Service, New York, New York 10017 (800) 253-9646; *Statistical Yearbook.*

U.S. Department of Transportation, Maritime Administration, 400 Seventh Street, SW, Washington, D.C. 20590(202) 366-5807; *A Statistical Analysis of the World's Merchant Fleets.*

MALDIVES - MINING - INDUSTRIAL PRODUCTION INDEX

Asian Development Bank, Post Office Box 789, 1099 Manila, Philippines; *Key Indicators of Developing Asian and Pacific Countries.*

MALDIVES - MONEY EXCHANGE RATE

Statistical Office of the United Nations, Publishing Service, New York, New York 10017 (800) 253-9646; *Statistical Yearbook.*

MALDIVES - MONEY SUPPLY

Asian Development Bank, Post Office Box 789, 1099 Manila, Philippines; *Key Indicators of Developing Asian and Pacific Countries.*

MALDIVES - MUSEUMS

United Nations Educational, Scientific and Cultural Organization (UNESCO), 7 Place de Fontenoy, F-75700 Paris, France (Telephone Number in U.S. (212) 963-5981); *Statistical Yearbook.*

MALDIVES - NATALITY - See MALDIVES - BIRTH RATES

MALDIVES - NATIONAL ACCOUNTS

Statistical Office of the United Nations, Publishing Service, New York, New York 10017 (800) 253-9646; *Statistical Yearbook for Asia and the Pacific.*

MALDIVES - NEWSPAPER - See MALDIVES - FORESTRY AND FOREST PRODUCTS

MALDIVES - PERIODICALS

United Nations Educational, Scientific and Cultural Organization (UNESCO), 7 Place de Fontenoy, F-75700 Paris, France (Telephone Number in U.S. (212) 963-5981); *Statistical Yearbook.*

MALDIVES - PESTICIDE USE

Food and Agricultural Organization of the United Nations (FAO), Via delle Terme di Caracalla, 00100 Rome, Italy (Telephone Number in U.S. (202) 653-2400); *The State of Food and Agriculture.*

MALDIVES - PETROLEUM INDUSTRY

Asian Development Bank, Post Office Box 789, 1099 Manila, Philippines; *Key Indicators of Developing Asian and Pacific Countries.*

Food and Agricultural Organization of the United Nations (FAO), Via delle Terme di Caracalla, 00100 Rome, Italy (Telephone Number in U.S. (202) 653-2400); *The State of Food and Agriculture.*

MALDIVES - POPULATION

Asian Development Bank, Post Office Box 789, 1099 Manila, Philippines; *Key Indicators of Developing Asian and Pacific Countries.*

Food and Agricultural Organization of the United Nations (FAO), Via delle Terme di Caracalla, 00100 Rome, Italy (Telephone Number in U.S. (202) 653-2400); *Production Yearbook.*

Statistical Office of the United Nations, Publishing Service, New York, New York 10017 (800) 253-9646; *Demographic Yearbook, Statistical Yearbook,* and *Statistical Yearbook for Asia and the Pacific.*

MALDIVES - PRICES

Asian Development Bank, Post Office Box 789, 1099 Manila, Philippines; *Key Indicators of Developing Asian and Pacific Countries.*

Food and Agricultural Organization of the United Nations (FAO), Via delle Terme di Caracalla, 00100 Rome, Italy (Telephone Number in U.S. (202) 653-2400); *Production Yearbook,* and *The State of Food and Agriculture.*

MALDIVES - RADIO BROADCASTING - See MALDIVES - BROADCASTING

MALDIVES - RICE PRODUCTION - See MALDIVES - CROPS

MALDIVES - ROOT AND TUBER PRODUCTION - See MALDIVES - CROPS

MALDIVES - SOCIAL DATA

Asian Development Bank, Post Office Box 789, 1099 Manila, Philippines; *Key Indicators of Developing Asian and Pacific Countries.*

MALDIVES - STOCKS - COMMODITY - MARKET PRICE - INDEX

Food and Agricultural Organization of the United Nations (FAO), Via delle Terme di Caracalla, 00100 Rome, Italy (Telephone Number in U.S. (202) 653-2400); *The State of Food and Agriculture.*

MALDIVES - TELEPHONES IN USE

American Telephone and Telegraph Company, 26 Parsippany Road, Whippany, New Jersey 07981 (800) 338-4038; *The World's Telephones.*

United Nations Educational, Scientific and Cultural Organization (UNESCO), 7 Place de Fontenoy, F-75700 Paris, France (Telephone Number in U.S. (212) 963-5981); *Statistical Yearbook.*

MALDIVES - TOURISM

World Tourism Organization, Calle Capitan Haya 42, E-28020 Madrid, Spain; *Yearbook of Tourism Statistics.*

MALDIVES - TRADE - See MALDIVES - FOREIGN TRADE

MALDIVES - TRANSPORTATION AND COMMUNICATIONS

Statistical Office of the United Nations, Publishing Service, New York, New York 10017 (800) 253-9646; *Statistical Yearbook for Asia and the Pacific.*

MALDIVES - VITAL STATISTICS

Statistical Office of the United Nations, Publishing Service, New York, New York 10017 (800) 253-9646; *Statistical Yearbook.*

World Health Organization, Office of Publications, Avenue Appia, CH-1211 Geneva 27, Switzerland (Telephone Number in U.S. (518) 436-9686); *World Health Statistics Annual.*

MALDIVES - WAGES AND PRICES

Statistical Office of the United Nations, Publishing Service, New York, New York 10017 (800) 253-9646; *Statistical Yearbook for Asia and the Pacific.*

MALDIVES - WHOLESALE PRICES - INDEX NUMBERS

Asian Development Bank, Post Office Box 789, 1099 Manila, Philippines; *Key Indicators of Developing Asian and Pacific Countries.*

MALE HOUSEHOLDER - See HOUSEHOLDS OR FAMILIES

Mali - National Statistical Office

Direction Nationale de L'Informatique, Ministere du Plan, B.P. 12, Bamako, Mali.

Mali- Primary Statistics Sources

Direction Nationale de la Statistique, BP12, Bamako, Mali; *Annuaire statistique du Mali* (Statistical Yearbook of Mali), *Bulletin Mensuel de Statistique,* (Monthly bulletin of statistics).

MALI - AGRICULTURE

Euromonitor Publications Limited, 87-88 Turnmill Street, London EC1M 5QU, England; *International Marketing Data and Statistics.*

Facts on File, 460 Park Avenue South, New York, New York 10016 (800) 443-8323; *The New Book of World Rankings.*

Food and Agricultural Organization of the United Nations (FAO), Via delle Terme di Caracalla, 00100 Rome, Italy (Telephone Number in U.S. (202) 653-2400); *The State of Food and Agriculture,* and *Trade Yearbook.*

G.K. Hall and Company, 70 Lincoln Street, Boston, Massachusetts 02111 (617) 423-3990; *The World in Figures.*

Statistical Office of the United Nations, Publishing Service, New York, New York 10017 (800) 253-9646; *Statistical Yearbook,* and *Survey of Economic and Social Conditions in Africa.*

Times Books, 201 East 50th Street, New York, New York 10022 (212) 751-2600; *The Economist Book of Vital World Statistics.*

United Nations Economic Commission for Africa, Africa Hall, Post Office Box 3001, Addis Ababa, Ethiopia (Telephone Number in U.S. (800) 253-9646); *African Statistical Yearbook.*

The World Bank, 1818 H Street, NW, Washington, D.C. 20433 (202) 477-1234; *World Tables.*

MALI - AIRLINE SERVICE

Facts on File, 460 Park Avenue South, New York, New York 10016 (800) 443-8323; *The New Book of World Rankings.*

G.K. Hall and Company, 70 Lincoln Street, Boston, Massachusetts 02111 (617) 423-3990; *The World in Figures.*

Statistical Office of the United Nations, Publishing Service, New York, New York 10017 (800) 253-9646; *Statistical Yearbook.*

United Nations Economic Commission for Africa, Africa Hall, Post Office Box 3001, Addis Ababa, Ethiopia (Telephone Number in U.S. (800) 253-9646); *African Statistical Yearbook.*

MALI - ALUMINUM PRODUCTION AND CONSUMPTION - See MALI - MINING AND MINERAL PRODUCTS

MALI - ANIMAL HEALTH

Food and Agricultural Organization of the United Nations (FAO), Via delle Terme di Caracalla, 00100 Rome, Italy (Telephone Number in U.S. (202) 653-2400); *Animal Health Yearbook.*

MALI - AREA AND DENSITY OF POPULATION

African Development Bank, 01 BP 1387, Abidjan 01, Cote d'Ivoire; *Selected Statistics on Regional Member Countries.*

Euromonitor Publications Limited, 87-88 Turnmill Street, London EC1M 5QU, England; *International Marketing Data and Statistics.*

Facts on File, 460 Park Avenue South, New York, New York 10016 (800) 443-8323; *The New Book of World Rankings.*

Food and Agricultural Organization of the United Nations (FAO), Via delle Terme di Caracalla, 00100 Rome, Italy (Telephone Number in U.S. (202) 653-2400); *The State of Food and Agriculture.*

G.K. Hall and Company, 70 Lincoln Street, Boston, Massachusetts 02111 (617) 423-3990; *The World in Figures.*

Statistical Office of the United Nations, Publishing Service, New York, New York 10017 (800) 253-9646; *Statistical Yearbook,* and *Survey of Economic and Social Conditions in Africa.*

Times Books, 201 East 50th Street, New York, New York 10022 (212) 751-2600; *The Economist Book of Vital World Statistics.*

MALI - ARMS EXPORTS AND IMPORTS

U.S. Arms Control and Disarmament Agency, 320 Twenty-first Street, NW, Washington, D.C. 20451 (202) 647-8677; *World Military Expenditures and Arms Transfers.*

MALI - BALANCE OF PAYMENTS

African Development Bank, 01 BP 1387, Abidjan 01, Cote d'Ivoire; *Selected Statistics on Regional Member Countries.*

The Economist Intelligence Unit, 111 West 57th Street, New York, New York 10019 (800) 938-4685; *The World Market Atlas.*

G.K. Hall and Company, 70 Lincoln Street, Boston, Massachusetts 02111 (617) 423-3990; *The World in Figures.*

International Monetary Fund, 700 Nineteenth Street, NW, Washington, D.C. 20431 (202) 623-7000; *Balance of Payments Yearbook.*

Times Books, 201 East 50th Street, New York, New York 10022 (212) 751-2600; *The Economist Book of Vital World Statistics.*

United Nations Economic Commission for Africa, Africa Hall, Post Office Box 3001, Addis Ababa, Ethiopia (Telephone Number in U.S. (800) 253-9646); *African Statistical Yearbook.*

The World Bank, 1818 H Street, NW, Washington, D.C. 20433 (202) 477-1234; *World Tables.*

MALI - BANKING

Facts on File, 460 Park Avenue South, New York, New York 10016 (800) 443-8323; *The New Book of World Rankings.*

G.K. Hall and Company, 70 Lincoln Street, Boston, Massachusetts 02111 (617) 423-3990; *The World in Figures.*

International Monetary Fund, 700 Nineteenth Street, NW, Washington, D.C. 20431 (202) 623-7000; *International Financial Statistics.*

United Nations Economic Commission for Africa, Africa Hall, Post Office Box 3001, Addis Ababa, Ethiopia (Telephone Number in U.S. (800) 253-9646); *African Statistical Yearbook.*

MALI - BARLEY PRODUCTION - See MALI - CROPS

MALI - BEER PRODUCTION

Facts on File, 460 Park Avenue South, New York, New York 10016 (800) 443-8323; *The New Book of World Rankings.*

Statistical Office of the United Nations, Publishing Service, New York, New York 10017 (800) 253-9646; *Statistical Yearbook.*

MALI - BIRTH RATES

Facts on File, 460 Park Avenue South, New York, New York 10016 (800) 443-8323; *The New Book of World Rankings*.

Statistical Office of the United Nations, Publishing Service, New York, New York 10017 (800) 253-9646; *Demographic Yearbook, Statistical Yearbook*, and *Survey of Economic and Social Conditions in Africa*.

Times Books, 201 East 50th Street, New York, New York 10022 (212) 751-2600; *The Economist Book of Vital World Statistics*.

The World Bank, 1818 H Street, NW, Washington, D.C. 20433 (202) 477-1234; *World Tables*.

MALI - BONDS

G.K. Hall and Company, 70 Lincoln Street, Boston, Massachusetts 02111 (617) 423-3990; *The World in Figures*.

International Monetary Fund, 700 Nineteenth Street, NW, Washington, D.C. 20431 (202) 623-7000; *Government Finance Statistics Yearbook*.

MALI - BOOK PRODUCTION

G.K. Hall and Company, 70 Lincoln Street, Boston, Massachusetts 02111 (617) 423-3990; *The World in Figures*.

United Nations Educational, Scientific and Cultural Organization (UNESCO), 7 Place de Fontenoy, F-75700 Paris, France (Telephone Number in U.S. (212) 963-5981); *Statistical Yearbook*.

MALI - BROADCASTING

Billboard Limited, Post Office Box 9027, 1006 AA Amsterdam, The Netherlands (Telephone Number in U.S. (212) 764-7300); *World Radio TV Handbook*.

Facts on File, 460 Park Avenue South, New York, New York 10016 (800) 443-8323; *The New Book of World Rankings*.

G.K. Hall and Company, 70 Lincoln Street, Boston, Massachusetts 02111 (617) 423-3990; *The World in Figures*.

Times Books, 201 East 50th Street, New York, New York 10022 (212) 751-2600; *The Economist Book of Vital World Statistics*.

MALI - BUSINESS

G.K. Hall and Company, 70 Lincoln Street, Boston, Massachusetts 02111 (617) 423-3990; *The World in Figures*.

MALI - BUSINESS AND PROPERTY TAXES

International Monetary Fund, 700 Nineteenth Street, NW, Washington, D.C. 20431 (202) 623-7000; *Government Finance Statistics Yearbook*.

MALI - BUTTER PRODUCTION - See MALI - DAIRY PRODUCTS

MALI - CALORIE SUPPLY

African Development Bank, 01 BP 1387, Abidjan 01, Cote d'Ivoire; *Selected Statistics on Regional Member Countries*.

Food and Agricultural Organization of the United Nations (FAO), Via delle Terme di Caracalla, 00100 Rome, Italy (Telephone Number in U.S. (202) 653-2400); *The State of Food and Agriculture*.

MALI - CAPITAL REVENUE

International Monetary Fund, 700 Nineteenth Street, NW, Washington, D.C. 20431 (202) 623-7000; *Government Finance Statistics Yearbook*.

MALI - CATTLE - See MALI - LIVESTOCK AND POULTRY

MALI - CEMENT PRODUCTION - See MALI - MINING AND MINERAL PRODUCTS

MALI - CHEMICAL (ORGANIC) PRODUCTION - See MALI - MINING AND MINERAL PRODUCTS

MALI - CHICKENS - See MALI - LIVESTOCK AND POULTRY

MALI - CLASS STRUCTURE

G.K. Hall and Company, 70 Lincoln Street, Boston, Massachusetts 02111 (617) 423-3990; *The World in Figures*.

MALI - CLIMATE

Facts on File, 460 Park Avenue South, New York, New York 10016 (800) 443-8323; *The New Book of World Rankings*.

G.K. Hall and Company, 70 Lincoln Street, Boston, Massachusetts 02111 (617) 423-3990; *The World in Figures*.

MALI - COAL PRODUCTION - See MALI - MINING AND MINERAL PRODUCTS

MALI - COFFEE PRODUCTION - See MALI - CROPS

MALI - COMMUNICATIONS

G.K. Hall and Company, 70 Lincoln Street, Boston, Massachusetts 02111 (617) 423-3990; *The World in Figures*.

United Nations Economic Commission for Africa, Africa Hall, Post Office Box 3001, Addis Ababa, Ethiopia (Telephone Number in U.S. (800) 253-9646); *African Statistical Yearbook*.

MALI - CONSTRUCTION INDUSTRY

Facts on File, 460 Park Avenue South, New York, New York 10016 (800) 443-8323; *The New Book of World Rankings*.

United Nations Economic Commission for Africa, Africa Hall, Post Office Box 3001, Addis Ababa, Ethiopia (Telephone Number in U.S. (800) 253-9646); *African Statistical Yearbook*.

MALI - CONSUMER PRICE INDEX

African Development Bank, 01 BP 1387, Abidjan 01, Cote d'Ivoire; *Selected Statistics on Regional Member Countries*.

G.K. Hall and Company, 70 Lincoln Street, Boston, Massachusetts 02111 (617) 423-3990; *The World in Figures*.

Statistical Office of the United Nations, Publishing Service, New York, New York 10017 (800) 253-9646; *Statistical Yearbook*, and *Survey of Economic and Social Conditions in Africa*.

Times Books, 201 East 50th Street, New York, New York 10022 (212) 751-2600; *The Economist Book of Vital World Statistics*.

United Nations Economic Commission for Africa, Africa Hall, Post Office Box 3001, Addis Ababa, Ethiopia (Telephone Number in U.S. (800) 253-9646); *African Statistical Yearbook.*

MALI - CONSUMER PRICES

International Labour Office, I.L.O. Publications, CH-1211, Geneva 22, Switzerland; *Yearbook of Labour Statistics.*

MALI - CONSUMPTION

African Development Bank, 01 BP 1387, Abidjan 01, Cote d'Ivoire; *Selected Statistics on Regional Member Countries.*

G.K. Hall and Company, 70 Lincoln Street, Boston, Massachusetts 02111 (617) 423-3990; *The World in Figures.*

Statistical Office of the United Nations, Publishing Service, New York, New York 10017 (800) 253-9646; *Survey of Economic and Social Conditions in Africa.*

MALI - COPPER PRODUCTION - See MALI - MINING AND MINERAL PRODUCTS

MALI - CORN PRODUCTION - See MALI - CROPS

MALI - CORPORATE TAXES - See MALI - TAXATION

MALI - COTTON - See MALI - CROPS

MALI - CROPS

Facts on File, 460 Park Avenue South, New York, New York 10016 (800) 443-8323; *The New Book of World Rankings.*

Food and Agricultural Organization of the United Nations (FAO), Via delle Terme di Caracalla, 00100 Rome, Italy (Telephone Number in U.S. (202) 653-2400); *Production Yearbook,* and *The State of Food and Agriculture.*

G.K. Hall and Company, 70 Lincoln Street, Boston, Massachusetts 02111 (617) 423-3990; *The World in Figures.*

International Monetary Fund, 700 Nineteenth Street, NW, Washington, D.C. 20431 (202) 623-7000; *International Financial Statistics.*

Statistical Office of the United Nations, Publishing Service, New York, New York 10017 (800) 253-9646; *Statistical Yearbook.*

United Nations Economic Commission for Africa, Africa Hall, Post Office Box 3001, Addis Ababa, Ethiopia (Telephone Number in U.S. (800) 253-9646); *African Statistical Yearbook.*

MALI - CUSTOMS DUTIES

G.K. Hall and Company, 70 Lincoln Street, Boston, Massachusetts 02111 (617) 423-3990; *The World in Figures.*

International Monetary Fund, 700 Nineteenth Street, NW, Washington, D.C. 20431 (202) 623-7000; *Government Finance Statistics Yearbook.*

MALI - DAIRY PRODUCTS

Facts on File, 460 Park Avenue South, New York, New York 10016 (800) 443-8323; *The New Book of World Rankings.*

Food and Agricultural Organization of the United Nations (FAO), Via delle Terme di Caracalla, 00100 Rome, Italy (Telephone Number in U.S. (202) 653-2400); *Production Yearbook,* and *The State of Food and Agriculture.*

Statistical Office of the United Nations, Publishing Service, New York, New York 10017 (800) 253-9646; *Statistical Yearbook.*

MALI - DEATH RATES

G.K. Hall and Company, 70 Lincoln Street, Boston, Massachusetts 02111 (617) 423-3990; *The World in Figures.*

Statistical Office of the United Nations, Publishing Service, New York, New York 10017 (800) 253-9646; *Statistical Yearbook,* and *Survey of Economic and Social Conditions in Africa.*

Times Books, 201 East 50th Street, New York, New York 10022 (212) 751-2600; *The Economist Book of Vital World Statistics.*

World Health Organization, Office of Publications, Avenue Appia, CH-1211 Geneva 27, Switzerland (Telephone Number in U.S. (518) 436-9686); *World Health Statistics Annual.*

MALI - DEFENSE EXPENDITURES

G.K. Hall and Company, 70 Lincoln Street, Boston, Massachusetts 02111 (617) 423-3990; *The World in Figures.*

International Monetary Fund, 700 Nineteenth Street, NW, Washington, D.C. 20431 (202) 623-7000; *Government Finance Statistics Yearbook.*

U.S. Arms Control and Disarmament Agency, 320 Twenty-first Street, NW, Washington, D.C. 20451 (202) 647-8677; *World Military Expenditures and Arms Transfers.*

MALI - DEMOGRAPHY

The Economist Intelligence Unit, 111 West 57th Street, New York, New York 10019 (800) 938-4685; *The World Market Atlas.*

Facts on File, 460 Park Avenue South, New York, New York 10016 (800) 443-8323; *The New Book of World Rankings.*

G.K. Hall and Company, 70 Lincoln Street, Boston, Massachusetts 02111 (617) 423-3990; *The World in Figures.*

Statistical Office of the United Nations, Publishing Service, New York, New York 10017 (800) 253-9646; *Survey of Economic and Social Conditions in Africa.*

MALI - DEVELOPMENT ASSISTANCE

G.K. Hall and Company, 70 Lincoln Street, Boston, Massachusetts 02111 (617) 423-3990; *The World in Figures.*

Statistical Office of the United Nations, Publishing Service, New York, New York 10017 (800) 253-9646; *Statistical Yearbook.*

MALI - DIAMOND PRODUCTION - See MALI - MINING AND MINERAL PRODUCTS

MALI - DISEASES

G.K. Hall and Company, 70 Lincoln Street, Boston, Massachusetts 02111 (617) 423-3990; *The World in Figures.*

World Health Organization, Office of Publications, Avenue Appia, CH-1211 Geneva 27, Switzerland (Telephone Number in U.S. (518) 436-9686); *World Health Statistics Annual.*

MALI - DIVORCE

Facts on File, 460 Park Avenue South, New York, New York 10016 (800) 443-8323; *The New Book of World Rankings.*

Statistical Office of the United Nations, Publishing Service, New York, New York 10017 (800) 253-9646; *Demographic Yearbook.*

MALI - DOMESTIC PRODUCT

G.K. Hall and Company, 70 Lincoln Street, Boston, Massachusetts 02111 (617) 423-3990; *The World in Figures.*

MALI - ECONOMY

African Development Bank, 01 BP 1387, Abidjan 01, Cote d'Ivoire; *Selected Statistics on Regional Member Countries.*

Euromonitor Publications Limited, 87-88 Turnmill Street, London EC1M 5QU, England; *International Marketing Data and Statistics.*

Facts on File, 460 Park Avenue South, New York, New York 10016 (800) 443-8323; *The New Book of World Rankings.*

G.K. Hall and Company, 70 Lincoln Street, Boston, Massachusetts 02111 (617) 423-3990; *The World in Figures*

MALI - EDUCATION

African Development Bank, 01 BP 1387, Abidjan 01, Cote d'Ivoire; *Selected Statistics on Regional Member Countries.*

The Economist Intelligence Unit, 111 West 57th Street, New York, New York 10019 (800) 938-4685; *The World Market Atlas.*

Facts on File, 460 Park Avenue South, New York, New York 10016 (800) 443-8323; *The New Book of World Rankings.*

G.K. Hall and Company, 70 Lincoln Street, Boston, Massachusetts 02111 (617) 423-3990; *The World in Figures.*

International Monetary Fund, 700 Nineteenth Street, NW, Washington, D.C. 20431 (202) 623-7000; *Government Finance Statistics Yearbook.*

Statistical Office of the United Nations, Publishing Service, New York, New York 10017 (800) 253-9646; *Survey of Economic and Social Conditions in Africa.*

Times Books, 201 East 50th Street, New York, New York 10022 (212) 751-2600; *The Economist Book of Vital World Statistics.*

United Nations Economic Commission for Africa, Africa Hall, Post Office Box 3001, Addis Ababa, Ethiopia (Telephone Number in U.S. (800) 253-9646); *African Statistical Yearbook.*

United Nations Educational, Scientific and Cultural Organization (UNESCO), 7 Place de Fontenoy, F-75700 Paris, France (Telephone Number in U.S. (212) 963-5981); *Statistical Yearbook.*

The World Bank, 1818 H Street, NW, Washington, D.C. 20433 (202) 477-1234; *World Tables.*

MALI - EGG PRODUCTION - See MALI - DAIRY PRODUCTS

MALI - ELECTRICITY

Facts on File, 460 Park Avenue South, New York, New York 10016 (800) 443-8323; *The New Book of World Rankings.*

Statistical Office of the United Nations, Publishing Service, New York, New York 10017 (800) 253-9646; *Statistical Yearbook,* and *Survey of Economic and Social Conditions in Africa.*

Times Books, 201 East 50th Street, New York, New York 10022 (212) 751-2600; *The Economist Book of Vital World Statistics.*

United Nations Economic Commission for Africa, Africa Hall, Post Office Box 3001, Addis Ababa, Ethiopia (Telephone Number in U.S. (800) 253-9646); *African Statistical Yearbook.*

MALI - EMPLOYMENT

Euromonitor Publications Limited, 87-88 Turnmill Street, London EC1M 5QU, England; *International Marketing Data and Statistics.*

Facts on File, 460 Park Avenue South, New York, New York 10016 (800) 443-8323; *The New Book of World Rankings.*

International Labour Office, I.L.O. Publications, CH-1211, Geneva 22, Switzerland, *Yearbook of Labour Statistics.*

Statistical Office of the United Nations, Publishing Service, New York, New York 10017 (800) 253-9646; *Statistical Yearbook,* and *Survey of Economic and Social Conditions in Africa.*

United Nations Economic Commission for Africa, Africa Hall, Post Office Box 3001, Addis Ababa, Ethiopia (Telephone Number in U.S. (800) 253-9646); *African Statistical Yearbook.*

MALI - ENERGY

Facts on File, 460 Park Avenue South, New York, New York 10016 (800) 443-8323; *The New Book of World Rankings.*

G.K. Hall and Company, 70 Lincoln Street, Boston, Massachusetts 02111 (617) 423-3990; *The World in Figures.*

Statistical Office of the United Nations, Publishing Service, New York, New York 10017 (800) 253-9646; *Energy Statistics Yearbook,* and *Statistical Yearbook.*

Times Books, 201 East 50th Street, New York, New York 10022 (212) 751-2600; *The Economist Book of Vital World Statistics.*

United Nations Economic Commission for Africa, Africa Hall, Post Office Box 3001, Addis Ababa, Ethiopia (Telephone Number in U.S. (800) 253-9646); *African Statistical Yearbook.*

MALI - EXCHANGE RATES

African Development Bank, 01 BP 1387, Abidjan 01, Cote d'Ivoire; *Selected Statistics on Regional Member Countries.*

Euromonitor Publications Limited, 87-88 Turnmill Street, London EC1M 5QU, England; *International Marketing Data and Statistics.*

International Monetary Fund, 700 Nineteenth Street, NW, Washington, D.C. 20431 (202) 623-7000; *International Financial Statistics.*

Statistical Office of the United Nations, Publishing Service, New York, New York 10017 (800) 253-9646; *Statistical Yearbook.*

MALI - EXCISE TAXES - See MALI - TAXATION

MALI - EXPORTS

African Development Bank, 01 BP 1387, Abidjan 01, Cote d'Ivoire; *Selected Statistics on Regional Member Countries.*

The Economist Intelligence Unit, 111 West 57th Street, New York, New York 10019 (800) 938-4685; *The World Market Atlas.*

Euromonitor Publications Limited, 87-88 Turnmill Street, London EC1M 5QU, England; *International Marketing Data and Statistics.*

Food and Agricultural Organization of the United Nations (FAO), Via delle Terme di Caracalla, 00100 Rome, Italy (Telephone Number in U.S. (202) 653-2400); *The State of Food and Agriculture.*

G.K. Hall and Company, 70 Lincoln Street, Boston, Massachusetts 02111 (617) 423-3990; *The World in Figures.*

International Monetary Fund, 700 Nineteenth Street, NW, Washington, D.C. 20431 (202) 623-7000; *Direction of Trade Statistics, Government Finance Statistics Yearbook,* and *International Financial Statistics.*

Statistical Office of the United Nations, Publishing Service, New York, New York 10017 (800) 253-9646; *Survey of Economic and Social Conditions in Africa.*

Times Books, 201 East 50th Street, New York, New York 10022 (212) 751-2600; *The Economist Book of Vital World Statistics.*

United Nations Economic Commission for Africa, Africa Hall, Post Office Box 3001, Addis Ababa, Ethiopia (Telephone Number in U.S. (800) 253-9646); *African Statistical Yearbook.*

The World Bank, 1818 H Street, NW, Washington, D.C. 20433 (202) 477-1234; *World Tables.*

MALI - EXTERNAL INDEBTEDNESS

African Development Bank, 01 BP 1387, Abidjan 01, Cote d'Ivoire; *Selected Statistics on Regional Member Countries.*

Statistical Office of the United Nations, Publishing Service, New York, New York 10017 (800) 253-9646; *Survey of Economic and Social Conditions in Africa.*

The World Bank, 1818 H Street, NW, Washington, D.C. 20433 (202) 477-1234; *World Tables.*

MALI - EXTERNAL TRADE

African Development Bank, 01 BP 1387, Abidjan 01, Cote d'Ivoire; *Selected Statistics on Regional Member Countries.*

Food and Agricultural Organization of the United Nations (FAO), Via delle Terme di Caracalla, 00100 Rome, Italy (Telephone Number in U.S. (202) 653-2400); *The State of Food and Agriculture,* and *Trade Yearbook.*

G.K. Hall and Company, 70 Lincoln Street, Boston, Massachusetts 02111 (617) 423-3990; *The World in Figures.*

Statistical Office of the United Nations, Publishing Service, New York, New York 10017 (800) 253-9646; *Statistical Yearbook.*

MALI - FARM CROPS - See MALI - CROPS

MALI - FEMALE WORKING POPULATION - See MALI - EMPLOYMENT

MALI - FERTILITY RATES

Facts on File, 460 Park Avenue South, New York, New York 10016 (800) 443-8323; *The New Book of World Rankings.*

Statistical Office of the United Nations, Publishing Service, New York, New York 10017 (800) 253-9646; *Survey of Economic and Social Conditions in Africa.*

Times Books, 201 East 50th Street, New York, New York 10022 (212) 751-2600; *The Economist Book of Vital World Statistics.*

The World Bank, 1818 H Street, NW, Washington, D.C. 20433 (202) 477-1234; *World Tables.*

MALI - FERTILIZER

Food and Agricultural Organization of the United Nations (FAO), Via delle Terme di Caracalla, 00100 Rome, Italy (Telephone Number in U.S. (202) 653-2400); *Fertilizer Yearbook,* and *The State of Food and Agriculture.*

Statistical Office of the United Nations, Publishing Service, New York, New York 10017 (800) 253-9646; *Statistical Yearbook.*

MALI - FETAL MORTALITY

Statistical Office of the United Nations, Publishing Service, New York, New York 10017 (800) 253-9646; *Demographic Yearbook.*

MALI - FINANCE

African Development Bank, 01 BP 1387, Abidjan 01, Cote d'Ivoire; *Selected Statistics on Regional Member Countries.*

Facts on File, 460 Park Avenue South, New York, New York 10016 (800) 443-8323; *The New Book of World Rankings.*

G.K. Hall and Company, 70 Lincoln Street, Boston, Massachusetts 02111 (617) 423-3990; *The World in Figures.*

International Monetary Fund, 700 Nineteenth Street, NW, Washington, D.C. 20431 (202) 623-7000; *Government Finance Statistics Yearbook,* and *International Financial Statistics.*

United Nations Economic Commission for Africa, Africa Hall, Post Office Box 3001, Addis Ababa, Ethiopia (Telephone Number in U.S. (800) 253-9646); *African Statistical Yearbook.*

MALI - FISHERIES

Facts on File, 460 Park Avenue South, New York, New York 10016 (800) 443-8323; *The New Book of World Rankings.*

Food and Agricultural Organization of the United Nations (FAO), Via delle Terme di Caracalla, 00100 Rome, Italy (Telephone Number in U.S. (202) 653-2400); *The State of Food and Agriculture,* and *Yearbook of Fishery Statistics.*

Statistical Office of the United Nations, Publishing Service, New York, New York 10017 (800) 253-9646; *Statistical Yearbook,* and *Survey of Economic and Social Conditions in Africa.*

United Nations Economic Commission for Africa, Africa Hall, Post Office Box 3001, Addis Ababa, Ethiopia (Telephone Number in U.S. (800) 253-9646); *African Statistical Yearbook.*

MALI - FOOD

African Development Bank, 01 BP 1387, Abidjan 01, Cote d'Ivoire; *Selected Statistics on Regional Member Countries*.

Food and Agricultural Organization of the United Nations (FAO), Via delle Terme di Caracalla, 00100 Rome, Italy (Telephone Number in U.S. (202) 653-2400); *Production Yearbook*, and *The State of Food and Agriculture*.

G.K. Hall and Company, 70 Lincoln Street, Boston, Massachusetts 02111 (617) 423-3990; *The World in Figures*.

MALI - FOREIGN AID

G.K. Hall and Company, 70 Lincoln Street, Boston, Massachusetts 02111 (617) 423-3990; *The World in Figures*.

MALI - FOREIGN TRADE

Euromonitor Publications Limited, 87-88 Turnmill Street, London EC1M 5QU, England; *International Marketing Data and Statistics*.

Facts on File, 460 Park Avenue South, New York, New York 10016 (800) 443-8323; *The New Book of World Rankings*.

Food and Agricultural Organization of the United Nations (FAO), Via delle Terme di Caracalla, 00100 Rome, Italy (Telephone Number in U.S. (202) 653-2400); *The State of Food and Agriculture*.

G.K. Hall and Company, 70 Lincoln Street, Boston, Massachusetts 02111 (617) 423-3990; *The World in Figures*.

International Monetary Fund, 700 Nineteenth Street, NW, Washington, D.C. 20431 (202) 623-7000; *International Financial Statistics*.

Statistical Office of the United Nations, Publishing Service, New York, New York 10017 (800) 253-9646; *Statistical Yearbook, International Trade Statistics Yearbook*, and *Trade in Manufactures of Developing Countries*.

United Nations Economic Commission for Africa, Africa Hall, Post Office Box 3001, Addis Ababa, Ethiopia (Telephone Number in U.S. (800) 253-9646); *African Statistical Yearbook*.

The World Bank, 1818 H Street, NW, Washington, D.C. 20433 (202) 477-1234; *World Tables*.

MALI - FORESTRY AND FOREST PRODUCTS

Facts on File, 460 Park Avenue South, New York, New York 10016 (800) 443-8323; *The New Book of World Rankings*.

Food and Agricultural Organization of the United Nations (FAO), Via delle Terme di Caracalla, 00100 Rome, Italy (Telephone Number in U.S. (202) 653-2400); *The State of Food and Agriculture*, and *Yearbook of Forest Products*.

G.K. Hall and Company, 70 Lincoln Street, Boston, Massachusetts 02111 (617) 423-3990; *The World in Figures*.

Statistical Office of the United Nations, Publishing Service, New York, New York 10017 (800) 253-9646; *Statistical Yearbook*.

United Nations Economic Commission for Africa, Africa Hall, Post Office Box 3001, Addis Ababa, Ethiopia (Telephone Number in U.S. (800) 253-9646); *African Statistical Yearbook*.

United Nations Educational, Scientific and Cultural Organization (UNESCO), 7 Place de Fontenoy, F-75700 Paris, France (Telephone Number in U.S. (212) 963-5981); *Statistical Yearbook*.

MALI - GAS PRODUCTION - See MALI - MINING AND MINERAL PRODUCTS

MALI - GENERAL MORTALITY

Statistical Office of the United Nations, Publishing Service, New York, New York 10017 (800) 253-9646; *Demographic Yearbook*.

MALI - GEOGRAPHIC DATA

Facts on File, 460 Park Avenue South, New York, New York 10016 (800) 443-8323; *The New Book of World Rankings*.

MALI - GOATS - See MALI - LIVESTOCK AND POULTRY

MALI - GOLD HOLDINGS

International Monetary Fund, 700 Nineteenth Street, NW, Washington, D.C. 20431 (202) 623-7000; *International Financial Statistics*.

Statistical Office of the United Nations, Publishing Service, New York, New York 10017 (800) 253-9646; *Statistical Yearbook*.

The World Bank, 1818 H Street, NW, Washington, D.C. 20433 (202) 477-1234; *World Tables*.

MALI - GOLD PRODUCTION AND CONSUMPTION - See MALI - MINING AND MINERAL PRODUCTS

MALI - GOVERNMENT

G.K. Hall and Company, 70 Lincoln Street, Boston, Massachusetts 02111 (617) 423-3990; *The World in Figures*.

MALI - GOVERNMENT EXPENDITURES

International Monetary Fund, 700 Nineteenth Street, NW, Washington, D.C. 20431 (202) 623-7000; *Government Finance Statistics Yearbook*.

Times Books, 201 East 50th Street, New York, New York 10022 (212) 751-2600; *The Economist Book of Vital World Statistics*.

The World Bank, 1818 H Street, NW, Washington, D.C. 20433 (202) 477-1234; *World Tables*.

MALI - GOVERNMENT FINANCES

International Monetary Fund, 700 Nineteenth Street, NW, Washington, D.C. 20431 (202) 623-7000; *International Financial Statistics*.

MALI - GOVERNMENT REVENUE

International Monetary Fund, 700 Nineteenth Street, NW, Washington, D.C. 20431 (202) 623-7000; *Government Finance Statistics Yearbook*.

Statistical Office of the United Nations, Publishing Service, New York, New York 10017 (800) 253-9646; *Survey of Economic and Social Conditions in Africa*.

Times Books, 201 East 50th Street, New York, New York 10022 (212) 751-2600; *The Economist Book of Vital World Statistics*.

The World Bank, 1818 H Street, NW, Washington, D.C. 20433 (202) 477-1234; *World Tables.*

MALI - GRAIN PRODUCTION - See MALI - CROPS

MALI - GRANTS

International Monetary Fund, 700 Nineteenth Street, NW, Washington, D.C. 20431 (202) 623-7000; *Government Finance Statistics Yearbook.*

MALI - GROSS DOMESTIC PRODUCT

African Development Bank, 01 BP 1387, Abidjan 01, Cote d'Ivoire; *Selected Statistics on Regional Member Countries.*

The Economist Intelligence Unit, 111 West 57th Street, New York, New York 10019 (800) 938-4685; *The World Market Atlas.*

Facts on File, 460 Park Avenue South, New York, New York 10016 (800) 443-8323; *The New Book of World Rankings.*

G.K. Hall and Company, 70 Lincoln Street, Boston, Massachusetts 02111 (617) 423-3990; *The World in Figures.*

International Monetary Fund, 700 Nineteenth Street, NW, Washington, D.C. 20431 (202) 623-7000; *International Financial Statistics.*

Statistical Office of the United Nations, Publishing Service, New York, New York 10017 (800) 253-9646; *Statistical Yearbook,* and *Survey of Economic and Social Conditions in Africa.*

Times Books, 201 East 50th Street, New York, New York 10022 (212) 751-2600; *The Economist Book of Vital World Statistics.*

United Nations Economic Commission for Africa, Africa Hall, Post Office Box 3001, Addis Ababa, Ethiopia (Telephone Number in U.S. (800) 253-9646); *African Statistical Yearbook.*

The World Bank, 1818 H Street, NW, Washington, D.C. 20433 (202) 477-1234; *World Tables.*

MALI - GROSS NATIONAL PRODUCT

Euromonitor Publications Limited, 87-88 Turnmill Street, London EC1M 5QU, England; *International Marketing Data and Statistics.*

U.S. Arms Control and Disarmament Agency, 320 Twenty-first Street, NW, Washington, D.C. 20451 (202) 647-8677; *World Military Expenditures and Arms Transfers.*

The World Bank, 1818 H Street, NW, Washington, D.C. 20433 (202) 477-1234; *World Tables.*

MALI - GROUNDNUTS - See MALI - CROPS

MALI - HEALTH

African Development Bank, 01 BP 1387, Abidjan 01, Cote d'Ivoire; *Selected Statistics on Regional Member Countries.*

Facts on File, 460 Park Avenue South, New York, New York 10016 (800) 443-8323; *The New Book of World Rankings.*

G.K. Hall and Company, 70 Lincoln Street, Boston, Massachusetts 02111 (617) 423-3990; *The World in Figures.*

Statistical Office of the United Nations, Publishing Service, New York, New York 10017 (800) 253-9646; *Statistical Yearbook.*

Times Books, 201 East 50th Street, New York, New York 10022 (212) 751-2600; *The Economist Book of Vital World Statistics.*

United Nations Economic Commission for Africa, Africa Hall, Post Office Box 3001, Addis Ababa, Ethiopia (Telephone Number in U.S. (800) 253-9646); *African Statistical Yearbook.*

World Health Organization, Office of Publications, Avenue Appia, CH-1211 Geneva 27, Switzerland (Telephone Number in U.S. (518) 436-9686); *World Health Statistics Annual.*

MALI - HEALTH EXPENDITURES

International Monetary Fund, 700 Nineteenth Street, NW, Washington, D.C. 20431 (202) 623-7000; *Government Finance Statistics Yearbook.*

MALI - HIDE PRODUCTION

Food and Agricultural Organization of the United Nations (FAO), Via delle Terme di Caracalla, 00100 Rome, Italy (Telephone Number in U.S. (202) 653-2400); *Production Yearbook.*

MALI - HIGHWAYS

G.K. Hall and Company, 70 Lincoln Street, Boston, Massachusetts 02111 (617) 423-3990; *The World in Figures.*

International Road Federation, 525 School Street, SW, Washington, D.C. 20024 (202) 554-2106; *World Road Statistics.*

Statistical Office of the United Nations, Publishing Service, New York, New York 10017 (800) 253-9646; *Survey of Economic and Social Conditions in Africa.*

United Nations Economic Commission for Africa, Africa Hall, Post Office Box 3001, Addis Ababa, Ethiopia (Telephone Number in U.S. (800) 253-9646); *African Statistical Yearbook.*

MALI - HORSES - See MALI - LIVESTOCK AND POULTRY

MALI - HOURS OF WORK - See MALI - EMPLOYMENT

MALI - HOUSING EXPENDITURES

Facts on File, 460 Park Avenue South, New York, New York 10016 (800) 443-8323; *The New Book of World Rankings.*

International Monetary Fund, 700 Nineteenth Street, NW, Washington, D.C. 20431 (202) 623-7000; *Government Finance Statistics Yearbook.*

MALI - ILLITERATE POPULATION

The Economist Intelligence Unit, 111 West 57th Street, New York, New York 10019 (800) 938-4685; *The World Market Atlas.*

G.K. Hall and Company, 70 Lincoln Street, Boston, Massachusetts 02111 (617) 423-3990; *The World in Figures.*

United Nations Educational, Scientific and Cultural Organization (UNESCO), 7 Place de Fontenoy, F-75700 Paris, France (Telephone Number in U.S. (212) 963-5981); *Statistical Yearbook.*

MALI - IMPORTS

African Development Bank, 01 BP 1387, Abidjan 01, Cote d'Ivoire; *Selected Statistics on Regional Member Countries.*

The Economist Intelligence Unit, 111 West 57th Street, New York, New York 10019 (800) 938-4685; *The World Market Atlas.*

Euromonitor Publications Limited, 87-88 Turnmill Street, London EC1M 5QU, England; *International Marketing Data and Statistics.*

Food and Agricultural Organization of the United Nations (FAO), Via delle Terme di Caracalla, 00100 Rome, Italy (Telephone Number in U.S. (202) 653-2400); *The State of Food and Agriculture.*

G.K. Hall and Company, 70 Lincoln Street, Boston, Massachusetts 02111 (617) 423-3990; *The World in Figures.*

International Monetary Fund, 700 Nineteenth Street, NW, Washington, D.C. 20431 (202) 623-7000; *Direction of Trade Statistics, Government Finance Statistics Yearbook,* and *International Financial Statistics.*

Statistical Office of the United Nations, Publishing Service, New York, New York 10017 (800) 253-9646; *Trade in Manufactures of Developing Countries.,* and *Survey of Economic and Social Conditions in Africa.*

Times Books, 201 East 50th Street, New York, New York 10022 (212) 751-2600; *The Economist Book of Vital World Statistics.*

United Nations Economic Commission for Africa, Africa Hall, Post Office Box 3001, Addis Ababa, Ethiopia (Telephone Number in U.S. (800) 253-9646); *African Statistical Yearbook.*

The World Bank, 1818 H Street, NW, Washington, D.C. 20433 (202) 477-1234; *World Tables.*

MALI - INCOME TAXES - See MALI - TAXATION

MALI - INDUSTRY

Euromonitor Publications Limited, 87-88 Turnmill Street, London EC1M 5QU, England; *International Marketing Data and Statistics.*

Facts on File, 460 Park Avenue South, New York, New York 10016 (800) 443-8323; *The New Book of World Rankings.*

G.K. Hall and Company, 70 Lincoln Street, Boston, Massachusetts 02111 (617) 423-3990; *The World in Figures.*

International Labour Office, I.L.O. Publications, CH-1211, Geneva 22, Switzerland; *Yearbook of Labour Statistics.*

Statistical Office of the United Nations, Publishing Service, New York, New York 10017 (800) 253-9646; *Survey of Economic and Social Conditions in Africa.*

Times Books, 201 East 50th Street, New York, New York 10022 (212) 751-2600; *The Economist Book of Vital World Statistics.*

United Nations Economic Commission for Africa, Africa Hall, Post Office Box 3001, Addis Ababa, Ethiopia (Telephone Number in U.S. (800) 253-9646); *African Statistical Yearbook.*

The World Bank, 1818 H Street, NW, Washington, D.C. 20433 (202) 477-1234; *World Tables.*

MALI - INFANT AND MATERNAL MORTALITY

Statistical Office of the United Nations, Publishing Service, New York, New York 10017 (800) 253-9646; *Demographic Yearbook, Statistical Yearbook,* and *Survey of Economic and Social Conditions in Africa.*

Times Books, 201 East 50th Street, New York, New York 10022 (212) 751-2600; *The Economist Book of Vital World Statistics.*

The World Bank, 1818 H Street, NW, Washington, D.C. 20433 (202) 477-1234; *World Tables.*

MALI - INTERNATIONAL LIQUIDITY

International Monetary Fund, 700 Nineteenth Street, NW, Washington, D.C. 20431 (202) 623-7000; *International Financial Statistics.*

MALI - INTERNATIONAL RESERVES EXCLUDING GOLD

African Development Bank, 01 BP 1387, Abidjan 01, Cote d'Ivoire; *Selected Statistics on Regional Member Countries.*

Statistical Office of the United Nations, Publishing Service, New York, New York 10017 (800) 253-9646; *Statistical Yearbook.*

The World Bank, 1818 H Street, NW, Washington, D.C. 20433 (202) 477-1234; *World Tables.*

MALI - IRON ORE PRODUCTION AND CONSUMPTION - See MALI - MINING AND MINERAL PRODUCTS

MALI - IRRIGATION

Euromonitor Publications Limited, 87-88 Turnmill Street, London EC1M 5QU, England; *International Marketing Data and Statistics.*

MALI - JUTE PRODUCTION - See MALI - CROPS

MALI - LABOR FORCE

African Development Bank, 01 BP 1387, Abidjan 01, Cote d'Ivoire; *Selected Statistics on Regional Member Countries.*

Euromonitor Publications Limited, 87-88 Turnmill Street, London EC1M 5QU, England; *International Marketing Data and Statistics.*

Facts on File, 460 Park Avenue South, New York, New York 10016 (800) 443-8323; *The New Book of World Rankings.*

Food and Agricultural Organization of the United Nations (FAO), Via delle Terme di Caracalla, 00100 Rome, Italy (Telephone Number in U.S. (202) 653-2400); *The State of Food and Agriculture.*

G.K. Hall and Company, 70 Lincoln Street, Boston, Massachusetts 02111 (617) 423-3990; *The World in Figures.*

The World Bank, 1818 H Street, NW, Washington, D.C. 20433 (202) 477-1234; *World Tables.*

MALI - LABOR PRODUCTIVITY

International Labour Office, I.L.O. Publications, CH-1211, Geneva 22, Switzerland; *Yearbook of Labour Statistics.*

MALI - LAND USE

Euromonitor Publications Limited, 87-88 Turnmill Street, London EC1M 5QU, England; *International Marketing Data and Statistics*.

Food and Agricultural Organization of the United Nations (FAO), Via delle Terme di Caracalla, 00100 Rome, Italy (Telephone Number in U.S. (202) 653-2400); *Production Yearbook*.

G.K. Hall and Company, 70 Lincoln Street, Boston, Massachusetts 02111 (617) 423-3990; *The World in Figures*.

MALI - LIBRARIES

Facts on File, 460 Park Avenue South, New York, New York 10016 (800) 443-8323; *The New Book of World Rankings*.

United Nations Educational, Scientific and Cultural Organization (UNESCO), 7 Place de Fontenoy, F-75700 Paris, France (Telephone Number in U.S. (212) 963-5981); *Statistical Yearbook*.

MALI - LIFE EXPECTANCY

African Development Bank, 01 BP 1387, Abidjan 01, Cote d'Ivoire; *Selected Statistics on Regional Member Countries*.

MALI - LITERACY RATE

Statistical Office of the United Nations, Publishing Service, New York, New York 10017 (800) 253-9646; *Survey of Economic and Social Conditions in Africa*.

MALI - LIVESTOCK AND POULTRY

Euromonitor Publications Limited, 87-88 Turnmill Street, London EC1M 5QU, England; *International Marketing Data and Statistics*.

Facts on File, 460 Park Avenue South, New York, New York 10016 (800) 443-8323; *The New Book of World Rankings*.

Food and Agricultural Organization of the United Nations (FAO), Via delle Terme di Caracalla, 00100 Rome, Italy (Telephone Number in U.S. (202) 653-2400); *Production Yearbook, and The State of Food and Agriculture*.

G.K. Hall and Company, 70 Lincoln Street, Boston, Massachusetts 02111 (617) 423-3990; *The World in Figures*.

Statistical Office of the United Nations, Publishing Service, New York, New York 10017 (800) 253-9646; *Statistical Yearbook, and Survey of Economic and Social Conditions in Africa*.

United Nations Economic Commission for Africa, Africa Hall, Post Office Box 3001, Addis Ababa, Ethiopia (Telephone Number in U.S. (800) 253-9646); *African Statistical Yearbook*.

MALI - LIVING LEVELS

G.K. Hall and Company, 70 Lincoln Street, Boston, Massachusetts 02111 (617) 423-3990; *The World in Figures*.

Times Books, 201 East 50th Street, New York, New York 10022 (212) 751-2600; *The Economist Book of Vital World Statistics*.

MALI - MAIL - NUMBER OF ITEMS SENT OR RECEIVED

Statistical Office of the United Nations, Publishing Service, New York, New York 10017 (800) 253-9646; *Statistical Yearbook*.

MALI - MANUFACTURING

Facts on File, 460 Park Avenue South, New York, New York 10016 (800) 443-8323; *The New Book of World Rankings*.

G.K. Hall and Company, 70 Lincoln Street, Boston, Massachusetts 02111 (617) 423-3990; *The World in Figures*.

Statistical Office of the United Nations, Publishing Service, New York, New York 10017 (800) 253-9646; *Survey of Economic and Social Conditions in Africa*.

United Nations Economic Commission for Africa, Africa Hall, Post Office Box 3001, Addis Ababa, Ethiopia (Telephone Number in U.S. (800) 253-9646); *African Statistical Yearbook*.

The World Bank, 1818 H Street, NW, Washington, D.C. 20433 (202) 477-1234; *World Tables*.

MALI - MARRIAGE RATES

Facts on File, 460 Park Avenue South, New York, New York 10016 (800) 443-8323; *The New Book of World Rankings*.

Statistical Office of the United Nations, Publishing Service, New York, New York 10017 (800) 253-9646; *Demographic Yearbook*.

MALI - MEAT PRODUCTION - See MALI - LIVESTOCK AND POULTRY

MALI - MERCHANT SHIPPING

G.K. Hall and Company, 70 Lincoln Street, Boston, Massachusetts 02111 (617) 423-3990; *The World in Figures*.

United Nations Economic Commission for Africa, Africa Hall, Post Office Box 3001, Addis Ababa, Ethiopia (Telephone Number in U.S. (800) 253-9646); *African Statistical Yearbook*.

MALI - MILITARY

Facts on File, 460 Park Avenue South, New York, New York 10016 (800) 443-8323; *The New Book of World Rankings*.

G.K. Hall and Company, 70 Lincoln Street, Boston, Massachusetts 02111 (617) 423-3990; *The World in Figures*.

The International Institute for Strategic Studies, 23 Tavistock Street, London WC2E 7NQ, England; *The Military Balance*.

U.S. Arms Control and Disarmament Agency, 320 Twenty-first Street, NW, Washington, D.C. 20451 (202) 647-8677; *World Military Expenditures and Arms Transfers*.

MALI - MILK PRODUCTION - See MALI - DAIRY PRODUCTS

MALI - MILLET PRODUCTION - See MALI - CROPS

MALI - MINING AND MINERAL PRODUCTS

Facts on File, 460 Park Avenue South, New York, New York 10016 (800) 443-8323; *The New Book of World Rankings*.

G.K. Hall and Company, 70 Lincoln Street, Boston, Massachusetts 02111 (617) 423-3990; *The World in Figures*.

Statistical Office of the United Nations, Publishing Service, New York, New York 10017 (800) 253-9646; *Statistical Yearbook*.

United Nations Economic Commission for Africa, Africa Hall, Post Office Box 3001, Addis Ababa, Ethiopia (Telephone Number in U.S. (800) 253-9646); *African Statistical Yearbook*.

MALI - MONEY EXCHANGE RATE

Euromonitor Publications Limited, 87-88 Turnmill Street, London EC1M 5QU, England; *International Marketing Data and Statistics*.

Statistical Office of the United Nations, Publishing Service, New York, New York 10017 (800) 253-9646; *Statistical Yearbook*.

MALI - MONEY RESERVES

Euromonitor Publications Limited, 87-88 Turnmill Street, London EC1M 5QU, England; *International Marketing Data and Statistics*.

MALI - MONEY SUPPLY

African Development Bank, 01 BP 1387, Abidjan 01, Cote d'Ivoire; *Selected Statistics on Regional Member Countries*.

Euromonitor Publications Limited, 87-88 Turnmill Street, London EC1M 5QU, England; *International Marketing Data and Statistics*.

G.K. Hall and Company, 70 Lincoln Street, Boston, Massachusetts 02111 (617) 423-3990; *The World in Figures*.

International Monetary Fund, 700 Nineteenth Street, NW, Washington, D.C. 20431 (202) 623-7000; *International Financial Statistics*.

Statistical Office of the United Nations, Publishing Service, New York, New York 10017 (800) 253-9646; *Statistical Yearbook*.

The World Bank, 1818 H Street, NW, Washington, D.C. 20433 (202) 477-1234; *World Tables*.

MALI - MOTOR VEHICLE TAXES - See MALI - TAXATION

MALI - MOTOR VEHICLES IN USE

G.K. Hall and Company, 70 Lincoln Street, Boston, Massachusetts 02111 (617) 423-3990; *The World in Figures*.

International Road Federation, 525 School Street, SW, Washington, D.C. 20024 (202) 554-2106; *World Road Statistics*.

Statistical Office of the United Nations, Publishing Service, New York, New York 10017 (800) 253-9646; *Statistical Yearbook*, and *Survey of Economic and Social Conditions in Africa*.

MALI - MUSEUMS

Facts on File, 460 Park Avenue South, New York, New York 10016 (800) 443-8323; *The New Book of World Rankings*.

Statistical Office of the United Nations, Publishing Service, New York, New York 10017 (800) 253-9646; *Statistical Yearbook*.

MALI - NATALITY - See MALI - BIRTH RATES

MALI - NATIONAL ACCOUNTS

African Development Bank, 01 BP 1387, Abidjan 01, Cote d'Ivoire; *Selected Statistics on Regional Member Countries*.

International Monetary Fund, 700 Nineteenth Street, NW, Washington, D.C. 20431 (202) 623-7000; *International Financial Statistics*.

Statistical Office of the United Nations, Publishing Service, New York, New York 10017 (800) 253-9646; *National Account Statistics*, and *Statistical Yearbook*.

United Nations Economic Commission for Africa, Africa Hall, Post Office Box 3001, Addis Ababa, Ethiopia (Telephone Number in U.S. (800) 253-9646); *African Statistical Yearbook*.

MALI - NATIONAL INCOME

Facts on File, 460 Park Avenue South, New York, New York 10016 (800) 443-8323; *The New Book of World Rankings*.

G.K. Hall and Company, 70 Lincoln Street, Boston, Massachusetts 02111 (617) 423-3990; *The World in Figures*.

Statistical Office of the United Nations, Publishing Service, New York, New York 10017 (800) 253-9646; *Statistical Yearbook*.

MALI - NATIONAL PRODUCT

Facts on File, 460 Park Avenue South, New York, New York 10016 (800) 443-8323; *The New Book of World Rankings*.

MALI - NATURAL GAS - PRODUCTION - See MALI - MINING AND MINERAL PRODUCTS

MALI - NEWSPAPER PRODUCTION - See MALI - FORESTRY AND FOREST PRODUCTS

MALI - NEWSPRINT - See MALI - FORESTRY AND FOREST PRODUCTS

MALI - OCCUPATIONS - See MALI - LABOR FORCE

MALI - PAPER - See MALI - FORESTRY AND FOREST PRODUCTS

MALI - PEANUT PRODUCTION - See MALI - CROPS

MALI - PERIODICALS

United Nations Educational, Scientific and Cultural Organization (UNESCO), 7 Place de Fontenoy, F-75700 Paris, France (Telephone Number in U.S. (212) 963-5981); *Statistical Yearbook*.

MALI - PESTICIDE USE

Food and Agricultural Organization of the United Nations (FAO), Via delle Terme di Caracalla, 00100 Rome, Italy (Telephone Number in U.S. (202) 653-2400); *The State of Food and Agriculture*.

MALI - PETROLEUM INDUSTRY

Facts on File, 460 Park Avenue South, New York, New York 10016 (800) 443-8323; *The New Book of World Rankings*.

Food and Agricultural Organization of the United Nations (FAO), Via delle Terme di Caracalla, 00100 Rome, Italy (Telephone Number in U.S. (202) 653-2400); *The State of Food and Agriculture*.

G.K. Hall and Company, 70 Lincoln Street, Boston, Massachusetts 02111 (617) 423-3990; *The World in Figures*.

MALI - PIGS - See MALI - LIVESTOCK AND POULTRY

MALI - POPULATION

African Development Bank, 01 BP 1387, Abidjan 01, Cote d'Ivoire; *Selected Statistics on Regional Member Countries*.

The Economist Intelligence Unit, 111 West 57th Street, New York, New York 10019 (800) 938-4685; *The World Market Atlas*.

Euromonitor Publications Limited, 87-88 Turnmill Street, London EC1M 5QU, England; *International Marketing Data and Statistics*.

Facts on File, 460 Park Avenue South, New York, New York 10016 (800) 443-8323; *The New Book of World Rankings*.

Food and Agricultural Organization of the United Nations (FAO), Via delle Terme di Caracalla, 00100 Rome, Italy (Telephone Number in U.S. (202) 653-2400); *Production Yearbook*.

G.K. Hall and Company, 70 Lincoln Street, Boston, Massachusetts 02111 (617) 423-3990; *The World in Figures*.

International Labour Office, I.L.O. Publications, CH-1211, Geneva 22, Switzerland; *Yearbook of Labour Statistics*.

Statistical Office of the United Nations, Publishing Service, New York, New York 10017 (800) 253-9646; *Demographic Yearbook, Statistical Yearbook*, and *Survey of Economic and Social Conditions in Africa*.

Times Books, 201 East 50th Street, New York, New York 10022 (212) 751-2600; *The Economist Book of Vital World Statistics*.

U.S. Arms Control and Disarmament Agency, 320 Twenty-first Street, NW, Washington, D.C. 20451 (202) 647-8677; *World Military Expenditures and Arms Transfers*.

World Health Organization, Office of Publications, Avenue Appia, CH-1211 Geneva 27, Switzerland (Telephone Number in U.S. (518) 436-9686); *World Health Statistics Annual*.

MALI - POST OFFICES

Facts on File, 460 Park Avenue South, New York, New York 10016 (800) 443-8323; *The New Book of World Rankings*.

MALI - POTATO PRODUCTION - See MALI- CROPS

MALI - PRICES

Facts on File, 460 Park Avenue South, New York, New York 10016 (800) 443-8323; *The New Book of World Rankings*.

Food and Agricultural Organization of the United Nations (FAO), Via delle Terme di Caracalla, 00100 Rome, Italy (Telephone Number in U.S. (202) 653-2400); *The State of Food and Agriculture*, and *Trade Yearbook*.

G.K. Hall and Company, 70 Lincoln Street, Boston, Massachusetts 02111 (617) 423-3990; *The World in Figures*.

International Labour Office, I.L.O. Publications, CH-1211, Geneva 22, Switzerland; *Yearbook of Labour Statistics*.

United Nations Economic Commission for Africa, Africa Hall, Post Office Box 3001, Addis Ababa, Ethiopia (Telephone Number in U.S. (800) 253-9646); *African Statistical Yearbook*.

MALI - PRINTING AND WRITING PAPER - See MALI - FORESTRY AND FOREST PRODUCTS

MALI - PRODUCTION

Facts on File, 460 Park Avenue South, New York, New York 10016 (800) 443-8323; *The New Book of World Rankings*.

G.K. Hall and Company, 70 Lincoln Street, Boston, Massachusetts 02111 (617) 423-3990; *The World in Figures*.

MALI - PRODUCTIVITY

Euromonitor Publications Limited, 87-88 Turnmill Street, London EC1M 5QU, England; *International Marketing Data and Statistics*.

MALI - PROPERTY TAXES

International Monetary Fund, 700 Nineteenth Street, NW, Washington, D.C. 20431 (202) 623-7000; *Government Finance Statistics Yearbook*.

MALI - PUBLIC FINANCE

Facts on File, 460 Park Avenue South, New York, New York 10016 (800) 443-8323; *The New Book of World Rankings*.

MALI - RADIO BROADCASTING - See MALI - BROADCASTING

MALI - RAILWAYS

G.K. Hall and Company, 70 Lincoln Street, Boston, Massachusetts 02111 (617) 423-3990; *The World in Figures*.

Jane's Information Group, Sentinel House, 163 Brighton Road, Coulsdon, Surrey CR5 2NH, England (Telephone Number in U.S. (703) 683-3700); *Jane's World Railways*.

Statistical Office of the United Nations, Publishing Service, New York, New York 10017 (800) 253-9646; *Statistical Yearbook*, and *Survey of Economic and Social Conditions in Africa*.

United Nations Economic Commission for Africa, Africa Hall, Post Office Box 3001, Addis Ababa, Ethiopia (Telephone Number in U.S. (800) 253-9646); *African Statistical Yearbook*.

MALI - RELIGION

Facts on File, 460 Park Avenue South, New York, New York 10016 (800) 443-8323; *The New Book of World Rankings*.

MALI - RETAIL TRADE

G.K. Hall and Company, 70 Lincoln Street, Boston, Massachusetts 02111 (617) 423-3990; *The World in Figures*.

MALI - RICE PRODUCTION - See MALI - CROPS

MALI - ROOT AND TUBER PRODUCTION - See MALI - CROPS

MALI - ROUNDWOOD PRODUCTION - See MALI - FORESTRY AND FOREST PRODUCTS

MALI - RUBBER PRODUCTION

Facts on File, 460 Park Avenue South, New York, New York 10016 (800) 443-8323; *The New Book of World Rankings*.

MALI - SALT PRODUCTION - See MALI - MINING AND MINERAL PRODUCTS

MALI - SAWNWOOD PRODUCTION - See MALI - FORESTRY AND FOREST PRODUCTS

MALI - SENIOR CITIZENS

Facts on File, 460 Park Avenue South, New York, New York 10016 (800) 443-8323; *The New Book of World Rankings.*

MALI - SHEEP - See MALI - LIVESTOCK AND POULTRY

MALI - SILVER PRODUCTION AND CONSUMPTION - See MALI - MINING AND MINERAL PRODUCTS

MALI - SOCIAL DATA

African Development Bank, 01 BP 1387, Abidjan 01, Cote d'Ivoire; *Selected Statistics on Regional Member Countries.*

Facts on File, 460 Park Avenue South, New York, New York 10016 (800) 443-8323; *The New Book of World Rankings.*

G.K. Hall and Company, 70 Lincoln Street, Boston, Massachusetts 02111 (617) 423-3990; *The World in Figures.*

MALI - SOCIAL SECURITY EXPENDITURES

International Monetary Fund, 700 Nineteenth Street, NW, Washington, D.C. 20431 (202) 623-7000; *Government Finance Statistics Yearbook.*

MALI - STAMP TAXES AND DUTIES - See MALI - TAXATION

MALI - STATE BUDGET

Euromonitor Publications Limited, 87-88 Turnmill Street, London EC1M 5QU, England; *International Marketing Data and Statistics.*

MALI - STEEL PRODUCTION - See MALI - MINING AND MINERAL PRODUCTS

MALI - STOCKS - COMMODITY - MARKET PRICE INDEX

Food and Agricultural Organization of the United Nations (FAO), Via delle Terme di Caracalla, 00100 Rome, Italy (Telephone Number in U.S. (202) 653-2400); *The State of Food and Agriculture.*

MALI - SUGAR PRODUCTION - See MALI - CROPS

MALI - TAXATION

G.K. Hall and Company, 70 Lincoln Street, Boston, Massachusetts 02111 (617) 423-3990; *The World in Figures.*

International Monetary Fund, 700 Nineteenth Street, NW, Washington, D.C. 20431 (202) 623-7000; *Government Finance Statistics Yearbook.*

International Road Federation, 525 School Street, SW, Washington, D.C. 20024 (202) 554-2106; *World Road Statistics.*

Times Books, 201 East 50th Street, New York, New York 10022 (212) 751-2600; *The Economist Book of Vital World Statistics.*

The World Bank, 1818 H Street, NW, Washington, D.C. 20433 (202) 477-1234; *World Tables.*

MALI - TELEPHONES IN USE

American Telephone and Telegraph Company, 26 Parsippany Road, Whippany, New Jersey 07981 (800) 338-4038; *The World's Telephones.*

G.K. Hall and Company, 70 Lincoln Street, Boston, Massachusetts 02111 (617) 423-3990; *The World in Figures.*

Statistical Office of the United Nations, Publishing Service, New York, New York 10017 (800) 253-9646; *Statistical Yearbook.*

MALI - TELEVISION BROADCASTING - See MALI - BROADCASTING

MALI - TEXTILE INDUSTRY

G.K. Hall and Company, 70 Lincoln Street, Boston, Massachusetts 02111 (617) 423-3990; *The World in Figures.*

MALI - TOBACCO PRODUCTION

Facts on File, 460 Park Avenue South, New York, New York 10016 (800) 443-8323; *The New Book of World Rankings.*

Statistical Office of the United Nations, Publishing Service, New York, New York 10017 (800) 253-9646; *Statistical Yearbook.*

MALI - TOURISM

Facts on File, 460 Park Avenue South, New York, New York 10016 (800) 443-8323; *The New Book of World Rankings.*

G.K. Hall and Company, 70 Lincoln Street, Boston, Massachusetts 02111 (617) 423-3990; *The World in Figures.*

Statistical Office of the United Nations, Publishing Service, New York, New York 10017 (800) 253-9646; *Statistical Yearbook.*

Times Books, 201 East 50th Street, New York, New York 10022 (212) 751-2600; *The Economist Book of Vital World Statistics.*

United Nations Economic Commission for Africa, Africa Hall, Post Office Box 3001, Addis Ababa, Ethiopia (Telephone Number in U.S. (800) 253-9646); *African Statistical Yearbook.*

World Tourism Organization, Calle Capitan Haya 42, E-28020 Madrid, Spain; *Yearbook of Tourism Statistics.*

MALI - TRACTORS IN USE

Statistical Office of the United Nations, Publishing Service, New York, New York 10017 (800) 253-9646; *Statistical Yearbook.*

MALI - TRADE - See MALI - FOREIGN TRADE

MALI - TRANSPORTATION AND COMMUNICATIONS

Facts on File, 460 Park Avenue South, New York, New York 10016 (800) 443-8323; *The New Book of World Rankings.*

G.K. Hall and Company, 70 Lincoln Street, Boston, Massachusetts 02111 (617) 423-3990; *The World in Figures.*

United Nations Economic Commission for Africa, Africa Hall, Post Office Box 3001, Addis Ababa, Ethiopia (Telephone Number in U.S. (800) 253-9646); *African Statistical Yearbook.*

MALI - TRAVEL FARES ABROAD

International Monetary Fund, 700 Nineteenth Street, NW, Washington, D.C. 20431 (202) 623-7000; *Government Finance Statistics Yearbook.*

MALI - UNEMPLOYMENT

Euromonitor Publications Limited, 87-88 Turnmill Street, London EC1M 5QU, England; *International Marketing Data and Statistics.*

International Labour Office, I.L.O. Publications, CH-1211, Geneva 22, Switzerland; *Yearbook of Labour Statistics.*

Statistical Office of the United Nations, Publishing Service, New York, New York 10017 (800) 253-9646; *Statistical Yearbook.*

MALI - VITAL STATISTICS

Euromonitor Publications Limited, 87-88 Turnmill Street, London EC1M 5QU, England; *International Marketing Data and Statistics.*

G.K. Hall and Company, 70 Lincoln Street, Boston, Massachusetts 02111 (617) 423-3990; *The World in Figures.*

Statistical Office of the United Nations, Publishing Service, New York, New York 10017 (800) 253-9646; *Statistical Yearbook.*

World Health Organization, Office of Publications, Avenue Appia, CH-1211 Geneva 27, Switzerland (Telephone Number in U.S. (518) 436-9686); *World Health Statistics Annual.*

MALI - WAGES

G.K. Hall and Company, 70 Lincoln Street, Boston, Massachusetts 02111 (617) 423-3990; *The World in Figures.*

International Labour Office, I.L.O. Publications, CH-1211, Geneva 22, Switzerland; *Yearbook of Labour Statistics.*

Statistical Office of the United Nations, Publishing Service, New York, New York 10017 (800) 253-9646; *Statistical Yearbook.*

MALI - WEATHER

Facts on File, 460 Park Avenue South, New York, New York 10016 (800) 443-8323; *The New Book of World Rankings.*

G.K. Hall and Company, 70 Lincoln Street, Boston, Massachusetts 02111 (617) 423-3990; *The World in Figures.*

MALI - WELFARE EXPENDITURES

International Monetary Fund, 700 Nineteenth Street, NW, Washington, D.C. 20431 (202) 623-7000; *Government Finance Statistics Yearbook.*

MALI - WHEAT PRODUCTION - See MALI - CROPS

MALI - WINE PRODUCTION

Facts on File, 460 Park Avenue South, New York, New York 10016 (800) 443-8323; *The New Book of World Rankings.*

MALI - WOOL PRODUCTION

Facts on File, 460 Park Avenue South, New York, New York 10016 (800) 443-8323; *The New Book of World Rankings.*

MALT BEVERAGES - See also BEVERAGES

U.S. Department of Agriculture, Economic Research Service, Fourteenth Street and Independence Avenue, SW, Washington, D.C. 20005-4789 (202) 219-1504; *Food Consumption, Prices, and Expenditures, Foreign Agricultural Trade of the United States,* and unpublished data.

U.S. Department of the Treasury, Bureau of Alcohol, Tobacco and Firearms, 650 Massachusetts Avenue, NW, Washington, D.C. 20226 (202) 927-8500; *Alcohol and Tobacco Summary Statistics.*

Malta - National Statistical Office

Central Office of Statistics, Auberge D'Italie, Valletta, Malta.

Malta - Primary Statistics Sources

Central Office of Statistics, Auberge D'Italie, Valletta, Malta; *Annual Abstract of Statistics* and *Quarterly Digest of Statistics.*

MALTA - AGRICULTURE

Food and Agricultural Organization of the United Nations (FAO), Via delle Terme di Caracalla, 00100 Rome, Italy (Telephone Number in U.S. (202) 653-2400); *Production Yearbook, The State of Food and Agriculture,* and *Trade Yearbook.*

Statistical Office of the United Nations, Publishing Service, New York, New York 10017 (800) 253-9646; *Statistical Yearbook.*

Times Books, 201 East 50th Street, New York, New York 10022 (212) 751-2600; *The Economist Book of Vital World Statistics.*

The World Bank, 1818 H Street, NW, Washington, D.C. 20433 (202) 477-1234; *World Tables.*

MALTA - AIRLINE SERVICE

International Civil Aviation Organization, 1000 Sherbrooke Street West, Suite 400, Montreal, Quebec H3A 2R2, Canada (514) 285-8219; *Civil Aviation Statistics of the World.*

Statistical Office of the United Nations, Publishing Service, New York, New York 10017 (800) 253-9646; *Statistical Yearbook.*

Times Books, 201 East 50th Street, New York, New York 10022 (212) 751-2600; *The Economist Book of Vital World Statistics.*

MALTA - ANIMAL HEALTH

Food and Agricultural Organization of the United Nations (FAO), Via delle Terme di Caracalla, 00100 Rome, Italy (Telephone Number in U.S. (202) 653-2400); *Animal Health Yearbook.*

MALTA - AREA AND DENSITY OF POPULATION

Food and Agricultural Organization of the United Nations (FAO), Via delle Terme di Caracalla, 00100 Rome, Italy (Telephone Number in U.S. (202) 653-2400); *The State of Food and Agriculture.*

Statistical Office of the United Nations, Publishing Service, New York, New York 10017 (800) 253-9646; *Statistical Yearbook.*

Times Books, 201 East 50th Street, New York, New York 10022 (212) 751-2600; *The Economist Book of Vital World Statistics.*

MALTA - ARMS EXPORTS AND IMPORTS

U.S. Arms Control and Disarmament Agency, 320 Twenty-first Street, NW, Washington, D.C. 20451 (202) 647-8677; *World Military Expenditures and Arms Transfers.*

MALTA - BALANCE OF PAYMENTS

International Monetary Fund, 700 Nineteenth Street, NW, Washington, D.C. 20431 (202) 623-7000; *Balance of Payments Yearbook.*

Times Books, 201 East 50th Street, New York, New York 10022 (212) 751-2600; *The Economist Book of Vital World Statistics.*

The World Bank, 1818 H Street, NW, Washington, D.C. 20433 (202) 477-1234; *World Tables.*

MALTA - BANKING

International Monetary Fund, 700 Nineteenth Street, NW, Washington, D.C. 20431 (202) 623-7000; *International Financial Statistics.*

MALTA - BARLEY PRODUCTION - See MALTA - CROPS

MALTA - BEER PRODUCTION

Statistical Office of the United Nations, Publishing Service, New York, New York 10017 (800) 253-9646; *Statistical Yearbook.*

MALTA - BIRTH RATES

Statistical Office of the United Nations, Publishing Service, New York, New York 10017 (800) 253-9646; *Demographic Yearbook, and Statistical Yearbook.*

Times Books, 201 East 50th Street, New York, New York 10022 (212) 751-2600; *The Economist Book of Vital World Statistics.*

The World Bank, 1818 H Street, NW, Washington, D.C. 20433 (202) 477-1234; *World Tables.*

World Health Organization, Office of Publications, Avenue Appia, CH-1211 Geneva 27, Switzerland (Telephone Number in U.S. (518) 436-9686); *World Health Statistics Annual.*

MALTA - BONDS

International Monetary Fund, 700 Nineteenth Street, NW, Washington, D.C. 20431 (202) 623-7000; *Government Finance Statistics Yearbook.*

MALTA - BOOK PRODUCTION

Euromonitor Publications Limited, 87-88 Turnmill Street, London EC1M 5QU, England; *European Marketing Data and Statistics.*

United Nations Educational, Scientific and Cultural Organization (UNESCO), 7 Place de Fontenoy, F-75700 Paris, France (Telephone Number in U.S. (212) 963-5981); *Statistical Yearbook.*

MALTA - BROADCASTING

Billboard Limited, Post Office Box 9027, 1006 AA Amsterdam, The Netherlands (Telephone Number in U.S. (212) 764-7300); *World Radio TV Handbook.*

Times Books, 201 East 50th Street, New York, New York 10022 (212) 751-2600; *The Economist Book of Vital World Statistics.*

United Nations Educational, Scientific and Cultural Organization (UNESCO), 7 Place de Fontenoy, F-75700 Paris, France (Telephone Number in U.S. (212) 963-5981); *Statistical Yearbook.*

MALTA - BUSINESS AND PROFESSIONAL LICENSES

International Monetary Fund, 700 Nineteenth Street, NW, Washington, D.C. 20431 (202) 623-7000; *Government Finance Statistics Yearbook.*

MALTA - CALORIE SUPPLY

Food and Agricultural Organization of the United Nations (FAO), Via delle Terme di Caracalla, 00100 Rome, Italy (Telephone Number in U.S. (202) 653-2400); *The State of Food and Agriculture.*

MALTA - CAPITAL REVENUE

International Monetary Fund, 700 Nineteenth Street, NW, Washington, D.C. 20431 (202) 623-7000; *Government Finance Statistics Yearbook.*

MALTA - CATTLE - See MALTA - LIVESTOCK AND POULTRY

MALTA - CEREAL PRODUCTION - See MALTA - CROPS

MALTA - CIGARETTE PRODUCTION - See MALTA - TOBACCO PRODUCTION

MALTA - CONSTRUCTION INDUSTRY

Statistical Office of the United Nations, Publishing Service, New York, New York 10017 (800) 253-9646; *Statistical Yearbook.*

MALTA - CONSUMER PRICE INDEX

Statistical Office of the United Nations, Publishing Service, New York, New York 10017 (800) 253-9646; *Statistical Yearbook.*

Times Books, 201 East 50th Street, New York, New York 10022 (212) 751-2600; *The Economist Book of Vital World Statistics.*

MALTA - CONSUMER PRICES

Euromonitor Publications Limited, 87-88 Turnmill Street, London EC1M 5QU, England; *European Marketing Data and Statistics.*

International Labour Office, I.L.O. Publications, CH-1211, Geneva 22, Switzerland; *Yearbook of Labour Statistics.*

International Monetary Fund, 700 Nineteenth Street, NW, Washington, D.C. 20431 (202) 623-7000; *International Financial Statistics.*

MALTA - CORN PRODUCTION - See MALTA - CROPS

MALTA - CORPORATE TAXES - See MALTA - TAXATION

MALTA - COTTON - See MALTA - CROPS

MALTA - CRIME

International Criminal Police Organization (INTERPOL), 26 rue Armengaud, 92210 Saint Cloud, France; *International Crime Statistics.*

Yale University Press, Yale Station, New Haven, Connecticut 06520 (203) 432-0940; *Violence and Crime in Cross-National Perspective.*

MALTA - CROPS

Euromonitor Publications Limited, 87-88 Turnmill Street, London EC1M 5QU, England; *European Marketing Data and Statistics.*

Food and Agricultural Organization of the United Nations (FAO), Via delle Terme di Caracalla, 00100 Rome, Italy (Telephone Number in U.S. (202) 653-2400); *Production Yearbook,* and *The State of Food and Agriculture.*

Statistical Office of the United Nations, Publishing Service, New York, New York 10017 (800) 253-9646; *Statistical Yearbook.*

MALTA - CUSTOMS DUTIES

International Monetary Fund, 700 Nineteenth Street, NW, Washington, D.C. 20431 (202) 623-7000; *Government Finance Statistics Yearbook.*

MALTA - DAIRY PRODUCTS

Food and Agricultural Organization of the United Nations (FAO), Via delle Terme di Caracalla, 00100 Rome, Italy (Telephone Number in U.S. (202) 653-2400); *Production Yearbook* and *The State of Food and Agriculture.*

Statistical Office of the United Nations, Publishing Service, New York, New York 10017 (800) 253-9646; *Statistical Yearbook.*

MALTA - DEATH RATES

Statistical Office of the United Nations, Publishing Service, New York, New York 10017 (800) 253-9646; *Statistical Yearbook.*

Times Books, 201 East 50th Street, New York, New York 10022 (212) 751-2600; *The Economist Book of Vital World Statistics.*

MALTA - DEFENSE EXPENDITURES

International Monetary Fund, 700 Nineteenth Street, NW, Washington, D.C. 20431 (202) 623-7000; *Government Finance Statistics Yearbook.*

U.S. Arms Control and Disarmament Agency, 320 Twenty-first Street, NW, Washington, D.C. 20451 (202) 647-8677; *World Military Expenditures and Arms Transfers.*

MALTA - DIVORCE

Statistical Office of the United Nations, Publishing Service, New York, New York 10017 (800) 253-9646; *Demographic Yearbook.*

MALTA - DUCKS - See MALTA - LIVESTOCK AND POULTRY

MALTA - ECONOMY

Euromonitor Publications Limited, 87-88 Turnmill Street, London EC1M 5QU, England; *European Marketing Data and Statistics.*

MALTA - EDUCATION

Euromonitor Publications Limited, 87-88 Turnmill Street, London EC1M 5QU, England; *European Marketing Data and Statistics.*

International Monetary Fund, 700 Nineteenth Street, NW, Washington, D.C. 20431 (202) 623-7000; *Government Finance*

Statistics Yearbook.

Times Books, 201 East 50th Street, New York, New York 10022 (212) 751-2600; *The Economist Book of Vital World Statistics.*

United Nations Educational, Scientific and Cultural Organization (UNESCO), 7 Place de Fontenoy, F-75700 Paris, France (Telephone Number in U.S. (212) 963-5981); *Statistical Yearbook.*

The World Bank, 1818 H Street, NW, Washington, D.C. 20433 (202) 477-1234; *World Tables.*

MALTA - EGG PRODUCTION AND CONSUMPTION - See MALTA - DAIRY PRODUCTS

MALTA - ELECTRICITY

Statistical Office of the United Nations, Publishing Service, New York, New York 10017 (800) 253-9646; *Statistical Yearbook.*

Times Books, 201 East 50th Street, New York, New York 10022 (212) 751-2600; *The Economist Book of Vital World Statistics.*

MALTA - EMPLOYMENT

Euromonitor Publications Limited, 87-88 Turnmill Street, London EC1M 5QU, England; *European Marketing Data and Statistics.*

International Labour Office, I.L.O. Publications, CH-1211, Geneva 22, Switzerland; *Yearbook of Labour Statistics.*

Statistical Office of the United Nations, Publishing Service, New York, New York 10017 (800) 253-9646; *Statistical Yearbook.*

MALTA - ENERGY

Euromonitor Publications Limited, 87-88 Turnmill Street, London EC1M 5QU, England; *European Marketing Data and Statistics.*

Food and Agricultural Organization of the United Nations (FAO), Via delle Terme di Caracalla, 00100 Rome, Italy (Telephone Number in U.S. (202) 653-2400); *The State of Food and Agriculture.*

Statistical Office of the United Nations, Publishing Service, New York, New York 10017 (800) 253-9646; *Energy Statistics Yearbook,* and *Statistical Yearbook.*

Times Books, 201 East 50th Street, New York, New York 10022 (212) 751-2600; *The Economist Book of Vital World Statistics.*

MALTA - EXCHANGE RATES

International Civil Aviation Organization, 1000 Sherbrooke Street West, Suite 400, Montreal, Quebec H3A 2R2, Canada (514) 285-8219; *Civil Aviation Statistics of the World.*

International Monetary Fund, 700 Nineteenth Street, NW, Washington, D.C. 20431 (202) 623-7000; *International Financial Statistics.*

Statistical Office of the United Nations, Publishing Service, New York, New York 10017 (800) 253-9646; *Statistical Yearbook.*

MALTA - EXCISE TAXES - See MALTA - TAXATION

MALTA - EXPORTS

Food and Agricultural Organization of the United Nations (FAO), Via delle Terme di Caracalla, 00100 Rome, Italy (Telephone Number in

U.S. (202) 653-2400); *The State of Food and Agriculture*.

International Monetary Fund, 700 Nineteenth Street, NW, Washington, D.C. 20431 (202) 623-7000; *Direction of Trade Statistics*.

Times Books, 201 East 50th Street, New York, New York 10022 (212) 751-2600; *The Economist Book of Vital World Statistics*.

The World Bank, 1818 H Street, NW, Washington, D.C. 20433 (202) 477-1234; *World Tables*.

MALTA - EXTERNAL INDEBTEDNESS

The World Bank, 1818 H Street, NW, Washington, D.C. 20433 (202) 477-1234; *World Tables*.

MALTA - EXTERNAL TRADE

Food and Agricultural Organization of the United Nations (FAO), Via delle Terme di Caracalla, 00100 Rome, Italy (Telephone Number in U.S. (202) 653-2400); *The State of Food and Agriculture*, and *Trade Yearbook*.

Statistical Office of the United Nations, Publishing Service, New York, New York 10017 (800) 253-9646; *Statistical Yearbook*.

MALTA - FARM CROPS - See MALTA - CROPS

MALTA - FERTILITY RATES

Times Books, 201 East 50th Street, New York, New York 10022 (212) 751-2600; *The Economist Book of Vital World Statistics*.

The World Bank, 1818 H Street, NW, Washington, D.C. 20433 (202) 477-1234; *World Tables*.

MALTA - FERTILIZER

Food and Agricultural Organization of the United Nations (FAO), Via delle Terme di Caracalla, 00100 Rome, Italy (Telephone Number in U.S. (202) 653-2400); *Fertilizer Yearbook*, and *The State of Food and Agriculture*.

Statistical Office of the United Nations, Publishing Service, New York, New York 10017 (800) 253-9646; *Statistical Yearbook*.

MALTA - FETAL MORTALITY

Statistical Office of the United Nations, Publishing Service, New York, New York 10017 (800) 253-9646; *Demographic Yearbook*.

World Health Organization, Office of Publications, Avenue Appia, CH-1211 Geneva 27, Switzerland (Telephone Number in U.S. (518) 436-9686); *World Health Statistics Annual*.

MALTA - FISHERIES

Euromonitor Publications Limited, 87-88 Turnmill Street, London EC1M 5QU, England; *European Marketing Data and Statistics*.

Food and Agricultural Organization of the United Nations (FAO), Via delle Terme di Caracalla, 00100 Rome, Italy (Telephone Number in U.S. (202) 653-2400); *The State of Food and Agriculture*, and *Yearbook of Fishery Statistics*.

International Monetary Fund, 700 Nineteenth Street, NW, Washington, D.C. 20431 (202) 623-7000; *Government Finance Statistics Yearbook*, and *International Financial Statistics*.

Statistical Office of the United Nations, Publishing Service, New York, New York 10017 (800) 253-9646; *Statistical Yearbook*.

MALTA - FLOUR PRODUCTION

Statistical Office of the United Nations, Publishing Service, New York, New York 10017 (800) 253-9646; *Statistical Yearbook*.

MALTA - FOOD

Food and Agricultural Organization of the United Nations (FAO), Via delle Terme di Caracalla, 00100 Rome, Italy (Telephone Number in U.S. (202) 653-2400); *Production Yearbook*, and *The State of Food and Agriculture*.

MALTA - FOREIGN DEBT

International Monetary Fund, 700 Nineteenth Street, NW, Washington, D.C. 20431 (202) 623-7000; *Government Finance Statistics Yearbook*.

MALTA - FOREIGN TRADE

Euromonitor Publications Limited, 87-88 Turnmill Street, London EC1M 5QU, England; *European Marketing Data and Statistics*.

Food and Agricultural Organization of the United Nations (FAO), Via delle Terme di Caracalla, 00100 Rome, Italy (Telephone Number in U.S. (202) 653-2400); *The State of Food and Agriculture*.

International Monetary Fund, 700 Nineteenth Street, NW, Washington, D.C. 20431 (202) 623-7000; *International Financial Statistics*.

Statistical Office of the United Nations, Publishing Service, New York, New York 10017 (800) 253-9646; *International Trade Statistics Yearbook*, and *Statistical Yearbook*.

The World Bank, 1818 H Street, NW, Washington, D.C. 20433 (202) 477-1234; *World Tables*.

MALTA - FORESTRY AND FOREST PRODUCTS

Euromonitor Publications Limited, 87-88 Turnmill Street, London EC1M 5QU, England; *European Marketing Data and Statistics*.

Food and Agricultural Organization of the United Nations (FAO), Via delle Terme di Caracalla, 00100 Rome, Italy (Telephone Number in U.S. (202) 653-2400); *The State of Food and Agriculture*, and *Yearbook of Forest Products*.

Statistical Office of the United Nations, Publishing Service, New York, New York 10017 (800) 253-9646; *Statistical Yearbook*.

United Nations Educational, Scientific and Cultural Organization (UNESCO), 7 Place de Fontenoy, F-75700 Paris, France (Telephone Number in U.S. (212) 963-5981); *Statistical Yearbook*.

MALTA - GAS PRODUCTION - See MALTA - MINING AND MINERAL PRODUCTS

MALTA - GENERAL INDUSTRIAL STATISTICS

Statistical Office of the United Nations, Publishing Service, New York, New York 10017 (800) 253-9646; *Industrial Statistics Yearbook*.

MALTA - GENERAL MORTALITY

Statistical Office of the United Nations, Publishing Service, New York, New York 10017 (800) 253-9646; *Demographic Yearbook.*

World Health Organization, Office of Publications, Avenue Appia, CH-1211 Geneva 27, Switzerland (Telephone Number in U.S. (518) 436-9686); *World Health Statistics Annual.*

MALTA - GOLD HOLDINGS

International Monetary Fund, 700 Nineteenth Street, NW, Washington, D.C. 20431 (202) 623-7000; *International Financial Statistics.*

Statistical Office of the United Nations, Publishing Service, New York, New York 10017 (800) 253-9646; *Statistical Yearbook.*

The World Bank, 1818 H Street, NW, Washington, D.C. 20433 (202) 477-1234; *World Tables.*

MALTA - GOVERNMENT EXPENDITURES

International Monetary Fund, 700 Nineteenth Street, NW, Washington, D.C. 20431 (202) 623-7000; *Government Finance Statistics Yearbook.*

Times Books, 201 East 50th Street, New York, New York 10022 (212) 751-2600; *The Economist Book of Vital World Statistics.*

The World Bank, 1818 H Street, NW, Washington, D.C. 20433 (202) 477-1234; *World Tables.*

MALTA - GOVERNMENT FINANCES

International Monetary Fund, 700 Nineteenth Street, NW, Washington, D.C. 20431 (202) 623-7000; *International Financial Statistics.*

MALTA - GOVERNMENT REVENUE

International Monetary Fund, 700 Nineteenth Street, NW, Washington, D.C. 20431 (202) 623-7000; *Government Finance Statistics Yearbook.*

Times Books, 201 East 50th Street, New York, New York 10022 (212) 751-2600; *The Economist Book of Vital World Statistics.*

The World Bank, 1818 H Street, NW, Washington, D.C. 20433 (202) 477-1234; *World Tables.*

MALTA - GRAIN PRODUCTION - See MALTA - CROPS

MALTA - GRANTS

International Monetary Fund, 700 Nineteenth Street, NW, Washington, D.C. 20431 (202) 623-7000; *Government Finance Statistics Yearbook.*

MALTA - GROSS DOMESTIC PRODUCT

Statistical Office of the United Nations, Publishing Service, New York, New York 10017 (800) 253-9646; *Statistical Yearbook.*

Times Books, 201 East 50th Street, New York, New York 10022 (212) 751-2600; *The Economist Book of Vital World Statistics.*

The World Bank, 1818 H Street, NW, Washington, D.C. 20433 (202) 477-1234; *World Tables.*

MALTA - GROSS NATIONAL PRODUCTION

U.S. Arms Control and Disarmament Agency, 320 Twenty-first Street, NW, Washington, D.C. 20451 (202) 647-8677; *World Military Expenditures and Arms Transfers.*

The World Bank, 1818 H Street, NW, Washington, D.C. 20433 (202) 477-1234; *World Tables.*

MALTA - HEALTH

Statistical Office of the United Nations, Publishing Service, New York, New York 10017 (800) 253-9646; *Statistical Yearbook.*

Times Books, 201 East 50th Street, New York, New York 10022 (212) 751-2600; *The Economist Book of Vital World Statistics.*

MALTA - HEALTH EXPENDITURES

International Monetary Fund, 700 Nineteenth Street, NW, Washington, D.C. 20431 (202) 623-7000; *Government Finance Statistics Yearbook.*

MALTA - HIDE PRODUCTION

Food and Agricultural Organization of the United Nations (FAO), Via delle Terme di Caracalla, 00100 Rome, Italy (Telephone Number in U.S. (202) 653-2400); *Production Yearbook.*

Statistical Office of the United Nations, Publishing Service, New York, New York 10017 (800) 253-9646; *Statistical Yearbook.*

MALTA - HIGHWAYS

International Road Federation, 525 School Street, SW, Washington, D.C. 20024 (202) 554-2106; *World Road Statistics.*

Statistical Office of the United Nations, Publishing Service, New York, New York 10017 (800) 253-9646; *Annual Bulletin of Transport Statistics for Europe.*

MALTA - HORSES - See MALTA - LIVESTOCK AND POULTRY

MALTA - HOURS OF WORK - See MALTA - EMPLOYMENT

MALTA - HOUSING EXPENDITURES

International Monetary Fund, 700 Nineteenth Street, NW, Washington, D.C. 20431 (202) 623-7000; *Government Finance Statistics Yearbook.*

MALTA - ILLITERATE POPULATION

United Nations Educational, Scientific and Cultural Organization (UNESCO), 7 Place de Fontenoy, F-75700 Paris, France (Telephone Number in U.S. (212) 963-5981); *Statistical Yearbook.*

MALTA - IMPORTS

Food and Agricultural Organization of the United Nations (FAO), Via delle Terme di Caracalla, 00100 Rome, Italy (Telephone Number in U.S. (202) 653-2400); *The State of Food and Agriculture.*

International Monetary Fund, 700 Nineteenth Street, NW, Washington, D.C. 20431 (202) 623-7000; *Direction of Trade Statistics,* and *Government Finance Statistics Yearbook.*

Times Books, 201 East 50th Street, New York, New York 10022 (212) 751-2600; *The Economist Book of Vital World Statistics.*

The World Bank, 1818 H Street, NW, Washington, D.C. 20433 (202) 477-1234; *World Tables*.

MALTA - INCOME TAXES - See MALTA - TAXATION

MALTA - INDUSTRY

International Labour Office, I.L.O. Publications, CH-1211, Geneva 22, Switzerland; *Yearbook of Labour Statistics*.

Statistical Office of the United Nations, Publishing Service, New York, New York 10017 (800) 253-9646; *Statistical Yearbook*.

The World Bank, 1818 H Street, NW, Washington, D.C. 20433 (202) 477-1234; *World Tables*.

World Intellectual Property Organization, 34 Chemin des Colombettes, CH-1211 Geneva 20, Switzerland; *Industrial Property Statistics*.

MALTA - INFANT AND MATERNAL MORTALITY

Statistical Office of the United Nations, Publishing Service, New York, New York 10017 (800) 253-9646; *Demographic Yearbook*, and *Statistical Yearbook*.

Times Books, 201 East 50th Street, New York, New York 10022 (212) 751-2600; *The Economist Book of Vital World Statistics*.

The World Bank, 1818 H Street, NW, Washington, D.C. 20433 (202) 477-1234; *World Tables*.

World Health Organization, Office of Publications, Avenue Appia, CH-1211 Geneva 27, Switzerland (Telephone Number in U.S. (518) 436-9686); *World Health Statistics Annual*.

MALTA - INTERNATIONAL LIQUIDITY

International Monetary Fund, 700 Nineteenth Street, NW, Washington, D.C. 20431 (202) 623-7000; *International Financial Statistics*.

MALTA - INTERNATIONAL RESERVES EXCLUDING GOLD

Statistical Office of the United Nations, Publishing Service, New York, New York 10017 (800) 253-9646; *Statistical Yearbook*.

The World Bank, 1818 H Street, NW, Washington, D.C. 20433 (202) 477-1234; *World Tables*.

MALTA - LABOR FORCE

Food and Agricultural Organization of the United Nations (FAO), Via delle Terme di Caracalla, 00100 Rome, Italy (Telephone Number in U.S. (202) 653-2400); *The State of Food and Agriculture*.

The World Bank, 1818 H Street, NW, Washington, D.C. 20433 (202) 477-1234; *World Tables*.

MALTA - LABOR PRODUCTIVITY

International Labour Office, I.L.O. Publications, CH-1211, Geneva 22, Switzerland; *Yearbook of Labour Statistics*.

MALTA - LAND USE

Euromonitor Publications Limited, 87-88 Turnmill Street, London EC1M 5QU, England; *European Marketing Data and Statistics*.

Food and Agricultural Organization of the United Nations (FAO), Via delle Terme di Caracalla, 00100 Rome, Italy (Telephone Number in U.S. (202) 653-2400); *Production Yearbook*.

MALTA - LIBRARIES

Euromonitor Publications Limited, 87-88 Turnmill Street, London EC1M 5QU, England; *European Marketing Data and Statistics*.

United Nations Educational, Scientific and Cultural Organization (UNESCO), 7 Place de Fontenoy, F-75700 Paris, France (Telephone Number in U.S. (212) 963-5981); *Statistical Yearbook*.

MALTA - LIVESTOCK AND POULTRY

Euromonitor Publications Limited, 87-88 Turnmill Street, London EC1M 5QU, England; *European Marketing Data and Statistics*.

Food and Agricultural Organization of the United Nations (FAO), Via delle Terme di Caracalla, 00100 Rome, Italy (Telephone Number in U.S. (202) 653-2400); *Production Yearbook*, and *The State of Food and Agriculture*.

Statistical Office of the United Nations, Publishing Service, New York, New York 10017 (800) 253-9646; *Statistical Yearbook*.

MALTA - LIVING LEVELS

Times Books, 201 East 50th Street, New York, New York 10022 (212) 751-2600; *The Economist Book of Vital World Statistics*.

MALTA - MAIL - NUMBER OF ITEMS SENT AND RECEIVED

Statistical Office of the United Nations, Publishing Service, New York, New York 10017 (800) 253-9646; *Statistical Yearbook*.

MALTA - MANUFACTURING

Statistical Office of the United Nations, Publishing Service, New York, New York 10017 (800) 253-9646; *Statistical Yearbook*.

The World Bank, 1818 H Street, NW, Washington, D.C. 20433 (202) 477-1234; *World Tables*.

MALTA - MARRIAGE RATES

Statistical Office of the United Nations, Publishing Service, New York, New York 10017 (800) 253-9646; *Demographic Yearbook*, and *Statistical Yearbook*.

MALTA - MEAT PRODUCTION - See MALTA - LIVESTOCK AND POULTRY

MALTA - MERCHANT SHIPPING

Lloyd's Register of Shipping, 17 Battery Place, New York, New York 10004 (212) 425-8050; *Register of Ships*.

Statistical Office of the United Nations, Publishing Service, New York, New York 10017 (800) 253-9646; *Statistical Yearbook*.

Times Books, 201 East 50th Street, New York, New York 10022 (212) 751-2600; *The Economist Book of Vital World Statistics*.

U.S. Department of Transportation, Maritime Administration, 400 Seventh Street, SW, Washington, D.C. 20590 (202) 366-5807; *A Statistical Analysis of the World's Merchant Fleets*.

MALTA - METAL PRODUCTS - See MALTA - MINING AND MINERAL PRODUCTS

MALTA - MILITARY

The International Institute for Strategic Studies, 23 Tavistock Street, London WC2E 7NQ, England; *The Military Balance*.

U.S. Arms Control and Disarmament Agency, 320 Twenty-first Street, NW, Washington, D.C. 20451 (202) 647-8677; *World Military Expenditures and Arms Transfers*.

MALTA - MILK PRODUCTION - See MALTA - DAIRY PRODUCTS

MALTA - MINING AND MINERAL PRODUCTS

Statistical Office of the United Nations, Publishing Service, New York, New York 10017 (800) 253-9646; *Statistical Yearbook*.

MALTA - MONEY EXCHANGE RATE

International Monetary Fund, 700 Nineteenth Street, NW, Washington, D.C. 20431 (202) 623-7000; *International Financial Statistics*.

Statistical Office of the United Nations, Publishing Service, New York, New York 10017 (800) 253-9646; *Statistical Yearbook*.

MALTA - MONEY SUPPLY

International Monetary Fund, 700 Nineteenth Street, NW, Washington, D.C. 20431 (202) 623-7000; *International Financial Statistics*.

Statistical Office of the United Nations, Publishing Service, New York, New York 10017 (800) 253-9646; *Statistical Yearbook*.

The World Bank, 1818 H Street, NW, Washington, D.C. 20433 (202) 477-1234; *World Tables*.

MALTA - MONUMENTS AND HISTORICAL SITES

United Nations Educational, Scientific and Cultural Organization (UNESCO), 7 Place de Fontenoy, F-75700 Paris, France (Telephone Number in U.S. (212) 963-5981); *Statistical Yearbook*.

MALTA - MOTION PICTURES

Statistical Office of the United Nations, Publishing Service, New York, New York 10017 (800) 253-9646; *Statistical Yearbook*.

MALTA - MOTOR VEHICLE TAXES - See MALTA - TAXATION

MALTA - MOTOR VEHICLES IN USE

International Road Federation, 525 School Street, SW, Washington, D.C. 20024 (202) 554-2106; *World Road Statistics*.

Statistical Office of the United Nations, Publishing Service, New York, New York 10017 (800) 253-9646; *Statistical Yearbook*.

MALTA - MULES - See MALTA - LIVESTOCK AND POULTRY

MALTA - MUSEUMS

Euromonitor Publications Limited, 87-88 Turnmill Street, London EC1M 5QU, England; *European Marketing Data and Statistics*.

United Nations Educational, Scientific and Cultural Organization (UNESCO), 7 Place de Fontenoy, F-75700 Paris, France (Telephone Number in U.S. (212) 963-5981); *Statistical Yearbook*.

MALTA - NATALITY - See MALTA - BIRTH RATES

MALTA - NATIONAL ACCOUNTS

Statistical Office of the United Nations, Publishing Service, New York, New York 10017 (800) 253-9646; *National Account Statistics*, and *Statistical Yearbook*.

MALTA - NATIONAL INCOME

Statistical Office of the United Nations, Publishing Service, New York, New York 10017 (800) 253-9646; *Statistical Yearbook*.

MALTA - NATIONAL PRODUCT

Statistical Office of the United Nations, Publishing Service, New York, New York 10017 (800) 253-9646; *Statistical Yearbook*.

MALTA - NEWSPAPER PRODUCTION - See MALTA - FORESTRY AND FOREST PRODUCTS

MALTA - PATENTS

Statistical Office of the United Nations, Publishing Service, New York, New York 10017 (800) 253-9646; *Statistical Yearbook*.

World Intellectual Property Organization, 34 Chemin des Colombettes, CH-1211 Geneva 20, Switzerland; *Industrial Property Statistics*.

MALTA - PERIODICALS

United Nations Educational, Scientific and Cultural Organization (UNESCO), 7 Place de Fontenoy, F-75700 Paris, France (Telephone Number in U.S. (212) 963-5981); *Statistical Yearbook*.

MALTA - PESTICIDE USE

Food and Agricultural Organization of the United Nations (FAO), Via delle Terme di Caracalla, 00100 Rome, Italy (Telephone Number in U.S. (202) 653-2400); *The State of Food and Agriculture*.

MALTA - PETROLEUM INDUSTRY

Euromonitor Publications Limited, 87-88 Turnmill Street, London EC1M 5QU, England; *European Marketing Data and Statistics*.

Food and Agricultural Organization of the United Nations (FAO), Via delle Terme di Caracalla, 00100 Rome, Italy (Telephone Number in U.S. (202) 653-2400); *The State of Food and Agriculture*.

MALTA - PIGS - See MALTA - LIVESTOCK AND POULTRY

MALTA - POPULATION

Euromonitor Publications Limited, 87-88 Turnmill Street, London EC1M 5QU, England; *European Marketing Data and Statistics*.

Food and Agricultural Organization of the United Nations (FAO), Via delle Terme di Caracalla, 00100 Rome, Italy (Telephone Number in U.S. (202) 653-2400); *Production Yearbook*.

International Labour Office, I.L.O. Publications, CH-1211, Geneva 22, Switzerland; *Yearbook of Labour Statistics*.

Statistical Office of the United Nations, Publishing Service, New York, New York 10017 (800) 253-9646; *Demographic Yearbook*, and *Statistical Yearbook*.

Times Books, 201 East 50th Street, New York, New York 10022 (212) 751-2600; *The Economist Book of Vital World Statistics*.

U.S. Arms Control and Disarmament Agency, 320 Twenty-first Street, NW, Washington, D.C. 20451 (202) 647-8677; *World Military Expenditures and Arms Transfers*.

World Health Organization, Office of Publications, Avenue Appia, CH-1211 Geneva 27, Switzerland (Telephone Number in U.S. (518) 436-9686); *World Health Statistics Annual*.

MALTA - POTATO PRODUCTION - See MALTA - CROPS

MALTA - PRICES

Food and Agricultural Organization of the United Nations (FAO), Via delle Terme di Caracalla, 00100 Rome, Italy (Telephone Number in U.S. (202) 653-2400); *Production Yearbook*, and *The State of Food and Agriculture*.

International Labour Office, I.L.O. Publications, CH-1211, Geneva 22, Switzerland; *Yearbook of Labour Statistics*.

International Monetary Fund, 700 Nineteenth Street, NW, Washington, D.C. 20431 (202) 623-7000; *International Financial Statistics*.

MALTA - PROPERTY TAXES

International Monetary Fund, 700 Nineteenth Street, NW, Washington, D.C. 20431 (202) 623-7000; *Government Finance Statistics Yearbook*.

MALTA - RADIO BROADCASTING - See MALTA - BROADCASTING

MALTA - RAILWAY USE

Euromonitor Publications Limited, 87-88 Turnmill Street, London EC1M 5QU, England; *European Marketing Data and Statistics*.

MALTA - RENT PRICES

International Labour Office, I.L.O. Publications, CH-1211, Geneva 22, Switzerland; *Yearbook of Labour Statistics*.

MALTA - ROOT AND TUBER PRODUCTION - See MALTA - CROPS

MALTA - ROUNDWOOD PRODUCTION - See MALTA - FORESTRY AND FOREST PRODUCTS

MALTA - SALT PRODUCTION - See MALTA - MINING AND MINERAL PRODUCTS

MALTA - SAWNWOOD PRODUCTION - See MALTA - FORESTRY AND FOREST PRODUCTS

MALTA - SCIENCE AND TECHNOLOGY - EXPENDITURE FOR RESEARCH

Statistical Office of the United Nations, Publishing Service, New York, New York 10017 (800) 253-9646; *Statistical Yearbook*.

MALTA - SCIENTISTS AND TECHNICIANS

Statistical Office of the United Nations, Publishing Service, New York, New York 10017 (800) 253-9646; *Statistical Yearbook*.

MALTA - SHEEP - See MALTA - LIVESTOCK AND POULTRY

MALTA - SOCIAL SECURITY EXPENDITURES

International Monetary Fund, 700 Nineteenth Street, NW, Washington, D.C. 20431 (202) 623-7000; *Government Finance Statistics Yearbook*.

MALTA - STAMP TAXES AND DUTIES - See MALTA - TAXATION

MALTA - STOCKS - COMMODITY - MARKET PRICE - INDEX

Food and Agricultural Organization of the United Nations (FAO), Via delle Terme di Caracalla, 00100 Rome, Italy (Telephone Number in U.S. (202) 653-2400); *The State of Food and Agriculture*.

MALTA - TAXATION

International Monetary Fund, 700 Nineteenth Street, NW, Washington, D.C. 20431 (202) 623-7000; *Government Finance Statistics Yearbook*.

International Road Federation, 525 School Street, SW, Washington, D.C. 20024 (202) 554-2106; *World Road Statistics*.

The World Bank, 1818 H Street, NW, Washington, D.C. 20433 (202) 477-1234; *World Tables*.

MALTA - TELEGRAPH SERVICE

Statistical Office of the United Nations, Publishing Service, New York, New York 10017 (800) 253-9646; *Statistical Yearbook*.

MALTA - TELEPHONES IN USE

American Telephone and Telegraph Company, 26 Parsippany Road, Whippany, New Jersey 07981 (800) 338-4038; *The World's Telephones*.

Statistical Office of the United Nations, Publishing Service, New York, New York 10017 (800) 253-9646; *Statistical Yearbook*.

MALTA - TELEVISION BROADCASTING - See MALTA - BROADCASTING

MALTA - TOBACCO PRODUCTION

Euromonitor Publications Limited, 87-88 Turnmill Street, London EC1M 5QU, England; *European Marketing Data and Statistics*.

Statistical Office of the United Nations, Publishing Service, New York, New York 10017 (800) 253-9646; *Statistical Yearbook*.

MALTA - TOURISM

Euromonitor Publications Limited, 87-88 Turnmill Street, London EC1M 5QU, England; *European Marketing Data and Statistics*.

Statistical Office of the United Nations, Publishing Service, New York, New York 10017 (800) 253-9646; *Statistical Yearbook*.

Times Books, 201 East 50th Street, New York, New York 10022 (212) 751-2600; *The Economist Book of Vital World Statistics*.

World Tourism Organization, Calle Capitan Haya 42, E-28020 Madrid, Spain; *Yearbook of Tourism Statistics*.

MALTA - TRACTORS IN USE

Statistical Office of the United Nations, Publishing Service, New York, New York 10017 (800) 253-9646; *Statistical Yearbook*.

MALTA - TRADE - See MALTA - FOREIGN TRADE

MALTA - TRADEMARKS AND SERVICE MARKS

Statistical Office of the United Nations, Publishing Service, New York, New York 10017 (800) 253-9646; *Statistical Yearbook*.

World Intellectual Property Organization, 34 Chemin des Colombettes, CH-1211 Geneva 20, Switzerland; *Industrial Property Statistics*.

MALTA - TURKEYS - See MALTA - LIVESTOCK AND POULTRY

MALTA - UNEMPLOYMENT

Euromonitor Publications Limited, 87-88 Turnmill Street, London EC1M 5QU, England; *European Marketing Data and Statistics*.

International Labour Office, I.L.O. Publications, CH-1211, Geneva 22, Switzerland; *Yearbook of Labour Statistics*.

Statistical Office of the United Nations, Publishing Service, New York, New York 10017 (800) 253-9646; *Statistical Yearbook*.

MALTA - VITAL STATISTICS

Statistical Office of the United Nations, Publishing Service, New York, New York 10017 (800) 253-9646; *Statistical Yearbook*.

World Health Organization, Office of Publications, Avenue Appia, CH-1211 Geneva 27, Switzerland (Telephone Number in U.S. (518) 436-9686); *World Health Statistics Annual*.

MALTA - WAGES

Euromonitor Publications Limited, 87-88 Turnmill Street, London EC1M 5QU, England; *European Marketing Data and Statistics*.

International Labour Office, I.L.O. Publications, CH-1211, Geneva 22, Switzerland; *Yearbook of Labour Statistics*.

MALTA - WELFARE EXPENDITURES

International Monetary Fund, 700 Nineteenth Street, NW, Washington, D.C. 20431 (202) 623-7000; *Government Finance Statistics Yearbook*.

MALTA - WHEAT PRODUCTION - See MALTA - CROPS

MALTA - WINE PRODUCTION

Statistical Office of the United Nations, Publishing Service, New York, New York 10017 (800) 253-9646; *Statistical Yearbook*.

MALTA - ZOOS AND BOTANICAL GARDENS

United Nations Educational, Scientific and Cultural Organization (UNESCO), 7 Place de Fontenoy, F-75700 Paris, France (Telephone Number in U.S. (212) 963-5981); *Statistical Yearbook*.

MAMMOGRAM

U.S. Department of Health and Human Services, National Center for Health Statistics, 3700 East-West Highway, Hyattsville, Maryland 20782 (301) 436-8500; *Health Promotion and Disease Prevention: U.S.*, and *Vital and Health Statistics*.

MANGANESE

U.S. Department of Defense, Defense Logistics Agency, Cameron Station, Washington, D.C. 22304 (703) 274-6000; *Statistical Supplement, Stockpile Report to the Congress*.

U.S. Department of the Interior, Bureau of Mines, 810 Seventh Street, NW, Washington, D.C. 20241 (202) 501-9649; *Annual Reports, Minerals Commodity Summaries*, and *Census of Mineral Industries*.

MANGANIFEROUS ORE

U.S. Department of the Interior, Bureau of Mines, 810 Seventh Street, NW, Washington, D.C. 20241 (202) 501-9649; *Annual Reports*, and *Mineral Commodity Summaries*.

MAN-MADE FIBERS AND FABRICS - See also Specific Items and FOREIGN TRADE

MAN-MADE FIBERS AND FABRICS

Fibre Economics Bureau, Incorporated, 101 Eisenhower Parkway, Roseland, New Jersey 07068 (201) 228-1107; *Textile Organon*.

MANUFACTURED PRODUCTS - See also Individual Products

MANUFACTURED PRODUCTS - EXPORTS - UNITED STATES AS COMPARED TO WORLD

U.S. Department of Commerce, International Trade Administration, Fourteenth Street between Constitution Avenue and E Street, NW, Washington, D.C. 20230 (202) 482-3809; *Business America, Market Share Reports*, and published data.

MANUFACTURED PRODUCTS - PRODUCTION INDEXES

Board of Governors of the Federal Reserve System, Twentieth Street and Constitution Avenue, NW, Washington, D.C. 20551 (202) 452-3000; *Federal Reserve Bulletin*.

MANUFACTURERS' EXCISE TAXES

U.S. Department of the Treasury, Internal Revenue Service, 1111 Constitution Avenue, NW, Washington, D.C. 20224 (202) 566-5000; *Annual Report of the Commissioner and Chief Counsel of the Internal Revenue Service*.

MANUFACTURING INDUSTRY - See also Individual Industries

MANUFACTURING INDUSTRY - CAPITAL

Board of Governors of the Federal Reserve System, Twentieth Street and Constitution Avenue, NW, Washington, D.C. 20551 (202) 452-3000; *Federal Reserve Bulletin*, and *Annual Statistical Digest*.

The Conference Board, 845 Third Avenue, New York, New York 10022 (212) 759-0900; *Quarterly Survey of Capital Investment and Supply Conditions in Manufacturing*.

U.S. Department of Commerce, Bureau of the Census, Suitland, Maryland 20233 (301) 763-4040; *Quarterly Financial Report for Manufacturing, Mining and Trade Corporations*.

MANUFACTURING INDUSTRY - COLLECTIVE BARGAINING SETTLEMENTS

U.S. Department of Labor, Bureau of Labor Statistics, Two Massachusetts Avenue, NE, Washington, D.C. 20212 (202) 606-7828; *Compensation and Working Conditions.*

MANUFACTURING INDUSTRY - EARNINGS

U.S. Department of Commerce, Bureau of Economic Analysis, Fourteenth Street between Constitution Avenue and E Street, NW, Washington, D.C. 20230 (202) 606-9900; *The National Income and Product Accounts of the United States,* and *Survey of Current Business.*

U.S. Department of Commerce, Bureau of the Census, Suitland, Maryland 20233 (301) 763-4040; *Census of Manufactures, Annual Survey of Manufactures, County Business Patterns, Current Industrial Reports, Manufacturing Technology,* and *Economic Census of Outlying Areas.*

U.S. Department of Labor, Bureau of Labor Statistics, Two Massachusetts Avenue, NE, Washington, D.C. 20212 (202) 606-7828; *Employment and Earnings,* and Bulletins 2370 and 2429.

MANUFACTURING INDUSTRY - ECONOMIC INDICATORS

U.S. Department of Commerce, Bureau of Economic Analysis, Fourteenth Street between Constitution Avenue and E Street, NW, Washington, D.C. 20230 (202) 606-9900; *Survey of Current Business.*

MANUFACTURING INDUSTRY - EMPLOYEES

U.S. Department of Commerce, Bureau of Economic Analysis, Fourteenth Street between Constitution Avenue and E Street, NW, Washington, D.C. 20230 (202) 606-9900; *Survey of Current Business.*

U.S. Department of Commerce, Bureau of the Census, Suitland, Maryland 20233 (301) 763-4040; *Annual Survey of Manufactures, Census of Manufactures, County Business Patterns, Current Industrial Reports, Manufacturing Technology,* and *Economic Census of Outlying Areas.*

U.S. Department of Labor, Bureau of Labor Statistics, Two Massachusetts Avenue, NE, Washington, D.C. 20212 (202) 606-7828; *Employment and Earnings, Monthly Labor Review,* and Bulletins 2370 and 2429.

U.S. Department of the Treasury, Internal Revenue Service, 1111 Constitution Avenue, NW, Washington, D.C. 20224 (202) 566-5000; *Statistics of Income,* various publications.

MANUFACTURING INDUSTRY - ESTABLISHMENTS

U.S. Department of Commerce, Bureau of the Census, Suitland, Maryland 20233 (301) 763-4040; *Annual Survey of Manufactures, County Business Patterns, Census of Manufactures,* and *Economic Census of Outlying Areas.*

MANUFACTURING INDUSTRY - FINANCES

Time Warner, 1675 Broadway, Rockefeller Center, New York, New York 10019 (212) 522-1212; *The Fortune Directories.*

U.S. Department of Commerce, Bureau of the Census, Suitland, Maryland 20233 (301) 763-4040; *Quarterly Financial Report for Manufacturing, Mining and Trade Corporations.*

U.S. Department of the Treasury, Internal Revenue Service, 1111 Constitution Avenue, NW, Washington, D.C. 20224 (202) 566-5000; *Statistics of Income, Corporation Income Tax Returns, Statistics of Income, Partnership Returns,* and *Statistics of Income Bulletin.*

MANUFACTURING INDUSTRY - FOREIGN COUNTRIES

Organization for Economic Cooperation and Development, 2001 L Street, NW, Washington, D.C. 20036 (202) 785-6323; *OECD Industrial Structure Statistics.*

Time Warner, 1675 Broadway, Rockefeller Center, New York, New York 10019 (212) 522-1212; *The Fortune Directories.*

U.S. Department of Labor, Bureau of Labor Statistics, Two Massachusetts Avenue, NE, Washington, D.C. 20212 (202) 606-7828; Report 844.

MANUFACTURING INDUSTRY - FOREIGN INVESTMENTS IN UNITED STATES

U.S. Department of Commerce, Bureau of Economic Analysis, Fourteenth Street between Constitution Avenue and E Street, NW, Washington, D.C. 20230 (202) 606-9900; *Survey of Current Business.*

MANUFACTURING INDUSTRY - FORM OF ORGANIZATION

U.S. Department of Commerce, Bureau of the Census, Suitland, Maryland 20233 (301) 763-4040; *Census of Manufactures,* and *Annual Survey of Manufactures.*

MANUFACTURING INDUSTRY - GROSS DOMESTIC PRODUCT ORIGINATING IN

U.S. Department of Commerce, Bureau of Economic Analysis, Fourteenth Street between Constitution Avenue and E Street, NW, Washington, D.C. 20230 (202) 606-9900; *The National Income and Product Accounts of the United States,* and *Survey of Current Business.*

MANUFACTURING INDUSTRY - INVENTORIES

U.S. Department of Commerce, Bureau of Economic Analysis, Fourteenth Street between Constitution Avenue and E Street, NW, Washington, D.C. 20230 (202) 606-9900; *The National Income and Product Accounts of the United States, Survey of Current Business,* and *Current Business Reports.*

U.S. Department of Commerce, Bureau of the Census, Suitland, Maryland 20233 (301) 763-4040; *Census of Manufactures, Annual Survey of Manufactures,* and *Current Industrial Reports, Manufacturers' Shipments, Inventories and Orders.*

MANUFACTURING INDUSTRY - INVESTMENT ABROAD

U.S. Department of Commerce, Bureau of Economic Analysis, Fourteenth Street between Constitution Avenue and E Street, NW, Washington, D.C. 20230 (202) 606-9900; *Survey of Current Business.*

MANUFACTURING INDUSTRY - OCCUPATIONAL SAFETY

National Safety Council, 1121 Spring Lake Drive, Itasca, Illinois 60143-3201 (708) 285-1121; *Accident Facts.*

U.S. Department of Labor, Bureau of Labor Statistics, Two Massachusetts Avenue, NE, Washington, D.C. 20212 (202) 606-7828; *Occupational Injuries and Illnesses in the United States by Industry.*

MANUFACTURING INDUSTRY - OUTLYING AREAS OF
UNITED STATES

U.S. Department of Commerce, Bureau of the Census, Suitland,
Maryland 20233 (301) 763-4040; *Economic Census of Outlying
Areas*, and *County Business Patterns*.

MANUFACTURING INDUSTRY - POLLUTION ABATEMENT

U.S. Department of Commerce, Bureau of the Census, Suitland,
Maryland 20233 (301) 763-4040; *Current Industrial Reports*.

MANUFACTURING INDUSTRY - PRODUCTIVITY

Board of Governors of the Federal Reserve System, Twentieth
Street and Constitution Avenue, NW, Washington, D.C. 20551 (202)
452-3000; *Federal Reserve Bulletin*, and *Capacity Utilization in
Manufacturing, Mining, Utilities, and Industrial Materials*.

U.S. Department of Labor, Bureau of Labor Statistics, Two
Massachusetts Avenue, NE, Washington, D.C. 20212 (202) 606-
7828; *Employment and Earnings, Productivity Measures for Selected
Industries and Government Services*, and unpublished data.

MANUFACTURING INDUSTRY - PROFITS

Time Warner, 1675 Broadway, Rockefeller Center, New York, New
York 10019 (212) 522-1212; *The Fortune Directories*.

U.S. Department of Commerce, Bureau of Economic Analysis,
Fourteenth Street between Constitution Avenue and E Street, NW,
Washington, D.C. 20230 (202) 606-9900 ; *Survey of Current
Business*, and *The National Income and Product Accounts of the
United States*.

U.S. Department of Commerce, Bureau of the Census, Suitland,
Maryland 20233 (301) 763-4040; *Quarterly Financial Report for
Manufacturing, Mining, and Trade Corporations*.

U.S. Department of the Treasury, Internal Revenue Service, 1111
Constitution Avenue, NW, Washington, D.C. 20224 (202) 566-5000;
Statistics of Income, various publications, and *Statistics of Income,
Corporation Income Tax Return*.

MANUFACTURING INDUSTRY - SALES, SHIPMENTS, RECEIPTS

Time Warner, 1675 Broadway, Rockefeller Center, New York, New
York 10019 (212) 522-1212; *The Fortune Directories*.

U.S. Department of Commerce, Bureau of Economic Analysis,
Fourteenth Street between Constitution Avenue and E Street, NW,
Washington, D.C. 20230 (202) 606-9900; *Survey of Current Business,
The National Income and Product Accounts of the United States*,
and unpublished data.

U.S. Department of Commerce, Bureau of the Census, Suitland,
Maryland 20233 (301) 763-4040; *Quarterly Financial Report for
Manufacturing, Mining, and Trade Corporations, Current Business
Reports, Manufacturing and Trade Inventories and Sales, Current
Industrial Reports, Manufactures' Shipments, Inventories, and
Orders, Census of Manufactures, Annual Survey of Manufactures*,
and unpublished data.

U.S. Department of the Treasury, Internal Revenue Service, 1111
Constitution Avenue, NW, Washington, D.C. 20224 (202) 566-5000;
Statistics of Income, various publications, and *Statistics of Income,
Corporation Income Tax Returns*.

MANUFACTURING INDUSTRY - UNION MEMBERSHIP

U.S. Department of Labor, Bureau of Labor Statistics, Two
Massachusetts Avenue, NE, Washington, D.C. 20212 (202) 606-7828;
Employment and Earnings.

MANUFACTURING INDUSTRY - VALUE ADDED

U.S. Department of Commerce, Bureau of the Census, Suitland,
Maryland 20233 (301) 763-4040; *Annual Survey of Manufactures,
Current Industrial Reports*, and *Census of Manufactures*.

MARGARINE

U.S. Department of Agriculture, Economic Research Service,
Fourteenth Street and Independence Avenue, SW, Washington, D.C.
20005-4789 (202) 219-1504; *Food Consumption, Prices, and
Expenditures*.

MARIHUANA - See also: DRUGS (ILLEGAL)

MARIHUANA - ARRESTS

U.S. Department of Justice, Federal Bureau of Investigation, Ninth
Street and Pennsylvania Avenue, NW, Washington, D.C. 20535 (202)
324-3000; *Crime in the United States*.

MARIHUANA - USE

U.S. Department of Health and Human Services, Substance Abuse
and Mental Health Administration, 5600 Fishers Lane, Rockville,
Maryland 20857 (301) 443-4797; *National Household Survey on Drug
Abuse*.

MARINE COMMUNICATION - PRIVATE RADIO STATIONS

U.S. Federal Communications Commission, 1919 M Street, NW,
Washington, D.C. 20554 (202) 632-7000; *Annual Report*, and
unpublished data.

MARINE CORPS

U.S. Department of Defense, Office of the Secretary, The Pentagon,
Washington, D.C. 20301 (703) 545-6700; *Selected Manpower
Statistics*.

MARITAL STATUS OF POPULATION

U.S. Department of Commerce, Bureau of the Census, Suitland,
Maryland 20233 (301) 763-4040; *Current Population Reports*.

U.S. Department of Health and Human Services, National Center for
Health Statistics, 3700 East-West Highway, Hyattsville, Maryland
20782 (301) 436-8500; *Vital Statistics of the United States, Monthly
Vital Statistics Report*, and unpublished data.

MARITAL STATUS OF POPULATION - BLACK POPULATION

U.S. Department of Commerce, Bureau of the Census, Suitland,
Maryland 20233 (301) 763-4040; *Current Population Reports*.

U.S. Department of Health and Human Services, National Center for
Health Statistics, 3700 East-West Highway, Hyattsville, Maryland
20782 (301) 436-8500; *Vital Statistics of the United States, Monthly
Vital Statistics Report*, and unpublished data.

MARITAL STATUS OF POPULATION - BY PRESENCE OF CHILDREN

U.S. Department of Commerce, Bureau of the Census, Suitland, Maryland 20233 (301) 763-4040; *Current Population Reports*, and unpublished data.

MARITAL STATUS OF POPULATION - COUPLES WITH OR WITHOUT OWN HOUSEHOLD

U.S. Department of Commerce, Bureau of the Census, Suitland, Maryland 20233 (301) 763-4040; *Current Population Reports*.

MARITAL STATUS OF POPULATION - ELDERLY

U.S. Department of Commerce, Bureau of the Census, Suitland, Maryland 20233 (301) 763-4040; *Current Population Reports*.

MARITAL STATUS OF POPULATION - EMPLOYED PERSONS

U.S. Department of Labor, Bureau of Labor Statistics, Two Massachusetts Avenue, NE, Washington, D.C. 20212 (202) 606-7828; *Employment and Earnings*, and unpublished data.

MARITAL STATUS OF POPULATION - FEMALE HOUSE HOLDER

U.S. Department of Commerce, Bureau of the Census, Suitland, Maryland 20233 (301) 763-4040; *Current Population Reports*, and unpublished data.

MARITAL STATUS OF POPULATION - HISPANIC ORIGIN POPULATION

U.S. Department of Commerce, Bureau of the Census, Suitland, Maryland 20233 (301) 763-4040; *Census of Population, Persons of Spanish Origin, Current Population Reports*, and unpublished data.

MARITAL STATUS OF POPULATION - HOUSEHOLDER STATUS

U.S. Department of Commerce, Bureau of the Census, Suitland, Maryland 20233 (301) 763-4040, *Current Population Reports*,

MARITAL STATUS OF POPULATION - LABOR FORCE - PARTICIPATION RATES

U.S. Department of Labor, Bureau of Labor Statistics, Two Massachusetts Avenue, NE, Washington, D.C. 20212 (202) 606-7828; *Monthly Labor Review*, Bulletin 2307, 2217 and 2340, and unpublished data.

MARITAL STATUS OF POPULATION - NONFAMILY HOUSEHOLDER

U.S. Department of Commerce, Bureau of the Census, Suitland, Maryland 20233 (301) 763-4040; *Current Population Reports*, and unpublished data.

MARITAL STATUS OF POPULATION - OUTLYING AREAS

U.S. Department of Commerce, Bureau of the Census, Suitland, Maryland 20233 (301) 763-4040; *Census of Population and Housing*.

MARITAL STATUS OF POPULATION - UNMARRIED COUPLES

U.S. Department of Commerce, Bureau of the Census, Suitland, Maryland 20233 (301) 763-4040; *Current Population Reports*.

MARITAL STATUS OF POPULATION - WOMEN IN THE LABOR FORCE

U.S. Department of Labor, Bureau of Labor Statistics, Two Massachusetts Avenue, NE, Washington, D.C. 20212 (202) 606-7828; Bulletin 2307, and unpublished data.

MARITAL STATUS OF POPULATION - WORK SCHEDULES

U.S. Department of Labor, Bureau of Labor Statistics, Two Massachusetts Avenue, NE, Washington, D.C. 20212 (202) 606-7828; *Monthly Labor Review, News*, and unpublished data.

MARRIAGE AND DIVORCE - See also MARITAL STATUS

U.S. Department of Commerce, Bureau of the Census, Suitland, Maryland 20233 (301) 763-4040; *Current Population Reports*.

U.S. Department of Health and Human Services, National Center for Health Statistics, 3700 East-West Highway, Hyattsville, Maryland 20782 (301) 436-8500; *Vital Statistics of the United States, Monthly Vital Statistics Report*, and unpublished data.

MARRIAGE AND DIVORCE - MEDIAN AGE AT MARRIAGE

U.S. Department of Health and Human Services, National Center for Health Statistics, 3700 East-West Highway, Hyattsville, Maryland 20782 (301) 436-8500 ; *Vital Statistics of the United States, Monthly Vital Statistics Report*, and unpublished data.

MARRIAGE AND DIVORCE - OUTLYING AREAS OF UNITED STATES

U.S. Department of Commerce, Bureau of the Census, Suitland, Maryland 20233 (301) 763-4040; *Census of Population*, and unpublished data

U.S. Department of Health and Human Services, National Center for Health Statistics, 3700 East-West Highway, Hyattsville, Maryland 20782 (301) 436-8500; *Vital Statistics of the United States*.

MARRIAGE AND DIVORCE - REMARRIAGES

U.S. Department of Health and Human Services, National Center for Health Statistics, 3700 East-West Highway, Hyattsville, Maryland 20782 (301) 436-8500; *Vital Statistics of the United States, Advance Data from Vital and Health Statistics, Monthly Vital Statistics Report*, and unpublished data.

MARRIED COUPLES - See HOUSEHOLDS OR FAMILIES

MARRIED PERSONS - See MARITAL STATUS OF POPULATION

Marshall Islands (Republic of) - National Statistical Office

Office of Planning and Statistics, Majuro, Republic of the Marshall Islands 96960.

MARSHALL ISLANDS - BROADCASTING

Billboard Limited, Post Office Box 9027, 1006 AA Amsterdam, The Netherlands (Telephone Number in U.S. (212) 764-7300); *World Radio TV Handbook*.

MARSHALL ISLANDS - TOURISM

World Tourism Organization, Calle Capitan Haya 42, E-28020 Madrid, Spain; *Yearbook of Tourism Statistics*.

Martinique - Primary Statistics Sources

Institut National de la Statistique et des Etudes Economiques, BP 863, 97175 Pointe-a-Pitre, France: *Annuaire statistique de la Martinique* (Statistical Yearbook of Martinique), *Bulletin Statistique* (Statistical bulletin), and *Tableaux Economiques Regionaux, Martinique.*

MARTINIQUE - AGRICULTURE

Food and Agricultural Organization of the United Nations (FAO), Via delle Terme di Caracalla, 00100 Rome, Italy (Telephone Number in U.S. (202) 653-2400); *Production Yearbook*, and *The State of Food and Agriculture.*

G.K. Hall and Company, 70 Lincoln Street, Boston, Massachusetts 02111 (617) 423-3990; *The World in Figures.*

Statistical Office of the United Nations, Publishing Service, New York, New York 10017 (800) 253-9646; *Statistical Yearbook.*

MARTINIQUE - AIRLINE SERVICE

G.K. Hall and Company, 70 Lincoln Street, Boston, Massachusetts 02111 (617) 423-3990; *The World in Figures.*

MARTINIQUE - AREA AND DENSITY OF POPULATION

Food and Agricultural Organization of the United Nations (FAO), Via delle Terme di Caracalla, 00100 Rome, Italy (Telephone Number in U.S. (202) 653-2400); *The State of Food and Agriculture.*

G.K. Hall and Company, 70 Lincoln Street, Boston, Massachusetts 02111 (617) 423-3990; *The World in Figures.*

Statistical Office of the United Nations, Publishing Service, New York, New York 10017 (800) 253-9646; *Statistical Yearbook.*

MARTINIQUE - BALANCE OF PAYMENTS

G.K. Hall and Company, 70 Lincoln Street, Boston, Massachusetts 02111 (617) 423-3990; *The World in Figures.*

MARTINIQUE - BANKING

G.K. Hall and Company, 70 Lincoln Street, Boston, Massachusetts 02111 (617) 423-3990; *The World in Figures.*

MARTINIQUE - BIRTH RATES

Statistical Office of the United Nations, Publishing Service, New York, New York 10017 (800) 253-9646; *Demographic Yearbook*, and *Statistical Yearbook.*

World Health Organization, Office of Publications, Avenue Appia, CH-1211 Geneva 27, Switzerland (Telephone Number in U.S. (518) 436-9686); *World Health Statistics Annual.*

MARTINIQUE - BONDS

G.K. Hall and Company, 70 Lincoln Street, Boston, Massachusetts 02111 (617) 423-3990; *The World in Figures.*

MARTINIQUE - BOOK PRODUCTION

G.K. Hall and Company, 70 Lincoln Street, Boston, Massachusetts 02111 (617) 423-3990; *The World in Figures.*

United Nations Educational, Scientific and Cultural Organization (UNESCO), 7 Place de Fontenoy, F-75700 Paris, France (Telephone Number in U.S. (212) 963-5981); *Statistical Yearbook.*

MARTINIQUE - BROADCASTING

Billboard Limited, Post Office Box 9027, 1006 AA Amsterdam, The Netherlands (Telephone Number in U.S. (212) 764-7300); *World Radio TV Handbook.*

G.K. Hall and Company, 70 Lincoln Street, Boston, Massachusetts 02111 (617) 423-3990; *The World in Figures.*

MARTINIQUE - BUSINESS

G.K. Hall and Company, 70 Lincoln Street, Boston, Massachusetts 02111 (617) 423-3990; *The World in Figures.*

MARTINIQUE - CALORIE SUPPLY

Food and Agricultural Organization of the United Nations (FAO), Via delle Terme di Caracalla, 00100 Rome, Italy (Telephone Number in U.S. (202) 653-2400); *The State of Food and Agriculture.*

MARTINIQUE - CATTLE - See MARTINIQUE - LIVESTOCK AND POULTRY

MARTINIQUE - CHEMICAL (ORGANIC) PRODUCTION - See MARTINIQUE - MINING AND MINERAL PRODUCTS

MARTINIQUE - CLASS STRUCTURE

G.K. Hall and Company, 70 Lincoln Street, Boston, Massachusetts 02111 (617) 423-3990; *The World in Figures.*

MARTINIQUE - CLIMATE

G.K. Hall and Company, 70 Lincoln Street, Boston, Massachusetts 02111 (617) 423-3990; *The World in Figures.*

MARTINIQUE - COAL PRODUCTION - See MARTINIQUE - MINING AND MINERAL PRODUCTS

MARTINIQUE - COCOA PRODUCTION

Statistical Office of the United Nations, Publishing Service, New York, New York 10017 (800) 253-9646; *Statistical Yearbook.*

MARTINIQUE - COMMUNICATIONS

G.K. Hall and Company, 70 Lincoln Street, Boston, Massachusetts 02111 (617) 423-3990; *The World in Figures.*

MARTINIQUE - CONSTRUCTION INDUSTRY

Statistical Office of the United Nations, Publishing Service, New York, New York 10017 (800) 253-9646; *Statistical Yearbook.*

MARTINIQUE - CONSTRUCTION INDUSTRY STATISTICS BY CATEGORY OF BUILDINGS

Statistical Office of the United Nations, Publishing Service, New York, New York 10017 (800) 253-9646; *Construction Statistics Yearbook.*

MARTINIQUE - CONSUMER PRICE INDEX

G.K. Hall and Company, 70 Lincoln Street, Boston, Massachusetts 02111 (617) 423-3990; *The World in Figures.*

Statistical Office of the United Nations, Publishing Service, New York, New York 10017 (800) 253-9646; *Statistical Yearbook.*

MARTINIQUE - CONSUMER PRICES

International Labour Office, I.L.O. Publications, CH-1211, Geneva 22, Switzerland; *Yearbook of Labour Statistics.*

MARTINIQUE - CONSUMPTION

G.K. Hall and Company, 70 Lincoln Street, Boston, Massachusetts 02111 (617) 423-3990; *The World in Figures.*

MARTINIQUE - CORN PRODUCTION - See MARTINIQUE - CROPS

MARTINIQUE - CORPORATE TAXES - See MARTINIQUE - TAXATION

MARTINIQUE - CROPS

Food and Agricultural Organization of the United Nations (FAO), Via delle Terme di Caracalla, 00100 Rome, Italy (Telephone Number in U.S. (202) 653-2400); *Production Yearbook,* and *The State of Food and Agriculture.*

G.K. Hall and Company, 70 Lincoln Street, Boston, Massachusetts 02111 (617) 423-3990; *The World in Figures.*

MARTINIQUE - CUSTOMS DUTIES

G.K. Hall and Company, 70 Lincoln Street, Boston, Massachusetts 02111 (617) 423-3990; *The World in Figures.*

MARTINIQUE - DAIRY PRODUCTS

Food and Agricultural Organization of the United Nations (FAO), Via delle Terme di Caracalla, 00100 Rome, Italy (Telephone Number in U.S. (202) 653-2400); *The State of Food and Agriculture.*

MARTINIQUE - DEATH RATES

G.K. Hall and Company, 70 Lincoln Street, Boston, Massachusetts 02111 (617) 423-3990; *The World in Figures.*

Statistical Office of the United Nations, Publishing Service, New York, New York 10017 (800) 253-9646; *Statistical Yearbook.*

World Health Organization, Office of Publications, Avenue Appia, CH-1211 Geneva 27, Switzerland (Telephone Number in U.S. (518) 436-9686); *World Health Statistics Annual.*

MARTINIQUE - DEFENSE EXPENDITURES

G.K. Hall and Company, 70 Lincoln Street, Boston, Massachusetts 02111 (617) 423-3990; *The World in Figures.*

MARTINIQUE - DEMOGRAPHY

G.K. Hall and Company, 70 Lincoln Street, Boston, Massachusetts 02111 (617) 423-3990; *The World in Figures.*

MARTINIQUE - DEVELOPMENT ASSISTANCE

G.K. Hall and Company, 70 Lincoln Street, Boston, Massachusetts 02111 (617) 423-3990; *The World in Figures.*

Statistical Office of the United Nations, Publishing Service, New York, New York 10017 (800) 253-9646; *Statistical Yearbook.*

MARTINIQUE - DISEASE

G.K. Hall and Company, 70 Lincoln Street, Boston, Massachusetts 02111 (617) 423-3990; *The World in Figures.*

World Health Organization, Office of Publications, Avenue Appia, CH-1211 Geneva 27, Switzerland (Telephone Number in U.S. (518) 436-9686); *World Health Statistics Annual.*

MARTINIQUE - DIVORCE

Statistical Office of the United Nations, Publishing Service, New York, New York 10017 (800) 253-9646; *Demographic Yearbook,* and *Statistical Yearbook.*

MARTINIQUE - DOMESTIC PRODUCT

G.K. Hall and Company, 70 Lincoln Street, Boston, Massachusetts 02111 (617) 423-3990; *The World in Figures.*

MARTINIQUE - DUCKS - See MARTINIQUE - LIVESTOCK AND POULTRY

MARTINIQUE - ECONOMY

G.K. Hall and Company, 70 Lincoln Street, Boston, Massachusetts 02111 (617) 423-3990; *The World in Figures.*

MARTINIQUE - EDUCATION

G.K. Hall and Company, 70 Lincoln Street, Boston, Massachusetts 02111 (617) 423-3990; *The World in Figures.*

MARTINIQUE - EGG PRODUCTION AND CONSUMPTION - See MARTINIQUE - DAIRY PRODUCTS

MARTINIQUE - ELECTRICITY

Statistical Office of the United Nations, Publishing Service, New York, New York 10017 (800) 253-9646; *Statistical Yearbook.*

MARTINIQUE - EMPLOYMENT

International Labour Office, I.L.O. Publications, CH-1211, Geneva 22, Switzerland; *Yearbook of Labour Statistics.*

MARTINIQUE - ENERGY

G.K. Hall and Company, 70 Lincoln Street, Boston, Massachusetts 02111 (617) 423-3990; *The World in Figures.*

Food and Agricultural Organization of the United Nations (FAO), Via delle Terme di Caracalla, 00100 Rome, Italy (Telephone Number in U.S. (202) 653-2400); *The State of Food and Agriculture.*

Statistical Office of the United Nations, Publishing Service, New York, New York 10017 (800) 253-9646; *Energy Statistics Yearbook,* and *Statistical Yearbook.*

MARTINIQUE - EXPORTS

Food and Agricultural Organization of the United Nations (FAO), Via delle Terme di Caracalla, 00100 Rome, Italy (Telephone Number in U.S. (202) 653-2400); *The State of Food and Agriculture.*

G.K. Hall and Company, 70 Lincoln Street, Boston, Massachusetts 02111 (617) 423-3990; *The World in Figures.*

International Monetary Fund, 700 Nineteenth Street, NW, Washington, D.C. 20431 (202) 623-7000; *Direction of Trade Statistics*.

MARTINIQUE - EXTERNAL TRADE

Food and Agricultural Organization of the United Nations (FAO), Via delle Terme di Caracalla, 00100 Rome, Italy (Telephone Number in U.S. (202) 653-2400); *The State of Food and Agriculture*, and *Trade Yearbook*.

G.K. Hall and Company, 70 Lincoln Street, Boston, Massachusetts 02111 (617) 423-3990; *The World in Figures*.

Statistical Office of the United Nations, Publishing Service, New York, New York 10017 (800) 253-9646; *Statistical Yearbook*.

MARTINIQUE - FARM CROPS - See MARTINIQUE - CROPS

MARTINIQUE - FERTILIZER

Food and Agricultural Organization of the United Nations (FAO), Via delle Terme di Caracalla, 00100 Rome, Italy (Telephone Number in U.S. (202) 653-2400); *Fertilizer Yearbook*, and *The State of Food and Agriculture*.

Statistical Office of the United Nations, Publishing Service, New York, New York 10017 (800) 253-9646; *Statistical Yearbook*.

MARTINIQUE - FETAL MORTALITY

Statistical Office of the United Nations, Publishing Service, New York, New York 10017 (800) 253-9646; *Demographic Yearbook*.

World Health Organization, Office of Publications, Avenue Appia, CH-1211 Geneva 27, Switzerland (Telephone Number in U.S. (518) 436-9686); *World Health Statistics Annual*.

MARTINIQUE - FINANCE

G.K. Hall and Company, 70 Lincoln Street, Boston, Massachusetts 02111 (617) 423-3990; *The World in Figures*.

MARTINIQUE - FISHERIES

Food and Agricultural Organization of the United Nations (FAO), Via delle Terme di Caracalla, 00100 Rome, Italy (Telephone Number in U.S. (202) 653-2400); *The State of Food and Agriculture*, and *Yearbook of Fishery Statistics*.

Statistical Office of the United Nations, Publishing Service, New York, New York 10017 (800) 253-9646; *Statistical Yearbook*.

MARTINIQUE - FOOD

Food and Agricultural Organization of the United Nations (FAO), Via delle Terme di Caracalla, 00100 Rome, Italy (Telephone Number in U.S. (202) 653-2400); *Production Yearbook*, and *The State of Food and Agriculture*.

G.K. Hall and Company, 70 Lincoln Street, Boston, Massachusetts 02111 (617) 423-3990; *The World in Figures*.

MARTINIQUE - FOREIGN AID

G.K. Hall and Company, 70 Lincoln Street, Boston, Massachusetts 02111 (617) 423-3990; *The World in Figures*.

MARTINIQUE - FOREIGN TRADE

Food and Agricultural Organization of the United Nations (FAO), Via delle Terme di Caracalla, 00100 Rome, Italy (Telephone Number in U.S. (202) 653-2400); *The State of Food and Agriculture*.

G.K. Hall and Company, 70 Lincoln Street, Boston, Massachusetts 02111 (617) 423-3990; *The World in Figures*.

Statistical Office of the United Nations, Publishing Service, New York, New York 10017 (800) 253-9646; *International Trade Statistics Yearbook*, and *Statistical Yearbook*.

MARTINIQUE - FORESTRY AND FOREST PRODUCTS

Food and Agricultural Organization of the United Nations (FAO), Via delle Terme di Caracalla, 00100 Rome, Italy (Telephone Number in U.S. (202) 653-2400); *The State of Food and Agriculture*, and *Yearbook of Forest Products*.

G.K. Hall and Company, 70 Lincoln Street, Boston, Massachusetts 02111 (617) 423-3990; *The World in Figures*.

Statistical Office of the United Nations, Publishing Service, New York, New York 10017 (800) 253-9646; *Statistical Yearbook*.

United Nations Educational, Scientific and Cultural Organization (UNESCO), 7 Place de Fontenoy, F-75700 Paris, France (Telephone Number in U.S. (212) 963-5981); *Statistical Yearbook*.

MARTINIQUE - GENERAL MORTALITY

Statistical Office of the United Nations, Publishing Service, New York, New York 10017 (800) 253-9646; *Demographic Yearbook*.

World Health Organization, Office of Publications, Avenue Appia, CH-1211 Geneva 27, Switzerland (Telephone Number in U.S. (518) 436-9686); *World Health Statistics Annual*.

MARTINIQUE - GOVERNMENT

G.K. Hall and Company, 70 Lincoln Street, Boston, Massachusetts 02111 (617) 423-3990; *The World in Figures*.

MARTINIQUE - GRAIN PRODUCTION - See MARTINIQUE - CROPS

MARTINIQUE - GROSS DOMESTIC PRODUCT

G.K. Hall and Company, 70 Lincoln Street, Boston, Massachusetts 02111 (617) 423-3990; *The World in Figures*.

Statistical Office of the United Nations, Publishing Service, New York, New York 10017 (800) 253-9646; *Statistical Yearbook*.

MARTINIQUE - HEALTH

G.K. Hall and Company, 70 Lincoln Street, Boston, Massachusetts 02111 (617) 423-3990; *The World in Figures*.

Statistical Office of the United Nations, Publishing Service, New York, New York 10017 (800) 253-9646; *Statistical Yearbook*.

World Health Organization, Office of Publications, Avenue Appia, CH-1211 Geneva 27, Switzerland (Telephone Number in U.S. (518) 436-9686); *World Health Statistics Annual*.

MARTINIQUE - HIDE PRODUCTION

Food and Agricultural Organization of the United Nations (FAO), Via delle Terme di Caracalla, 00100 Rome, Italy (Telephone Number in U.S. (202) 653-2400); *Production Yearbook*.

MARTINIQUE - HIGHWAYS

G.K. Hall and Company, 70 Lincoln Street, Boston, Massachusetts 02111 (617) 423-3990; *The World in Figures*.

MARTINIQUE - HORSES - See MARTINIQUE - LIVESTOCK AND POULTRY

MARTINIQUE - HOURS OF WORK - See MARTINIQUE - EMPLOYMENT

MARTINIQUE - ILLITERATE POPULATION

G.K. Hall and Company, 70 Lincoln Street, Boston, Massachusetts 02111 (617) 423-3990; *The World in Figures*.

United Nations Educational, Scientific and Cultural Organization (UNESCO), 7 Place de Fontenoy, F-75700 Paris, France (Telephone Number in U.S. (212) 963-5981); *Statistical Yearbook*.

MARTINIQUE - IMPORTS

Food and Agricultural Organization of the United Nations (FAO), Via delle Terme di Caracalla, 00100 Rome, Italy (Telephone Number in U.S. (202) 653-2400); *The State of Food and Agriculture*.

G.K. Hall and Company, 70 Lincoln Street, Boston, Massachusetts 02111 (617) 423-3990; *The World in Figures*.

International Monetary Fund, 700 Nineteenth Street, NW, Washington, D.C. 20431 (202) 623-7000; *Direction of Trade Statistics*.

Statistical Office of the United Nations, Publishing Service, New York, New York 10017 (800) 253-9646; *Trade in Manufactures of Developing Countries*.

MARTINIQUE - INDUSTRY

G.K. Hall and Company, 70 Lincoln Street, Boston, Massachusetts 02111 (617) 423-3990; *The World in Figures*.

International Labour Office, I.L.O. Publications, CH-1211, Geneva 22, Switzerland; *Yearbook of Labour Statistics*.

MARTINIQUE - INFANT AND MATERNAL MORTALITY

Statistical Office of the United Nations, Publishing Service, New York, New York 10017 (800) 253-9646; *Demographic Yearbook*, and *Statistical Yearbook*.

World Health Organization, Office of Publications, Avenue Appia, CH-1211 Geneva 27, Switzerland (Telephone Number in U.S. (518) 436-9686); *World Health Statistics Annual*.

MARTINIQUE - LABOR FORCE

Food and Agricultural Organization of the United Nations (FAO), Via delle Terme di Caracalla, 00100 Rome, Italy (Telephone Number in U.S. (202) 653-2400); *The State of Food and Agriculture*.

G.K. Hall and Company, 70 Lincoln Street, Boston, Massachusetts 02111 (617) 423-3990; *The World in Figures*.

MARTINIQUE - LABOR PRODUCTIVITY

International Labour Office, I.L.O. Publications, CH-1211, Geneva 22, Switzerland; *Yearbook of Labour Statistics*.

MARTINIQUE - LAND USE

Food and Agricultural Organization of the United Nations (FAO), Via delle Terme di Caracalla, 00100 Rome, Italy (Telephone Number in U.S. (202) 653-2400); *Production Yearbook*.

G.K. Hall and Company, 70 Lincoln Street, Boston, Massachusetts 02111 (617) 423-3990; *The World in Figures*.

MARTINIQUE - LIVESTOCK AND POULTRY

Food and Agricultural Organization of the United Nations (FAO), Via delle Terme di Caracalla, 00100 Rome, Italy (Telephone Number in U.S. (202) 653-2400); *Production Yearbook*, and *The State of Food and Agriculture*.

G.K. Hall and Company, 70 Lincoln Street, Boston, Massachusetts 02111 (617) 423-3990; *The World in Figures*.

Statistical Office of the United Nations, Publishing Service, New York, New York 10017 (800) 253-9646; *Statistical Yearbook*.

MARTINIQUE - LIVING LEVELS

G.K. Hall and Company, 70 Lincoln Street, Boston, Massachusetts 02111 (617) 423-3990; *The World in Figures*.

MARTINIQUE - MANUFACTURING

G.K. Hall and Company, 70 Lincoln Street, Boston, Massachusetts 02111 (617) 423-3990; *The World in Figures*.

MARTINIQUE - MARRIAGE RATES

Statistical Office of the United Nations, Publishing Service, New York, New York 10017 (800) 253-9646; *Demographic Yearbook*, and *Statistical Yearbook*.

MARTINIQUE - MEAT PRODUCTION - See MARTINIQUE - LIVESTOCK AND POULTRY

MARTINIQUE - MERCHANT SHIPPING

G.K. Hall and Company, 70 Lincoln Street, Boston, Massachusetts 02111 (617) 423-3990; *The World in Figures*.

Statistical Office of the United Nations, Publishing Service, New York, New York 10017 (800) 253-9646; *Statistical Yearbook*.

MARTINIQUE - MILITARY

G.K. Hall and Company, 70 Lincoln Street, Boston, Massachusetts 02111 (617) 423-3990; *The World in Figures*.

MARTINIQUE - MINING AND MINERAL PRODUCTS

G.K. Hall and Company, 70 Lincoln Street, Boston, Massachusetts 02111 (617) 423-3990; *The World in Figures*.

MARTINIQUE - MONEY SUPPLY

G.K. Hall and Company, 70 Lincoln Street, Boston, Massachusetts 02111 (617) 423-3990; *The World in Figures*.

MARTINIQUE - MOTOR VEHICLES IN USE

G.K. Hall and Company, 70 Lincoln Street, Boston, Massachusetts 02111 (617) 423-3990; *The World in Figures*.

Statistical Office of the United Nations, Publishing Service, New York, New York 10017 (800) 253-9646; *Statistical Yearbook*.

MARTINIQUE - NATALITY - See MARTINIQUE - BIRTH RATES

MARTINIQUE - NATIONAL ACCOUNTS

Statistical Office of the United Nations, Publishing Service, New York, New York 10017 (800) 253-9646; *Statistical Yearbook*, and *National Account Statistics*.

MARTINIQUE - NATIONAL INCOME

G.K. Hall and Company, 70 Lincoln Street, Boston, Massachusetts 02111 (617) 423-3990; *The World in Figures*.

Statistical Office of the United Nations, Publishing Service, New York, New York 10017 (800) 253-9646; *Statistical Yearbook*.

MARTINIQUE - NEWSPAPER PRODUCTION - See MARTINIQUE - FORESTRY AND FOREST PRODUCTS

MARTINIQUE - NEWSPRINT - See MARTINIQUE - FORESTRY AND FOREST PRODUCTS

MARTINIQUE - OCCUPATIONS - See MARTINIQUE - LABOR FORCE

MARTINIQUE - PAPER CONSUMPTION - See MARTINIQUE - FORESTRY AND FOREST PRODUCTS

MARTINIQUE - PERIODICALS

United Nations Educational, Scientific and Cultural Organization (UNESCO), 7 Place de Fontenoy, F-75700 Paris, France (Telephone Number in U.S. (212) 963-5981); *Statistical Yearbook*.

MARTINIQUE - PESTICIDE USE

Food and Agricultural Organization of the United Nations (FAO), Via delle Terme di Caracalla, 00100 Rome, Italy (Telephone Number in U.S. (202) 653-2400); *The State of Food and Agriculture*.

MARTINIQUE - PETROLEUM INDUSTRY

Food and Agricultural Organization of the United Nations (FAO), Via delle Terme di Caracalla, 00100 Rome, Italy (Telephone Number in U.S. (202) 653-2400); *The State of Food and Agriculture*.

G.K. Hall and Company, 70 Lincoln Street, Boston, Massachusetts 02111 (617) 423-3990; *The World in Figures*.

Statistical Office of the United Nations, Publishing Service, New York, New York 10017 (800) 253-9646; *Statistical Yearbook*.

MARTINIQUE - PIGS - SEE MARTINIQUE - LIVESTOCK AND POULTRY

MARTINIQUE - POPULATION

Food and Agricultural Organization of the United Nations (FAO), Via delle Terme di Caracalla, 00100 Rome, Italy (Telephone Number in U.S. (202) 653-2400); *Production Yearbook*.

G.K. Hall and Company, 70 Lincoln Street, Boston, Massachusetts 02111 (617) 423-3990; *The World in Figures*.

International Labour Office, I.L.O. Publications, CH-1211, Geneva 22, Switzerland; *Yearbook of Labour Statistics*.

Statistical Office of the United Nations, Publishing Service, New York, New York 10017 (800) 253-9646; *Demographic Yearbook*, and *Statistical Yearbook*.

World Health Organization, Office of Publications, Avenue Appia, CH-1211 Geneva 27, Switzerland (Telephone Number in U.S. (518) 436-9686); *World Health Statistics Annual*.

MARTINIQUE - PRICES

Food and Agricultural Organization of the United Nations (FAO), Via delle Terme di Caracalla, 00100 Rome, Italy (Telephone Number in U.S. (202) 653-2400); *Production Yearbook*, and *The State of Food and Agriculture*.

G.K. Hall and Company, 70 Lincoln Street, Boston, Massachusetts 02111 (617) 423-3990; *The World in Figures*.

International Labour Office, I.L.O. Publications, CH-1211, Geneva 22, Switzerland; *Yearbook of Labour Statistics*.

MARTINIQUE - PRINTING AND WRITING PAPER - See MARTINIQUE FORESTRY AND FOREST PRODUCTS

MARTINIQUE - PRODUCTION

G.K. Hall and Company, 70 Lincoln Street, Boston, Massachusetts 02111 (617) 423-3990; *The World in Figures*.

MARTINIQUE - RAILWAY USE

G.K. Hall and Company, 70 Lincoln Street, Boston, Massachusetts 02111 (617) 423-3990; *The World in Figures*.

MARTINIQUE - RENT PRICES

International Labour Office, I.L.O. Publications, CH-1211, Geneva 22, Switzerland; *Yearbook of Labour Statistics*.

MARTINIQUE - RETAIL TRADE

G.K. Hall and Company, 70 Lincoln Street, Boston, Massachusetts 02111 (617) 423-3990; *The World in Figures*.

MARTINIQUE - ROOT AND TUBER PRODUCTION - See MARTINIQUE - CROPS

MARTINIQUE - ROUNDWOOD PRODUCTION - See MARTINIQUE - FORESTRY AND FOREST PRODUCTS

MARTINIQUE - SALT PRODUCTION - See MARTINIQUE - MINING AND MINERAL PRODUCTS

MARTINIQUE - SAWNWOOD PRODUCTION - See MARTINIQUE - FORESTRY AND FOREST PRODUCTS

MARTINIQUE - SHEEP - See MARTINIQUE - LIVESTOCK AND POULTRY

MARTINIQUE - SOCIAL DATA

G.K. Hall and Company, 70 Lincoln Street, Boston, Massachusetts 02111 (617) 423-3990; *The World in Figures*.

MARTINIQUE - STOCKS - COMMODITY - MARKET PRICE - INDEX

Food and Agricultural Organization of the United Nations (FAO), Via delle Terme di Caracalla, 00100 Rome, Italy (Telephone Number in U.S. (202) 653-2400); *The State of Food and Agriculture*.

MARTINIQUE - SUGAR PRODUCTION AND CONSUMPTION - See MARTINIQUE - CROPS

MARTINIQUE - TAXATION

G.K. Hall and Company, 70 Lincoln Street, Boston, Massachusetts 02111 (617) 423-3990; *The World in Figures*.

MARTINIQUE - TELEPHONES IN USE

American Telephone and Telegraph Company, 26 Parsippany Road, Whippany, New Jersey 07981 (800) 338-4038; *The World's Telephones*.

G.K. Hall and Company, 70 Lincoln Street, Boston, Massachusetts 02111 (617) 423-3990; *The World in Figures*.

Statistical Office of the United Nations, Publishing Service, New York, New York 10017 (800) 253-9646; *Statistical Yearbook*.

MARTINIQUE - TEXTILE INDUSTRY

G.K. Hall and Company, 70 Lincoln Street, Boston, Massachusetts 02111 (617) 423-3990; *The World in Figures*.

MARTINIQUE - TOURISM

G.K. Hall and Company, 70 Lincoln Street, Boston, Massachusetts 02111 (617) 423-3990; *The World in Figures*.

World Tourism Organization, Calle Capitan Haya 42, E-28020 Madrid, Spain; *Yearbook of Tourism Statistics*.

MARTINIQUE - TRACTORS IN USE

Statistical Office of the United Nations, Publishing Service, New York, New York 10017 (800) 253-9646; *Statistical Yearbook*.

MARTINIQUE - TRADE - See MARTINIQUE - FOREIGN TRADE

MARTINIQUE - TRANSPORTATION AND COMMUNICATIONS

G.K. Hall and Company, 70 Lincoln Street, Boston, Massachusetts 02111 (617) 423-3990; *The World in Figures*.

MARTINIQUE - TURKEYS - See MARTINIQUE - LIVESTOCK AND POULTRY

MARTINIQUE - UNEMPLOYMENT

International Labour Office, I.L.O. Publications, CH-1211, Geneva 22, Switzerland; *Yearbook of Labour Statistics*.

MARTINIQUE - VITAL STATISTICS

G.K. Hall and Company, 70 Lincoln Street, Boston, Massachusetts 02111 (617) 423-3990; *The World in Figures*.

Statistical Office of the United Nations, Publishing Service, New York, New York 10017 (800) 253-9646; *Statistical Yearbook*.

World Health Organization, Office of Publications, Avenue Appia, CH-1211 Geneva 27, Switzerland (Telephone Number in U.S. (518) 436-9686); *World Health Statistics Annual*.

MARTINIQUE - WAGES

G.K. Hall and Company, 70 Lincoln Street, Boston, Massachusetts 02111 (617) 423-3990; *The World in Figures*.

International Labour Office, I.L.O. Publications, CH-1211, Geneva 22, Switzerland; *Yearbook of Labour Statistics*.

MARTINIQUE - WEATHER

G.K. Hall and Company, 70 Lincoln Street, Boston, Massachusetts 02111 (617) 423-3990; *The World in Figures*.

MARYLAND - See also STATE DATA (FOR INDIVIDUAL STATES)

Maryland - Primary Statistics Source

Department of Economic and Employment Development, 217 East Redwood Street, Baltimore, Maryland 21202 (410) 333-6953; *Maryland Statistical Abstract*.

Maryland - State Data Centers

Maryland Department of State Planning, 301 West Preston Street, Baltimore, Maryland 21201, Ms. Jane Traynham/Mr. Robert Dadd (410) 225-4450.

Computer Science Center, University of Maryland, College Park, Maryland 20742, Mr. John McNary (301) 405-3037.

State Library Resource Center, Pratt Library, 400 Cathedral Street, Baltimore, Maryland 21201, Mr. Jeff Korman (410) 396-1789.

Small Business Development Center, 217 East Redwood Street, 9th Floor, Baltimore, Maryland 21202, Mr. Michael E. Long (410) 333-6996.

MASSACHUSETTS - See also STATE DATA (FOR INDIVIDUAL STATES)

Massachusetts - Primary Statistics Source

Massachusetts Institute for Social and Economic Research, 128 Thompson Hall, University of Massachusetts, Amherst, Massachusetts 01003 (413) 545-3460; *Projected Total Population and Age Distribution for 2000 and 2005: Massachusetts Cities and Towns*.

Massachusetts - State Data Centers

Massachusetts Institute for Social and Economic Research, University of Massachusetts, 128 Thompson Hall, Amherst, Massachusetts 01003, Dr. Stephen Coelen, Director (413) 545-3460.

Massachusetts Institute for Social and Economic Research, Box 219, 100 Cambridge Street, Boston, Massachusetts 02133, Mr. William Murray (617) 727-4537.

Cape Cod Community Library, Library/Learning Resource Center, Route 132, West Barnstable, Massachusetts 02668, Ms. Jean Marie Fraser (508) 362-8638.

University of Massachusetts, Documents Library, 100 Morrissey Boulevard, Boston, Massachusetts 02125, Ms. Frances Schlisinger (617) 287-5935.

MATERNAL AND CHILD HEALTH SERVICES - EXPENDITURES FOR

U.S. Department of Health and Human Services, Health Care Financing Administration, 200 Independence Avenue,, SW, Washington, D.C. 20201; *Health Care Financing Review*.

U.S. Department of Health and Human Services, Social Security Administration, 6401 Security Boulevard, Baltimore, Maryland 21235; *Social Security Bulletin*.

MATHEMATICS - DEGREES CONFERRED

National Science Foundation, 4201 Wilson Boulevard, Arlington, Virginia 22230 (703) 366-1234; *Survey of Earned Doctorates, Selected Data on Science and Engineering Doctorate Awards* and *Characteristics of Recent Science and Engineering Graduates*.

U.S. Department of Education, 400 Maryland Avenue, SW, Washington, D.C. 20202 (202) 708-5366; *Digest of Education Statistics*.

MATHEMATICS - EMPLOYMENT

U.S. Department of Labor, Bureau of Labor Statistics, Two Massachusetts Avenue, NE, Washington, D.C. 20212 (202) 606-7828; *Monthly Labor Review*.

MATHEMATICS - SALARY OFFERS

College Placement Council, 62 Highland Avenue, Bethlehem, Pennsylvania 18017; *Salary Survey: A Study of Beginning Offers*.

Northwestern University, 633 Clark Street, Evanston, Illinois 60201; *The Northwestern Endicott-Lindquist Report*.

Mauritania - National Statistical Office

Direction de la Statistique et des Etudes Economiques (Department of Statistics and Economic Research), BP 240, Nouakchott, Mauritania.

Mauritania - Primary Statistics Sources

Direction de la Statistique, BP 240, Nouakchott, Mauritania; *Annuaire Statistique* (Statistical Yearbook); and *Bulletin Mensuel Statistique* (Monthly bulletin of statistics).

MAURITANIA - AGRICULTURE

Euromonitor Publications Limited, 87-88 Turnmill Street, London EC1M 5QU, England; *International Marketing Data and Statistics*.

Facts on File, 460 Park Avenue South, New York, New York 10016 (800) 443-8323; *The New Book of World Rankings*.

Food and Agricultural Organization of the United Nations (FAO), Via delle Terme di Caracalla, 00100 Rome, Italy (Telephone Number in U.S. (202) 653-2400); *Production Yearbook, The State of Food and Agriculture,* and *Trade Yearbook*.

G.K. Hall and Company, 70 Lincoln Street, Boston, Massachusetts 02111 (617) 423-3990; *The World in Figures*.

Statistical Office of the United Nations, Publishing Service, New York, New York 10017 (800) 253-9646; *Survey of Economic and Social Conditions in Africa*.

United Nations Economic Commission for Africa, Africa Hall, Post Office Box 3001, Addis Ababa, Ethiopia (Telephone Number in U.S. (800) 253-9646); *African Statistical Yearbook*.

The World Bank, 1818 H Street, NW, Washington, D.C. 20433 (202) 477-1234; *World Tables*.

MAURITANIA - AIRLINE SERVICE

Facts on File, 460 Park Avenue South, New York, New York 10016 (800) 443-8323; *The New Book of World Rankings*.

G.K. Hall and Company, 70 Lincoln Street, Boston, Massachusetts 02111 (617) 423-3990; *The World in Figures*.

International Civil Aviation Organization, 1000 Sherbrooke Street West, Suite 400, Montreal, Quebec H3A 2R2, Canada (514) 285-8219; *Civil Aviation Statistics of the World*.

Statistical Office of the United Nations, Publishing Service, New York, New York 10017 (800) 253-9646; *Statistical Yearbook*.

Times Books, 201 East 50th Street, New York, New York 10022 (212) 751-2600; *The Economist Book of Vital World Statistics*.

United Nations Economic Commission for Africa, Africa Hall, Post Office Box 3001, Addis Ababa, Ethiopia (Telephone Number in U.S. (800) 253-9646); *African Statistical Yearbook*.

MAURITANIA - ALUMINUM PRODUCTION AND CONSUMPTION - See MAURITANIA - MINING AND MINERAL PRODUCTS

MAURITANIA - ANIMAL HEALTH

Food and Agricultural Organization of the United Nations (FAO), Via delle Terme di Caracalla, 00100 Rome, Italy (Telephone Number in U.S. (202) 653-2400); *Animal Health Yearbook*.

MAURITANIA - AREA AND DENSITY OF POPULATION

African Development Bank, 01 BP 1387, Abidjan 01, Cote d'Ivoire; *Selected Statistics on Regional Member Countries*.

Euromonitor Publications Limited, 87-88 Turnmill Street, London EC1M 5QU, England; *International Marketing Data and Statistics*.

Facts on File, 460 Park Avenue South, New York, New York 10016 (800) 443-8323; *The New Book of World Rankings*.

Food and Agricultural Organization of the United Nations (FAO), Via delle Terme di Caracalla, 00100 Rome, Italy (Telephone Number in U.S. (202) 653-2400); *The State of Food and Agriculture*.

G.K. Hall and Company, 70 Lincoln Street, Boston, Massachusetts 02111 (617) 423-3990; *The World in Figures*.

Statistical Office of the United National, Publishing Service, New York, New York 10017 (800) 253-9646; *Survey of Economic and Social Conditions in Africa*.

Times Books, 201 East 50th Street, New York, New York 10022 (212) 751-2600; *The Economist Book of Vital World Statistics*.

MAURITANIA - ARMS EXPORTS AND IMPORTS

U.S. Arms Control and Disarmament Agency, 320 Twenty-first Street, NW, Washington, D.C. 20451 (202) 647-8677; *World Military Expenditures and Arms Transfers*.

MAURITANIA - BALANCE OF PAYMENTS

African Development Bank, 01 BP 1387, Abidjan 01, Cote d'Ivoire; *Selected Statistics on Regional Member Countries.*

The Economist Intelligence Unit, 111 West 57th Street, New York, New York 10019 (800) 938-4685; *The World Market Atlas.*

G.K. Hall and Company, 70 Lincoln Street, Boston, Massachusetts 02111 (617) 423-3990; *The World in Figures.*

International Monetary Fund, 700 Nineteenth Street, NW, Washington, D.C. 20431 (202) 623-7000; *Balance of Payments Yearbook.*

Times Books, 201 East 50th Street, New York, New York 10022 (212) 751-2600; *The Economist Book of Vital World Statistics.*

United Nations Economic Commission for Africa, Africa Hall, Post Office Box 3001, Addis Ababa, Ethiopia (Telephone Number in U.S. (800) 253-9646); *African Statistical Yearbook.*

The World Bank, 1818 H Street, NW, Washington, D.C. 20433 (202) 477-1234; *World Tables.*

MAURITANIA - BANKING

Facts on File, 460 Park Avenue South, New York, New York 10016 (800) 443-8323; *The New Book of World Rankings.*

G.K. Hall and Company, 70 Lincoln Street, Boston, Massachusetts 02111 (617) 423-3990; *The World in Figures.*

International Monetary Fund, 700 Nineteenth Street, NW, Washington, D.C. 20431 (202) 623-7000; *International Financial Statistics.*

Statistical Office of the United Nations, Publishing Service, New York, New York 10017 (800) 253-9646; *Statistical Yearbook.*

United Nations Economic Commission for Africa, Africa Hall, Post Office Box 3001, Addis Ababa, Ethiopia (Telephone Number in U.S. (800) 253-9646); *African Statistical Yearbook.*

MAURITANIA - BARLEY PRODUCTION - See MAURITANIA - CROPS

MAURITANIA - BEER PRODUCTION

Facts on File, 460 Park Avenue South, New York, New York 10016 (800) 443-8323; *The New Book of World Rankings.*

MAURITANIA - BIRTH RATES

Facts on File, 460 Park Avenue South, New York, New York 10016 (800) 443-8323; *The New Book of World Rankings.*

Statistical Office of the United Nations, Publishing Service, New York, New York 10017 (800) 253-9646; *Demographic Yearbook, Statistical Yearbook,* and *Survey of Economic and Social Conditions in Africa.*

Times Books, 201 East 50th Street, New York, New York 10022 (212) 751-2600; *The Economist Book of Vital World Statistics.*

The World Bank, 1818 H Street, NW, Washington, D.C. 20433 (202) 477-1234; *World Tables.*

MAURITANIA - BONDS

G.K. Hall and Company, 70 Lincoln Street, Boston, Massachusetts 02111 (617) 423-3990; *The World in Figures.*

MAURITANIA - BOOK PRODUCTION

G.K. Hall and Company, 70 Lincoln Street, Boston, Massachusetts 02111 (617) 423-3990; *The World in Figures.*

United Nations Educational, Scientific and Cultural Organization (UNESCO), 7 Place de Fontenoy, F-75700 Paris, France (Telephone Number in U.S. (212) 963-5981); *Statistical Yearbook.*

MAURITANIA - BROADCASTING

Billboard Limited, Post Office Box 9027, 1006 AA Amsterdam, The Netherlands (Telephone Number in U.S. (212) 764-7300); *World Radio TV Handbook.*

Facts on File, 460 Park Avenue South, New York, New York 10016 (800) 443-8323; *The New Book of World Rankings.*

G.K. Hall and Company, 70 Lincoln Street, Boston, Massachusetts 02111 (617) 423-3990; *The World in Figures.*

Times Books, 201 East 50th Street, New York, New York 10022 (212) 751-2600; *The Economist Book of Vital World Statistics.*

MAURITANIA - BUSINESS

G.K. Hall and Company, 70 Lincoln Street, Boston, Massachusetts 02111 (617) 423-3990; *The World in Figures.*

MAURITANIA - BUSINESS AND PROFESSIONAL LICENSES

International Monetary Fund, 700 Nineteenth Street, NW, Washington, D.C. 20431 (202) 623-7000; *Government Finance Statistics Yearbook.*

MAURITANIA - CALORIE SUPPLY

African Development Bank, 01 BP 1387, Abidjan 01, Cote d'Ivoire; *Selected Statistics on Regional Member Countries.*

Food and Agricultural Organization of the United Nations (FAO), Via delle Terme di Caracalla, 00100 Rome, Italy (Telephone Number in U.S. (202) 653-2400); *The State of Food and Agriculture.*

MAURITANIA - CAPITAL REVENUE

International Monetary Fund, 700 Nineteenth Street, NW, Washington, D.C. 20431 (202) 623-7000; *Government Finance Statistics Yearbook.*

MAURITANIA - CATTLE - See MAURITANIA - LIVESTOCK AND POULTRY

MAURITANIA - CEMENT PRODUCTION - See MAURITANIA - MINING AND MINERAL PRODUCTS

MAURITANIA - CHEESE PRODUCTION AND CONSUMPTION - See MAURITANIA - DAIRY PRODUCTS

MAURITANIA - CHEMICAL (ORGANIC) PRODUCTION - See MAURITANIA - MINING AND MINERAL PRODUCTS

MAURITANIA - CHICKENS - See MAURITANIA - LIVESTOCK AND POULTRY

MAURITANIA - CIGARETTE PRODUCTION - See MAURITANIA - TOBACCO PRODUCTION

MAURITANIA - CLASS STRUCTURE

G.K. Hall and Company, 70 Lincoln Street, Boston, Massachusetts 02111 (617) 423-3990; *The World in Figures.*

MAURITANIA - CLIMATE

Facts on File, 460 Park Avenue South, New York, New York 10016 (800) 443-8323; *The New Book of World Rankings.*

G.K. Hall and Company, 70 Lincoln Street, Boston, Massachusetts 02111 (617) 423-3990; *The World in Figures.*

MAURITANIA - COAL PRODUCTION - See MAURITANIA - MINING AND MINERAL PRODUCTS

MAURITANIA - COFFEE PRODUCTION AND CONSUMPTION - See MAURITANIA - CROPS

MAURITANIA - COMMUNICATIONS

G.K. Hall and Company, 70 Lincoln Street, Boston, Massachusetts 02111 (617) 423-3990; *The World in Figures.*

United Nations Economic Commission for Africa, Africa Hall, Post Office Box 3001, Addis Ababa, Ethiopia (Telephone Number in U.S. (800) 253-9646); *African Statistical Yearbook.*

MAURITANIA - CONSTRUCTION INDUSTRY

Facts on File, 460 Park Avenue South, New York, New York 10016 (800) 443-8323; *The New Book of World Rankings.*

United Nations Economic Commission for Africa, Africa Hall, Post Office Box 3001, Addis Ababa, Ethiopia (Telephone Number in U.S. (800) 253-9646); *African Statistical Yearbook.*

MAURITANIA - CONSUMER PRICE INDEX

African Development Bank, 01 BP 1387, Abidjan 01, Cote d'Ivoire; *Selected Statistics on Regional Member Countries.*

G.K. Hall and Company, 70 Lincoln Street, Boston, Massachusetts 02111 (617) 423-3990; *The World in Figures.*

Statistical Office of the United Nations, Publishing Service, New York, New York 10017 (800) 253-9646; *Statistical Yearbook,* and *Survey of Economic and Social Conditions in Africa.*

Times Books, 201 East 50th Street, New York, New York 10022 (212) 751-2600; *The Economist Book of Vital World Statistics.*

United Nations Economic Commission for Africa, Africa Hall, Post Office Box 3001, Addis Ababa, Ethiopia (Telephone Number in U.S. (800) 253-9646); *African Statistical Yearbook.*

MAURITANIA - CONSUMER PRICES

International Labour Office, I.L.O. Publications, CH-1211, Geneva 22, Switzerland; *Yearbook of Labour Statistics.*

International Monetary Fund, 700 Nineteenth Street, NW, Washington, D.C. 20431 (202) 623-7000; *International Financial Statistics.*

MAURITANIA - CONSUMPTION

African Development Bank, 01 BP 1387, Abidjan 01, Cote d'Ivoire; *Selected Statistics on Regional Member Countries.*

G.K. Hall and Company, 70 Lincoln Street, Boston, Massachusetts 02111 (617) 423-3990; *The World in Figures.*

Statistical Office of the United Nations, Publishing Service, New York, New York 10017 (800) 253-9646; *Survey of Economic and Social Conditions in Africa.*

MAURITANIA - COPPER AND COPPER ORE PRODUCTION AND CONSUMPTION - See MAURITANIA - MINING AND MINERAL PRODUCTS

MAURITANIA - CORN PRODUCTION - See MAURITANIA - CROPS

MAURITANIA - CORPORATE TAXES - See MAURITANIA - TAXATION

MAURITANIA - COTTON - See MAURITANIA - CROPS

MAURITANIA - CRIME

Yale University Press, Yale Station, New Haven, Connecticut 06520 (203) 432-0940; *Violence and Crime in Cross-National Perspective.*

MAURITANIA - CROPS

Facts on File, 460 Park Avenue South, New York, New York 10016 (800) 443-8323; *The New Book of World Rankings.*

Food and Agricultural Organization of the United Nations (FAO), Via delle Terme di Caracalla, 00100 Rome, Italy (Telephone Number in U.S. (202) 653-2400); *Production Yearbook,* and *The State of Food and Agriculture.*

G.K. Hall and Company, 70 Lincoln Street, Boston, Massachusetts 02111 (617) 423-3990; *The World in Figures.*

Statistical Office of the United Nations, Publishing Service, New York, New York 10017 (800) 253-9646; *Statistical Yearbook.*

United Nations Economic Commission for Africa, Africa Hall, Post Office Box 3001, Addis Ababa, Ethiopia (Telephone Number in U.S. (800) 253-9646); *African Statistical Yearbook.*

MAURITANIA - CUSTOMS DUTIES

G.K. Hall and Company, 70 Lincoln Street, Boston, Massachusetts 02111 (617) 423-3990; *The World in Figures.*

MAURITANIA - DAIRY PRODUCTS

Facts on File, 460 Park Avenue South, New York, New York 10016 (800) 443-8323; *The New Book of World Rankings.*

Food and Agricultural Organization of the United Nations (FAO), Via delle Terme di Caracalla, 00100 Rome, Italy (Telephone Number in U.S. (202) 653-2400); *Production Yearbook,* and *The State of Food and Agriculture.*

Statistical Office of the United Nations, Publishing Service, New York, New York 10017 (800) 253-9646; *Statistical Yearbook.*

MAURITANIA - DEATH RATES

G.K. Hall and Company, 70 Lincoln Street, Boston, Massachusetts 02111 (617) 423-3990; *The World in Figures.*

Statistical Office of the United Nations, Publishing Service, New York, New York 10017 (800) 253-9646; *Statistical Yearbook*, and *Survey of Economic and Social Conditions in Africa*.

Times Books, 201 East 50th Street, New York, New York 10022 (212) 751-2600; *The Economist Book of Vital World Statistics*.

MAURITANIA - DEFENSE EXPENDITURES

G.K. Hall and Company, 70 Lincoln Street, Boston, Massachusetts 02111 (617) 423-3990; *The World in Figures*.

International Monetary Fund, 700 Nineteenth Street, NW, Washington, D.C. 20431 (202) 623-7000; *Government Finance Statistics Yearbook*.

U.S. Arms Control and Disarmament Agency, 320 Twenty-first Street, NW, Washington, D.C. 20451 (202) 647-8677; *World Military Expenditures and Arms Transfers*.

MAURITANIA - DEMOGRAPHY

Facts on File, 460 Park Avenue South, New York, New York 10016 (800) 443-8323; *The New Book of World Rankings*.

G.K. Hall and Company, 70 Lincoln Street, Boston, Massachusetts 02111 (617) 423-3990; *The World in Figures*.

Statistical Office of the United Nations, Publishing Service, New York, New York 10017 (800) 253-9646; *Survey of Economic and Social Conditions in Africa*.

MAURITANIA - DEVELOPMENT ASSISTANCE

G.K. Hall and Company, 70 Lincoln Street, Boston, Massachusetts 02111 (617) 423-3990; *The World in Figures*.

Statistical Office of the United Nations, Publishing Service, New York, New York 10017 (800) 253-9646; *Statistical Yearbook*.

MAURITANIA - DIAMOND PRODUCTION - See MAURITANIA - MINING AND MINERAL PRODUCTS

MAURITANIA - DISCOUNT RATES

Statistical Office of the United Nations, Publishing Service, New York, New York 10017 (800) 253-9646; *Statistical Yearbook*.

MAURITANIA - DISEASE

G.K. Hall and Company, 70 Lincoln Street, Boston, Massachusetts 02111 (617) 423-3990; *The World in Figures*.

MAURITANIA - DIVORCE

Facts on File, 460 Park Avenue South, New York, New York 10016 (800) 443-8323; *The New Book of World Rankings*.

Statistical Office of the United Nations, Publishing Service, New York, New York 10017 (800) 253-9646; *Demographic Yearbook*.

MAURITANIA - DOMESTIC PRODUCT

G.K. Hall and Company, 70 Lincoln Street, Boston, Massachusetts 02111 (617) 423-3990; *The World in Figures*.

MAURITANIA - ECONOMY

African Development Bank, 01 BP 1387, Abidjan 01, Cote d'Ivoire; *Selected Statistics on Regional Member Countries*.

Euromonitor Publications Limited, 87-88 Turnmill Street, London EC1M 5QU, England; *International Marketing Data and Statistics*.

Facts on File, 460 Park Avenue South, New York, New York 10016 (800) 443-8323; *The New Book of World Rankings*.

G.K. Hall and Company, 70 Lincoln Street, Boston, Massachusetts 02111 (617) 423-3990; *The World in Figures*.

Statistical Office of the United Nations, Publishing Service, New York, New York 10017 (800) 253-9646; *Foreign Trade Statistics for Africa*.

MAURITANIA - EDUCATION

African Development Bank, 01 BP 1387, Abidjan 01, Cote d'Ivoire; *Selected Statistics on Regional Member Countries*.

The Economist Intelligence Unit, 111 West 57th Street, New York, New York 10019 (800) 938-4685; *The World Market Atlas*.

Facts on File, 460 Park Avenue South, New York, New York 10016 (800) 443-8323; *The New Book of World Rankings*.

G.K. Hall and Company, 70 Lincoln Street, Boston, Massachusetts 02111 (617) 423-3990; *The World in Figures*.

International Monetary Fund, 700 Nineteenth Street, NW, Washington, D.C. 20431 (202) 623-7000; *Government Finance Statistics Yearbook*.

Statistical Office of the United Nations, Publishing Service, New York, New York 10017 (800) 253-9646; *Survey of Economic and Social Conditions in Africa*.

Times Books, 201 East 50th Street, New York, New York 10022 (212) 751-2600; *The Economist Book of Vital World Statistics*.

United Nations Economic Commission for Africa, Africa Hall, Post Office Box 3001, Addis Ababa, Ethiopia (Telephone Number in U.S. (800) 253-9646); *African Statistical Yearbook*.

United Nations Educational, Scientific and Cultural Organization (UNESCO), 7 Place de Fontenoy, F-75700 Paris, France (Telephone Number in U.S. (212) 963-5981); *Statistical Yearbook*.

The World Bank, 1818 H Street, NW, Washington, D.C. 20433 (202) 477-1234; *World Tables*.

MAURITANIA - EGG PRODUCTION AND CONSUMPTION - See MAURITANIA - DAIRY PRODUCTS

MAURITANIA - ELECTRICITY

Facts on File, 460 Park Avenue South, New York, New York 10016 (800) 443-8323; *The New Book of World Rankings*.

Statistical Office of the United Nations, Publishing Service, New York, New York 10017 (800) 253-9646; *Statistical Yearbook*, and *Survey of Economic and Social Conditions in Africa*.

Times Books, 201 East 50th Street, New York, New York 10022 (212) 751-2600; *The Economist Book of Vital World Statistics*.

United Nations Economic Commission for Africa, Africa Hall, Post Office Box 3001, Addis Ababa, Ethiopia (Telephone Number in U.S. (800) 253-9646); *African Statistical Yearbook.*

MAURITANIA - EMPLOYMENT

Euromonitor Publications Limited, 87-88 Turnmill Street, London EC1M 5QU, England; *International Marketing Data and Statistics.*

Facts on File, 460 Park Avenue South, New York, New York 10016 (800) 443-8323; *The New Book of World Rankings.*

International Labour Office, I.L.O. Publications, CH-1211, Geneva 22, Switzerland; *Yearbook of Labour Statistics.*

Statistical Office of the United Nations, Publishing Service, New York, New York 10017 (800) 253-9646; *Survey of Economic and Social Conditions in Africa.*

United Nations Economic Commission for Africa, Africa Hall, Post Office Box 3001, Addis Ababa, Ethiopia (Telephone Number in U.S. (800) 253-9646); *African Statistical Yearbook.*

MAURITANIA - ENERGY

Facts on File, 460 Park Avenue South, New York, New York 10016 (800) 443-8323; *The New Book of World Rankings.*

Food and Agricultural Organization of the United Nations (FAO), Via delle Terme di Caracalla, 00100 Rome, Italy (Telephone Number in U.S. (202) 653-2400); *The State of Food and Agriculture.*

G.K. Hall and Company, 70 Lincoln Street, Boston, Massachusetts 02111 (617) 423-3990; *The World in Figures.*

Statistical Office of the United Nations, Publishing Service, New York, New York 10017 (800) 253-9646; *Energy Statistics Yearbook,* and *Statistical Yearbook.*

Times Books, 201 East 50th Street, New York, New York 10022 (212) 751-2600; *The Economist Book of Vital World Statistics.*

Statistical Office of the United Nations, Publishing Service, New York, New York 10017 (800) 253-9646; *World Energy Supplies.*

United Nations Economic Commission for Africa, Africa Hall, Post Office Box 3001, Addis Ababa, Ethiopia (Telephone Number in U.S. (800) 253-9646); *African Statistical Yearbook.*

MAURITANIA - EXCHANGE RATES

African Development Bank, 01 BP 1387, Abidjan 01, Cote d'Ivoire; *Selected Statistics on Regional Member Countries.*

Euromonitor Publications Limited, 87-88 Turnmill Street, London EC1M 5QU, England; *International Marketing Data and Statistics.*

International Civil Aviation Organization, 1000 Sherbrooke Street West, Suite 400, Montreal, Quebec H3A 2R2, Canada (514) 285-8219; *Civil Aviation Statistics of the World.*

International Monetary Fund, 700 Nineteenth Street, NW, Washington, D.C. 20431 (202) 623-7000; *International Financial Statistics.*

Statistical Office of the United Nations, Publishing Service, New York, New York 10017 (800) 253-9646; *Foreign Trade Statistics for Africa,* and *Statistical Yearbook.*

MAURITANIA - EXCISE TAXES - See MAURITANIA - TAXATION

MAURITANIA - EXPORTS

African Development Bank, 01 BP 1387, Abidjan 01, Cote d'Ivoire; *Selected Statistics on Regional Member Countries.*

The Economist Intelligence Unit, 111 West 57th Street, New York, New York 10019 (800) 938-4685; *The World Market Atlas.*

Euromonitor Publications Limited, 87-88 Turnmill Street, London EC1M 5QU, England; *International Marketing Data and Statistics.*

Food and Agricultural Organization of the United Nations (FAO), Via delle Terme di Caracalla, 00100 Rome, Italy (Telephone Number in U.S. (202) 653-2400); *The State of Food and Agriculture.*

G.K. Hall and Company, 70 Lincoln Street, Boston, Massachusetts 02111 (617) 423-3990; *The World in Figures.*

International Monetary Fund, 700 Nineteenth Street, NW, Washington, D.C. 20431 (202) 623-7000; *Direction of Trade Statistics, Government Finance Statistics Yearbook,* and *International Financial Statistics.*

Statistical Office of the United Nations, Publishing Service, New York, New York 10017 (800) 253-9646; *Foreign Trade Statistics for Africa,* and *Survey of Economic and Social Conditions in Africa.*

Times Books, 201 East 50th Street, New York, New York 10022 (212) 751-2600; *The Economist Book of Vital World Statistics.*

United Nations Economic Commission for Africa, Africa Hall, Post Office Box 3001, Addis Ababa, Ethiopia (Telephone Number in U.S. (800) 253-9646); *African Statistical Yearbook.*

The World Bank, 1818 H Street, NW, Washington, D.C. 20433 (202) 477-1234; *World Tables.*

MAURITANIA - EXTERNAL INDEBTEDNESS

African Development Bank, 01 BP 1387, Abidjan 01, Cote d'Ivoire; *Selected Statistics on Regional Member Countries.*

Statistical Office of the United Nations, Publishing Service, New York, New York 10017 (800) 253-9646; *Survey of Economic and Social Conditions in Africa.*

The World Bank, 1818 H Street, NW, Washington, D.C. 20433 (202) 477-1234; *World Tables.*

MAURITANIA - EXTERNAL TRADE

African Development Bank, 01 BP 1387, Abidjan 01, Cote d'Ivoire; *Selected Statistics on Regional Member Countries.*

Food and Agricultural Organization of the United Nations (FAO), Via delle Terme di Caracalla, 00100 Rome, Italy (Telephone Number in U.S. (202) 653-2400); *The State of Food and Agriculture,* and *Trade Yearbook.*

G.K. Hall and Company, 70 Lincoln Street, Boston, Massachusetts 02111 (617) 423-3990; *The World in Figures.*

Statistical Office of the United Nations, Publishing Service, New York, New York 10017 (800) 253-9646; *Statistical Yearbook.*

MAURITANIA - FARM CROPS - See MAURITANIA - CROPS

MAURITANIA - FEMALE WORKING POPULATION - See MAURITANIA - EMPLOYMENT

MAURITANIA - FERTILITY RATES

Facts on File, 460 Park Avenue South, New York, New York 10016 (800) 443-8323; *The New Book of World Rankings.*

Statistical Office of the United Nations, Publishing Service, New York, New York 10017 (800) 253-9646; *Survey of Economic and Social Conditions in Africa.*

Times Books, 201 East 50th Street, New York, New York 10022 (212) 751-2600; *The Economist Book of Vital World Statistics.*

The World Bank, 1818 H Street, NW, Washington, D.C. 20433 (202) 477-1234; *World Tables.*

MAURITANIA - FERTILIZER

Food and Agricultural Organization of the United Nations (FAO), Via delle Terme di Caracalla, 00100 Rome, Italy (Telephone Number in U.S. (202) 653-2400); *Fertilizer Yearbook,* and *The State of Food and Agriculture.*

Statistical Office of the United Nations, Publishing Service, New York, New York 10017 (000) 253-9646; *Statistical Yearbook.*

MAURITANIA - FETAL MORTALITY

Statistical Office of the United Nations, Publishing Service, New York, New York 10017 (800) 253-9646; *Demographic Yearbook.*

MAURITANIA - FINANCE

African Development Bank, 01 BP 1387, Abidjan 01, Cote d'Ivoire; *Selected Statistics on Regional Member Countries.*

Facts on File, 460 Park Avenue South, New York, New York 10016 (800) 443-8323; *The New Book of World Rankings.*

G.K. Hall and Company, 70 Lincoln Street, Boston, Massachusetts 02111 (617) 423-3990; *The World in Figures.*

International Monetary Fund, 700 Nineteenth Street, NW, Washington, D.C. 20431 (202) 623-7000; *Government Finance Statistics Yearbook,* and *International Financial Statistics.*

Statistical Office of the United Nations, Publishing Service, New York, New York 10017 (800) 253-9646; *Statistical Yearbook,* and *Survey of Economic and Social Conditions in Africa.*

United Nations Economic Commission for Africa, Africa Hall, Post Office Box 3001, Addis Ababa, Ethiopia (Telephone Number in U.S. (800) 253-9646); *African Statistical Yearbook.*

MAURITANIA - FISHERIES

Facts on File, 460 Park Avenue South, New York, New York 10016 (800) 443-8323; *The New Book of World Rankings.*

Food and Agricultural Organization of the United Nations (FAO), Via delle Terme di Caracalla, 00100 Rome, Italy (Telephone Number in U.S. (202) 653-2400); *The State of Food and Agriculture,* and *Yearbook of Fishery Statistics.*

International Monetary Fund, 700 Nineteenth Street, NW, Washington, D.C. 20431 (202) 623-7000; *International Financial Statistics.*

United Nations Economic Commission for Africa, Africa Hall, Post Office Box 3001, Addis Ababa, Ethiopia (Telephone Number in U.S. (800) 253-9646); *African Statistical Yearbook.*

MAURITANIA - FOOD

African Development Bank, 01 BP 1387, Abidjan 01, Cote d'Ivoire; *Selected Statistics on Regional Member Countries.*

Food and Agricultural Organization of the United Nations (FAO), Via delle Terme di Caracalla, 00100 Rome, Italy (Telephone Number in U.S. (202) 653-2400); *Production Yearbook,* and *The State of Food and Agriculture.*

G.K. Hall and Company, 70 Lincoln Street, Boston, Massachusetts 02111 (617) 423-3990; *The World in Figures.*

MAURITANIA - FOREIGN AID

G.K. Hall and Company, 70 Lincoln Street, Boston, Massachusetts 02111 (617) 423-3990; *The World in Figures.*

MAURITANIA - FOREIGN DEBT

International Monetary Fund, 700 Nineteenth Street, NW, Washington, D.C. 20431 (202) 623-7000; *Government Finance Statistics Yearbook.*

MAURITANIA - FOREIGN TRADE

Euromonitor Publications Limited, 87-88 Turnmill Street, London EC1M 5QU, England; *International Marketing Data and Statistics.*

Facts on File, 460 Park Avenue South, New York, New York 10016 (800) 443-8323; *The New Book of World Rankings.*

Food and Agricultural Organization of the United Nations (FAO), Via delle Terme di Caracalla, 00100 Rome, Italy (Telephone Number in U.S. (202) 653-2400); *The State of Food and Agriculture.*

G.K. Hall and Company, 70 Lincoln Street, Boston, Massachusetts 02111 (617) 423-3990; *The World in Figures.*

Statistical Office of the United Nations, Publishing Service, New York, New York 10017 (800) 253-9646; *Foreign Trade Statistics for Africa, International Trade Statistics Yearbook,* and *Statistical Yearbook.*

United Nations Economic Commission for Africa, Africa Hall, Post Office Box 3001, Addis Ababa, Ethiopia (Telephone Number in U.S. (800) 253-9646); *African Statistical Yearbook.*

The World Bank, 1818 H Street, NW, Washington, D.C. 20433 (202) 477-1234; *World Tables.*

MAURITANIA - FORESTRY AND FOREST PRODUCTS

Facts on File, 460 Park Avenue South, New York, New York 10016 (800) 443-8323; *The New Book of World Rankings.*

Food and Agricultural Organization of the United Nations (FAO), Via delle Terme di Caracalla, 00100 Rome, Italy (Telephone Number in U.S. (202) 653-2400); *The State of Food and Agriculture,* and *Yearbook of Forest Products.*

G.K. Hall and Company, 70 Lincoln Street, Boston, Massachusetts 02111 (617) 423-3990; *The World in Figures.*

Statistical Office of the United Nations, Publishing Service, New York, New York 10017 (800) 253-9646; *Statistical Yearbook*.

United Nations Economic Commission for Africa, Africa Hall, Post Office Box 3001, Addis Ababa, Ethiopia (Telephone Number in U.S. (800) 253-9646); *African Statistical Yearbook*.

MAURITANIA - GAS PRODUCTION - See MAURITANIA - MINING AND MINERAL PRODUCTS

MAURITANIA - GENERAL MORTALITY

Statistical Office of the United Nations, Publishing Service, New York, New York 10017 (800) 253-9646; *Demographic Yearbook*.

MAURITANIA - GEOGRAPHIC DATA

Facts on File, 460 Park Avenue South, New York, New York 10016 (800) 443-8323; *The New Book of World Rankings*.

MAURITANIA - GOATS - See MAURITANIA - LIVESTOCK AND POULTRY

MAURITANIA - GOLD HOLDINGS

International Monetary Fund, 700 Nineteenth Street, NW, Washington, D.C. 20431 (202) 623-7000; *International Financial Statistics*.

Statistical Office of the United Nations, Publishing Service, New York, New York 10017 (800) 253-9646; *Statistical Yearbook*.

The World Bank, 1818 H Street, NW, Washington, D.C. 20433 (202) 477-1234; *World Tables*.

MAURITANIA - GOLD PRODUCTION AND CONSUMPTION - See MAURITANIA - MINING AND MINERAL PRODUCTS

MAURITANIA - GOVERNMENT

G.K. Hall and Company, 70 Lincoln Street, Boston, Massachusetts 02111 (617) 423-3990; *The World in Figures*.

MAURITANIA - GOVERNMENT EXPENDITURES

International Monetary Fund, 700 Nineteenth Street, NW, Washington, D.C. 20431 (202) 623-7000; *Government Finance Statistics Yearbook*.

The World Bank, 1818 H Street, NW, Washington, D.C. 20433 (202) 477-1234; *World Tables*.

MAURITANIA - GOVERNMENT REVENUE

International Monetary Fund, 700 Nineteenth Street, NW, Washington, D.C. 20431 (202) 623-7000; *Government Finance Statistics Yearbook*.

Statistical Office of the United Nations, Publishing Service, New York, New York 10017 (800) 253-9646; *Survey of Economic and Social Conditions in Africa*.

The World Bank, 1818 H Street, NW, Washington, D.C. 20433 (202) 477-1234; *World Tables*.

MAURITANIA - GRAIN PRODUCTION - See MAURITANIA - CROPS

MAURITANIA - GRANTS

International Monetary Fund, 700 Nineteenth Street, NW, Washington, D.C. 20431 (202) 623-7000; *Government Finance Statistics Yearbook*.

MAURITANIA - GROSS DOMESTIC PRODUCT

African Development Bank, 01 BP 1387, Abidjan 01, Cote d'Ivoire; *Selected Statistics on Regional Member Countries*.

The Economist Intelligence Unit, 111 West 57th Street, New York, New York 10019 (800) 938-4685; *The World Market Atlas*.

Euromonitor Publications Limited, 87-88 Turnmill Street, London EC1M 5QU, England; *International Marketing Data and Statistics*.

Facts on File, 460 Park Avenue South, New York, New York 10016 (800) 443-8323; *The New Book of World Rankings*.

G.K. Hall and Company, 70 Lincoln Street, Boston, Massachusetts 02111 (617) 423-3990; *The World in Figures*.

Statistical Office of the United Nations, Publishing Service, New York, New York 10017 (800) 253-9646; *Statistical Yearbook*.

Times Books, 201 East 50th Street, New York, New York 10022 (212) 751-2600; *The Economist Book of Vital World Statistics*.

United Nations Economic Commission for Africa, Africa Hall, Post Office Box 3001, Addis Ababa, Ethiopia (Telephone Number in U.S. (800) 253-9646); *African Statistical Yearbook*.

The World Bank, 1818 H Street, NW, Washington, D.C. 20433 (202) 477-1234; *World Tables*.

MAURITANIA - GROSS DOMESTIC PRODUCT

Statistical Office of the United Nations, Publishing Service, New York, New York 10017 (800) 253-9646; *Survey of Economic and Social Conditions in Africa*.

MAURITANIA - GROSS NATIONAL PRODUCT

Euromonitor Publications Limited, 87-88 Turnmill Street, London EC1M 5QU, England; *International Marketing Data and Statistics*.

U.S. Arms Control and Disarmament Agency, 320 Twenty-first Street, NW, Washington, D.C. 20451 (202) 647-8677; *World Military Expenditures and Arms Transfers*.

The World Bank, 1818 H Street, NW, Washington, D.C. 20433 (202) 477-1234; *World Tables*.

MAURITANIA - GROUNDNUT PRODUCTION - See MAURITANIA - CROPS

MAURITANIA - HEALTH

African Development Bank, 01 BP 1387, Abidjan 01, Cote d'Ivoire; *Selected Statistics on Regional Member Countries*.

Facts on File, 460 Park Avenue South, New York, New York 10016 (800) 443-8323; *The New Book of World Rankings*.

G.K. Hall and Company, 70 Lincoln Street, Boston, Massachusetts 02111 (617) 423-3990; *The World in Figures*.

Statistical Office of the United Nations, Publishing Service, New York, New York 10017 (800) 253-9646; *Statistical Yearbook*.

Times Books, 201 East 50th Street, New York, New York 10022 (212) 751-2600; *The Economist Book of Vital World Statistics*.

United Nations Economic Commission for Africa, Africa Hall, Post Office Box 3001, Addis Ababa, Ethiopia (Telephone Number in U.S. (800) 253-9646); *African Statistical Yearbook*.

MAURITANIA - HEALTH EXPENDITURES

International Monetary Fund, 700 Nineteenth Street, NW, Washington, D.C. 20431 (202) 623-7000; *Government Finance Statistics Yearbook*.

MAURITANIA - HIDE PRODUCTION

Food and Agricultural Organization of the United Nations (FAO), Via delle Terme di Caracalla, 00100 Rome, Italy (Telephone Number in U.S. (202) 653-2400); *Production Yearbook*.

MAURITANIA - HIGHWAYS

G.K. Hall and Company, 70 Lincoln Street, Boston, Massachusetts 02111 (617) 423-3990; *The World in Figures*.

International Road Federation, 525 School Street, SW, Washington, D.C. 20024 (202) 554-2106; *World Road Statistics*.

Statistical Office of the United Nations, Publishing Service, New York, New York 10017 (800) 253-9646; *Survey of Economic and Social Conditions in Africa*.

United Nations Economic Commission for Africa, Africa Hall, Post Office Box 3001, Addis Ababa, Ethiopia (Telephone Number in U.S. (800) 253-9646); *African Statistical Yearbook*.

MAURITANIA - HORSES - See MAURITANIA - LIVESTOCK AND POULTRY

MAURITANIA - HOURS OF WORK - See MAURITANIA - EMPLOYMENT

MAURITANIA - HOUSING EXPENDITURES

Facts on File, 460 Park Avenue South, New York, New York 10016 (800) 443-8323; *The New Book of World Rankings*.

International Monetary Fund, 700 Nineteenth Street, NW, Washington, D.C. 20431 (202) 623-7000; *Government Finance Statistics Yearbook*.

MAURITANIA - ILLITERATE POPULATION

The Economist Intelligence Unit, 111 West 57th Street, New York, New York 10019 (800) 938-4685; *The World Market Atlas*.

G.K. Hall and Company, 70 Lincoln Street, Boston, Massachusetts 02111 (617) 423-3990; *The World in Figures*.

United Nations Educational, Scientific and Cultural Organization (UNESCO), 7 Place de Fontenoy, F-75700 Paris, France (Telephone Number in U.S. (212) 963-5981); *Statistical Yearbook*.

MAURITANIA - INDUSTRY

Facts on File, 460 Park Avenue South, New York, New York 10016 (800) 443-8323; *The New Book of World Rankings*.

MAURITANIA - IMPORTS

African Development Bank, 01 BP 1387, Abidjan 01, Cote d'Ivoire; *Selected Statistics on Regional Member Countries*.

The Economist Intelligence Unit, 111 West 57th Street, New York, New York 10019 (800) 938-4685; *The World Market Atlas*.

Euromonitor Publications Limited, 87-88 Turnmill Street, London EC1M 5QU, England; *International Marketing Data and Statistics*.

Food and Agricultural Organization of the United Nations (FAO), Via delle Terme di Caracalla, 00100 Rome, Italy (Telephone Number in U.S. (202) 653-2400); *The State of Food and Agriculture*.

G.K. Hall and Company, 70 Lincoln Street, Boston, Massachusetts 02111 (617) 423-3990; *The World in Figures*.

International Monetary Fund, 700 Nineteenth Street, NW, Washington, D.C. 20431 (202) 623-7000; *Direction of Trade Statistics, Government Finance Statistics Yearbook*, and *International Financial Statistics*.

Statistical Office of the United Nations, Publishing Service, New York, New York 10017 (800) 253-9646; *Foreign Trade Statistics for Africa, Foreign Trade Statistics for Africa*, and *Survey of Economic and Social Conditions in Africa*.

United Nations Economic Commission for Africa, Africa Hall, Post Office Box 3001, Addis Ababa, Ethiopia (Telephone Number in U.S. (800) 253-9646); *African Statistical Yearbook*.

The World Bank, 1818 H Street, NW, Washington, D.C. 20433 (202) 477-1234; *World Tables*.

MAURITANIA - INCOME TAXES - See MAURITANIA - TAXATION

MAURITANIA - INDUSTRY

G.K. Hall and Company, 70 Lincoln Street, Boston, Massachusetts 02111 (617) 423-3990; *The World in Figures*.

International Labour Office, I.L.O. Publications, CH-1211, Geneva 22, Switzerland; *Yearbook of Labour Statistics*.

Statistical Office of the United Nations, Publishing Service, New York, New York 10017 (800) 253-9646; *Survey of Economic and Social Conditions in Africa*.

Times Books, 201 East 50th Street, New York, New York 10022 (212) 751-2600; *The Economist Book of Vital World Statistics*.

United Nations Economic Commission for Africa, Africa Hall, Post Office Box 3001, Addis Ababa, Ethiopia (Telephone Number in U.S. (800) 253-9646); *African Statistical Yearbook*.

The World Bank, 1818 H Street, NW, Washington, D.C. 20433 (202) 477-1234; *World Tables*.

MAURITANIA - INFANT AND MATERNAL MORTALITY

Statistical Office of the United Nations, Publishing Service, New York, New York 10017 (800) 253-9646; *Demographic Yearbook, Statistical Yearbook*, and *Survey of Economic and Social Conditions in Africa*.

Times Books, 201 East 50th Street, New York, New York 10022 (212) 751-2600; *The Economist Book of Vital World Statistics*.

The World Bank, 1818 H Street, NW, Washington, D.C. 20433 (202) 477-1234; *World Tables.*

MAURITANIA - INTERNATIONAL LIQUIDITY

International Monetary Fund, 700 Nineteenth Street, NW, Washington, D.C. 20431 (202) 623-7000; *International Financial Statistics.*

MAURITANIA - INTERNATIONAL RESERVES EXCLUDING GOLD

African Development Bank, 01 BP 1387, Abidjan 01, Cote d'Ivoire; *Selected Statistics on Regional Member Countries.*

Statistical Office of the United Nations, Publishing Service, New York, New York 10017 (800) 253-9646; *Statistical Yearbook.*

The World Bank, 1818 H Street, NW, Washington, D.C. 20433 (202) 477-1234; *World Tables.*

MAURITANIA - IRON AND IRON ORE - See MAURITANIA - MINING AND MINERAL PRODUCTS

MAURITANIA - IRRIGATION

Euromonitor Publications Limited, 87-88 Turnmill Street, London EC1M 5QU, England; *International Marketing Data and Statistics.*

MAURITANIA - LABOR FORCE

African Development Bank, 01 BP 1387, Abidjan 01, Cote d'Ivoire; *Selected Statistics on Regional Member Countries.*

Euromonitor Publications Limited, 87-88 Turnmill Street, London EC1M 5QU, England; *International Marketing Data and Statistics.*

Facts on File, 460 Park Avenue South, New York, New York 10016 (800) 443-8323; *The New Book of World Rankings.*

Food and Agricultural Organization of the United Nations (FAO), Via delle Terme di Caracalla, 00100 Rome, Italy (Telephone Number in U.S. (202) 653-2400); *The State of Food and Agriculture.*

G.K. Hall and Company, 70 Lincoln Street, Boston, Massachusetts 02111 (617) 423-3990; *The World in Figures.*

The World Bank, 1818 H Street, NW, Washington, D.C. 20433 (202) 477-1234; *World Tables.*

MAURITANIA - LABOR PRODUCTIVITY

International Labour Office, I.L.O. Publications, CH-1211, Geneva 22, Switzerland; *Yearbook of Labour Statistics.*

MAURITANIA - LAND USE

Euromonitor Publications Limited, 87-88 Turnmill Street, London EC1M 5QU, England; *International Marketing Data and Statistics.*

Food and Agricultural Organization of the United Nations (FAO), Via delle Terme di Caracalla, 00100 Rome, Italy (Telephone Number in U.S. (202) 653-2400); *Production Yearbook.*

G.K. Hall and Company, 70 Lincoln Street, Boston, Massachusetts 02111 (617) 423-3990; *The World in Figures.*

MAURITANIA - LIBRARIES

Facts on File, 460 Park Avenue South, New York, New York 10016 (800) 443-8323; *The New Book of World Rankings.*

United Nations Educational, Scientific and Cultural Organization (UNESCO), 7 Place de Fontenoy, F-75700 Paris, France (Telephone Number in U.S. (212) 963-5981); *Statistical Yearbook.*

MAURITANIA - LIFE EXPECTANCY

African Development Bank, 01 BP 1387, Abidjan 01, Cote d'Ivoire; *Selected Statistics on Regional Member Countries.*

MAURITANIA - LITERACY RATE

Statistical Office of the United Nations, Publishing Service, New York, New York 10017 (800) 253-9646; *Survey of Economic and Social Conditions in Africa.*

MAURITANIA - LIVESTOCK AND POULTRY

Euromonitor Publications Limited, 87-88 Turnmill Street, London EC1M 5QU, England; *International Marketing Data and Statistics.*

Facts on File, 460 Park Avenue South, New York, New York 10016 (800) 443-8323; *The New Book of World Rankings.*

Food and Agricultural Organization of the United Nations (FAO), Via delle Terme di Caracalla, 00100 Rome, Italy (Telephone Number in U.S. (202) 653-2400); *Production Yearbook,* and *The State of Food and Agriculture.*

G.K. Hall and Company, 70 Lincoln Street, Boston, Massachusetts 02111 (617) 423-3990; *The World in Figures.*

Statistical Office of the United Nations, Publishing Service, New York, New York 10017 (800) 253-9646; *Statistical Yearbook,* and *Survey of Economic and Social Conditions in Africa.*

United Nations Economic Commission for Africa, Africa Hall, Post Office Box 3001, Addis Ababa, Ethiopia (Telephone Number in U.S. (800) 253-9646); *African Statistical Yearbook.*

MAURITANIA - LIVING LEVELS

G.K. Hall and Company, 70 Lincoln Street, Boston, Massachusetts 02111 (617) 423-3990; *The World in Figures.*

Times Books, 201 East 50th Street, New York, New York 10022 (212) 751-2600; *The Economist Book of Vital World Statistics.*

MAURITANIA - MAIL - NUMBER OF ITEMS SENT OR RECEIVED

Statistical Office of the United Nations, Publishing Service, New York, New York 10017 (800) 253-9646; *Statistical Yearbook.*

MAURITANIA - MANUFACTURING

Facts on File, 460 Park Avenue South, New York, New York 10016 (800) 443-8323; *The New Book of World Rankings.*

G.K. Hall and Company, 70 Lincoln Street, Boston, Massachusetts 02111 (617) 423-3990; *The World in Figures.*

Statistical Office of the United Nations, Publishing Service, New York, New York 10017 (800) 253-9646; *Survey of Economic and Social Conditions in Africa.*

United Nations Economic Commission for Africa, Africa Hall, Post Office Box 3001, Addis Ababa, Ethiopia (Telephone Number in U.S. (800) 253-9646); *African Statistical Yearbook*.

The World Bank, 1818 H Street, NW, Washington, D.C. 20433 (202) 477-1234; *World Tables*.

MAURITANIA - MARRIAGE

Facts on File, 460 Park Avenue South, New York, New York 10016 (800) 443-8323; *The New Book of World Rankings*.

Statistical Office of the United Nations, Publishing Service, New York, New York 10017 (800) 253-9646; *Demographic Yearbook*.

MAURITANIA - MEAT PRODUCTION - See MAURITANIA - LIVESTOCK AND POULTRY

MAURITANIA - MERCHANT SHIPPING

G.K. Hall and Company, 70 Lincoln Street, Boston, Massachusetts 02111 (617) 423-3990; *The World in Figures*.

Lloyd's Register of Shipping, 17 Battery Place, New York, New York 10004 (212) 425-8050; *Register of Ships*.

Statistical Office of the United Nations, Publishing Service, New York, New York 10017 (800) 253-9646; *Statistical Yearbook*.

Times Books, 201 East 50th Street, New York, New York 10022 (212) 751-2600; *The Economist Book of Vital World Statistics*.

United Nations Economic Commission for Africa, Africa Hall, Post Office Box 3001, Addis Ababa, Ethiopia (Telephone Number in U.S. (800) 253-9646); *African Statistical Yearbook*.

MAURITANIA - MILITARY

G.K. Hall and Company, 70 Lincoln Street, Boston, Massachusetts 02111 (617) 423-3990; *The World in Figures*.

The International Institute for Strategic Studies, 23 Tavistock Street, London WC2E 7NQ, England; *The Military Balance*.

U.S. Arms Control and Disarmament Agency, 320 Twenty-first Street, NW, Washington, D.C. 20451 (202) 647-8677; *World Military Expenditures and Arms Transfers*.

MAURITANIA - MILK PRODUCTION - See MAURITANIA - DAIRY PRODUCTS

MAURITANIA - MILLET PRODUCTION - See MAURITANIA - CROPS

MAURITANIA - MINING AND MINERAL PRODUCTS

Facts on File, 460 Park Avenue South, New York, New York 10016 (800) 443-8323; *The New Book of World Rankings*.

G.K. Hall and Company, 70 Lincoln Street, Boston, Massachusetts 02111 (617) 423-3990; *The World in Figures*.

International Monetary Fund, 700 Nineteenth Street, NW, Washington, D.C. 20431 (202) 623-7000; *International Financial Statistics*.

Statistical Office of the United Nations, Publishing Service, New York, New York 10017 (800) 253-9646; *Statistical Yearbook*.

United Nations Economic Commission for Africa, Africa Hall, Post Office Box 3001, Addis Ababa, Ethiopia (Telephone Number in U.S. (800) 253-9646); *African Statistical Yearbook*.

MAURITANIA - MONEY EXCHANGE RATE

Euromonitor Publications Limited, 87-88 Turnmill Street, London EC1M 5QU, England; *International Marketing Data and Statistics*.

International Monetary Fund, 700 Nineteenth Street, NW, Washington, D.C. 20431 (202) 623-7000; *International Financial Statistics*.

Statistical Office of the United Nations, Publishing Service, New York, New York 10017 (800) 253-9646; *Statistical Yearbook*.

MAURITANIA - MONEY RESERVES

Euromonitor Publications Limited, 87-88 Turnmill Street, London EC1M 5QU, England; *International Marketing Data and Statistics*.

MAURITANIA - MONEY SUPPLY

African Development Bank, 01 BP 1387, Abidjan 01, Cote d'Ivoire; *Selected Statistics on Regional Member Countries*.

Euromonitor Publications Limited, 87-88 Turnmill Street, London EC1M 5QU, England; *International Marketing Data and Statistics*.

G.K. Hall and Company, 70 Lincoln Street, Boston, Massachusetts 02111 (617) 423-3990; *The World in Figures*.

International Monetary Fund, 700 Nineteenth Street, NW, Washington, D.C. 20431 (202) 623-7000; *International Financial Statistics*.

Statistical Office of the United Nations, Publishing Service, New York, New York 10017 (800) 253-9646; *Statistical Yearbook*.

The World Bank, 1818 H Street, NW, Washington, D.C. 20433 (202) 477-1234; *World Tables*.

MAURITANIA - MOTOR VEHICLE TAXES - See MAURITANIA - TAXATION

MAURITANIA - MOTOR VEHICLES IN USE

G.K. Hall and Company, 70 Lincoln Street, Boston, Massachusetts 02111 (617) 423-3990; *The World in Figures*.

International Road Federation, 525 School Street, SW, Washington, D.C. 20024 (202) 554-2106; *World Road Statistics*.

Statistical Office of the United Nations, Publishing Service, New York, New York 10017 (800) 253-9646; *Statistical Yearbook*, and *Survey of Economic and Social Conditions in Africa*.

MAURITANIA - MUSEUMS

Facts on File, 460 Park Avenue South, New York, New York 10016 (800) 443-8323; *The New Book of World Rankings*.

United Nations Educational, Scientific and Cultural Organization (UNESCO), 7 Place de Fontenoy, F-75700 Paris, France (Telephone Number in U.S. (212) 963-5981); *Statistical Yearbook*.

MAURITANIA - NATALITY - See MAURITANIA - BIRTH RATES

MAURITANIA - NATIONAL ACCOUNTS

African Development Bank, 01 BP 1387, Abidjan 01, Cote d'Ivoire; *Selected Statistics on Regional Member Countries.*

Statistical Office of the United Nations, Publishing Service, New York, New York 10017 (800) 253-9646; *National Account Statistics,* and *Statistical Yearbook.*

United Nations Economic Commission for Africa, Africa Hall, Post Office Box 3001, Addis Ababa, Ethiopia (Telephone Number in U.S. (800) 253-9646); *African Statistical Yearbook.*

MAURITANIA - NATIONAL INCOME

Facts on File, 460 Park Avenue South, New York, New York 10016 (800) 443-8323; *The New Book of World Rankings.*

G.K. Hall and Company, 70 Lincoln Street, Boston, Massachusetts 02111 (617) 423-3990; *The World in Figures.*

Statistical Office of the United Nations, Publishing Service, New York, New York 10017 (800) 253-9646; *Statistical Yearbook.*

MAURITANIA - NATIONAL PRODUCT

Facts on File, 460 Park Avenue South, New York, New York 10016 (800) 443-8323; *The New Book of World Rankings.*

MAURITANIA - NATURAL GAS - PRODUCTION - See MAURITANIA - MINING AND MINERAL PRODUCTS

MAURITANIA - NEWSPAPER PRODUCTION - See MAURITANIA - FORESTRY AND FOREST PRODUCTS

MAURITANIA - OCCUPATIONS - See MAURITANIA - LABOR FORCE

MAURITANIA - PEANUT PRODUCTION - See MAURITANIA - CROPS

MAURITANIA - PESTICIDE USE

Food and Agricultural Organization of the United Nations (FAO), Via delle Terme di Caracalla, 00100 Rome, Italy (Telephone Number in U.S. (202) 653-2400); *The State of Food and Agriculture.*

MAURITANIA - PETROLEUM INDUSTRY

Facts on File, 460 Park Avenue South, New York, New York 10016 (800) 443-8323; *The New Book of World Rankings.*

Food and Agricultural Organization of the United Nations (FAO), Via delle Terme di Caracalla, 00100 Rome, Italy (Telephone Number in U.S. (202) 653-2400); *The State of Food and Agriculture.*

G.K. Hall and Company, 70 Lincoln Street, Boston, Massachusetts 02111 (617) 423-3990; *The World in Figures.*

MAURITANIA - PIGS - See MAURITANIA - LIVESTOCK AND POULTRY

MAURITANIA - POPULATION

African Development Bank, 01 BP 1387, Abidjan 01, Cote d'Ivoire; *Selected Statistics on Regional Member Countries.*

The Economist Intelligence Unit, 111 West 57th Street, New York, New York 10019 (800) 938-4685; *The World Market Atlas.*

Euromonitor Publications Limited, 87-88 Turnmill Street, London EC1M 5QU, England; *International Marketing Data and Statistics.*

Facts on File, 460 Park Avenue South, New York, New York 10016 (800) 443-8323; *The New Book of World Rankings.*

Food and Agricultural Organization of the United Nations (FAO), Via delle Terme di Caracalla, 00100 Rome, Italy (Telephone Number in U.S. (202) 653-2400); *Production Yearbook.*

G.K. Hall and Company, 70 Lincoln Street, Boston, Massachusetts 02111 (617) 423-3990; *The World in Figures.*

International Labour Office, I.L.O. Publications, CH-1211, Geneva 22, Switzerland; *Yearbook of Labour Statistics.*

Statistical Office of the United Nations, Publishing Service, New York, New York 10017; *Demographic Yearbook, Statistical Yearbook,* and *Survey of Economic and Social Conditions in Africa.*

Times Books, 201 East 50th Street, New York, New York 10022 (212) 751-2600; *The Economist Book of Vital World Statistics.*

U.S. Arms Control and Disarmament Agency, 320 Twenty-first Street, NW, Washington, D.C. 20451 (202) 647-8677; *World Military Expenditures and Arms Transfers.*

World Health Organization, Office of Publications, Avenue Appia, CH-1211 Geneva 27, Switzerland (Telephone in U.S. (518) 436-9686); *World Health Statistics Annual.*

MAURITANIA - POST OFFICES

Facts on File, 460 Park Avenue South, New York, New York 10016; *The New Book of World Rankings.*

MAURITANIA - POTATO PRODUCTION - See MAURITANIA - CROPS

MAURITANIA - PRICES

Facts on File, 460 Park Avenue South, New York, New York 10016 (800) 443-8323; *The New Book of World Rankings.*

Food and Agricultural Organization of the United Nations (FAO), Via delle Terme di Caracalla, 00100 Rome, Italy (Telephone Number in U.S. (202) 653-2400); *Production Yearbook,* and *The State of Food and Agriculture.*

G.K. Hall and Company, 70 Lincoln Street, Boston, Massachusetts 02111 (617) 423-3990; *The World in Figures.*

International Labour Office, I.L.O. Publications, CH-1211, Geneva 22, Switzerland; *Yearbook of Labour Statistics.*

International Monetary Fund, 700 Nineteenth Street, NW, Washington, D.C. 20431 (202) 623-7000; *International Financial Statistics.*

United Nations Economic Commission for Africa, Africa Hall, Post Office Box 3001, Addis Ababa, Ethiopia (Telephone Number in U.S. (800) 253-9646); *African Statistical Yearbook.*

MAURITANIA - PRODUCTION

Facts on File, 460 Park Avenue South, New York, New York 10016 (800) 443-8323; *The New Book of World Rankings.*

G.K. Hall and Company, 70 Lincoln Street, Boston, Massachusetts 02111 (617) 423-3990; *The World in Figures.*

MAURITANIA - PRODUCTIVITY

Euromonitor Publications Limited, 87-88 Turnmill Street, London EC1M 5QU, England; *International Marketing Data and Statistics.*

MAURITANIA - PROPERTY TAXES

International Monetary Fund, 700 Nineteenth Street, NW, Washington, D.C. 20431 (202) 623-7000; *Government Finance Statistics Yearbook.*

MAURITANIA - PUBLIC FINANCE

Facts on File, 460 Park Avenue South, New York, New York 10016 (800) 443-8323; *The New Book of World Rankings.*

MAURITANIA - RADIO BROADCASTING - See MAURITANIA - BROADCASTING

MAURITANIA - RAILWAY TRAFFIC

Statistical Office of the United Nations, Publishing Service, New York, New York 10017 (800) 253-9646; *Statistical Yearbook.*

MAURITANIA - RAILWAY USE

G.K. Hall and Company, 70 Lincoln Street, Boston, Massachusetts 02111 (617) 423-3990; *The World in Figures.*

Statistical Office of the United Nations, Publishing Service, New York, New York 10017 (800) 253-9646; *Survey of Economic and Social Conditions in Africa.*

MAURITANIA - RAILWAYS

Jane's Information Group, Sentinel House, 163 Brighton Road, Coulsdon, Surrey CR5 2NH, England (Telephone Number in U.S. (703) 683-3700); *Jane's World Railways.*

United Nations Economic Commission for Africa, Africa Hall, Post Office Box 3001, Addis Ababa, Ethiopia (Telephone Number in U.S. (800) 253-9646); *African Statistical Yearbook.*

MAURITANIA - RELIGION

Facts on File, 460 Park Avenue South, New York, New York 10016 (800) 443-8323; *The New Book of World Rankings.*

MAURITANIA - RETAIL TRADE

G.K. Hall and Company, 70 Lincoln Street, Boston, Massachusetts 02111 (617) 423-3990; *The World in Figures.*

Statistical Office of the United Nations, Publishing Service, New York, New York 10017 (800) 253-9646; *Statistical Yearbook.*

MAURITANIA - RICE PRODUCTION - See MAURITANIA - CROPS

MAURITANIA - ROOT AND TUBER PRODUCTION - See MAURITANIA - CROPS

MAURITANIA - ROUNDWOOD PRODUCTION - See MAURITANIA - FORESTRY AND FOREST PRODUCTS

MAURITANIA - RUBBER PRODUCTION AND CONSUMPTION

Facts on File, 460 Park Avenue South, New York, New York 10016 (800) 443-8323; *The New Book of World Rankings.*

MAURITANIA - SAWNWOOD PRODUCTION - See MAURITANIA - FORESTRY AND FOREST PRODUCTS

MAURITANIA - SENIOR CITIZENS

Facts on File, 460 Park Avenue South, New York, New York 10016 (800) 443-8323; *The New Book of World Rankings.*

MAURITANIA - SHEEP - See MAURITANIA - LIVESTOCK AND POULTRY

MAURITANIA - SILVER PRODUCTION AND CONSUMPTION - See MAURITANIA - MINING AND MINERAL PRODUCTS

MAURITANIA - SOCIAL DATA

African Development Bank, 01 BP 1387, Abidjan 01, Cote d'Ivoire; *Selected Statistics on Regional Member Countries.*

Facts on File, 460 Park Avenue South, New York, New York 10016 (800) 443-8323; *The New Book of World Rankings.*

G.K. Hall and Company, 70 Lincoln Street, Boston, Massachusetts 02111 (617) 423-3990; *The World in Figures.*

MAURITANIA - SOCIAL SECURITY EXPENDITURES

International Monetary Fund, 700 Nineteenth Street, NW, Washington, D.C. 20431 (202) 623-7000; *Government Finance Statistics Yearbook.*

MAURITANIA - STAMP TAXES AND DUTIES - See MAURITANIA - TAXATION

MAURITANIA - STATE BUDGET

Euromonitor Publications Limited, 87-88 Turnmill Street, London EC1M 5QU, England; *International Marketing Data and Statistics.*

MAURITANIA - STEEL PRODUCTION - See MAURITANIA - MINING AND MINERAL PRODUCTS

MAURITANIA - STOCKS - COMMODITY - MARKET PRICE - INDEX

Food and Agricultural Organization of the United Nations (FAO), Via delle Terme di Caracalla, 00100 Rome, Italy (Telephone Number in U.S. (202) 653-2400); *The State of Food and Agriculture.*

MAURITANIA - SUGAR PRODUCTION AND CONSUMPTION - See MAURITANIA - CROPS

MAURITANIA - TAXATION

G.K. Hall and Company, 70 Lincoln Street, Boston, Massachusetts 02111 (617) 423-3990; *The World in Figures.*

International Monetary Fund, 700 Nineteenth Street, NW, Washington, D.C. 20431 (202) 623-7000; *Government Finance Statistics Yearbook.*

International Road Federation, 525 School Street, SW, Washington, D.C. 20024 (202) 554-2106; *World Road Statistics.*

Times Books, 201 East 50th Street, New York, New York 10022 (212) 751-2600; *The Economist Book of Vital World Statistics.*

The World Bank, 1818 H Street, NW, Washington, D.C. 20433 (202) 477-1234; *World Tables.*

MAURITANIA - TELEPHONES IN USE

American Telephone and Telegraph Company, 26 Parsippany Road, Whippany, New Jersey 07981 (800) 338-4038; *The World's Telephones*.

G.K. Hall and Company, 70 Lincoln Street, Boston, Massachusetts 02111 (617) 423-3990; *The World in Figures*.

MAURITANIA - TELEVISION

Facts on File, 460 Park Avenue South, New York, New York 10016 (800) 443-8323; *The New Book of World Rankings*.

MAURITANIA - TEXTILE INDUSTRY

G.K. Hall and Company, 70 Lincoln Street, Boston, Massachusetts 02111 (617) 423-3990; *The World in Figures*.

MAURITANIA - TOBACCO PRODUCTION

Facts on File, 460 Park Avenue South, New York, New York 10016 (800) 443-8323; *The New Book of World Rankings*.

MAURITANIA - TOURISM

Facts on File, 460 Park Avenue South, New York, New York 10016 (800) 443-8323; *The New Book of World Rankings*.

G.K. Hall and Company, 70 Lincoln Street, Boston, Massachusetts 02111 (617) 423-3990; *The World in Figures*.

Statistical Office of the United Nations, Publishing Service, New York, New York 10017 (800) 253-9646; *Statistical Yearbook*.

United Nations Economic Commission for Africa, Africa Hall, Post Office Box 3001, Addis Ababa, Ethiopia (Telephone Number in U.S. (800) 253-9646); *African Statistical Yearbook*.

World Tourism Organization, Calle Capitan Haya 42, E-28020 Madrid, Spain; *Yearbook of Tourism Statistics*.

MAURITANIA - TRADE - See MAURITANIA - FOREIGN TRADE
MAURITANIA - TRANSPORTATION AND COMMUNICATIONS

Facts on File, 460 Park Avenue South, New York, New York 10016 (800) 443-8323; *The New Book of World Rankings*.

G.K. Hall and Company, 70 Lincoln Street, Boston, Massachusetts 02111 (617) 423-3990; *The World in Figures*.

United Nations Economic Commission for Africa, Africa Hall, Post Office Box 3001, Addis Ababa, Ethiopia (Telephone Number in U.S. (800) 253-9646); *African Statistical Yearbook*.

MAURITANIA - UNEMPLOYMENT

Euromonitor Publications Limited, 87-88 Turnmill Street, London EC1M 5QU, England; *International Marketing Data and Statistics*.

International Labour Office, I.L.O. Publications, CH-1211, Geneva 22, Switzerland; *Yearbook of Labour Statistics*.

MAURITANIA - VITAL STATISTICS

Euromonitor Publications Limited, 87-88 Turnmill Street, London EC1M 5QU, England; *International Marketing Data and Statistics*.

G.K. Hall and Company, 70 Lincoln Street, Boston, Massachusetts 02111 (617) 423-3990; *The World in Figures*.

Statistical Office of the United Nations, Publishing Service, New York, New York 10017 (800) 253-9646; *Statistical Yearbook*.

World Health Organization, Office of Publications, Avenue Appia, CH-1211 Geneva 27, Switzerland (Telephone in U.S. (518) 436-9686); *World Health Statistics Annual*.

MAURITANIA - WAGES

G.K. Hall and Company, 70 Lincoln Street, Boston, Massachusetts 02111 (617) 423-3990; *The World in Figures*.

International Labour Office, I.L.O. Publications, CH-1211, Geneva 22, Switzerland; *Yearbook of Labour Statistics*.

MAURITANIA - WATERMELON PRODUCTION - See MAURITANIA - CROPS

MAURITANIA - WEATHER

Facts on File, 460 Park Avenue South, New York, New York 10016 (800) 443-8323; *The New Book of World Rankings*.

G.K. Hall and Company, 70 Lincoln Street, Boston, Massachusetts 02111 (617) 423-3990; *The World in Figures*.

MAURITANIA - WELFARE EXPENDITURES

International Monetary Fund, 700 Nineteenth Street, NW, Washington, D.C. 20431 (202) 623-7000; *Government Finance Statistics Yearbook*.

MAURITANIA - WHEAT PRODUCTION - See MAURITANIA - CROPS

MAURITANIA - WINE PRODUCTION

Facts on File, 460 Park Avenue South, New York, New York 10016 (800) 443-8323; *The New Book of World Rankings*.

MAURITANIA - WOOL PRODUCTION

Facts on File, 460 Park Avenue South, New York, New York 10016 (800) 443-8323; *The New Book of World Rankings*.

Mauritius - National Statistical Office

Central Statistical Office, Ministry of Economic Planning and Development, Royal Road, Port Louis, Mauritius.

Mauritius - Primary Statistics Source

Central Statistical Office, Government Printer, Port Louis, Mauritius; *Annual Digest of Statistics*.

MAURITIUS - AGRICULTURE

Facts on File, 460 Park Avenue South, New York, New York 10016 (800) 443-8323; *The New Book of World Rankings*.

Food and Agricultural Organization of the United Nations (FAO), Via delle Terme di Caracalla, 00100 Rome, Italy (Telephone Number in U.S. (202) 653-2400); *The State of Food and Agriculture, Survey of Economic and Social Conditions in Africa*, and *Trade Yearbook*.

G.K. Hall and Company, 70 Lincoln Street, Boston, Massachusetts 02111 (617) 423-3990; *The World in Figures*.

Statistical Office of the United Nations, Publishing Service, New York, New York 10017 (800) 253-9646; *Statistical Yearbook*, and *Survey of Economic and Social Conditions in Africa*.

Times Books, 201 East 50th Street, New York, New York 10022 (212) 751-2600; *The Economist Book of Vital World Statistics*.

United Nations Economic Commission for Africa, Africa Hall, Post Office Box 3001, Addis Ababa, Ethiopia (Telephone Number in U.S. (800) 253-9646); *African Statistical Yearbook*.

The World Bank, 1818 H Street, NW, Washington, D.C. 20433 (202) 477-1234; *World Tables*.

MAURITIUS - AIRLINE SERVICE

Facts on File, 460 Park Avenue South, New York, New York 10016 (800) 443-8323; *The New Book of World Rankings*.

G.K. Hall and Company, 70 Lincoln Street, Boston, Massachusetts 02111 (617) 423-3990; *The World in Figures*.

International Civil Aviation Organization, 1000 Sherbrooke Street West, Suite 400, Montreal, Quebec H3A 2R2, Canada (514) 285-8219; *Civil Aviation Statistics of the World*.

Times Books, 201 East 50th Street, New York, New York 10022 (212) 751-2600; *The Economist Book of Vital World Statistics*.

United Nations Economic Commission for Africa, Africa Hall, Post Office Box 3001, Addis Ababa, Ethiopia (Telephone Number in U.S. (800) 253-9646); *African Statistical Yearbook*.

MAURITIUS - ALUMINUM PRODUCTION AND CONSUMPTION - See MAURITIUS - MINING AND MINERAL PRODUCTS

MAURITIUS - ANIMAL HEALTH

Food and Agricultural Organization of the United Nations (FAO), Via delle Terme di Caracalla, 00100 Rome, Italy (Telephone Number in U.S. (202) 653-2400); *Animal Health Yearbook*.

MAURITIUS - AREA AND DENSITY OF POPULATION

African Development Bank, 01 BP 1387, Abidjan 01, Cote d'Ivoire; *Selected Statistics on Regional Member Countries*.

Facts on File, 460 Park Avenue South, New York, New York 10016 (800) 443-8323; *The New Book of World Rankings*.

Food and Agricultural Organization of the United Nations (FAO), Via delle Terme di Caracalla, 00100 Rome, Italy (Telephone Number in U.S. (202) 653-2400); *The State of Food and Agriculture*.

G.K. Hall and Company, 70 Lincoln Street, Boston, Massachusetts 02111 (617) 423-3990; *The World in Figures*.

Statistical Office of the United Nations, Publishing Service, New York, New York 10017 (800) 253-9646; *Statistical Yearbook*, and *Survey of Economic and Social Conditions in Africa*.

Times Books, 201 East 50th Street, New York, New York 10022 (212) 751-2600; *The Economist Book of Vital World Statistics*.

MAURITIUS - ARMS EXPORTS AND IMPORTS

U.S. Arms Control and Disarmament Agency, 320 Twenty-first Street, NW, Washington, D.C. 20451 (202) 647-8677; *World Military Expenditures and Arms Transfers*.

MAURITIUS - BALANCE OF PAYMENTS

African Development Bank, 01 BP 1387, Abidjan 01, Cote d'Ivoire; *Selected Statistics on Regional Member Countries*.

G.K. Hall and Company, 70 Lincoln Street, Boston, Massachusetts 02111 (617) 423-3990; *The World in Figures*.

International Monetary Fund, 700 Nineteenth Street, NW, Washington, D.C. 20431 (202) 623-7000; *Balance of Payments Yearbook*.

Times Books, 201 East 50th Street, New York, New York 10022 (212) 751-2600; *The Economist Book of Vital World Statistics*.

United Nations Economic Commission for Africa, Africa Hall, Post Office Box 3001, Addis Ababa, Ethiopia (Telephone Number in U.S. (800) 253-9646); *African Statistical Yearbook*.

The World Bank, 1818 H Street, NW, Washington, D.C. 20433 (202) 477-1234; *World Tables*.

MAURITIUS - BANKING

Facts on File, 460 Park Avenue South, New York, New York 10016 (800) 443-8323; *The New Book of World Rankings*.

G.K. Hall and Company, 70 Lincoln Street, Boston, Massachusetts 02111 (617) 423-3990; *The World in Figures*.

International Monetary Fund, 700 Nineteenth Street, NW, Washington, D.C. 20431 (202) 623-7000; *Government Finance Statistics Yearbook*.

Statistical Office of the United Nations, Publishing Service, New York, New York 10017 (800) 253-9646; *Statistical Yearbook*.

United Nations Economic Commission for Africa, Africa Hall, Post Office Box 3001, Addis Ababa, Ethiopia (Telephone Number in U.S. (800) 253-9646); *African Statistical Yearbook*.

MAURITIUS - BARLEY PRODUCTION - See MAURITIUS - CROPS

MAURITIUS - BEER PRODUCTION

Facts on File, 460 Park Avenue South, New York, New York 10016 (800) 443-8323; *The New Book of World Rankings*.

Statistical Office of the United Nations, Publishing Service, New York, New York 10017 (800) 253-9646; *Statistical Yearbook*.

MAURITIUS - BIRTH RATES

Facts on File, 460 Park Avenue South, New York, New York 10016 (800) 443-8323; *The New Book of World Rankings*.

Statistical Office of the United Nations, Publishing Service, New York, New York 10017 (800) 253-9646; *Demographic Yearbook*, *Statistical Yearbook*, and *Survey of Economic and Social Conditions in Africa*.

Times Books, 201 East 50th Street, New York, New York 10022 (212) 751-2600; *The Economist Book of Vital World Statistics*.

The World Bank, 1818 H Street, NW, Washington, D.C. 20433 (202) 477-1234; *World Tables*.

World Health Organization, Office of Publications, Avenue Appia, CH-1211 Geneva 27, Switzerland (Telephone in U.S. (518) 436-9686); *World Health Statistics Annual*.

MAURITIUS - BONDS

G.K. Hall and Company, 70 Lincoln Street, Boston, Massachusetts 02111 (617) 423-3990; *The World in Figures*.

International Monetary Fund, 700 Nineteenth Street, NW, Washington, D.C. 20431 (202) 623-7000; *Government Finance Statistics Yearbook*.

MAURITIUS - BOOK PRODUCTION

G.K. Hall and Company, 70 Lincoln Street, Boston, Massachusetts 02111 (617) 423-3990; *The World in Figures*.

United Nations Educational, Scientific and Cultural Organization (UNESCO), 7 Place de Fontenoy, F-75700 Paris, France; *Statistical Yearbook*.

MAURITIUS - BROADCASTING

Billboard Limited, Post Office Box 9027, 1006 AA Amsterdam, The Netherlands (Telephone Number in U.S. (212) 764-7300); *World Radio TV Handbook*.

Facts on File, 460 Park Avenue South, New York, New York 10016 (800) 443-8323; *The New Book of World Rankings*.

G.K. Hall and Company, 70 Lincoln Street, Boston, Massachusetts 02111 (617) 423-3990; *The World in Figures*.

Times Books, 201 East 50th Street, New York, New York 10022 (212) 751-2600; *The Economist Book of Vital World Statistics*.

MAURITIUS - BUSINESS

G.K. Hall and Company, 70 Lincoln Street, Boston, Massachusetts 02111 (617) 423-3990; *The World in Figures*.

MAURITIUS - BUSINESS AND PROFESSIONAL LICENSES

International Monetary Fund, 700 Nineteenth Street, NW, Washington, D.C. 20431 (202) 623-7000; *Government Finance Statistics Yearbook*.

MAURITIUS - CALORIE SUPPLY

African Development Bank, 01 BP 1387, Abidjan 01, Cote d'Ivoire; *Selected Statistics on Regional Member Countries*.

Food and Agricultural Organization of the United Nations (FAO), Via delle Terme di Caracalla, 00100 Rome, Italy (Telephone Number in U.S. (202) 653-2400); *The State of Food and Agriculture*.

MAURITIUS - CAPITAL REVENUE

International Monetary Fund, 700 Nineteenth Street, NW, Washington, D.C. 20431 (202) 623-7000; *Government Finance Statistics Yearbook*.

MAURITIUS - CATTLE - See MAURITIUS - LIVESTOCK AND POULTRY

MAURITIUS - CEMENT PRODUCTION - See MAURITIUS - MINING AND MINERAL PRODUCTS

MAURITIUS - CHEMICAL (ORGANIC) PRODUCTION - See MAURITIUS - MINING AND MINERAL PRODUCTS

MAURITIUS - CHICKENS - See MAURITIUS - LIVESTOCK AND POULTRY

MAURITIUS - CIGARETTE PRODUCTION - See MAURITIUS - TOBACCO PRODUCTION

MAURITIUS - CLASS STRUCTURE

G.K. Hall and Company, 70 Lincoln Street, Boston, Massachusetts 02111 (617) 423-3990; *The World in Figures*.

MAURITIUS - CLIMATE

Facts on File, 460 Park Avenue South, New York, New York 10016 (800) 443-8323; *The New Book of World Rankings*.

G.K. Hall and Company, 70 Lincoln Street, Boston, Massachusetts 02111 (617) 423-3990; *The World in Figures*.

MAURITIUS - CLOTHING EXPORTS AND IMPORTS - See MAURITIUS TEXTILE INDUSTRY

MAURITIUS - COAL PRODUCTION - See MAURITIUS - MINING AND MINERAL PRODUCTS

MAURITIUS - COFFEE PRODUCTION AND CONSUMPTION - See MAURITIUS - CROPS

MAURITIUS - COMMUNICATIONS

G.K. Hall and Company, 70 Lincoln Street, Boston, Massachusetts 02111 (617) 423-3990; *The World in Figures*.

United Nations Economic Commission for Africa, Africa Hall, Post Office Box 3001, Addis Ababa, Ethiopia (Telephone Number in U.S. (800) 253-9646); *African Statistical Yearbook*.

MAURITIUS - CONSTRUCTION INDUSTRY

Facts on File, 460 Park Avenue South, New York, New York 10016 (800) 443-8323; *The New Book of World Rankings*.

Statistical Office of the United Nations, Publishing Service, New York, New York 10017 (800) 253-9646; *Statistical Yearbook*.

United Nations Economic Commission for Africa, Africa Hall, Post Office Box 3001, Addis Ababa, Ethiopia (Telephone Number in U.S. (800) 253-9646); *African Statistical Yearbook*.

MAURITIUS - CONSUMER PRICE INDEX

African Development Bank, 01 BP 1387, Abidjan 01, Cote d'Ivoire; *Selected Statistics on Regional Member Countries*.

G.K. Hall and Company, 70 Lincoln Street, Boston, Massachusetts 02111 (617) 423-3990; *The World in Figures*.

Statistical Office of the United Nations, Publishing Service, New York, New York 10017 (800) 253-9646; *Statistical Yearbook*, and *Survey of Economic and Social Conditions in Africa*.

United Nations Economic Commission for Africa, Africa Hall, Post Office Box 3001, Addis Ababa, Ethiopia (Telephone Number in U.S.

(800) 253-9646); *African Statistical Yearbook.*

MAURITIUS - CONSUMER PRICES

International Labour Office, I.L.O. Publications, CH-1211, Geneva 22, Switzerland; *Yearbook of Labour Statistics.*

International Monetary Fund, 700 Nineteenth Street, NW, Washington, D.C. 20431 (202) 623-7000; *International Financial Statistics.*

Times Books, 201 East 50th Street, New York, New York 10022 (212) 751-2600; *The Economist Book of Vital World Statistics.*

MAURITIUS - CONSUMPTION

African Development Bank, 01 BP 1387, Abidjan 01, Cote d'Ivoire; *Selected Statistics on Regional Member Countries.*

G.K. Hall and Company, 70 Lincoln Street, Boston, Massachusetts 02111 (617) 423-3990; *The World in Figures.*

Statistical Office of the United Nations, Publishing Service, New York, New York 10017 (800) 253-9646; *Survey of Economic and Social Conditions in Africa.*

MAURITIUS - COPPER PRODUCTION AND CONSUMPTION - See MAURITIUS - MINING AND MINERAL PRODUCTS

MAURITIUS - CORN PRODUCTION - See MAURITIUS - CROPS

MAURITIUS - CORPORATE TAXES - See MAURITIUS - TAXATION

MAURITIUS - COTTON PRODUCTION - See MAURITIUS - CROPS

MAURITIUS - CRIME

Yale University Press, Yale Station, New Haven, Connecticut 06520; *Violence and Crime in Cross-National Perspective.*

MAURITIUS - CROPS

Facts on File, 460 Park Avenue South, New York, New York 10016 (800) 443-8323; *The New Book of World Rankings.*

Food and Agricultural Organization of the United Nations (FAO), Via delle Terme di Caracalla, 00100 Rome, Italy (Telephone Number in U.S. (202) 653-2400); *Production Yearbook,* and *The State of Food and Agriculture.*

G.K. Hall and Company, 70 Lincoln Street, Boston, Massachusetts 02111 (617) 423-3990; *The World in Figures.*

International Monetary Fund, 700 Nineteenth Street, NW, Washington, D.C. 20431 (202) 623-7000; *International Financial Statistics.*

Statistical Office of the United Nations, Publishing Service, New York, New York 10017 (800) 253-9646; *Statistical Yearbook.*

United Nations Economic Commission for Africa, Africa Hall, Post Office Box 3001, Addis Ababa, Ethiopia (Telephone Number in U.S. (800) 253-9646); *African Statistical Yearbook.*

MAURITIUS - CUSTOMS DUTIES

G.K. Hall and Company, 70 Lincoln Street, Boston, Massachusetts 02111 (617) 423-3990; *The World in Figures.*

International Monetary Fund, 700 Nineteenth Street, NW, Washington, D.C. 20431 (202) 623-7000; *Government Finance Statistics Yearbook.*

MAURITIUS - DAIRY PRODUCTS

Facts on File, 460 Park Avenue South, New York, New York 10016 (800) 443-8323; *The New Book of World Rankings.*

Food and Agricultural Organization of the United Nations (FAO), Via delle Terme di Caracalla, 00100 Rome, Italy (Telephone Number in U.S. (202) 653-2400); *The State of Food and Agriculture.*

MAURITIUS - DEATH RATES

G.K. Hall and Company, 70 Lincoln Street, Boston, Massachusetts 02111 (617) 423-3990; *The World in Figures.*

Statistical Office of the United Nations, Publishing Service, New York, New York 10017 (800) 253-9646; *Statistical Yearbook,* and *Survey of Economic and Social Conditions in Africa.*

Times Books, 201 East 50th Street, New York, New York 10022 (212) 751-2600; *The Economist Book of Vital World Statistics.*

World Health Organization, Office of Publications, Avenue Appia, CH-1211 Geneva 27, Switzerland (Telephone in U.S. (518) 436-9686); *World Health Statistics Annual.*

MAURITIUS - DEFENSE EXPENDITURES

G.K. Hall and Company, 70 Lincoln Street, Boston, Massachusetts 02111 (617) 423-3990; *The World in Figures.*

International Monetary Fund, 700 Nineteenth Street, NW, Washington, D.C. 20431 (202) 623-7000; *Government Finance Statistics Yearbook.*

U.S. Arms Control and Disarmament Agency, 320 Twenty-first Street, NW, Washington, D.C. 20451 (202) 647-8677; *World Military Expenditures and Arms Transfers.*

MAURITIUS - DEMOGRAPHY

Facts on File, 460 Park Avenue South, New York, New York 10016 (800) 443-8323; *The New Book of World Rankings.*

G.K. Hall and Company, 70 Lincoln Street, Boston, Massachusetts 02111 (617) 423-3990; *The World in Figures.*

Statistical Office of the United Nations, Publishing Service, New York, New York 10017 (800) 253-9646; *Survey of Economic and Social Conditions in Africa.*

MAURITIUS - DEVELOPMENT ASSISTANCE

G.K. Hall and Company, 70 Lincoln Street, Boston, Massachusetts 02111 (617) 423-3990; *The World in Figures.*

Statistical Office of the United Nations, Publishing Service, New York, New York 10017 (800) 253-9646; *Statistical Yearbook.*

MAURITIUS - DIAMOND PRODUCTION - See MAURITIUS - MINING AND MINERAL PRODUCTS

MAURITIUS - DISCOUNT RATES

Statistical Office of the United Nations, Publishing Service, New York, New York 10017 (800) 253-9646; *Statistical Yearbook.*

MAURITIUS - DISEASE

G.K. Hall and Company, 70 Lincoln Street, Boston, Massachusetts 02111 (617) 423-3990; *The World in Figures*.

World Health Organization, Office of Publications, Avenue Appia, CH-1211 Geneva 27, Switzerland (Telephone in U.S. (518) 436-9686); *World Health Statistics Annual*.

MAURITIUS - DIVORCE

Facts on File, 460 Park Avenue South, New York, New York 10016 (800) 443-8323; *The New Book of World Rankings*.

Statistical Office of the United Nations, Publishing Service, New York, New York 10017 (800) 253-9646; *Demographic Yearbook*.

MAURITIUS - DOMESTIC PRODUCT

G.K. Hall and Company, 70 Lincoln Street, Boston, Massachusetts 02111 (617) 423-3990; *The World in Figures*.

MAURITIUS - DUCKS - See MAURITIUS - LIVESTOCK AND POULTRY

MAURITIUS - ECONOMY

African Development Bank, 01 BP 1387, Abidjan 01, Cote d'Ivoire; *Selected Statistics on Regional Member Countries*.

Facts on File, 460 Park Avenue South, New York, New York 10016 (800) 443-8323; *The New Book of World Rankings*.

G.K. Hall and Company, 70 Lincoln Street, Boston, Massachusetts 02111 (617) 423-3990; *The World in Figures*.

Statistical Office of the United Nations, Publishing Service, New York, New York 10017; *Foreign Trade Statistics for Africa*.

MAURITIUS - EDUCATION

African Development Bank, 01 BP 1387, Abidjan 01, Cote d'Ivoire; *Selected Statistics on Regional Member Countries*.

Facts on File, 460 Park Avenue South, New York, New York 10016 (800) 443-8323; *The New Book of World Rankings*.

G.K. Hall and Company, 70 Lincoln Street, Boston, Massachusetts 02111 (617) 423-3990; *The World in Figures*.

International Monetary Fund, 700 Nineteenth Street, NW, Washington, D.C. 20431 (202) 623-7000; *Government Finance Statistics Yearbook*.

Statistical Office of the United Nations, Publishing Service, New York, New York 10017 (800) 253-9646; *Survey of Economic and Social Conditions in Africa*.

Times Books, 201 East 50th Street, New York, New York 10022 (212) 751-2600; *The Economist Book of Vital World Statistics*.

United Nations Economic Commission for Africa, Africa Hall, Post Office Box 3001, Addis Ababa, Ethiopia (Telephone Number in U.S. (800) 253-9646); *African Statistical Yearbook*.

United Nations Educational, Scientific and Cultural Organization (UNESCO), 7 Place de Fontenoy, F-75700 Paris, France (Telephone Number in U.S. (212) 963-5981); *Statistical Yearbook*.

The World Bank, 1818 H Street, NW, Washington, D.C. 20433 (202) 477-1234; *World Tables*.

MAURITIUS - EGG PRODUCTION AND CONSUMPTION - See MAURITIUS - DAIRY PRODUCTS

MAURITIUS - ELECTRICITY

Facts on File, 460 Park Avenue South, New York, New York 10016 (800) 443-8323; *The New Book of World Rankings*.

Statistical Office of the United Nations, Publishing Service, New York, New York 10017 (800) 253-9646; *Statistical Yearbook*, and *Survey of Economic and Social Conditions in Africa*.

Times Books, 201 East 50th Street, New York, New York 10022 (212) 751-2600; *The Economist Book of Vital World Statistics*.

United Nations Economic Commission for Africa, Africa Hall, Post Office Box 3001, Addis Ababa, Ethiopia (Telephone Number in U.S. (800) 253-9646); *African Statistical Yearbook*.

MAURITIUS - EMPLOYMENT

Facts on File, 460 Park Avenue South, New York, New York 10016 (800) 443-8323; *The New Book of World Rankings*.

International Labour Office, I.L.O. Publications, CH-1211, Geneva 22, Switzerland; *Yearbook of Labour Statistics*.

Statistical Office of the United Nations, Publishing Service, New York, New York 10017 (800) 253-9646; *Statistical Yearbook*, and *Survey of Economic and Social Conditions in Africa*.

United Nations Economic Commission for Africa, Africa Hall, Post Office Box 3001, Addis Ababa, Ethiopia (Telephone Number in U.S. (800) 253-9646); *African Statistical Yearbook*.

MAURITIUS - ENERGY

Facts on File, 460 Park Avenue South, New York, New York 10016 (800) 443-8323; *The New Book of World Rankings*.

Food and Agricultural Organization of the United Nations (FAO), Via delle Terme di Caracalla, 00100 Rome, Italy (Telephone Number in U.S. (202) 653-2400); *The State of Food and Agriculture*.

G.K. Hall and Company, 70 Lincoln Street, Boston, Massachusetts 02111 (617) 423-3990; *The World in Figures*.

Statistical Office of the United Nations, Publishing Service, New York, New York 10017 (800) 253-9646; *Energy Statistics Yearbook*, and *Statistical Yearbook*.

Times Books, 201 East 50th Street, New York, New York 10022 (212) 751-2600; *The Economist Book of Vital World Statistics*.

United Nations Economic Commission for Africa, Africa Hall, Post Office Box 3001, Addis Ababa, Ethiopia (Telephone Number in U.S. (800) 253-9646); *African Statistical Yearbook*.

MAURITIUS - EXCHANGE RATES

African Development Bank, 01 BP 1387, Abidjan 01, Cote d'Ivoire; *Selected Statistics on Regional Member Countries*.

International Civil Aviation Organization, 1000 Sherbrooke Street West, Suite 400, Montreal, Quebec H3A 2R2, Canada (514) 285-8219; *Civil Aviation Statistics of the World*.

International Monetary Fund, 700 Nineteenth Street, NW, Washington, D.C. 20431 (202) 623-7000; *International Financial Statistics*.

Statistical Office of the United Nations, Publishing Service, New York, New York 10017 ((800) 253-9646; *Foreign Trade Statistics for Africa*, and *Statistical Yearbook*.

MAURITIUS - EXCISE TAXES - See MAURITIUS - TAXATION

MAURITIUS - EXPORTS

African Development Bank, 01 BP 1387, Abidjan 01, Cote d'Ivoire; *Selected Statistics on Regional Member Countries*.

Food and Agricultural Organization of the United Nations (FAO), Via delle Terme di Caracalla, 00100 Rome, Italy (Telephone Number in U.S. (202) 653-2400); *The State of Food and Agriculture*.

G.K. Hall and Company, 70 Lincoln Street, Boston, Massachusetts 02111 (617) 423-3990; *The World in Figures*.

International Monetary Fund, 700 Nineteenth Street, NW, Washington, D.C. 20431 (202) 623-7000; *Direction of Trade Statistics*, *Government Finance Statistics Yearbook*, and *International Financial Statistics*.

Statistical Office of the United Nations, Publishing Service, New York, New York 10017 (800) 253-9646; *Foreign Trade Statistics for Africa*, and *Survey of Economic and Social Conditions in Africa*.

Times Books, 201 East 50th Street, New York, New York 10022 (212) 751-2600; *The Economist Book of Vital World Statistics*.

United Nations Economic Commission for Africa, Africa Hall, Post Office Box 3001, Addis Ababa, Ethiopia (Telephone Number in U.S (800) 253-9646); *African Statistical Yearbook*.

The World Bank, 1818 H Street, NW, Washington, D.C. 20433 (202) 477-1234; *World Tables*.

MAURITIUS - EXTERNAL INDEBTEDNESS

African Development Bank, 01 BP 1387, Abidjan 01, Cote d'Ivoire; *Selected Statistics on Regional Member Countries*.

Statistical Office of the United Nations, Publishing Service, New York, New York 10017 (800) 253-9646; *Survey of Economic and Social Conditions in Africa*.

The World Bank, 1818 H Street, NW, Washington, D.C. 20433 (202) 477-1234; *World Tables*.

MAURITIUS - EXTERNAL TRADE

African Development Bank, 01 BP 1387, Abidjan 01, Cote d'Ivoire; *Selected Statistics on Regional Member Countries*.

Food and Agricultural Organization of the United Nations (FAO), Via delle Terme di Caracalla, 00100 Rome, Italy (Telephone Number in U.S. (202) 653-2400); *The State of Food and Agriculture*, and *Trade Yearbook*.

G.K. Hall and Company, 70 Lincoln Street, Boston, Massachusetts 02111 (617) 423-3990; *The World in Figures*.

Statistical Office of the United Nations, Publishing Service, New York, New York 10017 (800) 253-9646; *Statistical Yearbook*.

MAURITIUS - FARM CROPS - See MAURITIUS - CROPS

MAURITIUS - FERTILITY RATES

Facts on File, 460 Park Avenue South, New York, New York 10016 (800) 443-8323; *The New Book of World Rankings*.

Statistical Office of the United Nations, Publishing Service, New York, New York 10017 (800) 253-9646; *Survey of Economic and Social Conditions in Africa*.

Times Books, 201 East 50th Street, New York, New York 10022 (212) 751-2600; *The Economist Book of Vital World Statistics*.

The World Bank, 1818 H Street, NW, Washington, D.C. 20433 (202) 477-1234; *World Tables*.

MAURITIUS - FERTILIZER

Food and Agricultural Organization of the United Nations (FAO), Via delle Terme di Caracalla, 00100 Rome, Italy (Telephone Number in U.S. (202) 653-2400); *Fertilizer Yearbook*, and *The State of Food and Agriculture*.

Statistical Office of the United Nations, Publishing Service, New York, New York 10017 (800) 253-9646; *Statistical Yearbook*.

MAURITIUS - FETAL MORTALITY

Statistical Office of the United Nations, Publishing Service, New York, New York 10017 (000) 253-9646; *Demographic Yearbook*.

World Health Organization, Office of Publications, Avenue Appia, CH-1211 Geneva 27, Switzerland (Telephone in U.S. (518) 436-9686); *World Health Statistics Annual*.

MAURITIUS - FINANCE

African Development Bank, 01 BP 1387, Abidjan 01, Cote d'Ivoire; *Selected Statistics on Regional Member Countries*.

Facts on File, 460 Park Avenue South, New York, New York 10016 (800) 443-8323; *The New Book of World Rankings*.

G.K. Hall and Company, 70 Lincoln Street, Boston, Massachusetts 02111 (617) 423-3990; *The World in Figures*.

International Monetary Fund, 700 Nineteenth Street, NW, Washington, D.C. 20431 (202) 623-7000; *International Financial Statistics*.

United Nations Economic Commission for Africa, Africa Hall, Post Office Box 3001, Addis Ababa, Ethiopia (Telephone Number in U.S. (800) 253-9646); *African Statistical Yearbook*.

MAURITIUS - FISHERIES

Facts on File, 460 Park Avenue South, New York, New York 10016 (800) 443-8323; *The New Book of World Rankings*.

Food and Agricultural Organization of the United Nations (FAO), Via delle Terme di Caracalla, 00100 Rome, Italy (Telephone Number in U.S. (202) 653-2400); *The State of Food and Agriculture*, and *Yearbook of Fishery Statistics*.

Statistical Office of the United Nations, Publishing Service, New York, New York 10017 (800) 253-9646; *Statistical Yearbook*, and *Survey of Economic and Social Conditions in Africa*.

United Nations Economic Commission for Africa, Africa Hall, Post Office Box 3001, Addis Ababa, Ethiopia (Telephone Number in U.S. (800) 253-9646); *African Statistical Yearbook*.

MAURITIUS - FOOD

African Development Bank, 01 BP 1387, Abidjan 01, Cote d'Ivoire; *Selected Statistics on Regional Member Countries*.

Food and Agricultural Organization of the United Nations (FAO), Via delle Terme di Caracalla, 00100 Rome, Italy (Telephone Number in U.S. (202) 653-2400); *Production Yearbook*, and *The State of Food and Agriculture*.

G.K. Hall and Company, 70 Lincoln Street, Boston, Massachusetts 02111 (617) 423-3990; *The World in Figures*.

MAURITIUS - FOREIGN AID

G.K. Hall and Company, 70 Lincoln Street, Boston, Massachusetts 02111 (617) 423-3990; *The World in Figures*.

MAURITIUS - FOREIGN DEBT

International Monetary Fund, 700 Nineteenth Street, NW, Washington, D.C. 20431 (202) 623-7000; *Government Finance Statistics Yearbook*.

MAURITIUS - FOREIGN TRADE

Facts on File, 460 Park Avenue South, New York, New York 10016 (800) 443-8323; *The New Book of World Rankings*.

Food and Agricultural Organization of the United Nations (FAO), Via delle Terme di Caracalla, 00100 Rome, Italy (Telephone Number in U.S. (202) 653-2400); *The State of Food and Agriculture*.

G.K. Hall and Company, 70 Lincoln Street, Boston, Massachusetts 02111 (617) 423-3990; *The World in Figures*.

International Monetary Fund, 700 Nineteenth Street, NW, Washington, D.C. 20431 (202) 623-7000; *International Financial Statistics*.

Statistical Office of the United Nations, Publishing Service, New York, New York 10017 (800) 253-9646; *Foreign Trade Statistics for Africa, International Trade Statistics Yearbook*, and *Statistical Yearbook*.

United Nations Economic Commission for Africa, Africa Hall, Post Office Box 3001, Addis Ababa, Ethiopia (Telephone Number in U.S. (800) 253-9646); *African Statistical Yearbook*.

The World Bank, 1818 H Street, NW, Washington, D.C. 20433 (202) 477-1234; *World Tables*.

MAURITIUS - FORESTRY AND FOREST PRODUCTS

Facts on File, 460 Park Avenue South, New York, New York 10016 (800) 443-8323; *The New Book of World Rankings*.

Food and Agricultural Organization of the United Nations (FAO), Via delle Terme di Caracalla, 00100 Rome, Italy (Telephone Number in U.S. (202) 653-2400); *The State of Food and Agriculture*, and *Yearbook of Forest Products*.

G.K. Hall and Company, 70 Lincoln Street, Boston, Massachusetts 02111 (617) 423-3990; *The World in Figures*.

Statistical Office of the United Nations, Publishing Service, New York, New York 10017 (800) 253-9646; *Statistical Yearbook*.

United Nations Economic Commission for Africa, Africa Hall, Post Office Box 3001, Addis Ababa, Ethiopia (Telephone Number in U.S. (800) 253-9646); *African Statistical Yearbook*.

United Nations Educational, Scientific and Cultural Organization (UNESCO), 7 Place de Fontenoy, F-75700 Paris, France (Telephone Number in U.S. (212) 963-5981); *Statistical Yearbook*.

MAURITIUS - GAS PRODUCTION - See MAURITIUS - MINING AND MINERAL PRODUCTS

MAURITIUS - GENERAL INDUSTRIAL STATISTICS

Statistical Office of the United Nations, Publishing Service, New York, New York 10017 (800) 253-9646; *Industrial Statistics Yearbook*.

MAURITIUS - GENERAL MORTALITY

Statistical Office of the United Nations, Publishing Service, New York, New York 10017 (800) 253-9646; *Demographic Yearbook*.

World Health Organization, Office of Publications, Avenue Appia, CH-1211 Geneva 27, Switzerland (Telephone in U.S. (518) 436-9686); *World Health Statistics Annual*.

MAURITIUS - GEOGRAPHIC DATA

Facts on File, 460 Park Avenue South, New York, New York 10016 (800) 443-8323; *The New Book of World Rankings*.

MAURITIUS - GOATS - See MAURITIUS - LIVESTOCK AND POULTRY

MAURITIUS - GOLD HOLDINGS

International Monetary Fund, 700 Nineteenth Street, NW, Washington, D.C. 20431 (202) 623-7000; *International Financial Statistics*.

Statistical Office of the United Nations, Publishing Service, New York, New York 10017 (800) 253-9646; *Statistical Yearbook*.

The World Bank, 1818 H Street, NW, Washington, D.C. 20433 (202) 477-1234; *World Tables*.

MAURITIUS - GOLD PRODUCTION AND CONSUMPTION - See MAURITIUS - MINING AND MINERAL PRODUCTS

MAURITIUS - GOVERNMENT

G.K. Hall and Company, 70 Lincoln Street, Boston, Massachusetts 02111 (617) 423-3990; *The World in Figures*.

MAURITIUS - GOVERNMENT EXPENDITURES

International Monetary Fund, 700 Nineteenth Street, NW, Washington, D.C. 20431 (202) 623-7000; *Government Finance Statistics Yearbook*.

Times Books, 201 East 50th Street, New York, New York 10022 (212) 751-2600; *The Economist Book of Vital World Statistics*.

The World Bank, 1818 H Street, NW, Washington, D.C. 20433 (202) 477-1234; *World Tables*.

MAURITIUS - GOVERNMENT FINANCES

International Monetary Fund, 700 Nineteenth Street, NW, Washington, D.C. 20431 (202) 623-7000; *International Financial Statistics*.

MAURITIUS - GOVERNMENT REVENUES

International Monetary Fund, 700 Nineteenth Street, NW, Washington, D.C. 20431 (202) 623-7000; *Government Finance Statistics Yearbook*.

Statistical Office of the United Nations, Publishing Service, New York, New York 10017 (800) 253-9646; *Survey of Economic and Social Conditions in Africa*.

Times Books, 201 East 50th Street, New York, New York 10022 (212) 751-2600; *The Economist Book of Vital World Statistics*.

The World Bank, 1818 H Street, NW, Washington, D.C. 20433 (202) 477-1234; *World Tables*.

MAURITIUS - GRAIN PRODUCTION - See MAURITIUS - CROPS

MAURITIUS - GRANTS

International Monetary Fund, 700 Nineteenth Street, NW, Washington, D.C. 20431 (202) 623-7000; *Government Finance Statistics Yearbook*.

MAURITIUS - GROSS DOMESTIC PRODUCT

African Development Bank, 01 BP 1387, Abidjan 01, Cote d'Ivoire; *Selected Statistics on Regional Member Countries*.

Facts on File, 460 Park Avenue South, New York, New York 10016 (800) 443-8323; *The New Book of World Rankings*.

G.K. Hall and Company, 70 Lincoln Street, Boston, Massachusetts 02111 (617) 423-3990; *The World in Figures*.

Statistical Office of the United Nations, Publishing Service, New York, New York 10017 (800) 253-9646; *Statistical Yearbook*, and *Survey of Economic and Social Conditions in Africa*.

Times Books, 201 East 50th Street, New York, New York 10022 (212) 751-2600; *The Economist Book of Vital World Statistics*.

United Nations Economic Commission for Africa, Africa Hall, Post Office Box 3001, Addis Ababa, Ethiopia (Telephone Number in U.S. (800) 253-9646); *African Statistical Yearbook*.

The World Bank, 1818 H Street, NW, Washington, D.C. 20433 (202) 477-1234; *World Tables*.

MAURITIUS - GROSS NATIONAL PRODUCT

U.S. Arms Control and Disarmament Agency, 320 Twenty-first Street, NW, Washington, D.C. 20451 (202) 647-8677; *World Military Expenditures and Arms Transfers*.

The World Bank, 1818 H Street, NW, Washington, D.C. 20433 (202) 477-1234; *World Tables*.

MAURITIUS - GROUNDNUT PRODUCTION - See MAURITIUS - CROPS

MAURITIUS - HEALTH

African Development Bank, 01 BP 1387, Abidjan 01, Cote d'Ivoire; *Selected Statistics on Regional Member Countries*.

Facts on File, 460 Park Avenue South, New York, New York 10016 (800) 443-8323; *The New Book of World Rankings*.

G.K. Hall and Company, 70 Lincoln Street, Boston, Massachusetts 02111 (617) 423-3990; *The World in Figures*.

Statistical Office of the United Nations, Publishing Service, New York, New York 10017 (800) 253-9646; *Statistical Yearbook*.

Times Books, 201 East 50th Street, New York, New York 10022 (212) 751-2600; *The Economist Book of Vital World Statistics*.

United Nations Economic Commission for Africa, Africa Hall, Post Office Box 3001, Addis Ababa, Ethiopia (Telephone Number in U.S. (800) 253-9646); *African Statistical Yearbook*.

World Health Organization, Office of Publications, Avenue Appia, CH-1211 Geneva 27, Switzerland (Telephone in U.S. (518) 436-9686); *World Health Statistics Annual*.

MAURITIUS - HIDE PRODUCTION

Food and Agricultural Organization of the United Nations (FAO), Via delle Terme di Caracalla, 00100 Rome, Italy (Telephone Number in U.S. (202) 653-2400); *Production Yearbook*.

MAURITIUS - HIGHWAYS

G.K. Hall and Company, 70 Lincoln Street, Boston, Massachusetts 02111 (617) 423-3990; *The World in Figures*.

Statistical Office of the United Nations, Publishing Service, New York, New York 10017 (800) 253-9646; *Survey of Economic and Social Conditions in Africa*.

United Nations Economic Commission for Africa, Africa Hall, Post Office Box 3001, Addis Ababa, Ethiopia (Telephone Number in U.S. (800) 253-9646); *African Statistical Yearbook*.

MAURITIUS - HORSES - See MAURITIUS - LIVESTOCK AND POULTRY

MAURITIUS - HOURS OF WORK - See MAURITIUS - EMPLOYMENT

MAURITIUS - HOUSING EXPENDITURES

Facts on File, 460 Park Avenue South, New York, New York 10016 (800) 443-8323; *The New Book of World Rankings*.

International Monetary Fund, 700 Nineteenth Street, NW, Washington, D.C. 20431 (202) 623-7000; *Government Finance Statistics Yearbook*.

MAURITIUS - ILLITERATE POPULATION

G.K. Hall and Company, 70 Lincoln Street, Boston, Massachusetts 02111 (617) 423-3990; *The World in Figures*.

United Nations Educational, Scientific and Cultural Organization (UNESCO), 7 Place de Fontenoy, F-75700 Paris, France (Telephone Number in U.S. (212) 963-5981); *Statistical Yearbook*.

MAURITIUS - IMPORTS

African Development Bank, 01 BP 1387, Abidjan 01, Cote d'Ivoire; *Selected Statistics on Regional Member Countries.*

Food and Agricultural Organization of the United Nations (FAO), Via delle Terme di Caracalla, 00100 Rome, Italy (Telephone Number in U.S. (202) 653-2400); *The State of Food and Agriculture.*

G.K. Hall and Company, 70 Lincoln Street, Boston, Massachusetts 02111 (617) 423-3990; *The World in Figures.*

International Monetary Fund, 700 Nineteenth Street, NW, Washington, D.C. 20431 (202) 623-7000; *Direction of Trade Statistics, Government Finance Statistics Yearbook,* and *International Financial Statistics.*

Statistical Office of the United Nations, Publishing Service, New York, New York 10017 (800) 253-9646; *Foreign Trade Statistics for Africa,* and *Survey of Economic and Social Conditions in Africa.*

Times Books, 201 East 50th Street, New York, New York 10022 (212) 751-2600; *The Economist Book of Vital World Statistics.*

United Nations Economic Commission for Africa, Africa Hall, Post Office Box 3001, Addis Ababa, Ethiopia (Telephone Number in U.S. (800) 253-9646); *African Statistical Yearbook.*

The World Bank, 1818 H Street, NW, Washington, D.C. 20433 (202) 477-1234; *World Tables.*

MAURITIUS - INCOME TAXES - See MAURITIUS - TAXATION

MAURITIUS - INDUSTRY

Facts on File, 460 Park Avenue South, New York, New York 10016 (800) 443-8323; *The New Book of World Rankings.*

G.K. Hall and Company, 70 Lincoln Street, Boston, Massachusetts 02111 (617) 423-3990; *The World in Figures.*

International Labour Office, I.L.O. Publications, CH-1211, Geneva 22, Switzerland; *Yearbook of Labour Statistics.*

Statistical Office of the United Nations, Publishing Service, New York, New York 10017 (800) 253-9646; *Survey of Economic and Social Conditions in Africa.*

Times Books, 201 East 50th Street, New York, New York 10022 (212) 751-2600; *The Economist Book of Vital World Statistics.*

United Nations Economic Commission for Africa, Africa Hall, Post Office Box 3001, Addis Ababa, Ethiopia (Telephone Number in U.S. (800) 253-9646); *African Statistical Yearbook.*

The World Bank, 1818 H Street, NW, Washington, D.C. 20433 (202) 477-1234; *World Tables.*

World Intellectual Property Organization, 34 Chemin des Colombettes, CH-1211 Geneva 20, Switzerland; *Industrial Property Statistics.*

MAURITIUS - INFANT AND MATERNAL MORTALITY

Statistical Office of the United Nations, Publishing Service, New York, New York 10017 (800) 253-9646; *Demographic Yearbook, Statistical Yearbook,* and *Survey of Economic and Social Conditions in Africa.*

Times Books, 201 East 50th Street, New York, New York 10022 (212) 751-2600; *The Economist Book of Vital World Statistics.*

The World Bank, 1818 H Street, NW, Washington, D.C. 20433 (202) 477-1234; *World Tables.*

World Health Organization, Office of Publications, Avenue Appia, CH-1211 Geneva 27, Switzerland (Telephone in U.S. (518) 436-9686); *World Health Statistics Annual.*

MAURITIUS - INTERNATIONAL LIQUIDITY

International Monetary Fund, 700 Nineteenth Street, NW, Washington, D.C. 20431 (202) 623-7000; *International Financial Statistics.*

MAURITIUS - INTERNATIONAL RESERVES EXCLUDING GOLD

African Development Bank, 01 BP 1387, Abidjan 01, Cote d'Ivoire; *Selected Statistics on Regional Member Countries.*

Statistical Office of the United Nations, Publishing Service, New York, New York 10017 (800) 253-9646; *Statistical Yearbook.*

The World Bank, 1818 H Street, NW, Washington, D.C. 20433 (202) 477-1234; *World Tables.*

MAURITIUS - IRON ORE PRODUCTION AND CONSUMPTION - See MAURITIUS - MINING AND MINERAL PRODUCTS

MAURITIUS - LABOR FORCE

African Development Bank, 01 BP 1387, Abidjan 01, Cote d'Ivoire; *Selected Statistics on Regional Member Countries.*

Facts on File, 460 Park Avenue South, New York, New York 10016 (800) 443-8323; *The New Book of World Rankings.*

Food and Agricultural Organization of the United Nations (FAO), Via delle Terme di Caracalla, 00100 Rome, Italy (Telephone Number in U.S. (202) 653-2400); *The State of Food and Agriculture.*

G.K. Hall and Company, 70 Lincoln Street, Boston, Massachusetts 02111 (617) 423-3990; *The World in Figures.*

Times Books, 201 East 50th Street, New York, New York 10022 (212) 751-2600; *The Economist Book of Vital World Statistics.*

The World Bank, 1818 H Street, NW, Washington, D.C. 20433 (202) 477-1234; *World Tables.*

MAURITIUS - LABOR PRODUCTIVITY

International Labour Office, I.L.O. Publications, CH-1211, Geneva 22, Switzerland; *Yearbook of Labour Statistics.*

MAURITIUS - LAND USE

Food and Agricultural Organization of the United Nations (FAO), Via delle Terme di Caracalla, 00100 Rome, Italy (Telephone Number in U.S. (202) 653-2400); *Production Yearbook.*

G.K. Hall and Company, 70 Lincoln Street, Boston, Massachusetts 02111 (617) 423-3990; *The World in Figures.*

MAURITIUS - LIBRARIES

Facts on File, 460 Park Avenue South, New York, New York 10016 (800) 443-8323; *The New Book of World Rankings*.

United Nations Educational, Scientific and Cultural Organization (UNESCO), 7 Place de Fontenoy, F-75700 Paris, France (Telephone Number in U.S. (212) 963-5981); *Statistical Yearbook*.

MAURITIUS - LIFE EXPECTANCY

African Development Bank, 01 BP 1387, Abidjan 01, Cote d'Ivoire; *Selected Statistics on Regional Member Countries*.

MAURITIUS - LITERACY RATE

Statistical Office of the United Nations, Publishing Service, New York, New York 10017 (800) 253-9646; *Survey of Economic and Social Conditions in Africa*.

MAURITIUS - LIVESTOCK AND POULTRY

Facts on File, 460 Park Avenue South, New York, New York 10016 (800) 443-8323; *The New Book of World Rankings*.

Food and Agricultural Organization of the United Nations (FAO), Via delle Terme di Caracalla, 00100 Rome, Italy (Telephone Number in U.S. (202) 653-2400); *Production Yearbook*, and *The State of Food and Agriculture*.

G.K. Hall and Company, 70 Lincoln Street, Boston, Massachusetts 02111 (617) 423-3990; *The World in Figures*.

Statistical Office of the United Nations, Publishing Service, New York, New York 10017 (800) 253-9646; *Survey of Economic and Social Conditions in Africa*.

United Nations Economic Commission for Africa, Africa Hall, Post Office Box 3001, Addis Ababa, Ethiopia (Telephone Number in U.S. (800) 253-9646); *African Statistical Yearbook*.

MAURITIUS - LIVING LEVELS

G.K. Hall and Company, 70 Lincoln Street, Boston, Massachusetts 02111 (617) 423-3990; *The World in Figures*.

Times Books, 201 East 50th Street, New York, New York 10022 (212) 751-2600; *The Economist Book of Vital World Statistics*.

MAURITIUS - MAIL - PIECES SENT OR RECEIVED

Statistical Office of the United Nations, Publishing Service, New York, New York 10017 (800) 253-9646; *Statistical Yearbook*.

MAURITIUS - MANUFACTURING

Facts on File, 460 Park Avenue South, New York, New York 10016 (800) 443-8323; *The New Book of World Rankings*.

G.K. Hall and Company, 70 Lincoln Street, Boston, Massachusetts 02111 (617) 423-3990; *The World in Figures*.

Statistical Office of the United Nations, Publishing Service, New York, New York 10017 (800) 253-9646; *Statistical Yearbook*, and *Survey of Economic and Social Conditions in Africa*.

Times Books, 201 East 50th Street, New York, New York 10022 (212) 751-2600; *The Economist Book of Vital World Statistics*.

United Nations Economic Commission for Africa, Africa Hall, Post Office Box 3001, Addis Ababa, Ethiopia (Telephone Number in U.S. (800) 253-9646); *African Statistical Yearbook*.

The World Bank, 1818 H Street, NW, Washington, D.C. 20433 (202) 477-1234; *World Tables*.

MAURITIUS - MARRIAGE RATES

Facts on File, 460 Park Avenue South, New York, New York 10016 (800) 443-8323; *The New Book of World Rankings*.

Statistical Office of the United Nations, Publishing Service, New York, New York 10017 (800) 253-9646; *Demographic Yearbook*.

MAURITIUS - MEAT PRODUCTION - See - MAURITIUS - LIVESTOCK AND POULTRY

MAURITIUS - MERCHANT SHIPPING

G.K. Hall and Company, 70 Lincoln Street, Boston, Massachusetts 02111 (617) 423-3990; *The World in Figures*.

Lloyd's Register of Shipping, 17 Battery Place, New York, New York 10004 (212) 425-8050; *Register of Ships*.

Statistical Office of the United Nations, Publishing Service, New York, New York 10017 (800) 253-9646; *Statistical Yearbook*.

Times Books, 201 East 50th Street, New York, New York 10022 (212) 751-2000; *The Economist Book of Vital World Statistics*.

United Nations Economic Commission for Africa, Africa Hall, Post Office Box 3001, Addis Ababa, Ethiopia (Telephone Number in U.S. (800) 253-9646); *African Statistical Yearbook*.

U.S. Department of Transportation, Maritime Administration, 400 Seventh Street, SW, Washington, D.C. 20590; *A Statistical Analysis of the World's Merchant Fleets*.

MAURITIUS - MILITARY

G.K. Hall and Company, 70 Lincoln Street, Boston, Massachusetts 02111 (617) 423-3990; *The World in Figures*.

Facts on File, 460 Park Avenue South, New York, New York 10016 (800) 443-8323; *The New Book of World Rankings*.

U.S. Arms Control and Disarmament Agency, 320 Twenty-first Street, NW, Washington, D.C. 20451 (202) 647-8677; *World Military Expenditures and Arms Transfers*.

MAURITIUS - MINING AND MINERAL PRODUCTS

Facts on File, 460 Park Avenue South, New York, New York 10016 (800) 443-8323; *The New Book of World Rankings*.

G.K. Hall and Company, 70 Lincoln Street, Boston, Massachusetts 02111 (617) 423-3990; *The World in Figures*.

Statistical Office of the United Nations, Publishing Service, New York, New York 10017 (800) 253-9646; *Statistical Yearbook*.

United Nations Economic Commission for Africa, Africa Hall, Post Office Box 3001, Addis Ababa, Ethiopia (Telephone Number in U.S. (800) 253-9646); *African Statistical Yearbook*.

MAURITIUS - MONEY EXCHANGE RATE

International Monetary Fund, 700 Nineteenth Street, NW, Washington, D.C. 20431 (202) 623-7000; *International Financial Statistics*.

Statistical Office of the United Nations, Publishing Service, New York, New York 10017 (800) 253-9646; *Statistical Yearbook*.

MAURITIUS - MONEY SUPPLY

African Development Bank, 01 BP 1387, Abidjan 01, Cote d'Ivoire; *Selected Statistics on Regional Member Countries*.

G.K. Hall and Company, 70 Lincoln Street, Boston, Massachusetts 02111 (617) 423-3990; *The World in Figures*.

International Monetary Fund, 700 Nineteenth Street, NW, Washington, D.C. 20431 (202) 623-7000; *International Financial Statistics*.

The World Bank, 1818 H Street, NW, Washington, D.C. 20433 (202) 477-1234; *World Tables*.

MAURITIUS - MONUMENTS AND HISTORICAL SITES

United Nations Educational, Scientific and Cultural Organization (UNESCO), 7 Place de Fontenoy, F-75700 Paris, France (Telephone Number in U.S. (212) 963-5981); *Statistical Yearbook*.

MAURITIUS - MOTION PICTURES

Statistical Office of the United Nations, Publishing Service, New York, New York 10017 (800) 253-9646; *Statistical Yearbook*.

MAURITIUS - MOTOR VEHICLE TAXES - See MAURITIUS - TAXATION

MAURITIUS - MOTOR VEHICLES IN USE

G.K. Hall and Company, 70 Lincoln Street, Boston, Massachusetts 02111 (617) 423-3990; *The World in Figures*.

Statistical Office of the United Nations, Publishing Service, New York, New York 10017 (800) 253-9646; *Statistical Yearbook*, and *Survey of Economic and Social Conditions in Africa*.

Times Books, 201 East 50th Street, New York, New York 10022 (212) 751-2600; *The Economist Book of Vital World Statistics*.

MAURITIUS - MUSEUMS

Facts on File, 460 Park Avenue South, New York, New York 10016 (800) 443-8323; *The New Book of World Rankings*.

United Nations Educational, Scientific and Cultural Organization (UNESCO), 7 Place de Fontenoy, F-75700 Paris, France (Telephone Number in U.S. (212) 963-5981); *Statistical Yearbook*.

MAURITIUS - NATALITY - See MAURITIUS - BIRTH RATES

MAURITIUS - NATIONAL ACCOUNTS

African Development Bank, 01 BP 1387, Abidjan 01, Cote d'Ivoire; *Selected Statistics on Regional Member Countries*.

International Monetary Fund, 700 Nineteenth Street, NW, Washington, D.C. 20431 (202) 623-7000; *International Financial Statistics*.

Statistical Office of the United Nations, Publishing Service, New York, New York 10017 (800) 253-9646; *National Account Statistics*, and *Statistical Yearbook*.

United Nations Economic Commission for Africa, Africa Hall, Post Office Box 3001, Addis Ababa, Ethiopia (Telephone Number in U.S. (800) 253-9646); *African Statistical Yearbook*.

MAURITIUS - NATIONAL INCOME

Facts on File, 460 Park Avenue South, New York, New York 10016 (800) 443-8323; *The New Book of World Rankings*.

G.K. Hall and Company, 70 Lincoln Street, Boston, Massachusetts 02111 (617) 423-3990; *The World in Figures*.

Statistical Office of the United Nations, Publishing Service, New York, New York 10017 (800) 253-9646; *Statistical Yearbook*.

MAURITIUS - NATIONAL PRODUCT

Facts on File, 460 Park Avenue South, New York, New York 10016 (800) 443-8323; *The New Book of World Rankings*.

Statistical Office of the United Nations, Publishing Service, New York, New York 10017 (800) 253-9646; *Statistical Yearbook*.

MAURITIUS - NATURAL GAS - PRODUCTION - See MAURITIUS - MINING AND MINERAL PRODUCTS

MAURITIUS - NEWSPAPER PRODUCTION - See MAURITIUS - FORESTRY AND FOREST PRODUCTS

MAURITIUS - NEWSPRINT - See MAURITIUS - FORESTRY AND FOREST PRODUCTS

MAURITIUS - OCCUPATIONS - See MAURITIUS - LABOR FORCE

MAURITIUS - PAPER - See MAURITIUS - FORESTRY AND FOREST PRODUCTS

MAURITIUS - PATENTS

Statistical Office of the United Nations, Publishing Service, New York, New York 10017 (800) 253-9646; *Statistical Yearbook*.

World Intellectual Property Organization, 34 Chemin des Colombettes, CH-1211 Geneva 20, Switzerland; *Industrial Property Statistics*.

MAURITIUS - PEANUT PRODUCTION - See MAURITIUS - CROPS

MAURITIUS - PERIODICALS

United Nations Educational, Scientific and Cultural Organization (UNESCO), 7 Place de Fontenoy, F-75700 Paris, France (Telephone Number in U.S. (212) 963-5981); *Statistical Yearbook*.

MAURITIUS - PESTICIDE USE

Food and Agricultural Organization of the United Nations (FAO), Via delle Terme di Caracalla, 00100 Rome, Italy (Telephone Number in U.S. (202) 653-2400); *The State of Food and Agriculture*.

MAURITIUS - PETROLEUM INDUSTRY

Facts on File, 460 Park Avenue South, New York, New York 10016 (800) 443-8323; *The New Book of World Rankings*.

Food and Agricultural Organization of the United Nations (FAO), Via delle Terme di Caracalla, 00100 Rome, Italy (Telephone Number in U.S. (202) 653-2400); *The State of Food and Agriculture.*

G.K. Hall and Company, 70 Lincoln Street, Boston, Massachusetts 02111 (617) 423-3990; *The World in Figures.*

MAURITIUS - PIGS - See MAURITIUS - LIVESTOCK AND POULTRY

MAURITIUS - POPULATION

African Development Bank, 01 BP 1387, Abidjan 01, Cote d'Ivoire; *Selected Statistics on Regional Member Countries.*

Facts on File, 460 Park Avenue South, New York, New York 10016 (800) 443-8323; *The New Book of World Rankings.*

Food and Agricultural Organization of the United Nations (FAO), Via delle Terme di Caracalla, 00100 Rome, Italy (Telephone Number in U.S. (202) 653-2400); *Production Yearbook.*

G.K. Hall and Company, 70 Lincoln Street, Boston, Massachusetts 02111 (617) 423-3990; *The World in Figures.*

International Labour Office, I.L.O. Publications, CH-1211, Geneva 22, Switzerland; *Yearbook of Labour Statistics.*

Statistical Office of the United Nations, Publishing Service, New York, New York 10017 (800) 253-9646; *Demographic Yearbook, Statistical Yearbook,* and *Survey of Economic and Social Conditions in Africa.*

Times Books, 201 East 50th Street, New York, New York 10022 (212) 751-2600; *The Economist Book of Vital World Statistics.*

U.S. Arms Control and Disarmament Agency, 320 Twenty-First Street, NW, Washington, D.C. 20451 (202) 647-8677; *World Military Expenditures and Arms Transfers.*

World Health Organization, Office of Publications, Avenue Appia, CH-1211 Geneva 27, Switzerland (Telephone in U.S. (518) 436-9686); *World Health Statistics Annual.*

MAURITIUS - POST OFFICES

Facts on File, 460 Park Avenue South, New York, New York 10016 (800) 443-8323; *The New Book of World Rankings.*

MAURITIUS - POTATO PRODUCTION - See MAURITIUS - CROPS

MAURITIUS - POWER PRODUCTION INDUSTRY - ESTABLISHMENTS, PAYROLLS, VALUE ADDED, ETC.

Statistical Office of the United Nations, Publishing Service, New York, New York 10017 (800) 253-9646; *Statistical Yearbook.*

MAURITIUS - PRICES

Facts on File, 460 Park Avenue South, New York, New York 10016 (800) 443-8323; *The New Book of World Rankings.*

Food and Agricultural Organization of the United Nations (FAO), Via delle Terme di Caracalla, 00100 Rome, Italy (Telephone Number in U.S. (202) 653-2400); *Production Yearbook,* and *The State of Food and Agriculture.*

G.K. Hall and Company, 70 Lincoln Street, Boston, Massachusetts 02111 (617) 423-3990; *The World in Figures.*

International Labour Office, I.L.O. Publications, CH-1211, Geneva 22, Switzerland; *Yearbook of Labour Statistics.*

International Monetary Fund, 700 Nineteenth Street, NW, Washington, D.C. 20431 (202) 623-7000; *International Financial Statistics.*

United Nations Economic Commission for Africa, Africa Hall, Post Office Box 3001, Addis Ababa, Ethiopia (Telephone Number in U.S. (800) 253-9646); *African Statistical Yearbook.*

MAURITIUS - PRINTING AND WRITING PAPER - See MAURITIUS - FORESTRY AND FOREST PRODUCTS

MAURITIUS - PRODUCTION

Facts on File, 460 Park Avenue South, New York, New York 10016 (800) 443-8323; *The New Book of World Rankings.*

G.K. Hall and Company, 70 Lincoln Street, Boston, Massachusetts 02111 (617) 423-3990; *The World in Figures.*

MAURITIUS - PROPERTY TAXES

International Monetary Fund, 700 Nineteenth Street, NW, Washington, D.C. 20431 (202) 623-7000; *Government Finance Statistics Yearbook.*

MAURITIUS - PUBLIC FINANCE

Facts on File, 460 Park Avenue South, New York, New York 10016 (800) 443-8323; *The New Book of World Rankings.*

MAURITIUS - RADIO BROADCASTING - See MAURITIUS - BROADCASTING

MAURITIUS - RAILWAY USE

G.K. Hall and Company, 70 Lincoln Street, Boston, Massachusetts 02111 (617) 423-3990; *The World in Figures.*

United Nations Economic Commission for Africa, Africa Hall, Post Office Box 3001, Addis Ababa, Ethiopia (Telephone Number in U.S. (800) 253-9646); *African Statistical Yearbook.*

MAURITIUS - RELIGION

Facts on File, 460 Park Avenue South, New York, New York 10016 (800) 443-8323; *The New Book of World Rankings.*

MAURITIUS - RENT PRICES

International Labour Office, I.L.O. Publications, CH-1211, Geneva 22, Switzerland; *Yearbook of Labour Statistics.*

MAURITIUS - RETAIL TRADE

G.K. Hall and Company, 70 Lincoln Street, Boston, Massachusetts 02111 (617) 423-3990; *The World in Figures.*

Statistical Office of the United Nations, Publishing Service, New York, New York 10017 (800) 253-9646; *Statistical Yearbook.*

MAURITIUS - RICE PRODUCTION - See MAURITIUS - CROPS

MAURITIUS - ROOT AND TUBER PRODUCTION - See MAURITIUS - CROPS

STATISTICS SOURCES, Nineteenth Edition - 1996

MAURITIUS - ROUNDWOOD PRODUCTION - See MAURITIUS - FORESTRY AND FOREST PRODUCTS

MAURITIUS - RUBBER PRODUCTION

Facts on File, 460 Park Avenue South, New York, New York 10016 (800) 443-8323; *The New Book of World Rankings*.

MAURITIUS - SALT PRODUCTION - See MAURITIUS - MINING AND MINERAL PRODUCTS

MAURITIUS - SCIENCE AND TECHNOLOGY - EXPENDITURE FOR RESEARCH

Statistical Office of the United Nations, Publishing Service, New York, New York 10017 (800) 253-9646; *Statistical Yearbook*.

MAURITIUS - SCIENTISTS AND ENGINEERS

Statistical Office of the United Nations, Publishing Service, New York, New York 10017 (800) 253-9646; *Statistical Yearbook*.

United Nations Educational, Scientific and Cultural Organization (UNESCO), 7 Place de Fontenoy, F-75700 Paris, France (Telephone Number in U.S. (212) 963-5981); *Statistical Yearbook*.

MAURITIUS - SENIOR CITIZENS

Facts on File, 460 Park Avenue South, New York, New York 10016 (800) 443-8323; *The New Book of World Rankings*.

MAURITIUS - SHEEP - See MAURITIUS - LIVESTOCK AND POULTRY

MAURITIUS - SILVER PRODUCTION AND CONSUMPTION - See MAURITIUS - MINING AND MINERAL PRODUCTS

MAURITIUS - SOCIAL DATA

African Development Bank, 01 BP 1387, Abidjan 01, Cote d'Ivoire; *Selected Statistics on Regional Member Countries*.

Facts on File, 460 Park Avenue South, New York, New York 10016 (800) 443-8323; *The New Book of World Rankings*.

G.K. Hall and Company, 70 Lincoln Street, Boston, Massachusetts 02111 (617) 423-3990; *The World in Figures*.

MAURITIUS - STAMP TAXES AND DUTIES - See MAURITIUS - TAXATION

MAURITIUS - STEEL PRODUCTION - See MAURITIUS - MINING AND MINERAL PRODUCTS

MAURITIUS - STOCKS - COMMODITY - MARKET PRICE - INDEX

Food and Agricultural Organization of the United Nations (FAO), Via delle Terme di Caracalla, 00100 Rome, Italy (Telephone Number in U.S. (202) 653-2400); *The State of Food and Agriculture*.

MAURITIUS - SUGAR - See MAURITIUS - CROPS

MAURITIUS - TAXATION

G.K. Hall and Company, 70 Lincoln Street, Boston, Massachusetts 02111 (617) 423-3990; *The World in Figures*.

International Monetary Fund, 700 Nineteenth Street, NW, Washington, D.C. 20431 (202) 623-7000; *Government Finance Statistics Yearbook*.

The World Bank, 1818 H Street, NW, Washington, D.C. 20433 (202) 477-1234; *World Tables*.

MAURITIUS - TAX REVENUE - See MAURITIUS - TAXATION

MAURITIUS - TEA PRODUCTION - See MAURITIUS - CROPS

MAURITIUS - TELEPHONES IN USE

American Telephone and Telegraph Company, 26 Parsippany Road, Whippany, New Jersey 07981 (800) 338-4038; *The World's Telephones*.

G.K. Hall and Company, 70 Lincoln Street, Boston, Massachusetts 02111 (617) 423-3990; *The World in Figures*.

Statistical Office of the United Nations, Publishing Service, New York, New York 10017 (800) 253-9646; *Statistical Yearbook*.

MAURITIUS - TELEVISION BROADCASTING - See MAURITIUS - BROADCASTING

MAURITIUS - TEXTILE INDUSTRY

G.K. Hall and Company, 70 Lincoln Street, Boston, Massachusetts 02111 (617) 423-3990; *The World in Figures*.

Statistical Office of the United Nations, Publishing Service, New York, New York 10017 (800) 253-9646; *Trade in Manufactures of Developing Countries*.

MAURITIUS - TOBACCO PRODUCTION

Facts on File, 460 Park Avenue South, New York, New York 10016 (800) 443-8323; *The New Book of World Rankings*.

Statistical Office of the United Nations, Publishing Service, New York, New York 10017 (800) 253-9646; *Statistical Yearbook*.

MAURITIUS - TOURISM

Facts on File, 460 Park Avenue South, New York, New York 10016 (800) 443-8323; *The New Book of World Rankings*.

G.K. Hall and Company, 70 Lincoln Street, Boston, Massachusetts 02111 (617) 423-3990; *The World in Figures*.

Statistical Office of the United Nations, Publishing Service, New York, New York 10017 (800) 253-9646; *Statistical Yearbook*.

Times Books, 201 East 50th Street, New York, New York 10022 (212) 751-2600; *The Economist Book of Vital World Statistics*.

United Nations Economic Commission for Africa, Africa Hall, Post Office Box 3001, Addis Ababa, Ethiopia (Telephone Number in U.S. (800) 253-9646); *African Statistical Yearbook*.

MAURITIUS - TRACTORS IN USE

Statistical Office of the United Nations, Publishing Service, New York, New York 10017 (800) 253-9646; *Statistical Yearbook*.

MAURITIUS - TRADE - See MAURITIUS - FOREIGN TRADE

MAURITIUS - TRADEMARKS AND SERVICE MARKS

Statistical Office of the United Nations, Publishing Service, New York, New York 10017 (800) 253-9646; *Statistical Yearbook*.

World Intellectual Property Organization, 34 Chemin des Colombettes, CH-1211 Geneva 20, Switzerland; *Industrial Property Statistics.*

MAURITIUS - TRANSPORTATION AND COMMUNICATIONS

Facts on File, 460 Park Avenue South, New York, New York 10016 (800) 443-8323; *The New Book of World Rankings.*

G.K. Hall and Company, 70 Lincoln Street, Boston, Massachusetts 02111 (617) 423-3990; *The World in Figures.*

United Nations Economic Commission for Africa, Africa Hall, Post Office Box 3001, Addis Ababa, Ethiopia (Telephone Number in U.S. (800) 253-9646); *African Statistical Yearbook.*

MAURITIUS - TURKEYS - See MAURITIUS - LIVESTOCK AND POULTRY

MAURITIUS - UNEMPLOYMENT

International Labour Office, I.L.O. Publications, CH-1211, Geneva 22, Switzerland; *Yearbook of Labour Statistics.*

Statistical Office of the United Nations, Publishing Service, New York, New York 10017 (800) 253-9646; *Statistical Yearbook.*

MAURITIUS - VITAL STATISTICS

G.K. Hall and Company, 70 Lincoln Street, Boston, Massachusetts 02111 (617) 423-3990; *The World in Figures.*

Statistical Office of the United Nations, Publishing Service, New York, New York 10017 (800) 253-9646; *Statistical Yearbook.*

World Health Organization, Office of Publications, Avenue Appia, CH-1211 Geneva 27, Switzerland (Telephone in U.S. (518) 436-9686); *World Health Statistics Annual.*

MAURITIUS - WAGES

G.K. Hall and Company, 70 Lincoln Street, Boston, Massachusetts 02111 (617) 423-3990; *The World in Figures.*

International Labour Office, I.L.O. Publications, CH-1211, Geneva 22, Switzerland; *Yearbook of Labour Statistics.*

MAURITIUS - WAGES IN MANUFACTURING

Statistical Office of the United Nations, Publishing Service, New York, New York 10017 (800) 253-9646; *Statistical Yearbook.*

MAURITIUS - WEATHER

Facts on File, 460 Park Avenue South, New York, New York 10016 (800) 443-8323; *The New Book of World Rankings.*

G.K. Hall and Company, 70 Lincoln Street, Boston, Massachusetts 02111 (617) 423-3990; *The World in Figures.*

MAURITIUS - WHEAT PRODUCTION - See MAURITIUS - CROPS

MAURITIUS - WHOLESALE TRADE

Statistical Office of the United Nations, Publishing Service, New York, New York 10017 (800) 253-9646; *Statistical Yearbook.*

MAURITIUS - WINE PRODUCTION

Facts on File, 460 Park Avenue South, New York, New York 10016 (800) 443-8323; *The New Book of World Rankings.*

MAURITIUS - WOOL PRODUCTION

Facts on File, 460 Park Avenue South, New York, New York 10016 (800) 443-8323; *The New Book of World Rankings.*

MAURITIUS - YARN PRODUCTION

Statistical Office of the United Nations, Publishing Service, New York, New York 10017 (800) 253-9646; *Statistical Yearbook.*

MEASLES

U.S. Department of Health and Human Services, Center for Disease Control, 1600 Clifton Road, NE, Atlanta, Georgia 30333 (404) 639-3311; *Summary of Notifiable Diseases, U.S. Morbidity and Mortality Weekly Report,* and *National Health Interview Survey.*

MEAT AND MEAT PRODUCTS - See also FOOD AND KINDRED PRODUCTS and Individual Meats

MEAT AND MEAT PRODUCTS - CONSUMER EXPENDITURES

U.S. Department of Agriculture, Economic Research Service, Fourteenth Street and Independence Avenue, SW, Washington, D.C. 20005-4789 (202) 219-1504; *Food Consumption, Prices, and Expenditures, Food Cost Review, Food Review, Agricultural Statistics, Agricultural Outlook,* and unpublished data.

U.S. Department of Agriculture, National Agricultural Statistics Service, Fourteenth Street and Independence Avenue, SW, Washington, D.C. 20250 (202) 219-1504; *Livestock and Meat Statistics.*

U.S. Department of Labor, Bureau of Labor Statistics, Two Massachusetts Avenue, NE, Washington, D.C. 20212 (202) 606-7828; *Consumer Expenditures in 1992.*

MEAT AND MEAT PRODUCTS - CONSUMPTION

U.S. Department of Agriculture, Economic Research Service, Fourteenth Street and Independence Avenue, SW, Washington, D.C. 20005-4789 (202) 219-1504; *Food Consumption, Prices and Expenditures.*

U.S. Department of Agriculture, Foreign Agricultural Service, Fourteenth Street and Independence Avenue, SW, Washington, D.C. 20250 (202) 720-3448; *World Livestock Situation.*

MEAT AND MEAT PRODUCTS - EXPENDITURES

U.S. Department of Agriculture, Economic Research Service, Fourteenth Street and Independence Avenue, SW, Washington, D.C. 20005-4789 (202) 219-1504; *Food Cost Review, Food Review,* and *Agricultural Statistics.*

MEAT AND MEAT PRODUCTS - FOREIGN TRADE

U.S. Department of Agriculture, Economic Research Service, Fourteenth Street and Independence Avenue, SW, Washington, D.C. 20005-4789 (202) 219-1504; *Foreign Agricultural Trade of the United States, Agricultural Statistics,* and unpublished data.

U.S. Department of Agriculture, National Agricultural Statistics Service, Fourteenth Street and Independence Avenue, SW,

Washington, D.C. 20250 (202) 219-1504; *Livestock and Meat Statistics*, and *Agricultural Outlook*.

U.S. Department of Commerce, Bureau of the Census, Suitland, Maryland 20233 (301) 763-4040; *U.S. Merchandise Trade: Exports, General Imports, and Imports for Consumption*.

MEAT AND MEAT PRODUCTS - PRODUCTION

Food and Agriculture Organization of the United Nations (FAO), Via delle Terme di Caracalla, 00100 Rome, Italy (Telephone Number in U.S. (202) 653-2400); *FAO Production Yearbook*.

Statistical Office of the United Nations, Publishing Service, New York, New York 10017 (800) 253-9646; *Monthly Bulletin of Statistics*, and *Statistical Yearbook*.

U.S. Department of Agriculture, Economic Research Service, Fourteenth Street and Independence Avenue, SW, Washington, D.C. 20005-4789 (202) 219-1504; *World Agriculture Trends and Indicators*.

U.S. Department of Agriculture, National Agricultural Statistics Service, Fourteenth Street and Independence Avenue, SW, Washington, D.C, 20250 (202) 219-1504; *Livestock and Meat Statistics*, and *Agricultural Outlook*.

MEDIA - See also individual medium

Mediamark Research Incorporation, 708 Third Avenue, New York, New York 10017 (212) 599-0444; *Multimedia Audiences*.

Radio Advertising Bureau, 304 Park Avenue, South, New York, New York 10010 (212) 387-2100; *Radio Facts*.

Television Bureau of Advertising, Incorporated, 850 Third Avenue, New York, New York 10022 (212) 486-1111; *Trends in Television*.

Veronis, Suhler and Associates, 350 Park Avenue, New York, New York 10022 (212) 935-4990; *Communications Industry Forecast Report*.

MEDICAID - COVERAGE - RECIPIENTS

U.S. Department of Commerce, Bureau of the Census, Suitland, Maryland 20233 (301) 763-4040; *Current Population Reports*, and unpublished data.

U.S. Department of Health and Human Services, Health Care Financing Administration, 200 Independence Avenue, SW, Washington, D.C. 20201 (202) 245-6113; *Health Care Financing Review*.

U.S. Library of Congress, Congressional Research Service, 101 Independence Avenue, SE, Washington, D.C. 20540 (202) 707-5000; *Cash and Non-Cash Benefits for Persons With Limited Income: Eligibility Rules, Recipient and Expenditure Data*.

MEDICAID - EXPENDITURES

U.S. Department of Commerce, Bureau of the Census, Suitland, Maryland 20233 (301) 763-4040; *Current Population Reports*.

U.S. Department of Health and Human Services, Health Care Financing Administration, 200 Independence Avenue, SW, Washington, D.C. 20201 (202) 345-6113; *Health Care Financing Review*.

U.S. Department of Health and Human Services, Social Security Administration, 6401 Security Boulevard, Baltimore, Maryland 21235 (410) 965-1234; *Social Security Bulletin*.

U.S. Library of Congress, Congressional Research Service, 101 Independence Avenue, SE, Washington, D.C. 20540 (202) 707-5000; *Cash and Non-Cash Benefits for Persons with Limited Income: Eligibility Rules, Recipient and Expenditure Data*.

MEDICAID - NURSING HOMES

U.S. Department of Health and Human Services, Health Care Financing Administration, 200 Independence Avenue, SW, Washington, D.C. 20201 (202) 245-6113; *Health Care Financing Review*.

U.S. Department of Health and Human Services, National Center for Health Statistics, 3700 East-West Highway, Hyattsville, Maryland 20782 (301) 436-8500; *Advance Data from Vital and Health Statistics*, and unpublished data.

MEDICAID - STATE DATA

U.S. Department of Health and Human Services, Health Care Financing Administration, 200 Independence Avenue, SW, Washington, D.C. 20201 (202) 245-6113; unpublished data.

MEDICAL CARE - See also HEALTH SERVICES

MEDICAL CARE - EXPENDITURES FOR

U.S. Department of Health and Human Services, Health Care Financing Administration, 200 Independence Avenue, SW, Washington, D.C. 20201 (202) 245-6113; *Health Care Financing Review*, and unpublished data.

U.S. Department of Health and Human Services, Social Security Administration, 6401 Security Boulevard, Baltimore, Maryland 21235 (410) 965-1234; *Social Security Bulletin*.

U.S. Department of Labor, Bureau of Labor Statistics, Two Massachusetts Avenue, NE, Washington, D.C. 20212 (202) 606-7828; *Consumer Expenditures in 1992*.

MEDICAL CARE - INSURANCE BENEFITS

Health Insurance Association of America, 1025 Connecticut Avenue, NW, Suite 1200, Washington, D.C. 20036 (202) 223-7780; *Source Book of Health Insurance Data*.

U.S. Department of Health and Human Services, Health Care Financing Administration, 200 Independence Avenue, SW, Washington, D.C. 20201 (202) 245-6113; *Health Care Financing Review*, and unpublished data.

MEDICAL CARE - INSURANCE BENEFITS - EXPENDITURES FOR

U.S. Department of Health and Human Services, Health Care Financing Administration, 200 Independence Avenue, SW, Washington, D.C. 20201 (202) 245-6113; *Health Care Financing Review*.

MEDICAL CARE - PRICE INDEXES - CONSUMER

U.S. Department of Labor, Bureau of Labor Statistics, Two Massachusetts Avenue, NE, Washington, D.C. 20212 (202) 606-7828; *Consumer Price Index Detailed Report, Monthly Labor Review*, and *Handbook of Labor Statistics*.

MEDICAL RESEARCH

U.S. Department of Health and Human Services, Health Care Financing Administration, 200 Independence Avenue, SW, Washington, D.C. 20201 (202) 523-1327; *Health Care Financing Review*.

MEDICAL SCHOOLS - FOREIGN GRADUATES

U.S. Department of Health and Human Services, Health Resources and Services Administration, 5600 Fishers Lane, Rockville, Maryland 20857 (301) 443-2086; unpublished data.

MEDICAL SCHOOLS - NUMBER - STUDENTS - GRADUATES

U.S. Department of Education, 400 Maryland Avenue, SW, Washington, D.C. 20202 (202) 708-5366; *Digest of Education Statistics*, and unpublished data.

U.S. Department of Health and Human Services, Health Resources and Services Administration, 5600 Fishers Lane, Rockville, Maryland 20857 (301) 443-2086; unpublished data.

MEDICAL SCIENCES - EMPLOYMENT

U.S. Department of Labor, Bureau of Labor Statistics, Two Massachusetts Avenue, NE, Washington, D.C. 20212 (202) 606-7828; *Monthly Labor Review*, and *Employment and Earnings*.

MEDICAL SERVICES - See HEALTH SERVICES

MEDICARE - BENEFIT PAYMENTS EXPENDITURES

U.S. Department of Health and Human Services, Health Care Financing Administration, 200 Independence Avenue, SW, Washington, D.C. 20201 (202) 245-6113; *Health Care Financing Review*, and unpublished data.

U.S. Department of Health and Human Services, Social Security Administration, 6401 Security Boulevard, Baltimore, Maryland 21235 (410) 965-1234; *Social Security Bulletin*, and *Annual Statistical Supplement to the Social Security Bulletin*.

MEDICARE - CONTRIBUTIONS

U.S. Department of Health and Human Services, Social Security Administration, 6401 Security Boulevard, Baltimore, Maryland 21235 (410) 965-1234; *Social Security Bulletin*, *Annual Statistical Supplement to the Social Security Bulletin*, and *Annual Report of Board of Trustees, OASI, DI, HI, and SMI Trust Funds*.

MEDICARE - STATE DATA

U.S. Department of Health and Human Services, Health Care Financing Administration, 200 Independence Avenue, SW, Washington, D.C. 20210 (202) 245-6113; unpublished data.

MEDICARE - TRUST FUNDS

U.S. Department of Health and Human Services, Social Security Administration, 6401 Security Boulevard, Baltimore, Maryland 21235 (410) 965-1234; *Annual Statistical Supplement to the Social Security Bulletin*, *Social Security Bulletin*, *Annual Report of Board of Trustees, OASI, DI, HI, and SMI Trust Funds*, and unpublished data.

MEDICARE - UTILIZATION AND CHARGES

U.S. Department of Health and Human Services, Health Care Financing Administration, 200 Independence Avenue, SW, Washington, D.C. 20201 (202) 245-6113; *Medicare Program Statistics*, and unpublished data.

U.S. Department of Health and Human Services, Social Security Administration, 6401 Security Boulevard, Baltimore, Maryland 21235 (410) 965-1234; *Social Security Bulletin*.

MEDICINES - See DRUGS AND MEDICINES

MELONS

U.S. Department of Agriculture, National Agricultural Statistics Service, Fourteenth Street and Independence Avenue, SW, Washington, D.C. 20250 (202) 219-1504; *Agricultural Outlook*, *Agricultural Statistics*, *Economic Indicators of the Farm Sector: National Financial Summary*, *Food Consumption, Prices, and Expenditures*, and *Vegetables*.

MEMBERS OF CONGRESS - See CONGRESS, UNITED STATES

MEMBERSHIP ORGANIZATIONS - EARNINGS

U.S. Department of Commerce, Bureau of the Census, Suitland, Maryland 20233 (301) 763-4040; *Census of Service Industries*, and *County Business Patterns*.

U.S. Department of Labor, Bureau of Labor Statistics, Two Massachusetts Avenue, NE, Washington, D.C. 20212 (202) 606-7828; *Employment and Earnings*, and Bulletins 2370 and 2429.

MEMBERSHIP ORGANIZATIONS - EMPLOYEES

U.S. Department of Commerce, Bureau of Economic Analysis, Fourteenth Street between Constitution Avenue and E Street, NW, Washington, D.C. 20230 (202) 606-9900; *The National Income and Product Accounts of the United States*, and *Survey of Current Business*.

U.S. Department of Commerce, Bureau of the Census, Suitland, Maryland 20233 (301) 763-4040; *Census of Service Industries*, and *County Business Patterns*.

U.S. Department of Labor, Bureau of Labor Statistics, Two Massachusetts Avenue, NE, Washington, D.C. 20212 (202) 606-7828; *Monthly Labor Review*, *Employment and Earnings*, and Bulletins 2370 and 2429.

MEMBERSHIP ORGANIZATIONS - ESTABLISHMENTS

U.S. Department of Commerce, Bureau of the Census, Suitland, Maryland 20233 (301) 763-4040; *Census of Service Industries*, and *County Business Patterns*.

MEMBERSHIP ORGANIZATIONS - FINANCES

U.S. Department of Commerce, Bureau of the Census, Suitland, Maryland 20233 (301) 763-4040; *Census of Service Industries*.

MEMBERSHIP ORGANIZATIONS - GROSS NATIONAL PRODUCT

U.S. Department of Commerce, Bureau of Economic Analysis, Fourteenth Street between Constitution Avenue and E Street, NW, Washington, D.C. 20230 (202) 606-9900; *The National Income and Product Accounts of the United States*, and *Survey of Current Business*.

MENHADEN

U.S. Department of Commerce, National Oceanic and Atmospheric Administration, National Marine Fisheries Service, 1335 East-West Highway, Silver Spring, Maryland 20910 (301) 427-2239; *Fishery Statistics of the United States,* and *Fisheries of the United States.*

MENINGITIS

U.S. Department of Health and Human Services, Center for Disease Control, 1600 Clifton Road, NE, Atlanta, Georgia 30333 (404) 639-3311; *Summary of Notifiable Diseases, U.S. Morbidity and Mortality Weekly Report.*

U.S. Department of Health and Human Services, National Center for Health Statistics, 3700 East-West Highway, Hyattsville, Maryland 20782 (301) 436-8500; *Vital Statistics of the U.S, Monthly Vital Statistics Report,* and unpublished data.

MENTAL HEALTH

U.S. Department of Health and Human Services, Public Health Service, 200 Independence Avenue, SW, Washington, D.C. 20201 (202) 619-1296; *Health, United States, Vital and Health Statistics,* and unpublished data.

MENTAL HOSPITALS

American Hospital Association, 840 North Lake Shore Drive, Chicago, Illinois 60611 (312) 280-6000; *Hospital Statistics,* and unpublished data.

U.S. Department of Commerce, Bureau of the Census, Suitland, Maryland 20233 (301) 763-4040; *Census of Population, General Population Characteristics.*

U.S. Department of Health and Human Services, Substance Abuse and Mental Health Services Administration, 5600 Fishers Lane, Rockville, Maryland 20857 (301) 443-4797; unpublished data.

MENTAL RETARDATION FACILITIES

U.S. Department of Health and Human Services, Office of Human Development Services, 200 Independence Avenue, SW, Washington, D.C. 20201 (202) 245-7246; unpublished data.

MERCHANDISE - See FOREIGN TRADE and GENERAL MERCHANDISE STORES

MERCHANT VESSELS

Shipbuilders Council of America, 4301 North Fairfax Drive, Suite 330, Arlington, Virginia 22203 (703) 276-1700; unpublished data.

U.S. Department of Transportation, Maritime Administration, 400 Seventh Street, SW, Washington, D.C. 20590 (202) 366-5807; *New Ship Construction,* and *Employment Report of the U.S. Flag Merchant Fleet Ocean-Going Vessels 1,000 Gross Tons and Over.*

MERCHANT VESSELS - EMPLOYMENT AND WAGE SCALE

U.S. Department of Transportation, Maritime Administration, 400 Seventh Street, SW, Washington, D.C. 20590 (202) 366-5807; *United States Merchant Marine Data Sheet,* and unpublished data.

MERCHANT VESSELS - FOREIGN COUNTRIES

U.S. Department of Transportation, Maritime Administration, 400 Seventh Street, SW, Washington, D.C. 20590 (202) 366-5807; *Merchant Fleets of the World.*

MERCHANT VESSELS - NUMBER

Lloyd's Register of Shipping, 17 Battery Place, New York, New York 10036 (212) 789-1400, *Statistical Tables,* and *Annual Summary of Merchant Ships Completed in the World.*

U.S. Department of Transportation, Maritime Administration, 400 Seventh Street, SW, Washington, D.C. 20590 (202) 366-5807; *Merchant Fleets of the World, New Ship Construction,* and *Employment Report of the U.S. Flag Merchant Fleet Ocean-Going Vessels 1,000 Gross Tons and Over.*

MERCHANT VESSELS - NUMBER - HORSEPOWER

John A. Waring, 1320 South George Mason Drive, Arlington, Virginia 22204 (703) 521-1499; unpublished estimates.

MERCHANT VESSELS - NUMBER - LOST

Lloyd's Register of Shipping, 17 Battery Place, New York, New York 10036 (212) 789-1400; *Casualty Return.*

MERCHANT VESSELS - NUMBER - TONNAGE

U.S. Department of Transportation, Maritime Administration, 400 Seventh Street, SW, Washington, D.C. 20590 (202) 366-5807; *Employment Report of the United States Flag Merchant Fleet Ocean-Going Vessels 1,000 Gross Tons and Over.*

MERCHANT VESSELS - NUMBER - WORLD

Statistical Office of the United Nations, Publishing Service, New York, New York 10017 (800) 253-9646; *Monthly Bulletin of Statistics.*

U.S. Department of Transportation, Maritime Administration, 400 Seventh Street, SW, Washington, D.C. 20590 (202) 366-5807; *Merchant Fleets of the World.*

MERCURY

U.S. Department of the Interior, Bureau of Mines, 810 Seventh Street, NW, Washington, D.C. 20241 (202) 501-9649; *Annual Reports,* and *Mineral Commodity Summaries.*

MERGERS AND ACQUISITIONS

Securities Data Company, 1180 Raymond Boulevard, Newark, New Jersey 07102 (201) 622-3100; *Merger and Corporate Transactions Database.*

METAL INDUSTRIES - PRIMARY - MANUFACTURING - See also IRON AND STEEL

METAL INDUSTRIES - PRIMARY - MANUFACTURING - CAPITAL

U.S. Department of Commerce, Bureau of Economic Analysis, Fourteenth Street between Constitution Avenue and E Street, NW, Washington, D.C. 20230 (202) 606-9900; *Fixed Reproducible Tangible Wealth in the United States,* and *Survey of Current Business.*

METAL INDUSTRIES - PRIMARY - MANUFACTURING - EARNINGS

U.S. Department of the Census, Suitland, Maryland 20233 (301) 763-4040; *Census of Manufactures,* and *Annual Survey of Manufactures.*

U.S. Department of Labor, Bureau of Labor Statistics, Two Massachusetts Avenue, NE, Washington, D.C. 20212 (202) 606-7828; *Employment and Earnings*, and Bulletins 2370 and 2429.

METAL INDUSTRIES - PRIMARY - MANUFACTURING - EMPLOYEES

U.S. Department of Commerce, Bureau of Economic Analysis, Fourteenth Street between Constitution Avenue and E Street, NW, Washington, D.C. 20230 (202) 606-9900; *The National Income and Product Accounts of the United States, Fixed Reproducible Tangible Wealth in the United States*, and *Survey of Current Business*.

U.S. Department of Commerce, Bureau of the Census, Suitland, Maryland 20233 (301) 763-4040; *Census of Manufactures*, and *Annual Survey of Manufactures*.

U.S. Department of Commerce, International Trade Administration, Fourteenth Street between Constitution Avenue and E Street, NW, Washington, D.C. 20230 (202) 482-3809; *Industrial Outlook*.

U.S. Department of Labor, Bureau of Labor Statistics, Two Massachusetts Avenue, NE, Washington, D.C. 20212 (202) 606-7828; *Monthly Labor Review, Employment and Earnings*, and Bulletins 2370 and 2429.

METAL INDUSTRIES - PRIMARY - MANUFACTURING - ESTABLISHMENTS

U.S. Department of Commerce, Bureau of the Census, Suitland, Maryland 20233 (301) 763-4040; *Census of Manufactures* and *Annual Survey of Manufactures*.

METAL INDUSTRIES - PRIMARY - MANUFACTURING - FINANCE

American Iron and Steel Institute, 1101 Seventeenth Street, NW, Washington, D.C. 20036 (202) 452-7100; *Annual Statistical Report*.

METAL INDUSTRIES - PRIMARY - MANUFACTURING - FOREIGN TRADE

American Iron and Steel Institute, 1101 Seventeenth Street, NW, Washington, D.C. 20036 (202) 452-7100; *Annual Statistical Report*.

U.S. Department of Commerce, Bureau of the Census, Suitland, Maryland 20233 (301) 763-4040; *Census of Manufactures, Annual Survey of Manufactures*, and *U.S. Merchandise Trade*.

METAL INDUSTRIES - PRIMARY - MANUFACTURING - GROSS DOMESTIC PRODUCT

U.S. Department of Commerce, Bureau of Economic Analysis, Fourteenth Street between Constitution Avenue and E Street, NW, Washington, D.C. 20230 (202) 606-9900; *The National Income and Product Accounts of the United States*, and *Survey of Current Business*.

METAL INDUSTRIES - PRIMARY - MANUFACTURING - MERGERS AND ACQUISITIONS

Securities Data Company, 1180 Raymond Boulevard, Newark, New Jersey 07102 (201) 622-3100; *Merger and Corporate Transactions Database*.

METAL INDUSTRIES - PRIMARY - MANUFACTURING - OCCUPATIONAL SAFETY

U.S. Department of Labor, Bureau of Labor Statistics, Two Massachusetts Avenue, NE, Washington, D.C. 20212 (202) 606-

7828; *Occupational Injuries and Illnesses in the United States by Industry*.

METAL INDUSTRIES - PRIMARY - MANUFACTURING - PATENTS

U.S. Department of Commerce, Patent and Trademark Office, 2011 Crystal Drive, Arlington, Virginia 22202 (703) 305-8341; *Patenting Trends in the U.S., State Country Report*.

METAL INDUSTRIES - PRIMARY - MANUFACTURING - POLLUTION ABATEMENT

U.S. Department of Commerce, Bureau of Economic Analysis, Fourteenth Street between Constitution Avenue and E Street, NW, Washington, D.C. 20230 (202) 606-9900; *Survey of Current Business*, and unpublished data.

U.S. Department of Commerce, Bureau of the Census, Suitland, Maryland 20233 (301) 763-4040; *Current Industrial Reports*.

METAL INDUSTRIES - PRIMARY - MANUFACTURING - PRODUCTIVITY

Board of Governors of the Federal Reserve System, Twentieth Street and Constitution Avenue, NW, Washington, D.C. 20551 (202) 452-3000; *Federal Reserve Bulletin*.

U.S. Department of Labor, Bureau of Labor Statistics, Two Massachusetts Avenue, NE, Washington, D.C. 20212 (202) 606-7828; *Productivity Measures for Selected Industries and Government Services*, and unpublished data.

METAL INDUSTRIES - PRIMARY - MANUFACTURING - PROFITS

Forbes, Incorporated, 60 Fifth Avenue, New York, New York 10011 (212) 620-2200; *Forbes Annual Report on American Industry*.

Time Warner, 1675 Broadway, Rockefeller Center, New York, New York 10019 (212) 522-1212; *The Fortune Directories*.

U.S. Department of Commerce, Bureau of the Census, Suitland, Maryland 20233 (301) 763-4040; *Quarterly Financial Report for Manufacturing, Mining and Trade Corporations*.

METAL INDUSTRIES - PRIMARY - MANUFACTURING - SHIPMENTS

American Iron and Steel Institute, 1101 Seventeenth Street, NW, Washington, D.C. 20036 (202) 452-7100; *Annual Statistical Report*.

U.S. Department of Commerce, Bureau of the Census, Suitland, Maryland 20233 (301) 763-4040; *Current Industrial Reports, Census of Manufactures, Annual Survey of Manufactures*, and *Current Industrial Reports, Manufactures' Shipments, Inventories, and Orders*.

METAL INDUSTRIES - PRIMARY - MANUFACTURING - VALUE ADDED

U.S. Department of Commerce, Bureau of the Census, Suitland, Maryland 20233 (301) 763-4040; *Current Industrial Reports, Manufactures' Shipments, Inventories, and Orders*, and *Census of Manufactures*, and *Annual Survey of Manufactures*.

METAL MINING INDUSTRY - CAPITAL

U.S. Department of Commerce, Bureau of Economic Analysis, Fourteenth Street between Constitution Avenue and E Street, NW, Washington, D.C. 20230 (202) 606-9900; *Survey of Current Business*.

METAL MINING INDUSTRY - EARNINGS

U.S. Department of Commerce, Bureau of the Census, Suitland, Maryland 20233 (301) 763-4040; *Census of Manufactures*, and *Annual Survey of Manufactures*.

U.S. Department of Labor, Bureau of Labor Statistics, Two Massachusetts Avenue, NE, Washington, D.C. 20212 (202) 606-7828; *Employment and Earnings*, and Bulletins 2370 and 2429.

METAL MINING INDUSTRY - EMPLOYEES

U.S. Department of Commerce, Bureau of the Census, Suitland, Maryland 20233 (301) 763-4040; *Census of Manufactures*, and *Annual Survey of Manufactures*.

U.S. Department of Labor, Bureau of Labor Statistics, Two Massachusetts Avenue, NE, Washington, D.C. 20212 (202) 606-7828; *Employment and Earnings, Monthly Labor Review*, and Bulletins 2370 and 2429.

METAL MINING INDUSTRY - ESTABLISHMENTS

U.S. Department of Commerce, Bureau of the Census, Suitland, Maryland 20233 (301) 763-4040; *Census of Manufactures*, and *Annual Survey of Manufactures*.

METAL MINING INDUSTRY - GROSS DOMESTIC PRODUCT ORIGINATING IN

U.S. Department of Commerce, Bureau of Economic Analysis, Fourteenth Street between Constitution Avenue and E Street, NW, Washington, D.C. 20230 (202) 606-9900; *The National Income and Product Accounts of the United States*, and *Survey of Current Business*.

METAL MINING INDUSTRY - PRODUCTIVITY

Board of Governors of the Federal Reserve System, Twentieth Street and Constitution Avenue, NW, Washington, D.C. 20551 (202) 452-3000; *Federal Reserve Bulletin*.

METAL MINING INDUSTRY - SHIPMENTS

American Iron and Steel Institute, 1101 Seventeenth Street, NW, Washington, D.C. 20036 (202) 452-7100; *Annual Statistical Report*.

U.S. Department of Commerce, Bureau of the Census, Suitland, Maryland 20233 (301) 763-4040; *Current Industrial Reports, Current Industrial Reports, Manufactures, Shipments, Inventories, and Orders, Census of Manufactures*, and *Annual Survey of Manufactures*.

METAL MINING INDUSTRY - VALUE ADDED

U.S. Department of Commerce, Bureau of the Census, Suitland, Maryland 20233 (301) 763-4040; *Census of Manufactures*, and *Annual Survey of Manufactures*.

METAL WORKING MACHINERY

U.S. Department of Commerce, Bureau of the Census, Suitland, Maryland 20233 (301) 763-4040; *U.S. Merchandise Trade: Exports, General Imports, and Imports for Consumption, Census of Manufactures*, and *Annual Survey of Manufactures*.

U.S. Department of Labor, Bureau of Labor Statistics, Two Massachusetts Avenue, NE, Washington, D.C. 20212 (202) 606-7828; *Employment and Earnings*, and Bulletins 2370 and 2429.

METALS

U.S. Department of Commerce, Bureau of the Census, Suitland, Maryland 20233 (301) 763-4040; *Census of Mineral Industries*.

U.S. Department of the Interior, Bureau of Mines, 810 Seventh Street, NW, Washington, D.C. 20241 (202) 501-9649; *Annual Reports*, and *Mineral Commodity Summaries*.

METALS - FOREIGN TRADE

U.S. Department of Commerce, Bureau of the Census, Suitland, Maryland 20233 (301) 763-4040; *U.S. Merchandise Trade*, and *U.S. Merchandise Trade: Exports, General Imports, and Imports for Consumption*.

METALS - PRODUCTION AND VALUE

U.S. Department of the Interior, Bureau of Mines, 810 Seventh Street, NW, Washington, D.C. 20241 (202) 501-9649; *Annual Reports*, and *Mineral Commodity Summaries*.

METALS - PRODUCTION AND VALUE - INDEXES OF PRODUCTION

Board of Governors of the Federal Reserve System, Twentieth Street and Constitution Avenue, NW, Washington, D.C. 20551 (202) 452-3000; *Federal Reserve Bulletin*.

METALS - PRODUCTION AND VALUE - WORLD PRODUCTION

Statistical Office of the United Nations, Publishing Service, New York, New York 10017 (800) 253-9646; *Monthly Bulletin of Statistics*, and *Statistical Yearbook*.

U.S. Department of the Interior, Bureau of Mines, 810 Seventh Street, NW, Washington, D.C. 20241 (202) 501-9649; *Annual Reports*, and *Mineral Commodity Summaries*.

METALS - RAILROAD CAR LOADINGS OF

Association of American Railroads, American Railroads Building, 50 F Street, NW, Washington, D.C. 20001 (202) 639-2100; *Freight Commodity Statistics*, and *Weekly Railroad Traffic*.

METALS - SPOT MARKET PRICE INDEXES

Commodity Research Bureau, Incorporated, 75 Wall Street, New York, New York 10005 (212) 504-7754; *Commodity Research Bureau Commodity Index Report*.

METALS - STRATEGIC AND CRITICAL MATERIALS

U.S. Department of Defense, Defense Logistics Agency, Cameron Station, Alexandria, Virginia 22304-6100 (703) 274-6000; *Statistical Supplement, Stockpile Report to the Congress*.

METROPOLITAN AREAS - CIVILIAN LABOR FORCE

U.S. Department of Labor, Bureau of Labor Statistics, Two Massachusetts Avenue, NE, Washington, D.C. 20212 (202) 606-7828; *Employment and Earnings*.

METROPOLITAN AREAS - CONSUMER EXPENDITURES

U.S. Department of Labor, Bureau of Labor Statistics, Two Massachusetts Avenue, NE, Washington, D.C. 20212 (202) 606-7828; *Consumer Expenditures in 1992*.

METROPOLITAN AREAS - CONSUMER PRICE INDEX

American Chamber of Commerce Researchers Association, c/o American Chamber of Commerce Executives, 4232 King Street, Alexandria, Virginia 22302 (703) 998-0072; *Cost of Living Index.*

U.S. Department of Labor, Bureau of Labor Statistics, Two Massachusetts Avenue, NE, Washington, D.C. 20212 (202) 606-7828; *Monthly Labor Review*, and *CPI Detailed Report.*

METROPOLITAN AREAS - EARNINGS

U.S. Department of Labor, Bureau of Labor Statistics, Two Massachusetts Avenue, NE, Washington, D.C. 20212 (202) 606-7828; *Average Annual Pay Levels in Metropolitan Areas.*

METROPOLITAN AREAS - EMPLOYMENT - GOVERNMENT

U.S. Office of Personnel Management, 1900 E Street, NW, Washington, D.C. 20415 (202) 606-1800; *Federal Civilian Workforce Statistics - Employment and Trends*, and unpublished data.

METROPOLITAN AREAS - HOUSING - PRICES

National Association of Realtors, 430 North Michigan Avenue, Chicago, Illinois 60611 (312) 329-8200; *Real Estate Outlook: Market Trends and Insights.*

METROPOLITAN AREAS - HOUSING - VACANCIES

U.S. Department of Commerce, Bureau of the Census, Suitland, Maryland 20233 (301) 763-4040; *Current Housing Reports.*

METROPOLITAN AREAS - INCOME

U.S. Department of Commerce, Bureau of Economic Analysis, Fourteenth Street between Constitution Avenue and E Street, NW, Washington, D.C. 20230 (202) 606-9900; *Survey of Current Business*, and unpublished data.

METROPOLITAN AREAS - LAND AREA

U.S. Department of Commerce, Bureau of the Census, Suitland, Maryland 20233 (301) 763-4040; *Census of Population and Housing, Supplementary Report, Metropolitan Statistical Areas*, and press release.

METROPOLITAN AREAS - OFFICE SPACE

Society of Industrial and Office Realtors, 777 Fourteenth Street, NW, Suite 400, Washington, D.C. 20005 (202) 383-1150; *Comparative Statistics of Industrial and Office Real Estate Markets.*

METROPOLITAN AREAS - POPULATION

U.S. Department of Commerce, Bureau of the Census, Suitland, Maryland 20233 (301) 763-4040; *Census of Population and Housing, Supplementary Report, Metropolitan Statistical Areas, Current Population Reports*, and press release.

MEXICAN WAR - COST

U.S. Congress, The Capitol, Washington, D.C. 20510 (202) 224-3121; *The Military Budget and National Economic Priorities*, 91st Session, subsequently revised and updated by James L. Clayton, University of Utah, Salt Lake City, Utah.

Mexico - National Statistical Office

Instituto Nacional de Estadistica Geografia e Informatica, Patriotismo No. 711, PH, CP 03910 Mexico, DF, Mexico.

Mexico - Primary Statistics Sources

Instituto Nacional de Estadistica, Geografia e Informatica, CP 03910, Mexico; *Annuario Estadistico de los Estados Unidos Mexicanos*, and *Agenda estadistica.*

MEXICO - AGRICULTURE

The Economist Intelligence Unit, 111 West 57th Street, New York, New York 10019 (800) 938-4685; *The New Latin America Market Atlas.*

Euromonitor Publications Limited, 87-88 Turnmill Street, London EC1M 5QU, England; *International Marketing Data and Statistics.*

Facts on File, 460 Park Avenue South, New York, New York 10016 (800) 443-8323; *The New Book of World Rankings.*

Food and Agricultural Organization of the United Nations (FAO), Via delle Terme di Caracalla, 00100 Rome, Italy (Telephone Number in U.S. (202) 653-2400); *The State of Food and Agriculture.*

G.K. Hall and Company, 70 Lincoln Street, Boston, Massachusetts 02111 (617) 423-3990; *The World in Figures.*

Gale Research Incorporated, 835 Penobscot Building, Detroit, Michigan 48226 (800) 877-4253; *International Historical Statistics The Americas and Australasia.*

Inter-American Development Bank, 1300 New York Avenue, NW, Washington, D.C. 20577 (202) 872-1445; *Economic and Social Progress in Latin America.*

Statistical Office of the United Nations, Publishing Service, New York, New York 10017 (800) 253-9646; *Statistical Yearbook for Latin America and the Caribbean*, and *Statistical Yearbook.*

Times Books, 201 East 50th Street, New York, New York 10022 (212) 751-2600; *The Economist Book of Vital World Statistics.*

U.C.L.A. Latin American Center Publications, University of California, Los Angeles, California 90024 (310) 825-6634; *Statistical Abstract of Latin America.*

The World Bank, 1818 H Street, NW, Washington, D.C. 20433 (202) 477-1234; *World Tables.*

MEXICO - AIRLINE SERVICE

The Economist Intelligence Unit, 111 West 57th Street, New York, New York 10019 (800) 938-4685; *The New Latin America Market Atlas.*

Facts on File, 460 Park Avenue South, New York, New York 10016 (800) 443-8323; *The New Book of World Rankings.*

G.K. Hall and Company, 70 Lincoln Street, Boston, Massachusetts 02111 (617) 423-3990; *The World in Figures.*

International Civil Aviation Organization, 1000 Sherbrooke Street West, Suite 400, Montreal, Quebec H3A 2R2, Canada (514) 285-8219; *Civil Aviation Statistics of the World.*

Statistical Office of the United Nations, Publishing Service, New York, New York 10017 (800) 253-9646; *Statistical Yearbook.*

Times Books, 201 East 50th Street, New York, New York 10022 (212) 751-2600; *The Economist Book of Vital World Statistics.*

MEXICO - ALUMINUM PRODUCTION AND CONSUMPTION - See MEXICO - MINING AND MINERAL PRODUCTS

MEXICO - ANIMAL FEEDINGSTUFFS OF AQUATIC ANIMAL ORIGIN

Statistical Office of the United Nations, Publishing Service, New York, New York 10017 (800) 253-9646; *Statistical Yearbook.*

MEXICO - ANIMAL HEALTH

Food and Agricultural Organization of the United Nations (FAO), Via delle Terme di Caracalla, 00100 Rome, Italy (Telephone Number in U.S. (202) 653-2400); *Animal Health Yearbook.*

MEXICO - ANTIMONY AND ANTIMONY ORE PRODUCTION AND CONSUMPTION - See MEXICO - MINING AND MINERAL PRODUCTS

MEXICO - APPLES - See MEXICO - CROPS

MEXICO - AREA AND DENSITY OF POPULATION

Euromonitor Publications Limited, 87-88 Turnmill Street, London EC1M 5QU, England; *International Marketing Data and Statistics.*

Facts on File, 460 Park Avenue South, New York, New York 10016 (800) 443-8323; *The New Book of World Rankings.*

Food and Agricultural Organization of the United Nations (FAO), Via delle Terme di Caracalla, 00100 Rome, Italy (Telephone Number in U.S. (202) 653-2400); *The State of Food and Agriculture.*

G.K. Hall and Company, 70 Lincoln Street, Boston, Massachusetts 02111 (617) 423-3990; *The World in Figures.*

Inter-American Development Bank, 1300 New York Avenue, NW, Washington, D.C. 20577 (202) 872-1445; *Economic and Social Progress in Latin America.*

Statistical Office of the United Nations, Publishing Service, New York, New York 10017 (800) 253-9646; *Statistical Yearbook.*

Times Books, 201 East 50th Street, New York, New York 10022 (212) 751-2600; *The Economist Book of Vital World Statistics.*

United Nations Educational, Scientific and Cultural Organization (UNESCO), 7 Place de Fontenoy, F-75700 Paris, France (Telephone Number in U.S. (212) 963-5981); *Statistical Yearbook.*

MEXICO - ARMS EXPORTS AND IMPORTS

U.S. Arms Control and Disarmament Agency, 320 Twenty-first Street, NW, Washington, D.C. 20451 (202) 647-8677; *World Military Expenditures and Arms Transfers.*

MEXICO - ARSENIC PRODUCTION AND CONSUMPTION - See MEXICO - MINING AND MINERAL PRODUCTS

MEXICO - BALANCE OF PAYMENTS

The Economist Intelligence Unit, 111 West 57th Street, New York, New York 10019 (800) 938-4685; *The New Latin America Market Atlas,* and *The World Market Atlas.*

Euromonitor Publications Limited, 87-88 Turnmill Street, London EC1M 5QU, England; *Third World Economic Handbook.*

G.K. Hall and Company, 70 Lincoln Street, Boston, Massachusetts 02111 (617) 423-3990; *The World in Figures.*

Inter-American Development Bank, 1300 New York Avenue, NW, Washington, D.C. 20577 (202) 872-1445; *Economic and Social Progress in Latin America.*

International Monetary Fund, 700 Nineteenth Street, NW, Washington, D.C. 20431 (202) 623-7000; *Balance of Payments Yearbook,* and *International Financial Statistics.*

Organization of American States (OAS), General Secretariat, Washington, D.C. 20006 (202) 458-3533; *Statistical Bulletin of the OAS.*

Statistical Office of the United Nations, Publishing Service, New York, New York 10017 (800) 253-9646; *Economic Survey of Latin America and the Caribbean,* and *Statistical Yearbook for Latin America and the Caribbean.*

Times Books, 201 East 50th Street, New York, New York 10022 (212) 751-2600; *The Economist Book of Vital World Statistics.*

U.C.L.A. Latin American Center Publications, University of California, Los Angeles, California 90024 (310) 825-6634; *Statistical Abstract of Latin America.*

The World Bank, 1818 H Street, NW, Washington, D.C. 20433 (202) 477-1234; *World Tables.*

MEXICO - BANANA PRODUCTION - See MEXICO - CROPS

MEXICO - BANKING

Facts on File, 460 Park Avenue South, New York, New York 10016 (800) 443-8323; *The New Book of World Rankings.*

G.K. Hall and Company, 70 Lincoln Street, Boston, Massachusetts 02111 (617) 423-3990; *The World in Figures.*

Inter-American Development Bank, 1300 New York Avenue, NW, Washington, D.C. 20577 (202) 872-1445; *Economic and Social Progress in Latin America.*

International Monetary Fund, 700 Nineteenth Street, NW, Washington, D.C. 20431 (202) 623-7000; *International Financial Statistics.*

Statistical Office of the United Nations, Publishing Service, New York, New York 10017 (800) 253-9646; *Statistical Yearbook,* and *Statistical Yearbook for Latin America and the Caribbean.*

MEXICO - BARLEY PRODUCTION - See MEXICO - CROPS

MEXICO - BAUXITE PRODUCTION AND CONSUMPTION - See MEXICO - MINING AND MINERAL PRODUCTS

MEXICO - BEER PRODUCTION

Facts on File, 460 Park Avenue South, New York, New York 10016 (800) 443-8323; *The New Book of World Rankings.*

Statistical Office of the United Nations, Publishing Service, New York, New York 10017 (800) 253-9646; *Statistical Yearbook.*

MEXICO - BIRTH RATES

Euromonitor Publications Limited, 87-88 Turnmill Street, London EC1M 5QU, England; *Third World Economic Handbook*.

Facts on File, 460 Park Avenue South, New York, New York 10016 (800) 443-8323; *The New Book of World Rankings*.

Statistical Office of the United Nations, Publishing Service, New York, New York 10017 (800) 253-9646; *Demographic Yearbook, Statistical Yearbook*, and *Statistical Yearbook for Latin America and the Caribbean*.

Times Books, 201 East 50th Street, New York, New York 10022 (212) 751-2600; *The Economist Book of Vital World Statistics*.

The World Bank, 1818 H Street, NW, Washington, D.C. 20433 (202) 477-1234; *World Tables*.

World Health Organization, Office of Publications, Avenue Appia, CH-1211 Geneva 27, Switzerland (Telephone in U.S. (518) 436-9686); *World Health Statistics Annual*.

MEXICO - BISMUTH PRODUCTION AND CONSUMPTION - See MEXICO - MINING AND MINERAL PRODUCTS

MEXICO - BONDS

G.K. Hall and Company, 70 Lincoln Street, Boston, Massachusetts 02111 (617) 423-3990; *The World in Figures*.

Inter-American Development Bank, 1300 New York Avenue, NW, Washington, D.C. 20577 (202) 872-1445; *Economic and Social Progress in Latin America*.

International Monetary Fund, 700 Nineteenth Street, NW, Washington, D.C. 20431 (202) 623-7000; *Government Finance Statistics Yearbook*.

MEXICO - BOOK PRODUCTION

G.K. Hall and Company, 70 Lincoln Street, Boston, Massachusetts 02111 (617) 423-3990; *The World in Figures*.

MEXICO - BROADCASTING

Billboard Limited, Post Office Box 9027, 1006 AA Amsterdam, The Netherlands (Telephone Number in U.S. (212) 764-7300); *World Radio TV Handbook*.

Facts on File, 460 Park Avenue South, New York, New York 10016 (800) 443-8323; *The New Book of World Rankings*.

G.K. Hall and Company, 70 Lincoln Street, Boston, Massachusetts 02111 (617) 423-3990; *The World in Figures*.

Times Books, 201 East 50th Street, New York, New York 10022 (212) 751-2600; *The Economist Book of Vital World Statistics*.

United Nations Educational, Scientific and Cultural Organization (UNESCO), 7 Place de Fontenoy, F-75700 Paris, France (Telephone Number in U.S. (212) 963-5981); *Statistical Yearbook*.

MEXICO - BUSINESS

G.K. Hall and Company, 70 Lincoln Street, Boston, Massachusetts 02111 (617) 423-3990; *The World in Figures*.

Inter-American Development Bank, 1300 New York Avenue, NW, Washington, D.C. 20577 (202) 872-1445; *Economic and Social Progress in Latin America*.

MEXICO - BUSINESS AND PROFESSIONAL LICENSES

International Monetary Fund, 700 Nineteenth Street, NW, Washington, D.C. 20431 (202) 623-7000; *Government Finance Statistics Yearbook*.

MEXICO - BUTTER PRODUCTION - See MEXICO - DAIRY PRODUCTS

MEXICO - CADMIUM PRODUCTION AND CONSUMPTION - See MEXICO - MINING AND MINERAL PRODUCTS

MEXICO - CALORIE SUPPLY

Food and Agricultural Organization of the United Nations (FAO), Via delle Terme di Caracalla, 00100 Rome, Italy (Telephone Number in U.S. (202) 653-2400); *The State of Food and Agriculture*.

Statistical Office of the United Nations, Publishing Service, New York, New York 10017 (800) 253-9646; *Statistical Yearbook for Latin America and the Caribbean*.

MEXICO - CAPITAL INVESTMENT

Inter-American Development Bank, 1300 New York Avenue, NW, Washington, D.C. 20577 (202) 872-1445; *Economic and Social Progress in Latin America*.

MEXICO - CAPITAL REVENUE

Inter-American Development Bank, 1300 New York Avenue, NW, Washington, D.C. 20577 (202) 872-1445; *Economic and Social Progress in Latin America*.

International Monetary Fund, 700 Nineteenth Street, NW, Washington, D.C. 20431 (202) 623-7000; *Government Finance Statistics Yearbook*.

MEXICO - CASTOR BEAN PRODUCTION - See MEXICO - CROPS

MEXICO - CATTLE - See MEXICO - LIVESTOCK AND POULTRY

MEXICO - CAUSTIC SODA PRODUCTION

Statistical Office of the United Nations, Publishing Service, New York, New York 10017 (800) 253-9646; *Statistical Yearbook*.

MEXICO - CEMENT PRODUCTION - See MEXICO - MINING AND MINERAL PRODUCTS

MEXICO - CHEESE PRODUCTION AND CONSUMPTION - See MEXICO - DAIRY PRODUCTS

MEXICO - CHEMICAL (ORGANIC) PRODUCTION - See MEXICO - MINING AND MINERAL PRODUCTS

MEXICO - CHICK PEA PRODUCTION - See MEXICO - CROPS

MEXICO - CHICKENS - See MEXICO - LIVESTOCK AND POULTRY

MEXICO - CHROMITE PRODUCTION AND CONSUMPTION - See MEXICO - MINING AND MINERAL PRODUCTS

MEXICO - CHROMIUM ORE PRODUCTION AND CONSUMPTION - See MEXICO - MINING AND MINERAL PRODUCTS

MEXICO - CIGARETTE PRODUCTION - See MEXICO - TOBACCO PRODUCTION

MEXICO - CLASS STRUCTURE

G.K. Hall and Company, 70 Lincoln Street, Boston, Massachusetts 02111 (617) 423-3990; *The World in Figures.*

MEXICO - CLIMATE

Facts on File, 460 Park Avenue South, New York, New York 10016 (800) 443-8323; *The New Book of World Rankings.*

G.K. Hall and Company, 70 Lincoln Street, Boston, Massachusetts 02111 (617) 423-3990; *The World in Figures.*

MEXICO - CLOTHING EXPORTS TO DEVELOPED COUNTRIES

Euromonitor Publications Limited, 87-88 Turnmill Street, London EC1M 5QU, England; *Third World Economic Handbook.*

Statistical Office of the United Nations, Publishing Service, New York, New York 10017 (800) 253-9646; *Trade in Manufactures of Developing Countries.*

MEXICO - COAL PRODUCTION - See MEXICO - MINING AND MINERAL PRODUCTS

MEXICO - COBALT PRODUCTION AND CONSUMPTION - See MEXICO - MINING AND MINERAL PRODUCTS

MEXICO - COCOA (BEANS) PRODUCTION - See MEXICO - CROPS

MEXICO - COFFEE - See MEXICO - CROPS

MEXICO - COKE, COKE OVEN COKE AND COKE OVEN ORE PRODUCTION AND CONSUMPTION - See MEXICO - MINING AND MINERAL PRODUCTS

MEXICO - COMMUNICATIONS

Euromonitor Publications Limited, 87-88 Turnmill Street, London EC1M 5QU, England; *Third World Economic Handbook.*

Gale Research Incorporated, 835 Penobscot Building, Detroit, Michigan 48226 (800) 877-4253; *International Historical Statistics The Americas and Australasia.*

G.K. Hall and Company, 70 Lincoln Street, Boston, Massachusetts 02111 (617) 423-3990; *The World in Figures.*

Inter-American Development Bank, 1300 New York Avenue, NW, Washington, D.C. 20577 (202) 872-1445; *Economic and Social Progress in Latin America.*

U.C.L.A. Latin American Center Publications, University of California, Los Angeles, California 90024 (310) 825-6634; *Statistical Abstract of Latin America.*

MEXICO - CONSTRUCTION INDUSTRY

The Economist Intelligence Unit, 111 West 57th Street, New York, New York 10019 (800) 938-4685; *The New Latin America Market Atlas.*

Facts on File, 460 Park Avenue South, New York, New York 10016 (800) 443-8323; *The New Book of World Rankings.*

Inter-American Development Bank, 1300 New York Avenue, NW, Washington, D.C. 20577 (202) 872-1445; *Economic and Social Progress in Latin America.*

Statistical Office of the United Nations, Publishing Service, New York, New York 10017 (800) 253-9646; *Statistical Yearbook.*

U.C.L.A. Latin American Center Publications, University of California, Los Angeles, California 90024 (310) 825-6634; *Statistical Abstract of Latin America.*

MEXICO - CONSUMER PRICE INDEX

G.K. Hall and Company, 70 Lincoln Street, Boston, Massachusetts 02111 (617) 423-3990; *The World in Figures.*

Statistical Office of the United Nations, Publishing Service, New York, New York 10017 (800) 253-9646; *Statistical Yearbook.*

MEXICO - CONSUMER PRICES

The Economist Intelligence Unit, 111 West 57th Street, New York, New York 10019 (800) 938-4685; *The New Latin America Market Atlas.*

International Labour Office, I.L.O. Publications, CH-1211, Geneva 22, Switzerland; *Yearbook of Labour Statistics.*

International Monetary Fund, 700 Nineteenth Street, NW, Washington, D.C. 20431 (202) 623-7000; *International Financial Statistics.*

Organization of American States (OAS), General Secretariat, Washington, D.C. 20006 (202) 458-3533; *Statistical Bulletin of the OAS.*

Times Books, 201 East 50th Street, New York, New York 10022 (212) 751-2600; *The Economist Book of Vital World Statistics.*

U.C.L.A. Latin American Center Publications, University of California, Los Angeles, California 90024 (310) 825-6634; *Statistical Abstract of Latin America.*

MEXICO - CONSUMPTION

The Economist Intelligence Unit, 111 West 57th Street, New York, New York 10019 (800) 938-4685; *The New Latin America Market Atlas.*

G.K. Hall and Company, 70 Lincoln Street, Boston, Massachusetts 02111 (617) 423-3990; *The World in Figures.*

Inter-American Development Bank, 1300 New York Avenue, NW, Washington, D.C. 20577 (202) 872-1445; *Economic and Social Progress in Latin America.*

International Lead and Zinc Study Group, Metro House, 58 St. James's Street, London SW1A 1LD England; *Lead and Zinc Statistics.*

Statistical Office of the United Nations, Publishing Service, New York, New York 10017 (800) 253-9646; *Statistical Yearbook for Latin America and the Caribbean.*

MEXICO - COOPERATIVES

U.C.L.A. Latin American Center Publications, University of California, Los Angeles, California 90024 (310) 825-6634; *Statistical Abstract of Latin America.*

MEXICO - COPPER AND COPPER ORE PRODUCTION AND CONSUMPTION - See MEXICO - MINING AND MINERAL PRODUCTS

MEXICO - CORN PRODUCTION - See MEXICO - CROPS

MEXICO - CORPORATE INCOME TAXES - See MEXICO - TAXATION

MEXICO - CORPORATE TAXES - See MEXICO - TAXATION

MEXICO - COTTON - See MEXICO - CROPS

MEXICO - CRIME

Yale University Press, Yale Station, New Haven, Connecticut 06520 (203) 432-0940; *Violence and Crime in Cross-National Perspective.*

MEXICO - CROPS

Commodity Research Bureau, Incorporated, 75 Wall Street, New York, New York 10005 (212) 504-7754; *Commodity Year Book.*

The Economist Intelligence Unit, 111 West 57th Street, New York, New York 10019 (800) 938-4685; *The Now Latin America Market Atlas.*

Facts on File, 460 Park Avenue South, New York, New York 10016 (800) 443-8323; *The New Book of World Rankings.*

Food and Agricultural Organization of the United Nations (FAO), Via delle Terme di Caracalla, 00100 Rome, Italy (Telephone Number in U.S. (202) 653-2400); *Production Yearbook,* and *The State of Food and Agriculture.*

G.K. Hall and Company, 70 Lincoln Street, Boston, Massachusetts 02111 (617) 423-3990; *The World in Figures.*

International Lead and Zinc Study Group, Metro House, 58 St. James's Street, London SW1A 1LD England; *Lead and Zinc Statistics.*

International Monetary Fund, 700 Nineteenth Street, NW, Washington, D.C. 20431 (202) 623-7000; *International Financial Statistics.*

Organization of American States (OAS), General Secretariat, Washington, D.C. 20006 (202) 458-3533; *Statistical Bulletin of the OAS.*

Statistical Office of the United Nations, Publishing Service, New York, New York 10017 (800) 253-9646; *Statistical Yearbook.*

U.C.L.A. Latin American Center Publications, University of California, Los Angeles, California 90024 (310) 825-6634; *Statistical Abstract of Latin America.*

MEXICO - CUSTOMS DUTIES

G.K. Hall and Company, 70 Lincoln Street, Boston, Massachusetts 02111 (617) 423-3990; *The World in Figures.*

Inter-American Development Bank, 1300 New York Avenue, NW, Washington, D.C. 20577 (202) 872-1445; *Economic and Social Progress in Latin America.*

International Monetary Fund, 700 Nineteenth Street, NW, Washington, D.C. 20431 (202) 623-7000; *Government Finance Statistics Yearbook.*

MEXICO - DAIRY PRODUCTS

Facts on File, 460 Park Avenue South, New York, New York 10016 (800) 443-8323; *The New Book of World Rankings.*

Food and Agricultural Organization of the United Nations (FAO), Via delle Terme di Caracalla, 00100 Rome, Italy (Telephone Number in U.S. (202) 653-2400); *The State of Food and Agriculture.*

Statistical Office of the United Nations, Publishing Service, New York, New York 10017 (800) 253-9646; *Statistical Yearbook.*

U.C.L.A. Latin American Center Publications, University of California, Los Angeles, California 90024 (310) 825-6634; *Statistical Abstract of Latin America.*

MEXICO - DEATH RATES

Euromonitor Publications Limited, 87-88 Turnmill Street, London EC1M 5QU, England; *Third World Economic Handbook.*

G.K. Hall and Company, 70 Lincoln Street, Boston, Massachusetts 02111 (617) 423-3990; *The World in Figures.*

Statistical Office of the United Nations, Publishing Service, New York, New York 10017 (800) 253-9646; *Statistical Yearbook.*

Times Books, 201 East 50th Street, New York, New York 10022 (212) 751-2600; *The Economist Book of Vital World Statistics.*

World Health Organization, Office of Publications, Avenue Appia, CH-1211 Geneva 27, Switzerland (Telephone in U.S. (518) 436-9686); *World Health Statistics Annual.*

MEXICO - DEBT

The Economist Intelligence Unit, 111 West 57th Street, New York, New York 10019 (800) 938-4685; *The New Latin America Market Atlas.*

MEXICO - DEFENSE

The Economist Intelligence Unit, 111 West 57th Street, New York, New York 10019 (800) 938-4685; *The New Latin America Market Atlas.*

MEXICO - DEFENSE EXPENDITURES

G.K. Hall and Company, 70 Lincoln Street, Boston, Massachusetts 02111 (617) 423-3990; *The World in Figures.*

International Monetary Fund, 700 Nineteenth Street, NW, Washington, D.C. 20431 (202) 623-7000; *Government Finance Statistics Yearbook.*

U.S. Arms Control and Disarmament Agency, 320 Twenty-first Street, NW, Washington, D.C. 20451 (202) 647-8677; *World Military Expenditures and Arms Transfers.*

MEXICO - DEMOGRAPHY

The Economist Intelligence Unit, 111 West 57th Street, New York, New York 10019 (800) 938-4685; *The World Market Atlas.*

Facts on File, 460 Park Avenue South, New York, New York 10016 (800) 443-8323; *The New Book of World Rankings.*

G.K. Hall and Company, 70 Lincoln Street, Boston, Massachusetts 02111 (617) 423-3990; *The World in Figures.*

MEXICO - DEVELOPMENT ASSISTANCE

G.K. Hall and Company, 70 Lincoln Street, Boston, Massachusetts 02111 (617) 423-3990; *The World in Figures.*

Inter-American Development Bank, 1300 New York Avenue, NW, Washington, D.C. 20577 (202) 872-1445; *Economic and Social Progress in Latin America.*

Statistical Office of the United Nations, Publishing Service, New York, New York 10017 (800) 253-9646; *Statistical Yearbook.*

MEXICO - DIAMOND PRODUCTION - See MEXICO - MINING AND MINERAL PRODUCTS

MEXICO - DISCOUNT RATES

Inter-American Development Bank, 1300 New York Avenue, NW, Washington, D.C. 20577 (202) 872-1445; *Economic and Social Progress in Latin America.*

Statistical Office of the United Nations, Publishing Service, New York, New York 10017 (800) 253-9646; *Statistical Yearbook.*

MEXICO - DISEASES

G.K. Hall and Company, 70 Lincoln Street, Boston, Massachusetts 02111 (617) 423-3990; *The World in Figures.*

World Health Organization, Office of Publications, Avenue Appia, CH-1211 Geneva 27, Switzerland (Telephone in U.S. (518) 436-9686); *World Health Statistics Annual.*

MEXICO - DIVORCE

Facts on File, 460 Park Avenue South, New York, New York 10016 (800) 443-8323; *The New Book of World Rankings.*

Statistical Office of the United Nations, Publishing Service, New York, New York 10017 (800) 253-9646; *Demographic Yearbook,* and *Statistical Yearbook.*

MEXICO - DOMESTIC PRODUCT

G.K. Hall and Company, 70 Lincoln Street, Boston, Massachusetts 02111 (617) 423-3990; *The World in Figures.*

MEXICO - DUCKS - See MEXICO - LIVESTOCK AND POULTRY

MEXICO - ECONOMY

Euromonitor Publications Limited, 87-88 Turnmill Street, London EC1M 5QU, England; *Third World Economic Handbook.*

Facts on File, 460 Park Avenue South, New York, New York 10016 (800) 443-8323; *The New Book of World Rankings.*

G.K. Hall and Company, 70 Lincoln Street, Boston, Massachusetts 02111 (617) 423-3990; *The World in Figures.*

Inter-American Development Bank, 1300 New York Avenue, NW, Washington, D.C. 20577 (202) 872-1445; *Economic and Social Progress in Latin America, International Marketing Data and Statistics,* and *Third World Economic Handbook.*

Organization of American States (OAS), General Secretariat, Washington, D.C. 20006 (202) 458-3533; *Statistical Bulletin of the OAS.*

Statistical Office of the United Nations, Publishing Service, New York, New York 10017 (800) 253-9646; *Economic Survey for Latin America and the Caribbean.*

U.C.L.A. Latin American Center Publications, University of California, Los Angeles, California 90024 (310) 825-6634; *Statistical Abstract of Latin America.*

MEXICO - EDUCATION

The Economist Intelligence Unit, 111 West 57th Street, New York, New York 10019 (800) 938-4685; *The New Latin America Market Atlas,* and *The World Market Atlas.*

Facts on File, 460 Park Avenue South, New York, New York 10016 (800) 443-8323; *The New Book of World Rankings.*

Gale Research Incorporated, 835 Penobscot Building, Detroit, Michigan 48226 (800) 877-4253; *International Historical Statistics The Americas and Australasia.*

G.K. Hall and Company, 70 Lincoln Street, Boston, Massachusetts 02111 (617) 423-3990; *The World in Figures.*

International Monetary Fund, 700 Nineteenth Street, NW, Washington, D.C. 20431 (202) 623-7000; *Government Finance Statistics Yearbook.*

Times Books, 201 East 50th Street, New York, New York 10022 (212) 751-2600; *The Economist Book of Vital World Statistics.*

U.C.L.A. Latin American Center Publications, University of California, Los Angeles, California 90024 (310) 825-6634; *Statistical Abstract of Latin America.*

United Nations Educational, Scientific and Cultural Organization (UNESCO), 7 Place de Fontenoy, F-75700 Paris, France (Telephone Number in U.S. (212) 963-5981); *Statistical Yearbook.*

The World Bank, 1818 H Street, NW, Washington, D.C. 20433 (202) 477-1234; *World Tables.*

MEXICO - EGG PRODUCTION AND CONSUMPTION - See MEXICO - DAIRY PRODUCTS

MEXICO - EGGPLANT PRODUCTION - See MEXICO - CROPS

MEXICO - ELECTRICITY

The Economist Intelligence Unit, 111 West 57th Street, New York, New York 10019 (800) 938-4685; *The New Latin America Market Atlas.*

Facts on File, 460 Park Avenue South, New York, New York 10016 (800) 443-8323; *The New Book of World Rankings.*

Inter-American Development Bank, 1300 New York Avenue, NW, Washington, D.C. 20577 (202) 872-1445; *Economic and Social Progress in Latin America.*

Penn Well Publishing Company, 1421 South Sheridan Road, Post Office Box 1260, Tulsa, Oklahoma 74101 (800) 752-9764; *International Energy Statistics Sourcebook.*

Statistical Office of the United Nations, Publishing Service, New York, New York 10017 (800) 253-9646; *Statistical Yearbook.*

MEXICO - EMPLOYMENT

Euromonitor Publications Limited, 87-88 Turnmill Street, London EC1M 5QU, England; *International Marketing Data and Statistics.*

Facts on File, 460 Park Avenue South, New York, New York 10016 (800) 443-8323; *The New Book of World Rankings.*

International Labour Office, I.L.O. Publications, CH-1211, Geneva 22, Switzerland; *Yearbook of Labour Statistics.*

Statistical Office of the United Nations, Publishing Service, New York, New York 10017 (800) 253-9646; *Statistical Yearbook*, and *Statistical Yearbook for Latin America and the Caribbean.*

U.C.L.A. Latin American Center Publications, University of California, Los Angeles, California 90024 (310) 825-6634; *Statistical Abstracts of Latin America.*

MEXICO - ENERGY

The Economist Intelligence Unit, 111 West 57th Street, New York, New York 10019 (800) 938-4685; *The New Latin America Market Atlas.*

Facts on File, 460 Park Avenue South, New York, New York 10016 (800) 443-8323; *The New Book of World Rankings.*

Food and Agricultural Organization of the United Nations (FAO), Via delle Terme di Caracalla, 00100 Rome, Italy (Telephone Number in U.S. (202) 653-2400); *The State of Food and Agriculture.*

G.K. Hall and Company, 70 Lincoln Street, Boston, Massachusetts 02111 (617) 423-3990; *The World in Figures.*

Penn Well Publishing Company, 1421 South Sheridan Road, Post Office Box 1260, Tulsa, Oklahoma 74101 (800) 752-9764; *International Energy Statistics Sourcebook.*

Statistical Office of the United Nations, Publishing Service, New York, New York 10017 (800) 253-9646; *Energy Statistics Yearbook, Statistical Yearbook,* and *Statistical Yearbook for Latin America and the Caribbean.*

Times Books, 201 East 50th Street, New York, New York 10022 (212) 751-2600; *The Economist Book of Vital World Statistics.*

U.C.L.A. Latin American Center Publications, University of California, Los Angeles, California 90024 (310) 825-6634; *Statistical Abstract of Latin America.*

MEXICO - ENGINEERING AND METAL PRODUCTS EXPORTS AND IMPORTS

Statistical Office of the United Nations, Publishing Service, New York, New York 10017 (800) 253-9646; *Trade in Manufactures of Developing Countries.*

MEXICO - EXCHANGE RATES

Euromonitor Publications Limited, 87-88 Turnmill Street, London EC1M 5QU, England; *International Marketing Data and Statistics.*

Inter-American Development Bank, 1300 New York Avenue, NW, Washington, D.C. 20577 (202) 872-1445; *Economic and Social Progress in Latin America.*

International Civil Aviation Organization, 1000 Sherbrooke Street West, Suite 400, Montreal, Quebec H3A 2R2, Canada (514) 285-8219;

Civil Aviation Statistics of the World.

International Monetary Fund, 700 Nineteenth Street, NW, Washington, D.C. 20431 (202) 623-7000; *International Financial Statistics.*

Organization of American States (OAS), General Secretariat, Washington, D.C. 20006 (202) 458-3533; *Statistical Bulletin of the OAS.*

U.C.L.A. Latin American Center Publications, University of California, Los Angeles, California 90024 (310) 825-6634; *Statistical Abstract of Latin America.*

MEXICO - EXCISE TAXES - See MEXICO - TAXATION

MEXICO - EXPORTS

American Automobile Manufacturers Association, 1401 H Street, NW, Suite 900, Washington, D.C. 20005 (202) 326-5500; *World Motor Vehicle Data.*

The Economist Intelligence Unit, 111 West 57th Street, New York, New York 10019 (800) 938-4685; *The New Latin America Market Atlas,* and *The World Market Atlas.*

Euromonitor Publications Limited, 87-88 Turnmill Street, London EC1M 5QU, England; *Third World Economic Handbook.*

Food and Agricultural Organization of the United Nations (FAO), Via delle Terme di Caracalla, 00100 Rome, Italy (Telephone Number in U.S. (202) 653-2400); *The State of Food and Agriculture.*

G.K. Hall and Company, 70 Lincoln Street, Boston, Massachusetts 02111 (617) 423-3990; *The World in Figures.*

Inter-American Development Bank, 1300 New York Avenue, NW, Washington, D.C. 20577 (202) 872-1445; *Economic and Social Progress in Latin America.*

International Lead and Zinc Study Group, Metro House, 58 St. James's Street, London SW1A 1LD England; *Lead and Zinc Statistics.*

International Monetary Fund, 700 Nineteenth Street, NW, Washington, D.C. 20431 (202) 623-7000; *Direction of Trade Statistics, Government Finance Statistics Yearbook,* and *International Financial Statistics.*

Organization of American States (OAS), General Secretariat, Washington, D.C. 20006 (202) 458-3533; *Statistical Bulletin of the OAS.*

Statistical Office of the United Nations, Publishing Service, New York, New York 10017 (800) 253-9646; *Trade in Manufactures of Developing Countries.*

Times Books, 201 East 50th Street, New York, New York 10022 (212) 751-2600; *The Economist Book of Vital World Statistics.*

The World Bank, 1818 H Street, NW, Washington, D.C. 20433 (202) 477-1234; *World Tables.*

MEXICO - EXTERNAL FINANCING

Inter-American Development Bank, 1300 New York Avenue, NW, Washington, D.C. 20577 (202) 872-1445; *Economic and Social Progress in Latin America.*

Statistical Office of the United Nations, Publishing Service, New York, New York 10017 (800) 253-9646; *Statistical Yearbook for Latin America and the Caribbean.*

MEXICO - EXTERNAL INDEBTEDNESS

Euromonitor Publications Limited, 87-88 Turnmill Street, London EC1M 5QU, England; *Third World Economic Handbook.*

Inter-American Development Bank, 1300 New York Avenue, NW, Washington, D.C. 20577 (202) 872-1445; *Economic and Social Progress in Latin America.*

Statistical Office of the United Nations, Publishing Service, New York, New York 10017 (800) 253-9646; *Statistical Yearbook for Latin America and the Caribbean.*

The World Bank, 1818 H Street, NW, Washington, D.C. 20433 (202) 477-1234; *World Tables.*

MEXICO - EXTERNAL TRADE

Food and Agricultural Organization of the United Nations (FAO), Via delle Terme di Caracalla, 00100 Rome, Italy (Telephone Number in U.S. (202) 653-2400); *The State of Food and Agriculture*, and *Trade Yearbook.*

Gale Research Incorporated, 835 Penobscot Building, Detroit, Michigan 48226 (800) 877-4253; *International Historical Statistics The Americas and Australasia.*

G.K. Hall and Company, 70 Lincoln Street, Boston, Massachusetts 02111 (617) 423-3990; *The World in Figures.*

Inter-American Development Bank, 1300 New York Avenue, NW, Washington, D.C. 20577 (202) 872-1445; *Economic and Social Progress in Latin America.*

Statistical Office of the United Nations, Publishing Service, New York, New York 10017 (800) 253-9646; *Statistical Yearbook*, and *Statistical Yearbook for Latin America and the Caribbean.*

MEXICO - FABRIC PRODUCTION - See MEXICO - TEXTILE INDUSTRY

MEXICO - FAMILY PLANNING

U.C.L.A. Latin American Center Publications, University of California, Los Angeles, California 90024 (310) 825-6634; *Statistical Abstract of Latin America.*

MEXICO - FARM CROPS - See MEXICO - CROPS

MEXICO - FEMALE WORKING POPULATION - See MEXICO - EMPLOYMENT

MEXICO - FERTILITY RATES

Facts on File, 460 Park Avenue South, New York, New York 10016 (800) 443-8323; *The New Book of World Rankings.*

Times Books, 201 East 50th Street, New York, New York 10022 (212) 751-2600; *The Economist Book of Vital World Statistics.*

The World Bank, 1818 H Street, NW, Washington, D.C. 20433 (202) 477-1234; *World Tables.*

MEXICO - FERTILIZER

The Economist Intelligence Unit, 111 West 57th Street, New York, New York 10019 (800) 938-4685; *The New Latin America Market Atlas.*

Food and Agricultural Organization of the United Nations (FAO), Via delle Terme di Caracalla, 00100 Rome, Italy (Telephone Number in U.S. (202) 653-2400); *Fertilizer Yearbook*, and *The State of Food and Agriculture.*

Statistical Office of the United Nations, Publishing Service, New York, New York 10017 (800) 253-9646; *Statistical Yearbook.*

MEXICO - FETAL MORTALITY

Statistical Office of the United Nations, Publishing Service, New York, New York 10017 (800) 253-9646; *Demographic Yearbook.*

World Health Organization, Office of Publications, Avenue Appia, CH-1211 Geneva 27, Switzerland (Telephone in U.S. (518) 436-9686); *World Health Statistics Annual.*

MEXICO - FIBRE PRODUCTION - See MEXICO - TEXTILE INDUSTRY

MEXICO - FILAMENT PRODUCTION - See MEXICO - TEXTILE INDUSTRY

MEXICO - FILM - See MEXICO - MOTION PICTURES

MEXICO - FINANCE

Facts on File, 460 Park Avenue South, New York, New York 10016 (800) 443-8323; *The New Book of World Rankings.*

Gale Research Incorporated, 835 Penobscot Building, Detroit, Michigan 48226 (800) 877-4253; *International Historical Statistics The Americas and Australasia.*

G.K. Hall and Company, 70 Lincoln Street, Boston, Massachusetts 02111 (617) 423-3990; *The World in Figures.*

Inter-American Development Bank, 1300 New York Avenue, NW, Washington, D.C. 20577 (202) 872-1445; *Economic and Social Progress in Latin America.*

International Monetary Fund, 700 Nineteenth Street, NW, Washington, D.C. 20431 (202) 623-7000; *Government Finance Statistics Yearbook*, and *International Financial Statistics.*

Organization of American States (OAS), General Secretariat, Washington, D.C. 20006 (202) 458-3533; *Statistical Bulletin of the OAS.*

U.C.L.A. Latin American Center Publications, University of California, Los Angeles, California 90024 (310) 825-6634; *Statistical Abstract of Latin America.*

MEXICO - FISHERIES

Facts on File, 460 Park Avenue South, New York, New York 10016 (800) 443-8323; *The New Book of World Rankings.*

Food and Agricultural Organization of the United Nations (FAO), Via delle Terme di Caracalla, 00100 Rome, Italy (Telephone Number in U.S. (202) 653-2400); *The State of Food and Agriculture*, and *Yearbook of Fishery Statistics.*

Inter-American Development Bank, 1300 New York Avenue, NW, Washington, D.C. 20577 (202) 872-1445; *Economic and Social Progress in Latin America.*

Statistical Office of the United Nations, Publishing Service, New York, New York 10017 (800) 253-9646; *Statistical Yearbook.*

U.C.L.A. Latin American Center Publications, University of California, Los Angeles, California 90024 (310) 825-6634; *Statistical Abstract of Latin America.*

MEXICO - FLOUR PRODUCTION

Commodity Research Bureau, Incorporated, 75 Wall Street, New York, New York 10005 (212) 504-7754; *Commodity Year Book.*

Statistical Office of the United Nations, Publishing Service, New York, New York 10017 (800) 253-9646; *Statistical Yearbook.*

MEXICO - FOOD

Food and Agricultural Organization of the United Nations (FAO), Via delle Terme di Caracalla, 00100 Rome, Italy (Telephone Number in U.S. (202) 653-2400); *Production Yearbook,* and *The State of Food and Agriculture.*

G.K. Hall and Company, 70 Lincoln Street, Boston, Massachusetts 02111 (617) 423-3990; *The World in Figures.*

Statistical Office of the United Nations, Publishing Service, New York, New York 10017 (800) 253-9646; *Trade in Manufactures of Developing Countries.*

MEXICO - FOREIGN AID

G.K. Hall and Company, 70 Lincoln Street, Boston, Massachusetts 02111 (617) 423-3990; *The World in Figures.*

Inter-American Development Bank, 1300 New York Avenue, NW, Washington, D.C. 20577 (202) 872-1445; *Economic and Social Progress in Latin America.*

MEXICO - FOREIGN DEBT

The Economist Intelligence Unit, 111 West 57th Street, New York, New York 10019 (800) 938-4685; *The New Latin America Market Atlas.*

Inter-American Development Bank, 1300 New York Avenue, NW, Washington, D.C. 20577 (202) 872-1445; *Economic and Social Progress in Latin America.*

MEXICO - FOREIGN INDEBTEDNESS

Inter-American Development Bank, 1300 New York Avenue, NW, Washington, D.C. 20577 (202) 872-1445; *Economic and Social Progress in Latin America.*

Statistical Office of the United Nations, Publishing Service, New York, New York 10017 (800) 253-9646; *Economic Survey of Latin America and the Caribbean.*

MEXICO - FOREIGN INVESTMENT

The Economist Intelligence Unit, 111 West 57th Street, New York, New York 10019 (800) 938-4685; *The New Latin America Market Atlas.*

MEXICO - FOREIGN TRADE

The Economist Intelligence Unit, 111 West 57th Street, New York, New York 10019 (800) 938-4685; *The New Latin America Market Atlas.*

Euromonitor Publications Limited, 87-88 Turnmill Street, London EC1M 5QU, England; *International Marketing Data and Statistics,* and *Third World Economic Handbook.*

Facts on File, 460 Park Avenue South, New York, New York 10016 (800) 443-8323; *The New Book of World Rankings.*

Food and Agricultural Organization of the United Nations (FAO), Via delle Terme di Caracalla, 00100 Rome, Italy (Telephone Number in U.S. (202) 653-2400); *The State of Food and Agriculture.*

G.K. Hall and Company, 70 Lincoln Street, Boston, Massachusetts 02111 (617) 423-3990; *The World in Figures.*

Inter-American Development Bank, 1300 New York Avenue, NW, Washington, D.C. 20577 (202) 872-1445; *Economic and Social Progress in Latin America.*

International Monetary Fund, 700 Nineteenth Street, NW, Washington, D.C. 20431 (202) 623-7000; *International Financial Statistics.*

Statistical Office of the United Nations, Publishing Service, New York, New York 10017 (800) 253-9646; *Economic Survey of Latin America and the Caribbean, International Trade Statistics Yearbook,* and *Statistical Yearbook.*

U.C.L.A. Latin American Center Publications, University of California, Los Angeles, California 90024 (310) 825-6634; *Statistical Abstract of Latin America.*

The World Bank, 1818 H Street, NW, Washington, D.C. 20433 (202) 477-1234; *World Tables.*

MEXICO - FORESTRY AND FOREST PRODUCTS

American Forest and Paper Association, 1250 Connecticut Avenue, NW, Washington, D.C. 20036 (202) 463-2455; *Wood Pulp and Fiber Statistics.*

The Economist Intelligence Unit, 111 West 57th Street, New York, New York 10019 (800) 938-4685; *The New Latin America Market Atlas.*

Euromonitor Publications Limited, 87-88 Turnmill Street, London EC1M 5QU, England; *Third World Economic Handbook.*

Facts on File, 460 Park Avenue South, New York, New York 10016 (800) 443-8323; *The New Book of World Rankings.*

Food and Agricultural Organization of the United Nations (FAO), Via delle Terme di Caracalla, 00100 Rome, Italy (Telephone Number in U.S. (202) 653-2400); *The State of Food and Agriculture,* and *Yearbook of Forest Products.*

G.K. Hall and Company, 70 Lincoln Street, Boston, Massachusetts 02111 (617) 423-3990; *The World in Figures.*

Inter-American Development Bank, 1300 New York Avenue, NW, Washington, D.C. 20577 (202) 872-1445; *Economic and Social Progress in Latin America.*

Statistical Office of the United Nations, Publishing Service, New York, New York 10017 (800) 253-9646; *Statistical Yearbook.*

U.C.L.A. Latin American Center Publications, University of California, Los Angeles, California 90024 (310) 825-6634; *Statistical Abstract of Latin America.*

United Nations Educational, Scientific and Cultural Organization (UNESCO), 7 Place de Fontenoy, F-75700 Paris, France (Telephone Number in U.S. (212) 963-5981); *Statistical Yearbook.*

MEXICO - FURNITURE AND WOOD PRODUCTS EXPORTS TO DEVELOPED COUNTRIES

Statistical Office of the United Nations, Publishing Service, New York, New York 10017 (800) 253-9646; *Trade in Manufactures of Developing Countries.*

MEXICO - GARLIC PRODUCTION - See MEXICO - CROPS

MEXICO - GAS - See MEXICO - MINING AND MINERAL PRODUCTS

MEXICO - GENERAL INDUSTRIAL STATISTICS

Statistical Office of the United Nations, Publishing Service, New York, New York 10017 (800) 253-9646; *Industrial Statistics Yearbook.*

MEXICO - GENERAL MORTALITY

Statistical Office of the United Nations, Publishing Service, New York, New York 10017 (800) 253-9646; *Demographic Yearbook.*

World Health Organization, Office of Publications, Avenue Appia, CH-1211 Geneva 27, Switzerland (Telephone in U.S. (518) 436-9686); *World Health Statistics Annual.*

MEXICO - GEOGRAPHIC DATA

Facts on File, 460 Park Avenue South, New York, New York 10016 (800) 443-8323; *The New Book of World Rankings.*

U.C.L.A. Latin American Center Publications, University of California, Los Angeles, California 90024 (310) 825-6634; *Statistical Abstract of Latin America.*

MEXICO - GOATS - See MEXICO - LIVESTOCK AND POULTRY

MEXICO - GOLD HOLDINGS

International Monetary Fund, 700 Nineteenth Street, NW, Washington, D.C. 20431 (202) 623-7000; *International Financial Statistics.*

Statistical Office of the United Nations, Publishing Service, New York, New York 10017 (800) 253-9646; *Statistical Yearbook.*

The World Bank, 1818 H Street, NW, Washington, D.C. 20433 (202) 477-1234; *World Tables.*

MEXICO - GOLD PRODUCTION AND CONSUMPTION - See MEXICO - MINING AND MINERAL PRODUCTS

MEXICO - GOLD RESERVES

The Economist Intelligence Unit, 111 West 57th Street, New York, New York 10019 (800) 938-4685; *The New Latin America Market Atlas.*

MEXICO - GOVERNMENT

G.K. Hall and Company, 70 Lincoln Street, Boston, Massachusetts 02111 (617) 423-3990; *The World in Figures.*

Inter-American Development Bank, 1300 New York Avenue, NW, Washington, D.C. 20577 (202) 872-1445; *Economic and Social Progress in Latin America.*

MEXICO - GOVERNMENT CONSUMPTION

Inter-American Development Bank, 1300 New York Avenue, NW, Washington, D.C. 20577 (202) 872-1445; *Economic and Social Progress in Latin America.*

MEXICO - GOVERNMENT EXPENDITURES

Euromonitor Publications Limited, 87-88 Turnmill Street, London EC1M 5QU, England; *Third World Economic Handbook.*

Inter-American Development Bank, 1300 New York Avenue, NW, Washington, D.C. 20577 (202) 872-1445; *Economic and Social Progress in Latin America.*

International Monetary Fund, 700 Nineteenth Street, NW, Washington, D.C. 20431 (202) 623-7000; *Government Finance Statistics Yearbook.*

Times Books, 201 East 50th Street, New York, New York 10022 (212) 751-2600; *The Economist Book of Vital World Statistics.*

The World Bank, 1818 H Street, NW, Washington, D.C. 20433 (202) 477-1234; *World Tables.*

MEXICO - GOVERNMENT FINANCES

Inter-American Development Bank, 1300 New York Avenue, NW, Washington, D.C. 20577 (202) 872-1445; *Economic and Social Progress in Latin America.*

International Monetary Fund, 700 Nineteenth Street, NW, Washington, D.C. 20431 (202) 623-7000; *International Financial Statistics.*

MEXICO - GOVERNMENT REVENUE

Inter-American Development Bank, 1300 New York Avenue, NW, Washington, D.C. 20577 (202) 872-1445; *Economic and Social Progress in Latin America.*

International Monetary Fund, 700 Nineteenth Street, NW, Washington, D.C. 20431 (202) 623-7000; *Government Finance Statistics Yearbook.*

Times Books, 201 East 50th Street, New York, New York 10022 (212) 751-2600; *The Economist Book of Vital World Statistics.*

The World Bank, 1818 H Street, NW, Washington, D.C. 20433 (202) 477-1234; *World Tables.*

MEXICO - GRAIN PRODUCTION - See MEXICO - CROPS

MEXICO - GRANTS

International Monetary Fund, 700 Nineteenth Street, NW, Washington, D.C. 20431 (202) 623-7000; *Government Finance Statistics Yearbook.*

MEXICO - GREEN PEPPER AND CHILIE PRODUCTION - See MEXICO - CROPS

MEXICO - GROSS DOMESTIC PRODUCT

The Economist Intelligence Unit, 111 West 57th Street, New York, New York 10019 (800) 938-4685; *The New Latin America Market Atlas*, and *The World Market Atlas*.

Euromonitor Publications Limited, 87-88 Turnmill Street, London EC1M 5QU, England; *International Marketing Data and Statistics*, and *Third World Economic Handbook*.

Facts on File, 460 Park Avenue South, New York, New York 10016 (800) 443-8323; *The New Book of World Rankings*.

G.K. Hall and Company, 70 Lincoln Street, Boston, Massachusetts 02111 (617) 423-3990; *The World in Figures*.

Inter-American Development Bank, 1300 New York Avenue, NW, Washington, D.C. 20577 (202) 872-1445; *Economic and Social Progress in Latin America*.

Organization of American States (OAS), General Secretariat, Washington, D.C. 20006 (202) 458-3533; *Statistical Bulletin of the OAS*.

Statistical Office of the United Nations, Publishing Service, New York, New York 10017 (800) 253-9646; *Statistical Yearbook*, and *Statistical Yearbook for Latin America and the Caribbean*.

Times Books, 201 East 50th Street, New York, New York 10022 (212) 751-2600; *The Economist Book of Vital World Statistics*.

U.C.L.A. Latin American Center Publications, University of California, Los Angeles, California 90024 (310) 825-6634; *Statistical Abstract of Latin America*.

The World Bank, 1818 H Street, NW, Washington, D.C. 20433 (202) 477-1234; *World Tables*.

MEXICO - GROSS NATIONAL PRODUCT

Euromonitor Publications Limited, 87-88 Turnmill Street, London EC1M 5QU, England; *International Marketing Data and Statistics*, and *Third World Economic Handbook*.

Inter-American Development Bank, 1300 New York Avenue, NW, Washington, D.C. 20577 (202) 872-1445; *Economic and Social Progress in Latin America*.

U.S. Arms Control and Disarmament Agency, 320 Twenty-first Street, NW, Washington, D.C. 20451 (202) 647-8677; *World Military Expenditures and Arms Transfers*.

The World Bank, 1818 H Street, NW, Washington, D.C. 20433 (202) 477-1234; *World Tables*.

MEXICO - GROUNDNUT PRODUCTION - See MEXICO - CROPS

MEXICO - HEALTH

The Economist Intelligence Unit, 111 West 57th Street, New York, New York 10019 (800) 938-4685; *The New Latin America Market Atlas*.

Facts on File, 460 Park Avenue South, New York, New York 10016 (800) 443-8323; *The New Book of World Rankings*.

G.K. Hall and Company, 70 Lincoln Street, Boston, Massachusetts 02111 (617) 423-3990; *The World in Figures*.

Statistical Office of the United Nations, Publishing Service, New York, New York 10017 (800) 253-9646; *Statistical Yearbook*. and *Statistical Yearbook for Latin America and the Caribbean*.

Times Books, 201 East 50th Street, New York, New York 10022 (212) 751-2600; *The Economist Book of Vital World Statistics*.

U.C.L.A. Latin American Center Publications, University of California, Los Angeles, California 90024 (310) 825-6634; *Statistical Abstract of Latin America*.

World Health Organization, Office of Publications, Avenue Appia, CH-1211 Geneva 27, Switzerland (Telephone in U.S. (518) 436-9686); *World Health Statistics Annual*.

MEXICO - HIDE PRODUCTION

Commodity Research Bureau, Incorporated, 75 Wall Street, New York, New York 10005 (212) 504-7754; *Commodity Year Book*.

Food and Agricultural Organization of the United Nations (FAO), Via delle Terme di Caracalla, 00100 Rome, Italy (Telephone Number in U.S. (202) 653-2400); *Production Yearbook*.

MEXICO - HIGHWAYS

The Economist Intelligence Unit, 111 West 57th Street, New York, New York 10019 (800) 938-4685; *The New Latin America Market Atlas*.

G.K. Hall and Company, 70 Lincoln Street, Boston, Massachusetts 02111 (617) 423-3990; *The World in Figures*.

International Road Federation, 525 School Street, SW, Washington, D.C. 20024 (202) 554-2106; *World Road Statistics*.

MEXICO - HONEY PRODUCTION

Commodity Research Bureau, Incorporated, 75 Wall Street, New York, New York 10005 (212) 504-7754; *Commodity Year Book*.

MEXICO - HORSES - See MEXICO - LIVESTOCK AND POULTRY

MEXICO - HOURS OF WORK - See MEXICO - EMPLOYMENT

MEXICO - HOUSING AND HOUSING UNITS

Euromonitor Publications Limited, 87-88 Turnmill Street, London EC1M 5QU, England; *Third World Economic Handbook*.

Facts on File, 460 Park Avenue South, New York, New York 10016 (800) 443-8323; *The New Book of World Rankings*.

U.C.L.A. Latin American Center Publications, University of California, Los Angeles, California 90024 (310) 825-6634; *Statistical Abstract of Latin America*.

MEXICO - HYDROCHLORIC ACID PRODUCTION

Statistical Office of the United Nations, Publishing Service, New York, New York 10017 (800) 253-9646; *Statistical Yearbook*.

MEXICO - ILLITERACY RATES

The Economist Intelligence Unit, 111 West 57th Street, New York, New York 10019 (800) 938-4685; *The New Latin America Market*

Atlas.

MEXICO - ILLITERATE POPULATION

The Economist Intelligence Unit, 111 West 57th Street, New York, New York 10019 (800) 938-4685; *The World Market Atlas.*

G.K. Hall and Company, 70 Lincoln Street, Boston, Massachusetts 02111 (617) 423-3990; *The World in Figures.*

United Nations Educational, Scientific and Cultural Organization (UNESCO), 7 Place de Fontenoy, F-75700 Paris, France (Telephone Number in U.S. (212) 963-5981); *Statistical Yearbook.*

MEXICO - IMMIGRATION

U.C.L.A. Latin American Center Publications, University of California, Los Angeles, California 90024 (310) 825-6634; *Statistical Abstract of Latin America.*

MEXICO - IMPORTS

American Automobile Manufacturers Association, 1401 H Street, NW, Suite 900, Washington, D.C. 20005 (202) 326-5500; *World Motor Vehicle Data.*

The Economist Intelligence Unit, 111 West 57th Street, New York, New York 10019 (800) 938-4685; *The New Latin America Market Atlas,* and *The World Market Atlas.*

Euromonitor Publications Limited, 87-88 Turnmill Street, London EC1M 5QU, England; *International Marketing Data and Statistics,* and *Third World Economic Handbook.*

Food and Agricultural Organization of the United Nations (FAO), Via delle Terme di Caracalla, 00100 Rome, Italy (Telephone Number in U.S. (202) 653-2400); *The State of Food and Agriculture.*

G.K. Hall and Company, 70 Lincoln Street, Boston, Massachusetts 02111 (617) 423-3990; *The World in Figures.*

Inter-American Development Bank, 1300 New York Avenue, NW, Washington, D.C. 20577 (202) 872-1445; *Economic and Social Progress in Latin America.*

International Lead and Zinc Study Group, Metro House, 58 St. James's Street, London SW1A 1LD England; *Lead and Zinc Statistics.*

International Monetary Fund, 700 Nineteenth Street, NW, Washington, D.C. 20431 (202) 623-7000; *Direction of Trade Statistics, Government Finance Statistics Yearbook,* and *International Financial Statistics.*

Organization of American States (OAS), General Secretariat, Washington, D.C. 20006 (202) 458-3533; *Statistical Bulletin of the OAS.*

Times Books, 201 East 50th Street, New York, New York 10022 (212) 751-2600; *The Economist Book of Vital World Statistics.*

The World Bank, 1818 H Street, NW, Washington, D.C. 20433 (202) 477-1234; *World Tables.*

MEXICO - INCOME DISTRIBUTION

Statistical Office of the United Nations, Publishing Service, New York, New York 10017 (800) 253-9646; *Statistical Yearbook for Latin America and the Caribbean.*

U.C.L.A. Latin American Center Publications, University of California, Los Angeles, California 90024 (310) 825-6634; *Statistical Abstract of Latin America.*

MEXICO - INCOME TAXES - See MEXICO - TAXATION

MEXICO - INDUSTRIAL METALS PRODUCTION - See MEXICO - MINING AND MINERAL PRODUCTS

MEXICO - INDUSTRY

Euromonitor Publications Limited, 87-88 Turnmill Street, London EC1M 5QU, England; *International Marketing Data and Statistics.*

Facts on File, 460 Park Avenue South, New York, New York 10016 (800) 443-8323; *The New Book of World Rankings.*

Gale Research Incorporated, 835 Penobscot Building, Detroit, Michigan 48226 (800) 877-4253; *International Historical Statistics The Americas and Australasia.*

G.K. Hall and Company, 70 Lincoln Street, Boston, Massachusetts 02111 (617) 423-3990; *The World in Figures.*

International Labour Office, I.L.O. Publications, CH-1211, Geneva 22, Switzerland; *Yearbook of Labour Statistics.*

Statistical Office of the United Nations, Publishing Service, New York, New York 10017 (800) 253-9646; *Economic Survey of Latin America and the Caribbean,* and *Statistical Yearbook.*

Times Books, 201 East 50th Street, New York, New York 10022 (212) 751-2600; *The Economist Book of Vital World Statistics.*

U.C.L.A. Latin American Center Publications, University of California, Los Angeles, California 90024 (310) 825-6634; *Statistical Abstract of Latin America.*

The World Bank, 1818 H Street, NW, Washington, D.C. 20433 (202) 477-1234; *World Tables.*

World Intellectual Property Organization, 34 Chemin des Colombettes, CH-1211 Geneva 20, Switzerland; *Industrial Property Statistics.*

MEXICO - INFANT AND MATERNAL MORTALITY

The Economist Intelligence Unit, 111 West 57th Street, New York, New York 10019 (800) 938-4685; *The New Latin America Market Atlas.*

Statistical Office of the United Nations, Publishing Service, New York, New York 10017 (800) 253-9646; *Demographic Yearbook,* and *Statistical Yearbook.*

Times Books, 201 East 50th Street, New York, New York 10022 (212) 751-2600; *The Economist Book of Vital World Statistics.*

The World Bank, 1818 H Street, NW, Washington, D.C. 20433 (202) 477-1234; *World Tables.*

World Health Organization, Office of Publications, Avenue Appia, CH-1211 Geneva 27, Switzerland (Telephone in U.S. (518) 436-9686); *World Health Statistics Annual.*

MEXICO - INFLATIONARY FACTORS

Statistical Office of the United Nations, Publishing Service, New York, New York 10017 (800) 253-9646; *Economic Survey of Latin*

America and the Caribbean.

MEXICO - INTEREST RATES

Inter-American Development Bank, 1300 New York Avenue, NW, Washington, D.C. 20577 (202) 872-1445; *Economic and Social Progress in Latin America.*

Organization of American States (OAS), General Secretariat, Washington, D.C. 20006 (202) 458-3533; *Statistical Bulletin of the OAS.*

MEXICO - INTERNATIONAL FINANCE

Inter-American Development Bank, 1300 New York Avenue, NW, Washington, D.C. 20577 (202) 872-1445; *Economic and Social Progress in Latin America.*

U.C.L.A. Latin American Center Publications, University of California, Los Angeles, California 90024 (310) 825-6634; *Statistical Abstract of Latin America.*

MEXICO - INTERNATIONAL LIQUIDITY

Inter-American Development Bank, 1300 New York Avenue, NW, Washington, D.C. 20577 (202) 872-1445; *Economic and Social Progress in Latin America.*

International Monetary Fund, 700 Nineteenth Street, NW, Washington, D.C. 20431 (202) 623-7000; *International Financial Statistics.*

MEXICO - INTERNATIONAL RESERVES

Organization of American States (OAS), General Secretariat, Washington, D.C. 20006 (202) 458-3533; *Statistical Bulletin of the OAS.*

MEXICO - INTERNATIONAL RESERVES EXCLUDING GOLD

Inter-American Development Bank, 1300 New York Avenue, NW, Washington, D.C. 20577 (202) 872-1445; *Economic and Social Progress in Latin America.*

Statistical Office of the United Nations, Publishing Service, New York, New York 10017 (800) 253-9646; *Statistical Yearbook.*

The World Bank, 1818 H Street, NW, Washington, D.C. 20433 (202) 477-1234; *World Tables.*

MEXICO - INTERNATIONAL STATISTICS

Inter-American Development Bank, 1300 New York Avenue, NW, Washington, D.C. 20577 (202) 872-1445; *Economic and Social Progress in Latin America.*

U.C.L.A. Latin American Center Publications, University of California, Los Angeles, California 90024 (310) 825-6634; *Statistical Abstract of Latin America.*

MEXICO - INVESTMENTS

Inter-American Development Bank, 1300 New York Avenue, NW, Washington, D.C. 20577 (202) 872-1445; *Economic and Social Progress in Latin America.*

International Monetary Fund, 700 Nineteenth Street, NW, Washington, D.C. 20431 (202) 623-7000; *International Financial*

Statistics.

Statistical Office of the United Nations, Publishing Service, New York, New York 10017 (800) 253-9646; *Statistical Yearbook for Latin America and the Caribbean.*

MEXICO - IRON ORE PRODUCTION AND CONSUMPTION - See MEXICO - MINING AND MINERAL PRODUCTS

MEXICO - IRRIGATION

Euromonitor Publications Limited, 87-88 Turnmill Street, London EC1M 5QU, England; *International Marketing Data and Statistics.*

Inter-American Development Bank, 1300 New York Avenue, NW, Washington, D.C. 20577 (202) 872-1445; *Economic and Social Progress in Latin America.*

MEXICO - LABOR FORCE

The Economist Intelligence Unit, 111 West 57th Street, New York, New York 10019 (800) 938-4685; *The New Latin America Market Atlas.*

Euromonitor Publications Limited, 87-88 Turnmill Street, London EC1M 5QU, England; *International Marketing Data and Statistics.*

Facts on File, 460 Park Avenue South, New York, New York 10016 (800) 443-8323; *The New Book of World Rankings.*

Food and Agricultural Organization of the United Nations (FAO), Via delle Terme di Caracalla, 00100 Rome, Italy (Telephone Number in U.S. (202) 653-2400); *The State of Food and Agriculture.*

Gale Research Incorporated, 835 Penobscot Building, Detroit, Michigan 48226 (800) 877-4253; *International Historical Statistics The Americas and Australasia.*

G.K. Hall and Company, 70 Lincoln Street, Boston, Massachusetts 02111 (617) 423-3990; *The World in Figures.*

Times Books, 201 East 50th Street, New York, New York 10022 (212) 751-2600; *The Economist Book of Vital World Statistics.*

The World Bank, 1818 H Street, NW, Washington, D.C. 20433 (202) 477-1234; *World Tables.*

MEXICO - LABOR PRODUCTIVITY

International Labour Office, I.L.O. Publications, CH-1211, Geneva 22, Switzerland; *Yearbook of Labour Statistics.*

MEXICO - LAND AREA

The Economist Intelligence Unit, 111 West 57th Street, New York, New York 10019 (800) 938-4685; *The New Latin America Market Atlas.*

MEXICO - LAND USE

Euromonitor Publications Limited, 87-88 Turnmill Street, London EC1M 5QU, England; *International Marketing Data and Statistics.*

Food and Agricultural Organization of the United Nations (FAO), Via delle Terme di Caracalla, 00100 Rome, Italy (Telephone Number in U.S. (202) 653-2400); *Production Yearbook.*

G.K. Hall and Company, 70 Lincoln Street, Boston, Massachusetts 02111 (617) 423-3990; *The World in Figures.*

Inter-American Development Bank, 1300 New York Avenue, NW, Washington, D.C. 20577 (202) 872-1445; *Economic and Social Progress in Latin America.*

MEXICO - LEAD AND LEAD ORE PRODUCTION AND CONSUMPTION - See MEXICO - MINING AND MINERAL PRODUCTS

MEXICO - LEATHER AND FOOTWEAR EXPORTS AND IMPORTS

Statistical Office of the United Nations, Publishing Service, New York, New York 10017 (800) 253-9646; *Trade in Manufactures of Developing Countries.*

MEXICO - LIBRARIES

Facts on File, 460 Park Avenue South, New York, New York 10016 (800) 443-8323; *The New Book of World Rankings.*

United Nations Educational, Scientific and Cultural Organization (UNESCO), 7 Place de Fontenoy, F-75700 Paris, France (Telephone Number in U.S. (212) 963-5981); *Statistical Yearbook.*

MEXICO - LIFE EXPECTANCY RATE

The Economist Intelligence Unit, 111 West 57th Street, New York, New York 10019 (800) 938-4685; *The New Latin America Market Atlas.*

MEXICO - LIVESTOCK AND POULTRY

Commodity Research Bureau, Incorporated, 75 Wall Street, New York, New York 10005 (212) 504-7754; *Commodity Year Book.*

Euromonitor Publications Limited, 87-88 Turnmill Street, London EC1M 5QU, England; *International Marketing Data and Statistics.*

Facts on File, 460 Park Avenue South, New York, New York 10016 (800) 443-8323; *The New Book of World Rankings.*

Food and Agricultural Organization of the United Nations (FAO), Via delle Terme di Caracalla, 00100 Rome, Italy (Telephone Number in U.S. (202) 653-2400); *Production Yearbook,* and *The State of Food and Agriculture.*

G.K. Hall and Company, 70 Lincoln Street, Boston, Massachusetts 02111 (617) 423-3990; *The World in Figures.*

Statistical Office of the United Nations, Publishing Service, New York, New York 10017 (800) 253-9646; *Statistical Yearbook.*

MEXICO - LIVING LEVELS

G.K. Hall and Company, 70 Lincoln Street, Boston, Massachusetts 02111 (617) 423-3990; *The World in Figures.*

Statistical Office of the United Nations, Publishing Service, New York, New York 10017 (800) 253-9646; *Statistical Yearbook for Latin America and the Caribbean.*

Times Books, 201 East 50th Street, New York, New York 10022 (212) 751-2600; *The Economist Book of Vital World Statistics.*

MEXICO - MAGNESIUM PRODUCTION AND CONSUMPTION - See MEXICO - MINING AND MINERAL PRODUCTS

MEXICO - MAIL - NUMBER OF PIECES SENT OR RECEIVED

Statistical Office of the United Nations, Publishing Service, New York, New York 10017 (800) 253-9646; *Statistical Yearbook.*

MEXICO - MAIN ECONOMIC INDICATORS - See MEXICO - ECONOMY

MEXICO - MAIN INDICATORS - See MEXICO - ECONOMY

MEXICO - MANGANESE AND MANGANESE ORE PRODUCTION - See MEXICO - MINING AND MINERAL PRODUCTS

MEXICO - MANUFACTURING

American Automobile Manufacturers Association, 1401 H Street, NW, Suite 900, Washington, D.C. 20005 (202) 326-5500; *World Motor Vehicle Data.*

The Economist Intelligence Unit, 111 West 57th Street, New York, New York 10019 (800) 938-4685; *The New Latin America Market Atlas.*

Euromonitor Publications Limited, 87-88 Turnmill Street, London EC1M 5QU, England; *Third World Economic Handbook.*

Facts on File, 460 Park Avenue South, New York, New York 10016 (800) 443-8323; *The New Book of World Rankings.*

G.K. Hall and Company, 70 Lincoln Street, Boston, Massachusetts 02111 (617) 423-3990; *The World in Figures.*

Inter-American Development Bank, 1300 New York Avenue, NW, Washington, D.C. 20577 (202) 872-1445; *Economic and Social Progress in Latin America.*

Organization of American States (OAS), General Secretariat, Washington, D.C. 20006 (202) 458-3533; *Statistical Bulletin of the OAS.*

Statistical Office of the United Nations, Publishing Service, New York, New York 10017 (800) 253-9646; *Statistical Yearbook,* and *Statistical Yearbook for Latin America and the Caribbean.*

Times Books, 201 East 50th Street, New York, New York 10022 (212) 751-2600; *The Economist Book of Vital World Statistics.*

The World Bank, 1818 H Street, NW, Washington, D.C. 20433 (202) 477-1234; *World Tables.*

MEXICO - MARRIAGE RATES

Facts on File, 460 Park Avenue South, New York, New York 10016 (800) 443-8323; *The New Book of World Rankings.*

Statistical Office of the United Nations, Publishing Service, New York, New York 10017 (800) 253-9646; *Demographic Yearbook,* and *Statistical Yearbook.*

MEXICO - MEAT PRODUCTION - See MEXICO - LIVESTOCK AND POULTRY

MEXICO - MEDICAL PERSONNEL

U.C.L.A. Latin American Center Publications, University of California, Los Angeles, California 90024 (310) 825-6634; *Statistical Abstract of Latin America.*

MEXICO - MERCHANT SHIPPING

G.K. Hall and Company, 70 Lincoln Street, Boston, Massachusetts 02111 (617) 423-3990; *The World in Figures.*

Lloyd's Register of Shipping, 17 Battery Place, New York, New York 10004 (212) 425-8050; *Register of Ships.*

Statistical Office of the United Nations, Publishing Service, New York, New York 10017 (800) 253-9646; *Statistical Yearbook.*

Times Books, 201 East 50th Street, New York, New York 10022 (212) 751-2600; *The Economist Book of Vital World Statistics.*

U.S. Department of Transportation, Maritime Administration, 400 Seventh Street, SW, Washington, D.C. 20590; *A Statistical Analysis of the World's Merchant Fleets.*

MEXICO - MERCURY PRODUCTION AND CONSUMPTION - See MEXICO - MINING AND MINERAL PRODUCTS

MEXICO - MILK PRODUCTION - See MEXICO - DAIRY PRODUCTS

MEXICO - MILITARY

The Economist Intelligence Unit, 111 West 57th Street, New York, New York 10019 (800) 938-4685; *The New Latin America Market Atlas.*

G.K. Hall and Company, 70 Lincoln Street, Boston, Massachusetts 02111 (617) 423-3990; *The World in Figures.*

The International Institute for Strategic Studies, 23 Tavistock Street, London WC2E 7NQ, England; *The Military Balance.*

U.C.L.A. Latin American Center Publications, University of California, Los Angeles, California 90024 (310) 825-0034; *Statistical Abstract of Latin America.*

U.S. Arms Control and Disarmament Agency, 320 Twenty-first Street, NW, Washington, D.C. 20451 (202) 647-8677; *World Military Expenditures and Arms Transfers.*

MEXICO - MILK PRODUCTION - See MEXICO - DAIRY PRODUCTS

MEXICO - MINING AND MINERAL PRODUCTS

Commodity Research Bureau, Incorporated, 75 Wall Street, New York, New York 10005 (212) 504-7754; *Commodity Year Book.*

The Economist Intelligence Unit, 111 West 57th Street, New York, New York 10019 (800) 938-4685; *The New Latin America Market Atlas.*

Euromonitor Publications Limited, 87-88 Turnmill Street, London EC1M 5QU, England; *Third World Economic Handbook.*

Facts on File, 460 Park Avenue South, New York, New York 10016 (800) 443-8323; *The New Book of World Rankings.*

G.K. Hall and Company, 70 Lincoln Street, Boston, Massachusetts 02111 (617) 423-3990; *The World in Figures.*

Inter-American Development Bank, 1300 New York Avenue, NW, Washington, D.C. 20577 (202) 872-1445; *Economic and Social Progress in Latin America.*

International Lead and Zinc Study Group, Metro House, 58 St. James's Street, London SW1A 1LD England; *Lead and Zinc Statistics.*

Penn Well Publishing Company, 1421 South Sheridan Road, Post Office Box 1260, Tulsa, Oklahoma 74101 (800) 752-9764; *International Energy Statistics Sourcebook.*

Statistical Office of the United Nations, Publishing Service, New York, New York 10017 (800) 253-9646; *Statistical Yearbook,* and *Statistical Yearbook for Latin America and the Caribbean.*

U.C.L.A. Latin American Center Publications, University of California, Los Angeles, California 90024 (310) 825-6634; *Statistical Abstract of Latin America.*

MEXICO - MOLASSES PRODUCTION - See MEXICO - CROPS

MEXICO - MOLYBDENUM AND MOLYBDENUM ORE PRODUCTION AND CONSUMPTION - See MEXICO - MINING AND MINERAL PRODUCTS

MEXICO - MONEY EXCHANGE RATE

Euromonitor Publications Limited, 87-88 Turnmill Street, London EC1M 5QU, England; *International Marketing Data and Statistics.*

Inter-American Development Bank, 1300 New York Avenue, NW, Washington, D.C. 20577 (202) 872-1445; *Economic and Social Progress in Latin America.*

International Monetary Fund, 700 Nineteenth Street, NW, Washington, D.C. 20431 (202) 623-7000; *International Financial Statistics.*

Statistical Office of the United Nations, Publishing Service, New York, New York 10017 (800) 253-9646; *Statistical Yearbook.*

MEXICO - MONEY RATES MARKET

Inter-American Development Bank, 1300 New York Avenue, NW, Washington, D.C. 20577 (202) 872-1445; *Economic and Social Progress in Latin America.*

MEXICO - MONEY RESERVES

Euromonitor Publications Limited, 87-88 Turnmill Street, London EC1M 5QU, England; *International Marketing Data and Statistics.*

Inter-American Development Bank, 1300 New York Avenue, NW, Washington, D.C. 20577 (202) 872-1445; *Economic and Social Progress in Latin America.*

MEXICO - MONEY SUPPLY

Euromonitor Publications Limited, 87-88 Turnmill Street, London EC1M 5QU, England; *International Marketing Data and Statistics.*

G.K. Hall and Company, 70 Lincoln Street, Boston, Massachusetts 02111 (617) 423-3990; *The World in Figures.*

Inter-American Development Bank, 1300 New York Avenue, NW, Washington, D.C. 20577 (202) 872-1445; *Economic and Social Progress in Latin America.*

International Monetary Fund, 700 Nineteenth Street, NW, Washington, D.C. 20431 (202) 623-7000; *International Financial Statistics.*

Statistical Office of the United Nations, Publishing Service, New York, New York 10017 (800) 253-9646; *Statistical Yearbook.*

U.C.L.A. Latin American Center Publications, University of California, Los Angeles, California 90024 (310) 825-6634; *Statistical Abstract of Latin America.*

The World Bank, 1818 H Street, NW, Washington, D.C. 20433 (202) 477-1234; *World Tables.*

MEXICO - MONUMENTS AND HISTORICAL SITES

United Nations Educational, Scientific and Cultural Organization (UNESCO), 7 Place de Fontenoy, F-75700 Paris, France (Telephone Number in U.S. (212) 963-5981); *Statistical Yearbook.*

MEXICO - MOTION PICTURES

Statistical Office of the United Nations, Publishing Service, New York, New York 10017 (800) 253-9646; *Statistical Yearbook.*

United Nations Educational, Scientific and Cultural Organization (UNESCO), 7 Place de Fontenoy, F-75700 Paris, France (Telephone Number in U.S. (212) 963-5981); *Statistical Yearbook.*

MEXICO - MOTOR VEHICLE PRODUCTION

American Automobile Manufacturers Association, 1401 H Street, NW, Suite 900, Washington, D.C. 20005 (202) 326-5500; *World Motor Vehicle Data.*

MEXICO - MOTOR VEHICLE PRODUCTION AND ASSEMBLY

Statistical Office of the United Nations, Publishing Service, New York, New York 10017 (800) 253-9646; *Statistical Yearbook.*

MEXICO - MOTOR VEHICLE TAXES - See MEXICO - TAXATION

MEXICO - MOTOR VEHICLES

The Economist Intelligence Unit, 111 West 57th Street, New York, New York 10019 (800) 938-4685; *The New Latin America Market Atlas.*

MEXICO - MOTOR VEHICLES IN USE

American Automobile Manufacturers Association, 1401 H Street, NW, Suite 900, Washington, D.C. 20005 (202) 326-5500; *World Motor Vehicle Data.*

G.K. Hall and Company, 70 Lincoln Street, Boston, Massachusetts 02111 (617) 423-3990; *The World in Figures.*

International Road Federation, 525 School Street, SW, Washington, D.C. 20024 (202) 554-2106; *World Road Statistics.*

Statistical Office of the United Nations, Publishing Service, New York, New York 10017 (800) 253-9646; *Statistical Yearbook.*

Times Books, 201 East 50th Street, New York, New York 10022 (212) 751-2600; *The Economist Book of Vital World Statistics.*

MEXICO - MULES - See MEXICO - LIVESTOCK AND POULTRY

MEXICO - MUSEUMS

Facts on File, 460 Park Avenue South, New York, New York 10016 (800) 443-8323; *The New Book of World Rankings.*

United Nations Educational, Scientific and Cultural Organization (UNESCO), 7 Place de Fontenoy, F-75700 Paris, France (Telephone Number in U.S. (212) 963-5981); *Statistical Yearbook.*

MEXICO - NATALITY - See MEXICO - BIRTH RATES

MEXICO - NATIONAL ACCOUNTS

Gale Research Incorporated, 835 Penobscot Building, Detroit, Michigan 48226 (800) 877-4253; *International Historical Statistics The Americas and Australasia.*

Inter-American Development Bank, 1300 New York Avenue, NW, Washington, D.C. 20577 (202) 872-1445; *Economic and Social Progress in Latin America.*

International Monetary Fund, 700 Nineteenth Street, NW, Washington, D.C. 20431 (202) 623-7000; *International Financial Statistics.*

Organization of American States (OAS), General Secretariat, Washington, D.C. 20006 (202) 458-3533; *Statistical Bulletin of the OAS.*

Statistical Office of the United Nations, Publishing Service, New York, New York 10017 (800) 253-9646; *Statistical Yearbook.*

MEXICO - NATIONAL INCOME

Facts on File, 460 Park Avenue South, New York, New York 10016 (800) 443-8323; *The New Book of World Rankings.*

G.K. Hall and Company, 70 Lincoln Street, Boston, Massachusetts 02111 (617) 423-3990; *The World in Figures.*

Inter-American Development Bank, 1300 New York Avenue, NW, Washington, D.C. 20577 (202) 872-1445; *Economic and Social Progress in Latin America.*

Statistical Office of the United Nations, Publishing Service, New York, New York 10017 (800) 253-9646; *National Account Statistics, Statistical Yearbook,* and *Statistical Yearbook for Latin America and the Caribbean.*

U.C.L.A. Latin American Center Publications, University of California, Los Angeles, California 90024 (310) 825-6634; *Statistical Abstract of Latin America.*

MEXICO - NATIONAL PRODUCT

Facts on File, 460 Park Avenue South, New York, New York 10016 (800) 443-8323; *The New Book of World Rankings.*

Statistical Office of the United Nations, Publishing Service, New York, New York 10017 (800) 253-9646; *Statistical Yearbook.*

MEXICO - NATURAL GAS

Commodity Research Bureau, Incorporated, 75 Wall Street, New York, New York 10005 (212) 504-7754; *Commodity Year Book.*

Inter-American Development Bank, 1300 New York Avenue, NW, Washington, D.C. 20577 (202) 872-1445; *Economic and Social Progress in Latin America.*

Statistical Office of the United Nations, Publishing Service, New York, New York 10017 (800) 253-9646; *Statistical Yearbook.*

MEXICO - NATURAL GAS - PRODUCTION - See LUXEMBOURG - MINING AND MINERAL PRODUCTS

MEXICO - NEWSPAPER PRODUCTION - See MEXICO - FORESTRY AND FOREST PRODUCTION

MEXICO - NEWSPRINT - See MEXICO - FORESTRY AND FOREST PRODUCTS

MEXICO - NICKEL AND NICKEL ORE PRODUCTION AND CONSUMPTION - See MEXICO - MINING AND MINERAL PRODUCTS

MEXICO - NITRIC ACID PRODUCTION - See MEXICO - MINING AND MINERAL PRODUCTS

MEXICO - NUTRITION

Statistical Office of the United Nations, Publishing Service, New York, New York 10017 (800) 253-9646; *Statistical Yearbook for Latin America and the Caribbean*.

MEXICO - OATS PRODUCTION - See MEXICO - CROPS

MEXICO - OCCUPATIONS - See MEXICO - LABOR FORCE

MEXICO - ONION PRODUCTION - See MEXICO - CROPS

MEXICO - ORANGE PRODUCTION - See MEXICO - CROPS

MEXICO - PALM KERNELS PRODUCTION - See MEXICO - CROPS

MEXICO - PAPER - See MEXICO - FORESTRY AND FOREST PRODUCTS

MEXICO - PATENTS

Statistical Office of the United Nations, Publishing Service, New York, New York 10017 (800) 253-9646; *Statistical Yearbook*.

World Intellectual Property Organization, 34 Chemin des Colombettes, CH-1211 Geneva 20, Switzerland; *Industrial Property Statistics*.

MEXICO - PEANUT PRODUCTION - See MEXICO - CROPS

MEXICO - PERIODICALS

United Nations Educational, Scientific and Cultural Organization (UNESCO), 7 Place de Fontenoy, F-75700 Paris, France (Telephone Number in U.S. (212) 963-5981); *Statistical Yearbook*.

MEXICO - PESTICIDE USE

Food and Agricultural Organization of the United Nations (FAO), Via delle Terme di Caracalla, 00100 Rome, Italy (Telephone Number in U.S. (202) 653-2400); *The State of Food and Agriculture*.

MEXICO - PETROLEUM INDUSTRY

Commodity Research Bureau, 75 Wall Street, New York, New York 10005 (212) 504-7754; *Commodity Year Book*.

The Economist Intelligence Unit, 111 West 57th Street, New York, New York 10019 (800) 938-4685; *The New Latin America Market Atlas*.

Facts on File, 460 Park Avenue South, New York, New York 10016 (800) 443-8323; *The New Book of World Rankings*.

Food and Agricultural Organization of the United Nations (FAO), Via delle Terme di Caracalla, 00100 Rome, Italy (Telephone Number in U.S. (202) 653-2400); *The State of Food and Agriculture*.

G.K. Hall and Company, 70 Lincoln Street, Boston, Massachusetts 02111 (617) 423-3990; *The World in Figures*.

Inter-American Development Bank, 1300 New York Avenue, NW, Washington, D.C. 20577 (202) 872-1445; *Economic and Social Progress in Latin America*.

International Monetary Fund, 700 Nineteenth Street, NW, Washington, D.C. 20431 (202) 623-7000; *International Financial Statistics*.

Penn Well Publishing Company, 1421 South Sheridan Road, Post Office Box 1260, Tulsa, Oklahoma 74101 (800) 752-9764; *International Energy Statistics Sourcebook*.

Organization of American States (OAS), General Secretariat, Washington, D.C. 20006 (202) 458-3533; *Statistical Bulletin of the OAS*.

Statistical Office of the United Nations, Publishing Service, New York, New York 10017 (800) 253-9646; *Statistical Yearbook*.

MEXICO - PHOSPHATE ROCK PRODUCTION - See MEXICO - MINING AND MINERAL PRODUCTS

MEXICO - PIG-IRON AND FERRO-ALLOY PRODUCTION - See MEXICO - MINING AND MINERAL PRODUCTS

MEXICO - PIGS - See MEXICO - LIVESTOCK AND POULTRY

MEXICO - PLASTICS AND RESINS PRODUCTION

Euromonitor Publications Limited, 87-88 Turnmill Street, London EC1M 5QU, England; *Third World Economic Handbook*.

Statistical Office of the United Nations, Publishing Service, New York, New York 10017 (800) 253-9646; *Statistical Yearbook*.

MEXICO - PLATINUM PRODUCTION - See MEXICO - MINING AND MINERAL PRODUCTS

MEXICO - POLITICAL DATA

U.C.L.A. Latin American Center Publications, University of California, Los Angeles, California 90024 (310) 825-6634; *Statistical Abstract of Latin America*.

MEXICO - POPULATION

The Economist Intelligence Unit, 111 West 57th Street, New York, New York 10019 (800) 938-4685; *The New Latin America Market Atlas*, and *The World Market Atlas*.

Euromonitor Publications Limited, 87-88 Turnmill Street, London EC1M 5QU, England; *International Marketing Data and Statistics*, and *Third World Economic Handbook*.

Facts on File, 460 Park Avenue South, New York, New York 10016 (800) 443-8323; *The New Book of World Rankings*.

Food and Agricultural Organization of the United Nations (FAO), Via delle Terme di Caracalla, 00100 Rome, Italy (Telephone Number in U.S. (202) 653-2400); *Production Yearbook*.

Gale Research Incorporated, 835 Penobscot Building, Detroit, Michigan 48226 (800) 877-4253; *International Historical Statistics The Americas and Australasia*.

G.K. Hall and Company, 70 Lincoln Street, Boston, Massachusetts 02111 (617) 423-3990; *The World in Figures*.

Inter-American Development Bank, 1300 New York Avenue, NW, Washington, D.C. 20577 (202) 872-1445; *Economic and Social Progress in Latin America.*

International Labour Office, I.L.O. Publications, CH-1211, Geneva 22, Switzerland; *Yearbook of Labour Statistics.*

Organization of American States, (OAS), General Secretariat, Washington, D.C. 20006 (202) 458-3533; *Statistical Bulletin of the OAS.*

Statistical Office of the United Nations, Publishing Service, New York, New York 10017 (800) 253-9646; *Demographic Yearbook, Statistical Yearbook,* and *Statistical Yearbook for Latin America and the Caribbean.*

Times Books, 201 East 50th Street, New York, New York 10022 (212) 751-2600; *The Economist Book of Vital World Statistics.*

U.C.L.A. Latin American Center Publications, University of California, Los Angeles, California 90024 (310) 825-6634; *Statistical Abstract of Latin America.*

U.S. Arms Control and Disarmament Agency, 320 Twenty-first Street, NW, Washington, D.C. 20451 (202) 647-8677; *World Military Expenditures and Arms Transfers.*

World Health Organization, Office of Publications, Avenue Appia, CH-1211 Geneva 27, Switzerland (Telephone in U.S. (518) 436-9686); *World Health Statistics Annual.*

MEXICO - POST OFFICES

Facts on File, 460 Park Avenue South, New York, New York 10016 (800) 443-8323; *The New Book of World Rankings.*

MEXICO - POTATO PRODUCTION - See MEXICO - CROPS

MEXICO - PRICES

Facts on File, 460 Park Avenue South, New York, New York 10016 (800) 443-8323; *The New Book of World Rankings.*

Food and Agricultural Organization of the United Nations (FAO), Via delle Terme di Caracalla, 00100 Rome, Italy (Telephone Number in U.S. (202) 653-2400); *Production Yearbook,* and *The State of Food and Agriculture.*

Gale Research Incorporated, 835 Penobscot Building, Detroit, Michigan 48226 (800) 877-4253; *International Historical Statistics The Americas and Australasia.*

G.K. Hall and Company, 70 Lincoln Street, Boston, Massachusetts 02111 (617) 423-3990; *The World in Figures.*

International Labour Office, I.L.O. Publications, CH-1211, Geneva 22, Switzerland; *Yearbook of Labour Statistics.*

International Lead and Zinc Study Group, Metro House, 58 St. James's Street, London SW1A 1LD England; *Lead and Zinc Statistics.*

International Monetary Fund, 700 Nineteenth Street, NW, Washington, D.C. 20431 (202) 623-7000; *International Financial Statistics.*

Statistical Office of the United Nations, Publishing Service, New York, New York 10017 (800) 253-9646; *Economic Survey of Latin America and the Caribbean,* and *Statistical Yearbook for Latin America and the Caribbean.*

MEXICO - PRINTING AND WRITING PAPER - See MEXICO - FORESTRY AND FOREST PRODUCTS

MEXICO - PRODUCTION

American Automobile Manufacturers Association, 1401 H Street, NW, Suite 900, Washington, D.C. 20005 (202) 326-5500; *World Motor Vehicle Data.*

Euromonitor Publications Limited, 87-88 Turnmill Street, London EC1M 5QU, England; *Third World Economic Handbook.*

Facts on File, 460 Park Avenue South, New York, New York 10016 (800) 443-8323; *The New Book of World Rankings.*

G.K. Hall and Company, 70 Lincoln Street, Boston, Massachusetts 02111 (617) 423-3990; *The World in Figures.*

International Lead and Zinc Study Group, Metro House, 58 St. James's Street, London SW1A 1LD England; *Lead and Zinc Statistics.*

MEXICO - PRODUCTIVITY

Euromonitor Publications Limited, 87-88 Turnmill Street, London EC1M 5QU, England; *International Marketing Data and Statistics.*

MEXICO - PROPERTY TAXES

Inter-American Development Bank, 1300 New York Avenue, NW, Washington, D.C. 20577 (202) 872-1445; *Economic and Social Progress in Latin America.*

International Monetary Fund, 700 Nineteenth Street, NW, Washington, D.C. 20431 (202) 623-7000; *Government Finance Statistics Yearbook.*

MEXICO - PUBLIC CONSUMPTION FUND

Inter-American Development Bank, 1300 New York Avenue, NW, Washington, D.C. 20577 (202) 872-1445; *Economic and Social Progress in Latin America.*

MEXICO - PUBLIC EXPENDITURE

Inter-American Development Bank, 1300 New York Avenue, NW, Washington, D.C. 20577 (202) 872-1445; *Economic and Social Progress in Latin America.*

Organization of American States (OAS), General Secretariat, Washington, D.C. 20006 (202) 458-3533; *Statistical Bulletin of the OAS.*

Statistical Office of the United Nations, Publishing Service, New York, New York 10017 (800) 253-9646; *Statistical Yearbook for Latin America and the Caribbean.*

MEXICO - PUBLIC FINANCE

Facts on File, 460 Park Avenue South, New York, New York 10016 (800) 443-8323; *The New Book of World Rankings.*

Inter-American Development Bank, 1300 New York Avenue, NW, Washington, D.C. 20577 (202) 872-1445; *Economic and Social Progress in Latin America.*

Organization of American States (OAS), General Secretariat, Washington, D.C. 20006 (202) 458-3533; *Statistical Bulletin of the OAS.*

MEXICO - PUBLIC REVENUE

Inter-American Development Bank, 1300 New York Avenue, NW, Washington, D.C. 20577 (202) 872-1445; *Economic and Social Progress in Latin America.*

Organization of American States (OAS), General Secretariat, Washington, D.C. 20006 (202) 458-3533; *Statistical Bulletin of the OAS.*

MEXICO - RADIO BROADCASTING - See MEXICO - BROADCASTING

MEXICO - RADIO RECEIVER PRODUCTION

Statistical Office of the United Nations, Publishing Service, New York, New York 10017 (800) 253-9646; *Statistical Yearbook.*

MEXICO - RAILWAY USE

G.K. Hall and Company, 70 Lincoln Street, Boston, Massachusetts 02111 (617) 423-3990; *The World in Figures.*

Statistical Office of the United Nations, Publishing Service, New York, New York 10017 (800) 253-9646; *Statistical Yearbook.*

MEXICO - RAILWAYS

The Economist Intelligence Unit, 111 West 57th Street, New York, New York 10019 (800) 938-4685; *The New Latin America Market Atlas.*

Jane's Information Group, Sentinel House, 163 Brighton Road, Coulsdon, Surrey CR5 2NH, England (Telephone Number in U.S. (703) 683-3700); *Jane's World Railways.*

MEXICO - RANCHING

U.C.L.A. Latin American Center Publications, University of California, Los Angeles, California 90024 (310) 825-6634; *Statistical Abstract of Latin America.*

MEXICO - RAPESEED PRODUCTION - See MEXICO - CROPS

MEXICO - RELIGION

Facts on File, 460 Park Avenue South, New York, New York 10016 (800) 443-8323; *The New Book of World Rankings.*

U.C.L.A. Latin American Center Publications, University of California, Los Angeles, California 90024 (310) 825-6634; *Statistical Abstract of Latin America.*

MEXICO - RENT PRICES

International Labour Office, I.L.O. Publications, CH-1211, Geneva 22, Switzerland; *Yearbook of Labour Statistics.*

MEXICO - RESERVES EXCLUDING GOLD

The Economist Intelligence Unit, 111 West 57th Street, New York, New York 10019 (800) 938-4685; *The New Latin America Market Atlas.*

MEXICO - RETAIL TRADE

Euromonitor Publications Limited, 87-88 Turnmill Street, London EC1M 5QU, England; *Third World Economic Handbook.*

G.K. Hall and Company, 70 Lincoln Street, Boston, Massachusetts 02111 (617) 423-3990; *The World in Figures.*

Inter-American Development Bank, 1300 New York Avenue, NW, Washington, D.C. 20577 (202) 872-1445; *Economic and Social Progress in Latin America.*

Statistical Office of the United Nations, Publishing Service, New York, New York 10017 (800) 253-9646; *Statistical Yearbook.*

MEXICO - RICE PRODUCTION - See MEXICO - CROPS

MEXICO - ROOT AND TUBER PRODUCTION - See MEXICO - CROPS

MEXICO - ROUNDWOOD PRODUCTION - See MEXICO - FORESTRY AND FOREST PRODUCTS

MEXICO - RUBBER PRODUCTION AND CONSUMPTION

Euromonitor Publications Limited, 87-88 Turnmill Street, London EC1M 5QU, England; *Third World Economic Handbook.*

Facts on File, 460 Park Avenue South, New York, New York 10016 (800) 443-8323; *The New Book of World Rankings.*

Statistical Office of the United Nations, Publishing Service, New York, New York 10017 (800) 253-9646; *Statistical Yearbook.*

MEXICO - SAFFLOWER SEED PRODUCTION - See MEXICO - CROPS

MEXICO - SALT PRODUCTION - See MEXICO - MINING AND MINERAL PRODUCTS

MEXICO - SAWNWOOD PRODUCTION - See MEXICO - FORESTRY AND FOREST PRODUCTS

MEXICO - SCIENCE AND TECHNOLOGY

U.C.L.A. Latin American Center Publications, University of California, Los Angeles, California 90024 (310) 825-6634; *Statistical Abstract of Latin America.*

MEXICO - SCIENCE AND TECHNOLOGY - EXPENDITURE FOR RESEARCH

Statistical Office of the United Nations, Publishing Service, New York, New York 10017 (800) 253-9646; *Statistical Yearbook.*

MEXICO - SCIENTISTS AND TECHNICIANS

Statistical Office of the United Nations, Publishing Service, New York, New York 10017 (800) 253-9646; *Statistical Yearbook.*

MEXICO - SENIOR CITIZENS

Facts on File, 460 Park Avenue South, New York, New York 10016 (800) 443-8323; *The New Book of World Rankings.*

MEXICO - SESAME SEED PRODUCTION - See MEXICO - CROPS

MEXICO - SHEEP - See MEXICO - LIVESTOCK AND POULTRY

MEXICO - SHRIMP EXPORTS

International Monetary Fund, 700 Nineteenth Street, NW, Washington, D.C. 20431 (202) 623-7000; *International Financial Statistics.*

MEXICO - SILVER PRODUCTION AND CONSUMPTION - See MEXICO - MINING AND MINERAL PRODUCTS

MEXICO - SOCIAL DATA

Facts on File, 460 Park Avenue South, New York, New York 10016 (800) 443-8323; *The New Book of World Rankings.*

G.K. Hall and Company, 70 Lincoln Street, Boston, Massachusetts 02111 (617) 423-3990; *The World in Figures.*

U.C.L.A. Latin American Center Publications, University of California, Los Angeles, California 90024 (310) 825-6634; *Statistical Abstract of Latin America.*

MEXICO - SOCIAL SECURITY EXPENDITURES

Inter-American Development Bank, 1300 New York Avenue, NW, Washington, D.C. 20577 (202) 872-1445; *Economic and Social Progress in Latin America.*

International Monetary Fund, 700 Nineteenth Street, NW, Washington, D.C. 20431 (202) 623-7000; *Government Finance Statistics Yearbook.*

MEXICO - SOCIOECONOMIC DATA

Inter-American Development Bank, 1300 New York Avenue, NW, Washington, D.C. 20577 (202) 872-1445; *Economic and Social Progress in Latin America.*

U.C.L.A. Latin American Center Publications, University of California, Los Angeles, California 90024 (310) 825-6634; *Statistical Abstract of Latin America.*

MEXICO - SOYBEAN PRODUCTION - See MEXICO - CROPS

MEXICO - STAMP TAXES AND DUTIES - See MEXICO - TAXATION

MEXICO - STATE BUDGET REVENUE AND EXPENDITURES

Euromonitor Publications Limited, 87-88 Turnmill Street, London EC1M 5QU, England; *International Marketing Data and Statistics.*

Inter-American Development Bank, 1300 New York Avenue, NW, Washington, D.C. 20577 (202) 872-1445; *Economic and Social Progress in Latin America.*

MEXICO - STEEL - See MEXICO - MINING AND MINERAL PRODUCTS

MEXICO - STOCKS - COMMODITY - MARKET PRICE - INDEX

Food and Agricultural Organization of the United Nations (FAO), Via delle Terme di Caracalla, 00100 Rome, Italy (Telephone Number in U.S. (202) 653-2400); *The State of Food and Agriculture.*

International Lead and Zinc Study Group, Metro House, 58 St. James's Street, London SW1A 1LD England; *Lead and Zinc Statistics.*

MEXICO - SUGAR - See MEXICO - CROPS

MEXICO - SULPHUR AND SULPHURIC ACID PRODUCTION - See MEXICO - MINING AND MINERAL PRODUCTS

MEXICO - TAXATION

G.K. Hall and Company, 70 Lincoln Street, Boston, Massachusetts 02111 (617) 423-3990; *The World in Figures.*

Inter-American Development Bank, 1300 New York Avenue, NW, Washington, D.C. 20577 (202) 872-1445; *Economic and Social Progress in Latin America.*

International Monetary Fund, 700 Nineteenth Street, NW, Washington, D.C. 20431 (202) 623-7000; *Government Finance Statistics Yearbook.*

International Road Federation, 525 School Street, SW, Washington, D.C. 20024 (202) 554-2106; *World Road Statistics.*

Statistical Office of the United Nations, Publishing Service, New York, New York 10017 (800) 253-9646; *Statistical Yearbook for Latin America and the Caribbean.*

The World Bank, 1818 H Street, NW, Washington, D.C. 20433 (202) 477-1234; *World Tables.*

MEXICO - TAX REVENUE - See MEXICO - TAXATION

MEXICO - TELEGRAPH SERVICE

Statistical Office of the United Nations, Publishing Service, New York, New York 10017 (800) 253-9646; *Statistical Yearbook.*

MEXICO - TELEPHONES IN USE

American Telephone and Telegraph Company, 26 Parsippany Road, Whippany, New Jersey 07981 (800) 338-4038; *The World's Telephones.*

The Economist Intelligence Unit, 111 West 57th Street, New York, New York 10019 (800) 938-4685; *The New Latin America Market Atlas.*

Euromonitor Publications Limited, 87-88 Turnmill Street, London EC1M 5QU, England; *Third World Economic Handbook.*

G.K. Hall and Company, 70 Lincoln Street, Boston, Massachusetts 02111 (617) 423-3990; *The World in Figures.*

Statistical Office of the United Nations, Publishing Service, New York, New York 10017 (800) 253-9646; *Statistical Yearbook.*

MEXICO - TELEVISION BROADCASTING - See MEXICO - BROADCASTING

MEXICO - TELEVISION RECEIVER PRODUCTION

Statistical Office of the United Nations, Publishing Service, New York, New York 10017 (800) 253-9646; *Statistical Yearbook.*

MEXICO - TEXTILE INDUSTRY

American Forest and Paper Association, 1250 Connecticut Avenue, NW, Washington, D.C. 20036 (202) 463-2455; *Wood Pulp and Fiber Statistics.*

Euromonitor Publications Limited, 87-88 Turnmill Street, London EC1M 5QU, England; *Third World Economic Handbook.*

G.K. Hall and Company, 70 Lincoln Street, Boston, Massachusetts 02111 (617) 423-3990; *The World in Figures.*

Statistical Office of the United Nations, Publishing Service, New York, New York 10017 (800) 253-9646; *Trade in Manufactures of Developing Countries,* and *Statistical Yearbook.*

MEXICO - THEATRE

United Nations Educational, Scientific and Cultural Organization (UNESCO), 7 Place de Fontenoy, F-75700 Paris, France (Telephone Number in U.S. (212) 963-5981); *Statistical Yearbook.*

MEXICO - TIN - See MEXICO - MINING AND MINERAL PRODUCTS

MEXICO - TIRE (MOTOR VEHICLE) PRODUCTION

Statistical Office of the United Nations, Publishing Service, New York, New York 10017 (800) 253-9646; *Statistical Yearbook.*

MEXICO - TOBACCO PRODUCTION

Euromonitor Publications Limited, 87-88 Turnmill Street, London EC1M 5QU, England; *Third World Economic Handbook.*

Facts on File, 460 Park Avenue South, New York, New York 10016 (800) 443-8323; *The New Book of World Rankings.*

Statistical Office of the United Nations, Publishing Service, New York, New York 10017 (800) 253-9646; *Statistical Yearbook.*

U.C.L.A. Latin American Center Publications, University of California, Los Angeles, California 90024 (310) 825-6634; *Statistical Abstract of Latin America.*

MEXICO - TOURISM

The Economist Intelligence Unit, 111 West 57th Street, New York, New York 10019 (800) 938-4685; *The New Latin America Market Atlas.*

Euromonitor Publications Limited, 87-88 Turnmill Street, London EC1M 5QU, England; *Third World Economic Handbook.*

Facts on File, 460 Park Avenue South, New York, New York 10016 (800) 443-8323; *The New Book of World Rankings.*

G.K. Hall and Company, 70 Lincoln Street, Boston, Massachusetts 02111 (617) 423-3990; *The World in Figures.*

Organization of American States (OAS), General Secretariat, Washington, D.C. 20006 (202) 458-3533; *Statistical Bulletin of the OAS.*

Statistical Office of the United Nations, Publishing Service, New York, New York 10017 (800) 253-9646; *Statistical Yearbook.*

Times Books, 201 East 50th Street, New York, New York 10022 (212) 751-2600; *The Economist Book of Vital World Statistics.*

U.C.L.A. Latin American Center Publications, University of California, Los Angeles, California 90024 (310) 825-6634; *Statistical Abstract of Latin America.*

World Tourism Organization, Calle Capitan Haya 42, E-28020 Madrid, Spain; *Yearbook of Tourism Statistics.*

MEXICO - TRACTORS IN USE

The Economist Intelligence Unit, 111 West 57th Street, New York, New York 10019 (800) 938-4685; *The New Latin America Market Atlas.*

Statistical Office of the United Nations, Publishing Service, New York, New York 10017 (800) 253-9646; *Statistical Yearbook.*

MEXICO - TRADE - See MEXICO - FOREIGN TRADE

MEXICO - TRADEMARKS AND SERVICE MARKS

Statistical Office of the United Nations, Publishing Service, New York, New York 10017 (800) 253-9646; *Statistical Yearbook.*

World Intellectual Property Organization, 34 Chemin des Colombettes, CH-1211 Geneva 20, Switzerland; *Industrial Property Statistics.*

MEXICO - TRANSPORTATION AND COMMUNICATIONS

The Economist Intelligence Unit, 111 West 57th Street, New York, New York 10019 (800) 938-4685; *The New Latin America Market Atlas.*

Euromonitor Publications Limited, 87-88 Turnmill Street, London EC1M 5QU, England; *Third World Economic Handbook.*

Facts on File, 460 Park Avenue South, New York, New York 10016 (800) 443-8323; *The New Book of World Rankings.*

Gale Research Incorporated, 835 Penobscot Building, Detroit, Michigan 48226 (800) 877-4253; *International Historical Statistics The Americas and Australasia.*

G.K. Hall and Company, 70 Lincoln Street, Boston, Massachusetts 02111 (617) 423-3990; *The World in Figures.*

Inter-American Development Bank, 1300 New York Avenue, NW, Washington, D.C. 20577 (202) 872-1445; *Economic and Social Progress in Latin America.*

U.C.L.A. Latin American Center Publications, University of California, Los Angeles, California 90024 (310) 825-6634; *Statistical Abstract of Latin America.*

MEXICO - TUNGSTEN PRODUCTION AND CONSUMPTION - See MEXICO - MINING AND MINERAL PRODUCTS

MEXICO - TURKEYS - See MEXICO - LIVESTOCK AND POULTRY

MEXICO - UNEMPLOYMENT

The Economist Intelligence Unit, 111 West 57th Street, New York, New York 10019 (800) 938-4685; *The New Latin America Market Atlas.*

Euromonitor Publications Limited, 87-88 Turnmill Street, London EC1M 5QU, England; *International Marketing Data and Statistics.*

International Labour Office, I.L.O. Publications, CH-1211, Geneva 22, Switzerland; *Yearbook of Labour Statistics.*

Organization of American States (OAS), General Secretariat, Washington, D.C. 20006 (202) 458-3533; *Statistical Bulletin of the OAS.*

U.C.L.A. Latin American Center Publications, University of California, Los Angeles, California 90024 (310) 825-6634; *Statistical Abstract of Latin America*.

MEXICO - URANIUM PRODUCTION AND CONSUMPTION - See MEXICO - MINING AND MINERAL PRODUCTS

MEXICO - UTILITIES

U.C.L.A. Latin American Center Publications, University of California, Los Angeles, California 90024 (310) 825-6634; *Statistical Abstract of Latin America*.

MEXICO - VANADIUM AND VANADIUM ORE PRODUCTION AND CONSUMPTION - See MEXICO - MINING AND MINERAL PRODUCTS

MEXICO - VITAL STATISTICS

Euromonitor Publications Limited, 87-88 Turnmill Street, London EC1M 5QU, England; *International Marketing Data and Statistics*, and *Third World Economic Handbook*.

Gale Research Incorporated, 835 Penobscot Building, Detroit, Michigan 48226 (800) 877-4253; *International Historical Statistics The Americas and Australasia*.

G.K. Hall and Company, 70 Lincoln Street, Boston, Massachusetts 02111 (617) 423-3990; *The World in Figures*.

Statistical Office of the United Nations, Publishing Service, New York, New York 10017 (800) 253-9646; *Statistical Yearbook*.

World Health Organization, Office of Publications, Avenue Appia, CH-1211 Geneva 27, Switzerland (Telephone in U.S. (518) 436-9686); *World Health Statistics Annual*.

MEXICO - WAGES

G.K. Hall and Company, 70 Lincoln Street, Boston, Massachusetts 02111 (617) 423-3990; *The World in Figures*.

International Labour Office, I.L.O. Publications, CH-1211, Geneva 22, Switzerland; *Yearbook of Labour Statistics*.

Organization of American States (OAS), General Secretariat, Washington, D.C. 20006 (202) 458-3533; *Statistical Bulletin of the OAS*.

Statistical Office of the United Nations, Publishing Service, New York, New York 10017 (800) 253-9646; *Statistical Yearbook*.

U.C.L.A. Latin American Center Publications, University of California, Los Angeles, California 90024 (310) 825-6634; *Statistical Abstract of Latin America*.

MEXICO - WALNUT PRODUCTION - See MEXICO - CROPS

MEXICO - WATERMELON PRODUCTION - See MEXICO - CROPS

MEXICO - WEATHER

Facts on File, 460 Park Avenue South, New York, New York 10016 (800) 443-8323; *The New Book of World Rankings*.

G.K. Hall and Company, 70 Lincoln Street, Boston, Massachusetts 02111 (617) 423-3990; *The World in Figures*.

MEXICO - WELFARE

Inter-American Development Bank, 1300 New York Avenue, NW, Washington, D.C. 20577 (202) 872-1445; *Economic and Social Progress in Latin America*.

International Monetary Fund, 700 Nineteenth Street, NW, Washington, D.C. 20431 (202) 623-7000; *Government Finance Statistics Yearbook*.

MEXICO - WHEAT PRODUCTION - See MEXICO - CROPS

MEXICO - WHOLESALE PRICES

Inter-American Development Bank, 1300 New York Avenue, NW, Washington, D.C. 20577 (202) 872-1445; *Economic and Social Progress in Latin America*.

International Monetary Fund, 700 Nineteenth Street, NW, Washington, D.C. 20431 (202) 623-7000; *International Financial Statistics*.

Organization of American States (OAS), General Secretariat, Washington, D.C. 20006 (202) 458-3533; *Statistical Bulletin of the OAS*.

Statistical Office of the United Nations, Publishing Service, New York, New York 10017 (800) 253-9646; *Statistical Yearbook*.

MEXICO - WHOLESALE TRADE

Euromonitor Publications Limited, 87-88 Turnmill Street, London EC1M 5QU, England; *Third World Economic Handbook*.

Inter-American Development Bank, 1300 New York Avenue, NW, Washington, D.C. 20577 (202) 872-1445; *Economic and Social Progress in Latin America*.

Statistical Office of the United Nations, Publishing Service, New York, New York 10017 (800) 253-9646; *Statistical Yearbook*.

MEXICO - WINE PRODUCTION

Facts on File, 460 Park Avenue South, New York, New York 10016 (800) 443-8323; *The New Book of World Rankings*.

Statistical Office of the United Nations, Publishing Service, New York, New York 10017 (800) 253-9646; *Statistical Yearbook*.

MEXICO - WOOD AND WOOD PULP - See MEXICO - FORESTRY AND FOREST PRODUCTS

MEXICO - WOOL CONSUMPTION

Statistical Office of the United Nations, Publishing Service, New York, New York 10017 (800) 253-9646; *Statistical Yearbook*.

MEXICO - WOOL PRODUCTION

Facts on File, 460 Park Avenue South, New York, New York 10016 (800) 443-8323; *The New Book of World Rankings*.

MEXICO - YARN PRODUCTION

Statistical Office of the United Nations, Publishing Service, New York, New York 10017 (800) 253-9646; *Statistical Yearbook*.

MEXICO - ZINC AND ZINC ORE PRODUCTION AND CONSUMPTION - See MEXICO - MINING AND MINERAL PRODUCTS

MICA

U.S. Department of the Interior, Bureau of Mines, 810 Seventh Street, NW, Washington, D.C. 20241 (202) 501-9649; *Annual Reports*, and *Mineral Commodity Summaries*.

MICHIGAN - See also STATE DATA (FOR INDIVIDUAL STATES)

Michigan - Primary Statistics Source

School of Business Administration, Bureau of Business Research, Wayne State University, Detroit, Michigan 48202 (313) 872-4311; *Michigan Statistical Abstract*.

Michigan - State Data Centers

Michigan Information Center, Department of Management and Budget, Office of Revenue and Tax Analysis, Post Office Box 30026, Lansing, Michigan 48909, Mr. Eric Swanson (517) 373-7910.

MIMIC/Center for Urban Studies, Wayne State University, Faculty/Administration Building, 656 West Kirby, Detroit, Michigan 40802, Kurt Metzger (313) 577-8996.

The Library of Michigan, Government Documents Service, Post Office Box 30007, 717 West Allegan Street, Lansing, Michigan 48909, Ms. F. Anne Diamond (517) 373-0640.

MICROCOMPUTERS - See also: COMPUTERS

MICROCOMPUTERS - USE BY STUDENTS

Market Data Retrieval, 16 Progress Drive, Shelton, Connecticut 06484 (203) 926-4800; unpublished data.

U.S. Department of Education, 400 Maryland Avenue, SW, Washington, D.C. 20202 (202) 708-5366; *Digest of Education Statistics*.

University of Minnesota, Department of Sociology, Minneapolis, Minnesota 55455 (612) 625-5000; *IEA Computers in Education Study*.

MICROCONTROLLERS AND CHIPS

Dataquest, Incorporated, 1290 Ridder Park Drive, San Jose, California 95131 (408) 437-8000; unpublished data.

Micronesia (Federated States of) - National Statistical Office

Office of Planning and Statistics, Post Office Box PS4, National Government Federated States of Micronesia, Palikir, Pohnpei FM 96941.

MICRONESIA (FEDERATED STATES OF) - AGRICULTURE

Encyclopedia Britannica, Incorporated, 310 South Michigan Avenue, Chicago, Illinois 60604 (312) 347-7000; *"Britannica World Data."*

MICRONESIA (FEDERATED STATES OF) - AIRLINE SERVICE

Encyclopedia Britannica, Incorporated, 310 South Michigan Avenue, Chicago, Illinois 60604 (312) 347-7000; *"Britannica World Data."*

MICRONESIA (FEDERATED STATES OF) - BIRTH RATES

Encyclopedia Britannica, Incorporated, 310 South Michigan Avenue, Chicago, Illinois 60604 (312) 347-7000; *"Britannica World Data."*

MICRONESIA (FEDERATED STATES OF) - BROADCASTING

Billboard Limited, Post Office Box 9027, 1006 AA Amsterdam, The Netherlands (Telephone Number in U.S. (212) 764-7300); *World Radio TV Handbook*.

MICRONESIA (FEDERATED STATES OF) - CONSTRUCTION

Encyclopedia Britannica, Incorporated, 310 South Michigan Avenue, Chicago, Illinois 60604 (312) 347-7000; *"Britannica World Data."*

MICRONESIA (FEDERATED STATES OF) - DEMOGRAPHY

Encyclopedia Britannica, Incorporated, 310 South Michigan Avenue, Chicago, Illinois 60604 (312) 347-7000; *"Britannica World Data."*

MICRONESIA (FEDERATED STATES OF) - DIVORCE RATES

Encyclopedia Britannica, Incorporated, 310 South Michigan Avenue, Chicago, Illinois 60604 (312) 347-7000; *"Britannica World Data."*

MICRONESIA (FEDERATED STATES OF) - ECONOMY

Encyclopedia Britannica, Incorporated, 310 South Michigan Avenue, Chicago, Illinois 60604 (312) 347-7000; *"Britannica World Data."*

MICRONESIA (FEDERATED STATES OF) - EDUCATION

Encyclopedia Britannica, Incorporated, 310 South Michigan Avenue, Chicago, Illinois 60604 (312) 347-7000; *"Britannica World Data."*

MICRONESIA (FEDERATED STATES OF) - ENERGY

Encyclopedia Britannica, Incorporated, 310 South Michigan Avenue, Chicago, Illinois 60604 (312) 347-7000; *"Britannica World Data."*

MICRONESIA (FEDERATED STATES OF) - EXPORTS

Encyclopedia Britannica, Incorporated, 310 South Michigan Avenue, Chicago, Illinois 60604 (312) 347-7000; *"Britannica World Data."*

MICRONESIA (FEDERATED STATES OF) - FERTILITY RATES

Encyclopedia Britannica, Incorporated, 310 South Michigan Avenue, Chicago, Illinois 60604 (312) 347-7000; *"Britannica World Data."*

MICRONESIA (FEDERATED STATES OF) - FISHERIES

Encyclopedia Britannica, Incorporated, 310 South Michigan Avenue, Chicago, Illinois 60604 (312) 347-7000; *"Britannica World Data."*

MICRONESIA (FEDERATED STATES OF) - FOREIGN TRADE

Encyclopedia Britannica, Incorporated, 310 South Michigan Avenue, Chicago, Illinois 60604 (312) 347-7000; *"Britannica World Data."*

MICRONESIA (FEDERATED STATES OF) - FORESTRY AND FOREST PRODUCTS

Encyclopedia Britannica, Incorporated, 310 South Michigan Avenue, Chicago, Illinois 60604 (312) 347-7000; *"Britannica World Data."*

MICRONESIA (FEDERATED STATES OF) - HEALTH

Encyclopedia Britannica, Incorporated, 310 South Michigan Avenue, Chicago, Illinois 60604 (312) 347-7000; "*Britannica World Data.*"

MICRONESIA (FEDERATED STATES OF) - IMPORTS

Encyclopedia Britannica, Incorporated, 310 South Michigan Avenue, Chicago, Illinois 60604 (312) 347-7000; "*Britannica World Data.*"

MICRONESIA (FEDERATED STATES OF) - LAND USE

Encyclopedia Britannica, Incorporated, 310 South Michigan Avenue, Chicago, Illinois 60604 (312) 347-7000; "*Britannica World Data.*"

MICRONESIA (FEDERATED STATES OF) - LIVESTOCK AND POULTRY

Encyclopedia Britannica, Incorporated, 310 South Michigan Avenue, Chicago, Illinois 60604 (312) 347-7000; "*Britannica World Data.*"

MICRONESIA (FEDERATED STATES OF) - MANUFACTURING

Encyclopedia Britannica, Incorporated, 310 South Michigan Avenue, Chicago, Illinois 60604 (312) 347-7000; "*Britannica World Data.*"

MICRONESIA (FEDERATED STATES OF) - MARRIAGE RATES

Encyclopedia Britannica, Incorporated, 310 South Michigan Avenue, Chicago, Illinois 60604 (312) 347-7000; "*Britannica World Data.*"

MICRONESIA (FEDERATED STATES OF) - MILITARY

Encyclopedia Britannica, Incorporated, 310 South Michigan Avenue, Chicago, Illinois 60604 (312) 347-7000; "*Britannica World Data.*"

MICRONESIA (FEDERATED STATES OF) - MINING AND MINERAL PRODUCTS

Encyclopedia Britannica, Incorporated, 310 South Michigan Avenue, Chicago, Illinois 60604 (312) 347-7000; "*Britannica World Data.*"

MICRONESIA (FEDERATED STATES OF) - POPULATION

Encyclopedia Britannica, Incorporated, 310 South Michigan Avenue, Chicago, Illinois 60604 (312) 347-7000; "*Britannica World Data.*"

MICRONESIA (FEDERATED STATES OF) - RADIO RECEIVERS

Encyclopedia Britannica, Incorporated, 310 South Michigan Avenue, Chicago, Illinois 60604 (312) 347-7000; "*Britannica World Data.*"

MICRONESIA (FEDERATED STATES OF) - RAILWAYS

Encyclopedia Britannica, Incorporated, 310 South Michigan Avenue, Chicago, Illinois 60604 (312) 347-7000; "*Britannica World Data.*"

MICRONESIA (FEDERATED STATES OF) - ROADS

Encyclopedia Britannica, Incorporated, 310 South Michigan Avenue, Chicago, Illinois 60604 (312) 347-7000; "*Britannica World Data.*"

MICRONESIA (FEDERATED STATES OF) - TELEPHONES IN USE

Encyclopedia Britannica, Incorporated, 310 South Michigan Avenue, Chicago, Illinois 60604 (312) 347-7000; "*Britannica World Data.*"

MICRONESIA (FEDERATED STATES OF) - TELEVISION RECEIVERS

Encyclopedia Britannica, Incorporated, 310 South Michigan Avenue, Chicago, Illinois 60604 (312) 347-7000; "*Britannica World Data.*"

MICRONESIA (FEDERATED STATES OF) - TRANSPORTATION AND COMMUNICATIONS

Encyclopedia Britannica, Incorporated, 310 South Michigan Avenue, Chicago, Illinois 60604 (312) 347-7000; "*Britannica World Data.*"

MICRONESIA (FEDERATED STATES OF) - VITAL STATISTICS

Encyclopedia Britannica, Incorporated, 310 South Michigan Avenue, Chicago, Illinois 60604 (312) 347-7000; "*Britannica World Data.*"

MICROWAVE OVENS

Euromonitor Publications Limited, 87-88 Turnmill Street, London, EC1M 5QU, England; *European Marketing Data and Statistics.*

U.S. Department of Energy, Energy Information Administration, 1000 Independence Avenue, SW, Washington, D.C. 20585 (202) 586-8800; *Annual Energy Review.*

MIDWAY ISLANDS - AGRICULTURE

Food and Agricultural Organization of the United Nations (FAO), Via delle Terme di Caracalla, 00100 Rome, Italy (Telephone Number in U.S. (202) 653-2400); *Production Yearbook, The State of Food and Agriculture,* and *Trade Yearbook.*

MIDWAY ISLANDS - AREA AND DENSITY OF POPULATION

Food and Agricultural Organization of the United Nations (FAO), Via delle Terme di Caracalla, 00100 Rome, Italy (Telephone Number in U.S. (202) 653-2400); *The State of Food and Agriculture.*

Statistical Office of the United Nations, Publishing Service, New York, New York 10017 (800) 253-9646; *Statistical Yearbook.*

MIDWAY ISLANDS - BIRTH RATES

Statistical Office of the United Nations, Publishing Service, New York, New York 10017 (800) 253-9646; *Demographic Yearbook.*

MIDWAY ISLANDS - BROADCASTING

Billboard Limited, Post Office Box 9027, 1006 AA Amsterdam, The Netherlands (Telephone Number in U.S. (212) 764-7300); *World Radio TV Handbook.*

MIDWAY ISLANDS - CALORIE SUPPLY

Food and Agricultural Organization of the United Nations (FAO), Via delle Terme di Caracalla, 00100 Rome, Italy (Telephone Number in U.S. (202) 653-2400); *The State of Food and Agriculture.*

MIDWAY ISLANDS - CORN - See MIDWAY ISLANDS - CROPS

MIDWAY ISLANDS - CROPS

Food and Agricultural Organization of the United Nations (FAO), Via delle Terme di Caracalla, 00100 Rome, Italy (Telephone Number in U.S. (202) 653-2400); *The State of Food and Agriculture.*

MIDWAY ISLANDS - DAIRY PRODUCTS

Food and Agricultural Organization of the United Nations (FAO), Via delle Terme di Caracalla, 00100 Rome, Italy (Telephone Number in U.S. (202) 653-2400); *The State of Food and Agriculture*.

MIDWAY ISLANDS - DIVORCE

Statistical Office of the United Nations, Publishing Service, New York, New York 10017 (800) 253-9646; *Demographic Yearbook*.

MIDWAY ISLANDS - EGG PRODUCTION - See MIDWAY ISLANDS - DAIRY PRODUCTS

MIDWAY ISLANDS - ENERGY

Food and Agricultural Organization of the United Nations (FAO), Via delle Terme di Caracalla, 00100 Rome, Italy (Telephone Number in U.S. (202) 653-2400); *The State of Food and Agriculture*.

MIDWAY ISLANDS - EXPORTS

Food and Agricultural Organization of the United Nations (FAO), Via delle Terme di Caracalla, 00100 Rome, Italy (Telephone Number in U.S. (202) 653-2400); *The State of Food and Agriculture*.

MIDWAY ISLANDS - EXTERNAL TRADE

Food and Agricultural Organization of the United Nations (FAO), Via delle Terme di Caracalla, 00100 Rome, Italy (Telephone Number in U.S. (202) 653-2400); *The State of Food and Agriculture, and Trade Yearbook*.

MIDWAY ISLANDS - FARM CROPS - See MIDWAY ISLANDS - CROPS

MIDWAY ISLANDS - FERTILIZER

Food and Agricultural Organization of the United Nations (FAO), Via delle Terme di Caracalla, 00100 Rome, Italy (Telephone Number in U.S. (202) 653-2400); *The State of Food and Agriculture*.

MIDWAY ISLANDS - FETAL MORTALITY

Statistical Office of the United Nations, Publishing Service, New York, New York 10017 (800) 253-9646; *Demographic Yearbook*.

MIDWAY ISLANDS - FISHERIES

Food and Agricultural Organization of the United Nations (FAO), Via delle Terme di Caracalla, 00100 Rome, Italy (Telephone Number in U.S. (202) 653-2400); *The State of Food and Agriculture, and Yearbook of Fishery Statistics*.

MIDWAY ISLANDS - FOOD

Food and Agricultural Organization of the United Nations (FAO), Via delle Terme di Caracalla, 00100 Rome, Italy (Telephone Number in U.S. (202) 653-2400); *Production Yearbook, and The State of Food and Agriculture*.

MIDWAY ISLANDS - FOREIGN TRADE

Food and Agricultural Organization of the United Nations (FAO), Via delle Terme di Caracalla, 00100 Rome, Italy (Telephone Number in U.S. (202) 653-2400); *The State of Food and Agriculture*.

MIDWAY ISLANDS - FORESTRY AND FOREST PRODUCTS

Food and Agricultural Organization of the United Nations (FAO), Via delle Terme di Caracalla, 00100 Rome, Italy (Telephone Number in U.S. (202) 653-2400); *The State of Food and Agriculture*.

MIDWAY ISLANDS - GENERAL MORTALITY

Statistical Office of the United Nations, Publishing Service, New York, New York 10017 (800) 253-9646; *Demographic Yearbook*.

MIDWAY ISLANDS - GRAIN PRODUCTION - See MIDWAY ISLANDS - CROPS

MIDWAY ISLANDS - IMPORTS

Food and Agricultural Organization of the United Nations (FAO), Via delle Terme di Caracalla, 00100 Rome, Italy (Telephone Number in U.S. (202) 653-2400); *The State of Food and Agriculture*.

MIDWAY ISLANDS - INFANT AND MATERNAL MORTALITY

Statistical Office of the United Nations, Publishing Service, New York, New York 10017 (800) 253-9646; *Demographic Yearbook*.

MIDWAY ISLANDS - LABOR FORCE

Food and Agricultural Organization of the United Nations (FAO), Via delle Terme di Caracalla, 00100 Rome, Italy (Telephone Number in U.S. (202) 653-2400); *The State of Food and Agriculture*.

MIDWAY ISLANDS - LAND USE

Food and Agricultural Organization of the United Nations (FAO), Via delle Terme di Caracalla, 00100 Rome, Italy (Telephone Number in U.S. (202) 653-2400); *Production Yearbook*.

MIDWAY ISLANDS - LIVESTOCK AND POULTRY

Food and Agricultural Organization of the United Nations (FAO), Via delle Terme di Caracalla, 00100 Rome, Italy (Telephone Number in U.S. (202) 653-2400); *Production Yearbook, and The State of Food and Agriculture*.

MIDWAY ISLANDS - MARRIAGE RATES

Statistical Office of the United Nations, Publishing Service, New York, New York 10017 (800) 253-9646; *Demographic Yearbook*.

MIDWAY ISLANDS - MEAT PRODUCTION - See MIDWAY ISLANDS - LIVESTOCK AND POULTRY

MIDWAY ISLANDS - NATALITY - See MIDWAY ISLANDS - BIRTH RATES

MIDWAY ISLANDS - PESTICIDE USE

Food and Agricultural Organization of the United Nations (FAO), Via delle Terme di Caracalla, 00100 Rome, Italy (Telephone Number in U.S. (202) 653-2400); *The State of Food and Agriculture*.

MIDWAY ISLANDS - PETROLEUM INDUSTRY

Food and Agricultural Organization of the United Nations (FAO), Via delle Terme di Caracalla, 00100 Rome, Italy (Telephone Number in U.S. (202) 653-2400); *The State of Food and Agriculture*.

MIDWAY ISLANDS - POPULATION

Food and Agricultural Organization of the United Nations (FAO), Via delle Terme di Caracalla, 00100 Rome, Italy (Telephone Number in U.S. (202) 653-2400); *Production Yearbook.*

Statistical Office of the United Nations, Publishing Service, New York, New York 10017 (800) 253-9646; *Demographic Yearbook,* and *Statistical Yearbook.*

World Health Organization, Office of Publications, Avenue Appia, CH-1211 Geneva 27, Switzerland (Telephone in U.S. (518) 436-9686); *World Health Statistics Annual.*

MIDWAY ISLANDS - PRICES

Food and Agricultural Organization of the United Nations (FAO), Via delle Terme di Caracalla, 00100 Rome, Italy (Telephone Number in U.S. (202) 653-2400); *Production Yearbook,* and *The State of Food and Agriculture.*

MIDWAY ISLANDS - STOCKS - COMMODITY - MARKET PRICE - INDEX

Food and Agricultural Organization of the United Nations (FAO), Via delle Terme di Caracalla, 00100 Rome, Italy (Telephone Number in U.S. (202) 653-2400); *The State of Food and Agriculture.*

MIDWAY ISLANDS - TELEPHONES IN USE

American Telephone and Telegraph Company, 26 Parsippany Road, Whippany, New Jersey 07981 (800) 338-4038; *The World's Telephones.*

MIDWAY ISLANDS - TRADE - See MIDWAY ISLANDS - FOREIGN TRADE

MIDWAY ISLANDS - VITAL STATISTICS

World Health Organization, Office of Publications, Avenue Appia, CH-1211 Geneva 27, Switzerland (Telephone in U.S. (518) 436-9686); *World Health Statistics Annual.*

MIGRATION

U.S. Department of Commerce, Bureau of the Census, Suitland, Maryland 20233 (301) 763-4040; *Current Population Reports,* and unpublished data.

MILITARY BASES

Army Times Publishing Company, 6883 Commercial Drive, Springfield, Virginia 22159 (703) 750-9000; *Guide to Military Installations in the U.S.*

MILITARY EXPENDITURES - WORLDWIDE

U.S. Arms Control and Disarmament Agency, 320 Twenty-first Street, NW, Washington, D.C. 20541 (202) 647-8677; *World Military Expenditures and Arms Transfers.*

MILITARY EXPENDITURES - WORLDWIDE - FOREIGN COUNTRIES

U.S. Arms Control and Disarmament Agency, 320 Twenty-first Street, NW, Washington, D.C. 20541 (202) 647-8677; *World Military Expenditures and Arms Transfers.*

MILITARY SERVICES - BASIC PAY

U.S. Department of Defense, The Pentagon, Washington, D.C. 20301 (703) 545-6700; *Selected Manpower Statistics,* and unpublished data.

MILITARY SERVICES - CASUALTIES

The President's Commission on Veterans' Pensions, The White House Office, 1600 Pennsylvania Avenue, NW, Washington, D.C. 20500 (202) 233-4000; *Veterans' Benefits in the United States.*

National Archives and Records Administration, Seventh Street and Pennsylvania Avenue, NW, Washington, D.C. 20408 (202) 501-5400; unpublished data from Combat Area Casualties database.

U.S. Department of Defense, Office of the Secretary, The Pentagon, Washington, D.C. 20301 (703) 545-6700; *Selected Manpower Statistics,* and unpublished data.

MILITARY SERVICES - CASUALTIES - VIETNAM CONFLICT

National Archives and Records Administration, Seventh Street and Pennsylvania Avenue, NW, Washington, D.C. 20408 (202) 501-5400; unpublished data from Combat Area Casualties database.

MILITARY SERVICES - CONSTRUCTION - VALUE OF BUILDINGS

U.S. Department of Commerce, Bureau of the Census, Suitland, Maryland 20233 (301) 763-4040; *Current Construction Reports.*

MILITARY SERVICES - CONTRACT AWARDS

U.S. Department of Defense, Office of the Secretary, The Pentagon, Washington, D.C. 20301 (703) 545-6700; *Prime Contract Awards,* and *Atlas/Data Abstract for the United States and Selected Areas.*

MILITARY SERVICES - EXPENDITURES

Executive Office of the President, Office of Management and Budget, Executive Office Building, Washington, D.C. 20503 (202) 395-3080; *The Budget of the United States Government.*

U.S. Department of Defense, Office of the Secretary, The Pentagon, Washington, D.C. 20301 (703) 545-6700; *Atlas/Data Abstract for the U.S. and Selected Areas.*

MILITARY SERVICES - NATIONAL GUARD

U.S. National Guard Bureau, The Pentagon, Washington, D.C. 20301 (202) 443-5100; *Annual Review of the Chief, National Guard Bureau,* and unpublished data.

MILITARY SERVICES - PAYROLL

U.S. Department of Defense, Office of the Secretary, The Pentagon, Washington, D.C. 20301 (703) 545-6700; *Selected Manpower Statistics,* and *Atlas/State Data Abstract for the United States and Selected Areas.*

MILITARY SERVICES - PERSONNEL

U.S. Department of Defense, Office of the Secretary, The Pentagon, Washington, D.C. 20301 (703) 545-6700; *Selected Manpower Statistics, Atlas/State Data Abstract for the United States and Selected Areas,* and unpublished data.

MILITARY SERVICES - PERSONNEL - FOREIGN COUNTRIES

U.S. Department of Defense, Office of the Secretary, The Pentagon, Washington, D.C. 20301 (703) 545-6700; *Selected Manpower Statistics*, and unpublished data.

MILITARY SERVICES - RESERVES - BY BRANCH

U.S. Department of Defense, Office of the Secretary, The Pentagon, Washington, D.C. 20301 (703) 545-6700; *Official Guard and Manpower Strengths and Statistics*.

MILITARY SERVICES - RESERVES - BY BRANCH - COSTS - BY BRANCH

U.S. Department of Defense, Office of the Secretary, The Pentagon, Washington, D.C. 20301 (703) 545-6700; unpublished data.

MILITARY SERVICES - RETIREES

U.S. Department of Defense, Office of the Secretary, The Pentagon, Washington, D.C. 20301 (703) 545-6700; *Selected Manpower Statistics*.

MILITARY SERVICES - SELECTIVE SERVICE - INDUCTEES

U.S. Department of Defense, Office of the Secretary, The Pentagon, Washington, D.C. 20301 (703) 545-6700; *Selected Manpower Statistics*.

MILITARY SERVICES - SELECTIVE SERVICE - INDUCTEES - BY WAR

The President's Commission on Veteran's Pensions, The White House, 1600 Pennsylvania Avenue, NW, Washington, D.C. 20500 (202) 233-4000; *Veteran's Benefits in the United States*.

U.S. Department of Defense, The Pentagon, Washington, D.C. 20301 (703) 545-6700; unpublished data.

MILK - CREAM AND OTHER DAIRY PRODUCTS - CONSUMPTION

U.S. Department of Agriculture, Economic Research Service, Fourteenth Street and Independence Avenue, SW, Washington, D.C. 20005-4789 (202) 219-1504; *Food Consumption, Prices, and Expenditures, Agricultural Outlook*, and unpublished data.

MILK - PRICES

U.S. Department of Agriculture, National Agricultural Statistics Service, Fourteenth Street and Independence Avenue, SW, Washington, D.C. 20250 (202) 219-1504; *Dairy Products*, and *Milk Production, Disposition and Income*.

U.S. Department of Labor, Bureau of Labor Statistics, Two Massachusetts Avenue, NE, Washington, D.C. 20212 (202) 606-7828; *CPI Detailed Report*.

MILK - PRODUCTION

U.S. Department of Agriculture, National Agricultural Statistics Service, Fourteenth Street and Independence Avenue, SW, Washington, D.C. 20250 (202) 219-1504; *Dairy Products, Milk Production, Disposition, and Income*, and *Agricultural Outlook*.

MILK - SALES

U.S. Department of Agriculture, National Agricultural Statistics Service, Fourteenth Street and Independence Avenue, SW, Washington, D.C. 20250 (202) 219-1504; *Dairy Products*, and *Milk Production, Disposition, and Income*.

MILO - See SORGHUM FOR GRAIN

MINERAL FUELS

U.S. Department of Energy, Energy Information Administration, Washington, D.C. 20585 (202) 586-8800; *Annual Energy Review, Uranium Industry Annual, Petroleum Supply Annual, Natural Gas Annual*, and *Quarterly Coal Report*.

MINERAL LEASES, PUBLIC

U.S. Department of the Interior, Bureau of Land Management, C Street between Eighteenth and Nineteenth Streets, NW, Washington, D.C. 20240 (202) 208-3435; *Public Land Statistics*.

MINERALS - NON METALLIC - EXCEPT FUELS - MINING - CAPITAL

U.S. Department of Commerce, Bureau of the Census, Suitland, Maryland 20233 (301) 763-4040; *Census of Mineral Industries*.

MINERALS - NON METALLIC - EXCEPT FUELS - MINING - EARNINGS

U.S. Department of Commerce, Bureau of the Census, Suitland, Maryland 20233 (301) 763-4040; *County Business Patterns*, and *Census of Mineral Industries*.

U.S. Department of Labor, Bureau of Labor Statistics, Two Massachusetts Avenue, NE, Washington, D.C. 20212 (202) 606-7828; *Employment and Earnings*, and Bulletins 2370 and 2429.

MINERALS - NON METALLIC - EXCEPT FUELS - MINING - EMPLOYEES

U.S. Department of Commerce, Bureau of the Census, Suitland, Maryland 20233 (301) 763-4040; *County Business Patterns*, and *Census of Mineral Industries*.

U.S. Department of Labor, Bureau of Labor Statistics, Two Massachusetts Avenue, NE, Washington, D.C. 20212 (202) 606-7828; *Employment and Earnings*, and Bulletins 2370 and 2429.

MINERALS - NON METALLIC - EXCEPT FUELS - MINING - ESTABLISHMENTS

U.S. Department of Commerce, Bureau of the Census, Suitland, Maryland 20233 (301) 763-4040; *Census of Mineral Industries*.

MINERALS - NON METALLIC - EXCEPT FUELS - MINING - GROSS DOMESTIC PRODUCT

U.S. Department of Commerce, Bureau of Economic Analysis, Fourteenth Street between Constitution Avenue and E Street, NW, Washington, D.C. 20230 (202) 606-9900; *The National Income and Product Accounts of the United States*, and *Survey of Current Business*.

MINERALS - NON METALLIC - EXCEPT FUELS - MINING - OCCUPATIONAL SAFETY

U.S. Department of Labor, Bureau of Labor Statistics, Two Massachusetts Avenue, NE, Washington, D.C. 20212 (202) 606-7828; *Occupational Injuries and Illnesses in the United States by Industry*.

MINERALS - NON METALLIC - EXCEPT FUELS - MINING - PRODUCTIVITY

U.S. Department of Labor, Bureau of Labor Statistics, Two Massachusetts Avenue, NE, Washington, D.C. 20212 (202) 606-7828; *Productivity Measures for Selected Industries and Government Services*, and unpublished data.

MINERALS - NON METALLIC - EXCEPT FUELS - MINING - SHIPMENTS, RECEIPTS

U.S. Department of Commerce, Bureau of the Census, Suitland, Maryland 20233 (301) 763-4040; *Census of Mineral Industries*.

MINERALS - NON METALLIC - EXCEPT FUELS - MINING - VALUE ADDED

U.S. Department of Commerce, Bureau of the Census, Suitland, Maryland 20233 (301) 763-4040; *Census of Mineral Industries*.

MINERALS AND MINERAL PRODUCTS - See also MINING and Individual Minerals

MINERALS AND MINERAL PRODUCTS - FOREIGN TRADE

U.S. Department of Commerce, Bureau of the Census, Suitland, Maryland 20233 (301) 763-4040; *U.S. Imports for Consumption and General Imports, TSUSA Commodity and Country, U.S. Exports, Schedule B, Commodity and Country, U.S. Exports of Merchandise*, and *U.S. Imports of Merchandise*, compact discs.

U.S. Department of the Interior, Bureau of Mines, 810 Seventh Street, NW, Washington, D.C. 20241 (202) 501-9649; *Annual Reports*, and *Mineral Commodity Summaries*.

MINERALS AND MINERAL PRODUCTS - FOREIGN TRADE - WATERBORNE COMMERCE

U.S. Department of the Army, Corps of Engineers, The Pentagon, Washington, D.C. 20301 (202) 545-6700; *Waterborne Commerce of the United States*.

MINERALS AND MINERAL PRODUCTS - FUELS - PRODUCTION AND CONSUMPTION

U.S. Department of Energy, Energy Information Administration, Washington, D.C. 20585 (202) 586-8800; *Annual Energy Review*.

MINERALS AND MINERAL PRODUCTS - IMPORTS AS PERCENT OF CONSUMPTION

U.S. Department of Commerce, Bureau of the Census, Suitland, Maryland 20233 (301) 763-4040; import and export data.

U.S. Department of the Interior, Bureau of Mines, 810 Seventh Street, NW, Washington, D.C. 20241 (202) 501-9649; *Mineral Commodity Summaries*.

MINERALS AND MINERAL PRODUCTS - PRICE INDEXES

U.S. Department of Labor, Bureau of Labor Statistics, Two Massachusetts Avenue, NE, Washington, D.C. 20212 (202) 606-7828; *News*.

MINERALS AND MINERAL PRODUCTS - PRICES

U.S. Department of the Interior, Bureau of Mines, 810 Seventh Street, NW, Washington, D.C. 20241 (202) 501-9649; *Mineral Commodity Summaries*, and *Minerals Yearbook*.

MINERALS AND MINERAL PRODUCTS - PRODUCTION AND VALUE

Board of Governors of the Federal Reserve System, Twentieth Street and Constitution Avenue, NW, Washington, D.C. 20551 (202) 452-3000; *Federal Reserve Bulletin*.

U.S. Department of Commerce, Bureau of the Census, Suitland, Maryland 20233 (301) 763-4040; *Census of Mineral Industries*.

U.S. Department of Energy, Energy Information Administration, Washington, D.C. 20585 (202) 586-8800; *Annual Energy Review*.

U.S. Department of the Interior, Bureau of Mines, 810 Seventh Street, NW, Washington, D.C. 20241 (202) 501-9649; *Annual Reports*, and *Mineral Commodities Summaries*.

MINERALS AND MINERAL PRODUCTS - PRODUCTION AND VALUE - FOREIGN COUNTRIES

Statistical Office of the United Nations, Publishing Service, New York, New York 10017 (800) 253-9646; *Energy Statistics Yearbook*.

MINERALS AND MINERAL PRODUCTS - PRODUCTION - WORLD

U.S. Department of the Interior, Bureau of the Mines, 810 Seventh Street, NW, Washington, D.C. 20241 (202) 501-9649; *Annual Reports*, and *Mineral Commodities Summaries*.

MINERALS AND MINERAL PRODUCTS - STRATEGIC AND CRITICAL MATERIALS

U.S. Department of Defense, Defense Logistics Agency, Cameron Station, Alexandria, Virginia 22304 (703) 274-6000; *Statistical Supplement, Stockpile Report to the Congress*.

MINING INDUSTRY - See also MINERALS AND MINERAL PRODUCTS and Individual Minerals

MINING INDUSTRY - ASSETS

Time Warner, 1675 Broadway, Rockefeller Center, New York, New York 10019 (212) 522-1212; *The Fortune Directories*.

U.S. Department of Commerce, Bureau of the Census, Suitland, Maryland 20233 (301) 763-4040; *Census of Mineral Industries*.

U.S. Department of the Treasury, Internal Revenue Service, 1111 Constitution Avenue, NW, Washington, D.C. 20224 (202) 566-5000; *Statistics of Income, Corporation Income Tax Returns*.

MINING INDUSTRY - CAPITAL

U.S. Department of Commerce, Bureau of Economic Analysis, Fourteenth Street between Constitution Avenue and E Street, NW, Washington, D.C. 20230 (202) 606-9900; *Survey of Current Business*.

U.S. Department of Commerce, Bureau of the Census, Suitland, Maryland 20233 (301) 763-4040; *Census of Mineral Industries*.

MINING INDUSTRY - CAPITAL - EXPENDITURES

U.S. Department of Commerce, Bureau of the Census, Suitland, Maryland 20233 (301) 763-4040; *Census of Mineral Industries*, and *Plant and Equipment Expenditures and Plans*.

MINING INDUSTRY - EARNINGS

U.S. Department of Commerce, Bureau of Economic Analysis, Fourteenth Street between Constitution Avenue and E Street, NW,

Washington, D.C. 20230 (202) 606-9900; *The National Income and Product Accounts of the United States*, and *Survey of Current Business*.

U.S. Department of Commerce, Bureau of the Census, Suitland, Maryland 20233 (301) 763-4040; *Census of Mineral Industries, Census of Manufactures, Annual Survey of Manufactures*, and *County Business Patterns*.

U.S. Department of Labor, Bureau of Labor Statistics, Two Massachusetts Avenue, NE, Washington, D.C. 20212 (202) 606-7828; *Employment and Earnings*, and Bulletins 2370 and 2429.

MINING INDUSTRY - EMPLOYEES

U.S. Department of Commerce, Bureau of the Census, Suitland, Maryland 20233 (301) 763-4040; *Census of Mineral Industries, County Business Patterns, Census of Manufactures, Annual Survey of Manufactures, Origin of Exports of Manufactured Products*, and *Census of Mineral Industries*.

U.S. Department of Labor, Bureau of Labor Statistics, Two Massachusetts Avenue, NE, Washington, D.C. 20212 (202) 606-7828; *Employment and Earnings, Monthly Labor Review*, and Bulletins 2370 and 2429.

MINING INDUSTRY - ESTABLISHMENTS

U.S. Department of Commerce, Bureau of the Census, Suitland, Maryland 20233 (301) 763-4040; *Census of Mineral Industries*, and *County Business Patterns*.

MINING INDUSTRY - FINANCES

Time Warner, 1675 Broadway, Rockefeller Center, New York, New York 10019 (212) 522-1212; *The Fortune Directories*.

U.S. Department of Commerce, Bureau of the Census, Suitland, Maryland 20233 (301) 763-4040; *Census of Mineral Industries*.

U.S. Department of the Treasury, Internal Revenue Service, 1111 Constitution Avenue, NW, Washington, D.C. 20224 (202) 566-5000; *Statistics of Income, various publications*, and *Statistics of Income, Corporation Income Tax Returns*.

MINING INDUSTRY - FOREIGN INVESTMENTS IN THE UNITED STATES

U.S. Department of Commerce, Bureau of Economic Analysis, Fourteenth Street between Constitution Avenue and E Street, NW, Washington, D.C. 20230 (202) 606-9900; *Survey of Current Business*, and *Foreign Direct Investment in the United States, Operations of U.S. Affiliates of Foreign Countries*.

MINING INDUSTRY - GROSS DOMESTIC PRODUCT

U.S. Department of Commerce, Bureau of Economic Analysis, Fourteenth Street between Constitution Avenue and E Street, NW, Washington, D.C. 20230 (202) 606-9900; *The National Income and Product Accounts of the United States*, and *Survey of Current Business*.

MINING INDUSTRY - MERGERS AND ACQUISITIONS

Securities Data Company, 1180 Raymond Boulevard, Newark, New Jersey 07102 (201) 622-3100; *Merger and Corporate Transactions Database*.

MINING INDUSTRY - OCCUPATIONAL SAFETY

National Safety Council, 1121 Spring Lake Drive, Itasca, Illinois 60143-3201; *Accident Facts*.

U.S. Department of Labor, Bureau of Labor Statistics, Two Massachusetts Avenue, NE, Washington, D.C. 20212 (202) 606-7828; *Occupational Injuries and Illnesses in the United States by Industry*.

MINING INDUSTRY - PRODUCTIVITY

U.S. Department of Labor, Bureau of Labor Statistics, Two Massachusetts Avenue, NE, Washington, D.C. 20212 (202) 606-7828; *Productivity Measures for Selected Industries and Government Services*, and unpublished data.

MINING INDUSTRY - PROFITS

Time Warner, 1675 Broadway, Rockefeller Center, New York, New York 10019 (212) 522-1212; *The Fortune Directories*.

U.S. Department of the Treasury, Internal Revenue Service, 1111 Constitution Avenue, NW, Washington, D.C. 20224 (202) 566-5000; *Statistics of Income, Statistics of Income, Partnership Returns, Statistics of Income, Corporation Income Tax Returns*, and *Statistics of Income Bulletin*.

MINING INDUSTRY - RECEIPTS

Time Warner, 1675 Broadway, Rockefeller Center, New York, New York 10019 (212) 522-1212; *The Fortune Directories*.

U.S. Department of Commerce, Bureau of the Census, Suitland, Maryland 20233 (301) 763-4040; *Census of Mineral Industries*.

U.S. Department of the Treasury, Internal Revenue Service, 1111 Constitution Avenue, NW, Washington, D.C. 20224 (202) 566-5000; *Statistics of Income, various publications*.

MINING INDUSTRY - SHIPMENTS

U.S. Department of Commerce, Bureau of the Census, Suitland, Maryland 20233 (301) 763-4040; *Census of Mineral Industries*.

MINING INDUSTRY - UNION MEMBERSHIP

U.S. Department of Labor, Bureau of Labor Statistics, Two Massachusetts Avenue, NE, Washington, D.C. 20212 (202) 606-7828; *Employment and Earnings*.

MINING INDUSTRY - VALUE ADDED

U.S. Department of Commerce, Bureau of the Census, Suitland, Maryland 20233 (301) 763-4040; *Census of Mineral Industries*.

MINNESOTA - See also STATE DATA (FOR INDIVIDUAL STATES)

Minnesota - Primary Statistics Sources

Department of Trade and Economic Development, Business Development and Analysis Division, 500 Metro Square Building, St. Paul, Minnesota 55101 (612) 296-8283; *Compare Minnesota: An Economic and Statistical Factbook*, and *Economic Report to the Governor: State of Minnesota*.

Office of State Demographer, State Planning Agency, 300 Centennial Building, St. Paul, Minnesota 55155 (612) 296-2557; *Minnesota Population and Household Estimates*.

Minnesota - State Data Centers

State Demographer's Office, Minnesota Planning, 300 Centennial Office Building, 658 Cedar Street, St. Paul, Minnesota 55155, Mr. David Birkholz (612) 296-2557, Mr. David Rademacher (612) 297-3255.

Metropolitan Council Data Center, 230 East 5th Street, St. Paul, Minnesota 55101, Mr. Chuck Ballantine (612) 291-8140.

Interagency Resource and Information Center, Department of Education, 501 Capitol Square Building, St. Paul, Minnesota 55101, Ms. Patricia Tupper (612) 296-6684.

MINT - PEPPERMINT AND SPEARMINT

U.S. Department of Agriculture, National Agricultural Statistics Service, Fourteenth Street and Independence Avenue, SW, Washington, D.C. 20250 (202) 219-1504; *Agricultural Statistics*, and *Vegetables*.

MISSISSIPPI - See also STATE DATA (FOR INDIVIDUAL STATES)

Mississippi - Primary Statistics Source

Mississippi State University, College of Business and Industry, Division of Research, Mississippi State, Mississippi 39762 (601) 325-3817; *Mississippi Statistical Abstract*.

Mississippi - State Data Centers

Center for Population Studies, University of Mississippi, Bondurant Building, Room 3W, University, Mississippi 38677, Ms. Rachel McNeely, Manager (601) 232-7288.

Governor's Office of Federal-State Programs, Department of Community Development, 301 West Pearl Street, Jackson, Mississippi 39203-3096, Mr. Jim Catt (601) 949-2219.

Division of Research and Information Systems, Department of Economic and Community Development, 1200 Walter Sillas Building, Post Office Box 849, Jackson, Mississippi 39205, Mr. Bill Rigby (601) 359-2674.

MISSISSIPPI RIVER TRAFFIC

U.S. Department of the Army, Corps of Engineers, The Pentagon, Washington, D.C. 20301 (202) 545-6700; *Waterborne Commerce of the United States*.

MISSOURI - See also STATE DATA (FOR INDIVIDUAL STATES)

Missouri - Primary Statistics Source

Business and Public Administration Research Center, University of Missouri, Columbia, Missouri 65211 (314) 882-4805; *Statistical Abstract for Missouri*.

Missouri - State Data Centers

Missouri State Library, 600 West Main Street, Post Office Box 387, Jefferson City, Missouri 65102, Ms. Kate Graf (314) 751-1823.

Missouri Small Business Development Centers, 300 University Place, Columbia, Missouri 65211, Terry Maynard (314) 882-0344.

Office of Administration, 124 Capitol Building, Post Office Box 809, Jefferson City, Missouri 65102, Mr. Ryan Burson (314) 751-2345.

Office of Computing, University of Missouri-St. Louis, 8001 Natural Bridge Road, St. Louis, Missouri 63121, John Blodgett/Linda McDaniel (314) 553-6014.

Office of Social and Economic Data Analysis, University of Missouri-Columbia, 224 Lewis Hall, Columbia, Missouri 65211, Ms. Evelyn J. Cleveland (314) 882-7396.

Geographic Resources Center, University of Missouri-Columbia, 17 Stewart Hall, Columbia, Missouri 65211, Tim Haithcoat (314) 882-1404.

MOBILE HOMES

U.S. Department of Commerce, Bureau of the Census, Suitland, Maryland 20233 (301) 763-4040; *Current Construction Reports*, *Current Housing Reports*, and *American Housing Survey*.

MOBILE HOMES - CAPITAL STOCKS

U.S. Department of Commerce, Bureau of Economic Analysis, Fourteenth Street between Constitution Avenue and E Street, NW, Washington, D.C. 20230 (202) 606-9900; *Survey of Current Business* and *Fixed Reproducible Tangible Wealth in the United States*.

MOBILITY STATUS OF POPULATION

U.S. Department of Commerce, Bureau of the Census, Suitland, Maryland 20233 (301) 763-4040; *Current Population Reports*.

MOLDOVA - See also UNION OF SOVIET SOCIALIST REPUBLICS

MOLDOVA - AGRICULTURE

Business International Moscow, 23 Profsoyuznaya Ulitsa, 117859, Moscow (Telephone Number in U.S. (800) 938-4685); *The CIS Market Atlas*.

Encyclopedia Britannica, Incorporated, 310 South Michigan Avenue, Chicago, Illinois 60604 (312) 347-7000; *Britannica World Data*.

The World Bank, 1818 H Street, NW, Washington, D.C. 20433 (202) 477-1234; *Statistical Handbook: States of the Former USSR*.

MOLDOVA - AIRLINE SERVICE

Business International Moscow, 23 Profsoyuznaya Ulitsa, 117859, Moscow (Telephone Number in U.S. (800) 938-4685); *The CIS Market Atlas*.

Encyclopedia Britannica, Incorporated, 310 South Michigan Avenue, Chicago, Illinois 60604 (312) 347-7000; *Britannica World Data*.

MOLDOVA - AREA AND DENSITY OF POPULATION

Business International Moscow, 23 Profsoyuznaya Ulitsa, 117859, Moscow (Telephone Number in U.S. (800) 938-4685); *The CIS Market Atlas*.

MOLDOVA - BANKING

Business International Moscow, 23 Profsoyuznaya Ulitsa, 117859, Moscow (Telephone Number in U.S. (800) 938-4685); *The CIS Market Atlas*.

MOLDOVA - BIRTH RATES

Business International Moscow, 23 Profsoyuznaya Ulitsa, 117859, Moscow (Telephone Number in U.S. (800) 938-4685); *The CIS Market Atlas.*

Encyclopedia Britannica, Incorporated, 310 South Michigan Avenue, Chicago, Illinois 60604 (312) 347-7000; *Britannica World Data.*

MOLDOVA - BUDGET

Business International Moscow, 23 Profsoyuznaya Ulitsa, 117859, Moscow (Telephone Number in U.S. (800) 938-4685); *The CIS Market Atlas.*

MOLDOVA - CAPITAL INVESTMENT

The World Bank, 1818 H Street, NW, Washington, D.C. 20433 (202) 477-1234; *Statistical Handbook: States of the Former USSR.*

MOLDOVA - CATTLE - See MOLDOVA - LIVESTOCK AND POULTRY

MOLDOVA - CHEMICALS

Business International Moscow, 23 Profsoyuznaya Ulitsa, 117859, Moscow (Telephone Number in U.S. (800) 938-4685); *The CIS Market Atlas.*

MOLDOVA - COAL PRODUCTION AND CONSUMPTION - See MOLDOVA - MINING AND MINERAL PRODUCTS

MOLDOVA - COMMUNICATIONS

Business International Moscow, 23 Profsoyuznaya Ulitsa, 117859, Moscow (Telephone Number in U.S. (800) 938-4685); *The CIS Market Atlas.*

MOLDOVA - CONSTRUCTION INDUSTRY

Business International Moscow, 23 Profsoyuznaya Ulitsa, 117859, Moscow (Telephone Number in U.S. (800) 938-4685); *The CIS Market Atlas.*

Encyclopedia Britannica, Incorporated, 310 South Michigan Avenue, Chicago, Illinois 60604 (312) 347-7000; *Britannica World Data.*

MOLDOVA - CONSUMER PRODUCTS

Business International Moscow, 23 Profsoyuznaya Ulitsa, 117859, Moscow (Telephone Number in U.S. (800) 938-4685); *The CIS Market Atlas.*

MOLDOVA - CONSUMPTION

Business International Moscow, 23 Profsoyuznaya Ulitsa, 117859, Moscow (Telephone Number in U.S. (800) 938-4685); *The CIS Market Atlas.*

The World Bank, 1818 H Street, NW, Washington, D.C. 20433 (202) 477-1234; *Statistical Handbook: States of the Former USSR.*

MOLDOVA - COTTON PRODUCTION AND CONSUMPTION - See MOLDOVA - TEXTILE INDUSTRY

MOLDOVA - CROPS

The World Bank, 1818 H Street, NW, Washington, D.C. 20433 (202) 477-1234; *Statistical Handbook: States of the Former USSR.*

MOLDOVA - DEATH RATES

Business International Moscow, 23 Profsoyuznaya Ulitsa, 117859, Moscow (Telephone Number in U.S. (800) 938-4685); *The CIS Market Atlas.*

MOLDOVA - DEMOGRAPHY

Business International Moscow, 23 Profsoyuznaya Ulitsa, 117859, Moscow (Telephone Number in U.S. (800) 938-4685); *The CIS Market Atlas.*

Encyclopedia Britannica, Incorporated, 310 South Michigan Avenue, Chicago, Illinois 60604 (312) 347-7000; *Britannica World Data.*

The World Bank, 1818 H Street, NW, Washington, D.C. 20433 (202) 477-1234; *Statistical Handbook: States of the Former USSR.*

MOLDOVA - DISEASES

Business International Moscow, 23 Profsoyuznaya Ulitsa, 117859, Moscow (Telephone Number in U.S. (800) 938-4685); *The CIS Market Atlas.*

MOLDOVA - DIVORCE RATES

Encyclopedia Britannica, Incorporated, 310 South Michigan Avenue, Chicago, Illinois 60604 (312) 347-7000; *Britannica World Data.*

MOLDOVA - DOMESTIC INVESTMENT

Business International Moscow, 23 Profsoyuznaya Ulitsa, 117859, Moscow (Telephone Number in U.S. (800) 938-4685); *The CIS Market Atlas.*

MOLDOVA - ECONOMY

Business International Moscow, 23 Profsoyuznaya Ulitsa, 117859, Moscow (Telephone Number in U.S. (800) 938-4685); *The CIS Market Atlas.*

Encyclopedia Britannica, Incorporated, 310 South Michigan Avenue, Chicago, Illinois 60604 (312) 347-7000; *Britannica World Data.*

MOLDOVA - EDUCATION

Business International Moscow, 23 Profsoyuznaya Ulitsa, 117859, Moscow (Telephone Number in U.S. (800) 938-4685); *The CIS Market Atlas.*

Encyclopedia Britannica, Incorporated, 310 South Michigan Avenue, Chicago, Illinois 60604 (312) 347-7000; *Britannica World Data.*

MOLDOVA - ELECTRICITY

Business International Moscow, 23 Profsoyuznaya Ulitsa, 117859, Moscow (Telephone Number in U.S. (800) 938-4685); *The CIS Market Atlas.*

The World Bank, 1818 H Street, NW, Washington, D.C. 20433 (202) 477-1234; *Statistical Handbook: States of the Former USSR.*

MOLDOVA - EMPLOYMENT

The World Bank, 1818 H Street, NW, Washington, D.C. 20433 (202) 477-1234; *Statistical Handbook: States of the Former USSR.*

MOLDOVA - ENERGY

Business International Moscow, 23 Profsoyuznaya Ulitsa, 117859, Moscow (Telephone Number in U.S. (800) 938-4685); *The CIS Market Atlas.*

Encyclopedia Britannica, Incorporated, 310 South Michigan Avenue, Chicago, Illinois 60604 (312) 347-7000; *Britannica World Data.*

The World Bank, 1818 H Street, NW, Washington, D.C. 20433 (202) 477-1234; *Statistical Handbook: States of the Former USSR.*

MOLDOVA - ENVIRONMENT

Business International Moscow, 23 Profsoyuznaya Ulitsa, 117859, Moscow (Telephone Number in U.S. (800) 938-4685); *The CIS Market Atlas.*

MOLDOVA - EXPORTS

Business International Moscow, 23 Profsoyuznaya Ulitsa, 117859, Moscow (Telephone Number in U.S. (800) 938-4685); *The CIS Market Atlas.*

Encyclopedia Britannica, Incorporated, 310 South Michigan Avenue, Chicago, Illinois 60604 (312) 347-7000; *Britannica World Data.*

The World Bank, 1818 H Street, NW, Washington, D.C. 20433 (202) 477-1234; *Statistical Handbook: States of the Former USSR.*

MOLDOVA - EXTERNAL TRADE

The World Bank, 1818 H Street, NW, Washington, D.C. 20433 (202) 477-1234; *Statistical Handbook: States of the Former USSR.*

MOLDOVA - FABRIC PRODUCTION AND CONSUMPTION - See MOLDOVA - TEXTILE INDUSTRY

MOLDOVA - FERTILITY RATES

Encyclopedia Britannica, Incorporated, 310 South Michigan Avenue, Chicago, Illinois 60604 (312) 347-7000; *Britannica World Data.*

The World Bank, 1818 H Street, NW, Washington, D.C. 20433 (202) 477-1234; *Statistical Handbook: States of the Former USSR.*

MOLDOVA - FISHERIES

Encyclopedia Britannica, Incorporated, 310 South Michigan Avenue, Chicago, Illinois 60604 (312) 347-7000; *Britannica World Data.*

MOLDOVA - FOOTWEAR PRODUCTION AND CONSUMPTION - See MOLDOVA - TEXTILE INDUSTRY

MOLDOVA - FOREIGN INVESTMENT

Business International Moscow, 23 Profsoyuznaya Ulitsa, 117859, Moscow (Telephone Number in U.S. (800) 938-4685); *The CIS Market Atlas.*

MOLDOVA - FOREIGN TRADE

Business International Moscow, 23 Profsoyuznaya Ulitsa, 117859, Moscow (Telephone Number in U.S. (800) 938-4685); *The CIS Market Atlas.*

Encyclopedia Britannica, Incorporated, 310 South Michigan Avenue, Chicago, Illinois 60604 (312) 347-7000; *Britannica World Data.*

The World Bank, 1818 H Street, NW, Washington, D.C. 20433 (202) 477-1234; *Statistical Handbook: States of the Former USSR.*

MOLDOVA - FORESTRY AND FOREST PRODUCTS

Business International Moscow, 23 Profsoyuznaya Ulitsa, 117859, Moscow (Telephone Number in U.S. (800) 938-4685); *The CIS Market Atlas.*

Encyclopedia Britannica, Incorporated, 310 South Michigan Avenue, Chicago, Illinois 60604 (312) 347-7000; *Britannica World Data.*

MOLDOVA - GOATS - See MOLDOVA - LIVESTOCK AND POULTRY

MOLDOVA - GOVERNMENT EXPENDITURE

The World Bank, 1818 H Street, NW, Washington, D.C. 20433 (202) 477-1234; *Statistical Handbook: States of the Former USSR.*

MOLDOVA - GOVERNMENT REVENUE

The World Bank, 1818 H Street, NW, Washington, D.C. 20433 (202) 477-1234; *Statistical Handbook: States of the Former USSR.*

MOLDOVA - GROSS DOMESTIC PRODUCT

The World Bank, 1818 H Street, NW, Washington, D.C. 20433 (202) 477-1234; *Statistical Handbook: States of the Former USSR.*

MOLDOVA - HEALTH

Business International Moscow, 23 Profsoyuznaya Ulitsa, 117859, Moscow (Telephone Number in U.S. (800) 938-4685); *The CIS Market Atlas.*

Encyclopedia Britannica, Incorporated, 310 South Michigan Avenue, Chicago, Illinois 60604 (312) 347-7000; *Britannica World Data.*

MOLDOVA - HIGHWAYS

Business International Moscow, 23 Profsoyuznaya Ulitsa, 117859, Moscow (Telephone Number in U.S. (800) 938-4685); *The CIS Market Atlas.*

Encyclopedia Britannica, Incorporated, 310 South Michigan Avenue, Chicago, Illinois 60604 (312) 347-7000; *Britannica World Data.*

MOLDOVA - HOUSING AND HOUSING UNITS

Business International Moscow, 23 Profsoyuznaya Ulitsa, 117859, Moscow (Telephone Number in U.S. (800) 938-4685); *The CIS Market Atlas.*

MOLDOVA - IMPORTS

Business International Moscow, 23 Profsoyuznaya Ulitsa, 117859, Moscow (Telephone Number in U.S. (800) 938-4685); *The CIS Market Atlas.*

Encyclopedia Britannica, Incorporated, 310 South Michigan Avenue, Chicago, Illinois 60604 (312) 347-7000; *Britannica World Data.*

The World Bank, 1818 H Street, NW, Washington, D.C. 20433 (202) 477-1234; *Statistical Handbook: States of the Former USSR.*

MOLDOVA - INDUSTRY

Business International Moscow, 23 Profsoyuznaya Ulitsa, 117859, Moscow (Telephone Number in U.S. (800) 938-4685); *The CIS*

Market Atlas.

The World Bank, 1818 H Street, NW, Washington, D.C. 20433 (202) 477-1234; *Statistical Handbook: States of the Former USSR.*

MOLDOVA - INFANT MORTALITY RATE

Business International Moscow, 23 Profsoyuznaya Ulitsa, 117859, Moscow (Telephone Number in U.S. (800) 938-4685); *The CIS Market Atlas.*

MOLDOVA - LABOR FORCE

Business International Moscow, 23 Profsoyuznaya Ulitsa, 117859, Moscow (Telephone Number in U.S. (800) 938-4685); *The CIS Market Atlas.*

The World Bank, 1818 H Street, NW, Washington, D.C. 20433 (202) 477-1234; *Statistical Handbook: States of the Former USSR.*

MOLDOVA - LAND USE

Encyclopedia Britannica, Incorporated, 310 South Michigan Avenue, Chicago, Illinois 60604 (312) 347-7000; *Britannica World Data.*

MOLDOVA - LIFE EXPECTANCY

Business International Moscow, 23 Profsoyuznaya Ulitsa, 117859, Moscow (Telephone Number in U.S. (800) 938-4685); *The CIS Market Atlas.*

MOLDOVA - LIVESTOCK AND POULTRY

Business International Moscow, 23 Profsoyuznaya Ulitsa, 117859, Moscow (Telephone Number in U.S. (800) 938-4685); *The CIS Market Atlas.*

Encyclopedia Britannica, Incorporated, 310 South Michigan Avenue, Chicago, Illinois 60604 (312) 347-7000; *Britannica World Data.*

MOLDOVA - MANUFACTURING

Encyclopedia Britannica, Incorporated, 310 South Michigan Avenue, Chicago, Illinois 60604 (312) 347-7000; *Britannica World Data.*

MOLDOVA - MARRIAGE RATES

Encyclopedia Britannica, Incorporated, 310 South Michigan Avenue, Chicago, Illinois 60604 (312) 347-7000; *Britannica World Data.*

MOLDOVA - MEAT PRODUCTION - See MOLDOVA - LIVESTOCK AND POULTRY

MOLDOVA - MILITARY

The International Institute for Strategic Studies, 23 Tavistock Street, London WC2E 7NQ, England; *The Military Balance.*

MOLDOVA - MINING AND MINERAL PRODUCTS

Business International Moscow, 23 Profsoyuznaya Ulitsa, 117859, Moscow (Telephone Number in U.S. (800) 938-4685); *The CIS Market Atlas.*

Encyclopedia Britannica, Incorporated, 310 South Michigan Avenue, Chicago, Illinois 60604 (312) 347-7000; *Britannica World Data.*

MOLDOVA - MOTOR VEHICLES

Business International Moscow, 23 Profsoyuznaya Ulitsa, 117859, Moscow (Telephone Number in U.S. (800) 938-4685); *The CIS Market Atlas.*

MOLDOVA - NATIONAL ACCOUNTS

The World Bank, 1818 H Street, NW, Washington, D.C. 20433 (202) 477-1234; *Statistical Handbook: States of the Former USSR.*

MOLDOVA - NATIONAL INCOME

Business International Moscow, 23 Profsoyuznaya Ulitsa, 117859, Moscow (Telephone Number in U.S. (800) 938-4685); *The CIS Market Atlas.*

MOLDOVA - PIGS - See MOLDOVA - LIVESTOCK AND POULTRY

MOLDOVA - POPULATION

Business International Moscow, 23 Profsoyuznaya Ulitsa, 117859, Moscow (Telephone Number in U.S. (800) 938-4685); *The CIS Market Atlas.*

Encyclopedia Britannica, Incorporated, 310 South Michigan Avenue, Chicago, Illinois 60604 (312) 347-7000; *Britannica World Data.*

The World Bank, 1818 H Street, NW, Washington, D.C. 20433 (202) 477-1234; *Statistical Handbook: States of the Former USSR.*

MOLDOVA - POULTRY - See MOLDOVA - LIVESTOCK AND POULTRY

Business International Moscow, 23 Profsoyuznaya Ulitsa, 117859, Moscow (Telephone Number in U.S. (800) 938-4685); *The CIS Market Atlas.*

MOLDOVA - PRICES

The World Bank, 1818 H Street, NW, Washington, D.C. 20433 (202) 477-1234; *Statistical Handbook: States of the Former USSR.*

MOLDOVA - PRODUCTION

The World Bank, 1818 H Street, NW, Washington, D.C. 20433 (202) 477-1234; *Statistical Handbook: States of the Former USSR.*

MOLDOVA - PUBLIC FINANCE

The World Bank, 1818 H Street, NW, Washington, D.C. 20433 (202) 477-1234; *Statistical Handbook: States of the Former USSR.*

MOLDOVA - RADIO RECEIVERS

Encyclopedia Britannica, Incorporated, 310 South Michigan Avenue, Chicago, Illinois 60604 (312) 347-7000; *Britannica World Data.*

MOLDOVA - RAILWAYS

Business International Moscow, 23 Profsoyuznaya Ulitsa, 117859, Moscow (Telephone Number in U.S. (800) 938-4685); *The CIS Market Atlas.*

Encyclopedia Britannica, Incorporated, 310 South Michigan Avenue, Chicago, Illinois 60604 (312) 347-7000; *Britannica World Data.*

MOLDOVA - RETAIL TRADE

Business International Moscow, 23 Profsoyuznaya Ulitsa, 117859, Moscow (Telephone Number in U.S. (800) 938-4685); *The CIS Market Atlas.*

MOLDOVA - ROADS - See MOLDOVA - HIGHWAYS

MOLDOVA - ROUNDWOOD PRODUCTION AND CONSUMPTION - See MOLDOVA - FORESTRY AND FOREST PRODUCTS

MOLDOVA - SHEEP - See MOLDOVA - LIVESTOCK AND POULTRY

MOLDOVA - STEEL PRODUCTION AND CONSUMPTION - See MOLDOVA - MINING AND MINERAL PRODUCTS

MOLDOVA - TELEPHONES IN USE

Encyclopedia Britannica, Incorporated, 310 South Michigan Avenue, Chicago, Illinois 60604 (312) 347-7000; *Britannica World Data.*

MOLDOVA - TELEVISION RECEIVERS

Encyclopedia Britannica, Incorporated, 310 South Michigan Avenue, Chicago, Illinois 60604 (312) 347-7000; *Britannica World Data.*

MOLDOVA - TEXTILE INDUSTRY

Business International Moscow, 23 Profsoyuznaya Ulitsa, 117859, Moscow (Telephone Number in U.S. (800) 938-4685); *The CIS Market Atlas.*

MOLDOVA - TOURISM

Business International Moscow, 23 Profsoyuznaya Ulitsa, 117859, Moscow (Telephone Number in U.S. (800) 938-4685); *The CIS Market Atlas.*

MOLDOVA - TRANSPORTATION AND COMMUNICATIONS

Business International Moscow, 23 Profsoyuznaya Ulitsa, 117859, Moscow (Telephone Number in U.S. (800) 938-4685); *The CIS Market Atlas.*

Encyclopedia Britannica, Incorporated, 310 South Michigan Avenue, Chicago, Illinois 60604 (312) 347-7000; *Britannica World Data.*

MOLDOVA - VITAL STATISTICS

Encyclopedia Britannica, Incorporated, 310 South Michigan Avenue, Chicago, Illinois 60604 (312) 347-7000; *Britannica World Data.*

MOLDOVA - WAGES

Business International Moscow, 23 Profsoyuznaya Ulitsa, 117859, Moscow (Telephone Number in U.S. (800) 938-4685); *The CIS Market Atlas.*

The World Bank, 1818 H Street, NW, Washington, D.C. 20433 (202) 477-1234; *Statistical Handbook: States of the Former USSR.*

MOLDOVA - WOOL PRODUCTION AND CONSUMPTION - See MOLDOVA - TEXTILE INDUSTRY

MOLYBDENUM

U.S. Department of the Interior, Bureau of the Mines, 810 Seventh Street, NW, Washington, D.C. 20241 (202) 501-9649; *Annual Reports,* and *Mineral Commodity Summaries.*

Monaco - National Statistical Office

Services des Statistiques, et des Etudes Economiques, rue des Iris, Monte Carlo, Monaco.

Monaco - Primary Statistics Source

Services des Statistiques et des Etudes Economiques, 4 rue des Iris, Monte Carlo, Monaco; *Statistiques annuelles,* (Annual Statistics).

MONACO - AGRICULTURE

Facts on File, 460 Park Avenue South, New York, New York 10016 (800) 443-8323; *The New Book of World Rankings.*

Food and Agricultural Organization of the United Nations (FAO), Via delle Terme di Caracalla, 00100 Rome, Italy (Telephone Number in U.S. (202) 653-2400); *Production Yearbook, The State of Food and Agriculture,* and *Trade Yearbook.*

MONACO - AIRLINE SERVICE

Facts on File, 460 Park Avenue South, New York, New York 10016 (800) 443-8323; *The New Book of World Rankings.*

MONACO - ALUMINUM PRODUCTION AND CONSUMPTION - See MONACO - MINING AND MINERAL PRODUCTS

MONACO - AREA AND DENSITY OF POPULATION

Facts on File, 460 Park Avenue South, New York, New York 10016 (800) 443-8323; *The New Book of World Rankings.*

Food and Agricultural Organization of the United Nations (FAO), Via delle Terme di Caracalla, 00100 Rome, Italy (Telephone Number in U.S. (202) 653-2400); *The State of Food and Agriculture.*

Statistical Office of the United Nations, Publishing Service, New York, New York 10017 (800) 253-9646; *Statistical Yearbook.*

MONACO - BANKING

Facts on File, 460 Park Avenue South, New York, New York 10016 (800) 443-8323; *The New Book of World Rankings.*

MONACO - BARLEY PRODUCTION - See MONACO - CROPS

MONACO - BEER PRODUCTION

Facts on File, 460 Park Avenue South, New York, New York 10016 (800) 443-8323; *The New Book of World Rankings.*

MONACO - BIRTH RATES

Facts on File, 460 Park Avenue South, New York, New York 10016 (800) 443-8323; *The New Book of World Rankings.*

Statistical Office of the United Nations, Publishing Service, New York, New York 10017 (800) 253-9646; *Demographic Yearbook,* and *Statistical Yearbook.*

World Health Organization, Office of Publications, Avenue Appia, CH-1211 Geneva 27, Switzerland (Telephone Number in U.S. (518) 436-9686); *World Health Statistics Annual.*

MONACO - BROADCASTING

Billboard Limited, Post Office Box 9027, 1006 AA Amsterdam, The Netherlands (Telephone Number in U.S. (212) 764-7300); *World Radio TV Handbook.*

Facts on File, 460 Park Avenue South, New York, New York 10016 (800) 443-8323; *The New Book of World Rankings.*

United Nations Educational, Scientific and Cultural Organization (UNESCO), 7 Place de Fontenoy, F-75700 Paris, France (Telephone Number in U.S. (212) 963-5981); *Statistical Yearbook.*

MONACO - CALORIE SUPPLY

Food and Agricultural Organization of the United Nations (FAO), Via delle Terme di Caracalla, 00100 Rome, Italy (Telephone Number in U.S. (202) 653-2400); *The State of Food and Agriculture.*

MONACO - CATTLE - See MONACO - LIVESTOCK AND POULTRY

MONACO - CEMENT PRODUCTION - See MONACO - MINING AND MINERAL PRODUCTS

MONACO - CIGARETTE PRODUCTION - See MONACO - TOBACCO PRODUCTION

MONACO - CLIMATE

Facts on File, 460 Park Avenue South, New York, New York 10016 (800) 443-8323; *The New Book of World Rankings.*

MONACO - COAL PRODUCTION - See MONACO - MINING AND MINERAL PRODUCTS

MONACO - COFFEE PRODUCTION - See MONACO - CROPS

MONACO - CONSTRUCTION INDUSTRY

Facts on File, 460 Park Avenue South, New York, New York 10016 (800) 443-8323; *The New Book of World Rankings.*

MONACO - COPPER PRODUCTION AND CONSUMPTION - See MONACO - MINING AND MINERAL PRODUCTS

MONACO - CORN PRODUCTION - See MONACO - CROPS

MONACO - COTTON PRODUCTION - See MONACO - CROPS

MONACO - CRIME

International Criminal Police Organization (INTERPOL), 26 rue Armengaud, 92210 Saint Cloud, France; *International Crime Statistics.*

Yale University Press, Yale Station, New Haven, Connecticut 06520 (203) 432-0940; *Violence and Crime in Cross-National Perspective.*

MONACO - CROPS

Facts on File, 460 Park Avenue South, New York, New York 10016 (800) 443-8323; *The New Book of World Rankings.*

Food and Agricultural Organization of the United Nations (FAO), Via delle Terme di Caracalla, 00100 Rome, Italy (Telephone Number in U.S. (202) 653-2400); *The State of Food and Agriculture.*

MONACO - DAIRY PRODUCTS

Facts on File, 460 Park Avenue South, New York, New York 10016 (800) 443-8323; *The New Book of World Rankings.*

Food and Agricultural Organization of the United Nations (FAO), Via delle Terme di Caracalla, 00100 Rome, Italy (Telephone Number in U.S. (202) 653-2400); *The State of Food and Agriculture.*

MONACO - DEATH RATES

Statistical Office of the United Nations, Publishing Service, New York, New York 10017 (800) 253-9646; *Statistical Yearbook.*

MONACO - DEMOGRAPHY

Facts on File, 460 Park Avenue South, New York, New York 10016 (800) 443-8323; *The New Book of World Rankings.*

MONACO - DIAMOND PRODUCTION - See MONACO - MINING AND MINERAL PRODUCTS

MONACO - DIVORCE RATES

Facts on File, 460 Park Avenue South, New York, New York 10016 (800) 443-8323; *The New Book of World Rankings.*

Statistical Office of the United Nations, Publishing Service, New York, New York 10017 (800) 253-9646; *Demographic Yearbook,* and *Statistical Yearbook.*

MONACO - ECONOMY

Facts on File, 460 Park Avenue South, New York, New York 10016 (800) 443-8323; *The New Book of World Rankings.*

MONACO - EDUCATION

Facts on File, 460 Park Avenue South, New York, New York 10016 (800) 443-8323; *The New Book of World Rankings.*

United Nations Educational, Scientific and Cultural Organization (UNESCO), 7 Place de Fontenoy, F-75700 Paris, France (Telephone Number in U.S. (212) 963-5981); *Statistical Yearbook.*

MONACO - EGG PRODUCTION AND CONSUMPTION - See MONACO - DAIRY PRODUCTS

MONACO - ELECTRICITY, GAS AND WATER SUPPLY

Facts on File, 460 Park Avenue South, New York, New York 10016 (800) 443-8323; *The New Book of World Rankings.*

MONACO - EMPLOYMENT

Facts on File, 460 Park Avenue South, New York, New York 10016 (800) 443-8323; *The New Book of World Rankings.*

MONACO - ENERGY

Facts on File, 460 Park Avenue South, New York, New York 10016 (800) 443-8323; *The New Book of World Rankings.*

Food and Agricultural Organization of the United Nations (FAO), Via delle Terme di Caracalla, 00100 Rome, Italy (Telephone Number in U.S. (202) 653-2400); *The State of Food and Agriculture.*

MONACO - EXPORTS

Food and Agricultural Organization of the United Nations (FAO), Via delle Terme di Caracalla, 00100 Rome, Italy (Telephone Number in U.S. (202) 653-2400); *The State of Food and Agriculture.*

MONACO - EXTERNAL TRADE

Food and Agricultural Organization of the United Nations (FAO), Via delle Terme di Caracalla, 00100 Rome, Italy (Telephone Number in U.S. (202) 653-2400); *The State of Food and Agriculture,* and *Trade Yearbook.*

MONACO - FARM CROPS - See MONACO - CROPS

MONACO - FERTILITY RATES

Facts on File, 460 Park Avenue South, New York, New York 10016 (800) 443-8323; *The New Book of World Rankings.*

MONACO - FERTILIZER

Food and Agricultural Organization of the United Nations (FAO), Via delle Terme di Caracalla, 00100 Rome, Italy (Telephone Number in U.S. (202) 653-2400); *The State of Food and Agriculture.*

MONACO - FETAL MORTALITY

Statistical Office of the United Nations, Publishing Service, New York, New York 10017 (800) 253-9646; *Demographic Yearbook.*

MONACO - FINANCE

Facts on File, 460 Park Avenue South, New York, New York 10016 (800) 443-8323; *The New Book of World Rankings.*

MONACO - FISHERIES

Facts on File, 460 Park Avenue South, New York, New York 10016 (800) 443-8323; *The New Book of World Rankings.*

Food and Agricultural Organization of the United Nations (FAO), Via delle Terme di Caracalla, 00100 Rome, Italy (Telephone Number in U.S. (202) 653-2400); *The State of Food and Agriculture,* and *Yearbook of Fishery Statistics.*

MONACO - FOOD

Food and Agricultural Organization of the United Nations (FAO), Via delle Terme di Caracalla, 00100 Rome, Italy (Telephone Number in U.S. (202) 653-2400); *Production Yearbook,* and *The State of Food and Agriculture.*

MONACO - FOREIGN TRADE

Facts on File, 460 Park Avenue South, New York, New York 10016 (800) 443-8323; *The New Book of World Rankings.*

Food and Agricultural Organization of the United Nations (FAO), Via delle Terme di Caracalla, 00100 Rome, Italy (Telephone Number in U.S. (202) 653-2400); *The State of Food and Agriculture.*

MONACO - FORESTRY AND FOREST PRODUCTS

Facts on File, 460 Park Avenue South, New York, New York 10016 (800) 443-8323; *The New Book of World Rankings.*

Food and Agricultural Organization of the United Nations (FAO), Via delle Terme di Caracalla, 00100 Rome, Italy (Telephone Number

in U.S. (202) 653-2400); *The State of Food and Agriculture.*

Statistical Office of the United Nations, Publishing Service, New York, New York 10017 (800) 253-9646; *Statistical Yearbook.*

United Nations Educational, Scientific and Cultural Organization (UNESCO), 7 Place de Fontenoy, F-75700 Paris, France (Telephone Number in U.S. (212) 963-5981); *Statistical Yearbook.*

MONACO - GAS PRODUCTION - See MONACO - MINING AND MINERAL PRODUCTS

MONACO - GENERAL MORTALITY

Statistical Office of the United Nations, Publishing Service, New York, New York 10017 (800) 253-9646; *Demographic Yearbook.*

World Health Organization, Office of Publications, Avenue Appia, CH-1211 Geneva 27, Switzerland (Telephone Number in U.S. (518) 436-9686); *World Health Statistics Annual.*

MONACO - GEOGRAPHIC DATA

Facts on File, 460 Park Avenue South, New York, New York 10016 (800) 443-8323; *The New Book of World Rankings.*

MONACO - GOLD PRODUCTION AND CONSUMPTION - See MONACO - MINING AND MINERAL PRODUCTS

MONACO - GRAIN PRODUCTION - See MONACO - CROPS

MONACO - GROSS DOMESTIC PRODUCT

Facts on File, 460 Park Avenue South, New York, New York 10016 (800) 443-8323; *The New Book of World Rankings.*

MONACO - HEALTH

Facts on File, 460 Park Avenue South, New York, New York 10016 (800) 443-8323; *The New Book of World Rankings.*

Statistical Office of the United Nations, Publishing Service, New York, New York 10017 (800) 253-9646; *Statistical Yearbook.*

MONACO - HEALTH AND MEDICAL SERVICES

Statistical Office of the United Nations, Publishing Service, New York, New York 10017 (800) 253-9646; *Statistical Yearbook.*

MONACO - HORSES - See MONACO - LIVESTOCK AND POULTRY

MONACO - HOUSING

Facts on File, 460 Park Avenue South, New York, New York 10016 (800) 443-8323; *The New Book of World Rankings.*

MONACO - IMPORTS

Food and Agricultural Organization of the United Nations (FAO), Via delle Terme di Caracalla, 00100 Rome, Italy (Telephone Number in U.S. (202) 653-2400); *The State of Food and Agriculture.*

MONACO - INDUSTRY

Facts on File, 460 Park Avenue South, New York, New York 10016 (800) 443-8323; *The New Book of World Rankings.*

Statistical Office of the United Nations, Publishing Service, New York, New York 10017 (800) 253-9646; *Statistical Yearbook.*

World Intellectual Property Organization, 34 Chemin des Colombettes, CH-1211 Geneva 20, Switzerland; *Industrial Property Statistics*.

MONACO - INFANT AND MATERNAL MORTALITY

Statistical Office of the United Nations, Publishing Service, New York, New York 10017 (800) 253-9646; *Demographic Yearbook*, and *Statistical Yearbook*.

MONACO - IRON ORE PRODUCTION AND CONSUMPTION - See MONACO - MINING AND MINERAL PRODUCTS

MONACO - LABOR FORCE

Facts on File, 460 Park Avenue South, New York, New York 10016 (800) 443-8323; *The New Book of World Rankings*.

Food and Agricultural Organization of the United Nations (FAO), Via delle Terme di Caracalla, 00100 Rome, Italy (Telephone Number in U.S. (202) 653-2400); *The State of Food and Agriculture*.

MONACO - LAND USE

Food and Agricultural Organization of the United Nations (FAO), Via delle Terme di Caracalla, 00100 Rome, Italy (Telephone Number in U.S. (202) 653-2400); *Production Yearbook*.

MONACO - LIBRARIES

Facts on File, 460 Park Avenue South, New York, New York 10016 (800) 443-8323; *The New Book of World Rankings*.

United Nations Educational, Scientific and Cultural Organization (UNESCO), 7 Place de Fontenoy, F-75700 Paris, France (Telephone Number in U.S. (212) 963-5981); *Statistical Yearbook*.

MONACO - LIVESTOCK AND POULTRY

Facts on File, 460 Park Avenue South, New York, New York 10016 (800) 443-8323; *The New Book of World Rankings*.

Food and Agricultural Organization of the United Nations (FAO), Via delle Terme di Caracalla, 00100 Rome, Italy (Telephone Number in U.S. (202) 653-2400); *Production Yearbook*, and *The State of Food and Agriculture*.

MONACO - MANUFACTURING

Facts on File, 460 Park Avenue South, New York, New York 10016 (800) 443-8323; *The New Book of World Rankings*.

MONACO - MARRIAGE RATES

Facts on File, 460 Park Avenue South, New York, New York 10016 (800) 443-8323; *The New Book of World Rankings*.

Statistical Office of the United Nations, Publishing Service, New York, New York 10017 (800) 253-9646; *Demographic Yearbook*, and *Statistical Yearbook*.

MONACO - MEAT PRODUCTION - See MONACO - LIVESTOCK AND POULTRY

MONACO - MILK PRODUCTION - See MONACO - DAIRY PRODUCTS

MONACO - MINING AND MINERAL PRODUCTS

Facts on File, 460 Park Avenue South, New York, New York 10016 (800) 443-8323; *The New Book of World Rankings*.

MONACO - MOTION PICTURES

Statistical Office of the United Nations, Publishing Service, New York, New York 10017 (800) 253-9646; *Statistical Yearbook*.

MONACO - MUSEUMS

Facts on File, 460 Park Avenue South, New York, New York 10016 (800) 443-8323; *The New Book of World Rankings*.

United Nations Educational, Scientific and Cultural Organization (UNESCO), 7 Place de Fontenoy, F-75700 Paris, France (Telephone Number in U.S. (212) 963-5981); *Statistical Yearbook*.

MONACO - NATALITY - See MONACO - BIRTH RATES

MONACO - NATIONAL INCOME

Facts on File, 460 Park Avenue South, New York, New York 10016 (800) 443-8323; *The New Book of World Rankings*.

MONACO - NATIONAL PRODUCT

Facts on File, 460 Park Avenue South, New York, New York 10016 (800) 443-8323; *The New Book of World Rankings*

MONACO - NATURAL GAS - PRODUCTION - See MONACO - MINING AND MINERAL PRODUCTS

MONACO - NEWSPAPER PRODUCTION - See MONACO - FORESTRY AND FOREST PRODUCTS

MONACO - PATENTS

Statistical Office of the United Nations, Publishing Service, New York, New York 10017 (800) 253-9646; *Statistical Yearbook*.

World Intellectual Property Organization, 34 Chemin des Colombettes, CH-1211 Geneva 20, Switzerland; *Industrial Property Statistics*.

MONACO - PEANUT PRODUCTION - See MONACO - CROPS

MONACO - PERIODICALS

United Nations Educational, Scientific and Cultural Organization (UNESCO), 7 Place de Fontenoy, F-75700 Paris, France (Telephone Number in U.S. (212) 963-5981); *Statistical Yearbook*.

MONACO - PESTICIDE USE

Food and Agricultural Organization of the United Nations (FAO), Via delle Terme di Caracalla, 00100 Rome, Italy (Telephone Number in U.S. (202) 653-2400); *The State of Food and Agriculture*.

MONACO - PETROLEUM INDUSTRY

Facts on File, 460 Park Avenue South, New York, New York 10016 (800) 443-8323; *The New Book of World Rankings*.

Food and Agricultural Organization of the United Nations (FAO), Via delle Terme di Caracalla, 00100 Rome, Italy (Telephone Number in U.S. (202) 653-2400); *The State of Food and Agriculture*.

MONACO - PIGS - See MONACO - LIVESTOCK AND POULTRY

MONACO - POPULATION

Facts on File, 460 Park Avenue South, New York, New York 10016 (800) 443-8323; *The New Book of World Rankings*.

Food and Agricultural Organization of the United Nations (FAO), Via delle Terme di Caracalla, 00100 Rome, Italy (Telephone Number in U.S. (202) 653-2400); *Production Yearbook*.

International Labour Office, I.L.O. Publications, CH-1211, Geneva 22, Switzerland; *Yearbook of Labour Statistics*.

Statistical Office of the United Nations, Publishing Service, New York, New York 10017 (800) 253-9646; *Demographic Yearbook*, and *Statistical Yearbook*.

World Health Organization, Office of Publications, Avenue Appia, CH-1211 Geneva 27, Switzerland (Telephone Number in U.S. (518) 436-9686); *World Health Statistics Annual*.

MONACO - POST OFFICES

Facts on File, 460 Park Avenue South, New York, New York 10016 (800) 443-8323; *The New Book of World Rankings*.

MONACO - POTATO PRODUCTION - See MONACO - CROPS

MONACO - PRICES

Facts on File, 460 Park Avenue South, New York, New York 10016 (800) 443-8323; *The New Book of World Rankings*.

Food and Agricultural Organization of the United Nations (FAO), Via delle Terme di Caracalla, 00100 Rome, Italy (Telephone Number in U.S. (202) 653-2400); *Production Yearbook*, and *The State of Food and Agriculture*.

MONACO - PRODUCTION

Facts on File, 460 Park Avenue South, New York, New York 10016 (800) 443-8323; *The New Book of World Rankings*.

MONACO - PUBLIC FINANCE

Facts on File, 460 Park Avenue South, New York, New York 10016 (800) 443-8323; *The New Book of World Rankings*.

MONACO - RADIO BROADCASTING - See MONACO - BROADCASTING

MONACO - RELIGION

Facts on File, 460 Park Avenue South, New York, New York 10016 (800) 443-8323; *The New Book of World Rankings*.

MONACO - RICE PRODUCTION - See MONACO - CROPS

MONACO - RUBBER PRODUCTION AND CONSUMPTION

Facts on File, 460 Park Avenue South, New York, New York 10016 (800) 443-8323; *The New Book of World Rankings*.

MONACO - SENIOR CITIZENS

Facts on File, 460 Park Avenue South, New York, New York 10016 (800) 443-8323; *The New Book of World Rankings*.

MONACO - SHEEP - See MONACO - LIVESTOCK AND POULTRY

MONACO - SILVER PRODUCTION AND CONSUMPTION - See MONACO - MINING AND MINERAL PRODUCTS

MONACO - SOCIAL DATA

Facts on File, 460 Park Avenue South, New York, New York 10016 (800) 443-8323; *The New Book of World Rankings*.

MONACO - STEEL PRODUCTION - See MONACO - MINING AND MINERAL PRODUCTS

MONACO - STOCKS - COMMODITY - MARKET PRICE - INDEX

Food and Agricultural Organization of the United Nations (FAO), Via delle Terme di Caracalla, 00100 Rome, Italy (Telephone Number in U.S. (202) 653-2400); *The State of Food and Agriculture*.

MONACO - SUGAR PRODUCTION AND CONSUMPTION - See MONACO - CROPS

MONACO - TELEGRAPH SERVICE

Statistical Office of the United Nations, Publishing Service, New York, New York 10017 (800) 253-9646; *Statistical Yearbook*.

MONACO - TELEPHONES IN USE

American Telephone and Telegraph Company, 26 Parsippany Road, Whippany, New Jersey 07981 (800) 338-4038; *The World's Telephones*.

Statistical Office of the United Nations, Publishing Service, New York, New York 10017 (800) 253-9646; *Statistical Yearbook*.

MONACO - TELEVISION BROADCASTING - See MONACO - BROADCASTING

MONACO - THEATRE

United Nations Educational, Scientific and Cultural Organization (UNESCO), 7 Place de Fontenoy, F-75700 Paris, France (Telephone Number in U.S. (212) 963-5981); *Statistical Yearbook*.

MONACO - TOBACCO PRODUCTION

Facts on File, 460 Park Avenue South, New York, New York 10016 (800) 443-8323; *The New Book of World Rankings*.

MONACO - TOURISM

Facts on File, 460 Park Avenue South, New York, New York 10016 (800) 443-8323; *The New Book of World Rankings*.

Statistical Office of the United Nations, Publishing Service, New York, New York 10017 (800) 253-9646; *Statistical Yearbook*.

World Tourism Organization, Calle Capitan Haya 42, E-28020 Madrid, Spain; *Yearbook of Tourism Statistics*.

MONACO - TRADE - See MONACO - FOREIGN TRADE

MONACO - TRADEMARKS AND SERVICE MARKS

Statistical Office of the United Nations, Publishing Service, New York, New York 10017 (800) 253-9646; *Statistical Yearbook*.

World Intellectual Property Organization, 34 Chemin des Colombettes, CH-1211 Geneva 20, Switzerland; *Industrial Property Statistics.*

MONACO - TRANSPORTATION AND COMMUNICATIONS

Facts on File, 460 Park Avenue South, New York, New York 10016 (800) 443-8323; *The New Book of World Rankings.*

MONACO - VITAL STATISTICS

Statistical Office of the United Nations, Publishing Service, New York, New York 10017 (800) 253-9646; *Statistical Yearbook.*

World Health Organization, Office of Publications, Avenue Appia, CH-1211 Geneva 27, Switzerland (Telephone Number in U.S. (518) 436-9686); *World Health Statistics Annual.*

MONACO - WEATHER

Facts on File, 460 Park Avenue South, New York, New York 10016 (800) 443-8323; *The New Book of World Rankings.*

MONACO - WHEAT PRODUCTION - See MONACO - CROPS

MONACO - WINE PRODUCTION

Facts on File, 460 Park Avenue South, New York, New York 10016 (800) 443-8323; *The New Book of World Rankings.*

MONACO - WOOL PRODUCTION

Facts on File, 460 Park Avenue South, New York, New York 10016 (800) 443-8323; *The New Book of World Rankings.*

MONACO - ZOOS AND BOTANICAL GARDENS

United Nations Educational, Scientific and Cultural Organization (UNESCO), 7 Place de Fontenoy, F-75700 Paris, France (Telephone Number in U.S. (212) 963-5981); *Statistical Yearbook.*

MONETARY SYSTEM AND BANKS - FLOW OF FUNDS

Board of Governors of the Federal Reserve System, Twentieth Street and Constitution Avenue, NW, Washington, D.C. 20551 (202) 452-3000; *Annual Statistical Digest.*

MONEY MARKET ACCOUNTS - FUNDS

Board of Governors of the Federal Reserve System, Twentieth Street and Constitution Avenue, NW, Washington, D.C. 20551 (202) 452-3000; *Annual Statistical Digest, Money Stock, Liquid Assets, and Debt Measures, Federal Reserve Statistical Release,* and *Monthly Survey of Selected Deposits.*

MONEY MARKET ACCOUNTS - FUNDS - FAMILIES USING

Board of Governors of the Federal Reserve System, Twentieth Street and Constitution Avenue, NW, Washington, D.C. 20551 (202) 452-3000; *Annual Statistical Digest,* and *Federal Reserve Bulletin.*

MONEY MARKET RATES

Board of Governors of the Federal Reserve System, Twentieth Street and Constitution Avenue, NW, Washington, D.C. 20551 (202) 452-3000; *Federal Reserve Bulletin, Annual Statistical Digest, Money Stock, Liquid Assets, and Debt Measures, Federal Reserve Statistical Release,* and *Monthly Survey of Selected Deposits.*

Financial Rates, Inc., 860 U.S. Highway One, North Palm Beach, Florida 33408 (407) 627-7330; *Bank Rate Monitor.*

IBC/Donoghue Inc., 290 Eliot Street, Ashland, Massachusetts 01721 (508) 881-2800; *IBC/Donoghue's Money Market Insight.*

International Monetary Fund, 700 Nineteenth Street, NW, Washington, D.C. 20431 (202) 623-7000; *International Financial Statistics.*

MONEY ORDERS

Board of Governors of the Federal Reserve System, 20th Street and Constitution Avenue, NW, Washington, D.C. 20551 (202) 452-3000; *Federal Reserve Bulletin.*

U.S. Postal Service, 475 L'Enfant Plaza West, SW, Washington, D.C. 20549 (202) 433-5100; *Annual Report of the Postmaster General.*

MONEY SUPPLY - STOCK

Board of Governors of the Federal Reserve System, Twentieth Street and Constitution Avenue, NW, Washington, D.C. 20551 (202) 452-3000; *Federal Reserve Bulletin, Annual Statistical Digest, Money Stock, Liquid Assets, and Debt Measures Federal Reserve Statistical Release,* and *Monthly Survey of Selected Deposits.*

Mongolia - National Statistical Office

Central Statistical Office, Ulan Bator, Mongolia.

Mongolia - Primary Statistics Source

Central Statistical Office, Ulan Bator, Mongolia; *National Economy of the MPR for 60 Years.*

MONGOLIA - AGRICULTURE

Facts on File, 460 Park Avenue South, New York, New York 10016 (800) 443-8323; *The New Book of World Rankings.*

Food and Agricultural Organization of the United Nations (FAO), Via delle Terme di Caracalla, 00100 Rome, Italy (Telephone Number in U.S. (202) 653-2400); *Production Yearbook,* and *The State of Food and Agriculture, The State of Food and Agriculture,* and *Trade Yearbook.*

Statistical Office of the United Nations, Publishing Service, New York, New York 10017 (800) 253-9646; *Statistical Yearbook,* and *Statistical Yearbook for Asia and the Pacific.*

Times Books, 201 East 50th Street, New York, New York 10022 (212) 751-2600; *The Economist Book of Vital World Statistics.*

MONGOLIA - AIRLINE SERVICE

The Economist Intelligence Unit (Asia) Limited, 10th Floor, Luk Kwok Centre, 72 Gloucester Road, Wanchai, Hong Kong (Phone Number in U.S. (800) 938-4685); *Asian Market Atlas.*

Facts on File, 460 Park Avenue South, New York, New York 10016 (800) 443-8323; *The New Book of World Rankings.*

MONGOLIA - ALUMINUM PRODUCTION AND CONSUMPTION - See MONGOLIA - MINING AND MINERAL PRODUCTS

MONGOLIA - ANIMAL HEALTH

Food and Agricultural Organization of the United Nations (FAO), Via delle Terme di Caracalla, 00100 Rome, Italy (Telephone Number in U.S. (202) 653-2400); *Animal Health Yearbook.*

MONGOLIA - AREA AND DENSITY OF POPULATION

Facts on File, 460 Park Avenue South, New York, New York 10016 (800) 443-8323; *The New Book of World Rankings.*

Food and Agricultural Organization of the United Nations (FAO), Via delle Terme di Caracalla, 00100 Rome, Italy (Telephone Number in U.S. (202) 653-2400); *The State of Food and Agriculture.*

Statistical Office of the United Nations, Publishing Service, New York, New York 10017 (800) 253-9646; *Statistical Yearbook.*

Times Books, 201 East 50th Street, New York, New York 10022 (212) 751-2600; *The Economist Book of Vital World Statistics.*

MONGOLIA - ARMS EXPORTS AND IMPORTS

U.S. Arms Control and Disarmament Agency, 320 Twenty-first Street, NW, Washington, D.C. 20451 (202) 647-8677; *World Military Expenditures and Arms Transfers.*

MONGOLIA - BANKING

Facts on File, 460 Park Avenue South, New York, New York 10016 (800) 443-8323; *The New Book of World Rankings.*

MONGOLIA - BARLEY PRODUCTION - See MONGOLIA - CROPS

MONGOLIA - BEER PRODUCTION

Facts on File, 460 Park Avenue South, New York, New York 10016 (800) 443-8323; *The New Book of World Rankings.*

Statistical Office of the United Nations, Publishing Service, New York, New York 10017 (800) 253-9646; *Statistical Yearbook.*

MONGOLIA - BIRTH RATES

The Economist Intelligence Unit (Asia) Limited, 10th Floor, Luk Kwok Centre, 72 Gloucester Road, Wanchai, Hong Kong (Phone Number in U.S. (800) 938-4685); *Asian Market Atlas.*

Facts on File, 460 Park Avenue South, New York, New York 10016 (800) 443-8323; *The New Book of World Rankings.*

Statistical Office of the United Nations, Publishing Service, New York, New York 10017 (800) 253-9646; *Demographic Yearbook,* and *Statistical Yearbook.*

Times Books, 201 East 50th Street, New York, New York 10022 (212) 751-2600; *The Economist Book of Vital World Statistics.*

MONGOLIA - BROADCASTING

Billboard Limited, Post Office Box 9027, 1006 AA Amsterdam, The Netherlands (Telephone Number in U.S. (212) 764-7300); *World Radio TV Handbook.*

Times Books, 201 East 50th Street, New York, New York 10022 (212) 751-2600; *The Economist Book of Vital World Statistics.*

MONGOLIA - BUILDING CONSTRUCTION

Statistical Office of the United Nations, Publishing Service, New York, New York 10017 (800) 253-9646; *Statistical Yearbook.*

MONGOLIA - BUTTER PRODUCTION - See MONGOLIA - DAIRY PRODUCTS

MONGOLIA - CALORIE SUPPLY

Food and Agricultural Organization of the United Nations (FAO), Via delle Terme di Caracalla, 00100 Rome, Italy (Telephone Number in U.S. (202) 653-2400); *The State of Food and Agriculture.*

MONGOLIA - CATTLE - See MONGOLIA - LIVESTOCK AND POULTRY

MONGOLIA - CEMENT PRODUCTION - See MONGOLIA - MINING AND MINERAL PRODUCTS

MONGOLIA - CHEESE PRODUCTION AND CONSUMPTION - See MONGOLIA - DAIRY PRODUCTS

MONGOLIA - CIGARETTE PRODUCTION - See MONGOLIA - TOBACCO PRODUCTION

MONGOLIA - CLIMATE

Facts on File, 460 Park Avenue South, New York, New York 10016 (800) 443-8323; *The New Book of World Rankings.*

MONGOLIA - COAL PRODUCTION - See MONGOLIA - MINING AND MINERAL PRODUCTS

MONGOLIA - COFFEE PRODUCTION AND CONSUMPTION - See MONGOLIA - CROPS

MONGOLIA - COMMUNICATIONS

Statistical Office of the United Nations, Publishing Service, New York, New York 10017 (800) 253-9646; *Statistical Yearbook for Asia and the Pacific.*

MONGOLIA - CONSTRUCTION INDUSTRY

Facts on File, 460 Park Avenue South, New York, New York 10016 (800) 443-8323; *The New Book of World Rankings.*

Statistical Office of the United Nations, Publishing Service, New York, New York 10017 (800) 253-9646; *Statistical Yearbook.*

MONGOLIA - COPPER PRODUCTION AND CONSUMPTION - See MONGOLIA - MINING AND MINERAL PRODUCTS

MONGOLIA - CORN PRODUCTION - See MONGOLIA - CROPS

MONGOLIA - COTTON PRODUCTION - See MONGOLIA - CROPS

MONGOLIA - CROPS

The Economist Intelligence Unit (Asia) Limited, 10th Floor, Luk Kwok Centre, 72 Gloucester Road, Wanchai, Hong Kong (Phone Number in U.S. (800) 938-4685); *Asian Market Atlas.*

Facts on File, 460 Park Avenue South, New York, New York 10016 (800) 443-8323; *The New Book of World Rankings.*

Food and Agricultural Organization of the United Nations (FAO), Via delle Terme di Caracalla, 00100 Rome, Italy (Telephone Number in U.S. (202) 653-2400); *Production Yearbook,* and *The State of Food and Agriculture.*

Statistical Office of the United Nations, Publishing Service, New York, New York 10017 (800) 253-9646; *Statistical Yearbook.*

MONGOLIA - DAIRY PRODUCTS

Facts on File, 460 Park Avenue South, New York, New York 10016 (800) 443-8323; *The New Book of World Rankings.*

Food and Agricultural Organization of the United Nations (FAO), Via delle Terme di Caracalla, 00100 Rome, Italy (Telephone Number in U.S. (202) 653-2400); *Production Yearbook,* and *The State of Food and Agriculture.*

Statistical Office of the United Nations, Publishing Service, New York, New York 10017 (800) 253-9646; *Statistical Yearbook.*

MONGOLIA - DEATH RATES

The Economist Intelligence Unit (Asia) Limited, 10th Floor, Luk Kwok Centre, 72 Gloucester Road, Wanchai, Hong Kong (Phone Number in U.S. (800) 938-4685); *Asian Market Atlas.*

Statistical Office of the United Nations, Publishing Service, New York, New York 10017 (800) 253-9646; *Statistical Yearbook.*

Times Books, 201 East 50th Street, New York, New York 10022 (212) 751-2600; *The Economist Book of Vital World Statistics.*

MONGOLIA - DEFENSE EXPENDITURES

U.S. Arms Control and Disarmament Agency, 320 Twenty-first Street, NW, Washington, D.C. 20451 (202) 647-8677; *World Military Expenditures and Arms Transfers.*

MONGOLIA - DEMOGRAPHY

The Economist Intelligence Unit (Asia) Limited, 10th Floor, Luk Kwok Centre, 72 Gloucester Road, Wanchai, Hong Kong (Phone Number in U.S. (800) 938-4685); *Asian Market Atlas.*

Facts on File, 460 Park Avenue South, New York, New York 10016 (800) 443-8323; *The New Book of World Rankings.*

MONGOLIA - DIAMOND PRODUCTION - See MONGOLIA - MINING AND MINERAL PRODUCTS

MONGOLIA - DIVORCE RATES

Facts on File, 460 Park Avenue South, New York, New York 10016 (800) 443-8323; *The New Book of World Rankings.*

Statistical Office of the United Nations, Publishing Service, New York, New York 10017 (800) 253-9646; *Demographic Yearbook.*

MONGOLIA - ECONOMY

Facts on File, 460 Park Avenue South, New York, New York 10016 (800) 443-8323; *The New Book of World Rankings.*

MONGOLIA - EDUCATION

The Economist Intelligence Unit (Asia) Limited, 10th Floor, Luk Kwok Centre, 72 Gloucester Road, Wanchai, Hong Kong (Phone Number in U.S. (800) 938-4685); *Asian Market Atlas.*

Facts on File, 460 Park Avenue South, New York, New York 10016 (800) 443-8323; *The New Book of World Rankings.*

Statistical Office of the United Nations, Publishing Service, New York, New York 10017 (800) 253-9646; *Statistical Yearbook for Asia and the Pacific.*

Times Books, 201 East 50th Street, New York, New York 10022 (212) 751-2600; *The Economist Book of Vital World Statistics.*

United Nations Educational, Scientific and Cultural Organization (UNESCO), 7 Place de Fontenoy, F-75700 Paris, France (Telephone Number in U.S. (212) 963-5981); *Statistical Yearbook.*

MONGOLIA - EGG PRODUCTION AND CONSUMPTION - See MONGOLIA - DAIRY PRODUCTS

MONGOLIA - ELECTRICITY

Facts on File, 460 Park Avenue South, New York, New York 10016 (800) 443-8323; *The New Book of World Rankings.*

Statistical Office of the United Nations, Publishing Service, New York, New York 10017 (800) 253-9646; *Electric Power in Asia and the Pacific,* and *Statistical Yearbook.*

Times Books, 201 East 50th Street, New York, New York 10022 (212) 751-2600; *The Economist Book of Vital World Statistics.*

MONGOLIA EMPLOYMENT

Facts on File, 460 Park Avenue South, New York, New York 10016 (800) 443-8323; *The New Book of World Rankings.*

Statistical Office of the United Nations, Publishing Service, New York, New York 10017 (800) 253-9646; *Statistical Yearbook.*

MONGOLIA - ENERGY

Facts on File, 460 Park Avenue South, New York, New York 10016 (800) 443-8323; *The New Book of World Rankings.*

Food and Agricultural Organization of the United Nations (FAO), Via delle Terme di Caracalla, 00100 Rome, Italy (Telephone Number in U.S. (202) 653-2400); *The State of Food and Agriculture.*

Statistical Office of the United Nations, Publishing Service, New York, New York 10017 (800) 253-9646; *Energy Statistics Yearbook, Statistical Yearbook,* and *World Energy Supplies.*

Times Books, 201 East 50th Street, New York, New York 10022 (212) 751-2600; *The Economist Book of Vital World Statistics.*

MONGOLIA - EXCHANGE RATES

The Economist Intelligence Unit (Asia) Limited, 10th Floor, Luk Kwok Centre, 72 Gloucester Road, Wanchai, Hong Kong (Phone Number in U.S. (800) 938-4685); *Asian Market Atlas.*

Statistical Office of the United Nations, Publishing Service, New York, New York 10017 (800) 253-9646; *Statistical Yearbook.*

MONGOLIA - EXPORTS

The Economist Intelligence Unit (Asia) Limited, 10th Floor, Luk Kwok Centre, 72 Gloucester Road, Wanchai, Hong Kong (Phone Number in U.S. (800) 938-4685); *Asian Market Atlas.*

Food and Agricultural Organization of the United Nations (FAO), Via delle Terme di Caracalla, 00100 Rome, Italy (Telephone Number in U.S. (202) 653-2400); *The State of Food and Agriculture.*

International Monetary Fund, 700 Nineteenth Street, NW, Washington, D.C. 20431 (202) 623-7000; *Direction of Trade Statistics*.

MONGOLIA - EXTERNAL TRADE

Food and Agricultural Organization of the United Nations (FAO), Via delle Terme di Caracalla, 00100 Rome, Italy (Telephone Number in U.S. (202) 653-2400); *The State of Food and Agriculture*, and *Trade Yearbook*.

Statistical Office of the United Nations, Publishing Service, New York, New York 10017 (800) 253-9646; *Statistical Yearbook for Asia and the Pacific*.

MONGOLIA - FARM CROPS - See MONGOLIA - CROPS

MONGOLIA - FERTILITY RATES

Facts on File, 460 Park Avenue South, New York, New York 10016 (800) 443-8323; *The New Book of World Rankings*.

Times Books, 201 East 50th Street, New York, New York 10022 (212) 751-2600; *The Economist Book of Vital World Statistics*.

MONGOLIA - FERTILIZER

Food and Agricultural Organization of the United Nations (FAO), Via delle Terme di Caracalla, 00100 Rome, Italy (Telephone Number in U.S. (202) 653-2400); *Fertilizer Yearbook*, and *The State of Food and Agriculture*.

Statistical Office of the United Nations, Publishing Service, New York, New York 10017 (800) 253-9646; *Statistical Yearbook*.

MONGOLIA - FETAL MORTALITY

Statistical Office of the United Nations, Publishing Service, New York, New York 10017 (800) 253-9646; *Demographic Yearbook*.

MONGOLIA - FINANCE

Facts on File, 460 Park Avenue South, New York, New York 10016 (800) 443-8323; *The New Book of World Rankings*.

Statistical Office of the United Nations, Publishing Service, New York, New York 10017 (800) 253-9646; *Statistical Yearbook for Asia and the Pacific*.

MONGOLIA - FISHERIES

Facts on File, 460 Park Avenue South, New York, New York 10016 (800) 443-8323; *The New Book of World Rankings*.

Food and Agricultural Organization of the United Nations (FAO), Via delle Terme di Caracalla, 00100 Rome, Italy (Telephone Number in U.S. (202) 653-2400); *The State of Food and Agriculture*, and *Yearbook of Fishery Statistics*.

MONGOLIA - FLAX PRODUCTION - See MONGOLIA - TEXTILE INDUSTRY

MONGOLIA - FLOUR PRODUCTION

Statistical Office of the United Nations, Publishing Service, New York, New York 10017 (800) 253-9646; *Statistical Yearbook*.

MONGOLIA - FOOD

Food and Agricultural Organization of the United Nations (FAO), Via delle Terme di Caracalla, 00100 Rome, Italy (Telephone Number in U.S. (202) 653-2400); *Production Yearbook*, and *The State of Food and Agriculture*.

Statistical Office of the United Nations, Publishing Service, New York, New York 10017 (800) 253-9646; *Statistical Yearbook for Asia and the Pacific*.

MONGOLIA - FOREIGN TRADE

The Economist Intelligence Unit (Asia) Limited, 10th Floor, Luk Kwok Centre, 72 Gloucester Road, Wanchai, Hong Kong (Phone Number in U.S. (800) 938-4685); *Asian Market Atlas*.

Facts on File, 460 Park Avenue South, New York, New York 10016 (800) 443-8323; *The New Book of World Rankings*.

Food and Agricultural Organization of the United Nations (FAO), Via delle Terme di Caracalla, 00100 Rome, Italy (Telephone Number in U.S. (202) 653-2400); *The State of Food and Agriculture*.

Statistical Office of the United Nations, Publishing Service, New York, New York 10017 (800) 253-9646; *Statistical Yearbook*.

MONGOLIA - FORESTRY AND FOREST PRODUCTS

The Economist Intelligence Unit (Asia) Limited, 10th Floor, Luk Kwok Centre, 72 Gloucester Road, Wanchai, Hong Kong (Phone Number in U.S. (800) 938-4685); *Asian Market Atlas*.

Facts on File, 460 Park Avenue South, New York, New York 10016 (800) 443-8323; *The New Book of World Rankings*.

Food and Agricultural Organization of the United Nations (FAO), Via delle Terme di Caracalla, 00100 Rome, Italy (Telephone Number in U.S. (202) 653-2400); *The State of Food and Agriculture*, and *Yearbook of Forest Products*.

Statistical Office of the United Nations, Publishing Service, New York, New York 10017 (800) 253-9646; *Statistical Yearbook*.

United Nations Educational, Scientific and Cultural Organization (UNESCO), 7 Place de Fontenoy, F-75700 Paris, France (Telephone Number in U.S. (212) 963-5981); *Statistical Yearbook*.

MONGOLIA - GAS PRODUCTION - See MONGOLIA - MINING AND MINERAL PRODUCTS

MONGOLIA - GENERAL INDUSTRIAL STATISTICS

Statistical Office of the United Nations, Publishing Service, New York, New York 10017 (800) 253-9646; *Industrial Statistics Yearbook*.

MONGOLIA - GENERAL MORTALITY

Statistical Office of the United Nations, Publishing Service, New York, New York 10017 (800) 253-9640; *Demographic Yearbook*.

MONGOLIA - GEOGRAPHIC DATA

Facts on File, 460 Park Avenue South, New York, New York 10016 (800) 443-8323; *The New Book of World Rankings*.

MONGOLIA - GOLD PRODUCTION AND CONSUMPTION - See MONGOLIA - MINING AND MINERAL PRODUCTS

MONGOLIA - GRAIN PRODUCTION - See MONGOLIA - CROPS

MONGOLIA - GROSS DOMESTIC PRODUCT

The Economist Intelligence Unit (Asia) Limited, 10th Floor, Luk Kwok Centre, 72 Gloucester Road, Wanchai, Hong Kong (Phone Number in U.S. (800) 938-4685); *Asian Market Atlas*.

Facts on File, 460 Park Avenue South, New York, New York 10016 (800) 443-8323; *The New Book of World Rankings*.

Times Books, 201 East 50th Street, New York, New York 10022 (212) 751-2600; *The Economist Book of Vital World Statistics*.

MONGOLIA - GROSS NATIONAL PRODUCT

U.S. Arms Control and Disarmament Agency, 320 Twenty-first Street, NW, Washington, D.C. 20451 (202) 647-8677; *World Military Expenditures and Arms Transfers*.

MONGOLIA - HEALTH

The Economist Intelligence Unit (Asia) Limited, 10th Floor, Luk Kwok Centre, 72 Gloucester Road, Wanchai, Hong Kong (Phone Number in U.S. (800) 938-4685); *Asian Market Atlas*.

Facts on File, 460 Park Avenue South, New York, New York 10016 (800) 443-8323; *The New Book of World Rankings*.

Statistical Office of the United Nations, Publishing Service, New York, New York 10017 (800) 253-9646; *Statistical Yearbook*.

Times Books, 201 East 50th Street, New York, New York 10022 (212) 751-2600; *The Economist Book of Vital World Statistics*.

MONGOLIA - HEALTH AND MEDICAL SERVICES

Statistical Office of the United Nations, Publishing Service, New York, New York 10017 (800) 253-9646; *Statistical Yearbook*.

MONGOLIA - HIDE PRODUCTION

Food and Agricultural Organization of the United Nations (FAO), Via delle Terme di Caracalla, 00100 Rome, Italy (Telephone Number in U.S. (202) 653-2400); *Production Yearbook*.

MONGOLIA - HIGHWAYS

The Economist Intelligence Unit (Asia) Limited, 10th Floor, Luk Kwok Centre, 72 Gloucester Road, Wanchai, Hong Kong (Phone Number in U.S. (800) 938-4685); *Asian Market Atlas*.

MONGOLIA - HORSES - See MONGOLIA - LIVESTOCK AND POULTRY

MONGOLIA - HOUSING CONSTRUCTION - See MONGOLIA - CONSTRUCTION INDUSTRY

MONGOLIA - ILLITERATE POPULATION

United Nations Educational, Scientific and Cultural Organization (UNESCO), 7 Place de Fontenoy, F-75700 Paris, France (Telephone Number in U.S. (212) 963-5981); *Statistical Yearbook*.

MONGOLIA - IMPORTS

The Economist Intelligence Unit (Asia) Limited, 10th Floor, Luk Kwok Centre, 72 Gloucester Road, Wanchai, Hong Kong (Phone Number in U.S. (800) 938-4685); *Asian Market Atlas*.

Food and Agricultural Organization of the United Nations (FAO), Via delle Terme di Caracalla, 00100 Rome, Italy (Telephone Number in U.S. (202) 653-2400); *The State of Food and Agriculture*.

International Monetary Fund, 700 Nineteenth Street, NW, Washington, D.C. 20431 (202) 623-7000; *Direction of Trade Statistics*.

MONGOLIA - INDUSTRY

Facts on File, 460 Park Avenue South, New York, New York 10016 (800) 443-8323; *The New Book of World Rankings*.

Statistical Office of the United Nations, Publishing Service, New York, New York 10017 (800) 253-9646; *Statistical Yearbook*, and *Statistical Yearbook for Asia and the Pacific*.

World Intellectual Property Organization, 34 Chemin des Colombettes, CH-1211 Geneva 20, Switzerland; *Industrial Property Statistics*.

MONGOLIA - INFANT AND MATERNAL MORTALITY

The Economist Intelligence Unit (Asia) Limited, 10th Floor, Luk Kwok Centre, 72 Gloucester Road, Wanchai, Hong Kong (Phone Number in U.S. (800) 938-4685); *Asian Market Atlas*.

Statistical Office of the United Nations, Publishing Service, New York, New York 10017 (800) 253-9646; *Demographic Yearbook*.

Times Books, 201 East 50th Street, New York, New York 10022 (212) 751-2600; *The Economist Book of Vital World Statistics*.

MONGOLIA - INTERNAL TRADE

Statistical Office of the United Nations, Publishing Service, New York, New York 10017 (800) 253-9646; *Statistical Yearbook for Asia and the Pacific*.

MONGOLIA - IRON ORE PRODUCTION AND CONSUMPTION - See MONGOLIA - MINING AND MINERAL PRODUCTS

MONGOLIA - LABOR FORCE

The Economist Intelligence Unit (Asia) Limited, 10th Floor, Luk Kwok Centre, 72 Gloucester Road, Wanchai, Hong Kong (Phone Number in U.S. (800) 938-4685); *Asian Market Atlas*.

Facts on File, 460 Park Avenue South, New York, New York 10016 (800) 443-8323; *The New Book of World Rankings*.

Food and Agricultural Organization of the United Nations (FAO), Via delle Terme di Caracalla, 00100 Rome, Italy (Telephone Number in U.S. (202) 653-2400); *The State of Food and Agriculture*.

MONGOLIA - LAND USE

Food and Agricultural Organization of the United Nations (FAO), Via delle Terme di Caracalla, 00100 Rome, Italy (Telephone Number in U.S. (202) 653-2400); *Production Yearbook*.

MONGOLIA - LIBRARIES

Facts on File, 460 Park Avenue South, New York, New York 10016 (800) 443-8323; *The New Book of World Rankings*.

MONGOLIA - LIFE EXPECTANCY

The Economist Intelligence Unit (Asia) Limited, 10th Floor, Luk Kwok Centre, 72 Gloucester Road, Wanchai, Hong Kong (Phone

Number in U.S. (800) 938-4685); *Asian Market Atlas.*

MONGOLIA - LIGNITE PRODUCTION - See MONGOLIA - MINING AND MINERAL PRODUCTS

MONGOLIA - LIVESTOCK AND POULTRY

Facts on File, 460 Park Avenue South, New York, New York 10016 (800) 443-8323; *The New Book of World Rankings.*

Food and Agricultural Organization of the United Nations (FAO), Via delle Terme di Caracalla, 00100 Rome, Italy (Telephone Number in U.S. (202) 653-2400); *Production Yearbook,* and *The State of Food and Agriculture.*

Statistical Office of the United Nations, Publishing Service, New York, New York 10017 (800) 253-9646; *Statistical Yearbook.*

MONGOLIA - LIVING LEVELS

Times Books, 201 East 50th Street, New York, New York 10022 (212) 751-2600; *The Economist Book of Vital World Statistics.*

MONGOLIA - MANPOWER

Statistical Office of the United Nations, Publishing Service, New York, New York 10017 (800) 253-9646; *Statistical Yearbook for Asia and the Pacific.*

MONGOLIA - MANUFACTURING

Facts on File, 460 Park Avenue South, New York, New York 10016 (800) 443-8323; *The New Book of World Rankings.*

Statistical Office of the United Nations, Publishing Service, New York, New York 10017 (800) 253-9646; *Statistical Yearbook.*

MONGOLIA - MARRIAGE

Facts on File, 460 Park Avenue South, New York, New York 10016 (800) 443-8323; *The New Book of World Rankings.*

Statistical Office of the United Nations, Publishing Service, New York, New York 10017 (800) 253-9646; *Demographic Yearbook.*

MONGOLIA - MEAT PRODUCTION - See MONGOLIA - LIVESTOCK AND POULTRY

MONGOLIA - MERCHANT SHIPPING

Times Books, 201 East 50th Street, New York, New York 10022 (212) 751-2600; *The Economist Book of Vital World Statistics.*

MONGOLIA - MILK PRODUCTION - See MONGOLIA - DAIRY PRODUCTS

MONGOLIA - MINING AND MINERAL PRODUCTS

Facts on File, 460 Park Avenue South, New York, New York 10016 (800) 443-8323; *The New Book of World Rankings.*

Statistical Office of the United Nations, Publishing Service, New York, New York 10017 (800) 253-9646; *Statistical Yearbook.*

MONGOLIA - MILITARY

The Economist Intelligence Unit (Asia) Limited, 10th Floor, Luk Kwok Centre, 72 Gloucester Road, Wanchai, Hong Kong (Phone Number in U.S. (800) 938-4685); *Asian Market Atlas.*

The International Institute for Strategic Studies, 23 Tavistock Street, London WC2E 7NQ, England; *The Military Balance.*

U.S. Arms Control and Disarmament Agency, 320 Twenty-first Street, NW, Washington, D.C. 20451 (202) 647-8677; *World Military Expenditures and Arms Transfers.*

MONGOLIA - MONEY EXCHANGE RATE

Statistical Office of the United Nations, Publishing Service, New York, New York 10017 (800) 253-9646; *Statistical Yearbook.*

MONGOLIA - MOTION PICTURES

Statistical Office of the United Nations, Publishing Service, New York, New York 10017 (800) 253-9646; *Statistical Yearbook.*

MONGOLIA - MUSEUMS

Facts on File, 460 Park Avenue South, New York, New York 10016 (800) 443-8323; *The New Book of World Rankings.*

United Nations Educational, Scientific and Cultural Organization (UNESCO), 7 Place de Fontenoy, F-75700 Paris, France (Telephone Number in U.S. (212) 963-5981); *Statistical Yearbook.*

MONGOLIA - NATALITY - See MONGOLIA - BIRTH RATES

MONGOLIA - NATIONAL ACCOUNTS

Statistical Office of the United Nations, Publishing Service, New York, New York 10017 (800) 253-9646; *National Account Statistics,* and *Statistical Yearbook.*

MONGOLIA - NATIONAL INCOME - UTILIZATION OF

Facts on File, 460 Park Avenue South, New York, New York 10016 (800) 443-8323; *The New Book of World Rankings.*

MONGOLIA - NATIONAL PRODUCT

Facts on File, 460 Park Avenue South, New York, New York 10016 (800) 443-8323; *The New Book of World Rankings.*

Statistical Office of the United Nations, Publishing Service, New York, New York 10017 (800) 253-9646; *Statistical Yearbook.*

MONGOLIA - NATURAL GAS - PRODUCTION - See MONGOLIA - MINING AND MINERAL PRODUCTS

MONGOLIA - NET MATERIAL PRODUCT - AVERAGE ANNUAL GROWTH

Statistical Office of the United Nations, Publishing Service, New York, New York 10017 (800) 253-9646; *Statistical Yearbook.*

MONGOLIA - NEWSPAPER PRODUCTION - See MONGOLIA - FORESTRY AND FOREST PRODUCTS

MONGOLIA - NEWSPRINT - See MONGOLIA - FORESTRY AND FOREST PRODUCTS

MONGOLIA - OATS PRODUCTION - See MONGOLIA - CROPS

MONGOLIA - PAPER - See MONGOLIA - FORESTRY AND FOREST PRODUCTS

MONGOLIA - PATENTS

World Intellectual Property Organization, 34 Chemin des Colombettes, CH-1211 Geneva 20, Switzerland; *Industrial Property Statistics.*

MONGOLIA - PEANUT PRODUCTION - See MONGOLIA - CROPS

MONGOLIA - PESTICIDE USE

Food and Agricultural Organization of the United Nations (FAO), Via delle Terme di Caracalla, 00100 Rome, Italy (Telephone Number in U.S. (202) 653-2400); *The State of Food and Agriculture.*

MONGOLIA - PETROLEUM INDUSTRY

Facts on File, 460 Park Avenue South, New York, New York 10016 (800) 443-8323; *The New Book of World Rankings.*

Food and Agricultural Organization of the United Nations (FAO), Via delle Terme di Caracalla, 00100 Rome, Italy (Telephone Number in U.S. (202) 653-2400); *The State of Food and Agriculture.*

Statistical Office of the United Nations, Publishing Service, New York, New York 10017 (800) 253-9646; *Statistical Yearbook.*

MONGOLIA - PIGS - See MONGOLIA - LIVESTOCK AND POULTRY

MONGOLIA - POPULATION

The Economist Intelligence Unit (Asia) Limited, 10th Floor, Luk Kwok Centre, 72 Gloucester Road, Wanchai, Hong Kong (Phone Number in U.S. (800) 938-4685); *Asian Market Atlas.*

Facts on File, 460 Park Avenue South, New York, New York 10016 (800) 443-8323; *The New Book of World Rankings.*

Food and Agricultural Organization of the United Nations (FAO), Via delle Terme di Caracalla, 00100 Rome, Italy (Telephone Number in U.S. (202) 653-2400); *Production Yearbook.*

Statistical Office of the United Nations, Publishing Service, New York, New York 10017 (800) 253-9646; *Demographic Yearbook, Statistical Yearbook,* and *Statistical Yearbook for Asia and the Pacific.*

Times Books, 201 East 50th Street, New York, New York 10022 (212) 751-2600; *The Economist Book of Vital World Statistics.*

U.S. Arms Control and Disarmament Agency, 320 Twenty-first Street, NW, Washington, D.C. 20451 (202) 647-8677; *World Military Expenditures and Arms Transfers.*

World Health Organization, Office of Publications, Avenue Appia, CH-1211 Geneva 27, Switzerland (Telephone Number in U.S. (518) 436-9686); *World Health Statistics Annual.*

MONGOLIA - POST OFFICES

Facts on File, 460 Park Avenue South, New York, New York 10016 (800) 443-8323; *The New Book of World Rankings.*

MONGOLIA - POTATO PRODUCTION - See MONGOLIA - CROPS

MONGOLIA - POWER PRODUCTION INDUSTRY - ESTABLISHMENTS, PAYROLLS, VALUE ADDED, ETC.

Statistical Office of the United Nations, Publishing Service, New York, New York 10017 (800) 253-9646; *Electric Power in Asia and the Pacific.*

MONGOLIA - PRICES

Facts on File, 460 Park Avenue South, New York, New York 10016 (800) 443-8323; *The New Book of World Rankings.*

Food and Agricultural Organization of the United Nations (FAO), Via delle Terme di Caracalla, 00100 Rome, Italy (Telephone Number in U.S. (202) 653-2400); *Production Yearbook,* and *The State of Food and Agriculture.*

MONGOLIA - PRINTING AND WRITING PAPER - See MONGOLIA - FORESTRY AND FOREST PRODUCTS

MONGOLIA - PRODUCTION

Facts on File, 460 Park Avenue South, New York, New York 10016 (800) 443-8323; *The New Book of World Rankings.*

MONGOLIA - PUBLIC FINANCE

Facts on File, 460 Park Avenue South, New York, New York 10016 (800) 443-8323; *The New Book of World Rankings.*

MONGOLIA - RADIO

The Economist Intelligence Unit (Asia) Limited, 10th Floor, Luk Kwok Centre, 72 Gloucester Road, Wanchai, Hong Kong (Phone Number in U.S. (800) 938-4685); *Asian Market Atlas*

Facts on File, 460 Park Avenue South, New York, New York 10016 (800) 443-8323; *The New Book of World Rankings.*

Times Books, 201 East 50th Street, New York, New York 10022 (212) 751-2600; *The Economist Book of Vital World Statistics.*

MONGOLIA - RAILWAY USE

Statistical Office of the United Nations, Publishing Service, New York, New York 10017 (800) 253-9646; *Statistical Yearbook.*

MONGOLIA - RELIGION

Facts on File, 460 Park Avenue South, New York, New York 10016 (800) 443-8323; *The New Book of World Rankings.*

MONGOLIA - RETAIL TRADE

Statistical Office of the United Nations, Publishing Service, New York, New York 10017 (800) 253-9646; *Statistical Yearbook.*

MONGOLIA - RICE PRODUCTION - See MONGOLIA - CROPS

MONGOLIA - ROOT AND TUBER PRODUCTION - See MONGOLIA - CROPS

MONGOLIA - ROUNDWOOD PRODUCTION - See MONGOLIA - FORESTRY AND FOREST PRODUCTS

MONGOLIA - RUBBER PRODUCTION AND CONSUMPTION

Facts on File, 460 Park Avenue South, New York, New York 10016 (800) 443-8323; *The New Book of World Rankings.*

MONGOLIA - SALT PRODUCTION - See MONGOLIA - MINING AND MINERAL PRODUCTS

MONGOLIA - SAWNWOOD PRODUCTION - See MONGOLIA - FORESTRY AND FOREST PRODUCTS

MONGOLIA - SCIENCE AND TECHNOLOGY - EXPENDITURE FOR RESEARCH

Statistical Office of the United Nations, Publishing Service, New York, New York 10017 (800) 253-9646; *Statistical Yearbook.*

MONGOLIA - SCIENTISTS AND TECHNICIANS

Statistical Office of the United Nations, Publishing Service, New York, New York 10017 (800) 253-9646; *Statistical Yearbook.*

MONGOLIA - SENIOR CITIZENS

Facts on File, 460 Park Avenue South, New York, New York 10016 (800) 443-8323; *The New Book of World Rankings.*

MONGOLIA - SHEEP - See MONGOLIA - LIVESTOCK AND POULTRY

MONGOLIA - SILVER PRODUCTION AND CONSUMPTION - See MONGOLIA - MINING AND MINERAL PRODUCTS

MONGOLIA - SOCIAL DATA

Facts on File, 460 Park Avenue South, New York, New York 10016 (800) 443-8323; *The New Book of World Rankings.*

MONGOLIA - STEEL - See MONGOLIA - MINING AND MINERAL PRODUCTS

MONGOLIA - STOCKS - COMMODITY - MARKET PRICE - INDEX

Food and Agricultural Organization of the United Nations (FAO), Via delle Terme di Caracalla, 00100 Rome, Italy (Telephone Number in U.S. (202) 653-2400); *The State of Food and Agriculture.*

MONGOLIA - SUGAR PRODUCTION AND CONSUMPTION - See MONGOLIA - CROPS

MONGOLIA - TELEPHONES IN USE

American Telephone and Telegraph Company, 26 Parsippany Road, Whippany, New Jersey 07981 (800) 338-4038; *The World's Telephones.*

The Economist Intelligence Unit (Asia) Limited, 10th Floor, Luk Kwok Centre, 72 Gloucester Road, Wanchai, Hong Kong (Phone Number in U.S. (800) 938-4685); *Asian Market Atlas.*

Statistical Office of the United Nations, Publishing Service, New York, New York 10017 (800) 253-9646; *Statistical Yearbook.*

MONGOLIA - TELEVISION

The Economist Intelligence Unit (Asia) Limited, 10th Floor, Luk Kwok Centre, 72 Gloucester Road, Wanchai, Hong Kong (Phone Number in U.S. (800) 938-4685); *Asian Market Atlas.*

Facts on File, 460 Park Avenue South, New York, New York 10016 (800) 443-8323; *The New Book of World Rankings.*

MONGOLIA - TELEVISION BROADCASTING - See MONGOLIA - BROADCASTING

MONGOLIA - TEXTILE INDUSTRY

Statistical Office of the United Nations, Publishing Service, New York, New York 10017 (800) 253-9646; *Statistical Yearbook.*

MONGOLIA - TIMBER - See MONGOLIA - FORESTRY AND FOREST PRODUCTS

MONGOLIA - TOBACCO PRODUCTION

Facts on File, 460 Park Avenue South, New York, New York 10016 (800) 443-8323; *The New Book of World Rankings.*

MONGOLIA - TOURISM

Facts on File, 460 Park Avenue South, New York, New York 10016 (800) 443-8323; *The New Book of World Rankings.*

Times Books, 201 East 50th Street, New York, New York 10022 (212) 751-2600; *The Economist Book of Vital World Statistics.*

World Tourism Organization, Calle Capitan Haya 42, E-28020 Madrid, Spain; *Yearbook of Tourism Statistics.*

MONGOLIA - TRACTORS IN USE

Statistical Office of the United Nations, Publishing Service, New York, New York 10017 (800) 253-9646; *Statistical Yearbook.*

MONGOLIA - TRADE - See MONGOLIA - FOREIGN TRADE

MONGOLIA - TRADEMARKS AND SERVICE MARKS

World Intellectual Property Organization, 34 Chemin des Colombettes, CH-1211 Geneva 20, Switzerland; *Industrial Property Statistics.*

MONGOLIA - TRANSPORTATION AND COMMUNICATIONS

The Economist Intelligence Unit (Asia) Limited, 10th Floor, Luk Kwok Centre, 72 Gloucester Road, Wanchai, Hong Kong (Phone Number in U.S. (800) 938-4685); *Asian Market Atlas.*

Facts on File, 460 Park Avenue South, New York, New York 10016 (800) 443-8323; *The New Book of World Rankings.*

Statistical Office of the United Nations, Publishing Service, New York, New York 10017 (800) 253-9646; *Statistical Yearbook for Asia and the Pacific.*

MONGOLIA - UTILITIES

Statistical Office of the United Nations, Publishing Service, New York, New York 10017 (800) 253-9646; *Electric Power in Asia and the Pacific.*

MONGOLIA - VITAL STATISTICS

Statistical Office of the United Nations, Publishing Service, New York, New York 10017 (800) 253-9646; *Statistical Yearbook.*

World Health Organization, Office of Publications, Avenue Appia, CH-1211 Geneva 27, Switzerland (Telephone Number in U.S. (518) 436-9686); *World Health Statistics Annual.*

MONGOLIA - WAGES AND PRICES

Statistical Office of the United Nations, Publishing Service, New York, New York 10017 (800) 253-9646; *Statistical Yearbook for Asia and the Pacific.*

MONGOLIA - WEATHER

Facts on File, 460 Park Avenue South, New York, New York 10016 (800) 443-8323; *The New Book of World Rankings.*

MONGOLIA - WHEAT PRODUCTION - See MONGOLIA - CROPS

MONGOLIA - WHOLESALE TRADE

Statistical Office of the United Nations, Publishing Service, New York, New York 10017 (800) 253-9646; *Statistical Yearbook.*

MONGOLIA - WINE PRODUCTION

Facts on File, 460 Park Avenue South, New York, New York 10016 (800) 443-8323; *The New Book of World Rankings.*

MONGOLIA - WOOL PRODUCTION

Facts on File, 460 Park Avenue South, New York, New York 10016 (800) 443-8323; *The New Book of World Rankings.*

MONTANA - See also STATE DATA (FOR INDIVIDUAL STATES)

Montana - Primary Statistics Source

Montana Department of Commerce, Census and Economic Information Center, 1424 Ninth Avenue, Helena, Montana 59620 (406) 444-2896; Montana County Database.

Montana - State Data Centers

Census and Economic Information Center, Montana Department of Commerce, 1424 Ninth Avenue, Capitol Station, Helena, Montana 59620, Ms. Patricia Roberts (406) 444-2896.

Montana State Library, 1515 East 6th Avenue, Capitol Station, Helena, Montana 59620, Ms. Kathy Brown (406) 444-3004.

Bureau of Business and Economic Research, University of Montana, Missoula, Montana 59812, Mr. Jim Sylvester (406) 243-5113.

Research and Analysis Bureau, Employment Policy Division, Montana Department of Labor and Industry, Post Office Box 1728, Helena, Montana 59624, Cathy Shenkle (406) 444-2430.

MONTENEGRO - see Yugoslavia

Montserrat - National Statistical Office

Statistics Office, Chief Statistician, Government Headquarters, Plymouth, Montserrat.

Montserrat - Primary Statistics Source

Statistics Office, P.O. Box 292, Plymouth, Montserrat; *Statistical Digest.*

MONTSERRAT - AGRICULTURE

Food and Agricultural Organization of the United Nations (FAO), Via delle Terme di Caracalla, 00100 Rome, Italy (Telephone Number in U.S. (202) 653-2400); *Production Yearbook, The State of Food and Agriculture,* and *Trade Yearbook.*

G.K. Hall and Company, 70 Lincoln Street, Boston, Massachusetts 02111 (617) 423-3990; *The World in Figures.*

Statistical Office of the United Nations, Publishing Service, New York, New York 10017 (800) 253-9646; *Statistical Yearbook.*

MONTSERRAT - AIRLINE SERVICE

G.K. Hall and Company, 70 Lincoln Street, Boston, Massachusetts 02111 (617) 423-3990; *The World in Figures.*

MONTSERRAT - AREA AND DENSITY OF POPULATION

Food and Agricultural Organization of the United Nations (FAO), Via delle Terme di Caracalla, 00100 Rome, Italy (Telephone Number in U.S. (202) 653-2400); *The State of Food and Agriculture.*

G.K. Hall and Company, 70 Lincoln Street, Boston, Massachusetts 02111 (617) 423-3990; *The World in Figures.*

Statistical Office of the United Nations, Publishing Service, New York, New York 10017 (800) 253-9646; *Statistical Yearbook.*

MONTSERRAT - BALANCE OF PAYMENTS

G.K. Hall and Company, 70 Lincoln Street, Boston, Massachusetts 02111 (617) 423-3990; *The World in Figures.*

MONTSERRAT - BANKING

G.K. Hall and Company, 70 Lincoln Street, Boston, Massachusetts 02111 (617) 423-3990; *The World in Figures.*

MONTSERRAT - BIRTH RATES

Statistical Office of the United Nations, Publishing Service, New York, New York 10017 (800) 253-9646; *Demographic Yearbook,* and *Statistical Yearbook.*

World Health Organization, Office of Publications, Avenue Appia, CH-1211 Geneva 27, Switzerland (Telephone Number in U.S. (518) 436-9686); *World Health Statistics Annual.*

MONTSERRAT - BONDS

G.K. Hall and Company, 70 Lincoln Street, Boston, Massachusetts 02111 (617) 423-3990; *The World in Figures.*

MONTSERRAT - BOOK PRODUCTION

G.K. Hall and Company, 70 Lincoln Street, Boston, Massachusetts 02111 (617) 423-3990; *The World in Figures.*

MONTSERRAT - BROADCASTING

Billboard Limited, Post Office Box 9027, 1006 AA Amsterdam, The Netherlands (Telephone Number in U.S. (212) 764-7300); *World Radio TV Handbook.*

G.K. Hall and Company, 70 Lincoln Street, Boston, Massachusetts 02111 (617) 423-3990; *The World in Figures.*

MONTSERRAT - BUSINESS

G.K. Hall and Company, 70 Lincoln Street, Boston, Massachusetts 02111 (617) 423-3990; *The World in Figures.*

MONTSERRAT - CALORIE SUPPLY

Food and Agricultural Organization of the United Nations (FAO), Via delle Terme di Caracalla, 00100 Rome, Italy (Telephone Number in U.S. (202) 653-2400); *The State of Food and Agriculture.*

MONTSERRAT - CATTLE - See MONTSERRAT - LIVESTOCK AND POULTRY

MONTSERRAT - CHEMICAL (ORGANIC) PRODUCTION - See MONTSERRAT - MINING AND MINERAL PRODUCTS

MONTSERRAT - CLASS STRUCTURE

G.K. Hall and Company, 70 Lincoln Street, Boston, Massachusetts 02111 (617) 423-3990; *The World in Figures.*

MONTSERRAT - CLIMATE

G.K. Hall and Company, 70 Lincoln Street, Boston, Massachusetts 02111 (617) 423-3990; *The World in Figures.*

MONTSERRAT - COAL PRODUCTION - See MONTSERRAT - MINING AND MINERAL PRODUCTS

MONTSERRAT - COMMUNICATIONS

G.K. Hall and Company, 70 Lincoln Street, Boston, Massachusetts 02111 (617) 423-3990; *The World in Figures.*

MONTSERRAT - CONSUMER PRICE INDEX

G.K. Hall and Company, 70 Lincoln Street, Boston, Massachusetts 02111 (617) 423-3990; *The World in Figures.*

Statistical Office of the United Nations, Publishing Service, New York, New York 10017 (800) 253-9646; *Statistical Yearbook.*

MONTSERRAT - CONSUMER PRICES

International Labour Office, I.L.O. Publications, CH-1211, Geneva 22, Switzerland; *Yearbook of Labour Statistics.*

MONTSERRAT - CONSUMPTION

G.K. Hall and Company, 70 Lincoln Street, Boston, Massachusetts 02111 (617) 423-3990; *The World in Figures.*

MONTSERRAT - CORN PRODUCTION - See MONTSERRAT - CROPS

MONTSERRAT - CORPORATE TAXES - See MONTSERRAT - TAXATION

MONTSERRAT - CROPS

Food and Agricultural Organization of the United Nations (FAO), Via delle Terme di Caracalla, 00100 Rome, Italy (Telephone Number in U.S. (202) 653-2400); *The State of Food and Agriculture.*

G.K. Hall and Company, 70 Lincoln Street, Boston, Massachusetts 02111 (617) 423-3990; *The World in Figures.*

MONTSERRAT - CUSTOMS DUTIES

G.K. Hall and Company, 70 Lincoln Street, Boston, Massachusetts 02111 (617) 423-3990; *The World in Figures.*

MONTSERRAT - DAIRY PRODUCTS

Food and Agricultural Organization of the United Nations (FAO), Via delle Terme di Caracalla, 00100 Rome, Italy (Telephone Number in U.S. (202) 653-2400); *The State of Food and Agriculture.*

MONTSERRAT - DEATH RATES

G.K. Hall and Company, 70 Lincoln Street, Boston, Massachusetts 02111 (617) 423-3990; *The World in Figures.*

Statistical Office of the United Nations, Publishing Service, New York, New York 10017 (800) 253-9646; *Statistical Yearbook.*

World Health Organization, Office of Publications, Avenue Appia, CH-1211 Geneva 27, Switzerland (Telephone Number in U.S. (518) 436-9686); *World Health Statistics Annual.*

MONTSERRAT - DEFENSE EXPENDITURES

G.K. Hall and Company, 70 Lincoln Street, Boston, Massachusetts 02111 (617) 423-3990; *The World in Figures.*

MONTSERRAT - DEMOGRAPHY

G.K. Hall and Company, 70 Lincoln Street, Boston, Massachusetts 02111 (617) 423-3990; *The World in Figures.*

MONTSERRAT - DEVELOPMENT ASSISTANCE

G.K. Hall and Company, 70 Lincoln Street, Boston, Massachusetts 02111 (617) 423-3990; *The World in Figures.*

MONTSERRAT - DISEASES

G.K. Hall and Company, 70 Lincoln Street, Boston, Massachusetts 02111 (617) 423-3990; *The World in Figures.*

World Health Organization, Office of Publications, Avenue Appia, CH-1211 Geneva 27, Switzerland (Telephone Number in U.S. (518) 436-9686); *World Health Statistics Annual.*

MONTSERRAT - DIVORCE

Statistical Office of the United Nations, Publishing Service, New York, New York 10017 (800) 253-9646; *Demographic Yearbook*, and *Statistical Yearbook.*

MONTSERRAT - DOMESTIC PRODUCT

G.K. Hall and Company, 70 Lincoln Street, Boston, Massachusetts 02111 (617) 423-3990; *The World in Figures.*

MONTSERRAT - ECONOMY

G.K. Hall and Company, 70 Lincoln Street, Boston, Massachusetts 02111 (617) 423-3990; *The World in Figures.*

MONTSERRAT - EDUCATION

G.K. Hall and Company, 70 Lincoln Street, Boston, Massachusetts 02111 (617) 423-3990; *The World in Figures.*

United Nations Educational, Scientific and Cultural Organization (UNESCO), 7 Place de Fontenoy, F-75700 Paris, France (Telephone Number in U.S. (212) 963-5981); *Statistical Yearbook.*

MONTSERRAT - EGG PRODUCTION AND CONSUMPTION - See MONTSERRAT - DAIRY PRODUCTS

MONTSERRAT - EMPLOYMENT

International Labour Office, I.L.O. Publications, CH-1211, Geneva 22, Switzerland; *Yearbook of Labour Statistics.*

MONTSERRAT - ENERGY

Food and Agricultural Organization of the United Nations (FAO), Via delle Terme di Caracalla, 00100 Rome, Italy (Telephone Number in U.S. (202) 653-2400); *The State of Food and Agriculture.*

G.K. Hall and Company, 70 Lincoln Street, Boston, Massachusetts 02111 (617) 423-3990; *The World in Figures.*

Statistical Office of the United Nations, Publishing Service, New York, New York 10017 (800) 253-9646; *Statistical Yearbook*, and *World Energy Supplies.*

MONTSERRAT - EXPORTS

Food and Agricultural Organization of the United Nations (FAO), Via delle Terme di Caracalla, 00100 Rome, Italy (Telephone Number in U.S. (202) 653-2400); *The State of Food and Agriculture.*

G.K. Hall and Company, 70 Lincoln Street, Boston, Massachusetts 02111 (617) 423-3990; *The World in Figures.*

MONTSERRAT - EXTERNAL TRADE

Food and Agricultural Organization of the United Nations (FAO), Via delle Terme di Caracalla, 00100 Rome, Italy (Telephone Number in U.S. (202) 653-2400); *The State of Food and Agriculture*, and *Trade Yearbook.*

G.K. Hall and Company, 70 Lincoln Street, Boston, Massachusetts 02111 (617) 423-3990; *The World in Figures.*

MONTSERRAT - FARM CROPS - See MONTSERRAT - CROPS

MONTSERRAT - FERTILIZER

Food and Agricultural Organization of the United Nations (FAO), Via delle Terme di Caracalla, 00100 Rome, Italy (Telephone Number in U.S. (202) 653-2400); *The State of Food and Agriculture.*

MONTSERRAT - FETAL MORTALITY

Statistical Office of the United Nations, Publishing Service, New York, New York 10017 (800) 253-9646; *Demographic Yearbook.*

World Health Organization, Office of Publications, Avenue Appia, CH-1211 Geneva 27, Switzerland (Telephone Number in U.S. (518) 436-9686); *World Health Statistics Annual.*

MONTSERRAT - FINANCE

G.K. Hall and Company, 70 Lincoln Street, Boston, Massachusetts 02111 (617) 423-3990; *The World in Figures.*

MONTSERRAT - FISHERIES

Food and Agricultural Organization of the United Nations (FAO), Via delle Terme di Caracalla, 00100 Rome, Italy (Telephone Number in U.S. (202) 653-2400); *The State of Food and Agriculture*, and *Yearbook of Fishery Statistics.*

MONTSERRAT - FOOD

Food and Agricultural Organization of the United Nations (FAO), Via delle Terme di Caracalla, 00100 Rome, Italy (Telephone Number in U.S. (202) 653-2400); *Production Yearbook*, and *The State of Food and Agriculture.*

G.K. Hall and Company, 70 Lincoln Street, Boston, Massachusetts 02111 (617) 423-3990; *The World in Figures.*

MONTSERRAT - FOREIGN AID

G.K. Hall and Company, 70 Lincoln Street, Boston, Massachusetts 02111 (617) 423-3990; *The World in Figures.*

MONTSERRAT - FOREIGN TRADE

Food and Agricultural Organization of the United Nations (FAO), Via delle Terme di Caracalla, 00100 Rome, Italy (Telephone Number in U.S. (202) 653-2400); *The State of Food and Agriculture.*

G.K. Hall and Company, 70 Lincoln Street, Boston, Massachusetts 02111 (617) 423-3990; *The World in Figures.*

Statistical Office of the United Nations, Publishing Service, New York, New York 10017 (800) 253-9646; *International Trade Statistics Yearbook.*

MONTSERRAT - FORESTRY AND FOREST PRODUCTS

Food and Agricultural Organization of the United Nations (FAO), Via delle Terme di Caracalla, 00100 Rome, Italy (Telephone Number in U.S. (202) 653-2400); *The State of Food and Agriculture.*

G.K. Hall and Company, 70 Lincoln Street, Boston, Massachusetts 02111 (617) 423-3990; *The World in Figures.*

Statistical Office of the United Nations, Publishing Service, New York, New York 10017 (800) 253-9646; *Statistical Yearbook.*

MONTSERRAT - GENERAL MORTALITY

Statistical Office of the United Nations, Publishing Service, New York, New York 10017 (800) 253-9646; *Demographic Yearbook.*

World Health Organization, Office of Publications, Avenue Appia, CH-1211 Geneva 27, Switzerland (Telephone Number in U.S. (518) 436-9686); *World Health Statistics Annual.*

MONTSERRAT - GOVERNMENT

G.K. Hall and Company, 70 Lincoln Street, Boston, Massachusetts 02111 (617) 423-3990; *The World in Figures.*

MONTSERRAT - GRAIN PRODUCTION - See MONTSERRAT - CROPS

MONTSERRAT - GROSS DOMESTIC PRODUCT

G.K. Hall and Company, 70 Lincoln Street, Boston, Massachusetts 02111 (617) 423-3990; *The World in Figures.*

Statistical Office of the United Nations, Publishing Service, New York, New York 10017 (800) 253-9646; *Statistical Yearbook.*

MONTSERRAT - HEALTH

G.K. Hall and Company, 70 Lincoln Street, Boston, Massachusetts 02111 (617) 423-3990; *The World in Figures.*

Statistical Office of the United Nations, Publishing Service, New York, New York 10017 (800) 253-9646; *Statistical Yearbook*.

World Health Organization, Office of Publications, Avenue Appia, CH-1211 Geneva 27, Switzerland (Telephone Number in U.S. (518) 436-9686); *World Health Statistics Annual*.

MONTSERRAT - HEALTH AND MEDICAL SERVICES

Statistical Office of the United Nations, Publishing Service, New York, New York 10017 (800) 253-9646; *Statistical Yearbook*.

MONTSERRAT - HIDE PRODUCTION

Food and Agricultural Organization of the United Nations (FAO), Via delle Terme di Caracalla, 00100 Rome, Italy (Telephone Number in U.S. (202) 653-2400); *Production Yearbook*.

MONTSERRAT - HIGHWAYS

G.K. Hall and Company, 70 Lincoln Street, Boston, Massachusetts 02111 (617) 423-3990; *The World in Figures*.

MONTSERRAT - HOURS OF WORK - See MONTSERRAT - EMPLOYMENT

MONTSERRAT - ILLITERATE POPULATION

G.K. Hall and Company, 70 Lincoln Street, Boston, Massachusetts 02111 (617) 423-3990; *The World in Figures*.

United Nations Educational, Scientific and Cultural Organization (UNESCO), 7 Place de Fontenoy, F-75700 Paris, France (Telephone Number in U.S. (212) 963-5981); *Statistical Yearbook*.

MONTSERRAT - IMPORTS

Food and Agricultural Organization of the United Nations (FAO), Via delle Terme di Caracalla, 00100 Rome, Italy (Telephone Number in U.S. (202) 653-2400); *The State of Food and Agriculture*.

G.K. Hall and Company, 70 Lincoln Street, Boston, Massachusetts 02111 (617) 423-3990; *The World in Figures*.

MONTSERRAT - INDUSTRY

G.K. Hall and Company, 70 Lincoln Street, Boston, Massachusetts 02111 (617) 423-3990; *The World in Figures*.

International Labour Office, I.L.O. Publications, CH-1211, Geneva 22, Switzerland; *Yearbook of Labour Statistics*.

MONTSERRAT - INFANT AND MATERNAL MORTALITY

Statistical Office of the United Nations, Publishing Service, New York, New York 10017 (800) 253-9646; *Demographic Yearbook*, and *Statistical Yearbook*.

World Health Organization, Office of Publications, Avenue Appia, CH-1211 Geneva 27, Switzerland (Telephone Number in U.S. (518) 436-9686); *World Health Statistics Annual*.

MONTSERRAT - LABOR FORCE

Food and Agricultural Organization of the United Nations (FAO), Via delle Terme di Caracalla, 00100 Rome, Italy (Telephone Number in U.S. (202) 653-2400); *The State of Food and Agriculture*.

G.K. Hall and Company, 70 Lincoln Street, Boston, Massachusetts 02111 (617) 423-3990; *The World in Figures*.

MONTSERRAT - LABOR PRODUCTIVITY

International Labour Office, I.L.O. Publications, CH-1211, Geneva 22, Switzerland; *Yearbook of Labour Statistics*.

MONTSERRAT - LAND USE

Food and Agricultural Organization of the United Nations (FAO), Via delle Terme di Caracalla, 00100 Rome, Italy (Telephone Number in U.S. (202) 653-2400); *Production Yearbook*.

G.K. Hall and Company, 70 Lincoln Street, Boston, Massachusetts 02111 (617) 423-3990; *The World in Figures*.

MONTSERRAT - LIVESTOCK AND POULTRY

Food and Agricultural Organization of the United Nations (FAO), Via delle Terme di Caracalla, 00100 Rome, Italy (Telephone Number in U.S. (202) 653-2400); *Production Yearbook*, and *The State of Food and Agriculture*.

G.K. Hall and Company, 70 Lincoln Street, Boston, Massachusetts 02111 (617) 423-3990; *The World in Figures*.

Statistical Office of the United Nations, Publishing Service, New York, New York 10017 (800) 253-9646; *Statistical Yearbook*.

MONTSERRAT - LIVING LEVELS

G.K. Hall and Company, 70 Lincoln Street, Boston, Massachusetts 02111 (617) 423-3990; *The World in Figures*.

MONTSERRAT - MAIL - NUMBER OF ITEMS SENT AND RECEIVED

Statistical Office of the United Nations, Publishing Service, New York, New York 10017 (800) 253-9646; *Statistical Yearbook*.

MONTSERRAT - MANUFACTURING

G.K. Hall and Company, 70 Lincoln Street, Boston, Massachusetts 02111 (617) 423-3990; *The World in Figures*.

MONTSERRAT - MARRIAGE RATES

Statistical Office of the United Nations, Publishing Service, New York, New York 10017 (800) 253-9646; *Demographic Yearbook*, and *Statistical Yearbook*.

MONTSERRAT - MEAT PRODUCTION - See MONTSERRAT - LIVESTOCK AND POULTRY

MONTSERRAT - MERCHANT SHIPPING

G.K. Hall and Company, 70 Lincoln Street, Boston, Massachusetts 02111 (617) 423-3990; *The World in Figures*.

Statistical Office of the United Nations, Publishing Service, New York, New York 10017 (800) 253-9646; *Statistical Yearbook*.

MONTSERRAT - MILITARY

G.K. Hall and Company, 70 Lincoln Street, Boston, Massachusetts 02111 (617) 423-3990; *The World in Figures*.

MONTSERRAT - MINING AND MINERAL PRODUCTS

G.K. Hall and Company, 70 Lincoln Street, Boston, Massachusetts 02111 (617) 423-3990; *The World in Figures*.

MONTSERRAT - MONEY SUPPLY

G.K. Hall and Company, 70 Lincoln Street, Boston, Massachusetts 02111 (617) 423-3990; *The World in Figures*.

MONTSERRAT - MOTOR VEHICLES IN USE

G.K. Hall and Company, 70 Lincoln Street, Boston, Massachusetts 02111 (617) 423-3990; *The World in Figures*.

MONTSERRAT - NATALITY - See MONTSERRAT - BIRTH RATES

MONTSERRAT - NATIONAL ACCOUNTS

Statistical Office of the United Nations, Publishing Service, New York, New York 10017 (800) 253-9646; *Statistical Yearbook*, and *National Account Statistics*.

MONTSERRAT - NATIONAL INCOME

G.K. Hall and Company, 70 Lincoln Street, Boston, Massachusetts 02111 (617) 423-3990; *The World in Figures*.

Statistical Office of the United Nations, Publishing Service, New York, New York 10017 (800) 253-9646; *Statistical Yearbook*.

MONTSERRAT - NEWSPAPER PRODUCTION - See MONTSERRAT - FORESTRY AND FOREST PRODUCTS

MONTSERRAT - OCCUPATIONS - See MONTSERRAT - LABOR FORCE

MONTSERRAT - PERIODICALS

United Nations Educational, Scientific and Cultural Organization (UNESCO), 7 Place de Fontenoy, F-75700 Paris, France (Telephone Number in U.S. (212) 963-5981); *Statistical Yearbook*.

MONTSERRAT - PESTICIDE USE

Food and Agricultural Organization of the United Nations (FAO), Via delle Terme di Caracalla, 00100 Rome, Italy (Telephone Number in U.S. (202) 653-2400); *The State of Food and Agriculture*.

MONTSERRAT - PETROLEUM INDUSTRY

Food and Agricultural Organization of the United Nations (FAO), Via delle Terme di Caracalla, 00100 Rome, Italy (Telephone Number in U.S. (202) 653-2400); *The State of Food and Agriculture*.

G.K. Hall and Company, 70 Lincoln Street, Boston, Massachusetts 02111 (617) 423-3990; *The World in Figures*.

MONTSERRAT - PIGS - See MONTSERRAT - LIVESTOCK AND POULTRY

MONTSERRAT - POPULATION

Food and Agricultural Organization of the United Nations (FAO), Via delle Terme di Caracalla, 00100 Rome, Italy (Telephone Number in U.S. (202) 653-2400); *Production Yearbook*.

G.K. Hall and Company, 70 Lincoln Street, Boston, Massachusetts 02111 (617) 423-3990; *The World in Figures*.

International Labour Office, I.L.O. Publications, CH-1211, Geneva 22, Switzerland; *Yearbook of Labour Statistics*.

Statistical Office of the United Nations, Publishing Service, New York, New York 10017 (800) 253-9646; *Demographic Yearbook*, and *Statistical Yearbook*.

World Health Organization, Office of Publications, Avenue Appia, CH-1211 Geneva 27, Switzerland (Telephone Number in U.S. (518) 436-9686); *World Health Statistics Annual*.

MONTSERRAT - PRICES

Food and Agricultural Organization of the United Nations (FAO), Via delle Terme di Caracalla, 00100 Rome, Italy (Telephone Number in U.S. (202) 653-2400); *Production Yearbook*, and *The State of Food and Agriculture*.

G.K. Hall and Company, 70 Lincoln Street, Boston, Massachusetts 02111 (617) 423-3990; *The World in Figures*.

International Labour Office, I.L.O. Publications, CH-1211, Geneva 22, Switzerland; *Yearbook of Labour Statistics*.

MONTSERRAT - PRODUCTION

G.K. Hall and Company, 70 Lincoln Street, Boston, Massachusetts 02111 (617) 423-3990; *The World in Figures*.

MONTSERRAT - RAILWAY USE

G.K. Hall and Company, 70 Lincoln Street, Boston, Massachusetts 02111 (617) 423-3990; *The World in Figures*.

MONTSERRAT - RETAIL TRADE

G.K. Hall and Company, 70 Lincoln Street, Boston, Massachusetts 02111 (617) 423-3990; *The World in Figures*.

MONTSERRAT - ROUNDWOOD PRODUCTION - See MONTSERRAT - FORESTRY AND FOREST PRODUCTS

MONTSERRAT - SHEEP - See MONTSERRAT - LIVESTOCK AND POULTRY

MONTSERRAT - SOCIAL DATA

G.K. Hall and Company, 70 Lincoln Street, Boston, Massachusetts 02111 (617) 423-3990; *The World in Figures*.

MONTSERRAT - STOCKS - COMMODITY - MARKET PRICE - INDEX

Food and Agricultural Organization of the United Nations (FAO), Via delle Terme di Caracalla, 00100 Rome, Italy (Telephone Number in U.S. (202) 653-2400); *The State of Food and Agriculture*.

MONTSERRAT - TAXATION

G.K. Hall and Company, 70 Lincoln Street, Boston, Massachusetts 02111 (617) 423-3990; *The World in Figures*.

MONTSERRAT - TELEPHONES IN USE

American Telephone and Telegraph Company, 26 Parsippany Road, Whippany, New Jersey 07981 (800) 338-4038; *The World's Telephones*.

G.K. Hall and Company, 70 Lincoln Street, Boston, Massachusetts 02111 (617) 423-3990; *The World in Figures*.

Statistical Office of the United Nations, Publishing Service, New York, New York 10017 (800) 253-9646; *Statistical Yearbook.*

MONTSERRAT - TEXTILE INDUSTRY

G.K. Hall and Company, 70 Lincoln Street, Boston, Massachusetts 02111 (617) 423-3990; *The World in Figures.*

MONTSERRAT - THEATRE

United Nations Educational, Scientific and Cultural Organization (UNESCO), 7 Place de Fontenoy, F-75700 Paris, France (Telephone Number in U.S. (212) 963-5981); *Statistical Yearbook.*

MONTSERRAT - TOURISM

G.K. Hall and Company, 70 Lincoln Street, Boston, Massachusetts 02111 (617) 423-3990; *The World in Figures.*

World Tourism Organization, Calle Capitan Haya 42, E-28020 Madrid, Spain; *Yearbook of Tourism Statistics.*

MONTSERRAT - TRACTORS IN USE

Statistical Office of the United Nations, Publishing Service, New York, New York 10017 (800) 253-9646; *Statistical Yearbook.*

MONTSERRAT - TRADE - See MONTSERRAT - FOREIGN TRADE

MONTSERRAT - TRANSPORTATION AND COMMUNICATIONS

G.K. Hall and Company, 70 Lincoln Street, Boston, Massachusetts 02111 (617) 423-3990; *The World in Figures.*

MONTSERRAT - UNEMPLOYMENT

International Labour Office, I.L.O. Publications, CH-1211, Geneva 22, Switzerland; *Yearbook of Labour Statistics.*

MONTSERRAT - VITAL STATISTICS

G.K. Hall and Company, 70 Lincoln Street, Boston, Massachusetts 02111 (617) 423-3990; *The World in Figures.*

Statistical Office of the United Nations, Publishing Service, New York, New York 10017 (800) 253-9646; *Statistical Yearbook.*

World Health Organization, Office of Publications, Avenue Appia, CH-1211 Geneva 27, Switzerland (Telephone Number in U.S. (518) 436-9686); *World Health Statistics Annual.*

MONTSERRAT - WAGES

G.K. Hall and Company, 70 Lincoln Street, Boston, Massachusetts 02111 (617) 423-3990; *The World in Figures.*

International Labour Office, I.L.O. Publications, CH-1211, Geneva 22, Switzerland; *Yearbook of Labour Statistics.*

MONTSERRAT - WEATHER

G.K. Hall and Company, 70 Lincoln Street, Boston, Massachusetts 02111 (617) 423-3990; *The World in Figures.*

Morocco - National Statistical Offices

Direction de la Statistique, BP 178, Rabat, Morocco.
Office des Changes, Division des Etudes et de la Balance des Paiements, Place Moulay Hassan, BP 71, Rabat, Morocco.

Morocco - Primary Statistics Sources

Direction de la Statistique, BP 178, Rabat, Morocco; *Annuaire statistique du Maroc* (Statistical Yearbook of Morocco) and *Bulletin mensuel de statistique* (Monthly Bulletin of Statistics).

MOROCCO - AGRICULTURE

Euromonitor Publications Limited, 87-88 Turnmill Street, London EC1M 5QU, England; *International Marketing Data and Statistics,* and *Middle East Economic Handbook.*

Facts on File, 460 Park Avenue South, New York, New York 10016 (800) 443-8323; *The New Book of World Rankings.*

Food and Agricultural Organization of the United Nations (FAO), Via delle Terme di Caracalla, 00100 Rome, Italy (Telephone Number in U.S. (202) 653-2400); *Production Yearbook,* and *The State of Food and Agriculture.*

G.K. Hall and Company, 70 Lincoln Street, Boston, Massachusetts 02111 (617) 423-3990; *The World in Figures.*

Statistical Office of the United Nations, Publishing Service, New York, New York 10017 (800) 253-9646; *Statistical Yearbook,* and *Survey of Economic and Social Conditions in Africa.*

Times Books, 201 East 50th Street, New York, New York 10022 (212) 751-2600; *The Economist Book of Vital World Statistics.*

United Nations Economic Commission for Africa, Africa Hall, Post Office Box 3001, Addis Ababa, Ethiopia (Telephone Number in U.S. (800) 253-9646); *African Statistical Yearbook.*

The World Bank, 1818 H Street, NW, Washington, D.C. 20433 (202) 477-1234; *World Tables.*

MOROCCO - AIRLINE SERVICE

Facts on File, 460 Park Avenue South, New York, New York 10016 (800) 443-8323; *The New Book of World Rankings.*

G.K. Hall and Company, 70 Lincoln Street, Boston, Massachusetts 02111 (617) 423-3990; *The World in Figures.*

International Civil Aviation Organization, 1000 Sherbrooke Street West, Suite 400, Montreal, Quebec H3A 2R2, Canada (514) 285-8219; *Civil Aviation Statistics of the World.*

Statistical Office of the United Nations, Publishing Service, New York, New York 10017 (800) 253-9646; *Statistical Yearbook.*

Times Books, 201 East 50th Street, New York, New York 10022 (212) 751-2600; *The Economist Book of Vital World Statistics.*

United Nations Economic Commission for Africa, Africa Hall, Post Office Box 3001, Addis Ababa, Ethiopia (Telephone Number in U.S. (800) 253-9646); *African Statistical Yearbook.*

MOROCCO - ALMOND PRODUCTION - See MOROCCO - CROPS

MOROCCO - ALUMINUM PRODUCTION AND CONSUMPTION - See MOROCCO - MINING AND MINERAL PRODUCTS

MOROCCO - ANIMAL FEEDINGSTUFFS OF AQUATIC ANIMAL ORIGIN

Statistical Office of the United Nations, Publishing Service, New York, New York 10017 (800) 253-9646; *Statistical Yearbook.*

MOROCCO - ANIMAL HEALTH

Food and Agricultural Organization of the United Nations (FAO), Via delle Terme di Caracalla, 00100 Rome, Italy (Telephone Number in U.S. (202) 653-2400); *Animal Health Yearbook*.

MOROCCO - ANTIMONY AND ANTIMONY ORE PRODUCTION AND CONSUMPTION - See MOROCCO - MINING AND MINERAL PRODUCTS

MOROCCO - AREA AND DENSITY OF POPULATION

African Development Bank, 01 BP 1387, Abidjan 01, Cote d'Ivoire; *Selected Statistics on Regional Member Countries*.

Euromonitor Publications Limited, 87-88 Turnmill Street, London EC1M 5QU, England; *International Marketing Data and Statistics*, and *Middle East Economic Handbook*.

Facts on File, 460 Park Avenue South, New York, New York 10016 (800) 443-8323; *The New Book of World Rankings*.

Food and Agricultural Organization of the United Nations (FAO), Via delle Terme di Caracalla, 00100 Rome, Italy (Telephone Number in U.S. (202) 653-2400); *The State of Food and Agriculture*.

G.K. Hall and Company, 70 Lincoln Street, Boston, Massachusetts 02111 (617) 423-3990; *The World in Figures*.

Statistical Office of the United Nations, Publishing Service, New York, New York 10017 (800) 253-9646; *Statistical Yearbook*, and *Survey of Economic and Social Conditions in Africa*.

Times Books, 201 East 50th Street, New York, New York 10022 (212) 751-2600; *The Economist Book of Vital World Statistics*.

MOROCCO - ARMS EXPORTS AND IMPORTS

U.S. Arms Control and Disarmament Agency, 320 Twenty-first Street, NW, Washington, D.C. 20451 (202) 647-8677; *World Military Expenditures and Arms Transfers*.

MOROCCO - ARTICHOKE PRODUCTION

Food and Agricultural Organization of the United Nations (FAO), Via delle Terme di Caracalla, 00100 Rome, Italy (Telephone Number in U.S. (202) 653-2400); *Production Yearbook*.

MOROCCO - BALANCE OF PAYMENTS

African Development Bank, 01 BP 1387, Abidjan 01, Cote d'Ivoire; *Selected Statistics on Regional Member Countries*.

The Economist Intelligence Unit, 111 West 57th Street, New York, New York 10019 (800) 938-4685; *The World Market Atlas*.

G.K. Hall and Company, 70 Lincoln Street, Boston, Massachusetts 02111 (617) 423-3990; *The World in Figures*.

International Monetary Fund, 700 Nineteenth Street, NW, Washington, D.C. 20431 (202) 623-7000; *Balance of Payments Yearbook*, and *International Financial Statistics*.

Times Books, 201 East 50th Street, New York, New York 10022 (212) 751-2600; *The Economist Book of Vital World Statistics*.

United Nations Economic Commission for Africa, Africa Hall, Post Office Box 3001, Addis Ababa, Ethiopia (Telephone Number in U.S. (800) 253-9646; *African Statistical Yearbook*.

The World Bank, 1818 H Street, NW, Washington, D.C. 20433 (202) 477-1234; *World Tables*.

MOROCCO - BANKING

Facts on File, 460 Park Avenue South, New York, New York 10016 (800) 443-8323; *The New Book of World Rankings*.

G.K. Hall and Company, 70 Lincoln Street, Boston, Massachusetts 02111 (617) 423-3990; *The World in Figures*.

International Monetary Fund, 700 Nineteenth Street, NW, Washington, D.C. 20431 (202) 623-7000; *Government Finance Statistics Yearbook*, and *International Financial Statistics*.

Statistical Office of the United Nations, Publishing Service, New York, New York 10017 (800) 253-9646; *Statistical Yearbook*.

United Nations Economic Commission for Africa, Africa Hall, Post Office Box 3001, Addis Ababa, Ethiopia (Telephone Number in U.S. (800) 253-9646); *African Statistical Yearbook*.

MOROCCO - BARLEY PRODUCTION - See MOROCCO - CROPS

MOROCCO - BEER PRODUCTION

Facts on File, 460 Park Avenue South, New York, New York 10016 (000) 443-8323; *The New Book of World Rankings*.

Statistical Office of the United Nations, Publishing Service, New York, New York 10017 (000) 253-9646; *Statistical Yearbook*.

MOROCCO - BIRTH RATES

Euromonitor Publications Limited, 87-88 Turnmill Street, London EC1M 5QU, England; *Middle East Economic Handbook*.

Facts on File, 460 Park Avenue South, New York, New York 10016 (800) 443-8323; *The New Book of World Rankings*.

Statistical Office of the United Nations, Publishing Service, New York, New York 10017 (800) 253-9646; *Demographic Yearbook*, *Statistical Yearbook*, and *Survey of Economic and Social Conditions in Africa*.

Times Books, 201 East 50th Street, New York, New York 10022 (212) 751-2600; *The Economist Book of Vital World Statistics*.

The World Bank, 1818 H Street, NW, Washington, D.C. 20433 (202) 477-1234; *World Tables*.

MOROCCO - BONDS

G.K. Hall and Company, 70 Lincoln Street, Boston, Massachusetts 02111 (617) 423-3990; *The World in Figures*.

International Monetary Fund, 700 Nineteenth Street, NW, Washington, D.C. 20431 (202) 623-7000; *Government Finance Statistics Yearbook*.

MOROCCO - BOOK PRODUCTION

G.K. Hall and Company, 70 Lincoln Street, Boston, Massachusetts 02111 (617) 423-3990; *The World in Figures*.

MOROCCO - BROADCASTING

Billboard Limited, Post Office Box 9027, 1006 AA Amsterdam, The Netherlands (Telephone Number in U.S. (212) 764-7300); *World*

Radio TV Handbook.

Facts on File, 460 Park Avenue South, New York, New York 10016 (800) 443-8323; *The New Book of World Rankings.*

G.K. Hall and Company, 70 Lincoln Street, Boston, Massachusetts 02111 (617) 423-3990; *The World in Figures.*

Times Books, 201 East 50th Street, New York, New York 10022 (212) 751-2600; *The Economist Book of Vital World Statistics.*

United Nations Educational, Scientific and Cultural Organization (UNESCO), 7 Place de Fontenoy, F-75700 Paris, France (Telephone Number in U.S. (212) 963-5981); *Statistical Yearbook.*

MOROCCO - BUILDING CONSTRUCTION

Statistical Office of the United Nations, Publishing Service, New York, New York 10017 (800) 253-9646; *Statistical Yearbook.*

MOROCCO - BUSINESS

G.K. Hall and Company, 70 Lincoln Street, Boston, Massachusetts 02111 (617) 423-3990; *The World in Figures.*

MOROCCO - BUSINESS AND PROFESSIONAL LICENSES

International Monetary Fund, 700 Nineteenth Street, NW, Washington, D.C. 20431 (202) 623-7000; *Government Finance Statistics Yearbook.*

MOROCCO - BUTTER PRODUCTION - See MOROCCO - DAIRY PRODUCTS

MOROCCO - CALORIE SUPPLY

African Development Bank, 01 BP 1387, Abidjan 01, Cote d'Ivoire; *Selected Statistics on Regional Member Countries.*

Food and Agricultural Organization of the United Nations (FAO), Via delle Terme di Caracalla, 00100 Rome, Italy (Telephone Number in U.S. (202) 653-2400); *The State of Food and Agriculture.*

MOROCCO - CAPITAL REVENUE

International Monetary Fund, 700 Nineteenth Street, NW, Washington, D.C. 20431 (202) 623-7000; *Government Finance Statistics Yearbook.*

MOROCCO - CATTLE - See MOROCCO - LIVESTOCK AND POULTRY

MOROCCO - CEMENT PRODUCTION - See MOROCCO - MINING AND MINERAL PRODUCTS

MOROCCO - CHEESE PRODUCTION - See MOROCCO - DAIRY PRODUCTS

MOROCCO - CHEMICAL (ORGANIC) PRODUCTION - See MOROCCO - MINING AND MINERAL PRODUCTS

MOROCCO - CHICK PEA PRODUCTION - See MOROCCO - CROPS

MOROCCO - CIGAR PRODUCTION - See MOROCCO - TOBACCO PRODUCTION

MOROCCO - CIGARETTE PRODUCTION - See MOROCCO - TOBACCO PRODUCTION

MOROCCO - CLASS STRUCTURE

G.K. Hall and Company, 70 Lincoln Street, Boston, Massachusetts 02111 (617) 423-3990; *The World in Figures.*

MOROCCO - CLIMATE

Facts on File, 460 Park Avenue South, New York, New York 10016 (800) 443-8323; *The New Book of World Rankings.*

G.K. Hall and Company, 70 Lincoln Street, Boston, Massachusetts 02111 (617) 423-3990; *The World in Figures.*

MOROCCO - CLOTHING EXPORTS AND IMPORTS

Statistical Office of the United Nations, Publishing Service, New York, New York 10017 (800) 253-9646; *Trade in Manufactures of Developing Countries.*

MOROCCO - COAL PRODUCTION - See MOROCCO - MINING AND MINERAL PRODUCTS

MOROCCO - COBALT PRODUCTION AND CONSUMPTION - See MOROCCO - MINING AND MINERAL PRODUCTS

MOROCCO - COFFEE PRODUCTION AND CONSUMPTION - See MOROCCO - CROPS

MOROCCO - COMMUNICATIONS

G.K. Hall and Company, 70 Lincoln Street, Boston, Massachusetts 02111 (617) 423-3990; *The World in Figures.*

United Nations Economic Commission for Africa, Africa Hall, Post Office Box 3001, Addis Ababa, Ethiopia (Telephone Number in U.S. (800) 253-9646); *African Statistical Yearbook.*

MOROCCO - CONSTRUCTION INDUSTRY

Facts on File, 460 Park Avenue South, New York, New York 10016 (800) 443-8323; *The New Book of World Rankings.*

Statistical Office of the United Nations, Publishing Service, New York, New York 10017 (800) 253-9646; *Statistical Yearbook.*

United Nations Economic Commission for Africa, Africa Hall, Post Office Box 3001, Addis Ababa, Ethiopia (Telephone Number in U.S. (800) 253-9646); *African Statistical Yearbook.*

MOROCCO - CONSUMER PRICE INDEX

African Development Bank, 01 BP 1387, Abidjan 01, Cote d'Ivoire; *Selected Statistics on Regional Member Countries.*

G.K. Hall and Company, 70 Lincoln Street, Boston, Massachusetts 02111 (617) 423-3990; *The World in Figures.*

Statistical Office of the United Nations, Publishing Service, New York, New York 10017 (800) 253-9646; *Statistical Yearbook*, and *Survey of Economic and Social Conditions in Africa.*

United Nations Economic Commission for Africa, Africa Hall, Post Office Box 3001, Addis Ababa, Ethiopia (Telephone Number in U.S. (800) 253-9646); *African Statistical Yearbook.*

MOROCCO - CONSUMER PRICES

International Monetary Fund, 700 Nineteenth Street, NW, Washington, D.C. 20431 (202) 623-7000; *International Financial*

Statistics.

Times Books, 201 East 50th Street, New York, New York 10022 (212) 751-2600; *The Economist Book of Vital World Statistics.*

MOROCCO - CONSUMPTION

African Development Bank, 01 BP 1387, Abidjan 01, Cote d'Ivoire; *Selected Statistics on Regional Member Countries.*

Euromonitor Publications Limited, 87-88 Turnmill Street, London EC1M 5QU, England; *Middle East Economic Handbook.*

G.K. Hall and Company, 70 Lincoln Street, Boston, Massachusetts 02111 (617) 423-3990; *The World in Figures.*

International Lead and Zinc Study Group, Metro House, 58 St. James's Street, London SW1A 1LD England; *Lead and Zinc Statistics.*

Statistical Office of the United Nations, Publishing Service, New York, New York 10017 (800) 253-9646; *Survey of Economic and Social Conditions in Africa.*

MOROCCO - COPPER AND COPPER ORE PRODUCTION AND CONSUMPTION - See MOROCCO - MINING AND MINERAL PRODUCTS

MOROCCO - CORN PRODUCTION - See MOROCCO - CROPS

MOROCCO - CORPORATE TAXES - See MOROCCO - TAXATION

MOROCCO - COTTON - See MOROCCO - CROPS

MOROCCO - CRIME

International Criminal Police Organization (INTERPOL), 26 rue Armengaud, 92210 Saint Cloud, France; *International Crime Statistics.*

Yale University Press, Yale Station, New Haven, Connecticut 06520 (203) 432-0940; *Violence and Crime in Cross-National Perspective.*

MOROCCO - CROPS

Commodity Research Bureau, Incorporated, 75 Wall Street, New York, New York, 10005 (212) 504-7754; *Commodity Year Book.*

Facts on File, 460 Park Avenue South, New York, New York 10016 (800) 443-8323; *The New Book of World Rankings.*

Food and Agricultural Organization of the United Nations (FAO), Via delle Terme di Caracalla, 00100 Rome, Italy (Telephone Number in U.S. (202) 653-2400); *Production Yearbook,* and *The State of Food and Agriculture.*

G.K. Hall and Company, 70 Lincoln Street, Boston, Massachusetts 02111 (617) 423-3990; *The World in Figures.*

International Monetary Fund, 700 Nineteenth Street, NW, Washington, D.C. 20431 (202) 623-7000; *International Financial Statistics.*

Statistical Office of the United Nations, Publishing Service, New York, New York 10017 (800) 253-9646; *Statistical Yearbook.*

United Nations Economic Commission for Africa, Africa Hall, Post Office Box 3001, Addis Ababa, Ethiopia (Telephone Number in U.S. (800) 253-9646); *African Statistical Yearbook.*

MOROCCO - CUSTOMS DUTIES

G.K. Hall and Company, 70 Lincoln Street, Boston, Massachusetts 02111 (617) 423-3990; *The World in Figures.*

International Monetary Fund, 700 Nineteenth Street, NW, Washington, D.C. 20431 (202) 623-7000; *Government Finance Statistics Yearbook.*

MOROCCO - DAIRY PRODUCTS

Facts on File, 460 Park Avenue South, New York, New York 10016 (800) 443-8323; *The New Book of World Rankings.*

Food and Agricultural Organization of the United Nations (FAO), Via delle Terme di Caracalla, 00100 Rome, Italy (Telephone Number in U.S. (202) 653-2400); *Production Yearbook,* and *The State of Food and Agriculture.*

Statistical Office of the United Nations, Publishing Service, New York, New York 10017 (800) 253-9646; *Statistical Yearbook.*

MOROCCO - DEATH RATES

Euromonitor Publications Limited, 87-88 Turnmill Street, London EC1M 5QU, England; *Middle East Economic Handbook.*

G.K. Hall and Company, 70 Lincoln Street, Boston, Massachusetts 02111 (617) 423-3990; *The World in Figures.*

Statistical Office of the United Nations, Publishing Service, New York, New York 10017 (800) 253-9646; *Statistical Yearbook,* and *Survey of Economic and Social Conditions in Africa.*

Times Books, 201 East 50th Street, New York, New York 10022 (212) 751-2600; *The Economist Book of Vital World Statistics.*

MOROCCO - DEFENSE EXPENDITURES

G.K. Hall and Company, 70 Lincoln Street, Boston, Massachusetts 02111 (617) 423-3990; *The World in Figures.*

International Monetary Fund, 700 Nineteenth Street, NW, Washington, D.C. 20431 (202) 623-7000; *Government Finance Statistics Yearbook.*

U.S. Arms Control and Disarmament Agency, 320 Twenty-first Street, NW, Washington, D.C. 20451 (202) 647-8677; *World Military Expenditures and Arms Transfers.*

MOROCCO - DEMOGRAPHY

The Economist Intelligence Unit, 111 West 57th Street, New York, New York 10019 (800) 938-4685; *The World Market Atlas.*

Facts on File, 460 Park Avenue South, New York, New York 10016 (800) 443-8323; *The New Book of World Rankings.*

G.K. Hall and Company, 70 Lincoln Street, Boston, Massachusetts 02111 (617) 423-3990; *The World in Figures.*

Statistical Office of the United Nations, Publishing Service, New York, New York 10017 (800) 253-9646; *Survey of Economic and Social Conditions in Africa.*

MOROCCO - DEVELOPMENT ASSISTANCE

G.K. Hall and Company, 70 Lincoln Street, Boston, Massachusetts 02111 (617) 423-3990; *The World in Figures.*

Statistical Office of the United Nations, Publishing Service, New York, New York 10017 (800) 253-9646; *Statistical Yearbook.*

MOROCCO - DIAMOND PRODUCTION - See MOROCCO - MINING AND MINERAL PRODUCTS

MOROCCO - DISEASE

G.K. Hall and Company, 70 Lincoln Street, Boston, Massachusetts 02111 (617) 423-3990; *The World in Figures.*

MOROCCO - DIVORCE

Facts on File, 460 Park Avenue South, New York, New York 10016 (800) 443-8323; *The New Book of World Rankings.*

Statistical Office of the United Nations, Publishing Service, New York, New York 10017 (800) 253-9646; *Demographic Yearbook.*

MOROCCO - DOMESTIC PRODUCT

G.K. Hall and Company, 70 Lincoln Street, Boston, Massachusetts 02111 (617) 423-3990; *The World in Figures.*

MOROCCO - ECONOMY

African Development Bank, 01 BP 1387, Abidjan 01, Cote d'Ivoire; *Selected Statistics on Regional Member Countries.*

Euromonitor Publications Limited, 87-88 Turnmill Street, London EC1M 5QU, England; *International Marketing Data and Statistics.*

Facts on File, 460 Park Avenue South, New York, New York 10016 (800) 443-8323; *The New Book of World Rankings.*

G.K. Hall and Company, 70 Lincoln Street, Boston, Massachusetts 02111 (617) 423-3990; *The World in Figures.*

Statistical Office of the United Nations, Publishing Service, New York, New York 10017 (800) 253-9646; *Foreign Trade Statistics for Africa.*

MOROCCO - EDUCATION

African Development Bank, 01 BP 1387, Abidjan 01, Cote d'Ivoire; *Selected Statistics on Regional Member Countries.*

The Economist Intelligence Unit, 111 West 57th Street, New York, New York 10019 (800) 938-4685; *The World Market Atlas.*

Euromonitor Publications Limited, 87-88 Turnmill Street, London EC1M 5QU, England; *Middle East Economic Handbook.*

Facts on File, 460 Park Avenue South, New York, New York 10016 (800) 443-8323; *The New Book of World Rankings.*

G.K. Hall and Company, 70 Lincoln Street, Boston, Massachusetts 02111 (617) 423-3990; *The World in Figures.*

International Monetary Fund, 700 Nineteenth Street, NW, Washington, D.C. 20431 (202) 623-7000; *Government Finance Statistics Yearbook.*

Statistical Office of the United Nations, Publishing Service, New York, New York 10017 (800) 253-9646; *Survey of Economic and Social Conditions in Africa.*

Times Books, 201 East 50th Street, New York, New York 10022 (212) 751-2600; *The Economist Book of Vital World Statistics.*

United Nations Economic Commission for Africa, Africa Hall, Post Office Box 3001, Addis Ababa, Ethiopia (Telephone Number in U.S. (800) 253-9646); *African Statistical Yearbook.*

United Nations Educational, Scientific and Cultural Organization (UNESCO), 7 Place de Fontenoy, F-75700 Paris, France (Telephone Number in U.S. (212) 963-5981); *Statistical Yearbook.*

The World Bank, 1818 H Street, NW, Washington, D.C. 20433 (202) 477-1234; *World Tables.*

MOROCCO - EGG PRODUCTION AND CONSUMPTION - See MOROCCO - DAIRY PRODUCTS

MOROCCO - ELECTRICITY

Facts on File, 460 Park Avenue South, New York, New York 10016 (800) 443-8323; *The New Book of World Rankings.*

Penn Well Publishing Company, 1421 South Sheridan Road, Post Office Box 1260, Tulsa, Oklahoma 74101 (800) 752-9764; *International Energy Statistics Sourcebook.*

Statistical Office of the United Nations, Publishing Service, New York, New York 10017 (800) 253-9646; *Statistical Yearbook,* and *Survey of Economic and Social Conditions in Africa.*

Times Books, 201 East 50th Street, New York, New York 10022 (212) 751-2600; *The Economist Book of Vital World Statistics.*

United Nations Economic Commission for Africa, Africa Hall, Post Office Box 3001, Addis Ababa, Ethiopia (Telephone Number in U.S. (800) 253-9646); *African Statistical Yearbook.*

MOROCCO - EMPLOYMENT

Euromonitor Publications Limited, 87-88 Turnmill Street, London EC1M 5QU, England; *International Marketing Data and Statistics,* and *Middle East Economic Handbook.*

Facts on File, 460 Park Avenue South, New York, New York 10016 (800) 443-8323; *The New Book of World Rankings.*

Statistical Office of the United Nations, Publishing Service, New York, New York 10017 (800) 253-9646; *Survey of Economic and Social Conditions in Africa.*

United Nations Economic Commission for Africa, Africa Hall, Post Office Box 3001, Addis Ababa, Ethiopia (Telephone Number in U.S. (800) 253-9646); *African Statistical Yearbook.*

MOROCCO - ENERGY

Euromonitor Publications Limited, 87-88 Turnmill Street, London EC1M 5QU, England; *Middle East Economic Handbook.*

Facts on File, 460 Park Avenue South, New York, New York 10016 (800) 443-8323; *The New Book of World Rankings.*

Food and Agricultural Organization of the United Nations (FAO), Via delle Terme di Caracalla, 00100 Rome, Italy (Telephone Number in U.S. (202) 653-2400); *The State of Food and Agriculture.*

G.K. Hall and Company, 70 Lincoln Street, Boston, Massachusetts 02111 (617) 423-3990; *The World in Figures.*

Penn Well Publishing Company, 1421 South Sheridan Road, Post Office Box 1260, Tulsa, Oklahoma 74101 (800) 752-9764; *International Energy Statistics Sourcebook.*

Statistical Office of the United Nations, Publishing Service, New York, New York 10017 (800) 253-9646; *Energy Statistics Yearbook*, and *Statistical Yearbook*.

Times Books, 201 East 50th Street, New York, New York 10022 (212) 751-2600; *The Economist Book of Vital World Statistics*.

United Nations Economic Commission for Africa, Africa Hall, Post Office Box 3001, Addis Ababa, Ethiopia (Telephone Number in U.S. (800) 253-9646; *African Statistical Yearbook*.

MOROCCO - EXCHANGE RATES

African Development Bank, 01 BP 1387, Abidjan 01, Cote d'Ivoire; *Selected Statistics on Regional Member Countries*.

Euromonitor Publications Limited, 87-88 Turnmill Street, London EC1M 5QU, England; *International Marketing Data and Statistics*, and *Middle East Economic Handbook*.

International Civil Aviation Organization, 1000 Sherbrooke Street West, Suite 400, Montreal, Quebec H3A 2R2, Canada (514) 285-8219; *Civil Aviation Statistics of the World*.

International Monetary Fund, 700 Nineteenth Street, NW, Washington, D.C. 20431 (202) 623-7000; *International Financial Statistics*.

Statistical Office of the United Nations, Publishing Service, New York, New York 10017 (800) 253-9646; *Foreign Trade Statistics for Africa*, and *Statistical Yearbook*.

MOROCCO - EXCISE TAXES - See MOROCCO - TAXATION

MOROCCO - EXPORTS

African Development Bank, 01 BP 1387, Abidjan 01, Cote d'Ivoire; *Selected Statistics on Regional Member Countries*.

American Automobile Manufacturers Association, 1401 H Eye Street, NW, Suite 900, Washington, D.C. 20005 (202) 326-5500; *World Motor Vehicle Data*.

The Economist Intelligence Unit (Asia) Limited, 10th Floor, Luk Kwok Centre, 72 Gloucester Road, Wanchai, Hong Kong (Phone Number in U.S. (800) 938-4685); *Asian Market Atlas*.

Euromonitor Publications Limited, 87-88 Turnmill Street, London EC1M 5QU, England; *International Marketing Data and Statistics*, and *Middle East Economic Handbook*.

Food and Agricultural Organization of the United Nations (FAO), Via delle Terme di Caracalla, 00100 Rome, Italy (Telephone Number in U.S. (202) 653-2400); *The State of Food and Agriculture*.

G.K. Hall and Company, 70 Lincoln Street, Boston, Massachusetts 02111 (617) 423-3990; *The World in Figures*.

International Lead and Zinc Study Group, Metro House, 58 St. James's Street, London SW1A 1LD England; *Lead and Zinc Statistics*.

International Monetary Fund, 700 Nineteenth Street, NW, Washington, D.C. 20431 (202) 623-7000; *Direction of Trade Statistics*, *Government Finance Statistics Yearbook*, and *International Financial Statistics*.

Statistical Office of the United Nations, Publishing Service, New York, New York 10017 (800) 253-9646; *Foreign Trade Statistics for*

Africa, *Trade in Manufactures of Developing Countries*, and *Survey of Economic and Social Conditions in Africa*.

Times Books, 201 East 50th Street, New York, New York 10022 (212) 751-2600; *The Economist Book of Vital World Statistics*.

United Nations Economic Commission for Africa, Africa Hall, Post Office Box 3001, Addis Ababa, Ethiopia (Telephone Number in U.S. (800) 253-9646; *African Statistical Yearbook*.

The World Bank, 1818 H Street, NW, Washington, D.C. 20433 (202) 477-1234; *World Tables*.

MOROCCO - EXTERNAL INDEBTEDNESS

African Development Bank, 01 BP 1387, Abidjan 01, Cote d'Ivoire; *Selected Statistics on Regional Member Countries*.

Statistical Office of the United Nations, Publishing Service, New York, New York 10017 (800) 253-9646; *Survey of Economic and Social Conditions in Africa*.

The World Bank, 1818 H Street, NW, Washington, D.C. 20433 (202) 477-1234; *World Tables*.

MOROCCO - EXTERNAL TRADE

African Development Bank, 01 BP 1387, Abidjan 01, Cote d'Ivoire; *Selected Statistics on Regional Member Countries*.

Food and Agricultural Organization of the United Nations (FAO), Via delle Terme di Caracalla, 00100 Rome, Italy (Telephone Number in U.S. (202) 653-2400); *The State of Food and Agriculture*, and *Trade Yearbook*.

G.K. Hall and Company, 70 Lincoln Street, Boston, Massachusetts 02111 (617) 423-3990; *The World in Figures*.

Statistical Office of the United Nations, Publishing Service, New York, New York 10017 (800) 253-9646; *Statistical Yearbook*.

MOROCCO - FABRIC PRODUCTION - See MOROCCO - TEXTILE INDUSTRY

MOROCCO - FARM CROPS - See MOROCCO - CROPS

MOROCCO - FEMALE WORKING POPULATION - See MOROCCO - EMPLOYMENT

MOROCCO - FERTILITY RATES

Facts on File, 460 Park Avenue South, New York, New York 10016 (800) 443-8323; *The New Book of World Rankings*.

Statistical Office of the United Nations, Publishing Service, New York, New York 10017 (800) 253-9646; *Survey of Economic and Social Conditions in Africa*.

Times Books, 201 East 50th Street, New York, New York 10022 (212) 751-2600; *The Economist Book of Vital World Statistics*.

The World Bank, 1818 H Street, NW, Washington, D.C. 20433 (202) 477-1234; *World Tables*.

MOROCCO - FERTILIZER

Food and Agricultural Organization of the United Nations (FAO), Via delle Terme di Caracalla, 00100 Rome, Italy (Telephone Number in U.S. (202) 653-2400); *Fertilizer Yearbook*, and *The State of Food and*

Agriculture.

Statistical Office of the United Nations, Publishing Service, New York, New York 10017 (800) 253-9646; *Statistical Yearbook.*

MOROCCO - FETAL MORTALITY

Statistical Office of the United Nations, Publishing Service, New York, New York 10017 (800) 253-9646; *Demographic Yearbook.*

MOROCCO - FINANCE

African Development Bank, 01 BP 1387, Abidjan 01, Cote d'Ivoire; *Selected Statistics on Regional Member Countries.*

Euromonitor Publications Limited, 87-88 Turnmill Street, London EC1M 5QU, England; *Middle East Economic Handbook.*

Facts on File, 460 Park Avenue South, New York, New York 10016 (800) 443-8323; *The New Book of World Rankings.*

Food and Agricultural Organization of the United Nations (FAO), Via delle Terme di Caracalla, 00100 Rome, Italy (Telephone Number in U.S. (202) 653-2400); *The State of Food and Agriculture,* and *Yearbook of Fishery Statistics.*

G.K. Hall and Company, 70 Lincoln Street, Boston, Massachusetts 02111 (617) 423-3990; *The World in Figures.*

International Monetary Fund, 700 Nineteenth Street, NW, Washington, D.C. 20431 (202) 623-7000; *Government Finance Statistics Yearbook,* and *International Financial Statistics.*

Statistical Office of the United Nations, Publishing Service, New York, New York 10017 (800) 253-9646; *Statistical Yearbook,* and *Survey of Economic and Social Conditions in Africa.*

United Nations Economic Commission for Africa, Africa Hall, Post Office Box 3001, Addis Ababa, Ethiopia (Telephone Number in U.S. (800) 253-9646); *African Statistical Yearbook.*

MOROCCO - FISHERIES

United Nations Economic Commission for Africa, Africa Hall, Post Office Box 3001, Addis Ababa, Ethiopia (Telephone Number in U.S. (800) 253-9646); *African Statistical Yearbook.*

MOROCCO - FLOUR PRODUCTION

Statistical Office of the United Nations, Publishing Service, New York, New York 10017 (800) 253-9646; *Statistical Yearbook.*

MOROCCO - FOOD

African Development Bank, 01 BP 1387, Abidjan 01, Cote d'Ivoire; *Selected Statistics on Regional Member Countries.*

Food and Agricultural Organization of the United Nations (FAO), Via delle Terme di Caracalla, 00100 Rome, Italy (Telephone Number in U.S. (202) 653-2400); *Production Yearbook,* and *The State of Food and Agriculture.*

G.K. Hall and Company, 70 Lincoln Street, Boston, Massachusetts 02111 (617) 423-3990; *The World in Figures.*

Statistical Office of the United Nations, Publishing Service, New York, New York 10017 (800) 253-9646; *Trade in Manufactures of Developing Countries.*

MOROCCO - FOREIGN AID

G.K. Hall and Company, 70 Lincoln Street, Boston, Massachusetts 02111 (617) 423-3990; *The World in Figures.*

MOROCCO - FOREIGN DEBT

Euromonitor Publications Limited, 87-88 Turnmill Street, London EC1M 5QU, England; *Middle East Economic Handbook.*

International Monetary Fund, 700 Nineteenth Street, NW, Washington, D.C. 20431 (202) 623-7000; *Government Finance Statistics Yearbook.*

MOROCCO - FOREIGN TRADE

Euromonitor Publications Limited, 87-88 Turnmill Street, London EC1M 5QU, England; *International Marketing Data and Statistics,* and *Middle East Economic Handbook.*

Facts on File, 460 Park Avenue South, New York, New York 10016 (800) 443-8323; *The New Book of World Rankings.*

Food and Agricultural Organization of the United Nations (FAO), Via delle Terme di Caracalla, 00100 Rome, Italy (Telephone Number in U.S. (202) 653-2400); *The State of Food and Agriculture.*

G.K. Hall and Company, 70 Lincoln Street, Boston, Massachusetts 02111 (617) 423-3990; *The World in Figures.*

International Monetary Fund, 700 Nineteenth Street, NW, Washington, D.C. 20431 (202) 623-7000; *International Financial Statistics.*

Statistical Office of the United Nations, Publishing Service, New York, New York 10017 (800) 253-9646; *Foreign Trade Statistics for Africa, International Trade Statistics Yearbook,* and *Statistical Yearbook.*

United Nations Economic Commission for Africa, Africa Hall, Post Office Box 3001, Addis Ababa, Ethiopia (Telephone Number in U.S. (800) 253-9646); *African Statistical Yearbook.*

The World Bank, 1818 H Street, NW, Washington, D.C. 20433 (202) 477-1234; *World Tables.*

MOROCCO - FORESTRY AND FOREST PRODUCTS

Facts on File, 460 Park Avenue South, New York, New York 10016 (800) 443-8323; *The New Book of World Rankings.*

Food and Agricultural Organization of the United Nations (FAO), Via delle Terme di Caracalla, 00100 Rome, Italy (Telephone Number in U.S. (202) 653-2400); *The State of Food and Agriculture,* and *Yearbook of Forest Products.*

G.K. Hall and Company, 70 Lincoln Street, Boston, Massachusetts 02111 (617) 423-3990; *The World in Figures.*

Statistical Office of the United Nations, Publishing Service, New York, New York 10017 (800) 253-9646; *Statistical Yearbook.*

United Nations Economic Commission for Africa, Africa Hall, Post Office Box 3001, Addis Ababa, Ethiopia (Telephone Number in U.S. (800) 253-9646); *African Statistical Yearbook.*

United Nations Educational, Scientific and Cultural Organization (UNESCO), 7 Place de Fontenoy, F-75700 Paris, France (Telephone Number in U.S. (212) 963-5981); *Statistical Yearbook.*

MOROCCO - FRUIT EXPORTS

International Monetary Fund, 700 Nineteenth Street, NW, Washington, D.C. 20431 (202) 623-7000; *International Financial Statistics*.

MOROCCO - GAS PRODUCTION - See MOROCCO - MINING AND MINERAL PRODUCTS

MOROCCO - GENERAL MORTALITY

Statistical Office of the United Nations, Publishing Service, New York, New York 10017 (800) 253-9646; *Demographic Yearbook*.

MOROCCO - GEOGRAPHIC DATA

Facts on File, 460 Park Avenue South, New York, New York 10016 (800) 443-8323; *The New Book of World Rankings*.

MOROCCO - GOATS - See MOROCCO - LIVESTOCK AND POULTRY

MOROCCO - GOLD HOLDINGS

International Monetary Fund, 700 Nineteenth Street, NW, Washington, D.C. 20431 (202) 623-7000; *International Financial Statistics*.

Statistical Office of the United Nations, Publishing Service, New York, New York 10017 (800) 253-9646; *Statistical Yearbook*.

The World Bank, 1818 H Street, NW, Washington, D.C. 20433 (202) 477-1234; *World Tables*.

MOROCCO - GOLD PRODUCTION AND CONSUMPTION - See MOROCCO - MINING AND MINERAL PRODUCTS

MOROCCO - GOVERNMENT

G.K. Hall and Company, 70 Lincoln Street, Boston, Massachusetts 02111 (617) 423-3990; *The World in Figures*.

MOROCCO - GOVERNMENT EXPENDITURES

International Monetary Fund, 700 Nineteenth Street, NW, Washington, D.C. 20431 (202) 623-7000; *Government Finance Statistics Yearbook*.

Times Books, 201 East 50th Street, New York, New York 10022 (212) 751-2600; *The Economist Book of Vital World Statistics*.

The World Bank, 1818 H Street, NW, Washington, D.C. 20433 (202) 477-1234; *World Tables*.

MOROCCO - GOVERNMENT FINANCES

International Monetary Fund, 700 Nineteenth Street, NW, Washington, D.C. 20431 (202) 623-7000; *International Financial Statistics*.

MOROCCO - GOVERNMENT REVENUES

International Monetary Fund, 700 Nineteenth Street, NW, Washington, D.C. 20431 (202) 623-7000; *Government Finance Statistics Yearbook*.

Statistical Office of the United Nations, Publishing Service, New York, New York 10017 (800) 253-9646; *Survey of Economic and Social Conditions in Africa*.

Times Books, 201 East 50th Street, New York, New York 10022 (212) 751-2600; *The Economist Book of Vital World Statistics*.

The World Bank, 1818 H Street, NW, Washington, D.C. 20433 (202) 477-1234; *World Tables*.

MOROCCO - GRAIN PRODUCTION - See MOROCCO - CROPS

MOROCCO - GRANTS

International Monetary Fund, 700 Nineteenth Street, NW, Washington, D.C. 20431 (202) 623-7000; *Government Finance Statistics Yearbook*.

MOROCCO - GROSS DOMESTIC PRODUCT

African Development Bank, 01 BP 1387, Abidjan 01, Cote d'Ivoire; *Selected Statistics on Regional Member Countries*.

Euromonitor Publications Limited, 87-88 Turnmill Street, London EC1M 5QU, England; *International Marketing Data and Statistics*, and *Middle East Economic Handbook*.

Facts on File, 460 Park Avenue South, New York, New York 10016 (800) 443-8323; *The New Book of World Rankings*.

G.K. Hall and Company, 70 Lincoln Street, Boston, Massachusetts 02111 (617) 423-3990; *The World in Figures*.

Statistical Office of the United Nations, Publishing Service, New York, New York 10017 (800) 253-9646; *Statistical Yearbook*, and *Survey of Economic and Social Conditions in Africa*.

Times Books, 201 East 50th Street, New York, New York 10022 (212) 751-2600; *The Economist Book of Vital World Statistics*.

United Nations Economic Commission for Africa, Africa Hall, Post Office Box 3001, Addis Ababa, Ethiopia (Telephone Number in U.S. (800) 253-9646); *African Statistical Yearbook*.

The World Bank, 1818 H Street, NW, Washington, D.C. 20433 (202) 477-1234; *World Tables*.

MOROCCO - GROSS NATIONAL PRODUCT

Euromonitor Publications Limited, 87-88 Turnmill Street, London EC1M 5QU, England; *International Marketing Data and Statistics*.

U.S. Arms Control and Disarmament Agency, 320 Twenty-first Street, NW, Washington, D.C. 20451 (202) 647-8677; *World Military Expenditures and Arms Transfers*.

The World Bank, 1818 H Street, NW, Washington, D.C. 20433 (202) 477-1234; *World Tables*.

MOROCCO - GROUNDNUT PRODUCTION - See MOROCCO - CROPS

MOROCCO - HEALTH

African Development Bank, 01 BP 1387, Abidjan 01, Cote d'Ivoire; *Selected Statistics on Regional Member Countries*.

Euromonitor Publications Limited, 87-88 Turnmill Street, London EC1M 5QU, England; *Middle East Economic Handbook*.

Facts on File, 460 Park Avenue South, New York, New York 10016 (800) 443-8323; *The New Book of World Rankings*.

G.K. Hall and Company, 70 Lincoln Street, Boston, Massachusetts 02111 (617) 423-3990; *The World in Figures*.

Statistical Office of the United Nations, Publishing Service, New York, New York 10017 (800) 253-9646; *Statistical Yearbook*.

Times Books, 201 East 50th Street, New York, New York 10022 (212) 751-2600; *The Economist Book of Vital World Statistics*.

United Nations Economic Commission for Africa, Africa Hall, Post Office Box 3001, Addis Ababa, Ethiopia (Telephone Number in U.S. (800) 253-9646); *African Statistical Yearbook*.

MOROCCO - HEALTH AND MEDICAL SERVICES

Statistical Office of the United Nations, Publishing Service, New York, New York 10017 (800) 253-9646; *Statistical Yearbook*.

MOROCCO - HEALTH EXPENDITURES

International Monetary Fund, 700 Nineteenth Street, NW, Washington, D.C. 20431 (202) 623-7000; *Government Finance Statistics Yearbook*.

MOROCCO - HIDE PRODUCTION

Food and Agricultural Organization of the United Nations (FAO), Via delle Terme di Caracalla, 00100 Rome, Italy (Telephone Number in U.S. (202) 653-2400); *Production Yearbook*.

MOROCCO - HIGHWAYS

G.K. Hall and Company, 70 Lincoln Street, Boston, Massachusetts 02111 (617) 423-3990; *The World in Figures*.

Statistical Office of the United Nations, Publishing Service, New York, New York 10017 (800) 253-9646; *Survey of Economic and Social Conditions in Africa*.

United Nations Economic Commission for Africa, Africa Hall, Post Office Box 3001, Addis Ababa, Ethiopia (Telephone Number in U.S. (800) 253-9646); *African Statistical Yearbook*.

MOROCCO - HORSES - See MOROCCO - LIVESTOCK AND POULTRY

MOROCCO - HOURS OF WORK - See MOROCCO - EMPLOYMENT

MOROCCO - HOUSING EXPENDITURES

Facts on File, 460 Park Avenue South, New York, New York 10016 (800) 443-8323; *The New Book of World Rankings*.

International Monetary Fund, 700 Nineteenth Street, NW, Washington, D.C. 20431 (202) 623-7000; *Government Finance Statistics Yearbook*.

MOROCCO - ILLITERATE POPULATION

G.K. Hall and Company, 70 Lincoln Street, Boston, Massachusetts 02111 (617) 423-3990; *The World in Figures*.

United Nations Educational, Scientific and Cultural Organization (UNESCO), 7 Place de Fontenoy, F-75700 Paris, France (Telephone Number in U.S. (212) 963-5981); *Statistical Yearbook*.

MOROCCO - IMPORTS

African Development Bank, 01 BP 1387, Abidjan 01, Cote d'Ivoire; *Selected Statistics on Regional Member Countries*.

American Automobile Manufacturers Association, 1401 H Street, NW, Suite 900, Washington, D.C. 20005 (202) 326-5500; *World Motor Vehicle Data*.

The Economist Intelligence Unit, 111 West 57th Street, New York, New York 10019 (800) 938-4685; *The World Market Atlas*.

Euromonitor Publications Limited, 87-88 Turnmill Street, London EC1M 5QU, England; *International Marketing Data and Statistics*, and *Middle East Economic Handbook*.

Food and Agricultural Organization of the United Nations (FAO), Via delle Terme di Caracalla, 00100 Rome, Italy (Telephone Number in U.S. (202) 653-2400); *The State of Food and Agriculture*.

G.K. Hall and Company, 70 Lincoln Street, Boston, Massachusetts 02111 (617) 423-3990; *The World in Figures*.

International Lead and Zinc Study Group, Metro House, 58 St. James's Street, London SW1A 1LD England; *Lead and Zinc Statistics*.

International Monetary Fund, 700 Nineteenth Street, NW, Washington, D.C. 20431 (202) 623-7000; *Direction of Trade Statistics*, *Government Finance Statistics Yearbook*, and *International Financial Statistics*.

Statistical Office of the United Nations, Publishing Service, New York, New York 10017 (800) 253-9646; *Foreign Trade Statistics for Africa*, *Trade in Manufactures of Developing Countries*, and *Survey of Economic and Social Conditions in Africa*.

Times Books, 201 East 50th Street, New York, New York 10022 (212) 751-2600; *The Economist Book of Vital World Statistics*.

United Nations Economic Commission for Africa, Africa Hall, Post Office Box 3001, Addis Ababa, Ethiopia (Telephone Number in U.S. (800) 253-9646); *African Statistical Yearbook*.

The World Bank, 1818 H Street, NW, Washington, D.C. 20433 (202) 477-1234; *World Tables*.

MOROCCO - INCOME TAXES - See MOROCCO - TAXATION

MOROCCO - INDIVIDUAL INCOME TAXES

International Monetary Fund, 700 Nineteenth Street, NW, Washington, D.C. 20431 (202) 623-7000; *Government Finance Statistics Yearbook*.

MOROCCO - INDUSTRIAL METALS PRODUCTION - See MOROCCO - MINING AND MINERAL PRODUCTS

MOROCCO - INDUSTRY

Euromonitor Publications Limited, 87-88 Turnmill Street, London EC1M 5QU, England; *International Marketing Data and Statistics*.

Facts on File, 460 Park Avenue South, New York, New York 10016 (800) 443-8323; *The New Book of World Rankings*.

G.K. Hall and Company, 70 Lincoln Street, Boston, Massachusetts 02111 (617) 423-3990; *The World in Figures*.

Statistical Office of the United Nations, Publishing Service, New York, New York 10017 (800) 253-9646; *Statistical Yearbook*, and *Survey of Economic and Social Conditions in Africa*.

Times Books, 201 East 50th Street, New York, New York 10022 (212) 751-2600; *The Economist Book of Vital World Statistics*.

United Nations Economic Commission for Africa, Africa Hall, Post Office Box 3001, Addis Ababa, Ethiopia (Telephone Number in U.S. (800) 253-9646); *African Statistical Yearbook*.

The World Bank, 1818 H Street, NW, Washington, D.C. 20433 (202) 477-1234; *World Tables*.

World Intellectual Property Organization, 34 Chemin des Colombettes, CH-1211 Geneva 20, Switzerland; *Industrial Property Statistics*.

MOROCCO - INFANT AND MATERNAL MORTALITY

Statistical Office of the United Nations, Publishing Service, New York, New York 10017 (800) 253-9646; *Demographic Yearbook*, *Statistical Yearbook*, and *Survey of Economic and Social Conditions in Africa*.

Times Books, 201 East 50th Street, New York, New York 10022 (212) 751-2600; *The Economist Book of Vital World Statistics*.

The World Bank, 1818 H Street, NW, Washington, D.C. 20433 (202) 477-1234; *World Tables*.

MOROCCO - INTERNATIONAL LIQUIDITY

International Monetary Fund, 700 Nineteenth Street, NW, Washington, D.C. 20431 (202) 623-7000; *International Financial Statistics*.

MOROCCO - INTERNATIONAL RESERVES EXCLUDING GOLD

African Development Bank, 01 BP 1387, Abidjan 01, Cote d'Ivoire; *Selected Statistics on Regional Member Countries*.

Statistical Office of the United Nations, Publishing Service, New York, New York 10017 (800) 253-9646; *Statistical Yearbook*.

The World Bank, 1818 H Street, NW, Washington, D.C. 20433 (202) 477-1234; *World Tables*.

MOROCCO - INVESTMENTS

International Monetary Fund, 700 Nineteenth Street, NW, Washington, D.C. 20431 (202) 623-7000; *International Financial Statistics*.

MOROCCO - IRON ORE PRODUCTION AND CONSUMPTION - See MOROCCO - MINING AND MINERAL PRODUCTS

MOROCCO - IRRIGATION

Euromonitor Publications Limited, 87-88 Turnmill Street, London EC1M 5QU, England; *International Marketing Data and Statistics*.

MOROCCO - LABOR FORCE

African Development Bank, 01 BP 1387, Abidjan 01, Cote d'Ivoire; *Selected Statistics on Regional Member Countries*.

Euromonitor Publications Limited, 87-88 Turnmill Street, London EC1M 5QU, England; *International Marketing Data and Statistics*, and *Middle East Economic Handbook*.

Facts on File, 460 Park Avenue South, New York, New York 10016 (800) 443-8323; *The New Book of World Rankings*.

Food and Agricultural Organization of the United Nations (FAO), Via delle Terme di Caracalla, 00100 Rome, Italy (Telephone Number in U.S. (202) 653-2400); *The State of Food and Agriculture*.

G.K. Hall and Company, 70 Lincoln Street, Boston, Massachusetts 02111 (617) 423-3990; *The World in Figures*.

Times Books, 201 East 50th Street, New York, New York 10022 (212) 751-2600; *The Economist Book of Vital World Statistics*.

The World Bank, 1818 H Street, NW, Washington, D.C. 20433 (202) 477-1234; *World Tables*.

MOROCCO - LAND USE

Euromonitor Publications Limited, 87-88 Turnmill Street, London EC1M 5QU, England; *International Marketing Data and Statistics*.

Food and Agricultural Organization of the United Nations (FAO), Via delle Terme di Caracalla, 00100 Rome, Italy (Telephone Number in U.S. (202) 653-2400); *Production Yearbook*.

G.K. Hall and Company, 70 Lincoln Street, Boston, Massachusetts 02111 (617) 423-3990; *The World in Figures*.

MOROCCO - LEAD AND LEAD ORE PRODUCTION AND CONSUMPTION - See MOROCCO - MINING AND MINERAL PRODUCTS

MOROCCO - LIBRARIES

Facts on File, 460 Park Avenue South, New York, New York 10016 (800) 443-8323; *The New Book of World Rankings*.

United Nations Educational, Scientific and Cultural Organization (UNESCO), 7 Place de Fontenoy, F-75700 Paris, France (Telephone Number in U.S. (212) 963-5981); *Statistical Yearbook*.

MOROCCO - LIFE EXPECTANCY

African Development Bank, 01 BP 1387, Abidjan 01, Cote d'Ivoire; *Selected Statistics on Regional Member Countries*.

MOROCCO - LITERACY RATE

Statistical Office of the United Nations, Publishing Service, New York, New York 10017 (800) 253-9646; *Survey of Economic and Social Conditions in Africa*.

MOROCCO - LIVESTOCK AND POULTRY

Euromonitor Publications Limited, 87-88 Turnmill Street, London EC1M 5QU, England; *International Marketing Data and Statistics*.

Facts on File, 460 Park Avenue South, New York, New York 10016 (800) 443-8323; *The New Book of World Rankings*.

Food and Agricultural Organization of the United Nations (FAO), Via delle Terme di Caracalla, 00100 Rome, Italy (Telephone Number in U.S. (202) 653-2400); *Production Yearbook*, and *The State of Food and Agriculture*.

G.K. Hall and Company, 70 Lincoln Street, Boston, Massachusetts 02111 (617) 423-3990; *The World in Figures*.

Statistical Office of the United Nations, Publishing Service, New York, New York 10017 (800) 253-9646; *Statistical Yearbook*, and *Survey of Economic and Social Conditions in Africa*.

United Nations Economic Commission for Africa, Africa Hall, Post Office Box 3001, Addis Ababa, Ethiopia (Telephone Number in U.S. (800) 253-9646); *African Statistical Yearbook.*

MOROCCO - LIVING LEVELS

G.K. Hall and Company, 70 Lincoln Street, Boston, Massachusetts 02111 (617) 423-3990; *The World in Figures.*

Times Books, 201 East 50th Street, New York, New York 10022 (212) 751-2600; *The Economist Book of Vital World Statistics.*

MOROCCO - MAIL - NUMBER OF PIECES SENT OR RECEIVED

Statistical Office of the United Nations, Publishing Service, New York, New York 10017 (800) 253-9646; *Statistical Yearbook.*

MOROCCO - MANGANESE AND MANGANESE ORE PRODUCTION AND CONSUMPTION - See MOROCCO - MINING AND MINERAL PRODUCTS

MOROCCO - MANUFACTURING

American Automobile Manufacturers Association, 1401 H Street, NW, Suite 900, Washington, D.C. 20005 (202) 326-5500; *World Motor Vehicle Data.*

Facts on File, 460 Park Avenue South, New York, New York 10016 (800) 443-8323; *The New Book of World Rankings.*

G.K. Hall and Company, 70 Lincoln Street, Boston, Massachusetts 02111 (617) 423-3990; *The World in Figures.*

International Monetary Fund, 700 Nineteenth Street, NW, Washington, D.C. 20431 (202) 623-7000; *International Financial Statistics.*

Statistical Office of the United Nations, Publishing Service, New York, New York 10017 (800) 253-9646; *Statistical Yearbook,* and *Survey of Economic and Social Conditions in Africa.*

Times Books, 201 East 50th Street, New York, New York 10022 (212) 751-2600; *The Economist Book of Vital World Statistics.*

United Nations Economic Commission for Africa, Africa Hall, Post Office Box 3001, Addis Ababa, Ethiopia (Telephone Number in U.S. (800) 253-9646); *African Statistical Yearbook.*

The World Bank, 1818 H Street, NW, Washington, D.C. 20433 (202) 477-1234; *World Tables.*

MOROCCO - MARRIAGE

Facts on File, 460 Park Avenue South, New York, New York 10016 (800) 443-8323; *The New Book of World Rankings.*

Statistical Office of the United Nations, Publishing Service, New York, New York 10017 (800) 253-9646; *Demographic Yearbook.*

MOROCCO - MEAT PRODUCTION - See MOROCCO - LIVESTOCK AND POULTRY

MOROCCO - MERCHANT SHIPPING

G.K. Hall and Company, 70 Lincoln Street, Boston, Massachusetts 02111 (617) 423-3990; *The World in Figures.*

Lloyd's Register of Shipping, 17 Battery Place, New York, New York 10004 (212) 425-8050; *Register of Ships.*

Statistical Office of the United Nations, Publishing Service, New York, New York 10017 (800) 253-9646; *Statistical Yearbook.*

Times Books, 201 East 50th Street, New York, New York 10022 (212) 751-2600; *The Economist Book of Vital World Statistics.*

United Nations Economic Commission for Africa, Africa Hall, Post Office Box 3001, Addis Ababa, Ethiopia (Telephone Number in U.S. (800) 253-9646); *African Statistical Yearbook.*

U.S. Department of Transportation, Maritime Administration, 400 Seventh Street, SW, Washington, D.C. 20590; *A Statistical Analysis of the World's Merchant Fleets.*

MOROCCO - MILITARY

G.K. Hall and Company, 70 Lincoln Street, Boston, Massachusetts 02111 (617) 423-3990; *The World in Figures.*

The International Institute for Strategic Studies, 23 Tavistock Street, London WC2E 7NQ, England; *The Military Balance.*

U.S. Arms Control and Disarmament Agency, 320 Twenty-first Street, NW, Washington, D.C. 20451 (202) 647-8677; *World Military Expenditures and Arms Transfers.*

MOROCCO - MILK PRODUCTION - See MOROCCO - DAIRY PRODUCTS

MOROCCO - MILLET PRODUCTION - See MOROCCO - CROPS

MOROCCO - MINING AND MINERAL PRODUCTS

Commodity Research Bureau, Incorporated, 75 Wall Street, New York, New York, 10005 (212) 504-7754; *Commodity Year Book.*

Facts on File, 460 Park Avenue South, New York, New York 10016 (800) 443-8323; *The New Book of World Rankings.*

G.K. Hall and Company, 70 Lincoln Street, Boston, Massachusetts 02111 (617) 423-3990; *The World in Figures.*

International Lead and Zinc Study Group, Metro House, 58 St. James's Street, London SW1A 1LD England; *Lead and Zinc Statistics.*

Penn Well Publishing Company, 1421 South Sheridan Road, Post Office Box 1260, Tulsa, Oklahoma 74101 (800) 752-9764; *International Energy Statistics Sourcebook.*

Statistical Office of the United Nations, Publishing Service, New York, New York 10017 (800) 253-9646; *Statistical Yearbook.*

United Nations Economic Commission for Africa, Africa Hall, Post Office Box 3001, Addis Ababa, Ethiopia (Telephone Number in U.S. (800) 253-9646); *African Statistical Yearbook.*

MOROCCO - MONEY EXCHANGE RATE

Euromonitor Publications Limited, 87-88 Turnmill Street, London EC1M 5QU, England; *International Marketing Data and Statistics.*

International Monetary Fund, 700 Nineteenth Street, NW, Washington, D.C. 20431 (202) 623-7000; *International Financial Statistics.*

Statistical Office of the United Nations, Publishing Service, New York, New York 10017 (800) 253-9646; *Statistical Yearbook.*

MOROCCO - MONEY RESERVES

Euromonitor Publications Limited, 87-88 Turnmill Street, London EC1M 5QU, England; *International Marketing Data and Statistics*.

MOROCCO - MONEY SUPPLY

African Development Bank, 01 BP 1387, Abidjan 01, Cote d'Ivoire; *Selected Statistics on Regional Member Countries*.

Euromonitor Publications Limited, 87-88 Turnmill Street, London EC1M 5QU, England; *International Marketing Data and Statistics*.

G.K. Hall and Company, 70 Lincoln Street, Boston, Massachusetts 02111 (617) 423-3990; *The World in Figures*.

International Monetary Fund, 700 Nineteenth Street, NW, Washington, D.C. 20431 (202) 623-7000; *International Financial Statistics*.

Statistical Office of the United Nations, Publishing Service, New York, New York 10017 (800) 253-9646; *Statistical Yearbook*.

The World Bank, 1818 H Street, NW, Washington, D.C. 20433 (202) 477-1234; *World Tables*.

MOROCCO - MOTION PICTURES

Statistical Office of the United Nations, Publishing Service, New York, New York 10017 (800) 253-9646; *Statistical Yearbook*.

MOROCCO - MOTOR VEHICLE ASSEMBLY

Statistical Office of the United Nations, Publishing Service, New York, New York 10017 (800) 253-9646; *Statistical Yearbook*.

MOROCCO - MOTOR VEHICLE PRODUCTION

American Automobile Manufacturers Association, 1620 Eye Street, NW, Suite 900, Washington, D.C. 20005 (202) 326-5500; *World Motor Vehicle Data*.

MOROCCO - MOTOR VEHICLE TAXES - See MOROCCO - TAXATION

MOROCCO - MOTOR VEHICLES IN USE

American Automobile Manufacturers Association, 1401 H Street, NW, Suite 900, Washington, D.C. 20005 (202) 326-5500; *World Motor Vehicle Data*.

G.K. Hall and Company, 70 Lincoln Street, Boston, Massachusetts 02111 (617) 423-3990; *The World in Figures*.

Statistical Office of the United Nations, Publishing Service, New York, New York 10017 (800) 253-9646; *Statistical Yearbook*, and *Survey of Economic and Social Conditions in Africa*.

Times Books, 201 East 50th Street, New York, New York 10022 (212) 751-2600; *The Economist Book of Vital World Statistics*.

MOROCCO - MULES - See MOROCCO - LIVESTOCK AND POULTRY

MOROCCO - MUSEUMS

Facts on File, 460 Park Avenue South, New York, New York 10016 (800) 443-8323; *The New Book of World Rankings*.

MOROCCO - NATALITY - See MOROCCO - BIRTH RATES

MOROCCO - NATIONAL ACCOUNTS

African Development Bank, 01 BP 1387, Abidjan 01, Cote d'Ivoire; *Selected Statistics on Regional Member Countries*.

International Monetary Fund, 700 Nineteenth Street, NW, Washington, D.C. 20431 (202) 623-7000; *International Financial Statistics*.

Statistical Office of the United Nations, Publishing Service, New York, New York 10017 (800) 253-9646; *Statistical Yearbook*.

United Nations Economic Commission for Africa, Africa Hall, Post Office Box 3001, Addis Ababa, Ethiopia (Telephone Number in U.S. (800) 253-9646); *African Statistical Yearbook*.

MOROCCO - NATIONAL INCOME

Facts on File, 460 Park Avenue South, New York, New York 10016 (800) 443-8323; *The New Book of World Rankings*.

G.K. Hall and Company, 70 Lincoln Street, Boston, Massachusetts 02111 (617) 423-3990; *The World in Figures*.

Statistical Office of the United Nations, Publishing Service, New York, New York 10017 (800) 253-9646; *Statistical Yearbook*.

MOROCCO - NATIONAL PRODUCT

Facts on File, 460 Park Avenue South, New York, New York 10016 (800) 443-8323; *The New Book of World Rankings*.

Statistical Office of the United Nations, Publishing Service, New York, New York 10017 (800) 253-9646; *Statistical Yearbook*.

MOROCCO - NATURAL GAS - PRODUCTION - See MOROCCO - MINING AND MINERAL PRODUCTS

MOROCCO - NEWSPAPER PRODUCTION - See MOROCCO - FORESTRY AND FOREST PRODUCTS

MOROCCO - NEWSPRINT - See MOROCCO - FORESTRY AND FOREST PRODUCTS

MOROCCO - NICKEL AND NICKEL ORE PRODUCTION AND CONSUMPTION - See MOROCCO - MINING AND MINERAL PRODUCTS

MOROCCO - OATS PRODUCTION - See MOROCCO - CROPS

MOROCCO - OCCUPATIONS - See MOROCCO - LABOR FORCE

MOROCCO - ORANGES - See MOROCCO - CROPS

MOROCCO - PAPER - See MOROCCO - FORESTRY AND FOREST PRODUCTS

MOROCCO - PATENTS

Statistical Office of the United Nations, Publishing Service, New York, New York 10017 (800) 253-9646; *Statistical Yearbook*.

World Intellectual Property Organization, 34 Chemin des Colombettes, CH-1211 Geneva 20, Switzerland; *Industrial Property Statistics*.

MOROCCO - PEANUT PRODUCTION - See MOROCCO - CROPS

MOROCCO - PERIODICALS

United Nations Educational, Scientific and Cultural Organization (UNESCO), 7 Place de Fontenoy, F-75700 Paris, France (Telephone Number in U.S. (212) 963-5981); *Statistical Yearbook*.

MOROCCO - PESTICIDE USE

Food and Agricultural Organization of the United Nations (FAO), Via delle Terme di Caracalla, 00100 Rome, Italy (Telephone Number in U.S. (202) 653-2400); *The State of Food and Agriculture*.

MOROCCO - PETROLEUM INDUSTRY

Euromonitor Publications Limited, 87-88 Turnmill Street, London EC1M 5QU, England; *Middle East Economic Handbook*.

Facts on File, 460 Park Avenue South, New York, New York 10016 (800) 443-8323; *The New Book of World Rankings*.

Food and Agricultural Organization of the United Nations (FAO), Via delle Terme di Caracalla, 00100 Rome, Italy (Telephone Number in U.S. (202) 653-2400); *The State of Food and Agriculture*.

G.K. Hall and Company, 70 Lincoln Street, Boston, Massachusetts 02111 (617) 423-3990; *The World in Figures*.

Penn Well Publishing Company, 1421 South Sheridan Road, Post Office Box 1260, Tulsa, Oklahoma 74101 (800) 752-9764; *International Energy Statistics Sourcebook*.

Statistical Office of the United Nations, Publishing Service, New York, New York 10017 (800) 253-9646; *Statistical Yearbook*.

MOROCCO - PHOSPHATE EXPORTS

International Monetary Fund, 700 Nineteenth Street, NW, Washington, D.C. 20431 (202) 623-7000; *International Financial Statistics*.

MOROCCO - PHOSPHATE ROCK PRODUCTION - See MOROCCO - MINING AND MINERAL PRODUCTS

MOROCCO - PIG-IRON AND FERRO-ALLOY PRODUCTION - See MOROCCO - MINING AND MINERAL PRODUCTS

MOROCCO - PIGS - See MOROCCO - LIVESTOCK AND POULTRY

MOROCCO - POPULATION

African Development Bank, 01 BP 1387, Abidjan 01, Cote d'Ivoire; *Selected Statistics on Regional Member Countries*.

The Economist Intelligence Unit, 111 West 57th Street, New York, New York 10019 (800) 938-4685; *The World Market Atlas*.

Euromonitor Publications Limited, 87-88 Turnmill Street, London EC1M 5QU, England; *International Marketing Data and Statistics*, and *Middle East Economic Handbook*.

Facts on File, 460 Park Avenue South, New York, New York 10016 (800) 443-8323; *The New Book of World Rankings*.

Food and Agricultural Organization of the United Nations (FAO), Via delle Terme di Caracalla, 00100 Rome, Italy (Telephone Number in U.S. (202) 653-2400); *Production Yearbook*.

G.K. Hall and Company, 70 Lincoln Street, Boston, Massachusetts 02111 (617) 423-3990; *The World in Figures*.

Statistical Office of the United Nations, Publishing Service, New York, New York 10017 (800) 253-9646; *Demographic Yearbook*, *Statistical Yearbook*, and *Survey of Economic and Social Conditions in Africa*.

Times Books, 201 East 50th Street, New York, New York 10022 (212) 751-2600; *The Economist Book of Vital World Statistics*.

U.S. Arms Control and Disarmament Agency, 320 Twenty-first Street, NW, Washington, D.C. 20451 (202) 647-8677; *World Military Expenditures and Arms Transfers*.

World Health Organization, Office of Publications, Avenue Appia, CH-1211 Geneva 27, Switzerland (Telephone Number in U.S. (518) 436-9686); *World Health Statistics Annual*.

MOROCCO - POST OFFICES

Facts on File, 460 Park Avenue South, New York, New York 10016 (800) 443-8323; *The New Book of World Rankings*.

MOROCCO - POTATO PRODUCTION - See MOROCCO - CROPS

MOROCCO - PRICES

Facts on File, 460 Park Avenue South, New York, New York 10016 (800) 443-8323; *The New Book of World Rankings*.

Food and Agricultural Organization of the United Nations (FAO), Via delle Terme di Caracalla, 00100 Rome, Italy (Telephone Number in U.S. (202) 653-2400); *Production Yearbook*, and *The State of Food and Agriculture*.

G.K. Hall and Company, 70 Lincoln Street, Boston, Massachusetts 02111 (617) 423-3990; *The World in Figures*.

International Lead and Zinc Study Group, Metro House, 58 St. James's Street, London SW1A 1LD England; *Lead and Zinc Statistics*.

International Monetary Fund, 700 Nineteenth Street, NW, Washington, D.C. 20431 (202) 623-7000; *International Financial Statistics*.

United Nations Economic Commission for Africa, Africa Hall, Post Office Box 3001, Addis Ababa, Ethiopia (Telephone Number in U.S. (800) 253-9646); *African Statistical Yearbook*.

MOROCCO - PRINTING AND WRITING PAPER - See MOROCCO - FORESTRY AND FOREST PRODUCTS

MOROCCO - PRODUCTION

American Automobile Manufacturers Association, 1401 H Street, NW, Suite 900, Washington, D.C. 20005 (202) 326-5500; *World Motor Vehicle Data*.

Facts on File, 460 Park Avenue South, New York, New York 10016 (800) 443-8323; *The New Book of World Rankings*.

G.K. Hall and Company, 70 Lincoln Street, Boston, Massachusetts 02111 (617) 423-3990; *The World in Figures*.

International Lead and Zinc Study Group, Metro House, 58 St. James's Street, London SW1A 1LD England; *Lead and Zinc Statistics*.

MOROCCO - PRODUCTIVITY

International Monetary Fund, 700 Nineteenth Street, NW, Washington, D.C. 20431 (202) 623-7000; *International Financial Statistics*.

MOROCCO - PROPERTY TAXES

International Monetary Fund, 700 Nineteenth Street, NW, Washington, D.C. 20431 (202) 623-7000; *Government Finance Statistics Yearbook*.

MOROCCO - PUBLIC FINANCE

Facts on File, 460 Park Avenue South, New York, New York 10016 (800) 443-8323; *The New Book of World Rankings*.

MOROCCO - RADIO BROADCASTING - See MOROCCO - BROADCASTING

MOROCCO - RAILWAY USE

G.K. Hall and Company, 70 Lincoln Street, Boston, Massachusetts 02111; *The World in Figures*.

Statistical Office of the United Nations, Publishing Service, New York, New York 10017 (800) 253-9646; *Statistical Yearbook*.

MOROCCO - RAILWAYS

Jane's Information Group, Sentinel House, 163 Brighton Road, Coulsdon, Surrey CR5 2NH, England (Telephone Number in U.S. (703) 683-3700); *Jane's World Railways*.

United Nations Economic Commission for Africa, Africa Hall, Post Office Box 3001, Addis Ababa, Ethiopia (Telephone Number in U.S. (000) 253-9646); *African Statistical Yearbook*.

MOROCCO - RELIGION

Facts on File, 460 Park Avenue South, New York, New York 10016 (800) 443-8323; *The New Book of World Rankings*.

MOROCCO - RETAIL TRADE

G.K. Hall and Company, 70 Lincoln Street, Boston, Massachusetts 02111 (617) 423-3990; *The World in Figures*.

MOROCCO - RICE PRODUCTION - See MOROCCO - CROPS

MOROCCO - ROOT AND TUBER PRODUCTION - See MOROCCO - CROPS

MOROCCO - RUBBER PRODUCTION AND CONSUMPTION

Facts on File, 460 Park Avenue South, New York, New York 10016 (800) 443-8323; *The New Book of World Rankings*.

MOROCCO - SAFFLOWER SEED PRODUCTION - See MOROCCO - CROPS

MOROCCO - SALT PRODUCTION - See MOROCCO - MINING AND MINERAL PRODUCTS

MOROCCO - SAWNWOOD PRODUCTION - See MOROCCO - FORESTRY AND FOREST PRODUCTS

MOROCCO - SENIOR CITIZENS

Facts on File, 460 Park Avenue South, New York, New York 10016 (800) 443-8323; *The New Book of World Rankings*.

MOROCCO - SHEEP - See MOROCCO - LIVESTOCK AND POULTRY

MOROCCO - SILVER PRODUCTION AND CONSUMPTION - See MOROCCO - MINING AND MINERAL PRODUCTS

MOROCCO - SISAL PRODUCTION - See MOROCCO - CROPS

MOROCCO - SOCIAL DATA

African Development Bank, 01 BP 1387, Abidjan 01, Cote d'Ivoire; *Selected Statistics on Regional Member Countries*.

Facts on File, 460 Park Avenue South, New York, New York 10016 (800) 443-8323; *The New Book of World Rankings*.

G.K. Hall and Company, 70 Lincoln Street, Boston, Massachusetts 02111 (617) 423-3990; *The World in Figures*.

MOROCCO - SOCIAL SECURITY EXPENDITURES

International Monetary Fund, 700 Nineteenth Street, NW, Washington, D.C. 20431 (202) 623-7000; *Government Finance Statistics Yearbook*.

MOROCCO - STAMP TAXES AND DUTIES - See MOROCCO - TAXATION

MOROCCO - STATE BUDGET

Euromonitor Publications Limited, 87-88 Turnmill Street, London EC1M 5QU, England; *International Marketing Data and Statistics*.

MOROCCO - STEEL - See MOROCCO - MINING AND MINERAL PRODUCTS

MOROCCO - STOCKS - COMMODITY - MARKET PRICE - INDEX

Food and Agricultural Organization of the United Nations (FAO), Via delle Terme di Caracalla, 00100 Rome, Italy (Telephone Number in U.S. (202) 653-2400); *The State of Food and Agriculture*.

International Lead and Zinc Study Group, Metro House, 58 St. James's Street, London SW1A 1LD England; *Lead and Zinc Statistics*.

MOROCCO - SUGAR PRODUCTION AND CONSUMPTION - See MOROCCO - CROPS

MOROCCO - SULPHURIC ACID PRODUCTION - See MOROCCO - MINING AND MINERAL PRODUCTS

MOROCCO - TAXATION

G.K. Hall and Company, 70 Lincoln Street, Boston, Massachusetts 02111 (617) 423-3990; *The World in Figures*.

International Monetary Fund, 700 Nineteenth Street, NW, Washington, D.C. 20431 (202) 623-7000; *Government Finance Statistics Yearbook*.

The World Bank, 1818 H Street, NW, Washington, D.C. 20433 (202) 477-1234; *World Tables*.

MOROCCO - TAX REVENUE - See MOROCCO - TAXATION

MOROCCO - TEA CONSUMPTION - See MOROCCO - CROPS

MOROCCO - TELEGRAPH SERVICE

Statistical Office of the United Nations, Publishing Service, New York, New York 10017 (800) 253-9646; *Statistical Yearbook.*

MOROCCO - TELEPHONES IN USE

American Telephone and Telegraph Company, 26 Parsippany Road, Whippany, New Jersey 07981 (800) 338-4038; *The World's Telephones.*

Euromonitor Publications Limited, 87-88 Turnmill Street, London EC1M 5QU, England; *Middle East Economic Handbook.*

G.K. Hall and Company, 70 Lincoln Street, Boston, Massachusetts 02111 (617) 423-3990; *The World in Figures.*

Statistical Office of the United Nations, Publishing Service, New York, New York 10017 (800) 253-9646; *Statistical Yearbook.*

MOROCCO - TELEVISION BROADCASTING - See MOROCCO - BROADCASTING

MOROCCO - TEXTILE INDUSTRY

G.K. Hall and Company, 70 Lincoln Street, Boston, Massachusetts 02111 (617) 423-3990; *The World in Figures.*

Statistical Office of the United Nations, Publishing Service, New York, New York 10017 (800) 253-9646; *Statistical Yearbook,* and *Trade in Manufactures of Developing Countries.*

MOROCCO - TIN - See MOROCCO - MINING AND MINERAL PRODUCTS

MOROCCO - TIRE (MOTOR VEHICLE) PRODUCTION

Statistical Office of the United Nations, Publishing Service, New York, New York 10017 (800) 253-9646; *Statistical Yearbook.*

MOROCCO - TOBACCO PRODUCTION

Facts on File, 460 Park Avenue South, New York, New York 10016 (800) 443-8323; *The New Book of World Rankings.*

Statistical Office of the United Nations, Publishing Service, New York, New York 10017 (800) 253-9646; *Statistical Yearbook.*

MOROCCO - TOBACCO PRODUCTS

Statistical Office of the United Nations, Publishing Service, New York, New York 10017 (800) 253-9646; *Statistical Yearbook.*

MOROCCO - TOURISM

Euromonitor Publications Limited, 87-88 Turnmill Street, London EC1M 5QU, England; *Middle East Economic Handbook.*

Facts on File, 460 Park Avenue South, New York, New York 10016 (800) 443-8323; *The New Book of World Rankings.*

G.K. Hall and Company, 70 Lincoln Street, Boston, Massachusetts 02111 (617) 423-3990; *The World in Figures.*

Statistical Office of the United Nations, Publishing Service, New York, New York 10017 (800) 253-9646; *Statistical Yearbook.*

Times Books, 201 East 50th Street, New York, New York 10022 (212) 751-2600; *The Economist Book of Vital World Statistics.*

United Nations Economic Commission for Africa, Africa Hall, Post Office Box 3001, Addis Ababa, Ethiopia (Telephone Number in U.S. (800) 253-9646); *African Statistical Yearbook.*

World Tourism Organization, Calle Capitan Haya 42, E-28020 Madrid, Spain; *Yearbook of Tourism Statistics.*

MOROCCO - TRACTORS IN USE

Statistical Office of the United Nations, Publishing Service, New York, New York 10017 (800) 253-9646; *Statistical Yearbook.*

MOROCCO - TRADE - See MOROCCO - FOREIGN TRADE

MOROCCO - TRADEMARKS AND SERVICE MARKS

Statistical Office of the United Nations, Publishing Service, New York, New York 10017 (800) 253-9646; *Statistical Yearbook.*

World Intellectual Property Organization, 34 Chemin des Colombettes, CH-1211 Geneva 20, Switzerland; *Industrial Property Statistics.*

MOROCCO - TRANSPORTATION AND COMMUNICATIONS

Euromonitor Publications Limited, 87-88 Turnmill Street, London EC1M 5QU, England; *Middle East Economic Handbook.*

Facts on File, 460 Park Avenue South, New York, New York 10016 (800) 443-8323; *The New Book of World Rankings.*

G.K. Hall and Company, 70 Lincoln Street, Boston, Massachusetts 02111 (617) 423-3990; *The World in Figures.*

United Nations Economic Commission for Africa, Africa Hall, Post Office Box 3001, Addis Ababa, Ethiopia (Telephone Number in U.S. (800) 253-9646); *African Statistical Yearbook.*

MOROCCO - UNEMPLOYMENT

Euromonitor Publications Limited, 87-88 Turnmill Street, London EC1M 5QU, England; *International Marketing Data and Statistics,* and *Middle East Economic Handbook.*

Statistical Office of the United Nations, Publishing Service, New York, New York 10017 (800) 253-9646; *Statistical Yearbook.*

MOROCCO - VITAL STATISTICS

Euromonitor Publications Limited, 87-88 Turnmill Street, London EC1M 5QU, England; *International Marketing Data and Statistics,* and *Middle East Economic Handbook.*

G.K. Hall and Company, 70 Lincoln Street, Boston, Massachusetts 02111 (617) 423-3990; *The World in Figures.*

Statistical Office of the United Nations, Publishing Service, New York, New York 10017 (800) 253-9646; *Statistical Yearbook.*

World Health Organization, Office of Publications, Avenue Appia, CH-1211 Geneva 27, Switzerland (Telephone Number in U.S. (518) 436-9686); *World Health Statistics Annual.*

MOROCCO - WAGES

G.K. Hall and Company, 70 Lincoln Street, Boston, Massachusetts 02111 (617) 423-3990; *The World in Figures*.

MOROCCO - WAGES IN MANUFACTURING

Statistical Office of the United Nations, Publishing Service, New York, New York 10017 (800) 253-9646; *Statistical Yearbook*.

MOROCCO - WALNUT PRODUCTION - See MOROCCO - CROPS

MOROCCO - WATERMELON PRODUCTION - See MOROCCO - CROPS

MOROCCO - WEATHER

Facts on File, 460 Park Avenue South, New York, New York 10016 (800) 443-8323; *The New Book of World Rankings*.

G.K. Hall and Company, 70 Lincoln Street, Boston, Massachusetts 02111 (617) 423-3990; *The World in Figures*.

MOROCCO - WELFARE EXPENDITURES

International Monetary Fund, 700 Nineteenth Street, NW, Washington, D.C. 20431 (202) 623-7000; *Government Finance Statistics Yearbook*.

MOROCCO - WHEAT PRODUCTION - See MOROCCO - CROPS

MOROCCO - WHOLESALE PRICES - INDEX NUMBERS

Statistical Office of the United Nations, Publishing Service, New York, New York 10017 (800) 253-9646; *Statistical Yearbook*.

MOROCCO - WINE PRODUCTION

Facts on File, 460 Park Avenue South, New York, New York 10016 (800) 443-0323; *The New Book of World Rankings*.

Statistical Office of the United Nations, Publishing Service, New York, New York 10017 (800) 253-9646; *Statistical Yearbook*.

MOROCCO - WOOD PULP PRODUCTION - See MOROCCO - FORESTRY AND FOREST PRODUCTS

MOROCCO - WOOL PRODUCTION

Facts on File, 460 Park Avenue South, New York, New York 10016 (800) 443-8323; *The New Book of World Rankings*.

Statistical Office of the United Nations, Publishing Service, New York, New York 10017 (800) 253-9646; *Statistical Yearbook*.

MOROCCO - YARN PRODUCTION

Statistical Office of the United Nations, Publishing Service, New York, New York 10017 (800) 253-9646; *Statistical Yearbook*.

MOROCCO - ZINC AND ZINC ORE PRODUCTION AND CONSUMPTION - See MOROCCO - MINING AND MINERAL PRODUCTS

MORTGAGE POOLS AND TRUSTS

Board of Governors of the Federal Reserve System, Twentieth Street and Constitution Avenue, NW, Washington, D.C. 20551 (202) 452-3000; *Federal Reserve Bulletin*, and *Annual Statistical Digest*.

MORTGAGES - See LOANS AND MORTGAGES

MOTION PICTURES INDUSTRY - EARNINGS

U.S. Department of Commerce, Bureau of the Census, Suitland, Maryland 20233 (301) 763-4040; *Census of Service Industries*, and *County Business Patterns*.

U.S. Department of Labor, Bureau of Labor Statistics, Two Massachusetts Avenue, NE, Washington, D.C. 20212 (202) 606-7828; *Employment and Earnings*, and Bulletins 2370 and 2429.

MOTION PICTURES INDUSTRY - EMPLOYEES

U.S. Department of Commerce, Bureau of Economic Analysis, Fourteenth Street between Constitution Avenue and E Street, NW, Washington, D.C. 20230 (202) 606-9900; *The National Income and Product Accounts of the United States*, and *Survey of Current Business*.

U.S. Department of Commerce, Bureau of the Census, Suitland, Maryland 20233 (301) 763-4040; *County Business Patterns*, and *Census of Service Industries*.

U.S. Department of Labor, Bureau of Labor Statistics, Two Massachusetts Avenue, NE, Washington, D.C. 20212 (202) 606-7828; *Employment and Earnings*, and Bulletins 2370 and 2429.

MOTION PICTURES INDUSTRY - ESTABLISHMENTS

U.S. Department of Commerce, Bureau of the Census, Suitland, Maryland 20233 (301) 763-4040; *County Business Patterns*, and *Census of Service Industries*.

MOTION PICTURES INDUSTRY - GROSS DOMESTIC PRODUCT

U.S. Department of Commerce, Bureau of Economic Analysis, Fourteenth Street between Constitution Avenue and E Street, NW, Washington, D.C. 20230 (202) 606-9900; *The National Income and Product Accounts of the United States*, and *Survey of Current Business*.

MOTION PICTURES INDUSTRY - RECEIPTS

U.S. Department of Commerce, Bureau of the Census, Suitland, Maryland 20233 (301) 763-4040; *Current Business Reports, Service Annual Survey*, and *Census of Service Industries*.

MOTOR FUEL

U.S. Department of Energy, Energy Information Administration, Washington, D.C. 20202 (202) 586-8800; *Household Vehicles Energy Consumption, Monthly Energy Review, International Energy Annual, Annual Energy Review* and *Petroleum Supply Annual*.

U.S. Department of Transportation, Federal Highway Administration, 400 Seventh Street, SW, Washington, D.C. 20590 (202) 366-0660; *Highway Statistics*.

MOTOR FUEL - ADVERTISING EXPENDITURES

Television Bureau of Advertising, Incorporated, 850 Third Avenue, New York, New York 10022 (212) 872-1111; data compiled by Competitive Media Reporting, 11 West 42nd Street, New York, New York 10036.

MOTOR FUEL - CONSUMPTION - CIVIL AVIATION

U.S. Department of Transportation, Federal Aviation Administration, 800 Independence Avenue, SW, Washington, D.C. 20591 (202) 366-4000; *FAA Statistical Handbook of Aviation* and unpublished data.

MOTOR FUEL - CONSUMPTION - MOTOR VEHICLES

U.S. Department of Transportation, Federal Highway Administration, 400 Seventh Street, SW, Washington, D.C. 20590 (202) 366-0660; *Highway Statistics*.

MOTOR FUEL - SUPPLY

U.S. Department of Energy, Energy Information Administration, Washington, D.C. 20585 (202) 586-8800; *Monthly Energy Review*.

MOTOR FUEL - TAXES

U.S. Department of Commerce, Bureau of the Census, Suitland, Maryland 20233 (301) 763-4040; *State Government Finances*, and *State Government Tax Collections*.

MOTOR FUEL - TAXES - STATES

U.S. Department of Commerce, Bureau of the Census, Suitland, Maryland 20233 (301) 763-4040; *State Government Tax Collections*.

U.S. Department of Transportation, Federal Highway Administration, 400 Seventh Street, SW, Washington, D.C. 20590 (202) 366-0660; *Highway Statistics*.

MOTOR HOMES

American Automobile Manufacturers Association, 1401 H Street, NW, Suite 900, Washington, D.C. 20005 (202) 326-5500; *Motor Vehicle Facts and Figures*.

Recreation Vehicle Industry Association, Post Office Box 2999, 1896 Preston White Drive, Reston, Virginia 22090 (703) 620-6003; *RV's...The Family Camping Vehicle, A Year-End Report*.

MOTOR VEHICLE DEALERS - RETAIL - EARNINGS

National Automobile Dealers Association, 8400 Westpark Drive, McLean, Virginia 22102 (703) 827-7407; *NADA Data*.

U.S. Department of Commerce, Bureau of the Census, Suitland, Maryland 20233 (301) 763-4040; *Census of Retail Trade*, and *County Business Patterns*.

MOTOR VEHICLE DEALERS - RETAIL - EMPLOYEES

National Automobile Dealers Association, 8400 Westpark Drive, McLean, Virginia 22102 (301) 763-4040; *NADA Data*.

U.S. Department of Commerce, Bureau of the Census, Suitland, Maryland 20233 (301) 763-4040; *Census of Retail Trade*, and *County Business Patterns*.

MOTOR VEHICLE DEALERS - RETAIL - ESTABLISHMENTS

International Franchise Association, 1350 New York Avenue, Suite 900, Washington, D.C. 20005; *Franchising in the Economy*.

National Automobile Dealers Association, 8400 Westpark Drive, McLean, Virginia 22102 (703) 827-7407; *NADA Data*.

U.S. Department of Commerce, Bureau of the Census, Suitland, Maryland 20233 (301) 763-4040; *Census of Retail Trade*, and *County Business Patterns*.

MOTOR VEHICLE DEALERS - RETAIL - FINANCES

National Automobile Dealers Association, 8400 Westpark Drive, McLean, Virginia 22102 (703) 827-7407; *NADA Data*.

MOTOR VEHICLE DEALERS - RETAIL - FRANCHISES

International Franchise Association, 1350 New York Avenue, Suite 900, Washington, D.C. 20005 (202) 628-8000; *Franchising in the Economy*.

National Automobile Dealers Association, 8400 Westpark Drive, McLean, Virginia 22102 (703) 827-7407; *NADA Data*.

MOTOR VEHICLE DEALERS - RETAIL - INVENTORIES

National Automobile Dealers Association, 8400 Westpark Drive, McLean, Virginia 22102 (703) 827-7407; *NADA Data*.

U.S. Department of Commerce, Bureau of the Census, Suitland, Maryland 20233 (301) 763-4040; *Current Business Reports, Combined Annual and Revised Monthly Retail Trade*.

MOTOR VEHICLE DEALERS - RETAIL - PRODUCTIVITY

U.S. Department of Labor, Bureau of Labor Statistics, Washington, D.C. 20210 (202) 523-1327; *Productivity Measures for Selected Industries and Government Services*, and unpublished data.

MOTOR VEHICLE DEALERS - RETAIL - PROFITS

National Automobile Dealers Association, 8400 Westpark Drive, McLean, Virginia 22102 (703) 827-7407; *NADA Data*.

MOTOR VEHICLE DEALERS - RETAIL - SALES

International Franchise Association, 1350 New York Avenue, Suite 900, Washington, D.C. 20005 (202) 628-8000; *Franchising in the Economy*.

Market Statistics, 633 Third Avenue, New York, New York 10017 (212) 986-4000; *The Survey of Buying Power Data Service*.

National Automobile Dealers Association, 8400 Westpark Drive, McLean, Virginia 22102 (703) 827-7407; *NADA Data*.

U.S. Department of Commerce, Bureau of the Census, Suitland, Maryland 20233 (301) 763-4040; *Census of Retail Trade, Current Business Reports, Combined Annual and Revised Monthly Retail Trade*.

MOTOR VEHICLES - ACCIDENTS/DEATHS

National Safety Council, 1121 Spring Lake Drive, Itasca, Illinois 60143-3201; *Accident Facts*.

U.S. Department of Health and Human Services, Public Health Service, 200 Independence Avenue, SW, Washington, D.C. 20201 (202) 619-1296; *Vital Statistics of the United States*.

U.S. Department of Transportation, Bureau of Transportation Statistics, 400 Seventh Street, SW, Washington, D.C. 20590 (202) 366-DATA; *National Transportation Statistics Annual, Historical Compendium Information Report*.

U.S. Department of Transportation, Federal Highway Administration, 400 Seventh Street, SW, Washington, D.C. 20201 (202) 366-0660; *Fatal Accident Reporting System.*

MOTOR VEHICLES - ACCIDENTS/DEATHS - FOREIGN COUNTRIES

World Health Organization, Office of Publications, Avenue Appia, CH-1211 Geneva 27, Switzerland (Telephone Number in U.S. (518) 436-9686); *World Health Statistics Annual.*

MOTOR VEHICLES - ADVERTISING EXPENDITURES

Television Bureau of Advertising, Incorporated, 850 Third Avenue, New York, New York 10022 (212) 486-1111; from data compiled by Competitive Media Reporting, 11 West 42nd Street, New York 10036 (212) 789-4000.

MOTOR VEHICLES - COMMON CARRIERS

American Bus Association, 1100 New York Avenue, NW, Washington, D.C. 20005 (202) 842-1645; *Bus Facts*, and *Annual Report.*

American Public Transit Association, 1201 New York, NW, Suite 400, Washington, D.C. 20005 (202) 898-4000; *Transit Fact Book.*

Eno Transportation Foundation, 4421 Statestone Court, Lansdowne, Virginia 22075 (703) 729-7200; *Transportation in America.*

U.S. Department of Commerce, Bureau of the Census, Suitland, Maryland 20233 (301) 763-4040; *Current Business Reports, Motor Freight Transportation and Warehousing Survey.*

U.S. Interstate Commerce Commission, Twelfth Street and Constitution Avenue, NW, Washington, D.C. 20423 (202) 275-7119; *Transport Statistics in the United States.*

MOTOR VEHICLES - CONSUMER EXPENDITURES

U.S. Department of Labor, Bureau of Labor Statistics, Two Massachusetts Avenue, NE, Washington, D.C. 20212 (202) 606-7828; *Consumer Expenditures in 1992.*

MOTOR VEHICLES - DRIVERS LICENSES

U.S. Department of Justice, Bureau of Justice Statistics, 633 Indiana Avenue, NW, Washington, D.C. 20531 (800) 732-3277; *Drunk Driving, Special Report.*

U.S. Department of Transportation, Federal Highway Administration, 400 Seventh Street, SW, Washington, D.C. 20590 (202) 366-0660; *Selected Highway Statistics and Charts*, and *Highway Statistics.*

MOTOR VEHICLES - FARM EXPENDITURES

U.S. Department of Agriculture, Economic Research Service, Fourteenth Street and Independence Avenue, SW, Washington, D.C. 20005-4789 (202) 219-1504; *Agricultural Statistics*, and *Economic Indicators of the Farm Sector: National Financial Summary.*

MOTOR VEHICLES - FOREIGN TRADE

American Automobile Manufacturers Association, 1401 H Street, NW, Suite 900, Washington, D.C. 20005 (202) 326-5500; *Motor Vehicle Facts and Figures*, and *World Motor Vehicle Data Book.*

U.S. Department of Commerce, Bureau of the Census, Suitland, Maryland 20233 (301) 763-4040; *U.S. Merchandise Trade: Exports, General Imports, and Imports for Consumption.*

MOTOR VEHICLES - FUEL CONSUMED

U.S. Department of Transportation, Federal Highway Administration, 400 Seventh Street, SW, Washington, D.C. 20590 (202) 366-4000; *Highway Statistics.*

MOTOR VEHICLES - HORSEPOWER

John A. Waring, 1320 South George Mason Drive, Arlington, Virginia 22204 (703) 521-1499; unpublished estimates.

MOTOR VEHICLES - INSURANCE

U.S. Department of Commerce, International Trade Administration, Fourteenth Street between Constitution Avenue and E Street, NW, Washington, D.C. 20230 (202) 482-3809; *U.S. Industrial Outlook.*

MOTOR VEHICLES - MILES OF TRAVEL

U.S. Department of Transportation, Federal Highway Administration, 400 Seventh Street, Washington, D.C. 20590 (202) 366-0660; *Highway Statistics*, and *Selected Highway Statistics and Charts.*

MOTOR VEHICLES - NATIONAL INCOME ACCOUNTS

U.S. Department of Commerce, Bureau of Economic Analysis, Fourteenth Street between Constitution Avenue and E Street, NW, Washington, D.C. 20230 (202) 606-9900; *The National Income and Product Accounts of the United States*, and *Survey of Current Business.*

MOTOR VEHICLES - OWNERSHIP

U.S. Department of Energy, Energy Information Administration, Washington, D.C. 20585 (202) 586-8800; *Residential Energy Consumption Survey*, and *Household Vehicles Energy Consumption.*

MOTOR VEHICLES - PASSENGER OUTLAYS

Eno Transportation Foundation, 44211 Statestone Court, Lansdowne, Virginia 22075 (703) 729-7200; *Transportation in America.*

MOTOR VEHICLES - POLLUTANT EMISSIONS

U.S. Environmental Protection Agency, 401 M Street, SW, Washington, D.C. 20460 (202) 382-2090; *National Air Pollutant Emission Estimates.*

MOTOR VEHICLES - PRICE INDEXES - CONSUMER

U.S. Department of Labor, Bureau of Labor Statistics, Two Massachusetts Avenue, NE, Washington, D.C. 20212 (202) 606-7828; *Monthly Labor Review*, and *Consumer Price Indexes Detailed Report.*

MOTOR VEHICLES - PRICE INDEXES - CONSUMER - FIXED WEIGHT

U.S. Department of Commerce, Bureau of Economic Analysis, Fourteenth Street between Constitution Avenue and E Street, NW, Washington, D.C. 20230 (202) 606-9900; *The National Income and Product Accounts of the U.S.*, and *Survey of Current Business.*

MOTOR VEHICLES - PRODUCTION

American Automobile Manufacturers Association, 1401 H Street, NW, Suite 900, Washington, D.C. 20005 (202) 326-5500; *Motor Vehicle Facts and Figures*, and *World Motor Vehicle Data Book*.

MOTOR VEHICLES - PRODUCTION - WORLD PRODUCTION

Statistical Office of the United Nations, Publishing Service, New York, New York 10017 (800) 253-9646; *Monthly Bulletin of Statistics*.

MOTOR VEHICLES - RAILROAD - CAR LOADINGS

Association of American Railroads, American Railroads Building, 50 F Street, NW, Washington, D.C. 20001 (202) 639-2100; *Weekly Railroad Traffic*.

MOTOR VEHICLES - RECALLED FOR SAFETY DEFECTS

U.S. Department of Transportation, National Highway Traffic Safety Administration, 400 Seventh Street, SW, Washington, D.C. 20590 (202) 366-9550; *Motor Vehicles Defect Recall Campaigns*.

MOTOR VEHICLES - RECREATIONAL VEHICLES

American Automobile Manufacturers Association, 1401 H Street, NW, Suite 900, Washington, D.C. 20005 (202) 326-5500; *Motor Vehicle Facts and Figures*.

Recreation Vehicle Industry Association, Post Office Box 2999, 1896 Preston White Drive, Reston, Virginia 22090 (703) 620-6003; *RV's...The Family Camping Vehicle, A Year End Report*.

MOTOR VEHICLES - REGISTRATIONS

American Automobile Manufacturers Association, 1401 H Street, NW, Suite 900, Washington, D.C. 20005 (202) 326-5500; *Motor Vehicle Facts and Figures*, and *World Motor Vehicle Data Book*.

U.S. Department of Transportation, Federal Highway Administration, 400 Seventh Street, SW, Washington, D.C. 20590 (202) 366-9550; *Highway Statistics* and *Selected Highway Statistics and Charts*.

MOTOR VEHICLES - SALES

American Automobile Manufacturers Association, 1401 H Street, NW, Suite 900, Washington, D.C. 20005 (202) 326-5500; *Motor Vehicle Facts and Figures*.

U.S. Department of Commerce, Bureau of the Census, Suitland, Maryland 20233 (301) 763-4040 ; *Current Business Reports, Motor Freight Transportation and Warehousing Survey*, and *Census of Retail Trade, Merchandise Line Sales*.

MOTOR VEHICLES - SCRAPPED

American Automobile Manufacturers Association, 1401 H Street, NW, Suite 900, Washington, D.C. 20005 (202) 326-5500; *Motor Vehicle Facts and Figures*, and *World Motor Vehicle Data Book*.

MOTOR VEHICLES - SERVICE AND REPAIR SHOPS - See AUTOMOTIVE REPAIR, SERVICES AND PARKING

MOTOR VEHICLES - TAXES - LICENSES AND MOTOR FUEL

U.S. Department of Commerce, Bureau of the Census, Suitland, Maryland 20233 (301) 763-4040; *State Government Finances*.

MOTOR VEHICLES - THEFT

U.S. Department of Justice, Bureau of Justice Statistics, 633 Indiana Avenue, NW, Washington, D.C. 20531 (800) 732-3277; *Criminal Victimization in the United States, Crime and the Nation's Households*, and unpublished data.

U.S. Department of Justice, Federal Bureau of Investigation, Ninth Street and Pennsylvania Avenue, NW, Washington, D.C. 20535 (202) 324-3000; *Crime in the United States*, and *Population-at-Risk Rates and Selected Crime Indicators*.

MOTOR VEHICLES - TIRES AND BATTERIES

Battery Council International, 401 North Michigan Avenue, Chicago, Illinois 60611 (312) 644-6610.

Rubber Manufacturers Association, Inc., 1400 K Street, NW, Washington, D.C. 20005 (202) 682-4800; *RMA Monthly Tire Report*.

MOTOR VEHICLES - TRUCKS

American Automobile Manufacturers Association, 1401 H Street, NW, Suite 900, Washington, D.C. 20005 (202) 326-5500; *Motor Vehicle Facts and Figures*, and *World Motor Vehicle Data Book*.

U.S. Department of Transportation, Federal Highway Administration, 400 Seventh Street, Washington, D.C. 20590 (202) 366-9550; *Highway Statistics*.

MOTOR VEHICLES AND EQUIPMENT - MANUFACTURING - CAPITAL

U.S. Department of Commerce, Bureau of Economic Analysis, Fourteenth Street between Constitution Avenue and E Street, NW, Washington, D.C. 20230 (202) 606-9900; *Fixed Reproducible Tangible Wealth in the United States*, and *Survey of Current Business*.

MOTOR VEHICLES AND EQUIPMENT - MANUFACTURING - EARNINGS

U.S. Department of Commerce, Bureau of the Census, Suitland, Maryland 20233 (301) 763-4040; *Census of Manufactures*, and *Annual Survey of Manufactures*.

U.S. Department of Labor, Bureau of Labor Statistics, Two Massachusetts Avenue, NE, Washington, D.C. 20212 (202) 606-7828; *Employment and Earnings*, and Bulletins 2307 and 2429.

MOTOR VEHICLES AND EQUIPMENT - MANUFACTURING - EMPLOYEES

U.S. Department of Commerce, Bureau of the Census, Suitland, Maryland 20233 (301) 763-4040; *Census of Manufactures*, and *Annual Survey of Manufactures*.

U.S. Department of Labor, Bureau of Labor Statistics, Two Massachusetts Avenue, NE, Washington, D.C. 20212 (202) 606-7828; *Monthly Labor Review, Employment and Earnings*, and Bulletins 2307 and 2429.

MOTOR VEHICLES AND EQUIPMENT - MANUFACTURING - ESTABLISHMENTS

U.S. Department of Commerce, Bureau of the Census, Suitland, Maryland 20233 (301) 763-4040; *Census of Manufactures*, and *Annual Survey of Manufactures*.

MOTOR VEHICLES AND EQUIPMENT - MANUFACTURING - FOREIGN TRADE

U.S. Department of Commerce, Bureau of the Census, Suitland, Maryland 20233 (301) 763-4040; *U.S. Merchandise Trade*, and *U.S. Merchandise Trade: Exports, General Imports, and Imports for Consumption*.

MOTOR VEHICLES AND EQUIPMENT - MANUFACTURING - GROSS DOMESTIC PRODUCT

U.S. Department of Commerce, Bureau of Economic Analysis, Fourteenth Street between Constitution Avenue and E Street, NW, Washington, D.C. 20230 (202) 606-9900; *The National Income and Product Accounts of the United States*, and *Survey of Current Business*.

MOTOR VEHICLES AND EQUIPMENT - MANUFACTURING - INVENTORIES

U.S. Department of Commerce, Bureau of the Census, Suitland, Maryland 20233 (301) 763-4040; *Current Industrial Reports, Manufactures Shipments, Inventories, and Orders*.

MOTOR VEHICLES AND EQUIPMENT - MANUFACTURING - OCCUPATIONAL SAFETY

U.S. Department of Labor, Bureau of Labor Statistics, Two Massachusetts Avenue, NE, Washington, D.C. 20212 (202) 606-7828; *Occupational Injuries and Illnesses in the United States by Industry*.

MOTOR VEHICLES AND EQUIPMENT - MANUFACTURING - POLLUTION ABATEMENT

U.S. Department of Commerce, Bureau of Economic Analysis, Fourteenth Street between Constitution Avenue and E Street, NW, Washington, D.C. 20230 (202) 606-9900; *Survey of Current Business*.

U.S. Department of Commerce, Bureau of the Census, Suitland, Maryland 20233 (301) 763-4040; *Current Industrial Reports*.

MOTOR VEHICLES AND EQUIPMENT - MANUFACTURING - PRODUCTIVITY

Board of Governors of the Federal Reserve System, Twentieth Street and Constitution Avenue, NW, Washington, D.C. 20551 (202) 452-3000; *Federal Reserve Bulletin*.

U.S. Department of Labor, Bureau of Labor Statistics, Two Massachusetts Avenue, NE, Washington, D.C. 20212 (202) 606-7828; *Productivity Measures for Selected Industries and Government Services*, and unpublished data.

MOTOR VEHICLES AND EQUIPMENT - MANUFACTURING - PROFITS

Forbes, Incorporated, 60 Fifth Avenue, New York, New York 10011 (212) 620-2200; *Forbes Annual Report on American Industry*.

Time Warner, 1675 Broadway, Rockefeller Center, New York, New York 10019 (212) 522-1212; *The Fortune Directories*.

U.S. Department of Commerce, Bureau of the Census, Suitland, Maryland 20233 (301) 763-4040; *Quarterly Financial Report for Manufacturing, Mining and Trade Corporations*.

MOTOR VEHICLES AND EQUIPMENT - MANUFACTURING - RESEARCH AND DEVELOPMENT

U.S. National Science Foundation, 4201 Wilson Boulevard, Arlington, Virginia 22230 (703) 306-1234; *Research and Development in Industry*.

MOTOR VEHICLES AND EQUIPMENT - MANUFACTURING - SALES, SHIPMENTS, RECEIPTS

American Automobile Manufactures Association, 1401 H Street, NW, Suite 900, Washington, D.C. 20005 (202) 326-5500; *Motor Vehicle Facts and Figures*, and *World Motor Vehicle Data Book*.

International Iron and Steel Institute, 120, rue Colonel Bourg, B-1140 Brussels, Belgium; *Forbes Annual Report*.

Statistical Office of the United Nations, Publishing Service, New York, New York 10017 (800) 253-9646; *Monthly Bulletin of Statistics*.

U.S. Department of Commerce, Bureau of the Census, Suitland, Maryland 20233 (301) 763-4040; *Census of Manufactures, Annual Survey of Manufactures, Origin of Exports of Manufactured Products, and Current Industrial Reports, Manufactures' Shipments, Inventories and Orders*.

U.S. Department of Commerce, International Trade Administration, Fourteenth Street between Constitution Avenue and E Street, NW, Washington, D.C. 20230 (202) 482-3809; *Business America*, and unpublished data.

MOTOR VEHICLES AND EQUIPMENT - MANUFACTURING - VALUE ADDED

U.S. Department of Commerce, Bureau of the Census, Suitland, Maryland 20233 (301) 763-4040; *Census of Manufactures*, and *Annual Survey of Manufactures*.

MOTORCYCLES

National Safety Council, 1121 Spring Lake Drive, Itasca, Illinois 60143-3201 (708) 285-1121; *Accident Facts*.

U.S. Department of Commerce, Bureau of the Census, Suitland, Maryland 20233 (301) 763-4040; *U.S. Merchandise Trade*.

U.S. Department of Transportation, Federal Highway Administration, 400 Seventh Street, SW, Washington, D.C. 20590 (202) 366-9550; *Highway Statistics*, and *Selected Highway Statistics and Charts*.

U.S. Department of Transportation, National Highway Traffic Safety Administration, 400 Seventh Street, SW, Washington, D.C. 20490 (202) 366-4000; *Fatal Accident Reporting System*.

MOTORCYCLES - ACCIDENTS AND DEATHS

National Safety Council, 1121 Spring Lake Drive, Itasca, Illinois 60143-3201 (708) 285-1121; *Accident Facts*.

U.S. Department of Transportation, National Highway Traffic Safety Administration, 400 Seventh Street, SW, Washington, D.C. 20590 (202) 366-9550; *Fatal Accident Reporting System*.

MOTORCYCLES - FOREIGN TRADE

U.S. Department of Commerce, Bureau of the Census, Suitland, Maryland 20233 (301) 763-4040; *U.S. Merchandise Trade*.

MOTORCYCLES - HELMET LAW

National Safety Council, 1121 Spring Lake Drive, Itasca, Illinois 60143-3201 (708) 285-1121; *Accident Facts.*

Mozambique - National Statistical Office

National Directorate of Statistics, Ministerio do Plano, Av Ahmed Sekou Toure 21, CP 493, Maputo, Mozambique.

Mozambique - Primary Statistics Sources

Direccao Nacional de Estatistica, CP 493, Maputo, Mozambique; *Anuario estatistico* (Statistical Yearbook); and *Boletim Mensal de estatistics* (Monthly bulletin of statistics).

MOZAMBIQUE - AGRICULTURE

Euromonitor Publications Limited, 87-88 Turnmill Street, London EC1M 5QU, England; *International Marketing Data and Statistics.*

Facts on File, 460 Park Avenue South, New York, New York 10016 (800) 443-8323; *The New Book of World Rankings.*

Food and Agricultural Organization of the United Nations (FAO), Via delle Terme di Caracalla, 00100 Rome, Italy (Telephone Number in U.S. (202) 653-2400); *Production Yearbook, The State of Food and Agriculture,* and *Trade Yearbook.*

G.K. Hall and Company, 70 Lincoln Street, Boston, Massachusetts 02111 (617) 423-3990; *The World in Figures.*

Statistical Office of the United Nations, Publishing Service, New York, New York 10017 (800) 253-9646; *Statistical Yearbook,* and *Survey of Economic and Social Conditions in Africa.*

Times Books, 201 East 50th Street, New York, New York 10022 (212) 751-2600; *The Economist Book of Vital World Statistics.*

United Nations Economic Commission for Africa, Africa Hall, Post Office Box 3001, Addis Ababa, Ethiopia (Telephone Number in U.S. (800) 253-9646); *African Statistical Yearbook.*

The World Bank, 1818 H Street, NW, Washington, D.C. 20433 (202) 477-1234; *World Tables.*

MOZAMBIQUE - AIRLINE SERVICE

Facts on File, 460 Park Avenue South, New York, New York 10016 (800) 443-8323; *The New Book of World Rankings.*

G.K. Hall and Company, 70 Lincoln Street, Boston, Massachusetts 02111 (617) 423-3990; *The World in Figures.*

Times Books, 201 East 50th Street, New York, New York 10022 (212) 751-2600; *The Economist Book of Vital World Statistics.*

United Nations Economic Commission for Africa, Africa Hall, Post Office Box 3001, Addis Ababa, Ethiopia (Telephone Number in U.S. (800) 253-9646); *African Statistical Yearbook.*

MOZAMBIQUE - ALUMINUM PRODUCTION AND CONSUMPTION - See MOZAMBIQUE - MINING AND MINERAL PRODUCTS

MOZAMBIQUE - ANIMAL HEALTH

Food and Agricultural Organization of the United Nations (FAO), Via delle Terme di Caracalla, 00100 Rome, Italy (Telephone Number

in U.S. (202) 653-2400); *Animal Health Yearbook.*

MOZAMBIQUE - AREA AND DENSITY OF POPULATION

African Development Bank, 01 BP 1387, Abidjan 01, Cote d'Ivoire; *Selected Statistics on Regional Member Countries.*

Euromonitor Publications Limited, 87-88 Turnmill Street, London EC1M 5QU, England; *International Marketing Data and Statistics.*

Facts on File, 460 Park Avenue South, New York, New York 10016 (800) 443-8323; *The New Book of World Rankings.*

Food and Agricultural Organization of the United Nations (FAO), Via delle Terme di Caracalla, 00100 Rome, Italy (Telephone Number in U.S. (202) 653-2400); *The State of Food and Agriculture.*

G.K. Hall and Company, 70 Lincoln Street, Boston, Massachusetts 02111 (617) 423-3990; *The World in Figures.*

Statistical Office of the United Nations, Publishing Service, New York, New York 10017 (800) 253-9646; *Statistical Yearbook,* and *Survey of Economic and Social Conditions in Africa.*

Times Books, 201 East 50th Street, New York, New York 10022 (212) 751-2600; *The Economist Book of Vital World Statistics.*

MOZAMBIQUE - ARMS EXPORTS AND IMPORTS

U.S. Arms Control and Disarmament Agency, 320 Twenty-first Street, NW, Washington, D.C. 20451 (202) 647-8677; *World Military Expenditures and Arms Transfers.*

MOZAMBIQUE - BALANCE OF PAYMENTS

African Development Bank, 01 BP 1387, Abidjan 01, Cote d'Ivoire; *Selected Statistics on Regional Member Countries.*

The Economist Intelligence Unit, 111 West 57th Street, New York, New York 10019 (800) 938-4685; *The World Market Atlas.*

G.K. Hall and Company, 70 Lincoln Street, Boston, Massachusetts 02111 (617) 423-3990; *The World in Figures.*

The World Bank, 1818 H Street, NW, Washington, D.C. 20433 (202) 477-1234; *World Tables.*

MOZAMBIQUE - BANKING

Facts on File, 460 Park Avenue South, New York, New York 10016 (800) 443-8323; *The New Book of World Rankings.*

G.K. Hall and Company, 70 Lincoln Street, Boston, Massachusetts 02111 (617) 423-3990; *The World in Figures.*

MOZAMBIQUE - BARLEY PRODUCTION - See MOZAMBIQUE - CROPS

MOZAMBIQUE - BAUXITE PRODUCTION AND CONSUMPTION - See MOZAMBIQUE - MINING AND MINERAL PRODUCTS

MOZAMBIQUE - BEER PRODUCTION

Facts on File, 460 Park Avenue South, New York, New York 10016 (800) 443-8323; *The New Book of World Rankings.*

Statistical Office of the United Nations, Publishing Service, New York, New York 10017 (800) 253-9646; *Statistical Yearbook.*

MOZAMBIQUE - BIRTH RATES

Facts on File, 460 Park Avenue South, New York, New York 10016 (800) 443-8323; *The New Book of World Rankings*.

Statistical Office of the United Nations, Publishing Service, New York, New York 10017 (800) 253-9646; *Demographic Yearbook, Statistical Yearbook,* and *Survey of Economic and Social Conditions in Africa.*

Times Books, 201 East 50th Street, New York, New York 10022 (212) 751-2600; *The Economist Book of Vital World Statistics.*

The World Bank, 1818 H Street, NW, Washington, D.C. 20433 (202) 477-1234; *World Tables.*

MOZAMBIQUE - BONDS

G.K. Hall and Company, 70 Lincoln Street, Boston, Massachusetts 02111 (617) 423-3990; *The World in Figures.*

MOZAMBIQUE - BOOK PRODUCTION

G.K. Hall and Company, 70 Lincoln Street, Boston, Massachusetts 02111 (617) 423-3990; *The World in Figures.*

MOZAMBIQUE - BROADCASTING

Billboard Limited, Post Office Box 9027, 1006 AA Amsterdam, The Netherlands (Telephone Number in U.S. (212) 764-7300); *World Radio TV Handbook.*

Facts on File, 460 Park Avenue South, New York, New York 10016 (800) 443-8323; *The New Book of World Rankings.*

G.K. Hall and Company, 70 Lincoln Street, Boston, Massachusetts 02111 (617) 423-3990; *The World in Figures,*

Times Books, 201 East 50th Street, New York, New York 10022 (212) 751-2600; *The Economist Book of Vital World Statistics.*

MOZAMBIQUE - BUSINESS

G.K. Hall and Company, 70 Lincoln Street, Boston, Massachusetts 02111 (617) 423-3990; *The World in Figures.*

MOZAMBIQUE - CALORIE SUPPLY

African Development Bank, 01 BP 1387, Abidjan 01, Cote d'Ivoire; *Selected Statistics on Regional Member Countries.*

Food and Agricultural Organization of the United Nations (FAO), Via delle Terme di Caracalla, 00100 Rome, Italy (Telephone Number in U.S. (202) 653-2400); *The State of Food and Agriculture.*

MOZAMBIQUE - CASHEW NUT PRODUCTION - See MOZAMBIQUE - CROPS

MOZAMBIQUE - CASTOR BEAN PRODUCTION - See MOZAMBIQUE - CROPS

MOZAMBIQUE - CATTLE - See MOZAMBIQUE - LIVESTOCK AND POULTRY

MOZAMBIQUE - CEMENT PRODUCTION - See MOZAMBIQUE - MINING AND MINERAL PRODUCTS

MOZAMBIQUE - CHEMICAL (ORGANIC) PRODUCTION - See MOZAMBIQUE - MINING AND MINERAL PRODUCTS

MOZAMBIQUE - CHICKENS - See MOZAMBIQUE - LIVESTOCK AND POULTRY

MOZAMBIQUE - CIGARETTE PRODUCTION - See MOZAMBIQUE - TOBACCO PRODUCTION

MOZAMBIQUE - CLASS STRUCTURE

G.K. Hall and Company, 70 Lincoln Street, Boston, Massachusetts 02111 (617) 423-3990; *The World in Figures.*

MOZAMBIQUE - CLIMATE

Facts on File, 460 Park Avenue South, New York, New York 10016 (800) 443-8323; *The New Book of World Rankings.*

G.K. Hall and Company, 70 Lincoln Street, Boston, Massachusetts 02111 (617) 423-3990; *The World in Figures.*

MOZAMBIQUE - COAL PRODUCTION - See MOZAMBIQUE - MINING AND MINERAL PRODUCTS

MOZAMBIQUE - COFFEE PRODUCTION AND CONSUMPTION - See MOZAMBIQUE - CROPS

MOZAMBIQUE - COMMUNICATIONS

G.K. Hall and Company, 70 Lincoln Street, Boston, Massachusetts 02111 (617) 423-3990; *The World in Figures.*

United Nations Economic Commission for Africa, Africa Hall, Post Office Box 3001, Addis Ababa, Ethiopia (Telephone Number in U.S. (800) 253-9646); *African Statistical Yearbook.*

MOZAMBIQUE - CONSTRUCTION INDUSTRY

Facts on File, 460 Park Avenue South, New York, New York 10016 (800) 443-8323; *The New Book of World Rankings.*

Statistical Office of the United Nations, Publishing Service, New York, New York 10017 (800) 253-9646; *Construction Statistics Yearbook,* and *Statistical Yearbook.*

United Nations Economic Commission for Africa, Africa Hall, Post Office Box 3001, Addis Ababa, Ethiopia (Telephone Number in U.S. (800) 253-9646); *African Statistical Yearbook.*

MOZAMBIQUE - CONSUMER PRICE INDEX

African Development Bank, 01 BP 1387, Abidjan 01, Cote d'Ivoire; *Selected Statistics on Regional Member Countries.*

G.K. Hall and Company, 70 Lincoln Street, Boston, Massachusetts 02111 (617) 423-3990; *The World in Figures.*

Statistical Office of the United Nations, Publishing Service, New York, New York 10017 (800) 253-9646; *Statistical Yearbook,* and *Survey of Economic and Social Conditions in Africa.*

MOZAMBIQUE - CONSUMER PRICES

International Labour Office, I.L.O. Publications, CH-1211, Geneva 22, Switzerland; *Yearbook of Labour Statistics.*

MOZAMBIQUE - CONSUMPTION

African Development Bank, 01 BP 1387, Abidjan 01, Cote d'Ivoire; *Selected Statistics on Regional Member Countries.*

G.K. Hall and Company, 70 Lincoln Street, Boston, Massachusetts 02111 (617) 423-3990; *The World in Figures*.

Statistical Office of the United Nations, Publishing Service, New York, New York 10017 (800) 253-9646; *Survey of Economic and Social Conditions in Africa*.

MOZAMBIQUE - COPPER AND COPPER ORE PRODUCTION AND CONSUMPTION - See MOZAMBIQUE - MINING AND MINERAL PRODUCTS

MOZAMBIQUE - CORN PRODUCTION - See MOZAMBIQUE - CROPS

MOZAMBIQUE - CORPORATE TAXES - See MOZAMBIQUE - TAXATION

MOZAMBIQUE - COTTON - See MOZAMBIQUE - CROPS

MOZAMBIQUE - CROPS

Commodity Research Bureau, Incorporated, 75 Wall Street, New York, New York 10005 (212) 504-7754; *Commodity Year Book*.

Facts on File, 460 Park Avenue South, New York, New York 10016 (800) 443-8323; *The New Book of World Rankings*.

Food and Agricultural Organization of the United Nations (FAO), Via delle Terme di Caracalla, 00100 Rome, Italy (Telephone Number in U.S. (202) 653-2400); *Production Yearbook*, and *The State of Food and Agriculture*.

G.K. Hall and Company, 70 Lincoln Street, Boston, Massachusetts 02111 (617) 423-3990; *The World in Figures*.

Statistical Office of the United Nations, Publishing Service, New York, New York 10017 (800) 253-9646; *Statistical Yearbook*.

United Nations Economic Commission for Africa, Africa Hall, Post Office Box 3001, Addis Ababa, Ethiopia (Telephone Number in U.S. (800) 253-9646); *African Statistical Yearbook*.

MOZAMBIQUE - CUSTOMS DUTIES

G.K. Hall and Company, 70 Lincoln Street, Boston, Massachusetts 02111 (617) 423-3990; *The World in Figures*.

MOZAMBIQUE - DAIRY PRODUCTS

Facts on File, 460 Park Avenue South, New York, New York 10016 (800) 443-8323; *The New Book of World Rankings*.

Food and Agricultural Organization of the United Nations (FAO), Via delle Terme di Caracalla, 00100 Rome, Italy (Telephone Number in U.S. (202) 653-2400); *Production Yearbook*, and *The State of Food and Agriculture*.

Statistical Office of the United Nations, Publishing Service, New York, New York 10017 (800) 253-9646; *Statistical Yearbook*.

MOZAMBIQUE - DEATH RATES

G.K. Hall and Company, 70 Lincoln Street, Boston, Massachusetts 02111 (617) 423-3990; *The World in Figures*.

Statistical Office of the United Nations, Publishing Service, New York, New York 10017 (800) 253-9646; *Statistical Yearbook*, and *Survey of Economic and Social Conditions in Africa*.

Times Books, 201 East 50th Street, New York, New York 10022 (212) 751-2600; *The Economist Book of Vital World Statistics*.

World Health Organization, Office of Publications, Avenue Appia, CH-1211 Geneva 27, Switzerland (Telephone Number in U.S. (518) 436-9686); *World Health Statistics Annual*.

MOZAMBIQUE - DEFENSE EXPENDITURES

G.K. Hall and Company, 70 Lincoln Street, Boston, Massachusetts 02111 (617) 423-3990; *The World in Figures*.

U.S. Arms Control and Disarmament Agency, 320 Twenty-first Street, NW, Washington, D.C. 20451 (202) 647-8677; *World Military Expenditures and Arms Transfers*.

MOZAMBIQUE - DEMOGRAPHY

The Economist Intelligence Unit, 111 West 57th Street, New York, New York 10019 (800) 938-4685; *The World Market Atlas*.

Facts on File, 460 Park Avenue South, New York, New York 10016 (800) 443-8323; *The New Book of World Rankings*.

G.K. Hall and Company, 70 Lincoln Street, Boston, Massachusetts 02111 (617) 423-3990; *The World in Figures*.

Statistical Office of the United Nations, Publishing Service, New York, New York 10017 (800) 253-9646; *Survey of Economic and Social Conditions in Africa*.

MOZAMBIQUE - DEVELOPMENT ASSISTANCE

G.K. Hall and Company, 70 Lincoln Street, Boston, Massachusetts 02111 (617) 423-3990; *The World in Figures*.

Statistical Office of the United Nations, Publishing Service, New York, New York 10017 (800) 253-9646; *Statistical Yearbook*.

MOZAMBIQUE - DIAMOND PRODUCTION - See MOZAMBIQUE - MINING AND MINERAL PRODUCTS

MOZAMBIQUE - DISEASES

G.K. Hall and Company, 70 Lincoln Street, Boston, Massachusetts 02111 (617) 423-3990; *The World in Figures*.

World Health Organization, Office of Publications, Avenue Appia, CH-1211 Geneva 27, Switzerland (Telephone Number in U.S. (518) 436-9686); *World Health Statistics Annual*.

MOZAMBIQUE - DIVORCE RATES

Facts on File, 460 Park Avenue South, New York, New York 10016 (800) 443-8323; *The New Book of World Rankings*.

Statistical Office of the United Nations, Publishing Service, New York, New York 10017 (800) 253-9646; *Demographic Yearbook*.

MOZAMBIQUE - DOMESTIC PRODUCT

G.K. Hall and Company, 70 Lincoln Street, Boston, Massachusetts 02111 (617) 423-3990; *The World in Figures*.

MOZAMBIQUE - DUCKS - See MOZAMBIQUE - LIVESTOCK AND POULTRY

MOZAMBIQUE - ECONOMY

African Development Bank, 01 BP 1387, Abidjan 01, Cote d'Ivoire; *Selected Statistics on Regional Member Countries*.

Euromonitor Publications Limited, 87-88 Turnmill Street, London EC1M 5QU, England; *International Marketing Data and Statistics*.

Facts on File, 460 Park Avenue South, New York, New York 10016 (800) 443-8323; *The New Book of World Rankings*.

G.K. Hall and Company, 70 Lincoln Street, Boston, Massachusetts 02111 (617) 423-3990; *The World in Figures*.

Statistical Office of the United Nations, Publishing Service, New York, New York 10017 (800) 253-9646; *Foreign Trade Statistics for Africa*.

MOZAMBIQUE - EDUCATION

African Development Bank, 01 BP 1387, Abidjan 01, Cote d'Ivoire; *Selected Statistics on Regional Member Countries*.

The Economist Intelligence Unit, 111 West 57th Street, New York, New York 10019 (800) 938-4685; *The World Market Atlas*.

Facts on File, 460 Park Avenue South, New York, New York 10016 (800) 443-8323; *The New Book of World Rankings*.

G.K. Hall and Company, 70 Lincoln Street, Boston, Massachusetts 02111 (617) 423-3990; *The World in Figures*.

Statistical Office of the United Nations, Publishing Service, New York, New York 10017 (800) 253-9646; *Survey of Economic and Social Conditions in Africa*.

Times Books, 201 East 50th Street, New York, New York 10022 (212) 751-2600; *The Economist Book of Vital World Statistics*.

United Nations Economic Commission for Africa, Africa Hall, Post Office Box 3001, Addis Ababa, Ethiopia (Telephone Number in U.S. (800) 253-9646); *African Statistical Yearbook*.

The World Bank, 1818 H Street, NW, Washington, D.C. 20433 (202) 477-1234; *World Tables*.

MOZAMBIQUE - EGG PRODUCTION - See MOZAMBIQUE - DAIRY PRODUCTS

MOZAMBIQUE - ELECTRICITY

Facts on File, 460 Park Avenue South, New York, New York 10016 (800) 443-8323; *The New Book of World Rankings*.

Statistical Office of the United Nations, Publishing Service, New York, New York 10017 (800) 253-9646; *Statistical Yearbook*, and *Survey of Economic and Social Conditions in Africa*.

Times Books, 201 East 50th Street, New York, New York 10022 (212) 751-2600; *The Economist Book of Vital World Statistics*.

United Nations Economic Commission for Africa, Africa Hall, Post Office Box 3001, Addis Ababa, Ethiopia (Telephone Number in U.S. (800) 253-9646); *African Statistical Yearbook*.

MOZAMBIQUE - EMPLOYMENT

Euromonitor Publications Limited, 87-88 Turnmill Street, London EC1M 5QU, England; *International Marketing Data and Statistics*.

Facts on File, 460 Park Avenue South, New York, New York 10016 (800) 443-8323; *The New Book of World Rankings*.

International Labour Office, I.L.O. Publications, CH-1211, Geneva 22, Switzerland; *Yearbook of Labour Statistics*.

Statistical Office of the United Nations, Publishing Service, New York, New York 10017 (800) 253-9646; *Statistical Yearbook*, and *Survey of Economic and Social Conditions in Africa*.

United Nations Economic Commission for Africa, Africa Hall, Post Office Box 3001, Addis Ababa, Ethiopia (Telephone Number in U.S. (800) 253-9646); *African Statistical Yearbook*.

MOZAMBIQUE - ENERGY

Facts on File, 460 Park Avenue South, New York, New York 10016 (800) 443-8323; *The New Book of World Rankings*.

Food and Agricultural Organization of the United Nations (FAO), Via delle Terme di Caracalla, 00100 Rome, Italy (Telephone Number in U.S. (202) 653-2400); *The State of Food and Agriculture*.

G.K. Hall and Company, 70 Lincoln Street, Boston, Massachusetts 02111 (617) 423-3990; *The World in Figures*.

Statistical Office of the United Nations, Publishing Service, New York, New York 10017 (800) 253-9646; *Yearbook of World Energy*, and *Statistical Yearbook*.

Times Books, 201 East 50th Street, New York, New York 10022 (212) 751-2600; *The Economist Book of Vital World Statistics*.

United Nations Economic Commission for Africa, Africa Hall, Post Office Box 3001, Addis Ababa, Ethiopia (Telephone Number in U.S. (800) 253-9646); *African Statistical Yearbook*.

MOZAMBIQUE - EXCHANGE RATES

African Development Bank, 01 BP 1387, Abidjan 01, Cote d'Ivoire; *Selected Statistics on Regional Member Countries*.

Euromonitor Publications Limited, 87-88 Turnmill Street, London EC1M 5QU, England; *International Marketing Data and Statistics*.

Statistical Office of the United Nations, Publishing Service, New York, New York 10017 (800) 253-9646; *Foreign Trade Statistics for Africa*, and *Statistical Yearbook*.

MOZAMBIQUE - EXPORTS

African Development Bank, 01 BP 1387, Abidjan 01, Cote d'Ivoire; *Selected Statistics on Regional Member Countries*.

The Economist Intelligence Unit, 111 West 57th Street, New York, New York 10019 (800) 938-4685; *The World Market Atlas*.

Euromonitor Publications Limited, 87-88 Turnmill Street, London EC1M 5QU, England; *International Marketing Data and Statistics*.

Food and Agricultural Organization of the United Nations (FAO), Via delle Terme di Caracalla, 00100 Rome, Italy (Telephone Number in U.S. (202) 653-2400); *The State of Food and Agriculture*.

G.K. Hall and Company, 70 Lincoln Street, Boston, Massachusetts 02111 (617) 423-3990; *The World in Figures*.

International Monetary Fund, 700 Nineteenth Street, NW, Washington, D.C. 20431 (202) 623-7000; *Direction of Trade Statistics*.

Statistical Office of the United Nations, Publishing Service, New York, New York 10017 (800) 253-9646; *Foreign Trade Statistics for Africa*, and *Survey of Economic and Social Conditions in Africa*.

Times Books, 201 East 50th Street, New York, New York 10022 (212) 751-2600; *The Economist Book of Vital World Statistics*.

United Nations Economic Commission for Africa, Africa Hall, Post Office Box 3001, Addis Ababa, Ethiopia (Telephone Number in U.S. (800) 253-9646); *African Statistical Yearbook*.

The World Bank, 1818 H Street, NW, Washington, D.C. 20433 (202) 477-1234; *World Tables*.

MOZAMBIQUE - EXTERNAL INDEBTEDNESS

African Development Bank, 01 BP 1387, Abidjan 01, Cote d'Ivoire; *Selected Statistics on Regional Member Countries*.

Statistical Office of the United Nations, Publishing Service, New York, New York 10017 (800) 253-9646; *Survey of Economic and Social Conditions in Africa*.

MOZAMBIQUE - EXTERNAL TRADE

African Development Bank, 01 BP 1387, Abidjan 01, Cote d'Ivoire; *Selected Statistics on Regional Member Countries*.

Food and Agricultural Organization of the United Nations (FAO), Via delle Terme di Caracalla, 00100 Rome, Italy (Telephone Number in U.S. (202) 653-2400); *The State of Food and Agriculture*, and *Trade Yearbook*.

G.K. Hall and Company, 70 Lincoln Street, Boston, Massachusetts 02111 (617) 423-3990; *The World in Figures*.

Statistical Office of the United Nations, Publishing Service, New York, New York 10017 (800) 253-9646; *Statistical Yearbook*.

The World Bank, 1818 H Street, NW, Washington, D.C. 20433 (202) 477-1234; *World Tables*.

MOZAMBIQUE - FABRIC PRODUCTION - See MOZAMBIQUE - TEXTILE INDUSTRY

MOZAMBIQUE - FARM CROPS - See MOZAMBIQUE - CROPS

MOZAMBIQUE - FEMALE WORKING POPULATION - See MOZAMBIQUE - EMPLOYMENT

MOZAMBIQUE - FERTILITY RATES

Facts on File, 460 Park Avenue South, New York, New York 10016 (800) 443-8323; *The New Book of World Rankings*.

Statistical Office of the United Nations, Publishing Service, New York, New York 10017 (800) 253-9646; *Survey of Economic and Social Conditions in Africa*.

Times Books, 201 East 50th Street, New York, New York 10022 (212) 751-2600; *The Economist Book of Vital World Statistics*.

The World Bank, 1818 H Street, NW, Washington, D.C. 20433 (202) 477-1234; *World Tables*.

MOZAMBIQUE - FERTILIZER PRICES

Food and Agricultural Organization of the United Nations (FAO), Via delle Terme di Caracalla, 00100 Rome, Italy (Telephone Number

in U.S. (202) 653-2400); *The State of Food and Agriculture*.

MOZAMBIQUE - FERTILIZER PRODUCTION AND CONSUMPTION

Food and Agricultural Organization of the United Nations (FAO), Via delle Terme di Caracalla, 00100 Rome, Italy (Telephone Number in U.S. (202) 653-2400); *Fertilizer Yearbook*.

Statistical Office of the United Nations, Publishing Service, New York, New York 10017 (800) 253-9646; *Statistical Yearbook*.

MOZAMBIQUE - FETAL MORTALITY

Statistical Office of the United Nations, Publishing Service, New York, New York 10017 (800) 253-9646; *Demographic Yearbook*.

MOZAMBIQUE - FINANCE

African Development Bank, 01 BP 1387, Abidjan 01, Cote d'Ivoire; *Selected Statistics on Regional Member Countries*.

Facts on File, 460 Park Avenue South, New York, New York 10016 (800) 443-8323; *The New Book of World Rankings*.

G.K. Hall and Company, 70 Lincoln Street, Boston, Massachusetts 02111 (617) 423-3990; *The World in Figures*.

MOZAMBIQUE - FISHERIES

Facts on File, 460 Park Avenue South, New York, New York 10016 (800) 443-8323; *The New Book of World Rankings*.

Food and Agricultural Organization of the United Nations (FAO), Via delle Terme di Caracalla, 00100 Rome, Italy (Telephone Number in U.S. (202) 653-2400); *The State of Food and Agriculture*, and *Yearbook of Fishery Statistics*.

Statistical Office of the United Nations, Publishing Service, New York, New York 10017 (800) 253-9646; *Statistical Yearbook*, and *Survey of Economic and Social Conditions in Africa*.

United Nations Economic Commission for Africa, Africa Hall, Post Office Box 3001, Addis Ababa, Ethiopia (Telephone Number in U.S. (800) 253-9646); *African Statistical Yearbook*.

MOZAMBIQUE - FLOUR PRODUCTION

Statistical Office of the United Nations, Publishing Service, New York, New York 10017 (800) 253-9646; *Statistical Yearbook*.

MOZAMBIQUE - FOOD

African Development Bank, 01 BP 1387, Abidjan 01, Cote d'Ivoire; *Selected Statistics on Regional Member Countries*.

Food and Agricultural Organization of the United Nations (FAO), Via delle Terme di Caracalla, 00100 Rome, Italy (Telephone Number in U.S. (202) 653-2400); *Production Yearbook*, and *The State of Food and Agriculture*.

G.K. Hall and Company, 70 Lincoln Street, Boston, Massachusetts 02111 (617) 423-3990; *The World in Figures*.

MOZAMBIQUE - FOREIGN AID

G.K. Hall and Company, 70 Lincoln Street, Boston, Massachusetts 02111 (617) 423-3990; *The World in Figures*.

MOZAMBIQUE - FOREIGN TRADE

Euromonitor Publications Limited, 87-88 Turnmill Street, London EC1M 5QU, England; *International Marketing Data and Statistics*.

Facts on File, 460 Park Avenue South, New York, New York 10016 (800) 443-8323; *The New Book of World Rankings*.

Food and Agricultural Organization of the United Nations (FAO), Via delle Terme di Caracalla, 00100 Rome, Italy (Telephone Number in U.S. (202) 653-2400); *The State of Food and Agriculture*.

G.K. Hall and Company, 70 Lincoln Street, Boston, Massachusetts 02111 (617) 423-3990; *The World in Figures*.

Statistical Office of the United Nations, Publishing Service, New York, New York 10017 (800) 253-9646; *Foreign Trade Statistics for Africa*, *International Trade Statistics Yearbook*, and *Statistical Yearbook*.

United Nations Economic Commission for Africa, Africa Hall, Post Office Box 3001, Addis Ababa, Ethiopia (Telephone Number in U.S. (800) 253-9646); *African Statistical Yearbook*.

The World Bank, 1818 H Street, NW, Washington, D.C. 20433 (202) 477-1234; *World Tables*.

MOZAMBIQUE - FORESTRY AND FOREST PRODUCTS

Facts on File, 460 Park Avenue South, New York, New York 10016 (800) 443-8323; *The New Book of World Rankings*.

Food and Agricultural Organization of the United Nations (FAO), Via delle Terme di Caracalla, 00100 Rome, Italy (Telephone Number in U.S. (202) 653-2400), *The State of Food and Agriculture*, and *Yearbook of Forest Products*.

G.K. Hall and Company, 70 Lincoln Street, Boston, Massachusetts 02111 (617) 423-3990; *The World in Figures*.

Statistical Office of the United Nations, Publishing Service, New York, New York 10017 (800) 253-9646; *Statistical Yearbook*.

United Nations Economic Commission for Africa, Africa Hall, Post Office Box 3001, Addis Ababa, Ethiopia (Telephone Number in U.S. (800) 253-9646); *African Statistical Yearbook*.

United Nations Educational, Scientific and Cultural Organization (UNESCO), 7 Place de Fontenoy, F-75700 Paris, France (Telephone Number in U.S. (212) 963-5981); *Statistical Yearbook*.

MOZAMBIQUE - GENERAL MORTALITY

Statistical Office of the United Nations, Publishing Service, New York, New York 10017 (800) 253-9646; *Demographic Yearbook*.

MOZAMBIQUE - GAS PRODUCTION - See MOZAMBIQUE - MINING AND MINERAL PRODUCTS

MOZAMBIQUE - GEOGRAPHIC DATA

Facts on File, 460 Park Avenue South, New York, New York 10016 (800) 443-8323; *The New Book of World Rankings*.

MOZAMBIQUE - GOATS - See MOZAMBIQUE - LIVESTOCK AND POULTRY

MOZAMBIQUE - GOLD PRODUCTION AND CONSUMPTION - See MOZAMBIQUE - MINING AND MINERAL PRODUCTS

MOZAMBIQUE - GOVERNMENT

G.K. Hall and Company, 70 Lincoln Street, Boston, Massachusetts 02111 (617) 423-3990; *The World in Figures*.

MOZAMBIQUE - GOVERNMENT EXPENDITURE

The World Bank, 1818 H Street, NW, Washington, D.C. 20433 (202) 477-1234; *World Tables*.

MOZAMBIQUE - GOVERNMENT REVENUE

Statistical Office of the United Nations, Publishing Service, New York, New York 10017 (800) 253-9646; *Survey of Economic and Social Conditions in Africa*.

The World Bank, 1818 H Street, NW, Washington, D.C. 20433 (202) 477-1234; *World Tables*.

MOZAMBIQUE - GRAIN PRODUCTION

Food and Agricultural Organization of the United Nations (FAO), Via delle Terme di Caracalla, 00100 Rome, Italy (Telephone Number in U.S. (202) 653-2400); *The State of Food and Agriculture*.

MOZAMBIQUE - GROSS DOMESTIC PRODUCT

African Development Bank, 01 BP 1387, Abidjan 01, Cote d'Ivoire; *Selected Statistics on Regional Member Countries*.

The Economist Intelligence Unit, 111 West 57th Street, New York, New York 10019 (800) 938-4685; *The World Market Atlas*.

Euromonitor Publications Limited, 87-88 Turnmill Street, London EC1M 5QU, England; *International Marketing Data and Statistics*.

Facts on File, 460 Park Avenue South, New York, New York 10016 (800) 443-8323; *The New Book of World Rankings*.

G.K. Hall and Company, 70 Lincoln Street, Boston, Massachusetts 02111 (617) 423-3990; *The World in Figures*.

Statistical Office of the United Nations, Publishing Service, New York, New York 10017 (800) 253-9646; *Statistical Yearbook*, and *Survey of Economic and Social Conditions in Africa*.

Times Books, 201 East 50th Street, New York, New York 10022 (212) 751-2600; *The Economist Book of Vital World Statistics*.

United Nations Economic Commission for Africa, Africa Hall, Post Office Box 3001, Addis Ababa, Ethiopia (Telephone Number in U.S. (800) 253-9646); *African Statistical Yearbook*.

The World Bank, 1818 H Street, NW, Washington, D.C. 20433 (202) 477-1234; *World Tables*.

MOZAMBIQUE - GROSS NATIONAL PRODUCT

Euromonitor Publications Limited, 87-88 Turnmill Street, London EC1M 5QU, England; *International Marketing Data and Statistics*.

U.S. Arms Control and Disarmament Agency, 320 Twenty-first Street, NW, Washington, D.C. 20451 (202) 647-8677; *World Military Expenditures and Arms Transfers*.

The World Bank, 1818 H Street, NW, Washington, D.C. 20433 (202) 477-1234; *World Tables*.

MOZAMBIQUE - GROUNDNUT PRODUCTION - See MOZAMBIQUE - CROPS

MOZAMBIQUE - HEALTH

African Development Bank, 01 BP 1387, Abidjan 01, Cote d'Ivoire; *Selected Statistics on Regional Member Countries.*

Facts on File, 460 Park Avenue South, New York, New York 10016 (800) 443-8323; *The New Book of World Rankings.*

G.K. Hall and Company, 70 Lincoln Street, Boston, Massachusetts 02111 (617) 423-3990; *The World in Figures.*

Statistical Office of the United Nations, Publishing Service, New York, New York 10017 (800) 253-9646; *Statistical Yearbook.*

Times Books, 201 East 50th Street, New York, New York 10022 (212) 751-2600; *The Economist Book of Vital World Statistics.*

United Nations Economic Commission for Africa, Africa Hall, Post Office Box 3001, Addis Ababa, Ethiopia (Telephone Number in U.S. (800) 253-9646); *African Statistical Yearbook.*

World Health Organization, Office of Publications, Avenue Appia, CH-1211 Geneva 27, Switzerland (Telephone Number in U.S. (518) 436-9686); *World Health Statistics Annual.*

MOZAMBIQUE - HEALTH AND MEDICAL SERVICES

Statistical Office of the United Nations, Publishing Service, New York, New York 10017 (800) 253-9646; *Statistical Yearbook.*

MOZAMBIQUE - HIDE PRODUCTION

Food and Agricultural Organization of the United Nations (FAO), Via delle Terme di Caracalla, 00100 Rome, Italy (Telephone Number in U.S. (202) 653-2400); *Production Yearbook.*

MOZAMBIQUE - HIGHWAYS

G.K. Hall and Company, 70 Lincoln Street, Boston, Massachusetts 02111 (617) 423-3990; *The World in Figures.*

Statistical Office of the United Nations, Publishing Service, New York, New York 10017 (800) 253-9646; *Survey of Economic and Social Conditions in Africa.*

United Nations Economic Commission for Africa, Africa Hall, Post Office Box 3001, Addis Ababa, Ethiopia (Telephone Number in U.S. (800) 253-9646); *African Statistical Yearbook.*

MOZAMBIQUE - HORSES - See MOZAMBIQUE - LIVESTOCK AND POULTRY

MOZAMBIQUE - HOURS OF WORK - See MOZAMBIQUE - EMPLOYMENT

MOZAMBIQUE - HOUSING

Facts on File, 460 Park Avenue South, New York, New York 10016 (800) 443-8323; *The New Book of World Rankings.*

MOZAMBIQUE - ILLITERATE POPULATION

The Economist Intelligence Unit, 111 West 57th Street, New York, New York 10019 (800) 938-4685; *The World Market Atlas.*

G.K. Hall and Company, 70 Lincoln Street, Boston, Massachusetts 02111 (617) 423-3990; *The World in Figures.*

United Nations Educational, Scientific and Cultural Organization (UNESCO), 7 Place de Fontenoy, F-75700 Paris, France (Telephone Number in U.S. (212) 963-5981; *Statistical Yearbook.*

MOZAMBIQUE - IMPORTS

African Development Bank, 01 BP 1387, Abidjan 01, Cote d'Ivoire; *Selected Statistics on Regional Member Countries.*

The Economist Intelligence Unit, 111 West 57th Street, New York, New York 10019 (800) 938-4685; *The World Market Atlas.*

Euromonitor Publications Limited, 87-88 Turnmill Street, London EC1M 5QU, England; *International Marketing Data and Statistics.*

Food and Agricultural Organization of the United Nations (FAO), Via delle Terme di Caracalla, 00100 Rome, Italy (Telephone Number in U.S. (202) 653-2400); *The State of Food and Agriculture.*

G.K. Hall and Company, 70 Lincoln Street, Boston, Massachusetts 02111 (617) 423-3990; *The World in Figures.*

International Monetary Fund, 700 Nineteenth Street, NW, Washington, D.C. 20431 (202) 623-7000; *Direction of Trade Statistics.*

Statistical Office of the United Nations, Publishing Service, New York, New York 10017 (800) 253-9646; *Foreign Trade Statistics for Africa,* and *Survey of Economic and Social Conditions in Africa.*

United Nations Economic Commission for Africa, Africa Hall, Post Office Box 3001, Addis Ababa, Ethiopia (Telephone Number in U.S. (800) 253-9646); *African Statistical Yearbook.*

The World Bank, 1818 H Street, NW, Washington, D.C. 20433 (202) 477-1234; *World Tables.*

MOZAMBIQUE - INDUSTRIAL ACIDS PRODUCTION

Statistical Office of the United Nations, Publishing Service, New York, New York 10017 (800) 253-9646; *Statistical Yearbook.*

MOZAMBIQUE - INDUSTRY

Euromonitor Publications Limited, 87-88 Turnmill Street, London EC1M 5QU, England; *International Marketing Data and Statistics.*

Facts on File, 460 Park Avenue South, New York, New York 10016 (800) 443-8323; *The New Book of World Rankings.*

G.K. Hall and Company, 70 Lincoln Street, Boston, Massachusetts 02111 (617) 423-3990; *The World in Figures.*

International Labour Office, I.L.O. Publications, CH-1211, Geneva 22, Switzerland; *Yearbook of Labour Statistics.*

Statistical Office of the United Nations, Publishing Service, New York, New York 10017 (800) 253-9646; *Statistical Yearbook,* and *Survey of Economic and social Conditions in Africa.*

Times Books, 201 East 50th Street, New York, New York 10022 (212) 751-2600; *The Economist Book of Vital World Statistics.*

United Nations Economic Commission for Africa, Africa Hall, Post Office Box 3001, Addis Ababa, Ethiopia (Telephone Number in U.S. (800) 253-9646); *African Statistical Yearbook.*

The World Bank, 1818 H Street, NW, Washington, D.C. 20433 (202) 477-1234; *World Tables.*

MOZAMBIQUE - INFANT AND MATERNAL MORTALITY

Statistical Office of the United Nations, Publishing Service, New York, New York 10017 (800) 253-9646; *Demographic Yearbook, Statistical Yearbook,* and *Survey of Economic and Social Conditions in Africa.*

Times Books, 201 East 50th Street, New York, New York 10022 (212) 751-2600; *The Economist Book of Vital World Statistics.*

The World Bank, 1818 H Street, NW, Washington, D.C. 20433 (202) 477-1234; *World Tables.*

MOZAMBIQUE - INTERNATIONAL RESERVES EXCLUDING GOLD

African Development Bank, 01 BP 1387, Abidjan 01, Cote d'Ivoire; *Selected Statistics on Regional Member Countries.*

The World Bank, 1818 H Street, NW, Washington, D.C. 20433 (202) 477-1234; *World Tables.*

MOZAMBIQUE - IRON ORE PRODUCTION AND CONSUMPTION - See MOZAMBIQUE - MINING AND MINERAL PRODUCTS

MOZAMBIQUE - IRRIGATION

Euromonitor Publications Limited, 87-88 Turnmill Street, London EC1M 5QU, England; *International Marketing Data and Statistics.*

MOZAMBIQUE - JUTE PRODUCTION - See MOZAMBIQUE - CROPS

MOZAMBIQUE - LABOR FORCE

African Development Bank, 01 BP 1387, Abidjan 01, Cote d'Ivoire; *Selected Statistics on Regional Member Countries,*

Euromonitor Publications Limited, 87-88 Turnmill Street, London EC1M 5QU, England; *International Marketing Data and Statistics.*

Facts on File, 460 Park Avenue South, New York, New York 10016 (800) 443-8323; *The New Book of World Rankings.*

Food and Agricultural Organization of the United Nations (FAO), Via delle Terme di Caracalla, 00100 Rome, Italy (Telephone Number in U.S. (202) 653-2400); *The State of Food and Agriculture.*

G.K. Hall and Company, 70 Lincoln Street, Boston, Massachusetts 02111 (617) 423-3990; *The World in Figures.*

The World Bank, 1818 H Street, NW, Washington, D.C. 20433 (202) 477-1234; *World Tables.*

MOZAMBIQUE - LABOR PRODUCTIVITY

International Labour Office, I.L.O. Publications, CH-1211, Geneva 22, Switzerland; *Yearbook of Labour Statistics.*

MOZAMBIQUE - LAND USE

Euromonitor Publications Limited, 87-88 Turnmill Street, London EC1M 5QU, England; *International Marketing Data and Statistics.*

Food and Agricultural Organization of the United Nations (FAO), Via delle Terme di Caracalla, 00100 Rome, Italy (Telephone Number in U.S. (202) 653-2400); *Production Yearbook.*

G.K. Hall and Company, 70 Lincoln Street, Boston, Massachusetts 02111 (617) 423-3990; *The World in Figures.*

MOZAMBIQUE - LIBRARIES

Facts on File, 460 Park Avenue South, New York, New York 10016 (800) 443-8323; *The New Book of World Rankings.*

United Nations Educational, Scientific and Cultural Organization (UNESCO), 7 Place de Fontenoy, F-75700 Paris, France (Telephone Number in U.S. (212) 963-5981); *Statistical Yearbook.*

MOZAMBIQUE - LIFE EXPECTANCY

African Development Bank, 01 BP 1387, Abidjan 01, Cote d'Ivoire; *Selected Statistics on Regional Member Countries.*

MOZAMBIQUE - LIGNITE PRODUCTION - See MOZAMBIQUE - MINING AND MINERAL PRODUCTS

MOZAMBIQUE - LITERACY RATE

Statistical Office of the United Nations, Publishing Service, New York, New York 10017 (800) 253-9646; *Survey of Economic and Social Conditions in Africa.*

MOZAMBIQUE - LIVESTOCK AND POULTRY

Euromonitor Publications Limited, 87-88 Turnmill Street, London EC1M 5QU, England; *International Marketing Data and Statistics.*

Facts on File, 460 Park Avenue South, New York, New York 10016 (800) 443-8323; *The New Book of World Rankings.*

Food and Agricultural Organization of the United Nations (FAO), Via delle Terme di Caracalla, 00100 Rome, Italy (Telephone Number in U.S. (202) 653-2400); *Production Yearbook,* and *The State of Food and Agriculture.*

G.K. Hall and Company, 70 Lincoln Street, Boston, Massachusetts 02111 (617) 423-3990; *The World in Figures.*

Statistical Office of the United Nations, Publishing Service, New York, New York 10017 (800) 253-9646; *Statistical Yearbook,* and *Survey of Economic and Social Conditions in Africa.*

United Nations Economic Commission for Africa, Africa Hall, Post Office Box 3001, Addis Ababa, Ethiopia (Telephone Number in U.S. (800) 253-9646); *African Statistical Yearbook.*

MOZAMBIQUE - LIVING LEVELS

G.K. Hall and Company, 70 Lincoln Street, Boston, Massachusetts 02111 (617) 423-3990; *The World in Figures.*

Times Books, 201 East 50th Street, New York, New York 10022 (212) 751-2600; *The Economist Book of Vital World Statistics.*

MOZAMBIQUE - MAIL - NUMBER OF ITEMS SENT AND RECEIVED

Statistical Office of the United Nations, Publishing Service, New York, New York 10017 (800) 253-9646; *Statistical Yearbook.*

MOZAMBIQUE - MANUFACTURING

Facts on File, 460 Park Avenue South, New York, New York 10016 (800) 443-8323; *The New Book of World Rankings.*

G.K. Hall and Company, 70 Lincoln Street, Boston, Massachusetts 02111 (617) 423-3990; *The World in Figures.*

G.K. Hall and Company, 70 Lincoln Street, Boston, Massachusetts 02111 (617) 423-3990; *The World in Figures*.

Statistical Office of the United Nations, Publishing Service, New York, New York 10017 (800) 253-9646; *Statistical Yearbook*, and *Survey of Economic and Social Conditions in Africa*.

United Nations Economic Commission for Africa, Africa Hall, Post Office Box 3001, Addis Ababa, Ethiopia (Telephone Number in U.S. (800) 253-9646); *African Statistical Yearbook*.

The World Bank, 1818 H Street, NW, Washington, D.C. 20433 (202) 477-1234; *World Tables*.

MOZAMBIQUE - MARRIAGE RATES

Facts on File, 460 Park Avenue South, New York, New York 10016 (800) 443-8323; *The New Book of World Rankings*.

Statistical Office of the United Nations, Publishing Service, New York, New York 10017 (800) 253-9646; *Demographic Yearbook*.

MOZAMBIQUE - MEAT PRODUCTION - See MOZAMBIQUE - LIVESTOCK AND POULTRY

MOZAMBIQUE - MERCHANT SHIPPING

G.K. Hall and Company, 70 Lincoln Street, Boston, Massachusetts 02111 (617) 423-3990; *The World in Figures*.

Statistical Office of the United Nations, Publishing Service, New York, New York 10017 (800) 253-9646; *Statistical Yearbook*.

Times Books, 201 East 50th Street, New York, New York 10022 (212) 751-2600; *The Economist Book of Vital World Statistics*.

United Nations Economic Commission for Africa, Africa Hall, Post Office Box 3001, Addis Ababa, Ethiopia (Telephone Number in U.S. (800) 253-9646); *African Statistical Yearbook*.

U.S. Department of Transportation, Maritime Administration, 400 Seventh Street, SW, Washington, D.C. 20590 (202) 267-1587; *A Statistical Analysis of the World's Merchant Fleets*.

MOZAMBIQUE - MILITARY

G.K. Hall and Company, 70 Lincoln Street, Boston, Massachusetts 02111 (617) 423-3990; *The World in Figures*.

The International Institute for Strategic Studies, 23 Tavistock Street, London WC2E 7NQ, England; *The Military Balance*.

U.S. Arms Control and Disarmament Agency, 320 Twenty-first Street, NW, Washington, D.C. 20451 (202) 647-8677; *World Military Expenditures and Arms Transfers*.

MOZAMBIQUE - MILK PRODUCTION - See MOZAMBIQUE - DAIRY PRODUCTS

MOZAMBIQUE - MILLET PRODUCTION - See MOZAMBIQUE - CROPS

MOZAMBIQUE - MINING AND MINERAL PRODUCTS

Facts on File, 460 Park Avenue South, New York, New York 10016 (800) 443-8323; *The New Book of World Rankings*.

G.K. Hall and Company, 70 Lincoln Street, Boston, Massachusetts 02111 (617) 423-3990; *The World in Figures*.

Statistical Office of the United Nations, Publishing Service, New York, New York 10017 (800) 253-9646; *Statistical Yearbook*.

United Nations Economic Commission for Africa, Africa Hall, Post Office Box 3001, Addis Ababa, Ethiopia (Telephone Number in U.S. (800) 253-9646); *African Statistical Yearbook*.

The World Bank, 1818 H Street, NW, Washington, D.C. 20433 (202) 477-1234; *World Tables*.

MOZAMBIQUE - MONEY EXCHANGE RATES

Euromonitor Publications Limited, 87-88 Turnmill Street, London EC1M 5QU, England; *International Marketing Data and Statistics*.

Statistical Office of the United Nations, Publishing Service, New York, New York 10017 (800) 253-9646; *Statistical Yearbook*.

MOZAMBIQUE - MONEY RESERVES

Euromonitor Publications Limited, 87-88 Turnmill Street, London EC1M 5QU, England; *International Marketing Data and Statistics*.

MOZAMBIQUE - MONEY SUPPLY

African Development Bank, 01 BP 1387, Abidjan 01, Cote d'Ivoire; *Selected Statistics on Regional Member Countries*.

Euromonitor Publications Limited, 87-88 Turnmill Street, London EC1M 5QU, England; *International Marketing Data and Statistics*.

G.K. Hall and Company, 70 Lincoln Street, Boston, Massachusetts 02111 (617) 423-3990; *The World in Figures*.

The World Bank, 1818 H Street, NW, Washington, D.C. 20433 (202) 477-1234; *World Tables*.

MOZAMBIQUE - MOTOR VEHICLES IN USE

G.K. Hall and Company, 70 Lincoln Street, Boston, Massachusetts 02111 (617) 423-3990; *The World in Figures*.

Statistical Office of the United Nations, Publishing Service, New York, New York 10017 (800) 253-9646; *Statistical Yearbook*, and *Survey of Economic and Social Conditions in Africa*.

Times Books, 201 East 50th Street, New York, New York 10022 (212) 751-2600; *The Economist Book of Vital World Statistics*.

MOZAMBIQUE - MUSEUMS

Facts on File, 460 Park Avenue South, New York, New York 10016 (800) 443-8323; *The New Book of World Rankings*.

MOZAMBIQUE - NATALITY - See MOZAMBIQUE - BIRTH RATES

MOZAMBIQUE - NATIONAL ACCOUNTS

African Development Bank, 01 BP 1387, Abidjan 01, Cote d'Ivoire; *Selected Statistics on Regional Member Countries*.

Statistical Office of the United Nations, Publishing Service, New York, New York 10017 (800) 253-9646; *Statistical Yearbook*.

United Nations Economic Commission for Africa, Africa Hall, Post Office Box 3001, Addis Ababa, Ethiopia (Telephone Number in U.S. (800) 253-9646); *African Statistical Yearbook*.

MOZAMBIQUE - NATIONAL INCOME

Facts on File, 460 Park Avenue South, New York, New York 10016 (800) 443-8323; *The New Book of World Rankings.*

G.K. Hall and Company, 70 Lincoln Street, Boston, Massachusetts 02111 (617) 423-3990; *The World in Figures.*

MOZAMBIQUE - NATIONAL PRODUCT

Facts on File, 460 Park Avenue South, New York, New York 10016 (800) 443-8323; *The New Book of World Rankings.*

MOZAMBIQUE - NATURAL GAS - PRODUCTION - See MOZAMBIQUE - MINING AND MINERAL PRODUCTS

MOZAMBIQUE - NEWSPAPER PRODUCTION - See MOZAMBIQUE - FORESTRY AND FOREST PRODUCTS

MOZAMBIQUE - NEWSPRINT - See MOZAMBIQUE - FORESTRY AND FOREST PRODUCTS

MOZAMBIQUE - OCCUPATIONS - See MOZAMBIQUE - LABOR FORCE

MOZAMBIQUE - PAPER - See MOZAMBIQUE - FORESTRY AND FOREST PRODUCTS

MOZAMBIQUE - PEANUT PRODUCTION - See MOZAMBIQUE - CROPS

MOZAMBIQUE - PESTICIDE USE

Food and Agricultural Organization of the United Nations (FAO), Via delle Terme di Caracalla, 00100 Rome, Italy (Telephone Number in U.S. (202) 653-2400); *The State of Food and Agriculture.*

MOZAMBIQUE - PETROLEUM INDUSTRY

Facts on File, 460 Park Avenue South, New York, New York 10016 (800) 443-8323; *The New Book of World Rankings.*

Food and Agricultural Organization of the United Nations (FAO), Via delle Terme di Caracalla, 00100 Rome, Italy (Telephone Number in U.S. (202) 653-2400); *The State of Food and Agriculture.*

G.K. Hall and Company, 70 Lincoln Street, Boston, Massachusetts 02111 (617) 423-3990; *The World in Figures.*

Statistical Office of the United Nations, Publishing Service, New York, New York 10017 (800) 253-9646; *Statistical Yearbook.*

MOZAMBIQUE - PIGS - See MOZAMBIQUE - LIVESTOCK AND POULTRY

MOZAMBIQUE - POPULATION

African Development Bank, 01 BP 1387, Abidjan 01, Cote d'Ivoire; *Selected Statistics on Regional Member Countries.*

The Economist Intelligence Unit, 111 West 57th Street, New York, New York 10019 (800) 938-4685; *The World Market Atlas.*

Euromonitor Publications Limited, 87-88 Turnmill Street, London EC1M 5QU, England; *International Marketing Data and Statistics.*

Facts on File, 460 Park Avenue South, New York, New York 10016 (800) 443-8323; *The New Book of World Rankings.*

Food and Agricultural Organization of the United Nations (FAO), Via delle Terme di Caracalla, 00100 Rome, Italy (Telephone Number in U.S. (202) 653-2400); *Production Yearbook.*

G.K. Hall and Company, 70 Lincoln Street, Boston, Massachusetts 02111 (617) 423-3990; *The World in Figures.*

International Labour Office, I.L.O. Publications, CH-1211, Geneva 22, Switzerland; *Yearbook of Labour Statistics.*

Statistical Office of the United Nations, Publishing Service, New York, New York 10017 (800) 253-9646; *Demographic Yearbook, Statistical Yearbook,* and *Survey of Economic and Social Conditions in Africa.*

Times Books, 201 East 50th Street, New York, New York 10022 (212) 751-2600; *The Economist Book of Vital World Statistics.*

U.S. Arms Control and Disarmament Agency, 320 Twenty-first Street, NW, Washington, D.C. 20451 (202) 647-8677; *World Military Expenditures and Arms Transfers.*

World Health Organization, Office of Publications, Avenue Appia, CH-1211 Geneva 27, Switzerland (Telephone Number in U.S. (518) 436-9686); *World Health Statistics Annual.*

MOZAMBIQUE - POST OFFICES

Facts on File, 460 Park Avenue South, New York, New York 10016 (800) 443-8323; *The New Book of World Rankings.*

MOZAMBIQUE - POTATO PRODUCTION - See MOZAMBIQUE - CROPS

MOZAMBIQUE - POWER PRODUCTION INDUSTRY

Statistical Office of the United Nations, Publishing Service, New York, New York 10017 (800) 253-9646; *Statistical Yearbook.*

MOZAMBIQUE - PRICES

Facts on File, 460 Park Avenue South, New York, New York 10016 (800) 443-8323; *The New Book of World Rankings.*

Food and Agricultural Organization of the United Nations (FAO), Via delle Terme di Caracalla, 00100 Rome, Italy (Telephone Number in U.S. (202) 653-2400); *Production Yearbook,* and *The State of Food and Agriculture.*

G.K. Hall and Company, 70 Lincoln Street, Boston, Massachusetts 02111 (617) 423-3990; *The World in Figures.*

International Labour Office, I.L.O. Publications, CH-1211, Geneva 22, Switzerland; *Yearbook of Labour Statistics.*

MOZAMBIQUE - PRODUCTION

Facts on File, 460 Park Avenue South, New York, New York 10016 (800) 443-8323; *The New Book of World Rankings.*

G.K. Hall and Company, 70 Lincoln Street, Boston, Massachusetts 02111 (617) 423-3990; *The World in Figures.*

MOZAMBIQUE - PRODUCTIVITY

Euromonitor Publications Limited, 87-88 Turnmill Street, London EC1M 5QU, England; *International Marketing Data and Statistics.*

MOZAMBIQUE - PUBLIC FINANCE

Facts on File, 460 Park Avenue South, New York, New York 10016 (800) 443-8323; *The New Book of World Rankings*.

MOZAMBIQUE - RADIO BROADCASTING - See MOZAMBIQUE - BROADCASTING

MOZAMBIQUE - RADIO RECEIVER PRODUCTION

Statistical Office of the United Nations, Publishing Service, New York, New York 10017 (800) 253-9646; *Statistical Yearbook*.

MOZAMBIQUE - RAILWAY USE

G.K. Hall and Company, 70 Lincoln Street, Boston, Massachusetts 02111 (617) 423-3990; *The World in Figures*.

Statistical Office of the United Nations, Publishing Service, New York, New York 10017 (800) 253-9646; *Statistical Yearbook*, and *Survey of Economic and Social Conditions in Africa*.

MOZAMBIQUE - RAILWAYS

Jane's Information Group, Sentinel House, 163 Brighton Road, Coulsdon, Surrey CR5 2NH, England (Telephone Number in U.S. (703) 683-3700); *Jane's World Railways*.

United Nations Economic Commission for Africa, Africa Hall, Post Office Box 3001, Addis Ababa, Ethiopia (Telephone Number in U.S. (800) 253-9646); *African Statistical Yearbook*.

MOZAMBIQUE - RELIGION

Facts on File, 460 Park Avenue South, New York, New York 10016 (800) 443-8323; *The New Book of World Rankings*.

MOZAMBIQUE - RENT PRICES

International Labour Office, I.L.O. Publications, CH-1211, Geneva 22, Switzerland; *Yearbook of Labour Statistics*.

MOZAMBIQUE - RETAIL TRADE

G.K. Hall and Company, 70 Lincoln Street, Boston, Massachusetts 02111 (617) 423-3990; *The World in Figures*.

MOZAMBIQUE - RICE PRODUCTION - See MOZAMBIQUE - CROPS

MOZAMBIQUE - ROOT AND TUBER PRODUCTION - See MOZAMBIQUE - CROPS

MOZAMBIQUE - ROUNDWOOD PRODUCTION - See MOZAMBIQUE - FORESTRY AND FOREST PRODUCTS

MOZAMBIQUE - RUBBER PRODUCTION AND CONSUMPTION

Facts on File, 460 Park Avenue South, New York, New York 10016 (800) 443-8323; *The New Book of World Rankings*.

MOZAMBIQUE - SALT PRODUCTION - See MOZAMBIQUE - MINING AND MINERAL PRODUCTS

MOZAMBIQUE - SAWNWOOD PRODUCTION - See MOZAMBIQUE - FORESTRY AND FOREST PRODUCTS

MOZAMBIQUE - SENIOR CITIZENS

Facts on File, 460 Park Avenue South, New York, New York 10016 (800) 443-8323; *The New Book of World Rankings*.

MOZAMBIQUE - SESAME SEED PRODUCTION - See MOZAMBIQUE - CROPS

MOZAMBIQUE - SHEEP - See MOZAMBIQUE - LIVESTOCK AND POULTRY

MOZAMBIQUE - SILVER PRODUCTION AND CONSUMPTION - See MOZAMBIQUE - MINING AND MINERAL PRODUCTS

MOZAMBIQUE - SISAL PRODUCTION - See MOZAMBIQUE - CROPS

MOZAMBIQUE - SOCIAL DATA

African Development Bank, 01 BP 1387, Abidjan 01, Cote d'Ivoire; *Selected Statistics on Regional Member Countries*.

Facts on File, 460 Park Avenue South, New York, New York 10016 (800) 443-8323; *The New Book of World Rankings*.

G.K. Hall and Company, 70 Lincoln Street, Boston, Massachusetts 02111 (617) 423-3990; *The World in Figures*.

MOZAMBIQUE - STATE BUDGET

Euromonitor Publications Limited, 87-88 Turnmill Street, London EC1M 5QU, England; *International Marketing Data and Statistics*.

MOZAMBIQUE - STEEL - See MOZAMBIQUE - MINING AND MINERAL PRODUCTS

MOZAMBIQUE - STOCKS - COMMODITY - MARKET PRICE - INDEX

Food and Agricultural Organization of the United Nations (FAO), Via delle Terme di Caracalla, 00100 Rome, Italy (Telephone Number in U.S. (202) 653-2400); *The State of Food and Agriculture*.

MOZAMBIQUE - SUGAR PRODUCTION AND CONSUMPTION - See MOZAMBIQUE - CROPS

MOZAMBIQUE - SULPHURIC ACID - See MOZAMBIQUE - MINING AND MINERAL PRODUCTS

MOZAMBIQUE - TAXATION

G.K. Hall and Company, 70 Lincoln Street, Boston, Massachusetts 02111 (617) 423-3990; *The World in Figures*.

The World Bank, 1818 H Street, NW, Washington, D.C. 20433 (202) 477-1234; *World Tables*.

MOZAMBIQUE - TAX REVENUE - See MOZAMBIQUE - TAXATION

MOZAMBIQUE - TEA PRODUCTION - See MOZAMBIQUE - CROPS

MOZAMBIQUE - TELEPHONES IN USE

American Telephone and Telegraph Company, 26 Parsippany Road, Whippany, New Jersey 07981 (800) 338-4038; *The World's Telephones*.

G.K. Hall and Company, 70 Lincoln Street, Boston, Massachusetts 02111 (617) 423-3990; *The World in Figures*.

Statistical Office of the United Nations, Publishing Service, New York, New York 10017 (800) 253-9646; *Statistical Yearbook.*

MOZAMBIQUE - TELEVISION BROADCASTING - See MOZAMBIQUE - BROADCASTING

MOZAMBIQUE - TEXTILE INDUSTRY

G.K. Hall and Company, 70 Lincoln Street, Boston, Massachusetts 02111 (617) 423-3990; *The World in Figures.*

Statistical Office of the United Nations, Publishing Service, New York, New York 10017 (800) 253-9646; *Statistical Yearbook.*

MOZAMBIQUE - TOBACCO PRODUCTION

Facts on File, 460 Park Avenue South, New York, New York 10016 (800) 443-8323; *The New Book of World Rankings.*

Statistical Office of the United Nations, Publishing Service, New York, New York 10017 (800) 253-9646; *Statistical Yearbook.*

MOZAMBIQUE - TOURISM

Facts on File, 460 Park Avenue South, New York, New York 10016 (800) 443-8323; *The New Book of World Rankings.*

G.K. Hall and Company, 70 Lincoln Street, Boston, Massachusetts 02111 (617) 423-3990; *The World in Figures.*

United Nations Economic Commission for Africa, Africa Hall, Post Office Box 3001, Addis Ababa, Ethiopia (Telephone Number in U.S. (800) 253-9646); *African Statistical Yearbook.*

MOZAMBIQUE - TRACTORS IN USE

Statistical Office of the United Nations, Publishing Service, New York, New York 10017 (800) 253-9646; *Statistical Yearbook.*

MOZAMBIQUE - TRADE - See MOZAMBIQUE - FOREIGN TRADE

MOZAMBIQUE - TRANSPORTATION AND COMMUNICATIONS

Facts on File, 460 Park Avenue South, New York, New York 10016 (800) 443-8323; *The New Book of World Rankings.*

G.K. Hall and Company, 70 Lincoln Street, Boston, Massachusetts 02111 (617) 423-3990; *The World in Figures.*

United Nations Economic Commission for Africa, Africa Hall, Post Office Box 3001, Addis Ababa, Ethiopia (Telephone Number in U.S. (800) 253-9646); *African Statistical Yearbook.*

MOZAMBIQUE - UNEMPLOYMENT

International Labour Office, I.L.O. Publications, CH-1211, Geneva 22, Switzerland; *Yearbook of Labour Statistics.*

Statistical Office of the United Nations, Publishing Service, New York, New York 10017 (800) 253-9646; *Statistical Yearbook.*

MOZAMBIQUE - VITAL STATISTICS

Euromonitor Publications Limited, 87-88 Turnmill Street, London EC1M 5QU, England; *International Marketing Data and Statistics.*

G.K. Hall and Company, 70 Lincoln Street, Boston, Massachusetts 02111 (617) 423-3990; *The World in Figures.*

Statistical Office of the United Nations, Publishing Service, New York, New York 10017 (800) 253-9646; *Statistical Yearbook.*

World Health Organization, Office of Publications, Avenue Appia, CH-1211 Geneva 27, Switzerland (Telephone Number in U.S. (518) 436-9686); *World Health Statistics Annual.*

MOZAMBIQUE - WAGES

G.K. Hall and Company, 70 Lincoln Street, Boston, Massachusetts 02111 (617) 423-3990; *The World in Figures.*

International Labour Office, I.L.O. Publications, CH-1211, Geneva 22, Switzerland; *Yearbook of Labour Statistics.*

MOZAMBIQUE - WEATHER

Facts on File, 460 Park Avenue South, New York, New York 10016 (800) 443-8323; *The New Book of World Rankings.*

G.K. Hall and Company, 70 Lincoln Street, Boston, Massachusetts 02111 (617) 423-3990; *The World in Figures.*

MOZAMBIQUE - WHEAT PRODUCTION - See MOZAMBIQUE - CROPS

MOZAMBIQUE - WINE PRODUCTION

Facts on File, 460 Park Avenue South, New York, New York 10016 (800) 443-8323; *The New Book of World Rankings.*

MOZAMBIQUE - WOOL PRODUCTION

Facts on File, 460 Park Avenue South, New York, New York 10016 (800) 443-8323; *The New Book of World Rankings.*

MOZAMBIQUE - YARN PRODUCTION

Statistical Office of the United Nations, Publishing Service, New York, New York 10017 (800) 253-9646; *Statistical Yearbook.*

MULLET - CATCH

U.S. Department of Commerce, National Oceanic and Atmospheric Administration, National Marine Fisheries Service, 1335 East-West Highway, Silver Spring, Maryland 20910 (301) 427-2239; *Fishery Statistics of the United States,* and *Fisheries of the United States.*

MULTINATIONAL COMPANIES

U.S. Department of Commerce, Bureau of Economic Analysis, Fourteenth Street between Constitution Avenue and E Street, NW, Washington, D.C. 20230 (202) 606-9900; *Survey of Current Business.*

MUMPS

U.S. Department of Health and Human Services, Center for Disease Control, 1600 Clifton Road, NE, Atlanta, Georgia 30333 (404) 639-3311; *Summary of Notifiable Diseases, United States Morbidity and Mortality Weekly Report,* and *United States Immunization Survey.*

MUNICIPAL AND STATE BONDS

Board of Governors of the Federal Reserve System, Twentieth Street and Constitution Avenue, NW, Washington, D.C. 20551 (202) 452-3000; *Federal Reserve Bulletin,* and *Annual Statistical Digest.*

Moody's Investors Service, 99 Church Street, New York, New York 10007 (212) 553-0300.

Standard and Poor's Corporation, 25 Broadway, New York, New York 10004 (212) 208-8000; *Standard and Poor's Outlook.*

MUNICIPAL WASTE

Franklin Associates Limited, 4121 West Eighty-third Street, Suite 108, Prairie Village, Kansas 66208 (913) 649-2225; *Characterization of Municipal Solid Waste in the United States.*

MUNICIPALITIES - See CITIES and METROPOLITAN AREAS

MURDERS

U.S. Department of Health and Human Services, National Center for Health Statistics, 3700 East West Highway, Hyattsville, Maryland 20783 (301) 436-8500; *Vital Statistics of the United States.*

U.S. Department of Justice, Federal Bureau of Investigation, Ninth Street and Pennsylvania Avenue, NW, Washington, D.C. 20535 (202) 324-3000; *Crime in the United States.*

MUSEUMS - BOTANICAL - ZOOLOGICAL GARDENS - FEDERAL AID

U.S. National Endowment for the Arts, 1100 Pennsylvania Avenue, NW, Washington, D.C. 20506 (202) 682-5400; *Annual Report.*

U.S. National Endowment for the Humanities, 1100 Pennsylvania Avenue, NW, Washington, D.C. 20506 (202) 606-8438; *Annual Report.*

MUSEUMS - BOTANICAL - ZOOLOGICAL GARDENS - FINANCES

U.S. National Endowment for the Arts, 1100 Pennsylvania Avenue, NW, Washington, D.C. 20506 (202) 682-5400; *Annual Report.*

U.S. National Endowment for the Humanities, 1100 Pennsylvania Avenue, NW, Washington, D.C. 20506 (202) 606-8438; *Annual Report.*

MUSEUMS - BOTANICAL - ZOOLOGICAL GARDENS - OCCUPATIONAL SAFETY

U.S. Department of Labor, Bureau of Labor Statistics, Two Massachusetts Avenue, NE, Washington, D.C. 20212 (202) 606-7828; *Occupational Injuries and Illnesses in the United States by Industry.*

MUSEUMS - BOTANICAL - ZOOLOGICAL GARDENS - RECEIPTS

U.S. Department of Commerce, Bureau of the Census, Suitland, Maryland 20233 (301) 763-4040; *Census of Service Industries,* and *Current Business Reports, Service Annual Survey.*

MUSHROOMS

U.S. Department of Agriculture, National Agricultural Statistics Service, Fourteenth Street and Independence Avenue, SW, Washington, D.C. 20250 (202) 219-1504; *Economic Indicators of the Farm Sector: National Financial Summary, Vegetables, Agricultural Statistics,* and *Agricultural Outlook.*

MUSICIANS AND COMPOSERS

U.S. Department of Labor, Bureau of Labor Statistics, Two Massachusetts Avenue, NE, Washington, D.C. 20212 (202) 606-7828; *Employment and Earnings.*

MUSIC

Veronis, Suhler and Associates, 350 Park Avenue, New York, New York 10022 (212) 935-4990; *Communications Industry Forecast Report.*

MUTTON - See also MEAT AND MEAT PRODUCTS

MUTTON

U.S. Department of Agriculture, Economic Research Service, Fourteenth Street and Independence Avenue, SW, Washington, D.C. 20005-4789 (202) 219-1504; *Food Consumption, Prices, and Expenditures,* and unpublished data.

U.S. Department of Agriculture, National Agricultural Statistics Service, Fourteenth Street and Independence Avenue, SW, Washington, D.C. 20250 (202) 219-1504; *Livestock and Meat Statistics,* and *Agricultural Outlook.*

MUTUAL FUNDS

Access Research, Inc., 8 Griffin Road North, Windsor, Connecticut 06095 (203) 688-8821; *Marketplace Update.*

Board of Governors of the Federal Reserve System, Twentieth Street and Constitution Avenue, NW, Washington, D.C. 20551 (202) 452-3000; *Annual Statistical Digest,* and *Federal Reserve Bulletin.*

Investment Company Institute, 1600 M Street, NW, Washington, D.C. 20036 (202) 293-7700; *Mutual Fund Fact Book.*

Myanmar - National Statistical Office

Central Statistical Organization, Ministry of Planning and Finance, Six Storeyed Building, Strand Road, Yangon, Myanmar.

Myanmar - Primary Statistics Sources

Central Statistical and Economics Department, New Secretariat, Yangon, Myanmar; *Statistical Yearbook.*

Central Statistical Organization, Six Storeyed Building, Strand Road, Yangon, Myanmar; *Statistical Yearbook, Statistical Pocketbook,* and *Quarterly Bulletin of Statistics.*

MYANMAR - AGRICULTURE

Asian Development Bank, Post Office Box 789, Manila, 1099 Manila, Philippines; *Key Indicators of Developing Asian and Pacific Countries.*

Euromonitor Publications Limited, 87-88 Turnmill Street, London EC1M 5QU, England; *International Marketing Data and Statistics.*

Facts on File, 460 Park Avenue South, New York, New York 10016 (800) 443-8323; *The New Book of World Rankings.*

Federal Statistical Office, Gustav - Stresemann - Ring 11, D-6200 Wiesbaden, Germany; *Myanmar.*

Food and Agricultural Organization of the United Nations (FAO), Via delle Terme di Caracalla, 00100 Rome, Italy (Telephone Number in U.S. (202) 653-2400); *Production Yearbook, The State of Food and Agriculture,* and *Trade Yearbook.*

G.K. Hall and Company, 70 Lincoln Street, Boston, Massachusetts 02111 (617) 423-3990; *The World in Figures.*

Statistical Office of the United Nations, Publishing Service, New York, New York 10017 (800) 253-9646; *Statistical Yearbook.*

Times Books, 201 East 50th Street, New York, New York 10022 (212) 751-2600; *The Economist Book of Vital World Statistics.*

MYANMAR - AIRLINE SERVICE

The Economist Intelligence Unit (Asia) Limited, 10th Floor, Luk Kwok Centre, 72 Gloucester Road, Wanchai, Hong Kong (Phone Number in U.S. (800) 938-4685; *Asian Market Atlas.*

Facts on File, 460 Park Avenue South, New York, New York 10016 (800) 443-8323; *The New Book of World Rankings.*

G.K. Hall and Company, 70 Lincoln Street, Boston, Massachusetts 02111 (617) 423-3990; *The World in Figures.*

International Civil Aviation Organization, 1000 Sherbrooke Street West, Suite 400, Montreal, Quebec H3A 2R2, Canada (514) 285-8219; *Civil Aviation Statistics of the World.*

Statistical Office of the United Nations, Publishing Service, New York, New York 10017 (800) 253-9646; *Statistical Yearbook.*

Times Books, 201 East 50th Street, New York, New York 10022 (212) 751-2600; *The Economist Book of Vital World Statistics.*

MYANMAR - ALUMINUM PRODUCTION AND CONSUMPTION - See MYANMAR - MINING AND MINERAL PRODUCTS

MYANMAR - ANIMAL HEALTH

Food and Agricultural Organization of the United Nations (FAO), Via delle Terme di Caracalla, 00100, Rome, Italy (Telephone Number in U.S. (202) 653-2400); *Animal Health Yearbook.*

MYANMAR - ANTIMONY PRODUCTION - See MYANMAR - MINING AND MINERAL PRODUCTS

MYANMAR - AREA AND DENSITY OF POPULATION

Euromonitor Publications Limited, 87-88 Turnmill Street, London EC1M 5QU, England; *International Marketing Data and Statistics.*

Facts on File, 460 Park Avenue South, New York, New York 10016 (800) 443-8323; *The New Book of World Rankings.*

Federal Statistical Office, Gustav - Stresemann - Ring 11, D-6200 Wiesbaden, Germany; *Myanmar.*

Food and Agricultural Organization of the United Nations (FAO), Via delle Terme di Caracalla, 00100 Rome, Italy (Telephone Number in U.S. (202) 653-2400); *The State of Food and Agriculture.*

G.K. Hall and Company, 70 Lincoln Street, Boston, Massachusetts 02111 (617) 423-3990; *The World in Figures.*

Statistical Office of the United Nations, Publishing Service, New York, New York 10017 (800) 253-9646; *Statistical Yearbook.*

Times Books, 201 East 50th Street, New York, New York 10022 (212) 751-2600; *The Economist Book of Vital World Statistics.*

MYANMAR - ARMS EXPORTS AND IMPORTS

U.S. Arms Control and Disarmament Agency, 320 Twenty-first Street, NW, Washington, D.C. 20451 (202) 647-8677; *World Military Expenditures and Arms Transfers.*

MYANMAR - BALANCE OF PAYMENTS

The Economist Intelligence Unit, 111 West 57th Street, New York, New York 10019 (800) 938-4685; *The World Market Atlas.*

Federal Statistical Office, Gustav - Stresemann - Ring 11, D-6200 Wiesbaden, Germany; *Myanmar.*

G.K. Hall and Company, 70 Lincoln Street, Boston, Massachusetts 02111 (617) 423-3990; *The World in Figures.*

International Monetary Fund, Nineteenth and H Street, NW, Washington, D.C. 20431 (202) 623-7000; *International Financial Statistics.*

MYANMAR - BANKING

Asian Development Bank, Post Office Box 789, Manila, 1099 Manila, Philippines; *Key Indicators of Developing Asian and Pacific Countries.*

Facts on File, 460 Park Avenue South, New York, New York 10016 (800) 443-8323; *The New Book of World Rankings.*

G.K. Hall and Company, 70 Lincoln Street, Boston, Massachusetts 02111 (617) 423-3990; *The World in Figures.*

International Monetary Fund, Nineteenth and H Street, NW, Washington, D.C. 20431 (202) 623-7000; *International Financial Statistics.*

MYANMAR - BARLEY PRODUCTION - See MYANMAR - CROPS

MYANMAR - BEER PRODUCTION

Facts on File, 460 Park Avenue South, New York, New York 10016 (800) 443-8323; *The New Book of World Rankings.*

Statistical Office of the United Nations, Publishing Service, New York, New York 10017 (800) 253-9646; *Statistical Yearbook.*

MYANMAR - BIRTH RATES

The Economist Intelligence Unit (Asia) Limited, 10th Floor, Luk Kwok Centre, 72 Gloucester Road, Wanchai, Hong Kong (Phone Number in U.S. (800) 938-4685; *Asian Market Atlas.*

Facts on File, 460 Park Avenue South, New York, New York 10016 (800) 443-8323; *The New Book of World Rankings.*

Statistical Office of the United Nations, Publishing Service, New York, New York 10017 (800) 253-9646; *Demographic Yearbook,* and *Statistical Yearbook.*

Times Books, 201 East 50th Street, New York, New York 10022 (212) 751-2600; *The Economist Book of Vital World Statistics.*

MYANMAR - BONDS

Asian Development Bank, Post Office Box 789, Manila, 1099 Manila, Philippines; *Key Indicators of Developing Asian and Pacific Countries.*

G.K. Hall and Company, 70 Lincoln Street, Boston, Massachusetts 02111 (617) 423-3990; *The World in Figures.*

MYANMAR - BOOK PRODUCTION

G.K. Hall and Company, 70 Lincoln Street, Boston, Massachusetts 02111 (617) 423-3990; *The World in Figures*.

MYANMAR - BROADCASTING

Billboard Limited, Post Office Box 9027, 1006 AA Amsterdam, The Netherlands (Telephone Number in U.S. (212) 764-7300); *World Radio TV Handbook*.

The Economist Intelligence Unit (Asia) Limited, 10th Floor, Luk Kwok Centre, 72 Gloucester Road, Wanchai, Hong Kong (Phone Number in U.S. (800) 938-4685); *Asian Market Atlas*.

Facts on File, 460 Park Avenue South, New York, New York 10016 (800) 443-8323; *The New Book of World Rankings*.

G.K. Hall and Company, 70 Lincoln Street, Boston, Massachusetts 02111 (617) 423-3990; *The World in Figures*.

Times Books, 201 East 50th Street, New York, New York 10022 (212) 751-2600; *The Economist Book of Vital World Statistics*.

MYANMAR - BUSINESS

G.K. Hall and Company, 70 Lincoln Street, Boston, Massachusetts 02111 (617) 423-3990; *The World in Figures*.

MYANMAR - BUTTER PRODUCTION - See MYANMAR - DAIRY PRODUCTS

MYANMAR - CALORIE SUPPLY

Asian Development Bank, Post Office Box 789, Manila, 1099 Manila, Philippines; *Key Indicators of Developing Asian and Pacific Countries*.

Food and Agricultural Organization of the United Nations (FAO), Via delle Terme di Caracalla, 00100 Rome, Italy (Telephone Number in U.S. (202) 653-2400); *The State of Food and Agriculture*.

MYANMAR - CAPITAL INVESTMENT

Asian Development Bank, Post Office Box 789, Manila, 1099 Manila, Philippines; *Key Indicators of Developing Asian and Pacific Countries*.

MYANMAR - CAPITAL REVENUE

Asian Development Bank, Post Office Box 789, Manila, 1099 Manila, Philippines; *Key Indicators of Developing Asian and Pacific Countries*.

MYANMAR - CATTLE - See MYANMAR - LIVESTOCK AND POULTRY

MYANMAR - CEMENT PRODUCTION - See MYANMAR - MINING AND MINERAL PRODUCTS

MYANMAR - CHEESE PRODUCTION AND CONSUMPTION - See MYANMAR - DAIRY PRODUCTS

MYANMAR - CHEMICAL (ORGANIC) PRODUCTION - See MYANMAR - MINING AND MINERAL PRODUCTS

MYANMAR - CHICK PEA PRODUCTION - See MYANMAR - CROPS

MYANMAR - CHICKENS - See MYANMAR - LIVESTOCK AND POULTRY

MYANMAR - CIGAR AND CIGARETTE PRODUCTION - See MYANMAR - TOBACCO PRODUCTION

MYANMAR - CLASS STRUCTURE

G.K. Hall and Company, 70 Lincoln Street, Boston, Massachusetts 02111 (617) 423-3990; *The World in Figures*.

MYANMAR - CLIMATE

Facts on File, 460 Park Avenue South, New York, New York 10016 (800) 443-8323; *The New Book of World Rankings*.

G.K. Hall and Company, 70 Lincoln Street, Boston, Massachusetts 02111 (617) 423-3990; *The World in Figures*.

MYANMAR - COAL PRODUCTION - See MYANMAR - MINING AND MINERAL PRODUCTS

MYANMAR - COFFEE PRODUCTION AND CONSUMPTION - See MYANMAR - CROPS

MYANMAR - COMMUNICATIONS

Federal Statistical Office, Gustav - Stresemann - Ring 11, D-6200 Wiesbaden, Germany; *Myanmar*.

G.K. Hall and Company, 70 Lincoln Street, Boston, Massachusetts 02111 (617) 423-3990; *The World in Figures*.

Statistical Office of the United Nations, Publishing Service, New York, New York 10017 (800) 253-9646; *Statistical Yearbook for Asia and the Pacific*.

MYANMAR - CONSTRUCTION INDUSTRY

Facts on File, 460 Park Avenue South, New York, New York 10016 (800) 443-8323; *The New Book of World Rankings*.

Statistical Office of the United Nations, Publishing Service, New York, New York 10017 (800) 253-9646; *Statistical Yearbook*.

MYANMAR - CONSUMER PRICE INDEX

Asian Development Bank, Post Office Box 789, Manila, 1099 Manila, Philippines; *Key Indicators of Developing Asian and Pacific Countries*.

Federal Statistical Office, Gustav - Stresemann - Ring 11, D-6200 Wiesbaden, Germany; *Myanmar*.

G.K. Hall and Company, 70 Lincoln Street, Boston, Massachusetts 02111 (617) 423-3990; *The World in Figures*.

Statistical Office of the United Nations, Publishing Service, New York, New York 10017 (800) 253-9646; *Statistical Yearbook*.

MYANMAR - CONSUMER PRICES

Federal Statistical Office, Gustav - Stresemann - Ring 11, D-6200 Wiesbaden, Germany; *Myanmar*.

International Labour Office, I.L.O. Publications, CH-1211, Geneva 22, Switzerland; *Yearbook of Labour Statistics*.

International Monetary Fund, Nineteenth and H Street, NW, Washington, D.C. 20431 (202) 623-7000; *International Financial Statistics*.

Times Books, 201 East 50th Street, New York, New York 10022 (212) 751-2600; *The Economist Book of Vital World Statistics.*

MYANMAR - CONSUMPTION

G.K. Hall and Company, 70 Lincoln Street, Boston, Massachusetts 02111 (617) 423-3990; *The World in Figures.*

International Rubber Study Group, York House, Eighth Floor, Empire Way, Wembley, London HA9 0PA, England; *Rubber Statistical Bulletin.*

MYANMAR - COPPER AND COPPER ORE PRODUCTION AND CONSUMPTION - See MYANMAR - MINING AND MINERAL PRODUCTS

MYANMAR - CORN PRODUCTION - See MYANMAR - CROPS

MYANMAR - CORPORATE TAXES - See MYANMAR - TAXATION

MYANMAR - COTTON - See MYANMAR - CROPS

MYANMAR - CRIME

International Criminal Police Organization (INTERPOL), 26 rue Armengaud, 92210 Saint Cloud, France; *International Crime Statistics.*

Yale University Press, Yale Station, New Haven, Connecticut 06520 (203) 432-0940; *Violence and Crime in Cross-National Perspective.*

MYANMAR - CROPS

Asian Development Bank, Post Office Box 789, Manila, 1099 Manila, Philippines; *Key Indicators of Developing Asian and Pacific Countries.*

Commodity Research Bureau, Incorporated, 75 Wall Street, New York, New York 10005 (212) 504-7754; *Commodity Year Book.*

Facts on File, 460 Park Avenue South, New York, New York 10016 (800) 443-8323; *The New Book of World Rankings.*

Food and Agricultural Organization of the United Nations (FAO), Via delle Terme di Caracalla, 00100 Rome, Italy (Telephone Number in U.S. (202) 653-2400); *Production Yearbook,* and *The State of Food and Agriculture.*

G.K. Hall and Company, 70 Lincoln Street, Boston, Massachusetts 02111 (617) 423-3990; *The World in Figures.*

International Monetary Fund, Nineteenth and H Street, NW, Washington, D.C. 20431 (202) 623-7000; *International Financial Statistics.*

Statistical Office of the United Nations, Publishing Service, New York, New York 10017 (800) 253-9646; *Statistical Yearbook.*

MYANMAR - CUSTOMS DUTIES

G.K. Hall and Company, 70 Lincoln Street, Boston, Massachusetts 02111 (617) 423-3990; *The World in Figures.*

MYANMAR - DAIRY PRODUCTS

Facts on File, 460 Park Avenue South, New York, New York 10016 (800) 443-8323; *The New Book of World Rankings.*

Food and Agricultural Organization of the United Nations (FAO), Via delle Terme di Caracalla, 00100 Rome, Italy (Telephone Number in U.S. (202) 653-2400); *Production Yearbook,* and *The State of Food and Agriculture.*

Statistical Office of the United Nations, Publishing Service, New York, New York 10017 (800) 253-9646; *Statistical Yearbook.*

MYANMAR - DEATH RATES

The Economist Intelligence Unit (Asia) Limited, 10th Floor, Luk Kwok Centre, 72 Gloucester Road, Wanchai, Hong Kong (Phone Number in U.S. (800) 938-4685); *Asian Market Atlas.*

G.K. Hall and Company, 70 Lincoln Street, Boston, Massachusetts 02111 (617) 423-3990; *The World in Figures.*

Statistical Office of the United Nations, Publishing Service, New York, New York 10017 (800) 253-9646; *Statistical Yearbook.*

Times Books, 201 East 50th Street, New York, New York 10022 (212) 751-2600; *The Economist Book of Vital World Statistics.*

World Health Organization, Office of Publications, Avenue Appia, CH-1211 Geneva 27, Switzerland (Telephone Number in U.S. (518) 436-9686); *World Health Statistics Annual.*

MYANMAR - DEFENSE EXPENDITURES

G.K. Hall and Company, 70 Lincoln Street, Boston, Massachusetts 02111 (617) 423-3990; *The World in Figures.*

U.S. Arms Control and Disarmament Agency, 320 Twenty-first Street, NW, Washington, D.C. 20451 (202) 647-8677; *World Military Expenditures and Arms Transfers.*

MYANMAR - DEMOGRAPHY

The Economist Intelligence Unit, 111 West 57th Street, New York, New York 10019 (800) 938-4685; *The World Market Atlas.*

The Economist Intelligence Unit (Asia) Limited, 10th Floor, Luk Kwok Centre, 72 Gloucester Road, Wanchai, Hong Kong (Phone Number in U.S. (800) 938-4685); *Asian Market Atlas.*

Facts on File, 460 Park Avenue South, New York, New York 10016 (800) 443-8323; *The New Book of World Rankings.*

Federal Statistical Office, Gustav - Stresemann - Ring 11, D-6200 Wiesbaden, Germany; *Myanmar.*

G.K. Hall and Company, 70 Lincoln Street, Boston, Massachusetts 02111 (617) 423-3990; *The World in Figures.*

MYANMAR - DEVELOPMENT ASSISTANCE

Asian Development Bank, Post Office Box 789, Manila, 1099 Manila, Philippines; *Key Indicators of Developing Asian and Pacific Countries.*

G.K. Hall and Company, 70 Lincoln Street, Boston, Massachusetts 02111 (617) 423-3990; *The World in Figures.*

Statistical Office of the United Nations, Publishing Service, New York, New York 10017 (800) 253-9646; *Statistical Yearbook.*

MYANMAR - DIAMOND PRODUCTION - See MYANMAR - MINING AND MINERAL PRODUCTS

MYANMAR - DISEASES

G.K. Hall and Company, 70 Lincoln Street, Boston, Massachusetts 02111 (617) 423-3990; *The World in Figures.*

World Health Organization, Office of Publications, Avenue Appia, CH-1211 Geneva 27, Switzerland (Telephone Number in U.S. (518) 436-9686); *World Health Statistics Annual.*

MYANMAR - DIVORCE

Facts on File, 460 Park Avenue South, New York, New York 10016 (800) 443-8323; *The New Book of World Rankings.*

Statistical Office of the United Nations, Publishing Service, New York, New York 10017 (800) 253-9646; *Demographic Yearbook.*

MYANMAR - DOMESTIC PRODUCT

G.K. Hall and Company, 70 Lincoln Street, Boston, Massachusetts 02111 (617) 423-3990; *The World in Figures.*

MYANMAR - DUCKS - See MYANMAR - LIVESTOCK AND POULTRY

MYANMAR - ECONOMY

Asian Development Bank, Post Office Box 789, Manila, 1099 Manila, Philippines; *Key Indicators of Developing Asian and Pacific Countries.*

Euromonitor Publications Limited, 87-88 Turnmill Street, London EC1M 5QU, England; *International Marketing Data and Statistics.*

Facts on File, 460 Park Avenue South, New York, New York 10016 (800) 443-8323; *The New Book of World Rankings.*

Federal Statistical Office, Gustav - Stresemann - Ring 11, D-6200 Wiesbaden, Germany; *Myanmar.*

G.K. Hall and Company, 70 Lincoln Street, Boston, Massachusetts 02111 (617) 423-3990; *The World in Figures.*

MYANMAR - EDUCATION

The Economist Intelligence Unit, 111 West 57th Street, New York, New York 10019 (800) 938-4685; *The World Market Atlas.*

The Economist Intelligence Unit (Asia) Limited, 10th Floor, Luk Kwok Centre, 72 Gloucester Road, Wanchai, Hong Kong (Phone Number in U.S. (800) 938-4685); *Asian Market Atlas.*

Facts on File, 460 Park Avenue South, New York, New York 10016 (800) 443-8323; *The New Book of World Rankings.*

Federal Statistical Office, Gustav - Stresemann - Ring 11, D-6200 Wiesbaden, Germany; *Myanmar.*

G.K. Hall and Company, 70 Lincoln Street, Boston, Massachusetts 02111 (617) 423-3990; *The World in Figures.*

Statistical Office of the United Nations, Publishing Service, New York, New York 10017 (800) 253-9646; *Statistical Yearbook for Asia and the Pacific.*

Times Books, 201 East 50th Street, New York, New York 10022 (212) 751-2600; *The Economist Book of Vital World Statistics.*

United Nations Educational, Scientific and Cultural Organization (UNESCO), 7 Place de Fontenoy, F-75700 Paris, France (Telephone Number in U.S. (212) 963-5981); *Statistical Yearbook.*

MYANMAR - EGG PRODUCTION AND CONSUMPTION - See MYANMAR - DAIRY PRODUCTS

MYANMAR - ELECTRICITY

Asian Development Bank, Post Office Box 789, Manila, 1099 Manila, Philippines; *Key Indicators of Developing Asian and Pacific Countries.*

Facts on File, 460 Park Avenue South, New York, New York 10016 (800) 443-8323; *The New Book of World Rankings.*

Penn Well Publishing Company, 1421 South Sheridan Road, Post Office Box 1260, Tulsa, Oklahoma 74101 (800) 752-9764; *International Energy Statistics Sourcebook.*

Statistical Office of the United Nations, Publishing Service, New York, New York 10017 (800) 253-9646; *Electric Power in Asia and the Pacific,* and *Statistical Yearbook.*

Times Books, 201 East 50th Street, New York, New York 10022 (212) 751-2600; *The Economist Book of Vital World Statistics.*

MYANMAR - EMPLOYMENT

Euromonitor Publications Limited, 87-88 Turnmill Street, London EC1M 5QU, England; *International Marketing Data and Statistics.*

Facts on File, 460 Park Avenue South, New York, New York 10016 (800) 443-8323; *The New Book of World Rankings.*

Federal Statistical Office, Gustav - Stresemann - Ring 11, D-6200 Wiesbaden, Germany; *Myanmar.*

International Labour Office, I.L.O. Publications, CH-1211, Geneva 22, Switzerland; *Yearbook of Labour Statistics.*

Statistical Office of the United Nations, Publishing Service, New York, New York 10017 (800) 253-9646; *Statistical Yearbook.*

MYANMAR - ENERGY

Facts on File, 460 Park Avenue South, New York, New York 10016 (800) 443-8323; *The New Book of World Rankings.*

G.K. Hall and Company, 70 Lincoln Street, Boston, Massachusetts 02111 (617) 423-3990; *The World in Figures.*

Statistical Office of the United Nations, Publishing Service, New York, New York 10017 (800) 253-9646; *Energy Statistics Yearbook, Statistical Yearbook,* and *Statistical Yearbook for Asia and the Pacific.*

Penn Well Publishing Company, 1421 South Sheridan Road, Post Office Box 1260, Tulsa, Oklahoma 74101 (800) 752-9764; *International Energy Statistics Sourcebook.*

Times Books, 201 East 50th Street, New York, New York 10022 (212) 751-2600; *The Economist Book of Vital World Statistics.*

MYANMAR - EXCHANGE RATES

Asian Development Bank, Post Office Box 789, Manila, 1099 Manila, Philippines; *Key Indicators of Developing Asian and Pacific Countries.*

The Economist Intelligence Unit (Asia) Limited, 10th Floor, Luk Kwok Centre, 72 Gloucester Road, Wanchai, Hong Kong (Phone Number in U.S. (800) 938-4685); *Asian Market Atlas*.

Euromonitor Publications Limited, 87-88 Turnmill Street, London EC1M 5QU, England; *International Marketing Data and Statistics*.

International Civil Aviation Organization, 1000 Sherbrooke Street West, Suite 400, Montreal, Quebec H3A 2R2, Canada (514) 285-8219; *Civil Aviation Statistics of the World*.

International Monetary Fund, Nineteenth and H Street, NW, Washington, D.C. 20431 (202) 623-7000; *International Financial Statistics*.

MYANMAR - EXPORTS

Asian Development Bank, Post Office Box 789, Manila, 1099 Manila, Philippines; *Key Indicators of Developing Asian and Pacific Countries*.

The Economist Intelligence Unit, 111 West 57th Street, New York, New York 10019 (800) 938-4685; *The World Market Atlas*.

The Economist Intelligence Unit (Asia) Limited, 10th Floor, Luk Kwok Centre, 72 Gloucester Road, Wanchai, Hong Kong (Phone Number in U.S. (800) 938-4685); *Asian Market Atlas*.

Euromonitor Publications Limited, 87-88 Turnmill Street, London EC1M 5QU, England; *International Marketing Data and Statistics*.

Food and Agricultural Organization of the United Nations (FAO), Via delle Terme di Caracalla, 00100 Rome, Italy (Telephone Number in U.S. (202) 653-2400); *The State of Food and Agriculture*.

G.K. Hall and Company, 70 Lincoln Street, Boston, Massachusetts 02111 (617) 423-3990; *The World in Figures*.

International Monetary Fund, 700 Nineteenth Street, NW, Washington, D.C. 20431 (202) 623-7000; *Direction of Trade Statistics*, and *International Financial Statistics*.

International Rubber Study Group, York House, Eighth Floor, Empire Way, Wembley, London HA9 0PA, England; *Rubber Statistical Bulletin*.

Times Books, 201 East 50th Street, New York, New York 10022 (212) 751-2600; *The Economist Book of Vital World Statistics*.

MYANMAR - EXTERNAL FINANCING

Asian Development Bank, Post Office Box 789, Manila, 1099 Manila, Philippines; *Key Indicators of Developing Asian and Pacific Countries*.

MYANMAR - EXTERNAL INDEBTEDNESS

Asian Development Bank, Post Office Box 789, Manila, 1099 Manila, Philippines; *Key Indicators of Developing Asian and Pacific Countries*.

MYANMAR - EXTERNAL TRADE

Asian Development Bank, Post Office Box 789, Manila, 1099 Manila, Philippines; *Key Indicators of Developing Asian and Pacific Countries*.

Food and Agricultural Organization of the United Nations (FAO), Via delle Terme di Caracalla, 00100 Rome, Italy (Telephone Number

in U.S. (202) 653-2400); *The State of Food and Agriculture*, and *Trade Yearbook*.

G.K. Hall and Company, 70 Lincoln Street, Boston, Massachusetts 02111 (617) 423-3990; *The World in Figures*.

Statistical Office of the United Nations, Publishing Service, New York, New York 10017 (800) 253-9646; *Statistical Yearbook for Asia and the Pacific*.

MYANMAR - FABRIC PRODUCTION - See MYANMAR - TEXTILE INDUSTRY

MYANMAR - FARM CROPS - See MYANMAR - CROPS

MYANMAR - FEMALE WORKING POPULATION - See MYANMAR - EMPLOYMENT

MYANMAR - FERTILITY RATES

The Economist Intelligence Unit (Asia) Limited, 10th Floor, Luk Kwok Centre, 72 Gloucester Road, Wanchai, Hong Kong (Phone Number in U.S. (800) 938-4685); *Asian Market Atlas*.

Facts on File, 460 Park Avenue South, New York, New York 10016 (800) 443-8323; *The New Book of World Rankings*.

Times Books, 201 East 50th Street, New York, New York 10022 (212) 751-2600; *The Economist Book of Vital World Statistics*.

MYANMAR - FERTILIZER

Food and Agricultural Organization of the United Nations (FAO), Via delle Terme di Caracalla, 00100 Rome, Italy (Telephone Number in U.S. (202) 653-2400); *The State of Food and Agriculture*.

Statistical Office of the United Nations, Publishing Service, New York, New York 10017 (800) 253-9646; *Statistical Yearbook*.

MYANMAR - FETAL MORTALITY

Statistical Office of the United Nations, Publishing Service, New York, New York 10017 (800) 253-9646; *Demographic Yearbook*.

MYANMAR - FILMS PRODUCED - LONG - See MYANMAR - MOTION PICTURES

MYANMAR - FINANCE

Facts on File, 460 Park Avenue South, New York, New York 10016 (800) 443-8323; *The New Book of World Rankings*.

Federal Statistical Office, Gustav - Stresemann - Ring 11, D-6200 Wiesbaden, Germany; *Myanmar*.

G.K. Hall and Company, 70 Lincoln Street, Boston, Massachusetts 02111 (617) 423-3990; *The World in Figures*.

International Monetary Fund, Nineteenth and H Street, NW, Washington, D.C. 20431 (202) 623-7000; *International Financial Statistics*.

Statistical Office of the United Nations, Publishing Service, New York, New York 10017 (800) 253-9646; *Statistical Yearbook for Asia and the Pacific*.

MYANMAR - FISHERIES

Facts on File, 460 Park Avenue South, New York, New York 10016 (800) 443-8323; *The New Book of World Rankings*.

Federal Statistical Office, Gustav - Stresemann - Ring 11, D-6200 Wiesbaden, Germany; *Myanmar*.

Food and Agricultural Organization of the United Nations (FAO), Via delle Terme di Caracalla, 00100 Rome, Italy (Telephone Number in U.S. (202) 653-2400); *The State of Food and Agriculture*, and *Yearbook of Fishery Statistics*.

Statistical Office of the United Nations, Publishing Service, New York, New York 10017 (800) 253-9646; *Statistical Yearbook*.

MYANMAR - FLOUR PRODUCTION

Statistical Office of the United Nations, Publishing Service, New York, New York 10017 (800) 253-9646; *Statistical Yearbook*.

MYANMAR - FOOD

Food and Agricultural Organization of the United Nations (FAO), Via delle Terme di Caracalla, 00100 Rome, Italy (Telephone Number in U.S. (202) 653-2400); *Production Yearbook*, and *The State of Food and Agriculture*.

G.K. Hall and Company, 70 Lincoln Street, Boston, Massachusetts 02111 (617) 423-3990; *The World in Figures*.

Statistical Office of the United Nations, Publishing Service, New York, New York 10017 (800) 253-9646; *Statistical Yearbook for Asia and the Pacific*.

MYANMAR - FOREIGN AID

G.K. Hall and Company, 70 Lincoln Street, Boston, Massachusetts 02111 (617) 423-3990; *The World in Figures*.

MYANMAR - FOREIGN TRADE

Asian Development Bank, Post Office Box 789, Manila, 1099 Manila, Philippines; *Key Indicators of Developing Asian and Pacific Countries*.

The Economist Intelligence Unit (Asia) Limited, 10th Floor, Luk Kwok Centre, 72 Gloucester Road, Wanchai, Hong Kong (Phone Number in U.S. (800) 938-4685); *Asian Market Atlas*.

Euromonitor Publications Limited, 87-88 Turnmill Street, London EC1M 5QU, England; *International Marketing Data and Statistics*.

Facts on File, 460 Park Avenue South, New York, New York 10016 (800) 443-8323; *The New Book of World Rankings*.

Federal Statistical Office, Gustav - Stresemann - Ring 11, D-6200 Wiesbaden, Germany; *Myanmar*.

Food and Agricultural Organization of the United Nations (FAO), Via delle Terme di Caracalla, 00100 Rome, Italy (Telephone Number in U.S. (202) 653-2400); *The State of Food and Agriculture*.

G.K. Hall and Company, 70 Lincoln Street, Boston, Massachusetts 02111 (617) 423-3990; *The World in Figures*.

Organisation for Economic Co-operation and Development (OECD), 2 rue Andre-Pascal, 75 Paris 16, France (Telephone Number in U.S. (202) 785-6323); *Trade by Commodities*.

Statistical Office of the United Nations, Publishing Service, New York, New York 10017 (800) 253-9646; *International Trade Statistics Yearbook*, and *Statistical Yearbook*.

MYANMAR - FORESTRY AND FOREST PRODUCTS

The Economist Intelligence Unit (Asia) Limited, 10th Floor, Luk Kwok Centre, 72 Gloucester Road, Wanchai, Hong Kong (Phone Number in U.S. (800) 938-4685); *Asian Market Atlas*.

Facts on File, 460 Park Avenue South, New York, New York 10016 (800) 443-8323; *The New Book of World Rankings*.

Federal Statistical Office, Gustav - Stresemann - Ring 11, D-6200 Wiesbaden, Germany; *Myanmar*.

Food and Agricultural Organization of the United Nations (FAO), Via delle Terme di Caracalla, 00100 Rome, Italy (Telephone Number in U.S. (202) 653-2400); *The State of Food and Agriculture*, and *Yearbook of Forest Products*.

G.K. Hall and Company, 70 Lincoln Street, Boston, Massachusetts 02111 (617) 423-3990; *The World in Figures*.

Statistical Office of the United Nations, Publishing Service, New York, New York 10017 (800) 253-9646; *Statistical Yearbook*.

United Nations Educational, Scientific and Cultural Organization (UNESCO), 7 Place de Fontenoy, F-75700 Paris, France (Telephone Number in U.S. (212) 963-5981); *Statistical Yearbook*.

MYANMAR - GARLIC PRODUCTION - See MYANMAR - CROPS

MYANMAR - GAS PRODUCTION - See MYANMAR - MINING AND MINERAL PRODUCTS

MYANMAR - GENERAL INDUSTRIAL STATISTICS

Federal Statistical Office, Gustav - Stresemann - Ring 11, D-6200 Wiesbaden, Germany; *Myanmar*.

MYANMAR - GENERAL MORTALITY

Statistical Office of the United Nations, Publishing Service, New York, New York 10017 (800) 253-9646; *Demographic Yearbook*.

MYANMAR - GEOGRAPHIC DATA

Facts on File, 460 Park Avenue South, New York, New York 10016 (800) 443-8323; *The New Book of World Rankings*.

Federal Statistical Office, Gustav - Stresemann - Ring 11, D-6200 Wiesbaden, Germany; *Myanmar*.

MYANMAR - GOATS - See MYANMAR - LIVESTOCK AND POULTRY

MYANMAR - GOLD HOLDINGS

International Monetary Fund, Nineteenth and H Street, NW, Washington, D.C. 20431 (202) 623-7000; *International Financial Statistics*.

Statistical Office of the United Nations, Publishing Service, New York, New York 10017 (800) 253-9646; *Statistical Yearbook*.

MYANMAR - GOLD PRODUCTION AND CONSUMPTION - See MYANMAR - MINING AND MINERAL PRODUCTS

MYANMAR - GOVERNMENT

Asian Development Bank, Post Office Box 789, Manila, 1099 Manila, Philippines; *Key Indicators of Developing Asian and Pacific Countries*.

G.K. Hall and Company, 70 Lincoln Street, Boston, Massachusetts 02111 (617) 423-3990; *The World in Figures*.

MYANMAR - GOVERNMENT EXPENDITURE

Asian Development Bank, Post Office Box 789, Manila, 1099 Manila, Philippines; *Key Indicators of Developing Asian and Pacific Countries*.

MYANMAR - GOVERNMENT FINANCES

Asian Development Bank, Post Office Box 789, Manila, 1099 Manila, Philippines; *Key Indicators of Developing Asian and Pacific Countries*.

International Monetary Fund, Nineteenth and H Street, NW, Washington, D.C. 20431 (202) 623-7000; *International Financial Statistics*.

Statistical Office of the United Nations, Publishing Service, New York, New York 10017 (800) 253-9646; *Statistical Yearbook*.

MYANMAR - GOVERNMENT REVENUE

Asian Development Bank, Post Office Box 789, Manila, 1099 Manila, Philippines; *Key Indicators of Developing Asian and Pacific Countries*.

MYANMAR - GRAIN PRODUCTION

Food and Agricultural Organization of the United Nations (FAO), Via delle Terme di Caracalla, 00100 Rome, Italy (Telephone Number in U.S. (202) 653-2400); *The State of Food and Agriculture*.

MYANMAR - GROSS DOMESTIC PRODUCT

Asian Development Bank, Post Office Box 789, Manila, 1099 Manila, Philippines; *Key Indicators of Developing Asian and Pacific Countries*.

The Economist Intelligence Unit, 111 West 57th Street, New York, New York 10019 (800) 938-4685; *The World Market Atlas*.

The Economist Intelligence Unit (Asia) Limited, 10th Floor, Luk Kwok Centre, 72 Gloucester Road, Wanchai, Hong Kong (Phone Number in U.S. (800) 938-4685); *Asian Market Atlas*.

Euromonitor Publications Limited, 87-88 Turnmill Street, London EC1M 5QU, England; *International Marketing Data and Statistics*.

Facts on File, 460 Park Avenue South, New York, New York 10016 (800) 443-8323; *The New Book of World Rankings*.

G.K. Hall and Company, 70 Lincoln Street, Boston, Massachusetts 02111 (617) 423-3990; *The World in Figures*.

Statistical Office of the United Nations, Publishing Service, New York, New York 10017 (800) 253-9646; *Statistical Yearbook*.

Times Books, 201 East 50th Street, New York, New York 10022 (212) 751-2600; *The Economist Book of Vital World Statistics*.

MYANMAR - GROSS NATIONAL PRODUCT

Asian Development Bank, Post Office Box 789, Manila, 1099 Manila, Philippines; *Key Indicators of Developing Asian and Pacific Countries*.

Euromonitor Publications Limited, 87-88 Turnmill Street, London EC1M 5QU, England; *International Marketing Data and Statistics*.

U.S. Arms Control and Disarmament Agency, 320 Twenty-first Street, NW, Washington, D.C. 20451 (202) 647-8677; *World Military Expenditures and Arms Transfers*.

MYANMAR - GROUNDNUTS PRODUCTION - See MYANMAR - CROPS

MYANMAR - HEALTH

The Economist Intelligence Unit (Asia) Limited, 10th Floor, Luk Kwok Centre, 72 Gloucester Road, Wanchai, Hong Kong (Phone Number in U.S. (800) 938-4685); *Asian Market Atlas*.

Facts on File, 460 Park Avenue South, New York, New York 10016 (800) 443-8323; *The New Book of World Rankings*.

Federal Statistical Office, Gustav - Stresemann - Ring 11, D-6200 Wiesbaden, Germany; *Myanmar*.

G.K. Hall and Company, 70 Lincoln Street, Boston, Massachusetts 02111 (617) 423-3990; *The World in Figures*.

Statistical Office of the United Nations, Publishing Service, New York, New York 10017 (800) 253-9646; *Statistical Yearbook*.

Times Books, 201 East 50th Street, New York, New York 10022 (212) 751-2600; *The Economist Book of Vital World Statistics*.

World Health Organization, Office of Publications, Avenue Appia, CH-1211 Geneva 27, Switzerland (Telephone Number in U.S. (518) 436-9686); *World Health Statistics Annual*.

MYANMAR - HEALTH AND MEDICAL SERVICES

Federal Statistical Office, Gustav - Stresemann - Ring 11, D-6200 Wiesbaden, Germany; *Myanmar*.

Statistical Office of the United Nations, Publishing Service, New York, New York 10017 (800) 253-9646; *Statistical Yearbook*.

MYANMAR - HIDE PRODUCTION

Food and Agricultural Organization of the United Nations (FAO), Via delle Terme di Caracalla, 00100 Rome, Italy (Telephone Number in U.S. (202) 653-2400); *Production Yearbook*.

MYANMAR - HIGHWAYS

The Economist Intelligence Unit (Asia) Limited, 10th Floor, Luk Kwok Centre, 72 Gloucester Road, Wanchai, Hong Kong (Phone Number in U.S. (800) 938-4685); *Asian Market Atlas*.

G.K. Hall and Company, 70 Lincoln Street, Boston, Massachusetts 02111 (617) 423-3990; *The World in Figures*.

International Road Federation, 525 School Street, SW, Washington, D.C. 20024 (202) 554-2106; *World Road Statistics*.

MYANMAR - HORSES - See MYANMAR - LIVESTOCK AND POULTRY

MYANMAR - HOURS OF WORK - See MYANMAR - EMPLOYMENT

MYANMAR - HOUSING

Facts on File, 460 Park Avenue South, New York, New York 10016 (800) 443-8323; *The New Book of World Rankings*.

MYANMAR - ILLITERATE POPULATION

The Economist Intelligence Unit, 111 West 57th Street, New York, New York 10019 (800) 938-4685; *The World Market Atlas*.

G.K. Hall and Company, 70 Lincoln Street, Boston, Massachusetts 02111 (617) 423-3990; *The World in Figures*.

United Nations Educational, Scientific and Cultural Organization (UNESCO), 7 Place de Fontenoy, F-75700 Paris, France (Telephone Number in U.S. (212) 963-5981); *Statistical Yearbook*.

MYANMAR - IMPORTS

Asian Development Bank, Post Office Box 789, Manila, 1099 Manila, Philippines; *Key Indicators of Developing Asian and Pacific Countries*.

The Economist Intelligence Unit, 111 West 57th Street, New York, New York 10019 (800) 938-4685; *The World Market Atlas*.

The Economist Intelligence Unit (Asia) Limited, 10th Floor, Luk Kwok Centre, 72 Gloucester Road, Wanchai, Hong Kong (Phone Number in U.S. (800) 938-4685); *Asian Market Atlas*.

Euromonitor Publications Limited, 87-88 Turnmill Street, London EC1M 5QU, England; *International Marketing Data and Statistics*.

Food and Agricultural Organization of the United Nations (FAO), Via delle Terme di Caracalla, 00100 Rome, Italy (Telephone Number in U.S. (202) 653-2400); *The State of Food and Agriculture*.

G.K. Hall and Company, 70 Lincoln Street, Boston, Massachusetts 02111 (617) 423-3990; *The World in Figures*.

International Monetary Fund, 700 Nineteenth Street, NW, Washington, D.C. 20431 (202) 623-7000; *Direction of Trade Statistics*, and *International Financial Statistics*.

International Rubber Study Group, York House, Eighth Floor, Empire Way, Wembley, London HA9 0PA, England; *Rubber Statistical Bulletin*.

MYANMAR - IMPORTS FROM OTHER DEVELOPING COUNTRIES

Asian Development Bank, Post Office Box 789, Manila, 1099 Manila, Philippines; *Key Indicators of Developing Asian and Pacific Countries*.

MYANMAR - INDUSTRIAL METALS PRODUCTION - See MYANMAR - MINING AND MINERAL PRODUCTS

MYANMAR - INDUSTRY

Euromonitor Publications Limited, 87-88 Turnmill Street, London EC1M 5QU, England; *International Marketing Data and Statistics*.

Facts on File, 460 Park Avenue South, New York, New York 10016 (800) 443-8323; *The New Book of World Rankings*.

Federal Statistical Office, Gustav - Stresemann - Ring 11, D-6200 Wiesbaden, Germany; *Myanmar*.

G.K. Hall and Company, 70 Lincoln Street, Boston, Massachusetts 02111 (617) 423-3990; *The World in Figures*.

International Labour Office, I.L.O. Publications, CH-1211, Geneva 22, Switzerland; *Yearbook of Labour Statistics*.

Statistical Office of the United Nations, Publishing Service, New York, New York 10017 (800) 253-9646; *Statistical Yearbook for Asia and the Pacific*.

Times Books, 201 East 50th Street, New York, New York 10022 (212) 751-2600; *The Economist Book of Vital World Statistics*.

MYANMAR - INFANT AND MATERNAL MORTALITY

The Economist Intelligence Unit (Asia) Limited, 10th Floor, Luk Kwok Centre, 72 Gloucester Road, Wanchai, Hong Kong (Phone Number in U.S. (800) 938-4685); *Asian Market Atlas*.

Statistical Office of the United Nations, Publishing Service, New York, New York 10017 (800) 253-9646; *Demographic Yearbook*, and *Statistical Yearbook*.

Times Books, 201 East 50th Street, New York, New York 10022 (212) 751-2600; *The Economist Book of Vital World Statistics*.

MYANMAR - INTERNAL TRADE

Statistical Office of the United Nations, Publishing Service, New York, New York 10017 (800) 253-9646; *Statistical Yearbook for Asia and the Pacific*.

MYANMAR - INTERNATIONAL LIQUIDITY

International Monetary Fund, Nineteenth and H Street, NW, Washington, D.C. 20431 (202) 623-7000; *International Financial Statistics*.

MYANMAR - INTERNATIONAL RESERVES EXCLUDING GOLD

Asian Development Bank, Post Office Box 789, Manila, 1099 Manila, Philippines; *Key Indicators of Developing Asian and Pacific Countries*.

Statistical Office of the United Nations, Publishing Service, New York, New York 10017 (800) 253-9646; *Statistical Yearbook*.

MYANMAR - INTERNATIONAL STATISTICS

Asian Development Bank, Post Office Box 789, Manila, 1099 Manila, Philippines; *Key Indicators of Developing Asian and Pacific Countries*.

MYANMAR - INVESTMENTS

International Monetary Fund, Nineteenth and H Street, NW, Washington, D.C. 20431 (202) 623-7000; *International Financial Statistics*.

MYANMAR - IRON ORE PRODUCTION AND CONSUMPTION - See MYANMAR - MINING AND MINERAL PRODUCTS

MYANMAR - IRRIGATION

Euromonitor Publications Limited, 87-88 Turnmill Street, London EC1M 5QU, England; *International Marketing Data and Statistics*.

MYANMAR - JUTE PRODUCTION - See MYANMAR - CROPS

MYANMAR - LABOR FORCE

The Economist Intelligence Unit (Asia) Limited, 10th Floor, Luk Kwok Centre, 72 Gloucester Road, Wanchai, Hong Kong (Phone Number in U.S. (800) 938-4685); *Asian Market Atlas*.

Euromonitor Publications Limited, 87-88 Turnmill Street, London EC1M 5QU, England; *International Marketing Data and Statistics*.

Facts on File, 460 Park Avenue South, New York, New York 10016 (800) 443-8323; *The New Book of World Rankings*.

Food and Agricultural Organization of the United Nations (FAO), Via delle Terme di Caracalla, 00100 Rome, Italy (Telephone Number in U.S. (202) 653-2400); *The State of Food and Agriculture*.

G.K. Hall and Company, 70 Lincoln Street, Boston, Massachusetts 02111 (617) 423-3990; *The World in Figures*.

MYANMAR - LABOR PRODUCTIVITY

International Labour Office, I.L.O. Publications, CH-1211, Geneva 22, Switzerland; *Yearbook of Labour Statistics*.

MYANMAR - LAND USE

Euromonitor Publications Limited, 87-88 Turnmill Street, London EC1M 5QU, England; *International Marketing Data and Statistics*.

Food and Agricultural Organization of the United Nations (FAO), Via delle Terme di Caracalla, 00100 Rome, Italy (Telephone Number in U.S. (202) 653-2400); *Production Yearbook*.

G.K. Hall and Company, 70 Lincoln Street, Boston, Massachusetts 02111 (617) 423-3990; *The World in Figures*.

MYANMAR - LEAD AND LEAD ORE PRODUCTION AND CONSUMPTION - See MYANMAR - MINING AND MINERAL PRODUCTS

MYANMAR - LIBRARIES

Facts on File, 460 Park Avenue South, New York, New York 10016 (800) 443-8323; *The New Book of World Rankings*.

MYANMAR - LIFE EXPECTANCY

The Economist Intelligence Unit (Asia) Limited, 10th Floor, Luk Kwok Centre, 72 Gloucester Road, Wanchai, Hong Kong (Phone Number in U.S. (800) 938-4685); *Asian Market Atlas*.

MYANMAR - LIGNITE PRODUCTION - See MYANMAR - MINING AND MINERAL PRODUCTS

MYANMAR - LIVESTOCK AND POULTRY

Euromonitor Publications Limited, 87-88 Turnmill Street, London EC1M 5QU, England; *International Marketing Data and Statistics*.

Facts on File, 460 Park Avenue South, New York, New York 10016 (800) 443-8323; *The New Book of World Rankings*.

Food and Agricultural Organization of the United Nations (FAO), Via delle Terme di Caracalla, 00100 Rome, Italy (Telephone Number in U.S. (202) 653-2400); *Production Yearbook*, and *The State of Food and Agriculture*.

G.K. Hall and Company, 70 Lincoln Street, Boston, Massachusetts 02111 (617) 423-3990; *The World in Figures*.

Statistical Office of the United Nations, Publishing Service, New York, New York 10017 (800) 253-9646; *Statistical Yearbook*.

MYANMAR - LIVING LEVELS

G.K. Hall and Company, 70 Lincoln Street, Boston, Massachusetts 02111 (617) 423-3990; *The World in Figures*.

Times Books, 201 East 50th Street, New York, New York 10022 (212) 751-2600; *The Economist Book of Vital World Statistics*.

MYANMAR - MAIL - NUMBER OF PIECES SENT OR RECEIVED

Statistical Office of the United Nations, Publishing Service, New York, New York 10017 (800) 253-9646; *Statistical Yearbook*.

MYANMAR - MANPOWER

Statistical Office of the United Nations, Publishing Service, New York, New York 10017 (800) 253-9646; *Statistical Yearbook for Asia and the Pacific*.

MYANMAR - MANUFACTURING

Asian Development Bank, Post Office Box 789, Manila, 1099 Manila, Philippines; *Key Indicators of Developing Asian and Pacific Countries*.

Facts on File, 460 Park Avenue South, New York, New York 10016 (800) 443-8323; *The New Book of World Rankings*

G.K. Hall and Company, 70 Lincoln Street, Boston, Massachusetts 02111 (617) 423-3990; *The World in Figures*.

Statistical Office of the United Nations, Publishing Service, New York, New York 10017 (800) 253-9646; *Statistical Yearbook*.

MYANMAR - MARRIAGE RATES

Facts on File, 460 Park Avenue South, New York, New York 10016 (800) 443-8323; *The New Book of World Rankings*.

Statistical Office of the United Nations, Publishing Service, New York, New York 10017 (800) 253-9646; *Demographic Yearbook*.

MYANMAR - MEAT PRODUCTION - See MYANMAR - LIVESTOCK AND POULTRY

MYANMAR - MERCHANT SHIPPING

G.K. Hall and Company, 70 Lincoln Street, Boston, Massachusetts 02111 (617) 423-3990; *The World in Figures*.

Lloyd's Register of Shipping, 17 Battery Place, New York, New York 10004 (212) 425-8050; *Register of Ships*.

Statistical Office of the United Nations, Publishing Service, New York, New York 10017 (800) 253-9646; *Statistical Yearbook*.

Times Books, 201 East 50th Street, New York, New York 10022 (212) 751-2600; *The Economist Book of Vital World Statistics*.

U.S. Department of Transportation, Maritime Administration, 400 Seventh Street, SW, Washington, D.C. 20590; *A Statistical Analysis of the World's Merchant Fleets*.

MYANMAR - MILITARY

The Economist Intelligence Unit (Asia) Limited, 10th Floor, Luk Kwok Centre, 72 Gloucester Road, Wanchai, Hong Kong (Phone Number in U.S. (800) 938-4685); *Asian Market Atlas*.

G.K. Hall and Company, 70 Lincoln Street, Boston, Massachusetts 02111 (617) 423-3990; *The World in Figures*.

The International Institute for Strategic Studies, 23 Tavistock Street, London WC2E 7NQ, England; *The Military Balance*.

U.S. Arms Control and Disarmament Agency, 320 Twenty-first Street, NW, Washington, D.C. 20451 (202) 647-8677; *World Military Expenditures and Arms Transfers*.

MYANMAR - MILK PRODUCTION - See MYANMAR - DAIRY PRODUCTS

MYANMAR - MILLET PRODUCTION - See MYANMAR - CROPS

MYANMAR - MINING AND MINERAL PRODUCTS

Asian Development Bank, Post Office Box 789, Manila, 1099 Manila, Philippines; *Key Indicators of Developing Asian and Pacific Countries*.

Facts on File, 460 Park Avenue South, New York, New York 10016 (800) 443-8323; *The New Book of World Rankings*.

G.K. Hall and Company, 70 Lincoln Street, Boston, Massachusetts 02111 (617) 423-3990; *The World in Figures*.

Penn Well Publishing Company, 1421 South Sheridan Road, Post Office Box 1260, Tulsa, Oklahoma 74101 (800) 752-9764; *International Energy Statistics Sourcebook*.

Statistical Office of the United Nations, Publishing Service, New York, New York 10017 (800) 253-9646; *Statistical Yearbook*.

MYANMAR - MONEY EXCHANGE RATE

Euromonitor Publications Limited, 87-88 Turnmill Street, London EC1M 5QU, England; *International Marketing Data and Statistics*.

International Monetary Fund, Nineteenth and H Street, NW, Washington, D.C. 20431 (202) 623-7000; *International Financial Statistics*.

Statistical Office of the United Nations, Publishing Service, New York, New York 10017 (800) 253-9646; *Statistical Yearbook*.

MYANMAR - MONEY RESERVES

Euromonitor Publications Limited, 87-88 Turnmill Street, London EC1M 5QU, England; *International Marketing Data and Statistics*.

MYANMAR - MONEY SUPPLY

Asian Development Bank, Post Office Box 789, Manila, 1099 Manila, Philippines; *Key Indicators of Developing Asian and Pacific Countries*.

Euromonitor Publications Limited, 87-88 Turnmill Street, London EC1M 5QU, England; *International Marketing Data and Statistics*.

Federal Statistical Office, Gustav - Stresemann - Ring 11, D-6200 Wiesbaden, Germany; *Myanmar*.

G.K. Hall and Company, 70 Lincoln Street, Boston, Massachusetts 02111 (617) 423-3990; *The World in Figures*.

International Monetary Fund, Nineteenth and H Street, NW, Washington, D.C. 20431 (202) 623-7000; *International Financial Statistics*.

Statistical Office of the United Nations, Publishing Service, New York, New York 10017 (800) 253-9646; *Statistical Yearbook*.

MYANMAR - MOTION PICTURES

Statistical Office of the United Nations, Publishing Service, New York, New York 10017 (800) 253-9646; *Statistical Yearbook*.

United Nations Educational, Scientific and Cultural Organization (UNESCO), 7 Place de Fontenoy, F-75700 Paris, France (Telephone Number in U.S. (212) 963-5981); *Statistical Yearbook*.

MYANMAR - MOTOR VEHICLE PRODUCTION AND ASSEMBLY

Statistical Office of the United Nations, Publishing Service, New York, New York 10017 (800) 253-9646; *Statistical Yearbook*.

MYANMAR - MOTOR VEHICLES IN USE

G.K. Hall and Company, 70 Lincoln Street, Boston, Massachusetts 02111 (617) 423-3990; *The World in Figures*.

International Road Federation, 525 School Street, SW, Washington, D.C. 20024 (202) 554-2106; *World Road Statistics*.

Statistical Office of the United Nations, Publishing Service, New York, New York 10017 (800) 253-9646; *Statistical Yearbook*.

Times Books, 201 East 50th Street, New York, New York 10022 (212) 751-2600; *The Economist Book of Vital World Statistics*.

MYANMAR - MULES - See MYANMAR - LIVESTOCK AND POULTRY

MYANMAR - MUSEUMS

Facts on File, 460 Park Avenue South, New York, New York 10016 (800) 443-8323; *The New Book of World Rankings*.

United Nations Educational, Scientific and Cultural Organization (UNESCO), 7 Place de Fontenoy, F-75700 Paris, France (Telephone Number in U.S. (212) 963-5981); *Statistical Yearbook*.

MYANMAR - NATALITY - See MYANMAR - BIRTH RATES

MYANMAR - NATIONAL ACCOUNTS

Federal Statistical Office, Gustav - Stresemann - Ring 11, D-6200 Wiesbaden, Germany; *Myanmar*.

Statistical Office of the United Nations, Publishing Service, New York, New York 10017 (800) 253-9646; *National Accounts Statistics*, and *Statistical Yearbook*.

MYANMAR - NATIONAL INCOME

Facts on File, 460 Park Avenue South, New York, New York 10016 (800) 443-8323; *The New Book of World Rankings*.

G.K. Hall and Company, 70 Lincoln Street, Boston, Massachusetts 02111 (617) 423-3990; *The World in Figures*.

Statistical Office of the United Nations, Publishing Service, New York, New York 10017 (800) 253-9646; *Statistical Yearbook.*

MYANMAR - NATIONAL PRODUCT

Facts on File, 460 Park Avenue South, New York, New York 10016 (800) 443-8323; *The New Book of World Rankings.*

Statistical Office of the United Nations, Publishing Service, New York, New York 10017 (800) 253-9646; *Statistical Yearbook.*

MYANMAR - NATURAL GAS - PRODUCTION - See MYANMAR - MINING AND MINERAL PRODUCTS

MYANMAR - NATURAL RUBBER PRODUCTION

International Rubber Study Group, York House, Eighth Floor, Empire Way, Wembley, London HA9 0PA, England; *Rubber Statistical Bulletin.*

Statistical Office of the United Nations, Publishing Service, New York, New York 10017 (800) 253-9646; *Statistical Yearbook.*

MYANMAR - NEWSPAPER PRODUCTION - See MYANMAR - FORESTRY AND FOREST PRODUCTS

MYANMAR - MOTOR VEHICLE TAXES - See MYANMAR - TAXATION

MYANMAR - NEWSPRINT - See MYANMAR - FORESTRY AND FOREST PRODUCTS

MYANMAR - NICKEL ORE PRODUCTION AND CONSUMPTION - See MYANMAR - MINING AND MINERAL PRODUCTS

MYANMAR - OCCUPATIONS - See MYANMAR - LABOR FORCE

MYANMAR - OILCAKES EXPORTS

International Monetary Fund, Nineteenth and H Street, NW, Washington, D.C. 20431 (202) 623-7000; *International Financial Statistics.*

MYANMAR - PAPER - See MYANMAR - FORESTRY AND FOREST PRODUCTS

MYANMAR - PEANUT PRODUCTION - See MYANMAR - CROPS

MYANMAR - PERIODICALS

United Nations Educational, Scientific and Cultural Organization (UNESCO), 7 Place de Fontenoy, F-75700 Paris, France (Telephone Number in U.S. (212) 963-5981); *Statistical Yearbook.*

MYANMAR - PESTICIDE USE

Food and Agricultural Organization of the United Nations (FAO), Via delle Terme di Caracalla, 00100 Rome, Italy (Telephone Number in U.S. (202) 653-2400); *The State of Food and Agriculture.*

MYANMAR - PETROLEUM INDUSTRY

Asian Development Bank, Post Office Box 789, Manila, 1099 Manila, Philippines; *Key Indicators of Developing Asian and Pacific Countries.*

Facts on File, 460 Park Avenue South, New York, New York 10016 (800) 443-8323; *The New Book of World Rankings.*

Food and Agricultural Organization of the United Nations (FAO), Via delle Terme di Caracalla, 00100 Rome, Italy (Telephone Number in U.S. (202) 653-2400); *The State of Food and Agriculture.*

G.K. Hall and Company, 70 Lincoln Street, Boston, Massachusetts 02111 (617) 423-3990; *The World in Figures.*

Penn Well Publishing Company, 1421 South Sheridan Road, Post Office Box 1260, Tulsa, Oklahoma 74101 (800) 752-9764; *International Energy Statistics Sourcebook.*

Statistical Office of the United Nations, Publishing Service, New York, New York 10017 (800) 253-9646; *Statistical Yearbook.*

MYANMAR - PIGS - See MYANMAR - LIVESTOCK AND POULTRY

MYANMAR - POPULATION

Asian Development Bank, Post Office Box 789, Manila, 1099 Manila, Philippines; *Key Indicators of Developing Asian and Pacific Countries.*

The Economist Intelligence Unit, 111 West 57th Street, New York, New York 10019 (800) 938-4685; *The World Market Atlas.*

The Economist Intelligence Unit (Asia) Limited, 10th Floor, Luk Kwok Centre, 72 Gloucester Road, Wanchai, Hong Kong (Phone Number in U.S. (800) 938-4685); *Asian Market Atlas.*

Euromonitor Publications Limited, 87-88 Turnmill Street, London EC1M 5QU, England; *International Marketing Data and Statistics.*

Facts on File, 460 Park Avenue South, New York, New York 10016 (800) 443-8323; *The New Book of World Rankings.*

Federal Statistical Office, Gustav - Stresemann - Ring 11, D-6200 Wiesbaden, Germany; *Myanmar.*

Food and Agricultural Organization of the United Nations (FAO), Via delle Terme di Caracalla, 00100 Rome, Italy (Telephone Number in U.S. (202) 653-2400); *Production Yearbook.*

G.K. Hall and Company, 70 Lincoln Street, Boston, Massachusetts 02111 (617) 423-3990; *The World in Figures.*

International Labour Office, I.L.O. Publications, CH-1211, Geneva 22, Switzerland; *Yearbook of Labour Statistics.*

Statistical Office of the United Nations, Publishing Service, New York, New York 10017 (800) 253-9646; *Demographic Yearbook, Statistical Yearbook,* and *Statistical Yearbook for Asia and the Pacific.*

Times Books, 201 East 50th Street, New York, New York 10022 (212) 751-2600; *The Economist Book of Vital World Statistics.*

United Nations Educational, Scientific and Cultural Organization (UNESCO), 7 Place de Fontenoy, F-75700 Paris, France (Telephone Number in U.S. (212) 963-5981); *Statistical Yearbook.*

U.S. Arms Control and Disarmament Agency, 320 Twenty-first Street, NW, Washington, D.C. 20451 (202) 647-8677; *World Military Expenditures and Arms Transfers.*

World Health Organization, Office of Publications, Avenue Appia, CH-1211 Geneva 27, Switzerland (Telephone Number in U.S. (518) 436-9686); *World Health Statistics Annual.*

MYANMAR - POST OFFICES

Facts on File, 460 Park Avenue South, New York, New York 10016 (800) 443-8323; *The New Book of World Rankings*.

MYANMAR - POTATO PRODUCTION - See MYANMAR - CROPS

MYANMAR - POWER PRODUCTION INDUSTRY - ESTABLISHMENTS, PAYROLLS, VALUE ADDED, ETC.

Statistical Office of the United Nations, Publishing Service, New York, New York 10017 (800) 253-9646; *Electric Power in Asia and the Pacific*.

MYANMAR - PRICES

Asian Development Bank, Post Office Box 789, Manila, 1099 Manila, Philippines; *Key Indicators of Developing Asian and Pacific Countries*.

Facts on File, 460 Park Avenue South, New York, New York 10016 (800) 443-8323; *The New Book of World Rankings*.

Federal Statistical Office, Gustav - Stresemann - Ring 11, D-6200 Wiesbaden, Germany; *Myanmar*.

Food and Agricultural Organization of the United Nations (FAO), Via delle Terme di Caracalla, 00100 Rome, Italy (Telephone Number in U.S. (202) 653-2400); *Production Yearbook*, and *The State of Food and Agriculture*.

G.K. Hall and Company, 70 Lincoln Street, Boston, Massachusetts 02111 (617) 423-3990; *The World in Figures*.

International Labour Office, I.L.O. Publications, CH-1211, Geneva 22, Switzerland; *Yearbook of Labour Statistics*.

International Monetary Fund, Nineteenth and H Street, NW, Washington, D.C. 20431 (202) 623-7000; *International Financial Statistics*.

International Rubber Study Group, York House, Eighth Floor, Empire Way, Wembley, London HA9 0PA, England; *Rubber Statistical Bulletin*.

MYANMAR - PRINTING AND WRITING PAPER - See MYANMAR - FORESTRY AND FOREST PRODUCTS

MYANMAR - PRODUCTION

Facts on File, 460 Park Avenue South, New York, New York 10016 (800) 443-8323; *The New Book of World Rankings*.

G.K. Hall and Company, 70 Lincoln Street, Boston, Massachusetts 02111 (617) 423-3990; *The World in Figures*.

International Rubber Study Group, York House, Eighth Floor, Empire Way, Wembley, London HA9 0PA, England; *Rubber Statistical Bulletin*.

MYANMAR - PRODUCTIVITY

Euromonitor Publications Limited, 87-88 Turnmill Street, London EC1M 5QU, England; *International Marketing Data and Statistics*.

MYANMAR - PUBLIC FINANCE

Facts on File, 460 Park Avenue South, New York, New York 10016 (800) 443-8323; *The New Book of World Rankings*.

Federal Statistical Office, Gustav - Stresemann - Ring 11, D-6200 Wiesbaden, Germany; *Myanmar*.

MYANMAR - RADIO BROADCASTING - See MYANMAR - BROADCASTING

MYANMAR - RADIO RECEIVER PRODUCTION

Statistical Office of the United Nations, Publishing Service, New York, New York 10017 (800) 253-9646; *Statistical Yearbook*.

MYANMAR - RAILWAY USE

G.K. Hall and Company, 70 Lincoln Street, Boston, Massachusetts 02111 (617) 423-3990; *The World in Figures*.

Statistical Office of the United Nations, Publishing Service, New York, New York 10017 (800) 253-9646; *Statistical Yearbook*.

MYANMAR - RAPESEED PRODUCTION - See MYANMAR - CROPS

MYANMAR - RELIGION

Facts on File, 460 Park Avenue South, New York, New York 10016 (800) 443-8323; *The New Book of World Rankings*.

MYANMAR - RENT PRICES

International Labour Office, I.L.O. Publications, CH-1211, Geneva 22, Switzerland; *Yearbook of Labour Statistics*.

MYANMAR - RETAIL TRADE

G.K. Hall and Company, 70 Lincoln Street, Boston, Massachusetts 02111 (617) 423-3990; *The World in Figures*.

MYANMAR - RICE - See MYANMAR - CROPS

MYANMAR - ROOT AND TUBER PRODUCTION - See MYANMAR - CROPS

MYANMAR - ROUNDWOOD PRODUCTION - See MYANMAR - FORESTRY AND FOREST PRODUCTS

MYANMAR - RUBBER PRODUCTION AND CONSUMPTION

Facts on File, 460 Park Avenue South, New York, New York 10016 (800) 443-8323; *The New Book of World Rankings*.

International Rubber Study Group, York House, Eighth Floor, Empire Way, Wembley, London HA9 0PA, England; *Rubber Statistical Bulletin*.

Statistical Office of the United Nations, Publishing Service, New York, New York 10017 (800) 253-9646; *Statistical Yearbook*.

MYANMAR - SALT PRODUCTION - See MYANMAR - MINING AND MINERAL PRODUCTS

MYANMAR - SAWNWOOD PRODUCTION - See MYANMAR - FORESTRY AND FOREST PRODUCTS

MYANMAR - SCIENCE AND TECHNOLOGY - EXPENDITURE FOR RESEARCH

Statistical Office of the United Nations, Publishing Service, New York, New York 10017 (800) 253-9646; *Statistical Yearbook*.

MYANMAR - SCIENTISTS AND TECHNOLOGISTS

Statistical Office of the United Nations, Publishing Service, New York, New York 10017 (800) 253-9646; *Statistical Yearbook.*

MYANMAR - SENIOR CITIZENS

Facts on File, 460 Park Avenue South, New York, New York 10016 (800) 443-8323; *The New Book of World Rankings.*

MYANMAR - SESAME SEED PRODUCTION - See MYANMAR - CROPS

MYANMAR - SHEEP - See MYANMAR - LIVESTOCK AND POULTRY

MYANMAR - SILVER PRODUCTION AND CONSUMPTION - See MYANMAR - MINING AND MINERAL PRODUCTS

MYANMAR - SOCIAL DATA

Asian Development Bank, Post Office Box 789, Manila, 1099 Manila, Philippines; *Key Indicators of Developing Asian and Pacific Countries.*

Facts on File, 460 Park Avenue South, New York, New York 10016 (800) 443-8323; *The New Book of World Rankings.*

G.K. Hall and Company, 70 Lincoln Street, Boston, Massachusetts 02111 (617) 423-3990; *The World in Figures.*

MYANMAR - SOYBEAN PRODUCTION - See MYANMAR - CROPS

MYANMAR - STATE BUDGET

Euromonitor Publications Limited, 87-88 Turnmill Street, London EC1M 5QU, England; *International Marketing Data and Statistics.*

MYANMAR - STEEL - See MYANMAR - MINING AND MINERAL PRODUCTS

MYANMAR - STOCKS - COMMODITY - MARKET PRICE - INDEX

Food and Agricultural Organization of the United Nations (FAO), Via delle Terme di Caracalla, 00100 Rome, Italy (Telephone Number in U.S. (202) 653-2400); *The State of Food and Agriculture.*

MYANMAR - SUGAR PRODUCTION AND CONSUMPTION - See MYANMAR - CROPS

MYANMAR - TAXATION

G.K. Hall and Company, 70 Lincoln Street, Boston, Massachusetts 02111 (617) 423-3990; *The World in Figures.*

International Road Federation, 525 School Street, SW, Washington, D.C. 20024 (202) 554-2106; *World Road Statistics.*

MYANMAR - TEAK EXPORTS

International Monetary Fund, Nineteenth and H Street, NW, Washington, D.C. 20431 (202) 623-7000; *International Financial Statistics.*

MYANMAR - TELEGRAPH SERVICE

Statistical Office of the United Nations, Publishing Service, New York, New York 10017 (800) 253-9646; *Statistical Yearbook.*

MYANMAR - TELEPHONES IN USE

American Telephone and Telegraph Company, 26 Parsippany Road, Whippany, New Jersey 07981 (800) 338-4038; *The World's Telephones.*

The Economist Intelligence Unit (Asia) Limited, 10th Floor, Luk Kwok Centre, 72 Gloucester Road, Wanchai, Hong Kong (Phone Number in U.S. (800) 938-4685); *Asian Market Atlas.*

G.K. Hall and Company, 70 Lincoln Street, Boston, Massachusetts 02111 (617) 423-3990; *The World in Figures.*

Statistical Office of the United Nations, Publishing Service, New York, New York 10017 (800) 253-9646; *Statistical Yearbook.*

MYANMAR - TELEVISION BROADCASTING - See MYANMAR - BROADCASTING

MYANMAR - TEXTILE INDUSTRY

G.K. Hall and Company, 70 Lincoln Street, Boston, Massachusetts 02111 (617) 423-3990; *The World in Figures.*

Statistical Office of the United Nations, Publishing Service, New York, New York 10017 (800) 253-9646; *Statistical Yearbook.*

MYANMAR - TIN PRODUCTION - See MYANMAR - MINING AND MINERAL PRODUCTS

MYANMAR - TIRE (MOTOR VEHICLE) PRODUCTION

International Rubber Study Group, York House, Eighth Floor, Empire Way, Wembley, London HA9 0PA, England; *Rubber Statistical Bulletin.*

MYANMAR - TOBACCO PRODUCTION

Facts on File, 460 Park Avenue South, New York, New York 10016 (800) 443-8323; *The New Book of World Rankings.*

Statistical Office of the United Nations, Publishing Service, New York, New York 10017 (800) 253-9646; *Statistical Yearbook.*

MYANMAR - TOURISM

Facts on File, 460 Park Avenue South, New York, New York 10016 (800) 443-8323; *The New Book of World Rankings.*

Federal Statistical Office, Gustav - Stresemann - Ring 11, D-6200 Wiesbaden, Germany; *Myanmar.*

G.K. Hall and Company, 70 Lincoln Street, Boston, Massachusetts 02111 (617) 423-3990; *The World in Figures.*

Times Books, 201 East 50th Street, New York, New York 10022 (212) 751-2600; *The Economist Book of Vital World Statistics.*

MYANMAR - TRACTORS IN USE

Statistical Office of the United Nations, Publishing Service, New York, New York 10017 (800) 253-9646; *Statistical Yearbook.*

MYANMAR - TRADE - See MYANMAR - FOREIGN TRADE

MYANMAR - TRANSPORTATION AND COMMUNICATIONS

The Economist Intelligence Unit (Asia) Limited, 10th Floor, Luk Kwok Centre, 72 Gloucester Road, Wanchai, Hong Kong (Phone

Number in U.S. (800) 938-4685); *Asian Market Atlas*.

Facts on File, 460 Park Avenue South, New York, New York 10016 (800) 443-8323; *The New Book of World Rankings*.

Federal Statistical Office, Gustav - Stresemann - Ring 11, D-6200 Wiesbaden, Germany; *Myanmar*.

G.K. Hall and Company, 70 Lincoln Street, Boston, Massachusetts 02111 (617) 423-3990; *The World in Figures*.

Statistical Office of the United Nations, Publishing Service, New York, New York 10017 (800) 253-9646; *Statistical Yearbook for Asia and the Pacific*.

MYANMAR - TUNGSTEN PRODUCTION AND CONSUMPTION

Statistical Office of the United Nations, Publishing Service, New York, New York 10017 (800) 253-9646; *Statistical Yearbook*.

MYANMAR - TURKEYS - See MYANMAR - LIVESTOCK AND POULTRY

MYANMAR - UNEMPLOYMENT

Euromonitor Publications Limited, 87-88 Turnmill Street, London EC1M 5QU, England; *International Marketing Data and Statistics*.

International Labour Office, I.L.O. Publications, CH-1211, Geneva 22, Switzerland; *Yearbook of Labour Statistics*.

Statistical Office of the United Nations, Publishing Service, New York, New York 10017 (800) 253-9646; *Statistical Yearbook*.

MYANMAR - UTILITIES

Statistical Office of the United Nations, Publishing Service, New York, New York 10017 (800) 253-9646; *Electric Power in Asia and the Pacific*.

MYANMAR - VITAL STATISTICS

Euromonitor Publications Limited, 87-88 Turnmill Street, London EC1M 5QU, England; *International Marketing Data and Statistics*.

G.K. Hall and Company, 70 Lincoln Street, Boston, Massachusetts 02111 (617) 423-3990; *The World in Figures*.

Statistical Office of the United Nations, Publishing Service, New York, New York 10017 (800) 253-9646; *Statistical Yearbook*.

World Health Organization, Office of Publications, Avenue Appia, CH-1211 Geneva 27, Switzerland (Telephone Number in U.S. (518) 436-9686); *World Health Statistics Annual*.

MYANMAR - WAGES

Federal Statistical Office, Gustav - Stresemann - Ring 11, D-6200 Wiesbaden, Germany; *Myanmar*.

G.K. Hall and Company, 70 Lincoln Street, Boston, Massachusetts 02111 (617) 423-3990; *The World in Figures*.

International Labour Office, I.L.O. Publications, CH-1211, Geneva 22, Switzerland; *Yearbook of Labour Statistics*.

Statistical Office of the United Nations, Publishing Service, New York, New York 10017 (800) 253-9646; *Statistical Yearbook for Asia and the Pacific*.

MYANMAR - WEATHER

Facts on File, 460 Park Avenue South, New York, New York 10016 (800) 443-8323; *The New Book of World Rankings*.

G.K. Hall and Company, 70 Lincoln Street, Boston, Massachusetts 02111 (617) 423-3990; *The World in Figures*.

MYANMAR - WHEAT PRODUCTION - See MYANMAR - CROPS

MYANMAR - WHOLESALE PRICES - INDEX NUMBERS

Asian Development Bank, Post Office Box 789, Manila, 1099 Manila, Philippines; *Key Indicators of Developing Asian and Pacific Countries*.

MYANMAR - WINE PRODUCTION

Facts on File, 460 Park Avenue South, New York, New York 10016 (800) 443-8323; *The New Book of World Rankings*.

MYANMAR - WOOL PRODUCTION

Facts on File, 460 Park Avenue South, New York, New York 10016 (800) 443-8323; *The New Book of World Rankings*.

MYANMAR - YARN PRODUCTION

Statistical Office of the United Nations, Publishing Service, New York, New York 10017 (800) 253-9646; *Statistical Yearbook*.

MYANMAR - ZINC ORE PRODUCTION AND CONSUMPTION - See MYANMAR - MINING AND MINERAL PRODUCTS

N

Namibia - National Statistical Office

Central Statistical Office, National Planning Commission, Sixth Floor, Government Offices, Private Bag 13356, Windhoek, Namibia.

NAMIBIA - AGRICULTURE

Food and Agricultural Organization of the United Nations (FAO) Via delle Terme di Caracalla, 00100 Rome, Italy (Telephone Number in U.S. (202) 653-2400); *The State of Food and Agriculture*, and *Trade Yearbook*.

Statistical Office of the United Nations, Publishing Service, New York, New York 10017 (800) 253-9646; *Statistical Yearbook*.

Times Books, 201 East 50th Street, New York, New York 10022 (212) 751-2600, *The Economist Book of Vital World Statistics*.

United Nations Economic Commission for Africa, Africa Hall, Post Office Box 3001, Addis Ababa, Ethiopia (Telephone Number in U.S. (800) 253-9646); *African Statistical Yearbook*.

NAMIBIA - ANIMAL HEALTH

Food and Agricultural Organization of the United Nations (FAO), Via delle Terme di Caracalla, 00100 Rome, Italy (Telephone Number in U.S. (202) 653-2400); *Animal Health Yearbook*.

NAMIBIA - AREA AND DENSITY OF POPULATION

Food and Agricultural Organization of the United Nations (FAO) Via delle Terme di Caracalla, 00100 Rome, Italy (Telephone Number in U.S. (202) 653-2400); *The State of Food and Agriculture*.

Statistical Office of the United Nations, Publishing Service, New York, New York 10017 (800) 253-9646; *Statistical Yearbook*.

Times Books, 201 East 50th Street, New York, New York 10022 (212) 751-2600; *The Economist Book of Vital World Statistics*.

United Nations Educational, Scientific and Cultural Organization (UNESCO), 7 Place de Fontenoy, F-75700 Paris, France (Telephone Number in U.S. (212) 963-5981); *Statistical Yearbook*.

NAMIBIA - BALANCE OF PAYMENTS

The Economist Intelligence Unit, 111 West 57th Street, New York, New York 10019 (800) 938-4685; *The World Market Atlas*.

NAMIBIA - BEER PRODUCTION

Statistical Office of the United Nations, Publishing Service, New York, New York 10017 (800) 253-9646; *Statistical Yearbook*.

NAMIBIA - BIRTH RATES

Statistical Office of the United Nations, Publishing Service, New York, New York 10017 (800) 253-9646; *Demographic Yearbook*, and *Statistical Yearbook*.

Times Books, 201 East 50th Street, New York, New York 10022 (212) 751-2600; *The Economist Book of Vital World Statistics*.

NAMIBIA - BROADCASTING

Billboard Limited, Post Office Box 9027, 1006 AA Amsterdam, The Netherlands (Telephone Number in U.S. (212) 764-7300); *World Radio TV Handbook*.

Times Books, 201 East 50th Street, New York, New York 10022 (212) 751-2600; *The Economist Book of Vital World Statistics*.

NAMIBIA - BUTTER PRODUCTION - See NAMIBIA - DAIRY PRODUCTS

NAMIBIA - CALORIE SUPPLY

Food and Agricultural Organization of the United Nations (FAO) Via delle Terme di Caracalla, 00100 Rome, Italy (Telephone Number in U.S. (202) 653-2400); *The State of Food and Agriculture*.

NAMIBIA - CATTLE - See NAMIBIA - LIVESTOCK AND POULTRY

NAMIBIA - CONSTRUCTION INDUSTRY

United Nations Economic Commission for Africa, Africa Hall, Post Office Box 3001, Addis Ababa, Ethiopia (Telephone Number in U.S. (800) 253-9646); *African Statistical Yearbook*.

NAMIBIA - COPPER AND COPPER ORE PRODUCTION AND CONSUMPTION - See NAMIBIA - MINING AND MINERAL PRODUCTS

NAMIBIA - CORN PRODUCTION - See NAMIBIA - CROPS

NAMIBIA - CROPS

Food and Agricultural Organization of the United Nations (FAO) Via delle Terme di Caracalla, 00100 Rome, Italy (Telephone Number in U.S. (202) 653-2400); *The State of Food and Agriculture*, and *Production Yearbook*.

Statistical Office of the United Nations, Publishing Service, New York, New York 10017 (800) 253-9646; *Statistical Yearbook.*

United Nations Economic Commission for Africa, Africa Hall, Post Office Box 3001, Addis Ababa, Ethiopia (Telephone Number in U.S. (800) 253-9646); *African Statistical Yearbook.*

NAMIBIA - DAIRY PRODUCTS

Food and Agricultural Organization of the United Nations (FAO) Via delle Terme di Caracalla, 00100 Rome, Italy (Telephone Number in U.S. (202) 653-2400); *The State of Food and Agriculture.*

Statistical Office of the United Nations, Publishing Service, New York, New York 10017 (800) 253-9646; *Statistical Yearbook.*

NAMIBIA - DEATH RATES

Statistical Office of the United Nations, Publishing Service, New York, New York 10017 (800) 253-9646; *Statistical Yearbook.*

Times Books, 201 East 50th Street, New York, New York 10022 (212) 751-2600; *The Economist Book of Vital World Statistics.*

NAMIBIA - DEMOGRAPHY

The Economist Intelligence Unit, 111 West 57th Street, New York, New York 10019 (800) 938-4685; *The World Market Atlas.*

NAMIBIA - DIAMOND PRODUCTION - See NAMIBIA - MINING AND MINERAL PRODUCTS

NAMIBIA - DIVORCE

Statistical Office of the United Nations, Publishing Service, New York, New York 10017 (800) 253-9646; *Demographic Yearbook.*

NAMIBIA - EDUCATION

The Economist Intelligence Unit, 111 West 57th Street, New York, New York 10019 (800) 938-4685; *The World Market Atlas.*

Times Books, 201 East 50th Street, New York, New York 10022 (212) 751-2600; *The Economist Book of Vital World Statistics.*

United Nations Economic Commission for Africa, Africa Hall, Post Office Box 3001, Addis Ababa, Ethiopia (Telephone Number in U.S. (800) 253-9646); *African Statistical Yearbook.*

United Nations Educational, Scientific and Cultural Organization (UNESCO), 7 Place de Fontenoy, F-75700 Paris, France (Telephone Number in U.S. (212) 963-5981); *Statistical Yearbook.*

NAMIBIA - EGG PRODUCTION AND CONSUMPTION - See NAMIBIA - DAIRY PRODUCTS

NAMIBIA - ELECTRICITY

United Nations Economic Commission for Africa, Africa Hall, Post Office Box 3001, Addis Ababa, Ethiopia (Telephone Number in U.S. (800) 253-9646); *African Statistical Yearbook.*

NAMIBIA - EMPLOYMENT

United Nations Economic Commission for Africa, Africa Hall, Post Office Box 3001, Addis Ababa, Ethiopia (Telephone Number in U.S. (800) 253-9646); *African Statistical Yearbook.*

NAMIBIA - ENERGY

Food and Agricultural Organization of the United Nations (FAO) Via delle Terme di Caracalla, 00100 Rome, Italy (Telephone Number in U.S. (202) 653-2400); *The State of Food and Agriculture.*

Statistical Office of the United Nations, Publishing Service, New York, New York 10017 (800) 253-9646; *World Energy Supplies.*

United Nations Economic Commission for Africa, Africa Hall, Post Office Box 3001, Addis Ababa, Ethiopia (Telephone Number in U.S. (800) 253-9646); *African Statistical Yearbook.*

NAMIBIA - EXPORTS

The Economist Intelligence Unit, 111 West 57th Street, New York, New York 10019 (800) 938-4685; *The World Market Atlas.*

Food and Agricultural Organization of the United Nations (FAO) Via delle Terme di Caracalla, 00100 Rome, Italy (Telephone Number in U.S. (202) 653-2400); *The State of Food and Agriculture.*

International Monetary Fund, 700 Nineteenth Street, NW, Washington, D.C. 20431 (202) 623-7000; *Direction of Trade Statistics.*

Times Books, 201 East 50th Street, New York, New York 10022 (212) 751-2600; *The Economist Book of Vital World Statistics.*

NAMIBIA - EXTERNAL TRADE

Food and Agricultural Organization of the United Nations (FAO) Via delle Terme di Caracalla, 00100 Rome, Italy (Telephone Number in U.S. (202) 653-2400); *The State of Food and Agriculture*, and *Trade Yearbook.*

NAMIBIA - FARM CROPS - See NAMIBIA - CROPS

NAMIBIA - FETAL MORTALITY

Statistical Office of the United Nations, Publishing Service, New York, New York 10017 (800) 253-9646; *Demographic Yearbook.*

NAMIBIA - FERTILITY RATE

Times Books, 201 East 50th Street, New York, New York 10022 (212) 751-2600; *The Economist Book of Vital World Statistics.*

NAMIBIA - FERTILIZER

Food and Agricultural Organization of the United Nations (FAO) Via delle Terme di Caracalla, 00100 Rome, Italy (Telephone Number in U.S. (202) 653-2400); *The State of Food and Agriculture.*

NAMIBIA - FISHERIES

Food and Agricultural Organization of the United Nations (FAO) Via delle Terme di Caracalla, 00100 Rome, Italy (Telephone Number in U.S. (202) 653-2400); *The State of Food and Agriculture*, and *Yearbook of Fishery Statistics.*

Statistical Office of the United Nations, Publishing Service, New York, New York 10017 (800) 253-9646; *Statistical Yearbook.*

United Nations Economic Commission for Africa, Africa Hall, Post Office Box 3001, Addis Ababa, Ethiopia (Telephone Number in U.S. (800) 253-9646); *African Statistical Yearbook.*

NAMIBIA - FOOD

Food and Agricultural Organization of the United Nations (FAO), Via delle Terme di Caracalla, 00100 Rome, Italy (Telephone Number in U.S. (202) 653-2400); *Production Yearbook, and The State of Food and Agriculture.*

NAMIBIA - FORESTRY AND FOREST PRODUCTS

Food and Agricultural Organization of the United Nations (FAO) Via delle Terme di Caracalla, 00100 Rome, Italy (Telephone Number in U.S. (202) 653-2400); *The State of Food and Agriculture.*

Statistical Office of the United Nations, Publishing Service, New York, New York 10017 (800) 253-9646; *Statistical Yearbook.*

United Nations Economic Commission for Africa, Africa Hall, Post Office Box 3001, Addis Ababa, Ethiopia (Telephone Number in U.S. (800) 253-9646); *African Statistical Yearbook.*

United Nations Educational, Scientific and Cultural Organization (UNESCO), 7 Place de Fontenoy, F-75700 Paris, France (Telephone Number in U.S. (212) 963-5981); *Statistical Yearbook.*

NAMIBIA - GENERAL MORTALITY

Statistical Office of the United Nations, Publishing Service, New York, New York 10017 (800) 253-9646; *Demographic Yearbook.*

NAMIBIA - GRAIN PRODUCTION - See NAMIBIA - CROPS

NAMIBIA - GROSS DOMESTIC PRODUCT

The Economist Intelligence Unit, 111 West 57th Street, New York, New York 10019 (800) 938-4685; *The World Market Atlas.*

Times Books, 201 East 50th Street, New York, New York 10022 (212) 751-2600; *The Economist Book of Vital World Statistics.*

United Nations Economic Commission for Africa, Africa Hall, Post Office Box 3001, Addis Ababa, Ethiopia (Telephone Number in U.S. (800) 253-9646); *African Statistical Yearbook.*

NAMIBIA - HEALTH

Statistical Office of the United Nations, Publishing Service, New York, New York 10017 (800) 253-9646; *Statistical Yearbook.*

Times Books, 201 East 50th Street, New York, New York 10022 (212) 751-2600; *The Economist Book of Vital World Statistics.*

United Nations Economic Commission for Africa, Africa Hall, Post Office Box 3001, Addis Ababa, Ethiopia (Telephone Number in U.S. (800) 253-9646); *African Statistical Yearbook.*

NAMIBIA - HIDE PRODUCTION

Food and Agricultural Organization of the United Nations (FAO), Via delle Terme di Caracalla, 00100 Rome, Italy (Telephone Number in U.S. (202) 653-2400); *Production Yearbook.*

NAMIBIA - HORSES - See NAMIBIA - LIVESTOCK AND POULTRY

NAMIBIA - ILLITERATE POPULATION

The Economist Intelligence Unit, 111 West 57th Street, New York, New York 10019 (800) 938-4685; *The World Market Atlas.*

United Nations Educational, Scientific and Cultural Organization (UNESCO), 7 Place de Fontenoy, F-75700 Paris, France (Telephone Number in U.S. (212) 963-5981); *Statistical Yearbook.*

NAMIBIA - IMPORTS

The Economist Intelligence Unit, 111 West 57th Street, New York, New York 10019 (800) 938-4685; *The World Market Atlas.*

Food and Agricultural Organization of the United Nations (FAO) Via delle Terme di Caracalla, 00100 Rome, Italy (Telephone Number in U.S. (202) 653-2400); *The State of Food and Agriculture.*

International Monetary Fund, 700 Nineteenth Street, NW, Washington, D.C. 20431 (202) 623-7000; *Direction of Trade Statistics.*

Statistical Office of the United Nations, Publishing Service, New York, New York 10017 (800) 253-9646; *Statistical Yearbook.*

NAMIBIA - INDUSTRY

Times Books, 201 East 50th Street, New York, New York 10022 (212) 751-2600; *The Economist Book of Vital World Statistics.*

United Nations Economic Commission for Africa, Africa Hall, Post Office Box 3001, Addis Ababa, Ethiopia (Telephone Number in U.S. (800) 253-9646); *African Statistical Yearbook.*

World Intellectual Property Organization, 34 Chemin des Colombettes, CH-1211 Geneva 20, Switzerland; *Industrial Property Statistics.*

NAMIBIA - INFANT AND MATERNAL MORTALITY

Statistical Office of the United Nations, Publishing Service, New York, New York 10017 (800) 253-9646; *Demographic Yearbook.*

Times Books, 201 East 50th Street, New York, New York 10022 (212) 751-2600; *The Economist Book of Vital World Statistics.*

NAMIBIA - LABOR FORCE

Food and Agricultural Organization of the United Nations (FAO) Via delle Terme di Caracalla, 00100 Rome, Italy (Telephone Number in U.S. (202) 653-2400); *The State of Food and Agriculture.*

NAMIBIA - LAND USE

Food and Agricultural Organization of the United Nations (FAO), Via delle Terme di Caracalla, 00100 Rome, Italy (Telephone Number in U.S. (202) 653-2400); *Production Yearbook.*

NAMIBIA - LEAD AND LEAD ORE PRODUCTION AND CONSUMPTION - See NAMIBIA - MINING AND MINERAL PRODUCTS

NAMIBIA - LIVESTOCK AND POULTRY

Food and Agricultural Organization of the United Nations (FAO), Via delle Terme di Caracalla, 00100 Rome, Italy (Telephone Number in U.S. (202) 653-2400); *Production Yearbook, and The State of Food and Agriculture.*

Statistical Office of the United Nations, Publishing Service, New York, New York 10017 (800) 253-9646; *Statistical Yearbook.*

United Nations Economic Commission for Africa, Africa Hall, Post Office Box 3001, Addis Ababa, Ethiopia (Telephone Number in U.S. (800) 253-9646); *African Statistical Yearbook.*

NAMIBIA - LIVING LEVELS

Times Books, 201 East 50th Street, New York, New York 10022 (212) 751-2600; *The Economist Book of Vital World Statistics*.

NAMIBIA - MANGANESE ORE PRODUCTION AND CONSUMPTION - See NAMIBIA - MINING AND MINERAL PRODUCTS

NAMIBIA - MANUFACTURING

United Nations Economic Commission for Africa, Africa Hall, Post Office Box 3001, Addis Ababa, Ethiopia (Telephone Number in U.S. (800) 253-9646); *African Statistical Yearbook*.

NAMIBIA - MARRIAGE RATES

Statistical Office of the United Nations, Publishing Service, New York, New York 10017 (800) 253-9646; *Demographic Yearbook*.

NAMIBIA - MEAT PRODUCTION - ALL TYPES OF MEAT AND POULTRY

Food and Agricultural Organization of the United Nations (FAO), Via delle Terme di Caracalla, 00100 Rome, Italy (Telephone Number in U.S. (202) 653-2400); *Production Yearbook*, and *The State of Food and Agriculture*.

Statistical Office of the United Nations, Publishing Service, New York, New York 10017 (800) 253-9646; *Statistical Yearbook*.

NAMIBIA - MILITARY

The International Institute for Strategic Studies, 23 Tavistock Street, London WC2E 7NQ, England; *The Military Balance*.

NAMIBIA - MILK PRODUCTION - See NAMIBIA - DAIRY PRODUCTS

NAMIBIA - MILLET PRODUCTION - See NAMIBIA - CROPS

NAMIBIA - MINING AND MINERAL PRODUCTS

Commodity Research Bureau, Incorporated, 75 Wall Street, New York, New York 10005 (212) 504-7754; *Commodity Year Book*.

Statistical Office of the United Nations, Publishing Service, New York, New York 10017 (800) 253-9646; *Statistical Yearbook*.

United Nations Economic Commission for Africa, Africa Hall, Post Office Box 3001, Addis Ababa, Ethiopia (Telephone Number in U.S. (800) 253-9646); *African Statistical Yearbook*.

NAMIBIA - MULES - See NAMIBIA - LIVESTOCK AND POULTRY

NAMIBIA - NATALITY - See NAMIBIA - BIRTH RATES

NAMIBIA - NATIONAL ACCOUNTS

United Nations Economic Commission for Africa, Africa Hall, Post Office Box 3001, Addis Ababa, Ethiopia (Telephone Number in U.S. (800) 253-9646); *African Statistical Yearbook*.

NAMIBIA - NEWSPAPER PRODUCTION - See NAMIBIA - FORESTRY AND FOREST PRODUCTS

NAMIBIA - PATENTS

World Intellectual Property Organization, 34 Chemin des Colombettes, CH-1211 Geneva 20, Switzerland; *Industrial Property Statistics*.

NAMIBIA - PERIODICALS

United Nations Educational, Scientific and Cultural Organization (UNESCO), 7 Place de Fontenoy, F-75700 Paris, France (Telephone Number in U.S. (212) 963-5981); *Statistical Yearbook*.

NAMIBIA - PESTICIDE USE

Food and Agricultural Organization of the United Nations (FAO) Via delle Terme di Caracalla, 00100 Rome, Italy (Telephone Number in U.S. (202) 653-2400); *The State of Food and Agriculture*.

NAMIBIA - PETROLEUM INDUSTRY

Food and Agricultural Organization of the United Nations (FAO) Via delle Terme di Caracalla, 00100 Rome, Italy (Telephone Number in U.S. (202) 653-2400); *The State of Food and Agriculture*.

NAMIBIA - PIGS - See NAMIBIA - LIVESTOCK AND POULTRY

NAMIBIA - POPULATION

The Economist Intelligence Unit, 111 West 57th Street, New York, New York 10019 (800) 938-4685; *The World Market Atlas*.

Food and Agricultural Organization of the United Nations (FAO), Via delle Terme di Caracalla, 00100 Rome, Italy (Telephone Number in U.S. (202) 653-2400); *Production Yearbook*.

Statistical Office of the United Nations, Publishing Service, New York, New York 10017 (800) 253-9646; *Demographic Yearbook*, and *Statistical Yearbook*.

Times Books, 201 East 50th Street, New York, New York 10022 (212) 751-2600; *The Economist Book of Vital World Statistics*.

United Nations Educational, Scientific and Cultural Organization (UNESCO), 7 Place de Fontenoy, F-75700 Paris, France (Telephone Number in U.S. (212) 963-5981); *Statistical Yearbook*.

World Health Organization, Office of Publications, Avenue Appia, CH-1211 Geneva 27, Switzerland (Telephone Number in U.S. (518) 436-9686); *World Health Statistics Annual*.

NAMIBIA - PRICES

Food and Agricultural Organization of the United Nations (FAO), Via delle Terme di Caracalla, 00100 Rome, Italy (Telephone Number in U.S. (202) 653-2400); *Production Yearbook*, and *The State of Food and Agriculture*.

NAMIBIA - RADIO BROADCASTING - See NAMIBIA - BROADCASTING

NAMIBIA - ROOT AND TUBER PRODUCTION - See NAMIBIA - CROPS

NAMIBIA - SALT PRODUCTION - See NAMIBIA - MINING AND MINERAL PRODUCTS

NAMIBIA - SHEEP - See NAMIBIA - LIVESTOCK AND POULTRY

NAMIBIA - SILVER PRODUCTION AND CONSUMPTION - See NAMIBIA - MINING AND MINERAL PRODUCTS

NAMIBIA - STOCKS - COMMODITY - MARKET PRICE - INDEX

Food and Agricultural Organization of the United Nations (FAO) Via delle Terme di Caracalla, 00100 Rome, Italy (Telephone Number in

U.S. (202) 653-2400; *The State of Food and Agriculture.*

NAMIBIA - TELEPHONES IN USE

American Telephone and Telegraph Company, 26 Parsippany Road, Whippany, New Jersey 07981 (800) 338-4038; *The World's Telephones.*

Statistical Office of the United Nations, Publishing Service, New York, New York 10017 (800) 253-9646; *Statistical Yearbook.*

NAMIBIA - TELEVISION BROADCASTING - See NAMIBIA - BROADCASTING

NAMIBIA - TIN PRODUCTION - See NAMIBIA - MINING AND MINERAL PRODUCTS

NAMIBIA - TRACTORS IN USE

Statistical Office of the United Nations, Publishing Service, New York, New York 10017 (800) 253-9646; *Statistical Yearbook.*

NAMIBIA - TRADE

Food and Agricultural Organization of the United Nations (FAO) Via delle Terme di Caracalla, 00100 Rome, Italy (Telephone Number in U.S. (202) 653-2400); *The State of Food and Agriculture.*

NAMIBIA - TRADEMARKS AND SERVICE MARKS

World Intellectual Property Organization, 34 Chemin des Colombettes, CH-1211 Geneva 20, Switzerland; *Industrial Property Statistics.*

NAMIBIA - TUNGSTEN PRODUCTION AND CONSUMPTION - See NAMIBIA - MINING AND MINERAL PRODUCTS

NAMIBIA - URANIUM PRODUCTION AND CONSUMPTION - See NAMIBIA - MINING AND MINERAL PRODUCTS

NAMIBIA - VANADIUM ORE PRODUCTION AND CONSUMPTION - See NAMIBIA - MINING AND MINERAL PRODUCTS

NAMIBIA - VITAL STATISTICS

Statistical Office of the United Nations, Publishing Service, New York, New York 10017 (800) 253-9646; *Statistical Yearbook.*

World Health Organization, Office of Publications, Avenue Appia, CH-1211 Geneva 27, Switzerland (Telephone Number in U.S. (518) 436-9686); *World Health Statistics Annual.*

NAMIBIA - WHEAT PRODUCTION - See NAMIBIA - CROPS

NAMIBIA - ZINC ORE PRODUCTION AND CONSUMPTION - See NAMIBIA - MINING AND MINERAL PRODUCTS

NATIONAL AERONAUTICS AND SPACE ADMINISTRATION

U.S. National Science Foundation, 4201 Wilson Boulevard, Arlington, Virginia 22230 (703) 306-1234; *Federal Funds for Research and Development.*

NATIONAL AERONAUTICS AND SPACE ADMINISTRATION - BUDGET

U.S. National Aeronautics and Space Administration, 300 E Street, SW, Washington, D.C. 20546 (202) 358-1000; *1995 Budget Summary.*

NATIONAL AERONAUTICS AND SPACE ADMINISTRATION - EXPENDITURES - RESEARCH AND DEVELOPMENT

U.S. National Science Foundation, 4201 Wilson Boulevard, Arlington, Virginia 22230 (703) 306-1234; *National Patterns of Research and Development Resources,* and unpublished data.

NATIONAL AERONAUTICS AND SPACE ADMINISTRATION - EXPENDITURES - SPACE PROGRAM

U.S. National Aeronautics and Space Administration, 300 E Street, SW, Washington, D.C. 20546 (202) 358-1000; *Aeronautics and Space Report of the President, 1995 Budget Summary,* and *NASA News.*

NATIONAL AERONAUTICS AND SPACE ADMINISTRATION - SPACE LAUNCHES

U.S. Library of Congress, Congressional Research Service, Science Policy Research Division, 101 Independence Avenue, SE, Washington, D.C. 20540 (202) 707-5000; *Space Activities of the United States, CIS and Other Launching Countries/Organization.*

U.S. National Aeronautics and Space Administration, 300 E Street, SW, Washington, D.C. 20546 (202) 358-1000; *Payload Flight Assignments NASA Mixed Fleets,* and *Upcoming Shuttle Flights.*

NATIONAL ASSOCIATION OF SECURITIES DEALERS (NASDAQ)

National Association of Securities Dealers, 1735 K Street, NW, Washington, D.C. 20006 (202) 728-8000; *Fact Book.*

NATIONAL DEBT - See DEBT

NATIONAL DEFENSE - See also Individual Military Services

NATIONAL DEFENSE - CONTRACT AWARDS AND PAYROLLS

U.S. Department of Defense, Office of the Secretary, The Pentagon, Washington, D.C. 20301 (703) 545-6700; *Atlas/Data Abstract for the United States and Selected Areas.*

NATIONAL DEFENSE - COST OF AMERICAN WARS

U.S. Congress, Joint Economic Committee, The Capitol, Washington, D.C. 20510; *The Military Budget and National Economic Priorities,* 91st Congress, (Statement of James L. Clayton) subsequently revised and updated by James L. Clayton, University of Utah, Salt Lake City, Utah.

NATIONAL DEFENSE - EMPLOYMENT - DEFENSE-RELATED INDUSTRIES

U.S. Department of Labor, Bureau of Labor Statistics, Two Massachusetts Avenue, NE, Washington, D.C. 20212 (202) 606-7828; *Employment and Earnings.*

NATIONAL DEFENSE - EXPENDITURES - SPACE PROGRAM

U.S. National Aeronautics and Space Administration, 300 E Street, SW, Washington, D.C. 20546 (202) 358-1000; *Aeronautics and Space Report of the President.*

NATIONAL DEFENSE - EXPENDITURES - WORLD

U.S. Arms Control and Disarmament Agency, 320 Twenty-first Street, NW, Washington, D.C. 20451 (202) 647-8677; *World Military Expenditures and Arms Transfers*

NATIONAL DEFENSE - FEDERAL EMPLOYMENT AND
PAYROLLS

U.S. Department of Commerce, Bureau of the Census, Suitland,
Maryland 20233 (301) 763-4040; *Public Employment.*

NATIONAL DEFENSE - FEDERAL OUTLAYS

Executive Office of the President, Office of Management and
Budget, Executive Office Building, Washington, D.C. 20503 (202)
395-3080; *The Budget of the United States Government.*

NATIONAL DEFENSE - MILITARY FORCES

National Archives and Records Administration, Seventh Street and
Pennsylvania Avenue, NW, Washington, D.C. 20408 (202) 501-5400;
unpublished data from Combat Area Casualties Database.

U.S. Department of Defense, Office of the Secretary, The Pentagon,
Washington, D.C. 20301 (703) 545-6700; *Selected Manpower
Statistics,* and unpublished data.

U.S. Department of Transportation, United States Coast Guard, 2100
Second Street, SW, Washington, D.C. 20593 (202) 267-1587; *Annual
Report of the Secretary of Transportation.*

NATIONAL DEFENSE - MILITARY FORCES - ARMED
FORCES PERSONNEL, FOREIGN COUNTRIES

U.S. Arms Control and Disarmament Agency, 320 Twenty-first
Street, NW, Washington, D.C. 20451 (202) 647-8677; *World Military
Expenditures and Arms Transfers.*

NATIONAL DEFENSE - MILITARY FORCES - BRANCH OF
SERVICE

U.S. Department of Defense, Office of the Secretary, The Pentagon,
Washington, D.C. 20301 (703) 545-6700; *Selected Manpower
Statistics.*

NATIONAL DEFENSE - OUTLAYS

Executive Office of the President, Office of Management and
Budget, Executive Office Building, Washington, D.C. 20503 (202)
395-3080; *Budget of the United States Government.*

NATIONAL DEFENSE - READY RESERVES

U.S. Department of Defense, The Pentagon, Washington, D.C.
20301-1155 (703) 545-6700; *Official Guard and Reserve Manpower
Strengths and Statistics.*

NATIONAL DEFENSE - WORLDWIDE MILITARY
EXPENDITURES

U.S. Arms Control and Disarmament Agency, 320 Twenty-first
Street, NW, Washington, D.C. 20451 (202) 647-8677; *World Military
Expenditures and Arms Transfers.*

NATIONAL FORESTS - See FORESTS

NATIONAL GUARD

U.S. National Guard, The Pentagon, Washington, D.C. 20301 (202)
433-5100; *Annual Review of the Chief, National Guard Bureau,* and
unpublished data.

NATIONAL HEALTH EXPENDITURES

U.S. Department of Health and Human Services, Health Care
Financing Administration, 200 Independence Avenue, SW,
Washington, D.C. 20201 (202) 245-6113; *Health Care Financing
Review.*

NATIONAL INCOME - See also GROSS DOMESTIC PRODUCT

U.S. Department of Commerce, Bureau of Economic Analysis,
Fourteenth Street between Constitution Avenue and E Street, NW,
Washington, D.C. 20230 (202) 606-9900; *The National Income and
Product Accounts of the United States, Survey of Current Business,*
and unpublished data.

NATIONAL INCOME - BY SECTOR

U.S. Department of Commerce, Bureau of Economic Analysis,
Fourteenth Street between Constitution Avenue and E Street, NW,
Washington, D.C. 20230 (202) 606-9900; *The National Income and
Product Accounts of the United States,* and *Survey of Current
Business.*

NATIONAL INCOME - BY TYPE OF INCOME

U.S. Department of Commerce, Bureau of Economic Analysis,
Fourteenth Street between Constitution Avenue and E Street, NW,
Washington, D.C. 20230 (202) 606-9900; *The National Income and
Product Accounts of the United States,* and *Survey of Current
Business.*

NATIONAL INCOME - PERCENT DISTRIBUTION - PERCENT CHANGE

U.S. Department of Commerce, Bureau of Economic Analysis,
Fourteenth Street between Constitution Avenue and E Street, NW,
Washington, D.C. 20230 (202) 606-9900; *The National Income and
Product Accounts of the United States,* and *Survey of Current
Business.*

NATIONAL NONPROFIT ASSOCIATIONS - NUMBER, BY TYPE

Gale Research Incorporated, 835 Penobscot Building, Detroit,
Michigan 48226 (800) 877-4253; compiled from *Encyclopedia of
Associations.*

NATO COUNTRIES - MILITARY EXPENDITURES

U.S. Arms Control and Disarmament Agency, 320 Twenty-first
Street, NW, Washington, D.C. 20451 (202) 647-8677; *World Military
Expenditures and Arms Transfers.*

NATURAL GAS

U.S. Department of Energy, Energy Information Administration, 1000
Independence Avenue, SW, Washington, D.C. 20585 (202) 586-8800;
Annual Energy Review, and *Natural Gas Annual.*

NATURAL GAS PLANT LIQUIDS

U.S. Department of Energy, Energy Information Administration, 1000
Independence Avenue, SW, Washington, D.C. 20585 (202) 586-8800;
Energy Data Reports, Natural Gas Annual, and *Natural Gas Monthly.*

NATURAL RESOURCES - FEDERAL OUTLAYS

Executive Office of the President, Office of Management and Budget,
Executive Office Building, Washington, D.C. 20503 (202) 395-3080;
Budget of the United States Government.

NATURAL RESOURCES - GOVERNMENTAL FINANCES

U.S. Department of Commerce, Bureau of the Census, Suitland, Maryland 20233 (301) 763-4040; *Historical Statistics on Governmental Finances and Employment*, and *Government Finances*.

NATURAL RESOURCES - GOVERNMENTAL FINANCES - AID TO STATE AND LOCAL GOVERNMENTS

Executive Office of the President, Office of Management and Budget, Executive Office Building, Washington, D.C. 20503 (202) 395-3080; *Historical Tables, Budget of the United States Government*, and *Budget of the U.S. Government*.

NATURAL RESOURCES - GOVERNMENTAL FINANCES - GOVERNMENT EMPLOYMENT AND PAYROLLS

U.S. Department of Commerce, Bureau of the Census, Suitland, Maryland 20233 (301) 763-4040; *Public Employment*.

NATURAL RESOURCES - GOVERNMENTAL FINANCES - STATE AND LOCAL GOVERNMENT

U.S. Department of Commerce, Bureau of the Census, Suitland, Maryland 20233 (301) 763-4040; *Government Finances, Census of Governments*, and *Historical Statistics on Governmental Finances and Employment*.

NATURAL RESOURCES - GOVERNMENTAL FINANCES - STATE GOVERNMENTS

National Governors Association, Hall of the States, 444 North Capitol Street, NW, Washington, D.C. 20001 (202) 624-5300; *Fiscal Survey of the States*, and *NASBO State Expenditure Report*.

U.S. Department of Commerce, Bureau of the Census, Suitland, Maryland 20233 (301) 763-4040; *Census of Governments, Historical Statistics on Government Finances and Employment*, and *State Government Finances*.

NATURAL RESOURCES - GOVERNMENTAL REVENUE

U.S. Department of Commerce, Bureau of the Census, Suitland, Maryland 20233 (301) 763-4040; *Government Finances*.

NATURALIZATION

U.S. Department of Commerce, Bureau of the Census, Suitland, Maryland 20233 (301) 763-4040; *Census of Population*, and unpublished data.

NATURE STUDY (RECREATION)

U.S. Department of Agriculture, Forest Service, Fourteenth Street and Independence Avenue, SW, Washington, D.C. 20250 (202) 720-3760; unpublished data.

Nauru - National Statistical Office

Department of Island Development and Industry, Government Offices, Yaren District, Republic of Nauru, Central Pacific.

NAURU - AGRICULTURE

Facts on File, 460 Park Avenue South, New York, New York 10016 (800) 443-8323; *The New Book of World Rankings*.

Food and Agricultural Organization of the United Nations (FAO) Via delle Terme di Caracalla, 00100 Rome, Italy (Telephone Number in U.S. (202) 653-2400); *Production Yearbook, The State of Food and Agriculture*, and *Trade Yearbook*.

Statistical Office of the United Nations, Publishing Service, New York, New York 10017 (800) 253-9646; *Statistical Yearbook for Asia and the Pacific*.

NAURU - AIRLINE SERVICE

Facts on File, 460 Park Avenue South, New York, New York 10016 (800) 443-8323; *The New Book of World Rankings*.

NAURU - ALUMINUM PRODUCTION AND CONSUMPTION - See NAURU - MINING AND MINERAL PRODUCTS

NAURU - AREA AND DENSITY OF POPULATION

Facts on File, 460 Park Avenue South, New York, New York 10016 (800) 443-8323; *The New Book of World Rankings*.

Food and Agricultural Organization of the United Nations (FAO) Via delle Terme di Caracalla, 00100 Rome, Italy (Telephone Number in U.S. (202) 653-2400); *The State of Food and Agriculture*.

Statistical Office of the United Nations, Publishing Service, New York, New York 10017 (800) 253-9646; *Statistical Yearbook*.

United Nations Educational, Scientific and Cultural Organization (UNESCO), 7 Place de Fontenoy, F-75700 Paris, France (Telephone Number in U.S. (212) 963-5981); *Statistical Yearbook*.

NAURU - BANKING

Facts on File, 460 Park Avenue South, New York, New York 10016 (800) 443-8323; *The New Book of World Rankings*.

NAURU - BARLEY PRODUCTION - See NAURU - CROPS

NAURU - BEER PRODUCTION

Facts on File, 460 Park Avenue South, New York, New York 10016 (800) 443-8323; *The New Book of World Rankings*.

NAURU - BIRTH RATES

Facts on File, 460 Park Avenue South, New York, New York 10016 (800) 443-8323; *The New Book of World Rankings*.

Statistical Office of the United Nations, Publishing Service, New York, New York 10017 (800) 253-9646; *Demographic Yearbook*, and *Statistical Yearbook*.

World Health Organization, Office of Publications, Avenue Appia, CH-1211 Geneva 27, Switzerland (Telephone Number in U.S. (518) 436-9686); *World Health Statistics Annual*.

NAURU - BROADCASTING

Billboard Limited, Post Office Box 9027, 1006 AA Amsterdam, The Netherlands (Telephone Number in U.S. (212) 764-7300); *World Radio TV Handbook*.

Facts on File, 460 Park Avenue South, New York, New York 10016 (800) 443-8323; *The New Book of World Rankings*.

NAURU - CALORIE SUPPLY

Food and Agricultural Organization of the United Nations (FAO) Via delle Terme di Caracalla, 00100 Rome, Italy (Telephone Number in U.S. (202) 653-2400); *The State of Food and Agriculture.*

NAURU - CATTLE - See NAURU - LIVESTOCK AND POULTRY

NAURU - CEMENT PRODUCTION - See NAURU - MINING AND MINERAL PRODUCTS

NAURU - CIGARETTE PRODUCTION - See NAURU - TOBACCO PRODUCTION

NAURU - CLIMATE

Facts on File, 460 Park Avenue South, New York, New York 10016 (800) 443-8323; *The New Book of World Rankings.*

NAURU - CLOTHING EXPORTS AND IMPORTS

South Pacific Commission, Post Box D5, Noumea Cedex, New Caledonia; *Statistical Bulletin of the South Pacific: Retail Price Indexes.*

NAURU - COAL PRODUCTION - See NAURU - MINING AND MINERAL PRODUCTS

NAURU - COFFEE PRODUCTION AND CONSUMPTION - See NAURU CROPS

NAURU - COMMUNICATIONS

Statistical Office of the United Nations, Publishing Service, New York, New York 10017 (800) 253-9646; *Statistical Yearbook for Asia and the Pacific.*

NAURU - CONSTRUCTION

Facts on File, 460 Park Avenue South, New York, New York 10016 (800) 443-8323; *The New Book of World Rankings.*

NAURU - CONSUMPTION

South Pacific Commission, Post Box D5, Noumea Cedex, New Caledonia; *Statistical Bulletin of the South Pacific: Retail Price Indexes.*

NAURU - COPPER PRODUCTION AND CONSUMPTION - See NAURU - MINING AND MINERAL PRODUCTS

NAURU - CORN PRODUCTION - See NAURU - CROPS

NAURU - COTTON PRODUCTION - See NAURU - CROPS

NAURU - CROPS

Facts on File, 460 Park Avenue South, New York, New York 10016 (800) 443-8323; *The New Book of World Rankings.*

Food and Agricultural Organization of the United Nations (FAO) Via delle Terme di Caracalla, 00100 Rome, Italy (Telephone Number in U.S. (202) 653-2400); *The State of Food and Agriculture.*

NAURU - DAIRY PRODUCTS

Facts on File, 460 Park Avenue South, New York, New York 10016 (800) 443-8323; *The New Book of World Rankings.*

Food and Agricultural Organization of the United Nations (FAO) Via delle Terme di Caracalla, 00100 Rome, Italy (Telephone Number in U.S. (202) 653-2400); *The State of Food and Agriculture.*

NAURU - DEATH RATES

Statistical Office of the United Nations, Publishing Service, New York, New York 10017 (800) 253-9646; *Statistical Yearbook.*

NAURU - DEMOGRAPHY

Facts on File, 460 Park Avenue South, New York, New York 10016 (800) 443-8323; *The New Book of World Rankings.*

NAURU - DIAMOND PRODUCTION - See NAURU - MINING AND MINERAL PRODUCTS

NAURU - DIVORCE

Facts on File, 460 Park Avenue South, New York, New York 10016 (800) 443-8323; *The New Book of World Rankings.*

Statistical Office of the United Nations, Publishing Service, New York, New York 10017 (800) 253-9646; *Demographic Yearbook.*

NAURU - ECONOMY

Facts on File, 460 Park Avenue South, New York, New York 10016 (800) 443-8323; *The New Book of World Rankings.*

NAURU - EDUCATION

Facts on File, 460 Park Avenue South, New York, New York 10016 (800) 443-8323; *The New Book of World Rankings.*

Statistical Office of the United Nations, Publishing Service, New York, New York 10017 (800) 253-9646; *Statistical Yearbook for Asia and the Pacific.*

United Nations Educational, Scientific and Cultural Organization (UNESCO), 7 Place de Fontenoy, F-75700 Paris, France (Telephone Number in U.S. (212) 963-5981); *Statistical Yearbook.*

NAURU - EGG PRODUCTION AND CONSUMPTION - See NAURU - DAIRY PRODUCTS

NAURU - ELECTRICITY

Facts on File, 460 Park Avenue South, New York, New York 10016 (800) 443-8323; *The New Book of World Rankings.*

Statistical Office of the United Nations, Publishing Service, New York, New York 10017 (800) 253-9646; *Statistical Yearbook.*

NAURU - EMPLOYMENT

Facts on File, 460 Park Avenue South, New York, New York 10016 (800) 443-8323; *The New Book of World Rankings.*

NAURU - ENERGY

Facts on File, 460 Park Avenue South, New York, New York 10016 (800) 443-8323; *The New Book of World Rankings.*

Food and Agricultural Organization of the United Nations (FAO) Via delle Terme di Caracalla, 00100 Rome, Italy (Telephone Number in U.S. (202) 653-2400); *The State of Food and Agriculture.*

Statistical Office of the United Nations, Publishing Service, New York, New York 10017 (800) 253-9646; *Statistical Yearbook*, and *Statistical Yearbook for Asia and the Pacific*.

NAURU - EXPORTS

Food and Agricultural Organization of the United Nations (FAO) Via delle Terme di Caracalla, 00100 Rome, Italy (Telephone Number in U.S. (202) 653-2400); *The State of Food and Agriculture*.

International Monetary Fund, 700 Nineteenth Street, NW, Washington, D.C. 20431 (202) 623-7000; *Direction of Trade Statistics*.

South Pacific Commission, Post Box D5, Noumea Cedex, New Caledonia; *Statistical Bulletin of the South Pacific: Overseas Trade*.

NAURU - EXTERNAL TRADE

Food and Agricultural Organization of the United Nations (FAO) Via delle Terme di Caracalla, 00100 Rome, Italy (Telephone Number in U.S. (202) 653-2400); *The State of Food and Agriculture*, and *Trade Yearbook*.

Statistical Office of the United Nations, Publishing Service, New York, New York 10017 (800) 253-9646; *Statistical Yearbook for Asia and the Pacific*.

NAURU - FARM CROPS - See NAURU - CROPS

NAURU - FETAL MORTALITY

Statistical Office of the United Nations, Publishing Service, New York, New York 10017 (800) 253-9646; *Demographic Yearbook*.

NAURU - FERTILITY RATES

Facts on File, 460 Park Avenue South, New York, New York 10016 (800) 443-8323; *The New Book of World Rankings*.

NAURU - FERTILIZER

Food and Agricultural Organization of the United Nations (FAO) Via delle Terme di Caracalla, 00100 Rome, Italy (Telephone Number in U.S. (202) 653-2400); *The State of Food and Agriculture*.

NAURU - FINANCE

Facts on File, 460 Park Avenue South, New York, New York 10016 (800) 443-8323; *The New Book of World Rankings*.

Statistical Office of the United Nations, Publishing Service, New York, New York 10017 (800) 253-9646; *Statistical Yearbook for Asia and the Pacific*.

NAURU - FISHERIES

Facts on File, 460 Park Avenue South, New York, New York 10016 (800) 443-8323; *The New Book of World Rankings*.

Food and Agricultural Organization of the United Nations (FAO) Via delle Terme di Caracalla, 00100 Rome, Italy (Telephone Number in U.S. (202) 653-2400); *The State of Food and Agriculture*, and *Yearbook of Fishery Statistics*.

NAURU - FOOD

Food and Agricultural Organization of the United Nations (FAO), Via delle Terme di Caracalla, 00100 Rome, Italy (Telephone Number in U.S. (202) 653-2400); *Production Yearbook*, and *The State of Food and Agriculture*.

South Pacific Commission, Post Box D5, Noumea Cedex, New Caledonia; *Statistical Bulletin of the South Pacific: Retail Price Indexes*.

Statistical Office of the United Nations, Publishing Service, New York, New York 10017 (800) 253-9646; *Statistical Yearbook for Asia and the Pacific*.

NAURU - FOREIGN TRADE

Facts on File, 460 Park Avenue South, New York, New York 10016 (800) 443-8323; *The New Book of World Rankings*.

Food and Agricultural Organization of the United Nations (FAO) Via delle Terme di Caracalla, 00100 Rome, Italy (Telephone Number in U.S. (202) 653-2400); *The State of Food and Agriculture*.

South Pacific Commission, Post Box D5, Noumea Cedex, New Caledonia; *Statistical Bulletin of the South Pacific: Overseas Trade*.

NAURU - FORESTRY AND FOREST PRODUCTS

Facts on File, 460 Park Avenue South, New York, New York 10016 (800) 443-8323; *The New Book of World Rankings*.

Food and Agricultural Organization of the United Nations (FAO) Via delle Terme di Caracalla, 00100 Rome, Italy (Telephone Number in U.S. (202) 653-2400); *The State of Food and Agriculture*.

NAURU - GAS PRODUCTION - See NAURU - MINING AND MINERAL PRODUCTS

NAURU - GENERAL MORTALITY

Statistical Office of the United Nations, Publishing Service, New York, New York 10017 (800) 253-9646; *Demographic Yearbook*.

World Health Organization, Office of Publications, Avenue Appia, CH-1211 Geneva 27, Switzerland (Telephone Number in U.S. (518) 436-9686); *World Health Statistics Annual*.

NAURU - GEOGRAPHIC DATA

Facts on File, 460 Park Avenue South, New York, New York 10016 (800) 443-8323; *The New Book of World Rankings*.

NAURU - GOLD PRODUCTION AND CONSUMPTION - See NAURU - MINING AND MINERAL PRODUCTS

NAURU - GRAIN PRODUCTION - See NAURU - CROPS

NAURU - GROSS DOMESTIC PRODUCT

Facts on File, 460 Park Avenue South, New York, New York 10016 (800) 443-8323; *The New Book of World Rankings*.

NAURU - HEALTH

Facts on File, 460 Park Avenue South, New York, New York 10016 (800) 443-8323; *The New Book of World Rankings*.

South Pacific Commission, Post Box D5, Noumea Cedex, New Caledonia; *Statistical Bulletin of the South Pacific: Retail Price Indexes.*

Statistical Office of the United Nations, Publishing Service, New York, New York 10017 (800) 253-9646; *Statistical Yearbook.*

NAURU - HORSES - See NAURU - LIVESTOCK AND POULTRY

NAURU - HOUSING

Facts on File, 460 Park Avenue South, New York, New York 10016 (800) 443-8323; *The New Book of World Rankings.*

South Pacific Commission, Post Box D5, Noumea Cedex, New Caledonia; *Statistical Bulletin of the South Pacific: Retail Price Indexes.*

NAURU - HOUSING EXPENDITURES

South Pacific Commission, Post Box D5, Noumea Cedex, New Caledonia; *Statistical Bulletin of the South Pacific: Retail Price Indexes.*

NAURU - IMPORTS

Food and Agricultural Organization of the United Nations (FAO) Via delle Terme di Caracalla, 00100 Rome, Italy (Telephone Number in U.S. (202) 653-2400); *The State of Food and Agriculture.*

International Monetary Fund, 700 Nineteenth Street, NW, Washington, D.C. 20431 (202) 623-7000; *Direction of Trade Statistics.*

South Pacific Commission, Post Box D5, Noumea Cedex, New Caledonia; *Statistical Bulletin of the South Pacific: Overseas Trade.*

NAURU - INDUSTRY

Facts on File, 460 Park Avenue South, New York, New York 10016 (800) 443-8323; *The New Book of World Rankings.*

Statistical Office of the United Nations, Publishing Service, New York, New York 10017 (800) 253-9646; *Statistical Yearbook for Asia and the Pacific.*

NAURU - INFANT AND MATERNAL MORTALITY

Statistical Office of the United Nations, Publishing Service, New York, New York 10017 (800) 253-9646; *Demographic Yearbook.*

NAURU - INTERNAL TRADE

Statistical Office of the United Nations, Publishing Service, New York, New York 10017 (800) 253-9646; *Statistical Yearbook for Asia and the Pacific.*

NAURU - IRON ORE PRODUCTION AND CONSUMPTION - See NAURU - MINING AND MINERAL PRODUCTS

NAURU - LABOR FORCE

Facts on File, 460 Park Avenue South, New York, New York 10016 (800) 443-8323; *The New Book of World Rankings.*

Food and Agricultural Organization of the United Nations (FAO) Via delle Terme di Caracalla, 00100 Rome, Italy (Telephone Number in U.S. (202) 653-2400); *The State of Food and Agriculture.*

NAURU - LAND USE

Food and Agricultural Organization of the United Nations (FAO), Via delle Terme di Caracalla, 00100 Rome, Italy (Telephone Number in U.S. (202) 653-2400); *Production Yearbook.*

NAURU - LIBRARIES

Facts on File, 460 Park Avenue South, New York, New York 10016 (800) 443-8323; *The New Book of World Rankings.*

NAURU - LIVESTOCK AND POULTRY

Facts on File, 460 Park Avenue South, New York, New York 10016 (800) 443-8323; *The New Book of World Rankings.*

Food and Agricultural Organization of the United Nations (FAO), Via delle Terme di Caracalla, 00100 Rome, Italy (Telephone Number in U.S. (202) 653-2400); *Production Yearbook,* and *The State of Food and Agriculture.*

NAURU - MANPOWER

Statistical Office of the United Nations, Publishing Service, New York, New York 10017 (800) 253-9646; *Statistical Yearbook for Asia and the Pacific.*

NAURU - MANUFACTURING

Facts on File, 460 Park Avenue South, New York, New York 10016 (800) 443-8323; *The New Book of World Rankings.*

NAURU - MARRIAGE RATES

Facts on File, 460 Park Avenue South, New York, New York 10016 (800) 443-8323; *The New Book of World Rankings.*

Statistical Office of the United Nations, Publishing Service, New York, New York 10017 (800) 253-9646; *Demographic Yearbook,* and *Statistical Yearbook.*

NAURU - MEAT PRODUCTION - ALL TYPES OF MEAT AND POULTRY

Facts on File, 460 Park Avenue South, New York, New York 10016 (800) 443-8323; *The New Book of World Rankings.*

Food and Agricultural Organization of the United Nations (FAO) Via delle Terme di Caracalla, 00100 Rome, Italy (Telephone Number in U.S. (202) 653-2400); *The State of Food and Agriculture.*

NAURU - MERCHANT SHIPPING

Statistical Office of the United Nations, Publishing Service, New York, New York 10017 (800) 253-9646; *Statistical Yearbook.*

U.S. Department of Transportation, Maritime Administration, 400 Seventh Street, SW, Washington, D.C. 20590 (202) 366-5807; *A Statistical Analysis of the World's Merchant Fleets.*

NAURU - MILK PRODUCTION - See NAURU - DAIRY PRODUCTS

NAURU - MINING AND MINERAL PRODUCTS

Facts on File, 460 Park Avenue South, New York, New York 10016 (800) 443-8323; *The New Book of World Rankings.*

Statistical Office of the United Nations, Publishing Service, New York, New York 10017 (800) 253-9646; *Statistical Yearbook.*

NAURU - MOTION PICTURES

Statistical Office of the United Nations, Publishing Service, New York, New York 10017 (800) 253-9646; *Statistical Yearbook*.

NAURU - MUSEUMS

Facts on File, 460 Park Avenue South, New York, New York 10016 (800) 443-8323; *The New Book of World Rankings*.

NAURU - NATALITY - See NAURU - BIRTH RATES

NAURU - NATIONAL ACCOUNTS

Statistical Office of the United Nations, Publishing Service, New York, New York 10017 (800) 253-9646; *Statistical Yearbook for Asia and the Pacific*.

NAURU - NATIONAL INCOME

Facts on File, 460 Park Avenue South, New York, New York 10016 (800) 443-8323; *The New Book of World Rankings*.

NAURU - NATIONAL PRODUCT

Facts on File, 460 Park Avenue South, New York, New York 10016 (800) 443-8323; *The New Book of World Rankings*.

NAURU - NATURAL GAS PRODUCTION - See NAURU - MINING AND MINERAL PRODUCTS

NAURU - PEANUT PRODUCTION - See NAURU - CROPS

NAURU - PERIODICALS

United Nations Educational, Scientific and Cultural Organization (UNESCO), 7 Place de Fontenoy, F-75700 Paris, France (Telephone Number in U.S. (212) 963-5981); *Statistical Yearbook*.

NAURU - PESTICIDE USE

Food and Agricultural Organization of the United Nations (FAO) Via delle Terme di Caracalla, 00100 Rome, Italy (Telephone Number in U.S. (202) 653-2400); *The State of Food and Agriculture*.

NAURU - PETROLEUM INDUSTRY

Facts on File, 460 Park Avenue South, New York, New York 10016 (800) 443-8323; *The New Book of World Rankings*.

Food and Agricultural Organization of the United Nations (FAO) Via delle Terme di Caracalla, 00100 Rome, Italy (Telephone Number in U.S. (202) 653-2400); *The State of Food and Agriculture*.

NAURU - PHOSPHATE ROCK PRODUCTION - See NAURU - MINING AND MINERAL PRODUCTS

NAURU - PIGS - See NAURU - LIVESTOCK AND POULTRY

NAURU - POPULATION

Facts on File, 460 Park Avenue South, New York, New York 10016 (800) 443-8323; *The New Book of World Rankings*.

Food and Agricultural Organization of the United Nations (FAO), Via delle Terme di Caracalla, 00100 Rome, Italy (Telephone Number in U.S. (202) 653-2400); *Production Yearbook*.

Statistical Office of the United Nations, Publishing Service, New York, New York 10017 (800) 253-9646; *Demographic Yearbook*, *Statistical Yearbook*, and *Statistical Yearbook for Asia and the Pacific*.

United Nations Educational, Scientific and Cultural Organization (UNESCO), 7 Place de Fontenoy, F-75700 Paris, France (Telephone Number in U.S. (212) 963-5981); *Statistical Yearbook*.

World Health Organization, Office of Publications, Avenue Appia, CH-1211 Geneva 27, Switzerland (Telephone Number in U.S. (518) 436-9686); *World Health Statistics Annual*.

NAURU - POST OFFICES

Facts on File, 460 Park Avenue South, New York, New York 10016 (800) 443-8323; *The New Book of World Rankings*.

NAURU - POTATO PRODUCTION - See NAURU - CROPS

NAURU - PRICES

Facts on File, 460 Park Avenue South, New York, New York 10016 (800) 443-8323; *The New Book of World Rankings*.

Food and Agricultural Organization of the United Nations (FAO), Via delle Terme di Caracalla, 00100 Rome, Italy (Telephone Number in U.S. (202) 653-2400); *Production Yearbook*, and *The State of Food and Agriculture*.

South Pacific Commission, Post Box D5, Noumea Cedex, New Caledonia, *Statistical Bulletin of the South Pacific: Overseas Trade*, and *Statistical Bulletin of the South Pacific: Retail Price Indexes*.

NAURU - PRODUCTION

Facts on File, 460 Park Avenue South, New York, New York 10016 (800) 443-8323; *The New Book of World Rankings*.

NAURU - PUBLIC FINANCE

Facts on File, 460 Park Avenue South, New York, New York 10016 (800) 443-8323; *The New Book of World Rankings*.

NAURU - RADIO BROADCASTING - See NAURU - BROADCASTING

NAURU - RELIGION

Facts on File, 460 Park Avenue South, New York, New York 10016 (800) 443-8323; *The New Book of World Rankings*.

NAURU - RICE PRODUCTION - See NAURU - CROPS

NAURU - RUBBER PRODUCTION AND CONSUMPTION

Facts on File, 460 Park Avenue South, New York, New York 10016 (800) 443-8323; *The New Book of World Rankings*.

NAURU - SENIOR CITIZENS

Facts on File, 460 Park Avenue South, New York, New York 10016 (800) 443-8323; *The New Book of World Rankings*.

NAURU - SHEEP - See NAURU - LIVESTOCK AND POULTRY

NAURU - SILVER PRODUCTION AND CONSUMPTION - See NAURU - MINING AND MINERAL PRODUCTS

NAURU - SOCIAL PRODUCTION

Facts on File, 460 Park Avenue South, New York, New York 10016 (800) 443-8323; *The New Book of World Rankings*.

NAURU - STEEL PRODUCTION - See NAURU - MINING AND MINERAL PRODUCTS

NAURU - STOCKS - COMMODITY - MARKET PRICE - INDEX

Food and Agricultural Organization of the United Nations (FAO) Via delle Terme di Caracalla, 00100 Rome, Italy (Telephone Number in U.S. (202) 653-2400); *The State of Food and Agriculture*.

NAURU - SUGAR PRODUCTION AND CONSUMPTION - See NAURU - CROPS

NAURU - TELEPHONES IN USE

American Telephone and Telegraph Company, 26 Parsippany Road, Whippany, New Jersey 07981 (800) 338-4038; *The World's Telephones*.

NAURU - TELEVISION BROADCASTING - See NAURU - BROADCASTING

NAURU - TOBACCO PRODUCTION

Facts on File, 460 Park Avenue South, New York, New York 10016 (800) 443-8323; *The New Book of World Rankings*.

South Pacific Commission, Post Box D5, Noumea Cedex, New Caledonia; *Statistical Bulletin of the South Pacific: Retail Price Indexes*.

NAURU - TOURISM

Facts on File, 460 Park Avenue South, New York, New York 10016 (800) 443-8323; *The New Book of World Rankings*.

NAURU - TRADE - See NAURU - FOREIGN TRADE

NAURU - TRANSPORTATION AND COMMUNICATIONS

Facts on File, 460 Park Avenue South, New York, New York 10016 (800) 443-8323; *The New Book of World Rankings*.

South Pacific Commission, Post Box D5, Noumea Cedex, New Caledonia; *Statistical Bulletin of the South Pacific: Retail Price Indexes*.

Statistical Office of the United Nations, Publishing Service, New York, New York 10017 (800) 253-9646; *Statistical Yearbook for Asia and the Pacific*.

NAURU - VITAL STATISTICS

Statistical Office of the United Nations, Publishing Service, New York, New York 10017 (800) 253-9646; *Statistical Yearbook*.

World Health Organization, Office of Publications, Avenue Appia, CH-1211 Geneva 27, Switzerland (Telephone Number in U.S. (518) 436-9686); *World Health Statistics Annual*.

NAURU - WAGES AND PRICES

Statistical Office of the United Nations, Publishing Service, New York, New York 10017 (800) 253-9646; *Statistical Yearbook for Asia and the Pacific*.

NAURU - WEATHER

Facts on File, 460 Park Avenue South, New York, New York 10016 (800) 443-8323; *The New Book of World Rankings*.

NAURU - WHEAT PRODUCTION - See NAURU - CROPS

NAURU - WINE PRODUCTION

Facts on File, 460 Park Avenue South, New York, New York 10016 (800) 443-8323; *The New Book of World Rankings*.

NAURU - WOOL PRODUCTION

Facts on File, 460 Park Avenue South, New York, New York 10016 (800) 443-8323; *The New Book of World Rankings*.

NAVY

Executive Office of the President, Office of Management and Budget, Executive Office Building, Washington, D.C. 20503 (202) 395-3080; *The Budget of the United States Government*.

U.S. Department of Defense, Office of the Secretary, The Pentagon, Washington, D.C. 20301 (703) 545-6700; *Selected Manpower Statistics*.

NEBRASKA - See also STATE DATA (FOR INDIVIDUAL STATES)

Nebraska - Primary Statistics Source

Department of Economic Development, Division of Research, Box 94666, 301 Centennial Mall South, Lincoln, Nebraska 68509 (402) 471-3779; *Nebraska Statistical Handbook*.

Nebraska - State Data Centers

Center for Public Affairs Research, Peter Kiewit Conference Center, No. 232, The University of Nebraska - Omaha, Omaha, Nebraska 68182, Mr. Jerome Deichert (402) 595-2311.

Policy Research Office, Post Office Box 94601, State Capitol, Room 1319, Lincoln, Nebraska 68509-4601, Ms. Prem L. Bansal (402) 471-2414.

Federal Documents Librarian, Nebraska Library Commission, The Atrium, 1200 North Street, Suite 120, Lincoln, Nebraska 68508 (402) 471-2045.

Nebraska Department of Labor, 550 South 16th Street, Post Office Box 94600, Lincoln, Nebraska 68509-4600, Mr. Robert H. Shanahan (402) 471-2518.

The Central Data Processing Division, Department of Administration Services, 301 Centennial Mall South, Lower Level, Post Office Box 95045, Lincoln, Nebraska 68509-5045, Mr. Jerry Douglas (402) 471-4862.

Natural Resources Commission, 301 Centennial Mall South, Post Office Box 94876, Lincoln, Nebraska 68509-4876, Mr. Mahendra Bansal (402) 471-2081.

NECTARINES

U.S. Department of Agriculture, Economic Research Service, Fourteenth Street and Independence Avenue, SW, Washington, D.C. 20005-4789 (202) 219-1504; *Agricultural Outlook, Food Consumption, Prices, and Expenditures*, and unpublished data.

U.S. Department of Agriculture, National Agricultural Statistics Service, Fourteenth Street and Independence Avenue, SW, Washington, D.C. 20250 (202) 219-1504; *Noncitrus Fruits and Nuts*.

NEONATAL DEATHS - See also DEATHS AND DEATH RATES

NEONATAL DEATHS

U.S. Department of Health and Human Services, National Center for Health Statistics, 3700 East-West Highway, Hyattsville, Maryland 20782 (301) 436-8500; *Vital Statistics of the United States*, and *Monthly Vital Statistics Report*.

Nepal - National Statistical Office

Central Bureau of Statistics, National Planning Commission Secretariat, Ramshah Path, Thapathali, Kathmandu, Nepal.

Nepal - Primary Statistics Sources

Central Bureau of Statistics, National Planning Commission Secretariat, Ramshah Path, Thapathali, Kathmandu, Nepal; *Statistical Pocket Book*, and *Statistical Yearbook of Nepal*.

Consultancy Services Division, Nepal Industrial Development Corporation, Kathmandu, Nepal; *Statistical Abstract*.

Economic Planning Section, Program Office, US AID, Kathmandu, Nepal; *Economic Data Papers - Nepal*.

NEPAL - AGRICULTURE

Asian Development Bank, Post Office Box 789, 1099 Manila, Philippines; *Key Indicators of Developing Asian and Pacific Countries*.

Euromonitor Publications Limited, 87-88 Turnmill Street, London EC1M 5QU, England; *International Marketing Data and Statistics*.

Facts on File, 460 Park Avenue South, New York, New York 10016 (800) 443-8323; *The New Book of World Rankings*.

Food and Agricultural Organization of the United Nations (FAO) Via delle Terme di Caracalla, 00100 Rome, Italy (Telephone Number in U.S. (202) 653-2400); *Production Yearbook, The State of Food and Agriculture*, and *Trade Yearbook*.

Statistical Office of the United Nations, Publishing Service, New York, New York 10017 (800) 253-9646; *Statistical Yearbook*, and *Statistical Yearbook for Asia and the Pacific*.

Times Books, 201 East 50th Street, New York, New York 10022 (212) 751-2600; *The Economist Book of Vital World Statistics*.

The World Bank, 1818 H Street, NW, Washington, D.C. 20433 (202) 477-1234; *World Tables*.

NEPAL - AIRLINE SERVICE

The Economist Intelligence Unit (Asia) Limited, 10th Floor, Luk Kwok Centre, 72 Gloucester Road, Wanchai, Hong Kong (Phone Number in U.S. (800) 938-4685); *Asian Market Atlas*.

Facts on File, 460 Park Avenue South, New York, New York 10016 (800) 443-8323; *The New Book of World Rankings*.

International Civil Aviation Organization, 1000 Sherbrooke Street, West, Montreal, Quebec, Canada H3A 2R2 (514) 285-8219; *Civil Aviation Statistics of the World*.

Times Books, 201 East 50th Street, New York, New York 10022 (212) 751-2600; *The Economist Book of Vital World Statistics*.

NEPAL - ALUMINUM PRODUCTION AND CONSUMPTION - See NEPAL - MINING AND MINERAL PRODUCTS

NEPAL - ANIMAL HEALTH

Food and Agricultural Organization of the United Nations (FAO), Via delle Terme di Caracalla, 00100 Rome, Italy (Telephone Number in U.S. (202) 653-2400); *Animal Health Yearbook*.

NEPAL - AREA AND DENSITY OF POPULATION

Euromonitor Publications Limited, 87-88 Turnmill Street, London EC1M 5QU, England; *International Marketing Data and Statistics*.

Facts on File, 460 Park Avenue South, New York, New York 10016 (800) 443-8323; *The New Book of World Rankings*.

Food and Agricultural Organization of the United Nations (FAO) Via delle Terme di Caracalla, 00100 Rome, Italy (Telephone Number in U.S. (202) 653-2400); *The State of Food and Agriculture*.

Statistical Office of the United Nations, Publishing Service, New York, New York 10017 (800) 253-9646; *Statistical Yearbook*.

Times Books, 201 East 50th Street, New York, New York 10022 (212) 751-2600; *The Economist Book of Vital World Statistics*.

United Nations Educational, Scientific and Cultural Organization (UNESCO), 7 Place de Fontenoy, F-75700 Paris, France (Telephone Number in U.S. (212) 963-5981); *Statistical Yearbook*.

NEPAL - ARMS EXPORTS AND IMPORTS

U.S. Arms Control and Disarmament Agency, 320 Twenty-first Street, NW, Washington, D.C. 20451 (202) 647-8677; *World Military Expenditures and Arms Transfers*.

NEPAL - BALANCE OF PAYMENTS

The Economist Intelligence Unit, 111 West 57th Street, New York, New York 10019 (800) 938-4685; *The World Market Atlas*.

International Monetary Fund, 700 Nineteenth Street, NW, Washington, D.C. 20431 (202) 623-7000; *Balance of Payments Yearbook*.

Times Books, 201 East 50th Street, New York, New York 10022 (212) 751-2600; *The Economist Book of Vital World Statistics*.

The World Bank, 1818 H Street, NW, Washington, D.C. 20433 (202) 477-1234; *World Tables*.

NEPAL - BANKING

Asian Development Bank, Post Office Box 789, 1099 Manila, Philippines; *Key Indicators of Developing Asian and Pacific Countries*.

Facts on File, 460 Park Avenue South, New York, New York 10016 (800) 443-8323; *The New Book of World Rankings*.

International Monetary Fund, 700 Nineteenth Street, NW, Washington, D.C. 20431 (202) 623-7000; *Government Finance Statistics Yearbook*.

NEPAL - BARLEY PRODUCTION - See NEPAL - CROPS

NEPAL - BEER PRODUCTION

Facts on File, 460 Park Avenue South, New York, New York 10016 (800) 443-8323; *The New Book of World Rankings.*

Statistical Office of the United Nations, Publishing Service, New York, New York 10017 (800) 253-9646; *Statistical Yearbook.*

NEPAL - BIRTH RATES

The Economist Intelligence Unit (Asia) Limited, 10th Floor, Luk Kwok Centre, 72 Gloucester Road, Wanchai, Hong Kong (Phone Number in U.S. (800) 938-4685); *Asian Market Atlas.*

Facts on File, 460 Park Avenue South, New York, New York 10016 (800) 443-8323; *The New Book of World Rankings.*

Statistical Office of the United Nations, Publishing Service, New York, New York 10017 (800) 253-9646; *Demographic Yearbook,* and *Statistical Yearbook.*

Times Books, 201 East 50th Street, New York, New York 10022 (212) 751-2600; *The Economist Book of Vital World Statistics.*

The World Bank, 1818 H Street, NW, Washington, D.C. 20433 (202) 477-1234; *World Tables.*

NEPAL - BONDS

Asian Development Bank, Post Office Box 789, 1099 Manila, Philippines; *Key Indicators of Developing Asian and Pacific Countries.*

International Monetary Fund, 700 Nineteenth Street, NW, Washington, D.C. 20431 (202) 623-7000; *Government Finance Statistics Yearbook.*

NEPAL - BOOK PRODUCTION

United Nations Educational, Scientific and Cultural Organization (UNESCO), 7 Place de Fontenoy, F-75700 Paris, France (Telephone Number in U.S. (212) 963-5981); *Statistical Yearbook.*

NEPAL - BROADCASTING

Billboard Limited, Post Office Box 9027, 1006 AA Amsterdam, The Netherlands (Telephone Number in U.S. (212) 764-7300); *World Radio TV Handbook.*

The Economist Intelligence Unit (Asia) Limited, 10th Floor, Luk Kwok Centre, 72 Gloucester Road, Wanchai, Hong Kong (Phone Number in U.S. (800) 938-4685); *Asian Market Atlas.*

Facts on File, 460 Park Avenue South, New York, New York 10016 (800) 443-8323; *The New Book of World Rankings.*

Times Books, 201 East 50th Street, New York, New York 10022 (212) 751-2600; *The Economist Book of Vital World Statistics.*

United Nations Educational, Scientific and Cultural Organization (UNESCO), 7 Place de Fontenoy, F-75700 Paris, France (Telephone Number in U.S. (212) 963-5981); *Statistical Yearbook.*

NEPAL - BUSINESS AND PROFESSIONAL LICENSES

International Monetary Fund, 700 Nineteenth Street, NW, Washington, D.C. 20431 (202) 623-7000; *Government Finance*

Statistics Yearbook.

NEPAL - BUTTER PRODUCTION - See NEPAL - DAIRY PRODUCTS

NEPAL - CALORIE SUPPLY

Asian Development Bank, Post Office Box 789, 1099 Manila, Philippines; *Key Indicators of Developing Asian and Pacific Countries.*

Food and Agricultural Organization of the United Nations (FAO) Via delle Terme di Caracalla, 00100 Rome, Italy (Telephone Number in U.S. (202) 653-2400); *The State of Food and Agriculture.*

NEPAL - CAPITAL INVESTMENT

Asian Development Bank, Post Office Box 789, 1099 Manila, Philippines; *Key Indicators of Developing Asian and Pacific Countries.*

NEPAL - CAPITAL REVENUE

Asian Development Bank, Post Office Box 789, 1099 Manila, Philippines; *Key Indicators of Developing Asian and Pacific Countries.*

International Monetary Fund, 700 Nineteenth Street, NW, Washington, D.C. 20431 (202) 623-7000; *Government Finance Statistics Yearbook.*

NEPAL - CATTLE - See NEPAL - LIVESTOCK AND POULTRY

NEPAL - CEMENT PRODUCTION - See NEPAL - MINING AND MINERAL PRODUCTS

NEPAL - CHEESE PRODUCTION AND CONSUMPTION - See NEPAL - DAIRY PRODUCTS

NEPAL - CHICK PEA PRODUCTION - See NEPAL - CROPS

NEPAL - CHICKENS - See NEPAL - LIVESTOCK AND POULTRY

NEPAL - CIGARETTE PRODUCTION - See NEPAL - TOBACCO PRODUCTION

NEPAL - CLIMATE

Facts on File, 460 Park Avenue South, New York, New York 10016 (800) 443-8323; *The New Book of World Rankings.*

NEPAL - COAL PRODUCTION - See NEPAL - MINING AND MINERAL PRODUCTS

NEPAL - COFFEE PRODUCTION AND CONSUMPTION - See NEPAL - CROPS

NEPAL - COMMUNICATIONS

Statistical Office of the United Nations, Publishing Service, New York, New York 10017 (800) 253-9646; *Statistical Yearbook for Asia and the Pacific.*

NEPAL - CONSTRUCTION

Facts on File, 460 Park Avenue South, New York, New York 10016 (800) 443-8323; *The New Book of World Rankings.*

NEPAL - CONSUMER PRICE INDEX

Asian Development Bank, Post Office Box 789, 1099 Manila, Philippines; *Key Indicators of Developing Asian and Pacific Countries.*

NEPAL - CONSUMER PRICE INDEX NUMBERS

Statistical Office of the United Nations, Publishing Service, New York, New York 10017 (800) 253-9646; *Statistical Yearbook.*

NEPAL - CONSUMER PRICES

International Labour Office, I.L.O. Publications, CH-1211, Geneva 22, Switzerland; *Yearbook of Labour Statistics.*

Times Books, 201 East 50th Street, New York, New York 10022 (212) 751-2600; *The Economist Book of Vital World Statistics.*

NEPAL - COPPER PRODUCTION AND CONSUMPTION - See NEPAL - MINING AND MINERAL PRODUCTS

NEPAL - CORN PRODUCTION - See NEPAL - CROPS

NEPAL - CORPORATE TAXES - See NEPAL - TAXATION

NEPAL - COTTON PRODUCTION - See NEPAL - CROPS

NEPAL - CRIME

Yale University Press, Yale Station, New Haven, Connecticut 06520 (203) 432-0940; *Violence and Crime in Cross-National Perspective.*

NEPAL - CROPS

Asian Development Bank, Post Office Box 789, 1099 Manila, Philippines; *Key Indicators of Developing Asian and Pacific Countries.*

Facts on File, 460 Park Avenue South, New York, New York 10016 (800) 443-8323; *The New Book of World Rankings.*

Food and Agricultural Organization of the United Nations (FAO), Via delle Terme di Caracalla, 00100 Rome, Italy (Telephone Number in U.S. (202) 653-2400); *Production Yearbook,* and *The State of Food and Agriculture.*

Statistical Office of the United Nations, Publishing Service, New York, New York 10017 (800) 253-9646; *Statistical Yearbook.*

NEPAL - CUSTOMS DUTIES

International Monetary Fund, 700 Nineteenth Street, NW, Washington, D.C. 20431 (202) 623-7000; *Government Finance Statistics Yearbook.*

NEPAL - DAIRY PRODUCTS

Facts on File, 460 Park Avenue South, New York, New York 10016 (800) 443-8323; *The New Book of World Rankings.*

Food and Agricultural Organization of the United Nations (FAO) Via delle Terme di Caracalla, 00100 Rome, Italy (Telephone Number in U.S. (202) 653-2400); *The State of Food and Agriculture.*

Statistical Office of the United Nations, Publishing Service, New York, New York 10017 (800) 253-9646; *Statistical Yearbook.*

NEPAL - DEATH RATES

The Economist Intelligence Unit (Asia) Limited, 10th Floor, Luk Kwok Centre, 72 Gloucester Road, Wanchai, Hong Kong (Phone Number in U.S. (800) 938-4685); *Asian Market Atlas.*

Statistical Office of the United Nations, Publishing Service, New York, New York 10017 (800) 253-9646; *Statistical Yearbook.*

Times Books, 201 East 50th Street, New York, New York 10022 (212) 751-2600; *The Economist Book of Vital World Statistics.*

NEPAL - DEFENSE EXPENDITURES

International Monetary Fund, 700 Nineteenth Street, NW, Washington, D.C. 20431 (202) 623-7000; *Government Finance Statistics Yearbook.*

U.S. Arms Control and Disarmament Agency, 320 Twenty-first Street, NW, Washington, D.C. 20451 (202) 647-8677; *World Military Expenditures and Arms Transfers.*

NEPAL - DEMOGRAPHY

The Economist Intelligence Unit, 111 West 57th Street, New York, New York 10019 (800) 938-4685; *The World Market Atlas.*

The Economist Intelligence Unit (Asia) Limited, 10th Floor, Luk Kwok Centre, 72 Gloucester Road, Wanchai, Hong Kong (Phone Number in U.S. (800) 938-4685); *Asian Market Atlas.*

Facts on File, 460 Park Avenue South, New York, New York 10016 (800) 443-8323; *The New Book of World Rankings.*

NEPAL - DEVELOPMENT ASSISTANCE

Asian Development Bank, Post Office Box 789, 1099 Manila, Philippines; *Key Indicators of Developing Asian and Pacific Countries.*

Statistical Office of the United Nations, Publishing Service, New York, New York 10017 (800) 253-9646; *Statistical Yearbook.*

NEPAL - DIAMOND PRODUCTION - See NEPAL - MINING AND MINERAL PRODUCTS

NEPAL - DIVORCE

Facts on File, 460 Park Avenue South, New York, New York 10016 (800) 443-8323; *The New Book of World Rankings.*

Statistical Office of the United Nations, Publishing Service, New York, New York 10017 (800) 253-9646; *Demographic Yearbook.*

NEPAL - ECONOMY

Asian Development Bank, Post Office Box 789, 1099 Manila, Philippines; *Key Indicators of Developing Asian and Pacific Countries.*

Euromonitor Publications Limited, 87-88 Turnmill Street, London EC1M 5QU, England; *International Marketing Data and Statistics.*

Facts on File, 460 Park Avenue South, New York, New York 10016 (800) 443-8323; *The New Book of World Rankings.*

NEPAL - EDUCATION

The Economist Intelligence Unit, 111 West 57th Street, New York, New York 10019 (800) 938-4685; *The World Market Atlas.*

The Economist Intelligence Unit (Asia) Limited, 10th Floor, Luk Kwok Centre, 72 Gloucester Road, Wanchai, Hong Kong (Phone Number in U.S. (800) 938-4685); *Asian Market Atlas.*

Facts on File, 460 Park Avenue South, New York, New York 10016 (800) 443-8323; *The New Book of World Rankings.*

International Monetary Fund, 700 Nineteenth Street, NW, Washington, D.C. 20431 (202) 623-7000; *Government Finance Statistics Yearbook.*

Statistical Office of the United Nations, Publishing Service, New York, New York 10017 (800) 253-9646; *Statistical Yearbook for Asia and the Pacific.*

Times Books, 201 East 50th Street, New York, New York 10022 (212) 751-2600; *The Economist Book of Vital World Statistics.*

United Nations Educational, Scientific and Cultural Organization (UNESCO), 7 Place de Fontenoy, F-75700 Paris, France (Telephone Number in U.S. (212) 963-5981); *Statistical Yearbook.*

The World Bank, 1818 H Street, NW, Washington, D.C. 20433 (202) 477-1234; *World Tables.*

NEPAL - EGG PRODUCTION AND CONSUMPTION - See NEPAL - DAIRY PRODUCTS

NEPAL - ELECTRICITY

Asian Development Bank, Post Office Box 789, 1099 Manila, Philippines; *Key Indicators of Developing Asian and Pacific Countries.*

Facts on File, 460 Park Avenue South, New York, New York 10016 (800) 443-8323; *The New Book of World Rankings.*

Statistical Office of the United Nations, Publishing Service, New York, New York 10017 (800) 253-9646; *Electric Power in Asia and the Pacific* and *Statistical Yearbook.*

Times Books, 201 East 50th Street, New York, New York 10022 (212) 751-2600; *The Economist Book of Vital World Statistics.*

NEPAL - EMPLOYMENT

Euromonitor Publications Limited, 87-88 Turnmill Street, London EC1M 5QU, England; *International Marketing Data and Statistics.*

Facts on File, 460 Park Avenue South, New York, New York 10016 (800) 443-8323; *The New Book of World Rankings.*

International Labour Office, I.L.O. Publications, CH-1211, Geneva 22, Switzerland; *Yearbook of Labour Statistics.*

NEPAL - ENERGY

Facts on File, 460 Park Avenue South, New York, New York 10016 (800) 443-8323; *The New Book of World Rankings.*

Food and Agricultural Organization of the United Nations (FAO) Via delle Terme di Caracalla, 00100 Rome, Italy (Telephone Number in U.S. (202) 653-2400); *The State of Food and Agriculture.*

Statistical Office of the United Nations, Publishing Service, New York, New York 10017 (800) 253-9646; *Energy Statistics Yearbook, Statistical Yearbook,* and *Statistical Yearbook for Asia and the Pacific.*

Times Books, 201 East 50th Street, New York, New York 10022 (212) 751-2600; *The Economist Book of Vital World Statistics.*

NEPAL - EXCHANGE RATES

Asian Development Bank, Post Office Box 789, 1099 Manila, Philippines; *Key Indicators of Developing Asian and Pacific Countries.*

The Economist Intelligence Unit (Asia) Limited, 10th Floor, Luk Kwok Centre, 72 Gloucester Road, Wanchai, Hong Kong (Phone Number in U.S. (800) 938-4685); *Asian Market Atlas.*

Euromonitor Publications Limited, 87-88 Turnmill Street, London EC1M 5QU, England; *International Marketing Data and Statistics.*

International Civil Aviation Organization, 1000 Sherbrooke Street, West, Montreal, Quebec, Canada H3A 2R2 (514) 285-8219; *Civil Aviation Statistics of the World.*

Statistical Office of the United Nations, Publishing Service, New York, New York 10017 (800) 253-9646; *Statistical Yearbook.*

NEPAL - EXCISE TAXES - See NEPAL - TAXATION

NEPAL - EXPORTS

Asian Development Bank, Post Office Box 789, 1099 Manila, Philippines; *Key Indicators of Developing Asian and Pacific Countries.*

The Economist Intelligence Unit, 111 West 57th Street, New York, New York 10019 (800) 938-4685; *The World Market Atlas.*

The Economist Intelligence Unit (Asia) Limited, 10th Floor, Luk Kwok Centre, 72 Gloucester Road, Wanchai, Hong Kong (Phone Number in U.S. (800) 938-4685); *Asian Market Atlas.*

Euromonitor Publications Limited, 87-88 Turnmill Street, London EC1M 5QU, England; *International Marketing Data and Statistics.*

Food and Agricultural Organization of the United Nations (FAO) Via delle Terme di Caracalla, 00100 Rome, Italy (Telephone Number in U.S. (202) 653-2400); *The State of Food and Agriculture.*

International Monetary Fund, 700 Nineteenth Street, NW, Washington, D.C. 20431 (202) 623-7000; *Direction of Trade Statistics,* and *Government Finance Statistics Yearbook.*

Times Books, 201 East 50th Street, New York, New York 10022 (212) 751-2600; *The Economist Book of Vital World Statistics.*

The World Bank, 1818 H Street, NW, Washington, D.C. 20433 (202) 477-1234; *World Tables.*

NEPAL - EXTERNAL FINANCING

Asian Development Bank, Post Office Box 789, 1099 Manila, Philippines; *Key Indicators of Developing Asian and Pacific Countries.*

NEPAL - EXTERNAL INDEBTEDNESS

Asian Development Bank, Post Office Box 789, 1099 Manila, Philippines; *Key Indicators of Developing Asian and Pacific Countries.*

The World Bank, 1818 H Street, NW, Washington, D.C. 20433 (202) 477-1234; *World Tables.*

NEPAL - EXTERNAL TRADE

Asian Development Bank, Post Office Box 789, 1099 Manila, Philippines; *Key Indicators of Developing Asian and Pacific Countries.*

Food and Agricultural Organization of the United Nations (FAO) Via delle Terme di Caracalla, 00100 Rome, Italy (Telephone Number in U.S. (202) 653-2400); *The State of Food and Agriculture,* and *Trade Yearbook.*

Statistical Office of the United Nations, Publishing Service, New York, New York 10017 (800) 253-9646; *Statistical Yearbook for Asia and the Pacific.*

NEPAL - FARM CROPS - See NEPAL - CROPS

NEPAL - FEMALE WORKING POPULATION - See NEPAL - EMPLOYMENT

NEPAL - FERTILITY RATES

The Economist Intelligence Unit (Asia) Limited, 10th Floor, Luk Kwok Centre, 72 Gloucester Road, Wanchai, Hong Kong (Phone Number in U.S. (800) 938-4685); *Asian Market Atlas.*

Facts on File, 460 Park Avenue South, New York, New York 10016 (800) 443-8323; *The New Book of World Rankings.*

The World Bank, 1818 H Street, NW, Washington, D.C. 20433 (202) 477-1234; *World Tables.*

NEPAL - FERTILIZER

Food and Agricultural Organization of the United Nations (FAO) Via delle Terme di Caracalla, 00100 Rome, Italy (Telephone Number in U.S. (202) 653-2400); *The State of Food and Agriculture.*

Statistical Office of the United Nations, Publishing Service, New York, New York 10017 (800) 253-9646; *Statistical Yearbook.*

NEPAL - FETAL MORTALITY

Statistical Office of the United Nations, Publishing Service, New York, New York 10017 (800) 253-9646; *Demographic Yearbook.*

NEPAL - FINANCE

Asian Development Bank, Post Office Box 789, 1099 Manila, Philippines; *Key Indicators of Developing Asian and Pacific Countries.*

Facts on File, 460 Park Avenue South, New York, New York 10016 (800) 443-8323; *The New Book of World Rankings.*

International Monetary Fund, 700 Nineteenth Street, NW, Washington, D.C. 20431 (202) 623-7000; *Government Finance Statistics Yearbook,* and *International Financial Statistics.*

Statistical Office of the United Nations, Publishing Service, New York, New York 10017 (800) 253-9646; *Statistical Yearbook for Asia and the Pacific.*

NEPAL - FISHERIES

Facts on File, 460 Park Avenue South, New York, New York 10016 (800) 443-8323; *The New Book of World Rankings.*

Food and Agricultural Organization of the United Nations (FAO) Via delle Terme di Caracalla, 00100 Rome, Italy (Telephone Number in U.S. (202) 653-2400); *The State of Food and Agriculture,* and *Yearbook of Fishery Statistics.*

Statistical Office of the United Nations, Publishing Service, New York, New York 10017 (800) 253-9646; *Statistical Yearbook.*

NEPAL - FOOD

Food and Agricultural Organization of the United Nations (FAO), Via delle Terme di Caracalla, 00100 Rome, Italy (Telephone Number in U.S. (202) 653-2400); *Production Yearbook,* and *The State of Food and Agriculture.*

Statistical Office of the United Nations, Publishing Service, New York, New York 10017 (800) 253-9646; *Statistical Yearbook for Asia and the Pacific.*

NEPAL - FOREIGN DEBT

International Monetary Fund, 700 Nineteenth Street, NW, Washington, D.C. 20431 (202) 623-7000; *Government Finance Statistics Yearbook.*

NEPAL - FOREIGN TRADE

Asian Development Bank, Post Office Box 789, 1099 Manila, Philippines; *Key Indicators of Developing Asian and Pacific Countries.*

The Economist Intelligence Unit (Asia) Limited, 10th Floor, Luk Kwok Centre, 72 Gloucester Road, Wanchai, Hong Kong (Phone Number in U.S. (800) 938-4685); *Asian Market Atlas.*

Euromonitor Publications Limited, 87-88 Turnmill Street, London EC1M 5QU, England; *International Marketing Data and Statistics.*

Facts on File, 460 Park Avenue South, New York, New York 10016 (800) 443-8323; *The New Book of World Rankings.*

Food and Agricultural Organization of the United Nations (FAO) Via delle Terme di Caracalla, 00100 Rome, Italy (Telephone Number in U.S. (202) 653-2400); *The State of Food and Agriculture.*

Statistical Office of the United Nations, Publishing Service, New York, New York 10017 (800) 253-9646; *International Trade Statistics Yearbook,* and *Trade in Manufactures of Developing Countries.*

The World Bank, 1818 H Street, NW, Washington, D.C. 20433 (202) 477-1234; *World Tables.*

NEPAL - FORESTRY AND FOREST PRODUCTS

The Economist Intelligence Unit (Asia) Limited, 10th Floor, Luk Kwok Centre, 72 Gloucester Road, Wanchai, Hong Kong (Phone Number in U.S. (800) 938-4685); *Asian Market Atlas.*

Facts on File, 460 Park Avenue South, New York, New York 10016 (800) 443-8323; *The New Book of World Rankings.*

Food and Agricultural Organization of the United Nations (FAO) Via delle Terme di Caracalla, 00100 Rome, Italy (Telephone Number in U.S. (202) 653-2400); *The State of Food and Agriculture*, and *Yearbook of Forest Products*.

Statistical Office of the United Nations, Publishing Service, New York, New York 10017 (800) 253-9646; *Statistical Yearbook*.

United Nations Educational, Scientific and Cultural Organization (UNESCO), 7 Place de Fontenoy, F-75700 Paris, France (Telephone Number in U.S. (212) 963-5981); *Statistical Yearbook*.

NEPAL - GAS PRODUCTION - See NEPAL - MINING AND MINERAL PRODUCTS

NEPAL - GENERAL MORTALITY

Statistical Office of the United Nations, Publishing Service, New York, New York 10017 (800) 253-9646; *Demographic Yearbook*.

NEPAL - GEOGRAPHIC DATA

Facts on File, 460 Park Avenue South, New York, New York 10016 (800) 443-8323; *The New Book of World Rankings*.

NEPAL - GOATS - See NEPAL - LIVESTOCK AND POULTRY

NEPAL - GOLD HOLDINGS

Statistical Office of the United Nations, Publishing Service, New York, New York 10017 (800) 253-9646; *Statistical Yearbook*.

The World Bank, 1818 H Street, NW, Washington, D.C. 20433 (202) 477-1234; *World Tables*.

NEPAL - GOLD PRODUCTION AND CONSUMPTION - See NEPAL - MINING AND MINERAL PRODUCTS

NEPAL - GOVERNMENT

Asian Development Bank, Post Office Box 789, 1099 Manila, Philippines; *Key Indicators of Developing Asian and Pacific Countries*.

NEPAL - GOVERNMENT EXPENDITURES

Asian Development Bank, Post Office Box 789, 1099 Manila, Philippines; *Key Indicators of Developing Asian and Pacific Countries*.

International Monetary Fund, 700 Nineteenth Street, NW, Washington, D.C. 20431 (202) 623-7000; *Government Finance Statistics Yearbook*.

Times Books, 201 East 50th Street, New York, New York 10022 (212) 751-2600; *The Economist Book of Vital World Statistics*.

The World Bank, 1818 H Street, NW, Washington, D.C. 20433 (202) 477-1234; *World Tables*.

NEPAL - GOVERNMENT FINANCES

Asian Development Bank, Post Office Box 789, 1099 Manila, Philippines; *Key Indicators of Developing Asian and Pacific Countries*.

NEPAL - GOVERNMENT REVENUES

Asian Development Bank, Post Office Box 789, 1099 Manila, Philippines; *Key Indicators of Developing Asian and Pacific Countries*.

International Monetary Fund, 700 Nineteenth Street, NW, Washington, D.C. 20431 (202) 623-7000; *Government Finance Statistics Yearbook*.

Times Books, 201 East 50th Street, New York, New York 10022 (212) 751-2600; *The Economist Book of Vital World Statistics*.

The World Bank, 1818 H Street, NW, Washington, D.C. 20433 (202) 477-1234; *World Tables*.

NEPAL - GRAIN PRODUCTION - See NEPAL - CROPS

NEPAL - GRANTS

International Monetary Fund, 700 Nineteenth Street, NW, Washington, D.C. 20431 (202) 623-7000; *Government Finance Statistics Yearbook*.

NEPAL - GROSS DOMESTIC PRODUCT

Asian Development Bank, Post Office Box 789, 1099 Manila, Philippines; *Key Indicators of Developing Asian and Pacific Countries*.

The Economist Intelligence Unit, 111 West 57th Street, New York, New York 10019 (800) 938-4685; *The World Market Atlas*.

The Economist Intelligence Unit (Asia) Limited, 10th Floor, Luk Kwok Centre, 72 Gloucester Road, Wanchai, Hong Kong (Phone Number in U.S. (800) 938-4685); *Asian Market Atlas*.

Facts on File, 460 Park Avenue South, New York, New York 10016 (800) 443-8323; *The New Book of World Rankings*.

Euromonitor Publications Limited, 87-88 Turnmill Street, London EC1M 5QU, England; *International Marketing Data and Statistics*.

Statistical Office of the United Nations, Publishing Service, New York, New York 10017 (800) 253-9646; *Statistical Yearbook*.

Times Books, 201 East 50th Street, New York, New York 10022 (212) 751-2600; *The Economist Book of Vital World Statistics*.

The World Bank, 1818 H Street, NW, Washington, D.C. 20433 (202) 477-1234; *World Tables*.

NEPAL - GROSS NATIONAL PRODUCT

Asian Development Bank, Post Office Box 789, 1099 Manila, Philippines; *Key Indicators of Developing Asian and Pacific Countries*.

Euromonitor Publications Limited, 87-88 Turnmill Street, London EC1M 5QU, England; *International Marketing Data and Statistics*.

U.S. Arms Control and Disarmament Agency, 320 Twenty-first Street, NW, Washington, D.C. 20451 (202) 647-8677; *World Military Expenditures and Arms Transfers*.

The World Bank, 1818 H Street, NW, Washington, D.C. 20433 (202) 477-1234; *World Tables*.

NEPAL - HEALTH

The Economist Intelligence Unit (Asia) Limited, 10th Floor, Luk Kwok Centre, 72 Gloucester Road, Wanchai, Hong Kong (Phone Number in U.S. (800) 938-4685); *Asian Market Atlas*.

Facts on File, 460 Park Avenue South, New York, New York 10016 (800) 443-8323; *The New Book of World Rankings*.

Statistical Office of the United Nations, Publishing Service, New York, New York 10017 (800) 253-9646; *Statistical Yearbook*. personnel.

Times Books, 201 East 50th Street, New York, New York 10022 (212) 751-2600; *The Economist Book of Vital World Statistics*.

NEPAL - HEALTH EXPENDITURES

International Monetary Fund, 700 Nineteenth Street, NW, Washington, D.C. 20431 (202) 623-7000; *Government Finance Statistics Yearbook*.

NEPAL - HIDE PRODUCTION

Food and Agricultural Organization of the United Nations (FAO), Via delle Terme di Caracalla, 00100 Rome, Italy (Telephone Number in U.S. (202) 653-2400); *Production Yearbook*.

NEPAL - HIGHWAYS

The Economist Intelligence Unit (Asia) Limited, 10th Floor, Luk Kwok Centre, 72 Gloucester Road, Wanchai, Hong Kong (Phone Number in U.S. (800) 938-4685); *Asian Market Atlas*.

International Road Federation, 525 School Street, SW, Washington, D.C. 20024 (202) 554-2106; *World Road Statistics*.

NEPAL - HORSES - See NEPAL - LIVESTOCK AND POULTRY

NEPAL - HOURS OF WORK - See NEPAL - EMPLOYMENT

NEPAL - HOUSING

Facts on File, 460 Park Avenue South, New York, New York 10016 (800) 443-8323; *The New Book of World Rankings*.

NEPAL - HOUSING EXPENDITURES

International Monetary Fund, 700 Nineteenth Street, NW, Washington, D.C. 20431 (202) 623-7000; *Government Finance Statistics Yearbook*.

NEPAL - ILLITERATE POPULATION

United Nations Educational, Scientific and Cultural Organization (UNESCO), 7 Place de Fontenoy, F-75700 Paris, France (Telephone Number in U.S. (212) 963-5981); *Statistical Yearbook*.

NEPAL - IMPORTS

Asian Development Bank, Post Office Box 789, 1099 Manila, Philippines; *Key Indicators of Developing Asian and Pacific Countries*.

The Economist Intelligence Unit, 111 West 57th Street, New York, New York 10019 (800) 938-4685; *The World Market Atlas*.

The Economist Intelligence Unit (Asia) Limited, 10th Floor, Luk Kwok Centre, 72 Gloucester Road, Wanchai, Hong Kong (Phone

Number in U.S. (800) 938-4685); *Asian Market Atlas*.

Euromonitor Publications Limited, 87-88 Turnmill Street, London EC1M 5QU, England; *International Marketing Data and Statistics*.

Food and Agricultural Organization of the United Nations (FAO) Via delle Terme di Caracalla, 00100 Rome, Italy (Telephone Number in U.S. (202) 653-2400); *The State of Food and Agriculture*.

International Monetary Fund, 700 Nineteenth Street, NW, Washington, D.C. 20431 (202) 623-7000; *Direction of Trade Statistics*, and *Government Finance Statistics Yearbook*.

Times Books, 201 East 50th Street, New York, New York 10022 (212) 751-2600; *The Economist Book of Vital World Statistics*.

The World Bank, 1818 H Street, NW, Washington, D.C. 20433 (202) 477-1234; *World Tables*.

NEPAL - INCOME TAXES - See NEPAL - TAXATION

NEPAL - INDUSTRY

Euromonitor Publications Limited, 87-88 Turnmill Street, London EC1M 5QU, England; *International Marketing Data and Statistics*.

Facts on File, 460 Park Avenue South, New York, New York 10016 (800) 443-8323; *The New Book of World Rankings*.

International Labour Office, I.L.O. Publications, CH-1211, Geneva 22, Switzerland; *Yearbook of Labour Statistics*.

Times Books, 201 East 50th Street, New York, New York 10022 (212) 751-2600; *The Economist Book of Vital World Statistics*.

Statistical Office of the United Nations, Publishing Service, New York, New York 10017 (800) 253-9646; *Statistical Yearbook for Asia and the Pacific*.

The World Bank, 1818 H Street, NW, Washington, D.C. 20433 (202) 477-1234; *World Tables*.

World Intellectual Property Organization, 34 Chemin des Colombettes, CH-1211 Geneva 20, Switzerland; *Industrial Property Statistics*.

NEPAL - INFANT AND MATERNAL MORTALITY

The Economist Intelligence Unit (Asia) Limited, 10th Floor, Luk Kwok Centre, 72 Gloucester Road, Wanchai, Hong Kong (Phone Number in U.S. (800) 938-4685); *Asian Market Atlas*.

Statistical Office of the United Nations, Publishing Service, New York, New York 10017 (800) 253-9646; *Demographic Yearbook*.

Times Books, 201 East 50th Street, New York, New York 10022 (212) 751-2600; *The Economist Book of Vital World Statistics*.

The World Bank, 1818 H Street, NW, Washington, D.C. 20433 (202) 477-1234; *World Tables*.

NEPAL - INTERNAL TRADE

Statistical Office of the United Nations, Publishing Service, New York, New York 10017 (800) 253-9646; *Statistical Yearbook for Asia and the Pacific*.

NEPAL - INTERNATIONAL RESERVES EXCLUDING GOLD

Asian Development Bank, Post Office Box 789, 1099 Manila, Philippines; *Key Indicators of Developing Asian and Pacific Countries*.

Statistical Office of the United Nations, Publishing Service, New York, New York 10017 (800) 253-9646; *Statistical Yearbook*.

The World Bank, 1818 H Street, NW, Washington, D.C. 20433 (202) 477-1234; *World Tables*.

NEPAL - INTERNATIONAL STATISTICS

Asian Development Bank, Post Office Box 789, 1099 Manila, Philippines; *Key Indicators of Developing Asian and Pacific Countries*.

NEPAL - IRON ORE PRODUCTION AND CONSUMPTION - See NEPAL - MINING AND MINERAL PRODUCTS

NEPAL - IRRIGATION

Euromonitor Publications Limited, 87-88 Turnmill Street, London EC1M 5QU, England; *International Marketing Data and Statistics*.

NEPAL - JUTE PRODUCTION - See NEPAL - CROPS

NEPAL - LABOR FORCE

The Economist Intelligence Unit (Asia) Limited, 10th Floor, Luk Kwok Centre, 72 Gloucester Road, Wanchai, Hong Kong (Phone Number in U.S. (800) 938-4685); *Asian Market Atlas*.

Euromonitor Publications Limited, 87-88 Turnmill Street, London EC1M 5QU, England; *International Marketing Data and Statistics*.

Facts on File, 460 Park Avenue South, New York, New York 10016 (800) 443-8323; *The New Book of World Rankings*.

Food and Agricultural Organization of the United Nations (FAO) Via delle Terme di Caracalla, 00100 Rome, Italy (Telephone Number in U.S. (202) 653-2400); *The State of Food and Agriculture*.

Times Books, 201 East 50th Street, New York, New York 10022 (212) 751-2600; *The Economist Book of Vital World Statistics*.

The World Bank, 1818 H Street, NW, Washington, D.C. 20433 (202) 477-1234; *World Tables*.

NEPAL - LABOR PRODUCTIVITY

International Labour Office, I.L.O. Publications, CH-1211, Geneva 22, Switzerland; *Yearbook of Labour Statistics*.

NEPAL - LAND USE

Euromonitor Publications Limited, 87-88 Turnmill Street, London EC1M 5QU, England; *International Marketing Data and Statistics*.

Food and Agricultural Organization of the United Nations (FAO), Via delle Terme di Caracalla, 00100 Rome, Italy (Telephone Number in U.S. (202) 653-2400); *Production Yearbook*.

NEPAL - LIBRARIES

Facts on File, 460 Park Avenue South, New York, New York 10016 (800) 443-8323; *The New Book of World Rankings*.

NEPAL - LIFE EXPECTANCY

The Economist Intelligence Unit (Asia) Limited, 10th Floor, Luk Kwok Centre, 72 Gloucester Road, Wanchai, Hong Kong (Phone Number in U.S. (800) 938-4685); *Asian Market Atlas*.

NEPAL - LIVESTOCK AND POULTRY

Euromonitor Publications Limited, 87-88 Turnmill Street, London EC1M 5QU, England; *International Marketing Data and Statistics*.

Facts on File, 460 Park Avenue South, New York, New York 10016 (800) 443-8323; *The New Book of World Rankings*.

Food and Agricultural Organization of the United Nations (FAO), Via delle Terme di Caracalla, 00100 Rome, Italy (Telephone Number in U.S. (202) 653-2400); *Production Yearbook*, and *The State of Food and Agriculture*.

Statistical Office of the United Nations, Publishing Service, New York, New York 10017 (800) 253-9646; *Statistical Yearbook*.

NEPAL - LIVING LEVELS

Times Books, 201 East 50th Street, New York, New York 10022 (212) 751-2600; *The Economist Book of Vital World Statistics*.

NEPAL - MANPOWER

Statistical Office of the United Nations, Publishing Service, New York, New York 10017 (800) 253-9646; *Statistical Yearbook for Asia and the Pacific*.

NEPAL - MANUFACTURING

Asian Development Bank, Post Office Box 789, 1099 Manila, Philippines; *Key Indicators of Developing Asian and Pacific Countries*.

Facts on File, 460 Park Avenue South, New York, New York 10016 (800) 443-8323; *The New Book of World Rankings*.

The World Bank, 1818 H Street, NW, Washington, D.C. 20433 (202) 477-1234; *World Tables*.

NEPAL - MARRIAGE RATES

Facts on File, 460 Park Avenue South, New York, New York 10016 (800) 443-8323; *The New Book of World Rankings*.

Statistical Office of the United Nations, Publishing Service, New York, New York 10017 (800) 253-9646; *Demographic Yearbook*.

NEPAL - MEAT PRODUCTION - ALL TYPES OF MEAT AND POULTRY

Facts on File, 460 Park Avenue South, New York, New York 10016 (800) 443-8323; *The New Book of World Rankings*.

Food and Agricultural Organization of the United Nations (FAO) Via delle Terme di Caracalla, 00100 Rome, Italy (Telephone Number in U.S. (202) 653-2400); *The State of Food and Agriculture*.

Statistical Office of the United Nations, Publishing Service, New York, New York 10017 (800) 253-9646; *Statistical Yearbook*.

NEPAL - MILITARY

The Economist Intelligence Unit (Asia) Limited, 10th Floor, Luk Kwok Centre, 72 Gloucester Road, Wanchai, Hong Kong (Phone

Number in U.S. (800) 938-4685); *Asian Market Atlas.*

The International Institute for Strategic Studies, 23 Tavistock Street, London WC2E 7NQ, England; *The Military Balance.*

U.S. Arms Control and Disarmament Agency, 320 Twenty-first Street, NW, Washington, D.C. 20451 (202) 647-8677; *World Military Expenditures and Arms Transfers.*

NEPAL - MILK PRODUCTION - See NEPAL - DAIRY PRODUCTS

NEPAL - MILLET PRODUCTION - See NEPAL - CROPS

NEPAL - MINING AND MINERAL PRODUCTS

Asian Development Bank, Post Office Box 789, 1099 Manila, Philippines; *Key Indicators of Developing Asian and Pacific Countries.*

Facts on File, 460 Park Avenue South, New York, New York 10016 (800) 443-8323; *The New Book of World Rankings.*

NEPAL - MONEY EXCHANGE RATE

Euromonitor Publications Limited, 87-88 Turnmill Street, London EC1M 5QU, England; *International Marketing Data and Statistics.*

Statistical Office of the United Nations, Publishing Service, New York, New York 10017 (800) 253-9046; *Statistical Yearbook.*

NEPAL - MONEY RESERVES

Euromonitor Publications Limited, 87-80 Turnmill Street, London EC1M 5QU, England; *International Marketing Data and Statistics.*

NEPAL - MONEY SUPPLY

Asian Development Bank, Post Office Box 789, 1099 Manila, Philippines; *Key Indicators of Developing Asian and Pacific Countries.*

Euromonitor Publications Limited, 87-88 Turnmill Street, London EC1M 5QU, England; *International Marketing Data and Statistics.*

Statistical Office of the United Nations, Publishing Service, New York, New York 10017 (800) 253-9646; *Statistical Yearbook.*

The World Bank, 1818 H Street, NW, Washington, D.C. 20433 (202) 477-1234; *World Tables.*

NEPAL - MOTOR VEHICLE TAXES - See NEPAL - TAXATION

NEPAL - MOTOR VEHICLES IN USE

International Road Federation, 525 School Street, SW, Washington, D.C. 20024 (202) 554-2106; *World Road Statistics.*

Statistical Office of the United Nations, Publishing Service, New York, New York 10017 (800) 253-9646; *Statistical Yearbook.*

NEPAL - MUSEUMS

Facts on File, 460 Park Avenue South, New York, New York 10016 (800) 443-8323; *The New Book of World Rankings.*

NEPAL - NATALITY - See NEPAL - BIRTH RATES

NEPAL - NATIONAL ACCOUNTS

Statistical Office of the United Nations, Publishing Service, New York, New York 10017 (800) 253-9646; *National Accounts Statistics, Statistical Yearbook,* and *Statistical Yearbook for Asia and the Pacific.*

NEPAL - NATIONAL INCOME

Facts on File, 460 Park Avenue South, New York, New York 10016 (800) 443-8323; *The New Book of World Rankings.*

Statistical Office of the United Nations, Publishing Service, New York, New York 10017 (800) 253-9646; *Statistical Yearbook.*

NEPAL - NATIONAL PRODUCT

Facts on File, 460 Park Avenue South, New York, New York 10016 (800) 443-8323; *The New Book of World Rankings.*

Statistical Office of the United Nations, Publishing Service, New York, New York 10017 (800) 253-9646; *Statistical Yearbook.*

NEPAL - NATURAL GAS PRODUCTION - See NEPAL - MINING AND MINERAL PRODUCTS

NEPAL - NEWSPAPER PRODUCTION - See NEPAL - FORESTRY AND FOREST PRODUCTS

NEPAL - PATENTS

Statistical Office of the United Nations, Publishing Service, New York, New York 10017 (800) 253-9646; *Statistical Yearbook.*

World Intellectual Property Organization, 34 Chemin des Colombettes, CH 1211 Geneva 20, Switzerland; *Industrial Property Statistics.*

NEPAL - PEANUT PRODUCTION - See NEPAL - CROPS

NEPAL - PERIODICALS

United Nations Educational, Scientific and Cultural Organization (UNESCO), 7 Place de Fontenoy, F-75700 Paris, France (Telephone Number in U.S. (212) 963-5981); *Statistical Yearbook.*

NEPAL - PESTICIDE USE

Food and Agricultural Organization of the United Nations (FAO) Via delle Terme di Caracalla, 00100 Rome, Italy (Telephone Number in U.S. (202) 653-2400); *The State of Food and Agriculture.*

NEPAL - PETROLEUM INDUSTRY

Asian Development Bank, Post Office Box 789, 1099 Manila, Philippines; *Key Indicators of Developing Asian and Pacific Countries.*

Facts on File, 460 Park Avenue South, New York, New York 10016 (800) 443-8323; *The New Book of World Rankings.*

Food and Agricultural Organization of the United Nations (FAO) Via delle Terme di Caracalla, 00100 Rome, Italy (Telephone Number in U.S. (202) 653-2400); *The State of Food and Agriculture.*

NEPAL - PIGS - See NEPAL - LIVESTOCK AND POULTRY

NEPAL - POPULATION

Asian Development Bank, Post Office Box 789, 1099 Manila, Philippines; *Key Indicators of Developing Asian and Pacific Countries*.

The Economist Intelligence Unit, 111 West 57th Street, New York, New York 10019 (800) 938-4685; *The World Market Atlas*.

The Economist Intelligence Unit (Asia) Limited, 10th Floor, Luk Kwok Centre, 72 Gloucester Road, Wanchai, Hong Kong (Phone Number in U.S. (800) 938-4685); *Asian Market Atlas*.

Euromonitor Publications Limited, 87-88 Turnmill Street, London EC1M 5QU, England; *International Marketing Data and Statistics*.

Facts on File, 460 Park Avenue South, New York, New York 10016 (800) 443-8323; *The New Book of World Rankings*.

Food and Agricultural Organization of the United Nations (FAO), Via delle Terme di Caracalla, 00100 Rome, Italy (Telephone Number in U.S. (202) 653-2400); *Production Yearbook*.

International Labour Office, I.L.O. Publications, CH-1211, Geneva 22, Switzerland; *Yearbook of Labour Statistics*.

Statistical Office of the United Nations, Publishing Service, New York, New York 10017 (800) 253-9646; *Demographic Yearbook*, *Statistical Yearbook*, and *Statistical Yearbook for Asia and the Pacific*.

Times Books, 201 East 50th Street, New York, New York 10022 (212) 751-2600; *The Economist Book of Vital World Statistics*.

United Nations Educational, Scientific and Cultural Organization (UNESCO), 7 Place de Fontenoy, F-75700 Paris, France (Telephone Number in U.S. (212) 963-5981); *Statistical Yearbook*.

U.S. Arms Control and Disarmament Agency, 320 Twenty-first Street, NW, Washington, D.C. 20451 (202) 647-8677; *World Military Expenditures and Arms Transfers*.

World Health Organization, Office of Publications, Avenue Appia, CH-1211 Geneva 27, Switzerland (Telephone Number in U.S. (518) 436-9686); *World Health Statistics Annual*.

NEPAL - POST OFFICES

Facts on File, 460 Park Avenue South, New York, New York 10016 (800) 443-8323; *The New Book of World Rankings*.

NEPAL - POTATO PRODUCTION - See NEPAL - CROPS

NEPAL - POWER PRODUCTION INDUSTRY - ESTABLISHMENTS, PAYROLLS, VALUE ADDED, ETC.

Statistical Office of the United Nations, Publishing Service, New York, New York 10017 (800) 253-9646; *Electric Power in Asia and the Pacific*.

NEPAL - PRICES

Asian Development Bank, Post Office Box 789, 1099 Manila, Philippines; *Key Indicators of Developing Asian and Pacific Countries*.

Facts on File, 460 Park Avenue South, New York, New York 10016 (800) 443-8323; *The New Book of World Rankings*.

Food and Agricultural Organization of the United Nations (FAO), Via delle Terme di Caracalla, 00100 Rome, Italy (Telephone Number in U.S. (202) 653-2400); *Production Yearbook*, and *The State of Food and Agriculture*.

International Labour Office, I.L.O. Publications, CH-1211, Geneva 22, Switzerland; *Yearbook of Labour Statistics*.

NEPAL - PRODUCTION

Facts on File, 460 Park Avenue South, New York, New York 10016 (800) 443-8323; *The New Book of World Rankings*.

NEPAL - PRODUCTIVITY

Euromonitor Publications Limited, 87-88 Turnmill Street, London EC1M 5QU, England; *International Marketing Data and Statistics*.

NEPAL - PROPERTY TAXES

International Monetary Fund, 700 Nineteenth Street, NW, Washington, D.C. 20431 (202) 623-7000; *Government Finance Statistics Yearbook*.

NEPAL - PUBLIC FINANCE

Facts on File, 460 Park Avenue South, New York, New York 10016 (800) 443-8323; *The New Book of World Rankings*.

NEPAL - RADIO BROADCASTING - See NEPAL - BROADCASTING

NEPAL - RAILWAYS

Jane's Information Group, Sentinel House, 163 Brighton Road, Coulsdon, Surrey CR5 2NH, England (Telephone Number in U.S. (703) 683-3700); *Jane's World Railways*.

NEPAL - RELIGION

Facts on File, 460 Park Avenue South, New York, New York 10016 (800) 443-8323; *The New Book of World Rankings*.

NEPAL - RENT PRICES

International Labour Office, I.L.O. Publications, CH-1211, Geneva 22, Switzerland; *Yearbook of Labour Statistics*.

NEPAL - RICE PRODUCTION - See NEPAL - CROPS

NEPAL - ROOT AND TUBER PRODUCTION - See NEPAL - CROPS

NEPAL - ROUNDWOOD PRODUCTION - See NEPAL - FORESTRY AND FOREST PRODUCTS

NEPAL - RUBBER PRODUCTION AND CONSUMPTION

Facts on File, 460 Park Avenue South, New York, New York 10016 (800) 443-8323; *The New Book of World Rankings*.

NEPAL - SAWNWOOD PRODUCTION - See NEPAL - FORESTRY AND FOREST PRODUCTS

NEPAL - SENIOR CITIZENS

Facts on File, 460 Park Avenue South, New York, New York 10016 (800) 443-8323; *The New Book of World Rankings*.

NEPAL - SHEEP - See NEPAL - LIVESTOCK AND POULTRY

NEPAL - SILVER PRODUCTION AND CONSUMPTION - See NEPAL - MINING AND MINERAL PRODUCTS

NEPAL - SOCIAL DATA

Asian Development Bank, Post Office Box 789, 1099 Manila, Philippines; *Key Indicators of Developing Asian and Pacific Countries*.

Facts on File, 460 Park Avenue South, New York, New York 10016 (800) 443-8323; *The New Book of World Rankings*.

NEPAL - SOCIAL SECURITY

International Monetary Fund, 700 Nineteenth Street, NW, Washington, D.C. 20431 (202) 623-7000; *Government Finance Statistics Yearbook*.

NEPAL - STATE BUDGET REVENUE AND EXPENDITURES

Euromonitor Publications Limited, 87-88 Turnmill Street, London EC1M 5QU, England; *International Marketing Data and Statistics*.

NEPAL - STEEL PRODUCTION - See NEPAL - MINING AND MINERAL PRODUCTS

NEPAL - STOCKS - COMMODITY - MARKET PRICE - INDEX

Food and Agricultural Organization of the United Nations (FAO) Via delle Terme di Caracalla, 00100 Rome, Italy (Telephone Number in U.S. (202) 653-2400); *The State of Food and Agriculture*.

NEPAL - SUGAR PRODUCTION AND CONSUMPTION - See NEPAL - CROPS

NEPAL - TAXATION

International Monetary Fund, 700 Nineteenth Street, NW, Washington, D.C. 20431 (202) 623-7000; *Government Finance Statistics Yearbook*.

International Road Federation, 525 School Street, SW, Washington, D.C. 20024 (202) 554-2106; *World Road Statistics*.

The World Bank, 1818 H Street, NW, Washington, D.C. 20433 (202) 477-1234; *World Tables*.

NEPAL - TAX REVENUES - SEE NEPAL - TAXATION

NEPAL - TELEPHONES IN USE

American Telephone and Telegraph Company, 26 Parsippany Road, Whippany, New Jersey 07981 (800) 338-4038; *The World's Telephones*.

The Economist Intelligence Unit (Asia) Limited, 10th Floor, Luk Kwok Centre, 72 Gloucester Road, Wanchai, Hong Kong (Phone Number in U.S. (800) 938-4685); *Asian Market Atlas*.

Statistical Office of the United Nations, Publishing Service, New York, New York 10017 (800) 253-9646; *Statistical Yearbook*.

NEPAL - TELEVISION BROADCASTING - See NEPAL - BROADCASTING

NEPAL - THEATRE

United Nations Educational, Scientific and Cultural Organization (UNESCO), 7 Place de Fontenoy, F-75700 Paris, France (Telephone

Number in U.S. (212) 963-5981); *Statistical Yearbook*.

NEPAL - TOBACCO PRODUCTION

Facts on File, 460 Park Avenue South, New York, New York 10016 (800) 443-8323; *The New Book of World Rankings*.

Statistical Office of the United Nations, Publishing Service, New York, New York 10017 (800) 253-9646; *Statistical Yearbook*.

NEPAL - TOURISM

Facts on File, 460 Park Avenue South, New York, New York 10016 (800) 443-8323; *The New Book of World Rankings*.

Statistical Office of the United Nations, Publishing Service, New York, New York 10017 (800) 253-9646; *Statistical Yearbook*.

World Tourism Organization, Calle Capitan Haya 42, E-28020 Madrid, Spain; *Yearbook of Tourism Statistics*.

NEPAL - TRACTORS IN USE

Statistical Office of the United Nations, Publishing Service, New York, New York 10017 (800) 253-9646; *Statistical Yearbook*.

NEPAL - TRADE - See NEPAL - FOREIGN TRADE

NEPAL - TRADEMARKS AND SERVICE MARKS

Statistical Office of the United Nations, Publishing Service, New York, New York 10017 (800) 253-9646; *Statistical Yearbook*.

World Intellectual Property Organization, 34 Chemin des Colombettes, CH-1211 Geneva 20, Switzerland; *Industrial Property Statistics*.

NEPAL - TRANSPORTATION AND COMMUNICATIONS

The Economist Intelligence Unit (Asia) Limited, 10th Floor, Luk Kwok Centre, 72 Gloucester Road, Wanchai, Hong Kong (Phone Number in U.S. (800) 938-4685); *Asian Market Atlas*.

Facts on File, 460 Park Avenue South, New York, New York 10016 (800) 443-8323; *The New Book of World Rankings*.

Statistical Office of the United Nations, Publishing Service, New York, New York 10017 (800) 253-9646; *Statistical Yearbook for Asia and the Pacific*.

NEPAL - UNEMPLOYMENT

Euromonitor Publications Limited, 87-88 Turnmill Street, London EC1M 5QU, England; *International Marketing Data and Statistics*.

International Labour Office, I.L.O. Publications, CH-1211, Geneva 22, Switzerland; *Yearbook of Labour Statistics*.

NEPAL - UTILITIES

Statistical Office of the United Nations, Publishing Service, New York, New York 10017 (800) 253-9646; *Electric Power in Asia and the Pacific*.

NEPAL - VITAL STATISTICS

Euromonitor Publications Limited, 87-88 Turnmill Street, London EC1M 5QU, England; *International Marketing Data and Statistics*.

International Labour Office, I.L.O. Publications, CH-1211, Geneva 22, Switzerland; *Yearbook of Labour Statistics*.

Statistical Office of the United Nations, Publishing Service, New York, New York 10017 (800) 253-9646; *Statistical Yearbook*.

World Health Organization, Office of Publications, Avenue Appia, CH-1211 Geneva 27, Switzerland (Telephone Number in U.S. (518) 436-9686); *World Health Statistics Annual*.

NEPAL - WAGES AND PRICES

Statistical Office of the United Nations, Publishing Service, New York, New York 10017 (800) 253-9646; *Statistical Yearbook for Asia and the Pacific*.

NEPAL - WEATHER

Facts on File, 460 Park Avenue South, New York, New York 10016 (800) 443-8323; *The New Book of World Rankings*.

NEPAL - WELFARE

International Monetary Fund, 700 Nineteenth Street, NW, Washington, D.C. 20431 (202) 623-7000; *Government Finance Statistics Yearbook*.

NEPAL - WHEAT PRODUCTION AND PRICES - See NEPAL - CROPS

NEPAL - WHOLESALE PRICES

Asian Development Bank, Post Office Box 789, 1099 Manila, Philippines; *Key Indicators of Developing Asian and Pacific Countries*.

NEPAL - WINE PRODUCTION

Facts on File, 460 Park Avenue South, New York, New York 10016 (800) 443-8323; *The New Book of World Rankings*.

NEPAL - WOOL PRODUCTION

Facts on File, 460 Park Avenue South, New York, New York 10016 (800) 443-8323; *The New Book of World Rankings*.

Netherlands - National Statistical Office

Netherlands Central Bureau of Statistics, 428 Prises Beatrix laan, 2270 AZ Voorburg, The Hague, Netherlands.

Netherlands - Primary Statistics Sources

Netherlands Central Bureau of Statistics, 428 Prises Beatrix laan, 2270 AZ Voorburg, The Hague, Netherlands; *Statistical Pocketbook*, and *Statistical Yearbook of the Netherlands*.

NETHERLANDS - ABORTIONS

European Community Information Service, 2100 M Street, NW, Washington, D.C. 20037 (202) 862-9500; *Demographic Statistics*.

NETHERLANDS - AGRICULTURE

European Community Information Service, 2100 M Street, NW, Washington, D.C. 20037 (202) 862-9500; *Agriculture: Statistical Yearbook, Basic Statistics of the Community, Eurostatistics: Data for Short-term Economic Analysis, Labor Force Sample Survey*, and *Regions: Statistical Yearbook*.

Facts on File, 460 Park Avenue South, New York, New York 10016 (800) 443-8323; *The New Book of World Rankings*.

Food and Agricultural Organization of the United Nations (FAO) Via delle Terme di Caracalla, 00100 Rome, Italy (Telephone Number in U.S. (202) 653-2400); *Production Yearbook, The State of Food and Agriculture*, and *Trade Yearbook*.

Netherlands Central Bureau of Statistics, Staatsuitgeverij, The Hague, Netherlands; *Industrial Structure Statistics*, and *Statistical Yearbook of the Netherlands*.

Organisation for Economic Co-operation and Development (OECD), 2 rue Andre-Pascal, 75 Paris 16, France (Telephone Number in U.S. (202) 785-6323); *Economic Accounts for Agriculture, Indicators of Industrial Activity*, and *OECD Economic Surveys: Netherlands*.

Statistical Office of the United Nations, Publishing Service, New York, New York 10017 (800) 253-9646; *Statistical Yearbook*.

Times Books, 201 East 50th Street, New York, New York 10022 (212) 751-2600; *The Economist Book of Vital World Statistics*.

The World Bank, 1818 H Street, NW, Washington, D.C. 20433 (202) 477-1234; *World Tables*.

NETHERLANDS - AIRLINE SERVICE

Facts on File, 460 Park Avenue South, New York, New York 10016 (800) 443-8323; *The New Book of World Rankings*.

European Community Information Service, 2100 M Street, NW, Washington, D.C. 20037 (202) 862-9500; *Basic Statistics of the Community, Regions: Statistical Yearbook*, and *Transport Annual Statistics*.

International Civil Aviation Organization, 1000 Sherbrooke Street, West, Montreal, Quebec, Canada H3A 2R2 (514) 285-8219; *Civil Aviation Statistics of the World*.

Organisation for Economic Co-operation and Development (OECD), 2 rue Andre-Pascal, 75 Paris 16, France (Telephone Number in U.S. (202) 785-6323); *Tourism Policy and International Tourism in OECD Member Countries*.

Statistical Office of the United Nations, Publishing Service, New York, New York 10017 (800) 253-9646; *Statistical Yearbook*.

Times Books, 201 East 50th Street, New York, New York 10022 (212) 751-2600; *The Economist Book of Vital World Statistics*.

NETHERLANDS - ALMOND PRODUCTION - See NETHERLANDS - CROPS

NETHERLANDS - ALUMINUM PRODUCTION AND CONSUMPTION - See NETHERLANDS - MINING AND MINERAL PRODUCTS

NETHERLANDS - ANIMAL FEEDINGSTUFFS

Organisation for Economic Co-operation and Development (OECD), 2 rue Andre-Pascal, 75 Paris 16, France (Telephone Number in U.S. (202) 785-6323); *Foreign Trade by Commodities*.

Statistical Office of the United Nations, Publishing Service, New York, New York 10017 (800) 253-9646; *Statistical Yearbook*.

NETHERLANDS - ANIMAL HEALTH

Food and Agricultural Organization of the United Nations (FAO), Via delle Terme di Caracalla, 00100 Rome, Italy (Telephone Number in U.S. (202) 653-2400); *Animal Health Yearbook.*

NETHERLANDS - ANTIMONY AND ANTIMONY ORE PRODUCTION AND CONSUMPTION - See NETHERLANDS - MINING AND MINERAL PRODUCTS

NETHERLANDS - APPLES - See NETHERLANDS - CROPS

NETHERLANDS - AREA AND DENSITY OF POPULATION

European Community Information Service, 2100 M Street, NW, Washington, D.C. 20037 (202) 862-9500; *Basic Statistics of the Community,* and *Demographic Statistics.*

Food and Agricultural Organization of the United Nations (FAO) Via delle Terme di Caracalla, 00100 Rome, Italy (Telephone Number in U.S. (202) 653-2400); *The State of Food and Agriculture.*

Netherlands Central Bureau of Statistics, Staatsuitgeverij, The Hague, Netherlands; *Statistical Yearbook of the Netherlands.*

Statistical Office of the United Nations, Publishing Service, New York, New York 10017 (800) 253-9646; *Statistical Yearbook.*

Times Books, 201 East 50th Street, New York, New York 10022 (212) 751-2600; *The Economist Book of Vital World Statistics.*

United Nations Educational, Scientific and Cultural Organization (UNESCO), 7 Place de Fontenoy F-75700 Paris, France (Telephone Number in U.S. (212) 963-5981); *Statistical Yearbook.*

NETHERLANDS - ARMS EXPORTS AND IMPORTS

U.S. Arms Control and Disarmament Agency, 320 Twenty-first Street, NW, Washington, D.C. 20451 (202) 647-8677; *World Military Expenditures and Arms Transfers.*

NETHERLANDS - ARSENIC PRODUCTION AND CONSUMPTION - See NETHERLANDS - MINING AND MINERAL PRODUCTS

NETHERLANDS - BALANCE OF PAYMENTS

The Economist Intelligence Unit, 111 West 57th Street, New York, New York 10019 (800) 938-4685; *The World Market Atlas.*

European Community Information Service, 2100 M Street, NW, Washington, D.C. 20037 (202) 862-9500; *ACP: Basic Statistics, Basic Statistics of the Community, Energy Statistics Yearbook,* and *Eurostatistics: Data for Short-term Economic Analysis.*

International Monetary Fund, 700 Nineteenth Street, NW, Washington, D.C. 20431 (202) 623-7000; *Balance of Payments Yearbook,* and *International Financial Statistics.*

Netherlands Central Bureau of Statistics, Staatsuitgeverij, The Hague, Netherlands; *Statistical Yearbook of the Netherlands.*

Organisation for Economic Co-operation and Development (OECD), 2 rue Andre-Pascal, 75 Paris 16, France (Telephone Number in U.S. (202) 785-6323); *Economic Outlook, Geographical Distribution of Financial Flows to Developing Countries, Main Economic Indicators - Historical Statistics,* and *OECD Economic Surveys: Netherlands.*

Times Books, 201 East 50th Street, New York, New York 10022 (212) 751-2600; *The Economist Book of Vital World Statistics.*

The World Bank, 1818 H Street, NW, Washington, D.C. 20433 (202) 477-1234; *World Tables.*

NETHERLANDS - BANANA PRODUCTION - See NETHERLANDS - CROPS

NETHERLANDS - BANKING

European Community Information Service, 2100 M Street, NW, Washington, D.C. 20037 (202) 862-9500; *ACP: Basic Statistics.*

Facts on File, 460 Park Avenue South, New York, New York 10016 (800) 443-8323; *The New Book of World Rankings.*

International Monetary Fund, 700 Nineteenth Street, NW, Washington, D.C. 20431 (202) 623-7000; *Government Finance Statistics Yearbook,* and *International Financial Statistics.*

Netherlands Central Bureau of Statistics, Staatsuitgeverij, The Hague, Netherlands; *Statistical Yearbook of the Netherlands.*

Organisation for Economic Co-operation and Development (OECD), 2 rue Andre-Pascal, 75 Paris 16, France (Telephone Number in U.S. (202) 785-6323); *Economic Outlook, Financial Market Trends,* and *OECD Economic Surveys: Netherlands.*

Statistical Office of the United Nations, Publishing Service, New York, New York 10017 (800) 253-9646; *Statistical Yearbook.*

NETHERLANDS - BARLEY PRODUCTION - See NETHERLANDS - CROPS

NETHERLANDS - BAUXITE PRODUCTION AND CONSUMPTION - See NETHERLANDS - MINING AND MINERAL PRODUCTS

NETHERLANDS - BEER PRODUCTION

Facts on File, 460 Park Avenue South, New York, New York 10016 (800) 443-8323; *The New Book of World Rankings.*

Statistical Office of the United Nations, Publishing Service, New York, New York 10017 (800) 253-9646; *Statistical Yearbook.*

NETHERLANDS - BEVERAGES - PRODUCTION INDEX

Organisation for Economic Co-operation and Development (OECD), 2 rue Andre-Pascal, 75 Paris 16, France (Telephone Number in U.S. (202) 785-6323); *Indicators of Industrial Activity.*

NETHERLANDS - BIRTH RATES

European Community Information Service, 2100 M Street, NW, Washington, D.C. 20037 (202) 862-9500; *Basic Statistics of the Community,* and *Demographic Statistics.*

Facts on File, 460 Park Avenue South, New York, New York 10016 (800) 443-8323; *The New Book of World Rankings.*

Statistical Office of the United Nations, Publishing Service, New York, New York 10017 (800) 253-9646; *Demographic Yearbook,* and *Statistical Yearbook.*

Times Books, 201 East 50th Street, New York, New York 10022 (212) 751-2600; *The Economist Book of Vital World Statistics.*

The World Bank, 1818 H Street, NW, Washington, D.C. 20433 (202) 477-1234; *World Tables.*

World Health Organization, Office of Publications, Avenue Appia, CH-1211 Geneva 27, Switzerland (Telephone Number in U.S. (518) 436-9686); *World Health Statistics Annual.*

NETHERLANDS - BISMUTH PRODUCTION AND CONSUMPTION - See NETHERLANDS - MINING AND MINERAL PRODUCTS

NETHERLANDS - BONDS

European Community Information Service, 2100 M Street, NW, Washington, D.C. 20037 (202) 862-9500; *Basic Statistics of the Community.*

International Monetary Fund, 700 Nineteenth Street, NW, Washington, D.C. 20431 (202) 623-7000; *Government Finance Statistics Yearbook.*

Organisation for Economic Co-operation and Development (OECD), 2 rue Andre-Pascal, 75 Paris 16, France (Telephone Number in U.S. (202) 785-6323); *Financial Market Trends.*

Statistical Office of the United Nations, Publishing Service, New York, New York 10017 (800) 253-9646; *Statistical Yearbook.*

NETHERLANDS - BOOK PRODUCTION

Euromonitor Publications Limited, 87-88 Turnmill Street, London EC1M 5QU, England; *European Marketing Data and Statistics.*

Food and Agricultural Organization of the United Nations (FAO) Via delle Terme di Caracalla, 00100 Rome, Italy (Telephone Number in U.S. (202) 653-2400); *The State of Food and Agriculture.*

United Nations Educational, Scientific and Cultural Organization (UNESCO), 7 Place de Fontenoy, F-75700 Paris, France (Telephone Number in U.S. (212) 963-5981); *Statistical Yearbook.*

NETHERLANDS - BROADCASTING

Billboard Limited, Post Office Box 9027, 1006 AA Amsterdam, The Netherlands (Telephone Number in U.S. (212) 764-7300); *World Radio TV Handbook.*

European Community Information Service, 2100 M Street, NW, Washington, D.C. 20037 (202) 862-9500; *Basic Statistics of the Community.*

Facts on File, 460 Park Avenue South, New York, New York 10016 (800) 443-8323; *The New Book of World Rankings.*

Times Books, 201 East 50th Street, New York, New York 10022 (212) 751-2600; *The Economist Book of Vital World Statistics.*

United Nations Educational, Scientific and Cultural Organization (UNESCO), 7 Place de Fontenoy, F-75700 Paris, France (Telephone Number in U.S. (212) 963-5981); *Statistical Yearbook.*

NETHERLANDS - BUSINESS

European Community Information Service, 2100 M Street, NW, Washington, D.C. 20037 (202) 862-9500; *Basic Statistics of the Community.*

Organisation for Economic Co-operation and Development (OECD), 2 rue Andre-Pascal, 75 Paris 16, France (Telephone Number in U.S. (202) 785-6323); *Main Economic Indicators - Historical Statistics.*

NETHERLANDS - BUTTER - See NETHERLANDS - DAIRY PRODUCTS

NETHERLANDS - CABBAGE PRODUCTION - See NETHERLANDS - CROPS

NETHERLANDS - CADMIUM PRODUCTION AND CONSUMPTION - See NETHERLANDS - MINING AND MINERAL PRODUCTS

NETHERLANDS - CALORIE SUPPLY

Food and Agricultural Organization of the United Nations (FAO) Via delle Terme di Caracalla, 00100 Rome, Italy (Telephone Number in U.S. (202) 653-2400); *The State of Food and Agriculture.*

NETHERLANDS - CAPITAL INVESTMENT

Organisation for Economic Co-operation and Development (OECD), 2 rue Andre-Pascal, 75 Paris 16, France (Telephone Number in U.S. (202) 785-6323); *Economic Outlook,* and *Financial Market Trends.*

NETHERLANDS - CAPITAL REVENUE

International Monetary Fund, 700 Nineteenth Street, NW, Washington, D.C. 20431 (202) 623-7000; *Government Finance Statistics Yearbook.*

Organisation for Economic Co-operation and Development (OECD), 2 rue Andre-Pascal, 75 Paris 16, France (Telephone Number in U.S. (202) 785-6323); *Economic Outlook,* and *Financial Market Trends.*

NETHERLANDS - CASHEW NUT PRODUCTION - See NETHERLANDS - CROPS

NETHERLANDS - CASTOR BEAN PRODUCTION - See NETHERLANDS - CROPS

NETHERLANDS - CATTLE - See NETHERLANDS - LIVESTOCK AND POULTRY

NETHERLANDS - CAULIFLOWER PRODUCTION - See NETHERLANDS - CROPS

NETHERLANDS - CAUSTIC SODA PRODUCTION

European Community Information Service, 2100 M Street, NW, Washington, D.C. 20037 (202) 862-9500; *Basic Statistics of the Community.*

Organisation for Economic Co-operation and Development (OECD), 2 rue Andre-Pascal, 75 Paris 16, France (Telephone Number in U.S. (202) 785-6323); *Indicators of Industrial Activity.*

NETHERLANDS - CEMENT PRODUCTION - See NETHERLANDS - MINING AND MINERAL PRODUCTS

NETHERLANDS - CEREAL PRODUCTION - See NETHERLANDS - CROPS

NETHERLANDS - CHEESE - See NETHERLANDS - DAIRY PRODUCTS

NETHERLANDS - CHEMICAL INDUSTRY

European Community Information Service, 2100 M Street, NW, Washington, D.C. 20037 (202) 862-9500; *Industrial Production: Quarterly Statistics.*

NETHERLANDS - CHEMICAL (ORGANIC) PRODUCTION - See NETHERLANDS - MINING AND MINERAL PRODUCTS

NETHERLANDS - CHESTNUT PRODUCTION - See NETHERLANDS - CROPS

NETHERLANDS - CHICKENS - See NETHERLANDS - LIVESTOCK AND POULTRY

NETHERLANDS - CHROMITE PRODUCTION AND CONSUMPTION - See NETHERLANDS - MINING AND MINERAL PRODUCTS

NETHERLANDS - CHROMIUM ORE PRODUCTION AND CONSUMPTION - See NETHERLANDS - MINING AND MINERAL PRODUCTS

NETHERLANDS - CIGAR PRODUCTION - See NETHERLANDS - TOBACCO PRODUCTION

NETHERLANDS - CIGARETTE PRODUCTION - See NETHERLANDS - TOBACCO PRODUCTION

NETHERLANDS - CLASS STRUCTURE

European Community Information Service, 2100 M Street, NW, Washington, D.C. 20037 (202) 862-9500; *Basic Statistics of the Community*, and *Labor Force Sample Survey*.

NETHERLANDS - CLIMATE

Facts on File, 460 Park Avenue South, New York, New York 10016 (800) 443-8323; *The New Book of World Rankings*.

Netherlands Central Bureau of Statistics, Staatsuitgeverij, The Hague, Netherlands; *Statistical Yearbook of the Netherlands*.

NETHERLANDS - CLOTHING - PRODUCTION INDEX

Organisation for Economic Co-operation and Development (OECD), 2 rue Andre-Pascal, 75 Paris 16, France (Telephone Number in U.S. (202) 785-6323); *Indicators of Industrial Activity*.

NETHERLANDS - CLOTHING EXPORTS AND IMPORTS

European Community Information Service, 2100 M Street, NW, Washington, D.C. 20037 (202) 862-9500; *Basic Statistics of the Community*.

Organisation for Economic Co-operation and Development (OECD), 2 rue Andre-Pascal, 75 Paris 16, France (Telephone Number in U.S. (202) 785-6323); *Textile Industry in OECD Countries*.

Statistical Office of the United Nations, Publishing Service, New York, New York 10017 (800) 253-9646; *Trade in Manufactures of Developing Countries*.

NETHERLANDS - COAL PRODUCTION - See NETHERLANDS - MINING AND MINERAL PRODUCTS

NETHERLANDS - COBALT PRODUCTION AND CONSUMPTION - See NETHERLANDS - MINING AND MINERAL PRODUCTS

NETHERLANDS - COCOA (BEANS) PRODUCTION - See NETHERLANDS - CROPS

NETHERLANDS - COFFEE - See NETHERLANDS - CROPS

NETHERLANDS - COKE AND COKE OVEN COKE PRODUCTION AND CONSUMPTION - See NETHERLANDS - MINING AND MINERAL PRODUCTS

NETHERLANDS - COKE OVEN ORE PRODUCTION AND CONSUMPTION - See NETHERLANDS - MINING AND MINERAL PRODUCTS

NETHERLANDS - COMMERCE EMPLOYMENT - MALE AND FEMALE - See NETHERLANDS - EMPLOYMENT

NETHERLANDS - COMMUNICATION EMPLOYMENT - MALE AND FEMALE - See NETHERLANDS - EMPLOYMENT

NETHERLANDS - COMMUNICATIONS

European Community Information Service, 2100 M Street, NW, Washington, D.C. 20037 (202) 862-9500; *Basic Statistics of the Community*, and *Transport Annual Statistics*.

NETHERLANDS - CONSTRUCTION INDUSTRY

European Community Information Service, 2100 M Street, NW, Washington, D.C. 20037 (202) 862-9500; *Basic Statistics of the Community*.

Facts on File, 460 Park Avenue South, New York, New York 10016 (800) 443-8323; *The New Book of World Rankings*.

Organisation for Economic Co-operation and Development (OECD), 2 rue Andre-Pascal, 75 Paris 16, France (Telephone Number in U.S. (202) 785-6323); *Industrial Structure Statistics, The Iron and Steel Industry, Main Economic Indicators - Historical Statistics*, and *OECD Economic Surveys: Netherlands*.

Statistical Office of the United Nations, Publishing Service, New York, New York 10017 (800) 253-9646; *Statistical Yearbook*.

NETHERLANDS - CONSUMER PRICE INDEX

European Community Information Service, 2100 M Street, NW, Washington, D.C. 20037 (202) 862-9500; *Basic Statistics of the Community*.

Organisation for Economic Co-operation and Development (OECD), 2 rue Andre-Pascal, 75 Paris 16, France (Telephone Number in U.S. (202) 785-6323); *Economic Outlook*.

NETHERLANDS - CONSUMER PRICE INDEX NUMBERS

Statistical Office of the United Nations, Publishing Service, New York, New York 10017 (800) 253-9646; *Statistical Yearbook*.

NETHERLANDS - CONSUMER PRICES

Euromonitor Publications Limited, 87-88 Turnmill Street, London EC1M 5QU, England; *European Marketing Data and Statistics*.

European Community Information Service, 2100 M Street, NW, Washington, D.C. 20037 (202) 862-9500; *Basic Statistics of the Community, Eurostatistics: Data for Short-term Economic Analysis*, and *Money and Finance*.

International Labour Office, I.L.O. Publications, CH-1211, Geneva 22, Switzerland; *Yearbook of Labour Statistics*.

International Monetary Fund, 700 Nineteenth Street, NW, Washington, D.C. 20431 (202) 623-7000; *International Financial Statistics*.

Organisation for Economic Co-operation and Development (OECD), 2 rue Andre-Pascal, 75 Paris 16, France (Telephone Number in U.S. (202) 785-6323); *Economic Outlook*.

Times Books, 201 East 50th Street, New York, New York 10022 (212) 751-2600; *The Economist Book of Vital World Statistics*.

NETHERLANDS - CONSUMPTION

European Community Information Service, 2100 M Street, NW, Washington, D.C. 20037 (202) 862-9500; *Basic Statistics of the Community.*

International Iron and Steel Institute, 120, rue Colonel Bourg, B-1140 Brussels, Belgium; *Steel Statistical Yearbook.*

International Lead and Zinc Study Group, Metro House, 58 St. James's Street, London SW1A 1LD England; *Lead and Zinc Statistics.*

International Rubber Study Group, York House, Eighth Floor, Empire Way, Wembley, London HA9 0PA, England; *Rubber Statistical Bulletin.*

Organisation for Economic Co-operation and Development (OECD), 2 rue Andre-Pascal, 75 Paris 16, France (Telephone Number in U.S. (202) 785-6323); *The Footwear, Raw Hides and Skins, and Leather Industry in OECD Countries, The Iron and Steel Industry, Meat Balances in OECD Member Countries, The Non-Ferrous Metals Industry, The Pulp and Paper Industry,* and *Textile Industry in OECD Countries.*

NETHERLANDS - COPPER AND COPPER ORE PRODUCTION AND CONSUMPTION - See NETHERLANDS - MINING AND MINERAL PRODUCTS

NETHERLANDS - CORN PRODUCTION - See NETHERLANDS - CROPS

NETHERLANDS - CORPORATE INCOME TAXES - See NETHERLANDS - TAXATION

NETHERLANDS - CORPORATE TAXES - See NETHERLANDS - TAXATION

NETHERLANDS - COTTON - See NETHERLANDS - CROPS

NETHERLANDS - CRIME

International Criminal Police Organization (INTERPOL), 26 rue Armengaud, 92210 Saint Cloud, France; *International Crime Statistics.*

Yale University Press, Yale Station, New Haven, Connecticut 06520 (203) 432-0940; *Violence and Crime in Cross-National Perspective.*

NETHERLANDS - CROPS

Commodity Research Bureau, Incorporated, 75 Wall Street, New York, New York 10005 (212) 504-7754; *Commodity Year Book.*

Euromonitor Publications Limited, 87-88 Turnmill Street, London EC1M 5QU, England; *European Marketing Data and Statistics.*

European Community Information Service, 2100 M Street, NW, Washington, D.C. 20037 (202) 862-9500; *ACP: Basic Statistics, Agriculture: Statistical Yearbook, Basic Statistics of the Community, Crop Production: Quarterly Statistics, Eurostatistics: Data for Short-term Economic Analysis,* and *Regions: Statistical Yearbook.*

Facts on File, 460 Park Avenue South, New York, New York 10016 (800) 443-8323; *The New Book of World Rankings.*

Food and Agricultural Organization of the United Nations (FAO), Via delle Terme di Caracalla, 00100 Rome, Italy (Telephone Number in U.S. (202) 653-2400); *Production Yearbook,* and *The State of Food and Agriculture.*

Organisation for Economic Co-operation and Development (OECD), 2 rue Andre-Pascal, 75 Paris 16, France (Telephone Number in U.S. (202) 785-6323); *Economic Accounts for Agriculture, Foreign Trade by Commodities, Milk, Milk Products, and Egg Balances in OECD Member Countries,* and *Textile Industry in OECD Countries.*

Statistical Office of the United Nations, Publishing Service, New York, New York 10017 (800) 253-9646; *Statistical Yearbook.*

NETHERLANDS - CUSTOMS DUTIES

European Community Information Service, 2100 M Street, NW, Washington, D.C. 20037 (202) 862-9500; *Basic Statistics of the Community.*

International Monetary Fund, 700 Nineteenth Street, NW, Washington, D.C. 20431 (202) 623-7000; *Government Finance Statistics Yearbook.*

Organisation for Economic Co-operation and Development (OECD), 2 rue Andre-Pascal, 75 Paris 16, France (Telephone Number in U.S. (202) 785-6323); *The Non-Ferrous Metals Industry.*

NETHERLANDS - DAIRY PRODUCTS

Commodity Research Bureau, Incorporated, 75 Wall Street, New York, New York 10005 (212) 504-7754; *Commodity Year Book.*

European Community Information Service, 2100 M Street, NW, Washington, D.C. 20037 (202) 862-9500; *Basic Statistics of the Community,* and *Eurostatistics: Data for Short-term Economic Analysis.*

Facts on File, 460 Park Avenue South, New York, New York 10016 (800) 443-8323; *The New Book of World Rankings.*

Food and Agricultural Organization of the United Nations (FAO) Via delle Terme di Caracalla, 00100 Rome, Italy (Telephone Number in U.S. (202) 653-2400); *The State of Food and Agriculture.*

Organisation for Economic Co-operation and Development (OECD), 2 rue Andre-Pascal, 75 Paris 16, France (Telephone Number in U.S. (202) 785-6323); *Economic Accounts for Agriculture,* and *Milk, Milk Products, and Egg Balances in OECD Member Countries.*

Statistical Office of the United Nations, Publishing Service, New York, New York 10017 (800) 253-9646; *Statistical Yearbook.*

NETHERLANDS - DEATH RATES

European Community Information Service, 2100 M Street, NW, Washington, D.C. 20037 (202) 862-9500; *Basic Statistics of the Community,* and *Demographic Statistics.*

Statistical Office of the United Nations, Publishing Service, New York, New York 10017 (800) 253-9646; *Statistical Yearbook.*

Times Books, 201 East 50th Street, New York, New York 10022 (212) 751-2600; *The Economist Book of Vital World Statistics.*

World Health Organization, Office of Publications, Avenue Appia, CH-1211 Geneva 27, Switzerland (Telephone Number in U.S. (518) 436-9686); *World Health Statistics Annual.*

NETHERLANDS - DEFENSE EXPENDITURES

European Community Information Service, 2100 M Street, NW, Washington, D.C. 20037 (202) 862-9500; *Government Financing of Research and Development.*

International Monetary Fund, 700 Nineteenth Street, NW, Washington, D.C. 20431 (202) 623-7000; *Government Finance Statistics Yearbook.*

U.S. Arms Control and Disarmament Agency, 320 Twenty-first Street, NW, Washington, D.C. 20451 (202) 647-8677; *World Military Expenditures and Arms Transfers.*

NETHERLANDS - DEMOGRAPHY

The Economist Intelligence Unit, 111 West 57th Street, New York, New York 10019 (800) 938-4685; *The World Market Atlas.*

European Community Information Service, 2100 M Street, NW, Washington, D.C. 20037 (202) 862-9500; *Basic Statistics of the Community, Demographic Statistics, Employment and Unemployment,* and *Regions: Statistical Yearbook.*

Facts on File, 460 Park Avenue South, New York, New York 10016 (800) 443-8323; *The New Book of World Rankings.*

NETHERLANDS - DEVELOPMENT ASSISTANCE

European Community Information Service, 2100 M Street, NW, Washington, D.C. 20037 (202) 862-9500; *ACP: Basic Statistics, Basic Statistics of the Community,* and *Government Financing of Research and Development.*

Organisation for Economic Co-operation and Development (OECD), 2 rue Andre-Pascal, 75 Paris 16, France (Telephone Number in U.S. (202) 785-6323); *Geographical Distribution of Financial Flows to Developing Countries.*

Statistical Office of the United Nations, Publishing Service, New York, New York 10017 (800) 253-9646; *Statistical Yearbook.*

NETHERLANDS - DIAMOND EXPORTS - See NETHERLANDS - MINING AND MINERAL PRODUCTS

NETHERLANDS - DIAMOND PRODUCTION - See NETHERLANDS - MINING AND MINERAL PRODUCTS

NETHERLANDS - DISCOUNT RATES

Organisation for Economic Co-operation and Development (OECD), 2 rue Andre-Pascal, 75 Paris 16, France (Telephone Number in U.S. (202) 785-6323); *Financial Market Trends.*

Statistical Office of the United Nations, Publishing Service, New York, New York 10017 (800) 253-9646; *Statistical Yearbook.*

NETHERLANDS - DISEASE

World Health Organization, Office of Publications, Avenue Appia, CH-1211 Geneva 27, Switzerland (Telephone Number in U.S. (518) 436-9686); *World Health Statistics Annual.*

NETHERLANDS - DIVORCE RATES

European Community Information Service, 2100 M Street, NW, Washington, D.C. 20037 (202) 862-9500; *Demographic Statistics,* and *Eurostat Review.*

Facts on File, 460 Park Avenue South, New York, New York 10016 (800) 443-8323; *The New Book of World Rankings.*

Statistical Office of the United Nations, Publishing Service, New York, New York 10017 (800) 253-9646; *Demographic Yearbook,* and *Statistical Yearbook.*

NETHERLANDS - DOMESTIC PRODUCT

European Community Information Service, 2100 M Street, NW, Washington, D.C. 20037 (202) 862-9500; *Basic Statistics of the Community.*

NETHERLANDS - DUCKS - See NETHERLANDS - LIVESTOCK AND POULTRY

NETHERLANDS - ECONOMY

Euromonitor Publications Limited, 87-88 Turnmill Street, London EC1M 5QU, England; *European Marketing Data and Statistics.*

European Community Information Service, 2100 M Street, NW, Washington, D.C. 20037 (202) 862-9500; *ACP: Basic Statistics, Basic Statistics of the Community, Energy Statistics Yearbook, Labor Force Sample Survey,* and *Money and Finance.*

Facts on File, 460 Park Avenue South, New York, New York 10016 (800) 443-8323; *The New Book of World Rankings.*

Organisation for Economic Co-operation and Development (OECD), 2 rue Andre-Pascal, 75 Paris 16, France (Telephone Number in U.S. (202) 785-6323); *Economic Outlook, Geographical Distribution of Financial Flows to Developing Countries, OECD Economic Surveys: Netherlands,* and *OECD Employment Outlook.*

NETHERLANDS - EDUCATION

The Economist Intelligence Unit, 111 West 57th Street, New York, New York 10019 (800) 938-4685; *The World Market Atlas.*

Euromonitor Publications Limited, 87-88 Turnmill Street, London EC1M 5QU, England; *European Marketing Data and Statistics.*

European Community Information Service, 2100 M Street, NW, Washington, D.C. 20037 (202) 862-9500; *Basic Statistics of the Community,* and *Regions: Statistical Yearbook.*

Facts on File, 460 Park Avenue South, New York, New York 10016 (800) 443-8323; *The New Book of World Rankings.*

International Monetary Fund, 700 Nineteenth Street, NW, Washington, D.C. 20431 (202) 623-7000; *Government Finance Statistics Yearbook.*

Netherlands Central Bureau of Statistics, Staatsuitgeverij, The Hague, Netherlands; *Statistical Yearbook of the Netherlands.*

Organisation for Economic Co-operation and Development (OECD), 2 rue Andre-Pascal, 75 Paris 16, France (Telephone Number in U.S. (202) 785-6323); *Education in OECD Countries.*

Times Books, 201 East 50th Street, New York, New York 10022 (212) 751-2600; *The Economist Book of Vital World Statistics.*

United Nations Educational, Scientific and Cultural Organization (UNESCO), 7 Place de Fontenoy, F-75700 Paris, France (Telephone Number in U.S. (212) 963-5981); *Statistical Yearbook.*

The World Bank, 1818 H Street, NW, Washington, D.C. 20433 (202) 477-1234; *World Tables.*

NETHERLANDS - EGG PRODUCTION AND CONSUMPTION - See NETHERLANDS - DAIRY PRODUCTS

NETHERLANDS - ELECTRICITY

European Community Information Service, 2100 M Street, NW, Washington, D.C. 20037 (202) 862-9500; *Basic Statistics of the Community Energy: Monthly Statistics, Energy Statistics Yearbook, Eurostatistics: Data for Short-term Economic Analysis,* and *Regions: Statistical Yearbook.*

Facts on File, 460 Park Avenue South, New York, New York 10016 (800) 443-8323; *The New Book of World Rankings.*

Organisation for Economic Co-operation and Development (OECD), 2 rue Andre-Pascal, 75 Paris 16, France (Telephone Number in U.S. (202) 785-6323); *Coal Information, Energy Statistics of OECD Countries, Indicators of Industrial Activity, Industrial Structure Statistics,* and *Regions: Statistical Yearbook.*

Penn Well Publishing Company, 1421 South Sheridan Road, Post Office Box 1260, Tulsa, Oklahoma 74101 (800) 752-9764; *International Energy Statistics Sourcebook.*

Statistical Office of the United Nations, Publishing Service, New York, New York 10017 (800) 253-9646; *Statistical Yearbook.*

Times Books, 201 East 50th Street, New York, New York 10022 (212) 751-2600; *The Economist Book of Vital World Statistics.*

NETHERLANDS - EMPLOYMENT

Euromonitor Publications Limited, 87-88 Turnmill Street, London EC1M 5QU, England; *European Marketing Data and Statistics.*

European Community Information Service, 2100 M Street, NW, Washington, D.C. 20037 (202) 862-9500; *Basic Statistics of the Community, Earnings in Agriculture, Employment and Unemployment, Eurostatistics: Data for Short-term Economic Analysis, Iron and Steel: Statistical Yearbook, Labor Force Sample Survey,* and *Transport Annual Statistics.*

Facts on File, 460 Park Avenue South, New York, New York 10016 (800) 443-8323; *The New Book of World Rankings.*

International Labour Office, I.L.O. Publications, CH-1211, Geneva 22, Switzerland; *Yearbook of Labour Statistics.*

Organisation for Economic Co-operation and Development (OECD), 2 rue Andre-Pascal, 75 Paris 16, France (Telephone Number in U.S. (202) 785-6323); *Economic Outlook, The Iron and Steel Industry, OECD Economic Surveys: Netherlands, OECD Employment Outlook,* and *Textile Industry in OECD Countries.*

Statistical Office of the United Nations, Publishing Service, New York, New York 10017 (800) 253-9646; *Statistical Yearbook.*

NETHERLANDS - ENERGY

Euromonitor Publications Limited, 87-88 Turnmill Street, London EC1M 5QU, England; *European Marketing Data and Statistics.*

European Community Information Service, 2100 M Street, NW, Washington, D.C. 20037 (202) 862-9500; *Basic Statistics of the Community, Energy: Monthly Statistics, Energy Statistics Yearbook,* and *Transport Annual Statistics.*

Facts on File, 460 Park Avenue South, New York, New York 10016 (800) 443-8323; *The New Book of World Rankings.*

Food and Agricultural Organization of the United Nations (FAO) Via delle Terme di Caracalla, 00100 Rome, Italy (Telephone Number in

U.S. (202) 653-2400); *The State of Food and Agriculture.*

Organisation for Economic Co-operation and Development (OECD), 2 rue Andre-Pascal, 75 Paris 16, France (Telephone Number in U.S. (202) 785-6323); *Coal Information, Energy Statistics for OECD Countries, OECD Environmental Data,* and *Oil and Gas Information.*

Penn Well Publishing Company, 1421 South Sheridan Road, Post Office Box 1260, Tulsa, Oklahoma 74101 (800) 752-9764; *International Energy Statistics Sourcebook.*

Statistical Office of the United Nations, Publishing Service, New York, New York 10017 (800) 253-9646; *Energy Statistics Yearbook, Statistical Yearbook,* and *World Energy Supplies.*

Times Books, 201 East 50th Street, New York, New York 10022 (212) 751-2600; *The Economist Book of Vital World Statistics.*

NETHERLANDS - ENGINEERING AND METAL PRODUCTS - EXPORTS AND IMPORTS

European Community Information Service, 2100 M Street, NW, Washington, D.C. 20037 (202) 862-9500; *Basic Statistics of the Community, Energy: Monthly Statistics,* and *Industrial Production: Quarterly Statistics.*

Statistical Office of the United Nations, Publishing Service, New York, New York 10017 (800) 253-9646; *Trade in Manufactures of Developing Countries.*

NETHERLANDS - ENVIRONMENT

Organisation for Economic Co-operation and Development (OECD), 2 rue Andre-Pascal, 75 Paris 16, France (Telephone Number in U.S. (202) 785-6323); *OECD Environmental Data.*

NETHERLANDS - EXCHANGE RATES

European Community Information Service, 2100 M Street, NW, Washington, D.C. 20037 (202) 862-9500; *Eurostatistics: Data for Short-term Economic Analysis,* and *Money and Finance.*

International Civil Aviation Organization, 1000 Sherbrooke Street, West, Montreal, Quebec, Canada H3A 2R2 (514) 285-8219; *Civil Aviation Statistics of the World.*

International Monetary Fund, 700 Nineteenth Street, NW, Washington, D.C. 20431 (202) 623-7000; *International Financial Statistics.*

Organisation for Economic Co-operation and Development (OECD), 2 rue Andre-Pascal, 75 Paris 16, France (Telephone Number in U.S. (202) 785-6323); *Economic Outlook, Financial Market Trends, Revenue Statistics of OECD Member Countries,* and *Tourism Policy and International Tourism in OECD Member Countries.*

Statistical Office of the United Nations, Publishing Service, New York, New York 10017 (800) 253-9646; *Statistical Yearbook.*

NETHERLANDS - EXCISE TAXES - See NETHERLANDS - TAXATION

NETHERLANDS - EXPORTS

American Automobile Manufacturers Association, 1401 H Eye Street, NW, Suite 900, Washington, D.C. 20005 (202) 326-5500; *World Motor Vehicle Data.*

The Economist Intelligence Unit, 111 West 57th Street, New York, New York 10019 (800) 938-4685; *The World Market Atlas.*

European Community Information Service, 2100 M Street, NW, Washington, D.C. 20037 (202) 862-9500; *Basic Statistics of the Community, Energy Statistics Yearbook, Eurostatistics: Data for Short-term Economic Analysis, External Trade: Statistical Yearbook, External Trade: Monthly Statistics,* and *Fisheries: Yearly Statistics.*

Food and Agricultural Organization of the United Nations (FAO) Via delle Terme di Caracalla, 00100 Rome, Italy (Telephone Number in U.S. (202) 653-2400); *The State of Food and Agriculture.*

International Iron and Steel Institute, 120, rue Colonel Bourg, B-1140 Brussels, Belgium; *Steel Statistical Yearbook.*

International Lead and Zinc Study Group, Metro House, 58 St. James's Street, London SW1A 1LD England; *Lead and Zinc Statistics.*

International Monetary Fund, 700 Nineteenth Street, NW, Washington, D.C. 20431 (202) 623-7000; *Direction of Trade Statistics,* and *International Financial Statistics.*

International Rubber Study Group, York House, Eighth Floor, Empire Way, Wembley, London HA9 0PA, England; *Rubber Statistical Bulletin.*

Organisation for Economic Co-operation and Development (OECD), 2 rue Andre-Pascal, 75 Paris 16, France (Telephone Number in U.S. (202) 785-6323); *Economic Outlook, The Footwear, Raw Hides and Skins, and Leather Industry in OECD Countries, Foreign Trade by Commodities, Geographical Distribution of Financial Flows to Developing Countries, Industrial Structure Statistics, The Iron and Steel Industry, Milk, Milk Products, and Egg Balances in OECD Member Countries, OECD Economic Surveys: Netherlands, The Pulp and Paper Industry,* and *Review of Fisheries in OECD Member Countries.*

Times Books, 201 East 50th Street, New York, New York 10022 (212) 751-2600; *The Economist Book of Vital World Statistics.*

The World Bank, 1818 H Street, NW, Washington, D.C. 20433 (202) 477-1234; *World Tables.*

NETHERLANDS - EXTERNAL FINANCING

Organisation for Economic Co-operation and Development (OECD), 2 rue Andre-Pascal, 75 Paris 16, France (Telephone Number in U.S. (202) 785-6323); *Economic Outlook,* and *Financial Market Trends.*

NETHERLANDS - EXTERNAL INDEBTEDNESS

Organisation for Economic Co-operation and Development (OECD), 2 rue Andre-Pascal, 75 Paris 16, France (Telephone Number in U.S. (202) 785-6323); *Financial Market Trends,* and *Geographical Distribution of Financial Flows to Developing Countries.*

The World Bank, 1818 H Street, NW, Washington, D.C. 20433 (202) 477-1234; *World Tables.*

NETHERLANDS - EXTERNAL TRADE

European Community Information Service, 2100 M Street, NW, Washington, D.C. 20037 (202) 862-9500; *ACP: Basic Statistics, Basic Statistics of the Community, Eurostatistics: Data for Short-term Economic Analysis, External Trade: Statistical Yearbook,* and *External Trade: Monthly Statistics.*

Food and Agricultural Organization of the United Nations (FAO) Via delle Terme di Caracalla, 00100 Rome, Italy (Telephone Number in U.S. (202) 653-2400); *The State of Food and Agriculture,* and *Trade Yearbook.*

Statistical Office of the United Nations, Publishing Service, New York, New York 10017 (800) 253-9646; *Statistical Yearbook.*

NETHERLANDS - FABRIC PRODUCTION - See NETHERLANDS - TEXTILE INDUSTRY

NETHERLANDS - FARM CROPS - See NETHERLANDS - CROPS

NETHERLANDS - FEMALE WORKING POPULATION - See NETHERLANDS - EMPLOYMENT

NETHERLANDS - FERTILITY RATES

European Community Information Service, 2100 M Street, NW, Washington, D.C. 20037 (202) 862-9500; *Demographic Statistics.*

Facts on File, 460 Park Avenue South, New York, New York 10016 (800) 443-8323; *The New Book of World Rankings.*

Times Books, 201 East 50th Street, New York, New York 10022 (212) 751-2600; *The Economist Book of Vital World Statistics.*

The World Bank, 1818 H Street, NW, Washington, D.C. 20433 (202) 477-1234; *World Tables.*

NETHERLANDS - FERTILIZER

European Community Information Service, 2100 M Street, NW, Washington, D.C. 20037 (202) 862-9500; *Basic Statistics of the Community.*

Food and Agricultural Organization of the United Nations (FAO), Via delle Terme di Caracalla, 00100 Rome, Italy (Telephone Number in U.S. (202) 653-2400); *Fertilizer Yearbook,* and *The State of Food and Agriculture.*

Organisation for Economic Co-operation and Development (OECD), 2 rue Andre-Pascal, 75 Paris 16, France (Telephone Number in U.S. (202) 785-6323); *Economic Accounts for Agriculture,* and *Foreign Trade by Commodities.*

Statistical Office of the United Nations, Publishing Service, New York, New York 10017 (800) 253-9646; *Statistical Yearbook.*

NETHERLANDS - FETAL MORTALITY

European Community Information Service, 2100 M Street, NW, Washington, D.C. 20037 (202) 862-9500; *Basic Statistics of the Community,* and *Demographic Statistics.*

Statistical Office of the United Nations, Publishing Service, New York, New York 10017 (800) 253-9646; *Demographic Yearbook.*

World Health Organization, Office of Publications, Avenue Appia, CH-1211 Geneva 27, Switzerland (Telephone Number in U.S. (518) 436-9686); *World Health Statistics Annual.*

NETHERLANDS - FIBRE PRODUCTION - See NETHERLANDS - TEXTILE INDUSTRY

NETHERLANDS - FILAMENT PRODUCTION - See NETHERLANDS - TEXTILE INDUSTRY

NETHERLANDS - FILMS - See NETHERLANDS - MOTION PICTURES

NETHERLANDS - FINANCE

European Community Information Service, 2100 M Street, NW, Washington, D.C. 20037 (202) 862-9500; *ACP: Basic Statistics*, and *Basic Statistics of the Community, Eurostatistics: Data for Short-term Economic Analysis*, and *Money and Finance*.

Facts on File, 460 Park Avenue South, New York, New York 10016 (800) 443-8323; *The New Book of World Rankings*.

International Monetary Fund, 700 Nineteenth Street, NW, Washington, D.C. 20431 (202) 623-7000; *Government Finance Statistics Yearbook*, and *International Financial Statistics*.

Netherlands Central Bureau of Statistics, Staatsuitgeverij, The Hague, Netherlands; *Statistical Yearbook of the Netherlands*.

Organisation for Economic Co-operation and Development (OECD), 2 rue Andre-Pascal, 75 Paris 16, France (Telephone Number in U.S. (202) 785-6323); *Economic Outlook, Financial Market Trends, Geographical Distribution of Financial Flows to Developing Countries*, and *OECD Financial Statistics*.

NETHERLANDS - FISHERIES

Euromonitor Publications Limited, 87-88 Turnmill Street, London EC1M 5QU, England; *European Marketing Data and Statistics*.

European Community Information Service, 2100 M Street, NW, Washington, D.C. 20037 (202) 862-9500; *Agriculture: Statistical Yearbook*, and *Fisheries: Yearly Statistics*.

Facts on File, 460 Park Avenue South, New York, New York 10016 (800) 443-8323; *The New Book of World Rankings*.

Food and Agricultural Organization of the United Nations (FAO) Via delle Terme di Caracalla, 00100 Rome, Italy (Telephone Number in U.S. (202) 653-2400); *The State of Food and Agriculture*.

Netherlands Central Bureau of Statistics, Staatsuitgeverij, The Hague, Netherlands; *Statistical Yearbook of the Netherlands*.

Organisation for Economic Co-operation and Development (OECD), 2 rue Andre-Pascal, 75 Paris 16, France (Telephone Number in U.S. (202) 785-6323); *Foreign Trade by Commodities, Industrial Structure Statistics*, and *Review of Fisheries in OECD Member Countries*.

Statistical Office of the United Nations, Publishing Service, New York, New York 10017 (800) 253-9646; *Statistical Yearbook*.

NETHERLANDS - FLAX AND FLAX FIBRE PRODUCTION - See NETHERLANDS - TEXTILE INDUSTRY

NETHERLANDS - FLOUR PRODUCTION

European Community Information Service, 2100 M Street, NW, Washington, D.C. 20037 (202) 862-9500; *Basic Statistics of the Community*.

Statistical Office of the United Nations, Publishing Service, New York, New York 10017 (800) 253-9646; *Statistical Yearbook*.

NETHERLANDS - FOOD

European Community Information Service, 2100 M Street, NW, Washington, D.C. 20037 (202) 862-9500; *Basic Statistics of the Community*.

Food and Agricultural Organization of the United Nations (FAO), Via delle Terme di Caracalla, 00100 Rome, Italy (Telephone Number in U.S. (202) 653-2400); *Production Yearbook*, and *The State of Food and Agriculture*.

Organisation for Economic Co-operation and Development (OECD), 2 rue Andre-Pascal, 75 Paris 16, France (Telephone Number in U.S. (202) 785-6323); *Food Consumption Statistics*, and *Foreign Trade by Commodities*.

Statistical Office of the United Nations, Publishing Service, New York, New York 10017 (800) 253-9646; *Trade in Manufactures of Developing Countries*.

NETHERLANDS - FOOTWEAR - PRODUCTION INDEX

Organisation for Economic Co-operation and Development (OECD), 2 rue Andre-Pascal, 75 Paris 16, France (Telephone Number in U.S. (202) 785-6323); *Indicators of Industrial Activity*.

NETHERLANDS - FOREIGN DEBT

International Monetary Fund, 700 Nineteenth Street, NW, Washington, D.C. 20431 (202) 623-7000; *Government Finance Statistics Yearbook*.

Organisation for Economic Co-operation and Development (OECD), 2 rue Andre-Pascal, 75 Paris 16, France (Telephone Number in U.S. (202) 785-6323); *Economic Outlook*.

NETHERLANDS - FOREIGN FINANCE

Organisation for Economic Co-operation and Development (OECD), 2 rue Andre-Pascal, 75 Paris 16, France (Telephone Number in U.S. (202) 785-6323); *Economic Outlook, Financial Market Trends*, and *Main Economic Indicators - Historical Statistics*.

NETHERLANDS - FOREIGN INDEBTEDNESS

Organisation for Economic Co-operation and Development (OECD), 2 rue Andre-Pascal, 75 Paris 16, France (Telephone Number in U.S. (202) 785-6323); *Economic Outlook*, and *Financial Market Trends*.

NETHERLANDS - FOREIGN OFFICIAL RESERVES

European Community Information Service, 2100 M Street, NW, Washington, D.C. 20037 (202) 862-9500; *Money and Finance*.

NETHERLANDS - FOREIGN TRADE

Euromonitor Publications Limited, 87-88 Turnmill Street, London EC1M 5QU, England; *European Marketing Data and Statistics*.

European Community Information Service, 2100 M Street, NW, Washington, D.C. 20037 (202) 862-9500; *Basic Statistics of the Community, Energy Statistics Yearbook*, and *Iron and Steel: Statistical Yearbook*.

Facts on File, 460 Park Avenue South, New York, New York 10016 (800) 443-8323; *The New Book of World Rankings*.

Food and Agricultural Organization of the United Nations (FAO) Via delle Terme di Caracalla, 00100 Rome, Italy (Telephone Number in U.S. (202) 653-2400); *The State of Food and Agriculture*.

International Iron and Steel Institute, 120, rue Colonel Bourg, B-1140 Brussels, Belgium; *Steel Statistical Yearbook*.

Netherlands Central Bureau of Statistics, Staatsuitgeverij, The Hague, Netherlands; *Statistical Yearbook of the Netherlands*.

Organisation for Economic Co-operation and Development (OECD), 2 rue Andre-Pascal, 75 Paris 16, France (Telephone Number in U.S. (202) 785-6323); *Economic Outlook, The Footwear, Raw Hides and Skins, and Leather Industry in OECD Countries, Foreign Trade by Commodities, Main Economic Indicators - Historical Statistics, Maritime Transport, Meat Balances in OECD Member Countries*, and *OECD Economic Surveys: Netherlands*.

Statistical Office of the United Nations, Publishing Service, New York, New York 10017 (800) 253-9646; *International Trade Statistics Yearbook, Statistical Yearbook*, and *Trade in Manufactures of Developing Countries*.

The World Bank, 1818 H Street, NW, Washington, D.C. 20433 (202) 477-1234; *World Tables*.

World Bureau of Metal Statistics, 27-A High Street, Ware, Herts. SG12 9BA, England; *World Metal Statistics*.

NETHERLANDS - FORESTRY AND FOREST PRODUCTS

American Forest and Paper Association, 1250 Connecticut Avenue, NW, Washington, D.C. 20036 (202) 463-2455; *Wood Pulp and Fiber Statistics*.

Euromonitor Publications Limited, 87 80 Turnmill Street, London EC1M 5QU, England; *European Marketing Data and Statistics*.

European Community Information Service, 2100 M Street, NW, Washington, D.C. 20037 (202) 862-9500; *Agriculture: Statistical Yearbook, Basic Statistics of the Community*, and *Industrial Production: Quarterly Statistics*.

Facts on File, 460 Park Avenue South, New York, New York 10016 (800) 443-8323; *The New Book of World Rankings*.

Food and Agricultural Organization of the United Nations (FAO) Via delle Terme di Caracalla, 00100 Rome, Italy (Telephone Number in U.S. (202) 653-2400); *The State of Food and Agriculture*, and *Yearbook of Forest Products*.

Organisation for Economic Co-operation and Development (OECD), 2 rue Andre-Pascal, 75 Paris 16, France (Telephone Number in U.S. (202) 785-6323); *Foreign Trade by Commodities, Indicators of Industrial Activity, Industrial Structure Statistics*, and *The Pulp and Paper Industry*.

Statistical Office of the United Nations, Publishing Service, New York, New York 10017 (800) 253-9646; *Statistical Yearbook*.

United Nations Educational, Scientific and Cultural Organization (UNESCO), 7 Place de Fontenoy, F-75700 Paris, France (Telephone Number in U.S. (212) 963-5981); *Statistical Yearbook*.

NETHERLANDS - FRUIT PRODUCTION

European Community Information Service, 2100 M Street, NW, Washington, D.C. 20037 (202) 862-9500; *Basic Statistics of the Community*.

Organisation for Economic Co-operation and Development (OECD), 2 rue Andre-Pascal, 75 Paris 16, France (Telephone Number in U.S. (202) 785-6323); *Economic Accounts for Agriculture*, and *Foreign Trade by Commodities*.

NETHERLANDS - FURNITURE AND WOOD PRODUCTS - EXPORTS AND IMPORTS

European Community Information Service, 2100 M Street, NW, Washington, D.C. 20037 (202) 862-9500; *Basic Statistics of the Community*.

Organisation for Economic Co-operation and Development (OECD), 2 rue Andre-Pascal, 75 Paris 16, France (Telephone Number in U.S. (202) 785-6323); *Foreign Trade by Commodities*, and *Industrial Structure Statistics*.

Statistical Office of the United Nations, Publishing Service, New York, New York 10017 (800) 253-9646; *Trade in Manufactures of Developing Countries*.

NETHERLANDS - GARLIC PRODUCTION - See NETHERLANDS - CROPS

NETHERLANDS - GAS - See NETHERLANDS - MINING AND MINERAL PRODUCTS

NETHERLANDS - GENERAL INDUSTRIAL STATISTICS

European Community Information Service, 2100 M Street, NW, Washington, D.C. 20037 (202) 862-9500; *Basic Statistics of the Community*.

Statistical Office of the United Nations, Publishing Service, New York, New York 10017 (800) 253-9646; *Industrial Statistics Yearbook*.

NETHERLANDS - GENERAL MORTALITY

European Community Information Service, 2100 M Street, NW, Washington, D.C. 20037 (202) 862-9500; *Basic Statistics of the Community*, and *Demographic Statistics*.

Statistical Office of the United Nations, Publishing Service, New York, New York 10017 (800) 253-9646; *Demographic Yearbook*.

World Health Organization, Office of Publications, Avenue Appia, CH-1211 Geneva 27, Switzerland (Telephone Number in U.S. (518) 436-9686); *World Health Statistics Annual*.

NETHERLANDS - GEOGRAPHIC DATA

European Community Information Service, 2100 M Street, NW, Washington, D.C. 20037 (202) 862-9500; *Basic Statistics of the Community*.

Facts on File, 460 Park Avenue South, New York, New York 10016 (800) 443-8323; *The New Book of World Rankings*.

NETHERLANDS - GLASS AND GLASS PRODUCTS - PRODUCTION INDEX - See NETHERLANDS - MINING AND MINERAL PRODUCTS

NETHERLANDS - GOATS - See NETHERLANDS - LIVESTOCK AND POULTRY

NETHERLANDS - GOLD HOLDINGS

International Monetary Fund, 700 Nineteenth Street, NW, Washington, D.C. 20431 (202) 623-7000; *International Financial Statistics*.

Statistical Office of the United Nations, Publishing Service, New York, New York 10017 (800) 253-9646; *Statistical Yearbook*.

The World Bank, 1818 H Street, NW, Washington, D.C. 20433 (202) 477-1234; *World Tables.*

NETHERLANDS - GOLD PRODUCTION AND CONSUMPTION - See NETHERLANDS - MINING AND MINERAL PRODUCTS

NETHERLANDS - GOVERNMENT

European Community Information Service, 2100 M Street, NW, Washington, D.C. 20037 (202) 862-9500; *Basic Statistics of the Community.*

NETHERLANDS - GOVERNMENT CONSUMPTION

European Community Information Service, 2100 M Street, NW, Washington, D.C. 20037 (202) 862-9500; *Basic Statistics of the Community.*

NETHERLANDS - GOVERNMENT EXPENDITURES

European Community Information Service, 2100 M Street, NW, Washington, D.C. 20037 (202) 862-9500; *Basic Statistics of the Community,* and *Government Financing of Research and Development.*

International Monetary Fund, 700 Nineteenth Street, NW, Washington, D.C. 20431 (202) 623-7000; *Government Finance Statistics Yearbook.*

Organisation for Economic Co-operation and Development (OECD), 2 rue Andre-Pascal, 75 Paris 16, France (Telephone Number in U.S. (202) 785-6323); *Economic Outlook.*

Times Books, 201 East 50th Street, New York, New York 10022 (212) 751-2600; *The Economist Book of Vital World Statistics.*

The World Bank, 1818 H Street, NW, Washington, D.C. 20433 (202) 477-1234; *World Tables.*

NETHERLANDS - GOVERNMENT FINANCES

European Community Information Service, 2100 M Street, NW, Washington, D.C. 20037 (202) 862-9500; *Basic Statistics of the Community, Government Financing of Research and Development,* and *Money and Finance.*

International Monetary Fund, 700 Nineteenth Street, NW, Washington, D.C. 20431 (202) 623-7000; *International Financial Statistics.*

Organisation for Economic Co-operation and Development (OECD), 2 rue Andre-Pascal, 75 Paris 16, France (Telephone Number in U.S. (202) 785-6323); *Economic Outlook.*

Statistical Office of the United Nations, Publishing Service, New York, New York 10017 (800) 253-9646; *Statistical Yearbook.*

NETHERLANDS - GOVERNMENT REVENUES

European Community Information Service, 2100 M Street, NW, Washington, D.C. 20037 (202) 862-9500; *Basic Statistics of the Community,* and *Government Financing of Research and Development.*

International Monetary Fund, 700 Nineteenth Street, NW, Washington, D.C. 20431 (202) 623-7000; *Government Finance Statistics Yearbook.*

Organisation for Economic Co-operation and Development (OECD), 2 rue Andre-Pascal, 75 Paris 16, France (Telephone Number in U.S. (202) 785-6323); *Economic Outlook,* and *Revenue Statistics of OECD Member Countries.*

Times Books, 201 East 50th Street, New York, New York 10022 (212) 751-2600; *The Economist Book of Vital World Statistics.*

The World Bank, 1818 H Street, NW, Washington, D.C. 20433 (202) 477-1234; *World Tables.*

NETHERLANDS - GRAIN PRODUCTION

European Community Information Service, 2100 M Street, NW, Washington, D.C. 20037 (202) 862-9500; *Basic Statistics of the Community.*

Food and Agricultural Organization of the United Nations (FAO) Via delle Terme di Caracalla, 00100 Rome, Italy (Telephone Number in U.S. (202) 653-2400); *The State of Food and Agriculture.*

Organisation for Economic Co-operation and Development (OECD), 2 rue Andre-Pascal, 75 Paris 16, France (Telephone Number in U.S. (202) 785-6323); *Economic Accounts for Agriculture.*

NETHERLANDS - GRANTS

International Monetary Fund, 700 Nineteenth Street, NW, Washington, D.C. 20431 (202) 623-7000; *Government Finance Statistics Yearbook.*

Organisation for Economic Co-operation and Development (OECD), 2 rue Andre-Pascal, 75 Paris 16, France (Telephone Number in U.S. (202) 785-6323); *Geographical Distribution of Financial Flows to Developing Countries.*

NETHERLANDS - GREEN PEPPER AND CHILIE PRODUCTION - See NETHERLANDS - CROPS

NETHERLANDS - GROSS DOMESTIC PRODUCT

The Economist Intelligence Unit, 111 West 57th Street, New York, New York 10019 (800) 938-4685; *The World Market Atlas.*

European Community Information Service, 2100 M Street, NW, Washington, D.C. 20037 (202) 862-9500; *Basic Statistics of the Community, Eurostatistics: Data for Short-term Economic Analysis, Government Financing of Research and Development, Iron and Steel: Statistical Yearbook,* and *Money and Finance.*

Facts on File, 460 Park Avenue South, New York, New York 10016 (800) 443-8323; *The New Book of World Rankings.*

Organisation for Economic Co-operation and Development (OECD), 2 rue Andre-Pascal, 75 Paris 16, France (Telephone Number in U.S. (202) 785-6323); *Economic Outlook, Geographical Distribution of Financial Flows to Developing Countries,* and *Revenue Statistics of OECD Member Countries.*

Statistical Office of the United Nations, Publishing Service, New York, New York 10017 (800) 253-9646; *Statistical Yearbook.*

Times Books, 201 East 50th Street, New York, New York 10022 (212) 751-2600; *The Economist Book of Vital World Statistics.*

The World Bank, 1818 H Street, NW, Washington, D.C. 20433 (202) 477-1234; *World Tables.*

NETHERLANDS - GROSS INDUSTRIAL PRODUCT   -

European Community Information Service, 2100 M Street, NW, Washington, D.C. 20037 (202) 862-9500; *Government Financing of Research and Development*.

NETHERLANDS - GROSS NATIONAL PRODUCT

European Community Information Service, 2100 M Street, NW, Washington, D.C. 20037 (202) 862-9500; *ACP: Basic Statistics*, and *Basic Statistics of the Community*.

Organisation for Economic Co-operation and Development (OECD), 2 rue Andre-Pascal, 75 Paris 16, France (Telephone Number in U.S. (202) 785-6323); *Economic Outlook*, and *Geographical Distribution of Financial Flows to Developing Countries*.

U.S. Arms Control and Disarmament Agency, 320 Twenty-first Street, NW, Washington, D.C. 20451 (202) 647-8677; *World Military Expenditures and Arms Transfers*.

The World Bank, 1818 H Street, NW, Washington, D.C. 20433 (202) 477-1234; *World Tables*.

NETHERLANDS - GROUNDNUT PRODUCTION - See NETHERLANDS - CROPS

NETHERLANDS - HAY PRODUCTION - See NETHERLANDS - CROPS

NETHERLANDS - HAZELNUT PRODUCTION - See NETHERLANDS - CROPS

NETHERLANDS - HEALTH

European Community Information Service, 2100 M Street, NW, Washington, D.C. 20037 (202) 862-9500; *Basic Statistics of the Community*, and *Regions: Statistical Yearbook*.

Facts on File, 460 Park Avenue South, New York, New York 10016 (800) 443-8023; *The New Book of World Rankings*.

Netherlands Central Bureau of Statistics, Staatsuitgeverij, The Hague, Netherlands; *Statistical Yearbook of the Netherlands*.

Organisation for Economic Co-operation and Development (OECD), 2 rue Andre-Pascal, 75 Paris 16, France (Telephone Number in the U.S. (785-6323); *OECD Health Systems: Facts and Trends*.

Statistical Office of the United Nations, Publishing Service, New York, New York 10017 (800) 253-9646; *Statistical Yearbook*.

Times Books, 201 East 50th Street, New York, New York 10022 (212) 751-2600; *The Economist Book of Vital World Statistics*.

World Health Organization, Office of Publications, Avenue Appia, CH-1211 Geneva 27, Switzerland (Telephone Number in U.S. (518) 436-9686); *World Health Statistics Annual*.

NETHERLANDS - HEALTH EXPENDITURES

International Monetary Fund, 700 Nineteenth Street, NW, Washington, D.C. 20431 (202) 623-7000; *Government Finance Statistics Yearbook*.

NETHERLANDS - HEMP FIBRE PRODUCTION - See NETHERLANDS - TEXTILE INDUSTRY

NETHERLANDS - HIDE PRODUCTION

Food and Agricultural Organization of the United Nations (FAO), Via delle Terme di Caracalla, 00100 Rome, Italy (Telephone Number in U.S. (202) 653-2400); *Production Yearbook*.

Organisation for Economic Co-operation and Development (OECD), 2 rue Andre-Pascal, 75 Paris 16, France (Telephone Number in U.S. (202) 785-6323); *The Footwear, Raw Hides and Skins, and Leather Industry in OECD Countries, Foreign Trade by Commodities*, and *Indicators of Industrial Activity*.

NETHERLANDS - HIGHWAYS

European Community Information Service, 2100 M Street, NW, Washington, D.C. 20037 (202) 862-9500; *Basic Statistics of the Community*, and *Transport Annual Statistics*.

International Road Federation, 525 School Street, SW, Washington, D.C. 20024 (202) 554-2106; *World Road Statistics*.

Statistical Office of the United Nations, Publishing Service, New York, New York 10017 (800) 253-9646; *Annual Bulletin of Transport Statistics for Europe*.

NETHERLANDS - HOME FINANCE

Organisation for Economic Co-operation and Development (OECD), 2 rue Andre-Pascal, 75 Paris 16, France (Telephone Number in U.S. (202) 785-6323); *Main Economic Indicators - Historical Statistics*.

NETHERLANDS - HOPS PRODUCTION - See NETHERLANDS - CROPS

NETHERLANDS - HORSES - See NETHERLANDS - LIVESTOCK AND POULTRY

NETHERLANDS - HOURS OF WORK - See NETHERLANDS - EMPLOYMENT

NETHERLANDS - HOUSING AND HOUSING UNITS

European Community Information Service, 2100 M Street, NW, Washington, D.C. 20037 (202) 862-9500; *Basic Statistics of the Community, Labor Force Sample Survey*, and *Regions: Statistical Yearbook*.

Facts on File, 460 Park Avenue South, New York, New York 10016 (800) 443-8323; *The New Book of World Rankings*.

NETHERLANDS - HOUSING CONSTRUCTION - See NETHERLANDS - CONSTRUCTION INDUSTRY

NETHERLANDS - HOUSING EXPENDITURES

European Community Information Service, 2100 M Street, NW, Washington, D.C. 20037 (202) 862-9500; *Basic Statistics of the Community*.

International Monetary Fund, 700 Nineteenth Street, NW, Washington, D.C. 20431 (202) 623-7000; *Government Finance Statistics Yearbook*.

Netherlands Central Bureau of Statistics, Staatsuitgeverij, The Hague, Netherlands; *Statistical Yearbook of the Netherlands*.

NETHERLANDS - HYDROCHLORIC ACID PRODUCTION

European Community Information Service, 2100 M Street, NW, Washington, D.C. 20037 (202) 862-9500; *Basic Statistics of the*

Community.

Statistical Office of the United Nations, Publishing Service, New York, New York 10017 (800) 253-9646; *Statistical Yearbook.*

NETHERLANDS - ILLITERATE POPULATION

The Economist Intelligence Unit, 111 West 57th Street, New York, New York 10019 (800) 938-4685; *The World Market Atlas.*

NETHERLANDS - IMPORTS

American Automobile Manufacturers Association, 1401 H Street, NW, Suite 900, Washington, D.C. 20005 (202) 326-5500; *World Motor Vehicle Data.*

The Economist Intelligence Unit, 111 West 57th Street, New York, New York 10019 (800) 938-4685; *The World Market Atlas.*

European Community Information Service, 2100 M Street, NW, Washington, D.C. 20037 (202) 862-9500; *Basic Statistics of the Community, Energy: Monthly Statistics, Energy Statistics Yearbook, Eurostatistics: Data for Short-term Economic Analysis, External Trade: Statistical Yearbook, External Trade: Monthly Statistics,* and *Fisheries: Yearly Statistics.*

Food and Agricultural Organization of the United Nations (FAO) Via delle Terme di Caracalla, 00100 Rome, Italy (Telephone Number in U.S. (202) 653-2400); *The State of Food and Agriculture.*

International Iron and Steel Institute, 120, rue Colonel Bourg, B-1140 Brussels, Belgium; *Steel Statistical Yearbook.*

International Lead and Zinc Study Group, Metro House, 58 St. James's Street, London SW1A 1LD England; *Lead and Zinc Statistics.*

International Monetary Fund, 700 Nineteenth Street, NW, Washington, D.C. 20431 (202) 623-7000; *Direction of Trade Statistics, Government Finance Statistics Yearbook,* and *International Financial Statistics.*

International Rubber Study Group, York House, Eighth Floor, Empire Way, Wembley, London HA9 0PA, England; *Rubber Statistical Bulletin.*

Organisation for Economic Co-operation and Development (OECD), 2 rue Andre-Pascal, 75 Paris 16, France (Telephone Number in U.S. (202) 785-6323); *Economic Outlook, The Footwear, Raw Hides and Skins, and Leather Industry in OECD Countries, Industrial Structure Statistics, The Iron and Steel Industry, Milk, Milk Products, and Egg Balances in OECD Member Countries, OECD Economic Surveys: Netherlands, The Pulp and Paper Industry,* and *Review of Fisheries in OECD Member Countries.*

Times Books, 201 East 50th Street, New York, New York 10022 (212) 751-2600; *The Economist Book of Vital World Statistics.*

The World Bank, 1818 H Street, NW, Washington, D.C. 20433 (202) 477-1234; *World Tables.*

NETHERLANDS - INCOME TAXES - See NETHERLANDS - TAXATION

NETHERLANDS - INDUSTRIAL ACID PRODUCTION

European Community Information Service, 2100 M Street, NW, Washington, D.C. 20037 (202) 862-9500; *Basic Statistics of the Community.*

Statistical Office of the United Nations, Publishing Service, New York, New York 10017 (800) 253-9646; *Statistical Yearbook.*

NETHERLANDS - INDUSTRIAL METALS PRODUCTION - See NETHERLANDS - MINING AND MINERAL PRODUCTS

NETHERLANDS - INDUSTRY

European Community Information Service, 2100 M Street, NW, Washington, D.C. 20037 (202) 862-9500; *Basic Statistics of the Community, Employment and Unemployment, Eurostatistics: Data for Short-term Economic Analysis,* and *Labor Force Sample Survey.*

Facts on File, 460 Park Avenue South, New York, New York 10016 (800) 443-8323; *The New Book of World Rankings.*

International Labour Office, I.L.O. Publications, CH-1211, Geneva 22, Switzerland; *Yearbook of Labour Statistics.*

Organisation for Economic Co-operation and Development (OECD), 2 rue Andre-Pascal, 75 Paris 16, France (Telephone Number in U.S. (202) 785-6323); *Economic Outlook, Industrial Structure Statistics, Main Economic Indicators - Historical Statistics,* and *OECD Environmental Data.*

Statistical Office of the United Nations, Publishing Service, New York, New York 10017 (800) 253-9646; *Statistical Yearbook.*

Times Books, 201 East 50th Street, New York, New York 10022 (212) 751-2600; *The Economist Book of Vital World Statistics.*

The World Bank, 1818 H Street, NW, Washington, D.C. 20433 (202) 477-1234; *World Tables.*

World Intellectual Property Organization, 34 Chemin des Colombettes, CH-1211 Geneva 20, Switzerland; *Industrial Property Statistics.*

NETHERLANDS - INFANT AND MATERNAL MORTALITY

European Community Information Service, 2100 M Street, NW, Washington, D.C. 20037 (202) 862-9500; *Basic Statistics of the Community,* and *Demographic Statistics.*

Statistical Office of the United Nations, Publishing Service, New York, New York 10017 (800) 253-9646; *Demographic Yearbook,* and *Statistical Yearbook.*

Times Books, 201 East 50th Street, New York, New York 10022 (212) 751-2600; *The Economist Book of Vital World Statistics.*

The World Bank, 1818 H Street, NW, Washington, D.C. 20433 (202) 477-1234; *World Tables.*

World Health Organization, Office of Publications, Avenue Appia, CH-1211 Geneva 27, Switzerland (Telephone Number in U.S. (518) 436-9686); *World Health Statistics Annual.*

NETHERLANDS - INTEREST RATES

European Community Information Service, 2100 M Street, NW, Washington, D.C. 20037 (202) 862-9500; *Money and Finance.*

Organisation for Economic Co-operation and Development (OECD), 2 rue Andre-Pascal, 75 Paris 16, France (Telephone Number in U.S. (202) 785-6323); *Economic Outlook, Financial Market Trends, Main Economic Indicators - Historical Statistics,* and *OECD Financial Statistics.*

NETHERLANDS - INTERNAL TRADE

European Community Information Service, 2100 M Street, NW, Washington, D.C. 20037 (202) 862-9500; *Basic Statistics of the Community*.

Organisation for Economic Co-operation and Development (OECD), 2 rue Andre-Pascal, 75 Paris 16, France (Telephone Number in U.S. (202) 785-6323); *Main Economic Indicators - Historical Statistics*.

Statistical Office of the United Nations, Publishing Service, New York, New York 10017 (800) 253-9646; *Statistical Yearbook*.

NETHERLANDS - INTERNATIONAL FINANCE

European Community Information Service, 2100 M Street, NW, Washington, D.C. 20037 (202) 862-9500; *Basic Statistics of the Community*.

Organisation for Economic Co-operation and Development (OECD), 2 rue Andre-Pascal, 75 Paris 16, France (Telephone Number in U.S. (202) 785-6323); *Economic Outlook*, and *Financial Market Trends*.

NETHERLANDS - INTERNATIONAL LIQUIDITY

International Monetary Fund, 700 Nineteenth Street, NW, Washington, D.C. 20431 (202) 623-7000; *International Financial Statistics*.

Organisation for Economic Co-operation and Development (OECD), 2 rue Andre-Pascal, 75 Paris 16, France (Telephone Number in U.S. (202) 785-6323); *Economic Outlook*, and *Financial Market Trends*.

NETHERLANDS - INTERNATIONAL RESERVES EXCLUDING GOLD

Statistical Office of the United Nations, Publishing Service, New York, New York 10017 (800) 253-9646; *Statistical Yearbook*.

The World Bank, 1818 H Street, NW, Washington, D.C. 20433 (202) 477-1234; *World Tables*.

NETHERLANDS - INTERNATIONAL STATISTICS

Organisation for Economic Co-operation and Development (OECD), 2 rue Andre-Pascal, 75 Paris 16, France (Telephone Number in U.S. (202) 785-6323); *Financial Market Trends*, and *Tourism Policy and International Tourism in OECD Member Countries*.

NETHERLANDS - INVESTMENTS

International Monetary Fund, 700 Nineteenth Street, NW, Washington, D.C. 20431 (202) 623-7000; *International Financial Statistics*.

Organisation for Economic Co-operation and Development (OECD), 2 rue Andre-Pascal, 75 Paris 16, France (Telephone Number in U.S. (202) 785-6323); *Economic Outlook, Financial Market Trends, Industrial Structure Statistics, The Iron and Steel Industry*, and *Textile Industry in OECD Countries*.

NETHERLANDS - IRON ORE PRODUCTION AND CONSUMPTION - See NETHERLANDS - MINING AND MINERAL PRODUCTS

NETHERLANDS - JUTE PRODUCTION - See NETHERLANDS - CROPS

NETHERLANDS - LABOR FORCE

European Community Information Service, 2100 M Street, NW, Washington, D.C. 20037 (202) 862-9500; *Basic Statistics of the Community, Labor Force Sample Survey*, and *Regions: Statistical Yearbook*.

Facts on File, 460 Park Avenue South, New York, New York 10016 (800) 443-8323; *The New Book of World Rankings*.

Food and Agricultural Organization of the United Nations (FAO) Via delle Terme di Caracalla, 00100 Rome, Italy (Telephone Number in U.S. (202) 653-2400); *The State of Food and Agriculture*.

Netherlands Central Bureau of Statistics, Staatsuitgeverij, The Hague, Netherlands; *Statistical Yearbook of the Netherlands*.

Organisation for Economic Co-operation and Development (OECD), 2 rue Andre-Pascal, 75 Paris 16, France (Telephone Number in U.S. (202) 785-6323); *Economic Outlook, Main Economic Indicators - Historical Statistics, OECD Economic Surveys: Netherlands*, and *OECD Employment Outlook*.

Times Books, 201 East 50th Street, New York, New York 10022 (212) 751-2600; *The Economist Book of Vital World Statistics*.

The World Bank, 1818 H Street, NW, Washington, D.C. 20433 (202) 477-1234; *World Tables*.

NETHERLANDS - LABOR PRODUCTIVITY

International Labour Office, I.L.O. Publications, CH-1211, Geneva 22, Switzerland; *Yearbook of Labour Statistics*.

Organisation for Economic Co-operation and Development (OECD), 2 rue Andre-Pascal, 75 Paris 16, France (Telephone Number in U.S. (202) 785-6323); *Economic Outlook*, and *OECD Employment Outlook*.

NETHERLANDS - LAND USE

Euromonitor Publications Limited, 87-88 Turnmill Street, London EC1M 5QU, England; *European Marketing Data and Statistics*.

European Community Information Service, 2100 M Street, NW, Washington, D.C. 20037 (202) 862-9500; *Agriculture: Statistical Yearbook, Basic Statistics of the Community, Crop Production: Quarterly Statistics*, and *Regions: Statistical Yearbook*.

Food and Agricultural Organization of the United Nations (FAO), Via delle Terme di Caracalla, 00100 Rome, Italy (Telephone Number in U.S. (202) 653-2400); *Production Yearbook*.

NETHERLANDS - LEAD AND LEAD ORE PRODUCTION AND CONSUMPTION - See NETHERLANDS - MINING AND MINERAL PRODUCTS

NETHERLANDS - LEATHER AND FOOTWEAR EXPORTS AND IMPORTS

European Community Information Service, 2100 M Street, NW, Washington, D.C. 20037 (202) 862-9500; *Basic Statistics of the Community*.

Organisation for Economic Co-operation and Development (OECD), 2 rue Andre-Pascal, 75 Paris 16, France (Telephone Number in U.S. (202) 785-6323); *The Footwear, Raw Hides and Skins, and Leather Industry in OECD Countries*.

NETHERLANDS - LEATHER PRODUCTION INDEX

Organisation for Economic Co-operation and Development (OECD), 2 rue Andre-Pascal, 75 Paris 16, France (Telephone Number in U.S. (202) 785-6323); *Indicators of Industrial Activity.*

NETHERLANDS - LIBRARIES

Euromonitor Publications Limited, 87-88 Turnmill Street, London EC1M 5QU, England; *European Marketing Data and Statistics.*

Facts on File, 460 Park Avenue South, New York, New York 10016 (800) 443-8323; *The New Book of World Rankings.*

NETHERLANDS - LIGNITE PRODUCTION - See NETHERLANDS - MINING AND MINERAL PRODUCTS

NETHERLANDS - LIVESTOCK AND POULTRY

Euromonitor Publications Limited, 87-88 Turnmill Street, London EC1M 5QU, England; *European Marketing Data and Statistics.*

European Community Information Service, 2100 M Street, NW, Washington, D.C. 20037 (202) 862-9500; *Agriculture: Statistical Yearbook, Basic Statistics of the Community, Eurostatistics: Data for Short-term Economic Analysis,* and *Regions: Statistical Yearbook.*

Facts on File, 460 Park Avenue South, New York, New York 10016 (800) 443-8323; *The New Book of World Rankings.*

Food and Agricultural Organization of the United Nations (FAO), Via delle Terme di Caracalla, 00100 Rome, Italy (Telephone Number in U.S. (202) 653-2400); *Production Yearbook,* and *The State of Food and Agriculture.*

Organisation for Economic Co-operation and Development (OECD), 2 rue Andre-Pascal, 75 Paris 16, France (Telephone Number in U.S. (202) 785-6323); *Economic Accounts for Agriculture,* and *Meat Balances in OECD Member Countries.*

Statistical Office of the United Nations, Publishing Service, New York, New York 10017 (800) 253-9646; *Statistical Yearbook.*

NETHERLANDS - LIVING LEVELS

Organisation for Economic Co-operation and Development (OECD), 2 rue Andre-Pascal, 75 Paris 16, France (Telephone Number in U.S. (202) 785-6323); *Economic Outlook.*

Times Books, 201 East 50th Street, New York, New York 10022 (212) 751-2600; *The Economist Book of Vital World Statistics.*

NETHERLANDS - MACHINERY - PRODUCTION INDEX

Organisation for Economic Co-operation and Development (OECD), 2 rue Andre-Pascal, 75 Paris 16, France (Telephone Number in U.S. (202) 785-6323); *Indicators of Industrial Activity.*

NETHERLANDS - MAGNESIUM PRODUCTION AND CONSUMPTION - See NETHERLANDS - MINING AND MINERAL PRODUCTS

NETHERLANDS - MAIL - NUMBER OF PIECES SENT OR RECEIVED

European Community Information Service, 2100 M Street, NW, Washington, D.C. 20037 (202) 862-9500; *Transport Annual Statistics.*

Statistical Office of the United Nations, Publishing Service, New York, New York 10017 (800) 253-9646; *Statistical Yearbook.*

NETHERLANDS - MAIN ECONOMIC INDICATORS - See NETHERLANDS - ECONOMY

NETHERLANDS - MANGANESE PRODUCTION AND CONSUMPTION - See NETHERLANDS - MINING AND MINERAL PRODUCTS

NETHERLANDS - MANUFACTURING

American Automobile Manufacturers Association, 1401 H Street, NW, Suite 900, Washington, D.C. 20005 (202) 326-5500; *World Motor Vehicle Data.*

European Community Information Service, 2100 M Street, NW, Washington, D.C. 20037 (202) 862-9500; *Basic Statistics of the Community, Eurostatistics: Data for Short-term Economic Analysis, Industrial Production: Quarterly Statistics,* and *Labor Force Sample Survey.*

Facts on File, 460 Park Avenue South, New York, New York 10016 (800) 443-8323; *The New Book of World Rankings.*

Netherlands Central Bureau of Statistics, Staatsuitgeverij, The Hague, Netherlands; *Statistical Yearbook of the Netherlands.*

Organisation for Economic Co-operation and Development (OECD), 2 rue Andre-Pascal, 75 Paris 16, France (Telephone Number in U.S. (202) 785-6323); *Foreign Trade by Commodities, Indicators of Industrial Activity, Industrial Structure Statistics,* and *OECD Economic Surveys: Netherlands.*

Statistical Office of the United Nations, Publishing Service, New York, New York 10017 (800) 253-9646; *Statistical Yearbook.*

Times Books, 201 East 50th Street, New York, New York 10022 (212) 751-2600; *The Economist Book of Vital World Statistics.*

The World Bank, 1818 H Street, NW, Washington, D.C. 20433 (202) 477-1234; *World Tables.*

NETHERLANDS - MARRIAGE RATES

European Community Information Service, 2100 M Street, NW, Washington, D.C. 20037 (202) 862-9500; *Basic Statistics of the Community.*

Facts on File, 460 Park Avenue South, New York, New York 10016 (800) 443-8323; *The New Book of World Rankings.*

Statistical Office of the United Nations, Publishing Service, New York, New York 10017 (800) 253-9646; *Demographic Yearbook,* and *Statistical Yearbook.*

NETHERLANDS - MEAT PRODUCTION - See NETHERLANDS - LIVESTOCK AND POULTRY

NETHERLANDS - MERCHANT SHIPPING

European Community Information Service, 2100 M Street, NW, Washington, D.C. 20037 (202) 862-9500; *Basic Statistics of the Community, Fisheries: Yearly Statistics, Regions: Statistical Yearbook,* and *Transport Annual Statistics.*

Lloyd's Register of Shipping, 17 Battery Place, New York, New York 10004 (212) 425-8050; *Register of Ships.*

Organisation for Economic Co-operation and Development (OECD), 2 rue Andre-Pascal, 75 Paris 16, France (Telephone Number in U.S. (202) 785-6323); *Maritime Transport.*

Statistical Office of the United Nations, Publishing Service, New York, New York 10017 (800) 253-9646; *Statistical Yearbook*, and *Annual Bulletin of Transport Statistics for Europe.*

Times Books, 201 East 50th Street, New York, New York 10022 (212) 751-2600; *The Economist Book of Vital World Statistics.*

U.S. Department of Transportation, Maritime Administration, 400 Seventh Street, SW, Washington, D.C. 20590 (202) 366-5807; *A Statistical Analysis of the World's Merchant Fleets.*

NETHERLANDS - MERCURY PRODUCTION AND CONSUMPTION - See NETHERLANDS - MINING AND MINERAL PRODUCTS

NETHERLANDS - MILITARY

The International Institute for Strategic Studies, 23 Tavistock Street, London WC2E 7NQ, England; *The Military Balance.*

U.S. Arms Control and Disarmament Agency, 320 Twenty-first Street, NW, Washington, D.C. 20451 (202) 647-8677; *World Military Expenditures and Arms Transfers.*

NETHERLANDS - MILK PRODUCTION - See NETHERLANDS - DAIRY PRODUCTS

NETHERLANDS - MILLET PRODUCTION - See NETHERLANDS - CROPS

NETHERLANDS - MINING AND MINERAL PRODUCTS

Commodity Research Bureau, Incorporated, 75 Wall Street, New York, New York 10005 (212) 504-7754; *Commodity Year Book.*

European Community Information Service, 2100 M Street, NW, Washington, D.C. 20037 (202) 862-9500; *ACP: Basic Statistics, Basic Statistics of the Community, Energy: Monthly Statistics, Energy Statistics Yearbook, Eurostatistics: Data for Short-term Economic Analysis, Industrial Production: Quarterly Statistics, Iron and Steel: Statistical Yearbook*, and *Regions: Statistical Yearbook.*

Facts on File, 460 Park Avenue South, New York, New York 10016 (800) 443-8323; *The New Book of World Rankings.*

International Iron and Steel Institute, 120, rue Colonel Bourg, B-1140 Brussels, Belgium; *Steel Statistical Yearbook.*

International Lead and Zinc Study Group, Metro House, 58 St. James's Street, London SW1A 1LD England; *Lead and Zinc Statistics.*

Organisation for Economic Co-operation and Development (OECD), 2 rue Andre-Pascal, 75 Paris 16, France (Telephone Number in U.S. (202) 785-6323); *Coal Information, Energy Statistics of OECD Countries, Foreign Trade by Commodities, Indicators of Industrial Activity, Industrial Structure Statistics, The Iron and Steel Industry, The Non-Ferrous Metals Industry*, and *OECD Economic Surveys: Netherlands.*

Penn Well Publishing Company, 1421 South Sheridan Road, Post Office Box 1260, Tulsa, Oklahoma 74101 (800) 752-9764; *International Energy Statistics Sourcebook.*

Statistical Office of the United Nations, Publishing Service, New York, New York 10017 (800) 253-9646; *Statistical Yearbook.*

World Bureau of Metal Statistics, 27-A High Street, Ware, Herts. SG12 9BA, England; *World Metal Statistics.*

NETHERLANDS - MOLYBDENUM AND MOLYBDENUM ORE PRODUCTION AND CONSUMPTION - See NETHERLANDS - MINING AND MINERAL PRODUCTS

NETHERLANDS - MONEY AND CREDIT

Organization for Economic Co-operation and Development (OECD), 2 rue Andre-Pascal, 75 Paris 16, France (Telephone Number in U.S. (202) 785-6232); *OECD Economic Surveys: Netherlands.*

NETHERLANDS - MONEY EXCHANGE RATE

European Community Information Service, 2100 M Street, NW, Washington, D.C. 20037 (202) 862-9500; *Basic Statistics of the Community.*

International Monetary Fund, 700 Nineteenth Street, NW, Washington, D.C. 20431 (202) 623-7000; *International Financial Statistics.*

Organisation for Economic Co-operation and Development (OECD), 2 rue Andre-Pascal, 75 Paris 16, France (Telephone Number in U.S. (202) 785-6323); *Economic Outlook, Financial Market Trends*, and *Tourism Policy and International Tourism in OECD Member Countries.*

Statistical Office of the United Nations, Publishing Service, New York, New York 10017 (800) 253-9646; *Statistical Yearbook.*

NETHERLANDS - MONEY RATES - MARKET

European Community Information Service, 2100 M Street, NW, Washington, D.C. 20037 (202) 862-9500; *Basic Statistics of the Community.*

Organisation for Economic Co-operation and Development (OECD), 2 rue Andre Pascal, 75 Paris 16, France (Telephone Number in U.S. (202) 785-6323); *Economic Outlook*, and *Financial Market Trends.*

Statistical Office of the United Nations, Publishing Service, New York, New York 10017 (800) 253-9646; *Statistical Yearbook.*

NETHERLANDS - MONEY RESERVES

European Community Information Service, 2100 M Street, NW, Washington, D.C. 20037 (202) 862-9500; *Basic Statistics of the Community.*

Organisation for Economic Co-operation and Development (OECD), 2 rue Andre-Pascal, 75 Paris 16, France (Telephone Number in U.S. (202) 785-6323); *Economic Outlook*, and *Financial Market Trends.*

NETHERLANDS - MONEY SUPPLY

European Community Information Service, 2100 M Street, NW, Washington, D.C. 20037 (202) 862-9500; *Basic Statistics of the Community, Eurostatistics: Data for Short-term Economic Analysis*, and *Money and Finance.*

International Monetary Fund, 700 Nineteenth Street, NW, Washington, D.C. 20431 (202) 623-7000; *International Financial Statistics.*

Netherlands Central Bureau of Statistics, Staatsuitgeverij, The Hague, Netherlands; *Statistical Yearbook of the Netherlands.*

Organisation for Economic Co-operation and Development (OECD), 2 rue Andre-Pascal, 75 Paris 16, France (Telephone Number in U.S. (202) 785-6323); *Economic Outlook.*

Statistical Office of the United Nations, Publishing Service, New York, New York 10017 (800) 253-9646; *Statistical Yearbook.*

The World Bank, 1818 H Street, NW, Washington, D.C. 20433 (202) 477-1234; *World Tables.*

NETHERLANDS - MOTION PICTURES

Statistical Office of the United Nations, Publishing Service, New York, New York 10017 (800) 253-9646; *Statistical Yearbook.*

United Nations Educational, Scientific and Cultural Organization (UNESCO), 7 Place de Fontenoy, F-75700 Paris, France (Telephone Number in U.S. (212) 963-5981); *Statistical Yearbook.*

NETHERLANDS - MOTOR VEHICLE PRODUCTION

American Automobile Manufacturers Association, 1401 H Eye Street, NW, Suite 900, Washington, D.C. 20005 (202) 326-5500; *World Motor Vehicle Data.*

European Community Information Service, 2100 M Street, NW, Washington, D.C. 20037 (202) 862-9500; *Basic Statistics of the Community,* and *Eurostatistics: Data for Short-term Economic Analysis.*

Organisation for Economic Co-operation and Development (OECD), 2 rue Andre-Pascal, 75 Paris 16, France (Telephone Number in U.S. (202) 785-6323); *Foreign Trade by Commodities,* and *Indicators of Industrial Activity.*

NETHERLANDS - MOTOR VEHICLE PRODUCTION AND ASSEMBLY

Statistical Office of the United Nations, Publishing Service, New York, New York 10017 (800) 253-9646; *Statistical Yearbook.*

NETHERLANDS - MOTOR VEHICLE TAXES - See NETHERLANDS - TAXATION

NETHERLANDS - MOTOR VEHICLES IN USE

American Automobile Manufacturers Association, 1401 H Street, NW, Suite 900, Washington, D.C. 20005 (202) 326-5500; *World Motor Vehicle Data.*

European Community Information Service, 2100 M Street, NW, Washington, D.C. 20037 (202) 862-9500; *Basic Statistics of the Community,* and *Transport Annual Statistics.*

International Road Federation, 525 School Street, SW, Washington, D.C. 20024 (202) 554-2106; *World Road Statistics.*

Statistical Office of the United Nations, Publishing Service, New York, New York 10017 (800) 253-9646; *Statistical Yearbook.*

Times Books, 201 East 50th Street, New York, New York 10022 (212) 751-2600; *The Economist Book of Vital World Statistics.*

NETHERLANDS - MULES - See NETHERLANDS - LIVESTOCK AND POULTRY

NETHERLANDS - MUSEUMS

Euromonitor Publications Limited, 87-88 Turnmill Street, London EC1M 5QU, England; *European Marketing Data and Statistics.*

Facts on File, 460 Park Avenue South, New York, New York 10016 (800) 443-8323; *The New Book of World Rankings.*

United Nations Educational, Scientific and Cultural Organization (UNESCO), 7 Place de Fontenoy, F-75700 Paris, France (Telephone Number in U.S. (212) 963-5981); *Statistical Yearbook.*

NETHERLANDS - NATALITY - See NETHERLANDS - BIRTH RATES

NETHERLANDS - NATIONAL ACCOUNTS

European Community Information Service, 2100 M Street, NW, Washington, D.C. 20037 (202) 862-9500; *Basic Statistics of the Community,* and *Eurostatistics: Data for Short-term Economic Analysis.*

Netherlands Central Bureau of Statistics, Staatsuitgeverij, The Hague, Netherlands; *Statistical Yearbook of the Netherlands.*

Organisation for Economic Co-operation and Development (OECD), 2 rue Andre-Pascal, 75 Paris 16, France (Telephone Number in U.S. (202) 785-6323); *Economic Outlook.*

Statistical Office of the United Nations, Publishing Service, New York, New York 10017 (800) 253-9646; *National Accounts Statistics,* and *Statistical Yearbook.*

NETHERLANDS - NATIONAL INCOME

Facts on File, 460 Park Avenue South, New York, New York 10016 (800) 443-8323; *The New Book of World Rankings.*

Organisation for Economic Co-operation and Development (OECD), 2 rue Andre-Pascal, 75 Paris 16, France (Telephone Number in U.S. (202) 785-6323); *Economic Outlook.*

Statistical Office of the United Nations, Publishing Service, New York, New York 10017 (800) 253-9646; *Statistical Yearbook.*

NETHERLANDS - NATIONAL PRODUCT

European Community Information Service, 2100 M Street, NW, Washington, D.C. 20037 (202) 862-9500; *Basic Statistics of the Community.*

Facts on File, 460 Park Avenue South, New York, New York 10016 (800) 443-8323; *The New Book of World Rankings.*

Organisation for Economic Co-operation and Development (OECD), 2 rue Andre-Pascal, 75 Paris 16, France (Telephone Number in U.S. (202) 785-6323); *Economic Outlook,* and *Main Economic Indicators - Historical Statistics.*

Statistical Office of the United Nations, Publishing Service, New York, New York 10017 (800) 253-9646; *Statistical Yearbook.*

NETHERLANDS - NATURAL GAS PRODUCTION - See NETHERLANDS - MINING AND MINERAL PRODUCTS

NETHERLANDS - NATURAL RUBBER PRODUCTION

European Community Information Service, 2100 M Street, NW, Washington, D.C. 20037 (202) 862-9500; *Basic Statistics of the Community.*

International Rubber Study Group, York House, Eighth Floor, Empire Way, Wembley, London HA9 0PA, England; *Rubber Statistical Bulletin.*

NETHERLANDS - NEWSPAPER PRODUCTION - See NETHERLANDS - FORESTRY AND FOREST PRODUCTS

NETHERLANDS - NEWSPRINT - See NETHERLANDS - FORESTRY AND FOREST PRODUCTS

NETHERLANDS - NICKEL AND NICKEL ORE PRODUCTION AND CONSUMPTION - See NETHERLANDS - MINING AND MINERAL PRODUCTS

NETHERLANDS - NITRIC ACID PRODUCTION - See NETHERLANDS - MINING AND MINERAL PRODUCTS

NETHERLANDS - OATS PRODUCTION - See NETHERLANDS - CROPS

NETHERLANDS - OCCUPATIONS - See NETHERLANDS - LABOR FORCE

NETHERLANDS - OIL PRODUCING CROPS

European Community Information Service, 2100 M Street, NW, Washington, D.C. 20037 (202) 862-9500; *Basic Statistics of the Community.*

Organisation for Economic Co-operation and Development (OECD), 2 rue Andre-Pascal, 75 Paris 16, France (Telephone Number in U.S. (202) 785-6323; *Foreign Trade by Commodities.*

NETHERLANDS - ONION PRODUCTION - See NETHERLANDS - CROPS

NETHERLANDS - PALM KERNEL PRODUCTION See NETHERLANDS - CROPS

NETHERLANDS - PAPER - See NETHERLANDS - FORESTRY AND FOREST PRODUCTS

NETHERLANDS - PATENTS

Statistical Office of the United Nations, Publishing Service, New York, New York 10017 (800) 253-9646; *Statistical Yearbook.*

World Intellectual Property Organization, 34 Chemin des Colombettes, CH-1211 Geneva 20, Switzerland; *Industrial Property Statistics.*

NETHERLANDS - PEANUT PRODUCTION - See NETHERLANDS - CROPS

NETHERLANDS - PEPPER PRODUCTION - See NETHERLANDS - CROPS

NETHERLANDS - PESTICIDE USE

Food and Agricultural Organization of the United Nations (FAO) Via delle Terme di Caracalla, 00100 Rome, Italy (Telephone Number in U.S. (202) 653-2400); *The State of Food and Agriculture.*

NETHERLANDS - PETROLEUM INDUSTRY

Euromonitor Publications Limited, 87-88 Turnmill Street, London EC1M 5QU, England; *European Marketing Data and Statistics.*

European Community Information Service, 2100 M Street, NW, Washington, D.C. 20037 (202) 862-9500; *ACP: Basic Statistics, Basic Statistics of the Community,* and *Energy Statistics Yearbook.*

Facts on File, 460 Park Avenue South, New York, New York 10016 (800) 443-8323; *The New Book of World Rankings.*

Food and Agricultural Organization of the United Nations (FAO) Via delle Terme di Caracalla, 00100 Rome, Italy (Telephone Number in U.S. (202) 653-2400); *The State of Food and Agriculture.*

Organisation for Economic Co-operation and Development (OECD), 2 rue Andre-Pascal, 75 Paris 16, France (Telephone Number in U.S. (202) 785-6323); *Energy Statistics of OECD Countries, Foreign Trade by Commodities, Indicators of Industrial Activity,* and *Oil and Gas Information.*

Penn Well Publishing Company, 1421 South Sheridan Road, Post Office Box 1260, Tulsa, Oklahoma 74101 (800) 752-9764; *International Energy Statistics Sourcebook.*

Statistical Office of the United Nations, Publishing Service, New York, New York 10017 (800) 253-9646; *Statistical Yearbook.*

NETHERLANDS - PHOSPHATE ROCK PRODUCTION - See NETHERLANDS - MINING AND MINERAL PRODUCTS

NETHERLANDS - PHOSPHATES PRODUCTION - See NETHERLANDS - MINING AND MINERAL PRODUCTS

NETHERLANDS - PIG IRON AND FERRO-ALLOY PRODUCTION - See NETHERLANDS - MINING AND MINERAL PRODUCTS

NETHERLANDS - PIGS - See NETHERLANDS - LIVESTOCK AND POULTRY

NETHERLANDS - PIPELINES FOR OIL AND PETROLEUM PRODUCTS

European Community Information Service, 2100 M Street, NW, Washington, D.C. 20037 (202) 862-9500; *Transport Annual Statistics.*

Statistical Office of the United Nations, Publishing Service, New York, New York 10017 (800) 253-9646; *Annual Bulletin of Transport Statistics for Europe.*

NETHERLANDS - PLASTIC AND RESIN PRODUCTION

Commodity Research Bureau, Incorporated, 75 Wall Street, New York, New York 10005 (212) 504-7754; *Commodity Year Book.*

European Community Information Service, 2100 M Street, NW, Washington, D.C. 20037 (202) 862-9500; *Basic Statistics of the Community.*

Organisation for Economic Co-operation and Development (OECD), 2 rue Andre-Pascal, 75 Paris 16, France (Telephone Number in U.S. (202) 785-6323); *Foreign Trade by Commodities.*

Statistical Office of the United Nations, Publishing Service, New York, New York 10017 (800) 253-9646; *Statistical Yearbook.*

NETHERLANDS - PLATINUM PRODUCTION - See NETHERLANDS - MINING AND MINERAL PRODUCTS

NETHERLANDS - POPULATION

The Economist Intelligence Unit, 111 West 57th Street, New York, New York 10019 (800) 938-4685; *The World Market Atlas.*

Euromonitor Publications Limited, 87-88 Turnmill Street, London EC1M 5QU, England; *European Marketing Data and Statistics.*

European Community Information Service, 2100 M Street, NW, Washington, D.C. 20037 (202) 862-9500; *ACP: Basic Statistics, Basic Statistics of the Community, Demographic Statistics,*

Employment and Unemployment, Fisheries: Yearly Statistics, Iron and Steel: Statistical Yearbook, Labor Force Sample Survey, and *Regions: Statistical Yearbook.*

Facts on File, 460 Park Avenue South, New York, New York 10016 (800) 443-8323; *The New Book of World Rankings.*

Food and Agricultural Organization of the United Nations (FAO), Via delle Terme di Caracalla, 00100 Rome, Italy (Telephone Number in U.S. (202) 653-2400); *Production Yearbook.*

International Labour Office, I.L.O. Publications, CH-1211, Geneva 22, Switzerland; *Yearbook of Labour Statistics.*

Netherlands Central Bureau of Statistics, Staatsuitgeverij, The Hague, Netherlands; *Statistical Yearbook of the Netherlands.*

Statistical Office of the United Nations, Publishing Service, New York, New York 10017 (800) 253-9646; *Demographic Yearbook,* and *Statistical Yearbook.*

Times Books, 201 East 50th Street, New York, New York 10022 (212) 751-2600; *The Economist Book of Vital World Statistics.*

United Nations Educational, Scientific and Cultural Organization (UNESCO), 7 Place de Fontenoy, F-75700 Paris, France (Telephone Number in U.S. (212) 963-5981); *Statistical Yearbook.*

U.S. Arms Control and Disarmament Agency, 320 Twenty-first Street, NW, Washington, D.C. 20451 (202) 647-8677; *World Military Expenditures and Arms Transfers.*

NETHERLANDS - POST OFFICES

Facts on File, 460 Park Avenue South, New York, New York 10016 (800) 443-8323; *The New Book of World Rankings.*

NETHERLANDS - POTATO PRODUCTION - See NETHERLANDS - CROPS

NETHERLANDS - POWER PRODUCTION INDUSTRY

European Community Information Service, 2100 M Street, NW, Washington, D.C. 20037 (202) 862-9500; *Basic Statistics of the Community.*

Statistical Office of the United Nations, Publishing Service, New York, New York 10017 (800) 253-9646; *Statistical Yearbook.*

NETHERLANDS - PRICES

European Community Information Service, 2100 M Street, NW, Washington, D.C. 20037 (202) 862-9500; *Basic Statistics of the Community,* and *Eurostatistics: Data for Short-term Economic Analysis.*

Facts on File, 460 Park Avenue South, New York, New York 10016 (800) 443-8323; *The New Book of World Rankings.*

Food and Agricultural Organization of the United Nations (FAO), Via delle Terme di Caracalla, 00100 Rome, Italy (Telephone Number in U.S. (202) 653-2400); *Production Yearbook,* and *The State of Food and Agriculture.*

International Labour Office, I.L.O. Publications, CH-1211, Geneva 22, Switzerland; *Yearbook of Labour Statistics.*

International Lead and Zinc Study Group, Metro House, 58 St. James's Street, London SW1A 1LD England; *Lead and Zinc*

Statistics.

International Monetary Fund, 700 Nineteenth Street, NW, Washington, D.C. 20431 (202) 623-7000; *International Financial Statistics.*

International Rubber Study Group, York House, Eighth Floor, Empire Way, Wembley, London HA9 0PA, England; *Rubber Statistical Bulletin.*

Netherlands Central Bureau of Statistics, Staatsuitgeverij, The Hague, Netherlands; *Statistical Yearbook of the Netherlands.*

Organisation for Economic Co-operation and Development (OECD), 2 rue Andre-Pascal, 75 Paris 16, France (Telephone Number in U.S. (202) 785-6323); *Economic Outlook, The Footwear, Raw Hides and Skins, and Leather Industry in OECD Countries, Indicators of Industrial Activity, The Iron and Steel Industry, Main Economic Indicators - Historical Statistics,* and *The Pulp and Paper Industry.*

World Bureau of Metal Statistics, 27-A High Street, Ware, Herts. SG12 9BA, England; *World Metal Statistics.*

NETHERLANDS - PRINTING AND WRITING PAPER - See NETHERLANDS - FORESTRY AND FOREST PRODUCTS

NETHERLANDS - PRODUCTION

American Automobile Manufacturers Association, 1401 H Street, NW, Suite 900, Washington, D.C. 20005 (202) 326-5500; *World Motor Vehicle Data.*

European Community Information Service, 2100 M Street, NW, Washington, D.C. 20037 (202) 862-9500; *Basic Statistics of the Community, Eurostatistics: Data for Short-term Economic Analysis,* and *Fisheries: Yearly Statistics.*

Facts on File, 460 Park Avenue South, New York, New York 10016 (800) 443-8323; *The New Book of World Rankings.*

International Iron and Steel Institute, 120, rue Colonel Bourg, B-1140 Brussels, Belgium; *Steel Statistical Yearbook.*

International Lead and Zinc Study Group, Metro House, 58 St. James's Street, London SW1A 1LD England; *Lead and Zinc Statistics.*

International Rubber Study Group, York House, Eighth Floor, Empire Way, Wembley, London HA9 0PA, England; *Rubber Statistical Bulletin.*

Organisation for Economic Co-operation and Development (OECD), 2 rue Andre-Pascal, 75 Paris 16, France (Telephone Number in U.S. (202) 785-6323); *Economic Outlook, The Footwear, Raw Hides and Skins, and Leather Industry in OECD Countries, Indicators of Industrial Activity, Industrial Structure Statistics, The Iron and Steel Industry, Meat Balances in OECD Member Countries, Milk, Milk Products, and Egg Balances in OECD Member Countries, The Non-Ferrous Metals Industry, The Pulp and Paper Industry,* and *Textile Industry in OECD Countries.*

NETHERLANDS - PRODUCTIVITY

European Community Information Service, 2100 M Street, NW, Washington, D.C. 20037 (202) 862-9500; *Basic Statistics of the Community.*

Organisation for Economic Co-operation and Development (OECD), 2 rue Andre-Pascal, 75 Paris 16, France (Telephone Number in U.S.

(202) 785-6323); *Economic Outlook.*

NETHERLANDS - PROPERTY TAXES

European Community Information Service, 2100 M Street, NW, Washington, D.C. 20037 (202) 862-9500; *Basic Statistics of the Community.*

International Monetary Fund, 700 Nineteenth Street, NW, Washington, D.C. 20431 (202) 623-7000; *Government Finance Statistics Yearbook.*

Organisation for Economic Co-operation and Development (OECD), 2 rue Andre-Pascal, 75 Paris 16, France (Telephone Number in U.S. (202) 785-6323); *Revenue Statistics of OECD Member Countries.*

NETHERLANDS - PUBLIC CONSUMPTION FUND

European Community Information Service, 2100 M Street, NW, Washington, D.C. 20037 (202) 862-9500; *Basic Statistics of the Community.*

Organisation for Economic Co-operation and Development (OECD), 2 rue Andre-Pascal, 75 Paris 16, France (Telephone Number in U.S. (202) 785-6323); *Revenue Statistics of OECD Member Countries.*

NETHERLANDS - PUBLIC EXPENDITURES

European Community Information Service, 2100 M Street, NW, Washington, D.C. 20037 (202) 862-9500; *Basic Statistics of the Community.*

Organisation for Economic Co-operation and Development (OECD), 2 rue Andre-Pascal, 75 Paris 16, France (Telephone Number in U.S. (202) 785-6323); *Revenue Statistics of OECD Member Countries.*

NETHERLANDS - PUBLIC FINANCE

Facts on File, 460 Park Avenue South, New York, New York 10016 (800) 443-8323; *The New Book of World Rankings.*

Organisation for Economic Co-operation and Development (OECD), 2 rue Andre-Pascal, 75 Paris 16, France (Telephone Number in U.S. (202) 785-6323); *Revenue Statistics of OECD Member Countries.*

NETHERLANDS - PUBLIC HEALTH

European Community Information Service, 2100 M Street, NW, Washington, D.C. 20037 (202) 862-9500; *Basic Statistics of the Community.*

NETHERLANDS - PUBLIC REVENUES

Organisation for Economic Co-operation and Development (OECD), 2 rue Andre-Pascal, 75 Paris 16, France (Telephone Number in U.S. (202) 785-6323); *Revenue Statistics of OECD Member Countries.*

NETHERLANDS - RADIO BROADCASTING - See NETHERLANDS - BROADCASTING

NETHERLANDS - RAILWAYS

Euromonitor Publications Limited, 87-88 Turnmill Street, London EC1M 5QU, England; *European Marketing Data and Statistics.*

European Community Information Service, 2100 M Street, NW, Washington, D.C. 20037 (202) 862-9500; *Basic Statistics of the Community, Regions: Statistical Yearbook,* and *Transport Annual Statistics.*

Jane's Information Group, Sentinel House, 163 Brighton Road, Coulsdon, Surrey CR5 2NH, England (Telephone Number in U.S. (703) 683-3700); *Jane's World Railways.*

Statistical Office of the United Nations, Publishing Service, New York, New York 10017 (800) 253-9646; *Annual Bulletin of Transport Statistics for Europe,* and *Statistical Yearbook.*

NETHERLANDS - RANCHING

European Community Information Service, 2100 M Street, NW, Washington, D.C. 20037 (202) 862-9500; *Basic Statistics of the Community.*

NETHERLANDS - RAPESEED PRODUCTION - See NETHERLANDS - CROPS

NETHERLANDS - RELIGION

Facts on File, 460 Park Avenue South, New York, New York 10016 (800) 443-8323; *The New Book of World Rankings.*

NETHERLANDS - RENT PRICES

International Labour Office, I.L.O. Publications, CH-1211, Geneva 22, Switzerland; *Yearbook of Labour Statistics.*

NETHERLANDS - RETAIL TRADE

European Community Information Service, 2100 M Street, NW, Washington, D.C. 20037 (202) 862-9500; *Basic Statistics of the Community,* and *Eurostatistics. Data for Short-term Economic Analysis.*

Statistical Office of the United Nations, Publishing Service, New York, New York 10017 (800) 253-9646; *Statistical Yearbook.*

NETHERLANDS - RICE PRODUCTION - See NETHERLANDS - CROPS

NETHERLANDS - ROOT AND TUBER PRODUCTION - See NETHERLANDS - CROPS

NETHERLANDS - ROUNDWOOD PRODUCTION - See NETHERLANDS - FORESTRY AND FOREST PRODUCTS

NETHERLANDS - RUBBER PRODUCTION AND CONSUMPTION

European Community Information Service, 2100 M Street, NW, Washington, D.C. 20037 (202) 862-9500; *Basic Statistics of the Community.*

Facts on File, 460 Park Avenue South, New York, New York 10016 (800) 443-8323; *The New Book of World Rankings.*

International Rubber Study Group, York House, Eighth Floor, Empire Way, Wembley, London HA9 0PA, England; *Rubber Statistical Bulletin.*

Organisation for Economic Co-operation and Development (OECD), 2 rue Andre-Pascal, 75 Paris 16, France (Telephone Number in U.S. (202) 785-6323); *Foreign Trade by Commodities.*

Statistical Office of the United Nations, Publishing Service, New York, New York 10017 (800) 253-9646; *Statistical Yearbook.*

NETHERLANDS - RYE PRODUCTION - See NETHERLANDS - CROPS

NETHERLANDS - SAFFLOWER SEED PRODUCTION - See NETHERLANDS - CROPS

NETHERLANDS - SALES

Organisation for Economic Co-operation and Development (OECD), 2 rue Andre-Pascal, 75 Paris 16, France (Telephone Number in U.S. (202) 785-6323); *Main Economic Indicators - Historical Statistics.*

NETHERLANDS - SALT PRODUCTION - See NETHERLANDS - MINING AND MINERAL PRODUCTS

NETHERLANDS - SAVINGS ACCOUNT DEPOSITS

European Community Information Service, 2100 M Street, NW, Washington, D.C. 20037 (202) 862-9500; *Eurostatistics: Data for Short-term Economic Analysis.*

NETHERLANDS - SAWNWOOD PRODUCTION - See NETHERLANDS - FORESTRY AND FOREST PRODUCTS

NETHERLANDS - SCIENCE AND TECHNOLOGY

Netherlands Central Bureau of Statistics, Staatsuitgeverij, The Hague, Netherlands; *Statistical Yearbook of the Netherlands.*

NETHERLANDS - SCIENCE AND TECHNOLOGY - EXPENDITURE FOR RESEARCH

European Community Information Service, 2100 M Street, NW, Washington, D.C. 20037 (202) 862-9500; *Basic Statistics of the Community.*

Statistical Office of the United Nations, Publishing Service, New York, New York 10017 (800) 253-9646; *Statistical Yearbook.*

NETHERLANDS - SCIENTISTS AND ENGINEERS

European Community Information Service, 2100 M Street, NW, Washington, D.C. 20037 (202) 862-9500; *Basic Statistics of the Community.*

NETHERLANDS - SCIENTISTS AND TECHNICIANS

European Community Information Service, 2100 M Street, NW, Washington, D.C. 20037 (202) 862-9500; *Basic Statistics of the Community.*

Statistical Office of the United Nations, Publishing Service, New York, New York 10017 (800) 253-9646; *Statistical Yearbook.*

NETHERLANDS - SENIOR CITIZENS

Facts on File, 460 Park Avenue South, New York, New York 10016 (800) 443-8323; *The New Book of World Rankings.*

NETHERLANDS - SERVICES INDUSTRY EMPLOYMENT - MALE AND FEMALE

European Community Information Service, 2100 M Street, NW, Washington, D.C. 20037 (202) 862-9500; *Basic Statistics of the Community, Employment and Unemployment,* and *Labor Force Sample Survey.*

Organisation for Economic Co-operation and Development (OECD), 2 rue Andre-Pascal, 75 Paris 16, France (Telephone Number in U.S. (202) 785-6323); *OECD Employment Outlook.*

NETHERLANDS - SESAME SEED PRODUCTION - See NETHERLANDS - CROPS

NETHERLANDS - SHEEP - See NETHERLANDS - LIVESTOCK AND POULTRY

NETHERLANDS - SHIPBUILDING - PRODUCTION INDEX

Organisation for Economic Co-operation and Development (OECD), 2 rue Andre-Pascal, 75 Paris 16, France (Telephone Number in U.S. (202) 785-6323); *Indicators of Industrial Activity.*

NETHERLANDS - SILVER PRODUCTION AND CONSUMPTION - See NETHERLANDS - MINING AND MINERAL PRODUCTS

NETHERLANDS - SISAL PRODUCTION - See NETHERLANDS - CROPS

NETHERLANDS - SOCIAL DATA

European Community Information Service, 2100 M Street, NW, Washington, D.C. 20037 (202) 862-9500; *ACP: Basic Statistics, Basic Statistics of the Community.*

Facts on File, 460 Park Avenue South, New York, New York 10016 (800) 443-8323; *The New Book of World Rankings.*

NETHERLANDS - SOCIAL SECURITY

European Community Information Service, 2100 M Street, NW, Washington, D.C. 20037 (202) 862-9500; *Basic Statistics of the Community.*

International Monetary Fund, 700 Nineteenth Street, NW, Washington, D.C. 20431 (202) 623-7000; *Government Finance Statistics Yearbook.*

Organisation for Economic Co-operation and Development (OECD), 2 rue Andre-Pascal, 75 Paris 16, France (Telephone Number in U.S. (202) 785-6323); *Revenue Statistics of OECD Member Countries.*

NETHERLANDS - SOCIOECONOMIC DATA

European Community Information Service, 2100 M Street, NW, Washington, D.C. 20037 (202) 862-9500; *Basic Statistics of the Community.*

Organisation for Economic Co-operation and Development (OECD), 2 rue Andre-Pascal, 75 Paris 16, France (Telephone Number in U.S. (202) 785-6323); *Economic Outlook.*

NETHERLANDS - SOYBEAN PRODUCTION

European Community Information Service, 2100 M Street, NW, Washington, D.C. 20037 (202) 862-9500; *Basic Statistics of the Community.*

NETHERLANDS - STAMP TAXES AND DUTIES - See NETHERLANDS - TAXATION

NETHERLANDS - STEEL - See NETHERLANDS - MINING AND MINERAL PRODUCTS

NETHERLANDS - STOCKS - COMMODITY - MARKET PRICE - INDEXES

Food and Agricultural Organization of the United Nations (FAO) Via delle Terme di Caracalla, 00100 Rome, Italy (Telephone Number in U.S. (202) 653-2400); *The State of Food and Agriculture.*

International Lead and Zinc Study Group, Metro House, 58 St. James's Street, London SW1A 1LD England; *Lead and Zinc Statistics.*

Statistical Office of the United Nations, Publishing Service, New York, New York 10017 (800) 253-9646; *Statistical Yearbook.*

World Bureau of Metal Statistics, 27-A High Street, Ware, Herts. SG12 9BA, England; *World Metal Statistics.*

NETHERLANDS - STRAW PRODUCTION - See NETHERLANDS - CROPS

NETHERLANDS - SUGAR - See SUGAR - NETHERLANDS - CROPS

NETHERLANDS - SUGAR PRODUCTION AND CONSUMPTION

European Community Information Service, 2100 M Street, NW, Washington, D.C. 20037 (202) 862-9500; *ACP: Basic Statistics,* and *Basic Statistics of the Community.*

Facts on File, 460 Park Avenue South, New York, New York 10016 (800) 443-8323; *The New Book of World Rankings.*

Statistical Office of the United Nations, Publishing Service, New York, New York 10017 (800) 253-9646; *Statistical Yearbook.*

NETHERLANDS - SUGARBEET PRODUCTION

European Community Information Service, 2100 M Street, NW, Washington, D.C. 20037 (202) 862-9500; *Basic Statistics of the Community.*

NETHERLANDS - SULPHUR PRODUCTION - See NETHERLANDS - MINING AND MINERAL PRODUCTS

NETHERLANDS - SULPHURIC ACID - See NETHERLANDS - MINING AND MINERAL PRODUCTS

NETHERLANDS - SULPHURIC ACID PRODUCTION - See NETHERLANDS - MINING AND MINERAL PRODUCTS

NETHERLANDS - SUNFLOWER PRODUCTION - See NETHERLANDS - CROPS

NETHERLANDS - TAXATION

European Community Information Service, 2100 M Street, NW, Washington, D.C. 20037 (202) 862-9500; *Basic Statistics of the Community.*

International Monetary Fund, 700 Nineteenth Street, NW, Washington, D.C. 20431 (202) 623-7000; *Government Finance Statistics Yearbook.*

International Road Federation, 525 School Street, SW, Washington, D.C. 20024 (202) 554-2106; *World Road Statistics.*

Netherlands Central Bureau of Statistics, Staatsuitgeverij, The Hague, Netherlands; *Statistical Yearbook of the Netherlands.*

Organisation for Economic Co-operation and Development (OECD), 2 rue Andre-Pascal, 75 Paris 16, France (Telephone Number in U.S. (202) 785-6323; *Revenue Statistics of OECD Member Countries.*

The World Bank, 1818 H Street, NW, Washington, D.C. 20433 (202) 477-1234; *World Tables.*

NETHERLANDS - TAX REVENUE - See NETHERLANDS - TAXATION

NETHERLANDS - TEA PRODUCTION AND CONSUMPTION - See NETHERLANDS - CROPS

NETHERLANDS - TELEGRAPH SERVICE

NETHERLANDS - TELEPHONES IN USE

American Telephone and Telegraph Company, 26 Parsippany Road, Whippany, New Jersey 07981 (800) 338-4038; *The World's Telephones.*

European Community Information Service, 2100 M Street, NW, Washington, D.C. 20037 (202) 862-9500; *Basic Statistics of the Community,* and *Transport Annual Statistics.*

Statistical Office of the United Nations, Publishing Service, New York, New York 10017 (800) 253-9646; *Statistical Yearbook.*

World Health Organization, Office of Publications, Avenue Appia, CH-1211 Geneva 27, Switzerland (Telephone Number in U.S. (518) 436-9686); *World Health Statistics Annual.*

NETHERLANDS - TELEVISION BROADCASTING - See NETHERLANDS - BROADCASTING

NETHERLANDS - TELEVISION RECEIVER PRODUCTION

European Community Information Service, 2100 M Street, NW, Washington, D.C. 20037 (202) 862-9500; *Basic Statistics of the Community.*

NETHERLANDS - TEXTILE INDUSTRY

American Forest and Paper Association, 1250 Connecticut Avenue, NW, Washington, D.C. 20036 (202) 463-2455; *Wood Pulp and Fiber Statistics.*

European Community Information Service, 2100 M Street, NW, Washington, D.C. 20037 (202) 862-9500; *Basic Statistics of the Community, Eurostatistics: Data for Short-term Economic Analysis,* and *Industrial Production: Quarterly Statistics.*

Food and Agricultural Organization of the United Nations (FAO), Via delle Terme di Caracalla, 00100 Rome, Italy (Telephone Number in U.S. (202) 653-2400); *Production Yearbook.*

Organisation for Economic Co-operation and Development (OECD), 2 rue Andre-Pascal, 75 Paris 16, France (Telephone Number in U.S. (202) 785-6323); *Foreign Trade by Commodities, Indicators of Industrial Activity, Industrial Structure Statistics,* and *Textile Industry in OECD Countries.*

Statistical Office of the United Nations, Publishing Service, New York, New York 10017 (800) 253-9646; *Statistical Yearbook,* and *Trade in Manufactures of Developing Countries.*

NETHERLANDS - THEATRE

United Nations Educational, Scientific and Cultural Organization (UNESCO), 7 Place de Fontenoy, F-75700 Paris, France (Telephone Number in U.S. (212) 963-5981); *Statistical Yearbook.*

NETHERLANDS - TIMBER - See NETHERLANDS - FORESTRY AND FOREST PRODUCTS

NETHERLANDS - TIN - See NETHERLANDS - MINING AND MINERAL PRODUCTS

NETHERLANDS - TIRE (MOTOR VEHICLE) PRODUCTION

International Rubber Study Group, York House, Eighth Floor, Empire Way, Wembley, London HA9 0PA, England; *Rubber Statistical*

Bulletin.

NETHERLANDS - TOBACCO PRODUCTION

Euromonitor Publications Limited, 87-88 Turnmill Street, London EC1M 5QU, England; *European Marketing Data and Statistics.*

European Community Information Service, 2100 M Street, NW, Washington, D.C. 20037 (202) 862-9500; *Basic Statistics of the Community,* and *Industrial Production: Quarterly Statistics.*

Facts on File, 460 Park Avenue South, New York, New York 10016 (800) 443-8323; *The New Book of World Rankings.*

Organisation for Economic Co-operation and Development (OECD), 2 rue Andre-Pascal, 75 Paris 16, France (Telephone Number in U.S. (202) 785-6323); *Foreign Trade by Commodities, Indicators of Industrial Activity,* and *Industrial Structure Statistics.*

Statistical Office of the United Nations, Publishing Service, New York, New York 10017 (800) 253-9646; *Statistical Yearbook.*

NETHERLANDS - TOURISM

Euromonitor Publications Limited, 87-88 Turnmill Street, London EC1M 5QU, England; *European Marketing Data and Statistics.*

European Community Information Service, 2100 M Street, NW, Washington, D.C. 20037 (202) 862-9500; *Transport Annual Statistics.*

Facts on File, 460 Park Avenue South, New York, New York 10016 (800) 443-8323; *The New Book of World Rankings.*

Organisation for Economic Co-operation and Development (OECD), 2 rue Andre-Pascal, 75 Paris 16, France (Telephone Number in U.S. (202) 785-6323); *Tourism Policy and International Tourism in OECD Member Countries.*

Statistical Office of the United Nations, Publishing Service, New York, New York 10017 (800) 253-9646; *Statistical Yearbook.*

Times Books, 201 East 50th Street, New York, New York 10022 (212) 751-2600; *The Economist Book of Vital World Statistics.*

World Tourism Organization, Calle Capitan Haya 42, E-28020 Madrid, Spain; *Yearbook of Tourism Statistics.*

NETHERLANDS - TRACTORS IN USE

Statistical Office of the United Nations, Publishing Service, New York, New York 10017 (800) 253-9646; *Statistical Yearbook.*

NETHERLANDS - TRADE - See NETHERLANDS - FOREIGN TRADE

NETHERLANDS - TRADEMARKS AND SERVICE MARKS

Statistical Office of the United Nations, Publishing Service, New York, New York 10017 (800) 253-9646; *Statistical Yearbook.*

World Intellectual Property Organization, 34 Chemin des Colombettes, CH-1211 Geneva 20, Switzerland; *Industrial Property Statistics.*

NETHERLANDS - TRANSPORTATION AND COMMUNICATIONS

European Community Information Service, 2100 M Street, NW, Washington, D.C. 20037 (202) 862-9500; *Basic Statistics of the Community, Energy Statistics Yearbook, Regions: Statistical*

Yearbook, and *Transport Annual Statistics.*

Facts on File, 460 Park Avenue South, New York, New York 10016 (800) 443-8323; *The New Book of World Rankings.*

Netherlands Central Bureau of Statistics, Staatsuitgeverij, The Hague, Netherlands; *Statistical Yearbook of the Netherlands.*

NETHERLANDS - TRANSPORTATION EMPLOYMENT - MALE AND FEMALE - See NETHERLANDS - EMPLOYMENT

NETHERLANDS - TUNGSTEN PRODUCTION AND CONSUMPTION - See NETHERLANDS - MINING AND MINERAL PRODUCTS

NETHERLANDS - TURKEYS - See NETHERLANDS - LIVESTOCK AND POULTRY

NETHERLANDS - UNEMPLOYMENT

Euromonitor Publications Limited, 87-88 Turnmill Street, London EC1M 5QU, England; *European Marketing Data and Statistics.*

European Community Information Service, 2100 M Street, NW, Washington, D.C. 20037 (202) 862-9500; *Basic Statistics of the Community, Employment and Unemployment, Eurostatistics: Data for Short-term Economic Analysis, Labor Force Sample Survey,* and *Regions: Statistical Yearbook.*

International Labour Office, I.L.O. Publications, CH-1211, Geneva 22, Switzerland; *Yearbook of Labour Statistics.*

Organisation for Economic Co-operation and Development (OECD), 2 rue Andre-Pascal, 75 Paris 16, France (Telephone Number in U.S. (202) 785-6323); *Economic Outlook, OECD Economic Surveys: Netherlands,* and *OECD Employment Outlook.*

Statistical Office of the United Nations, Publishing Service, New York, New York 10017 (800) 253-9646; *Statistical Yearbook.*

NETHERLANDS - URANIUM PRODUCTION AND CONSUMPTION - See NETHERLANDS - MINING AND MINERAL PRODUCTS

NETHERLANDS - UTILITIES

European Community Information Service, 2100 M Street, NW, Washington, D.C. 20037 (202) 862-9500; *Basic Statistics of the Community.*

NETHERLANDS - VANADIUM AND VANADIUM ORE PRODUCTION AND CONSUMPTION - See NETHERLANDS - MINING AND MINERAL PRODUCTS

NETHERLANDS - VITAL STATISTICS

European Community Information Service, 2100 M Street, NW, Washington, D.C. 20037 (202) 862-9500; *Basic Statistics of the Community.*

Statistical Office of the United Nations, Publishing Service, New York, New York 10017 (800) 253-9646; *Statistical Yearbook.*

NETHERLANDS - WAGES

Euromonitor Publications Limited, 87-88 Turnmill Street, London EC1M 5QU, England; *European Marketing Data and Statistics.*

European Community Information Service, 2100 M Street, NW, Washington, D.C. 20037 (202) 862-9500; *Basic Statistics of the Community, Earnings in Agriculture,* and *Eurostatistics: Data for*

Short-term Economic Analysis.

International Labour Office, I.L.O. Publications, CH-1211, Geneva 22, Switzerland; *Yearbook of Labour Statistics.*

Organisation for Economic Co-operation and Development (OECD), 2 rue Andre-Pascal, 75 Paris 16, France (Telephone Number in U.S. (202) 785-6323); *Economic Outlook, Industrial Structure Statistics,* and *Main Economic Indicators - Historical Statistics.*

Statistical Office of the United Nations, Publishing Service, New York, New York 10017 (800) 253-9646; *Statistical Yearbook.*

NETHERLANDS - WALNUT PRODUCTION - See NETHERLANDS - CROPS

NETHERLANDS - WATERWAYS IN USE

European Community Information Service, 2100 M Street, NW, Washington, D.C. 20037 (202) 862-9500; *Basic Statistics of the Community,* and *Transport Annual Statistics.*

Organisation for Economic Co-operation and Development (OECD), 2 rue Andre-Pascal, 75 Paris 16, France (Telephone Number in U.S. (202) 785-6323); *Maritime Transport.*

Statistical Office of the United Nations, Publishing Service, New York, New York 10017 (800) 253-9646; *Annual Bulletin of Transport Statistics for Europe.*

NETHERLANDS - WEATHER

Facts on File, 460 Park Avenue South, New York, New York 10016 (800) 443-8323; *The New Book of World Rankings.*

NETHERLANDS - WELFARE

European Community Information Service, 2100 M Street, NW, Washington, D.C. 20037 (202) 862-9500; *Basic Statistics of the Community.*

International Monetary Fund, 700 Nineteenth Street, NW, Washington, D.C. 20431 (202) 623-7000; *Government Finance Statistics Yearbook.*

NETHERLANDS - WHEAT PRODUCTION AND PRICES - See NETHERLANDS CROPS

NETHERLANDS - WHOLESALE PRICES

European Community Information Service, 2100 M Street, NW, Washington, D.C. 20037 (202) 862-9500; *Basic Statistics of the Community.*

Statistical Office of the United Nations, Publishing Service, New York, New York 10017 (800) 253-9646; *Statistical Yearbook.*

NETHERLANDS - WHOLESALE TRADE

European Community Information Service, 2100 M Street, NW, Washington, D.C. 20037 (202) 862-9500; *Basic Statistics of the Community.*

Statistical Office of the United Nations, Publishing Service, New York, New York 10017 (800) 253-9646; *Statistical Yearbook.*

NETHERLANDS - WINE PRODUCTION

European Community Information Service, 2100 M Street, NW, Washington, D.C. 20037 (202) 862-9500; *Basic Statistics of the Community.*

Facts on File, 460 Park Avenue South, New York, New York 10016 (800) 443-8323; *The New Book of World Rankings.*

NETHERLANDS - WOOD AND WOOD PULP - See NETHERLANDS - FORESTRY AND FOREST PRODUCTS

NETHERLANDS - WOOL - INDUSTRIAL CONSUMPTION

Organisation for Economic Co-operation and Development (OECD), 2 rue Andre-Pascal, 75 Paris 16, France (Telephone Number in U.S. (202) 785-6323); *Textile Industry in OECD Countries.*

Statistical Office of the United Nations, Publishing Service, New York, New York 10017 (800) 253-9646; *Statistical Yearbook.*

NETHERLANDS - WOOL PRODUCTION

European Community Information Service, 2100 M Street, NW, Washington, D.C. 20037 (202) 862-9500; *Basic Statistics of the Community.*

Facts on File, 460 Park Avenue South, New York, New York 10016 (800) 443-8323; *The New Book of World Rankings.*

Organisation for Economic Co-operation and Development (OECD), 2 rue Andre-Pascal, 75 Paris 16, France (Telephone Number in U.S. (202) 785-6323); *Economic Accounts for Agriculture,* and *Textile Industry in OECD Countries.*

NETHERLANDS - YARN PRODUCTION

European Community Information Service, 2100 M Street, NW, Washington, D.C. 20037 (202) 862-9500; *Basic Statistics of the Community.*

Organisation for Economic Co-operation and Development (OECD), 2 rue Andre-Pascal, 75 Paris 16, France (Telephone Number in U.S. (202) 785-6323); *Foreign Trade by Commodities,* and *Textile Industry in OECD Countries.*

Statistical Office of the United Nations, Publishing Service, New York, New York 10017 (800) 253-9646; *Statistical Yearbook.*

NETHERLANDS - ZINC AND ZINC ORE PRODUCTION AND CONSUMPTION - See NETHERLANDS - MINING AND MINERAL PRODUCTS

NETHERLANDS - ZINC (SLAB) CONSUMPTION - See NETHERLANDS - MINING AND MINERAL PRODUCTS

Netherlands Antilles - National Statistical Office

Central Bureau of Statistics, Willemstad, Curacao, Netherlands Antilles.

Netherlands Antilles - Primary Statistics Source

Central Bureau of Statistics, Willemstad, Curacao, Netherlands Antilles; *Statistisch jaarboek: Nederlandse Antillen* (Statistical

Yearbook: Netherlands Antilles).

NETHERLANDS ANTILLES - AGRICULTURE

Food and Agricultural Organization of the United Nations (FAO) Via delle Terme di Caracalla, 00100 Rome, Italy (Telephone Number in U.S. (202) 653-2400); *Production Yearbook, The State of Food and Agriculture,* and *Trade Yearbook.*

G.K. Hall and Company, 70 Lincoln Street, Boston, Massachusetts 02111 (617) 423-3990; *The World in Figures.*

Statistical Office of the United Nations, Publishing Service, New York, New York 10017 (800) 253-9646; *Statistical Yearbook.*

NETHERLANDS ANTILLES - AIRLINE SERVICE

G.K. Hall and Company, 70 Lincoln Street, Boston, Massachusetts 02111 (617) 423-3990; *The World in Figures.*

NETHERLANDS ANTILLES - AREA AND DENSITY OF POPULATION

Food and Agricultural Organization of the United Nations (FAO) Via delle Terme di Caracalla, 00100 Rome, Italy (Telephone Number in U.S. (202) 653-2400); *The State of Food and Agriculture.*

G.K. Hall and Company, 70 Lincoln Street, Boston, Massachusetts 02111 (617) 423-3990; *The World in Figures.*

Statistical Office of the United Nations, Publishing Service, New York, New York 10017 (800) 253-9646; *Statistical Yearbook.*

Times Books, 201 East 50th Street, New York, New York 10022 (212) 751-2600; *The Economist Book of Vital World Statistics.*

United Nations Educational, Scientific and Cultural Organization (UNESCO), 7 Place de Fontenoy, F-75700 Paris, France (Telephone Number in U.S. (212) 963-5981); *Statistical Yearbook.*

NETHERLANDS ANTILLES - BALANCE OF PAYMENTS

The Economist Intelligence Unit, 111 West 57th Street, New York, New York 10019 (800) 938-4685; *The World Market Atlas.*

G.K. Hall and Company, 70 Lincoln Street, Boston, Massachusetts 02111 (617) 423-3990; *The World in Figures.*

International Monetary Fund, 700 Nineteenth Street, NW, Washington, D.C. 20431 (202) 623-7000; *Balance of Payments Yearbook.*

Times Books, 201 East 50th Street, New York, New York 10022 (212) 751-2600; *The Economist Book of Vital World Statistics.*

NETHERLANDS ANTILLES - BANKING

G.K. Hall and Company, 70 Lincoln Street, Boston, Massachusetts 02111 (617) 423-3990; *The World in Figures.*

International Monetary Fund, 700 Nineteenth Street, NW, Washington, D.C. 20431 (202) 623-7000; *Government Finance Statistics Yearbook,* and *International Financial Statistics.*

NETHERLANDS ANTILLES - BEER PRODUCTION

Statistical Office of the United Nations, Publishing Service, New York, New York 10017 (800) 253-9646; *Statistical Yearbook.*

NETHERLANDS ANTILLES - BIRTH RATES

Statistical Office of the United Nations, Publishing Service, New York, New York 10017 (800) 253-9646; *Demographic Yearbook,* and *Statistical Yearbook.*

NETHERLANDS ANTILLES - BONDS

G.K. Hall and Company, 70 Lincoln Street, Boston, Massachusetts 02111 (617) 423-3990; *The World in Figures.*

International Monetary Fund, 700 Nineteenth Street, NW, Washington, D.C. 20431 (202) 623-7000; *Government Finance Statistics Yearbook.*

NETHERLANDS ANTILLES - BOOK PRODUCTION

G.K. Hall and Company, 70 Lincoln Street, Boston, Massachusetts 02111 (617) 423-3990; *The World in Figures.*

United Nations Educational, Scientific and Cultural Organization (UNESCO), 7 Place de Fontenoy, F-75700 Paris, France (Telephone Number in U.S. (212) 963-5981); *Statistical Yearbook.*

NETHERLANDS ANTILLES - BROADCASTING

Billboard Limited, Post Office Box 9027, 1006 AA Amsterdam, The Netherlands (Telephone Number in U.S. (212) 764-7300); *World Radio TV Handbook.*

G.K. Hall and Company, 70 Lincoln Street, Boston, Massachusetts 02111 (617) 423-3990; *The World in Figures.*

Times Books, 201 East 50th Street, New York, New York 10022 (212) 751-2600; *The Economist Book of Vital World Statistics.*

NETHERLANDS ANTILLES - BUSINESS

G.K. Hall and Company, 70 Lincoln Street, Boston, Massachusetts 02111 (617) 423-3990; *The World in Figures.*

NETHERLANDS ANTILLES - CALORIE SUPPLY

Food and Agricultural Organization of the United Nations (FAO) Via delle Terme di Caracalla, 00100 Rome, Italy (Telephone Number in U.S. (202) 653-2400); *The State of Food and Agriculture.*

NETHERLANDS ANTILLES - CAPITAL REVENUE

International Monetary Fund, 700 Nineteenth Street, NW, Washington, D.C. 20431 (202) 623-7000; *Government Finance Statistics Yearbook.*

NETHERLANDS ANTILLES - CATTLE - See NETHERLANDS ANTILLES - LIVESTOCK AND POULTRY

NETHERLANDS ANTILLES - CHEMICAL (ORGANIC) PRODUCTION - See NETHERLANDS ANTILLES - MINING AND MINERAL PRODUCTS

NETHERLANDS ANTILLES - CLASS STRUCTURE

G.K. Hall and Company, 70 Lincoln Street, Boston, Massachusetts 02111 (617) 423-3990; *The World in Figures.*

NETHERLANDS ANTILLES - CLIMATE

G.K. Hall and Company, 70 Lincoln Street, Boston, Massachusetts 02111 (617) 423-3990; *The World in Figures.*

NETHERLANDS ANTILLES - COAL PRODUCTION - See NETHERLANDS ANTILLES - MINING AND MINERAL PRODUCTS

NETHERLANDS ANTILLES - COMMUNICATIONS

G.K. Hall and Company, 70 Lincoln Street, Boston, Massachusetts 02111 (617) 423-3990; *The World in Figures.*

NETHERLANDS ANTILLES - CONSTRUCTION INDUSTRY

Statistical Office of the United Nations, Publishing Service, New York, New York 10017 (800) 253-9646; *Construction Statistics Yearbook,* and *Statistical Yearbook.*

NETHERLANDS ANTILLES - CONSUMER PRICE INDEX

G.K. Hall and Company, 70 Lincoln Street, Boston, Massachusetts 02111 (617) 423-3990; *The World in Figures.*

Statistical Office of the United Nations, Publishing Service, New York, New York 10017 (800) 253-9646; *Statistical Yearbook.*

NETHERLANDS ANTILLES - CONSUMER PRICES

International Labour Office, I.L.O. Publications, CH-1211, Geneva 22, Switzerland; *Yearbook of Labour Statistics.*

International Monetary Fund, 700 Nineteenth Street, NW, Washington, D.C. 20431 (202) 623-7000; *International Financial Statistics.*

Times Books, 201 East 50th Street, New York, New York 10022 (212) 751-2600; *The Economist Book of Vital World Statistics.*

NETHERLANDS ANTILLES - CONSUMPTION

G.K. Hall and Company, 70 Lincoln Street, Boston, Massachusetts 02111 (617) 423-3990; *The World in Figures.*

NETHERLANDS ANTILLES - CORN PRODUCTION - See NETHERLANDS ANTILLES - CROPS

NETHERLANDS ANTILLES - CORPORATE TAXES - See NETHERLANDS ANTILLES - TAXATION

NETHERLANDS ANTILLES - CRIME

Yale University Press, Yale Station, New Haven, Connecticut 06520 (203) 432-0940; *Violence and Crime in Cross-National Perspective.*

NETHERLANDS ANTILLES - CROPS

Food and Agricultural Organization of the United Nations (FAO) Via delle Terme di Caracalla, 00100 Rome, Italy (Telephone Number in U.S. (202) 653-2400); *The State of Food and Agriculture.*

G.K. Hall and Company, 70 Lincoln Street, Boston, Massachusetts 02111 (617) 423-3990; *The World in Figures.*

NETHERLANDS ANTILLES - CUSTOMS DUTIES

G.K. Hall and Company, 70 Lincoln Street, Boston, Massachusetts 02111 (617) 423-3990; *The World in Figures.*

International Monetary Fund, 700 Nineteenth Street, NW, Washington, D.C. 20431 (202) 623-7000; *Government Finance Statistics Yearbook.*

NETHERLANDS ANTILLES - DAIRY PRODUCTS

Food and Agricultural Organization of the United Nations (FAO) Via delle Terme di Caracalla, 00100 Rome, Italy (Telephone Number in U.S. (202) 653-2400); *The State of Food and Agriculture.*

NETHERLANDS ANTILLES - DEATH RATES

G.K. Hall and Company, 70 Lincoln Street, Boston, Massachusetts 02111 (617) 423-3990; *The World in Figures.*

Statistical Office of the United Nations, Publishing Service, New York, New York 10017 (800) 253-9646; *Statistical Yearbook.*

NETHERLANDS ANTILLES - DEFENSE EXPENDITURES

G.K. Hall and Company, 70 Lincoln Street, Boston, Massachusetts 02111 (617) 423-3990; *The World in Figures.*

International Monetary Fund, 700 Nineteenth Street, NW, Washington, D.C. 20431 (202) 623-7000; *Government Finance Statistics Yearbook.*

NETHERLANDS ANTILLES - DEMOGRAPHY

The Economist Intelligence Unit, 111 West 57th Street, New York, New York 10019 (800) 938-4685; *The World Market Atlas.*

G.K. Hall and Company, 70 Lincoln Street, Boston, Massachusetts 02111 (617) 423-3990; *The World in Figures.*

NETHERLANDS ANTILLES - DEVELOPMENT ASSISTANCE

G.K. Hall and Company, 70 Lincoln Street, Boston, Massachusetts 02111 (617) 423-3990; *The World in Figures.*

Statistical Office of the United Nations, Publishing Service, New York, New York 10017 (800) 253-9646; *Statistical Yearbook.*

NETHERLANDS ANTILLES - DISEASE

G.K. Hall and Company, 70 Lincoln Street, Boston, Massachusetts 02111 (617) 423-3990; *The World in Figures.*

NETHERLANDS ANTILLES - DIVORCE RATES

Statistical Office of the United Nations, Publishing Service, New York, New York 10017 (800) 253-9646; *Demographic Yearbook,* and *Statistical Yearbook.*

NETHERLANDS ANTILLES - DOMESTIC PRODUCT

G.K. Hall and Company, 70 Lincoln Street, Boston, Massachusetts 02111 (617) 423-3990; *The World in Figures.*

NETHERLANDS ANTILLES - ECONOMY

G.K. Hall and Company, 70 Lincoln Street, Boston, Massachusetts 02111 (617) 423-3990; *The World in Figures.*

NETHERLANDS ANTILLES - EDUCATION

The Economist Intelligence Unit, 111 West 57th Street, New York, New York 10019 (800) 938-4685; *The World Market Atlas.*

G.K. Hall and Company, 70 Lincoln Street, Boston, Massachusetts 02111 (617) 423-3990; *The World in Figures.*

International Monetary Fund, 700 Nineteenth Street, NW, Washington, D.C. 20431 (202) 623-7000; *Government Finance Statistics Yearbook.*

Times Books, 201 East 50th Street, New York, New York 10022 (212) 751-2600; *The Economist Book of Vital World Statistics.*

United Nations Educational, Scientific and Cultural Organization (UNESCO), 7 Place de Fontenoy, F-75700 Paris, France (Telephone Number in U.S. (212) 963-5981); *Statistical Yearbook.*

NETHERLANDS ANTILLES - EGG PRODUCTION AND CONSUMPTION - See NETHERLANDS ANTILLES - DAIRY PRODUCTS

NETHERLANDS ANTILLES - ELECTRICITY

Statistical Office of the United Nations, Publishing Service, New York, New York 10017 (800) 253-9646; *Statistical Yearbook.*

NETHERLANDS ANTILLES - EMPLOYMENT

International Labour Office, I.L.O. Publications, CH-1211, Geneva 22, Switzerland; *Yearbook of Labour Statistics.*

NETHERLANDS ANTILLES - ENERGY

Food and Agricultural Organization of the United Nations (FAO) Via delle Terme di Caracalla, 00100 Rome, Italy (Telephone Number in U.S. (202) 653-2400); *The State of Food and Agriculture.*

G.K. Hall and Company, 70 Lincoln Street, Boston, Massachusetts 02111 (617) 423-3990; *The World in Figures.*

Statistical Office of the United Nations, Publishing Service, New York, New York 10017 (800) 253-9646; *Energy Statistics Yearbook,* and *Statistical Yearbook,* and *World Energy Supplies.*

Times Books, 201 East 50th Street, New York, New York 10022 (212) 751-2600; *The Economist Book of Vital World Statistics.*

NETHERLANDS ANTILLES - EXCHANGE RATES

International Monetary Fund, 700 Nineteenth Street, NW, Washington, D.C. 20431 (202) 623-7000; *International Financial Statistics.*

NETHERLANDS ANTILLES - EXCISE TAXES - See NETHERLANDS ANTILLES - TAXATION

NETHERLANDS ANTILLES - EXPORTS

The Economist Intelligence Unit, 111 West 57th Street, New York, New York 10019 (800) 938-4685; *The World Market Atlas.*

Food and Agricultural Organization of the United Nations (FAO) Via delle Terme di Caracalla, 00100 Rome, Italy (Telephone Number in U.S. (202) 653-2400); *The State of Food and Agriculture.*

G.K. Hall and Company, 70 Lincoln Street, Boston, Massachusetts 02111 (617) 423-3990; *The World in Figures.*

International Monetary Fund, 700 Nineteenth Street, NW, Washington, D.C. 20431 (202) 623-7000; *Direction of Trade Statistics.*

Statistical Office of the United Nations, Publishing Service, New York, New York 10017 (800) 253-9646; *Trade in Manufactures of Developing Countries.*

Times Books, 201 East 50th Street, New York, New York 10022 (212) 751-2600; *The Economist Book of Vital World Statistics.*

NETHERLANDS ANTILLES - EXTERNAL TRADE

Food and Agricultural Organization of the United Nations (FAO) Via delle Terme di Caracalla, 00100 Rome, Italy (Telephone Number in U.S. (202) 653-2400); *The State of Food and Agriculture,* and *Trade Yearbook.*

G.K. Hall and Company, 70 Lincoln Street, Boston, Massachusetts 02111 (617) 423-3990; *The World in Figures.*

Statistical Office of the United Nations, Publishing Service, New York, New York 10017 (800) 253-9646; *Statistical Yearbook.*

NETHERLANDS ANTILLES - FARM CROPS - See NETHERLANDS ANTILLES - CROPS

NETHERLANDS ANTILLES - FERTILIZER

Food and Agricultural Organization of the United Nations (FAO) Via delle Terme di Caracalla, 00100 Rome, Italy (Telephone Number in U.S. (202) 653-2400); *The State of Food and Agriculture.*

Statistical Office of the United Nations, Publishing Service, New York, New York 10017 (800) 253-9646; *Statistical Yearbook.*

NETHERLANDS ANTILLES - FETAL MORTALITY

Statistical Office of the United Nations, Publishing Service, New York, New York 10017 (800) 253-9646; *Demographic Yearbook.*

NETHERLANDS ANTILLES - FINANCE

G.K. Hall and Company, 70 Lincoln Street, Boston, Massachusetts 02111 (617) 423-3990; *The World in Figures.*

International Monetary Fund, 700 Nineteenth Street, NW, Washington, D.C. 20431 (202) 623-7000; *Government Finance Statistics Yearbook.*

NETHERLANDS ANTILLES - FISHERIES

Food and Agricultural Organization of the United Nations (FAO) Via delle Terme di Caracalla, 00100 Rome, Italy (Telephone Number in U.S. (202) 653-2400); *The State of Food and Agriculture,* and *Yearbook of Fishery Statistics.*

Statistical Office of the United Nations, Publishing Service, New York, New York 10017 (800) 253-9646; *Statistical Yearbook.*

NETHERLANDS ANTILLES - FOOD

Food and Agricultural Organization of the United Nations (FAO), Via delle Terme di Caracalla, 00100 Rome, Italy (Telephone Number in U.S. (202) 653-2400); *Production Yearbook,* and *The State of Food and Agriculture.*

G.K. Hall and Company, 70 Lincoln Street, Boston, Massachusetts 02111 (617) 423-3990; *The World in Figures.*

NETHERLANDS ANTILLES - FOREIGN AID

G.K. Hall and Company, 70 Lincoln Street, Boston, Massachusetts 02111 (617) 423-3990; *The World in Figures.*

NETHERLANDS ANTILLES - FOREIGN DEBT

International Monetary Fund, 700 Nineteenth Street, NW, Washington, D.C. 20431 (202) 623-7000; *Government Finance Statistics Yearbook*.

NETHERLANDS ANTILLES - FOREIGN TRADE

Food and Agricultural Organization of the United Nations (FAO) Via delle Terme di Caracalla, 00100 Rome, Italy (Telephone Number in U.S. (202) 653-2400); *The State of Food and Agriculture*.

G.K. Hall and Company, 70 Lincoln Street, Boston, Massachusetts 02111 (617) 423-3990; *The World in Figures*.

Statistical Office of the United Nations, Publishing Service, New York, New York 10017 (800) 253-9646; *International Trade Statistics Yearbook*, and *Statistical Yearbook*.

NETHERLANDS ANTILLES - FORESTRY AND FOREST PRODUCTS

Food and Agricultural Organization of the United Nations (FAO) Via delle Terme di Caracalla, 00100 Rome, Italy (Telephone Number in U.S. (202) 653-2400); *The State of Food and Agriculture*, and *Yearbook of Forest Products*.

G.K. Hall and Company, 70 Lincoln Street, Boston, Massachusetts 02111 (617) 423-3990; *The World in Figures*.

Statistical Office of the United Nations, Publishing Service, New York, New York 10017 (800) 253-9646; *Statistical Yearbook*.

United Nations Educational, Scientific and Cultural Organization (UNESCO), 7 Place de Fontenoy, F 75700 Paris, France (Telephone Number in U.S. (212) 963-5981); *Statistical Yearbook*.

NETHERLANDS ANTILLES - GENERAL MORTALITY

Statistical Office of the United Nations, Publishing Service, New York, New York 10017 (800) 253-9646; *Demographic Yearbook*.

NETHERLANDS ANTILLES - GOLD HOLDINGS

International Monetary Fund, 700 Nineteenth Street, NW, Washington, D.C. 20431 (202) 623-7000; *International Financial Statistics*.

NETHERLANDS ANTILLES - GOVERNMENT

G.K. Hall and Company, 70 Lincoln Street, Boston, Massachusetts 02111 (617) 423-3990; *The World in Figures*.

NETHERLANDS ANTILLES - GOVERNMENT EXPENDITURES

International Monetary Fund, 700 Nineteenth Street, NW, Washington, D.C. 20431 (202) 623-7000; *Government Finance Statistics Yearbook*.

Times Books, 201 East 50th Street, New York, New York 10022 (212) 751-2600; *The Economist Book of Vital World Statistics*.

NETHERLANDS ANTILLES - GOVERNMENT REVENUE

International Monetary Fund, 700 Nineteenth Street, NW, Washington, D.C. 20431 (202) 623-7000; *Government Finance Statistics Yearbook*.

Times Books, 201 East 50th Street, New York, New York 10022 (212) 751-2600; *The Economist Book of Vital World Statistics*.

NETHERLANDS ANTILLES - GRAIN PRODUCTION - See NETHERLANDS ANTILLES - CROPS

NETHERLANDS ANTILLES - GRANTS

International Monetary Fund, 700 Nineteenth Street, NW, Washington, D.C. 20431 (202) 623-7000; *Government Finance Statistics Yearbook*.

NETHERLANDS ANTILLES - GROSS DOMESTIC PRODUCT

The Economist Intelligence Unit, 111 West 57th Street, New York, New York 10019 (800) 938-4685; *The World Market Atlas*.

G.K. Hall and Company, 70 Lincoln Street, Boston, Massachusetts 02111 (617) 423-3990; *The World in Figures*.

Statistical Office of the United Nations, Publishing Service, New York, New York 10017 (800) 253-9646; *Statistical Yearbook*.

Times Books, 201 East 50th Street, New York, New York 10022 (212) 751-2600; *The Economist Book of Vital World Statistics*.

NETHERLANDS ANTILLES - HEALTH

G.K. Hall and Company, 70 Lincoln Street, Boston, Massachusetts 02111 (617) 423-3990; *The World in Figures*.

Statistical Office of the United Nations, Publishing Service, New York, New York 10017 (800) 253-9646; *Statistical Yearbook*.

NETHERLANDS ANTILLES - HEALTH EXPENDITURES

International Monetary Fund, 700 Nineteenth Street, NW, Washington, D.C. 20431 (202) 623-7000; *Government Finance Statistics Yearbook*.

NETHERLANDS ANTILLES - HIDE PRODUCTION

Food and Agricultural Organization of the United Nations (FAO), Via delle Terme di Caracalla, 00100 Rome, Italy (Telephone Number in U.S. (202) 653-2400); *Production Yearbook*.

NETHERLANDS ANTILLES - HIGHWAYS

G.K. Hall and Company, 70 Lincoln Street, Boston, Massachusetts 02111 (617) 423-3990; *The World in Figures*.

NETHERLANDS ANTILLES - HOURS OF WORK - See NETHERLANDS ANTILLES - EMPLOYMENT

NETHERLANDS ANTILLES - HOUSING EXPENDITURES

International Monetary Fund, 700 Nineteenth Street, NW, Washington, D.C. 20431 (202) 623-7000; *Government Finance Statistics Yearbook*.

NETHERLANDS ANTILLES - ILLITERATE POPULATION

The Economist Intelligence Unit, 111 West 57th Street, New York, New York 10019 (800) 938-4685; *The World Market Atlas*.

G.K. Hall and Company, 70 Lincoln Street, Boston, Massachusetts 02111 (617) 423-3990; *The World in Figures*.

United Nations Educational, Scientific and Cultural Organization (UNESCO), 7 Place de Fontenoy, F-75700 Paris, France (Telephone Number in U.S. (212) 963-5981); *Statistical Yearbook*.

NETHERLANDS ANTILLES - IMPORTS

The Economist Intelligence Unit, 111 West 57th Street, New York, New York 10019 (800) 938-4685; *The World Market Atlas*.

Food and Agricultural Organization of the United Nations (FAO) Via delle Terme di Caracalla, 00100 Rome, Italy (Telephone Number in U.S. (202) 653-2400); *The State of Food and Agriculture*.

G.K. Hall and Company, 70 Lincoln Street, Boston, Massachusetts 02111 (617) 423-3990; *The World in Figures*.

International Monetary Fund, 700 Nineteenth Street, NW, Washington, D.C. 20431 (202) 623-7000; *Direction of Trade Statistics*, and *Government Finance Statistics Yearbook*.

Statistical Office of the United Nations, Publishing Service, New York, New York 10017 (800) 253-9646; *Trade in Manufactures of Developing Countries*.

Times Books, 201 East 50th Street, New York, New York 10022 (212) 751-2600; *The Economist Book of Vital World Statistics*.

NETHERLANDS ANTILLES - INCOME TAXES - See NETHERLANDS ANTILLES - TAXATION

NETHERLANDS ANTILLES - INDUSTRY

G.K. Hall and Company, 70 Lincoln Street, Boston, Massachusetts 02111 (617) 423-3990; *The World in Figures*.

International Labour Office, I.L.O. Publications, CH-1211, Geneva 22, Switzerland; *Yearbook of Labour Statistics*.

Times Books, 201 East 50th Street, New York, New York 10022 (212) 751-2600; *The Economist Book of Vital World Statistics*.

NETHERLANDS ANTILLES - INFANT AND MATERNAL MORTALITY

Statistical Office of the United Nations, Publishing Service, New York, New York 10017 (800) 253-9646; *Demographic Yearbook*, and *Statistical Yearbook*.

NETHERLANDS ANTILLES - INTERNATIONAL LIQUIDITY

International Monetary Fund, 700 Nineteenth Street, NW, Washington, D.C. 20431 (202) 623-7000; *International Financial Statistics*.

NETHERLANDS ANTILLES - INTERNATIONAL RESERVES EXCLUDING GOLD

Statistical Office of the United Nations, Publishing Service, New York, New York 10017 (800) 253-9646; *Statistical Yearbook*.

NETHERLANDS ANTILLES - LABOR FORCE

Food and Agricultural Organization of the United Nations (FAO) Via delle Terme di Caracalla, 00100 Rome, Italy (Telephone Number in U.S. (202) 653-2400); *The State of Food and Agriculture*.

G.K. Hall and Company, 70 Lincoln Street, Boston, Massachusetts 02111 (617) 423-3990; *The World in Figures*.

Times Books, 201 East 50th Street, New York, New York 10022 (212) 751-2600; *The Economist Book of Vital World Statistics*.

NETHERLANDS ANTILLES - LABOR PRODUCTIVITY

International Labour Office, I.L.O. Publications, CH-1211, Geneva 22, Switzerland; *Yearbook of Labour Statistics*.

NETHERLANDS ANTILLES - LAND USE

Food and Agricultural Organization of the United Nations (FAO), Via delle Terme di Caracalla, 00100 Rome, Italy (Telephone Number in U.S. (202) 653-2400); *Production Yearbook*.

G.K. Hall and Company, 70 Lincoln Street, Boston, Massachusetts 02111 (617) 423-3990; *The World in Figures*.

NETHERLANDS ANTILLES - LIBRARIES

United Nations Educational, Scientific and Cultural Organization (UNESCO), 7 Place de Fontenoy, F-75700 Paris, France (Telephone Number in U.S. (212) 963-5981); *Statistical Yearbook*.

NETHERLANDS ANTILLES - LIVESTOCK AND POULTRY

Food and Agricultural Organization of the United Nations (FAO), Via delle Terme di Caracalla, 00100 Rome, Italy (Telephone Number in U.S. (202) 653-2400); *Production Yearbook*, and *The State of Food and Agriculture*.

G.K. Hall and Company, 70 Lincoln Street, Boston, Massachusetts 02111 (617) 423-3990; *The World in Figures*.

Statistical Office of the United Nations, Publishing Service, New York, New York 10017 (800) 253-9646; *Statistical Yearbook*.

NETHERLANDS ANTILLES - LIVING LEVELS

G.K. Hall and Company, 70 Lincoln Street, Boston, Massachusetts 02111 (617) 423-3990; *The World in Figures*.

NETHERLANDS ANTILLES - MAIL - PIECES SENT OR RECEIVED

Statistical Office of the United Nations, Publishing Service, New York, New York 10017 (800) 253-9646; *Statistical Yearbook*.

NETHERLANDS ANTILLES - MANUFACTURING

G.K. Hall and Company, 70 Lincoln Street, Boston, Massachusetts 02111 (617) 423-3990; *The World in Figures*.

Times Books, 201 East 50th Street, New York, New York 10022 (212) 751-2600; *The Economist Book of Vital World Statistics*.

NETHERLANDS ANTILLES - MARRIAGE RATES

Statistical Office of the United Nations, Publishing Service, New York, New York 10017 (800) 253-9646; *Demographic Yearbook*, and *Statistical Yearbook*.

NETHERLANDS ANTILLES - MEAT PRODUCTION - See - NETHERLANDS ANTILLES - LIVESTOCK AND POULTRY

NETHERLANDS ANTILLES - MERCHANT SHIPPING

G.K. Hall and Company, 70 Lincoln Street, Boston, Massachusetts 02111 (617) 423-3990; *The World in Figures*.

Statistical Office of the United Nations, Publishing Service, New York, New York 10017 (800) 253-9646; *Statistical Yearbook*.

Times Books, 201 East 50th Street, New York, New York 10022 (212) 751-2600; *The Economist Book of Vital World Statistics.*

NETHERLANDS ANTILLES - MILITARY

G.K. Hall and Company, 70 Lincoln Street, Boston, Massachusetts 02111 (617) 423-3990; *The World in Figures.*

NETHERLANDS ANTILLES - MINING AND MINERAL PRODUCTS

G.K. Hall and Company, 70 Lincoln Street, Boston, Massachusetts 02111 (617) 423-3990; *The World in Figures.*

Statistical Office of the United Nations, Publishing Service, New York, New York 10017 (800) 253-9646; *Statistical Yearbook.*

NETHERLANDS ANTILLES - MONEY EXCHANGE RATES

International Monetary Fund, 700 Nineteenth Street, NW, Washington, D.C. 20431 (202) 623-7000; *International Financial Statistics.*

NETHERLANDS ANTILLES - MONEY SUPPLY

G.K. Hall and Company, 70 Lincoln Street, Boston, Massachusetts 02111 (617) 423-3990; *The World in Figures.*

International Monetary Fund, 700 Nineteenth Street, NW, Washington, D.C. 20431 (202) 623-7000; *International Financial Statistics.*

NETHERLANDS ANTILLES - MOTOR VEHICLES IN USE

G.K. Hall and Company, 70 Lincoln Street, Boston, Massachusetts 02111 (617) 423-3990; *The World in Figures.*

Statistical Office of the United Nations, Publishing Service, New York, New York 10017 (800) 253-9646; *Statistical Yearbook.*

Times Books, 201 East 50th Street, New York, New York 10022 (212) 751-2600; *The Economist Book of Vital World Statistics.*

NETHERLANDS ANTILLES - NATALITY - See NETHERLANDS ANTILLES - BIRTH RATES

NETHERLANDS ANTILLES - NATIONAL ACCOUNTS

Statistical Office of the United Nations, Publishing Service, New York, New York 10017 (800) 253-9646; *National Accounts Statistics,* and *Statistical Yearbook.*

NETHERLANDS ANTILLES - NATIONAL INCOME

G.K. Hall and Company, 70 Lincoln Street, Boston, Massachusetts 02111 (617) 423-3990; *The World in Figures.*

Statistical Office of the United Nations, Publishing Service, New York, New York 10017 (800) 253-9646; *Statistical Yearbook.*

NETHERLANDS ANTILLES - NEWSPAPER PRODUCTION - See NETHERLANDS ANTILLES - FORESTRY AND FOREST PRODUCTS

NETHERLANDS ANTILLES - NEWSPRINT - See NETHERLANDS ANTILLES - FORESTRY AND FOREST PRODUCTS

NETHERLANDS ANTILLES - OCCUPATIONS - See NETHERLANDS ANTILLES - LABOR FORCE

NETHERLANDS ANTILLES - PAPER EXPORTS AND IMPORTS - See NETHERLANDS ANTILLES - FORESTRY AND FOREST PRODUCTS

NETHERLANDS ANTILLES - PESTICIDE USE

Food and Agricultural Organization of the United Nations (FAO) Via delle Terme di Caracalla, 00100 Rome, Italy (Telephone Number in U.S. (202) 653-2400); *The State of Food and Agriculture.*

NETHERLANDS ANTILLES - PETROLEUM INDUSTRY

Food and Agricultural Organization of the United Nations (FAO) Via delle Terme di Caracalla, 00100 Rome, Italy (Telephone Number in U.S. (202) 653-2400); *The State of Food and Agriculture.*

G.K. Hall and Company, 70 Lincoln Street, Boston, Massachusetts 02111 (617) 423-3990; *The World in Figures.*

Statistical Office of the United Nations, Publishing Service, New York, New York 10017 (800) 253-9646; *Statistical Yearbook.*

NETHERLANDS ANTILLES - PHOSPHATE ROCK PRODUCTION - See NETHERLANDS ANTILLES - MINING AND MINERAL PRODUCTS

NETHERLANDS ANTILLES - PIGS - See NETHERLANDS ANTILLES - LIVESTOCK AND POULTRY

NETHERLANDS ANTILLES - POPULATION

The Economist Intelligence Unit, 111 West 57th Street, New York, New York 10019 (800) 930-4055; *The World Market Atlas.*

Food and Agricultural Organization of the United Nations (FAO), Via delle Terme di Caracalla, 00100 Rome, Italy (Telephone Number in U.S. (202) 653-2400); *Production Yearbook.*

G.K. Hall and Company, 70 Lincoln Street, Boston, Massachusetts 02111 (617) 423-3990; *The World in Figures.*

International Labour Office, I.L.O. Publications, CH-1211, Geneva 22, Switzerland; *Yearbook of Labour Statistics.*

Statistical Office of the United Nations, Publishing Service, New York, New York 10017 (800) 253-9646; *Demographic Yearbook,* and *Statistical Yearbook.*

Times Books, 201 East 50th Street, New York, New York 10022 (212) 751-2600; *The Economist Book of Vital World Statistics.*

United Nations Educational, Scientific and Cultural Organization (UNESCO), 7 Place de Fontenoy, F-75700 Paris, France (Telephone Number in U.S. (212) 963-5981); *Statistical Yearbook.*

World Health Organization, Office of Publications, Avenue Appia, CH-1211 Geneva 27, Switzerland (Telephone Number in U.S. (518) 436-9686); *World Health Statistics Annual.*

NETHERLANDS ANTILLES - PRICES

Food and Agricultural Organization of the United Nations (FAO), Via delle Terme di Caracalla, 00100 Rome, Italy (Telephone Number in U.S. (202) 653-2400); *Production Yearbook,* and *The State of Food and Agriculture.*

G.K. Hall and Company, 70 Lincoln Street, Boston, Massachusetts 02111 (617) 423-3990; *The World in Figures.*

International Labour Office, I.L.O. Publications, CH-1211, Geneva 22, Switzerland; *Yearbook of Labour Statistics.*

International Monetary Fund, 700 Nineteenth Street, NW, Washington, D.C. 20431 (202) 623-7000; *International Financial Statistics.*

NETHERLANDS ANTILLES - PRINTING AND WRITING PAPER - See NETHERLANDS ANTILLES - FORESTRY AND FOREST PRODUCTS

NETHERLANDS ANTILLES - PRODUCTION

G.K. Hall and Company, 70 Lincoln Street, Boston, Massachusetts 02111 (617) 423-3990; *The World in Figures.*

NETHERLANDS ANTILLES - PROPERTY TAXES - See NETHERLANDS ANTILLES - TAXATION

NETHERLANDS ANTILLES - RADIO BROADCASTING - See NETHERLANDS ANTILLES - BROADCASTING

NETHERLANDS ANTILLES - RAILWAY USE

G.K. Hall and Company, 70 Lincoln Street, Boston, Massachusetts 02111 (617) 423-3990; *The World in Figures.*

NETHERLANDS ANTILLES - RENT PRICES

International Labour Office, I.L.O. Publications, CH-1211, Geneva 22, Switzerland; *Yearbook of Labour Statistics.*

NETHERLANDS ANTILLES - RETAIL TRADE

G.K. Hall and Company, 70 Lincoln Street, Boston, Massachusetts 02111 (617) 423-3990; *The World in Figures.*

NETHERLANDS ANTILLES - ROUNDWOOD PRODUCTION - See NETHERLANDS ANTILLES - FORESTRY AND FOREST PRODUCTS

NETHERLANDS ANTILLES - SALT PRODUCTION - See NETHERLANDS ANTILLES - MINING AND MINERAL PRODUCTS

NETHERLANDS ANTILLES - SAWNWOOD PRODUCTION - See NETHERLANDS ANTILLES - FORESTRY AND FOREST PRODUCTS

NETHERLANDS ANTILLES - SHEEP - See NETHERLANDS ANTILLES - LIVESTOCK AND POULTRY

NETHERLANDS ANTILLES - SOCIAL DATA

G.K. Hall and Company, 70 Lincoln Street, Boston, Massachusetts 02111 (617) 423-3990; *The World in Figures.*

NETHERLANDS ANTILLES - SOCIAL SECURITY

International Monetary Fund, 700 Nineteenth Street, NW, Washington, D.C. 20431 (202) 623-7000; *Government Finance Statistics Yearbook.*

NETHERLANDS ANTILLES - STAMP TAXES AND DUTIES - See NETHERLANDS ANTILLES - TAXATION

NETHERLANDS ANTILLES - STOCKS - COMMODITY - MARKET PRICE - INDEX

Food and Agricultural Organization of the United Nations (FAO) Via delle Terme di Caracalla, 00100 Rome, Italy (Telephone Number in U.S. (202) 653-2400; *The State of Food and Agriculture.*

NETHERLANDS ANTILLES - TAXATION

G.K. Hall and Company, 70 Lincoln Street, Boston, Massachusetts 02111 (617) 423-3990; *The World in Figures.*

International Monetary Fund, 700 Nineteenth Street, NW, Washington, D.C. 20431 (202) 623-7000; *Government Finance Statistics Yearbook.*

NETHERLANDS ANTILLES - TELEGRAPH SERVICE

Statistical Office of the United Nations, Publishing Service, New York, New York 10017 (800) 253-9646; *Statistical Yearbook.*

NETHERLANDS ANTILLES - TELEPHONES IN USE

American Telephone and Telegraph Company, 26 Parsippany Road, Whippany, New Jersey 07981 (800) 338-4038; *The World's Telephones.*

G.K. Hall and Company, 70 Lincoln Street, Boston, Massachusetts 02111 (617) 423-3990; *The World in Figures.*

Statistical Office of the United Nations, Publishing Service, New York, New York 10017 (800) 253-9646; *Statistical Yearbook.*

NETHERLANDS ANTILLES - TELEVISION BROADCASTING - See NETHERLANDS ANTILLES - BROADCASTING

NETHERLANDS ANTILLES - TEXTILE INDUSTRY

G.K. Hall and Company, 70 Lincoln Street, Boston, Massachusetts 02111 (617) 423-3990; *The World in Figures.*

NETHERLANDS ANTILLES - TOURISM

G.K. Hall and Company, 70 Lincoln Street, Boston, Massachusetts 02111 (617) 423-3990; *The World in Figures.*

Statistical Office of the United Nations, Publishing Service, New York, New York 10017 (800) 253-9646; *Statistical Yearbook.*

NETHERLANDS ANTILLES - TRACTORS IN USE

Statistical Office of the United Nations, Publishing Service, New York, New York 10017 (800) 253-9646; *Statistical Yearbook.*

NETHERLANDS ANTILLES - TRADE - See NETHERLANDS ANTILLES - FOREIGN TRADE

NETHERLANDS ANTILLES - TRANSPORTATION AND COMMUNICATIONS

G.K. Hall and Company, 70 Lincoln Street, Boston, Massachusetts 02111 (617) 423-3990; *The World in Figures.*

NETHERLANDS ANTILLES - UNEMPLOYMENT

International Labour Office, I.L.O. Publications, CH-1211, Geneva 22, Switzerland; *Yearbook of Labour Statistics.*

NETHERLANDS ANTILLES - VITAL STATISTICS

G.K. Hall and Company, 70 Lincoln Street, Boston, Massachusetts 02111 (617) 423-3990; *The World in Figures.*

Statistical Office of the United Nations, Publishing Service, New York, New York 10017 (800) 253-9646; *Statistical Yearbook.*

World Health Organization, Office of Publications, Avenue Appia, CH-1211 Geneva 27, Switzerland (Telephone Number in U.S. (518) 436-9686); *World Health Statistics Annual.*

NETHERLANDS ANTILLES - WAGES

G.K. Hall and Company, 70 Lincoln Street, Boston, Massachusetts 02111 (617) 423-3990; *The World in Figures.*

International Labour Office, I.L.O. Publications, CH-1211, Geneva 22, Switzerland; *Yearbook of Labour Statistics.*

Statistical Office of the United Nations, Publishing Service, New York, New York 10017 (800) 253-9646; *Statistical Yearbook.*

NETHERLANDS ANTILLES - WEATHER

G.K. Hall and Company, 70 Lincoln Street, Boston, Massachusetts 02111 (617) 423-3990; *The World in Figures.*

NETHERLANDS ANTILLES - WELFARE

International Monetary Fund, 700 Nineteenth Street, NW, Washington, D.C. 20431 (202) 623-7000; *Government Finance Statistics Yearbook.*

NEVADA - See also STATE DATA (FOR INDIVIDUAL STATES)

Nevada - Primary Statistics Source

Department of Administration, Budget and Planning Division, Capitol Complex, Carson City, Nevada 89710 (702) 687-4065, *Nevada Statistical Abstract.*

Nevada - State Data Center

Nevada State Library, Capitol Complex, 100 Stewart Street, Carson City, Nevada 89710, Ms. Patricia Deadder (702) 687-8327.

NEW BUSINESS INCORPORATIONS

Dun and Bradstreet Corporation, 299 Park Avenue, Twenty-fourth Floor, New York, New York 10171 (212) 593-6800; *Monthly Failure Report, New Business Incorporations,* and *Business Failure Record.*

New Caledonia - National Statistical Office

Direction Territoriale de la Statistique et des Etudes Economiques, BP 823, Noumea, New Caledonia.

New Caledonia - Primary Statistics Source

Direction Territoriale de la Statistique et des Etudes Economiques, BP 323, Noumea, New Caledonia, *Annuaire Statistique de la Nouvelle Caledonia et Dependances.*

NEW CALEDONIA - AGRICULTURE

Food and Agricultural Organization of the United Nations (FAO) Via delle Terme di Caracalla, 00100 Rome, Italy (Telephone Number in U.S. (202) 653-2400); *Production Yearbook, The State of Food and Agriculture,* and *Trade Yearbook.*

Statistical Office of the United Nations, Publishing Service, New York, New York 10017 (800) 253-9646; *Statistical Yearbook.*

NEW CALEDONIA - ANIMAL HEALTH

Food and Agricultural Organization of the United Nations (FAO), Via delle Terme di Caracalla, 00100 Rome, Italy (Telephone Number in U.S. (202) 653-2400); *Animal Health Yearbook.*

NEW CALEDONIA - AREA AND DENSITY OF POPULATION

Food and Agricultural Organization of the United Nations (FAO) Via delle Terme di Caracalla, 00100 Rome, Italy (Telephone Number in U.S. (202) 653-2400); *The State of Food and Agriculture.*

Statistical Office of the United Nations, Publishing Service, New York, New York 10017 (800) 253-9646; *Statistical Yearbook.*

United Nations Educational, Scientific and Cultural Organization (UNESCO), 7 Place de Fontenoy, F-75700 Paris, France (Telephone Number in U.S. (212) 963-5981); *Statistical Yearbook.*

NEW CALEDONIA - BEER PRODUCTION

Statistical Office of the United Nations, Publishing Service, New York, New York 10017 (800) 253-9646; *Statistical Yearbook.*

NEW CALEDONIA - BIRTH RATES

Statistical Office of the United Nations, Publishing Service, New York, New York 10017 (800) 253-9646; *Demographic Yearbook,* and *Statistical Yearbook.*

World Health Organization, Office of Publications, Avenue Appia, CH-1211 Geneva 27, Switzerland (Telephone Number in U.S. (518) 436-9686); *World Health Statistics Annual.*

NEW CALEDONIA - BROADCASTING

Billboard Limited, Post Office Box 9027, 1006 AA Amsterdam, The Netherlands (Telephone Number in U.S. (212) 764-7300); *World Radio TV Handbook.*

NEW CALEDONIA - CALORIE SUPPLY

Food and Agricultural Organization of the United Nations (FAO) Via delle Terme di Caracalla, 00100 Rome, Italy (Telephone Number in U.S. (202) 653-2400); *The State of Food and Agriculture.*

NEW CALEDONIA - CATTLE - See NEW CALEDONIA - LIVESTOCK AND POULTRY

NEW CALEDONIA - CEMENT PRODUCTION - See NEW CALEDONIA - MINING AND MINERAL PRODUCTS

NEW CALEDONIA - CLOTHING EXPORTS AND IMPORTS

South Pacific Commission, Post Box D5, Noumea Cedex, New Caledonia; *Statistical Bulletin of the South Pacific: Retail Price Indexes.*

NEW CALEDONIA - COAL PRODUCTION - See NEW CALEDONIA - MINING AND MINERAL PRODUCTS

NEW CALEDONIA - COBALT PRODUCTION AND CONSUMPTION - See NEW CALEDONIA - MINING AND MINERAL PRODUCTS

NEW CALEDONIA - CONSTRUCTION INDUSTRY

Statistical Office of the United Nations, Publishing Service, New York, New York 10017 (800) 253-9646; *Construction Statistics Yearbook,* and *Statistical Yearbook.*

NEW CALEDONIA - CONSUMER PRICE INDEX

Statistical Office of the United Nations, Publishing Service, New York, New York 10017 (800) 253-9646; *Statistical Yearbook.*

NEW CALEDONIA - CONSUMER PRICES

International Labour Office, I.L.O. Publications, CH-1211, Geneva 22, Switzerland; *Yearbook of Labour Statistics.*

NEW CALEDONIA - CORN PRODUCTION - See NEW CALEDONIA - CROPS

NEW CALEDONIA - CROPS

Food and Agricultural Organization of the United Nations (FAO) Via delle Terme di Caracalla, 00100 Rome, Italy (Telephone Number in U.S. (202) 653-2400); *Production Yearbook,* and *The State of Food and Agriculture.*

Statistical Office of the United Nations, Publishing Service, New York, New York 10017 (800) 253-9646; *Statistical Yearbook.*

NEW CALEDONIA - DAIRY PRODUCTS

Food and Agricultural Organization of the United Nations (FAO) Via delle Terme di Caracalla, 00100 Rome, Italy (Telephone Number in U.S. (202) 653-2400); *The State of Food and Agriculture.*

NEW CALEDONIA - DEATH RATES

Statistical Office of the United Nations, Publishing Service, New York, New York 10017 (800) 253-9646; *Statistical Yearbook.*

World Health Organization, Office of Publications, Avenue Appia, CH-1211 Geneva 27, Switzerland (Telephone Number in U.S. (518) 436-9686); *World Health Statistics Annual.*

NEW CALEDONIA - DEVELOPMENT ASSISTANCE

Statistical Office of the United Nations, Publishing Service, New York, New York 10017 (800) 253-9646; *Statistical Yearbook.*

NEW CALEDONIA - DISEASES

World Health Organization, Office of Publications, Avenue Appia, CH-1211 Geneva 27, Switzerland (Telephone Number in U.S. (518) 436-9686); *World Health Statistics Annual.*

NEW CALEDONIA - DIVORCE RATES

Statistical Office of the United Nations, Publishing Service, New York, New York 10017 (800) 253-9646; *Demographic Yearbook,* and *Statistical Yearbook.*

NEW CALEDONIA - EDUCATION

United Nations Educational, Scientific and Cultural Organization (UNESCO), 7 Place de Fontenoy, F-75700 Paris, France (Telephone Number in U.S. (212) 963-5981); *Statistical Yearbook.*

NEW CALEDONIA - EGG PRODUCTION AND CONSUMPTION - See NEW CALEDONIA - DAIRY PRODUCTS

NEW CALEDONIA - ELECTRICITY

Statistical Office of the United Nations, Publishing Service, New York, New York 10017 (800) 253-9646; *Statistical Yearbook.*

NEW CALEDONIA - EMPLOYMENT

International Labour Office, I.L.O. Publications, CH-1211, Geneva 22, Switzerland; *Yearbook of Labour Statistics.*

NEW CALEDONIA - ENERGY

Food and Agricultural Organization of the United Nations (FAO) Via delle Terme di Caracalla, 00100 Rome, Italy (Telephone Number in U.S. (202) 653-2400); *The State of Food and Agriculture.*

Statistical Office of the United Nations, Publishing Service, New York, New York 10017 (800) 253-9646; *Energy Statistics Yearbook, Statistical Yearbook,* and *World Energy Supplies.*

NEW CALEDONIA - EXPORTS

Food and Agricultural Organization of the United Nations (FAO) Via delle Terme di Caracalla, 00100 Rome, Italy (Telephone Number in U.S. (202) 653-2400); *The State of Food and Agriculture.*

International Monetary Fund, 700 Nineteenth Street, NW, Washington, D.C. 20431 (202) 623-7000; *Direction of Trade Statistics.*

South Pacific Commission, Post Box D5, Noumea Cedex, New Caledonia; *Statistical Bulletin of the South Pacific: Overseas Trade.*

Statistical Office of the United Nations, Publishing Service, New York, New York 10017 (800) 253-9646; *Trade in Manufactures of Developing Countries.*

NEW CALEDONIA - EXTERNAL TRADE

Food and Agricultural Organization of the United Nations (FAO) Via delle Terme di Caracalla, 00100 Rome, Italy (Telephone Number in U.S. (202) 653-2400); *The State of Food and Agriculture,* and *Trade Yearbook.*

Statistical Office of the United Nations, Publishing Service, New York, New York 10017 (800) 253-9646; *Statistical Yearbook.*

NEW CALEDONIA - FARM CROPS - See NEW CALEDONIA - CROPS

NEW CALEDONIA - FERTILIZER

Food and Agricultural Organization of the United Nations (FAO), Via delle Terme di Caracalla, 00100 Rome, Italy (Telephone Number in U.S. (202) 653-2400); *Fertilizer Yearbook,* and *The State of Food and Agriculture.*

Statistical Office of the United Nations, Publishing Service, New York, New York 10017 (800) 253-9646; *Statistical Yearbook.*

NEW CALEDONIA - FETAL MORTALITY

Statistical Office of the United Nations, Publishing Service, New York, New York 10017 (800) 253-9646; *Demographic Yearbook.*

World Health Organization, Office of Publications, Avenue Appia, CH-1211 Geneva 27, Switzerland (Telephone Number in U.S. (518) 436-9686); *World Health Statistics Annual.*

NEW CALEDONIA - FISHERIES

Food and Agricultural Organization of the United Nations (FAO) Via delle Terme di Caracalla, 00100 Rome, Italy (Telephone Number in U.S. (202) 653-2400); *The State of Food and Agriculture,* and *Yearbook of Fishery Statistics.*

NEW CALEDONIA - FOOD

Food and Agricultural Organization of the United Nations (FAO), Via delle Terme di Caracalla, 00100 Rome, Italy (Telephone Number in U.S. (202) 653-2400); *Production Yearbook,* and *The State of Food and Agriculture.*

South Pacific Commission, Post Box D5, Noumea Cedex, New Caledonia; *Statistical Bulletin of the South Pacific: Retail Price Indexes.*

NEW CALEDONIA - FOREIGN TRADE

Food and Agricultural Organization of the United Nations (FAO) Via delle Terme di Caracalla, 00100 Rome, Italy (Telephone Number in U.S. (202) 653-2400); *The State of Food and Agriculture.*

South Pacific Commission, Post Box D5, Noumea Cedex, New Caledonia; *Statistical Bulletin of the South Pacific: Overseas Trade.*

Statistical Office of the United Nations, Publishing Service, New York, New York 10017 (800) 253-9646; *International Trade Statistics Yearbook,* and *Statistical Yearbook.*

NEW CALEDONIA - FORESTRY AND FOREST PRODUCTS

Food and Agricultural Organization of the United Nations (FAO) Via delle Terme di Caracalla, 00100 Rome, Italy (Telephone Number in U.S. (202) 653-2400); *The State of Food and Agriculture,* and *Yearbook of Forest Products.*

NEW CALEDONIA - GENERAL MORTALITY

Statistical Office of the United Nations, Publishing Service, New York, New York 10017 (800) 253-9646; *Demographic Yearbook.*

World Health Organization, Office of Publications, Avenue Appia, CH-1211 Geneva 27, Switzerland (Telephone Number in U.S. (518) 436-9686); *World Health Statistics Annual.*

NEW CALEDONIA - GRAIN PRODUCTION - See NEW CALEDONIA - CROPS

NEW CALEDONIA - GROSS DOMESTIC PRODUCT

Statistical Office of the United Nations, Publishing Service, New York, New York 10017 (800) 253-9646; *Statistical Yearbook.*

NEW CALEDONIA - HEALTH

South Pacific Commission, Post Box D5, Noumea Cedex, New Caledonia; *Statistical Bulletin of the South Pacific: Retail Price Indexes.*

Statistical Office of the United Nations, Publishing Service, New York, New York 10017 (800) 253-9646; *Statistical Yearbook.*

World Health Organization, Office of Publications, Avenue Appia, CH-1211 Geneva 27, Switzerland (Telephone Number in U.S. (518) 436-9686); *World Health Statistics Annual.*

NEW CALEDONIA - HIDE PRODUCTION

Food and Agricultural Organization of the United Nations (FAO), Via delle Terme di Caracalla, 00100 Rome, Italy (Telephone Number in U.S. (202) 653-2400); *Production Yearbook.*

NEW CALEDONIA - HORSES - See NEW CALEDONIA - LIVESTOCK AND POULTRY

NEW CALEDONIA - HOURS OF WORK - See NEW CALEDONIA - EMPLOYMENT

NEW CALEDONIA - HOUSING AND HOUSING UNITS

South Pacific Commission, Post Box D5, Noumea Cedex, New Caledonia; *Statistical Bulletin of the South Pacific: Retail Price Indexes.*

NEW CALEDONIA - HOUSING EXPENDITURES

South Pacific Commission, Post Box D5, Noumea Cedex, New Caledonia; *Statistical Bulletin of the South Pacific: Retail Price Indexes.*

NEW CALEDONIA - ILLITERATE POPULATION

United Nations Educational, Scientific and Cultural Organization (UNESCO), 7 Place de Fontenoy, F-75700 Paris, France (Telephone Number in U.S. (212) 963-5981); *Statistical Yearbook.*

NEW CALEDONIA - IMPORTS

Food and Agricultural Organization of the United Nations (FAO) Via delle Terme di Caracalla, 00100 Rome, Italy (Telephone Number in U.S. (202) 653-2400); *The State of Food and Agriculture.*

International Monetary Fund, 700 Nineteenth Street, NW, Washington, D.C. 20431 (202) 623-7000; *Direction of Trade Statistics.*

South Pacific Commission, Post Box D5, Noumea Cedex, New Caledonia; *Statistical Bulletin of the South Pacific: Overseas Trade.*

NEW CALEDONIA - INDUSTRY

International Labour Office, I.L.O. Publications, CH-1211, Geneva 22, Switzerland; *Yearbook of Labour Statistics.*

NEW CALEDONIA - INFANT AND MATERNAL MORTALITY

Statistical Office of the United Nations, Publishing Service, New York, New York 10017 (800) 253-9646; *Demographic Yearbook,* and *Statistical Yearbook.*

World Health Organization, Office of Publications, Avenue Appia, CH-1211 Geneva 27, Switzerland (Telephone Number in U.S. (518) 436-9686); *World Health Statistics Annual.*

NEW CALEDONIA - IRON ORE PRODUCTION AND CONSUMPTION - See NEW CALEDONIA - MINING AND MINERAL PRODUCTS

NEW CALEDONIA - LABOR FORCE

Food and Agricultural Organization of the United Nations (FAO) Via delle Terme di Caracalla, 00100 Rome, Italy (Telephone Number in U.S. (202) 653-2400); *The State of Food and Agriculture.*

NEW CALEDONIA - LABOR PRODUCTIVITY

International Labour Office, I.L.O. Publications, CH-1211, Geneva 22, Switzerland; *Yearbook of Labour Statistics.*

NEW CALEDONIA - LAND USE

Food and Agricultural Organization of the United Nations (FAO), Via delle Terme di Caracalla, 00100 Rome, Italy (Telephone Number in U.S. (202) 653-2400); *Production Yearbook*.

NEW CALEDONIA - LIBRARIES

United Nations Educational, Scientific and Cultural Organization (UNESCO), 7 Place de Fontenoy, F-75700 Paris, France (Telephone Number in U.S. (212) 963-5981); *Statistical Yearbook*.

NEW CALEDONIA - LIVESTOCK AND POULTRY

Food and Agricultural Organization of the United Nations (FAO), Via delle Terme di Caracalla, 00100 Rome, Italy (Telephone Number in U.S. (202) 653-2400); *Production Yearbook*, and *The State of Food and Agriculture*.

Statistical Office of the United Nations, Publishing Service, New York, New York 10017 (800) 253-9646; *Statistical Yearbook*.

NEW CALEDONIA - MAIL - PIECES SENT OR RECEIVED

Statistical Office of the United Nations, Publishing Service, New York, New York 10017 (800) 253-9646; *Statistical Yearbook*.

NEW CALEDONIA - MARRIAGE RATES

Statistical Office of the United Nations, Publishing Service, New York, New York 10017 (800) 253-9646; *Demographic Yearbook*, and *Statistical Yearbook*.

NEW CALEDONIA - MEAT PRODUCTION - See NEW CALEDONIA - LIVESTOCK AND POULTRY

NEW CALEDONIA - MERCHANT SHIPPING

Statistical Office of the United Nations, Publishing Service, New York, New York 10017 (800) 253-9646; *Statistical Yearbook*.

NEW CALEDONIA - MINING AND MINERAL PRODUCTS

Commodity Research Bureau, Incorporated, 75 Wall Street, New York, New York 10005 (212) 504-7754; *Commodity Year Book*.

South Pacific Commission, Post Box D5, Noumea Cedex, New Caledonia; *Statistical Bulletin of the South Pacific: Retail Price Indexes*.

Statistical Office of the United Nations, Publishing Service, New York, New York 10017 (800) 253-9646; *Statistical Yearbook*.

NEW CALEDONIA - MOTION PICTURES

Statistical Office of the United Nations, Publishing Service, New York, New York 10017 (800) 253-9646; *Statistical Yearbook*.

NEW CALEDONIA - MOTOR VEHICLES IN USE

Statistical Office of the United Nations, Publishing Service, New York, New York 10017 (800) 253-9646; *Statistical Yearbook*.

NEW CALEDONIA - MUSEUMS

United Nations Educational, Scientific and Cultural Organization (UNESCO), 7 Place de Fontenoy, F-75700 Paris, France (Telephone Number in U.S. (212) 963-5981); *Statistical Yearbook*.

NEW CALEDONIA - NATALITY - See NEW CALEDONIA - BIRTH RATES

NEW CALEDONIA - NATIONAL ACCOUNTS

Statistical Office of the United Nations, Publishing Service, New York, New York 10017 (800) 253-9646; *National Accounts Statistics*, and *Statistical Yearbook*.

NEW CALEDONIA - NATIONAL INCOME

Statistical Office of the United Nations, Publishing Service, New York, New York 10017 (800) 253-9646; *Statistical Yearbook*.

NEW CALEDONIA - NEWSPAPER PRODUCTION

Statistical Office of the United Nations, Publishing Service, New York, New York 10017 (800) 253-9646; *Statistical Yearbook*.

United Nations Educational, Scientific and Cultural Organization (UNESCO), 7 Place de Fontenoy, F-75700 Paris, France (Telephone Number in U.S. (212) 963-5981); *Statistical Yearbook*.

NEW CALEDONIA - NICKEL AND NICKEL ORE PRODUCTION AND CONSUMPTION - See NEW CALEDONIA - MINING AND MINERAL PRODUCTS

NEW CALEDONIA - PERIODICALS

United Nations Educational, Scientific and Cultural Organization (UNESCO), 7 Place de Fontenoy, F-75700 Paris, France (Telephone Number in U.S. (212) 963-5981); *Statistical Yearbook*.

NEW CALEDONIA - PESTICIDE USE

Food and Agricultural Organization of the United Nations (FAO) Via delle Terme di Caracalla, 00100 Rome, Italy (Telephone Number in U.S. (202) 653-2400); *The State of Food and Agriculture*.

NEW CALEDONIA - PETROLEUM INDUSTRY

Food and Agricultural Organization of the United Nations (FAO) Via delle Terme di Caracalla, 00100 Rome, Italy (Telephone Number in U.S. (202) 653-2400); *The State of Food and Agriculture*.

NEW CALEDONIA - PIGS - See NEW CALEDONIA - LIVESTOCK AND POULTRY

NEW CALEDONIA - POPULATION

Food and Agricultural Organization of the United Nations (FAO), Via delle Terme di Caracalla, 00100 Rome, Italy (Telephone Number in U.S. (202) 653-2400); *Production Yearbook*.

International Labour Office, I.L.O. Publications, CH-1211, Geneva 22, Switzerland; *Yearbook of Labour Statistics*.

Statistical Office of the United Nations, Publishing Service, New York, New York 10017 (800) 253-9646; *Demographic Yearbook*, and *Statistical Yearbook*.

United Nations Educational, Scientific and Cultural Organization (UNESCO), 7 Place de Fontenoy, F-75700 Paris, France (Telephone Number in U.S. (212) 963-5981); *Statistical Yearbook*.

World Health Organization, Office of Publications, Avenue Appia, CH-1211 Geneva 27, Switzerland (Telephone Number in U.S. (518) 436-9686); *World Health Statistics Annual*.

NEW CALEDONIA - POTATO PRODUCTION - See NEW CALEDONIA - CROPS

NEW CALEDONIA - PRICES

Food and Agricultural Organization of the United Nations (FAO), Via delle Terme di Caracalla, 00100 Rome, Italy (Telephone Number in U.S. (202) 653-2400); *Production Yearbook*, and *The State of Food and Agriculture*.

International Labour Office, I.L.O. Publications, CH-1211, Geneva 22, Switzerland; *Yearbook of Labour Statistics*.

South Pacific Commission, Post Box D5, Noumea Cedex, New Caledonia; *Statistical Bulletin of the South Pacific: Overseas Trade*, and *Statistical Bulletin of the South Pacific: Retail Price Indexes*.

NEW CALEDONIA - RENT PRICES

International Labour Office, I.L.O. Publications, CH-1211, Geneva 22, Switzerland; *Yearbook of Labour Statistics*.

NEW CALEDONIA - ROOT AND TUBER PRODUCTION - See NEW CALEDONIA - CROPS

NEW CALEDONIA - ROUNDWOOD PRODUCTION - See NEW CALEDONIA - FORESTRY AND FOREST PRODUCTS

NEW CALEDONIA - SAWNWOOD PRODUCTION - See NEW CALEDONIA - FORESTRY AND FOREST PRODUCTS

NEW CALEDONIA - SCIENCE AND TECHNOLOGY - EXPENDITURE FOR RESEARCH

Statistical Office of the United Nations, Publishing Service, New York, New York 10017 (800) 253-9646; *Statistical Yearbook*.

NEW CALEDONIA - SCIENTISTS AND TECHNICIANS

Statistical Office of the United Nations, Publishing Service, New York, New York 10017 (800) 253-9646; *Statistical Yearbook*.

NEW CALEDONIA - SHEEP - See NEW CALEDONIA - LIVESTOCK AND POULTRY

NEW CALEDONIA - STOCKS - COMMODITY - MARKET PRICE - INDEX

Food and Agricultural Organization of the United Nations (FAO) Via delle Terme di Caracalla, 00100 Rome, Italy (Telephone Number in U.S. (202) 653-2400); *The State of Food and Agriculture*.

NEW CALEDONIA - TELEGRAPH SERVICE

Statistical Office of the United Nations, Publishing Service, New York, New York 10017 (800) 253-9646; *Statistical Yearbook*.

NEW CALEDONIA - TELEPHONES IN USE

American Telephone and Telegraph Company, 26 Parsippany Road, Whippany, New Jersey 07981 (800) 338-4038; *The World's Telephones*.

Statistical Office of the United Nations, Publishing Service, New York, New York 10017 (800) 253-9646; *Statistical Yearbook*.

NEW CALEDONIA - TELEVISION RECEIVERS - IN USE

Statistical Office of the United Nations, Publishing Service, New York, New York 10017 (800) 253-9646; *Statistical Yearbook*.

NEW CALEDONIA - TOBACCO PRODUCTION

South Pacific Commission, Post Box D5, Noumea Cedex, New Caledonia; *Statistical Bulletin of the South Pacific: Retail Price Indexes*.

NEW CALEDONIA - TOURISM

South Pacific Commission, Post Box D5, Noumea Cedex, New Caledonia; *Statistical Bulletin of the South Pacific: Retail Price Indexes*.

Statistical Office of the United Nations, Publishing Service, New York, New York 10017 (800) 253-9646; *Statistical Yearbook*.

World Tourism Organization, Calle Capitan Haya 42, E-28020 Madrid, Spain; *Yearbook of Tourism Statistics*.

NEW CALEDONIA - TRACTORS IN USE

Statistical Office of the United Nations, Publishing Service, New York, New York 10017 (800) 253-9646; *Statistical Yearbook*.

NEW CALEDONIA - TRADE - See NEW CALEDONIA - FOREIGN TRADE

NEW CALEDONIA - TRANSPORTATION AND COMMUNICATIONS

South Pacific Commission, Post Box D5, Noumea Cedex, New Caledonia; *Statistical Bulletin of the South Pacific: Retail Price Indexes*.

NEW CALEDONIA - UNEMPLOYMENT

International Labour Office, I.L.O. Publications, CH-1211, Geneva 22, Switzerland; *Yearbook of Labour Statistics*.

Statistical Office of the United Nations, Publishing Service, New York, New York 10017 (800) 253-9646; *Statistical Yearbook*.

NEW CALEDONIA - VITAL STATISTICS

Statistical Office of the United Nations, Publishing Service, New York, New York 10017 (800) 253-9646; *Statistical Yearbook*.

World Health Organization, Office of Publications, Avenue Appia, CH-1211 Geneva 27, Switzerland (Telephone Number in U.S. (518) 436-9686); *World Health Statistics Annual*.

NEW CALEDONIA - WAGES

International Labour Office, I.L.O. Publications, CH-1211, Geneva 22, Switzerland; *Yearbook of Labour Statistics*.

Statistical Office of the United Nations, Publishing Service, New York, New York 10017 (800) 253-9646; *Statistical Yearbook*.

NEW GUINEA - See PAPUA NEW GUINEA

NEW HAMPSHIRE - See also STATE DATA (FOR INDIVIDUAL STATES)

New Hampshire - Primary Statistics Source

Office of State Planning, 2 1/2 Beacon Street, Concord, New Hampshire 03301 (603) 271-2155; *Population Estimates for New Hampshire Cities and Towns, New Hampshire Population Projections for Cities and Towns,* and *Current Estimates and Trends in New Hampshire's Housing Supply.*

New Hampshire - State Data Centers

Office of State Planning, 2 1/2 Beacon Street, Concord, New Hampshire 03301, Mr. Tom Duffy (603) 271-2155.

New Hampshire State Library, 20 Park Street, Concord, New Hampshire 03301-6303, Mr. John McCormick (603) 271-2060.

Office of Biometrics, University of New Hampshire, Pettee Hall, Durham, New Hampshire 03824, Mr. Owen Durgin (603) 862-3930.

NEW JERSEY - See also STATE DATA (FOR INDIVIDUAL STATES)

New Jersey - Primary Statistics Source

New Jersey State Data Center, Department of Labor, CN 388, Trenton, New Jersey 08625 (609) 984-2593; *New Jersey Statistical Factbook,* and *New Jersey Source Book.*

New Jersey - State Data Centers

New Jersey Department of Labor, Division of Labor Market and Demographic Research, New Jersey Department of Labor, CN 388, John Fitch Plaza, Trenton, New Jersey 08625-0388, Ms. Connie O. Hughes (609) 984-2593.

New Jersey State Library, 185 West State Street, CN 520, Trenton, New Jersey 08625-0520, Ms. Beverly Railsback (609) 292-6259.

CIT - Information Services, Princeton University, 87 Prospect Avenue, Princeton, New Jersey 08544, Ms. Judith S. Rowe, (609) 258-6052.

Center for Computer and Information Services, Rutgers University, CCIS-Hill Center, Busch Campus, Post Office Box 879, Piscataway, New Jersey 08854, Mr. Chris Jarocha-Ernst (908) 932-0265.

Rutgers University-The State University, Kilmer Campus, Lucy Stone Hall, B Wing, New Brunswick, New Jersey 08903, Dr. James Hughes, Chair and Graduate Director (908) 932-3822.

NEW MEXICO - See also STATE DATA (FOR INDIVIDUAL STATES)

New Mexico - Primary Statistics Source

University of New Mexico, Bureau of Business and Economic Research, 1920 Lomas, NE, Albuquerque, New Mexico 87131 (505) 277-2216; *New Mexico Statistical Abstract,* and *County Profiles.*

New Mexico - State Data Centers

Economic Development Department, 1100 St. Francis Drive, Santa Fe, New Mexico 87503, Ms. Laurie Moye (505) 827-0182.

New Mexico State Library, 325 Don Gaspar Avenue, Post Office Box 1629, Santa Fe, New Mexico 87503, Ms. Laura Chaney (505) 827-3824.

Bureau of Business and Economic Research, University of New Mexico, 1920 Lomas NE, Albuquerque, New Mexico 87131, Mr. Kevin Kargacin (505) 277-6626/Mr. Bobby Leitch (505) 277-2216.

Department of Economics, New Mexico State University, Box 30001, Las Cruces, New Mexico 88003, Dr. Kathleen Brook (505) 646-2112.

NEW PRODUCT INTRODUCTIONS

Marketing Intelligence Service Limited, 33 Academy Street, Naples, New York 14512 (716) 374-6326; *Product Alert Weekly.*

NEW YORK - See also STATE DATA (FOR INDIVIDUAL STATES)

New York - Primary Statistics Source

Nelson Rockefeller Institute of Government, 411 State Street, Albany, New York 12203 (518) 443-5522; *New York State Statistical Yearbook.*

New York - State Data Centers

New York State Department of Economic Development, Division of Policy and Research, 1 Commerce Plaza, Room 905, 99 Washington Avenue, Albany, New York 12245, Staff (518) 474-1141.

Cornell University, CISER Data Archive, 201 Caldwell Hall, Ithaca, New York 14853, Ms. Ann Gray (607) 255-4801.

New York State Library, Cultural Education Center, Empire State Plaza, Albany, New York 12230, Ms. Mary Redmond (518) 474-3940.

Nelson A. Rockefeller Institute of Government, 411 State Street, Albany, New York 12203, Michael Cooper (518) 443-5258.

Division of Equalization and Assessment, 16 Sheridan Avenue, Albany, New York 12210, Mr. Wilfred B. Pauquette (518) 474-6742.

NEW YORK STOCK EXCHANGE

Board of Governors of the Federal Reserve System, Twentieth Street and Constitution Avenue, NW, Washington, D.C. 20551 (202) 452-3000; *Federal Reserve Bulletin,* and *Annual Statistical Digest.*

New York Stock Exchange, 11 Wall Street, New York, New York 10005 (212) 504-7754; *Fact Book.*

U.S. Securities and Exchange Commission, 450 Fifth Street, NW, Washington, D.C. 20549 (202) 272-3100; unpublished data.

New Zealand - National Statistical Office

Department of Statistics, Post Office Box 2922, Wellington, New Zealand.

New Zealand - Primary Statistics Sources

Government Bookshop, Mulgrave Street, Wellington, New Zealand; *New Zealand Official Yearbook, Monthly Abstracts of Statistics,* and *New Zealand Pocket Digest of Statistics.*

New Zealand - Databases

Information Network for Official Statistics (INFOS), New Zealand Department of Statistics, Post Office Box 2922, Wellington, New Zealand. Subject coverage: New Zealand national and regional statistical data.

Regional Population Database, New Zealand Department of Statistics, Head Office, Post Office Box 2922, Wellington, New Zealand. Subject coverage: Data for the entire country, local authorities and area units.

NEW ZEALAND - ABORTIONS

Statistical Office of the United Nations, Publishing Service, New York, New York 10017 (800) 253-9646; *Demographic Yearbook.*

NEW ZEALAND - AGRICULTURE

Euromonitor Publications Limited, 87-88 Turnmill Street, London EC1M 5QU, England; *International Marketing Data and Statistics,* and *The Pacific Basin: An Economic Handbook.*

Facts on File, 460 Park Avenue South, New York, New York 10016 (800) 443-8323; *The New Book of World Rankings.*

Food and Agricultural Organization of the United Nations (FAO) Via delle Terme di Caracalla, 00100 Rome, Italy (Telephone Number in U.S. (202) 653-2400); *Production Yearbook, The State of Food and Agriculture,* and *Trade Yearbook.*

Gale Research Incorporated, 835 Penobscot Building, Detroit, Michigan 48226 (800) 877-4253; *International Historical Statistics The Americas and Australasia.*

Organisation for Economic Co-operation and Development (OECD), 2 rue Andre-Pascal, 75 Paris 16, France (Telephone Number in U.S. (202) 785-6323); *Economic Accounts for Agriculture, Industrial Structure Statistics,* and *OECD Economic Surveys: New Zealand.*

Statistical Office of the United Nations, Publishing Service, New York, New York 10017 (800) 253-9646; *Statistical Yearbook,* and *Statistical Yearbook for Asia and the Pacific.*

Times Books, 201 East 50th Street, New York, New York 10022 (212) 751-2600; *The Economist Book of Vital World Statistics.*

The World Bank, 1818 H Street, NW, Washington, D.C. 20433 (202) 477-1234; *World Tables.*

NEW ZEALAND - AIRLINE SERVICE

The Economist Intelligence Unit (Asia) Limited, 10th Floor, Luk Kwok Centre, 72 Gloucester Road, Wanchai, Hong Kong (Phone Number in U.S. (800) 938-4685); *Asian Market Atlas.*

Facts on File, 460 Park Avenue South, New York, New York 10016 (800) 443-8323; *The New Book of World Rankings.*

International Civil Aviation Organization, 1000 Sherbrooke Street, West, Montreal, Quebec, Canada H3A 2R2 (514) 285-8219; *Civil Aviation Statistics of the World.*

Organisation for Economic Co-operation and Development (OECD), 2 rue Andre-Pascal, 75 Paris 16, France (Telephone Number in U.S. (202) 785-6323); *Tourism Policy and International Tourism in OECD Member Countries.*

Statistical Office of the United Nations, Publishing Service, New York, New York 10017 (800) 253-9646; *Statistical Yearbook.*

Times Books, 201 East 50th Street, New York, New York 10022 (212) 751-2600; *The Economist Book of Vital World Statistics.*

NEW ZEALAND - ALUMINUM PRODUCTION AND CONSUMPTION - See NEW ZEALAND - MINING AND MINERAL PRODUCTS

NEW ZEALAND - ANIMAL FEEDINGSTUFFS

Organisation for Economic Co-operation and Development (OECD), 2 rue Andre-Pascal, 75 Paris 16, France (Telephone Number in U.S. (202) 785-6323); *Foreign Trade by Commodities.*

NEW ZEALAND - ANIMAL HEALTH

Food and Agricultural Organization of the United Nations (FAO), Via delle Terme di Caracalla, 00100 Rome, Italy (Telephone Number in U.S. (202) 653-2400); *Animal Health Yearbook.*

NEW ZEALAND - AREA AND DENSITY OF POPULATION

Euromonitor Publications Limited, 87-88 Turnmill Street, London EC1M 5QU, England; *International Marketing Data and Statistics, The Pacific Basin: An Economic Handbook.*

Facts on File, 460 Park Avenue South, New York, New York 10016 (800) 443-8323; *The New Book of World Rankings.*

Food and Agricultural Organization of the United Nations (FAO) Via delle Terme di Caracalla, 00100 Rome, Italy (Telephone Number in U.S. (202) 653-2400); *The State of Food and Agriculture.*

Statistical Office of the United Nations, Publishing Service, New York, New York 10017 (800) 253-9646; *Statistical Yearbook.*

Times Books, 201 East 50th Street, New York, New York 10022 (212) 751-2600; *The Economist Book of Vital World Statistics.*

United Nations Educational, Scientific and Cultural Organization (UNESCO), 7 Place de Fontenoy, F-75700 Paris, France (Telephone Number in U.S. (212) 963-5981); *Statistical Yearbook.*

NEW ZEALAND - ARMS EXPORTS AND IMPORTS

U.S. Arms Control and Disarmament Agency, 320 Twenty-first Street, NW, Washington, D.C. 20451 (202) 647-8677; *World Military Expenditures and Arms Transfers.*

NEW ZEALAND - BALANCE OF PAYMENTS

The Economist Intelligence Unit, 111 West 57th Street, New York, New York 10019 (800) 938-4685; *The World Market Atlas.*

International Monetary Fund, 700 Nineteenth Street, NW, Washington, D.C. 20431 (202) 623-7000; *Balance of Payments Yearbook,* and *International Financial Statistics.*

Organisation for Economic Co-operation and Development (OECD), 2 rue Andre-Pascal, 75 Paris 16, France (Telephone Number in U.S. (202) 785-6323); *Economic Outlook, Geographical Distribution of Financial Flows to Developing Countries, Main Economic Indicators - Historical Statistics,* and *OECD Economic Surveys: New Zealand.*

Times Books, 201 East 50th Street, New York, New York 10022 (212) 751-2600; *The Economist Book of Vital World Statistics.*

The World Bank, 1818 H Street, NW, Washington, D.C. 20433 (202) 477-1234; *World Tables.*

NEW ZEALAND - BANKING

Facts on File, 460 Park Avenue South, New York, New York 10016 (800) 443-8323; *The New Book of World Rankings.*

International Monetary Fund, 700 Nineteenth Street, NW, Washington, D.C. 20431 (202) 623-7000; *Government Finance Statistics Yearbook.*

International Monetary Fund, 700 Nineteenth Street, NW, Washington, D.C. 20431 (202) 623-7000; *International Financial Statistics.*

Organisation for Economic Co-operation and Development (OECD), 2 rue Andre-Pascal, 75 Paris 16, France (Telephone Number in U.S. (202) 785-6323); *Economic Outlook, Financial Market Trends,* and *OECD Economic Surveys: New Zealand.*

Statistical Office of the United Nations, Publishing Service, New York, New York 10017 (800) 253-9646; *Statistical Yearbook.*

NEW ZEALAND - BARLEY PRODUCTION - See NEW ZEALAND - CROPS

NEW ZEALAND - BEEF EXPORTS - See NEW ZEALAND - LIVESTOCK AND POULTRY

NEW ZEALAND - BEER PRODUCTION

Facts on File, 460 Park Avenue South, New York, New York 10016 (800) 443-8323; *The New Book of World Rankings.*

Statistical Office of the United Nations, Publishing Service, New York, New York 10017 (800) 253-9646; *Statistical Yearbook.*

NEW ZEALAND - BIRTH RATES

The Economist Intelligence Unit (Asia) Limited, 10th Floor, Luk Kwok Centre, 72 Gloucester Road, Wanchai, Hong Kong (Phone Number in U.S. (800) 938-4685); *Asian Market Atlas.*

Euromonitor Publications Limited, 87-88 Turnmill Street, London EC1M 5QU, England; *The Pacific Basin: An Economic Handbook.*

Facts on File, 460 Park Avenue South, New York, New York 10016 (800) 443-8323; *The New Book of World Rankings.*

Statistical Office of the United Nations, Publishing Service, New York, New York 10017 (800) 253-9646; *Demographic Yearbook,* and *Statistical Yearbook.*

Times Books, 201 East 50th Street, New York, New York 10022 (212) 751-2600; *The Economist Book of Vital World Statistics.*

The World Bank, 1818 H Street, NW, Washington, D.C. 20433 (202) 477-1234; *World Tables.*

World Health Organization, Office of Publications, Avenue Appia, CH-1211 Geneva 27, Switzerland (Telephone Number in U.S. (518) 436-9686); *World Health Statistics Annual.*

NEW ZEALAND - BONDS

International Monetary Fund, 700 Nineteenth Street, NW, Washington, D.C. 20431 (202) 623-7000; *Government Finance Statistics Yearbook.*

Organisation for Economic Co-operation and Development (OECD), 2 rue Andre-Pascal, 75 Paris 16, France (Telephone Number in U.S. (202) 785-6323); *Financial Market Trends,* and *Main Economic Indicators - Historical Statistics.*

Statistical Office of the United Nations, Publishing Service, New York, New York 10017 (800) 253-9646; *Statistical Yearbook.*

NEW ZEALAND - BOOK PRODUCTION

United Nations Educational, Scientific and Cultural Organization (UNESCO), 7 Place de Fontenoy, F-75700 Paris, France (Telephone Number in U.S. (212) 963-5981); *Statistical Yearbook.*

NEW ZEALAND - BROADCASTING

Billboard Limited, Post Office Box 9027, 1006 AA Amsterdam, The Netherlands (Telephone Number in U.S. (212) 764-7300); *World Radio TV Handbook.*

The Economist Intelligence Unit (Asia) Limited, 10th Floor, Luk Kwok Centre, 72 Gloucester Road, Wanchai, Hong Kong (Phone Number in U.S. (800) 938-4685); *Asian Market Atlas.*

Facts on File, 460 Park Avenue South, New York, New York 10016 (800) 443-8323; *The New Book of World Rankings.*

Times Books, 201 East 50th Street, New York, New York 10022 (212) 751-2600; *The Economist Book of Vital World Statistics.*

NEW ZEALAND - BUTTER - See NEW ZEALAND - DAIRY PRODUCTS

NEW ZEALAND - CABBAGE PRODUCTION - See NEW ZEALAND - CROPS

NEW ZEALAND - CALORIE SUPPLY

Food and Agricultural Organization of the United Nations (FAO) Via delle Terme di Caracalla, 00100 Rome, Italy (Telephone Number in U.S. (202) 653-2400); *The State of Food and Agriculture.*

NEW ZEALAND - CAPITAL INVESTMENT

Organisation for Economic Co-operation and Development (OECD), 2 rue Andre-Pascal, 75 Paris 16, France (Telephone Number in U.S. (202) 785-6323); *Economic Outlook,* and *Financial Market Trends.*

NEW ZEALAND - CAPITAL REVENUE

International Monetary Fund, 700 Nineteenth Street, NW, Washington, D.C. 20431 (202) 623-7000; *Government Finance Statistics Yearbook.*

Organisation for Economic Co-operation and Development (OECD), 2 rue Andre-Pascal, 75 Paris 16, France (Telephone Number in U.S. (202) 785-6323); *Economic Outlook,* and *Financial Market Trends.*

NEW ZEALAND - CATTLE - See NEW ZEALAND - LIVESTOCK AND POULTRY

NEW ZEALAND - CAULIFLOWER PRODUCTION - See NEW ZEALAND - CROPS

NEW ZEALAND - CEMENT PRODUCTION - See NEW ZEALAND - MINING AND MINERAL PRODUCTS

NEW ZEALAND - CEREAL PRODUCTION - See NEW ZEALAND - CROPS

NEW ZEALAND - CHEESE - See NEW ZEALAND - DAIRY PRODUCTS

NEW ZEALAND - CHEMICAL (ORGANIC) PRODUCTION - See NEW ZEALAND - MINING AND MINERAL PRODUCTS

NEW ZEALAND - CHICKENS - See NEW ZEALAND - LIVESTOCK AND POULTRY

NEW ZEALAND - CIGARETTE PRODUCTION - See NEW ZEALAND - TOBACCO PRODUCTION

NEW ZEALAND - CLIMATE

Facts on File, 460 Park Avenue South, New York, New York 10016 (800) 443-8323; *The New Book of World Rankings.*

NEW ZEALAND - CLOTHING EXPORTS AND IMPORTS

Organisation for Economic Co-operation and Development (OECD), 2 rue Andre-Pascal, 75 Paris 16, France (Telephone Number in U.S. (202) 785-6323); *Textile Industry in OECD Countries.*

NEW ZEALAND - COAL PRODUCTION - See NEW ZEALAND - MINING AND MINERAL PRODUCTS

NEW ZEALAND - COBALT PRODUCTION AND CONSUMPTION - See NEW ZEALAND - MINING AND MINERAL PRODUCTS

NEW ZEALAND - COFFEE PRODUCTION AND CONSUMPTION - See NEW ZEALAND - CROPS

NEW ZEALAND - COKE, COKE OVEN COKE, AND COKE OVEN ORE PRODUCTION AND CONSUMPTION - See NEW ZEALAND - MINING AND MINERAL PRODUCTS

NEW ZEALAND - COMMUNICATIONS

Gale Research Incorporated, 835 Penobscot Building, Detroit, Michigan 48226 (800) 877-4253; *International Historical Statistics The Americas and Australasia.*

Statistical Office of the United Nations, Publishing Service, New York, New York 10017 (800) 253-9646; *Statistical Yearbook for Asia and the Pacific.*

NEW ZEALAND - CONSTRUCTION INDUSTRY

Facts on File, 460 Park Avenue South, New York, New York 10016 (800) 443-8323; *The New Book of World Rankings.*

Organisation for Economic Co-operation and Development (OECD), 2 rue Andre-Pascal, 75 Paris 16, France (Telephone Number in U.S. (202) 785-6323); *Industrial Structure Statistics, The Iron and Steel Industry, Main Economic Indicators - Historical Statistics,* and *OECD Economic Surveys: New Zealand.*

Statistical Office of the United Nations, Publishing Service, New York, New York 10017 (800) 253-9646; *Construction Statistics Yearbook,* and *Statistical Yearbook.*

NEW ZEALAND - CONSUMER PRICE INDEX

Organisation for Economic Co-operation and Development (OECD), 2 rue Andre-Pascal, 75 Paris 16, France (Telephone Number in U.S. (202) 785-6323); *Economic Outlook.*

Statistical Office of the United Nations, Publishing Service, New York, New York 10017 (800) 253-9646; *Statistical Yearbook.*

Times Books, 201 East 50th Street, New York, New York 10022 (212) 751-2600; *The Economist Book of Vital World Statistics.*

NEW ZEALAND - CONSUMER PRICES

International Labour Office, I.L.O. Publications, CH-1211, Geneva 22, Switzerland; *Yearbook of Labour Statistics.*

International Monetary Fund, 700 Nineteenth Street, NW, Washington, D.C. 20431 (202) 623-7000; *International Financial Statistics.*

Organisation for Economic Co-operation and Development (OECD), 2 rue Andre-Pascal, 75 Paris 16, France (Telephone Number in U.S. (202) 785-6323); *Economic Outlook,* and *Main Economic Indicators - Historical Statistics.*

NEW ZEALAND - CONSUMPTION

Euromonitor Publications Limited, 87-88 Turnmill Street, London EC1M 5QU, England; *The Pacific Basin: An Economic Handbook.*

Organisation for Economic Co-operation and Development (OECD), 2 rue Andre-Pascal, 75 Paris 16, France (Telephone Number in U.S. (202) 785-6323); *The Footwear, Raw Hides and Skins, and Leather Industry in OECD Countries, The Iron and Steel Industry, Meat Balances in OECD Member Countries, The Non-Ferrous Metals Industry, The Pulp and Paper Industry,* and *Textile Industry in OECD Countries.*

NEW ZEALAND - COPPER AND COPPER ORE PRODUCTION AND CONSUMPTION - See NEW ZEALAND - MINING AND MINERAL PRODUCTS

NEW ZEALAND - CORN PRODUCTION - See NEW ZEALAND - CROPS

NEW ZEALAND - CORPORATE INCOME TAXES - See NEW ZEALAND - TAXATION

NEW ZEALAND - CORPORATE TAXES - See NEW ZEALAND - TAXATION

NEW ZEALAND - COTTON - See NEW ZEALAND - CROPS

NEW ZEALAND - CRIME

International Criminal Police Organization (INTERPOL), 26 rue Armengaud, 92210 Saint Cloud, France; *International Crime Statistics.*

Yale University Press, Yale Station, New Haven, Connecticut 06520 (203) 432-0940; *Violence and Crime in Cross-National Perspective.*

NEW ZEALAND - CROPS

Facts on File, 460 Park Avenue South, New York, New York 10016 (800) 443-8323; *The New Book of World Rankings.*

Food and Agricultural Organization of the United Nations (FAO), Via delle Terme di Caracalla, 00100 Rome, Italy (Telephone Number in U.S. (202) 653-2400); *Production Yearbook,* and *The State of Food and Agriculture.*

Organisation for Economic Co-operation and Development (OECD), 2 rue Andre-Pascal, 75 Paris 16, France (Telephone Number in U.S. (202) 785-6323); *Economic Accounts for Agriculture, Foreign Trade by Commodities,* and *Textile Industry in OECD Countries.*

Statistical Office of the United Nations, Publishing Service, New York, New York 10017 (800) 253-9646; *Statistical Yearbook.*

NEW ZEALAND - CUSTOMS DUTIES

International Monetary Fund, 700 Nineteenth Street, NW, Washington, D.C. 20431 (202) 623-7000; *Government Finance Statistics Yearbook.*

Organisation for Economic Co-operation and Development (OECD), 2 rue Andre-Pascal, 75 Paris 16, France (Telephone Number in U.S. (202) 785-6323); *The Non-Ferrous Metals Industry*.

NEW ZEALAND - DAIRY PRODUCTS

Commodity Research Bureau, Incorporated, 75 Wall Street, New York, New York 10005 (212) 504-7754; *Commodity Year Book*.

Facts on File, 460 Park Avenue South, New York, New York 10016 (800) 443-8323; *The New Book of World Rankings*.

Food and Agricultural Organization of the United Nations (FAO), Via delle Terme di Caracalla, 00100 Rome, Italy (Telephone Number in U.S. (202) 653-2400); *Production Yearbook*, and *The State of Food and Agriculture*.

International Monetary Fund, 700 Nineteenth Street, NW, Washington, D.C. 20431 (202) 623-7000; *International Financial Statistics*.

Organisation for Economic Co-operation and Development (OECD), 2 rue Andre-Pascal, 75 Paris 16, France (Telephone Number in U.S. (202) 785-6323); *Economic Accounts for Agriculture*, and *Milk, Milk Products, and Egg Balances in OECD Member Countries*.

Statistical Office of the United Nations, Publishing Service, New York, New York 10017 (800) 253-9646; *Statistical Yearbook*.

NEW ZEALAND - DEATH RATES

The Economist Intelligence Unit (Asia) Limited, 10th Floor, Luk Kwok Centre, 72 Gloucester Road, Wanchai, Hong Kong (Phone Number in U.S. (800) 938-4685); *Asian Market Atlas*.

Euromonitor Publications Limited, 87-88 Turnmill Street, London EC1M 5QU, England; *The Pacific Basin: An Economic Handbook*.

Statistical Office of the United Nations, Publishing Service, New York, New York 10017 (800) 253-9646; *Statistical Yearbook*.

Times Books, 201 East 50th Street, New York, New York 10022 (212) 751-2600; *The Economist Book of Vital World Statistics*.

World Health Organization, Office of Publications, Avenue Appia, CH-1211 Geneva 27, Switzerland (Telephone Number in U.S. (518) 436-9686); *World Health Statistics Annual*.

NEW ZEALAND - DEFENSE EXPENDITURES

International Monetary Fund, 700 Nineteenth Street, NW, Washington, D.C. 20431 (202) 623-7000; *Government Finance Statistics Yearbook*.

U.S. Arms Control and Disarmament Agency, 320 Twenty-first Street, NW, Washington, D.C. 20451 (202) 647-8677; *World Military Expenditures and Arms Transfers*.

NEW ZEALAND - DEMOGRAPHY

The Economist Intelligence Unit (Asia) Limited, 10th Floor, Luk Kwok Centre, 72 Gloucester Road, Wanchai, Hong Kong (Phone Number in U.S. (800) 938-4685); *Asian Market Atlas*.

Facts on File, 460 Park Avenue South, New York, New York 10016 (800) 443-8323; *The New Book of World Rankings*.

NEW ZEALAND - DEVELOPMENT ASSISTANCE

Organisation for Economic Co-operation and Development (OECD), 2 rue Andre-Pascal, 75 Paris 16, France (Telephone Number in U.S. (202) 785-6323); *Geographical Distribution of Financial Flows to Developing Countries*.

Statistical Office of the United Nations, Publishing Service, New York, New York 10017 (800) 253-9646; *Statistical Yearbook*.

NEW ZEALAND - DIAMOND PRODUCTION - See NEW ZEALAND - MINING AND MINERAL PRODUCTS

NEW ZEALAND - DISCOUNT RATES

Organisation for Economic Co-operation and Development (OECD), 2 rue Andre-Pascal, 75 Paris 16, France (Telephone Number in U.S. (202) 785-6323); *Financial Market Trends*.

Statistical Office of the United Nations, Publishing Service, New York, New York 10017 (800) 253-9646; *Statistical Yearbook*.

NEW ZEALAND - DISEASES

World Health Organization, Office of Publications, Avenue Appia, CH-1211 Geneva 27, Switzerland (Telephone Number in U.S. (518) 436-9686); *World Health Statistics Annual*.

NEW ZEALAND - DIVORCE RATES

Facts on File, 460 Park Avenue South, New York, New York 10016 (800) 443-8323; *The New Book of World Rankings*.

Statistical Office of the United Nations, Publishing Service, New York, New York 10017 (800) 253-9646; *Demographic Yearbook*.

NEW ZEALAND - DUCKS - See NEW ZEALAND - LIVESTOCK AND POULTRY

NEW ZEALAND - ECONOMY

Euromonitor Publications Limited, 87-88 Turnmill Street, London EC1M 5QU, England; *International Marketing Data and Statistics*.

Facts on File, 460 Park Avenue South, New York, New York 10016 (800) 443-8323; *The New Book of World Rankings*.

Organisation for Economic Co-operation and Development (OECD), 2 rue Andre-Pascal, 75 Paris 16, France (Telephone Number in U.S. (202) 785-6323); *Economic Outlook, Geographical Distribution of Financial Flows to Developing Countries, Main Economic Indicators - Historical Statistics, OECD Economic Surveys: New Zealand*, and *OECD Employment Outlook*.

NEW ZEALAND - EDUCATION

The Economist Intelligence Unit, 111 West 57th Street, New York, New York 10019 (800) 938-4685; *The World Market Atlas*.

The Economist Intelligence Unit (Asia) Limited, 10th Floor, Luk Kwok Centre, 72 Gloucester Road, Wanchai, Hong Kong (Phone Number in U.S. (800) 938-4685); *Asian Market Atlas*.

Euromonitor Publications Limited, 87-88 Turnmill Street, London EC1M 5QU, England; *The Pacific Basin: An Economic Handbook*.

Facts on File, 460 Park Avenue South, New York, New York 10016 (800) 443-8323; *The New Book of World Rankings*.

Gale Research Incorporated, 835 Penobscot Building, Detroit, Michigan 48226 (800) 877-4253; *International Historical Statistics The Americas and Australasia.*

International Monetary Fund, 700 Nineteenth Street, NW, Washington, D.C. 20431 (202) 623-7000; *Government Finance Statistics Yearbook.*

Organisation for Economic Co-operation and Development (OECD), 2 rue Andre-Pascal, 75 Paris 16, France (Telephone Number in U.S. (202) 785-6323); *Education in OECD Countries.*

Statistical Office of the United Nations, Publishing Service, New York, New York 10017 (800) 253-9646; *Statistical Yearbook,* and *Statistical Yearbook for Asia and the Pacific.*

Times Books, 201 East 50th Street, New York, New York 10022 (212) 751-2600; *The Economist Book of Vital World Statistics.*

United Nations Educational, Scientific and Cultural Organization (UNESCO), 7 Place de Fontenoy, F-75700 Paris, France (Telephone Number in U.S. (212) 963-5981); *Statistical Yearbook.*

The World Bank, 1818 H Street, NW, Washington, D.C. 20433 (202) 477-1234; *World Tables.*

NEW ZEALAND - EGG PRODUCTION AND CONSUMPTION - See NEW ZEALAND - DAIRY PRODUCTS

NEW ZEALAND - ELECTRICITY

Facts on File, 460 Park Avenue South, New York, New York 10016 (800) 443-8323; *The New Book of World Rankings.*

Organisation for Economic Co-operation and Development (OECD), 2 rue Andre-Pascal, 75 Paris 16, France (Telephone Number in U.S. (202) 785-6323); *Coal Information, Energy Statistics of OECD Countries,* and *Industrial Structure Statistics.*

Penn Well Publishing Company, 1421 South Sheridan Road, Post Office Box 1260, Tulsa, Oklahoma 74101 (800) 752-9764; *International Energy Statistics Sourcebook.*

Statistical Office of the United Nations, Publishing Service, New York, New York 10017 (800) 253-9646; *Statistical Yearbook.*

Times Books, 201 East 50th Street, New York, New York 10022 (212) 751-2600; *The Economist Book of Vital World Statistics.*

NEW ZEALAND - EMPLOYMENT

Euromonitor Publications Limited, 87-88 Turnmill Street, London EC1M 5QU, England; *International Marketing Data and Statistics,* and *The Pacific Basin: An Economic Handbook.*

Facts on File, 460 Park Avenue South, New York, New York 10016 (800) 443-8323; *The New Book of World Rankings.*

International Labour Office, I.L.O. Publications, CH-1211, Geneva 22, Switzerland; *Yearbook of Labour Statistics.*

Organisation for Economic Co-operation and Development (OECD), 2 rue Andre-Pascal, 75 Paris 16, France (Telephone Number in U.S. (202) 785-6323); *The Iron and Steel Industry, OECD Economic Surveys: New Zealand, OECD Employment Outlook,* and *Textile Industry in OECD Countries.*

Statistical Office of the United Nations, Publishing Service, New York, New York 10017 (800) 253-9646; *Statistical Yearbook.*

NEW ZEALAND - ENERGY

Facts on File, 460 Park Avenue South, New York, New York 10016 (800) 443-8323; *The New Book of World Rankings.*

Food and Agricultural Organization of the United Nations (FAO) Via delle Terme di Caracalla, 00100 Rome, Italy (Telephone Number in U.S. (202) 653-2400); *The State of Food and Agriculture.*

Organisation for Economic Co-operation and Development (OECD), 2 rue Andre-Pascal, 75 Paris 16, France (Telephone Number in U.S. (202) 785-6323); *Coal Information, Energy Statistics of OECD Countries, OECD Environmental Data,* and *Oil and Gas Information.*

Penn Well Publishing Company, 1421 South Sheridan Road, Post Office Box 1260, Tulsa, Oklahoma 74101 (800) 752-9764; *International Energy Statistics Sourcebook.*

Statistical Office of the United Nations, Publishing Service, New York, New York 10017 (800) 253-9646; *Energy Statistics Yearbook, Statistical Yearbook, Statistical Yearbook for Asia and the Pacific,* and *World Energy Supplies.*

Times Books, 201 East 50th Street, New York, New York 10022 (212) 751-2600; *The Economist Book of Vital World Statistics.*

NEW ZEALAND - ENVIRONMENT

Organization for Economic Co-operation and Development (OECD), 2 rue Andre-Pascal, 75 Paris 16, France (Telephone Number in the U.S. (202) 785-6323); *OECD Environmental Data.*

NEW ZEALAND - EXCHANGE RATES

The Economist Intelligence Unit (Asia) Limited, 10th Floor, Luk Kwok Centre, 72 Gloucester Road, Wanchai, Hong Kong (Phone Number in U.S. (800) 938-4685); *Asian Market Atlas.*

Euromonitor Publications Limited, 87-88 Turnmill Street, London EC1M 5QU, England; *International Marketing Data and Statistics,* and *The Pacific Basin: An Economic Handbook.*

International Civil Aviation Organization, 1000 Sherbrooke Street, West, Montreal, Quebec, Canada H3A 2R2 (514) 285-8219; *Civil Aviation Statistics of the World.*

International Monetary Fund, 700 Nineteenth Street, NW, Washington, D.C. 20431 (202) 623-7000; *International Financial Statistics.*

Organisation for Economic Co-operation and Development (OECD), 2 rue Andre-Pascal, 75 Paris 16, France (Telephone Number in U.S. (202) 785-6323); *Economic Outlook, Financial Market Trends, Revenue Statistics of OECD Member Countries,* and *Tourism Policy and International Tourism in OECD Member Countries.*

Statistical Office of the United Nations, Publishing Service, New York, New York 10017 (800) 253-9646; *Statistical Yearbook.*

NEW ZEALAND - EXCISE TAXES - See NEW ZEALAND - TAXATION

NEW ZEALAND - EXPORTS

American Automobile Manufacturers Association, 1401 H Eye Street, NW, Suite 900, Washington, D.C. 20005 (202) 326-5500; *World Motor Vehicle Data.*

The Economist Intelligence Unit, 111 West 57th Street, New York, New York 10019 (800) 938-4685; *The World Market Atlas.*

The Economist Intelligence Unit (Asia) Limited, 10th Floor, Luk Kwok Centre, 72 Gloucester Road, Wanchai, Hong Kong (Phone Number in U.S. (800) 938-4685); *Asian Market Atlas*.

Euromonitor Publications Limited, 87-88 Turnmill Street, London EC1M 5QU, England; *International Marketing Data and Statistics*, and *The Pacific Basin: An Economic Handbook*.

Food and Agricultural Organization of the United Nations (FAO) Via delle Terme di Caracalla, 00100 Rome, Italy (Telephone Number in U.S. (202) 653-2400); *The State of Food and Agriculture*.

International Monetary Fund, 700 Nineteenth Street, NW, Washington, D.C. 20431 (202) 623-7000; *Direction of Trade Statistics*, and *International Financial Statistics*.

Organisation for Economic Co-operation and Development (OECD), 2 rue Andre-Pascal, 75 Paris 16, France (Telephone Number in U.S. (202) 785-6323); *Economic Outlook, The Footwear, Raw Hides and Skins, and Leather Industry in OECD Countries, Foreign Trade by Commodities, Geographical Distribution of Financial Flows to Developing Countries, Industrial Structure Statistics, The Iron and Steel Industry, Milk, Milk Products, and Egg Balances in OECD Member Countries, The Pulp and Paper Industry, OECD Economic Surveys: New Zealand*, and *Review of Fisheries in OECD Member Countries*.

Statistical Office of the United Nations, Publishing Service, New York, New York 10017 (800) 253-9646; *Foreign Trade Statistics of Asia and the Pacific*.

Times Books, 201 East 50th Street, New York, New York 10022 (212) 751-2600; *The Economist Book of Vital World Statistics*.

The World Bank, 1818 H Street, NW, Washington, D.C. 20433 (202) 477-1234; *World Tables*.

NEW ZEALAND - EXTERNAL FINANCING

Organisation for Economic Co-operation and Development (OECD), 2 rue Andre-Pascal, 75 Paris 16, France (Telephone Number in U.S. (202) 785-6323); *Economic Outlook*, and *Financial Market Trends*.

NEW ZEALAND - EXTERNAL INDEBTEDNESS

Organisation for Economic Co-operation and Development (OECD), 2 rue Andre-Pascal, 75 Paris 16, France (Telephone Number in U.S. (202) 785-6323); *Financial Market Trends*, and *Geographical Distribution of Financial Flows to Developing Countries*.

The World Bank, 1818 H Street, NW, Washington, D.C. 20433 (202) 477-1234; *World Tables*.

NEW ZEALAND - EXTERNAL TRADE

Food and Agricultural Organization of the United Nations (FAO) Via delle Terme di Caracalla, 00100 Rome, Italy (Telephone Number in U.S. (202) 653-2400); *The State of Food and Agriculture*, and *Trade Yearbook*.

Gale Research Incorporated, 835 Penobscot Building, Detroit, Michigan 48226 (800) 877-4253; *International Historical Statistics The Americas and Australasia*.

Statistical Office of the United Nations, Publishing Service, New York, New York 10017 (800) 253-9646; *Statistical Yearbook*, and *Statistical Yearbook for Asia and the Pacific*.

NEW ZEALAND - FABRIC PRODUCTION - See NEW ZEALAND - TEXTILE INDUSTRY

NEW ZEALAND - FARM CROPS - See NEW ZEALAND - CROPS

NEW ZEALAND - FEMALE WORKING POPULATION - See NEW ZEALAND - EMPLOYMENT

NEW ZEALAND - FERTILITY RATES

The Economist Intelligence Unit (Asia) Limited, 10th Floor, Luk Kwok Centre, 72 Gloucester Road, Wanchai, Hong Kong (Phone Number in U.S. (800) 938-4685); *Asian Market Atlas*.

Facts on File, 460 Park Avenue South, New York, New York 10016 (800) 443-8323; *The New Book of World Rankings*.

Times Books, 201 East 50th Street, New York, New York 10022 (212) 751-2600; *The Economist Book of Vital World Statistics*.

The World Bank, 1818 H Street, NW, Washington, D.C. 20433 (202) 477-1234; *World Tables*.

NEW ZEALAND - FERTILIZER

Food and Agricultural Organization of the United Nations (FAO) Via delle Terme di Caracalla, 00100 Rome, Italy (Telephone Number in U.S. (202) 653-2400); *The State of Food and Agriculture*.

Organisation for Economic Co-operation and Development (OECD), 2 rue Andre-Pascal, 75 Paris 16, France (Telephone Number in U.S. (202) 785-6323); *Economic Accounts for Agriculture*, and *Foreign Trade by Commodities*.

Statistical Office of the United Nations, Publishing Service, New York, New York 10017 (800) 253-9646; *Statistical Yearbook*.

NEW ZEALAND - FETAL MORTALITY

Statistical Office of the United Nations, Publishing Service, New York, New York 10017 (800) 253-9646; *Demographic Yearbook*.

World Health Organization, Office of Publications, Avenue Appia, CH-1211 Geneva 27, Switzerland (Telephone Number in U.S. (518) 436-9686); *World Health Statistics Annual*.

NEW ZEALAND - FIBRE PRODUCTION - See NEW ZEALAND - TEXTILE INDUSTRY

NEW ZEALAND - FILAMENT PRODUCTION - See NEW ZEALAND - TEXTILE INDUSTRY

NEW ZEALAND - FILMS PRODUCED - LONG - See NEW ZEALAND - MOTION PICTURES

NEW ZEALAND - FINANCE

Euromonitor Publications Limited, 87-88 Turnmill Street, London EC1M 5QU, England; *The Pacific Basin: An Economic Handbook*.

Facts on File, 460 Park Avenue South, New York, New York 10016 (800) 443-8323; *The New Book of World Rankings*.

Gale Research Incorporated, 835 Penobscot Building, Detroit, Michigan 48226 (800) 877-4253; *International Historical Statistics The Americas and Australasia*.

International Monetary Fund, 700 Nineteenth Street, NW, Washington, D.C. 20431 (202) 623-7000; *Government Finance*

Statistics Yearbook, and *International Financial Statistics*.

Organisation for Economic Co-operation and Development (OECD), 2 rue Andre-Pascal, 75 Paris 16, France (Telephone Number in U.S. (202) 785-6323); *Economic Outlook, Financial Market Trends, Geographical Distribution of Financial Flows to Developing Countries, Main Economic Indicators - Historical Statistics*, and *OECD Financial Statistics*.

Statistical Office of the United Nations, Publishing Service, New York, New York 10017 (800) 253-9646; *Statistical Yearbook for Asia and the Pacific*.

NEW ZEALAND - FISHERIES

Facts on File, 460 Park Avenue South, New York, New York 10016 (800) 443-8323; *The New Book of World Rankings*.

Food and Agricultural Organization of the United Nations (FAO) Via delle Terme di Caracalla, 00100 Rome, Italy (Telephone Number in U.S. (202) 653-2400); *The State of Food and Agriculture*, and *Yearbook of Fishery Statistics*.

Organisation for Economic Co-operation and Development (OECD), 2 rue Andre-Pascal, 75 Paris 16, France (Telephone Number in U.S. (202) 785-6323); *Foreign Trade by Commodities, Industrial Structure Statistics*, and *Review of Fisheries in OECD Member Countries*.

Statistical Office of the United Nations, Publishing Service, New York, New York 10017 (800) 253-9646; *Statistical Yearbook*.

NEW ZEALAND - FLOUR PRODUCTION

Statistical Office of the United Nations, Publishing Service, New York, New York 10017 (800) 253-9646; *Statistical Yearbook*.

NEW ZEALAND - FOOD

Food and Agricultural Organization of the United Nations (FAO), Via delle Terme di Caracalla, 00100 Rome, Italy (Telephone Number in U.S. (202) 653-2400); *Production Yearbook*, and *The State of Food and Agriculture*.

Organisation for Economic Co-operation and Development (OECD), 2 rue Andre-Pascal, 75 Paris 16, France (Telephone Number in U.S. (202) 785-6323); *Food Consumption Statistics*, and *Foreign Trade by Commodities*.

Statistical Office of the United Nations, Publishing Service, New York, New York 10017 (800) 253-9646; *Statistical Yearbook for Asia and the Pacific*.

NEW ZEALAND - FOREIGN DEBT

International Monetary Fund, 700 Nineteenth Street, NW, Washington, D.C. 20431 (202) 623-7000; *Government Finance Statistics Yearbook*.

Organisation for Economic Co-operation and Development (OECD), 2 rue Andre-Pascal, 75 Paris 16, France (Telephone Number in U.S. (202) 785-6323); *Economic Outlook*.

NEW ZEALAND - FOREIGN INDEBTEDNESS

Euromonitor Publications Limited, 87-88 Turnmill Street, London EC1M 5QU, England; *The Pacific Basin: An Economic Handbook*.

Organisation for Economic Co-operation and Development (OECD), 2 rue Andre-Pascal, 75 Paris 16, France (Telephone Number in U.S. (202) 785-6323); *Economic Outlook*, and *Financial Market Trends*.

NEW ZEALAND - FOREIGN TRADE

The Economist Intelligence Unit (Asia) Limited, 10th Floor, Luk Kwok Centre, 72 Gloucester Road, Wanchai, Hong Kong (Phone Number in U.S. (800) 938-4685); *Asian Market Atlas*.

Euromonitor Publications Limited, 87-88 Turnmill Street, London EC1M 5QU, England; *International Marketing Data and Statistics* and *The Pacific Basin: An Economic Handbook*.

Facts on File, 460 Park Avenue South, New York, New York 10016 (800) 443-8323; *The New Book of World Rankings*.

Food and Agricultural Organization of the United Nations (FAO) Via delle Terme di Caracalla, 00100 Rome, Italy (Telephone Number in U.S. (202) 653-2400); *The State of Food and Agriculture*.

Organisation for Economic Co-operation and Development (OECD), 2 rue Andre-Pascal, 75 Paris 16, France (Telephone Number in U.S. (202) 785-6323); *Economic Outlook, The Footwear, Raw Hides and Skins, and Leather Industry in OECD Countries, Foreign Trade by Commodities, Main Economic Indicators - Historical Statistics, Maritime Transport, Meat Balances in OECD Member Countries*, and *OECD Economic Surveys: New Zealand*.

Statistical Office of the United Nations, Publishing Service, New York, New York 10017 (800) 253-9646; *International Trade Statistics Yearbook, Statistical Yearbook*, and *Trade in Manufactures of Developing Countries*.

The World Bank, 1818 H Street, NW, Washington, D.C. 20433 (202) 477-1234; *World Tables*.

NEW ZEALAND - FORESTRY AND FOREST PRODUCTS

American Forest and Paper Association, 1250 Connecticut Avenue, NW, Washington, D.C. 20036 (202) 463-2455; *Wood Pulp and Fiber Statistics*.

Facts on File, 460 Park Avenue South, New York, New York 10016 (800) 443-8323; *The New Book of World Rankings*.

Food and Agricultural Organization of the United Nations (FAO) Via delle Terme di Caracalla, 00100 Rome, Italy (Telephone Number in U.S. (202) 653-2400); *The State of Food and Agriculture*, and *Yearbook of Forest Products*.

Organisation for Economic Co-operation and Development (OECD), 2 rue Andre-Pascal, 75 Paris 16, France (Telephone Number in U.S. (202) 785-6323); *Foreign Trade by Commodities, Industrial Structure Statistics*, and *The Pulp and Paper Industry*.

Statistical Office of the United Nations, Publishing Service, New York, New York 10017 (800) 253-9646; *Statistical Yearbook*.

NEW ZEALAND - FRUIT PRODUCTION - See NEW ZEALAND - CROPS

NEW ZEALAND - FURNITURE AND WOOD PRODUCTS - EXPORTS AND IMPORTS

Organisation for Economic Co-operation and Development (OECD), 2 rue Andre-Pascal, 75 Paris 16, France (Telephone Number in U.S. (202) 785-6323); *Foreign Trade by Commodities*, and *Industrial Structure Statistics*.

NEW ZEALAND - GAS PRODUCTION - See NEW ZEALAND - MINING AND MINERAL PRODUCTS

NEW ZEALAND - GENERAL INDUSTRIAL STATISTICS

Statistical Office of the United Nations, Publishing Service, New York, New York 10017 (800) 253-9646; *Industrial Statistics Yearbook.*

NEW ZEALAND - GENERAL MORTALITY

Statistical Office of the United Nations, Publishing Service, New York, New York 10017 (800) 253-9646; *Demographic Yearbook.*

World Health Organization, Office of Publications, Avenue Appia, CH-1211 Geneva 27, Switzerland (Telephone Number in U.S. (518) 436-9686); *World Health Statistics Annual.*

NEW ZEALAND - GEOGRAPHIC DATA

Facts on File, 460 Park Avenue South, New York, New York 10016 (800) 443-8323; *The New Book of World Rankings.*

NEW ZEALAND - GOATS - See NEW ZEALAND - LIVESTOCK AND POULTRY

NEW ZEALAND - GOLD HOLDINGS

International Monetary Fund, 700 Nineteenth Street, NW, Washington, D.C. 20431 (202) 623-7000; *International Financial Statistics.*

Statistical Office of the United Nations, Publishing Service, New York, New York 10017 (800) 253-9646; *Statistical Yearbook.*

The World Bank, 1818 H Street, NW, Washington, D.C. 20433 (202) 477-1234; *World Tables.*

NEW ZEALAND - GOLD PRODUCTION AND CONSUMPTION - See NEW ZEALAND - MINING AND MINERAL PRODUCTS

NEW ZEALAND - GOVERNMENT EXPENDITURES

International Monetary Fund, 700 Nineteenth Street, NW, Washington, D.C. 20431 (202) 623-7000; *Government Finance Statistics Yearbook.*

Organisation for Economic Co-operation and Development (OECD), 2 rue Andre-Pascal, 75 Paris 16, France (Telephone Number in U.S. (202) 785-6323); *Economic Outlook.*

Times Books, 201 East 50th Street, New York, New York 10022 (212) 751-2600; *The Economist Book of Vital World Statistics.*

The World Bank, 1818 H Street, NW, Washington, D.C. 20433 (202) 477-1234; *World Tables.*

NEW ZEALAND - GOVERNMENT FINANCES

International Monetary Fund, 700 Nineteenth Street, NW, Washington, D.C. 20431 (202) 623-7000; *International Financial Statistics.*

Organisation for Economic Co-operation and Development (OECD), 2 rue Andre-Pascal, 75 Paris 16, France (Telephone Number in U.S. (202) 785-6323); *Economic Outlook.*

Statistical Office of the United Nations, Publishing Service, New York, New York 10017 (800) 253-9646; *Statistical Yearbook.*

NEW ZEALAND - GOVERNMENT REVENUES

International Monetary Fund, 700 Nineteenth Street, NW, Washington, D.C. 20431 (202) 623-7000; *Government Finance Statistics Yearbook.*

Organisation for Economic Co-operation and Development (OECD), 2 rue Andre-Pascal, 75 Paris 16, France (Telephone Number in U.S. (202) 785-6323); *Economic Outlook,* and *Revenue Statistics of OECD Member Countries.*

Times Books, 201 East 50th Street, New York, New York 10022 (212) 751-2600; *The Economist Book of Vital World Statistics.*

The World Bank, 1818 H Street, NW, Washington, D.C. 20433 (202) 477-1234; *World Tables.*

NEW ZEALAND - GRAIN PRODUCTION - See NEW ZEALAND - CROPS

NEW ZEALAND - GRANTS

International Monetary Fund, 700 Nineteenth Street, NW, Washington, D.C. 20431 (202) 623-7000; *Government Finance Statistics Yearbook.*

Organisation for Economic Co-operation and Development (OECD), 2 rue Andre-Pascal, 75 Paris 16, France (Telephone Number in U.S. (202) 785-6323); *Geographical Distribution of Financial Flows to Developing Countries.*

NEW ZEALAND - GROSS DOMESTIC PRODUCT

The Economist Intelligence Unit, 111 West 57th Street, New York, New York 10019 (800) 938-4685; *The World Market Atlas.*

The Economist Intelligence Unit (Asia) Limited, 10th Floor, Luk Kwok Centre, 72 Gloucester Road, Wanchai, Hong Kong (Phone Number in U.S. (800) 938-4685); *Asian Market Atlas.*

Euromonitor Publications Limited, 87-88 Turnmill Street, London EC1M 5QU, England; *International Marketing Data and Statistics,* and *The Pacific Basin: An Economic Handbook.*

Facts on File, 460 Park Avenue South, New York, New York 10016 (800) 443-8323; *The New Book of World Rankings.*

Organisation for Economic Co-operation and Development (OECD), 2 rue Andre-Pascal, 75 Paris 16, France (Telephone Number in U.S. (202) 785-6323); *Economic Outlook, Geographical Distribution of Financial Flows to Developing Countries,* and *Revenue Statistics of OECD Member Countries.*

Statistical Office of the United Nations, Publishing Service, New York, New York 10017 (800) 253-9646; *Statistical Yearbook.*

Times Books, 201 East 50th Street, New York, New York 10022 (212) 751-2600; *The Economist Book of Vital World Statistics.*

The World Bank, 1818 H Street, NW, Washington, D.C. 20433 (202) 477-1234; *World Tables.*

NEW ZEALAND - GROSS NATIONAL PRODUCT

Euromonitor Publications Limited, 87-88 Turnmill Street, London EC1M 5QU, England; *International Marketing Data and Statistics.*

Organisation for Economic Co-operation and Development (OECD), 2 rue Andre-Pascal, 75 Paris 16, France (Telephone Number in U.S.

(202) 785-6323); *Economic Outlook,* and *Geographical Distribution of Financial Flows to Developing Countries.*

U.S. Arms Control and Disarmament Agency, 320 Twenty-first Street, NW, Washington, D.C. 20451 (202) 647-8677; *World Military Expenditures and Arms Transfers.*

The World Bank, 1818 H Street, NW, Washington, D.C. 20433 (202) 477-1234; *World Tables.*

NEW ZEALAND - HEALTH

The Economist Intelligence Unit (Asia) Limited, 10th Floor, Luk Kwok Centre, 72 Gloucester Road, Wanchai, Hong Kong (Phone Number in U.S. (800) 938-4685); *Asian Market Atlas.*

Euromonitor Publications Limited, 87-88 Turnmill Street, London EC1M 5QU, England; *The Pacific Basin: An Economic Handbook.*

Facts on File, 460 Park Avenue South, New York, New York 10016 (800) 443-8323; *The New Book of World Rankings.*

Organisation for Economic Co-operation and Development (OECD), 2 rue Andre-Pascal, 75 Paris 16, France (Telephone Number in U.S. (202) 785-6323); *OECD Health Systems: Facts and Trends.*

Statistical Office of the United Nations, Publishing Service, New York, New York 10017 (800) 253-9646; *Statistical Yearbook.*

Times Books, 201 East 50th Street, New York, New York 10022 (212) 751-2600; *The Economist Book of Vital World Statistics.*

World Health Organization, Office of Publications, Avenue Appia, CH-1211 Geneva 27, Switzerland (Telephone Number in U.S. (518) 436-9686); *World Health Statistics Annual.*

NEW ZEALAND - HEALTH EXPENDITURES

International Monetary Fund, 700 Nineteenth Street, NW, Washington, D.C. 20431 (202) 623-7000; *Government Finance Statistics Yearbook.*

NEW ZEALAND - HIDE PRODUCTION

Food and Agricultural Organization of the United Nations (FAO), Via delle Terme di Caracalla, 00100 Rome, Italy (Telephone Number in U.S. (202) 653-2400); *Production Yearbook.*

Organisation for Economic Co-operation and Development (OECD), 2 rue Andre-Pascal, 75 Paris 16, France (Telephone Number in U.S. (202) 785-6323); *The Footwear, Raw Hides and Skins, and Leather Industry in OECD Countries.*

Organisation for Economic Co-operation and Development (OECD), 2 rue Andre-Pascal, 75 Paris 16, France (Telephone Number in U.S. (202) 785-6323); *Foreign Trade by Commodities.*

NEW ZEALAND - HIGHWAYS

The Economist Intelligence Unit (Asia) Limited, 10th Floor, Luk Kwok Centre, 72 Gloucester Road, Wanchai, Hong Kong (Phone Number in U.S. (800) 938-4685); *Asian Market Atlas.*

International Road Federation, 525 School Street, SW, Washington, D.C. 20024 (202) 554-2106; *World Road Statistics.*

NEW ZEALAND - HOME FINANCE

Organisation for Economic Co-operation and Development (OECD), 2 rue Andre-Pascal, 75 Paris 16, France (Telephone Number in U.S. (202) 785-6323); *Main Economic Indicators - Historical Statistics.*

NEW ZEALAND - HORSES - See NEW ZEALAND - LIVESTOCK AND POULTRY

NEW ZEALAND - HOURS OF WORK - See NEW ZEALAND - EMPLOYMENT

NEW ZEALAND - HOUSING

Facts on File, 460 Park Avenue South, New York, New York 10016 (800) 443-8323; *The New Book of World Rankings.*

NEW ZEALAND - HOUSING CONSTRUCTION - See NEW ZEALAND - CONSTRUCTION INDUSTRY

NEW ZEALAND - HOUSING EXPENDITURES

International Monetary Fund, 700 Nineteenth Street, NW, Washington, D.C. 20431 (202) 623-7000; *Government Finance Statistics Yearbook.*

NEW ZEALAND - ILLITERATE POPULATION

The Economist Intelligence Unit, 111 West 57th Street, New York, New York 10019 (800) 938-4685; *The World Market Atlas.*

NEW ZEALAND - IMPORTS

American Automobile Manufacturers Association, 1401 H Street, NW, Suite 900, Washington, D.C. 20005 (202) 326-5500; *World Motor Vehicle Data.*

The Economist Intelligence Unit, 111 West 57th Street, New York, New York 10019 (800) 938-4685; *The World Market Atlas.*

The Economist Intelligence Unit (Asia) Limited, 10th Floor, Luk Kwok Centre, 72 Gloucester Road, Wanchai, Hong Kong (Phone Number in U.S. (800) 938-4685); *Asian Market Atlas.*

Euromonitor Publications Limited, 87-88 Turnmill Street, London EC1M 5QU, England; *International Marketing Data and Statistics,* and *The Pacific Basin: An Economic Handbook.*

Food and Agricultural Organization of the United Nations (FAO) Via delle Terme di Caracalla, 00100 Rome, Italy (Telephone Number in U.S. (202) 653-2400); *The State of Food and Agriculture.*

International Monetary Fund, 700 Nineteenth Street, NW, Washington, D.C. 20431 (202) 623-7000; *Direction of Trade Statistics, Government Finance Statistics Yearbook,* and *International Financial Statistics.*

Organisation for Economic Co-operation and Development (OECD), 2 rue Andre-Pascal, 75 Paris 16, France (Telephone Number in U.S. (202) 785-6323); *Economic Outlook, The Footwear, Raw Hides and Skins, and Leather Industry in OECD Countries, Industrial Structure Statistics, The Iron and Steel Industry, Milk, Milk Products, and Egg Balances in OECD Member Countries, The Pulp and Paper Industry, OECD Economic Surveys: New Zealand,* and *Review of Fisheries in OECD Member Countries.*

Statistical Office of the United Nations, Publishing Service, New York, New York 10017 (800) 253-9646; *Foreign Trade Statistics of Asia and the Pacific.*

Times Books, 201 East 50th Street, New York, New York 10022 (212) 751-2600; *The Economist Book of Vital World Statistics*.

The World Bank, 1818 H Street, NW, Washington, D.C. 20433 (202) 477-1234; *World Tables*.

NEW ZEALAND - INCOME TAXES - See NEW ZEALAND - TAXATION

NEW ZEALAND - INDUSTRY

Euromonitor Publications Limited, 87-88 Turnmill Street, London EC1M 5QU, England; *International Marketing Data and Statistics*.

Facts on File, 460 Park Avenue South, New York, New York 10016 (800) 443-8323; *The New Book of World Rankings*.

Gale Research Incorporated, 835 Penobscot Building, Detroit, Michigan 48226 (800) 877-4253; *International Historical Statistics The Americas and Australasia*.

International Labour Office, I.L.O. Publications, CH-1211, Geneva 22, Switzerland; *Yearbook of Labour Statistics*.

Organisation for Economic Co-operation and Development (OECD), 2 rue Andre-Pascal, 75 Paris 16, France (Telephone Number in U.S. (202) 785-6323); *Economic Outlook, Industrial Structure Statistics*, and *OECD Environmental Data*.

Statistical Office of the United Nations, Publishing Service, New York, New York 10017 (800) 253-9646; *Statistical Yearbook*, and *Statistical Yearbook for Asia and the Pacific*.

Times Books, 201 East 50th Street, New York, New York 10022 (212) 751-2600; *The Economist Book of Vital World Statistics*.

The World Bank, 1818 H Street, NW, Washington, D.C. 20433 (202) 477-1234; *World Tables*.

World Intellectual Property Organization, 34 Chemin des Colombettes, CH-1211 Geneva 20, Switzerland; *Industrial Property Statistics*.

NEW ZEALAND - INFANT AND MATERNAL MORTALITY

The Economist Intelligence Unit (Asia) Limited, 10th Floor, Luk Kwok Centre, 72 Gloucester Road, Wanchai, Hong Kong (Phone Number in U.S. (800) 938-4685); *Asian Market Atlas*.

Statistical Office of the United Nations, Publishing Service, New York, New York 10017 (800) 253-9646; *Demographic Yearbook*.

Times Books, 201 East 50th Street, New York, New York 10022 (212) 751-2600; *The Economist Book of Vital World Statistics*.

The World Bank, 1818 H Street, NW, Washington, D.C. 20433 (202) 477-1234; *World Tables*.

World Health Organization, Office of Publications, Avenue Appia, CH-1211 Geneva 27, Switzerland (Telephone Number in U.S. (518) 436-9686); *World Health Statistics Annual*.

NEW ZEALAND - INTEREST RATES

Euromonitor Publications Limited, 87-88 Turnmill Street, London EC1M 5QU, England; *The Pacific Basin: An Economic Handbook*.

Organisation for Economic Co-operation and Development (OECD), 2 rue Andre-Pascal, 75 Paris 16, France (Telephone Number in U.S. (202) 785-6323); *Economic Outlook, Financial Market Trends*, and

OECD Financial Statistics.

NEW ZEALAND - INTERNAL TRADE

Organisation for Economic Co-operation and Development (OECD), 2 rue Andre-Pascal, 75 Paris 16, France (Telephone Number in U.S. (202) 785-6323); *Main Economic Indicators - Historical Statistics*.

Statistical Office of the United Nations, Publishing Service, New York, New York 10017 (800) 253-9646; *Statistical Yearbook for Asia and the Pacific*.

NEW ZEALAND - INTERNATIONAL FINANCE

Organisation for Economic Co-operation and Development (OECD), 2 rue Andre-Pascal, 75 Paris 16, France (Telephone Number in U.S. (202) 785-6323); *Economic Outlook*, and *Financial Market Trends*.

NEW ZEALAND - INTERNATIONAL LIQUIDITY

International Monetary Fund, 700 Nineteenth Street, NW, Washington, D.C. 20431 (202) 623-7000; *International Financial Statistics*.

Organisation for Economic Co-operation and Development (OECD), 2 rue Andre-Pascal, 75 Paris 16, France (Telephone Number in U.S. (202) 785-6323); *Economic Outlook*, and *Financial Market Trends*.

NEW ZEALAND - INTERNATIONAL RESERVES EXCLUDING GOLD

Statistical Office of the United Nations, Publishing Service, New York, New York 10017 (800) 253-9646; *Statistical Yearbook*.

The World Bank, 1818 H Street, NW, Washington, D.C. 20433 (202) 477-1234; *World Tables*.

NEW ZEALAND - INTERNATIONAL STATISTICS

Organisation for Economic Co-operation and Development (OECD), 2 rue Andre-Pascal, 75 Paris 16, France (Telephone Number in U.S. (202) 785-6323); *Financial Market Trends*, and *Tourism Policy and International Tourism in OECD Member Countries*.

NEW ZEALAND - INVESTMENTS

International Monetary Fund, 700 Nineteenth Street, NW, Washington, D.C. 20431 (202) 623-7000; *International Financial Statistics*.

Organisation for Economic Co-operation and Development (OECD), 2 rue Andre-Pascal, 75 Paris 16, France (Telephone Number in U.S. (202) 785-6323); *Economic Outlook, Financial Market Trends, Industrial Structure Statistics, The Iron and Steel Industry*, and *Textile Industry in OECD Countries*.

NEW ZEALAND - IRON ORE PRODUCTION AND CONSUMPTION - See NEW ZEALAND - MINING AND MINERAL PRODUCTS

NEW ZEALAND - IRRIGATION

Euromonitor Publications Limited, 87-88 Turnmill Street, London EC1M 5QU, England; *International Marketing Data and Statistics*.

NEW ZEALAND - LABOR FORCE

The Economist Intelligence Unit (Asia) Limited, 10th Floor, Luk Kwok Centre, 72 Gloucester Road, Wanchai, Hong Kong (Phone Number in U.S. (800) 938-4685); *Asian Market Atlas*.

Euromonitor Publications Limited, 87-88 Turnmill Street, London EC1M 5QU, England; *International Marketing Data and Statistics,* and *The Pacific Basin: An Economic Handbook.*

Facts on File, 460 Park Avenue South, New York, New York 10016 (800) 443-8323; *The New Book of World Rankings.*

Food and Agricultural Organization of the United Nations (FAO) Via delle Terme di Caracalla, 00100 Rome, Italy (Telephone Number in U.S. (202) 653-2400; *The State of Food and Agriculture.*

Gale Research Incorporated, 835 Penobscot Building, Detroit, Michigan 48226 (800) 877-4253; *International Historical Statistics The Americas and Australasia.*

Organisation for Economic Co-operation and Development (OECD), 2 rue Andre-Pascal, 75 Paris 16, France (Telephone Number in U.S. (202) 785-6323); *Economic Outlook, Main Economic Indicators - Historical Statistics, Maritime Transport, OECD Economic Surveys: New Zealand, OECD Employment Outlook,* and *Textile Industry in OECD Countries.*

Times Books, 201 East 50th Street, New York, New York 10022 (212) 751-2600; *The Economist Book of Vital World Statistics.*

The World Bank, 1818 H Street, NW, Washington, D.C. 20433 (202) 477-1234; *World Tables.*

NEW ZEALAND - LABOR PRODUCTIVITY

International Labour Office, I.L.O. Publications, CH-1211, Geneva 22, Switzerland; *Yearbook of Labour Statistics.*

Organisation for Economic Co-operation and Development (OECD), 2 rue Andre-Pascal, 75 Paris 16, France (Telephone Number in U.S. (202) 785-6323); *Economic Outlook,* and *OECD Employment Outlook.*

NEW ZEALAND - LAMB AND MUTTON EXPORTS

International Monetary Fund, 700 Nineteenth Street, NW, Washington, D.C. 20431 (202) 623-7000; *International Financial Statistics.*

NEW ZEALAND - LAND USE

Euromonitor Publications Limited, 87-88 Turnmill Street, London EC1M 5QU, England; *International Marketing Data and Statistics.*

Food and Agricultural Organization of the United Nations (FAO), Via delle Terme di Caracalla, 00100 Rome, Italy (Telephone Number in U.S. (202) 653-2400; *Production Yearbook.*

NEW ZEALAND - LEAD AND LEAD ORE PRODUCTION AND CONSUMPTION - See NEW ZEALAND - MINING AND MINERAL PRODUCTS

NEW ZEALAND - LEATHER AND FOOTWEAR EXPORTS AND IMPORTS

Organisation for Economic Co-operation and Development (OECD), 2 rue Andre-Pascal, 75 Paris 16, France (Telephone Number in U.S. (202) 785-6323); *The Footwear, Raw Hides and Skins,* and *Leather Industry in OECD Countries.*

NEW ZEALAND - LIBRARIES

Facts on File, 460 Park Avenue South, New York, New York 10016 (800) 443-8323; *The New Book of World Rankings.*

United Nations Educational, Scientific and Cultural Organization (UNESCO), 7 Place de Fontenoy, F-75700 Paris, France (Telephone Number in U.S. (212) 963-5981); *Statistical Yearbook.*

NEW ZEALAND - LIFE EXPECTANCY

The Economist Intelligence Unit (Asia) Limited, 10th Floor, Luk Kwok Centre, 72 Gloucester Road, Wanchai, Hong Kong (Phone Number in U.S. (800) 938-4685); *Asian Market Atlas.*

NEW ZEALAND - LIGNITE PRODUCTION - See NEW ZEALAND - MINING AND MINERAL PRODUCTS

NEW ZEALAND - LIVESTOCK AND POULTRY

Commodity Research Bureau, Incorporated, 75 Wall Street, New York, New York 10005 (212) 504-7754; *Commodity Year Book.*

Euromonitor Publications Limited, 87-88 Turnmill Street, London EC1M 5QU, England; *International Marketing Data and Statistics.*

Facts on File, 460 Park Avenue South, New York, New York 10016 (800) 443-8323; *The New Book of World Rankings.*

Food and Agricultural Organization of the United Nations (FAO), Via delle Terme di Caracalla, 00100 Rome, Italy (Telephone Number in U.S. (202) 653-2400; *Production Yearbook,* and *The State of Food and Agriculture.*

International Monetary Fund, 700 Nineteenth Street, NW, Washington, D.C. 20431 (202) 623-7000; *International Financial Statistics.*

Organisation for Economic Co-operation and Development (OECD), 2 rue Andre-Pascal, 75 Paris 16, France (Telephone Number in U.S. (202) 785-6323); *Economic Accounts for Agriculture,* and *Meat Balances in OECD Member Countries.*

Statistical Office of the United Nations, Publishing Service, New York, New York 10017 (800) 253-9646; *Statistical Yearbook.*

NEW ZEALAND - LIVING LEVELS

Organisation for Economic Co-operation and Development (OECD), 2 rue Andre-Pascal, 75 Paris 16, France (Telephone Number in U.S. (202) 785-6323); *Economic Outlook.*

Times Books, 201 East 50th Street, New York, New York 10022 (212) 751-2600; *The Economist Book of Vital World Statistics.*

NEW ZEALAND - MAIL - NUMBER OF PIECES SENT OR RECEIVED

Statistical Office of the United Nations, Publishing Service, New York, New York 10017 (800) 253-9646; *Statistical Yearbook.*

NEW ZEALAND - MANGANESE PRODUCTION AND CONSUMPTION - See NEW ZEALAND - MINING AND MINERAL PRODUCTS

NEW ZEALAND - MANPOWER

Statistical Office of the United Nations, Publishing Service, New York, New York 10017 (800) 253-9646; *Statistical Yearbook for Asia and the Pacific.*

NEW ZEALAND - MANUFACTURING

American Automobile Manufacturers Association, 1401 H Eye Street, NW, Suite 900, Washington, D.C. 20005 (202) 326-5500; *World*

Motor Vehicle Data.

Facts on File, 460 Park Avenue South, New York, New York 10016 (800) 443-8323; *The New Book of World Rankings.*

Organisation for Economic Co-operation and Development (OECD), 2 rue Andre-Pascal, 75 Paris 16, France (Telephone Number in U.S. (202) 785-6323); *Foreign Trade by Commodities Industrial Structure Statistics*, and *OECD Economic Surveys: New Zealand.*

Statistical Office of the United Nations, Publishing Service, New York, New York 10017 (800) 253-9646; *Statistical Yearbook.*

Times Books, 201 East 50th Street, New York, New York 10022 (212) 751-2600; *The Economist Book of Vital World Statistics.*

The World Bank, 1818 H Street, NW, Washington, D.C. 20433 (202) 477-1234; *World Tables.*

NEW ZEALAND - MARRIAGE RATES

Facts on File, 460 Park Avenue South, New York, New York 10016 (800) 443-8323; *The New Book of World Rankings.*

Statistical Office of the United Nations, Publishing Service, New York, New York 10017 (800) 253-9646; *Demographic Yearbook.*

NEW ZEALAND - MEAT PRODUCTION - See NEW ZEALAND - LIVESTOCK AND POULTRY

NEW ZEALAND - MERCHANT SHIPPING

Lloyd's Register of Shipping, 17 Battery Place, New York, New York 10004; *Register of Ships.*

Organisation for Economic Co-operation and Development (OECD), 2 rue Andre-Pascal, 75 Paris 16, France (Telephone Number in U.S. (202) 785-6323); *Maritime Transport.*

Statistical Office of the United Nations, Publishing Service, New York, New York 10017 (800) 253-9646; *Statistical Yearbook.*

U.S. Department of Transportation, Maritime Administration, 400 Seventh Street, SW, Washington, D.C. 20590 (202) 366-5807; *A Statistical Analysis of the World's Merchant Fleets.*

NEW ZEALAND - MILITARY

The Economist Intelligence Unit (Asia) Limited, 10th Floor, Luk Kwok Centre, 72 Gloucester Road, Wanchai, Hong Kong (Phone Number in U.S. (800) 938-4685); *Asian Market Atlas.*

The International Institute for Strategic Studies, 23 Tavistock Street, London WC2E 7NQ, England; *The Military Balance.*

U.S. Arms Control and Disarmament Agency, 320 Twenty-first Street, NW, Washington, D.C. 20451 (202) 647-8677; *World Military Expenditures and Arms Transfers.*

NEW ZEALAND - MILK PRODUCTION - See NEW ZEALAND - DAIRY PRODUCTS

NEW ZEALAND - MINING AND MINERAL PRODUCTS

Facts on File, 460 Park Avenue South, New York, New York 10016 (800) 443-8323; *The New Book of World Rankings.*

Organisation for Economic Co-operation and Development (OECD), 2 rue Andre-Pascal, 75 Paris 16, France (Telephone Number in U.S.

(202) 785-6323); *Coal Information, Energy Statistics of OECD Countries, Foreign Trade by Commodities, Industrial Structure Statistics, The Iron and Steel Industry, The Non-Ferrous Metals Industry*, and *OECD Economic Surveys: New Zealand.*

Penn Well Publishing Company, 1421 South Sheridan Road, Post Office Box 1260, Tulsa, Oklahoma 74101 (800) 752-9764; *International Energy Statistics Sourcebook.*

Statistical Office of the United Nations, Publishing Service, New York, New York 10017 (800) 253-9646; *Statistical Yearbook.*

NEW ZEALAND - MONEY AND CREDIT

Organisation for Economic Co-operation and Development (OECD), 2 rue Andre-Pascal, 75 Paris 16, France (Telephone Number in U.S. (202) 785-6323); *OECD Economic Surveys: New Zealand.*

NEW ZEALAND - MONEY EXCHANGE RATE

Euromonitor Publications Limited, 87-88 Turnmill Street, London EC1M 5QU, England; *International Marketing Data and Statistics.*

International Monetary Fund, 700 Nineteenth Street, NW, Washington, D.C. 20431 (202) 623-7000; *International Financial Statistics.*

Organisation for Economic Co-operation and Development (OECD), 2 rue Andre-Pascal, 75 Paris 16, France (Telephone Number in U.S. (202) 785-6323); *Economic Outlook, Financial Market Trends*, and *Tourism Policy and International Tourism in OECD Member Countries.*

Statistical Office of the United Nations, Publishing Service, New York, New York 10017 (800) 253-9646; *Statistical Yearbook.*

NEW ZEALAND - MONEY RATES - MARKET

Organisation for Economic Co-operation and Development (OECD), 2 rue Andre-Pascal, 75 Paris 16, France (Telephone Number in U.S. (202) 785-6323); *Economic Outlook*, and *Financial Market Trends.*

NEW ZEALAND - MONEY RESERVES

Euromonitor Publications Limited, 87-88 Turnmill Street, London EC1M 5QU, England; *International Marketing Data and Statistics.*

Organisation for Economic Co-operation and Development (OECD), 2 rue Andre-Pascal, 75 Paris 16, France (Telephone Number in U.S. (202) 785-6323); *Economic Outlook*, and *Financial Market Trends.*

NEW ZEALAND - MONEY SUPPLY

Euromonitor Publications Limited, 87-88 Turnmill Street, London EC1M 5QU, England; *International Marketing Data and Statistics.*

International Monetary Fund, 700 Nineteenth Street, NW, Washington, D.C. 20431 (202) 623-7000; *International Financial Statistics.*

Organisation for Economic Co-operation and Development (OECD), 2 rue Andre-Pascal, 75 Paris 16, France (Telephone Number in U.S. (202) 785-6323); *Economic Outlook.*

Statistical Office of the United Nations, Publishing Service, New York, New York 10017 (800) 253-9646; *Statistical Yearbook.*

The World Bank, 1818 H Street, NW, Washington, D.C. 20433 (202) 477-1234; *World Tables.*

NEW ZEALAND - MOTION PICTURES

Statistical Office of the United Nations, Publishing Service, New York, New York 10017 (800) 253-9646; *Statistical Yearbook*.

United Nations Educational, Scientific and Cultural Organization (UNESCO), 7 Place de Fontenoy, F-75700 Paris, France (Telephone Number in U.S. (212) 963-5981); *Statistical Yearbook*.

NEW ZEALAND - MOTOR VEHICLE PRODUCTION

American Automobile Manufacturers Association, 1401 H Street, NW, Suite 900, Washington, D.C. 20005 (202) 326-5500; *World Motor Vehicle Data*.

Organisation for Economic Co-operation and Development (OECD), 2 rue Andre-Pascal, 75 Paris 16, France (Telephone Number in U.S. (202) 785-6323); *Foreign Trade by Commodities*.

NEW ZEALAND - MOTOR VEHICLE PRODUCTION AND ASSEMBLY

Statistical Office of the United Nations, Publishing Service, New York, New York 10017 (800) 253-9646; *Statistical Yearbook*.

NEW ZEALAND - MOTOR VEHICLE TAXES - See NEW ZEALAND - TAXATION

NEW ZEALAND - MOTOR VEHICLES IN USE

American Automobile Manufacturers Association, 1401 H Street, NW, Suite 900, Washington, D.C. 20005 (202) 326-5500; *World Motor Vehicle Data*.

International Road Federation, 525 School Street, SW, Washington, D.C. 20024 (202) 554-2106; *World Road Statistics*.

Statistical Office of the United Nations, Publishing Service, New York, New York 10017 (800) 253-9646; *Statistical Yearbook*.

Times Books, 201 East 50th Street, New York, New York 10022 (212) 751-2600; *The Economist Book of Vital World Statistics*.

NEW ZEALAND - MUSEUMS

Facts on File, 460 Park Avenue South, New York, New York 10016 (800) 443-8323; *The New Book of World Rankings*.

United Nations Educational, Scientific and Cultural Organization (UNESCO), 7 Place de Fontenoy, F-75700 Paris, France (Telephone Number in U.S. (212) 963-5981); *Statistical Yearbook*.

NEW ZEALAND - MUTTON AND LAMB EXPORTS

International Monetary Fund, 700 Nineteenth Street, NW, Washington, D.C. 20431 (202) 623-7000; *International Financial Statistics*.

NEW ZEALAND - NATALITY - See NEW ZEALAND - BIRTH RATES

NEW ZEALAND - NATIONAL ACCOUNTS

Gale Research Incorporated, 835 Penobscot Building, Detroit, Michigan 48226 (800) 877-4253; *International Historical Statistics The Americas and Australasia*.

Organisation for Economic Co-operation and Development (OECD), 2 rue Andre-Pascal, 75 Paris 16, France (Telephone Number in U.S. (202) 785-6323); *Economic Outlook*.

Statistical Office of the United Nations, Publishing Service, New York, New York 10017 (800) 253-9646; *National Accounts Statistics*, *Statistical Yearbook*.

NEW ZEALAND - NATIONAL INCOME

Facts on File, 460 Park Avenue South, New York, New York 10016 (800) 443-8323; *The New Book of World Rankings*.

Organisation for Economic Co-operation and Development (OECD), 2 rue Andre-Pascal, 75 Paris 16, France (Telephone Number in U.S. (202) 785-6323); *Economic Outlook*.

Statistical Office of the United Nations, Publishing Service, New York, New York 10017 (800) 253-9646; *Statistical Yearbook*.

NEW ZEALAND - NATIONAL PRODUCT

Facts on File, 460 Park Avenue South, New York, New York 10016 (800) 443-8323; *The New Book of World Rankings*.

Organisation for Economic Co-operation and Development (OECD), 2 rue Andre-Pascal, 75 Paris 16, France (Telephone Number in U.S. (202) 785-6323); *Economic Outlook*.

NEW ZEALAND - NATURAL GAS PRODUCTION - See NEW ZEALAND - MINING AND MINERAL PRODUCTS

NEW ZEALAND - NEWSPAPER PRODUCTION

The Economist Intelligence Unit (Asia) Limited, 10th Floor, Luk Kwok Centre, 72 Gloucester Road, Wanchai, Hong Kong (Phone Number in U.S. (800) 938-4685); *Asian Market Atlas*.

Statistical Office of the United Nations, Publishing Service, New York, New York 10017 (800) 253-9646; *Statistical Yearbook*.

United Nations Educational, Scientific and Cultural Organization (UNESCO), 7 Place de Fontenoy, F-75700 Paris, France (Telephone Number in U.S. (212) 963-5981); *Statistical Yearbook*.

NEW ZEALAND - NEWSPRINT PRODUCTION AND CONSUMPTION - See NEW ZEALAND - FORESTRY AND FOREST PRODUCTS

NEW ZEALAND - NICKEL PRODUCTION AND CONSUMPTION - See NEW ZEALAND - MINING AND MINERAL PRODUCTS

NEW ZEALAND - OIL PRODUCING CROPS - See NEW ZEALAND - CROPS

NEW ZEALAND - PAPER - See NEW ZEALAND - FORESTRY AND FOREST PRODUCTS

NEW ZEALAND - PATENTS

Statistical Office of the United Nations, Publishing Service, New York, New York 10017 (800) 253-9646; *Statistical Yearbook*.

World Intellectual Property Organization, 34 Chemin des Colombettes, CH-1211 Geneva 20, Switzerland; *Industrial Property Statistics*.

NEW ZEALAND - PEANUT PRODUCTION - See NEW ZEALAND - CROPS

NEW ZEALAND - PERIODICALS

United Nations Educational, Scientific and Cultural Organization (UNESCO), 7 Place de Fontenoy, F-75700 Paris, France (Telephone

Number in U.S. (212) 963-5981); *Statistical Yearbook.*

NEW ZEALAND - PESTICIDE USE

Food and Agricultural Organization of the United Nations (FAO) Via delle Terme di Caracalla, 00100 Rome, Italy (Telephone Number in U.S. (202) 653-2400); *The State of Food and Agriculture.*

NEW ZEALAND - PETROLEUM INDUSTRY

Facts on File, 460 Park Avenue South, New York, New York 10016 (800) 443-8323; *The New Book of World Rankings.*

Food and Agricultural Organization of the United Nations (FAO) Via delle Terme di Caracalla, 00100 Rome, Italy (Telephone Number in U.S. (202) 653-2400); *The State of Food and Agriculture.*

Organisation for Economic Co-operation and Development (OECD), 2 rue Andre-Pascal, 75 Paris 16, France (Telephone Number in U.S. (202) 785-6323); *Energy Statistics of OECD Countries, Foreign Trade by Commodities,* and *Oil and Gas Information.*

Penn Well Publishing Company, 1421 South Sheridan Road, Post Office Box 1260, Tulsa, Oklahoma 74101 (800) 752-9764; *International Energy Statistics Sourcebook.*

Statistical Office of the United Nations, Publishing Service, New York, New York 10017 (800) 253-9646; *Statistical Yearbook.*

NEW ZEALAND - PIG-IRON AND FERRO-ALLOY PRODUCTION

Organisation for Economic Co-operation and Development (OECD), 2 rue Andre-Pascal, 75 Paris 16, France (Telephone Number in U.S. (202) 785-6323); *The Iron and Steel Industry.*

NEW ZEALAND - PIGS - See NEW ZEALAND - LIVESTOCK AND POULTRY

NEW ZEALAND - PLASTIC AND RESIN PRODUCTION

Organisation for Economic Co-operation and Development (OECD), 2 rue Andre-Pascal, 75 Paris 16, France (Telephone Number in U.S. (202) 785-6323); *Foreign Trade by Commodities.*

NEW ZEALAND - POPULATION

The Economist Intelligence Unit, 111 West 57th Street, New York, New York 10019 (800) 938-4685; *The World Market Atlas.*

The Economist Intelligence Unit (Asia) Limited, 10th Floor, Luk Kwok Centre, 72 Gloucester Road, Wanchai, Hong Kong (Phone Number in U.S. (800) 938-4685; *Asian Market Atlas.*

Euromonitor Publications Limited, 87-88 Turnmill Street, London EC1M 5QU, England; *International Marketing Data and Statistics,* and *The Pacific Basin: An Economic Handbook.*

Facts on File, 460 Park Avenue South, New York, New York 10016 (800) 443-8323; *The New Book of World Rankings.*

Food and Agricultural Organization of the United Nations (FAO), Via delle Terme di Caracalla, 00100 Rome, Italy (Telephone Number in U.S. (202) 653-2400); *Production Yearbook.*

Gale Research Incorporated, 835 Penobscot Building, Detroit, Michigan 48226 (800) 877-4253; *International Historical Statistics The Americas and Australasia.*

International Labour Office, I.L.O. Publications, CH-1211, Geneva 22, Switzerland; *Yearbook of Labour Statistics.*

Statistical Office of the United Nations, Publishing Service, New York, New York 10017 (800) 253-9646; *Demographic Yearbook, Statistical Yearbook,* and *Statistical Yearbook for Asia and the Pacific.*

Times Books, 201 East 50th Street, New York, New York 10022 (212) 751-2600; *The Economist Book of Vital World Statistics.*

United Nations Educational, Scientific and Cultural Organization (UNESCO), 7 Place de Fontenoy, F-75700 Paris, France (Telephone Number in U.S. (212) 963-5981); *Statistical Yearbook.*

U.S. Arms Control and Disarmament Agency, 320 Twenty-first Street, NW, Washington, D.C. 20451 (202) 647-8677; *World Military Expenditures and Arms Transfers.*

World Health Organization, Office of Publications, Avenue Appia, CH-1211 Geneva 27, Switzerland (Telephone Number in U.S. (518) 436-9686); *World Health Statistics Annual.*

NEW ZEALAND - POST OFFICES

Facts on File, 460 Park Avenue South, New York, New York 10016 (800) 443-8323; *The New Book of World Rankings.*

NEW ZEALAND - POTATO PRODUCTION - See NEW ZEALAND - CROPS

NEW ZEALAND - POWER PRODUCTION INDUSTRY

Statistical Office of the United Nations, Publishing Service, New York, New York 10017 (800) 253-9646; *Statistical Yearbook.*

NEW ZEALAND - PRICES

Facts on File, 460 Park Avenue South, New York, New York 10016 (800) 443-8323; *The New Book of World Rankings.*

Food and Agricultural Organization of the United Nations (FAO), Via delle Terme di Caracalla, 00100 Rome, Italy (Telephone Number in U.S. (202) 653-2400); *Production Yearbook,* and *The State of Food and Agriculture.*

Gale Research Incorporated, 835 Penobscot Building, Detroit, Michigan 48226 (800) 877-4253; *International Historical Statistics The Americas and Australasia.*

International Labour Office, I.L.O. Publications, CH-1211, Geneva 22, Switzerland; *Yearbook of Labour Statistics.*

International Monetary Fund, 700 Nineteenth Street, NW, Washington, D.C. 20431 (202) 623-7000; *International Financial Statistics.*

Organisation for Economic Co-operation and Development (OECD), 2 rue Andre-Pascal, 75 Paris 16, France (Telephone Number in U.S. (202) 785-6323); *Economic Accounts for Agriculture, Economic Outlook, The Footwear, Raw Hides and Skins, and Leather Industry in OECD Countries, The Iron and Steel Industry,* and *The Pulp and Paper Industry.*

NEW ZEALAND - PRINTING AND WRITING PAPER PRODUCTION AND CONSUMPTION - See NEW ZEALAND - FORESTRY AND FOREST PRODUCTS

NEW ZEALAND - PRODUCTION

American Automobile Manufacturers Association, 1401 H Street, NW, Suite 900, Washington, D.C. 20005 (202) 326-5500; *World Motor Vehicle Data.*

Facts on File, 460 Park Avenue South, New York, New York 10016 (800) 443-8323; *The New Book of World Rankings.*

Organisation for Economic Co-operation and Development (OECD), 2 rue Andre-Pascal, 75 Paris 16, France (Telephone Number in U.S. (202) 785-6323); *Economic Outlook, The Footwear, Raw Hides and Skins, and Leather Industry in OECD Countries, Industrial Structure Statistics, The Iron and Steel Industry, Meat Balances in OECD Member Countries, Milk, Milk Products, and Egg Balances in OECD Member Countries, The Non-Ferrous Metals Industry, The Pulp and Paper Industry,* and *Textile Industry in OECD Countries.*

NEW ZEALAND - PRODUCTIVITY

Euromonitor Publications Limited, 87-88 Turnmill Street, London EC1M 5QU, England; *International Marketing Data and Statistics.*

Organisation for Economic Co-operation and Development (OECD), 2 rue Andre-Pascal, 75 Paris 16, France (Telephone Number in U.S. (202) 785-6323); *Economic Outlook.*

NEW ZEALAND - PROPERTY TAXES - See NEW ZEALAND - TAXATION

NEW ZEALAND - PUBLIC CONSUMPTION FUND

Organisation for Economic Co-operation and Development (OECD), 2 rue Andre-Pascal, 75 Paris 16, France (Telephone Number in U.S. (202) 785-6323); *Revenue Statistics of OECD Member Countries.*

NEW ZEALAND - PUBLIC EXPENDITURES

Organisation for Economic Co-operation and Development (OECD), 2 rue Andre-Pascal, 75 Paris 16, France (Telephone Number in U.S. (202) 785-6323); *Revenue Statistics of OECD Member Countries.*

NEW ZEALAND - PUBLIC FINANCE

Facts on File, 460 Park Avenue South, New York, New York 10016 (800) 443-8323; *The New Book of World Rankings.*

Organisation for Economic Co-operation and Development (OECD), 2 rue Andre-Pascal, 75 Paris 16, France (Telephone Number in U.S. (202) 785-6323); *Revenue Statistics of OECD Member Countries.*

NEW ZEALAND - PUBLIC REVENUES

Organisation for Economic Co-operation and Development (OECD), 2 rue Andre-Pascal, 75 Paris 16, France (Telephone Number in U.S. (202) 785-6323); *Revenue Statistics of OECD Member Countries.*

NEW ZEALAND - RADIO BROADCASTING - See NEW ZEALAND - BROADCASTING

NEW ZEALAND - RADIO RECEIVER PRODUCTION

Statistical Office of the United Nations, Publishing Service, New York, New York 10017 (800) 253-9646; *Statistical Yearbook.*

NEW ZEALAND - RAILWAYS

Jane's Information Group, Sentinel House, 163 Brighton Road, Coulsdon, Surrey CR5 2NH, England (Telephone Number in U.S.

(703) 683-3700); *Jane's World Railways.*

Statistical Office of the United Nations, Publishing Service, New York, New York 10017 (800) 253-9646; *Statistical Yearbook.*

NEW ZEALAND - RELIGION

Facts on File, 460 Park Avenue South, New York, New York 10016 (800) 443-8323; *The New Book of World Rankings.*

NEW ZEALAND - RENT PRICES

International Labour Office, I.L.O. Publications, CH-1211, Geneva 22, Switzerland; *Yearbook of Labour Statistics.*

NEW ZEALAND - RETAIL TRADE

Statistical Office of the United Nations, Publishing Service, New York, New York 10017 (800) 253-9646; *Statistical Yearbook.*

NEW ZEALAND - RICE PRODUCTION - See NEW ZEALAND - CROPS

NEW ZEALAND - ROOT AND TUBER PRODUCTION - See NEW ZEALAND - CROPS

NEW ZEALAND - ROUNDWOOD PRODUCTION - See NEW ZEALAND - FORESTRY AND FOREST PRODUCTS

NEW ZEALAND - RUBBER PRODUCTION AND CONSUMPTION

Facts on File, 460 Park Avenue South, New York, New York 10016 (800) 443-8323; *The New Book of World Rankings.*

Organisation for Economic Co-operation and Development (OECD), 2 rue Andre-Pascal, 75 Paris 16, France (Telephone Number in U.S. (202) 785-6323); *Foreign Trade by Commodities.*

NEW ZEALAND - SALT PRODUCTION - See NEW ZEALAND - MINING AND MINERAL PRODUCTS

NEW ZEALAND - SAWNWOOD PRODUCTION - See NEW ZEALAND - FORESTRY AND FOREST PRODUCTS

NEW ZEALAND - SCIENCE AND TECHNOLOGY - EXPENDITURE FOR RESEARCH

Statistical Office of the United Nations, Publishing Service, New York, New York 10017 (800) 253-9646; *Statistical Yearbook.*

NEW ZEALAND - SCIENTISTS AND TECHNICIANS

Statistical Office of the United Nations, Publishing Service, New York, New York 10017 (800) 253-9646; *Statistical Yearbook.*

NEW ZEALAND - SENIOR CITIZENS

Facts on File, 460 Park Avenue South, New York, New York 10016 (800) 443-8323; *The New Book of World Rankings.*

NEW ZEALAND - SERVICE INDUSTRY EMPLOYMENT - MALE AND FEMALE - See NEW ZEALAND - EMPLOYMENT

NEW ZEALAND - SHEEP - See NEW ZEALAND - LIVESTOCK AND POULTRY

NEW ZEALAND - SILVER PRODUCTION AND CONSUMPTION - See NEW ZEALAND - MINING AND MINERAL PRODUCTS

NEW ZEALAND - SOCIAL DATA

Facts on File, 460 Park Avenue South, New York, New York 10016 (800) 443-8323; *The New Book of World Rankings.*

NEW ZEALAND - SOCIAL SECURITY

International Monetary Fund, 700 Nineteenth Street, NW, Washington, D.C. 20431 (202) 623-7000; *Government Finance Statistics Yearbook.*

Organisation for Economic Co-operation and Development (OECD), 2 rue Andre-Pascal, 75 Paris 16, France (Telephone Number in U.S. (202) 785-6323); *Revenue Statistics of OECD Member Countries.*

NEW ZEALAND - SOCIOECONOMIC DATA

Organisation for Economic Co-operation and Development (OECD), 2 rue Andre-Pascal, 75 Paris 16, France (Telephone Number in U.S. (202) 785-6323); *Economic Outlook.*

NEW ZEALAND - STAMP TAXES AND DUTIES - See NEW ZEALAND - TAXATION

NEW ZEALAND - STATE BUDGET REVENUE AND EXPENDITURES

Euromonitor Publications Limited, 87-88 Turnmill Street, London EC1M 5QU, England; *International Marketing Data and Statistics.*

NEW ZEALAND - STEEL - See NEW ZEALAND - MINING AND MINERAL PRODUCTS

NEW ZEALAND - STOCKS - COMMODITY - MARKET PRICE - INDEXES

Food and Agricultural Organization of the United Nations (FAO) Via delle Terme di Caracalla, 00100 Rome, Italy (Telephone Number in U.S. (202) 653-2400); *The State of Food and Agriculture.*

Statistical Office of the United Nations, Publishing Service, New York, New York 10017 (800) 253-9646; *Statistical Yearbook.*

NEW ZEALAND - SUGAR - See NEW ZEALAND - CROPS

NEW ZEALAND - TAXATION

International Monetary Fund, 700 Nineteenth Street, NW, Washington, D.C. 20431 (202) 623-7000; *Government Finance Statistics Yearbook.*

International Road Federation, 525 School Street, SW, Washington, D.C. 20024 (202) 554-2106; *World Road Statistics.*

Organisation for Economic Co-operation and Development (OECD), 2 rue Andre-Pascal, 75 Paris 16, France (Telephone Number in U.S. (202) 785-6323); *Revenue Statistics of OECD Member Countries.*

The World Bank, 1818 H Street, NW, Washington, D.C. 20433 (202) 477-1234; *World Tables.*

NEW ZEALAND - TEA CONSUMPTION - See NEW ZEALAND - CROPS

NEW ZEALAND - TELEGRAPH SERVICE

Statistical Office of the United Nations, Publishing Service, New York, New York 10017 (800) 253-9646; *Statistical Yearbook.*

NEW ZEALAND - TELEPHONES IN USE

American Telephone and Telegraph Company, 26 Parsippany Road, Whippany, New Jersey 07981 (800) 338-4038; *The World's Telephones.*

The Economist Intelligence Unit (Asia) Limited, 10th Floor, Luk Kwok Centre, 72 Gloucester Road, Wanchai, Hong Kong (Phone Number in U.S. (800) 938-4685); *Asian Market Atlas.*

Euromonitor Publications Limited, 87-88 Turnmill Street, London EC1M 5QU, England; *The Pacific Basin: An Economic Handbook.*

Statistical Office of the United Nations, Publishing Service, New York, New York 10017 (800) 253-9646; *Statistical Yearbook.*

NEW ZEALAND - TELEVISION BROADCASTING - See NEW ZEALAND - BROADCASTING

NEW ZEALAND - TELEVISION RECEIVER PRODUCTION

Statistical Office of the United Nations, Publishing Service, New York, New York 10017 (800) 253-9646; *Statistical Yearbook.*

NEW ZEALAND - TEXTILE INDUSTRY

American Forest and Paper Association, 1250 Connecticut Avenue, NW, Washington, D.C. 20036 (202) 463-2455; *Wood Pulp and Fiber Statistics.*

Organisation for Economic Co-operation and Development (OECD), 2 rue Andre-Pascal, 75 Paris 16, France (Telephone Number in U.S. (202) 785-6323); *Foreign Trade by Commodities, Industrial Structure Statistics,* and *Textile Industry in OECD Countries.*

Statistical Office of the United Nations, Publishing Service, New York, New York 10017 (800) 253-9646; *Statistical Yearbook,* and *Trade in Manufactures of Developing Countries.*

NEW ZEALAND - THEATRE

United Nations Educational, Scientific and Cultural Organization (UNESCO), 7 Place de Fontenoy, F-75700 Paris, France (Telephone Number in U.S. (212) 963-5981); *Statistical Yearbook.*

NEW ZEALAND - TIN - See NEW ZEALAND - MINING AND MINERAL PRODUCTS

NEW ZEALAND - TIRE (MOTOR VEHICLE) PRODUCTION

Statistical Office of the United Nations, Publishing Service, New York, New York 10017 (800) 253-9646; *Statistical Yearbook.*

NEW ZEALAND - TOBACCO PRODUCTION

Facts on File, 460 Park Avenue South, New York, New York 10016 (800) 443-8323; *The New Book of World Rankings.*

Organisation for Economic Co-operation and Development (OECD), 2 rue Andre-Pascal, 75 Paris 16, France (Telephone Number in U.S. (202) 785-6323); *Foreign Trade by Commodities,* and *Industrial Structure Statistics.*

Statistical Office of the United Nations, Publishing Service, New York, New York 10017 (800) 253-9646; *Statistical Yearbook.*

NEW ZEALAND - TOURISM

Euromonitor Publications Limited, 87-88 Turnmill Street, London EC1M 5QU, England; *The Pacific Basin: An Economic Handbook.*

Facts on File, 460 Park Avenue South, New York, New York 10016 (800) 443-8323; *The New Book of World Rankings.*

Organisation for Economic Co-operation and Development (OECD), 2 rue Andre-Pascal, 75 Paris 16, France (Telephone Number in U.S. (202) 785-6323); *Tourism Policy and International Tourism in OECD Member Countries.*

Statistical Office of the United Nations, Publishing Service, New York, New York 10017 (800) 253-9646; *Statistical Yearbook.*

Times Books, 201 East 50th Street, New York, New York 10022 (212) 751-2600; *The Economist Book of Vital World Statistics.*

World Tourism Organization, Calle Capitan Haya 42, E-28020 Madrid, Spain; *Yearbook of Tourism Statistics.*

NEW ZEALAND - TRACTORS IN USE

Statistical Office of the United Nations, Publishing Service, New York, New York 10017 (800) 253-9646; *Statistical Yearbook.*

NEW ZEALAND - TRADE - See NEW ZEALAND - FOREIGN TRADE

NEW ZEALAND - TRADEMARKS AND SERVICE MARKS

Statistical Office of the United Nations, Publishing Service, New York, New York 10017 (800) 253-9646; *Statistical Yearbook.*

World Intellectual Property Organization, 34 Chemin des Colombettes, CH-1211 Geneva 20, Switzerland; *Industrial Property Statistics.*

NEW ZEALAND - TRANSPORTATION AND COMMUNICATIONS

The Economist Intelligence Unit (Asia) Limited, 10th Floor, Luk Kwok Centre, 72 Gloucester Road, Wanchai, Hong Kong (Phone Number in U.S. (800) 938-4685); *Asian Market Atlas.*

Euromonitor Publications Limited, 87-88 Turnmill Street, London EC1M 5QU, England; *The Pacific Basin: An Economic Handbook.*

Facts on File, 460 Park Avenue South, New York, New York 10016 (800) 443-8323; *The New Book of World Rankings.*

Gale Research Incorporated, 835 Penobscot Building, Detroit, Michigan 48226 (800) 877-4253; *International Historical Statistics The Americas and Australasia.*

Statistical Office of the United Nations, Publishing Service, New York, New York 10017 (800) 253-9646; *Statistical Yearbook for Asia and the Pacific.*

NEW ZEALAND - TUNGSTEN PRODUCTION AND CONSUMPTION - See NEW ZEALAND - MINING AND MINERAL PRODUCTS

NEW ZEALAND - TURKEYS - See NEW ZEALAND - LIVESTOCK AND POULTRY

NEW ZEALAND - UNEMPLOYMENT

Euromonitor Publications Limited, 87-88 Turnmill Street, London EC1M 5QU, England; *International Marketing Data and Statistics.*

International Labour Office, I.L.O. Publications, CH-1211, Geneva 22, Switzerland; *Yearbook of Labour Statistics.*

Organisation for Economic Co-operation and Development (OECD), 2 rue Andre-Pascal, 75 Paris 16, France (Telephone Number in U.S. (202) 785-6323); *Economic Outlook, OECD Economic Surveys: New Zealand,* and *OECD Employment Outlook.*

Statistical Office of the United Nations, Publishing Service, New York, New York 10017 (800) 253-9646; *Statistical Yearbook.*

NEW ZEALAND - VEAL EXPORTS

International Monetary Fund, 700 Nineteenth Street, NW, Washington, D.C. 20431 (202) 623-7000; *International Financial Statistics.*

NEW ZEALAND - VITAL STATISTICS

Euromonitor Publications Limited, 87-88 Turnmill Street, London EC1M 5QU, England; *International Marketing Data and Statistics.*

Gale Research Incorporated, 835 Penobscot Building, Detroit, Michigan 48226 (800) 877-4253; *International Historical Statistics The Americas and Australasia.*

World Health Organization, Office of Publications, Avenue Appia, CH-1211 Geneva 27, Switzerland (Telephone Number in U.S. (518) 436-9686); *World Health Statistics Annual.*

NEW ZEALAND - WAGES

International Labour Office, I.L.O. Publications, CH-1211, Geneva 22, Switzerland; *Yearbook of Labour Statistics.*

Organisation for Economic Co-operation and Development (OECD), 2 rue Andre-Pascal, 75 Paris 16, France (Telephone Number in U.S. (202) 785-6323); *Economic Outlook, Industrial Structure Statistics,* and *Main Economic Indicators - Historical Statistics.*

Statistical Office of the United Nations, Publishing Service, New York, New York 10017 (800) 253-9646; *Statistical Yearbook for Asia and the Pacific,* and *Statistical Yearbook.*

NEW ZEALAND - WALNUT PRODUCTION - See NEW ZEALAND - CROPS

NEW ZEALAND - WATERWAYS IN USE

Organisation for Economic Co-operation and Development (OECD), 2 rue Andre-Pascal, 75 Paris 16, France (Telephone Number in U.S. (202) 785-6323); *Maritime Transport.*

NEW ZEALAND - WEATHER

Facts on File, 460 Park Avenue South, New York, New York 10016 (800) 443-8323; *The New Book of World Rankings.*

NEW ZEALAND - WELFARE EXPENDITURES

International Monetary Fund, 700 Nineteenth Street, NW, Washington, D.C. 20431 (202) 623-7000; *Government Finance Statistics Yearbook.*

NEW ZEALAND - WHEAT PRODUCTION AND PRICES - See NEW ZEALAND - CROPS

NEW ZEALAND - WHOLESALE PRICES

Statistical Office of the United Nations, Publishing Service, New York, New York 10017 (800) 253-9646; *Statistical Yearbook.*

NEW ZEALAND - WHOLESALE TRADE

Statistical Office of the United Nations, Publishing Service, New York, New York 10017 (800) 253-9646; *Statistical Yearbook.*

NEW ZEALAND - WINE PRODUCTION

Facts on File, 460 Park Avenue South, New York, New York 10016 (800) 443-8323; *The New Book of World Rankings.*

Statistical Office of the United Nations, Publishing Service, New York, New York 10017 (800) 253-9646; *Statistical Yearbook.*

NEW ZEALAND - WOOD - See NEW ZEALAND - FORESTRY AND FOREST PRODUCTS

NEW ZEALAND - WOOL - INDUSTRIAL CONSUMPTION

Organisation for Economic Co-operation and Development (OECD), 2 rue Andre-Pascal, 75 Paris 16, France (Telephone Number in U.S. (202) 785-6323); *Textile Industry in OECD Countries.*

NEW ZEALAND - WOOL EXPORTS

International Monetary Fund, 700 Nineteenth Street, NW, Washington, D.C. 20431 (202) 623-7000; *International Financial Statistics.*

NEW ZEALAND - WOOL PRODUCTION

Commodity Research Bureau, Incorporated, 75 Wall Street, New York, New York 10005 (212) 504-7754; *Commodity Year Book.*

Facts on File, 460 Park Avenue South, New York, New York 10016 (800) 443-8323; *The New Book of World Rankings.*

Organisation for Economic Co-operation and Development (OECD), 2 rue Andre-Pascal, 75 Paris 16, France (Telephone Number in U.S. (202) 785-6323); *Economic Accounts in Agriculture,* and *Textile Industry in OECD Countries.*

Statistical Office of the United Nations, Publishing Service, New York, New York 10017 (800) 253-9646; *Statistical Yearbook.*

NEW ZEALAND - YARN PRODUCTION

Organisation for Economic Co-operation and Development (OECD), 2 rue Andre-Pascal, 75 Paris 16, France (Telephone Number in U.S. (202) 785-6323); *Foreign Trade by Commodities,* and *Textile Industry in OECD Countries.*

Statistical Office of the United Nations, Publishing Service, New York, New York 10017 (800) 253-9646; *Statistical Yearbook.*

NEW ZEALAND - ZINC AND ZINC ORE PRODUCTION AND CONSUMPTION - See NEW ZEALAND - MINING AND MINERAL PRODUCTS

NEWSPAPERS - ADVERTISING EXPENDITURES

McCann-Erickson, Incorporated, 750 Third Avenue, New York, New York 10017 (212) 697-6000; complied for Crain Communications, Incorporated, 740 North Rush Street, Chicago, Illinois 60611; in *Advertising Age.*

Television Bureau of Advertising, Incorporated, 850 Third Avenue, New York, New York 10022 (212) 486-1111; data compiled by Competitive Media Reporting, 11 West 42nd Street, New York, New York 10036 (212) 789-1400.

NEWSPAPERS - EXPENDITURES - CONSUMER

U.S. Department of Commerce, Bureau of Economic Analysis, Fourteenth Street between Constitution Avenue and E Street, NW, Washington, D.C. 20230 (202) 606-9900; *The National Income and Product Accounts of the United States,* and *Survey of Current Business.*

NEWSPAPERS - FREQUENCY OF PUBLICATION

Gale Research Incorporated, 835 Penobscot Building, Detroit, Michigan 48226 (800) 877-4253; *Gale Directory of Publications and Broadcast Media.*

NEWSPAPERS - MANUFACTURING - CAPITAL

U.S. Department of Commerce, Bureau of the Census, Suitland, Maryland 20233 (301) 763-4040; *Census of Manufactures,* and *Annual Survey of Manufactures.*

NEWSPAPERS - MANUFACTURING - EARNINGS

U.S. Department of Commerce, Bureau of the Census, Suitland, Maryland 20233 (301) 763-4040; *Census of Manufactures,* and *Annual Survey of Manufactures.*

U.S. Department of Labor, Bureau of Labor Statistics, Two Massachusetts Avenue, NE, Washington, D.C. 20212 (202) 606-7828; *Employment and Earnings,* and Bulletins 2370 and 2429.

NEWSPAPERS - MANUFACTURING - EMPLOYEES

U.S. Department of Commerce, Bureau of the Census, Suitland, Maryland 20233 (301) 763-4040; *Census of Manufactures,* and *Annual Survey of Manufactures.*

U.S. Department of Labor, Bureau of Labor Statistics, Two Massachusetts Avenue, NE, Washington, D.C. 20212 (202) 606-7828; *Employment and Earnings,* and Bulletins 2370 and 2429.

NEWSPAPERS - MANUFACTURING - ESTABLISHMENTS

U.S. Department of Commerce, Bureau of the Census, Suitland, Maryland 20233 (301) 763-4040; *Census of Manufactures,* and *Annual Survey of Manufactures.*

NEWSPAPERS - MANUFACTURING - FINANCES

U.S. Department of Commerce, Bureau of the Census, Suitland, Maryland 20233 (301) 763-4040; *Census of Manufactures,* and *Annual Survey of Manufactures.*

NEWSPAPERS - MANUFACTURING - INVENTORIES

U.S. Department of Commerce, Bureau of the Census, Suitland, Maryland 20233 (301) 763-4040; *Census of Manufactures,* and *Annual Survey of Manufactures.*

NEWSPAPERS - MANUFACTURING - SALES, SHIPMENTS, RECEIPTS

U.S. Department of Commerce, Bureau of the Census, Suitland, Maryland 20233 (301) 763-4040; *Census of Manufactures,* and *Annual Survey of Manufactures.*

NEWSPAPERS - MANUFACTURING - VALUE ADDED

U.S. Department of Commerce, Bureau of the Census, Suitland, Maryland 20233 (301) 763-4040; *Census of Manufactures*, and *Annual Survey of Manufactures*.

NEWSPAPERS - NUMBER AND CIRCULATION

Editor and Publisher Company, 11 West Nineteenth Street, New York, New York 10011 (212) 675-4380; *Editor and Publisher International Year Book*.

NEWSPAPERS - NUMBER AND CIRCULATION - FOREIGN COUNTRIES

Statistical Office of the United Nations, Publishing Service, New York, New York 10017 (800) 253-9646; *Statistical Yearbook*.

United Nations Educational, Scientific, and Cultural Organization (UNESCO), 7 Place de Fontenoy, F-75700 Paris, France (Telephone Number in U.S. (212) 963-5981); *Statistical Yearbook*.

NEWSPAPERS - READING

Mediamark Research, Incorporated, 708 Third Avenue, New York, New York 10017 (212) 599-0444; *Multimedia Audiences*.

Veronis, Suhler and Associates, 350 Park Avenue, New York, New York 10022 (212) 935-4990; *Communications Industry Forecast Report*.

NEWSPRINT

American Forest and Paper Association, 1250 Connecticut Avenue, NW, Washington, D.C. 20036 (202) 463-2455; *Statistics of Paper, Paperboard, and Woodpulp*, annual.

U.S. Department of Commerce, Bureau of Economic Analysis, Fourteenth Street between Constitution Avenue and E Streets, NW, Washington, D.C. 20230 (202) 606-9900; based on data from the Canadian Pulp and Paper Association, 1155 Metcalfe Street, 19th Floor, Montreal, Quebec H3B 4T6, Canada (514) 866-6621; and American Forest and Paper Association, 1250 Connecticut Avenue, NW, Washington, D.C. 20036 (202) 463-2455; monthly data in *Survey of Current Business*.

NEWSPRINT - WORLD PRODUCTION

Statistical Office of the United Nations, Publishing Service, New York, New York 10017 (800) 253-9646; *Monthly Bulletin of Statistics*.

Nicaragua - National Statistical Office

Instituto Nacional de Estadisdicas y Censos, Apartado 4031, Managua, Nicaragua.

Nicaragua - Primary Statistics Source

Instituto Nacional de Estadisticas y Censos, Apartado 4031, Managua, Nicaragua; *Anuario Estadistico de Nicaragua*, and *Boletin de Estadistica*.

NICARAGUA - AGRICULTURE

The Economist Intelligence Unit, 111 West 57th Street, New York, New York 10019 (800) 938-4685; *The New Latin America Market Atlas*.

Euromonitor Publications Limited, 87-88 Turnmill Street, London EC1M 5QU, England; *International Marketing Data and Statistics*.

Facts on File, 460 Park Avenue South, New York, New York 10016 (800) 443-8323; *The New Book of World Rankings*.

Food and Agricultural Organization of the United Nations (FAO) Via delle Terme di Caracalla, 00100 Rome, Italy (Telephone Number in U.S. (202) 653-2400); *Production Yearbook, The State of Food and Agriculture*, and *Trade Yearbook*.

Gale Research Incorporated, 835 Penobscot Building, Detroit, Michigan 48226 (800) 877-4253; *International Historical Statistics The Americas and Australasia*.

G.K. Hall and Company, 70 Lincoln Street, Boston, Massachusetts 02111 (617) 423-3990; *The World in Figures*.

Inter-American Development Bank, 1300 New York Avenue, NW, Washington, D.C. 20577 (202) 623-1753; *Economic and Social Progress in Latin America*.

Statistical Office of the United Nations, Publishing Service, New York, New York 10017 (800) 253-9646; *Statistical Yearbook*.

Times Books, 201 East 50th Street, New York, New York 10022 (212) 751-2600; *The Economist Book of Vital World Statistics*.

U.C.L.A. Latin American Center Publications, University of California, Los Angeles, California 90024 (310) 825-6634; *Statistical Abstract of Latin America*.

The World Bank, 1818 H Street, NW, Washington, D.C. 20433 (202) 477-1234; *World Tables*.

NICARAGUA - AIRLINE SERVICE

The Economist Intelligence Unit, 111 West 57th Street, New York, New York 10019 (800) 938-4685; *The New Latin America Market Atlas*.

Facts on File, 460 Park Avenue South, New York, New York 10016 (800) 443-8323; *The New Book of World Rankings*.

G.K. Hall and Company, 70 Lincoln Street, Boston, Massachusetts 02111 (617) 423-3990; *The World in Figures*.

Statistical Office of the United Nations, Publishing Service, New York, New York 10017 (800) 253-9646; *Statistical Yearbook*.

Times Books, 201 East 50th Street, New York, New York 10022 (212) 751-2600; *The Economist Book of Vital World Statistics*.

NICARAGUA - ALUMINUM PRODUCTION AND CONSUMPTION - See NICARAGUA - MINING AND MINERAL PRODUCTS

NICARAGUA - ANIMAL HEALTH

Food and Agricultural Organization of the United Nations (FAO), Via delle Terme di Caracalla, 00100 Rome, Italy (Telephone Number in U.S. (202) 653-2400); *Animal Health Yearbook*.

NICARAGUA - AREA AND DENSITY OF POPULATION

Euromonitor Publications Limited, 87-88 Turnmill Street, London EC1M 5QU, England; *International Marketing Data and Statistics*.

Facts on File, 460 Park Avenue South, New York, New York 10016 (800) 443-8323; *The New Book of World Rankings*.

Food and Agricultural Organization of the United Nations (FAO) Via delle Terme di Caracalla, 00100 Rome, Italy (Telephone Number in U.S. (202) 653-2400); *The State of Food and Agriculture.*

G.K. Hall and Company, 70 Lincoln Street, Boston, Massachusetts 02111 (617) 423-3990; *The World in Figures.*

Inter-American Development Bank, 1300 New York Avenue, NW, Washington, D.C. 20577 (202) 623-1753; *Economic and Social Progress in Latin America.*

Statistical Office of the United Nations, Publishing Service, New York, New York 10017 (800) 253-9646; *Statistical Yearbook.*

Times Books, 201 East 50th Street, New York, New York 10022 (212) 751-2600; *The Economist Book of Vital World Statistics.*

United Nations Educational, Scientific and Cultural Organization (UNESCO), 7 Place de Fontenoy, F-75700 Paris, France (Telephone Number in U.S. (212) 963-5981); *Statistical Yearbook.*

NICARAGUA - ARMS EXPORTS AND IMPORTS

U.S. Arms Control and Disarmament Agency, 320 Twenty-first Street, NW, Washington, D.C. 20451 (202) 647-8677; *World Military Expenditures and Arms Transfers.*

NICARAGUA - BALANCE OF PAYMENTS

The Economist Intelligence Unit, 111 West 57th Street, New York, New York 10019 (800) 938-4685; *The New Latin America Market Atlas,* and *The World Market Atlas.*

G.K. Hall and Company, 70 Lincoln Street, Boston, Massachusetts 02111 (617) 423-3990; *The World in Figures.*

Inter-American Development Bank, 1300 New York Avenue, NW, Washington, D.C. 20577 (202) 623-1753; *Economic and Social Progress in Latin America.*

International Monetary Fund, 700 Nineteenth Street, NW, Washington, D.C. 20431 (202) 623-7000; *Balance of Payments Yearbook.*

Statistical Office of the United Nations, Publishing Service, New York, New York 10017 (800) 253-9646; *Economic Survey of Latin America and the Caribbean.*

Times Books, 201 East 50th Street, New York, New York 10022 (212) 751-2600; *The Economist Book of Vital World Statistics.*

U.C.L.A. Latin American Center Publications, University of California, Los Angeles, California 90024 (310) 825-6634; *Statistical Abstract of Latin America.*

The World Bank, 1818 H Street, NW, Washington, D.C. 20433 (202) 477-1234; *World Tables.*

NICARAGUA - BANANA PRODUCTION - See NICARAGUA - CROPS

NICARAGUA - BANKING

Facts on File, 460 Park Avenue South, New York, New York 10016 (800) 443-8323; *The New Book of World Rankings.*

G.K. Hall and Company, 70 Lincoln Street, Boston, Massachusetts 02111 (617) 423-3990; *The World in Figures.*

Inter-American Development Bank, 1300 New York Avenue, NW, Washington, D.C. 20577 (202) 623-1753; *Economic and Social Progress in Latin America.*

International Monetary Fund, 700 Nineteenth Street, NW, Washington, D.C. 20431 (202) 623-7000; *International Financial Statistics.*

Statistical Office of the United Nations, Publishing Service, New York, New York 10017 (800) 253-9646; *Statistical Yearbook.*

NICARAGUA - BARLEY PRODUCTION - See NICARAGUA - CROPS

NICARAGUA - BEER PRODUCTION

Facts on File, 460 Park Avenue South, New York, New York 10016 (800) 443-8323; *The New Book of World Rankings.*

Statistical Office of the United Nations, Publishing Service, New York, New York 10017 (800) 253-9646; *Statistical Yearbook.*

NICARAGUA - BIRTH RATES

Facts on File, 460 Park Avenue South, New York, New York 10016 (800) 443-8323; *The New Book of World Rankings.*

Statistical Office of the United Nations, Publishing Service, New York, New York 10017 (800) 253-9646; *Demographic Yearbook,* and *Statistical Yearbook.*

Times Books, 201 East 50th Street, New York, New York 10022 (212) 751-2600; *The Economist Book of Vital World Statistics.*

The World Bank, 1818 H Street, NW, Washington, D.C. 20433 (202) 477-1234; *World Tables.*

World Health Organization, Office of Publications, Avenue Appia, CH-1211 Geneva 27, Switzerland (Telephone Number in U.S. (518) 436-9686); *World Health Statistics Annual.*

NICARAGUA - BONDS

G.K. Hall and Company, 70 Lincoln Street, Boston, Massachusetts 02111 (617) 423-3990; *The World in Figures.*

Inter-American Development Bank, 1300 New York Avenue, NW, Washington, D.C. 20577 (202) 623-1753; *Economic and Social Progress in Latin America.*

International Monetary Fund, 700 Nineteenth Street, NW, Washington, D.C. 20431 (202) 623-7000; *Government Finance Statistics Yearbook.*

NICARAGUA - BOOK PRODUCTION

G.K. Hall and Company, 70 Lincoln Street, Boston, Massachusetts 02111 (617) 423-3990; *The World in Figures.*

NICARAGUA - BROADCASTING

Billboard Limited, Post Office Box 9027, 1006 AA Amsterdam, The Netherlands (Telephone Number in U.S. (212) 764-7300); *World Radio TV Handbook.*

Facts on File, 460 Park Avenue South, New York, New York 10016 (800) 443-8323; *The New Book of World Rankings.*

G.K. Hall and Company, 70 Lincoln Street, Boston, Massachusetts 02111 (617) 423-3990; *The World in Figures.*

Times Books, 201 East 50th Street, New York, New York 10022 (212) 751-2600; *The Economist Book of Vital World Statistics*.

NICARAGUA - BUSINESS

G.K. Hall and Company, 70 Lincoln Street, Boston, Massachusetts 02111 (617) 423-3990; *The World in Figures*.

Inter-American Development Bank, 1300 New York Avenue, NW, Washington, D.C. 20577 (202) 623-1753; *Economic and Social Progress in Latin America*.

NICARAGUA - BUSINESS AND PROFESSIONAL LICENSES

International Monetary Fund, 700 Nineteenth Street, NW, Washington, D.C. 20431 (202) 623-7000; *Government Finance Statistics Yearbook*.

NICARAGUA - BUTTER PRODUCTION - See NICARAGUA - DAIRY PRODUCTS

NICARAGUA - CABBAGE PRODUCTION - See NICARAGUA - CROPS

NICARAGUA - CALORIE SUPPLY

Food and Agricultural Organization of the United Nations (FAO) Via delle Terme di Caracalla, 00100 Rome, Italy (Telephone Number in U.S. (202) 653-2400); *The State of Food and Agriculture*.

NICARAGUA - CAPITAL INVESTMENT

Inter-American Development Bank, 1300 New York Avenue, NW, Washington, D.C. 20577 (202) 623-1753; *Economic and Social Progress in Latin America*.

NICARAGUA - CAPITAL REVENUE

Inter-American Development Bank, 1300 New York Avenue, NW, Washington, D.C. 20577 (202) 623-1753; *Economic and Social Progress in Latin America*.

International Monetary Fund, 700 Nineteenth Street, NW, Washington, D.C. 20431 (202) 623-7000; *Government Finance Statistics Yearbook*.

NICARAGUA - CATTLE - See NICARAGUA - LIVESTOCK AND POULTRY

NICARAGUA - CEMENT PRODUCTION - See NICARAGUA - MINING AND MINERAL PRODUCTS

NICARAGUA - CHEESE PRODUCTION AND CONSUMPTION - See NICARAGUA - DAIRY PRODUCTS

NICARAGUA - CHEMICAL (ORGANIC) PRODUCTION - See NICARAGUA - MINING AND MINERAL PRODUCTS

NICARAGUA - CHICKENS - See NICARAGUA - LIVESTOCK AND POULTRY

NICARAGUA - CIGARETTE PRODUCTION - See NICARAGUA - TOBACCO PRODUCTION

NICARAGUA - CLASS STRUCTURE

G.K. Hall and Company, 70 Lincoln Street, Boston, Massachusetts 02111 (617) 423-3990; *The World in Figures*.

NICARAGUA - CLIMATE

Facts on File, 460 Park Avenue South, New York, New York 10016 (800) 443-8323; *The New Book of World Rankings*.

G.K. Hall and Company, 70 Lincoln Street, Boston, Massachusetts 02111 (617) 423-3990; *The World in Figures*.

NICARAGUA - COAL PRODUCTION - See NICARAGUA - MINING AND MINERAL PRODUCTS

NICARAGUA - COCOA PRODUCTION

Statistical Office of the United Nations, Publishing Service, New York, New York 10017 (800) 253-9646; *Statistical Yearbook*.

NICARAGUA - COCOA (BEANS) PRODUCTION - See NICARAGUA - CROPS

NICARAGUA - COFFEE - See NICARAGUA - CROPS

NICARAGUA - COMMUNICATIONS

Gale Research Incorporated, 835 Penobscot Building, Detroit, Michigan 48226 (800) 877-4253; *International Historical Statistics The Americas and Australasia*.

G.K. Hall and Company, 70 Lincoln Street, Boston, Massachusetts 02111 (617) 423-3990; *The World in Figures*.

Inter-American Development Bank, 1300 New York Avenue, NW, Washington, D.C. 20577 (202) 623-1753; *Economic and Social Progress in Latin America*.

U.C.L.A. Latin American Center Publications, University of California, Los Angeles, California 90024 (310) 825-6634; *Statistical Abstract of Latin America*.

NICARAGUA - CONSTRUCTION INDUSTRY

The Economist Intelligence Unit, 111 West 57th Street, New York, New York 10019 (800) 938-4685; *The New Latin America Market Atlas*.

Facts on File, 460 Park Avenue South, New York, New York 10016 (800) 443-8323; *The New Book of World Rankings*.

Inter-American Development Bank, 1300 New York Avenue, NW, Washington, D.C. 20577 (202) 623-1753; *Economic and Social Progress in Latin America*.

Statistical Office of the United Nations, Publishing Service, New York, New York 10017 (800) 253-9646; *Construction Statistics Yearbook*, and *Statistical Yearbook*.

U.C.L.A. Latin American Center Publications, University of California, Los Angeles, California 90024 (310) 825-6634; *Statistical Abstract of Latin America*.

NICARAGUA - CONSUMER PRICE INDEX

G.K. Hall and Company, 70 Lincoln Street, Boston, Massachusetts 02111 (617) 423-3990; *The World in Figures*.

Statistical Office of the United Nations, Publishing Service, New York, New York 10017 (800) 253-9646; *Statistical Yearbook*.

U.C.L.A. Latin American Center Publications, University of California, Los Angeles, California 90024 (310) 825-6634; *Statistical*

Abstract of Latin America.

NICARAGUA - CONSUMER PRICES

The Economist Intelligence Unit, 111 West 57th Street, New York, New York 10019 (800) 938-4685; *The New Latin America Market Atlas.*

International Labour Office, I.L.O. Publications, CH-1211, Geneva 22, Switzerland; *Yearbook of Labour Statistics.*

International Monetary Fund, 700 Nineteenth Street, NW, Washington, D.C. 20431 (202) 623-7000; *International Financial Statistics.*

Times Books, 201 East 50th Street, New York, New York 10022 (212) 751-2600; *The Economist Book of Vital World Statistics.*

NICARAGUA - CONSUMPTION

The Economist Intelligence Unit, 111 West 57th Street, New York, New York 10019 (800) 938-4685; *The New Latin America Market Atlas.*

G.K. Hall and Company, 70 Lincoln Street, Boston, Massachusetts 02111 (617) 423-3990; *The World in Figures.*

NICARAGUA - CONSUMPTION - GOVERNMENT

Inter-American Development Bank, 1300 New York Avenue, NW, Washington, D.C. 20577 (202) 623-1753; *Economic and Social Progress in Latin America.*

NICARAGUA - COOPERATIVES

U.C.L.A. Latin American Center Publications, University of California, Los Angeles, California 90024 (310) 825-6634; *Statistical Abstract of Latin America.*

NICARAGUA - COPPER AND COPPER ORE PRODUCTION AND CONSUMPTION - See NICARAGUA - MINING AND MINERAL PRODUCTS

NICARAGUA - CORN PRODUCTION - See NICARAGUA - CROPS

NICARAGUA - CORPORATE INCOME TAXES - See NICARAGUA - TAXATION

NICARAGUA - CORPORATE TAXES - See NICARAGUA - TAXATION

NICARAGUA - COTTON - See NICARAGUA - CROPS

NICARAGUA - CROPS

The Economist Intelligence Unit, 111 West 57th Street, New York, New York 10019 (800) 938-4685; *The New Latin America Market Atlas.*

Facts on File, 460 Park Avenue South, New York, New York 10016 (800) 443-8323; *The New Book of World Rankings.*

Food and Agricultural Organization of the United Nations (FAO), Via delle Terme di Caracalla, 00100 Rome, Italy (Telephone Number in U.S. (202) 653-2400); *Production Yearbook,* and *The State of Food and Agriculture.*

G.K. Hall and Company, 70 Lincoln Street, Boston, Massachusetts 02111 (617) 423-3990; *The World in Figures.*

International Monetary Fund, 700 Nineteenth Street, NW, Washington, D.C. 20431 (202) 623-7000; *International Financial Statistics.*

Statistical Office of the United Nations, Publishing Service, New York, New York 10017 (800) 253-9646; *Statistical Yearbook.*

U.C.L.A. Latin American Center Publications, University of California, Los Angeles, California 90024 (310) 825-6634; *Statistical Abstract of Latin America.*

NICARAGUA - CUSTOMS DUTIES

G.K. Hall and Company, 70 Lincoln Street, Boston, Massachusetts 02111 (617) 423-3990; *The World in Figures.*

Inter-American Development Bank, 1300 New York Avenue, NW, Washington, D.C. 20577 (202) 623-1753; *Economic and Social Progress in Latin America.*

International Monetary Fund, 700 Nineteenth Street, NW, Washington, D.C. 20431 (202) 623-7000; *Government Finance Statistics Yearbook.*

NICARAGUA - DAIRY PRODUCTS

Facts on File, 460 Park Avenue South, New York, New York 10016 (800) 443-8323; *The New Book of World Rankings.*

Food and Agricultural Organization of the United Nations (FAO) Via delle Terme di Caracalla, 00100 Rome, Italy (Telephone Number in U.S. (202) 653-2400); *Production Yearbook,* and *The State of Food and Agriculture.*

Statistical Office of the United Nations, Publishing Service, New York, New York 10017 (800) 253-9646; *Statistical Yearbook.*

U.C.L.A. Latin American Center Publications, University of California, Los Angeles, California 90024 (310) 825-6634; *Statistical Abstract of Latin America.*

NICARAGUA - DEATH RATES

G.K. Hall and Company, 70 Lincoln Street, Boston, Massachusetts 02111 (617) 423-3990; *The World in Figures.*

Statistical Office of the United Nations, Publishing Service, New York, New York 10017 (800) 253-9646; *Statistical Yearbook.*

Times Books, 201 East 50th Street, New York, New York 10022 (212) 751-2600; *The Economist Book of Vital World Statistics.*

World Health Organization, Office of Publications, Avenue Appia, CH-1211 Geneva 27, Switzerland (Telephone Number in U.S. (518) 436-9686); *World Health Statistics Annual.*

NICARAGUA - DEBT

The Economist Intelligence Unit, 111 West 57th Street, New York, New York 10019 (800) 938-4685; *The New Latin America Market Atlas.*

NICARAGUA - DEFENSE EXPENDITURES

The Economist Intelligence Unit, 111 West 57th Street, New York, New York 10019 (800) 938-4685; *The New Latin America Market Atlas.*

G.K. Hall and Company, 70 Lincoln Street, Boston, Massachusetts 02111 (617) 423-3990; *The World in Figures.*

International Monetary Fund, 700 Nineteenth Street, NW, Washington, D.C. 20431 (202) 623-7000; *Government Finance Statistics Yearbook.*

U.S. Arms Control and Disarmament Agency, 320 Twenty-first Street, NW, Washington, D.C. 20451 (202) 647-8677; *World Military Expenditures and Arms Transfers.*

NICARAGUA - DEMOGRAPHY

The Economist Intelligence Unit, 111 West 57th Street, New York, New York 10019 (800) 938-4685; *The World Market Atlas.*

Facts on File, 460 Park Avenue South, New York, New York 10016 (800) 443-8323; *The New Book of World Rankings.*

G.K. Hall and Company, 70 Lincoln Street, Boston, Massachusetts 02111 (617) 423-3990; *The World in Figures.*

NICARAGUA - DEVELOPMENT ASSISTANCE

G.K. Hall and Company, 70 Lincoln Street, Boston, Massachusetts 02111 (617) 423-3990; *The World in Figures.*

Inter-American Development Bank, 1300 New York Avenue, NW, Washington, D.C. 20577 (202) 623-1753; *Economic and Social Progress in Latin America:.*

Statistical Office of the United Nations, Publishing Service, New York, New York 10017 (800) 253-9646; *Statistical Yearbook.*

NICARAGUA - DIAMOND PRODUCTION - See NICARAGUA - MINING AND MINERAL PRODUCTS

NICARAGUA - DISCOUNT RATES

Inter-American Development Bank, 1300 New York Avenue, NW, Washington, D.C. 20577 (202) 623-1753; *Economic and Social Progress in Latin America.*

Statistical Office of the United Nations, Publishing Service, New York, New York 10017 (800) 253-9646; *Statistical Yearbook.*

NICARAGUA - DISEASE

G.K. Hall and Company, 70 Lincoln Street, Boston, Massachusetts 02111 (617) 423-3990; *The World in Figures.*

World Health Organization, Office of Publications, Avenue Appia, CH-1211 Geneva 27, Switzerland (Telephone Number in U.S. (518) 436-9686); *World Health Statistics Annual.*

NICARAGUA - DIVORCE RATES

Facts on File, 460 Park Avenue South, New York, New York 10016 (800) 443-8323; *The New Book of World Rankings.*

Statistical Office of the United Nations, Publishing Service, New York, New York 10017 (800) 253-9646; *Demographic Yearbook,* and *Statistical Yearbook.*

NICARAGUA - DOMESTIC PRODUCT

G.K. Hall and Company, 70 Lincoln Street, Boston, Massachusetts 02111 (617) 423-3990; *The World in Figures.*

NICARAGUA - ECONOMY

Euromonitor Publications Limited, 87-88 Turnmill Street, London EC1M 5QU, England; *International Marketing Data and Statistics.*

Facts on File, 460 Park Avenue South, New York, New York 10016 (800) 443-8323; *The New Book of World Rankings.*

G.K. Hall and Company, 70 Lincoln Street, Boston, Massachusetts 02111 (617) 423-3990; *The World in Figures.*

Inter-American Development Bank, 1300 New York Avenue, NW, Washington, D.C. 20577 (202) 623-1753; *Economic and Social Progress in Latin America.*

Statistical Office of the United Nations, Publishing Service, New York, New York 10017 (800) 253-9646; *Economic Survey of Latin America and the Caribbean.*

U.C.L.A. Latin American Center Publications, University of California, Los Angeles, California 90024 (310) 825-6634; *Statistical Abstract of Latin America.*

NICARAGUA - EDUCATION

The Economist Intelligence Unit, 111 West 57th Street, New York, New York 10019 (800) 938-4685; *The New Latin America Market Atlas,* and *The World Market Atlas.*

Facts on File, 460 Park Avenue South, New York, New York 10016 (800) 443-8323; *The New Book of World Rankings.*

Gale Research Incorporated, 835 Penobscot Building, Detroit, Michigan 48226 (800) 877-4253; *International Historical Statistics The Americas and Australasia.*

G.K. Hall and Company, 70 Lincoln Street, Boston, Massachusetts 02111 (617) 423-3990; *The World in Figures.*

International Monetary Fund, 700 Nineteenth Street, NW, Washington, D.C. 20431 (202) 623-7000; *Government Finance Statistics Yearbook.*

Times Books, 201 East 50th Street, New York, New York 10022 (212) 751-2600; *The Economist Book of Vital World Statistics.*

U.C.L.A. Latin American Center Publications, University of California, Los Angeles, California 90024 (310) 825-6634; *Statistical Abstract of Latin America.*

United Nations Educational, Scientific and Cultural Organization (UNESCO), 7 Place de Fontenoy, F-75700 Paris, France (Telephone Number in U.S. (212) 963-5981); *Statistical Yearbook.*

The World Bank, 1818 H Street, NW, Washington, D.C. 20433 (202) 477-1234; *World Tables.*

NICARAGUA - EGG PRODUCTION AND CONSUMPTION - See NICARAGUA - DAIRY PRODUCTS

NICARAGUA - ELECTRICITY

The Economist Intelligence Unit, 111 West 57th Street, New York, New York 10019 (800) 938-4685; *The New Latin America Market Atlas.*

Facts on File, 460 Park Avenue South, New York, New York 10016 (800) 443-8323; *The New Book of World Rankings.*

Inter-American Development Bank, 1300 New York Avenue, NW, Washington, D.C. 20577 (202) 623-1753; *Economic and Social Progress in Latin America*.

Statistical Office of the United Nations, Publishing Service, New York, New York 10017 (800) 253-9646; *Statistical Yearbook*.

NICARAGUA - EMPLOYMENT

Euromonitor Publications Limited, 87-88 Turnmill Street, London EC1M 5QU, England; *International Marketing Data and Statistics*.

Facts on File, 460 Park Avenue South, New York, New York 10016 (800) 443-8323; *The New Book of World Rankings*.

International Labour Office, I.L.O. Publications, CH-1211, Geneva 22, Switzerland; *Yearbook of Labour Statistics*.

U.C.L.A. Latin American Center Publications, University of California, Los Angeles, California 90024 (310) 825-6634; *Statistical Abstract of Latin America*.

NICARAGUA - ENERGY

The Economist Intelligence Unit, 111 West 57th Street, New York, New York 10019 (800) 938-4685; *The New Latin America Market Atlas*.

Facts on File, 460 Park Avenue South, New York, New York 10016 (800) 443-8323; *The New Book of World Rankings*.

Food and Agricultural Organization of the United Nations (FAO) Via delle Terme di Caracalla, 00100 Rome, Italy (Telephone Number in U.S. (202) 653-2400); *The State of Food and Agriculture*.

G.K. Hall and Company, 70 Lincoln Street, Boston, Massachusetts 02111 (617) 423-3990; *The World in Figures*.

Statistical Office of the United Nations, Publishing Service, New York, New York 10017 (800) 253-9646; *Energy Statistics Yearbook* and *Statistical Yearbook*.

Times Books, 201 East 50th Street, New York, New York 10022 (212) 751-2600; *The Economist Book of Vital World Statistics*.

U.C.L.A. Latin American Center Publications, University of California, Los Angeles, California 90024 (310) 825-6634; *Statistical Abstract of Latin America*.

NICARAGUA - EXCHANGE RATES

Euromonitor Publications Limited, 87-88 Turnmill Street, London EC1M 5QU, England; *International Marketing Data and Statistics*.

Inter-American Development Bank, 1300 New York Avenue, NW, Washington, D.C. 20577 (202) 623-1753; *Economic and Social Progress in Latin America*.

International Monetary Fund, 700 Nineteenth Street, NW, Washington, D.C. 20431 (202) 623-7000; *International Financial Statistics*.

Statistical Office of the United Nations, Publishing Service, New York, New York 10017 (800) 253-9646; *Statistical Yearbook*.

U.C.L.A. Latin American Center Publications, University of California, Los Angeles, California 90024 (310) 825-6634; *Statistical Abstract of Latin America*.

NICARAGUA - EXCISE TAXES - See NICARAGUA - TAXATION

NICARAGUA - EXPORTS

The Economist Intelligence Unit, 111 West 57th Street, New York, New York 10019 (800) 938-4685; *The New Latin America Market Atlas*, and *The World Market Atlas*.

Euromonitor Publications Limited, 87-88 Turnmill Street, London EC1M 5QU, England; *International Marketing Data and Statistics*.

Food and Agricultural Organization of the United Nations (FAO) Via delle Terme di Caracalla, 00100 Rome, Italy (Telephone Number in U.S. (202) 653-2400); *The State of Food and Agriculture*.

G.K. Hall and Company, 70 Lincoln Street, Boston, Massachusetts 02111 (617) 423-3990; *The World in Figures*.

Inter-American Development Bank, 1300 New York Avenue, NW, Washington, D.C. 20577 (202) 623-1753; *Economic and Social Progress in Latin America*.

International Monetary Fund, 700 Nineteenth Street, NW, Washington, D.C. 20431 (202) 623-7000; *Direction of Trade Statistics*, *Government Finance Statistics Yearbook*, and *International Financial Statistics*.

Times Books, 201 East 50th Street, New York, New York 10022 (212) 751-2600; *The Economist Book of Vital World Statistics*.

The World Bank, 1818 H Street, NW, Washington, D.C. 20433 (202) 477-1234; *World Tables*.

NICARAGUA - EXTERNAL FINANCING

Inter-American Development Bank, 1300 New York Avenue, NW, Washington, D.C. 20577 (202) 623-1753; *Economic and Social Progress in Latin America*.

NICARAGUA - EXTERNAL INDEBTEDNESS

Inter-American Development Bank, 1300 New York Avenue, NW, Washington, D.C. 20577 (202) 623-1753; *Economic and Social Progress in Latin America*.

The World Bank, 1818 H Street, NW, Washington, D.C. 20433 (202) 477-1234; *World Tables*.

NICARAGUA - EXTERNAL TRADE

Food and Agricultural Organization of the United Nations (FAO) Via delle Terme di Caracalla, 00100 Rome, Italy (Telephone Number in U.S. (202) 653-2400); *The State of Food and Agriculture*, and *Trade Yearbook*.

Gale Research Incorporated, 835 Penobscot Building, Detroit, Michigan 48226 (800) 877-4253; *International Historical Statistics The Americas and Australasia*.

G.K. Hall and Company, 70 Lincoln Street, Boston, Massachusetts 02111 (617) 423-3990; *The World in Figures*.

Inter-American Development Bank, 1300 New York Avenue, NW, Washington, D.C. 20577 (202) 623-1753; *Economic and Social Progress in Latin America*.

Statistical Office of the United Nations, Publishing Service, New York, New York 10017 (800) 253-9646; *Statistical Yearbook*.

NICARAGUA - FABRIC PRODUCTION - See NICARAGUA - TEXTILE INDUSTRY

NICARAGUA - FAMILY PLANNING

U.C.L.A. Latin American Center Publications, University of California, Los Angeles, California 90024 (310) 825-6634; *Statistical Abstract of Latin America.*

NICARAGUA - FARM CROPS - See NICARAGUA - CROPS

NICARAGUA - FEMALE WORKING POPULATION - See NICARAGUA - EMPLOYMENT

NICARAGUA - FERTILITY RATES

Facts on File, 460 Park Avenue South, New York, New York 10016 (800) 443-8323; *The New Book of World Rankings.*

Times Books, 201 East 50th Street, New York, New York 10022 (212) 751-2600; *The Economist Book of Vital World Statistics.*

The World Bank, 1818 H Street, NW, Washington, D.C. 20433 (202) 477-1234; *World Tables.*

NICARAGUA - FERTILIZER

The Economist Intelligence Unit, 111 West 57th Street, New York, New York 10019 (800) 938-4685; *The New Latin America Market Atlas.*

Food and Agricultural Organization of the United Nations (FAO), Via delle Terme di Caracalla, 00100 Rome, Italy (Telephone Number in U.S. (202) 653-2400); *Fertilizer Yearbook,* and *The State of Food and Agriculture.*

Statistical Office of the United Nations, Publishing Service, New York, New York 10017 (800) 253-9646; *Statistical Yearbook.*

NICARAGUA - FETAL MORTALITY

Statistical Office of the United Nations, Publishing Service, New York, New York 10017 (800) 253-9646; *Demographic Yearbook.*

World Health Organization, Office of Publications, Avenue Appia, CH-1211 Geneva 27, Switzerland (Telephone Number in U.S. (518) 436-9686); *World Health Statistics Annual.*

NICARAGUA - FINANCE

Facts on File, 460 Park Avenue South, New York, New York 10016 (800) 443-8323; *The New Book of World Rankings.*

Gale Research Incorporated, 835 Penobscot Building, Detroit, Michigan 48226 (800) 877-4253; *International Historical Statistics The Americas and Australasia.*

G.K. Hall and Company, 70 Lincoln Street, Boston, Massachusetts 02111 (617) 423-3990; *The World in Figures.*

Inter-American Development Bank, 1300 New York Avenue, NW, Washington, D.C. 20577 (202) 623-1753; *Economic and Social Progress in Latin America.*

International Monetary Fund, 700 Nineteenth Street, NW, Washington, D.C. 20431 (202) 623-7000; *Government Finance Statistics Yearbook,* and *International Financial Statistics.*

U.C.L.A. Latin American Center Publications, University of California, Los Angeles, California 90024 (310) 825-6634; *Statistical Abstract of Latin America.*

NICARAGUA - FISHERIES

Facts on File, 460 Park Avenue South, New York, New York 10016 (800) 443-8323; *The New Book of World Rankings.*

Food and Agricultural Organization of the United Nations (FAO) Via delle Terme di Caracalla, 00100 Rome, Italy (Telephone Number in U.S. (202) 653-2400); *The State of Food and Agriculture,* and *Yearbook of Fishery Statistics.*

Inter-American Development Bank, 1300 New York Avenue, NW, Washington, D.C. 20577 (202) 623-1753; *Economic and Social Progress in Latin America.*

Statistical Office of the United Nations, Publishing Service, New York, New York 10017 (800) 253-9646; *Statistical Yearbook.*

U.C.L.A. Latin American Center Publications, University of California, Los Angeles, California 90024 (310) 825-6634; *Statistical Abstract of Latin America.*

NICARAGUA - FLOUR PRODUCTION

Statistical Office of the United Nations, Publishing Service, New York, New York 10017 (800) 253-9646; *Statistical Yearbook.*

NICARAGUA - FOOD

Food and Agricultural Organization of the United Nations (FAO), Via delle Terme di Caracalla, 00100 Rome, Italy (Telephone Number in U.S. (202) 653-2400); *Production Yearbook,* and *The State of Food and Agriculture.*

G.K. Hall and Company, 70 Lincoln Street, Boston, Massachusetts 02111 (617) 423-3990; *The World in Figures.*

NICARAGUA - FOREIGN AID

G.K. Hall and Company, 70 Lincoln Street, Boston, Massachusetts 02111 (617) 423-3990; *The World in Figures.*

Inter-American Development Bank, 1300 New York Avenue, NW, Washington, D.C. 20577 (202) 623-1753; *Economic and Social Progress in Latin America.*

NICARAGUA - FOREIGN DEBT

The Economist Intelligence Unit, 111 West 57th Street, New York, New York 10019 (800) 938-4685; *The New Latin America Market Atlas.*

Inter-American Development Bank, 1300 New York Avenue, NW, Washington, D.C. 20577 (202) 623-1753; *Economic and Social Progress in Latin America.*

NICARAGUA - FOREIGN INDEBTEDNESS

Inter-American Development Bank, 1300 New York Avenue, NW, Washington, D.C. 20577 (202) 623-1753; *Economic and Social Progress in Latin America.*

Statistical Office of the United Nations, Publishing Service, New York, New York 10017 (800) 253-9646; *Economic Survey of Latin America and the Caribbean.*

NICARAGUA - FOREIGN INVESTMENT

The Economist Intelligence Unit, 111 West 57th Street, New York, New York 10019 (800) 938-4685; *The New Latin America Market Atlas.*

NICARAGUA - FOREIGN TRADE

The Economist Intelligence Unit, 111 West 57th Street, New York, New York 10019 (800) 938-4685; *The New Latin America Market Atlas.*

Euromonitor Publications Limited, 87-88 Turnmill Street, London EC1M 5QU, England; *International Marketing Data and Statistics.*

Facts on File, 460 Park Avenue South, New York, New York 10016 (800) 443-8323; *The New Book of World Rankings.*

Food and Agricultural Organization of the United Nations (FAO) Via delle Terme di Caracalla, 00100 Rome, Italy (Telephone Number in U.S. (202) 653-2400); *The State of Food and Agriculture.*

G.K. Hall and Company, 70 Lincoln Street, Boston, Massachusetts 02111 (617) 423-3990; *The World in Figures.*

Inter-American Development Bank, 1300 New York Avenue, NW, Washington, D.C. 20577 (202) 623-1753; *Economic and Social Progress in Latin America.*

Statistical Office of the United Nations, Publishing Service, New York, New York 10017 (800) 253-9646; *Economic Survey of Latin America and the Caribbean, International Trade Statistics Yearbook,* and *Statistical Yearbook.*

U.C.L.A. Latin American Center Publications, University of California, Los Angeles, California 90024 (310) 825-6634; *Statistical Abstract of Latin America.*

The World Bank, 1818 H Street, NW, Washington, D.C. 20433 (202) 477-1234; *World Tables.*

NICARAGUA - FORESTRY AND FOREST PRODUCTS

The Economist Intelligence Unit, 111 West 57th Street, New York, New York 10019 (800) 938-4685; *The New Latin America Market Atlas.*

Facts on File, 460 Park Avenue South, New York, New York 10016 (800) 443-8323; *The New Book of World Rankings.*

Food and Agricultural Organization of the United Nations (FAO) Via delle Terme di Caracalla, 00100 Rome, Italy (Telephone Number in U.S. (202) 653-2400); *The State of Food and Agriculture,* and *Yearbook of Forest Products.*

G.K. Hall and Company, 70 Lincoln Street, Boston, Massachusetts 02111 (617) 423-3990; *The World in Figures.*

Inter-American Development Bank, 1300 New York Avenue, NW, Washington, D.C. 20577 (202) 623-1753; *Economic and Social Progress in Latin America.*

Statistical Office of the United Nations, Publishing Service, New York, New York 10017 (800) 253-9646; *Statistical Yearbook.*

U.C.L.A. Latin American Center Publications, University of California, Los Angeles, California 90024 (310) 825-6634; *Statistical Abstract of Latin America.*

United Nations Educational, Scientific and Cultural Organization (UNESCO), 7 Place de Fontenoy, F-75700 Paris, France (Telephone Number in U.S. (212) 963-5981); *Statistical Yearbook.*

NICARAGUA - GAS PRODUCTION - See NICARAGUA - MINING AND MINERAL PRODUCTS

NICARAGUA - GENERAL INDUSTRIAL STATISTICS

Statistical Office of the United Nations, Publishing Service, New York, New York 10017 (800) 253-9646; *Industrial Statistics Yearbook.*

NICARAGUA - GENERAL MORTALITY

Statistical Office of the United Nations, Publishing Service, New York, New York 10017 (800) 253-9646; *Demographic Yearbook.*

NICARAGUA - GEOGRAPHIC DATA

Facts on File, 460 Park Avenue South, New York, New York 10016 (800) 443-8323; *The New Book of World Rankings.*

U.C.L.A. Latin American Center Publications, University of California, Los Angeles, California 90024 (310) 825-6634; *Statistical Abstract of Latin America.*

NICARAGUA - GOATS - See NICARAGUA - LIVESTOCK AND POULTRY

NICARAGUA - GOLD HOLDINGS

International Monetary Fund, 700 Nineteenth Street, NW, Washington, D.C. 20431 (202) 623-7000; *International Financial Statistics.*

Statistical Office of the United Nations, Publishing Service, New York, New York 10017 (800) 253-9646; *Statistical Yearbook.*

The World Bank, 1818 H Street, NW, Washington, D.C. 20433 (202) 477-1234; *World Tables.*

NICARAGUA - GOLD PRODUCTION AND CONSUMPTION - See NICARAGUA - MINING AND MINERAL PRODUCTS

NICARAGUA- GOLD RESERVES

The Economist Intelligence Unit, 111 West 57th Street, New York, New York 10019 (800) 938-4685; *The New Latin America Market Atlas.*

NICARAGUA - GOVERNMENT

G.K. Hall and Company, 70 Lincoln Street, Boston, Massachusetts 02111 (617) 423-3990; *The World in Figures.*

Inter-American Development Bank, 1300 New York Avenue, NW, Washington, D.C. 20577 (202) 623-1753; *Economic and Social Progress in Latin America.*

NICARAGUA - GOVERNMENT CONSUMPTION

Inter-American Development Bank, 1300 New York Avenue, NW, Washington, D.C. 20577 (202) 623-1753; *Economic and Social Progress in Latin America.*

NICARAGUA - GOVERNMENT EXPENDITURES

Inter-American Development Bank, 1300 New York Avenue, NW, Washington, D.C. 20577 (202) 623-1753; *Economic and Social Progress in Latin America.*

International Monetary Fund, 700 Nineteenth Street, NW, Washington, D.C. 20431 (202) 623-7000; *Government Finance Statistics Yearbook.*

The World Bank, 1818 H Street, NW, Washington, D.C. 20433 (202) 477-1234; *World Tables.*

NICARAGUA - GOVERNMENT FINANCE

Inter-American Development Bank, 1300 New York Avenue, NW, Washington, D.C. 20577 (202) 623-1753; *Economic and Social Progress in Latin America.*

International Monetary Fund, 700 Nineteenth Street, NW, Washington, D.C. 20431 (202) 623-7000; *International Financial Statistics.*

NICARAGUA - GOVERNMENT REVENUES

Inter-American Development Bank, 1300 New York Avenue, NW, Washington, D.C. 20577 (202) 623-1753; *Economic and Social Progress in Latin America.*

International Monetary Fund, 700 Nineteenth Street, NW, Washington, D.C. 20431 (202) 623-7000; *Government Finance Statistics Yearbook.*

Times Books, 201 East 50th Street, New York, New York 10022 (212) 751-2600; *The Economist Book of Vital World Statistics.*

The World Bank, 1818 H Street, NW, Washington, D.C. 20433 (202) 477-1234; *World Tables.*

NICARAGUA - GRAIN PRODUCTION - See NICARAGUA - CROPS

NICARAGUA - GRANTS

International Monetary Fund, 700 Nineteenth Street, NW, Washington, D.C. 20431 (202) 623-7000; *Government Finance Statistics Yearbook.*

NICARAGUA - GROSS DOMESTIC PRODUCT

The Economist Intelligence Unit, 111 West 57th Street, New York, New York 10019 (800) 938-4685; *The New Latin America Market Atlas,* and *The World Market Atlas.*

Euromonitor Publications Limited, 87-88 Turnmill Street, London EC1M 5QU, England; *International Marketing Data and Statistics.*

Facts on File, 460 Park Avenue South, New York, New York 10016 (800) 443-8323; *The New Book of World Rankings.*

G.K. Hall and Company, 70 Lincoln Street, Boston, Massachusetts 02111 (617) 423-3990; *The World in Figures.*

Inter-American Development Bank, 1300 New York Avenue, NW, Washington, D.C. 20577 (202) 623-1753; *Economic and Social Progress in Latin America.*

Statistical Office of the United Nations, Publishing Service, New York, New York 10017 (800) 253-9646; *Statistical Yearbook.*

Times Books, 201 East 50th Street, New York, New York 10022 (212) 751-2600; *The Economist Book of Vital World Statistics.*

U.C.L.A. Latin American Center Publications, University of California, Los Angeles, California 90024 (310) 825-6634; *Statistical Abstract of Latin America.*

U.S. Arms Control and Disarmament Agency, 320 Twenty-first Street, NW, Washington, D.C. 20451 (202) 647-8677; *World Military Expenditures and Arms Transfers.*

The World Bank, 1818 H Street, NW, Washington, D.C. 20433 (202) 477-1234; *World Tables.*

NICARAGUA - GROSS NATIONAL PRODUCT

Euromonitor Publications Limited, 87-88 Turnmill Street, London EC1M 5QU, England; *International Marketing Data and Statistics.*

Inter-American Development Bank, 1300 New York Avenue, NW, Washington, D.C. 20577 (202) 623-1753; *Economic and Social Progress in Latin America.*

U.S. Arms Control and Disarmament Agency, 320 Twenty-first Street, NW, Washington, D.C. 20451 (202) 647-8677; *World Military Expenditures and Arms Transfers.*

The World Bank, 1818 H Street, NW, Washington, D.C. 20433 (202) 477-1234; *World Tables.*

NICARAGUA - GROUNDNUT PRODUCTION - See NICARAGUA - CROPS

NICARAGUA - HEALTH

The Economist Intelligence Unit, 111 West 57th Street, New York, New York 10019 (800) 938-4685; *The New Latin America Market Atlas.*

Facts on File, 460 Park Avenue South, New York, New York 10016 (800) 443-8323; *The New Book of World Rankings.*

G.K. Hall and Company, 70 Lincoln Street, Boston, Massachusetts 02111 (617) 423-3990; *The World in Figures.*

Statistical Office of the United Nations, Publishing Service, New York, New York 10017 (800) 253-9646; *Statistical Yearbook.*

Times Books, 201 East 50th Street, New York, New York 10022 (212) 751-2600; *The Economist Book of Vital World Statistics.*

U.C.L.A. Latin American Center Publications, University of California, Los Angeles, California 90024 (310) 825-6634; *Statistical Abstract of Latin America.*

World Health Organization, Office of Publications, Avenue Appia, CH-1211 Geneva 27, Switzerland (Telephone Number in U.S. (518) 436-9686); *World Health Statistics Annual.*

NICARAGUA - HEALTH EXPENDITURES

International Monetary Fund, 700 Nineteenth Street, NW, Washington, D.C. 20431 (202) 623-7000; *Government Finance Statistics Yearbook.*

NICARAGUA - HIDE PRODUCTION

Food and Agricultural Organization of the United Nations (FAO), Via delle Terme di Caracalla, 00100 Rome, Italy (Telephone Number in

U.S. (202) 653-2400); *Production Yearbook.*

NICARAGUA - HIGHWAYS

The Economist Intelligence Unit, 111 West 57th Street, New York, New York 10019 (800) 938-4685; *The New Latin America Market Atlas.*

G.K. Hall and Company, 70 Lincoln Street, Boston, Massachusetts 02111 (617) 423-3990; *The World in Figures.*

International Road Federation, 525 School Street, SW, Washington, D.C. 20024 (202) 554-2106; *World Road Statistics.*

NICARAGUA - HORSES - See NICARAGUA - LIVESTOCK AND POULTRY

NICARAGUA - HOURS OF WORK - See NICARAGUA - EMPLOYMENT

NICARAGUA - HOUSING AND HOUSING UNITS

Facts on File, 460 Park Avenue South, New York, New York 10016 (800) 443-8323; *The New Book of World Rankings.*

U.C.L.A. Latin American Center Publications, University of California, Los Angeles, California 90024 (310) 825-6634; *Statistical Abstract of Latin America.*

NICARAGUA - HOUSING EXPENDITURES

International Monetary Fund, 700 Nineteenth Street, NW, Washington, D.C. 20431 (202) 623-7000; *Government Finance Statistics Yearbook.*

NICARAGUA - ILLITERACY RATES

The Economist Intelligence Unit, 111 West 57th Street, New York, New York 10019 (800) 938-4685; *The New Latin America Market Atlas.*

NICARAGUA - ILLITERATE POPULATION

The Economist Intelligence Unit, 111 West 57th Street, New York, New York 10019 (800) 938-4685; *The World Market Atlas.*

G.K. Hall and Company, 70 Lincoln Street, Boston, Massachusetts 02111 (617) 423-3990; *The World in Figures.*

United Nations Educational, Scientific and Cultural Organization (UNESCO), 7 Place de Fontenoy, F-75700 Paris, France (Telephone Number in U.S. (212) 963-5981); *Statistical Yearbook.*

NICARAGUA - IMMIGRATION

U.C.L.A. Latin American Center Publications, University of California, Los Angeles, California 90024 (310) 825-6634; *Statistical Abstract of Latin America.*

NICARAGUA - IMPORTS

The Economist Intelligence Unit, 111 West 57th Street, New York, New York 10019 (800) 938-4685; *The New Latin America Market Atlas,* and *The World Market Atlas.*

Euromonitor Publications Limited, 87-88 Turnmill Street, London EC1M 5QU, England; *International Marketing Data and Statistics.*

Food and Agricultural Organization of the United Nations (FAO) Via delle Terme di Caracalla, 00100 Rome, Italy (Telephone Number in

U.S. (202) 653-2400); *The State of Food and Agriculture.*

G.K. Hall and Company, 70 Lincoln Street, Boston, Massachusetts 02111 (617) 423-3990; *The World in Figures.*

Inter-American Development Bank, 1300 New York Avenue, NW, Washington, D.C. 20577 (202) 623-1753; *Economic and Social Progress in Latin America.*

International Monetary Fund, 700 Nineteenth Street, NW, Washington, D.C. 20431 (202) 623-7000; *Direction of Trade Statistics, Government Finance Statistics Yearbook,* and *International Financial Statistics.*

Statistical Office of the United Nations, Publishing Service, New York, New York 10017 (800) 253-9646; *Trade in Manufactures of Developing Countries.*

Times Books, 201 East 50th Street, New York, New York 10022 (212) 751-2600; *The Economist Book of Vital World Statistics.*

The World Bank, 1818 H Street, NW, Washington, D.C. 20433 (202) 477-1234; *World Tables.*

NICARAGUA - INCOME DISTRIBUTION

U.C.L.A. Latin American Center Publications, University of California, Los Angeles, California 90024 (310) 825-6634; *Statistical Abstract of Latin America.*

NICARAGUA - INCOME TAXES - See NICARAGUA - TAXATION

NICARAGUA - INDUSTRY

Euromonitor Publications Limited, 87-88 Turnmill Street, London EC1M 5QU, England; *International Marketing Data and Statistics.*

Facts on File, 460 Park Avenue South, New York, New York 10016 (800) 443-8323; *The New Book of World Rankings.*

Gale Research Incorporated, 835 Penobscot Building, Detroit, Michigan 48226 (800) 877-4253; *International Historical Statistics The Americas and Australasia.*

G.K. Hall and Company, 70 Lincoln Street, Boston, Massachusetts 02111 (617) 423-3990; *The World in Figures.*

International Labour Office, I.L.O. Publications, CH-1211, Geneva 22, Switzerland; *Yearbook of Labour Statistics.*

Statistical Office of the United Nations, Publishing Service, New York, New York 10017 (800) 253-9646; *Economic Survey of Latin America and the Caribbean.*

U.C.L.A. Latin American Center Publications, University of California, Los Angeles, California 90024 (310) 825-6634; *Statistical Abstract of Latin America.*

The World Bank, 1818 H Street, NW, Washington, D.C. 20433 (202) 477-1234; *World Tables.*

NICARAGUA - INFANT AND MATERNAL MORTALITY

The Economist Intelligence Unit, 111 West 57th Street, New York, New York 10019 (800) 938-4685; *The New Latin America Market Atlas.*

Statistical Office of the United Nations, Publishing Service, New York, New York 10017 (800) 253-9646; *Demographic Yearbook,* and

Statistical Yearbook.

Times Books, 201 East 50th Street, New York, New York 10022 (212) 751-2600; *The Economist Book of Vital World Statistics.*

The World Bank, 1818 H Street, NW, Washington, D.C. 20433 (202) 477-1234; *World Tables.*

World Health Organization, Office of Publications, Avenue Appia, CH-1211 Geneva 27, Switzerland (Telephone Number in U.S. (518) 436-9686); *World Health Statistics Annual.*

NICARAGUA - INFLATIONARY FACTORS

Statistical Office of the United Nations, Publishing Service, New York, New York 10017 (800) 253-9646; *Economic Survey of Latin America and the Caribbean.*

NICARAGUA - INTEREST RATES

Inter-American Development Bank, 1300 New York Avenue, NW, Washington, D.C. 20577 (202) 623-1753; *Economic and Social Progress in Latin America.*

NICARAGUA - INTERNATIONAL FINANCE

Inter-American Development Bank, 1300 New York Avenue, NW, Washington, D.C. 20577 (202) 623-1753; *Economic and Social Progress in Latin America.*

U.C.L.A. Latin American Center Publications, University of California, Los Angeles, California 90024 (310) 825-6634; *Statistical Abstract of Latin America.*

NICARAGUA - INTERNATIONAL LIQUIDITY

Inter-American Development Bank, 1300 New York Avenue, NW, Washington, D.C. 20577 (202) 623-1753; *Economic and Social Progress in Latin America.*

International Monetary Fund, 700 Nineteenth Street, NW, Washington, D.C. 20431 (202) 623-7000; *International Financial Statistics.*

NICARAGUA - INTERNATIONAL RESERVES EXCLUDING GOLD

Inter-American Development Bank, 1300 New York Avenue, NW, Washington, D.C. 20577 (202) 623-1753; *Economic and Social Progress in Latin America.*

Statistical Office of the United Nations, Publishing Service, New York, New York 10017 (800) 253-9646; *Statistical Yearbook.*

The World Bank, 1818 H Street, NW, Washington, D.C. 20433 (202) 477-1234; *World Tables.*

NICARAGUA - INTERNATIONAL STATISTICS

Inter-American Development Bank, 1300 New York Avenue, NW, Washington, D.C. 20577 (202) 623-1753; *Economic and Social Progress in Latin America.*

U.C.L.A. Latin American Center Publications, University of California, Los Angeles, California 90024 (310) 825-6634; *Statistical Abstract of Latin America.*

NICARAGUA - INVESTMENTS

Inter-American Development Bank, 1300 New York Avenue, NW, Washington, D.C. 20577 (202) 623-1753; *Economic and Social Progress in Latin America.*

NICARAGUA - IRON ORE PRODUCTION AND CONSUMPTION - See NICARAGUA - MINING AND MINERAL PRODUCTS

NICARAGUA - IRRIGATION

Euromonitor Publications Limited, 87-88 Turnmill Street, London EC1M 5QU, England; *International Marketing Data and Statistics.*

Inter-American Development Bank, 1300 New York Avenue, NW, Washington, D.C. 20577 (202) 623-1753; *Economic and Social Progress in Latin America.*

NICARAGUA - LABOR FORCE

The Economist Intelligence Unit, 111 West 57th Street, New York, New York 10019 (800) 938-4685; *The New Latin America Market Atlas.*

Euromonitor Publications Limited, 87-88 Turnmill Street, London EC1M 5QU, England; *International Marketing Data and Statistics.*

Facts on File, 460 Park Avenue South, New York, New York 10016 (800) 443-8323; *The New Book of World Rankings.*

Food and Agricultural Organization of the United Nations (FAO) Via delle Terme di Caracalla, 00100 Rome, Italy (Telephone Number in U.S. (202) 653-2400); *The State of Food and Agriculture.*

G.K. Hall and Company, 70 Lincoln Street, Boston, Massachusetts 02111 (617) 423-3990; *The World in Figures.*

Gale Research Incorporated, 835 Penobscot Building, Detroit, Michigan 48226 (800) 877-4253; *International Historical Statistics The Americas and Australasia.*

The World Bank, 1818 H Street, NW, Washington, D.C. 20433 (202) 477-1234; *World Tables.*

NICARAGUA - LABOR PRODUCTIVITY

International Labour Office, I.L.O. Publications, CH-1211, Geneva 22, Switzerland; *Yearbook of Labour Statistics.*

NICARAGUA - LAND AREA

The Economist Intelligence Unit, 111 West 57th Street, New York, New York 10019 (800) 938-4685; *The New Latin America Market Atlas.*

NICARAGUA - LAND USE

Euromonitor Publications Limited, 87-88 Turnmill Street, London EC1M 5QU, England; *International Marketing Data and Statistics.*

Food and Agricultural Organization of the United Nations (FAO), Via delle Terme di Caracalla, 00100 Rome, Italy (Telephone Number in U.S. (202) 653-2400); *Production Yearbook.*

G.K. Hall and Company, 70 Lincoln Street, Boston, Massachusetts 02111 (617) 423-3990; *The World in Figures.*

Inter-American Development Bank, 1300 New York Avenue, NW, Washington, D.C. 20577 (202) 623-1753; *Economic and Social*

Progress in Latin America.

NICARAGUA - LIBRARIES

Facts on File, 460 Park Avenue South, New York, New York 10016 (800) 443-8323; *The New Book of World Rankings.*

United Nations Educational, Scientific and Cultural Organization (UNESCO), 7 Place de Fontenoy, F-75700 Paris, France (Telephone Number in U.S. (212) 963-5981); *Statistical Yearbook.*

NICARAGUA - LIFE EXPECTANCY RATE

The Economist Intelligence Unit, 111 West 57th Street, New York, New York 10019 (800) 938-4685; *The New Latin America Market Atlas.*

NICARAGUA - LIVESTOCK AND POULTRY

Euromonitor Publications Limited, 87-88 Turnmill Street, London EC1M 5QU, England; *International Marketing Data and Statistics.*

Facts on File, 460 Park Avenue South, New York, New York 10016 (800) 443-8323; *The New Book of World Rankings.*

Food and Agricultural Organization of the United Nations (FAO), Via delle Terme di Caracalla, 00100 Rome, Italy (Telephone Number in U.S. (202) 653-2400); *Production Yearbook,* and *The State of Food and Agriculture.*

G.K. Hall and Company, 70 Lincoln Street, Boston, Massachusetts 02111 (617) 423-3990; *The World in Figures.*

International Monetary Fund, 700 Nineteenth Street, NW, Washington, D.C. 20431 (202) 623-7000; *International Financial Statistics.*

Statistical Office of the United Nations, Publishing Service, New York, New York 10017 (800) 253-9646; *Statistical Yearbook.*

NICARAGUA - LIVING LEVELS

G.K. Hall and Company, 70 Lincoln Street, Boston, Massachusetts 02111 (617) 423-3990; *The World in Figures.*

Times Books, 201 East 50th Street, New York, New York 10022 (212) 751-2600; *The Economist Book of Vital World Statistics.*

NICARAGUA - MAIL TRAFFIC

Statistical Office of the United Nations, Publishing Service, New York, New York 10017 (800) 253-9646; *Statistical Yearbook.*

NICARAGUA - MAIN ECONOMIC INDICATORS - See NICARAGUA - ECONOMY

NICARAGUA - MAIN INDICATORS - See NICARAGUA - ECONOMY

NICARAGUA - MANUFACTURING

The Economist Intelligence Unit, 111 West 57th Street, New York, New York 10019 (800) 938-4685; *The New Latin America Market Atlas.*

Facts on File, 460 Park Avenue South, New York, New York 10016 (800) 443-8323; *The New Book of World Rankings.*

G.K. Hall and Company, 70 Lincoln Street, Boston, Massachusetts 02111 (617) 423-3990; *The World in Figures.*

Inter-American Development Bank, 1300 New York Avenue, NW, Washington, D.C. 20577 (202) 623-1753; *Economic and Social Progress in Latin America.*

Statistical Office of the United Nations, Publishing Service, New York, New York 10017 (800) 253-9646; *Statistical Yearbook.*

Times Books, 201 East 50th Street, New York, New York 10022 (212) 751-2600; *The Economist Book of Vital World Statistics.*

The World Bank, 1818 H Street, NW, Washington, D.C. 20433 (202) 477-1234; *World Tables.*

NICARAGUA - MARRIAGE RATES

Facts on File, 460 Park Avenue South, New York, New York 10016 (800) 443-8323; *The New Book of World Rankings.*

Statistical Office of the United Nations, Publishing Service, New York, New York 10017 (800) 253-9646; *Demographic Yearbook,* and *Statistical Yearbook.*

NICARAGUA - MEAT - See NICARAGUA - LIVESTOCK AND POULTRY

NICARAGUA - MEDICAL PERSONNEL

U.C.L.A. Latin American Center Publications, University of California, Los Angeles, California 90024 (310) 825-6634; *Statistical Abstract of Latin America.*

NICARAGUA - MERCHANT FLEET SHIPPING

G.K. Hall and Company, 70 Lincoln Street, Boston, Massachusetts 02111 (617) 423-3990; *The World in Figures.*

Statistical Office of the United Nations, Publishing Service, New York, New York 10017 (800) 253-9646; *Statistical Yearbook.*

Times Books, 201 East 50th Street, New York, New York 10022 (212) 751-2600; *The Economist Book of Vital World Statistics.*

U.S. Department of Transportation, Maritime Administration, 400 Seventh Street, SW, Washington, D.C. 20590 (202) 366-5807; *A Statistical Analysis of the World's Merchant Fleets.*

NICARAGUA - MILITARY

The Economist Intelligence Unit, 111 West 57th Street, New York, New York 10019 (800) 938-4685; *The New Latin America Market Atlas.*

G.K. Hall and Company, 70 Lincoln Street, Boston, Massachusetts 02111 (617) 423-3990; *The World in Figures.*

The International Institute for Strategic Studies, 23 Tavistock Street, London WC2E 7NQ, England; *The Military Balance.*

U.C.L.A. Latin American Center Publications, University of California, Los Angeles, California 90024 (310) 825-6634; *Statistical Abstract of Latin America.*

U.S. Arms Control and Disarmament Agency, 320 Twenty-first Street, NW, Washington, D.C. 20451 (202) 647-8677; *World Military Expenditures and Arms Transfers.*

NICARAGUA - MILK PRODUCTION - See NICARAGUA - DAIRY PRODUCTS

NICARAGUA - MINING AND MINERAL PRODUCTS

Commodity Research Bureau, Incorporated, 75 Wall Street, New York, New York 10005 (212) 504-7754; *Commodity Year Book.*

The Economist Intelligence Unit, 111 West 57th Street, New York, New York 10019 (800) 938-4685; *The New Latin America Market Atlas.*

Facts on File, 460 Park Avenue South, New York, New York 10016 (800) 443-8323; *The New Book of World Rankings.*

G.K. Hall and Company, 70 Lincoln Street, Boston, Massachusetts 02111 (617) 423-3990; *The World in Figures.*

Inter-American Development Bank, 1300 New York Avenue, NW, Washington, D.C. 20577 (202) 623-1753; *Economic and Social Progress in Latin America.*

Statistical Office of the United Nations, Publishing Service, New York, New York 10017 (800) 253-9646; *Statistical Yearbook.*

U.C.L.A. Latin American Center Publications, University of California, Los Angeles, California 90024 (310) 825-6634; *Statistical Abstract of Latin America.*

NICARAGUA - MONEY EXCHANGE RATE

Euromonitor Publications Limited, 87-88 Turnmill Street, London EC1M 5QU, England; *International Marketing Data and Statistics.*

Inter-American Development Bank, 1300 New York Avenue, NW, Washington, D.C. 20577 (202) 623-1753; *Economic and Social Progress in Latin America.*

International Monetary Fund, 700 Nineteenth Street, NW, Washington, D.C. 20431 (202) 623-7000; *International Financial Statistics.*

Statistical Office of the United Nations, Publishing Service, New York, New York 10017 (800) 253-9646; *Statistical Yearbook.*

NICARAGUA - MONEY RATES - MARKET

Inter-American Development Bank, 1300 New York Avenue, NW, Washington, D.C. 20577 (202) 623-1753; *Economic and Social Progress in Latin America.*

NICARAGUA - MONEY RESERVES

Euromonitor Publications Limited, 87-88 Turnmill Street, London EC1M 5QU, England; *International Marketing Data and Statistics.*

Inter-American Development Bank, 1300 New York Avenue, NW, Washington, D.C. 20577 (202) 623-1753; *Economic and Social Progress in Latin America.*

NICARAGUA - MONEY SUPPLY

Euromonitor Publications Limited, 87-88 Turnmill Street, London EC1M 5QU, England; *International Marketing Data and Statistics.*

G.K. Hall and Company, 70 Lincoln Street, Boston, Massachusetts 02111 (617) 423-3990; *The World in Figures.*

Inter-American Development Bank, 1300 New York Avenue, NW, Washington, D.C. 20577 (202) 623-1753; *Economic and Social Progress in Latin America.*

International Monetary Fund, 700 Nineteenth Street, NW, Washington, D.C. 20431 (202) 623-7000; *International Financial Statistics.*

Statistical Office of the United Nations, Publishing Service, New York, New York 10017 (800) 253-9646; *Statistical Yearbook.*

U.C.L.A. Latin American Center Publications, University of California, Los Angeles, California 90024 (310) 825-6634; *Statistical Abstract of Latin America.*

The World Bank, 1818 H Street, NW, Washington, D.C. 20433 (202) 477-1234; *World Tables.*

NICARAGUA - MOTOR VEHICLE TAXES - See NICARAGUA - TAXATION

NICARAGUA - MOTOR VEHICLES IN USE

The Economist Intelligence Unit, 111 West 57th Street, New York, New York 10019 (800) 938-4685; *The New Latin America Market Atlas.*

G.K. Hall and Company, 70 Lincoln Street, Boston, Massachusetts 02111 (617) 423-3990; *The World in Figures.*

International Road Federation, 525 School Street, SW, Washington, D.C. 20024 (202) 554-2106; *World Road Statistics.*

Statistical Office of the United Nations, Publishing Service, New York, New York 10017 (800) 253-9646; *Statistical Yearbook.*

Times Books, 201 East 50th Street, New York, New York 10022 (212) 751-2600; *The Economist Book of Vital World Statistics.*

NICARAGUA - MULES - See NICARAGUA - LIVESTOCK AND POULTRY

NICARAGUA - MUSEUMS

Facts on File, 460 Park Avenue South, New York, New York 10016 (800) 443-8323; *The New Book of World Rankings.*

NICARAGUA - NATALITY - See NICARAGUA - BIRTH RATES

NICARAGUA - NATIONAL ACCOUNTS

Gale Research Incorporated, 835 Penobscot Building, Detroit, Michigan 48226 (800) 877-4253; *International Historical Statistics The Americas and Australasia.*

Inter-American Development Bank, 1300 New York Avenue, NW, Washington, D.C. 20577 (202) 623-1753; *Economic and Social Progress in Latin America.*

Statistical Office of the United Nations, Publishing Service, New York, New York 10017 (800) 253-9646; *National Accounts Statistics,* and *Statistical Yearbook.*

U.C.L.A. Latin American Center Publications, University of California, Los Angeles, California 90024 (310) 825-6634; *Statistical Abstract of Latin America.*

NICARAGUA - NATIONAL INCOME

Facts on File, 460 Park Avenue South, New York, New York 10016 (800) 443-8323; *The New Book of World Rankings.*

G.K. Hall and Company, 70 Lincoln Street, Boston, Massachusetts 02111 (617) 423-3990; *The World in Figures*.

Inter-American Development Bank, 1300 New York Avenue, NW, Washington, D.C. 20577 (202) 623-1753; *Economic and Social Progress in Latin America*.

Statistical Office of the United Nations, Publishing Service, New York, New York 10017 (800) 253-9646; *Statistical Yearbook*.

NICARAGUA - NATIONAL PRODUCT

Facts on File, 460 Park Avenue South, New York, New York 10016 (800) 443-8323; *The New Book of World Rankings*.

Statistical Office of the United Nations, Publishing Service, New York, New York 10017 (800) 253-9646; *Statistical Yearbook*.

NICARAGUA - NATURAL GAS PRODUCTION - See NICARAGUA - MINING AND MINERAL PRODUCTS

NICARAGUA - NEWSPAPER PRODUCTION - See NICARAGUA - FORESTRY AND FOREST PRODUCTS

NICARAGUA - NEWSPRINT - See NICARAGUA - FORESTRY AND FOREST PRODUCTS

NICARAGUA - OCCUPATIONS - See NICARAGUA - LABOR FORCE

NICARAGUA - ORANGES PRODUCTION - See NICARAGUA - CROPS

NICARAGUA - PAPER - See NICARAGUA - FORESTRY AND FOREST PRODUCTS

NICARAGUA - PATENTS

Statistical Office of the United Nations, Publishing Service, New York, New York 10017 (800) 253-9646; *Statistical Yearbook*.

NICARAGUA - PEANUT PRODUCTION - See NICARAGUA - CROPS

NICARAGUA - PESTICIDE USE

Food and Agricultural Organization of the United Nations (FAO) Via delle Terme di Caracalla, 00100 Rome, Italy (Telephone Number in U.S. (202) 653-2400); *The State of Food and Agriculture*.

NICARAGUA - PETROLEUM INDUSTRY

The Economist Intelligence Unit, 111 West 57th Street, New York, New York 10019 (800) 938-4685; *The New Latin America Market Atlas*.

Facts on File, 460 Park Avenue South, New York, New York 10016 (800) 443-8323; *The New Book of World Rankings*.

Food and Agricultural Organization of the United Nations (FAO) Via delle Terme di Caracalla, 00100 Rome, Italy (Telephone Number in U.S. (202) 653-2400); *The State of Food and Agriculture*.

G.K. Hall and Company, 70 Lincoln Street, Boston, Massachusetts 02111 (617) 423-3990; *The World in Figures*.

Inter-American Development Bank, 1300 New York Avenue, NW, Washington, D.C. 20577 (202) 623-1753; *Economic and Social Progress in Latin America*.

Statistical Office of the United Nations, Publishing Service, New York, New York 10017 (800) 253-9646; *Statistical Yearbook*.

NICARAGUA - PIG IRON AND FERRO-ALLOY PRODUCTION - See NICARAGUA - MINING AND MINERAL PRODUCTS

NICARAGUA - PIGS - See NICARAGUA - LIVESTOCK AND POULTRY

NICARAGUA - POLITICAL DATA

U.C.L.A. Latin American Center Publications, University of California, Los Angeles, California 90024 (310) 825-6634; *Statistical Abstract of Latin America*.

NICARAGUA - POPULATION

The Economist Intelligence Unit, 111 West 57th Street, New York, New York 10019 (800) 938-4685; *The New Latin America Market Atlas*, and *The World Market Atlas*.

Euromonitor Publications Limited, 87-88 Turnmill Street, London EC1M 5QU, England; *International Marketing Data and Statistics*.

Facts on File, 460 Park Avenue South, New York, New York 10016 (800) 443-8323; *The New Book of World Rankings*.

Food and Agricultural Organization of the United Nations (FAO), Via delle Terme di Caracalla, 00100 Rome, Italy (Telephone Number in U.S. (202) 653-2400); *Production Yearbook*.

Gale Research Incorporated, 835 Penobscot Building, Detroit, Michigan 48226 (800) 877-4253; *International Historical Statistics The Americas and Australasia*.

G.K. Hall and Company, 70 Lincoln Street, Boston, Massachusetts 02111 (617) 423-3990; *The World in Figures*.

Inter-American Development Bank, 1300 New York Avenue, NW, Washington, D.C. 20577 (202) 623-1753; *Economic and Social Progress in Latin America*.

International Labour Office, I.L.O. Publications, CH-1211, Geneva 22, Switzerland; *Yearbook of Labour Statistics*.

Statistical Office of the United Nations, Publishing Service, New York, New York 10017 (800) 253-9646; *Demographic Yearbook*, and *Statistical Yearbook*.

Times Books, 201 East 50th Street, New York, New York 10022 (212) 751-2600; *The Economist Book of Vital World Statistics*.

U.C.L.A. Latin American Center Publications, University of California, Los Angeles, California 90024 (310) 825-6634; *Statistical Abstract of Latin America*.

United Nations Educational, Scientific and Cultural Organization (UNESCO), 7 Place de Fontenoy, F-75700 Paris, France (Telephone Number in U.S. (212) 963-5981); *Statistical Yearbook*.

U.S. Arms Control and Disarmament Agency, 320 Twenty-first Street, NW, Washington, D.C. 20451 (202) 647-8677; *World Military Expenditures and Arms Transfers*.

World Health Organization, Office of Publications, Avenue Appia, CH-1211 Geneva 27, Switzerland (Telephone Number in U.S. (518) 436-9686); *World Health Statistics Annual*.

NICARAGUA - POST OFFICES

Facts on File, 460 Park Avenue South, New York, New York 10016 (800) 443-8323; *The New Book of World Rankings*.

NICARAGUA - POTATO PRODUCTION - See NICARAGUA - CROPS

NICARAGUA - PRICES

Facts on File, 460 Park Avenue South, New York, New York 10016 (800) 443-8323; *The New Book of World Rankings.*

Food and Agricultural Organization of the United Nations (FAO), Via delle Terme di Caracalla, 00100 Rome, Italy (Telephone Number in U.S. (202) 653-2400); *Production Yearbook,* and *The State of Food and Agriculture.*

Gale Research Incorporated, 835 Penobscot Building, Detroit, Michigan 48226 (800) 877-4253; *International Historical Statistics The Americas and Australasia.*

G.K. Hall and Company, 70 Lincoln Street, Boston, Massachusetts 02111 (617) 423-3990; *The World in Figures.*

International Labour Office, I.L.O. Publications, CH-1211, Geneva 22, Switzerland; *Yearbook of Labour Statistics.*

International Monetary Fund, 700 Nineteenth Street, NW, Washington, D.C. 20431 (202) 623-7000; *International Financial Statistics.*

Statistical Office of the United Nations, Publishing Service, New York, New York 10017 (800) 253-9646; *Economic Survey of Latin America and the Caribbean.*

NICARAGUA - PRINTING AND WRITING PAPER - See NICARAGUA - FORESTRY AND FOREST PRODUCTS

NICARAGUA - PRODUCTION

Facts on File, 460 Park Avenue South, New York, New York 10016 (800) 443-8323; *The New Book of World Rankings.*

G.K. Hall and Company, 70 Lincoln Street, Boston, Massachusetts 02111 (617) 423-3990; *The World in Figures.*

NICARAGUA - PRODUCTIVITY

Euromonitor Publications Limited, 87-88 Turnmill Street, London EC1M 5QU, England; *International Marketing Data and Statistics.*

NICARAGUA - PROPERTY TAXES - See NICARAGUA - TAXATION

NICARAGUA - PUBLIC CONSUMPTION FUND

Inter-American Development Bank, 1300 New York Avenue, NW, Washington, D.C. 20577 (202) 623-1753; *Economic and Social Progress in Latin America.*

NICARAGUA - PUBLIC EXPENDITURES

Inter-American Development Bank, 1300 New York Avenue, NW, Washington, D.C. 20577 (202) 623-1753; *Economic and Social Progress in Latin America.*

NICARAGUA - PUBLIC FINANCE

Facts on File, 460 Park Avenue South, New York, New York 10016 (800) 443-8323; *The New Book of World Rankings.*

Inter-American Development Bank, 1300 New York Avenue, NW, Washington, D.C. 20577 (202) 623-1753; *Economic and Social Progress in Latin America.*

NICARAGUA - PUBLIC REVENUES

Inter-American Development Bank, 1300 New York Avenue, NW, Washington, D.C. 20577 (202) 623-1753; *Economic and Social Progress in Latin America.*

NICARAGUA - RADIO BROADCASTING - See NICARAGUA - BROADCASTING

NICARAGUA - RADIO RECEIVER PRODUCTION

Statistical Office of the United Nations, Publishing Service, New York, New York 10017 (800) 253-9646; *Statistical Yearbook.*

NICARAGUA - RAILWAYS

The Economist Intelligence Unit, 111 West 57th Street, New York, New York 10019 (800) 938-4685; *The New Latin America Market Atlas.*

G.K. Hall and Company, 70 Lincoln Street, Boston, Massachusetts 02111 (617) 423-3990; *The World in Figures.*

Jane's Information Group, Sentinel House, 163 Brighton Road, Coulsdon, Surrey CR5 2NH, England (Telephone Number in U.S. (703) 683-3700); *Jane's World Railways.*

Statistical Office of the United Nations, Publishing Service, New York, New York 10017 (800) 253-9646; *Statistical Yearbook.*

NICARAGUA - RANCHING

U.C.L.A. Latin American Center Publications, University of California, Los Angeles, California 90024 (310) 825-6634; *Statistical Abstract of Latin America.*

NICARAGUA - RELIGION

Facts on File, 460 Park Avenue South, New York, New York 10016 (800) 443-8323; *The New Book of World Rankings.*

U.C.L.A. Latin American Center Publications, University of California, Los Angeles, California 90024 (310) 825-6634; *Statistical Abstract of Latin America.*

NICARAGUA - RENT PRICES

International Labour Office, I.L.O. Publications, CH-1211, Geneva 22, Switzerland; *Yearbook of Labour Statistics.*

NICARAGUA - RESERVES EXCLUDING GOLD

The Economist Intelligence Unit, 111 West 57th Street, New York, New York 10019 (800) 938-4685; *The New Latin America Market Atlas.*

NICARAGUA - RETAIL TRADE

G.K. Hall and Company, 70 Lincoln Street, Boston, Massachusetts 02111 (617) 423-3990; *The World in Figures.*

Inter-American Development Bank, 1300 New York Avenue, NW, Washington, D.C. 20577 (202) 623-1753; *Economic and Social Progress in Latin America.*

NICARAGUA - RICE PRODUCTION - See NICARAGUA - CROPS

NICARAGUA - ROOT AND TUBER PRODUCTION - See NICARAGUA - CROPS

NICARAGUA - ROUNDWOOD PRODUCTION - See NICARAGUA - FORESTRY AND FOREST PRODUCTS

NICARAGUA - RUBBER PRODUCTION AND CONSUMPTION

Facts on File, 460 Park Avenue South, New York, New York 10016 (800) 443-8323; *The New Book of World Rankings.*

NICARAGUA - SALT PRODUCTION - See NICARAGUA - MINING AND MINERAL PRODUCTS

NICARAGUA - SAWNWOOD PRODUCTION - See NICARAGUA - FORESTRY AND FOREST PRODUCTS

NICARAGUA - SCIENCE AND TECHNOLOGY

Statistical Office of the United Nations, Publishing Service, New York, New York 10017 (800) 253-9646; *Statistical Yearbook.*

U.C.L.A. Latin American Center Publications, University of California, Los Angeles, California 90024 (310) 825-6634; *Statistical Abstract of Latin America.*

NICARAGUA - SCIENTISTS AND TECHNICIANS

Statistical Office of the United Nations, Publishing Service, New York, New York 10017 (800) 253-9646; *Statistical Yearbook.*

NICARAGUA - SENIOR CITIZENS

Facts on File, 460 Park Avenue South, New York, New York 10016 (800) 443-8323; *The New Book of World Rankings.*

NICARAGUA - SESAME SEED PRODUCTION - See NICARAGUA - CROPS

NICARAGUA - SHEEP - See NICARAGUA - LIVESTOCK AND POULTRY

NICARAGUA - SILVER PRODUCTION AND CONSUMPTION - See NICARAGUA - MINING AND MINERAL PRODUCTS

NICARAGUA - SOCIAL DATA

Facts on File, 460 Park Avenue South, New York, New York 10016 (800) 443-8323; *The New Book of World Rankings.*

G.K. Hall and Company, 70 Lincoln Street, Boston, Massachusetts 02111 (617) 423-3990; *The World in Figures.*

U.C.L.A. Latin American Center Publications, University of California, Los Angeles, California 90024 (310) 825-6634; *Statistical Abstract of Latin America.*

NICARAGUA - SOCIAL SECURITY

Inter-American Development Bank, 1300 New York Avenue, NW, Washington, D.C. 20577 (202) 623-1753; *Economic and Social Progress in Latin America.*

International Monetary Fund, 700 Nineteenth Street, NW, Washington, D.C. 20431 (202) 623-7000; *Government Finance Statistics Yearbook.*

NICARAGUA - SOCIOECONOMIC DATA

Inter-American Development Bank, 1300 New York Avenue, NW, Washington, D.C. 20577 (202) 623-1753; *Economic and Social Progress in Latin America.*

U.C.L.A. Latin American Center Publications, University of California, Los Angeles, California 90024 (310) 825-6634; *Statistical Abstract of Latin America.*

NICARAGUA - SOYBEAN PRODUCTION - See NICARAGUA - CROPS

NICARAGUA - STAMP TAXES AND DUTIES - See NICARAGUA - TAXATION

NICARAGUA - STATE BUDGET REVENUE AND EXPENDITURES

Euromonitor Publications Limited, 87-88 Turnmill Street, London EC1M 5QU, England; *International Marketing Data and Statistics.*

Inter-American Development Bank, 1300 New York Avenue, NW, Washington, D.C. 20577 (202) 623-1753; *Economic and Social Progress in Latin America.*

NICARAGUA - STEEL - See NICARAGUA - MINING AND MINERAL PRODUCTS

NICARAGUA - STOCKS - COMMODITY - MARKET PRICE - INDEX

Food and Agricultural Organization of the United Nations (FAO) Via delle Terme di Caracalla, 00100 Rome, Italy (Telephone Number in U.S. (202) 653-2400); *The State of Food and Agriculture.*

NICARAGUA - SUGAR PRODUCTION AND CONSUMPTION - See NICARAGUA - CROPS

NICARAGUA - TAXATION

G.K. Hall and Company, 70 Lincoln Street, Boston, Massachusetts 02111 (617) 423-3990; *The World in Figures.*

Inter-American Development Bank, 1300 New York Avenue, NW, Washington, D.C. 20577 (202) 623-1753; *Economic and Social Progress in Latin America.*

International Monetary Fund, 700 Nineteenth Street, NW, Washington, D.C. 20431 (202) 623-7000; *Government Finance Statistics Yearbook.*

International Road Federation, 525 School Street, SW, Washington, D.C. 20024 (202) 554-2106; *World Road Statistics.*

The World Bank, 1818 H Street, NW, Washington, D.C. 20433 (202) 477-1234; *World Tables.*

NICARAGUA - TAX REVENUES - See NICARAGUA - TAXATION

NICARAGUA - TELEPHONES IN USE

American Telephone and Telegraph Company, 26 Parsippany Road, Whippany, New Jersey 07981 (800) 338-4038; *The World's Telephones.*

The Economist Intelligence Unit, 111 West 57th Street, New York, New York 10019 (800) 938-4685; *The New Latin America Market Atlas.*

G.K. Hall and Company, 70 Lincoln Street, Boston, Massachusetts 02111 (617) 423-3990; *The World in Figures.*

Statistical Office of the United Nations, Publishing Service, New York, New York 10017 (800) 253-9646; *Statistical Yearbook.*

NICARAGUA - TELEVISION BROADCASTING - See NICARAGUA - BROADCASTING

NICARAGUA - TELEVISION RECEIVER PRODUCTION

Statistical Office of the United Nations, Publishing Service, New York, New York 10017 (800) 253-9646; *Statistical Yearbook.*

NICARAGUA - TEXTILE INDUSTRY

G.K. Hall and Company, 70 Lincoln Street, Boston, Massachusetts 02111 (617) 423-3990; *The World in Figures.*

Statistical Office of the United Nations, Publishing Service, New York, New York 10017 (800) 253-9646; *Statistical Yearbook.*

NICARAGUA - TOBACCO PRODUCTION

Facts on File, 460 Park Avenue South, New York, New York 10016 (800) 443-8323; *The New Book of World Rankings.*

Statistical Office of the United Nations, Publishing Service, New York, New York 10017 (800) 253-9646; *Statistical Yearbook.*

U.C.L.A. Latin American Center Publications, University of California, Los Angeles, California 90024 (310) 825-6634; *Statistical Abstract of Latin America.*

NICARAGUA - TOURISM

The Economist Intelligence Unit, 111 West 57th Street, New York, New York 10019 (800) 938-4685; *The New Latin America Market Atlas.*

Facts on File, 460 Park Avenue South, New York, New York 10016 (800) 443-8323; *The New Book of World Rankings.*

G.K. Hall and Company, 70 Lincoln Street, Boston, Massachusetts 02111 (617) 423-3990; *The World in Figures.*

Statistical Office of the United Nations, Publishing Service, New York, New York 10017 (800) 253-9646; *Statistical Yearbook.*

U.C.L.A. Latin American Center Publications, University of California, Los Angeles, California 90024 (310) 825-6634; *Statistical Abstract of Latin America.*

NICARAGUA - TRACTORS IN USE

The Economist Intelligence Unit, 111 West 57th Street, New York, New York 10019 (800) 938-4685; *The New Latin America Market Atlas.*

NICARAGUA - TRADE - See NICARAGUA - FOREIGN TRADE

NICARAGUA - TRADEMARKS AND SERVICE MARKS

Statistical Office of the United Nations, Publishing Service, New York, New York 10017 (800) 253-9646; *Statistical Yearbook.*

NICARAGUA - TRANSPORTATION AND COMMUNICATIONS

The Economist Intelligence Unit, 111 West 57th Street, New York, New York 10019 (800) 938-4685; *The New Latin America Market Atlas.*

Facts on File, 460 Park Avenue South, New York, New York 10016 (800) 443-8323; *The New Book of World Rankings.*

Gale Research Incorporated, 835 Penobscot Building, Detroit, Michigan 48226 (800) 877-4253; *International Historical Statistics The Americas and Australasia.*

G.K. Hall and Company, 70 Lincoln Street, Boston, Massachusetts 02111 (617) 423-3990; *The World in Figures.*

Inter-American Development Bank, 1300 New York Avenue, NW, Washington, D.C. 20577 (202) 623-1753; *Economic and Social Progress in Latin America.*

U.C.L.A. Latin American Center Publications, University of California, Los Angeles, California 90024 (310) 825-6634; *Statistical Abstract of Latin America.*

NICARAGUA - UNEMPLOYMENT

The Economist Intelligence Unit, 111 West 57th Street, New York, New York 10019 (800) 938-4685; *The New Latin America Market Atlas.*

Euromonitor Publications Limited, 87-88 Turnmill Street, London EC1M 5QU, England; *International Marketing Data and Statistics.*

International Labour Office, I.L.O. Publications, CH-1211, Geneva 22, Switzerland; *Yearbook of Labour Statistics.*

Statistical Office of the United Nations, Publishing Service, New York, New York 10017 (800) 253-9646; *Statistical Yearbook.*

U.C.L.A. Latin American Center Publications, University of California, Los Angeles, California 90024 (310) 825-6634; *Statistical Abstract of Latin America.*

NICARAGUA - UTILITIES

U.C.L.A. Latin American Center Publications, University of California, Los Angeles, California 90024 (310) 825-6634; *Statistical Abstract of Latin America.*

NICARAGUA - VITAL STATISTICS

Euromonitor Publications Limited, 87-88 Turnmill Street, London EC1M 5QU, England; *International Marketing Data and Statistics.*

Gale Research Incorporated, 835 Penobscot Building, Detroit, Michigan 48226 (800) 877-4253; *International Historical Statistics The Americas and Australasia.*

G.K. Hall and Company, 70 Lincoln Street, Boston, Massachusetts 02111 (617) 423-3990; *The World in Figures.*

Statistical Office of the United Nations, Publishing Service, New York, New York 10017 (800) 253-9646; *Statistical Yearbook.*

World Health Organization, Office of Publications, Avenue Appia, CH-1211 Geneva 27, Switzerland (Telephone Number in U.S. (518) 436-9686); *World Health Statistics Annual.*

NICARAGUA - WAGES

G.K. Hall and Company, 70 Lincoln Street, Boston, Massachusetts 02111 (617) 423-3990; *The World in Figures.*

International Labour Office, I.L.O. Publications, CH-1211, Geneva 22, Switzerland; *Yearbook of Labour Statistics.*

Statistical Office of the United Nations, Publishing Service, New York, New York 10017 (800) 253-9646; *Statistical Yearbook.*

U.C.L.A. Latin American Center Publications, University of California, Los Angeles, California 90024 (310) 825-6634; *Statistical Abstract of Latin America.*

NICARAGUA - WEATHER

Facts on File, 460 Park Avenue South, New York, New York 10016 (800) 443-8323; *The New Book of World Rankings*.

G.K. Hall and Company, 70 Lincoln Street, Boston, Massachusetts 02111 (617) 423-3990; *The World in Figures*.

NICARAGUA - WELFARE

Inter-American Development Bank, 1300 New York Avenue, NW, Washington, D.C. 20577 (202) 623-1753; *Economic and Social Progress in Latin America*.

International Monetary Fund, 700 Nineteenth Street, NW, Washington, D.C. 20431 (202) 623-7000; *Government Finance Statistics Yearbook*.

NICARAGUA - WHEAT PRODUCTION AND PRICES - See NICARAGUA - CROPS

NICARAGUA - WHOLESALE PRICES

Inter-American Development Bank, 1300 New York Avenue, NW, Washington, D.C. 20577 (202) 623-1753; *Economic and Social Progress in Latin America*.

NICARAGUA - WHOLESALE TRADE

Inter-American Development Bank, 1300 New York Avenue, NW, Washington, D.C. 20577 (202) 623-1753; *Economic and Social Progress in Latin America*.

NICARAGUA - WINE PRODUCTION

Facts on File, 460 Park Avenue South, New York, New York 10016 (800) 443-8323; *The New Book of World Rankings*.

NICARAGUA - WOOD PULP PRODUCTION - See NICARAGUA - FORESTRY AND FOREST PRODUCTS

NICARAGUA - WOOL PRODUCTION

Facts on File, 460 Park Avenue South, New York, New York 10016 (800) 443-8323; *The New Book of World Rankings*.

NICKEL

U.S. Department of the Interior, Bureau of Mines, 810 Seventh Street, NW, Washington, D.C. 20241 (202) 501-9649; *Annual Reports*, and *Mineral Commodity Summaries*.

NICKEL - FOREIGN TRADE

U.S. Department of Commerce, Bureau of the Census, Suitland, Maryland 20233 (301) 763-4040; *U.S. Merchandise Trade*.

U.S. Department of the Interior, Bureau of Mines, 810 Seventh Street, NW, Washington, D.C. 20241 (202) 501-9649; *Annual Reports*, and *Mineral Commodity Summaries*.

NICKEL - PRICES

U.S. Department of the Interior, Bureau of Mines, 810 Seventh Street, NW, Washington, D.C. 20241 (202) 501-9649; *Annual Reports*, and *Mineral Commodity Summaries*.

NICKEL - WORLD PRODUCTION

U.S. Department of the Interior, Bureau of Mines, 810 Seventh Street, NW, Washington, D.C. 20241 (202) 501-9649; *Annual Reports*.

Niger - National Statistical Office

Direction de la Statistique, et de la Demographie, Ministere du Plan, BP 467 Niamey, Niger.

Niger - Primary Statistics Sources

Direction de la Statistique, Niamey, Niger; *Annuaire statistique* (Statistical Yearbook), and *Bulletin de statistique* (Statistical bulletin).

NIGER - AGRICULTURE

Euromonitor Publications Limited, 87-88 Turnmill Street, London EC1M 5QU, England; *International Marketing Data and Statistics*.

Facts on File, 460 Park Avenue South, New York, New York 10016 (800) 443-8323; *The New Book of World Rankings*.

Food and Agricultural Organization of the United Nations (FAO) Via delle Terme di Caracalla, 00100 Rome, Italy (Telephone Number in U.S. (202) 653-2400); *Production Yearbook, The State of Food and Agriculture*, and *Trade Yearbook*.

G.K. Hall and Company, 70 Lincoln Street, Boston, Massachusetts 02111 (617) 423-3990; *The World in Figures*.

Statistical Office of the United Nations, Publishing Service, New York, New York 10017 (800) 253-9646; *Statistical Yearbook*, and *Survey of Economic and Social Conditions in Africa*.

Times Books, 201 East 50th Street, New York, New York 10022 (212) 751-2600; *The Economist Book of Vital World Statistics*.

United Nations Economic Commission for Africa, Africa Hall, Post Office Box 3001, Addis Ababa, Ethiopia (Telephone Number in U.S. (800) 253-9646); *African Statistical Yearbook*.

The World Bank, 1818 H Street, NW, Washington, D.C. 20433 (202) 477-1234; *World Tables*.

NIGER - AIRLINE SERVICE

Facts on File, 460 Park Avenue South, New York, New York 10016 (800) 443-8323; *The New Book of World Rankings*.

G.K. Hall and Company, 70 Lincoln Street, Boston, Massachusetts 02111 (617) 423-3990; *The World in Figures*.

Statistical Office of the United Nations, Publishing Service, New York, New York 10017 (800) 253-9646; *Statistical Yearbook*.

Times Books, 201 East 50th Street, New York, New York 10022 (212) 751-2600; *The Economist Book of Vital World Statistics*.

United Nations Economic Commission for Africa, Africa Hall, Post Office Box 3001, Addis Ababa, Ethiopia (Telephone Number in U.S. (800) 253-9646); *African Statistical Yearbook*.

NIGER - ALUMINUM PRODUCTION AND CONSUMPTION - See NIGER - MINING AND MINERAL PRODUCTS

NIGER - ANIMAL HEALTH

Food and Agricultural Organization of the United Nations (FAO), Via delle Terme di Caracalla, 00100 Rome, Italy (Telephone Number in U.S. (202) 653-2400); *Animal Health Yearbook.*

NIGER - AREA AND DENSITY OF POPULATION

African Development Bank, 01 BP 1387, Abidjan 01, Cote d'Ivoire; *Selected Statistics on Regional Member Countries.*

Euromonitor Publications Limited, 87-88 Turnmill Street, London EC1M 5QU, England; *International Marketing Data and Statistics.*

Facts on File, 460 Park Avenue South, New York, New York 10016 (800) 443-8323; *The New Book of World Rankings.*

Food and Agricultural Organization of the United Nations (FAO) Via delle Terme di Caracalla, 00100 Rome, Italy (Telephone Number in U.S. (202) 653-2400); *The State of Food and Agriculture.*

G.K. Hall and Company, 70 Lincoln Street, Boston, Massachusetts 02111 (617) 423-3990; *The World in Figures.*

Statistical Office of the United Nations, Publishing Service, New York, New York 10017 (800) 253-9646; *Statistical Yearbook* and *Survey of Economic and Social Conditions in Africa.*

Times Books, 201 East 50th Street, New York, New York 10022 (212) 751-2600; *The Economist Book of Vital World Statistics.*

United Nations Educational, Scientific and Cultural Organization (UNESCO), 7 Place de Fontenoy, F-75700 Paris, France (Telephone Number in U.S. (212) 963-5981); *Statistical Yearbook.*

NIGER - ARMS EXPORTS AND IMPORTS

U.S. Arms Control and Disarmament Agency, 320 Twenty-first Street, NW, Washington, D.C. 20451 (202) 647-8677; *World Military Expenditures and Arms Transfers.*

NIGER - BALANCE OF PAYMENTS

African Development Bank, 01 BP 1387, Abidjan 01, Cote d'Ivoire; *Selected Statistics on Regional Member Countries.*

The Economist Intelligence Unit, 111 West 57th Street, New York, New York 10019 (800) 938-4685; *The World Market Atlas.*

G.K. Hall and Company, 70 Lincoln Street, Boston, Massachusetts 02111 (617) 423-3990; *The World in Figures.*

International Monetary Fund, 700 Nineteenth Street, NW, Washington, D.C. 20431 (202) 623-7000; *Balance of Payments Yearbook.*

Times Books, 201 East 50th Street, New York, New York 10022 (212) 751-2600; *The Economist Book of Vital World Statistics.*

United Nations Economic Commission for Africa, Africa Hall, Post Office Box 3001, Addis Ababa, Ethiopia (Telephone Number in U.S. (800) 253-9646); *African Statistical Yearbook.*

The World Bank, 1818 H Street, NW, Washington, D.C. 20433 (202) 477-1234; *World Tables.*

NIGER - BANKING

Facts on File, 460 Park Avenue South, New York, New York 10016 (800) 443-8323; *The New Book of World Rankings.*

G.K. Hall and Company, 70 Lincoln Street, Boston, Massachusetts 02111 (617) 423-3990; *The World in Figures.*

International Monetary Fund, 700 Nineteenth Street, NW, Washington, D.C. 20431 (202) 623-7000; *International Financial Statistics.*

Statistical Office of the United Nations, Publishing Service, New York, New York 10017 (800) 253-9646; *Statistical Yearbook.*

United Nations Economic Commission for Africa, Africa Hall, Post Office Box 3001, Addis Ababa, Ethiopia (Telephone Number in U.S. (800) 253-9646); *African Statistical Yearbook.*

NIGER - BARLEY PRODUCTION - See NIGER - CROPS

NIGER - BEER PRODUCTION

Facts on File, 460 Park Avenue South, New York, New York 10016 (800) 443-8323; *The New Book of World Rankings.*

Statistical Office of the United Nations, Publishing Service, New York, New York 10017 (800) 253-9646; *Statistical Yearbook.*

NIGER - BIRTH RATES

Facts on File, 460 Park Avenue South, New York, New York 10016 (800) 443-8323; *The New Book of World Rankings.*

Statistical Office of the United Nations, Publishing Service, New York, New York 10017 (800) 253-9646; *Demographic Yearbook, Statistical Yearbook,* and *Survey of Economic and Social Conditions in Africa.*

Times Books, 201 East 50th Street, New York, New York 10022 (212) 751-2600; *The Economist Book of Vital World Statistics.*

The World Bank, 1818 H Street, NW, Washington, D.C. 20433 (202) 477-1234; *World Tables.*

NIGER - BONDS

G.K. Hall and Company, 70 Lincoln Street, Boston, Massachusetts 02111 (617) 423-3990; *The World in Figures.*

NIGER - BOOK PRODUCTION

G.K. Hall and Company, 70 Lincoln Street, Boston, Massachusetts 02111 (617) 423-3990; *The World in Figures.*

United Nations Educational, Scientific and Cultural Organization (UNESCO), 7 Place de Fontenoy, F-75700 Paris, France (Telephone Number in U.S. (212) 963-5981); *Statistical Yearbook.*

NIGER - BROADCASTING

Billboard Limited, Post Office Box 9027, 1006 AA Amsterdam, The Netherlands (Telephone Number in U.S. (212) 764-7300); *World Radio TV Handbook.*

Facts on File, 460 Park Avenue South, New York, New York 10016 (800) 443-8323; *The New Book of World Rankings.*

G.K. Hall and Company, 70 Lincoln Street, Boston, Massachusetts 02111 (617) 423-3990; *The World in Figures.*

Times Books, 201 East 50th Street, New York, New York 10022 (212) 751-2600; *The Economist Book of Vital World Statistics.*

NIGER - BUSINESS

G.K. Hall and Company, 70 Lincoln Street, Boston, Massachusetts 02111 (617) 423-3990; *The World in Figures.*

NIGER - BUSINESS AND PROFESSIONAL LICENSES

International Monetary Fund, 700 Nineteenth Street, NW, Washington, D.C. 20431 (202) 623-7000; *Government Finance Statistics Yearbook.*

NIGER - BUTTER PRODUCTION - See NIGER - DAIRY PRODUCTS

NIGER - CALORIE SUPPLY

African Development Bank, 01 BP 1387, Abidjan 01, Cote d'Ivoire; *Selected Statistics on Regional Member Countries.*

Food and Agricultural Organization of the United Nations (FAO) Via delle Terme di Caracalla, 00100 Rome, Italy (Telephone Number in U.S. (202) 653-2400); *The State of Food and Agriculture.*

NIGER - CAPITAL REVENUE

International Monetary Fund, 700 Nineteenth Street, NW, Washington, D.C. 20431 (202) 623-7000; *Government Finance Statistics Yearbook.*

NIGER - CATTLE - See NIGER - LIVESTOCK AND POULTRY

NIGER - CEMENT PRODUCTION - See NIGER - MINING AND MINERAL PRODUCTS

NIGER - CHEESE PRODUCTION AND CONSUMPTION - See NIGER - DAIRY PRODUCTS

NIGER - CHEMICAL (ORGANIC) PRODUCTION - See NIGER - MINING AND MINERAL PRODUCTS

NIGER - CHICKENS - See NIGER - LIVESTOCK AND POULTRY

NIGER - CIGARETTE PRODUCTION - See NIGER - TOBACCO PRODUCTION

NIGER - CLASS STRUCTURE

G.K. Hall and Company, 70 Lincoln Street, Boston, Massachusetts 02111 (617) 423-3990; *The World in Figures.*

NIGER - CLIMATE

Facts on File, 460 Park Avenue South, New York, New York 10016 (800) 443-8323; *The New Book of World Rankings.*

G.K. Hall and Company, 70 Lincoln Street, Boston, Massachusetts 02111 (617) 423-3990; *The World in Figures.*

NIGER - COAL PRODUCTION - See NIGER - MINING AND MINERAL PRODUCTS

NIGER - COFFEE PRODUCTION AND CONSUMPTION - See NIGER - CROPS

NIGER - COMMUNICATIONS

G.K. Hall and Company, 70 Lincoln Street, Boston, Massachusetts 02111 (617) 423-3990; *The World in Figures.*

United Nations Economic Commission for Africa, Africa Hall, Post Office Box 3001, Addis Ababa, Ethiopia (Telephone Number in U.S. (800) 253-9646); *African Statistical Yearbook.*

NIGER - CONSTRUCTION INDUSTRY

Facts on File, 460 Park Avenue South, New York, New York 10016 (800) 443-8323; *The New Book of World Rankings.*

United Nations Economic Commission for Africa, Africa Hall, Post Office Box 3001, Addis Ababa, Ethiopia (Telephone Number in U.S. (800) 253-9646); *African Statistical Yearbook.*

NIGER - CONSUMER PRICE INDEX

African Development Bank, 01 BP 1387, Abidjan 01, Cote d'Ivoire; *Selected Statistics on Regional Member Countries.*

G.K. Hall and Company, 70 Lincoln Street, Boston, Massachusetts 02111 (617) 423-3990; *The World in Figures.*

Statistical Office of the United Nations, Publishing Service, New York, New York 10017 (800) 253-9646; *Statistical Yearbook* and *Survey of Economic and Social Conditions in Africa.*

Times Books, 201 East 50th Street, New York, New York 10022 (212) 751-2600; *The Economist Book of Vital World Statistics.*

United Nations Economic Commission for Africa, Africa Hall, Post Office Box 3001, Addis Ababa, Ethiopia (Telephone Number in U.S. (800) 253-9646); *African Statistical Yearbook.*

NIGER - CONSUMER PRICES

International Labour Office, I.L.O. Publications, CH-1211, Geneva 22, Switzerland; *Yearbook of Labour Statistics.*

International Monetary Fund, 700 Nineteenth Street, NW, Washington, D.C. 20431 (202) 623-7000; *International Financial Statistics.*

NIGER - CONSUMPTION

African Development Bank, 01 BP 1387, Abidjan 01, Cote d'Ivoire; *Selected Statistics on Regional Member Countries.*

G.K. Hall and Company, 70 Lincoln Street, Boston, Massachusetts 02111 (617) 423-3990; *The World in Figures.*

Statistical Office of the United Nations, Publishing Service, New York 10017 (800) 253-9646; *Survey of Economic and Social Conditions in Africa.*

NIGER - COPPER PRODUCTION AND CONSUMPTION - See NIGER - MINING AND MINERAL PRODUCTS

NIGER - CORN PRODUCTION - See NIGER - CROPS

NIGER - CORPORATE TAXES - See NIGER - TAXATION

NIGER - COTTON PRODUCTION - See NIGER - CROPS

NIGER - CROPS

Facts on File, 460 Park Avenue South, New York, New York 10016 (800) 443-8323; *The New Book of World Rankings.*

Food and Agricultural Organization of the United Nations (FAO) Via delle Terme di Caracalla, 00100 Rome, Italy (Telephone Number in U.S. (202) 653-2400); *Production Yearbook,* and *The State of Food and Agriculture.*

G.K. Hall and Company, 70 Lincoln Street, Boston, Massachusetts 02111 (617) 423-3990; *The World in Figures.*

Statistical Office of the United Nations, Publishing Service, New York, New York 10017 (800) 253-9646; *Statistical Yearbook.*

U.C.L.A. Latin American Center Publications, University of California, Los Angeles, California 90024 (310) 825-6634; *Statistical Abstract of Latin America.*

United Nations Economic Commission for Africa, Africa Hall, Post Office Box 3001, Addis Ababa, Ethiopia (Telephone Number in U.S. (800) 253-9646); *African Statistical Yearbook.*

NIGER - CUSTOMS DUTIES

G.K. Hall and Company, 70 Lincoln Street, Boston, Massachusetts 02111 (617) 423-3990; *The World in Figures.*

International Monetary Fund, 700 Nineteenth Street, NW, Washington, D.C. 20431 (202) 623-7000; *Government Finance Statistics Yearbook.*

NIGER - DAIRY PRODUCTS

Facts on File, 460 Park Avenue South, New York, New York 10016 (800) 443-8323; *The New Book of World Rankings.*

Food and Agricultural Organization of the United Nations (FAO) Via delle Terme di Caracalla, 00100 Rome, Italy (Telephone Number in U.S. (202) 653-2400); *Production Yearbook,* and *The State of Food and Agriculture.*

Statistical Office of the United Nations, Publishing Service, New York, New York 10017 (800) 253-9646; *Statistical Yearbook.*

NIGER - DEATH RATES

G.K. Hall and Company, 70 Lincoln Street, Boston, Massachusetts 02111 (617) 423-3990; *The World in Figures.*

Statistical Office of the United Nations, Publishing Service, New York, New York 10017 (800) 253-9646; *Statistical Yearbook* and *Survey of Economic and Social Conditions in Africa.*

Times Books, 201 East 50th Street, New York, New York 10022 (212) 751-2600; *The Economist Book of Vital World Statistics.*

World Health Organization, Office of Publications, Avenue Appia, CH-1211 Geneva 27, Switzerland (Telephone Number in U.S. (518) 436-9686); *World Health Statistics Annual.*

NIGER - DEFENSE EXPENDITURES

G.K. Hall and Company, 70 Lincoln Street, Boston, Massachusetts 02111 (617) 423-3990; *The World in Figures.*

International Monetary Fund, 700 Nineteenth Street, NW, Washington, D.C. 20431 (202) 623-7000; *Government Finance Statistics Yearbook.*

U.S. Arms Control and Disarmament Agency, 320 Twenty-first Street, NW, Washington, D.C. 20451 (202) 647-8677; *World Military Expenditures and Arms Transfers.*

NIGER - DEMOGRAPHY

Facts on File, 460 Park Avenue South, New York, New York 10016 (800) 443-8323; *The New Book of World Rankings.*

G.K. Hall and Company, 70 Lincoln Street, Boston, Massachusetts 02111 (617) 423-3990; *The World in Figures.*

Statistical Office of the United Nations, Publishing Service, New York, New York 10017 (800) 253-9646; *Survey of Economic and Social Conditions in Africa.*

NIGER - DEVELOPMENT ASSISTANCE

G.K. Hall and Company, 70 Lincoln Street, Boston, Massachusetts 02111 (617) 423-3990; *The World in Figures.*

Statistical Office of the United Nations, Publishing Service, New York, New York 10017 (800) 253-9646; *Statistical Yearbook.*

NIGER - DIAMOND PRODUCTION - See NIGER - MINING AND MINERAL PRODUCTS

NIGER - DISCOUNT RATES

Statistical Office of the United Nations, Publishing Service, New York, New York 10017 (800) 253-9646; *Statistical Yearbook.*

NIGER - DISEASES

G.K. Hall and Company, 70 Lincoln Street, Boston, Massachusetts 02111 (617) 423-3990; *The World in Figures.*

World Health Organization, Office of Publications, Avenue Appia, CH-1211 Geneva 27, Switzerland (Telephone Number in U.S. (518) 436-9686); *World Health Statistics Annual.*

NIGER - DIVORCE RATES

Facts on File, 460 Park Avenue South, New York, New York 10016 (800) 443-8323; *The New Book of World Rankings.*

Statistical Office of the United Nations, Publishing Service, New York, New York 10017 (800) 253-9646; *Demographic Yearbook.*

NIGER - DOMESTIC PRODUCT

G.K. Hall and Company, 70 Lincoln Street, Boston, Massachusetts 02111 (617) 423-3990; *The World in Figures.*

NIGER - ECONOMY

African Development Bank, 01 BP 1387, Abidjan 01, Cote d'Ivoire; *Selected Statistics on Regional Member Countries.*

Euromonitor Publications Limited, 87-88 Turnmill Street, London EC1M 5QU, England; *International Marketing Data and Statistics.*

Facts on File, 460 Park Avenue South, New York, New York 10016 (800) 443-8323; *The New Book of World Rankings.*

G.K. Hall and Company, 70 Lincoln Street, Boston, Massachusetts 02111 (617) 423-3990; *The World in Figures.*

Statistical Office of the United Nations, Publishing Service, New York, New York 10017 (800) 253-9646; *Foreign Trade Statistics for Africa*.

NIGER - EDUCATION

African Development Bank, 01 BP 1387, Abidjan 01, Cote d'Ivoire; *Selected Statistics on Regional Member Countries*.

The Economist Intelligence Unit, 111 West 57th Street, New York, New York 10019 (800) 938-4685; *The World Market Atlas*.

Facts on File, 460 Park Avenue South, New York, New York 10016 (800) 443-8323; *The New Book of World Rankings*.

G.K. Hall and Company, 70 Lincoln Street, Boston, Massachusetts 02111 (617) 423-3990; *The World in Figures*.

International Monetary Fund, 700 Nineteenth Street, NW, Washington, D.C. 20431 (202) 623-7000; *Government Finance Statistics Yearbook*.

Statistical Office of the United Nations, Publishing Service, New York 10017 (800) 253-9646; *Survey of Economic and Social Conditions in Africa*.

Times Books, 201 East 50th Street, New York, New York 10022 (212) 751-2600; *The Economist Book of Vital World Statistics*.

United Nations Economic Commission for Africa, Africa Hall, Post Office Box 3001, Addis Ababa, Ethiopia (Telephone Number in U.S. (800) 253-9646); *African Statistical Yearbook*.

United Nations Educational, Scientific and Cultural Organization (UNESCO), 7 Place de Fontenoy, F-75700 Paris, France (Telephone Number in U.S. (212) 963-5981); *Statistical Yearbook*.

The World Bank, 1818 H Street, NW, Washington, D.C. 20433 (202) 477-1234; *World Tables*.

NIGER - EGG PRODUCTION AND CONSUMPTION - See NIGER - DAIRY PRODUCTS

NIGER - ELECTRICITY

Facts on File, 460 Park Avenue South, New York, New York 10016 (800) 443-8323; *The New Book of World Rankings*.

Statistical Office of the United Nations, Publishing Service, New York, New York 10017 (800) 253-9646; *Statistical Yearbook* and *Survey of Economic and Social Conditions in Africa*.

Times Books, 201 East 50th Street, New York, New York 10022 (212) 751-2600; *The Economist Book of Vital World Statistics*.

United Nations Economic Commission for Africa, Africa Hall, Post Office Box 3001, Addis Ababa, Ethiopia (Telephone Number in U.S. (800) 253-9646); *African Statistical Yearbook*.

NIGER - EMPLOYMENT

Euromonitor Publications Limited, 87-88 Turnmill Street, London EC1M 5QU, England; *International Marketing Data and Statistics*.

Facts on File, 460 Park Avenue South, New York, New York 10016 (800) 443-8323; *The New Book of World Rankings*.

International Labour Office, I.L.O. Publications, CH-1211, Geneva 22, Switzerland; *Yearbook of Labour Statistics*.

Statistical Office of the United Nations, Publishing Service, New York, New York 10017 (800) 253-9646; *Statistical Yearbook*, and *Survey of Economic and Social Conditions in Africa*.

United Nations Economic Commission for Africa, Africa Hall, Post Office Box 3001, Addis Ababa, Ethiopia (Telephone Number in U.S. (800) 253-9646); *African Statistical Yearbook*.

NIGER - ENERGY

Facts on File, 460 Park Avenue South, New York, New York 10016 (800) 443-8323; *The New Book of World Rankings*.

Food and Agricultural Organization of the United Nations (FAO) Via delle Terme di Caracalla, 00100 Rome, Italy (Telephone Number in U.S. (202) 653-2400); *The State of Food and Agriculture*.

G.K. Hall and Company, 70 Lincoln Street, Boston, Massachusetts 02111 (617) 423-3990; *The World in Figures*.

Statistical Office of the United Nations, Publishing Service, New York, New York 10017 (800) 253-9646; *Energy Statistics Yearbook Statistical Yearbook*, and *World Energy Supplies*.

Times Books, 201 East 50th Street, New York, New York 10022 (212) 751-2600; *The Economist Book of Vital World Statistics*.

United Nations Economic Commission for Africa, Africa Hall, Post Office Box 3001, Addis Ababa, Ethiopia (Telephone Number in U.S. (800) 253-9646); *African Statistical Yearbook*.

NIGER - EXCHANGE RATES

African Development Bank, 01 BP 1387, Abidjan 01, Cote d'Ivoire; *Selected Statistics on Regional Member Countries*.

Euromonitor Publications Limited, 87-88 Turnmill Street, London EC1M 5QU, England; *International Marketing Data and Statistics*.

International Monetary Fund, 700 Nineteenth Street, NW, Washington, D.C. 20431 (202) 623-7000; *International Financial Statistics*.

Statistical Office of the United Nations, Publishing Service, New York, New York 10017 (800) 253-9646; *Foreign Trade Statistics for Africa*, and *Statistical Yearbook*.

NIGER - EXCISE TAXES - See NIGER - TAXATION

NIGER - EXPORTS

African Development Bank, 01 BP 1387, Abidjan 01, Cote d'Ivoire; *Selected Statistics on Regional Member Countries*.

The Economist Intelligence Unit, 111 West 57th Street, New York, New York 10019 (800) 938-4685; *The World Market Atlas*.

Euromonitor Publications Limited, 87-88 Turnmill Street, London EC1M 5QU, England; *International Marketing Data and Statistics*.

Food and Agricultural Organization of the United Nations (FAO) Via delle Terme di Caracalla, 00100 Rome, Italy (Telephone Number in U.S. (202) 653-2400); *The State of Food and Agriculture*.

G.K. Hall and Company, 70 Lincoln Street, Boston, Massachusetts 02111 (617) 423-3990; *The World in Figures*.

International Monetary Fund, 700 Nineteenth Street, NW, Washington, D.C. 20431 (202) 623-7000; *Direction of Trade*

Statistics, and *Government Finance Statistics Yearbook.*

Statistical Office of the United Nations, Publishing Service, New York, New York 10017 (800) 253-9646; *Foreign Trade Statistics for Africa,* and *Survey of Economic and Social Conditions in Africa.*

Times Books, 201 East 50th Street, New York, New York 10022 (212) 751-2600; *The Economist Book of Vital World Statistics.*

United Nations Economic Commission for Africa, Africa Hall, Post Office Box 3001, Addis Ababa, Ethiopia (Telephone Number in U.S. (800) 253-9646); *African Statistical Yearbook.*

The World Bank, 1818 H Street, NW, Washington, D.C. 20433 (202) 477-1234; *World Tables.*

NIGER - EXTERNAL INDEBTEDNESS

African Development Bank, 01 BP 1387, Abidjan 01, Cote d'Ivoire; *Selected Statistics on Regional Member Countries.*

Statistical Office of the United Nations, Publishing Service, New York 10017 (800) 253-9646; *Survey of Economic and Social Conditions in Africa.*

The World Bank, 1818 H Street, NW, Washington, D.C. 20433 (202) 477-1234; *World Tables.*

NIGER - EXTERNAL TRADE

African Development Bank, 01 BP 1387, Abidjan 01, Cote d'Ivoire; *Selected Statistics on Regional Member Countries.*

Food and Agricultural Organization of the United Nations (FAO) Via delle Terme di Caracalla, 00100 Rome, Italy (Telephone Number in U.S. (202) 653-2400; *The State of Food and Agriculture,* and *Trade Yearbook.*

G.K. Hall and Company, 70 Lincoln Street, Boston, Massachusetts 02111 (617) 423-3990; *The World in Figures.*

Statistical Office of the United Nations, Publishing Service, New York, New York 10017 (800) 253-9646; *Statistical Yearbook.*

NIGER - FARM CROPS - See NIGER - CROPS

NIGER - FEMALE WORKING POPULATION - See NIGER - EMPLOYMENT

NIGER - FERTILITY RATES

Facts on File, 460 Park Avenue South, New York, New York 10016 (800) 443-8323; *The New Book of World Rankings.*

Statistical Office of the United Nations, Publishing Service, New York 10017 (800) 253-9646; *Survey of Economic and Social Conditions in Africa.*

Times Books, 201 East 50th Street, New York, New York 10022 (212) 751-2600; *The Economist Book of Vital World Statistics.*

The World Bank, 1818 H Street, NW, Washington, D.C. 20433 (202) 477-1234; *World Tables.*

NIGER - FERTILIZER

Food and Agricultural Organization of the United Nations (FAO), Via delle Terme di Caracalla, 00100 Rome, Italy (Telephone Number in U.S. (202) 653-2400; *Fertilizer Yearbook,* and *The State of Food*

and Agriculture.

Statistical Office of the United Nations, Publishing Service, New York, New York 10017 (800) 253-9646; *Statistical Yearbook.*

NIGER - FETAL MORTALITY

Statistical Office of the United Nations, Publishing Service, New York, New York 10017 (800) 253-9646; *Demographic Yearbook.*

NIGER - FINANCE

African Development Bank, 01 BP 1387, Abidjan 01, Cote d'Ivoire; *Selected Statistics on Regional Member Countries.*

Facts on File, 460 Park Avenue South, New York, New York 10016 (800) 443-8323; *The New Book of World Rankings.*

G.K. Hall and Company, 70 Lincoln Street, Boston, Massachusetts 02111 (617) 423-3990; *The World in Figures.*

International Monetary Fund, 700 Nineteenth Street, NW, Washington, D.C. 20431 (202) 623-7000; *International Financial Statistics.*

United Nations Economic Commission for Africa, Africa Hall, Post Office Box 3001, Addis Ababa, Ethiopia (Telephone Number in U.S. (800) 253-9646); *African Statistical Yearbook.*

NIGER - FISHERIES

Facts on File, 460 Park Avenue South, New York, New York 10016 (800) 443-8323; *The New Book of World Rankings.*

Food and Agricultural Organization of the United Nations (FAO) Via delle Terme di Caracalla, 00100 Rome, Italy (Telephone Number in U.S. (202) 653-2400; *The State of Food and Agriculture,* and *Yearbook of Fishery Statistics.*

Statistical Office of the United Nations, Publishing Service, New York, New York 10017 (800) 253-9646; *Statistical Yearbook,* and *Survey of Economic and Social Conditions in Africa.*

United Nations Economic Commission for Africa, Africa Hall, Post Office Box 3001, Addis Ababa, Ethiopia (Telephone Number in U.S. (800) 253-9646); *African Statistical Yearbook.*

NIGER - FOOD

African Development Bank, 01 BP 1387, Abidjan 01, Cote d'Ivoire; *Selected Statistics on Regional Member Countries.*

Food and Agricultural Organization of the United Nations (FAO), Via delle Terme di Caracalla, 00100 Rome, Italy (Telephone Number in U.S. (202) 653-2400; *Production Yearbook,* and *The State of Food and Agriculture.*

G.K. Hall and Company, 70 Lincoln Street, Boston, Massachusetts 02111 (617) 423-3990; *The World in Figures.*

NIGER - FOREIGN AID

G.K. Hall and Company, 70 Lincoln Street, Boston, Massachusetts 02111 (617) 423-3990; *The World in Figures.*

NIGER - FOREIGN TRADE

Euromonitor Publications Limited, 87-88 Turnmill Street, London EC1M 5QU, England; *International Marketing Data and Statistics.*

Facts on File, 460 Park Avenue South, New York, New York 10016 (800) 443-8323; *The New Book of World Rankings*.

Food and Agricultural Organization of the United Nations (FAO) Via delle Terme di Caracalla, 00100 Rome, Italy (Telephone Number in U.S. (202) 653-2400); *The State of Food and Agriculture*.

G.K. Hall and Company, 70 Lincoln Street, Boston, Massachusetts 02111 (617) 423-3990; *The World in Figures*.

International Monetary Fund, 700 Nineteenth Street, NW, Washington, D.C. 20431 (202) 623-7000; *International Financial Statistics*.

Statistical Office of the United Nations, Publishing Service, New York, New York 10017 (800) 253-9646; *Foreign Trade Statistics for Africa, International Trade Statistics Yearbook, Statistical Yearbook,* and *Trade in Manufactures of Developing Countries*.

United Nations Economic Commission for Africa, Africa Hall, Post Office Box 3001, Addis Ababa, Ethiopia (Telephone Number in U.S. (800) 253-9646); *African Statistical Yearbook*.

The World Bank, 1818 H Street, NW, Washington, D.C. 20433 (202) 477-1234; *World Tables*.

NIGER - FORESTRY AND FOREST PRODUCTS

Facts on File, 460 Park Avenue South, New York, New York 10016 (800) 443-8323; *The New Book of World Rankings*.

Food and Agricultural Organization of the United Nations (FAO) Via delle Terme di Caracalla, 00100 Rome, Italy (Telephone Number in U.S. (202) 653-2400); *The State of Food and Agriculture*, and *Yearbook of Forest Products*.

G.K. Hall and Company, 70 Lincoln Street, Boston, Massachusetts 02111 (617) 423-3990; *The World in Figures*.

Statistical Office of the United Nations, Publishing Service, New York, New York 10017 (800) 253-9646; *Statistical Yearbook*.

United Nations Economic Commission for Africa, Africa Hall, Post Office Box 3001, Addis Ababa, Ethiopia (Telephone Number in U.S. (800) 253-9646); *African Statistical Yearbook*.

United Nations Educational, Scientific and Cultural Organization (UNESCO), 7 Place de Fontenoy, F-75700 Paris, France (Telephone Number in U.S. (212) 963-5981); *Statistical Yearbook*.

NIGER - GAS PRODUCTION - See NIGER - MINING AND MINERAL PRODUCTS

NIGER - GENERAL MORTALITY

Statistical Office of the United Nations, Publishing Service, New York, New York 10017 (800) 253-9646; *Demographic Yearbook*.

NIGER - GEOGRAPHIC DATA

Facts on File, 460 Park Avenue South, New York, New York 10016 (800) 443-8323; *The New Book of World Rankings*.

NIGER - GOATS - See NIGER - LIVESTOCK AND POULTRY

NIGER - GOLD HOLDINGS

International Monetary Fund, 700 Nineteenth Street, NW, Washington, D.C. 20431 (202) 623-7000; *International Financial Statistics*.

Statistical Office of the United Nations, Publishing Service, New York, New York 10017 (800) 253-9646; *Statistical Yearbook*.

The World Bank, 1818 H Street, NW, Washington, D.C. 20433 (202) 477-1234; *World Tables*.

NIGER - GOLD PRODUCTION AND CONSUMPTION - See NIGER - MINING AND MINERAL PRODUCTS

NIGER - GOVERNMENT

G.K. Hall and Company, 70 Lincoln Street, Boston, Massachusetts 02111 (617) 423-3990; *The World in Figures*.

NIGER - GOVERNMENT EXPENDITURES

International Monetary Fund, 700 Nineteenth Street, NW, Washington, D.C. 20431 (202) 623-7000; *Government Finance Statistics Yearbook*.

The World Bank, 1818 H Street, NW, Washington, D.C. 20433 (202) 477-1234; *World Tables*.

NIGER - GOVERNMENT FINANCES

International Monetary Fund, 700 Nineteenth Street, NW, Washington, D.C. 20431 (202) 623-7000; *International Financial Statistics*.

NIGER - GOVERNMENT REVENUES

International Monetary Fund, 700 Nineteenth Street, NW, Washington, D.C. 20431 (202) 623-7000; *Government Finance Statistics Yearbook*.

Statistical Office of the United Nations, Publishing Service, New York 10017 (800) 253-9646; *Survey of Economic and Social Conditions in Africa*.

Times Books, 201 East 50th Street, New York, New York 10022 (212) 751-2600; *The Economist Book of Vital World Statistics*.

The World Bank, 1818 H Street, NW, Washington, D.C. 20433 (202) 477-1234; *World Tables*.

NIGER - GRAIN PRODUCTION - See NIGER - CROPS

NIGER - GRANTS

International Monetary Fund, 700 Nineteenth Street, NW, Washington, D.C. 20431 (202) 623-7000; *Government Finance Statistics Yearbook*.

NIGER - GROSS DOMESTIC PRODUCT

African Development Bank, 01 BP 1387, Abidjan 01, Cote d'Ivoire; *Selected Statistics on Regional Member Countries*.

The Economist Intelligence Unit, 111 West 57th Street, New York, New York 10019 (800) 938-4685; *The World Market Atlas*.

Euromonitor Publications Limited, 87-88 Turnmill Street, London EC1M 5QU, England; *International Marketing Data and Statistics*.

Facts on File, 460 Park Avenue South, New York, New York 10016 (800) 443-8323; *The New Book of World Rankings*.

G.K. Hall and Company, 70 Lincoln Street, Boston, Massachusetts 02111 (617) 423-3990; *The World in Figures*.

Statistical Office of the United Nations, Publishing Service, New York, New York 10017 (800) 253-9646; *Statistical Yearbook*, and *Survey of Economic and Social Conditions in Africa*.

Times Books, 201 East 50th Street, New York, New York 10022 (212) 751-2600; *The Economist Book of Vital World Statistics*.

United Nations Economic Commission for Africa, Africa Hall, Post Office Box 3001, Addis Ababa, Ethiopia (Telephone Number in U.S. (800) 253-9646; *African Statistical Yearbook*.

The World Bank, 1818 H Street, NW, Washington, D.C. 20433 (202) 477-1234; *World Tables*.

NIGER - GROSS NATIONAL PRODUCT

Euromonitor Publications Limited, 87-88 Turnmill Street, London EC1M 5QU, England; *International Marketing Data and Statistics*.

U.S. Arms Control and Disarmament Agency, 320 Twenty-first Street, NW, Washington, D.C. 20451 (202) 647-8677; *World Military Expenditures and Arms Transfers*.

The World Bank, 1818 H Street, NW, Washington, D.C. 20433 (202) 477-1234; *World Tables*.

NIGER - GROUNDNUT PRODUCTION - See NIGER - CROPS

NIGER - HEALTH

African Development Bank, 01 BP 1387, Abidjan 01, Cote d'Ivoire; *Selected Statistics on Regional Member Countries*.

Facts on File, 460 Park Avenue South, New York, New York 10016 (800) 443-8323; *The New Book of World Rankings*.

G.K. Hall and Company, 70 Lincoln Street, Boston, Massachusetts 02111 (617) 423-3990; *The World in Figures*.

Statistical Office of the United Nations, Publishing Service, New York, New York 10017 (800) 253-9646; *Statistical Yearbook*.

Times Books, 201 East 50th Street, New York, New York 10022 (212) 751-2600; *The Economist Book of Vital World Statistics*.

United Nations Economic Commission for Africa, Africa Hall, Post Office Box 3001, Addis Ababa, Ethiopia (Telephone Number in U.S. (800) 253-9646; *African Statistical Yearbook*.

World Health Organization, Office of Publications, Avenue Appia, CH-1211 Geneva 27, Switzerland (Telephone Number in U.S. (518) 436-9686); *World Health Statistics Annual*.

NIGER - HEALTH EXPENDITURES

International Monetary Fund, 700 Nineteenth Street, NW, Washington, D.C. 20431 (202) 623-7000; *Government Finance Statistics Yearbook*.

NIGER - HIDE PRODUCTION

Food and Agricultural Organization of the United Nations (FAO), Via delle Terme di Caracalla, 00100 Rome, Italy (Telephone Number in U.S. (202) 653-2400; *Production Yearbook*.

NIGER - HIGHWAYS

G.K. Hall and Company, 70 Lincoln Street, Boston, Massachusetts 02111 (617) 423-3990; *The World in Figures*.

Statistical Office of the United Nations, Publishing Service, New York 10017 (800) 253-9646; *Survey of Economic and Social Conditions in Africa*.

United Nations Economic Commission for Africa, Africa Hall, Post Office Box 3001, Addis Ababa, Ethiopia (Telephone Number in U.S. (800) 253-9646; *African Statistical Yearbook*.

NIGER - HORSES - See NIGER - LIVESTOCK AND POULTRY

NIGER - HOURS OF WORK - See NIGER - EMPLOYMENT

NIGER - HOUSING EXPENDITURES

Facts on File, 460 Park Avenue South, New York, New York 10016 (800) 443-8323; *The New Book of World Rankings*.

International Monetary Fund, 700 Nineteenth Street, NW, Washington, D.C. 20431 (202) 623-7000; *Government Finance Statistics Yearbook*.

NIGER - ILLITERATE POPULATION

The Economist Intelligence Unit, 111 West 57th Street, New York, New York 10019 (800) 938-4685; *The World Market Atlas*.

G.K. Hall and Company, 70 Lincoln Street, Boston, Massachusetts 02111 (617) 423-3990; *The World in Figures*.

United Nations Educational, Scientific and Cultural Organization (UNESCO), 7 Place de Fontenoy, F-75700 Paris, France (Telephone Number in U.S. (212) 963-5981); *Statistical Yearbook*.

NIGER - IMPORTS

African Development Bank, 01 BP 1387, Abidjan 01, Cote d'Ivoire; *Selected Statistics on Regional Member Countries*.

The Economist Intelligence Unit, 111 West 57th Street, New York, New York 10019 (800) 938-4685; *The World Market Atlas*.

Euromonitor Publications Limited, 87-88 Turnmill Street, London EC1M 5QU, England; *International Marketing Data and Statistics*.

Food and Agricultural Organization of the United Nations (FAO) Via delle Terme di Caracalla, 00100 Rome, Italy (Telephone Number in U.S. (202) 653-2400); *The State of Food and Agriculture*.

G.K. Hall and Company, 70 Lincoln Street, Boston, Massachusetts 02111 (617) 423-3990; *The World in Figures*.

International Monetary Fund, 700 Nineteenth Street, NW, Washington, D.C. 20431 (202) 623-7000; *Direction of Trade Statistics*, and *Government Finance Statistics Yearbook*.

Statistical Office of the United Nations, Publishing Service, New York, New York 10017 (800) 253-9646; *Foreign Trade Statistics for Africa, Trade in Manufactures of Developing Countries* and *Survey of Economic and Social Conditions in Africa*.

Times Books, 201 East 50th Street, New York, New York 10022 (212) 751-2600; *The Economist Book of Vital World Statistics*.

United Nations Economic Commission for Africa, Africa Hall, Post Office Box 3001, Addis Ababa, Ethiopia (Telephone Number in U.S. (800) 253-9646); *African Statistical Yearbook.*

The World Bank, 1818 H Street, NW, Washington, D.C. 20433 (202) 477-1234; *World Tables.*

NIGER - INCOME TAXES - See NIGER - TAXATION

NIGER - INDUSTRY

Euromonitor Publications Limited, 87-88 Turnmill Street, London EC1M 5QU, England; *International Marketing Data and Statistics.*

Facts on File, 460 Park Avenue South, New York, New York 10016 (800) 443-8323; *The New Book of World Rankings.*

G.K. Hall and Company, 70 Lincoln Street, Boston, Massachusetts 02111 (617) 423-3990; *The World in Figures.*

International Labour Office, I.L.O. Publications, CH-1211, Geneva 22, Switzerland; *Yearbook of Labour Statistics.*

Times Books, 201 East 50th Street, New York, New York 10022 (212) 751-2600; *The Economist Book of Vital World Statistics.*

Statistical Office of the United Nations, Publishing Service, New York 10017 (800) 253-9646; *Survey of Economic and Social Conditions in Africa.*

United Nations Economic Commission for Africa, Africa Hall, Post Office Box 3001, Addis Ababa, Ethiopia (Telephone Number in U.S. (800) 253-9646); *African Statistical Yearbook.*

The World Bank, 1818 H Street, NW, Washington, D.C. 20433 (202) 477-1234; *World Tables.*

NIGER - INFANT AND MATERNAL MORTALITY

Statistical Office of the United Nations, Publishing Service, New York, New York 10017 (800) 253-9646; *Demographic Yearbook, Statistical Yearbook,* and *Survey of Economic and Social Conditions in Africa.*

Times Books, 201 East 50th Street, New York, New York 10022 (212) 751-2600; *The Economist Book of Vital World Statistics.*

The World Bank, 1818 H Street, NW, Washington, D.C. 20433 (202) 477-1234; *World Tables.*

NIGER - INTERNATIONAL LIQUIDITY

International Monetary Fund, 700 Nineteenth Street, NW, Washington, D.C. 20431 (202) 623-7000; *International Financial Statistics.*

NIGER - INTERNATIONAL RESERVES EXCLUDING GOLD

African Development Bank, 01 BP 1387, Abidjan 01, Cote d'Ivoire; *Selected Statistics on Regional Member Countries.*

Statistical Office of the United Nations, Publishing Service, New York, New York 10017 (800) 253-9646; *Statistical Yearbook.*

The World Bank, 1818 H Street, NW, Washington, D.C. 20433 (202) 477-1234; *World Tables.*

NIGER - IRON ORE PRODUCTION AND CONSUMPTION - See NIGER - MINING AND MINERAL PRODUCTS

NIGER - IRRIGATION

Euromonitor Publications Limited, 87-88 Turnmill Street, London EC1M 5QU, England; *International Marketing Data and Statistics.*

NIGER - LABOR FORCE

African Development Bank, 01 BP 1387, Abidjan 01, Cote d'Ivoire; *Selected Statistics on Regional Member Countries.*

Euromonitor Publications Limited, 87-88 Turnmill Street, London EC1M 5QU, England; *International Marketing Data and Statistics.*

Facts on File, 460 Park Avenue South, New York, New York 10016 (800) 443-8323; *The New Book of World Rankings.*

Food and Agricultural Organization of the United Nations (FAO) Via delle Terme di Caracalla, 00100 Rome, Italy (Telephone Number in U.S. (202) 653-2400); *The State of Food and Agriculture.*

G.K. Hall and Company, 70 Lincoln Street, Boston, Massachusetts 02111 (617) 423-3990; *The World in Figures.*

The World Bank, 1818 H Street, NW, Washington, D.C. 20433 (202) 477-1234; *World Tables.*

NIGER - LABOR PRODUCTIVITY

International Labour Office, I.L.O. Publications, CH-1211, Geneva 22, Switzerland; *Yearbook of Labour Statistics.*

NIGER - LAND USE

Euromonitor Publications Limited, 87-88 Turnmill Street, London EC1M 5QU, England; *International Marketing Data and Statistics.*

Food and Agricultural Organization of the United Nations (FAO), Via delle Terme di Caracalla, 00100 Rome, Italy (Telephone Number in U.S. (202) 653-2400); *Production Yearbook.*

G.K. Hall and Company, 70 Lincoln Street, Boston, Massachusetts 02111 (617) 423-3990; *The World in Figures.*

NIGER - LIBRARIES

Facts on File, 460 Park Avenue South, New York, New York 10016 (800) 443-8323; *The New Book of World Rankings.*

United Nations Educational, Scientific and Cultural Organization (UNESCO), 7 Place de Fontenoy, F-75700 Paris, France (Telephone Number in U.S. (212) 963-5981); *Statistical Yearbook.*

NIGER - LIFE EXPECTANCY

African Development Bank, 01 BP 1387, Abidjan 01, Cote d'Ivoire; *Selected Statistics on Regional Member Countries.*

NIGER - LITERACY RATE

Statistical Office of the United Nations, Publishing Service, New York, New York 10017 (800) 253-9646; *Survey of Economic and Social Conditions in Africa.*

NIGER - LIVESTOCK AND POULTRY

Euromonitor Publications Limited, 87-88 Turnmill Street, London EC1M 5QU, England; *International Marketing Data and Statistics.*

Facts on File, 460 Park Avenue South, New York, New York 10016 (800) 443-8323; *The New Book of World Rankings*.

Food and Agricultural Organization of the United Nations (FAO), Via delle Terme di Caracalla, 00100 Rome, Italy (Telephone Number in U.S. (202) 653-2400); *Production Yearbook*, and *The State of Food and Agriculture*.

G.K. Hall and Company, 70 Lincoln Street, Boston, Massachusetts 02111 (617) 423-3990; *The World in Figures*.

Statistical Office of the United Nations, Publishing Service, New York, New York 10017 (800) 253-9646; *Statistical Yearbook*, and *Survey of Economic and Social Conditions in Africa*.

United Nations Economic Commission for Africa, Africa Hall, Post Office Box 3001, Addis Ababa, Ethiopia (Telephone Number in U.S. (800) 253-9646); *African Statistical Yearbook*.

NIGER - LIVING LEVELS

G.K. Hall and Company, 70 Lincoln Street, Boston, Massachusetts 02111 (617) 423-3990; *The World in Figures*.

Times Books, 201 East 50th Street, New York, New York 10022 (212) 751-2600; *The Economist Book of Vital World Statistics*.

NIGER - MAIL - PIECES SENT OR RECEIVED

Statistical Office of the United Nations, Publishing Service, New York, New York 10017 (800) 253-9646; *Statistical Yearbook*.

NIGER - MANUFACTURING

Facts on File, 460 Park Avenue South, New York, New York 10016 (800) 443-8323; *The New Book of World Rankings*.

G.K. Hall and Company, 70 Lincoln Street, Boston, Massachusetts 02111 (617) 423-3990; *The World in Figures*.

Statistical Office of the United Nations, Publishing Service, New York, New York 10017 (800) 253-9646; *Statistical Yearbook*, and *Survey of Economic and Social Conditions in Africa*.

United Nations Economic Commission for Africa, Africa Hall, Post Office Box 3001, Addis Ababa, Ethiopia (Telephone Number in U.S. (800) 253-9646); *African Statistical Yearbook*.

The World Bank, 1818 H Street, NW, Washington, D.C. 20433 (202) 477-1234; *World Tables*.

NIGER - MARRIAGE RATES

Facts on File, 460 Park Avenue South, New York, New York 10016 (800) 443-8323; *The New Book of World Rankings*.

Statistical Office of the United Nations, Publishing Service, New York, New York 10017 (800) 253-9646; *Demographic Yearbook*.

NIGER - MEAT PRODUCTION - ALL TYPES OF MEAT AND POULTRY

Facts on File, 460 Park Avenue South, New York, New York 10016 (800) 443-8323; *The New Book of World Rankings*.

Food and Agricultural Organization of the United Nations (FAO), Via delle Terme di Caracalla, 00100 Rome, Italy (Telephone Number in U.S. (202) 653-2400); *Production Yearbook*, and *The State of Food and Agriculture*.

Statistical Office of the United Nations, Publishing Service, New York, New York 10017 (800) 253-9646; *Statistical Yearbook*.

NIGER - MERCHANT SHIPPING

G.K. Hall and Company, 70 Lincoln Street, Boston, Massachusetts 02111 (617) 423-3990; *The World in Figures*.

Times Books, 201 East 50th Street, New York, New York 10022 (212) 751-2600; *The Economist Book of Vital World Statistics*.

United Nations Economic Commission for Africa, Africa Hall, Post Office Box 3001, Addis Ababa, Ethiopia (Telephone Number in U.S. (800) 253-9646); *African Statistical Yearbook*.

NIGER - MILITARY

G.K. Hall and Company, 70 Lincoln Street, Boston, Massachusetts 02111 (617) 423-3990; *The World in Figures*.

The International Institute for Strategic Studies, 23 Tavistock Street, London WC2E 7NQ, England; *The Military Balance*.

U.S. Arms Control and Disarmament Agency, 320 Twenty-first Street, NW, Washington, D.C. 20451 (202) 647-8677; *World Military Expenditures and Arms Transfers*.

NIGER - MILK PRODUCTION - See NIGER - DAIRY PRODUCTS

NIGER - MILLET PRODUCTION - See NIGER - CROPS

NIGER - MINING AND MINERAL PRODUCTS

Commodity Research Bureau, Incorporated, 75 Wall Street, New York, New York 10005 (212) 504-7754; *Commodity Year Book*.

Facts on File, 460 Park Avenue South, New York, New York 10016 (800) 443-8323; *The New Book of World Rankings*.

G.K. Hall and Company, 70 Lincoln Street, Boston, Massachusetts 02111 (617) 423-3990; *The World in Figures*.

Statistical Office of the United Nations, Publishing Service, New York, New York 10017 (800) 253-9646; *Statistical Yearbook*.

United Nations Economic Commission for Africa, Africa Hall, Post Office Box 3001, Addis Ababa, Ethiopia (Telephone Number in U.S. (800) 253-9646); *African Statistical Yearbook*.

NIGER - MONEY EXCHANGE RATE

Euromonitor Publications Limited, 87-88 Turnmill Street, London EC1M 5QU, England; *International Marketing Data and Statistics*.

International Monetary Fund, 700 Nineteenth Street, NW, Washington, D.C. 20431 (202) 623-7000; *International Financial Statistics*.

Statistical Office of the United Nations, Publishing Service, New York, New York 10017 (800) 253-9646; *Statistical Yearbook*.

NIGER - MONEY RESERVES

Euromonitor Publications Limited, 87-88 Turnmill Street, London EC1M 5QU, England; *International Marketing Data and Statistics*.

NIGER - MONEY SUPPLY

African Development Bank, 01 BP 1387, Abidjan 01, Cote d'Ivoire; *Selected Statistics on Regional Member Countries*.

Euromonitor Publications Limited, 87-88 Turnmill Street, London EC1M 5QU, England; *International Marketing Data and Statistics*.

G.K. Hall and Company, 70 Lincoln Street, Boston, Massachusetts 02111 (617) 423-3990; *The World in Figures*.

International Monetary Fund, 700 Nineteenth Street, NW, Washington, D.C. 20431 (202) 623-7000; *International Financial Statistics*.

Statistical Office of the United Nations, Publishing Service, New York, New York 10017 (800) 253-9646; *Statistical Yearbook*.

The World Bank, 1818 H Street, NW, Washington, D.C. 20433 (202) 477-1234; *World Tables*.

NIGER - MOTOR VEHICLE TAXES - See NIGER - TAXATION

NIGER - MOTOR VEHICLES IN USE

G.K. Hall and Company, 70 Lincoln Street, Boston, Massachusetts 02111 (617) 423-3990; *The World in Figures*.

Statistical Office of the United Nations, Publishing Service, New York, New York 10017 (800) 253-9646; *Statistical Yearbook*, and *Survey of Economic and Social Conditions in Africa*.

Times Books, 201 East 50th Street, New York, New York 10022 (212) 751-2600; *The Economist Book of Vital World Statistics*.

NIGER - MUSEUMS

Facts on File, 460 Park Avenue South, New York, New York 10016 (800) 443-8323; *The New Book of World Rankings*.

United Nations Educational, Scientific and Cultural Organization (UNESCO), 7 Place de Fontenoy, F-75700 Paris, France (Telephone Number in U.S. (212) 963-5981); *Statistical Yearbook*.

NIGER - NATALITY - See NIGER - BIRTH RATES

NIGER - NATIONAL ACCOUNTS

African Development Bank, 01 BP 1387, Abidjan 01, Cote d'Ivoire; *Selected Statistics on Regional Member Countries*.

International Monetary Fund, 700 Nineteenth Street, NW, Washington, D.C. 20431 (202) 623-7000; *International Financial Statistics*.

Statistical Office of the United Nations, Publishing Service, New York, New York 10017 (800) 253-9646; *Statistical Yearbook*.

United Nations Economic Commission for Africa, Africa Hall, Post Office Box 3001, Addis Ababa, Ethiopia (Telephone Number in U.S. (800) 253-9646); *African Statistical Yearbook*.

NIGER - NATIONAL INCOME

Facts on File, 460 Park Avenue South, New York, New York 10016 (800) 443-8323; *The New Book of World Rankings*.

G.K. Hall and Company, 70 Lincoln Street, Boston, Massachusetts 02111 (617) 423-3990; *The World in Figures*.

Statistical Office of the United Nations, Publishing Service, New York, New York 10017 (800) 253-9646; *Statistical Yearbook*.

NIGER - NATIONAL PRODUCT

Facts on File, 460 Park Avenue South, New York, New York 10016 (800) 443-8323; *The New Book of World Rankings*.

NIGER - NATURAL GAS PRODUCTION - See NIGER - MINING AND MINERAL PRODUCTS

NIGER - NEWSPAPER PRODUCTION - See NIGER - FORESTRY AND FOREST PRODUCTS

NIGER - NEWSPRINT - See NIGER - FORESTRY AND FOREST PRODUCTS

NIGER - OCCUPATIONS - See NIGER - LABOR FORCE

NIGER - PAPER - See NIGER - FORESTRY AND FOREST PRODUCTS

NIGER - PEANUT PRODUCTION - See NIGER - CROPS

NIGER - PERIODICALS

United Nations Educational, Scientific and Cultural Organization (UNESCO), 7 Place de Fontenoy, F-75700 Paris, France (Telephone Number in U.S. (212) 963-5981); *Statistical Yearbook*.

NIGER - PESTICIDE USE

Food and Agricultural Organization of the United Nations (FAO) Via delle Terme di Caracalla, 00100 Rome, Italy (Telephone Number in U.S. (202) 653-2400); *The State of Food and Agriculture*.

NIGER - PETROLEUM INDUSTRY

Facts on File, 460 Park Avenue South, New York, New York 10016 (800) 443-8323; *The New Book of World Rankings*.

Food and Agricultural Organization of the United Nations (FAO) Via delle Terme di Caracalla, 00100 Rome, Italy (Telephone Number in U.S. (202) 653-2400); *The State of Food and Agriculture*.

G.K. Hall and Company, 70 Lincoln Street, Boston, Massachusetts 02111 (617) 423-3990; *The World in Figures*.

NIGER - PIGS - See NIGER - LIVESTOCK AND POULTRY

NIGER - POPULATION

African Development Bank, 01 BP 1387, Abidjan 01, Cote d'Ivoire; *Selected Statistics on Regional Member Countries*.

The Economist Intelligence Unit, 111 West 57th Street, New York, New York 10019 (800) 938-4685; *The World Market Atlas*.

Euromonitor Publications Limited, 87-88 Turnmill Street, London EC1M 5QU, England; *International Marketing Data and Statistics*.

Facts on File, 460 Park Avenue South, New York, New York 10016 (800) 443-8323; *The New Book of World Rankings*.

Food and Agricultural Organization of the United Nations (FAO), Via delle Terme di Caracalla, 00100 Rome, Italy (Telephone Number in U.S. (202) 653-2400); *Production Yearbook*.

G.K. Hall and Company, 70 Lincoln Street, Boston, Massachusetts 02111 (617) 423-3990; *The World in Figures*.

International Labour Office, I.L.O. Publications, CH-1211, Geneva 22, Switzerland; *Yearbook of Labour Statistics.*

Statistical Office of the United Nations, Publishing Service, New York, New York 10017 (800) 253-9646; *Demographic Yearbook, Statistical Yearbook,* and *Survey of Economic and Social Conditions in Africa.*

Times Books, 201 East 50th Street, New York, New York 10022 (212) 751-2600; *The Economist Book of Vital World Statistics.*

United Nations Educational, Scientific and Cultural Organization (UNESCO), 7 Place de Fontenoy, F-75700 Paris, France (Telephone Number in U.S. (212) 963-5981); *Statistical Yearbook.*

U.S. Arms Control and Disarmament Agency, 320 Twenty-first Street, NW, Washington, D.C. 20451 (202) 647-8677; *World Military Expenditures and Arms Transfers.*

World Health Organization, Office of Publications, Avenue Appia, CH-1211 Geneva 27, Switzerland (Telephone Number in U.S. (518) 436-9686); *World Health Statistics Annual.*

NIGER - POST OFFICES

Facts on File, 460 Park Avenue South, New York, New York 10016 (800) 443-8323; *The New Book of World Rankings.*

NIGER - POTATO PRODUCTION - See NIGER - CROPS

NIGER - PRICES

Facts on File, 460 Park Avenue South, New York, New York 10016 (800) 443-8323; *The New Book of World Rankings.*

Food and Agricultural Organization of the United Nations (FAO), Via delle Terme di Caracalla, 00100 Rome, Italy (Telephone Number in U.S. (202) 653-2400); *Production Yearbook,* and *The State of Food and Agriculture.*

G.K. Hall and Company, 70 Lincoln Street, Boston, Massachusetts 02111 (617) 423-3990; *The World in Figures.*

International Labour Office, I.L.O. Publications, CH-1211, Geneva 22, Switzerland; *Yearbook of Labour Statistics.*

International Monetary Fund, 700 Nineteenth Street, NW, Washington, D.C. 20431 (202) 623-7000; *International Financial Statistics.*

United Nations Economic Commission for Africa, Africa Hall, Post Office Box 3001, Addis Ababa, Ethiopia (Telephone Number in U.S. (800) 253-9646); *African Statistical Yearbook.*

NIGER - PRINTING AND WRITING PAPER - See NIGER - FORESTRY AND FOREST PRODUCTS

NIGER - PRODUCTION

Facts on File, 460 Park Avenue South, New York, New York 10016 (800) 443-8323; *The New Book of World Rankings.*

G.K. Hall and Company, 70 Lincoln Street, Boston, Massachusetts 02111 (617) 423-3990; *The World in Figures.*

NIGER - PRODUCTIVITY

Euromonitor Publications Limited, 87-88 Turnmill Street, London EC1M 5QU, England; *International Marketing Data and Statistics.*

NIGER - PROPERTY TAXES

International Monetary Fund, 700 Nineteenth Street, NW, Washington, D.C. 20431 (202) 623-7000; *Government Finance Statistics Yearbook.*

NIGER - PUBLIC FINANCE

Facts on File, 460 Park Avenue South, New York, New York 10016 (800) 443-8323; *The New Book of World Rankings.*

NIGER - RADIO BROADCASTING - See NIGER - BROADCASTING

NIGER - RAILWAYS

G.K. Hall and Company, 70 Lincoln Street, Boston, Massachusetts 02111 (617) 423-3990; *The World in Figures.*

United Nations Economic Commission for Africa, Africa Hall, Post Office Box 3001, Addis Ababa, Ethiopia (Telephone Number in U.S. (800) 253-9646); *African Statistical Yearbook.*

NIGER - RELIGION

Facts on File, 460 Park Avenue South, New York, New York 10016 (800) 443-8323; *The New Book of World Rankings.*

NIGER - RETAIL TRADE

G.K. Hall and Company, 70 Lincoln Street, Boston, Massachusetts 02111 (617) 423-3990; *The World in Figures.*

NIGER - RICE PRODUCTION - See NIGER - CROPS

NIGER - ROOT AND TUBER PRODUCTION - See NIGER - CROPS

NIGER - ROUNDWOOD PRODUCTION - See NIGER - FORESTRY AND FOREST PRODUCTS

NIGER - RUBBER PRODUCTION AND CONSUMPTION

Facts on File, 460 Park Avenue South, New York, New York 10016 (800) 443-8323; *The New Book of World Rankings.*

NIGER - SALT PRODUCTION - See NIGER - MINING AND MINERAL PRODUCTS

NIGER - SAWNWOOD PRODUCTION - See NIGER - FORESTRY AND FOREST PRODUCTS

NIGER - SCIENCE AND TECHNOLOGY - EXPENDITURE FOR RESEARCH

Statistical Office of the United Nations, Publishing Service, New York, New York 10017 (800) 253-9646; *Statistical Yearbook.*

NIGER - SCIENTISTS AND TECHNICIANS

Statistical Office of the United Nations, Publishing Service, New York, New York 10017 (800) 253-9646; *Statistical Yearbook.*

NIGER - SENIOR CITIZENS

Facts on File, 460 Park Avenue South, New York, New York 10016 (800) 443-8323; *The New Book of World Rankings.*

NIGER - SHEEP - See NIGER - LIVESTOCK AND POULTRY

NIGER - SILVER PRODUCTION AND CONSUMPTION - See NIGER - MINING AND MINERAL PRODUCTS

NIGER - SOCIAL DATA

African Development Bank, 01 BP 1387, Abidjan 01, Cote d'Ivoire; *Selected Statistics on Regional Member Countries.*

Facts on File, 460 Park Avenue South, New York, New York 10016 (800) 443-8323; *The New Book of World Rankings.*

G.K. Hall and Company, 70 Lincoln Street, Boston, Massachusetts 02111 (617) 423-3990; *The World in Figures.*

NIGER - SOCIAL SECURITY

International Monetary Fund, 700 Nineteenth Street, NW, Washington, D.C. 20431 (202) 623-7000; *Government Finance Statistics Yearbook.*

NIGER - STAMP TAXES AND DUTIES - See NIGER - TAXATION

NIGER - STATE BUDGET REVENUE AND EXPENDITURES

Euromonitor Publications Limited, 87-88 Turnmill Street, London EC1M 5QU, England; *International Marketing Data and Statistics.*

NIGER - STEEL PRODUCTION - See NIGER - MINING AND MINERAL PRODUCTS

NIGER - STOCKS - COMMODITY - MARKET PRICE - INDEX

Food and Agricultural Organization of the United Nations (FAO) Via delle Terme di Caracalla, 00100 Rome, Italy (Telephone Number in U.S. (202) 653-2400); *The State of Food and Agriculture.*

NIGER - SUGAR PRODUCTION AND CONSUMPTION - See NIGER - CROPS

NIGER - TAXATION

G.K. Hall and Company, 70 Lincoln Street, Boston, Massachusetts 02111 (617) 423-3990; *The World in Figures.*

International Monetary Fund, 700 Nineteenth Street, NW, Washington, D.C. 20431 (202) 623-7000; *Government Finance Statistics Yearbook.*

The World Bank, 1818 H Street, NW, Washington, D.C. 20433 (202) 477-1234; *World Tables.*

NIGER - TAX REVENUES - See NIGER - TAXATION

NIGER - TELEGRAPH SERVICE

Statistical Office of the United Nations, Publishing Service, New York, New York 10017 (800) 253-9646; *Statistical Yearbook.*

NIGER - TELEPHONES IN USE

American Telephone and Telegraph Company, 26 Parsippany Road, Whippany, New Jersey 07981 (800) 338-4038; *The World's Telephones.*

G.K. Hall and Company, 70 Lincoln Street, Boston, Massachusetts 02111 (617) 423-3990; *The World in Figures.*

Statistical Office of the United Nations, Publishing Service, New York, New York 10017 (800) 253-9646; *Statistical Yearbook.*

NIGER - TELEVISION PRODUCTION

Facts on File, 460 Park Avenue South, New York, New York 10016 (800) 443-8323; *The New Book of World Rankings.*

NIGER - TEXTILE INDUSTRY

G.K. Hall and Company, 70 Lincoln Street, Boston, Massachusetts 02111 (617) 423-3990; *The World in Figures.*

NIGER - TIN PRODUCTION AND CONSUMPTION - See NIGER - MINING AND MINERAL PRODUCTS

NIGER - TOBACCO PRODUCTION

Facts on File, 460 Park Avenue South, New York, New York 10016 (800) 443-8323; *The New Book of World Rankings.*

Statistical Office of the United Nations, Publishing Service, New York, New York 10017 (800) 253-9646; *Statistical Yearbook.*

NIGER - TOURISM

Facts on File, 460 Park Avenue South, New York, New York 10016 (800) 443-8323; *The New Book of World Rankings.*

G.K. Hall and Company, 70 Lincoln Street, Boston, Massachusetts 02111 (617) 423-3990; *The World in Figures.*

Times Books, 201 East 50th Street, New York, New York 10022 (212) 751-2600; *The Economist Book of Vital World Statistics.*

United Nations Economic Commission for Africa, Africa Hall, Post Office Box 3001, Addis Ababa, Ethiopia (Telephone Number in U.S. (800) 253-9646); *African Statistical Yearbook.*

World Tourism Organization, Calle Capitan Haya 42, E-28020 Madrid, Spain; *Yearbook of Tourism Statistics.*

NIGER - TRACTORS IN USE

Statistical Office of the United Nations, Publishing Service, New York, New York 10017 (800) 253-9646; *Statistical Yearbook.*

NIGER - TRADE - See NIGER - FOREIGN TRADE

NIGER - TRANSPORTATION AND COMMUNICATIONS

Facts on File, 460 Park Avenue South, New York, New York 10016 (800) 443-8323; *The New Book of World Rankings.*

G.K. Hall and Company, 70 Lincoln Street, Boston, Massachusetts 02111 (617) 423-3990; *The World in Figures.*

United Nations Economic Commission for Africa, Africa Hall, Post Office Box 3001, Addis Ababa, Ethiopia (Telephone Number in U.S. (800) 253-9646); *African Statistical Yearbook.*

NIGER - UNEMPLOYMENT

Euromonitor Publications Limited, 87-88 Turnmill Street, London EC1M 5QU, England; *International Marketing Data and Statistics.*

International Labour Office, I.L.O. Publications, CH-1211, Geneva 22, Switzerland; *Yearbook of Labour Statistics.*

Statistical Office of the United Nations, Publishing Service, New York, New York 10017 (800) 253-9646; *Statistical Yearbook.*

NIGER - URANIUM PRODUCTION AND CONSUMPTION - See NIGER - MINING AND MINERAL PRODUCTS

NIGER - VITAL STATISTICS

Euromonitor Publications Limited, 87-88 Turnmill Street, London EC1M 5QU, England; *International Marketing Data and Statistics.*

G.K. Hall and Company, 70 Lincoln Street, Boston, Massachusetts 02111 (617) 423-3990; *The World in Figures.*

Statistical Office of the United Nations, Publishing Service, New York, New York 10017 (800) 253-9646; *Statistical Yearbook.*

World Health Organization, Office of Publications, Avenue Appia, CH-1211 Geneva 27, Switzerland (Telephone Number in U.S. (518) 436-9686); *World Health Statistics Annual.*

NIGER - WAGES

G.K. Hall and Company, 70 Lincoln Street, Boston, Massachusetts 02111 (617) 423-3990; *The World in Figures.*

International Labour Office, I.L.O. Publications, CH-1211, Geneva 22, Switzerland; *Yearbook of Labour Statistics.*

NIGER - WEATHER

Facts on File, 460 Park Avenue South, New York, New York 10016 (800) 443-8323; *The New Book of World Rankings.*

G.K. Hall and Company, 70 Lincoln Street, Boston, Massachusetts 02111 (617) 423-3990; *The World in Figures.*

NIGER - WELFARE

International Monetary Fund, 700 Nineteenth Street, NW, Washington, D.C. 20431 (202) 623-7000; *Government Finance Statistics Yearbook.*

NIGER - WHEAT PRODUCTION AND PRICES - See NIGER - CROPS

NIGER - WINE PRODUCTION

Facts on File, 460 Park Avenue South, New York, New York 10016 (800) 443-8323; *The New Book of World Rankings.*

NIGER - WOOL PRODUCTION

Facts on File, 460 Park Avenue South, New York, New York 10016 (800) 443-8323; *The New Book of World Rankings.*

Nigeria - National Statistical Office

Federal Office of Statistics, 36-38 Broad Street, PM Bag 12528, Lagos, Nigeria.

Nigeria - Primary Statistics Sources

Federal Office of Statistics, 36 - 38 Broad Street, PM Bag 12528, Lagos, Nigeria; *Annual Abstract of Statistics,* and *Digest of Statistics,* quarterly.

NIGERIA - AGRICULTURE

Euromonitor Publications Limited, 87-88 Turnmill Street, London EC1M 5QU, England; *International Marketing Data and Statistics,* and *Third World Economic Handbook.*

Facts on File, 460 Park Avenue South, New York, New York 10016 (800) 443-8323; *The New Book of World Rankings.*

Food and Agricultural Organization of the United Nations (FAO) Via delle Terme di Caracalla, 00100 Rome, Italy (Telephone Number in U.S. (202) 653-2400); *Production Yearbook, The State of Food and Agriculture,* and *Trade Yearbook.*

Statistical Office of the United Nations, Publishing Service, New York, New York 10017 (800) 253-9646; *Statistical Yearbook,* and *Survey of Economic and Social Conditions in Africa.*

Times Books, 201 East 50th Street, New York, New York 10022 (212) 751-2600; *The Economist Book of Vital World Statistics.*

United Nations Economic Commission for Africa, Africa Hall, Post Office Box 3001, Addis Ababa, Ethiopia (Telephone Number in U.S. (800) 253-9646); *African Statistical Yearbook.*

The World Bank, 1818 H Street, NW, Washington, D.C. 20433 (202) 477-1234; *World Tables.*

NIGERIA - AIRLINE SERVICE

Facts on File, 460 Park Avenue South, New York, New York 10016 (800) 443-8323; *The New Book of World Rankings.*

Statistical Office of the United Nations, Publishing Service, New York, New York 10017 (800) 253-9646; *Statistical Yearbook.*

Times Books, 201 East 50th Street, New York, New York 10022 (212) 751-2600; *The Economist Book of Vital World Statistics.*

United Nations Economic Commission for Africa, Africa Hall, Post Office Box 3001, Addis Ababa, Ethiopia (Telephone Number in U.S. (800) 253-9646); *African Statistical Yearbook.*

NIGERIA - ALUMINUM PRODUCTION AND CONSUMPTION - See NIGERIA - MINING AND MINERAL PRODUCTS

NIGERIA - ANIMAL HEALTH

Food and Agricultural Organization of the United Nations (FAO), Via delle Terme di Caracalla, 00100 Rome, Italy (Telephone Number in U.S. (202) 653-2400); *Animal Health Yearbook.*

NIGERIA - AREA AND DENSITY OF POPULATION

African Development Bank, 01 BP 1387, Abidjan 01, Cote d'Ivoire; *Selected Statistics on Regional Member Countries.*

Euromonitor Publications Limited, 87-88 Turnmill Street, London EC1M 5QU, England; *International Marketing Data and Statistics.*

Facts on File, 460 Park Avenue South, New York, New York 10016 (800) 443-8323; *The New Book of World Rankings.*

Food and Agricultural Organization of the United Nations (FAO) Via delle Terme di Caracalla, 00100 Rome, Italy (Telephone Number in U.S. (202) 653-2400); *The State of Food and Agriculture.*

Statistical Office of the United Nations, Publishing Service, New York, New York 10017 (800) 253-9646; *Statistical Yearbook,* and *Survey of Economic and Social Conditions in Africa.*

Times Books, 201 East 50th Street, New York, New York 10022 (212) 751-2600; *The Economist Book of Vital World Statistics.*

United Nations Educational, Scientific and Cultural Organization (UNESCO), 7 Place de Fontenoy, F-75700 Paris, France (Telephone Number in U.S. (212) 963-5981); *Statistical Yearbook.*

NIGERIA - ARMS EXPORTS AND IMPORTS

U.S. Arms Control and Disarmament Agency, 320 Twenty-first Street, NW, Washington, D.C. 20451 (202) 647-8677; *World Military Expenditures and Arms Transfers.*

NIGERIA - BALANCE OF PAYMENTS

African Development Bank, 01 BP 1387, Abidjan 01, Cote d'Ivoire; *Selected Statistics on Regional Member Countries.*

The Economist Intelligence Unit, 111 West 57th Street, New York, New York 10019 (800) 938-4685; *The World Market Atlas.*

Euromonitor Publications Limited, 87-88 Turnmill Street, London EC1M 5QU, England; *Third World Economic Handbook.*

International Monetary Fund, 700 Nineteenth Street, NW, Washington, D.C. 20431 (202) 623-7000; *Balance of Payments Yearbook.*

Times Books, 201 East 50th Street, New York, New York 10022 (212) 751-2600; *The Economist Book of Vital World Statistics.*

United Nations Economic Commission for Africa, Africa Hall, Post Office Box 3001, Addis Ababa, Ethiopia (Telephone Number in U.S. (800) 253-9646); *African Statistical Yearbook.*

The World Bank, 1818 H Street, NW, Washington, D.C. 20433 (202) 477-1234; *World Tables.*

NIGERIA - BANKING

Facts on File, 460 Park Avenue South, New York, New York 10016 (800) 443-8323; *The New Book of World Rankings.*

International Monetary Fund, 700 Nineteenth Street, NW, Washington, D.C. 20431 (202) 623-7000; *International Financial Statistics.*

Statistical Office of the United Nations, Publishing Service, New York, New York 10017 (800) 253-9646; *Statistical Yearbook.*

United Nations Economic Commission for Africa, Africa Hall, Post Office Box 3001, Addis Ababa, Ethiopia (Telephone Number in U.S. (800) 253-9646); *African Statistical Yearbook.*

NIGERIA - BARLEY PRODUCTION - See NIGERIA - CROPS

NIGERIA - BEER PRODUCTION

Facts on File, 460 Park Avenue South, New York, New York 10016 (800) 443-8323; *The New Book of World Rankings.*

Statistical Office of the United Nations, Publishing Service, New York, New York 10017 (800) 253-9646; *Statistical Yearbook.*

NIGERIA - BIRTH RATES

Euromonitor Publications Limited, 87-88 Turnmill Street, London EC1M 5QU, England; *Third World Economic Handbook.*

Facts on File, 460 Park Avenue South, New York, New York 10016 (800) 443-8323; *The New Book of World Rankings.*

Statistical Office of the United Nations, Publishing Service, New York, New York 10017 (800) 253-9646; *Demographic Yearbook, Statistical Yearbook,* and *Survey of Economic and Social Conditions in Africa.*

Times Books, 201 East 50th Street, New York, New York 10022 (212) 751-2600; *The Economist Book of Vital World Statistics.*

The World Bank, 1818 H Street, NW, Washington, D.C. 20433 (202) 477-1234; *World Tables.*

NIGERIA - BONDS

International Monetary Fund, 700 Nineteenth Street, NW, Washington, D.C. 20431 (202) 623-7000; *Government Finance Statistics Yearbook.*

NIGERIA - BOOK PRODUCTION

United Nations Educational, Scientific and Cultural Organization (UNESCO), 7 Place de Fontenoy, F-75700 Paris, France (Telephone Number in U.S. (212) 963-5981); *Statistical Yearbook.*

NIGERIA - BROADCASTING

Billboard Limited, Post Office Box 9027, 1006 AA Amsterdam, The Netherlands (Telephone Number in U.S. (212) 764-7300); *World Radio TV Handbook.*

Facts on File, 460 Park Avenue South, New York, New York 10016 (800) 443-8323; *The New Book of World Rankings.*

Times Books, 201 East 50th Street, New York, New York 10022 (212) 751-2600; *The Economist Book of Vital World Statistics.*

NIGERIA - BUSINESS AND PROFESSIONAL LICENSES

International Monetary Fund, 700 Nineteenth Street, NW, Washington, D.C. 20431 (202) 623-7000; *Government Finance Statistics Yearbook.*

NIGERIA - BUTTER PRODUCTION - See NIGERIA - DAIRY PRODUCTS

NIGERIA - CACAO EXPORTS

International Monetary Fund, 700 Nineteenth Street, NW, Washington, D.C. 20431 (202) 623-7000; *International Financial Statistics.*

NIGERIA - CALORIE SUPPLY

African Development Bank, 01 BP 1387, Abidjan 01, Cote d'Ivoire; *Selected Statistics on Regional Member Countries.*

Food and Agricultural Organization of the United Nations (FAO) Via delle Terme di Caracalla, 00100 Rome, Italy (Telephone Number in U.S. (202) 653-2400); *The State of Food and Agriculture.*

NIGERIA - CAPITAL REVENUE

International Monetary Fund, 700 Nineteenth Street, NW, Washington, D.C. 20431 (202) 623-7000; *Government Finance Statistics Yearbook.*

NIGERIA - CATTLE - See NIGERIA - LIVESTOCK AND POULTRY

NIGERIA - CEMENT PRODUCTION - See NIGERIA - MINING AND MINERAL PRODUCTS

NIGERIA - CHEESE PRODUCTION AND CONSUMPTION - See NIGERIA - DAIRY PRODUCTS

NIGERIA - CHICKENS - See NIGERIA - LIVESTOCK AND POULTRY

NIGERIA - CIGARETTE PRODUCTION - See NIGERIA - TOBACCO PRODUCTION

NIGERIA - CLIMATE

Facts on File, 460 Park Avenue South, New York, New York 10016 (800) 443-8323; *The New Book of World Rankings.*

NIGERIA - CLOTHING EXPORTS AND IMPORTS

Euromonitor Publications Limited, 87-88 Turnmill Street, London EC1M 5QU, England; *Third World Economic Handbook.*

NIGERIA - COAL PRODUCTION - See NIGERIA -MINING AND MINERAL PRODUCTS

NIGERIA - COCOA (BEANS) PRODUCTION - See NIGERIA - CROPS

NIGERIA - COFFEE PRODUCTION AND CONSUMPTION - See NIGERIA - CROPS

NIGERIA - COMMUNICATIONS

Euromonitor Publications Limited, 87-88 Turnmill Street, London EC1M 5QU, England; *Third World Economic Handbook.*

United Nations Economic Commission for Africa, Africa Hall, Post Office Box 3001, Addis Ababa, Ethiopia (Telephone Number in U.S. (800) 253-9646); *African Statistical Yearbook.*

NIGERIA - CONSTRUCTION INDUSTRY

Facts on File, 460 Park Avenue South, New York, New York 10016 (800) 443-8323; *The New Book of World Rankings.*

Statistical Office of the United Nations, Publishing Service, New York, New York 10017 (800) 253-9646; *Statistical Yearbook.*

United Nations Economic Commission for Africa, Africa Hall, Post Office Box 3001, Addis Ababa, Ethiopia (Telephone Number in U.S. (800) 253-9646); *African Statistical Yearbook.*

NIGERIA - CONSUMER PRICE INDEX

African Development Bank, 01 BP 1387, Abidjan 01, Cote d'Ivoire; *Selected Statistics on Regional Member Countries.*

Statistical Office of the United Nations, Publishing Service, New York, New York 10017 (800) 253-9646; *Statistical Yearbook,* and *Survey of Economic and Social Conditions in Africa.*

United Nations Economic Commission for Africa, Africa Hall, Post Office Box 3001, Addis Ababa, Ethiopia (Telephone Number in U.S. (800) 253-9646); *African Statistical Yearbook.*

NIGERIA - CONSUMER PRICES

International Labour Office, I.L.O. Publications, CH-1211, Geneva 22, Switzerland; *Yearbook of Labour Statistics.*

International Monetary Fund, 700 Nineteenth Street, NW, Washington, D.C. 20431 (202) 623-7000; *International Financial Statistics.*

Times Books, 201 East 50th Street, New York, New York 10022 (212) 751-2600; *The Economist Book of Vital World Statistics.*

NIGERIA - CONSUMPTION

African Development Bank, 01 BP 1387, Abidjan 01, Cote d'Ivoire; *Selected Statistics on Regional Member Countries.*

International Rubber Study Group, York House, Eighth Floor, Empire Way, Wembley, London HA9 0PA, England; *Rubber Statistical Bulletin.*

Statistical Office of the United Nations, Publishing Service, New York 10017 (800) 253-9646; *Survey of Economic and Social Conditions in Africa.*

NIGERIA - COPPER PRODUCTION AND CONSUMPTION - See NIGERIA - MINING AND MINERAL PRODUCTS

NIGERIA - CORN PRODUCTION - See NIGERIA - CROPS

NIGERIA - CORPORATE TAXES - See NIGERIA - TAXATION

NIGERIA - COTTON - See NIGERIA - CROPS

NIGERIA - CRIME

International Criminal Police Organization (INTERPOL), 26 rue Armengaud, 92210 Saint Cloud, France; *International Crime Statistics.*

Yale University Press, Yale Station, New Haven, Connecticut 06520 (203) 432 0040, *Violence and Crime in Cross-National Perspective.*

NIGERIA - CROPS

Commodity Research Bureau, Incorporated, 75 Wall Street, New York, New York 10005 (212) 504-7754; *Commodity Year Book.*

Facts on File, 460 Park Avenue South, New York, New York 10016 (800) 443-8323; *The New Book of World Rankings.*

Food and Agricultural Organization of the United Nations (FAO) Via delle Terme di Caracalla, 00100 Rome, Italy (Telephone Number in U.S. (202) 653-2400); *The State of Food and Agriculture,* and *Production Yearbook.*

Statistical Office of the United Nations, Publishing Service, New York, New York 10017 (800) 253-9646; *Statistical Yearbook.*

United Nations Economic Commission for Africa, Africa Hall, Post Office Box 3001, Addis Ababa, Ethiopia (Telephone Number in U.S. (800) 253-9646); *African Statistical Yearbook.*

NIGERIA - CUSTOMS DUTIES

International Monetary Fund, 700 Nineteenth Street, NW, Washington, D.C. 20431 (202) 623-7000; *Government Finance Statistics Yearbook.*

NIGERIA - DAIRY PRODUCTS

Facts on File, 460 Park Avenue South, New York, New York 10016 (800) 443-8323; *The New Book of World Rankings.*

Food and Agricultural Organization of the United Nations (FAO) Via delle Terme di Caracalla, 00100 Rome, Italy (Telephone Number in U.S. (202) 653-2400); *The State of Food and Agriculture.*

Statistical Office of the United Nations, Publishing Service, New York, New York 10017 (800) 253-9646; *Statistical Yearbook.*

NIGERIA - DEATH RATES

Euromonitor Publications Limited, 87-88 Turnmill Street, London EC1M 5QU, England; *Third World Economic Handbook.*

Statistical Office of the United Nations, Publishing Service, New York, New York 10017 (800) 253-9646; *Statistical Yearbook,* and *Survey of Economic and Social Conditions in Africa.*

Times Books, 201 East 50th Street, New York, New York 10022 (212) 751-2600; *The Economist Book of Vital World Statistics.*

World Health Organization, Office of Publications, Avenue Appia, CH-1211 Geneva 27, Switzerland (Telephone Number in U.S. (518) 436-9686); *World Health Statistics Annual.*

NIGERIA - DEFENSE EXPENDITURES

International Monetary Fund, 700 Nineteenth Street, NW, Washington, D.C. 20431 (202) 623-7000; *Government Finance Statistics Yearbook.*

U.S. Arms Control and Disarmament Agency, 320 Twenty-first Street, NW, Washington, D.C. 20451 (202) 647-8677; *World Military Expenditures and Arms Transfers.*

NIGERIA - DEMOGRAPHY

The Economist Intelligence Unit, 111 West 57th Street, New York, New York 10019 (800) 938-4685; *The World Market Atlas.*

Facts on File, 460 Park Avenue South, New York, New York 10016 (800) 443-8323; *The New Book of World Rankings.*

Statistical Office of the United Nations, Publishing Service, New York 10017 (800) 253-9646; *Survey of Economic and Social Conditions in Africa.*

NIGERIA - DEVELOPMENT ASSISTANCE

Statistical Office of the United Nations, Publishing Service, New York, New York 10017 (800) 253-9646; *Statistical Yearbook.*

NIGERIA - DIAMOND PRODUCTION - See NIGERIA - MINING AND MINERAL PRODUCTS

NIGERIA - DISCOUNT RATES

Statistical Office of the United Nations, Publishing Service, New York, New York 10017 (800) 253-9646; *Statistical Yearbook.*

NIGERIA - DISEASE

World Health Organization, Office of Publications, Avenue Appia, CH-1211 Geneva 27, Switzerland (Telephone Number in U.S. (518) 436-9686); *World Health Statistics Annual.*

NIGERIA - DIVORCE RATES

Facts on File, 460 Park Avenue South, New York, New York 10016 (800) 443-8323; *The New Book of World Rankings.*

Statistical Office of the United Nations, Publishing Service, New York, New York 10017 (800) 253-9646; *Demographic Yearbook.*

NIGERIA - ECONOMY

African Development Bank, 01 BP 1387, Abidjan 01, Cote d'Ivoire; *Selected Statistics on Regional Member Countries.*

Euromonitor Publications Limited, 87-88 Turnmill Street, London EC1M 5QU, England; *International Marketing Data and Statistics,* and *Third World Economic Handbook.*

Facts on File, 460 Park Avenue South, New York, New York 10016 (800) 443-8323; *The New Book of World Rankings.*

Statistical Office of the United Nations, Publishing Service, New York, New York 10017 (800) 253-9646; *Foreign Trade Statistics for Africa.*

NIGERIA - EDUCATION

African Development Bank, 01 BP 1387, Abidjan 01, Cote d'Ivoire; *Selected Statistics on Regional Member Countries.*

The Economist Intelligence Unit, 111 West 57th Street, New York, New York 10019 (800) 938-4685; *The World Market Atlas.*

Facts on File, 460 Park Avenue South, New York, New York 10016 (800) 443-8323; *The New Book of World Rankings.*

International Monetary Fund, 700 Nineteenth Street, NW, Washington, D.C. 20431 (202) 623-7000; *Government Finance Statistics Yearbook.*

Statistical Office of the United Nations, Publishing Service, New York 10017 (800) 253-9646; *Survey of Economic and Social Conditions in Africa.*

Times Books, 201 East 50th Street, New York, New York 10022 (212) 751-2600; *The Economist Book of Vital World Statistics.*

United Nations Economic Commission for Africa, Africa Hall, Post Office Box 3001, Addis Ababa, Ethiopia (Telephone Number in U.S. (800) 253-9646); *African Statistical Yearbook.*

United Nations Educational, Scientific and Cultural Organization (UNESCO), 7 Place de Fontenoy, F-75700 Paris, France (Telephone Number in U.S. (212) 963-5981); *Statistical Yearbook.*

The World Bank, 1818 H Street, NW, Washington, D.C. 20433 (202) 477-1234; *World Tables.*

NIGERIA - EGG PRODUCTION AND CONSUMPTION - See NIGERIA - DAIRY PRODUCTS

NIGERIA - ELECTRICITY

Facts on File, 460 Park Avenue South, New York, New York 10016 (800) 443-8323; *The New Book of World Rankings.*

Penn Well Publishing Company, 1421 South Sheridan Road, Post Office Box 1260, Tulsa, Oklahoma 74101 (800) 752-9764; *International Energy Statistics Sourcebook.*

Statistical Office of the United Nations, Publishing Service, New York, New York 10017 (800) 253-9646; *Statistical Yearbook,* and *Survey of Economic and Social Conditions in Africa.*

Times Books, 201 East 50th Street, New York, New York 10022 (212) 751-2600; *The Economist Book of Vital World Statistics.*

United Nations Economic Commission for Africa, Africa Hall, Post Office Box 3001, Addis Ababa, Ethiopia (Telephone Number in U.S. (800) 253-9646); *African Statistical Yearbook.*

NIGERIA - EMPLOYMENT

Euromonitor Publications Limited, 87-88 Turnmill Street, London EC1M 5QU, England; *International Marketing Data and Statistics.*

Facts on File, 460 Park Avenue South, New York, New York 10016 (800) 443-8323; *The New Book of World Rankings.*

International Labour Office, I.L.O. Publications, CH-1211, Geneva 22, Switzerland; *Yearbook of Labour Statistics.*

Statistical Office of the United Nations, Publishing Service, New York, New York 10017 (800) 253-9646; *Statistical Yearbook,* and *Survey of Economic and Social Conditions in Africa.*

United Nations Economic Commission for Africa, Africa Hall, Post Office Box 3001, Addis Ababa, Ethiopia (Telephone Number in U.S. (800) 253-9646); *African Statistical Yearbook.*

NIGERIA - ENERGY

Facts on File, 460 Park Avenue South, New York, New York 10016 (800) 443-8323; *The New Book of World Rankings.*

Food and Agricultural Organization of the United Nations (FAO) Via delle Terme di Caracalla, 00100 Rome, Italy (Telephone Number in U.S. (202) 653-2400); *The State of Food and Agriculture.*

Penn Well Publishing Company, 1421 South Sheridan Road, Post Office Box 1260, Tulsa, Oklahoma 74101 (800) 752-9764; *International Energy Statistics Sourcebook.*

Statistical Office of the United Nations, Publishing Service, New York, New York 10017 (800) 253-9646; *Energy Statistics Yearbook* and *Statistical Yearbook.*

Times Books, 201 East 50th Street, New York, New York 10022 (212) 751-2600; *The Economist Book of Vital World Statistics.*

United Nations Economic Commission for Africa, Africa Hall, Post Office Box 3001, Addis Ababa, Ethiopia (Telephone Number in U.S. (800) 253-9646); *African Statistical Yearbook.*

NIGERIA - EXCHANGE RATES

African Development Bank, 01 BP 1387, Abidjan 01, Cote d'Ivoire; *Selected Statistics on Regional Member Countries.*

Euromonitor Publications Limited, 87-88 Turnmill Street, London EC1M 5QU, England; *International Marketing Data and Statistics.*

International Monetary Fund, 700 Nineteenth Street, NW, Washington, D.C. 20431 (202) 623-7000; *International Financial Statistics.*

Organization of Petroleum Exporting Countries, Obere Donaustrasse 93, 1020 Vienna 2, Austria; *OPEC Annual Statistical Bulletin.*

Statistical Office of the United Nations, Publishing Service, New York, New York 10017 (800) 253-9646; *Foreign Trade Statistics for Africa,* and *Statistical Yearbook.*

NIGERIA - EXCISE TAXES - See NIGERIA - TAXATION

NIGERIA - EXPORT DUTIES

International Monetary Fund, 700 Nineteenth Street, NW, Washington, D.C. 20431 (202) 623-7000; *Government Finance Statistics Yearbook.*

NIGERIA - EXPORTS

African Development Bank, 01 BP 1387, Abidjan 01, Cote d'Ivoire; *Selected Statistics on Regional Member Countries.*

American Automobile Manufacturers Association, 1401 H Street, NW, Suite 900, Washington, D.C. 20005 (202) 326-5500; *World Motor Vehicle Data.*

The Economist Intelligence Unit, 111 West 57th Street, New York, New York 10019 (800) 938-4685; *The World Market Atlas.*

Euromonitor Publications Limited, 87-88 Turnmill Street, London EC1M 5QU, England; *International Marketing Data and Statistics,* and *Third World Economic Handbook.*

Food and Agricultural Organization of the United Nations (FAO) Via delle Terme di Caracalla, 00100 Rome, Italy (Telephone Number in U.S. (202) 653-2400); *The State of Food and Agriculture.*

International Monetary Fund, 700 Nineteenth Street, NW, Washington, D.C. 20431 (202) 623-7000; *Direction of Trade Statistics,* and *International Financial Statistics.*

International Rubber Study Group, York House, Eighth Floor, Empire Way, Wembley, London HA9 0PA, England; *Rubber Statistical Bulletin.*

Organization of Petroleum Exporting Countries, Obere Donaustrasse 93, 1020 Vienna 2, Austria; *OPEC Annual Statistical Bulletin.*

Statistical Office of the United Nations, Publishing Service, New York, New York 10017 (800) 253-9646; *Foreign Trade Statistics for Africa, Trade in Manufactures of Developing Countries,* and *Survey of Economic and Social Conditions in Africa.*

Times Books, 201 East 50th Street, New York, New York 10022 (212) 751-2600; *The Economist Book of Vital World Statistics.*

United Nations Economic Commission for Africa, Africa Hall, Post Office Box 3001, Addis Ababa, Ethiopia (Telephone Number in U.S. (800) 253-9646); *African Statistical Yearbook.*

The World Bank, 1818 H Street, NW, Washington, D.C. 20433 (202) 477-1234; *World Tables.*

NIGERIA - EXTERNAL INDEBTEDNESS

African Development Bank, 01 BP 1387, Abidjan 01, Cote d'Ivoire; *Selected Statistics on Regional Member Countries.*

Euromonitor Publications Limited, 87-88 Turnmill Street, London EC1M 5QU, England; *Third World Economic Handbook.*

Statistical Office of the United Nations, Publishing Service, New York, New York 10017 (800) 253-9646; *Statistical Yearbook,* and *Survey of Economic and Social Conditions in Africa.*

The World Bank, 1818 H Street, NW, Washington, D.C. 20433 (202) 477-1234; *World Tables.*

NIGERIA - EXTERNAL TRADE

African Development Bank, 01 BP 1387, Abidjan 01, Cote d'Ivoire; *Selected Statistics on Regional Member Countries.*

Food and Agricultural Organization of the United Nations (FAO) Via delle Terme di Caracalla, 00100 Rome, Italy (Telephone Number in U.S. (202) 653-2400); *The State of Food and Agriculture,* and *Trade Yearbook.*

Statistical Office of the United Nations, Publishing Service, New York, New York 10017 (800) 253-9646; *Statistical Yearbook.*

NIGERIA - FABRIC PRODUCTION - See NIGERIA - TEXTILE INDUSTRY

NIGERIA - FARM CROPS - See NIGERIA - CROPS

NIGERIA - FEMALE WORKING POPULATION - See NIGERIA - EMPLOYMENT

NIGERIA - FERTILITY RATES

Facts on File, 460 Park Avenue South, New York, New York 10016 (800) 443-8323; *The New Book of World Rankings.*

Times Books, 201 East 50th Street, New York, New York 10022 (212) 751-2600; *The Economist Book of Vital World Statistics.*

Statistical Office of the United Nations, Publishing Service, New York 10017 (800) 253-9646; *Survey of Economic and Social Conditions in Africa.*

The World Bank, 1818 H Street, NW, Washington, D.C. 20433 (202) 477-1234; *World Tables.*

NIGERIA - FERTILIZER

Food and Agricultural Organization of the United Nations (FAO), Via delle Terme di Caracalla, 00100 Rome, Italy (Telephone Number in U.S. (202) 653-2400); *Fertilizer Yearbook,* and *The State of Food and Agriculture.*

Statistical Office of the United Nations, Publishing Service, New York, New York 10017 (800) 253-9646; *Statistical Yearbook.*

NIGERIA - FETAL MORTALITY

Statistical Office of the United Nations, Publishing Service, New York, New York 10017 (800) 253-9646; *Demographic Yearbook.*

NIGERIA - FILMS PRODUCED - LONG - See NIGERIA - MOTION PICTURES

NIGERIA - FINANCE

African Development Bank, 01 BP 1387, Abidjan 01, Cote d'Ivoire; *Selected Statistics on Regional Member Countries.*

Facts on File, 460 Park Avenue South, New York, New York 10016 (800) 443-8323; *The New Book of World Rankings.*

International Monetary Fund, 700 Nineteenth Street, NW, Washington, D.C. 20431 (202) 623-7000; *Government Finance Statistics Yearbook,* and *International Financial Statistics.*

United Nations Economic Commission for Africa, Africa Hall, Post Office Box 3001, Addis Ababa, Ethiopia (Telephone Number in U.S. (800) 253-9646); *African Statistical Yearbook.*

NIGERIA - FISHERIES

Facts on File, 460 Park Avenue South, New York, New York 10016 (800) 443-8323; *The New Book of World Rankings.*

Food and Agricultural Organization of the United Nations (FAO) Via delle Terme di Caracalla, 00100 Rome, Italy (Telephone Number in U.S. (202) 653-2400); *The State of Food and Agriculture,* and *Yearbook of Fishery Statistics.*

Statistical Office of the United Nations, Publishing Service, New York, New York 10017 (800) 253-9646; *Statistical Yearbook,* and *Survey of Economic and Social Conditions in Africa.*

United Nations Economic Commission for Africa, Africa Hall, Post Office Box 3001, Addis Ababa, Ethiopia (Telephone Number in U.S. (800) 253-9646); *African Statistical Yearbook.*

NIGERIA - FLOUR PRODUCTION

Statistical Office of the United Nations, Publishing Service, New York, New York 10017 (800) 253-9646; *Statistical Yearbook.*

NIGERIA - FOOD

African Development Bank, 01 BP 1387, Abidjan 01, Cote d'Ivoire; *Selected Statistics on Regional Member Countries.*

Food and Agricultural Organization of the United Nations (FAO), Via delle Terme di Caracalla, 00100 Rome, Italy (Telephone Number in U.S. (202) 653-2400); *Production Yearbook,* and *The State of Food and Agriculture.*

Statistical Office of the United Nations, Publishing Service, New York, New York 10017 (800) 253-9646; *Trade in Manufactures of Developing Countries.*

NIGERIA - FOREIGN TRADE

Euromonitor Publications Limited, 87-88 Turnmill Street, London EC1M 5QU, England; *International Marketing Data and Statistics,* and *Third World Economic Handbook.*

Facts on File, 460 Park Avenue South, New York, New York 10016 (800) 443-8323; *The New Book of World Rankings.*

Food and Agricultural Organization of the United Nations (FAO) Via delle Terme di Caracalla, 00100 Rome, Italy (Telephone Number in U.S. (202) 653-2400); *The State of Food and Agriculture.*

International Monetary Fund, 700 Nineteenth Street, NW, Washington, D.C. 20431 (202) 623-7000; *International Financial Statistics.*

Statistical Office of the United Nations, Publishing Service, New York, New York 10017 (800) 253-9646; *International Trade Statistics Yearbook, Foreign Trade Statistics for Africa,* and *Statistical Yearbook.*

United Nations Economic Commission for Africa, Africa Hall, Post Office Box 3001, Addis Ababa, Ethiopia (Telephone Number in U.S. (800) 253-9646); *African Statistical Yearbook.*

The World Bank, 1818 H Street, NW, Washington, D.C. 20433 (202) 477-1234; *World Tables.*

NIGERIA - FORESTRY AND FOREST PRODUCTS

Euromonitor Publications Limited, 87-88 Turnmill Street, London EC1M 5QU, England; *Third World Economic Handbook.*

Facts on File, 460 Park Avenue South, New York, New York 10016 (800) 443-8323; *The New Book of World Rankings.*

Food and Agricultural Organization of the United Nations (FAO) Via delle Terme di Caracalla, 00100 Rome, Italy (Telephone Number in U.S. (202) 653-2400); *The State of Food and Agriculture*, and *Yearbook of Forest Products.*

Statistical Office of the United Nations, Publishing Service, New York, New York 10017 (800) 253-9646; *Statistical Yearbook.*

United Nations Economic Commission for Africa, Africa Hall, Post Office Box 3001, Addis Ababa, Ethiopia (Telephone Number in U.S. (800) 253-9646); *African Statistical Yearbook.*

United Nations Educational, Scientific and Cultural Organization (UNESCO), 7 Place de Fontenoy, F-75700 Paris, France (Telephone Number in U.S. (212) 963-5981); *Statistical Yearbook.*

NIGERIA - GAS PRODUCTION - See NIGERIA - MINING AND MINERAL PRODUCTS

NIGERIA - GENERAL INDUSTRIAL STATISTICS

Statistical Office of the United Nations, Publishing Service, New York, New York 10017 (800) 253-9646; *Industrial Statistics Yearbook.*

NIGERIA - GENERAL MORTALITY

Statistical Office of the United Nations, Publishing Service, New York, New York 10017 (800) 253-9646; *Demographic Yearbook.*

NIGERIA - GEOGRAPHIC DATA

Facts on File, 460 Park Avenue South, New York, New York 10016 (800) 443-8323; *The New Book of World Rankings.*

NIGERIA - GOATS - See NIGERIA - LIVESTOCK AND POULTRY

NIGERIA - GOLD HOLDINGS

International Monetary Fund, 700 Nineteenth Street, NW, Washington, D.C. 20431 (202) 623-7000; *International Financial Statistics.*

Statistical Office of the United Nations, Publishing Service, New York, New York 10017 (800) 253-9646; *Statistical Yearbook.*

The World Bank, 1818 H Street, NW, Washington, D.C. 20433 (202) 477-1234; *World Tables.*

NIGERIA - GOLD PRODUCTION AND CONSUMPTION - See NIGERIA - MINING AND MINERAL PRODUCTS

NIGERIA - GOVERNMENT EXPENDITURES

Euromonitor Publications Limited, 87-88 Turnmill Street, London EC1M 5QU, England; *Third World Economic Handbook.*

International Monetary Fund, 700 Nineteenth Street, NW, Washington, D.C. 20431 (202) 623-7000; *Government Finance Statistics Yearbook.*

Times Books, 201 East 50th Street, New York, New York 10022 (212) 751-2600; *The Economist Book of Vital World Statistics.*

The World Bank, 1818 H Street, NW, Washington, D.C. 20433 (202) 477-1234; *World Tables.*

NIGERIA - GOVERNMENT FINANCES

Statistical Office of the United Nations, Publishing Service, New York, New York 10017 (800) 253-9646; *Statistical Yearbook.*

NIGERIA - GOVERNMENT REVENUES

International Monetary Fund, 700 Nineteenth Street, NW, Washington, D.C. 20431 (202) 623-7000; *Government Finance Statistics Yearbook.*

Statistical Office of the United Nations, Publishing Service, New York 10017 (800) 253-9646; *Survey of Economic and Social Conditions in Africa.*

Times Books, 201 East 50th Street, New York, New York 10022 (212) 751-2600; *The Economist Book of Vital World Statistics.*

The World Bank, 1818 H Street, NW, Washington, D.C. 20433 (202) 477-1234; *World Tables.*

NIGERIA - GRAIN PRODUCTION - See NIGERIA - CROPS

NIGERIA - GRANTS

International Monetary Fund, 700 Nineteenth Street, NW, Washington, D.C. 20431 (202) 623-7000; *Government Finance Statistics Yearbook.*

NIGERIA - GREEN PEPPER AND CHILIE PRODUCTION - See NIGERIA - CROPS

NIGERIA - GROSS DOMESTIC PRODUCT

African Development Bank, 01 BP 1387, Abidjan 01, Cote d'Ivoire; *Selected Statistics on Regional Member Countries.*

The Economist Intelligence Unit, 111 West 57th Street, New York, New York 10019 (800) 938-4685; *The World Market Atlas.*

Euromonitor Publications Limited, 87-88 Turnmill Street, London EC1M 5QU, England; *International Marketing Data and Statistics*, and *Third World Economic Handbook.*

Facts on File, 460 Park Avenue South, New York, New York 10016 (800) 443-8323; *The New Book of World Rankings.*

Statistical Office of the United Nations, Publishing Service, New York, New York 10017 (800) 253-9646; *Statistical Yearbook*, and *Survey of Economic and Social Conditions in Africa.*

Times Books, 201 East 50th Street, New York, New York 10022 (212) 751-2600; *The Economist Book of Vital World Statistics.*

United Nations Economic Commission for Africa, Africa Hall, Post Office Box 3001, Addis Ababa, Ethiopia (Telephone Number in U.S. (800) 253-9646); *African Statistical Yearbook.*

The World Bank, 1818 H Street, NW, Washington, D.C. 20433 (202) 477-1234; *World Tables.*

NIGERIA - GROSS INDUSTRIAL PRODUCT - BY CATEGORIES OF GOODS

Euromonitor Publications Limited, 87-88 Turnmill Street, London EC1M 5QU, England; *Third World Economic Handbook.*

NIGERIA - GROSS NATIONAL PRODUCT

Euromonitor Publications Limited, 87-88 Turnmill Street, London EC1M 5QU, England; *International Marketing Data and Statistics,* and *Third World Economic Handbook.*

Organization of Petroleum Exporting Countries, Obere Donaustrasse 93, 1020 Vienna 2, Austria; *OPEC Annual Statistical Bulletin.*

U.S. Arms Control and Disarmament Agency, 320 Twenty-first Street, NW, Washington, D.C. 20451 (202) 647-8677; *World Military Expenditures and Arms Transfers.*

The World Bank, 1818 H Street, NW, Washington, D.C. 20433 (202) 477-1234; *World Tables.*

NIGERIA - GROUNDNUTS PRODUCTION - See NIGERIA - CROPS

NIGERIA - HEALTH

African Development Bank, 01 BP 1387, Abidjan 01, Cote d'Ivoire; *Selected Statistics on Regional Member Countries.*

Facts on File, 460 Park Avenue South, New York, New York 10016 (800) 443-8323; *The New Book of World Rankings.*

Statistical Office of the United Nations, Publishing Service, New York, New York 10017 (800) 253-9646; *Statistical Yearbook.*

Times Books, 201 East 50th Street, New York, New York 10022 (212) 751-2600; *The Economist Book of Vital World Statistics.*

United Nations Economic Commission for Africa, Africa Hall, Post Office Box 3001, Addis Ababa, Ethiopia (Telephone Number in U.S. (800) 253-9646); *African Statistical Yearbook.*

World Health Organization, Office of Publications, Avenue Appia, CH-1211 Geneva 27, Switzerland (Telephone Number in U.S. (518) 436-9686); *World Health Statistics Annual.*

NIGERIA - HEALTH EXPENDITURES

International Monetary Fund, 700 Nineteenth Street, NW, Washington, D.C. 20431 (202) 623-7000; *Government Finance Statistics Yearbook.*

NIGERIA - HIDE PRODUCTION

Food and Agricultural Organization of the United Nations (FAO), Via delle Terme di Caracalla, 00100 Rome, Italy (Telephone Number in U.S. (202) 653-2400); *Production Yearbook.*

NIGERIA - HIGHWAYS

Statistical Office of the United Nations, Publishing Service, New York 10017 (800) 253-9646; *Survey of Economic and Social Conditions in Africa.*

United Nations Economic Commission for Africa, Africa Hall, Post Office Box 3001, Addis Ababa, Ethiopia (Telephone Number in U.S. (800) 253-9646); *African Statistical Yearbook.*

NIGERIA - HORSES - See NIGERIA - LIVESTOCK AND POULTRY

NIGERIA - HOURS OF WORK - See NIGERIA - EMPLOYMENT

NIGERIA - HOUSING AND HOUSING UNITS

Euromonitor Publications Limited, 87-88 Turnmill Street, London EC1M 5QU, England; *Third World Economic Handbook.*

Facts on File, 460 Park Avenue South, New York, New York 10016 (800) 443-8323; *The New Book of World Rankings.*

NIGERIA - HOUSING EXPENDITURES

International Monetary Fund, 700 Nineteenth Street, NW, Washington, D.C. 20431 (202) 623-7000; *Government Finance Statistics Yearbook.*

NIGERIA - ILLITERATE POPULATION

The Economist Intelligence Unit, 111 West 57th Street, New York, New York 10019 (800) 938-4685; *The World Market Atlas.*

United Nations Educational, Scientific and Cultural Organization (UNESCO), 7 Place de Fontenoy, F-75700 Paris, France (Telephone Number in U.S. (212) 963-5981); *Statistical Yearbook.*

NIGERIA - IMPORTS

African Development Bank, 01 BP 1387, Abidjan 01, Cote d'Ivoire; *Selected Statistics on Regional Member Countries.*

American Automobile Manufacturers Association, 1401 H Street, NW, Suite 900, Washington, D.C. 20005 (202) 326-5500; *World Motor Vehicle Data.*

Euromonitor Publications Limited, 87-88 Turnmill Street, London EC1M 5QU, England; *International Marketing Data and Statistics,* and *Third World Economic Handbook.*

Food and Agricultural Organization of the United Nations (FAO) Via delle Terme di Caracalla, 00100 Rome, Italy (Telephone Number in U.S. (202) 653-2400); *The State of Food and Agriculture.*

International Monetary Fund, 700 Nineteenth Street, NW, Washington, D.C. 20431 (202) 623-7000; *Direction of Trade Statistics, Government Finance Statistics Yearbook,* and *International Financial Statistics.*

International Rubber Study Group, York House, Eighth Floor, Empire Way, Wembley, London HA9 0PA, England; *Rubber Statistical Bulletin.*

Statistical Office of the United Nations, Publishing Service, New York, New York 10017 (800) 253-9646; *Foreign Trade Statistics for Africa, Trade in Manufactures of Developing Countries,* and *Survey of Economic and Social Conditions in Africa.*

United Nations Economic Commission for Africa, Africa Hall, Post Office Box 3001, Addis Ababa, Ethiopia (Telephone Number in U.S. (800) 253-9646); *African Statistical Yearbook.*

The World Bank, 1818 H Street, NW, Washington, D.C. 20433 (202) 477-1234; *World Tables.*

NIGERIA - INCOME TAXES - See NIGERIA - TAXATION

NIGERIA - INDUSTRIAL METALS PRODUCTION - See NIGERIA - MINING AND MINERAL PRODUCTS

NIGERIA - INDUSTRY

Euromonitor Publications Limited, 87-88 Turnmill Street, London EC1M 5QU, England; *International Marketing Data and Statistics*, and *Third World Economic Handbook*.

Facts on File, 460 Park Avenue South, New York, New York 10016 (800) 443-8323; *The New Book of World Rankings*.

International Labour Office, I.L.O. Publications, CH-1211, Geneva 22, Switzerland; *Yearbook of Labour Statistics*.

Statistical Office of the United Nations, Publishing Service, New York, New York 10017 (800) 253-9646; *Statistical Yearbook*, and *Survey of Economic and Social Conditions in Africa*.

Times Books, 201 East 50th Street, New York, New York 10022 (212) 751-2600; *The Economist Book of Vital World Statistics*.

United Nations Economic Commission for Africa, Africa Hall, Post Office Box 3001, Addis Ababa, Ethiopia (Telephone Number in U.S. (800) 253-9646); *African Statistical Yearbook*.

The World Bank, 1818 H Street, NW, Washington, D.C. 20433 (202) 477-1234; *World Tables*.

NIGERIA - INFANT AND MATERNAL MORTALITY

Statistical Office of the United Nations, Publishing Service, New York, New York 10017 (800) 253-9646; *Demographic Yearbook*, and *Survey of Economic and Social Conditions in Africa*.

Times Books, 201 East 50th Street, New York, New York 10022 (212) 751-2600; *The Economist Book of Vital World Statistics*.

The World Bank, 1818 H Street, NW, Washington, D.C. 20433 (202) 477-1234; *World Tables*.

NIGERIA - INTERNATIONAL LIQUIDITY

International Monetary Fund, 700 Nineteenth Street, NW, Washington, D.C. 20431 (202) 623-7000; *International Financial Statistics*.

NIGERIA - INTERNATIONAL RESERVES EXCLUDING GOLD

African Development Bank, 01 BP 1387, Abidjan 01, Cote d'Ivoire; *Selected Statistics on Regional Member Countries*.

Statistical Office of the United Nations, Publishing Service, New York, New York 10017 (800) 253-9646; *Statistical Yearbook*.

The World Bank, 1818 H Street, NW, Washington, D.C. 20433 (202) 477-1234; *World Tables*.

NIGERIA - IRON ORE PRODUCTION AND CONSUMPTION - See NIGERIA - MINING AND MINERAL PRODUCTS

NIGERIA - IRRIGATION

Euromonitor Publications Limited, 87-88 Turnmill Street, London EC1M 5QU, England; *International Marketing Data and Statistics*.

NIGERIA - LABOR FORCE

African Development Bank, 01 BP 1387, Abidjan 01, Cote d'Ivoire; *Selected Statistics on Regional Member Countries*.

Euromonitor Publications Limited, 87-88 Turnmill Street, London EC1M 5QU, England; *International Marketing Data and Statistics*.

Facts on File, 460 Park Avenue South, New York, New York 10016 (800) 443-8323; *The New Book of World Rankings*.

Food and Agricultural Organization of the United Nations (FAO) Via delle Terme di Caracalla, 00100 Rome, Italy (Telephone Number in U.S. (202) 653-2400); *The State of Food and Agriculture*.

The World Bank, 1818 H Street, NW, Washington, D.C. 20433 (202) 477-1234; *World Tables*.

NIGERIA - LABOR PRODUCTIVITY

International Labour Office, I.L.O. Publications, CH-1211, Geneva 22, Switzerland; *Yearbook of Labour Statistics*.

NIGERIA - LAND USE

Euromonitor Publications Limited, 87-88 Turnmill Street, London EC1M 5QU, England; *International Marketing Data and Statistics*.

Food and Agricultural Organization of the United Nations (FAO), Via delle Terme di Caracalla, 00100 Rome, Italy (Telephone Number in U.S. (202) 653-2400); *Production Yearbook*.

NIGERIA - LEAD ORE PRODUCTION AND CONSUMPTION - See NIGERIA - MINING AND MINERAL PRODUCTS

NIGERIA - LEATHER AND FOOTWEAR - EXPORTS AND IMPORTS

Statistical Office of the United Nations, Publishing Service, New York, New York 10017 (800) 253-9646; *Trade in Manufactures of Developing Countries*.

NIGERIA - LIBRARIES

Facts on File, 460 Park Avenue South, New York, New York 10016 (800) 443-8323; *The New Book of World Rankings*.

United Nations Educational, Scientific and Cultural Organization (UNESCO), 7 Place de Fontenoy, F-75700 Paris, France (Telephone Number in U.S. (212) 963-5981); *Statistical Yearbook*.

NIGERIA - LIFE EXPECTANCY

African Development Bank, 01 BP 1387, Abidjan 01, Cote d'Ivoire; *Selected Statistics on Regional Member Countries*.

NIGERIA - LIGNITE PRODUCTION - See NIGERIA - MINING AND MINERAL PRODUCTS

NIGERIA - LITERACY RATE

Statistical Office of the United Nations, Publishing Service, New York 10017 (800) 253-9646; *Survey of Economic and Social Conditions in Africa*.

NIGERIA - LIVESTOCK AND POULTRY

Euromonitor Publications Limited, 87-88 Turnmill Street, London EC1M 5QU, England; *International Marketing Data and Statistics*.

Facts on File, 460 Park Avenue South, New York, New York 10016 (800) 443-8323; *The New Book of World Rankings*.

Food and Agricultural Organization of the United Nations (FAO), Via delle Terme di Caracalla, 00100 Rome, Italy (Telephone Number in

U.S. (202) 653-2400); *Production Yearbook*, and *The State of Food and Agriculture*.

Statistical Office of the United Nations, Publishing Service, New York, New York 10017 (800) 253-9646; *Statistical Yearbook*, and *Survey of Economic and Social Conditions in Africa*.

United Nations Economic Commission for Africa, Africa Hall, Post Office Box 3001, Addis Ababa, Ethiopia (Telephone Number in U.S. (800) 253-9646); *African Statistical Yearbook*.

NIGERIA - LIVING LEVELS

Times Books, 201 East 50th Street, New York, New York 10022 (212) 751-2600; *The Economist Book of Vital World Statistics*.

NIGERIA - MAIL - NUMBER OF PIECES SENT OR RECEIVED

Statistical Office of the United Nations, Publishing Service, New York, New York 10017 (800) 253-9646; *Statistical Yearbook*.

NIGERIA - MANUFACTURING

American Automobile Manufacturers Association, 1401 H Street, NW, Suite 900, Washington, D.C. 20005 (202) 326-5500; *World Motor Vehicle Data*.

Euromonitor Publications Limited, 87-88 Turnmill Street, London EC1M 5QU, England; *Third World Economic Handbook*.

Facts on File, 460 Park Avenue South, New York, New York 10016 (800) 443-8323; *The New Book of World Rankings*.

Statistical Office of the United Nations, Publishing Service, New York, New York 10017 (800) 253-9646; *Statistical Yearbook*, and *Survey of Economic and Social Conditions in Africa*.

United Nations Economic Commission for Africa, Africa Hall, Post Office Box 3001, Addis Ababa, Ethiopia (Telephone Number in U.S. (800) 253-9646); *African Statistical Yearbook*.

The World Bank, 1818 H Street, NW, Washington, D.C. 20433 (202) 477-1234; *World Tables*.

NIGERIA - MARRIAGE RATES

Facts on File, 460 Park Avenue South, New York, New York 10016 (800) 443-8323; *The New Book of World Rankings*.

Statistical Office of the United Nations, Publishing Service, New York, New York 10017 (800) 253-9646; *Demographic Yearbook*.

NIGERIA - MEAT PRODUCTION - See NIGERIA - LIVESTOCK AND POULTRY

NIGERIA - MERCHANT SHIPPING

Lloyd's Register of Shipping, 17 Battery Place, New York, New York 10004 (212) 425-8050; *Register of Ships*.

Organization of Petroleum Exporting Countries, Obere Donaustrasse 93, 1020 Vienna 2, Austria; *OPEC Annual Statistical Bulletin*.

Statistical Office of the United Nations, Publishing Service, New York, New York 10017 (800) 253-9646; *Statistical Yearbook*.

Times Books, 201 East 50th Street, New York, New York 10022 (212) 751-2600; *The Economist Book of Vital World Statistics*.

United Nations Economic Commission for Africa, Africa Hall, Post Office Box 3001, Addis Ababa, Ethiopia (Telephone Number in U.S. (800) 253-9646); *African Statistical Yearbook*.

U.S. Department of Transportation, Maritime Administration, 400 Seventh Street, SW, Washington, D.C. 20590 (202) 366-5807; *A Statistical Analysis of the World's Merchant Fleets*.

NIGERIA - MILITARY

The International Institute for Strategic Studies, 23 Tavistock Street, London WC2E 7NQ, England; *The Military Balance*.

U.S. Arms Control and Disarmament Agency, 320 Twenty-first Street, NW, Washington, D.C. 20451 (202) 647-8677; *World Military Expenditures and Arms Transfers*.

NIGERIA - MILK PRODUCTION - See NIGERIA - DAIRY PRODUCTS

NIGERIA - MILLET PRODUCTION - See NIGERIA - CROPS

NIGERIA - MINING AND MINERAL PRODUCTS

Euromonitor Publications Limited, 87-88 Turnmill Street, London EC1M 5QU, England; *Third World Economic Handbook*.

Facts on File, 460 Park Avenue South, New York, New York 10016 (800) 443-8323; *The New Book of World Rankings*.

Organization of Petroleum Exporting Countries, Obere Donaustrasse 93, 1020 Vienna 2, Austria; *OPEC Annual Statistical Bulletin*.

Penn Well Publishing Company, 1421 South Sheridan Road, Post Office Box 1260, Tulsa, Oklahoma 74101 (800) 752-9764; *International Energy Statistics Sourcebook*.

Statistical Office of the United Nations, Publishing Service, New York, New York 10017 (800) 253-9646; *Statistical Yearbook*.

United Nations Economic Commission for Africa, Africa Hall, Post Office Box 3001, Addis Ababa, Ethiopia (Telephone Number in U.S. (800) 253-9646); *African Statistical Yearbook*.

NIGERIA - MONEY EXCHANGE RATE

Euromonitor Publications Limited, 87-88 Turnmill Street, London EC1M 5QU, England; *International Marketing Data and Statistics*.

International Monetary Fund, 700 Nineteenth Street, NW, Washington, D.C. 20431 (202) 623-7000; *International Financial Statistics*.

Statistical Office of the United Nations, Publishing Service, New York, New York 10017 (800) 253-9646; *Statistical Yearbook*.

NIGERIA - MONEY RESERVES

Euromonitor Publications Limited, 87-88 Turnmill Street, London EC1M 5QU, England; *International Marketing Data and Statistics*.

NIGERIA - MONEY SUPPLY

African Development Bank, 01 BP 1387, Abidjan 01, Cote d'Ivoire; *Selected Statistics on Regional Member Countries*.

Euromonitor Publications Limited, 87-88 Turnmill Street, London EC1M 5QU, England; *International Marketing Data and Statistics*.

International Monetary Fund, 700 Nineteenth Street, NW, Washington, D.C. 20431 (202) 623-7000; *International Financial Statistics*.

Statistical Office of the United Nations, Publishing Service, New York, New York 10017 (800) 253-9646; *Statistical Yearbook*.

The World Bank, 1818 H Street, NW, Washington, D.C. 20433 (202) 477-1234; *World Tables*.

NIGERIA - MOTION PICTURES

Statistical Office of the United Nations, Publishing Service, New York, New York 10017 (800) 253-9646; *Statistical Yearbook*.

United Nations Educational, Scientific and Cultural Organization (UNESCO), 7 Place de Fontenoy, F-75700 Paris, France (Telephone Number in U.S. (212) 963-5981); *Statistical Yearbook*.

NIGERIA - MOTOR VEHICLE ASSEMBLY

Statistical Office of the United Nations, Publishing Service, New York, New York 10017 (800) 253-9646; *Statistical Yearbook*.

NIGERIA - MOTOR VEHICLE PRODUCTION

American Automobile Manufacturers Association, 1401 H Street, NW, Suite 900, Washington, D.C. 20005 (202) 326-5500; *World Motor Vehicle Data*.

NIGERIA - MOTOR VEHICLES IN USE

American Automobile Manufacturers Association, 1401 H Street, NW, Suite 900, Washington, D.C. 20005 (202) 326-5500; *World Motor Vehicle Data*.

Statistical Office of the United Nations, Publishing Service, New York, New York 10017 (800) 253-9646; *Statistical Yearbook*, and *Survey of Economic and Social Conditions in Africa*.

Times Books, 201 East 50th Street, New York, New York 10022 (212) 751-2600; *The Economist Book of Vital World Statistics*.

NIGERIA - MUSEUMS

Facts on File, 460 Park Avenue South, New York, New York 10016 (800) 443-8323; *The New Book of World Rankings*.

NIGERIA - NATALITY - See NIGERIA - BIRTH RATES

NIGERIA - NATIONAL ACCOUNTS

African Development Bank, 01 BP 1387, Abidjan 01, Cote d'Ivoire; *Selected Statistics on Regional Member Countries*.

International Monetary Fund, 700 Nineteenth Street, NW, Washington, D.C. 20431 (202) 623-7000; *International Financial Statistics*.

Statistical Office of the United Nations, Publishing Service, New York, New York 10017 (800) 253-9646; *National Accounts Statistics*, and *Statistical Yearbook*.

United Nations Economic Commission for Africa, Africa Hall, Post Office Box 3001, Addis Ababa, Ethiopia (Telephone Number in U.S. (800) 253-9646); *African Statistical Yearbook*.

NIGERIA - NATIONAL INCOME

Facts on File, 460 Park Avenue South, New York, New York 10016 (800) 443-8323; *The New Book of World Rankings*.

Statistical Office of the United Nations, Publishing Service, New York, New York 10017 (800) 253-9646; *Statistical Yearbook*.

NIGERIA - NATIONAL PRODUCT

Facts on File, 460 Park Avenue South, New York, New York 10016 (800) 443-8323; *The New Book of World Rankings*.

Statistical Office of the United Nations, Publishing Service, New York, New York 10017 (800) 253-9646; *Statistical Yearbook*.

NIGERIA - NATURAL GAS PRODUCTION - See NIGERIA - MINING AND MINERAL PRODUCTS

NIGERIA - NATURAL RUBBER PRODUCTION

International Rubber Study Group, York House, Eighth Floor, Empire Way, Wembley, London HA9 0PA, England; *Rubber Statistical Bulletin*.

Statistical Office of the United Nations, Publishing Service, New York, New York 10017 (800) 253-9646; *Statistical Yearbook*.

NIGERIA - NEWSPAPER PRODUCTION - See NIGERIA - FORESTRY AND FOREST PRODUCTS

NIGERIA - NEWSPRINT - See NIGERIA - FORESTRY AND FOREST PRODUCTS

NIGERIA - PALM OIL AND PALM KERNELS PRODUCTION - See NIGERIA - CROPS

NIGERIA - PAPER - See NIGERIA - FORESTRY AND FOREST PRODUCTS

NIGERIA - PATENTS

Statistical Office of the United Nations, Publishing Service, New York, New York 10017 (800) 253-9646; *Statistical Yearbook*.

NIGERIA - PEANUT PRODUCTION - See NIGERIA - CROPS

NIGERIA - PESTICIDE USE

Food and Agricultural Organization of the United Nations (FAO) Via delle Terme di Caracalla, 00100 Rome, Italy (Telephone Number in U.S. (202) 653-2400); *The State of Food and Agriculture*.

NIGERIA - PETROLEUM INDUSTRY

Commodity Research Bureau, Incorporated, 75 Wall Street, New York, New York 10005 (212) 504-7754; *Commodity Year Book*.

Facts on File, 460 Park Avenue South, New York, New York 10016 (800) 443-8323; *The New Book of World Rankings*.

Food and Agricultural Organization of the United Nations (FAO) Via delle Terme di Caracalla, 00100 Rome, Italy (Telephone Number in U.S. (202) 653-2400); *The State of Food and Agriculture*.

Organization of Petroleum Exporting Countries, Obere Donaustrasse 93, 1020 Vienna 2, Austria; *OPEC Annual Statistical Bulletin*.

Penn Well Publishing Company, 1421 South Sheridan Road, Post Office Box 1260, Tulsa, Oklahoma 74101 (800) 752-9764; *International Energy Statistics Sourcebook.*

Statistical Office of the United Nations, Publishing Service, New York, New York 10017 (800) 253-9646; *Statistical Yearbook.*

NIGERIA - PIGS - See NIGERIA - LIVESTOCK AND POULTRY

NIGERIA - PIPELINES FOR OIL AND PETROLEUM PRODUCTS

Organization of Petroleum Exporting Countries, Obere Donaustrasse 93, 1020 Vienna 2, Austria; *OPEC Annual Statistical Bulletin.*

NIGERIA - PLASTIC AND RESIN PRODUCTION

Euromonitor Publications Limited, 87-88 Turnmill Street, London EC1M 5QU, England; *Third World Economic Handbook.*

NIGERIA - POPULATION

African Development Bank, 01 BP 1387, Abidjan 01, Cote d'Ivoire; *Selected Statistics on Regional Member Countries.*

The Economist Intelligence Unit, 111 West 57th Street, New York, New York 10019 (800) 938-4685; *The World Market Atlas.*

Euromonitor Publications Limited, 87-88 Turnmill Street, London EC1M 5QU, England; *International Marketing Data and Statistics.,* and *Third World Economic Handbook.*

Facts on File, 460 Park Avenue South, New York, New York 10016 (800) 443-8323; *The New Book of World Rankings.*

Food and Agricultural Organization of the United Nations (FAO), Via delle Terme di Caracalla, 00100 Rome, Italy (Telephone Number in U.S. (202) 653-2400); *Production Yearbook.*

International Labour Office, I.L.O. Publications, CH-1211, Geneva 22, Switzerland; *Yearbook of Labour Statistics.*

Statistical Office of the United Nations, Publishing Service, New York, New York 10017 (800) 253-9646; *Demographic Yearbook, Statistical Yearbook,* and *Survey of Economic and Social Conditions in Africa.*

Times Books, 201 East 50th Street, New York, New York 10022 (212) 751-2600; *The Economist Book of Vital World Statistics.*

United Nations Educational, Scientific and Cultural Organization (UNESCO), 7 Place de Fontenoy, F-75700 Paris, France (Telephone Number in U.S. (212) 963-5981); *Statistical Yearbook.*

U.S. Arms Control and Disarmament Agency, 320 Twenty-first Street, NW, Washington, D.C. 20451 (202) 647-8677; *World Military Expenditures and Arms Transfers.*

World Health Organization, Office of Publications, Avenue Appia, CH-1211 Geneva 27, Switzerland (Telephone Number in U.S. (518) 436-9686); *World Health Statistics Annual.*

NIGERIA - POST OFFICES

Facts on File, 460 Park Avenue South, New York, New York 10016 (800) 443-8323; *The New Book of World Rankings.*

NIGERIA - POTATO PRODUCTION - See NIGERIA - CROPS

NIGERIA - PRICES

Facts on File, 460 Park Avenue South, New York, New York 10016 (800) 443-8323; *The New Book of World Rankings.*

Food and Agricultural Organization of the United Nations (FAO), Via delle Terme di Caracalla, 00100 Rome, Italy (Telephone Number in U.S. (202) 653-2400); *Production Yearbook,* and *The State of Food and Agriculture.*

International Labour Office, I.L.O. Publications, CH-1211, Geneva 22, Switzerland; *Yearbook of Labour Statistics.*

International Monetary Fund, 700 Nineteenth Street, NW, Washington, D.C. 20431 (202) 623-7000; *International Financial Statistics.*

International Rubber Study Group, York House, Eighth Floor, Empire Way, Wembley, London HA9 0PA, England; *Rubber Statistical Bulletin.*

United Nations Economic Commission for Africa, Africa Hall, Post Office Box 3001, Addis Ababa, Ethiopia (Telephone Number in U.S. (800) 253-9646); *African Statistical Yearbook.*

NIGERIA - PRINTING AND WRITING PAPER - See NIGERIA - FORESTRY AND FOREST PRODUCTS

NIGERIA - PRODUCTION

American Automobile Manufacturers Association, 1401 H Street, NW, Suite 900, Washington, D.C. 20005 (202) 326-5500; *World Motor Vehicle Data.*

Euromonitor Publications Limited, 87-88 Turnmill Street, London EC1M 5QU, England; *Third World Economic Handbook.*

Facts on File, 460 Park Avenue South, New York, New York 10016 (800) 443-8323; *The New Book of World Rankings.*

International Rubber Study Group, York House, Eighth Floor, Empire Way, Wembley, London HA9 0PA, England; *Rubber Statistical Bulletin.*

NIGERIA - PRODUCTIVITY

Euromonitor Publications Limited, 87-88 Turnmill Street, London EC1M 5QU, England; *International Marketing Data and Statistics.*

NIGERIA - PROPERTY TAXES

International Monetary Fund, 700 Nineteenth Street, NW, Washington, D.C. 20431 (202) 623-7000; *Government Finance Statistics Yearbook.*

NIGERIA - RADIO BROADCASTING - See NIGERIA - BROADCASTING

NIGERIA - RADIO RECEIVER PRODUCTION

Statistical Office of the United Nations, Publishing Service, New York, New York 10017 (800) 253-9646; *Statistical Yearbook.*

NIGERIA - RAILWAYS

Jane's Information Group, Sentinel House, 163 Brighton Road, Coulsdon, Surrey CR5 2NH, England (Telephone Number in U.S. (703) 683-3700); *Jane's World Railways.*

Statistical Office of the United Nations, Publishing Service, New York, New York 10017 (800) 253-9646; *Statistical Yearbook*, and *Survey of Economic and Social Conditions in Africa*.

United Nations Economic Commission for Africa, Africa Hall, Post Office Box 3001, Addis Ababa, Ethiopia (Telephone Number in U.S. (800) 253-9646); *African Statistical Yearbook*.

NIGERIA - RELIGION

Facts on File, 460 Park Avenue South, New York, New York 10016 (800) 443-8323; *The New Book of World Rankings*.

NIGERIA - RENT PRICES

International Labour Office, I.L.O. Publications, CH-1211, Geneva 22, Switzerland; *Yearbook of Labour Statistics*.

NIGERIA - RETAIL TRADE

Euromonitor Publications Limited, 87-88 Turnmill Street, London EC1M 5QU, England; *Third World Economic Handbook*.

NIGERIA - RICE PRODUCTION - See NIGERIA - CROPS

NIGERIA - ROOT AND TUBER PRODUCTION - See NIGERIA - CROPS

NIGERIA - ROUNDWOOD PRODUCTION - See NIGERIA - FORESTRY AND FOREST PRODUCTS

NIGERIA - RUBBER PRODUCTION AND CONSUMPTION

Euromonitor Publications Limited, 87-88 Turnmill Street, London EC1M 5QU, England; *Third World Economic Handbook*.

Facts on File, 460 Park Avenue South, New York, New York 10016 (800) 443-8323; *The New Book of World Rankings*.

International Rubber Study Group, York House, Eighth Floor, Empire Way, Wembley, London HA9 0PA, England; *Rubber Statistical Bulletin*.

Statistical Office of the United Nations, Publishing Service, New York, New York 10017 (800) 253-9646; *Statistical Yearbook*.

NIGERIA - SAWNWOOD PRODUCTION - See NIGERIA - FORESTRY AND FOREST PRODUCTS

NIGERIA - SCIENCE AND TECHNOLOGY - EXPENDITURE FOR RESEARCH

Statistical Office of the United Nations, Publishing Service, New York, New York 10017 (800) 253-9646; *Statistical Yearbook*.

NIGERIA - SCIENTISTS AND TECHNICIANS

Statistical Office of the United Nations, Publishing Service, New York, New York 10017 (800) 253-9646; *Statistical Yearbook*.

United Nations Educational, Scientific and Cultural Organization (UNESCO), 7 Place de Fontenoy, F-75700 Paris, France (Telephone Number in U.S. (212) 963-5981); *Statistical Yearbook*.

NIGERIA - SENIOR CITIZENS

Facts on File, 460 Park Avenue South, New York, New York 10016 (800) 443-8323; *The New Book of World Rankings*.

NIGERIA - SESAME SEED PRODUCTION - See NIGERIA - CROPS

NIGERIA - SHEEP - See NIGERIA - LIVESTOCK AND POULTRY

NIGERIA - SILVER PRODUCTION AND CONSUMPTION - See NIGERIA - MINING AND MINERAL PRODUCTS

NIGERIA - SOCIAL DATA

African Development Bank, 01 BP 1387, Abidjan 01, Cote d'Ivoire; *Selected Statistics on Regional Member Countries*.

Facts on File, 460 Park Avenue South, New York, New York 10016 (800) 443-8323; *The New Book of World Rankings*.

NIGERIA - SOCIAL SECURITY

International Monetary Fund, 700 Nineteenth Street, NW, Washington, D.C. 20431 (202) 623-7000; *Government Finance Statistics Yearbook*.

NIGERIA - SOYBEAN PRODUCTION - See NIGERIA - CROPS

NIGERIA - STAMP TAXES AND DUTIES - See NIGERIA - TAXATION

NIGERIA - STATE BUDGET REVENUE AND EXPENDITURES

Euromonitor Publications Limited, 87-88 Turnmill Street, London EC1M 5QU, England; *International Marketing Data and Statistics*.

NIGERIA - STEEL - See NIGERIA - MINING AND MINERAL PRODUCTS

NIGERIA - STOCKS - COMMODITY - MARKET PRICE - INDEX

Facts on File, 460 Park Avenue South, New York, New York 10016 (800) 443-8323; *The New Book of World Rankings*.

Food and Agricultural Organization of the United Nations (FAO) Via delle Terme di Caracalla, 00100 Rome, Italy (Telephone Number in U.S. (202) 653-2400); *The State of Food and Agriculture*.

NIGERIA - SUGAR PRODUCTION AND CONSUMPTION - See NIGERIA - CROPS

NIGERIA - TAXATION

International Monetary Fund, 700 Nineteenth Street, NW, Washington, D.C. 20431 (202) 623-7000; *Government Finance Statistics Yearbook*.

The World Bank, 1818 H Street, NW, Washington, D.C. 20433 (202) 477-1234; *World Tables*.

NIGERIA - TAX REVENUES - See NIGERIA - TAXATION

NIGERIA - TELEGRAPH SERVICE

Statistical Office of the United Nations, Publishing Service, New York, New York 10017 (800) 253-9646; *Statistical Yearbook*.

NIGERIA - TELEPHONES IN USE

American Telephone and Telegraph Company, 26 Parsippany Road, Whippany, New Jersey 07981 (800) 338-4038; *The World's Telephones*.

Euromonitor Publications Limited, 87-88 Turnmill Street, London EC1M 5QU, England; *Third World Economic Handbook*.

Statistical Office of the United Nations, Publishing Service, New York, New York 10017 (800) 253-9646; *Statistical Yearbook*.

NIGERIA - TELEVISION BROADCASTING - See NIGERIA - BROADCASTING

NIGERIA - TEXTILE INDUSTRY

Euromonitor Publications Limited, 87-88 Turnmill Street, London EC1M 5QU, England; *Third World Economic Handbook*.

Statistical Office of the United Nations, Publishing Service, New York, New York 10017 (800) 253-9646; *Statistical Yearbook*.

NIGERIA - TIN - See NIGERIA - MINING AND MINERAL PRODUCTS

NIGERIA - TIRE (MOTOR VEHICLE) PRODUCTION

International Rubber Study Group, York House, Eighth Floor, Empire Way, Wembley, London HA9 0PA, England; *Rubber Statistical Bulletin*.

Statistical Office of the United Nations, Publishing Service, New York, New York 10017 (800) 253-9646; *Statistical Yearbook*.

NIGERIA - TOBACCO PRODUCTION

Euromonitor Publications Limited, 87-88 Turnmill Street, London EC1M 5QU, England; *Third World Economic Handbook*.

Facts on File, 460 Park Avenue South, New York, New York 10016 (800) 443-8323; *The New Book of World Rankings*.

Statistical Office of the United Nations, Publishing Service, New York, New York 10017 (800) 253-9646; *Statistical Yearbook*.

NIGERIA - TOURISM

Euromonitor Publications Limited, 87-88 Turnmill Street, London EC1M 5QU, England; *Third World Economic Handbook*.

Facts on File, 460 Park Avenue South, New York, New York 10016 (800) 443-8323; *The New Book of World Rankings*.

Statistical Office of the United Nations, Publishing Service, New York, New York 10017 (800) 253-9646; *Statistical Yearbook*.

Times Books, 201 East 50th Street, New York, New York 10022 (212) 751-2600; *The Economist Book of Vital World Statistics*.

United Nations Economic Commission for Africa, Africa Hall, Post Office Box 3001, Addis Ababa, Ethiopia (Telephone Number in U.S. (800) 253-9646); *African Statistical Yearbook*.

NIGERIA - TRACTORS IN USE

Statistical Office of the United Nations, Publishing Service, New York, New York 10017 (800) 253-9646; *Statistical Yearbook*.

NIGERIA - TRADE - See NIGERIA - FOREIGN TRADE

NIGERIA - TRADEMARKS AND SERVICE MARKS

Statistical Office of the United Nations, Publishing Service, New York, New York 10017 (800) 253-9646; *Statistical Yearbook*.

NIGERIA - TRANSPORTATION AND COMMUNICATIONS

Euromonitor Publications Limited, 87-88 Turnmill Street, London EC1M 5QU, England; *Third World Economic Handbook*.

Facts on File, 460 Park Avenue South, New York, New York 10016 (800) 443-8323; *The New Book of World Rankings*.

United Nations Economic Commission for Africa, Africa Hall, Post Office Box 3001, Addis Ababa, Ethiopia (Telephone Number in U.S. (800) 253-9646); *African Statistical Yearbook*.

NIGERIA - UNEMPLOYMENT

Euromonitor Publications Limited, 87-88 Turnmill Street, London EC1M 5QU, England; *International Marketing Data and Statistics*.

International Labour Office, I.L.O. Publications, CH-1211, Geneva 22, Switzerland; *Yearbook of Labour Statistics*.

Statistical Office of the United Nations, Publishing Service, New York, New York 10017 (800) 253-9646; *Statistical Yearbook*.

NIGERIA - VITAL STATISTICS

Euromonitor Publications Limited, 87-88 Turnmill Street, London EC1M 5QU, England; *International Marketing Data and Statistics*, and *Third World Economic Handbook*.

Statistical Office of the United Nations, Publishing Service, New York, New York 10017 (800) 253-9646; *Statistical Yearbook*.

World Health Organization, Office of Publications, Avenue Appia, CH-1211 Geneva 27, Switzerland (Telephone Number in U.S. (518) 436-9686); *World Health Statistics Annual*.

NIGERIA - WAGES

International Labour Office, I.L.O. Publications, CH-1211, Geneva 22, Switzerland; *Yearbook of Labour Statistics*.

Statistical Office of the United Nations, Publishing Service, New York, New York 10017 (800) 253-9646; *Statistical Yearbook*.

NIGERIA - WEATHER

Facts on File, 460 Park Avenue South, New York, New York 10016 (800) 443-8323; *The New Book of World Rankings*.

NIGERIA - WELFARE

International Monetary Fund, 700 Nineteenth Street, NW, Washington, D.C. 20431 (202) 623-7000; *Government Finance Statistics Yearbook*.

NIGERIA - WHEAT PRODUCTION AND PRICES - See NIGERIA - CROPS

NIGERIA - WHOLESALE TRADE

Euromonitor Publications Limited, 87-88 Turnmill Street, London EC1M 5QU, England; *Third World Economic Handbook*.

NIGERIA - WINE PRODUCTION

Facts on File, 460 Park Avenue South, New York, New York 10016 (800) 443-8323; *The New Book of World Rankings*.

NIGERIA - WOOD PULP PRODUCTION - See NIGERIA - FORESTRY AND FOREST PRODUCTS

NIGERIA - WOOL PRODUCTION

Facts on File, 460 Park Avenue South, New York, New York 10016 (800) 443-8323; *The New Book of World Rankings.*

NIGERIA - YARN PRODUCTION

Statistical Office of the United Nations, Publishing Service, New York, New York 10017 (800) 253-9646; *Statistical Yearbook.*

NITROGEN IN AMMONIA - WORLD PRODUCTION

U.S. Department of the Interior, Bureau of the Mines, 810 Seventh Street, NW, Washington, D.C. 20241 (202) 501-9649; *Annual Reports,* and *Mineral Commodities Summaries.*

Niue - National Statistical Office

Government of Niue, Post Office Box 67, Alofi, Niue, South Pacific.

Niue - Primary Statistics Source

Department of Economic Development, Statistics Unit, Post Office Box 42, Niue Island, Niue; *Abstract of Statistics.*

NIUE - AGRICULTURE

Food and Agricultural Organization of the United Nations (FAO) Via delle Terme di Caracalla, 00100 Rome, Italy (Telephone Number in U.S. (202) 653-2400); *Production Yearbook, The State of Food and Agriculture,* and *Trade Yearbook.*

Statistical Office of the United Nations, Publishing Service, New York, New York 10017 (800) 253-9646; *Statistical Yearbook,* and *Statistical Yearbook for Asia and the Pacific.*

NIUE - AREA AND DENSITY OF POPULATION

Food and Agricultural Organization of the United Nations (FAO) Via delle Terme di Caracalla, 00100 Rome, Italy (Telephone Number in U.S. (202) 653-2400); *The State of Food and Agriculture.*

Statistical Office of the United Nations, Publishing Service, New York, New York 10017 (800) 253-9646; *Statistical Yearbook.*

NIUE - BIRTH RATES

Statistical Office of the United Nations, Publishing Service, New York, New York 10017 (800) 253-9646; *Demographic Yearbook,* and *Statistical Yearbook.*

World Health Organization, Office of Publications, Avenue Appia, CH-1211 Geneva 27, Switzerland (Telephone Number in U.S. (518) 436-9686); *World Health Statistics Annual.*

NIUE - BROADCASTING

Billboard Limited, Post Office Box 9027, 1006 AA Amsterdam, The Netherlands (Telephone Number in U.S. (212) 764-7300); *World Radio TV Handbook.*

United Nations Educational, Scientific and Cultural Organization (UNESCO), 7 Place de Fontenoy, F-75700 Paris, France (Telephone Number in U.S. (212) 963-5981); *Statistical Yearbook.*

NIUE - CALORIE SUPPLY

Food and Agricultural Organization of the United Nations (FAO) Via delle Terme di Caracalla, 00100 Rome, Italy (Telephone Number in U.S. (202) 653-2400); *The State of Food and Agriculture.*

NIUE - CATTLE - See NIUE - LIVESTOCK AND POULTRY

NIUE - CLOTHING EXPORTS AND IMPORTS

South Pacific Commission, Post Box D5, Noumea Cedex, New Caledonia; *Statistical Bulletin of the South Pacific: Retail Price Indexes.*

NIUE - COMMUNICATIONS

Statistical Office of the United Nations, Publishing Service, New York, New York 10017 (800) 253-9646; *Statistical Yearbook for Asia and the Pacific.*

NIUE - CONSUMER PRICE INDEX

Statistical Office of the United Nations, Publishing Service, New York, New York 10017 (800) 253-9646; *Statistical Yearbook.*

NIUE - CONSUMER PRICES

International Labour Office, I.L.O. Publications, CH-1211, Geneva 22, Switzerland; *Yearbook of Labour Statistics.*

NIUE - CONSUMPTION

South Pacific Commission, Post Box D5, Noumea Cedex, New Caledonia; *Statistical Bulletin of the South Pacific: Retail Price Indexes.*

NIUE - CORN PRODUCTION - See NIUE - CROPS

NIUE - CROPS

Food and Agricultural Organization of the United Nations (FAO) Via delle Terme di Caracalla, 00100 Rome, Italy (Telephone Number in U.S. (202) 653-2400); *Production Yearbook,* and *The State of Food and Agriculture.*

NIUE - DAIRY PRODUCTS

Food and Agricultural Organization of the United Nations (FAO) Via delle Terme di Caracalla, 00100 Rome, Italy (Telephone Number in U.S. (202) 653-2400); *The State of Food and Agriculture.*

NIUE - DEATH RATES

Statistical Office of the United Nations, Publishing Service, New York, New York 10017 (800) 253-9646; *Statistical Yearbook.*

NIUE - DEVELOPMENT ASSISTANCE

Statistical Office of the United Nations, Publishing Service, New York, New York 10017 (800) 253-9646; *Statistical Yearbook.*

NIUE - DIVORCE RATES

Statistical Office of the United Nations, Publishing Service, New York, New York 10017 (800) 253-9646; *Demographic Yearbook,* and *Statistical Yearbook.*

NIUE - EDUCATION

Statistical Office of the United Nations, Publishing Service, New York, New York 10017 (800) 253-9646; *Statistical Yearbook for Asia and the Pacific.*

United Nations Educational, Scientific and Cultural Organization (UNESCO), 7 Place de Fontenoy, F-75700 Paris, France (Telephone Number in U.S. (212) 963-5981); *Statistical Yearbook.*

NIUE - EGG PRODUCTION AND CONSUMPTION - See NIUE - DAIRY PRODUCTS

NIUE - ELECTRICITY

Statistical Office of the United Nations, Publishing Service, New York, New York 10017 (800) 253-9646; *Electric Power in Asia and the Pacific.*

NIUE - EMPLOYMENT

International Labour Office, I.L.O. Publications, CH-1211, Geneva 22, Switzerland; *Yearbook of Labour Statistics.*

NIUE - ENERGY SUPPLIES

Food and Agricultural Organization of the United Nations (FAO) Via delle Terme di Caracalla, 00100 Rome, Italy (Telephone Number in U.S. (202) 653-2400); *The State of Food and Agriculture.*

Statistical Office of the United Nations, Publishing Service, New York, New York 10017 (800) 253-9646; *Statistical Yearbook for Asia and the Pacific.*

NIUE - EXPORTS

Food and Agricultural Organization of the United Nations (FAO) Via delle Terme di Caracalla, 00100 Rome, Italy (Telephone Number in U.S. (202) 653-2400); *The State of Food and Agriculture.*

South Pacific Commission, Post Box D5, Noumea Cedex, New Caledonia; *Statistical Bulletin of the South Pacific: Overseas Trade.*

NIUE - EXTERNAL TRADE

Food and Agricultural Organization of the United Nations (FAO) Via delle Terme di Caracalla, 00100 Rome, Italy (Telephone Number in U.S. (202) 653-2400); *The State of Food and Agriculture*, and *Trade Yearbook.*

Statistical Office of the United Nations, Publishing Service, New York, New York 10017 (800) 253-9646; *Statistical Yearbook for Asia and the Pacific.*

NIUE - FARM CROPS - See NIUE - CROPS

NIUE - FETAL MORTALITY

Statistical Office of the United Nations, Publishing Service, New York, New York 10017 (800) 253-9646; *Demographic Yearbook.*

NIUE - FERTILIZER

Food and Agricultural Organization of the United Nations (FAO) Via delle Terme di Caracalla, 00100 Rome, Italy (Telephone Number in U.S. (202) 653-2400); *The State of Food and Agriculture.*

NIUE - FINANCE

Statistical Office of the United Nations, Publishing Service, New York, New York 10017 (800) 253-9646; *Statistical Yearbook for Asia and the Pacific.*

NIUE - FISHERIES

Food and Agricultural Organization of the United Nations (FAO) Via delle Terme di Caracalla, 00100 Rome, Italy (Telephone Number in U.S. (202) 653-2400); *The State of Food and Agriculture,* and *Yearbook of Fishery Statistics.*

NIUE - FOOD

Food and Agricultural Organization of the United Nations (FAO), Via delle Terme di Caracalla, 00100 Rome, Italy (Telephone Number in U.S. (202) 653-2400); *Production Yearbook,* and *The State of Food and Agriculture.*

South Pacific Commission, Post Box D5, Noumea Cedex, New Caledonia; *Statistical Bulletin of the South Pacific: Retail Price Indexes.*

Statistical Office of the United Nations, Publishing Service, New York, New York 10017 (800) 253-9646; *Statistical Yearbook for Asia and the Pacific.*

NIUE - FOREIGN TRADE

Food and Agricultural Organization of the United Nations (FAO) Via delle Terme di Caracalla, 00100 Rome, Italy (Telephone Number in U.S. (202) 653-2400); *The State of Food and Agriculture.*

South Pacific Commission, Post Box D5, Noumea Cedex, New Caledonia; *Statistical Bulletin of the South Pacific: Overseas Trade.*

Statistical Office of the United Nations, Publishing Service, New York, New York 10017 (800) 253-9646; *International Trade Statistics Yearbook.*

NIUE - FORESTRY AND FOREST PRODUCTS

Food and Agricultural Organization of the United Nations (FAO) Via delle Terme di Caracalla, 00100 Rome, Italy (Telephone Number in U.S. (202) 653-2400); *The State of Food and Agriculture.*

Statistical Office of the United Nations, Publishing Service, New York, New York 10017 (800) 253-9646; *Statistical Yearbook.*

NIUE - GENERAL MORTALITY

Statistical Office of the United Nations, Publishing Service, New York, New York 10017 (800) 253-9646; *Demographic Yearbook.*

World Health Organization, Office of Publications, Avenue Appia, CH-1211 Geneva 27, Switzerland (Telephone Number in U.S. (518) 436-9686); *World Health Statistics Annual.*

NIUE - GRAIN PRODUCTION - See NIUE - CROPS

NIUE - HEALTH

South Pacific Commission, Post Box D5, Noumea Cedex, New Caledonia; *Statistical Bulletin of the South Pacific: Retail Price Indexes.*

Statistical Office of the United Nations, Publishing Service, New York, New York 10017 (800) 253-9646; *Statistical Yearbook.*

NIUE - HIDE PRODUCTION

Food and Agricultural Organization of the United Nations (FAO), Via delle Terme di Caracalla, 00100 Rome, Italy (Telephone Number in U.S. (202) 653-2400); *Production Yearbook.*

NIUE - HOURS OF WORK - See NIUE - EMPLOYMENT

NIUE - HOUSING AND HOUSING UNITS

South Pacific Commission, Post Box D5, Noumea Cedex, New Caledonia; *Statistical Bulletin of the South Pacific: Retail Price Indexes.*

NIUE - HOUSING EXPENDITURES

South Pacific Commission, Post Box D5, Noumea Cedex, New Caledonia; *Statistical Bulletin of the South Pacific: Retail Price Indexes.*

NIUE - ILLITERATE POPULATION

United Nations Educational, Scientific and Cultural Organization (UNESCO), 7 Place de Fontenoy, F-75700 Paris, France (Telephone Number in U.S. (212) 963-5981); *Statistical Yearbook.*

NIUE - IMPORTS

Food and Agricultural Organization of the United Nations (FAO) Via delle Terme di Caracalla, 00100 Rome, Italy (Telephone Number in U.S (203) 653-2400); *The State of Food and Agriculture.*

South Pacific Commission, Post Box D5, Noumea Cedex, New Caledonia; *Statistical Bulletin of the South Pacific: Overseas Trade.*

NIUE - INDUSTRY

International Labour Office, I.L.O. Publications, CH-1211, Geneva 22, Switzerland; *Yearbook of Labour Statistics.*

Statistical Office of the United Nations, Publishing Service, New York, New York 10017 (800) 253-9646; *Statistical Yearbook for Asia and the Pacific.*

NIUE - INFANT AND MATERNAL MORTALITY

Statistical Office of the United Nations, Publishing Service, New York, New York 10017 (800) 253-9646; *Demographic Yearbook,* and *Statistical Yearbook.*

NIUE - INTERNAL TRADE

Statistical Office of the United Nations, Publishing Service, New York, New York 10017 (800) 253-9646; *Statistical Yearbook for Asia and the Pacific.*

NIUE - LABOR FORCE

Food and Agricultural Organization of the United Nations (FAO) Via delle Terme di Caracalla, 00100 Rome, Italy (Telephone Number in U.S. (202) 653-2400); *The State of Food and Agriculture.*

NIUE - LABOR PRODUCTIVITY

International Labour Office, I.L.O. Publications, CH-1211, Geneva 22, Switzerland; *Yearbook of Labour Statistics.*

NIUE - LAND USE

Food and Agricultural Organization of the United Nations (FAO), Via delle Terme di Caracalla, 00100 Rome, Italy (Telephone Number in U.S. (202) 653-2400); *Production Yearbook.*

NIUE - LIBRARIES

United Nations Educational, Scientific and Cultural Organization (UNESCO), 7 Place de Fontenoy, F-75700 Paris, France (Telephone Number in U.S. (212) 963-5981); *Statistical Yearbook.*

NIUE - LIVESTOCK AND POULTRY

Food and Agricultural Organization of the United Nations (FAO), Via delle Terme di Caracalla, 00100 Rome, Italy (Telephone Number in U.S. (202) 653-2400); *Production Yearbook,* and *The State of Food and Agriculture.*

Statistical Office of the United Nations, Publishing Service, New York, New York 10017 (800) 253-9646; *Statistical Yearbook.*

NIUE - MANPOWER

Statistical Office of the United Nations, Publishing Service, New York, New York 10017 (800) 253-9646; *Statistical Yearbook for Asia and the Pacific.*

NIUE - MARRIAGE RATES

Statistical Office of the United Nations, Publishing Service, New York, New York 10017 (800) 253-9646; *Demographic Yearbook,* and *Statistical Yearbook.*

NIUE - MEAT PRODUCTION - See NIUE - LIVESTOCK AND POULTRY

NIUE - MOTION PICTURE THEATRES

Statistical Office of the United Nations, Publishing Service, New York, New York 10017 (800) 253-9646; *Statistical Yearbook.*

NIUE - NATALITY - See NIUE - BIRTH RATES

NIUE - NATIONAL ACCOUNTS

Statistical Office of the United Nations, Publishing Service, New York, New York 10017 (800) 253-9646; *Statistical Yearbook for Asia and the Pacific.*

NIUE - NEWSPAPER PRODUCTION - See NIUE - FORESTRY AND FOREST PRODUCTS

NIUE - PERIODICALS

United Nations Educational, Scientific and Cultural Organization (UNESCO), 7 Place de Fontenoy, F-75700 Paris, France (Telephone Number in U.S. (212) 963-5981); *Statistical Yearbook.*

NIUE - PESTICIDE USE

Food and Agricultural Organization of the United Nations (FAO) Via delle Terme di Caracalla, 00100 Rome, Italy (Telephone Number in U.S. (202) 653-2400); *The State of Food and Agriculture.*

NIUE - PETROLEUM INDUSTRY

Food and Agricultural Organization of the United Nations (FAO) Via delle Terme di Caracalla, 00100 Rome, Italy (Telephone Number in U.S. (202) 653-2400); *The State of Food and Agriculture.*

NIUE - PIGS - See NIUE - LIVESTOCK AND POULTRY

NIUE - POPULATION

Food and Agricultural Organization of the United Nations (FAO), Via delle Terme di Caracalla, 00100 Rome, Italy (Telephone Number in U.S. (202) 653-2400); *Production Yearbook.*

International Labour Office, I.L.O. Publications, CH-1211, Geneva 22, Switzerland; *Yearbook of Labour Statistics.*

Statistical Office of the United Nations, Publishing Service, New York, New York 10017 (800) 253-9646; *Demographic Yearbook,* and *Statistical Yearbook for Asia and the Pacific.*

World Health Organization, Office of Publications, Avenue Appia, CH-1211 Geneva 27, Switzerland (Telephone Number in U.S. (518) 436-9686); *World Health Statistics Annual.*

NIUE - POWER PRODUCTION INDUSTRY

Statistical Office of the United Nations, Publishing Service, New York, New York 10017 (800) 253-9646; *Electric Power in Asia and the Pacific.*

NIUE - PRICES

Food and Agricultural Organization of the United Nations (FAO), Via delle Terme di Caracalla, 00100 Rome, Italy (Telephone Number in U.S. (202) 653-2400); *Production Yearbook.*

International Labour Office, I.L.O. Publications, CH-1211, Geneva 22, Switzerland; *Yearbook of Labour Statistics.*

South Pacific Commission, Post Box D5, Noumea Cedex, New Caledonia; *Statistical Bulletin of the South Pacific: Overseas Trade,* and *Statistical Bulletin of the South Pacific: Retail Price Indexes.*

NIUE - RADIO BROADCASTING - See NIUE - BROADCASTING

NIUE - ROOT AND TUBER PRODUCTION - NIUE - CROPS

NIUE - SCIENTISTS AND TECHNICIANS

Statistical Office of the United Nations, Publishing Service, New York, New York 10017 (800) 253-9646; *Statistical Yearbook.*

NIUE - STOCKS - COMMODITY - MARKET PRICE - INDEX

Food and Agricultural Organization of the United Nations (FAO) Via delle Terme di Caracalla, 00100 Rome, Italy (Telephone Number in U.S. (202) 653-2400); *The State of Food and Agriculture.*

NIUE - TELEPHONES IN USE

American Telephone and Telegraph Company, 26 Parsippany Road, Whippany, New Jersey 07981 (800) 338-4038; *The World's Telephones.*

NIUE - TOBACCO PRODUCTION

South Pacific Commission, Post Box D5, Noumea Cedex, New Caledonia; *Statistical Bulletin of the South Pacific: Retail Price Indexes.*

NIUE - TOURISM

World Tourism Organization, Calle Capitan Haya 42, E-28020 Madrid, Spain; *Yearbook of Tourism Statistics.*

NIUE - TRACTORS IN USE

Statistical Office of the United Nations, Publishing Service, New York, New York 10017 (800) 253-9646; *Statistical Yearbook.*

NIUE - TRADE - See NIUE - FOREIGN TRADE

NIUE - TRANSPORTATION AND COMMUNICATIONS

South Pacific Commission, Post Box D5, Noumea Cedex, New Caledonia; *Statistical Bulletin of the South Pacific: Retail Price Indexes.*

Statistical Office of the United Nations, Publishing Service, New York, New York 10017 (800) 253-9646; *Statistical Yearbook for Asia and the Pacific.*

NIUE - UTILITIES

Statistical Office of the United Nations, Publishing Service, New York, New York 10017 (800) 253-9646; *Electric Power in Asia and the Pacific.*

NIUE - VITAL STATISTICS

Statistical Office of the United Nations, Publishing Service, New York, New York 10017 (800) 253-9646; *Statistical Yearbook.*

World Health Organization, Office of Publications, Avenue Appia, CH-1211 Geneva 27, Switzerland (Telephone Number in U.S. (518) 436-9686); *World Health Statistics Annual.*

NOBEL PRIZE LAUREATES

National Science Foundation, 4201 Wilson Boulevard, Arlington, Virginia 22230 (703) 306-1234; unpublished data.

NONFERROUS METALS AND PRODUCTS - See METALS

NONFINANCIAL CORPORATIONS - See CORPORATIONS

NONPROFIT ASSOCIATIONS

Gale Research Incorporated, 835 Penobscot Building, Detroit, Michigan 48226 (800) 877-4253; compiled from *Encyclopedia of Associations.*

Norfolk Island - Primary Statistics Source

Australian Government Publishing Service, Post Office Box 84, Canberra ACT 26010, Australia; *Annual Report of the Territory of Norfolk Island.*

NORFOLK ISLAND - AGRICULTURE

Food and Agricultural Organization of the United Nations (FAO) Via delle Terme di Caracalla, 00100 Rome, Italy (Telephone Number in U.S. (202) 653-2400); *Production Yearbook, The State of Food and Agriculture,* and *Trade Yearbook.*

Statistical Office of the United Nations, Publishing Service, New York, New York 10017 (800) 253-9646; *Statistical Yearbook.*

NORFOLK ISLAND - AREA AND DENSITY OF POPULATION

Food and Agricultural Organization of the United Nations (FAO) Via delle Terme di Caracalla, 00100 Rome, Italy (Telephone Number in U.S. (202) 653-2400); *The State of Food and Agriculture*.

Statistical Office of the United Nations, Publishing Service, New York, New York 10017 (800) 253-9646; *Statistical Yearbook*.

NORFOLK ISLAND - BIRTH RATES

Statistical Office of the United Nations, Publishing Service, New York, New York 10017 (800) 253-9646; *Demographic Yearbook*, and *Statistical Yearbook*.

World Health Organization, Office of Publications, Avenue Appia, CH-1211 Geneva 27, Switzerland (Telephone Number in U.S. (518) 436-9686); *World Health Statistics Annual*.

NORFOLK ISLAND - BOOK PRODUCTION

United Nations Educational, Scientific and Cultural Organization (UNESCO), 7 Place de Fontenoy, F-75700 Paris, France (Telephone Number in U.S. (212) 963-5981); *Statistical Yearbook*.

NORFOLK ISLAND - BROADCASTING

Billboard Limited, Post Office Box 9027, 1006 AA Amsterdam, The Netherlands (Telephone Number in U.S. (212) 764-7300); *World Radio TV Handbook*.

NORFOLK ISLAND - CALORIE SUPPLY

Food and Agricultural Organization of the United Nations (FAO) Via delle Terme di Caracalla, 00100 Rome, Italy (Telephone Number in U.S. (202) 653-2400); *The State of Food and Agriculture*.

NORFOLK ISLAND - CATTLE - See NORFOLK ISLAND - LIVESTOCK AND POULTRY

NORFOLK ISLAND - CORN PRODUCTION - See NORFOLK ISLAND - CROPS

NORFOLK ISLAND - CROPS

Food and Agricultural Organization of the United Nations (FAO) Via delle Terme di Caracalla, 00100 Rome, Italy (Telephone Number in U.S. (202) 653-2400); *The State of Food and Agriculture*.

NORFOLK ISLAND - DAIRY PRODUCTS

Food and Agricultural Organization of the United Nations (FAO) Via delle Terme di Caracalla, 00100 Rome, Italy (Telephone Number in U.S. (202) 653-2400); *The State of Food and Agriculture*.

NORFOLK ISLAND - DEATH RATES

Statistical Office of the United Nations, Publishing Service, New York, New York 10017 (800) 253-9646; *Statistical Yearbook*.

NORFOLK ISLAND - DIVORCE RATES

Statistical Office of the United Nations, Publishing Service, New York, New York 10017 (800) 253-9646; *Demographic Yearbook*.

NORFOLK ISLAND - EDUCATION

United Nations Educational, Scientific and Cultural Organization (UNESCO), 7 Place de Fontenoy, F-75700 Paris, France (Telephone Number in U.S. (212) 963-5981); *Statistical Yearbook*.

NORFOLK ISLAND - EGG PRODUCTION AND CONSUMPTION - See NORFOLK ISLAND - DAIRY PRODUCTS

NORFOLK ISLAND - ENERGY

Food and Agricultural Organization of the United Nations (FAO) Via delle Terme di Caracalla, 00100 Rome, Italy (Telephone Number in U.S. (202) 653-2400); *The State of Food and Agriculture*.

NORFOLK ISLAND - EXPORTS

Food and Agricultural Organization of the United Nations (FAO) Via delle Terme di Caracalla, 00100 Rome, Italy (Telephone Number in U.S. (202) 653-2400); *The State of Food and Agriculture*.

NORFOLK ISLAND - EXTERNAL TRADE

Food and Agricultural Organization of the United Nations (FAO) Via delle Terme di Caracalla, 00100 Rome, Italy (Telephone Number in U.S. (202) 653-2400); *The State of Food and Agriculture*, and *Trade Yearbook*.

NORFOLK ISLAND - FARM CROPS - See NORFOLK ISLAND - CROPS

NORFOLK ISLAND - FETAL MORTALITY

Statistical Office of the United Nations, Publishing Service, New York, New York 10017 (800) 253-9646; *Demographic Yearbook*.

NORFOLK ISLAND - FERTILIZER

Food and Agricultural Organization of the United Nations (FAO) Via delle Terme di Caracalla, 00100 Rome, Italy (Telephone Number in U.S. (202) 653-2400); *The State of Food and Agriculture*.

NORFOLK ISLAND - FISHERIES

Food and Agricultural Organization of the United Nations (FAO) Via delle Terme di Caracalla, 00100 Rome, Italy (Telephone Number in U.S. (202) 653-2400); *The State of Food and Agriculture*, and *Yearbook of Fishery Statistics*.

NORFOLK ISLAND - FOOD

Food and Agricultural Organization of the United Nations (FAO), Via delle Terme di Caracalla, 00100 Rome, Italy (Telephone Number in U.S. (202) 653-2400); *Production Yearbook*, and *The State of Food and Agriculture*.

NORFOLK ISLAND - FOREIGN TRADE

Food and Agricultural Organization of the United Nations (FAO) Via delle Terme di Caracalla, 00100 Rome, Italy (Telephone Number in U.S. (202) 653-2400); *The State of Food and Agriculture*.

NORFOLK ISLAND - FORESTRY AND FOREST PRODUCTS

Food and Agricultural Organization of the United Nations (FAO) Via delle Terme di Caracalla, 00100 Rome, Italy (Telephone Number in U.S. (202) 653-2400); *The State of Food and Agriculture*.

Statistical Office of the United Nations, Publishing Service, New York, New York 10017 (800) 253-9646; *Statistical Yearbook*.

NORFOLK ISLAND - GENERAL MORTALITY

Statistical Office of the United Nations, Publishing Service, New York, New York 10017 (800) 253-9646; *Demographic Yearbook.*

World Health Organization, Office of Publications, Avenue Appia, CH-1211 Geneva 27, Switzerland (Telephone Number in U.S. (518) 436-9686); *World Health Statistics Annual.*

NORFOLK ISLAND - GRAIN PRODUCTION - See NORFOLK ISLAND - CROPS

NORFOLK ISLAND - HOUSING AND HOUSING UNITS

Statistical Office of the United Nations, Publishing Service, New York, New York 10017 (800) 253-9646; *Statistical Yearbook.*

NORFOLK ISLAND - IMPORTS

Food and Agricultural Organization of the United Nations (FAO) Via delle Terme di Caracalla, 00100 Rome, Italy (Telephone Number in U.S. (202) 653-2400); *The State of Food and Agriculture.*

NORFOLK ISLAND - INFANT AND MATERNAL MORTALITY

Statistical Office of the United Nations, Publishing Service, New York, New York 10017 (800) 253-9646; *Demographic Yearbook.*

NORFOLK ISLAND - LABOR FORCE

Food and Agricultural Organization of the United Nations (FAO) Via delle Terme di Caracalla, 00100 Rome, Italy (Telephone Number in U.S. (202) 653-2400); *The State of Food and Agriculture.*

NORFOLK ISLAND - LAND USE

Food and Agricultural Organization of the United Nations (FAO), Via delle Terme di Caracalla, 00100 Rome, Italy (Telephone Number in U.S. (202) 653-2400); *Production Yearbook.*

NORFOLK ISLAND - LIBRARIES

United Nations Educational, Scientific and Cultural Organization (UNESCO), 7 Place de Fontenoy, F-75700 Paris, France (Telephone Number in U.S. (212) 963-5981); *Statistical Yearbook.*

NORFOLK ISLAND - LIVESTOCK AND POULTRY

Food and Agricultural Organization of the United Nations (FAO), Via delle Terme di Caracalla, 00100 Rome, Italy (Telephone Number in U.S. (202) 653-2400); *Production Yearbook,* and *The State of Food and Agriculture.*

Statistical Office of the United Nations, Publishing Service, New York, New York 10017 (800) 253-9646; *Statistical Yearbook.*

NORFOLK ISLAND - MAIL - NUMBER OF ITEMS SENT OR RECEIVED

Statistical Office of the United Nations, Publishing Service, New York, New York 10017 (800) 253-9646; *Statistical Yearbook.*

NORFOLK ISLAND - MARRIAGE RATES

Statistical Office of the United Nations, Publishing Service, New York, New York 10017 (800) 253-9646; *Demographic Yearbook,* and *Statistical Yearbook.*

NORFOLK ISLAND - MEAT PRODUCTION - See NORFOLK ISLAND - LIVESTOCK AND POULTRY

NORFOLK ISLAND - MONUMENTS AND HISTORICAL SITES

United Nations Educational, Scientific and Cultural Organization (UNESCO), 7 Place de Fontenoy, F-75700 Paris, France (Telephone Number in U.S. (212) 963-5981); *Statistical Yearbook.*

NORFOLK ISLAND - MOTION PICTURE THEATRES

Statistical Office of the United Nations, Publishing Service, New York, New York 10017 (800) 253-9646; *Statistical Yearbook.*

NORFOLK ISLAND - MUSEUMS

United Nations Educational, Scientific and Cultural Organization (UNESCO), 7 Place de Fontenoy, F-75700 Paris, France (Telephone Number in U.S. (212) 963-5981); *Statistical Yearbook.*

NORFOLK ISLAND - NATALITY - See NORFOLK ISLAND - BIRTH RATES

NORFOLK ISLAND - NEWSPAPER PRODUCTION - See NORFOLK ISLAND - FORESTRY AND FOREST PRODUCTS

NORFOLK ISLAND - PERIODICALS

United Nations Educational, Scientific and Cultural Organization (UNESCO), 7 Place de Fontenoy, F-75700 Paris, France (Telephone Number in U.S. (212) 963-5981); *Statistical Yearbook.*

NORFOLK ISLAND - PESTICIDE USE

Food and Agricultural Organization of the United Nations (FAO) Via delle Terme di Caracalla, 00100 Rome, Italy (Telephone Number in U.S. (202) 653-2400); *The State of Food and Agriculture.*

NORFOLK ISLAND - PETROLEUM INDUSTRY

Food and Agricultural Organization of the United Nations (FAO) Via delle Terme di Caracalla, 00100 Rome, Italy (Telephone Number in U.S. (202) 653-2400); *The State of Food and Agriculture.*

NORFOLK ISLAND - POPULATION

Food and Agricultural Organization of the United Nations (FAO), Via delle Terme di Caracalla, 00100 Rome, Italy (Telephone Number in U.S. (202) 653-2400); *Production Yearbook.*

Statistical Office of the United Nations, Publishing Service, New York, New York 10017 (800) 253-9646; *Demographic Yearbook,* and *Statistical Yearbook.*

World Health Organization, Office of Publications, Avenue Appia, CH-1211 Geneva 27, Switzerland (Telephone Number in U.S. (518) 436-9686); *World Health Statistics Annual.*

NORFOLK ISLAND - PRICES

Food and Agricultural Organization of the United Nations (FAO), Via delle Terme di Caracalla, 00100 Rome, Italy (Telephone Number in U.S. (202) 653-2400); *Production Yearbook,* and *The State of Food and Agriculture.*

NORFOLK ISLAND - SCIENTISTS AND TECHNICIANS

Statistical Office of the United Nations, Publishing Service, New York, New York 10017 (800) 253-9646; *Statistical Yearbook.*

NORFOLK ISLAND - STOCKS - COMMODITY - MARKET
PRICE - INDEX

Food and Agricultural Organization of the United Nations (FAO) Via delle Terme di Caracalla, 00100 Rome, Italy (Telephone Number in U.S. (202) 653-2400); *The State of Food and Agriculture.*

NORFOLK ISLAND - TELEPHONES IN USE

American Telephone and Telegraph Company, 26 Parsippany Road, Whippany, New Jersey 07981 (800) 338-4038; *The World's Telephones.*

NORFOLK ISLAND - THEATRE

United Nations Educational, Scientific and Cultural Organization (UNESCO), 7 Place de Fontenoy, F-75700 Paris, France (Telephone Number in U.S. (212) 963-5981); *Statistical Yearbook.*

NORFOLK ISLAND - TRACTORS IN USE

Statistical Office of the United Nations, Publishing Service, New York, New York 10017 (800) 253-9646; *Statistical Yearbook.*

NORFOLK ISLAND - TRADE - See NORFOLK ISLAND - FOREIGN TRADE

NORFOLK ISLAND - VITAL STATISTICS

World Health Organization, Office of Publications, Avenue Appia, CH-1211 Geneva 27, Switzerland (Telephone Number in U.S. (518) 436-9686); *World Health Statistics Annual.*

NORTH CAROLINA - See also STATE DATA (FOR INDIVIDUAL STATES)

North Carolina - Primary Statistics Sources

Office of the Governor, Office of State Planning, 116 West Jones Street, Raleigh, North Carolina 27603 (919) 733-4131; *Statistical Abstract of North Carolina Counties.*

North Carolina - State Data Centers

North Carolina Office of State Planning, 116 West Jones Street, Raleigh, North Carolina 27603-8005, Staff (919) 733-3683.

Division of State Library, 109 East Jones Street, Raleigh, North Carolina 27611, Mr. Joel Sigmon (919) 733-3683.

Institute for Research in Social Science, University of North Carolina, Manning Hall CB 3355, Chapel Hill, North Carolina 27599-3355, Mr. Ed Bachmann (919) 962-0512.

Center for Geographic Information, Office of State Planning, Post Office Box 27687, Raleigh, North Carolina 27611, Ms. Karen Siderelis/Tim Johnson (919) 733-2090.

NORTH DAKOTA - See also STATE DATA (FOR INDIVIDUAL STATES)

North Dakota - Primary Statistics Sources

Bureau of Business and Economic Research, University of North Dakota, Grand Forks, North Dakota 58202 (701) 777-2637; *The Statistical Abstract of North Dakota.*

North Dakota - State Data Centers

Department of Agricultural Economics, North Dakota State University, Morrill Hall, Room 224, Post Office Box 5636, Fargo, North Dakota 58105, Dr. Richard Rathge (701) 237-8621.

Office of Intergovernmental Assistance, State Capitol, 14th Floor, Bismarck, North Dakota 58505, Mr. Jim Boyd (701) 224-2094.

Department of Geography, University of North Dakota, Grand Forks, North Dakota 58202, Mohammad Hemmasi (701) 777-4246.

North Dakota State Library, Liberty Memorial Building, Capitol Grounds, Bismarck, North Dakota 58505, Ms. Susan Pahimeyer (701) 224-2490.

NORTHERN IRELAND - See UNITED KINGDOM

Northern Mariana Islands - National Statistical Office

Department of Commerce and Labor, Saipan, M.P. 96950, Commonwealth of the Northern Mariana Islands.

NORTHERN MARIANA ISLANDS - BROADCASTING

Billboard Limited, Post Office Box 9027, 1006 AA Amsterdam, The Netherlands (Telephone Number in U.S. (212) 764-7300); *World Radio TV Handbook.*

NORTHERN MARIANA ISLANDS - TOURISM

World Tourism Organization, Calle Capitan Haya 42, E-28020 Madrid, Spain; *Yearbook of Tourism Statistics.*

Norway - National Statistical Office

Statistisk Sentralbyra, Skippergate 15, Postboks 8131, DEP N-0033, Oslo 1, Norway.

Norway - Primary Statistics Sources

Statistisk Sentralbyra (Central Bureau of Statistics), Skippergate 15, P.B. 8131, DEP N-0033, Oslo 1, Norway; *Statistisk monedshefte* (Monthly Bulletin of Statistics), *Okonomisk utsyn* (Economic Survey), and *Statistisk arbok* (Statistical Yearbook).

Norway - Databases

Norwegian Social Science Data Services (NSD), Hans Holmboesgate 22, N-5007 Bergen, Norway. Subject coverage: Norwegian social science data with some coverage of Scandinavian and European data.

SSB-DATA, Norway Ministry of Finances and Customs, Statistics Norway, Kongensgt 6, Post Office Box 4131 DEP, N-0033 Oslo, Norway. Subject coverage: Norwegian statistics.

NORWAY - ABORTIONS

Nordic Council of Ministers, Store Strandstraede 18, DK-1255 Copenhagen K, Denmark and the Nordic Statistical Secretariat, Postboks 2550, DK-2100 Copenhagen 0, Denmark; *The Yearbook of Nordic Statistics.*

Statistical Office of the United Nations, Publishing Service, New York, New York 10017 (800) 253-9646; *Demographic Yearbook.*

NORWAY - AGRICULTURE

Facts on File, 460 Park Avenue South, New York, New York 10016 (800) 443-8323; *The New Book of World Rankings*.

Food and Agricultural Organization of the United Nations (FAO) Via delle Terme di Caracalla, 00100 Rome, Italy (Telephone Number in U.S. (202) 653-2400); *Production Yearbook, The State of Food and Agriculture*, and *Trade Yearbook*.

Nordic Council of Ministers, Store Strandstraede 18, DK-1255 Copenhagen K, Denmark and the Nordic Statistical Secretariat, Postboks 2550, DK-2100 Copenhagen 0, Denmark; *The Yearbook of Nordic Statistics*.

Organisation for Economic Co-operation and Development (OECD), 2 rue Andre-Pascal, 75 Paris 16, France (Telephone Number in U.S. (202) 785-6323); *Economic Accounts for Agriculture, Indicators of Industrial Activity, Industrial Structure Statistics*, and *OECD Economic Surveys: Norway*.

Statistical Office of the United Nations, Publishing Service, New York, New York 10017 (800) 253-9646; *Statistical Yearbook*.

Times Books, 201 East 50th Street, New York, New York 10022 (212) 751-2600; *The Economist Book of Vital World Statistics*.

The World Bank, 1818 H Street, NW, Washington, D.C. 20433 (202) 477-1234; *World Tables*.

NORWAY - AIRLINE SERVICE

Facts on File, 460 Park Avenue South, New York, New York 10016 (800) 443-8323; *The New Book of World Rankings*.

International Civil Aviation Organization, 1000 Sherbrooke Street, West, Montreal, Quebec, Canada H3A 2R2 (514) 285-8219; *Civil Aviation Statistics of the World*.

Nordic Council of Ministers, Store Strandstraede 18, D-K-1255 Copenhagen k, Denmark and the Nordic Statistical Secretariat, Postboks 2550, DK-2100 Copenhagen O, Denmark; *The Yearbook of Nordic Statistics*.

Organisation for Economic Co-operation and Development (OECD), 2 rue Andre-Pascal, 75 Paris 16, France (Telephone Number in U.S. (202) 785-6323); *Tourism Policy and International Tourism in OECD Member Countries*.

Statistical Office of the United Nations, Publishing Service, New York, New York 10017 (800) 253-9646; *Statistical Yearbook*.

Times Books, 201 East 50th Street, New York, New York 10022 (212) 751-2600; *The Economist Book of Vital World Statistics*.

NORWAY - ALUMINUM EXPORTS

International Monetary Fund, 700 Nineteenth Street, NW, Washington, D.C. 20431 (202) 623-7000; *International Financial Statistics*.

NORWAY - ALUMINUM PRODUCTION AND CONSUMPTION - See NORWAY - MINING AND MINERAL PRODUCTS

NORWAY - ANIMAL FEEDINGSTUFFS

Organisation for Economic Co-operation and Development (OECD), 2 rue Andre-Pascal, 75 Paris 16, France (Telephone Number in U.S. (202) 785-6323); *Foreign Trade by Commodities*.

Statistical Office of the United Nations, Publishing Service, New York, New York 10017 (800) 253-9646; *Statistical Yearbook*.

NORWAY - ANIMAL HEALTH

Food and Agricultural Organization of the United Nations (FAO), Via delle Terme di Caracalla, 00100 Rome, Italy (Telephone Number in U.S. (202) 653-2400); *Animal Health Yearbook*.

NORWAY - ANTIMONY AND ANTIMONY ORE PRODUCTION AND CONSUMPTION - See NORWAY - MINING AND MINERAL PRODUCTS

NORWAY - AREA AND DENSITY OF POPULATION

Facts on File, 460 Park Avenue South, New York, New York 10016 (800) 443-8323; *The New Book of World Rankings*.

Food and Agricultural Organization of the United Nations (FAO) Via delle Terme di Caracalla, 00100 Rome, Italy (Telephone Number in U.S. (202) 653-2400); *The State of Food and Agriculture*.

Nordic Council of Ministers, Store Strandstraede 18, DK-1255 Copenhagen K, Denmark and the Nordic Statistical Secretariat, Postboks 2550, DK-2100 Copenhagen 0, Denmark; *The Yearbook of Nordic Statistics*.

Statistical Office of the United Nations, Publishing Service, New York, New York 10017 (800) 253-9646; *Statistical Yearbook*.

Times Books, 201 East 50th Street, New York, New York 10022 (212) 751-2600; *The Economist Book of Vital World Statistics*.

United Nations Educational, Scientific and Cultural Organization (UNESCO), 7 Place de Fontenoy, F-75700 Paris, France (Telephone Number in U.S. (212) 963-5981); *Statistical Yearbook*.

NORWAY - ARMS EXPORTS AND IMPORTS

U.S. Arms Control and Disarmament Agency, 320 Twenty-first Street, NW, Washington, D.C. 20451 (202) 647-8677; *World Military Expenditures and Arms Transfers*.

NORWAY - ARSENIC PRODUCTION AND CONSUMPTION - See NORWAY - MINING AND MINERAL PRODUCTS

NORWAY - BALANCE OF PAYMENTS

The Economist Intelligence Unit, 111 West 57th Street, New York, New York 10019 (800) 938-4685; *The World Market Atlas*.

International Monetary Fund, 700 Nineteenth Street, NW, Washington, D.C. 20431 (202) 623-7000; *International Financial Statistics*.

Nordic Council of Ministers, Store Strandstraede 18, DK-1255 Copenhagen K, Denmark and the Nordic Statistical Secretariat, Postboks 2550, DK-2100 Copenhagen 0, Denmark; *The Yearbook of Nordic Statistics*.

Organisation for Economic Co-operation and Development (OECD), 2 rue Andre-Pascal, 75 Paris 16, France (Telephone Number in U.S. (202) 785-6323); *Economic Outlook, Geographical Distribution of Financial Flows to Developing Countries, Main Economic Indicators - Historical Statistics*, and *OECD Economic Surveys: Norway*.

Times Books, 201 East 50th Street, New York, New York 10022 (212) 751-2600; *The Economist Book of Vital World Statistics*.

The World Bank, 1818 H Street, NW, Washington, D.C. 20433 (202) 477-1234; *World Tables*.

NORWAY - BANKING

Facts on File, 460 Park Avenue South, New York, New York 10016 (800) 443-8323; *The New Book of World Rankings*.

International Monetary Fund, 700 Nineteenth Street, NW, Washington, D.C. 20431 (202) 623-7000; *Government Finance Statistics Yearbook*, and *International Financial Statistics*.

Nordic Council of Ministers, Store Strandstraede 18, DK-1255 Copenhagen K, Denmark and the Nordic Statistical Secretariat, Postboks 2550, DK-2100 Copenhagen 0, Denmark; *The Yearbook of Nordic Statistics*.

Organisation for Economic Co-operation and Development (OECD), 2 rue Andre-Pascal, 75 Paris 16, France (Telephone Number in U.S. (202) 785-6323); *Economic Outlook, Financial Market Trends*, and *OECD Economic Surveys: Norway*.

Statistical Office of the United Nations, Publishing Service, New York, New York 10017 (800) 253-9646; *Statistical Yearbook*.

NORWAY - BARLEY PRODUCTION - See NORWAY - CROPS

NORWAY - BAUXITE PRODUCTION AND CONSUMPTION - See NORWAY - MINING AND MINERAL PRODUCTS

NORWAY - BEER PRODUCTION

Facts on File, 460 Park Avenue South, New York, New York 10016 (800) 443-8323; *The New Book of World Rankings*.

Statistical Office of the United Nations, Publishing Service, New York, New York 10017 (800) 253-9646; *Statistical Yearbook*.

NORWAY - BEVERAGES - PRODUCTION INDEX

Organisation for Economic Co-operation and Development (OECD), 2 rue Andre-Pascal, 75 Paris 16, France (Telephone Number in U.S. (202) 785-6323); *Indicators of Industrial Activity*.

NORWAY - BIRTH RATE

Facts on File, 460 Park Avenue South, New York, New York 10016 (800) 443-8323; *The New Book of World Rankings*.

Nordic Council of Ministers, Store Strandstraede 18, DK-1255 Copenhagen K, Denmark and the Nordic Statistical Secretariat, Postboks 2550, DK-2100 Copenhagen 0, Denmark; *The Yearbook of Nordic Statistics*.

Statistical Office of the United Nations, Publishing Service, New York, New York 10017 (800) 253-9646; *Demographic Yearbook*, and *Statistical Yearbook*.

Times Books, 201 East 50th Street, New York, New York 10022 (212) 751-2600; *The Economist Book of Vital World Statistics*.

The World Bank, 1818 H Street, NW, Washington, D.C. 20433 (202) 477-1234; *World Tables*.

World Health Organization, Office of Publications, Avenue Appia, CH-1211 Geneva 27, Switzerland (Telephone Number in U.S. (518) 436-9686); *World Health Statistics Annual*.

NORWAY - BISMUTH PRODUCTION AND CONSUMPTION

Organisation for Economic Co-operation and Development (OECD), 2 rue Andre-Pascal, 75 Paris 16, France (Telephone Number in U.S. (202) 785-6323); *Indicators of Industrial Activity*.

NORWAY - BONDS

International Monetary Fund, 700 Nineteenth Street, NW, Washington, D.C. 20431 (202) 623-7000; *Government Finance Statistics Yearbook*.

Organisation for Economic Co-operation and Development (OECD), 2 rue Andre-Pascal, 75 Paris 16, France (Telephone Number in U.S. (202) 785-6323); *Financial Market Trends*, and *Main Economic - Historical Statistics*.

Statistical Office of the United Nations, Publishing Service, New York, New York 10017 (800) 253-9646; *Statistical Yearbook*.

NORWAY - BOOK PRODUCTION

Nordic Council of Ministers, Store Strandstraede 18, DK-1255 Copenhagen K, Denmark and the Nordic Statistical Secretariat, Postboks 2550, DK-2100 Copenhagen 0, Denmark; *The Yearbook of Nordic Statistics*.

Organisation for Economic Co-operation and Development (OECD), 2 rue Andre-Pascal, 75 Paris 16, France (Telephone Number in U.S. (202) 785-6323); *Indicators of Industrial Activity*.

United Nations Educational, Scientific and Cultural Organization (UNESCO), 7 Place de Fontenoy, F-75700 Paris, France (Telephone Number in U.S. (212) 963-5981); *Statistical Yearbook*.

NORWAY - BROADCASTING

Billboard Limited, Post Office Box 9027, 1006 AA Amsterdam, The Netherlands (Telephone Number in U.S. (212) 764-7300); *World Radio TV Handbook*.

Facts on File, 460 Park Avenue South, New York, New York 10016 (800) 443-8323; *The New Book of World Rankings*.

Nordic Council of Ministers, Store Strandstraede 18, DK-1255 Copenhagen K, Denmark and the Nordic Statistical Secretariat, Postboks 2550, DK-2100 Copenhagen 0, Denmark; *The Yearbook of Nordic Statistics*.

Times Books, 201 East 50th Street, New York, New York 10022 (212) 751-2600; *The Economist Book of Vital World Statistics*.

United Nations Educational, Scientific and Cultural Organization (UNESCO), 7 Place de Fontenoy, F-75700 Paris, France (Telephone Number in U.S. (212) 963-5981); *Statistical Yearbook*.

NORWAY - BUSINESS

Organisation for Economic Co-operation and Development (OECD), 2 rue Andre-Pascal, 75 Paris 16, France (Telephone Number in U.S. (202) 785-6323); *Main Economic Indicators - Historical Statistics*.

NORWAY - BUSINESS AND PROFESSIONAL LICENSES

International Monetary Fund, 700 Nineteenth Street, NW, Washington, D.C. 20431 (202) 623-7000; *Government Finance Statistics Yearbook*.

NORWAY - BUTTER - See NORWAY - DAIRY PRODUCTS

NORWAY - CABBAGE PRODUCTION - See NORWAY - CROPS

NORWAY - CADMIUM PRODUCTION AND CONSUMPTION - See NORWAY - MINING AND MINERAL PRODUCTS

NORWAY - CALORIE SUPPLY

Food and Agricultural Organization of the United Nations (FAO) Via delle Terme di Caracalla, 00100 Rome, Italy (Telephone Number in U.S. (202) 653-2400); *The State of Food and Agriculture.*

NORWAY - CAPITAL INVESTMENT

Organisation for Economic Co-operation and Development (OECD), 2 rue Andre-Pascal, 75 Paris 16, France (Telephone Number in U.S. (202) 785-6323); *Economic Outlook,* and *Financial Market Trends.*

NORWAY - CAPITAL REVENUE

International Monetary Fund, 700 Nineteenth Street, NW, Washington, D.C. 20431 (202) 623-7000; *Government Finance Statistics Yearbook.*

Organisation for Economic Co-operation and Development (OECD), 2 rue Andre-Pascal, 75 Paris 16, France (Telephone Number in U.S. (202) 785-6323); *Economic Outlook,* and *Financial Market Trends.*

NORWAY - CATTLE - See NORWAY - LIVESTOCK AND POULTRY

NORWAY - CAULIFLOWER PRODUCTION - See NORWAY - CROPS

NORWAY - CAUSTIC SODA PRODUCTION

Organisation for Economic Co-operation and Development (OECD), 2 rue Andre-Pascal, 75 Paris 16, France (Telephone Number in U.S. (202) 785-6323); *Indicators of Industrial Activity.*

Statistical Office of the United Nations, Publishing Service, New York, New York 10017 (800) 253-9646; *Statistical Yearbook.*

NORWAY - CEMENT PRODUCTION - See NORWAY - MINING AND MINERAL PRODUCTS

NORWAY - CEREAL PRODUCTION - See NORWAY - CROPS

NORWAY - CHEESE - See NORWAY - DAIRY PRODUCTS

NORWAY - CHEMICAL (ORGANIC) PRODUCTION - See NORWAY - MINING AND MINERAL PRODUCTS

NORWAY - CHROMITE PRODUCTION AND CONSUMPTION - See NORWAY - MINING AND MINERAL PRODUCTS

NORWAY - CHROMIUM ORE PRODUCTION AND CONSUMPTION - See NORWAY - MINING AND MINERAL PRODUCTS

NORWAY - CIGARETTE PRODUCTION - See NORWAY - TOBACCO PRODUCTION

NORWAY - CLIMATE

Facts on File, 460 Park Avenue South, New York, New York 10016 (800) 443-8323; *The New Book of World Rankings.*

NORWAY - CLOTHING - PRODUCTION INDEX

Organisation for Economic Co-operation and Development (OECD), 2 rue Andre-Pascal, 75 Paris 16, France (Telephone Number in U.S. (202) 785-6323); *Indicators of Industrial Activity.*

NORWAY - CLOTHING EXPORTS AND IMPORTS

Organisation for Economic Co-operation and Development (OECD), 2 rue Andre-Pascal, 75 Paris 16, France (Telephone Number in U.S. (202) 785-6323); *Textile Industry in OECD Countries.*

Statistical Office of the United Nations, Publishing Service, New York, New York 10017 (800) 253-9646; *Trade in Manufactures of Developing Countries.*

NORWAY - COAL PRODUCTION - See NORWAY - MINING AND MINERAL PRODUCTS

NORWAY - COBALT PRODUCTION AND CONSUMPTION - See NORWAY - MINING AND MINERAL PRODUCTS

NORWAY - COFFEE PRODUCTION AND CONSUMPTION - See NORWAY - CROPS

NORWAY - COKE AND COKE OVEN COKE PRODUCTION AND CONSUMPTION - See NORWAY - MINING AND MINERAL PRODUCTS

NORWAY - COKE OVEN ORE PRODUCTION AND CONSUMPTION - See NORWAY - MINING AND MINERAL PRODUCTS

NORWAY - CONSTRUCTION INDUSTRY

Facts on File, 460 Park Avenue South, New York, New York 10016 (800) 443-8323; *The New Book of World Rankings.*

Nordic Council of Ministers, Store Strandstraede 18, DK-1255 Copenhagen K, Denmark and the Nordic Statistical Secretariat, Postboks 2550, DK-2100 Copenhagen 0, Denmark; *The Yearbook of Nordic Statistics.*

Organisation for Economic Co-operation and Development (OECD), 2 rue Andre-Pascal, 75 Paris 16, France (Telephone Number in U.S. (202) 785-6323); *Industrial Structure Statistics, The Iron and Steel Industry, Main Economic Indicators - Historical Statistics,* and *OECD Economic Surveys: Norway.*

Statistical Office of the United Nations, Publishing Service, New York, New York 10017 (800) 253-9646; *Construction Statistics Yearbook,* and *Statistical Yearbook.*

NORWAY - CONSUMER PRICE INDEX

Nordic Council of Ministers, Store Strandstraede 18, DK-1255 Copenhagen K, Denmark and the Nordic Statistical Secretariat, Postboks 2550, DK-2100 Copenhagen 0, Denmark; *The Yearbook of Nordic Statistics.*

Organisation for Economic Co-operation and Development (OECD), 2 rue Andre-Pascal, 75 Paris 16, France (Telephone Number in U.S. (202) 785-6323); *Economic Outlook.*

Statistical Office of the United Nations, Publishing Service, New York, New York 10017 (800) 253-9646; *Statistical Yearbook.*

Times Books, 201 East 50th Street, New York, New York 10022 (212) 751-2600; *The Economist Book of Vital World Statistics.*

NORWAY - CONSUMER PRICES

International Labour Office, I.L.O. Publications, CH-1211, Geneva 22, Switzerland; *Yearbook of Labour Statistics.*

International Monetary Fund, 700 Nineteenth Street, NW, Washington, D.C. 20431 (202) 623-7000; *International Financial Statistics.*

Organisation for Economic Co-operation and Development (OECD), 2 rue Andre-Pascal, 75 Paris 16, France (Telephone Number in U.S. (202) 785-6323); *Economic Outlook.*

NORWAY - CONSUMPTION

International Lead and Zinc Study Group, Metro House, 58 St. James's Street, London SW1A 1LD England; *Lead and Zinc Statistics.*

Nordic Council of Ministers, Store Strandstraede 18, DK-1255 Copenhagen K, Denmark and the Nordic Statistical Secretariat, Postboks 2550, DK-2100 Copenhagen 0, Denmark; *The Yearbook of Nordic Statistics.*

Organisation for Economic Co-operation and Development (OECD), 2 rue Andre-Pascal, 75 Paris 16, France (Telephone Number in U.S. (202) 785-6323); *The Footwear, Raw Hides and Skins, and Leather Industry in OECD Countries, The Iron and Steel Industry, Meat Balances in OECD Member Countries, The Non-Ferrous Metals Industry, The Pulp and Paper Industry,* and *Textile Industry in OECD Countries.*

NORWAY - COPPER AND COPPER ORE PRODUCTION AND CONSUMPTION - See NORWAY - MINING AND MINERAL PRODUCTS

NORWAY - CORN PRODUCTION - See NORWAY - CROPS

NORWAY - CORPORATE INCOME TAXES - See NORWAY - TAXATION

NORWAY - CORPORATE TAXES - See NORWAY - TAXATION

NORWAY - COTTON - See NORWAY - CROPS

NORWAY - CRIME

International Criminal Police Organization (INTERPOL), 26 rue Armengaud, 92210 Saint Cloud, France; *International Crime Statistics.*

Nordic Council of Ministers, Store Strandstraede 18, DK-1255 Copenhagen K, Denmark and the Nordic Statistical Secretariat, Postboks 2550, DK-2100 Copenhagen 0, Denmark; *The Yearbook of Nordic Statistics.*

Yale University Press, Yale Station, New Haven, Connecticut 06520 (203) 432-0940; *Violence and Crime in Cross-National Perspective.*

NORWAY - CROPS

Facts on File, 460 Park Avenue South, New York, New York 10016 (800) 443-8323; *The New Book of World Rankings.*

Food and Agricultural Organization of the United Nations (FAO), Via delle Terme di Caracalla, 00100 Rome, Italy (Telephone Number in U.S. (202) 653-2400); *Production Yearbook,* and *The State of Food and Agriculture.*

Organisation for Economic Co-operation and Development (OECD), 2 rue Andre-Pascal, 75 Paris 16, France (Telephone Number in U.S. (202) 785-6323); *Economic Accounts for Agriculture, Foreign Trade by Commodities,* and *Textile Industry in OECD Countries.*

Statistical Office of the United Nations, Publishing Service, New York, New York 10017 (800) 253-9646; *Statistical Yearbook.*

NORWAY - CUSTOMS DUTIES

International Monetary Fund, 700 Nineteenth Street, NW, Washington, D.C. 20431 (202) 623-7000; *Government Finance Statistics Yearbook.*

Organisation for Economic Co-operation and Development (OECD), 2 rue Andre-Pascal, 75 Paris 16, France (Telephone Number in U.S. (202) 785-6323); *The Non-Ferrous Metals Industry.*

NORWAY - DAIRY PRODUCTS

Facts on File, 460 Park Avenue South, New York, New York 10016 (800) 443-8323; *The New Book of World Rankings.*

Food and Agricultural Organization of the United Nations (FAO) Via delle Terme di Caracalla, 00100 Rome, Italy (Telephone Number in U.S. (202) 653-2400); *Production Yearbook,* and *The State of Food and Agriculture.*

Nordic Council of Ministers, Store Strandstraede 18, DK-1255 Copenhagen K, Denmark and the Nordic Statistical Secretariat, Postboks 2550, DK-2100 Copenhagen 0, Denmark; *The Yearbook of Nordic Statistics.*

Organisation for Economic Co-operation and Development (OECD), 2 rue Andre-Pascal, 75 Paris 16, France (Telephone Number in U.S. (202) 785-6323); *Economic Accounts for Agriculture,* and *Milk, Milk Products, and Egg Balances in OECD Member Countries.*

Statistical Office of the United Nations, Publishing Service, New York, New York 10017 (800) 253-9646; *Statistical Yearbook.*

NORWAY - DEATH RATES

Nordic Council of Ministers, Store Strandstraede 18, DK-1255 Copenhagen K, Denmark and the Nordic Statistical Secretariat, Postboks 2550, DK-2100 Copenhagen 0, Denmark; *The Yearbook of Nordic Statistics.*

Statistical Office of the United Nations, Publishing Service, New York, New York 10017 (800) 253-9646; *Statistical Yearbook.*

Times Books, 201 East 50th Street, New York, New York 10022 (212) 751-2600; *The Economist Book of Vital World Statistics.*

World Health Organization, Office of Publications, Avenue Appia, CH-1211 Geneva 27, Switzerland (Telephone Number in U.S. (518) 436-9686); *World Health Statistics Annual.*

NORWAY - DEFENSE EXPENDITURES

U.S. Arms Control and Disarmament Agency, 320 Twenty-first Street, NW, Washington, D.C. 20451 (202) 647-8677; *World Military Expenditures and Arms Transfers.*

NORWAY - DEMOGRAPHY

The Economist Intelligence Unit, 111 West 57th Street, New York, New York 10019 (800) 938-4685; *The World Market Atlas.*

Facts on File, 460 Park Avenue South, New York, New York 10016 (800) 443-8323; *The New Book of World Rankings.*

Nordic Council of Ministers, Store Strandstraede 18, DK-1255 Copenhagen K, Denmark and the Nordic Statistical Secretariat, Postboks 2550, DK-2100 Copenhagen 0, Denmark; *The Yearbook of Nordic Statistics.*

NORWAY - DEVELOPMENT ASSISTANCE

Organisation for Economic Co-operation and Development (OECD), 2 rue Andre-Pascal, 75 Paris 16, France (Telephone Number in U.S. (202) 785-6323); *Geographical Distribution of Financial Flows to Developing Countries.*

Statistical Office of the United Nations, Publishing Service, New York, New York 10017 (800) 253-9646; *Statistical Yearbook.*

NORWAY - DIAMOND PRODUCTION - See NORWAY - MINING AND MINERAL PRODUCTS

NORWAY - DISCOUNT RATES

Organisation for Economic Co-operation and Development (OECD), 2 rue Andre-Pascal, 75 Paris 16, France (Telephone Number in U.S. (202) 785-6323); *Financial Market Trends.*

Statistical Office of the United Nations, Publishing Service, New York, New York 10017 (800) 253-9646; *Statistical Yearbook.*

NORWAY - DISEASES

World Health Organization, Office of Publications, Avenue Appia, CH-1211 Geneva 27, Switzerland (Telephone Number in U.S. (518) 436-9686); *World Health Statistics Annual.*

NORWAY - DIVORCE RATES

Facts on File, 460 Park Avenue South, New York, New York 10016 (800) 443-8323; *The New Book of World Rankings.*

Nordic Council of Ministers, Store Strandstraede 18, DK-1255 Copenhagen K, Denmark and the Nordic Statistical Secretariat, Postboks 2550, DK-2100 Copenhagen 0, Denmark; *The Yearbook of Nordic Statistics.*

Statistical Office of the United Nations, Publishing Service, New York, New York 10017 (800) 253-9646; *Demographic Yearbook,* and *Statistical Yearbook.*

NORWAY - DUCKS - See NORWAY - LIVESTOCK AND POULTRY

NORWAY - ECONOMY

Facts on File, 460 Park Avenue South, New York, New York 10016 (800) 443-8323; *The New Book of World Rankings.*

Organisation for Economic Co-operation and Development (OECD), 2 rue Andre-Pascal, 75 Paris 16, France (Telephone Number in U.S. (202) 785-6323); *Economic Outlook, Geographical Distribution of Financial Flows to Developing Countries, Main Economic Indicators - Historical Statistics, OECD Economic Surveys: Norway,* and *OECD Employment Outlook.*

NORWAY - EDUCATION

The Economist Intelligence Unit, 111 West 57th Street, New York, New York 10019 (800) 938-4685; *The World Market Atlas.*

Facts on File, 460 Park Avenue South, New York, New York 10016 (800) 443-8323; *The New Book of World Rankings.*

International Monetary Fund, 700 Nineteenth Street, NW, Washington, D.C. 20431 (202) 623-7000; *Government Finance Statistics Yearbook.*

Nordic Council of Ministers, Store Strandstraede 18, DK-1255 Copenhagen K, Denmark and the Nordic Statistical Secretariat, Postboks 2550, DK-2100 Copenhagen 0, Denmark; *The Yearbook of Nordic Statistics.*

Organisation for Economic Co-operation and Development (OECD), 2 rue Andre-Pascal, 75 Paris 16, France (Telephone Number in U.S. (202) 785-6323); *Education in OECD.*

Times Books, 201 East 50th Street, New York, New York 10022 (212) 751-2600; *The Economist Book of Vital World Statistics.*

United Nations Educational, Scientific and Cultural Organization (UNESCO), 7 Place de Fontenoy, F-75700 Paris, France (Telephone Number in U.S. (212) 963-5981); *Statistical Yearbook.*

The World Bank, 1818 H Street, NW, Washington, D.C. 20433 (202) 477-1234; *World Tables.*

NORWAY - EGG PRODUCTION AND CONSUMPTION - See NORWAY DAIRY PRODUCTS

NORWAY - ELECTRICITY

Commodity Research Bureau, Incorporated, 75 Wall Street, New York, New York 10005 (212) 504-7754; *Commodity Year Book.*

Facts on File, 460 Park Avenue South, New York, New York 10016 (800) 443-8323; *The New Book of World Rankings.*

Nordic Council of Ministers, Store Strandstraede 18, DK-1255 Copenhagen K, Denmark and the Nordic Statistical Secretariat, Postboks 2550, DK-2100 Copenhagen 0, Denmark; *The Yearbook of Nordic Statistics.*

Organisation for Economic Co-operation and Development (OECD), 2 rue Andre-Pascal, 75 Paris 16, France (Telephone Number in U.S. (202) 785-6323); *Coal Information, Energy Statistics of OECD Countries, Indicators of Industrial Activity,* and *Industrial Structure Statistics.*

Penn Well Publishing Company, 1421 South Sheridan Road, Post Office Box 1260, Tulsa, Oklahoma 74101 (800) 752-9764; *International Energy Statistics Sourcebook.*

Statistical Office of the United Nations, Publishing Service, New York, New York 10017 (800) 253-9646; *Statistical Yearbook.*

Times Books, 201 East 50th Street, New York, New York 10022 (212) 751-2600; *The Economist Book of Vital World Statistics.*

NORWAY - EMPLOYMENT

Facts on File, 460 Park Avenue South, New York, New York 10016 (800) 443-8323; *The New Book of World Rankings.*

International Labour Office, I.L.O. Publications, CH-1211, Geneva 22, Switzerland; *Yearbook of Labour Statistics.*

Nordic Council of Ministers, Store Strandstraede 18, DK-1255 Copenhagen K, Denmark and the Nordic Statistical Secretariat, Postboks 2550, DK-2100 Copenhagen 0, Denmark; *The Yearbook of*

Nordic Statistics.

Organisation for Economic Co-operation and Development (OECD), 2 rue Andre-Pascal, 75 Paris 16, France (Telephone Number in U.S. (202) 785-6323); *Economic Outlook, The Iron and Steel Industry, OECD Economic Surveys: Norway, OECD Employment Outlook,* and *Textile Industry in OECD Countries.*

Statistical Office of the United Nations, Publishing Service, New York, New York 10017 (800) 253-9646; *Statistical Yearbook.*

NORWAY - ENERGY

Facts on File, 460 Park Avenue South, New York, New York 10016 (800) 443-8323; *The New Book of World Rankings.*

Food and Agricultural Organization of the United Nations (FAO) Via delle Terme di Caracalla, 00100 Rome, Italy (Telephone Number in U.S. (202) 653-2400); *The State of Food and Agriculture.*

Nordic Council of Ministers, Store Strandstraede 18, DK-1255 Copenhagen K, Denmark and the Nordic Statistical Secretariat, Postboks 2550, DK-2100 Copenhagen 0, Denmark; *The Yearbook of Nordic Statistics.*

Organisation for Economic Co-operation and Development (OECD), 2 rue Andre-Pascal, 75 Paris 16, France (Telephone Number in U.S. (202) 785-6323); *Coal Information, Energy Statistics of OECD Countries,* and *Oil and Gas Information.*

Penn Well Publishing Company, 1421 South Sheridan Road, Post Office Box 1260, Tulsa, Oklahoma 74101 (800) 752-9764; *International Energy Statistics Sourcebook.*

Statistical Office of the United Nations, Publishing Service, New York, New York 10017 (800) 253-9646; *Energy Statistics Yearbook, OECD Environmental Data, Statistical Yearbook,* and *World Energy Supplies.*

Times Books, 201 East 50th Street, New York, New York 10022 (212) 751-2600; *The Economist Book of Vital World Statistics.*

NORWAY - EXCHANGE RATES

International Civil Aviation Organization, 1000 Sherbrooke Street, West, Montreal, Quebec, Canada H3A 2R2 (514) 285-8219; *Civil Aviation Statistics of the World.*

International Monetary Fund, 700 Nineteenth Street, NW, Washington, D.C. 20431 (202) 623-7000; *International Financial Statistics.*

Nordic Council of Ministers, Store Strandstraede 18, DK-1255 Copenhagen K, Denmark and the Nordic Statistical Secretariat, Postboks 2550, DK-2100 Copenhagen 0, Denmark; *The Yearbook of Nordic Statistics.*

Organisation for Economic Co-operation and Development (OECD), 2 rue Andre-Pascal, 75 Paris 16, France (Telephone Number in U.S. (202) 785-6323); *Economic Outlook, Financial Market Trends, Revenue Statistics of OECD Member Countries,* and *Tourism Policy and International Tourism in OECD Member Countries.*

Statistical Office of the United Nations, Publishing Service, New York, New York 10017 (800) 253-9646; *Statistical Yearbook.*

NORWAY - EXCISE TAXES - See NORWAY - TAXATION

NORWAY - EXPORTS

American Automobile Manufacturers Association, 1401 H Street, NW, Suite 900, Washington, D.C. 20005 (202) 326-5500; *World Motor Vehicle Data.*

The Economist Intelligence Unit, 111 West 57th Street, New York, New York 10019 (800) 938-4685; *The World Market Atlas.*

Food and Agricultural Organization of the United Nations (FAO) Via delle Terme di Caracalla, 00100 Rome, Italy (Telephone Number in U.S. (202) 653-2400); *The State of Food and Agriculture.*

International Lead and Zinc Study Group, Metro House, 58 St. James's Street, London SW1A 1LD England; *Lead and Zinc Statistics.*

International Monetary Fund, 700 Nineteenth Street, NW, Washington, D.C. 20431 (202) 623-7000; *Direction of Trade Statistics, Government Finance Statistics Yearbook,* and *International Financial Statistics.*

Nordic Council of Ministers, Store Strandstraede 18, DK-1255 Copenhagen K, Denmark and the Nordic Statistical Secretariat, Postboks 2550, DK-2100 Copenhagen 0, Denmark; *The Yearbook of Nordic Statistics.*

Organisation for Economic Co-operation and Development (OECD), 2 rue Andre-Pascal, 75 Paris 16, France (Telephone Number in U.S. (202) 785-6323); *Economic Outlook, The Footwear, Raw Hides and Skins, and Leather Industry in OECD Countries, Foreign Trade by Commodities, Geographical Distribution of Financial Flows to Developing Countries, Industrial Structure Statistics, The Iron and Steel Industry, Milk, Milk Products, and Egg Balances in OECD Member Countries, The Pulp and Paper Industry, OECD Economic Surveys: Norway,* and *Review of Fisheries in OECD Member Countries.*

Times Books, 201 East 50th Street, New York, New York 10022 (212) 751-2600; *The Economist Book of Vital World Statistics.*

The World Bank, 1818 H Street, NW, Washington, D.C. 20433 (202) 477-1234; *World Tables.*

NORWAY - EXTERNAL FINANCING

Organisation for Economic Co-operation and Development (OECD), 2 rue Andre-Pascal, 75 Paris 16, France (Telephone Number in U.S. (202) 785-6323); *Economic Outlook,* and *Financial Market Trends.*

NORWAY - EXTERNAL INDEBTEDNESS

Organisation for Economic Co-operation and Development (OECD), 2 rue Andre-Pascal, 75 Paris 16, France (Telephone Number in U.S. (202) 785-6323); *Financial Market Trends,* and *Geographical Distribution of Financial Flows to Developing Countries.*

The World Bank, 1818 H Street, NW, Washington, D.C. 20433 (202) 477-1234; *World Tables.*

NORWAY - EXTERNAL TRADE

Food and Agricultural Organization of the United Nations (FAO) Via delle Terme di Caracalla, 00100 Rome, Italy (Telephone Number in U.S. (202) 653-2400); *The State of Food and Agriculture,* and *Trade Yearbook.*

Nordic Council of Ministers, Store Strandstraede 18, DK-1255 Copenhagen K, Denmark and the Nordic Statistical Secretariat,

Postboks 2550, DK-2100 Copenhagen 0, Denmark; *The Yearbook of Nordic Statistics*.

Statistical Office of the United Nations, Publishing Service, New York, New York 10017 (800) 253-9646; *Statistical Yearbook*.

NORWAY - FABRIC PRODUCTION - See NORWAY - TEXTILE INDUSTRY

NORWAY - FARM CROPS - See NORWAY - CROPS

NORWAY - FERTILITY RATES

Facts on File, 460 Park Avenue South, New York, New York 10016 (800) 443-8323; *The New Book of World Rankings*.

Nordic Council of Ministers, Store Strandstraede 18, DK-1255 Copenhagen K, Denmark and the Nordic Statistical Secretariat, Postboks 2550, DK-2100 Copenhagen 0, Denmark; *The Yearbook of Nordic Statistics*.

Times Books, 201 East 50th Street, New York, New York 10022 (212) 751-2600; *The Economist Book of Vital World Statistics*.

The World Bank, 1818 H Street, NW, Washington, D.C. 20433 (202) 477-1234; *World Tables*.

NORWAY - FERTILIZER

Food and Agricultural Organization of the United Nations (FAO), Via delle Terme di Caracalla, 00100 Rome, Italy (Telephone Number in U.S. (202) 653-2400); *Fertilizer Yearbook*, and *The State of Food and Agriculture*.

Organisation for Economic Co-operation and Development (OECD), 2 rue Andre-Pascal, 75 Paris 16, France (Telephone Number in U.S. (202) 785-6323); *Economic Accounts for Agriculture*, and *Foreign Trade by Commodities*.

Statistical Office of the United Nations, Publishing Service, New York, New York 10017 (800) 253-9646; *Statistical Yearbook*.

NORWAY - FETAL MORTALITY

Nordic Council of Ministers, Store Strandstraede 18, DK-1255 Copenhagen K, Denmark and the Nordic Statistical Secretariat, Postboks 2550, DK-2100 Copenhagen 0, Denmark; *The Yearbook of Nordic Statistics*.

Statistical Office of the United Nations, Publishing Service, New York, New York 10017 (800) 253-9646; *Demographic Yearbook*.

World Health Organization, Office of Publications, Avenue Appia, CH-1211 Geneva 27, Switzerland (Telephone Number in U.S. (518) 436-9686); *World Health Statistics Annual*.

NORWAY - FILAMENT PRODUCTION - See NORWAY - TEXTILE INDUSTRY

NORWAY - FILMS PRODUCED - LONG - See NORWAY - MOTION PICTURES

NORWAY - FINANCE

Facts on File, 460 Park Avenue South, New York, New York 10016 (800) 443-8323; *The New Book of World Rankings*.

International Monetary Fund, 700 Nineteenth Street, NW, Washington, D.C. 20431 (202) 623-7000; *Government Finance Statistics Yearbook*, and *International Financial Statistics*.

Organisation for Economic Co-operation and Development (OECD), 2 rue Andre-Pascal, 75 Paris 16, France (Telephone Number in U.S. (202) 785-6323); *Economic Outlook, Financial Market Trends, Geographical Distribution of Financial Flows to Developing Countries, Main Economic Indicators - Historical Statistics*, and *OECD Financial Statistics*.

NORWAY - FISHERIES

Facts on File, 460 Park Avenue South, New York, New York 10016 (800) 443-8323; *The New Book of World Rankings*.

Food and Agricultural Organization of the United Nations (FAO) Via delle Terme di Caracalla, 00100 Rome, Italy (Telephone Number in U.S. (202) 653-2400); *The State of Food and Agriculture*, and *Yearbook of Fishery Statistics*.

International Monetary Fund, 700 Nineteenth Street, NW, Washington, D.C. 20431 (202) 623-7000; *International Financial Statistics*.

Nordic Council of Ministers, Store Strandstraede 18, DK-1255 Copenhagen K, Denmark and the Nordic Statistical Secretariat, Postboks 2550, DK-2100 Copenhagen 0, Denmark; *The Yearbook of Nordic Statistics*.

Organisation for Economic Co-operation and Development (OECD), 2 rue Andre-Pascal, 75 Paris 16, France (Telephone Number in U.S. (202) 785-6323); *Foreign Trade by Commodities, Industrial Structure Statistics*, and *Review of Fisheries in OECD Member Countries*.

Statistical Office of the United Nations, Publishing Service, New York, New York 10017 (800) 253-9646; *Statistical Yearbook*.

NORWAY - FLOUR PRODUCTION

Statistical Office of the United Nations, Publishing Service, New York, New York 10017 (800) 253-9646; *Statistical Yearbook*.

NORWAY - FOOD

Food and Agricultural Organization of the United Nations (FAO) Via delle Terme di Caracalla, 00100 Rome, Italy (Telephone Number in U.S. (202) 653-2400); *The State of Food and Agriculture*, and *Production Yearbook*.

Organisation for Economic Co-operation and Development (OECD), 2 rue Andre-Pascal, 75 Paris 16, France (Telephone Number in U.S. (202) 785-6323); *Food Consumption Statistics*, and *Foreign Trade by Commodities*.

NORWAY - FOOTWEAR - PRODUCTION INDEX

Organisation for Economic Co-operation and Development (OECD), 2 rue Andre-Pascal, 75 Paris 16, France (Telephone Number in U.S. (202) 785-6323); *Indicators of Industrial Activity*.

NORWAY - FOREIGN DEBT

International Monetary Fund, 700 Nineteenth Street, NW, Washington, D.C. 20431 (202) 623-7000; *Government Finance Statistics Yearbook*.

Organisation for Economic Co-operation and Development (OECD), 2 rue Andre-Pascal, 75 Paris 16, France (Telephone Number in U.S. (202) 785-6323); *Economic Outlook*.

NORWAY - FOREIGN INDEBTEDNESS

Organisation for Economic Co-operation and Development (OECD), 2 rue Andre-Pascal, 75 Paris 16, France (Telephone Number in U.S. (202) 785-6323); *Economic Outlook*, and *Financial Market Trends*.

NORWAY - FOREIGN TRADE

Facts on File, 460 Park Avenue South, New York, New York 10016 (800) 443-8323; *The New Book of World Rankings*.

Food and Agricultural Organization of the United Nations (FAO) Via delle Terme di Caracalla, 00100 Rome, Italy (Telephone Number in U.S. (202) 653-2400); *The State of Food and Agriculture*.

International Monetary Fund, 700 Nineteenth Street, NW, Washington, D.C. 20431 (202) 623-7000; *International Financial Statistics*.

Organisation for Economic Co-operation and Development (OECD), 2 rue Andre-Pascal, 75 Paris 16, France (Telephone Number in U.S. (202) 785-6323); *Economic Outlook, The Footwear, Raw Hides and Skins, and Leather Industry in OECD Countries, Foreign Trade by Commodities, Main Economic Indicators - Historical Statistics, Maritime Transport, Meat Balances in OECD Member Countries*, and *OECD Economic Surveys: Norway*.

Statistical Office of the United Nations, Publishing Service, New York, New York 10017 (800) 253-9646; *International Trade Statistics Yearbook, Statistical Yearbook* and *Trade in Manufactures of Developing Countries* .

The World Bank, 1818 H Street, NW, Washington, D.C. 20433 (202) 477-1234; *World Tables*.

World Bureau of Metal Statistics, 27-A High Street, Ware, Herts. SG12 9BA, England; *World Metal Statistics*.

NORWAY - FORESTRY AND FOREST PRODUCTS

Facts on File, 460 Park Avenue South, New York, New York 10016 (800) 443-8323; *The New Book of World Rankings*.

Food and Agricultural Organization of the United Nations (FAO) Via delle Terme di Caracalla, 00100 Rome, Italy (Telephone Number in U.S. (202) 653-2400); *The State of Food and Agriculture*, and *Yearbook of Forest Products*.

International Monetary Fund, 700 Nineteenth Street, NW, Washington, D.C. 20431 (202) 623-7000; *International Financial Statistics*.

Nordic Council of Ministers, Store Strandstraede 18, DK-1255 Copenhagen K, Denmark and the Nordic Statistical Secretariat, Postboks 2550, DK-2100 Copenhagen 0, Denmark; *The Yearbook of Nordic Statistics*.

Organisation for Economic Co-operation and Development (OECD), 2 rue Andre-Pascal, 75 Paris 16, France (Telephone Number in U.S. (202) 785-6323); *Foreign Trade by Commodities, Indicators of Industrial Activity, Industrial Structure Statistics*, and *The Pulp and Paper Industry*.

Statistical Office of the United Nations, Publishing Service, New York, New York 10017 (800) 253-9646; *Statistical Yearbook*.

United Nations Educational, Scientific and Cultural Organization (UNESCO), 7 Place de Fontenoy, F-75700 Paris, France (Telephone Number in U.S. (212) 963-5981); *Statistical Yearbook*.

NORWAY - FRUIT PRODUCTION - See NORWAY - CROPS

NORWAY - FURNITURE AND WOOD PRODUCTS - EXPORTS AND IMPORTS

Organisation for Economic Co-operation and Development (OECD), 2 rue Andre-Pascal, 75 Paris 16, France (Telephone Number in U.S. (202) 785-6323); *Foreign Trade by Commodities*, and *Industrial Structure Statistics*.

NORWAY - GAS - See NORWAY - MINING AND MINERAL PRODUCTS

NORWAY - GENERAL INDUSTRIAL STATISTICS

Statistical Office of the United Nations, Publishing Service, New York, New York 10017 (800) 253-9646; *Industrial Statistics Yearbook*.

NORWAY - GENERAL MORTALITY

Nordic Council of Ministers, Store Strandstraede 18, DK-1255 Copenhagen K, Denmark and the Nordic Statistical Secretariat, Postboks 2550, DK-2100 Copenhagen 0, Denmark; *The Yearbook of Nordic Statistics*.

Statistical Office of the United Nations, Publishing Service, New York, New York 10017 (800) 253-9646; *Demographic Yearbook*.

World Health Organization, Office of Publications, Avenue Appia, CH-1211 Geneva 27, Switzerland (Telephone Number in U.S. (518) 436-9686); *World Health Statistics Annual*.

NORWAY - GEOGRAPHIC DATA

Facts on File, 460 Park Avenue South, New York, New York 10016 (800) 443-8323; *The New Book of World Rankings*.

NORWAY - GLASS AND GLASS PRODUCTS - PRODUCTION INDEX

Organisation for Economic Co-operation and Development (OECD), 2 rue Andre-Pascal, 75 Paris 16, France (Telephone Number in U.S. (202) 785-6323); *Indicators of Industrial Activity*.

NORWAY - GOATS - See NORWAY - LIVESTOCK AND POULTRY

NORWAY - GOLD HOLDINGS

International Monetary Fund, 700 Nineteenth Street, NW, Washington, D.C. 20431 (202) 623-7000; *International Financial Statistics*.

Statistical Office of the United Nations, Publishing Service, New York, New York 10017 (800) 253-9646; *Statistical Yearbook*.

The World Bank, 1818 H Street, NW, Washington, D.C. 20433 (202) 477-1234; *World Tables*.

NORWAY - GOLD PRODUCTION AND CONSUMPTION - See NORWAY - MINING AND MINERAL PRODUCTS

NORWAY - GOVERNMENT EXPENDITURES

International Monetary Fund, 700 Nineteenth Street, NW, Washington, D.C. 20431 (202) 623-7000; *Government Finance Statistics Yearbook*.

Nordic Council of Ministers, Store Strandstraede 18, DK-1255 Copenhagen K, Denmark and the Nordic Statistical Secretariat, Postboks 2550, DK-2100 Copenhagen 0, Denmark; *The Yearbook of*

Nordic Statistics.

Organisation for Economic Co-operation and Development (OECD), 2 rue Andre-Pascal, 75 Paris 16, France (Telephone Number in U.S. (202) 785-6323); *Economic Outlook.*

Times Books, 201 East 50th Street, New York, New York 10022 (212) 751-2600; *The Economist Book of Vital World Statistics.*

The World Bank, 1818 H Street, NW, Washington, D.C. 20433 (202) 477-1234; *World Tables.*

NORWAY - GOVERNMENT FINANCES

Organisation for Economic Co-operation and Development (OECD), 2 rue Andre-Pascal, 75 Paris 16, France (Telephone Number in U.S. (202) 785-6323); *Economic Outlook.*

Statistical Office of the United Nations, Publishing Service, New York, New York 10017 (800) 253-9646; *Statistical Yearbook.*

NORWAY - GOVERNMENT REVENUES

International Monetary Fund, 700 Nineteenth Street, NW, Washington, D.C. 20431 (202) 623-7000; *Government Finance Statistics Yearbook.*

Nordic Council of Ministers, Store Strandstraede 18, DK-1255 Copenhagen K, Denmark and the Nordic Statistical Secretariat, Postboks 2550, DK-2100 Copenhagen 0, Denmark; *The Yearbook of Nordic Statistics.*

Organisation for Economic Co-operation and Development (OECD), 2 rue Andre-Pascal, 75 Paris 16, France (Telephone Number in U.S. (202) 785-6323); *Economic Outlook,* and *Revenue Statistics of OECD Member Countries.*

Times Books, 201 East 50th Street, New York, New York 10022 (212) 751-2600; *The Economist Book of Vital World Statistics.*

The World Bank, 1818 H Street, NW, Washington, D.C. 20433 (202) 477-1234; *World Tables.*

NORWAY - GRAIN PRODUCTION - See NORWAY - CROPS

NORWAY - GRANTS

International Monetary Fund, 700 Nineteenth Street, NW, Washington, D.C. 20431 (202) 623-7000; *Government Finance Statistics Yearbook.*

Organisation for Economic Co-operation and Development (OECD), 2 rue Andre-Pascal, 75 Paris 16, France (Telephone Number in U.S. (202) 785-6323); *Geographical Distribution of Financial Flows to Developing Countries.*

NORWAY - GROSS DOMESTIC PRODUCT

The Economist Intelligence Unit, 111 West 57th Street, New York, New York 10019 (800) 938-4685; *The World Market Atlas.*

Facts on File, 460 Park Avenue South, New York, New York 10016 (800) 443-8323; *The New Book of World Rankings.*

Nordic Council of Ministers, Store Strandstraede 18, DK-1255 Copenhagen K, Denmark and the Nordic Statistical Secretariat, Postboks 2550, DK-2100 Copenhagen 0, Denmark; *The Yearbook of Nordic Statistics.*

Organisation for Economic Co-operation and Development (OECD), 2 rue Andre-Pascal, 75 Paris 16, France (Telephone Number in U.S. (202) 785-6323); *Economic Outlook, Geographical Distribution of Financial Flows to Developing Countries,* and *Revenue Statistics of OECD Member Countries.*

Statistical Office of the United Nations, Publishing Service, New York, New York 10017 (800) 253-9646; *Statistical Yearbook.*

Times Books, 201 East 50th Street, New York, New York 10022 (212) 751-2600; *The Economist Book of Vital World Statistics.*

The World Bank, 1818 H Street, NW, Washington, D.C. 20433 (202) 477-1234; *World Tables.*

NORWAY - GROSS NATIONAL PRODUCT

Organisation for Economic Co-operation and Development (OECD), 2 rue Andre-Pascal, 75 Paris 16, France (Telephone Number in U.S. (202) 785-6323); *Economic Outlook,* and *Geographical Distribution of Financial Flows to Developing Countries.*

U.S. Arms Control and Disarmament Agency, 320 Twenty-first Street, NW, Washington, D.C. 20451 (202) 647-8677; *World Military Expenditures and Arms Transfers.*

The World Bank, 1818 H Street, NW, Washington, D.C. 20433 (202) 477-1234; *World Tables.*

NORWAY - HEALTH

Facts on File, 460 Park Avenue South, New York, New York 10016 (800) 443-8323; *The New Book of World Rankings.*

Nordic Council of Ministers, Store Strandstraede 18, DK-1255 Copenhagen K, Denmark and the Nordic Statistical Secretariat, Postboks 2550, DK-2100 Copenhagen 0, Denmark; *The Yearbook of Nordic Statistics.*

Organisation for Economic Co-operation and Development (OECD), 2 rue Andre-Pascal, 75 Paris 16, France (Telephone Number in U.S. (202) 785-6323); *OECD Health Systems: Facts and Trends.*

Statistical Office of the United Nations, Publishing Service, New York, New York 10017 (800) 253-9646; *Statistical Yearbook.*

Times Books, 201 East 50th Street, New York, New York 10022 (212) 751-2600; *The Economist Book of Vital World Statistics.*

World Health Organization, Office of Publications, Avenue Appia, CH-1211 Geneva 27, Switzerland (Telephone Number in U.S. (518) 436-9686); *World Health Statistics Annual.*

NORWAY - HEALTH EXPENDITURES

International Monetary Fund, 700 Nineteenth Street, NW, Washington, D.C. 20431 (202) 623-7000; *Government Finance Statistics Yearbook.*

NORWAY - HIDE PRODUCTION

Food and Agricultural Organization of the United Nations (FAO), Via delle Terme di Caracalla, 00100 Rome, Italy (Telephone Number in U.S. (202) 653-2400); *Production Yearbook.*

Organisation for Economic Co-operation and Development (OECD), 2 rue Andre-Pascal, 75 Paris 16, France (Telephone Number in U.S. (202) 785-6323); *The Footwear, Raw Hides and Skins, and Leather Industry in OECD Countries, Foreign Trade by Commodities,* and

Indicators of Industrial Activity.

NORWAY - HIGHWAYS

International Road Federation, 525 School Street, SW, Washington, D.C. 20024 (202) 554-2106; *World Road Statistics.*

Nordic Council of Ministers, Store Strandstraede 18, DK-1255 Copenhagen K, Denmark and the Nordic Statistical Secretariat, Postboks 2550, DK-2100 Copenhagen 0, Denmark; *The Yearbook of Nordic Statistics.*

Statistical Office of the United Nations, Publishing Service, New York, New York 10017 (800) 253-9646; *Annual Bulletin of Transport Statistics for Europe.*

NORWAY - HOME FINANCE

Organisation for Economic Co-operation and Development (OECD), 2 rue Andre-Pascal, 75 Paris 16, France (Telephone Number in U.S. (202) 785-6323); *Main Economic Indicators - Historical Statistics.*

NORWAY - HORSES - See NORWAY - LIVESTOCK AND POULTRY

NORWAY - HOURS OF WORK - See NORWAY - EMPLOYMENT

NORWAY - HOUSING

Facts on File, 460 Park Avenue South, New York, New York 10016 (800) 443-8323; *The New Book of World Rankings.*

Nordic Council of Ministers, Store Strandstraede 18, DK-1255 Copenhagen K, Denmark and the Nordic Statistical Secretariat, Postboks 2550, DK-2100 Copenhagen 0, Denmark; *The Yearbook of Nordic Statistics.*

NORWAY - HOUSING CONSTRUCTION - See NORWAY - CONSTRUCTION INDUSTRY

NORWAY - HOUSING EXPENDITURES

International Monetary Fund, 700 Nineteenth Street, NW, Washington, D.C. 20431 (202) 623-7000; *Government Finance Statistics Yearbook.*

NORWAY - HYDROCHLORIC ACID PRODUCTION

Statistical Office of the United Nations, Publishing Service, New York, New York 10017 (800) 253-9646; *Statistical Yearbook.*

NORWAY - ILLITERATE POPULATION

The Economist Intelligence Unit, 111 West 57th Street, New York, New York 10019 (800) 938-4685; *The World Market Atlas.*

NORWAY - IMPORTS

American Automobile Manufacturers Association, 1401 H Street, NW, Suite 900, Washington, D.C. 20005 (202) 326-5500; *World Motor Vehicle Data.*

The Economist Intelligence Unit, 111 West 57th Street, New York, New York 10019 (800) 938-4685; *The World Market Atlas.*

Food and Agricultural Organization of the United Nations (FAO) Via delle Terme di Caracalla, 00100 Rome, Italy (Telephone Number in U.S. (202) 653-2400); *The State of Food and Agriculture.*

International Lead and Zinc Study Group, Metro House, 58 St. James's Street, London SW1A 1LD England; *Lead and Zinc Statistics.*

International Monetary Fund, 700 Nineteenth Street, NW, Washington, D.C. 20431 (202) 623-7000; *Direction of Trade Statistics, Government Finance Statistics Yearbook,* and *International Financial Statistics.*

Nordic Council of Ministers, Store Strandstraede 18, DK-1255 Copenhagen K, Denmark and the Nordic Statistical Secretariat, Postboks 2550, DK-2100 Copenhagen 0, Denmark; *The Yearbook of Nordic Statistics.*

Organisation for Economic Co-operation and Development (OECD), 2 rue Andre-Pascal, 75 Paris 16, France (Telephone Number in U.S. (202) 785-6323); *Economic Outlook, The Footwear, Raw Hides and Skins, and Leather Industry in OECD Countries, Industrial Structure Statistics, The Iron and Steel Industry, Milk, Milk Products, and Egg Balances in OECD Member Countries, OECD Economic Surveys: Norway, The Pulp and Paper Industry,* and *Review of Fisheries in OECD Member Countries.*

Times Books, 201 East 50th Street, New York, New York 10022 (212) 751-2600; *The Economist Book of Vital World Statistics.*

The World Bank, 1818 H Street, NW, Washington, D.C. 20433 (202) 477-1234; *World Tables.*

NORWAY - INCOME TAXES - See NORWAY - TAXATION

NORWAY - INDUSTRIAL METALS PRODUCTION - See NORWAY - MINING AND MINERAL PRODUCTS

NORWAY - INDUSTRY

Facts on File, 460 Park Avenue South, New York, New York 10016 (800) 443-8323; *The New Book of World Rankings.*

International Labour Office, I.L.O. Publications, CH-1211, Geneva 22, Switzerland; *Yearbook of Labour Statistics.*

Nordic Council of Ministers, Store Strandstraede 18, DK-1255 Copenhagen K, Denmark and the Nordic Statistical Secretariat, Postboks 2550, DK-2100 Copenhagen 0, Denmark; *The Yearbook of Nordic Statistics.*

Organisation for Economic Co-operation and Development (OECD), 2 rue Andre-Pascal, 75 Paris 16, France (Telephone Number in U.S. (202) 785-6323); *Economic Outlook, Indicators of Industrial Activity, Industrial Structure Statistics,* and *Main Economic Indicators - Historical Statistics.*

Statistical Office of the United Nations, Publishing Service, New York, New York 10017 (800) 253-9646; *Statistical Yearbook.*

Times Books, 201 East 50th Street, New York, New York 10022 (212) 751-2600; *The Economist Book of Vital World Statistics.*

The World Bank, 1818 H Street, NW, Washington, D.C. 20433 (202) 477-1234; *World Tables.*

World Intellectual Property Organization, 34 Chemin des Colombettes, CH-1211 Geneva 20, Switzerland; *Industrial Property Statistics.*

NORWAY - INFANT AND MATERNAL MORTALITY

Nordic Council of Ministers, Store Strandstraede 18, DK-1255 Copenhagen K, Denmark and the Nordic Statistical Secretariat, Postboks 2550, DK-2100 Copenhagen 0, Denmark; *The Yearbook of Nordic Statistics.*

Statistical Office of the United Nations, Publishing Service, New York, New York 10017 (800) 253-9646; *Demographic Yearbook,* and *Statistical Yearbook.*

Times Books, 201 East 50th Street, New York, New York 10022 (212) 751-2600; *The Economist Book of Vital World Statistics.*

The World Bank, 1818 H Street, NW, Washington, D.C. 20433 (202) 477-1234; *World Tables.*

World Health Organization, Office of Publications, Avenue Appia, CH-1211 Geneva 27, Switzerland (Telephone Number in U.S. (518) 436-9686); *World Health Statistics Annual.*

NORWAY - INTEREST RATES

Organisation for Economic Co-operation and Development (OECD), 2 rue Andre-Pascal, 75 Paris 16, France (Telephone Number in U.S. (202) 785-6323); *Economic Outlook, Financial Market Trends,* and *OECD Financial Statistics.*

NORWAY - INTERNAL TRADE

Nordic Council of Ministers, Store Strandstraede 18, DK-1255 Copenhagen K, Denmark and the Nordic Statistical Secretariat, Postboks 2550, DK-2100 Copenhagen 0, Denmark; *The Yearbook of Nordic Statistics.*

Organisation for Economic Co-operation and Development (OECD), 2 rue Andre-Pascal, 75 Paris 16, France (Telephone Number in U.S. (202) 785-6323); *Main Economic Indicators - Historical Statistics.*

NORWAY - INTERNATIONAL FINANCE

Organisation for Economic Co-operation and Development (OECD), 2 rue Andre-Pascal, 75 Paris 16, France (Telephone Number in U.S. (202) 785-6323); *Economic Outlook,* and *Financial Market Trends.*

NORWAY - INTERNATIONAL LIQUIDITY

International Monetary Fund, 700 Nineteenth Street, NW, Washington, D.C. 20431 (202) 623-7000; *International Financial Statistics.*

Organisation for Economic Co-operation and Development (OECD), 2 rue Andre-Pascal, 75 Paris 16, France (Telephone Number in U.S. (202) 785-6323); *Economic Outlook,* and *Financial Market Trends.*

NORWAY - INTERNATIONAL RESERVES EXCLUDING GOLD

Statistical Office of the United Nations, Publishing Service, New York, New York 10017 (800) 253-9646; *Statistical Yearbook.*

The World Bank, 1818 H Street, NW, Washington, D.C. 20433 (202) 477-1234; *World Tables.*

NORWAY - INTERNATIONAL STATISTICS

Organisation for Economic Co-operation and Development (OECD), 2 rue Andre-Pascal, 75 Paris 16, France (Telephone Number in U.S. (202) 785-6323); *Financial Market Trends,* and *Tourism Policy and International Tourism in OECD Member Countries.*

NORWAY - INVESTMENTS

International Monetary Fund, 700 Nineteenth Street, NW, Washington, D.C. 20431 (202) 623-7000; *International Financial Statistics.*

Organisation for Economic Co-operation and Development (OECD), 2 rue Andre-Pascal, 75 Paris 16, France (Telephone Number in U.S. (202) 785-6323); *Economic Outlook, Financial Market Trends, Industrial Structure Statistics, The Iron and Steel Industry,* and *Textile Industry in OECD Countries.*

NORWAY - IRON ORE PRODUCTION AND CONSUMPTION - See NORWAY - MINING AND MINERAL PRODUCTS

NORWAY - LABOR FORCE

Facts on File, 460 Park Avenue South, New York, New York 10016 (800) 443-8323; *The New Book of World Rankings.*

Food and Agricultural Organization of the United Nations (FAO) Via delle Terme di Caracalla, 00100 Rome, Italy (Telephone Number in U.S. (202) 653-2400); *The State of Food and Agriculture.*

Nordic Council of Ministers, Store Strandstraede 18, DK-1255 Copenhagen K, Denmark and the Nordic Statistical Secretariat, Postboks 2550, DK-2100 Copenhagen 0, Denmark; *The Yearbook of Nordic Statistics.*

Organisation for Economic Co-operation and Development (OECD), 2 rue Andre-Pascal, 75 Paris 16, France (Telephone Number in U.S. (202) 785-6323); *Economic Outlook, The Iron and Steel Industry, Maritime Transport, OECD Economic Surveys: Norway, OECD Employment Outlook,* and *Textile Industry in OECD Countries.*

Times Books, 201 East 50th Street, New York, New York 10022 (212) 751-2600; *The Economist Book of Vital World Statistics.*

The World Bank, 1818 H Street, NW, Washington, D.C. 20433 (202) 477-1234; *World Tables.*

NORWAY - LABOR PRODUCTIVITY

International Labour Office, I.L.O. Publications, CH-1211, Geneva 22, Switzerland; *Yearbook of Labour Statistics.*

Organisation for Economic Co-operation and Development (OECD), 2 rue Andre-Pascal, 75 Paris 16, France (Telephone Number in U.S. (202) 785-6323); *Economic Outlook,* and *OECD Employment Outlook.*

NORWAY - LAND USE

Food and Agricultural Organization of the United Nations (FAO), Via delle Terme di Caracalla, 00100 Rome, Italy (Telephone Number in U.S. (202) 653-2400); *Production Yearbook.*

NORWAY - LEAD - See NORWAY - MINING AND MINERAL PRODUCTS

NORWAY - LEATHER - PRODUCTION INDEX

Organisation for Economic Co-operation and Development (OECD), 2 rue Andre-Pascal, 75 Paris 16, France (Telephone Number in U.S. (202) 785-6323); *Indicators of Industrial Activity.*

NORWAY - LEATHER AND FOOTWEAR - EXPORTS AND IMPORTS

Organisation for Economic Co-operation and Development (OECD), 2 rue Andre-Pascal, 75 Paris 16, France (Telephone Number in U.S.

(202) 785-6323); *The Footwear, Raw Hides and Skins, and Leather Industry in OECD Countries.*

NORWAY - LIBRARIES

Facts on File, 460 Park Avenue South, New York, New York 10016 (800) 443-8323; *The New Book of World Rankings.*

Nordic Council of Ministers, Store Strandstraede 18, DK-1255 Copenhagen K, Denmark and the Nordic Statistical Secretariat, Postboks 2550, DK-2100 Copenhagen 0, Denmark; *The Yearbook of Nordic Statistics.*

Statistical Office of the United Nations, Publishing Service, New York, New York 10017 (800) 253-9646; *Statistical Yearbook.*

NORWAY - LIGNITE PRODUCTION - See NORWAY - MINING AND MINERAL PRODUCTS

NORWAY - LIVESTOCK AND POULTRY

Facts on File, 460 Park Avenue South, New York, New York 10016 (800) 443-8323; *The New Book of World Rankings.*

Food and Agricultural Organization of the United Nations (FAO) Via delle Terme di Caracalla, 00100 Rome, Italy (Telephone Number in U.S. (202) 653-2400); *Production Yearbook,* and *The State of Food and Agriculture.*

Nordic Council of Ministers, Store Strandstraede 18, DK-1255 Copenhagen K, Denmark and the Nordic Statistical Secretariat, Postboks 2550, DK-2100 Copenhagen 0, Denmark; *The Yearbook of Nordic Statistics.*

Organisation for Economic Co-operation and Development (OECD), 2 rue Andre-Pascal, 75 Paris 16, France (Telephone Number in U.S. (202) 785-6323); *Economic Accounts in Agriculture,* and *Meat Balances in OECD Member Countries.*

Statistical Office of the United Nations, Publishing Service, New York, New York 10017 (800) 253-9646; *Statistical Yearbook.*

NORWAY - LIVING LEVELS

Organisation for Economic Co-operation and Development (OECD), 2 rue Andre-Pascal, 75 Paris 16, France (Telephone Number in U.S. (202) 785-6323); *Economic Outlook.*

Times Books, 201 East 50th Street, New York, New York 10022 (212) 751-2600; *The Economist Book of Vital World Statistics.*

NORWAY - MACHINERY - PRODUCTION INDEX

Organisation for Economic Co-operation and Development (OECD), 2 rue Andre-Pascal, 75 Paris 16, France (Telephone Number in U.S. (202) 785-6323); *Indicators of Industrial Activity.*

NORWAY - MAGNESIUM PRODUCTION AND CONSUMPTION - See NORWAY - MINING AND MINERAL PRODUCTS

NORWAY - MAIL - NUMBER OF PIECES SENT OR RECEIVED

Nordic Council of Ministers, Store Strandstraede 18, DK-1255 Copenhagen K, Denmark and the Nordic Statistical Secretariat, Postboks 2550, DK-2100 Copenhagen 0, Denmark; *The Yearbook of Nordic Statistics.*

Statistical Office of the United Nations, Publishing Service, New York, New York 10017 (800) 253-9646; *Statistical Yearbook.*

NORWAY - MANGANESE PRODUCTION AND CONSUMPTION - See NORWAY - MINING AND MINERAL PRODUCTS

NORWAY - MANUFACTURING

American Automobile Manufacturers Association, 1401 H Street, NW, Suite 900, Washington, D.C. 20005 (202) 326-5500; *World Motor Vehicle Data.*

Facts on File, 460 Park Avenue South, New York, New York 10016 (800) 443-8323; *The New Book of World Rankings.*

Nordic Council of Ministers, Store Strandstraede 18, DK-1255 Copenhagen K, Denmark and the Nordic Statistical Secretariat, Postboks 2550, DK-2100 Copenhagen 0, Denmark; *The Yearbook of Nordic Statistics.*

Organisation for Economic Co-operation and Development (OECD), 2 rue Andre-Pascal, 75 Paris 16, France (Telephone Number in U.S. (202) 785-6323); *Foreign Trade by Commodities, Indicators of Industrial Activity, Industrial Structure Statistics,* and *OECD Economic Surveys: Norway.*

Statistical Office of the United Nations, Publishing Service, New York, New York 10017 (800) 253-9646; *Statistical Yearbook.*

Times Books, 201 East 50th Street, New York, New York 10022 (212) 751-2600; *The Economist Book of Vital World Statistics.*

The World Bank, 1818 H Street, NW, Washington, D.C. 20433 (202) 477-1234; *World Tables.*

NORWAY - MARRIAGE RATES

Facts on File, 460 Park Avenue South, New York, New York 10016 (800) 443-8323; *The New Book of World Rankings.*

Nordic Council of Ministers, Store Strandstraede 18, DK-1255 Copenhagen K, Denmark and the Nordic Statistical Secretariat, Postboks 2550, DK-2100 Copenhagen 0, Denmark; *The Yearbook of Nordic Statistics.*

Statistical Office of the United Nations, Publishing Service, New York, New York 10017 (800) 253-9646; *Demographic Yearbook,* and *Statistical Yearbook.*

NORWAY - MEAT PRODUCTION - See NORWAY - LIVESTOCK AND POULTRY

NORWAY - MERCHANT SHIPPING

Lloyd's Register of Shipping, 17 Battery Place, New York, New York 10004 (212) 425-8050; *Register of Ships.*

Nordic Council of Ministers, Store Strandstraede 18, DK-1255 Copenhagen K, Denmark and the Nordic Statistical Secretariat, Postboks 2550, DK-2100 Copenhagen 0, Denmark; *The Yearbook of Nordic Statistics.*

Organisation for Economic Co-operation and Development (OECD), 2 rue Andre-Pascal, 75 Paris 16, France (Telephone Number in U.S. (202) 785-6323); *Maritime Transport.*

Statistical Office of the United Nations, Publishing Service, New York, New York 10017 (800) 253-9646; *Statistical Yearbook.*

Times Books, 201 East 50th Street, New York, New York 10022 (212) 751-2600; *The Economist Book of Vital World Statistics.*

U.S. Department of Transportation, Maritime Administration, 400 Seventh Street, SW, Washington, D.C. 20590 (202) 366-5807; *A Statistical Analysis of the World's Merchant Fleets*.

NORWAY - MERCURY PRODUCTION AND CONSUMPTION - See NORWAY - MINING AND MINERAL PRODUCTS

NORWAY - MILITARY

The International Institute for Strategic Studies, 23 Tavistock Street, London WC2E 7NQ, England; *The Military Balance*.

Nordic Council of Ministers, Store Strandstraede 18, DK-1255 Copenhagen K, Denmark and the Nordic Statistical Secretariat, Postboks 2550, DK-2100 Copenhagen 0, Denmark; *The Yearbook of Nordic Statistics*.

U.S. Arms Control and Disarmament Agency, 320 Twenty-first Street, NW, Washington, D.C. 20451 (202) 647-8677; *World Military Expenditures and Arms Transfers*.

NORWAY - MILK PRODUCTION - See NORWAY - DAIRY PRODUCTS

NORWAY - MINING AND MINERAL PRODUCTS

Commodity Research Bureau, Incorporated, 75 Wall Street, New York, New York 10005 (212) 504-7754; *Commodity Year Book*.

Facts on File, 460 Park Avenue South, New York, New York 10016 (800) 443-8323; *The New Book of World Rankings*.

International Lead and Zinc Study Group, Metro House, 58 St. James's Street, London SW1A 1LD England; *Lead and Zinc Statistics*.

Nordic Council of Ministers, Store Strandstraede 18, DK-1255 Copenhagen K, Denmark and the Nordic Statistical Secretariat, Postboks 2550, DK-2100 Copenhagen 0, Denmark; *The Yearbook of Nordic Statistics*.

Organisation for Economic Co-operation and Development (OECD), 2 rue Andre-Pascal, 75 Paris 16, France (Telephone Number in U.S. (202) 785-6323); *Coal Information, Energy Statistics of OECD Countries, Foreign Trade by Commodities, Indicators of Industrial Activity, Industrial Structure Statistics, The Iron and Steel Industry, The Non-Ferrous Metals Industry*, and *OECD Economic Surveys: Norway*.

Penn Well Publishing Company, 1421 South Sheridan Road, Post Office Box 1260, Tulsa, Oklahoma 74101 (800) 752-9764; *International Energy Statistics Sourcebook*.

Statistical Office of the United Nations, Publishing Service, New York, New York 10017 (800) 253-9646; *Statistical Yearbook*.

World Bureau of Metal Statistics, 27-A High Street, Ware, Herts. SG12 9BA, England; *World Metal Statistics*.

NORWAY - MOLYBDENUM - See NORWAY - MINING AND MINERAL PRODUCTS

NORWAY - MINING AND MINERAL PRODUCTS

NORWAY - MONEY AND CREDIT

Organisation for Economic Co-operation and Development (OECD), 2 rue Andre-Pascal, 75 Paris 16, France (Telephone Number in U.S. (202) 785-6323); *OECD Economic Surveys: Norway*.

NORWAY - MONEY EXCHANGE RATE

International Monetary Fund, 700 Nineteenth Street, NW, Washington, D.C. 20431 (202) 623-7000; *International Financial Statistics*.

Organisation for Economic Co-operation and Development (OECD), 2 rue Andre-Pascal, 75 Paris 16, France (Telephone Number in U.S. (202) 785-6323); *Economic Outlook, Financial Market Trends*, and *Tourism Policy and International Tourism in OECD Member Countries*.

Statistical Office of the United Nations, Publishing Service, New York, New York 10017 (800) 253-9646; *Statistical Yearbook*.

NORWAY - MONEY RATES - MARKET

Organisation for Economic Co-operation and Development (OECD), 2 rue Andre-Pascal, 75 Paris 16, France (Telephone Number in U.S. (202) 785-6323); *Economic Outlook*, and *Financial Market Trends*.

NORWAY - MONEY RESERVES

Organisation for Economic Co-operation and Development (OECD), 2 rue Andre-Pascal, 75 Paris 16, France (Telephone Number in U.S. (202) 785-6323); *Economic Outlook*, and *Financial Market Trends*.

NORWAY - MONEY SUPPLY

International Monetary Fund, 700 Nineteenth Street, NW, Washington, D.C. 20431 (202) 623-7000; *International Financial Statistics*.

Nordic Council of Ministers, Store Strandstraede 18, DK-1255 Copenhagen K, Denmark and the Nordic Statistical Secretariat, Postboks 2550, DK-2100 Copenhagen 0, Denmark; *The Yearbook of Nordic Statistics*.

Organisation for Economic Co-operation and Development (OECD), 2 rue Andre-Pascal, 75 Paris 16, France (Telephone Number in U.S. (202) 785-6323); *Economic Outlook*.

Statistical Office of the United Nations, Publishing Service, New York, New York 10017 (800) 253-9646; *Statistical Yearbook*.

The World Bank, 1818 H Street, NW, Washington, D.C. 20433 (202) 477-1234; *World Tables*.

NORWAY - MOTION PICTURES

Statistical Office of the United Nations, Publishing Service, New York, New York 10017 (800) 253-9646; *Statistical Yearbook*.

United Nations Educational, Scientific and Cultural Organization (UNESCO), 7 Place de Fontenoy, F-75700 Paris, France (Telephone Number in U.S. (212) 963-5981); *Statistical Yearbook*.

NORWAY - MOTOR VEHICLE PRODUCTION

American Automobile Manufacturers Association, 1401 H Street, NW, Suite 900, Washington, D.C. 20005 (202) 326-5500; *World Motor Vehicle Data*.

Nordic Council of Ministers, Store Strandstraede 18, DK-1255 Copenhagen K, Denmark and the Nordic Statistical Secretariat, Postboks 2550, DK-2100 Copenhagen 0, Denmark; *The Yearbook of Nordic Statistics*.

Organisation for Economic Co-operation and Development (OECD), 2 rue Andre-Pascal, 75 Paris 16, France (Telephone Number in U.S. (202) 785-6323); *Foreign Trade by Commodities*, and *Indicators of Industrial Activity*.

Times Books, 201 East 50th Street, New York, New York 10022 (212) 751-2600; *The Economist Book of Vital World Statistics*.

NORWAY - MOTOR VEHICLE TAXES - See NORWAY - TAXATION

NORWAY - MOTOR VEHICLES IN USE

American Automobile Manufacturers Association, 1401 H Street, NW, Suite 900, Washington, D.C. 20005 (202) 326-5500; *World Motor Vehicle Data*.

International Road Federation, 525 School Street, SW, Washington, D.C. 20024 (202) 554-2106; *World Road Statistics*.

Statistical Office of the United Nations, Publishing Service, New York, New York 10017 (800) 253-9646; *Statistical Yearbook*.

NORWAY - MUSEUMS

Facts on File, 460 Park Avenue South, New York, New York 10016 (800) 443-8323; *The New Book of World Rankings*.

Nordic Council of Ministers, Store Strandstraede 18, DK-1255 Copenhagen K, Denmark and the Nordic Statistical Secretariat, Postboks 2550, DK-2100 Copenhagen 0, Denmark; *The Yearbook of Nordic Statistics*.

United Nations Educational, Scientific and Cultural Organization (UNESCO), 7 Place de Fontenoy, F-75700 Paris, France (Telephone Number in U.S. (212) 963-5981); *Statistical Yearbook*.

NORWAY - NATALITY - See NORWAY - BIRTH RATES

NORWAY - NATIONAL ACCOUNTS

International Monetary Fund, 700 Nineteenth Street, NW, Washington, D.C. 20431 (202) 623-7000; *International Financial Statistics*.

Nordic Council of Ministers, Store Strandstraede 18, DK-1255 Copenhagen K, Denmark and the Nordic Statistical Secretariat, Postboks 2550, DK-2100 Copenhagen 0, Denmark; *The Yearbook of Nordic Statistics*.

Organisation for Economic Co-operation and Development (OECD), 2 rue Andre-Pascal, 75 Paris 16, France (Telephone Number in U.S. (202) 785-6323); *Economic Outlook*.

Statistical Office of the United Nations, Publishing Service, New York, New York 10017 (800) 253-9646; *National Accounts Statistics*, and *Statistical Yearbook*.

NORWAY - NATIONAL INCOME

Facts on File, 460 Park Avenue South, New York, New York 10016 (800) 443-8323; *The New Book of World Rankings*.

Nordic Council of Ministers, Store Strandstraede 18, DK-1255 Copenhagen K, Denmark and the Nordic Statistical Secretariat, Postboks 2550, DK-2100 Copenhagen 0, Denmark; *The Yearbook of Nordic Statistics*.

Organisation for Economic Co-operation and Development (OECD), 2 rue Andre-Pascal, 75 Paris 16, France (Telephone Number in U.S.

(202) 785-6323); *Economic Outlook*.

Statistical Office of the United Nations, Publishing Service, New York, New York 10017 (800) 253-9646; *Statistical Yearbook*.

NORWAY - NATIONAL PRODUCT

Facts on File, 460 Park Avenue South, New York, New York 10016 (800) 443-8323; *The New Book of World Rankings*.

Organisation for Economic Co-operation and Development (OECD), 2 rue Andre-Pascal, 75 Paris 16, France (Telephone Number in U.S. (202) 785-6323); *Economic Outlook*, and *Main Economic Indicators - Historical Statistics*.

Statistical Office of the United Nations, Publishing Service, New York, New York 10017 (800) 253-9646; *Statistical Yearbook*.

NORWAY - NATURAL GAS PRODUCTION - See NORWAY - MINING AND MINERAL PRODUCTS

NORWAY - NEWSPAPER PRODUCTION - See NORWAY - FORESTRY AND FOREST PRODUCTS

NORWAY - NEWSPRINT PRODUCTION AND CONSUMPTION - See NORWAY - FORESTRY AND FOREST PRODUCTS

NORWAY - NICKEL - See NORWAY - MINING AND MINERAL PRODUCTS

NORWAY - NITRIC ACID PRODUCTION - See NORWAY - MINING AND MINERAL PRODUCTS

NORWAY - OATS PRODUCTION - See NORWAY - CROPS

NORWAY - OIL PRODUCING CROPS

Organisation for Economic Co-operation and Development (OECD), 2 rue Andre-Pascal, 75 Paris 16, France (Telephone Number in U.S. (202) 785-6323); *Foreign Trade by Commodities*.

NORWAY - PAPER - See NORWAY - FORESTRY AND FOREST PRODUCTS

NORWAY - PATENTS

Nordic Council of Ministers, Store Strandstraede 18, DK-1255 Copenhagen K, Denmark and the Nordic Statistical Secretariat, Postboks 2550, DK-2100 Copenhagen 0, Denmark; *The Yearbook of Nordic Statistics*.

Statistical Office of the United Nations, Publishing Service, New York, New York 10017 (800) 253-9646; *Statistical Yearbook*.

World Intellectual Property Organization, 34 Chemin des Colombettes, CH-1211 Geneva 20, Switzerland; *Industrial Property Statistics*.

NORWAY - PEANUT PRODUCTION - See NORWAY - CROPS

NORWAY - PERIODICALS

United Nations Educational, Scientific and Cultural Organization (UNESCO), 7 Place de Fontenoy, F-75700 Paris, France (Telephone Number in U.S. (212) 963-5981); *Statistical Yearbook*.

NORWAY - PESTICIDE USE

Food and Agricultural Organization of the United Nations (FAO) Via delle Terme di Caracalla, 00100 Rome, Italy (Telephone Number in U.S. (202) 653-2400); *The State of Food and Agriculture.*

NORWAY - PETROLEUM INDUSTRY

Facts on File, 460 Park Avenue South, New York, New York 10016 (800) 443-8323; *The New Book of World Rankings.*

Food and Agricultural Organization of the United Nations (FAO) Via delle Terme di Caracalla, 00100 Rome, Italy (Telephone Number in U.S. (202) 653-2400); *The State of Food and Agriculture.*

Organisation for Economic Co-operation and Development (OECD), 2 rue Andre-Pascal, 75 Paris 16, France (Telephone Number in U.S. (202) 785-6323); *Energy Statistics of OECD Countries, Foreign Trade by Commodities, Indicators of Industrial Activity, Oil and Gas Information.*

Penn Well Publishing Company, 1421 South Sheridan Road, Post Office Box 1260, Tulsa, Oklahoma 74101 (800) 752-9764; *International Energy Statistics Sourcebook.*

Statistical Office of the United Nations, Publishing Service, New York, New York 10017 (800) 253-9646; *Statistical Yearbook.*

NORWAY - PHOSPHATES PRODUCTION - See NORWAY - MINING AND MINERAL PRODUCTS

NORWAY - PHOSPHATES ROCK PRODUCTION - See NORWAY - MINING AND MINERAL PRODUCTS

NORWAY - PIG-IRON AND FERRO-ALLOY PRODUCTION - See NORWAY - MINING AND MINERAL PRODUCTS

NORWAY - PIGS - See NORWAY - LIVESTOCK AND POULTRY

NORWAY - PIPELINES FOR OIL AND PETROLEUM PRODUCTS

Statistical Office of the United Nations, Publishing Service, New York, New York 10017 (800) 253-9646; *Annual Bulletin of Transport Statistics for Europe.*

NORWAY - PLASTIC AND RESIN PRODUCTION

Organisation for Economic Co-operation and Development (OECD), 2 rue Andre-Pascal, 75 Paris 16, France (Telephone Number in U.S. (202) 785-6323); *Foreign Trade by Commodities.*

Statistical Office of the United Nations, Publishing Service, New York, New York 10017 (800) 253-9646; *Statistical Yearbook.*

NORWAY - PLATINUM PRODUCTION - See NORWAY - MINING AND MINERAL PRODUCTS

NORWAY - POPULATION

Facts on File, 460 Park Avenue South, New York, New York 10016 (800) 443-8323; *The New Book of World Rankings.*

Food and Agricultural Organization of the United Nations (FAO), Via delle Terme di Caracalla, 00100 Rome, Italy (Telephone Number in U.S. (202) 653-2400); *Production Yearbook.*

International Labour Office, I.L.O. Publications, CH-1211, Geneva 22, Switzerland; *Yearbook of Labour Statistics.*

Nordic Council of Ministers, Store Strandstraede 18, DK-1255 Copenhagen K, Denmark and the Nordic Statistical Secretariat, Postboks 2550, DK-2100 Copenhagen 0, Denmark; *The Yearbook of Nordic Statistics.*

Statistical Office of the United Nations, Publishing Service, New York, New York 10017 (800) 253-9646; *Demographic Yearbook,* and *Statistical Yearbook.*

Times Books, 201 East 50th Street, New York, New York 10022 (212) 751-2600; *The Economist Book of Vital World Statistics.*

United Nations Educational, Scientific and Cultural Organization (UNESCO), 7 Place de Fontenoy, F-75700 Paris, France (Telephone Number in U.S. (212) 963-5981); *Statistical Yearbook.*

U.S. Arms Control and Disarmament Agency, 320 Twenty-first Street, NW, Washington, D.C. 20451 (202) 647-8677; *World Military Expenditures and Arms Transfers.*

World Health Organization, Office of Publications, Avenue Appia, CH-1211 Geneva 27, Switzerland (Telephone Number in U.S. (518) 436-9686); *World Health Statistics Annual.*

NORWAY - POST OFFICES

Facts on File, 460 Park Avenue South, New York, New York 10016 (800) 443-8323; *The New Book of World Rankings.*

NORWAY - POTATO PRODUCTION - See NORWAY - CROPS

NORWAY - POWER PRODUCTION INDUSTRY

Statistical Office of the United Nations, Publishing Service, New York, New York 10017 (800) 253-9646; *Statistical Yearbook.*

NORWAY - PRICES

Facts on File, 460 Park Avenue South, New York, New York 10016 (800) 443-8323; *The New Book of World Rankings.*

Food and Agricultural Organization of the United Nations (FAO), Via delle Terme di Caracalla, 00100 Rome, Italy (Telephone Number in U.S. (202) 653-2400); *Production Yearbook,* and *The State of Food and Agriculture.*

International Labour Office, I.L.O. Publications, CH-1211, Geneva 22, Switzerland; *Yearbook of Labour Statistics.*

International Lead and Zinc Study Group, Metro House, 58 St. James's Street, London SW1A 1LD England; *Lead and Zinc Statistics.*

International Monetary Fund, 700 Nineteenth Street, NW, Washington, D.C. 20431 (202) 623-7000; *International Financial Statistics.*

Nordic Council of Ministers, Store Strandstraede 18, DK-1255 Copenhagen K, Denmark and the Nordic Statistical Secretariat, Postboks 2550, DK-2100 Copenhagen 0, Denmark; *The Yearbook of Nordic Statistics.*

Organisation for Economic Co-operation and Development (OECD), 2 rue Andre-Pascal, 75 Paris 16, France (Telephone Number in U.S. (202) 785-6323); *Economic Outlook, The Footwear, Raw Hides and Skins, and Leather Industry in OECD Countries, Indicators of Industrial Activity, The Iron and Steel Industry, Main Economic Indicators - Historical Statistics,* and *The Pulp and Paper Industry.*

World Bureau of Metal Statistics, 27-A High Street, Ware, Herts. SG12 9BA, England; *World Metal Statistics.*

NORWAY - PRINTING AND WRITING PAPER PRODUCTION AND CONSUMPTION - See NORWAY - FORESTRY AND FOREST INDUSTRY

NORWAY - PRODUCTION

American Automobile Manufacturers Association, 1401 H Street, NW, Suite 900, Washington, D.C. 20005 (202) 326-5500; *World Motor Vehicle Data.*

Facts on File, 460 Park Avenue South, New York, New York 10016 (800) 443-8323; *The New Book of World Rankings.*

International Lead and Zinc Study Group, Metro House, 58 St. James's Street, London SW1A 1LD England; *Lead and Zinc Statistics.*

Organisation for Economic Co-operation and Development (OECD), 2 rue Andre-Pascal, 75 Paris 16, France (Telephone Number in U.S. (202) 785-6323); *Economic Outlook, The Footwear, Raw Hides and Skins, and Leather Industry in OECD Countries, Indicators of Industrial Activity, Industrial Structure Statistics, The Iron and Steel Industry, Meat Balances in OECD Member Countries, Milk, Milk Products, and Egg Balances in OECD Member Countries, The Non-Ferrous Metals Industry, The Pulp and Paper Industry,* and *Textile Industry in OECD Countries.*

NORWAY - PRODUCTIVITY

Organisation for Economic Co-operation and Development (OECD), 2 rue Andre-Pascal, 75 Paris 16, France (Telephone Number in U.S. (202) 785-6323); *Economic Outlook.*

NORWAY - PROPERTY TAXES

International Monetary Fund, 700 Nineteenth Street, NW, Washington, D.C. 20431 (202) 623-7000; *Government Finance Statistics Yearbook.*

Organisation for Economic Co-operation and Development (OECD), 2 rue Andre-Pascal, 75 Paris 16, France (Telephone Number in U.S. (202) 785-6323); *Revenue Statistics of OECD Member Countries.*

NORWAY - PUBLIC CONSUMPTION FUND

Organisation for Economic Co-operation and Development (OECD), 2 rue Andre-Pascal, 75 Paris 16, France (Telephone Number in U.S. (202) 785-6323); *Revenue Statistics of OECD Member Countries.*

NORWAY - PUBLIC EXPENDITURES

Organisation for Economic Co-operation and Development (OECD), 2 rue Andre-Pascal, 75 Paris 16, France (Telephone Number in U.S. (202) 785-6323); *Revenue Statistics of OECD Member Countries.*

NORWAY - PUBLIC FINANCE

Facts on File, 460 Park Avenue South, New York, New York 10016 (800) 443-8323; *The New Book of World Rankings.*

Nordic Council of Ministers, Store Strandstraede 18, DK-1255 Copenhagen K, Denmark and the Nordic Statistical Secretariat, Postboks 2550, DK-2100 Copenhagen 0, Denmark; *The Yearbook of Nordic Statistics.*

Organisation for Economic Co-operation and Development (OECD), 2 rue Andre-Pascal, 75 Paris 16, France (Telephone Number in U.S.

(202) 785-6323); *Revenue Statistics of OECD Member Countries.*

NORWAY - PUBLIC REVENUES

Organisation for Economic Co-operation and Development (OECD), 2 rue Andre-Pascal, 75 Paris 16, France (Telephone Number in U.S. (202) 785-6323); *Revenue Statistics of OECD Member Countries.*

NORWAY - RADIO BROADCASTING - See NORWAY - BROADCASTING

NORWAY - RADIO RECEIVER PRODUCTION

Statistical Office of the United Nations, Publishing Service, New York, New York 10017 (800) 253-9646; *Statistical Yearbook.*

NORWAY - RAILWAYS

Jane's Information Group, Sentinel House, 163 Brighton Road, Coulsdon, Surrey CR5 2NH, England (Telephone Number in U.S. (703) 683-3700); *Jane's World Railways.*

Nordic Council of Ministers, Store Strandstraede 18, DK-1255 Copenhagen K, Denmark and the Nordic Statistical Secretariat, Postboks 2550, DK-2100 Copenhagen 0, Denmark; *The Yearbook of Nordic Statistics.*

Statistical Office of the United Nations, Publishing Service, New York, New York 10017 (800) 253-9646; *Annual Bulletin of Transport Statistics for Europe,* and *Statistical Yearbook.*

NORWAY - RAPESEED PRODUCTION - See NORWAY - CROPS

NORWAY - RELIGION

Facts on File, 460 Park Avenue South, New York, New York 10016 (800) 443-8323; *The New Book of World Rankings.*

NORWAY - RENT PRICES

International Labour Office, I.L.O. Publications, CH-1211, Geneva 22, Switzerland; *Yearbook of Labour Statistics.*

NORWAY - RETAIL TRADE

Statistical Office of the United Nations, Publishing Service, New York, New York 10017 (800) 253-9646; *Statistical Yearbook.*

NORWAY - RICE PRODUCTION - See NORWAY - CROPS

NORWAY - ROOT AND TUBER PRODUCTION - See NORWAY - CROPS

NORWAY - ROUNDWOOD PRODUCTION - See NORWAY - FORESTRY AND FOREST PRODUCTS

NORWAY - RUBBER PRODUCTION AND CONSUMPTION

Facts on File, 460 Park Avenue South, New York, New York 10016 (800) 443-8323; *The New Book of World Rankings.*

Organisation for Economic Co-operation and Development (OECD), 2 rue Andre-Pascal, 75 Paris 16, France (Telephone Number in U.S. (202) 785-6323); *Foreign Trade by Commodities.*

NORWAY - SALT PRODUCTION - See NORWAY - MINING AND MINERAL PRODUCTS

NORWAY - SAWNWOOD PRODUCTION - See NORWAY - FORESTRY AND FOREST PRODUCTS

NORWAY - SCIENCE AND TECHNOLOGY - EXPENDITURE FOR RESEARCH

Statistical Office of the United Nations, Publishing Service, New York, New York 10017 (800) 253-9646; *Statistical Yearbook*.

NORWAY - SCIENTISTS AND TECHNICIANS

Statistical Office of the United Nations, Publishing Service, New York, New York 10017 (800) 253-9646; *Statistical Yearbook*.

NORWAY - SENIOR CITIZENS

Facts on File, 460 Park Avenue South, New York, New York 10016 (800) 443-8323; *The New Book of World Rankings*.

NORWAY - SHEEP - See NORWAY - LIVESTOCK AND POULTRY

NORWAY - SHIP EXPORTS

International Monetary Fund, 700 Nineteenth Street, NW, Washington, D.C. 20431 (202) 623-7000; *International Financial Statistics*.

NORWAY - SHIPBUILDING - PRODUCTION INDEX

Organisation for Economic Co-operation and Development (OECD), 2 rue Andre-Pascal, 75 Paris 16, France (Telephone Number in U.S. (202) 785-6323); *Indicators of Industrial Activity*.

NORWAY - SILVER PRODUCTION AND CONSUMPTION - See NORWAY - MINING AND MINERAL PRODUCTS

NORWAY - SOCIAL DATA

Facts on File, 460 Park Avenue South, New York, New York 10016 (800) 443-8323; *The New Book of World Rankings*.

NORWAY - SOCIAL SECURITY

Nordic Council of Ministers, Store Strandstraede 18, DK-1255 Copenhagen K, Denmark and the Nordic Statistical Secretariat, Postboks 2550, DK-2100 Copenhagen 0, Denmark; *The Yearbook of Nordic Statistics*.

Organisation for Economic Co-operation and Development (OECD), 2 rue Andre-Pascal, 75 Paris 16, France (Telephone Number in U.S. (202) 785-6323); *Revenue Statistics of OECD Member Countries*.

NORWAY - SOCIOECONOMIC DATA

Organisation for Economic Co-operation and Development (OECD), 2 rue Andre-Pascal, 75 Paris 16, France (Telephone Number in U.S. (202) 785-6323); *Economic Outlook*.

NORWAY - STEEL - See NORWAY - MINING AND MINERAL PRODUCTS

NORWAY - STOCKS - COMMODITY - MARKET PRICE - INDEXES

Food and Agricultural Organization of the United Nations (FAO) Via delle Terme di Caracalla, 00100 Rome, Italy (Telephone Number in U.S. (202) 653-2400); *The State of Food and Agriculture*.

International Lead and Zinc Study Group, Metro House, 58 St. James's Street, London SW1A 1LD England; *Lead and Zinc Statistics*.

Statistical Office of the United Nations, Publishing Service, New York, New York 10017 (800) 253-9646; *Statistical Yearbook*.

World Bureau of Metal Statistics, 27-A High Street, Ware, Herts. SG12 9BA, England; *World Metal Statistics*.

NORWAY - SUGAR - See NORWAY - CROPS

NORWAY - SULPHUR PRODUCTION - See NORWAY - MINING AND MINERAL PRODUCTS

NORWAY - TAXATION

International Monetary Fund, 700 Nineteenth Street, NW, Washington, D.C. 20431 (202) 623-7000; *Government Finance Statistics Yearbook*.

International Road Federation, 525 School Street, SW, Washington, D.C. 20024 (202) 554-2106; *World Road Statistics*.

Nordic Council of Ministers, Store Strandstraede 18, DK-1255 Copenhagen K, Denmark and the Nordic Statistical Secretariat, Postboks 2550, DK-2100 Copenhagen 0, Denmark; *The Yearbook of Nordic Statistics*.

Organisation for Economic Co-operation and Development (OECD), 2 rue Andre-Pascal, 75 Paris 16, France (Telephone Number in U.S. (202) 785-6323); *Revenue Statistics of OECD Member Countries*.

The World Bank, 1818 H Street, NW, Washington, D.C. 20433 (202) 477-1234; *World Tables*.

NORWAY - TAX REVENUES - See NORWAY - TAXATION

NORWAY - TELEGRAPH SERVICE

Nordic Council of Ministers, Store Strandstraede 18, DK-1255 Copenhagen K, Denmark and the Nordic Statistical Secretariat, Postboks 2550, DK-2100 Copenhagen 0, Denmark; *The Yearbook of Nordic Statistics*.

Statistical Office of the United Nations, Publishing Service, New York, New York 10017 (800) 253-9646; *Statistical Yearbook*.

NORWAY - TELEPHONES IN USE

American Telephone and Telegraph Company, 26 Parsippany Road, Whippany, New Jersey 07981 (800) 338-4038; *The World's Telephones*.

Nordic Council of Ministers, Store Strandstraede 18, DK-1255 Copenhagen K, Denmark and the Nordic Statistical Secretariat, Postboks 2550, DK-2100 Copenhagen 0, Denmark; *The Yearbook of Nordic Statistics*.

Statistical Office of the United Nations, Publishing Service, New York, New York 10017 (800) 253-9646; *Statistical Yearbook*.

NORWAY - TELEVISION BROADCASTING - See NORWAY - BROADCASTING

NORWAY - TELEVISION RECEIVER PRODUCTION

Statistical Office of the United Nations, Publishing Service, New York, New York 10017 (800) 253-9646; *Statistical Yearbook*.

NORWAY - TEXTILE INDUSTRY

Organisation for Economic Co-operation and Development (OECD), 2 rue Andre-Pascal, 75 Paris 16, France (Telephone Number in U.S. (202) 785-6323); *Foreign Trade by Commodities, Indicators of Industrial Activity, Industrial Structure Statistics,* and *Textile Industry in OECD Countries.*

Statistical Office of the United Nations, Publishing Service, New York, New York 10017 (800) 253-9646; *Statistical Yearbook.*

NORWAY - THEATRE

United Nations Educational, Scientific and Cultural Organization (UNESCO), 7 Place de Fontenoy, F-75700 Paris, France (Telephone Number in U.S. (212) 963-5981); *Statistical Yearbook.*

NORWAY - TIN - INDUSTRIAL CONSUMPTION - See NORWAY - MINING AND MINERAL PRODUCTS

NORWAY - TIN PRODUCTION AND CONSUMPTION - See NORWAY - MINING AND MINERAL PRODUCTS

NORWAY - TOBACCO PRODUCTION

Facts on File, 460 Park Avenue South, New York, New York 10016 (800) 443-8323; *The New Book of World Rankings.*

Organisation for Economic Co-operation and Development (OECD), 2 rue Andre-Pascal, 75 Paris 16, France (Telephone Number in U.S. (202) 785-6323); *Foreign Trade by Commodities, Indicators of Industrial Activity,* and *Industrial Structure Statistics.*

Statistical Office of the United Nations, Publishing Service, New York, New York 10017 (800) 253-9646; *Statistical Yearbook.*

NORWAY - TOURISM

Facts on File, 460 Park Avenue South, New York, New York 10016 (800) 443-8323; *The New Book of World Rankings.*

Organisation for Economic Co-operation and Development (OECD), 2 rue Andre-Pascal, 75 Paris 16, France (Telephone Number in U.S. (202) 785-6323); *Tourism Policy and International Tourism in OECD Member Countries.*

Statistical Office of the United Nations, Publishing Service, New York, New York 10017 (800) 253-9646; *Statistical Yearbook.*

Times Books, 201 East 50th Street, New York, New York 10022 (212) 751-2600; *The Economist Book of Vital World Statistics.*

World Tourism Organization, Calle Capitan Haya 42, E-28020 Madrid, Spain; *Yearbook of Tourism Statistics.*

NORWAY - TRACTORS IN USE

Statistical Office of the United Nations, Publishing Service, New York, New York 10017 (800) 253-9646; *Statistical Yearbook.*

NORWAY - TRADE - See NORWAY - FOREIGN TRADE

NORWAY - TRADEMARKS AND SERVICE MARKS

Statistical Office of the United Nations, Publishing Service, New York, New York 10017 (800) 253-9646; *Statistical Yearbook.*

World Intellectual Property Organization, 34 Chemin des Colombettes, CH-1211 Geneva 20, Switzerland; *Industrial Property Statistics.*

NORWAY - TRANSPORTATION AND COMMUNICATIONS

Nordic Council of Ministers, Store Strandstraede 18, DK-1255 Copenhagen K, Denmark and the Nordic Statistical Secretariat, Postboks 2550, DK-2100 Copenhagen 0, Denmark; *The Yearbook of Nordic Statistics.*

NORWAY - TUNGSTEN PRODUCTION AND CONSUMPTION - See NORWAY - MINING AND MINERAL PRODUCTS

NORWAY - TURKEYS - See NORWAY - LIVESTOCK AND POULTRY

NORWAY - UNEMPLOYMENT

International Labour Office, I.L.O. Publications, CH-1211, Geneva 22, Switzerland; *Yearbook of Labour Statistics.*

Nordic Council of Ministers, Store Strandstraede 18, DK-1255 Copenhagen K, Denmark and the Nordic Statistical Secretariat, Postboks 2550, DK-2100 Copenhagen 0, Denmark; *The Yearbook of Nordic Statistics.*

Organisation for Economic Co-operation and Development (OECD), 2 rue Andre-Pascal, 75 Paris 16, France (Telephone Number in U.S. (202) 785-6323); *Economic Outlook, OECD Economic Surveys: Norway,* and *OECD Employment Outlook.*

Statistical Office of the United Nations, Publishing Service, New York, New York 10017 (800) 253-9646; *Statistical Yearbook.*

NORWAY - URANIUM PRODUCTION AND CONSUMPTION - See NORWAY - MINING AND MINERAL PRODUCTS

NORWAY - VANADIUM AND VANADIUM ORE PRODUCTION AND CONSUMPTION - See NORWAY - MINING AND MINERAL PRODUCTS

NORWAY - VITAL STATISTICS

Nordic Council of Ministers, Store Strandstraede 18, DK-1255 Copenhagen K, Denmark and the Nordic Statistical Secretariat, Postboks 2550, DK-2100 Copenhagen 0, Denmark; *The Yearbook of Nordic Statistics.*

Statistical Office of the United Nations, Publishing Service, New York, New York 10017 (800) 253-9646; *Statistical Yearbook.*

World Health Organization, Office of Publications, Avenue Appia, CH-1211 Geneva 27, Switzerland (Telephone Number in U.S. (518) 436-9686); *World Health Statistics Annual.*

NORWAY - WAGES

International Labour Office, I.L.O. Publications, CH-1211, Geneva 22, Switzerland; *Yearbook of Labour Statistics.*

Nordic Council of Ministers, Store Strandstraede 18, DK-1255 Copenhagen K, Denmark and the Nordic Statistical Secretariat, Postboks 2550, DK-2100 Copenhagen 0, Denmark; *The Yearbook of Nordic Statistics.*

Organisation for Economic Co-operation and Development (OECD), 2 rue Andre-Pascal, 75 Paris 16, France (Telephone Number in U.S. (202) 785-6323); *Economic Outlook, Industrial Structure Statistics,* and *Main Economic Indicators - Historical Statistics.*

Statistical Office of the United Nations, Publishing Service, New York, New York 10017 (800) 253-9646; *Statistical Yearbook.*

NORWAY - WATERWAYS IN USE

Organisation for Economic Co-operation and Development (OECD), 2 rue Andre-Pascal, 75 Paris 16, France (Telephone Number in U.S. (202) 785-6323); *Maritime Transport.*

NORWAY - WEATHER

Facts on File, 460 Park Avenue South, New York, New York 10016 (800) 443-8323; *The New Book of World Rankings.*

Nordic Council of Ministers, Store Strandstraede 18, DK-1255 Copenhagen K, Denmark and the Nordic Statistical Secretariat, Postboks 2550, DK-2100 Copenhagen 0, Denmark; *The Yearbook of Nordic Statistics.*

NORWAY - WELFARE

Nordic Council of Ministers, Store Strandstraede 18, DK-1255 Copenhagen K, Denmark and the Nordic Statistical Secretariat, Postboks 2550, DK-2100 Copenhagen 0, Denmark; *The Yearbook of Nordic Statistics.*

NORWAY - WHALE AND SPERM OIL PRODUCTION

Statistical Office of the United Nations, Publishing Service, New York, New York 10017 (800) 253-9646; *Statistical Yearbook.*

NORWAY - WHALES CAUGHT

Statistical Office of the United Nations, Publishing Service, New York, New York 10017 (800) 253-9646; *Statistical Yearbook.*

NORWAY - WHALING APPARATUS IN OPERATION

Statistical Office of the United Nations, Publishing Service, New York, New York 10017 (800) 253-9646; *Statistical Yearbook.*

NORWAY - WHEAT PRODUCTION AND PRICES - See NORWAY - CROPS

NORWAY - WHOLESALE PRICES - INDEX NUMBERS

Nordic Council of Ministers, Store Strandstraede 18, DK-1255 Copenhagen K, Denmark and the Nordic Statistical Secretariat, Postboks 2550, DK-2100 Copenhagen 0, Denmark; *The Yearbook of Nordic Statistics.*

Statistical Office of the United Nations, Publishing Service, New York, New York 10017 (800) 253-9646; *Statistical Yearbook.*

NORWAY - WHOLESALE TRADE

Statistical Office of the United Nations, Publishing Service, New York, New York 10017 (800) 253-9646; *Statistical Yearbook.*

NORWAY - WINE PRODUCTION

Facts on File, 460 Park Avenue South, New York, New York 10016 (800) 443-8323; *The New Book of World Rankings.*

NORWAY - WOOD AND WOOD PULP - See NORWAY - FORESTRY AND FOREST PRODUCTS

NORWAY - WOOL - INDUSTRIAL CONSUMPTION

Organisation for Economic Co-operation and Development (OECD), 2 rue Andre-Pascal, 75 Paris 16, France (Telephone Number in U.S. (202) 785-6323); *Textile Industry in OECD Countries.*

Statistical Office of the United Nations, Publishing Service, New York, New York 10017 (800) 253-9646; *Statistical Yearbook.*

NORWAY - WOOL PRODUCTION

Facts on File, 460 Park Avenue South, New York, New York 10016 (800) 443-8323; *The New Book of World Rankings.*

Organisation for Economic Co-operation and Development (OECD), 2 rue Andre-Pascal, 75 Paris 16, France (Telephone Number in U.S. (202) 785-6323); *Economic Accounts for Agriculture,* and *Textile Industry in OECD Countries.*

NORWAY - YARN PRODUCTION

Organisation for Economic Co-operation and Development (OECD), 2 rue Andre-Pascal, 75 Paris 16, France (Telephone Number in U.S. (202) 785-6323); *Foreign Trade by Commodities,* and *Textile Industry in OECD Countries.*

Statistical Office of the United Nations, Publishing Service, New York, New York 10017 (800) 253-9646; *Statistical Yearbook.*

NORWAY - ZINC - See NORWAY - MINING AND MINERAL PRODUCTS

NUCLEAR POWER

U.S. Department of Energy, Energy Information Administration, 1000 Independence Avenue, SW, Washington, D.C. 20585 (202) 586-8000; *Annual Energy Review, Uranium Industry Annual,* and unpublished data.

NUCLEAR POWER - CAPABILITY

McGraw-Hill, Incorporated, 1221 Avenue of the Americas, New York, New York 10020 (212) 512-2000; *Nucleonics Week.*

U.S. Department of Energy, Energy Information Administration, Washington, D.C. 20585 (202) 586-8000; *Electric Power Annual, Electric Power Monthly, Annual Energy Review,* and unpublished data.

NUCLEAR POWER - COMMERCIAL GENERATION - BY COUNTRY

McGraw-Hill, Incorporated, 1221 Avenue of the Americas, New York, New York 10020 (212) 512-2000; *Nucleonics Week.*

NUCLEAR POWER - CONSUMPTION

U.S. Department of Energy, Energy Information Administration, Washington, D.C. 20585 (202) 586-8000; *State Energy Data Report, Annual Energy Review, Monthly Energy Review,* and unpublished data.

NUCLEAR POWER - PRODUCTION

McGraw-Hill Incorporated, 1221 Avenue of the Americas, New York, New York 10020 (212) 512-2000; *Nucleonics Week.*

U.S. Department of Energy, Energy Information Administration, Washington, D.C. 20585 (202) 586-8000; *Annual Energy Review, Monthly Energy Review, Electric Power Monthly, International Energy Annual,* and unpublished data.

NUCLEAR POWER - REACTORS

McGraw-Hill, Incorporated, 1221 Avenue of the Americas, New York, New York 10020 (212) 512-2000; *Nucleonics Week.*

U.S. Department of Energy, Energy Information Administration, Washington, D.C. 20585 (202) 586-8000; *Annual Energy Review*.

NUCLEAR POWER - STATE DATA

U.S. Department of Energy, Energy Information Administration, Washington, D.C. 20585 (202) 586-8000; *Electric Power Monthly*, and *Electric Power Annual*.

NUCLEAR POWER - WASTE DISCHARGED FUEL

U.S. Department of Energy, Energy Information Administration, Washington, D.C. 20585 (202) 586-8000; *Annual Energy Review, Uranium Industry Annual*, and unpublished data.

NURSERY AND GREENHOUSE PRODUCTS

U.S. Department of Agriculture, Economic Research Service, Fourteenth Street and Independence Avenue, SW, Washington, D.C. 20005-4789 (202) 219-1504; *Economic Indicators of the Farm Sector: National Financial Summary*, and unpublished data.

NURSING AND PERSONAL CARE FACILITIES - EARNINGS

U.S. Department of Commerce, Bureau of the Census, Suitland, Maryland 20233 (301) 763-4040; *Census of Service Industries*, and *County Business Patterns*.

NURSING AND PERSONAL CARE FACILITIES - EMPLOYEES

U.S. Department of Commerce, Bureau of the Census, Suitland, Maryland 20233 (301) 763-4040; *Census of Service Industries*, and *County Business Patterns*.

U.S. Department of Health and Human Services, National Center for Health Statistics, 3700 East West Highway, Hyattsville, Maryland 20782 (301) 436-8500; *Advanced Data from Vital and Health Statistics*, and unpublished data.

U.S. Department of Labor, Bureau of Labor Statistics, Two Massachusetts Avenue, NE, Washington, D.C. 20212 (202) 606-7828; *Monthly Labor Review, Employment and Earnings*, and Bulletins 2370 and 2429.

NURSING AND PERSONAL CARE FACILITIES - ESTABLISHMENTS

U.S. Department of Commerce, Bureau of the Census, Suitland, Maryland 20233 (301) 763-4040; *Census of Service Industries*, and *County Business Patterns*.

U.S. Department of Health and Human Services, National Center for Health Statistics, 3700 East West Highway, Hyattsville, Maryland 20782 (301) 436-8500; *Advance Data from Vital and Health Statistics*, and unpublished data.

NURSING AND PERSONAL CARE FACILITIES - EXPENDITURES

U.S. Department of Health and Human Services, Health Care Financing Administration, 200 Independence Avenue, SW, Washington, D.C. 20201 (202) 245-6113; *Health Care Financing Review*.

NURSING AND PERSONAL CARE FACILITIES - EXPENDITURES - CONSUMER

U.S. Department of Health and Human Services, Health Care Financing Administration, 200 Independence Avenue, SW, Washington, D.C. 20201 (202) 245-6113; *Health Care Financing Review*.

NURSING AND PERSONAL CARE FACILITIES - FINANCES

U.S. Department of Commerce, Bureau of the Census, Suitland, Maryland 20233 (301) 763-4040; *Census of Service Industries, Current Business Reports*, and *Service Annual Survey*.

NURSING AND PERSONAL CARE FACILITIES - RECEIPTS

U.S. Department of Commerce, Bureau of the Census, Suitland, Maryland 20233 (301) 763-4040; *Census of Service Industries, Current Business Reports*, and *Service Annual Survey*.

NURSING AND PERSONAL CARE FACILITIES - RESIDENTS

U.S. Department of Health and Human Services, National Center for Health Statistics, 3700 East West Highway, Hyattsville, Maryland 20782 (301) 436-8500; *Advance Data from Vital and Health Statistics*, and unpublished data.

NURSING PERSONNEL

American Hospital Association, 840 North Lake Shore Drive, Chicago, Illinois 60611 (312) 280-6000; *Report of the Hospital Nursing Personnel Survey*.

National League for Nursing, 350 Hudson Street, New York, New York 10014 (212) 989-9393; *NLN Data Book*.

U.S. Department of Health and Human Services, Health Resources and Services Administration, 5600 Fishers Lane, Rockville, Maryland 20857 (301) 443-2086; unpublished data.

U.S. Department of Health and Human Services, National Center for Health Statistics, 3700 East West Highway, Hyattsville, Maryland 20782 (301) 436-8500; *Advance Data from Vital and Health Statistics*, and unpublished data.

NURSING PERSONNEL - EMPLOYMENT

American Hospital Association, 840 North Lake Shore Drive, Chicago, Illinois 60611 (312) 280-6000; *Report of the Hospital Nursing Personnel Survey*.

U.S. Department of Labor, Bureau of Labor Statistics, Two Massachusetts Avenue, NE, Washington, D.C. 20212 (202) 606-7828; *Employment and Earnings*.

NURSING PERSONNEL - EMPLOYMENT - PROJECTIONS

U.S. Department of Labor, Bureau of Labor Statistics, Two Massachusetts Avenue, NE, Washington, D.C. 20212 (202) 606-7828; *Monthly Labor Review*.

NURSING PROGRAMS - STUDENTS AND GRADUATES

National League for Nursing, 350 Hudson Street, New York, New York 10014 (212) 989-9393; *NLN Data Book*, and *State Approved Schools of Nursing, RN*.

U.S. Department of Health and Human Services, National Center for Health Statistics, 3700 East West Highway, Hyattsville, Maryland 20782 (301) 436-8500; unpublished data.

NUTRITION - CONSUMPTION OF MAJOR COMMODITIES

U.S. Department of Agriculture, Economic Research Service, Fourteenth Street and Independence Avenue, SW, Washington, D.C. 20005-4789 (202) 219-1504; *Food Consumption, Prices, and Expenditures*, and unpublished data.

NUTRITION - NUTRIENTS AND NUTRITIONAL INTAKE

U.S. Department of Agriculture, Human Nutrition Information Service, Hyattsville, Maryland 20782 (301) 436-7725; data published by U.S. Department of Agriculture, Economic Research Service; *Food Consumption, Prices and Expenditures*, and *National Food Review*.

U.S. Department of Health and Human Services, Public Health Service, 200 Independence Avenue, SW, Washington, D.C. 20201 (202) 619-1296; *Advanced Data from Vital and Health Statistics*.

NUTS - ACREAGE

U.S. Department of Agriculture, National Agricultural Statistics Service, Fourteenth Street and Independence Avenue, SW, Washington, D.C. 20250 (202) 219-1504; *Noncitrus Fruits and Nuts*.

NUTS - CASH RECEIPTS - MARKETING

U.S. Department of Agriculture, Economic Research Service, Fourteenth Street and Independence Avenue, SW, Washington, D.C. 20005-4789 (202) 219-1504; *Economic Indicators of the Farm Sector: National Financial Summary*.

NUTS - FOREIGN TRADE

U.S. Department of Agriculture, Economic Research Service, Fourteenth Street and Independence Avenue, SW, Washington, D.C. 20005-4789 (202) 219-1504; *Agricultural Statistics*, and *Foreign Agricultural Trade of the U.S.*

NUTS - PRODUCTION

U.S. Department of Agriculture, Economic Research Service, Fourteenth Street and Independence Avenue, SW, Washington, D.C. 20005-4789 (202) 219-1504; *Agricultural Outlook*.

U.S. Department of Agriculture, National Agricultural Statistics Service, Fourteenth Street and Independence Avenue, SW, Washington, D.C. 20250 (202) 219-1504; *Noncitrus Fruit and Nuts*.

O

OATS

U.S. Department of Agriculture, Economic Research Service, Fourteenth Street and Independence Avenue, SW, Washington, D.C. 20005-4789 (202) 219-1504; *Economic Indicators of the Farm Sector: National Financial Summary*.

OBSTETRICIANS

American Medical Association, 515 North State Street, Chicago, Illinois 60610 (312) 464-4818; *Physician Characteristics and Distribution in the United States*.

OCCUPATIONAL SAFETY

U.S. Department of Labor, Bureau of Labor Statistics, Two Massachusetts Avenue, NE, Washington, D.C. 20212 (202) 606-7828; *Occupational Injuries and Illnesses in the United States By Industry*.

OCCUPATIONS - See also Individual Occupations

OCCUPATIONS - BLACK POPULATION

U.S. Department of Labor, Bureau of Labor Statistics, Two Massachusetts Avenue, NE, Washington, D.C. 20212 (202) 606-7828; *Employment and Earnings*, and unpublished data.

OCCUPATIONS - EARNINGS

U.S. Department of Commerce, Bureau of the Census, Suitland, Maryland 20233 (301) 763-4040; *Current Population Reports*.

U.S. Department of Labor, Bureau of Labor Statistics, Two Massachusetts Avenue, NE, Washington, D.C. 20212 (202) 606-7828; *Employment and Earnings*, and Bulletin 2307.

OCCUPATIONS - EMPLOYMENT - BLACK POPULATION

U.S. Department of Labor, Bureau of Labor Statistics, Two Massachusetts Avenue, NE, Washington, D.C. 20212 (202) 606-7828; *Employment and Earnings*, and unpublished data.

OCCUPATIONS - EMPLOYMENT - HISPANIC ORIGIN POPULATION

U.S. Department of Labor, Bureau of Labor Statistics, Two Massachusetts Avenue, NE, Washington, D.C. 20212 (202) 606-7828; *Employment and Earnings*.

OCCUPATIONS - EMPLOYMENT - PROJECTIONS

U.S. Department of Labor, Bureau of Labor Statistics, Two Massachusetts Avenue, NE, Washington, D.C. 20212 (202) 606-7828; *Monthly Labor Review*.

OCCUPATIONS - EMPLOYMENT - RACE

U.S. Department of Labor, Bureau of Labor Statistics, Two Massachusetts Avenue, NE, Washington, D.C. 20212 (202) 606-7828; *Employment and Earnings*.

OCCUPATIONS - EMPLOYMENT - SEX

U.S. Department of Labor, Bureau of Labor Statistics, Two Massachusetts Avenue, NE, Washington, D.C. 20212 (202) 606-7828; *Employment and Earnings*, and unpublished data.

OCCUPATIONS - EMPLOYMENT COST INDEX

U.S. Department of Labor, Bureau of Labor Statistics, Two Massachusetts Avenue, NE, Washington, D.C. 20212 (202) 606-7828; *News, Employment Cost Index*.

OCCUPATIONS - FOREIGN BORN POPULATION

U.S. Department of Commerce, Bureau of the Census, Suitland, Maryland 20233 (301) 763-4040; *Census of Population*, and *The Foreign Born Population in the U.S.*

OCCUPATIONS - HISPANIC ORIGIN POPULATION

U.S. Department of Labor, Bureau of Labor Statistics, Two Massachusetts Avenue, NE, Washington, D.C. 20212 (202) 606-7828; *Employment and Earnings*.

OCCUPATIONS - INCOME

U.S. Department of Commerce, Bureau of the Census, Suitland, Maryland 20233 (301) 763-4040; *Current Population Reports*.

OCCUPATIONS - LABOR UNION MEMBERSHIP

U.S. Department of Labor, Bureau of Labor Statistics, Two Massachusetts Avenue, NE, Washington, D.C. 20212 (202) 606-7828; *Employment and Earnings*.

OCCUPATIONS - PENSION PLAN - HEALTH PLAN COVERAGE

U.S. Department of Commerce, Bureau of the Census, Suitland, Maryland 20233 (301) 763-4040; *Current Population Reports*, and unpublished data.

OCCUPATIONS - SEX AND EDUCATIONAL ATTAINMENT

U.S. Department of Labor, Bureau of Labor Statistics, Two Massachusetts Avenue, NE, Washington, D.C. 20212 (202) 606-7828; unpublished data.

OCCUPATIONS - WHITE-COLLAR AND BLUE-COLLAR WORKERS

U.S. Department of Labor, Bureau of Labor Statistics, Two Massachusetts Avenue, NE, Washington, D.C. 20212 (202) 606-7828; *Employment and Earnings*, and *Monthly Labor Review*.

U.S. Office of Personnel Management, 1900 E Street, NW, Washington, D.C. 20415 (202) 606-1800; *Federal Civilian Workforce Statistics - Employment and Trends, Pay Structure of the Federal Civil Service*, and unpublished data.

OCEAN PERCH - ATLANTIC

U.S. Department of Commerce, National Oceanic and Atmospheric Administration, National Marine Fisheries Service, 1335 East-West Highway, Silver Spring, Maryland 20910 (301) 427-2239; *Fisheries of the United States*.

OFFICE BUILDINGS - See also COMMERCIAL BUILDINGS

U.S. Department of Commerce, Bureau of the Census, Suitland, Maryland 20233 (301) 763-4040; *Current Construction Reports*.

OFFICE BUILDINGS - CONSTRUCTION

ONCOR International, 3040 Post Oak Boulevard, Houston, Texas 77056 (713) 961-0600; *Office Market Data Book*.

OFFICE BUILDINGS - VACANCY RATES

ONCOR International, 3040 Post Oak Boulevard, Houston, Texas 77056 (713) 961-0600; *Office Market Data Book*.

OFFICE EQUIPMENT - See COMPUTER AND OFFICE EQUIPMENT

OFFSHORE LEASES

U.S. Department of the Interior, Minerals Management Service, Eighteenth and C Streets, NW, Washington, D.C. 20240 (202) 208-3983; *Federal Offshore Statistics*.

OHIO - See also STATE DATA (FOR INDIVIDUAL STATES)

Ohio - Primary Statistics Sources

Department of Development, Ohio Data Users Center (ODUC), Post Office Box 1001, Columbus, Ohio 43266-0101 (614) 466-2115; *Research Products and Services*, updated continuously.

The Ohio State University, School of Public Policy and Management, 1775 College Road, Columbus, Ohio 43210-1399 (614) 292-8696; *Benchmark Ohio*.

Ohio - State Data Centers

Ohio Data Users Center, Ohio Department of Development, Post Office Box 1001, 77 High Street, 27th Floor, Columbus, Ohio 43266-0101, Mr. Barry Bennett (614) 466-2115.

State Library of Ohio, 65 South Front Street, Columbus, Ohio 43215, Mr. Clyde Hordusky (614) 644-7051.

Cleveland State University, Northern Ohio Data and Information Service, 1737 Euclid Avenue, Room 45, Cleveland, Ohio 44115, Mr. Mark Salling (216) 687-2209.

Ohio State University Library/Census Data Center, 126 Main Library, 1858 Neil Avenue Mall, Columbus, Ohio 43210, Brian Martin (614) 292-6175.

University of Cincinnati, Southwest Ohio Regional Data Center, Institute for Policy Research, Mail Loc 132, Cincinnati, Ohio 45221, Steven Howe (513) 556-5082.

OIL AND GAS EXTRACTION - See also PETROLEUM AND PRODUCTS and GAS

OIL AND GAS EXTRACTION INDUSTRY - CAPITAL

Time Warner, 1675 Broadway, Rockefeller Center, New York, New York 10019 (212) 522-1212; *The Fortune Directories*.

U.S. Department of Commerce, Bureau of Economic Analysis, Fourteenth Street between Constitution Avenue and E Street, NW, Washington, D.C. 20230 (202) 606-9900; *Fixed Reproducible Tangible Wealth in the United States*, and *Survey of Current Business*.

U.S. Department of Commerce, Bureau of the Census, Suitland, Maryland 20233 (301) 763-4040; *Census of Mineral Industries*.

OIL AND GAS EXTRACTION INDUSTRY - EARNINGS

U.S. Department of Commerce, Bureau of the Census, Suitland, Maryland 20233 (301) 763-4040; *Census of Mineral Industries*.

U.S. Department of Labor, Bureau of Labor Statistics, Two Massachusetts Avenue, NE, Washington, D.C. 20212 (202) 606-7828; *Employment and Earnings*, and Bulletins 2370 and 2429.

OIL AND GAS EXTRACTION INDUSTRY - EMPLOYEES

U.S. Department of Commerce, Bureau of the Census, Suitland, Maryland 20233 (301) 763-4040; *Census of Mineral Industries*.

U.S. Department of Labor, Bureau of Labor Statistics, Two Massachusetts Avenue, NE, Washington, D.C. 20212 (202) 606-7828; *Employment and Earnings*, and Bulletins 2370 and 2429.

OIL AND GAS EXTRACTION INDUSTRY - ESTABLISHMENTS

U.S. Department of Commerce, Bureau of the Census, Suitland, Maryland 20233 (301) 763-4040; *Census of Mineral Industries*.

OIL AND GAS EXTRACTION INDUSTRY - GROSS DOMESTIC PRODUCT

U.S. Department of Commerce, Bureau of Economic Analysis, Fourteenth Street between Constitution Avenue and E Street, NW, Washington, D.C. 20230 (202) 606-9900; *The National Income and Product Accounts of the United States*, and *Survey of Current Business*.

OIL AND GAS EXTRACTION INDUSTRY - OCCUPATIONAL SAFETY

U.S. Department of Labor, Bureau of Labor Statistics, Two Massachusetts Avenue, NE, Washington, D.C. 20212 (202) 606-7828; *Occupational Injuries and Illnesses in the United States by Industry*.

OIL AND GAS EXTRACTION INDUSTRY - OUTPUT

Board of Governors of the Federal Reserve System, Twentieth Street and Constitution Avenue, NW, Washington, D.C. 20551 (202) 452-3000; *Federal Reserve Bulletin*.

OIL AND GAS EXTRACTION INDUSTRY - PARTNERSHIPS

U.S. Department of the Treasury, Internal Revenue Service, 1111 Constitution Avenue, NW, Washington, D.C. 20224 (202) 566-5000; *Statistics of Income, Partnership Returns*, and *Statistics of Income Bulletin*.

OIL AND GAS EXTRACTION INDUSTRY - PATENTS

U.S. Department of Commerce, Patent and Trademark Office, 2011 Crystal Drive, Arlington, Virginia 22202 (703) 305-8341; *Patenting Trends in the United States, State Country Report*.

OIL AND GAS EXTRACTION INDUSTRY - PRODUCTION INDEXES

Board of Governors of the Federal Reserve System, Twentieth Street and Constitution Avenue, NW, Washington, D.C. 20551 (202) 452-3000; *Federal Reserve Bulletin*.

OIL AND GAS EXTRACTION INDUSTRY - SHIPMENTS, RECEIPTS

U.S. Department of Commerce, Bureau of the Census, Suitland, Maryland 20233 (301) 763-4040; *Census of Mineral Industries*.

OIL AND GAS EXTRACTION INDUSTRY - VALUE ADDED

U.S. Department of Commerce, Bureau of the Census, Suitland, Maryland 20233 (301) 763-4040; *Census of Mineral Industries*.

OIL CROPS

U.S. Department of Agriculture, Economic Research Service, Fourteenth Street and Independence Avenue, SW, Washington, D.C. 20005-4789 (202) 219-1504; *Agricultural Outlook, Economic Indicators of the Farm Sector: National Financial Summary*, and *Foreign Agricultural Trade of the United States*.

U.S. Department of Agriculture, National Agricultural Statistics Service, Fourteenth Street and Independence Avenue, SW, Washington, D.C. 20250 (202) 219-1504; *Crop Production* and *Crop Values*, and *Agricultural Prices: Annual Summary*.

OIL SPILLS

Tanker Advisory Center, 10 East End Avenue, New York, New York 10028 (212) 628-7686; *Worldwide Tanker Casualty Returns*.

OILS - ANIMAL (OILS AND FATS)

U.S. Department of Agriculture, Economic Research Service, Fourteenth Street and Independence Avenue, SW, Washington, D.C. 20005-4789 (202) 219-1504; *Food Consumption, Prices and Expenditures, Agricultural Statistics*, and *Foreign Agricultural Trade of the U.S.*

OILS - ANIMAL AND VEGETABLE - FOREIGN TRADE

U.S. Department of Agriculture, Economic Research Service, Fourteenth Street and Independence Avenue, SW, Washington, D.C. 20005-4789 (202) 219-1504; *Agricultural Outlook, Agricultural Statistics*, and *Foreign Agricultural Trade of the U.S.*

U.S. Department of Agriculture, Foreign Agricultural Service, Fourteenth Street and Independence Avenue, SW, Washington, D.C. 20250 (202) 720-3448; *Foreign Agricultural Commodity Circular Series*.

U.S. Department of Commerce, Bureau of the Census, Suitland, Maryland 20233 (301) 763-4040; *U.S. Merchandise Trade: Exports, General Imports, and Imports for Consumption*.

OILS - FISH

U.S. Department of Commerce, National Oceanic and Atmospheric Administration, National Marine Fisheries Service, 1335 East-West Highway, Silver Spring, Maryland 20910 (301) 427-2239; *Fishery Statistics of the United States* and *Fisheries of the United States*.

OILS - VEGETABLE - FOREIGN TRADE

U.S. Department of Agriculture, Economic Research Service, Fourteenth Street and Independence Avenue, SW, Washington, D.C. 20005-4789 (202) 219-1504; *Agricultural Outlook, Agricultural Statistics*, and *Foreign Agricultural Trade of the U.S.*

U.S. Department of Agriculture, Foreign Agricultural Service, Fourteenth Street and Independence Avenue, SW, Washington, D.C. 20250 (202) 720-3448; *Foreign Agricultural Commodity Circular Series*.

U.S. Department of Commerce, Bureau of the Census, Suitland, Maryland 20233 (301) 763-4040; *U.S. Merchandise Trade: Exports, General Imports, and Imports for Consumption*.

OILS - VEGETABLE - PRODUCTION, CONSUMPTION, AND STOCKS

U.S. Department of Agriculture, Economic Research Service, Fourteenth Street and Independence Avenue, SW, Washington, D.C. 20005-4789 (202) 219-1504; *Food Consumption, Prices, and Expenditures*, and unpublished data.

U.S. Department of Agriculture, Foreign Agricultural Service, Fourteenth Street and Independence Avenue, SW, Washington, D.C. 20250 (202) 720-3448; *Foreign Agricultural Commodity Circular Series*.

OKLAHOMA - See also STATE DATE (FOR INDIVIDUAL STATES)

Oklahoma - Primary Statistics Source

Center for Economic and Management Research, University of Oklahoma, 307 West Brooks Street, Room 4, Norman, Oklahoma 73109 (405) 325-2931; *Statistical Abstract of Oklahoma*.

Oklahoma - State Data Centers

Oklahoma State Data Center, Oklahoma Department of Commerce, 6601 Broadway Extension, P.O. Box 26980, Oklahoma City, Oklahoma 73126-0980, Mr. Jeff Wallace (405) 841-5184.

Oklahoma Department of Libraries, 200 N.E. 18th Street, Oklahoma City, Oklahoma 73105, Mr. Steve Beleu (405) 521-2502.

OLD-AGE ASSISTANCE, PUBLIC

U.S. Department of Health and Human Services, Administration for Children and Families, 370 L'Enfant Promenade, SW, Washington, D.C. 20447 (202) 401-9200; *Quarterly Public Assistance Statistics*.

U.S. Department of Health and Human Services, Social Security Administration, 6401 Security Boulevard, Baltimore, Maryland 21235 (410) 965-1234; *Social Security Bulletin*, and *Annual Statistical Summary to the Social Security Bulletin*.

OLD-AGE PENSIONS - See PENSIONS AND RETIREMENT BENEFITS

OLD-AGE, SURVIVORS, DISABILITY, AND HEALTH
INSURANCE - See SOCIAL INSURANCE

OLIVES

U.S. Department of Agriculture, National Agricultural Statistics Service, Fourteenth Street and Independence Avenue, SW, Washington, D.C. 20250 (202) 219-1504; *Noncitrus Fruits and Nuts*.

Oman - National Statistical Office

Directorate General of National Statistics, Development Council, Post Office Box 881, Muscat, Oman.

Oman - Primary Statistics Source

Directorate General of National Statistics, Development Council, P.O. Box 881, Muscat, Oman; *Statistical Year Book*.

OMAN - AGRICULTURE

Economic Commission for Western Asia, Post Office Box 27, Baghdad, Iraq; *Statistical Abstract of Western Asia*.

Euromonitor Publications Limited, 87-88 Turnmill Street, London EC1M 5QU, England; *International Marketing Data and Statistics*, and *Middle East Economic Handbook*.

Facts on File, 460 Park Avenue South, New York, New York 10016 (800) 443-8323; *The New Book of World Rankings*.

Federal Statistical Office, Gustav - Stresemann - Ring 11, D-6200 Wiesbaden, Germany; *Oman*.

Food and Agricultural Organization of the United Nations (FAO), Via delle Terme di Caracalla, 00100 Rome, Italy (Telephone Number in U.S. (202) 653-2400); *Production Yearbook, The State of Food and Agriculture*, and *Trade Yearbook*.

Times Books, 201 East 50th Street, New York, New York 10022 (212) 751-2600; *The Economist Book of Vital World Statistics*.

The World Bank, 1818 H Street, NW, Washington, D.C. 20433 (202) 477-1234; *World Tables*.

OMAN - AIRLINE SERVICE

Economic Commission for Western Asia, Post Office Box 27, Baghdad, Iraq; *Statistical Abstract of Western Asia*.

Facts on File, 460 Park Avenue South, New York, New York 10016 (800) 443-8323; *The New Book of World Rankings*.

Times Books, 201 East 50th Street, New York, New York 10022 (212) 751-2600; *The Economist Book of Vital World Statistics*.

OMAN - ALUMINUM PRODUCTION AND CONSUMPTION - See
OMAN - MINING AND MINERAL PRODUCTS

OMAN - ANIMAL HEALTH

Food and Agricultural Organization of the United Nations (FAO), Via delle Terme di Caracalla, 00100 Rome, Italy (Telephone Number in U.S. (202) 653-2400); *Animal Health Yearbook*.

OMAN - AREA AND DENSITY OF POPULATION

Economic Commission for Western Asia, Post Office Box 27, Baghdad, Iraq; *Statistical Abstract of Western Asia*.

Euromonitor Publications Limited, 87-88 Turnmill Street, London EC1M 5QU, England; *International Marketing Data and Statistics*, and *Middle East Economic Handbook*.

Facts on File, 460 Park Avenue South, New York, New York 10016 (800) 443-8323; *The New Book of World Rankings*.

Federal Statistical Office, Gustav - Stresemann - Ring 11, D-6200 Wiesbaden, Germany; *Oman*.

Food and Agricultural Organization of the United Nations (FAO) Via delle Terme di Caracalla, 00100 Rome, Italy (Telephone Number in U.S. (202) 653-2400); *The State of Food and Agriculture*.

Statistical Office of the United Nations, Publishing Service, New York, New York 10017 (800) 253-9646; *Statistical Yearbook*.

Times Books, 201 East 50th Street, New York, New York 10022 (212) 751-2600; *The Economist Book of Vital World Statistics*.

OMAN - ARMS EXPORTS AND IMPORTS

U.S. Arms Control and Disarmament Agency, 320 Twenty-first Street, NW, Washington, D.C. 20451 (202) 647-8677; *World Military Expenditures and Arms Transfers*.

OMAN - BALANCE OF PAYMENTS

Economic Commission for Western Asia, Post Office Box 27, Baghdad, Iraq; *Statistical Abstract of Western Asia*.

The Economist Intelligence Unit, 111 West 57th Street, New York, New York 10019 (800) 938-4685; *The World Market Atlas*.

Federal Statistical Office, Gustav - Stresemann - Ring 11, D-6200 Wiesbaden, Germany; *Oman*.

International Monetary Fund, 700 Nineteenth Street, NW, Washington, D.C. 20431 (202) 623-7000; *Balance of Payments Yearbook*.

Times Books, 201 East 50th Street, New York, New York 10022 (212) 751-2600; *The Economist Book of Vital World Statistics*.

The World Bank, 1818 H Street, NW, Washington, D.C. 20433 (202) 477-1234; *World Tables*.

OMAN - BALANCE OF TRADE

Economic Commission for Western Asia, Post Office Box 27, Baghdad, Iraq; *Statistical Abstract of Western Asia*.

OMAN - BANKING

Economic Commission for Western Asia, Post Office Box 27, Baghdad, Iraq; *Statistical Abstract of Western Asia*.

Facts on File, 460 Park Avenue South, New York, New York 10016 (800) 443-8323; *The New Book of World Rankings.*

International Monetary Fund, 700 Nineteenth Street, NW, Washington, D.C. 20431 (202) 623-7000; *Government Finance Statistics Yearbook,* and *International Financial Statistics.*

OMAN - BARLEY PRODUCTION - See OMAN - CROPS

OMAN - BEER PRODUCTION

Facts on File, 460 Park Avenue South, New York, New York 10016 (800) 443-8323; *The New Book of World Rankings.*

OMAN - BIRTH RATES

Euromonitor Publications Limited, 87-88 Turnmill Street, London EC1M 5QU, England; *Middle East Economic Handbook.*

Facts on File, 460 Park Avenue South, New York, New York 10016 (800) 443-8323; *The New Book of World Rankings.*

Statistical Office of the United Nations, Publishing Service, New York, New York 10017 (800) 253-9646; *Demographic Yearbook.*

Times Books, 201 East 50th Street, New York, New York 10022 (212) 751-2600; *The Economist Book of Vital World Statistics.*

The World Bank, 1818 H Street, NW, Washington, D.C. 20433 (202) 477-1234; *World Tables.*

OMAN - BIRTH RATES

Facts on File, 460 Park Avenue South, New York, New York 10016 (800) 443-8323; *The New Book of World Rankings.*

OMAN - BROADCASTING

Billboard Limited, Post Office Box 9027, 1006 AA Amsterdam, The Netherlands (Telephone Number in U.S. (212) 764-7300); *World Radio TV Handbook.*

Facts on File, 460 Park Avenue South, New York, New York 10016 (800) 443-8323; *The New Book of World Rankings.*

Times Books, 201 East 50th Street, New York, New York 10022 (212) 751-2600; *The Economist Book of Vital World Statistics.*

OMAN - BUSINESS AND PROFESSIONAL LICENSES

International Monetary Fund, 700 Nineteenth Street, NW, Washington, D.C. 20431 (202) 623-7000; *Government Finance Statistics Yearbook.*

OMAN - BUTTER PRODUCTION - See OMAN - DAIRY PRODUCTS

OMAN - CALORIE SUPPLY

Food and Agricultural Organization of the United Nations (FAO) Via delle Terme di Caracalla, 00100 Rome, Italy (Telephone Number in U.S. (202) 653-2400); *The State of Food and Agriculture.*

OMAN - CAPITAL REVENUE

International Monetary Fund, 700 Nineteenth Street, NW, Washington, D.C. 20431 (202) 623-7000; *Government Finance Statistics Yearbook.*

OMAN - CATTLE - See OMAN - LIVESTOCK AND POULTRY

OMAN - CEMENT PRODUCTION - See OMAN - MINING AND MINERAL PRODUCTS

OMAN - CHICKENS - See OMAN - LIVESTOCK AND POULTRY

OMAN - CIGARETTE PRODUCTION - See OMAN - TOBACCO PRODUCTION

OMAN - CLIMATE

Facts on File, 460 Park Avenue South, New York, New York 10016 (800) 443-8323; *The New Book of World Rankings.*

OMAN - COAL PRODUCTION - See OMAN - MINING AND MINERAL PRODUCTS

OMAN - COFFEE PRODUCTION AND CONSUMPTION - See OMAN - CROPS

OMAN - CONSTRUCTION

Facts on File, 460 Park Avenue South, New York, New York 10016 (800) 443-8323; *The New Book of World Rankings.*

OMAN - COMMUNICATIONS

Economic Commission for Western Asia, Post Office Box 27, Baghdad, Iraq; *Statistical Abstract of Western Asia.*

Federal Statistical Office, Gustav - Stresemann - Ring 11, D-6200 Wiesbaden, Germany; *Oman.*

OMAN - CONSTRUCTION INDUSTRY

Statistical Office of the United Nations, Publishing Service, New York, New York 10017 (800) 253-9646; *Construction Statistics Yearbook.*

OMAN - CONSUMER PRICES

Times Books, 201 East 50th Street, New York, New York 10022 (212) 751-2600; *The Economist Book of Vital World Statistics.*

OMAN - CONSUMPTION

Euromonitor Publications Limited, 87-88 Turnmill Street, London EC1M 5QU, England; *Middle East Economic Handbook.*

OMAN - COPPER PRODUCTION AND CONSUMPTION - See OMAN - MINING AND MINERAL PRODUCTS

OMAN - CORN PRODUCTION - See OMAN - CROPS

OMAN - CORPORATE TAXES - See OMAN - TAXATION

OMAN - COTTON PRODUCTION - See OMAN - CROPS

OMAN - CRIME

International Criminal Police Organization (INTERPOL), 26 rue Armengaud, 92210 Saint Cloud, France; *International Crime Statistics.*

OMAN - CROPS

Facts on File, 460 Park Avenue South, New York, New York 10016 (800) 443-8323; *The New Book of World Rankings.*

Food and Agricultural Organization of the United Nations (FAO) Via delle Terme di Caracalla, 00100 Rome, Italy (Telephone Number in U.S. (202) 653-2400); *The State of Food and Agriculture.*

Statistical Office of the United Nations, Publishing Service, New York, New York 10017 (800) 253-9646; *Statistical Yearbook.*

OMAN - CUSTOMS DUTIES

International Monetary Fund, 700 Nineteenth Street, NW, Washington, D.C. 20431 (202) 623-7000; *Government Finance Statistics Yearbook.*

OMAN - DAIRY PRODUCTS

Economic Commission for Western Asia, Post Office Box 27, Baghdad, Iraq; *Statistical Abstract of Western Asia.*

Facts on File, 460 Park Avenue South, New York, New York 10016 (800) 443-8323; *The New Book of World Rankings.*

Food and Agricultural Organization of the United Nations (FAO) Via delle Terme di Caracalla, 00100 Rome, Italy (Telephone Number in U.S. (202) 653-2400); *Production Yearbook,* and *The State of Food and Agriculture.*

Statistical Office of the United Nations, Publishing Service, New York, New York 10017 (800) 253-9646; *Statistical Yearbook.*

OMAN - DEATH RATES

Euromonitor Publications Limited, 87-88 Turnmill Street, London EC1M 5QU, England; *Middle East Economic Handbook.*

Times Books, 201 East 50th Street, New York, New York 10022 (212) 751-2600; *The Economist Book of Vital World Statistics.*

World Health Organization, Office of Publications, Avenue Appia, CH-1211 Geneva 27, Switzerland (Telephone Number in U.S. (518) 436-9686); *World Health Statistics Annual.*

OMAN - DEFENSE EXPENDITURES

International Monetary Fund, 700 Nineteenth Street, NW, Washington, D.C. 20431 (202) 623-7000; *Government Finance Statistics Yearbook.*

U.S. Arms Control and Disarmament Agency, 320 Twenty-first Street, NW, Washington, D.C. 20451 (202) 647-8677; *World Military Expenditures and Arms Transfers.*

OMAN - DEMOGRAPHY

The Economist Intelligence Unit, 111 West 57th Street, New York, New York 10019 (800) 938-4685; *The World Market Atlas.*

Facts on File, 460 Park Avenue South, New York, New York 10016 (800) 443-8323; *The New Book of World Rankings.*

OMAN - DEVELOPMENT ASSISTANCE

Statistical Office of the United Nations, Publishing Service, New York, New York 10017 (800) 253-9646; *Statistical Yearbook.*

OMAN - DIAMOND PRODUCTION - See OMAN - MINING AND MINERAL PRODUCTS

OMAN - DISEASES

World Health Organization, Office of Publications, Avenue Appia, CH-1211 Geneva 27, Switzerland (Telephone Number in U.S. (518) 436-9686); *World Health Statistics Annual.*

OMAN - DIVORCE RATES

Facts on File, 460 Park Avenue South, New York, New York 10016 (800) 443-8323; *The New Book of World Rankings.*

Statistical Office of the United Nations, Publishing Service, New York, New York 10017 (800) 253-9646; *Demographic Yearbook.*

OMAN - ECONOMY

Euromonitor Publications Limited, 87-88 Turnmill Street, London EC1M 5QU, England; *International Marketing Data and Statistics.*

Facts on File, 460 Park Avenue South, New York, New York 10016 (800) 443-8323; *The New Book of World Rankings.*

OMAN - EDUCATION

Economic Commission for Western Asia, Post Office Box 27, Baghdad, Iraq; *Statistical Abstract of Western Asia.*

The Economist Intelligence Unit, 111 West 57th Street, New York, New York 10019 (800) 938-4685; *The World Market Atlas.*

Euromonitor Publications Limited, 87-88 Turnmill Street, London EC1M 5QU, England; *Middle East Economic Handbook.*

Facts on File, 460 Park Avenue South, New York, New York 10016 (800) 443-8323; *The New Book of World Rankings.*

Federal Statistical Office, Gustav - Stresemann - Ring 11, D-6200 Wiesbaden, Germany; *Oman.*

International Monetary Fund, 700 Nineteenth Street, NW, Washington, D.C. 20431 (202) 623-7000; *Government Finance Statistics Yearbook.*

Times Books, 201 East 50th Street, New York, New York 10022 (212) 751-2600; *The Economist Book of Vital World Statistics.*

United Nations Educational, Scientific and Cultural Organization (UNESCO), 7 Place de Fontenoy, F-75700 Paris, France (Telephone Number in U.S. (212) 963-5981); *Statistical Yearbook.*

The World Bank, 1818 H Street, NW, Washington, D.C. 20433 (202) 477-1234; *World Tables.*

OMAN - EGG PRODUCTION AND CONSUMPTION - See OMAN - DAIRY PRODUCTS

OMAN - ELECTRICITY

Facts on File, 460 Park Avenue South, New York, New York 10016 (800) 443-8323; *The New Book of World Rankings.*

Penn Well Publishing Company, 1421 South Sheridan Road, Post Office Box 1260, Tulsa, Oklahoma 74101 (800) 752-9764; *International Energy Statistics Sourcebook.*

Statistical Office of the United Nations, Publishing Service, New York, New York 10017 (800) 253-9646; *Statistical Yearbook.*

Times Books, 201 East 50th Street, New York, New York 10022 (212) 751-2600; *The Economist Book of Vital World Statistics*.

OMAN - EMPLOYMENT

Economic Commission for Western Asia, Post Office Box 27, Baghdad, Iraq; *Statistical Abstract of Western Asia*.

Euromonitor Publications Limited, 87-88 Turnmill Street, London EC1M 5QU, England; *International Marketing Data and Statistics*, and *Middle East Economic Handbook*.

Facts on File, 460 Park Avenue South, New York, New York 10016 (800) 443-8323; *The New Book of World Rankings*.

Federal Statistical Office, Gustav - Stresemann - Ring 11, D-6200 Wiesbaden, Germany; *Oman*.

OMAN - ENERGY

Economic Commission for Western Asia, Post Office Box 27, Baghdad, Iraq; *Statistical Abstract of Western Asia*.

Euromonitor Publications Limited, 87-88 Turnmill Street, London EC1M 5QU, England; *Middle East Economic Handbook*.

Facts on File, 460 Park Avenue South, New York, New York 10016 (800) 443-8323; *The New Book of World Rankings*.

Food and Agricultural Organization of the United Nations (FAO) Via delle Terme di Caracalla, 00100 Rome, Italy (Telephone Number in U.S. (202) 653-2400); *The State of Food and Agriculture*.

Penn Well Publishing Company, 1421 South Sheridan Road, Post Office Box 1260, Tulsa, Oklahoma 74101 (800) 752-9764; *International Energy Statistics Sourcebook*.

Statistical Office of the United Nations, Publishing Service, New York, New York 10017 (800) 253-9646; *Energy Statistics Yearbook* and *Statistical Yearbook*.

Times Books, 201 East 50th Street, New York, New York 10022 (212) 751-2600; *The Economist Book of Vital World Statistics*.

OMAN - EXCHANGE RATES

Euromonitor Publications Limited, 87-88 Turnmill Street, London EC1M 5QU, England; *International Marketing Data and Statistics*, and *Middle East Economic Handbook*.

International Monetary Fund, 700 Nineteenth Street, NW, Washington, D.C. 20431 (202) 623-7000; *International Financial Statistics*.

Statistical Office of the United Nations, Publishing Service, New York, New York 10017 (800) 253-9646; *Statistical Yearbook*.

OMAN - EXPORTS

American Automobile Manufacturers Association, 1401 H Street, NW, Suite 900, Washington, D.C. 20005 (202) 326-5500; *World Motor Vehicle Data*.

Economic Commission for Western Asia, Post Office Box 27, Baghdad, Iraq; *Statistical Abstract of Western Asia*.

The Economist Intelligence Unit, 111 West 57th Street, New York, New York 10019 (800) 938-4685; *The World Market Atlas*.

Euromonitor Publications Limited, 87-88 Turnmill Street, London EC1M 5QU, England; *International Marketing Data and Statistics*, and *Middle East Economic Handbook*.

Food and Agricultural Organization of the United Nations (FAO) Via delle Terme di Caracalla, 00100 Rome, Italy (Telephone Number in U.S. (202) 653-2400); *The State of Food and Agriculture*.

International Monetary Fund, 700 Nineteenth Street, NW, Washington, D.C. 20431 (202) 623-7000; *Direction of Trade Statistics*, and *International Financial Statistics*.

Times Books, 201 East 50th Street, New York, New York 10022 (212) 751-2600; *The Economist Book of Vital World Statistics*.

The World Bank, 1818 H Street, NW, Washington, D.C. 20433 (202) 477-1234; *World Tables*.

OMAN - EXTERNAL TRADE

Food and Agricultural Organization of the United Nations (FAO) Via delle Terme di Caracalla, 00100 Rome, Italy (Telephone Number in U.S. (202) 653-2400); *The State of Food and Agriculture*, and *Trade Yearbook*.

Statistical Office of the United Nations, Publishing Service, New York, New York 10017 (800) 253-9646; *Statistical Yearbook*.

OMAN - FARM CROPS - See OMAN - CROPS

OMAN - FEMALE WORKING POPULATION - See OMAN - EMPLOYMENT

OMAN - FERTILITY RATES

Facts on File, 460 Park Avenue South, New York, New York 10016 (800) 443-8323; *The New Book of World Rankings*.

Times Books, 201 East 50th Street, New York, New York 10022 (212) 751-2600; *The Economist Book of Vital World Statistics*.

The World Bank, 1818 H Street, NW, Washington, D.C. 20433 (202) 477-1234; *World Tables*.

OMAN - FERTILIZER

Food and Agricultural Organization of the United Nations (FAO) Via delle Terme di Caracalla, 00100 Rome, Italy (Telephone Number in U.S. (202) 653-2400); *The State of Food and Agriculture*.

Statistical Office of the United Nations, Publishing Service, New York, New York 10017 (800) 253-9646; *Statistical Yearbook*.

OMAN - FETAL MORTALITY

Statistical Office of the United Nations, Publishing Service, New York, New York 10017 (800) 253-9646; *Demographic Yearbook*.

OMAN - FINANCE

Economic Commission for Western Asia, Post Office Box 27, Baghdad, Iraq; *Statistical Abstract of Western Asia*.

Euromonitor Publications Limited, 87-88 Turnmill Street, London EC1M 5QU, England; *Middle East Economic Handbook*.

Facts on File, 460 Park Avenue South, New York, New York 10016 (800) 443-8323; *The New Book of World Rankings*.

Federal Statistical Office, Gustav - Stresemann - Ring 11, D-6200 Wiesbaden, Germany; *Oman.*

International Monetary Fund, 700 Nineteenth Street, NW, Washington, D.C. 20431 (202) 623-7000; *Government Finance Statistics Yearbook,* and *International Financial Statistics.*

OMAN - FISHERIES

Economic Commission for Western Asia, Post Office Box 27, Baghdad, Iraq; *Statistical Abstract of Western Asia.*

Facts on File, 460 Park Avenue South, New York, New York 10016 (800) 443-8323; *The New Book of World Rankings.*

Federal Statistical Office, Gustav - Stresemann - Ring 11, D-6200 Wiesbaden, Germany; *Oman.*

Food and Agricultural Organization of the United Nations (FAO) Via delle Terme di Caracalla, 00100 Rome, Italy (Telephone Number in U.S. (202) 653-2400); *The State of Food and Agriculture,* and *Yearbook of Fishery Statistics.*

Statistical Office of the United Nations, Publishing Service, New York, New York 10017 (800) 253-9646; *Statistical Yearbook.*

OMAN - FOOD

Food and Agricultural Organization of the United Nations (FAO), Via delle Terme di Caracalla, 00100 Rome, Italy (Telephone Number in U.S. (202) 653-2400); *Production Yearbook,* and *The State of Food and Agriculture.*

OMAN - FOREIGN DEBT

International Monetary Fund, 700 Nineteenth Street, NW, Washington, D.C. 20431 (202) 623-7000; *Government Finance Statistics Yearbook.*

OMAN - FOREIGN INDEBTEDNESS

Euromonitor Publications Limited, 87-88 Turnmill Street, London EC1M 5QU, England; *Middle East Economic Handbook.*

OMAN - FOREIGN TRADE

Economic Commission for Western Asia, Post Office Box 27, Baghdad, Iraq; *Statistical Abstract of Western Asia.*

Euromonitor Publications Limited, 87-88 Turnmill Street, London EC1M 5QU, England; *International Marketing Data and Statistics* and *Middle East Economic Handbook.*

Facts on File, 460 Park Avenue South, New York, New York 10016 (800) 443-8323; *The New Book of World Rankings.*

Federal Statistical Office, Gustav - Stresemann - Ring 11, D-6200 Wiesbaden, Germany; *Oman.*

Food and Agricultural Organization of the United Nations (FAO) Via delle Terme di Caracalla, 00100 Rome, Italy (Telephone Number in U.S. (202) 653-2400); *The State of Food and Agriculture.*

Statistical Office of the United Nations, Publishing Service, New York, New York 10017 (800) 253-9646; *International Trade Statistics Yearbook,* and *Statistical Yearbook.*

The World Bank, 1818 H Street, NW, Washington, D.C. 20433 (202) 477-1234; *World Tables.*

OMAN - FOREIGN TRADE - INDEX NUMBERS

Economic Commission for Western Asia, Post Office Box 27, Baghdad, Iraq; *Statistical Abstract of Western Asia.*

OMAN - FORESTRY AND FOREST PRODUCTS

Facts on File, 460 Park Avenue South, New York, New York 10016 (800) 443-8323; *The New Book of World Rankings.*

Food and Agricultural Organization of the United Nations (FAO) Via delle Terme di Caracalla, 00100 Rome, Italy (Telephone Number in U.S. (202) 653-2400); *The State of Food and Agriculture,* and *Yearbook of Forest Products.*

OMAN - GAS (NATURAL) PRODUCTION - See OMAN - MINING AND MINERAL PRODUCTS

OMAN - GENERAL MORTALITY

Facts on File, 460 Park Avenue South, New York, New York 10016 (800) 443-8323; *The New Book of World Rankings.*

Statistical Office of the United Nations, Publishing Service, New York, New York 10017 (800) 253-9646; *Demographic Yearbook.*

OMAN - GOLD HOLDINGS

International Monetary Fund, 700 Nineteenth Street, NW, Washington, D.C. 20431 (202) 623-7000; *International Financial Statistics.*

Statistical Office of the United Nations, Publishing Service, New York, New York 10017 (800) 253-9646; *Statistical Yearbook.*

The World Bank, 1818 H Street, NW, Washington, D.C. 20433 (202) 477-1234; *World Tables.*

OMAN - GOLD PRODUCTION AND CONSUMPTION - See OMAN - MINING AND MINERAL PRODUCTS

OMAN - GOVERNMENT EXPENDITURES

Economic Commission for Western Asia, Post Office Box 27, Baghdad, Iraq; *Statistical Abstract of Western Asia.*

International Monetary Fund, 700 Nineteenth Street, NW, Washington, D.C. 20431 (202) 623-7000; *Government Finance Statistics Yearbook.*

Times Books, 201 East 50th Street, New York, New York 10022 (212) 751-2600; *The Economist Book of Vital World Statistics.*

The World Bank, 1818 H Street, NW, Washington, D.C. 20433 (202) 477-1234; *World Tables.*

OMAN - GOVERNMENT REVENUES

Economic Commission for Western Asia, Post Office Box 27, Baghdad, Iraq; *Statistical Abstract of Western Asia.*

International Monetary Fund, 700 Nineteenth Street, NW, Washington, D.C. 20431 (202) 623-7000; *Government Finance Statistics Yearbook.*

Times Books, 201 East 50th Street, New York, New York 10022 (212) 751-2600; *The Economist Book of Vital World Statistics.*

The World Bank, 1818 H Street, NW, Washington, D.C. 20433 (202) 477-1234; *World Tables*.

OMAN - GRAIN PRODUCTION - See OMAN - CROPS

OMAN - GRANTS

International Monetary Fund, 700 Nineteenth Street, NW, Washington, D.C. 20431 (202) 623-7000; *Government Finance Statistics Yearbook*.

OMAN - GROSS DOMESTIC PRODUCT

Economic Commission for Western Asia, Post Office Box 27, Baghdad, Iraq; *Statistical Abstract of Western Asia*.

The Economist Intelligence Unit, 111 West 57th Street, New York, New York 10019 (800) 938-4685; *The World Market Atlas*.

Euromonitor Publications Limited, 87-88 Turnmill Street, London EC1M 5QU, England; *International Marketing Data and Statistics*, and *Middle East Economic Handbook*.

Facts on File, 460 Park Avenue South, New York, New York 10016 (800) 443-8323; *The New Book of World Rankings*.

Statistical Office of the United Nations, Publishing Service, New York, New York 10017 (800) 253-9646; *Statistical Yearbook*.

Times Books, 201 East 50th Street, New York, New York 10022 (212) 751-2600; *The Economist Book of Vital World Statistics*.

The World Bank, 1818 H Street, NW, Washington, D.C. 20433 (202) 477-1234; *World Tables*.

OMAN - GROSS NATIONAL PRODUCT

Euromonitor Publications Limited, 87-88 Turnmill Street, London EC1M 5QU, England; *International Marketing Data and Statistics*.

U.S. Arms Control and Disarmament Agency, 320 Twenty-first Street, NW, Washington, D.C. 20451 (202) 647-8677; *World Military Expenditures and Arms Transfers*.

The World Bank, 1818 H Street, NW, Washington, D.C. 20433 (202) 477-1234; *World Tables*.

OMAN - HEALTH

Economic Commission for Western Asia, Post Office Box 27, Baghdad, Iraq; *Statistical Abstract of Western Asia*.

Euromonitor Publications Limited, 87-88 Turnmill Street, London EC1M 5QU, England; *Middle East Economic Handbook*.

Facts on File, 460 Park Avenue South, New York, New York 10016 (800) 443-8323; *The New Book of World Rankings*.

Federal Statistical Office, Gustav - Stresemann - Ring 11, D-6200 Wiesbaden, Germany; *Oman*.

Statistical Office of the United Nations, Publishing Service, New York, New York 10017 (800) 253-9646; *Statistical Yearbook*.

Times Books, 201 East 50th Street, New York, New York 10022 (212) 751-2600; *The Economist Book of Vital World Statistics*.

World Health Organization, Office of Publications, Avenue Appia, CH-1211 Geneva 27, Switzerland (Telephone Number in U.S. (518) 436-9686); *World Health Statistics Annual*.

OMAN - HEALTH EXPENDITURES

International Monetary Fund, 700 Nineteenth Street, NW, Washington, D.C. 20431 (202) 623-7000; *Government Finance Statistics Yearbook*.

OMAN - HIDE PRODUCTION

Food and Agricultural Organization of the United Nations (FAO), Via delle Terme di Caracalla, 00100 Rome, Italy (Telephone Number in U.S. (202) 653-2400); *Production Yearbook*.

OMAN - HIGHWAYS

Economic Commission for Western Asia, Post Office Box 27, Baghdad, Iraq; *Statistical Abstract of Western Asia*.

OMAN - HORSES - See OMAN - LIVESTOCK AND POULTRY

OMAN - HOURS OF WORK - See OMAN - EMPLOYMENT

OMAN - HOUSING EXPENDITURES

Facts on File, 460 Park Avenue South, New York, New York 10016 (800) 443-8323; *The New Book of World Rankings*.

International Monetary Fund, 700 Nineteenth Street, NW, Washington, D.C. 20431 (202) 623-7000; *Government Finance Statistics Yearbook*.

OMAN - ILLITERATE POPULATION

The Economist Intelligence Unit, 111 West 57th Street, New York, New York 10019 (800) 938-4685; *The World Market Atlas*.

OMAN - IMPORTS

American Automobile Manufacturers Association, 1401 H Street, NW, Suite 900, Washington, D.C. 20005 (202) 326-5500; *World Motor Vehicle Data*.

Economic Commission for Western Asia, Post Office Box 27, Baghdad, Iraq; *Statistical Abstract of Western Asia*.

The Economist Intelligence Unit, 111 West 57th Street, New York, New York 10019 (800) 938-4685; *The World Market Atlas*.

Euromonitor Publications Limited, 87-88 Turnmill Street, London EC1M 5QU, England; *International Marketing Data and Statistics*, and *Middle East Economic Handbook*.

Food and Agricultural Organization of the United Nations (FAO) Via delle Terme di Caracalla, 00100 Rome, Italy (Telephone Number in U.S. (202) 653-2400); *The State of Food and Agriculture*.

International Monetary Fund, 700 Nineteenth Street, NW, Washington, D.C. 20431 (202) 623-7000; *Direction of Trade Statistics*, *Government Finance Statistics Yearbook*, and *International Financial Statistics*.

Times Books, 201 East 50th Street, New York, New York 10022 (212) 751-2600; *The Economist Book of Vital World Statistics*.

The World Bank, 1818 H Street, NW, Washington, D.C. 20433 (202) 477-1234; *World Tables*.

OMAN - INDUSTRY

Euromonitor Publications Limited, 87-88 Turnmill Street, London EC1M 5QU, England; *International Marketing Data and Statistics*.

Facts on File, 460 Park Avenue South, New York, New York 10016 (800) 443-8323; *The New Book of World Rankings*.

Federal Statistical Office, Gustav - Stresemann - Ring 11, D-6200 Wiesbaden, Germany; *Oman*.

Times Books, 201 East 50th Street, New York, New York 10022 (212) 751-2600; *The Economist Book of Vital World Statistics*.

The World Bank, 1818 H Street, NW, Washington, D.C. 20433 (202) 477-1234; *World Tables*.

OMAN - INFANT AND MATERNAL MORTALITY

Statistical Office of the United Nations, Publishing Service, New York, New York 10017 (800) 253-9646; *Demographic Yearbook*.

Times Books, 201 East 50th Street, New York, New York 10022 (212) 751-2600; *The Economist Book of Vital World Statistics*.

The World Bank, 1818 H Street, NW, Washington, D.C. 20433 (202) 477-1234; *World Tables*.

OMAN - INTERNATIONAL LIQUIDITY

International Monetary Fund, 700 Nineteenth Street, NW, Washington, D.C. 20431 (202) 623-7000; *International Financial Statistics*.

OMAN - INTERNATIONAL RESERVES EXCLUDING GOLD

Statistical Office of the United Nations, Publishing Service, New York, New York 10017 (800) 253-9646; *Statistical Yearbook*.

The World Bank, 1818 H Street, NW, Washington, D.C. 20433 (202) 477-1234; *World Tables*.

OMAN - IRON ORE PRODUCTION AND CONSUMPTION - See OMAN - MINING AND MINERAL PRODUCTS

OMAN - IRRIGATION

Euromonitor Publications Limited, 87-88 Turnmill Street, London EC1M 5QU, England; *International Marketing Data and Statistics*.

OMAN - LABOR FORCE

Economic Commission for Western Asia, Post Office Box 27, Baghdad, Iraq; *Statistical Abstract of Western Asia*.

Euromonitor Publications Limited, 87-88 Turnmill Street, London EC1M 5QU, England; *International Marketing Data and Statistics*, and *Middle East Economic Handbook*.

Facts on File, 460 Park Avenue South, New York, New York 10016 (800) 443-8323; *The New Book of World Rankings*.

Food and Agricultural Organization of the United Nations (FAO) Via delle Terme di Caracalla, 00100 Rome, Italy (Telephone Number in U.S. (202) 653-2400); *The State of Food and Agriculture*.

The World Bank, 1818 H Street, NW, Washington, D.C. 20433 (202) 477-1234; *World Tables*.

OMAN - LAND USE

Economic Commission for Western Asia, Post Office Box 27, Baghdad, Iraq; *Statistical Abstract of Western Asia*.

Euromonitor Publications Limited, 87-88 Turnmill Street, London EC1M 5QU, England; *International Marketing Data and Statistics*.

Food and Agricultural Organization of the United Nations (FAO), Via delle Terme di Caracalla, 00100 Rome, Italy (Telephone Number in U.S. (202) 653-2400); *Production Yearbook*.

OMAN - LIBRARIES

Facts on File, 460 Park Avenue South, New York, New York 10016 (800) 443-8323; *The New Book of World Rankings*.

OMAN - LIVESTOCK AND POULTRY

Economic Commission for Western Asia, Post Office Box 27, Baghdad, Iraq; *Statistical Abstract of Western Asia*.

Euromonitor Publications Limited, 87-88 Turnmill Street, London EC1M 5QU, England; *International Marketing Data and Statistics*.

Facts on File, 460 Park Avenue South, New York, New York 10016 (800) 443-8323; *The New Book of World Rankings*.

Food and Agricultural Organization of the United Nations (FAO), Via delle Terme di Caracalla, 00100 Rome, Italy (Telephone Number in U.S. (202) 653-2400); *Production Yearbook*, and *The State of Food and Agriculture*.

Statistical Office of the United Nations, Publishing Service, New York, New York 10017 (800) 253-9646; *Statistical Yearbook*.

OMAN - LIVING LEVELS

Times Books, 201 East 50th Street, New York, New York 10022 (212) 751-2600; *The Economist Book of Vital World Statistics*.

OMAN - MANUFACTURING

American Automobile Manufacturers Association, 1401 H Street, NW, Suite 900, Washington, D.C. 20005 (202) 326-5500; *World Motor Vehicle Data*.

Facts on File, 460 Park Avenue South, New York, New York 10016 (800) 443-8323; *The New Book of World Rankings*.

Times Books, 201 East 50th Street, New York, New York 10022 (212) 751-2600; *The Economist Book of Vital World Statistics*.

The World Bank, 1818 H Street, NW, Washington, D.C. 20433 (202) 477-1234; *World Tables*.

OMAN - MARRIAGE RATES

Facts on File, 460 Park Avenue South, New York, New York 10016 (800) 443-8323; *The New Book of World Rankings*.

Statistical Office of the United Nations, Publishing Service, New York, New York 10017 (800) 253-9646; *Demographic Yearbook*.

OMAN - MEAT PRODUCTION - See OMAN - LIVESTOCK AND POULTRY

OMAN - MERCHANT FLEET CHARACTERISTICS

Lloyd's Register of Shipping, 17 Battery Place, New York, New York 10004 (212) 425-8050; *Register of Ships*.

OMAN - MERCHANT SHIPPING

Economic Commission for Western Asia, Post Office Box 27, Baghdad, Iraq; *Statistical Abstract of Western Asia*.

Lloyd's Register of Shipping, 17 Battery Place, New York, New York 10004 (212) 425-8050; *Register of Ships*.

Statistical Office of the United Nations, Publishing Service, New York, New York 10017 (800) 253-9646; *Statistical Yearbook*.

Times Books, 201 East 50th Street, New York, New York 10022 (212) 751-2600; *The Economist Book of Vital World Statistics*.

OMAN - MILITARY

The International Institute for Strategic Studies, 23 Tavistock Street, London WC2E 7NQ, England; *The Military Balance*.

U.S. Arms Control and Disarmament Agency, 320 Twenty-first Street, NW, Washington, D.C. 20451 (202) 647-8677; *World Military Expenditures and Arms Transfers*.

OMAN - MILK PRODUCTION - See OMAN - DAIRY PRODUCTS

OMAN - MINING AND MINERAL PRODUCTS

Economic Commission for Western Asia, Post Office Box 27, Baghdad, Iraq; *Statistical Abstract of Western Asia*.

Facts on File, 460 Park Avenue South, New York, New York 10016 (800) 443-8323; *The New Book of World Rankings*.

Penn Well Publishing Company, 1421 South Sheridan Road, Post Office Box 1260, Tulsa, Oklahoma 74101 (800) 752-9764; *International Energy Statistics Sourcebook*.

Statistical Office of the United Nations, Publishing Service, New York, New York 10017 (800) 253-9646; *Statistical Yearbook*.

OMAN - MONEY EXCHANGE RATES

Euromonitor Publications Limited, 87-88 Turnmill Street, London EC1M 5QU, England; *International Marketing Data and Statistics*.

International Monetary Fund, 700 Nineteenth Street, NW, Washington, D.C. 20431 (202) 623-7000; *International Financial Statistics*.

Statistical Office of the United Nations, Publishing Service, New York, New York 10017 (800) 253-9646; *Statistical Yearbook*.

OMAN - MONEY RESERVES

Euromonitor Publications Limited, 87-88 Turnmill Street, London EC1M 5QU, England; *International Marketing Data and Statistics*.

OMAN - MONEY SUPPLY

Economic Commission for Western Asia, Post Office Box 27, Baghdad, Iraq; *Statistical Abstract of Western Asia*.

Euromonitor Publications Limited, 87-88 Turnmill Street, London EC1M 5QU, England; *International Marketing Data and Statistics*.

International Monetary Fund, 700 Nineteenth Street, NW, Washington, D.C. 20431 (202) 623-7000; *International Financial Statistics*.

The World Bank, 1818 H Street, NW, Washington, D.C. 20433 (202) 477-1234; *World Tables*.

OMAN - MOTION PICTURES

Statistical Office of the United Nations, Publishing Service, New York, New York 10017 (800) 253-9646; *Statistical Yearbook*.

OMAN - MOTOR VEHICLE PRODUCTION

American Automobile Manufacturers Association, 1401 H Street, NW, Suite 900, Washington, D.C. 20005 (202) 326-5500; *World Motor Vehicle Data*.

OMAN - MOTOR VEHICLE TAXES - See OMAN - TAXATION

OMAN - MOTOR VEHICLES

Economic Commission for Western Asia, Post Office Box 27, Baghdad, Iraq; *Statistical Abstract of Western Asia*.

OMAN - MOTOR VEHICLES IN USE

American Automobile Manufacturers Association, 1401 H Street, NW, Suite 900, Washington, D.C. 20005 (202) 326-5500; *World Motor Vehicle Data*.

Times Books, 201 East 50th Street, New York, New York 10022 (212) 751-2600; *The Economist Book of Vital World Statistics*.

OMAN - MUSEUMS

Facts on File, 460 Park Avenue South, New York, New York 10016 (800) 443-8323; *The New Book of World Rankings*.

OMAN - NATALITY - See OMAN - BIRTH RATES

OMAN - NATIONAL ACCOUNTS

Economic Commission for Western Asia, Post Office Box 27, Baghdad, Iraq; *Statistical Abstract of Western Asia*.

Federal Statistical Office, Gustav - Stresemann - Ring 11, D-6200 Wiesbaden, Germany; *Oman*.

Statistical Office of the United Nations, Publishing Service, New York, New York 10017 (800) 253-9646; *Statistical Yearbook*.

OMAN - NATIONAL INCOME

Facts on File, 460 Park Avenue South, New York, New York 10016 (800) 443-8323; *The New Book of World Rankings*.

Statistical Office of the United Nations, Publishing Service, New York, New York 10017 (800) 253-9646; *Statistical Yearbook*.

OMAN - NATIONAL PRODUCT

Facts on File, 460 Park Avenue South, New York, New York 10016 (800) 443-8323; *The New Book of World Rankings*.

OMAN - NATURAL GAS PRODUCTION - See OMAN - MINING AND MINERAL PRODUCTS

OMAN - PEANUT PRODUCTION - See OMAN - CROPS

OMAN - PESTICIDE USE

Food and Agricultural Organization of the United Nations (FAO) Via delle Terme di Caracalla, 00100 Rome, Italy (Telephone Number in U.S. (202) 653-2400); *The State of Food and Agriculture.*

OMAN - PETROLEUM INDUSTRY

Euromonitor Publications Limited, 87-88 Turnmill Street, London EC1M 5QU, England; *Middle East Economic Handbook.*

Facts on File, 460 Park Avenue South, New York, New York 10016 (800) 443-8323; *The New Book of World Rankings.*

Food and Agricultural Organization of the United Nations (FAO) Via delle Terme di Caracalla, 00100 Rome, Italy (Telephone Number in U.S. (202) 653-2400); *The State of Food and Agriculture.*

Penn Well Publishing Company, 1421 South Sheridan Road, Post Office Box 1260, Tulsa, Oklahoma 74101 (800) 752-9764; *International Energy Statistics Sourcebook.*

Statistical Office of the United Nations, Publishing Service, New York, New York 10017 (800) 253-9646; *Statistical Yearbook.*

OMAN - PIGS - See OMAN - LIVESTOCK AND POULTRY

OMAN - POPULATION

Economic Commission for Western Asia, Post Office Box 27, Baghdad, Iraq; *Statistical Abstract of Western Asia.*

The Economist Intelligence Unit, 111 West 57th Street, New York, New York 10019 (800) 938-4685; *The World Market Atlas.*

Euromonitor Publications Limited, 87-88 Turnmill Street, London EC1M 5QU, England; *International Marketing Data and Statistics,* and *Middle East Economic Handbook.*

Facts on File, 460 Park Avenue South, New York, New York 10016 (800) 443-8323; *The New Book of World Rankings.*

Federal Statistical Office, Gustav - Stresemann - Ring 11, D-6200 Wiesbaden, Germany; *Oman.*

Food and Agricultural Organization of the United Nations (FAO), Via delle Terme di Caracalla, 00100 Rome, Italy (Telephone Number in U.S. (202) 653-2400); *Production Yearbook.*

Statistical Office of the United Nations, Publishing Service, New York, New York 10017 (800) 253-9646; *Demographic Yearbook,* and *Statistical Yearbook.*

Times Books, 201 East 50th Street, New York, New York 10022 (212) 751-2600; *The Economist Book of Vital World Statistics.*

U.S. Arms Control and Disarmament Agency, 320 Twenty-first Street, NW, Washington, D.C. 20451 (202) 647-8677; *World Military Expenditures and Arms Transfers.*

World Health Organization, Office of Publications, Avenue Appia, CH-1211 Geneva 27, Switzerland (Telephone Number in U.S. (518) 436-9686); *World Health Statistics Annual.*

OMAN - POST OFFICES

Facts on File, 460 Park Avenue South, New York, New York 10016 (800) 443-8323; *The New Book of World Rankings.*

OMAN - POTATO PRODUCTION - See OMAN - CROPS

OMAN - PRICES

Economic Commission for Western Asia, Post Office Box 27, Baghdad, Iraq; *Statistical Abstract of Western Asia.*

Facts on File, 460 Park Avenue South, New York, New York 10016 (800) 443-8323; *The New Book of World Rankings.*

Federal Statistical Office, Gustav - Stresemann - Ring 11, D-6200 Wiesbaden, Germany; *Oman.*

Food and Agricultural Organization of the United Nations (FAO), Via delle Terme di Caracalla, 00100 Rome, Italy (Telephone Number in U.S. (202) 653-2400); *Production Yearbook,* and *The State of Food and Agriculture.*

OMAN - PRODUCTION

American Automobile Manufacturers Association, 1401 H Street, NW, Suite 900, Washington, D.C. 20005 (202) 326-5500; *World Motor Vehicle Data.*

Facts on File, 460 Park Avenue South, New York, New York 10016 (800) 443-8323; *The New Book of World Rankings.*

OMAN - PRODUCTIVITY

Euromonitor Publications Limited, 87-88 Turnmill Street, London EC1M 5QU, England; *International Marketing Data and Statistics.*

OMAN - PROPERTY TAXES

International Monetary Fund, 700 Nineteenth Street, NW, Washington, D.C. 20431 (202) 623-7000; *Government Finance Statistics Yearbook.*

OMAN - PUBLIC FINANCE

Facts on File, 460 Park Avenue South, New York, New York 10016 (800) 443-8323; *The New Book of World Rankings.*

OMAN - RADIO BROADCASTING - See OMAN - BROADCASTING

OMAN - RELIGION

Facts on File, 460 Park Avenue South, New York, New York 10016 (800) 443-8323; *The New Book of World Rankings.*

OMAN - RICE PRODUCTION - See OMAN - CROPS

OMAN - ROUNDWOOD PRODUCTION - See OMAN - FORESTRY AND FOREST PRODUCTS

OMAN - RUBBER PRODUCTION AND CONSUMPTION

Facts on File, 460 Park Avenue South, New York, New York 10016 (800) 443-8323; *The New Book of World Rankings.*

OMAN - SAWNWOOD PRODUCTION - See OMAN - FORESTRY AND FOREST PRODUCTS

OMAN - SENIOR CITIZENS

Facts on File, 460 Park Avenue South, New York, New York 10016 (800) 443-8323; *The New Book of World Rankings.*

OMAN - SHEEP - See OMAN - LIVESTOCK AND POULTRY

OMAN - SILVER PRODUCTION AND CONSUMPTION - See OMAN - MINING AND MINERAL PRODUCTS

OMAN - SOCIAL DATA

Facts on File, 460 Park Avenue South, New York, New York 10016 (800) 443-8323; *The New Book of World Rankings*.

OMAN - SOCIAL SECURITY

International Monetary Fund, 700 Nineteenth Street, NW, Washington, D.C. 20431 (202) 623-7000; *Government Finance Statistics Yearbook*.

OMAN - STATE BUDGET REVENUE AND EXPENDITURES

Euromonitor Publications Limited, 87-88 Turnmill Street, London EC1M 5QU, England; *International Marketing Data and Statistics*.

OMAN - STEEL PRODUCTION - See OMAN - MINING AND MINERAL PRODUCTS

OMAN - STOCKS - COMMODITY - MARKET PRICE - INDEX

Food and Agricultural Organization of the United Nations (FAO) Via delle Terme di Caracalla, 00100 Rome, Italy (Telephone Number in U.S. (202) 653-2400); *The State of Food and Agriculture*.

OMAN - SUGAR PRODUCTION AND CONSUMPTION - See OMAN - CROPS

OMAN - TAXATION

International Monetary Fund, 700 Nineteenth Street, NW, Washington, D.C. 20431 (202) 623-7000; *Government Finance Statistics Yearbook*.

The World Bank, 1818 H Street, NW, Washington, D.C. 20433 (202) 477-1234; *World Tables*.

OMAN - TAX REVENUES - See OMAN - TAXATION

OMAN - TELEPHONES IN USE

American Telephone and Telegraph Company, 26 Parsippany Road, Whippany, New Jersey 07981 (800) 338-4038; *The World's Telephones*.

Euromonitor Publications Limited, 87-88 Turnmill Street, London EC1M 5QU, England; *Middle East Economic Handbook*.

Statistical Office of the United Nations, Publishing Service, New York, New York 10017 (800) 253-9646; *Statistical Yearbook*.

OMAN - TELEVISION BROADCASTING - See OMAN - BROADCASTING

OMAN - TOBACCO PRODUCTION

Facts on File, 460 Park Avenue South, New York, New York 10016 (800) 443-8323; *The New Book of World Rankings*.

Statistical Office of the United Nations, Publishing Service, New York, New York 10017 (800) 253-9646; *Statistical Yearbook*.

OMAN - TOURISM

Economic Commission for Western Asia, Post Office Box 27, Baghdad, Iraq; *Statistical Abstract of Western Asia*.

Euromonitor Publications Limited, 87-88 Turnmill Street, London EC1M 5QU, England; *Middle East Economic Handbook*.

Facts on File, 460 Park Avenue South, New York, New York 10016 (800) 443-8323; *The New Book of World Rankings*.

Federal Statistical Office, Gustav - Stresemann - Ring 11, D-6200 Wiesbaden, Germany; *Oman*.

Times Books, 201 East 50th Street, New York, New York 10022 (212) 751-2600; *The Economist Book of Vital World Statistics*.

World Tourism Organization, Calle Capitan Haya 42, E-28020 Madrid, Spain; *Yearbook of Tourism Statistics*.

OMAN - TRADE - See OMAN - FOREIGN TRADE

OMAN - TRANSPORTATION AND COMMUNICATIONS

Economic Commission for Western Asia, Post Office Box 27, Baghdad, Iraq; *Statistical Abstract of Western Asia*.

Euromonitor Publications Limited, 87-88 Turnmill Street, London EC1M 5QU, England; *Middle East Economic Handbook*.

Facts on File, 460 Park Avenue South, New York, New York 10016 (800) 443-8323; *The New Book of World Rankings*.

Federal Statistical Office, Gustav - Stresemann - Ring 11, D-6200 Wiesbaden, Germany; *Oman*.

OMAN - UNEMPLOYMENT

Euromonitor Publications Limited, 87-88 Turnmill Street, London EC1M 5QU, England; *International Marketing Data and Statistics*, and *Middle East Economic Handbook*.

OMAN - VITAL STATISTICS

Euromonitor Publications Limited, 87-88 Turnmill Street, London EC1M 5QU, England; *International Marketing Data and Statistics*, and *Middle East Economic Handbook*.

World Health Organization, Office of Publications, Avenue Appia, CH-1211 Geneva 27, Switzerland (Telephone Number in U.S. (518) 436-9686); *World Health Statistics Annual*.

OMAN - WAGES

Federal Statistical Office, Gustav - Stresemann - Ring 11, D-6200 Wiesbaden, Germany; *Oman*.

OMAN - WEATHER

Facts on File, 460 Park Avenue South, New York, New York 10016 (800) 443-8323; *The New Book of World Rankings*.

OMAN - WELFARE

International Monetary Fund, 700 Nineteenth Street, NW, Washington, D.C. 20431 (202) 623-7000; *Government Finance Statistics Yearbook*.

OMAN - WHEAT PRODUCTION AND CONSUMPTION - See OMAN - CROPS

OMAN - WINE PRODUCTION

Facts on File, 460 Park Avenue South, New York, New York 10016 (800) 443-8323; *The New Book of World Rankings*.

OMAN - WOOL PRODUCTION

Facts on File, 460 Park Avenue South, New York, New York 10016 (800) 443-8323; *The New Book of World Rankings*.

ONIONS

U.S. Department of Agriculture, Economic Research Service, Fourteenth Street and Independence Avenue, SW, Washington, D.C. 20005-4789 (202) 219-1504; *Food Consumption, Prices, and Expenditures, Agricultural Outlook*, and *Economic Indicators of the Farm Sector, National Financial Summary*.

U.S. Department of Agriculture, National Agricultural Statistics Service, Fourteenth Street and Independence Avenue, SW, Washington, D.C. 20250 (202) 219-1504; *Agricultural Statistics*, and *Vegetables*.

OPERA

Opera America, 777 Fourteenth Street, NW, Suite 520, Washington, D.C. 20005 (202) 347-9262; unpublished data.

OPERATIONS PERFORMED - MEDICAL

U.S. Department of Health and Human Services, National Center for Health Statistics, 3700 East-West Highway, Hyattsville, Maryland 20782 (301) 436-8500; *Vital and Health Statistics*, and unpublished data.

OPHTHALMOLOGISTS

American Medical Association, 515 North State Street, Chicago, Illinois 60610 (312) 464-4818; *Physician Characteristics and Distribution in the United States*.

OPTOMETRISTS

U.S. Department of Commerce, Bureau of the Census, Suitland, Maryland 20233 (301) 763-4040; *County Business Patterns*.

U.S. Department of Health and Human Services, Health Care Financing Administration, 200 Independence Avenue, SW, Washington, D.C. 20201 (202) 245-6113; *Health Care Financing Review*.

ORANGES

U.S. Department of Agriculture, Economic Research Service, Fourteenth Street and Independence Avenue, SW, Washington, D.C. 20005-4789 (202) 219-1504; *Economic Indicators of the Farm Sector: National Financial Summary, Food Consumption, Prices and Expenditures*, and *Agricultural Outlook*.

U.S. Department of Agriculture, National Agricultural Statistics Service, Fourteenth Street and Independence Avenue, SW, Washington, D.C 20250 (202) 219-1504; *Citrus Fruits*.

OREGON - See also STATE DATA (FOR INDIVIDUAL STATES)

Oregon - Primary Statistics Source

Oregon Secretary of State, Room 136, State Capitol, Salem, Oregon 97310; *Oregon Blue Book*.

Oregon - State Data Centers

Center for Population Research and Census, Portland State University, Post Office Box 751, Portland, Oregon 97207-0751, Mr. David Gardner (503) 725-5159.

Oregon State Library, State Library Building, Salem, Oregon 97310, Mr. Craig Smith (503) 378-4277.

Bureau of Governmental Research and Service, University of Oregon, Hendricks Hall, Room 331, 1408 University Street, Post Office Box 3177, Eugene, Oregon 97403, Ms. Karen Seidel (503) 346-5235.

Oregon Housing Agency, 1600 State Street Suite 100, Salem, Oregon 97310-0161, Mr. Mike Murphy (503) 378-4730.

State Service Center for Geographic Information Systems, Department of Energy Building, 625 Marion Street, NE, Salem, Oregon 97310, Mr. Kenneth C. Yingling (503) 378-4036.

ORES, CRUDE - See also Individual Ores

ORES - CRUDE - FOREIGN TRADE

U.S. Department of the Interior, Bureau of Mines, 810 Seventh Street, NW, Washington, D.C. 20241 (202) 501-9649; *Annual Reports*.

ORES - CRUDE - WORLD PRODUCTION

U.S. Department of the Interior, Bureau of Mines, 810 Seventh Street, NW, Washington, D.C. 20241 (202) 501-9649; *Annual Reports*, and *Mineral Commodity Summaries*.

ORGAN TRANSPLANTS

American Association of Tissue Banks, 1350 Beverly Road, Suite 220-A, McLean, Virginia 22101 (703) 827-9582.

American Hospital Association, 840 North Lake Shore Drive, Chicago, Illinois 60611 (312) 280-6000; *Hospital Statistics*, and *Annual Survey of Hospitals*.

Eye Bank Association of America, 1001 Connecticut Avenue, NW, Suite 601, Washington, D.C. 20036-5504 (202) 775-4999.

U.S. Department of Health and Human Services, Public Health Service, Division of Organ Transplantation, 200 Independence Avenue, SW, Washington, D.C. 20201 (202) 619-1296; unpublished data.

ORPHANS

U.S. Department of Justice, Immigration and Naturalization, 425 I Street, NW, Washington, D.C. 20536 (202) 514-4316; *Statistical Yearbook*.

OSTEOPATHS - See also PHYSICIANS

American Medical Association, 515 North State Street, Chicago, Illinois 60610 (312) 464-4818; *Physician Characteristics and Distribution in the United States*.

American Osteopathic Association, 142 East Ontario Street, Chicago, Illinois 60611 (312) 280-5800.

U.S. Department of Health and Human Services, Health Resources and Services Administration, 5600 Fishers Lane, Rockville, Maryland 20857 (301) 443-2086; unpublished data.

OUTDOOR RECREATION ACTIVITIES - See also AMUSEMENTS, AND RECREATIONAL SERVICES, RECREATION, and Specific Forms of Recreation

National Endowment for the Arts, 1100 Pennsylvania Avenue, NW, Washington, D.C. 20506 (202) 682-5400; *Arts Participation in America: 1982-1992.*

National Sporting Goods Association, Lake Center Plaza Building, 1699 Wall Street, Mount Prospect, Illinois 60056-5780 (708) 439-4000; *Sports Participation in 1992: Series I.*

U.S. Department of Agriculture, Forest Service, Fourteenth Street and Independence Avenue, SW, Washington, D.C. 20250 (202) 720-3760; unpublished data.

OUTLAYS - FEDERAL BUDGET

Executive Office of the President, Office of Management and Budget, Executive Office Building, Washington, D.C. 20503 (202) 395-3080; *Budget of the United States Government.*

OUTLYING AREAS - ACCESSION

U.S. Department of Commerce, Bureau of the Census, Suitland, Maryland 20233 (301) 763-4040; unpublished data.

OUTLYING AREAS - AGRICULTURE - SUMMARY

U.S. Department of Commerce, Bureau of the Census, Suitland, Maryland 20233 (301) 763-4040; *Census of Agriculture.*

OUTLYING AREAS - AID BY UNITED STATES GOVERNMENT

U.S. Department of Commerce, Bureau of Economic Analysis, Fourteenth Street between Constitution Avenue and E Street, NW, Washington, D.C. 20230 (202) 606-9900; press releases and unpublished data.

OUTLYING AREAS - AREA

U.S. Department of Commerce, Bureau of the Census, Suitland, Maryland 20233 (301) 763-4040; *Census of Population and Housing,* and unpublished data.

OUTLYING AREAS - BANKS AND BANKING

Puerto Rico Planning Board, San Juan Puerto Rico; *Income and Product,* and *Socioeconomic Statistics.*

U.S. Federal Deposit Insurance Corporation, 550 Seventeenth Street, NW, Washington, D.C. 20429 (202) 393-8400; *Statistics on Banking, Annual Report,* and *FDIC Quarterly Banking Profile.*

OUTLYING AREAS - BIRTHS AND DEATHS

U.S. Department of Commerce, Bureau of the Census, Suitland, Maryland 20233 (301) 763-4040; *Current Population Reports.*

U.S. Department of Health and Human Services, National Center for Health Statistics, 3700 East-West Highway, Hyattsville, Maryland 20782 (301) 436-8500; *Vital Statistics of the United States.*

OUTLYING AREAS - BUSINESS SUMMARY

U.S. Department of Commerce, Bureau of the Census, Suitland, Maryland 20233 (301) 763-4040; *Economic Census of Outlying Areas,* and *County Business Patterns.*

OUTLYING AREAS - CLIMATE (PUERTO RICO)

U.S. Department of Commerce, National Oceanic and Atmospheric Administration, National Climatic Data Center, Federal Building, Asheville, North Carolina 28801 (704) 259-2850; *Climatography of the United States,* and *Comparative Climatic Data.*

OUTLYING AREAS - COMMERCE

U.S. Department of Commerce, Bureau of the Census, Suitland, Maryland 20233 (301) 763-4040; *Foreign Commerce and Navigation of the United States, United States Trade with Puerto Rico and United States Possessions, Highlights of U.S. Export and Import Trade,* and *FT990.*

OUTLYING AREAS - EARNINGS

U.S. Department of Commerce, Bureau of the Census, Suitland, Maryland 20233 (301) 763-4040; *County Business Patterns,* and *Economic Census of Outlying Areas.*

OUTLYING AREAS - EDUCATION

Puerto Rico Planning Board, San Juan, Puerto Rico; *Socioeconomic Statistics,* and *Income and Product.*

U.S. Department of Education, Center for Education Statistics, 400 Maryland Avenue, SW, Washington, D.C. 20202 (202) 708-5366; *Digest of Education Statistics,* and unpublished data.

OUTLYING AREAS - EDUCATION - ATTAINMENT

U.S. Department of Commerce, Bureau of the Census, Suitland, Maryland 20233 (301) 763-4040; *Census of Population and Housing.*

OUTLYING AREAS - EDUCATION - ENROLLMENT

U.S. Department of Education, Center for Education Statistics, 400 Maryland Avenue, SW, Washington, D.C. 20202 (202) 708-5366; unpublished data.

OUTLYING AREAS - EMPLOYEES

U.S. Department of Commerce, Bureau of the Census, Suitland, Maryland 20233 (301) 763-4040; *County Business Patterns,* and *Economic Census of Outlying Areas.*

OUTLYING AREAS - ESTABLISHMENTS

U.S. Department of Commerce, Bureau of the Census, Suitland, Maryland 20233 (301) 763-4040; *County Business Patterns,* and *Economic Census of Outlying Areas.*

OUTLYING AREAS - FEDERAL PAYMENT TO INDIVIDUALS

U.S. Department of Commerce, Bureau of the Census, Suitland, Maryland 20233 (301) 763-4040; *Federal Expenditures by State for Fiscal Year.*

OUTLYING AREAS - FINANCES

Puerto Rico Planning Board, San Juan, Puerto Rico; *Income and Product,* and *Socioeconomic Statistics,* and *Economic Report of the Governor.*

OUTLYING AREAS - FOREIGN INVESTMENT

U.S. Department of Commerce, Bureau of Economic Analysis, Fourteenth Street between Constitution Avenue and E Street, NW,

Washington, D.C. 20230 (202) 606-9900; *Survey of Current Business*, and *Foreign Direct Investment in the United States, Operations of U.S. Affiliates of Foreign Companies*.

OUTLYING AREAS - GEOGRAPHIC DATA

U.S. Department of the Interior, Geological Survey, National Center, 12201 Sunrise Valley Drive, Reston, Virginia 22092 (703) 648-4460; *Elevations and Distances in the United States*.

OUTLYING AREAS - GROSS DOMESTIC PRODUCT

Puerto Rico Planning Board, San Juan, Puerto Rico; *Economic Report of the Governor*.

OUTLYING AREAS - HOSPITAL FACILITIES

American Hospital Association, 840 North Lake Shore Drive, Chicago, Illinois 60611 (312) 280-6000; *Hospital Statistics*.

OUTLYING AREAS - INCOME

Puerto Rico Planning Board, San Juan, Puerto Rico; *Income and Product*, and *Socioeconomic Statistics*.

OUTLYING AREAS - LABOR FORCE AND EMPLOYMENT

Puerto Rico Department of Labor and Human Resources, Bureau of Labor Statistics, San Juan, Puerto Rico.

Puerto Rico Planning Board, San Juan, Puerto Rico; *Income and Product*, and *Socioeconomic Statistics*.

U.S. Department of Commerce, Bureau of the Census, Suitland, Maryland 20233 (301) 763-4040; *Census of Population and Housing*, and unpublished data.

OUTLYING AREAS - MARRIAGE AND DIVORCE

U.S. Department of Health and Human Services, National Center for Health Statistics 3700 East-West Highway, Hyattsville, Maryland 20782 (301) 436-8500; *Vital Statistics of the United States*.

OUTLYING AREAS - POPULATION AND/OR AREA

Puerto Rico Planning Board, San Juan, Puerto Rico; *Socioeconomic Statistics*, and *Income and Product*.

U.S. Department of Commerce, Bureau of the Census, Suitland, Maryland 20233 (301) 763-4040; *World Population Profile*.

OUTLYING AREAS - PUBLIC AID

U.S. Department of Health and Human Services, Administration for Children and Families, 370 L'Enfant Promenade, SW, Washington, D.C. 20447 (202) 401-9200; *Quarterly Public Assistance Statistics*.

U.S. Department of Health and Human Services, Social Security Administration, 6401 Security Boulevard, Baltimore, Maryland 21235

(410) 965-1234; *Annual Statistical Supplement to the Social Security Bulletin*, and *Social Security Bulletin*.

OUTLYING AREAS - PUBLIC LIBRARIES

R.R. Bowker Company, 121 Chanlon Road, New Providence, New Jersey 07974 (908) 464-6800; *The Bowker Annual: Library and Book Trade Almanac*, and *American Library Directory*.

OUTLYING AREAS - SALES, SHIPMENTS, RECEIPTS

U.S. Department of Commerce, Bureau of the Census, Suitland, Maryland 20233 (301) 763-4040; *Census of Agriculture*, and *Economic Census of Outlying Areas*.

OUTLYING AREAS - SOCIAL INSURANCE

U.S. Department of Health and Human Services, Social Security Administration, 6401 Security Boulevard, Baltimore, Maryland 21235 (410) 965-1234; *Social Security Bulletin*.

OUTLYING AREAS - TOURISM

Puerto Rico Planning Board, San Juan, Puerto Rico; *Income and Product*, and *Socioeconomic Statistics*.

OUTLYING AREAS - UNEMPLOYMENT INSURANCE

U.S. Department of Labor, Employment and Training Administration, 200 Constitution Avenue, NW, Washington, D.C. 20210 (202) 219-0600; *Unemployment Insurance Data Summary*.

OUTLYING AREAS - VITAL STATISTICS

U.S. Department of Commerce, Bureau of the Census, Suitland, Maryland 20233 (301) 763-4040; *Current Population Reports*.

U.S. Department of Health and Human Services, National Center for Health Statistics, 3700 East-West Highway, Hyattsville, Maryland 20782 (301) 436-8500; *Vital Statistics of the United States*.

OUTPATIENT CARE FACILITIES

American Hospital Association, 840 North Lake Shore Drive, Chicago, Illinois 60611 (312) 280-6000; *Hospital Statistics*, and *Annual Survey of Hospitals*.

OUTPATIENT CARE FACILITIES - VISITS

American Hospital Association, 840 North Lake Shore Drive, Chicago, Illinois 60611 (312) 280-6000; *Hospital Statistics*.

OYSTERS

U.S. Department of Commerce, National Marine Fisheries Service, 1335 East-West Highway, Silver Spring, Maryland 20910 (301) 427-2239; *Fishery Statistics of the United States*, and *Fisheries of the United States*.

P

PACIFIC ISLANDER POPULATION

U.S. Department of Commerce, Bureau of the Census, Suitland, Maryland 20233 (301) 763-4040; *Census of Population*, and *Current Population Reports*.

PACIFIC ISLANDER POPULATION - DEGREES CONFERRED

U.S. National Science Foundation, 4201 Wilson Boulevard, Arlington, Virginia 22230 (703) 306-1234; *Survey of Earned Doctorates, Selected Data on Science and Engineering Doctorate Awards*.

Pacific Islands - Primary Statistics Source

Superintendent of Documents, U.S. Government Printing Office, Washington, D.C. 20402; *Annual Report to the United Nations on the Administration of the Trust Territory of the Pacific Islands*.

PACIFIC ISLANDS - AGRICULTURE

Food and Agricultural Organization of the United Nations (FAO) Via delle Terme di Caracalla, 00100 Rome, Italy (Telephone Number in U.S. (202) 653-2400); *Production Yearbook, The State of Food and Agriculture*, and *Trade Yearbook*.

G.K. Hall and Company, 70 Lincoln Street, Boston, Massachusetts 02111 (617) 423-3990; *The World in Figures*.

Statistical Office of the United Nations, Publishing Service, New York, New York 10017 (800) 253-9646; *Statistical Yearbook*, and *Statistical Yearbook for Asia and the Pacific*.

PACIFIC ISLANDS - AIRLINE SERVICE

G.K. Hall and Company, 70 Lincoln Street, Boston, Massachusetts 02111 (617) 423-3990; *The World in Figures*.

PACIFIC ISLANDS - AREA AND DENSITY OF POPULATION

Food and Agricultural Organization of the United Nations (FAO) Via delle Terme di Caracalla, 00100 Rome, Italy (Telephone Number in U.S. (202) 653-2400); *The State of Food and Agriculture*.

G.K. Hall and Company, 70 Lincoln Street, Boston, Massachusetts 02111 (617) 423-3990; *The World in Figures*.

Statistical Office of the United Nations, Publishing Service, New York, New York 10017 (800) 253-9646; *Statistical Yearbook*.

United Nations Educational, Scientific and Cultural Organization (UNESCO), 7 Place de Fontenoy, F-75700 Paris, France (Telephone Number in U.S. (212) 963-5981); *Statistical Yearbook*.

PACIFIC ISLANDS - BALANCE OF PAYMENTS

G.K. Hall and Company, 70 Lincoln Street, Boston, Massachusetts 02111 (617) 423-3990; *The World in Figures*.

PACIFIC ISLANDS - BANKING

G.K. Hall and Company, 70 Lincoln Street, Boston, Massachusetts 02111 (617) 423-3990; *The World in Figures*.

PACIFIC ISLANDS - BIRTH RATES

Statistical Office of the United Nations, Publishing Service, New York, New York 10017 (800) 253-9646; *Demographic Yearbook*, and *Statistical Yearbook*.

World Health Organization, Office of Publications, Avenue Appia, CH-1211 Geneva 27, Switzerland (Telephone Number in U.S. (518) 436-9686); *World Health Statistics Annual*.

PACIFIC ISLANDS - BONDS

G.K. Hall and Company, 70 Lincoln Street, Boston, Massachusetts 02111 (617) 423-3990; *The World in Figures*.

PACIFIC ISLANDS - BOOK PRODUCTION

G.K. Hall and Company, 70 Lincoln Street, Boston, Massachusetts 02111 (617) 423-3990; *The World in Figures*.

United Nations Educational, Scientific and Cultural Organization (UNESCO), 7 Place de Fontenoy, F-75700 Paris, France (Telephone Number in U.S. (212) 963-5981); *Statistical Yearbook*.

PACIFIC ISLANDS - BROADCASTING

G.K. Hall and Company, 70 Lincoln Street, Boston, Massachusetts 02111 (617) 423-3990; *The World in Figures*.

PACIFIC ISLANDS - BUSINESS

G.K. Hall and Company, 70 Lincoln Street, Boston, Massachusetts 02111 (617) 423-3990; *The World in Figures*.

PACIFIC ISLANDS - CALORIE SUPPLY

Food and Agricultural Organization of the United Nations (FAO) Via delle Terme di Caracalla, 00100 Rome, Italy (Telephone Number in U.S. (202) 653-2400); *The State of Food and Agriculture*.

PACIFIC ISLANDS - CATTLE - See PACIFIC ISLANDS - LIVESTOCK AND POULTRY

PACIFIC ISLANDS - CHEMICAL (ORGANIC) PRODUCTION - See PACIFIC ISLANDS - MINING AND MINERAL PRODUCTS

PACIFIC ISLANDS - CLASS STRUCTURE

G.K. Hall and Company, 70 Lincoln Street, Boston, Massachusetts 02111 (617) 423-3990; *The World in Figures.*

PACIFIC ISLANDS - CLIMATE

G.K. Hall and Company, 70 Lincoln Street, Boston, Massachusetts 02111 (617) 423-3990; *The World in Figures.*

PACIFIC ISLANDS - COAL PRODUCTION - See PACIFIC ISLANDS - MINING AND MINERAL PRODUCTS

PACIFIC ISLANDS - COMMUNICATIONS

G.K. Hall and Company, 70 Lincoln Street, Boston, Massachusetts 02111 (617) 423-3990; *The World in Figures.*

Statistical Office of the United Nations, Publishing Service, New York, New York 10017 (800) 253-9646; *Statistical Yearbook for Asia and the Pacific.*

PACIFIC ISLANDS - CONSUMER PRICE INDEX

G.K. Hall and Company, 70 Lincoln Street, Boston, Massachusetts 02111 (617) 423-3990; *The World in Figures.*

PACIFIC ISLANDS - CONSUMPTION

G.K. Hall and Company, 70 Lincoln Street, Boston, Massachusetts 02111 (617) 423-3990; *The World in Figures.*

PACIFIC ISLANDS - CORN PRODUCTION - See PACIFIC ISLANDS - CROPS

PACIFIC ISLANDS - CORPORATE TAXES - See PACIFIC ISLANDS - TAXATION

PACIFIC ISLANDS - CROPS

Food and Agricultural Organization of the United Nations (FAO) Via delle Terme di Caracalla, 00100 Rome, Italy (Telephone Number in U.S. (202) 653-2400); *Production Yearbook,* and *The State of Food and Agriculture.*

G.K. Hall and Company, 70 Lincoln Street, Boston, Massachusetts 02111 (617) 423-3990; *The World in Figures.*

PACIFIC ISLANDS - CUSTOMS DUTIES

G.K. Hall and Company, 70 Lincoln Street, Boston, Massachusetts 02111 (617) 423-3990; *The World in Figures.*

PACIFIC ISLANDS - DAIRY PRODUCTS

Food and Agricultural Organization of the United Nations (FAO) Via delle Terme di Caracalla, 00100 Rome, Italy (Telephone Number in U.S. (202) 653-2400); *The State of Food and Agriculture.*

PACIFIC ISLANDS - DEATH RATES

G.K. Hall and Company, 70 Lincoln Street, Boston, Massachusetts 02111 (617) 423-3990; *The World in Figures.*

Statistical Office of the United Nations, Publishing Service, New York, New York 10017 (800) 253-9646; *Statistical Yearbook.*

World Health Organization, Office of Publications, Avenue Appia, CH-1211 Geneva 27, Switzerland (Telephone Number in U.S. (518) 436-9686); *World Health Statistics Annual.*

PACIFIC ISLANDS - DEFENSE EXPENDITURES

G.K. Hall and Company, 70 Lincoln Street, Boston, Massachusetts 02111 (617) 423-3990; *The World in Figures.*

PACIFIC ISLANDS - DEMOGRAPHY

G.K. Hall and Company, 70 Lincoln Street, Boston, Massachusetts 02111 (617) 423-3990; *The World in Figures.*

PACIFIC ISLANDS - DEVELOPMENT ASSISTANCE

G.K. Hall and Company, 70 Lincoln Street, Boston, Massachusetts 02111 (617) 423-3990; *The World in Figures.*

Statistical Office of the United Nations, Publishing Service, New York, New York 10017 (800) 253-9646; *Statistical Yearbook.*

PACIFIC ISLANDS - DISEASES

G.K. Hall and Company, 70 Lincoln Street, Boston, Massachusetts 02111 (617) 423-3990; *The World in Figures.*

World Health Organization, Office of Publications, Avenue Appia, CH-1211 Geneva 27, Switzerland (Telephone Number in U.S. (518) 436-9686); *World Health Statistics Annual.*

PACIFIC ISLANDS - DIVORCE RATES

Statistical Office of the United Nations, Publishing Service, New York, New York 10017 (800) 253-9646; *Demographic Yearbook,* and *Statistical Yearbook.*

PACIFIC ISLANDS - DOMESTIC PRODUCT

G.K. Hall and Company, 70 Lincoln Street, Boston, Massachusetts 02111 (617) 423-3990; *The World in Figures.*

PACIFIC ISLANDS - DUCKS - See PACIFIC ISLANDS - LIVESTOCK AND POULTRY

PACIFIC ISLANDS - ECONOMY

G.K. Hall and Company, 70 Lincoln Street, Boston, Massachusetts 02111 (617) 423-3990; *The World in Figures.*

PACIFIC ISLANDS - EDUCATION

G.K. Hall and Company, 70 Lincoln Street, Boston, Massachusetts 02111 (617) 423-3990; *The World in Figures.*

Statistical Office of the United Nations, Publishing Service, New York, New York 10017 (800) 253-9646; *Statistical Yearbook for Asia and the Pacific.*

United Nations Educational, Scientific and Cultural Organization (UNESCO), 7 Place de Fontenoy, F-75700 Paris, France (Telephone Number in U.S. (212) 963-5981); *Statistical Yearbook.*

PACIFIC ISLANDS - EGG PRODUCTION AND CONSUMPTION - See PACIFIC ISLANDS - DAIRY PRODUCTS

PACIFIC ISLANDS - ELECTRICITY

Statistical Office of the United Nations, Publishing Service, New York, New York 10017 (800) 253-9646; *Statistical Yearbook.*

PACIFIC ISLANDS - ENERGY

Food and Agricultural Organization of the United Nations (FAO) Via delle Terme di Caracalla, 00100 Rome, Italy (Telephone Number in U.S. (202) 653-2400); *The State of Food and Agriculture.*

G.K. Hall and Company, 70 Lincoln Street, Boston, Massachusetts 02111 (617) 423-3990; *The World in Figures.*

Statistical Office of the United Nations, Publishing Service, New York, New York 10017 (800) 253-9646; *Energy Statistics Yearbook, Statistical Yearbook, Statistical Yearbook for Asia and the Pacific,* and *World Energy Supplies.*

PACIFIC ISLANDS - EXPORTS

Food and Agricultural Organization of the United Nations (FAO) Via delle Terme di Caracalla, 00100 Rome, Italy (Telephone Number in U.S. (202) 653-2400); *The State of Food and Agriculture.*

G.K. Hall and Company, 70 Lincoln Street, Boston, Massachusetts 02111 (617) 423-3990; *The World in Figures.*

South Pacific Commission, Post Box D5, Noumea Cedex, New Caledonia; *Statistical Bulletin of the South Pacific: Overseas Trade.*

PACIFIC ISLANDS - EXTERNAL TRADE

Food and Agricultural Organization of the United Nations (FAO) Via delle Terme di Caracalla, 00100 Rome, Italy (Telephone Number in U.S. (202) 653-2400); *The State of Food and Agriculture,* and *Trade Yearbook.*

G.K. Hall and Company, 70 Lincoln Street, Boston, Massachusetts 02111 (617) 423-3990; *The World in Figures.*

Statistical Office of the United Nations, Publishing Service, New York, New York 10017 (800) 253-9646; *Statistical Yearbook for Asia and the Pacific.*

PACIFIC ISLANDS - FARM CROPS - See PACIFIC ISLANDS - CROPS

PACIFIC ISLANDS - FERTILIZER

Food and Agricultural Organization of the United Nations (FAO) Via delle Terme di Caracalla, 00100 Rome, Italy (Telephone Number in U.S. (202) 653-2400); *The State of Food and Agriculture.*

PACIFIC ISLANDS - FETAL MORTALITY

Statistical Office of the United Nations, Publishing Service, New York, New York 10017 (800) 253-9646; *Demographic Yearbook.*

World Health Organization, Office of Publications, Avenue Appia, CH-1211 Geneva 27, Switzerland (Telephone Number in U.S. (518) 436-9686); *World Health Statistics Annual.*

PACIFIC ISLANDS - FINANCE

G.K. Hall and Company, 70 Lincoln Street, Boston, Massachusetts 02111 (617) 423-3990; *The World in Figures.*

Statistical Office of the United Nations, Publishing Service, New York, New York 10017 (800) 253-9646; *Statistical Yearbook for Asia and the Pacific.*

PACIFIC ISLANDS - FISHERIES

Food and Agricultural Organization of the United Nations (FAO) Via delle Terme di Caracalla, 00100 Rome, Italy (Telephone Number in U.S. (202) 653-2400); *The State of Food and Agriculture,* and *Trade Yearbook.*

Statistical Office of the United Nations, Publishing Service, New York, New York 10017 (800) 253-9646; *Statistical Yearbook.*

PACIFIC ISLANDS - FOOD

Food and Agricultural Organization of the United Nations (FAO) Via delle Terme di Caracalla, 00100 Rome, Italy (Telephone Number in U.S. (202) 653-2400); *Production Yearbook,* and *The State of Food and Agriculture.*

G.K. Hall and Company, 70 Lincoln Street, Boston, Massachusetts 02111 (617) 423-3990; *The World in Figures.*

Statistical Office of the United Nations, Publishing Service, New York, New York 10017 (800) 253-9646; *Statistical Yearbook for Asia and the Pacific.*

PACIFIC ISLANDS - FORESTRY AND FOREST PRODUCTS

Food and Agricultural Organization of the United Nations (FAO) Via delle Terme di Caracalla, 00100 Rome, Italy (Telephone Number in U.S. (202) 653-2400); *The State of Food and Agriculture.*

G.K. Hall and Company, 70 Lincoln Street, Boston, Massachusetts 02111 (617) 423-3990; *The World in Figures.*

Statistical Office of the United Nations, Publishing Service, New York, New York 10017 (800) 253-9646; *Statistical Yearbook.*

PACIFIC ISLANDS - FOREIGN AID

G.K. Hall and Company, 70 Lincoln Street, Boston, Massachusetts 02111 (617) 423-3990; *The World in Figures.*

PACIFIC ISLANDS - FOREIGN TRADE

Food and Agricultural Organization of the United Nations (FAO) Via delle Terme di Caracalla, 00100 Rome, Italy (Telephone Number in U.S. (202) 653-2400); *The State of Food and Agriculture.*

G.K. Hall and Company, 70 Lincoln Street, Boston, Massachusetts 02111 (617) 423-3990; *The World in Figures.*

South Pacific Commission, Post Box D5, Noumea Cedex, New Caledonia; *Statistical Bulletin of the South Pacific: Overseas Trade.*

PACIFIC ISLANDS - GENERAL MORTALITY

Statistical Office of the United Nations, Publishing Service, New York, New York 10017 (800) 253-9646; *Demographic Yearbook.*

World Health Organization, Office of Publications, Avenue Appia, CH-1211 Geneva 27, Switzerland (Telephone Number in U.S. (518) 436-9686); *World Health Statistics Annual.*

PACIFIC ISLANDS - GOVERNMENT

G.K. Hall and Company, 70 Lincoln Street, Boston, Massachusetts 02111 (617) 423-3990; *The World in Figures*.

PACIFIC ISLANDS - GRAIN PRODUCTION - See PACIFIC ISLANDS - CROPS

PACIFIC ISLANDS - GROSS DOMESTIC PRODUCT

G.K. Hall and Company, 70 Lincoln Street, Boston, Massachusetts 02111 (617) 423-3990; *The World in Figures*.

PACIFIC ISLANDS - HEALTH

G.K. Hall and Company, 70 Lincoln Street, Boston, Massachusetts 02111 (617) 423-3990; *The World in Figures*.

Statistical Office of the United Nations, Publishing Service, New York, New York 10017 (800) 253-9646; *Statistical Yearbook*.

World Health Organization, Office of Publications, Avenue Appia, CH-1211 Geneva 27, Switzerland (Telephone Number in U.S. (518) 436-9686); *World Health Statistics Annual*.

PACIFIC ISLANDS - HIDE PRODUCTION

Food and Agricultural Organization of the United Nations (FAO), Via delle Terme di Caracalla, 00100 Rome, Italy (Telephone Number in U.S. (202) 653-2400); *Production Yearbook*.

PACIFIC ISLANDS - HIGHWAYS

G.K. Hall and Company, 70 Lincoln Street, Boston, Massachusetts 02111 (617) 423-3990; *The World in Figures*.

PACIFIC ISLANDS - ILLITERATE POPULATION

G.K. Hall and Company, 70 Lincoln Street, Boston, Massachusetts 02111 (617) 423-3990; *The World in Figures*.

PACIFIC ISLANDS - IMPORTS

Food and Agricultural Organization of the United Nations (FAO) Via delle Terme di Caracalla, 00100 Rome, Italy (Telephone Number in U.S. (202) 653-2400); *The State of Food and Agriculture*.

G.K. Hall and Company, 70 Lincoln Street, Boston, Massachusetts 02111 (617) 423-3990; *The World in Figures*.

South Pacific Commission, Post Box D5, Noumea Cedex, New Caledonia; *Statistical Bulletin of the South Pacific: Overseas Trade*.

PACIFIC ISLANDS - INDUSTRY

G.K. Hall and Company, 70 Lincoln Street, Boston, Massachusetts 02111 (617) 423-3990; *The World in Figures*.

Statistical Office of the United Nations, Publishing Service, New York, New York 10017 (800) 253-9646; *Statistical Yearbook for Asia and the Pacific*.

PACIFIC ISLANDS - INFANT AND MATERNAL MORTALITY

Statistical Office of the United Nations, Publishing Service, New York, New York 10017 (800) 253-9646; *Demographic Yearbook*, and *Statistical Yearbook*.

World Health Organization, Office of Publications, Avenue Appia, CH-1211 Geneva 27, Switzerland (Telephone Number in U.S. (518) 436-9686); *World Health Statistics Annual*.

PACIFIC ISLANDS - INTERNAL TRADE

Statistical Office of the United Nations, Publishing Service, New York, New York 10017 (800) 253-9646; *Statistical Yearbook for Asia and the Pacific*.

PACIFIC ISLANDS - LABOR FORCE

Food and Agricultural Organization of the United Nations (FAO) Via delle Terme di Caracalla, 00100 Rome, Italy (Telephone Number in U.S. (202) 653-2400); *The State of Food and Agriculture*.

G.K. Hall and Company, 70 Lincoln Street, Boston, Massachusetts 02111 (617) 423-3990; *The World in Figures*.

PACIFIC ISLANDS - LAND USE

Food and Agricultural Organization of the United Nations (FAO), Via delle Terme di Caracalla, 00100 Rome, Italy (Telephone Number in U.S. (202) 653-2400); *Production Yearbook*.

G.K. Hall and Company, 70 Lincoln Street, Boston, Massachusetts 02111 (617) 423-3990; *The World in Figures*.

PACIFIC ISLANDS - LIBRARIES

United Nations Educational, Scientific and Cultural Organization (UNESCO), 7 Place de Fontenoy, F-75700 Paris, France (Telephone Number in U.S. (212) 963-5981); *Statistical Yearbook*.

PACIFIC ISLANDS - LIVESTOCK AND POULTRY

Food and Agricultural Organization of the United Nations (FAO), Via delle Terme di Caracalla, 00100 Rome, Italy (Telephone Number in U.S. (202) 653-2400); *Production Yearbook*, and *The State of Food and Agriculture*.

G.K. Hall and Company, 70 Lincoln Street, Boston, Massachusetts 02111 (617) 423-3990; *The World in Figures*.

Statistical Office of the United Nations, Publishing Service, New York, New York 10017 (800) 253-9646; *Statistical Yearbook*.

PACIFIC ISLANDS - LIVING LEVELS

G.K. Hall and Company, 70 Lincoln Street, Boston, Massachusetts 02111 (617) 423-3990; *The World in Figures*.

PACIFIC ISLANDS - MANPOWER

Statistical Office of the United Nations, Publishing Service, New York, New York 10017 (800) 253-9646; *Statistical Yearbook for Asia and the Pacific*.

PACIFIC ISLANDS - MANUFACTURING

G.K. Hall and Company, 70 Lincoln Street, Boston, Massachusetts 02111 (617) 423-3990; *The World in Figures*.

PACIFIC ISLANDS - MARRIAGE RATES

Statistical Office of the United Nations, Publishing Service, New York, New York 10017 (800) 253-9646; *Demographic Yearbook*.

PACIFIC ISLANDS - MEAT PRODUCTION - See PACIFIC ISLANDS - LIVESTOCK AND POULTRY

PACIFIC ISLANDS - MERCHANT SHIPPING

G.K. Hall and Company, 70 Lincoln Street, Boston, Massachusetts 02111 (617) 423-3990; *The World in Figures.*

Statistical Office of the United Nations, Publishing Service, New York, New York 10017 (800) 253-9646; *Statistical Yearbook.*

PACIFIC ISLANDS - MILITARY

G.K. Hall and Company, 70 Lincoln Street, Boston, Massachusetts 02111 (617) 423-3990; *The World in Figures.*

PACIFIC ISLANDS - MINING AND MINERAL PRODUCTS

G.K. Hall and Company, 70 Lincoln Street, Boston, Massachusetts 02111 (617) 423-3990; *The World in Figures.*

PACIFIC ISLANDS - MONEY SUPPLY

G.K. Hall and Company, 70 Lincoln Street, Boston, Massachusetts 02111 (617) 423-3990; *The World in Figures.*

PACIFIC ISLANDS - MOTION PICTURES

Statistical Office of the United Nations, Publishing Service, New York, New York 10017 (800) 253-9646; *Statistical Yearbook.*

PACIFIC ISLANDS - MOTOR VEHICLES IN USE

G.K. Hall and Company, 70 Lincoln Street, Boston, Massachusetts 02111 (617) 423-3990; *The World in Figures.*

PACIFIC ISLANDS - MUSEUMS

United Nations Educational, Scientific and Cultural Organization (UNESCO), 7 Place de Fontenoy, F-75700 Paris, France (Telephone Number in U.S. (212) 963-5981); *Statistical Yearbook.*

PACIFIC ISLANDS - NATALITY - See PACIFIC ISLANDS - BIRTH RATES

PACIFIC ISLANDS - NATIONAL ACCOUNTS

Statistical Office of the United Nations, Publishing Service, New York, New York 10017 (800) 253-9646; *Statistical Yearbook for Asia and the Pacific.*

PACIFIC ISLANDS - NATIONAL INCOME

G.K. Hall and Company, 70 Lincoln Street, Boston, Massachusetts 02111 (617) 423-3990; *The World in Figures.*

PACIFIC ISLANDS - NEWSPAPER PRODUCTION - See PACIFIC ISLANDS - FORESTRY AND FOREST PRODUCTS

PACIFIC ISLANDS - OCCUPATIONS - See PACIFIC ISLANDS - LABOR FORCE

PACIFIC ISLANDS - PERIODICALS

United Nations Educational, Scientific and Cultural Organization (UNESCO), 7 Place de Fontenoy, F-75700 Paris, France (Telephone Number in U.S. (212) 963-5981); *Statistical Yearbook.*

PACIFIC ISLANDS - PESTICIDE USE

Food and Agricultural Organization of the United Nations (FAO) Via delle Terme di Caracalla, 00100 Rome, Italy (Telephone Number in U.S. (202) 653-2400); *The State of Food and Agriculture.*

PACIFIC ISLANDS - PETROLEUM INDUSTRY

Food and Agricultural Organization of the United Nations (FAO) Via delle Terme di Caracalla, 00100 Rome, Italy (Telephone Number in U.S. (202) 653-2400); *The State of Food and Agriculture.*

G.K. Hall and Company, 70 Lincoln Street, Boston, Massachusetts 02111 (617) 423-3990; *The World in Figures.*

PACIFIC ISLANDS - PIGS - See PACIFIC ISLANDS - LIVESTOCK AND POULTRY

PACIFIC ISLANDS - POPULATION

Food and Agricultural Organization of the United Nations (FAO), Via delle Terme di Caracalla, 00100 Rome, Italy (Telephone Number in U.S. (202) 653-2400); *Production Yearbook.*

G.K. Hall and Company, 70 Lincoln Street, Boston, Massachusetts 02111 (617) 423-3990; *The World in Figures.*

Statistical Office of the United Nations, Publishing Service, New York, New York 10017 (800) 253-9646; *Demographic Yearbook, Statistical Yearbook,* and *Statistical Yearbook for Asia and the Pacific.*

United Nations Educational, Scientific and Cultural Organization (UNESCO), 7 Place de Fontenoy, F-75700 Paris, France (Telephone Number in U.S. (212) 963-5981); *Statistical Yearbook.*

World Health Organization, Office of Publications, Avenue Appia, CH-1211 Geneva 27, Switzerland (Telephone Number in U.S. (518) 436-9686); *World Health Statistics Annual.*

PACIFIC ISLANDS - PRICES

Food and Agricultural Organization of the United Nations (FAO), Via delle Terme di Caracalla, 00100 Rome, Italy (Telephone Number in U.S. (202) 653-2400); *Production Yearbook,* and *The State of Food and Agriculture.*

G.K. Hall and Company, 70 Lincoln Street, Boston, Massachusetts 02111 (617) 423-3990; *The World in Figures.*

South Pacific Commission, Post Box D5, Noumea Cedex, New Caledonia; *Statistical Bulletin of the South Pacific: Overseas Trade.*

PACIFIC ISLANDS - PRODUCTION

G.K. Hall and Company, 70 Lincoln Street, Boston, Massachusetts 02111 (617) 423-3990; *The World in Figures.*

PACIFIC ISLANDS - RAILWAYS

G.K. Hall and Company, 70 Lincoln Street, Boston, Massachusetts 02111 (617) 423-3990; *The World in Figures.*

PACIFIC ISLANDS - RETAIL TRADE

G.K. Hall and Company, 70 Lincoln Street, Boston, Massachusetts 02111 (617) 423-3990; *The World in Figures.*

PACIFIC ISLANDS - ROOT AND TUBER PRODUCTION - See PACIFIC ISLANDS - CROPS

PACIFIC ISLANDS - SCIENTISTS AND TECHNICIANS

Statistical Office of the United Nations, Publishing Service, New York, New York 10017 (800) 253-9646; *Statistical Yearbook.*

PACIFIC ISLANDS - SOCIAL DATA

G.K. Hall and Company, 70 Lincoln Street, Boston, Massachusetts 02111 (617) 423-3990; *The World in Figures.*

PACIFIC ISLANDS - STOCKS - COMMODITY - MARKET PRICE - INDEX

Food and Agricultural Organization of the United Nations (FAO) Via delle Terme di Caracalla, 00100 Rome, Italy (Telephone Number in U.S. (202) 653-2400); *The State of Food and Agriculture.*

PACIFIC ISLANDS - TAXATION

G.K. Hall and Company, 70 Lincoln Street, Boston, Massachusetts 02111 (617) 423-3990; *The World in Figures.*

PACIFIC ISLANDS - TELEPHONES IN USE

G.K. Hall and Company, 70 Lincoln Street, Boston, Massachusetts 02111 (617) 423-3990; *The World in Figures.*

PACIFIC ISLANDS - TEXTILE INDUSTRY

G.K. Hall and Company, 70 Lincoln Street, Boston, Massachusetts 02111 (617) 423-3990; *The World in Figures.*

PACIFIC ISLANDS - TOURISM

G.K. Hall and Company, 70 Lincoln Street, Boston, Massachusetts 02111 (617) 423-3990; *The World in Figures.*

PACIFIC ISLANDS - TRACTORS IN USE

Statistical Office of the United Nations, Publishing Service, New York, New York 10017 (800) 253-9646; *Statistical Yearbook.*

PACIFIC ISLANDS - TRADE - See PACIFIC ISLANDS - FOREIGN TRADE

PACIFIC ISLANDS - TRANSPORTATION AND COMMUNICATIONS

G.K. Hall and Company, 70 Lincoln Street, Boston, Massachusetts 02111 (617) 423-3990; *The World in Figures.*

Statistical Office of the United Nations, Publishing Service, New York, New York 10017 (800) 253-9646; *Statistical Yearbook for Asia and the Pacific.*

PACIFIC ISLANDS - VITAL STATISTICS

G.K. Hall and Company, 70 Lincoln Street, Boston, Massachusetts 02111 (617) 423-3990; *The World in Figures.*

Statistical Office of the United Nations, Publishing Service, New York, New York 10017 (800) 253-9646; *Statistical Yearbook.*

World Health Organization, Office of Publications, Avenue Appia, CH-1211 Geneva 27, Switzerland (Telephone Number in U.S. (518) 436-9686); *World Health Statistics Annual.*

PACIFIC ISLANDS - WAGES

G.K. Hall and Company, 70 Lincoln Street, Boston, Massachusetts 02111 (617) 423-3990; *The World in Figures.*

PACIFIC ISLANDS - WAGES AND PRICES

Statistical Office of the United Nations, Publishing Service, New York, New York 10017 (800) 253-9646; *Statistical Yearbook for Asia and the Pacific.*

PACIFIC ISLANDS - WEATHER

G.K. Hall and Company, 70 Lincoln Street, Boston, Massachusetts 02111 (617) 423-3990; *The World in Figures.*

Pakistan - National Statistical Office

Federal Bureau of Statistics, Ministry of Finance and Economic Affairs, S-SLIC Building Blue Area, F-6/4, Islamabad, Pakistan.

Pakistan - Primary Statistics Sources

Manager of Publications, Government of Pakistan, Block Number 44, Shahrah-e-iraq, Karachi, Pakistan; *Statistical Pocketbook of Pakistan, Statistical Bulletin,* and *Pakistan Statistical Yearbook.*

PAKISTAN - AGRICULTURE

Asian Development Bank, Post Office Box 789, 1099 Manila, Philippines; *Key Indicators of Developing Asian and Pacific Countries.*

Euromonitor Publications Limited, 87-88 Turnmill Street, London EC1M 5QU, England; *International Marketing Data and Statistics.*

Facts on File, 460 Park Avenue South, New York, New York 10016 (800) 443-8323; *The New Book of World Rankings.*

Food and Agricultural Organization of the United Nations (FAO) Via delle Terme di Caracalla, 00100 Rome, Italy (Telephone Number in U.S. (202) 653-2400); *Production Yearbook, The State of Food and Agriculture,* and *Trade Yearbook.*

G.K. Hall and Company, 70 Lincoln Street, Boston, Massachusetts 02111 (617) 423-3990; *The World in Figures.*

Statistical Office of the United Nations, Publishing Service, New York, New York 10017 (800) 253-9646; *Statistical Yearbook,* and *Statistical Yearbook for Asia and the Pacific.*

Times Books, 201 East 50th Street, New York, New York 10022 (212) 751-2600; *The Economist Book of Vital World Statistics.*

The World Bank, 1818 H Street, NW, Washington, D.C. 20433 (202) 477-1234; *World Tables.*

PAKISTAN - AIRLINE SERVICE

The Economist Intelligence Unit (Asia) Limited, 10th Floor, Luk Kwok Centre, 72 Gloucester Road, Wanchai, Hong Kong (Phone Number in U.S. (800) 938-4685); *Asian Market Atlas.*

Facts on File, 460 Park Avenue South, New York, New York 10016 (800) 443-8323; *The New Book of World Rankings.*

G.K. Hall and Company, 70 Lincoln Street, Boston, Massachusetts 02111 (617) 423-3990; *The World in Figures.*

International Civil Aviation Organization, 1000 Sherbrooke Street, West, Montreal, Quebec, Canada H3A 2R2 (514) 285-8219; *Civil Aviation Statistics of the World.*

Statistical Office of the United Nations, Publishing Service, New York, New York 10017 (800) 253-9646; *Statistical Yearbook.*

Times Books, 201 East 50th Street, New York, New York 10022 (212) 751-2600; *The Economist Book of Vital World Statistics.*

PAKISTAN - ALUMINUM PRODUCTION AND CONSUMPTION - See PAKISTAN - MINING AND MINERAL PRODUCTS

PAKISTAN - ANIMAL HEALTH

Food and Agricultural Organization of the United Nations (FAO), Via delle Terme di Caracalla, 00100 Rome, Italy (Telephone Number in U.S. (202) 653-2400); *Animal Health Yearbook.*

PAKISTAN - AREA AND DENSITY OF POPULATION

Euromonitor Publications Limited, 87-88 Turnmill Street, London EC1M 5QU, England; *International Marketing Data and Statistics.*

Facts on File, 460 Park Avenue South, New York, New York 10016 (800) 443-8323; *The New Book of World Rankings.*

Food and Agricultural Organization of the United Nations (FAO) Via delle Terme di Caracalla, 00100 Rome, Italy (Telephone Number in U.S. (202) 653-2400); *The State of Food and Agriculture.*

G.K. Hall and Company, 70 Lincoln Street, Boston, Massachusetts 02111 (617) 423-3990; *The World in Figures.*

Statistical Office of the United Nations, Publishing Service, New York, New York 10017 (800) 253-9646; *Statistical Yearbook.*

Times Books, 201 East 50th Street, New York, New York 10022 (212) 751-2600; *The Economist Book of Vital World Statistics.*

United Nations Educational, Scientific and Cultural Organization (UNESCO), 7 Place de Fontenoy, F-75700 Paris, France (Telephone Number in U.S. (212) 963-5981); *Statistical Yearbook.*

PAKISTAN - ARMS EXPORTS AND IMPORTS

U.S. Arms Control and Disarmament Agency, 320 Twenty-first Street, NW, Washington, D.C. 20451 (202) 647-8677; *World Military Expenditures and Arms Transfers.*

PAKISTAN - BALANCE OF PAYMENTS

The Economist Intelligence Unit, 111 West 57th Street, New York, New York 10019 (800) 938-4685; *The World Market Atlas.*

G.K. Hall and Company, 70 Lincoln Street, Boston, Massachusetts 02111 (617) 423-3990; *The World in Figures.*

International Monetary Fund, 700 Nineteenth Street, NW, Washington, D.C. 20431 (202) 623-7000; *Balance of Payments Yearbook,* and *International Financial Statistics.*

Times Books, 201 East 50th Street, New York, New York 10022 (212) 751-2600; *The Economist Book of Vital World Statistics.*

The World Bank, 1818 H Street, NW, Washington, D.C. 20433 (202) 477-1234; *World Tables.*

PAKISTAN - BANKING

Asian Development Bank, Post Office Box 789, 1099 Manila, Philippines; *Key Indicators of Developing Asian and Pacific Countries.*

Facts on File, 460 Park Avenue South, New York, New York 10016 (800) 443-8323; *The New Book of World Rankings.*

G.K. Hall and Company, 70 Lincoln Street, Boston, Massachusetts 02111 (617) 423-3990; *The World in Figures.*

International Monetary Fund, 700 Nineteenth Street, NW, Washington, D.C. 20431 (202) 623-7000; *Government Finance Statistics Yearbook,* and *International Financial Statistics.*

Statistical Office of the United Nations, Publishing Service, New York, New York 10017 (800) 253-9646; *Statistical Yearbook.*

PAKISTAN - BARLEY PRODUCTION - See PAKISTAN - CROPS

PAKISTAN - BEER PRODUCTION

Facts on File, 460 Park Avenue South, New York, New York 10016 (800) 443-8323; *The New Book of World Rankings.*

Statistical Office of the United Nations, Publishing Service, New York, New York 10017 (800) 253-9646; *Statistical Yearbook.*

PAKISTAN - BIRTH RATES

The Economist Intelligence Unit (Asia) Limited, 10th Floor, Luk Kwok Centre, 72 Gloucester Road, Wanchai, Hong Kong (Phone Number in U.S. (800) 938-4685); *Asian Market Atlas.*

Facts on File, 460 Park Avenue South, New York, New York 10016 (800) 443-8323; *The New Book of World Rankings.*

Statistical Office of the United Nations, Publishing Service, New York, New York 10017 (800) 253-9646; *Demographic Yearbook,* and *Statistical Yearbook.*

Times Books, 201 East 50th Street, New York, New York 10022 (212) 751-2600; *The Economist Book of Vital World Statistics.*

The World Bank, 1818 H Street, NW, Washington, D.C. 20433 (202) 477-1234; *World Tables.*

PAKISTAN - BONDS

Asian Development Bank, Post Office Box 789, 1099 Manila, Philippines; *Key Indicators of Developing Asian and Pacific Countries.*

G.K. Hall and Company, 70 Lincoln Street, Boston, Massachusetts 02111 (617) 423-3990; *The World in Figures.*

International Monetary Fund, 700 Nineteenth Street, NW, Washington, D.C. 20431 (202) 623-7000; *Government Finance Statistics Yearbook.*

Statistical Office of the United Nations, Publishing Service, New York, New York 10017 (800) 253-9646; *Statistical Yearbook.*

PAKISTAN - BOOK PRODUCTION

G.K. Hall and Company, 70 Lincoln Street, Boston, Massachusetts 02111 (617) 423-3990; *The World in Figures.*

United Nations Educational, Scientific and Cultural Organization (UNESCO), 7 Place de Fontenoy, F-75700 Paris, France (Telephone Number in U.S. (212) 963-5981); *Statistical Yearbook.*

PAKISTAN - BROADCASTING

Billboard Limited, Post Office Box 9027, 1006 AA Amsterdam, The Netherlands (Telephone Number in U.S. (212) 764-7300); *World Radio TV Handbook.*

The Economist Intelligence Unit (Asia) Limited, 10th Floor, Luk Kwok Centre, 72 Gloucester Road, Wanchai, Hong Kong (Phone Number in U.S. (800) 938-4685); *Asian Market Atlas.*

Facts on File, 460 Park Avenue South, New York, New York 10016 (800) 443-8323; *The New Book of World Rankings.*

G.K. Hall and Company, 70 Lincoln Street, Boston, Massachusetts 02111 (617) 423-3990; *The World in Figures.*

Times Books, 201 East 50th Street, New York, New York 10022 (212) 751-2600; *The Economist Book of Vital World Statistics.*

United Nations Educational, Scientific and Cultural Organization (UNESCO), 7 Place de Fontenoy, F-75700 Paris, France (Telephone Number in U.S. (212) 963-5981); *Statistical Yearbook.*

PAKISTAN - BUSINESS

G.K. Hall and Company, 70 Lincoln Street, Boston, Massachusetts 02111 (617) 423-3990; *The World in Figures.*

PAKISTAN - BUTTER PRODUCTION - See PAKISTAN - DAIRY PRODUCTS

PAKISTAN - CALORIE SUPPLY

Asian Development Bank, Post Office Box 789, 1099 Manila, Philippines; *Key Indicators of Developing Asian and Pacific Countries.*

Food and Agricultural Organization of the United Nations (FAO) Via delle Terme di Caracalla, 00100 Rome, Italy (Telephone Number in U.S. (202) 653-2400); *The State of Food and Agriculture.*

PAKISTAN - CAPITAL INVESTMENT

Asian Development Bank, Post Office Box 789, 1099 Manila, Philippines; *Key Indicators of Developing Asian and Pacific Countries.*

PAKISTAN - CAPITAL REVENUE

Asian Development Bank, Post Office Box 789, 1099 Manila, Philippines; *Key Indicators of Developing Asian and Pacific Countries.*

International Monetary Fund, 700 Nineteenth Street, NW, Washington, D.C. 20431 (202) 623-7000; *Government Finance Statistics Yearbook.*

PAKISTAN - CASTOR BEAN PRODUCTION - See PAKISTAN - CROPS

PAKISTAN - CATTLE - See PAKISTAN - LIVESTOCK AND POULTRY

PAKISTAN - CAUSTIC SODA PRODUCTION

Statistical Office of the United Nations, Publishing Service, New York, New York 10017 (800) 253-9646; *Statistical Yearbook.*

PAKISTAN - CEMENT PRODUCTION - See PAKISTAN - MINING AND MINERAL PRODUCTS

PAKISTAN - CHEMICAL (ORGANIC) PRODUCTION - See PAKISTAN - MINING AND MINERAL PRODUCTS

PAKISTAN - CHICK PEA PRODUCTION - See PAKISTAN - CROPS

PAKISTAN - CHICKENS - See PAKISTAN - LIVESTOCK AND POULTRY

PAKISTAN - CHROMITE PRODUCTION AND CONSUMPTION - See PAKISTAN - MINING AND MINERAL PRODUCTS

PAKISTAN - CHROMIUM ORE PRODUCTION AND CONSUMPTION - See PAKISTAN - MINING AND MINERAL PRODUCTS

PAKISTAN - CIGARETTE PRODUCTION - See PAKISTAN - TOBACCO PRODUCTION

PAKISTAN - CLASS STRUCTURE

G.K. Hall and Company, 70 Lincoln Street, Boston, Massachusetts 02111 (617) 423-3990; *The World in Figures.*

PAKISTAN - CLIMATE

Facts on File, 460 Park Avenue South, New York, New York 10016 (800) 443-8323; *The New Book of World Rankings.*

G.K. Hall and Company, 70 Lincoln Street, Boston, Massachusetts 02111 (617) 423-3990; *The World in Figures.*

PAKISTAN - CLOTHING EXPORTS AND IMPORTS

Statistical Office of the United Nations, Publishing Service, New York, New York 10017 (800) 253-9646; *Trade in Manufactures of Developing Countries.*

PAKISTAN - COAL PRODUCTION - See PAKISTAN - MINING AND MINERAL PRODUCTS

PAKISTAN - COFFEE PRODUCTION AND CONSUMPTION - See PAKISTAN - CROPS

PAKISTAN - COMMUNICATIONS

G.K. Hall and Company, 70 Lincoln Street, Boston, Massachusetts 02111 (617) 423-3990; *The World in Figures.*

Statistical Office of the United Nations, Publishing Service, New York, New York 10017 (800) 253-9646; *Statistical Yearbook for Asia and the Pacific.*

PAKISTAN - CONSTRUCTION INDUSTRY

Facts on File, 460 Park Avenue South, New York, New York 10016 (800) 443-8323; *The New Book of World Rankings.*

Statistical Office of the United Nations, Publishing Service, New York, New York 10017 (800) 253-9646; *Construction Statistics Yearbook*, and *Statistical Yearbook.*

PAKISTAN - CONSUMER PRICE INDEX

Asian Development Bank, Post Office Box 789, 1099 Manila, Philippines; *Key Indicators of Developing Asian and Pacific Countries.*

G.K. Hall and Company, 70 Lincoln Street, Boston, Massachusetts 02111 (617) 423-3990; *The World in Figures*.

Statistical Office of the United Nations, Publishing Service, New York, New York 10017 (800) 253-9646; *Statistical Yearbook*.

PAKISTAN - CONSUMER PRICES

International Labour Office, I.L.O. Publications, CH-1211, Geneva 22, Switzerland; *Yearbook of Labour Statistics*.

International Monetary Fund, 700 Nineteenth Street, NW, Washington, D.C. 20431 (202) 623-7000; *International Financial Statistics*.

Times Books, 201 East 50th Street, New York, New York 10022 (212) 751-2600; *The Economist Book of Vital World Statistics*.

PAKISTAN - CONSUMPTION

G.K. Hall and Company, 70 Lincoln Street, Boston, Massachusetts 02111 (617) 423-3990; *The World in Figures*.

PAKISTAN - COPPER PRODUCTION AND CONSUMPTION - See PAKISTAN - MINING AND MINERAL PRODUCTS

PAKISTAN - CORN PRODUCTION - See PAKISTAN - CROPS

PAKISTAN - CORPORATE TAXES - See PAKISTAN - TAXATION

PAKISTAN - COTTON - See PAKISTAN - CROPS

PAKISTAN - CRIME

Yale University Press, Yale Station, New Haven, Connecticut 06520 (203) 432-0940; *Violence and Crime in Cross-National Perspective*.

PAKISTAN - CROPS

Asian Development Bank, Post Office Box 789, 1099 Manila, Philippines; *Key Indicators of Developing Asian and Pacific Countries*.

Commodity Research Bureau, Incorporated, 75 Wall Street, New York, New York 10005 (212) 504-7754; *Commodity Year Book*.

Facts on File, 460 Park Avenue South, New York, New York 10016 (800) 443-8323; *The New Book of World Rankings*.

Food and Agricultural Organization of the United Nations (FAO), Via delle Terme di Caracalla, 00100 Rome, Italy (Telephone Number in U.S. (202) 653-2400); *Production Yearbook*, and *The State of Food and Agriculture*.

G.K. Hall and Company, 70 Lincoln Street, Boston, Massachusetts 02111 (617) 423-3990; *The World in Figures*.

International Monetary Fund, 700 Nineteenth Street, NW, Washington, D.C. 20431 (202) 623-7000; *International Financial Statistics*.

Statistical Office of the United Nations, Publishing Service, New York, New York 10017 (800) 253-9646; *Statistical Yearbook*.

PAKISTAN - CUSTOMS DUTIES

G.K. Hall and Company, 70 Lincoln Street, Boston, Massachusetts 02111 (617) 423-3990; *The World in Figures*.

PAKISTAN - DAIRY PRODUCTS

Facts on File, 460 Park Avenue South, New York, New York 10016 (800) 443-8323; *The New Book of World Rankings*.

Food and Agricultural Organization of the United Nations (FAO), Via delle Terme di Caracalla, 00100 Rome, Italy (Telephone Number in U.S. (202) 653-2400); *Production Yearbook*, and *The State of Food and Agriculture*.

Statistical Office of the United Nations, Publishing Service, New York, New York 10017 (800) 253-9646; *Statistical Yearbook*.

PAKISTAN - DEATH RATES

The Economist Intelligence Unit (Asia) Limited, 10th Floor, Luk Kwok Centre, 72 Gloucester Road, Wanchai, Hong Kong (Phone Number in U.S. (800) 938-4685); *Asian Market Atlas*.

G.K. Hall and Company, 70 Lincoln Street, Boston, Massachusetts 02111 (617) 423-3990; *The World in Figures*.

Statistical Office of the United Nations, Publishing Service, New York, New York 10017 (800) 253-9646; *Statistical Yearbook*.

Times Books, 201 East 50th Street, New York, New York 10022 (212) 751-2600; *The Economist Book of Vital World Statistics*.

World Health Organization, Office of Publications, Avenue Appia, CH-1211 Geneva 27, Switzerland (Telephone Number in U.S. (518) 436-9686); *World Health Statistics Annual*.

PAKISTAN - DEFENSE EXPENDITURES

G.K. Hall and Company, 70 Lincoln Street, Boston, Massachusetts 02111 (617) 423-3990; *The World in Figures*.

International Monetary Fund, 700 Nineteenth Street, NW, Washington, D.C. 20431 (202) 623-7000; *Government Finance Statistics Yearbook*.

U.S. Arms Control and Disarmament Agency, 320 Twenty-first Street, NW, Washington, D.C. 20451 (202) 647-8677; *World Military Expenditures and Arms Transfers*.

PAKISTAN - DEMOGRAPHY

The Economist Intelligence Unit, 111 West 57th Street, New York, New York 10019 (800) 938-4685; *The World Market Atlas*.

The Economist Intelligence Unit (Asia) Limited, 10th Floor, Luk Kwok Centre, 72 Gloucester Road, Wanchai, Hong Kong (Phone Number in U.S. (800) 938-4685); *Asian Market Atlas*.

Facts on File, 460 Park Avenue South, New York, New York 10016 (800) 443-8323; *The New Book of World Rankings*.

G.K. Hall and Company, 70 Lincoln Street, Boston, Massachusetts 02111 (617) 423-3990; *The World in Figures*.

PAKISTAN - DEVELOPMENT ASSISTANCE

Asian Development Bank, Post Office Box 789, 1099 Manila, Philippines; *Key Indicators of Developing Asian and Pacific Countries*.

G.K. Hall and Company, 70 Lincoln Street, Boston, Massachusetts 02111 (617) 423-3990; *The World in Figures*.

Statistical Office of the United Nations, Publishing Service, New York, New York 10017 (800) 253-9646; *Statistical Yearbook.*

PAKISTAN - DIAMOND PRODUCTION - See PAKISTAN - MINING AND MINERAL PRODUCTS

PAKISTAN - DISCOUNT RATES

Statistical Office of the United Nations, Publishing Service, New York, New York 10017 (800) 253-9646; *Statistical Yearbook.*

PAKISTAN - DISEASES

G.K. Hall and Company, 70 Lincoln Street, Boston, Massachusetts 02111 (617) 423-3990; *The World in Figures.*

World Health Organization, Office of Publications, Avenue Appia, CH-1211 Geneva 27, Switzerland (Telephone Number in U.S. (518) 436-9686); *World Health Statistics Annual.*

PAKISTAN - DIVORCE RATES

Facts on File, 460 Park Avenue South, New York, New York 10016 (800) 443-8323; *The New Book of World Rankings.*

Statistical Office of the United Nations, Publishing Service, New York, New York 10017 (800) 253-9646; *Demographic Yearbook.*

PAKISTAN - DOMESTIC PRODUCT

G.K. Hall and Company, 70 Lincoln Street, Boston, Massachusetts 02111 (617) 423-3990; *The World in Figures.*

PAKISTAN - DUCKS - See PAKISTAN - LIVESTOCK AND POULTRY

PAKISTAN - ECONOMY

Asian Development Bank, Post Office Box 789, 1099 Manila, Philippines; *Key Indicators of Developing Asian and Pacific Countries.*

Euromonitor Publications Limited, 87-88 Turnmill Street, London EC1M 5QU, England; *International Marketing Data and Statistics.*

Facts on File, 460 Park Avenue South, New York, New York 10016 (800) 443-8323; *The New Book of World Rankings.*

G.K. Hall and Company, 70 Lincoln Street, Boston, Massachusetts 02111 (617) 423-3990; *The World in Figures.*

PAKISTAN - EDUCATION

The Economist Intelligence Unit, 111 West 57th Street, New York, New York 10019 (800) 938-4685; *The World Market Atlas.*

The Economist Intelligence Unit (Asia) Limited, 10th Floor, Luk Kwok Centre, 72 Gloucester Road, Wanchai, Hong Kong (Phone Number in U.S. (800) 938-4685); *Asian Market Atlas.*

Facts on File, 460 Park Avenue South, New York, New York 10016 (800) 443-8323; *The New Book of World Rankings.*

G.K. Hall and Company, 70 Lincoln Street, Boston, Massachusetts 02111 (617) 423-3990; *The World in Figures.*

International Monetary Fund, 700 Nineteenth Street, NW, Washington, D.C. 20431 (202) 623-7000; *Government Finance Statistics Yearbook.*

Statistical Office of the United Nations, Publishing Service, New York, New York 10017 (800) 253-9646; *Statistical Yearbook for Asia and the Pacific.*

Times Books, 201 East 50th Street, New York, New York 10022 (212) 751-2600; *The Economist Book of Vital World Statistics.*

United Nations Educational, Scientific and Cultural Organization (UNESCO), 7 Place de Fontenoy, F-75700 Paris, France (Telephone Number in U.S. (212) 963-5981); *Statistical Yearbook.*

The World Bank, 1818 H Street, NW, Washington, D.C. 20433 (202) 477-1234; *World Tables.*

PAKISTAN - EGG PRODUCTION AND CONSUMPTION - See PAKISTAN - DAIRY PRODUCTS

PAKISTAN - ELECTRICITY

Asian Development Bank, Post Office Box 789, 1099 Manila, Philippines; *Key Indicators of Developing Asian and Pacific Countries.*

Facts on File, 460 Park Avenue South, New York, New York 10016 (800) 443-8323; *The New Book of World Rankings.*

Penn Well Publishing Company, 1421 South Sheridan Road, Post Office Box 1260, Tulsa, Oklahoma 74101 (800) 752-9764; *International Energy Statistics Sourcebook.*

Statistical Office of the United Nations, Publishing Service, New York, New York 10017 (800) 253-9646; *Electric Power in Asia and the Pacific,* and *Statistical Yearbook.*

Times Books, 201 East 50th Street, New York, New York 10022 (212) 751-2600; *The Economist Book of Vital World Statistics.*

PAKISTAN - EMPLOYMENT

Euromonitor Publications Limited, 87-88 Turnmill Street, London EC1M 5QU, England; *International Marketing Data and Statistics.*

Facts on File, 460 Park Avenue South, New York, New York 10016 (800) 443-8323; *The New Book of World Rankings.*

International Labour Office, I.L.O. Publications, CH-1211, Geneva 22, Switzerland; *Yearbook of Labour Statistics.*

Statistical Office of the United Nations, Publishing Service, New York, New York 10017 (800) 253-9646; *Statistical Yearbook.*

PAKISTAN - ENERGY

Facts on File, 460 Park Avenue South, New York, New York 10016 (800) 443-8323; *The New Book of World Rankings.*

Food and Agricultural Organization of the United Nations (FAO) Via delle Terme di Caracalla, 00100 Rome, Italy (Telephone Number in U.S. (202) 653-2400); *The State of Food and Agriculture.*

G.K. Hall and Company, 70 Lincoln Street, Boston, Massachusetts 02111 (617) 423-3990; *The World in Figures.*

Penn Well Publishing Company, 1421 South Sheridan Road, Post Office Box 1260, Tulsa, Oklahoma 74101 (800) 752-9764; *International Energy Statistics Sourcebook.*

Statistical Office of the United Nations, Publishing Service, New York, New York 10017 (800) 253-9646; *Foreign Trade Statistics of*

Asia and the Pacific, Statistical Yearbook, Statistical Yearbook for Asia and the Pacific, and *World Energy Supplies.*

Times Books, 201 East 50th Street, New York, New York 10022 (212) 751-2600; *The Economist Book of Vital World Statistics.*

PAKISTAN - EXCHANGE RATES

Asian Development Bank, Post Office Box 789, 1099 Manila, Philippines; *Key Indicators of Developing Asian and Pacific Countries.*

The Economist Intelligence Unit (Asia) Limited, 10th Floor, Luk Kwok Centre, 72 Gloucester Road, Wanchai, Hong Kong (Phone Number in U.S. (800) 938-4685); *Asian Market Atlas.*

Euromonitor Publications Limited, 87-88 Turnmill Street, London EC1M 5QU, England; *International Marketing Data and Statistics.*

International Civil Aviation Organization, 1000 Sherbrooke Street, West, Montreal, Quebec, Canada H3A 2R2 (514) 285-8219; *Civil Aviation Statistics of the World.*

International Monetary Fund, 700 Nineteenth Street, NW, Washington, D.C. 20431 (202) 623-7000; *International Financial Statistics.*

Statistical Office of the United Nations, Publishing Service, New York, New York 10017 (800) 253-9646; *Statistical Yearbook.*

PAKISTAN - EXCISE TAXES - See PAKISTAN - TAXATION

PAKISTAN - EXPORTS

Asian Development Bank, Post Office Box 789, 1099 Manila, Philippines; *Key Indicators of Developing Asian and Pacific Countries.*

The Economist Intelligence Unit, 111 West 57th Street, New York, New York 10019 (800) 938-4685; *The World Market Atlas.*

The Economist Intelligence Unit (Asia) Limited, 10th Floor, Luk Kwok Centre, 72 Gloucester Road, Wanchai, Hong Kong (Phone Number in U.S. (800) 938-4685); *Asian Market Atlas.*

Euromonitor Publications Limited, 87-88 Turnmill Street, London EC1M 5QU, England; *International Marketing Data and Statistics.*

Food and Agricultural Organization of the United Nations (FAO) Via delle Terme di Caracalla, 00100 Rome, Italy (Telephone Number in U.S. (202) 653-2400); *The State of Food and Agriculture.*

G.K. Hall and Company, 70 Lincoln Street, Boston, Massachusetts 02111 (617) 423-3990; *The World in Figures.*

International Monetary Fund, 700 Nineteenth Street, NW, Washington, D.C. 20431 (202) 623-7000; *Direction of Trade Statistics,* and *Government Finance Statistics Yearbook.*

Statistical Office of the United Nations, Publishing Service, New York, New York 10017 (800) 253-9646; *Foreign Trade Statistics of Asia and the Pacific,* and *Trade in Manufactures of Developing Countries.*

Times Books, 201 East 50th Street, New York, New York 10022 (212) 751-2600; *The Economist Book of Vital World Statistics.*

The World Bank, 1818 H Street, NW, Washington, D.C. 20433 (202) 477-1234; *World Tables.*

PAKISTAN - EXTERNAL FINANCING

Asian Development Bank, Post Office Box 789, 1099 Manila, Philippines; *Key Indicators of Developing Asian and Pacific Countries.*

PAKISTAN - EXTERNAL INDEBTEDNESS

Asian Development Bank, Post Office Box 789, 1099 Manila, Philippines; *Key Indicators of Developing Asian and Pacific Countries.*

The World Bank, 1818 H Street, NW, Washington, D.C. 20433 (202) 477-1234; *World Tables.*

PAKISTAN - EXTERNAL TRADE

Asian Development Bank, Post Office Box 789, 1099 Manila, Philippines; *Key Indicators of Developing Asian and Pacific Countries.*

Food and Agricultural Organization of the United Nations (FAO) Via delle Terme di Caracalla, 00100 Rome, Italy (Telephone Number in U.S. (202) 653-2400); *The State of Food and Agriculture,* and *Trade Yearbook.*

G.K. Hall and Company, 70 Lincoln Street, Boston, Massachusetts 02111 (617) 423-3990; *The World in Figures.*

Statistical Office of the United Nations, Publishing Service, New York, New York 10017 (800) 253-9646; *Statistical Yearbook,* and *Statistical Yearbook for Asia and the Pacific.*

PAKISTAN - FABRIC PRODUCTION - See PAKISTAN - TEXTILE INDUSTRY

PAKISTAN - FARM CROPS - See PAKISTAN - CROPS

PAKISTAN - FEMALE WORKING POPULATION - See PAKISTAN - EMPLOYMENT

PAKISTAN - FERTILITY RATES

The Economist Intelligence Unit (Asia) Limited, 10th Floor, Luk Kwok Centre, 72 Gloucester Road, Wanchai, Hong Kong (Phone Number in U.S. (800) 938-4685); *Asian Market Atlas.*

Facts on File, 460 Park Avenue South, New York, New York 10016 (800) 443-8323; *The New Book of World Rankings.*

Times Books, 201 East 50th Street, New York, New York 10022 (212) 751-2600; *The Economist Book of Vital World Statistics.*

The World Bank, 1818 H Street, NW, Washington, D.C. 20433 (202) 477-1234; *World Tables.*

PAKISTAN - FERTILIZER

Food and Agricultural Organization of the United Nations (FAO), Via delle Terme di Caracalla, 00100 Rome, Italy (Telephone Number in U.S. (202) 653-2400); *Fertilizer Yearbook,* and *The State of Food and Agriculture.*

Statistical Office of the United Nations, Publishing Service, New York, New York 10017 (800) 253-9646; *Statistical Yearbook.*

PAKISTAN - FETAL MORTALITY

Statistical Office of the United Nations, Publishing Service, New York, New York 10017 (800) 253-9646; *Demographic Yearbook.*

PAKISTAN - FIBRE PRODUCTION - See PAKISTAN - TEXTILE INDUSTRY

PAKISTAN - FILAMENT PRODUCTION - See PAKISTAN - TEXTILE INDUSTRY

PAKISTAN - FILMS - See PAKISTAN - MOTION PICTURES

PAKISTAN - FINANCE

Asian Development Bank, Post Office Box 789, 1099 Manila, Philippines; *Key Indicators of Developing Asian and Pacific Countries.*

Facts on File, 460 Park Avenue South, New York, New York 10016 (800) 443-8323; *The New Book of World Rankings.*

G.K. Hall and Company, 70 Lincoln Street, Boston, Massachusetts 02111 (617) 423-3990; *The World in Figures.*

International Monetary Fund, 700 Nineteenth Street, NW, Washington, D.C. 20431 (202) 623-7000; *Government Finance Statistics Yearbook*, and *International Financial Statistics.*

Statistical Office of the United Nations, Publishing Service, New York, New York 10017 (800) 253-9646; *Statistical Yearbook for Asia and the Pacific.*

PAKISTAN - FISHERIES

Facts on File, 460 Park Avenue South, New York, New York 10016 (800) 443-8323; *The New Book of World Rankings.*

Food and Agricultural Organization of the United Nations (FAO) Via delle Terme di Caracalla, 00100 Rome, Italy (Telephone Number in U.S. (202) 653-2400); *The State of Food and Agriculture*, and *Yearbook of Fishery Statistics.*

Statistical Office of the United Nations, Publishing Service, New York, New York 10017 (800) 253-9646; *Statistical Yearbook.*

PAKISTAN - FOOD

Food and Agricultural Organization of the United Nations (FAO) Via delle Terme di Caracalla, 00100 Rome, Italy (Telephone Number in U.S. (202) 653-2400); *Production Yearbook*, and *The State of Food and Agriculture.*

G.K. Hall and Company, 70 Lincoln Street, Boston, Massachusetts 02111 (617) 423-3990; *The World in Figures.*

Statistical Office of the United Nations, Publishing Service, New York, New York 10017 (800) 253-9646; *Statistical Yearbook for Asia and the Pacific.*

PAKISTAN - FOREIGN AID

G.K. Hall and Company, 70 Lincoln Street, Boston, Massachusetts 02111 (617) 423-3990; *The World in Figures.*

PAKISTAN - FOREIGN DEBT

International Monetary Fund, 700 Nineteenth Street, NW, Washington, D.C. 20431 (202) 623-7000; *Government Finance*

Statistics Yearbook.

PAKISTAN - FOREIGN TRADE

Asian Development Bank, Post Office Box 789, 1099 Manila, Philippines; *Key Indicators of Developing Asian and Pacific Countries.*

The Economist Intelligence Unit (Asia) Limited, 10th Floor, Luk Kwok Centre, 72 Gloucester Road, Wanchai, Hong Kong (Phone Number in U.S. (800) 938-4685); *Asian Market Atlas.*

Euromonitor Publications Limited, 87-88 Turnmill Street, London EC1M 5QU, England; *International Marketing Data and Statistics.*

Facts on File, 460 Park Avenue South, New York, New York 10016 (800) 443-8323; *The New Book of World Rankings.*

Food and Agricultural Organization of the United Nations (FAO) Via delle Terme di Caracalla, 00100 Rome, Italy (Telephone Number in U.S. (202) 653-2400); *The State of Food and Agriculture.*

G.K. Hall and Company, 70 Lincoln Street, Boston, Massachusetts 02111 (617) 423-3990; *The World in Figures.*

International Monetary Fund, 700 Nineteenth Street, NW, Washington, D.C. 20431 (202) 623-7000; *International Financial Statistics.*

Statistical Office of the United Nations, Publishing Service, New York, New York 10017 (800) 253-9646; *International Trade Statistics Yearbook*, and *Statistical Yearbook.*

The World Bank, 1818 H Street, NW, Washington, D.C. 20433 (202) 477-1234; *World Tables.*

PAKISTAN - FORESTRY AND FOREST PRODUCTS

American Forest and Paper Association, 1250 Connecticut Avenue, NW, Washington, D.C. 20036 (202) 463-2455; *Wood Pulp and Fiber Statistics.*

The Economist Intelligence Unit (Asia) Limited, 10th Floor, Luk Kwok Centre, 72 Gloucester Road, Wanchai, Hong Kong (Phone Number in U.S. (800) 938-4685); *Asian Market Atlas.*

Facts on File, 460 Park Avenue South, New York, New York 10016 (800) 443-8323; *The New Book of World Rankings.*

Food and Agricultural Organization of the United Nations (FAO) Via delle Terme di Caracalla, 00100 Rome, Italy (Telephone Number in U.S. (202) 653-2400); *The State of Food and Agriculture*, and *Yearbook of Forest Products.*

G.K. Hall and Company, 70 Lincoln Street, Boston, Massachusetts 02111 (617) 423-3990; *The World in Figures.*

Statistical Office of the United Nations, Publishing Service, New York, New York 10017 (800) 253-9646; *Statistical Yearbook.*

United Nations Educational, Scientific and Cultural Organization (UNESCO), 7 Place de Fontenoy, F-75700 Paris, France (Telephone Number in U.S. (212) 963-5981); *Statistical Yearbook.*

PAKISTAN - GARLIC PRODUCTION - See PAKISTAN - CROPS

PAKISTAN - GAS PRODUCTION - See PAKISTAN - MINING AND MINERAL PRODUCTS

PAKISTAN - GENERAL MORTALITY

Statistical Office of the United Nations, Publishing Service, New York, New York 10017 (800) 253-9646; *Demographic Yearbook.*

PAKISTAN - GEOGRAPHIC DATA

Facts on File, 460 Park Avenue South, New York, New York 10016 (800) 443-8323; *The New Book of World Rankings.*

PAKISTAN - GOATS - See PAKISTAN - LIVESTOCK AND POULTRY

PAKISTAN - GOLD HOLDINGS

International Monetary Fund, 700 Nineteenth Street, NW, Washington, D.C. 20431 (202) 623-7000; *International Financial Statistics.*

Statistical Office of the United Nations, Publishing Service, New York, New York 10017 (800) 253-9646; *Statistical Yearbook.*

The World Bank, 1818 H Street, NW, Washington, D.C. 20433 (202) 477-1234; *World Tables.*

PAKISTAN - GOLD PRODUCTION AND CONSUMPTION - See PAKISTAN - MINING AND MINERAL PRODUCTS

PAKISTAN - GOVERNMENT

Asian Development Bank, Post Office Box 789, 1099 Manila, Philippines; *Key Indicators of Developing Asian and Pacific Countries.*

G.K. Hall and Company, 70 Lincoln Street, Boston, Massachusetts 02111 (617) 423-3990; *The World in Figures.*

PAKISTAN - GOVERNMENT EXPENDITURES

Asian Development Bank, Post Office Box 789, 1099 Manila, Philippines; *Key Indicators of Developing Asian and Pacific Countries.*

International Monetary Fund, 700 Nineteenth Street, NW, Washington, D.C. 20431 (202) 623-7000; *Government Finance Statistics Yearbook.*

Times Books, 201 East 50th Street, New York, New York 10022 (212) 751-2600; *The Economist Book of Vital World Statistics.*

The World Bank, 1818 H Street, NW, Washington, D.C. 20433 (202) 477-1234; *World Tables.*

PAKISTAN - GOVERNMENT FINANCES

Asian Development Bank, Post Office Box 789, 1099 Manila, Philippines; *Key Indicators of Developing Asian and Pacific Countries.*

International Monetary Fund, 700 Nineteenth Street, NW, Washington, D.C. 20431 (202) 623-7000; *International Financial Statistics.*

PAKISTAN - GOVERNMENT REVENUES

Asian Development Bank, Post Office Box 789, 1099 Manila, Philippines; *Key Indicators of Developing Asian and Pacific Countries.*

International Monetary Fund, 700 Nineteenth Street, NW, Washington, D.C. 20431 (202) 623-7000; *Government Finance Statistics Yearbook.*

Times Books, 201 East 50th Street, New York, New York 10022 (212) 751-2600; *The Economist Book of Vital World Statistics.*

The World Bank, 1818 H Street, NW, Washington, D.C. 20433 (202) 477-1234; *World Tables.*

PAKISTAN - GRAIN PRODUCTION - See PAKISTAN - CROPS

PAKISTAN - GRANTS

International Monetary Fund, 700 Nineteenth Street, NW, Washington, D.C. 20431 (202) 623-7000; *Government Finance Statistics Yearbook.*

PAKISTAN - GREEN PEPPER AND CHILIE PRODUCTION - See PAKISTAN - CROPS

PAKISTAN - GROSS DOMESTIC PRODUCT

Asian Development Bank, Post Office Box 789, 1099 Manila, Philippines; *Key Indicators of Developing Asian and Pacific Countries.*

The Economist Intelligence Unit, 111 West 57th Street, New York, New York 10019 (800) 938-4685; *The World Market Atlas.*

The Economist Intelligence Unit (Asia) Limited, 10th Floor, Luk Kwok Centre, 72 Gloucester Road, Wanchai, Hong Kong (Phone Number in U.S. (800) 938-4685); *Asian Market Atlas.*

Euromonitor Publications Limited, 87-88 Turnmill Street, London EC1M 5QU, England; *International Marketing Data and Statistics,* and *The World in Figures.*

Facts on File, 460 Park Avenue South, New York, New York 10016 (800) 443-8323; *The New Book of World Rankings.*

Statistical Office of the United Nations, Publishing Service, New York, New York 10017 (800) 253-9646; *Statistical Yearbook.*

Times Books, 201 East 50th Street, New York, New York 10022 (212) 751-2600; *The Economist Book of Vital World Statistics.*

The World Bank, 1818 H Street, NW, Washington, D.C. 20433 (202) 477-1234; *World Tables.*

PAKISTAN - GROSS NATIONAL PRODUCT

Asian Development Bank, Post Office Box 789, 1099 Manila, Philippines; *Key Indicators of Developing Asian and Pacific Countries.*

Euromonitor Publications Limited, 87-88 Turnmill Street, London EC1M 5QU, England; *International Marketing Data and Statistics.*

U.S. Arms Control and Disarmament Agency, 320 Twenty-first Street, NW, Washington, D.C. 20451 (202) 647-8677; *World Military Expenditures and Arms Transfers.*

The World Bank, 1818 H Street, NW, Washington, D.C. 20433 (202) 477-1234; *World Tables.*

PAKISTAN - GROUNDNUTS PRODUCTION - See PAKISTAN - CROPS

PAKISTAN - HEALTH

The Economist Intelligence Unit (Asia) Limited, 10th Floor, Luk Kwok Centre, 72 Gloucester Road, Wanchai, Hong Kong (Phone Number in U.S. (800) 938-4685); *Asian Market Atlas*.

Facts on File, 460 Park Avenue South, New York, New York 10016 (800) 443-8323; *The New Book of World Rankings*.

G.K. Hall and Company, 70 Lincoln Street, Boston, Massachusetts 02111 (617) 423-3990; *The World in Figures*.

Statistical Office of the United Nations, Publishing Service, New York, New York 10017 (800) 253-9646; *Statistical Yearbook*.

Times Books, 201 East 50th Street, New York, New York 10022 (212) 751-2600; *The Economist Book of Vital World Statistics*.

World Health Organization, Office of Publications, Avenue Appia, CH-1211 Geneva 27, Switzerland (Telephone Number in U.S. (518) 436-9686); *World Health Statistics Annual*.

PAKISTAN - HEALTH EXPENDITURES

International Monetary Fund, 700 Nineteenth Street, NW, Washington, D.C. 20431 (202) 623-7000; *Government Finance Statistics Yearbook*.

PAKISTAN - HEMP FIBRE PRODUCTION - See PAKISTAN - TEXTILE INDUSTRY

PAKISTAN - HIDE PRODUCTION

Food and Agricultural Organization of the United Nations (FAO), Via delle Terme di Caracalla, 00100 Rome, Italy (Telephone Number in U.S. (202) 653-2400); *Production Yearbook*.

PAKISTAN - HIGHWAYS

The Economist Intelligence Unit (Asia) Limited, 10th Floor, Luk Kwok Centre, 72 Gloucester Road, Wanchai, Hong Kong (Phone Number in U.S. (800) 938-4685); *Asian Market Atlas*.

G.K. Hall and Company, 70 Lincoln Street, Boston, Massachusetts 02111 (617) 423-3990; *The World in Figures*.

International Road Federation, 525 School Street, SW, Washington, D.C. 20024 (202) 554-2106; *World Road Statistics*.

PAKISTAN - HORSES - See PAKISTAN - LIVESTOCK AND POULTRY

PAKISTAN - HOURS OF WORK - See PAKISTAN - EMPLOYMENT

PAKISTAN - HOUSING EXPENDITURES

Facts on File, 460 Park Avenue South, New York, New York 10016 (800) 443-8323; *The New Book of World Rankings*.

International Monetary Fund, 700 Nineteenth Street, NW, Washington, D.C. 20431 (202) 623-7000; *Government Finance Statistics Yearbook*.

PAKISTAN - ILLITERATE POPULATION

The Economist Intelligence Unit, 111 West 57th Street, New York, New York 10019 (800) 938-4685; *The World Market Atlas*.

G.K. Hall and Company, 70 Lincoln Street, Boston, Massachusetts 02111 (617) 423-3990; *The World in Figures*.

United Nations Educational, Scientific and Cultural Organization (UNESCO), 7 Place de Fontenoy, F-75700 Paris, France (Telephone Number in U.S. (212) 963-5981); *Statistical Yearbook*.

PAKISTAN - IMPORTS

Asian Development Bank, Post Office Box 789, 1099 Manila, Philippines; *Key Indicators of Developing Asian and Pacific Countries*.

The Economist Intelligence Unit, 111 West 57th Street, New York, New York 10019 (800) 938-4685; *The World Market Atlas*.

The Economist Intelligence Unit (Asia) Limited, 10th Floor, Luk Kwok Centre, 72 Gloucester Road, Wanchai, Hong Kong (Phone Number in U.S. (800) 938-4685); *Asian Market Atlas*.

Euromonitor Publications Limited, 87-88 Turnmill Street, London EC1M 5QU, England; *International Marketing Data and Statistics*.

Food and Agricultural Organization of the United Nations (FAO) Via delle Terme di Caracalla, 00100 Rome, Italy (Telephone Number in U.S. (202) 653-2400); *The State of Food and Agriculture*.

G.K. Hall and Company, 70 Lincoln Street, Boston, Massachusetts 02111 (617) 423-3990; *The World in Figures*.

International Monetary Fund, 700 Nineteenth Street, NW, Washington, D.C. 20431 (202) 623-7000; *Direction of Trade Statistics, Government Finance Statistics Yearbook*, and *International Financial Statistics*.

Statistical Office of the United Nations, Publishing Service, New York, New York 10017 (800) 253-9646; *Foreign Trade Statistics of Asia and the Pacific*, and *Trade in Manufactures of Developing Countries*.

Times Books, 201 East 50th Street, New York, New York 10022 (212) 751-2600; *The Economist Book of Vital World Statistics*.

The World Bank, 1818 H Street, NW, Washington, D.C. 20433 (202) 477-1234; *World Tables*.

PAKISTAN - INCOME TAXES - See PAKISTAN - TAXATION

PAKISTAN - INDUSTRIAL METALS PRODUCTION - See PAKISTAN - MINING AND MINERAL PRODUCTS

PAKISTAN - INDUSTRY

Euromonitor Publications Limited, 87-88 Turnmill Street, London EC1M 5QU, England; *International Marketing Data and Statistics*.

Facts on File, 460 Park Avenue South, New York, New York 10016 (800) 443-8323; *The New Book of World Rankings*.

G.K. Hall and Company, 70 Lincoln Street, Boston, Massachusetts 02111 (617) 423-3990; *The World in Figures*.

International Labour Office, I.L.O. Publications, CH-1211, Geneva 22, Switzerland; *Yearbook of Labour Statistics*.

Statistical Office of the United Nations, Publishing Service, New York, New York 10017 (800) 253-9646; *Statistical Yearbook*, and *Statistical Yearbook for Asia and the Pacific*.

Times Books, 201 East 50th Street, New York, New York 10022 (212) 751-2600; *The Economist Book of Vital World Statistics*.

The World Bank, 1818 H Street, NW, Washington, D.C. 20433 (202) 477-1234; *World Tables*.

World Intellectual Property Organization, 34 Chemin des Colombettes, CH-1211 Geneva 20, Switzerland; *Industrial Property Statistics*.

PAKISTAN - INFANT AND MATERNAL MORTALITY

The Economist Intelligence Unit (Asia) Limited, 10th Floor, Luk Kwok Centre, 72 Gloucester Road, Wanchai, Hong Kong (Phone Number in U.S. (800) 938-4685); *Asian Market Atlas*.

Statistical Office of the United Nations, Publishing Service, New York, New York 10017 (800) 253-9646; *Demographic Yearbook*, and *Statistical Yearbook*.

Times Books, 201 East 50th Street, New York, New York 10022 (212) 751-2600; *The Economist Book of Vital World Statistics*.

The World Bank, 1818 H Street, NW, Washington, D.C. 20433 (202) 477-1234; *World Tables*.

PAKISTAN - INTERNAL TRADE

Statistical Office of the United Nations, Publishing Service, New York, New York 10017 (800) 253-9646; *Statistical Yearbook for Asia and the Pacific*.

PAKISTAN - INTERNATIONAL LIQUIDITY

International Monetary Fund, 700 Nineteenth Street, NW, Washington, D.C. 20431 (202) 623-7000; *International Financial Statistics*.

PAKISTAN - INTERNATIONAL RESERVES EXCLUDING GOLD

Asian Development Bank, Post Office Box 789, 1099 Manila, Philippines; *Key Indicators of Developing Asian and Pacific Countries*.

Statistical Office of the United Nations, Publishing Service, New York, New York 10017 (800) 253-9646; *Statistical Yearbook*.

The World Bank, 1818 H Street, NW, Washington, D.C. 20433 (202) 477-1234; *World Tables*.

PAKISTAN - INTERNATIONAL STATISTICS

Asian Development Bank, Post Office Box 789, 1099 Manila, Philippines; *Key Indicators of Developing Asian and Pacific Countries*.

PAKISTAN - INVESTMENTS

International Monetary Fund, 700 Nineteenth Street, NW, Washington, D.C. 20431 (202) 623-7000; *International Financial Statistics*.

PAKISTAN - IRON ORE PRODUCTION AND CONSUMPTION - See PAKISTAN - MINING AND MINERAL PRODUCTS

PAKISTAN - IRRIGATION

Euromonitor Publications Limited, 87-88 Turnmill Street, London EC1M 5QU, England; *International Marketing Data and Statistics*.

PAKISTAN - JUTE PRODUCTION - See PAKISTAN - CROPS

PAKISTAN - LABOR FORCE

The Economist Intelligence Unit (Asia) Limited, 10th Floor, Luk Kwok Centre, 72 Gloucester Road, Wanchai, Hong Kong (Phone Number in U.S. (800) 938-4685); *Asian Market Atlas*.

Euromonitor Publications Limited, 87-88 Turnmill Street, London EC1M 5QU, England; *International Marketing Data and Statistics*.

Facts on File, 460 Park Avenue South, New York, New York 10016 (800) 443-8323; *The New Book of World Rankings*.

Food and Agricultural Organization of the United Nations (FAO) Via delle Terme di Caracalla, 00100 Rome, Italy (Telephone Number in U.S. (202) 653-2400); *The State of Food and Agriculture*.

G.K. Hall and Company, 70 Lincoln Street, Boston, Massachusetts 02111 (617) 423-3990; *The World in Figures*.

Times Books, 201 East 50th Street, New York, New York 10022 (212) 751-2600; *The Economist Book of Vital World Statistics*.

The World Bank, 1818 H Street, NW, Washington, D.C. 20433 (202) 477-1234; *World Tables*.

PAKISTAN - LABOR PRODUCTIVITY

International Labour Office, I.L.O. Publications, CH-1211, Geneva 22, Switzerland; *Yearbook of Labour Statistics*.

PAKISTAN - LAND USE

Euromonitor Publications Limited, 87-88 Turnmill Street, London EC1M 5QU, England; *International Marketing Data and Statistics*.

Food and Agricultural Organization of the United Nations (FAO), Via delle Terme di Caracalla, 00100 Rome, Italy (Telephone Number in U.S. (202) 653-2400); *Production Yearbook*.

G.K. Hall and Company, 70 Lincoln Street, Boston, Massachusetts 02111 (617) 423-3990; *The World in Figures*.

PAKISTAN - LEATHER AND FOOTWEAR - EXPORTS AND IMPORTS

Statistical Office of the United Nations, Publishing Service, New York, New York 10017 (800) 253-9646; *Trade in Manufactures of Developing Countries*.

PAKISTAN - LIBRARIES

Facts on File, 460 Park Avenue South, New York, New York 10016 (800) 443-8323; *The New Book of World Rankings*.

United Nations Educational, Scientific and Cultural Organization (UNESCO), 7 Place de Fontenoy, F-75700 Paris, France (Telephone Number in U.S. (212) 963-5981); *Statistical Yearbook*.

PAKISTAN - LIFE EXPECTANCY

The Economist Intelligence Unit (Asia) Limited, 10th Floor, Luk Kwok Centre, 72 Gloucester Road, Wanchai, Hong Kong (Phone Number in U.S. (800) 938-4685); *Asian Market Atlas*.

PAKISTAN - LIGNITE PRODUCTION - See PAKISTAN - MINING AND MINERAL PRODUCTS

PAKISTAN - LIVESTOCK AND POULTRY

Euromonitor Publications Limited, 87-88 Turnmill Street, London EC1M 5QU, England; *International Marketing Data and Statistics*.

Facts on File, 460 Park Avenue South, New York, New York 10016 (800) 443-8323; *The New Book of World Rankings*.

Food and Agricultural Organization of the United Nations (FAO), Via delle Terme di Caracalla, 00100 Rome, Italy (Telephone Number in U.S. (202) 653-2400); *Production Yearbook*, and *The State of Food and Agriculture*.

G.K. Hall and Company, 70 Lincoln Street, Boston, Massachusetts 02111 (617) 423-3990; *The World in Figures*.

Statistical Office of the United Nations, Publishing Service, New York, New York 10017 (800) 253-9646; *Statistical Yearbook*.

PAKISTAN - LIVING LEVELS

G.K. Hall and Company, 70 Lincoln Street, Boston, Massachusetts 02111 (617) 423-3990; *The World in Figures*.

Times Books, 201 East 50th Street, New York, New York 10022 (212) 751-2600; *The Economist Book of Vital World Statistics*.

PAKISTAN - MAIL - NUMBER OF PIECES SENT OR RECEIVED

Statistical Office of the United Nations, Publishing Service, New York, New York 10017 (800) 253-9646; *Statistical Yearbook*.

PAKISTAN - MANGANESE ORE PRODUCTION AND CONSUMPTION - See PAKISTAN - MINING AND MINERAL PRODUCTS

PAKISTAN - MANPOWER

Statistical Office of the United Nations, Publishing Service, New York, New York 10017 (800) 253-9646; *Statistical Yearbook for Asia and the Pacific*.

PAKISTAN - MANUFACTURING

Asian Development Bank, Post Office Box 789, 1099 Manila, Philippines; *Key Indicators of Developing Asian and Pacific Countries*.

Facts on File, 460 Park Avenue South, New York, New York 10016 (800) 443-8323; *The New Book of World Rankings*.

G.K. Hall and Company, 70 Lincoln Street, Boston, Massachusetts 02111 (617) 423-3990; *The World in Figures*.

Statistical Office of the United Nations, Publishing Service, New York, New York 10017 (800) 253-9646; *Statistical Yearbook*.

Times Books, 201 East 50th Street, New York, New York 10022 (212) 751-2600; *The Economist Book of Vital World Statistics*.

The World Bank, 1818 H Street, NW, Washington, D.C. 20433 (202) 477-1234; *World Tables*.

PAKISTAN - MARRIAGE RATES

Facts on File, 460 Park Avenue South, New York, New York 10016 (800) 443-8323; *The New Book of World Rankings*.

Statistical Office of the United Nations, Publishing Service, New York, New York 10017 (800) 253-9646; *Demographic Yearbook*.

PAKISTAN - MEAT PRODUCTION - See PAKISTAN - LIVESTOCK AND POULTRY

PAKISTAN - MERCHANT SHIPPING

G.K. Hall and Company, 70 Lincoln Street, Boston, Massachusetts 02111 (617) 423-3990; *The World in Figures*.

Lloyd's Register of Shipping, 17 Battery Place, New York, New York 10004 (212) 425-8050; *Register of Ships*.

Statistical Office of the United Nations, Publishing Service, New York, New York 10017 (800) 253-9646; *Statistical Yearbook*.

Times Books, 201 East 50th Street, New York, New York 10022 (212) 751-2600; *The Economist Book of Vital World Statistics*.

U.S. Department of Transportation, Maritime Administration, 400 Seventh Street, SW, Washington, D.C. 20590 (202) 366-5807; *A Statistical Analysis of the World's Merchant Fleets*.

PAKISTAN - MILITARY

The Economist Intelligence Unit (Asia) Limited, 10th Floor, Luk Kwok Centre, 72 Gloucester Road, Wanchai, Hong Kong (Phone Number in U.S. (800) 938-4685); *Asian Market Atlas*.

G.K. Hall and Company, 70 Lincoln Street, Boston, Massachusetts 02111 (617) 423-3990; *The World in Figures*.

The International Institute for Strategic Studies, 23 Tavistock Street, London WC2E 7NQ, England; *The Military Balance*.

U.S. Arms Control and Disarmament Agency, 320 Twenty-first Street, NW, Washington, D.C. 20451 (202) 647-8677; *World Military Expenditures and Arms Transfers*.

PAKISTAN - MILK PRODUCTION - See PAKISTAN - DAIRY PRODUCTS

PAKISTAN - MILLET PRODUCTION - See PAKISTAN - CROPS

PAKISTAN - MINING AND MINERAL PRODUCTS

Asian Development Bank, Post Office Box 789, 1099 Manila, Philippines; *Key Indicators of Developing Asian and Pacific Countries*.

Commodity Research Bureau, Incorporated, 75 Wall Street, New York, New York 10005 (212) 504-7754; *Commodity Year Book*.

Facts on File, 460 Park Avenue South, New York, New York 10016 (800) 443-8323; *The New Book of World Rankings*.

G.K. Hall and Company, 70 Lincoln Street, Boston, Massachusetts 02111 (617) 423-3990; *The World in Figures*.

Penn Well Publishing Company, 1421 South Sheridan Road, Post Office Box 1260, Tulsa, Oklahoma 74101 (800) 752-9764; *International Energy Statistics Sourcebook*.

Statistical Office of the United Nations, Publishing Service, New York, New York 10017 (800) 253-9646; *Statistical Yearbook*.

PAKISTAN - MONEY EXCHANGE RATE

Euromonitor Publications Limited, 87-88 Turnmill Street, London EC1M 5QU, England; *International Marketing Data and Statistics*.

International Monetary Fund, 700 Nineteenth Street, NW, Washington, D.C. 20431 (202) 623-7000; *International Financial Statistics*.

Statistical Office of the United Nations, Publishing Service, New York, New York 10017 (800) 253-9646; *Statistical Yearbook*.

PAKISTAN - MONEY MARKET RATES

Statistical Office of the United Nations, Publishing Service, New York, New York 10017 (800) 253-9646; *Statistical Yearbook*.

PAKISTAN - MONEY RESERVES

Euromonitor Publications Limited, 87-88 Turnmill Street, London EC1M 5QU, England; *International Marketing Data and Statistics*.

PAKISTAN - MONEY SUPPLY

Asian Development Bank, Post Office Box 789, 1099 Manila, Philippines; *Key Indicators of Developing Asian and Pacific Countries*.

Euromonitor Publications Limited, 87-88 Turnmill Street, London EC1M 5QU, England; *International Marketing Data and Statistics*.

G.K. Hall and Company, 70 Lincoln Street, Boston, Massachusetts 02111 (617) 423-3990; *The World in Figures*.

International Monetary Fund, 700 Nineteenth Street, NW, Washington, D.C. 20431 (202) 623-7000; *International Financial Statistics*.

Statistical Office of the United Nations, Publishing Service, New York, New York 10017 (800) 253-9646; *Statistical Yearbook*.

The World Bank, 1818 H Street, NW, Washington, D.C. 20433 (202) 477-1234; *World Tables*.

PAKISTAN - MOTION PICTURES

Statistical Office of the United Nations, Publishing Service, New York, New York 10017 (800) 253-9646; *Statistical Yearbook*.

United Nations Educational, Scientific and Cultural Organization (UNESCO), 7 Place de Fontenoy, F-75700 Paris, France (Telephone Number in U.S. (212) 963-5981); *Statistical Yearbook*.

PAKISTAN - MOTOR VEHICLE TAXES - See PAKISTAN - TAXATION

PAKISTAN - MOTOR VEHICLES IN USE

G.K. Hall and Company, 70 Lincoln Street, Boston, Massachusetts 02111 (617) 423-3990; *The World in Figures*.

International Road Federation, 525 School Street, SW, Washington, D.C. 20024 (202) 554-2106; *World Road Statistics*.

Statistical Office of the United Nations, Publishing Service, New York, New York 10017 (800) 253-9646; *Statistical Yearbook*.

Times Books, 201 East 50th Street, New York, New York 10022 (212) 751-2600; *The Economist Book of Vital World Statistics*.

PAKISTAN - MULES - See PAKISTAN - LIVESTOCK AND POULTRY

PAKISTAN - MUSEUMS

Facts on File, 460 Park Avenue South, New York, New York 10016 (800) 443-8323; *The New Book of World Rankings*.

United Nations Educational, Scientific and Cultural Organization (UNESCO), 7 Place de Fontenoy, F-75700 Paris, France (Telephone Number in U.S. (212) 963-5981); *Statistical Yearbook*.

PAKISTAN - NATALITY - See PAKISTAN - BIRTH RATES

PAKISTAN - NATIONAL ACCOUNTS

International Monetary Fund, 700 Nineteenth Street, NW, Washington, D.C. 20431 (202) 623-7000; *International Financial Statistics*.

Statistical Office of the United Nations, Publishing Service, New York, New York 10017 (800) 253-9646; *National Accounts Statistics, Statistical Yearbook*, and *Statistical Yearbook for Asia and the Pacific*.

PAKISTAN - NATIONAL INCOME

Facts on File, 460 Park Avenue South, New York, New York 10016 (800) 443-8323; *The New Book of World Rankings*.

G.K. Hall and Company, 70 Lincoln Street, Boston, Massachusetts 02111 (617) 423-3990; *The World in Figures*.

Statistical Office of the United Nations, Publishing Service, New York, New York 10017 (800) 253-9646; *Statistical Yearbook*.

PAKISTAN - NATIONAL PRODUCT

Facts on File, 460 Park Avenue South, New York, New York 10016 (800) 443-8323; *The New Book of World Rankings*.

Statistical Office of the United Nations, Publishing Service, New York, New York 10017 (800) 253-9646; *Statistical Yearbook*.

PAKISTAN - NATURAL GAS - PRODUCTION - See PAKISTAN - MINING AND MINERAL PRODUCTS

PAKISTAN - NEWSPAPER PRODUCTION AND CONSUMPTION - See PAKISTAN - FORESTRY AND FOREST PRODUCTS

PAKISTAN - NEWSPRINT - See PAKISTAN - FORESTRY AND FOREST PRODUCTS

PAKISTAN - OCCUPATIONS - See PAKISTAN - LABOR FORCE

PAKISTAN - PAPER - See PAKISTAN - FORESTRY AND FOREST PRODUCTS

PAKISTAN - PATENTS

Statistical Office of the United Nations, Publishing Service, New York, New York 10017 (800) 253-9646; *Statistical Yearbook*.

World Intellectual Property Organization, 34 Chemin des Colombettes, CH-1211 Geneva 20, Switzerland; *Industrial Property Statistics*.

PAKISTAN - PEANUT PRODUCTION - See PAKISTAN - CROPS

PAKISTAN - PERIODICALS

United Nations Educational, Scientific and Cultural Organization (UNESCO), 7 Place de Fontenoy, F-75700 Paris, France (Telephone Number in U.S. (212) 963-5981); *Statistical Yearbook*.

PAKISTAN - PESTICIDE USE

Food and Agricultural Organization of the United Nations (FAO) Via delle Terme di Caracalla, 00100 Rome, Italy (Telephone Number in U.S. (202) 653-2400); *The State of Food and Agriculture*.

PAKISTAN - PETROLEUM INDUSTRY

Asian Development Bank, Post Office Box 789, 1099 Manila, Philippines; *Key Indicators of Developing Asian and Pacific Countries*.

Facts on File, 460 Park Avenue South, New York, New York 10016 (800) 443-8323; *The New Book of World Rankings*.

Food and Agricultural Organization of the United Nations (FAO) Via delle Terme di Caracalla, 00100 Rome, Italy (Telephone Number in U.S. (202) 653-2400); *The State of Food and Agriculture*.

G.K. Hall and Company, 70 Lincoln Street, Boston, Massachusetts 02111 (617) 423-3990; *The World in Figures*.

Penn Well Publishing Company, 1421 South Sheridan Road, Post Office Box 1260, Tulsa, Oklahoma 74101 (800) 752-9764; *International Energy Statistics Sourcebook*.

Statistical Office of the United Nations, Publishing Service, New York, New York 10017 (800) 253-9646; *Statistical Yearbook*.

PAKISTAN - PHOSPHATE ROCK PRODUCTION - See PAKISTAN - MINING AND MINERAL PRODUCTS

PAKISTAN - PIGS - See PAKISTAN - LIVESTOCK AND POULTRY

PAKISTAN - POPULATION

Asian Development Bank, Post Office Box 789, 1099 Manila, Philippines; *Key Indicators of Developing Asian and Pacific Countries*.

The Economist Intelligence Unit, 111 West 57th Street, New York, New York 10019 (800) 938-4685; *The World Market Atlas*.

The Economist Intelligence Unit (Asia) Limited, 10th Floor, Luk Kwok Centre, 72 Gloucester Road, Wanchai, Hong Kong (Phone Number in U.S. (800) 938-4685); *Asian Market Atlas*.

Euromonitor Publications Limited, 87-88 Turnmill Street, London EC1M 5QU, England; *International Marketing Data and Statistics*.

Facts on File, 460 Park Avenue South, New York, New York 10016 (800) 443-8323; *The New Book of World Rankings*.

Food and Agricultural Organization of the United Nations (FAO), Via delle Terme di Caracalla, 00100 Rome, Italy (Telephone Number in U.S. (202) 653-2400); *Production Yearbook*.

G.K. Hall and Company, 70 Lincoln Street, Boston, Massachusetts 02111 (617) 423-3990; *The World in Figures*.

International Labour Office, I.L.O. Publications, CH-1211, Geneva 22, Switzerland; *Yearbook of Labour Statistics*.

Statistical Office of the United Nations, Publishing Service, New York, New York 10017 (800) 253-9646; *Demographic Yearbook, Statistical Yearbook*, and *Statistical Yearbook for Asia and the Pacific*.

Times Books, 201 East 50th Street, New York, New York 10022 (212) 751-2600; *The Economist Book of Vital World Statistics*.

United Nations Educational, Scientific and Cultural Organization (UNESCO), 7 Place de Fontenoy, F-75700 Paris, France (Telephone Number in U.S. (212) 963-5981); *Statistical Yearbook*.

U.S. Arms Control and Disarmament Agency, 320 Twenty-first Street, NW, Washington, D.C. 20451 (202) 647-8677; *World Military Expenditures and Arms Transfers*.

PAKISTAN - POST OFFICES

Facts on File, 460 Park Avenue South, New York, New York 10016 (800) 443-8323; *The New Book of World Rankings*.

PAKISTAN - POTATO PRODUCTION - See PAKISTAN - CROPS

PAKISTAN - POWER PRODUCTION INDUSTRY

Statistical Office of the United Nations, Publishing Service, New York, New York 10017 (800) 253-9646; *Electric Power in Asia and the Pacific*.

PAKISTAN - PRICES

Asian Development Bank, Post Office Box 789, 1099 Manila, Philippines; *Key Indicators of Developing Asian and Pacific Countries*.

Facts on File, 460 Park Avenue South, New York, New York 10016 (800) 443-8323; *The New Book of World Rankings*.

Food and Agricultural Organization of the United Nations (FAO), Via delle Terme di Caracalla, 00100 Rome, Italy (Telephone Number in U.S. (202) 653-2400); *Production Yearbook*, and *The State of Food and Agriculture*.

G.K. Hall and Company, 70 Lincoln Street, Boston, Massachusetts 02111 (617) 423-3990; *The World in Figures*.

International Labour Office, I.L.O. Publications, CH-1211, Geneva 22, Switzerland; *Yearbook of Labour Statistics*.

International Monetary Fund, 700 Nineteenth Street, NW, Washington, D.C. 20431 (202) 623-7000; *International Financial Statistics*.

PAKISTAN - PRINTING AND WRITING PAPER - See PAKISTAN - FORESTRY AND FOREST PRODUCTS

PAKISTAN - PRODUCTION

Facts on File, 460 Park Avenue South, New York, New York 10016 (800) 443-8323; *The New Book of World Rankings*.

G.K. Hall and Company, 70 Lincoln Street, Boston, Massachusetts 02111 (617) 423-3990; *The World in Figures*.

PAKISTAN - PRODUCTIVITY

Euromonitor Publications Limited, 87-88 Turnmill Street, London EC1M 5QU, England; *International Marketing Data and Statistics*.

PAKISTAN - PROPERTY TAXES

International Monetary Fund, 700 Nineteenth Street, NW, Washington, D.C. 20431 (202) 623-7000; *Government Finance Statistics Yearbook*.

PAKISTAN - PUBLIC FINANCE

Facts on File, 460 Park Avenue South, New York, New York 10016 (800) 443-8323; *The New Book of World Rankings*.

PAKISTAN - RADIO BROADCASTING - See PAKISTAN - BROADCASTING

PAKISTAN - RAILWAYS

G.K. Hall and Company, 70 Lincoln Street, Boston, Massachusetts 02111 (617) 423-3990; *The World in Figures*.

Jane's Information Group, Sentinel House, 163 Brighton Road, Coulsdon, Surrey CR5 2NH, England (Telephone Number in U.S. (703) 683-3700); *Jane's World Railways*.

Statistical Office of the United Nations, Publishing Service, New York, New York 10017 (800) 253-9646; *Statistical Yearbook*.

PAKISTAN - RAPESEED PRODUCTION - See PAKISTAN - CROPS

PAKISTAN - RELIGION

Facts on File, 460 Park Avenue South, New York, New York 10016 (800) 443-8323; *The New Book of World Rankings*.

PAKISTAN - RENT PRICES

International Labour Office, I.L.O. Publications, CH-1211, Geneva 22, Switzerland; *Yearbook of Labour Statistics*.

PAKISTAN - RETAIL TRADE

G.K. Hall and Company, 70 Lincoln Street, Boston, Massachusetts 02111 (617) 423-3990; *The World in Figures*.

PAKISTAN - RICE - See PAKISTAN - CROPS

PAKISTAN - ROOT AND TUBER PRODUCTION - See PAKISTAN - CROPS

PAKISTAN - ROUNDWOOD PRODUCTION - See PAKISTAN - FORESTRY AND FOREST PRODUCTS

PAKISTAN - RUBBER PRODUCTION AND CONSUMPTION

Facts on File, 460 Park Avenue South, New York, New York 10016 (800) 443-8323; *The New Book of World Rankings*.

PAKISTAN - SALT PRODUCTION - See PAKISTAN - MINING AND MINERAL PRODUCTS

PAKISTAN - SAWNWOOD PRODUCTION - See PAKISTAN - FORESTRY AND FOREST PRODUCTS

PAKISTAN - SCIENCE AND TECHNOLOGY - EXPENDITURE FOR RESEARCH

Statistical Office of the United Nations, Publishing Service, New York, New York 10017 (800) 253-9646; *Statistical Yearbook*.

PAKISTAN - SCIENTISTS AND TECHNICIANS

Statistical Office of the United Nations, Publishing Service, New York, New York 10017 (800) 253-9646; *Statistical Yearbook*.

United Nations Educational, Scientific and Cultural Organization (UNESCO), 7 Place de Fontenoy, F-75700 Paris, France (Telephone Number in U.S. (212) 963-5981); *Statistical Yearbook*.

PAKISTAN - SENIOR CITIZENS

Facts on File, 460 Park Avenue South, New York, New York 10016 (800) 443-8323; *The New Book of World Rankings*.

PAKISTAN - SESAME SEED PRODUCTION - See PAKISTAN - CROPS

PAKISTAN - SHEEP - See PAKISTAN - LIVESTOCK AND POULTRY

PAKISTAN - SILVER PRODUCTION AND CONSUMPTION - See PAKISTAN - MINING AND MINERAL PRODUCTS

PAKISTAN - SOCIAL DATA

Asian Development Bank, Post Office Box 789, 1099 Manila, Philippines; *Key Indicators of Developing Asian and Pacific Countries*.

Facts on File, 460 Park Avenue South, New York, New York 10016 (800) 443-8323; *The New Book of World Rankings*.

G.K. Hall and Company, 70 Lincoln Street, Boston, Massachusetts 02111 (617) 423-3990; *The World in Figures*.

PAKISTAN - SOCIAL SECURITY

International Monetary Fund, 700 Nineteenth Street, NW, Washington, D.C. 20431 (202) 623-7000; *Government Finance Statistics Yearbook*.

PAKISTAN - STATE BUDGET REVENUE AND EXPENDITURES

Euromonitor Publications Limited, 87-88 Turnmill Street, London EC1M 5QU, England; *International Marketing Data and Statistics*.

PAKISTAN - STEEL - See PAKISTAN - MINING AND MINERAL PRODUCTS

PAKISTAN - STOCKS - COMMODITY - MARKET PRICE - INDEX

Food and Agricultural Organization of the United Nations (FAO) Via delle Terme di Caracalla, 00100 Rome, Italy (Telephone Number in U.S. (202) 653-2400); *The State of Food and Agriculture*.

PAKISTAN - SUGAR PRODUCTION AND CONSUMPTION - See PAKISTAN - CROPS

PAKISTAN - SULPHURIC ACID PRODUCTION - See PAKISTAN - MINING AND MINERAL PRODUCTS

PAKISTAN - TAXATION

G.K. Hall and Company, 70 Lincoln Street, Boston, Massachusetts 02111 (617) 423-3990; *The World in Figures*.

International Monetary Fund, 700 Nineteenth Street, NW, Washington, D.C. 20431 (202) 623-7000; *Government Finance Statistics Yearbook*.

International Road Federation, 525 School Street, SW, Washington, D.C. 20024 (202) 554-2106; *World Road Statistics*.

The World Bank, 1818 H Street, NW, Washington, D.C. 20433 (202) 477-1234; *World Tables*.

PAKISTAN - TAX REVENUES - See PAKISTAN - TAXATION

PAKISTAN - TEA PRODUCTION AND CONSUMPTION - See PAKISTAN - CROPS

PAKISTAN - TELEGRAPH SERVICE

Statistical Office of the United Nations, Publishing Service, New York, New York 10017 (800) 253-9646; *Statistical Yearbook*.

PAKISTAN - TELEPHONES IN USE

American Telephone and Telegraph Company, 26 Parsippany Road, Whippany, New Jersey 07981 (800) 338-4038; *The World's Telephones*.

The Economist Intelligence Unit (Asia) Limited, 10th Floor, Luk Kwok Centre, 72 Gloucester Road, Wanchai, Hong Kong (Phone Number in U.S. (800) 938-4685); *Asian Market Atlas*.

G.K. Hall and Company, 70 Lincoln Street, Boston, Massachusetts 02111 (617) 423-3990; *The World in Figures*.

Statistical Office of the United Nations, Publishing Service, New York, New York 10017 (800) 253-9646; *Statistical Yearbook*.

PAKISTAN - TELEVISION BROADCASTING - See PAKISTAN - BROADCASTING

PAKISTAN - TEXTILE INDUSTRY

American Forest and Paper Association, 1250 Connecticut Avenue, NW, Washington, D.C. 20036 (202) 463-2455; *Wood Pulp and Fiber Statistics*.

Food and Agricultural Organization of the United Nations (FAO), Via delle Terme di Caracalla, 00100 Rome, Italy (Telephone Number in U.S. (202) 653-2400); *Production Yearbook*.

G.K. Hall and Company, 70 Lincoln Street, Boston, Massachusetts 02111 (617) 423-3990; *The World in Figures*.

Statistical Office of the United Nations, Publishing Service, New York, New York 10017 (800) 253-9646; *Statistical Yearbook, and Trade in Manufactures of Developing Countries*.

PAKISTAN - THEATRE

United Nations Educational, Scientific and Cultural Organization (UNESCO), 7 Place de Fontenoy, F-75700 Paris, France (Telephone Number in U.S. (212) 963-5981); *Statistical Yearbook*.

PAKISTAN - TIN - INDUSTRIAL CONSUMPTION - See PAKISTAN - MINING AND MINERAL PRODUCTS

PAKISTAN - TIRE (MOTOR VEHICLE) PRODUCTION

Statistical Office of the United Nations, Publishing Service, New York, New York 10017 (800) 253-9646; *Statistical Yearbook*.

PAKISTAN - TOBACCO PRODUCTION

Commodity Research Bureau, Incorporated, 75 Wall Street, New York, New York 10005 (212) 504-7754; *Commodity Year Book*.

Facts on File, 460 Park Avenue South, New York, New York 10016 (800) 443-8323; *The New Book of World Rankings*.

Statistical Office of the United Nations, Publishing Service, New York, New York 10017 (800) 253-9646; *Statistical Yearbook*.

PAKISTAN - TOURISM

Facts on File, 460 Park Avenue South, New York, New York 10016 (800) 443-8323; *The New Book of World Rankings*.

G.K. Hall and Company, 70 Lincoln Street, Boston, Massachusetts 02111 (617) 423-3990; *The World in Figures*.

Statistical Office of the United Nations, Publishing Service, New York, New York 10017 (800) 253-9646; *Statistical Yearbook*.

Times Books, 201 East 50th Street, New York, New York 10022 (212) 751-2600; *The Economist Book of Vital World Statistics*.

World Tourism Organization, Calle Capitan Haya 42, E-28020 Madrid, Spain; *Yearbook of Tourism Statistics*.

PAKISTAN - TRACTORS IN USE

Statistical Office of the United Nations, Publishing Service, New York, New York 10017 (800) 253-9646; *Statistical Yearbook*.

PAKISTAN - TRADE - See PAKISTAN - FOREIGN TRADE

PAKISTAN - TRADEMARKS AND SERVICE MARKS

Statistical Office of the United Nations, Publishing Service, New York, New York 10017 (800) 253-9646; *Statistical Yearbook*.

World Intellectual Property Organization, 34 Chemin des Colombettes, CH-1211 Geneva 20, Switzerland; *Industrial Property Statistics*.

PAKISTAN - TRANSPORTATION AND COMMUNICATIONS

The Economist Intelligence Unit (Asia) Limited, 10th Floor, Luk Kwok Centre, 72 Gloucester Road, Wanchai, Hong Kong (Phone Number in U.S. (800) 938-4685); *Asian Market Atlas*.

Facts on File, 460 Park Avenue South, New York, New York 10016 (800) 443-8323; *The New Book of World Rankings*.

G.K. Hall and Company, 70 Lincoln Street, Boston, Massachusetts 02111 (617) 423-3990; *The World in Figures*.

Statistical Office of the United Nations, Publishing Service, New York, New York 10017 (800) 253-9646; *Statistical Yearbook for Asia and the Pacific*.

PAKISTAN - UNEMPLOYMENT

Euromonitor Publications Limited, 87-88 Turnmill Street, London EC1M 5QU, England; *International Marketing Data and Statistics*.

International Labour Office, I.L.O. Publications, CH-1211, Geneva 22, Switzerland; *Yearbook of Labour Statistics*.

Statistical Office of the United Nations, Publishing Service, New York, New York 10017 (800) 253-9646; *Statistical Yearbook*.

PAKISTAN - UTILITIES

Statistical Office of the United Nations, Publishing Service, New York, New York 10017 (800) 253-9646; *Electric Power in Asia and the Pacific*.

PAKISTAN - VITAL STATISTICS

Euromonitor Publications Limited, 87-88 Turnmill Street, London EC1M 5QU, England; *International Marketing Data and Statistics*.

G.K. Hall and Company, 70 Lincoln Street, Boston, Massachusetts 02111 (617) 423-3990; *The World in Figures*.

Statistical Office of the United Nations, Publishing Service, New York, New York 10017 (800) 253-9646; *Statistical Yearbook*.

PAKISTAN - WAGES

G.K. Hall and Company, 70 Lincoln Street, Boston, Massachusetts 02111 (617) 423-3990; *The World in Figures*.

International Labour Office, I.L.O. Publications, CH-1211, Geneva 22, Switzerland; *Yearbook of Labour Statistics*.

Statistical Office of the United Nations, Publishing Service, New York, New York 10017 (800) 253-9646; *Statistical Yearbook*.

PAKISTAN - WAGES AND PRICES

Statistical Office of the United Nations, Publishing Service, New York, New York 10017 (800) 253-9646; *Statistical Yearbook for Asia and the Pacific*.

PAKISTAN - WEATHER

Facts on File, 460 Park Avenue South, New York, New York 10016 (800) 443-8323; *The New Book of World Rankings*.

G.K. Hall and Company, 70 Lincoln Street, Boston, Massachusetts 02111 (617) 423-3990; *The World in Figures*.

PAKISTAN - WELFARE

International Monetary Fund, 700 Nineteenth Street, NW, Washington, D.C. 20431 (202) 623-7000; *Government Finance Statistics Yearbook*.

PAKISTAN - WHEAT PRODUCTION AND PRICES - See PAKISTAN - CROPS

PAKISTAN - WHOLESALE PRICES

Asian Development Bank, Post Office Box 789, 1099 Manila, Philippines; *Key Indicators of Developing Asian and Pacific Countries*.

International Monetary Fund, 700 Nineteenth Street, NW, Washington, D.C. 20431 (202) 623-7000; *International Financial Statistics*.

Statistical Office of the United Nations, Publishing Service, New York, New York 10017 (800) 253-9646; *Statistical Yearbook*.

PAKISTAN - WINE PRODUCTION

Facts on File, 460 Park Avenue South, New York, New York 10016 (800) 443-8323; *The New Book of World Rankings*.

PAKISTAN - WOOD AND WOOD PULP - See FORESTRY AND FOREST PRODUCTS

PAKISTAN - WOOL CONSUMPTION

Statistical Office of the United Nations, Publishing Service, New York, New York 10017 (800) 253-9646; *Statistical Yearbook*.

PAKISTAN - WOOL PRODUCTION

Facts on File, 460 Park Avenue South, New York, New York 10016 (800) 443-8323; *The New Book of World Rankings*.

Statistical Office of the United Nations, Publishing Service, New York, New York 10017 (800) 253-9646; *Statistical Yearbook*.

PAKISTAN - YARN PRODUCTION

Statistical Office of the United Nations, Publishing Service, New York, New York 10017 (800) 253-9646; *Statistical Yearbook*.

Palau (Republic of) - National Statistical Office

Office of Planning and Statistics, Post Office Box 100, Koror, Republic of Palau, Western Caroline Islands 96940.

PALAU - BROADCASTING

Billboard Limited, Post Office Box 9027, 1006 AA Amsterdam, The Netherlands (Telephone Number in U.S. (212) 764-7300); *World Radio TV Handbook*.

Palestine - Primary Statistics Source

Palestine Liberation Organization, Economic Department, Central Bureau of Statistics, Damascus, Syria; *Palestinian Statistical Abstract*.

PALESTINE - AGRICULTURE

Economic Commission for Western Asia, Post Office Box 27, Baghdad, Iraq; *Statistical Abstract of Western Asia*.

Food and Agricultural Organization of the United Nations (FAO) Via delle Terme di Caracalla, 00100 Rome, Italy (Telephone Number in U.S. (202) 653-2400); *Production Yearbook, The State of Food and Agriculture*, and *Trade Yearbook*.

G.K. Hall and Company, 70 Lincoln Street, Boston, Massachusetts 02111 (617) 423-3990; *The World in Figures*.

PALESTINE - AIRLINE SERVICE

G.K. Hall and Company, 70 Lincoln Street, Boston, Massachusetts 02111 (617) 423-3990; *The World in Figures*.

Economic Commission for Western Asia, Post Office Box 27, Baghdad, Iraq; *Statistical Abstract of Western Asia*.

PALESTINE - AREA AND DENSITY OF POPULATION

Economic Commission for Western Asia, Post Office Box 27, Baghdad, Iraq; *Statistical Abstract of Western Asia*.

Food and Agricultural Organization of the United Nations (FAO) Via delle Terme di Caracalla, 00100 Rome, Italy (Telephone Number in U.S. (202) 653-2400); *The State of Food and Agriculture.*

G.K. Hall and Company, 70 Lincoln Street, Boston, Massachusetts 02111 (617) 423-3990; *The World in Figures.*

Statistical Office of the United Nations, Publishing Service, New York, New York 10017 (800) 253-9646; *Statistical Yearbook.*

PALESTINE - BALANCE OF PAYMENTS

Economic Commission for Western Asia, Post Office Box 27, Baghdad, Iraq; *Statistical Abstract of Western Asia.*

G.K. Hall and Company, 70 Lincoln Street, Boston, Massachusetts 02111 (617) 423-3990; *The World in Figures.*

PALESTINE - BALANCE OF TRADE

Economic Commission for Western Asia, Post Office Box 27, Baghdad, Iraq; *Statistical Abstract of Western Asia.*

PALESTINE - BANKING

Economic Commission for Western Asia, Post Office Box 27, Baghdad, Iraq; *Statistical Abstract of Western Asia.*

G.K. Hall and Company, 70 Lincoln Street, Boston, Massachusetts 02111 (617) 423-3990; *The World in Figures.*

PALESTINE - BIRTH RATES

Statistical Office of the United Nations, Publishing Service, New York, New York 10017 (800) 253-9646; *Demographic Yearbook.*

PALESTINE - BONDS

G.K. Hall and Company, 70 Lincoln Street, Boston, Massachusetts 02111 (617) 423-3990; *The World in Figures.*

PALESTINE - BOOK PRODUCTION

G.K. Hall and Company, 70 Lincoln Street, Boston, Massachusetts 02111 (617) 423-3990; *The World in Figures.*

PALESTINE - BROADCASTING

G.K. Hall and Company, 70 Lincoln Street, Boston, Massachusetts 02111 (617) 423-3990; *The World in Figures.*

PALESTINE - BUSINESS

G.K. Hall and Company, 70 Lincoln Street, Boston, Massachusetts 02111 (617) 423-3990; *The World in Figures.*

PALESTINE - CALORIE SUPPLY

Food and Agricultural Organization of the United Nations (FAO) Via delle Terme di Caracalla, 00100 Rome, Italy (Telephone Number in U.S. (202) 653-2400); *The State of Food and Agriculture.*

PALESTINE - CHEMICAL (ORGANIC) PRODUCTION - See PALESTINE - MINING AND MINERAL PRODUCTS

PALESTINE - CLASS STRUCTURE

G.K. Hall and Company, 70 Lincoln Street, Boston, Massachusetts 02111 (617) 423-3990; *The World in Figures.*

PALESTINE - CLIMATE

G.K. Hall and Company, 70 Lincoln Street, Boston, Massachusetts 02111 (617) 423-3990; *The World in Figures.*

PALESTINE - COAL PRODUCTION - See PALESTINE - MINING AND MINERAL PRODUCTS

PALESTINE - COMMUNICATIONS

Economic Commission for Western Asia, Post Office Box 27, Baghdad, Iraq; *Statistical Abstract of Western Asia.*

G.K. Hall and Company, 70 Lincoln Street, Boston, Massachusetts 02111 (617) 423-3990; *The World in Figures.*

PALESTINE - CONSUMER PRICE INDEX

G.K. Hall and Company, 70 Lincoln Street, Boston, Massachusetts 02111 (617) 423-3990; *The World in Figures.*

PALESTINE - CONSUMPTION

G.K. Hall and Company, 70 Lincoln Street, Boston, Massachusetts 02111 (617) 423-3990; *The World in Figures.*

PALESTINE - CORN PRODUCTION - See PALESTINE - CROPS

PALESTINE - CORPORATE TAXES - See PALESTINE - TAXATION

PALESTINE - CROPS

Food and Agricultural Organization of the United Nations (FAO) Via delle Terme di Caracalla, 00100 Rome, Italy (Telephone Number in U.S. (202) 653-2400); *The State of Food and Agriculture.*

G.K. Hall and Company, 70 Lincoln Street, Boston, Massachusetts 02111 (617) 423-3990; *The World in Figures.*

PALESTINE - CUSTOMS DUTIES

G.K. Hall and Company, 70 Lincoln Street, Boston, Massachusetts 02111 (617) 423-3990; *The World in Figures.*

PALESTINE - DAIRY PRODUCTS

Economic Commission for Western Asia, Post Office Box 27, Baghdad, Iraq; *Statistical Abstract of Western Asia.*

Food and Agricultural Organization of the United Nations (FAO) Via delle Terme di Caracalla, 00100 Rome, Italy (Telephone Number in U.S. (202) 653-2400); *The State of Food and Agriculture.*

PALESTINE - DEATH RATES

G.K. Hall and Company, 70 Lincoln Street, Boston, Massachusetts 02111 (617) 423-3990; *The World in Figures.*

Statistical Office of the United Nations, Publishing Service, New York, New York 10017 (800) 253-9646; *Statistical Yearbook.*

PALESTINE - DEFENSE EXPENDITURES

G.K. Hall and Company, 70 Lincoln Street, Boston, Massachusetts 02111 (617) 423-3990; *The World in Figures.*

PALESTINE - DEMOGRAPHY

G.K. Hall and Company, 70 Lincoln Street, Boston, Massachusetts 02111 (617) 423-3990; *The World in Figures*.

PALESTINE - DEVELOPMENT ASSISTANCE

G.K. Hall and Company, 70 Lincoln Street, Boston, Massachusetts 02111 (617) 423-3990; *The World in Figures*.

PALESTINE - DISEASE

G.K. Hall and Company, 70 Lincoln Street, Boston, Massachusetts 02111 (617) 423-3990; *The World in Figures*.

PALESTINE - DIVORCE RATES

Statistical Office of the United Nations, Publishing Service, New York, New York 10017 (800) 253-9646; *Demographic Yearbook*, and *Statistical Yearbook*.

PALESTINE - DOMESTIC PRODUCT

G.K. Hall and Company, 70 Lincoln Street, Boston, Massachusetts 02111 (617) 423-3990; *The World in Figures*.

PALESTINE - ECONOMY

G.K. Hall and Company, 70 Lincoln Street, Boston, Massachusetts 02111 (617) 423-3990; *The World in Figures*.

PALESTINE - EDUCATION

Economic Commission for Western Asia, Post Office Box 27, Baghdad, Iraq; *Statistical Abstract of Western Asia*.

G.K. Hall and Company, 70 Lincoln Street, Boston, Massachusetts 02111 (617) 423-3990; *The World in Figures*.

PALESTINE - EGG PRODUCTION AND CONSUMPTION - See PALESTINE - DAIRY PRODUCTS

PALESTINE - EMPLOYMENT

Economic Commission for Western Asia, Post Office Box 27, Baghdad, Iraq; *Statistical Abstract of Western Asia*.

PALESTINE - ENERGY

Economic Commission for Western Asia, Post Office Box 27, Baghdad, Iraq; *Statistical Abstract of Western Asia*.

Food and Agricultural Organization of the United Nations (FAO) Via delle Terme di Caracalla, 00100 Rome, Italy (Telephone Number in U.S. (202) 653-2400); *The State of Food and Agriculture*.

G.K. Hall and Company, 70 Lincoln Street, Boston, Massachusetts 02111 (617) 423-3990; *The World in Figures*.

PALESTINE - EXPORTS

Economic Commission for Western Asia, Post Office Box 27, Baghdad, Iraq; *Statistical Abstract of Western Asia*.

Food and Agricultural Organization of the United Nations (FAO) Via delle Terme di Caracalla, 00100 Rome, Italy (Telephone Number in U.S. (202) 653-2400); *The State of Food and Agriculture*.

G.K. Hall and Company, 70 Lincoln Street, Boston, Massachusetts 02111 (617) 423-3990; *The World in Figures*.

PALESTINE - EXTERNAL TRADE

Food and Agricultural Organization of the United Nations (FAO) Via delle Terme di Caracalla, 00100 Rome, Italy (Telephone Number in U.S. (202) 653-2400); *The State of Food and Agriculture*, and *Trade Yearbook*.

G.K. Hall and Company, 70 Lincoln Street, Boston, Massachusetts 02111 (617) 423-3990; *The World in Figures*.

PALESTINE - FARM CROPS - See PALESTINE - CROPS

PALESTINE - FERTILIZER

Food and Agricultural Organization of the United Nations (FAO) Via delle Terme di Caracalla, 00100 Rome, Italy (Telephone Number in U.S. (202) 653-2400); *The State of Food and Agriculture*.

PALESTINE - FETAL MORTALITY

Statistical Office of the United Nations, Publishing Service, New York, New York 10017 (800) 253-9646; *Demographic Yearbook*.

PALESTINE - FINANCE

Economic Commission for Western Asia, Post Office Box 27, Baghdad, Iraq; *Statistical Abstract of Western Asia*.

G.K. Hall and Company, 70 Lincoln Street, Boston, Massachusetts 02111 (617) 423-3990; *The World in Figures*.

PALESTINE - FISHERIES

Economic Commission for Western Asia, Post Office Box 27, Baghdad, Iraq; *Statistical Abstract of Western Asia*.

Food and Agricultural Organization of the United Nations (FAO) Via delle Terme di Caracalla, 00100 Rome, Italy (Telephone Number in U.S. (202) 653-2400); *The State of Food and Agriculture*, and *Yearbook of Fishery Statistics*.

PALESTINE - FOOD

Food and Agricultural Organization of the United Nations (FAO) Via delle Terme di Caracalla, 00100 Rome, Italy (Telephone Number in U.S. (202) 653-2400); *Production Yearbook*, and *The State of Food and Agriculture*.

G.K. Hall and Company, 70 Lincoln Street, Boston, Massachusetts 02111 (617) 423-3990; *The World in Figures*.

PALESTINE - FOREIGN AID

G.K. Hall and Company, 70 Lincoln Street, Boston, Massachusetts 02111 (617) 423-3990; *The World in Figures*.

PALESTINE - FOREIGN TRADE

Economic Commission for Western Asia, Post Office Box 27, Baghdad, Iraq; *Statistical Abstract of Western Asia*.

Food and Agricultural Organization of the United Nations (FAO) Via delle Terme di Caracalla, 00100 Rome, Italy (Telephone Number in U.S. (202) 653-2400); *The State of Food and Agriculture*.

G.K. Hall and Company, 70 Lincoln Street, Boston, Massachusetts 02111 (617) 423-3990; *The World in Figures.*

PALESTINE - FORESTRY AND FOREST PRODUCTS

Food and Agricultural Organization of the United Nations (FAO) Via delle Terme di Caracalla, 00100 Rome, Italy (Telephone Number in U.S. (202) 653-2400); *The State of Food and Agriculture.*

G.K. Hall and Company, 70 Lincoln Street, Boston, Massachusetts 02111 (617) 423-3990; *The World in Figures.*

PALESTINE - GENERAL MORTALITY

Statistical Office of the United Nations, Publishing Service, New York, New York 10017 (800) 253-9646; *Demographic Yearbook.*

PALESTINE - GOVERNMENT

G.K. Hall and Company, 70 Lincoln Street, Boston, Massachusetts 02111 (617) 423-3990; *The World in Figures.*

PALESTINE - GOVERNMENT EXPENDITURE

Economic Commission for Western Asia, Post Office Box 27, Baghdad, Iraq; *Statistical Abstract of Western Asia.*

PALESTINE - GOVERNMENT REVENUE

Economic Commission for Western Asia, Post Office Box 27, Baghdad, Iraq; *Statistical Abstract of Western Asia.*

PALESTINE - GRAIN PRODUCTION - See PALESTINE - CROPS

PALESTINE - GROSS DOMESTIC PRODUCT

Economic Commission for Western Asia, Post Office Box 27, Baghdad, Iraq; *Statistical Abstract of Western Asia.*

G.K. Hall and Company, 70 Lincoln Street, Boston, Massachusetts 02111 (617) 423-3990; *The World in Figures.*

PALESTINE - HEALTH

Economic Commission for Western Asia, Post Office Box 27, Baghdad, Iraq; *Statistical Abstract of Western Asia.*

G.K. Hall and Company, 70 Lincoln Street, Boston, Massachusetts 02111 (617) 423-3990; *The World in Figures.*

PALESTINE - HIGHWAYS

Economic Commission for Western Asia, Post Office Box 27, Baghdad, Iraq; *Statistical Abstract of Western Asia.*

G.K. Hall and Company, 70 Lincoln Street, Boston, Massachusetts 02111 (617) 423-3990; *The World in Figures.*

PALESTINE - ILLITERATE POPULATION

G.K. Hall and Company, 70 Lincoln Street, Boston, Massachusetts 02111 (617) 423-3990; *The World in Figures.*

PALESTINE - IMPORTS

Economic Commission for Western Asia, Post Office Box 27, Baghdad, Iraq; *Statistical Abstract of Western Asia.*

Food and Agricultural Organization of the United Nations (FAO) Via delle Terme di Caracalla, 00100 Rome, Italy (Telephone Number in U.S. (202) 653-2400); *The State of Food and Agriculture.*

G.K. Hall and Company, 70 Lincoln Street, Boston, Massachusetts 02111 (617) 423-3990; *The World in Figures.*

PALESTINE - INDUSTRY

G.K. Hall and Company, 70 Lincoln Street, Boston, Massachusetts 02111 (617) 423-3990; *The World in Figures.*

PALESTINE - INFANT AND MATERNAL MORTALITY

Statistical Office of the United Nations, Publishing Service, New York, New York 10017 (800) 253-9646; *Demographic Yearbook.*

PALESTINE - LABOR FORCE

Economic Commission for Western Asia, Post Office Box 27, Baghdad, Iraq; *Statistical Abstract of Western Asia.*

Food and Agricultural Organization of the United Nations (FAO) Via delle Terme di Caracalla, 00100 Rome, Italy (Telephone Number in U.S. (202) 653-2400); *The State of Food and Agriculture.*

G.K. Hall and Company, 70 Lincoln Street, Boston, Massachusetts 02111 (617) 423-3990; *The World in Figures.*

PALESTINE - LAND USE

Economic Commission for Western Asia, Post Office Box 27, Baghdad, Iraq; *Statistical Abstract of Western Asia.*

Food and Agricultural Organization of the United Nations (FAO), Via delle Terme di Caracalla, 00100 Rome, Italy (Telephone Number in U.S. (202) 653-2400); *Production Yearbook.*

G.K. Hall and Company, 70 Lincoln Street, Boston, Massachusetts 02111 (617) 423-3990; *The World in Figures.*

PALESTINE - LIVESTOCK AND POULTRY

Economic Commission for Western Asia, Post Office Box 27, Baghdad, Iraq; *Statistical Abstract of Western Asia.*

Food and Agricultural Organization of the United Nations (FAO), Via delle Terme di Caracalla, 00100 Rome, Italy (Telephone Number in U.S. (202) 653-2400); *Production Yearbook*, and *The State of Food and Agriculture.*

G.K. Hall and Company, 70 Lincoln Street, Boston, Massachusetts 02111 (617) 423-3990; *The World in Figures.*

PALESTINE - LIVING LEVELS

G.K. Hall and Company, 70 Lincoln Street, Boston, Massachusetts 02111 (617) 423-3990; *The World in Figures.*

PALESTINE - MANUFACTURING

G.K. Hall and Company, 70 Lincoln Street, Boston, Massachusetts 02111 (617) 423-3990; *The World in Figures.*

PALESTINE - MARRIAGE RATES

Statistical Office of the United Nations, Publishing Service, New York, New York 10017 (800) 253-9646; *Demographic Yearbook*, and *Statistical Yearbook.*

PALESTINE - MEAT PRODUCTION - See PALESTINE - LIVESTOCK AND POULTRY

PALESTINE - MERCHANT SHIPPING

Economic Commission for Western Asia, Post Office Box 27, Baghdad, Iraq; *Statistical Abstract of Western Asia*.

G.K. Hall and Company, 70 Lincoln Street, Boston, Massachusetts 02111 (617) 423-3990; *The World in Figures*.

PALESTINE - MILITARY

G.K. Hall and Company, 70 Lincoln Street, Boston, Massachusetts 02111 (617) 423-3990; *The World in Figures*.

PALESTINE - MILK PRODUCTION - See PALESTINE - DAIRY PRODUCTS

PALESTINE - MINING AND MINERAL PRODUCTS

Economic Commission for Western Asia, Post Office Box 27, Baghdad, Iraq; *Statistical Abstract of Western Asia*.

G.K. Hall and Company, 70 Lincoln Street, Boston, Massachusetts 02111 (617) 423-3990; *The World in Figures*.

PALESTINE - MONEY SUPPLY

Economic Commission for Western Asia, Post Office Box 27, Baghdad, Iraq; *Statistical Abstract of Western Asia*.

G.K. Hall and Company, 70 Lincoln Street, Boston, Massachusetts 02111 (617) 423-3990; *The World in Figures*.

PALESTINE - MOTOR VEHICLES

Economic Commission for Western Asia, Post Office Box 27, Baghdad, Iraq; *Statistical Abstract of Western Asia*.

PALESTINE - MOTOR VEHICLES IN USE

G.K. Hall and Company, 70 Lincoln Street, Boston, Massachusetts 02111 (617) 423-3990; *The World in Figures*.

PALESTINE - NATALITY - See PALESTINE - BIRTH RATES

PALESTINE - NATIONAL ACCOUNTS

Economic Commission for Western Asia, Post Office Box 27, Baghdad, Iraq; *Statistical Abstract of Western Asia*.

PALESTINE - NATIONAL INCOME

G.K. Hall and Company, 70 Lincoln Street, Boston, Massachusetts 02111 (617) 423-3990; *The World in Figures*.

PALESTINE - NEWSPAPER PRODUCTION - See PALESTINE - FORESTRY AND FOREST PRODUCTS

PALESTINE - OCCUPATIONS - See PALESTINE - LABOR FORCE

PALESTINE - PESTICIDE USE

Food and Agricultural Organization of the United Nations (FAO) Via delle Terme di Caracalla, 00100 Rome, Italy (Telephone Number in U.S. (202) 653-2400); *The State of Food and Agriculture*.

PALESTINE - PETROLEUM INDUSTRY

Food and Agricultural Organization of the United Nations (FAO) Via delle Terme di Caracalla, 00100 Rome, Italy (Telephone Number in U.S. (202) 653-2400); *The State of Food and Agriculture*.

G.K. Hall and Company, 70 Lincoln Street, Boston, Massachusetts 02111 (617) 423-3990; *The World in Figures*.

PALESTINE - POPULATION

Economic Commission for Western Asia, Post Office Box 27, Baghdad, Iraq; *Statistical Abstract of Western Asia*.

Food and Agricultural Organization of the United Nations (FAO), Via delle Terme di Caracalla, 00100 Rome, Italy (Telephone Number in U.S. (202) 653-2400); *Production Yearbook*.

G.K. Hall and Company, 70 Lincoln Street, Boston, Massachusetts 02111 (617) 423-3990; *The World in Figures*.

Statistical Office of the United Nations, Publishing Service, New York, New York 10017 (800) 253-9646; *Demographic Yearbook*, and *Statistical Yearbook*.

World Health Organization, Office of Publications, Avenue Appia, CH-1211 Geneva 27, Switzerland (Telephone Number in U.S. (518) 436-9686); *World Health Statistics Annual*.

PALESTINE - PRICES

Economic Commission for Western Asia, Post Office Box 27, Baghdad, Iraq; *Statistical Abstract of Western Asia*.

Food and Agricultural Organization of the United Nations (FAO), Via delle Terme di Caracalla, 00100 Rome, Italy (Telephone Number in U.S. (202) 653-2400); *Production Yearbook*, and *The State of Food and Agriculture*.

G.K. Hall and Company, 70 Lincoln Street, Boston, Massachusetts 02111 (617) 423-3990; *The World in Figures*.

PALESTINE - PRODUCTION

G.K. Hall and Company, 70 Lincoln Street, Boston, Massachusetts 02111 (617) 423-3990; *The World in Figures*.

PALESTINE - RAILWAY USE

G.K. Hall and Company, 70 Lincoln Street, Boston, Massachusetts 02111 (617) 423-3990; *The World in Figures*.

PALESTINE - RETAIL TRADE

G.K. Hall and Company, 70 Lincoln Street, Boston, Massachusetts 02111 (617) 423-3990; *The World in Figures*.

PALESTINE - SOCIAL DATA

G.K. Hall and Company, 70 Lincoln Street, Boston, Massachusetts 02111 (617) 423-3990; *The World in Figures*.

PALESTINE - STOCKS - COMMODITY - MARKET PRICE - INDEX

Food and Agricultural Organization of the United Nations (FAO) Via delle Terme di Caracalla, 00100 Rome, Italy (Telephone Number in U.S. (202) 653-2400); *The State of Food and Agriculture*.

PALESTINE - TAXATION

G.K. Hall and Company, 70 Lincoln Street, Boston, Massachusetts 02111 (617) 423-3990; *The World in Figures.*

PALESTINE - TELEPHONES IN USE

G.K. Hall and Company, 70 Lincoln Street, Boston, Massachusetts 02111 (617) 423-3990; *The World in Figures.*

PALESTINE - TEXTILE INDUSTRY

G.K. Hall and Company, 70 Lincoln Street, Boston, Massachusetts 02111 (617) 423-3990; *The World in Figures.*

PALESTINE - TOURISM

Economic Commission for Western Asia, Post Office Box 27, Baghdad, Iraq; *Statistical Abstract of Western Asia.*

G.K. Hall and Company, 70 Lincoln Street, Boston, Massachusetts 02111 (617) 423-3990; *The World in Figures.*

PALESTINE - TRADE - See PALESTINE - FOREIGN TRADE

PALESTINE - TRANSPORTATION AND COMMUNICATIONS

Economic Commission for Western Asia, Post Office Box 27, Baghdad, Iraq; *Statistical Abstract of Western Asia.*

G.K. Hall and Company, 70 Lincoln Street, Boston, Massachusetts 02111 (617) 423-3990; *The World in Figures.*

PALESTINE - VITAL STATISTICS

G.K. Hall and Company, 70 Lincoln Street, Boston, Massachusetts 02111 (617) 423-3990; *The World in Figures.*

Statistical Office of the United Nations, Publishing Service, New York, New York 10017 (800) 253-9646; *Statistical Yearbook.*

World Health Organization, Office of Publications, Avenue Appia, CH-1211 Geneva 27, Switzerland (Telephone Number in U.S. (518) 436-9686); *World Health Statistics Annual.*

PALESTINE - WAGES

G.K. Hall and Company, 70 Lincoln Street, Boston, Massachusetts 02111 (617) 423-3990; *The World in Figures.*

PALESTINE - WEATHER

G.K. Hall and Company, 70 Lincoln Street, Boston, Massachusetts 02111 (617) 423-3990; *The World in Figures.*

Panama - National Statistical Office

Direccion de Estadistica y Censo, Apartado 5213, Panama 5, Panama.

Panama - Primary Statistics Source

Direccion de Estadistica y Censo, Apartado 5213, Panama 5, Panama; *Panama en Cifras* (Panama in figures).

PANAMA - ABORTIONS

Statistical Office of the United Nations, Publishing Service, New York, New York 10017 (800) 253-9646; *Demographic Yearbook.*

PANAMA - AGRICULTURE

The Economist Intelligence Unit, 111 West 57th Street, New York, New York 10019 (800) 938-4685; *The New Latin America Market Atlas.*

Euromonitor Publications Limited, 87-88 Turnmill Street, London EC1M 5QU, England; *International Marketing Data and Statistics.*

Facts on File, 460 Park Avenue South, New York, New York 10016 (800) 443-8323; *The New Book of World Rankings.*

Food and Agricultural Organization of the United Nations (FAO) Via delle Terme di Caracalla, 00100 Rome, Italy (Telephone Number in U.S. (202) 653-2400); *Production Yearbook,* and *The State of Food and Agriculture,* and *Trade Yearbook.*

Gale Research Incorporated, 835 Penobscot Building, Detroit, Michigan 48226 (800) 877-4253; *International Historical Statistics The Americas and Australasia.*

G.K. Hall and Company, 70 Lincoln Street, Boston, Massachusetts 02111 (617) 423-3990; *The World in Figures.*

Inter-American Development Bank, 1300 New York Avenue, NW, Washington, D.C. 20577 (202) 623-1753; *Economic and Social Progress in Latin America.*

Statistical Office of the United Nations, Publishing Service, New York, New York 10017 (800) 253-9646; *Statistical Yearbook,* and *Statistical Yearbook for Latin America and the Caribbean.*

Times Books, 201 East 50th Street, New York, New York 10022 (212) 751-2600; *The Economist Book of Vital World Statistics.*

U.C.L.A. Latin American Center Publications, University of California, Los Angeles, California 90024 (310) 825-6634; *Statistical Abstract of Latin America.*

The World Bank, 1818 H Street, NW, Washington, D.C. 20433 (202) 477-1234; *World Tables.*

PANAMA - AIRLINE SERVICE

The Economist Intelligence Unit, 111 West 57th Street, New York, New York 10019 (800) 938-4685; *The New Latin America Market Atlas.*

Facts on File, 460 Park Avenue South, New York, New York 10016 (800) 443-8323; *The New Book of World Rankings.*

G.K. Hall and Company, 70 Lincoln Street, Boston, Massachusetts 02111 (617) 423-3990; *The World in Figures.*

International Civil Aviation Organization, 1000 Sherbrooke Street, West, Montreal, Quebec, Canada H3A 2R2 (514) 285-8219; *Civil Aviation Statistics of the World.*

Statistical Office of the United Nations, Publishing Service, New York, New York 10017 (800) 253-9646; *Statistical Yearbook.*

Times Books, 201 East 50th Street, New York, New York 10022 (212) 751-2600; *The Economist Book of Vital World Statistics.*

PANAMA - ALUMINUM PRODUCTION AND CONSUMPTION - See PANAMA - MINING AND MINERAL PRODUCTS

PANAMA - ANIMAL HEALTH

Food and Agricultural Organization of the United Nations (FAO), Via delle Terme di Caracalla, 00100 Rome, Italy (Telephone Number in U.S. (202) 653-2400); *Animal Health Yearbook.*

PANAMA - AREA AND DENSITY OF POPULATION

Euromonitor Publications Limited, 87-88 Turnmill Street, London EC1M 5QU, England; *International Marketing Data and Statistics.*

Facts on File, 460 Park Avenue South, New York, New York 10016 (800) 443-8323; *The New Book of World Rankings.*

Food and Agricultural Organization of the United Nations (FAO) Via delle Terme di Caracalla, 00100 Rome, Italy (Telephone Number in U.S. (202) 653-2400); *The State of Food and Agriculture.*

G.K. Hall and Company, 70 Lincoln Street, Boston, Massachusetts 02111 (617) 423-3990; *The World in Figures.*

Inter-American Development Bank, 1300 New York Avenue, NW, Washington, D.C. 20577 (202) 623-1753; *Economic and Social Progress in Latin America.*

Statistical Office of the United Nations, Publishing Service, New York, New York 10017 (800) 253-9646; *Statistical Yearbook.*

Times Books, 201 East 50th Street, New York, New York 10022 (212) 751-2600; *The Economist Book of Vital World Statistics.*

United Nations Educational, Scientific and Cultural Organization (UNESCO), 7 Place de Fontenoy, F-75700 Paris, France (Telephone Number in U.S. (212) 963-5981); *Statistical Yearbook.*

PANAMA - ARMS EXPORTS AND IMPORTS

U.S. Arms Control and Disarmament Agency, 320 Twenty-first Street, NW, Washington, D.C. 20451 (202) 647-8677; *World Military Expenditures and Arms Transfers.*

PANAMA - BALANCE OF PAYMENTS

The Economist Intelligence Unit, 111 West 57th Street, New York, New York 10019 (800) 938-4685; *The New Latin America Market Atlas*, and *The World Market Atlas.*

G.K. Hall and Company, 70 Lincoln Street, Boston, Massachusetts 02111 (617) 423-3990; *The World in Figures.*

Inter-American Development Bank, 1300 New York Avenue, NW, Washington, D.C. 20577 (202) 623-1753; *Economic and Social Progress in Latin America.*

International Monetary Fund, 700 Nineteenth Street, NW, Washington, D.C. 20431 (202) 623-7000; *Balance of Payments Yearbook.*

Organization of American States (OAS), General Secretariat, Washington, D.C. 20006 (202) 458-3533; *Statistical Bulletin of the OAS.*

Statistical Office of the United Nations, Publishing Service, New York, New York 10017 (800) 253-9646; *Economic Survey of Latin America and the Caribbean*, and *Statistical Yearbook for Latin America and the Caribbean.*

Times Books, 201 East 50th Street, New York, New York 10022 (212) 751-2600; *The Economist Book of Vital World Statistics.*

U.C.L.A. Latin American Center Publications, University of California, Los Angeles, California 90024 (310) 825-6634; *Statistical Abstract of Latin America.*

The World Bank, 1818 H Street, NW, Washington, D.C. 20433 (202) 477-1234; *World Tables.*

PANAMA - BANANAS - See PANAMA - CROPS

PANAMA - BANKING

Facts on File, 460 Park Avenue South, New York, New York 10016 (800) 443-8323; *The New Book of World Rankings.*

G.K. Hall and Company, 70 Lincoln Street, Boston, Massachusetts 02111 (617) 423-3990; *The World in Figures.*

Inter-American Development Bank, 1300 New York Avenue, NW, Washington, D.C. 20577 (202) 623-1753; *Economic and Social Progress in Latin America.*

International Monetary Fund, 700 Nineteenth Street, NW, Washington, D.C. 20431 (202) 623-7000; *Government Finance Statistics Yearbook*, and *International Financial Statistics.*

Statistical Office of the United Nations, Publishing Service, New York, New York 10017 (800) 253-9646; *Statistical Yearbook for Latin America and the Caribbean.*

PANAMA - BARLEY PRODUCTION - See PANAMA - CROPS

PANAMA - BEER PRODUCTION

Facts on File, 460 Park Avenue South, New York, New York 10016 (800) 443-8323; *The New Book of World Rankings.*

Statistical Office of the United Nations, Publishing Service, New York, New York 10017 (800) 253-9646; *Statistical Yearbook.*

PANAMA - BIRTH RATE

Facts on File, 460 Park Avenue South, New York, New York 10016 (800) 443-8323; *The New Book of World Rankings.*

Statistical Office of the United Nations, Publishing Service, New York, New York 10017 (800) 253-9646; *Demographic Yearbook*, *Statistical Yearbook*, and *Statistical Yearbook for Latin America and the Caribbean.*

Times Books, 201 East 50th Street, New York, New York 10022 (212) 751-2600; *The Economist Book of Vital World Statistics.*

The World Bank, 1818 H Street, NW, Washington, D.C. 20433 (202) 477-1234; *World Tables.*

World Health Organization, Office of Publications, Avenue Appia, CH-1211 Geneva 27, Switzerland (Telephone Number in U.S. (518) 436-9686); *World Health Statistics Annual.*

PANAMA - BONDS

G.K. Hall and Company, 70 Lincoln Street, Boston, Massachusetts 02111 (617) 423-3990; *The World in Figures.*

Inter-American Development Bank, 1300 New York Avenue, NW, Washington, D.C. 20577 (202) 623-1753; *Economic and Social*

Progress in Latin America.

International Monetary Fund, 700 Nineteenth Street, NW, Washington, D.C. 20431 (202) 623-7000; *Government Finance Statistics Yearbook.*

PANAMA - BOOK PRODUCTION

G.K. Hall and Company, 70 Lincoln Street, Boston, Massachusetts 02111 (617) 423-3990; *The World in Figures.*

United Nations Educational, Scientific and Cultural Organization (UNESCO), 7 Place de Fontenoy, F-75700 Paris, France (Telephone Number in U.S. (212) 963-5981); *Statistical Yearbook.*

PANAMA - BROADCASTING

Billboard Limited, Post Office Box 9027, 1006 AA Amsterdam, The Netherlands (Telephone Number in U.S. (212) 764-7300); *World Radio TV Handbook.*

Facts on File, 460 Park Avenue South, New York, New York 10016 (800) 443-8323; *The New Book of World Rankings.*

G.K. Hall and Company, 70 Lincoln Street, Boston, Massachusetts 02111 (617) 423-3990; *The World in Figures.*

Times Books, 201 East 50th Street, New York, New York 10022 (212) 751-2600; *The Economist Book of Vital World Statistics.*

United Nations Educational, Scientific and Cultural Organization (UNESCO), 7 Place de Fontenoy, F-75700 Paris, France (Telephone Number in U.S. (212) 963-5981); *Statistical Yearbook.*

PANAMA - BUSINESS

G.K. Hall and Company, 70 Lincoln Street, Boston, Massachusetts 02111 (617) 423-3990; *The World in Figures.*

Inter-American Development Bank, 1300 New York Avenue, NW, Washington, D.C. 20577 (202) 623-1753; *Economic and Social Progress in Latin America.*

PANAMA - BUSINESS AND PROFESSIONAL LICENSES

International Monetary Fund, 700 Nineteenth Street, NW, Washington, D.C. 20431 (202) 623-7000; *Government Finance Statistics Yearbook.*

PANAMA - BUTTER PRODUCTION - See PANAMA - DAIRY PRODUCTS

PANAMA - CALORIE SUPPLY

Food and Agricultural Organization of the United Nations (FAO) Via delle Terme di Caracalla, 00100 Rome, Italy (Telephone Number in U.S. (202) 653-2400); *The State of Food and Agriculture.*

Statistical Office of the United Nations, Publishing Service, New York, New York 10017 (800) 253-9646; *Statistical Yearbook for Latin America and the Caribbean.*

PANAMA - CAPITAL INVESTMENT

Inter-American Development Bank, 1300 New York Avenue, NW, Washington, D.C. 20577 (202) 623-1753; *Economic and Social Progress in Latin America.*

PANAMA - CAPITAL REVENUE

Inter-American Development Bank, 1300 New York Avenue, NW, Washington, D.C. 20577 (202) 623-1753; *Economic and Social Progress in Latin America.*

International Monetary Fund, 700 Nineteenth Street, NW, Washington, D.C. 20431 (202) 623-7000; *Government Finance Statistics Yearbook.*

PANAMA - CATTLE - See PANAMA - LIVESTOCK AND POULTRY

PANAMA - CEMENT PRODUCTION - See PANAMA - MINING AND MINERAL PRODUCTS

PANAMA - CHEESE PRODUCTION AND CONSUMPTION - See PANAMA - DAIRY PRODUCTS

PANAMA - CHEMICAL (ORGANIC) PRODUCTION - See PANAMA - MINING AND MINERAL PRODUCTS

PANAMA - CHICKENS - See PANAMA - LIVESTOCK AND POULTRY

PANAMA - CIGARETTE PRODUCTION - See PANAMA - TOBACCO PRODUCTION

PANAMA - CLASS STRUCTURE

G.K. Hall and Company, 70 Lincoln Street, Boston, Massachusetts 02111 (617) 423-3990; *The World in Figures.*

PANAMA - CLIMATE

Facts on File, 460 Park Avenue South, New York, New York 10016 (800) 443-8323; *The New Book of World Rankings.*

G.K. Hall and Company, 70 Lincoln Street, Boston, Massachusetts 02111 (617) 423-3990; *The World in Figures.*

PANAMA - COAL PRODUCTION - See PANAMA - MINING AND MINERAL PRODUCTS

PANAMA - COCOA (BEANS) PRODUCTION - See PANAMA - CROPS

PANAMA - COFFEE PRODUCTION AND CONSUMPTION - See PANAMA - CROPS

PANAMA - COMMUNICATIONS

Gale Research Incorporated, 835 Penobscot Building, Detroit, Michigan 48226 (800) 877-4253; *International Historical Statistics The Americas and Australasia.*

G.K. Hall and Company, 70 Lincoln Street, Boston, Massachusetts 02111 (617) 423-3990; *The World in Figures.*

Inter-American Development Bank, 1300 New York Avenue, NW, Washington, D.C. 20577 (202) 623-1753; *Economic and Social Progress in Latin America: Natural Resources.*

U.C.L.A. Latin American Center Publications, University of California, Los Angeles, California 90024 (310) 825-6634; *Statistical Abstract of Latin America.*

PANAMA - CONSTRUCTION INDUSTRY

The Economist Intelligence Unit, 111 West 57th Street, New York, New York 10019 (800) 938-4685; *The New Latin America Market Atlas.*

Facts on File, 460 Park Avenue South, New York, New York 10016 (800) 443-8323; *The New Book of World Rankings*.

Inter-American Development Bank, 1300 New York Avenue, NW, Washington, D.C. 20577 (202) 623-1753; *Economic and Social Progress in Latin America*.

Statistical Office of the United Nations, Publishing Service, New York, New York 10017 (800) 253-9646; *Statistical Yearbook*.

U.C.L.A. Latin American Center Publications, University of California, Los Angeles, California 90024 (310) 825-6634; *Statistical Abstract of Latin America*.

PANAMA - CONSUMER PRICE INDEX

G.K. Hall and Company, 70 Lincoln Street, Boston, Massachusetts 02111 (617) 423-3990; *The World in Figures*.

Statistical Office of the United Nations, Publishing Service, New York, New York 10017 (800) 253-9646; *Statistical Yearbook*.

PANAMA - CONSUMER PRICES

The Economist Intelligence Unit, 111 West 57th Street, New York, New York 10019 (800) 938-4685; *The New Latin America Market Atlas*.

International Labour Office, I.L.O. Publications, CH-1211, Geneva 22, Switzerland; *Yearbook of Labour Statistics*.

International Monetary Fund, 700 Nineteenth Street, NW, Washington, D.C. 20431 (202) 623-7000; *International Financial Statistics*.

Organization of American States (OAS), General Secretariat, Washington, D.C. 20006 (202) 458-3533; *Statistical Bulletin of the OAS*.

Times Books, 201 East 50th Street, New York, New York 10022 (212) 751-2600; *The Economist Book of Vital World Statistics*.

U.C.L.A. Latin American Center Publications, University of California, Los Angeles, California 90024 (310) 825-6634; *Statistical Abstract of Latin America*.

PANAMA - CONSUMPTION

The Economist Intelligence Unit, 111 West 57th Street, New York, New York 10019 (800) 938-4685; *The New Latin America Market Atlas*.

G.K. Hall and Company, 70 Lincoln Street, Boston, Massachusetts 02111 (617) 423-3990; *The World in Figures*.

Inter-American Development Bank, 1300 New York Avenue, NW, Washington, D.C. 20577 (202) 623-1753; *Economic and Social Progress in Latin America*.

Statistical Office of the United Nations, Publishing Service, New York, New York 10017 (800) 253-9646; *Statistical Yearbook for Latin America and the Caribbean*.

PANAMA - COOPERATIVES

U.C.L.A. Latin American Center Publications, University of California, Los Angeles, California 90024 (310) 825-6634; *Statistical Abstract of Latin America*.

PANAMA - COPPER PRODUCTION AND CONSUMPTION - See PAKISTAN - MINING AND MINERAL PRODUCTS

PANAMA - CORN PRODUCTION - See PANAMA - CROPS

PANAMA - CORPORATE INCOME TAXES - See PANAMA - TAXATION

PANAMA - CORPORATE TAXES - See PANAMA - TAXATION

PANAMA - COTTON PRODUCTION - See PANAMA - CROPS

PANAMA - CRIME

Yale University Press, Yale Station, New Haven, Connecticut 06520 (203) 432-0940; *Violence and Crime in Cross-National Perspective*.

PANAMA - CROPS

The Economist Intelligence Unit, 111 West 57th Street, New York, New York 10019 (800) 938-4685; *The New Latin America Market Atlas*.

Facts on File, 460 Park Avenue South, New York, New York 10016 (800) 443-8323; *The New Book of World Rankings*.

Food and Agricultural Organization of the United Nations (FAO) Via delle Terme di Caracalla, 00100 Rome, Italy (Telephone Number in U.S. (202) 653-2400; *Production Yearbook, and The State of Food and Agriculture*.

G.K. Hall and Company, 70 Lincoln Street, Boston, Massachusetts 02111 (617) 423-3990; *The World in Figures*

International Monetary Fund, 700 Nineteenth Street, NW, Washington, D.C. 20431 (202) 623-7000; *International Financial Statistics*.

Organization of American States (OAS), General Secretariat, Washington, D.C. 20006 (202) 458-3533; *Statistical Bulletin of the OAS*.

Statistical Office of the United Nations, Publishing Service, New York, New York 10017 (800) 253-9646; *Statistical Yearbook*.

U.C.L.A. Latin American Center Publications, University of California, Los Angeles, California 90024 (310) 825-6634; *Statistical Abstract of Latin America*.

PANAMA - CUSTOMS DUTIES

G.K. Hall and Company, 70 Lincoln Street, Boston, Massachusetts 02111 (617) 423-3990; *The World in Figures*.

Inter-American Development Bank, 1300 New York Avenue, NW, Washington, D.C. 20577 (202) 623-1753; *Economic and Social Progress in Latin America*.

International Monetary Fund, 700 Nineteenth Street, NW, Washington, D.C. 20431 (202) 623-7000; *Government Finance Statistics Yearbook*.

PANAMA - DAIRY PRODUCTS

Facts on File, 460 Park Avenue South, New York, New York 10016 (800) 443-8323; *The New Book of World Rankings*.

Food and Agricultural Organization of the United Nations (FAO) Via delle Terme di Caracalla, 00100 Rome, Italy (Telephone Number in

U.S. (202) 653-2400); *Production Yearbook*, and *The State of Food and Agriculture*.

Statistical Office of the United Nations, Publishing Service, New York, New York 10017 (800) 253-9646; *Statistical Yearbook*.

U.C.L.A. Latin American Center Publications, University of California, Los Angeles, California 90024 (310) 825-6634; *Statistical Abstract of Latin America*.

PANAMA - DEATH RATES

G.K. Hall and Company, 70 Lincoln Street, Boston, Massachusetts 02111 (617) 423-3990; *The World in Figures*.

Statistical Office of the United Nations, Publishing Service, New York, New York 10017 (800) 253-9646; *Statistical Yearbook*, and *Statistical Yearbook for Latin America and the Caribbean*.

Times Books, 201 East 50th Street, New York, New York 10022 (212) 751-2600; *The Economist Book of Vital World Statistics*.

World Health Organization, Office of Publications, Avenue Appia, CH-1211 Geneva 27, Switzerland (Telephone Number in U.S. (518) 436-9686); *World Health Statistics Annual*.

PANAMA - DEBT

The Economist Intelligence Unit, 111 West 57th Street, New York, New York 10019 (800) 938-4685; *The New Latin America Market Atlas*.

PANAMA - DEFENSE

The Economist Intelligence Unit, 111 West 57th Street, New York, New York 10019 (800) 938-4685; *The New Latin America Market Atlas*.

PANAMA - DEFENSE EXPENDITURES

G.K. Hall and Company, 70 Lincoln Street, Boston, Massachusetts 02111 (617) 423-3990; *The World in Figures*.

International Monetary Fund, 700 Nineteenth Street, NW, Washington, D.C. 20431 (202) 623-7000; *Government Finance Statistics Yearbook*.

U.S. Arms Control and Disarmament Agency, 320 Twenty-first Street, NW, Washington, D.C. 20451 (202) 647-8677; *World Military Expenditures and Arms Transfers*.

PANAMA - DEMOGRAPHY

The Economist Intelligence Unit, 111 West 57th Street, New York, New York 10019 (800) 938-4685; *The World Market Atlas*.

Facts on File, 460 Park Avenue South, New York, New York 10016 (800) 443-8323; *The New Book of World Rankings*.

G.K. Hall and Company, 70 Lincoln Street, Boston, Massachusetts 02111 (617) 423-3990; *The World in Figures*.

PANAMA - DEVELOPMENT ASSISTANCE

G.K. Hall and Company, 70 Lincoln Street, Boston, Massachusetts 02111 (617) 423-3990; *The World in Figures*.

Inter-American Development Bank, 1300 New York Avenue, NW, Washington, D.C. 20577 (202) 623-1753; *Economic and Social*

Progress in Latin America.

Statistical Office of the United Nations, Publishing Service, New York, New York 10017 (800) 253-9646; *Statistical Yearbook*.

PANAMA - DIAMOND PRODUCTION - See PANAMA - MINING AND MINERAL PRODUCTS

PANAMA - DISCOUNT RATES

Inter-American Development Bank, 1300 New York Avenue, NW, Washington, D.C. 20577 (202) 623-1753; *Economic and Social Progress in Latin America*.

PANAMA - DISEASES

G.K. Hall and Company, 70 Lincoln Street, Boston, Massachusetts 02111 (617) 423-3990; *The World in Figures*.

World Health Organization, Office of Publications, Avenue Appia, CH-1211 Geneva 27, Switzerland (Telephone Number in U.S. (518) 436-9686); *World Health Statistics Annual*.

PANAMA - DIVORCE RATES

Facts on File, 460 Park Avenue South, New York, New York 10016 (800) 443-8323; *The New Book of World Rankings*.

Statistical Office of the United Nations, Publishing Service, New York, New York 10017 (800) 253-9646; *Demographic Yearbook*, and *Statistical Yearbook*.

PANAMA - DUCKS - See PANAMA - LIVESTOCK AND POULTRY

PANAMA - ECONOMY

Euromonitor Publications Limited, 87-88 Turnmill Street, London EC1M 5QU, England; *International Marketing Data and Statistics*.

Facts on File, 460 Park Avenue South, New York, New York 10016 (800) 443-8323; *The New Book of World Rankings*.

G.K. Hall and Company, 70 Lincoln Street, Boston, Massachusetts 02111 (617) 423-3990; *The World in Figures*.

Inter-American Development Bank, 1300 New York Avenue, NW, Washington, D.C. 20577 (202) 623-1753; *Economic and Social Progress in Latin America*.

Organization of American States (OAS), General Secretariat, Washington, D.C. 20006 (202) 458-3533; *Statistical Bulletin of the OAS*.

Statistical Office of the United Nations, Publishing Service, New York, New York 10017 (800) 253-9646; *Economic Survey of Latin America and the Caribbean*.

U.C.L.A. Latin American Center Publications, University of California, Los Angeles, California 90024 (310) 825-6634; *Statistical Abstract of Latin America*.

PANAMA - EDUCATION

The Economist Intelligence Unit, 111 West 57th Street, New York, New York 10019 (800) 938-4685; *The New Latin America Market Atlas*, and *The World Market Atlas*.

Facts on File, 460 Park Avenue South, New York, New York 10016 (800) 443-8323; *The New Book of World Rankings*.

Gale Research Incorporated, 835 Penobscot Building, Detroit, Michigan 48226 (800) 877-4253; *International Historical Statistics The Americas and Australasia.*

G.K. Hall and Company, 70 Lincoln Street, Boston, Massachusetts 02111 (617) 423-3990; *The World in Figures.*

International Monetary Fund, 700 Nineteenth Street, NW, Washington, D.C. 20431 (202) 623-7000; *Government Finance Statistics Yearbook.*

Statistical Office of the United Nations, Publishing Service, New York, New York 10017 (800) 253-9646; *Statistical Yearbook for Latin America and the Caribbean.*

Times Books, 201 East 50th Street, New York, New York 10022 (212) 751-2600; *The Economist Book of Vital World Statistics.*

U.C.L.A. Latin American Center Publications, University of California, Los Angeles, California 90024 (310) 825-6634; *Statistical Abstract of Latin America.*

United Nations Educational, Scientific and Cultural Organization (UNESCO), 7 Place de Fontenoy, F-75700 Paris, France (Telephone Number in U.S. (212) 963-5981); *Statistical Yearbook.*

The World Bank, 1818 H Street, NW, Washington, D.C. 20433 (202) 477-1234; *World Tables.*

PANAMA - EGG PRODUCTION AND CONSUMPTION - See PANAMA - DAIRY PRODUCTS

PANAMA - ELECTRICITY

The Economist Intelligence Unit, 111 West 57th Street, New York, New York 10019 (800) 938-4685; *The New Latin America Market Atlas.*

Facts on File, 460 Park Avenue South, New York, New York 10016 (800) 443-8323; *The New Book of World Rankings.*

Inter-American Development Bank, 1300 New York Avenue, NW, Washington, D.C. 20577 (202) 623-1753; *Economic and Social Progress in Latin America.*

Organization of American States (OAS), General Secretariat, Washington, D.C. 20006 (202) 458-3533; *Statistical Bulletin of the OAS.*

Statistical Office of the United Nations, Publishing Service, New York, New York 10017 (800) 253-9646; *Statistical Yearbook.*

PANAMA - EMPLOYMENT

Euromonitor Publications Limited, 87-88 Turnmill Street, London EC1M 5QU, England; *International Marketing Data and Statistics.*

Facts on File, 460 Park Avenue South, New York, New York 10016 (800) 443-8323; *The New Book of World Rankings.*

International Labour Office, I.L.O. Publications, CH-1211, Geneva 22, Switzerland; *Yearbook of Labour Statistics.*

Statistical Office of the United Nations, Publishing Service, New York, New York 10017 (800) 253-9646; *Statistical Yearbook,* and *Statistical Yearbook for Latin America and the Caribbean.*

U.C.L.A. Latin American Center Publications, University of California, Los Angeles, California 90024 (310) 825-6634; *Statistical*

Abstract of Latin America.

PANAMA - ENERGY

The Economist Intelligence Unit, 111 West 57th Street, New York, New York 10019 (800) 938-4685; *The New Latin America Market Atlas.*

Facts on File, 460 Park Avenue South, New York, New York 10016 (800) 443-8323; *The New Book of World Rankings.*

Food and Agricultural Organization of the United Nations (FAO) Via delle Terme di Caracalla, 00100 Rome, Italy (Telephone Number in U.S. (202) 653-2400); *The State of Food and Agriculture.*

G.K. Hall and Company, 70 Lincoln Street, Boston, Massachusetts 02111 (617) 423-3990; *The World in Figures.*

Statistical Office of the United Nations, Publishing Service, New York, New York 10017 (800) 253-9646; *Energy Statistics Yearbook, Statistical Yearbook, Statistical Yearbook for Latin America and the Caribbean,* and *World Energy Supplies.*

Times Books, 201 East 50th Street, New York, New York 10022 (212) 751-2600; *The Economist Book of Vital World Statistics.*

U.C.L.A. Latin American Center Publications, University of California, Los Angeles, California 90024 (310) 825-6634; *Statistical Abstract of Latin America.*

PANAMA - EXCHANGE RATES

Euromonitor Publications Limited, 87-88 Turnmill Street, London EC1M 5QU, England; *International Marketing Data and Statistics.*

Inter-American Development Bank, 1300 New York Avenue, NW, Washington, D.C. 20577 (202) 623-1753; *Economic and Social Progress in Latin America.*

International Civil Aviation Organization, 1000 Sherbrooke Street, West, Montreal, Quebec, Canada H3A 2R2 (514) 285-8219; *Civil Aviation Statistics of the World.*

International Monetary Fund, 700 Nineteenth Street, NW, Washington, D.C. 20431 (202) 623-7000; *International Financial Statistics.*

Organization of American States (OAS), General Secretariat, Washington, D.C. 20006 (202) 458-3533; *Statistical Bulletin of the OAS.*

Statistical Office of the United Nations, Publishing Service, New York, New York 10017 (800) 253-9646; *Statistical Yearbook.*

U.C.L.A. Latin American Center Publications, University of California, Los Angeles, California 90024 (310) 825-6634; *Statistical Abstract of Latin America.*

PANAMA - EXCHANGE TAXES

International Monetary Fund, 700 Nineteenth Street, NW, Washington, D.C. 20431 (202) 623-7000; *Government Finance Statistics Yearbook.*

PANAMA - EXCISE TAXES - See PANAMA - TAXATION

PANAMA - EXPENDITURES

Organization of American States (OAS), General Secretariat, Washington, D.C. 20006 (202) 458-3533; *Statistical Bulletin of the OAS*.

PANAMA - EXPORTS

The Economist Intelligence Unit, 111 West 57th Street, New York, New York 10019 (800) 938-4685; *The New Latin America Market Atlas*, and *The World Market Atlas*.

Euromonitor Publications Limited, 87-88 Turnmill Street, London EC1M 5QU, England; *International Marketing Data and Statistics*.

Food and Agricultural Organization of the United Nations (FAO) Via delle Terme di Caracalla, 00100 Rome, Italy (Telephone Number in U.S. (202) 653-2400); *The State of Food and Agriculture*.

G.K. Hall and Company, 70 Lincoln Street, Boston, Massachusetts 02111 (617) 423-3990; *The World in Figures*.

Inter-American Development Bank, 1300 New York Avenue, NW, Washington, D.C. 20577 (202) 623-1753; *Economic and Social Progress in Latin America*.

International Monetary Fund, 700 Nineteenth Street, NW, Washington, D.C. 20431 (202) 623-7000; *Direction of Trade Statistics*, *Government Finance Statistics Yearbook*, and *International Financial Statistics*.

Organization of American States (OAS), General Secretariat, Washington, D.C. 20006 (202) 458-3533; *Statistical Bulletin of the OAS*.

Statistical Office of the United Nations, Publishing Service, New York, New York 10017 (800) 253-9646; *Statistical Yearbook for Latin America and the Caribbean*.

Times Books, 201 East 50th Street, New York, New York 10022 (212) 751-2600; *The Economist Book of Vital World Statistics*.

The World Bank, 1818 H Street, NW, Washington, D.C. 20433 (202) 477-1234; *World Tables*.

PANAMA - EXTERNAL FINANCING

Inter-American Development Bank, 1300 New York Avenue, NW, Washington, D.C. 20577 (202) 623-1753; *Economic and Social Progress in Latin America*.

Statistical Office of the United Nations, Publishing Service, New York, New York 10017 (800) 253-9646; *Statistical Yearbook for Latin America and the Caribbean*.

PANAMA - EXTERNAL INDEBTEDNESS

Inter-American Development Bank, 1300 New York Avenue, NW, Washington, D.C. 20577 (202) 623-1753; *Economic and Social Progress in Latin America*.

Statistical Office of the United Nations, Publishing Service, New York, New York 10017 (800) 253-9646; *Statistical Yearbook for Latin America and the Caribbean*.

The World Bank, 1818 H Street, NW, Washington, D.C. 20433 (202) 477-1234; *World Tables*.

PANAMA - EXTERNAL TRADE

Food and Agricultural Organization of the United Nations (FAO) Via delle Terme di Caracalla, 00100 Rome, Italy (Telephone Number in U.S. (202) 653-2400); *The State of Food and Agriculture*, and *Trade Yearbook*.

Gale Research Incorporated, 835 Penobscot Building, Detroit, Michigan 48226 (800) 877-4253; *International Historical Statistics The Americas and Australasia*.

G.K. Hall and Company, 70 Lincoln Street, Boston, Massachusetts 02111 (617) 423-3990; *The World in Figures*.

Inter-American Development Bank, 1300 New York Avenue, NW, Washington, D.C. 20577 (202) 623-1753; *Economic and Social Progress in Latin America*.

Statistical Office of the United Nations, Publishing Service, New York, New York 10017 (800) 253-9646; *Statistical Yearbook*, and *Statistical Yearbook for Latin America and the Caribbean*.

PANAMA - FAMILY PLANNING

U.C.L.A. Latin American Center Publications, University of California, Los Angeles, California 90024 (310) 825-6634; *Statistical Abstract of Latin America*.

PANAMA - FARM CROPS - See PANAMA - CROPS

PANAMA - FEMALE WORKING POPULATION - See PANAMA - EMPLOYMENT

PANAMA - FERTILITY RATES

Facts on File, 460 Park Avenue South, New York, New York 10016 (800) 443-8323; *The New Book of World Rankings*.

Times Books, 201 East 50th Street, New York, New York 10022 (212) 751-2600; *The Economist Book of Vital World Statistics*.

The World Bank, 1818 H Street, NW, Washington, D.C. 20433 (202) 477-1234; *World Tables*.

PANAMA - FERTILIZER

The Economist Intelligence Unit, 111 West 57th Street, New York, New York 10019 (800) 938-4685; *The New Latin America Market Atlas*.

Food and Agricultural Organization of the United Nations (FAO), Via delle Terme di Caracalla, 00100 Rome, Italy (Telephone Number in U.S. (202) 653-2400); *Fertilizer Yearbook*, and *The State of Food and Agriculture*.

Statistical Office of the United Nations, Publishing Service, New York, New York 10017 (800) 253-9646; *Statistical Yearbook*.

PANAMA - FETAL MORTALITY

Statistical Office of the United Nations, Publishing Service, New York, New York 10017 (800) 253-9646; *Demographic Yearbook*.

World Health Organization, Office of Publications, Avenue Appia, CH-1211 Geneva 27, Switzerland (Telephone Number in U.S. (518) 436-9686); *World Health Statistics Annual*.

PANAMA - FINANCE

Facts on File, 460 Park Avenue South, New York, New York 10016 (800) 443-8323; *The New Book of World Rankings.*

Gale Research Incorporated, 835 Penobscot Building, Detroit, Michigan 48226 (800) 877-4253; *International Historical Statistics The Americas and Australasia.*

G.K. Hall and Company, 70 Lincoln Street, Boston, Massachusetts 02111 (617) 423-3990; *The World in Figures.*

Inter-American Development Bank, 1300 New York Avenue, NW, Washington, D.C. 20577 (202) 623-1753; *Economic and Social Progress in Latin America.*

International Monetary Fund, 700 Nineteenth Street, NW, Washington, D.C. 20431 (202) 623-7000; *Government Finance Statistics Yearbook,* and *International Financial Statistics.*

Organization of American States (OAS), General Secretariat, Washington, D.C. 20006 (202) 458-3533; *Statistical Bulletin of the OAS.*

U.C.L.A. Latin American Center Publications, University of California, Los Angeles, California 90024 (310) 825-6634; *Statistical Abstract of Latin America.*

PANAMA - FISHERIES

Facts on File, 460 Park Avenue South, New York, New York 10016 (800) 443-8323; *The New Book of World Rankings.*

Food and Agricultural Organization of the United Nations (FAO) Via delle Terme di Caracalla, 00100 Rome, Italy (Telephone Number in U.S. (202) 653-2400); *The State of Food and Agriculture,* and *Yearbook of Fishery Statistics.*

Inter-American Development Bank, 1300 New York Avenue, NW, Washington, D.C. 20577 (202) 623-1753; *Economic and Social Progress in Latin America.*

Statistical Office of the United Nations, Publishing Service, New York, New York 10017 (800) 253-9646; *Statistical Yearbook.*

U.C.L.A. Latin American Center Publications, University of California, Los Angeles, California 90024 (310) 825-6634; *Statistical Abstract of Latin America.*

PANAMA - FLOUR PRODUCTION

Statistical Office of the United Nations, Publishing Service, New York, New York 10017 (800) 253-9646; *Statistical Yearbook.*

PANAMA - FOOD

Food and Agricultural Organization of the United Nations (FAO) Via delle Terme di Caracalla, 00100 Rome, Italy (Telephone Number in U.S. (202) 653-2400); *Production Yearbook,* and *The State of Food and Agriculture.*

G.K. Hall and Company, 70 Lincoln Street, Boston, Massachusetts 02111 (617) 423-3990; *The World in Figures.*

PANAMA - FOOTWEAR PRODUCTION

Statistical Office of the United Nations, Publishing Service, New York, New York 10017 (800) 253-9646; *Statistical Yearbook.*

PANAMA - FOREIGN AID

G.K. Hall and Company, 70 Lincoln Street, Boston, Massachusetts 02111 (617) 423-3990; *The World in Figures.*

Inter-American Development Bank, 1300 New York Avenue, NW, Washington, D.C. 20577 (202) 623-1753; *Economic and Social Progress in Latin America.*

PANAMA - FOREIGN DEBT

The Economist Intelligence Unit, 111 West 57th Street, New York, New York 10019 (800) 938-4685; *The New Latin America Market Atlas.*

Inter-American Development Bank, 1300 New York Avenue, NW, Washington, D.C. 20577 (202) 623-1753; *Economic and Social Progress in Latin America.*

International Monetary Fund, 700 Nineteenth Street, NW, Washington, D.C. 20431 (202) 623-7000; *Government Finance Statistics Yearbook.*

PANAMA - FOREIGN INDEBTEDNESS

Inter-American Development Bank, 1300 New York Avenue, NW, Washington, D.C. 20577 (202) 623-1753; *Economic and Social Progress in Latin America.*

Statistical Office of the United Nations, Publishing Service, New York, New York 10017 (800) 253-9646; *Economic Survey of Latin America and the Caribbean.*

PANAMA - FOREIGN INVESTMENT

The Economist Intelligence Unit, 111 West 57th Street, New York, New York 10019 (800) 938-4685; *The New Latin America Market Atlas.*

PANAMA - FOREIGN TRADE

The Economist Intelligence Unit, 111 West 57th Street, New York, New York 10019 (800) 938-4685; *The New Latin America Market Atlas.*

Euromonitor Publications Limited, 87-88 Turnmill Street, London EC1M 5QU, England; *International Marketing Data and Statistics.*

Facts on File, 460 Park Avenue South, New York, New York 10016 (800) 443-8323; *The New Book of World Rankings.*

Food and Agricultural Organization of the United Nations (FAO) Via delle Terme di Caracalla, 00100 Rome, Italy (Telephone Number in U.S. (202) 653-2400); *The State of Food and Agriculture.*

G.K. Hall and Company, 70 Lincoln Street, Boston, Massachusetts 02111 (617) 423-3990; *The World in Figures.*

Inter-American Development Bank, 1300 New York Avenue, NW, Washington, D.C. 20577 (202) 623-1753; *Economic and Social Progress in Latin America.*

International Monetary Fund, 700 Nineteenth Street, NW, Washington, D.C. 20431 (202) 623-7000; *International Financial Statistics.*

Statistical Office of the United Nations, Publishing Service, New York, New York 10017 (800) 253-9646; *Economic Survey of Latin America and the Caribbean, International Trade Statistics Yearbook,* and *Statistical Yearbook.*

U.C.L.A. Latin American Center Publications, University of California, Los Angeles, California 90024 (310) 825-6634; *Statistical Abstract of Latin America.*

The World Bank, 1818 H Street, NW, Washington, D.C. 20433 (202) 477-1234; *World Tables.*

PANAMA - FORESTRY AND FOREST PRODUCTS

The Economist Intelligence Unit, 111 West 57th Street, New York, New York 10019 (800) 938-4685; *The New Latin America Market Atlas.*

Facts on File, 460 Park Avenue South, New York, New York 10016 (800) 443-8323; *The New Book of World Rankings.*

Food and Agricultural Organization of the United Nations (FAO) Via delle Terme di Caracalla, 00100 Rome, Italy (Telephone Number in U.S. (202) 653-2400); *The State of Food and Agriculture,* and *Yearbook of Forest Products.*

G.K. Hall and Company, 70 Lincoln Street, Boston, Massachusetts 02111 (617) 423-3990; *The World in Figures.*

Inter-American Development Bank, 1300 New York Avenue, NW, Washington, D.C. 20577 (202) 623-1753; *Economic and Social Progress in Latin America.*

Statistical Office of the United Nations, Publishing Service, New York, New York 10017 (800) 253-9646; *Statistical Yearbook.*

U.C.L.A. Latin American Center Publications, University of California, Los Angeles, California 90024 (310) 825-6634; *Statistical Abstract of Latin America.*

United Nations Educational, Scientific and Cultural Organization (UNESCO), 7 Place de Fontenoy, F-75700 Paris, France (Telephone Number in U.S. (212) 963-5981); *Statistical Yearbook.*

PANAMA - GAS PRODUCTION - See PANAMA - MINING AND MINERAL PRODUCTS

PANAMA - GENERAL INDUSTRIAL STATISTICS

Statistical Office of the United Nations, Publishing Service, New York, New York 10017 (800) 253-9646; *Industrial Statistics Yearbook.*

PANAMA - GENERAL MORTALITY

Statistical Office of the United Nations, Publishing Service, New York, New York 10017 (800) 253-9646; *Demographic Yearbook.*

World Health Organization, Office of Publications, Avenue Appia, CH-1211 Geneva 27, Switzerland (Telephone Number in U.S. (518) 436-9686); *World Health Statistics Annual.*

PANAMA - GEOGRAPHIC DATA

Facts on File, 460 Park Avenue South, New York, New York 10016 (800) 443-8323; *The New Book of World Rankings.*

U.C.L.A. Latin American Center Publications, University of California, Los Angeles, California 90024 (310) 825-6634; *Statistical Abstract of Latin America.*

PANAMA - GOATS - See PANAMA - LIVESTOCK AND POULTRY

PANAMA - GOLD HOLDINGS

International Monetary Fund, 700 Nineteenth Street, NW, Washington, D.C. 20431 (202) 623-7000; *International Financial Statistics.*

Statistical Office of the United Nations, Publishing Service, New York, New York 10017 (800) 253-9646; *Statistical Yearbook.*

The World Bank, 1818 H Street, NW, Washington, D.C. 20433 (202) 477-1234; *World Tables.*

PANAMA - GOLD PRODUCTION AND CONSUMPTION - See PANAMA - MINING AND MINERAL PRODUCTS

PANAMA - GOLD RESERVES

The Economist Intelligence Unit, 111 West 57th Street, New York, New York 10019 (800) 938-4685; *The New Latin America Market Atlas.*

PANAMA - GOVERNMENT

G.K. Hall and Company, 70 Lincoln Street, Boston, Massachusetts 02111 (617) 423-3990; *The World in Figures.*

Inter-American Development Bank, 1300 New York Avenue, NW, Washington, D.C. 20577 (202) 623-1753; *Economic and Social Progress in Latin America.*

PANAMA - GOVERNMENT CONSUMPTION

Inter-American Development Bank, 1300 New York Avenue, NW, Washington, D.C. 20577 (202) 623-1753; *Economic and Social Progress in Latin America.*

PANAMA - GOVERNMENT EXPENDITURES

Inter-American Development Bank, 1300 New York Avenue, NW, Washington, D.C. 20577 (202) 623-1753; *Economic and Social Progress in Latin America.*

International Monetary Fund, 700 Nineteenth Street, NW, Washington, D.C. 20431 (202) 623-7000; *Government Finance Statistics Yearbook.*

Times Books, 201 East 50th Street, New York, New York 10022 (212) 751-2600; *The Economist Book of Vital World Statistics.*

The World Bank, 1818 H Street, NW, Washington, D.C. 20433 (202) 477-1234; *World Tables.*

PANAMA - GOVERNMENT FINANCES

Inter-American Development Bank, 1300 New York Avenue, NW, Washington, D.C. 20577 (202) 623-1753; *Economic and Social Progress in Latin America.*

International Monetary Fund, 700 Nineteenth Street, NW, Washington, D.C. 20431 (202) 623-7000; *International Financial Statistics.*

Statistical Office of the United Nations, Publishing Service, New York, New York 10017 (800) 253-9646; *Statistical Yearbook.*

PANAMA - GOVERNMENT REVENUES

Inter-American Development Bank, 1300 New York Avenue, NW, Washington, D.C. 20577 (202) 623-1753; *Economic and Social Progress in Latin America.*

International Monetary Fund, 700 Nineteenth Street, NW, Washington, D.C. 20431 (202) 623-7000; *Government Finance Statistics Yearbook.*

The World Bank, 1818 H Street, NW, Washington, D.C. 20433 (202) 477-1234; *World Tables.*

PANAMA - GRAIN PRODUCTION - See PANAMA - CROPS

PANAMA - GRANTS

International Monetary Fund, 700 Nineteenth Street, NW, Washington, D.C. 20431 (202) 623-7000; *Government Finance Statistics Yearbook.*

PANAMA - GROSS DOMESTIC PRODUCT

The Economist Intelligence Unit, 111 West 57th Street, New York, New York 10019 (800) 938-4685; *The New Latin America Market Atlas,* and *The World Market Atlas.*

Euromonitor Publications Limited, 87-88 Turnmill Street, London EC1M 5QU, England; *International Marketing Data and Statistics.*

Facts on File, 460 Park Avenue South, New York, New York 10016 (800) 443-8323; *The New Book of World Rankings.*

G.K. Hall and Company, 70 Lincoln Street, Boston, Massachusetts 02111 (617) 423-3990; *The World in Figures.*

Inter-American Development Bank, 1300 New York Avenue, NW, Washington, D.C. 20577 (202) 623-1753; *Economic and Social Progress in Latin America.*

Organization of American States (OAS), General Secretariat, Washington, D.C. 20006 (202) 458-3533; *Statistical Bulletin of the OAS.*

Statistical Office of the United Nations, Publishing Service, New York, New York 10017 (800) 253-9646; *Statistical Yearbook,* and *Statistical Yearbook for Latin America and the Caribbean.*

Times Books, 201 East 50th Street, New York, New York 10022 (212) 751-2600; *The Economist Book of Vital World Statistics.*

U.C.L.A. Latin American Center Publications, University of California, Los Angeles, California 90024 (310) 825-6634; *Statistical Abstract of Latin America.*

The World Bank, 1818 H Street, NW, Washington, D.C. 20433 (202) 477-1234; *World Tables.*

PANAMA - GROSS NATIONAL PRODUCT

Euromonitor Publications Limited, 87-88 Turnmill Street, London EC1M 5QU, England; *International Marketing Data and Statistics.*

Inter-American Development Bank, 1300 New York Avenue, NW, Washington, D.C. 20577 (202) 623-1753; *Economic and Social Progress in Latin America.*

U.S. Arms Control and Disarmament Agency, 320 Twenty-first Street, NW, Washington, D.C. 20451 (202) 647-8677; *World Military*

Expenditures and Arms Transfers.

The World Bank, 1818 H Street, NW, Washington, D.C. 20433 (202) 477-1234; *World Tables.*

PANAMA - HEALTH

The Economist Intelligence Unit, 111 West 57th Street, New York, New York 10019 (800) 938-4685; *The New Latin America Market Atlas.*

Facts on File, 460 Park Avenue South, New York, New York 10016 (800) 443-8323; *The New Book of World Rankings.*

G.K. Hall and Company, 70 Lincoln Street, Boston, Massachusetts 02111 (617) 423-3990; *The World in Figures.*

Statistical Office of the United Nations, Publishing Service, New York, New York 10017 (800) 253-9646; *Statistical Yearbook,* and *Statistical Yearbook for Latin America and the Caribbean.*

Times Books, 201 East 50th Street, New York, New York 10022 (212) 751-2600; *The Economist Book of Vital World Statistics.*

U.C.L.A. Latin American Center Publications, University of California, Los Angeles, California 90024 (310) 825-6634; *Statistical Abstract of Latin America.*

World Health Organization, Office of Publications, Avenue Appia, CH-1211 Geneva 27, Switzerland (Telephone Number in U.S. (518) 436-9686); *World Health Statistics Annual.*

PANAMA - HEALTH EXPENDITURES

International Monetary Fund, 700 Nineteenth Street, NW, Washington, D.C. 20431 (202) 623-7000; *Government Finance Statistics Yearbook.*

PANAMA - HIDE PRODUCTION

Food and Agricultural Organization of the United Nations (FAO), Via delle Terme di Caracalla, 00100 Rome, Italy (Telephone Number in U.S. (202) 653-2400); *Production Yearbook.*

PANAMA - HIGHWAYS

The Economist Intelligence Unit, 111 West 57th Street, New York, New York 10019 (800) 938-4685; *The New Latin America Market Atlas.*

G.K. Hall and Company, 70 Lincoln Street, Boston, Massachusetts 02111 (617) 423-3990; *The World in Figures.*

International Road Federation, 525 School Street, SW, Washington, D.C. 20024 (202) 554-2106; *World Road Statistics.*

PANAMA - HORSES - See PANAMA - LIVESTOCK AND POULTRY

PANAMA - HOURS OF WORK - See PANAMA - EMPLOYMENT

PANAMA - HOUSING AND HOUSING UNITS

Facts on File, 460 Park Avenue South, New York, New York 10016 (800) 443-8323; *The New Book of World Rankings.*

Statistical Office of the United Nations, Publishing Service, New York, New York 10017 (800) 253-9646; *Statistical Yearbook for Latin America and the Caribbean.*

U.C.L.A. Latin American Center Publications, University of California, Los Angeles, California 90024 (310) 825-6634; *Statistical Abstract of Latin America.*

PANAMA - HOUSING EXPENDITURES

International Monetary Fund, 700 Nineteenth Street, NW, Washington, D.C. 20431 (202) 623-7000; *Government Finance Statistics Yearbook.*

PANAMA - ILLITERACY RATES

The Economist Intelligence Unit, 111 West 57th Street, New York, New York 10019 (800) 938-4685; *The New Latin America Market Atlas.*

PANAMA - ILLITERATE POPULATION

The Economist Intelligence Unit, 111 West 57th Street, New York, New York 10019 (800) 938-4685; *The World Market Atlas.*

G.K. Hall and Company, 70 Lincoln Street, Boston, Massachusetts 02111 (617) 423-3990; *The World in Figures.*

Statistical Office of the United Nations, Publishing Service, New York, New York 10017 (800) 253-9646; *Statistical Yearbook for Latin America and the Caribbean.*

United Nations Educational, Scientific and Cultural Organization (UNESCO), 7 Place de Fontenoy, F-75700 Paris, France (Telephone Number in U.S. (212) 963-5981); *Statistical Yearbook.*

PANAMA - IMMIGRATION

U.C.L.A. Latin American Center Publications, University of California, Los Angeles, California 90024 (310) 825-6634; *Statistical Abstract of Latin America.*

PANAMA - IMPORTS

The Economist Intelligence Unit, 111 West 57th Street, New York, New York 10019 (800) 938-4685; *The New Latin America Market Atlas*, and *The World Market Atlas.*

Euromonitor Publications Limited, 87-88 Turnmill Street, London EC1M 5QU, England; *International Marketing Data and Statistics.*

Food and Agricultural Organization of the United Nations (FAO) Via delle Terme di Caracalla, 00100 Rome, Italy (Telephone Number in U.S. (202) 653-2400); *The State of Food and Agriculture.*

G.K. Hall and Company, 70 Lincoln Street, Boston, Massachusetts 02111 (617) 423-3990; *The World in Figures.*

Inter-American Development Bank, 1300 New York Avenue, NW, Washington, D.C. 20577 (202) 623-1753; *Economic and Social Progress in Latin America.*

International Monetary Fund, 700 Nineteenth Street, NW, Washington, D.C. 20431 (202) 623-7000; *Direction of Trade Statistics, Government Finance Statistics Yearbook*, and *International Financial Statistics.*

Organization of American States (OAS), General Secretariat, Washington, D.C. 20006 (202) 458-3533; *Statistical Bulletin of the OAS.*

Statistical Office of the United Nations, Publishing Service, New York, New York 10017 (800) 253-9646; *Statistical Yearbook for*

Latin America and the Caribbean, and *Trade in Manufactures of Developing Countries.*

Times Books, 201 East 50th Street, New York, New York 10022 (212) 751-2600; *The Economist Book of Vital World Statistics.*

The World Bank, 1818 H Street, NW, Washington, D.C. 20433 (202) 477-1234; *World Tables.*

PANAMA - INCOME DISTRIBUTION

Statistical Office of the United Nations, Publishing Service, New York, New York 10017 (800) 253-9646; *Statistical Yearbook for Latin America and the Caribbean.*

U.C.L.A. Latin American Center Publications, University of California, Los Angeles, California 90024 (310) 825-6634; *Statistical Abstract of Latin America.*

PANAMA - INCOME TAXES - See PANAMA - TAXATION

PANAMA - INDUSTRY

Euromonitor Publications Limited, 87-88 Turnmill Street, London EC1M 5QU, England; *International Marketing Data and Statistics.*

Facts on File, 460 Park Avenue South, New York, New York 10016 (800) 443-8323; *The New Book of World Rankings.*

Gale Research Incorporated, 835 Penobscot Building, Detroit, Michigan 48226 (800) 877-4253; *International Historical Statistics The Americas and Australasia.*

G.K. Hall and Company, 70 Lincoln Street, Boston, Massachusetts 02111 (617) 423-3990; *The World in Figures.*

International Labour Office, I.L.O. Publications, CH-1211, Geneva 22, Switzerland; *Yearbook of Labour Statistics.*

Statistical Office of the United Nations, Publishing Service, New York, New York 10017 (800) 253-9646; *Economic Survey of Latin America and the Caribbean*, and *Statistical Yearbook.*

Times Books, 201 East 50th Street, New York, New York 10022 (212) 751-2600; *The Economist Book of Vital World Statistics.*

U.C.L.A. Latin American Center Publications, University of California, Los Angeles, California 90024 (310) 825-6634; *Statistical Abstract of Latin America.*

The World Bank, 1818 H Street, NW, Washington, D.C. 20433 (202) 477-1234; *World Tables.*

World Intellectual Property Organization, 34 Chemin des Colombettes, CH-1211 Geneva 20, Switzerland; *Industrial Property Statistics.*

PANAMA - INFANT AND MATERNAL MORTALITY

The Economist Intelligence Unit, 111 West 57th Street, New York, New York 10019 (800) 938-4685; *The New Latin America Market Atlas.*

Statistical Office of the United Nations, Publishing Service, New York, New York 10017 (800) 253-9646; *Demographic Yearbook*, and *Statistical Yearbook.*

The World Bank, 1818 H Street, NW, Washington, D.C. 20433 (202) 477-1234; *World Tables.*

World Health Organization, Office of Publications, Avenue Appia, CH-1211 Geneva 27, Switzerland (Telephone Number in U.S. (518) 436-9686); *World Health Statistics Annual.*

PANAMA - INFLATIONARY FACTORS

Statistical Office of the United Nations, Publishing Service, New York, New York 10017 (800) 253-9646; *Economic Survey of Latin America and the Caribbean.*

PANAMA - INTEREST RATES

Inter-American Development Bank, 1300 New York Avenue, NW, Washington, D.C. 20577 (202) 623-1753; *Economic and Social Progress in Latin America.*

PANAMA - INTERNAL TRADE

Statistical Office of the United Nations, Publishing Service, New York, New York 10017 (800) 253-9646; *Statistical Yearbook.*

PANAMA - INTERNATIONAL FINANCE

Inter-American Development Bank, 1300 New York Avenue, NW, Washington, D.C. 20577 (202) 623-1753; *Economic and Social Progress in Latin America.*

U.C.L.A. Latin American Center Publications, University of California, Los Angeles, California 90024 (310) 825-6634; *Statistical Abstract of Latin America.*

PANAMA - INTERNATIONAL LIQUIDITY

Inter-American Development Bank, 1300 New York Avenue, NW, Washington, D.C. 20577 (202) 623-1753; *Economic and Social Progress in Latin America.*

International Monetary Fund, 700 Nineteenth Street, NW, Washington, D.C. 20431 (202) 623-7000; *International Financial Statistics.*

PANAMA - INTERNATIONAL RESERVES

Organization of American States (OAS), General Secretariat, Washington, D.C. 20006 (202) 458-3533; *Statistical Bulletin of the OAS.*

PANAMA - INTERNATIONAL RESERVES EXCLUDING GOLD

Inter-American Development Bank, 1300 New York Avenue, NW, Washington, D.C. 20577 (202) 623-1753; *Economic and Social Progress in Latin America.*

Statistical Office of the United Nations, Publishing Service, New York, New York 10017 (800) 253-9646; *Statistical Yearbook.*

The World Bank, 1818 H Street, NW, Washington, D.C. 20433 (202) 477-1234; *World Tables.*

PANAMA - INTERNATIONAL STATISTICS

Inter-American Development Bank, 1300 New York Avenue, NW, Washington, D.C. 20577 (202) 623-1753; *Economic and Social Progress in Latin America.*

U.C.L.A. Latin American Center Publications, University of California, Los Angeles, California 90024 (310) 825-6634; *Statistical Abstract of Latin America.*

PANAMA - INVESTMENTS

Inter-American Development Bank, 1300 New York Avenue, NW, Washington, D.C. 20577 (202) 623-1753; *Economic and Social Progress in Latin America.*

International Monetary Fund, 700 Nineteenth Street, NW, Washington, D.C. 20431 (202) 623-7000; *International Financial Statistics.*

Statistical Office of the United Nations, Publishing Service, New York, New York 10017 (800) 253-9646; *Statistical Yearbook for Latin America and the Caribbean.*

PANAMA - IRON ORE PRODUCTION AND CONSUMPTION - See PANAMA - MINING AND MINERAL PRODUCTS

PANAMA - IRRIGATION

Euromonitor Publications Limited, 87-88 Turnmill Street, London EC1M 5QU, England; *International Marketing Data and Statistics.*

Inter-American Development Bank, 1300 New York Avenue, NW, Washington, D.C. 20577 (202) 623-1753; *Economic and Social Progress in Latin America.*

PANAMA - LABOR FORCE

The Economist Intelligence Unit, 111 West 57th Street, New York, New York 10019 (800) 938-4685; *The New Latin America Market Atlas.*

Euromonitor Publications Limited, 87-88 Turnmill Street, London EC1M 5QU, England; *International Marketing Data and Statistics.*

Facts on File, 460 Park Avenue South, New York, New York 10016 (800) 443-8323; *The New Book of World Rankings.*

Food and Agricultural Organization of the United Nations (FAO) Via delle Terme di Caracalla, 00100 Rome, Italy (Telephone Number in U.S. (202) 653-2400); *The State of Food and Agriculture.*

Gale Research Incorporated, 835 Penobscot Building, Detroit, Michigan 48226 (800) 877-4253; *International Historical Statistics The Americas and Australasia.*

G.K. Hall and Company, 70 Lincoln Street, Boston, Massachusetts 02111 (617) 423-3990; *The World in Figures.*

The World Bank, 1818 H Street, NW, Washington, D.C. 20433 (202) 477-1234; *World Tables.*

PANAMA - LABOR PRODUCTIVITY

International Labour Office, I.L.O. Publications, CH-1211, Geneva 22, Switzerland; *Yearbook of Labour Statistics.*

PANAMA - LAND AREA

The Economist Intelligence Unit, 111 West 57th Street, New York, New York 10019 (800) 938-4685; *The New Latin America Market Atlas.*

PANAMA - LAND USE

Euromonitor Publications Limited, 87-88 Turnmill Street, London EC1M 5QU, England; *International Marketing Data and Statistics.*

Food and Agricultural Organization of the United Nations (FAO), Via delle Terme di Caracalla, 00100 Rome, Italy (Telephone Number in U.S. (202) 653-2400); *Production Yearbook*.

G.K. Hall and Company, 70 Lincoln Street, Boston, Massachusetts 02111 (617) 423-3990; *The World in Figures*.

Inter-American Development Bank, 1300 New York Avenue, NW, Washington, D.C. 20577 (202) 623-1753; *Economic and Social Progress in Latin America*.

PANAMA - LIBRARIES

Facts on File, 460 Park Avenue South, New York, New York 10016 (800) 443-8323; *The New Book of World Rankings*.

United Nations Educational, Scientific and Cultural Organization (UNESCO), 7 Place de Fontenoy, F-75700 Paris, France (Telephone Number in U.S. (212) 963-5981); *Statistical Yearbook*.

PANAMA - LIFE EXPECTANCY RATE

The Economist Intelligence Unit, 111 West 57th Street, New York, New York 10019 (800) 938-4685; *The New Latin America Market Atlas*.

PANAMA - LIVESTOCK AND POULTRY

Euromonitor Publications Limited, 87-88 Turnmill Street, London EC1M 5QU, England; *International Marketing Data and Statistics*.

Facts on File, 460 Park Avenue South, New York, New York 10016 (800) 443-8323; *The New Book of World Rankings*.

Food and Agricultural Organization of the United Nations (FAO), Via delle Terme di Caracalla, 00100 Rome, Italy (Telephone Number in U.S. (202) 653-2400); *Production Yearbook*, and *The State of Food and Agriculture*.

G.K. Hall and Company, 70 Lincoln Street, Boston, Massachusetts 02111 (617) 423-3990; *The World in Figures*.

Statistical Office of the United Nations, Publishing Service, New York, New York 10017 (800) 253-9646; *Statistical Yearbook*.

PANAMA - LIVING LEVELS

G.K. Hall and Company, 70 Lincoln Street, Boston, Massachusetts 02111 (617) 423-3990; *The World in Figures*.

Statistical Office of the United Nations, Publishing Service, New York, New York 10017 (800) 253-9646; *Statistical Yearbook for Latin America and the Caribbean*.

Times Books, 201 East 50th Street, New York, New York 10022 (212) 751-2600; *The Economist Book of Vital World Statistics*.

PANAMA - MAIL - NUMBER OF ITEMS SENT AND RECEIVED

Statistical Office of the United Nations, Publishing Service, New York, New York 10017 (800) 253-9646; *Statistical Yearbook*.

PANAMA - MAIN ECONOMIC INDICATORS - See PANAMA - ECONOMY

PANAMA - MANUFACTURING

The Economist Intelligence Unit, 111 West 57th Street, New York, New York 10019 (800) 938-4685; *The New Latin America Market Atlas*.

Facts on File, 460 Park Avenue South, New York, New York 10016 (800) 443-8323; *The New Book of World Rankings*.

G.K. Hall and Company, 70 Lincoln Street, Boston, Massachusetts 02111 (617) 423-3990; *The World in Figures*.

Inter-American Development Bank, 1300 New York Avenue, NW, Washington, D.C. 20577 (202) 623-1753; *Economic and Social Progress in Latin America*.

Statistical Office of the United Nations, Publishing Service, New York, New York 10017 (800) 253-9646; *Statistical Yearbook*, and *Statistical Yearbook for Latin America and the Caribbean*.

Times Books, 201 East 50th Street, New York, New York 10022 (212) 751-2600; *The Economist Book of Vital World Statistics*.

The World Bank, 1818 H Street, NW, Washington, D.C. 20433 (202) 477-1234; *World Tables*.

PANAMA - MARRIAGE RATES

Facts on File, 460 Park Avenue South, New York, New York 10016 (800) 443-8323; *The New Book of World Rankings*.

Statistical Office of the United Nations, Publishing Service, New York, New York 10017 (800) 253-9646; *Demographic Yearbook*, and *Statistical Yearbook*.

PANAMA - MEAT PRODUCTION - See PANAMA - LIVESTOCK AND POULTRY

PANAMA - MEDICAL PERSONNEL

U.C.L.A. Latin American Center Publications, University of California, Los Angeles, California 90024 (310) 825-6634; *Statistical Abstract of Latin America*.

PANAMA - MERCHANT SHIPPING

G.K. Hall and Company, 70 Lincoln Street, Boston, Massachusetts 02111 (617) 423-3990; *The World in Figures*.

Lloyd's Register of Shipping, 17 Battery Place, New York, New York 10004 (212) 425-8050; *Register of Ships*.

Statistical Office of the United Nations, Publishing Service, New York, New York 10017 (800) 253-9646; *Statistical Yearbook*.

Times Books, 201 East 50th Street, New York, New York 10022 (212) 751-2600; *The Economist Book of Vital World Statistics*.

U.S. Department of Transportation, Maritime Administration, 400 Seventh Street, SW, Washington, D.C. 20590 (202) 366-5807; *A Statistical Analysis of the World's Merchant Fleets*.

PANAMA - MILITARY

The Economist Intelligence Unit, 111 West 57th Street, New York, New York 10019 (800) 938-4685; *The New Latin America Market Atlas*.

G.K. Hall and Company, 70 Lincoln Street, Boston, Massachusetts 02111 (617) 423-3990; *The World in Figures*.

The International Institute for Strategic Studies, 23 Tavistock Street, London WC2E 7NQ, England; *The Military Balance*.

U.S. Arms Control and Disarmament Agency, 320 Twenty-first Street, NW, Washington, D.C. 20451 (202) 647-8677; *World Military Expenditures and Arms Transfers*.

U.C.L.A. Latin American Center Publications, University of California, Los Angeles, California 90024 (310) 825-6634; *Statistical Abstract of Latin America*.

PANAMA - MILK PRODUCTION - See PANAMA - DAIRY PRODUCTS

PANAMA - MINING AND MINERAL PRODUCTS

The Economist Intelligence Unit, 111 West 57th Street, New York, New York 10019 (800) 938-4685; *The New Latin America Market Atlas*.

Facts on File, 460 Park Avenue South, New York, New York 10016 (800) 443-8323; *The New Book of World Rankings*.

G.K. Hall and Company, 70 Lincoln Street, Boston, Massachusetts 02111 (617) 423-3990; *The World in Figures*.

Inter-American Development Bank, 1300 New York Avenue, NW, Washington, D.C. 20577 (202) 623-1753; *Economic and Social Progress in Latin America*.

Statistical Office of the United Nations, Publishing Service, New York, New York 10017 (800) 253-9646; *Statistical Yearbook*, and *Statistical Yearbook for Latin America and the Caribbean*.

U.C.L.A. Latin American Center Publications, University of California, Los Angeles, California 90024 (310) 825-6634; *Statistical Abstract of Latin America*.

PANAMA - MONEY EXCHANGE RATE

Euromonitor Publications Limited, 87-88 Turnmill Street, London EC1M 5QU, England; *International Marketing Data and Statistics*.

Inter-American Development Bank, 1300 New York Avenue, NW, Washington, D.C. 20577 (202) 623-1753; *Economic and Social Progress in Latin America*.

International Monetary Fund, 700 Nineteenth Street, NW, Washington, D.C. 20431 (202) 623-7000; *International Financial Statistics*.

Statistical Office of the United Nations, Publishing Service, New York, New York 10017 (800) 253-9646; *Statistical Yearbook*.

PANAMA - MONEY RESERVES

Euromonitor Publications Limited, 87-88 Turnmill Street, London EC1M 5QU, England; *International Marketing Data and Statistics*.

Inter-American Development Bank, 1300 New York Avenue, NW, Washington, D.C. 20577 (202) 623-1753; *Economic and Social Progress in Latin America*.

PANAMA - MONEY SUPPLY

Euromonitor Publications Limited, 87-88 Turnmill Street, London EC1M 5QU, England; *International Marketing Data and Statistics*.

G.K. Hall and Company, 70 Lincoln Street, Boston, Massachusetts 02111 (617) 423-3990; *The World in Figures*.

Inter-American Development Bank, 1300 New York Avenue, NW, Washington, D.C. 20577 (202) 623-1753; *Economic and Social*

Progress in Latin America.

International Monetary Fund, 700 Nineteenth Street, NW, Washington, D.C. 20431 (202) 623-7000; *International Financial Statistics*.

Statistical Office of the United Nations, Publishing Service, New York, New York 10017 (800) 253-9646; *Statistical Yearbook*.

U.C.L.A. Latin American Center Publications, University of California, Los Angeles, California 90024 (310) 825-6634; *Statistical Abstract of Latin America*.

The World Bank, 1818 H Street, NW, Washington, D.C. 20433 (202) 477-1234; *World Tables*.

PANAMA - MOTION PICTURES

Statistical Office of the United Nations, Publishing Service, New York, New York 10017 (800) 253-9646; *Statistical Yearbook*.

PANAMA - MOTOR VEHICLE TAXES - See PANAMA - TAXATION

PANAMA - MOTOR VEHICLES IN USE

The Economist Intelligence Unit, 111 West 57th Street, New York, New York 10019 (800) 938-4685; *The New Latin America Market Atlas*.

G.K. Hall and Company, 70 Lincoln Street, Boston, Massachusetts 02111 (617) 423-3990; *The World in Figures*.

International Road Federation, 525 School Street, SW, Washington, D.C. 20024 (202) 554-2106; *World Road Statistics*.

Statistical Office of the United Nations, Publishing Service, New York, New York 10017 (800) 253-9646; *Statistical Yearbook*.

Times Books, 201 East 50th Street, New York, New York 10022 (212) 751-2600; *The Economist Book of Vital World Statistics*.

PANAMA - MULES - See PANAMA - LIVESTOCK AND POULTRY

PANAMA - MUSEUMS

Facts on File, 460 Park Avenue South, New York, New York 10016 (800) 443-8323; *The New Book of World Rankings*.

PANAMA - NATALITY - See PANAMA - BIRTH RATES

PANAMA - NATIONAL ACCOUNTS

Gale Research Incorporated, 835 Penobscot Building, Detroit, Michigan 48226 (800) 877-4253; *International Historical Statistics The Americas and Australasia*.

Inter-American Development Bank, 1300 New York Avenue, NW, Washington, D.C. 20577 (202) 623-1753; *Economic and Social Progress in Latin America*.

Organization of American States (OAS), General Secretariat, Washington, D.C. 20006 (202) 458-3533; *Statistical Bulletin of the OAS*.

Statistical Office of the United Nations, Publishing Service, New York, New York 10017 (800) 253-9646; *National Accounts Statistics*, and *Statistical Yearbook*.

U.C.L.A. Latin American Center Publications, University of California, Los Angeles, California 90024 (310) 825-6634; *Statistical Abstract of Latin America*.

PANAMA - NATIONAL INCOME

Facts on File, 460 Park Avenue South, New York, New York 10016 (800) 443-8323; *The New Book of World Rankings*.

G.K. Hall and Company, 70 Lincoln Street, Boston, Massachusetts 02111 (617) 423-3990; *The World in Figures*.

Inter-American Development Bank, 1300 New York Avenue, NW, Washington, D.C. 20577 (202) 623-1753; *Economic and Social Progress in Latin America*.

Statistical Office of the United Nations, Publishing Service, New York, New York 10017 (800) 253-9646; *Statistical Yearbook*, and *Statistical Yearbook for Latin America and the Caribbean*.

PANAMA - NATIONAL PRODUCT

Facts on File, 460 Park Avenue South, New York, New York 10016 (800) 443-8323; *The New Book of World Rankings*.

Statistical Office of the United Nations, Publishing Service, New York, New York 10017 (800) 253-9646; *Statistical Yearbook*.

PANAMA - NATURAL GAS PRODUCTION - See PANAMA - MINING AND MINERAL PRODUCTS

PANAMA - NEWSPAPER PRODUCTION - See PANAMA - FORESTRY AND FOREST PRODUCTS

PANAMA - NEWSPRINT - See PANAMA - FORESTRY AND FOREST PRODUCTS

PANAMA - NUTRITION

Statistical Office of the United Nations, Publishing Service, New York, New York 10017 (800) 253-9646; *Statistical Yearbook for Latin America and the Caribbean*.

PANAMA - OCCUPATIONS - See PANAMA - LABOR FORCE

PANAMA - ORANGES PRODUCTION - See PANAMA - CROPS

PANAMA - PAPER - See PANAMA - FORESTRY AND FOREST PRODUCTS

PANAMA - PATENTS

Statistical Office of the United Nations, Publishing Service, New York, New York 10017 (800) 253-9646; *Statistical Yearbook*.

World Intellectual Property Organization, 34 Chemin des Colombettes, CH-1211 Geneva 20, Switzerland; *Industrial Property Statistics*.

PANAMA - PEANUT PRODUCTION - See PANAMA - CROPS

PANAMA - PERIODICALS

Statistical Office of the United Nations, Publishing Service, New York, New York 10017 (800) 253-9646; *Statistical Yearbook*.

PANAMA - PESTICIDE USE

Food and Agricultural Organization of the United Nations (FAO) Via delle Terme di Caracalla, 00100 Rome, Italy (Telephone Number in U.S. (202) 653-2400); *The State of Food and Agriculture*.

PANAMA - PETROLEUM INDUSTRY

The Economist Intelligence Unit, 111 West 57th Street, New York, New York 10019 (800) 938-4685; *The New Latin America Market Atlas*.

Facts on File, 460 Park Avenue South, New York, New York 10016 (800) 443-8323; *The New Book of World Rankings*.

Food and Agricultural Organization of the United Nations (FAO) Via delle Terme di Caracalla, 00100 Rome, Italy (Telephone Number in U.S. (202) 653-2400); *The State of Food and Agriculture*.

G.K. Hall and Company, 70 Lincoln Street, Boston, Massachusetts 02111 (617) 423-3990; *The World in Figures*.

Inter-American Development Bank, 1300 New York Avenue, NW, Washington, D.C. 20577 (202) 623-1753; *Economic and Social Progress in Latin America*.

Organization of American States (OAS), General Secretariat, Washington, D.C. 20006 (202) 458-3533; *Statistical Bulletin of the OAS*.

Statistical Office of the United Nations, Publishing Service, New York, New York 10017 (800) 253-9646; *Statistical Yearbook*.

PANAMA - PIG-IRON AND FERRO-ALLOY PRODUCTION - See PAKISTAN - MINING AND MINERAL PRODUCTS

PANAMA - PIGS - See PANAMA - LIVESTOCK AND POULTRY

PANAMA - POLITICAL DATA

U.C.L.A. Latin American Center Publications, University of California, Los Angeles, California 90024 (310) 825-6634; *Statistical Abstract of Latin America*.

PANAMA - POPULATION

The Economist Intelligence Unit, 111 West 57th Street, New York, New York 10019 (800) 938-4685; *The New Latin America Market Atlas*, and *The World Market Atlas*.

Euromonitor Publications Limited, 87-88 Turnmill Street, London EC1M 5QU, England; *International Marketing Data and Statistics*.

Facts on File, 460 Park Avenue South, New York, New York 10016 (800) 443-8323; *The New Book of World Rankings*.

Food and Agricultural Organization of the United Nations (FAO), Via delle Terme di Caracalla, 00100 Rome, Italy (Telephone Number in U.S. (202) 653-2400); *Production Yearbook*.

Gale Research Incorporated, 835 Penobscot Building, Detroit, Michigan 48226 (800) 877-4253; *International Historical Statistics The Americas and Australasia*.

G.K. Hall and Company, 70 Lincoln Street, Boston, Massachusetts 02111 (617) 423-3990; *The World in Figures*.

Inter-American Development Bank, 1300 New York Avenue, NW, Washington, D.C. 20577 (202) 623-1753; *Economic and Social*

Progress in Latin America.

International Labour Office, I.L.O. Publications, CH-1211, Geneva 22, Switzerland; *Yearbook of Labour Statistics.*

Organization of American States (OAS), General Secretariat, Washington, D.C. 20006 (202) 458-3533; *Statistical Bulletin of the OAS.*

Statistical Office of the United Nations, Publishing Service, New York, New York 10017 (800) 253-9646; *Demographic Yearbook, Statistical Yearbook*, and *Statistical Yearbook for Latin America and the Caribbean.*

Times Books, 201 East 50th Street, New York, New York 10022 (212) 751-2600; *The Economist Book of Vital World Statistics.*

U.C.L.A. Latin American Center Publications, University of California, Los Angeles, California 90024 (310) 825-6634; *Statistical Abstract of Latin America.*

United Nations Educational, Scientific and Cultural Organization (UNESCO), 7 Place de Fontenoy, F-75700 Paris, France (Telephone Number in U.S. (212) 963-5981); *Statistical Yearbook.*

U.S. Arms Control and Disarmament Agency, 320 Twenty-first Street, NW, Washington, D.C. 20451 (202) 647-8677; *World Military Expenditures and Arms Transfers.*

World Health Organization, Office of Publications, Avenue Appia, CH-1211 Geneva 27, Switzerland (Telephone Number in U.S. (518) 436-9686); *World Health Statistics Annual.*

PANAMA - POST OFFICES

Facts on File, 460 Park Avenue South, New York, New York 10016 (800) 443-8323; *The New Book of World Rankings.*

PANAMA - POTATO PRODUCTION - See PANAMA - CROPS

PANAMA - POWER PRODUCTION INDUSTRY

Statistical Office of the United Nations, Publishing Service, New York, New York 10017 (800) 253-9646; *Statistical Yearbook.*

PANAMA - PRICES

Facts on File, 460 Park Avenue South, New York, New York 10016 (800) 443-8323; *The New Book of World Rankings.*

Food and Agricultural Organization of the United Nations (FAO), Via delle Terme di Caracalla, 00100 Rome, Italy (Telephone Number in U.S. (202) 653-2400); *Production Yearbook*, and *The State of Food and Agriculture.*

Gale Research Incorporated, 835 Penobscot Building, Detroit, Michigan 48226 (800) 877-4253; *International Historical Statistics The Americas and Australasia.*

G.K. Hall and Company, 70 Lincoln Street, Boston, Massachusetts 02111 (617) 423-3990; *The World in Figures.*

International Labour Office, I.L.O. Publications, CH-1211, Geneva 22, Switzerland; *Yearbook of Labour Statistics.*

International Monetary Fund, 700 Nineteenth Street, NW, Washington, D.C. 20431 (202) 623-7000; *International Financial Statistics.*

Statistical Office of the United Nations, Publishing Service, New York, New York 10017 (800) 253-9646; *Economic Survey of Latin America and the Caribbean*, and *Statistical Yearbook for Latin America and the Caribbean.*

PANAMA - PRINTING AND WRITING PAPER - See PANAMA - FORESTRY AND FOREST PRODUCTS

PANAMA - PRODUCTION

Facts on File, 460 Park Avenue South, New York, New York 10016 (800) 443-8323; *The New Book of World Rankings.*

G.K. Hall and Company, 70 Lincoln Street, Boston, Massachusetts 02111 (617) 423-3990; *The World in Figures.*

PANAMA - PRODUCTIVITY

Euromonitor Publications Limited, 87-88 Turnmill Street, London EC1M 5QU, England; *International Marketing Data and Statistics.*

PANAMA - PROPERTY TAXES

Inter-American Development Bank, 1300 New York Avenue, NW, Washington, D.C. 20577 (202) 623-1753; *Economic and Social Progress in Latin America.*

International Monetary Fund, 700 Nineteenth Street, NW, Washington, D.C. 20431 (202) 623-7000; *Government Finance Statistics Yearbook.*

PANAMA - PUBLIC CONSUMPTION FUND

Inter-American Development Bank, 1300 New York Avenue, NW, Washington, D.C. 20577 (202) 623-1753; *Economic and Social Progress in Latin America.*

PANAMA - PUBLIC EXPENDITURE

Inter-American Development Bank, 1300 New York Avenue, NW, Washington, D.C. 20577 (202) 623-1753; *Economic and Social Progress in Latin America.*

Organization of American States (OAS), General Secretariat, Washington, D.C. 20006 (202) 458-3533; *Statistical Bulletin of the OAS.*

Statistical Office of the United Nations, Publishing Service, New York, New York 10017 (800) 253-9646; *Statistical Yearbook for Latin America and the Caribbean.*

PANAMA - PUBLIC FINANCES

Facts on File, 460 Park Avenue South, New York, New York 10016 (800) 443-8323; *The New Book of World Rankings.*

Inter-American Development Bank, 1300 New York Avenue, NW, Washington, D.C. 20577 (202) 623-1753; *Economic and Social Progress in Latin America.*

Organization of American States (OAS), General Secretariat, Washington, D.C. 20006 (202) 458-3533; *Statistical Bulletin of the OAS.*

PANAMA - PUBLIC REVENUE

Inter-American Development Bank, 1300 New York Avenue, NW, Washington, D.C. 20577 (202) 623-1753; *Economic and Social Progress in Latin America.*

Organization of American States (OAS), General Secretariat, Washington, D.C. 20006 (202) 458-3533; *Statistical Bulletin of the OAS.*

PANAMA - RADIO BROADCASTING - See PANAMA - BROADCASTING

PANAMA - RAILWAYS

The Economist Intelligence Unit, 111 West 57th Street, New York, New York 10019 (800) 938-4685; *The New Latin America Market Atlas.*

G.K. Hall and Company, 70 Lincoln Street, Boston, Massachusetts 02111 (617) 423-3990; *The World in Figures.*

Jane's Information Group, Sentinel House, 163 Brighton Road, Coulsdon, Surrey CR5 2NH, England (Telephone Number in U.S. (703) 683-3700); *Jane's World Railways.*

PANAMA - RANCHING

U.C.L.A. Latin American Center Publications, University of California, Los Angeles, California 90024 (310) 825-6634; *Statistical Abstract of Latin America.*

PANAMA - RELIGION

Facts on File, 460 Park Avenue South, New York, New York 10016 (800) 443-8323; *The New Book of World Rankings.*

U.C.L.A. Latin American Center Publications, University of California, Los Angeles, California 90024 (310) 825-6634; *Statistical Abstract of Latin America.*

PANAMA - RENT PRICES

International Labour Office, I.L.O. Publications, CH-1211, Geneva 22, Switzerland; *Yearbook of Labour Statistics.*

PANAMA - RESERVES EXCLUDING GOLD

The Economist Intelligence Unit, 111 West 57th Street, New York, New York 10019 (800) 938-4685; *The New Latin America Market Atlas.*

PANAMA - RETAIL TRADE

G.K. Hall and Company, 70 Lincoln Street, Boston, Massachusetts 02111 (617) 423-3990; *The World in Figures.*

Inter-American Development Bank, 1300 New York Avenue, NW, Washington, D.C. 20577 (202) 623-1753; *Economic and Social Progress in Latin America.*

Statistical Office of the United Nations, Publishing Service, New York, New York 10017 (800) 253-9646; *Statistical Yearbook.*

PANAMA - REVENUES

Organization of American States (OAS), General Secretariat, Washington, D.C. 20006 (202) 458-3533; *Statistical Bulletin of the OAS.*

PANAMA - RICE PRODUCTION - See PANAMA - CROPS

PANAMA - ROOT AND TUBER PRODUCTION - See PANAMA - CROPS

PANAMA - ROUNDWOOD PRODUCTION - See PANAMA - FORESTRY AND FOREST PRODUCTS

PANAMA - RUBBER PRODUCTION AND CONSUMPTION

Facts on File, 460 Park Avenue South, New York, New York 10016 (800) 443-8323; *The New Book of World Rankings.*

PANAMA - SALT PRODUCTION - See PANAMA - MINING AND MINERAL PRODUCTS

PANAMA - SAWNWOOD PRODUCTION - See PANAMA - FORESTRY AND FOREST PRODUCTS

PANAMA - SCIENCE AND TECHNOLOGY

Statistical Office of the United Nations, Publishing Service, New York, New York 10017 (800) 253-9646; *Statistical Yearbook.*

U.C.L.A. Latin American Center Publications, University of California, Los Angeles, California 90024 (310) 825-6634; *Statistical Abstract of Latin America.*

PANAMA - SCIENTISTS AND TECHNICIANS

Statistical Office of the United Nations, Publishing Service, New York, New York 10017 (800) 253-9646; *Statistical Yearbook.*

PANAMA - SENIOR CITIZENS

Facts on File, 460 Park Avenue South, New York, New York 10016 (800) 443-8323; *The New Book of World Rankings.*

PANAMA - SHEEP - See PANAMA - LIVESTOCK AND POULTRY

PANAMA - SHRIMP EXPORTS

International Monetary Fund, 700 Nineteenth Street, NW, Washington, D.C. 20431 (202) 623-7000; *International Financial Statistics.*

PANAMA - SILVER PRODUCTION AND CONSUMPTION - See PANAMA - MINING AND MINERAL PRODUCTS

PANAMA - SOCIAL DATA

Facts on File, 460 Park Avenue South, New York, New York 10016 (800) 443-8323; *The New Book of World Rankings.*

G.K. Hall and Company, 70 Lincoln Street, Boston, Massachusetts 02111 (617) 423-3990; *The World in Figures.*

U.C.L.A. Latin American Center Publications, University of California, Los Angeles, California 90024 (310) 825-6634; *Statistical Abstract of Latin America.*

PANAMA - SOCIAL SECURITY

Inter-American Development Bank, 1300 New York Avenue, NW, Washington, D.C. 20577 (202) 623-1753; *Economic and Social Progress in Latin America.*

International Monetary Fund, 700 Nineteenth Street, NW, Washington, D.C. 20431 (202) 623-7000; *Government Finance Statistics Yearbook.*

PANAMA - SOCIOECONOMIC DATA

Inter-American Development Bank, 1300 New York Avenue, NW, Washington, D.C. 20577 (202) 623-1753; *Economic and Social Progress in Latin America.*

U.C.L.A. Latin American Center Publications, University of California, Los Angeles, California 90024 (310) 825-6634; *Statistical Abstract of Latin America.*

PANAMA - SOYBEAN PRODUCTION - See PANAMA - CROPS

PANAMA - STAMP TAXES AND DUTIES - See PANAMA - TAXATION

PANAMA - STATE BUDGET REVENUE AND EXPENDITURES

Euromonitor Publications Limited, 87-88 Turnmill Street, London EC1M 5QU, England; *International Marketing Data and Statistics.*

Inter-American Development Bank, 1300 New York Avenue, NW, Washington, D.C. 20577 (202) 623-1753; *Economic and Social Progress in Latin America.*

PANAMA - STEEL - See PANAMA - MINING AND MINERAL PRODUCTS

PANAMA - STOCKS - COMMODITY - MARKET PRICE - INDEX

Food and Agricultural Organisation of the United Nations (FAO) Via delle Terme di Caracalla, 00100 Rome, Italy (Telephone Number in U.S. (202) 653-2400); *The State of Food and Agriculture.*

PANAMA - SUGAR - See PANAMA - CROPS

PANAMA - TAXATION

G.K. Hall and Company, 70 Lincoln Street, Boston, Massachusetts 02111 (617) 423-3990; *The World in Figures.*

Inter-American Development Bank, 1300 New York Avenue, NW, Washington, D.C. 20577 (202) 623-1753; *Economic and Social Progress in Latin America.*

International Monetary Fund, 700 Nineteenth Street, NW, Washington, D.C. 20431 (202) 623-7000; *Government Finance Statistics Yearbook.*

International Road Federation, 525 School Street, SW, Washington, D.C. 20024 (202) 554-2106; *World Road Statistics.*

Statistical Office of the United Nations, Publishing Service, New York, New York 10017 (800) 253-9646; *Statistical Yearbook for Latin America and the Caribbean.*

The World Bank, 1818 H Street, NW, Washington, D.C. 20433 (202) 477-1234; *World Tables.*

PANAMA - TAX REVENUES - See PANAMA - TAXATION

PANAMA - TELEPHONES IN USE

American Telephone and Telegraph Company, 26 Parsippany Road, Whippany, New Jersey 07981 (800) 338-4038; *The World's Telephones.*

The Economist Intelligence Unit, 111 West 57th Street, New York, New York 10019 (800) 938-4685; *The New Latin America Market Atlas.*

G.K. Hall and Company, 70 Lincoln Street, Boston, Massachusetts 02111 (617) 423-3990; *The World in Figures.*

Statistical Office of the United Nations, Publishing Service, New York, New York 10017 (800) 253-9646; *Statistical Yearbook.*

PANAMA - TELEVISION BROADCASTING - See PANAMA - BROADCASTING

PANAMA - TEXTILE INDUSTRY

G.K. Hall and Company, 70 Lincoln Street, Boston, Massachusetts 02111 (617) 423-3990; *The World in Figures.*

Statistical Office of the United Nations, Publishing Service, New York, New York 10017 (800) 253-9646; *Statistical Yearbook.*

PANAMA - THEATRE

United Nations Educational, Scientific and Cultural Organization (UNESCO), 7 Place de Fontenoy, F-75700 Paris, France (Telephone Number in U.S. (212) 963-5981); *Statistical Yearbook.*

PANAMA - TIRE (MOTOR VEHICLE) PRODUCTION

Statistical Office of the United Nations, Publishing Service, New York, New York 10017 (800) 253-9646; *Statistical Yearbook.*

PANAMA - TOBACCO PRODUCTION

Facts on File, 460 Park Avenue South, New York, New York 10016 (800) 443-8323; *The New Book of World Rankings.*

Statistical Office of the United Nations, Publishing Service, New York, New York 10017 (800) 253-9646; *Statistical Yearbook.*

U.C.L.A. Latin American Center Publications, University of California, Los Angeles, California 90024 (310) 825-6634; *Statistical Abstract of Latin America.*

PANAMA - TOURISM

The Economist Intelligence Unit, 111 West 57th Street, New York, New York 10019 (800) 938-4685; *The New Latin America Market Atlas.*

Facts on File, 460 Park Avenue South, New York, New York 10016 (800) 443-8323; *The New Book of World Rankings.*

G.K. Hall and Company, 70 Lincoln Street, Boston, Massachusetts 02111 (617) 423-3990; *The World in Figures.*

Organization of American States (OAS), General Secretariat, Washington, D.C. 20006 (202) 458-3533; *Statistical Bulletin of the OAS.*

Statistical Office of the United Nations, Publishing Service, New York, New York 10017 (800) 253-9646; *Statistical Yearbook*, and *Statistical Yearbook for Latin America and the Caribbean.*

Times Books, 201 East 50th Street, New York, New York 10022 (212) 751-2600; *The Economist Book of Vital World Statistics.*

U.C.L.A. Latin American Center Publications, University of California, Los Angeles, California 90024 (310) 825-6634; *Statistical Abstract of Latin America.*

World Tourism Organization, Calle Capitan Haya 42, E-28020 Madrid, Spain; *Yearbook of Tourism Statistics.*

PANAMA - TRACTORS IN USE

The Economist Intelligence Unit, 111 West 57th Street, New York, New York 10019 (800) 938-4685; *The New Latin America Market Atlas.*

Statistical Office of the United Nations, Publishing Service, New York, New York 10017 (800) 253-9646; *Statistical Yearbook.*

PANAMA - TRADE - See PANAMA - FOREIGN TRADE

PANAMA - TRADEMARKS AND SERVICE MARKS

World Intellectual Property Organization, 34 Chemin des Colombettes, CH-1211 Geneva 20, Switzerland; *Industrial Property Statistics.*

PANAMA - TRANSPORTATION AND COMMUNICATIONS

The Economist Intelligence Unit, 111 West 57th Street, New York, New York 10019 (800) 938-4685; *The New Latin America Market Atlas.*

Facts on File, 460 Park Avenue South, New York, New York 10016 (800) 443-8323; *The New Book of World Rankings.*

Gale Research Incorporated, 835 Penobscot Building, Detroit, Michigan 48226 (800) 877-4253; *International Historical Statistics The Americas and Australasia.*

G.K. Hall and Company, 70 Lincoln Street, Boston, Massachusetts 02111 (617) 423-3990; *The World in Figures.*

Inter-American Development Bank, 1300 New York Avenue, NW, Washington, D.C. 20577 (202) 623-1753; *Economic and Social Progress in Latin America.*

Statistical Office of the United Nations, Publishing Service, New York, New York 10017 (800) 253-9646; *Statistical Yearbook for Latin America and the Caribbean.*

U.C.L.A. Latin American Center Publications, University of California, Los Angeles, California 90024 (310) 825-6634; *Statistical Abstract of Latin America.*

PANAMA - TURKEYS - See PANAMA - LIVESTOCK AND POULTRY

PANAMA - UNEMPLOYMENT

The Economist Intelligence Unit, 111 West 57th Street, New York, New York 10019 (800) 938-4685; *The New Latin America Market Atlas.*

Euromonitor Publications Limited, 87-88 Turnmill Street, London EC1M 5QU, England; *International Marketing Data and Statistics.*

International Labour Office, I.L.O. Publications, CH-1211, Geneva 22, Switzerland; *Yearbook of Labour Statistics.*

Organization of American States (OAS), General Secretariat, Washington, D.C. 20006 (202) 458-3533; *Statistical Bulletin of the OAS.*

Statistical Office of the United Nations, Publishing Service, New York, New York 10017 (800) 253-9646; *Statistical Yearbook.*

U.C.L.A. Latin American Center Publications, University of California, Los Angeles, California 90024 (310) 825-6634; *Statistical Abstract of Latin America.*

PANAMA - UTILITIES

U.C.L.A. Latin American Center Publications, University of California, Los Angeles, California 90024 (310) 825-6634; *Statistical Abstract of Latin America.*

PANAMA - VITAL STATISTICS

Euromonitor Publications Limited, 87-88 Turnmill Street, London EC1M 5QU, England; *International Marketing Data and Statistics.*

Gale Research Incorporated, 835 Penobscot Building, Detroit, Michigan 48226 (800) 877-4253; *International Historical Statistics The Americas and Australasia.*

G.K. Hall and Company, 70 Lincoln Street, Boston, Massachusetts 02111 (617) 423-3990; *The World in Figures.*

Statistical Office of the United Nations, Publishing Service, New York, New York 10017 (800) 253-9646; *Statistical Yearbook.*

World Health Organization, Office of Publications, Avenue Appia, CH-1211 Geneva 27, Switzerland (Telephone Number in U.S. (518) 436-9686); *World Health Statistics Annual.*

PANAMA - WAGES

G.K. Hall and Company, 70 Lincoln Street, Boston, Massachusetts 02111 (617) 423-3990; *The World in Figures.*

International Labour Office, I.L.O. Publications, CH-1211, Geneva 22, Switzerland; *Yearbook of Labour Statistics.*

Statistical Office of the United Nations, Publishing Service, New York, New York 10017 (800) 253-9646; *Statistical Yearbook.*

U.C.L.A. Latin American Center Publications, University of California, Los Angeles, California 90024 (310) 825-6634; *Statistical Abstract of Latin America.*

PANAMA - WEATHER

Facts on File, 460 Park Avenue South, New York, New York 10016 (800) 443-8323; *The New Book of World Rankings.*

G.K. Hall and Company, 70 Lincoln Street, Boston, Massachusetts 02111 (617) 423-3990; *The World in Figures.*

PANAMA - WELFARE

Inter-American Development Bank, 1300 New York Avenue, NW, Washington, D.C. 20577 (202) 623-1753; *Economic and Social Progress in Latin America.*

International Monetary Fund, 700 Nineteenth Street, NW, Washington, D.C. 20431 (202) 623-7000; *Government Finance Statistics Yearbook.*

PANAMA - WHEAT PRODUCTION AND PRICES - See PANAMA - CROPS

PANAMA - WHOLESALE PRICES

Inter-American Development Bank, 1300 New York Avenue, NW, Washington, D.C. 20577 (202) 623-1753; *Economic and Social Progress in Latin America.*

International Monetary Fund, 700 Nineteenth Street, NW, Washington, D.C. 20431 (202) 623-7000; *International Financial*

Statistics.

Organization of American States (OAS), General Secretariat, Washington, D.C. 20006 (202) 458-3533; *Statistical Bulletin of the OAS*.

Statistical Office of the United Nations, Publishing Service, New York, New York 10017 (800) 253-9646; *Statistical Yearbook*.

PANAMA - WHOLESALE TRADE

Inter-American Development Bank, 1300 New York Avenue, NW, Washington, D.C. 20577 (202) 623-1753; *Economic and Social Progress in Latin America*.

Statistical Office of the United Nations, Publishing Service, New York, New York 10017 (800) 253-9646; *Statistical Yearbook*.

PANAMA - WINE PRODUCTION

Facts on File, 460 Park Avenue South, New York, New York 10016 (800) 443-8323; *The New Book of World Rankings*.

PANAMA - WOOD PULP PRODUCTION - See PANAMA - FORESTRY AND FOREST PRODUCTS

PANAMA - WOOL PRODUCTION

Facts on File, 460 Park Avenue South, New York, New York 10016 (800) 443-8323; *The New Book of World Rankings*.

PAPAYAS

U.S. Department of Agriculture, National Agricultural Statistics Service, Fourteenth Street and Independence Avenue, SW, Washington, D.C. 20250 (202) 219-1504; *Noncitrus Fruits and Nuts*, and unpublished data.

PAPER AND ALLIED PRODUCTS INDUSTRY - MANUFACTURING - CAPITAL

U.S. Department of Commerce, Bureau of Economic Analysis, Fourteenth Street between Constitution Avenue and E Street, NW, Washington, D.C. 20230 (202) 606-9900; *Survey of Current Business*, and *Fixed Reproducible Tangible Wealth in the United States*.

U.S. Department of Commerce, Bureau of the Census, Suitland, Maryland 20233 (301) 763-4040; *Plant and Equipment Expenditures and Plans*, and *Current Industrial Reports*.

PAPER AND ALLIED PRODUCTS INDUSTRY - MANUFACTURING - EARNINGS

U.S. Department of Commerce, Bureau of the Census, Suitland, Maryland 20233 (301) 763-4040; *Census of Manufactures, County Business Patterns*, and *Annual Survey of Manufactures*.

U.S. Department of Labor, Bureau of Labor Statistics, Two Massachusetts Avenue, NE, Washington, D.C. 20212 (202) 606-7828; *Employment and Earnings*, and Bulletins 2370 2429.

PAPER AND ALLIED PRODUCTS INDUSTRY - MANUFACTURING - EMPLOYEES

U.S. Department of Commerce, Bureau of the Census, Suitland, Maryland 20233 (301) 763-4040; *Census of Manufactures, Annual Survey of Manufactures*, and *County Business Patterns*.

U.S. Department of Labor, Bureau of Labor Statistics, Two Massachusetts Avenue, NE, Washington, D.C. 20212 (202) 606-7828; *Employment and Earnings*, and Bulletins 2370 and 2429.

PAPER AND ALLIED PRODUCTS INDUSTRY - MANUFACTURING - ESTABLISHMENTS

U.S. Department of Commerce, Bureau of the Census, Suitland, Maryland 20233 (301) 763-4040; *Census of Manufactures, Annual Survey of Manufactures*, and *County Business Patterns*.

PAPER AND ALLIED PRODUCTS INDUSTRY - MANUFACTURING - GROSS DOMESTIC PRODUCT

U.S. Department of Commerce, Bureau of Economic Analysis, Fourteenth Street between Constitution Avenue and E Street, NW, Washington, D.C. 20230 (202) 606-9900; *The National Income and Product Accounts of the United States*, and *Survey of Current Business*.

PAPER AND ALLIED PRODUCTS INDUSTRY - MANUFACTURING - MERGERS AND ACQUISITIONS

Securities Data Company, 1180 Raymond Boulevard, Newark, New Jersey 07102 (201) 622-3100; *Merger and Corporate Transactions Database*.

PAPER AND ALLIED PRODUCTS INDUSTRY - MANUFACTURING - OCCUPATIONAL SAFETY

U.S. Department of Labor, Bureau of Labor Statistics, Two Massachusetts Avenue, NE, Washington, D.C. 20212 (202) 606-7828; *Occupational Injuries and Illnesses in the United States by Industry*.

PAPER AND ALLIED PRODUCTS INDUSTRY - MANUFACTURING - OUTPUT

American Forest and Paper Association, 1250 Connecticut Avenue, NW, Washington, D.C. 20036 (202) 463-2455; *Statistics of Paper, Paperboard, and Wood Pulp*.

PAPER AND ALLIED PRODUCTS INDUSTRY - MANUFACTURING - POLLUTION ABATEMENT

U.S. Department of Commerce, Bureau of the Census, Suitland, Maryland 20233 (301) 763-4040; *Current Industrial Reports*.

PAPER AND ALLIED PRODUCTS INDUSTRY - MANUFACTURING - PRODUCTIVITY

American Forest and Paper Association, 1250 Connecticut Avenue, NW, Washington, D.C. 20036 (202) 463-2455; *Statistics of Paper, Paperboard, and Woodpulp*.

Board of Governors of the Federal Reserve System, Twentieth Street and Constitution Avenue, NW, Washington, D.C. 20551 (202) 452-3000; *Federal Reserve Bulletin*.

U.S. Department of Labor, Bureau of Labor Statistics, Two Massachusetts Avenue, NE, Washington, D.C. 20212 (202) 606-7828; *Productivity Measures for Selected Industries and Government Services*, and unpublished data.

PAPER AND ALLIED PRODUCTS INDUSTRY - MANUFACTURING - RESEARCH AND DEVELOPMENT

U.S. National Science Foundation, 4201 Wilson Boulevard, Arlington, Virginia 22230 (703) 306-1234; *Research and Development in Industry*.

PAPER AND ALLIED PRODUCTS INDUSTRY - MANUFACTURING - SALES, SHIPMENTS, RECEIPTS

U.S. Department of Commerce, Bureau of the Census, Suitland, Maryland 20233 (301) 763-4040; *Census of Manufactures, Annual Survey of Manufactures*, and *Current Industrial Reports, Manufactures' Shipments, Inventories and Orders*.

U.S. Department of Commerce, International Trade Administration, Fourteenth Street between Constitution Avenue, and E Street, NW, Washington, D.C. 20230 (202) 482-3809; *U.S. Industrial Outlook*.

PAPER AND PAPERBOARD PRODUCTS

Franklin Associates Limited, 4121 West 83rd Street, Suite 108, Prairie Village, Kansas 66208 (913) 649-2225; *Characterization of Municipal Solid Waste in the United States*.

PAPER AND PAPERBOARD PRODUCTS - FOREIGN TRADE

U.S. Department of Commerce, Bureau of the Census, Suitland, Maryland 20233 (301) 763-4040; *U.S. Merchandise Trade: Exports, General Imports, and Imports for Consumption*, and *U.S. Merchandise Trade*.

PAPER AND PAPERBOARD PRODUCTS - PRODUCTION

American Forest and Paper Association, 1250 Connecticut Avenue, NW, Washington, D.C. 20036 (202) 463-2455; *Statistics of Paper, Paperboard, and Woodpulp*.

U.S. Department of Commerce, Bureau of Economic Analysis, Fourteenth Street between Constitution Avenue and E Street, NW, Washington, D.C. 20230 (202) 606-9900; *Survey of Current Business*.

PAPER AND PAPERBOARD PRODUCTS - RAILROAD CAR LOADINGS

Association of American Railroads, American Railroads Building, 50 F Street, NW, Washington, D.C. 20001 (202) 639-2100; *Freight Commodity Statistics*, and *Weekly Railroad Traffic*.

PAPER AND PAPERBOARD PRODUCTS - RECYCLING

American Forest and Paper Association, 1250 Connecticut Avenue, NW, Washington, D.C. 20036 (202) 463-2455; *Statistics of Paper, Paperboard, and Woodpulp*, and unpublished data.

Papua New Guinea - National Statistical Office

National Statistics Office, Central Government Offices, Post Office Wards Strip, Waigani, Papua New Guinea.

Papua New Guinea - Primary Statistics Sources

National Statistics Office, Central Government Offices, Post Office Wards Strip, Waigani, Papua New Guinea; *Statistical Digest*, and *Abstract of Statistics*.

PAPUA NEW GUINEA - AGRICULTURE

Asian Development Bank, Post Office Box 789, 1099 Manila, Philippines; *Key Indicators of Developing Asian and Pacific Countries*.

Euromonitor Publications Limited, 87-88 Turnmill Street, London EC1M 5QU, England; *International Marketing Data and Statistics*.

Facts on File, 460 Park Avenue South, New York, New York 10016 (800) 443-8323; *The New Book of World Rankings*.

Federal Statistical Office, Gustav - Stresemann - Ring 11, D-6200 Wiesbaden, Germany; *Papua New Guinea*.

Food and Agricultural Organization of the United Nations (FAO), Via delle Terme di Caracalla, 00100 Rome, Italy (Telephone Number in U.S. (202) 653-2400); *Production Yearbook, The State of Food and Agriculture*, and *Trade Yearbook*.

G.K. Hall and Company, 70 Lincoln Street, Boston, Massachusetts 02111 (617) 423-3990; *The World in Figures*.

Statistical Office of the United Nations, Publishing Service, New York, New York 10017 (800) 253-9646; *Statistical Yearbook*, and *Statistical Yearbook for Asia and the Pacific*.

Times Books, 201 East 50th Street, New York, New York 10022 (212) 751-2600; *The Economist Book of Vital World Statistics*.

The World Bank, 1818 H Street, NW, Washington, D.C. 20433 (202) 477-1234; *World Tables*.

PAPUA NEW GUINEA - AIRLINE SERVICE

The Economist Intelligence Unit (Asia) Limited, 10th Floor, Luk Kwok Centre, 72 Gloucester Road, Wanchai, Hong Kong (Phone Number in U.S. (800) 938-4685); *Asian Market Atlas*.

Facts on File, 460 Park Avenue South, New York, New York 10016 (800) 443-8323; *The New Book of World Rankings*.

G.K. Hall and Company, 70 Lincoln Street, Boston, Massachusetts 02111 (617) 423-3990; *The World in Figures*.

International Civil Aviation Organization, 1000 Sherbrooke Street, West, Montreal, Quebec, Canada H3A 2R2 (514) 285-8219; *Civil Aviation Statistics of the World*.

Times Books, 201 East 50th Street, New York, New York 10022 (212) 751-2600; *The Economist Book of Vital World Statistics*.

PAPUA NEW GUINEA - ALUMINUM PRODUCTION AND CONSUMPTION - See PAPUA NEW GUINEA - MINING AND MINERAL PRODUCTS

PAPUA NEW GUINEA - ANTIMONY AND ANTIMONY ORE PRODUCTION AND CONSUMPTION - See PAPUA NEW GUINEA - MINING AND MINERAL PRODUCTS

PAPUA NEW GUINEA - AREA AND DENSITY OF POPULATION

Euromonitor Publications Limited, 87-88 Turnmill Street, London EC1M 5QU, England; *International Marketing Data and Statistics*.

Facts on File, 460 Park Avenue South, New York, New York 10016 (800) 443-8323; *The New Book of World Rankings*.

Federal Statistical Office, Gustav - Stresemann - Ring 11, D-6200 Wiesbaden, Germany; *Papua New Guinea*.

Food and Agricultural Organization of the United Nations (FAO) Via delle Terme di Caracalla, 00100 Rome, Italy (Telephone Number in U.S. (202) 653-2400); *The State of Food and Agriculture*.

G.K. Hall and Company, 70 Lincoln Street, Boston, Massachusetts 02111 (617) 423-3990; *The World in Figures*.

Statistical Office of the United Nations, Publishing Service, New York, New York 10017 (800) 253-9646; *Statistical Yearbook*.

Times Books, 201 East 50th Street, New York, New York 10022 (212) 751-2600; *The Economist Book of Vital World Statistics*.

United Nations Educational, Scientific and Cultural Organization (UNESCO), 7 Place de Fontenoy, F-75700 Paris, France (Telephone Number in U.S. (212) 963-5981); *Statistical Yearbook*.

PAPUA NEW GUINEA - ARMS EXPORTS AND IMPORTS

U.S. Arms Control and Disarmament Agency, 320 Twenty-first Street, NW, Washington, D.C. 20451 (202) 647-8677; *World Military Expenditures and Arms Transfers*.

PAPUA NEW GUINEA - BALANCE OF PAYMENTS

The Economist Intelligence Unit, 111 West 57th Street, New York, New York 10019 (800) 938-4685; *The World Market Atlas*.

Federal Statistical Office, Gustav - Stresemann - Ring 11, D-6200 Wiesbaden, Germany; *Papua New Guinea*.

G.K. Hall and Company, 70 Lincoln Street, Boston, Massachusetts 02111 (617) 423-3990; *The World in Figures*.

International Monetary Fund, 700 Nineteenth Street, NW, Washington, D.C. 20431 (202) 623-7000; *Balance of Payments Yearbook*.

Times Books, 201 East 50th Street, New York, New York 10022 (212) 751-2600; *The Economist Book of Vital World Statistics*.

The World Bank, 1818 H Street, NW, Washington, D.C. 20433 (202) 477-1234; *World Tables*.

PAPUA NEW GUINEA - BANKING

Asian Development Bank, Post Office Box 789, 1099 Manila, Philippines; *Key Indicators of Developing Asian and Pacific Countries*.

Facts on File, 460 Park Avenue South, New York, New York 10016 (800) 443-8323; *The New Book of World Rankings*.

G.K. Hall and Company, 70 Lincoln Street, Boston, Massachusetts 02111 (617) 423-3990; *The World in Figures*.

International Monetary Fund, 700 Nineteenth Street, NW, Washington, D.C. 20431 (202) 623-7000; *International Financial Statistics*.

PAPUA NEW GUINEA - BARLEY PRODUCTION - See PAPUA NEW GUINEA - CROPS

PAPUA NEW GUINEA - BAUXITE PRODUCTION AND CONSUMPTION - See PAPUA NEW GUINEA - MINING AND MINERAL PRODUCTS

PAPUA NEW GUINEA - BEER PRODUCTION

Facts on File, 460 Park Avenue South, New York, New York 10016 (800) 443-8323; *The New Book of World Rankings*.

PAPUA NEW GUINEA - BIRTH RATES

The Economist Intelligence Unit (Asia) Limited, 10th Floor, Luk Kwok Centre, 72 Gloucester Road, Wanchai, Hong Kong (Phone

Number in U.S. (800) 938-4685); *Asian Market Atlas*.

Facts on File, 460 Park Avenue South, New York, New York 10016 (800) 443-8323; *The New Book of World Rankings*.

Statistical Office of the United Nations, Publishing Service, New York, New York 10017 (800) 253-9646; *Demographic Yearbook*, and *Statistical Yearbook*.

Times Books, 201 East 50th Street, New York, New York 10022 (212) 751-2600; *The Economist Book of Vital World Statistics*.

The World Bank, 1818 H Street, NW, Washington, D.C. 20433 (202) 477-1234; *World Tables*.

World Health Organization, Office of Publications, Avenue Appia, CH-1211 Geneva 27, Switzerland (Telephone Number in U.S. (518) 436-9686); *World Health Statistics Annual*.

PAPUA NEW GUINEA - BONDS

Asian Development Bank, Post Office Box 789, 1099 Manila, Philippines; *Key Indicators of Developing Asian and Pacific Countries*.

G.K. Hall and Company, 70 Lincoln Street, Boston, Massachusetts 02111 (617) 423-3990; *The World in Figures*

International Monetary Fund, 700 Nineteenth Street, NW, Washington, D.C. 20431 (202) 623-7000; *Government Finance Statistics Yearbook*.

PAPUA NEW GUINEA - BOOK PRODUCTION

G.K. Hall and Company, 70 Lincoln Street, Boston, Massachusetts 02111 (617) 423-3990; *The World in Figures*.

PAPUA NEW GUINEA - BROADCASTING

Billboard Limited, Post Office Box 9027, 1006 AA Amsterdam, The Netherlands (Telephone Number in U.S. (212) 764-7300); *World Radio TV Handbook*.

The Economist Intelligence Unit (Asia) Limited, 10th Floor, Luk Kwok Centre, 72 Gloucester Road, Wanchai, Hong Kong (Phone Number in U.S. (800) 938-4685); *Asian Market Atlas*.

Facts on File, 460 Park Avenue South, New York, New York 10016 (800) 443-8323; *The New Book of World Rankings*.

G.K. Hall and Company, 70 Lincoln Street, Boston, Massachusetts 02111 (617) 423-3990; *The World in Figures*.

Times Books, 201 East 50th Street, New York, New York 10022 (212) 751-2600; *The Economist Book of Vital World Statistics*.

United Nations Educational, Scientific and Cultural Organization (UNESCO), 7 Place de Fontenoy, F-75700 Paris, France (Telephone Number in U.S. (212) 963-5981); *Statistical Yearbook*.

PAPUA NEW GUINEA - BUSINESS

G.K. Hall and Company, 70 Lincoln Street, Boston, Massachusetts 02111 (617) 423-3990; *The World in Figures*.

PAPUA NEW GUINEA - BUSINESS AND PROFESSIONAL LICENSES

International Monetary Fund, 700 Nineteenth Street, NW, Washington, D.C. 20431 (202) 623-7000; *Government Finance Statistics Yearbook.*

PAPUA NEW GUINEA - CACAO EXPORTS

International Monetary Fund, 700 Nineteenth Street, NW, Washington, D.C. 20431 (202) 623-7000; *International Financial Statistics.*

PAPUA NEW GUINEA - CADMIUM PRODUCTION AND CONSUMPTION - See PAPUA NEW GUINEA - MINING AND MINERAL PRODUCTS

PAPUA NEW GUINEA - CALORIE SUPPLY

Asian Development Bank, Post Office Box 789, 1099 Manila, Philippines; *Key Indicators of Developing Asian and Pacific Countries.*

Food and Agricultural Organization of the United Nations (FAO) Via delle Terme di Caracalla, 00100 Rome, Italy (Telephone Number in U.S. (202) 653-2400); *The State of Food and Agriculture.*

PAPUA NEW GUINEA - CAPITAL INVESTMENT

Asian Development Bank, Post Office Box 789, 1099 Manila, Philippines; *Key Indicators of Developing Asian and Pacific Countries.*

PAPUA NEW GUINEA - CAPITAL REVENUE

Asian Development Bank, Post Office Box 789, 1099 Manila, Philippines; *Key Indicators of Developing Asian and Pacific Countries.*

International Monetary Fund, 700 Nineteenth Street, NW, Washington, D.C. 20431 (202) 623-7000; *Government Finance Statistics Yearbook.*

PAPUA NEW GUINEA - CATTLE - See PAPUA NEW GUINEA - LIVESTOCK AND POULTRY

PAPUA NEW GUINEA - CEMENT PRODUCTION - See PAPUA NEW GUINEA - MINING AND MINERAL PRODUCTS

PAPUA NEW GUINEA - CHEMICAL (ORGANIC) PRODUCTION - See PAPUA NEW GUINEA - MINING AND MINERAL PRODUCTS

PAPUA NEW GUINEA - CHICKENS - See PAPUA NEW GUINEA - LIVESTOCK AND POULTRY

PAPUA NEW GUINEA - CIGARETTE PRODUCTION - See PAPUA NEW GUINEA - TOBACCO PRODUCTION

PAPUA NEW GUINEA - CLASS STRUCTURE

G.K. Hall and Company, 70 Lincoln Street, Boston, Massachusetts 02111 (617) 423-3990; *The World in Figures.*

PAPUA NEW GUINEA - CLIMATE

Facts on File, 460 Park Avenue South, New York, New York 10016 (800) 443-8323; *The New Book of World Rankings.*

G.K. Hall and Company, 70 Lincoln Street, Boston, Massachusetts 02111 (617) 423-3990; *The World in Figures.*

PAPUA NEW GUINEA - CLOTHING EXPORTS AND IMPORTS

South Pacific Commission, Post Box D5, Noumea Cedex, New Caledonia; *Statistical Bulletin of the South Pacific: Retail Price Indexes.*

PAPUA NEW GUINEA - COAL PRODUCTION - See PAPUA NEW GUINEA - MINING AND MINERAL PRODUCTS

PAPUA NEW GUINEA - COCOA PRODUCTION - See PAPUA NEW GUINEA - CROPS

PAPUA NEW GUINEA - COFFEE - See PAPUA NEW GUINEA - CROPS

PAPUA NEW GUINEA - COMMUNICATIONS

Federal Statistical Office, Gustav - Stresemann - Ring 11, D-6200 Wiesbaden, Germany; *Papua New Guinea.*

G.K. Hall and Company, 70 Lincoln Street, Boston, Massachusetts 02111 (617) 423-3990; *The World in Figures.*

Statistical Office of the United Nations, Publishing Service, New York, New York 10017 (800) 253-9646; *Statistical Yearbook for Asia and the Pacific.*

PAPUA NEW GUINEA - CONSTRUCTION INDUSTRY

Facts on File, 460 Park Avenue South, New York, New York 10016 (800) 443-8323; *The New Book of World Rankings.*

Statistical Office of the United Nations, Publishing Service, New York, New York 10017 (800) 253-9646; *Construction Statistics Yearbook,* and *Statistical Yearbook.*

PAPUA NEW GUINEA - CONSUMER PRICE INDEX

Asian Development Bank, Post Office Box 789, 1099 Manila, Philippines; *Key Indicators of Developing Asian and Pacific Countries.*

G.K. Hall and Company, 70 Lincoln Street, Boston, Massachusetts 02111 (617) 423-3990; *The World in Figures.*

Statistical Office of the United Nations, Publishing Service, New York, New York 10017 (800) 253-9646; *Statistical Yearbook.*

Times Books, 201 East 50th Street, New York, New York 10022 (212) 751-2600; *The Economist Book of Vital World Statistics.*

PAPUA NEW GUINEA - CONSUMER PRICES

International Labour Office, I.L.O. Publications, CH-1211, Geneva 22, Switzerland; *Yearbook of Labour Statistics.*

International Monetary Fund, 700 Nineteenth Street, NW, Washington, D.C. 20431 (202) 623-7000; *International Financial Statistics.*

PAPUA NEW GUINEA - CONSUMPTION

G.K. Hall and Company, 70 Lincoln Street, Boston, Massachusetts 02111 (617) 423-3990; *The World in Figures.*

South Pacific Commission, Post Box D5, Noumea Cedex, New Caledonia; *Statistical Bulletin of the South Pacific: Retail Price*

Indexes.

PAPUA NEW GUINEA - COPPER - See **PAPUA NEW GUINEA - MINING AND MINERAL PRODUCTS**

PAPUA NEW GUINEA - COPRA EXPORTS

International Monetary Fund, 700 Nineteenth Street, NW, Washington, D.C. 20431 (202) 623-7000; *International Financial Statistics.*

PAPUA NEW GUINEA - CORN PRODUCTION - See **PAPUA NEW GUINEA - CROPS**

PAPUA NEW GUINEA - CORPORATE TAXES - See **PAPUA NEW GUINEA - TAXATION**

PAPUA NEW GUINEA - COTTON PRODUCTION - See **PAPUA NEW GUINEA - CROPS**

PAPUA NEW GUINEA - CRIME

International Criminal Police Organization (INTERPOL), 26 rue Armengaud, 92210 Saint Cloud, France; *International Crime Statistics.*

PAPUA NEW GUINEA - CROPS

Asian Development Bank, Post Office Box 789, 1099 Manila, Philippines; *Key Indicators of Developing Asian and Pacific Countries.*

Facts on File, 460 Park Avenue South, New York, New York 10016 (800) 443-8323; *The New Book of World Rankings.*

Food and Agricultural Organization of the United Nations (FAO) Via delle Terme di Caracalla, 00100 Rome, Italy (Telephone Number in U.S. (202) 653-2400; *Production Yearbook,* and *The State of Food and Agriculture.*

International Monetary Fund, 700 Nineteenth Street, NW, Washington, D.C. 20431 (202) 623-7000; *International Financial Statistics.*

Statistical Office of the United Nations, Publishing Service, New York, New York 10017 (800) 253-9646; *Statistical Yearbook.*

PAPUA NEW GUINEA - CUSTOMS DUTIES

G.K. Hall and Company, 70 Lincoln Street, Boston, Massachusetts 02111 (617) 423-3990; *The World in Figures.*

International Monetary Fund, 700 Nineteenth Street, NW, Washington, D.C. 20431 (202) 623-7000; *Government Finance Statistics Yearbook.*

PAPUA NEW GUINEA - DAIRY PRODUCTS

Facts on File, 460 Park Avenue South, New York, New York 10016 (800) 443-8323; *The New Book of World Rankings.*

Food and Agricultural Organization of the United Nations (FAO), Via delle Terme di Caracalla, 00100 Rome, Italy (Telephone Number in U.S. (202) 653-2400); *Production Yearbook,* and *The State of Food and Agriculture.*

PAPUA NEW GUINEA - DEATH RATES

The Economist Intelligence Unit (Asia) Limited, 10th Floor, Luk Kwok Centre, 72 Gloucester Road, Wanchai, Hong Kong (Phone Number in U.S. (800) 938-4685); *Asian Market Atlas.*

G.K. Hall and Company, 70 Lincoln Street, Boston, Massachusetts 02111 (617) 423-3990; *The World in Figures.*

Statistical Office of the United Nations, Publishing Service, New York, New York 10017 (800) 253-9646; *Statistical Yearbook.*

Times Books, 201 East 50th Street, New York, New York 10022 (212) 751-2600; *The Economist Book of Vital World Statistics.*

World Health Organization, Office of Publications, Avenue Appia, CH-1211 Geneva 27, Switzerland (Telephone Number in U.S. (518) 436-9686); *World Health Statistics Annual.*

PAPUA NEW GUINEA - DEFENSE EXPENDITURES

G.K. Hall and Company, 70 Lincoln Street, Boston, Massachusetts 02111 (617) 423-3990; *The World in Figures.*

International Monetary Fund, 700 Nineteenth Street, NW, Washington, D.C. 20431 (202) 623-7000; *Government Finance Statistics Yearbook.*

U.S. Arms Control and Disarmament Agency, 320 Twenty first Street, NW, Washington, D.C. 20451 (202) 647-8677; *World Military Expenditures and Arms Transfers.*

PAPUA NEW GUINEA - DEMOGRAPHY

The Economist Intelligence Unit (Asia) Limited, 10th Floor, Luk Kwok Centre, 72 Gloucester Road, Wanchai, Hong Kong (Phone Number in U.S. (800) 938-4685); *Asian Market Atlas.*

Facts on File, 460 Park Avenue South, New York, New York 10016 (800) 443-8323; *The New Book of World Rankings.*

G.K. Hall and Company, 70 Lincoln Street, Boston, Massachusetts 02111 (617) 423-3990; *The World in Figures.*

PAPUA NEW GUINEA - DEVELOPMENT ASSISTANCE

Asian Development Bank, Post Office Box 789, 1099 Manila, Philippines; *Key Indicators of Developing Asian and Pacific Countries.*

G.K. Hall and Company, 70 Lincoln Street, Boston, Massachusetts 02111 (617) 423-3990; *The World in Figures.*

Statistical Office of the United Nations, Publishing Service, New York, New York 10017 (800) 253-9646; *Statistical Yearbook.*

PAPUA NEW GUINEA - DIAMOND PRODUCTION - See **PAPUA NEW GUINEA - MINING AND MINERAL PRODUCTS**

PAPUA NEW GUINEA - DISEASES

G.K. Hall and Company, 70 Lincoln Street, Boston, Massachusetts 02111 (617) 423-3990; *The World in Figures.*

World Health Organization, Office of Publications, Avenue Appia, CH-1211 Geneva 27, Switzerland (Telephone Number in U.S. (518) 436-9686); *World Health Statistics Annual.*

PAPUA NEW GUINEA - DIVORCE RATES

Facts on File, 460 Park Avenue South, New York, New York 10016 (800) 443-8323; *The New Book of World Rankings*.

Statistical Office of the United Nations, Publishing Service, New York, New York 10017 (800) 253-9646; *Demographic Yearbook*.

PAPUA NEW GUINEA - DOMESTIC PRODUCT

G.K. Hall and Company, 70 Lincoln Street, Boston, Massachusetts 02111 (617) 423-3990; *The World in Figures*.

PAPUA NEW GUINEA - DUCKS - See PAPUA NEW GUINEA - LIVESTOCK AND POULTRY

PAPUA NEW GUINEA - ECONOMY

Asian Development Bank, Post Office Box 789, 1099 Manila, Philippines; *Key Indicators of Developing Asian and Pacific Countries*.

Euromonitor Publications Limited, 87-88 Turnmill Street, London EC1M 5QU, England; *International Marketing Data and Statistics*.

Facts on File, 460 Park Avenue South, New York, New York 10016 (800) 443-8323; *The New Book of World Rankings*.

G.K. Hall and Company, 70 Lincoln Street, Boston, Massachusetts 02111 (617) 423-3990; *The World in Figures*.

PAPUA NEW GUINEA - EDUCATION

The Economist Intelligence Unit, 111 West 57th Street, New York, New York 10019 (800) 938-4685; *The World Market Atlas*.

The Economist Intelligence Unit (Asia) Limited, 10th Floor, Luk Kwok Centre, 72 Gloucester Road, Wanchai, Hong Kong (Phone Number in U.S. (800) 938-4685); *Asian Market Atlas*.

Facts on File, 460 Park Avenue South, New York, New York 10016 (800) 443-8323; *The New Book of World Rankings*.

Federal Statistical Office, Gustav - Stresemann - Ring 11, D-6200 Wiesbaden, Germany; *Papua New Guinea*.

G.K. Hall and Company, 70 Lincoln Street, Boston, Massachusetts 02111 (617) 423-3990; *The World in Figures*.

International Monetary Fund, 700 Nineteenth Street, NW, Washington, D.C. 20431 (202) 623-7000; *Government Finance Statistics Yearbook*.

Statistical Office of the United Nations, Publishing Service, New York, New York 10017 (800) 253-9646; *Statistical Yearbook for Asia and the Pacific*.

Times Books, 201 East 50th Street, New York, New York 10022 (212) 751-2600; *The Economist Book of Vital World Statistics*.

United Nations Educational, Scientific and Cultural Organization (UNESCO), 7 Place de Fontenoy, F-75700 Paris, France (Telephone Number in U.S. (212) 963-5981); *Statistical Yearbook*.

The World Bank, 1818 H Street, NW, Washington, D.C. 20433 (202) 477-1234; *World Tables*.

PAPUA NEW GUINEA - EGG PRODUCTION AND CONSUMPTION - See PAPUA NEW GUINEA - DAIRY PRODUCTS

PAPUA NEW GUINEA - ELECTRICITY

Asian Development Bank, Post Office Box 789, 1099 Manila, Philippines; *Key Indicators of Developing Asian and Pacific Countries*.

Facts on File, 460 Park Avenue South, New York, New York 10016 (800) 443-8323; *The New Book of World Rankings*.

Penn Well Publishing Company, 1421 South Sheridan Road, Post Office Box 1260, Tulsa, Oklahoma 74101 (800) 752-9764; *International Energy Statistics Sourcebook*.

Statistical Office of the United Nations, Publishing Service, New York, New York 10017 (800) 253-9646; *Statistical Yearbook*.

Times Books, 201 East 50th Street, New York, New York 10022 (212) 751-2600; *The Economist Book of Vital World Statistics*.

PAPUA NEW GUINEA - EMPLOYMENT

Euromonitor Publications Limited, 87-88 Turnmill Street, London EC1M 5QU, England; *International Marketing Data and Statistics*.

Facts on File, 460 Park Avenue South, New York, New York 10016 (800) 443-8323; *The New Book of World Rankings*.

Federal Statistical Office, Gustav - Stresemann - Ring 11, D-6200 Wiesbaden, Germany; *Papua New Guinea*.

International Labour Office, I.L.O. Publications, CH-1211, Geneva 22, Switzerland; *Yearbook of Labour Statistics*.

Statistical Office of the United Nations, Publishing Service, New York, New York 10017 (800) 253-9646; *Statistical Yearbook*.

PAPUA NEW GUINEA - ENERGY

Facts on File, 460 Park Avenue South, New York, New York 10016 (800) 443-8323; *The New Book of World Rankings*.

Food and Agricultural Organization of the United Nations (FAO) Via delle Terme di Caracalla, 00100 Rome, Italy (Telephone Number in U.S. (202) 653-2400); *The State of Food and Agriculture*.

G.K. Hall and Company, 70 Lincoln Street, Boston, Massachusetts 02111 (617) 423-3990; *The World in Figures*.

Penn Well Publishing Company, 1421 South Sheridan Road, Post Office Box 1260, Tulsa, Oklahoma 74101 (800) 752-9764; *International Energy Statistics Sourcebook*.

Statistical Office of the United Nations, Publishing Service, New York, New York 10017 (800) 253-9646; *Energy Statistics Yearbook, Statistical Yearbook, Statistical Yearbook for Asia and the Pacific, and World Energy Supplies*.

Times Books, 201 East 50th Street, New York, New York 10022 (212) 751-2600; *The Economist Book of Vital World Statistics*.

PAPUA NEW GUINEA - EXCHANGE RATES

Asian Development Bank, Post Office Box 789, 1099 Manila, Philippines; *Key Indicators of Developing Asian and Pacific Countries*.

The Economist Intelligence Unit (Asia) Limited, 10th Floor, Luk Kwok Centre, 72 Gloucester Road, Wanchai, Hong Kong (Phone Number in U.S. (800) 938-4685); *Asian Market Atlas*.

Euromonitor Publications Limited, 87-88 Turnmill Street, London EC1M 5QU, England; *International Marketing Data and Statistics*.

International Civil Aviation Organization, 1000 Sherbrooke Street, West, Montreal, Quebec, Canada H3A 2R2 (514) 285-8219; *Civil Aviation Statistics of the World*.

International Monetary Fund, 700 Nineteenth Street, NW, Washington, D.C. 20431 (202) 623-7000; *International Financial Statistics*.

Statistical Office of the United Nations, Publishing Service, New York, New York 10017 (800) 253-9646; *Statistical Yearbook*.

PAPUA NEW GUINEA - EXCISE TAXES - See PAPUA NEW GUINEA - TAXATION

PAPUA NEW GUINEA - EXPORTS

American Automobile Manufacturers Association, 1401 H Street, NW, Suite 900, Washington, D.C. 20005 (202) 326-5500; *World Motor Vehicle Data*.

Asian Development Bank, Post Office Box 789, 1099 Manila, Philippines; *Key Indicators of Developing Asian and Pacific Countries*.

The Economist Intelligence Unit, 111 West 57th Street, New York, New York 10019 (800) 938-4685; *The World Market Atlas*.

The Economist Intelligence Unit (Asia) Limited, 10th Floor, Luk Kwok Centre, 72 Gloucester Road, Wanchai, Hong Kong (Phone Number in U.S. (800) 938-4685); *Asian Market Atlas*.

Euromonitor Publications Limited, 87-88 Turnmill Street, London EC1M 5QU, England; *International Marketing Data and Statistics*.

Food and Agricultural Organization of the United Nations (FAO) Via delle Terme di Caracalla, 00100 Rome, Italy (Telephone Number in U.S. (202) 653-2400); *The State of Food and Agriculture*.

G.K. Hall and Company, 70 Lincoln Street, Boston, Massachusetts 02111 (617) 423-3990; *The World in Figures*.

International Monetary Fund, 700 Nineteenth Street, NW, Washington, D.C. 20431 (202) 623-7000; *Direction of Trade Statistics, Government Finance Statistics Yearbook*, and *International Financial Statistics*.

South Pacific Commission, Post Box D5, Noumea Cedex, New Caledonia; *Statistical Bulletin of the South Pacific: Overseas Trade*.

Times Books, 201 East 50th Street, New York, New York 10022 (212) 751-2600; *The Economist Book of Vital World Statistics*.

The World Bank, 1818 H Street, NW, Washington, D.C. 20433 (202) 477-1234; *World Tables*.

PAPUA NEW GUINEA - EXTERNAL FINANCING

Asian Development Bank, Post Office Box 789, 1099 Manila, Philippines; *Key Indicators of Developing Asian and Pacific Countries*.

PAPUA NEW GUINEA - EXTERNAL INDEBTEDNESS

Asian Development Bank, Post Office Box 789, 1099 Manila, Philippines; *Key Indicators of Developing Asian and Pacific Countries*.

PAPUA NEW GUINEA - EXTERNAL TRADE

Asian Development Bank, Post Office Box 789, 1099 Manila, Philippines; *Key Indicators of Developing Asian and Pacific Countries*.

Food and Agricultural Organization of the United Nations (FAO) Via delle Terme di Caracalla, 00100 Rome, Italy (Telephone Number in U.S. (202) 653-2400); *The State of Food and Agriculture*, and *Trade Yearbook*.

G.K. Hall and Company, 70 Lincoln Street, Boston, Massachusetts 02111 (617) 423-3990; *The World in Figures*.

Statistical Office of the United Nations, Publishing Service, New York, New York 10017 (800) 253-9646; *Statistical Yearbook*, and *Statistical Yearbook for Asia and the Pacific*.

PAPUA NEW GUINEA - FARM CROPS - See PAPUA NEW GUINEA - CROPS

PAPUA NEW GUINEA - FEMALE WORKING POPULATION - See PAPUA NEW GUINEA - EMPLOYMENT

PAPUA NEW GUINEA - FERTILITY RATES

The Economist Intelligence Unit (Asia) Limited, 10th Floor, Luk Kwok Centre, 72 Gloucester Road, Wanchai, Hong Kong (Phone Number in U.S. (800) 938-4685); *Asian Market Atlas*.

Facts on File, 460 Park Avenue South, New York, New York 10016 (800) 443-8323; *The New Book of World Rankings*.

Times Books, 201 East 50th Street, New York, New York 10022 (212) 751-2600; *The Economist Book of Vital World Statistics*.

The World Bank, 1818 H Street, NW, Washington, D.C. 20433 (202) 477-1234; *World Tables*.

PAPUA NEW GUINEA - FERTILIZER

Food and Agricultural Organization of the United Nations (FAO), Via delle Terme di Caracalla, 00100 Rome, Italy (Telephone Number in U.S. (202) 653-2400); *Fertilizer Yearbook*, and *The State of Food and Agriculture*.

Statistical Office of the United Nations, Publishing Service, New York, New York 10017 (800) 253-9646; *Statistical Yearbook*.

PAPUA NEW GUINEA - FETAL MORTALITY

Statistical Office of the United Nations, Publishing Service, New York, New York 10017 (800) 253-9646; *Demographic Yearbook*.

PAPUA NEW GUINEA - FINANCE

Asian Development Bank, Post Office Box 789, 1099 Manila, Philippines; *Key Indicators of Developing Asian and Pacific Countries*.

Facts on File, 460 Park Avenue South, New York, New York 10016 (800) 443-8323; *The New Book of World Rankings*.

Federal Statistical Office, Gustav - Stresemann - Ring 11, D-6200 Wiesbaden, Germany; *Papua New Guinea*.

G.K. Hall and Company, 70 Lincoln Street, Boston, Massachusetts 02111 (617) 423-3990; *The World in Figures.*

International Monetary Fund, 700 Nineteenth Street, NW, Washington, D.C. 20431 (202) 623-7000; *Government Finance Statistics Yearbook,* and *International Financial Statistics.*

Statistical Office of the United Nations, Publishing Service, New York, New York 10017 (800) 253-9646; *Statistical Yearbook for Asia and the Pacific.*

PAPUA NEW GUINEA - FISHERIES

Facts on File, 460 Park Avenue South, New York, New York 10016 (800) 443-8323; *The New Book of World Rankings.*

Federal Statistical Office, Gustav - Stresemann - Ring 11, D-6200 Wiesbaden, Germany; *Papua New Guinea.*

Food and Agricultural Organization of the United Nations (FAO) Via delle Terme di Caracalla, 00100 Rome, Italy (Telephone Number in U.S. (202) 653-2400); *The State of Food and Agriculture,* and *Yearbook of Fishery Statistics.*

Statistical Office of the United Nations, Publishing Service, New York, New York 10017 (800) 253-9646; *Statistical Yearbook.*

PAPUA NEW GUINEA - FOOD

Food and Agricultural Organization of the United Nations (FAO), Via delle Terme di Caracalla, 00100 Rome, Italy (Telephone Number in U.S. (202) 653-2400); *Production Yearbook,* and *The State of Food and Agriculture.*

G.K. Hall and Company, 70 Lincoln Street, Boston, Massachusetts 02111 (617) 423-3990; *The World in Figures.*

South Pacific Commission, Post Box D5, Noumea Cedex, New Caledonia; *Statistical Bulletin of the South Pacific: Retail Price Indexes.*

Statistical Office of the United Nations, Publishing Service, New York, New York 10017 (800) 253-9646; *Statistical Yearbook for Asia and the Pacific.*

PAPUA NEW GUINEA - FOREIGN AID

G.K. Hall and Company, 70 Lincoln Street, Boston, Massachusetts 02111 (617) 423-3990; *The World in Figures.*

PAPUA NEW GUINEA - FOREIGN DEBT

International Monetary Fund, 700 Nineteenth Street, NW, Washington, D.C. 20431 (202) 623-7000; *Government Finance Statistics Yearbook.*

PAPUA NEW GUINEA - FOREIGN TRADE

Asian Development Bank, Post Office Box 789, 1099 Manila, Philippines; *Key Indicators of Developing Asian and Pacific Countries.*

The Economist Intelligence Unit (Asia) Limited, 10th Floor, Luk Kwok Centre, 72 Gloucester Road, Wanchai, Hong Kong (Phone Number in U.S. (800) 938-4685); *Asian Market Atlas.*

Euromonitor Publications Limited, 87-88 Turnmill Street, London EC1M 5QU, England; *International Marketing Data and Statistics.*

Facts on File, 460 Park Avenue South, New York, New York 10016 (800) 443-8323; *The New Book of World Rankings.*

Federal Statistical Office, Gustav - Stresemann - Ring 11, D-6200 Wiesbaden, Germany; *Papua New Guinea.*

Food and Agricultural Organization of the United Nations (FAO) Via delle Terme di Caracalla, 00100 Rome, Italy (Telephone Number in U.S. (202) 653-2400); *The State of Food and Agriculture.*

G.K. Hall and Company, 70 Lincoln Street, Boston, Massachusetts 02111 (617) 423-3990; *The World in Figures.*

South Pacific Commission, Post Box D5, Noumea Cedex, New Caledonia; *Statistical Bulletin of the South Pacific: Overseas Trade.*

Statistical Office of the United Nations, Publishing Service, New York, New York 10017 (800) 253-9646; *International Trade Statistics Yearbook,* and *Statistical Yearbook.*

The World Bank, 1818 H Street, NW, Washington, D.C. 20433 (202) 477-1234; *World Metal Statistics,* and *World Tables.*

PAPUA NEW GUINEA - FORESTRY AND FOREST PRODUCTS

The Economist Intelligence Unit (Asia) Limited, 10th Floor, Luk Kwok Centre, 72 Gloucester Road, Wanchai, Hong Kong (Phone Number in U.S. (800) 938-4685); *Asian Market Atlas.*

Facts on File, 460 Park Avenue South, New York, New York 10016 (800) 443-8323; *The New Book of World Rankings.*

Federal Statistical Office, Gustav - Stresemann - Ring 11, D-6200 Wiesbaden, Germany; *Papua New Guinea.*

Food and Agricultural Organization of the United Nations (FAO) Via delle Terme di Caracalla, 00100 Rome, Italy (Telephone Number in U.S. (202) 653-2400); *The State of Food and Agriculture,* and *Yearbook of Forest Products.*

G.K. Hall and Company, 70 Lincoln Street, Boston, Massachusetts 02111 (617) 423-3990; *The World in Figures.*

Statistical Office of the United Nations, Publishing Service, New York, New York 10017 (800) 253-9646; *Statistical Yearbook.*

United Nations Educational, Scientific and Cultural Organization (UNESCO), 7 Place de Fontenoy, F-75700 Paris, France (Telephone Number in U.S. (212) 963-5981); *Statistical Yearbook.*

PAPUA NEW GUINEA - GAS PRODUCTION - See PAPUA NEW GUINEA - MINING AND MINERAL PRODUCTS

PAPUA NEW GUINEA - GENERAL INDUSTRIAL STATISTICS

Statistical Office of the United Nations, Publishing Service, New York, New York 10017 (800) 253-9646; *Industrial Statistics Yearbook.*

PAPUA NEW GUINEA - GENERAL MORTALITY

Statistical Office of the United Nations, Publishing Service, New York, New York 10017 (800) 253-9646; *Demographic Yearbook.*

World Health Organization, Office of Publications, Avenue Appia, CH-1211 Geneva 27, Switzerland (Telephone Number in U.S. (518) 436-9686); *World Health Statistics Annual.*

PAPUA NEW GUINEA - GEOGRAPHIC DATA

Facts on File, 460 Park Avenue South, New York, New York 10016 (800) 443-8323; *The New Book of World Rankings*.

PAPUA NEW GUINEA - GOATS - See PAPUA NEW GUINEA - LIVESTOCK AND POULTRY

PAPUA NEW GUINEA - GOLD HOLDINGS

International Monetary Fund, 700 Nineteenth Street, NW, Washington, D.C. 20431 (202) 623-7000; *International Financial Statistics*.

Statistical Office of the United Nations, Publishing Service, New York, New York 10017 (800) 253-9646; *Statistical Yearbook*.

The World Bank, 1818 H Street, NW, Washington, D.C. 20433 (202) 477-1234; *World Tables*.

PAPUA NEW GUINEA - GOLD PRODUCTION AND CONSUMPTION - See PAPUA NEW GUINEA - MINING AND MINERAL PRODUCTS

PAPUA NEW GUINEA - GOVERNMENT

Asian Development Bank, Post Office Box 789, 1099 Manila, Philippines; *Key Indicators of Developing Asian and Pacific Countries*.

G.K. Hall and Company, 70 Lincoln Street, Boston, Massachusetts 02111 (617) 423-3990; *The World in Figures*.

PAPUA NEW GUINEA - GOVERNMENT EXPENDITURES

Asian Development Bank, Post Office Box 789, 1099 Manila, Philippines; *Key Indicators of Developing Asian and Pacific Countries*.

International Monetary Fund, 700 Nineteenth Street, NW, Washington, D.C. 20431 (202) 623-7000; *Government Finance Statistics Yearbook*.

Times Books, 201 East 50th Street, New York, New York 10022 (212) 751-2600; *The Economist Book of Vital World Statistics*.

The World Bank, 1818 H Street, NW, Washington, D.C. 20433 (202) 477-1234; *World Tables*.

PAPUA NEW GUINEA - GOVERNMENT FINANCES

Asian Development Bank, Post Office Box 789, 1099 Manila, Philippines; *Key Indicators of Developing Asian and Pacific Countries*.

PAPUA NEW GUINEA - GOVERNMENT REVENUES

Asian Development Bank, Post Office Box 789, 1099 Manila, Philippines; *Key Indicators of Developing Asian and Pacific Countries*.

International Monetary Fund, 700 Nineteenth Street, NW, Washington, D.C. 20431 (202) 623-7000; *Government Finance Statistics Yearbook*.

Times Books, 201 East 50th Street, New York, New York 10022 (212) 751-2600; *The Economist Book of Vital World Statistics*.

The World Bank, 1818 H Street, NW, Washington, D.C. 20433 (202) 477-1234; *World Tables*.

PAPUA NEW GUINEA - GRAIN PRODUCTION - See PAPUA NEW GUINEA - CROPS

PAPUA NEW GUINEA - GRANTS

International Monetary Fund, 700 Nineteenth Street, NW, Washington, D.C. 20431 (202) 623-7000; *Government Finance Statistics Yearbook*.

PAPUA NEW GUINEA - GROSS DOMESTIC PRODUCT

Asian Development Bank, Post Office Box 789, 1099 Manila, Philippines; *Key Indicators of Developing Asian and Pacific Countries*.

The Economist Intelligence Unit, 111 West 57th Street, New York, New York 10019 (800) 938-4685; *The World Market Atlas*.

The Economist Intelligence Unit (Asia) Limited, 10th Floor, Luk Kwok Centre, 72 Gloucester Road, Wanchai, Hong Kong (Phone Number in U.S. (800) 938-4685); *Asian Market Atlas*.

Euromonitor Publications Limited, 87-88 Turnmill Street, London EC1M 5QU, England; *International Marketing Data and Statistics*.

Facts on File, 460 Park Avenue South, New York, New York 10016 (800) 443-8323; *The New Book of World Rankings*.

G.K. Hall and Company, 70 Lincoln Street, Boston, Massachusetts 02111 (617) 423-3990; *The World in Figures*.

Statistical Office of the United Nations, Publishing Service, New York, New York 10017 (800) 253-9646; *Statistical Yearbook*.

Times Books, 201 East 50th Street, New York, New York 10022 (212) 751-2600; *The Economist Book of Vital World Statistics*.

The World Bank, 1818 H Street, NW, Washington, D.C. 20433 (202) 477-1234; *World Tables*.

PAPUA NEW GUINEA - GROSS NATIONAL PRODUCT

Asian Development Bank, Post Office Box 789, 1099 Manila, Philippines; *Key Indicators of Developing Asian and Pacific Countries*.

Euromonitor Publications Limited, 87-88 Turnmill Street, London EC1M 5QU, England; *International Marketing Data and Statistics*.

U.S. Arms Control and Disarmament Agency, 320 Twenty-first Street, NW, Washington, D.C. 20451 (202) 647-8677; *World Military Expenditures and Arms Transfers*.

The World Bank, 1818 H Street, NW, Washington, D.C. 20433 (202) 477-1234; *World Tables*.

PAPUA NEW GUINEA - GROUNDNUT PRODUCTION - See PAPUA NEW GUINEA - CROPS

PAPUA NEW GUINEA - HEALTH

The Economist Intelligence Unit (Asia) Limited, 10th Floor, Luk Kwok Centre, 72 Gloucester Road, Wanchai, Hong Kong (Phone Number in U.S. (800) 938-4685); *Asian Market Atlas*.

Facts on File, 460 Park Avenue South, New York, New York 10016 (800) 443-8323; *The New Book of World Rankings*.

Federal Statistical Office, Gustav - Stresemann - Ring 11, D-6200 Wiesbaden, Germany; *Papua New Guinea.*

G.K. Hall and Company, 70 Lincoln Street, Boston, Massachusetts 02111 (617) 423-3990; *The World in Figures.*

South Pacific Commission, Post Box D5, Noumea Cedex, New Caledonia; *Statistical Bulletin of the South Pacific: Retail Price Indexes.*

Statistical Office of the United Nations, Publishing Service, New York, New York 10017 (800) 253-9646; *Statistical Yearbook.*

Times Books, 201 East 50th Street, New York, New York 10022 (212) 751-2600; *The Economist Book of Vital World Statistics.*

World Health Organization, Office of Publications, Avenue Appia, CH-1211 Geneva 27, Switzerland (Telephone Number in U.S. (518) 436-9686); *World Health Statistics Annual.*

PAPUA NEW GUINEA - HEALTH EXPENDITURES

International Monetary Fund, 700 Nineteenth Street, NW, Washington, D.C. 20431 (202) 623-7000; *Government Finance Statistics Yearbook.*

PAPUA NEW GUINEA - HIDE PRODUCTION

Food and Agricultural Organization of the United Nations (FAO), Via delle Terme di Caracalla, 00100 Rome, Italy (Telephone Number in U.S. (202) 653-2400); *Production Yearbook.*

PAPUA NEW GUINEA - HIGHWAYS

The Economist Intelligence Unit (Asia) Limited, 10th Floor, Luk Kwok Centre, 72 Gloucester Road, Wanchai, Hong Kong (Phone Number in U.S. (800) 938-4685); *Asian Market Atlas.*

G.K. Hall and Company, 70 Lincoln Street, Boston, Massachusetts 02111 (617) 423-3990; *The World in Figures.*

PAPUA NEW GUINEA - HORSES - See PAPUA NEW GUINEA - LIVESTOCK AND POULTRY

PAPUA NEW GUINEA - HOURS OF WORK - See PAPUA NEW GUINEA - EMPLOYMENT

PAPUA NEW GUINEA - HOUSING AND HOUSING UNITS

Facts on File, 460 Park Avenue South, New York, New York 10016 (800) 443-8323; *The New Book of World Rankings.*

South Pacific Commission, Post Box D5, Noumea Cedex, New Caledonia; *Statistical Bulletin of the South Pacific: Retail Price Indexes.*

PAPUA NEW GUINEA - HOUSING EXPENDITURES

International Monetary Fund, 700 Nineteenth Street, NW, Washington, D.C. 20431 (202) 623-7000; *Government Finance Statistics Yearbook.*

South Pacific Commission, Post Box D5, Noumea Cedex, New Caledonia; *Statistical Bulletin of the South Pacific: Retail Price Indexes.*

PAPUA NEW GUINEA - ILLITERATE POPULATION

The Economist Intelligence Unit, 111 West 57th Street, New York, New York 10019 (800) 938-4685; *The World Market Atlas.*

G.K. Hall and Company, 70 Lincoln Street, Boston, Massachusetts 02111 (617) 423-3990; *The World in Figures.*

PAPUA NEW GUINEA - IMPORTS

American Automobile Manufacturers Association, 1401 H Street, NW, Suite 900, Washington, D.C. 20005 (202) 326-5500; *World Motor Vehicle Data.*

Asian Development Bank, Post Office Box 789, 1099 Manila, Philippines; *Key Indicators of Developing Asian and Pacific Countries.*

The Economist Intelligence Unit, 111 West 57th Street, New York, New York 10019 (800) 938-4685; *The World Market Atlas.*

The Economist Intelligence Unit (Asia) Limited, 10th Floor, Luk Kwok Centre, 72 Gloucester Road, Wanchai, Hong Kong (Phone Number in U.S. (800) 938-4685); *Asian Market Atlas.*

Euromonitor Publications Limited, 87-88 Turnmill Street, London EC1M 5QU, England; *International Marketing Data and Statistics.*

Food and Agricultural Organization of the United Nations (FAO) Via delle Terme di Caracalla, 00100 Rome, Italy (Telephone Number in U.S. (202) 653-2400); *The State of Food and Agriculture.*

G.K. Hall and Company, 70 Lincoln Street, Boston, Massachusetts 02111 (617) 423-3990; *The World in Figures.*

International Monetary Fund, 700 Nineteenth Street, NW, Washington, D.C. 20431 (202) 623-7000; *Direction of Trade Statistics, Government Finance Statistics Yearbook,* and *International Financial Statistics.*

South Pacific Commission, Post Box D5, Noumea Cedex, New Caledonia; *Statistical Bulletin of the South Pacific: Overseas Trade.*

Times Books, 201 East 50th Street, New York, New York 10022 (212) 751-2600; *The Economist Book of Vital World Statistics.*

The World Bank, 1818 H Street, NW, Washington, D.C. 20433 (202) 477-1234; *World Tables.*

PAPUA NEW GUINEA - INCOME TAXES - See PAPUA NEW GUINEA - TAXATION

PAPUA NEW GUINEA - INDUSTRY

Euromonitor Publications Limited, 87-88 Turnmill Street, London EC1M 5QU, England; *Industrial Marketing Data and Statistics.*

Facts on File, 460 Park Avenue South, New York, New York 10016 (800) 443-8323; *The New Book of World Rankings.*

Federal Statistical Office, Gustav - Stresemann - Ring 11, D-6200 Wiesbaden, Germany; *Papua New Guinea.*

G.K. Hall and Company, 70 Lincoln Street, Boston, Massachusetts 02111 (617) 423-3990; *The World in Figures.*

International Labour Office, I.L.O. Publications, CH-1211, Geneva 22, Switzerland; *Yearbook of Labour Statistics.*

Times Books, 201 East 50th Street, New York, New York 10022 (212) 751-2600; *The Economist Book of Vital World Statistics*.

Statistical Office of the United Nations, Publishing Service, New York, New York 10017 (800) 253-9646; *Statistical Yearbook for Asia and the Pacific*.

The World Bank, 1818 H Street, NW, Washington, D.C. 20433 (202) 477-1234; *World Tables*.

PAPUA NEW GUINEA - INFANT AND MATERNAL MORTALITY

The Economist Intelligence Unit (Asia) Limited, 10th Floor, Luk Kwok Centre, 72 Gloucester Road, Wanchai, Hong Kong (Phone Number in U.S. (800) 938-4685); *Asian Market Atlas*.

Statistical Office of the United Nations, Publishing Service, New York, New York 10017 (800) 253-9646; *Demographic Yearbook*.

Times Books, 201 East 50th Street, New York, New York 10022 (212) 751-2600; *The Economist Book of Vital World Statistics*.

The World Bank, 1818 H Street, NW, Washington, D.C. 20433 (202) 477-1234; *World Tables*.

PAPUA NEW GUINEA - INTERNAL TRADE

Statistical Office of the United Nations, Publishing Service, New York, New York 10017 (800) 253-9646; *Statistical Yearbook Asia and the Pacific*.

PAPUA NEW GUINEA - INTERNATIONAL LIQUIDITY

International Monetary Fund, 700 Nineteenth Street, NW, Washington, D.C. 20431 (202) 623-7000; *International Financial Statistics*.

PAPUA NEW GUINEA - INTERNATIONAL RESERVES EXCLUDING GOLD

Asian Development Bank, Post Office Box 789, 1099 Manila, Philippines; *Key Indicators of Developing Asian and Pacific Countries*.

Statistical Office of the United Nations, Publishing Service, New York, New York 10017 (800) 253-9646; *Statistical Yearbook*.

The World Bank, 1818 H Street, NW, Washington, D.C. 20433 (202) 477-1234; *World Tables*.

PAPUA NEW GUINEA - INTERNATIONAL STATISTICS

Asian Development Bank, Post Office Box 789, 1099 Manila, Philippines; *Key Indicators of Developing Asian and Pacific Countries*.

PAPUA NEW GUINEA - IRON ORE PRODUCTION AND CONSUMPTION - See PAPUA NEW GUINEA - MINING AND MINERAL PRODUCTS

PAPUA NEW GUINEA - IRRIGATION

Euromonitor Publications Limited, 87-88 Turnmill Street, London EC1M 5QU, England; *International Marketing Data and Statistics*.

PAPUA NEW GUINEA - LABOR FORCE

The Economist Intelligence Unit (Asia) Limited, 10th Floor, Luk Kwok Centre, 72 Gloucester Road, Wanchai, Hong Kong (Phone

Number in U.S. (800) 938-4685); *Asian Market Atlas*.

Euromonitor Publications Limited, 87-88 Turnmill Street, London EC1M 5QU, England; *International Marketing Data and Statistics*.

Facts on File, 460 Park Avenue South, New York, New York 10016 (800) 443-8323; *The New Book of World Rankings*.

Food and Agricultural Organization of the United Nations (FAO) Via delle Terme di Caracalla, 00100 Rome, Italy (Telephone Number in U.S. (202) 653-2400); *The State of Food and Agriculture*.

G.K. Hall and Company, 70 Lincoln Street, Boston, Massachusetts 02111 (617) 423-3990; *The World in Figures*.

The World Bank, 1818 H Street, NW, Washington, D.C. 20433 (202) 477-1234; *World Tables*.

PAPUA NEW GUINEA - LABOR PRODUCTIVITY

International Labour Office, I.L.O. Publications, CH-1211, Geneva 22, Switzerland; *Yearbook of Labour Statistics*.

PAPUA NEW GUINEA - LAND USE

Euromonitor Publications Limited, 87-88 Turnmill Street, London EC1M 5QU, England; *International Marketing Data and Statistics*.

Food and Agricultural Organization of the United Nations (FAO), Via delle Terme di Caracalla, 00100 Rome, Italy (Telephone Number in U.S. (202) 653-2400); *Production Yearbook*.

G.K. Hall and Company, 70 Lincoln Street, Boston, Massachusetts 02111 (617) 423-3990; *The World in Figures*

PAPUA NEW GUINEA - LEAD AND LEAD ORE PRODUCTION AND CONSUMPTION - See PAPUA NEW GUINEA - MINING AND MINERAL PRODUCTS

PAPUA NEW GUINEA - LIBRARIES

Facts on File, 460 Park Avenue South, New York, New York 10016 (800) 443-8323; *The New Book of World Rankings*.

United Nations Educational, Scientific and Cultural Organization (UNESCO), 7 Place de Fontenoy, F-75700 Paris, France (Telephone Number in U.S. (212) 963-5981); *Statistical Yearbook*.

PAPUA NEW GUINEA - LIFE EXPECTANCY

The Economist Intelligence Unit (Asia) Limited, 10th Floor, Luk Kwok Centre, 72 Gloucester Road, Wanchai, Hong Kong (Phone Number in U.S. (800) 938-4685); *Asian Market Atlas*.

PAPUA NEW GUINEA - LIVESTOCK AND POULTRY

Euromonitor Publications Limited, 87-88 Turnmill Street, London EC1M 5QU, England; *International Marketing Data and Statistics*.

Facts on File, 460 Park Avenue South, New York, New York 10016 (800) 443-8323; *The New Book of World Rankings*.

Food and Agricultural Organization of the United Nations (FAO), Via delle Terme di Caracalla, 00100 Rome, Italy (Telephone Number in U.S. (202) 653-2400); *Production Yearbook*, and *The State of Food and Agriculture*.

G.K. Hall and Company, 70 Lincoln Street, Boston, Massachusetts 02111 (617) 423-3990; *The World in Figures*.

Statistical Office of the United Nations, Publishing Service, New York, New York 10017 (800) 253-9646; *Statistical Yearbook.*

PAPUA NEW GUINEA - LIVING LEVELS

G.K. Hall and Company, 70 Lincoln Street, Boston, Massachusetts 02111 (617) 423-3990; *The World in Figures.*

Times Books, 201 East 50th Street, New York, New York 10022 (212) 751-2600; *The Economist Book of Vital World Statistics.*

PAPUA NEW GUINEA - MANPOWER

Statistical Office of the United Nations, Publishing Service, New York, New York 10017 (800) 253-9646; *Statistical Yearbook for Asia and the Pacific.*

PAPUA NEW GUINEA - MANUFACTURING

American Automobile Manufacturers Association, 1401 H Street, NW, Suite 900, Washington, D.C. 20005 (202) 326-5500; *World Motor Vehicle Data.*

Asian Development Bank, Post Office Box 789, 1099 Manila, Philippines; *Key Indicators of Developing Asian and Pacific Countries.*

Facts on File, 460 Park Avenue South, New York, New York 10016 (800) 443-8323; *The New Book of World Rankings.*

G.K. Hall and Company, 70 Lincoln Street, Boston, Massachusetts 02111 (617) 423-3990; *The World in Figures.*

Statistical Office of the United Nations, Publishing Service, New York, New York 10017 (800) 253-9646; *Statistical Yearbook.*

Times Books, 201 East 50th Street, New York, New York 10022 (212) 751-2600; *The Economist Book of Vital World Statistics.*

The World Bank, 1818 H Street, NW, Washington, D.C. 20433 (202) 477-1234; *World Tables.*

PAPUA NEW GUINEA - MARRIAGE RATES

Facts on File, 460 Park Avenue South, New York, New York 10016 (800) 443-8323; *The New Book of World Rankings.*

Statistical Office of the United Nations, Publishing Service, New York, New York 10017 (800) 253-9646; *Demographic Yearbook.*

PAPUA NEW GUINEA - MEAT PRODUCTION - See PAPUA NEW GUINEA - LIVESTOCK AND POULTRY

PAPUA NEW GUINEA - MERCHANT SHIPPING

G.K. Hall and Company, 70 Lincoln Street, Boston, Massachusetts 02111 (617) 423-3990; *The World in Figures.*

Lloyd's Register of Shipping, 17 Battery Place, New York, New York 10004 (212) 425-8050; *Register of Ships.*

Statistical Office of the United Nations, Publishing Service, New York, New York 10017 (800) 253-9646; *Statistical Yearbook.*

Times Books, 201 East 50th Street, New York, New York 10022 (212) 751-2600; *The Economist Book of Vital World Statistics.*

PAPUA NEW GUINEA - MILITARY

The Economist Intelligence Unit (Asia) Limited, 10th Floor, Luk Kwok Centre, 72 Gloucester Road, Wanchai, Hong Kong (Phone Number in U.S. (800) 938-4685); *Asian Market Atlas.*

G.K. Hall and Company, 70 Lincoln Street, Boston, Massachusetts 02111 (617) 423-3990; *The World in Figures.*

The International Institute for Strategic Studies, 23 Tavistock Street, London WC2E 7NQ, England; *The Military Balance.*

U.S. Arms Control and Disarmament Agency, 320 Twenty-first Street, NW, Washington, D.C. 20451 (202) 647-8677; *World Military Expenditures and Arms Transfers.*

PAPUA NEW GUINEA - MILK PRODUCTION - See PAPUA NEW GUINEA - DAIRY PRODUCTS

PAPUA NEW GUINEA - MINING AND MINERAL PRODUCTS

Asian Development Bank, Post Office Box 789, 1099 Manila, Philippines; *Key Indicators of Developing Asian and Pacific Countries.*

Facts on File, 460 Park Avenue South, New York, New York 10016 (800) 443-8323; *The New Book of World Rankings.*

G.K. Hall and Company, 70 Lincoln Street, Boston, Massachusetts 02111 (617) 423-3990; *The World in Figures.*

International Monetary Fund, 700 Nineteenth Street, NW, Washington, D.C. 20431 (202) 623-7000; *International Financial Statistics.*

Penn Well Publishing Company, 1421 South Sheridan Road, Post Office Box 1260, Tulsa, Oklahoma 74101 (800) 752-9764; *International Energy Statistics Sourcebook.*

Statistical Office of the United Nations, Publishing Service, New York, New York 10017 (800) 253-9646; *Statistical Yearbook.*

World Bureau of Metal Statistics, 27-A High Street, Ware, Herts. SG12 9BA, England; *World Metal Statistics.*

PAPUA NEW GUINEA - MOLYBDENUM - See PAPUA NEW GUINEA - MINING AND MINERAL PRODUCTS

PAPUA NEW GUINEA - MONEY EXCHANGE RATES

Euromonitor Publications Limited, 87-88 Turnmill Street, London EC1M 5QU, England; *International Marketing Data and Statistics.*

Statistical Office of the United Nations, Publishing Service, New York, New York 10017 (800) 253-9646; *Statistical Yearbook.*

PAPUA NEW GUINEA - MONEY RESERVES

Euromonitor Publications Limited, 87-88 Turnmill Street, London EC1M 5QU, England; *International Marketing Data and Statistics.*

PAPUA NEW GUINEA - MONEY SUPPLY

Asian Development Bank, Post Office Box 789, 1099 Manila, Philippines; *Key Indicators of Developing Asian and Pacific Countries.*

Euromonitor Publications Limited, 87-88 Turnmill Street, London EC1M 5QU, England; *International Marketing Data and Statistics.*

G.K. Hall and Company, 70 Lincoln Street, Boston, Massachusetts 02111 (617) 423-3990; *The World in Figures.*

The World Bank, 1818 H Street, NW, Washington, D.C. 20433 (202) 477-1234; *World Tables.*

PAPUA NEW GUINEA - MOTION PICTURES

Statistical Office of the United Nations, Publishing Service, New York, New York 10017 (800) 253-9646; *Statistical Yearbook.*

PAPUA NEW GUINEA - MOTOR VEHICLE PRODUCTION

American Automobile Manufacturers Association, 1401 H Street, NW, Suite 900, Washington, D.C. 20005 (202) 326-5500; *World Motor Vehicle Data.*

Times Books, 201 East 50th Street, New York, New York 10022 (212) 751-2600; *The Economist Book of Vital World Statistics.*

PAPUA NEW GUINEA - MOTOR VEHICLE TAXES - See PAPUA NEW GUINEA - TAXATION

PAPUA NEW GUINEA - MOTOR VEHICLES IN USE

American Automobile Manufacturers Association, 1401 H Street, NW, Suite 900, Washington, D.C. 20005 (202) 326-5500; *World Motor Vehicle Data.*

G.K. Hall and Company, 70 Lincoln Street, Boston, Massachusetts 02111 (617) 423-3990; *The World in Figures.*

Statistical Office of the United Nations, Publishing Service, New York, New York 10017 (800) 253-9646; *Statistical Yearbook.*

PAPUA NEW GUINEA - MUSEUMS

Facts on File, 460 Park Avenue South, New York, New York 10016 (800) 443-8323; *The New Book of World Rankings.*

United Nations Educational, Scientific and Cultural Organization (UNESCO), 7 Place de Fontenoy, F-75700 Paris, France (Telephone Number in U.S. (212) 963-5981); *Statistical Yearbook.*

PAPUA NEW GUINEA - NATALITY - See PAPUA NEW GUINEA - BIRTH RATES

PAPUA NEW GUINEA - NATIONAL ACCOUNTS

Federal Statistical Office, Gustav - Stresemann - Ring 11, D-6200 Wiesbaden, Germany; *Papua New Guinea.*

Statistical Office of the United Nations, Publishing Service, New York, New York 10017 (800) 253-9646; *National Accounts Statistics, Statistical Yearbook,* and *Statistical Yearbook for Asia and the Pacific.*

PAPUA NEW GUINEA - NATIONAL INCOME

Facts on File, 460 Park Avenue South, New York, New York 10016 (800) 443-8323; *The New Book of World Rankings.*

G.K. Hall and Company, 70 Lincoln Street, Boston, Massachusetts 02111 (617) 423-3990; *The World in Figures.*

Statistical Office of the United Nations, Publishing Service, New York, New York 10017 (800) 253-9646; *Statistical Yearbook.*

PAPUA NEW GUINEA - NATIONAL PRODUCT

Facts on File, 460 Park Avenue South, New York, New York 10016 (800) 443-8323; *The New Book of World Rankings.*

Statistical Office of the United Nations, Publishing Service, New York, New York 10017 (800) 253-9646; *Statistical Yearbook.*

PAPUA NEW GUINEA - NATURAL GAS PRODUCTION - See PAPUA NEW GUINEA - MINING AND MINERAL PRODUCTS

PAPUA NEW GUINEA - NATURAL RUBBER PRODUCTION

Statistical Office of the United Nations, Publishing Service, New York, New York 10017 (800) 253-9646; *Statistical Yearbook.*

PAPUA NEW GUINEA - NEWSPAPER PRODUCTION AND CONSUMPTION - See PAPUA NEW GUINEA - FORESTRY AND FOREST PRODUCTS

PAPUA NEW GUINEA - NEWSPRINT PRODUCTION AND CONSUMPTION - See PAPUA NEW GUINEA - FORESTRY AND FOREST INDUSTRY

PAPUA NEW GUINEA - NICKEL AND NICKEL ORE PRODUCTION AND CONSUMPTION - See PAPUA NEW GUINEA - MINING AND MINERAL PRODUCTS

PAPUA NEW GUINEA - OCCUPATIONS - See PAPUA NEW GUINEA - LABOR FORCE

PAPUA NEW GUINEA - PALM KERNELS AND PALM OIL - See PAPUA NEW GUINEA - CROPS

PAPUA NEW GUINEA - PEANUT PRODUCTION - See PAPUA NEW GUINEA - CROPS

PAPUA NEW GUINEA - PERIODICALS

United Nations Educational, Scientific and Cultural Organization (UNESCO), 7 Place de Fontenoy, F-75700 Paris, France (Telephone Number in U.S. (212) 963-5981); *Statistical Yearbook.*

PAPUA NEW GUINEA - PESTICIDE USE

Food and Agricultural Organization of the United Nations (FAO) Via delle Terme di Caracalla, 00100 Rome, Italy (Telephone Number in U.S. (202) 653-2400); *The State of Food and Agriculture.*

PAPUA NEW GUINEA - PETROLEUM INDUSTRY

Asian Development Bank, Post Office Box 789, 1099 Manila, Philippines; *Key Indicators of Developing Asian and Pacific Countries.*

Facts on File, 460 Park Avenue South, New York, New York 10016 (800) 443-8323; *The New Book of World Rankings.*

Food and Agricultural Organization of the United Nations (FAO) Via delle Terme di Caracalla, 00100 Rome, Italy (Telephone Number in U.S. (202) 653-2400); *The State of Food and Agriculture.*

G.K. Hall and Company, 70 Lincoln Street, Boston, Massachusetts 02111 (617) 423-3990; *The World in Figures.*

Penn Well Publishing Company, 1421 South Sheridan Road, Post Office Box 1260, Tulsa, Oklahoma 74101 (800) 752-9764; *International Energy Statistics Sourcebook.*

PAPUA NEW GUINEA - PIGS - See PAPUA NEW GUINEA - LIVESTOCK AND POULTRY

PAPUA NEW GUINEA - POPULATION

Asian Development Bank, Post Office Box 789, 1099 Manila, Philippines; *Key Indicators of Developing Asian and Pacific Countries.*

The Economist Intelligence Unit, 111 West 57th Street, New York, New York 10019 (800) 938-4685; *The World Market Atlas.*

The Economist Intelligence Unit (Asia) Limited, 10th Floor, Luk Kwok Centre, 72 Gloucester Road, Wanchai, Hong Kong (Phone Number in U.S. (800) 938-4685); *Asian Market Atlas.*

Euromonitor Publications Limited, 87-88 Turnmill Street, London EC1M 5QU, England; *International Marketing Data and Statistics.*

Facts on File, 460 Park Avenue South, New York, New York 10016 (800) 443-8323; *The New Book of World Rankings.*

Federal Statistical Office, Gustav - Stresemann - Ring 11, D-6200 Wiesbaden, Germany; *Papua New Guinea.*

Food and Agricultural Organization of the United Nations (FAO), Via delle Terme di Caracalla, 00100 Rome, Italy (Telephone Number in U.S. (202) 653-2400); *Production Yearbook.*

G.K. Hall and Company, 70 Lincoln Street, Boston, Massachusetts 02111 (617) 423-3990; *The World in Figures.*

International Labour Office, I.L.O. Publications, CH-1211, Geneva 22, Switzerland; *Yearbook of Labour Statistics.*

Statistical Office of the United Nations, Publishing Service, New York, New York 10017 (800) 253-9646; *Demographic Yearbook, Statistical Yearbook,* and *Statistical Yearbook for Asia and the Pacific.*

Times Books, 201 East 50th Street, New York, New York 10022 (212) 751-2600; *The Economist Book of Vital World Statistics.*

United Nations Educational, Scientific and Cultural Organization (UNESCO), 7 Place de Fontenoy, F-75700 Paris, France (Telephone Number in U.S. (212) 963-5981); *Statistical Yearbook.*

U.S. Arms Control and Disarmament Agency, 320 Twenty-first Street, NW, Washington, D.C. 20451 (202) 647-8677; *World Military Expenditures and Arms Transfers.*

World Health Organization, Office of Publications, Avenue Appia, CH-1211 Geneva 27, Switzerland (Telephone Number in U.S. (518) 436-9686); *World Health Statistics Annual.*

PAPUA NEW GUINEA - POST OFFICES

Facts on File, 460 Park Avenue South, New York, New York 10016 (800) 443-8323; *The New Book of World Rankings.*

PAPUA NEW GUINEA - POTATO PRODUCTION - See PAPUA NEW GUINEA - CROPS

PAPUA NEW GUINEA - PRICES

Asian Development Bank, Post Office Box 789, 1099 Manila, Philippines; *Key Indicators of Developing Asian and Pacific Countries.*

Facts on File, 460 Park Avenue South, New York, New York 10016 (800) 443-8323; *The New Book of World Rankings.*

Food and Agricultural Organization of the United Nations (FAO), Via delle Terme di Caracalla, 00100 Rome, Italy (Telephone Number in U.S. (202) 653-2400); *Production Yearbook,* and *The State of Food and Agriculture.*

G.K. Hall and Company, 70 Lincoln Street, Boston, Massachusetts 02111 (617) 423-3990; *The World in Figures.*

International Labour Office, I.L.O. Publications, CH-1211, Geneva 22, Switzerland; *Yearbook of Labour Statistics.*

International Monetary Fund, 700 Nineteenth Street, NW, Washington, D.C. 20431 (202) 623-7000; *International Financial Statistics.*

South Pacific Commission, Post Box D5, Noumea Cedex, New Caledonia; *Statistical Bulletin of the South Pacific: Overseas Trade,* and *Statistical Bulletin of the South Pacific: Retail Price Indexes.*

World Bureau of Metal Statistics, 27-A High Street, Ware, Herts. SG12 9BA, England; *World Metal Statistics.*

PAPUA NEW GUINEA - PRODUCTION

American Automobile Manufacturers Association, 1401 H Street, NW, Suite 900, Washington, D.C. 20005 (202) 326-5500; *World Motor Vehicle Data.*

Facts on File, 460 Park Avenue South, New York, New York 10016 (800) 443-8323; *The New Book of World Rankings.*

G.K. Hall and Company, 70 Lincoln Street, Boston, Massachusetts 02111 (617) 423-3990; *The World in Figures.*

PAPUA NEW GUINEA - PRODUCTIVITY

Euromonitor Publications Limited, 87-88 Turnmill Street, London EC1M 5QU, England; *International Marketing Data and Statistics.*

PAPUA NEW GUINEA - PROPERTY TAXES - See PAPUA NEW GUINEA - TAXATION

PAPUA NEW GUINEA - PUBLIC FINANCE

Facts on File, 460 Park Avenue South, New York, New York 10016 (800) 443-8323; *The New Book of World Rankings.*

PAPUA NEW GUINEA - RADIO BROADCASTING - See PAPUA NEW GUINEA - BROADCASTING

PAPUA NEW GUINEA - RAILWAYS

G.K. Hall and Company, 70 Lincoln Street, Boston, Massachusetts 02111 (617) 423-3990; *The World in Figures.*

PAPUA NEW GUINEA - RELIGION

Facts on File, 460 Park Avenue South, New York, New York 10016 (800) 443-8323; *The New Book of World Rankings.*

PAPUA NEW GUINEA - RENT PRICES

International Labour Office, I.L.O. Publications, CH-1211, Geneva 22, Switzerland; *Yearbook of Labour Statistics.*

PAPUA NEW GUINEA - RETAIL TRADE

G.K. Hall and Company, 70 Lincoln Street, Boston, Massachusetts 02111 (617) 423-3990; *The World in Figures.*

Statistical Office of the United Nations, Publishing Service, New York, New York 10017 (800) 253-9646; *Statistical Yearbook.*

PAPUA NEW GUINEA - RICE PRODUCTION - See PAPUA NEW GUINEA - CROPS

PAPUA NEW GUINEA - ROOT AND TUBER PRODUCTION - See PAPUA NEW GUINEA - CROPS

PAPUA NEW GUINEA - ROUNDWOOD PRODUCTION - See PAPUA NEW GUINEA - FORESTRY AND FOREST PRODUCTS

PAPUA NEW GUINEA - RUBBER PRODUCTION AND CONSUMPTION

Facts on File, 460 Park Avenue South, New York, New York 10016 (800) 443-8323; *The New Book of World Rankings.*

Statistical Office of the United Nations, Publishing Service, New York, New York 10017 (800) 253-9646; *Statistical Yearbook.*

PAPUA NEW GUINEA - SAWNWOOD PRODUCTION - PAPUA NEW GUINEA - FORESTRY AND FOREST PRODUCTS

PAPUA NEW GUINEA - SENIOR CITIZENS

Facts on File, 460 Park Avenue South, New York, New York 10016 (800) 443-8323; *The New Book of World Rankings.*

PAPUA NEW GUINEA - SHEEP - See PAPUA NEW GUINEA - LIVESTOCK AND POULTRY

PAPUA NEW GUINEA - SILVER PRODUCTION AND CONSUMPTION - See PAPUA NEW GUINEA - MINING AND MINERAL PRODUCTS

PAPUA NEW GUINEA - SOCIAL DATA

Asian Development Bank, Post Office Box 789, 1099 Manila, Philippines; *Key Indicators of Developing Asian and Pacific Countries.*

Facts on File, 460 Park Avenue South, New York, New York 10016 (800) 443-8323; *The New Book of World Rankings.*

G.K. Hall and Company, 70 Lincoln Street, Boston, Massachusetts 02111 (617) 423-3990; *The World in Figures.*

PAPUA NEW GUINEA - SOCIAL SECURITY

International Monetary Fund, 700 Nineteenth Street, NW, Washington, D.C. 20431 (202) 623-7000; *Government Finance Statistics Yearbook.*

PAPUA NEW GUINEA - STAMP TAXES AND DUTIES - See PAPUA NEW GUINEA - TAXATION

PAPUA NEW GUINEA - STATE BUDGET REVENUE AND EXPENDITURES

Euromonitor Publications Limited, 87-88 Turnmill Street, London EC1M 5QU, England; *International Marketing Data and Statistics.*

PAPUA NEW GUINEA - STEEL PRODUCTION - See PAPUA NEW GUINEA - MINING AND MINERAL PRODUCTS

PAPUA NEW GUINEA - STOCKS - COMMODITY - MARKET PRICE -INDEX

Food and Agricultural Organization of the United Nations (FAO) Via delle Terme di Caracalla, 00100 Rome, Italy (Telephone Number in U.S. (202) 653-2400); *The State of Food and Agriculture.*

World Bureau of Metal Statistics, 27-A High Street, Ware, Herts. SG12 9BA, England; *World Metal Statistics.*

PAPUA NEW GUINEA - SUGAR PRODUCTION AND CONSUMPTION - See PAPUA NEW GUINEA - CROPS

PAPUA NEW GUINEA - TAXATION

G.K. Hall and Company, 70 Lincoln Street, Boston, Massachusetts 02111 (617) 423-3990; *The World in Figures.*

International Monetary Fund, 700 Nineteenth Street, NW, Washington, D.C. 20431 (202) 623-7000; *Government Finance Statistics Yearbook.*

The World Bank, 1818 H Street, NW, Washington, D.C. 20433 (202) 477-1234; *World Tables.*

PAPUA NEW GUINEA - TAX REVENUES - See PAPUA NEW GUINEA - TAXATION

PAPUA NEW GUINEA - TEA PRODUCTION - See PAPUA NEW GUINEA - CROPS

PAPUA NEW GUINEA - TELEPHONES IN USE

American Telephone and Telegraph Company, 26 Parsippany Road, Whippany, New Jersey 07981 (800) 338-4038; *The World's Telephones.*

The Economist Intelligence Unit (Asia) Limited, 10th Floor, Luk Kwok Centre, 72 Gloucester Road, Wanchai, Hong Kong (Phone Number in U.S. (800) 938-4685); *Asian Market Atlas.*

G.K. Hall and Company, 70 Lincoln Street, Boston, Massachusetts 02111 (617) 423-3990; *The World in Figures.*

Statistical Office of the United Nations, Publishing Service, New York, New York 10017 (800) 253-9646; *Statistical Yearbook.*

PAPUA NEW GUINEA - TELEVISION

The Economist Intelligence Unit (Asia) Limited, 10th Floor, Luk Kwok Centre, 72 Gloucester Road, Wanchai, Hong Kong (Phone Number in U.S. (800) 938-4685); *Asian Market Atlas.*

Facts on File, 460 Park Avenue South, New York, New York 10016 (800) 443-8323; *The New Book of World Rankings.*

PAPUA NEW GUINEA - TELEVISION BROADCASTING - See PAPUA NEW GUINEA - BROADCASTING

PAPUA NEW GUINEA - TEXTILE INDUSTRY

G.K. Hall and Company, 70 Lincoln Street, Boston, Massachusetts 02111 (617) 423-3990; *The World in Figures.*

PAPUA NEW GUINEA - THEATRE

United Nations Educational, Scientific and Cultural Organization (UNESCO), 7 Place de Fontenoy, F-75700 Paris, France (Telephone Number in U.S. (212) 963-5981); *Statistical Yearbook.*

PAPUA NEW GUINEA - TIN - See PAPUA NEW GUINEA - MINING AND MINERAL PRODUCTS

PAPUA NEW GUINEA - TOBACCO PRODUCTION

Facts on File, 460 Park Avenue South, New York, New York 10016 (800) 443-8323; *The New Book of World Rankings*.

South Pacific Commission, Post Box D5, Noumea Cedex, New Caledonia; *Statistical Bulletin of the South Pacific: Retail Price Indexes*.

PAPUA NEW GUINEA - TOURISM

Facts on File, 460 Park Avenue South, New York, New York 10016 (800) 443-8323; *The New Book of World Rankings*.

Federal Statistical Office, Gustav - Stresemann - Ring 11, D-6200 Wiesbaden, Germany; *Papua New Guinea*.

G.K. Hall and Company, 70 Lincoln Street, Boston, Massachusetts 02111 (617) 423-3990; *The World in Figures*.

Statistical Office of the United Nations, Publishing Service, New York, New York 10017 (800) 253-9646; *Statistical Yearbook*.

Times Books, 201 East 50th Street, New York, New York 10022 (212) 751-2600; *The Economist Book of Vital World Statistics*.

World Tourism Organization, Calle Capitan Haya 42, E-28020 Madrid, Spain; *Yearbook of Tourism Statistics*.

PAPUA NEW GUINEA - TRACTORS IN USE

Statistical Office of the United Nations, Publishing Service, New York, New York 10017 (800) 253-9646; *Statistical Yearbook*.

PAPUA NEW GUINEA - TRADE - See PAPUA NEW GUINEA - FOREIGN TRADE

PAPUA NEW GUINEA - TRANSPORTATION AND COMMUNICATIONS

The Economist Intelligence Unit (Asia) Limited, 10th Floor, Luk Kwok Centre, 72 Gloucester Road, Wanchai, Hong Kong (Phone Number in U.S. (800) 938-4685); *Asian Market Atlas*.

Facts on File, 460 Park Avenue South, New York, New York 10016 (800) 443-8323; *The New Book of World Rankings*.

Federal Statistical Office, Gustav - Stresemann - Ring 11, D-6200 Wiesbaden, Germany; *Papua New Guinea*.

G.K. Hall and Company, 70 Lincoln Street, Boston, Massachusetts 02111 (617) 423-3990; *The World in Figures*.

South Pacific Commission, Post Box D5, Noumea Cedex, New Caledonia; *Statistical Bulletin of the South Pacific: Retail Price Indexes*.

Statistical Office of the United Nations, Publishing Service, New York, New York 10017 (800) 253-9646; *Statistical Yearbook for Asia and the Pacific*.

PAPUA NEW GUINEA - UNEMPLOYMENT

Euromonitor Publications Limited, 87-88 Turnmill Street, London EC1M 5QU, England; *International Marketing Data and Statistics*.

International Labour Office, I.L.O. Publications, CH-1211, Geneva 22, Switzerland; *Yearbook of Labour Statistics*.

PAPUA NEW GUINEA - VITAL STATISTICS

Euromonitor Publications Limited, 87-88 Turnmill Street, London EC1M 5QU, England; *International Marketing Data and Statistics*.

G.K. Hall and Company, 70 Lincoln Street, Boston, Massachusetts 02111 (617) 423-3990; *The World in Figures*.

Statistical Office of the United Nations, Publishing Service, New York, New York 10017 (800) 253-9646; *Statistical Yearbook*.

World Health Organization, Office of Publications, Avenue Appia, CH-1211 Geneva 27, Switzerland (Telephone Number in U.S. (518) 436-9686); *World Health Statistics Annual*.

PAPUA NEW GUINEA - WAGES

Federal Statistical Office, Gustav - Stresemann - Ring 11, D-6200 Wiesbaden, Germany; *Papua New Guinea*.

G.K. Hall and Company, 70 Lincoln Street, Boston, Massachusetts 02111 (617) 423-3990; *The World in Figures*.

International Labour Office, I.L.O. Publications, CH-1211, Geneva 22, Switzerland; *Yearbook of Labour Statistics*.

PAPUA NEW GUINEA - WAGES AND PRICES

Federal Statistical Office, Gustav - Stresemann - Ring 11, D-6200 Wiesbaden, Germany; *Papua New Guinea*.

Statistical Office of the United Nations, Publishing Service, New York, New York 10017 (800) 253-9646; *Statistical Yearbook for Asia and the Pacific*.

PAPUA NEW GUINEA - WEATHER

Facts on File, 460 Park Avenue South, New York, New York 10016 (800) 443-8323; *The New Book of World Rankings*.

G.K. Hall and Company, 70 Lincoln Street, Boston, Massachusetts 02111 (617) 423-3990; *The World in Figures*.

PAPUA NEW GUINEA - WELFARE

International Monetary Fund, 700 Nineteenth Street, NW, Washington, D.C. 20431 (202) 623-7000; *Government Finance Statistics Yearbook*.

PAPUA NEW GUINEA - WHEAT PRODUCTION AND CONSUMPTION - See PAPUA NEW GUINEA - CROPS

PAPUA NEW GUINEA - WHOLESALE PRICES - INDEX NUMBERS

Asian Development Bank, Post Office Box 789, 1099 Manila, Philippines; *Key Indicators of Developing Asian and Pacific Countries*.

PAPUA NEW GUINEA - WHOLESALE TRADE

Statistical Office of the United Nations, Publishing Service, New York, New York 10017 (800) 253-9646; *Statistical Yearbook*.

PAPUA NEW GUINEA - WINE PRODUCTION

Facts on File, 460 Park Avenue South, New York, New York 10016 (800) 443-8323; *The New Book of World Rankings*.

PAPUA NEW GUINEA - WOOL PRODUCTION

Facts on File, 460 Park Avenue South, New York, New York 10016 (800) 443-8323; *The New Book of World Rankings*.

PAPUA NEW GUINEA - ZINC - See PAPUA NEW GUINEA - MINING AND MINERAL PRODUCTS

Paraguay - National Statistical Offices

Departmento de Estudios Economicos del Banco Central del Paraguay, Pablo VI y San Rafael, Barrio Santa Domingo, Asuncion, Paraguay; economic and trade monthly statistics.

Direccion General de Estadistica y Censos, Humaita 473, Asuncion, Paraguay; general statistics.

Paraguay - Primary Statistics Source

Direccion General de Estadistica y Censos, Humaita 473, Asuncion, Paraguay; *Annuario estadistico del Paraguay* (Statistical Yearbook of Paraguay).

PARAGUAY - AGRICULTURE

The Economist Intelligence Unit, 111 West 57th Street, New York, New York 10019 (800) 938-4685; *The New Latin America Market Atlas*.

Euromonitor Publications Limited, 87-88 Turnmill Street, London EC1M 5QU, England; *International Marketing Data and Statistics*.

Facts on File, 460 Park Avenue South, New York, New York 10016 (800) 443-8323; *The New Book of World Rankings*.

Food and Agricultural Organization of the United Nations (FAO), Via delle Terme di Caracalla, 00100 Rome, Italy (Telephone Number in U.S. (202) 653-2400); *Production Yearbook*, *The State of Food and Agriculture*, and *Trade Yearbook*.

Gale Research Incorporated, 835 Penobscot Building, Detroit, Michigan 48226 (800) 877-4253; *International Historical Statistics The Americas and Australasia*.

G.K. Hall and Company, 70 Lincoln Street, Boston, Massachusetts 02111 (617) 423-3990; *The World in Figures*.

Inter-American Development Bank, 1300 New York Avenue, NW, Washington, D.C. 20577 (202) 623-1753; *Economic and Social Progress in Latin America*.

Statistical Office of the United Nations, Publishing Service, New York, New York 10017 (800) 253-9646; *Statistical Yearbook*, and *Statistical Yearbook for Latin America and the Caribbean*.

Times Books, 201 East 50th Street, New York, New York 10022 (212) 751-2600; *The Economist Book of Vital World Statistics*.

U.C.L.A. Latin American Center Publications, University of California, Los Angeles, California 90024 (310) 825-6634; *Statistical Abstract of Latin America*.

The World Bank, 1818 H Street, NW, Washington, D.C. 20433 (202) 477-1234; *World Tables*.

PARAGUAY - AIRLINE SERVICE

The Economist Intelligence Unit, 111 West 57th Street, New York, New York 10019 (800) 938-4685; *The New Latin America Market Atlas*.

Facts on File, 460 Park Avenue South, New York, New York 10016 (800) 443-8323; *The New Book of World Rankings*.

G.K. Hall and Company, 70 Lincoln Street, Boston, Massachusetts 02111 (617) 423-3990; *The World in Figures*.

Times Books, 201 East 50th Street, New York, New York 10022 (212) 751-2600; *The Economist Book of Vital World Statistics*.

PARAGUAY - ALUMINUM PRODUCTION AND CONSUMPTION - See PARAGUAY - MINING AND MINERAL PRODUCTS

PARAGUAY - ANIMAL HEALTH

Food and Agricultural Organization of the United Nations (FAO), Via delle Terme di Caracalla, 00100 Rome, Italy (Telephone Number in U.S. (202) 653-2400); *Animal Health Yearbook*.

PARAGUAY - AREA AND DENSITY OF POPULATION

Euromonitor Publications Limited, 87-88 Turnmill Street, London EC1M 5QU, England; *International Marketing Data and Statistics*.

Facts on File, 460 Park Avenue South, New York, New York 10016 (800) 443-8323; *The New Book of World Rankings*.

Food and Agricultural Organization of the United Nations (FAO) Via delle Terme di Caracalla, 00100 Rome, Italy (Telephone Number in U.S. (202) 653-2400); *The State of Food and Agriculture*.

G.K. Hall and Company, 70 Lincoln Street, Boston, Massachusetts 02111 (617) 423-3990; *The World in Figures*.

Inter-American Development Bank, 1300 New York Avenue, NW, Washington, D.C. 20577 (202) 623-1753; *Economic and Social Progress in Latin America*.

Statistical Office of the United Nations, Publishing Service, New York, New York 10017 (800) 253-9646; *Statistical Yearbook*.

Times Books, 201 East 50th Street, New York, New York 10022 (212) 751-2600; *The Economist Book of Vital World Statistics*.

United Nations Educational, Scientific and Cultural Organization (UNESCO), 7 Place de Fontenoy, F-75700 Paris, France (Telephone Number in U.S. (212) 963-5981); *Statistical Yearbook*.

PARAGUAY - ARMS EXPORTS AND IMPORTS

U.S. Arms Control and Disarmament Agency, 320 Twenty-first Street, NW, Washington, D.C. 20451 (202) 647-8677; *World Military Expenditures and Arms Transfers*.

PARAGUAY - BALANCE OF PAYMENTS

The Economist Intelligence Unit, 111 West 57th Street, New York, New York 10019 (800) 938-4685; *The New Latin America Market Atlas*, and *The World Market Atlas*.

G.K. Hall and Company, 70 Lincoln Street, Boston, Massachusetts 02111 (617) 423-3990; *The World in Figures.*

Inter-American Development Bank, 1300 New York Avenue, NW, Washington, D.C. 20577 (202) 623-1753; *Economic and Social Progress in Latin America.*

International Monetary Fund, 700 Nineteenth Street, NW, Washington, D.C. 20431 (202) 623-7000; *Balance of Payments Yearbook,* and *International Financial Statistics.*

Organization of American States (OAS), General Secretariat, Washington, D.C. 20006 (202) 458-3533; *Statistical Bulletin of the OAS.*

Statistical Office of the United Nations, Publishing Service, New York, New York 10017 (800) 253-9646; *Economic Survey of Latin America and the Caribbean,* and *Statistical Yearbook for Latin America and the Caribbean.*

Times Books, 201 East 50th Street, New York, New York 10022 (212) 751-2600; *The Economist Book of Vital World Statistics.*

U.C.L.A. Latin American Center Publications, University of California, Los Angeles, California 90024 (310) 825-6634; *Statistical Abstract of Latin America.*

The World Bank, 1818 H Street, NW, Washington, D.C. 20433 (202) 477-1234; *World Tables.*

PARAGUAY - BANANA PRODUCTION - See PARAGUAY - CROPS

PARAGUAY - BANKING

Facts on File, 460 Park Avenue South, New York, New York 10016 (800) 443-8323; *The New Book of World Rankings.*

G.K. Hall and Company, 70 Lincoln Street, Boston, Massachusetts 02111 (617) 423-3990; *The World in Figures.*

Inter-American Development Bank, 1300 New York Avenue, NW, Washington, D.C. 20577 (202) 623-1753; *Economic and Social Progress in Latin America.*

International Monetary Fund, 700 Nineteenth Street, NW, Washington, D.C. 20431 (202) 623-7000; *Government Finance Statistics Yearbook,* and *International Financial Statistics.*

Statistical Office of the United Nations, Publishing Service, New York, New York 10017 (800) 253-9646; *Statistical Yearbook for Latin America and the Caribbean.*

PARAGUAY - BARLEY PRODUCTION - See PARAGUAY - CROPS

PARAGUAY - BEER PRODUCTION

Facts on File, 460 Park Avenue South, New York, New York 10016 (800) 443-8323; *The New Book of World Rankings.*

Statistical Office of the United Nations, Publishing Service, New York, New York 10017 (800) 253-9646; *Statistical Yearbook.*

PARAGUAY - BIRTH RATES

Facts on File, 460 Park Avenue South, New York, New York 10016 (800) 443-8323; *The New Book of World Rankings.*

Statistical Office of the United Nations, Publishing Service, New York, New York 10017 (800) 253-9646; *Demographic Yearbook,*

Statistical Yearbook, and *Statistical Yearbook for Latin America and the Caribbean.*

Times Books, 201 East 50th Street, New York, New York 10022 (212) 751-2600; *The Economist Book of Vital World Statistics.*

The World Bank, 1818 H Street, NW, Washington, D.C. 20433 (202) 477-1234; *World Tables.*

World Health Organization, Office of Publications, Avenue Appia, CH-1211 Geneva 27, Switzerland (Telephone Number in U.S. (518) 436-9686); *World Health Statistics Annual.*

PARAGUAY - BONDS

G.K. Hall and Company, 70 Lincoln Street, Boston, Massachusetts 02111 (617) 423-3990; *The World in Figures.*

Inter-American Development Bank, 1300 New York Avenue, NW, Washington, D.C. 20577 (202) 623-1753; *Economic and Social Progress in Latin America.*

International Monetary Fund, 700 Nineteenth Street, NW, Washington, D.C. 20431 (202) 623-7000; *Government Finance Statistics Yearbook.*

PARAGUAY - BOOK PRODUCTION

G.K. Hall and Company, 70 Lincoln Street, Boston, Massachusetts 02111 (617) 423-3990; *The World in Figures.*

PARAGUAY - BROADCASTING

Billboard Limited, Post Office Box 9027, 1006 AA Amsterdam, The Netherlands (Telephone Number in U.S. (212) 764-7300); *World Radio TV Handbook.*

Facts on File, 460 Park Avenue South, New York, New York 10016 (800) 443-8323; *The New Book of World Rankings.*

G.K. Hall and Company, 70 Lincoln Street, Boston, Massachusetts 02111 (617) 423-3990; *The World in Figures.*

Times Books, 201 East 50th Street, New York, New York 10022 (212) 751-2600; *The Economist Book of Vital World Statistics.*

PARAGUAY - BUSINESS

G.K. Hall and Company, 70 Lincoln Street, Boston, Massachusetts 02111 (617) 423-3990; *The World in Figures.*

Inter-American Development Bank, 1300 New York Avenue, NW, Washington, D.C. 20577 (202) 623-1753; *Economic and Social Progress in Latin America.*

PARAGUAY - BUTTER PRODUCTION - See PARAGUAY - DAIRY PRODUCTS

PARAGUAY - CALORIE SUPPLY

Food and Agricultural Organization of the United Nations (FAO) Via delle Terme di Caracalla, 00100 Rome, Italy (Telephone Number in U.S. (202) 653-2400); *The State of Food and Agriculture.*

Statistical Office of the United Nations, Publishing Service, New York, New York 10017 (800) 253-9646; *Statistical Yearbook for Latin America and the Caribbean.*

PARAGUAY - CAPITAL INVESTMENT

Inter-American Development Bank, 1300 New York Avenue, NW, Washington, D.C. 20577 (202) 623-1753; *Economic and Social Progress in Latin America.*

PARAGUAY - CAPITAL REVENUE

Inter-American Development Bank, 1300 New York Avenue, NW, Washington, D.C. 20577 (202) 623-1753; *Economic and Social Progress in Latin America.*

International Monetary Fund, 700 Nineteenth Street, NW, Washington, D.C. 20431 (202) 623-7000; *Government Finance Statistics Yearbook.*

PARAGUAY - CASTOR BEAN PRODUCTION - See PARAGUAY - CROPS

PARAGUAY - CATTLE - See PARAGUAY - LIVESTOCK AND POULTRY

PARAGUAY - CEMENT PRODUCTION - See PARAGUAY - MINING AND MINERAL PRODUCTS

PARAGUAY - CHEESE PRODUCTION AND CONSUMPTION - See PARAGUAY - DAIRY PRODUCTS

PARAGUAY - CHEMICAL (ORGANIC) PRODUCTION - See PARAGUAY - MINING AND MINERAL PRODUCTS

PARAGUAY - CHICKENS - See PARAGUAY - LIVESTOCK AND POULTRY

PARAGUAY - CIGAR PRODUCTION - See PARAGUAY - TOBACCO PRODUCTION

PARAGUAY - CIGARETTE PRODUCTION - See PARAGUAY - TOBACCO PRODUCTION

PARAGUAY - CLASS STRUCTURE

G.K. Hall and Company, 70 Lincoln Street, Boston, Massachusetts 02111 (617) 423-3990; *The World in Figures.*

PARAGUAY - CLIMATE

Facts on File, 460 Park Avenue South, New York, New York 10016 (800) 443-8323; *The New Book of World Rankings.*

G.K. Hall and Company, 70 Lincoln Street, Boston, Massachusetts 02111 (617) 423-3990; *The World in Figures.*

PARAGUAY - COAL PRODUCTION - See PARAGUAY - MINING AND MINERAL PRODUCTS

PARAGUAY - COCOA (BEANS) PRODUCTION - See PARAGUAY - CROPS

PARAGUAY - COFFEE - See PARAGUAY - CROPS

PARAGUAY - COMMUNICATIONS

Gale Research Incorporated, 835 Penobscot Building, Detroit, Michigan 48226 (800) 877-4253; *International Historical Statistics The Americas and Australasia.*

G.K. Hall and Company, 70 Lincoln Street, Boston, Massachusetts 02111 (617) 423-3990; *The World in Figures.*

Inter-American Development Bank, 1300 New York Avenue, NW, Washington, D.C. 20577 (202) 623-1753; *Economic and Social Progress in Latin America.*

U.C.L.A. Latin American Center Publications, University of California, Los Angeles, California 90024 (310) 825-6634; *Statistical Abstract of Latin America.*

PARAGUAY - CONSTRUCTION INDUSTRY

The Economist Intelligence Unit, 111 West 57th Street, New York, New York 10019 (800) 938-4685; *The New Latin America Market Atlas.*

Facts on File, 460 Park Avenue South, New York, New York 10016 (800) 443-8323; *The New Book of World Rankings.*

Inter-American Development Bank, 1300 New York Avenue, NW, Washington, D.C. 20577 (202) 623-1753; *Economic and Social Progress in Latin America.*

Statistical Office of the United Nations, Publishing Service, New York, New York 10017 (800) 253-9646; *Statistical Yearbook.*

U.C.L.A. Latin American Center Publications, University of California, Los Angeles, California 90024 (310) 825-6634; *Statistical Abstract of Latin America.*

PARAGUAY - CONSUMER PRICE INDEX

G.K. Hall and Company, 70 Lincoln Street, Boston, Massachusetts 02111 (617) 423-3990; *The World in Figures.*

Statistical Office of the United Nations, Publishing Service, New York, New York 10017 (800) 253-9646; *Statistical Yearbook.*

U.C.L.A. Latin American Center Publications, University of California, Los Angeles, California 90024 (310) 825-6634; *Statistical Abstract of Latin America.*

PARAGUAY - CONSUMER PRICES

The Economist Intelligence Unit, 111 West 57th Street, New York, New York 10019 (800) 938-4685; *The New Latin America Market Atlas.*

International Labour Office, I.L.O. Publications, CH-1211, Geneva 22, Switzerland; *Yearbook of Labour Statistics.*

International Monetary Fund, 700 Nineteenth Street, NW, Washington, D.C. 20431 (202) 623-7000; *International Financial Statistics.*

Organization of American States (OAS), General Secretariat, Washington, D.C. 20006 (202) 458-3533; *Statistical Bulletin of the OAS.*

Times Books, 201 East 50th Street, New York, New York 10022 (212) 751-2600; *The Economist Book of Vital World Statistics.*

PARAGUAY - CONSUMPTION

The Economist Intelligence Unit, 111 West 57th Street, New York, New York 10019 (800) 938-4685; *The New Latin America Market Atlas.*

G.K. Hall and Company, 70 Lincoln Street, Boston, Massachusetts 02111 (617) 423-3990; *The World in Figures.*

Inter-American Development Bank, 1300 New York Avenue, NW, Washington, D.C. 20577 (202) 623-1753; *Economic and Social Progress in Latin America.*

Statistical Office of the United Nations, Publishing Service, New York, New York 10017 (800) 253-9646; *Statistical Yearbook for Latin America and the Caribbean.*

PARAGUAY - COOPERATIVES

U.C.L.A. Latin American Center Publications, University of California, Los Angeles, California 90024 (310) 825-6634; *Statistical Abstract of Latin America.*

PARAGUAY - COPPER PRODUCTION AND CONSUMPTION - See PARAGUAY - MINING AND MINERAL PRODUCTS

PARAGUAY - CORN PRODUCTION - See PARAGUAY - CROPS

PARAGUAY - CORPORATE INCOME TAXES - See PARAGUAY - TAXATION

PARAGUAY - CORPORATE TAXES - See PARAGUAY - TAXATION

PARAGUAY - COTTON - See PARAGUAY - CROPS

PARAGUAY - CROPS

The Economist Intelligence Unit, 111 West 57th Street, New York, New York 10019 (800) 938-4685; *The New Latin America Market Atlas.*

Facts on File, 460 Park Avenue South, New York, New York 10016 (800) 443-8323; *The New Book of World Rankings.*

Food and Agricultural Organization of the United Nations (FAO), Via delle Terme di Caracalla, 00100 Rome, Italy (Telephone Number in U.S. (202) 653-2400); *Production Yearbook,* and *The State of Food and Agriculture.*

International Monetary Fund, 700 Nineteenth Street, NW, Washington, D.C. 20431 (202) 623-7000; *International Financial Statistics.*

Organization of American States (OAS), General Secretariat, Washington, D.C. 20006 (202) 458-3533; *Statistical Bulletin of the OAS.*

Statistical Office of the United Nations, Publishing Service, New York, New York 10017 (800) 253-9646; *Statistical Yearbook.*

U.C.L.A. Latin American Center Publications, University of California, Los Angeles, California 90024 (310) 825-6634; *Statistical Abstract of Latin America.*

PARAGUAY - CUSTOMS DUTIES

G.K. Hall and Company, 70 Lincoln Street, Boston, Massachusetts 02111 (617) 423-3990; *The World in Figures.*

Inter-American Development Bank, 1300 New York Avenue, NW, Washington, D.C. 20577 (202) 623-1753; *Economic and Social Progress in Latin America.*

International Monetary Fund, 700 Nineteenth Street, NW, Washington, D.C. 20431 (202) 623-7000; *Government Finance Statistics Yearbook.*

PARAGUAY - DAIRY PRODUCTS

Facts on File, 460 Park Avenue South, New York, New York 10016 (800) 443-8323; *The New Book of World Rankings.*

Food and Agricultural Organization of the United Nations (FAO), Via delle Terme di Caracalla, 00100 Rome, Italy (Telephone Number in U.S. (202) 653-2400); *Production Yearbook,* and *The State of Food and Agriculture.*

Statistical Office of the United Nations, Publishing Service, New York, New York 10017 (800) 253-9646; *Statistical Yearbook.*

U.C.L.A. Latin American Center Publications, University of California, Los Angeles, California 90024 (310) 825-6634; *Statistical Abstract of Latin America.*

PARAGUAY - DEATH RATES

G.K. Hall and Company, 70 Lincoln Street, Boston, Massachusetts 02111 (617) 423-3990; *The World in Figures.*

Statistical Office of the United Nations, Publishing Service, New York, New York 10017 (800) 253-9646; *Statistical Yearbook,* and *Statistical Yearbook for Latin America and the Caribbean.*

Times Books, 201 East 50th Street, New York, New York 10022 (212) 751-2600; *The Economist Book of Vital World Statistics.*

World Health Organization, Office of Publications, Avenue Appia, CH-1211 Geneva 27, Switzerland (Telephone Number in U.S. (518) 436-9686); *World Health Statistics Annual.*

PARAGUAY - DEBT

The Economist Intelligence Unit, 111 West 57th Street, New York, New York 10019 (800) 938-4685; *The New Latin America Market Atlas.*

PARAGUAY - DEFENSE EXPENDITURES

The Economist Intelligence Unit, 111 West 57th Street, New York, New York 10019 (800) 938-4685; *The New Latin America Market Atlas.*

G.K. Hall and Company, 70 Lincoln Street, Boston, Massachusetts 02111 (617) 423-3990; *The World in Figures.*

International Monetary Fund, 700 Nineteenth Street, NW, Washington, D.C. 20431 (202) 623-7000; *Government Finance Statistics Yearbook.*

U.S. Arms Control and Disarmament Agency, 320 Twenty-first Street, NW, Washington, D.C. 20451 (202) 647-8677; *World Military Expenditures and Arms Transfers.*

PARAGUAY - DEMOGRAPHY

The Economist Intelligence Unit, 111 West 57th Street, New York, New York 10019 (800) 938-4685; *The World Market Atlas.*

Facts on File, 460 Park Avenue South, New York, New York 10016 (800) 443-8323; *The New Book of World Rankings.*

G.K. Hall and Company, 70 Lincoln Street, Boston, Massachusetts 02111 (617) 423-3990; *The World in Figures.*

PARAGUAY - DEVELOPMENT ASSISTANCE

G.K. Hall and Company, 70 Lincoln Street, Boston, Massachusetts 02111 (617) 423-3990; *The World in Figures.*

Inter-American Development Bank, 1300 New York Avenue, NW, Washington, D.C. 20577 (202) 623-1753; *Economic and Social Progress in Latin America.*

Statistical Office of the United Nations, Publishing Service, New York, New York 10017 (800) 253-9646; *Statistical Yearbook.*

PARAGUAY - DIAMOND PRODUCTION - See PARAGUAY - MINING AND MINERAL PRODUCTS

PARAGUAY - DISCOUNT RATES

Inter-American Development Bank, 1300 New York Avenue, NW, Washington, D.C. 20577 (202) 623-1753; *Economic and Social Progress in Latin America.*

PARAGUAY - DISEASES

G.K. Hall and Company, 70 Lincoln Street, Boston, Massachusetts 02111 (617) 423-3990; *The World in Figures.*

World Health Organization, Office of Publications, Avenue Appia, CH-1211 Geneva 27, Switzerland (Telephone Number in U.S. (518) 436-9686), *World Health Statistics Annual.*

PARAGUAY - DIVORCE RATES

Facts on File, 460 Park Avenue South, New York, New York 10016 (800) 443-8323; *The New Book of World Rankings.*

Statistical Office of the United Nations, Publishing Service, New York, New York 10017 (800) 253-9646; *Demographic Yearbook.*

PARAGUAY - DOMESTIC PRODUCT

G.K. Hall and Company, 70 Lincoln Street, Boston, Massachusetts 02111 (617) 423-3990; *The World in Figures.*

PARAGUAY - DUCKS - See PARAGUAY - LIVESTOCK AND POULTRY

PARAGUAY - ECONOMY

Euromonitor Publications Limited, 87-88 Turnmill Street, London EC1M 5QU, England; *International Marketing Data and Statistics.*

Facts on File, 460 Park Avenue South, New York, New York 10016 (800) 443-8323; *The New Book of World Rankings.*

G.K. Hall and Company, 70 Lincoln Street, Boston, Massachusetts 02111 (617) 423-3990; *The World in Figures.*

Inter-American Development Bank, 1300 New York Avenue, NW, Washington, D.C. 20577 (202) 623-1753; *Economic and Social Progress in Latin America.*

Organization of American States (OAS), General Secretariat, Washington, D.C. 20006 (202) 458-3533; *Statistical Bulletin of the OAS.*

Statistical Office of the United Nations, Publishing Service, New York, New York 10017 (800) 253-9646; *Economic Survey of Latin America and the Caribbean.*

U.C.L.A. Latin American Center Publications, University of California, Los Angeles, California 90024 (310) 825-6634; *Statistical Abstract of Latin America.*

PARAGUAY - EDUCATION

The Economist Intelligence Unit, 111 West 57th Street, New York, New York 10019 (800) 938-4685; *The New Latin America Market Atlas*, and *The World Market Atlas.*

Facts on File, 460 Park Avenue South, New York, New York 10016 (800) 443-8323; *The New Book of World Rankings.*

Gale Research Incorporated, 835 Penobscot Building, Detroit, Michigan 48226 (800) 877-4253; *International Historical Statistics The Americas and Australasia.*

G.K. Hall and Company, 70 Lincoln Street, Boston, Massachusetts 02111 (617) 423-3990; *The World in Figures.*

International Monetary Fund, 700 Nineteenth Street, NW, Washington, D.C. 20431 (202) 623-7000; *Government Finance Statistics Yearbook.*

Statistical Office of the United Nations, Publishing Service, New York, New York 10017 (800) 253-9646; *Statistical Yearbook for Latin America and the Caribbean.*

Times Books, 201 East 50th Street, New York, New York 10022 (212) 751-2600; *The Economist Book of Vital World Statistics.*

U.C.L.A. Latin American Center Publications, University of California, Los Angeles, California 90024 (310) 825-6634; *Statistical Abstract of Latin America.*

United Nations Educational, Scientific and Cultural Organization (UNESCO), 7 Place de Fontenoy, F-75700 Paris, France (Telephone Number in U.S. (212) 963-5981); *Statistical Yearbook.*

The World Bank, 1818 H Street, NW, Washington, D.C. 20433 (202) 477-1234; *World Tables.*

PARAGUAY - EGG PRODUCTION AND CONSUMPTION - See PARAGUAY - DAIRY PRODUCTS

PARAGUAY - ELECTRICITY

The Economist Intelligence Unit, 111 West 57th Street, New York, New York 10019 (800) 938-4685; *The New Latin America Market Atlas.*

Facts on File, 460 Park Avenue South, New York, New York 10016 (800) 443-8323; *The New Book of World Rankings.*

Inter-American Development Bank, 1300 New York Avenue, NW, Washington, D.C. 20577 (202) 623-1753; *Economic and Social Progress in Latin America.*

Statistical Office of the United Nations, Publishing Service, New York, New York 10017 (800) 253-9646; *Statistical Yearbook.*

Times Books, 201 East 50th Street, New York, New York 10022 (212) 751-2600; *The Economist Book of Vital World Statistics.*

PARAGUAY - EMPLOYMENT

Euromonitor Publications Limited, 87-88 Turnmill Street, London EC1M 5QU, England; *International Marketing Data and Statistics.*

Facts on File, 460 Park Avenue South, New York, New York 10016 (800) 443-8323; *The New Book of World Rankings*.

International Labour Office, I.L.O. Publications, CH-1211, Geneva 22, Switzerland; *Yearbook of Labour Statistics*.

Statistical Office of the United Nations, Publishing Service, New York, New York 10017 (800) 253-9646; *Statistical Yearbook for Latin America and the Caribbean*.

U.C.L.A. Latin American Center Publications, University of California, Los Angeles, California 90024 (310) 825-6634; *Statistical Abstract of Latin America*.

PARAGUAY - ENERGY

The Economist Intelligence Unit, 111 West 57th Street, New York, New York 10019 (800) 938-4685; *The New Latin America Market Atlas*.

Facts on File, 460 Park Avenue South, New York, New York 10016 (800) 443-8323; *The New Book of World Rankings*.

Food and Agricultural Organization of the United Nations (FAO) Via delle Terme di Caracalla, 00100 Rome, Italy (Telephone Number in U.S. (202) 653-2400); *The State of Food and Agriculture*.

G.K. Hall and Company, 70 Lincoln Street, Boston, Massachusetts 02111 (617) 423-3990; *The World in Figures*.

Statistical Office of the United Nations, Publishing Service, New York, New York 10017 (800) 253-9646; *Energy Statistics Yearbook, Statistical Yearbook,* and *Statistical Yearbook for Latin America and the Caribbean*.

Times Books, 201 East 50th Street, New York, New York 10022 (212) 751-2600; *The Economist Book of Vital World Statistics*.

U.C.L.A. Latin American Center Publications, University of California, Los Angeles, California 90024 (310) 825-6634; *Statistical Abstract of Latin America*.

PARAGUAY - EXCHANGE RATES

Euromonitor Publications Limited, 87-88 Turnmill Street, London EC1M 5QU, England; *International Marketing Data and Statistics*.

Inter-American Development Bank, 1300 New York Avenue, NW, Washington, D.C. 20577 (202) 623-1753; *Economic and Social Progress in Latin America*.

International Monetary Fund, 700 Nineteenth Street, NW, Washington, D.C. 20431 (202) 623-7000; *Government Finance Statistics Yearbook,* and *International Financial Statistics*.

Organization of American States (OAS), General Secretariat, Washington, D.C. 20006 (202) 458-3533; *Statistical Bulletin of the OAS*.

Statistical Office of the United Nations, Publishing Service, New York, New York 10017 (800) 253-9646; *Statistical Yearbook*.

U.C.L.A. Latin American Center Publications, University of California, Los Angeles, California 90024 (310) 825-6634; *Statistical Abstract of Latin America*.

PARAGUAY - EXCISE TAXES - See PARAGUAY - TAXATION

PARAGUAY - EXPENDITURES

Organization of American States (OAS), General Secretariat, Washington, D.C. 20006 (202) 458-3533; *Statistical Bulletin of the OAS*.

PARAGUAY - EXPORTS

The Economist Intelligence Unit, 111 West 57th Street, New York, New York 10019 (800) 938-4685; *The New Latin America Market Atlas,* and *The World Market Atlas*.

Euromonitor Publications Limited, 87-88 Turnmill Street, London EC1M 5QU, England; *International Marketing Data and Statistics*.

Food and Agricultural Organization of the United Nations (FAO) Via delle Terme di Caracalla, 00100 Rome, Italy (Telephone Number in U.S. (202) 653-2400); *The State of Food and Agriculture*.

G.K. Hall and Company, 70 Lincoln Street, Boston, Massachusetts 02111 (617) 423-3990; *The World in Figures*.

Inter-American Development Bank, 1300 New York Avenue, NW, Washington, D.C. 20577 (202) 623-1753; *Economic and Social Progress in Latin America*.

International Monetary Fund, 700 Nineteenth Street, NW, Washington, D.C. 20431 (202) 623-7000; *Direction of Trade Statistics, Government Finance Statistics Yearbook,* and *International Financial Statistics*.

Organization of American States (OAS), General Secretariat, Washington, D.C. 20006 (202) 458-3533; *Statistical Bulletin of the OAS*.

Statistical Office of the United Nations, Publishing Service, New York, New York 10017 (800) 253-9646; *Statistical Yearbook for Latin America and the Caribbean*.

Times Books, 201 East 50th Street, New York, New York 10022 (212) 751-2600; *The Economist Book of Vital World Statistics*.

The World Bank, 1818 H Street, NW, Washington, D.C. 20433 (202) 477-1234; *World Tables*.

PARAGUAY - EXTERNAL FINANCING

Inter-American Development Bank, 1300 New York Avenue, NW, Washington, D.C. 20577 (202) 623-1753; *Economic and Social Progress in Latin America*.

Statistical Office of the United Nations, Publishing Service, New York, New York 10017 (800) 253-9646; *Statistical Yearbook for Latin America and the Caribbean*.

PARAGUAY - EXTERNAL INDEBTEDNESS

Inter-American Development Bank, 1300 New York Avenue, NW, Washington, D.C. 20577 (202) 623-1753; *Economic and Social Progress in Latin America*.

Statistical Office of the United Nations, Publishing Service, New York, New York 10017 (800) 253-9646; *Statistical Yearbook for Latin America and the Caribbean*.

The World Bank, 1818 H Street, NW, Washington, D.C. 20433 (202) 477-1234; *World Tables*.

PARAGUAY - EXTERNAL TRADE

Food and Agricultural Organization of the United Nations (FAO) Via delle Terme di Caracalla, 00100 Rome, Italy (Telephone Number in U.S. (202) 653-2400); *The State of Food and Agriculture*, and *Trade Yearbook*.

Gale Research Incorporated, 835 Penobscot Building, Detroit, Michigan 48226 (800) 877-4253; *International Historical Statistics The Americas and Australasia*.

G.K. Hall and Company, 70 Lincoln Street, Boston, Massachusetts 02111 (617) 423-3990; *The World in Figures*.

Inter-American Development Bank, 1300 New York Avenue, NW, Washington, D.C. 20577 (202) 623-1753; *Economic and Social Progress in Latin America*.

Statistical Office of the United Nations, Publishing Service, New York, New York 10017 (800) 253-9646; *Statistical Yearbook*, and *Statistical Yearbook for Latin America and the Caribbean*.

PARAGUAY - FABRIC PRODUCTION - See PARAGUAY - TEXTILE INDUSTRY

PARAGUAY - FAMILY PLANNING

Food and Agricultural Organization of the United Nations (FAO) Via delle Terme di Caracalla, 00100 Rome, Italy (Telephone Number in U.S. (202) 653-2400); *The State of Food and Agriculture*.

U.C.L.A. Latin American Center Publications, University of California, Los Angeles, California 90024 (310) 825-6634; *Statistical Abstract of Latin America*.

PARAGUAY - FARM CROPS - See PARAGUAY - CROPS

PARAGUAY - FEMALE WORKING POPULATION - See PARAGUAY - EMPLOYMENT

PARAGUAY - FERTILITY RATES

Facts on File, 460 Park Avenue South, New York, New York 10016 (800) 443-8323; *The New Book of World Rankings*.

Times Books, 201 East 50th Street, New York, New York 10022 (212) 751-2600; *The Economist Book of Vital World Statistics*.

The World Bank, 1818 H Street, NW, Washington, D.C. 20433 (202) 477-1234; *World Tables*.

PARAGUAY - FERTILIZER

The Economist Intelligence Unit, 111 West 57th Street, New York, New York 10019 (800) 938-4685; *The New Latin America Market Atlas*.

Food and Agricultural Organization of the United Nations (FAO), Via delle Terme di Caracalla, 00100 Rome, Italy (Telephone Number in U.S. (202) 653-2400); *Fertilizer Yearbook*, and *The State of Food and Agriculture*.

Statistical Office of the United Nations, Publishing Service, New York, New York 10017 (800) 253-9646; *Statistical Yearbook*.

PARAGUAY - FETAL MORTALITY

Statistical Office of the United Nations, Publishing Service, New York, New York 10017 (800) 253-9646; *Demographic Yearbook*.

World Health Organization, Office of Publications, Avenue Appia, CH-1211 Geneva 27, Switzerland (Telephone Number in U.S. (518) 436-9686); *World Health Statistics Annual*.

PARAGUAY - FINANCE

Facts on File, 460 Park Avenue South, New York, New York 10016 (800) 443-8323; *The New Book of World Rankings*.

Gale Research Incorporated, 835 Penobscot Building, Detroit, Michigan 48226 (800) 877-4253; *International Historical Statistics The Americas and Australasia*.

G.K. Hall and Company, 70 Lincoln Street, Boston, Massachusetts 02111 (617) 423-3990; *The World in Figures*.

Inter-American Development Bank, 1300 New York Avenue, NW, Washington, D.C. 20577 (202) 623-1753; *Economic and Social Progress in Latin America*, and *Statistical Bulletin of the OAS*.

International Monetary Fund, 700 Nineteenth Street, NW, Washington, D.C. 20431 (202) 623-7000; *Government Finance Statistics Yearbook*, and *International Financial Statistics*.

U.C.L.A. Latin American Center Publications, University of California, Los Angeles, California 90024 (310) 825-6634; *Statistical Abstract of Latin America*.

PARAGUAY - FISHERIES

Facts on File, 460 Park Avenue South, New York, New York 10016 (800) 443-8323; *The New Book of World Rankings*.

Food and Agricultural Organization of the United Nations (FAO) Via delle Terme di Caracalla, 00100 Rome, Italy (Telephone Number in U.S. (202) 653-2400); *The State of Food and Agriculture*, and *Yearbook of Fishery Statistics*.

Inter-American Development Bank, 1300 New York Avenue, NW, Washington, D.C. 20577 (202) 623-1753; *Economic and Social Progress in Latin America*.

Statistical Office of the United Nations, Publishing Service, New York, New York 10017 (800) 253-9646; *Statistical Yearbook*.

U.C.L.A. Latin American Center Publications, University of California, Los Angeles, California 90024 (310) 825-6634; *Statistical Abstract of Latin America*.

PARAGUAY - FLOUR PRODUCTION

Statistical Office of the United Nations, Publishing Service, New York, New York 10017 (800) 253-9646; *Statistical Yearbook*.

PARAGUAY - FOOD

Food and Agricultural Organization of the United Nations (FAO), Via delle Terme di Caracalla, 00100 Rome, Italy (Telephone Number in U.S. (202) 653-2400); *Production Yearbook*, and *The State of Food and Agriculture*.

G.K. Hall and Company, 70 Lincoln Street, Boston, Massachusetts 02111 (617) 423-3990; *The World in Figures*.

Statistical Office of the United Nations, Publishing Service, New York, New York 10017 (800) 253-9646; *Trade in Manufactures of Developing Countries*.

PARAGUAY - FOREIGN AID

G.K. Hall and Company, 70 Lincoln Street, Boston, Massachusetts 02111 (617) 423-3990; *The World in Figures*.

Inter-American Development Bank, 1300 New York Avenue, NW, Washington, D.C. 20577 (202) 623-1753; *Economic and Social Progress in Latin America*.

PARAGUAY - FOREIGN DEBT

The Economist Intelligence Unit, 111 West 57th Street, New York, New York 10019 (800) 938-4685; *The New Latin America Market Atlas*.

Inter-American Development Bank, 1300 New York Avenue, NW, Washington, D.C. 20577 (202) 623-1753; *Economic and Social Progress in Latin America*.

International Monetary Fund, 700 Nineteenth Street, NW, Washington, D.C. 20431 (202) 623-7000; *Government Finance Statistics Yearbook*.

PARAGUAY - FOREIGN INDEBTEDNESS

Inter-American Development Bank, 1300 New York Avenue, NW, Washington, D.C. 20577 (202) 623-1753; *Economic and Social Progress in Latin America*.

Statistical Office of the United Nations, Publishing Service, New York, New York 10017 (800) 253-9646; *Economic Survey of Latin America and the Caribbean*.

PARAGUAY - FOREIGN INVESTMENT

The Economist Intelligence Unit, 111 West 57th Street, New York, New York 10019 (800) 938-4685; *The New Latin America Market Atlas*.

PARAGUAY - FOREIGN TRADE

The Economist Intelligence Unit, 111 West 57th Street, New York, New York 10019 (800) 938-4685; *The New Latin America Market Atlas*.

Euromonitor Publications Limited, 87-88 Turnmill Street, London EC1M 5QU, England; *International Marketing Data and Statistics*.

Facts on File, 460 Park Avenue South, New York, New York 10016 (800) 443-8323; *The New Book of World Rankings*.

Food and Agricultural Organization of the United Nations (FAO) Via delle Terme di Caracalla, 00100 Rome, Italy (Telephone Number in U.S. (202) 653-2400); *The State of Food and Agriculture*.

G.K. Hall and Company, 70 Lincoln Street, Boston, Massachusetts 02111 (617) 423-3990; *The World in Figures*.

Inter-American Development Bank, 1300 New York Avenue, NW, Washington, D.C. 20577 (202) 623-1753; *Economic and Social Progress in Latin America*.

International Monetary Fund, 700 Nineteenth Street, NW, Washington, D.C. 20431 (202) 623-7000; *International Financial Statistics*.

Statistical Office of the United Nations, Publishing Service, New York, New York 10017 (800) 253-9646; *Economic Survey of Latin America and the Caribbean, International Trade Statistics Yearbook*, and *Statistical Yearbook*.

U.C.L.A. Latin American Center Publications, University of California, Los Angeles, California 90024 (310) 825-6634; *Statistical Abstract of Latin America*.

The World Bank, 1818 H Street, NW, Washington, D.C. 20433 (202) 477-1234; *World Tables*.

PARAGUAY - FORESTRY AND FOREST PRODUCTS

The Economist Intelligence Unit, 111 West 57th Street, New York, New York 10019 (800) 938-4685; *The New Latin America Market Atlas*.

Facts on File, 460 Park Avenue South, New York, New York 10016 (800) 443-8323; *The New Book of World Rankings*.

Food and Agricultural Organization of the United Nations (FAO) Via delle Terme di Caracalla, 00100 Rome, Italy (Telephone Number in U.S. (202) 653-2400); *The State of Food and Agriculture*, and *Yearbook of Forest Products*.

G.K. Hall and Company, 70 Lincoln Street, Boston, Massachusetts 02111 (617) 423-3990; *The World in Figures*.

Inter-American Development Bank, 1300 New York Avenue, NW, Washington, D.C. 20577 (202) 623-1753; *Economic and Social Progress in Latin America*.

International Monetary Fund, 700 Nineteenth Street, NW, Washington, D.C. 20431 (202) 623-7000; *International Financial Statistics*.

Statistical Office of the United Nations, Publishing Service, New York, New York 10017 (800) 253-9646; *Statistical Yearbook*.

U.C.L.A. Latin American Center Publications, University of California, Los Angeles, California 90024 (310) 825-6634; *Statistical Abstract of Latin America*.

United Nations Educational, Scientific and Cultural Organization (UNESCO), 7 Place de Fontenoy, F-75700 Paris, France (Telephone Number in U.S. (212) 963-5981); *Statistical Yearbook*.

PARAGUAY - GARLIC PRODUCTION - See PARAGUAY - CROPS

PARAGUAY - GAS PRODUCTION - See PARAGUAY - MINING AND MINERAL PRODUCTS

PARAGUAY - GENERAL MORTALITY

Statistical Office of the United Nations, Publishing Service, New York, New York 10017 (800) 253-9646; *Demographic Yearbook*.

World Health Organization, Office of Publications, Avenue Appia, CH-1211 Geneva 27, Switzerland (Telephone Number in U.S. (518) 436-9686); *World Health Statistics Annual*.

PARAGUAY - GEOGRAPHIC DATA

Facts on File, 460 Park Avenue South, New York, New York 10016 (800) 443-8323; *The New Book of World Rankings*.

U.C.L.A. Latin American Center Publications, University of California, Los Angeles, California 90024 (310) 825-6634; *Statistical Abstract of Latin America*.

PARAGUAY - GOATS - See PARAGUAY - LIVESTOCK AND POULTRY

PARAGUAY - GOLD HOLDINGS

International Monetary Fund, 700 Nineteenth Street, NW, Washington, D.C. 20431 (202) 623-7000; *International Financial Statistics*.

Statistical Office of the United Nations, Publishing Service, New York, New York 10017 (800) 253-9646; *Statistical Yearbook*.

The World Bank, 1818 H Street, NW, Washington, D.C. 20433 (202) 477-1234; *World Tables*.

PARAGUAY - GOLD PRODUCTION AND CONSUMPTION - See PARAGUAY - MINING AND MINERAL PRODUCTS

PARAGUAY - GOLD RESERVES

The Economist Intelligence Unit, 111 West 57th Street, New York, New York 10019 (800) 938-4685; *The New Latin America Market Atlas*.

PARAGUAY - GOVERNMENT

G.K. Hall and Company, 70 Lincoln Street, Boston, Massachusetts 02111 (617) 423-3990; *The World in Figures*.

Inter-American Development Bank, 1300 New York Avenue, NW, Washington, D.C. 20577 (202) 623-1753; *Economic and Social Progress in Latin America*.

PARAGUAY - GOVERNMENT CONSUMPTION

Inter-American Development Bank, 1300 New York Avenue, NW, Washington, D.C. 20577 (202) 623-1753; *Economic and Social Progress in Latin America*.

PARAGUAY - GOVERNMENT EXPENDITURES

Inter-American Development Bank, 1300 New York Avenue, NW, Washington, D.C. 20577 (202) 623-1753; *Economic and Social Progress in Latin America*.

International Monetary Fund, 700 Nineteenth Street, NW, Washington, D.C. 20431 (202) 623-7000; *Government Finance Statistics Yearbook*.

Times Books, 201 East 50th Street, New York, New York 10022 (212) 751-2600; *The Economist Book of Vital World Statistics*.

The World Bank, 1818 H Street, NW, Washington, D.C. 20433 (202) 477-1234; *World Tables*.

PARAGUAY - GOVERNMENT FINANCES

Inter-American Development Bank, 1300 New York Avenue, NW, Washington, D.C. 20577 (202) 623-1753; *Economic and Social Progress in Latin America*.

International Monetary Fund, 700 Nineteenth Street, NW, Washington, D.C. 20431 (202) 623-7000; *International Financial Statistics*.

Statistical Office of the United Nations, Publishing Service, New York, New York 10017 (800) 253-9646; *Statistical Yearbook*.

PARAGUAY - GOVERNMENT REVENUES

Inter-American Development Bank, 1300 New York Avenue, NW, Washington, D.C. 20577 (202) 623-1753; *Economic and Social Progress in Latin America*.

International Monetary Fund, 700 Nineteenth Street, NW, Washington, D.C. 20431 (202) 623-7000; *Government Finance Statistics Yearbook*.

Times Books, 201 East 50th Street, New York, New York 10022 (212) 751-2600; *The Economist Book of Vital World Statistics*.

The World Bank, 1818 H Street, NW, Washington, D.C. 20433 (202) 477-1234; *World Tables*.

PARAGUAY - GRAIN PRODUCTION - See PARAGUAY - CROPS

PARAGUAY - GRANTS

International Monetary Fund, 700 Nineteenth Street, NW, Washington, D.C. 20431 (202) 623-7000; *Government Finance Statistics Yearbook*.

PARAGUAY - GROSS DOMESTIC PRODUCT

The Economist Intelligence Unit, 111 West 57th Street, New York, New York 10019 (800) 938-4685; *The New Latin America Market Atlas*, and *The World Market Atlas*.

Euromonitor Publications Limited, 87-88 Turnmill Street, London EC1M 5QU, England; *International Marketing Data and Statistics*.

Facts on File, 460 Park Avenue South, New York, New York 10016 (800) 443-8323; *The New Book of World Rankings*.

G.K. Hall and Company, 70 Lincoln Street, Boston, Massachusetts 02111 (617) 423-3990; *The World in Figures*.

Inter-American Development Bank, 1300 New York Avenue, NW, Washington, D.C. 20577 (202) 623-1753; *Economic and Social Progress in Latin America*.

Organization of American States (OAS), General Secretariat, Washington, D.C. 20006 (202) 458-3533; *Statistical Bulletin of the OAS*.

Statistical Office of the United Nations, Publishing Service, New York, New York 10017 (800) 253-9646; *Statistical Yearbook*, and *Statistical Yearbook for Latin America and the Caribbean*.

Times Books, 201 East 50th Street, New York, New York 10022 (212) 751-2600; *The Economist Book of Vital World Statistics*.

U.C.L.A. Latin American Center Publications, University of California, Los Angeles, California 90024 (310) 825-6634; *Statistical Abstract of Latin America*.

The World Bank, 1818 H Street, NW, Washington, D.C. 20433 (202) 477-1234; *World Tables*.

PARAGUAY - GROSS NATIONAL PRODUCT

Euromonitor Publications Limited, 87-88 Turnmill Street, London EC1M 5QU, England; *International Marketing Data and Statistics*.

Inter-American Development Bank, 1300 New York Avenue, NW, Washington, D.C. 20577 (202) 623-1753; *Economic and Social Progress in Latin America*.

U.S. Arms Control and Disarmament Agency, 320 Twenty-first Street, NW, Washington, D.C. 20451 (202) 647-8677; *World Military Expenditures and Arms Transfers*.

The World Bank, 1818 H Street, NW, Washington, D.C. 20433 (202) 477-1234; *World Tables*.

PARAGUAY - GROUNDNUTS PRODUCTION - See PARAGUAY - CROPS

PARAGUAY - HEALTH

The Economist Intelligence Unit, 111 West 57th Street, New York, New York 10019 (800) 938-4685; *The New Latin America Market Atlas*.

Facts on File, 460 Park Avenue South, New York, New York 10016 (800) 443-8323; *The New Book of World Rankings*.

G.K. Hall and Company, 70 Lincoln Street, Boston, Massachusetts 02111 (617) 423-3990; *The World in Figures*.

Statistical Office of the United Nations, Publishing Service, New York, New York 10017 (800) 253-9646; *Statistical Yearbook for Latin America and the Caribbean*, and *Statistical Yearbook*.

Times Books, 201 East 50th Street, New York, New York 10022 (212) 751-2600; *The Economist Book of Vital World Statistics*.

U.C.L.A. Latin American Center Publications, University of California, Los Angeles, California 90024 (310) 825-6634; *Statistical Abstract of Latin America*.

World Health Organization, Office of Publications, Avenue Appia, CH-1211 Geneva 27, Switzerland (Telephone Number in U.S. (518) 436-9686); *World Health Statistics Annual*.

PARAGUAY - HEALTH EXPENDITURES

International Monetary Fund, 700 Nineteenth Street, NW, Washington, D.C. 20431 (202) 623-7000; *Government Finance Statistics Yearbook*.

PARAGUAY - HIDE PRODUCTION

Food and Agricultural Organization of the United Nations (FAO), Via delle Terme di Caracalla, 00100 Rome, Italy (Telephone Number in U.S. (202) 653-2400); *Production Yearbook*.

PARAGUAY - HIDES EXPORTS

International Monetary Fund, 700 Nineteenth Street, NW, Washington, D.C. 20431 (202) 623-7000; *International Financial Statistics*.

PARAGUAY - HIGHWAYS

The Economist Intelligence Unit, 111 West 57th Street, New York, New York 10019 (800) 938-4685; *The New Latin America Market Atlas*.

G.K. Hall and Company, 70 Lincoln Street, Boston, Massachusetts 02111 (617) 423-3990; *The World in Figures*.

International Road Federation, 525 School Street, SW, Washington, D.C. 20024 (202) 554-2106; *World Road Statistics*.

PARAGUAY - HORSES - See PARAGUAY - LIVESTOCK AND POULTRY

PARAGUAY - HOURS OF WORK - See PARAGUAY - EMPLOYMENT

PARAGUAY - HOUSING

Facts on File, 460 Park Avenue South, New York, New York 10016 (800) 443-8323; *The New Book of World Rankings*.

Statistical Office of the United Nations, Publishing Service, New York, New York 10017 (800) 253-9646; *Statistical Yearbook for Latin America and the Caribbean*.

U.C.L.A. Latin American Center Publications, University of California, Los Angeles, California 90024 (310) 825-6634; *Statistical Abstract of Latin America*.

PARAGUAY - HOUSING EXPENDITURES

International Monetary Fund, 700 Nineteenth Street, NW, Washington, D.C. 20431 (202) 623-7000; *Government Finance Statistics Yearbook*.

PARAGUAY - ILLITERACY RATES

The Economist Intelligence Unit, 111 West 57th Street, New York, New York 10019 (800) 938-4685; *The New Latin America Market Atlas*.

PARAGUAY - ILLITERATE POPULATION

The Economist Intelligence Unit, 111 West 57th Street, New York, New York 10019 (800) 938-4685; *The World Market Atlas*.

G.K. Hall and Company, 70 Lincoln Street, Boston, Massachusetts 02111 (617) 423-3990; *The World in Figures*.

Statistical Office of the United Nations, Publishing Service, New York, New York 10017 (800) 253-9646; *Statistical Yearbook for Latin America and the Caribbean*.

United Nations Educational, Scientific and Cultural Organization (UNESCO), 7 Place de Fontenoy, F-75700 Paris, France (Telephone Number in U.S. (212) 963-5981); *Statistical Yearbook*.

PARAGUAY - IMMIGRATION

U.C.L.A. Latin American Center Publications, University of California, Los Angeles, California 90024 (310) 825-6634; *Statistical Abstract of Latin America*.

PARAGUAY - IMPORTS

The Economist Intelligence Unit, 111 West 57th Street, New York, New York 10019 (800) 938-4685; *The New Latin America Market Atlas*, and *The World Market Atlas*.

Euromonitor Publications Limited, 87-88 Turnmill Street, London EC1M 5QU, England; *International Marketing Data and Statistics*.

Food and Agricultural Organization of the United Nations (FAO) Via delle Terme di Caracalla, 00100 Rome, Italy (Telephone Number in U.S. (202) 653-2400); *The State of Food and Agriculture*.

G.K. Hall and Company, 70 Lincoln Street, Boston, Massachusetts 02111 (617) 423-3990; *The World in Figures*.

Inter-American Development Bank, 1300 New York Avenue, NW, Washington, D.C. 20577 (202) 623-1753; *Economic and Social Progress in Latin America*.

International Monetary Fund, 700 Nineteenth Street, NW, Washington, D.C. 20431 (202) 623-7000; *Direction of Trade Statistics*, and *Government Finance Statistics Yearbook*.

Organization of American States (OAS), General Secretariat, Washington, D.C. 20006 (202) 458-3533; *Statistical Bulletin of the OAS*.

Statistical Office of the United Nations, Publishing Service, New York, New York 10017 (800) 253-9646; *Statistical Yearbook for Latin America and the Caribbean*.

Times Books, 201 East 50th Street, New York, New York 10022 (212) 751-2600; *The Economist Book of Vital World Statistics*.

The World Bank, 1818 H Street, NW, Washington, D.C. 20433 (202) 477-1234; *World Tables*.

PARAGUAY - INCOME DISTRIBUTION

Statistical Office of the United Nations, Publishing Service, New York, New York 10017 (800) 253-9646; *Statistical Yearbook for Latin America and the Caribbean*.

U.C.L.A. Latin American Center Publications, University of California, Los Angeles, California 90024 (310) 825-6634; *Statistical Abstract of Latin America*.

PARAGUAY - INCOME TAXES - See PARAGUAY - TAXATION

PARAGUAY - INDUSTRY

Euromonitor Publications Limited, 87-88 Turnmill Street, London EC1M 5QU, England; *International Marketing Data and Statistics*.

Facts on File, 460 Park Avenue South, New York, New York 10016 (800) 443-8323; *The New Book of World Rankings*.

G.K. Hall and Company, 70 Lincoln Street, Boston, Massachusetts 02111 (617) 423-3990; *The World in Figures*.

International Labour Office, I.L.O. Publications, CH 1211, Geneva 22, Switzerland; *Yearbook of Labour Statistics*.

Statistical Office of the United Nations, Publishing Service, New York, New York 10017 (800) 253-9646; *Economic Survey of Latin America and the Caribbean*, and *Statistical Yearbook*.

Times Books, 201 East 50th Street, New York, New York 10022 (212) 751-2600; *The Economist Book of Vital World Statistics*.

U.C.L.A. Latin American Center Publications, University of California, Los Angeles, California 90024 (310) 825-6634; *Statistical Abstract of Latin America*.

The World Bank, 1818 H Street, NW, Washington, D.C. 20433 (202) 477-1234; *World Tables*.

PARAGUAY - INFANT AND MATERNAL MORTALITY

The Economist Intelligence Unit, 111 West 57th Street, New York, New York 10019 (800) 938-4685; *The New Latin America Market Atlas*.

Statistical Office of the United Nations, Publishing Service, New York, New York 10017 (800) 253-9646; *Demographic Yearbook*, and *Statistical Yearbook*.

Times Books, 201 East 50th Street, New York, New York 10022 (212) 751-2600; *The Economist Book of Vital World Statistics*.

The World Bank, 1818 H Street, NW, Washington, D.C. 20433 (202) 477-1234; *World Tables*.

World Health Organization, Office of Publications, Avenue Appia, CH-1211 Geneva 27, Switzerland (Telephone Number in U.S. (518) 436-9686); *World Health Statistics Annual*.

PARAGUAY - INFLATIONARY FACTORS

Statistical Office of the United Nations, Publishing Service, New York, New York 10017 (800) 253-9646; *Economic Survey of Latin America and the Caribbean*.

PARAGUAY - INTEREST RATES

Inter-American Development Bank, 1300 New York Avenue, NW, Washington, D.C. 20577 (202) 623-1753; *Economic and Social Progress in Latin America*.

PARAGUAY - INTERNATIONAL FINANCE

Inter-American Development Bank, 1300 New York Avenue, NW, Washington, D.C. 20577 (202) 623-1753; *Economic and Social Progress in Latin America*.

U.C.L.A. Latin American Center Publications, University of California, Los Angeles, California 90024 (310) 825-6634; *Statistical Abstract of Latin America*.

PARAGUAY - INTERNATIONAL LIQUIDITY

Inter-American Development Bank, 1300 New York Avenue, NW, Washington, D.C. 20577 (202) 623-1753; *Economic and Social Progress in Latin America*.

International Monetary Fund, 700 Nineteenth Street, NW, Washington, D.C. 20431 (202) 623-7000; *International Financial Statistics*.

PARAGUAY - INTERNATIONAL RESERVES

Organization of American States (OAS), General Secretariat, Washington, D.C. 20006 (202) 458-3533; *Statistical Bulletin of the OAS*.

PARAGUAY - INTERNATIONAL RESERVES EXCLUDING GOLD

Inter-American Development Bank, 1300 New York Avenue, NW, Washington, D.C. 20577 (202) 623-1753; *Economic and Social Progress in Latin America*.

Statistical Office of the United Nations, Publishing Service, New York, New York 10017 (800) 253-9646; *Statistical Yearbook*.

PARAGUAY - INTERNATIONAL STATISTICS

Inter-American Development Bank, 1300 New York Avenue, NW, Washington, D.C. 20577 (202) 623-1753; *Economic and Social Progress in Latin America*.

U.C.L.A. Latin American Center Publications, University of California, Los Angeles, California 90024 (310) 825-6634; *Statistical Abstract of Latin America*.

PARAGUAY - INVESTMENT

Inter-American Development Bank, 1300 New York Avenue, NW, Washington, D.C. 20577 (202) 623-1753; *Economic and Social Progress in Latin America.*

Statistical Office of the United Nations, Publishing Service, New York, New York 10017 (800) 253-9646; *Statistical Yearbook for Latin America and the Caribbean.*

PARAGUAY - IRON ORE PRODUCTION AND CONSUMPTION - See PARAGUAY - MINING AND MINERAL PRODUCTS

PARAGUAY - IRRIGATION

Euromonitor Publications Limited, 87-88 Turnmill Street, London EC1M 5QU, England; *International Marketing Data and Statistics.*

Inter-American Development Bank, 1300 New York Avenue, NW, Washington, D.C. 20577 (202) 623-1753; *Economic and Social Progress in Latin America.*

PARAGUAY - LABOR FORCE

The Economist Intelligence Unit, 111 West 57th Street, New York, New York 10019 (800) 938-4685; *The New Latin America Market Atlas.*

Euromonitor Publications Limited, 87-88 Turnmill Street, London EC1M 5QU, England; *International Marketing Data and Statistics.*

Facts on File, 460 Park Avenue South, New York, New York 10016 (800) 443-8323; *The New Book of World Rankings.*

Food and Agricultural Organization of the United Nations (FAO) Via delle Terme di Caracalla, 00100 Rome, Italy (Telephone Number in U.S. (202) 653-2400); *The State of Food and Agriculture.*

G.K. Hall and Company, 70 Lincoln Street, Boston, Massachusetts 02111 (617) 423-3990; *The World in Figures.*

Gale Research Incorporated, 835 Penobscot Building, Detroit, Michigan 48226 (800) 877-4253; *International Historical Statistics The Americas and Australasia.*

Times Books, 201 East 50th Street, New York, New York 10022 (212) 751-2600; *The Economist Book of Vital World Statistics.*

The World Bank, 1818 H Street, NW, Washington, D.C. 20433 (202) 477-1234; *World Tables.*

PARAGUAY - LABOR PRODUCTIVITY

International Labour Office, I.L.O. Publications, CH-1211, Geneva 22, Switzerland; *Yearbook of Labour Statistics.*

PARAGUAY - LAND AREA

The Economist Intelligence Unit, 111 West 57th Street, New York, New York 10019 (800) 938-4685; *The New Latin America Market Atlas.*

PARAGUAY - LAND USE

Euromonitor Publications Limited, 87-88 Turnmill Street, London EC1M 5QU, England; *International Marketing Data and Statistics.*

Food and Agricultural Organization of the United Nations (FAO), Via delle Terme di Caracalla, 00100 Rome, Italy (Telephone Number

in U.S. (202) 653-2400); *Production Yearbook.*

G.K. Hall and Company, 70 Lincoln Street, Boston, Massachusetts 02111 (617) 423-3990; *The World in Figures.*

Inter-American Development Bank, 1300 New York Avenue, NW, Washington, D.C. 20577 (202) 623-1753; *Economic and Social Progress in Latin America.*

PARAGUAY - LIBRARIES

Facts on File, 460 Park Avenue South, New York, New York 10016 (800) 443-8323; *The New Book of World Rankings.*

PARAGUAY - LIFE EXPECTANCY

The Economist Intelligence Unit, 111 West 57th Street, New York, New York 10019 (800) 938-4685; *The New Latin America Market Atlas.*

PARAGUAY - LIVESTOCK AND POULTRY

Euromonitor Publications Limited, 87-88 Turnmill Street, London EC1M 5QU, England; *International Marketing Data and Statistics.*

Facts on File, 460 Park Avenue South, New York, New York 10016 (800) 443-8323; *The New Book of World Rankings.*

Food and Agricultural Organization of the United Nations (FAO), Via delle Terme di Caracalla, 00100 Rome, Italy (Telephone Number in U.S. (202) 653-2400); *Production Yearbook*, and *The State of Food and Agriculture.*

G.K. Hall and Company, 70 Lincoln Street, Boston, Massachusetts 02111 (617) 423-3990; *The World in Figures.*

International Monetary Fund, 700 Nineteenth Street, NW, Washington, D.C. 20431 (202) 623-7000; *International Financial Statistics.*

Organization of American States (OAS), General Secretariat, Washington, D.C. 20006 (202) 458-3533; *Statistical Bulletin of the OAS.*

Statistical Office of the United Nations, Publishing Service, New York, New York 10017 (800) 253-9646; *Statistical Yearbook.*

PARAGUAY - LIVING LEVELS

G.K. Hall and Company, 70 Lincoln Street, Boston, Massachusetts 02111 (617) 423-3990; *The World in Figures.*

Statistical Office of the United Nations, Publishing Service, New York, New York 10017 (800) 253-9646; *Statistical Yearbook for Latin America and the Caribbean.*

Times Books, 201 East 50th Street, New York, New York 10022 (212) 751-2600; *The Economist Book of Vital World Statistics.*

PARAGUAY - MAIN ECONOMIC INDICATORS - See PARAGUAY - ECONOMY

PARAGUAY - MANUFACTURING

The Economist Intelligence Unit, 111 West 57th Street, New York, New York 10019 (800) 938-4685; *The New Latin America Market Atlas.*

Facts on File, 460 Park Avenue South, New York, New York 10016 (800) 443-8323; *The New Book of World Rankings.*

G.K. Hall and Company, 70 Lincoln Street, Boston, Massachusetts 02111 (617) 423-3990; *The World in Figures.*

Inter-American Development Bank, 1300 New York Avenue, NW, Washington, D.C. 20577 (202) 623-1753; *Economic and Social Progress in Latin America.*

Statistical Office of the United Nations, Publishing Service, New York, New York 10017 (800) 253-9646; *Statistical Yearbook for Latin America and the Caribbean.*

Times Books, 201 East 50th Street, New York, New York 10022 (212) 751-2600; *The Economist Book of Vital World Statistics.*

The World Bank, 1818 H Street, NW, Washington, D.C. 20433 (202) 477-1234; *World Tables.*

PARAGUAY - MARRIAGE RATES

Facts on File, 460 Park Avenue South, New York, New York 10016 (800) 443-8323; *The New Book of World Rankings.*

Statistical Office of the United Nations, Publishing Service, New York, New York 10017 (800) 253-9646; *Demographic Yearbook,* and *Statistical Yearbook.*

PARAGUAY - MEAT PRODUCTION - See PARAGUAY - LIVESTOCK AND POULTRY

PARAGUAY - MEDICAL PERSONNEL

U.C.L.A. Latin American Center Publications, University of California, Los Angeles, California 90024 (310) 825-6634; *Statistical Abstract of Latin America.*

PARAGUAY - MERCHANT SHIPPING

Times Books, 201 East 50th Street, New York, New York 10022 (212) 751-2600; *The Economist Book of Vital World Statistics.*

PARAGUAY - MILITARY

The Economist Intelligence Unit, 111 West 57th Street, New York, New York 10019 (800) 938-4685; *The New Latin America Market Atlas.*

G.K. Hall and Company, 70 Lincoln Street, Boston, Massachusetts 02111 (617) 423-3990; *The World in Figures.*

The International Institute for Strategic Studies, 23 Tavistock Street, London WC2E 7NQ, England; *The Military Balance.*

U.C.L.A. Latin American Center Publications, University of California, Los Angeles, California 90024 (310) 825-6634; *Statistical Abstract of Latin America.*

U.S. Arms Control and Disarmament Agency, 320 Twenty-first Street, NW, Washington, D.C. 20451 (202) 647-8677; *World Military Expenditures and Arms Transfers.*

PARAGUAY - MILK PRODUCTION - ALL TYPES OF MILK

Facts on File, 460 Park Avenue South, New York, New York 10016 (800) 443-8323; *The New Book of World Rankings.*

Statistical Office of the United Nations, Publishing Service, New York, New York 10017 (800) 253-9646; *Statistical Yearbook.*

PARAGUAY - MINING AND MINERAL PRODUCTS

The Economist Intelligence Unit, 111 West 57th Street, New York, New York 10019 (800) 938-4685; *The New Latin America Market Atlas.*

Facts on File, 460 Park Avenue South, New York, New York 10016 (800) 443-8323; *The New Book of World Rankings.*

G.K. Hall and Company, 70 Lincoln Street, Boston, Massachusetts 02111 (617) 423-3990; *The World in Figures.*

Inter-American Development Bank, 1300 New York Avenue, NW, Washington, D.C. 20577 (202) 623-1753; *Economic and Social Progress in Latin America.*

Statistical Office of the United Nations, Publishing Service, New York, New York 10017 (800) 253-9646; *Statistical Yearbook,* and *Statistical Yearbook for Latin America and the Caribbean.*

U.C.L.A. Latin American Center Publications, University of California, Los Angeles, California 90024 (310) 825-6634; *Statistical Abstract of Latin America.*

PARAGUAY - MONEY EXCHANGE RATES

Euromonitor Publications Limited, 87-88 Turnmill Street, London EC1M 5QU, England; *International Marketing Data and Statistics.*

Inter-American Development Bank, 1300 New York Avenue, NW, Washington, D.C. 20577 (202) 623-1753; *Economic and Social Progress in Latin America.*

International Monetary Fund, 700 Nineteenth Street, NW, Washington, D.C. 20431 (202) 623-7000; *International Financial Statistics.*

Statistical Office of the United Nations, Publishing Service, New York, New York 10017 (800) 253-9646; *Statistical Yearbook.*

PARAGUAY - MONEY RATES - MARKET

Inter-American Development Bank, 1300 New York Avenue, NW, Washington, D.C. 20577 (202) 623-1753; *Economic and Social Progress in Latin America.*

PARAGUAY - MONEY RESERVES

Euromonitor Publications Limited, 87-88 Turnmill Street, London EC1M 5QU, England; *International Marketing Data and Statistics.*

Inter-American Development Bank, 1300 New York Avenue, NW, Washington, D.C. 20577 (202) 623-1753; *Economic and Social Progress in Latin America.*

PARAGUAY - MONEY SUPPLY

Euromonitor Publications Limited, 87-88 Turnmill Street, London EC1M 5QU, England; *International Marketing Data and Statistics.*

G.K. Hall and Company, 70 Lincoln Street, Boston, Massachusetts 02111 (617) 423-3990; *The World in Figures.*

Inter-American Development Bank, 1300 New York Avenue, NW, Washington, D.C. 20577 (202) 623-1753; *Economic and Social Progress in Latin America.*

International Monetary Fund, 700 Nineteenth Street, NW, Washington, D.C. 20431 (202) 623-7000; *International Financial Statistics*.

Statistical Office of the United Nations, Publishing Service, New York, New York 10017 (800) 253-9646; *Statistical Yearbook*.

U.C.L.A. Latin American Center Publications, University of California, Los Angeles, California 90024 (310) 825-6634; *Statistical Abstract of Latin America*.

The World Bank, 1818 H Street, NW, Washington, D.C. 20433 (202) 477-1234; *World Tables*.

PARAGUAY - MOTOR VEHICLE TAXES - See PARAGUAY - TAXATION

PARAGUAY - MOTOR VEHICLES IN USE

The Economist Intelligence Unit, 111 West 57th Street, New York, New York 10019 (800) 938-4685; *The New Latin America Market Atlas*.

G.K. Hall and Company, 70 Lincoln Street, Boston, Massachusetts 02111 (617) 423-3990; *The World in Figures*.

International Road Federation, 525 School Street, SW, Washington, D.C. 20024 (202) 554-2106; *World Road Statistics*.

Statistical Office of the United Nations, Publishing Service, New York, New York 10017 (800) 253-9646; *Statistical Yearbook*.

Times Books, 201 East 50th Street, New York, New York 10022 (212) 751-2600; *The Economist Book of Vital World Statistics*.

PARAGUAY - MULES - See PARAGUAY - LIVESTOCK AND POULTRY

PARAGUAY - MUSEUMS

Facts on File, 460 Park Avenue South, New York, New York 10016 (800) 443-8323; *The New Book of World Rankings*.

PARAGUAY - NATALITY - See PARAGUAY - BIRTH RATES

PARAGUAY - NATIONAL ACCOUNTS

Gale Research Incorporated, 835 Penobscot Building, Detroit, Michigan 48226 (800) 877-4253; *International Historical Statistics The Americas and Australasia*.

Inter-American Development Bank, 1300 New York Avenue, NW, Washington, D.C. 20577 (202) 623-1753; *Economic and Social Progress in Latin America*.

International Monetary Fund, 700 Nineteenth Street, NW, Washington, D.C. 20431 (202) 623-7000; *International Financial Statistics*.

Organization of American States (OAS), General Secretariat, Washington, D.C. 20006 (202) 458-3533; *Statistical Bulletin of the OAS*.

Statistical Office of the United Nations, Publishing Service, New York, New York 10017 (800) 253-9646; *National Accounts Statistics*, and *Statistical Yearbook*.

U.C.L.A. Latin American Center Publications, University of California, Los Angeles, California 90024 (310) 825-6634; *Statistical Abstract of Latin America*.

PARAGUAY - NATIONAL INCOME

Facts on File, 460 Park Avenue South, New York, New York 10016 (800) 443-8323; *The New Book of World Rankings*.

G.K. Hall and Company, 70 Lincoln Street, Boston, Massachusetts 02111 (617) 423-3990; *The World in Figures*.

Inter-American Development Bank, 1300 New York Avenue, NW, Washington, D.C. 20577 (202) 623-1753; *Economic and Social Progress in Latin America*.

Statistical Office of the United Nations, Publishing Service, New York, New York 10017 (800) 253-9646; *Statistical Yearbook*, and *Statistical Yearbook for Latin America and the Caribbean*.

PARAGUAY - NATIONAL PRODUCT

Facts on File, 460 Park Avenue South, New York, New York 10016 (800) 443-8323; *The New Book of World Rankings*.

Statistical Office of the United Nations, Publishing Service, New York, New York 10017 (800) 253-9646; *Statistical Yearbook*.

PARAGUAY - NATURAL GAS PRODUCTION - See PARAGUAY - MINING AND MINERAL PRODUCTS

PARAGUAY - NEWSPAPER PRODUCTION - See PARAGUAY - FORESTRY AND FOREST PRODUCTS

PARAGUAY - NEWSPRINT - See PARAGUAY - FORESTRY AND FOREST PRODUCTS

PARAGUAY - NUTRITION

Statistical Office of the United Nations, Publishing Service, New York, New York 10017 (800) 253-9646; *Statistical Yearbook for Latin America and the Caribbean*.

PARAGUAY - OCCUPATIONS - See PARAGUAY - LABOR FORCE

PARAGUAY - ORANGES PRODUCTION - See PARAGUAY - CROPS

PARAGUAY - PALM KERNELS PRODUCTION - See PARAGUAY - CROPS

PARAGUAY - PAPER - See PARAGUAY - FORESTRY AND FOREST PRODUCTS

PARAGUAY - PEANUT PRODUCTION - See PARAGUAY - CROPS

PARAGUAY - PESTICIDE USE

Food and Agricultural Organization of the United Nations (FAO) Via delle Terme di Caracalla, 00100 Rome, Italy (Telephone Number in U.S. (202) 653-2400); *The State of Food and Agriculture*.

PARAGUAY - PETROLEUM INDUSTRY

The Economist Intelligence Unit, 111 West 57th Street, New York, New York 10019 (800) 938-4685; *The New Latin America Market Atlas*.

Facts on File, 460 Park Avenue South, New York, New York 10016 (800) 443-8323; *The New Book of World Rankings*.

Food and Agricultural Organization of the United Nations (FAO) Via delle Terme di Caracalla, 00100 Rome, Italy (Telephone Number in U.S. (202) 653-2400); *The State of Food and Agriculture*.

G.K. Hall and Company, 70 Lincoln Street, Boston, Massachusetts 02111 (617) 423-3990; *The World in Figures*.

Inter-American Development Bank, 1300 New York Avenue, NW, Washington, D.C. 20577 (202) 623-1753; *Economic and Social Progress in Latin America*.

Statistical Office of the United Nations, Publishing Service, New York, New York 10017 (800) 253-9646; *Statistical Yearbook*.

PARAGUAY - PIG-IRON AND FERRO-ALLOY PRODUCTION - See PARAGUAY - MINING AND MINERAL PRODUCTS

PARAGUAY - PIGS - See PARAGUAY - LIVESTOCK AND POULTRY

PARAGUAY - POLITICAL DATA

U.C.L.A. Latin American Center Publications, University of California, Los Angeles, California 90024 (310) 825-6634; *Statistical Abstract of Latin America*.

PARAGUAY - POPULATION

The Economist Intelligence Unit, 111 West 57th Street, New York, New York 10019 (800) 938-4685; *The New Latin America Market Atlas*, and *The World Market Atlas*.

Euromonitor Publications Limited, 87-88 Turnmill Street, London EC1M 5QU, England; *International Marketing Data and Statistics*.

Facts on File, 460 Park Avenue South, New York, New York 10016 (800) 443-8323; *The New Book of World Rankings*.

Food and Agricultural Organization of the United Nations (FAO), Via delle Terme di Caracalla, 00100 Rome, Italy (Telephone Number in U.S. (202) 653-2400); *Production Yearbook*.

Gale Research Incorporated, 835 Penobscot Building, Detroit, Michigan 48226 (800) 877-4253; *International Historical Statistics The Americas and Australasia*.

G.K. Hall and Company, 70 Lincoln Street, Boston, Massachusetts 02111 (617) 423-3990; *The World in Figures*.

Inter-American Development Bank, 1300 New York Avenue, NW, Washington, D.C. 20577 (202) 623-1753; *Economic and Social Progress in Latin America*.

International Labour Office, I.L.O. Publications, CH-1211, Geneva 22, Switzerland; *Yearbook of Labour Statistics*.

Organization of American States (OAS), General Secretariat, Washington, D.C. 20006 (202) 458-3533; *Statistical Bulletin of the OAS*.

Statistical Office of the United Nations, Publishing Service, New York, New York 10017 (800) 253-9646; *Demographic Yearbook, Statistical Yearbook*, and *Statistical Yearbook for Latin America and the Caribbean*.

Times Books, 201 East 50th Street, New York, New York 10022 (212) 751-2600; *The Economist Book of Vital World Statistics*.

U.C.L.A. Latin American Center Publications, University of California, Los Angeles, California 90024 (310) 825-6634; *Statistical Abstract of Latin America*.

United Nations Educational, Scientific and Cultural Organization (UNESCO), 7 Place de Fontenoy, F-75700 Paris, France (Telephone

Number in U.S. (212) 963-5981); *Statistical Yearbook*.

U.S. Arms Control and Disarmament Agency, 320 Twenty-first Street, NW, Washington, D.C. 20451 (202) 647-8677; *World Military Expenditures and Arms Transfers*.

World Health Organization, Office of Publications, Avenue Appia, CH-1211 Geneva 27, Switzerland (Telephone Number in U.S. (518) 436-9686); *World Health Statistics Annual*.

PARAGUAY - POST OFFICES

Facts on File, 460 Park Avenue South, New York, New York 10016 (800) 443-8323; *The New Book of World Rankings*.

PARAGUAY - POTATO PRODUCTION - See PARAGUAY - CROPS

PARAGUAY - PRICES

Facts on File, 460 Park Avenue South, New York, New York 10016 (800) 443-8323; *The New Book of World Rankings*.

Food and Agricultural Organization of the United Nations (FAO), Via delle Terme di Caracalla, 00100 Rome, Italy (Telephone Number in U.S. (202) 653-2400); *Production Yearbook*, and *The State of Food and Agriculture*.

Gale Research Incorporated, 835 Penobscot Building, Detroit, Michigan 48226 (800) 877-4253; *International Historical Statistics The Americas and Australasia*.

G.K. Hall and Company, 70 Lincoln Street, Boston, Massachusetts 02111 (617) 423-3990; *The World in Figures*.

International Labour Office, I.L.O. Publications, CH-1211, Geneva 22, Switzerland; *Yearbook of Labour Statistics*.

International Monetary Fund, 700 Nineteenth Street, NW, Washington, D.C. 20431 (202) 623-7000; *International Financial Statistics*.

Statistical Office of the United Nations, Publishing Service, New York, New York 10017 (800) 253-9646; *Economic Survey of Latin America and the Caribbean*, and *Statistical Yearbook for Latin America and the Caribbean*.

PARAGUAY - PRINTING AND WRITING PAPER - See PARAGUAY - FORESTRY AND FOREST PRODUCTS

PARAGUAY - PRODUCTION

Facts on File, 460 Park Avenue South, New York, New York 10016 (800) 443-8323; *The New Book of World Rankings*.

G.K. Hall and Company, 70 Lincoln Street, Boston, Massachusetts 02111 (617) 423-3990; *The World in Figures*.

PARAGUAY - PRODUCTIVITY

Euromonitor Publications Limited, 87-88 Turnmill Street, London EC1M 5QU, England; *International Marketing Data and Statistics*.

PARAGUAY - PROPERTY TAXES - See PARAGUAY - TAXATION

PARAGUAY - PUBLIC CONSUMPTION FUND

Inter-American Development Bank, 1300 New York Avenue, NW, Washington, D.C. 20577 (202) 623-1753; *Economic and Social Progress in Latin America*.

PARAGUAY - PUBLIC EXPENDITURE

Inter-American Development Bank, 1300 New York Avenue, NW, Washington, D.C. 20577 (202) 623-1753; *Economic and Social Progress in Latin America.*

Organization of American States (OAS), General Secretariat, Washington, D.C. 20006 (202) 458-3533; *Statistical Bulletin of the OAS.*

Statistical Office of the United Nations, Publishing Service, New York, New York 10017 (800) 253-9646; *Statistical Yearbook for Latin America and the Caribbean.*

PARAGUAY - PUBLIC FINANCE

Facts on File, 460 Park Avenue South, New York, New York 10016 (800) 443-8323; *The New Book of World Rankings.*

Inter-American Development Bank, 1300 New York Avenue, NW, Washington, D.C. 20577 (202) 623-1753; *Economic and Social Progress in Latin America.*

Organization of American States (OAS), General Secretariat, Washington, D.C. 20006 (202) 458-3533; *Statistical Bulletin of the OAS.*

PARAGUAY - PUBLIC REVENUE

Inter-American Development Bank, 1300 New York Avenue, NW, Washington, D.C. 20577 (202) 623-1753; *Economic and Social Progress in Latin America.*

Organization of American States (OAS), General Secretariat, Washington, D.C. 20006 (202) 458-3533; *Statistical Bulletin of the OAS.*

PARAGUAY - RADIO BROADCASTING - See PARAGUAY - BROADCASTING

PARAGUAY - RAILWAYS

The Economist Intelligence Unit, 111 West 57th Street, New York, New York 10019 (800) 938-4685; *The New Latin America Market Atlas.*

G.K. Hall and Company, 70 Lincoln Street, Boston, Massachusetts 02111 (617) 423-3990; *The World in Figures.*

Jane's Information Group, Sentinel House, 163 Brighton Road, Coulsdon, Surrey CR5 2NH, England (Telephone Number in U.S. (703) 683-3700); *Jane's World Railways.*

Statistical Office of the United Nations, Publishing Service, New York, New York 10017 (800) 253-9646; *Statistical Yearbook.*

PARAGUAY - RANCHING

U.C.L.A. Latin American Center Publications, University of California, Los Angeles, California 90024 (310) 825-6634; *Statistical Abstract of Latin America.*

PARAGUAY - RELIGION

Facts on File, 460 Park Avenue South, New York, New York 10016 (800) 443-8323; *The New Book of World Rankings.*

U.C.L.A. Latin American Center Publications, University of California, Los Angeles, California 90024 (310) 825-6634; *Statistical*

Abstract of Latin America.

PARAGUAY - RENT PRICES

International Labour Office, I.L.O. Publications, CH-1211, Geneva 22, Switzerland; *Yearbook of Labour Statistics.*

PARAGUAY - RESERVES EXCLUDING GOLD

The Economist Intelligence Unit, 111 West 57th Street, New York, New York 10019 (800) 938-4685; *The New Latin America Market Atlas.*

PARAGUAY - RETAIL TRADE

G.K. Hall and Company, 70 Lincoln Street, Boston, Massachusetts 02111 (617) 423-3990; *The World in Figures.*

Inter-American Development Bank, 1300 New York Avenue, NW, Washington, D.C. 20577 (202) 623-1753; *Economic and Social Progress in Latin America.*

PARAGUAY - REVENUE

Organization of American States (OAS), General Secretariat, Washington, D.C. 20006 (202) 458-3533; *Statistical Bulletin of the OAS.*

PARAGUAY - RICE PRODUCTION - See PARAGUAY - CROPS

PARAGUAY - ROOT AND TUBER PRODUCTION - See PARAGUAY - CROPS

PARAGUAY - ROUNDWOOD PRODUCTION - See PARAGUAY - FORESTRY AND FOREST PRODUCTS

PARAGUAY - RUBBER PRODUCTION AND CONSUMPTION

Facts on File, 460 Park Avenue South, New York, New York 10016 (800) 443-8323; *The New Book of World Rankings.*

PARAGUAY - SAWNWOOD PRODUCTION - See PARAGUAY - FORESTRY AND FOREST PRODUCTS

PARAGUAY - SCIENCE AND TECHNOLOGY

Statistical Office of the United Nations, Publishing Service, New York, New York 10017 (800) 253-9646; *Statistical Yearbook.*

U.C.L.A. Latin American Center Publications, University of California, Los Angeles, California 90024 (310) 825-6634; *Statistical Abstract of Latin America.*

PARAGUAY - SCIENTISTS AND TECHNICIANS

Statistical Office of the United Nations, Publishing Service, New York, New York 10017 (800) 253-9646; *Statistical Yearbook.*

PARAGUAY - SENIOR CITIZENS

Facts on File, 460 Park Avenue South, New York, New York 10016 (800) 443-8323; *The New Book of World Rankings.*

PARAGUAY - SHEEP - See PARAGUAY - LIVESTOCK AND POULTRY

PARAGUAY - SILVER PRODUCTION AND CONSUMPTION - See PAPUA NEW GUINEA - MINING AND MINERAL PRODUCTS

PARAGUAY - SOCIAL DATA

Facts on File, 460 Park Avenue South, New York, New York 10016 (800) 443-8323; *The New Book of World Rankings*.

G.K. Hall and Company, 70 Lincoln Street, Boston, Massachusetts 02111 (617) 423-3990; *The World in Figures*.

U.C.L.A. Latin American Center Publications, University of California, Los Angeles, California 90024 (310) 825-6634; *Statistical Abstract of Latin America*.

PARAGUAY - SOCIAL SECURITY

Inter-American Development Bank, 1300 New York Avenue, NW, Washington, D.C. 20577 (202) 623-1753; *Economic and Social Progress in Latin America*.

International Monetary Fund, 700 Nineteenth Street, NW, Washington, D.C. 20431 (202) 623-7000; *Government Finance Statistics Yearbook*.

PARAGUAY - SOCIOECONOMIC DATA

Inter-American Development Bank, 1300 New York Avenue, NW, Washington, D.C. 20577 (202) 623-1753; *Economic and Social Progress in Latin America*.

U.C.L.A. Latin American Center Publications, University of California, Los Angeles, California 90024 (310) 825-6634; *Statistical Abstract of Latin America*.

PARAGUAY - SOYBEANS - See PARAGUAY - CROPS

PARAGUAY - STAMP TAXES AND DUTIES - See PARAGUAY - TAXATION

PARAGUAY - STATE BUDGET REVENUE AND EXPENDITURES

Euromonitor Publications Limited, 87-88 Turnmill Street, London EC1M 5QU, England; *International Marketing Data and Statistics*.

Inter-American Development Bank, 1300 New York Avenue, NW, Washington, D.C. 20577 (202) 623-1753; *Economic and Social Progress in Latin America*.

PARAGUAY - STEEL - See PARAGUAY - MINING AND MINERAL PRODUCTS

PARAGUAY - STOCKS - COMMODITY - MARKET PRICE - INDEX

Food and Agricultural Organization of the United Nations (FAO) Via delle Terme di Caracalla, 00100 Rome, Italy (Telephone Number in U.S. (202) 653-2400); *The State of Food and Agriculture*.

PARAGUAY - SUGAR PRODUCTION AND CONSUMPTION - See PARAGUAY - CROPS

PARAGUAY - TAXATION

G.K. Hall and Company, 70 Lincoln Street, Boston, Massachusetts 02111 (617) 423-3990; *The World in Figures*.

Inter-American Development Bank, 1300 New York Avenue, NW, Washington, D.C. 20577 (202) 623-1753; *Economic and Social Progress in Latin America*.

International Monetary Fund, 700 Nineteenth Street, NW, Washington, D.C. 20431 (202) 623-7000; *Government Finance*

Statistics Yearbook.

International Road Federation, 525 School Street, SW, Washington, D.C. 20024 (202) 554-2106; *World Road Statistics*.

Statistical Office of the United Nations, Publishing Service, New York, New York 10017 (800) 253-9646; *Statistical Yearbook for Latin America and the Caribbean*.

The World Bank, 1818 H Street, NW, Washington, D.C. 20433 (202) 477-1234; *World Tables*.

PARAGUAY - TAX REVENUE - See PARAGUAY - TAXATION

PARAGUAY - TELEGRAPH SERVICE

Statistical Office of the United Nations, Publishing Service, New York, New York 10017 (800) 253-9646; *Statistical Yearbook*.

PARAGUAY - TELEPHONES IN USE

American Telephone and Telegraph Company, 26 Parsippany Road, Whippany, New Jersey 07981 (800) 338-4038; *The World's Telephones*.

The Economist Intelligence Unit, 111 West 57th Street, New York, New York 10019 (800) 938-4685; *The New Latin America Market Atlas*.

G.K. Hall and Company, 70 Lincoln Street, Boston, Massachusetts 02111 (617) 423-3990; *The World in Figures*.

Statistical Office of the United Nations, Publishing Service, New York, New York 10017 (800) 253-9646; *Statistical Yearbook*.

PARAGUAY - TELEVISION BROADCASTING - See PARAGUAY - BROADCASTING

PARAGUAY - TEXTILE INDUSTRY

G.K. Hall and Company, 70 Lincoln Street, Boston, Massachusetts 02111 (617) 423-3990; *The World in Figures*.

Statistical Office of the United Nations, Publishing Service, New York, New York 10017 (800) 253-9646; *Statistical Yearbook*.

PARAGUAY - TIMBER EXPORTS - See PARAGUAY - FORESTRY AND FOREST PRODUCTS

PARAGUAY - TOBACCO EXPORTS

International Monetary Fund, 700 Nineteenth Street, NW, Washington, D.C. 20431 (202) 623-7000; *International Financial Statistics*.

PARAGUAY - TOBACCO PRODUCTION

Facts on File, 460 Park Avenue South, New York, New York 10016 (800) 443-8323; *The New Book of World Rankings*.

Statistical Office of the United Nations, Publishing Service, New York, New York 10017 (800) 253-9646; *Statistical Yearbook*.

U.C.L.A. Latin American Center Publications, University of California, Los Angeles, California 90024 (310) 825-6634; *Statistical Abstract of Latin America*.

PARAGUAY - TOURISM

The Economist Intelligence Unit, 111 West 57th Street, New York, New York 10019 (800) 938-4685; *The New Latin America Market Atlas*.

Facts on File, 460 Park Avenue South, New York, New York 10016 (800) 443-8323; *The New Book of World Rankings*.

G.K. Hall and Company, 70 Lincoln Street, Boston, Massachusetts 02111 (617) 423-3990; *The World in Figures*.

Organization of American States (OAS), General Secretariat, Washington, D.C. 20006 (202) 458-3533; *Statistical Bulletin of the OAS*.

Statistical Office of the United Nations, Publishing Service, New York, New York 10017 (800) 253-9646; *Statistical Yearbook*, and *Statistical Yearbook for Latin America and the Caribbean*.

Times Books, 201 East 50th Street, New York, New York 10022 (212) 751-2600; *The Economist Book of Vital World Statistics*.

U.C.L.A. Latin American Center Publications, University of California, Los Angeles, California 90024 (310) 825-6634; *Statistical Abstract of Latin America*.

World Tourism Organization, Calle Capitan Haya 42, E-28020 Madrid, Spain; *Yearbook of Tourism Statistics*.

PARAGUAY - TRACTORS IN USE

The Economist Intelligence Unit, 111 West 57th Street, New York, New York 10019 (800) 938-4685; *The New Latin America Market Atlas*.

Statistical Office of the United Nations, Publishing Service, New York, New York 10017 (800) 253-9646; *Statistical Yearbook*.

PARAGUAY - TRADE - See PARAGUAY - FOREIGN TRADE

PARAGUAY - TRANSPORTATION AND COMMUNICATIONS

The Economist Intelligence Unit, 111 West 57th Street, New York, New York 10019 (800) 938-4685; *The New Latin America Market Atlas*.

Facts on File, 460 Park Avenue South, New York, New York 10016 (800) 443-8323; *The New Book of World Rankings*.

Gale Research Incorporated, 835 Penobscot Building, Detroit, Michigan 48226 (800) 877-4253; *International Historical Statistics The Americas and Australasia*.

G.K. Hall and Company, 70 Lincoln Street, Boston, Massachusetts 02111 (617) 423-3990; *The World in Figures*.

Inter-American Development Bank, 1300 New York Avenue, NW, Washington, D.C. 20577 (202) 623-1753; *Economic and Social Progress in Latin America*.

Statistical Office of the United Nations, Publishing Service, New York, New York 10017 (800) 253-9646; *Statistical Yearbook for Latin America and the Caribbean*.

U.C.L.A. Latin American Center Publications, University of California, Los Angeles, California 90024 (310) 825-6634; *Statistical Abstract of Latin America*.

PARAGUAY - TRAVEL FARES ABROAD

International Monetary Fund, 700 Nineteenth Street, NW, Washington, D.C. 20431 (202) 623-7000; *Government Finance Statistics Yearbook*.

PARAGUAY - TURKEYS - See PARAGUAY - LIVESTOCK AND POULTRY

PARAGUAY - UNEMPLOYMENT

The Economist Intelligence Unit, 111 West 57th Street, New York, New York 10019 (800) 938-4685; *The New Latin America Market Atlas*.

Euromonitor Publications Limited, 87-88 Turnmill Street, London EC1M 5QU, England; *International Marketing Data and Statistics*.

International Labour Office, I.L.O. Publications, CH-1211, Geneva 22, Switzerland; *Yearbook of Labour Statistics*.

U.C.L.A. Latin American Center Publications, University of California, Los Angeles, California 90024 (310) 825-6634; *Statistical Abstract of Latin America*.

PARAGUAY - UTILITIES

U.C.L.A. Latin American Center Publications, University of California, Los Angeles, California 90024 (310) 825-6634; *Statistical Abstract of Latin America*.

PARAGUAY - VEGETABLE OIL EXPORTS

International Monetary Fund, 700 Nineteenth Street, NW, Washington, D.C. 20431 (202) 623-7000; *International Financial Statistics*.

PARAGUAY - VITAL STATISTICS

Euromonitor Publications Limited, 87-88 Turnmill Street, London EC1M 5QU, England; *International Marketing Data and Statistics*.

Gale Research Incorporated, 835 Penobscot Building, Detroit, Michigan 48226 (800) 877-4253; *International Historical Statistics The Americas and Australasia*.

G.K. Hall and Company, 70 Lincoln Street, Boston, Massachusetts 02111 (617) 423-3990; *The World in Figures*.

Statistical Office of the United Nations, Publishing Service, New York, New York 10017 (800) 253-9646; *Statistical Yearbook*.

World Health Organization, Office of Publications, Avenue Appia, CH-1211 Geneva 27, Switzerland (Telephone Number in U.S. (518) 436-9686); *World Health Statistics Annual*.

PARAGUAY - WAGES

G.K. Hall and Company, 70 Lincoln Street, Boston, Massachusetts 02111 (617) 423-3990; *The World in Figures*.

International Labour Office, I.L.O. Publications, CH-1211, Geneva 22, Switzerland; *Yearbook of Labour Statistics*.

Organization of American States (OAS), General Secretariat, Washington, D.C. 20006 (202) 458-3533; *Statistical Bulletin of the OAS*.

U.C.L.A. Latin American Center Publications, University of California, Los Angeles, California 90024 (310) 825-6634; *Statistical Abstract of Latin America*.

PARAGUAY - WATERMELON PRODUCTION - See PARAGUAY - CROPS

PARAGUAY - WEATHER

Facts on File, 460 Park Avenue South, New York, New York 10016 (800) 443-8323; *The New Book of World Rankings*.

G.K. Hall and Company, 70 Lincoln Street, Boston, Massachusetts 02111 (617) 423-3990; *The World in Figures*.

PARAGUAY - WELFARE

Inter-American Development Bank, 1300 New York Avenue, NW, Washington, D.C. 20577 (202) 623-1753; *Economic and Social Progress in Latin America*.

International Monetary Fund, 700 Nineteenth Street, NW, Washington, D.C. 20431 (202) 623-7000; *Government Finance Statistics Yearbook*.

PARAGUAY - WHEAT PRODUCTION AND PRICES - See PARAGUAY - CROPS

PARAGUAY - WHOLESALE PRICES

Inter-American Development Bank, 1300 New York Avenue, NW, Washington, D.C. 20577 (202) 623-1753; *Economic and Social Progress in Latin America*.

International Monetary Fund, 700 Nineteenth Street, NW, Washington, D.C. 20431 (202) 623-7000; *International Financial Statistics*.

Organization of American States (OAS), General Secretariat, Washington, D.C. 20006 (202) 458-3533; *Statistical Bulletin of the OAS*.

PARAGUAY - WHOLESALE TRADE

Inter-American Development Bank, 1300 New York Avenue, NW, Washington, D.C. 20577 (202) 623-1753; *Economic and Social Progress in Latin America*.

PARAGUAY - WINE PRODUCTION

Facts on File, 460 Park Avenue South, New York, New York 10016 (800) 443-8323; *The New Book of World Rankings*.

Statistical Office of the United Nations, Publishing Service, New York, New York 10017 (800) 253-9646; *Statistical Yearbook*.

PARAGUAY - WOOD PULP PRODUCTION - See PARAGUAY - FORESTRY AND FOREST PRODUCTS

PARAGUAY - WOOL PRODUCTION

Facts on File, 460 Park Avenue South, New York, New York 10016 (800) 443-8323; *The New Book of World Rankings*.

PARAGUAY - YARN PRODUCTION

Statistical Office of the United Nations, Publishing Service, New York, New York 10017 (800) 253-9646; *Statistical Yearbook*.

PARKS

National Association of State Park Directors, 126 Mill Branch Road, Tallahassee, Florida 32312 (904) 893-4959; *Annual Information Exchange*.

U.S. Department of the Interior, National Park Service, C Street between Eighteenth and Nineteenth Streets, NW, Washington, D.C. 20240 (202) 208-6843; *National Park Statistical Abstract*.

PARKS - FINANCES

U.S. Department of the Interior, National Park Service, C Street between Eighteenth and Nineteenth Streets, NW, Washington, D.C. 20240 (202) 208-6843; *National Park Statistical Abstract*.

PARKS - GOVERNMENT EMPLOYMENT AND PAYROLLS

U.S. Department of Commerce, Bureau of the Census, Suitland, Maryland 20233 (301) 763-4040; *Public Employment*.

PARKS - NATIONAL

U.S. Department of the Interior, National Park Service, C Street between Eighteenth and Nineteenth Streets, NW, Washington, D.C. 20240 (202) 208-6843; *National Park Statistical Abstract*.

PARKS - STATE

National Association of State Park Directors, 126 Mill Branch Road, Tallahassee, Florida 32312 (904) 893-4959; *Annual Information Exchange*.

PAROLEES - See also CORRECTIONAL INSTITUTIONS and PRISONS AND PRISONERS

U.S. Department of Justice, Bureau of Justice Statistics, 633 Indiana Avenue, NW, Washington, D.C. 20531 (800) 732-3277; *Correctional Populations in the United States*.

PARTIES, POLITICAL - See POLITICAL PARTIES

PARTNERSHIPS - ESTABLISHMENTS AND FINANCES

U.S. Department of Commerce, Bureau of Economic Analysis, Fourteenth Street between Constitution Avenue and E Street, NW, Washington, D.C. 20230 (202) 606-9900; *The National Income and Product Accounts of the United States*, and *Survey of Current Business*.

U.S. Department of the Treasury, Internal Revenue Service, 1111 Constitution Avenue, NW, Washington, D.C. 20224 (202) 566-5000; *Statistics of Income, Statistics of Income, Partnership Returns, Statistics of Income Bulletin*, various publications and unpublished data.

PASSENGER TRANSIT INDUSTRY - See also PASSENGERS

PASSENGER TRANSIT INDUSTRY - EARNINGS

U.S. Department of Labor, Bureau of Labor Statistics, Two Massachusetts Avenue, NE, Washington, D.C. 20212 (202) 606-7828; *Employment and Earnings*, and Bulletins 2370 and 2429.

PASSENGER TRANSIT INDUSTRY - EMPLOYEES

U.S. Department of Labor, Bureau of Labor Statistics, Two Massachusetts Avenue, NE, Washington, D.C. 20212 (202) 606-7828; *Employment and Earnings*, and Bulletins 2370 and 2429.

PASSENGER TRANSIT INDUSTRY - OCCUPATIONAL SAFETY

U.S. Department of Labor, Bureau of Labor Statistics, Two Massachusetts Avenue, NE, Washington, D.C. 20212 (202) 606-7828; *Occupational Injuries and Illnesses in the United States by Industry.*

PASSENGER TRANSIT INDUSTRY - PRODUCTIVITY

U.S. Department of Labor, Bureau of Labor Statistics, Two Massachusetts Avenue, NE, Washington, D.C. 20212 (202) 606-7828; *Productivity Measures for Selected Industries and Government Services,* and unpublished data.

PASSENGERS - See also PASSENGER TRANSIT INDUSTRY and Various Transportation Modes

PASSENGERS - ARRIVING FROM OVERSEAS

U.S. Department of Commerce, Bureau of Economic Analysis, Fourteenth Street between Constitution Avenue and E Street, NW, Washington, D.C. 20230 (202) 606-9900; *Survey of Current Business.*

U.S. Department of Commerce, Travel and Tourism Administration, Washington, D.C. 20230 (202) 482-3811; unpublished data.

U.S. Department of Justice, Immigration and Naturalization Service, 425 I Street, NW, Washington, D.C. 20536 (202) 514-4316; *Statistical Yearbook.*

PASSENGERS - CARRIER OPERATION - SUMMARY

Air Transport Association of America, 1301 Pennsylvania, Suite 1100, Washington, D.C. 20004-7017 (202) 626-4000; *Air Transport,* and *Air Transport, Facts and Figures.*

American Bus Association, 1100 New York Avenue, NW, Washington, D.C. 20005 (202) 842-1645; *Bus Facts,* and *Annual Report.*

American Public Transit Association, 1201 New York Avenue, NW, Washington, D.C. 20005 (202) 898-4000; *Transit Fact Book.*

Association of American Railroads, American Railroads Building, 50 F Street, NW, Washington, D.C. 20001 (202) 639-2100; *Railroad Facts, Statistics of Railroads of Class I,* and *Analysis of Class I Railroads.*

Regional Airline Association, 1101 Connecticut Avenue, NW, Suite 700, Washington, D.C. 20036 (202) 857-1170; *Annual Report of the Regional Airline Industry.*

U.S. Department of Energy, Energy Information Administration, 1000 Independence Avenue, SW, Washington, D.C. 20585 (202) 586-8800; *Household Vehicles Energy Consumption.*

U.S. Department of Transportation, Federal Aviation Administration, 800 Independence Avenue, SW, Washington, D.C. 20591 (202) 366-4000; *Air Carrier Traffic Statistics,* and *Air Carrier Financial Statistics.*

U.S. Interstate Commerce Commission, Twelfth Street and Constitution Avenue, NW, Washington, D.C. 20433 (202) 275-7119; *Transport Statistics in the United States.*

PASSENGERS - CARRIER OPERATION SUMMARY - AIR

Air Transport Association of America, 1301 Pennsylvania, Suite 1100, Washington, D.C. 20004-7017 (202) 626-4000; *Air Transport,* and *Air Transport, Facts and Figures.*

Regional Airline Association, 1101 Connecticut Avenue, NW, Washington, D.C. 20036 (202) 857-1170; *Annual Report of the Regional Airline Industry.*

U.S. Department of Transportation, Federal Aviation Administration, 400 Seventh Street, SW, Washington, D.C. 20591 (202) 366-4000; *FAA Statistical Handbook of Aviation, Air Carrier Financial Statistics,* and *Air Carrier Traffic Statistics.*

PASSENGERS - CARRIER OPERATION SUMMARY - RAIL

Association of American Railroads, American Railroads Building, 50 F Street, NW, Washington, D.C. 20001 (202) 639-2100; *Railroad Facts, Statistics of Railroads of Class I,* and *Analysis of Class I Railroads.*

U.S. Department of Transportation, Federal Railroad Administration, 400 Seventh Street, SW, Washington, D.C. 20590 (202) 366-0881; *Accident Bulletin.*

PASSENGERS - OUTLAYS - BY TYPE OF TRANSPORT

Eno Transportation Foundation, 44211 Statestone Court, Lansdowne, Virginia 22075 (703) 729-7200; *Transportation in America.*

PASSENGERS - PASSENGER TRAFFIC - VOLUME

Eno Transportation Foundation, 44211 Statestone Court, Lansdowne, Virginia 22075 (703) 729-7200; *Transportation in America.*

PASSENGERS - RAILROADS - BY TYPE

Association of American Railroads, American Railroads Building, 50 F Street, N.W. Washington, D.C. 20001 (202) 639-2100; *Railroad Facts, Statistics of Railroads of Class I,* and *Analysis of Class I Railroads.*

U.S. Department of Transportation, Federal Railroad Administration, 400 Seventh Street, SW, Washington, D.C. 20590 (202) 366-0881; *Accident Bulletin.*

PASTORS - NUMBER WITH CHARGES

National Council of the Churches of Christ in the United States of America, 475 Riverside Drive, New York, New York 10115 (212) 870-2227; *Yearbook of American and Canadian Churches.*

PATENTS AND TRADEMARKS

U.S. Department of Commerce, Patent and Trademark Office, 2011 Crystal Drive, Arlington, Virginia 22202 (703) 305-8341; *Commissioner of Patents and Trademarks Annual Report, Patenting Trends in the United States, State Country Report,* and Technology Assessment and Forecast Database.

PATHOLOGISTS

American Medical Association, 515 North State Street, Chicago, Illinois 60610 (312) 464-4818; *Physician Characteristics and Distribution in the United States.*

PEACHES

U.S. Department of Agriculture, Economic Research Service, Fourteenth Street and Independence Avenue, SW, Washington, D.C. 20005-4789 (202) 219-1504; *Agricultural Outlook, Food Consumption, Prices, and Expenditures, Economic Indicators of the Farm Sector: National Financial Summary,* and unpublished data.

U.S. Department of Agriculture, National Agricultural Statistics Service, Fourteenth Street and Independence Avenue, SW, Washington, D.C. 20250 (202) 219-1504; *Noncitrus Fruits and Nuts.*

PEANUTS

Statistical Office of the United Nations, Publishing Service, New York, New York 10017 (800) 253-9646; *Monthly Bulletin of Statistics.*

U.S. Department of Agriculture, Agricultural Stabilization and Conservation Service, Fourteenth Street and Independence Avenue, SW, Washington, D.C. 20250 (202) 720-5237; *Commodity Credit Corporation Report of Financial Condition and Operations,* and *Agricultural Outlook.*

U.S. Department of Agriculture, Economic Research Service, Fourteenth Street and Independence Avenue, SW, Washington, D.C. 20005-4789 (202) 219-1504; *Food Consumption, Prices and Expenditures, Economic Indicators of the Farm Sector: National Financial Summary,* and unpublished data.

PEARS

U.S. Department of Agriculture, Economic Research Service, Fourteenth Street and Independence Avenue, SW, Washington, D.C. 20005-4789 (202) 219-1504; *Agricultural Outlook, Food Consumption, Prices, and Expenditures, Economic Indicators of the Farm Sector: National Financial Summary,* and unpublished data.

U.S. Department of Agriculture, National Agricultural Statistics Service, Fourteenth Street and Independence Avenue, SW, Washington, D.C. 20250 (202) 219-1504; *Noncitrus Fruits and Nuts.*

PEAS

U.S. Department of Agriculture, National Agricultural Statistics Service, Fourteenth Street and Independence Avenue, SW, Washington, D.C. 20250 (202) 219-1504; *Vegetables, Agricultural Statistics,* and unpublished data.

PEAT

U.S. Department of the Interior, Bureau of Mines, 810 Seventh Street, NW, Washington, D.C. 20241 (202) 501-9649; *Annual Reports,* and *Mineral Commodity Summaries.*

PECANS

U.S. Department of Agriculture, National Agricultural Statistics Service, Fourteenth Street and Independence Avenue, SW, Washington, D.C. 20250 (202) 1504; *Economic Indicators of the Farm Sector: National Financial Summary,* and *Noncitrus Fruit and Nuts.*

PEDIATRICIANS - See also PHYSICIANS

American Medical Association, 515 North State Street, Chicago, Illinois 60610 (312) 464-4818; *Physician Characteristics and Distribution in the United States,* and *Socioeconomic Characteristics of Medical Practice.*

PENNSYLVANIA - See also STATE DATA (FOR INDIVIDUAL STATES)

Pennsylvania - Primary Statistics Source

Pennsylvania State Data Center, Pennsylvania State University at Harrisburg, 777 West Harrisburg Pike, Middletown, Pennsylvania 15057 (717) 948-6336; *Pennsylvania Statistical Abstract.*

Pennsylvania - State Data Centers

Pennsylvania State Data Center, Institute of State and Regional Affairs, Pennsylvania State University at Harrisburg, 777 West Harrisburg Pike, Middletown, Pennsylvania 17057, Mr. Michael Behney (717) 948-6336.

Pennsylvania State Library, Forum Building, Harrisburg, Pennsylvania 17105, Mr. John Gerswindt (717) 787-2327.

PENS, PENCILS, OFFICE AND ART SUPPLIES - MANUFACTURING - EARNINGS

U.S. Department of Commerce, Bureau of the Census, Suitland, Maryland 20233 (301) 763-4040; *Census of Manufactures,* and *Annual Survey of Manufactures.*

U.S. Department of Labor, Bureau of Labor Statistics, Two Massachusetts Avenue, NE, Washington, D.C. 20212 (202) 606-7828; *Employment and Earnings,* and Bulletins 2370 and 2429.

PENS, PENCILS, OFFICE AND ART SUPPLIES - MANUFACTURING - EMPLOYEES

U.S. Department of Commerce, Bureau of the Census, Suitland, Maryland 20233 (301) 763-4040; *Census of Manufactures,* and *Annual Survey of Manufactures.*

U.S. Department of Labor, Bureau of Labor Statistics, Two Massachusetts Avenue, NE, Washington, D.C. 20212 (202) 606-7828; *Employment and Earnings,* and Bulletins 2370 and 2429.

PENS, PENCILS, OFFICE AND ART SUPPLIES - MANUFACTURING - ESTABLISHMENTS

U.S. Department of Commerce, Bureau of the Census, Suitland, Maryland 20233 (301) 763-4040; *Census of Manufactures,* and *Annual Survey of Manufactures.*

PENS, PENCILS, OFFICE AND ART SUPPLIES - MANUFACTURING - SALES, SHIPMENTS, RECEIPTS

U.S. Department of Commerce, Bureau of the Census, Suitland, Maryland 20233 (301) 763-4040; *Census of Manufactures,* and *Annual Survey of Manufactures.*

PENS, PENCILS, OFFICE AND ART SUPPLIES - MANUFACTURING - VALUE ADDED

U.S. Department of Commerce, Bureau of the Census, Suitland, Maryland 20233 (301) 763-4040; *Census of Manufactures,* and *Annual Survey of Manufactures.*

PENSIONS AND RETIREMENT BENEFITS - See also SOCIAL INSURANCE

PENSIONS AND RETIREMENT BENEFITS - EXPENDITURES

Employee Benefit Research Institute, 2121 K Street, NW, Suite 600, Washington, D.C. 20037 (202) 659-0670; *EBRI Databook on*

Employee Benefits.

U.S. Department of Health and Human Services, Social Security Administration, 6401 Security Boulevard, Baltimore, Maryland 21235 (410) 965-1234; *Annual Statistical Supplement to the Social Security Bulletin.*

U.S. Department of Labor, Bureau of Labor Statistics, Two Massachusetts Avenue, NE, Washington, D.C. 20212 (202) 606-7828; *Consumer Expenditures in 1992.*

PENSIONS AND RETIREMENT BENEFITS - FUNDS - FLOW OF FUNDS

Board of Governors of the Federal Reserve System, Twentieth Street and Constitution Avenue, NW, Washington, D.C. 20551 (202) 452-3000; *Annual Statistical Digest.*

PENSIONS AND RETIREMENT BENEFITS - GOVERNMENT EMPLOYEES

Employee Benefit Research Institute, 2121 K Street, NW, Suite 600, Washington, D.C. 20037 (202) 659-0670; *EBRI Databook on Employee Benefits.*

U.S. Department of Commerce, Bureau of the Census, Suitland, Maryland 20233 (301) 763-4040; *Finances of Employee - Retirement Systems of State and Local Governments.*

U.S. Department of Health and Human Services, Social Security Administration, 6401 Security Boulevard, Baltimore, Maryland 21235 (410) 965-1234; *Social Security Bulletin, Annual Statistical Supplement to the Social Security Bulletin,* and unpublished data.

U.S. Department of Labor, Bureau of Labor Statistics, Two Massachusetts Avenue, NE, Washington, D.C. 20212 (202) 606-7828; *Employee Benefits in State and Local Governments.*

U.S. Office of Personnel Management, 1900 E Street, NW, Washington, D.C. 20415 (202) 606-1800; *Compensation Report.*

PENSIONS AND RETIREMENT BENEFITS - PENSION PLANS

Access Research, Inc., 8 Griffin Road North, Windsor, Connecticut 06095 (203) 688-8821; *Marketplace Update.*

Employee Benefit Research Institute, 2121 K Street, NW, Suite 600, Washington, D.C. 20037 (202) 659-0670; *EBRI Databook on Employee Benefits.*

U.S. Department of Commerce, Bureau of the Census, Suitland, Maryland 20233 (301) 763-4040; unpublished data.

U.S. Department of Labor, Pension and Welfare Benefits Administration, 200 Constitution Avenue, NW, Washington, D.C. 20210 (202) 219-8921; *Private Pension Plan Bulletin.*

PENSIONS AND RETIREMENT BENEFITS - RAILROAD

U.S. Department of Health and Human Services, Social Security Administration, 6401 Security Boulevard, Baltimore, Maryland 21235 (410) 965-1234; *Social Security Bulletin, Annual Statistical Supplement to the Social Security Bulletin,* and unpublished data.

PENSIONS AND RETIREMENT BENEFITS - RETIREMENT AND SAVINGS PLANS

Access Research, Inc., 8 Griffin Road North, Windsor, Connecticut 06095 (203) 688-8821; *Marketplace Update.*

Employee Benefit Research Institute, 2121 K Street, NW, Suite 600, Washington, D.C. 20037 (202) 659-0670; *EBRI Databook on Employee Benefits.*

U.S. Department of Labor, Bureau of Labor Statistics, Two Massachusetts Avenue, NE, Washington, D.C. 20212 (202) 606-7828; *Employee Benefits in Medium and Large Private Establishments, Employee Benefits in State and Local Governments,* and *Employee Benefits in Small Private Establishments.*

PENSIONS AND RETIREMENT BENEFITS - VETERANS

U.S. Department of Health and Human Services, Social Security Administration, 6401 Security Boulevard, Baltimore, Maryland 21235 (410) 965-1234; *Social Security Bulletin,* and unpublished data.

PERCH

U.S. Department of Commerce, National Oceanic and Atmospheric Administration, National Marine Fisheries Service, 1335 East-West Highway, Silver Spring, Maryland 20910 (301) 427-2239; *Fishery Statistics of the United States,* and *Fisheries of the United States.*

PERFORMING ARTS - SELECTED DATA

American Symphony Orchestra League, 777 Fourteenth Street, NW, Suite 700, Washington, D.C. 20005 (202) 628-0099.

Opera America, 777 Fourteenth Street, NW, Suite 520, Washington, D.C. 20005 (202) 347-9262; *Opera America - Profile.*

Theatre Communications Group, 355 Lexington Avenue, New York, New York 10017 (212) 697-5230.

Variety, Inc., 249 West Seventeenth Street, New York, New York 10011 (212) 779-1100.

PERIODICALS - See PRINTING AND PUBLISHING INDUSTRIES

PERLITE

U.S. Department of the Interior, Bureau of Mines, 810 Seventh Street, NW, Washington, D.C. 20241 (202) 501-9649; *Annual Reports,* and *Mineral Commodity Summaries.*

PERSONAL CONSUMPTION EXPENDITURES

U.S. Department of Commerce, Bureau of Economic Analysis, Fourteenth Street between Constitution Avenue and E Street, NW, Washington, D.C. 20230 (202) 606-9900; *The National Income and Product Accounts of the United States,* and *Survey of Current Business.*

PERSONAL CONSUMPTION EXPENDITURES - FOOD AND BEVERAGES - FOREIGN COUNTRIES

U.S. Department of Agriculture, Economic Research Service, Fourteenth Street and Independence Avenue, SW, Washington, D.C. 20005-4789 (202) 219-1504; based on data from the United Nations, New York, New York; *National Accounts Statistics.*

PERSONAL CONSUMPTION EXPENDITURES - RECREATION

U.S. Department of Commerce, Bureau of Economic Analysis, Fourteenth Street between Constitution Avenue and E Street, NW, Washington, D.C. 20230 (202) 606-9900; *The National Income and Product Accounts of the United States,* and *Survey of Current Business.*

PERSONAL HEALTH CARE

U.S. Department of Health and Human Services, Health Care Financing Administration, 200 Independence Avenue, SW, Washington, D.C. 20201 (202) 245-6113; *Health Care Financing Review*.

PERSONAL INCOME

U.S. Department of Commerce, Bureau of Economic Analysis, Fourteenth Street between Constitution Avenue and E Street, NW, Washington, D.C. 20230 (202) 606-9900; *The National Income and Product Accounts of the United States, Survey of Current Business*, and unpublished data.

PERSONAL SAVINGS

Board of Governors of the Federal Reserve System, Twentieth Street and Constitution Avenue, NW, Washington, D.C. 20551 (202) 452-3000; *Flow of Funds Accounts*.

U.S. Department of Commerce, Bureau of Economic Analysis, Fourteenth Street between Constitution Avenue and E Street, NW, Washington, D.C. 20230 (202) 606-9900; *The National Income and Product Accounts of the United States*, and *Survey of Current Business*.

PERSONAL SERVICES INDUSTRY - EARNINGS

U.S. Department of Commerce, Bureau of the Census, Suitland, Maryland 20233 (301) 763-4040; *County Business Patterns*, and *Census of Service Industries*.

U.S. Department of Labor, Bureau of Labor Statistics, Two Massachusetts Avenue, NE, Washington, D.C. 20212 (202) 606-7828; *Employment and Earnings*, and Bulletins 2370 and 2429.

PERSONAL SERVICES INDUSTRY - EMPLOYEES

U.S. Department of Commerce, Bureau of the Census, Suitland, Maryland 20233 (301) 763-4040; *County Business Patterns*, and *Census of Service Industries*.

U.S. Department of Labor, Bureau of Labor Statistics, Two Massachusetts Avenue, NE, Washington, D.C. 20212 (202) 606-7828; *Employment and Earnings*, and Bulletins 2370 and 2429.

PERSONAL SERVICES INDUSTRY - ESTABLISHMENTS

U.S. Department of Commerce, Bureau of Economic Analysis, Fourteenth Street between Constitution Avenue and E Street, NW, Washington, D.C. 20230 (202) 606-9900; *The National Income and Product Accounts of the United States*, and *Survey of Current Business*.

U.S. Department of Commerce, Bureau of the Census, Suitland, Maryland 20233 (301) 763-4040; *Census of Service Industries*, and *County Business Patterns*.

PERSONAL SERVICES INDUSTRY - GROSS NATIONAL PRODUCT

U.S. Department of Commerce, Bureau of Economic Analysis, Fourteenth Street between Constitution Avenue and E Street, NW, Washington, D.C. 20230 (202) 606-9900; *The National Income and Product Accounts of the United States*, and *Survey of Current Business*.

PERSONAL SERVICES INDUSTRY - OCCUPATIONAL SAFETY

U.S. Department of Labor, Bureau of Labor Statistics, Two Massachusetts Avenue, NE, Washington, D.C. 20212 (202) 606-7828; *Occupational Injuries and Illnesses in the United States by Industry*.

PERSONAL SERVICES INDUSTRY - PRODUCTIVITY

U.S. Department of Labor, Bureau of Labor Statistics, Two Massachusetts Avenue, NE, Washington, D.C. 20212 (202) 606-7828; *Productivity Measures for Selected Industries and Government Services*, and unpublished data.

PERSONAL SERVICES INDUSTRY - RECEIPTS

U.S. Department of Commerce, Bureau of the Census, Suitland, Maryland 20233 (301) 763-4040; *Current Business Reports, Service Annual Survey*, and *Census of Service Industries*.

PERSONNEL SUPPLY SERVICES INDUSTRY - EARNINGS

U.S. Department of Commerce, Bureau of the Census, Suitland, Maryland 20233 (301) 763-4040; *Census of Service Industries*, and *County Business Patterns*.

U.S. Department of Labor, Bureau of Labor Statistics, Two Massachusetts Avenue, NE, Washington, D.C. 20212 (202) 606-7828; *Employment and Earnings*, and Bulletins 2370 and 2429.

PERSONNEL SUPPLY SERVICES INDUSTRY - EMPLOYEES

U.S. Department of Commerce, Bureau of the Census, Suitland, Maryland 20233 (301) 763-4040; *Census of Service Industries*, and *County Business Patterns*.

U.S. Department of Labor, Bureau of Labor Statistics, Two Massachusetts Avenue, NE, Washington, D.C. 20212 (202) 606-7828; *Employment and Earnings, Monthly Labor Review*, and Bulletins 2370 and 2429.

PERSONNEL SUPPLY SERVICES INDUSTRY - ESTABLISHMENTS

U.S. Department of Commerce, Bureau of the Census, Suitland, Maryland 20233 (301) 763-4040; *Census of Service Industries*, and *County Business Patterns*.

International Franchise Association, 1350 New York Avenue, Suite 900, Washington, D.C. 20005 (202) 628-8000; *Franchising in the Economy*.

PERSONNEL SUPPLY SERVICES INDUSTRY - RECEIPTS

U.S. Department of Commerce, Bureau of the Census, Suitland, Maryland 20233 (301) 763-4040; *Census of Service Industries, Current Business Reports*, and *Service Annual Survey*.

International Franchise Association, 1350 New York Avenue, Suite 900, Washington, D.C. 20005 (202) 628-8000; *Franchising in the Economy*.

Peru - National Statistical Office

Instituto Nacional de Estadistica, Avenida 28 de Julio 1056, Lima 1, Peru.

Peru - Primary Statistics Source

Direccion General de Estadistica y Censos, Instituto Nacional de Estadistica, Avenida 28 de Julio 1056, Lima 1, Peru; *Anuario estadistico del Peru* (Statistical Yearbook of Peru), *Compendio estadistico*, and *Informe estadistico*.

PERU - AGRICULTURE

The Economist Intelligence Unit, 111 West 57th Street, New York, New York 10019 (800) 938-4685; *The New Latin America Market Atlas*.

Euromonitor Publications Limited, 87-88 Turnmill Street, London EC1M 5QU, England; *International Marketing Data and Statistics*.

Facts on File, 460 Park Avenue South, New York, New York 10016 (800) 443-8323; *The New Book of World Rankings*.

Food and Agricultural Organization of the United Nations (FAO) Via delle Terme di Caracalla, 00100 Rome, Italy (Telephone Number in U.S. (202) 653-2400); *Production Yearbook*, and *The State of Food and Agriculture*, and *Trade Yearbook*.

Gale Research Incorporated, 835 Penobscot Building, Detroit, Michigan 48226 (800) 877-4253; *International Historical Statistics The Americas and Australasia*.

G.K. Hall and Company, 70 Lincoln Street, Boston, Massachusetts 02111 (617) 423-3990; *The World in Figures*.

Inter-American Development Bank, 1300 New York Avenue, NW, Washington, D.C. 20577 (202) 623-1753; *Economic and Social Progress in Latin America*.

Statistical Office of the United Nations, Publishing Service, New York, New York 10017 (800) 253-9646; *Statistical Yearbook*, and *Statistical Yearbook for Latin America and the Caribbean*.

Times Books, 201 East 50th Street, New York, New York 10022 (212) 751-2600; *The Economist Book of Vital World Statistics*.

U.C.L.A. Latin American Center Publications, University of California, Los Angeles, California 90024 (310) 825-6634; *Statistical Abstract of Latin America*.

The World Bank, 1818 H Street, NW, Washington, D.C. 20433 (202) 477-1234; *World Tables*.

PERU - AIRLINE SERVICE

The Economist Intelligence Unit, 111 West 57th Street, New York, New York 10019 (800) 938-4685; *The New Latin America Market Atlas*.

Facts on File, 460 Park Avenue South, New York, New York 10016 (800) 443-8323; *The New Book of World Rankings*.

G.K. Hall and Company, 70 Lincoln Street, Boston, Massachusetts 02111 (617) 423-3990; *The World in Figures*.

International Civil Aviation Organization, 1000 Sherbrooke Street, West, Montreal, Quebec, Canada H3A 2R2 (514) 285-8219; *Civil Aviation Statistics of the World*.

Statistical Office of the United Nations, Publishing Service, New York, New York 10017 (800) 253-9646; *Statistical Yearbook*.

PERU - ARMS EXPORTS AND IMPORTS

U.S. Arms Control and Disarmament Agency, 320 Twenty-first Street, NW, Washington, D.C. 20451 (202) 647-8677; *World Military Expenditures and Arms Transfers*.

PERU - ALUMINUM PRODUCTION AND CONSUMPTION - See PERU - MINING AND MINERAL PRODUCTS

PERU - ANIMAL FEEDINGSTUFFS OF AQUATIC ANIMAL ORIGIN

Statistical Office of the United Nations, Publishing Service, New York, New York 10017 (800) 253-9646; *Statistical Yearbook*.

PERU - ANIMAL HEALTH

Food and Agricultural Organization of the United Nations (FAO), Via delle Terme di Caracalla, 00100 Rome, Italy (Telephone Number in U.S. (202) 653-2400); *Animal Health Yearbook*.

PERU - ANTIMONY AND ANTIMONY ORE PRODUCTION AND CONSUMPTION - See PERU - MINING AND MINERAL PRODUCTS

PERU - AREA AND DENSITY OF POPULATION

Euromonitor Publications Limited, 87-88 Turnmill Street, London EC1M 5QU, England; *International Marketing Data and Statistics*.

Facts on File, 460 Park Avenue South, New York, New York 10016 (800) 443-8323; *The New Book of World Rankings*.

Food and Agricultural Organization of the United Nations (FAO) Via delle Terme di Caracalla, 00100 Rome, Italy (Telephone Number in U.S. (202) 653-2400); *The State of Food and Agriculture*.

G.K. Hall and Company, 70 Lincoln Street, Boston, Massachusetts 02111 (617) 423-3990; *The World in Figures*.

Inter-American Development Bank, 1300 New York Avenue, NW, Washington, D.C. 20577 (202) 623-1753; *Economic and Social Progress in Latin America*.

Statistical Office of the United Nations, Publishing Service, New York, New York 10017 (800) 253-9646; *Statistical Yearbook*.

Times Books, 201 East 50th Street, New York, New York 10022 (212) 751-2600; *The Economist Book of Vital World Statistics*.

United Nations Educational, Scientific and Cultural Organization (UNESCO), 7 Place de Fontenoy, F-75700 Paris, France (Telephone Number in U.S. (212) 963-5981); *Statistical Yearbook*.

PERU - ARSENIC PRODUCTION AND CONSUMPTION - See PERU - MINING AND MINERAL PRODUCTS

PERU - BALANCE OF PAYMENTS

The Economist Intelligence Unit, 111 West 57th Street, New York, New York 10019 (800) 938-4685; *The New Latin America Market Atlas*, and *The World Market Atlas*.

G.K. Hall and Company, 70 Lincoln Street, Boston, Massachusetts 02111 (617) 423-3990; *The World in Figures*.

Inter-American Development Bank, 1300 New York Avenue, NW, Washington, D.C. 20577 (202) 623-1753; *Economic and Social Progress in Latin America*.

International Monetary Fund, 700 Nineteenth Street, NW, Washington, D.C. 20431 (202) 623-7000; *Balance of Payments Yearbook*, and *International Financial Statistics*.

Organization of American States (OAS), General Secretariat, Washington, D.C. 20006 (202) 458-3533; *Statistical Bulletin of the OAS*.

Statistical Office of the United Nations, Publishing Service, New York, New York 10017 (800) 253-9646; *Economic Survey of Latin America and the Caribbean*, and *Statistical Yearbook for Latin America and the Caribbean*.

Times Books, 201 East 50th Street, New York, New York 10022 (212) 751-2600; *The Economist Book of Vital World Statistics*.

U.C.L.A. Latin American Center Publications, University of California, Los Angeles, California 90024 (310) 825-6634; *Statistical Abstract of Latin America*.

The World Bank, 1818 H Street, NW, Washington, D.C. 20433 (202) 477-1234; *World Tables*.

PERU - BANANA PRODUCTION - See PERU - CROPS

PERU - BANKING

Facts on File, 460 Park Avenue South, New York, New York 10016 (800) 443-8323; *The New Book of World Rankings*.

G.K. Hall and Company, 70 Lincoln Street, Boston, Massachusetts 02111 (617) 423-3990; *The World in Figures*.

Inter-American Development Bank, 1300 New York Avenue, NW, Washington, D.C. 20577 (202) 623-1753; *Economic and Social Progress in Latin America*.

International Monetary Fund, 700 Nineteenth Street, NW, Washington, D.C. 20431 (202) 623-7000; *International Financial Statistics*.

Statistical Office of the United Nations, Publishing Service, New York, New York 10017 (800) 253-9646; *Statistical Yearbook*, and *Statistical Yearbook for Latin America and the Caribbean*.

PERU - BARLEY PRODUCTION - See PERU - CROPS

PERU - BAUXITE PRODUCTION AND CONSUMPTION - See PERU - MINING AND MINERAL PRODUCTS

PERU - BEER PRODUCTION

Facts on File, 460 Park Avenue South, New York, New York 10016 (800) 443-8323; *The New Book of World Rankings*.

Statistical Office of the United Nations, Publishing Service, New York, New York 10017 (800) 253-9646; *Statistical Yearbook*.

PERU - BIRTH RATES

Facts on File, 460 Park Avenue South, New York, New York 10016 (800) 443-8323; *The New Book of World Rankings*.

Statistical Office of the United Nations, Publishing Service, New York, New York 10017 (800) 253-9646; *Demographic Yearbook*, *Statistical Yearbook*, and *Statistical Yearbook for Latin America and the Caribbean*.

Times Books, 201 East 50th Street, New York, New York 10022 (212) 751-2600; *The Economist Book of Vital World Statistics*.

The World Bank, 1818 H Street, NW, Washington, D.C. 20433 (202) 477-1234; *World Tables*.

PERU - BISMUTH PRODUCTION AND CONSUMPTION

Commodity Research Bureau, Incorporated, 75 Wall Street, New York, New York 10005 (212) 504-7754; *Commodity Year Book*.

PERU - BONDS

G.K. Hall and Company, 70 Lincoln Street, Boston, Massachusetts 02111 (617) 423-3990; *The World in Figures*.

Inter-American Development Bank, 1300 New York Avenue, NW, Washington, D.C. 20577 (202) 623-1753; *Economic and Social Progress in Latin America*.

PERU - BOOK PRODUCTION

G.K. Hall and Company, 70 Lincoln Street, Boston, Massachusetts 02111 (617) 423-3990; *The World in Figures*.

United Nations Educational, Scientific and Cultural Organization (UNESCO), 7 Place de Fontenoy, F-75700 Paris, France (Telephone Number in U.S. (212) 963-5981); *Statistical Yearbook*.

PERU - BROADCASTING

Billboard Limited, Post Office Box 9027, 1006 AA Amsterdam, The Netherlands (Telephone Number in U.S. (212) 764-7300); *World Radio TV Handbook*.

Facts on File, 460 Park Avenue South, New York, New York 10016 (800) 443-8323; *The New Book of World Rankings*.

G.K. Hall and Company, 70 Lincoln Street, Boston, Massachusetts 02111 (617) 423-3990; *The World in Figures*.

Times Books, 201 East 50th Street, New York, New York 10022 (212) 751-2600; *The Economist Book of Vital World Statistics*.

United Nations Educational, Scientific and Cultural Organization (UNESCO), 7 Place de Fontenoy, F-75700 Paris, France (Telephone Number in U.S. (212) 963-5981); *Statistical Yearbook*.

PERU - BUSINESS

G.K. Hall and Company, 70 Lincoln Street, Boston, Massachusetts 02111 (617) 423-3990; *The World in Figures*.

Inter-American Development Bank, 1300 New York Avenue, NW, Washington, D.C. 20577 (202) 623-1753; *Economic and Social Progress in Latin America*.

PERU - BUTTER PRODUCTION - See PERU - DAIRY PRODUCTS

PERU - CABBAGE PRODUCTION - See PERU - CROPS

PERU - CADMIUM PRODUCTION AND CONSUMPTION - See PERU - MINING AND MINERAL PRODUCTS

PERU - CALORIE SUPPLY

Food and Agricultural Organization of the United Nations (FAO) Via delle Terme di Caracalla, 00100 Rome, Italy (Telephone Number in U.S. (202) 653-2400); *The State of Food and Agriculture*.

Statistical Office of the United Nations, Publishing Service, New York, New York 10017 (800) 253-9646; *Statistical Yearbook for Latin America and the Caribbean.*

PERU - CAPITAL INVESTMENT

Inter-American Development Bank, 1300 New York Avenue, NW, Washington, D.C. 20577 (202) 623-1753; *Economic and Social Progress in Latin America.*

PERU - CAPITAL REVENUE

Inter-American Development Bank, 1300 New York Avenue, NW, Washington, D.C. 20577 (202) 623-1753; *Economic and Social Progress in Latin America.*

International Monetary Fund, 700 Nineteenth Street, NW, Washington, D.C. 20431 (202) 623-7000; *Government Finance Statistics Yearbook.*

PERU - CATTLE - See PERU - LIVESTOCK AND POULTRY

PERU - CAULIFLOWER PRODUCTION - See PERU - CROPS

PERU - CAUSTIC SODA PRODUCTION

Statistical Office of the United Nations, Publishing Service, New York, New York 10017 (800) 253-9646; *Statistical Yearbook.*

PERU - CEMENT PRODUCTION - See PERU - MINING AND MINERAL PRODUCTS

PERU - CHEESE PRODUCTION AND CONSUMPTION - See PERU - DAIRY PRODUCTS

PERU - CHEMICAL (ORGANIC) PRODUCTION - See PERU - MINING AND MINERAL PRODUCTS

PERU - CHICK PEA PRODUCTION - See PERU - CROPS

PERU - CHICKENS - See PERU - LIVESTOCK AND POULTRY

PERU - CHROMITE PRODUCTION AND CONSUMPTION - See PERU - MINING AND MINERAL PRODUCTS

PERU - CHROMIUM ORE PRODUCTION AND CONSUMPTION - See PERU - MINING AND MINERAL PRODUCTS

PERU - CIGAR AND CIGARETTE PRODUCTION - See PERU - TOBACCO PRODUCTION

PERU - CLASS STRUCTURE

G.K. Hall and Company, 70 Lincoln Street, Boston, Massachusetts 02111 (617) 423-3990; *The World in Figures.*

PERU - CLIMATE

Facts on File, 460 Park Avenue South, New York, New York 10016 (800) 443-8323; *The New Book of World Rankings.*

G.K. Hall and Company, 70 Lincoln Street, Boston, Massachusetts 02111 (617) 423-3990; *The World in Figures.*

PERU - COAL PRODUCTION - See PERU - MINING AND MINERAL PRODUCTS

PERU - COBALT PRODUCTION AND CONSUMPTION - See PERU - MINING AND MINERAL PRODUCTS

PERU - COCOA (BEANS) PRODUCTION - See PERU - CROPS

PERU - COFFEE - See PERU - CROPS

PERU - COKE, COKE OVEN ORE, AND COKE OVEN COKE PRODUCTION AND CONSUMPTION - See PERU - MINING AND MINERAL PRODUCTS

PERU - COMMUNICATIONS

Gale Research Incorporated, 835 Penobscot Building, Detroit, Michigan 48226 (800) 877-4253; *International Historical Statistics The Americas and Australasia.*

G.K. Hall and Company, 70 Lincoln Street, Boston, Massachusetts 02111 (617) 423-3990; *The World in Figures.*

Inter-American Development Bank, 1300 New York Avenue, NW, Washington, D.C. 20577 (202) 623-1753; *Economic and Social Progress in Latin America.*

U.C.L.A. Latin American Center Publications, University of California, Los Angeles, California 90024 (310) 825-6634; *Statistical Abstract of Latin America.*

PERU - CONSTRUCTION INDUSTRY

The Economist Intelligence Unit, 111 West 57th Street, New York, New York 10019 (800) 938-4685; *The New Latin America Market Atlas.*

Facts on File, 460 Park Avenue South, New York, New York 10016 (800) 443-8323; *The New Book of World Rankings.*

Inter-American Development Bank, 1300 New York Avenue, NW, Washington, D.C. 20577 (202) 623-1753; *Economic and Social Progress in Latin America.*

Statistical Office of the United Nations, Publishing Service, New York, New York 10017 (800) 253-9646; *Statistical Yearbook.*

U.C.L.A. Latin American Center Publications, University of California, Los Angeles, California 90024 (310) 825-6634; *Statistical Abstract of Latin America.*

PERU - CONSUMER PRICE INDEX

G.K. Hall and Company, 70 Lincoln Street, Boston, Massachusetts 02111 (617) 423-3990; *The World in Figures.*

Statistical Office of the United Nations, Publishing Service, New York, New York 10017 (800) 253-9646; *Statistical Yearbook.*

U.C.L.A. Latin American Center Publications, University of California, Los Angeles, California 90024 (310) 825-6634; *Statistical Abstract of Latin America.*

PERU - CONSUMER PRICES

The Economist Intelligence Unit, 111 West 57th Street, New York, New York 10019 (800) 938-4685; *The New Latin America Market Atlas.*

International Labour Office, I.L.O. Publications, CH-1211, Geneva 22, Switzerland; *Yearbook of Labour Statistics.*

International Monetary Fund, 700 Nineteenth Street, NW, Washington, D.C. 20431 (202) 623-7000; *International Financial Statistics.*

Organization of American States (OAS), General Secretariat, Washington, D.C. 20006 (202) 458-3533; *Statistical Bulletin of the OAS.*

Times Books, 201 East 50th Street, New York, New York 10022 (212) 751-2600; *The Economist Book of Vital World Statistics.*

PERU - CONSUMPTION

The Economist Intelligence Unit, 111 West 57th Street, New York, New York 10019 (800) 938-4685; *The New Latin America Market Atlas.*

G.K. Hall and Company, 70 Lincoln Street, Boston, Massachusetts 02111 (617) 423-3990; *The World in Figures.*

Inter-American Development Bank, 1300 New York Avenue, NW, Washington, D.C. 20577 (202) 623-1753; *Economic and Social Progress in Latin America.*

International Lead and Zinc Study Group, Metro House, 58 St. James's Street, London SW1A 1LD, England; *Lead and Zinc Statistics.*

Statistical Office of the United Nations, Publishing Service, New York, New York 10017 (800) 253-9646; *Statistical Yearbook for Latin America and the Caribbean.*

PERU - COOPERATIVES

U.C.L.A. Latin American Center Publications, University of California, Los Angeles, California 90024 (310) 825-6634; *Statistical Abstract of Latin America.*

PERU - COPPER AND COPPER ORE PRODUCTION AND CONSUMPTION - See PERU - MINING AND MINERAL PRODUCTS

PERU - CORN PRODUCTION - See PERU - CROPS

PERU - CORPORATE TAXES - See PERU - TAXATION

PERU - COTTON - See PERU - CROPS

Facts on File, 460 Park Avenue South, New York, New York 10016 (800) 443-8323; *The New Book of World Rankings.*

International Monetary Fund, 700 Nineteenth Street, NW, Washington, D.C. 20431 (202) 623-7000; *International Financial Statistics.*

Organization of American States (OAS), General Secretariat, Washington, D.C. 20006 (202) 458-3533; *Statistical Bulletin of the OAS.*

Statistical Office of the United Nations, Publishing Service, New York, New York 10017 (800) 253-9646; *Statistical Yearbook.*

U.C.L.A. Latin American Center Publications, University of California, Los Angeles, California 90024 (310) 825-6634; *Statistical Abstract of Latin America.*

PERU - CRIME

International Criminal Police Organization (INTERPOL), 26 rue Armengaud, 92210 Saint Cloud, France; *International Crime Statistics.*

Yale University Press, Yale Station, New Haven, Connecticut 06520 (203) 432-0940; *Violence and Crime in Cross-National Perspective.*

PERU - CROPS

The Economist Intelligence Unit, 111 West 57th Street, New York, New York 10019 (800) 938-4685; *The New Latin America Market Atlas.*

Facts on File, 460 Park Avenue South, New York, New York 10016 (800) 443-8323; *The New Book of World Rankings.*

Food and Agricultural Organization of the United Nations (FAO), Via delle Terme di Caracalla, 00100 Rome, Italy (Telephone Number in U.S. (202) 653-2400); *Production Yearbook,* and *The State of Food and Agriculture.*

G.K. Hall and Company, 70 Lincoln Street, Boston, Massachusetts 02111 (617) 423-3990; *The World in Figures.*

International Monetary Fund, 700 Nineteenth Street, NW, Washington, D.C. 20431 (202) 623-7000; *International Financial Statistics.*

Organization of American States (OAS), General Secretariat, Washington, D.C. 20006 (202) 458-3533; *Statistical Bulletin of the OAS.*

Statistical Office of the United Nations, Publishing Service, New York, New York 10017 (800) 253-9646; *Statistical Yearbook.*

U.C.L.A. Latin American Center Publications, University of California, Los Angeles, California 90024 (310) 825-6634; *Statistical Abstract of Latin America.*

PERU - CUSTOMS DUTIES

G.K. Hall and Company, 70 Lincoln Street, Boston, Massachusetts 02111 (617) 423-3990; *The World in Figures.*

Inter-American Development Bank, 1300 New York Avenue, NW, Washington, D.C. 20577 (202) 623-1753; *Economic and Social Progress in Latin America.*

International Monetary Fund, 700 Nineteenth Street, NW, Washington, D.C. 20431 (202) 623-7000; *Government Finance Statistics Yearbook.*

PERU - DAIRY PRODUCTS

Facts on File, 460 Park Avenue South, New York, New York 10016 (800) 443-8323; *The New Book of World Rankings.*

Food and Agricultural Organization of the United Nations (FAO) Via delle Terme di Caracalla, 00100 Rome, Italy (Telephone Number in U.S. (202) 653-2400); *Production Yearbook,* and *The State of Food and Agriculture.*

Statistical Office of the United Nations, Publishing Service, New York, New York 10017 (800) 253-9646; *Statistical Yearbook.*

U.C.L.A. Latin American Center Publications, University of California, Los Angeles, California 90024 (310) 825-6634; *Statistical Abstract of Latin America.*

PERU - DEATH RATES

G.K. Hall and Company, 70 Lincoln Street, Boston, Massachusetts 02111 (617) 423-3990; *The World in Figures.*

Statistical Office of the United Nations, Publishing Service, New York, New York 10017 (800) 253-9646; *Statistical Yearbook,* and

Statistical Yearbook for Latin America and the Caribbean.

Times Books, 201 East 50th Street, New York, New York 10022 (212) 751-2600; *The Economist Book of Vital World Statistics.*

World Health Organization, Office of Publications, Avenue Appia, CH-1211 Geneva 27, Switzerland (Telephone Number in U.S. (518) 436-9686); *World Health Statistics Annual.*

PERU - DEBT

The Economist Intelligence Unit, 111 West 57th Street, New York, New York 10019 (800) 938-4685; *The New Latin America Market Atlas.*

PERU - DEFENSE EXPENDITURES

The Economist Intelligence Unit, 111 West 57th Street, New York, New York 10019 (800) 938-4685; *The New Latin America Market Atlas.*

G.K. Hall and Company, 70 Lincoln Street, Boston, Massachusetts 02111 (617) 423-3990; *The World in Figures.*

International Monetary Fund, 700 Nineteenth Street, NW, Washington, D.C. 20431 (202) 623-7000; *Government Finance Statistics Yearbook.*

U.S. Arms Control and Disarmament Agency, 320 Twenty-first Street, NW, Washington, D.C. 20451 (202) 647-8677; *World Military Expenditures and Arms Transfers.*

PERU - DEMOGRAPHY

The Economist Intelligence Unit, 111 West 57th Street, New York, New York 10019 (800) 938-4685; *The World Market Atlas.*

Facts on File, 460 Park Avenue South, New York, New York 10016 (800) 443-8323; *The New Book of World Rankings.*

G.K. Hall and Company, 70 Lincoln Street, Boston, Massachusetts 02111 (617) 423-3990; *The World in Figures.*

PERU - DEVELOPMENT ASSISTANCE

G.K. Hall and Company, 70 Lincoln Street, Boston, Massachusetts 02111 (617) 423-3990; *The World in Figures.*

Inter-American Development Bank, 1300 New York Avenue, NW, Washington, D.C. 20577 (202) 623-1753; *Economic and Social Progress in Latin America.*

Statistical Office of the United Nations, Publishing Service, New York, New York 10017 (800) 253-9646; *Statistical Yearbook.*

PERU - DIAMOND PRODUCTION - See PERU - MINING AND MINERAL PRODUCTS

PERU - DISCOUNT RATES

Inter-American Development Bank, 1300 New York Avenue, NW, Washington, D.C. 20577 (202) 623-1753; *Economic and Social Progress in Latin America.*

Statistical Office of the United Nations, Publishing Service, New York, New York 10017 (800) 253-9646; *Statistical Yearbook.*

PERU - DISEASES

G.K. Hall and Company, 70 Lincoln Street, Boston, Massachusetts 02111 (617) 423-3990; *The World in Figures.*

World Health Organization, Office of Publications, Avenue Appia, CH-1211 Geneva 27, Switzerland (Telephone Number in U.S. (518) 436-9686); *World Health Statistics Annual.*

PERU - DIVORCE RATES

Facts on File, 460 Park Avenue South, New York, New York 10016 (800) 443-8323; *The New Book of World Rankings.*

Statistical Office of the United Nations, Publishing Service, New York, New York 10017 (800) 253-9646; *Demographic Yearbook,* and *Statistical Yearbook.*

PERU - DOMESTIC PRODUCT

G.K. Hall and Company, 70 Lincoln Street, Boston, Massachusetts 02111 (617) 423-3990; *The World in Figures.*

PERU - ECONOMY

Euromonitor Publications Limited, 87-88 Turnmill Street, London EC1M 5QU, England; *International Marketing Data and Statistics.*

Facts on File, 460 Park Avenue South, New York, New York 10016 (800) 443-8323; *The New Book of World Rankings.*

G.K. Hall and Company, 70 Lincoln Street, Boston, Massachusetts 02111 (617) 423-3990; *The World in Figures.*

Inter-American Development Bank, 1300 New York Avenue, NW, Washington, D.C. 20577 (202) 623-1753; *Economic and Social Progress in Latin America.*

Statistical Office of the United Nations, Publishing Service, New York, New York 10017 (800) 253-9646; *Economic Survey of Latin America and the Caribbean.*

Organization of American States (OAS), General Secretariat, Washington, D.C. 20006 (202) 458-3533; *Statistical Bulletin of the OAS.*

U.C.L.A. Latin American Center Publications, University of California, Los Angeles, California 90024 (310) 825-6634; *Statistical Abstract of Latin America.*

PERU - EDUCATION

The Economist Intelligence Unit, 111 West 57th Street, New York, New York 10019 (800) 938-4685; *The New Latin America Market Atlas,* and *The World Market Atlas.*

Facts on File, 460 Park Avenue South, New York, New York 10016 (800) 443-8323; *The New Book of World Rankings.*

Gale Research Incorporated, 835 Penobscot Building, Detroit, Michigan 48226 (800) 877-4253; *International Historical Statistics The Americas and Australasia.*

G.K. Hall and Company, 70 Lincoln Street, Boston, Massachusetts 02111 (617) 423-3990; *The World in Figures.*

International Monetary Fund, 700 Nineteenth Street, NW, Washington, D.C. 20431 (202) 623-7000; *Government Finance Statistics Yearbook.*

Statistical Office of the United Nations, Publishing Service, New York, New York 10017 (800) 253-9646; *Statistical Yearbook for Latin America and the Caribbean.*

Times Books, 201 East 50th Street, New York, New York 10022 (212) 751-2600; *The Economist Book of Vital World Statistics.*

U.C.L.A. Latin American Center Publications, University of California, Los Angeles, California 90024 (310) 825-6634; *Statistical Abstract of Latin America.*

United Nations Educational, Scientific and Cultural Organization (UNESCO), 7 Place de Fontenoy, F-75700 Paris, France (Telephone Number in U.S. (212) 963-5981); *Statistical Yearbook.*

The World Bank, 1818 H Street, NW, Washington, D.C. 20433 (202) 477-1234; *World Tables.*

PERU - EGG PRODUCTION AND CONSUMPTION - See PERU - DAIRY PRODUCTS

PERU - ELECTRICITY

The Economist Intelligence Unit, 111 West 57th Street, New York, New York 10019 (800) 938-4685; *The New Latin America Market Atlas.*

Facts on File, 460 Park Avenue South, New York, New York 10016 (800) 443-8323; *The New Book of World Rankings.*

Inter-American Development Bank, 1300 New York Avenue, NW, Washington, D.C. 20577 (202) 623-1753; *Economic and Social Progress in Latin America.*

Penn Well Publishing Company, 1421 South Sheridan Road, Post Office Box 1260, Tulsa, Oklahoma 74101 (800) 752-9764; *International Energy Statistics Sourcebook.*

Statistical Office of the United Nations, Publishing Service, New York, New York 10017 (800) 253-9646; *Statistical Yearbook.*

Times Books, 201 East 50th Street, New York, New York 10022 (212) 751-2600; *The Economist Book of Vital World Statistics.*

PERU - EMPLOYMENT

Euromonitor Publications Limited, 87-88 Turnmill Street, London EC1M 5QU, England; *International Marketing Data and Statistics.*

Facts on File, 460 Park Avenue South, New York, New York 10016 (800) 443-8323; *The New Book of World Rankings.*

International Labour Office, I.L.O. Publications, CH-1211, Geneva 22, Switzerland; *Yearbook of Labour Statistics.*

Statistical Office of the United Nations, Publishing Service, New York, New York 10017 (800) 253-9646; *Statistical Yearbook*, and *Statistical Yearbook for Latin America and the Caribbean.*

U.C.L.A. Latin American Center Publications, University of California, Los Angeles, California 90024 (310) 825-6634; *Statistical Abstract of Latin America.*

PERU - ENERGY

The Economist Intelligence Unit, 111 West 57th Street, New York, New York 10019 (800) 938-4685; *The New Latin America Market Atlas.*

Facts on File, 460 Park Avenue South, New York, New York 10016 (800) 443-8323; *The New Book of World Rankings.*

Food and Agricultural Organization of the United Nations (FAO) Via delle Terme di Caracalla, 00100 Rome, Italy (Telephone Number in U.S. (202) 653-2400); *The State of Food and Agriculture.*

G.K. Hall and Company, 70 Lincoln Street, Boston, Massachusetts 02111 (617) 423-3990; *The World in Figures.*

Penn Well Publishing Company, 1421 South Sheridan Road, Post Office Box 1260, Tulsa, Oklahoma 74101 (800) 752-9764; *International Energy Statistics Sourcebook.*

Statistical Office of the United Nations, Publishing Service, New York, New York 10017 (800) 253-9646; *Energy Statistics Yearbook, Statistical Yearbook*, and *Statistical Yearbook for Latin America and the Caribbean.*

Times Books, 201 East 50th Street, New York, New York 10022 (212) 751-2600; *The Economist Book of Vital World Statistics.*

U.C.L.A. Latin American Center Publications, University of California, Los Angeles, California 90024 (310) 825-6634; *Statistical Abstract of Latin America.*

PERU - EXCHANGE RATES

Euromonitor Publications Limited, 87-88 Turnmill Street, London EC1M 5QU, England; *International Marketing Data and Statistics.*

Inter-American Development Bank, 1300 New York Avenue, NW, Washington, D.C. 20577 (202) 623-1753; *Economic and Social Progress in Latin America.*

International Civil Aviation Organization, 1000 Sherbrooke Street, West, Montreal, Quebec, Canada H3A 2R2 (514) 285-8219; *Civil Aviation Statistics of the World.*

International Monetary Fund, 700 Nineteenth Street, NW, Washington, D.C. 20431 (202) 623-7000; *International Financial Statistics.*

Organization of American States (OAS), General Secretariat, Washington, D.C. 20006 (202) 458-3533; *Statistical Bulletin of the OAS.*

U.C.L.A. Latin American Center Publications, University of California, Los Angeles, California 90024 (310) 825-6634; *Statistical Abstract of Latin America.*

PERU - EXCISE TAXES - See PERU - TAXATION

PERU - EXPENDITURES

Organization of American States (OAS), General Secretariat, Washington, D.C. 20006 (202) 458-3533; *Statistical Bulletin of the OAS.*

PERU - EXPORTS

American Automobile Manufacturers Association, 1401 H Street, NW, Suite 900, Washington, D.C. 20005 (202) 326-5500; *World Motor Vehicle Data.*

The Economist Intelligence Unit, 111 West 57th Street, New York, New York 10019 (800) 938-4685; *The New Latin America Market Atlas*, and *The World Market Atlas.*

Euromonitor Publications Limited, 87-88 Turnmill Street, London EC1M 5QU, England; *International Marketing Data and Statistics.*

Food and Agricultural Organization of the United Nations (FAO) Via delle Terme di Caracalla, 00100 Rome, Italy (Telephone Number in U.S. (202) 653-2400); *The State of Food and Agriculture.*

G.K. Hall and Company, 70 Lincoln Street, Boston, Massachusetts 02111 (617) 423-3990; *The World in Figures.*

Inter-American Development Bank, 1300 New York Avenue, NW, Washington, D.C. 20577 (202) 623-1753; *Economic and Social Progress in Latin America.*

International Lead and Zinc Study Group, Metro House, 58 St. James's Street, London SW1A 1LD, England; *Lead and Zinc Statistics.*

International Monetary Fund, 700 Nineteenth Street, NW, Washington, D.C. 20431 (202) 623-7000; *Direction of Trade Statistics, Government Finance Statistics Yearbook,* and *International Financial Statistics.*

Organization of American States (OAS), General Secretariat, Washington, D.C. 20006 (202) 458-3533; *Statistical Bulletin of the OAS.*

Statistical Office of the United Nations, Publishing Service, New York, New York 10017 (800) 253-9646; *Statistical Yearbook for Latin America and the Caribbean.*

Times Books, 201 East 50th Street, New York, New York 10022 (212) 751-2600; *The Economist Book of Vital World Statistics.*

The World Bank, 1818 H Street, NW, Washington, D.C. 20433 (202) 477-1234; *World Tables.*

PERU - EXTERNAL FINANCING

Inter-American Development Bank, 1300 New York Avenue, NW, Washington, D.C. 20577 (202) 623-1753; *Economic and Social Progress in Latin America.*

Statistical Office of the United Nations, Publishing Service, New York, New York 10017 (800) 253-9646; *Statistical Yearbook for Latin America and the Caribbean.*

PERU - EXTERNAL INDEBTEDNESS

Inter-American Development Bank, 1300 New York Avenue, NW, Washington, D.C. 20577 (202) 623-1753; *Economic and Social Progress in Latin America.*

Statistical Office of the United Nations, Publishing Service, New York, New York 10017 (800) 253-9646; *Statistical Yearbook for Latin America and the Caribbean.*

The World Bank, 1818 H Street, NW, Washington, D.C. 20433 (202) 477-1234; *World Tables.*

PERU - EXTERNAL TRADE

Food and Agricultural Organization of the United Nations (FAO) Via delle Terme di Caracalla, 00100 Rome, Italy (Telephone Number in U.S. (202) 653-2400); *The State of Food and Agriculture,* and *Trade Yearbook.*

Gale Research Incorporated, 835 Penobscot Building, Detroit, Michigan 48226 (800) 877-4253; *International Historical Statistics*

The Americas and Australasia.

G.K. Hall and Company, 70 Lincoln Street, Boston, Massachusetts 02111 (617) 423-3990; *The World in Figures.*

Inter-American Development Bank, 1300 New York Avenue, NW, Washington, D.C. 20577 (202) 623-1753; *Economic and Social Progress in Latin America.*

Statistical Office of the United Nations, Publishing Service, New York, New York 10017 (800) 253-9646; *Statistical Yearbook,* and *Statistical Yearbook for Latin America and the Caribbean.*

PERU - FABRIC PRODUCTION - See PERU - TEXTILE INDUSTRY

PERU - FAMILY PLANNING

U.C.L.A. Latin American Center Publications, University of California, Los Angeles, California 90024 (310) 825-6634; *Statistical Abstract of Latin America.*

PERU - FARM CROPS - See PERU - CROPS

PERU - FEMALE WORKING POPULATION - See PERU - EMPLOYMENT

PERU - FERTILITY RATES

Facts on File, 460 Park Avenue South, New York, New York 10016 (800) 443-8323; *The New Book of World Rankings.*

Times Books, 201 East 50th Street, New York, New York 10022 (212) 751-2600; *The Economist Book of Vital World Statistics.*

The World Bank, 1818 H Street, NW, Washington, D.C. 20433 (202) 477-1234; *World Tables.*

PERU - FERTILIZER

The Economist Intelligence Unit, 111 West 57th Street, New York, New York 10019 (800) 938-4685; *The New Latin America Market Atlas.*

Food and Agricultural Organization of the United Nations (FAO), Via delle Terme di Caracalla, 00100 Rome, Italy (Telephone Number in U.S. (202) 653-2400); *Fertilizer Yearbook,* and *The State of Food and Agriculture.*

Statistical Office of the United Nations, Publishing Service, New York, New York 10017 (800) 253-9646; *Statistical Yearbook.*

PERU - FETAL MORTALITY

Statistical Office of the United Nations, Publishing Service, New York, New York 10017 (800) 253-9646; *Demographic Yearbook.*

PERU - FIBRE PRODUCTION - See PERU - TEXTILE INDUSTRY

PERU - FILAMENT PRODUCTION - See PERU - TEXTILE INDUSTRY

PERU - FILM - See PERU - MOTION PICTURES

PERU - FINANCE

Facts on File, 460 Park Avenue South, New York, New York 10016 (800) 443-8323; *The New Book of World Rankings.*

Gale Research Incorporated, 835 Penobscot Building, Detroit, Michigan 48226 (800) 877-4253; *International Historical Statistics*

The Americas and Australasia.

G.K. Hall and Company, 70 Lincoln Street, Boston, Massachusetts 02111 (617) 423-3990; *The World in Figures.*

Inter-American Development Bank, 1300 New York Avenue, NW, Washington, D.C. 20577 (202) 623-1753; *Economic and Social Progress in Latin America.*

International Monetary Fund, 700 Nineteenth Street, NW, Washington, D.C. 20431 (202) 623-7000; *International Financial Statistics.*

Organization of American States (OAS), General Secretariat, Washington, D.C. 20006 (202) 458-3533; *Statistical Bulletin of the OAS.*

U.C.L.A. Latin American Center Publications, University of California, Los Angeles, California 90024 (310) 825-6634; *Statistical Abstract of Latin America.*

PERU - FISHERIES

Facts on File, 460 Park Avenue South, New York, New York 10016 (800) 443-8323; *The New Book of World Rankings.*

Food and Agricultural Organization of the United Nations (FAO) Via delle Terme di Caracalla, 00100 Rome, Italy (Telephone Number in U.S. (202) 653-2400); *The State of Food and Agriculture,* and *Yearbook of Fishery Statistics.*

Inter-American Development Bank, 1300 New York Avenue, NW, Washington, D.C. 20577 (202) 623-1753; *Economic and Social Progress in Latin America.*

International Monetary Fund, 700 Nineteenth Street, NW, Washington, D.C. 20431 (202) 623-7000; *International Financial Statistics.*

Statistical Office of the United Nations, Publishing Service, New York, New York 10017 (800) 253-9646; *Statistical Yearbook.*

U.C.L.A. Latin American Center Publications, University of California, Los Angeles, California 90024 (310) 825-6634; *Statistical Abstract of Latin America.*

PERU - FLOUR PRODUCTION

Statistical Office of the United Nations, Publishing Service, New York, New York 10017 (800) 253-9646; *Statistical Yearbook.*

PERU - FOOD

Food and Agricultural Organization of the United Nations (FAO) Via delle Terme di Caracalla, 00100 Rome, Italy (Telephone Number in U.S. (202) 653-2400); *Production Yearbook,* and *The State of Food and Agriculture.*

G.K. Hall and Company, 70 Lincoln Street, Boston, Massachusetts 02111 (617) 423-3990; *The World in Figures.*

PERU - FOREIGN AID

G.K. Hall and Company, 70 Lincoln Street, Boston, Massachusetts 02111 (617) 423-3990; *The World in Figures.*

Inter-American Development Bank, 1300 New York Avenue, NW, Washington, D.C. 20577 (202) 623-1753; *Economic and Social Progress in Latin America.*

PERU - FOREIGN DEBT

The Economist Intelligence Unit, 111 West 57th Street, New York, New York 10019 (800) 938-4685; *The New Latin America Market Atlas.*

Inter-American Development Bank, 1300 New York Avenue, NW, Washington, D.C. 20577 (202) 623-1753; *Economic and Social Progress in Latin America.*

PERU - FOREIGN INDEBTEDNESS

Inter-American Development Bank, 1300 New York Avenue, NW, Washington, D.C. 20577 (202) 623-1753; *Economic and Social Progress in Latin America.*

Statistical Office of the United Nations, Publishing Service, New York, New York 10017 (800) 253-9646; *Economic Survey of Latin America and the Caribbean.*

PERU - FOREIGN INVESTMENT

The Economist Intelligence Unit, 111 West 57th Street, New York, New York 10019 (800) 938-4685; *The New Latin America Market Atlas.*

PERU - FOREIGN TRADE

The Economist Intelligence Unit, 111 West 57th Street, New York, New York 10019 (800) 938-4685; *The New Latin America Market Atlas.*

Euromonitor Publications Limited, 87-88 Turnmill Street, London EC1M 5QU, England; *International Marketing Data and Statistics.*

Facts on File, 460 Park Avenue South, New York, New York 10016 (800) 443-8323; *The New Book of World Rankings.*

Food and Agricultural Organization of the United Nations (FAO) Via delle Terme di Caracalla, 00100 Rome, Italy (Telephone Number in U.S. (202) 653-2400); *The State of Food and Agriculture.*

G.K. Hall and Company, 70 Lincoln Street, Boston, Massachusetts 02111 (617) 423-3990; *The World in Figures.*

Inter-American Development Bank, 1300 New York Avenue, NW, Washington, D.C. 20577 (202) 623-1753; *Economic and Social Progress in Latin America.*

International Monetary Fund, 700 Nineteenth Street, NW, Washington, D.C. 20431 (202) 623-7000; *International Financial Statistics.*

Statistical Office of the United Nations, Publishing Service, New York, New York 10017 (800) 253-9646; *Economic Survey of Latin America and the Caribbean, International Trade Statistics Yearbook,* and *Statistical Yearbook.*

U.C.L.A. Latin American Center Publications, University of California, Los Angeles, California 90024 (310) 825-6634; *Statistical Abstract of Latin America.*

The World Bank, 1818 H Street, NW, Washington, D.C. 20433 (202) 477-1234; *World Tables.*

World Bureau of Metal Statistics, 27-A High Street, Ware, Herts. SG12 9BA, England; *World Metal Statistics.*

PERU - FORESTRY AND FOREST PRODUCTS

American Forest and Paper Association, 1250 Connecticut Avenue, NW, Washington, D.C. 20036 (202) 463-2455; *Wood Pulp and Fiber Statistics.*

The Economist Intelligence Unit, 111 West 57th Street, New York, New York 10019 (800) 938-4685; *The New Latin America Market Atlas.*

Facts on File, 460 Park Avenue South, New York, New York 10016 (800) 443-8323; *The New Book of World Rankings.*

Food and Agricultural Organization of the United Nations (FAO) Via delle Terme di Caracalla, 00100 Rome, Italy (Telephone Number in U.S. (202) 653-2400); *The State of Food and Agriculture,* and *Yearbook of Forest Products.*

G.K. Hall and Company, 70 Lincoln Street, Boston, Massachusetts 02111 (617) 423-3990; *The World in Figures.*

Inter-American Development Bank, 1300 New York Avenue, NW, Washington, D.C. 20577 (202) 623-1753; *Economic and Social Progress in Latin America.*

Statistical Office of the United Nations, Publishing Service, New York, New York 10017 (800) 253-9646; *Statistical Yearbook.*

U.C.L.A. Latin American Center Publications, University of California, Los Angeles, California 90024 (310) 825-6634; *Statistical Abstract of Latin America.*

United Nations Educational, Scientific and Cultural Organization (UNESCO), 7 Place de Fontenoy, F-75700 Paris, France (Telephone Number in U.S. (212) 963-5981); *Statistical Yearbook.*

PERU - GARLIC PRODUCTION - See PERU - CROPS

PERU - GAS AND GAS LIQUIDS PRODUCTION - See PERU - MINING AND MINERAL PRODUCTS

PERU - GENERAL INDUSTRIAL STATISTICS

Statistical Office of the United Nations, Publishing Service, New York, New York 10017 (800) 253-9646; *Industrial Statistics Yearbook.*

PERU - GENERAL MORTALITY

Statistical Office of the United Nations, Publishing Service, New York, New York 10017 (800) 253-9646; *Demographic Yearbook.*

PERU - GEOGRAPHIC DATA

Facts on File, 460 Park Avenue South, New York, New York 10016 (800) 443-8323; *The New Book of World Rankings.*

U.C.L.A. Latin American Center Publications, University of California, Los Angeles, California 90024 (310) 825-6634; *Statistical Abstract of Latin America.*

PERU - GOATS - See PERU - LIVESTOCK AND POULTRY

PERU - GOLD HOLDINGS

International Monetary Fund, 700 Nineteenth Street, NW, Washington, D.C. 20431 (202) 623-7000; *International Financial Statistics.*

Statistical Office of the United Nations, Publishing Service, New York, New York 10017 (800) 253-9646; *Statistical Yearbook.*

The World Bank, 1818 H Street, NW, Washington, D.C. 20433 (202) 477-1234; *World Tables.*

PERU - GOLD PRODUCTION AND CONSUMPTION - See PERU - MINING AND MINERAL PRODUCTS

PERU - GOLD RESERVES

The Economist Intelligence Unit, 111 West 57th Street, New York, New York 10019 (800) 938-4685; *The New Latin America Market Atlas.*

PERU - GOVERNMENT

G.K. Hall and Company, 70 Lincoln Street, Boston, Massachusetts 02111 (617) 423-3990; *The World in Figures.*

Inter-American Development Bank, 1300 New York Avenue, NW, Washington, D.C. 20577 (202) 623-1753; *Economic and Social Progress in Latin America.*

PERU - GOVERNMENT CONSUMPTION

Inter-American Development Bank, 1300 New York Avenue, NW, Washington, D.C. 20577 (202) 623-1753; *Economic and Social Progress in Latin America.*

PERU - GOVERNMENT EXPENDITURES

Inter-American Development Bank, 1300 New York Avenue, NW, Washington, D.C. 20577 (202) 623-1753; *Economic and Social Progress in Latin America.*

International Monetary Fund, 700 Nineteenth Street, NW, Washington, D.C. 20431 (202) 623-7000; *Government Finance Statistics Yearbook.*

Times Books, 201 East 50th Street, New York, New York 10022 (212) 751-2600; *The Economist Book of Vital World Statistics.*

The World Bank, 1818 H Street, NW, Washington, D.C. 20433 (202) 477-1234; *World Tables.*

PERU - GOVERNMENT FINANCES

Inter-American Development Bank, 1300 New York Avenue, NW, Washington, D.C. 20577 (202) 623-1753; *Economic and Social Progress in Latin America.*

International Monetary Fund, 700 Nineteenth Street, NW, Washington, D.C. 20431 (202) 623-7000; *International Financial Statistics.*

Statistical Office of the United Nations, Publishing Service, New York, New York 10017 (800) 253-9646; *Statistical Yearbook.*

PERU - GOVERNMENT REVENUE

Inter-American Development Bank, 1300 New York Avenue, NW, Washington, D.C. 20577 (202) 623-1753; *Economic and Social Progress in Latin America.*

International Monetary Fund, 700 Nineteenth Street, NW, Washington, D.C. 20431 (202) 623-7000; *Government Finance Statistics Yearbook.*

Times Books, 201 East 50th Street, New York, New York 10022 (212) 751-2600; *The Economist Book of Vital World Statistics.*

The World Bank, 1818 H Street, NW, Washington, D.C. 20433 (202) 477-1234; *World Tables.*

PERU - GRAIN PRODUCTION - See PERU - CROPS

PERU - GRANTS

International Monetary Fund, 700 Nineteenth Street, NW, Washington, D.C. 20431 (202) 623-7000; *Government Finance Statistics Yearbook.*

PERU - GREEN PEPPER AND CHILIE PRODUCTION - See PERU - CROPS

PERU - GROSS DOMESTIC PRODUCT

The Economist Intelligence Unit, 111 West 57th Street, New York, New York 10019 (800) 938-4685; *The New Latin America Market Atlas,* and *The World Market Atlas.*

Euromonitor Publications Limited, 87-88 Turnmill Street, London EC1M 5QU, England; *International Marketing Data and Statistics.*

Facts on File, 460 Park Avenue South, New York, New York 10016 (800) 443-8323; *The New Book of World Rankings.*

G.K. Hall and Company, 70 Lincoln Street, Boston, Massachusetts 02111 (617) 423-3990; *The World in Figures.*

Inter-American Development Bank, 1300 New York Avenue, NW, Washington, D.C. 20577 (202) 623-1753; *Economic and Social Progress in Latin America.*

Organization of American States (OAS), General Secretariat, Washington, D.C. 20006 (202) 458-3533; *Statistical Bulletin of the OAS.*

Statistical Office of the United Nations, Publishing Service, New York, New York 10017 (800) 253-9646; *Statistical Yearbook,* and *Statistical Yearbook for Latin America and the Caribbean.*

Times Books, 201 East 50th Street, New York, New York 10022 (212) 751-2600; *The Economist Book of Vital World Statistics.*

U.C.L.A. Latin American Center Publications, University of California, Los Angeles, California 90024 (310) 825-6634; *Statistical Abstract of Latin America.*

The World Bank, 1818 H Street, NW, Washington, D.C. 20433 (202) 477-1234; *World Tables.*

PERU - GROSS NATIONAL PRODUCT

Euromonitor Publications Limited, 87-88 Turnmill Street, London EC1M 5QU, England; *International Marketing Data and Statistics.*

Inter-American Development Bank, 1300 New York Avenue, NW, Washington, D.C. 20577 (202) 623-1753; *Economic and Social Progress in Latin America.*

U.S. Arms Control and Disarmament Agency, 320 Twenty-first Street, NW, Washington, D.C. 20451 (202) 647-8677; *World Military Expenditures and Arms Transfers.*

The World Bank, 1818 H Street, NW, Washington, D.C. 20433 (202) 477-1234; *World Tables.*

PERU - GROUNDNUT PRODUCTION - See PERU - CROPS

PERU - HEALTH

The Economist Intelligence Unit, 111 West 57th Street, New York, New York 10019 (800) 938-4685; *The New Latin America Market Atlas.*

Facts on File, 460 Park Avenue South, New York, New York 10016 (800) 443-8323; *The New Book of World Rankings.*

G.K. Hall and Company, 70 Lincoln Street, Boston, Massachusetts 02111 (617) 423-3990; *The World in Figures.*

Statistical Office of the United Nations, Publishing Service, New York, New York 10017 (800) 253-9646; *Statistical Yearbook,* and *Statistical Yearbook for Latin America and the Caribbean.*

Times Books, 201 East 50th Street, New York, New York 10022 (212) 751-2600; *The Economist Book of Vital World Statistics.*

World Health Organization, Office of Publications, Avenue Appia, CH-1211 Geneva 27, Switzerland (Telephone Number in U.S. (518) 436-9686); *World Health Statistics Annual.*

PERU - HEALTH EXPENDITURES

International Monetary Fund, 700 Nineteenth Street, NW, Washington, D.C. 20431 (202) 623-7000; *Government Finance Statistics Yearbook.*

PERU - HIDE PRODUCTION

Food and Agricultural Organization of the United Nations (FAO), Via delle Terme di Caracalla, 00100 Rome, Italy (Telephone Number in U.S. (202) 653-2400); *Production Yearbook.*

PERU - HIGHWAYS

The Economist Intelligence Unit, 111 West 57th Street, New York, New York 10019 (800) 938-4685; *The New Latin America Market Atlas.*

G.K. Hall and Company, 70 Lincoln Street, Boston, Massachusetts 02111 (617) 423-3990; *The World in Figures.*

International Road Federation, 525 School Street, SW, Washington, D.C. 20024 (202) 554-2106; *World Road Statistics.*

PERU - HORSES - See PERU - LIVESTOCK AND POULTRY

PERU - HOURS OF WORK - See PERU - EMPLOYMENT

PERU - HOUSING AND HOUSING UNITS

Facts on File, 460 Park Avenue South, New York, New York 10016 (800) 443-8323; *The New Book of World Rankings.*

Statistical Office of the United Nations, Publishing Service, New York, New York 10017 (800) 253-9646; *Statistical Yearbook for Latin America and the Caribbean.*

U.C.L.A. Latin American Center Publications, University of California, Los Angeles, California 90024 (310) 825-6634; *Statistical Abstract of Latin America.*

PERU - ILLITERATE POPULATION

The Economist Intelligence Unit, 111 West 57th Street, New York, New York 10019 (800) 938-4685; *The New Latin American Market Atlas*, and *The World Market Atlas*.

G.K. Hall and Company, 70 Lincoln Street, Boston, Massachusetts 02111 (617) 423-3990; *The World in Figures*.

Statistical Office of the United Nations, Publishing Service, New York, New York 10017 (800) 253-9646; *Statistical Yearbook for Latin America and the Caribbean*.

United Nations Educational, Scientific and Cultural Organization (UNESCO), 7 Place de Fontenoy, F-75700 Paris, France (Telephone Number in U.S. (212) 963-5981); *Statistical Yearbook*.

PERU - IMMIGRATION

U.C.L.A. Latin American Center Publications, University of California, Los Angeles, California 90024 (310) 825-6634; *Statistical Abstract of Latin America*.

PERU - IMPORTS

American Automobile Manufacturers Association, 1401 H Street, NW, Suite 900, Washington, D.C. 20005 (202) 326-5500; *World Motor Vehicle Data*.

The Economist Intelligence Unit, 111 West 57th Street, New York, New York 10019 (800) 938-4685; *The New Latin America Market Atlas*, and *The World Market Atlas*.

Euromonitor Publications Limited, 87-88 Turnmill Street, London EC1M 5QU, England; *International Marketing Data and Statistics*.

Food and Agricultural Organization of the United Nations (FAO) Via delle Terme di Caracalla, 00100 Rome, Italy (Telephone Number in U.S. (202) 653-2400); *The State of Food and Agriculture*.

G.K. Hall and Company, 70 Lincoln Street, Boston, Massachusetts 02111 (617) 423-3990; *The World in Figures*.

Inter-American Development Bank, 1300 New York Avenue, NW, Washington, D.C. 20577 (202) 623-1753; *Economic and Social Progress in Latin America*.

International Lead and Zinc Study Group, Metro House, 58 St. James's Street, London SW1A 1LD, England; *Lead and Zinc Statistics*.

International Monetary Fund, 700 Nineteenth Street, NW, Washington, D.C. 20431 (202) 623-7000; *Direction of Trade Statistics, Government Finance Statistics Yearbook*, and *International Financial Statistics*.

Organization of American States (OAS), General Secretariat, Washington, D.C. 20006 (202) 458-3533; *Statistical Bulletin of the OAS*.

Statistical Office of the United Nations, Publishing Service, New York, New York 10017 (800) 253-9646; *Statistical Yearbook for Latin America and the Caribbean*.

Times Books, 201 East 50th Street, New York, New York 10022 (212) 751-2600; *The Economist Book of Vital World Statistics*.

The World Bank, 1818 H Street, NW, Washington, D.C. 20433 (202) 477-1234; *World Tables*.

PERU - INCOME DISTRIBUTION

Statistical Office of the United Nations, Publishing Service, New York, New York 10017 (800) 253-9646; *Statistical Yearbook for Latin America and the Caribbean*.

U.C.L.A. Latin American Center Publications, University of California, Los Angeles, California 90024 (310) 825-6634; *Statistical Abstract of Latin America*.

PERU - INCOME TAXES - See PERU - TAXATION

PERU - INDUSTRIAL METALS PRODUCTION - See PERU - MINING AND MINERAL PRODUCTS

PERU - INDUSTRY

Euromonitor Publications Limited, 87-88 Turnmill Street, London EC1M 5QU, England; *International Marketing Data and Statistics*.

Facts on File, 460 Park Avenue South, New York, New York 10016 (800) 443-8323; *The New Book of World Rankings*.

Gale Research Incorporated, 835 Penobscot Building, Detroit, Michigan 48226 (800) 877-4253; *International Historical Statistics The Americas and Australasia*.

G.K. Hall and Company, 70 Lincoln Street, Boston, Massachusetts 02111 (617) 423-3990; *The World in Figures*.

International Labour Office, I.L.O. Publications, CH-1211, Geneva 22, Switzerland; *Yearbook of Labour Statistics*.

Statistical Office of the United Nations, Publishing Service, New York, New York 10017 (800) 253-9646; *Economic Survey of Latin America and the Caribbean*, and *Statistical Yearbook*.

Times Books, 201 East 50th Street, New York, New York 10022 (212) 751-2600; *The Economist Book of Vital World Statistics*.

U.C.L.A. Latin American Center Publications, University of California, Los Angeles, California 90024 (310) 825-6634; *Statistical Abstract of Latin America*.

The World Bank, 1818 H Street, NW, Washington, D.C. 20433 (202) 477-1234; *World Tables*.

World Intellectual Property Organization, 34 Chemin des Colombettes, CH-1211 Geneva 20, Switzerland; *Industrial Property Statistics*.

PERU - INFANT AND MATERNAL MORTALITY

The Economist Intelligence Unit, 111 West 57th Street, New York, New York 10019 (800) 938-4685; *The New Latin America Market Atlas*.

Statistical Office of the United Nations, Publishing Service, New York, New York 10017 (800) 253-9646; *Demographic Yearbook*, and *Statistical Yearbook*.

Times Books, 201 East 50th Street, New York, New York 10022 (212) 751-2600; *The Economist Book of Vital World Statistics*.

The World Bank, 1818 H Street, NW, Washington, D.C. 20433 (202) 477-1234; *World Tables*.

PERU - INFLATIONARY FACTORS

Statistical Office of the United Nations, Publishing Service, New York, New York 10017 (800) 253-9646; *Economic Survey of Latin America and the Caribbean.*

PERU - INTEREST RATES

Inter-American Development Bank, 1300 New York Avenue, NW, Washington, D.C. 20577 (202) 623-1753; *Economic and Social Progress in Latin America.*

Organization of American States (OAS), General Secretariat, Washington, D.C. 20006 (202) 458-3533; *Statistical Bulletin of the OAS.*

PERU - INTERNATIONAL FINANCE

Inter-American Development Bank, 1300 New York Avenue, NW, Washington, D.C. 20577 (202) 623-1753; *Economic and Social Progress in Latin America.*

U.C.L.A. Latin American Center Publications, University of California, Los Angeles, California 90024 (310) 825-6634; *Statistical Abstract of Latin America.*

PERU - INTERNATIONAL LIQUIDITY

Inter-American Development Bank, 1300 New York Avenue, NW, Washington, D.C. 20577 (202) 623-1753; *Economic and Social Progress in Latin America.*

International Monetary Fund, 700 Nineteenth Street, NW, Washington, D.C. 20431 (202) 623-7000; *International Financial Statistics.*

PERU - INTERNATIONAL RESERVES

Inter-American Development Bank, 1300 New York Avenue, NW, Washington, D.C. 20577 (202) 623-1753; *Economic and Social Progress in Latin America.*

Organization of American States (OAS), General Secretariat, Washington, D.C. 20006 (202) 458-3533; *Statistical Bulletin of the OAS.*

Statistical Office of the United Nations, Publishing Service, New York, New York 10017 (800) 253-9646; *Statistical Yearbook.*

PERU - INTERNATIONAL RESERVES EXCLUDING GOLD

The World Bank, 1818 H Street, NW, Washington, D.C. 20433 (202) 477-1234; *World Tables.*

PERU - INTERNATIONAL STATISTICS

Inter-American Development Bank, 1300 New York Avenue, NW, Washington, D.C. 20577 (202) 623-1753; *Economic and Social Progress in Latin America.*

U.C.L.A. Latin American Center Publications, University of California, Los Angeles, California 90024 (310) 825-6634; *Statistical Abstract of Latin America.*

PERU - INVESTMENTS

Inter-American Development Bank, 1300 New York Avenue, NW, Washington, D.C. 20577 (202) 623-1753; *Economic and Social Progress in Latin America.*

International Monetary Fund, 700 Nineteenth Street, NW, Washington, D.C. 20431 (202) 623-7000; *International Financial Statistics.*

Statistical Office of the United Nations, Publishing Service, New York, New York 10017 (800) 253-9646; *Statistical Yearbook for Latin America and the Caribbean.*

PERU - IRON ORE - See PERU - MINING AND MINERAL PRODUCTS

PERU - IRRIGATION

Euromonitor Publications Limited, 87-88 Turnmill Street, London EC1M 5QU, England; *International Marketing Data and Statistics.*

Inter-American Development Bank, 1300 New York Avenue, NW, Washington, D.C. 20577 (202) 623-1753; *Economic and Social Progress in Latin America.*

PERU - JUTE PRODUCTION - See PERU - CROPS

PERU - LABOR FORCE

The Economist Intelligence Unit, 111 West 57th Street, New York, New York 10019 (800) 938-4685; *The New Latin America Market Atlas.*

Euromonitor Publications Limited, 87-88 Turnmill Street, London EC1M 5QU, England; *International Marketing Data and Statistics.*

Facts on File, 460 Park Avenue South, New York, New York 10016 (800) 443-8323; *The New Book of World Rankings.*

Food and Agricultural Organization of the United Nations (FAO) Via delle Terme di Caracalla, 00100 Rome, Italy (Telephone Number in U.S. (202) 653-2400); *The State of Food and Agriculture.*

Gale Research Incorporated, 835 Penobscot Building, Detroit, Michigan 18226 (000) 077-4253, *International Historical Statistics The Americas and Australasia.*

G.K. Hall and Company, 70 Lincoln Street, Boston, Massachusetts 02111 (617) 423-3990; *The World in Figures.*

Times Books, 201 East 50th Street, New York, New York 10022 (212) 751-2600; *The Economist Book of Vital World Statistics.*

The World Bank, 1818 H Street, NW, Washington, D.C. 20433 (202) 477-1234; *World Tables.*

PERU - LABOR PRODUCTIVITY

International Labour Office, I.L.O. Publications, CH-1211, Geneva 22, Switzerland; *Yearbook of Labour Statistics.*

PERU - LAND AREA

The Economist Intelligence Unit, 111 West 57th Street, New York, New York 10019 (800) 938-4685; *The New Latin America Market Atlas.*

PERU - LAND USE

Euromonitor Publications Limited, 87-88 Turnmill Street, London EC1M 5QU, England; *International Marketing Data and Statistics.*

Food and Agricultural Organization of the United Nations (FAO), Via delle Terme di Caracalla, 00100 Rome, Italy (Telephone Number in U.S. (202) 653-2400), *Production Yearbook.*

G.K. Hall and Company, 70 Lincoln Street, Boston, Massachusetts 02111 (617) 423-3990; *The World in Figures*.

Inter-American Development Bank, 1300 New York Avenue, NW, Washington, D.C. 20577 (202) 623-1753; *Economic and Social Progress in Latin America*.

PERU - LEAD AND LEAD ORE PRODUCTION AND CONSUMPTION - See PERU - MINING AND MINERAL PRODUCTS

PERU - LIBRARIES

Facts on File, 460 Park Avenue South, New York, New York 10016 (800) 443-8323; *The New Book of World Rankings*.

PERU - LIBRARIES - HIGHER EDUCATION

United Nations Educational, Scientific and Cultural Organization (UNESCO), 7 Place de Fontenoy, F-75700 Paris, France (Telephone Number in U.S. (212) 963-5981); *Statistical Yearbook*.

PERU - LIFE EXPECTANCY

The Economist Intelligence Unit, 111 West 57th Street, New York, New York 10019 (800) 938-4685; *The New Latin America Market Atlas*.

PERU - LIGNITE PRODUCTION - See PERU - MINING AND MINERAL PRODUCTS

PERU - LIVESTOCK AND POULTRY

Commodity Research Bureau, Incorporated, 75 Wall Street, New York, New York 10005 (212) 504-7754; *Commodity Year Book*.

Euromonitor Publications Limited, 87-88 Turnmill Street, London EC1M 5QU, England; *International Marketing Data and Statistics*.

Facts on File, 460 Park Avenue South, New York, New York 10016 (800) 443-8323; *The New Book of World Rankings*.

Food and Agricultural Organization of the United Nations (FAO), Via delle Terme di Caracalla, 00100 Rome, Italy (Telephone Number in U.S. (202) 653-2400); *Production Yearbook*, and *The State of Food and Agriculture*.

G.K. Hall and Company, 70 Lincoln Street, Boston, Massachusetts 02111 (617) 423-3990; *The World in Figures*.

Statistical Office of the United Nations, Publishing Service, New York, New York 10017 (800) 253-9646; *Statistical Yearbook*.

PERU - LIVING LEVELS

G.K. Hall and Company, 70 Lincoln Street, Boston, Massachusetts 02111 (617) 423-3990; *The World in Figures*.

Statistical Office of the United Nations, Publishing Service, New York, New York 10017 (800) 253-9646; *Statistical Yearbook for Latin America and the Caribbean*.

Times Books, 201 East 50th Street, New York, New York 10022 (212) 751-2600; *The Economist Book of Vital World Statistics*.

PERU - MAGNESIUM PRODUCTION AND CONSUMPTION - See PERU - MINING AND MINERAL PRODUCTS

PERU - MAIN ECONOMIC INDICATORS - See PERU - ECONOMY

PERU - MANGANESE AND MANGANESE ORE PRODUCTION AND CONSUMPTION - See PERU - MINING AND MINERAL PRODUCTS

PERU - MANUFACTURING

American Automobile Manufacturers Association, 1401 H Street, NW, Suite 900, Washington, D.C. 20005 (202) 326-5500; *World Motor Vehicle Data*.

The Economist Intelligence Unit, 111 West 57th Street, New York, New York 10019 (800) 938-4685; *The New Latin America Market Atlas*.

Facts on File, 460 Park Avenue South, New York, New York 10016 (800) 443-8323; *The New Book of World Rankings*.

G.K. Hall and Company, 70 Lincoln Street, Boston, Massachusetts 02111 (617) 423-3990; *The World in Figures*.

Inter-American Development Bank, 1300 New York Avenue, NW, Washington, D.C. 20577 (202) 623-1753; *Economic and Social Progress in Latin America*.

Statistical Office of the United Nations, Publishing Service, New York, New York 10017 (800) 253-9646; *Statistical Yearbook*, and *Statistical Yearbook for Latin America and the Caribbean*.

Times Books, 201 East 50th Street, New York, New York 10022 (212) 751-2600; *The Economist Book of Vital World Statistics*.

The World Bank, 1818 H Street, NW, Washington, D.C. 20433 (202) 477-1234; *World Tables*.

PERU - MARGARINE PRODUCTION

Statistical Office of the United Nations, Publishing Service, New York, New York 10017 (800) 253-9646; *Statistical Yearbook*.

PERU - MARRIAGE RATES

Facts on File, 460 Park Avenue South, New York, New York 10016 (800) 443-8323; *The New Book of World Rankings*.

Statistical Office of the United Nations, Publishing Service, New York, New York 10017 (800) 253-9646; *Demographic Yearbook*, and *Statistical Yearbook*.

PERU - MEAT PRODUCTION - See PERU - LIVESTOCK AND POULTRY

PERU - MEDICAL PERSONNEL

U.C.L.A. Latin American Center Publications, University of California, Los Angeles, California 90024 (310) 825-6634; *Statistical Abstract of Latin America*.

PERU - MERCHANT SHIPPING

G.K. Hall and Company, 70 Lincoln Street, Boston, Massachusetts 02111 (617) 423-3990; *The World in Figures*.

Lloyd's Register of Shipping, 17 Battery Place, New York, New York 10004 (212) 425-8050; *Register of Ships*.

Statistical Office of the United Nations, Publishing Service, New York, New York 10017 (800) 253-9646; *Statistical Yearbook*.

Times Books, 201 East 50th Street, New York, New York 10022 (212) 751-2600; *The Economist Book of Vital World Statistics*.

U.S. Department of Transportation, Maritime Administration, 400 Seventh Street, SW, Washington, D.C. 20590 (202) 366-5807; *A Statistical Analysis of the World's Merchant Fleets.*

PERU - MERCURY PRODUCTION AND CONSUMPTION - See PERU - MINING AND MINERAL PRODUCTS

PERU - MILITARY

The Economist Intelligence Unit, 111 West 57th Street, New York, New York 10019 (800) 938-4685; *The New Latin America Market Atlas.*

G.K. Hall and Company, 70 Lincoln Street, Boston, Massachusetts 02111 (617) 423-3990; *The World in Figures.*

The International Institute for Strategic Studies, 23 Tavistock Street, London WC2E 7NQ, England; *The Military Balance.*

U.C.L.A. Latin American Center Publications, University of California, Los Angeles, California 90024 (310) 825-6634; *Statistical Abstract of Latin America.*

U.S. Arms Control and Disarmament Agency, 320 Twenty-first Street, NW, Washington, D.C. 20451 (202) 647-8677; *World Military Expenditures and Arms Transfers.*

PERU - MILK PRODUCTION - See PERU - DAIRY PRODUCTS

PERU - MINING AND MINERAL PRODUCTS

Commodity Research Bureau, Incorporated, 75 Wall Street, New York, New York 10005 (212) 504-7754; *Commodity Year Book.*

The Economist Intelligence Unit, 111 West 57th Street, New York, New York 10019 (800) 938-4685; *The New Latin America Market Atlas.*

Facts on File, 460 Park Avenue South, New York, New York 10016 (800) 443-8323; *The New Book of World Rankings.*

G.K. Hall and Company, 70 Lincoln Street, Boston, Massachusetts 02111 (617) 423-3990; *The World in Figures.*

Inter-American Development Bank, 1300 New York Avenue, NW, Washington, D.C. 20577 (202) 623-1753; *Economic and Social Progress in Latin America.*

International Lead and Zinc Study Group, Metro House, 58 St. James's Street, London SW1A 1LD, England; *Lead and Zinc Statistics.*

International Monetary Fund, 700 Nineteenth Street, NW, Washington, D.C. 20431 (202) 623-7000; *International Financial Statistics.*

Organization of American States (OAS), General Secretariat, Washington, D.C. 20006 (202) 458-3533; *Statistical Bulletin of the OAS.*

Penn Well Publishing Company, 1421 South Sheridan Road, Post Office Box 1260, Tulsa, Oklahoma 74101 (800) 752-9764; *International Energy Statistics Sourcebook.*

Statistical Office of the United Nations, Publishing Service, New York, New York 10017 (800) 253-9646; *Statistical Yearbook,* and *Statistical Yearbook for Latin America and the Caribbean.*

U.C.L.A. Latin American Center Publications, University of California, Los Angeles, California 90024 (310) 825-6634; *Statistical Abstract of Latin America.*

World Bureau of Metal Statistics, 27-A High Street, Ware, Herts. SG12 9BA, England; *World Metal Statistics.*

PERU - MOLYBDENUM AND MOLYBDENUM ORE PRODUCTION AND CONSUMPTION - See PERU - MINING AND MINERAL PRODUCTS

PERU - MONEY EXCHANGE RATE

Euromonitor Publications Limited, 87-88 Turnmill Street, London EC1M 5QU, England; *International Marketing Data and Statistics.*

Inter-American Development Bank, 1300 New York Avenue, NW, Washington, D.C. 20577 (202) 623-1753; *Economic and Social Progress in Latin America.*

International Monetary Fund, 700 Nineteenth Street, NW, Washington, D.C. 20431 (202) 623-7000; *International Financial Statistics.*

Statistical Office of the United Nations, Publishing Service, New York, New York 10017 (800) 253-9646; *Statistical Yearbook.*

PERU - MONEY RATES - MARKET

Inter-American Development Bank, 1300 New York Avenue, NW, Washington, D.C. 20577 (202) 623-1753; *Economic and Social Progress in Latin America.*

PERU - MONEY RESERVES

Euromonitor Publications Limited, 87-88 Turnmill Street, London EC1M 5QU, England; *International Marketing Data and Statistics.*

Inter-American Development Bank, 1300 New York Avenue, NW, Washington, D.C. 20577 (202) 623-1753; *Economic and Social Progress in Latin America.*

PERU - MONEY SUPPLY

Euromonitor Publications Limited, 87-88 Turnmill Street, London EC1M 5QU, England; *International Marketing Data and Statistics.*

G.K. Hall and Company, 70 Lincoln Street, Boston, Massachusetts 02111 (617) 423-3990; *The World in Figures.*

Inter-American Development Bank, 1300 New York Avenue, NW, Washington, D.C. 20577 (202) 623-1753; *Economic and Social Progress in Latin America.*

International Monetary Fund, 700 Nineteenth Street, NW, Washington, D.C. 20431 (202) 623-7000; *International Financial Statistics.*

Statistical Office of the United Nations, Publishing Service, New York, New York 10017 (800) 253-9646; *Statistical Yearbook.*

U.C.L.A. Latin American Center Publications, University of California, Los Angeles, California 90024 (310) 825-6634; *Statistical Abstract of Latin America.*

The World Bank, 1818 H Street, NW, Washington, D.C. 20433 (202) 477-1234; *World Tables.*

PERU - MONUMENTS AND HISTORICAL SITES

United Nations Educational, Scientific and Cultural Organization (UNESCO), 7 Place de Fontenoy, F-75700 Paris, France (Telephone Number in U.S. (212) 963-5981); *Statistical Yearbook*.

PERU - MOTION PICTURES

Statistical Office of the United Nations, Publishing Service, New York, New York 10017 (800) 253-9646; *Statistical Yearbook*.

United Nations Educational, Scientific and Cultural Organization (UNESCO), 7 Place de Fontenoy, F-75700 Paris, France (Telephone Number in U.S. (212) 963-5981); *Statistical Yearbook*.

PERU - MOTOR VEHICLE PRODUCTION

American Automobile Manufacturers Association, 1401 H Street, NW, Suite 900, Washington, D.C. 20005 (202) 326-5500; *World Motor Vehicle Data*.

The Economist Intelligence Unit, 111 West 57th Street, New York, New York 10019 (800) 938-4685; *The New Latin America Market Atlas*.

Statistical Office of the United Nations, Publishing Service, New York, New York 10017 (800) 253-9646; *Statistical Yearbook*.

PERU - MOTOR VEHICLE TAXES - See PERU - TAXATION

PERU - MOTOR VEHICLES IN USE

American Automobile Manufacturers Association, 1401 H Street, NW, Suite 900, Washington, D.C. 20005 (202) 326-5500; *World Motor Vehicle Data*.

G.K. Hall and Company, 70 Lincoln Street, Boston, Massachusetts 02111 (617) 423-3990; *The World in Figures*.

International Road Federation, 525 School Street, SW, Washington, D.C. 20024 (202) 554-2106; *World Road Statistics*.

Statistical Office of the United Nations, Publishing Service, New York, New York 10017 (800) 253-9646; *Statistical Yearbook*.

Times Books, 201 East 50th Street, New York, New York 10022 (212) 751-2600; *The Economist Book of Vital World Statistics*.

PERU - MULES - See PERU - LIVESTOCK AND POULTRY

PERU - MUSEUMS

Facts on File, 460 Park Avenue South, New York, New York 10016 (800) 443-8323; *The New Book of World Rankings*.

United Nations Educational, Scientific and Cultural Organization (UNESCO), 7 Place de Fontenoy, F-75700 Paris, France (Telephone Number in U.S. (212) 963-5981); *Statistical Yearbook*.

PERU - NATALITY - See PERU - BIRTH RATES

PERU - NATIONAL ACCOUNTS

Gale Research Incorporated, 835 Penobscot Building, Detroit, Michigan 48226 (800) 877-4253; *International Historical Statistics The Americas and Australasia*.

Inter-American Development Bank, 1300 New York Avenue, NW, Washington, D.C. 20577 (202) 623-1753; *Economic and Social Progress in Latin America*.

International Monetary Fund, 700 Nineteenth Street, NW, Washington, D.C. 20431 (202) 623-7000; *International Financial Statistics*.

Organization of American States (OAS), General Secretariat, Washington, D.C. 20006 (202) 458-3533; *Statistical Bulletin of the OAS*.

Statistical Office of the United Nations, Publishing Service, New York, New York 10017 (800) 253-9646; *National Accounts Statistics*, and *Statistical Yearbook*.

U.C.L.A. Latin American Center Publications, University of California, Los Angeles, California 90024 (310) 825-6634; *Statistical Abstract of Latin America*.

PERU - NATIONAL INCOME

Facts on File, 460 Park Avenue South, New York, New York 10016 (800) 443-8323; *The New Book of World Rankings*.

G.K. Hall and Company, 70 Lincoln Street, Boston, Massachusetts 02111 (617) 423-3990; *The World in Figures*.

Inter-American Development Bank, 1300 New York Avenue, NW, Washington, D.C. 20577 (202) 623-1753; *Economic and Social Progress in Latin America*.

Statistical Office of the United Nations, Publishing Service, New York, New York 10017 (800) 253-9646; *Statistical Yearbook*.

PERU - NATIONAL PRODUCT

Facts on File, 460 Park Avenue South, New York, New York 10016 (800) 443-8323; *The New Book of World Rankings*.

Statistical Office of the United Nations, Publishing Service, New York, New York 10017 (800) 253-9646; *Statistical Yearbook*.

PERU - NATURAL GAS PRODUCTION - See PERU - MINING AND MINERAL PRODUCTS

PERU - NEWSPAPER PRODUCTION - See PERU - FORESTRY AND FOREST PRODUCTS

PERU - NEWSPRINT - See PERU - FORESTRY AND FOREST PRODUCTS

PERU - NICKEL - See PERU - MINING AND MINERAL PRODUCTS

PERU - NITRIC ACID PRODUCTION - See PERU - MINING AND MINERAL PRODUCTS

PERU - NUTRITION

Statistical Office of the United Nations, Publishing Service, New York, New York 10017 (800) 253-9646; *Statistical Yearbook for Latin America and the Caribbean*.

PERU - OATS PRODUCTION - See PERU - CROPS

PERU - OCCUPATIONS - See PERU - LABOR FORCE

PERU - ORANGES PRODUCTION - See PERU - CROPS

PERU - PALM KERNELS AND PALM OIL PRODUCTION - See PERU - CROPS

PERU - PAPER - See PERU - FORESTRY AND FOREST PRODUCTS

PERU - PATENTS

Statistical Office of the United Nations, Publishing Service, New York, New York 10017 (800) 253-9646; *Statistical Yearbook.*

World Intellectual Property Organization, 34 Chemin des Colombettes, CH-1211 Geneva 20, Switzerland; *Industrial Property Statistics.*

PERU - PEANUT PRODUCTION - See PERU - CROPS

PERU - PERIODICALS

United Nations Educational, Scientific and Cultural Organization (UNESCO), 7 Place de Fontenoy, F-75700 Paris, France (Telephone Number in U.S. (212) 963-5981); *Statistical Yearbook.*

PERU - PESTICIDE USE

Food and Agricultural Organization of the United Nations (FAO) Via delle Terme di Caracalla, 00100 Rome, Italy (Telephone Number in U.S. (202) 653-2400); *The State of Food and Agriculture.*

PERU - PETROLEUM INDUSTRY

The Economist Intelligence Unit, 111 West 57th Street, New York, New York 10019 (800) 938-4685; *The New Latin America Market Atlas.*

Facts on File, 460 Park Avenue South, New York, New York 10016 (800) 443-8323; *The New Book of World Rankings.*

Food and Agricultural Organization of the United Nations (FAO) Via delle Terme di Caracalla, 00100 Rome, Italy (Telephone Number in U.S. (202) 653-2400); *The State of Food and Agriculture.*

G.K. Hall and Company, 70 Lincoln Street, Boston, Massachusetts 02111 (617) 423-3990; *The World in Figures.*

Inter-American Development Bank, 1300 New York Avenue, NW, Washington, D.C. 20577 (202) 623-1753; *Economic and Social Progress in Latin America.*

Penn Well Publishing Company, 1421 South Sheridan Road, Post Office Box 1260, Tulsa, Oklahoma 74101 (800) 752-9764; *International Energy Statistics Sourcebook.*

Statistical Office of the United Nations, Publishing Service, New York, New York 10017 (800) 253-9646; *Statistical Yearbook.*

PERU - PHOSPHATE ROCK PRODUCTION - See PERU - MINING AND MINERAL PRODUCTS

PERU - PIG-IRON AND FERRO-ALLOYS PRODUCTION - See PERU - MINING AND MINERAL PRODUCTS

PERU - PIGS - See PERU - LIVESTOCK AND POULTRY

PERU - PLATINUM PRODUCTION AND CONSUMPTION - See PERU - MINING AND MINERAL PRODUCTS

PERU - POLITICAL DATA

U.C.L.A. Latin American Center Publications, University of California, Los Angeles, California 90024 (310) 825-6634; *Statistical Abstract of Latin America.*

PERU - POPULATION

The Economist Intelligence Unit, 111 West 57th Street, New York, New York 10019 (800) 938-4685; *The New Latin America Market Atlas,* and *The World Market Atlas.*

Euromonitor Publications Limited, 87-88 Turnmill Street, London EC1M 5QU, England; *International Marketing Data and Statistics.*

Facts on File, 460 Park Avenue South, New York, New York 10016 (800) 443-8323; *The New Book of World Rankings.*

Food and Agricultural Organization of the United Nations (FAO), Via delle Terme di Caracalla, 00100 Rome, Italy (Telephone Number in U.S. (202) 653-2400); *Production Yearbook.*

Gale Research Incorporated, 835 Penobscot Building, Detroit, Michigan 48226 (800) 877-4253; *International Historical Statistics The Americas and Australasia.*

G.K. Hall and Company, 70 Lincoln Street, Boston, Massachusetts 02111 (617) 423-3990; *The World in Figures.*

Inter-American Development Bank, 1300 New York Avenue, NW, Washington, D.C. 20577 (202) 623-1753; *Economic and Social Progress in Latin America.*

International Labour Office, I.L.O. Publications, CH-1211, Geneva 22, Switzerland; *Yearbook of Labour Statistics.*

Organization of American States (OAS), General Secretariat, Washington, D.C. 20006 (202) 458-3533; *Statistical Bulletin of the OAS*

Statistical Office of the United Nations, Publishing Service, New York, New York 10017 (800) 253-9646; *Demographic Yearbook, Statistical Yearbook,* and *Statistical Yearbook for Latin America and the Caribbean.*

Times Books, 201 East 50th Street, New York, New York 10022 (212) 751-2600; *The Economist Book of Vital World Statistics.*

U.C.L.A. Latin American Center Publications, University of California, Los Angeles, California 90024 (310) 825-6634; *Statistical Abstract of Latin America.*

United Nations Educational, Scientific and Cultural Organization (UNESCO), 7 Place de Fontenoy, F-75700 Paris, France (Telephone Number in U.S. (212) 963-5981); *Statistical Yearbook.*

U.S. Arms Control and Disarmament Agency, 320 Twenty-first Street, NW, Washington, D.C. 20451 (202) 647-8677; *World Military Expenditures and Arms Transfers.*

World Health Organization, Office of Publications, Avenue Appia, CH-1211 Geneva 27, Switzerland (Telephone Number in U.S. (518) 436-9686); *World Health Statistics Annual.*

PERU - POST OFFICES

Facts on File, 460 Park Avenue South, New York, New York 10016 (800) 443-8323; *The New Book of World Rankings.*

PERU - POTATO PRODUCTION - See PERU - CROPS

PERU - POWER PRODUCTION INDUSTRY

Statistical Office of the United Nations, Publishing Service, New York, New York 10017 (800) 253-9646; *Statistical Yearbook.*

PERU - PRICES

Facts on File, 460 Park Avenue South, New York, New York 10016 (800) 443-8323; *The New Book of World Rankings.*

Food and Agricultural Organization of the United Nations (FAO), Via delle Terme di Caracalla, 00100 Rome, Italy (Telephone Number in U.S. (202) 653-2400); *Production Yearbook,* and *The State of Food and Agriculture.*

Gale Research Incorporated, 835 Penobscot Building, Detroit, Michigan 48226 (800) 877-4253; *International Historical Statistics The Americas and Australasia.*

G.K. Hall and Company, 70 Lincoln Street, Boston, Massachusetts 02111 (617) 423-3990; *The World in Figures.*

International Labour Office, I.L.O. Publications, CH-1211, Geneva 22, Switzerland; *Yearbook of Labour Statistics.*

International Lead and Zinc Study Group, Metro House, 58 St. James's Street, London SW1A 1LD, England; *Lead and Zinc Statistics.*

International Monetary Fund, 700 Nineteenth Street, NW, Washington, D.C. 20431 (202) 623-7000; *International Financial Statistics.*

Statistical Office of the United Nations, Publishing Service, New York, New York 10017 (800) 253-9646; *Economic Survey of Latin America and the Caribbean,* and *Statistical Yearbook for Latin America and the Caribbean.*

World Bureau of Metal Statistics, 27-A High Street, Ware, Herts. SG12 9BA, England; *World Metal Statistics.*

PERU - PRINTING AND WRITING PAPER - See PERU - FORESTRY AND FOREST PRODUCTS

PERU - PRODUCTION

American Automobile Manufacturers Association, 1401 H Street, NW, Suite 900, Washington, D.C. 20005 (202) 326-5500; *World Motor Vehicle Data.*

Facts on File, 460 Park Avenue South, New York, New York 10016 (800) 443-8323; *The New Book of World Rankings.*

G.K. Hall and Company, 70 Lincoln Street, Boston, Massachusetts 02111 (617) 423-3990; *The World in Figures.*

International Lead and Zinc Study Group, Metro House, 58 St. James's Street, London SW1A 1LD, England; *Lead and Zinc Statistics.*

PERU - PRODUCTIVITY

Euromonitor Publications Limited, 87-88 Turnmill Street, London EC1M 5QU, England; *International Marketing Data and Statistics.*

PERU - PROPERTY TAXES - See PERU - TAXATION

PERU - PUBLIC CONSUMPTION FUND

Inter-American Development Bank, 1300 New York Avenue, NW, Washington, D.C. 20577 (202) 623-1753; *Economic and Social Progress in Latin America.*

PERU - PUBLIC EXPENDITURES

Inter-American Development Bank, 1300 New York Avenue, NW, Washington, D.C. 20577 (202) 623-1753; *Economic and Social Progress in Latin America.*

Organization of American States (OAS), General Secretariat, Washington, D.C. 20006 (202) 458-3533; *Statistical Bulletin of the OAS.*

Statistical Office of the United Nations, Publishing Service, New York, New York 10017 (800) 253-9646; *Statistical Yearbook for Latin America and the Caribbean.*

PERU - PUBLIC FINANCE

Facts on File, 460 Park Avenue South, New York, New York 10016 (800) 443-8323; *The New Book of World Rankings.*

Inter-American Development Bank, 1300 New York Avenue, NW, Washington, D.C. 20577 (202) 623-1753; *Economic and Social Progress in Latin America.*

Organization of American States (OAS), General Secretariat, Washington, D.C. 20006 (202) 458-3533; *Statistical Bulletin of the OAS.*

PERU - PUBLIC REVENUE

Inter-American Development Bank, 1300 New York Avenue, NW, Washington, D.C. 20577 (202) 623-1753; *Economic and Social Progress in Latin America.*

Organization of American States (OAS), General Secretariat, Washington, D.C. 20006 (202) 458-3533; *Statistical Bulletin of the OAS.*

PERU - RADIO BROADCASTING - See PERU - BROADCASTING

PERU - RADIO RECEIVER PRODUCTION

Statistical Office of the United Nations, Publishing Service, New York, New York 10017 (800) 253-9646; *Statistical Yearbook.*

PERU - RAILWAYS

The Economist Intelligence Unit, 111 West 57th Street, New York, New York 10019 (800) 938-4685; *The New Latin America Market Atlas.*

G.K. Hall and Company, 70 Lincoln Street, Boston, Massachusetts 02111 (617) 423-3990; *The World in Figures.*

Jane's Information Group, Sentinel House, 163 Brighton Road, Coulsdon, Surrey CR5 2NH, England (Telephone Number in U.S. (703) 683-3700); *Jane's World Railways.*

Statistical Office of the United Nations, Publishing Service, New York, New York 10017 (800) 253-9646; *Statistical Yearbook.*

PERU - RANCHING

U.C.L.A. Latin American Center Publications, University of California, Los Angeles, California 90024 (310) 825-6634; *Statistical Abstract of Latin America.*

PERU - RELIGION

Facts on File, 460 Park Avenue South, New York, New York 10016 (800) 443-8323; *The New Book of World Rankings*.

U.C.L.A. Latin American Center Publications, University of California, Los Angeles, California 90024 (310) 825-6634; *Statistical Abstract of Latin America*.

PERU - RENT PRICES

International Labour Office, I.L.O. Publications, CH-1211, Geneva 22, Switzerland; *Yearbook of Labour Statistics*.

PERU - RESERVES EXCLUDING GOLD

The Economist Intelligence Unit, 111 West 57th Street, New York, New York 10019 (800) 938-4685; *The New Latin America Market Atlas*.

PERU - RETAIL TRADE

G.K. Hall and Company, 70 Lincoln Street, Boston, Massachusetts 02111 (617) 423-3990; *The World in Figures*.

Inter-American Development Bank, 1300 New York Avenue, NW, Washington, D.C. 20577 (202) 623-1753; *Economic and Social Progress in Latin America*.

PERU - REVENUES

Organization of American States (OAS), General Secretariat, Washington, D.C. 20006 (202) 458-3533; *Statistical Bulletin of the OAS*.

PERU - RICE PRODUCTION - See PERU - CROPS

PERU - ROOT AND TUBER PRODUCTION - See PERU - CROPS

PERU - ROUNDWOOD PRODUCTION - See PERU - FORESTRY AND FORESTRY PRODUCTS

PERU - RUBBER PRODUCTION AND CONSUMPTION

Facts on File, 460 Park Avenue South, New York, New York 10016 (800) 443-8323; *The New Book of World Rankings*.

PERU - SALT PRODUCTION - See PERU - MINING AND MINERAL PRODUCTS

PERU - SAWNWOOD PRODUCTION - See PERU - FORESTRY AND FOREST PRODUCTS

PERU - SCIENCE AND TECHNOLOGY

Statistical Office of the United Nations, Publishing Service, New York, New York 10017 (800) 253-9646; *Statistical Yearbook*.

U.C.L.A. Latin American Center Publications, University of California, Los Angeles, California 90024 (310) 825-6634; *Statistical Abstract of Latin America*.

PERU - SCIENTISTS AND TECHNICIANS

Statistical Office of the United Nations, Publishing Service, New York, New York 10017 (800) 253-9646; *Statistical Yearbook*.

United Nations Educational, Scientific and Cultural Organization (UNESCO), 7 Place de Fontenoy, F-75700 Paris, France (Telephone

Number in U.S. (212) 963-5981); *Statistical Yearbook*.

PERU - SENIOR CITIZENS

Facts on File, 460 Park Avenue South, New York, New York 10016 (800) 443-8323; *The New Book of World Rankings*.

PERU - SHEEP - See PERU - LIVESTOCK AND POULTRY

PERU - SILVER EXPORTS - See PERU - MINING AND MINERAL PRODUCTS

PERU - SILVER PRODUCTION AND CONSUMPTION - See PERU - MINING AND MINERAL PRODUCTS

PERU - SOCIAL DATA

Facts on File, 460 Park Avenue South, New York, New York 10016 (800) 443-8323; *The New Book of World Rankings*.

G.K. Hall and Company, 70 Lincoln Street, Boston, Massachusetts 02111 (617) 423-3990; *The World in Figures*.

U.C.L.A. Latin American Center Publications, University of California, Los Angeles, California 90024 (310) 825-6634; *Statistical Abstract of Latin America*.

PERU - SOCIAL SECURITY

Inter-American Development Bank, 1300 New York Avenue, NW, Washington, D.C. 20577 (202) 623-1753; *Economic and Social Progress in Latin America*.

International Monetary Fund, 700 Nineteenth Street, NW, Washington, D.C. 20431 (202) 623-7000; *Government Finance Statistics Yearbook*.

PERU - SOCIOECONOMIC DATA

Inter-American Development Bank, 1300 New York Avenue, NW, Washington, D.C. 20577 (202) 623-1753; *Economic and Social Progress in Latin America*.

U.C.L.A. Latin American Center Publications, University of California, Los Angeles, California 90024 (310) 825-6634; *Statistical Abstract of Latin America*.

PERU - SOYBEAN PRODUCTION - See PERU - CROPS

PERU - STAMP TAXES AND DUTIES - See PERU - TAXATION

PERU - STATE BUDGET REVENUE AND EXPENDITURES

Euromonitor Publications Limited, 87-88 Turnmill Street, London EC1M 5QU, England; *International Marketing Data and Statistics*.

Inter-American Development Bank, 1300 New York Avenue, NW, Washington, D.C. 20577 (202) 623-1753; *Economic and Social Progress in Latin America*.

PERU - STEEL - See PERU - MINING AND MINERAL PRODUCTS

PERU - STOCKS - COMMODITY - MARKET PRICE - INDEXES

Food and Agricultural Organization of the United Nations (FAO) Via delle Terme di Caracalla, 00100 Rome, Italy (Telephone Number in U.S. (202) 653-2400); *The State of Food and Agriculture*.

International Lead and Zinc Study Group, Metro House, 58 St. James's Street, London SW1A 1LD, England; *Lead and Zinc Statistics*.

Statistical Office of the United Nations, Publishing Service, New York, New York 10017 (800) 253-9646; *Statistical Yearbook*.

World Bureau of Metal Statistics, 27-A High Street, Ware, Herts. SG12 9BA, England; *World Metal Statistics*.

PERU - SUGAR PRODUCTION - See PERU - CROPS

PERU - SULPHURIC ACID PRODUCTION - See PERU - MINING AND MINERAL PRODUCTS

PERU - TAXATION

G.K. Hall and Company, 70 Lincoln Street, Boston, Massachusetts 02111 (617) 423-3990; *The World in Figures*.

Inter-American Development Bank, 1300 New York Avenue, NW, Washington, D.C. 20577 (202) 623-1753; *Economic and Social Progress in Latin America*.

International Monetary Fund, 700 Nineteenth Street, NW, Washington, D.C. 20431 (202) 623-7000; *Government Finance Statistics Yearbook*.

International Road Federation, 525 School Street, SW, Washington, D.C. 20024 (202) 554-2106; *World Road Statistics*.

Statistical Office of the United Nations, Publishing Service, New York, New York 10017 (800) 253-9646; *Statistical Yearbook for Latin America and the Caribbean*.

The World Bank, 1818 H Street, NW, Washington, D.C. 20433 (202) 477-1234; *World Tables*.

PERU - TEA PRODUCTION - See PERU - CROPS

PERU - TELEGRAPH SERVICE

Statistical Office of the United Nations, Publishing Service, New York, New York 10017 (800) 253-9646; *Statistical Yearbook*.

PERU - TELEPHONES IN USE

American Telephone and Telegraph Company, 26 Parsippany Road, Whippany, New Jersey 07981 (800) 338-4038; *The World's Telephones*.

The Economist Intelligence Unit, 111 West 57th Street, New York, New York 10019 (800) 938-4685; *The New Latin America Market Atlas*.

G.K. Hall and Company, 70 Lincoln Street, Boston, Massachusetts 02111 (617) 423-3990; *The World in Figures*.

Statistical Office of the United Nations, Publishing Service, New York, New York 10017 (800) 253-9646; *Statistical Yearbook*.

PERU - TELEVISION BROADCASTING - See PERU - BROADCASTING

PERU - TELEVISION RECEIVER PRODUCTION

Statistical Office of the United Nations, Publishing Service, New York, New York 10017 (800) 253-9646; *Statistical Yearbook*.

PERU - TEXTILE INDUSTRY

American Forest and Paper Association, 1250 Connecticut Avenue, NW, Washington, D.C. 20036 (202) 463-2455; *Wood Pulp and Fiber Statistics*.

G.K. Hall and Company, 70 Lincoln Street, Boston, Massachusetts 02111 (617) 423-3990; *The World in Figures*.

Statistical Office of the United Nations, Publishing Service, New York, New York 10017 (800) 253-9646; *Statistical Yearbook*.

PERU - THEATRE

United Nations Educational, Scientific and Cultural Organization (UNESCO), 7 Place de Fontenoy, F-75700 Paris, France (Telephone Number in U.S. (212) 963-5981); *Statistical Yearbook*.

PERU - TIN PRODUCTION AND CONSUMPTION - See PERU - MINING AND MINERAL PRODUCTS

PERU - TIRE (MOTOR VEHICLE) PRODUCTION

Statistical Office of the United Nations, Publishing Service, New York, New York 10017 (800) 253-9646; *Statistical Yearbook*.

PERU - TOBACCO PRODUCTION

Facts on File, 460 Park Avenue South, New York, New York 10016 (800) 443-8323; *The New Book of World Rankings*.

Statistical Office of the United Nations, Publishing Service, New York, New York 10017 (800) 253-9646; *Statistical Yearbook*.

U.C.L.A. Latin American Center Publications, University of California, Los Angeles, California 90024 (310) 825-6634; *Statistical Abstract of Latin America*.

PERU - TOURISM

The Economist Intelligence Unit, 111 West 57th Street, New York, New York 10019 (800) 938-4685; *The New Latin America Market Atlas*.

Facts on File, 460 Park Avenue South, New York, New York 10016 (800) 443-8323; *The New Book of World Rankings*.

G.K. Hall and Company, 70 Lincoln Street, Boston, Massachusetts 02111 (617) 423-3990; *The World in Figures*.

Statistical Office of the United Nations, Publishing Service, New York, New York 10017 (800) 253-9646; *Statistical Yearbook*, and *Statistical Yearbook for Latin America and the Caribbean*.

Times Books, 201 East 50th Street, New York, New York 10022 (212) 751-2600; *The Economist Book of Vital World Statistics*.

U.C.L.A. Latin American Center Publications, University of California, Los Angeles, California 90024 (310) 825-6634; *Statistical Abstract of Latin America*.

PERU - TRACTORS IN USE

The Economist Intelligence Unit, 111 West 57th Street, New York, New York 10019 (800) 938-4685; *The New Latin America Market Atlas*.

Statistical Office of the United Nations, Publishing Service, New York, New York 10017 (800) 253-9646; *Statistical Yearbook*.

PERU - TRADE - See PERU - FOREIGN TRADE

PERU - TRADEMARKS AND SERVICE MARKS

Statistical Office of the United Nations, Publishing Service, New York, New York 10017 (800) 253-9646; *Statistical Yearbook.*

World Intellectual Property Organization, 34 Chemin des Colombettes, CH-1211 Geneva 20, Switzerland; *Industrial Property Statistics.*

PERU - TRANSPORTATION AND COMMUNICATIONS

The Economist Intelligence Unit, 111 West 57th Street, New York, New York 10019 (800) 938-4685; *The New Latin America Market Atlas.*

Facts on File, 460 Park Avenue South, New York, New York 10016 (800) 443-8323; *The New Book of World Rankings.*

Gale Research Incorporated, 835 Penobscot Building, Detroit, Michigan 48226 (800) 877-4253; *International Historical Statistics The Americas and Australasia.*

G.K. Hall and Company, 70 Lincoln Street, Boston, Massachusetts 02111 (617) 423-3990; *The World in Figures.*

Inter-American Development Bank, 1300 New York Avenue, NW, Washington, D.C. 20577 (202) 623-1753; *Economic and Social Progress in Latin America.*

Statistical Office of the United Nations, Publishing Service, New York, New York 10017 (800) 253-9646; *Statistical Yearbook for Latin America and the Caribbean.*

U.C.L.A. Latin American Center Publications, University of California, Los Angeles, California 90024 (310) 825-6634; *Statistical Abstract of Latin America.*

PERU - TUNGSTEN PRODUCTION AND CONSUMPTION - See PERU - MINING AND MINERAL PRODUCTS

PERU - UNEMPLOYMENT

The Economist Intelligence Unit, 111 West 57th Street, New York, New York 10019 (800) 938-4685; *The New Latin America Market Atlas.*

Euromonitor Publications Limited, 87-88 Turnmill Street, London EC1M 5QU, England; *International Marketing Data and Statistics.*

International Labour Office, I.L.O. Publications, CH-1211, Geneva 22, Switzerland; *Yearbook of Labour Statistics.*

Statistical Office of the United Nations, Publishing Service, New York, New York 10017 (800) 253-9646; *Statistical Yearbook.*

U.C.L.A. Latin American Center Publications, University of California, Los Angeles, California 90024 (310) 825-6634; *Statistical Abstract of Latin America.*

PERU - URANIUM PRODUCTION AND CONSUMPTION - See PERU - MINING AND MINERAL PRODUCTS

PERU - UTILITIES

U.C.L.A. Latin American Center Publications, University of California, Los Angeles, California 90024 (310) 825-6634; *Statistical Abstract of Latin America.*

PERU - VANADIUM AND VANADIUM ORE PRODUCTION AND CONSUMPTION - See PERU - MINING AND MINERAL PRODUCTS

PERU - VITAL STATISTICS

Euromonitor Publications Limited, 87-88 Turnmill Street, London EC1M 5QU, England; *International Marketing Data and Statistics.*

Gale Research Incorporated, 835 Penobscot Building, Detroit, Michigan 48226 (800) 877-4253; *International Historical Statistics The Americas and Australasia.*

G.K. Hall and Company, 70 Lincoln Street, Boston, Massachusetts 02111 (617) 423-3990; *The World in Figures.*

Statistical Office of the United Nations, Publishing Service, New York, New York 10017 (800) 253-9646; *Statistical Yearbook.*

World Health Organization, Office of Publications, Avenue Appia, CH-1211 Geneva 27, Switzerland (Telephone Number in U.S. (518) 436-9686); *World Health Statistics Annual.*

PERU - WAGES

G.K. Hall and Company, 70 Lincoln Street, Boston, Massachusetts 02111 (617) 423-3990; *The World in Figures.*

International Labour Office, I.L.O. Publications, CH-1211, Geneva 22, Switzerland; *Yearbook of Labour Statistics.*

Statistical Office of the United Nations, Publishing Service, New York, New York 10017 (800) 253-9646; *Statistical Yearbook.*

U.C.L.A. Latin American Center Publications, University of California, Los Angeles, California 90024 (310) 825-6634; *Statistical Abstract of Latin America.*

PERU - WATERMELON PRODUCTION - See PERU - CROPS

PERU - WEATHER

Facts on File, 460 Park Avenue South, New York, New York 10016 (800) 443-8323; *The New Book of World Rankings.*

G.K. Hall and Company, 70 Lincoln Street, Boston, Massachusetts 02111 (617) 423-3990; *The World in Figures.*

PERU - WELFARE

Inter-American Development Bank, 1300 New York Avenue, NW, Washington, D.C. 20577 (202) 623-1753; *Economic and Social Progress in Latin America.*

International Monetary Fund, 700 Nineteenth Street, NW, Washington, D.C. 20431 (202) 623-7000; *Government Finance Statistics Yearbook.*

PERU - WHALE AND SPERM OIL PRODUCTION

Statistical Office of the United Nations, Publishing Service, New York, New York 10017 (800) 253-9646; *Statistical Yearbook.*

PERU - WHALES CAUGHT

Statistical Office of the United Nations, Publishing Service, New York, New York 10017 (800) 253-9646; *Statistical Yearbook.*

PERU - WHALING APPARATUS IN OPERATION

Statistical Office of the United Nations, Publishing Service, New York, New York 10017 (800) 253-9646; *Statistical Yearbook*.

PERU - WHEAT PRODUCTION AND PRICES - See PERU - CROPS

PERU - WHOLESALE PRICES

Inter-American Development Bank, 1300 New York Avenue, NW, Washington, D.C. 20577 (202) 623-1753; *Economic and Social Progress in Latin America*.

Statistical Office of the United Nations, Publishing Service, New York, New York 10017 (800) 253-9646; *Statistical Yearbook*.

PERU - WHOLESALE TRADE

Inter-American Development Bank, 1300 New York Avenue, NW, Washington, D.C. 20577 (202) 623-1753; *Economic and Social Progress in Latin America*.

PERU - WINE PRODUCTION

Facts on File, 460 Park Avenue South, New York, New York 10016 (800) 443-8323; *The New Book of World Rankings*.

Statistical Office of the United Nations, Publishing Service, New York, New York 10017 (800) 253-9646; *Statistical Yearbook*.

PERU - WOOD AND WOOD PULP - SEE PERU - FORESTRY AND FOREST PRODUCTS

PERU - WOOL PRODUCTION

Facts on File, 460 Park Avenue South, New York, New York 10016 (800) 443-8323; *The New Book of World Rankings*.

Statistical Office of the United Nations, Publishing Service, New York, New York 10017 (800) 253-9646; *Statistical Yearbook*.

PERU - ZINC - See PERU - MINING AND MINERAL PRODUCTS

PESTICIDES

U.S. Department of Agriculture, Economic Research Service, Fourteenth Street and Independence Avenue, SW, Washington, D.C. 20005-4789 (202) 219-1504; *Economic Indicators of the Farm Sector: National Financial Summary*.

PET OWNERSHIP/SUPPLIES

American Veterinary Medical Association, 930 North Meacham Road, Schaumburg, Illinois 60196 (708) 605-8070; *U.S. Pet Ownership and Demographics Sourcebook*.

PET PRODUCTS

Television Bureau of Advertising, Incorporated, 850 Third Avenue, New York, New York 10022 (212) 486-1111; from data compiled by Competitive Media Reporting, 11 West 42nd Street, New York, New York 10036 (212) 789-1400.

PETROLEUM AND REFINING PRODUCTS - MANUFACTURING - CAPITAL

U.S. Department of Commerce, Bureau of Economic Analysis, Fourteenth Street between Constitution Avenue and E Street, NW, Washington, D.C. 20230 (202) 606-9900; *Fixed Reproducible*

Tangible Wealth in the United States, and *Survey of Current Business*.

U.S. Department of Commerce, Bureau of the Census, Suitland, Maryland 20233 (301) 763-4040; *Plant and Equipment Expenditures and Plans*.

PETROLEUM AND REFINING PRODUCTS - MANUFACTURING - EARNINGS

U.S. Department of Labor, Bureau of Labor Statistics, Two Massachusetts Avenue, NE, Washington, D.C. 20212 (202) 606-7828; *Employment and Earnings*, and Bulletins 2370 and 2429.

PETROLEUM AND REFINING PRODUCTS - MANUFACTURING - EMPLOYEES

U.S. Department of Commerce, Bureau of the Census, Suitland, Maryland 20233 (301) 763-4040; *Annual Survey of Manufactures*, *Census of Manufactures*, and *County Business Patterns*.

U.S. Department of Labor, Bureau of Labor Statistics, Two Massachusetts Avenue, NE, Washington, D.C. 20212 (202) 606-7828; *Employment and Earnings*, *Monthly Labor Review*, and Bulletins 2370 and 2429.

PETROLEUM AND REFINING PRODUCTS - MANUFACTURING - ESTABLISHMENTS

U.S. Department of Commerce, Bureau of the Census, Suitland, Maryland 20233 (301) 763-4040; *Annual Survey of Manufactures*, *Census of Manufactures*, and *County Business Patterns*.

PETROLEUM AND REFINING PRODUCTS - MANUFACTURING - FINANCES

Carl H. Pforzheimer and Company, 70 Pine Street, New York, New York 10270 (212) 422-5484; *Comparative Oil Company Statements*.

U.S. Department of Energy, Energy Information Administration, 1000 Independence Avenue, SW, Washington, D.C. 20585 (202) 586-8800; *Performance Profiles of Major Energy Producers*.

PETROLEUM AND REFINING PRODUCTS - MANUFACTURING - FOREIGN INVESTMENTS IN UNITED STATES

U.S. Department of Commerce, Bureau of Economic Analysis, Fourteenth Street between Constitution Avenue and E Street, NW, Washington, D.C. 20230 (202) 606-9900; *Foreign Direct Investment in the United States, Operations of U.S. Affiliates of Foreign Countries*, and *Survey of Current Business*.

PETROLEUM AND REFINING PRODUCTS - MANUFACTURING - OCCUPATIONAL SAFETY

U.S. Department of Labor, Bureau of Labor Statistics, Two Massachusetts Avenue, NE, Washington, D.C. 20212 (202) 606-7828; *Occupational Injuries and Illnesses in the United States by Industry*.

PETROLEUM AND REFINING PRODUCTS - MANUFACTURING - POLLUTION ABATEMENT

U.S. Department of Commerce, Bureau of the Census, Suitland, Maryland 20233 (301) 763-4040; *Current Industrial Reports*.

PETROLEUM AND REFINING PRODUCTS - MANUFACTURING - PRODUCTIVITY

U.S. Department of Labor, Bureau of Labor Statistics, Two Massachusetts Avenue, NE, Washington, D.C. 20212 (202) 606-7828; *Productivity Measures for Selected Industries and Government Services*, and unpublished data.

PETROLEUM AND REFINING PRODUCTS - MANUFACTURING - PROFITS

Carl H. Pforzheimer and Company, 70 Pine Street, New York, New York 10270 (212) 422-5484; *Comparative Oil Company Statements*.

U.S. Department of Commerce, Bureau of Economic Analysis, Fourteenth Street between Constitution Avenue and E Street, NW, Washington, D.C. 20230 (202) 606-9900; *The National Income and Product Accounts of the United States*, and *Survey of Current Business*.

U.S. Department of Commerce, Bureau of the Census, Suitland, Maryland 20233 (301) 763-4040; *Quarterly Financial Report for Manufacturing, Mining and Trade Corporations*.

U.S. Department of Energy, Energy Information Administration, Washington, D.C. 20585 (202) 586-8800; *Performance Profiles of Major Energy Producers*, and unpublished data.

PETROLEUM AND REFINING PRODUCTS - MANUFACTURING - RESEARCH AND DEVELOPMENT

U.S. National Science Foundation, 4201 Wilson Boulevard, Arlington, Virginia 22230 (703) 306-1234; *Research and Development in Industry*.

PETROLEUM AND REFINING PRODUCTS - MANUFACTURING - SHIPMENTS

U.S. Department of Commerce, Bureau of the Census, Suitland, Maryland 20233 (301) 763-4040; *Census of Mineral Industries, Census of Manufactures, Annual Survey of Manufactures*, and *Current Industrial Reports, Manufactures' Shipments, Inventories, and Orders*.

PETROLEUM AND REFINING PRODUCTS - MANUFACTURING - TAXES

U.S. Department of Commerce, Bureau of the Census, Suitland, Maryland 20233 (301) 763-4040; *Quarterly Financial Report for Manufacturing, Mining, and Trade Corporations*.

PETROLEUM AND REFINING PRODUCTS - MANUFACTURING - VALUE ADDED

U.S. Department of Commerce, Bureau of the Census, Suitland, Maryland 20233 (301) 763-4040; *Annual Survey of Manufactures*, and *Census of Manufactures*.

PETROLEUM AND PRODUCTS - CONSUMPTION

U.S. Department of Energy, Energy Information Administration, Washington, D.C. 20585 (202) 586-8800; *Annual Energy Review, Monthly Energy Review*, and *State Energy Data Report*.

U.S. Department of the Interior, Bureau of Mines, 810 Seventh Street, NW, Washington, D.C. 20241 (202) 501-9649; *Mineral Commodity Summaries*.

PETROLEUM AND PRODUCTS - CONSUMPTION - FOREIGN TRADE

U.S. Department of Commerce, Bureau of the Census, Suitland, Maryland 20233 (301) 763-4040; *U.S. Merchandise Trade: Exports, General Imports, and Imports for Consumption*, and *U.S. Merchandise Trade*.

U.S. Department of the Interior, Bureau of Mines, 810 Seventh Street, NW, Washington, D.C. 20241 (202) 501-9649; *Mineral Commodity Summaries*.

PETROLEUM AND PRODUCTS - CONSUMPTION - STATES

U.S. Department of Energy, Energy Information Administration, Washington, D.C. 20585 (202) 586-8800; *State Energy Data Report*.

PETROLEUM AND PRODUCTS - CRUDE OIL - DRILLING COSTS

American Petroleum Institute, 1220 L Street, NW, Washington, D.C. 20005 (202) 682-8000; Independent Petroleum Association of America, 1101 Sixteenth Street, NW, Washington, D.C. 20036 (202) 857-4722; Mid-Continent Oil and Gas Association, 801 Pennsylvania Avenue, NW, Suite 840, Washington, D.C. 20004 (202) 638-4400; *Joint Association Survey on Drilling Costs*.

PETROLEUM AND PRODUCTS - CRUDE OIL - FOREIGN TRADE

U.S. Department of Commerce, Bureau of the Census, Suitland, Maryland 20233 (301) 763-4040; *U.S. Exports of Merchandise*, and *U.S. Imports of Merchandise*, compact discs.

U.S. Department of Energy, Energy Information Administration, Washington, D.C. 20585 (202) 586-8800; *Annual Energy Review, Monthly Energy Review, Petroleum Supply Annual*, and *International Energy Annual*.

U.S. Department of the Interior, Bureau of Mines, 810 Seventh Street, NW, Washington, D.C. 20241 (202) 501-9649; *Annual Reports*.

PETROLEUM AND PRODUCTS - CRUDE OIL - LEASE REVENUES

U.S. Department of Energy, Energy Information Administration, Washington, D.C. 20585 (202) 586-8800; *Petroleum Supply Annual*.

U.S. Department of the Interior, Minerals Management Service, C Street between Eighteenth Street and Nineteenth Streets, NW, Washington, D.C. 20240 (202) 3983; *Federal Offshore Statistics*.

PETROLEUM AND PRODUCTS - CRUDE OIL - PRICES

U.S. Department of Energy, Energy Information Administration, Washington, D.C. 20585 (202) 586-8800; *Monthly Energy Review, Annual Energy Review*, and *Petroleum Supply Annual*.

U.S. Department of Labor, Bureau of Labor Statistics, Two Massachusetts Avenue, NE, Washington, D.C. 20212 (202) 606-7828; *Producer Price Indexes*.

U.S. Department of the Interior, Bureau of Mines, 810 Seventh Street, NW, Washington, D.C. 20241 (202) 501-9649; *Annual Reports*, and *Mineral Commodity Summaries*.

PETROLEUM AND PRODUCTS - CRUDE OIL - PRODUCTION

U.S. Department of Energy, Energy Information Administration, Washington, D.C. 20585 (202) 586-8800; *Petroleum Supply Annual, Monthly Energy Review, Annual Energy Review, Natural Gas*

Monthly, Natural Gas Annual, Energy Data Reports, and *International Energy Annual.*

U.S. Department of the Interior, Bureau of Mines, 810 Seventh Street, NW, Washington, D.C. 20241 (202) 501-9649; *Annual Reports,* and *Mineral Commodity Summaries.*

U.S. Department of the Interior, Minerals Management Service, C Street between Eighteenth and Nineteenth Streets, NW, Washington, D.C. 20240 (202) 208-3983; *Federal Offshore Statistics.*

PETROLEUM AND PRODUCTS - CRUDE OIL - PRODUCTION - FOREIGN COUNTRIES

Statistical Office of the United Nations, Publishing Service, New York, New York 10017 (800) 253-9646; *Energy Statistics Yearbook.*

U.S. Department of the Interior, Bureau of Mines, 810 Seventh Street, NW, Washington, D.C. 20241 (202) 501-9649; *Mineral Commodity Summaries.*

PETROLEUM AND PRODUCTS - FOREIGN TRADE

U.S. Department of Commerce, Bureau of the Census, Suitland, Maryland 20233 (301) 763-4040; *U.S. Merchandise Trade: Exports, General Imports,* and *Imports for Consumption,* and *U.S. Merchandise Trade.*

U.S. Department of Energy, Energy Information Administration, Washington, D.C. 20585 (202) 586-8800; *Annual Energy Review, Monthly Energy Review, Petroleum Supply Annual, Petroleum Supply Monthly,* and *International Energy Annual.*

PETROLEUM AND PRODUCTS - INTERNATIONAL INVESTMENTS

U. S. Department of Commerce, Bureau of Economic Analysis, Fourteenth Street between Constitution Avenue and E Street, NW, Washington, D.C. 20230 (202) 606-9900; *Survey of Current Business.*

PETROLEUM AND PRODUCTS - NATURAL GAS PLANT LIQUID

U.S. Department of Energy, Energy Information Administration, Washington, D.C. 20585 (202) 586-8800; *International Energy Annual, Energy Data Reports, Petroleum Supply Annual, Natural Gas Annual,* and *Natural Gas Monthly.*

PETROLEUM AND PRODUCTS - RAILROAD - CARLOADINGS OF

Association of American Railroads, American Railroads Building, 50 F Street, NW, Washington, D.C. 20001 (202) 639-2100; *Freight Commodity Statistics,* and *Weekly Railroad Traffic.*

PETROLEUM AND PRODUCTS - REFINERIES

U.S. Department of Energy, Energy Information Administration, Washington, D.C. 20585 (202) 5868800; *Annual Energy Review,* and *Petroleum Supply Annual.*

PETROLEUM AND PRODUCTS - RESERVES

U.S. Department of the Interior, Minerals Management Service, C Street between Eighteenth and Nineteenth Street, NW, Washington, D.C. 20240 (202) 208-3983; *Federal Offshore Statistics.*

PETROLEUM AND PRODUCTS - STOCKS

U.S. Department of Energy, Energy Information Administration, Washington, D.C. 20585 (202) 586-8800; *Monthly Energy Review,*

Annual Energy Review, and *Petroleum Supply Annual.*

PETROLEUM AND PRODUCTS - WELLS

American Petroleum Institute, 1220 L Street, NW, Washington, D.C. 20005 (202) 682-8000; Independent Petroleum Association of America, 1101 Sixteenth, NW, Washington, D.C. 20036 (202) 857-4722; Mid-Continent Oil and Gas Association, 801 Pennsylvania Avenue, NW, Suite 840, Washington, D.C. 20004 (202) 638-4400; *Joint Association Survey on Drilling Costs.*

U.S. Department of Energy, Energy Information Administration, Washington, D.C. 20585 (202) 586-8800; *Natural Gas Annual, Natural Gas Monthly, Petroleum Statement,* and *Petroleum Supply Annual,* and *Annual Energy Review.*

U.S. Department of Interior, Minerals Management Service, C Street between Eighteenth and Nineteenth Street, NW, Washington, D.C. 20240 (202) 208-3983; *Federal Offshore Statistics.*

PETROLEUM AND PRODUCTS - WELLS - DRILLING COSTS

American Petroleum Institute, 1220 L Street, NW, Washington, D.C. 20005 (202) 682-8000; Independent Petroleum Association of America, 1101 Sixteenth Street, NW, Washington, D.C. 20036 (202) 857-4722; Mid-Continent Oil and Gas Association, 801 Pennsylvania Avenue, NW, Suite 840, Washington, D.C. 20004 (202) 638-4400; *Joint Association Survey on Drilling Costs.*

PETROLEUM AND PRODUCTS - WELLS - LEASES AND PRODUCTION

U.S. Department of the Interior, Minerals Management Service, C Street between Eighteenth and Nineteenth Streets, NW, Washington, D.C. 20240 (202) 208-3983; *Federal Offshore Statistics.*

PETROLEUM AND PRODUCTS - WELLS - NUMBER AND PRODUCTION (OIL)

American Petroleum Institute, 1220 L Street, NW, Washington, D.C. 20005 (202) 682-8000; Independent Petroleum Association of America, 1101 Sixteenth Street, NW, Washington, D.C. 20036 (202) 857-4722; Mid-Continent Oil and Gas Association, 801 Pennsylvania Avenue, NW, Suite 840, Washington, D.C. 20004 (202) 638-4400; *Joint Association Survey on Drilling Costs.*

U.S. Department of the Interior, Minerals Management Service, C Street between Eighteenth and Nineteenth Streets, NW, Washington, D.C. 20240 (202) 208-3983; *Federal Offshore Statistics.*

PHARMACEUTICAL PREPS

U.S. Department of Commerce, Bureau of the Census, Suitland, Maryland 20233 (301) 763-4040; *Current Industrial Reports.*

PHARMACISTS

U.S. Department of Labor, Bureau of Labor Statistics, Two Massachusetts Avenue, NE, Washington, D.C. 20212 (202) 606-7828; *Employment and Earnings.*

PHILANTHROPY

American Association of Fund Raising Counsel Trust for Philanthropy, 25 West 43rd Street, Suite 820, New York, New York 10036 (212) 354-5799; *Giving U.S.A.*

The Conference Board, 845 Third Avenue, New York, New York 10022 (212) 759-0900; *Annual Survey of Corporate Contributions.*

The Foundation Center, 79 Fifth Avenue, New York, New York 10003 (212) 620-4230; *Foundation Grants Index*, and *Guide to U.S. Foundations*.

Independent Sector, 1828 L Street, NW, Washington, D.C. 20036 (202) 223-8100; *Giving and Volunteering in the United States*.

PHILANTHROPY - CORPORATE

The Conference Board, Incorporated, 845 Third Avenue, New York, New York 10022 (212) 759-0900; *Annual Survey of Corporate Contributions*.

PHILANTHROPY - EXPENDITURES - HEALTH

U.S. Department of Health and Human Services, Health Care Financing Administration, 200 Independence Avenue, SW, Washington, D.C. 20201 (202) 245-6113; *Health Care Financing Review*.

Philippines - National Statistical Office

National Statistical Coordination Board, Marvin Plaza Building, 2153 Pasong Tamo Street, Makati, Metro Manila, Republic of the Philippines.

Philippines - Primary Statistics Sources

Publications Division, Bureau of the Census and Statistics, Post Office Box 779, Manila, Philippines; *Statistical Pocketbook of the Philippines, Journal of Philippine Statistics, Philippine Statistical Yearbook*, and *Philippine Yearbook*.

PHILIPPINES - AGRICULTURE

Asian Development Bank, Post Office Box 789, 1099 Manila, Philippines; *Key Indicators of Developing Asian and Pacific Countries*.

Euromonitor Publications Limited, 87-88 Turnmill Street, London EC1M 5QU, England; *International Marketing Data and Statistics*, and *The Pacific Basin: An Economic Handbook*.

Facts on File, 460 Park Avenue South, New York, New York 10016 (800) 443-8323; *The New Book of World Rankings*.

Food and Agricultural Organization of the United Nations (FAO), Via delle Terme di Caracalla, 00100 Rome, Italy (Telephone Number in U.S. (202) 653-2400); *Production Yearbook, The State of Food and Agriculture*, and *Trade Yearbook*.

G.K. Hall and Company, 70 Lincoln Street, Boston, Massachusetts 02111 (617) 423-3990; *The World in Figures*.

Statistical Office of the United Nations, Publishing Service, New York, New York 10017 (800) 253-9646; *Statistical Yearbook*, and *Statistical Yearbook for Asia and the Pacific*.

Times Books, 201 East 50th Street, New York, New York 10022 (212) 751-2600; *The Economist Book of Vital World Statistics*.

The World Bank, 1818 H Street, NW, Washington, D.C. 20433 (202) 477-1234; *World Tables*.

PHILIPPINES - AIRLINE SERVICE

The Economist Intelligence Unit (Asia) Limited, 10th Floor, Luk Kwok Centre, 72 Gloucester Road, Wanchai, Hong Kong (Phone

Number in U.S. (800) 938-4685); *Asian Market Atlas*.

Facts on File, 460 Park Avenue South, New York, New York 10016 (800) 443-8323; *The New Book of World Rankings*.

G.K. Hall and Company, 70 Lincoln Street, Boston, Massachusetts 02111 (617) 423-3990; *The World in Figures*.

International Civil Aviation Organization, 1000 Sherbrooke Street, West, Montreal, Quebec, Canada H3A 2R2 (514) 285-8219; *Civil Aviation Statistics of the World*.

Statistical Office of the United Nations, Publishing Service, New York, New York 10017 (800) 253-9646; *Statistical Yearbook*.

Times Books, 201 East 50th Street, New York, New York 10022 (212) 751-2600; *The Economist Book of Vital World Statistics*.

PHILIPPINES - ALUMINUM PRODUCTION AND CONSUMPTION - See PHILIPPINES - MINING AND MINERAL PRODUCTS

PHILIPPINES - ANIMAL HEALTH

Food and Agricultural Organization of the United Nations (FAO), Via delle Terme di Caracalla, 00100 Rome, Italy (Telephone Number in U.S. (202) 653-2400); *Animal Health Yearbook*.

PHILIPPINES - ANTIMONY AND ANTIMONY ORE PRODUCTION AND CONSUMPTION - See PHILIPPINES - MINING AND MINERAL PRODUCTS

PHILIPPINES - AREA AND DENSITY OF POPULATION

Euromonitor Publications Limited, 87-88 Turnmill Street, London EC1M 5QU, England; *International Marketing Data and Statistics*, and *The Pacific Basin: An Economic Handbook*.

Facts on File, 460 Park Avenue South, New York, New York 10016 (800) 443-8323; *The New Book of World Rankings*.

Food and Agricultural Organization of the United Nations (FAO) Via delle Terme di Caracalla, 00100 Rome, Italy (Telephone Number in U.S. (202) 653-2400); *The State of Food and Agriculture*.

G.K. Hall and Company, 70 Lincoln Street, Boston, Massachusetts 02111 (617) 423-3990; *The World in Figures*.

Statistical Office of the United Nations, Publishing Service, New York, New York 10017 (800) 253-9646; *Statistical Yearbook*.

Times Books, 201 East 50th Street, New York, New York 10022 (212) 751-2600; *The Economist Book of Vital World Statistics*.

United Nations Educational, Scientific and Cultural Organization (UNESCO), 7 Place de Fontenoy, F-75700 Paris, France (Telephone Number in U.S. (212) 963-5981); *Statistical Yearbook*.

PHILIPPINES - ARMS EXPORTS AND IMPORTS

U.S. Arms Control and Disarmament Agency, 320 Twenty-first Street, NW, Washington, D.C. 20451 (202) 647-8677; *World Military Expenditures and Arms Transfers*.

PHILIPPINES - BALANCE OF PAYMENTS

The Economist Intelligence Unit, 111 West 57th Street, New York, New York 10019 (800) 938-4685; *The World Market Atlas*.

G.K. Hall and Company, 70 Lincoln Street, Boston, Massachusetts 02111 (617) 423-3990; *The World in Figures.*

International Monetary Fund, 700 Nineteenth Street, NW, Washington, D.C. 20431 (202) 623-7000; *Balance of Payments Yearbook*, and *International Financial Statistics.*

Times Books, 201 East 50th Street, New York, New York 10022 (212) 751-2600; *The Economist Book of Vital World Statistics.*

The World Bank, 1818 H Street, NW, Washington, D.C. 20433 (202) 477-1234; *World Tables.*

PHILIPPINES - BANKING

Asian Development Bank, Post Office Box 789, Manila, 1099 Manila, Philippines; *Key Indicators of Developing Asian and Pacific Countries.*

Facts on File, 460 Park Avenue South, New York, New York 10016 (800) 443-8323; *The New Book of World Rankings.*

G.K. Hall and Company, 70 Lincoln Street, Boston, Massachusetts 02111 (617) 423-3990; *The World in Figures.*

International Monetary Fund, 700 Nineteenth Street, NW, Washington, D.C. 20431 (202) 623-7000; *International Financial Statistics.*

Statistical Office of the United Nations, Publishing Service, New York, New York 10017 (800) 253-9646; *Statistical Yearbook.*

PHILIPPINES - BARLEY PRODUCTION - See PHILIPPINES - CROPS

PHILIPPINES - BAUXITE PRODUCTION AND CONSUMPTION - See PHILIPPINES - MINING AND MINERAL PRODUCTS

PHILIPPINES - BEER PRODUCTION

Facts on File, 460 Park Avenue South, New York, New York 10016 (800) 443-8323; *The New Book of World Rankings.*

Statistical Office of the United Nations, Publishing Service, New York, New York 10017 (800) 253-9646; *Statistical Yearbook.*

PHILIPPINES - BIRTH RATES

The Economist Intelligence Unit (Asia) Limited, 10th Floor, Luk Kwok Centre, 72 Gloucester Road, Wanchai, Hong Kong (Phone Number in U.S. (800) 938-4685); *Asian Market Atlas.*

Euromonitor Publications Limited, 87-88 Turnmill Street, London EC1M 5QU, England; *The Pacific Basin: An Economic Handbook.*

Facts on File, 460 Park Avenue South, New York, New York 10016 (800) 443-8323; *The New Book of World Rankings.*

Statistical Office of the United Nations, Publishing Service, New York, New York 10017 (800) 253-9646; *Demographic Yearbook*, and *Statistical Yearbook.*

Times Books, 201 East 50th Street, New York, New York 10022 (212) 751-2600; *The Economist Book of Vital World Statistics.*

The World Bank, 1818 H Street, NW, Washington, D.C. 20433 (202) 477-1234; *World Tables.*

World Health Organization, Office of Publications, Avenue Appia, CH-1211 Geneva 27, Switzerland (Telephone Number in U.S. (518)

436-9686); *World Health Statistics Annual.*

PHILIPPINES - BONDS

Asian Development Bank, Post Office Box 789, Manila, 1099 Manila, Philippines; *Key Indicators of Developing Asian and Pacific Countries.*

G.K. Hall and Company, 70 Lincoln Street, Boston, Massachusetts 02111 (617) 423-3990; *The World in Figures.*

International Monetary Fund, 700 Nineteenth Street, NW, Washington, D.C. 20431 (202) 623-7000; *Government Finance Statistics Yearbook.*

PHILIPPINES - BOOK PRODUCTION

United Nations Educational, Scientific and Cultural Organization (UNESCO), 7 Place de Fontenoy, F-75700 Paris, France (Telephone Number in U.S. (212) 963-5981); *Statistical Yearbook.*

PHILIPPINES - BROADCASTING

Billboard Limited, Post Office Box 9027, 1006 AA Amsterdam, The Netherlands (Telephone Number in U.S. (212) 764-7300); *World Radio TV Handbook.*

The Economist Intelligence Unit (Asia) Limited, 10th Floor, Luk Kwok Centre, 72 Gloucester Road, Wanchai, Hong Kong (Phone Number in U.S. (800) 938-4685); *Asian Market Atlas.*

Facts on File, 460 Park Avenue South, New York, New York 10016 (800) 443-8323; *The New Book of World Rankings.*

G.K. Hall and Company, 70 Lincoln Street, Boston, Massachusetts 02111 (617) 423-3990; *The World in Figures.*

Times Books, 201 East 50th Street, New York, New York 10022 (212) 751-2600; *The Economist Book of Vital World Statistics.*

PHILIPPINES - BUSINESS

G.K. Hall and Company, 70 Lincoln Street, Boston, Massachusetts 02111 (617) 423-3990; *The World in Figures.*

PHILIPPINES - BUSINESS AND PROFESSIONAL LICENSES

International Monetary Fund, 700 Nineteenth Street, NW, Washington, D.C. 20431 (202) 623-7000; *Government Finance Statistics Yearbook.*

PHILIPPINES - CABBAGE PRODUCTION - See PHILIPPINES - CROPS

PHILIPPINES - CADMIUM PRODUCTION AND CONSUMPTION - See PHILIPPINES - MINING AND MINERAL PRODUCTS

PHILIPPINES - CALORIE SUPPLY

Asian Development Bank, Post Office Box 789, Manila, 1099 Manila, Philippines; *Key Indicators of Developing Asian and Pacific Countries.*

Food and Agricultural Organization of the United Nations (FAO) Via delle Terme di Caracalla, 00100 Rome, Italy (Telephone Number in U.S. (202) 653-2400); *The State of Food and Agriculture.*

PHILIPPINES - CAPITAL INVESTMENT

Asian Development Bank, Post Office Box 789, Manila, 1099 Manila, Philippines; *Key Indicators of Developing Asian and Pacific Countries.*

PHILIPPINES - CAPITAL REVENUE

Asian Development Bank, Post Office Box 789, Manila, 1099 Manila, Philippines; *Key Indicators of Developing Asian and Pacific Countries.*

International Monetary Fund, 700 Nineteenth Street, NW, Washington, D.C. 20431 (202) 623-7000; *Government Finance Statistics Yearbook.*

PHILIPPINES - CASHEW NUT PRODUCTION - See PHILIPPINES - CROPS

PHILIPPINES - CASTOR BEAN PRODUCTION - See PHILIPPINES - CROPS

PHILIPPINES - CATTLE - See PHILIPPINES - LIVESTOCK AND POULTRY

PHILIPPINES - CAUSTIC SODA PRODUCTION

Statistical Office of the United Nations, Publishing Service, New York, New York 10017 (800) 253-9646; *Statistical Yearbook.*

PHILIPPINES - CEMENT PRODUCTION - See PHILIPPINES - MINING AND MINERAL PRODUCTS

PHILIPPINES - CHEMICAL (ORGANIC) PRODUCTION - See PHILIPPINES - MINING AND MINERAL PRODUCTS

PHILIPPINES - CHICKENS - See PHILIPPINES - LIVESTOCK AND POULTRY

PHILIPPINES - CHROMITE PRODUCTION AND CONSUMPTION - See PHILIPPINES - MINING AND MINERAL PRODUCTS

PHILIPPINES - CHROMIUM ORE PRODUCTION AND CONSUMPTION - See PHILIPPINES - MINING AND MINERAL PRODUCTS

PHILIPPINES - CIGAR AND CIGARETTE PRODUCTION - See PHILIPPINES - TOBACCO PRODUCTION

PHILIPPINES - CLASS STRUCTURE

G.K. Hall and Company, 70 Lincoln Street, Boston, Massachusetts 02111 (617) 423-3990; *The World in Figures.*

PHILIPPINES - CLIMATE

Facts on File, 460 Park Avenue South, New York, New York 10016 (800) 443-8323; *The New Book of World Rankings.*

G.K. Hall and Company, 70 Lincoln Street, Boston, Massachusetts 02111 (617) 423-3990; *The World in Figures.*

PHILIPPINES - CLOTHING EXPORTS AND IMPORTS

Statistical Office of the United Nations, Publishing Service, New York, New York 10017 (800) 253-9646; *Trade in Manufactures of Developing Countries.*

PHILIPPINES - COAL PRODUCTION - See PHILIPPINES - MINING AND MINERAL PRODUCTS

PHILIPPINES - COBALT PRODUCTION AND CONSUMPTION - See PHILIPPINES - MINING AND MINERAL PRODUCTS

PHILIPPINES - COCOA (BEANS) PRODUCTION - See PHILIPPINES - CROPS

PHILIPPINES - COCONUT PRODUCTS EXPORTS

International Monetary Fund, 700 Nineteenth Street, NW, Washington, D.C. 20431 (202) 623-7000; *International Financial Statistics.*

PHILIPPINES - COFFEE PRODUCTION AND CONSUMPTION - See PHILIPPINES - CROPS

PHILIPPINES - COMMUNICATIONS

G.K. Hall and Company, 70 Lincoln Street, Boston, Massachusetts 02111 (617) 423-3990; *The World in Figures.*

Statistical Office of the United Nations, Publishing Service, New York, New York 10017 (800) 253-9646; *Statistical Yearbook for Asia and the Pacific.*

PHILIPPINES - CONSTRUCTION INDUSTRY

Facts on File, 460 Park Avenue South, New York, New York 10016 (800) 443-8323; *The New Book of World Rankings.*

Statistical Office of the United Nations, Publishing Service, New York, New York 10017 (800) 253-9646; *Statistical Yearbook.*

PHILIPPINES - CONSUMER PRICE INDEX

Asian Development Bank, Post Office Box 789, Manila, 1099 Manila, Philippines; *Key Indicators of Developing Asian and Pacific Countries.*

G.K. Hall and Company, 70 Lincoln Street, Boston, Massachusetts 02111 (617) 423-3990; *The World in Figures.*

PHILIPPINES - CONSUMER PRICES

Times Books, 201 East 50th Street, New York, New York 10022 (212) 751-2600; *The Economist Book of Vital World Statistics.*

PHILIPPINES - CONSUMPTION

Euromonitor Publications Limited, 87-88 Turnmill Street, London EC1M 5QU, England; *The Pacific Basin: An Economic Handbook.*

G.K. Hall and Company, 70 Lincoln Street, Boston, Massachusetts 02111 (617) 423-3990; *The World in Figures.*

International Monetary Fund, 700 Nineteenth Street, NW, Washington, D.C. 20431 (202) 623-7000; *International Financial Statistics.*

PHILIPPINES - COPPER AND COPPER ORE PRODUCTION AND CONSUMPTION - See PHILIPPINES - MINING AND MINERAL PRODUCTS

PHILIPPINES - CORN PRODUCTION - See PHILIPPINES - CROPS

PHILIPPINES - CORPORATE TAXES - See PHILIPPINES - TAXATION

PHILIPPINES - COTTON - See PHILIPPINES - CROPS

PHILIPPINES - CRIME

International Criminal Police Organization (INTERPOL), 26 rue Armengaud, 92210 Saint Cloud, France; *International Crime Statistics*.

Yale University Press, Yale Station, New Haven, Connecticut 06520 (203) 432-0940; *Violence and Crime in Cross-National Perspective*.

PHILIPPINES - CROPS

Asian Development Bank, Post Office Box 789, Manila, 1099 Manila, Philippines; *Key Indicators of Developing Asian and Pacific Countries*.

Commodity Research Bureau, Incorporated, 75 Wall Street, New York, New York 10005 (212) 504-7754; *Commodity Year Book*.

Facts on File, 460 Park Avenue South, New York, New York 10016 (800) 443-8323; *The New Book of World Rankings*.

Food and Agricultural Organization of the United Nations (FAO) Via delle Terme di Caracalla, 00100 Rome, Italy (Telephone Number in U.S. (202) 653-2400); *Production Yearbook*, and *The State of Food and Agriculture*.

G.K. Hall and Company, 70 Lincoln Street, Boston, Massachusetts 02111 (617) 423-3990; *The World in Figures*.

Statistical Office of the United Nations, Publishing Service, New York, New York 10017 (800) 253-9646; *Statistical Yearbook*.

PHILIPPINES - CUSTOMS DUTIES

G.K. Hall and Company, 70 Lincoln Street, Boston, Massachusetts 02111 (617) 423-3990; *The World in Figures*.

International Monetary Fund, 700 Nineteenth Street, NW, Washington, D.C. 20431 (202) 623-7000; *Government Finance Statistics Yearbook*.

PHILIPPINES - DAIRY PRODUCTS

Facts on File, 460 Park Avenue South, New York, New York 10016 (800) 443-8323; *The New Book of World Rankings*.

Food and Agricultural Organization of the United Nations (FAO) Via delle Terme di Caracalla, 00100 Rome, Italy (Telephone Number in U.S. (202) 653-2400); *Production Yearbook*, and *The State of Food and Agriculture*.

PHILIPPINES - DEATH RATES

The Economist Intelligence Unit (Asia) Limited, 10th Floor, Luk Kwok Centre, 72 Gloucester Road, Wanchai, Hong Kong (Phone Number in U.S. (800) 938-4685); *Asian Market Atlas*.

Euromonitor Publications Limited, 87-88 Turnmill Street, London EC1M 5QU, England; *The Pacific Basin: An Economic Handbook*.

G.K. Hall and Company, 70 Lincoln Street, Boston, Massachusetts 02111 (617) 423-3990; *The World in Figures*.

Statistical Office of the United Nations, Publishing Service, New York, New York 10017 (800) 253-9646; *Statistical Yearbook*.

Times Books, 201 East 50th Street, New York, New York 10022 (212) 751-2600; *The Economist Book of Vital World Statistics*.

World Health Organization, Office of Publications, Avenue Appia, CH-1211 Geneva 27, Switzerland (Telephone Number in U.S. (518) 436-9686); *World Health Statistics Annual*.

PHILIPPINES - DEFENSE EXPENDITURES

G.K. Hall and Company, 70 Lincoln Street, Boston, Massachusetts 02111 (617) 423-3990; *The World in Figures*.

International Monetary Fund, 700 Nineteenth Street, NW, Washington, D.C. 20431 (202) 623-7000; *Government Finance Statistics Yearbook*.

U.S. Arms Control and Disarmament Agency, 320 Twenty-first Street, NW, Washington, D.C. 20451 (202) 647-8677; *World Military Expenditures and Arms Transfers*.

PHILIPPINES - DEMOGRAPHY

The Economist Intelligence Unit, 111 West 57th Street, New York, New York 10019 (800) 938-4685; *The World Market Atlas*.

The Economist Intelligence Unit (Asia) Limited, 10th Floor, Luk Kwok Centre, 72 Gloucester Road, Wanchai, Hong Kong (Phone Number in U.S. (800) 938-4685); *Asian Market Atlas*.

Facts on File, 460 Park Avenue South, New York, New York 10016 (800) 443-8323; *The New Book of World Rankings*.

G.K. Hall and Company, 70 Lincoln Street, Boston, Massachusetts 02111 (617) 423-3990; *The World in Figures*.

PHILIPPINES - DEVELOPMENT ASSISTANCE

Asian Development Bank, Post Office Box 789, Manila, 1099 Manila, Philippines; *Key Indicators of Developing Asian and Pacific Countries*.

G.K. Hall and Company, 70 Lincoln Street, Boston, Massachusetts 02111 (617) 423-3990; *The World in Figures*.

Statistical Office of the United Nations, Publishing Service, New York, New York 10017 (800) 253-9646; *Statistical Yearbook*.

PHILIPPINES - DIAMOND PRODUCTION - See PHILIPPINES - MINING AND MINERAL PRODUCTS

PHILIPPINES - DISEASES

G.K. Hall and Company, 70 Lincoln Street, Boston, Massachusetts 02111 (617) 423-3990; *The World in Figures*.

World Health Organization, Office of Publications, Avenue Appia, CH-1211 Geneva 27, Switzerland (Telephone Number in U.S. (518) 436-9686); *World Health Statistics Annual*.

PHILIPPINES - DIVORCE RATES

Facts on File, 460 Park Avenue South, New York, New York 10016 (800) 443-8323; *The New Book of World Rankings*.

Statistical Office of the United Nations, Publishing Service, New York, New York 10017 (800) 253-9646; *Demographic Yearbook*.

PHILIPPINES - DOMESTIC PRODUCT

G.K. Hall and Company, 70 Lincoln Street, Boston, Massachusetts 02111 (617) 423-3990; *The World in Figures.*

PHILIPPINES - DUCKS - See PHILIPPINES - LIVESTOCK AND POULTRY

PHILIPPINES - ECONOMY

Asian Development Bank, Post Office Box 789, Manila, 1099 Manila, Philippines; *Key Indicators of Developing Asian and Pacific Countries.*

Euromonitor Publications Limited, 87-88 Turnmill Street, London EC1M 5QU, England; *International Marketing Data and Statistics.*

Facts on File, 460 Park Avenue South, New York, New York 10016 (800) 443-8323; *The New Book of World Rankings.*

G.K. Hall and Company, 70 Lincoln Street, Boston, Massachusetts 02111 (617) 423-3990; *The World in Figures.*

PHILIPPINES - EDUCATION

The Economist Intelligence Unit, 111 West 57th Street, New York, New York 10019 (800) 938-4685; *The World Market Atlas.*

The Economist Intelligence Unit (Asia) Limited, 10th Floor, Luk Kwok Centre, 72 Gloucester Road, Wanchai, Hong Kong (Phone Number in U.S. (800) 938-4685); *Asian Market Atlas.*

Euromonitor Publications Limited, 87-88 Turnmill Street, London EC1M 5QU, England; *The Pacific Basin: An Economic Handbook.*

Facts on File, 460 Park Avenue South, New York, New York 10016 (800) 443-8323; *The New Book of World Rankings.*

G.K. Hall and Company, 70 Lincoln Street, Boston, Massachusetts 02111 (817) 423-3990; *The World in Figures.*

International Monetary Fund, 700 Nineteenth Street, NW, Washington, D.C. 20431 (202) 623-7000; *Government Finance Statistics Yearbook.*

Statistical Office of the United Nations, Publishing Service, New York, New York 10017 (800) 253-9646; *Statistical Yearbook for Asia and the Pacific.*

Times Books, 201 East 50th Street, New York, New York 10022 (212) 751-2600; *The Economist Book of Vital World Statistics.*

United Nations Educational, Scientific and Cultural Organization (UNESCO), 7 Place de Fontenoy, F-75700 Paris, France (Telephone Number in U.S. (212) 963-5981); *Statistical Yearbook.*

The World Bank, 1818 H Street, NW, Washington, D.C. 20433 (202) 477-1234; *World Tables.*

PHILIPPINES - EGG PRODUCTION AND CONSUMPTION - See PHILIPPINES - DAIRY PRODUCTS

PHILIPPINES - EGGPLANT PRODUCTION

Food and Agricultural Organization of the United Nations (FAO), Via delle Terme di Caracalla, 00100 Rome, Italy (Telephone Number in U.S. (202) 653-2400); *Production Yearbook.*

PHILIPPINES - ELECTRICITY

Asian Development Bank, Post Office Box 789, Manila, 1099 Manila, Philippines; *Key Indicators of Developing Asian and Pacific Countries.*

Facts on File, 460 Park Avenue South, New York, New York 10016 (800) 443-8323; *The New Book of World Rankings.*

Penn Well Publishing Company, 1421 South Sheridan Road, Post Office Box 1260, Tulsa, Oklahoma 74101 (800) 752-9764; *International Energy Statistics Sourcebook.*

Statistical Office of the United Nations, Publishing Service, New York, New York 10017 (800) 253-9646; *Statistical Yearbook.*

Times Books, 201 East 50th Street, New York, New York 10022 (212) 751-2600; *The Economist Book of Vital World Statistics.*

PHILIPPINES - EMPLOYMENT

Euromonitor Publications Limited, 87-88 Turnmill Street, London EC1M 5QU, England; *International Marketing Data and Statistics,* and *The Pacific Basin: An Economic Handbook.*

Facts on File, 460 Park Avenue South, New York, New York 10016 (800) 443-8323; *The New Book of World Rankings.*

International Labour Office, I.L.O. Publications, CH-1211, Geneva 22, Switzerland; *Yearbook of Labour Statistics.*

Statistical Office of the United Nations, Publishing Service, New York, New York 10017 (800) 253-9646; *Statistical Yearbook.*

PHILIPPINES - ENERGY

Facts on File, 460 Park Avenue South, New York, New York 10016 (800) 443-8323; *The New Book of World Rankings.*

Food and Agricultural Organization of the United Nations (FAO) Via delle Terme di Caracalla, 00100 Rome, Italy (Telephone Number in U.S. (202) 653-2400); *The State of Food and Agriculture.*

G.K. Hall and Company, 70 Lincoln Street, Boston, Massachusetts 02111 (617) 423-3990; *The World in Figures.*

Penn Well Publishing Company, 1421 South Sheridan Road, Post Office Box 1260, Tulsa, Oklahoma 74101 (800) 752-9764; *International Energy Statistics Sourcebook.*

Statistical Office of the United Nations, Publishing Service, New York, New York 10017 (800) 253-9646; *Energy Statistics Yearbook,* *Statistical Yearbook,* and *Statistical Yearbook for Asia and the Pacific.*

Times Books, 201 East 50th Street, New York, New York 10022 (212) 751-2600; *The Economist Book of Vital World Statistics.*

PHILIPPINES - ENGINEERING AND METAL PRODUCTS - EXPORTS AND IMPORTS

Statistical Office of the United Nations, Publishing Service, New York, New York 10017 (800) 253-9646; *Trade in Manufactures of Developing Countries.*

PHILIPPINES - EXCHANGE RATE

Asian Development Bank, Post Office Box 789, Manila, 1099 Manila, Philippines; *Key Indicators of Developing Asian and Pacific*

Countries.

The Economist Intelligence Unit (Asia) Limited, 10th Floor, Luk Kwok Centre, 72 Gloucester Road, Wanchai, Hong Kong (Phone Number in U.S. (800) 938-4685); *Asian Market Atlas.*

Euromonitor Publications Limited, 87-88 Turnmill Street, London EC1M 5QU, England; *International Marketing Data and Statistics,* and *The Pacific Basin: An Economic Handbook.*

International Civil Aviation Organization, 1000 Sherbrooke Street, West, Montreal, Quebec, Canada H3A 2R2 (514) 285-8219; *Civil Aviation Statistics of the World.*

International Monetary Fund, 700 Nineteenth Street, NW, Washington, D.C. 20431 (202) 623-7000; *International Financial Statistics.*

Statistical Office of the United Nations, Publishing Service, New York, New York 10017 (800) 253-9646; *Statistical Yearbook.*

PHILIPPINES - EXCISE TAXES - See PHILIPPINES - TAXATION

PHILIPPINES - EXPORTS

American Automobile Manufacturers Association, 1401 H Street, NW, Suite 900, Washington, D.C. 20005 (202) 326-5500; *World Motor Vehicle Data.*

Asian Development Bank, Post Office Box 789, Manila, 1099 Manila, Philippines; *Key Indicators of Developing Asian and Pacific Countries.*

The Economist Intelligence Unit, 111 West 57th Street, New York, New York 10019 (800) 938-4685; *The World Market Atlas.*

The Economist Intelligence Unit (Asia) Limited, 10th Floor, Luk Kwok Centre, 72 Gloucester Road, Wanchai, Hong Kong (Phone Number in U.S. (800) 938-4685); *Asian Market Atlas.*

Euromonitor Publications Limited, 87-88 Turnmill Street, London EC1M 5QU, England; *International Marketing Data and Statistics,* and *The Pacific Basin: An Economic Handbook.*

Food and Agricultural Organization of the United Nations (FAO) Via delle Terme di Caracalla, 00100 Rome, Italy (Telephone Number in U.S. (202) 653-2400); *The State of Food and Agriculture.*

G.K. Hall and Company, 70 Lincoln Street, Boston, Massachusetts 02111 (617) 423-3990; *The World in Figures.*

International Monetary Fund, 700 Nineteenth Street, NW, Washington, D.C. 20431 (202) 623-7000; *Direction of Trade Statistics, Government Finance Statistics Yearbook,* and *International Financial Statistics.*

Statistical Office of the United Nations, Publishing Service, New York, New York 10017 (800) 253-9646; *Foreign Trade Statistics of Asia and the Pacific.*

Times Books, 201 East 50th Street, New York, New York 10022 (212) 751-2600; *The Economist Book of Vital World Statistics.*

The World Bank, 1818 H Street, NW, Washington, D.C. 20433 (202) 477-1234; *World Tables.*

PHILIPPINES - EXTERNAL FINANCING

Asian Development Bank, Post Office Box 789, Manila, 1099 Manila, Philippines; *Key Indicators of Developing Asian and Pacific Countries.*

PHILIPPINES - EXTERNAL INDEBTEDNESS

Asian Development Bank, Post Office Box 789, Manila, 1099 Manila, Philippines; *Key Indicators of Developing Asian and Pacific Countries.*

The World Bank, 1818 H Street, NW, Washington, D.C. 20433 (202) 477-1234; *World Tables.*

PHILIPPINES - EXTERNAL TRADE

Asian Development Bank, Post Office Box 789, Manila, 1099 Manila, Philippines; *Key Indicators of Developing Asian and Pacific Countries.*

Food and Agricultural Organization of the United Nations (FAO), Via delle Terme di Caracalla, 00100 Rome, Italy (Telephone Number in U.S. (202) 653-2400); *Production Yearbook, The State of Food and Agriculture,* and *Trade Yearbook.*

G.K. Hall and Company, 70 Lincoln Street, Boston, Massachusetts 02111 (617) 423-3990; *The World in Figures.*

Statistical Office of the United Nations, Publishing Service, New York, New York 10017 (800) 253-9646; *Statistical Yearbook,* and *Statistical Yearbook for Asia and the Pacific.*

PHILIPPINES - FABRIC PRODUCTION - See PHILIPPINES - TEXTILE INDUSTRY

PHILIPPINES - FARM CROPS - See PHILIPPINES - CROPS

PHILIPPINES - FEMALE WORKING POPULATION - See PHILIPPINES - EMPLOYMENT

PHILIPPINES - FERTILITY RATES

The Economist Intelligence Unit (Asia) Limited, 10th Floor, Luk Kwok Centre, 72 Gloucester Road, Wanchai, Hong Kong (Phone Number in U.S. (800) 938-4685); *Asian Market Atlas.*

Facts on File, 460 Park Avenue South, New York, New York 10016 (800) 443-8323; *The New Book of World Rankings.*

Times Books, 201 East 50th Street, New York, New York 10022 (212) 751-2600; *The Economist Book of Vital World Statistics.*

The World Bank, 1818 H Street, NW, Washington, D.C. 20433 (202) 477-1234; *World Tables.*

PHILIPPINES - FERTILIZER

Food and Agricultural Organization of the United Nations (FAO), Via delle Terme di Caracalla, 00100 Rome, Italy (Telephone Number in U.S. (202) 653-2400); *Fertilizer Yearbook,* and *The State of Food and Agriculture.*

Statistical Office of the United Nations, Publishing Service, New York, New York 10017 (800) 253-9646; *Statistical Yearbook.*

PHILIPPINES - FETAL MORTALITY

Statistical Office of the United Nations, Publishing Service, New York, New York 10017 (800) 253-9646; *Demographic Yearbook.*

World Health Organization, Office of Publications, Avenue Appia, CH-1211 Geneva 27, Switzerland (Telephone Number in U.S. (518) 436-9686); *World Health Statistics Annual.*

PHILIPPINES - FIBRE PRODUCTION - See PHILIPPINES - TEXTILE INDUSTRY

PHILIPPINES - FILAMENT PRODUCTION - See PHILIPPINES - TEXTILE INDUSTRY

PHILIPPINES - FILM - See PHILIPPINES - MOTION PICTURES

PHILIPPINES - FINANCE

Asian Development Bank, Post Office Box 789, Manila, 1099 Manila, Philippines; *Key Indicators of Developing Asian and Pacific Countries.*

Euromonitor Publications Limited, 87-88 Turnmill Street, London EC1M 5QU, England; *The Pacific Basin: An Economic Handbook.*

Facts on File, 460 Park Avenue South, New York, New York 10016 (800) 443-8323; *The New Book of World Rankings.*

G.K. Hall and Company, 70 Lincoln Street, Boston, Massachusetts 02111 (617) 423-3990; *The World in Figures.*

International Monetary Fund, 700 Nineteenth Street, NW, Washington, D.C. 20431 (202) 623-7000; *Government Finance Statistics Yearbook.*

Statistical Office of the United Nations, Publishing Service, New York, New York 10017 (800) 253-9646; *Statistical Yearbook for Asia and the Pacific.*

PHILIPPINES - FISHERIES

Facts on File, 460 Park Avenue South, New York, New York 10016 (800) 443-8323; *The New Book of World Rankings.*

Food and Agricultural Organization of the United Nations (FAO) Via delle Terme di Caracalla, 00100 Rome, Italy (Telephone Number in U.S. (202) 653-2400); *The State of Food and Agriculture,* and *Yearbook of Fishery Statistics.*

Statistical Office of the United Nations, Publishing Service, New York, New York 10017 (800) 253-9646; *Statistical Yearbook.*

PHILIPPINES - FLOUR PRODUCTION

Statistical Office of the United Nations, Publishing Service, New York, New York 10017 (800) 253-9646; *Statistical Yearbook.*

PHILIPPINES - FOOD

Food and Agricultural Organization of the United Nations (FAO) Via delle Terme di Caracalla, 00100 Rome, Italy (Telephone Number in U.S. (202) 653-2400); *Production Yearbook,* and *The State of Food and Agriculture.*

G.K. Hall and Company, 70 Lincoln Street, Boston, Massachusetts 02111 (617) 423-3990; *The World in Figures.*

Statistical Office of the United Nations, Publishing Service, New York, New York 10017 (800) 253-9646; *Statistical Yearbook for Asia and the Pacific,* and *Trade in Manufactures of Developing Countries.*

PHILIPPINES - FOREIGN AID

G.K. Hall and Company, 70 Lincoln Street, Boston, Massachusetts 02111 (617) 423-3990; *The World in Figures.*

PHILIPPINES - FOREIGN DEBT

International Monetary Fund, 700 Nineteenth Street, NW, Washington, D.C. 20431 (202) 623-7000; *Government Finance Statistics Yearbook.*

PHILIPPINES - FOREIGN INDEBTEDNESS

Euromonitor Publications Limited, 87-88 Turnmill Street, London EC1M 5QU, England; *The Pacific Basin: An Economic Handbook.*

PHILIPPINES - FOREIGN TRADE

Asian Development Bank, Post Office Box 789, Manila, 1099 Manila, Philippines; *Key Indicators of Developing Asian and Pacific Countries.*

The Economist Intelligence Unit (Asia) Limited, 10th Floor, Luk Kwok Centre, 72 Gloucester Road, Wanchai, Hong Kong (Phone Number in U.S. (800) 938-4685); *Asian Market Atlas.*

Euromonitor Publications Limited, 87-88 Turnmill Street, London EC1M 5QU, England; *International Marketing Data and Statistics,* and *The Pacific Basin: An Economic Handbook.*

Facts on File, 460 Park Avenue South, New York, New York 10016 (800) 443-8323; *The New Book of World Rankings.*

Food and Agricultural Organization of the United Nations (FAO) Via delle Terme di Caracalla, 00100 Rome, Italy (Telephone Number in U.S. (202) 653-2400); *The State of Food and Agriculture.*

G.K. Hall and Company, 70 Lincoln Street, Boston, Massachusetts 02111 (617) 423-3990; *The World in Figures.*

Statistical Office of the United Nations, Publishing Service, New York, New York 10017 (800) 253-9646; *International Trade Statistics Yearbook,* and *Statistical Yearbook.*

The World Bank, 1818 H Street, NW, Washington, D.C. 20433 (202) 477-1234; *World Tables.*

World Bureau of Metal Statistics, 27-A High Street, Ware, Herts. SG12 9BA, England; *World Metal Statistics.*

PHILIPPINES - FORESTRY AND FOREST PRODUCTS

The Economist Intelligence Unit (Asia) Limited, 10th Floor, Luk Kwok Centre, 72 Gloucester Road, Wanchai, Hong Kong (Phone Number in U.S. (800) 938-4685); *Asian Market Atlas.*

Facts on File, 460 Park Avenue South, New York, New York 10016 (800) 443-8323; *The New Book of World Rankings.*

Food and Agricultural Organization of the United Nations (FAO) Via delle Terme di Caracalla, 00100 Rome, Italy (Telephone Number in U.S. (202) 653-2400); *The State of Food and Agriculture,* and *Yearbook of Forest Products.*

G.K. Hall and Company, 70 Lincoln Street, Boston, Massachusetts 02111 (617) 423-3990; *The World in Figures.*

Statistical Office of the United Nations, Publishing Service, New York, New York 10017 (800) 253-9646; *Statistical Yearbook.*

United Nations Educational, Scientific and Cultural Organization (UNESCO), 7 Place de Fontenoy, F-75700 Paris, France (Telephone Number in U.S. (212) 963-5981); *Statistical Yearbook.*

PHILIPPINES - FURNITURE AND WOOD PRODUCTS - EXPORTS AND IMPORTS

Statistical Office of the United Nations, Publishing Service, New York, New York 10017 (800) 253-9646; *Trade in Manufactures of Developing Countries.*

PHILIPPINES - GARLIC PRODUCTION - See PHILIPPINES - CROPS

PHILIPPINES - GAS PRODUCTION - See PHILIPPINES - MINING AND MINERAL PRODUCTS

PHILIPPINES - GENERAL INDUSTRIAL STATISTICS

Statistical Office of the United Nations, Publishing Service, New York, New York 10017 (800) 253-9646; *Industrial Statistics Yearbook.*

PHILIPPINES - GENERAL MORTALITY

Statistical Office of the United Nations, Publishing Service, New York, New York 10017 (800) 253-9646; *Demographic Yearbook.*

World Health Organization, Office of Publications, Avenue Appia, CH-1211 Geneva 27, Switzerland (Telephone Number in U.S. (518) 436-9686); *World Health Statistics Annual.*

PHILIPPINES - GEOGRAPHIC DATA

Facts on File, 460 Park Avenue South, New York, New York 10016 (800) 443-8323; *The New Book of World Rankings.*

PHILIPPINES - GOATS - See PHILIPPINES - LIVESTOCK AND POULTRY

PHILIPPINES - GOLD HOLDINGS

International Monetary Fund, 700 Nineteenth Street, NW, Washington, D.C. 20431 (202) 623-7000; *International Financial Statistics.*

Statistical Office of the United Nations, Publishing Service, New York, New York 10017 (800) 253-9646; *Statistical Yearbook.*

The World Bank, 1818 H Street, NW, Washington, D.C. 20433 (202) 477-1234; *World Tables.*

PHILIPPINES - GOLD PRODUCTION AND CONSUMPTION - See PHILIPPINES - MINING AND MINERAL PRODUCTS

PHILIPPINES - GOVERNMENT

Asian Development Bank, Post Office Box 789, Manila, 1099 Manila, Philippines; *Key Indicators of Developing Asian and Pacific Countries.*

G.K. Hall and Company, 70 Lincoln Street, Boston, Massachusetts 02111 (617) 423-3990; *The World in Figures.*

PHILIPPINES - GOVERNMENT CONSUMPTION

International Monetary Fund, 700 Nineteenth Street, NW, Washington, D.C. 20431 (202) 623-7000; *International Financial Statistics.*

PHILIPPINES - GOVERNMENT EXPENDITURES

Asian Development Bank, Post Office Box 789, Manila, 1099 Manila, Philippines; *Key Indicators of Developing Asian and Pacific Countries.*

International Monetary Fund, 700 Nineteenth Street, NW, Washington, D.C. 20431 (202) 623-7000; *Government Finance Statistics Yearbook.*

Times Books, 201 East 50th Street, New York, New York 10022 (212) 751-2600; *The Economist Book of Vital World Statistics.*

The World Bank, 1818 H Street, NW, Washington, D.C. 20433 (202) 477-1234; *World Tables.*

PHILIPPINES - GOVERNMENT FINANCES

Asian Development Bank, Post Office Box 789, Manila, 1099 Manila, Philippines; *Key Indicators of Developing Asian and Pacific Countries.*

International Monetary Fund, 700 Nineteenth Street, NW, Washington, D.C. 20431 (202) 623-7000; *International Financial Statistics.*

Statistical Office of the United Nations, Publishing Service, New York, New York 10017 (800) 253-9646; *Statistical Yearbook.*

PHILIPPINES - GOVERNMENT REVENUE

Asian Development Bank, Post Office Box 789, Manila, 1099 Manila, Philippines; *Key Indicators of Developing Asian and Pacific Countries.*

International Monetary Fund, 700 Nineteenth Street, NW, Washington, D.C. 20431 (202) 623-7000; *Government Finance Statistics Yearbook.*

Times Books, 201 East 50th Street, New York, New York 10022 (212) 751-2600; *The Economist Book of Vital World Statistics.*

The World Bank, 1818 H Street, NW, Washington, D.C. 20433 (202) 477-1234; *World Tables.*

PHILIPPINES - GRAIN PRODUCTION - See PHILIPPINES - CROPS

PHILIPPINES - GRANTS

International Monetary Fund, 700 Nineteenth Street, NW, Washington, D.C. 20431 (202) 623-7000; *Government Finance Statistics Yearbook.*

PHILIPPINES - GROSS DOMESTIC PRODUCT

Asian Development Bank, Post Office Box 789, Manila, 1099 Manila, Philippines; *Key Indicators of Developing Asian and Pacific Countries.*

The Economist Intelligence Unit, 111 West 57th Street, New York, New York 10019 (800) 938-4685; *The World Market Atlas.*

The Economist Intelligence Unit (Asia) Limited, 10th Floor, Luk Kwok Centre, 72 Gloucester Road, Wanchai, Hong Kong (Phone Number in U.S. (800) 938-4685); *Asian Market Atlas*.

Facts on File, 460 Park Avenue South, New York, New York 10016 (800) 443-8323; *The New Book of World Rankings*.

Euromonitor Publications Limited, 87-88 Turnmill Street, London EC1M 5QU, England; *International Marketing Data and Statistics*, and *The Pacific Basin: An Economic Handbook*.

G.K. Hall and Company, 70 Lincoln Street, Boston, Massachusetts 02111 (617) 423-3990; *The World in Figures*.

International Monetary Fund, 700 Nineteenth Street, NW, Washington, D.C. 20431 (202) 623-7000; *International Financial Statistics*.

Statistical Office of the United Nations, Publishing Service, New York, New York 10017 (800) 253-9646; *Statistical Yearbook*.

Times Books, 201 East 50th Street, New York, New York 10022 (212) 751-2600; *The Economist Book of Vital World Statistics*.

The World Bank, 1818 H Street, NW, Washington, D.C. 20433 (202) 477-1234; *World Tables*.

PHILIPPINES - GROSS NATIONAL PRODUCT

Asian Development Bank, Post Office Box 789, Manila, 1099 Manila, Philippines; *Key Indicators of Developing Asian and Pacific Countries*.

Euromonitor Publications Limited, 07-00 Turnmill Street, London EC1M 5QU, England; *International Marketing Data and Statistics*.

U.S. Arms Control and Disarmament Agency, 320 Twenty-first Street, NW, Washington, D.C. 20451 (202) 647-8677; *World Military Expenditures and Arms Transfers*.

The World Bank, 1818 H Street, NW, Washington, D.C. 20433 (202) 477-1234; *World Tables*.

PHILIPPINES - GROUNDNUT PRODUCTION - PHILIPPINES - CROPS

PHILIPPINES - HEALTH

The Economist Intelligence Unit (Asia) Limited, 10th Floor, Luk Kwok Centre, 72 Gloucester Road, Wanchai, Hong Kong (Phone Number in U.S. (800) 938-4685); *Asian Market Atlas*.

Euromonitor Publications Limited, 87-88 Turnmill Street, London EC1M 5QU, England; *The Pacific Basin: An Economic Handbook*.

Facts on File, 460 Park Avenue South, New York, New York 10016 (800) 443-8323; *The New Book of World Rankings*.

G.K. Hall and Company, 70 Lincoln Street, Boston, Massachusetts 02111 (617) 423-3990; *The World in Figures*.

Statistical Office of the United Nations, Publishing Service, New York, New York 10017 (800) 253-9646; *Statistical Yearbook*.

Times Books, 201 East 50th Street, New York, New York 10022 (212) 751-2600; *The Economist Book of Vital World Statistics*.

World Health Organization, Office of Publications, Avenue Appia, CH-1211 Geneva 27, Switzerland (Telephone Number in U.S. (518) 436-9686); *World Health Statistics Annual*.

PHILIPPINES - HEALTH EXPENDITURES

International Monetary Fund, 700 Nineteenth Street, NW, Washington, D.C. 20431 (202) 623-7000; *Government Finance Statistics Yearbook*.

PHILIPPINES - HIDE PRODUCTION

Food and Agricultural Organization of the United Nations (FAO), Via delle Terme di Caracalla, 00100 Rome, Italy (Telephone Number in U.S. (202) 653-2400); *Production Yearbook*.

PHILIPPINES - HIGHWAYS

The Economist Intelligence Unit (Asia) Limited, 10th Floor, Luk Kwok Centre, 72 Gloucester Road, Wanchai, Hong Kong (Phone Number in U.S. (800) 938-4685); *Asian Market Atlas*.

G.K. Hall and Company, 70 Lincoln Street, Boston, Massachusetts 02111 (617) 423-3990; *The World in Figures*.

International Road Federation, 525 School Street, SW, Washington, D.C. 20024 (202) 554-2106; *World Road Statistics*.

PHILIPPINES - HORSES - See PHILIPPINES - LIVESTOCK AND POULTRY

PHILIPPINES - HOURS OF WORK - See PHILIPPINES - EMPLOYMENT

PHILIPPINES - HOUSING AND HOUSING UNITS

Facts on File, 460 Park Avenue South, New York, New York 10016 (000) 443-0023; *The New Book of World Rankings*.

PHILIPPINES - HOUSING EXPENDITURES

International Monetary Fund, 700 Nineteenth Street, NW, Washington, D.C. 20431 (202) 623-7000; *Government Finance Statistics Yearbook*.

PHILIPPINES - HYDROCHLORIC ACID PRODUCTION

Statistical Office of the United Nations, Publishing Service, New York, New York 10017 (800) 253-9646; *Statistical Yearbook*.

PHILIPPINES - ILLITERATE POPULATION

The Economist Intelligence Unit, 111 West 57th Street, New York, New York 10019 (800) 938-4685; *The World Market Atlas*.

G.K. Hall and Company, 70 Lincoln Street, Boston, Massachusetts 02111 (617) 423-3990; *The World in Figures*.

United Nations Educational, Scientific and Cultural Organization (UNESCO), 7 Place de Fontenoy, F-75700 Paris, France (Telephone Number in U.S. (212) 963-5981); *Statistical Yearbook*.

PHILIPPINES - IMPORTS

American Automobile Manufacturers Association, 1401 H Street, NW, Suite 900, Washington, D.C. 20005 (202) 326-5500; *World Motor Vehicle Data*.

Asian Development Bank, Post Office Box 789, Manila, 1099 Manila, Philippines; *Key Indicators of Developing Asian and Pacific Countries*.

The Economist Intelligence Unit, 111 West 57th Street, New York, New York 10019 (800) 938-4685; *The World Market Atlas*.

The Economist Intelligence Unit (Asia) Limited, 10th Floor, Luk Kwok Centre, 72 Gloucester Road, Wanchai, Hong Kong (Phone Number in U.S. (800) 938-4685); *Asian Market Atlas.*

Euromonitor Publications Limited, 87-88 Turnmill Street, London EC1M 5QU, England; *International Marketing Data and Statistics, and The Pacific Basin: An Economic Handbook.*

Food and Agricultural Organization of the United Nations (FAO) Via delle Terme di Caracalla, 00100 Rome, Italy (Telephone Number in U.S. (202) 653-2400); *The State of Food and Agriculture.*

G.K. Hall and Company, 70 Lincoln Street, Boston, Massachusetts 02111 (617) 423-3990; *The World in Figures.*

International Monetary Fund, 700 Nineteenth Street, NW, Washington, D.C. 20431 (202) 623-7000; *Direction of Trade Statistics, Government Finance Statistics Yearbook,* and *International Financial Statistics.*

Statistical Office of the United Nations, Publishing Service, New York, New York 10017 (800) 253-9646; *Foreign Trade Statistics of Asia and the Pacific,* and *Trade in Manufactures of Developing Countries.*

Times Books, 201 East 50th Street, New York, New York 10022 (212) 751-2600; *The Economist Book of Vital World Statistics.*

The World Bank, 1818 H Street, NW, Washington, D.C. 20433 (202) 477-1234; *World Tables.*

PHILIPPINES - INCOME TAXES - See PHILIPPINES - TAXATION

PHILIPPINES - INDUSTRY

Euromonitor Publications Limited, 87-88 Turnmill Street, London EC1M 5QU, England; *International Marketing Data and Statistics.*

Facts on File, 460 Park Avenue South, New York, New York 10016 (800) 443-8323; *The New Book of World Rankings.*

G.K. Hall and Company, 70 Lincoln Street, Boston, Massachusetts 02111 (617) 423-3990; *The World in Figures.*

International Labour Office, I.L.O. Publications, CH-1211, Geneva 22, Switzerland; *Yearbook of Labour Statistics.*

Statistical Office of the United Nations, Publishing Service, New York, New York 10017 (800) 253-9646; *Statistical Yearbook,* and *Statistical Yearbook for Asia and the Pacific.*

Times Books, 201 East 50th Street, New York, New York 10022 (212) 751-2600; *The Economist Book of Vital World Statistics.*

The World Bank, 1818 H Street, NW, Washington, D.C. 20433 (202) 477-1234; *World Tables.*

World Intellectual Property Organization, 34 Chemin des Colombettes, CH-1211 Geneva 20, Switzerland; *Industrial Property Statistics.*

PHILIPPINES - INFANT AND MATERNAL MORTALITY

The Economist Intelligence Unit (Asia) Limited, 10th Floor, Luk Kwok Centre, 72 Gloucester Road, Wanchai, Hong Kong (Phone Number in U.S. (800) 938-4685); *Asian Market Atlas.*

Statistical Office of the United Nations, Publishing Service, New York, New York 10017 (800) 253-9646; *Demographic Yearbook,* and

Statistical Yearbook.

Times Books, 201 East 50th Street, New York, New York 10022 (212) 751-2600; *The Economist Book of Vital World Statistics.*

The World Bank, 1818 H Street, NW, Washington, D.C. 20433 (202) 477-1234; *World Tables.*

World Health Organization, Office of Publications, Avenue Appia, CH-1211 Geneva 27, Switzerland (Telephone Number in U.S. (518) 436-9686); *World Health Statistics Annual.*

PHILIPPINES - INTEREST RATES

Euromonitor Publications Limited, 87-88 Turnmill Street, London EC1M 5QU, England; *The Pacific Basin: An Economic Handbook.*

PHILIPPINES - INTERNAL TRADE

Statistical Office of the United Nations, Publishing Service, New York, New York 10017 (800) 253-9646; *Statistical Yearbook for Asia and the Pacific.*

PHILIPPINES - INTERNATIONAL LIQUIDITY

International Monetary Fund, 700 Nineteenth Street, NW, Washington, D.C. 20431 (202) 623-7000; *International Financial Statistics.*

PHILIPPINES - INTERNATIONAL RESERVES EXCLUDING GOLD

Asian Development Bank, Post Office Box 789, Manila, 1099 Manila, Philippines; *Key Indicators of Developing Asian and Pacific Countries.*

Statistical Office of the United Nations, Publishing Service, New York, New York 10017 (800) 253-9646; *Statistical Yearbook.*

The World Bank, 1818 H Street, NW, Washington, D.C. 20433 (202) 477-1234; *World Tables.*

PHILIPPINES - INTERNATIONAL STATISTICS

Asian Development Bank, Post Office Box 789, Manila, 1099 Manila, Philippines; *Key Indicators of Developing Asian and Pacific Countries.*

PHILIPPINES - INVESTMENTS

International Monetary Fund, 700 Nineteenth Street, NW, Washington, D.C. 20431 (202) 623-7000; *International Financial Statistics.*

PHILIPPINES - IRON ORE PRODUCTION AND CONSUMPTION - See PHILIPPINES - MINING AND MINERAL PRODUCTS

PHILIPPINES - IRRIGATION

Euromonitor Publications Limited, 87-88 Turnmill Street, London EC1M 5QU, England; *International Marketing Data and Statistics.*

PHILIPPINES - LABOR FORCE

The Economist Intelligence Unit (Asia) Limited, 10th Floor, Luk Kwok Centre, 72 Gloucester Road, Wanchai, Hong Kong (Phone Number in U.S. (800) 938-4685); *Asian Market Atlas.*

Euromonitor Publications Limited, 87-88 Turnmill Street, London EC1M 5QU, England; *International Marketing Data and Statistics*, and *The Pacific Basin: An Economic Handbook*.

Facts on File, 460 Park Avenue South, New York, New York 10016 (800) 443-8323; *The New Book of World Rankings*.

Food and Agricultural Organization of the United Nations (FAO) Via delle Terme di Caracalla, 00100 Rome, Italy (Telephone Number in U.S. (202) 653-2400); *The State of Food and Agriculture*.

G.K. Hall and Company, 70 Lincoln Street, Boston, Massachusetts 02111 (617) 423-3990; *The World in Figures*.

Times Books, 201 East 50th Street, New York, New York 10022 (212) 751-2600; *The Economist Book of Vital World Statistics*.

The World Bank, 1818 H Street, NW, Washington, D.C. 20433 (202) 477-1234; *World Tables*.

PHILIPPINES - LABOR PRODUCTIVITY

International Labour Office, I.L.O. Publications, CH-1211, Geneva 22, Switzerland; *Yearbook of Labour Statistics*.

PHILIPPINES - LAND USE

Euromonitor Publications Limited, 87-88 Turnmill Street, London EC1M 5QU, England; *International Marketing Data and Statistics*.

Food and Agricultural Organization of the United Nations (FAO), Via delle Terme di Caracalla, 00100 Rome, Italy (Telephone Number in U.S. (202) 653-2400); *Production Yearbook*.

G.K. Hall and Company, 70 Lincoln Street, Boston, Massachusetts 02111 (617) 423-3990; *The World in Figures*.

PHILIPPINES - LEAD AND LEAD ORE PRODUCTION AND CONSUMPTION - See PHILIPPINES - MINING AND MINERAL PRODUCTS

PHILIPPINES - LIBRARIES

Facts on File, 460 Park Avenue South, New York, New York 10016 (800) 443-8323; *The New Book of World Rankings*.

United Nations Educational, Scientific and Cultural Organization (UNESCO), 7 Place de Fontenoy, F-75700 Paris, France (Telephone Number in U.S. (212) 963-5981); *Statistical Yearbook*.

PHILIPPINES - LIFE EXPECTANCY

The Economist Intelligence Unit (Asia) Limited, 10th Floor, Luk Kwok Centre, 72 Gloucester Road, Wanchai, Hong Kong (Phone Number in U.S. (800) 938-4685); *Asian Market Atlas*.

PHILIPPINES - LIGNITE PRODUCTION - See PHILIPPINES - MINING AND MINERAL PRODUCTS

PHILIPPINES - LIVESTOCK AND POULTRY

Commodity Research Bureau, Incorporated, 75 Wall Street, New York, New York 10005 (212) 504-7754; *Commodity Year Book*.

Euromonitor Publications Limited, 87-88 Turnmill Street, London EC1M 5QU, England; *International Marketing Data and Statistics*.

Facts on File, 460 Park Avenue South, New York, New York 10016 (800) 443-8323; *The New Book of World Rankings*.

Food and Agricultural Organization of the United Nations (FAO), Via delle Terme di Caracalla, 00100 Rome, Italy (Telephone Number in U.S. (202) 653-2400); *Production Yearbook*, and *The State of Food and Agriculture*.

G.K. Hall and Company, 70 Lincoln Street, Boston, Massachusetts 02111 (617) 423-3990; *The World in Figures*.

Statistical Office of the United Nations, Publishing Service, New York, New York 10017 (800) 253-9646; *Statistical Yearbook*.

PHILIPPINES - LIVING LEVELS

G.K. Hall and Company, 70 Lincoln Street, Boston, Massachusetts 02111 (617) 423-3990; *The World in Figures*.

Times Books, 201 East 50th Street, New York, New York 10022 (212) 751-2600; *The Economist Book of Vital World Statistics*.

PHILIPPINES - MANGANESE ORE PRODUCTION AND CONSUMPTION - See PHILIPPINES - MINING AND MINERAL PRODUCTS

PHILIPPINES - MANPOWER

Statistical Office of the United Nations, Publishing Service, New York, New York 10017 (800) 253-9646; *Statistical Yearbook for Asia and the Pacific*.

PHILIPPINES - MANUFACTURING

American Automobile Manufacturers Association, 1401 H Street, NW, Suite 900, Washington, D.C. 20005 (202) 326-5500; *World Motor Vehicle Data*.

Facts on File, 460 Park Avenue South, New York, New York 10016 (800) 443-8323; *The New Book of World Rankings*.

G.K. Hall and Company, 70 Lincoln Street, Boston, Massachusetts 02111 (617) 423-3990; *The World in Figures*.

Statistical Office of the United Nations, Publishing Service, New York, New York 10017 (800) 253-9646; *Statistical Yearbook*.

Times Books, 201 East 50th Street, New York, New York 10022 (212) 751-2600; *The Economist Book of Vital World Statistics*.

The World Bank, 1818 H Street, NW, Washington, D.C. 20433 (202) 477-1234; *World Tables*.

PHILIPPINES - MARRIAGE RATES

Facts on File, 460 Park Avenue South, New York, New York 10016 (800) 443-8323; *The New Book of World Rankings*.

Statistical Office of the United Nations, Publishing Service, New York, New York 10017 (800) 253-9646; *Demographic Yearbook*, and *Statistical Yearbook*.

PHILIPPINES - MEAT PRODUCTION - See PHILIPPINES - LIVESTOCK AND POULTRY

PHILIPPINES - MERCHANT SHIPPING

G.K. Hall and Company, 70 Lincoln Street, Boston, Massachusetts 02111 (617) 423-3990; *The World in Figures*.

Lloyd's Register of Shipping, 17 Battery Place, New York, New York 10004 (212) 425-8050; *Register of Ships*.

Statistical Office of the United Nations, Publishing Service, New York, New York 10017 (800) 253-9646; *Statistical Yearbook.*

Times Books, 201 East 50th Street, New York, New York 10022 (212) 751-2600; *The Economist Book of Vital World Statistics.*

U.S. Department of Transportation, Maritime Administration, 400 Seventh Street, SW, Washington, D.C. 20590 (202) 366-5807; *A Statistical Analysis of the World's Merchant Fleets.*

PHILIPPINES - MERCURY PRODUCTION AND CONSUMPTION - See PHILIPPINES - MINING AND MINERAL PRODUCTS

PHILIPPINES - MILITARY

The Economist Intelligence Unit (Asia) Limited, 10th Floor, Luk Kwok Centre, 72 Gloucester Road, Wanchai, Hong Kong (Phone Number in U.S. (800) 938-4685); *Asian Market Atlas.*

G.K. Hall and Company, 70 Lincoln Street, Boston, Massachusetts 02111 (617) 423-3990; *The World in Figures.*

The International Institute for Strategic Studies, 23 Tavistock Street, London WC2E 7NQ, England; *The Military Balance.*

U.S. Arms Control and Disarmament Agency, 320 Twenty-first Street, NW, Washington, D.C. 20451 (202) 647-8677; *World Military Expenditures and Arms Transfers.*

PHILIPPINES - MILK PRODUCTION - See PHILIPPINES - DAIRY PRODUCTS

PHILIPPINES - MINING AND MINERAL PRODUCTS

Asian Development Bank, Post Office Box 789, Manila, 1099 Manila, Philippines; *Key Indicators of Developing Asian and Pacific Countries.*

Commodity Research Bureau, Incorporated, 75 Wall Street, New York, New York 10005 (212) 504-7754; *Commodity Year Book.*

Facts on File, 460 Park Avenue South, New York, New York 10016 (800) 443-8323; *The New Book of World Rankings.*

G.K. Hall and Company, 70 Lincoln Street, Boston, Massachusetts 02111 (617) 423-3990; *The World in Figures.*

International Monetary Fund, 700 Nineteenth Street, NW, Washington, D.C. 20431 (202) 623-7000; *International Financial Statistics.*

Penn Well Publishing Company, 1421 South Sheridan Road, Post Office Box 1260, Tulsa, Oklahoma 74101 (800) 752-9764; *International Energy Statistics Sourcebook.*

Statistical Office of the United Nations, Publishing Service, New York, New York 10017 (800) 253-9646; *Statistical Yearbook.*

World Bureau of Metal Statistics, 27-A High Street, Ware, Herts. SG12 9BA, England; *World Metal Statistics.*

PHILIPPINES - MOLASSES PRODUCTION - See PHILIPPINES - CROPS

PHILIPPINES - MOLYBDENUM AND MOLYBDENUM ORE PRODUCTION AND CONSUMPTION - See PHILIPPINES - MINING AND MINERAL PRODUCTS

PHILIPPINES - MONEY EXCHANGE RATE

Euromonitor Publications Limited, 87-88 Turnmill Street, London EC1M 5QU, England; *International Marketing Data and Statistics.*

International Monetary Fund, 700 Nineteenth Street, NW, Washington, D.C. 20431 (202) 623-7000; *International Financial Statistics.*

Statistical Office of the United Nations, Publishing Service, New York, New York 10017 (800) 253-9646; *Statistical Yearbook.*

PHILIPPINES - MONEY RESERVES

Euromonitor Publications Limited, 87-88 Turnmill Street, London EC1M 5QU, England; *International Marketing Data and Statistics.*

PHILIPPINES - MONEY SUPPLY

Asian Development Bank, Post Office Box 789, Manila, 1099 Manila, Philippines; *Key Indicators of Developing Asian and Pacific Countries.*

Euromonitor Publications Limited, 87-88 Turnmill Street, London EC1M 5QU, England; *International Marketing Data and Statistics.*

G.K. Hall and Company, 70 Lincoln Street, Boston, Massachusetts 02111 (617) 423-3990; *The World in Figures.*

International Monetary Fund, 700 Nineteenth Street, NW, Washington, D.C. 20431 (202) 623-7000; *International Financial Statistics.*

Statistical Office of the United Nations, Publishing Service, New York, New York 10017 (800) 253-9646; *Statistical Yearbook.*

The World Bank, 1818 H Street, NW, Washington, D.C. 20433 (202) 477-1234; *World Tables.*

PHILIPPINES - MONUMENTS AND HISTORICAL SITES

United Nations Educational, Scientific and Cultural Organization (UNESCO), 7 Place de Fontenoy, F-75700 Paris, France (Telephone Number in U.S. (212) 963-5981); *Statistical Yearbook.*

PHILIPPINES - MOTION PICTURES

Statistical Office of the United Nations, Publishing Service, New York, New York 10017 (800) 253-9646; *Statistical Yearbook.*

United Nations Educational, Scientific and Cultural Organization (UNESCO), 7 Place de Fontenoy, F-75700 Paris, France (Telephone Number in U.S. (212) 963-5981); *Statistical Yearbook.*

PHILIPPINES - MOTOR VEHICLE PRODUCTION

American Automobile Manufacturers Association, 1401 H Street, NW, Suite 900, Washington, D.C. 20005 (202) 326-5500; *World Motor Vehicle Data.*

Statistical Office of the United Nations, Publishing Service, New York, New York 10017 (800) 253-9646; *Statistical Yearbook.*

PHILIPPINES - MOTOR VEHICLE TAXES - See PHILIPPINES - TAXATION

PHILIPPINES - MOTOR VEHICLES IN USE

American Automobile Manufacturers Association, 1401 H Street, NW, Suite 900, Washington, D.C. 20005 (202) 326-5500; *World Motor Vehicle Data.*

G.K. Hall and Company, 70 Lincoln Street, Boston, Massachusetts 02111 (617) 423-3990; *The World in Figures.*

International Road Federation, 525 School Street, SW, Washington, D.C. 20024 (202) 554-2106; *World Road Statistics.*

Statistical Office of the United Nations, Publishing Service, New York, New York 10017 (800) 253-9646; *Statistical Yearbook.*

Times Books, 201 East 50th Street, New York, New York 10022 (212) 751-2600; *The Economist Book of Vital World Statistics.*

PHILIPPINES - MUSEUMS

Facts on File, 460 Park Avenue South, New York, New York 10016 (800) 443-8323; *The New Book of World Rankings.*

United Nations Educational, Scientific and Cultural Organization (UNESCO), 7 Place de Fontenoy, F-75700 Paris, France (Telephone Number in U.S. (212) 963-5981); *Statistical Yearbook.*

PHILIPPINES - NATALITY - See PHILIPPINES - BIRTH RATES

PHILIPPINES - NATIONAL ACCOUNTS

International Monetary Fund, 700 Nineteenth Street, NW, Washington, D.C. 20401 (202) 020-7000; *International Financial Statistics.*

Statistical Office of the United Nations, Publishing Service, New York, New York 10017 (800) 253-9646; *National Accounts Statistics, Statistical Yearbook,* and *Statistical Yearbook for Asia and the Pacific.*

PHILIPPINES - NATIONAL INCOME

Facts on File, 460 Park Avenue South, New York, New York 10016 (800) 443-8323; *The New Book of World Rankings.*

G.K. Hall and Company, 70 Lincoln Street, Boston, Massachusetts 02111 (617) 423-3990; *The World in Figures.*

Statistical Office of the United Nations, Publishing Service, New York, New York 10017 (800) 253-9646; *Statistical Yearbook.*

PHILIPPINES - NATIONAL PRODUCT

Facts on File, 460 Park Avenue South, New York, New York 10016 (800) 443-8323; *The New Book of World Rankings.*

Statistical Office of the United Nations, Publishing Service, New York, New York 10017 (800) 253-9646; *Statistical Yearbook.*

PHILIPPINES - NATURAL GAS PRODUCTION - See PHILIPPINES - MINING AND MINERAL PRODUCTS

PHILIPPINES - NATURAL RUBBER PRODUCTION

Statistical Office of the United Nations, Publishing Service, New York, New York 10017 (800) 253-9646; *Statistical Yearbook.*

PHILIPPINES - NEWSPAPER PRODUCTION - See PHILIPPINES - FORESTRY AND FOREST PRODUCTS

PHILIPPINES - NEWSPRINT - See PHILIPPINES - FORESTRY AND FOREST PRODUCTS

PHILIPPINES - NICKEL - See PHILIPPINES - MINING AND MINERAL PRODUCTS

PHILIPPINES - OCCUPATIONS - See PHILIPPINES - LABOR FORCE

PHILIPPINES - PALM KERNELS AND PALM OIL PRODUCTION - See PHILIPPINES - CROPS

PHILIPPINES - PAPER - See PHILIPPINES - FORESTRY AND FOREST PRODUCTS

PHILIPPINES - PATENTS

Statistical Office of the United Nations, Publishing Service, New York, New York 10017 (800) 253-9646; *Statistical Yearbook.*

World Intellectual Property Organization, 34 Chemin des Colombettes, CH-1211 Geneva 20, Switzerland; *Industrial Property Statistics.*

PHILIPPINES - PEANUT PRODUCTION - See PHILIPPINES - CROPS

PHILIPPINES - PERIODICALS

United Nations Educational, Scientific and Cultural Organization (UNESCO), 7 Place de Fontenoy, F-75700 Paris, France (Telephone Number in U.S. (212) 963-5981); *Statistical Yearbook.*

PHILIPPINES - PESTICIDE USE

Food and Agricultural Organization of the United Nations (FAO) Via delle Terme di Caracalla, 00100 Rome, Italy (Telephone Number in U.S. (202) 653-2400); *The State of Food and Agriculture.*

PHILIPPINES - PETROLEUM INDUSTRY

Asian Development Bank, Post Office Box 789, Manila, 1099 Manila, Philippines; *Key Indicators of Developing Asian and Pacific Countries.*

Facts on File, 460 Park Avenue South, New York, New York 10016 (800) 443-8323; *The New Book of World Rankings.*

Food and Agricultural Organization of the United Nations (FAO) Via delle Terme di Caracalla, 00100 Rome, Italy (Telephone Number in U.S. (202) 653-2400); *The State of Food and Agriculture.*

G.K. Hall and Company, 70 Lincoln Street, Boston, Massachusetts 02111 (617) 423-3990; *The World in Figures.*

Penn Well Publishing Company, 1421 South Sheridan Road, Post Office Box 1260, Tulsa, Oklahoma 74101 (800) 752-9764; *International Energy Statistics Sourcebook.*

Statistical Office of the United Nations, Publishing Service, New York, New York 10017 (800) 253-9646; *Statistical Yearbook.*

PHILIPPINES - PHOSPHATE ROCK PRODUCTION - See PHILIPPINES - MINING AND MINERAL PRODUCTS

PHILIPPINES - PIGS - See PHILIPPINES - LIVESTOCK AND POULTRY

PHILIPPINES - PLASTIC AND RESIN PRODUCTION

Statistical Office of the United Nations, Publishing Service, New York, New York 10017 (800) 253-9646; *Statistical Yearbook.*

PHILIPPINES - PLATINUM PRODUCTION AND CONSUMPTION - See PHILIPPINES - MINING AND MINERAL PRODUCTS

PHILIPPINES - POPULATION

Asian Development Bank, Post Office Box 789, Manila, 1099 Manila, Philippines; *Key Indicators of Developing Asian and Pacific Countries.*

The Economist Intelligence Unit, 111 West 57th Street, New York, New York 10019 (800) 938-4685; *The World Market Atlas.*

The Economist Intelligence Unit (Asia) Limited, 10th Floor, Luk Kwok Centre, 72 Gloucester Road, Wanchai, Hong Kong (Phone Number in U.S. (800) 938-4685; *Asian Market Atlas.*

Euromonitor Publications Limited, 87-88 Turnmill Street, London EC1M 5QU, England; *International Marketing Data and Statistics,* and *The Pacific Basin: An Economic Handbook.*

Facts on File, 460 Park Avenue South, New York, New York 10016 (800) 443-8323; *The New Book of World Rankings.*

Food and Agricultural Organization of the United Nations (FAO), Via delle Terme di Caracalla, 00100 Rome, Italy (Telephone Number in U.S. (202) 653-2400); *Production Yearbook.*

G.K. Hall and Company, 70 Lincoln Street, Boston, Massachusetts 02111 (617) 423-3990; *The World in Figures.*

International Labour Office, I.L.O. Publications, CH-1211, Geneva 22, Switzerland; *Yearbook of Labour Statistics.*

Statistical Office of the United Nations, Publishing Service, New York, New York 10017 (800) 253-9646; *Demographic Yearbook, Statistical Yearbook,* and *Statistical Yearbook for Asia and the Pacific.*

Times Books, 201 East 50th Street, New York, New York 10022 (212) 751-2600; *The Economist Book of Vital World Statistics.*

United Nations Educational, Scientific and Cultural Organization (UNESCO), 7 Place de Fontenoy, F-75700 Paris, France (Telephone Number in U.S. (212) 963-5981); *Statistical Yearbook.*

U.S. Arms Control and Disarmament Agency, 320 Twenty-first Street, NW, Washington, D.C. 20451 (202) 647-8677; *World Military Expenditures and Arms Transfers.*

World Health Organization, Office of Publications, Avenue Appia, CH-1211 Geneva 27, Switzerland (Telephone Number in U.S. (518) 436-9686); *World Health Statistics Annual.*

PHILIPPINES - POST OFFICES

Facts on File, 460 Park Avenue South, New York, New York 10016 (800) 443-8323; *The New Book of World Rankings.*

PHILIPPINES - POTATO PRODUCTION - See PHILIPPINES - CROPS

PHILIPPINES - PRICES

Asian Development Bank, Post Office Box 789, Manila, 1099 Manila, Philippines; *Key Indicators of Developing Asian and Pacific Countries.*

Facts on File, 460 Park Avenue South, New York, New York 10016 (800) 443-8323; *The New Book of World Rankings.*

Food and Agricultural Organization of the United Nations (FAO), Via delle Terme di Caracalla, 00100 Rome, Italy (Telephone Number in U.S. (202) 653-2400); *Production Yearbook,* and *The State of Food and Agriculture.*

G.K. Hall and Company, 70 Lincoln Street, Boston, Massachusetts 02111 (617) 423-3990; *The World in Figures.*

International Labour Office, I.L.O. Publications, CH-1211, Geneva 22, Switzerland; *Yearbook of Labour Statistics.*

International Monetary Fund, 700 Nineteenth Street, NW, Washington, D.C. 20431 (202) 623-7000; *International Financial Statistics.*

World Bureau of Metal Statistics, 27-A High Street, Ware, Herts. SG12 9BA, England; *World Metal Statistics.*

PHILIPPINES - PRINTING AND WRITING PAPER - See PHILIPPINES - FORESTRY AND FOREST PRODUCTS

PHILIPPINES - PRODUCTION

American Automobile Manufacturers Association, 1401 H Street, NW, Suite 900, Washington, D.C. 20005 (202) 326-5500; *World Motor Vehicle Data.*

Facts on File, 460 Park Avenue South, New York, New York 10016 (800) 443-8323; *The New Book of World Rankings.*

G.K. Hall and Company, 70 Lincoln Street, Boston, Massachusetts 02111 (617) 423-3990; *The World in Figures.*

PHILIPPINES - PRODUCTIVITY

Euromonitor Publications Limited, 87-88 Turnmill Street, London EC1M 5QU, England; *International Marketing Data and Statistics.*

PHILIPPINES - PROPERTY TAXES - See PHILIPPINES - TAXATION

PHILIPPINES - PUBLIC FINANCE

Facts on File, 460 Park Avenue South, New York, New York 10016 (800) 443-8323; *The New Book of World Rankings.*

PHILIPPINES - RADIO BROADCASTING - See PHILIPPINES - BROADCASTING

PHILIPPINES - RADIO RECEIVER PRODUCTION

Statistical Office of the United Nations, Publishing Service, New York, New York 10017 (800) 253-9646; *Statistical Yearbook.*

PHILIPPINES - RAILWAYS

G.K. Hall and Company, 70 Lincoln Street, Boston, Massachusetts 02111 (617) 423-3990; *The World in Figures.*

Jane's Information Group, Sentinel House, 163 Brighton Road, Coulsdon, Surrey CR5 2NH, England (Telephone Number in U.S. (703) 683-3700); *Jane's World Railways.*

Statistical Office of the United Nations, Publishing Service, New York, New York 10017 (800) 253-9646; *Statistical Yearbook.*

PHILIPPINES - RELIGION

Facts on File, 460 Park Avenue South, New York, New York 10016 (800) 443-8323; *The New Book of World Rankings.*

PHILIPPINES - RENT PRICES

International Labour Office, I.L.O. Publications, CH-1211, Geneva 22, Switzerland; *Yearbook of Labour Statistics.*

PHILIPPINES - RETAIL TRADE

G.K. Hall and Company, 70 Lincoln Street, Boston, Massachusetts 02111 (617) 423-3990; *The World in Figures.*

Statistical Office of the United Nations, Publishing Service, New York, New York 10017 (800) 253-9646; *Statistical Yearbook.*

PHILIPPINES - RICE PRODUCTION - See PHILIPPINES - CROPS

PHILIPPINES - ROOT AND TUBER PRODUCTION - See PHILIPPINES - CROPS

PHILIPPINES - ROUNDWOOD PRODUCTION - See PHILIPPINES - FORESTRY AND FOREST PRODUCTS

PHILIPPINES - RUBBER PRODUCTION AND CONSUMPTION

Facts on File, 460 Park Avenue South, New York, New York 10016 (800) 443-8323; *The New Book of World Rankings.*

Statistical Office of the United Nations, Publishing Service, New York, New York 10017 (800) 253-9646; *Statistical Yearbook.*

PHILIPPINES - SALT PRODUCTION - See PHILIPPINES - MINING AND MINERAL PRODUCTS

PHILIPPINES - SAWNWOOD PRODUCTION - See PHILIPPINES - FORESTRY AND FOREST PRODUCTS

PHILIPPINES - SCIENCE AND TECHNOLOGY - EXPENDITURE FOR RESEARCH

Statistical Office of the United Nations, Publishing Service, New York, New York 10017 (800) 253-9646; *Statistical Yearbook.*

PHILIPPINES - SCIENTISTS AND TECHNICIANS

Statistical Office of the United Nations, Publishing Service, New York, New York 10017 (800) 253-9646; *Statistical Yearbook.*

United Nations Educational, Scientific and Cultural Organization (UNESCO), 7 Place de Fontenoy, F-75700 Paris, France (Telephone Number in U.S. (212) 963-5981); *Statistical Yearbook.*

PHILIPPINES - SENIOR CITIZENS

Facts on File, 460 Park Avenue South, New York, New York 10016 (800) 443-8323; *The New Book of World Rankings.*

PHILIPPINES - SHEEP - See PHILIPPINES - LIVESTOCK AND POULTRY

PHILIPPINES - SILVER PRODUCTION AND CONSUMPTION - See PHILIPPINES - MINING AND MINERAL PRODUCTS

PHILIPPINES - SOCIAL DATA

Asian Development Bank, Post Office Box 789, Manila, 1099 Manila, Philippines; *Key Indicators of Developing Asian and Pacific Countries.*

Facts on File, 460 Park Avenue South, New York, New York 10016 (800) 443-8323; *The New Book of World Rankings.*

G.K. Hall and Company, 70 Lincoln Street, Boston, Massachusetts 02111 (617) 423-3990; *The World in Figures.*

PHILIPPINES - SOCIAL SECURITY

International Monetary Fund, 700 Nineteenth Street, NW, Washington, D.C. 20431 (202) 623-7000; *Government Finance Statistics Yearbook.*

PHILIPPINES - SOYBEAN PRODUCTION - See PHILIPPINES - CROPS

PHILIPPINES - STAMP TAXES AND DUTIES - See PHILIPPINES - TAXATION

PHILIPPINES - STATE BUDGET REVENUE AND EXPENDITURES

Euromonitor Publications Limited, 87-88 Turnmill Street, London EC1M 5QU, England; *International Marketing Data and Statistics.*

PHILIPPINES - STEEL - See PHILIPPINES - MINING AND MINERAL PRODUCTS

PHILIPPINES - STOCKS - COMMODITY - MARKET PRICE - INDEX

Food and Agricultural Organization of the United Nations (FAO) Via delle Terme di Caracalla, 00100 Rome, Italy (Telephone Number in U.S. (202) 653-2400); *The State of Food and Agriculture.*

World Bureau of Metal Statistics, 27 A High Street, Ware, Herts. SG12 9BA, England; *World Metal Statistics.*

PHILIPPINES - SUGAR PRODUCTION AND CONSUMPTION - See PHILIPPINES - CROPS

PHILIPPINES - SULPHURIC ACID PRODUCTION - See PHILIPPINES - MINING AND MINERAL PRODUCTS

PHILIPPINES - TAXATION

G.K. Hall and Company, 70 Lincoln Street, Boston, Massachusetts 02111 (617) 423-3990; *The World in Figures.*

International Monetary Fund, 700 Nineteenth Street, NW, Washington, D.C. 20431 (202) 623-7000; *Government Finance Statistics Yearbook.*

International Road Federation, 525 School Street, SW, Washington, D.C. 20024 (202) 554-2106; *World Road Statistics.*

The World Bank, 1818 H Street, NW, Washington, D.C. 20433 (202) 477-1234; *World Tables.*

PHILIPPINES - TELEPHONES IN USE

American Telephone and Telegraph Company, 26 Parsippany Road, Whippany, New Jersey 07981 (800) 338-4038; *The World's Telephones.*

The Economist Intelligence Unit (Asia) Limited, 10th Floor, Luk Kwok Centre, 72 Gloucester Road, Wanchai, Hong Kong (Phone Number in U.S. (800) 938-4685); *Asian Market Atlas.*

Euromonitor Publications Limited, 87-88 Turnmill Street, London EC1M 5QU, England; *The Pacific Basin: An Economic Handbook.*

G.K. Hall and Company, 70 Lincoln Street, Boston, Massachusetts 02111 (617) 423-3990; *The World in Figures.*

Statistical Office of the United Nations, Publishing Service, New York, New York 10017 (800) 253-9646; *Statistical Yearbook.*

PHILIPPINES - TELEVISION BROADCASTING - See PHILIPPINES - BROADCASTING

PHILIPPINES - TELEVISION RECEIVER PRODUCTION

Statistical Office of the United Nations, Publishing Service, New York, New York 10017 (800) 253-9646; *Statistical Yearbook.*

PHILIPPINES - TEXTILE INDUSTRY

American Forest and Paper Association, 1250 Connecticut Avenue, NW, Washington, D.C. 20036 (202) 463-2455; *Wood Pulp and Fiber Statistics.*

G.K. Hall and Company, 70 Lincoln Street, Boston, Massachusetts 02111 (617) 423-3990; *The World in Figures.*

Statistical Office of the United Nations, Publishing Service, New York, New York 10017 (800) 253-9646; *Statistical Yearbook,* and *Trade in Manufactures of Developing Countries.*

PHILIPPINES - THEATRE

United Nations Educational, Scientific and Cultural Organization (UNESCO), 7 Place de Fontenoy, F-75700 Paris, France (Telephone Number in U.S. (212) 963-5981); *Statistical Yearbook.*

PHILIPPINES - TIN PRODUCTION AND CONSUMPTION - See PHILIPPINES - MINING AND MINERAL PRODUCTS

PHILIPPINES - TIRE (MOTOR VEHICLE) PRODUCTION

Statistical Office of the United Nations, Publishing Service, New York, New York 10017 (800) 253-9646; *Statistical Yearbook.*

PHILIPPINES - TOBACCO PRODUCTION

Commodity Research Bureau, Incorporated, 75 Wall Street, New York, New York 10005 (212) 504-7754; *Commodity Year Book.*

Facts on File, 460 Park Avenue South, New York, New York 10016 (800) 443-8323; *The New Book of World Rankings.*

Statistical Office of the United Nations, Publishing Service, New York, New York 10017 (800) 253-9646; *Statistical Yearbook.*

PHILIPPINES - TOURISM

Euromonitor Publications Limited, 87-88 Turnmill Street, London EC1M 5QU, England; *The Pacific Basin: An Economic Handbook.*

Facts on File, 460 Park Avenue South, New York, New York 10016 (800) 443-8323; *The New Book of World Rankings.*

G.K. Hall and Company, 70 Lincoln Street, Boston, Massachusetts 02111 (617) 423-3990; *The World in Figures.*

Statistical Office of the United Nations, Publishing Service, New York, New York 10017 (800) 253-9646; *Statistical Yearbook.*

Times Books, 201 East 50th Street, New York, New York 10022 (212) 751-2600; *The Economist Book of Vital World Statistics.*

World Tourism Organization, Calle Capitan Haya 42, E-28020 Madrid, Spain; *Yearbook of Tourism Statistics.*

PHILIPPINES - TRACTORS IN USE

Statistical Office of the United Nations, Publishing Service, New York, New York 10017 (800) 253-9646; *Statistical Yearbook.*

PHILIPPINES - TRADE - See PHILIPPINES - FOREIGN TRADE

PHILIPPINES - TRADEMARKS AND SERVICE MARKS

Statistical Office of the United Nations, Publishing Service, New York, New York 10017 (800) 253-9646; *Statistical Yearbook.*

World Intellectual Property Organization, 34 Chemin des Colombettes, CH-1211 Geneva 20, Switzerland; *Industrial Property Statistics.*

PHILIPPINES - TRANSPORTATION AND COMMUNICATIONS

The Economist Intelligence Unit (Asia) Limited, 10th Floor, Luk Kwok Centre, 72 Gloucester Road, Wanchai, Hong Kong (Phone Number in U.S. (800) 938-4685); *Asian Market Atlas.*

Euromonitor Publications Limited, 87-88 Turnmill Street, London EC1M 5QU, England; *The Pacific Basin: An Economic Handbook.*

Facts on File, 460 Park Avenue South, New York, New York 10016 (800) 443-8323; *The New Book of World Rankings.*

G.K. Hall and Company, 70 Lincoln Street, Boston, Massachusetts 02111 (617) 423-3990; *The World in Figures.*

Statistical Office of the United Nations, Publishing Service, New York, New York 10017 (800) 253-9646; *Statistical Yearbook for Asia and the Pacific.*

PHILIPPINES - TURKEYS - See PHILIPPINES - LIVESTOCK AND POULTRY

PHILIPPINES - UNEMPLOYMENT

Euromonitor Publications Limited, 87-88 Turnmill Street, London EC1M 5QU, England; *International Marketing Data and Statistics,* and *The Pacific Basin: An Economic Handbook.*

International Labour Office, I.L.O. Publications, CH-1211, Geneva 22, Switzerland; *Yearbook of Labour Statistics.*

Statistical Office of the United Nations, Publishing Service, New York, New York 10017 (800) 253-9646; *Statistical Yearbook.*

PHILIPPINES - URANIUM PRODUCTION AND CONSUMPTION - See PHILIPPINES - MINING AND MINERAL PRODUCTS

PHILIPPINES - VITAL STATISTICS

Euromonitor Publications Limited, 87-88 Turnmill Street, London EC1M 5QU, England; *International Marketing Data and Statistics,* and *The Pacific Basin: An Economic Handbook.*

G.K. Hall and Company, 70 Lincoln Street, Boston, Massachusetts 02111 (617) 423-3990; *The World in Figures.*

Statistical Office of the United Nations, Publishing Service, New York, New York 10017 (800) 253-9646; *Statistical Yearbook.*

World Health Organization, Office of Publications, Avenue Appia, CH-1211 Geneva 27, Switzerland (Telephone Number in U.S. (518) 436-9686); *World Health Statistics Annual.*

PHILIPPINES - WAGES

G.K. Hall and Company, 70 Lincoln Street, Boston, Massachusetts 02111 (617) 423-3990; *The World in Figures.*

International Labour Office, I.L.O. Publications, CH-1211, Geneva 22, Switzerland; *Yearbook of Labour Statistics.*

Statistical Office of the United Nations, Publishing Service, New York, New York 10017 (800) 253-9646; *Statistical Yearbook,* and *Statistical Yearbook for Asia and the Pacific.*

PHILIPPINES - WATERMELON PRODUCTION - See PHILIPPINES - CROPS

PHILIPPINES - WEATHER

Facts on File, 460 Park Avenue South, New York, New York 10016 (800) 443-8323; *The New Book of World Rankings.*

G.K. Hall and Company, 70 Lincoln Street, Boston, Massachusetts 02111 (617) 423-3990; *The World in Figures.*

PHILIPPINES - WELFARE

International Monetary Fund, 700 Nineteenth Street, NW, Washington, D.C. 20431 (202) 623-7000; *Government Finance Statistics Yearbook.*

PHILIPPINES - WHEAT PRODUCTION AND PRICES - See PHILIPPINES - CROPS

PHILIPPINES - WHOLESALE PRICES

Asian Development Bank, Post Office Box 789, 1099 Manila, Philippines; *Key Indicators of Developing Asian and Pacific Countries*

International Monetary Fund, 700 Nineteenth Street, NW, Washington, D.C. 20431 (202) 623-7000; *International Financial Statistics.*

Statistical Office of the United Nations, Publishing Service, New York, New York 10017 (800) 253-9646; *Statistical Yearbook.*

PHILIPPINES - WHOLESALE TRADE

Statistical Office of the United Nations, Publishing Service, New York, New York 10017 (800) 253-9646; *Statistical Yearbook.*

PHILIPPINES - WINE PRODUCTION

Facts on File, 460 Park Avenue South, New York, New York 10016 (800) 443-8323; *The New Book of World Rankings.*

PHILIPPINES - WOOD AND WOOD PULP - See PHILIPPINES - FORESTRY AND FOREST PRODUCTS

PHILIPPINES - WOOL PRODUCTION

Facts on File, 460 Park Avenue South, New York, New York 10016 (800) 443-8323; *The New Book of World Rankings.*

PHILIPPINES - YARN PRODUCTION

Statistical Office of the United Nations, Publishing Service, New York, New York 10017 (800) 253-9646; *Statistical Yearbook.*

PHILIPPINES - ZINC AND ZINC ORE PRODUCTION AND CONSUMPTION - See PHILIPPINES - MINING AND MINERAL PRODUCTS

PHONOGRAPH RECORDS AND TAPES

Recording Industry Association of America, 1020 Nineteenth Street, NW, Suite 200, Washington, D.C. 20036 (202) 775-0101; *Inside the Recording Industry: A Statistical Overview.*

PHOSPHATE ROCK - CONSUMPTION

U.S. Department of the Interior, Bureau of Mines, 810 Seventh Street, NW, Washington, D.C. 20241 (202) 501-9649; *Mineral Commodity Summaries.*

PHOSPHATE ROCK - EMPLOYMENT

U.S. Department of the Interior, Bureau of Mines, 810 Seventh Street, NW, Washington, D.C. 20241 (202) 501-9649; *Mineral Commodity Summaries.*

PHOSPHATE ROCK - FOREIGN TRADE

U.S. Department of the Interior, Bureau of Mines, 810 Seventh Street, NW, Washington, D.C. 20241 (202) 501-9649; *Mineral Commodity Summaries.*

PHOSPHATE ROCK - PRICES

U.S. Department of the Interior, Bureau of Mines, 810 Seventh Street, NW, Washington, D.C. 20241 (202) 501-9649; *Mineral Commodity Summaries.*

PHOSPHATE ROCK - PRODUCTION AND VALUE

U.S. Department of the Interior, Bureau of Mines, 810 Seventh Street, NW, Washington, D.C. 20241 (202) 501-9649; *Annual Reports,* and *Mineral Commodity Summaries.*

PHOSPHATE ROCK - WORLD PRODUCTION

Statistical Office of the United Nations, Publishing Service, New York, New York 10017 (800) 253-9646; *Energy Statistics Yearbook.*

U.S. Department of the Interior, Bureau of Mines, 810 Seventh Street, NW, Washington, D.C. 20241 (202) 501-9649; *Mineral Commodity Summaries,* and *Annual Reports.*

PHOTOGRAPHIC EQUIPMENT AND SUPPLIES

U.S. Department of Commerce, Bureau of the Census, Suitland, Maryland 20233 (301) 763-4040; *U.S. Merchandise Trade: Exports, General Imports, and Imports for Consumption,* and *U.S. Merchandise Trade: Selected Highlights.*

PHYSICAL SCIENCES

U.S. National Science Foundation, 4201 Wilson Boulevard, Arlington, Virginia 22230 (703) 306-1234; *Characteristics of Doctoral Scientists and Engineers in the U.S.*

PHYSICAL SCIENCES - DEGREES CONFERRED

U.S. Department of Education, 400 Maryland Avenue, SW, Washington, D.C. 20202 (202) 708-5366, *Digest of Education Statistics.*

U.S. National Science Foundation, Division of Science Resources Studies, 4201 Wilson Boulevard, Arlington, Virginia 22230 (703) 306-1234; *Survey of Earned Doctorates, Selected Data on Science and Engineering Doctorate Awards,* and *Characteristics of Recent Science and Engineering Graduates.*

PHYSICAL SCIENCES - EMPLOYEES

U.S. Department of Labor, Bureau of Labor Statistics, Two Massachusetts Avenue, NE, Washington, D.C. 20212 (202) 606-7828; *Monthly Labor Review,* and *Employment and Earnings.*

PHYSICIANS

American Medical Association, 515 North State Street, Chicago, Illinois 60610 (312) 464-4818; *Physician Characteristics and Distribution in the United States.*

U.S. Department of Health and Human Services, Health Resources and Services Administration, 5600 Fishers Lane, Rockville, Maryland 20857 (301) 443-2086; unpublished data.

U.S. Department of Health and Human Services, National Center for Health Statistics, 3700 East-West Highway, Hyattsville, Maryland 20782 (301) 436-8500; *Vital and Health Statistics,* and unpublished data.

PHYSICIANS - DEGREES CONFERRED

U.S. Department of Education, 400 Maryland Avenue, SW, Washington, D.C. 20202 (202) 708-5366; *Digest of Education Statistics.*

PHYSICIANS - EARNINGS

American Medical Association, 515 North State Street, Chicago, Illinois 60610 (312) 464-4818; *Socioeconomic Characteristics of Medical Practice.*

PHYSICIANS - EMPLOYMENT

American Medical Association, 515 North State Street, Chicago, Illinois 60610 (312) 464-4818; *Physician Characteristics and Distribution in the United States.*

U.S. Department of Labor, Bureau of Labor Statistics, Two Massachusetts Avenue, NE, Washington, D.C. 20212 (202) 606-7828; *Employment and Earnings.*

PHYSICIANS - EMPLOYMENT - PROJECTIONS

U.S. Department of Labor, Bureau of Labor Statistics, Two Massachusetts Avenue, NE, Washington, D.C. 20212 (202) 606-7828; *Monthly Labor Review.*

PHYSICIANS - EXPENDITURES FOR

U.S. Department of Health and Human Services, Health Care Financing Administration, 200 Independence Avenue, SW, Washington, D.C. 20201 (202) 245-6113; *Health Care Financing Review.*

PHYSICIANS - FOREIGN MEDICAL SCHOOL GRADUATES

American Medical Association, 515 North State Street, Chicago, Illinois 60610 (312) 464-4818; *Physician Characteristics and Distribution in the United States.*

PHYSICIANS - MEDICAL SCHOOLS - STUDENTS AND GRADUATES

American Medical Association, 515 North State Street, Chicago, Illinois 60610 (312) 464-4818; *Physician Characteristics and Distribution in the United States.*

U.S. Department of Education, 400 Maryland Avenue, SW, Washington, D.C. 20202 (202) 708-5366; *Digest of Education Statistics.*

PHYSICIANS - OFFICES

U.S. Department of Commerce, Bureau of the Census, Suitland, Maryland 20233 (301) 763-4040; *County Business Patterns, Census of Service Industries,* and *Current Business Reports.*

PHYSICIANS - PRICE INDEX

U.S Department of Labor, Bureau of Labor Statistics, Two Massachusetts Avenue, NE, Washington, D.C. 20212 (202) 606-7828; *CPI Detailed Report,* and unpublished data.

PHYSICIANS - SPECIALTY AND PROFESSIONAL ACTIVITY

American Medical Association, 515 North State Street, Chicago, Illinois 60610 (312) 464-4818; *Physician Characteristics and Distribution in the United States.*

PHYSICIANS - TYPE OF PRACTICE

American Medical Association, 515 North State Street, Chicago, Illinois 60610 (312) 464-4818; *Physician Characteristics and Distribution in the United States.*

American Osteopathic Association, 142 East Ontario Street, Chicago, Illinois 60611 (312) 280-5800.

PHYSICIANS - VISITS TO

U.S. Department of Health and Human Services, National Center for Health Statistics, 3700 East-West Highway, Hyattsville, Maryland 20782 (301) 436-8500; *Vital and Health Statistics, Health, U.S.,* and unpublished data.

PHYSICS - See also PHYSICAL SCIENCES

PHYSICS - NOBEL PRIZE LAUREATES

U.S. National Science Foundation, 4201 Wilson Boulevard, Arlington, Virginia 22230 (703) 306-1234; unpublished data.

PHYSICS - SALARY OFFERS

College Placement Council, 62 Highland Avenue, Bethlehem, Pennsylvania 18017 (212) 868-1421; *Salary Survey: A Study of Beginning Offers.*

PHYSIOLOGY - NOBEL PRIZE LAUREATES

U.S. National Science Foundation, 4201 Wilson Boulevard, Arlington, Virginia 22230 (703) 306-1234; unpublished data.

PIG IRON - See IRON

PIGGYBACK - RAILROAD CARLOADS

Association of American Railroads, American Railroads Building, 50 F Street, NW, Washington, D.C. 20001 (202) 639-2100; *Weekly Railroad Traffic.*

PIGS - See HOGS

PILCHARD - See SARDINES

PINEAPPLES

U.S. Department of Agriculture, Economic Research Service, Fourteenth Street and Independence Avenue, SW, Washington, D.C. 20005-4789 (202) 219-1504; *Agricultural Outlook, Food Consumption, Prices, and Expenditures*, and unpublished data.

U.S. Department of Agriculture, National Agricultural Statistics Service, Fourteenth Street and Independence Avenue, SW, Washington, D.C. 20250 (202) 219-1504; *Citrus Fruits*.

PIPELINES - EXCEPT NATURAL GAS - CAPITAL

Pennwell Publishing Company, 1421 South Sheridan Road, Tulsa, Oklahoma 74101 (800) 752-9764; *Oil and Gas Journal*.

U.S. Department of Commerce, Bureau of Economic Analysis, Fourteenth Street between Constitution Avenue and E Street, NW, Washington, D.C. 20230 (202) 606-9900; *Fixed Reproducible Tangible Wealth in the United States*, and *Survey of Current Business*.

PIPELINES - EXCEPT NATURAL GAS - EARNINGS

U.S. Department of Labor, Bureau of Labor Statistics, Two Massachusetts Avenue, NE, Washington, D.C. 20212 (202) 606-7828; *Employment and Earnings*, and Bulletins 2370 and 2429.

PIPELINES - EXCEPT NATURAL GAS - EMPLOYEES

U.S. Department of Labor, Bureau of Labor Statistics, Two Massachusetts Avenue, NE, Washington, D.C. 20212 (202) 606-7828; *Employment and Earnings*, and Bulletins 2370 and 2429.

PIPELINES - EXCEPT NATURAL GAS - FINANCES

Pennwell Publishing Company, 1421 South Sheridan Road, Tulsa, Oklahoma 74101 (800) 752-9764; *Oil and Gas Journal*.

PIPELINES - EXCEPT NATURAL GAS - OCCUPATIONAL SAFETY

U.S. Department of Labor, Bureau of Labor Statistics, Two Massachusetts Avenue, NE, Washington, D.C. 20212 (202) 606-7828; *Occupational Injuries and Illnesses in the United States by Industry*.

PIPELINES - EXCEPT NATURAL GAS - OUTPUT

Pennwell Publishing Company, 1421 South Sheridan Road, Tulsa, Oklahoma 74101 (800) 752-9764; *Oil and Gas Journal*.

PIPELINES - EXCEPT NATURAL GAS - PRODUCTIVITY

U.S. Department of Labor, Bureau of Labor Statistics, Two Massachusetts Avenue, NE, Washington, D.C. 20212 (202) 606-7828; *Productivity Measures for Selected Industries and Government Services*, and unpublished data.

PISTACHIOS

U.S. Department of Agriculture, National Agricultural Statistics Service, Fourteenth Street and Independence Avenue, SW, Washington, D.C. 20250 (202) 219-1504; *Noncitrus Fruits and Nuts*.

PISTOLS - See FIREARMS

PITCAIRN ISLAND - AGRICULTURE

Food and Agricultural Organization of the United Nations (FAO) Via delle Terme di Caracalla, 00100 Rome, Italy (Telephone Number in U.S. (202) 653-2400); *Production Yearbook, The State of Food and Agriculture*, and *Trade Yearbook*.

G.K. Hall and Company, 70 Lincoln Street, Boston, Massachusetts 02111 (617) 423-3990; *The World in Figures*.

PITCAIRN ISLAND - AIRLINE SERVICE

G.K. Hall and Company, 70 Lincoln Street, Boston, Massachusetts 02111 (617) 423-3990; *The World in Figures*.

PITCAIRN ISLAND - AREA AND DENSITY OF POPULATION

Food and Agricultural Organization of the United Nations (FAO) Via delle Terme di Caracalla, 00100 Rome, Italy (Telephone Number in U.S. (202) 653-2400); *The State of Food and Agriculture*.

G.K. Hall and Company, 70 Lincoln Street, Boston, Massachusetts 02111 (617) 423-3990; *The World in Figures*.

Statistical Office of the United Nations, Publishing Service, New York, New York 10017 (800) 253-9646; *Statistical Yearbook*.

PITCAIRN ISLAND - BALANCE OF PAYMENTS

G.K. Hall and Company, 70 Lincoln Street, Boston, Massachusetts 02111 (617) 423-3990; *The World in Figures*.

PITCAIRN ISLAND - BANKING

G.K. Hall and Company, 70 Lincoln Street, Boston, Massachusetts 02111 (617) 423-3990; *The World in Figures*.

PITCAIRN ISLAND - BIRTH RATES

Statistical Office of the United Nations, Publishing Service, New York, New York 10017 (800) 253-9646; *Demographic Yearbook*, and *Statistical Yearbook*.

PITCAIRN ISLAND - BONDS

G.K. Hall and Company, 70 Lincoln Street, Boston, Massachusetts 02111 (617) 423-3990; *The World in Figures*.

PITCAIRN ISLAND - BOOK PRODUCTION

G.K. Hall and Company, 70 Lincoln Street, Boston, Massachusetts 02111 (617) 423-3990; *The World in Figures*.

PITCAIRN ISLAND - BROADCASTING

G.K. Hall and Company, 70 Lincoln Street, Boston, Massachusetts 02111 (617) 423-3990; *The World in Figures*.

PITCAIRN ISLAND - BUSINESS

G.K. Hall and Company, 70 Lincoln Street, Boston, Massachusetts 02111 (617) 423-3990; *The World in Figures*.

PITCAIRN ISLAND - CALORIE SUPPLY

Food and Agricultural Organization of the United Nations (FAO) Via delle Terme di Caracalla, 00100 Rome, Italy (Telephone Number in U.S. (202) 653-2400); *The State of Food and Agriculture*.

PITCAIRN ISLAND - CHEMICAL (ORGANIC) PRODUCTION - See PITCAIRN ISLAND - MINING AND MINERAL PRODUCTS

PITCAIRN ISLAND - CLASS STRUCTURE

G.K. Hall and Company, 70 Lincoln Street, Boston, Massachusetts 02111 (617) 423-3990; *The World in Figures*.

PITCAIRN ISLAND - CLIMATE

G.K. Hall and Company, 70 Lincoln Street, Boston, Massachusetts 02111 (617) 423-3990; *The World in Figures*.

PITCAIRN ISLAND - COAL PRODUCTION - See PITCAIRN ISLANDS - MINING AND MINERAL PRODUCTS

PITCAIRN ISLAND - COMMUNICATIONS

G.K. Hall and Company, 70 Lincoln Street, Boston, Massachusetts 02111 (617) 423-3990; *The World in Figures*.

PITCAIRN ISLAND - CONSUMER PRICE INDEX

G.K. Hall and Company, 70 Lincoln Street, Boston, Massachusetts 02111 (617) 423-3990; *The World in Figures*.

PITCAIRN ISLAND - CONSUMPTION

G.K. Hall and Company, 70 Lincoln Street, Boston, Massachusetts 02111 (617) 423-3990; *The World in Figures*.

PITCAIRN ISLAND - CORN PRODUCTION - See PITCAIRN ISLAND - CROPS

PITCAIRN ISLAND - CORPORATE TAXES - See PITCAIRN ISLAND - TAXATION

PITCAIRN ISLAND - CROPS

Food and Agricultural Organization of the United Nations (FAO) Via delle Terme di Caracalla, 00100 Rome, Italy (Telephone Number in U.S. (202) 653-2400); *The State of Food and Agriculture*.

G.K. Hall and Company, 70 Lincoln Street, Boston, Massachusetts 02111 (617) 423-3990; *The World in Figures*.

PITCAIRN ISLAND - CUSTOMS DUTIES

G.K. Hall and Company, 70 Lincoln Street, Boston, Massachusetts 02111 (617) 423-3990; *The World in Figures*.

PITCAIRN ISLAND - DAIRY PRODUCTS

Food and Agricultural Organization of the United Nations (FAO) Via delle Terme di Caracalla, 00100 Rome, Italy (Telephone Number in U.S. (202) 653-2400); *The State of Food and Agriculture*.

PITCAIRN ISLAND - DEATH RATES

G.K. Hall and Company, 70 Lincoln Street, Boston, Massachusetts 02111 (617) 423-3990; *The World in Figures*.

Statistical Office of the United Nations, Publishing Service, New York, New York 10017 (800) 253-9646; *Statistical Yearbook*.

PITCAIRN ISLAND - DEFENSE EXPENDITURES

G.K. Hall and Company, 70 Lincoln Street, Boston, Massachusetts 02111 (617) 423-3990; *The World in Figures*.

PITCAIRN ISLAND - DEMOGRAPHY

G.K. Hall and Company, 70 Lincoln Street, Boston, Massachusetts 02111 (617) 423-3990; *The World in Figures*.

PITCAIRN ISLAND - DEVELOPMENT ASSISTANCE

G.K. Hall and Company, 70 Lincoln Street, Boston, Massachusetts 02111 (617) 423-3990; *The World in Figures*.

PITCAIRN ISLAND - DISEASE

G.K. Hall and Company, 70 Lincoln Street, Boston, Massachusetts 02111 (617) 423-3990; *The World in Figures*.

PITCAIRN ISLAND - DIVORCE RATES

Statistical Office of the United Nations, Publishing Service, New York, New York 10017 (800) 253-9646; *Demographic Yearbook*.

PITCAIRN ISLAND - DOMESTIC PRODUCT

G.K. Hall and Company, 70 Lincoln Street, Boston, Massachusetts 02111 (617) 423-3990; *The World in Figures*.

PITCAIRN ISLAND - ECONOMY

G.K. Hall and Company, 70 Lincoln Street, Boston, Massachusetts 02111 (617) 423-3990; *The World in Figures*.

PITCAIRN ISLAND - EDUCATION

G.K. Hall and Company, 70 Lincoln Street, Boston, Massachusetts 02111 (617) 423-3990; *The World in Figures*.

PITCAIRN ISLAND - EGG PRODUCTION AND CONSUMPTION - See PITCAIRN ISLAND - DAIRY PRODUCTS

PITCAIRN ISLAND - ENERGY

Food and Agricultural Organization of the United Nations (FAO) Via delle Terme di Caracalla, 00100 Rome, Italy (Telephone Number in U.S. (202) 653-2400); *The State of Food and Agriculture*.

G.K. Hall and Company, 70 Lincoln Street, Boston, Massachusetts 02111 (617) 423-3990; *The World in Figures*.

PITCAIRN ISLAND - EXPORTS

Food and Agricultural Organization of the United Nations (FAO) Via delle Terme di Caracalla, 00100 Rome, Italy (Telephone Number in U.S. (202) 653-2400); *The State of Food and Agriculture*.

G.K. Hall and Company, 70 Lincoln Street, Boston, Massachusetts 02111 (617) 423-3990; *The World in Figures*.

PITCAIRN ISLAND - EXTERNAL TRADE

Food and Agricultural Organization of the United Nations (FAO) Via delle Terme di Caracalla, 00100 Rome, Italy (Telephone Number in U.S. (202) 653-2400); *The State of Food and Agriculture*, and *Trade Yearbook*.

G.K. Hall and Company, 70 Lincoln Street, Boston, Massachusetts 02111 (617) 423-3990; *The World in Figures*.

PITCAIRN ISLAND - FARM CROPS - See PITCAIRN ISLAND - CROPS

PITCAIRN ISLAND - FETAL MORTALITY

Statistical Office of the United Nations, Publishing Service, New York, New York 10017 (800) 253-9646; *Demographic Yearbook*.

PITCAIRN ISLAND - FERTILIZER

Food and Agricultural Organization of the United Nations (FAO) Via delle Terme di Caracalla, 00100 Rome, Italy (Telephone Number in U.S. (202) 653-2400); *The State of Food and Agriculture*.

PITCAIRN ISLAND - FINANCE

G.K. Hall and Company, 70 Lincoln Street, Boston, Massachusetts 02111 (617) 423-3990; *The World in Figures*.

PITCAIRN ISLAND - FISHERIES

Food and Agricultural Organization of the United Nations (FAO) Via delle Terme di Caracalla, 00100 Rome, Italy (Telephone Number in U.S. (202) 653-2400); *The State of Food and Agriculture*, and *Yearbook of Fishery Statistics*.

PITCAIRN ISLAND - FOOD

Food and Agricultural Organization of the United Nations (FAO), Via delle Terme di Caracalla, 00100 Rome, Italy (Telephone Number in U.S. (202) 653-2400); *Production Yearbook*, and *The State of Food and Agriculture*.

G.K. Hall and Company, 70 Lincoln Street, Boston, Massachusetts 02111 (617) 423-3990; *The World in Figures*.

PITCAIRN ISLAND FOREIGN AID

G.K. Hall and Company, 70 Lincoln Street, Boston, Massachusetts 02111 (617) 423-3990; *The World in Figures*.

PITCAIRN ISLAND - FOREIGN TRADE

G.K. Hall and Company, 70 Lincoln Street, Boston, Massachusetts 02111 (617) 423-3990; *The World in Figures*.

PITCAIRN ISLAND - FORESTRY AND FOREST PRODUCTS

Food and Agricultural Organization of the United Nations (FAO) Via delle Terme di Caracalla, 00100 Rome, Italy (Telephone Number in U.S. (202) 653-2400); *The State of Food and Agriculture*.

G.K. Hall and Company, 70 Lincoln Street, Boston, Massachusetts 02111 (617) 423-3990; *The World in Figures*.

PITCAIRN ISLAND - GENERAL MORTALITY

Statistical Office of the United Nations, Publishing Service, New York, New York 10017 (800) 253-9646; *Demographic Yearbook*.

PITCAIRN ISLAND - GOVERNMENT

G.K. Hall and Company, 70 Lincoln Street, Boston, Massachusetts 02111 (617) 423-3990; *The World in Figures*.

PITCAIRN ISLAND - GRAIN PRODUCTION - See PITCAIRN ISLAND - CROPS

PITCAIRN ISLAND - GROSS DOMESTIC PRODUCT

G.K. Hall and Company, 70 Lincoln Street, Boston, Massachusetts 02111 (617) 423-3990; *The World in Figures*.

PITCAIRN ISLAND - HEALTH

G.K. Hall and Company, 70 Lincoln Street, Boston, Massachusetts 02111 (617) 423-3990; *The World in Figures*.

PITCAIRN ISLAND - HIGHWAYS

G.K. Hall and Company, 70 Lincoln Street, Boston, Massachusetts 02111 (617) 423-3990; *The World in Figures*.

PITCAIRN ISLAND - ILLITERATE POPULATION

G.K. Hall and Company, 70 Lincoln Street, Boston, Massachusetts 02111 (617) 423-3990; *The World in Figures*.

PITCAIRN ISLAND - IMPORTS

Food and Agricultural Organization of the United Nations (FAO) Via delle Terme di Caracalla, 00100 Rome, Italy (Telephone Number in U.S. (202) 653-2400); *The State of Food and Agriculture*.

G.K. Hall and Company, 70 Lincoln Street, Boston, Massachusetts 02111 (617) 423-3990; *The World in Figures*.

PITCAIRN ISLAND - INDUSTRY

G.K. Hall and Company, 70 Lincoln Street, Boston, Massachusetts 02111 (617) 423-3990; *The World in Figures*.

PITCAIRN ISLAND - INFANT AND MATERNAL MORTALITY

Statistical Office of the United Nations, Publishing Service, New York, New York 10017 (800) 253-9646; *Demographic Yearbook*.

PITCAIRN ISLAND - LABOR FORCE

Food and Agricultural Organization of the United Nations (FAO) Via delle Terme di Caracalla, 00100 Rome, Italy (Telephone Number in U.S. (202) 653-2400); *The State of Food and Agriculture*.

G.K. Hall and Company, 70 Lincoln Street, Boston, Massachusetts 02111 (617) 423-3990; *The World in Figures*.

PITCAIRN ISLAND - LAND USE

Food and Agricultural Organization of the United Nations (FAO), Via delle Terme di Caracalla, 00100 Rome, Italy (Telephone Number in U.S. (202) 653-2400); *Production Yearbook*.

G.K. Hall and Company, 70 Lincoln Street, Boston, Massachusetts 02111 (617) 423-3990; *The World in Figures*.

PITCAIRN ISLAND - LIVESTOCK AND POULTRY

Food and Agricultural Organization of the United Nations (FAO), Via delle Terme di Caracalla, 00100 Rome, Italy (Telephone Number in U.S. (202) 653-2400); *Production Yearbook*, and *The State of Food and Agriculture*.

G.K. Hall and Company, 70 Lincoln Street, Boston, Massachusetts 02111 (617) 423-3990; *The World in Figures*.

PITCAIRN ISLAND - LIVING LEVELS

G.K. Hall and Company, 70 Lincoln Street, Boston, Massachusetts 02111 (617) 423-3990; *The World in Figures*.

PITCAIRN ISLAND - MANUFACTURING

G.K. Hall and Company, 70 Lincoln Street, Boston, Massachusetts 02111 (617) 423-3990; *The World in Figures.*

PITCAIRN ISLAND - MARRIAGE RATES

Statistical Office of the United Nations, Publishing Service, New York, New York 10017 (800) 253-9646; *Demographic Yearbook.*

PITCAIRN ISLAND - MEAT PRODUCTION - See PITCAIRN ISLAND - LIVESTOCK AND POULTRY

PITCAIRN ISLAND - MERCHANT SHIPPING

G.K. Hall and Company, 70 Lincoln Street, Boston, Massachusetts 02111 (617) 423-3990; *The World in Figures.*

PITCAIRN ISLAND - MILITARY

G.K. Hall and Company, 70 Lincoln Street, Boston, Massachusetts 02111 (617) 423-3990; *The World in Figures.*

PITCAIRN ISLAND - MINING AND MINERAL PRODUCTS

G.K. Hall and Company, 70 Lincoln Street, Boston, Massachusetts 02111 (617) 423-3990; *The World in Figures.*

PITCAIRN ISLAND - MONEY SUPPLY

G.K. Hall and Company, 70 Lincoln Street, Boston, Massachusetts 02111 (617) 423-3990; *The World in Figures.*

PITCAIRN ISLAND - MOTOR VEHICLES IN USE

G.K. Hall and Company, 70 Lincoln Street, Boston, Massachusetts 02111 (617) 423-3990; *The World in Figures.*

PITCAIRN ISLAND - NATALITY - See PITCAIRN ISLAND - BIRTH RATES

PITCAIRN ISLAND - NATIONAL INCOME

G.K. Hall and Company, 70 Lincoln Street, Boston, Massachusetts 02111 (617) 423-3990; *The World in Figures.*

PITCAIRN ISLAND - NEWSPAPER PRODUCTION - See PITCAIRN ISLAND - FORESTRY AND FOREST PRODUCTS

PITCAIRN ISLAND - OCCUPATIONS - See PITCAIRN ISLAND - LABOR FORCE

PITCAIRN ISLAND - PESTICIDE USE

Food and Agricultural Organization of the United Nations (FAO) Via delle Terme di Caracalla, 00100 Rome, Italy (Telephone Number in U.S. (202) 653-2400); *The State of Food and Agriculture.*

PITCAIRN ISLAND - PETROLEUM INDUSTRY

Food and Agricultural Organization of the United Nations (FAO) Via delle Terme di Caracalla, 00100 Rome, Italy (Telephone Number in U.S. (202) 653-2400); *The State of Food and Agriculture.*

G.K. Hall and Company, 70 Lincoln Street, Boston, Massachusetts 02111 (617) 423-3990; *The World in Figures.*

PITCAIRN ISLAND - POPULATION

Food and Agricultural Organization of the United Nations (FAO), Via delle Terme di Caracalla, 00100 Rome, Italy (Telephone Number in U.S. (202) 653-2400); *Production Yearbook.*

G.K. Hall and Company, 70 Lincoln Street, Boston, Massachusetts 02111 (617) 423-3990; *The World in Figures.*

Statistical Office of the United Nations, Publishing Service, New York, New York 10017 (800) 253-9646; *Demographic Yearbook,* and *Statistical Yearbook.*

World Health Organization, Office of Publications, Avenue Appia, CH-1211 Geneva 27, Switzerland (Telephone Number in U.S. (518) 436-9686); *World Health Statistics Annual.*

PITCAIRN ISLAND - PRICES

Food and Agricultural Organization of the United Nations (FAO), Via delle Terme di Caracalla, 00100 Rome, Italy (Telephone Number in U.S. (202) 653-2400); *Production Yearbook,* and *The State of Food and Agriculture.*

G.K. Hall and Company, 70 Lincoln Street, Boston, Massachusetts 02111 (617) 423-3990; *The World in Figures.*

PITCAIRN ISLAND - PRODUCTION

G.K. Hall and Company, 70 Lincoln Street, Boston, Massachusetts 02111 (617) 423-3990; *The World in Figures.*

PITCAIRN ISLAND - RAILWAYS

G.K. Hall and Company, 70 Lincoln Street, Boston, Massachusetts 02111 (617) 423-3990; *The World in Figures.*

PITCAIRN ISLAND - RETAIL TRADE

G.K. Hall and Company, 70 Lincoln Street, Boston, Massachusetts 02111 (617) 423-3990; *The World in Figures.*

PITCAIRN ISLAND - SOCIAL DATA

G.K. Hall and Company, 70 Lincoln Street, Boston, Massachusetts 02111 (617) 423-3990; *The World in Figures.*

PITCAIRN ISLAND - STOCKS - COMMODITY - MARKET PRICE - INDEX

Food and Agricultural Organization of the United Nations (FAO) Via delle Terme di Caracalla, 00100 Rome, Italy (Telephone Number in U.S. (202) 653-2400); *The State of Food and Agriculture.*

PITCAIRN ISLAND - TAXATION

G.K. Hall and Company, 70 Lincoln Street, Boston, Massachusetts 02111 (617) 423-3990; *The World in Figures.*

PITCAIRN ISLAND - TELEPHONES IN USE

G.K. Hall and Company, 70 Lincoln Street, Boston, Massachusetts 02111 (617) 423-3990; *The World in Figures.*

PITCAIRN ISLAND - TEXTILE INDUSTRY

G.K. Hall and Company, 70 Lincoln Street, Boston, Massachusetts 02111 (617) 423-3990; *The World in Figures.*

PITCAIRN ISLAND - TOURISM

G.K. Hall and Company, 70 Lincoln Street, Boston, Massachusetts 02111 (617) 423-3990; *The World in Figures.*

PITCAIRN ISLAND - TRADE

Food and Agricultural Organization of the United Nations (FAO) Via delle Terme di Caracalla, 00100 Rome, Italy (Telephone Number in U.S. (202) 653-2400); *The State of Food and Agriculture.*

PITCAIRN ISLAND - TRANSPORTATION AND COMMUNICATIONS

G.K. Hall and Company, 70 Lincoln Street, Boston, Massachusetts 02111 (617) 423-3990; *The World in Figures.*

PITCAIRN ISLAND - VITAL STATISTICS

G.K. Hall and Company, 70 Lincoln Street, Boston, Massachusetts 02111 (617) 423-3990; *The World in Figures.*

World Health Organization, Office of Publications, Avenue Appia, CH-1211 Geneva 27, Switzerland (Telephone Number in U.S. (518) 436-9686); *World Health Statistics Annual.*

PITCAIRN ISLAND - WAGES

G.K. Hall and Company, 70 Lincoln Street, Boston, Massachusetts 02111 (617) 423-3990; *The World in Figures.*

PITCAIRN ISLAND - WEATHER

G.K. Hall and Company, 70 Lincoln Street, Boston, Massachusetts 02111 (617) 423-3990; *The World in Figures.*

PLANTS

National Gardening Association, 180 Flynn Avenue, Burlington, Vermont 05401 (802) 863-1308; *National Gardening Survey.*

U.S. Department of Agriculture, Economic Research Service, Fourteenth Street and Independence Avenue, SW, Washington, D.C. 20005-4789 (202) 219-1504; unpublished data.

PLATINUM GROUP METALS

U.S. Department of the Interior, Bureau of Mines, 810 Seventh Street, NW, Washington, D.C. 20241 (202) 501-9649; *Mineral Commodity Summaries.*

PLATINUM GROUP METALS - CONSUMPTION

U.S. Department of the Interior, Bureau of Mines, 810 Seventh Street, NW, Washington, D.C. 20241 (202) 501-9649; *Annual Reports,* and *Mineral Commodity Summaries.*

PLATINUM GROUP METALS - EMPLOYMENT

U.S. Department of the Interior, Bureau of Mines, 810 Seventh Street, NW, Washington, D.C. 20241 (202) 501-9649; *Mineral Commodity Summaries.*

PLATINUM GROUP METALS - FOREIGN TRADE

U.S. Department of the Interior, Bureau of Mines, 810 Seventh Street, NW, Washington, D.C. 20241 (202) 501-9649; *Annual Reports,* and *Mineral Commodity Summaries.*

PLATINUM GROUP METALS - PRICES

U.S. Department of the Interior, Bureau of Mines, 810 Seventh Street, NW, Washington, D.C. 20241 (202) 501-9649; *Mineral Commodity Summaries.*

PLATINUM GROUP METALS - PRODUCTION

U.S. Department of the Interior, Bureau of Mines, 810 Seventh Street, NW, Washington, D.C. 20241 (202) 501-9649; *Annual Reports,* and *Mineral Commodity Summaries.*

PLATINUM GROUP METALS - STRATEGIC AND CRITICAL MATERIALS

U.S. Department of Defense, Defense Logistics Agency, Cameron Station, Alexandria, Virginia 22304-6100 (703) 274-6000; *Statistical Supplement, Stockpile Report to the Congress.*

PLUMS AND PRUNES

U.S. Department of Agriculture, Economic Research Service, Fourteenth Street and Independence Avenue, SW, Washington, D.C. 20005-4789 (202) 219-1504; *Agricultural Outlook, Food Consumption, Prices, and Expenditures, Economic Indicators of the Farm Sector: National Financial Summary,* and unpublished data.

U.S. Department of Agriculture, National Agricultural Statistics Service, Fourteenth Street and Independence Avenue, SW, Washington, D.C. 20250 (202) 219-1504; *Noncitrus Fruits and Nuts.*

PLYWOOD - CONSUMPTION

U.S. Department of Agriculture, Forest Service, Fourteenth Street and Independence Avenue, SW, Washington, D.C. 20250 (202) 720-3760; *United States Timber Production, Trade, Consumption, and Price Statistics.*

U.S. Department of Commerce, Bureau of the Census, Suitland, Maryland 20233 (301) 763-4040; *Current Industrial Reports.*

PLYWOOD - FOREIGN TRADE

U.S. Department of Agriculture, Forest Service, Fourteenth Street and Independence Avenue, SW, Washington, D.C. 20250 (202) 720-3760; *United States Timber Production, Trade, Consumption, and Price Statistics.*

PLYWOOD - OUTPUT

U.S. Department of Agriculture, Forest Service, Fourteenth Street and Independence Avenue, SW, Washington, D.C. 20250 (202) 720-3760; *United States Timber Production, Trade, Consumption, and Price Statistics.*

U.S. Department of Commerce, Bureau of the Census, Suitland, Maryland 20233 (301) 763-4040; *Current Industrial Reports.*

PLYWOOD - PRODUCER PRICE INDEXES

U.S. Department of Labor, Bureau of Labor Statistics, Two Massachusetts Avenue, NE, Washington, D.C. 20212 (202) 606-7828; *Producer Price Indexes.*

PNEUMONIA

U.S. Department of Health and Human Services, National Center for Health Statistics, 3700 East-West Highway, Hyattsville, Maryland 20782 (301) 436-8500; *Vital Statistics of the United States, Monthly*

Vital Statistics Report, and unpublished data.

POISONING - DEATHS FROM

U.S. Department of Health and Human Services, National Center for Health Statistics, 3700 East-West Highway, Hyattsville, Maryland 20782 (301) 436-8500; *Vital Statistics of the United States.*

Poland - National Statistical Office

Glowny Urzad Statystyczny (Central Statistical Office), Al Niepodleglosci 208, 00-925 Warsaw, Poland.

Poland - Primary Statistics Sources

Glowny Urzad Statystyczny (Central Statistical Office), Al Niepodleglosci 208, 00-925 Warsaw, Poland; *Rocznik statystyczny* (Statistical Yearbook); *Maly rocznik statystyczny* (Concise Statistical Yearbook); *Biuletyn statystyczny* (Statistical Bulletin); and *Concise Statistical Yearbook of Poland.*

POLAND - ABORTIONS

Statistical Office of the United Nations, Publishing Service, New York, New York 10017 (800) 253-9646; *Demographic Yearbook.*

POLAND - AGRICULTURE

Columbia University Press, 562 West 113th Street, New York, New York 10014 (212) 316-7100; *East European and Soviet Data Book.*

Facts on File, 460 Park Avenue South, New York, New York 10016 (800) 443-8323; *The New Book of World Rankings.*

Food and Agricultural Organization of the United Nations (FAO), Via delle Terme di Caracalla, 00100 Rome, Italy (Telephone Number in U.S. (202) 653-2400); *Production Yearbook, The State of Food and Agriculture,* and *Trade Yearbook.*

G.K. Hall and Company, 70 Lincoln Street, Boston, Massachusetts 02111 (617) 423-3990; *The World in Figures.*

Statistical Office of the United Nations, Publishing Service, New York, New York 10017 (800) 253-9646; *Statistical Yearbook.*

Times Books, 201 East 50th Street, New York, New York 10022 (212) 751-2600; *The Economist Book of Vital World Statistics.*

The World Bank, 1818 H Street, NW, Washington, D.C. 20433 (202) 477-1234; *World Tables.*

POLAND - AIRLINE SERVICE

Facts on File, 460 Park Avenue South, New York, New York 10016 (800) 443-8323; *The New Book of World Rankings.*

G.K. Hall and Company, 70 Lincoln Street, Boston, Massachusetts 02111 (617) 423-3990; *The World in Figures.*

Statistical Office of the United Nations, Publishing Service, New York, New York 10017 (800) 253-9646; *Statistical Yearbook.*

Times Books, 201 East 50th Street, New York, New York 10022 (212) 751-2600; *The Economist Book of Vital World Statistics.*

POLAND - ALUMINUM PRODUCTION AND CONSUMPTION - See POLAND - MINING AND MINERAL PRODUCTS

POLAND - ANIMAL FEEDINGSTUFFS OF AQUATIC ANIMAL ORIGIN

Statistical Office of the United Nations, Publishing Service, New York, New York 10017 (800) 253-9646; *Statistical Yearbook.*

POLAND - AREA AND DENSITY OF POPULATION

Facts on File, 460 Park Avenue South, New York, New York 10016 (800) 443-8323; *The New Book of World Rankings.*

Food and Agricultural Organization of the United Nations (FAO) Via delle Terme di Caracalla, 00100 Rome, Italy (Telephone Number in U.S. (202) 653-2400); *The State of Food and Agriculture.*

G.K. Hall and Company, 70 Lincoln Street, Boston, Massachusetts 02111 (617) 423-3990; *The World in Figures.*

Statistical Office of the United Nations, Publishing Service, New York, New York 10017 (800) 253-9646; *Statistical Yearbook.*

Times Books, 201 East 50th Street, New York, New York 10022 (212) 751-2600; *The Economist Book of Vital World Statistics.*

United Nations Educational, Scientific and Cultural Organization (UNESCO), 7 Place de Fontenoy, F-75700 Paris, France (Telephone Number in U.S. (212) 963-5981); *Statistical Yearbook.*

POLAND - ARMS EXPORTS AND IMPORTS

U.S. Arms Control and Disarmament Agency, 320 Twenty-first Street, NW, Washington, D.C. 20451 (202) 647-8677; *World Military Expenditures and Arms Transfers.*

POLAND - BALANCE OF PAYMENTS

The Economist Intelligence Unit, 111 West 57th Street, New York, New York 10019 (800) 938-4685; *The World Market Atlas.*

G.K. Hall and Company, 70 Lincoln Street, Boston, Massachusetts 02111 (617) 423-3990; *The World in Figures.*

Times Books, 201 East 50th Street, New York, New York 10022 (212) 751-2600; *The Economist Book of Vital World Statistics.*

The World Bank, 1818 H Street, NW, Washington, D.C. 20433 (202) 477-1234; *World Tables.*

POLAND - BANKING

Facts on File, 460 Park Avenue South, New York, New York 10016 (800) 443-8323; *The New Book of World Rankings.*

G.K. Hall and Company, 70 Lincoln Street, Boston, Massachusetts 02111 (617) 423-3990; *The World in Figures.*

POLAND - BARLEY PRODUCTION

Facts on File, 460 Park Avenue South, New York, New York 10016 (800) 443-8323; *The New Book of World Rankings.*

Statistical Office of the United Nations, Publishing Service, New York, New York 10017 (800) 253-9646; *Statistical Yearbook.*

POLAND - BEER PRODUCTION

Facts on File, 460 Park Avenue South, New York, New York 10016 (800) 443-8323; *The New Book of World Rankings.*

Statistical Office of the United Nations, Publishing Service, New York, New York 10017 (800) 253-9646; *Statistical Yearbook.*

POLAND - BIRTH RATES

Facts on File, 460 Park Avenue South, New York, New York 10016 (800) 443-8323; *The New Book of World Rankings.*

Statistical Office of the United Nations, Publishing Service, New York, New York 10017 (800) 253-9646; *Demographic Yearbook,* and *Statistical Yearbook.*

Times Books, 201 East 50th Street, New York, New York 10022 (212) 751-2600; *The Economist Book of Vital World Statistics.*

The World Bank, 1818 H Street, NW, Washington, D.C. 20433 (202) 477-1234; *World Tables.*

World Health Organization, Office of Publications, Avenue Appia, CH-1211 Geneva 27, Switzerland (Telephone Number in U.S. (518) 436-9686); *World Health Statistics Annual.*

POLAND - BONDS

G.K. Hall and Company, 70 Lincoln Street, Boston, Massachusetts 02111 (617) 423-3990; *The World in Figures.*

POLAND - BOOK PRODUCTION

Euromonitor Publications Limited, 87-88 Turnmill Street, London EC1M 5QU, England; *European Marketing Data and Statistics.*

G.K. Hall and Company, 70 Lincoln Street, Boston, Massachusetts 02111 (617) 423-3990; *The World in Figures.*

United Nations Educational, Scientific and Cultural Organization (UNESCO), 7 Place de Fontenoy, F-75700 Paris, France (Telephone Number in U.S. (212) 963-5981); *Statistical Yearbook.*

POLAND - BROADCASTING

Billboard Limited, Post Office Box 9027, 1006 AA Amsterdam, The Netherlands (Telephone Number in U.S. (212) 764-7300); *World Radio TV Handbook.*

Facts on File, 460 Park Avenue South, New York, New York 10016 (800) 443-8323; *The New Book of World Rankings.*

G.K. Hall and Company, 70 Lincoln Street, Boston, Massachusetts 02111 (617) 423-3990; *The World in Figures.*

Times Books, 201 East 50th Street, New York, New York 10022 (212) 751-2600; *The Economist Book of Vital World Statistics.*

United Nations Educational, Scientific and Cultural Organization (UNESCO), 7 Place de Fontenoy, F-75700 Paris, France (Telephone Number in U.S. (212) 963-5981); *Statistical Yearbook.*

POLAND - BUSINESS

G.K. Hall and Company, 70 Lincoln Street, Boston, Massachusetts 02111 (617) 423-3990; *The World in Figures.*

POLAND - BUTTER PRODUCTION - See POLAND - DAIRY PRODUCTS

POLAND - CABBAGE PRODUCTION - See POLAND - CROPS

POLAND - CADMIUM PRODUCTION AND CONSUMPTION - See POLAND - MINING AND MINERAL PRODUCTS

POLAND - CALORIE SUPPLY

Food and Agricultural Organization of the United Nations (FAO) Via delle Terme di Caracalla, 00100 Rome, Italy (Telephone Number in U.S. (202) 653-2400); *The State of Food and Agriculture.*

POLAND - CATTLE - See POLAND - LIVESTOCK AND POULTRY

POLAND - CAULIFLOWER PRODUCTION - See POLAND - CROPS

POLAND - CAUSTIC SODA PRODUCTION

Statistical Office of the United Nations, Publishing Service, New York, New York 10017 (800) 253-9646; *Statistical Yearbook.*

POLAND - CEMENT PRODUCTION - See POLAND - MINING AND MINERAL PRODUCTS

POLAND - CEREALS PRODUCTION - See POLAND - CROPS

POLAND - CHEESE PRODUCTION AND CONSUMPTION - See POLAND - DAIRY PRODUCTS

POLAND - CHEMICAL (ORGANIC) PRODUCTION - See POLAND - MINING AND MINERAL PRODUCTS

POLAND - CIGAR AND CIGARETTE PRODUCTION - See POLAND - TOBACCO PRODUCTION

POLAND - CLASS STRUCTURE

Columbia University Press, 562 West 113th Street, New York, New York 10014 (212) 316-7100; *East European and Soviet Data Book.*

G.K. Hall and Company, 70 Lincoln Street, Boston, Massachusetts 02111 (617) 423-3990; *The World in Figures.*

POLAND - CLIMATE

Facts on File, 460 Park Avenue South, New York, New York 10016 (800) 443-8323; *The New Book of World Rankings.*

G.K. Hall and Company, 70 Lincoln Street, Boston, Massachusetts 02111 (617) 423-3990; *The World in Figures.*

POLAND - COAL PRODUCTION - See POLAND - MINING AND MINERAL PRODUCTS

POLAND - COFFEE PRODUCTION AND CONSUMPTION - See POLAND - CROPS

POLAND - COKE OVEN COKE PRODUCTION AND CONSUMPTION - See POLAND - MINING AND MINERAL PRODUCTS

POLAND - COMMUNICATIONS

G.K. Hall and Company, 70 Lincoln Street, Boston, Massachusetts 02111 (617) 423-3990; *The World in Figures.*

POLAND - CONSTRUCTION INDUSTRY

Facts on File, 460 Park Avenue South, New York, New York 10016 (800) 443-8323; *The New Book of World Rankings.*

Statistical Office of the United Nations, Publishing Service, New York, New York 10017 (800) 253-9646; *Construction Statistics Yearbook,* and *Statistical Yearbook*

POLAND - CONSUMER PRICE INDEX

G.K. Hall and Company, 70 Lincoln Street, Boston, Massachusetts 02111 (617) 423-3990; *The World in Figures*.

Statistical Office of the United Nations, Publishing Service, New York, New York 10017 (800) 253-9646; *Statistical Yearbook*.

POLAND - CONSUMER PRICES

Euromonitor Publications Limited, 87-88 Turnmill Street, London EC1M 5QU, England; *European Marketing Data and Statistics*.

International Labour Office, I.L.O. Publications, CH-1211, Geneva 22, Switzerland; *Yearbook of Labour Statistics*.

Times Books, 201 East 50th Street, New York, New York 10022 (212) 751-2600; *The Economist Book of Vital World Statistics*.

POLAND - CONSUMPTION

G.K. Hall and Company, 70 Lincoln Street, Boston, Massachusetts 02111 (617) 423-3990; *The World in Figures*.

International Lead and Zinc Study Group, Metro House, 58 St. James's Street, London SW1A 1LD, England; *Lead and Zinc Statistics*.

International Rubber Study Group, York House, Eighth Floor, Empire Way, Wembley, London HA9 0PA, England; *Rubber Statistical Bulletin*.

POLAND - COPPER AND COPPER ORE PRODUCTION AND CONSUMPTION - See POLAND - MINING AND MINERAL PRODUCTS

POLAND - CORN PRODUCTION - See POLAND - CROPS

POLAND - CORPORATE TAXES - See POLAND - TAXATION

POLAND - COTTON - See POLAND - CROPS

POLAND - CRIME

Yale University Press, Yale Station, New Haven, Connecticut 06520 (203) 432-0940; *Violence and Crime in Cross-National Perspective*.

POLAND - CROPS

Commodity Research Bureau, Incorporated, 75 Wall Street, New York, New York 10005 (212) 504-7754; *Commodity Year Book*.

Euromonitor Publications Limited, 87-88 Turnmill Street, London EC1M 5QU, England; *European Marketing Data and Statistics*.

Facts on File, 460 Park Avenue South, New York, New York 10016 (800) 443-8323; *The New Book of World Rankings*.

Food and Agricultural Organization of the United Nations (FAO), Via delle Terme di Caracalla, 00100 Rome, Italy (Telephone Number in U.S. (202) 653-2400); *Production Yearbook*, and *The State of Food and Agriculture*.

Statistical Office of the United Nations, Publishing Service, New York, New York 10017 (800) 253-9646; *Statistical Yearbook*.

POLAND - CUSTOMS DUTIES

G.K. Hall and Company, 70 Lincoln Street, Boston, Massachusetts 02111 (617) 423-3990; *The World in Figures*.

POLAND - DAIRY PRODUCTS

Commodity Research Bureau, Incorporated, 75 Wall Street, New York, New York 10005 (212) 504-7754; *Commodity Year Book*.

Facts on File, 460 Park Avenue South, New York, New York 10016 (800) 443-8323; *The New Book of World Rankings*.

Food and Agricultural Organization of the United Nations (FAO) Via delle Terme di Caracalla, 00100 Rome, Italy (Telephone Number in U.S. (202) 653-2400); *Production Yearbook*, and *The State of Food and Agriculture*.

Statistical Office of the United Nations, Publishing Service, New York, New York 10017 (800) 253-9646; *Statistical Yearbook*.

POLAND - DEATH RATES

G.K. Hall and Company, 70 Lincoln Street, Boston, Massachusetts 02111 (617) 423-3990; *The World in Figures*.

Statistical Office of the United Nations, Publishing Service, New York, New York 10017 (800) 253-9646; *Statistical Yearbook*.

Times Books, 201 East 50th Street, New York, New York 10022 (212) 751-2600; *The Economist Book of Vital World Statistics*.

World Health Organization, Office of Publications, Avenue Appia, CH-1211 Geneva 27, Switzerland (Telephone Number in U.S. (518) 436-9686); *World Health Statistics Annual*.

POLAND - DEFENSE EXPENDITURES

G.K. Hall and Company, 70 Lincoln Street, Boston, Massachusetts 02111 (617) 423-3990; *The World in Figures*.

U.S. Arms Control and Disarmament Agency, 320 Twenty-first Street, NW, Washington, D.C. 20451 (202) 647-8677; *World Military Expenditures and Arms Transfers*.

POLAND - DEMOGRAPHY

The Economist Intelligence Unit, 111 West 57th Street, New York, New York 10019 (800) 938-4685; *The World Market Atlas*.

Facts on File, 460 Park Avenue South, New York, New York 10016 (800) 443-8323; *The New Book of World Rankings*.

G.K. Hall and Company, 70 Lincoln Street, Boston, Massachusetts 02111 (617) 423-3990; *The World in Figures*.

POLAND - DEVELOPMENT ASSISTANCE

G.K. Hall and Company, 70 Lincoln Street, Boston, Massachusetts 02111 (617) 423-3990; *The World in Figures*.

Statistical Office of the United Nations, Publishing Service, New York, New York 10017 (800) 253-9646; *Statistical Yearbook*.

POLAND - DIAMOND PRODUCTION - See POLAND - MINING AND MINERAL PRODUCTS

POLAND - DISEASES

G.K. Hall and Company, 70 Lincoln Street, Boston, Massachusetts 02111 (617) 423-3990; *The World in Figures*.

World Health Organization, Office of Publications, Avenue Appia, CH-1211 Geneva 27, Switzerland (Telephone Number in U.S. (518)

436-9686); *World Health Statistics Annual.*

POLAND - DIVORCE RATES

Facts on File, 460 Park Avenue South, New York, New York 10016 (800) 443-8323; *The New Book of World Rankings.*

Statistical Office of the United Nations, Publishing Service, New York, New York 10017 (800) 253-9646; *Demographic Yearbook,* and *Statistical Yearbook.*

POLAND - DOMESTIC PRODUCT

G.K. Hall and Company, 70 Lincoln Street, Boston, Massachusetts 02111 (617) 423-3990; *The World in Figures.*

POLAND - DUCKS - See POLAND - LIVESTOCK AND POULTRY

POLAND - ECONOMY

Euromonitor Publications Limited, 87-88 Turnmill Street, London EC1M 5QU, England; *European Marketing Data and Statistics.*

Facts on File, 460 Park Avenue South, New York, New York 10016 (800) 443-8323; *The New Book of World Rankings.*

G K Hall and Company, 70 Lincoln Street, Boston, Massachusetts 02111 (617) 423-3990; *The World in Figures.*

POLAND - EDUCATION

Columbia University Press, 562 West 113th Street, New York, New York 10014 (212) 316-7100; *East European and Soviet Data Book.*

The Economist Intelligence Unit, 111 West 57th Street, New York, New York 10019 (800) 938-4685; *The World Market Atlas.*

Euromonitor Publications Limited, 87-88 Turnmill Street, London EC1M 5QU, England; *European Marketing Data and Statistics.*

Facts on File, 460 Park Avenue South, New York, New York 10016 (800) 443-8323; *The New Book of World Rankings*

G.K. Hall and Company, 70 Lincoln Street, Boston, Massachusetts 02111 (617) 423-3990; *The World in Figures.*

Times Books, 201 East 50th Street, New York, New York 10022 (212) 751-2600; *The Economist Book of Vital World Statistics.*

United Nations Educational, Scientific and Cultural Organization (UNESCO), 7 Place de Fontenoy, F-75700 Paris, France (Telephone Number in U.S. (212) 963-5981); *Statistical Yearbook.*

The World Bank, 1818 H Street, NW, Washington, D.C. 20433 (202) 477-1234; *World Tables.*

POLAND - EGG PRODUCTION AND CONSUMPTION - See POLAND - DAIRY PRODUCTS

POLAND - ELECTRICITY

Commodity Research Bureau, Incorporated, 75 Wall Street, New York, New York 10005 (212) 504-7754; *Commodity Year Book.*

Facts on File, 460 Park Avenue South, New York, New York 10016 (800) 443-8323; *The New Book of World Rankings.*

Penn Well Publishing Company, 1421 South Sheridan Road, Post Office Box 1260, Tulsa, Oklahoma 74101 (800) 752-9764;

International Energy Statistics Sourcebook.

Statistical Office of the United Nations, Publishing Service, New York, New York 10017 (800) 253-9646; *Statistical Yearbook.*

Times Books, 201 East 50th Street, New York, New York 10022 (212) 751-2600; *The Economist Book of Vital World Statistics.*

POLAND - EMPLOYMENT

Columbia University Press, 562 West 113th Street, New York, New York 10014 (212) 316-7100; *East European and Soviet Data Book.*

Euromonitor Publications Limited, 87-88 Turnmill Street, London EC1M 5QU, England; *European Marketing Data and Statistics.*

Facts on File, 460 Park Avenue South, New York, New York 10016 (800) 443-8323; *The New Book of World Rankings.*

International Labour Office, I.L.O. Publications, CH-1211, Geneva 22, Switzerland; *Yearbook of Labour Statistics.*

Statistical Office of the United Nations, Publishing Service, New York, Now York 10017 (800) 253-9646; *Statistical Yearbook.*

POLAND - ENERGY

Euromonitor Publications Limited, 87-88 Turnmill Street, London EC1M 5QU, England; *European Marketing Data and Statistics.*

Facts on File, 460 Park Avenue South, New York, New York 10016 (800) 443-8323; *The New Book of World Rankings.*

Food and Agricultural Organization of the United Nations (FAO) Via delle Terme di Caracalla, 00100 Rome, Italy (Telephone Number in U.S. (202) 653-2400); *The State of Food and Agriculture.*

G.K. Hall and Company, 70 Lincoln Street, Boston, Massachusetts 02111 (617) 423-3990; *The World in Figures.*

Penn Well Publishing Company, 1421 South Sheridan Road, Post Office Box 1260, Tulsa, Oklahoma 74101 (800) 752-9764; *International Energy Statistics Sourcebook.*

Statistical Office of the United Nations, Publishing Service, New York, New York 10017 (800) 253-9646; *Energy Statistics Yearbook, Statistical Yearbook,* and *World Energy Supplies.*

Times Books, 201 East 50th Street, New York, New York 10022 (212) 751-2600; *The Economist Book of Vital World Statistics.*

POLAND - EXCHANGE RATES

Statistical Office of the United Nations, Publishing Service, New York, New York 10017 (800) 253-9646; *Statistical Yearbook.*

POLAND - EXPORTS

American Automobile Manufacturers Association, 1401 H Eye Street, NW, Suite 900, Washington, D.C. 20005 (202) 326-5500; *World Motor Vehicle Data.*

The Economist Intelligence Unit, 111 West 57th Street, New York, New York 10019 (800) 938-4685; *The World Market Atlas.*

Food and Agricultural Organization of the United Nations (FAO) Via delle Terme di Caracalla, 00100 Rome, Italy (Telephone Number in U.S. (202) 653-2400); *The State of Food and Agriculture.*

G.K. Hall and Company, 70 Lincoln Street, Boston, Massachusetts 02111 (617) 423-3990; *The World in Figures.*

International Lead and Zinc Study Group, Metro House, 58 St. James's Street, London SW1A 1LD, England; *Lead and Zinc Statistics.*

International Monetary Fund, 700 Nineteenth Street, NW, Washington, D.C. 20431 (202) 623-7000; *Direction of Trade Statistics.*

International Rubber Study Group, York House, Eighth Floor, Empire Way, Wembley, London HA9 0PA, England; *Rubber Statistical Bulletin.*

Times Books, 201 East 50th Street, New York, New York 10022 (212) 751-2600; *The Economist Book of Vital World Statistics.*

POLAND - EXTERNAL INDEBTEDNESS

The World Bank, 1818 H Street, NW, Washington, D.C. 20433 (202) 477-1234; *World Tables.*

POLAND - EXTERNAL TRADE

Food and Agricultural Organization of the United Nations (FAO) Via delle Terme di Caracalla, 00100 Rome, Italy (Telephone Number in U.S. (202) 653-2400); *The State of Food and Agriculture,* and *Trade Yearbook.*

G.K. Hall and Company, 70 Lincoln Street, Boston, Massachusetts 02111 (617) 423-3990; *The World in Figures.*

Statistical Office of the United Nations, Publishing Service, New York, New York 10017 (800) 253-9646; *Statistical Yearbook.*

POLAND - FABRIC PRODUCTION - See POLAND - TEXTILE INDUSTRY

POLAND - FARM CROPS

Facts on File, 460 Park Avenue South, New York, New York 10016 (800) 443-8323; *The New Book of World Rankings.*

Food and Agricultural Organization of the United Nations (FAO) Via delle Terme di Caracalla, 00100 Rome, Italy (Telephone Number in U.S. (202) 653-2400); *The State of Food and Agriculture.*

G.K. Hall and Company, 70 Lincoln Street, Boston, Massachusetts 02111 (617) 423-3990; *The World in Figures.*

POLAND - FERTILITY RATES

Columbia University Press, 562 West 113th Street, New York, New York 10014 (212) 316-7100; *East European and Soviet Data Book.*

Facts on File, 460 Park Avenue South, New York, New York 10016 (800) 443-8323; *The New Book of World Rankings.*

Times Books, 201 East 50th Street, New York, New York 10022 (212) 751-2600; *The Economist Book of Vital World Statistics.*

The World Bank, 1818 H Street, NW, Washington, D.C. 20433 (202) 477-1234; *World Tables.*

POLAND - FERTILIZER

Food and Agricultural Organization of the United Nations (FAO), Via delle Terme di Caracalla, 00100 Rome, Italy (Telephone Number

in U.S. (202) 653-2400); *Fertilizer Yearbook,* and *The State of Food and Agriculture.*

Statistical Office of the United Nations, Publishing Service, New York, New York 10017 (800) 253-9646; *Statistical Yearbook.*

POLAND - FETAL MORTALITY

Statistical Office of the United Nations, Publishing Service, New York, New York 10017 (800) 253-9646; *Demographic Yearbook.*

World Health Organization, Office of Publications, Avenue Appia, CH-1211 Geneva 27, Switzerland (Telephone Number in U.S. (518) 436-9686); *World Health Statistics Annual.*

POLAND - FIBRE PRODUCTION - See POLAND - TEXTILE INDUSTRY

POLAND - FILAMENT PRODUCTION - See POLAND - TEXTILE INDUSTRY

POLAND - FILM - See POLAND - MOTION PICTURES

POLAND - FINANCE

Facts on File, 460 Park Avenue South, New York, New York 10016 (800) 443-8323; *The New Book of World Rankings.*

G.K. Hall and Company, 70 Lincoln Street, Boston, Massachusetts 02111 (617) 423-3990; *The World in Figures.*

POLAND - FISHERIES

Euromonitor Publications Limited, 87-88 Turnmill Street, London EC1M 5QU, England; *European Marketing Data and Statistics.*

Facts on File, 460 Park Avenue South, New York, New York 10016 (800) 443-8323; *The New Book of World Rankings.*

Food and Agricultural Organization of the United Nations (FAO) Via delle Terme di Caracalla, 00100 Rome, Italy (Telephone Number in U.S. (202) 653-2400); *The State of Food and Agriculture,* and *Yearbook of Fishery Statistics.*

Statistical Office of the United Nations, Publishing Service, New York, New York 10017 (800) 253-9646; *Statistical Yearbook.*

POLAND - FLAX AND FLAX FIBRE PRODUCTION - See POLAND - TEXTILE INDUSTRY

POLAND - FLOUR PRODUCTION

Commodity Research Bureau, Incorporated, 75 Wall Street, New York, New York 10005 (212) 504-7754; *Commodity Year Book.*

Statistical Office of the United Nations, Publishing Service, New York, New York 10017 (800) 253-9646; *Statistical Yearbook.*

POLAND - FOOD

Food and Agricultural Organization of the United Nations (FAO), Via delle Terme di Caracalla, 00100 Rome, Italy (Telephone Number in U.S. (202) 653-2400); *Production Yearbook,* and *The State of Food and Agriculture.*

G.K. Hall and Company, 70 Lincoln Street, Boston, Massachusetts 02111 (617) 423-3990; *The World in Figures.*

POLAND - FOREIGN AID

G.K. Hall and Company, 70 Lincoln Street, Boston, Massachusetts 02111 (617) 423-3990; *The World in Figures.*

POLAND - FOREIGN TRADE

Facts on File, 460 Park Avenue South, New York, New York 10016 (800) 443-8323; *The New Book of World Rankings.*

G.K. Hall and Company, 70 Lincoln Street, Boston, Massachusetts 02111 (617) 423-3990; *The World in Figures.*

Statistical Office of the United Nations, Publishing Service, New York, New York 10017 (800) 253-9646; *International Trade Statistics Yearbook,* and *Statistical Yearbook.*

The World Bank, 1818 H Street, NW, Washington, D.C. 20433 (202) 477-1234; *World Tables.*

POLAND - FORESTRY AND FOREST PRODUCTS

Euromonitor Publications Limited, 87-88 Turnmill Street, London EC1M 5QU, England; *European Marketing Data and Statistics.*

Facts on File, 460 Park Avenue South, New York, New York 10016 (800) 443-8323; *The New Book of World Rankings*

Food and Agricultural Organization of the United Nations (FAO) Via delle Terme di Caracalla, 00100 Rome, Italy (Telephone Number in U.S. (202) 653-2400); *The State of Food and Agriculture,* and *Yearbook of Forest Products.*

G.K. Hall and Company, 70 Lincoln Street, Boston, Massachusetts 02111 (617) 423-3990; *The World in Figures.*

Statistical Office of the United Nations, Publishing Service, New York, New York 10017 (800) 253-9646; *Statistical Yearbook.*

United Nations Educational, Scientific and Cultural Organization (UNESCO), 7 Place de Fontenoy, F-75700 Paris, France (Telephone Number in U.S. (212) 963-5981); *Statistical Yearbook.*

POLAND - GAS AND GAS LIQUIDS - See POLAND - MINING AND MINERAL PRODUCTS

POLAND - GENERAL INDUSTRIAL STATISTICS

Statistical Office of the United Nations, Publishing Service, New York, New York 10017 (800) 253-9646; *Industrial Statistics Yearbook.*

POLAND - GENERAL MORTALITY

Statistical Office of the United Nations, Publishing Service, New York, New York 10017 (800) 253-9646; *Demographic Yearbook.*

World Health Organization, Office of Publications, Avenue Appia, CH-1211 Geneva 27, Switzerland (Telephone Number in U.S. (518) 436-9686); *World Health Statistics Annual.*

POLAND - GEOGRAPHIC DATA

Facts on File, 460 Park Avenue South, New York, New York 10016 (800) 443-8323; *The New Book of World Rankings.*

POLAND - GOLD HOLDINGS

The World Bank, 1818 H Street, NW, Washington, D.C. 20433 (202) 477-1234; *World Tables.*

POLAND - GOLD PRODUCTION AND CONSUMPTION - See POLAND - MINING AND MINERAL PRODUCTS

POLAND - GOVERNMENT

G.K. Hall and Company, 70 Lincoln Street, Boston, Massachusetts 02111 (617) 423-3990; *The World in Figures.*

POLAND - GOVERNMENT EXPENDITURE

The World Bank, 1818 H Street, NW, Washington, D.C. 20433 (202) 477-1234; *World Tables.*

POLAND - GOVERNMENT REVENUE

Times Books, 201 East 50th Street, New York, New York 10022 (212) 751-2600; *The Economist Book of Vital World Statistics.*

The World Bank, 1818 H Street, NW, Washington, D.C. 20433 (202) 477-1234; *World Tables.*

POLAND - GOVERNMENT FINANCES

Statistical Office of the United Nations, Publishing Service, New York, New York 10017 (800) 253-9646; *Statistical Yearbook.*

POLAND - GRAIN PRODUCTION - See POLAND - CROPS

POLAND - GROSS DOMESTIC PRODUCT

The Economist Intelligence Unit, 111 West 57th Street, New York, New York 10019 (800) 938-4685; *The World Market Atlas.*

Facts on File, 460 Park Avenue South, New York, New York 10016 (800) 443-8323; *The New Book of World Rankings.*

G.K. Hall and Company, 70 Lincoln Street, Boston, Massachusetts 02111 (617) 423-3990; *The World in Figures.*

Statistical Office of the United Nations, Publishing Service, New York, New York 10017 (800) 253-9646; *Statistical Yearbook.*

Times Books, 201 East 50th Street, New York, New York 10022 (212) 751-2600; *The Economist Book of Vital World Statistics.*

The World Bank, 1818 H Street, NW, Washington, D.C. 20433 (202) 477-1234; *World Tables.*

POLAND - GROSS NATIONAL PRODUCT

U.S. Arms Control and Disarmament Agency, 320 Twenty-first Street, NW, Washington, D.C. 20451 (202) 647-8677; *World Military Expenditures and Arms Transfers.*

The World Bank, 1818 H Street, NW, Washington, D.C. 20433 (202) 477-1234; *World Tables.*

POLAND - HEALTH

Facts on File, 460 Park Avenue South, New York, New York 10016 (800) 443-8323; *The New Book of World Rankings.*

G.K. Hall and Company, 70 Lincoln Street, Boston, Massachusetts 02111 (617) 423-3990; *The World in Figures.*

Statistical Office of the United Nations, Publishing Service, New York, New York 10017 (800) 253-9646; *Statistical Yearbook.*

Times Books, 201 East 50th Street, New York, New York 10022 (212) 751-2600; *The Economist Book of Vital World Statistics.*

World Health Organization, Office of Publications, Avenue Appia, CH-1211 Geneva 27, Switzerland (Telephone Number in U.S. (518) 436-9686); *World Health Statistics Annual.*

POLAND - HEMP FIBRE PRODUCTION - See POLAND - TEXTILE INDUSTRY

POLAND - HIDE PRODUCTION

Food and Agricultural Organization of the United Nations (FAO), Via delle Terme di Caracalla, 00100 Rome, Italy (Telephone Number in U.S. (202) 653-2400); *Production Yearbook.*

POLAND - HIGHWAYS

G.K. Hall and Company, 70 Lincoln Street, Boston, Massachusetts 02111 (617) 423-3990; *The World in Figures.*

International Road Federation, 525 School Street, SW, Washington, D.C. 20024 (202) 554-2106; *World Road Statistics.*

Statistical Office of the United Nations, Publishing Service, New York, New York 10017 (800) 253-9646; *Annual Bulletin of Transport Statistics for Europe.*

POLAND - HONEY PRODUCTION

Commodity Research Bureau, Incorporated, 75 Wall Street, New York, New York 10005 (212) 504-7754; *Commodity Year Book.*

POLAND - HOPS PRODUCTION - See POLAND - CROPS

POLAND - HORSES - See POLAND - LIVESTOCK AND POULTRY

POLAND - HOURS OF WORK - See POLAND - EMPLOYMENT

POLAND - HOUSING AND HOUSING UNITS

Columbia University Press, 562 West 113th Street, New York, New York 10014 (212) 316-7100; *East European and Soviet Data Book.*

Facts on File, 460 Park Avenue South, New York, New York 10016 (800) 443-8323; *The New Book of World Rankings.*

POLAND - HYDROCHLORIC ACID PRODUCTION

Statistical Office of the United Nations, Publishing Service, New York, New York 10017 (800) 253-9646; *Statistical Yearbook.*

POLAND - ILLITERATE POPULATION

Columbia University Press, 562 West 113th Street, New York, New York 10014 (212) 316-7100; *East European and Soviet Data Book.*

The Economist Intelligence Unit, 111 West 57th Street, New York, New York 10019 (800) 938-4685; *The World Market Atlas.*

G.K. Hall and Company, 70 Lincoln Street, Boston, Massachusetts 02111 (617) 423-3990; *The World in Figures.*

United Nations Educational, Scientific and Cultural Organization (UNESCO), 7 Place de Fontenoy, F-75700 Paris, France (Telephone Number in U.S. (212) 963-5981); *Statistical Yearbook.*

POLAND - IMPORTS

American Automobile Manufacturers Association, 1401 H Eye Street, NW, Suite 900, Washington, D.C. 20005 (202) 326-5500; *World Motor Vehicle Data.*

The Economist Intelligence Unit, 111 West 57th Street, New York, New York 10019 (800) 938-4685; *The World Market Atlas.*

Food and Agricultural Organization of the United Nations (FAO) Via delle Terme di Caracalla, 00100 Rome, Italy (Telephone Number in U.S. (202) 653-2400); *The State of Food and Agriculture.*

G.K. Hall and Company, 70 Lincoln Street, Boston, Massachusetts 02111 (617) 423-3990; *The World in Figures.*

International Lead and Zinc Study Group, Metro House, 58 St. James's Street, London SW1A 1LD, England; *Lead and Zinc Statistics.*

International Monetary Fund, 700 Nineteenth Street, NW, Washington, D.C. 20431 (202) 623-7000; *Direction of Trade Statistics.*

International Rubber Study Group, York House, Eighth Floor, Empire Way, Wembley, London HA9 0PA, England; *Rubber Statistical Bulletin.*

Times Books, 201 East 50th Street, New York, New York 10022 (212) 751-2600; *The Economist Book of Vital World Statistics.*

The World Bank, 1818 H Street, NW, Washington, D.C. 20433 (202) 477-1234; *World Tables.*

POLAND - INDUSTRIAL METALS PRODUCTION - See POLAND - MINING AND MINERAL PRODUCTS

POLAND - INDUSTRY

Facts on File, 460 Park Avenue South, New York, New York 10016 (800) 443-8323; *The New Book of World Rankings.*

G.K. Hall and Company, 70 Lincoln Street, Boston, Massachusetts 02111 (617) 423-3990; *The World in Figures.*

International Labour Office, I.L.O. Publications, CH-1211, Geneva 22, Switzerland; *Yearbook of Labour Statistics.*

Statistical Office of the United Nations, Publishing Service, New York, New York 10017 (800) 253-9646; *Statistical Yearbook.*

Times Books, 201 East 50th Street, New York, New York 10022 (212) 751-2600; *The Economist Book of Vital World Statistics.*

The World Bank, 1818 H Street, NW, Washington, D.C. 20433 (202) 477-1234; *World Tables.*

World Intellectual Property Organization, 34 Chemin des Colombettes, CH-1211 Geneva 20, Switzerland; *Industrial Property Statistics.*

POLAND - INFANT AND MATERNAL MORTALITY

Statistical Office of the United Nations, Publishing Service, New York, New York 10017 (800) 253-9646; *Demographic Yearbook,* and *Statistical Yearbook.*

Times Books, 201 East 50th Street, New York, New York 10022 (212) 751-2600; *The Economist Book of Vital World Statistics.*

The World Bank, 1818 H Street, NW, Washington, D.C. 20433 (202) 477-1234; *World Tables*.

World Health Organization, Office of Publications, Avenue Appia, CH-1211 Geneva 27, Switzerland (Telephone Number in U.S. (518) 436-9686); *World Health Statistics Annual*.

POLAND - INTERNAL TRADE

Statistical Office of the United Nations, Publishing Service, New York, New York 10017 (800) 253-9646; *Statistical Yearbook*.

POLAND - INTERNATIONAL RESERVES EXCLUDING GOLD

The World Bank, 1818 H Street, NW, Washington, D.C. 20433 (202) 477-1234; *World Tables*.

POLAND - IRON ORE PRODUCTION AND CONSUMPTION - See POLAND - MINING AND MINERAL PRODUCTS

POLAND - LABOR FORCE

Columbia University Press, 562 West 113th Street, New York, New York 10014 (212) 316-7100; *East European and Soviet Data Book*.

Facts on File, 460 Park Avenue South, New York, New York 10016 (800) 443-8323; *The New Book of World Rankings*.

Food and Agricultural Organization of the United Nations (FAO) Via delle Terme di Caracalla, 00100 Rome, Italy (Telephone Number in U.S. (202) 653-2400); *The State of Food and Agriculture*.

G.K. Hall and Company, 70 Lincoln Street, Boston, Massachusetts 02111 (617) 423-3990; *The World in Figures*.

The World Bank, 1818 H Street, NW, Washington, D.C. 20433 (202) 477-1234; *World Tables*.

POLAND - LABOR PRODUCTIVITY

International Labour Office, I.L.O. Publications, CH-1211, Geneva 22, Switzerland; *Yearbook of Labour Statistics*.

POLAND - LAND USE

Euromonitor Publications Limited, 87-88 Turnmill Street, London EC1M 5QU, England; *European Marketing Data and Statistics*.

Food and Agricultural Organization of the United Nations (FAO), Via delle Terme di Caracalla, 00100 Rome, Italy (Telephone Number in U.S. (202) 653-2400); *Production Yearbook*.

G.K. Hall and Company, 70 Lincoln Street, Boston, Massachusetts 02111 (617) 423-3990; *The World in Figures*.

POLAND - LEAD AND LEAD ORE PRODUCTION AND CONSUMPTION - See POLAND - MINING AND MINERAL PRODUCTS

POLAND - LIBRARIES

Euromonitor Publications Limited, 87-88 Turnmill Street, London EC1M 5QU, England; *European Marketing Data and Statistics*.

Facts on File, 460 Park Avenue South, New York, New York 10016 (800) 443-8323; *The New Book of World Rankings*.

United Nations Educational, Scientific and Cultural Organization (UNESCO), 7 Place de Fontenoy, F-75700 Paris, France (Telephone Number in U.S. (212) 963-5981); *Statistical Yearbook*.

POLAND - LIGNITE PRODUCTION - See POLAND - MINING AND MINERAL PRODUCTS

POLAND - LIVESTOCK AND POULTRY

Commodity Research Bureau, Incorporated, 75 Wall Street, New York, New York 10005 (212) 504-7754; *Commodity Year Book*.

Euromonitor Publications Limited, 87-88 Turnmill Street, London EC1M 5QU, England; *European Marketing Data and Statistics*.

Facts on File, 460 Park Avenue South, New York, New York 10016 (800) 443-8323; *The New Book of World Rankings*.

Food and Agricultural Organization of the United Nations (FAO), Via delle Terme di Caracalla, 00100 Rome, Italy (Telephone Number in U.S. (202) 653-2400); *Production Yearbook*, and *The State of Food and Agriculture*.

G.K. Hall and Company, 70 Lincoln Street, Boston, Massachusetts 02111 (617) 423-3990; *The World in Figures*.

Statistical Office of the United Nations, Publishing Service, New York, New York 10017 (800) 253-9646; *Statistical Yearbook*.

POLAND - LIVING LEVELS

G.K. Hall and Company, 70 Lincoln Street, Boston, Massachusetts 02111 (617) 423-3990; *The World in Figures*.

Times Books, 201 East 50th Street, New York, New York 10022 (212) 751-2600; *The Economist Book of Vital World Statistics*.

POLAND - MAGNESIUM PRODUCTION AND CONSUMPTION - See POLAND - MINING AND MINERAL PRODUCTS

POLAND - MAIL - NUMBER OF ITEMS SENT OR RECEIVED

Statistical Office of the United Nations, Publishing Service, New York, New York 10017 (800) 253-9646; *Statistical Yearbook*.

POLAND - MANUFACTURING

American Automobile Manufacturers Association, 1401 H Eye Street, NW, Suite 900, Washington, D.C. 20005 (202) 326-5500; *World Motor Vehicle Data*.

Facts on File, 460 Park Avenue South, New York, New York 10016 (800) 443-8323; *The New Book of World Rankings*.

G.K. Hall and Company, 70 Lincoln Street, Boston, Massachusetts 02111 (617) 423-3990; *The World in Figures*.

Statistical Office of the United Nations, Publishing Service, New York, New York 10017 (800) 253-9646; *Statistical Yearbook*.

Times Books, 201 East 50th Street, New York, New York 10022 (212) 751-2600; *The Economist Book of Vital World Statistics*.

The World Bank, 1818 H Street, NW, Washington, D.C. 20433 (202) 477-1234; *World Tables*.

POLAND - MARRIAGE RATES

Facts on File, 460 Park Avenue South, New York, New York 10016 (800) 443-8323; *The New Book of World Rankings*.

Statistical Office of the United Nations, Publishing Service, New York, New York 10017 (800) 253-9646; *Demographic Yearbook*, and

Statistical Yearbook.

POLAND - MEAT PRODUCTION - See POLAND - LIVESTOCK AND POULTRY

POLAND - MERCHANT SHIPPING

G.K. Hall and Company, 70 Lincoln Street, Boston, Massachusetts 02111 (617) 423-3990; *The World in Figures.*

Lloyd's Register of Shipping, 17 Battery Place, New York, New York 10004 (212) 425-8050; *Register of Ships.*

Statistical Office of the United Nations, Publishing Service, New York, New York 10017 (800) 253-9646; *Annual Bulletin of Transport Statistics for Europe,* and *Statistical Yearbook.*

Times Books, 201 East 50th Street, New York, New York 10022 (212) 751-2600; *The Economist Book of Vital World Statistics.*

U.S. Department of Transportation, Maritime Administration, 400 Seventh Street, SW, Washington, D.C. 20590 (202) 366-5807; *A Statistical Analysis of the World's Merchant Fleets.*

POLAND - MILITARY

The International Institute for Strategic Studies, 23 Tavistock Street, London WC2E 7NQ, England; *The Military Balance.*

G.K. Hall and Company, 70 Lincoln Street, Boston, Massachusetts 02111 (617) 423-3990; *The World in Figures.*

U.S. Arms Control and Disarmament Agency, 320 Twenty-first Street, NW, Washington, D.C. 20451 (202) 647-8677; *World Military Expenditures and Arms Transfers.*

POLAND - MILK PRODUCTION - See POLAND - DAIRY PRODUCTS

POLAND - MILLET PRODUCTION - See POLAND - CROPS

POLAND - MINING AND MINERAL PRODUCTS

Commodity Research Bureau, Incorporated, 75 Wall Street, New York, New York 10005 (212) 504-7754; *Commodity Year Book.*

Facts on File, 460 Park Avenue South, New York, New York 10016 (800) 443-8323; *The New Book of World Rankings.*

G.K. Hall and Company, 70 Lincoln Street, Boston, Massachusetts 02111 (617) 423-3990; *The World in Figures.*

International Lead and Zinc Study Group, Metro House, 58 St. James's Street, London SW1A 1LD, England; *Lead and Zinc Statistics.*

Penn Well Publishing Company, 1421 South Sheridan Road, Post Office Box 1260, Tulsa, Oklahoma 74101 (800) 752-9764; *International Energy Statistics Sourcebook.*

Statistical Office of the United Nations, Publishing Service, New York, New York 10017 (800) 253-9646; *Statistical Yearbook.*

POLAND - MOLASSES PRODUCTION - See POLAND - CROPS

POLAND - MONEY EXCHANGE RATES

Statistical Office of the United Nations, Publishing Service, New York, New York 10017 (800) 253-9646; *Statistical Yearbook.*

POLAND - MONEY SUPPLY

G.K. Hall and Company, 70 Lincoln Street, Boston, Massachusetts 02111 (617) 423-3990; *The World in Figures.*

The World Bank, 1818 H Street, NW, Washington, D.C. 20433 (202) 477-1234; *World Tables.*

POLAND - MOTION PICTURES

Statistical Office of the United Nations, Publishing Service, New York, New York 10017 (800) 253-9646; *Statistical Yearbook.*

United Nations Educational, Scientific and Cultural Organization (UNESCO), 7 Place de Fontenoy, F-75700 Paris, France (Telephone Number in U.S. (212) 963-5981); *Statistical Yearbook.*

POLAND - MOTOR VEHICLE PRODUCTION AND ASSEMBLY

American Automobile Manufacturers Association, 1401 H Street, NW, Suite 900, Washington, D.C. 20005 (202) 326-5500; *World Motor Vehicle Data.*

Statistical Office of the United Nations, Publishing Service, New York, New York 10017 (800) 253-9646; *Statistical Yearbook.*

POLAND - MOTOR VEHICLE TAXES - See POLAND - TAXATION

POLAND - MOTOR VEHICLES IN USE

American Automobile Manufacturers Association, 1401 H Street, NW, Suite 900, Washington, D.C. 20005 (202) 326-5500; *World Motor Vehicle Data.*

G.K. Hall and Company, 70 Lincoln Street, Boston, Massachusetts 02111 (617) 423-3990; *The World in Figures.*

International Road Federation, 525 School Street, SW, Washington, D.C. 20024 (202) 554-2106; *World Road Statistics.*

Statistical Office of the United Nations, Publishing Service, New York, New York 10017 (800) 253-9646; *Statistical Yearbook.*

Times Books, 201 East 50th Street, New York, New York 10022 (212) 751-2600; *The Economist Book of Vital World Statistics.*

POLAND - MUSEUMS

Euromonitor Publications Limited, 87-88 Turnmill Street, London EC1M 5QU, England; *European Marketing Data and Statistics.*

Facts on File, 460 Park Avenue South, New York, New York 10016 (800) 443-8323; *The New Book of World Rankings.*

United Nations Educational, Scientific and Cultural Organization (UNESCO), 7 Place de Fontenoy, F-75700 Paris, France (Telephone Number in U.S. (212) 963-5981); *Statistical Yearbook.*

POLAND - NATALITY - See POLAND - BIRTH RATES

POLAND - NATIONAL ACCOUNTS

Statistical Office of the United Nations, Publishing Service, New York, New York 10017 (800) 253-9646; *National Accounts Statistics,* and *Statistical Yearbook.*

POLAND - NATIONAL INCOME

Facts on File, 460 Park Avenue South, New York, New York 10016 (800) 443-8323; *The New Book of World Rankings*.

G.K. Hall and Company, 70 Lincoln Street, Boston, Massachusetts 02111 (617) 423-3990; *The World in Figures*.

Statistical Office of the United Nations, Publishing Service, New York, New York 10017 (800) 253-9646; *Statistical Yearbook*.

POLAND - NATIONAL PRODUCT

Facts on File, 460 Park Avenue South, New York, New York 10016 (800) 443-8323; *The New Book of World Rankings*.

Statistical Office of the United Nations, Publishing Service, New York, New York 10017 (800) 253-9646; *Statistical Yearbook*.

POLAND - NATURAL GAS PRODUCTION - See POLAND - MINING AND MINERAL PRODUCTS

POLAND - NATURAL RUBBER PRODUCTION

International Rubber Study Group, York House, Eighth Floor, Empire Way, Wembley, London IIA9 0PA, England; *Rubber Statistical Bulletin*.

POLAND - NET MATERIAL PRODUCT

Statistical Office of the United Nations, Publishing Service, New York, New York 10017 (800) 253-9646; *Statistical Yearbook*.

POLAND - NEWSPAPER PRODUCTION - See POLAND - FORESTRY AND FOREST PRODUCTS

POLAND - NEWSPRINT PRODUCTION AND CONSUMPTION - See POLAND - FORESTRY AND FOREST PRODUCTS

POLAND - NICKEL AND NICKEL ORE PRODUCTION AND CONSUMPTION - See POLAND - MINING AND MINERAL PRODUCTS

POLAND - NITRIC ACID PRODUCTION - See POLAND - MINING AND MINERAL PRODUCTS

POLAND - OATS PRODUCTION - See POLAND - CROPS

POLAND - OCCUPATIONS - See POLAND - LABOR FORCE

POLAND - ONION PRODUCTION - See POLAND - CROPS

POLAND - PAPER PRODUCTION - See POLAND - FORESTRY AND FOREST PRODUCTS

POLAND - PARTY LEADERS

Columbia University Press, 562 West 113th Street, New York, New York 10014 (212) 316-7100; *East European and Soviet Data Book*.

POLAND - PARTY MEMBERSHIP

Columbia University Press, 562 West 113th Street, New York, New York 10014 (212) 316-7100; *East European and Soviet Data Book*.

POLAND - PATENTS

Statistical Office of the United Nations, Publishing Service, New York, New York 10017 (800) 253-9646; *Statistical Yearbook*.

World Intellectual Property Organization, 34 Chemin des Colombettes, CH-1211 Geneva 20, Switzerland; *Industrial Property Statistics*.

POLAND - PEANUT PRODUCTION - See POLAND - CROPS

POLAND - PERIODICALS

United Nations Educational, Scientific and Cultural Organization (UNESCO), 7 Place de Fontenoy, F-75700 Paris, France (Telephone Number in U.S. (212) 963-5981); *Statistical Yearbook*.

POLAND - PESTICIDE USE

Food and Agricultural Organization of the United Nations (FAO) Via delle Terme di Caracalla, 00100 Rome, Italy (Telephone Number in U.S. (202) 653-2400); *The State of Food and Agriculture*.

POLAND - PETROLEUM INDUSTRY

Euromonitor Publications Limited, 87-88 Turnmill Street, London EC1M 5QU, England; *European Marketing Data and Statistics*.

Facts on File, 460 Park Avenue South, New York, New York 10016 (800) 443-8323; *The New Book of World Rankings*.

Food and Agricultural Organization of the United Nations (FAO) Via delle Terme di Caracalla, 00100 Rome, Italy (Telephone Number in U.S. (202) 653-2400); *The State of Food and Agriculture*.

G.K. Hall and Company, 70 Lincoln Street, Boston, Massachusetts 02111 (617) 423-3990; *The World in Figures*.

Penn Well Publishing Company, 1421 South Sheridan Road, Post Office Box 1260, Tulsa, Oklahoma 74101 (800) 752-9764; *International Energy Statistics Sourcebook*.

Statistical Office of the United Nations, Publishing Service, New York, New York 10017 (800) 253-9646; *Statistical Yearbook*.

POLAND - PHOSPHATE ROCK PRODUCTION - See POLAND - MINING AND MINERAL PRODUCTS

POLAND - PIG-IRON AND FERRO-ALLOY PRODUCTION - See POLAND - MINING AND MINERAL PRODUCTS

POLAND - PIGS - See POLAND - LIVESTOCK AND POULTRY

POLAND - PIPELINES FOR OIL AND PETROLEUM PRODUCTS

Statistical Office of the United Nations, Publishing Service, New York, New York 10017 (800) 253-9646; *Annual Bulletin of Transport Statistics for Europe*.

POLAND - PLASTIC AND RESIN PRODUCTION

Commodity Research Bureau, Incorporated, 75 Wall Street, New York, New York 10005 (212) 504-7754; *Commodity Year Book*.

Statistical Office of the United Nations, Publishing Service, New York, New York 10017 (800) 253-9646; *Statistical Yearbook*.

POLAND - POPULATION

Columbia University Press, 562 West 113th Street, New York, New York 10014 (212) 316-7100; *East European and Soviet Data Book*.

The Economist Intelligence Unit, 111 West 57th Street, New York, New York 10019 (800) 938-4685; *The World Market Atlas*.

Euromonitor Publications Limited, 87-88 Turnmill Street, London EC1M 5QU, England; *European Marketing Data and Statistics*.

Facts on File, 460 Park Avenue South, New York, New York 10016 (800) 443-8323; *The New Book of World Rankings*.

Food and Agricultural Organization of the United Nations (FAO), Via delle Terme di Caracalla, 00100 Rome, Italy (Telephone Number in U.S. (202) 653-2400); *Production Yearbook*.

G.K. Hall and Company, 70 Lincoln Street, Boston, Massachusetts 02111 (617) 423-3990; *The World in Figures*.

International Labour Office, I.L.O. Publications, CH-1211, Geneva 22, Switzerland; *Yearbook of Labour Statistics*.

Statistical Office of the United Nations, Publishing Service, New York, New York 10017 (800) 253-9646; *Demographic Yearbook*, and *Statistical Yearbook*.

Times Books, 201 East 50th Street, New York, New York 10022 (212) 751-2600; *The Economist Book of Vital World Statistics*.

United Nations Educational, Scientific and Cultural Organization (UNESCO), 7 Place de Fontenoy, F-75700 Paris, France (Telephone Number in U.S. (212) 963-5981); *Statistical Yearbook*.

U.S. Arms Control and Disarmament Agency, 320 Twenty-first Street, NW, Washington, D.C. 20451 (202) 647-8677; *World Military Expenditures and Arms Transfers*.

World Health Organization, Office of Publications, Avenue Appia, CH-1211 Geneva 27, Switzerland (Telephone Number in U.S. (518) 436-9686); *World Health Statistics Annual*.

POLAND - POST OFFICES

Facts on File, 460 Park Avenue South, New York, New York 10016 (800) 443-8323; *The New Book of World Rankings*.

POLAND - POTATO PRODUCTION - See POLAND - CROPS

POLAND - POWER PRODUCTION INDUSTRY

Statistical Office of the United Nations, Publishing Service, New York, New York 10017 (800) 253-9646; *Statistical Yearbook*.

POLAND - PRICES

Facts on File, 460 Park Avenue South, New York, New York 10016 (800) 443-8323; *The New Book of World Rankings*.

Food and Agricultural Organization of the United Nations (FAO), Via delle Terme di Caracalla, 00100 Rome, Italy (Telephone Number in U.S. (202) 653-2400); *Production Yearbook*, and *The State of Food and Agriculture*.

G.K. Hall and Company, 70 Lincoln Street, Boston, Massachusetts 02111 (617) 423-3990; *The World in Figures*.

International Labour Office, I.L.O. Publications, CH-1211, Geneva 22, Switzerland; *Yearbook of Labour Statistics*.

International Lead and Zinc Study Group, Metro House, 58 St. James's Street, London SW1A 1LD, England; *Lead and Zinc Statistics*.

International Rubber Study Group, York House, Eighth Floor, Empire Way, Wembley, London HA9 0PA, England; *Rubber Statistical Bulletin*.

POLAND - PRODUCTION

American Automobile Manufacturers Association, 1401 H Street, NW, Suite 900, Washington, D.C. 20005 (202) 326-5500; *World Motor Vehicle Data*.

Facts on File, 460 Park Avenue South, New York, New York 10016 (800) 443-8323; *The New Book of World Rankings*.

G.K. Hall and Company, 70 Lincoln Street, Boston, Massachusetts 02111 (617) 423-3990; *The World in Figures*.

International Lead and Zinc Study Group, Metro House, 58 St. James's Street, London SW1A 1LD, England; *Lead and Zinc Statistics*.

International Rubber Study Group, York House, Eighth Floor, Empire Way, Wembley, London HA9 0PA, England; *Rubber Statistical Bulletin*.

POLAND - PUBLIC FINANCE

Facts on File, 460 Park Avenue South, New York, New York 10016 (800) 443-8323; *The New Book of World Rankings*.

POLAND - RADIO BROADCASTING - See POLAND - BROADCASTING

POLAND - RADIO RECEIVER PRODUCTION

Statistical Office of the United Nations, Publishing Service, New York, New York 10017 (800) 253-9646; *Statistical Yearbook*.

POLAND - RAILWAYS

Euromonitor Publications Limited, 87-88 Turnmill Street, London EC1M 5QU, England; *European Marketing Data and Statistics*.

G.K. Hall and Company, 70 Lincoln Street, Boston, Massachusetts 02111 (617) 423-3990; *The World in Figures*.

Jane's Information Group, Sentinel House, 163 Brighton Road, Coulsdon, Surrey CR5 2NH, England (Telephone Number in U.S. (703) 683-3700); *Jane's World Railways*.

Statistical Office of the United Nations, Publishing Service, New York, New York 10017 (800) 253-9646; *Annual Bulletin of Transport Statistics for Europe*, and *Statistical Yearbook*.

POLAND - RAPESEED PRODUCTION - See POLAND - CROPS

POLAND - RELIGION

Facts on File, 460 Park Avenue South, New York, New York 10016 (800) 443-8323; *The New Book of World Rankings*.

POLAND - RETAIL TRADE

G.K. Hall and Company, 70 Lincoln Street, Boston, Massachusetts 02111 (617) 423-3990; *The World in Figures*.

Statistical Office of the United Nations, Publishing Service, New York, New York 10017 (800) 253-9646; *Statistical Yearbook*.

POLAND - RICE PRODUCTION - See POLAND - CROPS

POLAND - ROOT AND TUBER PRODUCTION - See POLAND - CROPS

POLAND - ROUNDWOOD PRODUCTION - See POLAND - FORESTRY AND FOREST PRODUCTS

POLAND - RUBBER PRODUCTION AND CONSUMPTION

Commodity Research Bureau, Incorporated, 75 Wall Street, New York, New York 10005 (212) 504-7754; *Commodity Year Book*.

Facts on File, 460 Park Avenue South, New York, New York 10016 (800) 443-8323; *The New Book of World Rankings*.

International Rubber Study Group, York House, Eighth Floor, Empire Way, Wembley, London HA9 0PA, England; *Rubber Statistical Bulletin*.

Statistical Office of the United Nations, Publishing Service, New York, New York 10017 (800) 253-9646; *Statistical Yearbook*.

POLAND - RYE PRODUCTION - See POLAND - CROPS

POLAND - SALT PRODUCTION - See POLAND - MINING AND MINERAL PRODUCTS

POLAND - SAWNWOOD PRODUCTION - See POLAND - FORESTRY AND FOREST PRODUCTS

POLAND - SCIENCE AND TECHNOLOGY - EXPENDITURE FOR RESEARCH

Statistical Office of the United Nations, Publishing Service, New York, New York 10017 (800) 253-9646; *Statistical Yearbook*.

POLAND - SCIENTISTS AND TECHNICIANS

Statistical Office of the United Nations, Publishing Service, New York, New York 10017 (800) 253-9646; *Statistical Yearbook*.

United Nations Educational, Scientific and Cultural Organization (UNESCO), 7 Place de Fontenoy, F-75700 Paris, France (Telephone Number in U.S. (212) 063-5081); *Statistical Yearbook*.

POLAND - SENIOR CITIZENS

Facts on File, 460 Park Avenue South, New York, New York 10016 (800) 443-8323; *The New Book of World Rankings*.

POLAND - SHEEP - See POLAND - LIVESTOCK AND POULTRY

POLAND - SILVER PRODUCTION AND CONSUMPTION - See POLAND - MINING AND MINERAL PRODUCTS

POLAND - SOCIAL DATA

Facts on File, 460 Park Avenue South, New York, New York 10016 (800) 443-8323; *The New Book of World Rankings*.

G.K. Hall and Company, 70 Lincoln Street, Boston, Massachusetts 02111 (617) 423-3990; *The World in Figures*.

POLAND - STEEL - See POLAND - MINING AND MINERAL PRODUCTS

POLAND - STOCKS - COMMODITY - MARKET PRICE - INDEX

Food and Agricultural Organization of the United Nations (FAO) Via delle Terme di Caracalla, 00100 Rome, Italy (Telephone Number in U.S. (202) 653-2400); *The State of Food and Agriculture*.

International Lead and Zinc Study Group, Metro House, 58 St. James's Street, London SW1A 1LD, England; *Lead and Zinc Statistics*.

POLAND - SUGAR PRODUCTION AND CONSUMPTION - See POLAND - CROPS

POLAND - SULPHUR AND SULPHURIC ACID PRODUCTION - See POLAND - MINING AND MINERAL PRODUCTS

POLAND - TAXATION

G.K. Hall and Company, 70 Lincoln Street, Boston, Massachusetts 02111 (617) 423-3990; *The World in Figures*.

International Road Federation, 525 School Street, SW, Washington, D.C. 20024 (202) 554-2106; *World Road Statistics*.

The World Bank, 1818 H Street, NW, Washington, D.C. 20433 (202) 477-1234; *World Tables*.

POLAND - TEA CONSUMPTION - See POLAND - CROPS

POLAND - TELEGRAPH SERVICE

Statistical Office of the United Nations, Publishing Service, New York, New York 10017 (800) 253-9646; *Statistical Yearbook*.

POLAND - TELEPHONES IN USE

American Telephone and Telegraph Company, 26 Parsippany Road, Whippany, New Jersey 07981 (800) 338-4038; *The World's Telephones*.

G.K. Hall and Company, 70 Lincoln Street, Boston, Massachusetts 02111 (617) 423-3990; *The World in Figures*.

Statistical Office of the United Nations, Publishing Service, New York, New York 10017 (800) 253-9646; *Statistical Yearbook*.

POLAND - TELEVISION BROADCASTING - See POLAND - BROADCASTING

POLAND - TELEVISION RECEIVER PRODUCTION

Statistical Office of the United Nations, Publishing Service, New York, New York 10017 (800) 253-9646; *Statistical Yearbook*.

POLAND - TEXTILE INDUSTRY

Food and Agricultural Organization of the United Nations (FAO), Via delle Terme di Caracalla, 00100 Rome, Italy (Telephone Number in U.S. (202) 653-2400); *Production Yearbook*.

G.K. Hall and Company, 70 Lincoln Street, Boston, Massachusetts 02111 (617) 423-3990; *The World in Figures*.

Statistical Office of the United Nations, Publishing Service, New York, New York 10017 (800) 253-9646; *Statistical Yearbook*.

POLAND - THEATRE

United Nations Educational, Scientific and Cultural Organization (UNESCO), 7 Place de Fontenoy, F-75700 Paris, France (Telephone Number in U.S. (212) 963-5981); *Statistical Yearbook*.

POLAND - TIMBER RESOURCE FORESTS - See POLAND - FORESTRY AND FOREST PRODUCTS

POLAND - TIN - INDUSTRIAL CONSUMPTION - See POLAND - MINING AND MINERAL PRODUCTS

POLAND - TIRE (MOTOR VEHICLE) PRODUCTION

International Rubber Study Group, York House, Eighth Floor, Empire Way, Wembley, London HA9 0PA, England; *Rubber Statistical Bulletin.*

Statistical Office of the United Nations, Publishing Service, New York, New York 10017 (800) 253-9646; *Statistical Yearbook.*

POLAND - TOBACCO PRODUCTION

Euromonitor Publications Limited, 87-88 Turnmill Street, London EC1M 5QU, England; *European Marketing Data and Statistics.*

Facts on File, 460 Park Avenue South, New York, New York 10016 (800) 443-8323; *The New Book of World Rankings.*

Statistical Office of the United Nations, Publishing Service, New York, New York 10017 (800) 253-9646; *Statistical Yearbook.*

POLAND - TOURISM

Euromonitor Publications Limited, 87-88 Turnmill Street, London EC1M 5QU, England; *European Marketing Data and Statistics.*

Facts on File, 460 Park Avenue South, New York, New York 10016 (800) 443-8323; *The New Book of World Rankings.*

G.K. Hall and Company, 70 Lincoln Street, Boston, Massachusetts 02111 (617) 423-3990; *The World in Figures.*

Statistical Office of the United Nations, Publishing Service, New York, New York 10017 (800) 253-9646; *Statistical Yearbook.*

Times Books, 201 East 50th Street, New York, New York 10022 (212) 751-2600; *The Economist Book of Vital World Statistics.*

World Tourism Organization, Calle Capitan Haya 42, E-28020 Madrid, Spain; *Yearbook of Tourism Statistics.*

POLAND - TRACTORS IN USE

Statistical Office of the United Nations, Publishing Service, New York, New York 10017 (800) 253-9646; *Statistical Yearbook.*

POLAND - TRADE

Euromonitor Publications Limited, 87-88 Turnmill Street, London EC1M 5QU, England; *European Marketing Data and Statistics.*

Food and Agricultural Organization of the United Nations (FAO) Via delle Terme di Caracalla, 00100 Rome, Italy (Telephone Number in U.S. (202) 653-2400); *The State of Food and Agriculture.*

POLAND - TRADEMARKS AND SERVICE MARKS

Statistical Office of the United Nations, Publishing Service, New York, New York 10017 (800) 253-9646; *Statistical Yearbook.*

World Intellectual Property Organization, 34 Chemin des Colombettes, CH-1211 Geneva 20, Switzerland; *Industrial Property Statistics.*

POLAND - TRANSPORTATION AND COMMUNICATIONS

Facts on File, 460 Park Avenue South, New York, New York 10016 (800) 443-8323; *The New Book of World Rankings.*

G.K. Hall and Company, 70 Lincoln Street, Boston, Massachusetts 02111 (617) 423-3990; *The World in Figures.*

POLAND - TURKEYS - See POLAND - LIVESTOCK AND POULTRY

POLAND - UNEMPLOYMENT

Euromonitor Publications Limited, 87-88 Turnmill Street, London EC1M 5QU, England; *European Marketing Data and Statistics.*

International Labour Office, I.L.O. Publications, CH-1211, Geneva 22, Switzerland; *Yearbook of Labour Statistics.*

POLAND - VITAL STATISTICS

G.K. Hall and Company, 70 Lincoln Street, Boston, Massachusetts 02111 (617) 423-3990; *The World in Figures.*

Statistical Office of the United Nations, Publishing Service, New York, New York 10017 (800) 253-9646; *Statistical Yearbook.*

World Health Organization, Office of Publications, Avenue Appia, CH-1211 Geneva 27, Switzerland (Telephone Number in U.S. (518) 436-9686); *World Health Statistics Annual.*

POLAND - WAGES

Euromonitor Publications Limited, 87-88 Turnmill Street, London EC1M 5QU, England; *European Marketing Data and Statistics.*

G.K. Hall and Company, 70 Lincoln Street, Boston, Massachusetts 02111 (617) 423-3990; *The World in Figures.*

International Labour Office, I.L.O. Publications, CH-1211, Geneva 22, Switzerland; *Yearbook of Labour Statistics.*

Statistical Office of the United Nations, Publishing Service, New York, New York 10017 (800) 253-9646; *Statistical Yearbook.*

POLAND - WATERWAYS IN USE

Statistical Office of the United Nations, Publishing Service, New York, New York 10017 (800) 253-9646; *Annual Bulletin of Transport Statistics for Europe.*

POLAND - WEATHER

Facts on File, 460 Park Avenue South, New York, New York 10016 (800) 443-8323; *The New Book of World Rankings.*

G.K. Hall and Company, 70 Lincoln Street, Boston, Massachusetts 02111 (617) 423-3990; *The World in Figures.*

POLAND - WHEAT PRODUCTION AND PRICES - See POLAND - CROPS

POLAND - WHOLESALE TRADE

Statistical Office of the United Nations, Publishing Service, New York, New York 10017 (800) 253-9646; *Statistical Yearbook.*

POLAND - WINE PRODUCTION

Facts on File, 460 Park Avenue South, New York, New York 10016 (800) 443-8323; *The New Book of World Rankings.*

POLAND - WOOD PULP PRODUCTION - See POLAND - FORESTRY AND FOREST PRODUCTS

POLAND - WOOL PRODUCTION

Facts on File, 460 Park Avenue South, New York, New York 10016 (800) 443-8323; *The New Book of World Rankings.*

POLAND - YARN PRODUCTION

Statistical Office of the United Nations, Publishing Service, New York, New York 10017 (800) 253-9646; *Statistical Yearbook.*

POLAND - ZINC AND ZINC ORE PRODUCTION AND CONSUMPTION - See POLAND - MINING AND MINERAL PRODUCTS

POLICE - See LAW ENFORCEMENT and PUBLIC SAFETY

POLIOMYELITIS

U.S. Department of Health and Human Services, Center for Disease Control, 1000 Clifton Road, NE, Atlanta, Georgia 30333 (404) 639-3311; *Summary of Notifiable Diseases, United States Morbidity and Mortality Weekly Report,* and *National Health Interview Survey.*

POLITICAL ACTION COMMITTEES

U.S. Federal Election Commission, 999 E Street, NW, Washington, D.C. 20463 (800) 424-9530; *FEC Reports on Financial Activity, United States Senate and House Campaigns, Party and Non-Party Political Committees,* and press releases.

POLITICAL PARTIES - CAMPAIGN FINANCES

U.S. Federal Election Commission, 999 E Street, NW, Washington, D.C. 20463 (800) 424-9530; *FEC Reports on Financial Activity, Final Report, Party and Non-Party Political Committees, FEC Reports on Financial Activity, Final Report, Presidential Pre-Nomination Campaigns,* and *FEC Reports on Financial Activity, Final Report, U.S. Senate and House Campaigns.*

POLITICAL PARTIES - CAMPAIGN FINANCES - POLITICAL ACTION COMMITTEES

U.S. Federal Election Commission, 999 E Street, NW, Washington, D.C. 20463 (800) 424-9530; *FEC Reports on Financial Activity, Final Report, United States Senate and House Campaigns,* and press releases.

POLITICAL PARTIES - CONGRESS - COMPOSITION OF

U.S. Congress, Joint Committee on Printing, North Capitol and H Streets, NW, Washington, D.C. 20401 (202) 275-2051; *Congressional Directory,* and unpublished data.

POLITICAL PARTIES - CONGRESSIONAL DISTRICTS

Congressional Quarterly, Incorporated, 1414 22nd Street, NW, Washington, D.C. 20037 (202) 887-8500; *Congressional Quarterly Weekly Report.*

Elections Research Center, 558 Greystone Street, Chevy Chase, Maryland 20815 (202) 659-9490; *America Votes.*

POLITICAL PARTIES - GOVERNORS - BY PARTY AFFILIATION

National Governors' Association, Hall of the States, 444 North Capitol, Washington, D.C. 20001 (202) 624-5300; *Directory of Governors of the American States, Commonwealths, and Territories.*

POLITICAL PARTIES - STATE LEGISLATURES - COMPOSITION OF

Council of State Governments, Post Office Box 11910, Iron Works Pike, Lexington, Kentucky 40578 (606) 231-1939; *State Elective Officials and the Legislatures.*

National Conference of State Legislatures, 1050 Seventeenth Street, Suite 2100, Denver, Colorado 80265 (303) 623-7800; *State Legislatures.*

POLITICAL PARTIES - VOTER REGISTRATION

Center for Political Studies, University of Michigan, Post Office Box 1248, Ann Arbor, Michigan 48106 (313) 764-8363; unpublished data.

POLITICAL PARTIES - VOTES

Elections Research Center, 558 Greystone Street, Chevy Chase, Maryland 20815 (202) 659-9490; *America Votes.*

POLITICAL TV ADVERTISING

Television Bureau of Advertising, Incorporated, 850 Third Avenue, New York, New York 10022 (212) 486-1111; data compiled by Competitive Media Reporting, 11 West 42nd Street, New York, New York 10036 (212) 789-1400.

POLLOCK

U.S. Department of Commerce, National Oceanic and Atmospheric Administration, National Marine Fisheries Service, 1335 East-West Highway, Silver Spring, Maryland 20910 (301) 427-2239; *Fisheries of the United States,* and *Fishery Statistics of the United States.*

POLLUTION - ABATEMENT EXPENDITURES

U.S. Department of Commerce, Bureau of Economic Analysis, Fourteenth between Constitution Avenue and E Street, NW, Washington, D.C. 20230 (202) 606-9900; *Survey of Current Business,* and unpublished data.

U.S. Department of Commerce, Bureau of the Census, Suitland, Maryland 20233 (301) 763-4040; *Current Industrial Reports.*

POLLUTION - AIR

U.S. Department of Commerce, Bureau of Economic Analysis, Fourteenth Street between Constitution Avenue and E Street, NW, Washington, D.C. 20230 (202) 606-9900; *Survey of Current Business,* and unpublished data.

U.S. Department of Commerce, Bureau of the Census, Suitland, Maryland 20233 (301) 763-4040; *Current Industrial Reports.*

U.S. Environmental Protection Agency, 401 M Street, SW, Washington, D.C. 20460 (202) 382-2090; *National Air Quality and Emissions Trends Report, National Air Pollutant Emission Trends,* and *Air Quality Update.*

POLLUTION - HAZARDOUS WASTE SITES

U.S. Environmental Protection Agency, 401 M Street, SW, Washington, D.C. 20460 (202) 382-2090; *Supplementary Materials: National Priorities List, Proposed Rule.*

POLLUTION - MOTOR VEHICLE EMISSIONS

U.S. Environmental Protection Agency, 401 M Street, SW, Washington, D.C. 20460 (202) 382-2090; *National Air Pollutant Emission Trends.*

POLLUTION - WATER

U.S. Department of Commerce, Bureau of Economic Analysis, Fourteenth Street between Constitution Avenue and E Street, NW, Washington, D.C. 20230 (202) 606-9900; *Survey of Current Business,* and unpublished data.

U.S. Department of Commerce, Bureau of the Census, Suitland, Maryland 20233 (301) 763-4040; *Current Industrial Reports.*

U.S. Department of Transportation, United States Coast Guard, 2100 Second Street, SW, Washington, D.C. 20593 (202) 267-1587; unpublished data from the *Marine Safety Information System.*

POOR PERSONS - See INCOME and POVERTY

POPULATION - See also VITAL STATISTICS

POPULATION - ABROAD - U.S. POPULATION

U.S. Department of Commerce, Bureau of the Census, Suitland, Maryland 20233 (301) 763-4040; *Census of Population.*

U.S. Department of State, 2201 C Street, NW, Washington, D.C. 20520 (202) 647-4000; unpublished data.

POPULATION - AGE - AMERICAN INDIAN, ESKIMO, ALEUT POPULATION

U.S. Department of Commerce, Bureau of the Census, Suitland, Maryland 20233 (301) 763-4040; *Current Population Reports.*

POPULATION - AGE - ASIAN AND PACIFIC ISLANDER POPULATION

U.S. Department of Commerce, Bureau of the Census, Suitland, Maryland 20233 (301) 763-4040; *Current Population Reports,* and unpublished data.

POPULATION - AGE - BLACK POPULATION

U.S. Department of Commerce, Bureau of the Census, Suitland, Maryland 20233 (301) 763-4040; *Current Population Reports.*

POPULATION - AGE - DISTRIBUTION

U.S. Department of Commerce, Bureau of the Census, Suitland, Maryland 20233 (301) 763-4040; *Current Population Reports.*

POPULATION - AGE - HISPANIC POPULATION

U.S. Department of Commerce, Bureau of the Census, Suitland, Maryland 20233 (301) 763-4040; *Current Population Reports,* and unpublished data.

POPULATION - AGE - OUTLYING AREAS

U.S. Department of Commerce, Bureau of the Census, Suitland, Maryland 20233 (301) 763-4040; *Census of Population,* and *Characteristics of the Population.*

POPULATION - AGE - RACE

U.S. Department of Commerce, Bureau of the Census, Suitland, Maryland 20233 (301) 763-4040; *Current Population Reports,* and *Census of Population.*

POPULATION - AGE - SCHOOL ENROLLMENT

U.S. Department of Commerce, Bureau of the Census, Suitland, Maryland 20233 (301) 763-4040; *Current Population Reports.*

U.S. Department of Education, National Center for Education Statistics, 400 Maryland Avenue, SW, Washington, D.C. 20202 (202) 708-5366; *Digest of Education Statistics,* and *Projections of Educational Statistics.*

POPULATION - AGE - SEX

U.S. Department of Commerce, Bureau of the Census, Suitland, Maryland 20233 (301) 763-4040; *Current Population Reports,* and *Census of Population.*

POPULATION - AGE - VOTING-AGE POPULATION - VOTES

Elections Research Center, 558 Greystone Street, Chevy Chase, Maryland 20815 (202) 659-9490; *America Votes.*

U.S. Department of Commerce, Bureau of the Census, Suitland, Maryland 20233 (301) 763-4040; *Current Population Reports.*

POPULATION - ANCESTRY

U.S. Department of Commerce, Bureau of the Census, Suitland, Maryland 20233 (301) 763-4040; *Census of Population, Supplementary Reports, Detailed Ancestry Groups for States.*

POPULATION - CENTER

U.S. Department of Commerce, Bureau of the Census, Suitland, Maryland 20233 (301) 763-4040; unpublished data.

POPULATION - CITIES

U.S. Department of Commerce, Bureau of the Census, Suitland, Maryland 20233 (301) 763-4040; *Census of Population and Housing.*

POPULATION - CIVILIAN

U.S. Department of Commerce, Bureau of the Census, Suitland, Maryland 20233 (301) 763-4040; *Current Population Reports.*

POPULATION - COASTAL

U.S. Department of Commerce, Bureau of the Census, Suitland, Maryland 20233 (301) 763-4040; *Census of Population and Housing,* and unpublished data.

POPULATION - DENSITY

U.S. Department of Commerce, Bureau of the Census, Suitland, Maryland 20233 (301) 763-4040; *Area Measurement Reports, Current Population Reports,* and *Census of Population and Housing.*

POPULATION - DENSITY - FOREIGN COUNTRIES

Statistical Office of the United Nations, Publishing Service, New York, New York 10017 (800) 253-9646; *Demographic Yearbook.*

U.S. Department of Commerce, Bureau of the Census, Suitland, Maryland 20233 (301) 763-4040; *World Population Profile.*

POPULATION - ELDERLY

U.S. Department of Commerce, Bureau of the Census, Suitland, Maryland 20233 (301) 763-4040; *Census of Population, Current Population Reports*, and unpublished data.

POPULATION - ETHNIC ORIGIN

U.S. Department of Commerce, Bureau of the Census, Suitland, Maryland 20233 (301) 763-4040; *Census of Population, The Foreign Born Population in the U.S.*

POPULATION - FERTILITY

U.S. Department of Commerce, Bureau of the Census, Suitland, Maryland 20233 (301) 763-4040; *Current Population Reports.*

U.S. Department of Health and Human Services, Public Health Service, 200 Independence Avenue, SW, Washington, D.C. 20201 (202) 619-1296; *Vital Statistics of the United States*, and unpublished data.

POPULATION - FOREIGN BORN

U.S. Department of Commerce, Bureau of the Census, Suitland, Maryland 20233 (301) 763-4040; *Census of Population, The Foreign Born Population in the U.S.*, and *Census of Population, Supplementary Reports, Detailed Ancestry Groups for States.*

POPULATION - FOREIGN COUNTRIES

Statistical Office of the United Nations, Publishing Service, New York, New York 10017 (800) 253-9646; *Demographic Yearbook.*

U.S. Department of Commerce, Bureau of the Census, Suitland, Maryland 20233 (301) 763-4040; *International Data Base and World Population Profile.*

POPULATION - GROUP QUARTERS

U.S. Department of Commerce, Bureau of the Census, Suitland, Maryland 20233 (301) 763-4040; *Census of Population, General Population Characteristics.*

POPULATION - HISPANIC ORIGIN - See HISPANIC ORIGIN POPULATION

POPULATION - HOUSEHOLDS AND/OR FAMILIES - See HOUSEHOLDS OR FAMILIES

POPULATION - IMMIGRANTS

U.S. Department of Justice, Immigration and Naturalization Service, 425 I Street, NW, Washington, D.C. 20536 (202) 514-4316; *Statistical Yearbook*, and releases.

POPULATION - INSTITUTIONAL

U.S. Department of Commerce, Bureau of the Census, Suitland, Maryland 20233 (301) 763-4040; *Census of Population, General Population Characteristics.*

POPULATION - LABOR FORCE - See LABOR FORCE EMPLOYMENT AND EARNINGS

POPULATION - MARITAL STATUS - See MARITAL STATUS OF POPULATION

POPULATION - METROPOLITAN AREAS

U.S. Department of Commerce, Bureau of the Census, Suitland, Maryland 20233 (301) 763-4040; *Census of Population, Supplementary Report, Metropolitan Statistical Areas*, and *Census of Population and Housing, Supplementary Reports, Metropolitan Areas as Defined by the Office of Management and Budget.*

POPULATION - MIGRATION

U.S. Department of Commerce, Bureau of the Census, Suitland, Maryland 20233 (301) 763-4040; *Current Population Reports*, and unpublished data.

POPULATION - MOBILITY

U.S. Department of Commerce, Bureau of the Census, Suitland, Maryland 20233 (301) 763-4040; *Current Population Reports.*

POPULATION - NATIVITY

U.S. Department of Commerce, Bureau of the Census, Suitland, Maryland 20233 (301) 763-4040; *Census of Population, The Foreign Born Population in the U.S.*

POPULATION - NATURALIZATIONS

U.S. Department of Commerce, Bureau of the Census, Suitland, Maryland 20233 (301) 763-4040; *Census of Population, The Foreign Born Population in the U.S.*

POPULATION - OUTLYING AREAS OF UNITED STATES

Puerto Rico Planning Board, San Juan, Puerto Rico, *Socioeconomic Statistics.*

U.S. Department of Commerce, Bureau of the Census, Suitland, Maryland 20233 (301) 763-4040; *Census of Population and Housing, Current Population Reports, Characteristics of the Population*, and *World Population Profile.*

POPULATION - PLACE OF BIRTH

U.S. Department of Commerce, Bureau of the Census, Suitland, Maryland 20233 (301) 763-4040; *Census of Population, The Foreign Born Population in the U.S.*

POPULATION - PROJECTIONS

U.S. Department of Commerce, Bureau of the Census, Suitland, Maryland 20233 (301) 763-4040; *Census of Population, Current Population Reports*, and unpublished data.

POPULATION - RACE

U.S. Department of Commerce, Bureau of the Census, Suitland, Maryland 20233 (301) 763-4040; *Census of Population*, and *Current Population Reports.*

POPULATION - RESIDENT

U.S. Department of Commerce, Bureau of the Census, Suitland, Maryland 20233 (301) 763-4040; *Census of Population, Areas of the*

United States, Area Measurement Reports, and *Current Population Reports.*

POPULATION - SEX

U.S. Department of Commerce, Bureau of the Census, Suitland, Maryland 20233 (301) 763-4040; *Census of Population, Characteristics of the Population, Current Population Reports,* and unpublished data.

POPULATION - SEX - OUTLYING AREAS

U.S. Department of Commerce, Bureau of the Census, Suitland, Maryland 20233 (301) 763-4040; *Census of Population,* and *Characteristics of the Population.*

POPULATION - STATES

U.S. Department of Commerce, Bureau of the Census, Suitland, Maryland 20233 (301) 763-4040; *Census of Population, Current Population Reports,* and unpublished data.

POPULATION - STATES - DENSITY

U.S. Department of Commerce, Bureau of the Census, Suitland, Maryland 20233 (301) 763-4040; *Census of Population,* and *Current Population Reports.*

POPULATION - STATES - VOTING AGE

U.S. Department of Commerce, Bureau of the Census, Suitland, Maryland 20233 (301) 763-4040; *Current Population Reports.*

POPULATION - TOTAL - INCLUDING ARMED FORCES OVERSEAS

U.S. Department of Commerce, Bureau of the Census, Suitland, Maryland 20233 (301) 763-4040; *Current Population Reports.*

POPULATION - TOWNSHIPS AND SPECIAL DISTRICTS

U.S. Department of Commerce, Bureau of the Census, Suitland, Maryland 20233 (301) 763-4040; *Census of Governments, Government Organization.*

POPULATION - WORLD

Population Division of the United Nations, New York, New York 10017 (800) 253-9646; *Demographic Yearbook.*

Statistical Office of the United Nations, Publishing Service, New York, New York 10017 (800) 253-9646; *Monthly Bulletin of Statistics.*

U.S. Department of Commerce, Bureau of the Census, Suitland, Maryland 20233 (301) 763-4040; International Data Base and *World Population Profile.*

PORK - See also MEAT AND MEAT PRODUCTS

PORK - CONSUMPTION

U.S. Department of Agriculture, Economic Research Service, Fourteenth Street and Independence Avenue, SW, Washington, D.C. 20005-4789 (202) 219-1504; *Food Consumption, Prices, and Expenditures, Livestock and Meat Statistics,* and *Agricultural Outlook.*

U.S. Department of Agriculture, Foreign Agricultural Service, Fourteenth Street and Independence Avenue, SW, Washington,

D.C. 20250 (202) 720-3448; *World Livestock Situation.*

PORK - FOREIGN TRADE

U.S. Department of Agriculture, Economic Research Service, Fourteenth Street and Independence Avenue, SW, Washington, D.C. 20005-4789 (202) 219-1504; *Foreign Agricultural Trade of the United States, Livestock and Meat Statistics,* and *Agricultural Outlook.*

PORK - PRODUCTION

U.S. Department of Agriculture, Economic Research Service, Fourteenth Street and Independence Avenue, SW, Washington, D.C. 20005-4789 (202) 219-1504; *Livestock and Meat Statistics,* and *Agricultural Outlook.*

U.S. Department of Agriculture, National Agricultural Statistics Service, Fourteenth Street and Independence Avenue, SW, Washington, D.C. 20250 (202) 219-1504; *Meat Animals - Production, Disposition and Income,* and *Agricultural Statistics.*

PORK - SUPPLY

U.S. Department of Agriculture, Economic Research Service, Fourteenth Street and Independence Avenue, SW, Washington, D.C. 20005-4789 (202) 219-1504; *Livestock and Meat Statistics,* and *Agricultural Outlook.*

PORTLAND CEMENT

U.S. Department of the Interior, Bureau of Mines, 810 Seventh Street, NW, Washington, D.C. 20241 (202) 501-9649; *Annual Reports,* and *Mineral Commodities Summaries.*

Portugal - National Statistical Office

Instituto Nacional de Estatistica, Avenida Antonio Jose de Almeida, 1078 Lisbon 1, Portugal.

Portugal - Primary Statistics Sources

Instituto Nacional de Estatistica (National Statistical Institute), Avenida Antonio Jose de Almeida, 1078 Lisbon 1, Portugal; *Anuario estatistico* (Statistical Yearbook) and *Boletin mensal de estatistica* (Monthly Bulletin of Statistics).

PORTUGAL - ABORTIONS

European Community Information Service, 2100 M Street, NW, Washington, D.C. 20037 (202) 862-9500; *Demographic Statistics.*

PORTUGAL - AGRICULTURE

European Community Information Service, 2100 M Street, NW, Washington, D.C. 20037 (202) 862-9500; *Agriculture: Statistical Yearbook, Basic Statistics of the Community, Eurostatistics: Data for Short-Term Economic Analysis, Labor Force Sample Survey,* and *Regions: Statistical Yearbook.*

Facts on File, 460 Park Avenue South, New York, New York 10016 (800) 443-8323; *The New Book of World Rankings.*

Federal Statistical Office, Gustav - Stresemann - Ring 11, D-6200 Wiesbaden, Germany; *Portugal.*

Food and Agricultural Organization of the United Nations (FAO) Via delle Terme di Caracalla, 00100 Rome, Italy (Telephone Number in U.S. (202) 653-2400); *Production Yearbook, The State of Food and*

Agriculture, and *Trade Yearbook.*

G.K. Hall and Company, 70 Lincoln Street, Boston, Massachusetts 02111 (617) 423-3990; *The World in Figures.*

Organisation for Economic Co-operation and Development (OECD), 2 rue Andre-Pascal, 75 Paris 16, France (Telephone Number in U.S. (202) 785-6323); *Economic Accounts for Agriculture, Indicators of Industrial Activity, Industrial Structure Statistics,* and *OECD Economic Surveys: Portugal.*

Statistical Office of the United Nations, Publishing Service, New York, New York 10017 (800) 253-9646; *Statistical Yearbook.*

Time Books, 201 East 50th Street, New York, New York 10022 (212) 751-2600; *The Economist Book of Vital World Statistics.*

The World Bank, 1818 H Street, NW, Washington, D.C. 20433 (202) 477-1234; *World Tables.*

PORTUGAL - AIRLINE SERVICE

European Community Information Service, 2100 M Street, NW, Washington, D.C. 20037 (202) 862-9500; *Basic Statistics of the Community, Regions: Statistical Yearbook,* and *Transport Annual Statistics.*

Facts on File, 460 Park Avenue South, New York, New York 10016 (800) 443-8323; *The New Book of World Rankings.*

G.K. Hall and Company, 70 Lincoln Street, Boston, Massachusetts 02111 (617) 423-3990; *The World in Figures.*

International Civil Aviation Organization, 1000 Sherbrooke Street West, Suite 400, Montreal, Quebec, Canada H3A 2R2 (514) 285-8219; *Civil Aviation Statistics of the World.*

Organisation for Economic Co-operation and Development (OECD), 2 rue Andre-Pascal, 75 Paris 16, France (Telephone Number in U.S. (202) 785-6323); *Tourism Policy and International Tourism in OECD Member Countries.*

Statistical Office of the United Nations, Publishing Service, New York, New York 10017 (800) 253-9646; *Statistical Yearbook.* services.

Time Books, 201 East 50th Street, New York, New York 10022 (212) 751-2600; *The Economist Book of Vital World Statistics.*

PORTUGAL - ALMOND PRODUCTION - See PORTUGAL - CROPS

PORTUGAL - ALUMINUM PRODUCTION AND CONSUMPTION - See PORTUGAL - MINING AND MINERAL PRODUCTS

PORTUGAL - ANIMAL FEEDINGSTUFFS OF AQUATIC ANIMAL ORIGIN

Organisation for Economic Co-operation and Development (OECD), 2 rue Andre-Pascal, 75 Paris 16, France (Telephone Number in U.S. (202) 785-6323); *Foreign Trade by Commodities.*

Statistical Office of the United Nations, Publishing Service, New York, New York 10017 (800) 253-9646; *Statistical Yearbook.* animal origin.

PORTUGAL - ANIMAL HEALTH

Food and Agricultural Organization of the United Nations (FAO), Via delle Terme di Caracalla, 00100 Rome, Italy (Telephone Number in U.S. (202) 653-2400; *Animal Health Yearbook.*

PORTUGAL - ANTIMONY AND ANTIMONY ORE PRODUCTION AND CONSUMPTION - See PORTUGAL - MINING AND MINERAL PRODUCTS

PORTUGAL - AREA AND DENSITY OF POPULATION

European Community Information Service, 2100 M Street, NW, Washington, D.C. 20037 (202) 862-9500; *Basic Statistics of the Community,* and *Demographic Statistics.*

Facts on File, 460 Park Avenue South, New York, New York 10016 (800) 443-8323; *The New Book of World Rankings.*

Federal Statistical Office, Gustav - Stresemann - Ring 11, D-6200 Wiesbaden, Germany; *Portugal.*

Food and Agricultural Organization of the United Nations (FAO) Via delle Terme di Caracalla, 00100 Rome, Italy (Telephone Number in U.S. (202) 653-2400; *The State of Food and Agriculture.*

G.K. Hall and Company, 70 Lincoln Street, Boston, Massachusetts 02111 (617) 423-3990; *The World in Figures.*

Statistical Office of the United Nations, Publishing Service, New York, New York 10017 (800) 253-9646; *Statistical Yearbook.*

Time Books, 201 East 50th Street, New York, New York 10022 (212) 751-2600; *The Economist Book of Vital World Statistics.*

United Nations Educational, Scientific and Cultural Organization (UNESCO), 7 Place de Fontenoy, F-75700 Paris, France (Telephone Number in U.S. (212) 963-5981); *Statistical Yearbook.*

PORTUGAL - ARMS EXPORTS AND IMPORTS

U.S. Arms Control and Disarmament Agency, 320 Twenty-first Street, NW, Washington, D.C. 20451 (202) 647-8677; *World Military Expenditures and Arms Transfers.*

PORTUGAL - ARSENIC PRODUCTION AND CONSUMPTION - See PORTUGAL - MINING AND MINERAL PRODUCTS

PORTUGAL - BALANCE OF PAYMENTS

The Economist Intelligence Unit, 111 West 57th Street, New York, New York 10019 (800) 938-4685; *The World Market Atlas.*

European Community Information Service, 2100 M Street, NW, Washington, D.C. 20037 (202) 862-9500; *ACP: Basic Statistics, Basic Statistics of the Community, Energy Statistics Yearbook,* and *Eurostatistics: Data for Short-Term Economic Analysis.*

Federal Statistical Office, Gustav - Stresemann - Ring 11, D-6200 Wiesbaden, Germany; *Portugal.*

G.K. Hall and Company, 70 Lincoln Street, Boston, Massachusetts 02111 (617) 423-3990; *The World in Figures.*

International Monetary Fund, 700 Nineteenth Street, NW, Washington, D.C. 20431 (202) 623-7000; *Balance of Payments Yearbook,* and *International Financial Statistics.*

Organisation for Economic Co-operation and Development (OECD), 2 rue Andre-Pascal, 75 Paris 16, France (Telephone Number in U.S. (202) 785-6323); *Economic Outlook, Geographical Distribution of Financial Flows to Developing Countries, Main Economic Indicators - Historical Statistics,* and *OECD Economic Surveys: Portugal.*

Time Books, 201 East 50th Street, New York, New York 10022 (212) 751-2600; *The Economist Book of Vital World Statistics*.

The World Bank, 1818 H Street, NW, Washington, D.C. 20433 (202) 477-1234; *World Tables*.

PORTUGAL - BANKING

European Community Information Service, 2100 M Street, NW, Washington, D.C. 20037 (202) 862-9500; *ACP: Basic Statistics*.

Facts on File, 460 Park Avenue South, New York, New York 10016 (800) 443-8323; *The New Book of World Rankings*.

G.K. Hall and Company, 70 Lincoln Street, Boston, Massachusetts 02111 (617) 423-3990; *The World in Figures*.

International Monetary Fund, 700 Nineteenth Street, NW, Washington, D.C. 20431 (202) 623-7000; *International Financial Statistics*.

Organisation for Economic Co-operation and Development (OECD), 2 rue Andre-Pascal, 75 Paris 16, France (Telephone Number in U.S. (202) 785-6323); *Economic Outlook, Financial Market Trends*, and *OECD Economic Surveys: Portugal*.

Statistical Office of the United Nations, Publishing Service, New York, New York 10017 (800) 253-9646; *Statistical Yearbook*.

PORTUGAL - BARLEY PRODUCTION - See PORTUGAL - CROPS

PORTUGAL - BAUXITE PRODUCTION AND CONSUMPTION - See PORTUGAL - MINING AND MINERAL PRODUCTS

PORTUGAL - BEER PRODUCTION

Facts on File, 460 Park Avenue South, New York, New York 10016 (800) 443-8323; *The New Book of World Rankings*.

Statistical Office of the United Nations, Publishing Service, New York, New York 10017 (800) 253-9646; *Statistical Yearbook*.

PORTUGAL - BEVERAGES - PRODUCTION INDEX

Organisation for Economic Co-operation and Development (OECD), 2 rue Andre-Pascal, 75 Paris 16, France (Telephone Number in U.S. (202) 785-6323); *Indicators of Industrial Activity*.

PORTUGAL - BIRTH RATES

European Community Information Service, 2100 M Street, NW, Washington, D.C. 20037 (202) 862-9500; *Basic Statistics of the Community*, and *Demographic Statistics*.

Facts on File, 460 Park Avenue South, New York, New York 10016 (800) 443-8323; *The New Book of World Rankings*.

Statistical Office of the United Nations, Publishing Service, New York, New York 10017 (800) 253-9646; *Demographic Yearbook*, and *Statistical Yearbook*.

Time Books, 201 East 50th Street, New York, New York 10022 (212) 751-2600; *The Economist Book of Vital World Statistics*.

The World Bank, 1818 H Street, NW, Washington, D.C. 20433 (202) 477-1234; *World Tables*.

World Health Organization, Office of Publications, Avenue Appia, CH-1211 Geneva 27, Switzerland (Telephone Number in U.S. (518) 436-9686); *World Health Statistics Annual*.

PORTUGAL - BISMUTH PRODUCTION AND CONSUMPTION

Food and Agricultural Organization of the United Nations (FAO) Via delle Terme di Caracalla, 00100 Rome, Italy (Telephone Number in U.S. (202) 653-2400); *The State of Food and Agriculture*.

PORTUGAL - BONDS

European Community Information Service, 2100 M Street, NW, Washington, D.C. 20037 (202) 862-9500; *Basic Statistics of the Community*.

G.K. Hall and Company, 70 Lincoln Street, Boston, Massachusetts 02111 (617) 423-3990; *The World in Figures*.

Organisation for Economic Co-operation and Development (OECD), 2 rue Andre-Pascal, 75 Paris 16, France (Telephone Number in U.S. (202) 785-6323); *Financial Market Trends*.

Statistical Office of the United Nations, Publishing Service, New York, New York 10017 (800) 253-9646; *Statistical Yearbook*.

PORTUGAL - BOOK PRODUCTION

Euromonitor Publications Limited, 87-88 Turnmill Street, London EC1M 5QU, England; *European Marketing Data and Statistics*.

G.K. Hall and Company, 70 Lincoln Street, Boston, Massachusetts 02111 (617) 423-3990; *The World in Figures*.

Organisation for Economic Co-operation and Development (OECD), 2 rue Andre-Pascal, 75 Paris 16, France (Telephone Number in U.S. (202) 785-6323); *Indicators of Industrial Activity*.

PORTUGAL - BROADCASTING

Billboard Limited, Post Office Box 9027, 1006 AA Amsterdam, The Netherlands (Telephone Number in U.S. (212) 764-7300); *World Radio TV Handbook*.

European Community Information Service, 2100 M Street, NW, Washington, D.C. 20037 (202) 862-9500; *Basic Statistics of the Community*.

Facts on File, 460 Park Avenue South, New York, New York 10016 (800) 443-8323; *The New Book of World Rankings*.

G.K. Hall and Company, 70 Lincoln Street, Boston, Massachusetts 02111 (617) 423-3990; *The World in Figures*.

Time Books, 201 East 50th Street, New York, New York 10022 (212) 751-2600; *The Economist Book of Vital World Statistics*.

United Nations Educational, Scientific and Cultural Organization (UNESCO), 7 Place de Fontenoy, F-75700 Paris, France (Telephone Number in U.S. (212) 963-5981); *Statistical Yearbook*.

PORTUGAL - BUSINESS

European Community Information Service, 2100 M Street, NW, Washington, D.C. 20037 (202) 862-9500; *Basic Statistics of the Community*.

G.K. Hall and Company, 70 Lincoln Street, Boston, Massachusetts 02111 (617) 423-3990; *The World in Figures*.

PORTUGAL - BUSINESS AND PROFESSIONAL LICENSES

International Monetary Fund, 700 Nineteenth Street, NW, Washington, D.C. 20431 (202) 623-7000; *Government Finance Statistics Yearbook.*

PORTUGAL - BUTTER PRODUCTION - See PORTUGAL - DAIRY PRODUCTS

PORTUGAL - CABBAGE PRODUCTION - See PORTUGAL - CROPS

PORTUGAL - CADMIUM PRODUCTION - See PORTUGAL - MINING AND MINERAL PRODUCTS

PORTUGAL - CALORIE SUPPLY

Food and Agricultural Organization of the United Nations (FAO) Via delle Terme di Caracalla, 00100 Rome, Italy (Telephone Number in U.S. (202) 653-2400); *The State of Food and Agriculture.*

PORTUGAL - CAPITAL INVESTMENT

Organisation for Economic Co-operation and Development (OECD), 2 rue Andre-Pascal, 75 Paris 16, France (Telephone Number in U.S. (202) 785-6323); *Economic Outlook,* and *Financial Market Trends.*

PORTUGAL - CAPITAL REVENUE

International Monetary Fund, 700 Nineteenth Street, NW, Washington, D.C. 20431 (202) 623-7000; *Government Finance Statistics Yearbook.*

Organisation for Economic Co-operation and Development (OECD), 2 rue Andre-Pascal, 75 Paris 16, France (Telephone Number in U.S. (202) 785-6323); *Economic Outlook,* and *Financial Market Trends.*

PORTUGAL - CAPITAL STRUCTURE

Organisation for Economic Co-operation and Development (OECD), 2 rue Andre-Pascal, 75 Paris 16, France (Telephone Number in U.S. (202) 785-6323); *Financial Market Trends.*

PORTUGAL - CATTLE - See PORTUGAL - LIVESTOCK AND POULTRY

PORTUGAL - CAUSTIC SODA PRODUCTION

European Community Information Service, 2100 M Street, NW, Washington, D.C. 20037 (202) 862-9500; *Basic Statistics of the Community.*

Organisation for Economic Co-operation and Development (OECD), 2 rue Andre-Pascal, 75 Paris 16, France (Telephone Number in U.S. (202) 785-6323); *Indicators of Industrial Activity.*

PORTUGAL - CEMENT PRODUCTION - See PORTUGAL - MINING AND MINERAL PRODUCTS

PORTUGAL - CEREALS PRODUCTION - See PORTUGAL - CROPS

PORTUGAL - CHEESE PRODUCTION AND CONSUMPTION - See PORTUGAL - DAIRY PRODUCTS

PORTUGAL - CHEMICAL INDUSTRY

European Community Information Service, 2100 M Street, NW, Washington, D.C. 20037 (202) 862-9500; *Industrial Production: Quarterly.*

PORTUGAL - CHEMICAL (ORGANIC) PRODUCTION - See PORTUGAL - MINING AND MINERAL PRODUCTS

PORTUGAL - CHESTNUT PRODUCTION - See PORTUGAL - CROPS

PORTUGAL - CHICK PEA PRODUCTION - See PORTUGAL - CROPS

PORTUGAL - CHROMITE PRODUCTION AND CONSUMPTION - See PORTUGAL - MINING AND MINERAL PRODUCTS

PORTUGAL - CHROMIUM ORE PRODUCTION AND CONSUMPTION - See PORTUGAL - MINING AND MINERAL PRODUCTS

PORTUGAL - CIGAR AND CIGARETTE PRODUCTION - See PORTUGAL - TOBACCO PRODUCTION

PORTUGAL - CLASS STRUCTURE

European Community Information Service, 2100 M Street, NW, Washington, D.C. 20037 (202) 862-9500; *Basic Statistics of the Community.*

G.K. Hall and Company, 70 Lincoln Street, Boston, Massachusetts 02111 (617) 423-3990; *The World in Figures.*

PORTUGAL - CLIMATE

Facts on File, 460 Park Avenue South, New York, New York 10016 (800) 443-8323; *The New Book of World Rankings.*

G.K. Hall and Company, 70 Lincoln Street, Boston, Massachusetts 02111 (617) 423-3990; *The World in Figures.*

Statistical Office of the United Nations, Publishing Service, New York, New York 10017 (800) 253-9646; *Statistical Yearbook.*

PORTUGAL - CLOTHING - PRODUCTION INDEX

Organisation for Economic Co-operation and Development (OECD), 2 rue Andre-Pascal, 75 Paris 16, France (Telephone Number in U.S. (202) 785-6323); *Indicators of Industrial Activity.*

PORTUGAL - CLOTHING EXPORTS AND IMPORTS

European Community Information Service, 2100 M Street, NW, Washington, D.C. 20037 (202) 862-9500; *Basic Statistics of the Community.*

Organisation for Economic Co-operation and Development (OECD), 2 rue Andre-Pascal, 75 Paris 16, France (Telephone Number in U.S. (202) 785-6323); *Textile Industry in OECD Countries.*

PORTUGAL - COAL PRODUCTION - See PORTUGAL - MINING AND MINERAL PRODUCTS

PORTUGAL - COBALT PRODUCTION AND CONSUMPTION - See PORTUGAL - MINING AND MINERAL PRODUCTS

PORTUGAL - COFFEE PRODUCTION AND CONSUMPTION - See PORTUGAL - CROPS

PORTUGAL - COKE, COKE OVEN ORE, AND COKE OVEN COKE PRODUCTION AND CONSUMPTION - See PORTUGAL - MINING AND MINERAL PRODUCTS

PORTUGAL - COMMUNICATIONS

European Community Information Service, 2100 M Street, NW, Washington, D.C. 20037 (202) 862-9500; *Basic Statistics of the*

Community, and Transport Annual Statistics.

Federal Statistical Office, Gustav - Stresemann - Ring 11, D-6200 Wiesbaden, Germany; *Portugal.*

G.K. Hall and Company, 70 Lincoln Street, Boston, Massachusetts 02111 (617) 423-3990; *The World in Figures.*

PORTUGAL - CONSTRUCTION INDUSTRY

European Community Information Service, 2100 M Street, NW, Washington, D.C. 20037 (202) 862-9500; *Basic Statistics of the Community, and Labor Force Sample Survey.*

Facts on File, 460 Park Avenue South, New York, New York 10016 (800) 443-8323; *The New Book of World Rankings.*

Organisation for Economic Co-operation and Development (OECD), 2 rue Andre-Pascal, 75 Paris 16, France (Telephone Number in U.S. (202) 785-6323); *Industrial Structure Statistics, The Iron and Steel Industry, Main Economic Indicators - Historical Statistics,* and *OECD Economic Surveys: Portugal.*

Statistical Office of the United Nations, Publishing Service, New York, New York 10017 (800) 253-9646; *Statistical Yearbook.*

PORTUGAL - CONSUMER PRICE INDEX

European Community Information Service, 2100 M Street, NW, Washington, D.C. 20037 (202) 862-9500; *Basic Statistics of the Community,* and *Eurostatistics: Data for Short-Term Economic Analysis.*

G.K. Hall and Company, 70 Lincoln Street, Boston, Massachusetts 02111 (617) 423-3990; *The World in Figures.*

Organisation for Economic Co-operation and Development (OECD), 2 rue Andre-Pascal, 75 Paris 16, France (Telephone Number in U.S. (202) 785-6323); *Economic Outlook.*

Statistical Office of the United Nations, Publishing Service, New York, New York 10017 (800) 253-9646; *Statistical Yearbook.*

PORTUGAL - CONSUMER PRICES

Euromonitor Publications Limited, 87-88 Turnmill Street, London EC1M 5QU, England; *European Marketing Data and Statistics.*

European Community Information Service, 2100 M Street, NW, Washington, D.C. 20037 (202) 862-9500; *Basic Statistics for the Community, Eurostatistics: Data for Short-Term Economic Analysis,* and *Money and Finance.*

International Labour Office, I.L.O. Publications, CH-1211, Geneva 22, Switzerland; *Yearbook of Labour Statistics.*

International Monetary Fund, 700 Nineteenth Street, NW, Washington, D.C. 20431 (202) 623-7000; *International Financial Statistics.*

Organisation for Economic Co-operation and Development (OECD), 2 rue Andre-Pascal, 75 Paris 16, France (Telephone Number in U.S. (202) 785-6323); *Economic Outlook.*

Time Books, 201 East 50th Street, New York, New York 10022 (212) 751-2600; *The Economist Book of Vital World Statistics.*

PORTUGAL - CONSUMPTION

European Community Information Service, 2100 M Street, NW, Washington, D.C. 20037 (202) 862-9500; *Basic Statistics of the Community.*

G.K. Hall and Company, 70 Lincoln Street, Boston, Massachusetts 02111 (617) 423-3990; *The World in Figures.*

Organisation for Economic Co-operation and Development (OECD), 2 rue Andre-Pascal, 75 Paris 16, France (Telephone Number in U.S. (202) 785-6323); *The Footwear, Raw Hides and Skins, and Leather Industry in OECD Countries, The Iron and Steel Industry, Meat Balances in OECD Member Countries, The Pulp and Paper Industry,* and *Textile Industry in OECD Countries.*

PORTUGAL - COPPER AND COPPER ORE PRODUCTION AND CONSUMPTION - See PORTUGAL - MINING AND MINERAL PRODUCTS

PORTUGAL - CORK EXPORTS

International Monetary Fund, 700 Nineteenth Street, NW, Washington, D.C. 20431 (202) 623-7000; *International Financial Statistics.*

PORTUGAL - CORN PRODUCTION - See PORTUGAL - CROPS

PORTUGAL - CORPORATE TAXES - See PORTUGAL - TAXATION

PORTUGAL - COTTON - See PORTUGAL - CROPS

PORTUGAL - CRIME

International Criminal Police Organization (INTERPOL), 26 rue Armengaud, 92210 Saint Cloud, France; *International Crime Statistics.*

Yale University Press, Yale Station, New Haven, Connecticut 06520 (203) 432-0940; *Violence and Crime in Cross-National Perspective.*

PORTUGAL - CROPS

Euromonitor Publications Limited, 87-88 Turnmill Street, London EC1M 5QU, England; *European Marketing Data and Statistics.*

European Community Information Service, 2100 M Street, NW, Washington, D.C. 20037 (202) 862-9500; *ACP: Basis Statistics, Agriculture: Statistical Yearbook, Basic Statistics of the Community, Crop Production: Quarterly Statistics, Eurostatistics: Data for Short-Term Economic Analysis,* and *Regions: Statistical Yearbook.*

Facts on File, 460 Park Avenue South, New York, New York 10016 (800) 443-8323; *The New Book of World Rankings.*

Food and Agricultural Organization of the United Nations (FAO), Via delle Terme di Caracalla, 00100 Rome, Italy (Telephone Number in U.S. (202) 653-2400); *Production Yearbook,* and *The State of Food and Agriculture.*

Organisation for Economic Co-operation and Development (OECD), 2 rue Andre-Pascal, 75 Paris 16, France (Telephone Number in U.S. (202) 785-6323); *Economic Accounts for Agriculture, Foreign Trade by Commodities, The Non-Ferrous Metals Industry,* and *Textile Industry in OECD Countries.*

Statistical Office of the United Nations, Publishing Service, New York, New York 10017 (800) 253-9646; *Statistical Yearbook.*

PORTUGAL - CUSTOMS DUTIES

European Community Information Service, 2100 M Street, NW, Washington, D.C. 20037 (202) 862-9500; *Basic Statistics of the Community.*

G.K. Hall and Company, 70 Lincoln Street, Boston, Massachusetts 02111 (617) 423-3990; *The World in Figures.*

International Monetary Fund, 700 Nineteenth Street, NW, Washington, D.C. 20431 (202) 623-7000; *Government Finance Statistics Yearbook.*

Organisation for Economic Co-operation and Development (OECD), 2 rue Andre-Pascal, 75 Paris 16, France (Telephone Number in U.S. (202) 785-6323); *The Non-Ferrous Metals Industry.*

PORTUGAL - DAIRY PRODUCTS

European Community Information Service, 2100 M Street, NW, Washington, D.C. 20037 (202) 862-9500; *Eurostatistics: Data for Short-Term Economic Analysis.*

Facts on File, 460 Park Avenue South, New York, New York 10016 (800) 443-8323; *The New Book of World Rankings.*

Food and Agricultural Organization of the United Nations (FAO) Via delle Terme di Caracalla, 00100 Rome, Italy (Telephone Number in U.S. (202) 653-2400); *The State of Food and Agriculture.*

Organisation for Economic Co-operation and Development (OECD), 2 rue Andre-Pascal, 75 Paris 16, France (Telephone Number in U.S. (202) 785-6323); *Economic Accounts for Agriculture,* and *Milk, Milk Products, and Egg Balances in OECD Member Countries.*

Statistical Office of the United Nations, Publishing Service, New York, New York 10017 (800) 253-9646; *Statistical Yearbook.*

PORTUGAL - DEATH RATES

European Community Information Service, 2100 M Street, NW, Washington, D.C. 20037 (202) 862-9500; *Basic Statistics of the Community,* and *Demographic Statistics.*

G.K. Hall and Company, 70 Lincoln Street, Boston, Massachusetts 02111 (617) 423-3990; *The World in Figures.*

Statistical Office of the United Nations, Publishing Service, New York, New York 10017 (800) 253-9646; *Statistical Yearbook.*

Time Books, 201 East 50th Street, New York, New York 10022 (212) 751-2600; *The Economist Book of Vital World Statistics.*

World Health Organization, Office of Publications, Avenue Appia, CH-1211 Geneva 27, Switzerland (Telephone Number in U.S. (518) 436-9686); *World Health Statistics Annual.*

PORTUGAL - DEFENSE EXPENDITURES

European Community Information Service, 2100 M Street, NW, Washington, D.C. 20037 (202) 862-9500; *Government Financing of Research and Development.*

G.K. Hall and Company, 70 Lincoln Street, Boston, Massachusetts 02111 (617) 423-3990; *The World in Figures.*

International Monetary Fund, 700 Nineteenth Street, NW, Washington, D.C. 20431 (202) 623-7000; *Government Finance Statistics Yearbook.*

U.S. Arms Control and Disarmament Agency, 320 Twenty-first Street, NW, Washington, D.C. 20451 (202) 647-8677; *World Military Expenditures and Arms Transfers.*

PORTUGAL - DEMOGRAPHY

The Economist Intelligence Unit, 111 West 57th Street, New York, New York 10019 (800) 938-4685; *The World Market Atlas.*

European Community Information Service, 2100 M Street, NW, Washington, D.C. 20037 (202) 862-9500; *Basic Statistics of the Community, Demographic Statistics, Employment and Unemployment,* and *Regions: Statistical Yearbook.*

Facts on File, 460 Park Avenue South, New York, New York 10016 (800) 443-8323; *The New Book of World Rankings.*

G.K. Hall and Company, 70 Lincoln Street, Boston, Massachusetts 02111 (617) 423-3990; *The World in Figures.*

PORTUGAL - DEVELOPMENT ASSISTANCE

European Community Information Service, 2100 M Street, NW, Washington, D.C. 20037 (202) 862-9500; *ACP: Basic Statistics, Basis Statistics of the Community,* and *Government Financing of Research and Development.*

G.K. Hall and Company, 70 Lincoln Street, Boston, Massachusetts 02111 (617) 423-3990; *The World in Figures.*

Organisation for Economic Co-operation and Development (OECD), 2 rue Andre-Pascal, 75 Paris 16, France (Telephone Number in U.S. (202) 785-6323); *Geographical Distribution of Financial Flows to Developing Countries.*

Statistical Office of the United Nations, Publishing Service, New York, New York 10017 (800) 253-9646; *Statistical Yearbook.*

PORTUGAL - DIAMOND PRODUCTION - See PORTUGAL - MINING AND MINERAL PRODUCTS

PORTUGAL - DISCOUNT RATES

Organisation for Economic Co-operation and Development (OECD), 2 rue Andre-Pascal, 75 Paris 16, France (Telephone Number in U.S. (202) 785-6323); *Financial Market Trends.*

Statistical Office of the United Nations, Publishing Service, New York, New York 10017 (800) 253-9646; *Statistical Yearbook.*

PORTUGAL - DISEASES

G.K. Hall and Company, 70 Lincoln Street, Boston, Massachusetts 02111 (617) 423-3990; *The World in Figures.*

World Health Organization, Office of Publications, Avenue Appia, CH-1211 Geneva 27, Switzerland (Telephone Number in U.S. (518) 436-9686); *World Health Statistics Annual.*

PORTUGAL - DIVORCE RATES

European Community Information Service, 2100 M Street, NW, Washington, D.C. 20037 (202) 862-9500; *Demographic Statistics.*

Facts on File, 460 Park Avenue South, New York, New York 10016 (800) 443-8323; *The New Book of World Rankings.*

Statistical Office of the United Nations, Publishing Service, New York, New York 10017 (800) 253-9646; *Demographic Yearbook,* and

Statistical Yearbook.

PORTUGAL - DOMESTIC PRODUCT

European Community Information Service, 2100 M Street, NW, Washington, D.C. 20037 (202) 862-9500; *Basic Statistics of the Community.*

G.K. Hall and Company, 70 Lincoln Street, Boston, Massachusetts 02111 (617) 423-3990; *The World in Figures.*

PORTUGAL - ECONOMY

Euromonitor Publications Limited, 87-88 Turnmill Street, London EC1M 5QU, England; *ACP: Basic Statistics, Basic Statistics of the Community, Energy Statistics Yearbook, European Marketing Data and Statistics,* and *Labor Force Sample Survey.*

European Community Information Service, 2100 M Street, NW, Washington, D.C. 20037 (202) 862-9500; *Money and Finance.*

Facts on File, 460 Park Avenue South, New York, New York 10016 (800) 443-8323; *The New Book of World Rankings.*

G.K. Hall and Company, 70 Lincoln Street, Boston, Massachusetts 02111 (617) 423-3990; *The World in Figures.*

Organisation for Economic Co-operation and Development (OECD), 2 rue Andre-Pascal, 75 Paris 16, France (Telephone Number in U.S. (202) 785-6323); *Economic Outlook, Geographical Distribution of Financial Flows to Developing Countries, Main Economic Indicators, OECD Economic Surveys: Portugal,* and *OECD Employment Outlook.*

PORTUGAL - EDUCATION

The Economist Intelligence Unit, 111 West 57th Street, New York, New York 10019 (800) 938-4685; *The World Market Atlas.*

Euromonitor Publications Limited, 87-88 Turnmill Street, London EC1M 5QU, England; *European Marketing Data and Statistics.*

European Community Information Service, 2100 M Street, NW, Washington, D.C. 20037 (202) 862-9500; *Basic Statistics of the Community,* and *Regions: Statistical Yearbook.*

Facts on File, 460 Park Avenue South, New York, New York 10016 (800) 443-8323; *The New Book of World Rankings.*

Federal Statistical Office, Gustav - Stresemann - Ring 11, D-6200 Wiesbaden, Germany; *Portugal.*

G.K. Hall and Company, 70 Lincoln Street, Boston, Massachusetts 02111 (617) 423-3990; *The World in Figures.*

International Monetary Fund, 700 Nineteenth Street, NW, Washington, D.C. 20431 (202) 623-7000; *Government Finance Statistics Yearbook.*

Organisation for Economic Co-operation and Development (OECD), 2 rue Andre-Pascal, 75 Paris 16, France (Telephone Number in U.S. (202) 785-6323); *Education in OECD.*

United Nations Educational, Scientific and Cultural Organization (UNESCO), 7 Place de Fontenoy, F-75700 Paris, France (Telephone Number in U.S. (212) 963-5981); *Statistical Yearbook.*

The World Bank, 1818 H Street, NW, Washington, D.C. 20433 (202) 477-1234; *World Tables.*

PORTUGAL - EGG PRODUCTION AND CONSUMPTION - See PORTUGAL - DAIRY PRODUCTS

PORTUGAL - ELECTRICITY

European Community Information Service, 2100 M Street, NW, Washington, D.C. 20037 (202) 862-9500; *Basic Statistics of the Community, Energy: Monthly Statistics, Energy Statistics Yearbook, Eurostatistics: Data for Short-Term Economic Analysis,* and *Regions: Statistical Yearbook.*

Facts on File, 460 Park Avenue South, New York, New York 10016 (800) 443-8323; *The New Book of World Rankings.*

Organisation for Economic Co-operation and Development (OECD), 2 rue Andre-Pascal, 75 Paris 16, France (Telephone Number in U.S. (202) 785-6323); *Coal Information, Energy Statistics of OECD Countries, Indicators of Industrial Activity,* and *Industrial Structure Statistics.*

Statistical Office of the United Nations, Publishing Service, New York, New York 10017 (800) 253-9646; *Statistical Yearbook.*

Time Books, 201 East 50th Street, New York, New York 10022 (212) 751-2600; *The Economist Book of Vital World Statistics.*

PORTUGAL - EMPLOYMENT

European Community Information Service, 2100 M Street, NW, Washington, D.C. 20037 (202) 862-9500; *Basic Statistics of the Community, Earnings in Agriculture, Employment and Unemployment,* and *Eurostatistics: Data for Short-Term Economic Analysis.*

European Community Information Service, 2100 M Street, NW, Washington, D.C. 20037 (202) 862-9500; *Iron and Steel: Statistical Yearbook.*

Euromonitor Publications Limited, 87-88 Turnmill Street, London EC1M 5QU, England; *European Marketing Data and Statistics.*

Facts on File, 460 Park Avenue South, New York, New York 10016 (800) 443-8323; *The New Book of World Rankings.*

Federal Statistical Office, Gustav - Stresemann - Ring 11, D-6200 Wiesbaden, Germany; *Portugal.*

International Labour Office, I.L.O. Publications, CH-1211, Geneva 22, Switzerland; *Yearbook of Labour Statistics.*

Organisation for Economic Co-operation and Development (OECD), 2 rue Andre-Pascal, 75 Paris 16, France (Telephone Number in U.S. (202) 785-6323); *Economic Outlook, The Iron and Steel Industry, OECD Economic Surveys: Portugal, OECD Employment Outlook,* and *Textile Industry in OECD Countries.*

Statistical Office of the United Nations, Publishing Service, New York, New York 10017 (800) 253-9646; *Statistical Yearbook.*

PORTUGAL - ENERGY

European Community Information Service, 2100 M Street, NW, Washington, D.C. 20037 (202) 862-9500; *Basic Statistics of the Community, Energy: Monthly Statistics, Energy Statistics Yearbook, Regions: Statistical Yearbook,* and *Transport Annual Statistics.*

Euromonitor Publications Limited, 87-88 Turnmill Street, London EC1M 5QU, England; *European Marketing Data and Statistics.*

Facts on File, 460 Park Avenue South, New York, New York 10016 (800) 443-8323; *The New Book of World Rankings.*

Food and Agricultural Organization of the United Nations (FAO) Via delle Terme di Caracalla, 00100 Rome, Italy (Telephone Number in U.S. (202) 653-2400); *The State of Food and Agriculture.*

G.K. Hall and Company, 70 Lincoln Street, Boston, Massachusetts 02111 (617) 423-3990; *The World in Figures.*

Organisation for Economic Co-operation and Development (OECD), 2 rue Andre-Pascal, 75 Paris 16, France (Telephone Number in U.S. (202) 785-6323); *Coal Information, Energy Statistics of OECD Countries, OECD Environmental Data,* and *Oil and Gas Information.*

Statistical Office of the United Nations, Publishing Service, New York, New York 10017 (800) 253-9646; *Energy Statistics Yearbook, Statistical Yearbook,* and *World Energy Supplies.*

Time Books, 201 East 50th Street, New York, New York 10022 (212) 751-2600; *The Economist Book of Vital World Statistics.*

PORTUGAL - ENGINEERING - METAL PRODUCTS

European Community Information Service, 2100 M Street, NW, Washington, D.C. 20037 (202) 862-9500; *Basic Statistics of the Community,* and *Industrial Production: Quarterly.*

PORTUGAL - ENVIRONMENT

Organisation for Economic Co-operation and Development (OECD), 2 rue Andre-Pascal, 75 Paris 16, France (Telephone Number in U.S. (202) 785-6323); *OECD Environmental Data.*

PORTUGAL - EXCHANGE RATES

European Community Information Service, 2100 M Street, NW, Washington, D.C. 20037 (202) 862-9500; *Eurostatistics: Data for Short-Term Economic Analysis,* and *Money and Finance.*

International Civil Aviation Organization, 1000 Sherbrooke Street West, Suite 400, Montreal, Quebec, Canada H3A 2R2 (514) 285-8219; *Civil Aviation Statistics of the World.*

International Monetary Fund, 700 Nineteenth Street, NW, Washington, D.C. 20431 (202) 623-7000; *International Financial Statistics.*

Organisation for Economic Co-operation and Development (OECD), 2 rue Andre-Pascal, 75 Paris 16, France (Telephone Number in U.S. (202) 785-6323); *Economic Outlook, Financial Market Trends, Revenue Statistics of OECD Member Countries,* and *Tourism Policy and International Tourism in OECD Member Countries.*

Statistical Office of the United Nations, Publishing Service, New York, New York 10017 (800) 253-9646; *Statistical Yearbook.*

PORTUGAL - EXCISE TAXES - See PORTUGAL - TAXATION

PORTUGAL - EXPORTS

American Automobile Manufacturers Association, 1401 H Street, NW, Suite 900, Washington, D.C. 20005 (202) 326-5500; *World Motor Vehicle Data.*

The Economist Intelligence Unit, 111 West 57th Street, New York, New York 10019 (800) 938-4685; *The World Market Atlas.*

European Community Information Service, 2100 M Street, NW, Washington, D.C. 20037 (202) 862-9500; *Basic Statistics of the Community, Energy: Monthly Statistics, Energy Statistics Yearbook, Eurostatistics: Data for Short-Term Economic Analysis, External Trade: Statistical Yearbook, External Trade: Monthly Statistics,* and *Fisheries: Yearly Statistics.*

Food and Agricultural Organization of the United Nations (FAO) Via delle Terme di Caracalla, 00100 Rome, Italy (Telephone Number in U.S. (202) 653-2400); *The State of Food and Agriculture.*

G.K. Hall and Company, 70 Lincoln Street, Boston, Massachusetts 02111 (617) 423-3990; *The World in Figures.*

International Monetary Fund, 700 Nineteenth Street, NW, Washington, D.C. 20431 (202) 623-7000; *Direction of Trade, Government Finance Statistics Yearbook,* and *International Financial Statistics.*

Organisation for Economic Co-operation and Development (OECD), 2 rue Andre-Pascal, 75 Paris 16, France (Telephone Number in U.S. (202) 785-6323); *Economic Outlook, The Footwear, Raw Hides and Skins, and Leather Industry in OECD Countries, Foreign Trade by Commodities, Geographical Distribution of Financial Flows to Developing Countries, Industrial Structure Statistics, The Iron and Steel Industry, Milk, Milk Products, and Egg Balances in OECD Member Countries, The Pulp and Paper Industry, OECD Economic Surveys: Portugal,* and *Review of Fisheries in OECD Member Countries.*

Time Books, 201 East 50th Street, New York, New York 10022 (212) 751-2600; *The Economist Book of Vital World Statistics.*

The World Bank, 1818 H Street, NW, Washington, D.C. 20433 (202) 477-1234; *World Tables.*

PORTUGAL - EXTERNAL FINANCING

Organisation for Economic Co-operation and Development (OECD), 2 rue Andre-Pascal, 75 Paris 16, France (Telephone Number in U.S. (202) 785-6323); *Economic Outlook,* and *Financial Market Trends.*

PORTUGAL - EXTERNAL INDEBTEDNESS

Organisation for Economic Co-operation and Development (OECD), 2 rue Andre-Pascal, 75 Paris 16, France (Telephone Number in U.S. (202) 785-6323); *Financial Market Trends,* and *Geographical Distribution of Financial Flows to Developing Countries.*

The World Bank, 1818 H Street, NW, Washington, D.C. 20433 (202) 477-1234; *World Tables.*

PORTUGAL - EXTERNAL TRADE

European Community Information Service, 2100 M Street, NW, Washington, D.C. 20037 (202) 862-9500; *ACP: Basic Statistics, Basic Statistics of the Community, Eurostatistics: Data for Short-Term Economic Analysis, External Trade: Statistical Yearbook, External Trade: Monthly Statistics,* and *Foreign Trade of the People's Republic of China.*

Food and Agricultural Organization of the United Nations (FAO) Via delle Terme di Caracalla, 00100 Rome, Italy (Telephone Number in U.S. (202) 653-2400); *The State of Food and Agriculture,* and *Trade Yearbook.*

G.K. Hall and Company, 70 Lincoln Street, Boston, Massachusetts 02111 (617) 423-3990; *The World in Figures.*

Statistical Office of the United Nations, Publishing Service, New York, New York 10017 (800) 253-9646; *Statistical Yearbook.*

PORTUGAL - FABRIC PRODUCTION - See PORTUGAL - TEXTILE INDUSTRY

PORTUGAL - FARM CROPS - See PORTUGAL - CROPS

PORTUGAL - FEMALE WORKING POPULATION - See PORTUGAL - EMPLOYMENT

PORTUGAL - FERTILITY RATES

European Community Information Service, 2100 M Street, NW, Washington, D.C. 20037 (202) 862-9500; *Demographic Statistics.*

Facts on File, 460 Park Avenue South, New York, New York 10016 (800) 443-8323; *The New Book of World Rankings.*

Time Books, 201 East 50th Street, New York, New York 10022 (212) 751-2600; *The Economist Book of Vital World Statistics.*

The World Bank, 1818 H Street, NW, Washington, D.C. 20433 (202) 477-1234; *World Tables.*

PORTUGAL - FERTILIZER

European Community Information Service, 2100 M Street, NW, Washington, D.C. 20037 (202) 862-9500; *Basic Statistics of the Community.*

Food and Agricultural Organization of the United Nations (FAO), Via delle Terme di Caracalla, 00100 Rome, Italy (Telephone Number in U.S. (202) 653-2400); *Fertilizer Yearbook,* and *The State of Food and Agriculture.*

Organisation for Economic Co-operation and Development (OECD), 2 rue Andre-Pascal, 75 Paris 16, France (Telephone Number in U.S. (202) 785-6323); *Economic Accounts for Agriculture,* and *Foreign Trade by Commodities.*

Statistical Office of the United Nations, Publishing Service, New York, New York 10017 (800) 253-9646; *Statistical Yearbook.*

PORTUGAL - FETAL MORTALITY

European Community Information Service, 2100 M Street, NW, Washington, D.C. 20037 (202) 862-9500; *Basic Statistics of the Community,* and *Demographic Statistics.*

Statistical Office of the United Nations, Publishing Service, New York, New York 10017 (800) 253-9646; *Demographic Yearbook.*

World Health Organization, Office of Publications, Avenue Appia, CH-1211 Geneva 27, Switzerland (Telephone Number in U.S. (518) 436-9686); *World Health Statistics Annual.*

PORTUGAL - FIBRE PRODUCTION - See PORTUGAL - TEXTILE INDUSTRY

PORTUGAL - FILAMENT PRODUCTION - See PORTUGAL - TEXTILE INDUSTRY

PORTUGAL - FILM - See PORTUGAL - MOTION PICTURES

PORTUGAL - FINANCE

European Community Information Service, 2100 M Street, NW, Washington, D.C. 20037 (202) 862-9500; *ACP: Basic Statistics, Basic*

Statistics of the Community, Eurostatistics: Data for Short-Term Economic Analysis, and *Money and Finance.*

Facts on File, 460 Park Avenue South, New York, New York 10016 (800) 443-8323; *The New Book of World Rankings.*

Federal Statistical Office, Gustav - Stresemann - Ring 11, D-6200 Wiesbaden, Germany; *Portugal.*

G.K. Hall and Company, 70 Lincoln Street, Boston, Massachusetts 02111 (617) 423-3990; *The World in Figures.*

International Monetary Fund, 700 Nineteenth Street, NW, Washington, D.C. 20431 (202) 623-7000; *International Financial Statistics.*

Organisation for Economic Co-operation and Development (OECD), 2 rue Andre-Pascal, 75 Paris 16, France (Telephone Number in U.S. (202) 785-6323); *Economic Outlook, Financial Market Trends, Geographical Distribution of Financial Flows to Developing Countries, Main Economic Indicators - Historical Statistics,* and *OECD Financial Statistics.*

PORTUGAL - FISHERIES

European Community Information Service, 2100 M Street, NW, Washington, D.C. 20037 (202) 862-9500; *Agriculture: Statistical Yearbook,* and *Fisheries: Yearly Statistics.*

Euromonitor Publications Limited, 87-88 Turnmill Street, London EC1M 5QU, England; *European Marketing Data and Statistics.*

Facts on File, 460 Park Avenue South, New York, New York 10016 (800) 443-8323; *The New Book of World Rankings.*

Federal Statistical Office, Gustav - Stresemann - Ring 11, D-6200 Wiesbaden, Germany; *Portugal.*

Food and Agricultural Organization of the United Nations (FAO) Via delle Terme di Caracalla, 00100 Rome, Italy (Telephone Number in U.S. (202) 653-2400); *The State of Food and Agriculture,* and *Yearbook of Fishery Statistics.*

Organisation for Economic Co-operation and Development (OECD), 2 rue Andre-Pascal, 75 Paris 16, France (Telephone Number in U.S. (202) 785-6323); *Foreign Trade by Commodities, Industrial Structure Statistics,* and *Review of Fisheries in OECD Member Countries.*

PORTUGAL - FLOUR PRODUCTION

European Community Information Service, 2100 M Street, NW, Washington, D.C. 20037 (202) 862-9500; *Basic Statistics of the Community.*

Statistical Office of the United Nations, Publishing Service, New York, New York 10017 (800) 253-9646; *Statistical Yearbook.*

PORTUGAL - FOOD

Food and Agricultural Organization of the United Nations (FAO), Via delle Terme di Caracalla, 00100 Rome, Italy (Telephone Number in U.S. (202) 653-2400); *Production Yearbook,* and *The State of Food and Agriculture.*

G.K. Hall and Company, 70 Lincoln Street, Boston, Massachusetts 02111 (617) 423-3990; *The World in Figures.*

Organisation for Economic Co-operation and Development (OECD), 2 rue Andre-Pascal, 75 Paris 16, France (Telephone Number in U.S.

(202) 785-6323); *Food Consumption Statistics*, and *Foreign Trade by Commodities*.

PORTUGAL - FOOTWEAR - PRODUCTION INDEX

Organisation for Economic Co-operation and Development (OECD), 2 rue Andre-Pascal, 75 Paris 16, France (Telephone Number in U.S. (202) 785-6323); *Indicators of Industrial Activity*.

PORTUGAL - FOREIGN AID

G.K. Hall and Company, 70 Lincoln Street, Boston, Massachusetts 02111 (617) 423-3990; *The World in Figures*.

PORTUGAL - FOREIGN DEBT

Organisation for Economic Co-operation and Development (OECD), 2 rue Andre-Pascal, 75 Paris 16, France (Telephone Number in U.S. (202) 785-6323); *Economic Outlook*.

PORTUGAL - FOREIGN INDEBTEDNESS

Organisation for Economic Co-operation and Development (OECD), 2 rue Andre-Pascal, 75 Paris 16, France (Telephone Number in U.S. (202) 785-6323); *Economic Outlook*, and *Financial Market Trends*.

PORTUGAL - FOREIGN OFFICIAL RESERVES

European Community Information Service, 2100 M Street, NW, Washington, D.C. 20037 (202) 862-9500; *Money and Finance*.

PORTUGAL - FOREIGN TRADE

Euromonitor Publications Limited, 87-88 Turnmill Street, London EC1M 5QU, England; *European Marketing Data and Statistics*.

European Community Information Service, 2100 M Street, NW, Washington, D.C. 20037 (202) 862-9500; *Basic Statistics of the Community*, *Energy Statistics Yearbook*, *Foreign Trade of the People's Republic of China*, and *Iron and Steel: Statistical Yearbook*.

Facts on File, 460 Park Avenue South, New York, New York 10016 (800) 443-8323; *The New Book of World Rankings*.

Federal Statistical Office, Gustav - Stresemann - Ring 11, D-6200 Wiesbaden, Germany; *Portugal*.

Food and Agricultural Organization of the United Nations (FAO) Via delle Terme di Caracalla, 00100 Rome, Italy (Telephone Number in U.S. (202) 653-2400); *The State of Food and Agriculture*.

G.K. Hall and Company, 70 Lincoln Street, Boston, Massachusetts 02111 (617) 423-3990; *The World in Figures*.

International Monetary Fund, 700 Nineteenth Street, NW, Washington, D.C. 20431 (202) 623-7000; *International Financial Statistics*.

Organisation for Economic Co-operation and Development (OECD), 2 rue Andre-Pascal, 75 Paris 16, France (Telephone Number in U.S. (202) 785-6323); *Economic Outlook, The Footwear, Raw Hides and Skins, and Leather Industry in OECD Countries, Foreign Trade by Commodities, Main Economic Indicators - Historical Statistics, Maritime Transport, Meat Balances in OECD Member Countries*, and *OECD Economic Surveys: Portugal*.

Statistical Office of the United Nations, Publishing Service, New York, New York 10017 (800) 253-9646; *International Trade Statistics Yearbook, Statistical Yearbook*, and *Trade in Manufactures of Developing Countries*.

The World Bank, 1818 H Street, NW, Washington, D.C. 20433 (202) 477-1234; *World Tables*.

PORTUGAL - FORESTRY AND FOREST PRODUCTS

American Forest and Paper Association, 1250 Connecticut Avenue, NW, Washington, D.C. 20036 (202) 463-2455; *Wood Pulp and Fiber Statistics*.

Euromonitor Publications Limited, 87-88 Turnmill Street, London EC1M 5QU, England; *European Marketing Data and Statistics*.

European Community Information Service, 2100 M Street, NW, Washington, D.C. 20037 (202) 862-9500; *Agriculture: Statistical Yearbook, Basic Statistics of the Community*, and *Industrial Production: Quarterly*.

Facts on File, 460 Park Avenue South, New York, New York 10016 (800) 443-8323; *The New Book of World Rankings*.

Federal Statistical Office, Gustav - Stresemann - Ring 11, D-6200 Wiesbaden, Germany; *Portugal*.

Food and Agricultural Organization of the United Nations (FAO) Via delle Terme di Caracalla, 00100 Rome, Italy (Telephone Number in U.S. (202) 653-2400); *The State of Food and Agriculture*, and *Yearbook of Forest Products*.

G.K. Hall and Company, 70 Lincoln Street, Boston, Massachusetts 02111 (617) 423-3990; *The World in Figures*.

Organisation for Economic Co-operation and Development (OECD), 2 rue Andre-Pascal, 75 Paris 16, France (Telephone Number in U.S. (202) 785-6323); *Foreign Trade by Commodities, Indicators of Industrial Activity*, and *The Pulp and Paper Industry*.

Statistical Office of the United Nations, Publishing Service, New York, New York 10017 (800) 253-9646; *Statistical Yearbook*.

United Nations Educational, Scientific and Cultural Organization (UNESCO), 7 Place de Fontenoy, F-75700 Paris, France (Telephone Number in U.S. (212) 963-5981); *Statistical Yearbook*.

PORTUGAL - FRUIT PRODUCTION - See PORTUGAL - CROPS

PORTUGAL - FURNITURE AND WOOD PRODUCTS - EXPORTS AND IMPORTS

European Community Information Service, 2100 M Street, NW, Washington, D.C. 20037 (202) 862-9500; *Basic Statistics of the Community*.

Organisation for Economic Co-operation and Development (OECD), 2 rue Andre-Pascal, 75 Paris 16, France (Telephone Number in U.S. (202) 785-6323); *Foreign Trade by Commodities*, and *Industrial Structure Statistics*.

PORTUGAL - GAS AND GAS LIQUIDS PRODUCTION - See PORTUGAL - MINING AND MINERAL PRODUCTS

PORTUGAL - GENERAL INDUSTRIAL STATISTICS

European Community Information Service, 2100 M Street, NW, Washington, D.C. 20037 (202) 862-9500; *Basic Statistics of the Community*.

Statistical Office of the United Nations, Publishing Service, New York, New York 10017 (800) 253-9646; *Industrial Statistics Yearbook*.

PORTUGAL - GENERAL MORTALITY

European Community Information Service, 2100 M Street, NW, Washington, D.C. 20037 (202) 862-9500; *Basic Statistics of the Community*, and *Demographic Statistics*.

Statistical Office of the United Nations, Publishing Service, New York, New York 10017 (800) 253-9646; *Demographic Yearbook*.

World Health Organization, Office of Publications, Avenue Appia, CH-1211 Geneva 27, Switzerland (Telephone Number in U.S. (518) 436-9686); *World Health Statistics Annual*.

PORTUGAL - GEOGRAPHIC DATA

European Community Information Service, 2100 M Street, NW, Washington, D.C. 20037 (202) 862-9500; *Basic Statistics of the Community*.

Facts on File, 460 Park Avenue South, New York, New York 10016 (800) 443-8323; *The New Book of World Rankings*.

PORTUGAL - GLASS AND GLASS PRODUCTS - PRODUCTION INDEX

Organisation for Economic Co-operation and Development (OECD), 2 rue Andre-Pascal, 75 Paris 16, France (Telephone Number in U.S. (202) 785-6323); *Indicators of Industrial Activity*.

PORTUGAL - GOATS - See PORTUGAL - LIVESTOCK AND POULTRY

PORTUGAL - GOLD HOLDINGS

International Monetary Fund, 700 Nineteenth Street, NW, Washington, D.C. 20431 (202) 623-7000; *International Financial Statistics*.

Statistical Office of the United Nations, Publishing Service, New York, New York 10017 (800) 253-9646; *Statistical Yearbook*.

The World Bank, 1818 H Street, NW, Washington, D.C. 20433 (202) 477-1234; *World Tables*.

PORTUGAL - GOLD PRODUCTION AND CONSUMPTION - See PORTUGAL - MINING AND MINERAL PRODUCTS

PORTUGAL - GOVERNMENT

European Community Information Service, 2100 M Street, NW, Washington, D.C. 20037 (202) 862-9500; *Basic Statistics of the Community*.

G.K. Hall and Company, 70 Lincoln Street, Boston, Massachusetts 02111 (617) 423-3990; *The World in Figures*.

PORTUGAL - GOVERNMENT CONSUMPTION

European Community Information Service, 2100 M Street, NW, Washington, D.C. 20037 (202) 862-9500; *Basic Statistics of the Community*, and *Government Financing of Research and Development*.

PORTUGAL - GOVERNMENT EXPENDITURES

International Monetary Fund, 700 Nineteenth Street, NW, Washington, D.C. 20431 (202) 623-7000; *Government Finance*

Statistics Yearbook.

Organisation for Economic Co-operation and Development (OECD), 2 rue Andre-Pascal, 75 Paris 16, France (Telephone Number in U.S. (202) 785-6323); *Economic Outlook*.

Time Books, 201 East 50th Street, New York, New York 10022 (212) 751-2600; *The Economist Book of Vital World Statistics*.

The World Bank, 1818 H Street, NW, Washington, D.C. 20433 (202) 477-1234; *World Tables*.

PORTUGAL - GOVERNMENT FINANCES

European Community Information Service, 2100 M Street, NW, Washington, D.C. 20037 (202) 862-9500; *Basic Statistics of the Community*, *Government Financing of Research and Development*, and *Money and Finance*.

Organisation for Economic Co-operation and Development (OECD), 2 rue Andre-Pascal, 75 Paris 16, France (Telephone Number in U.S. (202) 785-6323); *Economic Outlook*.

Statistical Office of the United Nations, Publishing Service, New York, New York 10017 (800) 253-9646; *Statistical Yearbook*.

PORTUGAL - GOVERNMENT REVENUE

European Community Information Service, 2100 M Street, NW, Washington, D.C. 20037 (202) 862-9500; *Basic Statistics of the Community*, and *Government Financing of Research and Development*.

International Monetary Fund, 700 Nineteenth Street, NW, Washington, D.C. 20431 (202) 623-7000; *Government Finance Statistics Yearbook*.

Organisation for Economic Co-operation and Development (OECD), 2 rue Andre-Pascal, 75 Paris 16, France (Telephone Number in U.S. (202) 785-6323); *Economic Outlook*, and *Revenue Statistics of OECD Member Countries*.

Time Books, 201 East 50th Street, New York, New York 10022 (212) 751-2600; *The Economist Book of Vital World Statistics*.

The World Bank, 1818 H Street, NW, Washington, D.C. 20433 (202) 477-1234; *World Tables*.

PORTUGAL - GRAIN PRODUCTION - See PORTUGAL - CROPS

PORTUGAL - GRANTS

International Monetary Fund, 700 Nineteenth Street, NW, Washington, D.C. 20431 (202) 623-7000; *Government Finance Statistics Yearbook*.

Organisation for Economic Co-operation and Development (OECD), 2 rue Andre-Pascal, 75 Paris 16, France (Telephone Number in U.S. (202) 785-6323); *Geographical Distribution of Financial Flows to Developing Countries*.

PORTUGAL - GROSS DOMESTIC PRODUCT

The Economist Intelligence Unit, 111 West 57th Street, New York, New York 10019 (800) 938-4685; *The World Market Atlas*.

European Community Information Service, 2100 M Street, NW, Washington, D.C. 20037 (202) 862-9500; *Basic Statistics of the Community, Eurostatistics: Data for Short-Term Economic Analysis*,

Government Financing of Research and Development, Iron and Steel: Statistical Yearbook, and *Money and Finance.*

Facts on File, 460 Park Avenue South, New York, New York 10016 (800) 443-8323; *The New Book of World Rankings.*

G.K. Hall and Company, 70 Lincoln Street, Boston, Massachusetts 02111 (617) 423-3990; *The World in Figures.*

Organisation for Economic Co-operation and Development (OECD), 2 rue Andre-Pascal, 75 Paris 16, France (Telephone Number in U.S. (202) 785-6323); *Economic Outlook, Geographical Distribution of Financial Flows to Developing Countries,* and *Revenue Statistics of OECD Member Countries.*

Statistical Office of the United Nations, Publishing Service, New York, New York 10017 (800) 253-9646; *Statistical Yearbook.*

Time Books, 201 East 50th Street, New York, New York 10022 (212) 751-2600; *The Economist Book of Vital World Statistics.*

The World Bank, 1818 H Street, NW, Washington, D.C. 20433 (202) 477-1234; *World Tables.*

PORTUGAL - GROSS INDUSTRIAL PRODUCT

European Community Information Service, 2100 M Street, NW, Washington, D.C. 20037 (202) 862-9500; *Government Financing of Research and Development.*

PORTUGAL - GROSS NATIONAL PRODUCT

European Community Information Service, 2100 M Street, NW, Washington, D.C. 20037 (202) 862-9500; *ACP: Basic Statistics,* and *Basic Statistics of the Community.*

Organisation for Economic Co-operation and Development (OECD), 2 rue Andre-Pascal, 75 Paris 16, France (Telephone Number in U.S. (202) 785-6323); *Economic Outlook,* and *Geographical Distribution of Financial Flows to Developing Countries.*

U.S. Arms Control and Disarmament Agency, 320 Twenty-first Street, NW, Washington, D.C. 20451 (202) 647-8677; *World Military Expenditures and Arms Transfers.*

The World Bank, 1818 H Street, NW, Washington, D.C. 20433 (202) 477-1234; *World Tables.*

PORTUGAL - HAZELNUT PRODUCTION - See PORTUGAL - CROPS

PORTUGAL - HEALTH

European Community Information Service, 2100 M Street, NW, Washington, D.C. 20037 (202) 862-9500; *Basic Statistics of the Community,* and *Regions: Statistical Yearbook.*

Facts on File, 460 Park Avenue South, New York, New York 10016 (800) 443-8323; *The New Book of World Rankings.*

Federal Statistical Office, Gustav - Stresemann - Ring 11, D-6200 Wiesbaden, Germany; *Portugal.*

G.K. Hall and Company, 70 Lincoln Street, Boston, Massachusetts 02111 (617) 423-3990; *The World in Figures.*

Organisation for Economic Co-operation and Development (OECD), 2 rue Andre-Pascal, 75 Paris 16, France (Telephone Number in U.S. (202) 785-6323); *OECD Health Systems: Facts and Trends.*

Statistical Office of the United Nations, Publishing Service, New York, New York 10017 (800) 253-9646; *Statistical Yearbook.*

Time Books, 201 East 50th Street, New York, New York 10022 (212) 751-2600; *The Economist Book of Vital World Statistics.*

World Health Organization, Office of Publications, Avenue Appia, CH-1211 Geneva 27, Switzerland (Telephone Number in U.S. (518) 436-9686); *World Health Statistics Annual.*

PORTUGAL - HEALTH EXPENDITURES

International Monetary Fund, 700 Nineteenth Street, NW, Washington, D.C. 20431 (202) 623-7000; *Government Finance Statistics Yearbook.*

PORTUGAL - HIDE PRODUCTION

Food and Agricultural Organization of the United Nations (FAO), Via delle Terme di Caracalla, 00100 Rome, Italy (Telephone Number in U.S. (202) 653-2400); *Production Yearbook.*

Organisation for Economic Co-operation and Development (OECD), 2 rue Andre-Pascal, 75 Paris 16, France (Telephone Number in U.S. (202) 785-6323); *The Footwear, Raw Hides and Skins,* and *Leather Industry in OECD Countries, Foreign Trade by Commodities,* and *Indicators of Industrial Activity.*

PORTUGAL - HIGHWAYS

European Community Information Service, 2100 M Street, NW, Washington, D.C. 20037 (202) 862-9500; *Basic Statistics of the Community* and *Transport Annual Statistics.*

G.K. Hall and Company, 70 Lincoln Street, Boston, Massachusetts 02111 (617) 423-3990; *The World in Figures.*

International Road Federation, 525 School Street, SW, Washington, D.C. 20024 (202) 554-2106; *World Road Statistics.*

PORTUGAL - HOME FINANCE

Organisation for Economic Co-operation and Development (OECD), 2 rue Andre-Pascal, 75 Paris 16, France (Telephone Number in U.S. (202) 785-6323); *Main Economic Indicators - Historical Statistics.*

PORTUGAL - HORSES - See PORTUGAL - LIVESTOCK AND POULTRY

PORTUGAL - HOURS OF WORK - See PORTUGAL - EMPLOYMENT

PORTUGAL - HOUSING AND HOUSING UNITS

European Community Information Service, 2100 M Street, NW, Washington, D.C. 20037 (202) 862-9500; *Basic Statistics of the Community, Labor Force Sample Survey,* and *Regions: Statistical Yearbook.*

Facts on File, 460 Park Avenue South, New York, New York 10016 (800) 443-8323; *The New Book of World Rankings.*

PORTUGAL - HOUSING CONSTRUCTION - See PORTUGAL - CONSTRUCTION INDUSTRY

PORTUGAL - HOUSING EXPENDITURES

European Community Information Service, 2100 M Street, NW, Washington, D.C. 20037 (202) 862-9500; *Basic Statistics of the Community.*

International Monetary Fund, 700 Nineteenth Street, NW, Washington, D.C. 20431 (202) 623-7000; *Government Finance Statistics Yearbook.*

PORTUGAL - HYDROCHLORIC ACID PRODUCTION

Statistical Office of the United Nations, Publishing Service, New York, New York 10017 (800) 253-9646; *Statistical Yearbook.*

PORTUGAL - ILLITERATE POPULATION

The Economist Intelligence Unit, 111 West 57th Street, New York, New York 10019 (800) 938-4685; *The World Market Atlas.*

G.K. Hall and Company, 70 Lincoln Street, Boston, Massachusetts 02111 (617) 423-3990; *The World in Figures.*

PORTUGAL - IMPORTS

American Automobile Manufacturers Association, 1401 H Street, NW, Suite 900, Washington, D.C. 20005 (202) 326-5500; *World Motor Vehicle Data.*

The Economist Intelligence Unit, 111 West 57th Street, New York, New York 10019 (800) 938-4685; *The World Market Atlas.*

European Community Information Service, 2100 M Street, NW, Washington, D.C. 20037 (202) 862-9500; *Basic Statistics of the Community, Energy: Monthly Statistics, Energy Statistics Yearbook, Eurostatistics: Data for Short-Term Economic Analysis, External Trade: Statistical Yearbook, External Trade: Monthly Statistics,* and *Fisheries: Yearly Statistics.*

Food and Agricultural Organization of the United Nations (FAO) Via delle Terme di Caracalla, 00100 Rome, Italy (Telephone Number in U.S. (202) 653-2400); *The State of Food and Agriculture.*

G.K. Hall and Company, 70 Lincoln Street, Boston, Massachusetts 02111 (617) 423-3990; *The World in Figures.*

International Monetary Fund, 700 Nineteenth Street, NW, Washington, D.C. 20431 (202) 623-7000; *Direction of Trade,* and *International Financial Statistics.*

Organisation for Economic Co-operation and Development (OECD), 2 rue Andre-Pascal, 75 Paris 16, France (Telephone Number in U.S. (202) 785-6323); *Economic Outlook.*

Organisation for Economic Co-operation and Development (OECD), 2 rue Andre-Pascal, 75 Paris 16, France (Telephone Number in U.S. (202) 785-6323); *The Footwear, Raw Hides and Skins, and Leather Industry in OECD Countries, Industrial Structure Statistics, The Iron and Steel Industry, Milk, Milk Products, and Egg Balances in OECD Member Countries, The Pulp and Paper Industry, OECD Economic Surveys: Portugal,* and *Review of Fisheries in OECD Member Countries.*

Time Books, 201 East 50th Street, New York, New York 10022 (212) 751-2600; *The Economist Book of Vital World Statistics.*

The World Bank, 1818 H Street, NW, Washington, D.C. 20433 (202) 477-1234; *World Tables.*

PORTUGAL - INCOME TAXES - See PORTUGAL - TAXATION

PORTUGAL - INDUSTRIAL ACID PRODUCTION

Statistical Office of the United Nations, Publishing Service, New York, New York 10017 (800) 253-9646; *Statistical Yearbook.*

PORTUGAL - INDUSTRY

European Community Information Service, 2100 M Street, NW, Washington, D.C. 20037 (202) 862-9500; *Basic Statistics of the Community, Employment and Unemployment, Eurostatistics: Data for Short-Term Economic Analysis,* and *Labor Force Sample Survey.*

Facts on File, 460 Park Avenue South, New York, New York 10016 (800) 443-8323; *The New Book of World Rankings.*

Federal Statistical Office, Gustav - Stresemann - Ring 11, D-6200 Wiesbaden, Germany; *Portugal.*

G.K. Hall and Company, 70 Lincoln Street, Boston, Massachusetts 02111 (617) 423-3990; *The World in Figures.*

International Labour Office, I.L.O. Publications, CH-1211, Geneva 22, Switzerland; *Yearbook of Labour Statistics.*

Organisation for Economic Co-operation and Development (OECD), 2 rue Andre-Pascal, 75 Paris 16, France (Telephone Number in U.S. (202) 785-6323); *Economic Outlook, Indicators of Industrial Activity, Industrial Structure Statistics, Main Economic Indicators - Historical Statistics,* and *OECD Environmental Data.*

Statistical Office of the United Nations, Publishing Service, New York, New York 10017 (800) 253-9646; *Statistical Yearbook.*

Time Books, 201 East 50th Street, New York, New York 10022 (212) 751-2600; *The Economist Book of Vital World Statistics.*

The World Bank, 1818 H Street, NW, Washington, D.C. 20433 (202) 477-1234; *World Tables.*

World Intellectual Property Organization, 34 Chemin des Colombettes, CH-1211 Geneva 20, Switzerland; *Industrial Property Statistics.*

PORTUGAL - INFANT AND MATERNAL MORTALITY

European Community Information Service, 2100 M Street, NW, Washington, D.C. 20037 (202) 862-9500; *Basic Statistics of the Community,* and *Demographic Statistics.*

Statistical Office of the United Nations, Publishing Service, New York, New York 10017 (800) 253-9646; *Demographic Yearbook,* and *Statistical Yearbook.*

Time Books, 201 East 50th Street, New York, New York 10022 (212) 751-2600; *The Economist Book of Vital World Statistics.*

The World Bank, 1818 H Street, NW, Washington, D.C. 20433 (202) 477-1234; *World Tables.*

World Health Organization, Office of Publications, Avenue Appia, CH-1211 Geneva 27, Switzerland (Telephone Number in U.S. (518) 436-9686); *World Health Statistics Annual.*

PORTUGAL - INTEREST RATES

European Community Information Service, 2100 M Street, NW, Washington, D.C. 20037 (202) 862-9500; *Money and Finance.*

Organisation for Economic Co-operation and Development (OECD), 2 rue Andre-Pascal, 75 Paris 16, France (Telephone Number in U.S. (202) 785-6323); *Economic Outlook, Financial Market Trends,* and *OECD Financial Statistics.*

PORTUGAL - INTERNAL TRADE

European Community Information Service, 2100 M Street, NW, Washington, D.C. 20037 (202) 862-9500; *Basic Statistics of the Community*.

Statistical Office of the United Nations, Publishing Service, New York, New York 10017 (800) 253-9646; *Statistical Yearbook*.

PORTUGAL - INTERNATIONAL FINANCE

European Community Information Service, 2100 M Street, NW, Washington, D.C. 20037 (202) 862-9500; *Basic Statistics of the Community*.

Organisation for Economic Co-operation and Development (OECD), 2 rue Andre-Pascal, 75 Paris 16, France (Telephone Number in U.S. (202) 785-6323); *Economic Outlook*, and *Financial Market Trends*.

PORTUGAL - INTERNATIONAL LIQUIDITY

International Monetary Fund, 700 Nineteenth Street, NW, Washington, D.C. 20431 (202) 623-7000; *International Financial Statistics*.

Organisation for Economic Co-operation and Development (OECD), 2 rue Andre-Pascal, 75 Paris 16, France (Telephone Number in U.S. (202) 785-6323); *Economic Outlook*, and *Financial Market Trends*.

PORTUGAL - INTERNATIONAL RESERVES EXCLUDING GOLD

Statistical Office of the United Nations, Publishing Service, New York, New York 10017 (800) 253-9646; *Statistical Yearbook*.

The World Bank, 1818 H Street, NW, Washington, D.C. 20433 (202) 477-1234; *World Tables*.

PORTUGAL - INTERNATIONAL STATISTICS

Organisation for Economic Co-operation and Development (OECD), 2 rue Andre-Pascal, 75 Paris 16, France (Telephone Number in U.S. (202) 785-6323); *Financial Market Trends*, and *Tourism Policy and International Tourism in OECD Member Countries*.

PORTUGAL - INVESTMENTS

International Monetary Fund, 700 Nineteenth Street, NW, Washington, D.C. 20431 (202) 623-7000; *International Financial Statistics*.

Organisation for Economic Co-operation and Development (OECD), 2 rue Andre-Pascal, 75 Paris 16, France (Telephone Number in U.S. (202) 785-6323); *Economic Outlook, Financial Market Trends, Industrial Structure Statistics, The Iron and Steel Industry*, and *Textile Industry in OECD Countries*.

PORTUGAL - IRON ORE PRODUCTION AND CONSUMPTION - See PORTUGAL - MINING AND MINERAL PRODUCTS

PORTUGAL - LABOR FORCE

European Community Information Service, 2100 M Street, NW, Washington, D.C. 20037 (202) 862-9500; *Basic Statistics of the Community, Labor Force Sample Survey*, and *Regions: Statistical Yearbook*.

Facts on File, 460 Park Avenue South, New York, New York 10016 (800) 443-8323; *The New Book of World Rankings*.

Food and Agricultural Organization of the United Nations (FAO) Via delle Terme di Caracalla, 00100 Rome, Italy (Telephone Number in U.S. (202) 653-2400); *The State of Food and Agriculture*.

G.K. Hall and Company, 70 Lincoln Street, Boston, Massachusetts 02111 (617) 423-3990; *The World in Figures*.

Organisation for Economic Co-operation and Development (OECD), 2 rue Andre-Pascal, 75 Paris 16, France (Telephone Number in U.S. (202) 785-6323); *Economic Outlook, The Iron and Steel Industry, Maritime Transport, OECD Economic Surveys: Portugal, OECD Employment Outlook*, and *Textile Industry in OECD Countries*.

Time Books, 201 East 50th Street, New York, New York 10022 (212) 751-2600; *The Economist Book of Vital World Statistics*.

The World Bank, 1818 H Street, NW, Washington, D.C. 20433 (202) 477-1234; *World Tables*.

PORTUGAL - LABOR PRODUCTIVITY

International Labour Office, I.L.O. Publications, CH-1211, Geneva 22, Switzerland; *Yearbook of Labour Statistics*.

Organisation for Economic Co-operation and Development (OECD), 2 rue Andre-Pascal, 75 Paris 16, France (Telephone Number in U.S. (202) 785-6323); *Economic Outlook, OECD Economic Surveys: Portugal*, and *OECD Employment Outlook*.

PORTUGAL - LAND USE

Euromonitor Publications Limited, 87-88 Turnmill Street, London EC1M 5QU, England; *European Marketing Data and Statistics*.

European Community Information Service, 2100 M Street, NW, Washington, D.C. 20037 (202) 862-9500; *Agriculture: Statistical Yearbook, Basic Statistics of the Community, Crop Production: Quarterly Statistics*, and *Regions: Statistical Yearbook*.

Food and Agricultural Organization of the United Nations (FAO), Via delle Terme di Caracalla, 00100 Rome, Italy (Telephone Number in U.S. (202) 653-2400); *Production Yearbook*.

G.K. Hall and Company, 70 Lincoln Street, Boston, Massachusetts 02111 (617) 423-3990; *The World in Figures*.

PORTUGAL - LEAD AND LEAD ORE PRODUCTION AND CONSUMPTION - See PORTUGAL - MINING AND MINERAL PRODUCTS

PORTUGAL - LEATHER - PRODUCTION INDEX

Organisation for Economic Co-operation and Development (OECD), 2 rue Andre-Pascal, 75 Paris 16, France (Telephone Number in U.S. (202) 785-6323); *Indicators of Industrial Activity*.

PORTUGAL - LEATHER AND FOOTWEAR EXPORTS AND IMPORTS

European Community Information Service, 2100 M Street, NW, Washington, D.C. 20037 (202) 862-9500; *Basic Statistics of the Community*.

Organisation for Economic Co-operation and Development (OECD), 2 rue Andre-Pascal, 75 Paris 16, France (Telephone Number in U.S. (202) 785-6323); *The Footwear, Raw Hides and Skins*, and *Leather Industry in OECD Countries*.

PORTUGAL - LIBRARIES

Euromonitor Publications Limited, 87-88 Turnmill Street, London EC1M 5QU, England; *European Marketing Data and Statistics.*

Facts on File, 460 Park Avenue South, New York, New York 10016 (800) 443-8323; *The New Book of World Rankings.*

United Nations Educational, Scientific and Cultural Organization (UNESCO), 7 Place de Fontenoy, F-75700 Paris, France (Telephone Number in U.S. (212) 963-5981); *Statistical Yearbook.*

PORTUGAL - LIGNITE PRODUCTION - See PORTUGAL - MINING AND MINERAL PRODUCTS

PORTUGAL - LIVESTOCK AND POULTRY

Euromonitor Publications Limited, 87-88 Turnmill Street, London EC1M 5QU, England; *European Marketing Data and Statistics.*

European Community Information Service, 2100 M Street, NW, Washington, D.C. 20037 (202) 862-9500; *Agriculture: Statistical Yearbook, Basic Statistics of the Community, Eurostatistics: Data for Short-Term Economic Analysis,* and *Regions: Statistical Yearbook.*

Facts on File, 460 Park Avenue South, New York, New York 10016 (800) 443-8323; *The New Book of World Rankings.*

Food and Agricultural Organization of the United Nations (FAO), Via delle Terme di Caracalla, 00100 Rome, Italy (Telephone Number in U.S. (202) 653-2400); *Production Yearbook,* and *The State of Food and Agriculture.*

G.K. Hall and Company, 70 Lincoln Street, Boston, Massachusetts 02111 (617) 423-3990; *The World in Figures.*

Organisation for Economic Co-operation and Development (OECD), 2 rue Andre-Pascal, 75 Paris 16, France (Telephone Number in U.S. (202) 785-6323); *Economic Accounts for Agriculture,* and *Meat Balances in OECD Member Countries.*

Statistical Office of the United Nations, Publishing Service, New York, New York 10017 (800) 253-9646; *Statistical Yearbook.*

PORTUGAL - LIVING LEVELS

G.K. Hall and Company, 70 Lincoln Street, Boston, Massachusetts 02111 (617) 423-3990; *The World in Figures.*

Organisation for Economic Co-operation and Development (OECD), 2 rue Andre-Pascal, 75 Paris 16, France (Telephone Number in U.S. (202) 785-6323); *Economic Outlook.*

Time Books, 201 East 50th Street, New York, New York 10022 (212) 751-2600; *The Economist Book of Vital World Statistics.*

PORTUGAL - MACHINERY - PRODUCTION INDEX

Organisation for Economic Co-operation and Development (OECD), 2 rue Andre-Pascal, 75 Paris 16, France (Telephone Number in U.S. (202) 785-6323); *Indicators of Industrial Activity.*

PORTUGAL - MAGNESIUM PRODUCTION AND CONSUMPTION - See PORTUGAL - MINING AND MINERAL PRODUCTS

PORTUGAL - MAIL - NUMBER OF PIECES SENT OR RECEIVED

European Community Information Service, 2100 M Street, NW, Washington, D.C. 20037 (202) 862-9500; *Transport Annual Statistics.*

Statistical Office of the United Nations, Publishing Service, New York, New York 10017 (800) 253-9646; *Statistical Yearbook.*

PORTUGAL - MAIN ECONOMIC INDICATORS - See PORTUGAL - ECONOMY

PORTUGAL - MANGANESE AND MANGANESE ORE PRODUCTION AND CONSUMPTION - See PORTUGAL - MINING AND MINERAL PRODUCTS

PORTUGAL - MANUFACTURING

American Automobile Manufacturers Association, 1401 H Street, NW, Suite 900, Washington, D.C. 20005 (202) 326-5500; *World Motor Vehicle Data.*

European Community Information Service, 2100 M Street, NW, Washington, D.C. 20037 (202) 862-9500; *Basic Statistics of the Community, Eurostatistics: Data for Short-Term Economic Analysis,* and *Industrial Production: Quarterly.*

Facts on File, 460 Park Avenue South, New York, New York 10016 (800) 443-8323; *The New Book of World Rankings.*

G.K. Hall and Company, 70 Lincoln Street, Boston, Massachusetts 02111 (617) 423-3990; *The World in Figures.*

Organisation for Economic Co-operation and Development (OECD), 2 rue Andre-Pascal, 75 Paris 16, France (Telephone Number in U.S. (202) 785-6323); *Foreign Trade by Commodities, Indicators of Industrial Activity, Indicators of Industrial Activity, Industrial Structure Statistics, OECD Economic Surveys: Portugal,* and *Statistical Yearbook.*

Statistical Office of the United Nations, Publishing Service, New York, New York 10017 (800) 253-9646; *Statistical Yearbook.*

Time Books, 201 East 50th Street, New York, New York 10022 (212) 751-2600; *The Economist Book of Vital World Statistics.*

The World Bank, 1818 H Street, NW, Washington, D.C. 20433 (202) 477-1234; *World Tables.*

PORTUGAL - MARRIAGE RATES

European Community Information Service, 2100 M Street, NW, Washington, D.C. 20037 (202) 862-9500; *Basic Statistics of the Community.*

Facts on File, 460 Park Avenue South, New York, New York 10016 (800) 443-8323; *The New Book of World Rankings.*

Statistical Office of the United Nations, Publishing Service, New York, New York 10017 (800) 253-9646; *Demographic Yearbook,* and *Statistical Yearbook.*

PORTUGAL - MEAT PRODUCTION - See PORTUGAL - LIVESTOCK AND POULTRY

PORTUGAL - MERCHANT SHIPPING

European Community Information Service, 2100 M Street, NW, Washington, D.C. 20037 (202) 862-9500; *Basic Statistics of the Community, Fisheries: Yearly Statistics, Regions: Statistical Yearbook,* and *Transport Annual Statistics.*

G.K. Hall and Company, 70 Lincoln Street, Boston, Massachusetts 02111 (617) 423-3990; *The World in Figures.*

Lloyd's Register of Shipping, 17 Battery Place, New York, New York 10004 (212) 425-8050; *Register of Ships.*

Organisation for Economic Co-operation and Development (OECD), 2 rue Andre-Pascal, 75 Paris 16, France (Telephone Number in U.S. (202) 785-6323); *Maritime Transport.*

Statistical Office of the United Nations, Publishing Service, New York, New York 10017 (800) 253-9646; *Statistical Yearbook.*

U.S. Department of Transportation, Maritime Administration, 400 Seventh Street, SW, Washington, D.C. 20590 (202) 366-5807; *A Statistical Analysis of the World's Merchant Fleets.*

PORTUGAL - MERCURY PRODUCTION AND CONSUMPTION - See PORTUGAL - MINING AND MINERAL PRODUCTS

PORTUGAL - MILITARY

G.K. Hall and Company, 70 Lincoln Street, Boston, Massachusetts 02111 (617) 423-3990; *The World in Figures.*

The International Institute for Strategic Studies, 23 Tavistock Street, London WC2E 7NQ, England; *The Military Balance.*

U.S. Arms Control and Disarmament Agency, 320 Twenty-first Street, NW, Washington, D.C. 20451 (202) 647-8677; *World Military Expenditures and Arms Transfers.*

PORTUGAL - MILK PRODUCTION - See PORTUGAL - DAIRY PRODUCTS

PORTUGAL - MILLET PRODUCTION - See PORTUGAL - CROPS

PORTUGAL - MINING AND MINERAL PRODUCTS

Commodity Research Bureau, Incorporated, 75 Wall Street, New York, New York 10005 (212) 504-7754; *Commodity Year Book.*

European Community Information Service, 2100 M Street, NW, Washington, D.C. 20037 (202) 862-9500; *ACP: Basic Statistics, Basic Statistics of the Community, Energy: Monthly Statistics, Energy Statistics Yearbook, Eurostatistics: Data for Short-Term Economic Analysis, Industrial Production: Quarterly, Iron and Steel: Statistical Yearbook, Labor Force Sample Survey,* and *Regions: Statistical Yearbook.*

Facts on File, 460 Park Avenue South, New York, New York 10016 (800) 443-8323; *The New Book of World Rankings.*

Food and Agricultural Organization of the United Nations (FAO), Via delle Terme di Caracalla, 00100 Rome, Italy (Telephone Number in U.S. (202) 653-2400); *Production Yearbook.*

G.K. Hall and Company, 70 Lincoln Street, Boston, Massachusetts 02111 (617) 423-3990; *The World in Figures.*

Organisation for Economic Co-operation and Development (OECD), 2 rue Andre-Pascal, 75 Paris 16, France (Telephone Number in U.S. (202) 785-6323); *Coal Information, Energy Statistics of OECD Countries, Foreign Trade by Commodities, Indicators of Industrial Activity, Industrial Structure Statistics, The Iron and Steel Industry, The Non-Ferrous Metals Industry,* and *OECD Economic Surveys: Portugal.*

Statistical Office of the United Nations, Publishing Service, New York, New York 10017 (800) 253-9646; *Statistical Yearbook.*

PORTUGAL - MOLYBDENUM AND MOLYBDENUM ORE PRODUCTION AND CONSUMPTION - See PORTUGAL - MINING AND MINERAL PRODUCTS

PORTUGAL - MONEY AND CREDIT

Organisation for Economic Co-operation and Development (OECD), 2 rue Andre-Pascal, 75 Paris 16, France (Telephone Number in U.S. (202) 785-6323); *OECD Economic Surveys: Portugal.*

PORTUGAL - MONEY EXCHANGE RATE

European Community Information Service, 2100 M Street, NW, Washington, D.C. 20037 (202) 862-9500; *Basic Statistics of the Community.*

International Monetary Fund, 700 Nineteenth Street, NW, Washington, D.C. 20431 (202) 623-7000; *International Financial Statistics.*

Organisation for Economic Co-operation and Development (OECD), 2 rue Andre-Pascal, 75 Paris 16, France (Telephone Number in U.S. (202) 785-6323); *Economic Outlook, Financial Market Trends,* and *Tourism Policy and International Tourism in OECD Member Countries.*

Statistical Office of the United Nations, Publishing Service, New York, New York 10017 (800) 253-9646; *Statistical Yearbook.*

PORTUGAL - MONEY RATES - MARKET

European Community Information Service, 2100 M Street, NW, Washington, D.C. 20037 (202) 862-9500; *Basic Statistics of the Community.*

Organisation for Economic Co-operation and Development (OECD), 2 rue Andre-Pascal, 75 Paris 16, France (Telephone Number in U.S. (202) 785-6323); *Economic Outlook,* and *Financial Market Trends.*

PORTUGAL - MONEY RESERVES

European Community Information Service, 2100 M Street, NW, Washington, D.C. 20037 (202) 862-9500; *Basic Statistics of the Community.*

Organisation for Economic Co-operation and Development (OECD), 2 rue Andre-Pascal, 75 Paris 16, France (Telephone Number in U.S. (202) 785-6323); *Economic Outlook,* and *Financial Market Trends.*

PORTUGAL - MONEY SUPPLY

European Community Information Service, 2100 M Street, NW, Washington, D.C. 20037 (202) 862-9500; *Basic Statistics of the Community, Eurostatistics: Data for Short-Term Economic Analysis,* and *Money and Finance.*

G.K. Hall and Company, 70 Lincoln Street, Boston, Massachusetts 02111 (617) 423-3990; *The World in Figures.*

International Monetary Fund, 700 Nineteenth Street, NW, Washington, D.C. 20431 (202) 623-7000; *International Financial Statistics.*

Organisation for Economic Co-operation and Development (OECD), 2 rue Andre-Pascal, 75 Paris 16, France (Telephone Number in U.S. (202) 785-6323); *Economic Outlook.*

Statistical Office of the United Nations, Publishing Service, New York, New York 10017 (800) 253-9646; *Statistical Yearbook*.

The World Bank, 1818 H Street, NW, Washington, D.C. 20433 (202) 477-1234; *World Tables*.

PORTUGAL - MOTION PICTURES

Statistical Office of the United Nations, Publishing Service, New York, New York 10017 (800) 253-9646; *Statistical Yearbook*.

United Nations Educational, Scientific and Cultural Organization (UNESCO), 7 Place de Fontenoy, F-75700 Paris, France (Telephone Number in U.S. (212) 963-5981); *Statistical Yearbook*.

PORTUGAL - MOTOR VEHICLE PRODUCTION

American Automobile Manufacturers Association, 1401 H Street, NW, Suite 900, Washington, D.C. 20005 (202) 326-5500; *World Motor Vehicle Data*.

European Community Information Service, 2100 M Street, NW, Washington, D.C. 20037 (202) 862-9500; *Basic Statistics of the Community*, and *Eurostatistics: Data for Short-Term Economic Analysis*.

Organisation for Economic Co-operation and Development (OECD), 2 rue Andre-Pascal, 75 Paris 16, France (Telephone Number in U.S. (202) 785-6323); *Foreign Trade by Commodities*, and *Indicators of Industrial Activity*.

Statistical Office of the United Nations, Publishing Service, New York, New York 10017 (800) 253-9646; *Statistical Yearbook*.

PORTUGAL - MOTOR VEHICLE TAXES - See PORTUGAL - TAXATION

PORTUGAL - MOTOR VEHICLES IN USE

American Automobile Manufacturers Association, 1401 H Street, NW, Suite 900, Washington, D.C. 20005 (202) 326-5500; *World Motor Vehicle Data*.

European Community Information Service, 2100 M Street, NW, Washington, D.C. 20037 (202) 862-9500; *Basic Statistics of the Community*, and *Transport Annual Statistics*.

G.K. Hall and Company, 70 Lincoln Street, Boston, Massachusetts 02111 (617) 423-3990; *The World in Figures*.

International Road Federation, 525 School Street, SW, Washington, D.C. 20024 (202) 554-2106; *World Road Statistics*.

Statistical Office of the United Nations, Publishing Service, New York, New York 10017 (800) 253-9646; *Statistical Yearbook*.

Time Books, 201 East 50th Street, New York, New York 10022 (212) 751-2600; *The Economist Book of Vital World Statistics*.

PORTUGAL - MULES - See PORTUGAL - LIVESTOCK AND POULTRY

PORTUGAL - MUSEUMS

Euromonitor Publications Limited, 87-88 Turnmill Street, London EC1M 5QU, England; *European Marketing Data and Statistics*.

Facts on File, 460 Park Avenue South, New York, New York 10016 (800) 443-8323; *The New Book of World Rankings*.

United Nations Educational, Scientific and Cultural Organization (UNESCO), 7 Place de Fontenoy, F-75700 Paris, France (Telephone Number in U.S. (212) 963-5981); *Statistical Yearbook*.

PORTUGAL - NATALITY - See PORTUGAL - BIRTH RATES

PORTUGAL - NATIONAL ACCOUNTS

European Community Information Service, 2100 M Street, NW, Washington, D.C. 20037 (202) 862-9500; *Basic Statistics of the Community*, and *Eurostatistics: Data for Short-Term Economic Analysis*.

Federal Statistical Office, Gustav - Stresemann - Ring 11, D-6200 Wiesbaden, Germany; *Portugal*.

Organisation for Economic Co-operation and Development (OECD), 2 rue Andre-Pascal, 75 Paris 16, France (Telephone Number in U.S. (202) 785-6323); *Economic Outlook*.

Statistical Office of the United Nations, Publishing Service, New York, New York 10017 (800) 253-9646; *National Accounts Statistics*, and *Statistical Yearbook*.

PORTUGAL - NATIONAL INCOME

Facts on File, 460 Park Avenue South, New York, New York 10016 (800) 443-8323; *The New Book of World Rankings*.

G.K. Hall and Company, 70 Lincoln Street, Boston, Massachusetts 02111 (617) 423-3990; *The World in Figures*.

Organisation for Economic Co-operation and Development (OECD), 2 rue Andre-Pascal, 75 Paris 16, France (Telephone Number in U.S. (202) 785-6323); *Economic Outlook*.

Statistical Office of the United Nations, Publishing Service, New York, New York 10017 (800) 253-9646; *Statistical Yearbook*.

PORTUGAL - NATIONAL PRODUCT

European Community Information Service, 2100 M Street, NW, Washington, D.C. 20037 (202) 862-9500; *Basic Statistics of the Community*.

Facts on File, 460 Park Avenue South, New York, New York 10016 (800) 443-8323; *The New Book of World Rankings*.

Organisation for Economic Co-operation and Development (OECD), 2 rue Andre-Pascal, 75 Paris 16, France (Telephone Number in U.S. (202) 785-6323); *Economic Outlook*.

Statistical Office of the United Nations, Publishing Service, New York, New York 10017 (800) 253-9646; *Statistical Yearbook*.

PORTUGAL - NATURAL GAS PRODUCTION - See PORTUGAL - MINING AND MINERAL PRODUCTS

PORTUGAL - NEWSPAPER PRODUCTION - See PORTUGAL - FORESTRY AND FOREST PRODUCTS

PORTUGAL - NEWSPRINT PRODUCTION AND CONSUMPTION - See PORTUGAL - FORESTRY AND FOREST PRODUCTS

PORTUGAL - NICKEL AND NICKEL ORE PRODUCTION AND CONSUMPTION - See PORTUGAL - MINING AND MINERAL PRODUCTS

PORTUGAL - NITRIC ACID PRODUCTION - See PORTUGAL - MINING AND MINERAL PRODUCTS

PORTUGAL - OATS PRODUCTION - See PORTUGAL - CROPS

PORTUGAL - OCCUPATIONS AND EDUCATION

G.K. Hall and Company, 70 Lincoln Street, Boston, Massachusetts 02111 (617) 423-3990; *The World in Figures.*

PORTUGAL - OIL PRODUCING CROPS

European Community Information Service, 2100 M Street, NW, Washington, D.C. 20037 (202) 862-9500; *Basic Statistics of the Community.*

Organisation for Economic Co-operation and Development (OECD), 2 rue Andre-Pascal, 75 Paris 16, France (Telephone Number in U.S. (202) 785-6323); *Foreign Trade by Commodities.*

PORTUGAL - PAPER - See PORTUGAL - FORESTRY AND FOREST PRODUCTS

PORTUGAL - PATENTS

Statistical Office of the United Nations, Publishing Service, New York, New York 10017 (800) 253-9646; *Statistical Yearbook.*

World Intellectual Property Organization, 34 Chemin des Colombettes, CH 1211 Geneva 20, Switzerland; *Industrial Property Statistics.*

PORTUGAL - PEANUT PRODUCTION - See PORTUGAL - CROPS

PORTUGAL - PERIODICALS

United Nations Educational, Scientific and Cultural Organization (UNESCO), 7 Place de Fontenoy, F-75700 Paris, France (Telephone Number in U.S. (212) 963-5981); *Statistical Yearbook.*

PORTUGAL - PESTICIDE USE

Food and Agricultural Organization of the United Nations (FAO) Via delle Terme di Caracalla, 00100 Rome, Italy (Telephone Number in U.S. (202) 653-2400); *The State of Food and Agriculture.*

PORTUGAL - PETROLEUM INDUSTRY

Euromonitor Publications Limited, 87-88 Turnmill Street, London EC1M 5QU, England; *European Marketing Data and Statistics.*

European Community Information Service, 2100 M Street, NW, Washington, D.C. 20037 (202) 862-9500; *ACP: Basic Statistics, Basic Statistics of the Community,* and *Energy Statistics Yearbook.*

Facts on File, 460 Park Avenue South, New York, New York 10016 (800) 443-8323; *The New Book of World Rankings.*

Food and Agricultural Organization of the United Nations (FAO) Via delle Terme di Caracalla, 00100 Rome, Italy (Telephone Number in U.S. (202) 653-2400); *The State of Food and Agriculture.*

G.K. Hall and Company, 70 Lincoln Street, Boston, Massachusetts 02111 (617) 423-3990; *The World in Figures.*

Organisation for Economic Co-operation and Development (OECD), 2 rue Andre-Pascal, 75 Paris 16, France (Telephone Number in U.S. (202) 785-6323); *Energy Statistics of OECD Countries, Foreign Trade by Commodities, Indicators of Industrial Activity,* and *Oil and Gas Information.*

Statistical Office of the United Nations, Publishing Service, New York, New York 10017 (800) 253-9646; *Statistical Yearbook.*

PORTUGAL - PHOSPHATE ROCK PRODUCTION - See PORTUGAL - MINING AND MINERAL PRODUCTS

PORTUGAL - PHOSPHATES PRODUCTION - See PORTUGAL - MINING AND MINERAL PRODUCTS

PORTUGAL - PIG-IRON AND FERRO-ALLOY PRODUCTION - See PORTUGAL - MINING AND MINERAL PRODUCTS

PORTUGAL - PIGS - See PORTUGAL - LIVESTOCK AND POULTRY

PORTUGAL - PLASTIC RESIN PRODUCTION

Organisation for Economic Co-operation and Development (OECD), 2 rue Andre-Pascal, 75 Paris 16, France (Telephone Number in U.S. (202) 785-6323); *Foreign Trade by Commodities.*

Statistical Office of the United Nations, Publishing Service, New York, New York 10017 (800) 253-9646; *Statistical Yearbook.*

PORTUGAL - PLATINUM PRODUCTION - See PORTUGAL - MINING AND MINERAL PRODUCTS

PORTUGAL - POPULATION

The Economist Intelligence Unit, 111 West 57th Street, New York, New York 10019 (800) 938-4685; *The World Market Atlas.*

Euromonitor Publications Limited, 87-88 Turnmill Street, London EC1M 5QU, England; *European Marketing Data and Statistics.*

European Community Information Service, 2100 M Street, NW, Washington, D.C. 20037 (202) 862-9500; *ACP: Basic Statistics, Basic Statistics of the Community, Demographic Statistics, Employment and Unemployment, Fisheries: Yearly Statistics, Iron and Steel: Statistical Yearbook, Labor Force Sample Survey,* and *Regions: Statistical Yearbook.*

Facts on File, 460 Park Avenue South, New York, New York 10016 (800) 443-8323; *The New Book of World Rankings.*

Federal Statistical Office, Gustav - Stresemann - Ring 11, D-6200 Wiesbaden, Germany; *Portugal.*

Food and Agricultural Organization of the United Nations (FAO), Via delle Terme di Caracalla, 00100 Rome, Italy (Telephone Number in U.S. (202) 653-2400); *Production Yearbook.*

G.K. Hall and Company, 70 Lincoln Street, Boston, Massachusetts 02111 (617) 423-3990; *The World in Figures.*

International Labour Office, I.L.O. Publications, CH-1211, Geneva 22, Switzerland; *Yearbook of Labour Statistics.*

Statistical Office of the United Nations, Publishing Service, New York, New York 10017 (800) 253-9646; *Demographic Yearbook,* and *Statistical Yearbook.*

Time Books, 201 East 50th Street, New York, New York 10022 (212) 751-2600; *The Economist Book of Vital World Statistics.*

United Nations Educational, Scientific and Cultural Organization (UNESCO), 7 Place de Fontenoy, F-75700 Paris, France (Telephone Number in U.S. (212) 963-5981); *Statistical Yearbook.*

U.S. Arms Control and Disarmament Agency, 320 Twenty-first Street, NW, Washington, D.C. 20451 (202) 647-8677; *World Military Expenditures and Arms Transfers.*

World Health Organization, Office of Publications, Avenue Appia, CH-1211 Geneva 27, Switzerland (Telephone Number in U.S. (518) 436-9686); *World Health Statistics Annual.*

PORTUGAL - POST OFFICES

Facts on File, 460 Park Avenue South, New York, New York 10016 (800) 443-8323; *The New Book of World Rankings.*

PORTUGAL - POTATO PRODUCTION - See PORTUGAL - CROPS

PORTUGAL - POWER PRODUCTION INDUSTRY - EMPLOYMENT

European Community Information Service, 2100 M Street, NW, Washington, D.C. 20037 (202) 862-9500; *Basic Statistics of the Community.*

Statistical Office of the United Nations, Publishing Service, New York, New York 10017 (800) 253-9646; *Statistical Yearbook.*

PORTUGAL - PRICES

European Community Information Service, 2100 M Street, NW, Washington, D.C. 20037 (202) 862-9500; *Basic Statistics of the Community, Eurostatistics: Data for Short-Term Economic Analysis.*

Facts on File, 460 Park Avenue South, New York, New York 10016 (800) 443-8323; *The New Book of World Rankings.*

Food and Agricultural Organization of the United Nations (FAO), Via delle Terme di Caracalla, 00100 Rome, Italy (Telephone Number in U.S. (202) 653-2400); *Production Yearbook,* and *The State of Food and Agriculture.*

G.K. Hall and Company, 70 Lincoln Street, Boston, Massachusetts 02111 (617) 423-3990; *The World in Figures.*

International Labour Office, I.L.O. Publications, CH-1211, Geneva 22, Switzerland; *Yearbook of Labour Statistics.*

International Monetary Fund, 700 Nineteenth Street, NW, Washington, D.C. 20431 (202) 623-7000; *International Financial Statistics.*

Organisation for Economic Co-operation and Development (OECD), 2 rue Andre-Pascal, 75 Paris 16, France (Telephone Number in U.S. (202) 785-6323); *Economic Outlook, The Footwear, Raw Hides and Skins, and Leather Industry in OECD Countries, Indicators of Industrial Activity, The Iron and Steel Industry, Main Economic Indicators - Historical Statistics,* and *The Pulp and Paper Industry.*

PORTUGAL - PRINTING AND WRITING PAPER PRODUCTION - See PORTUGAL - FORESTRY AND FOREST PRODUCTS

PORTUGAL - PRODUCTION

American Automobile Manufacturers Association, 1401 H Street, NW, Suite 900, Washington, D.C. 20005 (202) 326-5500; *World Motor Vehicle Data.*

European Community Information Service, 2100 M Street, NW, Washington, D.C. 20037 (202) 862-9500; *Basic Statistics of the Community, Eurostatistics: Data for Short-Term Economic Analysis,* and *Fisheries: Yearly Statistics.*

Facts on File, 460 Park Avenue South, New York, New York 10016 (800) 443-8323; *The New Book of World Rankings.*

G.K. Hall and Company, 70 Lincoln Street, Boston, Massachusetts 02111 (617) 423-3990; *The World in Figures.*

Organisation for Economic Co-operation and Development (OECD), 2 rue Andre-Pascal, 75 Paris 16, France (Telephone Number in U.S. (202) 785-6323); *Economic Outlook, The Footwear, Raw Hides and Skins, and Leather Industry in OECD Countries, Indicators of Industrial Activity, Industrial Structure Statistics, The Iron and Steel Industry, Meat Balances in OECD Member Countries, Milk, Milk Products, and Egg Balances in OECD Member Countries, The Non-Ferrous Metals Industry, The Pulp and Paper Industry,* and *Textile Industry in OECD Countries.*

PORTUGAL - PRODUCTIVITY

European Community Information Service, 2100 M Street, NW, Washington, D.C. 20037 (202) 862-9500; *Basic Statistics of the Community.*

Organisation for Economic Co-operation and Development (OECD), 2 rue Andre-Pascal, 75 Paris 16, France (Telephone Number in U.S. (202) 785-6323); *Economic Outlook.*

PORTUGAL - PROPERTY TAXES - See PORTUGAL - TAXATION

PORTUGAL - PUBLIC CONSUMPTION FUND

European Community Information Service, 2100 M Street, NW, Washington, D.C. 20037 (202) 862-9500; *Basic Statistics of the Community.*

Organisation for Economic Co-operation and Development (OECD), 2 rue Andre-Pascal, 75 Paris 16, France (Telephone Number in U.S. (202) 785-6323); *Revenue Statistics of OECD Member Countries.*

PORTUGAL - PUBLIC EXPENDITURES

European Community Information Service, 2100 M Street, NW, Washington, D.C. 20037 (202) 862-9500; *Basic Statistics of the Community.*

Organisation for Economic Co-operation and Development (OECD), 2 rue Andre-Pascal, 75 Paris 16, France (Telephone Number in U.S. (202) 785-6323); *Revenue Statistics of OECD Member Countries.*

PORTUGAL - PUBLIC FINANCE

Facts on File, 460 Park Avenue South, New York, New York 10016 (800) 443-8323; *The New Book of World Rankings.*

Organisation for Economic Co-operation and Development (OECD), 2 rue Andre-Pascal, 75 Paris 16, France (Telephone Number in U.S. (202) 785-6323); *Revenue Statistics of OECD Member Countries.*

PORTUGAL - PUBLIC HEALTH

European Community Information Service, 2100 M Street, NW, Washington, D.C. 20037 (202) 862-9500; *Basic Statistics of the Community.*

PORTUGAL - PUBLIC REVENUES

Organisation for Economic Co-operation and Development (OECD), 2 rue Andre-Pascal, 75 Paris 16, France (Telephone Number in U.S. (202) 785-6323); *Revenue Statistics of OECD Member Countries.*

PORTUGAL - RADIO BROADCASTING - See PORTUGAL - BROADCASTING

PORTUGAL - RADIO RECEIVER PRODUCTION

Statistical Office of the United Nations, Publishing Service, New York, New York 10017 (800) 253-9646; *Statistical Yearbook*.

PORTUGAL - RAILWAYS

Euromonitor Publications Limited, 87-88 Turnmill Street, London EC1M 5QU, England; *European Marketing Data and Statistics*.

European Community Information Service, 2100 M Street, NW, Washington, D.C. 20037 (202) 862-9500; *Basic Statistics of the Community, Regions: Statistical Yearbook*, and *Transport Annual Statistics*.

G.K. Hall and Company, 70 Lincoln Street, Boston, Massachusetts 02111 (617) 423-3990; *The World in Figures*.

Jane's Information Group, Sentinel House, 163 Brighton Road, Coulsdon, Surrey CR5 2NH, England (Telephone Number in U.S. (703) 683-3700); *Jane's World Railways*.

Statistical Office of the United Nations, Publishing Service, New York, New York 10017 (800) 253-9646; *Statistical Yearbook*, and *Annual Bulletin of Transport Statistics for Europe*.

PORTUGAL - RANCHING

European Community Information Service, 2100 M Street, NW, Washington, D.C. 20037 (202) 862-9500; *Basic Statistics of the Community*.

PORTUGAL - RELIGION

Facts on File, 460 Park Avenue South, New York, New York 10016 (800) 443-8323; *The New Book of World Rankings*.

PORTUGAL - RENT PRICES

International Labour Office, I.L.O. Publications, CH-1211, Geneva 22, Switzerland; *Yearbook of Labour Statistics*.

PORTUGAL - RETAIL TRADE

European Community Information Service, 2100 M Street, NW, Washington, D.C. 20037 (202) 862-9500; *Basic Statistics of the Community*, and *Eurostatistics: Data for Short-Term Economic Analysis*.

G.K. Hall and Company, 70 Lincoln Street, Boston, Massachusetts 02111 (617) 423-3990; *The World in Figures*.

Statistical Office of the United Nations, Publishing Service, New York, New York 10017 (800) 253-9646; *Statistical Yearbook*.

PORTUGAL - RICE PRODUCTION - See PORTUGAL - CROPS

PORTUGAL - ROOT AND TUBER PRODUCTION - See PORTUGAL - CROPS

PORTUGAL - ROUNDWOOD PRODUCTION - See PORTUGAL - FORESTRY AND FOREST PRODUCTS

PORTUGAL - RUBBER PRODUCTION AND CONSUMPTION

European Community Information Service, 2100 M Street, NW, Washington, D.C. 20037 (202) 862-9500; *Basic Statistics of the Community*.

Facts on File, 460 Park Avenue South, New York, New York 10016 (800) 443-8323; *The New Book of World Rankings*.

Organisation for Economic Co-operation and Development (OECD), 2 rue Andre-Pascal, 75 Paris 16, France (Telephone Number in U.S. (202) 785-6323); *Foreign Trade by Commodities*.

Statistical Office of the United Nations, Publishing Service, New York, New York 10017 (800) 253-9646; *Statistical Yearbook*.

PORTUGAL - SAFFLOWER SEED PRODUCTION - See PORTUGAL - CROPS

PORTUGAL - SALT PRODUCTION - See PORTUGAL - MINING AND MINERAL PRODUCTS

PORTUGAL - SAVINGS ACCOUNT DEPOSITS

European Community Information Service, 2100 M Street, NW, Washington, D.C. 20037 (202) 862-9500; *Eurostatistics: Data for Short-Term Economic Analysis*.

PORTUGAL - SAWNWOOD PRODUCTION - See PORTUGAL - FORESTRY AND FOREST PRODUCTS

PORTUGAL - SCIENCE AND TECHNOLOGY - EXPENDITURE FOR RESEARCH

European Community Information Service, 2100 M Street, NW, Washington, D.C. 20037 (202) 862-9500; *Basic Statistics of the Community*.

Statistical Office of the United Nations, Publishing Service, New York, New York 10017 (800) 253-9646; *Statistical Yearbook*.

PORTUGAL - SCIENTISTS AND TECHNICIANS

European Community Information Service, 2100 M Street, NW, Washington, D.C. 20037 (202) 862-9500; *Basic Statistics of the Community*.

Statistical Office of the United Nations, Publishing Service, New York, New York 10017 (800) 253-9646; *Statistical Yearbook*.

United Nations Educational, Scientific and Cultural Organization (UNESCO), 7 Place de Fontenoy, F-75700 Paris, France (Telephone Number in U.S. (212) 963-5981); *Statistical Yearbook*.

PORTUGAL - SENIOR CITIZENS

Facts on File, 460 Park Avenue South, New York, New York 10016 (800) 443-8323; *The New Book of World Rankings*.

PORTUGAL - SERVICES INDUSTRY EMPLOYMENT - MALE AND FEMALE

Organisation for Economic Co-operation and Development (OECD), 2 rue Andre-Pascal, 75 Paris 16, France (Telephone Number in U.S. (202) 785-6323); *OECD Employment Outlook*.

PORTUGAL - SHEEP - See PORTUGAL - LIVESTOCK AND POULTRY

PORTUGAL - SHIPBUILDING - PRODUCTION INDEX

Organisation for Economic Co-operation and Development (OECD), 2 rue Andre-Pascal, 75 Paris 16, France (Telephone Number in U.S. (202) 785-6323); *Indicators of Industrial Activity.*

PORTUGAL - SILVER PRODUCTION AND CONSUMPTION - See PORTUGAL - MINING AND MINERAL PRODUCTS

PORTUGAL - SOCIAL DATA

European Community Information Service, 2100 M Street, NW, Washington, D.C. 20037 (202) 862-9500; *Basic Statistics of the Community.*

Facts on File, 460 Park Avenue South, New York, New York 10016 (800) 443-8323; *The New Book of World Rankings.*

G.K. Hall and Company, 70 Lincoln Street, Boston, Massachusetts 02111 (617) 423-3990; *The World in Figures.*

PORTUGAL - SOCIAL SECURITY

European Community Information Service, 2100 M Street, NW, Washington, D.C. 20037 (202) 862-9500; *Basic Statistics of the Community.*

International Monetary Fund, 700 Nineteenth Street, NW, Washington, D.C. 20431 (202) 623-7000; *Government Finance Statistics Yearbook.*

Organisation for Economic Co-operation and Development (OECD), 2 rue Andre-Pascal, 75 Paris 16, France (Telephone Number in U.S. (202) 785-6323); *Revenue statistics of OECD Member Countries.*

PORTUGAL - SOCIOECONOMIC DATA

European Community Information Service, 2100 M Street, NW, Washington, D.C. 20037 (202) 862-9500; *Basic Statistics of the Community.*

Organisation for Economic Co-operation and Development (OECD), 2 rue Andre-Pascal, 75 Paris 16, France (Telephone Number in U.S. (202) 785-6323); *Economic Outlook.*

PORTUGAL - STAMP TAXES AND DUTIES - See PORTUGAL - TAXATION

PORTUGAL - STEEL - See PORTUGAL - MINING AND MINERAL PRODUCTS

PORTUGAL - STOCKS - COMMODITY - MARKET PRICE - INDEXES

European Community Information Service, 2100 M Street, NW, Washington, D.C. 20037 (202) 862-9500; *Basic Statistics of the Community.*

Statistical Office of the United Nations, Publishing Service, New York, New York 10017 (800) 253-9646; *Statistical Yearbook.*

PORTUGAL - SUGAR - See PORTUGAL - CROPS

PORTUGAL - SULPHUR AND SULPHURIC ACID PRODUCTION - See PORTUGAL - MINING AND MINERAL PRODUCTS

PORTUGAL - TAXATION

European Community Information Service, 2100 M Street, NW, Washington, D.C. 20037 (202) 862-9500; *Basic Statistics of the Community.*

G.K. Hall and Company, 70 Lincoln Street, Boston, Massachusetts 02111 (617) 423-3990; *The World in Figures.*

International Monetary Fund, 700 Nineteenth Street, NW, Washington, D.C. 20431 (202) 623-7000; *Government Finance Statistics Yearbook.*

International Road Federation, 525 School Street, SW, Washington, D.C. 20024 (202) 554-2106; *World Road Statistics.*

Organisation for Economic Co-operation and Development (OECD), 2 rue Andre-Pascal, 75 Paris 16, France (Telephone Number in U.S. (202) 785-6323); *Revenue Statistics of OECD Member Countries.*

The World Bank, 1818 H Street, NW, Washington, D.C. 20433 (202) 477-1234; *World Tables.*

PORTUGAL - TAX REVENUE - See PORTUGAL - TAXATION

PORTUGAL - TELEGRAPH SERVICE

Statistical Office of the United Nations, Publishing Service, New York, New York 10017 (800) 253-9646; *Statistical Yearbook.*

PORTUGAL - TELEPHONES IN USE

American Telephone and Telegraph Company, 26 Parsippany Road, Whippany, New Jersey 07981 (800) 338-4038; *The World's Telephones.*

European Community Information Service, 2100 M Street, NW, Washington, D.C. 20037 (202) 862-9500; *Basic Statistics of the Community,* and *Transport Annual Statistics.*

G.K. Hall and Company, 70 Lincoln Street, Boston, Massachusetts 02111 (617) 423-3990; *The World in Figures.*

Statistical Office of the United Nations, Publishing Service, New York, New York 10017 (800) 253-9646; *Statistical Yearbook.*

PORTUGAL - TELEVISION BROADCASTING - See PORTUGAL - BROADCASTING

PORTUGAL - TELEVISION RECEIVER PRODUCTION

European Community Information Service, 2100 M Street, NW, Washington, D.C. 20037 (202) 862-9500; *Basic Statistics of the Community.*

Statistical Office of the United Nations, Publishing Service, New York, New York 10017 (800) 253-9646; *Statistical Yearbook.*

PORTUGAL - TEXTILE INDUSTRY

American Forest and Paper Association, 1250 Connecticut Avenue, NW, Washington, D.C. 20036 (202) 463-2455; *Wood Pulp and Fiber Statistics.*

European Community Information Service, 2100 M Street, NW, Washington, D.C. 20037 (202) 862-9500; *Basic Statistics of the Community, Eurostatistics: Data for Short-Term Economic Analysis,* and *Industrial Production: Quarterly.*

G.K. Hall and Company, 70 Lincoln Street, Boston, Massachusetts 02111 (617) 423-3990; *The World in Figures*.

Organisation for Economic Co-operation and Development (OECD), 2 rue Andre-Pascal, 75 Paris 16, France (Telephone Number in U.S. (202) 785-6323); *Foreign Trade by Commodities, Indicators of Industrial Activity, Industrial Structure Statistics*, and *Textile Industry in OECD Countries*.

Statistical Office of the United Nations, Publishing Service, New York, New York 10017 (800) 253-9646; *Statistical Yearbook*.

PORTUGAL - THEATRE

United Nations Educational, Scientific and Cultural Organization (UNESCO), 7 Place de Fontenoy, F-75700 Paris, France (Telephone Number in U.S. (212) 963-5981); *Statistical Yearbook*.

PORTUGAL - TIN - See PORTUGAL - MINING AND MINERAL PRODUCTS

PORTUGAL - TIRE (MOTOR VEHICLE) PRODUCTION

Statistical Office of the United Nations, Publishing Service, New York, New York 10017 (800) 253-9646; *Statistical Yearbook*.

PORTUGAL - TOBACCO PRODUCTION

European Community Information Service, 2100 M Street, NW, Washington, D.C. 20037 (202) 862-9500; *Basic Statistics of the Community*, and *Industrial Production: Quarterly*.

Euromonitor Publications Limited, 87-88 Turnmill Street, London EC1M 5QU, England; *European Marketing Data and Statistics*.

Facts on File, 460 Park Avenue South, New York, New York 10016 (800) 443-8323; *The New Book of World Rankings*.

Organisation for Economic Co-operation and Development (OECD), 2 rue Andre-Pascal, 75 Paris 16, France (Telephone Number in U S (202) 785-6323); *Foreign Trade by Commodities, Indicators of Industrial Activity*, and *Industrial Structure Statistics*.

Statistical Office of the United Nations, Publishing Service, New York, New York 10017 (800) 253-9646; *Statistical Yearbook*.

PORTUGAL - TOURISM

European Community Information Service, 2100 M Street, NW, Washington, D.C. 20037 (202) 862-9500; *Transport Annual Statistics*.

Euromonitor Publications Limited, 87-88 Turnmill Street, London EC1M 5QU, England; *European Marketing Data and Statistics*.

Facts on File, 460 Park Avenue South, New York, New York 10016 (800) 443-8323; *The New Book of World Rankings*.

Federal Statistical Office, Gustav - Stresemann - Ring 11, D-6200 Wiesbaden, Germany; *Portugal*.

G.K. Hall and Company, 70 Lincoln Street, Boston, Massachusetts 02111 (617) 423-3990; *The World in Figures*.

Organisation for Economic Co-operation and Development (OECD), 2 rue Andre-Pascal, 75 Paris 16, France (Telephone Number in U.S. (202) 785-6323); *Tourism Policy and International Tourism in OECD Member Countries*.

Statistical Office of the United Nations, Publishing Service, New York, New York 10017 (800) 253-9646; *Statistical Yearbook*.

Time Books, 201 East 50th Street, New York, New York 10022 (212) 751-2600; *The Economist Book of Vital World Statistics*.

World Tourism Organization, Calle Capitan Haya 42, E-28020 Madrid, Spain; *Yearbook of Tourism Statistics*.

PORTUGAL - TRACTORS IN USE

European Community Information Service, 2100 M Street, NW, Washington, D.C. 20037 (202) 862-9500; *Transport Annual Statistics*.

Statistical Office of the United Nations, Publishing Service, New York, New York 10017 (800) 253-9646; *Statistical Yearbook*.

PORTUGAL - TRADE - See PORTUGAL - FOREIGN TRADE

PORTUGAL - TRADEMARKS AND SERVICE MARKS

Statistical Office of the United Nations, Publishing Service, New York, New York 10017 (800) 253-9646; *Statistical Yearbook*.

World Intellectual Property Organization, 34 Chemin des Colombettes, CH-1211 Geneva 20, Switzerland; *Industrial Property Statistics*.

PORTUGAL - TRANSPORTATION AND COMMUNICATIONS

European Community Information Service, 2100 M Street, NW, Washington, D.C. 20037 (202) 862-9500; *Basic Statistics of the Community, Energy Statistics Yearbook, Regions: Statistical Yearbook*, and *Transport Annual Statistics*.

Facts on File, 460 Park Avenue South, New York, New York 10016 (800) 443-8323; *The New Book of World Rankings*.

Federal Statistical Office, Gustav - Stresemann - Ring 11, D-6200 Wiesbaden, Germany; *Portugal*.

G.K. Hall and Company, 70 Lincoln Street, Boston, Massachusetts 02111 (617) 423-3990; *The World in Figures*.

PORTUGAL - TRANSPORTATION EMPLOYMENT - MALE AND FEMALE - See PORTUGAL - EMPLOYMENT

PORTUGAL - TUNGSTEN PRODUCTION AND CONSUMPTION - See PORTUGAL - MINING AND MINERAL PRODUCTS

PORTUGAL - UNEMPLOYMENT

Euromonitor Publications Limited, 87-88 Turnmill Street, London EC1M 5QU, England; *European Marketing Data and Statistics*.

European Community Information Service, 2100 M Street, NW, Washington, D.C. 20037 (202) 862-9500; *Basic Statistics of the Community, Employment and Unemployment, Eurostatistics: Data for Short-Term Economic Analysis, Labor Force Sample Survey*, and *Regions: Statistical Yearbook*.

International Labour Office, I.L.O. Publications, CH-1211, Geneva 22, Switzerland; *Yearbook of Labour Statistics*.

Organisation for Economic Co-operation and Development (OECD), 2 rue Andre-Pascal, 75 Paris 16, France (Telephone Number in U.S. (202) 785-6323); *Economic Outlook, OECD Economic Surveys: Portugal, OECD Employment Outlook*, and *Statistical Yearbook*.

PORTUGAL - URANIUM PRODUCTION AND CONSUMPTION - See PORTUGAL - MINING AND MINERAL PRODUCTS

PORTUGAL - VANADIUM AND VANADIUM ORE PRODUCTION AND CONSUMPTION - See PORTUGAL - MINING AND MINERAL PRODUCTS

PORTUGAL - VITAL STATISTICS

European Community Information Service, 2100 M Street, NW, Washington, D.C. 20037 (202) 862-9500; *Basic Statistics of the Community*.

G.K. Hall and Company, 70 Lincoln Street, Boston, Massachusetts 02111 (617) 423-3990; *The World in Figures*.

Statistical Office of the United Nations, Publishing Service, New York, New York 10017 (800) 253-9646; *Statistical Yearbook*.

World Health Organization, Office of Publications, Avenue Appia, CH-1211 Geneva 27, Switzerland (Telephone Number in U.S. (518) 436-9686); *World Health Statistics Annual*.

PORTUGAL - WAGES

Euromonitor Publications Limited, 87-88 Turnmill Street, London EC1M 5QU, England; *European Marketing Data and Statistics*.

European Community Information Service, 2100 M Street, NW, Washington, D.C. 20037 (202) 862-9500; *Basic Statistics of the Community, Earnings in Agriculture*, and *Eurostatistics: Data for Short-Term Economic Analysis*.

Federal Statistical Office, Gustav - Stresemann - Ring 11, D-6200 Wiesbaden, Germany; *Portugal*.

G.K. Hall and Company, 70 Lincoln Street, Boston, Massachusetts 02111 (617) 423-3990; *The World in Figures*.

International Labour Office, I.L.O. Publications, CH-1211, Geneva 22, Switzerland; *Yearbook of Labour Statistics*.

Organisation for Economic Co-operation and Development (OECD), 2 rue Andre-Pascal, 75 Paris 16, France (Telephone Number in U.S. (202) 785-6323); *Economic Outlook*, and *Industrial Structure Statistics*.

Statistical Office of the United Nations, Publishing Service, New York, New York 10017 (800) 253-9646; *Statistical Yearbook*.

PORTUGAL - WALNUT PRODUCTION - See PORTUGAL - CROPS

PORTUGAL - WATERWAYS IN USE

European Community Information Service, 2100 M Street, NW, Washington, D.C. 20037 (202) 862-9500; *Basic Statistics of the Community*, and *Transport Annual Statistics*.

Organisation for Economic Co-operation and Development (OECD), 2 rue Andre-Pascal, 75 Paris 16, France (Telephone Number in U.S. (202) 785-6323); *Maritime Transport*.

Statistical Office of the United Nations, Publishing Service, New York, New York 10017 (800) 253-9646; *Annual Bulletin of Transport Statistics for Europe*.

PORTUGAL - WEATHER

Facts on File, 460 Park Avenue South, New York, New York 10016 (800) 443-8323; *The New Book of World Rankings*.

G.K. Hall and Company, 70 Lincoln Street, Boston, Massachusetts 02111 (617) 423-3990; *The World in Figures*.

PORTUGAL - WELFARE

European Community Information Service, 2100 M Street, NW, Washington, D.C. 20037 (202) 862-9500; *Basic Statistics of the Community*.

International Monetary Fund, 700 Nineteenth Street, NW, Washington, D.C. 20431 (202) 623-7000; *Government Finance Statistics Yearbook*.

PORTUGAL - WHALE AND SPERM OIL PRODUCTION

Statistical Office of the United Nations, Publishing Service, New York, New York 10017 (800) 253-9646; *Statistical Yearbook*.

PORTUGAL - WHALES CAUGHT

Statistical Office of the United Nations, Publishing Service, New York, New York 10017 (800) 253-9646; *Statistical Yearbook*.

PORTUGAL - WHEAT PRODUCTION AND PRICES - See PORTUGAL - CROPS

PORTUGAL - WHOLESALE PRICES - INDEX NUMBERS

European Community Information Service, 2100 M Street, NW, Washington, D.C. 20037 (202) 862-9500; *Basic Statistics of the Community*.

Statistical Office of the United Nations, Publishing Service, New York, New York 10017 (800) 253-9646; *Statistical Yearbook*.

PORTUGAL - WHOLESALE TRADE

Statistical Office of the United Nations, Publishing Service, New York, New York 10017 (800) 253-9646; *Statistical Yearbook*.

PORTUGAL - WINE EXPORTS

International Monetary Fund, 700 Nineteenth Street, NW, Washington, D.C. 20431 (202) 623-7000; *International Financial Statistics*.

PORTUGAL - WINE PRODUCTION

European Community Information Service, 2100 M Street, NW, Washington, D.C. 20037 (202) 862-9500; *Basic Statistics of the Community*.

Facts on File, 460 Park Avenue South, New York, New York 10016 (800) 443-8323; *The New Book of World Rankings*.

Statistical Office of the United Nations, Publishing Service, New York, New York 10017 (800) 253-9646; *Statistical Yearbook*.

PORTUGAL - WOOD - See PORTUGAL - FORESTRY AND FOREST PRODUCTS

PORTUGAL - WOOL - INDUSTRIAL CONSUMPTION

Organisation for Economic Co-operation and Development (OECD), 2 rue Andre-Pascal, 75 Paris 16, France (Telephone Number in U.S. (202) 785-6323); *Textile Industry in OECD Countries*.

Statistical Office of the United Nations, Publishing Service, New York, New York 10017 (800) 253-9646; *Statistical Yearbook*.

PORTUGAL - WOOL PRODUCTION

European Community Information Service, 2100 M Street, NW, Washington, D.C. 20037 (202) 862-9500; *Basic Statistics of the Community*.

Facts on File, 460 Park Avenue South, New York, New York 10016 (800) 443-8323; *The New Book of World Rankings*.

Organisation for Economic Co-operation and Development (OECD), 2 rue Andre-Pascal, 75 Paris 16, France (Telephone Number in U.S. (202) 785-6323); *Economic Accounts for Agriculture*, and *Textile Industry in OECD Countries*.

Statistical Office of the United Nations, Publishing Service, New York, New York 10017 (800) 253-9646; *Statistical Yearbook*.

PORTUGAL - YARN PRODUCTION

European Community Information Service, 2100 M Street, NW, Washington, D.C. 20037 (202) 862-9500; *Basic Statistics of the Community*.

Organisation for Economic Co-operation and Development (OECD), 2 rue Andre-Pascal, 75 Paris 16, France (Telephone Number in U.S. (202) 785-6323); *Foreign Trade by Commodities*, and *Textile Industry in OECD Countries*.

Statistical Office of the United Nations, Publishing Service, New York, New York 10017 (800) 253-9646; *Statistical Yearbook*.

PORTUGAL - ZINC AND ZINC ORE PRODUCTION AND CONSUMPTION - See PORTUGAL - MINING AND MINERAL PRODUCTS

POSTAL RATES

U.S. Postal Service, 475 L'Enfant Plaza West, SW, Washington, D.C. 20260-0010 (202) 268-2000; *United States Domestic Postage Rates: Recent History*, and unpublished data.

POSTAL SERVICE

U.S. Postal Service, 475 L'Enfant Plaza West, SW, Washington, D.C. 20260-0010 (202) 268-2000; *Annual Report of the Postmaster General, United States Domestic Postage Rates: Recent History*, and unpublished data.

POTASH (POTASSIUM SALTS)

U.S. Department of the Interior, Bureau of Mines, 810 Seventh Street, NW, Washington, D.C. 20241 (202) 501-9649; *Annual Reports*, and *Mineral Commodity Summaries*.

POTASSIUM - FOREIGN TRADE

U.S. Department of the Interior, Bureau of Mines, 810 Seventh Street, NW, Washington, D.C. 20241 (202) 501-9649; *Mineral Commodity Summaries*.

POTATOES - ACREAGE

U.S. Department of Agriculture, National Agricultural Statistics Service, Fourteenth Street and Independence Avenue, SW, Washington, D.C. 20250 (202) 219-1504; *Agricultural Statistics*, and *Vegetables*.

POTATOES - CONSUMPTION

U.S. Department of Agriculture, Economic Research Service, Fourteenth Street and Independence Avenue, SW, Washington, D.C. 20005-4789 (202) 219-1504; *Food Consumption, Prices, and Expenditures*, and unpublished data.

POTATOES - FARM MARKETINGS, SALES

U.S. Department of Agriculture, Economic Research Service, Fourteenth Street and Independence Avenue, SW, Washington, D.C. 20005-4789 (202) 219-1504; *Economic Indicators of the Farm Sector: National Financial Summary*.

POTATOES - PRODUCTION

U.S. Department of Agriculture, National Agricultural Statistics Service, Fourteenth Street and Independence Avenue, SW, Washington, D.C. 20250 (202) 219-1504; *Vegetables* and *Agricultural Statistics*.

POTATOES - WORLD PRODUCTION

Statistical Office of the United Nations, Publishing Service, New York, New York 10017 (800) 253-9646; *Statistical Yearbook*, and *Monthly Bulletin of Statistics*.

POULTRY - See also EGGS

POULTRY - CONSUMER EXPENDITURES

U.S. Department of Agriculture, Economic Research Service, Fourteenth Street and Independence Avenue, SW, Washington, D.C. 20005-4789 (202) 219-1504; *Food Cost Review, Food Consumption, Prices, Expenditures, Agricultural Statistics*, and *Food Review*.

POULTRY - CONSUMPTION

U.S. Department of Agriculture, Economic Research Service, Fourteenth Street and Independence Avenue, SW, Washington, D.C. 20005-4789 (202) 219-1504; *Food Consumption, Prices, and Expenditures*, and unpublished data.

U.S. Department of Agriculture, Foreign Agricultural Service, Fourteenth Street and Independence Avenue, SW, Washington, D.C. 20250 (202) 720-3448; *World Poultry Situation*.

POULTRY - FARM MARKETINGS, SALES

U.S. Department of Agriculture, Economic Research Service, Fourteenth Street and Independence Avenue, SW, Washington, D.C. 20005-4789 (202) 219-1504; *Economic Indicators of the Farm Sector: National Financial Summary*.

POULTRY - FOREIGN TRADE

U.S. Department of Agriculture, Economic Research Service, Fourteenth Street and Independence Avenue, SW, Washington, D.C. 20005-4789 (202) 219-1504; *Foreign Agricultural Trade of the U.S.*, and *Agricultural Statistics*.

POULTRY - NUMBER ON FARMS

U.S. Department of Agriculture, National Agricultural Statistics Service, Fourteenth Street and Independence Avenue, SW, Washington, D.C. 20250 (202) 219-1504; *Poultry - Production and Value, Turkeys*, and *Layers and Egg Production*.

POULTRY - PRICES

U.S. Department of Agriculture, National Agricultural Statistics Service, Fourteenth Street and Independence Avenue, SW, Washington, D.C. 20250 (202) 219-1504; *Layers and Egg Production, Poultry-Production and Value, Turkeys*, and *Agricultural Prices: Annual Summary*.

POULTRY - PRODUCTION AND SALES

U.S. Department of Agriculture, Economic Research Service, Fourteenth Street and Independence Avenue, SW, Washington, D.C. 20005-4789 (202) 219-1504; *Agricultural Outlook*.

U.S. Department of Agriculture, National Agricultural Statistics Service, Fourteenth Street and Independence Avenue, SW, Washington, D.C. 20250 (202) 219-1504; *Poultry - Production and Value, Turkeys*, and *Layers and Egg Production*.

POULTRY - VALUE

U.S. Department of Agriculture, National Agricultural Statistics Service, Fourteenth Street and Independence Avenue, SW, Washington, D.C. 20250 (202) 219-1504; *Poultry Production and Value, Turkeys*, and *Layers and Egg Production*.

POVERTY

U.S. Department of Commerce, Bureau of the Census, Suitland, Maryland 20233 (301) 763-4040; *Current Population Reports*.

POVERTY - CHILDREN

National Center for Children in Poverty, Columbia University, 154 Haven Avenue, Manhattan, New York 10032 (212) 927-8793; unpublished data.

U.S. Department of Commerce, Bureau of the Census, Suitland, Maryland 20233 (301) 763-4040; *Current Population Reports*.

POVERTY - FAMILIES

Congressional Budget Office, 2nd and D Streets, SW, Washington, D.C. 20515 (202) 226-2621; *Trends in Family Income*, and unpublished data.

U.S. Department of Commerce, Bureau of the Census, Suitland, Maryland 20233 (301) 763-4040; *Current Population Reports*, and *Census of Population*.

POVERTY - FAMILIES - AGE OF HOUSEHOLDER

U.S. Department of Commerce, Bureau of the Census, Suitland, Maryland 20233 (301) 763-4040; *Current Population Reports*.

POVERTY - FAMILIES - ASIAN AND PACIFIC ISLANDER POPULATION

U.S. Department of Commerce, Bureau of the Census, Suitland, Maryland 20233 (301) 763-4040; *Current Population Reports*, and unpublished data.

POVERTY - FAMILIES - BLACK POPULATION

U.S. Department of Commerce, Bureau of the Census, Suitland, Maryland 20233 (301) 763-4040; *Current Population Reports*.

POVERTY - FAMILIES - EDUCATIONAL ATTAINMENT

U.S. Department of Commerce, Bureau of the Census, Suitland, Maryland 20233 (301) 763-4040; *Current Population Reports*.

POVERTY - FAMILIES - ELDERLY

U.S. Department of Commerce, Bureau of the Census, Suitland, Maryland 20233 (301) 763-4040; *Current Population Reports*, and unpublished data.

POVERTY - FAMILIES - HISPANIC ORIGIN POPULATION

U.S. Department of Commerce, Bureau of the Census, Suitland, Maryland 20233 (301) 763-4040; *Current Population Reports*.

POVERTY - FAMILIES - HOUSING

U.S. Department of Commerce, Bureau of the Census, Suitland, Maryland 20233 (301) 763-4040; *Current Housing Reports*.

POVERTY - FAMILIES - LABOR FORCE PARTICIPATION

U.S. Department of Commerce, Bureau of the Census, Suitland, Maryland 20233 (301) 763-4040; *Current Population Reports*.

POVERTY - PERSONS

U.S. Department of Commerce, Bureau of the Census, Suitland, Maryland 20233 (301) 763-4040; *Current Population Reports*, and *Census of Population*.

POVERTY - PERSONS - AGE

U.S. Department of Commerce, Bureau of the Census, Suitland, Maryland 20233 (301) 763-4040; *Current Population Reports*.

POVERTY - PERSONS - BLACK POPULATION

U.S. Department of Commerce, Bureau of the Census, Suitland, Maryland 20233 (301) 763-4040; *Current Population Reports*, and unpublished data.

POVERTY - PERSONS - CHILDREN

National Center for Children in Poverty, Columbia University, 154 Haven Avenue, Manhattan, New York 10032 (212) 927-8793; unpublished data.

U.S. Department of Commerce, Bureau of the Census, Suitland, Maryland 20233 (301) 763-4040; *Current Population Reports*.

POVERTY - PERSONS - ELDERLY

U.S. Department of Commerce, Bureau of the Census, Suitland, Maryland 20233 (301) 763-4040; *Current Population Reports*.

POVERTY - PERSONS - HISPANIC ORIGIN POPULATION

U.S. Department of Commerce, Bureau of the Census, Suitland, Maryland 20233 (301) 763-4040; *Current Population Reports*, and *Census of Population*.

POWER - See also ELECTRIC LIGHT AND POWER INDUSTRY

POWER - ELECTRIC

Edison Electric Institute, 701 Pennsylvania Avenue, NW, Washington, D.C. 20004 (202) 508-5000; *Statistical Yearbook of the Electric Utility Industry.*

U.S. Department of Energy, Energy Information Administration, 1000 Independence Avenue, SW, Washington, D.C. 20585 (202) 586-8800; *Electric Power Annual, Inventory of Power Plants in the U.S., Electric Power Monthly, Annual Energy Review, Financial Statistics of Major U.S Investor-owned Electric Utilities,* and unpublished data.

POWER - ELECTRIC - NUCLEAR ENERGY CAPACITY

U.S. Department of Energy, Energy Information Administration, 1000 Independence Avenue, SW, Washington, D.C. 20585 (202) 586-8800; *Annual Energy Review.*

POWER - ELECTRIC - PRICES

U.S. Department of Energy, Energy Information Administration, 1000 Independence Avenue, SW, Washington, D.C. 20585 (202) 586-8800; *Monthly Energy Review, State Energy Price and Expenditure Report,* and *Annual Energy Review.*

POWER - HORSEPOWER

John A. Waring, 1320 South George Mason Drive, Arlington, Virginia 22204 (703) 521-1499; unpublished estimates.

POWER - HYDRO

U.S. Department of Energy, Energy Information Administration, 1000 Independence Avenue, SW, Washington, D.C. 20585 (202) 586-8800; *Electric Power Annual, Annual Energy Review,* and unpublished data.

POWER - NUCLEAR

McGraw-Hill Incorporated, 1221 Avenue of the Americas, New York, New York 10020 (212) 512-2000; *Nucleonics Week.*

U.S. Department of Energy, Energy Information Administration, 1000 Independence Avenue, SW, Washington, D.C. 20585 (202) 586-8800; *Electric Power Annual, Annual Energy Review,* and unpublished data.

POWER - PRICES

U.S. Department of Energy, Energy Information Administration, 1000 Independence Avenue, SW, Washington, D.C. 20585 (202) 586-2363; *Monthly Energy Review, State Energy Price and Expenditure Report,* and *Annual Energy Review.*

POWER - TRACTIVE EFFORT OF RAILROAD LOCOMOTIVES

Association of American Railroads, American Railroads Building, 50 F Street, NW, Washington, D.C. 20001 (202) 639-2100; *Railroad Facts, Statistics of Railroads of Class I,* and *Analysis of Class I Railroads.*

POWER - WATER

U.S. Department of Energy, Federal Energy Regulatory Commission, 1000 Independence Avenue, SW, Washington, D.C. 20585 (202) 208-0300; *Hydroelectric Power Resources of the United States, Developed and Undeveloped,* and unpublished data.

POWER PLANTS - See ELECTRIC LIGHT AND POWER INDUSTRY

PRECIPITATION - SELECTED CITIES

U.S. Department of Commerce, National Oceanic and Atmospheric Administration, National Climatic Data Center, Federal Building, Asheville, North Carolina 28801 (704) 259-2850; *Climatography of the United States,* and *Comparative Climatic Data.*

PREGNANCIES

U.S. Department of Health and Human Services, National Center for Health Statistics, 3700 East-West Highway, Hyattsville, Maryland 20782 (301) 436-8500; *Monthly Vital Statistics Report.*

PRENATAL CARE

U.S. Department of Health and Human Services, National Center for Health Statistics, 3700 East-West Highway, Hyattsville, Maryland 20782 (301) 436-8500; *Monthly Vital Statistics Report, Vital Statistics of the United States,* and unpublished data.

PRESIDENT, UNITED STATES - ELECTIONS FOR

Center for Political Studies, University of Michigan, Post Office Box 1248, Ann Arbor, Michigan 48106 (313) 764-8363; unpublished data.

Committee for the Study of the American Electorate, 421 New Jersey Avenue, SE, Washington, D.C. 20003 (202) 546-3221; unpublished data.

Elections Research Center, 5508 Greystone Street, Chevy Chase, Maryland 20815 (202) 659-9490; *America Votes.*

U.S. Department of Commerce, Bureau of the Census, Suitland, Maryland 20233 (301) 763-4040; *Current Population Reports.*

PRESIDENT, UNITED STATES - ELECTIONS FOR - CAMPAIGN FINANCES

Federal Election Commission, 999 E Street, NW, Washington, D.C. 20463 (800) 424-9530; *FEC Reports on Financial Activity, Final Report, Presidential Pre-Nomination Campaigns, FEC Index of Independent Expenditures,* and press releases.

PRICES - See also Individual Commodities

PRICES - BONDS

Board of Governors of the Federal Reserve System, Twentieth Street and Constitution Avenue, NW, Washington, D.C. 20551 (202) 452-3000; *Federal Reserve Bulletin,* and *Annual Statistics Digest.*

Dow Jones and Company, Incorporated, 200 Liberty Street, New York, New York 10006 (212) 416-2000.

New York Stock Exchange, 11 Wall Street, New York, New York 10005 (212) 656-3000; *Fact Book.*

PRICES - BOOKS AND PERIODICALS

R.R. Bowker Company, 121 Chanlon Road, New Providence, New Jersey 07974 (908) 464-6800; *Publishers Weekly, Bowker Annual: Library and Book Trade Almanac,* and *Library Journal.*

PRICES - ELECTRICITY

U.S. Department of Energy, Energy Information Administration, 1000 Independence Avenue, SW, Washington, D.C. 20585 (202) 586-8800; *Monthly Energy Review, State Energy Price and Expenditure Report,* and *Annual Energy Review.*

PRICES - ENERGY

U.S. Department of Energy, Energy Information Administration, 1000 Independence Avenue, SW, Washington, D.C. 20585 (202) 586-8800; *International Energy Annual, Household Energy Consumption and Expenditures,* and *Annual Energy Review.*

PRICES - FISH, BY SPECIES

U.S. Department of Commerce, National Oceanic and Atmospheric Administration, National Marine Fisheries Service, 1335 East-West Highway, Silver Spring, Maryland 20910 (301) 427-2239; *Fishery Statistics of the United States,* and *Fisheries of the United States.*

PRICES - FOOD

U.S. Department of Agriculture, Human Nutrition Information Service, Hyattsville, Maryland 20782 (301) 436-7725; *Administrative Bulletin Number 329.*

U.S. Department of Labor, Bureau of Labor Statistics, Two Massachusetts Avenue, NE, Washington, D.C. 20212 (202) 606-7828; *Consumer Price Index, Detailed Report.*

PRICES - FOREIGN COUNTRIES

International Monetary Fund, 700 Nineteenth Street, NW, Washington, D.C. 20431 (202) 623-7000; *International Financial Statistics.*

Organization for Economic Co-operation and Development, Publication and Information Center, 2001 L Street, NW, Washington, D.C. 20036 (202) 785-6323; *Main Economic Indicators.*

U.S. Department of Energy, Energy Information Administration, 1000 Independence Avenue, SW, Washington, D.C. 20585 (202) 586-8800; *International Energy Annual.*

PRICES - HOUSING

Chicago Title Insurance Company, 111 West Washington Street, Chicago, Illinois 60602 (312) 630-2000; *The Guarantor.*

National Association of Realtors, 430 North Michigan Avenue, Chicago, Illinois 60611-4087 (312) 329-8200; *Real Estate Outlook: Market Trends and Insights..*

U.S. Department of Commerce, Bureau of the Census, Suitland, Maryland 20233 (301) 763-4040; *Current Construction Reports, Characteristics of New Housing,* and *New One-Family Houses Sold.*

PRICES - INDEXES - AIRLINE COST

Air Transport Association of America, 1301 Pennsylvania Avenue, NW, Washington, D.C. 20004 (202) 626-4000; *Air Transport,* and unpublished data.

PRICES - INDEXES - CONSTRUCTION MATERIALS

U.S. Department of Labor, Bureau of Labor Statistics, Two Massachusetts Avenue, NE, Washington, D.C. 20212 (202) 606-7828; *Producer Price Indexes.*

PRICES - INDEXES - CONSUMER PRICE

International Monetary Fund, 700 Nineteenth Street, NW, Washington, D.C. 20431 (202) 623-7000; *International Financial Statistics.*

U.S. Department of Labor, Bureau of Labor Statistics, Two Massachusetts Avenue, NE, Washington, D.C. 20212 (202) 606-7828; *Monthly Labor Review, Consumer Price Index, Detailed Report,* and *Handbook of Labor Statistics.*

PRICES - INDEXES - CONSUMER PRICE - FOREIGN COUNTRIES

International Monetary Fund, 700 Nineteenth Street, NW, Washington, D.C. 20431 (202) 623-7000; *International Financial Statistics.*

PRICES - INDEXES - CONSUMER PRICE - MEDICAL CARE

U.S. Department of Labor, Bureau of Labor Statistics, Two Massachusetts Avenue, NE, Washington, D.C. 20212 (202) 606-7828; *Consumer Price Index Detailed Report,* and unpublished data.

PRICES - INDEXES - CONSUMER PRICE - SELECTED METRO AREAS

American Chamber of Commerce Research Association, Post Office Box 6749, Louisville, Kentucky 40206; *Cost of Living Index.*

U.S. Department of Labor, Bureau of Labor Statistics, Two Massachusetts Avenue, NE, Washington, D.C. 20212 (202) 606-7828; *Monthly Labor Review,* and *Consumer Price Index Detailed Report.*

PRICES - INDEXES - EXPORTS

U.S. Department of Labor, Bureau of Labor Statistics, Two Massachusetts Avenue, NE, Washington, D.C. 20212 (202) 606-7828; *News.*

PRICES - INDEXES - FIXED WEIGHTED

U.S. Department of Commerce, Bureau of Economic Analysis, Fourteenth Street between Constitution Avenue and E Street, NW, Washington, D.C. 20230 (202) 606-9900; *The National Income and Product Accounts of the United States,* and *Survey of Current Business.*

PRICES - INDEXES - HOUSES - ONE-FAMILY

U.S. Department of Commerce, Bureau of the Census, Suitland, Maryland 20233 (301) 763-4040; *Current Construction Reports.*

PRICES - INDEXES - IMPORTS

Commodity Research Bureau, Incorporated, 75 Wall Street, New York, New York 10005 (212) 504-7754; *Commodity Research Bureau Commodity Index Report.*

U.S. Department of Labor, Bureau of Labor Statistics, Two Massachusetts Avenue, NE, Washington, D.C. 20212 (202) 606-7828; *News.*

PRICES - INDEXES - NEWSPRINT

U.S. Department of Commerce, Bureau of Economic Analysis, Fourteenth Street between Constitution Avenue and E Street, NW, Washington, D.C. 20230 (202) 606-9900; *Survey of Current Business,* monthly, based on data from the American Forest and Paper Association, 1250 Connecticut Avenue, NW, Washington, D.C. 20036 (202) 463-2455; and the Canadian Pulp and Paper Association, 1155

Metcalfe Street, 23rd Floor, Montreal, Quebec H3B 2X9, Canada.

PRICES - INDEXES - NEWSPRINT - TIMBER

U.S. Department of Labor, Bureau of Labor Statistics, Two Massachusetts Avenue, NE, Washington, D.C. 20212 (202) 606-7828; *Producer Price Indexes*.

PRICES - INDEXES - PRODUCER PRICES

U.S. Department of Labor, Bureau of Labor Statistics, Two Massachusetts Avenue, NE, Washington, D.C. 20212 (202) 606-7828; *Producer Price Indexes*, and *Monthly Labor Review*.

PRICES - INDEXES - PRODUCER PRICES - COMMODITY GROUPS

U.S. Department of Labor, Bureau of Labor Statistics, Two Massachusetts Avenue, NE, Washington, D.C. 20212 (202) 606-7828; *Producer Price Indexes*.

PRICES - INDEXES - PRODUCER PRICES - CONSTRUCTION MATERIALS

U.S. Department of Labor, Bureau of Labor Statistics, Two Massachusetts Avenue, NE, Washington, D.C. 20212 (202) 606-7828; *Producer Price Indexes*.

PRICES - INDEXES - PURCHASING POWER OF THE DOLLAR

U.S. Department of Commerce, Bureau of Economic Analysis, Fourteenth Street between Constitution Avenue and E Street, NW, Washington, D.C. 20230 (202) 606-9900; *Survey of Current Business*.

PRICES - INDEXES - RAILROAD FREIGHT

U.S. Department of Labor, Bureau of Labor Statistics, Two Massachusetts Avenue, NE, Washington, D.C. 20212 (202) 606-7828; *Producer Price Indexes*.

PRICES - INDEXES - SCHOOL EXPENDITURES

Research Associates of Washington, 2605 Klingle Road, NW, Washington, D.C. 20008 (202) 966-3326; *Inflation Measures for Schools and Colleges*.

U.S. Department of Education, 400 Maryland Avenue, SW, Washington, D.C. 20202 (202) 708-5366; *Digest of Education Statistics, Financial Statistics of Institutions of Higher Education*, and *Projections of Education Statistics*.

PRICES - INDEXES - SPOT MARKET PRICE

Commodity Research Bureau, Incorporated, 75 Wall Street, New York, New York 10005 (212) 504-7754; *Commodity Research Bureau Commodity Index Report*.

PRICES - LUMBER AND STUMPAGE

U.S. Department of Agriculture, Forest Service, Fourteenth Street and Independence Avenue, SW, Washington, D.C. 20250 (202) 720-3760; *United States Timber Production, Trade Consumption, and Price Statistics*.

PRICES - MINERAL PRODUCTS - See also Individual Minerals

U.S. Department of the Interior, Bureau of Mines, 810 Seventh Street, NW, Washington, D.C. 20241 (202) 501-9649; *Minerals*

Yearbook, and *Mineral Commodity Summaries*.

PRICES - RECEIVED BY FARMERS - CROPS

U.S. Department of Agriculture, Economic Research Service, Fourteenth Street and Independence Avenue, SW, Washington, D.C. 20005-4789 (202) 219-1504; *Feed Situation, Fats and Oils Situation, Wheat Situation, Tobacco Situation, Cotton and Wool Outlook Statistics, Agricultural Supply and Demand Estimates*, and *Foreign Agricultural Trade of the United States*.

U.S. Department of Agriculture, National Agricultural Statistics Service, Fourteenth Street and Independence Avenue, SW, Washington, D.C. 20250 (202) 219-1504; *Agricultural Statistics, Crop Production, Field Crops, Crop Values*, and *Agricultural Outlook*.

PRICES - RECEIVED BY FARMERS - INDEXES

U.S. Department of Agriculture, National Agricultural Statistics Service, Fourteenth Street and Independence Avenue, SW, Washington, D.C. 20250 (202) 219-1504; *Agricultural Prices: Annual Summary*.

PRICES - RECEIVED BY FARMERS - LIVESTOCK AND PRODUCTS - POULTRY

U.S. Department of Agriculture, National Agricultural Statistics Service, Fourteenth Street and Independence Avenue, SW, Washington, D.C. 20250 (202) 219-1504; *Agricultural Statistics, Agricultural Prices: Annual Summary, Meat Animals - Production Disposition and Income, Layers and Egg Production - Annual, Poultry - Production and Value*, and *Turkeys*.

PRICES - STOCKS

Board of Governors of the Federal Reserve System, Twentieth Street and Constitution Avenue, NW, Washington, D.C. 20551 (202) 452-3000; *Federal Reserve Bulletin*, and *Annual Statistical Digest*.

National Association of Securities Dealers, 1735 K Street, NW, Washington, D.C. 20006 (202) 728-8000; *Fact Book*.

New York Stock Exchange, 11 Wall Street, New York, New York 10005 (212) 656-3000; *Fact Book*.

PRIMARIES - PRESIDENTIAL PREFERENCE

Committee for the Study of the American Electorate, 421 New Jersey Avenue, SE, Washington, D.C. 20003 (202) 546-3221; unpublished data.

Elections Research Center, 5508 Greystone Street, Chevy Chase, Maryland 20815 (202) 659-9490; *America Votes*.

Federal Election Commission, 999 E Street, NW, Washington, D.C. 20463 (800) 424-9530; *FEC Reports on Financial Activity, Final Report, Presidential Pre-Nomination Campaigns*.

PRIME MOVERS

John A. Waring, 1320 South George Mason Drive, Arlington, Virginia 22204 (703) 521-1499; unpublished estimates.

PRINTING AND PUBLISHING INDUSTRIES - CAPITAL

U.S. Department of Commerce, Bureau of the Census, Suitland, Maryland 20233 (301) 763-4040; *Census of Manufactures*, and *Annual Survey of Manufactures*.

PRINTING AND PUBLISHING INDUSTRIES - EARNINGS

U.S. Department of Commerce, Bureau of the Census, Suitland, Maryland 20233 (301) 763-4040; *Census of Manufactures*, and *Annual Survey of Manufactures*.

U.S. Department of Labor, Bureau of Labor Statistics, Two Massachusetts Avenue, NE, Washington, D.C. 20212 (202) 606-7828; *Employment and Earnings*, and Bulletins 2370 and 2429.

PRINTING AND PUBLISHING INDUSTRIES - EMPLOYEES

U.S. Department of Commerce, Bureau of the Census, Suitland, Maryland 20233 (301) 763-4040; *Census of Manufactures*, and *Annual Survey of Manufactures, Origin of Exports of Manufactured Products*.

U.S. Department of Commerce, International Trade Administration, Fourteenth Street between Constitution Avenue, and E Street, NW, Washington, D.C. 20230 (202) 482-3809; *U.S. Industrial Outlook*.

U.S. Department of Labor, Bureau of Labor Statistics, Two Massachusetts Avenue, NE, Washington, D.C. 20212 (202) 606-7828; *Employment and Earnings, Monthly Labor Review*, and Bulletins 2370 and 2429.

PRINTING AND PUBLISHING INDUSTRIES - ESTABLISHMENTS

U.S. Department of Commerce, Bureau of the Census, Suitland, Maryland 20233 (301) 763-4040; *Census of Manufactures*, and *Annual Survey of Manufactures*.

U.S. Department of Labor, Bureau of Labor Statistics, Two Massachusetts Avenue, NE, Washington, D.C. 20212 (202) 606-7828; *Employment and Earnings*.

PRINTING AND PUBLISHING INDUSTRIES - FINANCES

U.S. Department of Commerce, Bureau of the Census, Suitland, Maryland 20233 (301) 763-4040; *Annual Survey of Manufactures*, and *Census of Manufactures*.

PRINTING AND PUBLISHING INDUSTRIES - FOREIGN TRADE

U.S. Department of Commerce, Bureau of the Census, Suitland, Maryland 20233 (301) 763-4040; *U.S. Merchandise Trade: Selected Highlights*.

PRINTING AND PUBLISHING INDUSTRIES - GROSS DOMESTIC PRODUCT

U.S. Department of Commerce, Bureau of Economic Analysis, Fourteenth Street between Constitution Avenue and E Street, NW, Washington, D.C. 20230 (202) 606-9900; *The National Income and Product Accounts of the U.S.*, and *Survey of Current Business*.

PRINTING AND PUBLISHING INDUSTRIES - OCCUPATIONAL SAFETY

U.S. Department of Labor, Bureau of Labor Statistics, Two Massachusetts Avenue, NE, Washington, D.C. 20212 (202) 606-7828; *Occupational Injuries and Illnesses in the United States by Industry*.

PRINTING AND PUBLISHING INDUSTRIES - PRODUCTIVITY

Board of Governors of the Federal Reserve System, Twentieth Street and Constitution Avenue, NW, Washington, D.C. 20551 (202) 452-3000; *Federal Reserve Bulletin*.

PRINTING AND PUBLISHING INDUSTRIES - SALES, SHIPMENTS, RECEIPTS

Forbes, Incorporated, 60 Fifth Avenue, New York, New York 10011 (212) 620-2200; *Forbes Annual Report on American Industry*.

U.S. Department of Commerce, Bureau of the Census, Suitland, Maryland 20233 (301) 763-4040; *Census of Manufactures*, and *Annual Survey of Manufactures*.

U.S. Department of Commerce, International Trade Administration, Fourteenth Street between Constitution Avenue, and E Street, NW, Washington, D.C. 20230 (202) 482-3809; *U.S. Industrial Outlook*.

PRINTING AND PUBLISHING INDUSTRIES - VALUE ADDED

U.S. Department of Commerce, Bureau of the Census, Suitland, Maryland 20233 (301) 763-4040; *Census of Manufactures*, and *Annual Survey of Manufactures*.

PRISONS AND PRISONERS - See also CORRECTIONAL INSTITUTIONS

U.S. Department of Justice, Bureau of Justice Statistics, 633 Indiana Avenue, NW, Washington, D.C. 20531 (800) 732-3277; *Prisoners in State and Federal Institutions on December 31, Probation and Parole, Correctional Populations in the United States, Capital Punishment, Survey of State Prison Inmates*, and *Prisoners in 1991*.

PRISONS AND PRISONERS - DEATH SENTENCE

U.S. Department of Justice, Bureau of Justice Statistics, 633 Indiana Avenue, NW, Washington, D.C. 20531 (800) 732-3277; *Capital Punishment*, and *Correctional Populations in the United States*.

PRISONS AND PRISONERS - EXECUTIONS

U.S. Department of Justice, Bureau of Justice Statistics, 633 Indiana Avenue, NW, Washington, D.C. 20531 (800) 732-3277; *Capital Punishment*, and *Correctional Projections in the United States*.

PRISONS AND PRISONERS - INMATE CHARACTERISTICS

U.S. Department of Justice, Bureau of Justice Statistics, 633 Indiana Avenue, NW, Washington, D.C. 20531 (800) 732-3277; *Survey of State Prison Inmates*.

PRISONS AND PRISONERS - SENTENCE - BY OFFENSE

U.S. Department of Justice, Bureau of Justice Statistics, 633 Indiana Avenue, NW, Washington, D.C. 20531 (800) 732-3277; *Federal Criminal Case Processing*.

PROBATION

U.S. Department of Justice, Bureau of Justice Statistics, 633 Indiana Avenue, NW, Washington, D.C. 20531 (800) 732-3277, *Correctional Populations in the United States*.

PRODUCER PRICE INDEXES

U.S. Department of Labor, Bureau of Labor Statistics, Two Massachusetts Avenue, NE, Washington, D.C. 20212 (202) 606-7828; *Producer Price Indexes*, and *Monthly Labor Review*.

PRODUCER PRICE INDEXES - CONSTRUCTION MATERIALS

U.S. Department of Labor, Bureau of Labor Statistics, Two Massachusetts Avenue, NE, Washington, D.C. 20212 (202) 606-7828; *Producer Price Indexes*.

PRODUCER PRICE INDEXES - NEWSPRINT

U.S. Department of Commerce, Bureau of Economic Analysis, Fourteenth Street between Constitution Avenue and E Street, NW, Washington, D.C. 20230 (202) 606-9900; *Survey of Current Business* data from American Forest and Paper Association, 1250 Connecticut Avenue, NW, Washington, D.C. 20036 (202) 463-2455 and Canadian Pulp and Paper Association, 1155 Metcalfe Street, 19th Floor, Montreal, Quebec H3B 4T6, Canada (514) 866-6621.

PRODUCER PRICE INDEXES - RAILROAD FREIGHT

U.S. Department of Labor, Bureau of Labor Statistics, Two Massachusetts Avenue, NE, Washington, D.C. 20212 (202) 606-7828; *Producer Price Indexes*.

PRODUCER PRICE INDEXES - STAGE - OF PROCESSING

U.S. Department of Labor, Bureau of Labor Statistics, Two Massachusetts Avenue, NE, Washington, D.C. 20212 (202) 606-7828; *Producer Price Indexes*, and *Monthly Labor Review*.

PRODUCER PRICE INDEXES - TIMBER

U.S. Department of Labor, Bureau of Labor Statistics, Two Massachusetts Avenue, NE, Washington, D.C. 20212 (202) 606-7828; *Producer Price Indexes*.

PRODUCTIVITY - See also Individual Industries

PRODUCTIVITY - CAPACITY UTILIZATION

Board of Governors of the Federal Reserve System, Twentieth Street and Constitution Avenue, NW, Washington, D.C. 20551 (202) 452-3000; *Capacity Utilization in Manufacturing, Mining, Utilities, and Industrial Materials*.

PRODUCTIVITY - FARM OUTPUT

U.S. Department of Agriculture, Economic Research Service, Fourteenth Street and Independence Avenue, SW, Washington, D.C. 20005-4789 (202) 219-1504; *Agricultural Statistics*, and *Agricultural Resources: Cropland, Water, and Conservation Situation and Outlook Report*.

PRODUCTIVITY - LABOR

U.S. Department of Labor, Bureau of Labor Statistics, Two Massachusetts Avenue, NE, Washington, D.C. 20212 (202) 606-7828; *Productivity Measures for Selected Industries and Government Services, Employment and Earnings*, Report 844, *Monthly Labor Review*, and *News Release*.

PRODUCTIVITY - MINING INDUSTRIES

U.S. Department of Energy, Energy Information Administration, 1000 Independence Avenue, SW, Washington, D.C. 20585 (202) 586-8800; *Coal Production, Quarterly Coal Report*, and *Annual Energy Review*.

PROFITS - CORPORATIONS

Executive Office of the President, Council of Economic Advisers, Old Executive Office Building, Washington, D.C. 20500 (202) 395-5084; *Economic Report of the President*.

Time Warner, 1675 Broadway, Rockefeller Center, New York, New York 10019 (212) 522-1212; *The Fortune Directories*.

U.S. Department of Commerce, Bureau of Economic Analysis, Fourteenth Street between Constitution Avenue and E Street, NW, Washington, D.C. 20230 (202) 606-9900; *The National Income and Product Accounts of the United States*, and *Survey of Current Business*.

U.S. Department of Commerce, Bureau of the Census, Suitland, Maryland 20233 (301) 763-4040; *Quarterly Financial Report for Manufacturing, Mining and Trade Corporations*.

U.S. Department of the Treasury, Internal Revenue Service, 1111 Constitution Avenue, NW, Washington, D.C. 20224 (202) 566-5000; *Statistics of Income*, various publications, *Statistics of Income Bulletin*, and *Statistics of Income, Corporation Income Tax Returns*.

PROFITS - PARTNERSHIPS AND PROPRIETORSHIPS

U.S. Department of the Treasury, Internal Revenue Service, 1111 Constitution Avenue, NW, Washington, D.C. 20224 (202) 566-5000; *Statistics of Income*, various publications.

PROJECTIONS - BIRTHS

U.S. Department of Commerce, Bureau of the Census, Suitland, Maryland 20233 (301) 763-4040; *Current Population Reports*, and unpublished data.

PROJECTIONS - COLLEGE ENROLLMENT

U.S. Department of Education, 400 Maryland Avenue, SW, Washington, D.C. 20202 (202) 708-5366; *Projections of Education Statistics, Digest of Education Statistics*, and unpublished data.

PROJECTIONS - DEATHS

U.S. Department of Commerce, Bureau of the Census, Suitland, Maryland 20233 (301) 763-4040; *Current Population Reports*.

PROJECTIONS - EMPLOYMENT

U.S. Department of Labor, Bureau of Labor Statistics, Two Massachusetts Avenue, NE, Washington, D.C. 20212 (202) 606-7828; *Monthly Labor Review*.

PROJECTIONS - LABOR FORCE

U.S. Department of Labor, Bureau of Labor Statistics, Two Massachusetts Avenue, NE, Washington, D.C. 20212 (202) 606-7828; *Employment and Earnings, Monthly Labor Review*, and unpublished data.

PROJECTIONS - LIFE EXPECTANCY

U.S. Department of Health and Human Services, National Center for Health Statistics, 3700 East-West Highway, Hyattsville, Maryland 20782 (301) 436-8500; *Vital Statistics of the United States*, and unpublished data.

PROJECTIONS - SCHOOL ENROLLMENT

U.S. Department of Education, 400 Maryland Avenue, SW, Washington, D.C. 20202 (202) 708-5366; *Projections of Education Statistics, Digest of Education Statistics*, and unpublished data.

PROJECTIONS - TEACHERS

U.S. Department of Education, 400 Maryland Avenue, SW, Washington, D.C. 20202 (202) 708-5366; *Digest of Education Statistics*, and *Projections of Education Statistics*.

U.S. Department of Labor, Bureau of Labor Statistics, Two Massachusetts Avenue, NE, Washington, D.C. 20212 (202) 606-7828; *Monthly Labor Review.*

PROPERTY AND CASUALTY INSURANCE

U.S. Department of Commerce, International Trade Administration, Fourteenth Street between Constitution Avenue and E Street, NW, Washington, D.C. 20230 (202) 482-3809; *U.S. Industrial Outlook.*

PROPERTY TAX

U.S. Department of Commerce, Bureau of the Census, Suitland, Maryland 20233 (301) 763-4040; *Government Finances, City Government Finances,* and *State Government Finances.*

PROPERTY TAX - RATES - SELECTED CITIES

Government of the District of Columbia, Department of Finance and Revenue, 300 Indiana Avenue, NW, Washington, D.C. 20001 (202) 727-6103; *Tax Rates and Tax Burdens in the District of Columbia: A Nationwide Comparison.*

PROPERTY TAX - STATE AND LOCAL GOVERNMENT

U.S. Department of Commerce, Bureau of the Census, Suitland, Maryland 20233 (301) 763-4040; *Historical Statistics on Governmental Finances and Employment, Government Finances, State Government Finances,* and *Census of Governments.*

PROPRIETORS' INCOME

U.S. Department of Commerce, Bureau of Economic Analysis, Fourteenth Street between Constitution Avenue and E Street, NW, Washington, D.C. 20230 (202) 606-9900; *The National Income and Product Accounts of the United States,* and *Survey of Current Business.*

PROPRIETORSHIPS

U.S. Department of the Treasury, Internal Revenue Service, 1111 Constitution Avenue, NW, Washington, D.C. 20224 (202) 566-5000; *Statistics of Income, Statistics of Income Bulletin,* and various publications

PROSTITUTION AND COMMERCIALIZED VICE

U.S. Department of Justice, Federal Bureau of Investigation, Ninth Street and Pennsylvania Avenue, NW, Washington, D.C. 20535 (202) 324-3000; *Crime in the United States.*

PROTECTIVE SERVICE WORKERS - See PUBLIC SAFETY

PROTEIN AVAILABLE FOR CONSUMPTION

U.S. Department of Agriculture, Economic Research Service, Fourteenth Street and Independence Avenue, SW, Washington, D.C. 20005-4789 (202) 219-1504; *Food Consumption, Prices, and Expenditures,* and *National Food Review.*

PROTESTANTS - See RELIGION

PRUNES AND PLUMS

U.S. Department of Agriculture, National Agricultural Statistics Service, Fourteenth Street and Independence Avenue, SW, Washington, D.C. 20250 (202) 219-1504; *Food Consumption, Prices and Expenditures,* and *Noncitrus Fruits and Nuts.*

PSYCHIATRIC CARE AND INSTITUTIONS - See MENTAL HEALTH

PSYCHOLOGY - DEGREES CONFERRED

U.S. Department of Education, 400 Maryland Avenue, SW, Washington, D.C. 20202 (202) 708-5366; *Digest of Education Statistics,* and unpublished data.

U.S. National Science Foundation, Division of Science Resource Studies, 4201 Wilson Boulevard, Arlington, Virginia 22230 (703) 306-1234; *Survey of Earned Doctorates, Selected Data on Science and Engineering Doctorate Awards,* and *Characteristics of Recent Science and Engineering Graduates.*

PSYCHOLOGY - EMPLOYMENT

U.S. National Science Foundation, 4201 Wilson Boulevard, Arlington, Virginia 22230 (703) 306-1234; *United States Scientists and Engineers,* and *Women and Minorities in Science and Engineering.*

PSYCHOLOGY - RESEARCH - UNITED STATES GOVERNMENT OBLIGATIONS FOR

U.S. National Science Foundation, 4201 Wilson Boulevard, Arlington, Virginia 22230 (703) 306-1234; *Federal Funds for Research and Development.*

PSYCHOTHERAPEUTIC DRUGS - NONMEDICAL USE

U.S. Department of Health and Human Services, Substance Abuse and Mental Health Services Administration, 5600 Fishers Lane, Rockville, Maryland 20857 (301) 443-4797; *National Household Survey on Drug Abuse.*

PUBLIC ADMINISTRATION - See GOVERNMENT

PUBLIC AID ASSISTANCE

Executive Office of the President, Office of Management and Budget, Executive Office Building, Washington, D.C. 20503 (202) 395-3080; *The Budget of the United States Government.*

U.S. Department of Health and Human Services, Administration for Children and Families, 370 L'Enfant Promenade, SW, Washington, D.C. 20447 (202) 401-9200; *Quarterly Public Assistance Statistics.*

U.S. Department of Health and Human Services, Social Security Administration, 6401 Security Boulevard, Baltimore, Maryland 21235 (410) 965-1234; *Social Security Bulletin, Annual Statistical Supplement to the Social Security Bulletin,* and unpublished data.

U.S. Library of Congress, Congressional Research Service, 10 First Street, SE, Washington, D.C. 20540 (202) 707-5000; *Cash and Non-Cash Benefits for Persons With Limited Income: Eligibility Rules, Recipient and Expenditure Data.*

PUBLIC AID ASSISTANCE - BENEFITS PAID

Executive Office of the President, Office of Management and Budget, Executive Office Building, Washington, D.C. 20503 (202) 395-3080; *The Budget of the United States Government.*

U.S. Department of Health and Human Services, Administration for Children and Families, 370 L'Enfant Promenade, SW, Washington, D.C. 20447 (202) 401-9200; *Quarterly Public Assistance Statistics.*

U.S. Department of Health and Human Services, Health Care Financing Administration, 200 Independence Avenue, SW, Washington, D.C. 20201 (202) 245-6113; unpublished data.

U.S. Department of Health and Human Services, Social Security Administration, 6401 Security Boulevard, Baltimore, Maryland 21235 (410) 965-1234; *Social Security Bulletin, Annual Statistical Supplement to the Social Security Bulletin,* and unpublished data.

U.S. Library of Congress, Congressional Research Service, 10 First Street, SE, Washington, D.C. 20540 (202) 707-5000; *Cash and Non-Cash Benefits for Persons With Limited Income: Eligibility Rules, Recipient and Expenditure Data.*

PUBLIC AID ASSISTANCE - FEDERAL AID TO STATE AND LOCAL GOVERNMENTS

Executive Office of the President, Office of Management and Budget, Executive Office Building, Washington, D.C. 20503 (202) 395-3080; *Historical Tables, Budget of the United States Government,* and *Budget of the U.S. Government.*

U.S. Department of Commerce, Bureau of the Census, Suitland, Maryland 20233 (301) 763-4040; *Federal Expenditures by State for Fiscal Year.*

PUBLIC AID ASSISTANCE - FEDERAL EXPENDITURES

Executive Office of the President, Office of Management and Budget, Executive Office Building, Washington, D.C. 20503 (202) 395-3080; *Budget of the United States Government.*

U.S. Department of Health and Human Services, Health Care Financing Administration, 200 Independence Avenue, SW, Washington, D.C. 20201 (202) 245-6113; *Health Care Financing Review,* and unpublished data.

U.S. Department of Health and Human Services, Social Security Administration, 6401 Security Boulevard, Baltimore, Maryland 21235 (410) 965-1234; *Social Security Bulletin.*

U.S. Library of Congress, Congressional Research Service, 10 First Street, SE, Washington, D.C. 20540 (202) 707-5000; *Cash and Non-Cash Benefits for Persons With Limited Income. Eligibility Rules, Recipient and Expenditure Data.*

PUBLIC AID ASSISTANCE - HEALTH EXPENDITURES

Executive Office of the President, Office of Management and Budget, Executive Office Building, Washington, D.C. 20503 (202) 395-3080; *The Budget of the United States Government.*

U.S. Department of Commerce, Bureau of the Census, Suitland, Maryland 20233 (301) 763-4040; *Current Population Reports.*

U.S. Department of Health and Human Services, Health Care Financing Administration, 200 Independence Avenue, SW, Washington, D.C. 20201 (202) 245-6113; *Health Care Financing Review,* and unpublished data.

U.S. Department of Health and Human Services, Social Security Administration, 6401 Security Boulevard, Baltimore, Maryland 21235 (410) 965-1234; *Social Security Bulletin.*

U.S. Library of Congress, Congressional Research Service, 10 First Street, SE, Washington, D.C. 20540 (202) 707-5000; *Cash and Non-cash Benefits for Persons With Limited Income: Eligibility Rules, Recipient and Expenditure Data.*

PUBLIC AID ASSISTANCE - RECIPIENTS

U.S. Department of Commerce, Bureau of the Census, Suitland, Maryland 20233 (301) 763-4040; *Current Population Reports.*

U.S. Department of Health and Human Services, Administration for Children and Families, 370 L'Enfant Promenade, SW, Washington, D.C. 20447 (202) 401-9200; *Quarterly Public Assistance Statistics.*

U.S. Department of Health and Human Services, Social Security Administration, 6401 Security Boulevard, Baltimore, Maryland 21235 (410) 965-1234; *Social Security Bulletin, Annual Statistical Supplement to the Social Security Bulletin,* and unpublished data.

U.S. Library of Congress, Congressional Research Service, 10 First Street, SE, Washington, D.C. 20540 (202) 707-5000; *Cash and Non-Cash Benefits for Persons With Limited Income: Eligibility Rules, Recipient and Expenditure Data.*

PUBLIC BROADCASTING STATIONS

Corporation for Public Broadcasting, 901 E Street, NW, Washington, D.C. 20004-2006 (202) 879-9600; *PTV Programming Survey, Public Broadcasting Income, Fiscal Year 1992,* and unpublished data.

PUBLIC DOMAIN - See PUBLIC LANDS

PUBLIC HOUSING

U.S. Department of Commerce, Bureau of the Census, Suitland, Maryland 20233 (301) 763-4040; *Current Population Reports, Federal Expenditures by State for Fiscal Year, Census of Housing, Current Housing Reports,* and *Annual Housing Survey.*

U.S. Department of Housing and Urban Development, 451 Seventh Street, SW, Washington, D.C. 20410 (202) 708-1422; unpublished data based on the Field Office Report Monitoring System.

PUBLIC LANDS - See also FORESTS

PUBLIC LANDS - AREA

U.S. Department of the Interior, Bureau of Land Management, C Street between Eighteenth and Nineteenth Streets, NW, Washington, D.C. 20240 (202) 208-3435; *Areas of Acquisitions to the Territory of the United States.*

U.S. General Services Administration, General Services Building, Eighteenth and F Streets, NW, Washington, D.C. 20405; *Inventory Report on Real Property Owned by the United States Throughout the World.*

PUBLIC LANDS - COST AND USAGE

U.S. General Services Administration, General Services Building, Eighteenth and F Streets, NW, Washington, D.C. 20405 (202) 708-5082; *Inventory Report on Real Property Owned by the United States Throughout the World.*

PUBLIC LANDS - FOREST LAND - AREA

U.S. Department of Agriculture, Forest Service, Fourteenth Street and Independence Avenue, SW, Washington, D.C. 20250 (202) 720-3760; *Forest Resources of the U.S., Land Areas of the National Forest System,* and unpublished data.

PUBLIC LANDS - LEASES, PERMITS, AND LICENSES

U.S. Department of the Interior, Bureau of Land Management, C Street between Eighteenth and Nineteenth Streets, NW, Washington, D.C. 20240 (202) 208-3435; *Public Land Statistics.*

U.S. Department of the Interior, Minerals Management Service, C Street between Eighteenth and Nineteenth Streets, NW,

Washington, D.C. 20240 (202) 208-3983; *Federal Offshore Statistics.*

PUBLIC LANDS - NATIONAL PARK SYSTEM

U.S. Department of the Interior, National Park Service, C Street between Eighteenth and Nineteenth Streets, NW, Washington, D.C. 20240 (202) 208-6843; *National Park Statistical Abstract,* and unpublished data.

PUBLIC LANDS - OWNERSHIP

U.S. General Services Administration, General Services Building, Eighteenth and F Streets, NW, Washington, D.C. 20405 (202) 708-5082; *Inventory Report on Real Property Owned by the United States Throughout the World.*

PUBLIC LANDS - RECREATION

U.S. Department of the Interior, Bureau of Land Management, C Street between 18th and 19th Streets, NW, Washington, D.C. 20240 (202) 208-3435; *Public Land Statistics.*

U.S. Department of the Interior, National Park Service, C Street between Eighteenth and Nineteenth Streets, NW, Washington, D.C. 20204 (202) 208-6843; *National Park Statistical Abstract,* and unpublished data.

PUBLIC OFFICIALS - PROSECUTIONS

U.S. Department of Justice, Constitution Avenue and Tenth Street, NW, Washington, D.C. 20530 (202) 514-2000; *Report to Congress on the Activities and Operations of the Public Integrity Section.*

PUBLIC ROADS - See HIGHWAYS

PUBLIC SAFETY - See also LAW ENFORCEMENT

PUBLIC SAFETY - COMMUNICATION - PRIVATE RADIO STATIONS

U.S. Federal Communications Commission, 1919 M Street, NW, Washington, D.C. 20554 (202) 632-7000; *Annual Report,* and unpublished data.

PUBLIC SAFETY - EMPLOYMENT

U.S. Department of Commerce, Bureau of the Census, Suitland, Maryland 20233 (301) 763-4040; *Public Employment,* and *Government Finances.*

U.S. Department of Justice, Bureau of Justice Statistics, 633 Indiana Avenue, NW, Washington, D.C. 20531 (800) 732-3277; *Justice Expenditure and Employment in the U.S.*

U.S. Department of Labor, Bureau of Labor Statistics, Two Massachusetts Avenue, NE, Washington, D.C. 20212 (202) 606-7828; *Monthly Labor Review,* and *Employment and Earnings.*

PUBLIC SAFETY - EMPLOYMENT - CITY GOVERNMENT

U.S. Department of Commerce, Bureau of the Census, Suitland, Maryland 20233 (301) 763-4040; *City Employment,* and *Compendium of Public Employment.*

PUBLIC SAFETY - EMPLOYMENT - FIRE PROTECTION

U.S. Department of Commerce, Bureau of the Census, Suitland, Maryland 20233 (301) 763-4040; *Public Employment.*

PUBLIC SAFETY - EMPLOYMENT - POLICE PROTECTION AND CORRECTION

U.S. Department of Commerce, Bureau of the Census, Suitland, Maryland 20233 (301) 763-4040; *Public Employment, Government Finances,* and *Historical Statistics on Governmental Finances and Employment.*

U.S. Department of Justice, Bureau of Justice Statistics, 633 Indiana Avenue, NW, Washington, D.C. 20531 (800) 732-3277; *Justice Expenditure and Employment in the U.S.*

PUBLIC SAFETY - EXPENDITURES

U.S. Department of Commerce, Bureau of the Census, Suitland, Maryland 20233 (301) 763-4040; *Government Finances, City Government Finances, Historical Statistics on Governmental Finances and Employment,* and *Public Employment.*

U.S. Department of Justice, Bureau of Justice Statistics, 633 Indiana Avenue, NW, Washington, D.C. 20531 (800) 732-3277; *Justice Expenditure and Employment in the U.S.*

PUBLIC SAFETY - EXPENDITURES - CITY GOVERNMENTS

U.S. Department of Commerce, Bureau of the Census, Suitland, Maryland 20233 (301) 763-4040; *City Government Finances.*

PUBLIC SAFETY - EXPENDITURES - STATE AND LOCAL GOVERNMENT

U.S. Department of Commerce, Bureau of the Census, Suitland, Maryland 20233 (301) 763-4040; *Historical Statistics on Government Finances and Employment,* and *Government Finances.*

PUBLIC SAFETY - EXPENDITURES - STATE GOVERNMENT

U.S. Department of Commerce, Bureau of the Census, Suitland, Maryland 20233 (301) 763-4040; *Historical Statistics on Governmental Finances and Employment,* and *State Government Finances.*

PUBLIC SCHOOLS - See EDUCATION

PUBLISHING INDUSTRY - See PRINTING AND PUBLISHING INDUSTRIES

Puerto Rico - National Statistical Office

Planning Board, Commonwealth of Puerto Rico, North Building, Box 41119, San Juan, Puerto Rico 00940.

Puerto Rico - Primary Statistics Source

Puerto Rico Planning Board, North Building, Box 41119, San Juan, Puerto Rico 00940; *Anuario estastistico* (Statistical Yearbook).

Puerto Rico - State Data Centers

Puerto Rico Planning Board, Minillas Government Center, North Building, Avenida De Diego, Post Office Box 41119, San Juan, Puerto Rico 00940-9985, Sr. Jose Jiminez (809) 728-4430.

Recinto Universitario De Mayaguez, Edificio Anexo Pineiro, Carretera Num 2, Mayaguez, Puerto Rico 00708, Sra. Marta Segarra (809) 832-4040.

Departmeno de Educacion, Post Office Box 759, Hato Rey, Puerto Rico 00919, Sra. Carmen Martinez and Sra. Nayada Pratts (809) 724-1046.

Universidad Interamiricana, Recinto de Guayama, Post Office Box 1559, Guayama, Puerto Rico 00785, Angel Rivera (809) 864-2222.

PUERTO RICO - AGRICULTURE

Euromonitor Publications Limited, 87-88 Turnmill Street, London EC1M 5QU, England; *International Marketing Data and Statistics.*

Food and Agricultural Organization of the United Nations (FAO), Via delle Terme di Caracalla, 00100 Rome, Italy (Telephone Number in U.S. (202) 653-2400); *Production Yearbook,* and *The State of Food and Agriculture,* and *Trade Yearbook.*

Gale Research Incorporated, 835 Penobscot Building, Detroit, Michigan 48226 (800) 877-4253; *International Historical Statistics The Americas and Australasia.*

G.K. Hall and Company, 70 Lincoln Street, Boston, Massachusetts 02111 (617) 423-3990; *The World in Figures.*

Organisation for Economic Co-operation and Development (OECD), 2 rue Andre-Pascal, 75 Paris 16, France (Telephone Number in U.S. (202) 785-6323); *Indicators of Industrial Activity.*

Statistical Office of the United Nations, Publishing Service, New York, New York 10017 (800) 253-9646; *Statistical Yearbook.*

Time Books, 201 East 50th Street, New York, New York 10022 (212) 751-2600; *The Economist Book of Vital World Statistics.*

PUERTO RICO - AIRLINE SERVICE

G.K. Hall and Company, 70 Lincoln Street, Boston, Massachusetts 02111 (617) 423-3990; *The World in Figures.*

Time Books, 201 East 50th Street, New York, New York 10022 (212) 751-2600; *The Economist Book of Vital World Statistics.*

PUERTO RICO - AREA AND DENSITY OF POPULATION

Euromonitor Publications Limited, 87-88 Turnmill Street, London EC1M 5QU, England; *International Marketing Data and Statistics.*

Food and Agricultural Organization of the United Nations (FAO) Via delle Terme di Caracalla, 00100 Rome, Italy (Telephone Number in U.S. (202) 653-2400); *The State of Food and Agriculture.*

G.K. Hall and Company, 70 Lincoln Street, Boston, Massachusetts 02111 (617) 423-3990; *The World in Figures.*

Statistical Office of the United Nations, Publishing Service, New York, New York 10017 (800) 253-9646; *Statistical Yearbook.*

Time Books, 201 East 50th Street, New York, New York 10022 (212) 751-2600; *The Economist Book of Vital World Statistics.*

United Nations Educational, Scientific and Cultural Organization (UNESCO), 7 Place de Fontenoy, F-75700 Paris, France (Telephone Number in U.S. (212) 963-5981); *Statistical Yearbook.*

PUERTO RICO - BALANCE OF PAYMENTS

G.K. Hall and Company, 70 Lincoln Street, Boston, Massachusetts 02111 (617) 423-3990; *The World in Figures.*

International Monetary Fund, 700 Nineteenth Street, NW, Washington, D.C. 20431 (202) 623-7000; *Balance of Payments Yearbook.*

Time Books, 201 East 50th Street, New York, New York 10022 (212) 751-2600; *The Economist Book of Vital World Statistics.*

PUERTO RICO - BANKING

G.K. Hall and Company, 70 Lincoln Street, Boston, Massachusetts 02111 (617) 423-3990; *The World in Figures.*

PUERTO RICO - BEER PRODUCTION

Statistical Office of the United Nations, Publishing Service, New York, New York 10017 (800) 253-9646; *Statistical Yearbook.*

PUERTO RICO - BIRTH RATES

Statistical Office of the United Nations, Publishing Service, New York, New York 10017 (800) 253-9646; *Demographic Yearbook,* and *Statistical Yearbook.*

Time Books, 201 East 50th Street, New York, New York 10022 (212) 751-2600; *The Economist Book of Vital World Statistics.*

World Health Organization, Office of Publications, Avenue Appia, CH-1211 Geneva 27, Switzerland (Telephone Number in U.S. (518) 436-9686); *World Health Statistics Annual.*

PUERTO RICO - BONDS

G.K. Hall and Company, 70 Lincoln Street, Boston, Massachusetts 02111 (617) 423-3990; *The World in Figures.*

PUERTO RICO - BOOK PRODUCTION

G.K. Hall and Company, 70 Lincoln Street, Boston, Massachusetts 02111 (617) 423-3990; *The World in Figures.*

PUERTO RICO - BROADCASTING

Billboard Limited, Post Office Box 9027, 1006 AA Amsterdam, The Netherlands (Telephone Number in U.S. (212) 764-7300); *World Radio TV Handbook.*

G.K. Hall and Company, 70 Lincoln Street, Boston, Massachusetts 02111 (617) 423-3990; *The World in Figures.*

Time Books, 201 East 50th Street, New York, New York 10022 (212) 751-2600; *The Economist Book of Vital World Statistics.*

United Nations Educational, Scientific and Cultural Organization (UNESCO), 7 Place de Fontenoy, F-75700 Paris, France (Telephone Number in U.S. (212) 963-5981); *Statistical Yearbook.*

PUERTO RICO - BUSINESS

G.K. Hall and Company, 70 Lincoln Street, Boston, Massachusetts 02111 (617) 423-3990; *The World in Figures.*

PUERTO RICO - BUTTER PRODUCTION - See PUERTO RICO - DAIRY PRODUCTS

PUERTO RICO - CALORIE SUPPLY

Food and Agricultural Organization of the United Nations (FAO) Via delle Terme di Caracalla, 00100 Rome, Italy (Telephone Number in U.S. (202) 653-2400); *The State of Food and Agriculture.*

PUERTO RICO - CATTLE - See PUERTO RICO - LIVESTOCK AND POULTRY

PUERTO RICO - CEMENT PRODUCTION - See PUERTO RICO - MINING AND MINERAL PRODUCTS

PUERTO RICO - CHEMICAL (ORGANIC) PRODUCTION - See PUERTO RICO - MINING AND MINERAL PRODUCTS

PUERTO RICO - CHICKENS - See PUERTO RICO - LIVESTOCK AND POULTRY

PUERTO RICO - CLASS STRUCTURE

G.K. Hall and Company, 70 Lincoln Street, Boston, Massachusetts 02111 (617) 423-3990; *The World in Figures*.

PUERTO RICO - CLIMATE

G.K. Hall and Company, 70 Lincoln Street, Boston, Massachusetts 02111 (617) 423-3990; *The World in Figures*.

PUERTO RICO - COAL PRODUCTION - See PUERTO RICO - MINING AND MINERAL PRODUCTS

PUERTO RICO - COFFEE PRODUCTION AND CONSUMPTION - See PUERTO RICO - CROPS

PUERTO RICO - COMMUNICATIONS

Gale Research Incorporated, 835 Penobscot Building, Detroit, Michigan 48226 (800) 877-4253; *International Historical Statistics The Americas and Australasia*.

G.K. Hall and Company, 70 Lincoln Street, Boston, Massachusetts 02111 (617) 423-3990; *The World in Figures*.

PUERTO RICO - CONSTRUCTION INDUSTRY

Statistical Office of the United Nations, Publishing Service, New York, New York 10017 (800) 253-9646; *Construction Statistics Yearbook*, and *Statistical Yearbook*.

PUERTO RICO - CONSUMER PRICE INDEX

G.K. Hall and Company, 70 Lincoln Street, Boston, Massachusetts 02111 (617) 423-3990; *The World in Figures*.

Statistical Office of the United Nations, Publishing Service, New York, New York 10017 (800) 253-9646; *Statistical Yearbook*.

PUERTO RICO - CONSUMER PRICES

International Labour Office, I.L.O. Publications, CH-1211, Geneva 22, Switzerland; *Yearbook of Labour Statistics*.

Time Books, 201 East 50th Street, New York, New York 10022 (212) 751-2600; *The Economist Book of Vital World Statistics*.

PUERTO RICO - CONSUMPTION

G.K. Hall and Company, 70 Lincoln Street, Boston, Massachusetts 02111 (617) 423-3990; *The World in Figures*.

PUERTO RICO - CORN PRODUCTION - See PUERTO RICO - CROPS

PUERTO RICO - CORPORATE TAXES - See PUERTO RICO - TAXATION

PUERTO RICO - CRIME

Yale University Press, Yale Station, New Haven, Connecticut 06520 (203) 432-0940; *Violence and Crime in Cross-National Perspective*.

PUERTO RICO - CROPS

Food and Agricultural Organization of the United Nations (FAO) Via delle Terme di Caracalla, 00100 Rome, Italy (Telephone Number in U.S. (202) 653-2400); *Production Yearbook*, and *The State of Food and Agriculture*.

G.K. Hall and Company, 70 Lincoln Street, Boston, Massachusetts 02111 (617) 423-3990; *The World in Figures*.

Statistical Office of the United Nations, Publishing Service, New York, New York 10017 (800) 253-9646; *Statistical Yearbook*.

PUERTO RICO - CUSTOMS DUTIES

G.K. Hall and Company, 70 Lincoln Street, Boston, Massachusetts 02111 (617) 423-3990; *The World in Figures*.

PUERTO RICO - DAIRY PRODUCTS

Food and Agricultural Organization of the United Nations (FAO) Via delle Terme di Caracalla, 00100 Rome, Italy (Telephone Number in U.S. (202) 653-2400); *The State of Food and Agriculture*.

Statistical Office of the United Nations, Publishing Service, New York, New York 10017 (800) 253-9646; *Statistical Yearbook*.

PUERTO RICO - DEATH RATE

G.K. Hall and Company, 70 Lincoln Street, Boston, Massachusetts 02111 (617) 423-3990; *The World in Figures*.

Statistical Office of the United Nations, Publishing Service, New York, New York 10017 (800) 253-9646; *Statistical Yearbook*.

Time Books, 201 East 50th Street, New York, New York 10022 (212) 751-2600; *The Economist Book of Vital World Statistics*.

World Health Organization, Office of Publications, Avenue Appia, CH-1211 Geneva 27, Switzerland (Telephone Number in U.S. (518) 436-9686); *World Health Statistics Annual*.

PUERTO RICO - DEFENSE EXPENDITURES

G.K. Hall and Company, 70 Lincoln Street, Boston, Massachusetts 02111 (617) 423-3990; *The World in Figures*.

PUERTO RICO - DEMOGRAPHY

G.K. Hall and Company, 70 Lincoln Street, Boston, Massachusetts 02111 (617) 423-3990; *The World in Figures*.

PUERTO RICO - DEVELOPMENT ASSISTANCE

G.K. Hall and Company, 70 Lincoln Street, Boston, Massachusetts 02111 (617) 423-3990; *The World in Figures*.

PUERTO RICO - DISEASES

G.K. Hall and Company, 70 Lincoln Street, Boston, Massachusetts 02111 (617) 423-3990; *The World in Figures*.

World Health Organization, Office of Publications, Avenue Appia, CH-1211 Geneva 27, Switzerland (Telephone Number in U.S. (518)

436-9686); *World Health Statistics Annual.*

PUERTO RICO - DIVORCE RATES

Statistical Office of the United Nations, Publishing Service, New York, New York 10017 (800) 253-9646; *Demographic Yearbook,* and *Statistical Yearbook.*

PUERTO RICO - DOMESTIC PRODUCT

G.K. Hall and Company, 70 Lincoln Street, Boston, Massachusetts 02111 (617) 423-3990; *The World in Figures.*

PUERTO RICO - ECONOMY

Euromonitor Publications Limited, 87-88 Turnmill Street, London EC1M 5QU, England; *International Marketing Data and Statistics.*

G.K. Hall and Company, 70 Lincoln Street, Boston, Massachusetts 02111 (617) 423-3990; *The World in Figures.*

PUERTO RICO - EDUCATION

Gale Research Incorporated, 835 Penobscot Building, Detroit, Michigan 48226 (800) 877-4253; *International Historical Statistics The Americas and Australasia.*

G.K. Hall and Company, 70 Lincoln Street, Boston, Massachusetts 02111 (617) 423-3990; *The World in Figures.*

Time Books, 201 East 50th Street, New York, New York 10022 (212) 751-2600; *The Economist Book of Vital World Statistics.*

United Nations Educational, Scientific and Cultural Organization (UNESCO), 7 Place de Fontenoy, F-75700 Paris, France (Telephone Number in U.S. (212) 963-5981); *Statistical Yearbook.*

PUERTO RICO - EGG PRODUCTION AND CONSUMPTION - See PUERTO RICO - DAIRY PRODUCTS

PUERTO RICO - ELECTRICITY

Statistical Office of the United Nations, Publishing Service, New York, New York 10017 (800) 253-9646; *Statistical Yearbook.*

PUERTO RICO - EMPLOYMENT

Euromonitor Publications Limited, 87-88 Turnmill Street, London EC1M 5QU, England; *International Marketing Data and Statistics.*

International Labour Office, I.L.O. Publications, CH-1211, Geneva 22, Switzerland; *Yearbook of Labour Statistics.*

Statistical Office of the United Nations, Publishing Service, New York, New York 10017 (800) 253-9646; *Statistical Yearbook.*

PUERTO RICO - ENERGY

G.K. Hall and Company, 70 Lincoln Street, Boston, Massachusetts 02111 (617) 423-3990; *The World in Figures.*

Food and Agricultural Organization of the United Nations (FAO) Via delle Terme di Caracalla, 00100 Rome, Italy (Telephone Number in U.S. (202) 653-2400); *The State of Food and Agriculture.*

Statistical Office of the United Nations, Publishing Service, New York, New York 10017 (800) 253-9646; *Energy Statistics Yearbook,* and *Statistical Yearbook.*

Time Books, 201 East 50th Street, New York, New York 10022 (212) 751-2600; *The Economist Book of Vital World Statistics.*

PUERTO RICO - EXCHANGE RATES

Euromonitor Publications Limited, 87-88 Turnmill Street, London EC1M 5QU, England; *International Marketing Data and Statistics.*

PUERTO RICO - EXPORTS

American Automobile Manufacturers Association, 1401 H Street, NW, Suite 900, Washington, D.C. 20005 (202) 326-5500; *World Motor Vehicle Data.*

Euromonitor Publications Limited, 87-88 Turnmill Street, London EC1M 5QU, England; *International Marketing Data and Statistics.*

Food and Agricultural Organization of the United Nations (FAO) Via delle Terme di Caracalla, 00100 Rome, Italy (Telephone Number in U.S. (202) 653-2400); *The State of Food and Agriculture.*

G.K. Hall and Company, 70 Lincoln Street, Boston, Massachusetts 02111 (617) 423-3990; *The World in Figures.*

Time Books, 201 East 50th Street, New York, New York 10022 (212) 751-2600; *The Economist Book of Vital World Statistics.*

PUERTO RICO - EXTERNAL TRADE

Food and Agricultural Organization of the United Nations (FAO) Via delle Terme di Caracalla, 00100 Rome, Italy (Telephone Number in U.S. (202) 653-2400); *The State of Food and Agriculture,* and *Trade Yearbook.*

Gale Research Incorporated, 835 Penobscot Building, Detroit, Michigan 48226 (800) 877-4253; *International Historical Statistics The Americas and Australasia.*

G.K. Hall and Company, 70 Lincoln Street, Boston, Massachusetts 02111 (617) 423-3990; *The World in Figures.*

PUERTO RICO - FARM CROPS - See PUERTO RICO - CROPS

PUERTO RICO - FEMALE WORKING POPULATION - See PUERTO RICO - EMPLOYMENT

PUERTO RICO - FERTILITY RATE

Time Books, 201 East 50th Street, New York, New York 10022 (212) 751-2600; *The Economist Book of Vital World Statistics.*

PUERTO RICO - FERTILIZER

Food and Agricultural Organization of the United Nations (FAO) Via delle Terme di Caracalla, 00100 Rome, Italy (Telephone Number in U.S. (202) 653-2400); *The State of Food and Agriculture.*

PUERTO RICO - FETAL MORTALITY

Statistical Office of the United Nations, Publishing Service, New York, New York 10017 (800) 253-9646; *Demographic Yearbook.*

World Health Organization, Office of Publications, Avenue Appia, CH-1211 Geneva 27, Switzerland (Telephone Number in U.S. (518) 436-9686); *World Health Statistics Annual.*

PUERTO RICO - FINANCE

Gale Research Incorporated, 835 Penobscot Building, Detroit, Michigan 48226 (800) 877-4253; *International Historical Statistics The Americas and Australasia.*

G.K. Hall and Company, 70 Lincoln Street, Boston, Massachusetts 02111 (617) 423-3990; *The World in Figures.*

PUERTO RICO - FISHERIES

Food and Agricultural Organization of the United Nations (FAO) Via delle Terme di Caracalla, 00100 Rome, Italy (Telephone Number in U.S. (202) 653-2400); *The State of Food and Agriculture,* and *Yearbook of Fishery Statistics.*

Statistical Office of the United Nations, Publishing Service, New York, New York 10017 (800) 253-9646; *Statistical Yearbook.*

PUERTO RICO - FOOD

Food and Agricultural Organization of the United Nations (FAO), Via delle Terme di Caracalla, 00100 Rome, Italy (Telephone Number in U.S. (202) 653-2400); *Production Yearbook,* and *The State of Food and Agriculture.*

G.K. Hall and Company, 70 Lincoln Street, Boston, Massachusetts 02111 (617) 423-3990; *The World in Figures.*

PUERTO RICO - FOREIGN AID

G.K. Hall and Company, 70 Lincoln Street, Boston, Massachusetts 02111 (617) 423-3990; *The World in Figures.*

PUERTO RICO - FOREIGN TRADE

Euromonitor Publications Limited, 87-88 Turnmill Street, London EC1M 5QU, England; *International Marketing Data and Statistics.*

Food and Agricultural Organization of the United Nations (FAO) Via delle Terme di Caracalla, 00100 Rome, Italy (Telephone Number in U.S. (202) 653-2400); *The State of Food and Agriculture.*

G.K. Hall and Company, 70 Lincoln Street, Boston, Massachusetts 02111 (617) 423-3990; *The World in Figures.*

PUERTO RICO - FORESTRY AND FOREST PRODUCTS

Food and Agricultural Organization of the United Nations (FAO) Via delle Terme di Caracalla, 00100 Rome, Italy (Telephone Number in U.S. (202) 653-2400); *The State of Food and Agriculture.*

G.K. Hall and Company, 70 Lincoln Street, Boston, Massachusetts 02111 (617) 423-3990; *The World in Figures.*

Statistical Office of the United Nations, Publishing Service, New York, New York 10017 (800) 253-9646; *Statistical Yearbook.*

United Nations Educational, Scientific and Cultural Organization (UNESCO), 7 Place de Fontenoy, F-75700 Paris, France (Telephone Number in U.S. (212) 963-5981); *Statistical Yearbook.*

PUERTO RICO - GENERAL INDUSTRIAL STATISTICS

Statistical Office of the United Nations, Publishing Service, New York, New York 10017 (800) 253-9646; *Industrial Statistics Yearbook.*

PUERTO RICO - GENERAL MORTALITY

Statistical Office of the United Nations, Publishing Service, New York, New York 10017 (800) 253-9646; *Demographic Yearbook.*

World Health Organization, Office of Publications, Avenue Appia, CH-1211 Geneva 27, Switzerland (Telephone Number in U.S. (518) 436-9686); *World Health Statistics Annual.*

PUERTO RICO - GOATS - See PUERTO RICO - LIVESTOCK AND POULTRY

PUERTO RICO - GOVERNMENT

G.K. Hall and Company, 70 Lincoln Street, Boston, Massachusetts 02111 (617) 423-3990; *The World in Figures.*

PUERTO RICO - GRAIN PRODUCTION - See PUERTO RICO - CROPS

PUERTO RICO - GREEN PEPPER AND CHILIE PRODUCTION - See PUERTO RICO - CROPS

PUERTO RICO - GROSS DOMESTIC PRODUCT

Euromonitor Publications Limited, 87-88 Turnmill Street, London EC1M 5QU, England; *International Marketing Data and Statistics.*

G.K. Hall and Company, 70 Lincoln Street, Boston, Massachusetts 02111 (617) 423-3990; *The World in Figures.*

Statistical Office of the United Nations, Publishing Service, New York, New York 10017 (800) 253-9646; *Statistical Yearbook.*

Time Books, 201 East 50th Street, New York, New York 10022 (212) 751-2600; *The Economist Book of Vital World Statistics.*

PUERTO RICO - GROSS NATIONAL PRODUCT

Euromonitor Publications Limited, 87-88 Turnmill Street, London EC1M 5QU, England; *International Marketing Data and Statistics.*

PUERTO RICO - HEALTH

G.K. Hall and Company, 70 Lincoln Street, Boston, Massachusetts 02111 (617) 423-3990; *The World in Figures.*

Statistical Office of the United Nations, Publishing Service, New York, New York 10017 (800) 253-9646; *Statistical Yearbook.*

Time Books, 201 East 50th Street, New York, New York 10022 (212) 751-2600; *The Economist Book of Vital World Statistics.*

World Health Organization, Office of Publications, Avenue Appia, CH-1211 Geneva 27, Switzerland (Telephone Number in U.S. (518) 436-9686); *World Health Statistics Annual.*

PUERTO RICO - HIDE PRODUCTION

Food and Agricultural Organization of the United Nations (FAO), Via delle Terme di Caracalla, 00100 Rome, Italy (Telephone Number in U.S. (202) 653-2400); *Production Yearbook.*

PUERTO RICO - HIGHWAYS

G.K. Hall and Company, 70 Lincoln Street, Boston, Massachusetts 02111 (617) 423-3990; *The World in Figures.*

PUERTO RICO - HORSES - See PUERTO RICO - LIVESTOCK AND POULTRY

PUERTO RICO - HOURS OF WORK - See PUERTO RICO - EMPLOYMENT

PUERTO RICO - ILLITERATE POPULATION

G.K. Hall and Company, 70 Lincoln Street, Boston, Massachusetts 02111 (617) 423-3990; *The World in Figures.*

United Nations Educational, Scientific and Cultural Organization (UNESCO), 7 Place de Fontenoy, F-75700 Paris, France (Telephone Number in U.S. (212) 963-5981); *Statistical Yearbook.*

PUERTO RICO - IMPORTS

American Automobile Manufacturers Association, 1401 H Street, NW, Suite 900, Washington, D.C. 20005 (202) 326-5500; *World Motor Vehicle Data.*

Euromonitor Publications Limited, 87-88 Turnmill Street, London EC1M 5QU, England; *International Marketing Data and Statistics.*

Food and Agricultural Organization of the United Nations (FAO) Via delle Terme di Caracalla, 00100 Rome, Italy (Telephone Number in U.S. (202) 653-2400); *The State of Food and Agriculture.*

G.K. Hall and Company, 70 Lincoln Street, Boston, Massachusetts 02111 (617) 423-3990; *The World in Figures.*

PUERTO RICO - INDUSTRY

Euromonitor Publications Limited, 87-88 Turnmill Street, London EC1M 5QU, England; *International Marketing Data and Statistics.*

Gale Research Incorporated, 835 Penobscot Building, Detroit, Michigan 48226 (800) 877-4253; *International Historical Statistics The Americas and Australasia.*

G.K. Hall and Company, 70 Lincoln Street, Boston, Massachusetts 02111 (617) 423-3990; *The World in Figures.*

International Labour Office, I.L.O. Publications, CH-1211, Geneva 22, Switzerland; *Yearbook of Labour Statistics.*

Time Books, 201 East 50th Street, New York, New York 10022 (212) 751-2600; *The Economist Book of Vital World Statistics.*

PUERTO RICO - INFANT AND MATERNAL MORTALITY

Statistical Office of the United Nations, Publishing Service, New York, New York 10017 (800) 253-9646; *Demographic Yearbook*, and *Statistical Yearbook.*

Time Books, 201 East 50th Street, New York, New York 10022 (212) 751-2600; *The Economist Book of Vital World Statistics.*

World Health Organization, Office of Publications, Avenue Appia, CH-1211 Geneva 27, Switzerland (Telephone Number in U.S. (518) 436-9686); *World Health Statistics Annual.*

PUERTO RICO - INTERNAL TRADE

Statistical Office of the United Nations, Publishing Service, New York, New York 10017 (800) 253-9646; *Statistical Yearbook.*

PUERTO RICO - IRRIGATION

Euromonitor Publications Limited, 87-88 Turnmill Street, London EC1M 5QU, England; *International Marketing Data and Statistics.*

PUERTO RICO - LABOR FORCE

Euromonitor Publications Limited, 87-88 Turnmill Street, London EC1M 5QU, England; *International Marketing Data and Statistics.*

Food and Agricultural Organization of the United Nations (FAO) Via delle Terme di Caracalla, 00100 Rome, Italy (Telephone Number in U.S. (202) 653-2400); *The State of Food and Agriculture.*

Gale Research Incorporated, 835 Penobscot Building, Detroit, Michigan 48226 (800) 877-4253; *International Historical Statistics The Americas and Australasia.*

G.K. Hall and Company, 70 Lincoln Street, Boston, Massachusetts 02111 (617) 423-3990; *The World in Figures.*

PUERTO RICO - LABOR PRODUCTIVITY

International Labour Office, I.L.O. Publications, CH-1211, Geneva 22, Switzerland; *Yearbook of Labour Statistics.*

PUERTO RICO - LAND USE

Euromonitor Publications Limited, 87-88 Turnmill Street, London EC1M 5QU, England; *International Marketing Data and Statistics.*

Food and Agricultural Organization of the United Nations (FAO), Via delle Terme di Caracalla, 00100 Rome, Italy (Telephone Number in U.S. (202) 653-2400); *Production Yearbook.*

G.K. Hall and Company, 70 Lincoln Street, Boston, Massachusetts 02111 (617) 423-3990; *The World in Figures.*

PUERTO RICO - LIBRARIES

United Nations Educational, Scientific and Cultural Organization (UNESCO), 7 Place de Fontenoy, F-75700 Paris, France (Telephone Number in U.S. (212) 963-5981); *Statistical Yearbook.*

PUERTO RICO - LIVESTOCK AND POULTRY

Euromonitor Publications Limited, 87-88 Turnmill Street, London EC1M 5QU, England; *European Marketing Data and Statistics*, and *International Marketing Data and Statistics.*

Facts on File, 460 Park Avenue South, New York, New York 10016 (800) 443-8323; *The New Book of World Rankings.*

Food and Agricultural Organization of the United Nations (FAO), Via delle Terme di Caracalla, 00100 Rome, Italy (Telephone Number in U.S. (202) 653-2400); *Production Yearbook*, and *The State of Food and Agriculture.*

G.K. Hall and Company, 70 Lincoln Street, Boston, Massachusetts 02111 (617) 423-3990; *The World in Figures.*

Organisation for Economic Co-operation and Development (OECD), 2 rue Andre-Pascal, 75 Paris 16, France (Telephone Number in U.S. (202) 785-6323); *Economic Accounts for Agriculture*, and *Meat Balances in OECD Member Countries.*

Statistical Office of the United Nations, Publishing Service, New York, New York 10017 (800) 253-9646; *Statistical Yearbook.*

PUERTO RICO - LIVING LEVELS

G.K. Hall and Company, 70 Lincoln Street, Boston, Massachusetts 02111 (617) 423-3990; *The World in Figures.*

Time Books, 201 East 50th Street, New York, New York 10022 (212) 751-2600; *The Economist Book of Vital World Statistics*.

PUERTO RICO - MANUFACTURING

American Automobile Manufacturers Association, 1401 H Street, NW, Suite 900, Washington, D.C. 20005 (202) 326-5500; *World Motor Vehicle Data*.

G.K. Hall and Company, 70 Lincoln Street, Boston, Massachusetts 02111 (617) 423-3990; *The World in Figures*.

Statistical Office of the United Nations, Publishing Service, New York, New York 10017 (800) 253-9646; *Statistical Yearbook*.

PUERTO RICO - MARRIAGE RATES

Statistical Office of the United Nations, Publishing Service, New York, New York 10017 (800) 253-9646; *Demographic Yearbook*, and *Statistical Yearbook*.

PUERTO RICO - MEAT PRODUCTION - See PUERTO RICO - LIVESTOCK AND POULTRY

PUERTO RICO - MERCHANT SHIPPING

G.K. Hall and Company, 70 Lincoln Street, Boston, Massachusetts 02111 (617) 423-3990; *The World in Figures*.

Time Books, 201 East 50th Street, New York, New York 10022 (212) 751-2600; *The Economist Book of Vital World Statistics*.

PUERTO RICO - MILITARY

G.K. Hall and Company, 70 Lincoln Street, Boston, Massachusetts 02111 (617) 423-3990; *The World in Figures*.

PUERTO RICO - MILK PRODUCTION - See PUERTO RICO - DAIRY PRODUCTS

PUERTO RICO - MINING AND MINERAL PRODUCTS

G.K. Hall and Company, 70 Lincoln Street, Boston, Massachusetts 02111 (617) 423-3990; *The World in Figures*.

Statistical Office of the United Nations, Publishing Service, New York, New York 10017 (800) 253-9646; *Statistical Yearbook*.

PUERTO RICO - MONEY EXCHANGE RATES

Euromonitor Publications Limited, 87-88 Turnmill Street, London EC1M 5QU, England; *International Marketing Data and Statistics*.

PUERTO RICO - MONEY RESERVES

Euromonitor Publications Limited, 87-88 Turnmill Street, London EC1M 5QU, England; *International Marketing Data and Statistics*.

PUERTO RICO - MONEY SUPPLY

Euromonitor Publications Limited, 87-88 Turnmill Street, London EC1M 5QU, England; *International Marketing Data and Statistics*.

G.K. Hall and Company, 70 Lincoln Street, Boston, Massachusetts 02111 (617) 423-3990; *The World in Figures*.

PUERTO RICO - MOTION PICTURES

Statistical Office of the United Nations, Publishing Service, New York, New York 10017 (800) 253-9646; *Statistical Yearbook*.

PUERTO RICO - MOTOR VEHICLE PRODUCTION

American Automobile Manufacturers Association, 1401 H Street, NW, Suite 900, Washington, D.C. 20005 (202) 326-5500; *World Motor Vehicle Data*.

PUERTO RICO - MOTOR VEHICLES IN USE

American Automobile Manufacturers Association, 1401 H Street, NW, Suite 900, Washington, D.C. 20005 (202) 326-5500; *World Motor Vehicle Data*.

G.K. Hall and Company, 70 Lincoln Street, Boston, Massachusetts 02111 (617) 423-3990; *The World in Figures*.

Statistical Office of the United Nations, Publishing Service, New York, New York 10017 (800) 253-9646; *Statistical Yearbook*.

Time Books, 201 East 50th Street, New York, New York 10022 (212) 751-2600; *The Economist Book of Vital World Statistics*.

PUERTO RICO - MULES

PUERTO RICO - MUSEUMS

United Nations Educational, Scientific and Cultural Organization (UNESCO), 7 Place de Fontenoy, F-75700 Paris, France (Telephone Number in U.S. (212) 963-5981); *Statistical Yearbook*.

PUERTO RICO - NATALITY - See PUERTO RICO - BIRTH RATES

PUERTO RICO - NATIONAL ACCOUNTS

Gale Research Incorporated, 835 Penobscot Building, Detroit, Michigan 48226 (800) 877-4253; *International Historical Statistics The Americas and Australasia*.

Statistical Office of the United Nations, Publishing Service, New York, New York 10017 (800) 253-9646; *National Accounts Statistics*, and *Statistical Yearbook*.

PUERTO RICO - NATIONAL INCOME

G.K. Hall and Company, 70 Lincoln Street, Boston, Massachusetts 02111 (617) 423-3990; *The World in Figures*.

Statistical Office of the United Nations, Publishing Service, New York, New York 10017 (800) 253-9646; *Statistical Yearbook*.

PUERTO RICO - NATIONAL PRODUCT

Statistical Office of the United Nations, Publishing Service, New York, New York 10017 (800) 253-9646; *Statistical Yearbook*.

PUERTO RICO - NEWSPAPER PRODUCTION - See PUERTO RICO - FORESTRY AND FOREST PRODUCTS

PUERTO RICO - OCCUPATIONS - See PUERTO RICO - LABOR FORCE

PUERTO RICO - PESTICIDE USE

Food and Agricultural Organization of the United Nations (FAO) Via delle Terme di Caracalla, 00100 Rome, Italy (Telephone Number in U.S. (202) 653-2400); *The State of Food and Agriculture*.

PUERTO RICO - PETROLEUM INDUSTRY

Food and Agricultural Organization of the United Nations (FAO) Via delle Terme di Caracalla, 00100 Rome, Italy (Telephone Number in U.S. (202) 653-2400); *The State of Food and Agriculture.*

G.K. Hall and Company, 70 Lincoln Street, Boston, Massachusetts 02111 (617) 423-3990; *The World in Figures.*

Statistical Office of the United Nations, Publishing Service, New York, New York 10017 (800) 253-9646; *Statistical Yearbook.*

PUERTO RICO - PIGS - See PUERTO RICO - LIVESTOCK AND POULTRY

PUERTO RICO - POPULATION

Euromonitor Publications Limited, 87-88 Turnmill Street, London EC1M 5QU, England; *International Marketing Data and Statistics.*

Food and Agricultural Organization of the United Nations (FAO), Via delle Terme di Caracalla, 00100 Rome, Italy (Telephone Number in U.S. (202) 653-2400); *Production Yearbook.*

Gale Research Incorporated, 835 Penobscot Building, Detroit, Michigan 48226 (800) 877-4253; *International Historical Statistics The Americas and Australasia.*

G.K. Hall and Company, 70 Lincoln Street, Boston, Massachusetts 02111 (617) 423-3990; *The World in Figures.*

International Labour Office, I.L.O. Publications, CH-1211, Geneva 22, Switzerland; *Yearbook of Labour Statistics.*

Statistical Office of the United Nations, Publishing Service, New York, New York 10017 (800) 253-9646; *Demographic Yearbook,* and *Statistical Yearbook.*

Time Books, 201 East 50th Street, New York, New York 10022 (212) 751-2600; *The Economist Book of Vital World Statistics.*

United Nations Educational, Scientific and Cultural Organization (UNESCO), 7 Place de Fontenoy, F-75700 Paris, France (Telephone Number in U.S. (212) 963-5981); *Statistical Yearbook.*

World Health Organization, Office of Publications, Avenue Appia, CH-1211 Geneva 27, Switzerland (Telephone Number in U.S. (518) 436-9686); *World Health Statistics Annual.*

PUERTO RICO - PRICES

Food and Agricultural Organization of the United Nations (FAO), Via delle Terme di Caracalla, 00100 Rome, Italy (Telephone Number in U.S. (202) 653-2400); *Production Yearbook,* and *The State of Food and Agriculture.*

Gale Research Incorporated, 835 Penobscot Building, Detroit, Michigan 48226 (800) 877-4253; *International Historical Statistics The Americas and Australasia.*

G.K. Hall and Company, 70 Lincoln Street, Boston, Massachusetts 02111 (617) 423-3990; *The World in Figures.*

International Labour Office, I.L.O. Publications, CH-1211, Geneva 22, Switzerland; *Yearbook of Labour Statistics.*

PUERTO RICO - PRODUCTION

American Automobile Manufacturers Association, 1401 H Street, NW, Suite 900, Washington, D.C. 20005 (202) 326-5500; *World Motor Vehicle Data.*

G.K. Hall and Company, 70 Lincoln Street, Boston, Massachusetts 02111 (617) 423-3990; *The World in Figures.*

PUERTO RICO - PRODUCTIVITY

Euromonitor Publications Limited, 87-88 Turnmill Street, London EC1M 5QU, England; *International Marketing Data and Statistics.*

PUERTO RICO - RADIO BROADCASTING - See PUERTO RICO - BROADCASTING

PUERTO RICO - RAILWAYS

G.K. Hall and Company, 70 Lincoln Street, Boston, Massachusetts 02111 (617) 423-3990; *The World in Figures.*

PUERTO RICO - RENT PRICES

International Labour Office, I.L.O. Publications, CH-1211, Geneva 22, Switzerland; *Yearbook of Labour Statistics.*

PUERTO RICO - RETAIL TRADE

G.K. Hall and Company, 70 Lincoln Street, Boston, Massachusetts 02111 (617) 423-3990; *The World in Figures.*

Statistical Office of the United Nations, Publishing Service, New York, New York 10017 (800) 253-9646; *Statistical Yearbook.*

PUERTO RICO - RICE PRODUCTION - See PUERTO RICO - CROPS

PUERTO RICO - ROOT AND TUBER PRODUCTION - See PUERTO RICO - CROPS

PUERTO RICO - SALT PRODUCTION - See PUERTO RICO - MINING AND MINERAL PRODUCTS

PUERTO RICO - SHEEP - See PUERTO RICO - LIVESTOCK AND POULTRY

PUERTO RICO - SOCIAL DATA

G.K. Hall and Company, 70 Lincoln Street, Boston, Massachusetts 02111 (617) 423-3990; *The World in Figures.*

PUERTO RICO - STATE BUDGET REVENUE AND EXPENDITURES

Euromonitor Publications Limited, 87-88 Turnmill Street, London EC1M 5QU, England; *International Marketing Data and Statistics.*

PUERTO RICO - STOCKS - COMMODITY - MARKET PRICE - INDEX

Food and Agricultural Organization of the United Nations (FAO) Via delle Terme di Caracalla, 00100 Rome, Italy (Telephone Number in U.S. (202) 653-2400); *The State of Food and Agriculture.*

PUERTO RICO - SUGAR PRODUCTION AND CONSUMPTION - See PUERTO RICO - CROPS

PUERTO RICO - TAXATION

G.K. Hall and Company, 70 Lincoln Street, Boston, Massachusetts 02111 (617) 423-3990; *The World in Figures.*

PUERTO RICO - TAX REVENUE - See PUERTO RICO - TAXATION

PUERTO RICO - TELEPHONES IN USE

American Telephone and Telegraph Company, 26 Parsippany Road, Whippany, New Jersey 07981 (800) 338-4038; *The World's Telephones*.

G.K. Hall and Company, 70 Lincoln Street, Boston, Massachusetts 02111 (617) 423-3990; *The World in Figures*.

Statistical Office of the United Nations, Publishing Service, New York, New York 10017 (800) 253-9646; *Statistical Yearbook*.

PUERTO RICO - TELEVISION BROADCASTING - See PUERTO RICO - BROADCASTING

PUERTO RICO - TEXTILE INDUSTRY

G.K. Hall and Company, 70 Lincoln Street, Boston, Massachusetts 02111 (617) 423-3990; *The World in Figures*.

PUERTO RICO - TOBACCO PRODUCTION

Statistical Office of the United Nations, Publishing Service, New York, New York 10017 (800) 253-9646; *Statistical Yearbook*.

PUERTO RICO - TOURISM

G.K. Hall and Company, 70 Lincoln Street, Boston, Massachusetts 02111 (617) 423-3990; *The World in Figures*.

Statistical Office of the United Nations, Publishing Service, New York, New York 10017 (800) 253-9646; *Statistical Yearbook*.

Time Books, 201 East 50th Street, New York, New York 10022 (212) 751-2600; *The Economist Book of Vital World Statistics*.

World Tourism Organization, Calle Capitan Haya 42, E-28020 Madrid, Spain; *Yearbook of Tourism Statistics*.

PUERTO RICO - TRACTORS IN USE

Statistical Office of the United Nations, Publishing Service, New York, New York 10017 (800) 253-9646; *Statistical Yearbook*.

PUERTO RICO - TRADE - See PUERTO RICO - FOREIGN TRADE

PUERTO RICO - TRANSPORTATION AND COMMUNICATIONS

Gale Research Incorporated, 835 Penobscot Building, Detroit, Michigan 48226 (800) 877-4253; *International Historical Statistics The Americas and Australasia*.

G.K. Hall and Company, 70 Lincoln Street, Boston, Massachusetts 02111 (617) 423-3990; *The World in Figures*.

PUERTO RICO - UNEMPLOYMENT

Euromonitor Publications Limited, 87-88 Turnmill Street, London EC1M 5QU, England; *International Marketing Data and Statistics*.

International Labour Office, I.L.O. Publications, CH-1211, Geneva 22, Switzerland; *Yearbook of Labour Statistics*.

Statistical Office of the United Nations, Publishing Service, New York, New York 10017 (800) 253-9646; *Statistical Yearbook*.

PUERTO RICO - VITAL STATISTICS

Euromonitor Publications Limited, 87-88 Turnmill Street, London EC1M 5QU, England; *International Marketing Data and Statistics*.

Gale Research Incorporated, 835 Penobscot Building, Detroit, Michigan 48226 (800) 877-4253; *International Historical Statistics The Americas and Australasia*.

G.K. Hall and Company, 70 Lincoln Street, Boston, Massachusetts 02111 (617) 423-3990; *The World in Figures*.

Statistical Office of the United Nations, Publishing Service, New York, New York 10017 (800) 253-9646; *Statistical Yearbook*.

World Health Organization, Office of Publications, Avenue Appia, CH-1211 Geneva 27, Switzerland (Telephone Number in U.S. (518) 436-9686); *World Health Statistics Annual*.

PUERTO RICO - WAGES

G.K. Hall and Company, 70 Lincoln Street, Boston, Massachusetts 02111 (617) 423-3990; *The World in Figures*.

International Labour Office, I.L.O. Publications, CH-1211, Geneva 22, Switzerland; *Yearbook of Labour Statistics*.

Statistical Office of the United Nations, Publishing Service, New York, New York 10017 (800) 253-9646; *Statistical Yearbook*.

PUERTO RICO - WEATHER

G.K. Hall and Company, 70 Lincoln Street, Boston, Massachusetts 02111 (617) 423-3990; *The World in Figures*.

PUERTO RICO - WHOLESALE PRICES

Statistical Office of the United Nations, Publishing Service, New York, New York 10017 (800) 253-9646; *Statistical Yearbook*.

PUERTO RICO - WHOLESALE TRADE

Statistical Office of the United Nations, Publishing Service, New York, New York 10017 (800) 253-9646; *Statistical Yearbook*.

PULMONARY DISEASES

U.S. Department of Health and Human Services, Centers for Disease Control, 1600 Clifton Road, NE, Atlanta, Georgia 30333 (404) 639-3311; *Summary of Notifiable Disease, United States, Morbidity and Mortality Weekly Report*.

U.S. Department of Health and Human Services, National Center for Health Statistics, 3700 East-West Highway, Hyattsville, Maryland 20782 (301) 436-8500; *Vital and Health Statistics, Vital Statistics of the United States, Health, United States, Monthly Vital Statistics Report*, and unpublished data.

PULPWOOD

U.S. Department of Agriculture, Forest Service, Fourteenth Street and Independence Avenue, SW, Washington, D.C. 20250 (202) 720-3760; *United States Timber Production, Trade, Consumption, and Price Statistics*.

U.S. Department of Commerce, Bureau of the Census, Suitland, Maryland 20233 (301) 763-4040; *Current Industrial Reports, Census of Manufactures*, and *Annual Survey of Manufactures*.

PUMICE AND PUMICITE

U.S. Department of the Interior, Bureau of Mines, 810 Seventh Street, NW, Washington, D.C. 20241 (202) 501-9649; *Annual Report*, and *Mineral Commodities Summaries*.

PUMPS AND COMPRESSORS

U.S. Department of Commerce, Bureau of the Census, Suitland, Maryland 20233 (301) 763-4040; *Current Industrial Reports*.

PURCHASING POWER OF THE DOLLAR

U.S. Department of Commerce, Bureau of Economic Analysis, Fourteenth Street between Constitution Avenue and E Street, NW, Washington, D.C. 20230 (202) 606-9900; *Survey of Current Business*.

PYRITES

U.S. Department of the Interior, Bureau of Mines, 810 Seventh Street, NW, Washington, D.C. 20241 (202) 501-9649; *Annual Report*, and *Mineral Commodities Summaries*.

Q

Qatar - National Statistical Office

Central Statistical Organisation, Post Office Box 7283, Doha, Qatar.

Qatar - Primary Statistics Source

Central Statistical Organization, Post Office Box 7283, Doha, Qatar; *Annual Statistical Abstract*.

QATAR - AGRICULTURE

Economic Commission for Western Asia, Post Office Box 27, Baghdad, Iraq; *Statistical Abstract of Western Asia*.

Euromonitor Publications Limited, 87-88 Turnmill Street, London EC1M 5QU, England; *Middle East Economic Handbook*.

Facts on File, 460 Park Avenue South, New York, New York 10016 (800) 443-8323; *The New Book of World Rankings*.

Federal Statistical Office, Gustav - Stresemann - Ring 11, D-6200 Wiesbaden, Germany; *Qatar*.

Food and Agricultural Organization of the United Nations (FAO) Via delle Terme di Caracalla, 00100 Rome, Italy (Telephone Number in U.S. (202) 653-2400); *Production Yearbook, The State of Food and Agriculture*, and *Trade Yearbook*.

G.K. Hall and Company, 70 Lincoln Street, Boston, Massachusetts 02111 (617) 423-3990; *The World in Figures*.

Presidency of the Council of Ministers, Central Statistical Organisation, Doha, Qatar; *Annual Statistical Abstract State of Qatar*.

Times Books, 201 East 50th Street, New York, New York 10022 (212) 751-2600; *The Economist Book of Vital World Statistics*.

QATAR - AIRLINE SERVICE

Economic Commission for Western Asia, Post Office Box 27, Baghdad, Iraq; *Statistical Abstract of Western Asia*.

Facts on File, 460 Park Avenue South, New York, New York 10016 (800) 443-8323; *The New Book of World Rankings*.

G.K. Hall and Company, 70 Lincoln Street, Boston, Massachusetts 02111 (617) 423-3990; *The World in Figures*.

Times Books, 201 East 50th Street, New York, New York 10022 (212) 751-2600; *The Economist Book of Vital World Statistics*.

QATAR - ALUMINUM PRODUCTION AND CONSUMPTION - See QATAR - MINING AND MINERAL PRODUCTS

QATAR - ANIMAL HEALTH

Food and Agricultural Organization of the United Nations (FAO), Via delle Terme di Caracalla, 00100 Rome, Italy (Telephone Number in U.S. (202) 653-2400); *Animal Health Yearbook*.

QATAR - AREA AND DENSITY OF POPULATION

Euromonitor Publications Limited, 87-88 Turnmill Street, London EC1M 5QU, England; *Middle East Economic Handbook*.

Economic Commission for Western Asia, Post Office Box 27, Baghdad, Iraq; *Statistical Abstract of Western Asia*.

Facts on File, 460 Park Avenue South, New York, New York 10016 (800) 443-8323; *The New Book of World Rankings*.

Federal Statistical Office, Gustav - Stresemann - Ring 11, D-6200 Wiesbaden, Germany; *Qatar*.

Food and Agricultural Organization of the United Nations (FAO) Via delle Terme di Caracalla, 00100 Rome, Italy (Telephone Number in U.S. (202) 653-2400); *The State of Food and Agriculture*.

G.K. Hall and Company, 70 Lincoln Street, Boston, Massachusetts 02111 (617) 423-3990; *The World in Figures*.

Statistical Office of the United Nations, Publishing Service, New York, New York 10017 (800) 253-9646; *Statistical Yearbook*.

Times Books, 201 East 50th Street, New York, New York 10022 (212) 751-2600; *The Economist Book of Vital World Statistics*.

United Nations Educational, Scientific and Cultural Organization (UNESCO), 7 Place de Fontenoy, F-75700 Paris, France (Telephone Number in U.S. (212) 963-5981); *Statistical Yearbook*.

QATAR - ARMS EXPORTS AND IMPORTS

U.S. Arms Control and Disarmament Agency, 320 Twenty-first Street, NW, Washington, D.C. 20451 (202) 647-8677; *World Military Expenditures and Arms Transfers*.

QATAR - BALANCE OF PAYMENTS

Economic Commission for Western Asia, Post Office Box 27, Baghdad, Iraq; *Statistical Abstract of Western Asia*.

The Economist Intelligence Unit, 111 West 57th Street, New York, New York 10019 (800) 938-4685; *The World Market Atlas.*

Federal Statistical Office, Gustav - Stresemann - Ring 11, D-6200 Wiesbaden, Germany; *Qatar.*

G.K. Hall and Company, 70 Lincoln Street, Boston, Massachusetts 02111 (617) 423-3990; *The World in Figures.*

QATAR - BALANCE OF TRADE

Economic Commission for Western Asia, Post Office Box 27, Baghdad, Iraq; *Statistical Abstract of Western Asia.*

QATAR - BANKING

Economic Commission for Western Asia, Post Office Box 27, Baghdad, Iraq; *Statistical Abstract of Western Asia.*

Facts on File, 460 Park Avenue South, New York, New York 10016 (800) 443-8323; *The New Book of World Rankings.*

G.K. Hall and Company, 70 Lincoln Street, Boston, Massachusetts 02111 (617) 423-3990; *The World in Figures.*

International Monetary Fund, 700 Nineteenth Street, NW, Washington, D.C. 20431 (202) 623-7000; *International Financial Statistics.*

Presidency of the Council of Ministers, Central Statistical Organisation, Doha, Qatar; *Annual Statistical Abstract State of Qatar.*

QATAR - BARLEY PRODUCTION - See QATAR - CROPS

QATAR - BEER PRODUCTION

Facts on File, 460 Park Avenue South, New York, New York 10016 (800) 443-8323; *The New Book of World Rankings.*

QATAR - BIRTH RATES

Euromonitor Publications Limited, 87-88 Turnmill Street, London EC1M 5QU, England; *Middle East Economic Handbook.*

Facts on File, 460 Park Avenue South, New York, New York 10016 (800) 443-8323; *The New Book of World Rankings.*

Statistical Office of the United Nations, Publishing Service, New York, New York 10017 (800) 253-9646; *Demographic Yearbook.*

Times Books, 201 East 50th Street, New York, New York 10022 (212) 751-2600; *The Economist Book of Vital World Statistics.*

QATAR - BONDS

G.K. Hall and Company, 70 Lincoln Street, Boston, Massachusetts 02111 (617) 423-3990; *The World in Figures.*

QATAR - BOOK PRODUCTION

G.K. Hall and Company, 70 Lincoln Street, Boston, Massachusetts 02111 (617) 423-3990; *The World in Figures.*

United Nations Educational, Scientific and Cultural Organization (UNESCO), 7 Place de Fontenoy, F-75700 Paris, France (Telephone Number in U.S. (212) 963-5981); *Statistical Yearbook.*

QATAR - BROADCASTING

Billboard Limited, Post Office Box 9027, 1006 AA Amsterdam, The Netherlands (Telephone Number in U.S. (212) 764-7300); *World Radio TV Handbook.*

Facts on File, 460 Park Avenue South, New York, New York 10016 (800) 443-8323; *The New Book of World Rankings.*

G.K. Hall and Company, 70 Lincoln Street, Boston, Massachusetts 02111 (617) 423-3990; *The World in Figures.*

Times Books, 201 East 50th Street, New York, New York 10022 (212) 751-2600; *The Economist Book of Vital World Statistics.*

United Nations Educational, Scientific and Cultural Organization (UNESCO), 7 Place de Fontenoy, F-75700 Paris, France (Telephone Number in U.S. (212) 963-5981); *Statistical Yearbook.*

QATAR - BUSINESS

G.K. Hall and Company, 70 Lincoln Street, Boston, Massachusetts 02111 (617) 423-3990; *The World in Figures.*

QATAR - CALORIE SUPPLY

Food and Agricultural Organization of the United Nations (FAO) Via delle Terme di Caracalla, 00100 Rome, Italy (Telephone Number in U.S. (202) 653-2400); *The State of Food and Agriculture.*

QATAR - CATTLE - See QATAR - LIVESTOCK AND POULTRY

QATAR - CEMENT PRODUCTION - See QATAR - MINING AND MINERAL PRODUCTS

QATAR - CHEMICAL (ORGANIC) PRODUCTION - See QATAR - MINING AND MINERAL PRODUCTS

QATAR - CIGARETTE PRODUCTION - See QATAR - TOBACCO PRODUCTION

QATAR - CLASS STRUCTURE

G.K. Hall and Company, 70 Lincoln Street, Boston, Massachusetts 02111 (617) 423-3990; *The World in Figures.*

QATAR - CLIMATE

Facts on File, 460 Park Avenue South, New York, New York 10016 (800) 443-8323; *The New Book of World Rankings.*

G.K. Hall and Company, 70 Lincoln Street, Boston, Massachusetts 02111 (617) 423-3990; *The World in Figures.*

QATAR - COAL PRODUCTION - See QATAR - MINING AND MINERAL PRODUCTS

QATAR - COFFEE PRODUCTION AND CONSUMPTION - See QATAR CROPS

QATAR - COMMUNICATIONS

Economic Commission for Western Asia, Post Office Box 27, Baghdad, Iraq; *Statistical Abstract of Western Asia.*

Federal Statistical Office, Gustav - Stresemann - Ring 11, D-6200 Wiesbaden, Germany; *Qatar.*

G.K. Hall and Company, 70 Lincoln Street, Boston, Massachusetts 02111 (617) 423-3990; *The World in Figures*.

Presidency of the Council of Ministers, Central Statistical Organisation, Doha, Qatar; *Annual Statistical Abstract State of Qatar*.

QATAR - CONSTRUCTION

Facts on File, 460 Park Avenue South, New York, New York 10016 (800) 443-8323; *The New Book of World Rankings*.

QATAR - CONSUMER PRICE INDEX

G.K. Hall and Company, 70 Lincoln Street, Boston, Massachusetts 02111 (617) 423-3990; *The World in Figures*.

QATAR - CONSUMER PRICES

Times Books, 201 East 50th Street, New York, New York 10022 (212) 751-2600; *The Economist Book of Vital World Statistics*.

QATAR - CONSUMPTION

Euromonitor Publications Limited, 87-88 Turnmill Street, London EC1M 5QU, England; *Middle East Economic Handbook*.

G.K. Hall and Company, 70 Lincoln Street, Boston, Massachusetts 02111 (617) 423-3990; *The World in Figures*.

QATAR - COPPER PRODUCTION AND CONSUMPTION - See QATAR - MINING AND MINERAL PRODUCTS

QATAR - CORN PRODUCTION - See QATAR - CROPS

QATAR - CORPORATE TAXES - See QATAR - TAXATION

QATAR - COTTON PRODUCTION - See QATAR - CROPS

QATAR - CRIME

International Criminal Police Organization (INTERPOL), 26 rue Armengaud, 92210 Saint Cloud, France; *International Crime Statistics*.

Yale University Press, Yale Station, New Haven, Connecticut 06520 (203) 432-0940; *Violence and Crime in Cross-National Perspective*.

QATAR - CROPS

Facts on File, 460 Park Avenue South, New York, New York 10016 (800) 443-8323; *The New Book of World Rankings*.

Food and Agricultural Organization of the United Nations (FAO) Via delle Terme di Caracalla, 00100 Rome, Italy (Telephone Number in U.S. (202) 653-2400); *The State of Food and Agriculture*.

G.K. Hall and Company, 70 Lincoln Street, Boston, Massachusetts 02111 (617) 423-3990; *The World in Figures*.

QATAR - CUSTOMS DUTIES

G.K. Hall and Company, 70 Lincoln Street, Boston, Massachusetts 02111 (617) 423-3990; *The World in Figures*.

QATAR - DAIRY PRODUCTS

Economic Commission for Western Asia, Post Office Box 27, Baghdad, Iraq; *Statistical Abstract of Western Asia*.

Facts on File, 460 Park Avenue South, New York, New York 10016 (800) 443-8323; *The New Book of World Rankings*.

Food and Agricultural Organization of the United Nations (FAO) Via delle Terme di Caracalla, 00100 Rome, Italy (Telephone Number in U.S. (202) 653-2400); *Production Yearbook*, and *The State of Food and Agriculture*.

QATAR - DEATH RATES

Euromonitor Publications Limited, 87-88 Turnmill Street, London EC1M 5QU, England; *Middle East Economic Handbook*.

G.K. Hall and Company, 70 Lincoln Street, Boston, Massachusetts 02111 (617) 423-3990; *The World in Figures*.

Times Books, 201 East 50th Street, New York, New York 10022 (212) 751-2600; *The Economist Book of Vital World Statistics*.

World Health Organization, Office of Publications, Avenue Appia, CH-1211 Geneva 27, Switzerland (Telephone Number in U.S. (518) 436-9686); *World Health Statistics Annual*.

QATAR - DEFENSE EXPENDITURES

G.K. Hall and Company, 70 Lincoln Street, Boston, Massachusetts 02111 (617) 423-3990; *The World in Figures*.

U.S. Arms Control and Disarmament Agency, 320 Twenty-first Street, NW, Washington, D.C. 20451 (202) 647-8677; *World Military Expenditures and Arms Transfers*.

QATAR - DEMOGRAPHY

Facts on File, 460 Park Avenue South, New York, New York 10016 (800) 443-8323; *The New Book of World Rankings*.

G.K. Hall and Company, 70 Lincoln Street, Boston, Massachusetts 02111 (617) 423-3990; *The World in Figures*.

QATAR - DEVELOPMENT ASSISTANCE

G.K. Hall and Company, 70 Lincoln Street, Boston, Massachusetts 02111 (617) 423-3990; *The World in Figures*.

Statistical Office of the United Nations, Publishing Service, New York, New York 10017 (800) 253-9646; *Statistical Yearbook*.

QATAR - DIAMOND PRODUCTION - See QATAR - MINING AND MINERAL PRODUCTS

QATAR - DISEASE

G.K. Hall and Company, 70 Lincoln Street, Boston, Massachusetts 02111 (617) 423-3990; *The World in Figures*.

QATAR - DIVORCE RATES

Facts on File, 460 Park Avenue South, New York, New York 10016 (800) 443-8323; *The New Book of World Rankings*.

Statistical Office of the United Nations, Publishing Service, New York, New York 10017 (800) 253-9646; *Demographic Yearbook*.

QATAR - DOMESTIC PRODUCT

G.K. Hall and Company, 70 Lincoln Street, Boston, Massachusetts 02111 (617) 423-3990; *The World in Figures*.

QATAR - ECONOMY

Facts on File, 460 Park Avenue South, New York, New York 10016 (800) 443-8323; *The New Book of World Rankings*.

G.K. Hall and Company, 70 Lincoln Street, Boston, Massachusetts 02111 (617) 423-3990; *The World in Figures*.

QATAR - EDUCATION

Economic Commission for Western Asia, Post Office Box 27, Baghdad, Iraq; *Statistical Abstract of Western Asia*.

The Economist Intelligence Unit, 111 West 57th Street, New York, New York 10019 (800) 938-4685; *The World Market Atlas*.

Euromonitor Publications Limited, 87-88 Turnmill Street, London EC1M 5QU, England; *Middle East Economic Handbook*.

Facts on File, 460 Park Avenue South, New York, New York 10016 (800) 443-8323; *The New Book of World Rankings*.

Federal Statistical Office, Gustav - Stresemann - Ring 11, D-6200 Wiesbaden, Germany; *Qatar*.

G.K. Hall and Company, 70 Lincoln Street, Boston, Massachusetts 02111 (617) 423-3990; *The World in Figures*.

Presidency of the Council of Ministers, Central Statistical Organisation, Doha, Qatar; *Annual Statistical Abstract State of Qatar*.

Times Books, 201 East 50th Street, New York, New York 10022 (212) 751-2600; *The Economist Book of Vital World Statistics*.

United Nations Educational, Scientific and Cultural Organization (UNESCO), 7 Place de Fontenoy, F-75700 Paris, France (Telephone Number in U.S. (212) 963-5981); *Statistical Yearbook*.

QATAR - EGG PRODUCTION AND CONSUMPTION - See QATAR - DAIRY PRODUCTS

QATAR - ELECTRICITY

Facts on File, 460 Park Avenue South, New York, New York 10016 (800) 443-8323; *The New Book of World Rankings*.

Penn Well Publishing Company, 1421 South Sheridan Road, Post Office Box 1260, Tulsa, Oklahoma 74101 (800) 752-9764; *International Energy Statistics Sourcebook*.

Presidency of the Council of Ministers, Central Statistical Organisation, Doha, Qatar; *Annual Statistical Abstract State of Qatar*.

Statistical Office of the United Nations, Publishing Service, New York, New York 10017 (800) 253-9646; *Statistical Yearbook*.

Times Books, 201 East 50th Street, New York, New York 10022 (212) 751-2600; *The Economist Book of Vital World Statistics*.

QATAR - EMPLOYMENT

Economic Commission for Western Asia, Post Office Box 27, Baghdad, Iraq; *Statistical Abstract of Western Asia*.

Euromonitor Publications Limited, 87-88 Turnmill Street, London EC1M 5QU, England; *Middle East Economic Handbook*.

Facts on File, 460 Park Avenue South, New York, New York 10016 (800) 443-8323; *The New Book of World Rankings*.

Federal Statistical Office, Gustav - Stresemann - Ring 11, D-6200 Wiesbaden, Germany; *Qatar*.

International Labour Office, I.L.O. Publications, CH-1211, Geneva 22, Switzerland; *Yearbook of Labour Statistics*.

QATAR - ENERGY

Economic Commission for Western Asia, Post Office Box 27, Baghdad, Iraq; *Statistical Abstract of Western Asia*.

Euromonitor Publications Limited, 87-88 Turnmill Street, London EC1M 5QU, England; *Middle East Economic Handbook*.

Facts on File, 460 Park Avenue South, New York, New York 10016 (800) 443-8323; *The New Book of World Rankings*.

Food and Agricultural Organization of the United Nations (FAO) Via delle Terme di Caracalla, 00100 Rome, Italy (Telephone Number in U.S. (202) 653-2400); *The State of Food and Agriculture*.

G.K. Hall and Company, 70 Lincoln Street, Boston, Massachusetts 02111 (617) 423-3990; *The World in Figures*.

Penn Well Publishing Company, 1421 South Sheridan Road, Post Office Box 1260, Tulsa, Oklahoma 74101 (800) 752-9764; *International Energy Statistics Sourcebook*.

Statistical Office of the United Nations, Publishing Service, New York, New York 10017 (800) 253-9646; *Energy Statistics Yearbook*, and *Statistical Yearbook*.

Times Books, 201 East 50th Street, New York, New York 10022 (212) 751-2600; *The Economist Book of Vital World Statistics*.

QATAR - EXCHANGE RATES

Euromonitor Publications Limited, 87-88 Turnmill Street, London EC1M 5QU, England; *Middle East Economic Handbook*.

International Monetary Fund, 700 Nineteenth Street, NW, Washington, D.C. 20431 (202) 623-7000; *International Financial Statistics*.

Organization of Petroleum Exporting Countries, Obere Donaustrasse 93, 1020 Vienna 2, Austria; *OPEC Annual Statistical Bulletin*.

Statistical Office of the United Nations, Publishing Service, New York, New York 10017 (800) 253-9646; *Statistical Yearbook*.

QATAR - EXPORTS

Economic Commission for Western Asia, Post Office Box 27, Baghdad, Iraq; *Statistical Abstract of Western Asia*.

The Economist Intelligence Unit, 111 West 57th Street, New York, New York 10019 (800) 938-4685; *The World Market Atlas*.

Euromonitor Publications Limited, 87-88 Turnmill Street, London EC1M 5QU, England; *Middle East Economic Handbook*.

Food and Agricultural Organization of the United Nations (FAO) Via delle Terme di Caracalla, 00100 Rome, Italy (Telephone Number in U.S. (202) 653-2400); *The State of Food and Agriculture*.

G.K. Hall and Company, 70 Lincoln Street, Boston, Massachusetts 02111 (617) 423-3990; *The World in Figures*.

International Monetary Fund, 700 Nineteenth Street, NW, Washington, D.C. 20431 (202) 623-7000; *Direction of Trade Statistics*, and *International Financial Statistics*.

Organization of Petroleum Exporting Countries, Obere Donaustrasse 93, 1020 Vienna 2, Austria; *OPEC Annual Statistical Bulletin*.

Times Books, 201 East 50th Street, New York, New York 10022 (212) 751-2600; *The Economist Book of Vital World Statistics*.

QATAR - EXTERNAL TRADE

Food and Agricultural Organization of the United Nations (FAO) Via delle Terme di Caracalla, 00100 Rome, Italy (Telephone Number in U.S. (202) 653-2400); *The State of Food and Agriculture*, and *Trade Yearbook*.

G.K. Hall and Company, 70 Lincoln Street, Boston, Massachusetts 02111 (617) 423-3990; *The World in Figures*.

QATAR - FARM CROPS - See QATAR - CROPS

QATAR - FERTILITY RATE

Facts on File, 460 Park Avenue South, New York, New York 10016 (800) 443-8323; *The New Book of World Rankings*.

Times Books, 201 East 50th Street, New York, New York 10022 (212) 751-2600; *The Economist Book of Vital World Statistics*.

QATAR - FERTILIZER

Food and Agricultural Organization of the United Nations (FAO), Via delle Terme di Caracalla, 00100 Rome, Italy (Telephone Number in U.S. (202) 653-2400); *Fertilizer Yearbook*, and *The State of Food and Agriculture*.

Statistical Office of the United Nations, Publishing Service, New York, New York 10017 (800) 253-9646; *Statistical Yearbook*.

QATAR - FETAL MORTALITY

Statistical Office of the United Nations, Publishing Service, New York, New York 10017 (800) 253-9646; *Demographic Yearbook*.

QATAR - FILM - See QATAR - MOTION PICTURES

QATAR - FINANCE

Economic Commission for Western Asia, Post Office Box 27, Baghdad, Iraq; *Statistical Abstract of Western Asia*.

Euromonitor Publications Limited, 87-88 Turnmill Street, London EC1M 5QU, England; *Middle East Economic Handbook*.

Facts on File, 460 Park Avenue South, New York, New York 10016 (800) 443-8323; *The New Book of World Rankings*.

Federal Statistical Office, Gustav - Stresemann - Ring 11, D-6200 Wiesbaden, Germany; *Qatar*.

G.K. Hall and Company, 70 Lincoln Street, Boston, Massachusetts 02111 (617) 423-3990; *The World in Figures*.

International Monetary Fund, 700 Nineteenth Street, NW, Washington, D.C. 20431 (202) 623-7000; *International Financial Statistics*.

QATAR - FISHERIES

Economic Commission for Western Asia, Post Office Box 27, Baghdad, Iraq; *Statistical Abstract of Western Asia*.

Facts on File, 460 Park Avenue South, New York, New York 10016 (800) 443-8323; *The New Book of World Rankings*.

Federal Statistical Office, Gustav - Stresemann - Ring 11, D-6200 Wiesbaden, Germany; *Qatar*.

Food and Agricultural Organization of the United Nations (FAO) Via delle Terme di Caracalla, 00100 Rome, Italy (Telephone Number in U.S. (202) 653-2400); *The State of Food and Agriculture*, and *Yearbook of Fishery Statistics*.

Statistical Office of the United Nations, Publishing Service, New York, New York 10017 (800) 253-9646; *Statistical Yearbook*.

QATAR - FOOD

Food and Agricultural Organization of the United Nations (FAO), Via delle Terme di Caracalla, 00100 Rome, Italy (Telephone Number in U.S. (202) 653-2400); *Production Yearbook*, and *The State of Food and Agriculture*.

G.K. Hall and Company, 70 Lincoln Street, Boston, Massachusetts 02111 (617) 423-3990; *The World in Figures*

QATAR - FOREIGN AID

G.K. Hall and Company, 70 Lincoln Street, Boston, Massachusetts 02111 (617) 423-3990; *The World in Figures*.

QATAR - FOREIGN INDEBTEDNESS

Euromonitor Publications Limited, 87-88 Turnmill Street, London EC1M 5QU, England; *Middle East Economic Handbook*.

QATAR - FOREIGN TRADE

Economic Commission for Western Asia, Post Office Box 27, Baghdad, Iraq; *Statistical Abstract of Western Asia*.

Euromonitor Publications Limited, 87-88 Turnmill Street, London EC1M 5QU, England; *Middle East Economic Handbook*.

Facts on File, 460 Park Avenue South, New York, New York 10016 (800) 443-8323; *The New Book of World Rankings*.

Federal Statistical Office, Gustav - Stresemann - Ring 11, D-6200 Wiesbaden, Germany; *Qatar*.

Food and Agricultural Organization of the United Nations (FAO) Via delle Terme di Caracalla, 00100 Rome, Italy (Telephone Number in U.S. (202) 653-2400); *The State of Food and Agriculture*.

G.K. Hall and Company, 70 Lincoln Street, Boston, Massachusetts 02111 (617) 423-3990; *The World in Figures*.

Presidency of the Council of Ministers, Central Statistical Organisation, Doha, Qatar; *Annual Statistical Abstract State of Qatar*.

Statistical Office of the United Nations, Publishing Service, New York, New York 10017 (800) 253-9646; *International Trade Statistics Yearbook*, and *Statistical Yearbook*.

QATAR - FORESTRY AND FOREST PRODUCTS

Facts on File, 460 Park Avenue South, New York, New York 10016 (800) 443-8323; *The New Book of World Rankings*.

Federal Statistical Office, Gustav - Stresemann - Ring 11, D-6200 Wiesbaden, Germany; *Qatar*.

Food and Agricultural Organization of the United Nations (FAO) Via delle Terme di Caracalla, 00100 Rome, Italy (Telephone Number in U.S. (202) 653-2400); *The State of Food and Agriculture*, and *Yearbook of Forest Products*.

G.K. Hall and Company, 70 Lincoln Street, Boston, Massachusetts 02111 (617) 423-3990; *The World in Figures*.

United Nations Educational, Scientific and Cultural Organization (UNESCO), 7 Place de Fontenoy, F-75700 Paris, France (Telephone Number in U.S. (212) 963-5981); *Statistical Yearbook*.

QATAR - GAS PRODUCTION - See QATAR - MINING AND MINERAL PRODUCTS

QATAR - GENERAL MORTALITY

Statistical Office of the United Nations, Publishing Service, New York, New York 10017 (800) 253-9646; *Demographic Yearbook*.

QATAR - GEOGRAPHIC DATA

Facts on File, 460 Park Avenue South, New York, New York 10016 (800) 443-8323; *The New Book of World Rankings*.

QATAR - GOLD HOLDINGS

International Monetary Fund, 700 Nineteenth Street, NW, Washington, D.C. 20431 (202) 623-7000; *International Financial Statistics*.

Statistical Office of the United Nations, Publishing Service, New York, New York 10017 (800) 253-9646; *Statistical Yearbook*.

QATAR - GOLD PRODUCTION AND CONSUMPTION - See QATAR - MINING AND MINERAL PRODUCTS

QATAR - GOVERNMENT

G.K. Hall and Company, 70 Lincoln Street, Boston, Massachusetts 02111 (617) 423-3990; *The World in Figures*.

QATAR - GOVERNMENT EXPENDITURE

Economic Commission for Western Asia, Post Office Box 27, Baghdad, Iraq; *Statistical Abstract of Western Asia*.

QATAR - GOVERNMENT REVENUE

Economic Commission for Western Asia, Post Office Box 27, Baghdad, Iraq; *Statistical Abstract of Western Asia*.

QATAR - GRAIN PRODUCTION - See QATAR - CROPS

QATAR - GROSS DOMESTIC PRODUCT

Economic Commission for Western Asia, Post Office Box 27, Baghdad, Iraq; *Statistical Abstract of Western Asia*.

The Economist Intelligence Unit, 111 West 57th Street, New York, New York 10019 (800) 938-4685; *The World Market Atlas*.

Euromonitor Publications Limited, 87-88 Turnmill Street, London EC1M 5QU, England; *Middle East Economic Handbook*.

Facts on File, 460 Park Avenue South, New York, New York 10016 (800) 443-8323; *The New Book of World Rankings*.

G.K. Hall and Company, 70 Lincoln Street, Boston, Massachusetts 02111 (617) 423-3990; *The World in Figures*.

Times Books, 201 East 50th Street, New York, New York 10022 (212) 751-2600; *The Economist Book of Vital World Statistics*.

QATAR - GROSS NATIONAL PRODUCT

Organization of Petroleum Exporting Countries, Obere Donaustrasse 93, 1020 Vienna 2, Austria; *OPEC Annual Statistical Bulletin*.

U.S. Arms Control and Disarmament Agency, 320 Twenty-first Street, NW, Washington, D.C. 20451 (202) 647-8677; *World Military Expenditures and Arms Transfers*.

QATAR - HEALTH

Economic Commission for Western Asia, Post Office Box 27, Baghdad, Iraq; *Statistical Abstract of Western Asia*.

Euromonitor Publications Limited, 87-88 Turnmill Street, London EC1M 5QU, England; *Middle East Economic Handbook*.

Facts on File, 460 Park Avenue South, New York, New York 10016 (800) 443-8323; *The New Book of World Rankings*.

Federal Statistical Office, Gustav - Stresemann - Ring 11, D-6200 Wiesbaden, Germany; *Qatar*.

G.K. Hall and Company, 70 Lincoln Street, Boston, Massachusetts 02111 (617) 423-3990; *The World in Figures*.

Presidency of the Council of Ministers, Central Statistical Organisation, Doha, Qatar; *Annual Statistical Abstract State of Qatar*.

Statistical Office of the United Nations, Publishing Service, New York, New York 10017 (800) 253-9646; *Statistical Yearbook*.

Times Books, 201 East 50th Street, New York, New York 10022 (212) 751-2600; *The Economist Book of Vital World Statistics*.

World Health Organization, Office of Publications, Avenue Appia, CH-1211 Geneva 27, Switzerland (Telephone Number in U.S. (518) 436-9686); *World Health Statistics Annual*.

QATAR - HIDE PRODUCTION

Food and Agricultural Organization of the United Nations (FAO), Via delle Terme di Caracalla, 00100 Rome, Italy (Telephone Number in U.S. (202) 653-2400); *Production Yearbook*.

QATAR - HIGHWAYS

Economic Commission for Western Asia, Post Office Box 27, Baghdad, Iraq; *Statistical Abstract of Western Asia.*

G.K. Hall and Company, 70 Lincoln Street, Boston, Massachusetts 02111 (617) 423-3990; *The World in Figures.*

QATAR - HORSES - See QATAR - LIVESTOCK AND POULTRY

QATAR - HOURS OF WORK - See QATAR - EMPLOYMENT

QATAR - HOUSING

Facts on File, 460 Park Avenue South, New York, New York 10016 (800) 443-8323; *The New Book of World Rankings.*

QATAR - ILLITERATE POPULATION

The Economist Intelligence Unit, 111 West 57th Street, New York, New York 10019 (800) 938-4685; *The World Market Atlas.*

G.K. Hall and Company, 70 Lincoln Street, Boston, Massachusetts 02111 (617) 423-3990; *The World in Figures.*

QATAR - IMPORTS

Economic Commission for Western Asia, Post Office Box 27, Baghdad, Iraq; *Statistical Abstract of Western Asia.*

The Economist Intelligence Unit, 111 West 57th Street, New York, New York 10019 (800) 938-4685; *The World Market Atlas.*

Euromonitor Publications Limited, 87-88 Turnmill Street, London EC1M 5QU, England; *Middle East Economic Handbook.*

Food and Agricultural Organization of the United Nations (FAO) Via delle Terme di Caracalla, 00100 Rome, Italy (Telephone Number in U.S. (202) 653-2400); *The State of Food and Agriculture.*

G.K. Hall and Company, 70 Lincoln Street, Boston, Massachusetts 02111 (617) 423-3990; *The World in Figures.*

International Monetary Fund, 700 Nineteenth Street, NW, Washington, D.C. 20431 (202) 623-7000; *Direction of Trade Statistics,* and *International Financial Statistics.*

Times Books, 201 East 50th Street, New York, New York 10022 (212) 751-2600; *The Economist Book of Vital World Statistics.*

QATAR - INDUSTRY

Facts on File, 460 Park Avenue South, New York, New York 10016 (800) 443-8323; *The New Book of World Rankings.*

Federal Statistical Office, Gustav - Stresemann - Ring 11, D-6200 Wiesbaden, Germany; *Qatar.*

G.K. Hall and Company, 70 Lincoln Street, Boston, Massachusetts 02111 (617) 423-3990; *The World in Figures.*

Presidency of the Council of Ministers, Central Statistical Organisation, Doha, Qatar; *Annual Statistical Abstract State of Qatar.*

Times Books, 201 East 50th Street, New York, New York 10022 (212) 751-2600; *The Economist Book of Vital World Statistics.*

QATAR - INFANT AND MATERNAL MORTALITY

Statistical Office of the United Nations, Publishing Service, New York, New York 10017 (800) 253-9646; *Demographic Yearbook.*

Times Books, 201 East 50th Street, New York, New York 10022 (212) 751-2600; *The Economist Book of Vital World Statistics.*

QATAR - INTERNATIONAL LIQUIDITY

International Monetary Fund, 700 Nineteenth Street, NW, Washington, D.C. 20431 (202) 623-7000; *International Financial Statistics.*

QATAR - INTERNATIONAL RESERVES EXCLUDING GOLD

Statistical Office of the United Nations, Publishing Service, New York, New York 10017 (800) 253-9646; *Statistical Yearbook.*

QATAR - IRON ORE PRODUCTION AND CONSUMPTION - See QATAR - MINING AND MINERAL PRODUCTS

QATAR - LABOR FORCE

Economic Commission for Western Asia, Post Office Box 27, Baghdad, Iraq; *Statistical Abstract of Western Asia.*

Euromonitor Publications Limited, 87-88 Turnmill Street, London EC1M 5QU, England; *Middle East Economic Handbook.*

Facts on File, 460 Park Avenue South, New York, New York 10016 (800) 443-8323; *The New Book of World Rankings*

Food and Agricultural Organization of the United Nations (FAO) Via delle Terme di Caracalla, 00100 Rome, Italy (Telephone Number in U.S. (202) 653-2400); *The State of Food and Agriculture.*

G.K. Hall and Company, 70 Lincoln Street, Boston, Massachusetts 02111 (617) 423-3990; *The World in Figures.*

QATAR - LAND USE

Economic Commission for Western Asia, Post Office Box 27, Baghdad, Iraq; *Statistical Abstract of Western Asia.*

Food and Agricultural Organization of the United Nations (FAO), Via delle Terme di Caracalla, 00100 Rome, Italy (Telephone Number in U.S. (202) 653-2400); *Production Yearbook.*

G.K. Hall and Company, 70 Lincoln Street, Boston, Massachusetts 02111 (617) 423-3990; *The World in Figures.*

QATAR - LIBRARIES

Facts on File, 460 Park Avenue South, New York, New York 10016 (800) 443-8323; *The New Book of World Rankings.*

United Nations Educational, Scientific and Cultural Organization (UNESCO), 7 Place de Fontenoy, F-75700 Paris, France (Telephone Number in U.S. (212) 963-5981); *Statistical Yearbook.*

QATAR - LIVESTOCK AND POULTRY

Economic Commission for Western Asia, Post Office Box 27, Baghdad, Iraq; *Statistical Abstract of Western Asia.*

Facts on File, 460 Park Avenue South, New York, New York 10016 (800) 443-8323; *The New Book of World Rankings.*

Food and Agricultural Organization of the United Nations (FAO), Via delle Terme di Caracalla, 00100 Rome, Italy (Telephone Number in U.S. (202) 653-2400); *Production Yearbook*, and *The State of Food and Agriculture*.

G.K. Hall and Company, 70 Lincoln Street, Boston, Massachusetts 02111 (617) 423-3990; *The World in Figures*.

Statistical Office of the United Nations, Publishing Service, New York, New York 10017 (800) 253-9646; *Statistical Yearbook*.

QATAR - LIVING LEVELS

G.K. Hall and Company, 70 Lincoln Street, Boston, Massachusetts 02111 (617) 423-3990; *The World in Figures*.

Times Books, 201 East 50th Street, New York, New York 10022 (212) 751-2600; *The Economist Book of Vital World Statistics*.

QATAR - MANPOWER

Presidency of the Council of Ministers, Central Statistical Organisation, Doha, Qatar; *Annual Statistical Abstract State of Qatar*.

QATAR - MANUFACTURING

Facts on File, 460 Park Avenue South, New York, New York 10016 (800) 443-8323; *The New Book of World Rankings*.

G.K. Hall and Company, 70 Lincoln Street, Boston, Massachusetts 02111 (617) 423-3990; *The World in Figures*.

QATAR - MARRIAGE RATES

Facts on File, 460 Park Avenue South, New York, New York 10016 (800) 443-8323; *The New Book of World Rankings*.

Statistical Office of the United Nations, Publishing Service, New York, New York 10017 (800) 253-9646; *Demographic Yearbook*.

QATAR - MEAT PRODUCTION - See QATAR - LIVESTOCK AND POULTRY

QATAR - MERCHANT SHIPPING

Economic Commission for Western Asia, Post Office Box 27, Baghdad, Iraq; *Statistical Abstract of Western Asia*.

G.K. Hall and Company, 70 Lincoln Street, Boston, Massachusetts 02111 (617) 423-3990; *The World in Figures*.

Organization of Petroleum Exporting Countries, Obere Donaustrasse 93, 1020 Vienna 2, Austria; *OPEC Annual Statistical Bulletin*.

Statistical Office of the United Nations, Publishing Service, New York, New York 10017 (800) 253-9646; *Statistical Yearbook*.

Times Books, 201 East 50th Street, New York, New York 10022 (212) 751-2600; *The Economist Book of Vital World Statistics*.

QATAR - MILITARY

G.K. Hall and Company, 70 Lincoln Street, Boston, Massachusetts 02111 (617) 423-3990; *The World in Figures*.

The International Institute for Strategic Studies, 23 Tavistock Street, London WC2E 7NQ, England; *The Military Balance*.

U.S. Arms Control and Disarmament Agency, 320 Twenty-first Street, NW, Washington, D.C. 20451 (202) 647-8677; *World Military Expenditures and Arms Transfers*.

QATAR - MILK PRODUCTION - See QATAR - DAIRY PRODUCTS

QATAR - MINING AND MINERAL PRODUCTS

Economic Commission for Western Asia, Post Office Box 27, Baghdad, Iraq; *Statistical Abstract of Western Asia*.

Facts on File, 460 Park Avenue South, New York, New York 10016 (800) 443-8323; *The New Book of World Rankings*.

G.K. Hall and Company, 70 Lincoln Street, Boston, Massachusetts 02111 (617) 423-3990; *The World in Figures*.

Organization of Petroleum Exporting Countries, Obere Donaustrasse 93, 1020 Vienna 2, Austria; *OPEC Annual Statistical Bulletin*.

Penn Well Publishing Company, 1421 South Sheridan Road, Post Office Box 1260, Tulsa, Oklahoma 74101 (800) 752-9764; *International Energy Statistics Sourcebook*.

Statistical Office of the United Nations, Publishing Service, New York, New York 10017 (800) 253-9646; *Statistical Yearbook*.

QATAR - MONEY EXCHANGE RATES

International Monetary Fund, 700 Nineteenth Street, NW, Washington, D.C. 20431 (202) 623-7000; *International Financial Statistics*.

Statistical Office of the United Nations, Publishing Service, New York, New York 10017 (800) 253-9646; *Statistical Yearbook*.

QATAR - MONEY SUPPLY

G.K. Hall and Company, 70 Lincoln Street, Boston, Massachusetts 02111 (617) 423-3990; *The World in Figures*.

International Monetary Fund, 700 Nineteenth Street, NW, Washington, D.C. 20431 (202) 623-7000; *International Financial Statistics*.

Statistical Office of the United Nations, Publishing Service, New York, New York 10017 (800) 253-9646; *Statistical Yearbook*.

QATAR - MOTION PICTURES

United Nations Educational, Scientific and Cultural Organization (UNESCO), 7 Place de Fontenoy, F-75700 Paris, France (Telephone Number in U.S. (212) 963-5981); *Statistical Yearbook*.

QATAR - MOTOR VEHICLES

Economic Commission for Western Asia, Post Office Box 27, Baghdad, Iraq; *Statistical Abstract of Western Asia*.

QATAR - MOTOR VEHICLES IN USE

G.K. Hall and Company, 70 Lincoln Street, Boston, Massachusetts 02111 (617) 423-3990; *The World in Figures*.

Times Books, 201 East 50th Street, New York, New York 10022 (212) 751-2600; *The Economist Book of Vital World Statistics*.

QATAR - MUSEUMS

Facts on File, 460 Park Avenue South, New York, New York 10016 (800) 443-8323; *The New Book of World Rankings.*

United Nations Educational, Scientific and Cultural Organization (UNESCO), 7 Place de Fontenoy, F-75700 Paris, France (Telephone Number in U.S. (212) 963-5981); *Statistical Yearbook.*

QATAR - NATALITY - See QATAR - BIRTH RATES

QATAR - NATIONAL ACCOUNTS

Economic Commission for Western Asia, Post Office Box 27, Baghdad, Iraq; *Statistical Abstract of Western Asia.*

Federal Statistical Office, Gustav - Stresemann - Ring 11, D-6200 Wiesbaden, Germany; *Qatar.*

QATAR - NATIONAL INCOME

Facts on File, 460 Park Avenue South, New York, New York 10016 (800) 443-8323; *The New Book of World Rankings.*

G.K. Hall and Company, 70 Lincoln Street, Boston, Massachusetts 02111 (617) 423-3990; *The World in Figures.*

Presidency of the Council of Ministers, Central Statistical Organisation, Doha, Qatar; *Annual Statistical Abstract State of Qatar.*

Statistical Office of the United Nations, Publishing Service, New York, New York 10017 (800) 253-9646; *Statistical Yearbook.*

QATAR - NATURAL GAS PRODUCTION - See QATAR - MINING AND MINERAL PRODUCTS

QATAR - NEWSPAPER PRODUCTION - See QATAR - FORESTRY AND FOREST PRODUCTS

QATAR - OCCUPATIONS - See QATAR - LABOR FORCE

QATAR - PAPER - See QATAR - FORESTRY AND FOREST PRODUCTS

QATAR - PEANUT PRODUCTION - See QATAR - CROPS

QATAR - PERIODICALS

United Nations Educational, Scientific and Cultural Organization (UNESCO), 7 Place de Fontenoy, F-75700 Paris, France (Telephone Number in U.S. (212) 963-5981); *Statistical Yearbook.*

QATAR - PESTICIDE USE

Food and Agricultural Organization of the United Nations (FAO) Via delle Terme di Caracalla, 00100 Rome, Italy (Telephone Number in U.S. (202) 653-2400); *The State of Food and Agriculture.*

QATAR - PETROLEUM INDUSTRY

Euromonitor Publications Limited, 87-88 Turnmill Street, London EC1M 5QU, England; *Middle East Economic Handbook.*

Facts on File, 460 Park Avenue South, New York, New York 10016 (800) 443-8323; *The New Book of World Rankings.*

Food and Agricultural Organization of the United Nations (FAO) Via delle Terme di Caracalla, 00100 Rome, Italy (Telephone Number in U.S. (202) 653-2400); *The State of Food and Agriculture.*

G.K. Hall and Company, 70 Lincoln Street, Boston, Massachusetts 02111 (617) 423-3990; *The World in Figures.*

Organization of Petroleum Exporting Countries, Obere Donaustrasse 93, 1020 Vienna 2, Austria; *OPEC Annual Statistical Bulletin.*

Penn Well Publishing Company, 1421 South Sheridan Road, Post Office Box 1260, Tulsa, Oklahoma 74101 (800) 752-9764; *International Energy Statistics Sourcebook.*

Presidency of the Council of Ministers, Central Statistical Organisation, Doha, Qatar; *Annual Statistical Abstract State of Qatar.*

Statistical Office of the United Nations, Publishing Service, New York, New York 10017 (800) 253-9646; *Statistical Yearbook.*

QATAR - PIGS - See QATAR - LIVESTOCK AND POULTRY

QATAR - PIPELINES FOR OIL AND PETROLEUM PRODUCTS

Organization of Petroleum Exporting Countries, Obere Donaustrasse 93, 1020 Vienna 2, Austria; *OPEC Annual Statistical Bulletin.*

QATAR - POPULATION

Economic Commission for Western Asia, Post Office Box 27, Baghdad, Iraq; *Statistical Abstract of Western Asia.*

The Economist Intelligence Unit, 111 West 57th Street, New York, New York 10019 (800) 938-4685; *The World Market Atlas.*

Euromonitor Publications Limited, 87-88 Turnmill Street, London EC1M 5QU, England; *Middle East Economic Handbook.*

Facts on File, 460 Park Avenue South, New York, New York 10016 (800) 443-8323; *The New Book of World Rankings.*

Federal Statistical Office, Gustav - Stresemann - Ring 11, D-6200 Wiesbaden, Germany; *Qatar.*

Food and Agricultural Organization of the United Nations (FAO), Via delle Terme di Caracalla, 00100 Rome, Italy (Telephone Number in U.S. (202) 653-2400); *Production Yearbook.*

G.K. Hall and Company, 70 Lincoln Street, Boston, Massachusetts 02111 (617) 423-3990; *The World in Figures.*

Presidency of the Council of Ministers, Central Statistical Organisation, Doha, Qatar; *Annual Statistical Abstract State of Qatar.*

Statistical Office of the United Nations, Publishing Service, New York, New York 10017 (800) 253-9646; *Demographic Yearbook,* and *Statistical Yearbook.*

Times Books, 201 East 50th Street, New York, New York 10022 (212) 751-2600; *The Economist Book of Vital World Statistics.*

United Nations Educational, Scientific and Cultural Organization (UNESCO), 7 Place de Fontenoy, F-75700 Paris, France (Telephone Number in U.S. (212) 963-5981); *Statistical Yearbook.*

U.S. Arms Control and Disarmament Agency, 320 Twenty-first Street, NW, Washington, D.C. 20451 (202) 647-8677; *World Military Expenditures and Arms Transfers*

World Health Organization, Office of Publications, Avenue Appia, CH-1211 Geneva 27, Switzerland (Telephone Number in U.S. (518) 436-9686); *World Health Statistics Annual.*

QATAR - POST OFFICES

Facts on File, 460 Park Avenue South, New York, New York 10016 (800) 443-8323; *The New Book of World Rankings.*

QATAR - POTATO PRODUCTION - See QATAR - CROPS

QATAR - PRICES

Economic Commission for Western Asia, Post Office Box 27, Baghdad, Iraq; *Statistical Abstract of Western Asia.*

Facts on File, 460 Park Avenue South, New York, New York 10016 (800) 443-8323; *The New Book of World Rankings.*

Federal Statistical Office, Gustav - Stresemann - Ring 11, D-6200 Wiesbaden, Germany; *Qatar.*

Food and Agricultural Organization of the United Nations (FAO) Via delle Terme di Caracalla, 00100 Rome, Italy (Telephone Number in U.S. (202) 653-2400); *The State of Food and Agriculture.*

G.K. Hall and Company, 70 Lincoln Street, Boston, Massachusetts 02111 (617) 423-3990; *The World in Figures.*

Presidency of the Council of Ministers, Central Statistical Organisation, Doha, Qatar; *Annual Statistical Abstract State of Qatar.*

QATAR - PRODUCTION

Facts on File, 460 Park Avenue South, New York, New York 10016 (800) 443-8323; *The New Book of World Rankings.*

G.K. Hall and Company, 70 Lincoln Street, Boston, Massachusetts 02111 (617) 423-3990; *The World in Figures.*

QATAR - PUBLIC FINANCE

Facts on File, 460 Park Avenue South, New York, New York 10016 (800) 443-8323; *The New Book of World Rankings.*

QATAR - RADIO BROADCASTING - See QATAR - BROADCASTING

QATAR - RAILWAYS

G.K. Hall and Company, 70 Lincoln Street, Boston, Massachusetts 02111 (617) 423-3990; *The World in Figures.*

QATAR - RELIGION

Facts on File, 460 Park Avenue South, New York, New York 10016 (800) 443-8323; *The New Book of World Rankings.*

QATAR - RETAIL TRADE

G.K. Hall and Company, 70 Lincoln Street, Boston, Massachusetts 02111 (617) 423-3990; *The World in Figures.*

QATAR - RICE PRODUCTION - See QATAR - CROPS

QATAR - RUBBER PRODUCTION AND CONSUMPTION

Facts on File, 460 Park Avenue South, New York, New York 10016 (800) 443-8323; *The New Book of World Rankings.*

QATAR - SCIENTISTS AND TECHNICIANS

Statistical Office of the United Nations, Publishing Service, New York, New York 10017 (800) 253-9646; *Statistical Yearbook.*

QATAR - SENIOR CITIZENS

Facts on File, 460 Park Avenue South, New York, New York 10016 (800) 443-8323; *The New Book of World Rankings.*

QATAR - SHEEP - See QATAR - LIVESTOCK AND POULTRY

QATAR - SILVER PRODUCTION AND CONSUMPTION - See QATAR - MINING AND MINERAL PRODUCTS

QATAR - SOCIAL DATA

Facts on File, 460 Park Avenue South, New York, New York 10016 (800) 443-8323; *The New Book of World Rankings.*

G.K. Hall and Company, 70 Lincoln Street, Boston, Massachusetts 02111 (617) 423-3990; *The World in Figures.*

QATAR - STEEL PRODUCTION - See QATAR - MINING AND MINERAL PRODUCTS

QATAR - STOCKS - COMMODITY - MARKET PRICE - INDEX

Food and Agricultural Organization of the United Nations (FAO) Via delle Terme di Caracalla, 00100 Rome, Italy (Telephone Number in U.S. (202) 653-2400); *The State of Food and Agriculture.*

QATAR - SUGAR PRODUCTION AND CONSUMPTION - See QATAR - CROPS

QATAR - TAXATION

G.K. Hall and Company, 70 Lincoln Street, Boston, Massachusetts 02111 (617) 423-3990; *The World in Figures.*

QATAR - TELEPHONES IN USE

American Telephone and Telegraph Company, 26 Parsippany Road, Whippany, New Jersey 07981 (800) 338-4038; *The World's Telephones.*

Euromonitor Publications Limited, 87-88 Turnmill Street, London EC1M 5QU, England; *Middle East Economic Handbook.*

G.K. Hall and Company, 70 Lincoln Street, Boston, Massachusetts 02111 (617) 423-3990; *The World in Figures.*

Statistical Office of the United Nations, Publishing Service, New York, New York 10017 (800) 253-9646; *Statistical Yearbook.*

QATAR - TELEVISION BROADCASTING - See QATAR - BROADCASTING

QATAR - TEXTILE INDUSTRY

G.K. Hall and Company, 70 Lincoln Street, Boston, Massachusetts 02111 (617) 423-3990; *The World in Figures.*

QATAR - THEATRE

United Nations Educational, Scientific and Cultural Organization (UNESCO), 7 Place de Fontenoy, F-75700 Paris, France (Telephone Number in U.S. (212) 963-5981); *Statistical Yearbook.*

QATAR - TOBACCO PRODUCTION

Facts on File, 460 Park Avenue South, New York, New York 10016 (800) 443-8323; *The New Book of World Rankings*.

QATAR - TOURISM

Economic Commission for Western Asia, Post Office Box 27, Baghdad, Iraq; *Statistical Abstract of Western Asia*.

Euromonitor Publications Limited, 87-88 Turnmill Street, London EC1M 5QU, England; *Middle East Economic Handbook*.

Facts on File, 460 Park Avenue South, New York, New York 10016 (800) 443-8323; *The New Book of World Rankings*.

Federal Statistical Office, Gustav - Stresemann - Ring 11, D-6200 Wiesbaden, Germany; *Qatar*.

G.K. Hall and Company, 70 Lincoln Street, Boston, Massachusetts 02111 (617) 423-3990; *The World in Figures*.

Presidency of the Council of Ministers, Central Statistical Organisation, Doha, Qatar; *Annual Statistical Abstract State of Qatar*.

Times Books, 201 East 50th Street, New York, New York 10022 (212) 751-2600; *The Economist Book of Vital World Statistics*.

QATAR - TRADE - See QATAR - FOREIGN TRADE

QATAR - TRANSPORTATION AND COMMUNICATIONS

Economic Commission for Western Asia, Post Office Box 27, Baghdad, Iraq; *Statistical Abstract of Western Asia*.

Euromonitor Publications Limited, 87-88 Turnmill Street, London EC1M 5QU, England; *Middle East Economic Handbook*.

Facts on File, 460 Park Avenue South, New York, New York 10016 (800) 443-8323; *The New Book of World Rankings*.

Federal Statistical Office, Gustav - Stresemann - Ring 11, D-6200 Wiesbaden, Germany; *Qatar*.

G.K. Hall and Company, 70 Lincoln Street, Boston, Massachusetts 02111 (617) 423-3990; *The World in Figures*.

Presidency of the Council of Ministers, Central Statistical Organisation, Doha, Qatar; *Annual Statistical Abstract State of Qatar*.

QATAR - UNEMPLOYMENT

Euromonitor Publications Limited, 87-88 Turnmill Street, London EC1M 5QU, England; *Middle East Economic Handbook*.

QATAR - VITAL STATISTICS

Euromonitor Publications Limited, 87-88 Turnmill Street, London EC1M 5QU, England; *Middle East Economic Handbook*.

G.K. Hall and Company, 70 Lincoln Street, Boston, Massachusetts 02111 (617) 423-3990; *The World in Figures*.

Presidency of the Council of Ministers, Central Statistical Organisation, Doha, Qatar; *Annual Statistical Abstract State of Qatar*.

World Health Organization, Office of Publications, Avenue Appia, CH-1211 Geneva 27, Switzerland (Telephone Number in U.S. (518) 436-9686); *World Health Statistics Annual*.

QATAR - WAGES

Federal Statistical Office, Gustav - Stresemann - Ring 11, D-6200 Wiesbaden, Germany; *Qatar*.

G.K. Hall and Company, 70 Lincoln Street, Boston, Massachusetts 02111 (617) 423-3990; *The World in Figures*.

QATAR - WEATHER

Facts on File, 460 Park Avenue South, New York, New York 10016 (800) 443-8323; *The New Book of World Rankings*.

G.K. Hall and Company, 70 Lincoln Street, Boston, Massachusetts 02111 (617) 423-3990; *The World in Figures*.

QATAR - WHEAT PRODUCTION AND PRICES - See QATAR - CROPS

QATAR - WINE PRODUCTION

Facts on File, 460 Park Avenue South, New York, New York 10016 (800) 443-8323; *The New Book of World Rankings*.

QATAR - WOOL PRODUCTION

Facts on File, 460 Park Avenue South, New York, New York 10016 (800) 443-8323; *The New Book of World Rankings*.

QUARRIES - See MINING INDUSTRY

QUICKSILVER (MERCURY)

U.S. Department of the Interior, Bureau of Mines, 810 Seventh Street, NW, Washington, D.C. 20241 (202) 501-9649; *Annual Reports*, and *Mineral Commodities Summaries*.

R

RABIES

U.S. Department of Health and Human Services, Centers for Disease Control, 1600 Clifton Road, NE, Atlanta, Georgia 30333 (404) 639-3311; *Summary of Notifiable Diseases, United States Morbidity and Mortality Weekly Report.*

RACETRACK OPERATIONS - BUSINESS SUMMARY

Association of Racing Commissioners International, Incorporated, 4067 Iron Works Pike, Lexington, Kentucky 40511 (606) 254-4060.

RACQUETBALL

National Sporting Goods Association, Lake Center Plaza Building, 1699 Wall Street, Mt. Prospect, Illinois 60056 (708) 439-4000; *Sports Participation in 1992: Series I.*

RADIOLOGISTS

American Medical Association, 515 North State Street, Chicago, Illinois 60610 (312) 464-4818; *Physician Characteristics and Distribution in the United States.*

RADIO BROADCASTING STATIONS - ADVERTISING EXPENDITURES

McCann-Erickson, Incorporated, 750 Third Avenue, New York, New York 10017 (212) 697-6000; compiled for Crain Communications, Incorporated, 740 North Rush Street, Chicago, Illinois 60611; *Advertising Age.*

RADIO BROADCASTING STATIONS - EARNINGS

U.S. Department of Labor, Bureau of Labor Statistics, Two Massachusetts Avenue, NE, Washington, D.C. 20212 (202) 606-7828; *Employment and Earnings,* and Bulletins 2370 and 2429.

RADIO BROADCASTING STATIONS - EMPLOYEES

U.S. Department of Labor, Bureau of Labor Statistics, Two Massachusetts Avenue, NE, Washington, D.C. 20212 (202) 606-7828; *Employment and Earnings,* and Bulletins 2370 and 2429.

RADIO BROADCASTING STATIONS - FINANCES

U.S. Department of Commerce, Bureau of the Census, Suitland, Maryland 20233 (301) 763-4040; *Annual Survey of Communication Services.*

Veronis, Suhler and Associates, 350 Park Avenue, New York, New York 10022 (212) 935-4990; *Communications Industry Forecast Report.*

RADIO BROADCASTING STATIONS - STATIONS

Broadcasting Publications, Incorporated, 1705 DeSales Street, NW, Washington, D.C. 20036 (202) 659-2340; *The Broadcasting Yearbook.*

Radio Advertising Bureau, 304 Park Avenue, South, New York, New York 10010 (212) 254-4800; *Radio Facts.*

U.S. Federal Communications Commission, 1919 M Street, NW, Washington, D.C. 20554 (202) 632-7000; *Annual Report,* and unpublished data.

RADIOS - AUDIENCE CHARACTERISTICS

Mediamark Research, Incorporated, 708 Third Avenue, New York, New York 10017 (212) 599-0444; *Multimedia Audiences.*

RADIOS - HOUSEHOLDS WITH

Euromonitor Publications Limited, 87-88 Turnmill Street, London EC1M 5QU, England; *European Marketing Data and Statistics.*

International Telecommunications Union, Palais des Nations, CH-1211 Geneva 20, Switzerland; *World Telecom Indicators.*

Statistical Office of the United Nations, Publishing Service, New York, New York 10017 (800) 253-9646; *Statistical Yearbook.*

United Nations Educational, Scientific and Cultural Organization, (UNESCO). 7 Place de Fontenoy, F-75700 Paris, France (Telephone Number in U.S. (212) 963-5981); *Statistical Yearbook.*

RAILROAD EMPLOYEES RETIREMENT FUNDS

Executive Office of the President, Office of Management and Budget, Executive Office Building, Washington, D.C. 20503 (202) 395-3080; *Budget of the United States Government.*

U.S. Department of Health and Human Services, Social Security Administration, 6401 Security Boulevard, Baltimore, Maryland 21235 (410) 965-1234; *Social Security Bulletin, Annual Statistical Supplement to the Social Security Bulletin,* and unpublished data.

RAILROAD RETIREMENT BOARD

U.S. Department of Health and Human Services, Social Security Administration, 6401 Security Boulevard, Baltimore, Maryland 21235

(410) 965-1234; *Social Security Bulletin, Annual Statistical Supplement to the Social Security Bulletin,* and unpublished data.

RAILROADS - AMTRAK

Association of American Railroads, American Railroads Building, 50 F Street, NW, Washington, D.C. 20001 (202) 639-2100; *Railroad Facts, Statistics of Railroads of Class I,* and *Analysis of Class I Railroads.*

U.S. Department of Transportation, Federal Railroad Administration, 400 Seventh Street, SW, Washington, D.C. 20590 (202) 366-0881; *Accident Bulletin.*

RAILROADS - CAR LOADINGS - BY COMMODITY

Association of American Railroads, American Railroads Building, 50 F Street, NW, Washington, D.C. 20001 (202) 639-2100; *Freight Commodity Statistics,* and *Weekly Railroad Traffic.*

RAILROADS - CONSTRUCTION VALUE

U.S. Department of Commerce, Bureau of the Census, Suitland, Maryland 20233 (301) 763-4040; *Current Construction Reports.*

RAILROADS - EARNINGS

Association of American Railroads, American Railroads Building, 50 F Street, NW, Washington, D.C. 20001 (202) 639-2222; *Railroad Facts, Statistics of Railroads of Class I,* and *Analysis of Class I Railroads.*

U.S. Department of Labor, Bureau of Labor Statistics, Two Massachusetts Avenue, NE, Washington, D.C. 20212 (202) 606-7828; *Employment and Earnings,* and Bulletin 2370.

RAILROADS - EMPLOYEES

Association of American Railroads, American Railroads Building, 50 F Street, NW, Washington, D.C. 20001 (202) 639-2100; *Railroad Facts Statistics of Railroads of Class I,* and *Analysis of Class I Railroads.*

U.S. Department of Labor, Bureau of Labor Statistics, Two Massachusetts Avenue, NE, Washington, D.C. 20212 (202) 606-7828; *Employment and Earnings,* and Bulletins 2370 and 2429.

RAILROADS - EQUIPMENT IN SERVICE

Association of American Railroads, American Railroads Building, 50 F Street, NW, Washington, D.C. 20001 (202) 639-2100; *Analysis of Class I Railroads, Railroad Facts, Statistics of Railroads of Class I.*

RAILROADS - FINANCES

Association of American Railroads, American Railroads Building, 50 F Street, NW, Washington, D.C. 20001 (202) 639-2100; *Analysis of Class I Railroads,* and *Railroad Facts, Statistics of Railroads of Class I.*

Board of Governors of the Federal Reserve System, Twentieth Street and Constitution Avenue, NW, Washington, D.C. 20551 (202) 452-3000; *Federal Reserve Bulletin.*

U.S. Department of Commerce, Bureau of Economic Analysis, Fourteenth Street between Constitution Avenue and E Street, NW, Washington, D.C. 20230 (202) 606-9900; *Fixed Reproducible Tangible Wealth in the U.S.,* and *Survey of Current Business.*

U.S. Department of Transportation, Bureau of Transportation Statistics, 400 Seventh Street, SW, Washington, D.C. 20590 (202) 366-DATA; *National Transportation Statistics Annual, Historical Compendium Information Report.*

RAILROADS - FREIGHT PRICE INDEXES

U.S. Department of Labor, Bureau of Labor Statistics, Two Massachusetts Avenue, NE, Washington, D.C. 20212 (202) 606-7828; *Producer Price Indexes.*

RAILROADS - FREIGHT TRAFFIC

Association of American Railroads, American Railroads Building, 50 F Street, NW, Washington, D.C. 20001 (202) 639-2100; *Railroad Facts, Statistics of Railroads of Class I, Analysis of Class I Railroads, Freight Commodity Statistics,* and *Weekly Railroad Traffic.*

Eno Transportation Foundation, 44211 Statestone Court, Lansdowne, Virginia 22075 (703) 729-7200; *Transportation in America.*

RAILROADS - HORSEPOWER

John A. Waring, 1320 South George Mason Drive, Arlington, Virginia 22204 (703) 521-1499; unpublished estimates.

RAILROADS - MILEAGE OWNED AND OPERATED

Association of American Railroads, American Railroads Building, 50 F Street, NW, Washington, D.C. 20001 (202) 639-2100; *Railroad Facts, Statistics of Railroads of Class I,* and *Analysis of Class I Railroads.*

RAILROADS - OCCUPATIONAL SAFETY

U.S. Department of Labor, Bureau of Labor Statistics, Two Massachusetts Avenue, NE, Washington, D.C. 20212 (202) 606-7828; *Compensation and Working Conditions.*

U.S. Department of Transportation, Bureau of Transportation Statistics, 400 Seventh Street, SW, Washington, D.C. 20590 (202) 366-DATA; *National Transportation Statistics Annual, Historical Compendium Information Report.*

U.S. Department of Transportation, Federal Railroad Administration, 400 Seventh Street, SW, Washington, D.C. 20590 (202) 366-0881 *Accident Bulletin.*

RAILROADS - PASSENGER TRAFFIC AND REVENUE

Association of American Railroads, American Railroads Building, 50 F Street, NW, Washington, D.C. 20001 (202) 639-2100; *Railroad Facts, Statistics of Railroads of Class I,* and *Analysis of Class I Railroads.*

Eno Transportation Foundation, 44211 Statestone Court, Lansdowne, Virginia 22075 (703) 729-7200; *Transportation in America.*

RAILROADS - PIGGYBACK

Association of American Railroads, American Railroads Building, 50 F Street, NW, Washington, D.C. 20001 (202) 639-2100; *Freight Commodity Statistics,* and *Weekly Railroad Traffic.*

RAILROADS - RECEIPTS

United States Travel Data Center, Two Lafayette Center, 1133 Twenty-first Street, NW, Washington, D.C. 20036 (202) 293-1040; *Impact of Travel on State Economies.*

RAINFALL - SELECTED CITIES

U.S. Department of Commerce, National Oceanic and Atmospheric Administration, National Climatic Data Center, Federal Building, Asheville, North Carolina 28801 (704) 259-2850; *Climatography of the United States,* and *Comparative Climatic Data.*

RANGES - See STOVES AND RANGES

RANKINGS - AIRPORT TRAFFIC

U.S. Department of Transportation, Federal Aviation Administration, 800 Independence Avenue, SW, Washington, D.C. 20591 (202) 366-4000; *Airport Activity Statistics.*

RANKINGS - CITIES - POPULATION

U.S. Department of Commerce, Bureau of the Census, Suitland, Maryland 20233 (301) 763-4040; *Census of Population, Current Population Reports,* and unpublished data.

RANKINGS - CITIES - RESIDENTIAL PROPERTY TAX

Government of the District of Columbia, Department of Finance and Revenue, 300 Indiana Avenue, NW, Washington, D.C. 20001 (202) 727-6103; *Tax Rates and Tax Burdens in the District of Columbia: A Nationwide Comparison.*

RANKINGS - CITIES - WORLD POPULATION

Statistical Office of the United Nations, Publishing Service, New York, New York 10017 (800) 253-9646; *Demographic Yearbook.*

U.S. Department of Commerce, Bureau of the Census, Suitland, Maryland 20233 (301) 763-4040; *International Data Base,* and *World Population Profile.*

RANKINGS - COUNTRIES - CONSUMPTION OF BEEF, PORK, POULTRY

U.S. Department of Agriculture, Foreign Agricultural Service, Fourteenth Street and Independence Avenue, SW, Washington, D.C. 20250 (202) 720-3448; *World Livestock Situation,* and *World Poultry Situation.*

RANKINGS - COUNTRIES - EXPORTS AND IMPORTS OF WHEAT, RICE AND CORN

Organization for Economic Cooperation and Development, Publication and Information Center, 2001 L Street, NW, Washington, D.C. 20036 (202) 785-6323; *National Accounts of OECD Countries.*

RANKINGS - COUNTRIES - POPULATION

Statistical Office of the United Nations, Publishing Service, New York, New York 10017 (800) 253-9646; *Demographic Yearbook.*

U.S. Department of Commerce, Bureau of the Census, Suitland, Maryland 20233 (301) 763-4040; *International Data Base,* and *World Population Profile.*

RANKINGS - FEDERAL RESEARCH AND DEVELOPMENT OBLIGATIONS TO HIGHER EDUCATION

National Science Foundation, 4201 Wilson Boulevard, Arlington, Virginia 22230 (703) 306-1234; *Federal Support to Universities and Colleges and Selected Non-Profit Institutions.*

RANKINGS - METROPOLITAN AREAS - POPULATION

U.S. Department of Commerce, Bureau of the Census, Suitland, Maryland 20233 (301) 763-4040; *Census of Population and Housing, Supplementary Reports, Metropolitan Areas as Defined by the OMB, Current Population Reports,* and press release.

RANKINGS - STATE - DOMESTIC TRAVEL EXPENDITURES

United States Travel Data Center, Two Lafayette Center, 1133 Twenty-first Street, NW, Washington, D.C. 20036 (202) 293-1040; *Impact of Travel on State Economies.*

RANKINGS - STATE - FARM MARKETINGS

U.S. Department of Agriculture, National Agricultural Statistics Service, Fourteenth Street and Independence Avenue, SW, Washington, D.C. 20250 (202) 219-1504; *Economic Indicators of the Farm Sector: State Financial Summary.*

RANKINGS - STATE - FOREIGN TRADE

U.S. Department of Agriculture, Economic Research Service, Fourteenth Street and Independence Avenue, SW, Washington, D.C. 20005-4789 (202) 219-1504; *Foreign Agricultural Trade of the U.S.*

U.S. Department of Commerce, Bureau of the Census, Suitland, Maryland 20233 (301) 763-4040; *U.S. Merchandise Trade, Selected Highlights,* series FT 920.

RANKINGS - STATE - GOVERNMENT FINANCES

U.S. Department of Commerce, Bureau of the Census, Suitland, Maryland 20233 (301) 763-4040; *State Governmental Finances, Historical Statistics on Governmental Finances and Employment,* and *Government Finances.*

RANKINGS - STATE - PERSONAL INCOME PER CAPITA

U.S. Department of Commerce, Bureau of Economic Analysis, Fourteenth Street between Constitution Avenue and E Street, NW, Washington, D.C. 20230 (202) 606-9900; *Survey of Current Business.*

RANKINGS - STATE - PERSONAL INCOME PER CAPITA - DISPOSABLE

U.S. Department of Commerce, Bureau of Economic Analysis, Fourteenth Street between Constitution Avenue and E Street, NW, Washington, D.C. 20230 (202) 606-9900; *Survey of Current Business.*

RANKINGS - STATE - POPULATION

U.S. Department of Commerce, Bureau of the Census, Suitland, Maryland 20233 (301) 763-4040; *Census of Population and Housing, Population and Housing Unit Counts,* and *Current Population Reports.*

RANKINGS - STATE - PUBLIC ELEMENTARY - SECONDARY SCHOOL FINANCES

National Education Association, 1201 Sixteenth Street, NW, Washington, D.C. 20036 (202) 833-4000; *Estimates of School Statistics,* and unpublished data.

RAPE - FORCIBLE

U.S. Department of Justice, Bureau of Justice Statistics, 633 Indiana Avenue, NW, Washington, D.C. 20531 (800) 732-3277; *Criminal Victimization in the United States,* and *Crime and the Nation's*

Households.

U.S. Department of Justice, Federal Bureau of Investigation, Ninth Street and Pennsylvania Avenue, NW, Washington, D.C. 20535 (202) 324-3000; *Crime in the United States,* and *Population-at-Risk Rates and Selected Crime Indicators.*

RARE - EARTH MINERALS

U.S. Department of the Interior, Bureau of Mines, 810 Seventh Street, NW, Washington, D.C. 20241 (202) 501-9649; *Mineral Commodity Summaries.*

RAW MATERIALS - See CRUDE MATERIALS

READING - See also BOOKS and LIBRARIES AND LIBRARIANS

Book Industry Study Group, 160 Fifth Avenue, New York, New York 10010 (212) 929-1393; *Book Industry Trends.*

U.S. Department of Labor, Bureau of Labor Statistics, Two Massachusetts Avenue, NE, Washington, D.C. 20212 (202) 606-7828; *Consumer Expenditure Survey.*

REAL ESTATE ASSESSMENTS

U.S. Department of Commerce, Bureau of the Census, Suitland, Maryland 20233 (301) 763-4040; *Census of Governments, Property Values Subject to Local General Property Taxation in the United States,* and *Government Finances.*

REAL ESTATE INDUSTRY - EARNINGS

U.S. Department of Commerce, Bureau of the Census, Suitland, Maryland 20233 (301) 763-4040; *County Business Patterns.*

U.S. Department of Labor, Bureau of Labor Statistics, Two Massachusetts Avenue, NE, Washington, D.C. 20212 (202) 606-7828; *Employment and Earnings,* and Bulletins 2370 and 2429.

REAL ESTATE INDUSTRY - EMPLOYEES

U.S. Department of Commerce, Bureau of Economic Analysis, Fourteenth Street between Constitution Avenue and E Street, NW, Washington, D.C. 20230 (202) 606-9900; *The National Income and Product Accounts of the United States,* and *Survey of Current Business.*

U.S. Department of Commerce, Bureau of the Census, Suitland, Maryland 20233 (301) 763-4040; *County Business Patterns.*

U.S. Department of Labor, Bureau of Labor Statistics, Two Massachusetts Avenue, NE, Washington, D.C. 20212 (202) 606-7828; *Employment and Earnings,* and Bulletins 2370 and 2429.

REAL ESTATE INDUSTRY - ESTABLISHMENTS

U.S. Department of Commerce, Bureau of the Census, Suitland, Maryland 20233 (301) 763-4040; *County Business Patterns.*

International Franchise Association, 1350 New York Avenue, Suite 900, Washington, D.C. 20005 (202) 628-8000; *Franchising in the Economy.*

REAL ESTATE INDUSTRY - GROSS DOMESTIC PRODUCT

U.S. Department of Commerce, Bureau of Economic Analysis, Fourteenth Street between Constitution Avenue and E Street, NW, Washington, D.C. 20230 (202) 606-9900; *The National Income and Product Accounts of the United States,* and *Survey of Current Business.*

U.S. Department of Commerce, Bureau of the Census, Suitland, Maryland 20233 (301) 763-4040; *County Business Patterns.*

REAL ESTATE INDUSTRY - RECEIPTS

U.S. Department of Commerce, Bureau of the Census, Suitland, Maryland 20233 (301) 763-4040; *Current Business Reports,* and *Service Annual Survey.*

REAL ESTATE INDUSTRY - SALES

International Franchise Association, 1350 New York Avenue, Suite 900, Washington, D.C. 20005 (202) 628-8000; *Franchising in the Economy.*

RECEIPTS - See also Individual Industries and TAX RECEIPTS

RECEIPTS

U.S. Department of Commerce, Bureau of the Census, Suitland, Maryland 20233 (301) 763-4040; *Current Business Reports, Service Annual Survey, Census of Service Industries,* and *County Business Patterns.*

RECEIPTS - CORPORATIONS - PARTNERSHIPS AND PROPRIETORSHIPS

U.S. Department of the Treasury, Internal Revenue Service, 1111 Constitution Avenue, NW, Washington, D.C. 20224 (202) 566-5000; *Statistics of Income, Corporation Income Tax Returns, Statistics of Income, Partnership Returns, Statistics of Income,* various publications, *Statistics of Income Bulletin,* and unpublished data.

RECEIPTS - INTERNATIONAL TRANSPORTATION

U.S. Department of Commerce, Bureau of Economic Analysis, Fourteenth Street between Constitution Avenue and E Street, NW, Washington, D.C. 20230 (202) 606-9900; *Survey of Current Business,* and unpublished data.

RECEIPTS - REVENUE - LOCAL GOVERNMENTS

U.S. Department of Commerce, Bureau of the Census, Suitland, Maryland 20233 (301) 763-4040; *Government Finances,* and *Historical Statistics on Governmental Finances and Employment.*

RECEIPTS - REVENUE - LOCAL GOVERNMENTS - CITY GOVERNMENTS

U.S. Department of Commerce, Bureau of the Census, Suitland, Maryland 20233 (301) 763-4040; *City Government Finances.*

RECEIPTS - REVENUE - STATE AND LOCAL GOVERNMENTS COMBINED

U.S. Department of Commerce, Bureau of Economic Analysis, Fourteenth Street between Constitution Avenue and E Street, NW, Washington, D.C. 20230 (202) 606-9900; *The National Income and Product Accounts of the United States,* and *Survey of Current Business.*

U.S. Department of Commerce, Bureau of the Census, Suitland, Maryland 20233 (301) 763-4040; *Historical Statistics on Governmental Finances and Employment, Government Finances, State Government Finances,* and unpublished data.

RECEIPTS - REVENUE - STATE GOVERNMENTS

National Governors' Association, Hall of the States, 444 North Capitol Street, NW, Washington, D.C. 20001 (202) 624-5300; *Fiscal Survey of the States*, and *NASBO State Expenditure Report*.

U.S. Department of Commerce, Bureau of the Census, Suitland, Maryland 20233 (301) 763-4040; *Historical Statistics on Government Finances and Employment, Government Finances, State Government Finances, State Government Tax Collections*.

RECEIPTS - REVENUE - STATE GOVERNMENTS - TAX COLLECTIONS

U.S. Department of Commerce, Bureau of the Census, Suitland, Maryland 20233 (301) 763-4040; *State Government Tax Collections*.

RECEIPTS - TRUST FUNDS

Executive Office of the President, Office of Management and Budget, Executive Office Building, Washington, D.C. 20503 (202) 395-3080; *Budget of the United States Government*.

RECEIPTS - UNITED STATES GOVERNMENT

Executive Office of the President, Office of Management and Budget, Executive Office Building, Washington, D.C. 20503 (202) 395-3080; *The Budget of the United States Government*.

U.S. Department of Commerce, Bureau of the Census, Suitland, Maryland 20233 (301) 763-4040; *Historical Statistics on Government Finances and Employment* and *Government Finances*.

U.S. Department of the Treasury, Internal Revenue Service, 1111 Constitution Avenue, NW, Washington, D.C. 20224 (202) 566-5000; *Annual Report of the Commissioner and Chief Counsel of the Internal Revenue Service*.

RECEIPTS - UNITED STATES GOVERNMENT - FROM NATIONAL FORESTS

U.S. Department of Agriculture, Forest Service, Fourteenth Street and Independence Avenue, SW, Washington, D.C. 20250 (202) 720-3760; *Agricultural Statistics*, and unpublished data.

RECREATION - See also AMUSEMENTS AND RECREATIONAL SERVICES

RECREATION - ACTIVITIES

Boy Scouts of America, 1325 Walnut Hill Lane, P.O. Box 152079, Irving, Texas 75015 (214) 580-2000; *Annual Report*.

Girls Scouts of the United States of America, 420 Fifth Avenue and 51st Street, New York, New York 10018-2702 (212) 852-8000; *Annual Report*.

National Association of State Park Directors, 126 Mill Branch Road, Tallahassee, Florida 32312 (904) 893-4959; *Annual Information Exchange*.

National Endowment for the Arts, 1100 Pennsylvania Avenue, NW, Washington, D.C. 20506 (202) 682-5400; *Arts Participation in America: 1982-1992*.

The National Gardening Association, 180 Flynn Avenue, Burlington, Vermont 05401 (802) 863-1308; *National Gardening Survey*.

National Sporting Goods Association, Lake Center Plaza Building, 1699 Wall Street, Mount Prospect, Illinois 60056 (708) 439-4000; *Sports Participation in 1992: Series I*.

U.S. Department of Agriculture, Forest Service, Fourteenth Street and Independence Avenue, SW, Washington, D.C. 20250 (202) 720-3760; unpublished data.

U.S. Department of the Interior, Bureau of Land Management, C Street between Eighteenth and Nineteenth Streets, NW, Washington, D.C. 20240 (202) 208-3435; *Public Land Statistics*.

U.S. Department of the Interior, Fish and Wildlife Service, C Street between Eighteenth and Nineteenth Streets, NW, Washington, D.C. 20240 (202) 208-5634; *Federal Aid in Fish and Wildlife Restoration*, and *National Survey of Fishing, Hunting, and Wildlife-Associated Recreation*.

U.S. Department of the Interior, National Park Service, C Street between Eighteenth and Nineteenth Streets, NW, Washington, D.C. 20240 (202) 208-6843; *National Park Statistical Abstract*, and unpublished data.

RECREATION - BUILDING CONSTRUCTION - VALUE

F.W. Dodge Division, McGraw-Hill Information Systems Company, 1221 Avenue of the Americas, New York, New York 10020 (212) 512-2000; *Dodge Construction Potentials*.

RECREATION - CONSUMER EXPENDITURES

Book Industry Study Group, 160 Fifth Avenue, New York, New York 10010 (212) 929-1393; *Book Industry Trends*.

National Sporting Goods Association, Lake Center Plaza Building, 1699 Wall Street, Mount Prospect, Illinois 60056 (708) 439-4000; *The Sporting Goods Market in 1993*.

U.S. Department of Commerce, Bureau of Economic Analysis, Fourteenth Street between Constitution Avenue and E Street, NW, Washington, D.C. 20230 (202) 606-9900; *The National Income and Product Accounts of the United States*, and *Survey of Current Business*.

U.S. Department of Labor, Bureau of Labor Statistics, Two Massachusetts Avenue, NE, Washington, D.C. 20212 (202) 606-7828; *Consumer Expenditure Survey*.

RECREATION - CONSUMER PRICE INDEXES

U.S. Department of Labor, Bureau of Labor Statistics, Two Massachusetts Avenue, NE, Washington, D.C. 20212 (202) 606-7828; *Monthly Labor Review*, and *Consumer Price Indexes, Detailed Report*.

RECREATION - EMPLOYMENT AND EXPENDITURES - GOVERNMENT

Executive Office of the President, U.S. Office of Management and Budget, Executive Office Building, Washington, D.C. 20503 (202) 395-3080; *Budget of the United States Government*.

RECREATION - EMPLOYMENT AND EXPENDITURES - GOVERNMENT - CITY GOVERNMENTS

U.S. Department of Commerce, Bureau of the Census, Suitland, Maryland 20233 (301) 763-4040; *City Government Finances, Public Employment*, and *City Employment*.

RECREATION - PARKS - GOVERNMENT EXPENDITURES

U.S. Department of Commerce, Bureau of the Census, Suitland, Maryland 20233 (301) 763-4040; *Government Finances*, and *Historical Statistics on Governmental Finances and Employment*.

RECREATION - PARKS - NATIONAL

U.S. Department of the Interior, National Park Service, C Street between Eighteenth and Nineteenth Streets, NW, Washington, D.C. 20240 (202) 208-6843; *National Park Statistical Abstract*, and unpublished data.

RECREATION - PARKS - NATIONAL - VISITS

National Association of State Park Directors, 126 Mill Branch Road, Tallahassee, Florida 32312 (904) 893-4959; *Annual Information Exchange*.

U.S. Department of the Interior, National Park Service, C Street between Eighteenth and Nineteenth Streets, NW, Washington, D.C. 20240 (202) 208-6843; *National Park Statistical Abstract*, and unpublished data.

RECREATION - PARTICIPATION

Amateur Softball Association of America, 2801 NE 50th Street, Oklahoma City, Oklahoma 73111-7203 (405) 424-5266.

American Bowling Congress, 5301 South 76th Street, Greendale, Wisconsin 53129 (414) 421-6400.

Bicycle Manufacturers Association of America, Incorporated, 3050 K Street, NW, Suite 400, Washington, D.C. 20007 (202) 944-9297.

The Gallup Organization Incorporated, 100 Palmer Square, Princeton, New Jersey 08542 (609) 924-9600.

Motion Picture Association of America, Incorporated, 1600 Eye Street, NW, Washington, D.C. 20006 (202) 293-1966.

Motorcycle Industry Council, Incorporated, Two Jenner Street, Suite 150, Irvine, California 92718 (714) 727-4211.

National Bowling Council, 2300 Clarendon Boulevard, No. 1107, Arlington, Virginia 22201 (703) 841-1660.

National Marine Manufacturers Association, 401 North Michigan Avenue, Suite 1150, Chicago, Illinois 60611 (312) 836-4747.

National Sporting Goods Association, Lake Center Plaza Building, 1699 Wall Street, Mt. Prospect, Illinois 60056 (708) 439-4000; *Sports Participation in 1990: Series I*.

Specialty Vehicles Institute of America, Two Jenner Street, Suite 150, Irvine, California 92718 (714) 727-3727.

United States Tennis Association, 1212 Avenue of the Americas, New York, New York 10036 (212) 302-3322.

U.S. Department of Labor, Bureau of Labor Statistics, Two Massachusetts Avenue, NE, Washington, D.C. 20212 (202) 606-7828; *Consumer Expenditure Survey*.

RECREATION - PERFORMING ARTS

American Symphony Orchestra League, 777 Fourteenth Street, NW, Washington, D.C. 20005 (202) 628-0099.

Opera America, 777 Fourteenth Street, NW, Washington, D.C. 20005 (202) 347-9262.

Variety, 249 West Seventeenth Street, New York, New York 10011 (212) 779-1100.

RECREATION - TRAVEL

U.S. Department of Commerce, Bureau of Economic Analysis, Fourteenth Street between Constitution Avenue and E Street, NW, Washington, D.C. 20230 (202) 606-9900; *Survey of Current Business*.

U.S. Department of Commerce, Travel and Tourism Administration, Washington, D.C. 20230 (202) 482-3811; unpublished data.

U.S. Travel Data Center, Two Lafayette Center, 1133 Twenty-first Street, NW, Washington, D.C. 20036 (202) 293-1040; *Impact of Travel on State Economies*, *The Economic Review of Travel in America*, and *National Travel Survey*.

RECREATION - VOLUNTEERS

Independent Sector, 1828 L Street, NW, Washington, D.C. 20036 (202) 223-8100; *Giving and Volunteering in the United States*.

RECREATIONAL VEHICLES

American Automobile Manufacturers Association, 1401 H Street, NW, Suite 900, Washington, D.C. 20005 (202) 326-5500; *Motor Vehicle Facts and Figures*.

National Sporting Goods Association, Lake Center Plaza Building, 1699 Wall Street, Mount Prospect, Illinois 60056 (708) 439-4000; *The Sporting Goods Market in 1993*.

Recreation Vehicle Industry Association, Post Office Box 2999, 1896 Preston White Drive, Reston, Virginia 22090 (703) 620-6003; *Recreational Vehicles...The Family Camping Vehicle, A Year-End Report*.

Specialty Vehicles Institute of America, Two Jenner Street, Suite 150, Irvine, California 92718 (714) 727-3727.

U.S. Department of Commerce, Bureau of the Census, Suitland, Maryland 20233 (301) 763-4040; *Census of Retail Trade*.

RECYCLING WASTE

Franklin Associates Limited, 4121 West Eighty-third Street, Suite 108, Prairie Village, Kansas 66208 (913) 649-2225; *Characterization of Municipal Solid Waste in the United States*.

REFRIGERATORS AND REFRIGERATION EQUIPMENT

U.S. Department of Commerce, Bureau of the Census, Suitland, Maryland 20233 (301) 763-4040; *Current Industrial Reports*.

REFUGEES

U.S. Department of Justice, Immigration and Naturalization Service, 425 I Street, NW, Washington, D.C. 20536 (202) 514-4316; *Statistical Yearbook*, and releases.

RELIGION

American Jewish Committee, c/o Institute of Human Relations, 165 East 56th Street, New York, New York 10022 (212) 751-4000; and the Jewish Publication Society, 1930 Chestnut Street, Philadelphia, Pennsylvania 19103-4599 (215) 564-5925; *American Jewish Year*

Book.

Encyclopedia Britannica, Incorporated, 310 South Michigan Avenue, Chicago, Illinois 60604 (312) 347-7000; *Britannica Book of the Year.*

National Council of the Churches of Christ in the United States of America, 475 Riverside Drive, New York, New York 10115 (212) 870-2227; *Yearbook of American and Canadian Churches.*

Princeton Religion Research Center, 47 Hulfish Street, Princeton, New Jersey 08542 (609) 921-8112; *Emerging Trends,* based on surveys conducted by The Gallup Organization, Inc., 100 Palmer Square, Princeton, New Jersey 08542 (609) 924-9600.

RELIGION - CATHOLICS

National Council of the Churches of Christ in the United States of America, 475 Riverside Drive, New York, New York 10115 (212) 870-2227; *Yearbook of American and Canadian Churches.*

Princeton Religion Research Center, 47 Hulfish Street, Princeton, New Jersey 08542 (609) 921-8112; *Emerging Trends,* based on surveys conducted by The Gallup Organization, Inc., 100 Palmer Square, Princeton, New Jersey 08542 (609) 924-9600.

RELIGION - CHARITABLE CONTRIBUTIONS

American Association of Fund Raising Council, 25 West Forty-third Street, Suite 1519, New York, New York 10036 (212) 354-5799; *Giving USA.*

Independent Sector, 1828 L Street, NW, Washington, D.C. 20036 (202) 223-8100; *Giving and Volunteering in the United States.*

RELIGION - CHURCH - SYNAGOGUE ATTENDANCE

Princeton Religion Research Center, 47 Hulfish Street, Princeton, New Jersey 08542 (609) 921-8112; *Emerging Trends,* based on surveys conducted by The Gallup Organization, Inc., 100 Palmer Square, Princeton, New Jersey 08542 (609) 924-9600.

RELIGION - JEWS

American Jewish Committee, c/o Institute of Human Relations, 165 East Fifty-sixth Street, New York, New York 10022 (212) 751-4000; and the Jewish Publication Society, 1930 Chestnut Street, Philadelphia, Pennsylvania 19103 (215) 564-5925; *American Jewish Yearbook.*

National Council of the Churches of Christ in the United States of America, 475 Riverside Drive, New York, New York 10115 (212) 870-2227; *Yearbook of American and Canadian Churches.*

RELIGION - PHILANTHROPY

American Association of Fund Raising Counsel, 25 West Forty-third Street, Suite 1519, New York, New York 10036 (212) 354-5799; *Giving USA.*

The Foundation Center, 79 Fifth Avenue, New York, New York 10003 (212) 620-4230; *Foundation Grants Index.*

Independent Sector, 1828 L Street, NW, Washington, D.C. 20036 (202) 223-8100; *Giving and Volunteering in the United States.*

RELIGION - PROTESTANTS

National Council of the Churches of Christ in the United States of America, 475 Riverside Drive, New York, New York 10115 (212)

870-2227; *Yearbook of American and Canadian Churches.*

Princeton Religion Research Center, 47 Hulfish Street, Princeton, New Jersey 08542 (609) 921-8112; *Emerging Trends,* based on surveys conducted by The Gallup Organization, Inc., 100 Palmer Square, Princeton, New Jersey 08542 (609) 924-9600.

RELIGIOUS ORGANIZATIONS

Encyclopedia Britannica, Incorporated, 310 South Michigan Avenue, Chicago, Illinois 60604 (312) 347-7000; *Britannica Book of the Year.*

Gale Research Incorporated, 835 Penobscot Building, Detroit, Michigan 48226 (800) 877-4253; *Encyclopedia of Associations.*

U.S. Department of Commerce, Bureau of the Census, Suitland, Maryland 20233 (301) 763-4040; *County Business Patterns.*

RELIGIOUS ORGANIZATIONS - VOLUNTEERS

Independent Sector, 1828 L Street, NW, Washington, D.C. 20036 (202) 223-8100; *Giving and Volunteering in the U.S.*

RELIGIOUS PREFERENCE

Princeton Religion Research Center, 47 Hulfish Street, Princeton, New Jersey 08542 (609) 921-8112; *Emerging Trends,* based on surveys conducted by The Gallup Organization, Inc., 100 Palmer Square, Princeton, New Jersey 08542 (609) 924-9600.

RENTS

U.S. Department of Labor, Bureau of Labor Statistics, Two Massachusetts Avenue, NE, Washington, D.C. 20212 (202) 606-7828; *Monthly Labor Review,* and *Consumer Price Indexes, Detailed Report.*

REPAIR SERVICES - See AUTOMOTIVE REPAIR, SERVICES AND PARKING

REPRESENTATIVES, UNITED STATES - See CONGRESS, UNITED STATES

RESEARCH AND DEVELOPMENT - EMPLOYMENT

U.S. National Science Foundation, 4201 Wilson Boulevard, Arlington, Virginia 22230 (703) 306-1234; *National Patterns of Research and Development Resources,* and *Research and Development in Industry.*

RESEARCH AND DEVELOPMENT - EXPENDITURES - BY COUNTRY

U.S. National Science Foundation, 4201 Wilson Boulevard, Arlington, Virginia 22230 (703) 306-1234; *Science Indicators, National Patterns of Research and Development Resources.*

RESEARCH AND DEVELOPMENT - EXPENDITURES - COLLEGES AND UNIVERSITIES

U.S. Department of Education, 400 Maryland Avenue, SW, Washington, D.C. 20202 (202) 708-5366; *Financial Statistics of Institutions of Higher Education,* and *Digest of Education Statistics.*

U.S. National Science Foundation, 4201 Wilson Boulevard, Arlington, Virginia 22230 (703) 306-1234; *Survey of Scientific and Engineering Expenditures of Universities and Colleges, Science and Engineering Indicators,* and *National Patterns of Research and Development Resources.*

RESEARCH AND DEVELOPMENT - EXPENDITURES - FEDERAL

U.S. National Science Foundation, 4201 Wilson Boulevard, Arlington, Virginia 22230 (703) 306-1234; *National Patterns of Research and Development Resources, Federal Funds for Research and Development, Federal Research and Development Funding by Budget Function, Science and Engineering Indicators*, and *Survey of Federal Support to Universities, Colleges, and Nonprofit Institutions*.

RESEARCH AND DEVELOPMENT - EXPENDITURES - INDUSTRY

U.S. National Science Foundation, 4201 Wilson Boulevard, Arlington, Virginia 22230 (703) 306-1234; *National Patterns of Research and Development Resources*, and *Research and Development in Industry*.

RESEARCH AND DEVELOPMENT - EXPENDITURES -
NATIONAL DEFENSE

Executive Office of the President, Office of Management and Budget, Executive Office Building, Washington, D.C. 20503 (202) 395-3080; *The Budget of the United States Government*.

U.S. National Science Foundation, 4201 Wilson Boulevard, Arlington, Virginia 22230 (703) 306-1234; *National Patterns of Research and Development Resources*.

RESEARCH AND DEVELOPMENT - EXPENDITURES - SPACE
PROGRAM

Executive Office of the President, Office of Management and Budget, Executive Office Building, Washington, D.C. 20503 (202) 395-3080; *The Budget of the United States Government*.

National Aeronautics and Space Administration, 600 Independence Avenue, SW, Washington, D.C. 20546 (202) 453-1000; *1995 Budget Summary*.

RESEARCH AND DEVELOPMENT - STATES - BY SECTOR

U.S. National Science Foundation, 4201 Wilson Boulevard, Arlington, Virginia 22230 (703) 306-1234; *National Patterns of Research and Development Resources*.

RESIDENTIAL BUILDINGS - See CONSTRUCTION INDUSTRY
and HOUSING AND HOUSING UNITS

RESIDENTIAL CAPITAL

U.S. Department of Commerce, Bureau of Economic Analysis, Fourteenth Street between Constitution Avenue and E Street, NW, Washington, D.C. 20230 (202) 606-9900; *Survey of Current Business*, and *Fixed Reproducible Tangible Wealth in the United States*.

RESTAURANTS - See EATING AND DRINKING PLACES

RETAIL TRADE - COLLECTIVE BARGAINING SETTLEMENTS

U.S. Department of Labor, Bureau of Labor Statistics, Two Massachusetts Avenue, NE, Washington, D.C. 20212 (202) 606-7828; *Compensation and Working Conditions*.

RETAIL TRADE - EARNINGS

U.S. Department of Commerce, Bureau of Economic Analysis, Fourteenth Street between Constitution Avenue and E Street, NW, Washington, D.C. 20230 (202) 606-9900; *The National Income and Products Accounts of the United States*, and *Survey of Current Business*.

U.S. Department of Commerce, Bureau of the Census, Suitland, Maryland 20233 (301) 763-4040; *Economic Census of Outlying Areas, Census of Retail Trade*, and *County Business Patterns*.

U.S. Department of Labor, Bureau of Labor Statistics, Two Massachusetts Avenue, NE, Washington, D.C. 20212 (202) 606-7828; *Employment and Earnings*, and Bulletins 2370 and 2429.

RETAIL TRADE - EMPLOYEES

U.S. Department of Commerce, Bureau of Economic Analysis, Fourteenth Street between Constitution Avenue and E Street, NW, Washington, D.C. 20230 (202) 606-9900; *The National Income and Product Accounts of the United States*, and *Survey of Current Business*.

U.S. Department of Commerce, Bureau of the Census, Suitland, Maryland 20233 (301) 763-4040; *Census of Retail Trade County Business Patterns*, and *Economic Census of Outlying Areas*.

U.S. Department of Labor, Bureau of Labor Statistics, Two Massachusetts Avenue, NE, Washington, D.C. 20212 (202) 606-7828; *Employment and Earnings, Monthly Labor Review*, and Bulletins 2370 and 2429, and unpublished data.

RETAIL TRADE - ESTABLISHMENTS

International Franchise Association, 1350 New York Avenue, Suite 900, Washington, D.C. 20005 (202) 628-8000; *Franchising in the Economy*.

U.S. Department of Commerce, Bureau of the Census, Suitland, Maryland 20233 (301) 763-4040; *Census of Retail Trade, Economic Census of Outlying Areas*, and *County Business Patterns*.

RETAIL TRADE - FINANCES

Board of Governors of the Federal Reserve System, 20th Street and Constitution Avenue, NW, Washington, D.C. 20551 (202) 452-3000; *Federal Reserve Bulletin*, and *Annual Statistical Digest*.

Time Warner, 1675 Broadway, Rockefeller Center, New York, New York 10019 (212) 522-1212; *The Fortune Directories*.

U.S. Department of the Treasury, Internal Revenue Service, 1111 Constitution Avenue, NW, Washington, D.C. 20224 (202) 566-5000; *Statistics of Income, Statistics of Income Bulletin*, and various publications.

RETAIL TRADE - FOREIGN INVESTMENTS IN THE UNITED STATES

U.S. Department of Commerce, Bureau of Economic Analysis, Fourteenth Street between Constitution Avenue and E Street, NW, Washington, D.C. 20230 (202) 606-9900; *Survey of Current Business*, and *Foreign Direct Investment in the United States, Operations of U.S. Affiliates of Foreign Companies*.

RETAIL TRADE - FRANCHISES

International Franchise Association, 1350 New York Avenue, Suite 900, Washington, D.C. 20005 (202) 628-8000; *Franchising in the Economy*.

RETAIL TRADE - GROSS DOMESTIC PRODUCT

Puerto Rico Planning Board, North Building, Box 41119, Santurce, Puerto Rico 00940; *Economic Report of the Governor.*

U.S. Department of Commerce, Bureau of Economic Analysis, Fourteenth Street between Constitution Avenue and E Street, NW, Washington, D.C. 20230 (202) 606-9900; *The National Income and Product Accounts of the United States,* and *Survey of Current Business.*

RETAIL TRADE - INVENTORIES

U.S. Department of Commerce, Bureau of Economic Analysis, Fourteenth Street between Constitution Avenue and E Street, NW, Washington, D.C. 20230 (202) 606-9900; *The National Income and Product Accounts of the United States, Survey of Current Business,* and unpublished data.

U.S. Department of Commerce, Bureau of the Census, Suitland, Maryland 20233 (301) 763-4040; *Current Business Reports, Combined Annual and Revised Monthly Retail Trade,* and *Manufacturing and Trade Inventories and Sales.*

RETAIL TRADE - MERGERS AND ACQUISITIONS

Securities Data Company, 1180 Raymond Boulevard, Newark, New Jersey 07102 (201) 622-3100; *Merger and Corporate Transactions Database.*

RETAIL TRADE - OCCUPATIONAL SAFETY

U.S. Department of Labor, Bureau of Labor Statistics, Two Massachusetts Avenue, NE, Washington, D.C. 20212 (202) 606-7828; *Occupational Injuries and Illnesses in the United States by Industry.*

RETAIL TRADE - SALES

International Franchise Association, 1350 New York Avenue, Suite 900, Washington, D.C. 20005 (202) 628-8000; *Franchising in the Economy.*

Market Statistics, 633 Third Avenue, New York, New York 10017 (212) 986-4000; *The Survey of Buying Power Data Service.*

Time Warner, 1675 Broadway, Rockefeller Center, New York, New York 10019 (212) 522-1212; *The Fortune Directories.*

U.S. Department of Commerce, Bureau of Economic Analysis, Fourteenth Street between Constitution Avenue and E Street, NW, Washington, D.C. 20230 (202) 606-9900; *Survey of Current Business, Business Conditions Digest,* and *The National Income and Product Accounts of the United States.*

U.S. Department of Commerce, Bureau of the Census, Suitland, Maryland 20233 (301) 763-4040; *Census of Retail Trade, Current Business Reports, Combined Annual and Revised Monthly Retail Trade, Manufacturing and Trade Inventories and Sales, Merchandise Line Sales, Current Business Reports, Revised Monthly Retail Sales and Inventories,* and *Economic Census of Outlying Areas.*

RETIREMENT SYSTEM - BENEFITS PAID

Employment Benefit Research Institute, 2121 K Street, NW, Suite 600, Washington, D.C. 20037 (202) 659-0670; *EBRI Databook on Employee Benefits.*

U.S. Department of Health and Human Services, Social Security Administration, 6401 Security Boulevard, Baltimore, Maryland 21235 (410) 965-1234; *Social Security Bulletin, Annual Statistical Supplement to the Social Security Bulletin,* and unpublished data.

U.S. Department of Labor, Bureau of Labor Statistics, Two Massachusetts Avenue, NE, Washington, D.C. 20212 (202) 606-7828; *Employee Benefits in Medium and Large Private Establishments,* and *Employee Benefits in Small Private Establishments.*

RETIREMENT SYSTEM - CIVIL SERVICE

Board of Governors of the Federal Reserve System, Twentieth Street and Constitution Avenue, NW, Washington, D.C. 20551 (202) 452-3000; *Annual Statistical Digest,* and unpublished data.

U.S. Department of Health and Human Services, Social Security Administration, 6401 Security Boulevard, Baltimore, Maryland 21235 (410) 965-1234; *Social Security Bulletin, Annual Statistical Supplement to the Social Security Bulletin,* and unpublished data.

U.S. Office of Personnel Management, 1900 E Street, NW, Washington, D.C. 20415 (202) 606-1800; *Compensation Report.*

RETIREMENT SYSTEM - FEDERAL - OTHER THAN CIVIL SERVICE

Board of Governors of the Federal Reserve System, Twentieth Street and Constitution Avenue, NW, Washington, D.C. 20551 (202) 452-3000; *Annual Statistical Digest,* and unpublished data.

U.S. Department of Health and Human Services, Social Security Administration, 6401 Security Boulevard, Baltimore, Maryland 21235 (410) 965-1234; *Annual Statistical Supplement to the Social Security Bulletin, Social Security Bulletin,* and unpublished data.

RETIREMENT SYSTEM - OLD AGE, SURVIVORS, DISABILITY, AND HEALTH INSURANCE - See SOCIAL INSURANCE

RETIREMENT SYSTEM - PENSION PLANS

Board of Governors of the Federal Reserve System, Twentieth Street and Constitution Avenue, NW, Washington, D.C. 20551 (202) 452-3000; *Annual Statistical Digest,* and unpublished data.

U.S. Department of Health and Human Services, Social Security Administration, 6401 Security Boulevard, Baltimore, Maryland 21235 (410) 965-1234; *Social Security Bulletin, Annual Statistical Supplement to the Social Security Bulletin,* and unpublished data.

U.S. Department of Labor, Pension and Welfare Benefits Administration, 200 Constitution Avenue, NW, Washington, D.C. 20210 (202) 219-8771; *Private Pension Plan Benefits.*

RETIREMENT SYSTEM - RAILROAD

Board of Governors of the Federal Reserve System, Twentieth Street and Constitution Avenue, NW, Washington, D.C. 20551 (202) 452-3000; *Annual Statistical Digest,* and unpublished data.

U.S. Department of Health and Human Services, Social Security Administration, 6401 Security Boulevard, Baltimore, Maryland 21235 (410) 965-1234; *Social Security Bulletin, Annual Statistical Supplement to the Social Security Bulletin,* and unpublished data.

RETIREMENT SYSTEM - SOCIAL SECURITY TRUST FUNDS

U.S. Department of Health and Human Services, Social Security Administration, 6401 Security Boulevard, Baltimore, Maryland 21235

(410) 965-1234; *Annual Report of Board of Trustees, OASI, DI, HI, and SMI Trust Funds, Annual Statistical Supplement to the Social Security Bulletin,* and unpublished data.

RETIREMENT SYSTEM - STATE AND LOCAL GOVERNMENT

Board of Governors of the Federal Reserve System, Twentieth Street and Constitution Avenue, NW, Washington, D.C. 20551 (202) 452-3000; *Annual Statistical Digest,* and unpublished data.

Executive Office of the President, Office of Management and Budget, Executive Office Building, Washington, D.C. 20503 (202) 395-3080; *The Budget of the United States Government.*

U.S. Department of Commerce, Bureau of the Census, Suitland, Maryland 20233 (301) 763-4040; *Historical Statistics on Governmental Finances and Employment, Government Finances,* and *Public Employment.*

U.S. Department of Health and Human Services, Social Security Administration, 6401 Security Boulevard, Baltimore, Maryland 21235 (410) 965-1234; *Social Security Bulletin, Annual Statistical Supplement to the Social Security Bulletin,* and unpublished data.

RETIREMENT SYSTEM - TRUST FUNDS

Executive Office of the President, Office of Management and Budget, Executive Office Building, Washington, D.C. 20503 (202) 395-3080; *Budget of the United States Government.*

Reunion - Primary Statistics Sources

Institut National de la Statistique et des Etudes Economiques (France), 4 rue de l'Ecole, Sainte, Clothilde, Reunion 97490; *Tableau Economique de La Reunion.*

REUNION - ABORTIONS

Statistical Office of the United Nations, Publishing Service, New York, New York 10017 (800) 253-9646; *Demographic Yearbook.*

REUNION - AGRICULTURE

Food and Agricultural Organization of the United Nations (FAO) Via delle Terme di Caracalla, 00100 Rome, Italy (Telephone Number in U.S. (202) 653-2400); *Production Yearbook, The State of Food and Agriculture,* and *Trade Yearbook.*

G.K. Hall and Company, 70 Lincoln Street, Boston, Massachusetts 02111 (617) 423-3990; *The World in Figures.*

REUNION - AIRLINE SERVICE

G.K. Hall and Company, 70 Lincoln Street, Boston, Massachusetts 02111 (617) 423-3990; *The World in Figures.*

REUNION - ANIMAL HEALTH

Food and Agricultural Organization of the United Nations (FAO), Via delle Terme di Caracalla, 00100, Rome, Italy (Telephone Number in U.S. (202) 653-2400); *Animal Health Yearbook.*

REUNION - AREA AND DENSITY OF POPULATION

Food and Agricultural Organization of the United Nations (FAO) Via delle Terme di Caracalla, 00100 Rome, Italy (Telephone Number in U.S. (202) 653-2400); *The State of Food and Agriculture.*

G.K. Hall and Company, 70 Lincoln Street, Boston, Massachusetts 02111 (617) 423-3990; *The World in Figures.*

Statistical Office of the United Nations, Publishing Service, New York, New York 10017 (800) 253-9646; *Statistical Yearbook.*

United Nations Educational, Scientific and Cultural Organization (UNESCO), 7 Place de Fontenoy, F-75700 Paris, France (Telephone Number in U.S. (212) 963-5981); *Statistical Yearbook.*

REUNION - BALANCE OF PAYMENTS

G.K. Hall and Company, 70 Lincoln Street, Boston, Massachusetts 02111 (617) 423-3990; *The World in Figures.*

REUNION - BANKING

G.K. Hall and Company, 70 Lincoln Street, Boston, Massachusetts 02111 (617) 423-3990; *The World in Figures.*

REUNION - BIRTH RATES

Statistical Office of the United Nations, Publishing Service, New York, New York 10017 (800) 253-9646; *Demographic Yearbook,* and *Statistical Yearbook.*

World Health Organization, Office of Publications, Avenue Appia, CH-1211 Geneva 27, Switzerland (Telephone Number in U.S. (518) 436-9686); *World Health Statistics Annual.*

REUNION - BONDS

G.K. Hall and Company, 70 Lincoln Street, Boston, Massachusetts 02111 (617) 423-3990; *The World in Figures.*

REUNION - BOOK PRODUCTION

G.K. Hall and Company, 70 Lincoln Street, Boston, Massachusetts 02111 (617) 423-3990; *The World in Figures.*

United Nations Educational, Scientific and Cultural Organization (UNESCO), 7 Place de Fontenoy, F-75700 Paris, France (Telephone Number in U.S. (212) 963-5981); *Statistical Yearbook.*

REUNION - BROADCASTING

Billboard Limited, P.O. Box 9027, 1006 AA Amsterdam, The Netherlands (Telephone Number in U.S. (212) 764-7300); *World Radio TV Handbook.*

G.K. Hall and Company, 70 Lincoln Street, Boston, Massachusetts 02111 (617) 423-3990; *The World in Figures.*

REUNION - BUSINESS

G.K. Hall and Company, 70 Lincoln Street, Boston, Massachusetts 02111 (617) 423-3990; *The World in Figures.*

REUNION - CALORIE SUPPLY

Food and Agricultural Organization of the United Nations (FAO) Via delle Terme di Caracalla, 00100 Rome, Italy (Telephone Number in U.S. (202) 653-2400); *The State of Food and Agriculture.*

REUNION - CATTLE - See REUNION - LIVESTOCK AND POULTRY

REUNION - CHEMICAL (ORGANIC) PRODUCTION - See REUNION - MINING AND MINERAL PRODUCTS

REUNION - CLASS STRUCTURE

G.K. Hall and Company, 70 Lincoln Street, Boston, Massachusetts 02111 (617) 423-3990; *The World in Figures.*

REUNION - CLIMATE

G.K. Hall and Company, 70 Lincoln Street, Boston, Massachusetts 02111 (617) 423-3990; *The World in Figures.*

REUNION - COAL PRODUCTION - See REUNION - MINING AND MINERAL PRODUCTS

REUNION - COMMUNICATIONS

G.K. Hall and Company, 70 Lincoln Street, Boston, Massachusetts 02111 (617) 423-3990; *The World in Figures.*

REUNION - CONSTRUCTION INDUSTRY

Statistical Office of the United Nations, Publishing Service, New York, New York 10017 (800) 253-9646; *Construction Statistics Yearbook.*

United Nations Economic Commission for Africa, Africa Hall, P.O. Box 3001, Addis Ababa, Ethiopia (Telephone Number in U.S. (800) 253-9646); *African Statistical Yearbook.*

REUNION - CONSUMER PRICE INDEX

G.K. Hall and Company, 70 Lincoln Street, Boston, Massachusetts 02111 (617) 423-3990; *The World in Figures.*

Statistical Office of the United Nations, Publishing Service, New York, New York 10017 (800) 253-9646; *Statistical Yearbook.*

REUNION - CONSUMER PRICES

International Labour Office, I.L.O. Publications, CH-1211, Geneva 22, Switzerland; *Yearbook of Labour Statistics.*

REUNION - CONSUMPTION

G.K. Hall and Company, 70 Lincoln Street, Boston, Massachusetts 02111 (617) 423-3990; *The World in Figures.*

REUNION - CORN PRODUCTION - See REUNION - CROPS

REUNION - CORPORATE TAXES - See REUNION - TAXATION

REUNION - CROPS

Food and Agricultural Organization of the United Nations (FAO) Via delle Terme di Caracalla, 00100 Rome, Italy (Telephone Number in U.S. (202) 653-2400); *Production Yearbook,* and *The State of Food and Agriculture.*

G.K. Hall and Company, 70 Lincoln Street, Boston, Massachusetts 02111 (617) 423-3990; *The World in Figures.*

Statistical Office of the United Nations, Publishing Service, New York, New York 10017 (800) 253-9646; *Statistical Yearbook.*

REUNION - CUSTOMS DUTIES

G.K. Hall and Company, 70 Lincoln Street, Boston, Massachusetts 02111 (617) 423-3990; *The World in Figures.*

REUNION - DAIRY PRODUCTS

Food and Agricultural Organization of the United Nations (FAO) Via delle Terme di Caracalla, 00100 Rome, Italy (Telephone Number in U.S. (202) 653-2400); *The State of Food and Agriculture.*

Statistical Office of the United Nations, Publishing Service, New York, New York 10017 (800) 253-9646; *Statistical Yearbook.*

REUNION - DEATH RATES

G.K. Hall and Company, 70 Lincoln Street, Boston, Massachusetts 02111 (617) 423-3990; *The World in Figures.*

Statistical Office of the United Nations, Publishing Service, New York, New York 10017 (800) 253-9646; *Statistical Yearbook.*

World Health Organization, Office of Publications, Avenue Appia, CH-1211 Geneva 27, Switzerland (Telephone Number in U.S. (518) 436-9686); *World Health Statistics Annual.*

REUNION - DEFENSE EXPENDITURES

G.K. Hall and Company, 70 Lincoln Street, Boston, Massachusetts 02111 (617) 423-3990; *The World in Figures.*

REUNION - DEMOGRAPHY

G.K. Hall and Company, 70 Lincoln Street, Boston, Massachusetts 02111 (617) 423-3990; *The World in Figures.*

REUNION - DEVELOPMENT ASSISTANCE

G.K. Hall and Company, 70 Lincoln Street, Boston, Massachusetts 02111 (617) 423-3990; *The World in Figures.*

Statistical Office of the United Nations, Publishing Service, New York, New York 10017 (800) 253-9646; *Statistical Yearbook.*

REUNION - DISEASE

G.K. Hall and Company, 70 Lincoln Street, Boston, Massachusetts 02111 (617) 423-3990; *The World in Figures.*

World Health Organization, Office of Publications, Avenue Appia, CH-1211 Geneva 27, Switzerland (Telephone Number in U.S. (518) 436-9686); *World Health Statistics Annual.*

REUNION - DIVORCE RATES

Statistical Office of the United Nations, Publishing Service, New York, New York 10017 (800) 253-9646; *Demographic Yearbook,* and *Statistical Yearbook.*

REUNION - DOMESTIC PRODUCT

G.K. Hall and Company, 70 Lincoln Street, Boston, Massachusetts 02111 (617) 423-3990; *The World in Figures.*

REUNION - ECONOMY

G.K. Hall and Company, 70 Lincoln Street, Boston, Massachusetts 02111 (617) 423-3990; *The World in Figures.*

REUNION - EDUCATION

G.K. Hall and Company, 70 Lincoln Street, Boston, Massachusetts 02111 (617) 423-3990; *The World in Figures.*

United Nations Educational, Scientific and Cultural Organization (UNESCO), 7 Place de Fontenoy, F-75700 Paris, France (Telephone Number in U.S. (212) 963-5981); *Statistical Yearbook.*

REUNION - EGG PRODUCTION AND CONSUMPTION - See REUNION - DAIRY PRODUCTS

REUNION - ELECTRICITY

Statistical Office of the United Nations, Publishing Service, New York, New York 10017 (800) 253-9646; *Statistical Yearbook.*

United Nations Economic Commission for Africa, Africa Hall, P.O. Box 3001, Addis Ababa, Ethiopia (Telephone Number in U.S. (800) 253-9646); *African Statistical Yearbook.*

REUNION - EMPLOYMENT

International Labour Office, I.L.O. Publications, CH-1211, Geneva 22, Switzerland; *Yearbook of Labour Statistics.*

United Nations Economic Commission for Africa, Africa Hall, P.O. Box 3001, Addis Ababa, Ethiopia (Telephone Number in U.S. (800) 253-9646); *African Statistical Yearbook.*

REUNION - ENERGY

Food and Agricultural Organization of the United Nations (FAO) Via delle Terme di Caracalla, 00100 Rome, Italy (Telephone Number in U.S. (202) 653-2400); *The State of Food and Agriculture.*

G.K. Hall and Company, 70 Lincoln Street, Boston, Massachusetts 02111 (617) 423-3990; *The World in Figures.*

Statistical Office of the United Nations, Publishing Service, New York, New York 10017 (800) 253-9646; *Energy Statistics Yearbook,* and *Statistical Yearbook.*

United Nations Economic Commission for Africa, Africa Hall, P.O. Box 3001, Addis Ababa, Ethiopia (Telephone Number in U.S. (800) 253-9646); *African Statistical Yearbook.*

REUNION - EXPORTS

Food and Agricultural Organization of the United Nations (FAO) Via delle Terme di Caracalla, 00100 Rome, Italy (Telephone Number in U.S. (202) 653-2400); *The State of Food and Agriculture.*

G.K. Hall and Company, 70 Lincoln Street, Boston, Massachusetts 02111 (617) 423-3990; *The World in Figures.*

International Monetary Fund, 700 Nineteenth Street, NW, Washington, D.C. 20431 (202) 623-7000; *Direction of Trade Statistics.*

United Nations Economic Commission for Africa, Africa Hall, P.O. Box 3001, Addis Ababa, Ethiopia (Telephone Number in U.S. (800) 253-9646); *African Statistical Yearbook.*

REUNION - EXTERNAL TRADE

Food and Agricultural Organization of the United Nations (FAO) Via delle Terme di Caracalla, 00100 Rome, Italy (Telephone Number in U.S. (202) 653-2400); *The State of Food and Agriculture,* and *Trade Yearbook.*

G.K. Hall and Company, 70 Lincoln Street, Boston, Massachusetts 02111 (617) 423-3990; *The World in Figures.*

Statistical Office of the United Nations, Publishing Service, New York, New York 10017 (800) 253-9646; *Statistical Yearbook.*

REUNION - FARM CROPS - See REUNION - CROPS

REUNION - FERTILIZER

Food and Agricultural Organization of the United Nations (FAO), Via delle Terme di Caracalla, 00100, Rome, Italy (Telephone Number in U.S. (202) 653-2400); *Fertilizer Yearbook,* and *The State of Food and Agriculture.*

Statistical Office of the United Nations, Publishing Service, New York, New York 10017 (800) 253-9646; *Statistical Yearbook.*

REUNION - FETAL MORTALITY

Statistical Office of the United Nations, Publishing Service, New York, New York 10017 (800) 253-9646; *Demographic Yearbook.*

World Health Organization, Office of Publications, Avenue Appia, CH-1211 Geneva 27, Switzerland (Telephone Number in U.S. (518) 436-9686); *World Health Statistics Annual.*

REUNION - FISHERIES

Food and Agricultural Organization of the United Nations (FAO) Via delle Terme di Caracalla, 00100 Rome, Italy (Telephone Number in U.S. (202) 653-2400); *The State of Food and Agriculture,* and *Yearbook of Fishery Statistics.*

Statistical Office of the United Nations, Publishing Service, New York, New York 10017 (800) 253-9646; *Statistical Yearbook.*

REUNION - FINANCE

G.K. Hall and Company, 70 Lincoln Street, Boston, Massachusetts 02111 (617) 423-3990; *The World in Figures.*

REUNION - FOOD

Food and Agricultural Organization of the United Nations (FAO) Via delle Terme di Caracalla, 00100 Rome, Italy (Telephone Number in U.S. (202) 653-2400); *The State of Food and Agriculture.*

REUNION - FOOD SUPPLY

Food and Agricultural Organization of the United Nations (FAO), Via delle Terme di Caracalla, 00100, Rome, Italy (Telephone Number in U.S. (202) 653-2400); *Production Yearbook,* and *The State of Food and Agriculture.*

G.K. Hall and Company, 70 Lincoln Street, Boston, Massachusetts 02111 (617) 423-3990; *The World in Figures.*

REUNION - FOREIGN AID

G.K. Hall and Company, 70 Lincoln Street, Boston, Massachusetts 02111 (617) 423-3990; *The World in Figures.*

REUNION - FOREIGN TRADE

Food and Agricultural Organization of the United Nations (FAO) Via delle Terme di Caracalla, 00100 Rome, Italy (Telephone Number in U.S. (202) 653-2400); *The State of Food and Agriculture.*

G.K. Hall and Company, 70 Lincoln Street, Boston, Massachusetts 02111 (617) 423-3990; *The World in Figures.*

Statistical Office of the United Nations, Publishing Service, New York, New York 10017 (800) 253-9646; *International Trade Statistics,* and *Statistical Yearbook.*

United Nations Economic Commission for Africa, Africa Hall, P.O. Box 3001, Addis Ababa, Ethiopia (Telephone Number in U.S. (800) 253-9646); *African Statistical Yearbook.*

REUNION - FORESTRY AND FOREST PRODUCTS

Food and Agricultural Organization of the United Nations (FAO) Via delle Terme di Caracalla, 00100 Rome, Italy (Telephone Number in U.S. (202) 653-2400); *The State of Food and Agriculture,* and *Yearbook of Forest Products.*

G.K. Hall and Company, 70 Lincoln Street, Boston, Massachusetts 02111 (617) 423-3990; *The World in Figures.*

Statistical Office of the United Nations, Publishing Service, New York, New York 10017 (800) 253-9646; *Statistical Yearbook.*

United Nations Educational, Scientific and Cultural Organization (UNESCO), 7 Place de Fontenoy, F-75700 Paris, France (Telephone Number in U.S. (212) 963-5981); *Statistical Yearbook.*

REUNION - GENERAL MORTALITY

Statistical Office of the United Nations, Publishing Service, New York, New York 10017 (800) 253-9646; *Demographic Yearbook.*

World Health Organization, Office of Publications, Avenue Appia, CH-1211 Geneva 27, Switzerland (Telephone Number in U.S. (518) 436-9686); *World Health Statistics Annual.*

REUNION - GOVERNMENT

G.K. Hall and Company, 70 Lincoln Street, Boston, Massachusetts 02111 (617) 423-3990; *The World in Figures.*

REUNION - GRAIN PRODUCTION - See REUNION - CROPS

REUNION - GROSS DOMESTIC PRODUCT

G.K. Hall and Company, 70 Lincoln Street, Boston, Massachusetts 02111 (617) 423-3990; *The World in Figures.*

Statistical Office of the United Nations, Publishing Service, New York, New York 10017 (800) 253-9646; *Statistical Yearbook.*

United Nations Economic Commission for Africa, Africa Hall, P.O. Box 3001, Addis Ababa, Ethiopia (Telephone Number in U.S. (800) 253-9646); *African Statistical Yearbook.*

REUNION - GROUNDNUT PRODUCTION - See REUNION - CROPS

REUNION - HEALTH

G.K. Hall and Company, 70 Lincoln Street, Boston, Massachusetts 02111 (617) 423-3990; *The World in Figures.*

Statistical Office of the United Nations, Publishing Service, New York, New York 10017 (800) 253-9646; *Statistical Yearbook.*

World Health Organization, Office of Publications, Avenue Appia, CH-1211 Geneva 27, Switzerland (Telephone Number in U.S. (518) 436-9686); *World Health Statistics Annual.*

REUNION - HIDE PRODUCTION

Food and Agricultural Organization of the United Nations (FAO), Via delle Terme di Caracalla, 00100, Rome, Italy (Telephone Number in U.S. (202) 653-2400); *Production Yearbook.*

REUNION - HIGHWAYS

G.K. Hall and Company, 70 Lincoln Street, Boston, Massachusetts 02111 (617) 423-3990; *The World in Figures.*

REUNION - HOURS OF WORK - See REUNION - EMPLOYMENT

REUNION - ILLITERATE POPULATION

G.K. Hall and Company, 70 Lincoln Street, Boston, Massachusetts 02111 (617) 423-3990; *The World in Figures.*

United Nations Educational, Scientific and Cultural Organization (UNESCO), 7 Place de Fontenoy, F-75700 Paris, France (Telephone Number in U.S. (212) 963-5981); *Statistical Yearbook.*

REUNION - IMPORTS

Food and Agricultural Organization of the United Nations (FAO) Via delle Terme di Caracalla, 00100 Rome, Italy (Telephone Number in U.S. (202) 653-2400); *The State of Food and Agriculture.*

G.K. Hall and Company, 70 Lincoln Street, Boston, Massachusetts 02111 (617) 423-3990; *The World in Figures.*

International Labour Office, I.L.O. Publications, CH-1211, Geneva 22, Switzerland; *Direction of Trade.*

Statistical Office of the United Nations, Publishing Service, New York, New York 10017 (800) 253-9646; *Trade in Manufactures of Developing Countries.*

United Nations Economic Commission for Africa, Africa Hall, P.O. Box 3001, Addis Ababa, Ethiopia (Telephone Number in U.S. (000) 253-9646); *African Statistical Yearbook.*

REUNION - INDUSTRY

G.K. Hall and Company, 70 Lincoln Street, Boston, Massachusetts 02111 (617) 423-3990; *The World in Figures.*

International Labour Office, I.L.O. Publications, CH-1211, Geneva 22, Switzerland; *Yearbook of Labour Statistics.*

United Nations Economic Commission for Africa, Africa Hall, P.O. Box 3001, Addis Ababa, Ethiopia (Telephone Number in U.S. (800) 253-9646); *African Statistical Yearbook.*

REUNION - INFANT AND MATERNAL MORTALITY

Statistical Office of the United Nations, Publishing Service, New York, New York 10017 (800) 253-9646; *Demographic Yearbook,* and *Statistical Yearbook.*

World Health Organization, Office of Publications, Avenue Appia, CH-1211 Geneva 27, Switzerland (Telephone Number in U.S. (518) 436-9686); *World Health Statistics Annual.*

REUNION - LABOR FORCE

Food and Agricultural Organization of the United Nations (FAO) Via delle Terme di Caracalla, 00100 Rome, Italy (Telephone Number in U.S. (202) 653-2400); *The State of Food and Agriculture.*

G.K. Hall and Company, 70 Lincoln Street, Boston, Massachusetts 02111 (617) 423-3990; *The World in Figures*.

REUNION - LABOR PRODUCTIVITY

International Labour Office, I.L.O. Publications, CH-1211, Geneva 22, Switzerland; *Yearbook of Labour Statistics*.

REUNION - LAND USE

Food and Agricultural Organization of the United Nations (FAO), Via delle Terme di Caracalla, 00100, Rome, Italy (Telephone Number in U.S. (202) 653-2400); *Production Yearbook*.

G.K. Hall and Company, 70 Lincoln Street, Boston, Massachusetts 02111 (617) 423-3990; *The World in Figures*.

REUNION - LIBRARIES

United Nations Educational, Scientific and Cultural Organization (UNESCO), 7 Place de Fontenoy, F-75700 Paris, France (Telephone Number in U.S. (212) 963-5981); *Statistical Yearbook*.

REUNION - LIVESTOCK AND POULTRY

Food and Agricultural Organization of the United Nations (FAO), Via delle Terme di Caracalla, 00100, Rome, Italy (Telephone Number in U.S. (202) 653-2400); *Production Yearbook*, and *The State of Food and Agriculture*.

G.K. Hall and Company, 70 Lincoln Street, Boston, Massachusetts 02111 (617) 423-3990; *The World in Figures*.

Statistical Office of the United Nations, Publishing Service, New York, New York 10017 (800) 253-9646; *Statistical Yearbook*.

REUNION - LIVING LEVELS

G.K. Hall and Company, 70 Lincoln Street, Boston, Massachusetts 02111 (617) 423-3990; *The World in Figures*.

REUNION - MANUFACTURING

G.K. Hall and Company, 70 Lincoln Street, Boston, Massachusetts 02111 (617) 423-3990; *The World in Figures*.

Statistical Office of the United Nations, Publishing Service, New York, New York 10017 (800) 253-9646; *Statistical Yearbook*.

United Nations Economic Commission for Africa, Africa Hall, P.O. Box 3001, Addis Ababa, Ethiopia (Telephone Number in U.S. (800) 253-9646); *African Statistical Yearbook*.

REUNION - MARRIAGE RATES

Statistical Office of the United Nations, Publishing Service, New York, New York 10017 (800) 253-9646; *Demographic Yearbook*, and *Statistical Yearbook*.

REUNION - MEAT PRODUCTION - See REUNION - LIVESTOCK AND POULTRY

REUNION - MERCHANT SHIPPING

G.K. Hall and Company, 70 Lincoln Street, Boston, Massachusetts 02111 (617) 423-3990; *The World in Figures*.

Statistical Office of the United Nations, Publishing Service, New York, New York 10017 (800) 253-9646; *Statistical Yearbook*.

REUNION - MILITARY

G.K. Hall and Company, 70 Lincoln Street, Boston, Massachusetts 02111 (617) 423-3990; *The World in Figures*.

REUNION - MINING AND MINERAL PRODUCTS

G.K. Hall and Company, 70 Lincoln Street, Boston, Massachusetts 02111 (617) 423-3990; *The World in Figures*.

United Nations Economic Commission for Africa, Africa Hall, P.O. Box 3001, Addis Ababa, Ethiopia (Telephone Number in U.S. (800) 253-9646); *African Statistical Yearbook*.

REUNION - MONEY SUPPLY

G.K. Hall and Company, 70 Lincoln Street, Boston, Massachusetts 02111 (617) 423-3990; *The World in Figures*.

REUNION - MOTION PICTURES

Statistical Office of the United Nations, Publishing Service, New York, New York 10017 (800) 253-9646; *Statistical Yearbook*.

REUNION - MOTOR VEHICLES IN USE

G.K. Hall and Company, 70 Lincoln Street, Boston, Massachusetts 02111 (617) 423-3990; *The World in Figures*.

Statistical Office of the United Nations, Publishing Service, New York, New York 10017 (800) 253-9646; *Statistical Yearbook*.

REUNION - MULES - See REUNION - LIVESTOCK AND POULTRY

REUNION - MUSEUMS

United Nations Educational, Scientific and Cultural Organization (UNESCO), 7 Place de Fontenoy, F-75700 Paris, France (Telephone Number in U.S. (212) 963-5981); *Statistical Yearbook*.

REUNION - NATALITY - See REUNION - BIRTH RATE

REUNION - NATIONAL ACCOUNTS

Statistical Office of the United Nations, Publishing Service, New York, New York 10017 (800) 253-9646; *National Accounts Statistics*, and *Statistical Yearbook*.

United Nations Economic Commission for Africa, Africa Hall, P.O. Box 3001, Addis Ababa, Ethiopia (Telephone Number in U.S. (800) 253-9646); *African Statistical Yearbook*.

REUNION - NATIONAL INCOME

G.K. Hall and Company, 70 Lincoln Street, Boston, Massachusetts 02111 (617) 423-3990; *The World in Figures*.

Statistical Office of the United Nations, Publishing Service, New York, New York 10017 (800) 253-9646; *Statistical Yearbook*.

REUNION - NEWSPAPER PRODUCTION - See REUNION - FORESTRY AND FOREST PRODUCTS

REUNION - NEWSPRINT - See REUNION - FORESTRY AND FOREST PRODUCTS

REUNION - OCCUPATIONS - See REUNION - LABOR FORCE

REUNION - PAPER - See REUNION - FORESTRY AND FOREST PRODUCTS

REUNION - PERIODICALS

United Nations Educational, Scientific and Cultural Organization (UNESCO), 7 Place de Fontenoy, F-75700 Paris, France (Telephone Number in U.S. (212) 963-5981); *Statistical Yearbook.*

REUNION - PESTICIDE USE

Food and Agricultural Organization of the United Nations (FAO) Via delle Terme di Caracalla, 00100 Rome, Italy (Telephone Number in U.S. (202) 653-2400); *The State of Food and Agriculture.*

REUNION - PETROLEUM INDUSTRY

Food and Agricultural Organization of the United Nations (FAO) Via delle Terme di Caracalla, 00100 Rome, Italy (Telephone Number in U.S. (202) 653-2400); *The State of Food and Agriculture.*

G.K. Hall and Company, 70 Lincoln Street, Boston, Massachusetts 02111 (617) 423-3990; *The World in Figures.*

REUNION - PIGS - See REUNION - LIVESTOCK AND POULTRY

REUNION - POPULATION

Food and Agricultural Organization of the United Nations (FAO), Via delle Terme di Caracalla, 00100, Rome, Italy (Telephone Number in U.S. (202) 653-2400); *Production Yearbook.*

G.K. Hall and Company, 70 Lincoln Street, Boston, Massachusetts 02111 (617) 423-3990; *The World in Figures.*

International Labour Office, I.L.O. Publications, CH-1211, Geneva 22, Switzerland; *Yearbook of Labour Statistics.*

Statistical Office of the United Nations, Publishing Service, New York, New York 10017 (800) 253-9646; *Demographic Yearbook,* and *Statistical Yearbook.*

United Nations Educational, Scientific and Cultural Organization (UNESCO), 7 Place de Fontenoy, F-75700 Paris, France (Telephone Number in U.S. (212) 963-5981); *Statistical Yearbook.*

World Health Organization, Office of Publications, Avenue Appia, CH-1211 Geneva 27, Switzerland (Telephone Number in U.S. (518) 436-9686); *World Health Statistics Annual.*

REUNION - POTATO PRODUCTION - See REUNION - CROPS

REUNION - PRICES

Food and Agricultural Organization of the United Nations (FAO), Via delle Terme di Caracalla, 00100, Rome, Italy (Telephone Number in U.S. (202) 653-2400); *Production Yearbook,* and *The State of Food and Agriculture.*

G.K. Hall and Company, 70 Lincoln Street, Boston, Massachusetts 02111 (617) 423-3990; *The World in Figures.*

International Labour Office, I.L.O. Publications, CH-1211, Geneva 22, Switzerland; *Yearbook of Labour Statistics.*

REUNION - PRINTING AND WRITING PAPER - See REUNION - FORESTRY AND FOREST PRODUCTS

REUNION - PRODUCTION

G.K. Hall and Company, 70 Lincoln Street, Boston, Massachusetts 02111 (617) 423-3990; *The World in Figures.*

REUNION - RAILWAYS

G.K. Hall and Company, 70 Lincoln Street, Boston, Massachusetts 02111 (617) 423-3990; *The World in Figures.*

REUNION - RENT PRICES

International Labour Office, I.L.O. Publications, CH-1211, Geneva 22, Switzerland; *Yearbook of Labour Statistics.*

REUNION - RETAIL TRADE

G.K. Hall and Company, 70 Lincoln Street, Boston, Massachusetts 02111 (617) 423-3990; *The World in Figures.*

REUNION - ROOT AND TUBER PRODUCTION - See REUNION - CROPS

REUNION - ROUNDWOOD PRODUCTION - See REUNION - FORESTRY AND FOREST PRODUCTS

REUNION - SAWNWOOD PRODUCTION - See REUNION - FORESTRY AND FOREST PRODUCTS

REUNION - SHEEP - See REUNION - LIVESTOCK AND POULTRY

REUNION - SOCIAL DATA

G.K. Hall and Company, 70 Lincoln Street, Boston, Massachusetts 02111 (617) 423-3990; *The World in Figures.*

REUNION - STOCKS - COMMODITY - MARKET PRICE - INDEX

Food and Agricultural Organization of the United Nations (FAO) Via delle Terme di Caracalla, 00100 Rome, Italy (Telephone Number in U.S. (202) 653-2400); *The State of Food and Agriculture.*

REUNION - SUGAR - See REUNION - CROPS

REUNION - TAXATION

G.K. Hall and Company, 70 Lincoln Street, Boston, Massachusetts 02111 (617) 423-3990; *The World in Figures.*

REUNION - TELEPHONES IN USE

American Telephone and Telegraph Company, 26 Parsippany Road, Whippany, New Jersey 07981 (800) 338-4038; *The World's Telephones.*

G.K. Hall and Company, 70 Lincoln Street, Boston, Massachusetts 02111 (617) 423-3990; *The World in Figures.*

Statistical Office of the United Nations, Publishing Service, New York, New York 10017 (800) 253-9646; *Statistical Yearbook.*

REUNION - TEXTILE INDUSTRY

G.K. Hall and Company, 70 Lincoln Street, Boston, Massachusetts 02111 (617) 423-3990; *The World in Figures.*

REUNION - TOURISM

G.K. Hall and Company, 70 Lincoln Street, Boston, Massachusetts 02111 (617) 423-3990; *The World in Figures*.

REUNION - TRADE - See REUNION - FOREIGN TRADE

REUNION - TRANSPORTATION AND COMMUNICATIONS

G.K. Hall and Company, 70 Lincoln Street, Boston, Massachusetts 02111 (617) 423-3990; *The World in Figures*.

REUNION - UNEMPLOYMENT

International Labour Office, I.L.O. Publications, CH-1211, Geneva 22, Switzerland; *Yearbook of Labour Statistics*.

REUNION - VITAL STATISTICS

G.K. Hall and Company, 70 Lincoln Street, Boston, Massachusetts 02111 (617) 423-3990; *The World in Figures*.

Statistical Office of the United Nations, Publishing Service, New York, New York 10017 (800) 253-9646; *Statistical Yearbook*.

World Health Organization, Office of Publications, Avenue Appia, CH-1211 Geneva 27, Switzerland (Telephone Number in U.S. (518) 436-9686); *World Health Statistics Annual*.

REUNION - WAGES

G.K. Hall and Company, 70 Lincoln Street, Boston, Massachusetts 02111 (617) 423-3990; *The World in Figures*.

International Labour Office, I.L.O. Publications, CH-1211, Geneva 22, Switzerland; *Yearbook of Labour Statistics*.

REUNION - WEATHER

G.K. Hall and Company, 70 Lincoln Street, Boston, Massachusetts 02111 (617) 423-3990; *The World in Figures*.

REVOLVERS - See FIREARMS

RHEUMATIC FEVER

U.S. Department of Health and Human Services, Centers for Disease Control, 1600 Clifton Road, NE, Atlanta, Georgia 30333 (404) 639-3311; *Summary of Notifiable Diseases, United States, Morbidity and Mortality Weekly Report*.

RHODE ISLAND - See also STATE DATA (FOR INDIVIDUAL STATES)

Rhode Island - Primary Statistics Source

Department of Economic Development, 7 Jackson Walkway, Providence, Rhode Island 02903 (401) 277-2601; *Rhode Island Basic Economic Statistics*.

Rhode Island - State Data Centers

Department of Administration, Office of Municipal Affairs, One Capitol Hill, Providence, Rhode Island 02908-5873, Mr. Paul Egan (401) 277-6493.

Rhode Island Department of State, Library Services, 300 Richmond Street, Providence, Rhode Island 02903, Mr. Frank Iacona (401) 277-

2726.

Social Science Data Center, Brown University, Post Office Box 1916, Providence, Rhode Island 02912, Mr. James McNally (401) 863-3459.

United Way of Rhode Island, 229 Waterman Street, Providence, Rhode Island 02908, Jane Nugent (401) 521-9000.

Office of Health Statistics, Rhode Island Department of Health, 3 Capitol Hill, Providence, Rhode Island 02908, Dr. Jay Buechner (401) 277-2550.

Rhode Island Department of Education, 22 Hayes Street, Providence, Rhode Island 02908, Mr. James P. Karon (401) 277-3126.

Rhode Island Department of Economic Development, 7 Jackson Walkway, Providence, Rhode Island 02903, Mr. Vincent Harrington (401) 277-2601.

RICE - ACREAGE

U.S. Department of Agriculture, National Agricultural Statistics Service, Fourteenth Street and Independence Avenue, SW, Washington, D.C. 20250 (202) 219-1504; *Agricultural Statistics, Crop Production Field Crops, Crop Values*, and *Agricultural Outlook*.

RICE - COMMODITY CREDIT CORPORATION TRANSACTIONS

U.S. Department of Agriculture, Agricultural Stabilization and Conservation Service, Fourteenth Street and Independence Avenue, SW, Washington, D.C. 20250 (202) 720-5237; *Commodity Credit Corporation Report of Financial Condition and Operations*, and *Agricultural Outlook*.

RICE - CONSUMPTION

U.S. Department of Agriculture, Economic Research Service, Fourteenth Street and Independence Avenue, SW, Washington, D.C. 20250-4789 (202) 219-1504; *Food Consumption, Prices and Expenditures*, and unpublished data.

RICE - FARM MARKETINGS - SALES

U.S. Department of Agriculture, Economic Research Service, Fourteenth Street and Independence Avenue, SW, Washington, D.C. 20250-4789 (202) 219-1504; *Economic Indicators of the Farm Sector: National Financial Summary*.

RICE - FOREIGN TRADE

Food and Agricultural Organization of the United Nations (FAO), Via delle Terme di Caracalla, 00100 Rome, Italy (Telephone Number in U.S. (202) 653-2400); *FAO Trade Yearbook*.

U.S. Department of Agriculture, Economic Research Service, Fourteenth Street and Independence Avenue, SW, Washington, D.C. 20250-4789 (202) 219-1504; *Agricultural Statistics, Foreign Agricultural Trade of the United States*, and *Agricultural Outlook*.

U.S. Department of Agriculture, Foreign Agricultural Service, Fourteenth Street and Independence Avenue, SW, Washington, D.C. 20250 (202) 720-3448; *Foreign Agricultural Commodity Circular Series*.

RICE - PRICES

U.S. Department of Agriculture, National Agricultural Statistics Service, Fourteenth Street and Independence Avenue, SW, Washington, D.C. 20250 (202) 219-1504; *Agricultural Statistics, Crop*

Production, Crop Values, Field Crops, and *Agricultural Outlook.*

RICE - PRODUCTION

U.S. Department of Agriculture, Foreign Agricultural Service, Fourteenth Street and Independence Avenue, SW, Washington, D.C. 20250 (202) 720-3448; *Foreign Agricultural Commodity Circular Series.*

U.S. Department of Agriculture, National Agricultural Statistics Service, Fourteenth Street and Independence Avenue, SW, Washington, D.C. 20250 (202) 219-1504; *Agricultural Statistics, Crop Production, Crop Values, Field Crops,* and *Agricultural Outlook.*

RICE - PRODUCTION - WORLD

Statistical Office of the United Nations, Publishing Service, New York, New York 10017 (800) 253-9646; *Monthly Bulletin of Statistics,* and *Statistical Yearbook.*

U.S. Department of Agriculture, Foreign Agricultural Service, Fourteenth Street and Independence Avenue, SW, Washington, D.C. 20250 (202) 720-3448; *Foreign Agricultural Commodity Circular Series,* and *World Agriculture - Trends and Indicators.*

RICE - SUPPLY AND DISAPPEARANCE

U.S. Department of Agriculture, Economic Research Service, Fourteenth Street and Independence Avenue, SW, Washington, D.C. 20250-4789 (202) 219-1504; *Agricultural Supply and Demand Estimates, Agricultural Outlook* and *Agricultural Statistics.*

RIVERS, CANALS, HARBORS, ETC. - COMMERCE - DOMESTIC AND FOREIGN

U.S. Department of the Army, Corps of Engineers, The Pentagon, Washington, D.C. 20310 (202) 545-6700; *Waterborne Commerce of the United States.*

RIVERS, CANALS, HARBORS, ETC. - DRAINAGE AREA AND FLOW

U.S. Department of the Interior, Geological Survey, National Center, 12201 Sunrise Valley Drive, Reston, Virginia 22092 (703) 648-4460; *Largest Rivers in the United States, Open File Report 87-242.*

RIVERS, CANALS, HARBORS, ETC. - FEDERAL EXPENDITURES FOR

U.S. Department of the Army, Corps of Engineers, The Pentagon, Washington, D.C. 20310 (202) 545-6700; *Report of Civil Works Expenditures by State and Fiscal Year.*

RIVERS, CANALS, HARBORS, ETC. - LENGTH OF PRINCIPAL RIVERS

U.S. Department of the Interior, Geological Survey, National Center, 12201 Sunrise Valley Drive, Reston, Virginia 22092 (703) 648-4460; *Largest Rivers in the United States, in Open File Report 87-242.*

RIVERS, CANALS, HARBORS, ETC. - WATER QUALITY

U.S. Department of the Interior, Geological Survey, National Center, 12201 Sunrise Valley Drive, Reston, Virginia 22092 (703) 648-4460; *Water - Data Report,* and unpublished data.

ROADS, PUBLIC - See HIGHWAYS

ROADWAY CONGESTION

Texas Transportation Institute, Texas A&M University, Riverside Campus, Building 7751, Safety Division, College Station, Texas 77843 (409) 845-8408; *Roadway Congestion in Major Urban Areas.*

ROBBERY

U.S. Department of Justice, Bureau of Justice Statistics, 633 Indiana Avenue, NW, Washington, D.C. 20531 (800) 732-3277; *Criminal Victimization in the United States.*

U.S. Department of Justice, Federal Bureau of Investigation, Ninth Street and Pennsylvania Avenue, NW, Washington, D.C. 20535 (202) 324-3000; *Crime in the United States,* and *Population-at-Risk Rates and Selected Crime Indicators.*

ROBOTICS

U.S. Department of Commerce, Bureau of the Census, Suitland, Maryland 20233 (301) 763-4040; *Current Industrial Reports,* and *U.S. Merchandise Trade.*

ROCKFISH

U.S. Department of Commerce, National Oceanic and Atmospheric Administration, National Marine Fisheries Service, 1335 East West Highway, Silver Spring, Maryland 20910 (301) 427-2239; *Fisheries of the United States,* and *Fishery Statistics of the United States.*

RODEOS

Professional Rodeo Cowboys Association, 101 Prorodeo Drive, Colorado Springs, Colorado 80910 (719) 593-8840; *Official Professional Rodeo Media Guide.*

Romania - National Statistical Office

Directia Centrala de Statistica, Str. Stavropoleos Number 6, Bucharest, Romania.

Romania - Primary Statistics Source

Comisia Nationala Pentru Statistica, Bucharest, Romania; *Anuarul Statistic Al Romaniei.*

ROMANIA - AGRICULTURE

Columbia University Press, 562 West 113th Street, New York, New York 10014 (212) 316-7100; *East European and Soviet Data Book.*

Facts on File, 460 Park Avenue South, New York, New York 10016 (800) 443-8323; *The New Book of World Rankings.*

Food and Agricultural Organization of the United Nations (FAO) Via delle Terme di Caracalla, 00100 Rome, Italy (Telephone Number in U.S. (202) 653-2400); *Production Yearbook, The State of Food and Agriculture,* and *Trade Yearbook.*

G.K. Hall and Company, 70 Lincoln Street, Boston, Massachusetts 02111 (617) 423-3990; *The World in Figures.*

Statistical Office of the United Nations, Publishing Service, New York, New York 10017 (800) 253-9646; *Statistical Yearbook.*

Times Books, 201 East 50th Street, New York, New York 10022 (212) 751-2600; *The Economist Book of Vital World Statistics.*

ROMANIA - AIRLINE SERVICE

Facts on File, 460 Park Avenue South, New York, New York 10016 (800) 443-8323; *The New Book of World Rankings*.

G.K. Hall and Company, 70 Lincoln Street, Boston, Massachusetts 02111 (617) 423-3990; *The World in Figures*.

Statistical Office of the United Nations, Publishing Service, New York, New York 10017 (800) 253-9646; *Statistical Yearbook*.

Times Books, 201 East 50th Street, New York, New York 10022 (212) 751-2600; *The Economist Book of Vital World Statistics*.

ROMANIA - ALUMINUM PRODUCTION AND CONSUMPTION - See ROMANIA - MINING AND MINERAL PRODUCTS

ROMANIA - ANIMAL HEALTH

Food and Agricultural Organization of the United Nations (FAO), Via delle Terme di Caracalla, 00100, Rome, Italy (Telephone Number in U.S. (202) 653-2400); *Animal Health Yearbook*.

ROMANIA - AREA AND DENSITY OF POPULATION

Facts on File, 460 Park Avenue South, New York, New York 10016 (800) 443-8323; *The New Book of World Rankings*.

Food and Agricultural Organization of the United Nations (FAO) Via delle Terme di Caracalla, 00100 Rome, Italy (Telephone Number in U.S. (202) 653-2400); *The State of Food and Agriculture*.

G.K. Hall and Company, 70 Lincoln Street, Boston, Massachusetts 02111 (617) 423-3990; *The World in Figures*.

Statistical Office of the United Nations, Publishing Service, New York, New York 10017 (800) 253-9646; *Statistical Yearbook*.

Times Books, 201 East 50th Street, New York, New York 10022 (212) 751-2600; *The Economist Book of Vital World Statistics*.

United Nations Educational, Scientific and Cultural Organization (UNESCO), 7 Place de Fontenoy, F-75700 Paris, France (Telephone Number in U.S. (212) 963-5981); *Statistical Yearbook*.

ROMANIA - ARMS EXPORTS AND IMPORTS

U.S. Arms Control and Disarmament Agency, 320 Twenty-first Street, NW, Washington, D.C. 20451 (202) 647-8677; *World Military Expenditures and Arms Transfers*.

ROMANIA - BALANCE OF PAYMENTS

The Economist Intelligence Unit, 111 West 57th Street, New York, New York 10019 (800) 938-4685; *The World Market Atlas*.

G.K. Hall and Company, 70 Lincoln Street, Boston, Massachusetts 02111 (617) 423-3990; *The World in Figures*.

International Monetary Fund, 700 Nineteenth Street, NW, Washington, D.C. 20431 (202) 623-7000; *Balance of Payments Yearbook*.

Times Books, 201 East 50th Street, New York, New York 10022 (212) 751-2600; *The Economist Book of Vital World Statistics*.

ROMANIA - BANKING

Facts on File, 460 Park Avenue South, New York, New York 10016 (800) 443-8323; *The New Book of World Rankings*.

G.K. Hall and Company, 70 Lincoln Street, Boston, Massachusetts 02111 (617) 423-3990; *The World in Figures*.

International Monetary Fund, 700 Nineteenth Street, NW, Washington, D.C. 20431 (202) 623-7000; *International Financial Statistics*.

ROMANIA - BARLEY PRODUCTION - See ROMANIA - CROPS

ROMANIA - BAUXITE PRODUCTION AND CONSUMPTION - See ROMANIA - MINING AND MINERAL PRODUCTS

ROMANIA - BEER PRODUCTION

Facts on File, 460 Park Avenue South, New York, New York 10016 (800) 443-8323; *The New Book of World Rankings*.

Statistical Office of the United Nations, Publishing Service, New York, New York 10017 (800) 253-9646; *Statistical Yearbook*.

ROMANIA - BIRTH RATE

Facts on File, 460 Park Avenue South, New York, New York 10016 (800) 443-8323; *The New Book of World Rankings*.

Statistical Office of the United Nations, Publishing Service, New York, New York 10017 (800) 253-9646; *Demographic Yearbook*, and *Statistical Yearbook*.

Times Books, 201 East 50th Street, New York, New York 10022 (212) 751-2600; *The Economist Book of Vital World Statistics*.

World Health Organization, Office of Publications, Avenue Appia, CH-1211 Geneva 27, Switzerland (Telephone Number in U.S. (518) 436-9686); *World Health Statistics Annual*.

ROMANIA - BISMUTH PRODUCTION AND CONSUMPTION - See ROMANIA - MINING AND MINERAL PRODUCTS

ROMANIA - BONDS

G.K. Hall and Company, 70 Lincoln Street, Boston, Massachusetts 02111 (617) 423-3990; *The World in Figures*.

ROMANIA - BOOK PRODUCTION

Euromonitor Publications Limited, 87-88 Turnmill Street, London EC1M 5QU, England; *European Marketing Data and Statistics*.

G.K. Hall and Company, 70 Lincoln Street, Boston, Massachusetts 02111 (617) 423-3990; *The World in Figures*.

United Nations Educational, Scientific and Cultural Organization (UNESCO), 7 Place de Fontenoy, F-75700 Paris, France (Telephone Number in U.S. (212) 963-5981); *Statistical Yearbook*.

ROMANIA - BROADCASTING

Billboard Limited, P.O. Box 9027, 1006 AA Amsterdam, The Netherlands (Telephone Number in U.S. (212) 764-7300); *World Radio TV Handbook*.

Facts on File, 460 Park Avenue South, New York, New York 10016 (800) 443-8323; *The New Book of World Rankings*.

G.K. Hall and Company, 70 Lincoln Street, Boston, Massachusetts 02111 (617) 423-3990; *The World in Figures*.

Times Books, 201 East 50th Street, New York, New York 10022 (212) 751-2600; *The Economist Book of Vital World Statistics*.

ROMANIA - BUSINESS

G.K. Hall and Company, 70 Lincoln Street, Boston, Massachusetts 02111 (617) 423-3990; *The World in Figures*.

ROMANIA - BUTTER PRODUCTION - See ROMANIA - DAIRY PRODUCTS

ROMANIA - CABBAGE PRODUCTION - See ROMANIA - CROPS

ROMANIA - CALORIE SUPPLY

Food and Agricultural Organization of the United Nations (FAO) Via delle Terme di Caracalla, 00100 Rome, Italy (Telephone Number in U.S. (202) 653-2400); *The State of Food and Agriculture*.

ROMANIA - CAPITAL REVENUE

International Monetary Fund, 700 Nineteenth Street, NW, Washington, D.C. 20431 (202) 623-7000; *Government Finance Statistics Yearbook*.

ROMANIA - CASTOR BEAN PRODUCTION - See ROMANIA - CROPS

ROMANIA - CATTLE - See ROMANIA - LIVESTOCK AND POULTRY

ROMANIA - CAUSTIC SODA PRODUCTION

Statistical Office of the United Nations, Publishing Service, New York, New York 10017 (800) 253-9646; *Statistical Yearbook*.

ROMANIA - CEMENT PRODUCTION - See ROMANIA - MINING AND MINERAL PRODUCTS

ROMANIA - CEREALS PRODUCTION - See ROMANIA - CROPS

ROMANIA - CHEESE PRODUCTION AND CONSUMPTION - See ROMANIA - DAIRY PRODUCTS

ROMANIA - CHEMICAL (ORGANIC) PRODUCTION - See ROMANIA - MINING AND MINERAL PRODUCTS

ROMANIA - CIGARETTE PRODUCTION - See ROMANIA - TOBACCO PRODUCTION

ROMANIA - CLASS STRUCTURE

Columbia University Press, 562 West 113th Street, New York, New York 10014 (212) 316-7100; *East European and Soviet Data Book*.

G.K. Hall and Company, 70 Lincoln Street, Boston, Massachusetts 02111 (617) 423-3990; *The World in Figures*.

ROMANIA - CLIMATE

Facts on File, 460 Park Avenue South, New York, New York 10016 (800) 443-8323; *The New Book of World Rankings*.

G.K. Hall and Company, 70 Lincoln Street, Boston, Massachusetts 02111 (617) 423-3990; *The World in Figures*.

ROMANIA - COAL PRODUCTION - See ROMANIA - MINING AND MINERAL PRODUCTS

ROMANIA - COFFEE PRODUCTION AND CONSUMPTION - See ROMANIA - CROPS

ROMANIA - COKE OVEN COKE PRODUCTION AND CONSUMPTION - See ROMANIA - MINING AND MINERAL PRODUCTS

ROMANIA - COMMUNICATIONS

G.K. Hall and Company, 70 Lincoln Street, Boston, Massachusetts 02111 (617) 423-3990; *The World in Figures*.

ROMANIA - CONSTRUCTION INDUSTRY

Facts on File, 460 Park Avenue South, New York, New York 10016 (800) 443-8323; *The New Book of World Rankings*.

Statistical Office of the United Nations, Publishing Service, New York, New York 10017 (800) 253-9646; *Statistical Yearbook*.

ROMANIA - CONSUMER PRICE INDEX

G.K. Hall and Company, 70 Lincoln Street, Boston, Massachusetts 02111 (617) 423-3990; *The World in Figures*.

Statistical Office of the United Nations, Publishing Service, New York, New York 10017 (800) 253-9646; *Statistical Yearbook*.

ROMANIA - CONSUMER PRICES

Euromonitor Publications Limited, 87-88 Turnmill Street, London EC1M 5QU, England; *European Marketing Data and Statistics*.

International Labour Office, I.L.O. Publications, CH-1211, Geneva 22, Switzerland; *Yearbook of Labour Statistics*.

International Monetary Fund, 700 Nineteenth Street, NW, Washington, D.C. 20431 (202) 623-7000; *International Financial Statistics*.

ROMANIA - CONSUMPTION

G.K. Hall and Company, 70 Lincoln Street, Boston, Massachusetts 02111 (617) 423-3990; *The World in Figures*.

ROMANIA - COPPER PRODUCTION AND CONSUMPTION - See ROMANIA - MINING AND MINERAL PRODUCTS

ROMANIA - CORN PRODUCTION - See ROMANIA - CROPS

ROMANIA - CORPORATE TAXES - See ROMANIA - TAXATION

ROMANIA - COTTON - See ROMANIA - CROPS

ROMANIA - CRIME

Statistical Office of the United Nations, Publishing Service, New York, New York 10017 (800) 253-9646; *Foreign Trade Statistics for Africa*.

Yale University Press, Yale Station, New Haven, Connecticut 06520 (203) 432-0940; *Violence and Crime in Cross-National Perspective*.

ROMANIA - CROPS

Commodity Research Bureau, Incorporated, 75 Wall Street, New York, New York 10005 (212) 504-7754; *Commodity Year Book*.

Euromonitor Publications Limited, 87-88 Turnmill Street, London EC1M 5QU, England; *European Marketing Data and Statistics*.

Facts on File, 460 Park Avenue South, New York, New York 10016 (800) 443-8323; *The New Book of World Rankings*.

Food and Agricultural Organization of the United Nations (FAO) Via delle Terme di Caracalla, 00100 Rome, Italy (Telephone Number in U.S. (202) 653-2400); *Production Yearbook*, and *The State of Food and Agriculture*.

G.K. Hall and Company, 70 Lincoln Street, Boston, Massachusetts 02111 (617) 423-3990; *The World in Figures*.

Statistical Office of the United Nations, Publishing Service, New York, New York 10017 (800) 253-9646; *Statistical Yearbook*.

Times Books, 201 East 50th Street, New York, New York 10022 (212) 751-2600; *The Economist Book of Vital World Statistics*.

ROMANIA - CUSTOMS DUTIES

G.K. Hall and Company, 70 Lincoln Street, Boston, Massachusetts 02111 (617) 423-3990; *The World in Figures*.

ROMANIA - DAIRY PRODUCTS

Facts on File, 460 Park Avenue South, New York, New York 10016 (800) 443-8323; *The New Book of World Rankings*.

Food and Agricultural Organization of the United Nations (FAO), Via delle Terme di Caracalla, 00100 Rome, Italy (Telephone Number in U.S. (202) 653-2400); *Production Yearbook*, and *The State of Food and Agriculture*.

Statistical Office of the United Nations, Publishing Service, New York, New York 10017 (800) 253-9646; *Statistical Yearbook*.

ROMANIA - DEATH RATE

G.K. Hall and Company, 70 Lincoln Street, Boston, Massachusetts 02111 (617) 423-3990; *The World in Figures*.

Statistical Office of the United Nations, Publishing Service, New York, New York 10017 (800) 253-9646; *Statistical Yearbook*.

Times Books, 201 East 50th Street, New York, New York 10022 (212) 751-2600; *The Economist Book of Vital World Statistics*.

World Health Organization, Office of Publications, Avenue Appia, CH-1211 Geneva 27, Switzerland (Telephone Number in U.S. (518) 436-9686); *World Health Statistics Annual*.

ROMANIA - DEFENSE EXPENDITURES

G.K. Hall and Company, 70 Lincoln Street, Boston, Massachusetts 02111 (617) 423-3990; *The World in Figures*.

International Monetary Fund, 700 Nineteenth Street, NW, Washington, D.C. 20431 (202) 623-7000; *Government Finance Statistics Yearbook*.

U.S. Arms Control and Disarmament Agency, 320 Twenty-first Street, NW, Washington, D.C. 20451 (202) 647-8677; *World Military Expenditures and Arms Transfers*.

ROMANIA - DEMOGRAPHY

The Economist Intelligence Unit, 111 West 57th Street, New York, New York 10019 (800) 938-4685; *The World Market Atlas*.

Facts on File, 460 Park Avenue South, New York, New York 10016 (800) 443-8323; *The New Book of World Rankings*.

G.K. Hall and Company, 70 Lincoln Street, Boston, Massachusetts 02111 (617) 423-3990; *The World in Figures*.

ROMANIA - DEVELOPMENT ASSISTANCE

G.K. Hall and Company, 70 Lincoln Street, Boston, Massachusetts 02111 (617) 423-3990; *The World in Figures*.

Statistical Office of the United Nations, Publishing Service, New York, New York 10017 (800) 253-9646; *Statistical Yearbook*.

ROMANIA - DIAMOND PRODUCTION - See ROMANIA - MINING AND MINERAL PRODUCTS

ROMANIA - DISEASE

G.K. Hall and Company, 70 Lincoln Street, Boston, Massachusetts 02111 (617) 423-3990; *The World in Figures*.

World Health Organization, Office of Publications, Avenue Appia, CH-1211 Geneva 27, Switzerland (Telephone Number in U.S. (518) 436-9686); *World Health Statistics Annual*.

ROMANIA - DIVORCE RATES

Facts on File, 460 Park Avenue South, New York, New York 10016 (800) 443-8323; *The New Book of World Rankings*.

Statistical Office of the United Nations, Publishing Service, New York, New York 10017 (800) 253-9646; *Demographic Yearbook*, and *Statistical Yearbook*.

ROMANIA - DOMESTIC PRODUCT

G.K. Hall and Company, 70 Lincoln Street, Boston, Massachusetts 02111 (617) 423-3990; *The World in Figures*.

ROMANIA - ECONOMY

Euromonitor Publications Limited, 87-88 Turnmill Street, London EC1M 5QU, England; *European Marketing Data and Statistics*.

Facts on File, 460 Park Avenue South, New York, New York 10016 (800) 443-8323; *The New Book of World Rankings*.

G.K. Hall and Company, 70 Lincoln Street, Boston, Massachusetts 02111 (617) 423-3990; *The World in Figures*.

ROMANIA - EDUCATION

Columbia University Press, 562 West 113th Street, New York, New York 10014 (212) 316-7100; *East European and Soviet Data Book*.

The Economist Intelligence Unit, 111 West 57th Street, New York, New York 10019 (800) 938-4685; *The World Market Atlas*.

Euromonitor Publications Limited, 87-88 Turnmill Street, London EC1M 5QU, England; *European Marketing Data and Statistics*.

Facts on File, 460 Park Avenue South, New York, New York 10016 (800) 443-8323; *The New Book of World Rankings*.

G.K. Hall and Company, 70 Lincoln Street, Boston, Massachusetts 02111 (617) 423-3990; *The World in Figures*.

International Monetary Fund, 700 Nineteenth Street, NW, Washington, D.C. 20431 (202) 623-7000; *Government Finance Statistics Yearbook.*

Times Books, 201 East 50th Street, New York, New York 10022 (212) 751-2600; *The Economist Book of Vital World Statistics.*

United Nations Educational, Scientific and Cultural Organization (UNESCO), 7 Place de Fontenoy, F-75700 Paris, France (Telephone Number in U.S. (212) 963-5981); *Statistical Yearbook.*

ROMANIA - EGG PRODUCTION AND CONSUMPTION - See ROMANIA - DAIRY PRODUCTS

ROMANIA - ELECTRICITY

Facts on File, 460 Park Avenue South, New York, New York 10016 (800) 443-8323; *The New Book of World Rankings.*

Penn Well Publishing Company, 1421 South Sheridan Road, P.O. Box 1260, Tulsa, Oklahoma 74101 (800) 752-9764; *International Energy Statistics Sourcebook.*

Statistical Office of the United Nations, Publishing Service, New York, New York 10017 (800) 253-9646; *Statistical Yearbook.*

Times Books, 201 East 50th Street, New York, New York 10022 (212) 751-2600; *The Economist Book of Vital World Statistics.*

ROMANIA - EMPLOYMENT

Columbia University Press, 562 West 113th Street, New York, New York 10014 (212) 316-7100; *East European and Soviet Data Book.*

Euromonitor Publications Limited, 87-88 Turnmill Street, London EC1M 5QU, England; *European Marketing Data and Statistics.*

Facts on File, 460 Park Avenue South, New York, New York 10016 (800) 443-8323; *The New Book of World Rankings.*

International Labour Office, I.L.O. Publications, CH-1211, Geneva 22, Switzerland; *Yearbook of Labour Statistics.*

Statistical Office of the United Nations, Publishing Service, New York, New York 10017 (800) 253-9646; *Statistical Yearbook.*

ROMANIA - ENERGY

Euromonitor Publications Limited, 87-88 Turnmill Street, London EC1M 5QU, England; *European Marketing Data and Statistics.*

Facts on File, 460 Park Avenue South, New York, New York 10016 (800) 443-8323; *The New Book of World Rankings.*

Food and Agricultural Organization of the United Nations (FAO) Via delle Terme di Caracalla, 00100 Rome, Italy (Telephone Number in U.S. (202) 653-2400); *The State of Food and Agriculture.*

G.K. Hall and Company, 70 Lincoln Street, Boston, Massachusetts 02111 (617) 423-3990; *The World in Figures.*

Penn Well Publishing Company, 1421 South Sheridan Road, P.O. Box 1260, Tulsa, Oklahoma 74101 (800) 752-9764; *International Energy Statistics Sourcebook.*

Statistical Office of the United Nations, Publishing Service, New York, New York 10017 (800) 253-9646; *Energy Statistics Yearbook, Statistical Yearbook,* and *World Energy Supplies.*

Times Books, 201 East 50th Street, New York, New York 10022 (212) 751-2600; *The Economist Book of Vital World Statistics.*

ROMANIA - EXCHANGE RATES

International Monetary Fund, 700 Nineteenth Street, NW, Washington, D.C. 20431 (202) 623-7000; *International Financial Statistics.*

Statistical Office of the United Nations, Publishing Service, New York, New York 10017 (800) 253-9646; *Statistical Yearbook.*

ROMANIA - EXPORTS

The Economist Intelligence Unit, 111 West 57th Street, New York, New York 10019 (800) 938-4685; *The World Market Atlas.*

Food and Agricultural Organization of the United Nations (FAO) Via delle Terme di Caracalla, 00100 Rome, Italy (Telephone Number in U.S. (202) 653-2400); *The State of Food and Agriculture.*

G.K. Hall and Company, 70 Lincoln Street, Boston, Massachusetts 02111 (617) 423-3990; *The World in Figures.*

International Monetary Fund, 700 Nineteenth Street, NW, Washington, D.C. 20431 (202) 623-7000; *Direction of Trade Statistics.*

Times Books, 201 East 50th Street, New York, New York 10022 (212) 751-2600; *The Economist Book of Vital World Statistics.*

ROMANIA - EXTERNAL TRADE

Food and Agricultural Organization of the United Nations (FAO) Via delle Terme di Caracalla, 00100 Rome, Italy (Telephone Number in U.S. (202) 653-2400); *The State of Food and Agriculture,* and *Trade Yearbook.*

G.K. Hall and Company, 70 Lincoln Street, Boston, Massachusetts 02111 (617) 423-3990; *The World in Figures.*

Statistical Office of the United Nations, Publishing Service, New York, New York 10017 (800) 253-9646; *Statistical Yearbook.*

ROMANIA - FABRIC PRODUCTION - See ROMANIA - TEXTILE INDUSTRY

ROMANIA - FARM CROPS - See ROMANIA - CROPS

ROMANIA - FERTILITY RATES

Columbia University Press, 562 West 113th Street, New York, New York 10014 (212) 316-7100; *East European and Soviet Data Book.*

Facts on File, 460 Park Avenue South, New York, New York 10016 (800) 443-8323; *The New Book of World Rankings.*

Times Books, 201 East 50th Street, New York, New York 10022 (212) 751-2600; *The Economist Book of Vital World Statistics.*

ROMANIA - FERTILIZER

Food and Agricultural Organization of the United Nations (FAO) Via delle Terme di Caracalla, 00100 Rome, Italy (Telephone Number in U.S. (202) 653-2400); *The State of Food and Agriculture.*

Statistical Office of the United Nations, Publishing Service, New York, New York 10017 (800) 253-9646; *Statistical Yearbook.*

ROMANIA - FETAL MORTALITY

Statistical Office of the United Nations, Publishing Service, New York, New York 10017 (800) 253-9646; *Demographic Yearbook*.

World Health Organization, Office of Publications, Avenue Appia, CH-1211 Geneva 27, Switzerland (Telephone Number in U.S. (518) 436-9686); *World Health Statistics Annual*.

ROMANIA - FIBRE PRODUCTION - See ROMANIA - TEXTILE INDUSTRY

ROMANIA - FILAMENT PRODUCTION - See ROMANIA - TEXTILE INDUSTRY

ROMANIA - FILM - See ROMANIA - MOTION PICTURES

ROMANIA - FINANCE

Facts on File, 460 Park Avenue South, New York, New York 10016 (800) 443-8323; *The New Book of World Rankings*.

G.K. Hall and Company, 70 Lincoln Street, Boston, Massachusetts 02111 (617) 423-3990; *The World in Figures*.

International Monetary Fund, 700 Nineteenth Street, NW, Washington, D.C. 20431 (202) 623-7000; *International Financial Statistics*.

ROMANIA - FISHERIES

Euromonitor Publications Limited, 87-88 Turnmill Street, London EC1M 5QU, England; *European Marketing Data and Statistics*.

Facts on File, 460 Park Avenue South, New York, New York 10016 (800) 443-8323; *The New Book of World Rankings*.

Food and Agricultural Organization of the United Nations (FAO) Via delle Terme di Caracalla, 00100 Rome, Italy (Telephone Number in U.S. (202) 653-2400); *The State of Food and Agriculture*, and *Yearbook of Fishery Statistics*.

Statistical Office of the United Nations, Publishing Service, New York, New York 10017 (800) 253-9646; *Statistical Yearbook*.

ROMANIA - FLAX PRODUCTION - See ROMANIA - TEXTILE INDUSTRY

ROMANIA - FLOUR PRODUCTION

Statistical Office of the United Nations, Publishing Service, New York, New York 10017 (800) 253-9646; *Statistical Yearbook*.

ROMANIA - FOOD

Food and Agricultural Organization of the United Nations (FAO) Via delle Terme di Caracalla, 00100 Rome, Italy (Telephone Number in U.S. (202) 653-2400); *Production Yearbook*, and *The State of Food and Agriculture*.

G.K. Hall and Company, 70 Lincoln Street, Boston, Massachusetts 02111 (617) 423-3990; *The World in Figures*.

ROMANIA - FOREIGN AID

G.K. Hall and Company, 70 Lincoln Street, Boston, Massachusetts 02111 (617) 423-3990; *The World in Figures*.

ROMANIA - FOREIGN TRADE

Facts on File, 460 Park Avenue South, New York, New York 10016 (800) 443-8323; *The New Book of World Rankings*.

G.K. Hall and Company, 70 Lincoln Street, Boston, Massachusetts 02111 (617) 423-3990; *The World in Figures*.

Statistical Office of the United Nations, Publishing Service, New York, New York 10017 (800) 253-9646; *International Trade Statistics Yearbook*, and *Statistical Yearbook*.

ROMANIA - FORESTRY AND FOREST PRODUCTS

Euromonitor Publications Limited, 87-88 Turnmill Street, London EC1M 5QU, England; *European Marketing Data and Statistics*.

Facts on File, 460 Park Avenue South, New York, New York 10016 (800) 443-8323; *The New Book of World Rankings*.

Food and Agricultural Organization of the United Nations (FAO) Via delle Terme di Caracalla, 00100 Rome, Italy (Telephone Number in U.S. (202) 653-2400); *The State of Food and Agriculture*, and *Yearbook of Forest Products*.

G.K. Hall and Company, 70 Lincoln Street, Boston, Massachusetts 02111 (617) 423-3990; *The World in Figures*.

Statistical Office of the United Nations, Publishing Service, New York, New York 10017 (800) 253-9646; *Statistical Yearbook*.

United Nations Educational, Scientific and Cultural Organization (UNESCO), 7 Place de Fontenoy, F-75700 Paris, France (Telephone Number in U.S. (212) 963-5981); *Statistical Yearbook*.

ROMANIA - GARLIC PRODUCTION - See ROMANIA - CROPS

ROMANIA - GAS LIQUIDS (NATURAL) PRODUCTION - See ROMANIA - MINING AND MINERAL PRODUCTS

ROMANIA - GAS PRODUCTION - See ROMANIA - MINING AND MINERAL PRODUCTS

ROMANIA - GENERAL INDUSTRIAL STATISTICS

Statistical Office of the United Nations, Publishing Service, New York, New York 10017 (800) 253-9646; *Industrial Statistics Yearbook*.

ROMANIA - GENERAL MORTALITY

Statistical Office of the United Nations, Publishing Service, New York, New York 10017 (800) 253-9646; *Demographic Yearbook*.

World Health Organization, Office of Publications, Avenue Appia, CH-1211 Geneva 27, Switzerland (Telephone Number in U.S. (518) 436-9686); *World Health Statistics Annual*.

ROMANIA - GEOGRAPHIC DATA

Facts on File, 460 Park Avenue South, New York, New York 10016 (800) 443-8323; *The New Book of World Rankings*.

ROMANIA - GOLD HOLDINGS

International Monetary Fund, 700 Nineteenth Street, NW, Washington, D.C. 20431 (202) 623-7000; *International Financial Statistics*.

ROMANIA - GOLD PRODUCTION AND CONSUMPTION - See ROMANIA - MINING AND MINERAL PRODUCTS

ROMANIA - GOVERNMENT

G.K. Hall and Company, 70 Lincoln Street, Boston, Massachusetts 02111 (617) 423-3990; *The World in Figures*.

ROMANIA - GOVERNMENT EXPENDITURES

International Monetary Fund, 700 Nineteenth Street, NW, Washington, D.C. 20431 (202) 623-7000; *Government Finance Statistics Yearbook*.

Times Books, 201 East 50th Street, New York, New York 10022 (212) 751-2600; *The Economist Book of Vital World Statistics*.

ROMANIA - GOVERNMENT FINANCES

International Monetary Fund, 700 Nineteenth Street, NW, Washington, D.C. 20431 (202) 623-7000; *International Financial Statistics*.

Statistical Office of the United Nations, Publishing Service, New York, New York 10017 (800) 253-9646; *Statistical Yearbook*.

ROMANIA - GOVERNMENT REVENUE

International Monetary Fund, 700 Nineteenth Street, NW, Washington, D.C. 20431 (202) 623-7000; *Government Finance Statistics Yearbook*.

Times Books, 201 East 50th Street, New York, New York 10022 (212) 751-2600; *The Economist Book of Vital World Statistics*.

ROMANIA - GRAIN PRODUCTION - See ROMANIA - CROPS

ROMANIA - GRANTS

International Monetary Fund, 700 Nineteenth Street, NW, Washington, D.C. 20431 (202) 623-7000; *Government Finance Statistics Yearbook*.

ROMANIA - GREEN PEPPER AND CHILIE PRODUCTION - See ROMANIA - CROPS

ROMANIA - GROSS DOMESTIC PRODUCT

The Economist Intelligence Unit, 111 West 57th Street, New York, New York 10019 (800) 938-4685; *The World Market Atlas*.

Facts on File, 460 Park Avenue South, New York, New York 10016 (800) 443-8323; *The New Book of World Rankings*.

G.K. Hall and Company, 70 Lincoln Street, Boston, Massachusetts 02111 (617) 423-3990; *The World in Figures*.

Statistical Office of the United Nations, Publishing Service, New York, New York 10017 (800) 253-9646; *Statistical Yearbook*.

Times Books, 201 East 50th Street, New York, New York 10022 (212) 751-2600; *The Economist Book of Vital World Statistics*.

ROMANIA - GROSS NATIONAL PRODUCT

U.S. Arms Control and Disarmament Agency, 320 Twenty-first Street, NW, Washington, D.C. 20451 (202) 647-8677; *World Military Expenditures and Arms Transfers*.

ROMANIA - HEALTH

Facts on File, 460 Park Avenue South, New York, New York 10016 (800) 443-8323; *The New Book of World Rankings*.

G.K. Hall and Company, 70 Lincoln Street, Boston, Massachusetts 02111 (617) 423-3990; *The World in Figures*.

Statistical Office of the United Nations, Publishing Service, New York, New York 10017 (800) 253-9646; *Statistical Yearbook*.

Times Books, 201 East 50th Street, New York, New York 10022 (212) 751-2600; *The Economist Book of Vital World Statistics*.

World Health Organization, Office of Publications, Avenue Appia, CH-1211 Geneva 27, Switzerland (Telephone Number in U.S. (518) 436-9686); *World Health Statistics Annual*.

ROMANIA - HEALTH EXPENDITURES

International Monetary Fund, 700 Nineteenth Street, NW, Washington, D.C. 20431 (202) 623-7000; *Government Finance Statistics Yearbook*.

ROMANIA - HEMP FIBRE PRODUCTION - See ROMANIA - TEXTILE INDUSTRY

ROMANIA - HIDE PRODUCTION

Food and Agricultural Organization of the United Nations (FAO), Via delle Terme di Caracalla, 00100 Rome, Italy (Telephone Number in U.S. (202) 653-2400); *Production Yearbook*

ROMANIA - HIGHWAYS

G.K. Hall and Company, 70 Lincoln Street, Boston, Massachusetts 02111 (617) 423-3990; *The World in Figures*.

International Road Federation, 525 School Street, SW, Washington, D.C. 20024 (202) 554-2106; *World Road Statistics*.

Statistical Office of the United Nations, Publishing Service, New York, New York 10017 (800) 253-9646; *Annual Bulletin of Transport Statistics for Europe*.

ROMANIA - HOPS PRODUCTION - See ROMANIA - CROPS

ROMANIA - HORSES - See ROMANIA - LIVESTOCK AND POULTRY

ROMANIA - HOURS OF WORK - See ROMANIA - EMPLOYMENT

ROMANIA - HOUSING AND HOUSING UNITS

Columbia University Press, 562 West 113th Street, New York, New York 10014 (212) 316-7100; *East European and Soviet Data Book*.

Facts on File, 460 Park Avenue South, New York, New York 10016 (800) 443-8323; *The New Book of World Rankings*.

ROMANIA - HYDROCHLORIC ACID PRODUCTION

Statistical Office of the United Nations, Publishing Service, New York, New York 10017 (800) 253-9646; *Statistical Yearbook*.

ROMANIA - ILLITERATE POPULATION

Columbia University Press, 562 West 113th Street, New York, New York 10014 (212) 316-7100; *East European and Soviet Data Book*.

The Economist Intelligence Unit, 111 West 57th Street, New York, New York 10019 (800) 938-4685; *The World Market Atlas*.

G.K. Hall and Company, 70 Lincoln Street, Boston, Massachusetts 02111 (617) 423-3990; *The World in Figures*.

United Nations Educational, Scientific and Cultural Organization (UNESCO), 7 Place de Fontenoy, F-75700 Paris, France (Telephone Number in U.S. (212) 963-5981); *Statistical Yearbook*.

ROMANIA - IMPORTS

The Economist Intelligence Unit, 111 West 57th Street, New York, New York 10019 (800) 938-4685; *The World Market Atlas*.

Food and Agricultural Organization of the United Nations (FAO) Via delle Terme di Caracalla, 00100 Rome, Italy (Telephone Number in U.S. (202) 653-2400); *The State of Food and Agriculture*.

G.K. Hall and Company, 70 Lincoln Street, Boston, Massachusetts 02111 (617) 423-3990; *The World in Figures*.

International Monetary Fund, 700 Nineteenth Street, NW, Washington, D.C. 20431 (202) 623-7000; *Direction of Trade Statistics*.

ROMANIA - INCOME TAXES - See ROMANIA - TAXATION

ROMANIA - INDUSTRIAL METALS PRODUCTION - See ROMANIA - MINING AND MINERAL PRODUCTS

ROMANIA - INDUSTRY

Facts on File, 460 Park Avenue South, New York, New York 10016 (800) 443-8323; *The New Book of World Rankings*.

G.K. Hall and Company, 70 Lincoln Street, Boston, Massachusetts 02111 (617) 423-3990; *The World in Figures*.

International Labour Office, I.L.O. Publications, CH-1211, Geneva 22, Switzerland; *Yearbook of Labour Statistics*.

Statistical Office of the United Nations, Publishing Service, New York, New York 10017 (800) 253-9646; *Statistical Yearbook*.

Times Books, 201 East 50th Street, New York, New York 10022 (212) 751-2600; *The Economist Book of Vital World Statistics*.

World Intellectual Property Organization, 34 Chemin des Colombettes, CH-1211 Geneva 20. Switzerland; *Industrial Property Statistics*.

ROMANIA - INFANT AND MATERNAL MORTALITY

Statistical Office of the United Nations, Publishing Service, New York, New York 10017 (800) 253-9646; *Demographic Yearbook*.

Times Books, 201 East 50th Street, New York, New York 10022 (212) 751-2600; *The Economist Book of Vital World Statistics*.

World Health Organization, Office of Publications, Avenue Appia, CH-1211 Geneva 27, Switzerland (Telephone Number in U.S. (518) 436-9686); *World Health Statistics Annual*.

ROMANIA - INTERNATIONAL LIQUIDITY

International Monetary Fund, 700 Nineteenth Street, NW, Washington, D.C. 20431 (202) 623-7000; *International Financial Statistics*.

ROMANIA - INTERNATIONAL RESERVES EXCLUDING GOLD

Statistical Office of the United Nations, Publishing Service, New York, New York 10017 (800) 253-9646; *Statistical Yearbook*.

ROMANIA - IRON ORE PRODUCTION AND CONSUMPTION - See ROMANIA - MINING AND MINERAL PRODUCTS

ROMANIA - LABOR FORCE

Columbia University Press, 562 West 113th Street, New York, New York 10014 (212) 316-7100; *East European and Soviet Data Book*.

Facts on File, 460 Park Avenue South, New York, New York 10016 (800) 443-8323; *The New Book of World Rankings*.

Food and Agricultural Organization of the United Nations (FAO) Via delle Terme di Caracalla, 00100 Rome, Italy (Telephone Number in U.S. (202) 653-2400); *The State of Food and Agriculture*.

G.K. Hall and Company, 70 Lincoln Street, Boston, Massachusetts 02111 (617) 423-3990; *The World in Figures*.

ROMANIA - LABOR PRODUCTIVITY

International Labour Office, I.L.O. Publications, CH-1211, Geneva 22, Switzerland; *Yearbook of Labour Statistics*.

ROMANIA - LAND USE

Euromonitor Publications Limited, 87-88 Turnmill Street, London EC1M 5QU, England; *European Marketing Data and Statistics*.

Food and Agricultural Organization of the United Nations (FAO), Via delle Terme di Caracalla, 00100 Rome, Italy (Telephone Number in U.S. (202) 653-2400); *Production Yearbook*.

G.K. Hall and Company, 70 Lincoln Street, Boston, Massachusetts 02111 (617) 423-3990; *The World in Figures*.

ROMANIA - LEAD AND LEAD ORE PRODUCTION AND CONSUMPTION - See ROMANIA - MINING AND MINERAL PRODUCTS

ROMANIA - LIBRARIES

Euromonitor Publications Limited, 87-88 Turnmill Street, London EC1M 5QU, England; *European Marketing Data and Statistics*.

Facts on File, 460 Park Avenue South, New York, New York 10016 (800) 443-8323; *The New Book of World Rankings*.

Statistical Office of the United Nations, Publishing Service, New York, New York 10017 (800) 253-9646; *Statistical Yearbook*.

United Nations Educational, Scientific and Cultural Organization (UNESCO), 7 Place de Fontenoy, F-75700 Paris, France (Telephone Number in U.S. (212) 963-5981); *Statistical Yearbook*.

ROMANIA - LIGNITE PRODUCTION - See ROMANIA - MINING AND MINERAL PRODUCTS

ROMANIA - LIVESTOCK AND POULTRY

Euromonitor Publications Limited, 87-88 Turnmill Street, London EC1M 5QU, England; *European Marketing Data and Statistics*.

Facts on File, 460 Park Avenue South, New York, New York 10016 (800) 443-8323; *The New Book of World Rankings*.

Food and Agricultural Organization of the United Nations (FAO), Via delle Terme di Caracalla, 00100 Rome, Italy (Telephone Number in U.S. (202) 653-2400); *Production Yearbook*, and *The State of Food and Agriculture*.

G.K. Hall and Company, 70 Lincoln Street, Boston, Massachusetts 02111 (617) 423-3990; *The World in Figures*.

Statistical Office of the United Nations, Publishing Service, New York, New York 10017 (800) 253-9646; *Statistical Yearbook*.

ROMANIA - LIVING LEVELS

G.K. Hall and Company, 70 Lincoln Street, Boston, Massachusetts 02111 (617) 423-3990; *The World in Figures*.

Times Books, 201 East 50th Street, New York, New York 10022 (212) 751-2600; *The Economist Book of Vital World Statistics*.

ROMANIA - MAIL - NUMBER OF PIECES SENT OR RECEIVED

Statistical Office of the United Nations, Publishing Service, New York, New York 10017 (800) 253-9646; *Statistical Yearbook*.

ROMANIA - MANGANESE ORE PRODUCTION AND CONSUMPTION - See ROMANIA - MINING AND MINERAL PRODUCTS

ROMANIA - MANUFACTURING

Facts on File, 460 Park Avenue South, New York, New York 10016 (800) 443-8323; *The New Book of World Rankings*.

G.K. Hall and Company, 70 Lincoln Street, Boston, Massachusetts 02111 (617) 423-3990; *The World in Figures*.

Statistical Office of the United Nations, Publishing Service, New York, New York 10017 (800) 253-9646; *Statistical Yearbook*.

Times Books, 201 East 50th Street, New York, New York 10022 (212) 751-2600; *The Economist Book of Vital World Statistics*.

ROMANIA - MARRIAGE RATES

Facts on File, 460 Park Avenue South, New York, New York 10016 (800) 443-8323; *The New Book of World Rankings*.

Statistical Office of the United Nations, Publishing Service, New York, New York 10017 (800) 253-9646; *Demographic Yearbook*, and *Statistical Yearbook*.

ROMANIA - MEAT PRODUCTION - See ROMANIA - LIVESTOCK AND POULTRY

ROMANIA - MERCHANT SHIPPING

G.K. Hall and Company, 70 Lincoln Street, Boston, Massachusetts 02111 (617) 423-3990; *The World in Figures*.

Lloyd's Register of Shipping, 17 Battery Place, New York, New York 10004 (212) 425-8050; *Register of Ships*.

Statistical Office of the United Nations, Publishing Service, New York, New York 10017 (800) 253-9646; *Annual Bulletin of Transport Statistics for Europe*, and *Statistical Yearbook*.

Times Books, 201 East 50th Street, New York, New York 10022 (212) 751-2600; *The Economist Book of Vital World Statistics*.

U.S. Department of Transportation, Maritime Administration, 400 Seventh Street, SW, Washington, D.C. 20590 (202) 366-5807; *A Statistical Analysis of the World's Merchant Fleets*.

ROMANIA - MILITARY

G.K. Hall and Company, 70 Lincoln Street, Boston, Massachusetts 02111 (617) 423-3990; *The World in Figures*.

The International Institute for Strategic Studies, 23 Tavistock Street, London WC2E 7NQ, England; *The Military Balance*.

U.S. Arms Control and Disarmament Agency, 320 Twenty-first Street, NW, Washington, D.C. 20451 (202) 647-8677; *World Military Expenditures and Arms Transfers*.

ROMANIA - MILK - See ROMANIA - DAIRY PRODUCTS

ROMANIA - MINING AND MINERAL PRODUCTS

Commodity Research Bureau, Incorporated, 75 Wall Street, New York, New York 10005 (212) 504-7754; *Commodity Year Book*.

Facts on File, 460 Park Avenue South, New York, New York 10016 (800) 443-8323; *The New Book of World Rankings*.

G.K. Hall and Company, 70 Lincoln Street, Boston, Massachusetts 02111 (617) 423-3990; *The World in Figures*.

Penn Well Publishing Company, 1421 South Sheridan Road, P.O. Box 1260, Tulsa, Oklahoma 74101 (800) 752-9764; *International Energy Statistics Sourcebook*.

Statistical Office of the United Nations, Publishing Service, New York, New York 10017 (800) 253-9646; *Statistical Yearbook*.

ROMANIA - MONEY EXCHANGE RATES

International Monetary Fund, 700 Nineteenth Street, NW, Washington, D.C. 20431 (202) 623-7000; *International Financial Statistics*.

Statistical Office of the United Nations, Publishing Service, New York, New York 10017 (800) 253-9646; *Statistical Yearbook*.

ROMANIA - MONEY SUPPLY

G.K. Hall and Company, 70 Lincoln Street, Boston, Massachusetts 02111 (617) 423-3990; *The World in Figures*.

International Monetary Fund, 700 Nineteenth Street, NW, Washington, D.C. 20431 (202) 623-7000; *International Financial Statistics*.

ROMANIA - MOTION PICTURES

Statistical Office of the United Nations, Publishing Service, New York, New York 10017 (800) 253-9646; *Statistical Yearbook*.

United Nations Educational, Scientific and Cultural Organization (UNESCO), 7 Place de Fontenoy, F-75700 Paris, France (Telephone Number in U.S. (212) 963-5981); *Statistical Yearbook*.

ROMANIA - MOTOR VEHICLE PRODUCTION AND ASSEMBLY

Statistical Office of the United Nations, Publishing Service, New York, New York 10017 (800) 253-9646; *Statistical Yearbook*.

ROMANIA - MOTOR VEHICLE TAXES - See ROMANIA - TAXATION

ROMANIA - MOTOR VEHICLES IN USE

G.K. Hall and Company, 70 Lincoln Street, Boston, Massachusetts 02111 (617) 423-3990; *The World in Figures*.

International Road Federation, 525 School Street, SW, Washington, D.C. 20024 (202) 554-2106; *World Road Statistics*.

Statistical Office of the United Nations, Publishing Service, New York, New York 10017 (800) 253-9646; *Statistical Yearbook*.

Times Books, 201 East 50th Street, New York, New York 10022 (212) 751-2600; *The Economist Book of Vital World Statistics*.

ROMANIA - MUSEUMS

Euromonitor Publications Limited, 87-88 Turnmill Street, London EC1M 5QU, England; *European Marketing Data and Statistics*.

Facts on File, 460 Park Avenue South, New York, New York 10016 (800) 443-8323; *The New Book of World Rankings*.

United Nations Educational, Scientific and Cultural Organization (UNESCO), 7 Place de Fontenoy, F-75700 Paris, France (Telephone Number in U.S. (212) 963-5981); *Statistical Yearbook*.

ROMANIA - NATALITY - See ROMANIA - BIRTH RATE

ROMANIA - NATIONAL ACCOUNTS

Statistical Office of the United Nations, Publishing Service, New York, New York 10017 (800) 253-9646; *National Accounts Statistics*, and *Statistical Yearbook*.

ROMANIA - NATIONAL INCOME

Facts on File, 460 Park Avenue South, New York, New York 10016 (800) 443-8323; *The New Book of World Rankings*.

G.K. Hall and Company, 70 Lincoln Street, Boston, Massachusetts 02111 (617) 423-3990; *The World in Figures*.

Statistical Office of the United Nations, Publishing Service, New York, New York 10017 (800) 253-9646; *Statistical Yearbook*.

ROMANIA - NATIONAL PRODUCT

Facts on File, 460 Park Avenue South, New York, New York 10016 (800) 443-8323; *The New Book of World Rankings*.

Statistical Office of the United Nations, Publishing Service, New York, New York 10017 (800) 253-9646; *Statistical Yearbook*.

ROMANIA - NATURAL GAS PRODUCTION - See ROMANIA - MINING AND MINERAL PRODUCTS

ROMANIA - NET MATERIAL PRODUCT

Statistical Office of the United Nations, Publishing Service, New York, New York 10017 (800) 253-9646; *Statistical Yearbook*.

ROMANIA - NEWSPAPER PRODUCTION - See ROMANIA - FORESTRY AND FOREST PRODUCTS

ROMANIA - NEWSPRINT PRODUCTION AND CONSUMPTION - See ROMANIA - FORESTRY AND FOREST PRODUCTS

ROMANIA - NITRIC ACID PRODUCTION - See ROMANIA - MINING AND MINERAL PRODUCTS

ROMANIA - OATS PRODUCTION - See ROMANIA - CROPS

ROMANIA - OCCUPATIONS - See ROMANIA - LABOR FORCE

ROMANIA - ONION PRODUCTION - See ROMANIA - CROPS

ROMANIA - PAPER PRODUCTION - See ROMANIA - FORESTRY AND FOREST PRODUCTS

ROMANIA - PARTY LEADERS

Columbia University Press, 562 West 113th Street, New York, New York 10014 (212) 316-7100; *East European and Soviet Data Book*.

ROMANIA - PARTY MEMBERSHIP

Columbia University Press, 562 West 113th Street, New York, New York 10014 (212) 316-7100; *East European and Soviet Data Book*.

ROMANIA - PATENTS

Statistical Office of the United Nations, Publishing Service, New York, New York 10017 (800) 253-9646; *Statistical Yearbook*.

World Intellectual Property Organization, 34 Chemin des Colombettes, CH-1211 Geneva 20. Switzerland; *Industrial Property Statistics*.

ROMANIA - PEANUT PRODUCTION - See ROMANIA - CROPS

ROMANIA - PERIODICALS

United Nations Educational, Scientific and Cultural Organization (UNESCO), 7 Place de Fontenoy, F-75700 Paris, France (Telephone Number in U.S. (212) 963-5981); *Statistical Yearbook*.

ROMANIA - PESTICIDE USE

Food and Agricultural Organization of the United Nations (FAO) Via delle Terme di Caracalla, 00100 Rome, Italy (Telephone Number in U.S. (202) 653-2400); *The State of Food and Agriculture*.

ROMANIA - PETROLEUM INDUSTRY

Commodity Research Bureau, Incorporated, 75 Wall Street, New York, New York 10005 (212) 504-7754; *Commodity Year Book*.

Euromonitor Publications Limited, 87-88 Turnmill Street, London EC1M 5QU, England; *European Marketing Data and Statistics*.

Facts on File, 460 Park Avenue South, New York, New York 10016 (800) 443-8323; *The New Book of World Rankings*.

Food and Agricultural Organization of the United Nations (FAO) Via delle Terme di Caracalla, 00100 Rome, Italy (Telephone Number in U.S. (202) 653-2400); *The State of Food and Agriculture*.

G.K. Hall and Company, 70 Lincoln Street, Boston, Massachusetts 02111 (617) 423-3990; *The World in Figures*.

Penn Well Publishing Company, 1421 South Sheridan Road, P.O. Box 1260, Tulsa, Oklahoma 74101 (800) 752-9764; *International Energy Statistics Sourcebook*.

Statistical Office of the United Nations, Publishing Service, New York, New York 10017 (800) 253-9646; *Statistical Yearbook*.

ROMANIA - PIG-IRON AND FERRO-ALLOYS PRODUCTION - See ROMANIA - MINING AND MINERAL PRODUCTS

ROMANIA - PIGS - See ROMANIA - LIVESTOCK AND POULTRY

ROMANIA - PIPELINES FOR OIL AND PETROLEUM PRODUCTS

Statistical Office of the United Nations, Publishing Service, New York, New York 10017 (800) 253-9646; *Annual Bulletin of Transport Statistics for Europe*.

ROMANIA - PLASTIC AND RESIN PRODUCTION

Statistical Office of the United Nations, Publishing Service, New York, New York 10017 (800) 253-9646; *Statistical Yearbook*.

ROMANIA - POPULATION

Columbia University Press, 562 West 113th Street, New York, New York 10014 (212) 316-7100; *East European and Soviet Data Book*.

The Economist Intelligence Unit, 111 West 57th Street, New York, New York 10019 (800) 938-4685; *The World Market Atlas*.

Euromonitor Publications Limited, 87-88 Turnmill Street, London EC1M 5QU, England; *European Marketing Data and Statistics*.

Facts on File, 460 Park Avenue South, New York, New York 10016 (800) 443-8323; *The New Book of World Rankings*.

Food and Agricultural Organization of the United Nations (FAO), Via delle Terme di Caracalla, 00100 Rome, Italy (Telephone Number in U.S. (202) 653-2400); *Production Yearbook*.

G.K. Hall and Company, 70 Lincoln Street, Boston, Massachusetts 02111 (617) 423-3990; *The World in Figures*.

International Labour Office, I.L.O. Publications, CH-1211, Geneva 22, Switzerland; *Yearbook of Labour Statistics*.

Statistical Office of the United Nations, Publishing Service, New York, New York 10017 (800) 253-9646; *Demographic Yearbook*, and *Statistical Yearbook*.

Times Books, 201 East 50th Street, New York, New York 10022 (212) 751-2600; *The Economist Book of Vital World Statistics*.

United Nations Educational, Scientific and Cultural Organization (UNESCO), 7 Place de Fontenoy, F-75700 Paris, France (Telephone Number in U.S. (212) 963-5981); *Statistical Yearbook*.

U.S. Arms Control and Disarmament Agency, 320 Twenty-first Street, NW, Washington, D.C. 20451 (202) 647-8677; *World Military Expenditures and Arms Transfers*.

World Health Organization, Office of Publications, Avenue Appia, CH-1211 Geneva 27, Switzerland (Telephone Number in U.S. (518) 436-9686); *World Health Statistics Annual*.

ROMANIA - POST OFFICES

Facts on File, 460 Park Avenue South, New York, New York 10016 (800) 443-8323; *The New Book of World Rankings*.

ROMANIA - POTATO PRODUCTION - See ROMANIA - CROPS

ROMANIA - POWER PRODUCTION INDUSTRY

Statistical Office of the United Nations, Publishing Service, New York, New York 10017 (800) 253-9646; *Statistical Yearbook*.

ROMANIA - PRICES

Facts on File, 460 Park Avenue South, New York, New York 10016 (800) 443-8323; *The New Book of World Rankings*.

Food and Agricultural Organization of the United Nations (FAO), Via delle Terme di Caracalla, 00100 Rome, Italy (Telephone Number in U.S. (202) 653-2400); *Production Yearbook*, and *The State of Food and Agriculture*.

G.K. Hall and Company, 70 Lincoln Street, Boston, Massachusetts 02111 (617) 423-3990; *The World in Figures*.

International Labour Office, I.L.O. Publications, CH-1211, Geneva 22, Switzerland; *Yearbook of Labour Statistics*.

International Monetary Fund, 700 Nineteenth Street, NW, Washington, D.C. 20431 (202) 623-7000; *International Financial Statistics*.

ROMANIA - PRODUCTION

Facts on File, 460 Park Avenue South, New York, New York 10016 (800) 443-8323; *The New Book of World Rankings*.

G.K. Hall and Company, 70 Lincoln Street, Boston, Massachusetts 02111 (617) 423-3990; *The World in Figures*.

ROMANIA - PROPERTY TAXES - See ROMANIA - TAXATION

ROMANIA - PUBLIC FINANCE

Facts on File, 460 Park Avenue South, New York, New York 10016 (800) 443-8323; *The New Book of World Rankings*.

ROMANIA - RADIO BROADCASTING - See ROMANIA - BROADCASTING

ROMANIA - RADIO RECEIVER PRODUCTION

Statistical Office of the United Nations, Publishing Service, New York, New York 10017 (800) 253-9646; *Statistical Yearbook*.

ROMANIA - RAILWAYS

Euromonitor Publications Limited, 87-88 Turnmill Street, London EC1M 5QU, England; *European Marketing Data and Statistics*.

G.K. Hall and Company, 70 Lincoln Street, Boston, Massachusetts 02111 (617) 423-3990; *The World in Figures*.

Jane's Information Group, Sentinel House, 163 Brighton Road, Coulsdon, Surrey CR5 2NH, England (Telephone Number in U.S. (703) 683-3700); *Jane's World Railways*.

Statistical Office of the United Nations, Publishing Service, New York, New York 10017 (800) 253-9646; *Annual Bulletin of Transport Statistics for Europe*, and *Statistical Yearbook*.

ROMANIA - RAPESEED PRODUCTION - See ROMANIA - CROPS

ROMANIA - RELIGION

Facts on File, 460 Park Avenue South, New York, New York 10016 (800) 443-8323; *The New Book of World Rankings*.

ROMANIA - RENT PRICES

International Labour Office, I.L.O. Publications, CH-1211, Geneva 22, Switzerland; *Yearbook of Labour Statistics*.

ROMANIA - RETAIL TRADE

G.K. Hall and Company, 70 Lincoln Street, Boston, Massachusetts 02111 (617) 423-3990; *The World in Figures*.

Statistical Office of the United Nations, Publishing Service, New York, New York 10017 (800) 253-9646; *Statistical Yearbook*.

ROMANIA - RICE PRODUCTION - See ROMANIA - CROPS

ROMANIA - ROOT AND TUBER PRODUCTION - See ROMANIA - CROPS

ROMANIA - ROUNDWOOD PRODUCTION - See ROMANIA - FORESTRY AND FOREST PRODUCTS

ROMANIA - RUBBER PRODUCTION AND CONSUMPTION

Facts on File, 460 Park Avenue South, New York, New York 10016 (800) 443-8323; *The New Book of World Rankings*.

Statistical Office of the United Nations, Publishing Service, New York, New York 10017 (800) 253-9646; *Statistical Yearbook*.

ROMANIA - SALT PRODUCTION - See ROMANIA - MINING AND MINERAL PRODUCTS

ROMANIA - SAWNWOOD PRODUCTION - See ROMANIA - FORESTRY AND FOREST PRODUCTS

ROMANIA - SCIENCE AND TECHNOLOGY - EXPENDITURE FOR RESEARCH

Statistical Office of the United Nations, Publishing Service, New York, New York 10017 (800) 253-9646; *Statistical Yearbook*.

ROMANIA - SCIENTISTS AND TECHNICIANS

Statistical Office of the United Nations, Publishing Service, New York, New York 10017 (800) 253-9646; *Statistical Yearbook*.

United Nations Educational, Scientific and Cultural Organization (UNESCO), 7 Place de Fontenoy, F-75700 Paris, France (Telephone Number in U.S. (212) 963-5981); *Statistical Yearbook*.

ROMANIA - SENIOR CITIZENS

Facts on File, 460 Park Avenue South, New York, New York 10016 (800) 443-8323; *The New Book of World Rankings*.

ROMANIA - SHEEP - See ROMANIA - LIVESTOCK AND POULTRY

ROMANIA - SILVER PRODUCTION AND CONSUMPTION - See ROMANIA - MINING AND MINERAL PRODUCTS

ROMANIA - SOCIAL DATA

Facts on File, 460 Park Avenue South, New York, New York 10016 (800) 443-8323; *The New Book of World Rankings*.

G.K. Hall and Company, 70 Lincoln Street, Boston, Massachusetts 02111 (617) 423-3990; *The World in Figures*.

ROMANIA - SOCIAL SECURITY

International Monetary Fund, 700 Nineteenth Street, NW, Washington, D.C. 20431 (202) 623-7000; *Government Finance Statistics Yearbook*.

ROMANIA - SOYBEAN PRODUCTION - See ROMANIA - CROPS

ROMANIA - STEEL - See ROMANIA - MINING AND MINERAL PRODUCTS

ROMANIA - STOCKS - COMMODITY - MARKET PRICE - INDEX

Food and Agricultural Organization of the United Nations (FAO) Via delle Terme di Caracalla, 00100 Rome, Italy (Telephone Number in U.S. (202) 653-2400); *The State of Food and Agriculture*.

ROMANIA - SUGAR PRODUCTION AND CONSUMPTION - See ROMANIA - CROPS

ROMANIA - SULPHURIC ACID PRODUCTION - See ROMANIA - MINING AND MINERAL PRODUCTS

ROMANIA - TAXATION

G.K. Hall and Company, 70 Lincoln Street, Boston, Massachusetts 02111 (617) 423-3990; *The World in Figures*.

International Monetary Fund, 700 Nineteenth Street, NW, Washington, D.C. 20431 (202) 623-7000; *Government Finance Statistics Yearbook*.

International Road Federation, 525 School Street, SW, Washington, D.C. 20024 (202) 554-2106; *World Road Statistics*.

ROMANIA - TELEPHONES IN USE

American Telephone and Telegraph Company, 26 Parsippany Road, Whippany, New Jersey 07981 (800) 338-4038; *The World's Telephones*.

G.K. Hall and Company, 70 Lincoln Street, Boston, Massachusetts 02111 (617) 423-3990; *The World in Figures*.

Statistical Office of the United Nations, Publishing Service, New York, New York 10017 (800) 253-9646; *Statistical Yearbook*.

ROMANIA - TELEVISION BROADCASTING - See ROMANIA - BROADCASTING

ROMANIA - TELEVISION RECEIVER PRODUCTION

Statistical Office of the United Nations, Publishing Service, New York, New York 10017 (800) 253-9646; *Statistical Yearbook*.

ROMANIA - TEXTILE INDUSTRY

Food and Agricultural Organization of the United Nations (FAO), Via delle Terme di Caracalla, 00100 Rome, Italy (Telephone Number in U.S. (202) 653-2400); *Production Yearbook*.

G.K. Hall and Company, 70 Lincoln Street, Boston, Massachusetts 02111 (617) 423-3990; *The World in Figures*.

Statistical Office of the United Nations, Publishing Service, New York, New York 10017 (800) 253-9646; *Statistical Yearbook.*

ROMANIA - THEATRE

United Nations Educational, Scientific and Cultural Organization (UNESCO), 7 Place de Fontenoy, F-75700 Paris, France (Telephone Number in U.S. (212) 963-5981); *Statistical Yearbook.*

ROMANIA - TIMBER - RESOURCE FORESTS - See ROMANIA - FORESTRY AND FOREST PRODUCTS

ROMANIA - TIN - INDUSTRIAL CONSUMPTION - See ROMANIA - MINING AND MINERAL PRODUCTS

ROMANIA - TIRE (MOTOR VEHICLE) PRODUCTION

Statistical Office of the United Nations, Publishing Service, New York, New York 10017 (800) 253-9646; *Statistical Yearbook.*

ROMANIA - TOBACCO PRODUCTION

Euromonitor Publications Limited, 87-88 Turnmill Street, London EC1M 5QU, England; *European Marketing Data and Statistics.*

Facts on File, 460 Park Avenue South, New York, New York 10016 (800) 443-8323; *The New Book of World Rankings.*

Statistical Office of the United Nations, Publishing Service, New York, New York 10017 (800) 253-9646; *Statistical Yearbook.*

ROMANIA - TOURISM

Euromonitor Publications Limited, 87-88 Turnmill Street, London EC1M 5QU, England; *European Marketing Data and Statistics.*

Facts on File, 460 Park Avenue South, New York, New York 10016 (800) 443-8323; *The New Book of World Rankings.*

G.K. Hall and Company, 70 Lincoln Street, Boston, Massachusetts 02111 (617) 423-3990; *The World in Figures.*

Statistical Office of the United Nations, Publishing Service, New York, New York 10017 (800) 253-9646; *Statistical Yearbook.*

Times Books, 201 East 50th Street, New York, New York 10022 (212) 751-2600; *The Economist Book of Vital World Statistics.*

World Tourism Organization, Calle Capitan Haya 42, E-28020 Madrid, Spain; *Yearbook of Tourism Statistics.*

ROMANIA - TRACTORS IN USE

Statistical Office of the United Nations, Publishing Service, New York, New York 10017 (800) 253-9646; *Statistical Yearbook.*

ROMANIA - TRADE

Euromonitor Publications Limited, 87-88 Turnmill Street, London EC1M 5QU, England; *European Marketing Data and Statistics.*

Food and Agricultural Organization of the United Nations (FAO) Via delle Terme di Caracalla, 00100 Rome, Italy (Telephone Number in U.S. (202) 653-2400); *The State of Food and Agriculture.*

Statistical Office of the United Nations, Publishing Service, New York, New York 10017 (800) 253-9646; *Statistical Yearbook.*

ROMANIA - TRADEMARKS AND SERVICE MARKS

Statistical Office of the United Nations, Publishing Service, New York, New York 10017 (800) 253-9646; *Statistical Yearbook.*

World Intellectual Property Organization, 34 Chemin des Colombettes, CH-1211 Geneva 20. Switzerland; *Industrial Property Statistics.*

ROMANIA - TRANSPORTATION AND COMMUNICATIONS

Facts on File, 460 Park Avenue South, New York, New York 10016 (800) 443-8323; *The New Book of World Rankings.*

G.K. Hall and Company, 70 Lincoln Street, Boston, Massachusetts 02111 (617) 423-3990; *The World in Figures.*

ROMANIA - UNEMPLOYMENT

Euromonitor Publications Limited, 87-88 Turnmill Street, London EC1M 5QU, England; *European Marketing Data and Statistics.*

International Labour Office, I.L.O. Publications, CH-1211, Geneva 22, Switzerland; *Yearbook of Labour Statistics.*

ROMANIA - VITAL STATISTICS

G.K. Hall and Company, 70 Lincoln Street, Boston, Massachusetts 02111 (617) 423-3990; *The World in Figures.*

Statistical Office of the United Nations, Publishing Service, New York, New York 10017 (800) 253-9646; *Statistical Yearbook.*

ROMANIA - WAGES

Euromonitor Publications Limited, 87-88 Turnmill Street, London EC1M 5QU, England; *European Marketing Data and Statistics.*

G.K. Hall and Company, 70 Lincoln Street, Boston, Massachusetts 02111 (617) 423-3990; *The World in Figures.*

International Labour Office, I.L.O. Publications, CH-1211, Geneva 22, Switzerland; *Yearbook of Labour Statistics.*

Statistical Office of the United Nations, Publishing Service, New York, New York 10017 (800) 253-9646; *Statistical Yearbook.*

ROMANIA - WALNUT PRODUCTION - See ROMANIA - CROPS

ROMANIA - WATERWAYS IN USE

Statistical Office of the United Nations, Publishing Service, New York, New York 10017 (800) 253-9646; *Annual Bulletin of Transport Statistics for Europe.*

ROMANIA - WEATHER

G.K. Hall and Company, 70 Lincoln Street, Boston, Massachusetts 02111 (617) 423-3990; *The World in Figures.*

ROMANIA - WELFARE

International Monetary Fund, 700 Nineteenth Street, NW, Washington, D.C. 20431 (202) 623-7000; *Government Finance Statistics Yearbook.*

ROMANIA - WHEAT PRODUCTION AND CONSUMPTION - See ROMANIA - CROPS

ROMANIA - WINE PRODUCTION

Statistical Office of the United Nations, Publishing Service, New York, New York 10017 (800) 253-9646; *Statistical Yearbook.*

ROMANIA - WOOD PULP PRODUCTION - See ROMANIA - FORESTRY AND FOREST PRODUCTS

ROMANIA - WOOL PRODUCTION

Facts on File, 460 Park Avenue South, New York, New York 10016 (800) 443-8323; *The New Book of World Rankings.*

ROMANIA - YARN PRODUCTION

Statistical Office of the United Nations, Publishing Service, New York, New York 10017 (800) 253-9646; *Statistical Yearbook.*

RUBBER AND MISCELLANEOUS PLASTICS - MANUFACTURING - CAPITAL

U.S. Department of Commerce, Bureau of Economic Analysis, Fourteenth Street between Constitution Avenue and E Street, NW, Washington, D.C. 20230 (202) 606-9900; *Survey of Current Business,* and *Fixed Reproducible Tangible Wealth in the United States.*

U.S. Department of Commerce, Bureau of the Census, Suitland, Maryland 20233 (301) 763-4040; *Census of Manufactures, Annual Survey of Manufactures,* and *Plant and Equipment Expenditures and Plans.*

RUBBER AND MISCELLANEOUS PLASTICS - MANUFACTURING - EARNINGS

U.S. Department of Commerce, Bureau of the Census, Suitland, Maryland 20233 (301) 763-4040; *Census of Manufactures, Annual Survey of Manufactures,* and *County Business Patterns.*

U.S. Department of Labor, Bureau of Labor Statistics, Two Massachusetts Avenue, NE, Washington, D.C. 20212 (202) 606-7828; *Employment and Earnings,* and Bulletins 2370 and 2429.

RUBBER AND MISCELLANEOUS PLASTICS - MANUFACTURING - EMPLOYEES

U.S. Department of Commerce, Bureau of the Census, Suitland, Maryland 20233 (301) 763-4040; *Census of Manufactures, Annual Survey of Manufactures, Annual Survey of Manufactures, Origin of Exports of Manufactured Products,* and *County Business Patterns.*

U.S. Department of Labor, Bureau of Labor Statistics, Two Massachusetts Avenue, NE, Washington, D.C. 20212 (202) 606-7828; *Employment and Earnings, Monthly Labor Review,* and Bulletins 2370 and 2429.

RUBBER AND MISCELLANEOUS PLASTICS - MANUFACTURING - ESTABLISHMENTS

U.S. Department of Commerce, Bureau of the Census, Suitland, Maryland 20233 (301) 763-4040; *Census of Manufactures, Annual Survey of Manufactures,* and *County Business Patterns.*

RUBBER AND MISCELLANEOUS PLASTICS - MANUFACTURING - FOREIGN TRADE

U.S. Department of Commerce, Bureau of the Census, Suitland, Maryland 20233 (301) 763-4040; *U.S. Merchandise Trade, Selected Highlights.*

RUBBER AND MISCELLANEOUS PLASTICS - MANUFACTURING - GROSS DOMESTIC PRODUCT

U.S. Department of Commerce, Bureau of Economic Analysis, Fourteenth Street between Constitution Avenue and E Street, NW, Washington, D.C. 20230 (202) 606-9900; *The National Income and Product Accounts of the United States,* and *Survey of Current Business.*

RUBBER AND MISCELLANEOUS PLASTICS - MANUFACTURING - INVENTORIES

U.S. Department of Commerce, Bureau of the Census, Suitland, Maryland 20233 (301) 763-4040; *Current Industrial Reports, Manufactures' Shipments, Inventories, and Orders.*

RUBBER AND MISCELLANEOUS PLASTICS - MANUFACTURING - MERGERS AND ACQUISITIONS

Securities Data Company, 1180 Raymond Boulevard, Newark, New Jersey 07102 (201) 622-3100; *Merger and Corporate Transactions Database.*

RUBBER AND MISCELLANEOUS PLASTICS - MANUFACTURING - OCCUPATIONAL SAFETY

U.S. Department of Labor, Bureau of Labor Statistics, Two Massachusetts Avenue, NE, Washington, D.C. 20212 (202) 606-7828; *Occupational Injuries and Illnesses in the United States by Industry.*

RUBBER AND MISCELLANEOUS PLASTICS - MANUFACTURING - PATENTS

U.S. Department of Commerce, Patent and Trademark Office, 2011 Crystal Drive, Arlington, Virginia 22202 (703) 305-8341; *Patenting Trends in the United States, State Country Report.*

RUBBER AND MISCELLANEOUS PLASTICS - MANUFACTURING - PRODUCTIVITY

U.S. Department of Labor, Bureau of Labor Statistics, Two Massachusetts Avenue, NE, Washington, D.C. 20212 (202) 606-7828; *Productivity Measures for Selected Industries and Government Services,* and unpublished data.

RUBBER AND MISCELLANEOUS PLASTICS - MANUFACTURING - PROFITS

Time Warner, 1675 Broadway, Rockefeller Center, New York, New York 10019 (212) 522-1212; *The Fortune Directories.*

RUBBER AND MISCELLANEOUS PLASTICS - MANUFACTURING - SALES, SHIPMENTS, RECEIPTS

Time Warner, 1675 Broadway, Rockefeller Center, New York, New York 10019 (212) 522-1212; *The Fortune Directories.*

U.S. Department of Commerce, Bureau of the Census, Suitland, Maryland 20233 (301) 763-4040; *Current Industrial Reports, Manufactures' Shipments, Inventories, and Orders, Census of Manufactures,* and *Annual Survey of Manufactures, Origin of Exports of Manufactured Products.*

RUBBER AND MISCELLANEOUS PLASTICS - MANUFACTURING - VALUE ADDED

U.S. Department of Commerce, Bureau of the Census, Suitland, Maryland 20233 (301) 763-4040; *Census of Manufactures,* and *Annual Survey of Manufactures.*

RUBBER PRODUCTS

U.S. Department of Commerce, Bureau of the Census, Suitland, Maryland 20233 (301) 763-4040; *Current Industrial Reports, U.S. Merchandise Trade,* and *U.S. Merchandise Trade, Exports, General Imports, and Imports for Consumption.*

RUBELLA

U.S. Department of Health and Human Services, Centers for Disease Control, 1600 Clifton Road, NE, Atlanta, Georgia 30333 (404) 639-3311; *National Health Interview Survey,* and *Summary of Notifiable Diseases, United States, Morbidity and Mortality Weekly Report.*

RUGS - See FLOOR COVERINGS

RURAL POPULATION - See POPULATION

RUSSIA - See also UNION OF SOVIET SOCIALIST REPUBLICS

Russia - Primary Statistics Source

Gosudarstvennyi Komitet Rossiiskoi Federatsii Po Statistike, Moscow, Russia; *Narodnoe Khoziaistvo Rossiiskoi Federatsii: Statisticheskii Ezhegodnik.*

RUSSIA - AGRICULTURE

Business International Moscow, 23 Profsoyuznaya Ulitsa, 117859, Moscow (Telephone Number in U.S. (800) 938-4685); *The CIS Market Atlas.*

Encyclopedia Britannica, Incorporated, 310 South Michigan Avenue, Chicago, Illinois 60004 (312) 347-7000; *Britannica World Data.*

The World Bank, 1818 H Street, NW, Washington, D.C. 20433 (202) 477-1234; *Statistical Handbook: States of the Former USSR.*

RUSSIA - AIRLINE SERVICE

Business International Moscow, 23 Profsoyuznaya Ulitsa, 117859, Moscow (Telephone Number in U.S. (800) 938-4685); *The CIS Market Atlas.*

Encyclopedia Britannica, Incorporated, 310 South Michigan Avenue, Chicago, Illinois 60604 (312) 347-7000; *Britannica World Data.*

RUSSIA - AREA AND DENSITY OF POPULATION

Business International Moscow, 23 Profsoyuznaya Ulitsa, 117859, Moscow (Telephone Number in U.S. (800) 938-4685); *The CIS Market Atlas.*

RUSSIA - BANKING

Business International Moscow, 23 Profsoyuznaya Ulitsa, 117859, Moscow (Telephone Number in U.S. (800) 938-4685); *The CIS Market Atlas.*

RUSSIA - BIRTH RATES

Business International Moscow, 23 Profsoyuznaya Ulitsa, 117859, Moscow (Telephone Number in U.S. (800) 938-4685); *The CIS Market Atlas.*

Encyclopedia Britannica, Incorporated, 310 South Michigan Avenue, Chicago, Illinois 60604 (312) 347-7000; *Britannica World Data.*

RUSSIA - BUDGET

Business International Moscow, 23 Profsoyuznaya Ulitsa, 117859, Moscow (Telephone Number in U.S. (800) 938-4685); *The CIS Market Atlas.*

RUSSIA - CAPITAL INVESTMENT

The World Bank, 1818 H Street, NW, Washington, D.C. 20433 (202) 477-1234; *Statistical Handbook: States of the Former USSR.*

RUSSIA - CATTLE - See RUSSIA - LIVESTOCK AND POULTRY

RUSSIA - CHEMICALS

Business International Moscow, 23 Profsoyuznaya Ulitsa, 117859, Moscow (Telephone Number in U.S. (800) 938-4685); *The CIS Market Atlas.*

RUSSIA - COAL PRODUCTION AND CONSUMPTION - See RUSSIA - MINING AND MINERAL PRODUCTS

RUSSIA - COMMUNICATIONS

Business International Moscow, 23 Profsoyuznaya Ulitsa, 117859, Moscow (Telephone Number in U.S. (800) 938-4685); *The CIS Market Atlas.*

RUSSIA - CONSTRUCTION INDUSTRY

Business International Moscow, 23 Profsoyuznaya Ulitsa, 117859, Moscow (Telephone Number in U.S. (800) 938-4685); *The CIS Market Atlas.*

Encyclopedia Britannica, Incorporated, 310 South Michigan Avenue, Chicago, Illinois 60604 (312) 347-7000; *Britannica World Data.*

RUSSIA - CONSUMER PRODUCTS

Business International Moscow, 23 Profsoyuznaya Ulitsa, 117859, Moscow (Telephone Number in U.S. (800) 938-4685); *The CIS Market Atlas.*

RUSSIA - CONSUMPTION

Business International Moscow, 23 Profsoyuznaya Ulitsa, 117859, Moscow (Telephone Number in U.S. (800) 938-4685); *The CIS Market Atlas.*

The World Bank, 1818 H Street, NW, Washington, D.C. 20433 (202) 477-1234; *Statistical Handbook: States of the Former USSR.*

RUSSIA - COTTON PRODUCTION AND CONSUMPTION - See RUSSIA - CROPS

RUSSIA - CROPS

Business International Moscow, 23 Profsoyuznaya Ulitsa, 117859, Moscow (Telephone Number in U.S. (800) 938-4685); *The CIS Market Atlas.*

The World Bank, 1818 H Street, NW, Washington, D.C. 20433 (202) 477-1234; *Statistical Handbook: States of the Former USSR.*

RUSSIA - DEATH RATES

Business International Moscow, 23 Profsoyuznaya Ulitsa, 117859, Moscow (Telephone Number in U.S. (800) 938-4685); *The CIS Market Atlas.*

RUSSIA - DEMOGRAPHY

Business International Moscow, 23 Profsoyuznaya Ulitsa, 117859, Moscow (Telephone Number in U.S. (800) 938-4685); *The CIS Market Atlas.*

Encyclopedia Britannica, Incorporated, 310 South Michigan Avenue, Chicago, Illinois 60604 (312) 347-7000; *Britannica World Data.*

The World Bank, 1818 H Street, NW, Washington, D.C. 20433 (202) 477-1234; *Statistical Handbook: States of the Former USSR.*

RUSSIA - DISEASES

Business International Moscow, 23 Profsoyuznaya Ulitsa, 117859, Moscow (Telephone Number in U.S. (800) 938-4685); *The CIS Market Atlas.*

RUSSIA - DIVORCE RATES

Encyclopedia Britannica, Incorporated, 310 South Michigan Avenue, Chicago, Illinois 60604 (312) 347-7000; *Britannica World Data.*

RUSSIA - DOMESTIC INVESTMENT

Business International Moscow, 23 Profsoyuznaya Ulitsa, 117859, Moscow (Telephone Number in U.S. (800) 938-4685); *The CIS Market Atlas.*

RUSSIA - ECONOMY

Business International Moscow, 23 Profsoyuznaya Ulitsa, 117859, Moscow (Telephone Number in U.S. (800) 938-4685); *The CIS Market Atlas.*

Encyclopedia Britannica, Incorporated, 310 South Michigan Avenue, Chicago, Illinois 60604 (312) 347-7000; *Britannica World Data.*

RUSSIA - EDUCATION

Business International Moscow, 23 Profsoyuznaya Ulitsa, 117859, Moscow (Telephone Number in U.S. (800) 938-4685); *The CIS Market Atlas.*

Encyclopedia Britannica, Incorporated, 310 South Michigan Avenue, Chicago, Illinois 60604 (312) 347-7000; *Britannica World Data.*

RUSSIA - ELECTRICITY

Business International Moscow, 23 Profsoyuznaya Ulitsa, 117859, Moscow (Telephone Number in U.S. (800) 938-4685); *The CIS Market Atlas.*

The World Bank, 1818 H Street, NW, Washington, D.C. 20433 (202) 477-1234; *Statistical Handbook: States of the Former USSR.*

RUSSIA - EMPLOYMENT

The World Bank, 1818 H Street, NW, Washington, D.C. 20433 (202) 477-1234; *Statistical Handbook: States of the Former USSR.*

RUSSIA - ENERGY

Business International Moscow, 23 Profsoyuznaya Ulitsa, 117859, Moscow (Telephone Number in U.S. (800) 938-4685); *The CIS Market Atlas.*

Encyclopedia Britannica, Incorporated, 310 South Michigan Avenue, Chicago, Illinois 60604 (312) 347-7000; *Britannica World Data.*

The World Bank, 1818 H Street, NW, Washington, D.C. 20433 (202) 477-1234; *Statistical Handbook: States of the Former USSR.*

RUSSIA - ENVIRONMENT

Business International Moscow, 23 Profsoyuznaya Ulitsa, 117859, Moscow (Telephone Number in U.S. (800) 938-4685); *The CIS Market Atlas.*

RUSSIA - EXPORTS

Business International Moscow, 23 Profsoyuznaya Ulitsa, 117859, Moscow (Telephone Number in U.S. (800) 938-4685); *The CIS Market Atlas.*

Encyclopedia Britannica, Incorporated, 310 South Michigan Avenue, Chicago, Illinois 60604 (312) 347-7000; *Britannica World Data.*

The World Bank, 1818 H Street, NW, Washington, D.C. 20433 (202) 477-1234; *Statistical Handbook: States of the Former USSR.*

RUSSIA - EXTERNAL TRADE

The World Bank, 1818 H Street, NW, Washington, D.C. 20433 (202) 477-1234; *Statistical Handbook: States of the Former USSR.*

RUSSIA - FABRIC PRODUCTION AND CONSUMPTION - See RUSSIA - TEXTILE INDUSTRY

RUSSIA - FERTILITY RATES

Encyclopedia Britannica, Incorporated, 310 South Michigan Avenue, Chicago, Illinois 60604 (312) 347-7000; *Britannica World Data.*

The World Bank, 1818 H Street, NW, Washington, D.C. 20433 (202) 477-1234; *Statistical Handbook: States of the Former USSR.*

RUSSIA - FISHERIES

Encyclopedia Britannica, Incorporated, 310 South Michigan Avenue, Chicago, Illinois 60604 (312) 347-7000; *Britannica World Data.*

RUSSIA - FOOTWEAR PRODUCTION AND CONSUMPTION - See RUSSIA - TEXTILE INDUSTRY

RUSSIA - FOREIGN INVESTMENT

Business International Moscow, 23 Profsoyuznaya Ulitsa, 117859, Moscow (Telephone Number in U.S. (800) 938-4685); *The CIS Market Atlas.*

RUSSIA - FOREIGN TRADE

Business International Moscow, 23 Profsoyuznaya Ulitsa, 117859, Moscow (Telephone Number in U.S. (800) 938-4685); *The CIS Market Atlas.*

Encyclopedia Britannica, Incorporated, 310 South Michigan Avenue, Chicago, Illinois 60604 (312) 347-7000; *Britannica World Data.*

The World Bank, 1818 H Street, NW, Washington, D.C. 20433 (202) 477-1234; *Statistical Handbook: States of the Former USSR.*

RUSSIA - FORESTRY AND FOREST PRODUCTS

Business International Moscow, 23 Profsoyuznaya Ulitsa, 117859, Moscow (Telephone Number in U.S. (800) 938-4685); *The CIS Market Atlas.*

Encyclopedia Britannica, Incorporated, 310 South Michigan Avenue, Chicago, Illinois 60604 (312) 347-7000; *Britannica World Data.*

RUSSIA - GOATS - See RUSSIA - LIVESTOCK AND POULTRY

RUSSIA - GOVERNMENT EXPENDITURE

The World Bank, 1818 H Street, NW, Washington, D.C. 20433 (202) 477-1234; *Statistical Handbook: States of the Former USSR.*

RUSSIA - GOVERNMENT REVENUE

The World Bank, 1818 H Street, NW, Washington, D.C. 20433 (202) 477-1234; *Statistical Handbook: States of the Former USSR.*

RUSSIA - GROSS DOMESTIC PRODUCT

The World Bank, 1818 H Street, NW, Washington, D.C. 20433 (202) 477-1234; *Statistical Handbook: States of the Former USSR.*

RUSSIA - HEALTH

Business International Moscow, 23 Profsoyuznaya Ulitsa, 117859, Moscow (Telephone Number in U.S. (800) 938-4685); *The CIS Market Atlas.*

Encyclopedia Britannica, Incorporated, 310 South Michigan Avenue, Chicago, Illinois 60604 (312) 347-7000; *Britannica World Data.*

RUSSIA - HIGHWAYS

Business International Moscow, 23 Profsoyuznaya Ulitsa, 117859, Moscow (Telephone Number in U.S. (800) 938-4685); *The CIS Market Atlas.*

Encyclopedia Britannica, Incorporated, 310 South Michigan Avenue, Chicago, Illinois 60604 (312) 347-7000; *Britannica World Data.*

RUSSIA - HOUSING AND HOUSING UNITS

Business International Moscow, 23 Profsoyuznaya Ulitsa, 117859, Moscow (Telephone Number in U.S. (800) 938-4685); *The CIS Market Atlas.*

RUSSIA - IMPORTS

Business International Moscow, 23 Profsoyuznaya Ulitsa, 117859, Moscow (Telephone Number in U.S. (800) 938-4685); *The CIS Market Atlas.*

Encyclopedia Britannica, Incorporated, 310 South Michigan Avenue, Chicago, Illinois 60604 (312) 347-7000; *Britannica World Data.*

The World Bank, 1818 H Street, NW, Washington, D.C. 20433 (202) 477-1234; *Statistical Handbook: States of the Former USSR.*

RUSSIA - INDUSTRY

Business International Moscow, 23 Profsoyuznaya Ulitsa, 117859, Moscow (Telephone Number in U.S. (800) 938-4685); *The CIS Market Atlas.*

The World Bank, 1818 H Street, NW, Washington, D.C. 20433 (202) 477-1234; *Statistical Handbook: States of the Former USSR.*

RUSSIA - INFANT MORTALITY

Business International Moscow, 23 Profsoyuznaya Ulitsa, 117859, Moscow (Telephone Number in U.S. (800) 938-4685); *The CIS*

RUSSIA - LABOR FORCE

Business International Moscow, 23 Profsoyuznaya Ulitsa, 117859, Moscow (Telephone Number in U.S. (800) 938-4685); *The CIS Market Atlas.*

The World Bank, 1818 H Street, NW, Washington, D.C. 20433 (202) 477-1234; *Statistical Handbook: States of the Former USSR.*

RUSSIA - LAND USE

Encyclopedia Britannica, Incorporated, 310 South Michigan Avenue, Chicago, Illinois 60604 (312) 347-7000; *Britannica World Data.*

RUSSIA - LIFE EXPECTANCY

Business International Moscow, 23 Profsoyuznaya Ulitsa, 117859, Moscow (Telephone Number in U.S. (800) 938-4685); *The CIS Market Atlas.*

RUSSIA - LIVESTOCK AND POULTRY

Business International Moscow, 23 Profsoyuznaya Ulitsa, 117859, Moscow (Telephone Number in U.S. (800) 938-4685); *The CIS Market Atlas*

Encyclopedia Britannica, Incorporated, 310 South Michigan Avenue, Chicago, Illinois 60604 (312) 347-7000; *Britannica World Data.*

RUSSIA - MANUFACTURING

Encyclopedia Britannica, Incorporated, 310 South Michigan Avenue, Chicago, Illinois 60604 (312) 347-7000; *Britannica World Data.*

RUSSIA - MARRIAGE RATES

Encyclopedia Britannica, Incorporated, 310 South Michigan Avenue, Chicago, Illinois 60604 (312) 347-7000; *Britannica World Data.*

RUSSIA - MEAT PRODUCTION - See RUSSIA - LIVESTOCK AND POULTRY

RUSSIA - MILITARY

The International Institute for Strategic Studies, 23 Tavistock Street, London WC2E 7NQ, England; *The Military Balance.*

RUSSIA - MINING AND MINERAL PRODUCTS

Business International Moscow, 23 Profsoyuznaya Ulitsa, 117859, Moscow (Telephone Number in U.S. (800) 938-4685); *The CIS Market Atlas.*

Encyclopedia Britannica, Incorporated, 310 South Michigan Avenue, Chicago, Illinois 60604 (312) 347-7000; *Britannica World Data.*

RUSSIA - MOTOR VEHICLES

Business International Moscow, 23 Profsoyuznaya Ulitsa, 117859, Moscow (Telephone Number in U.S. (800) 938-4685); *The CIS Market Atlas.*

RUSSIA - NATIONAL ACCOUNTS

The World Bank, 1818 H Street, NW, Washington, D.C. 20433 (202) 477-1234; *Statistical Handbook: States of the Former USSR.*

RUSSIA - NATIONAL INCOME

Business International Moscow, 23 Profsoyuznaya Ulitsa, 117859, Moscow (Telephone Number in U.S. (800) 938-4685); *The CIS Market Atlas*.

RUSSIA - PIGS - See RUSSIA - LIVESTOCK AND POULTRY

RUSSIA - POPULATION

Business International Moscow, 23 Profsoyuznaya Ulitsa, 117859, Moscow (Telephone Number in U.S. (800) 938-4685); *The CIS Market Atlas*.

Encyclopedia Britannica, Incorporated, 310 South Michigan Avenue, Chicago, Illinois 60604 (312) 347-7000; *Britannica World Data*.

The World Bank, 1818 H Street, NW, Washington, D.C. 20433 (202) 477-1234; *Statistical Handbook: States of the Former USSR*.

RUSSIA - POULTRY - See RUSSIA - LIVESTOCK AND POULTRY

RUSSIA - PRICES

The World Bank, 1818 H Street, NW, Washington, D.C. 20433 (202) 477-1234; *Statistical Handbook: States of the Former USSR*.

RUSSIA - PRODUCTION

The World Bank, 1818 H Street, NW, Washington, D.C. 20433 (202) 477-1234; *Statistical Handbook: States of the Former USSR*.

RUSSIA - PUBLIC FINANCE

The World Bank, 1818 H Street, NW, Washington, D.C. 20433 (202) 477-1234; *Statistical Handbook: States of the Former USSR*.

RUSSIA - RADIO RECEIVERS

Encyclopedia Britannica, Incorporated, 310 South Michigan Avenue, Chicago, Illinois 60604 (312) 347-7000; *Britannica World Data*.

RUSSIA - RAILWAYS

Business International Moscow, 23 Profsoyuznaya Ulitsa, 117859, Moscow (Telephone Number in U.S. (800) 938-4685); *The CIS Market Atlas*.

Encyclopedia Britannica, Incorporated, 310 South Michigan Avenue, Chicago, Illinois 60604 (312) 347-7000; *Britannica World Data*.

RUSSIA - RETAIL TRADE

Business International Moscow, 23 Profsoyuznaya Ulitsa, 117859, Moscow (Telephone Number in U.S. (800) 938-4685); *The CIS Market Atlas*.

RUSSIA - ROADS - See RUSSIA - HIGHWAYS

RUSSIA - ROUNDWOOD PRODUCTION AND CONSUMPTION - See RUSSIA - FORESTRY AND FOREST PRODUCTS

RUSSIA - SHEEP - See RUSSIA - LIVESTOCK AND POULTRY

RUSSIA - STEEL PRODUCTION AND CONSUMPTION - See RUSSIA - MINING AND MINERAL PRODUCTS

RUSSIA - TELEPHONES IN USE

Encyclopedia Britannica, Incorporated, 310 South Michigan Avenue, Chicago, Illinois 60604 (312) 347-7000; *Britannica World Data*.

RUSSIA - TELEVISION RECEIVERS

Encyclopedia Britannica, Incorporated, 310 South Michigan Avenue, Chicago, Illinois 60604 (312) 347-7000; *Britannica World Data*.

RUSSIA - TEXTILE INDUSTRY

Business International Moscow, 23 Profsoyuznaya Ulitsa, 117859, Moscow (Telephone Number in U.S. (800) 938-4685); *The CIS Market Atlas*.

RUSSIA - TOURISM

Business International Moscow, 23 Profsoyuznaya Ulitsa, 117859, Moscow (Telephone Number in U.S. (800) 938-4685); *The CIS Market Atlas*.

RUSSIA - TRANSPORTATION AND COMMUNICATIONS

Business International Moscow, 23 Profsoyuznaya Ulitsa, 117859, Moscow (Telephone Number in U.S. (800) 938-4685); *The CIS Market Atlas*.

Encyclopedia Britannica, Incorporated, 310 South Michigan Avenue, Chicago, Illinois 60604 (312) 347-7000; *Britannica World Data*.

RUSSIA - VITAL STATISTICS

Encyclopedia Britannica, Incorporated, 310 South Michigan Avenue, Chicago, Illinois 60604 (312) 347-7000; *Britannica World Data*.

RUSSIA - WAGES

Business International Moscow, 23 Profsoyuznaya Ulitsa, 117859, Moscow (Telephone Number in U.S. (800) 938-4685); *The CIS Market Atlas*.

The World Bank, 1818 H Street, NW, Washington, D.C. 20433 (202) 477-1234; *Statistical Handbook: States of the Former USSR*.

RUSSIA - WOOL PRODUCTION AND CONSUMPTION - See RUSSIA - TEXTILE INDUSTRY

Rwanda - National Statistical Office

Direction Generale de la Statistiques, Ministere du Plan, BP 46, Kigali, Rwanda.

Rwanda - Primary Statistics Source

Direction Generale de la Statistiques, BP 46, Kigali, Rwanda; *Bulletin de Statistique* (Statistical Bulletin).

RWANDA - AGRICULTURE

Euromonitor Publications Limited, 87-88 Turnmill Street, London EC1M 5QU, England; *International Marketing Data and Statistics*.

Facts on File, 460 Park Avenue South, New York, New York 10016 (800) 443-8323; *The New Book of World Rankings*.

Food and Agricultural Organization of the United Nations (FAO) Via delle Terme di Caracalla, 00100 Rome, Italy (Telephone Number in

U.S. (202) 653-2400); *Production Yearbook, The State of Food and Agriculture,* and *Trade Yearbook.*

G.K. Hall and Company, 70 Lincoln Street, Boston, Massachusetts 02111 (617) 423-3990; *The World in Figures.*

Statistical Office of the United Nations, Publishing Service, New York, New York 10017 (800) 253-9646; *Statistical Yearbook,* and *Survey of Economic and Social Conditions in Africa.*

Times Books, 201 East 50th Street, New York, New York 10022 (212) 751-2600; *The Economist Book of Vital World Statistics.*

United Nations Economic Commission for Africa, Africa Hall, P.O. Box 3001, Addis Ababa, Ethiopia (Telephone Number in U.S. (800) 253-9646); *African Statistical Yearbook.*

The World Bank, 1818 H Street, N.W., Washington, D.C. 20433 (202) 477-1234; *World Tables.*

RWANDA - AIRLINE SERVICE

Facts on File, 460 Park Avenue South, New York, New York 10016 (800) 443-8323; *The New Book of World Rankings.*

G.K. Hall and Company, 70 Lincoln Street, Boston, Massachusetts 02111 (617) 423-3990; *The World in Figures.*

Times Books, 201 East 50th Street, New York, New York 10022 (212) 751-2600; *The Economist Book of Vital World Statistics.*

United Nations Economic Commission for Africa, Africa Hall, P.O. Box 3001, Addis Ababa, Ethiopia (Telephone Number in U.S. (800) 253-9646); *African Statistical Yearbook.*

RWANDA - ALUMINUM PRODUCTION AND CONSUMPTION - See RWANDA - MINING AND MINERAL PRODUCTS

RWANDA - ANIMAL HEALTH

Food and Agricultural Organization of the United Nations (FAO), Via delle Terme di Caracalla, 00100, Rome, Italy (Telephone Number in U.S. (202) 653-2400); *Animal Health Yearbook.*

RWANDA - AREA AND DENSITY OF POPULATION

African Development Bank, 01 BP 1387, Abidjan 01, Cote d'Ivoire; *Selected Statistics on Regional Member Countries.*

Euromonitor Publications Limited, 87-88 Turnmill Street, London EC1M 5QU, England; *International Marketing Data and Statistics.*

Facts on File, 460 Park Avenue South, New York, New York 10016 (800) 443-8323; *The New Book of World Rankings.*

Food and Agricultural Organization of the United Nations (FAO) Via delle Terme di Caracalla, 00100 Rome, Italy (Telephone Number in U.S. (202) 653-2400); *The State of Food and Agriculture.*

G.K. Hall and Company, 70 Lincoln Street, Boston, Massachusetts 02111 (617) 423-3990; *The World in Figures.*

Statistical Office of the United Nations, Publishing Service, New York, New York 10017 (800) 253-9646; *Statistical Yearbook,* and *Survey of Economic and Social Conditions in Africa.*

Times Books, 201 East 50th Street, New York, New York 10022 (212) 751-2600; *The Economist Book of Vital World Statistics.*

United Nations Educational, Scientific and Cultural Organization (UNESCO), 7 Place de Fontenoy, F-75700 Paris, France (Telephone Number in U.S. (212) 963-5981); *Statistical Yearbook.*

RWANDA - ARMS EXPORTS AND IMPORTS

U.S. Arms Control and Disarmament Agency, 320 Twenty-first Street, NW, Washington, D.C. 20451 (202) 647-8677; *World Military Expenditures and Arms Transfers.*

RWANDA - BALANCE OF PAYMENTS

African Development Bank, 01 BP 1387, Abidjan 01, Cote d'Ivoire; *Selected Statistics on Regional Member Countries.*

The Economist Intelligence Unit, 111 West 57th Street, New York, New York 10019 (800) 938-4685; *The World Market Atlas.*

G.K. Hall and Company, 70 Lincoln Street, Boston, Massachusetts 02111 (617) 423-3990; *The World in Figures.*

International Monetary Fund, 700 Nineteenth Street, NW, Washington, D.C. 20431 (202) 623-7000; *Balance of Payments Yearbook,* and *International Financial Statistics.*

Times Books, 201 East 50th Street, New York, New York 10022 (212) 751-2600; *The Economist Book of Vital World Statistics.*

United Nations Economic Commission for Africa, Africa Hall, P.O. Box 3001, Addis Ababa, Ethiopia (Telephone Number in U.S. (800) 253-9646); *African Statistical Yearbook.*

The World Bank, 1818 H Street, N.W., Washington, D.C. 20433 (202) 477-1234; *World Tables.*

RWANDA - BANKING

Facts on File, 460 Park Avenue South, New York, New York 10016 (800) 443-8323; *The New Book of World Rankings.*

G.K. Hall and Company, 70 Lincoln Street, Boston, Massachusetts 02111 (617) 423-3990; *The World in Figures.*

International Monetary Fund, 700 Nineteenth Street, NW, Washington, D.C. 20431 (202) 623-7000; *International Financial Statistics.*

Statistical Office of the United Nations, Publishing Service, New York, New York 10017 (800) 253-9646; *Statistical Yearbook.*

United Nations Economic Commission for Africa, Africa Hall, P.O. Box 3001, Addis Ababa, Ethiopia (Telephone Number in U.S. (800) 253-9646); *African Statistical Yearbook.*

RWANDA - BARLEY PRODUCTION - See RWANDA - CROPS

RWANDA - BEER PRODUCTION

Facts on File, 460 Park Avenue South, New York, New York 10016 (800) 443-8323; *The New Book of World Rankings.*

Statistical Office of the United Nations, Publishing Service, New York, New York 10017 (800) 253-9646; *Statistical Yearbook.*

RWANDA - BIRTH RATES

Facts on File, 460 Park Avenue South, New York, New York 10016 (800) 443-8323; *The New Book of World Rankings.*

Statistical Office of the United Nations, Publishing Service, New York, New York 10017 (800) 253-9646; *Demographic Yearbook,* and *Statistical Yearbook,* and *Survey of Economic and Social Conditions in Africa.*

Times Books, 201 East 50th Street, New York, New York 10022 (212) 751-2600; *The Economist Book of Vital World Statistics.*

The World Bank, 1818 H Street, N.W., Washington, D.C. 20433 (202) 477-1234; *World Tables.*

World Health Organization, Office of Publications, Avenue Appia, CH-1211 Geneva 27, Switzerland (Telephone Number in U.S. (518) 436-9686); *World Health Statistics Annual.*

RWANDA - BONDS

G.K. Hall and Company, 70 Lincoln Street, Boston, Massachusetts 02111 (617) 423-3990; *The World in Figures.*

International Monetary Fund, 700 Nineteenth Street, NW, Washington, D.C. 20431 (202) 623-7000; *Government Finance Statistics Yearbook.*

RWANDA - BOOK PRODUCTION

G.K. Hall and Company, 70 Lincoln Street, Boston, Massachusetts 02111 (617) 423-3990; *The World in Figures.*

RWANDA - BROADCASTING

Billboard Limited, P.O. Box 9027, 1006 AA Amsterdam, The Netherlands (Telephone Number in U.S. (212) 764-7300); *World Radio TV Handbook.*

Facts on File, 460 Park Avenue South, New York, New York 10016 (800) 443-8323; *The New Book of World Rankings.*

G.K. Hall and Company, 70 Lincoln Street, Boston, Massachusetts 02111 (617) 423-3990; *The World in Figures.*

Times Books, 201 East 50th Street, New York, New York 10022 (212) 751-2600; *The Economist Book of Vital World Statistics.*

RWANDA - BUSINESS

G.K. Hall and Company, 70 Lincoln Street, Boston, Massachusetts 02111 (617) 423-3990; *The World in Figures.*

RWANDA - BUSINESS AND PROFESSIONAL LICENSES

International Monetary Fund, 700 Nineteenth Street, NW, Washington, D.C. 20431 (202) 623-7000; *Government Finance Statistics Yearbook.*

RWANDA - CALORIE SUPPLY

African Development Bank, 01 BP 1387, Abidjan 01, Cote d'Ivoire; *Selected Statistics on Regional Member Countries.*

Food and Agricultural Organization of the United Nations (FAO) Via delle Terme di Caracalla, 00100 Rome, Italy (Telephone Number in U.S. (202) 653-2400); *The State of Food and Agriculture.*

RWANDA - CAPITAL REVENUE

International Monetary Fund, 700 Nineteenth Street, NW, Washington, D.C. 20431 (202) 623-7000; *Government Finance Statistics Yearbook.*

RWANDA - CATTLE - See RWANDA - LIVESTOCK AND POULTRY

RWANDA - CEMENT PRODUCTION - See RWANDA - MINING AND MINERAL PRODUCTS

RWANDA - CHEMICAL (ORGANIC) PRODUCTION - See RWANDA - MINING AND MINERAL PRODUCTS

RWANDA - CHICKENS - See RWANDA - LIVESTOCK AND POULTRY

RWANDA - CIGARETTE PRODUCTION - See RWANDA - TOBACCO PRODUCTION

RWANDA - CLASS STRUCTURE

G.K. Hall and Company, 70 Lincoln Street, Boston, Massachusetts 02111 (617) 423-3990; *The World in Figures.*

RWANDA - CLIMATE

Facts on File, 460 Park Avenue South, New York, New York 10016 (800) 443-8323; *The New Book of World Rankings.*

G.K. Hall and Company, 70 Lincoln Street, Boston, Massachusetts 02111 (617) 423-3990; *The World in Figures.*

RWANDA - COAL PRODUCTION - See RWANDA - MINING AND MINERAL PRODUCTS

RWANDA - COFFEE - See RWANDA - CROPS

RWANDA - COMMUNICATIONS

G.K. Hall and Company, 70 Lincoln Street, Boston, Massachusetts 02111 (617) 423-3990; *The World in Figures.*

United Nations Economic Commission for Africa, Africa Hall, P.O. Box 3001, Addis Ababa, Ethiopia (Telephone Number in U.S. (800) 253-9646); *African Statistical Yearbook.*

RWANDA - CONSTRUCTION INDUSTRY

Facts on File, 460 Park Avenue South, New York, New York 10016 (800) 443-8323; *The New Book of World Rankings.*

Statistical Office of the United Nations, Publishing Service, New York, New York 10017 (800) 253-9646; *Statistical Yearbook.*

United Nations Economic Commission for Africa, Africa Hall, P.O. Box 3001, Addis Ababa, Ethiopia (Telephone Number in U.S. (800) 253-9646); *African Statistical Yearbook.*

RWANDA - CONSUMER PRICE INDEX

African Development Bank, 01 BP 1387, Abidjan 01, Cote d'Ivoire; *Selected Statistics on Regional Member Countries.*

G.K. Hall and Company, 70 Lincoln Street, Boston, Massachusetts 02111 (617) 423-3990; *The World in Figures.*

Statistical Office of the United Nations, Publishing Service, New York, New York 10017 (800) 253-9646; *Statistical Yearbook,* and *Survey of Economic and Social Conditions in Africa.*

United Nations Economic Commission for Africa, Africa Hall, P.O. Box 3001, Addis Ababa, Ethiopia (Telephone Number in U.S. (800) 253-9646); *African Statistical Yearbook.*

RWANDA - CONSUMER PRICES

International Labour Office, I.L.O. Publications, CH-1211, Geneva 22, Switzerland; *Yearbook of Labour Statistics*.

International Monetary Fund, 700 Nineteenth Street, NW, Washington, D.C. 20431 (202) 623-7000; *International Financial Statistics*.

Times Books, 201 East 50th Street, New York, New York 10022 (212) 751-2600; *The Economist Book of Vital World Statistics*.

RWANDA - CONSUMPTION

African Development Bank, 01 BP 1387, Abidjan 01, Cote d'Ivoire; *Selected Statistics on Regional Member Countries*.

G.K. Hall and Company, 70 Lincoln Street, Boston, Massachusetts 02111 (617) 423-3990; *The World in Figures*.

Statistical Office of the United Nations, Publishing Service, New York 10017 (800) 253-9646; *Survey of Economic and Social Conditions in Africa*.

RWANDA - COPPER PRODUCTION AND CONSUMPTION - See RWANDA - MINING AND MINERAL PRODUCTS

RWANDA - CORN PRODUCTION - See RWANDA - CROPS

RWANDA - CORPORATE TAXES - See RWANDA - TAXATION

RWANDA - COTTON PRODUCTION - See RWANDA - CROPS

RWANDA - CRIME

International Criminal Police Organization (INTERPOL), 26 rue Armengaud, 02210 Saint Cloud, France; *International Crime Statistics*.

RWANDA - CROPS

Facts on File, 460 Park Avenue South, New York, New York 10016 (800) 443-8323; *The New Book of World Rankings*.

Food and Agricultural Organization of the United Nations (FAO) Via delle Terme di Caracalla, 00100 Rome, Italy (Telephone Number in U.S. (202) 653-2400); *Production Yearbook*, and *The State of Food and Agriculture*.

G.K. Hall and Company, 70 Lincoln Street, Boston, Massachusetts 02111 (617) 423-3990; *The World in Figures*.

International Monetary Fund, 700 Nineteenth Street, NW, Washington, D.C. 20431 (202) 623-7000; *International Financial Statistics*.

Statistical Office of the United Nations, Publishing Service, New York, New York 10017 (800) 253-9646; *Statistical Yearbook*.

United Nations Economic Commission for Africa, Africa Hall, P.O. Box 3001, Addis Ababa, Ethiopia (Telephone Number in U.S. (800) 253-9646); *African Statistical Yearbook*.

RWANDA - CUSTOMS DUTIES

G.K. Hall and Company, 70 Lincoln Street, Boston, Massachusetts 02111 (617) 423-3990; *The World in Figures*.

International Monetary Fund, 700 Nineteenth Street, NW, Washington, D.C. 20431 (202) 623-7000; *Government Finance Statistics Yearbook*.

RWANDA - DAIRY PRODUCTS

Facts on File, 460 Park Avenue South, New York, New York 10016 (800) 443-8323; *The New Book of World Rankings*.

Food and Agricultural Organization of the United Nations (FAO) Via delle Terme di Caracalla, 00100 Rome, Italy (Telephone Number in U.S. (202) 653-2400); *The State of Food and Agriculture*.

RWANDA - DEATH RATES

G.K. Hall and Company, 70 Lincoln Street, Boston, Massachusetts 02111 (617) 423-3990; *The World in Figures*.

Statistical Office of the United Nations, Publishing Service, New York, New York 10017 (800) 253-9646; *Statistical Yearbook*, and *Survey of Economic and Social Conditions in Africa*.

Times Books, 201 East 50th Street, New York, New York 10022 (212) 751-2800; *The Economist Book of Vital World Statistics*.

World Health Organization, Office of Publications, Avenue Appia, CH-1211 Geneva 27, Switzerland (Telephone Number in U.S. (518) 436-9686); *World Health Statistics Annual*.

RWANDA - DEFENSE EXPENDITURES

G.K. Hall and Company, 70 Lincoln Street, Boston, Massachusetts 02111 (617) 423-3990; *The World in Figures*.

International Monetary Fund, 700 Nineteenth Street, NW, Washington, D.C. 20431 (202) 623-7000; *Government Finance Statistics Yearbook*.

U.S. Arms Control and Disarmament Agency, 320 Twenty-first Street, NW, Washington, D.C. 20451 (202) 647-8677; *World Military Expenditures and Arms Transfers*.

RWANDA - DEMOGRAPHY

The Economist Intelligence Unit, 111 West 57th Street, New York, New York 10019 (800) 938-4685; *The World Market Atlas*.

Facts on File, 460 Park Avenue South, New York, New York 10016 (800) 443-8323; *The New Book of World Rankings*.

G.K. Hall and Company, 70 Lincoln Street, Boston, Massachusetts 02111 (617) 423-3990; *The World in Figures*.

Statistical Office of the United Nations, Publishing Service, New York 10017 (800) 253-9646; *Survey of Economic and Social Conditions in Africa*.

RWANDA - DEVELOPMENT ASSISTANCE

G.K. Hall and Company, 70 Lincoln Street, Boston, Massachusetts 02111 (617) 423-3990; *The World in Figures*.

Statistical Office of the United Nations, Publishing Service, New York, New York 10017 (800) 253-9646; *Statistical Yearbook*.

RWANDA - DIAMOND PRODUCTION - See RWANDA - MINING AND MINERAL PRODUCTS

RWANDA - DISCOUNT RATES

Statistical Office of the United Nations, Publishing Service, New York, New York 10017 (800) 253-9646; *Statistical Yearbook.*

RWANDA - DISEASE

G.K. Hall and Company, 70 Lincoln Street, Boston, Massachusetts 02111 (617) 423-3990; *The World in Figures.*

World Health Organization, Office of Publications, Avenue Appia, CH-1211 Geneva 27, Switzerland (Telephone Number in U.S. (518) 436-9686); *World Health Statistics Annual.*

RWANDA - DIVORCE RATES

Facts on File, 460 Park Avenue South, New York, New York 10016 (800) 443-8323; *The New Book of World Rankings.*

Statistical Office of the United Nations, Publishing Service, New York, New York 10017 (800) 253-9646; *Demographic Yearbook,* and *Statistical Yearbook.*

RWANDA - DOMESTIC PRODUCT

G.K. Hall and Company, 70 Lincoln Street, Boston, Massachusetts 02111 (617) 423-3990; *The World in Figures.*

RWANDA - ECONOMY

African Development Bank, 01 BP 1387, Abidjan 01, Cote d'Ivoire; *Selected Statistics on Regional Member Countries.*

Euromonitor Publications Limited, 87-88 Turnmill Street, London EC1M 5QU, England; *International Marketing Data and Statistics.*

Facts on File, 460 Park Avenue South, New York, New York 10016 (800) 443-8323; *The New Book of World Rankings.*

G.K. Hall and Company, 70 Lincoln Street, Boston, Massachusetts 02111 (617) 423-3990; *The World in Figures.*

Statistical Office of the United Nations, Publishing Service, New York, New York 10017 (800) 253-9646; *Foreign Trade Statistics for Africa.*

RWANDA - EDUCATION

African Development Bank, 01 BP 1387, Abidjan 01, Cote d'Ivoire; *Selected Statistics on Regional Member Countries.*

The Economist Intelligence Unit, 111 West 57th Street, New York, New York 10019 (800) 938-4685; *The World Market Atlas.*

Facts on File, 460 Park Avenue South, New York, New York 10016 (800) 443-8323; *The New Book of World Rankings.*

G.K. Hall and Company, 70 Lincoln Street, Boston, Massachusetts 02111 (617) 423-3990; *The World in Figures.*

International Monetary Fund, 700 Nineteenth Street, NW, Washington, D.C. 20431 (202) 623-7000; *Government Finance Statistics Yearbook.*

Statistical Office of the United Nations, Publishing Service, New York 10017 (800) 253-9646; *Survey of Economic and Social Conditions in Africa.*

Times Books, 201 East 50th Street, New York, New York 10022 (212) 751-2600; *The Economist Book of Vital World Statistics.*

United Nations Economic Commission for Africa, Africa Hall, P.O. Box 3001, Addis Ababa, Ethiopia (Telephone Number in U.S. (800) 253-9646); *African Statistical Yearbook.*

United Nations Educational, Scientific and Cultural Organization (UNESCO), 7 Place de Fontenoy, F-75700 Paris, France (Telephone Number in U.S. (212) 963-5981); *Statistical Yearbook.*

The World Bank, 1818 H Street, N.W., Washington, D.C. 20433 (202) 477-1234; *World Tables.*

RWANDA - EGG PRODUCTION AND CONSUMPTION - See RWANDA - DAIRY PRODUCTS

RWANDA - ELECTRICITY

Facts on File, 460 Park Avenue South, New York, New York 10016 (800) 443-8323; *The New Book of World Rankings.*

Statistical Office of the United Nations, Publishing Service, New York, New York 10017 (800) 253-9646; *Statistical Yearbook,* and *Survey of Economic and Social Conditions in Africa.*

Times Books, 201 East 50th Street, New York, New York 10022 (212) 751-2600; *The Economist Book of Vital World Statistics.*

United Nations Economic Commission for Africa, Africa Hall, P.O. Box 3001, Addis Ababa, Ethiopia (Telephone Number in U.S. (800) 253-9646); *African Statistical Yearbook.*

RWANDA - EMPLOYMENT

Euromonitor Publications Limited, 87-88 Turnmill Street, London EC1M 5QU, England; *International Marketing Data and Statistics.*

Facts on File, 460 Park Avenue South, New York, New York 10016 (800) 443-8323; *The New Book of World Rankings.*

International Labour Office, I.L.O. Publications, CH-1211, Geneva 22, Switzerland; *Yearbook of Labour Statistics.*

Statistical Office of the United Nations, Publishing Service, New York, New York 10017 (800) 253-9646; *Statistical Yearbook,* and *Survey of Economic and Social Conditions in Africa.*

United Nations Economic Commission for Africa, Africa Hall, P.O. Box 3001, Addis Ababa, Ethiopia (Telephone Number in U.S. (800) 253-9646); *African Statistical Yearbook.*

RWANDA - ENERGY

Facts on File, 460 Park Avenue South, New York, New York 10016 (800) 443-8323; *The New Book of World Rankings.*

Food and Agricultural Organization of the United Nations (FAO) Via delle Terme di Caracalla, 00100 Rome, Italy (Telephone Number in U.S. (202) 653-2400); *The State of Food and Agriculture.*

G.K. Hall and Company, 70 Lincoln Street, Boston, Massachusetts 02111 (617) 423-3990; *The World in Figures.*

Statistical Office of the United Nations, Publishing Service, New York, New York 10017 (800) 253-9646; *Energy Statistics Yearbook,* and *Statistical Yearbook.*

Times Books, 201 East 50th Street, New York, New York 10022 (212) 751-2600; *The Economist Book of Vital World Statistics*.

United Nations Economic Commission for Africa, Africa Hall, P.O. Box 3001, Addis Ababa, Ethiopia (Telephone Number in U.S. (800) 253-9646); *African Statistical Yearbook*.

RWANDA - EXCHANGE RATES

African Development Bank, 01 BP 1387, Abidjan 01, Cote d'Ivoire; *Selected Statistics on Regional Member Countries*.

Euromonitor Publications Limited, 87-88 Turnmill Street, London EC1M 5QU, England; *International Marketing Data and Statistics*.

International Monetary Fund, 700 Nineteenth Street, NW, Washington, D.C. 20431 (202) 623-7000; *International Financial Statistics*.

Statistical Office of the United Nations, Publishing Service, New York, New York 10017 (800) 253-9646; *Foreign Trade Statistics for Africa*, and *Statistical Yearbook*.

RWANDA - EXCISE TAXES - See RWANDA - TAXATION

RWANDA - EXPORTS

African Development Bank, 01 BP 1387, Abidjan 01, Cote d'Ivoire; *Selected Statistics on Regional Member Countries*.

The Economist Intelligence Unit, 111 West 57th Street, New York, New York 10019 (800) 938-4685; *The World Market Atlas*.

Euromonitor Publications Limited, 87-88 Turnmill Street, London EC1M 5QU, England; *International Marketing Data and Statistics*.

Food and Agricultural Organization of the United Nations (FAO) Via delle Terme di Caracalla, 00100 Rome, Italy (Telephone Number in U.S. (202) 653-2400); *The State of Food and Agriculture*.

G.K. Hall and Company, 70 Lincoln Street, Boston, Massachusetts 02111 (617) 423-3990; *The World in Figures*.

International Monetary Fund, 700 Nineteenth Street, NW, Washington, D.C. 20431 (202) 623-7000; *Direction of Trade Statistics, Government Finance Statistics Yearbook*, and *International Financial Statistics*.

Statistical Office of the United Nations, Publishing Service, New York, New York 10017 (800) 253-9646; *Foreign Trade Statistics for Africa*, and *Survey of Economic and Social Conditions in Africa*.

Times Books, 201 East 50th Street, New York, New York 10022 (212) 751-2600; *The Economist Book of Vital World Statistics*.

United Nations Economic Commission for Africa, Africa Hall, P.O. Box 3001, Addis Ababa, Ethiopia (Telephone Number in U.S. (800) 253-9646); *African Statistical Yearbook*.

The World Bank, 1818 H Street, N.W., Washington, D.C. 20433 (202) 477-1234; *World Tables*.

RWANDA - EXTERNAL INDEBTEDNESS

African Development Bank, 01 BP 1387, Abidjan 01, Cote d'Ivoire; *Selected Statistics on Regional Member Countries*.

Statistical Office of the United Nations, Publishing Service, New York 10017 (800) 253-9646; *Survey of Economic and Social Conditions in Africa*.

The World Bank, 1818 H Street, N.W., Washington, D.C. 20433 (202) 477-1234; *World Tables*.

RWANDA - EXTERNAL TRADE

African Development Bank, 01 BP 1387, Abidjan 01, Cote d'Ivoire; *Selected Statistics on Regional Member Countries*.

Food and Agricultural Organization of the United Nations (FAO) Via delle Terme di Caracalla, 00100 Rome, Italy (Telephone Number in U.S. (202) 653-2400); *The State of Food and Agriculture*, and *Trade Yearbook*.

G.K. Hall and Company, 70 Lincoln Street, Boston, Massachusetts 02111 (617) 423-3990; *The World in Figures*.

Statistical Office of the United Nations, Publishing Service, New York, New York 10017 (800) 253-9646; *Statistical Yearbook*.

RWANDA - FARM CROPS - See RWANDA - CROPS

RWANDA - FEMALE WORKING POPULATION - See RWANDA - EMPLOYMENT

RWANDA - FERTILITY RATES

Facts on File, 460 Park Avenue South, New York, New York 10016 (800) 443-8323; *The New Book of World Rankings*.

Statistical Office of the United Nations, Publishing Service, New York 10017 (800) 253-9646; *Survey of Economic and Social Conditions in Africa*.

Times Books, 201 East 50th Street, New York, New York 10022 (212) 751-2600; *The Economist Book of Vital World Statistics*.

The World Bank, 1818 H Street, N.W., Washington, D.C. 20433 (202) 477-1234; *World Tables*.

RWANDA - FERTILIZER

Food and Agricultural Organization of the United Nations (FAO), Via delle Terme di Caracalla, 00100 Rome, Italy (Telephone Number in U.S. (202) 653-2400); *Fertilizer Yearbook*, and *The State of Food and Agriculture*.

Statistical Office of the United Nations, Publishing Service, New York, New York 10017 (800) 253-9646; *Statistical Yearbook*.

RWANDA - FETAL MORTALITY

Statistical Office of the United Nations, Publishing Service, New York, New York 10017 (800) 253-9646; *Demographic Yearbook*.

RWANDA - FINANCE

African Development Bank, 01 BP 1387, Abidjan 01, Cote d'Ivoire; *Selected Statistics on Regional Member Countries*.

Facts on File, 460 Park Avenue South, New York, New York 10016 (800) 443-8323; *The New Book of World Rankings*.

G.K. Hall and Company, 70 Lincoln Street, Boston, Massachusetts 02111 (617) 423-3990; *The World in Figures*.

International Monetary Fund, 700 Nineteenth Street, NW, Washington, D.C. 20431 (202) 623-7000; *Government Finance*

Statistics Yearbook, and *International Financial Statistics.*

United Nations Economic Commission for Africa, Africa Hall, P.O. Box 3001, Addis Ababa, Ethiopia (Telephone Number in U.S. (800) 253-9646); *African Statistical Yearbook.*

RWANDA - FISHERIES

Facts on File, 460 Park Avenue South, New York, New York 10016 (800) 443-8323; *The New Book of World Rankings.*

Food and Agricultural Organization of the United Nations (FAO) Via delle Terme di Caracalla, 00100 Rome, Italy (Telephone Number in U.S. (202) 653-2400); *The State of Food and Agriculture,* and *Yearbook of Fishery Statistics.*

Statistical Office of the United Nations, Publishing Service, New York, New York 10017 (800) 253-9646; *Statistical Yearbook,* and *Survey of Economic and Social Conditions in Africa.*

United Nations Economic Commission for Africa, Africa Hall, P.O. Box 3001, Addis Ababa, Ethiopia (Telephone Number in U.S. (800) 253-9646); *African Statistical Yearbook.*

RWANDA - FOOD

African Development Bank, 01 BP 1387, Abidjan 01, Cote d'Ivoire; *Selected Statistics on Regional Member Countries.*

Food and Agricultural Organization of the United Nations (FAO) Via delle Terme di Caracalla, 00100 Rome, Italy (Telephone Number in U.S. (202) 653-2400); *Production Yearbook,* and *The State of Food and Agriculture.*

G.K. Hall and Company, 70 Lincoln Street, Boston, Massachusetts 02111 (617) 423-3990; *The World in Figures.*

RWANDA - FOREIGN AID

G.K. Hall and Company, 70 Lincoln Street, Boston, Massachusetts 02111 (617) 423-3990; *The World in Figures.*

RWANDA - FOREIGN DEBT

International Monetary Fund, 700 Nineteenth Street, NW, Washington, D.C. 20431 (202) 623-7000; *Government Finance Statistics Yearbook.*

RWANDA - FOREIGN TRADE

Euromonitor Publications Limited, 87-88 Turnmill Street, London EC1M 5QU, England; *International Marketing Data and Statistics.*

Facts on File, 460 Park Avenue South, New York, New York 10016 (800) 443-8323; *The New Book of World Rankings.*

Food and Agricultural Organization of the United Nations (FAO) Via delle Terme di Caracalla, 00100 Rome, Italy (Telephone Number in U.S. (202) 653-2400); *The State of Food and Agriculture.*

G.K. Hall and Company, 70 Lincoln Street, Boston, Massachusetts 02111 (617) 423-3990; *The World in Figures.*

International Monetary Fund, 700 Nineteenth Street, NW, Washington, D.C. 20431 (202) 623-7000; *International Financial Statistics.*

Statistical Office of the United Nations, Publishing Service, New York, New York 10017 (800) 253-9646; *Foreign Trade Statistics for Africa, International Trade Statistics Yearbook, Statistical Yearbook,* and *Trade in Manufactures of Developing Countries.*

United Nations Economic Commission for Africa, Africa Hall, P.O. Box 3001, Addis Ababa, Ethiopia (Telephone Number in U.S. (800) 253-9646); *African Statistical Yearbook.*

The World Bank, 1818 H Street, N.W., Washington, D.C. 20433 (202) 477-1234; *World Tables.*

RWANDA - FORESTRY AND FOREST PRODUCTS

Facts on File, 460 Park Avenue South, New York, New York 10016 (800) 443-8323; *The New Book of World Rankings.*

Food and Agricultural Organization of the United Nations (FAO) Via delle Terme di Caracalla, 00100 Rome, Italy (Telephone Number in U.S. (202) 653-2400); *The State of Food and Agriculture,* and *Yearbook of Forest Products.*

G.K. Hall and Company, 70 Lincoln Street, Boston, Massachusetts 02111 (617) 423-3990; *The World in Figures.*

Statistical Office of the United Nations, Publishing Service, New York, New York 10017 (800) 253-9646; *Statistical Yearbook.*

United Nations Economic Commission for Africa, Africa Hall, P.O. Box 3001, Addis Ababa, Ethiopia (Telephone Number in U.S. (800) 253-9646); *African Statistical Yearbook.*

RWANDA - GAS (NATURAL) PRODUCTION - See RWANDA - MINING AND MINERAL PRODUCTS

RWANDA - GENERAL INDUSTRIAL STATISTICS

Statistical Office of the United Nations, Publishing Service, New York, New York 10017 (800) 253-9646; *Industrial Statistics Yearbook.*

RWANDA - GENERAL MORTALITY

Statistical Office of the United Nations, Publishing Service, New York, New York 10017 (800) 253-9646; *Demographic Yearbook.*

World Health Organization, Office of Publications, Avenue Appia, CH-1211 Geneva 27, Switzerland (Telephone Number in U.S. (518) 436-9686); *World Health Statistics Annual.*

RWANDA - GEOGRAPHIC DATA

Facts on File, 460 Park Avenue South, New York, New York 10016 (800) 443-8323; *The New Book of World Rankings.*

RWANDA - GOATS - See RWANDA - LIVESTOCK AND POULTRY

RWANDA - GOLD HOLDINGS

International Monetary Fund, 700 Nineteenth Street, NW, Washington, D.C. 20431 (202) 623-7000; *International Financial Statistics.*

Statistical Office of the United Nations, Publishing Service, New York, New York 10017 (800) 253-9646; *Statistical Yearbook.*

The World Bank, 1818 H Street, N.W., Washington, D.C. 20433 (202) 477-1234; *World Tables.*

RWANDA - GOLD PRODUCTION AND CONSUMPTION - See RWANDA - MINING AND MINERAL PRODUCTS

RWANDA - GOVERNMENT

G.K. Hall and Company, 70 Lincoln Street, Boston, Massachusetts 02111 (617) 423-3990; *The World in Figures.*

RWANDA - GOVERNMENT EXPENDITURES

International Monetary Fund, 700 Nineteenth Street, NW, Washington, D.C. 20431 (202) 623-7000; *Government Finance Statistics Yearbook.*

The World Bank, 1818 H Street, N.W., Washington, D.C. 20433 (202) 477-1234; *World Tables.*

RWANDA - GOVERNMENT FINANCES

International Monetary Fund, 700 Nineteenth Street, NW, Washington, D.C. 20431 (202) 623-7000; *International Financial Statistics.*

RWANDA - GOVERNMENT REVENUE

International Monetary Fund, 700 Nineteenth Street, NW, Washington, D.C. 20431 (202) 623-7000; *Government Finance Statistics Yearbook.*

Statistical Office of the United Nations, Publishing Service, New York 10017 (800) 253-9646; *Survey of Economic and Social Conditions in Africa.*

The World Bank, 1818 H Street, N.W., Washington, D.C. 20433 (202) 477-1234; *World Tables.*

RWANDA - GRAIN PRODUCTION - See RWANDA - CROPS

RWANDA - GRANTS

International Monetary Fund, 700 Nineteenth Street, NW, Washington, D.C. 20431 (202) 623-7000; *Government Finance Statistics Yearbook.*

RWANDA - GROSS DOMESTIC PRODUCT

African Development Bank, 01 BP 1387, Abidjan 01, Cote d'Ivoire; *Selected Statistics on Regional Member Countries.*

The Economist Intelligence Unit, 111 West 57th Street, New York, New York 10019 (800) 938-4685; *The World Market Atlas.*

Euromonitor Publications Limited, 87-88 Turnmill Street, London EC1M 5QU, England; *International Marketing Data and Statistics.*

Facts on File, 460 Park Avenue South, New York, New York 10016 (800) 443-8323; *The New Book of World Rankings.*

G.K. Hall and Company, 70 Lincoln Street, Boston, Massachusetts 02111 (617) 423-3990; *The World in Figures.*

Statistical Office of the United Nations, Publishing Service, New York, New York 10017 (800) 253-9646; *Statistical Yearbook,* and *Survey of Economic and Social Conditions in Africa.*

United Nations Economic Commission for Africa, Africa Hall, P.O. Box 3001, Addis Ababa, Ethiopia (Telephone Number in U.S. (800) 253-9646); *African Statistical Yearbook.*

Times Books, 201 East 50th Street, New York, New York 10022 (212) 751-2600; *The Economist Book of Vital World Statistics.*

The World Bank, 1818 H Street, N.W., Washington, D.C. 20433 (202) 477-1234; *World Tables.*

RWANDA - GROSS NATIONAL PRODUCT

Euromonitor Publications Limited, 87-88 Turnmill Street, London EC1M 5QU, England; *International Marketing Data and Statistics.*

U.S. Arms Control and Disarmament Agency, 320 Twenty-first Street, NW, Washington, D.C. 20451 (202) 647-8677; *World Military Expenditures and Arms Transfers.*

The World Bank, 1818 H Street, N.W., Washington, D.C. 20433 (202) 477-1234; *World Tables.*

RWANDA - GROUNDNUTS PRODUCTION - See RWANDA - CROPS

RWANDA - HEALTH

African Development Bank, 01 BP 1387, Abidjan 01, Cote d'Ivoire; *Selected Statistics on Regional Member Countries.*

Facts on File, 460 Park Avenue South, New York, New York 10016 (800) 443-8323; *The New Book of World Rankings.*

G.K. Hall and Company, 70 Lincoln Street, Boston, Massachusetts 02111 (617) 423-3990; *The World in Figures.*

Statistical Office of the United Nations, Publishing Service, New York, New York 10017 (800) 253-9646; *Statistical Yearbook.*

Times Books, 201 East 50th Street, New York, New York 10022 (212) 751-2600; *The Economist Book of Vital World Statistics.*

United Nations Economic Commission for Africa, Africa Hall, P.O. Box 3001, Addis Ababa, Ethiopia (Telephone Number in U.S. (800) 253-9646); *African Statistical Yearbook.*

World Health Organization, Office of Publications, Avenue Appia, CH-1211 Geneva 27, Switzerland (Telephone Number in U.S. (518) 436-9686); *World Health Statistics Annual.*

RWANDA - HEALTH EXPENDITURES

International Monetary Fund, 700 Nineteenth Street, NW, Washington, D.C. 20431 (202) 623-7000; *Government Finance Statistics Yearbook.*

RWANDA - HIDE PRODUCTION

Food and Agricultural Organization of the United Nations (FAO), Via delle Terme di Caracalla, 00100 Rome, Italy (Telephone Number in U.S. (202) 653-2400); *Production Yearbook.*

RWANDA - HIGHWAYS

G.K. Hall and Company, 70 Lincoln Street, Boston, Massachusetts 02111 (617) 423-3990; *The World in Figures.*

International Road Federation, 525 School Street, SW, Washington, D.C. 20024 (202) 554-2106; *World Road Statistics.*

Statistical Office of the United Nations, Publishing Service, New York 10017 (800) 253-9646; *Survey of Economic and Social Conditions in Africa.*

United Nations Economic Commission for Africa, Africa Hall, P.O. Box 3001, Addis Ababa, Ethiopia (Telephone Number in U.S. (800) 253-9646); *African Statistical Yearbook.*

RWANDA - HORSES - See RWANDA - LIVESTOCK AND POULTRY

RWANDA - HOURS OF WORK - See RWANDA - EMPLOYMENT

RWANDA - HOUSING AND HOUSING UNITS

Facts on File, 460 Park Avenue South, New York, New York 10016 (800) 443-8323; *The New Book of World Rankings*.

RWANDA - HOUSING EXPENDITURES

International Monetary Fund, 700 Nineteenth Street, NW, Washington, D.C. 20431 (202) 623-7000; *Government Finance Statistics Yearbook*.

RWANDA - ILLITERATE POPULATION

The Economist Intelligence Unit, 111 West 57th Street, New York, New York 10019 (800) 938-4685; *The World Market Atlas*.

G.K. Hall and Company, 70 Lincoln Street, Boston, Massachusetts 02111 (617) 423-3990; *The World in Figures*.

United Nations Educational, Scientific and Cultural Organization (UNESCO), 7 Place de Fontenoy, F-75700 Paris, France (Telephone Number in U.S. (212) 963-5981); *Statistical Yearbook*.

RWANDA - IMPORTS

African Development Bank, 01 BP 1387, Abidjan 01, Cote d'Ivoire; *Selected Statistics on Regional Member Countries*.

The Economist Intelligence Unit, 111 West 57th Street, New York, New York 10019 (800) 938-4685; *The World Market Atlas*.

Euromonitor Publications Limited, 87-88 Turnmill Street, London EC1M 5QU, England; *International Marketing Data and Statistics*.

Food and Agricultural Organization of the United Nations (FAO) Via delle Terme di Caracalla, 00100 Rome, Italy (Telephone Number in U.S. (202) 653-2400); *The State of Food and Agriculture*.

G.K. Hall and Company, 70 Lincoln Street, Boston, Massachusetts 02111 (617) 423-3990; *The World in Figures*.

International Monetary Fund, 700 Nineteenth Street, NW, Washington, D.C. 20431 (202) 623-7000; *Direction of Trade Statistics, Government Finance Statistics Yearbook, and International Financial Statistics*.

Statistical Office of the United Nations, Publishing Service, New York, New York 10017 (800) 253-9646; *Foreign Trade Statistics for Africa, and Survey of Economic and Social Conditions in Africa*.

United Nations Economic Commission for Africa, Africa Hall, P.O. Box 3001, Addis Ababa, Ethiopia (Telephone Number in U.S. (800) 253-9646); *African Statistical Yearbook*.

The World Bank, 1818 H Street, N.W., Washington, D.C. 20433 (202) 477-1234; *World Tables*.

RWANDA - INCOME TAXES - See RWANDA - TAXATION

RWANDA - INDUSTRY

Euromonitor Publications Limited, 87-88 Turnmill Street, London EC1M 5QU, England; *International Marketing Data and Statistics*.

Facts on File, 460 Park Avenue South, New York, New York 10016 (800) 443-8323; *The New Book of World Rankings*.

G.K. Hall and Company, 70 Lincoln Street, Boston, Massachusetts 02111 (617) 423-3990; *The World in Figures*.

International Labour Office, I.L.O. Publications, CH-1211, Geneva 22, Switzerland; *Yearbook of Labour Statistics*.

Statistical Office of the United Nations, Publishing Service, New York 10017 (800) 253-9646; *Survey of Economic and Social Conditions in Africa*.

Times Books, 201 East 50th Street, New York, New York 10022 (212) 751-2600; *The Economist Book of Vital World Statistics*.

United Nations Economic Commission for Africa, Africa Hall, P.O. Box 3001, Addis Ababa, Ethiopia (Telephone Number in U.S. (800) 253-9646); *African Statistical Yearbook*.

The World Bank, 1818 H Street, N.W., Washington, D.C. 20433 (202) 477-1234; *World Tables*.

World Intellectual Property Organization, 34 Chemin des Colombettes, CH-1211 Geneva 20. Switzerland; *Industrial Property Statistics*.

RWANDA - INFANT AND MATERNAL MORTALITY

Statistical Office of the United Nations, Publishing Service, New York, New York 10017 (800) 253-9646; *Demographic Yearbook, and Statistical Yearbook, and Survey of Economic and Social Conditions in Africa*.

Times Books, 201 East 50th Street, New York, New York 10022 (212) 751-2600; *The Economist Book of Vital World Statistics*.

The World Bank, 1818 H Street, N.W., Washington, D.C. 20433 (202) 477-1234; *World Tables*.

RWANDA - INTERNATIONAL RESERVES EXCLUDING GOLD

African Development Bank, 01 BP 1387, Abidjan 01, Cote d'Ivoire; *Selected Statistics on Regional Member Countries*.

Statistical Office of the United Nations, Publishing Service, New York, New York 10017 (800) 253-9646; *Statistical Yearbook*.

The World Bank, 1818 H Street, N.W., Washington, D.C. 20433 (202) 477-1234; *World Tables*.

RWANDA - INVESTMENTS

International Monetary Fund, 700 Nineteenth Street, NW, Washington, D.C. 20431 (202) 623-7000; *International Financial Statistics*.

RWANDA - IRON ORE PRODUCTION AND CONSUMPTION - See RWANDA - MINING AND MINERAL PRODUCTS

RWANDA - IRRIGATION

Euromonitor Publications Limited, 87-88 Turnmill Street, London EC1M 5QU, England; *International Marketing Data and Statistics*.

RWANDA - LABOR FORCE

African Development Bank, 01 BP 1387, Abidjan 01, Cote d'Ivoire; *Selected Statistics on Regional Member Countries*.

Euromonitor Publications Limited, 87-88 Turnmill Street, London EC1M 5QU, England; *International Marketing Data and Statistics*.

Facts on File, 460 Park Avenue South, New York, New York 10016 (800) 443-8323; *The New Book of World Rankings*.

Food and Agricultural Organization of the United Nations (FAO) Via delle Terme di Caracalla, 00100 Rome, Italy (Telephone Number in U.S. (202) 653-2400); *The State of Food and Agriculture*.

G.K. Hall and Company, 70 Lincoln Street, Boston, Massachusetts 02111 (617) 423-3990; *The World in Figures*.

The World Bank, 1818 H Street, N.W., Washington, D.C. 20433 (202) 477-1234; *World Tables*.

RWANDA - LABOR PRODUCTIVITY

International Labour Office, I.L.O. Publications, CH-1211, Geneva 22, Switzerland; *Yearbook of Labour Statistics*.

RWANDA - LAND USE

Euromonitor Publications Limited, 87-88 Turnmill Street, London EC1M 5QU, England; *International Marketing Data and Statistics*.

Food and Agricultural Organization of the United Nations (FAO), Via delle Terme di Caracalla, 00100 Rome, Italy (Telephone Number in U.S. (202) 653-2400); *Production Yearbook*.

G.K. Hall and Company, 70 Lincoln Street, Boston, Massachusetts 02111 (617) 423-3990; *The World in Figures*.

RWANDA - LIBRARIES

Facts on File, 460 Park Avenue South, New York, New York 10016 (800) 443-8323; *The New Book of World Rankings*.

United Nations Educational, Scientific and Cultural Organization (UNESCO), 7 Place de Fontenoy, F-75700 Paris, France (Telephone Number in U.S. (212) 963-5981); *Statistical Yearbook*.

RWANDA - LIFE EXPECTANCY

African Development Bank, 01 BP 1387, Abidjan 01, Cote d'Ivoire; *Selected Statistics on Regional Member Countries*.

RWANDA - LITERACY RATE

Statistical Office of the United Nations, Publishing Service, New York 10017 (800) 253-9646; *Survey of Economic and Social Conditions in Africa*.

RWANDA - LIVESTOCK AND POULTRY

Euromonitor Publications Limited, 87-88 Turnmill Street, London EC1M 5QU, England; *International Marketing Data and Statistics*.

Facts on File, 460 Park Avenue South, New York, New York 10016 (800) 443-8323; *The New Book of World Rankings*.

Food and Agricultural Organization of the United Nations (FAO), Via delle Terme di Caracalla, 00100 Rome, Italy (Telephone Number in U.S. (202) 653-2400); *Production Yearbook*, and *The State of Food and Agriculture*.

G.K. Hall and Company, 70 Lincoln Street, Boston, Massachusetts 02111 (617) 423-3990; *The World in Figures*.

Statistical Office of the United Nations, Publishing Service, New York, New York 10017 (800) 253-9646; *Statistical Yearbook*, and *Survey of Economic and Social Conditions in Africa*.

United Nations Economic Commission for Africa, Africa Hall, P.O. Box 3001, Addis Ababa, Ethiopia (Telephone Number in U.S. (800) 253-9646); *African Statistical Yearbook*.

RWANDA - LIVING LEVELS

G.K. Hall and Company, 70 Lincoln Street, Boston, Massachusetts 02111 (617) 423-3990; *The World in Figures*.

Times Books, 201 East 50th Street, New York, New York 10022 (212) 751-2600; *The Economist Book of Vital World Statistics*.

RWANDA - MAIL - NUMBER OF PIECES SENT OR RECEIVED

Statistical Office of the United Nations, Publishing Service, New York, New York 10017 (800) 253-9646; *Statistical Yearbook*.

RWANDA - MANUFACTURING

Facts on File, 460 Park Avenue South, New York, New York 10016 (800) 443-8323; *The New Book of World Rankings*.

G.K. Hall and Company, 70 Lincoln Street, Boston, Massachusetts 02111 (617) 423-3990; *The World in Figures*.

Statistical Office of the United Nations, Publishing Service, New York, New York 10017 (800) 253-9646; *Statistical Yearbook*, and *Survey of Economic and Social Conditions in Africa*.

Times Books, 201 East 50th Street, New York, New York 10022 (212) 751-2600; *The Economist Book of Vital World Statistics*.

United Nations Economic Commission for Africa, Africa Hall, P.O. Box 3001, Addis Ababa, Ethiopia (Telephone Number in U.S. (800) 253-9646); *African Statistical Yearbook*.

The World Bank, 1818 H Street, N.W., Washington, D.C. 20433 (202) 477-1234; *World Tables*.

RWANDA - MARRIAGE RATES

Facts on File, 460 Park Avenue South, New York, New York 10016 (800) 443-8323; *The New Book of World Rankings*.

Statistical Office of the United Nations, Publishing Service, New York, New York 10017 (800) 253-9646; *Demographic Yearbook*, and *Statistical Yearbook*.

RWANDA - MEAT PRODUCTION - See RWANDA - LIVESTOCK AND POULTRY

RWANDA - MERCHANT SHIPPING

G.K. Hall and Company, 70 Lincoln Street, Boston, Massachusetts 02111 (617) 423-3990; *The World in Figures*.

United Nations Economic Commission for Africa, Africa Hall, P.O. Box 3001, Addis Ababa, Ethiopia (Telephone Number in U.S. (800) 253-9646); *African Statistical Yearbook*.

RWANDA - MILITARY

G.K. Hall and Company, 70 Lincoln Street, Boston, Massachusetts 02111 (617) 423-3990; *The World in Figures*.

The International Institute for Strategic Studies, 23 Tavistock Street, London WC2E 7NQ, England; *The Military Balance*.

U.S. Arms Control and Disarmament Agency, 320 Twenty-first Street, NW, Washington, D.C. 20451 (202) 647-8677; *World Military Expenditures and Arms Transfers*.

RWANDA - MILK PRODUCTION - See RWANDA - DAIRY PRODUCTS

RWANDA - MILLET PRODUCTION

Food and Agricultural Organization of the United Nations (FAO), Via delle Terme di Caracalla, 00100 Rome, Italy (Telephone Number in U.S. (202) 653-2400); *Production Yearbook*.

RWANDA - MINING AND MINERAL PRODUCTS

Facts on File, 460 Park Avenue South, New York, New York 10016 (800) 443-8323; *The New Book of World Rankings*.

G.K. Hall and Company, 70 Lincoln Street, Boston, Massachusetts 02111 (617) 423-3990; *The World in Figures*.

Statistical Office of the United Nations, Publishing Service, New York, New York 10017 (800) 253-9646; *Statistical Yearbook*.

United Nations Economic Commission for Africa, Africa Hall, P.O. Box 3001, Addis Ababa, Ethiopia (Telephone Number in U.S. (800) 253-9646); *African Statistical Yearbook*.

RWANDA - MONEY EXCHANGE RATE

Euromonitor Publications Limited, 87-88 Turnmill Street, London EC1M 5QU, England; *International Marketing Data and Statistics*.

International Monetary Fund, 700 Nineteenth Street, NW, Washington, D.C. 20431 (202) 623-7000; *International Financial Statistics*.

Statistical Office of the United Nations, Publishing Service, New York, New York 10017 (800) 253-9646; *Statistical Yearbook*.

RWANDA - MONEY RESERVES

Euromonitor Publications Limited, 87-88 Turnmill Street, London EC1M 5QU, England; *International Marketing Data and Statistics*.

RWANDA - MONEY SUPPLY

African Development Bank, 01 BP 1387, Abidjan 01, Cote d'Ivoire; *Selected Statistics on Regional Member Countries*.

Euromonitor Publications Limited, 87-88 Turnmill Street, London EC1M 5QU, England; *International Marketing Data and Statistics*.

G.K. Hall and Company, 70 Lincoln Street, Boston, Massachusetts 02111 (617) 423-3990; *The World in Figures*.

International Monetary Fund, 700 Nineteenth Street, NW, Washington, D.C. 20431 (202) 623-7000; *International Financial Statistics*.

Statistical Office of the United Nations, Publishing Service, New York, New York 10017 (800) 253-9646; *Statistical Yearbook*.

The World Bank, 1818 H Street, N.W., Washington, D.C. 20433 (202) 477-1234; *World Tables*.

RWANDA - MOTION PICTURES

Statistical Office of the United Nations, Publishing Service, New York, New York 10017 (800) 253-9646; *Statistical Yearbook*.

RWANDA - MOTOR VEHICLE TAXES - See RWANDA - TAXATION

RWANDA - MOTOR VEHICLES IN USE

G.K. Hall and Company, 70 Lincoln Street, Boston, Massachusetts 02111 (617) 423-3990; *The World in Figures*.

International Road Federation, 525 School Street, SW, Washington, D.C. 20024 (202) 554-2106; *World Road Statistics*.

Statistical Office of the United Nations, Publishing Service, New York, New York 10017 (800) 253-9646; *Statistical Yearbook*, and *Survey of Economic and Social Conditions in Africa*.

Times Books, 201 East 50th Street, New York, New York 10022 (212) 751-2600; *The Economist Book of Vital World Statistics*.

RWANDA - MUSEUMS

Facts on File, 460 Park Avenue South, New York, New York 10016 (800) 443-8323; *The New Book of World Rankings*.

United Nations Educational, Scientific and Cultural Organization (UNESCO), 7 Place de Fontenoy, F-75700 Paris, France (Telephone Number in U.S. (212) 963-5981); *Statistical Yearbook*.

RWANDA - NATALITY - See RWANDA - BIRTH RATE

RWANDA - NATIONAL ACCOUNTS

African Development Bank, 01 BP 1387, Abidjan 01, Cote d'Ivoire; *Selected Statistics on Regional Member Countries*.

Statistical Office of the United Nations, Publishing Service, New York, New York 10017 (800) 253-9646; *National Accounts Statistics*, and *Statistical Yearbook*.

United Nations Economic Commission for Africa, Africa Hall, P.O. Box 3001, Addis Ababa, Ethiopia (Telephone Number in U.S. (800) 253-9646); *African Statistical Yearbook*.

RWANDA - NATIONAL INCOME

Facts on File, 460 Park Avenue South, New York, New York 10016 (800) 443-8323; *The New Book of World Rankings*.

G.K. Hall and Company, 70 Lincoln Street, Boston, Massachusetts 02111 (617) 423-3990; *The World in Figures*.

Statistical Office of the United Nations, Publishing Service, New York, New York 10017 (800) 253-9646; *Statistical Yearbook*.

RWANDA - NATIONAL PRODUCT

Facts on File, 460 Park Avenue South, New York, New York 10016 (800) 443-8323; *The New Book of World Rankings*.

Statistical Office of the United Nations, Publishing Service, New York, New York 10017 (800) 253-9646; *Statistical Yearbook*.

RWANDA - NATURAL GAS PRODUCTION

Facts on File, 460 Park Avenue South, New York, New York 10016 (800) 443-8323; *The New Book of World Rankings*.

Statistical Office of the United Nations, Publishing Service, New York, New York 10017 (800) 253-9646; *Statistical Yearbook.*

RWANDA - NEWSPAPER PRODUCTION - See RWANDA - FORESTRY AND FOREST PRODUCTS

RWANDA - OCCUPATIONS - See RWANDA - LABOR FORCE

RWANDA - PATENTS

Statistical Office of the United Nations, Publishing Service, New York, New York 10017 (800) 253-9646; *Statistical Yearbook.*

World Intellectual Property Organization, 34 Chemin des Colombettes, CH-1211 Geneva 20. Switzerland; *Industrial Property Statistics.*

RWANDA - PERIODICALS

United Nations Educational, Scientific and Cultural Organization (UNESCO), 7 Place de Fontenoy, F-75700 Paris, France (Telephone Number in U.S. (212) 963-5981); *Statistical Yearbook.*

RWANDA - PEANUT PRODUCTION - See RWANDA - CROPS

RWANDA - PESTICIDE USE

Food and Agricultural Organization of the United Nations (FAO) Via delle Terme di Caracalla, 00100 Rome, Italy (Telephone Number in U.S. (202) 653-2400); *The State of Food and Agriculture.*

RWANDA - PETROLEUM INDUSTRY

Facts on File, 460 Park Avenue South, New York, New York 10016 (800) 443-8323; *The New Book of World Rankings.*

Food and Agricultural Organization of the United Nations (FAO) Via delle Terme di Caracalla, 00100 Rome, Italy (Telephone Number in U.S. (202) 653-2400); *The State of Food and Agriculture.*

G.K. Hall and Company, 70 Lincoln Street, Boston, Massachusetts 02111 (617) 423-3990; *The World in Figures.*

RWANDA - PIGS - See RWANDA - LIVESTOCK AND POULTRY

RWANDA - POPULATION

African Development Bank, 01 BP 1387, Abidjan 01, Cote d'Ivoire; *Selected Statistics on Regional Member Countries.*

The Economist Intelligence Unit, 111 West 57th Street, New York, New York 10019 (800) 938-4685; *The World Market Atlas.*

Euromonitor Publications Limited, 87-88 Turnmill Street, London EC1M 5QU, England; *International Marketing Data and Statistics.*

Facts on File, 460 Park Avenue South, New York, New York 10016 (800) 443-8323; *The New Book of World Rankings.*

Food and Agricultural Organization of the United Nations (FAO), Via delle Terme di Caracalla, 00100 Rome, Italy (Telephone Number in U.S. (202) 653-2400); *Production Yearbook.*

G.K. Hall and Company, 70 Lincoln Street, Boston, Massachusetts 02111 (617) 423-3990; *The World in Figures.*

International Labour Office, I.L.O. Publications, CH-1211, Geneva 22, Switzerland; *Yearbook of Labour Statistics.*

Statistical Office of the United Nations, Publishing Service, New York, New York 10017 (800) 253-9646; *Demographic Yearbook, Statistical Yearbook,* and *Survey of Economic and Social Conditions in Africa.*

Times Books, 201 East 50th Street, New York, New York 10022 (212) 751-2600; *The Economist Book of Vital World Statistics.*

United Nations Educational, Scientific and Cultural Organization (UNESCO), 7 Place de Fontenoy, F-75700 Paris, France (Telephone Number in U.S. (212) 963-5981); *Statistical Yearbook.*

U.S. Arms Control and Disarmament Agency, 320 Twenty-first Street, NW, Washington, D.C. 20451 (202) 647-8677; *World Military Expenditures and Arms Transfers.*

World Health Organization, Office of Publications, Avenue Appia, CH-1211 Geneva 27, Switzerland (Telephone Number in U.S. (518) 436-9686); *World Health Statistics Annual.*

RWANDA - POST OFFICES

Facts on File, 460 Park Avenue South, New York, New York 10016 (800) 443-8323; *The New Book of World Rankings.*

RWANDA - POTATO PRODUCTION - See RWANDA - CROPS

RWANDA - PRICES

Facts on File, 460 Park Avenue South, New York, New York 10016 (800) 443-8323; *The New Book of World Rankings.*

Food and Agricultural Organization of the United Nations (FAO), Via delle Terme di Caracalla, 00100 Rome, Italy (Telephone Number in U.S. (202) 653-2400); *Production Yearbook,* and *The State of Food and Agriculture.*

G.K. Hall and Company, 70 Lincoln Street, Boston, Massachusetts 02111 (617) 423-3990; *The World in Figures.*

International Labour Office, I.L.O. Publications, CH-1211, Geneva 22, Switzerland; *Yearbook of Labour Statistics.*

International Monetary Fund, 700 Nineteenth Street, NW, Washington, D.C. 20431 (202) 623-7000; *International Financial Statistics.*

United Nations Economic Commission for Africa, Africa Hall, P.O. Box 3001, Addis Ababa, Ethiopia (Telephone Number in U.S. (800) 253-9646); *African Statistical Yearbook.*

RWANDA - PRODUCTION

Facts on File, 460 Park Avenue South, New York, New York 10016 (800) 443-8323; *The New Book of World Rankings.*

G.K. Hall and Company, 70 Lincoln Street, Boston, Massachusetts 02111 (617) 423-3990; *The World in Figures.*

RWANDA - PRODUCTIVITY

Euromonitor Publications Limited, 87-88 Turnmill Street, London EC1M 5QU, England; *International Marketing Data and Statistics.*

RWANDA - PROPERTY TAXES - See RWANDA - TAXATION

RWANDA - PUBLIC FINANCE

Facts on File, 460 Park Avenue South, New York, New York 10016 (800) 443-8323; *The New Book of World Rankings.*

RWANDA - RADIO BROADCASTING - See RWANDA - BROADCASTING

RWANDA - RADIO RECEIVER PRODUCTION

Statistical Office of the United Nations, Publishing Service, New York, New York 10017 (800) 253-9646; *Statistical Yearbook.*

RWANDA - RAILWAYS

G.K. Hall and Company, 70 Lincoln Street, Boston, Massachusetts 02111 (617) 423-3990; *The World in Figures.*

United Nations Economic Commission for Africa, Africa Hall, P.O. Box 3001, Addis Ababa, Ethiopia (Telephone Number in U.S. (800) 253-9646); *African Statistical Yearbook.*

RWANDA - RELIGION

Facts on File, 460 Park Avenue South, New York, New York 10016 (800) 443-8323; *The New Book of World Rankings.*

RWANDA - RETAIL TRADE

G.K. Hall and Company, 70 Lincoln Street, Boston, Massachusetts 02111 (617) 423-3990; *The World in Figures.*

RWANDA - RICE PRODUCTION - See RWANDA - CROPS

RWANDA - ROOT AND TUBER PRODUCTION - See RWANDA - CROPS

RWANDA - ROUNDWOOD PRODUCTION - See RWANDA - FORESTRY AND FOREST PRODUCTS

RWANDA - RUBBER PRODUCTION AND CONSUMPTION

Facts on File, 460 Park Avenue South, New York, New York 10016 (800) 443-8323; *The New Book of World Rankings.*

RWANDA - SAWNWOOD PRODUCTION - See RWANDA - FORESTRY AND FOREST PRODUCTS

RWANDA - SCIENTISTS AND ENGINEERS

Statistical Office of the United Nations, Publishing Service, New York, New York 10017 (800) 253-9646; *Statistical Yearbook.*

United Nations Educational, Scientific and Cultural Organization (UNESCO), 7 Place de Fontenoy, F-75700 Paris, France (Telephone Number in U.S. (212) 963-5981); *Statistical Yearbook.*

RWANDA - SENIOR CITIZENS

Facts on File, 460 Park Avenue South, New York, New York 10016 (800) 443-8323; *The New Book of World Rankings.*

RWANDA - SHEEP - See RWANDA - LIVESTOCK AND POULTRY

RWANDA - SILVER PRODUCTION AND CONSUMPTION - See RWANDA - MINING AND MINERAL PRODUCTS

RWANDA - SOCIAL DATA

African Development Bank, 01 BP 1387, Abidjan 01, Cote d'Ivoire; *Selected Statistics on Regional Member Countries.*

Facts on File, 460 Park Avenue South, New York, New York 10016 (800) 443-8323; *The New Book of World Rankings.*

G.K. Hall and Company, 70 Lincoln Street, Boston, Massachusetts 02111 (617) 423-3990; *The World in Figures.*

RWANDA - SOCIAL SECURITY

International Monetary Fund, 700 Nineteenth Street, NW, Washington, D.C. 20431 (202) 623-7000; *Government Finance Statistics Yearbook.*

RWANDA - SOYBEAN PRODUCTION - See RWANDA - CROPS

RWANDA - STATE BUDGET REVENUE AND EXPENDITURES

Euromonitor Publications Limited, 87-88 Turnmill Street, London EC1M 5QU, England; *International Marketing Data and Statistics.*

RWANDA - STEEL - See RWANDA - MINING AND MINERAL PRODUCTS

RWANDA - STOCKS - COMMODITY - MARKET PRICE - INDEX

Food and Agricultural Organization of the United Nations (FAO) Via delle Terme di Caracalla, 00100 Rome, Italy (Telephone Number in U.S. (202) 653-2400); *The State of Food and Agriculture.*

RWANDA - SUGAR PRODUCTION AND CONSUMPTION - See RWANDA - CROPS

RWANDA - TAXATION

G.K. Hall and Company, 70 Lincoln Street, Boston, Massachusetts 02111 (617) 423-3990; *The World in Figures.*

International Monetary Fund, 700 Nineteenth Street, NW, Washington, D.C. 20431 (202) 623-7000; *Government Finance Statistics Yearbook.*

International Road Federation, 525 School Street, SW, Washington, D.C. 20024 (202) 554-2106; *World Road Statistics.*

The World Bank, 1818 H Street, N.W., Washington, D.C. 20433 (202) 477-1234; *World Tables.*

RWANDA - TAX REVENUE - See RWANDA - TAXATION

RWANDA - TEA EXPORTS - See RWANDA - CROPS

RWANDA - TELEPHONES IN USE

American Telephone and Telegraph Company, 26 Parsippany Road, Whippany, New Jersey 07981 (800) 338-4038; *The World's Telephones.*

G.K. Hall and Company, 70 Lincoln Street, Boston, Massachusetts 02111 (617) 423-3990; *The World in Figures.*

Statistical Office of the United Nations, Publishing Service, New York, New York 10017 (800) 253-9646; *Statistical Yearbook.*

RWANDA - TELEVISION BROADCASTING - See RWANDA - BROADCASTING

RWANDA - TEXTILE INDUSTRY

G.K. Hall and Company, 70 Lincoln Street, Boston, Massachusetts 02111 (617) 423-3990; *The World in Figures.*

RWANDA - TIN PRODUCTION - See RWANDA - MINING AND MINERAL PRODUCTS

RWANDA - TOBACCO PRODUCTION

Facts on File, 460 Park Avenue South, New York, New York 10016 (800) 443-8323; *The New Book of World Rankings.*

Statistical Office of the United Nations, Publishing Service, New York, New York 10017 (800) 253-9646; *Statistical Yearbook.*

RWANDA - TOURISM

Facts on File, 460 Park Avenue South, New York, New York 10016 (800) 443-8323; *The New Book of World Rankings.*

G.K. Hall and Company, 70 Lincoln Street, Boston, Massachusetts 02111 (617) 423-3990; *The World in Figures.*

Times Books, 201 East 50th Street, New York, New York 10022 (212) 751-2600; *The Economist Book of Vital World Statistics.*

United Nations Economic Commission for Africa, Africa Hall, P.O. Box 3001, Addis Ababa, Ethiopia (Telephone Number in U.S. (800) 253-9646); *African Statistical Yearbook.*

RWANDA - TRACTORS IN USE

Statistical Office of the United Nations, Publishing Service, New York, New York 10017 (800) 253-9646; *Statistical Yearbook*

RWANDA - TRADE - See RWANDA - FOREIGN TRADE

RWANDA - TRADEMARKS AND SERVICE MARKS

Statistical Office of the United Nations, Publishing Service, New York, New York 10017 (800) 253-9646; *Statistical Yearbook.*

World Intellectual Property Organization, 34 Chemin des Colombettes, CH-1211 Geneva 20. Switzerland; *Industrial Property Statistics.*

RWANDA - TRANSPORTATION AND COMMUNICATIONS

Facts on File, 460 Park Avenue South, New York, New York 10016 (800) 443-8323; *The New Book of World Rankings.*

G.K. Hall and Company, 70 Lincoln Street, Boston, Massachusetts 02111 (617) 423-3990; *The World in Figures.*

United Nations Economic Commission for Africa, Africa Hall, P.O. Box 3001, Addis Ababa, Ethiopia (Telephone Number in U.S. (800) 253-9646); *African Statistical Yearbook.*

RWANDA - TUNGSTEN PRODUCTION AND CONSUMPTION - See RWANDA - MINING AND MINERAL PRODUCTS

RWANDA - UNEMPLOYMENT

Euromonitor Publications Limited, 87-88 Turnmill Street, London EC1M 5QU, England; *International Marketing Data and Statistics.*

International Labour Office, I.L.O. Publications, CH-1211, Geneva 22, Switzerland; *Yearbook of Labour Statistics.*

RWANDA - VITAL STATISTICS

Euromonitor Publications Limited, 87-88 Turnmill Street, London EC1M 5QU, England; *International Marketing Data and Statistics.*

G.K. Hall and Company, 70 Lincoln Street, Boston, Massachusetts 02111 (617) 423-3990; *The World in Figures.*

Statistical Office of the United Nations, Publishing Service, New York, New York 10017 (800) 253-9646; *Statistical Yearbook.*

World Health Organization, Office of Publications, Avenue Appia, CH-1211 Geneva 27, Switzerland (Telephone Number in U.S. (518) 436-9686); *World Health Statistics Annual.*

RWANDA - WAGES

G.K. Hall and Company, 70 Lincoln Street, Boston, Massachusetts 02111 (617) 423-3990; *The World in Figures.*

International Labour Office, I.L.O. Publications, CH-1211, Geneva 22, Switzerland; *Yearbook of Labour Statistics.*

RWANDA - WEATHER

Facts on File, 460 Park Avenue South, New York, New York 10016 (800) 443-8323; *The New Book of World Rankings.*

G.K. Hall and Company, 70 Lincoln Street, Boston, Massachusetts 02111 (617) 423-3990; *The World in Figures.*

RWANDA - WELFARE

International Monetary Fund, 700 Nineteenth Street, NW, Washington, D.C. 20431 (202) 623-7000; *Government Finance Statistics Yearbook.*

RWANDA - WHEAT PRODUCTION AND PRICES - See RWANDA - CROPS

RWANDA - WINE PRODUCTION

Facts on File, 460 Park Avenue South, New York, New York 10016 (800) 443-8323; *The New Book of World Rankings.*

RWANDA - WOOL PRODUCTION

Facts on File, 460 Park Avenue South, New York, New York 10016 (800) 443-8323; *The New Book of World Rankings.*

S

SABLEFISH

U.S. Department of Commerce, National Oceanic and Atmospheric Administration, National Marine Fisheries Service, 1335 East-West Highway, Silver Spring, Maryland 20910 (301) 427-2239; *Fisheries of the United States*.

SACCHARIN CONSUMPTION

U.S. Department of Agriculture, Economic Research Service, Fourteenth Street and Independence Avenue, SW, Washington, D.C. 20250-4709 (202) 219-1504, *Food Consumption, Prices, and Expenditures*, and unpublished data.

Saint Helena - National Statistical Office

Information Officer, Broadway House, Saint Helena.

Saint Helena - Primary Statistics Source

HM Stationery Office, Post Office Box 569, London SE1, England: *Saint Helena: Report for the Years....*

SAINT HELENA - AGRICULTURE

Food and Agricultural Organization of the United Nations (FAO) Via delle Terme di Caracalla, 00100 Rome, Italy (Telephone Number in U.S. (202) 653-2400); *Production Yearbook, The State of Food and Agriculture*, and *Trade Yearbook*.

G.K. Hall and Company, 70 Lincoln Street, Boston, Massachusetts 02111 (617) 423-3990; *The World in Figures*.

SAINT HELENA - AIRLINE SERVICE

G.K. Hall and Company, 70 Lincoln Street, Boston, Massachusetts 02111 (617) 423-3990; *The World in Figures*.

SAINT HELENA - AREA AND DENSITY OF POPULATION

Food and Agricultural Organization of the United Nations (FAO) Via delle Terme di Caracalla, 00100 Rome, Italy (Telephone Number in U.S. (202) 653-2400); *The State of Food and Agriculture*.

G.K. Hall and Company, 70 Lincoln Street, Boston, Massachusetts 02111 (617) 423-3990; *The World in Figures*.

Statistical Office of the United Nations, Publishing Service, New York, New York 10017 (800) 253-9646; *Statistical Yearbook*.

United Nations Educational, Scientific and Cultural Organization (UNESCO), 7 Place de Fontenoy, F-75700 Paris, France (Telephone Number in U.S. (212) 963-5981); *Statistical Yearbook*.

SAINT HELENA - BALANCE OF PAYMENTS

G.K. Hall and Company, 70 Lincoln Street, Boston, Massachusetts 02111 (617) 423-3990; *The World in Figures*.

SAINT HELENA - BANKING

G.K. Hall and Company, 70 Lincoln Street, Boston, Massachusetts 02111 (617) 423-3990; *The World in Figures*.

SAINT HELENA - BIRTH RATES

Statistical Office of the United Nations, Publishing Service, New York, New York 10017 (800) 253-9646; *Demographic Yearbook*, and *Statistical Yearbook*.

World Health Organization, Office of Publications, Avenue Appia, CH-1211 Geneva 27, Switzerland (Telephone Number in U.S. (518) 436-9686); *World Health Statistics Annual*.

SAINT HELENA - BONDS

G.K. Hall and Company, 70 Lincoln Street, Boston, Massachusetts 02111 (617) 423-3990; *The World in Figures*.

SAINT HELENA - BOOK PRODUCTION

G.K. Hall and Company, 70 Lincoln Street, Boston, Massachusetts 02111 (617) 423-3990; *The World in Figures*.

SAINT HELENA - BROADCASTING

Billboard Limited, P.O. Box 9027, 1006 AA Amsterdam, The Netherlands (Telephone Number in U.S. (212) 764-7300); *World Radio TV Handbook*.

G.K. Hall and Company, 70 Lincoln Street, Boston, Massachusetts 02111 (617) 423-3990; *The World in Figures*.

SAINT HELENA - BUSINESS

G.K. Hall and Company, 70 Lincoln Street, Boston, Massachusetts 02111 (617) 423-3990; *The World in Figures*.

SAINT HELENA - CALORIE SUPPLY

Food and Agricultural Organization of the United Nations (FAO) Via delle Terme di Caracalla, 00100 Rome, Italy (Telephone Number in

U.S. (202) 653-2400); *The State of Food and Agriculture*.

SAINT HELENA - CATTLE - See SAINT HELENA - LIVESTOCK AND POULTRY

SAINT HELENA - CHEMICAL (ORGANIC) PRODUCTION - See SAINT HELENA - MINING AND MINERAL PRODUCTS

SAINT HELENA - CLASS STRUCTURE

G.K. Hall and Company, 70 Lincoln Street, Boston, Massachusetts 02111 (617) 423-3990; *The World in Figures*.

SAINT HELENA - CLIMATE

G.K. Hall and Company, 70 Lincoln Street, Boston, Massachusetts 02111 (617) 423-3990; *The World in Figures*.

SAINT HELENA - COAL PRODUCTION - See SAINT HELENA - MINING AND MINERAL PRODUCTS

SAINT HELENA - COMMUNICATIONS

G.K. Hall and Company, 70 Lincoln Street, Boston, Massachusetts 02111 (617) 423-3990; *The World in Figures*.

SAINT HELENA - CONSUMER PRICE INDEX

G.K. Hall and Company, 70 Lincoln Street, Boston, Massachusetts 02111 (617) 423-3990; *The World in Figures*.

SAINT HELENA - CONSUMPTION

G.K. Hall and Company, 70 Lincoln Street, Boston, Massachusetts 02111 (617) 423-3990; *The World in Figures*.

SAINT HELENA - CORN PRODUCTION - See SAINT HELENA - CROPS

SAINT HELENA - CORPORATE TAXES - See SAINT HELENA - TAXATION

SAINT HELENA - CROPS

Food and Agricultural Organization of the United Nations (FAO) Via delle Terme di Caracalla, 00100 Rome, Italy (Telephone Number in U.S. (202) 653-2400); *The State of Food and Agriculture*.

G.K. Hall and Company, 70 Lincoln Street, Boston, Massachusetts 02111 (617) 423-3990; *The World in Figures*.

SAINT HELENA - CUSTOMS DUTIES

G.K. Hall and Company, 70 Lincoln Street, Boston, Massachusetts 02111 (617) 423-3990; *The World in Figures*.

SAINT HELENA - DAIRY PRODUCTS

Food and Agricultural Organization of the United Nations (FAO) Via delle Terme di Caracalla, 00100 Rome, Italy (Telephone Number in U.S. (202) 653-2400); *The State of Food and Agriculture*.

SAINT HELENA - DEATH RATES

G.K. Hall and Company, 70 Lincoln Street, Boston, Massachusetts 02111 (617) 423-3990; *The World in Figures*.

Statistical Office of the United Nations, Publishing Service, New York, New York 10017 (800) 253-9646; *Statistical Yearbook*.

SAINT HELENA - DEFENSE EXPENDITURES

G.K. Hall and Company, 70 Lincoln Street, Boston, Massachusetts 02111 (617) 423-3990; *The World in Figures*.

SAINT HELENA - DEMOGRAPHY

G.K. Hall and Company, 70 Lincoln Street, Boston, Massachusetts 02111 (617) 423-3990; *The World in Figures*.

SAINT HELENA - DEVELOPMENT ASSISTANCE

G.K. Hall and Company, 70 Lincoln Street, Boston, Massachusetts 02111 (617) 423-3990; *The World in Figures*.

Statistical Office of the United Nations, Publishing Service, New York, New York 10017 (800) 253-9646; *Statistical Yearbook*.

SAINT HELENA - DISEASE

G.K. Hall and Company, 70 Lincoln Street, Boston, Massachusetts 02111 (617) 423-3990; *The World in Figures*.

SAINT HELENA - DIVORCE RATES

Statistical Office of the United Nations, Publishing Service, New York, New York 10017 (800) 253-9646; *Demographic Yearbook*, and *Statistical Yearbook*.

SAINT HELENA - DOMESTIC PRODUCT

G.K. Hall and Company, 70 Lincoln Street, Boston, Massachusetts 02111 (617) 423-3990; *The World in Figures*.

SAINT HELENA - ECONOMY

G.K. Hall and Company, 70 Lincoln Street, Boston, Massachusetts 02111 (617) 423-3990; *The World in Figures*.

SAINT HELENA - EDUCATION

G.K. Hall and Company, 70 Lincoln Street, Boston, Massachusetts 02111 (617) 423-3990; *The World in Figures*.

United Nations Educational, Scientific and Cultural Organization (UNESCO), 7 Place de Fontenoy, F-75700 Paris, France (Telephone Number in U.S. (212) 963-5981); *Statistical Yearbook*.

SAINT HELENA - EGG PRODUCTION AND CONSUMPTION - See SAINT HELENA - DAIRY PRODUCTS

SAINT HELENA - EMPLOYMENT

International Labour Office, I.L.O. Publications, CH-1211, Geneva 22, Switzerland; *Yearbook of Labour Statistics*.

SAINT HELENA - ENERGY

Food and Agricultural Organization of the United Nations (FAO) Via delle Terme di Caracalla, 00100 Rome, Italy (Telephone Number in U.S. (202) 653-2400); *The State of Food and Agriculture*.

G.K. Hall and Company, 70 Lincoln Street, Boston, Massachusetts 02111 (617) 423-3990; *The World in Figures*.

Statistical Office of the United Nations, Publishing Service, New York, New York 10017 (800) 253-9646; *Energy Statistics Yearbook*.

SAINT HELENA - EXPORTS

Food and Agricultural Organization of the United Nations (FAO) Via delle Terme di Caracalla, 00100 Rome, Italy (Telephone Number in U.S. (202) 653-2400); *The State of Food and Agriculture.*

G.K. Hall and Company, 70 Lincoln Street, Boston, Massachusetts 02111 (617) 423-3990; *The World in Figures.*

International Monetary Fund, 700 Nineteenth Street, NW, Washington, D.C. 20431 (202) 623-7000; *Direction of Trade Statistics.*

SAINT HELENA - EXTERNAL TRADE

Food and Agricultural Organization of the United Nations (FAO) Via delle Terme di Caracalla, 00100 Rome, Italy (Telephone Number in U.S. (202) 653-2400); *The State of Food and Agriculture,* and *Trade Yearbook.*

G.K. Hall and Company, 70 Lincoln Street, Boston, Massachusetts 02111 (617) 423-3990; *The World in Figures.*

SAINT HELENA - FARM CROPS - See SAINT HELENA - CROPS

SAINT HELENA - FERTILIZER

Food and Agricultural Organization of the United Nations (FAO) Via delle Terme di Caracalla, 00100 Rome, Italy (Telephone Number in U.S. (202) 653-2400); *The State of Food and Agriculture.*

SAINT HELENA - FETAL MORTALITY

Statistical Office of the United Nations, Publishing Service, New York, New York 10017 (800) 253-9646; *Demographic Yearbook.*

SAINT HELENA - FINANCE

G.K. Hall and Company, 70 Lincoln Street, Boston, Massachusetts 02111 (617) 423-3990; *The World in Figures.*

SAINT HELENA - FISHERIES

Food and Agricultural Organization of the United Nations (FAO) Via delle Terme di Caracalla, 00100 Rome, Italy (Telephone Number in U.S. (202) 653-2400); *The State of Food and Agriculture,* and *Yearbook of Fishery Statistics.*

SAINT HELENA - FOOD

Food and Agricultural Organization of the United Nations (FAO), Via delle Terme di Caracalla, 00100 Rome, Italy (Telephone Number in U.S. (202) 653-2400); *Production Yearbook,* and *The State of Food and Agriculture.*

SAINT HELENA - FOREIGN AID

G.K. Hall and Company, 70 Lincoln Street, Boston, Massachusetts 02111 (617) 423-3990; *The World in Figures.*

SAINT HELENA - FOREIGN TRADE

Food and Agricultural Organization of the United Nations (FAO) Via delle Terme di Caracalla, 00100 Rome, Italy (Telephone Number in U.S. (202) 653-2400); *The State of Food and Agriculture.*

G.K. Hall and Company, 70 Lincoln Street, Boston, Massachusetts 02111 (617) 423-3990; *The World in Figures.*

SAINT HELENA - FORESTRY AND FOREST PRODUCTS

Food and Agricultural Organization of the United Nations (FAO) Via delle Terme di Caracalla, 00100 Rome, Italy (Telephone Number in U.S. (202) 653-2400); *The State of Food and Agriculture.*

G.K. Hall and Company, 70 Lincoln Street, Boston, Massachusetts 02111 (617) 423-3990; *The World in Figures.*

SAINT HELENA - GENERAL MORTALITY

Statistical Office of the United Nations, Publishing Service, New York, New York 10017 (800) 253-9646; *Demographic Yearbook.*

World Health Organization, Office of Publications, Avenue Appia, CH-1211 Geneva 27, Switzerland (Telephone Number in U.S. (518) 436-9686); *World Health Statistics Annual.*

SAINT HELENA - GOVERNMENT

G.K. Hall and Company, 70 Lincoln Street, Boston, Massachusetts 02111 (617) 423-3990; *The World in Figures.*

SAINT HELENA - GRAIN PRODUCTION - See SAINT HELENA - CROPS

SAINT HELENA - GROSS DOMESTIC PRODUCT

G.K. Hall and Company, 70 Lincoln Street, Boston, Massachusetts 02111 (617) 423-3990; *The World in Figures.*

SAINT HELENA - GROUNDNUT PRODUCTION - See SAINT HELENA - CROPS

SAINT HELENA - HEALTH

G.K. Hall and Company, 70 Lincoln Street, Boston, Massachusetts 02111 (617) 423-3990; *The World in Figures.*

Statistical Office of the United Nations, Publishing Service, New York, New York 10017 (800) 253-9646; *Statistical Yearbook.*

SAINT HELENA - HIGHWAYS

G.K. Hall and Company, 70 Lincoln Street, Boston, Massachusetts 02111 (617) 423-3990; *The World in Figures.*

SAINT HELENA - HOURS OF WORK - See SAINT HELENA - EMPLOYMENT

SAINT HELENA - ILLITERATE POPULATION

G.K. Hall and Company, 70 Lincoln Street, Boston, Massachusetts 02111 (617) 423-3990; *The World in Figures.*

United Nations Educational, Scientific and Cultural Organization (UNESCO), 7 Place de Fontenoy, F-75700 Paris, France (Telephone Number in U.S. (212) 963-5981); *Statistical Yearbook.*

SAINT HELENA - IMPORTS

Food and Agricultural Organization of the United Nations (FAO) Via delle Terme di Caracalla, 00100 Rome, Italy (Telephone Number in U.S. (202) 653-2400); *The State of Food and Agriculture.*

G.K. Hall and Company, 70 Lincoln Street, Boston, Massachusetts 02111 (617) 423-3990; *The World in Figures.*

International Monetary Fund, 700 Nineteenth Street, NW, Washington, D.C. 20431 (202) 623-7000; *Direction of Trade Statistics*.

SAINT HELENA - INDUSTRY

G.K. Hall and Company, 70 Lincoln Street, Boston, Massachusetts 02111 (617) 423-3990; *The World in Figures*.

SAINT HELENA - INFANT AND MATERNAL MORTALITY

Statistical Office of the United Nations, Publishing Service, New York, New York 10017 (800) 253-9646; *Demographic Yearbook*, and *Statistical Yearbook*.

SAINT HELENA - LABOR FORCE

Food and Agricultural Organization of the United Nations (FAO) Via delle Terme di Caracalla, 00100 Rome, Italy (Telephone Number in U.S. (202) 653-2400); *The State of Food and Agriculture*.

G.K. Hall and Company, 70 Lincoln Street, Boston, Massachusetts 02111 (617) 423-3990; *The World in Figures*.

SAINT HELENA - LAND USE

Food and Agricultural Organization of the United Nations (FAO), Via delle Terme di Caracalla, 00100 Rome, Italy (Telephone Number in U.S. (202) 653-2400); *Production Yearbook*.

G.K. Hall and Company, 70 Lincoln Street, Boston, Massachusetts 02111 (617) 423-3990; *The World in Figures*.

SAINT HELENA - LIBRARIES

United Nations Educational, Scientific and Cultural Organization (UNESCO), 7 Place de Fontenoy, F-75700 Paris, France (Telephone Number in U.S. (212) 963-5981); *Statistical Yearbook*.

SAINT HELENA - LIVESTOCK AND POULTRY

Food and Agricultural Organization of the United Nations (FAO), Via delle Terme di Caracalla, 00100 Rome, Italy (Telephone Number in U.S. (202) 653-2400); *Production Yearbook*, and *The State of Food and Agriculture*.

G.K. Hall and Company, 70 Lincoln Street, Boston, Massachusetts 02111 (617) 423-3990; *The World in Figures*.

Statistical Office of the United Nations, Publishing Service, New York, New York 10017 (800) 253-9646; *Statistical Yearbook*.

SAINT HELENA - LIVING LEVELS

G.K. Hall and Company, 70 Lincoln Street, Boston, Massachusetts 02111 (617) 423-3990; *The World in Figures*.

SAINT HELENA - MAIL - NUMBER OF ITEMS SENT AND RECEIVED

Statistical Office of the United Nations, Publishing Service, New York, New York 10017 (800) 253-9646; *Statistical Yearbook*.

SAINT HELENA - MANUFACTURING

G.K. Hall and Company, 70 Lincoln Street, Boston, Massachusetts 02111 (617) 423-3990; *The World in Figures*.

SAINT HELENA - MARRIAGE RATES

Statistical Office of the United Nations, Publishing Service, New York, New York 10017 (800) 253-9646; *Demographic Yearbook*, and *Statistical Yearbook*.

SAINT HELENA - MEAT PRODUCTION - See SAINT HELENA - LIVESTOCK AND POULTRY

SAINT HELENA - MERCHANT SHIPPING

G.K. Hall and Company, 70 Lincoln Street, Boston, Massachusetts 02111 (617) 423-3990; *The World in Figures*.

Statistical Office of the United Nations, Publishing Service, New York, New York 10017 (800) 253-9646; *Statistical Yearbook*.

SAINT HELENA - MILITARY

G.K. Hall and Company, 70 Lincoln Street, Boston, Massachusetts 02111 (617) 423-3990; *The World in Figures*.

SAINT HELENA - MINING AND MINERAL PRODUCTS

G.K. Hall and Company, 70 Lincoln Street, Boston, Massachusetts 02111 (617) 423-3990; *The World in Figures*.

SAINT HELENA - MONEY SUPPLY

G.K. Hall and Company, 70 Lincoln Street, Boston, Massachusetts 02111 (617) 423-3990; *The World in Figures*.

SAINT HELENA - MOTION PICTURES

Statistical Office of the United Nations, Publishing Service, New York, New York 10017 (800) 253-9646; *Statistical Yearbook*.

SAINT HELENA - MOTOR VEHICLES IN USE

G.K. Hall and Company, 70 Lincoln Street, Boston, Massachusetts 02111 (617) 423-3990; *The World in Figures*.

SAINT HELENA - MUSEUMS

United Nations Educational, Scientific and Cultural Organization (UNESCO), 7 Place de Fontenoy, F-75700 Paris, France (Telephone Number in U.S. (212) 963-5981); *Statistical Yearbook*.

SAINT HELENA - NATALITY - See SAINT HELENA - BIRTH RATE

SAINT HELENA - NATIONAL INCOME

G.K. Hall and Company, 70 Lincoln Street, Boston, Massachusetts 02111 (617) 423-3990; *The World in Figures*.

SAINT HELENA - NEWSPAPER PRODUCTION - See SAINT HELENA - FORESTRY AND FOREST PRODUCTS

SAINT HELENA - OCCUPATIONS - See SAINT HELENA - LABOR FORCE

SAINT HELENA - PERIODICALS

United Nations Educational, Scientific and Cultural Organization (UNESCO), 7 Place de Fontenoy, F-75700 Paris, France (Telephone Number in U.S. (212) 963-5981); *Statistical Yearbook*.

SAINT HELENA - PESTICIDE USE

Food and Agricultural Organization of the United Nations (FAO) Via delle Terme di Caracalla, 00100 Rome, Italy (Telephone Number in U.S. (202) 653-2400); *The State of Food and Agriculture.*

SAINT HELENA - PETROLEUM INDUSTRY

Food and Agricultural Organization of the United Nations (FAO) Via delle Terme di Caracalla, 00100 Rome, Italy (Telephone Number in U.S. (202) 653-2400); *The State of Food and Agriculture.*

G.K. Hall and Company, 70 Lincoln Street, Boston, Massachusetts 02111 (617) 423-3990; *The World in Figures.*

SAINT HELENA - PIGS - See SAINT HELENA - LIVESTOCK AND POULTRY

SAINT HELENA - POPULATION

Food and Agricultural Organization of the United Nations (FAO), Via delle Terme di Caracalla, 00100 Rome, Italy (Telephone Number in U.S. (202) 653-2400); *Production Yearbook.*

G.K. Hall and Company, 70 Lincoln Street, Boston, Massachusetts 02111 (617) 423-3990; *The World in Figures.*

Statistical Office of the United Nations, Publishing Service, New York, New York 10017 (000) 253-9646; *Demographic Yearbook,* and *Statistical Yearbook.*

United Nations Educational, Scientific and Cultural Organization (UNESCO), 7 Place de Fontenoy, F-75700 Paris, France (Telephone Number in U.S. (212) 963-5981); *Statistical Yearbook.*

World Health Organization, Office of Publications, Avenue Appia, CH-1211 Geneva 27, Switzerland (Telephone Number in U.S. (518) 436-9686); *World Health Statistics Annual.*

SAINT HELENA - PRICES

Food and Agricultural Organization of the United Nations (FAO), Via delle Terme di Caracalla, 00100 Rome, Italy (Telephone Number in U.S. (202) 653-2400); *Production Yearbook,* and *The State of Food and Agriculture.*

G.K. Hall and Company, 70 Lincoln Street, Boston, Massachusetts 02111 (617) 423-3990; *The World in Figures.*

SAINT HELENA - PRODUCTION

G.K. Hall and Company, 70 Lincoln Street, Boston, Massachusetts 02111 (617) 423-3990; *The World in Figures.*

SAINT HELENA - RAILWAY USE

G.K. Hall and Company, 70 Lincoln Street, Boston, Massachusetts 02111 (617) 423-3990; *The World in Figures.*

SAINT HELENA - RETAIL TRADE

G.K. Hall and Company, 70 Lincoln Street, Boston, Massachusetts 02111 (617) 423-3990; *The World in Figures.*

SAINT HELENA - SHEEP - See SAINT HELENA - LIVESTOCK AND POULTRY

SAINT HELENA - SOCIAL DATA

G.K. Hall and Company, 70 Lincoln Street, Boston, Massachusetts 02111 (617) 423-3990; *The World in Figures.*

SAINT HELENA - STOCKS - COMMODITY - MARKET PRICE - INDEX

Food and Agricultural Organization of the United Nations (FAO) Via delle Terme di Caracalla, 00100 Rome, Italy (Telephone Number in U.S. (202) 653-2400); *The State of Food and Agriculture.*

SAINT HELENA - TAXATION

G.K. Hall and Company, 70 Lincoln Street, Boston, Massachusetts 02111 (617) 423-3990; *The World in Figures.*

SAINT HELENA - TELEPHONES IN USE

G.K. Hall and Company, 70 Lincoln Street, Boston, Massachusetts 02111 (617) 423-3990; *The World in Figures.*

SAINT HELENA - TEXTILE INDUSTRY

G.K. Hall and Company, 70 Lincoln Street, Boston, Massachusetts 02111 (617) 423-3990; *The World in Figures.*

SAINT HELENA - TOURISM

G.K. Hall and Company, 70 Lincoln Street, Boston, Massachusetts 02111 (617) 423-3990; *The World in Figures.*

SAINT HELENA - TRADE - See SAINT HELENA - FOREIGN TRADE

SAINT HELENA - TRANSPORTATION AND COMMUNICATIONS

G.K. Hall and Company, 70 Lincoln Street, Boston, Massachusetts 02111 (617) 423-3990; *The World in Figures.*

SAINT HELENA - VITAL STATISTICS

G.K. Hall and Company, 70 Lincoln Street, Boston, Massachusetts 02111 (617) 423-3990; *The World in Figures.*

Statistical Office of the United Nations, Publishing Service, New York, New York 10017 (800) 253-9646; *Statistical Yearbook.*

World Health Organization, Office of Publications, Avenue Appia, CH-1211 Geneva 27, Switzerland (Telephone Number in U.S. (518) 436-9686); *World Health Statistics Annual.*

SAINT HELENA - WAGES

G.K. Hall and Company, 70 Lincoln Street, Boston, Massachusetts 02111 (617) 423-3990; *The World in Figures.*

SAINT HELENA - WEATHER

G.K. Hall and Company, 70 Lincoln Street, Boston, Massachusetts 02111 (617) 423-3990; *The World in Figures.*

Saint Kitts and Nevis - National Statistical Office

Statistics Division, Planning Unit, Ministry of Finance, Church Street, Post Office Box 186, Basseterre, Saint Kitts and Nevis.

Saint Kitts and Nevis - Primary Statistics Source

HM Stationery Office, Post Office Box 569, London SE1 9NH, England; *Saint Kitts and Nevis: Report.*

SAINT KITTS AND NEVIS - AGRICULTURE

Food and Agricultural Organization of the United Nations (FAO) Via delle Terme di Caracalla, 00100 Rome, Italy (Telephone Number in U.S. (202) 653-2400); *Production Yearbook,* and *The State of Food and Agriculture,* and *Trade Yearbook.*

G.K. Hall and Company, 70 Lincoln Street, Boston, Massachusetts 02111 (617) 423-3990; *The World in Figures.*

Statistical Office of the United Nations, Publishing Service, New York, New York 10017 (800) 253-9646; *Statistical Yearbook.*

The World Bank, 1818 H Street, NW, Washington, D.C. 20433 (202) 477-1234; *World Tables.*

SAINT KITTS AND NEVIS - AIRLINE SERVICE

G.K. Hall and Company, 70 Lincoln Street, Boston, Massachusetts 02111 (617) 423-3990; *The World in Figures.*

SAINT KITTS AND NEVIS - AREA AND DENSITY OF POPULATION

Food and Agricultural Organization of the United Nations (FAO) Via delle Terme di Caracalla, 00100 Rome, Italy (Telephone Number in U.S. (202) 653-2400); *The State of Food and Agriculture.*

G.K. Hall and Company, 70 Lincoln Street, Boston, Massachusetts 02111 (617) 423-3990; *The World in Figures.*

Statistical Office of the United Nations, Publishing Service, New York, New York 10017 (800) 253-9646; *Statistical Yearbook.*

United Nations Educational, Scientific and Cultural Organization (UNESCO), 7 Place de Fontenoy, F-75700 Paris, France (Telephone Number in U.S. (212) 963-5981); *Statistical Yearbook.*

SAINT KITTS AND NEVIS - BALANCE OF PAYMENTS

G.K. Hall and Company, 70 Lincoln Street, Boston, Massachusetts 02111 (617) 423-3990; *The World in Figures.*

The World Bank, 1818 H Street, NW, Washington, D.C. 20433 (202) 477-1234; *World Tables.*

SAINT KITTS AND NEVIS - BANKING

G.K. Hall and Company, 70 Lincoln Street, Boston, Massachusetts 02111 (617) 423-3990; *The World in Figures.*

SAINT KITTS AND NEVIS - BIRTH RATES

Statistical Office of the United Nations, Publishing Service, New York, New York 10017 (800) 253-9646; *Demographic Yearbook,* and *Statistical Yearbook.*

The World Bank, 1818 H Street, NW, Washington, D.C. 20433 (202) 477-1234; *World Tables.*

World Health Organization, Office of Publications, Avenue Appia, CH-1211 Geneva 27, Switzerland (Telephone Number in U.S. (518)

436-9686); *World Health Statistics Annual.*

SAINT KITTS AND NEVIS - BONDS

G.K. Hall and Company, 70 Lincoln Street, Boston, Massachusetts 02111 (617) 423-3990; *The World in Figures.*

SAINT KITTS AND NEVIS - BOOK PRODUCTION

G.K. Hall and Company, 70 Lincoln Street, Boston, Massachusetts 02111 (617) 423-3990; *The World in Figures.*

United Nations Educational, Scientific and Cultural Organization (UNESCO), 7 Place de Fontenoy, F-75700 Paris, France (Telephone Number in U.S. (212) 963-5981); *Statistical Yearbook.*

SAINT KITTS AND NEVIS - BROADCASTING

Billboard Limited, P.O. Box 9027, 1006 AA Amsterdam, The Netherlands (Telephone Number in U.S. (212) 764-7300); *World Radio TV Handbook.*

G.K. Hall and Company, 70 Lincoln Street, Boston, Massachusetts 02111 (617) 423-3990; *The World in Figures.*

SAINT KITTS AND NEVIS - BUSINESS

G.K. Hall and Company, 70 Lincoln Street, Boston, Massachusetts 02111 (617) 423-3990; *The World in Figures.*

SAINT KITTS AND NEVIS - CALORIE SUPPLY

Food and Agricultural Organization of the United Nations (FAO) Via delle Terme di Caracalla, 00100 Rome, Italy (Telephone Number in U.S. (202) 653-2400); *The State of Food and Agriculture.*

SAINT KITTS AND NEVIS - CATTLE - See SAINT KITTS AND NEVIS - LIVESTOCK AND POULTRY

SAINT KITTS AND NEVIS - CHEMICAL (ORGANIC) PRODUCTION - See SAINT KITTS AND NEVIS - MINING AND MINERAL PRODUCTS

SAINT KITTS AND NEVIS - CLASS STRUCTURE

G.K. Hall and Company, 70 Lincoln Street, Boston, Massachusetts 02111 (617) 423-3990; *The World in Figures.*

SAINT KITTS AND NEVIS - CLIMATE

G.K. Hall and Company, 70 Lincoln Street, Boston, Massachusetts 02111 (617) 423-3990; *The World in Figures.*

SAINT KITTS AND NEVIS - COAL PRODUCTION - See SAINT KITTS AND NEVIS - MINING AND MINERAL PRODUCTS

SAINT KITTS AND NEVIS - COMMUNICATIONS

G.K. Hall and Company, 70 Lincoln Street, Boston, Massachusetts 02111 (617) 423-3990; *The World in Figures.*

SAINT KITTS AND NEVIS - CONSUMER PRICE INDEX

G.K. Hall and Company, 70 Lincoln Street, Boston, Massachusetts 02111 (617) 423-3990; *The World in Figures.*

Statistical Office of the United Nations, Publishing Service, New York, New York 10017 (800) 253-9646; *Statistical Yearbook.*

SAINT KITTS AND NEVIS - CONSUMER PRICES

International Labour Office, I.L.O. Publications, CH-1211, Geneva 22, Switzerland; *Yearbook of Labour Statistics.*

SAINT KITTS AND NEVIS - CONSUMPTION

G.K. Hall and Company, 70 Lincoln Street, Boston, Massachusetts 02111 (617) 423-3990; *The World in Figures.*

SAINT KITTS AND NEVIS - CORN PRODUCTION - See SAINT KITTS AND NEVIS - CROPS

SAINT KITTS AND NEVIS - CORPORATE TAXES - See SAINT KITTS AND NEVIS - TAXATION

SAINT KITTS AND NEVIS - CROPS

Food and Agricultural Organization of the United Nations (FAO) Via delle Terme di Caracalla, 00100 Rome, Italy (Telephone Number in U.S. (202) 653-2400); *The State of Food and Agriculture.*

G.K. Hall and Company, 70 Lincoln Street, Boston, Massachusetts 02111 (617) 423-3990; *The World in Figures.*

Statistical Office of the United Nations, Publishing Service, New York, New York 10017 (800) 253-9646; *Statistical Yearbook.*

SAINT KITTS AND NEVIS - CUSTOMS DUTIES

G.K. Hall and Company, 70 Lincoln Street, Boston, Massachusetts 02111 (617) 423-3990; *The World in Figures.*

SAINT KITTS AND NEVIS   DAIRY PRODUCTS

Food and Agricultural Organization of the United Nations (FAO) Via delle Terme di Caracalla, 00100 Rome, Italy (Telephone Number in U.S. (202) 653-2400); *The State of Food and Agriculture.*

SAINT KITTS AND NEVIS - DEATH RATES

G.K. Hall and Company, 70 Lincoln Street, Boston, Massachusetts 02111 (617) 423-3990; *The World in Figures.*

Statistical Office of the United Nations, Publishing Service, New York, New York 10017 (800) 253-9646; *Statistical Yearbook.*

World Health Organization, Office of Publications, Avenue Appia, CH-1211 Geneva 27, Switzerland (Telephone Number in U.S. (518) 436-9686); *World Health Statistics Annual.*

SAINT KITTS AND NEVIS - DEFENSE EXPENDITURES

G.K. Hall and Company, 70 Lincoln Street, Boston, Massachusetts 02111 (617) 423-3990; *The World in Figures.*

SAINT KITTS AND NEVIS - DEMOGRAPHY

G.K. Hall and Company, 70 Lincoln Street, Boston, Massachusetts 02111 (617) 423-3990; *The World in Figures.*

SAINT KITTS AND NEVIS - DEVELOPMENT ASSISTANCE

G.K. Hall and Company, 70 Lincoln Street, Boston, Massachusetts 02111 (617) 423-3990; *The World in Figures.*

SAINT KITTS AND NEVIS - DISEASES

G.K. Hall and Company, 70 Lincoln Street, Boston, Massachusetts 02111 (617) 423-3990; *The World in Figures.*

World Health Organization, Office of Publications, Avenue Appia, CH-1211 Geneva 27, Switzerland (Telephone Number in U.S. (518) 436-9686); *World Health Statistics Annual.*

SAINT KITTS AND NEVIS - DIVORCE RATES

Statistical Office of the United Nations, Publishing Service, New York, New York 10017 (800) 253-9646; *Demographic Yearbook,* and *Statistical Yearbook.*

SAINT KITTS AND NEVIS - DOMESTIC PRODUCT

G.K. Hall and Company, 70 Lincoln Street, Boston, Massachusetts 02111 (617) 423-3990; *The World in Figures.*

SAINT KITTS AND NEVIS - ECONOMY

G.K. Hall and Company, 70 Lincoln Street, Boston, Massachusetts 02111 (617) 423-3990; *The World in Figures.*

SAINT KITTS AND NEVIS - EDUCATION

G.K. Hall and Company, 70 Lincoln Street, Boston, Massachusetts 02111 (617) 423-3990; *The World in Figures.*

United Nations Educational, Scientific and Cultural Organization (UNESCO), 7 Place de Fontenoy, F-75700 Paris, France (Telephone Number in U.S. (212) 963-5981); *Statistical Yearbook.*

The World Bank, 1818 H Street, NW, Washington, D.C. 20433 (202) 477-1234; *World Tables.*

SAINT KITTS AND NEVIS - EGG PRODUCTION - See SAINT KITTS AND NEVIS - DAIRY PRODUCTS

SAINT KITTS AND NEVIS - ELECTRICITY

Statistical Office of the United Nations, Publishing Service, New York, New York 10017 (800) 253-9646; *Statistical Yearbook.*

SAINT KITTS AND NEVIS - EMPLOYMENT

International Labour Office, I.L.O. Publications, CH-1211, Geneva 22, Switzerland; *Yearbook of Labour Statistics.*

SAINT KITTS AND NEVIS - ENERGY

Food and Agricultural Organization of the United Nations (FAO) Via delle Terme di Caracalla, 00100 Rome, Italy (Telephone Number in U.S. (202) 653-2400); *The State of Food and Agriculture.*

G.K. Hall and Company, 70 Lincoln Street, Boston, Massachusetts 02111 (617) 423-3990; *The World in Figures.*

Statistical Office of the United Nations, Publishing Service, New York, New York 10017 (800) 253-9646; *Statistical Yearbook.*

SAINT KITTS AND NEVIS - EXPORTS

Food and Agricultural Organization of the United Nations (FAO) Via delle Terme di Caracalla, 00100 Rome, Italy (Telephone Number in U.S. (202) 653-2400); *The State of Food and Agriculture.*

G.K. Hall and Company, 70 Lincoln Street, Boston, Massachusetts 02111 (617) 423-3990; *The World in Figures.*

International Monetary Fund, 700 Nineteenth Street, NW, Washington, D.C. 20431 (202) 623-7000; *Direction of Trade Statistics.*

The World Bank, 1818 H Street, NW, Washington, D.C. 20433 (202) 477-1234; *World Tables.*

SAINT KITTS AND NEVIS - EXTERNAL INDEBTEDNESS

The World Bank, 1818 H Street, NW, Washington, D.C. 20433 (202) 477-1234; *World Tables.*

SAINT KITTS AND NEVIS - EXTERNAL TRADE

Food and Agricultural Organization of the United Nations (FAO) Via delle Terme di Caracalla, 00100 Rome, Italy (Telephone Number in U.S. (202) 653-2400); *The State of Food and Agriculture,* and *Trade Yearbook.*

G.K. Hall and Company, 70 Lincoln Street, Boston, Massachusetts 02111 (617) 423-3990; *The World in Figures.*

SAINT KITTS AND NEVIS - FARM CROPS - See SAINT KITTS AND NEVIS - CROPS

SAINT KITTS AND NEVIS - FERTILITY RATES

The World Bank, 1818 H Street, NW, Washington, D.C. 20433 (202) 477-1234; *World Tables.*

SAINT KITTS AND NEVIS - FERTILIZER

Food and Agricultural Organization of the United Nations (FAO) Via delle Terme di Caracalla, 00100 Rome, Italy (Telephone Number in U.S. (202) 653-2400); *The State of Food and Agriculture.*

Statistical Office of the United Nations, Publishing Service, New York, New York 10017 (800) 253-9646; *Statistical Yearbook.*

SAINT KITTS AND NEVIS - FETAL MORTALITY

Statistical Office of the United Nations, Publishing Service, New York, New York 10017 (800) 253-9646; *Demographic Yearbook.*

World Health Organization, Office of Publications, Avenue Appia, CH-1211 Geneva 27, Switzerland (Telephone Number in U.S. (518) 436-9686); *World Health Statistics Annual.*

SAINT KITTS AND NEVIS - FINANCE

G.K. Hall and Company, 70 Lincoln Street, Boston, Massachusetts 02111 (617) 423-3990; *The World in Figures.*

SAINT KITTS AND NEVIS - FISHERIES

Food and Agricultural Organization of the United Nations (FAO) Via delle Terme di Caracalla, 00100 Rome, Italy (Telephone Number in U.S. (202) 653-2400); *The State of Food and Agriculture,* and *Yearbook of Fishery Statistics.*

SAINT KITTS AND NEVIS - FOOD

Food and Agricultural Organization of the United Nations (FAO) Via delle Terme di Caracalla, 00100 Rome, Italy (Telephone Number in U.S. (202) 653-2400); *The State of Food and Agriculture.*

SAINT KITTS AND NEVIS - FOREIGN AID

G.K. Hall and Company, 70 Lincoln Street, Boston, Massachusetts 02111 (617) 423-3990; *The World in Figures.*

SAINT KITTS AND NEVIS - FOREIGN TRADE

Food and Agricultural Organization of the United Nations (FAO) Via delle Terme di Caracalla, 00100 Rome, Italy (Telephone Number in U.S. (202) 653-2400); *The State of Food and Agriculture.*

G.K. Hall and Company, 70 Lincoln Street, Boston, Massachusetts 02111 (617) 423-3990; *The World in Figures.*

Statistical Office of the United Nations, Publishing Service, New York, New York 10017 (800) 253-9646; *Statistical Yearbook.*

The World Bank, 1818 H Street, NW, Washington, D.C. 20433 (202) 477-1234; *World Tables.*

SAINT KITTS AND NEVIS - FORESTRY AND FOREST PRODUCTS

Food and Agricultural Organization of the United Nations (FAO) Via delle Terme di Caracalla, 00100 Rome, Italy (Telephone Number in U.S. (202) 653-2400); *The State of Food and Agriculture.*

G.K. Hall and Company, 70 Lincoln Street, Boston, Massachusetts 02111 (617) 423-3990; *The World in Figures.*

Statistical Office of the United Nations, Publishing Service, New York, New York 10017 (800) 253-9646; *Statistical Yearbook.*

United Nations Educational, Scientific and Cultural Organization (UNESCO), 7 Place de Fontenoy, F-75700 Paris, France (Telephone Number in U.S. (212) 963-5981); *Statistical Yearbook.*

SAINT KITTS AND NEVIS - GENERAL MORTALITY

Statistical Office of the United Nations, Publishing Service, New York, New York 10017 (800) 253-9646; *Demographic Yearbook.*

World Health Organization, Office of Publications, Avenue Appia, CH-1211 Geneva 27, Switzerland (Telephone Number in U.S. (518) 436-9686); *World Health Statistics Annual.*

SAINT KITTS AND NEVIS - GOLD HOLDINGS

The World Bank, 1818 H Street, NW, Washington, D.C. 20433 (202) 477-1234; *World Tables.*

SAINT KITTS AND NEVIS - GOVERNMENT

G.K. Hall and Company, 70 Lincoln Street, Boston, Massachusetts 02111 (617) 423-3990; *The World in Figures.*

SAINT KITTS AND NEVIS - GOVERNMENT EXPENDITURE

The World Bank, 1818 H Street, NW, Washington, D.C. 20433 (202) 477-1234; *World Tables.*

SAINT KITTS AND NEVIS - GOVERNMENT REVENUE

The World Bank, 1818 H Street, NW, Washington, D.C. 20433 (202) 477-1234; *World Tables.*

SAINT KITTS AND NEVIS - GRAIN PRODUCTION - See SAINT KITTS AND NEVIS - CROPS

SAINT KITTS AND NEVIS - GROSS DOMESTIC PRODUCT

G.K. Hall and Company, 70 Lincoln Street, Boston, Massachusetts 02111 (617) 423-3990; *The World in Figures.*

Statistical Office of the United Nations, Publishing Service, New York, New York 10017 (800) 253-9646; *Statistical Yearbook.*

The World Bank, 1818 H Street, NW, Washington, D.C. 20433 (202) 477-1234; *World Tables.*

SAINT KITTS AND NEVIS - GROSS NATIONAL PRODUCT

The World Bank, 1818 H Street, NW, Washington, D.C. 20433 (202) 477-1234; *World Tables.*

SAINT KITTS AND NEVIS - GROUNDNUT PRODUCTION - See SAINT KITTS AND NEVIS - CROPS

SAINT KITTS AND NEVIS - HEALTH

G.K. Hall and Company, 70 Lincoln Street, Boston, Massachusetts 02111 (617) 423-3990; *The World in Figures.*

Statistical Office of the United Nations, Publishing Service, New York, New York 10017 (800) 253-9646; *Statistical Yearbook.*

World Health Organization, Office of Publications, Avenue Appia, CH-1211 Geneva 27, Switzerland (Telephone Number in U.S. (518) 436-9686); *World Health Statistics Annual.*

SAINT KITTS AND NEVIS - HIGHWAYS

G.K. Hall and Company, 70 Lincoln Street, Boston, Massachusetts 02111 (617) 423-3990; *The World in Figures.*

SAINT KITTS AND NEVIS - HOURS OF WORK - See SAINT KITTS AND NEVIS - EMPLOYMENT

SAINT KITTS AND NEVIS - ILLITERATE POPULATION

G.K. Hall and Company, 70 Lincoln Street, Boston, Massachusetts 02111 (617) 423-3990; *The World in Figures.*

United Nations Educational, Scientific and Cultural Organization (UNESCO), 7 Place de Fontenoy, F-75700 Paris, France (Telephone Number in U.S. (212) 963-5981); *Statistical Yearbook.*

SAINT KITTS AND NEVIS - IMPORTS

Food and Agricultural Organization of the United Nations (FAO) Via delle Terme di Caracalla, 00100 Rome, Italy (Telephone Number in U.S. (202) 653-2400); *The State of Food and Agriculture.*

G.K. Hall and Company, 70 Lincoln Street, Boston, Massachusetts 02111 (617) 423-3990; *The World in Figures.*

International Monetary Fund, 700 Nineteenth Street, NW, Washington, D.C. 20431 (202) 623-7000; *Direction of Trade Statistics.*

The World Bank, 1818 H Street, NW, Washington, D.C. 20433 (202) 477-1234; *World Tables.*

SAINT KITTS AND NEVIS - INDUSTRY

G.K. Hall and Company, 70 Lincoln Street, Boston, Massachusetts 02111 (617) 423-3990; *The World in Figures.*

International Labour Office, I.L.O. Publications, CH-1211, Geneva 22, Switzerland; *Yearbook of Labour Statistics.*

The World Bank, 1818 H Street, NW, Washington, D.C. 20433 (202) 477-1234; *World Tables.*

SAINT KITTS AND NEVIS - INFANT AND MATERNAL MORTALITY

Statistical Office of the United Nations, Publishing Service, New York, New York 10017 (800) 253-9646; *Demographic Yearbook,* and *Statistical Yearbook.*

The World Bank, 1818 H Street, NW, Washington, D.C. 20433 (202) 477-1234; *World Tables.*

World Health Organization, Office of Publications, Avenue Appia, CH-1211 Geneva 27, Switzerland (Telephone Number in U.S. (518) 436-9686); *World Health Statistics Annual.*

SAINT KITTS AND NEVIS - INTERNATIONAL RESERVES EXCLUDING GOLD

The World Bank, 1818 H Street, NW, Washington, D.C. 20433 (202) 477-1234; *World Tables.*

SAINT KITTS AND NEVIS - LABOR FORCE

Food and Agricultural Organization of the United Nations (FAO) Via delle Terme di Caracalla, 00100 Rome, Italy (Telephone Number in U.S. (202) 653-2400); *The State of Food and Agriculture.*

G.K. Hall and Company, 70 Lincoln Street, Boston, Massachusetts 02111 (617) 423-3990; *The World in Figures.*

The World Bank, 1818 H Street, NW, Washington, D.C. 20433 (202) 477-1234; *World Tables.*

SAINT KITTS AND NEVIS - LABOR PRODUCTIVITY

International Labour Office, I.L.O. Publications, CH-1211, Geneva 22, Switzerland; *Yearbook of Labour Statistics.*

SAINT KITTS AND NEVIS - LAND USE

Food and Agricultural Organization of the United Nations (FAO), Via delle Terme di Caracalla, 00100 Rome, Italy (Telephone Number in U.S. (202) 653-2400); *Production Yearbook.*

G.K. Hall and Company, 70 Lincoln Street, Boston, Massachusetts 02111 (617) 423-3990; *The World in Figures.*

SAINT KITTS AND NEVIS - LIVESTOCK AND POULTRY

Food and Agricultural Organization of the United Nations (FAO), Via delle Terme di Caracalla, 00100 Rome, Italy (Telephone Number in U.S. (202) 653-2400); *Production Yearbook,* and *The State of Food and Agriculture.*

G.K. Hall and Company, 70 Lincoln Street, Boston, Massachusetts 02111 (617) 423-3990; *The World in Figures.*

Statistical Office of the United Nations, Publishing Service, New York, New York 10017 (800) 253-9646; *Statistical Yearbook.*

SAINT KITTS AND NEVIS - LIVING LEVELS

G.K. Hall and Company, 70 Lincoln Street, Boston, Massachusetts 02111 (617) 423-3990; *The World in Figures.*

SAINT KITTS AND NEVIS - MAIL - NUMBER OF ITEMS SENT AND RECEIVED

Statistical Office of the United Nations, Publishing Service, New York, New York 10017 (800) 253-9646; *Statistical Yearbook*.

SAINT KITTS AND NEVIS - MANUFACTURING

G.K. Hall and Company, 70 Lincoln Street, Boston, Massachusetts 02111 (617) 423-3990; *The World in Figures*.

The World Bank, 1818 H Street, NW, Washington, D.C. 20433 (202) 477-1234; *World Tables*.

SAINT KITTS AND NEVIS - MARRIAGE RATES

Statistical Office of the United Nations, Publishing Service, New York, New York 10017 (800) 253-9646; *Demographic Yearbook*, and *Statistical Yearbook*.

SAINT KITTS AND NEVIS - MEAT PRODUCTION - See SAINT KITTS AND NEVIS - LIVESTOCK AND POULTRY

SAINT KITTS AND NEVIS - MERCHANT SHIPPING

G.K. Hall and Company, 70 Lincoln Street, Boston, Massachusetts 02111 (617) 423-3990; *The World in Figures*.

Statistical Office of the United Nations, Publishing Service, New York, New York 10017 (800) 253-9646; *Statistical Yearbook*.

SAINT KITTS AND NEVIS - MILITARY

G.K. Hall and Company, 70 Lincoln Street, Boston, Massachusetts 02111 (617) 423-3990; *The World in Figures*.

SAINT KITTS AND NEVIS - MINING AND MINERAL PRODUCTS

G.K. Hall and Company, 70 Lincoln Street, Boston, Massachusetts 02111 (617) 423-3990; *The World in Figures*.

SAINT KITTS AND NEVIS - MONEY SUPPLY

G.K. Hall and Company, 70 Lincoln Street, Boston, Massachusetts 02111 (617) 423-3990; *The World in Figures*.

The World Bank, 1818 H Street, NW, Washington, D.C. 20433 (202) 477-1234; *World Tables*.

SAINT KITTS AND NEVIS - MOTOR VEHICLES IN USE

G.K. Hall and Company, 70 Lincoln Street, Boston, Massachusetts 02111 (617) 423-3990; *The World in Figures*.

Statistical Office of the United Nations, Publishing Service, New York, New York 10017 (800) 253-9646; *Statistical Yearbook*.

SAINT KITTS AND NEVIS - NATALITY - See SAINT KITTS AND NEVIS - BIRTH RATE

SAINT KITTS AND NEVIS - NATIONAL ACCOUNTS

Statistical Office of the United Nations, Publishing Service, New York, New York 10017 (800) 253-9646; *Statistical Yearbook*.

SAINT KITTS AND NEVIS - NATIONAL INCOME

G.K. Hall and Company, 70 Lincoln Street, Boston, Massachusetts 02111 (617) 423-3990; *The World in Figures*.

Statistical Office of the United Nations, Publishing Service, New York, New York 10017 (800) 253-9646; *Statistical Yearbook*.

SAINT KITTS AND NEVIS - NEWSPAPER PRODUCTION - See SAINT KITTS AND NEVIS - FORESTRY AND FOREST PRODUCTS

SAINT KITTS AND NEVIS - OCCUPATIONS - See SAINT KITTS AND NEVIS - LABOR FORCE

SAINT KITTS AND NEVIS - PESTICIDE USE

Food and Agricultural Organization of the United Nations (FAO) Via delle Terme di Caracalla, 00100 Rome, Italy (Telephone Number in U.S. (202) 653-2400); *The State of Food and Agriculture*.

SAINT KITTS AND NEVIS - PETROLEUM INDUSTRY

Food and Agricultural Organization of the United Nations (FAO) Via delle Terme di Caracalla, 00100 Rome, Italy (Telephone Number in U.S. (202) 653-2400); *The State of Food and Agriculture*.

G.K. Hall and Company, 70 Lincoln Street, Boston, Massachusetts 02111 (617) 423-3990; *The World in Figures*.

SAINT KITTS AND NEVIS - PIGS - See SAINT KITTS AND NEVIS - LIVESTOCK AND POULTRY

SAINT KITTS AND NEVIS - POPULATION

Food and Agricultural Organization of the United Nations (FAO), Via delle Terme di Caracalla, 00100 Rome, Italy (Telephone Number in U.S. (202) 653-2400); *Production Yearbook*.

G.K. Hall and Company, 70 Lincoln Street, Boston, Massachusetts 02111 (617) 423-3990; *The World in Figures*.

International Labour Office, I.L.O. Publications, CH-1211, Geneva 22, Switzerland; *Yearbook of Labour Statistics*.

Statistical Office of the United Nations, Publishing Service, New York, New York 10017 (800) 253-9646; *Demographic Yearbook*, and *Statistical Yearbook*.

United Nations Educational, Scientific and Cultural Organization (UNESCO), 7 Place de Fontenoy, F-75700 Paris, France (Telephone Number in U.S. (212) 963-5981); *Statistical Yearbook*.

World Health Organization, Office of Publications, Avenue Appia, CH-1211 Geneva 27, Switzerland (Telephone Number in U.S. (518) 436-9686); *World Health Statistics Annual*.

SAINT KITTS AND NEVIS - PRICES

Food and Agricultural Organization of the United Nations (FAO), Via delle Terme di Caracalla, 00100 Rome, Italy (Telephone Number in U.S. (202) 653-2400); *Production Yearbook*, and *The State of Food and Agriculture*.

G.K. Hall and Company, 70 Lincoln Street, Boston, Massachusetts 02111 (617) 423-3990; *The World in Figures*.

International Labour Office, I.L.O. Publications, CH-1211, Geneva 22, Switzerland; *Yearbook of Labour Statistics*.

SAINT KITTS AND NEVIS - PRODUCTION

G.K. Hall and Company, 70 Lincoln Street, Boston, Massachusetts 02111 (617) 423-3990; *The World in Figures*.

SAINT KITTS AND NEVIS - RAILWAY USE

G.K. Hall and Company, 70 Lincoln Street, Boston, Massachusetts 02111 (617) 423-3990; *The World in Figures*.

SAINT KITTS AND NEVIS - RETAIL TRADE

G.K. Hall and Company, 70 Lincoln Street, Boston, Massachusetts 02111 (617) 423-3990; *The World in Figures*.

SAINT KITTS AND NEVIS - SHEEP - See SAINT KITTS AND NEVIS - LIVESTOCK AND POULTRY

SAINT KITTS AND NEVIS - SOCIAL DATA

G.K. Hall and Company, 70 Lincoln Street, Boston, Massachusetts 02111 (617) 423-3990; *The World in Figures*.

SAINT KITTS AND NEVIS - STOCKS - COMMODITY - MARKET PRICE - INDEX

Food and Agricultural Organization of the United Nations (FAO) Via delle Terme di Caracalla, 00100 Rome, Italy (Telephone Number in U.S. (202) 653-2400); *The State of Food and Agriculture*.

SAINT KITTS AND NEVIS - SUGAR - See SAINT KITTS AND NEVIS - CROPS

SAINT KITTS AND NEVIS - TAXATION

G.K. Hall and Company, 70 Lincoln Street, Boston, Massachusetts 02111 (617) 423-3990; *The World in Figures*.

The World Bank, 1818 H Street, NW, Washington, D.C. 20433 (202) 477-1234; *World Tables*.

SAINT KITTS AND NEVIS - TELEPHONES IN USE

American Telephone and Telegraph Company, 26 Parsippany Road, Whippany, New Jersey 07981 (800) 338-4038; *The World's Telephones*.

G.K. Hall and Company, 70 Lincoln Street, Boston, Massachusetts 02111 (617) 423-3990; *The World in Figures*.

Statistical Office of the United Nations, Publishing Service, New York, New York 10017 (800) 253-9646; *Statistical Yearbook*.

SAINT KITTS AND NEVIS - TEXTILE INDUSTRY

G.K. Hall and Company, 70 Lincoln Street, Boston, Massachusetts 02111 (617) 423-3990; *The World in Figures*.

SAINT KITTS AND NEVIS - TOURISM

G.K. Hall and Company, 70 Lincoln Street, Boston, Massachusetts 02111 (617) 423-3990; *The World in Figures*.

World Tourism Organization, Calle Capitan Haya 42, E-28020 Madrid, Spain; *Yearbook of Tourism Statistics*.

SAINT KITTS AND NEVIS - TRACTORS IN USE

Statistical Office of the United Nations, Publishing Service, New York, New York 10017 (800) 253-9646; *Statistical Yearbook*.

SAINT KITTS AND NEVIS - TRADE - See SAINT KITTS AND NEVIS - FOREIGN TRADE

SAINT KITTS AND NEVIS - TRANSPORTATION AND COMMUNICATIONS

G.K. Hall and Company, 70 Lincoln Street, Boston, Massachusetts 02111 (617) 423-3990; *The World in Figures*.

SAINT KITTS AND NEVIS - UNEMPLOYMENT

International Labour Office, I.L.O. Publications, CH-1211, Geneva 22, Switzerland; *Yearbook of Labour Statistics*.

SAINT KITTS AND NEVIS - VITAL STATISTICS

G.K. Hall and Company, 70 Lincoln Street, Boston, Massachusetts 02111 (617) 423-3990; *The World in Figures*.

Statistical Office of the United Nations, Publishing Service, New York, New York 10017 (800) 253-9646; *Statistical Yearbook*.

World Health Organization, Office of Publications, Avenue Appia, CH-1211 Geneva 27, Switzerland (Telephone Number in U.S. (518) 436-9686); *World Health Statistics Annual*.

SAINT KITTS AND NEVIS - WAGES

G.K. Hall and Company, 70 Lincoln Street, Boston, Massachusetts 02111 (617) 423-3990; *The World in Figures*.

International Labour Office, I.L.O. Publications, CH-1211, Geneva 22, Switzerland; *Yearbook of Labour Statistics*.

SAINT KITTS AND NEVIS - WEATHER

G.K. Hall and Company, 70 Lincoln Street, Boston, Massachusetts 02111 (617) 423-3990; *The World in Figures*.

Saint Lucia - National Statistical Office

Statistical Department, Ministry of Trade, Industry, and Tourism, Post Office Building, Castries, Saint Lucia.

Saint Lucia - Primary Statistics Source

Development, Planning and Statistics Division, Premier's Office, Post Office Building, Castries, Saint Lucia; *Annual Statistical Digest*.

SAINT LUCIA - AGRICULTURE

Food and Agricultural Organization of the United Nations (FAO) Via delle Terme di Caracalla, 00100 Rome, Italy (Telephone Number in U.S. (202) 653-2400); *Production Yearbook, The State of Food and Agriculture,* and *Trade Yearbook*.

G.K. Hall and Company, 70 Lincoln Street, Boston, Massachusetts 02111 (617) 423-3990; *The World in Figures*.

Statistical Office of the United Nations, Publishing Service, New York, New York 10017 (800) 253-9646; *Statistical Yearbook*.

The World Bank, 1818 H Street, NW, Washington, D.C. 20433 (202) 477-1234; *World Tables*.

SAINT LUCIA - AIRLINE SERVICE

G.K. Hall and Company, 70 Lincoln Street, Boston, Massachusetts 02111 (617) 423-3990; *The World in Figures*.

SAINT LUCIA - ANIMAL HEALTH

Food and Agricultural Organization of the United Nations (FAO), Via delle Terme di Caracalla, 00100, Rome, Italy (Telephone Number in U.S. (202) 653-2400); *Animal Health Yearbook*.

SAINT LUCIA - AREA AND DENSITY OF POPULATION

Food and Agricultural Organization of the United Nations (FAO) Via delle Terme di Caracalla, 00100 Rome, Italy (Telephone Number in U.S. (202) 653-2400); *The State of Food and Agriculture*.

G.K. Hall and Company, 70 Lincoln Street, Boston, Massachusetts 02111 (617) 423-3990; *The World in Figures*.

Statistical Office of the United Nations, Publishing Service, New York, New York 10017 (800) 253-9646; *Statistical Yearbook*.

United Nations Educational, Scientific and Cultural Organization (UNESCO), 7 Place de Fontenoy, F-75700 Paris, France (Telephone Number in U.S. (212) 963-5981); *Statistical Yearbook*.

SAINT LUCIA - BALANCE OF PAYMENTS

G.K. Hall and Company, 70 Lincoln Street, Boston, Massachusetts 02111 (617) 423-3990; *The World in Figures*.

The World Bank, 1818 H Street, NW, Washington, D.C. 20433 (202) 477-1234; *World Tables*.

SAINT LUCIA - BANKING

G.K. Hall and Company, 70 Lincoln Street, Boston, Massachusetts 02111 (617) 423-3990; *The World in Figures*.

SAINT LUCIA - BIRTH RATES

Statistical Office of the United Nations, Publishing Service, New York, New York 10017 (800) 253-9646; *Demographic Yearbook*, and *Statistical Yearbook*.

The World Bank, 1818 H Street, NW, Washington, D.C. 20433 (202) 477-1234; *World Tables*.

World Health Organization, Office of Publications, Avenue Appia, CH-1211 Geneva 27, Switzerland (Telephone Number in U.S. (518) 436-9686); *World Health Statistics Annual*.

SAINT LUCIA - BONDS

G.K. Hall and Company, 70 Lincoln Street, Boston, Massachusetts 02111 (617) 423-3990; *The World in Figures*.

SAINT LUCIA - BOOK PRODUCTION

G.K. Hall and Company, 70 Lincoln Street, Boston, Massachusetts 02111 (617) 423-3990; *The World in Figures*.

SAINT LUCIA - BROADCASTING

Billboard Limited, P.O. Box 9027, 1006 AA Amsterdam, The Netherlands (Telephone Number in U.S. (212) 764-7300); *World Radio TV Handbook*.

G.K. Hall and Company, 70 Lincoln Street, Boston, Massachusetts 02111 (617) 423-3990; *The World in Figures*.

SAINT LUCIA - BUSINESS

G.K. Hall and Company, 70 Lincoln Street, Boston, Massachusetts 02111 (617) 423-3990; *The World in Figures*.

SAINT LUCIA - CALORIE SUPPLY

Food and Agricultural Organization of the United Nations (FAO) Via delle Terme di Caracalla, 00100 Rome, Italy (Telephone Number in U.S. (202) 653-2400); *The State of Food and Agriculture*.

SAINT LUCIA - CATTLE - See SAINT LUCIA - LIVESTOCK AND POULTRY

SAINT LUCIA - COCOA PRODUCTION - See SAINT LUCIA - CROPS

SAINT LUCIA - CHEMICAL (ORGANIC) PRODUCTION - See SAINT LUCIA - MINING AND MINERAL PRODUCTS

SAINT LUCIA - CLASS STRUCTURE

G.K. Hall and Company, 70 Lincoln Street, Boston, Massachusetts 02111 (617) 423-3990; *The World in Figures*.

SAINT LUCIA - CLIMATE

G.K. Hall and Company, 70 Lincoln Street, Boston, Massachusetts 02111 (617) 423-3990; *The World in Figures*.

SAINT LUCIA - COAL PRODUCTION - See SAINT LUCIA - MINING AND MINERAL PRODUCTS

SAINT LUCIA - COMMUNICATIONS

G.K. Hall and Company, 70 Lincoln Street, Boston, Massachusetts 02111 (617) 423-3990; *The World in Figures*.

SAINT LUCIA - CONSUMER PRICE INDEX

G.K. Hall and Company, 70 Lincoln Street, Boston, Massachusetts 02111 (617) 423-3990; *The World in Figures*.

Statistical Office of the United Nations, Publishing Service, New York, New York 10017 (800) 253-9646; *Statistical Yearbook*.

SAINT LUCIA - CONSUMER PRICES

International Labour Office, I.L.O. Publications, CH-1211, Geneva 22, Switzerland; *Yearbook of Labour Statistics*.

SAINT LUCIA - CONSUMPTION

G.K. Hall and Company, 70 Lincoln Street, Boston, Massachusetts 02111 (617) 423-3990; *The World in Figures*.

SAINT LUCIA - CORN PRODUCTION - See SAINT LUCIA - CROPS

SAINT LUCIA - CORPORATE TAXES - See SAINT LUCIA - TAXATION

SAINT LUCIA - CROPS

Food and Agricultural Organization of the United Nations (FAO) Via delle Terme di Caracalla, 00100 Rome, Italy (Telephone Number in U.S. (202) 653-2400); *The State of Food and Agriculture*.

G.K. Hall and Company, 70 Lincoln Street, Boston, Massachusetts 02111 (617) 423-3990; *The World in Figures*.

Statistical Office of the United Nations, Publishing Service, New York, New York 10017 (800) 253-9646; *Statistical Yearbook*.

SAINT LUCIA - CUSTOMS DUTIES

G.K. Hall and Company, 70 Lincoln Street, Boston, Massachusetts 02111 (617) 423-3990; *The World in Figures*.

SAINT LUCIA - DAIRY PRODUCTS

Food and Agricultural Organization of the United Nations (FAO) Via delle Terme di Caracalla, 00100 Rome, Italy (Telephone Number in U.S. (202) 653-2400); *The State of Food and Agriculture*.

SAINT LUCIA - DEATH RATES

G.K. Hall and Company, 70 Lincoln Street, Boston, Massachusetts 02111 (617) 423-3990; *The World in Figures*.

Statistical Office of the United Nations, Publishing Service, New York, New York 10017 (800) 253-9646; *Statistical Yearbook*.

World Health Organization, Office of Publications, Avenue Appia, CH-1211 Geneva 27, Switzerland (Telephone Number in U.S. (518) 436-9686); *World Health Statistics Annual*.

SAINT LUCIA - DEFENSE EXPENDITURES

G.K. Hall and Company, 70 Lincoln Street, Boston, Massachusetts 02111 (617) 423-3990; *The World in Figures*.

SAINT LUCIA - DEMOGRAPHY

G.K. Hall and Company, 70 Lincoln Street, Boston, Massachusetts 02111 (617) 423-3990; *The World in Figures*.

SAINT LUCIA - DEVELOPMENT ASSISTANCE

G.K. Hall and Company, 70 Lincoln Street, Boston, Massachusetts 02111 (617) 423-3990; *The World in Figures*.

SAINT LUCIA - DISEASES

G.K. Hall and Company, 70 Lincoln Street, Boston, Massachusetts 02111 (617) 423-3990; *The World in Figures*.

World Health Organization, Office of Publications, Avenue Appia, CH-1211 Geneva 27, Switzerland (Telephone Number in U.S. (518) 436-9686); *World Health Statistics Annual*.

SAINT LUCIA - DIVORCE RATES

Statistical Office of the United Nations, Publishing Service, New York, New York 10017 (800) 253-9646; *Demographic Yearbook*.

SAINT LUCIA - DOMESTIC PRODUCT

G.K. Hall and Company, 70 Lincoln Street, Boston, Massachusetts 02111 (617) 423-3990; *The World in Figures*.

SAINT LUCIA - ECONOMY

G.K. Hall and Company, 70 Lincoln Street, Boston, Massachusetts 02111 (617) 423-3990; *The World in Figures*.

SAINT LUCIA - EDUCATION

G.K. Hall and Company, 70 Lincoln Street, Boston, Massachusetts 02111 (617) 423-3990; *The World in Figures*.

United Nations Educational, Scientific and Cultural Organization (UNESCO), 7 Place de Fontenoy, F-75700 Paris, France (Telephone Number in U.S. (212) 963-5981); *Statistical Yearbook*.

The World Bank, 1818 H Street, NW, Washington, D.C. 20433 (202) 477-1234; *World Tables*.

SAINT LUCIA - EGG PRODUCTION - See SAINT LUCIA - DAIRY PRODUCTS

SAINT LUCIA - ELECTRICITY

Statistical Office of the United Nations, Publishing Service, New York, New York 10017 (800) 253-9646; *Statistical Yearbook*.

SAINT LUCIA - EMPLOYMENT

International Labour Office, I.L.O. Publications, CH-1211, Geneva 22, Switzerland; *Yearbook of Labour Statistics*.

SAINT LUCIA - ENERGY

Food and Agricultural Organization of the United Nations (FAO) Via delle Terme di Caracalla, 00100 Rome, Italy (Telephone Number in U.S. (202) 653-2400); *The State of Food and Agriculture*.

G.K. Hall and Company, 70 Lincoln Street, Boston, Massachusetts 02111 (617) 423-3990; *The World in Figures*.

Statistical Office of the United Nations, Publishing Service, New York, New York 10017 (800) 253-9646; *Energy Statistics Yearbook*, and *Statistical Yearbook*.

SAINT LUCIA - EXPORTS

Food and Agricultural Organization of the United Nations (FAO) Via delle Terme di Caracalla, 00100 Rome, Italy (Telephone Number in U.S. (202) 653-2400); *The State of Food and Agriculture*.

G.K. Hall and Company, 70 Lincoln Street, Boston, Massachusetts 02111 (617) 423-3990; *The World in Figures*.

The World Bank, 1818 H Street, NW, Washington, D.C. 20433 (202) 477-1234; *World Tables*.

SAINT LUCIA - EXTERNAL INDEBTEDNESS

The World Bank, 1818 H Street, NW, Washington, D.C. 20433 (202) 477-1234; *World Tables*.

SAINT LUCIA - EXTERNAL TRADE

Food and Agricultural Organization of the United Nations (FAO) Via delle Terme di Caracalla, 00100 Rome, Italy (Telephone Number in U.S. (202) 653-2400); *The State of Food and Agriculture*, and *Trade Yearbook*.

G.K. Hall and Company, 70 Lincoln Street, Boston, Massachusetts 02111 (617) 423-3990; *The World in Figures*.

Statistical Office of the United Nations, Publishing Service, New York, New York 10017 (800) 253-9646; *Statistical Yearbook*.

SAINT LUCIA - FARM CROPS - See SAINT LUCIA - CROPS

SAINT LUCIA - FERTILITY RATES

The World Bank, 1818 H Street, NW, Washington, D.C. 20433 (202) 477-1234; *World Tables*.

SAINT LUCIA - FERTILIZER

Food and Agricultural Organization of the United Nations (FAO) Via delle Terme di Caracalla, 00100 Rome, Italy (Telephone Number in U.S. (202) 653-2400); *The State of Food and Agriculture.*

Statistical Office of the United Nations, Publishing Service, New York, New York 10017 (800) 253-9646; *Statistical Yearbook.*

SAINT LUCIA - FETAL MORTALITY

Statistical Office of the United Nations, Publishing Service, New York, New York 10017 (800) 253-9646; *Demographic Yearbook.*

World Health Organization, Office of Publications, Avenue Appia, CH-1211 Geneva 27, Switzerland (Telephone Number in U.S. (518) 436-9686); *World Health Statistics Annual.*

SAINT LUCIA - FINANCE

G.K. Hall and Company, 70 Lincoln Street, Boston, Massachusetts 02111 (617) 423-3990; *The World in Figures.*

SAINT LUCIA - FISHERIES

Food and Agricultural Organization of the United Nations (FAO) Via delle Terme di Caracalla, 00100 Rome, Italy (Telephone Number in U.S. (202) 653-2400); *The State of Food and Agriculture,* and *Yearbook of Fishery Statistics.*

Statistical Office of the United Nations, Publishing Service, New York, New York 10017 (800) 253-9646; *Statistical Yearbook.*

SAINT LUCIA - FOOD

Food and Agricultural Organization of the United Nations (FAO), Via delle Terme di Caracalla, 00100 Rome, Italy (Telephone Number in U.S. (202) 653-2400); *Production Yearbook,* and *The State of Food and Agriculture.*

G.K. Hall and Company, 70 Lincoln Street, Boston, Massachusetts 02111 (617) 423-3990; *The World in Figures.*

SAINT LUCIA - FOREIGN AID

G.K. Hall and Company, 70 Lincoln Street, Boston, Massachusetts 02111 (617) 423-3990; *The World in Figures.*

SAINT LUCIA - FOREIGN TRADE

Food and Agricultural Organization of the United Nations (FAO) Via delle Terme di Caracalla, 00100 Rome, Italy (Telephone Number in U.S. (202) 653-2400); *The State of Food and Agriculture.*

G.K. Hall and Company, 70 Lincoln Street, Boston, Massachusetts 02111 (617) 423-3990; *The World in Figures.*

Statistical Office of the United Nations, Publishing Service, New York, New York 10017 (800) 253-9646; *International Trade Statistics Yearbook,* and *Statistical Yearbook.*

The World Bank, 1818 H Street, NW, Washington, D.C. 20433 (202) 477-1234; *World Tables.*

SAINT LUCIA - FORESTRY AND FOREST PRODUCTS

Food and Agricultural Organization of the United Nations (FAO) Via delle Terme di Caracalla, 00100 Rome, Italy (Telephone Number in U.S. (202) 653-2400); *The State of Food and Agriculture.*

G.K. Hall and Company, 70 Lincoln Street, Boston, Massachusetts 02111 (617) 423-3990; *The World in Figures.*

Statistical Office of the United Nations, Publishing Service, New York, New York 10017 (800) 253-9646; *Statistical Yearbook.*

United Nations Educational, Scientific and Cultural Organization (UNESCO), 7 Place de Fontenoy, F-75700 Paris, France (Telephone Number in U.S. (212) 963-5981); *Statistical Yearbook.*

SAINT LUCIA - GENERAL MORTALITY

Statistical Office of the United Nations, Publishing Service, New York, New York 10017 (800) 253-9646; *Demographic Yearbook.*

World Health Organization, Office of Publications, Avenue Appia, CH-1211 Geneva 27, Switzerland (Telephone Number in U.S. (518) 436-9686); *World Health Statistics Annual.*

SAINT LUCIA - GOLD HOLDINGS

The World Bank, 1818 H Street, NW, Washington, D.C. 20433 (202) 477-1234; *World Tables.*

SAINT LUCIA - GOVERNMENT

G.K. Hall and Company, 70 Lincoln Street, Boston, Massachusetts 02111 (617) 423-3990; *The World in Figures.*

SAINT LUCIA - GOVERNMENT EXPENDITURES

The World Bank, 1818 H Street, NW, Washington, D.C. 20433 (202) 477-1234; *World Tables.*

SAINT LUCIA - GOVERNMENT REVENUES

The World Bank, 1818 H Street, NW, Washington, D.C. 20433 (202) 477-1234; *World Tables.*

SAINT LUCIA - GRAIN PRODUCTION - See SAINT LUCIA - CROPS

SAINT LUCIA - GROSS DOMESTIC PRODUCT

G.K. Hall and Company, 70 Lincoln Street, Boston, Massachusetts 02111 (617) 423-3990; *The World in Figures.*

Statistical Office of the United Nations, Publishing Service, New York, New York 10017 (800) 253-9646; *Statistical Yearbook.*

The World Bank, 1818 H Street, NW, Washington, D.C. 20433 (202) 477-1234; *World Tables.*

SAINT LUCIA - GROSS NATIONAL PRODUCT

The World Bank, 1818 H Street, NW, Washington, D.C. 20433 (202) 477-1234; *World Tables.*

SAINT LUCIA - HEALTH

G.K. Hall and Company, 70 Lincoln Street, Boston, Massachusetts 02111 (617) 423-3990; *The World in Figures.*

Statistical Office of the United Nations, Publishing Service, New York, New York 10017 (800) 253-9646; *Statistical Yearbook.*

World Health Organization, Office of Publications, Avenue Appia, CH-1211 Geneva 27, Switzerland (Telephone Number in U.S. (518) 436-9686); *World Health Statistics Annual.*

SAINT LUCIA - HIGHWAYS

G.K. Hall and Company, 70 Lincoln Street, Boston, Massachusetts 02111 (617) 423-3990; *The World in Figures*.

SAINT LUCIA - HORSES - See SAINT LUCIA - LIVESTOCK AND POULTRY

SAINT LUCIA - HOURS OF WORK - See SAINT LUCIA - EMPLOYMENT

SAINT LUCIA - ILLITERATE POPULATION

G.K. Hall and Company, 70 Lincoln Street, Boston, Massachusetts 02111 (617) 423-3990; *The World in Figures*.

United Nations Educational, Scientific and Cultural Organization (UNESCO), 7 Place de Fontenoy, F-75700 Paris, France (Telephone Number in U.S. (212) 963-5981); *Statistical Yearbook*.

SAINT LUCIA - IMPORTS

Food and Agricultural Organization of the United Nations (FAO) Via dollo Tormo di Caracalla, 00100 Romo, Italy (Tolophono Number in U.S. (202) 653-2400); *The State of Food and Agriculture*.

G.K. Hall and Company, 70 Lincoln Street, Boston, Massachusetts 02111 (617) 423-3990; *The World in Figures*.

The World Bank, 1818 H Street, NW, Washington, D.C. 20433 (202) 477-1234; *World Tables*.

SAINT LUCIA - INDUSTRY

G.K. Hall and Company, 70 Lincoln Street, Boston, Massachusetts 02111 (617) 423-3990; *The World in Figures*.

International Labour Office, I.L.O. Publications, CH-1211, Geneva 22, Switzerland; *Yearbook of Labour Statistics*.

The World Bank, 1818 H Street, NW, Washington, D.C. 20433 (202) 477-1234; *World Tables*.

SAINT LUCIA - INFANT AND MATERNAL MORTALITY

Statistical Office of the United Nations, Publishing Service, New York, New York 10017 (800) 253-9646; *Demographic Yearbook*, and *Statistical Yearbook*.

The World Bank, 1818 H Street, NW, Washington, D.C. 20433 (202) 477-1234; *World Tables*.

World Health Organization, Office of Publications, Avenue Appia, CH-1211 Geneva 27, Switzerland (Telephone Number in U.S. (518) 436-9686); *World Health Statistics Annual*.

SAINT LUCIA - INTERNATIONAL RESERVES EXCLUDING GOLD

The World Bank, 1818 H Street, NW, Washington, D.C. 20433 (202) 477-1234; *World Tables*.

SAINT LUCIA - LABOR FORCE

Food and Agricultural Organization of the United Nations (FAO) Via delle Terme di Caracalla, 00100 Rome, Italy (Telephone Number in U.S. (202) 653-2400); *The State of Food and Agriculture*.

G.K. Hall and Company, 70 Lincoln Street, Boston, Massachusetts 02111 (617) 423-3990; *The World in Figures*.

The World Bank, 1818 H Street, NW, Washington, D.C. 20433 (202) 477-1234; *World Tables*.

SAINT LUCIA - LABOR PRODUCTIVITY

International Labour Office, I.L.O. Publications, CH-1211, Geneva 22, Switzerland; *Yearbook of Labour Statistics*.

SAINT LUCIA - LAND USE

Food and Agricultural Organization of the United Nations (FAO), Via delle Terme di Caracalla, 00100 Rome, Italy (Telephone Number in U.S. (202) 653-2400); *Production Yearbook*.

G.K. Hall and Company, 70 Lincoln Street, Boston, Massachusetts 02111 (617) 423-3990; *The World in Figures*.

SAINT LUCIA - LIBRARIES

United Nations Educational, Scientific and Cultural Organization (UNESCO), 7 Place de Fontenoy, F-75700 Paris, France (Telephone Number in U.S. (212) 963-5981); *Statistical Yearbook*.

SAINT LUCIA - LIVESTOCK AND POULTRY

Food and Agricultural Organization of the United Nations (FAO), Via delle Terme di Caracalla, 00100 Rome, Italy (Telephone Number in U.S. (202) 653-2400); *Production Yearbook*, and *The State of Food and Agriculture*.

G.K. Hall and Company, 70 Lincoln Street, Boston, Massachusetts 02111 (617) 423-3990; *The World in Figures*.

Statistical Office of the United Nations, Publishing Service, New York, New York 10017 (800) 253-9646; *Statistical Yearbook*.

SAINT LUCIA - LIVING LEVELS

G.K. Hall and Company, 70 Lincoln Street, Boston, Massachusetts 02111 (617) 423-3990; *The World in Figures*.

SAINT LUCIA - MAIL TRAFFIC - NUMBER OF ITEMS SENT AND RECEIVED

Statistical Office of the United Nations, Publishing Service, New York, New York 10017 (800) 253-9646; *Statistical Yearbook*.

SAINT LUCIA - MANUFACTURING

G.K. Hall and Company, 70 Lincoln Street, Boston, Massachusetts 02111 (617) 423-3990; *The World in Figures*.

The World Bank, 1818 H Street, NW, Washington, D.C. 20433 (202) 477-1234; *World Tables*.

SAINT LUCIA - MARRIAGE RATES

Statistical Office of the United Nations, Publishing Service, New York, New York 10017 (800) 253-9646; *Demographic Yearbook*, and *Statistical Yearbook*.

SAINT LUCIA - MEAT PRODUCTION - See SAINT LUCIA - LIVESTOCK AND POULTRY

SAINT LUCIA - MERCHANT SHIPPING

G.K. Hall and Company, 70 Lincoln Street, Boston, Massachusetts 02111 (617) 423-3990; *The World in Figures*.

Statistical Office of the United Nations, Publishing Service, New York, New York 10017 (800) 253-9646; *Statistical Yearbook*.

SAINT LUCIA - MILITARY

G.K. Hall and Company, 70 Lincoln Street, Boston, Massachusetts 02111 (617) 423-3990; *The World in Figures*.

SAINT LUCIA - MINING AND MINERAL PRODUCTS

G.K. Hall and Company, 70 Lincoln Street, Boston, Massachusetts 02111 (617) 423-3990; *The World in Figures*.

SAINT LUCIA - MONEY SUPPLY

G.K. Hall and Company, 70 Lincoln Street, Boston, Massachusetts 02111 (617) 423-3990; *The World in Figures*.

The World Bank, 1818 H Street, NW, Washington, D.C. 20433 (202) 477-1234; *World Tables*.

SAINT LUCIA - MOTOR VEHICLES - IN USE

G.K. Hall and Company, 70 Lincoln Street, Boston, Massachusetts 02111 (617) 423-3990; *The World in Figures*.

Statistical Office of the United Nations, Publishing Service, New York, New York 10017 (800) 253-9646; *Statistical Yearbook*.

SAINT LUCIA - MULES - See SAINT LUCIA - LIVESTOCK AND POULTRY

SAINT LUCIA - MUSEUMS

United Nations Educational, Scientific and Cultural Organization (UNESCO), 7 Place de Fontenoy, F-75700 Paris, France (Telephone Number in U.S. (212) 963-5981); *Statistical Yearbook*.

SAINT LUCIA - NATALITY - See SAINT LUCIA - BIRTH RATE

SAINT LUCIA - NATIONAL ACCOUNTS

Statistical Office of the United Nations, Publishing Service, New York, New York 10017 (800) 253-9646; *National Accounts Statistics*, and *Statistical Yearbook*.

SAINT LUCIA - NATIONAL INCOME

G.K. Hall and Company, 70 Lincoln Street, Boston, Massachusetts 02111 (617) 423-3990; *The World in Figures*.

Statistical Office of the United Nations, Publishing Service, New York, New York 10017 (800) 253-9646; *Statistical Yearbook*.

SAINT LUCIA - NEWSPAPER PRODUCTION - See SAINT LUCIA - FORESTRY AND FOREST PRODUCTS

SAINT LUCIA - OCCUPATIONS - See SAINT LUCIA - LABOR FORCE

SAINT LUCIA - PESTICIDE USE

Food and Agricultural Organization of the United Nations (FAO) Via delle Terme di Caracalla, 00100 Rome, Italy (Telephone Number in U.S. (202) 653-2400); *The State of Food and Agriculture*.

SAINT LUCIA - PETROLEUM INDUSTRY

Food and Agricultural Organization of the United Nations (FAO) Via delle Terme di Caracalla, 00100 Rome, Italy (Telephone Number in U.S. (202) 653-2400); *The State of Food and Agriculture*.

G.K. Hall and Company, 70 Lincoln Street, Boston, Massachusetts 02111 (617) 423-3990; *The World in Figures*.

SAINT LUCIA - PIGS - See SAINT LUCIA - LIVESTOCK AND POULTRY

SAINT LUCIA - POPULATION

Food and Agricultural Organization of the United Nations (FAO), Via delle Terme di Caracalla, 00100 Rome, Italy (Telephone Number in U.S. (202) 653-2400); *Production Yearbook*.

G.K. Hall and Company, 70 Lincoln Street, Boston, Massachusetts 02111 (617) 423-3990; *The World in Figures*.

International Labour Office, I.L.O. Publications, CH-1211, Geneva 22, Switzerland; *Yearbook of Labour Statistics*.

Statistical Office of the United Nations, Publishing Service, New York, New York 10017 (800) 253-9646; *Demographic Yearbook*, and *Statistical Yearbook*.

United Nations Educational, Scientific and Cultural Organization (UNESCO), 7 Place de Fontenoy, F-75700 Paris, France (Telephone Number in U.S. (212) 963-5981); *Statistical Yearbook*.

World Health Organization, Office of Publications, Avenue Appia, CH-1211 Geneva 27, Switzerland (Telephone Number in U.S. (518) 436-9686); *World Health Statistics Annual*.

SAINT LUCIA - PRICES

Food and Agricultural Organization of the United Nations (FAO), Via delle Terme di Caracalla, 00100 Rome, Italy (Telephone Number in U.S. (202) 653-2400); *Production Yearbook*, and *The State of Food and Agriculture*.

G.K. Hall and Company, 70 Lincoln Street, Boston, Massachusetts 02111 (617) 423-3990; *The World in Figures*.

International Labour Office, I.L.O. Publications, CH-1211, Geneva 22, Switzerland; *Yearbook of Labour Statistics*.

SAINT LUCIA - PRODUCTION

G.K. Hall and Company, 70 Lincoln Street, Boston, Massachusetts 02111 (617) 423-3990; *The World in Figures*.

SAINT LUCIA - RAILWAY USE

G.K. Hall and Company, 70 Lincoln Street, Boston, Massachusetts 02111 (617) 423-3990; *The World in Figures*.

SAINT LUCIA - RENT PRICES

International Labour Office, I.L.O. Publications, CH-1211, Geneva 22, Switzerland; *Yearbook of Labour Statistics*.

SAINT LUCIA - RETAIL TRADE

G.K. Hall and Company, 70 Lincoln Street, Boston, Massachusetts 02111 (617) 423-3990; *The World in Figures*.

SAINT LUCIA - SHEEP - See SAINT LUCIA - LIVESTOCK AND POULTRY

SAINT LUCIA - SOCIAL DATA

G.K. Hall and Company, 70 Lincoln Street, Boston, Massachusetts 02111 (617) 423-3990; *The World in Figures.*

SAINT LUCIA - STOCKS - COMMODITY - MARKET PRICE - INDEX

Food and Agricultural Organization of the United Nations (FAO) Via delle Terme di Caracalla, 00100 Rome, Italy (Telephone Number in U.S. (202) 653-2400); *The State of Food and Agriculture.*

SAINT LUCIA - TAXATION

G.K. Hall and Company, 70 Lincoln Street, Boston, Massachusetts 02111 (617) 423-3990; *The World in Figures.*

The World Bank, 1818 H Street, NW, Washington, D.C. 20433 (202) 477-1234; *World Tables.*

SAINT LUCIA - TELEPHONES IN USE

American Telephone and Telegraph Company, 26 Parsippany Road, Whippany, New Jersey 07981 (800) 338-4038; *The World's Telephones.*

G.K. Hall and Company, 70 Lincoln Street, Boston, Massachusetts 02111 (617) 423-3990; *The World in Figures.*

Statistical Office of the United Nations, Publishing Service, New York, New York 10017 (800) 253-9646; *Statistical Yearbook.*

SAINT LUCIA - TEXTILE INDUSTRY

G.K. Hall and Company, 70 Lincoln Street, Boston, Massachusetts 02111 (617) 423-3990; *The World in Figures.*

SAINT LUCIA - TOURISM

G.K. Hall and Company, 70 Lincoln Street, Boston, Massachusetts 02111 (617) 423-3990; *The World in Figures.*

World Tourism Organization, Calle Capitan Haya 42, E-28020 Madrid, Spain; *Yearbook of Tourism Statistics.*

SAINT LUCIA - TRACTORS IN USE

Statistical Office of the United Nations, Publishing Service, New York, New York 10017 (800) 253-9646; *Statistical Yearbook.*

SAINT LUCIA - TRADE - See SAINT LUCIA - FOREIGN TRADE

SAINT LUCIA - TRANSPORTATION AND COMMUNICATIONS

G.K. Hall and Company, 70 Lincoln Street, Boston, Massachusetts 02111 (617) 423-3990; *The World in Figures.*

SAINT LUCIA - UNEMPLOYMENT

International Labour Office, I.L.O. Publications, CH-1211, Geneva 22, Switzerland; *Yearbook of Labour Statistics.*

SAINT LUCIA - VITAL STATISTICS

G.K. Hall and Company, 70 Lincoln Street, Boston, Massachusetts 02111 (617) 423-3990; *The World in Figures.*

Statistical Office of the United Nations, Publishing Service, New York, New York 10017 (800) 253-9646; *Statistical Yearbook.*

World Health Organization, Office of Publications, Avenue Appia, CH-1211 Geneva 27, Switzerland (Telephone Number in U.S. (518) 436-9686); *World Health Statistics Annual.*

SAINT LUCIA - WAGES

G.K. Hall and Company, 70 Lincoln Street, Boston, Massachusetts 02111 (617) 423-3990; *The World in Figures.*

International Labour Office, I.L.O. Publications, CH-1211, Geneva 22, Switzerland; *Yearbook of Labour Statistics.*

SAINT LUCIA - WEATHER

G.K. Hall and Company, 70 Lincoln Street, Boston, Massachusetts 02111 (617) 423-3990; *The World in Figures.*

Saint Pierre and Miquelon - Primary Statistics Sources

Institut National de la Statistique et des Etudes Economiques (INSEE), 18 boulevard Adolphe Pinard, 75675 Paris Cedex 14, France; *Annuaire Statistique des territoires d'outre mer* (Statistical yearbook of overseas territories).

SAINT PIERRE AND MIQUELON - AGRICULTURE

Food and Agricultural Organization of the United Nations (FAO) Via delle Terme di Caracalla, 00100 Rome, Italy (Telephone Number in U.S. (202) 653-2400); *Production Yearbook, The State of Food and Agriculture,* and *Trade Yearbook.*

G.K. Hall and Company, 70 Lincoln Street, Boston, Massachusetts 02111 (617) 423-3990; *The World in Figures.*

SAINT PIERRE AND MIQUELON - AIRLINE SERVICE

G.K. Hall and Company, 70 Lincoln Street, Boston, Massachusetts 02111 (617) 423-3990; *The World in Figures.*

SAINT PIERRE AND MIQUELON - AREA AND DENSITY OF POPULATION

Food and Agricultural Organization of the United Nations (FAO) Via delle Terme di Caracalla, 00100 Rome, Italy (Telephone Number in U.S. (202) 653-2400); *The State of Food and Agriculture.*

G.K. Hall and Company, 70 Lincoln Street, Boston, Massachusetts 02111 (617) 423-3990; *The World in Figures.*

Statistical Office of the United Nations, Publishing Service, New York, New York 10017 (800) 253-9646; *Statistical Yearbook.*

United Nations Educational, Scientific and Cultural Organization (UNESCO), 7 Place de Fontenoy, F-75700 Paris, France (Telephone Number in U.S. (212) 963-5981); *Statistical Yearbook.*

SAINT PIERRE AND MIQUELON - BALANCE OF PAYMENTS

G.K. Hall and Company, 70 Lincoln Street, Boston, Massachusetts 02111 (617) 423-3990; *The World in Figures.*

SAINT PIERRE AND MIQUELON - BANKING

G.K. Hall and Company, 70 Lincoln Street, Boston, Massachusetts 02111 (617) 423-3990; *The World in Figures.*

SAINT PIERRE AND MIQUELON - BIRTH RATES

Statistical Office of the United Nations, Publishing Service, New York, New York 10017 (800) 253-9646; *Demographic Yearbook*, and *Statistical Yearbook*.

World Health Organization, Office of Publications, Avenue Appia, CH-1211 Geneva 27, Switzerland (Telephone Number in U.S. (518) 436-9686); *World Health Statistics Annual*.

SAINT PIERRE AND MIQUELON - BONDS

G.K. Hall and Company, 70 Lincoln Street, Boston, Massachusetts 02111 (617) 423-3990; *The World in Figures*.

SAINT PIERRE AND MIQUELON - BOOK PRODUCTION

G.K. Hall and Company, 70 Lincoln Street, Boston, Massachusetts 02111 (617) 423-3990; *The World in Figures*.

SAINT PIERRE AND MIQUELON - BROADCASTING

Billboard Limited, P.O. Box 9027, 1006 AA Amsterdam, The Netherlands (Telephone Number in U.S. (212) 764-7300); *World Radio TV Handbook*.

G.K. Hall and Company, 70 Lincoln Street, Boston, Massachusetts 02111 (617) 423-3990; *The World in Figures*.

United Nations Educational, Scientific and Cultural Organization (UNESCO), 7 Place de Fontenoy, F-75700 Paris, France (Telephone Number in U.S. (212) 963-5981); *Statistical Yearbook*.

SAINT PIERRE AND MIQUELON - BUSINESS

G.K. Hall and Company, 70 Lincoln Street, Boston, Massachusetts 02111 (617) 423-3990; *The World in Figures*.

SAINT PIERRE AND MIQUELON - CALORIE SUPPLY

Food and Agricultural Organization of the United Nations (FAO) Via delle Terme di Caracalla, 00100 Rome, Italy (Telephone Number in U.S. (202) 653-2400); *The State of Food and Agriculture*.

SAINT PIERRE AND MIQUELON - CHEMICAL (ORGANIC) PRODUCTION - See SAINT PIERRE AND MIQUELON - MINING AND MINERAL PRODUCTS

SAINT PIERRE AND MIQUELON - CLASS STRUCTURE

G.K. Hall and Company, 70 Lincoln Street, Boston, Massachusetts 02111 (617) 423-3990; *The World in Figures*.

SAINT PIERRE AND MIQUELON - CLIMATE

G.K. Hall and Company, 70 Lincoln Street, Boston, Massachusetts 02111 (617) 423-3990; *The World in Figures*.

SAINT PIERRE AND MIQUELON - COAL PRODUCTION - See SAINT PIERRE AND MIQUELON - MINING AND MINERAL PRODUCTS

SAINT PIERRE AND MIQUELON - COMMUNICATIONS

G.K. Hall and Company, 70 Lincoln Street, Boston, Massachusetts 02111 (617) 423-3990; *The World in Figures*.

SAINT PIERRE AND MIQUELON - CONSUMER PRICE INDEX

G.K. Hall and Company, 70 Lincoln Street, Boston, Massachusetts 02111 (617) 423-3990; *The World in Figures*.

SAINT PIERRE AND MIQUELON - CONSUMER PRICES

International Labour Office, I.L.O. Publications, CH-1211, Geneva 22, Switzerland; *Yearbook of Labour Statistics*.

SAINT PIERRE AND MIQUELON - CONSUMPTION

G.K. Hall and Company, 70 Lincoln Street, Boston, Massachusetts 02111 (617) 423-3990; *The World in Figures*.

SAINT PIERRE AND MIQUELON - CORN PRODUCTION - SAINT PIERRE AND MIQUELON

SAINT PIERRE AND MIQUELON - CORPORATE TAXES - See SAINT PIERRE AND MIQUELON - TAXATION

SAINT PIERRE AND MIQUELON - CUSTOMS DUTIES

G.K. Hall and Company, 70 Lincoln Street, Boston, Massachusetts 02111 (617) 423-3990; *The World in Figures*.

SAINT PIERRE AND MIQUELON - CROPS

Food and Agricultural Organization of the United Nations (FAO) Via delle Terme di Caracalla, 00100 Rome, Italy (Telephone Number in U.S. (202) 653-2400); *The State of Food and Agriculture*.

G.K. Hall and Company, 70 Lincoln Street, Boston, Massachusetts 02111 (617) 423-3990; *The World in Figures*.

SAINT PIERRE AND MIQUELON - DAIRY PRODUCTS

Food and Agricultural Organization of the United Nations (FAO) Via delle Terme di Caracalla, 00100 Rome, Italy (Telephone Number in U.S. (202) 653-2400); *The State of Food and Agriculture*.

SAINT PIERRE AND MIQUELON - DEATH RATES

G.K. Hall and Company, 70 Lincoln Street, Boston, Massachusetts 02111 (617) 423-3990; *The World in Figures*.

Statistical Office of the United Nations, Publishing Service, New York, New York 10017 (800) 253-9646; *Statistical Yearbook*.

SAINT PIERRE AND MIQUELON - DEFENSE EXPENDITURES

G.K. Hall and Company, 70 Lincoln Street, Boston, Massachusetts 02111 (617) 423-3990; *The World in Figures*.

SAINT PIERRE AND MIQUELON - DEMOGRAPHY

G.K. Hall and Company, 70 Lincoln Street, Boston, Massachusetts 02111 (617) 423-3990; *The World in Figures*.

SAINT PIERRE AND MIQUELON - DEVELOPMENT ASSISTANCE

G.K. Hall and Company, 70 Lincoln Street, Boston, Massachusetts 02111 (617) 423-3990; *The World in Figures*.

Statistical Office of the United Nations, Publishing Service, New York, New York 10017 (800) 253-9646; *Statistical Yearbook*.

SAINT PIERRE AND MIQUELON - DISEASE

G.K. Hall and Company, 70 Lincoln Street, Boston, Massachusetts 02111 (617) 423-3990; *The World in Figures*.

SAINT PIERRE AND MIQUELON - DIVORCE RATES

Statistical Office of the United Nations, Publishing Service, New York, New York 10017 (800) 253-9646; *Demographic Yearbook*, and *Statistical Yearbook*.

SAINT PIERRE AND MIQUELON - DOMESTIC PRODUCT

G.K. Hall and Company, 70 Lincoln Street, Boston, Massachusetts 02111 (617) 423-3990; *The World in Figures*.

SAINT PIERRE AND MIQUELON - ECONOMY

G.K. Hall and Company, 70 Lincoln Street, Boston, Massachusetts 02111 (617) 423-3990; *The World in Figures*.

SAINT PIERRE AND MIQUELON - EDUCATION

G.K. Hall and Company, 70 Lincoln Street, Boston, Massachusetts 02111 (617) 423-3990; *The World in Figures*.

SAINT PIERRE AND MIQUELON - EGG PRODUCTION AND CONSUMPTION - See SAINT PIERRE AND MIQUELON - DAIRY PRODUCTS

SAINT PIERRE AND MIQUELON - EMPLOYMENT

International Labour Office, I.L.O. Publications, CH-1211, Geneva 22, Switzerland; *Yearbook of Labour Statistics*.

SAINT PIERRE AND MIQUELON - ENERGY

Food and Agricultural Organization of the United Nations (FAO) Via delle Terme di Caracalla, 00100 Rome, Italy (Telephone Number in U.S. (202) 653-2400); *The State of Food and Agriculture*.

G.K. Hall and Company, 70 Lincoln Street, Boston, Massachusetts 02111 (617) 423-3990; *The World in Figures*.

Statistical Office of the United Nations, Publishing Service, New York, New York 10017 (800) 253-9646; *Energy Statistics Yearbook*, and *Statistical Yearbook*.

SAINT PIERRE AND MIQUELON - EXPORTS

Food and Agricultural Organization of the United Nations (FAO) Via delle Terme di Caracalla, 00100 Rome, Italy (Telephone Number in U.S. (202) 653-2400); *The State of Food and Agriculture*.

G.K. Hall and Company, 70 Lincoln Street, Boston, Massachusetts 02111 (617) 423-3990; *The World in Figures*.

International Monetary Fund, 700 Nineteenth Street, NW, Washington, D.C. 20431 (202) 623-7000; *Direction of Trade Statistics*.

SAINT PIERRE AND MIQUELON - EXTERNAL TRADE

Food and Agricultural Organization of the United Nations (FAO) Via delle Terme di Caracalla, 00100 Rome, Italy (Telephone Number in U.S. (202) 653-2400); *The State of Food and Agriculture*, and *Trade Yearbook*.

G.K. Hall and Company, 70 Lincoln Street, Boston, Massachusetts 02111 (617) 423-3990; *The World in Figures*.

Statistical Office of the United Nations, Publishing Service, New York, New York 10017 (800) 253-9646; *Statistical Yearbook*.

SAINT PIERRE AND MIQUELON - FARM CROPS - See SAINT PIERRE AND MIQUELON

SAINT PIERRE AND MIQUELON - FETAL MORTALITY

Statistical Office of the United Nations, Publishing Service, New York, New York 10017 (800) 253-9646; *Demographic Yearbook*.

World Health Organization, Office of Publications, Avenue Appia, CH-1211 Geneva 27, Switzerland (Telephone Number in U.S. (518) 436-9686); *World Health Statistics Annual*.

SAINT PIERRE AND MIQUELON - FERTILIZER

Food and Agricultural Organization of the United Nations (FAO) Via delle Terme di Caracalla, 00100 Rome, Italy (Telephone Number in U.S. (202) 653-2400); *The State of Food and Agriculture*.

SAINT PIERRE AND MIQUELON - FINANCE

G.K. Hall and Company, 70 Lincoln Street, Boston, Massachusetts 02111 (617) 423-3990; *The World in Figures*.

SAINT PIERRE AND MIQUELON - FISHERIES

Food and Agricultural Organization of the United Nations (FAO) Via delle Terme di Caracalla, 00100 Rome, Italy (Telephone Number in U.S. (202) 653-2400); *The State of Food and Agriculture*, and *Yearbook of Fishery Statistics*.

Statistical Office of the United Nations, Publishing Service, New York, New York 10017 (800) 253-9646; *Statistical Yearbook*.

SAINT PIERRE AND MIQUELON - FOOD

Food and Agricultural Organization of the United Nations (FAO), Via delle Terme di Caracalla, 00100 Rome, Italy (Telephone Number in U.S. (202) 653-2400); *Production Yearbook*, and *The State of Food and Agriculture*.

G.K. Hall and Company, 70 Lincoln Street, Boston, Massachusetts 02111 (617) 423-3990; *The World in Figures*.

SAINT PIERRE AND MIQUELON - FOREIGN AID

G.K. Hall and Company, 70 Lincoln Street, Boston, Massachusetts 02111 (617) 423-3990; *The World in Figures*.

SAINT PIERRE AND MIQUELON - FOREIGN TRADE

Food and Agricultural Organization of the United Nations (FAO) Via delle Terme di Caracalla, 00100 Rome, Italy (Telephone Number in U.S. (202) 653-2400); *The State of Food and Agriculture*.

G.K. Hall and Company, 70 Lincoln Street, Boston, Massachusetts 02111 (617) 423-3990; *The World in Figures*.

Statistical Office of the United Nations, Publishing Service, New York, New York 10017 (800) 253-9646; *International Trade Statistics Yearbook*.

SAINT PIERRE AND MIQUELON - FORESTRY AND FOREST PRODUCTS

Food and Agricultural Organization of the United Nations (FAO) Via delle Terme di Caracalla, 00100 Rome, Italy (Telephone Number in U.S. (202) 653-2400); *The State of Food and Agriculture*.

G.K. Hall and Company, 70 Lincoln Street, Boston, Massachusetts 02111 (617) 423-3990; *The World in Figures*.

SAINT PIERRE AND MIQUELON - GENERAL MORTALITY

Statistical Office of the United Nations, Publishing Service, New York, New York 10017 (800) 253-9646; *Demographic Yearbook*.

World Health Organization, Office of Publications, Avenue Appia, CH-1211 Geneva 27, Switzerland (Telephone Number in U.S. (518) 436-9686); *World Health Statistics Annual*.

SAINT PIERRE AND MIQUELON - GOVERNMENT

G.K. Hall and Company, 70 Lincoln Street, Boston, Massachusetts 02111 (617) 423-3990; *The World in Figures*.

SAINT PIERRE AND MIQUELON - GRAIN PRODUCTION - SAINT HELENA - CROPS

SAINT PIERRE AND MIQUELON - GROSS DOMESTIC PRODUCT

G.K. Hall and Company, 70 Lincoln Street, Boston, Massachusetts 02111 (617) 423-3990; *The World in Figures*.

SAINT PIERRE AND MIQUELON - HEALTH

G.K. Hall and Company, 70 Lincoln Street, Boston, Massachusetts 02111 (617) 423-3990; *The World in Figures*.

Statistical Office of the United Nations, Publishing Service, New York, New York 10017 (800) 253-9646; *Statistical Yearbook*.

SAINT PIERRE AND MIQUELON - HIGHWAYS

G.K. Hall and Company, 70 Lincoln Street, Boston, Massachusetts 02111 (617) 423-3990; *The World in Figures*.

SAINT PIERRE AND MIQUELON - HOURS OF WORK - See SAINT PIERRE AND MIQUELON - EMPLOYMENT

SAINT PIERRE AND MIQUELON - ILLITERATE POPULATION

G.K. Hall and Company, 70 Lincoln Street, Boston, Massachusetts 02111 (617) 423-3990; *The World in Figures*.

United Nations Educational, Scientific and Cultural Organization (UNESCO), 7 Place de Fontenoy, F-75700 Paris, France (Telephone Number in U.S. (212) 963-5981); *Statistical Yearbook*.

SAINT PIERRE AND MIQUELON - IMPORTS

Food and Agricultural Organization of the United Nations (FAO) Via delle Terme di Caracalla, 00100 Rome, Italy (Telephone Number in U.S. (202) 653-2400); *The State of Food and Agriculture*.

G.K. Hall and Company, 70 Lincoln Street, Boston, Massachusetts 02111 (617) 423-3990; *The World in Figures*.

International Monetary Fund, 700 Nineteenth Street, NW, Washington, D.C. 20431 (202) 623-7000; *Direction of Trade Statistics*.

SAINT PIERRE AND MIQUELON - INDUSTRY

G.K. Hall and Company, 70 Lincoln Street, Boston, Massachusetts 02111 (617) 423-3990; *The World in Figures*.

International Labour Office, I.L.O. Publications, CH-1211, Geneva 22, Switzerland; *Yearbook of Labour Statistics*.

SAINT PIERRE AND MIQUELON - INFANT AND MATERNAL MORTALITY

Statistical Office of the United Nations, Publishing Service, New York, New York 10017 (800) 253-9646; *Demographic Yearbook*, and *Statistical Yearbook*.

World Health Organization, Office of Publications, Avenue Appia, CH-1211 Geneva 27, Switzerland (Telephone Number in U.S. (518) 436-9686); *World Health Statistics Annual*.

SAINT PIERRE AND MIQUELON - LABOR FORCE

Food and Agricultural Organization of the United Nations (FAO) Via delle Terme di Caracalla, 00100 Rome, Italy (Telephone Number in U.S. (202) 653-2400); *The State of Food and Agriculture*.

G.K. Hall and Company, 70 Lincoln Street, Boston, Massachusetts 02111 (617) 423-3990; *The World in Figures*.

SAINT PIERRE AND MIQUELON - LABOR PRODUCTIVITY

International Labour Office, I.L.O. Publications, CH-1211, Geneva 22, Switzerland; *Yearbook of Labour Statistics*.

SAINT PIERRE AND MIQUELON - LAND USE

Food and Agricultural Organization of the United Nations (FAO), Via delle Terme di Caracalla, 00100 Rome, Italy (Telephone Number in U.S. (202) 653-2400); *Production Yearbook*.

G.K. Hall and Company, 70 Lincoln Street, Boston, Massachusetts 02111 (617) 423-3990; *The World in Figures*.

SAINT PIERRE AND MIQUELON - LIBRARIES

United Nations Educational, Scientific and Cultural Organization (UNESCO), 7 Place de Fontenoy, F-75700 Paris, France (Telephone Number in U.S. (212) 963-5981); *Statistical Yearbook*.

SAINT PIERRE AND MIQUELON - LIVESTOCK AND POULTRY

Food and Agricultural Organization of the United Nations (FAO), Via delle Terme di Caracalla, 00100 Rome, Italy (Telephone Number in U.S. (202) 653-2400); *Production Yearbook*, and *The State of Food and Agriculture*.

G.K. Hall and Company, 70 Lincoln Street, Boston, Massachusetts 02111 (617) 423-3990; *The World in Figures*.

SAINT PIERRE AND MIQUELON - LIVING LEVELS

G.K. Hall and Company, 70 Lincoln Street, Boston, Massachusetts 02111 (617) 423-3990; *The World in Figures*.

SAINT PIERRE AND MIQUELON - MAIL - NUMBER OF ITEMS SENT AND RECEIVED

Statistical Office of the United Nations, Publishing Service, New York, New York 10017 (800) 253-9646; *Statistical Yearbook*.

SAINT PIERRE AND MIQUELON - MANUFACTURING

G.K. Hall and Company, 70 Lincoln Street, Boston, Massachusetts 02111 (617) 423-3990; *The World in Figures*.

SAINT PIERRE AND MIQUELON - MARRIAGE RATES

Statistical Office of the United Nations, Publishing Service, New York, New York 10017 (800) 253-9646; *Demographic Yearbook*, and *Statistical Yearbook*.

SAINT PIERRE AND MIQUELON - MEAT PRODUCTION - See SAINT PIERRE AND MIQUELON - LIVESTOCK AND POULTRY

SAINT PIERRE AND MIQUELON - MERCHANT SHIPPING

G.K. Hall and Company, 70 Lincoln Street, Boston, Massachusetts 02111 (617) 423-3990; *The World in Figures*.

Statistical Office of the United Nations, Publishing Service, New York, New York 10017 (800) 253-9646; *Statistical Yearbook*.

SAINT PIERRE AND MIQUELON - MILITARY

G.K. Hall and Company, 70 Lincoln Street, Boston, Massachusetts 02111 (617) 423-3990; *The World in Figures*.

SAINT PIERRE AND MIQUELON - MINING AND MINERAL PRODUCTS

G.K. Hall and Company, 70 Lincoln Street, Boston, Massachusetts 02111 (617) 423-3990; *The World in Figures*.

SAINT PIERRE AND MIQUELON - MONEY SUPPLY

G.K. Hall and Company, 70 Lincoln Street, Boston, Massachusetts 02111 (617) 423-3990; *The World in Figures*.

SAINT PIERRE AND MIQUELON - MOTION PICTURES

Statistical Office of the United Nations, Publishing Service, New York, New York 10017 (800) 253-9646; *Statistical Yearbook*.

SAINT PIERRE AND MIQUELON - MOTOR VEHICLES IN USE

G.K. Hall and Company, 70 Lincoln Street, Boston, Massachusetts 02111 (617) 423-3990; *The World in Figures*.

SAINT PIERRE AND MIQUELON - MUSEUMS

United Nations Educational, Scientific and Cultural Organization (UNESCO), 7 Place de Fontenoy, F-75700 Paris, France (Telephone Number in U.S. (212) 963-5981); *Statistical Yearbook*.

SAINT PIERRE AND MIQUELON - NATALITY - See SAINT PIERRE AND MIQUELON - BIRTH RATE

SAINT PIERRE AND MIQUELON - NATIONAL INCOME

G.K. Hall and Company, 70 Lincoln Street, Boston, Massachusetts 02111 (617) 423-3990; *The World in Figures*.

SAINT PIERRE AND MIQUELON - NEWSPAPER PRODUCTION - See SAINT PIERRE AND MIQUELON - FORESTRY AND FOREST PRODUCTS

SAINT PIERRE AND MIQUELON - OCCUPATIONS - See SAINT PIERRE AND MIQUELON - LABOR FORCE

SAINT PIERRE AND MIQUELON - PESTICIDE USE

Food and Agricultural Organization of the United Nations (FAO) Via delle Terme di Caracalla, 00100 Rome, Italy (Telephone Number in U.S. (202) 653-2400); *The State of Food and Agriculture*.

SAINT PIERRE AND MIQUELON - PETROLEUM INDUSTRY

Food and Agricultural Organization of the United Nations (FAO) Via delle Terme di Caracalla, 00100 Rome, Italy (Telephone Number in U.S. (202) 653-2400); *The State of Food and Agriculture*.

G.K. Hall and Company, 70 Lincoln Street, Boston, Massachusetts 02111 (617) 423-3990; *The World in Figures*.

SAINT PIERRE AND MIQUELON - POPULATION

Food and Agricultural Organization of the United Nations (FAO), Via delle Terme di Caracalla, 00100 Rome, Italy (Telephone Number in U.S. (202) 653-2400); *Production Yearbook*.

G.K. Hall and Company, 70 Lincoln Street, Boston, Massachusetts 02111 (617) 423-3990; *The World in Figures*.

International Labour Office, I.L.O. Publications, CH-1211, Geneva 22, Switzerland; *Yearbook of Labour Statistics*.

Statistical Office of the United Nations, Publishing Service, New York, New York 10017 (800) 253-9646; *Demographic Yearbook*, and *Statistical Yearbook*.

United Nations Educational, Scientific and Cultural Organization (UNESCO), 7 Place de Fontenoy, F-75700 Paris, France (Telephone Number in U.S. (212) 963-5981); *Statistical Yearbook*.

World Health Organization, Office of Publications, Avenue Appia, CH-1211 Geneva 27, Switzerland (Telephone Number in U.S. (618) 436-9686); *World Health Statistics Annual*.

SAINT PIERRE AND MIQUELON - PRICES

Food and Agricultural Organization of the United Nations (FAO), Via delle Terme di Caracalla, 00100 Rome, Italy (Telephone Number in U.S. (202) 653-2400); *Production Yearbook*, and *The State of Food and Agriculture*.

G.K. Hall and Company, 70 Lincoln Street, Boston, Massachusetts 02111 (617) 423-3990; *The World in Figures*.

International Labour Office, I.L.O. Publications, CH-1211, Geneva 22, Switzerland; *Yearbook of Labour Statistics*.

SAINT PIERRE AND MIQUELON - PRODUCTION

G.K. Hall and Company, 70 Lincoln Street, Boston, Massachusetts 02111 (617) 423-3990; *The World in Figures*.

SAINT PIERRE AND MIQUELON - RADIO BROADCASTING - See SAINT PIERRE AND MIQUELON - BROADCASTING

SAINT PIERRE AND MIQUELON - RAILWAY USE

G.K. Hall and Company, 70 Lincoln Street, Boston, Massachusetts 02111 (617) 423-3990; *The World in Figures*.

SAINT PIERRE AND MIQUELON - RENT PRICES

International Labour Office, I.L.O. Publications, CH-1211, Geneva 22, Switzerland; *Yearbook of Labour Statistics*.

SAINT PIERRE AND MIQUELON - RETAIL TRADE

G.K. Hall and Company, 70 Lincoln Street, Boston, Massachusetts 02111 (617) 423-3990; *The World in Figures.*

SAINT PIERRE AND MIQUELON - SCIENCE AND TECHNOLOGY - EXPENDITURE FOR RESEARCH

Statistical Office of the United Nations, Publishing Service, New York, New York 10017 (800) 253-9646; *Statistical Yearbook.*

SAINT PIERRE AND MIQUELON - SCIENTISTS AND TECHNICIANS

Statistical Office of the United Nations, Publishing Service, New York, New York 10017 (800) 253-9646; *Statistical Yearbook.*

SAINT PIERRE AND MIQUELON - SOCIAL DATA

G.K. Hall and Company, 70 Lincoln Street, Boston, Massachusetts 02111 (617) 423-3990; *The World in Figures.*

SAINT PIERRE AND MIQUELON - STOCKS - COMMODITY - MARKET PRICE - INDEX

Food and Agricultural Organization of the United Nations (FAO) Via delle Terme di Caracalla, 00100 Rome, Italy (Telephone Number in U.S. (202) 653-2400); *The State of Food and Agriculture.*

SAINT PIERRE AND MIQUELON - TAXATION

G.K. Hall and Company, 70 Lincoln Street, Boston, Massachusetts 02111 (617) 423-3990; *The World in Figures.*

SAINT PIERRE AND MIQUELON - TELEPHONES IN USE

American Telephone and Telegraph Company, 26 Parsippany Road, Whippany, New Jersey 07981 (800) 338-4038; *The World's Telephones.*

G.K. Hall and Company, 70 Lincoln Street, Boston, Massachusetts 02111 (617) 423-3990; *The World in Figures.*

SAINT PIERRE AND MIQUELON - TELEVISION BROADCASTING - See SAINT PIERRE AND MIQUELON - BROADCASTING

SAINT PIERRE AND MIQUELON - TEXTILE INDUSTRY

G.K. Hall and Company, 70 Lincoln Street, Boston, Massachusetts 02111 (617) 423-3990; *The World in Figures.*

SAINT PIERRE AND MIQUELON - TOURISM

G.K. Hall and Company, 70 Lincoln Street, Boston, Massachusetts 02111 (617) 423-3990; *The World in Figures.*

SAINT PIERRE AND MIQUELON - TRADE - See SAINT PIERRE AND MIQUELON - FOREIGN TRADE

SAINT PIERRE AND MIQUELON - TRANSPORTATION AND COMMUNICATIONS

G.K. Hall and Company, 70 Lincoln Street, Boston, Massachusetts 02111 (617) 423-3990; *The World in Figures.*

SAINT PIERRE AND MIQUELON - UNEMPLOYMENT

International Labour Office, I.L.O. Publications, CH-1211, Geneva 22, Switzerland; *Yearbook of Labour Statistics.*

SAINT PIERRE AND MIQUELON - VITAL STATISTICS

G.K. Hall and Company, 70 Lincoln Street, Boston, Massachusetts 02111 (617) 423-3990; *The World in Figures.*

Statistical Office of the United Nations, Publishing Service, New York, New York 10017 (800) 253-9646; *Statistical Yearbook.*

World Health Organization, Office of Publications, Avenue Appia, CH-1211 Geneva 27, Switzerland (Telephone Number in U.S. (518) 436-9686); *World Health Statistics Annual.*

SAINT PIERRE AND MIQUELON - WAGES

G.K. Hall and Company, 70 Lincoln Street, Boston, Massachusetts 02111 (617) 423-3990; *The World in Figures.*

International Labour Office, I.L.O. Publications, CH-1211, Geneva 22, Switzerland; *Yearbook of Labour Statistics.*

SAINT PIERRE AND MIQUELON - WEATHER

G.K. Hall and Company, 70 Lincoln Street, Boston, Massachusetts 02111 (617) 423-3990; *The World in Figures.*

Saint Vincent and The Grenadines - National Statistical Office

Statistical Office, Ministry of Finance, Kingstown, Saint Vincent and The Grenadines.

Saint Vincent and The Grenadines - Primary Statistics Source

Statistical Office, Ministry of Finance, Kingstown, Saint Vincent and The Grenadines; *Digest of Statistics.*

SAINT VINCENT AND THE GRENADINES - AGRICULTURE

Food and Agricultural Organization of the United Nations (FAO) Via delle Terme di Caracalla, 00100 Rome, Italy (Telephone Number in U.S. (202) 653-2400); *Production Yearbook, The State of Food and Agriculture,* and *Trade Yearbook.*

G.K. Hall and Company, 70 Lincoln Street, Boston, Massachusetts 02111 (617) 423-3990; *The World in Figures.*

Statistical Office of the United Nations, Publishing Service, New York, New York 10017 (800) 253-9646; *Statistical Yearbook.*

The World Bank, 1818 H Street, NW, Washington, D.C. 20433 (202) 477-1234; *World Tables.*

SAINT VINCENT AND THE GRENADINES - AIRLINE SERVICE

G.K. Hall and Company, 70 Lincoln Street, Boston, Massachusetts 02111 (617) 423-3990; *The World in Figures.*

SAINT VINCENT AND THE GRENADINES - ANIMAL HEALTH

Food and Agricultural Organization of the United Nations (FAO), Via delle Terme di Caracalla, 00100, Rome, Italy (Telephone Number in

U.S. (202) 653-2400); *Animal Health Yearbook.*

SAINT VINCENT AND THE GRENADINES - AREA AND DENSITY OF POPULATION

Food and Agricultural Organization of the United Nations (FAO) Via delle Terme di Caracalla, 00100 Rome, Italy (Telephone Number in U.S. (202) 653-2400); *The State of Food and Agriculture.*

G.K. Hall and Company, 70 Lincoln Street, Boston, Massachusetts 02111 (617) 423-3990; *The World in Figures.*

Statistical Office of the United Nations, Publishing Service, New York, New York 10017 (800) 253-9646; *Statistical Yearbook.*

United Nations Educational, Scientific and Cultural Organization (UNESCO), 7 Place de Fontenoy, F-75700 Paris, France (Telephone Number in U.S. (212) 963-5981); *Statistical Yearbook.*

SAINT VINCENT AND THE GRENADINES - BALANCE OF PAYMENTS

G.K. Hall and Company, 70 Lincoln Street, Boston, Massachusetts 02111 (617) 423-3990; *The World in Figures.*

The World Bank, 1818 H Street, NW, Washington, D.C. 20433 (202) 477-1234; *World Tables.*

SAINT VINCENT AND THE GRENADINES - BANKING

G.K. Hall and Company, 70 Lincoln Street, Boston, Massachusetts 02111 (617) 423-3990; *The World in Figures.*

SAINT VINCENT AND THE GRENADINES - BIRTH RATES

Statistical Office of the United Nations, Publishing Service, New York, New York 10017 (800) 253-9646; *Demographic Yearbook,* and *Statistical Yearbook.*

The World Bank, 1818 H Street, NW, Washington, D.C. 20433 (202) 477-1234; *World Tables.*

World Health Organization, Office of Publications, Avenue Appia, CH-1211 Geneva 27, Switzerland (Telephone Number in U.S. (518) 436-9686); *World Health Statistics Annual.*

SAINT VINCENT AND THE GRENADINES - BONDS

G.K. Hall and Company, 70 Lincoln Street, Boston, Massachusetts 02111 (617) 423-3990; *The World in Figures.*

SAINT VINCENT AND THE GRENADINES - BOOK PRODUCTION

G.K. Hall and Company, 70 Lincoln Street, Boston, Massachusetts 02111 (617) 423-3990; *The World in Figures.*

SAINT VINCENT AND THE GRENADINES - BROADCASTING

Billboard Limited, P.O. Box 9027, 1006 AA Amsterdam, The Netherlands (Telephone Number in U.S. (212) 764-7300); *World Radio TV Handbook.*

G.K. Hall and Company, 70 Lincoln Street, Boston, Massachusetts 02111 (617) 423-3990; *The World in Figures.*

SAINT VINCENT AND THE GRENADINES - BUSINESS

G.K. Hall and Company, 70 Lincoln Street, Boston, Massachusetts 02111 (617) 423-3990; *The World in Figures.*

SAINT VINCENT AND THE GRENADINES - CALORIE SUPPLY

Food and Agricultural Organization of the United Nations (FAO) Via delle Terme di Caracalla, 00100 Rome, Italy (Telephone Number in U.S. (202) 653-2400); *The State of Food and Agriculture.*

SAINT VINCENT AND THE GRENADINES - CATTLE - See SAINT VINCENT AND THE GRENADINES - LIVESTOCK AND POULTRY

SAINT VINCENT AND THE GRENADINES - CHEMICAL (ORGANIC) PRODUCTION - See SAINT VINCENT AND THE GRENADINES - MINING AND MINERAL PRODUCTS

SAINT VINCENT AND THE GRENADINES - CLASS STRUCTURE

G.K. Hall and Company, 70 Lincoln Street, Boston, Massachusetts 02111 (617) 423-3990; *The World in Figures.*

SAINT VINCENT AND THE GRENADINES - CLIMATE

G.K. Hall and Company, 70 Lincoln Street, Boston, Massachusetts 02111 (617) 423-3990; *The World in Figures.*

SAINT VINCENT AND THE GRENADINES - COAL PRODUCTION - See SAINT VINCENT AND THE GRENADINES - MINING AND MINERAL PRODUCTS

SAINT VINCENT AND THE GRENADINES - COCOA PRODUCTION - See SAINT VINCENT AND THE GRENADINES - CROPS

SAINT VINCENT AND THE GRENADINES - COMMUNICATIONS

G.K. Hall and Company, 70 Lincoln Street, Boston, Massachusetts 02111 (617) 423-3990; *The World in Figures.*

SAINT VINCENT AND THE GRENADINES - CONSUMER PRICE INDEX

G.K. Hall and Company, 70 Lincoln Street, Boston, Massachusetts 02111 (617) 423-3990; *The World in Figures.*

SAINT VINCENT AND THE GRENADINES - CONSUMER PRICES

International Labour Office, I.L.O. Publications, CH-1211, Geneva 22, Switzerland; *Yearbook of Labour Statistics.*

SAINT VINCENT AND THE GRENADINES - CONSUMPTION

G.K. Hall and Company, 70 Lincoln Street, Boston, Massachusetts 02111 (617) 423-3990; *The World in Figures.*

SAINT VINCENT AND THE GRENADINES - CORN PRODUCTION - See SAINT VINCENT AND THE GRENADINES - CROPS

SAINT VINCENT AND THE GRENADINES - CORPORATE TAXES - See SAINT VINCENT AND THE GRENADINES - TAXATION

SAINT VINCENT AND THE GRENADINES - CROPS

Food and Agricultural Organization of the United Nations (FAO) Via delle Terme di Caracalla, 00100 Rome, Italy (Telephone Number in U.S. (202) 653-2400); *The State of Food and Agriculture.*

G.K. Hall and Company, 70 Lincoln Street, Boston, Massachusetts 02111 (617) 423-3990; *The World in Figures.*

Statistical Office of the United Nations, Publishing Service, New York, New York 10017 (800) 253-9646; *Statistical Yearbook*

SAINT VINCENT AND THE GRENADINES - CUSTOMS DUTIES

G.K. Hall and Company, 70 Lincoln Street, Boston, Massachusetts 02111 (617) 423-3990; *The World in Figures.*

SAINT VINCENT AND THE GRENADINES - DAIRY PRODUCTS

Food and Agricultural Organization of the United Nations (FAO) Via delle Terme di Caracalla, 00100 Rome, Italy (Telephone Number in U.S. (202) 653-2400); *The State of Food and Agriculture.*

SAINT VINCENT AND THE GRENADINES - DEATH RATES

G.K. Hall and Company, 70 Lincoln Street, Boston, Massachusetts 02111 (617) 423-3990; *The World in Figures.*

Statistical Office of the United Nations, Publishing Service, New York, New York 10017 (800) 253-9646; *Statistical Yearbook.*

World Health Organization, Office of Publications, Avenue Appia, CH-1211 Geneva 27, Switzerland (Telephone Number in U.S. (518) 436-9686); *World Health Statistics Annual.*

SAINT VINCENT AND THE GRENADINES - DEFENSE EXPENDITURES

G.K. Hall and Company, 70 Lincoln Street, Boston, Massachusetts 02111 (617) 423-3990; *The World in Figures.*

SAINT VINCENT AND THE GRENADINES - DEMOGRAPHY

G.K. Hall and Company, 70 Lincoln Street, Boston, Massachusetts 02111 (617) 423-3990; *The World in Figures.*

SAINT VINCENT AND THE GRENADINES - DEVELOPMENT ASSISTANCE

G.K. Hall and Company, 70 Lincoln Street, Boston, Massachusetts 02111 (617) 423-3990; *The World in Figures.*

SAINT VINCENT AND THE GRENADINES - DISEASES

G.K. Hall and Company, 70 Lincoln Street, Boston, Massachusetts 02111 (617) 423-3990; *The World in Figures.*

World Health Organization, Office of Publications, Avenue Appia, CH-1211 Geneva 27, Switzerland (Telephone Number in U.S. (518) 436-9686); *World Health Statistics Annual.*

SAINT VINCENT AND THE GRENADINES - DIVORCE RATES

Statistical Office of the United Nations, Publishing Service, New York, New York 10017 (800) 253-9646; *Demographic Yearbook,* and *Statistical Yearbook.*

SAINT VINCENT AND THE GRENADINES - DOMESTIC PRODUCT

G.K. Hall and Company, 70 Lincoln Street, Boston, Massachusetts 02111 (617) 423-3990; *The World in Figures.*

SAINT VINCENT AND THE GRENADINES - ECONOMY

G.K. Hall and Company, 70 Lincoln Street, Boston, Massachusetts 02111 (617) 423-3990; *The World in Figures.*

SAINT VINCENT AND THE GRENADINES - EDUCATION

G.K. Hall and Company, 70 Lincoln Street, Boston, Massachusetts 02111 (617) 423-3990; *The World in Figures.*

United Nations Educational, Scientific and Cultural Organization (UNESCO), 7 Place de Fontenoy, F-75700 Paris, France (Telephone Number in U.S. (212) 963-5981); *Statistical Yearbook.*

The World Bank, 1818 H Street, NW, Washington, D.C. 20433 (202) 477-1234; *World Tables.*

SAINT VINCENT AND THE GRENADINES - EGG PRODUCTION AND CONSUMPTION - See SAINT VINCENT AND THE GRENADINES - DAIRY PRODUCTS

SAINT VINCENT AND THE GRENADINES - EMPLOYMENT

International Labour Office, I.L.O. Publications, CH-1211, Geneva 22, Switzerland; *Yearbook of Labour Statistics.*

SAINT VINCENT AND THE GRENADINES - ENERGY

Food and Agricultural Organization of the United Nations (FAO) Via delle Terme di Caracalla, 00100 Rome, Italy (Telephone Number in U.S. (202) 653-2400); *The State of Food and Agriculture.*

G.K. Hall and Company, 70 Lincoln Street, Boston, Massachusetts 02111 (617) 423-3990; *The World in Figures.*

Statistical Office of the United Nations, Publishing Service, New York, New York 10017 (800) 253-9646; *Energy Statistics Yearbook,* and *Statistical Yearbook.*

SAINT VINCENT AND THE GRENADINES - EXPORTS

Food and Agricultural Organization of the United Nations (FAO) Via delle Terme di Caracalla, 00100 Rome, Italy (Telephone Number in U.S. (202) 653-2400); *The State of Food and Agriculture.*

G.K. Hall and Company, 70 Lincoln Street, Boston, Massachusetts 02111 (617) 423-3990; *The World in Figures.*

The World Bank, 1818 H Street, NW, Washington, D.C. 20433 (202) 477-1234; *World Tables.*

SAINT VINCENT AND THE GRENADINES - EXTERNAL INDEBTEDNESS

The World Bank, 1818 H Street, NW, Washington, D.C. 20433 (202) 477-1234; *World Tables.*

SAINT VINCENT AND THE GRENADINES - EXTERNAL TRADE

Food and Agricultural Organization of the United Nations (FAO) Via delle Terme di Caracalla, 00100 Rome, Italy (Telephone Number in U.S. (202) 653-2400); *The State of Food and Agriculture,* and *Trade Yearbook.*

G.K. Hall and Company, 70 Lincoln Street, Boston, Massachusetts 02111 (617) 423-3990; *The World in Figures.*

Statistical Office of the United Nations, Publishing Service, New York, New York 10017 (800) 253-9646; *Statistical Yearbook.*

SAINT VINCENT AND THE GRENADINES - FARM CROPS - See SAINT VINCENT AND THE GRENADINES - CROPS

SAINT VINCENT AND THE GRENADINES - FERTILITY RATES

The World Bank, 1818 H Street, NW, Washington, D.C. 20433 (202) 477-1234; *World Tables.*

SAINT VINCENT AND THE GRENADINES - FERTILIZER

Food and Agricultural Organization of the United Nations (FAO) Via delle Terme di Caracalla, 00100 Rome, Italy (Telephone Number in U.S. (202) 653-2400); *The State of Food and Agriculture.*

Statistical Office of the United Nations, Publishing Service, New York, New York 10017 (800) 253-9646; *Statistical Yearbook.*

SAINT VINCENT AND THE GRENADINES - FETAL MORTALITY

Statistical Office of the United Nations, Publishing Service, New York, New York 10017 (800) 253-9646; *Demographic Yearbook.*

World Health Organization, Office of Publications, Avenue Appia, CH-1211 Geneva 27, Switzerland (Telephone Number in U.S. (518) 436-9686); *World Health Statistics Annual.*

SAINT VINCENT AND THE GRENADINES - FINANCE

G.K. Hall and Company, 70 Lincoln Street, Boston, Massachusetts 02111 (617) 423-3990; *The World in Figures.*

SAINT VINCENT AND THE GRENADINES - FISHERIES

Food and Agricultural Organization of the United Nations (FAO) Via delle Terme di Caracalla, 00100 Rome, Italy (Telephone Number in U.S. (202) 653-2400); *The State of Food and Agriculture,* and *Yearbook of Fishery Statistics.*

SAINT VINCENT AND THE GRENADINES - FOOD

Food and Agricultural Organization of the United Nations (FAO), Via delle Terme di Caracalla, 00100 Rome, Italy (Telephone Number in U.S. (202) 653-2400); *Production Yearbook,* and *The State of Food and Agriculture.*

G.K. Hall and Company, 70 Lincoln Street, Boston, Massachusetts 02111 (617) 423-3990; *The World in Figures.*

SAINT VINCENT AND THE GRENADINES - FOREIGN AID

G.K. Hall and Company, 70 Lincoln Street, Boston, Massachusetts 02111 (617) 423-3990; *The World in Figures.*

SAINT VINCENT AND THE GRENADINES - FOREIGN TRADE

Food and Agricultural Organization of the United Nations (FAO) Via delle Terme di Caracalla, 00100 Rome, Italy (Telephone Number in U.S. (202) 653-2400); *The State of Food and Agriculture.*

G.K. Hall and Company, 70 Lincoln Street, Boston, Massachusetts 02111 (617) 423-3990; *The World in Figures.*

Statistical Office of the United Nations, Publishing Service, New York, New York 10017 (800) 253-9646; *International Trade Statistics Yearbook,* and *Statistical Yearbook.*

The World Bank, 1818 H Street, NW, Washington, D.C. 20433 (202) 477-1234; *World Tables.*

SAINT VINCENT AND THE GRENADINES - FORESTRY AND FOREST PRODUCTS

Food and Agricultural Organization of the United Nations (FAO) Via delle Terme di Caracalla, 00100 Rome, Italy (Telephone Number in U.S. (202) 653-2400); *The State of Food and Agriculture.*

G.K. Hall and Company, 70 Lincoln Street, Boston, Massachusetts 02111 (617) 423-3990; *The World in Figures.*

Statistical Office of the United Nations, Publishing Service, New York, New York 10017 (800) 253-9646; *Statistical Yearbook.*

SAINT VINCENT AND THE GRENADINES - GENERAL MORTALITY

Statistical Office of the United Nations, Publishing Service, New York, New York 10017 (800) 253-9646; *Demographic Yearbook.*

World Health Organization, Office of Publications, Avenue Appia, CH-1211 Geneva 27, Switzerland (Telephone Number in U.S. (518) 436-9686); *World Health Statistics Annual.*

SAINT VINCENT AND THE GRENADINES - GOLD HOLDINGS

The World Bank, 1818 H Street, NW, Washington, D.C. 20433 (202) 477-1234; *World Tables.*

SAINT VINCENT AND THE GRENADINES - GOVERNMENT

G.K. Hall and Company, 70 Lincoln Street, Boston, Massachusetts 02111 (617) 423-3990; *The World in Figures.*

SAINT VINCENT AND THE GRENADINES - GOVERNMENT EXPENDITURE

The World Bank, 1818 H Street, NW, Washington, D.C. 20433 (202) 477-1234; *World Tables.*

SAINT VINCENT AND THE GRENADINES - GOVERNMENT REVENUE

The World Bank, 1818 H Street, NW, Washington, D.C. 20433 (202) 477-1234; *World Tables.*

SAINT VINCENT AND THE GRENADINES - GRAIN PRODUCTION - See SAINT VINCENT AND THE GRENADINES - CROPS

SAINT VINCENT AND THE GRENADINES - GROSS DOMESTIC PRODUCT

G.K. Hall and Company, 70 Lincoln Street, Boston, Massachusetts 02111 (617) 423-3990; *The World in Figures.*

Statistical Office of the United Nations, Publishing Service, New York, New York 10017 (800) 253-9646; *Statistical Yearbook.*

The World Bank, 1818 H Street, NW, Washington, D.C. 20433 (202) 477-1234; *World Tables.*

SAINT VINCENT AND THE GRENADINES - GROSS NATIONAL PRODUCT

The World Bank, 1818 H Street, NW, Washington, D.C. 20433 (202) 477-1234; *World Tables.*

SAINT VINCENT AND THE GRENADINES - GROUNDNUT PRODUCTION - See SAINT VINCENT AND THE GRENADINES - CROPS

SAINT VINCENT AND THE GRENADINES - HEALTH

G.K. Hall and Company, 70 Lincoln Street, Boston, Massachusetts 02111 (617) 423-3990; *The World in Figures.*

Statistical Office of the United Nations, Publishing Service, New York, New York 10017 (800) 253-9646; *Statistical Yearbook.*

World Health Organization, Office of Publications, Avenue Appia, CH-1211 Geneva 27, Switzerland (Telephone Number in U.S. (518) 436-9686); *World Health Statistics Annual*.

SAINT VINCENT AND THE GRENADINES - HIGHWAYS

G.K. Hall and Company, 70 Lincoln Street, Boston, Massachusetts 02111 (617) 423-3990; *The World in Figures*.

SAINT VINCENT AND THE GRENADINES - HOURS OF WORK - See SAINT VINCENT AND THE GRENADINES - EMPLOYMENT

SAINT VINCENT AND THE GRENADINES - ILLITERATE POPULATION

G.K. Hall and Company, 70 Lincoln Street, Boston, Massachusetts 02111 (617) 423-3990; *The World in Figures*.

United Nations Educational, Scientific and Cultural Organization (UNESCO), 7 Place de Fontenoy, F-75700 Paris, France (Telephone Number in U.S. (212) 963-5981); *Statistical Yearbook*.

SAINT VINCENT AND THE GRENADINES - IMPORTS

Food and Agricultural Organization of the United Nations (FAO) Via delle Terme di Caracalla, 00100 Rome, Italy (Telephone Number in U.S. (202) 653-2400); *The State of Food and Agriculture*.

G.K. Hall and Company, 70 Lincoln Street, Boston, Massachusetts 02111 (617) 423-3990; *The World in Figures*.

The World Bank, 1818 H Street, NW, Washington, D.C. 20433 (202) 477-1234; *World Tables*.

SAINT VINCENT AND THE GRENADINES - INDUSTRY

G.K. Hall and Company, 70 Lincoln Street, Boston, Massachusetts 02111 (617) 423-3990; *The World in Figures*.

International Labour Office, I.L.O. Publications, CH-1211, Geneva 22, Switzerland; *Yearbook of Labour Statistics*.

The World Bank, 1818 H Street, NW, Washington, D.C. 20433 (202) 477-1234; *World Tables*.

SAINT VINCENT AND THE GRENADINES - INFANT AND MATERNAL MORTALITY

Statistical Office of the United Nations, Publishing Service, New York, New York 10017 (800) 253-9646; *Demographic Yearbook*, and *Statistical Yearbook*.

The World Bank, 1818 H Street, NW, Washington, D.C. 20433 (202) 477-1234; *World Tables*.

World Health Organization, Office of Publications, Avenue Appia, CH-1211 Geneva 27, Switzerland (Telephone Number in U.S. (518) 436-9686); *World Health Statistics Annual*.

SAINT VINCENT AND THE GRENADINES - INTERNATIONAL RESERVES EXCLUDING GOLD

The World Bank, 1818 H Street, NW, Washington, D.C. 20433 (202) 477-1234; *World Tables*.

SAINT VINCENT AND THE GRENADINES - LABOR FORCE

Food and Agricultural Organization of the United Nations (FAO) Via delle Terme di Caracalla, 00100 Rome, Italy (Telephone Number in

U.S. (202) 653-2400); *The State of Food and Agriculture*.

G.K. Hall and Company, 70 Lincoln Street, Boston, Massachusetts 02111 (617) 423-3990; *The World in Figures*.

The World Bank, 1818 H Street, NW, Washington, D.C. 20433 (202) 477-1234; *World Tables*.

SAINT VINCENT AND THE GRENADINES - LABOR PRODUCTIVITY

International Labour Office, I.L.O. Publications, CH-1211, Geneva 22, Switzerland; *Yearbook of Labour Statistics*.

SAINT VINCENT AND THE GRENADINES - LAND USE

Food and Agricultural Organization of the United Nations (FAO), Via delle Terme di Caracalla, 00100 Rome, Italy (Telephone Number in U.S. (202) 653-2400); *Production Yearbook*.

G.K. Hall and Company, 70 Lincoln Street, Boston, Massachusetts 02111 (617) 423-3990; *The World in Figures*.

SAINT VINCENT AND THE GRENADINES - LIBRARIES

United Nations Educational, Scientific and Cultural Organization (UNESCO), 7 Place de Fontenoy, F-75700 Paris, France (Telephone Number in U.S. (212) 963-5981); *Statistical Yearbook*.

SAINT VINCENT AND THE GRENADINES - LIVESTOCK AND POULTRY

Food and Agricultural Organization of the United Nations (FAO), Via delle Terme di Caracalla, 00100 Rome, Italy (Telephone Number in U.S. (202) 653-2400); *Production Yearbook*, and *The State of Food and Agriculture*.

G.K. Hall and Company, 70 Lincoln Street, Boston, Massachusetts 02111 (617) 423-3990; *The World in Figures*.

Statistical Office of the United Nations, Publishing Service, New York, New York 10017 (800) 253-9646; *Statistical Yearbook*.

SAINT VINCENT AND THE GRENADINES - LIVING LEVELS

G.K. Hall and Company, 70 Lincoln Street, Boston, Massachusetts 02111 (617) 423-3990; *The World in Figures*.

SAINT VINCENT AND THE GRENADINES - MANUFACTURING

G.K. Hall and Company, 70 Lincoln Street, Boston, Massachusetts 02111 (617) 423-3990; *The World in Figures*.

The World Bank, 1818 H Street, NW, Washington, D.C. 20433 (202) 477-1234; *World Tables*.

SAINT VINCENT AND THE GRENADINES - MARRIAGE RATES

Statistical Office of the United Nations, Publishing Service, New York, New York 10017 (800) 253-9646; *Demographic Yearbook*, and *Statistical Yearbook*.

SAINT VINCENT AND THE GRENADINES - MEAT PRODUCTION - See SAINT VINCENT AND THE GRENADINES - LIVESTOCK AND POULTRY

SAINT VINCENT AND THE GRENADINES - MERCHANT SHIPPING

G.K. Hall and Company, 70 Lincoln Street, Boston, Massachusetts 02111 (617) 423-3990; *The World in Figures*.

Statistical Office of the United Nations, Publishing Service, New York, New York 10017 (800) 253-9646; *Statistical Yearbook*.

SAINT VINCENT AND THE GRENADINES - MILITARY

G.K. Hall and Company, 70 Lincoln Street, Boston, Massachusetts 02111 (617) 423-3990; *The World in Figures*.

SAINT VINCENT AND THE GRENADINES - MINING AND MINERAL PRODUCTS

G.K. Hall and Company, 70 Lincoln Street, Boston, Massachusetts 02111 (617) 423-3990; *The World in Figures*.

SAINT VINCENT AND THE GRENADINES - MONEY SUPPLY

G.K. Hall and Company, 70 Lincoln Street, Boston, Massachusetts 02111 (617) 423-3990; *The World in Figures*.

The World Bank, 1818 H Street, NW, Washington, D.C. 20433 (202) 477-1234; *World Tables*.

SAINT VINCENT AND THE GRENADINES - MOTION PICTURES

Statistical Office of the United Nations, Publishing Service, New York, New York 10017 (800) 253-9646; *Statistical Yearbook*.

SAINT VINCENT AND THE GRENADINES - MOTOR VEHICLES IN USE

G.K. Hall and Company, 70 Lincoln Street, Boston, Massachusetts 02111 (617) 423-3990; *The World in Figures*.

Statistical Office of the United Nations, Publishing Service, New York, New York 10017 (800) 253-9646; *Statistical Yearbook*.

SAINT VINCENT AND THE GRENADINES - NATALITY - See SAINT VINCENT AND THE GRENADINES - BIRTH RATE

SAINT VINCENT AND THE GRENADINES - NATIONAL ACCOUNTS

Statistical Office of the United Nations, Publishing Service, New York, New York 10017 (800) 253-9646; *National Accounts Statistics*, and *Statistical Yearbook*.

SAINT VINCENT AND THE GRENADINES - NATIONAL INCOME

G.K. Hall and Company, 70 Lincoln Street, Boston, Massachusetts 02111 (617) 423-3990; *The World in Figures*.

Statistical Office of the United Nations, Publishing Service, New York, New York 10017 (800) 253-9646; *Statistical Yearbook*.

SAINT VINCENT AND THE GRENADINES - NEWSPAPER PRODUCTION - See SAINT VINCENT AND THE GRENADINES - FORESTRY AND FOREST PRODUCTS

SAINT VINCENT AND THE GRENADINES - OCCUPATIONS - See SAINT VINCENT AND THE GRENADINES - LABOR FORCE

SAINT VINCENT AND THE GRENADINES - PESTICIDE USE

Food and Agricultural Organization of the United Nations (FAO) Via delle Terme di Caracalla, 00100 Rome, Italy (Telephone Number in U.S. (202) 653-2400); *The State of Food and Agriculture*.

SAINT VINCENT AND THE GRENADINES - PETROLEUM INDUSTRY

Food and Agricultural Organization of the United Nations (FAO) Via delle Terme di Caracalla, 00100 Rome, Italy (Telephone Number in U.S. (202) 653-2400); *The State of Food and Agriculture*.

G.K. Hall and Company, 70 Lincoln Street, Boston, Massachusetts 02111 (617) 423-3990; *The World in Figures*.

SAINT VINCENT AND THE GRENADINES - PIGS - See SAINT VINCENT AND THE GRENADINES - LIVESTOCK AND POULTRY

SAINT VINCENT AND THE GRENADINES - POPULATION

Food and Agricultural Organization of the United Nations (FAO), Via delle Terme di Caracalla, 00100 Rome, Italy (Telephone Number in U.S. (202) 653-2400); *Production Yearbook*.

G.K. Hall and Company, 70 Lincoln Street, Boston, Massachusetts 02111 (617) 423-3990; *The World in Figures*.

International Labour Office, I.L.O. Publications, CH-1211, Geneva 22, Switzerland; *Yearbook of Labour Statistics*.

Statistical Office of the United Nations, Publishing Service, New York, New York 10017 (800) 253-9646; *Demographic Yearbook*, and *Statistical Yearbook*.

United Nations Educational, Scientific and Cultural Organization (UNESCO), 7 Place de Fontenoy, F-75700 Paris, France (Telephone Number in U.S. (212) 963-5981); *Statistical Yearbook*.

World Health Organization, Office of Publications, Avenue Appia, CH-1211 Geneva 27, Switzerland (Telephone Number in U.S. (518) 436-9686); *World Health Statistics Annual*.

SAINT VINCENT AND THE GRENADINES - PRICES

Food and Agricultural Organization of the United Nations (FAO), Via delle Terme di Caracalla, 00100 Rome, Italy (Telephone Number in U.S. (202) 653-2400); *Production Yearbook*, and *The State of Food and Agriculture*.

G.K. Hall and Company, 70 Lincoln Street, Boston, Massachusetts 02111 (617) 423-3990; *The World in Figures*.

International Labour Office, I.L.O. Publications, CH-1211, Geneva 22, Switzerland; *Yearbook of Labour Statistics*.

SAINT VINCENT AND THE GRENADINES - PRODUCTION

G.K. Hall and Company, 70 Lincoln Street, Boston, Massachusetts 02111 (617) 423-3990; *The World in Figures*.

SAINT VINCENT AND THE GRENADINES - RAILWAY USE

G.K. Hall and Company, 70 Lincoln Street, Boston, Massachusetts 02111 (617) 423-3990; *The World in Figures*.

SAINT VINCENT AND THE GRENADINES - RETAIL TRADE

G.K. Hall and Company, 70 Lincoln Street, Boston, Massachusetts 02111 (617) 423-3990; *The World in Figures*.

SAINT VINCENT AND THE GRENADINES - SHEEP - See SAINT VINCENT AND THE GRENADINES - LIVESTOCK AND POULTRY

SAINT VINCENT AND THE GRENADINES - SOCIAL DATA

G.K. Hall and Company, 70 Lincoln Street, Boston, Massachusetts 02111 (617) 423-3990; *The World in Figures.*

SAINT VINCENT AND THE GRENADINES - STOCKS - COMMODITY - MARKET PRICE - INDEX

Food and Agricultural Organization of the United Nations (FAO) Via delle Terme di Caracalla, 00100 Rome, Italy (Telephone Number in U.S. (202) 653-2400); *The State of Food and Agriculture.*

SAINT VINCENT AND THE GRENADINES - TAXATION

G.K. Hall and Company, 70 Lincoln Street, Boston, Massachusetts 02111 (617) 423-3990; *The World in Figures.*

The World Bank, 1818 H Street, NW, Washington, D.C. 20433 (202) 477-1234; *World Tables.*

SAINT VINCENT AND THE GRENADINES - TELEPHONES IN USE

American Telephone and Telegraph Company, 26 Parsippany Road, Whippany, New Jersey 07981 (800) 338-4038; *The World's Telephones.*

G.K. Hall and Company, 70 Lincoln Street, Boston, Massachusetts 02111 (617) 423-3990; *The World in Figures.*

Statistical Office of the United Nations, Publishing Service, New York, New York 10017 (800) 253-9646; *Statistical Yearbook.*

SAINT VINCENT AND THE GRENADINES - TEXTILE INDUSTRY

G.K. Hall and Company, 70 Lincoln Street, Boston, Massachusetts 02111 (617) 423-3990; *The World in Figures.*

SAINT VINCENT AND THE GRENADINES - TOURISM

G.K. Hall and Company, 70 Lincoln Street, Boston, Massachusetts 02111 (617) 423-3990; *The World in Figures.*

World Tourism Organization, Calle Capitan Haya 42, E-28020 Madrid, Spain; *Yearbook of Tourism Statistics.*

SAINT VINCENT AND THE GRENADINES - TRACTORS IN USE

Statistical Office of the United Nations, Publishing Service, New York, New York 10017 (800) 253-9646; *Statistical Yearbook.*

SAINT VINCENT AND THE GRENADINES - TRADE - See SAINT VINCENT AND THE GRENADINES - FOREIGN TRADE

SAINT VINCENT AND THE GRENADINES - TRANSPORTATION AND COMMUNICATIONS

G.K. Hall and Company, 70 Lincoln Street, Boston, Massachusetts 02111 (617) 423-3990; *The World in Figures.*

SAINT VINCENT AND THE GRENADINES - UNEMPLOYMENT

International Labour Office, I.L.O. Publications, CH-1211, Geneva 22, Switzerland; *Yearbook of Labour Statistics.*

SAINT VINCENT AND THE GRENADINES - VITAL STATISTICS

G.K. Hall and Company, 70 Lincoln Street, Boston, Massachusetts 02111 (617) 423-3990; *The World in Figures.*

Statistical Office of the United Nations, Publishing Service, New York, New York 10017 (800) 253-9646; *Statistical Yearbook.*

World Health Organization, Office of Publications, Avenue Appia, CH-1211 Geneva 27, Switzerland (Telephone Number in U.S. (518) 436-9686); *World Health Statistics Annual.*

SAINT VINCENT AND THE GRENADINES - WAGES

G.K. Hall and Company, 70 Lincoln Street, Boston, Massachusetts 02111 (617) 423-3990; *The World in Figures.*

International Labour Office, I.L.O. Publications, CH-1211, Geneva 22, Switzerland; *Yearbook of Labour Statistics.*

SAINT VINCENT AND THE GRENADINES - WEATHER

G.K. Hall and Company, 70 Lincoln Street, Boston, Massachusetts 02111 (617) 423-3990; *The World in Figures.*

SALAD AND COOKING OILS - CONSUMPTION

U.S. Department of Agriculture, Economic Research Service, Fourteenth Street and Independence Avenue, SW, Washington, D.C. 20005-4789 (202) 219-1504; *Food Consumption, Prices, and Expenditures,* and unpublished data.

SALARIES AND WAGES - See EARNINGS

SALES - See Individual Commodities and Industries

SALESWORKERS

U.S. Department of Labor, Bureau of Labor Statistics, Two Massachusetts Avenue, NE, Washington, D.C. 20212 (202) 606-7828; *Employment and Earnings.*

SALMON

U.S. Department of Commerce, National Oceanic and Atmospheric Administration, National Marine Fisheries Service, 1335 East-West Highway, Silver Spring, Maryland 20910 (301) 427-2239; *Fisheries of the United States,* and *Fishery Statistics of the United States.*

SALMON - CANNED

U.S. Department of Commerce, National Oceanic and Atmospheric Administration, National Marine Fisheries Service, 1335 East-West Highway, Silver Spring, Maryland 20910 (301) 427-2239; *Fishery Statistics of the United States,* and *Fisheries of the United States.*

SALT - PRODUCTION AND VALUE

U.S. Department of the Interior, Bureau of Mines, 810 Seventh Street, NW, Washington, D.C. 20241 (202) 501-9649; *Annual Reports,* and *Mineral Commodities Summaries.*

Samoa - National Statistical Office

Department of Statistics, Post Office Box 1151, Apia, Samoa.

SAMOA - AGRICULTURE

Food and Agricultural Organization of the United Nations (FAO) Via delle Terme di Caracalla, 00100 Rome, Italy (Telephone Number in U.S. (202) 653-2400); *Production Yearbook, The State of Food and Agriculture,* and *Trade Yearbook.*

G.K. Hall and Company, 70 Lincoln Street, Boston, Massachusetts 02111 (617) 423-3990; *The World in Figures.*

Statistical Office of the United Nations, Publishing Service, New York, New York 10017 (800) 253-9646; *Statistical Yearbook*, and *Statistical Yearbook for Asia and the Pacific.*

SAMOA - AIRLINE SERVICE

G.K. Hall and Company, 70 Lincoln Street, Boston, Massachusetts 02111 (617) 423-3990; *The World in Figures.*

SAMOA - AREA AND DENSITY OF POPULATION

Food and Agricultural Organization of the United Nations (FAO) Via delle Terme di Caracalla, 00100 Rome, Italy (Telephone Number in U.S. (202) 653-2400); *The State of Food and Agriculture.*

G.K. Hall and Company, 70 Lincoln Street, Boston, Massachusetts 02111 (617) 423-3990; *The World in Figures.*

Statistical Office of the United Nations, Publishing Service, New York, New York 10017 (800) 253-9646; *Statistical Yearbook.*

SAMOA - BALANCE OF PAYMENTS

G.K. Hall and Company, 70 Lincoln Street, Boston, Massachusetts 02111 (617) 423-3990; *The World in Figures.*

SAMOA - BANKING

G.K. Hall and Company, 70 Lincoln Street, Boston, Massachusetts 02111 (617) 423-3990; *The World in Figures.*

SAMOA - BIRTH RATES

Statistical Office of the United Nations, Publishing Service, New York, New York 10017 (800) 253-9646; *Demographic Yearbook*, and *Statistical Yearbook.*

World Health Organization, Office of Publications, Avenue Appia, CH-1211 Geneva 27, Switzerland (Telephone Number in U.S. (518) 436-9686); *World Health Statistics Annual.*

SAMOA - BONDS

G.K. Hall and Company, 70 Lincoln Street, Boston, Massachusetts 02111 (617) 423-3990; *The World in Figures.*

SAMOA - BOOK PRODUCTION

G.K. Hall and Company, 70 Lincoln Street, Boston, Massachusetts 02111 (617) 423-3990; *The World in Figures.*

United Nations Educational, Scientific and Cultural Organization (UNESCO), 7 Place de Fontenoy, F-75700 Paris, France (Telephone Number in U.S. (212) 963-5981); *Statistical Yearbook.*

SAMOA - BROADCASTING

Billboard Limited, P.O. Box 9027, 1006 AA Amsterdam, The Netherlands (Telephone Number in U.S. (212) 764-7300); *World Radio TV Handbook.*

G.K. Hall and Company, 70 Lincoln Street, Boston, Massachusetts 02111 (617) 423-3990; *The World in Figures.*

United Nations Educational, Scientific and Cultural Organization (UNESCO), 7 Place de Fontenoy, F-75700 Paris, France (Telephone

Number in U.S. (212) 963-5981); *Statistical Yearbook.*

SAMOA - BUSINESS

G.K. Hall and Company, 70 Lincoln Street, Boston, Massachusetts 02111 (617) 423-3990; *The World in Figures.*

SAMOA - CALORIE SUPPLY

Food and Agricultural Organization of the United Nations (FAO) Via delle Terme di Caracalla, 00100 Rome, Italy (Telephone Number in U.S. (202) 653-2400); *The State of Food and Agriculture.*

SAMOA - CATTLE - See SAMOA - LIVESTOCK AND POULTRY

SAMOA - CHEMICAL (ORGANIC) PRODUCTION - See SAMOA - MINING AND MINERAL PRODUCTS

SAMOA - CLASS STRUCTURE

G.K. Hall and Company, 70 Lincoln Street, Boston, Massachusetts 02111 (617) 423-3990; *The World in Figures.*

SAMOA - CLIMATE

G.K. Hall and Company, 70 Lincoln Street, Boston, Massachusetts 02111 (617) 423-3990; *The World in Figures.*

SAMOA - COAL PRODUCTION - See SAMOA - MINING AND MINERAL PRODUCTS

SAMOA - COCOA PRODUCTION - See SAMOA - CROPS

SAMOA - COMMUNICATIONS

G.K. Hall and Company, 70 Lincoln Street, Boston, Massachusetts 02111 (617) 423-3990; *The World in Figures.*

Statistical Office of the United Nations, Publishing Service, New York, New York 10017 (800) 253-9646; *Statistical Yearbook for Asia and the Pacific.*

SAMOA - CONSTRUCTION INDUSTRY

Statistical Office of the United Nations, Publishing Service, New York, New York 10017 (800) 253-9646; *Construction Statistics Yearbook*, and *Statistical Yearbook.*

SAMOA - CONSUMER PRICE INDEX

G.K. Hall and Company, 70 Lincoln Street, Boston, Massachusetts 02111 (617) 423-3990; *The World in Figures.*

Statistical Office of the United Nations, Publishing Service, New York, New York 10017 (800) 253-9646; *Statistical Yearbook.*

SAMOA - CONSUMER PRICES

International Labour Office, I.L.O. Publications, CH-1211, Geneva 22, Switzerland; *Yearbook of Labour Statistics.*

SAMOA - CONSUMPTION

G.K. Hall and Company, 70 Lincoln Street, Boston, Massachusetts 02111 (617) 423-3990; *The World in Figures.*

SAMOA - CORN PRODUCTION - See SAMOA - CROPS

SAMOA - CORPORATE TAXES - See SAMOA - TAXATION

SAMOA - CROPS

Food and Agricultural Organization of the United Nations (FAO) Via delle Terme di Caracalla, 00100 Rome, Italy (Telephone Number in U.S. (202) 653-2400); *The State of Food and Agriculture.*

G.K. Hall and Company, 70 Lincoln Street, Boston, Massachusetts 02111 (617) 423-3990; *The World in Figures.*

Statistical Office of the United Nations, Publishing Service, New York, New York 10017 (800) 253-9646; *Statistical Yearbook.*

SAMOA - CUSTOMS DUTIES

G.K. Hall and Company, 70 Lincoln Street, Boston, Massachusetts 02111 (617) 423-3990; *The World in Figures.*

SAMOA - DAIRY PRODUCTS

Food and Agricultural Organization of the United Nations (FAO) Via delle Terme di Caracalla, 00100 Rome, Italy (Telephone Number in U.S. (202) 653-2400); *The State of Food and Agriculture.*

SAMOA - DEATH RATES

G.K. Hall and Company, 70 Lincoln Street, Boston, Massachusetts 02111 (617) 423-3990; *The World in Figures.*

Statistical Office of the United Nations, Publishing Service, New York, New York 10017 (800) 253-9646; *Statistical Yearbook.*

World Health Organization, Office of Publications, Avenue Appia, CH-1211 Geneva 27, Switzerland (Telephone Number in U.S. (518) 436-9686); *World Health Statistics Annual.*

SAMOA - DEFENSE EXPENDITURES

G.K. Hall and Company, 70 Lincoln Street, Boston, Massachusetts 02111 (617) 423-3990; *The World in Figures.*

SAMOA - DEMOGRAPHY

G.K. Hall and Company, 70 Lincoln Street, Boston, Massachusetts 02111 (617) 423-3990; *The World in Figures.*

SAMOA - DEVELOPMENT ASSISTANCE

G.K. Hall and Company, 70 Lincoln Street, Boston, Massachusetts 02111 (617) 423-3990; *The World in Figures.*

Statistical Office of the United Nations, Publishing Service, New York, New York 10017 (800) 253-9646; *Statistical Yearbook.*

SAMOA - DISEASES

G.K. Hall and Company, 70 Lincoln Street, Boston, Massachusetts 02111 (617) 423-3990; *The World in Figures.*

World Health Organization, Office of Publications, Avenue Appia, CH-1211 Geneva 27, Switzerland (Telephone Number in U.S. (518) 436-9686); *World Health Statistics Annual.*

SAMOA - DIVORCE RATES

Statistical Office of the United Nations, Publishing Service, New York, New York 10017 (800) 253-9646; *Demographic Yearbook,* and *Statistical Yearbook.*

SAMOA - DOMESTIC PRODUCT

G.K. Hall and Company, 70 Lincoln Street, Boston, Massachusetts 02111 (617) 423-3990; *The World in Figures.*

SAMOA - ECONOMY

G.K. Hall and Company, 70 Lincoln Street, Boston, Massachusetts 02111 (617) 423-3990; *The World in Figures.*

SAMOA - EDUCATION

G.K. Hall and Company, 70 Lincoln Street, Boston, Massachusetts 02111 (617) 423-3990; *The World in Figures.*

Statistical Office of the United Nations, Publishing Service, New York, New York 10017 (800) 253-9646; *Statistical Yearbook for Asia and the Pacific.*

United Nations Educational, Scientific and Cultural Organization (UNESCO), 7 Place de Fontenoy, F-75700 Paris, France (Telephone Number in U.S. (212) 963-5981); *Statistical Yearbook.*

SAMOA - EGG PRODUCTION AND CONSUMPTION - See SAMOA - DAIRY PRODUCTS

SAMOA - ELECTRICITY

Statistical Office of the United Nations, Publishing Service, New York, New York 10017 (800) 253-9646; *Electric Power in Asia and the Pacific.*

SAMOA - EMPLOYMENT

International Labour Office, I.L.O. Publications, CH-1211, Geneva 22, Switzerland; *Yearbook of Labour Statistics.*

SAMOA - ENERGY

Food and Agricultural Organization of the United Nations (FAO) Via delle Terme di Caracalla, 00100 Rome, Italy (Telephone Number in U.S. (202) 653-2400); *The State of Food and Agriculture.*

G.K. Hall and Company, 70 Lincoln Street, Boston, Massachusetts 02111 (617) 423-3990; *The World in Figures.*

Statistical Office of the United Nations, Publishing Service, New York, New York 10017 (800) 253-9646; *Energy Statistics Yearbook, Statistical Yearbook,* and *Statistical Yearbook for Asia and the Pacific.*

SAMOA - EXCHANGE RATES

Statistical Office of the United Nations, Publishing Service, New York, New York 10017 (800) 253-9646; *Statistical Yearbook.*

SAMOA - EXPORTS

Food and Agricultural Organization of the United Nations (FAO) Via delle Terme di Caracalla, 00100 Rome, Italy (Telephone Number in U.S. (202) 653-2400); *The State of Food and Agriculture.*

G.K. Hall and Company, 70 Lincoln Street, Boston, Massachusetts 02111 (617) 423-3990; *The World in Figures.*

International Monetary Fund, 700 Nineteenth Street, NW, Washington, D.C. 20431 (202) 623-7000; *Direction of Trade Statistics.*

SAMOA - EXTERNAL TRADE

Food and Agricultural Organization of the United Nations (FAO) Via delle Terme di Caracalla, 00100 Rome, Italy (Telephone Number in U.S. (202) 653-2400); *The State of Food and Agriculture*, and *Trade Yearbook*.

G.K. Hall and Company, 70 Lincoln Street, Boston, Massachusetts 02111 (617) 423-3990; *The World in Figures*.

Statistical Office of the United Nations, Publishing Service, New York, New York 10017 (800) 253-9646; *Statistical Yearbook*, and *Statistical Yearbook for Asia and the Pacific*.

SAMOA - FARM CROPS - See SAMOA - CROPS

SAMOA - FETAL MORTALITY

World Health Organization, Office of Publications, Avenue Appia, CH-1211 Geneva 27, Switzerland (Telephone Number in U.S. (518) 436-9686); *World Health Statistics Annual*.

SAMOA - FERTILIZER

Food and Agricultural Organization of the United Nations (FAO) Via delle Terme di Caracalla, 00100 Rome, Italy (Telephone Number in U.S. (202) 653-2400); *The State of Food and Agriculture*.

SAMOA - FINANCE

G.K. Hall and Company, 70 Lincoln Street, Boston, Massachusetts 02111 (617) 423-3990; *The World in Figures*.

Statistical Office of the United Nations, Publishing Service, New York, New York 10017 (800) 253-9646; *Statistical Yearbook for Asia and the Pacific*.

SAMOA - FISHERIES

Food and Agricultural Organization of the United Nations (FAO) Via delle Terme di Caracalla, 00100 Rome, Italy (Telephone Number in U.S. (202) 653-2400); *The State of Food and Agriculture*, and *Yearbook of Fishery Statistics*.

Statistical Office of the United Nations, Publishing Service, New York, New York 10017 (800) 253-9646; *Statistical Yearbook*.

SAMOA - FOOD

Food and Agricultural Organization of the United Nations (FAO) Via delle Terme di Caracalla, 00100 Rome, Italy (Telephone Number in U.S. (202) 653-2400); *Production Yearbook*, and *The State of Food and Agriculture*.

G.K. Hall and Company, 70 Lincoln Street, Boston, Massachusetts 02111 (617) 423-3990; *The World in Figures*.

Statistical Office of the United Nations, Publishing Service, New York, New York 10017 (800) 253-9646; *Statistical Yearbook for Asia and the Pacific*.

SAMOA - FOREIGN AID

G.K. Hall and Company, 70 Lincoln Street, Boston, Massachusetts 02111 (617) 423-3990; *The World in Figures*.

SAMOA - FOREIGN TRADE

Food and Agricultural Organization of the United Nations (FAO) Via delle Terme di Caracalla, 00100 Rome, Italy (Telephone Number in U.S. (202) 653-2400); *The State of Food and Agriculture*.

G.K. Hall and Company, 70 Lincoln Street, Boston, Massachusetts 02111 (617) 423-3990; *The World in Figures*.

Statistical Office of the United Nations, Publishing Service, New York, New York 10017 (800) 253-9646; *International Trade Statistics Yearbook, Statistical Yearbook*, and *Trade in Manufactures of Developing Countries*.

SAMOA - FORESTRY AND FOREST PRODUCTS

Food and Agricultural Organization of the United Nations (FAO) Via delle Terme di Caracalla, 00100 Rome, Italy (Telephone Number in U.S. (202) 653-2400); *The State of Food and Agriculture*, and *Yearbook of Forest Products*.

G.K. Hall and Company, 70 Lincoln Street, Boston, Massachusetts 02111 (617) 423-3990; *The World in Figures*.

Statistical Office of the United Nations, Publishing Service, New York, New York 10017 (800) 253-9646; *Statistical Yearbook*.

SAMOA - GENERAL MORTALITY

Statistical Office of the United Nations, Publishing Service, New York, New York 10017 (800) 253-9646; *Demographic Yearbook*.

World Health Organization, Office of Publications, Avenue Appia, CH-1211 Geneva 27, Switzerland (Telephone Number in U.S. (518) 436-9686); *World Health Statistics Annual*.

SAMOA - GOLD HOLDINGS

Statistical Office of the United Nations, Publishing Service, New York, New York 10017 (800) 253-9646; *Statistical Yearbook*.

SAMOA - GOVERNMENT

G.K. Hall and Company, 70 Lincoln Street, Boston, Massachusetts 02111 (617) 423-3990; *The World in Figures*.

SAMOA - GRAIN PRODUCTION - See SAMOA - CROPS

SAMOA - GROSS DOMESTIC PRODUCT

G.K. Hall and Company, 70 Lincoln Street, Boston, Massachusetts 02111 (617) 423-3990; *The World in Figures*.

Statistical Office of the United Nations, Publishing Service, New York, New York 10017 (800) 253-9646; *Statistical Yearbook*.

SAMOA - HEALTH

G.K. Hall and Company, 70 Lincoln Street, Boston, Massachusetts 02111 (617) 423-3990; *The World in Figures*.

Statistical Office of the United Nations, Publishing Service, New York, New York 10017 (800) 253-9646; *Statistical Yearbook*.

World Health Organization, Office of Publications, Avenue Appia, CH-1211 Geneva 27, Switzerland (Telephone Number in U.S. (518) 436-9686); *World Health Statistics Annual*.

SAMOA - HIGHWAYS

G.K. Hall and Company, 70 Lincoln Street, Boston, Massachusetts 02111 (617) 423-3990; *The World in Figures.*

SAMOA - HORSES - See SAMOA - LIVESTOCK AND POULTRY

SAMOA - HOURS OF WORK - See SAMOA - EMPLOYMENT

SAMOA - ILLITERATE POPULATION

G.K. Hall and Company, 70 Lincoln Street, Boston, Massachusetts 02111 (617) 423-3990; *The World in Figures.*

SAMOA - IMPORTS

Food and Agricultural Organization of the United Nations (FAO) Via delle Terme di Caracalla, 00100 Rome, Italy (Telephone Number in U.S. (202) 653-2400); *The State of Food and Agriculture.*

G.K. Hall and Company, 70 Lincoln Street, Boston, Massachusetts 02111 (617) 423-3990; *The World in Figures.*

International Monetary Fund, 700 Nineteenth Street, NW, Washington, D.C. 20431 (202) 623-7000; *Direction of Trade Statistics.*

SAMOA - INDUSTRY

G.K. Hall and Company, 70 Lincoln Street, Boston, Massachusetts 02111 (617) 423-3990; *The World in Figures.*

International Labour Office, I.L.O. Publications, CH-1211, Geneva 22, Switzerland; *Yearbook of Labour Statistics.*

Statistical Office of the United Nations, Publishing Service, New York, New York 10017 (800) 253-9646; *Statistical Yearbook for Asia and the Pacific.*

SAMOA - INFANT AND MATERNAL MORTALITY

Statistical Office of the United Nations, Publishing Service, New York, New York 10017 (800) 253-9646; *Demographic Yearbook,* and *Statistical Yearbook.*

World Health Organization, Office of Publications, Avenue Appia, CH-1211 Geneva 27, Switzerland (Telephone Number in U.S. (518) 436-9686); *World Health Statistics Annual.*

SAMOA - INTERNAL TRADE

Statistical Office of the United Nations, Publishing Service, New York, New York 10017 (800) 253-9646; *Statistical Yearbook for Asia and the Pacific.*

SAMOA - INTERNATIONAL RESERVES EXCLUDING GOLD

Statistical Office of the United Nations, Publishing Service, New York, New York 10017 (800) 253-9646; *Statistical Yearbook.*

SAMOA - LABOR FORCE

Food and Agricultural Organization of the United Nations (FAO) Via delle Terme di Caracalla, 00100 Rome, Italy (Telephone Number in U.S. (202) 653-2400); *The State of Food and Agriculture.*

G.K. Hall and Company, 70 Lincoln Street, Boston, Massachusetts 02111 (617) 423-3990; *The World in Figures.*

SAMOA - LABOR PRODUCTIVITY

International Labour Office, I.L.O. Publications, CH-1211, Geneva 22, Switzerland; *Yearbook of Labour Statistics.*

SAMOA - LAND USE

Food and Agricultural Organization of the United Nations (FAO), Via delle Terme di Caracalla, 00100 Rome, Italy (Telephone Number in U.S. (202) 653-2400); *Production Yearbook.*

G.K. Hall and Company, 70 Lincoln Street, Boston, Massachusetts 02111 (617) 423-3990; *The World in Figures.*

SAMOA - LIBRARIES

United Nations Educational, Scientific and Cultural Organization (UNESCO), 7 Place de Fontenoy, F-75700 Paris, France (Telephone Number in U.S. (212) 963-5981); *Statistical Yearbook.*

SAMOA - LIVESTOCK AND POULTRY

Food and Agricultural Organization of the United Nations (FAO), Via delle Terme di Caracalla, 00100 Rome, Italy (Telephone Number in U.S. (202) 653-2400); *Production Yearbook,* and *The State of Food and Agriculture.*

G.K. Hall and Company, 70 Lincoln Street, Boston, Massachusetts 02111 (617) 423-3990; *The World in Figures.*

Statistical Office of the United Nations, Publishing Service, New York, New York 10017 (800) 253-9646; *Statistical Yearbook.*

SAMOA - LIVING LEVELS

G.K. Hall and Company, 70 Lincoln Street, Boston, Massachusetts 02111 (617) 423-3990; *The World in Figures.*

SAMOA - MAIL TRAFFIC - NUMBER OF ITEMS SENT AND RECEIVED

Statistical Office of the United Nations, Publishing Service, New York, New York 10017 (800) 253-9646; *Statistical Yearbook.*

SAMOA - MANPOWER

Statistical Office of the United Nations, Publishing Service, New York, New York 10017 (800) 253-9646; *Statistical Yearbook for Asia and the Pacific.*

SAMOA - MANUFACTURING

G.K. Hall and Company, 70 Lincoln Street, Boston, Massachusetts 02111 (617) 423-3990; *The World in Figures.*

SAMOA - MARRIAGE RATES

Statistical Office of the United Nations, Publishing Service, New York, New York 10017 (800) 253-9646; *Demographic Yearbook,* and *Statistical Yearbook.*

SAMOA - MEAT PRODUCTION - See SAMOA - LIVESTOCK AND POULTRY

SAMOA - MERCHANT SHIPPING

G.K. Hall and Company, 70 Lincoln Street, Boston, Massachusetts 02111 (617) 423-3990; *The World in Figures.*

Statistical Office of the United Nations, Publishing Service, New York, New York 10017 (800) 253-9646; *Statistical Yearbook.*

SAMOA - MILITARY

G.K. Hall and Company, 70 Lincoln Street, Boston, Massachusetts 02111 (617) 423-3990; *The World in Figures.*

SAMOA - MINING AND MINERAL PRODUCTS

G.K. Hall and Company, 70 Lincoln Street, Boston, Massachusetts 02111 (617) 423-3990; *The World in Figures.*

SAMOA - MONEY EXCHANGE RATES

Statistical Office of the United Nations, Publishing Service, New York, New York 10017 (800) 253-9646; *Statistical Yearbook.*

SAMOA - MONEY SUPPLY

G.K. Hall and Company, 70 Lincoln Street, Boston, Massachusetts 02111 (617) 423-3990; *The World in Figures.*

Statistical Office of the United Nations, Publishing Service, New York, New York 10017 (800) 253-9646; *Statistical Yearbook.*

SAMOA - MOTION PICTURES

Statistical Office of the United Nations, Publishing Service, New York, New York 10017 (800) 253-9646; *Statistical Yearbook.*

SAMOA - MOTOR VEHICLES IN USE

G.K. Hall and Company, 70 Lincoln Street, Boston, Massachusetts 02111 (617) 423-3990; *The World in Figures.*

Statistical Office of the United Nations, Publishing Service, New York, New York 10017 (800) 253-9646; *Statistical Yearbook.*

SAMOA - NATALITY - See SAMOA - BIRTH RATE

SAMOA - NATIONAL ACCOUNTS

Statistical Office of the United Nations, Publishing Service, New York, New York 10017 (800) 253-9646; *National Accounts Statistics,* and *Statistical Yearbook for Asia and the Pacific.*

SAMOA - NATIONAL INCOME

G.K. Hall and Company, 70 Lincoln Street, Boston, Massachusetts 02111 (617) 423-3990; *The World in Figures.*

Statistical Office of the United Nations, Publishing Service, New York, New York 10017 (800) 253-9646; *Statistical Yearbook.*

SAMOA - NEWSPAPER PRODUCTION - See SAMOA - FORESTRY AND FOREST PRODUCTS

SAMOA - NEWSPRINT - See SAMOA - FORESTRY AND FOREST PRODUCTS

SAMOA - OCCUPATIONS - See SAMOA - LABOR FORCE

SAMOA - PATENTS

Statistical Office of the United Nations, Publishing Service, New York, New York 10017 (800) 253-9646; *Statistical Yearbook.*

SAMOA - PERIODICALS

United Nations Educational, Scientific and Cultural Organization (UNESCO), 7 Place de Fontenoy, F-75700 Paris, France (Telephone Number in U.S. (212) 963-5981); *Statistical Yearbook.*

SAMOA - PESTICIDE USE

Food and Agricultural Organization of the United Nations (FAO) Via delle Terme di Caracalla, 00100 Rome, Italy (Telephone Number in U.S. (202) 653-2400); *The State of Food and Agriculture.*

SAMOA - PETROLEUM INDUSTRY

Food and Agricultural Organization of the United Nations (FAO) Via delle Terme di Caracalla, 00100 Rome, Italy (Telephone Number in U.S. (202) 653-2400); *The State of Food and Agriculture.*

G.K. Hall and Company, 70 Lincoln Street, Boston, Massachusetts 02111 (617) 423-3990; *The World in Figures.*

SAMOA - PIGS - See SAMOA - LIVESTOCK AND POULTRY

SAMOA - POPULATION

Food and Agricultural Organization of the United Nations (FAO), Via delle Terme di Caracalla, 00100 Rome, Italy (Telephone Number in U.S. (202) 653-2400); *Production Yearbook.*

G.K. Hall and Company, 70 Lincoln Street, Boston, Massachusetts 02111 (617) 423-3990; *The World in Figures.*

International Labour Office, I.L.O. Publications, CH-1211, Geneva 22, Switzerland; *Yearbook of Labour Statistics.*

Statistical Office of the United Nations, Publishing Service, New York, New York 10017 (800) 253-9646; *Demographic Yearbook,* and *Statistical Yearbook,* and *Statistical Yearbook for Asia and the Pacific.*

World Health Organization, Office of Publications, Avenue Appia, CH-1211 Geneva 27, Switzerland (Telephone Number in U.S. (518) 436-9686); *World Health Statistics Annual.*

SAMOA - POWER PRODUCTION INDUSTRY

Statistical Office of the United Nations, Publishing Service, New York, New York 10017 (800) 253-9646; *Electric Power in Asia and the Pacific.*

SAMOA - PRICES

Food and Agricultural Organization of the United Nations (FAO), Via delle Terme di Caracalla, 00100 Rome, Italy (Telephone Number in U.S. (202) 653-2400); *Production Yearbook,* and *The State of Food and Agriculture.*

G.K. Hall and Company, 70 Lincoln Street, Boston, Massachusetts 02111 (617) 423-3990; *The World in Figures.*

International Labour Office, I.L.O. Publications, CH-1211, Geneva 22, Switzerland; *Yearbook of Labour Statistics.*

SAMOA - PRODUCTION

G.K. Hall and Company, 70 Lincoln Street, Boston, Massachusetts 02111 (617) 423-3990; *The World in Figures.*

SAMOA - RADIO BROADCASTING - See SAMOA - BROADCASTING

SAMOA - RAILWAYS

G.K. Hall and Company, 70 Lincoln Street, Boston, Massachusetts 02111 (617) 423-3990; *The World in Figures*.

SAMOA - RETAIL TRADE

G.K. Hall and Company, 70 Lincoln Street, Boston, Massachusetts 02111 (617) 423-3990; *The World in Figures*.

SAMOA - ROUNDWOOD PRODUCTION - See SAMOA - FORESTRY AND FOREST PRODUCTS

SAMOA - SAWNWOOD PRODUCTION - See SAMOA - FORESTRY AND FOREST PRODUCTS

SAMOA - SCIENCE AND TECHNOLOGY - EXPENDITURE FOR RESEARCH

Statistical Office of the United Nations, Publishing Service, New York, New York 10017 (800) 253-9646; *Statistical Yearbook*.

SAMOA - SCIENTISTS AND TECHNICIANS

Statistical Office of the United Nations, Publishing Service, New York, New York 10017 (800) 253-9646; *Statistical Yearbook*.

SAMOA - SOCIAL DATA

G.K. Hall and Company, 70 Lincoln Street, Boston, Massachusetts 02111 (617) 423-3990; *The World in Figures*.

SAMOA - STOCKS - COMMODITY - MARKET PRICE - INDEX

Food and Agricultural Organization of the United Nations (FAO) Via delle Terme di Caracalla, 00100 Rome, Italy (Telephone Number in U.S. (202) 653-2400); *The State of Food and Agriculture*.

SAMOA - TAXATION

G.K. Hall and Company, 70 Lincoln Street, Boston, Massachusetts 02111 (617) 423-3990; *The World in Figures*.

SAMOA - TELEPHONES IN USE

G.K. Hall and Company, 70 Lincoln Street, Boston, Massachusetts 02111 (617) 423-3990; *The World in Figures*.

Statistical Office of the United Nations, Publishing Service, New York, New York 10017 (800) 253-9646; *Statistical Yearbook*.

SAMOA - TEXTILE INDUSTRY

G.K. Hall and Company, 70 Lincoln Street, Boston, Massachusetts 02111 (617) 423-3990; *The World in Figures*.

SAMOA - THEATRE

United Nations Educational, Scientific and Cultural Organization (UNESCO), 7 Place de Fontenoy, F-75700 Paris, France (Telephone Number in U.S. (212) 963-5981); *Statistical Yearbook*.

SAMOA - TOBACCO PRODUCTION

Statistical Office of the United Nations, Publishing Service, New York, New York 10017 (800) 253-9646; *Statistical Yearbook*.

SAMOA - TOURISM

G.K. Hall and Company, 70 Lincoln Street, Boston, Massachusetts 02111 (617) 423-3990; *The World in Figures*.

Statistical Office of the United Nations, Publishing Service, New York, New York 10017 (800) 253-9646; *Statistical Yearbook*.

World Tourism Organization, Calle Capitan Haya 42, E-28020 Madrid, Spain; *Yearbook of Tourism Statistics*.

SAMOA - TRACTORS IN USE

Statistical Office of the United Nations, Publishing Service, New York, New York 10017 (800) 253-9646; *Statistical Yearbook*.

SAMOA - TRADE - See SAMOA - FOREIGN TRADE

SAMOA - TRADEMARKS AND SERVICE MARKS

Statistical Office of the United Nations, Publishing Service, New York, New York 10017 (800) 253-9646; *Statistical Yearbook*.

SAMOA - TRANSPORTATION AND COMMUNICATIONS

G.K. Hall and Company, 70 Lincoln Street, Boston, Massachusetts 02111 (617) 423-3990; *The World in Figures*.

Statistical Office of the United Nations, Publishing Service, New York, New York 10017 (800) 253-9646; *Statistical Yearbook for Asia and the Pacific*.

SAMOA - UNEMPLOYMENT

International Labour Office, I.L.O. Publications, CH-1211, Geneva 22, Switzerland; *Yearbook of Labour Statistics*.

SAMOA - UTILITIES

Statistical Office of the United Nations, Publishing Service, New York, New York 10017 (800) 253-9646; *Electric Power in Asia and the Pacific*.

SAMOA - VITAL STATISTICS

G.K. Hall and Company, 70 Lincoln Street, Boston, Massachusetts 02111 (617) 423-3990; *The World in Figures*.

Statistical Office of the United Nations, Publishing Service, New York, New York 10017 (800) 253-9646; *Statistical Yearbook*.

World Health Organization, Office of Publications, Avenue Appia, CH-1211 Geneva 27, Switzerland (Telephone Number in U.S. (518) 436-9686); *World Health Statistics Annual*.

SAMOA - WAGES

G.K. Hall and Company, 70 Lincoln Street, Boston, Massachusetts 02111 (617) 423-3990; *The World in Figures*.

International Labour Office, I.L.O. Publications, CH-1211, Geneva 22, Switzerland; *Yearbook of Labour Statistics*.

Statistical Office of the United Nations, Publishing Service, New York, New York 10017 (800) 253-9646; *Statistical Yearbook for Asia and the Pacific*.

SAMOA - WEATHER

G.K. Hall and Company, 70 Lincoln Street, Boston, Massachusetts 02111 (617) 423-3990; *The World in Figures.*

SAMOAN POPULATION

U.S. Department of Commerce, Bureau of the Census, Suitland, Maryland 20233 (301) 763-4040; *Census of Population, General Population Characteristics, United States,* and press release.

San Marino - National Statistical Office

Ufficio Statale di Statistica, Via Antonio Onofri 87, Repubblica de San Marino.

San Marino - Primary Statistics Sources

Servicio Statale di Statistica, Via G Carducci 145, Repubblica de San Marino; *Sintesi Statistica Socio-economica* (Socio-economic statistical analysis); *Bollettino di statistica* (Statistical bulletin), and *Annuario Statistico* (Statistical Yearbook).

SAN MARINO - AGRICULTURE

Food and Agricultural Organization of the United Nations (FAO) Via delle Terme di Caracalla, 00100 Rome, Italy (Telephone Number in U.S. (202) 653-2400); *Production Yearbook, The State of Food and Agriculture,* and *Trade Yearbook.*

G.K. Hall and Company, 70 Lincoln Street, Boston, Massachusetts 02111 (617) 423-3990; *The World in Figures.*

SAN MARINO - AIRLINE SERVICE

G.K. Hall and Company, 70 Lincoln Street, Boston, Massachusetts 02111 (617) 423-3990; *The World in Figures.*

SAN MARINO - AREA AND DENSITY OF POPULATION

Food and Agricultural Organization of the United Nations (FAO) Via delle Terme di Caracalla, 00100 Rome, Italy (Telephone Number in U.S. (202) 653-2400); *The State of Food and Agriculture.*

G.K. Hall and Company, 70 Lincoln Street, Boston, Massachusetts 02111 (617) 423-3990; *The World in Figures.*

Statistical Office of the United Nations, Publishing Service, New York, New York 10017 (800) 253-9646; *Statistical Yearbook.*

SAN MARINO - BALANCE OF PAYMENTS

G.K. Hall and Company, 70 Lincoln Street, Boston, Massachusetts 02111 (617) 423-3990; *The World in Figures.*

SAN MARINO - BANKING

G.K. Hall and Company, 70 Lincoln Street, Boston, Massachusetts 02111 (617) 423-3990; *The World in Figures.*

SAN MARINO - BIRTH RATES

Statistical Office of the United Nations, Publishing Service, New York, New York 10017 (800) 253-9646; *Demographic Yearbook,* and *Statistical Yearbook.*

World Health Organization, Office of Publications, Avenue Appia, CH-1211 Geneva 27, Switzerland (Telephone Number in U.S. (518)

436-9686); *World Health Statistics Annual.*

SAN MARINO - BONDS

G.K. Hall and Company, 70 Lincoln Street, Boston, Massachusetts 02111 (617) 423-3990; *The World in Figures.*

SAN MARINO - BOOK PRODUCTION

G.K. Hall and Company, 70 Lincoln Street, Boston, Massachusetts 02111 (617) 423-3990; *The World in Figures.*

United Nations Educational, Scientific and Cultural Organization (UNESCO), 7 Place de Fontenoy, F-75700 Paris, France (Telephone Number in U.S. (212) 963-5981); *Statistical Yearbook.*

SAN MARINO - BROADCASTING

Billboard Limited, P.O. Box 9027, 1006 AA Amsterdam, The Netherlands (Telephone Number in U.S. (212) 764-7300); *World Radio TV Handbook.*

G.K. Hall and Company, 70 Lincoln Street, Boston, Massachusetts 02111 (617) 423-3990; *The World in Figures.*

SAN MARINO - BUSINESS

G.K. Hall and Company, 70 Lincoln Street, Boston, Massachusetts 02111 (617) 423-3990; *The World in Figures.*

SAN MARINO - CALORIE SUPPLY

Food and Agricultural Organization of the United Nations (FAO) Via delle Terme di Caracalla, 00100 Rome, Italy (Telephone Number in U.S. (202) 653-2400); *The State of Food and Agriculture.*

SAN MARINO - CHEMICAL (ORGANIC) PRODUCTION - See SAN MARINO - MINING AND MINERAL PRODUCTS

SAN MARINO - CLASS STRUCTURE

G.K. Hall and Company, 70 Lincoln Street, Boston, Massachusetts 02111 (617) 423-3990; *The World in Figures.*

SAN MARINO - CLIMATE

G.K. Hall and Company, 70 Lincoln Street, Boston, Massachusetts 02111 (617) 423-3990; *The World in Figures.*

SAN MARINO - COAL PRODUCTION - See SAN MARINO - MINING AND MINERAL PRODUCTS

G.K. Hall and Company, 70 Lincoln Street, Boston, Massachusetts 02111 (617) 423-3990; *The World in Figures.*

SAN MARINO - COMMUNICATIONS

G.K. Hall and Company, 70 Lincoln Street, Boston, Massachusetts 02111 (617) 423-3990; *The World in Figures.*

SAN MARINO - CONSTRUCTION INDUSTRY

Statistical Office of the United Nations, Publishing Service, New York, New York 10017 (800) 253-9646; *Construction Statistics Yearbook,* and *Statistical Yearbook.*

SAN MARINO - CONSUMER PRICE INDEX

G.K. Hall and Company, 70 Lincoln Street, Boston, Massachusetts 02111 (617) 423-3990; *The World in Figures*.

SAN MARINO - CONSUMPTION

G.K. Hall and Company, 70 Lincoln Street, Boston, Massachusetts 02111 (617) 423-3990; *The World in Figures*.

SAN MARINO - CORN PRODUCTION - See SAN MARINO - CROPS

SAN MARINO - CORPORATE TAXES - See SAN MARINO - TAXATION

SAN MARINO - CROPS

Food and Agricultural Organization of the United Nations (FAO) Via delle Terme di Caracalla, 00100 Rome, Italy (Telephone Number in U.S. (202) 653-2400); *The State of Food and Agriculture*.

G.K. Hall and Company, 70 Lincoln Street, Boston, Massachusetts 02111 (617) 423-3990; *The World in Figures*.

SAN MARINO - CUSTOMS DUTIES

G.K. Hall and Company, 70 Lincoln Street, Boston, Massachusetts 02111 (617) 423-3990; *The World in Figures*.

SAN MARINO - DAIRY PRODUCTS

Food and Agricultural Organization of the United Nations (FAO) Via delle Terme di Caracalla, 00100 Rome, Italy (Telephone Number in U.S. (202) 653-2400); *The State of Food and Agriculture*.

SAN MARINO - DEATH RATES

G.K. Hall and Company, 70 Lincoln Street, Boston, Massachusetts 02111 (617) 423-3990; *The World in Figures*.

Statistical Office of the United Nations, Publishing Service, New York, New York 10017 (800) 253-9646; *Statistical Yearbook*.

SAN MARINO - DEFENSE EXPENDITURES

G.K. Hall and Company, 70 Lincoln Street, Boston, Massachusetts 02111 (617) 423-3990; *The World in Figures*.

SAN MARINO - DEMOGRAPHY

G.K. Hall and Company, 70 Lincoln Street, Boston, Massachusetts 02111 (617) 423-3990; *The World in Figures*.

SAN MARINO - DEVELOPMENT ASSISTANCE

G.K. Hall and Company, 70 Lincoln Street, Boston, Massachusetts 02111 (617) 423-3990; *The World in Figures*.

SAN MARINO - DISEASE

G.K. Hall and Company, 70 Lincoln Street, Boston, Massachusetts 02111 (617) 423-3990; *The World in Figures*.

SAN MARINO - DIVORCE RATES

Statistical Office of the United Nations, Publishing Service, New York, New York 10017 (800) 253-9646; *Demographic Yearbook*.

SAN MARINO - DOMESTIC PRODUCT

G.K. Hall and Company, 70 Lincoln Street, Boston, Massachusetts 02111 (617) 423-3990; *The World in Figures*.

SAN MARINO - ECONOMY

G.K. Hall and Company, 70 Lincoln Street, Boston, Massachusetts 02111 (617) 423-3990; *The World in Figures*.

SAN MARINO - EDUCATION

G.K. Hall and Company, 70 Lincoln Street, Boston, Massachusetts 02111 (617) 423-3990; *The World in Figures*.

United Nations Educational, Scientific and Cultural Organization (UNESCO), 7 Place de Fontenoy, F-75700 Paris, France (Telephone Number in U.S. (212) 963-5981); *Statistical Yearbook*.

SAN MARINO - EGG PRODUCTION AND CONSUMPTION - See SAN MARINO - DAIRY PRODUCTS

SAN MARINO - ENERGY

Food and Agricultural Organization of the United Nations (FAO) Via delle Terme di Caracalla, 00100 Rome, Italy (Telephone Number in U.S. (202) 653-2400); *The State of Food and Agriculture*.

G.K. Hall and Company, 70 Lincoln Street, Boston, Massachusetts 02111 (617) 423-3990; *The World in Figures*.

SAN MARINO - EXPORTS

Food and Agricultural Organization of the United Nations (FAO) Via delle Terme di Caracalla, 00100 Rome, Italy (Telephone Number in U.S. (202) 653-2400); *The State of Food and Agriculture*.

G.K. Hall and Company, 70 Lincoln Street, Boston, Massachusetts 02111 (617) 423-3990; *The World in Figures*.

SAN MARINO - EXTERNAL TRADE

Food and Agricultural Organization of the United Nations (FAO) Via delle Terme di Caracalla, 00100 Rome, Italy (Telephone Number in U.S. (202) 653-2400); *The State of Food and Agriculture*, and *Trade Yearbook*.

G.K. Hall and Company, 70 Lincoln Street, Boston, Massachusetts 02111 (617) 423-3990; *The World in Figures*.

SAN MARINO - FARM CROPS - See SAN MARINO - CROPS

SAN MARINO - FETAL MORTALITY

Statistical Office of the United Nations, Publishing Service, New York, New York 10017 (800) 253-9646; *Demographic Yearbook*.

World Health Organization, Office of Publications, Avenue Appia, CH-1211 Geneva 27, Switzerland (Telephone Number in U.S. (518) 436-9686); *World Health Statistics Annual*.

SAN MARINO - FINANCE

G.K. Hall and Company, 70 Lincoln Street, Boston, Massachusetts 02111 (617) 423-3990; *The World in Figures*.

SAN MARINO - FISHERIES

Food and Agricultural Organization of the United Nations (FAO) Via delle Terme di Caracalla, 00100 Rome, Italy (Telephone Number in U.S. (202) 653-2400); *The State of Food and Agriculture*, and *Yearbook of Fishery Statistics*.

SAN MARINO - FOOD

Food and Agricultural Organization of the United Nations (FAO) Via delle Terme di Caracalla, 00100 Rome, Italy (Telephone Number in U.S. (202) 653-2400); *Production Yearbook*, and *The State of Food and Agriculture*.

G.K. Hall and Company, 70 Lincoln Street, Boston, Massachusetts 02111 (617) 423-3990; *The World in Figures*.

SAN MARINO - FOREIGN AID

G.K. Hall and Company, 70 Lincoln Street, Boston, Massachusetts 02111 (617) 423-3990; *The World in Figures*.

SAN MARINO - FOREIGN TRADE

Food and Agricultural Organization of the United Nations (FAO) Via delle Terme di Caracalla, 00100 Rome, Italy (Telephone Number in U.S. (202) 653-2400); *The State of Food and Agriculture*.

G.K. Hall and Company, 70 Lincoln Street, Boston, Massachusetts 02111 (617) 423-3990; *The World in Figures*.

SAN MARINO - FORESTRY AND FOREST PRODUCTS

G.K. Hall and Company, 70 Lincoln Street, Boston, Massachusetts 02111 (617) 423-3990; *The World in Figures*.

Statistical Office of the United Nations, Publishing Service, New York, New York 10017 (800) 253-9646; *Statistical Yearbook*.

United Nations Educational, Scientific and Cultural Organization (UNESCO), 7 Place de Fontenoy, F-75700 Paris, France (Telephone Number in U.S. (212) 963-5981); *Statistical Yearbook*.

SAN MARINO - GENERAL MORTALITY

Statistical Office of the United Nations, Publishing Service, New York, New York 10017 (800) 253-9646; *Demographic Yearbook*.

World Health Organization, Office of Publications, Avenue Appia, CH-1211 Geneva 27, Switzerland (Telephone Number in U.S. (518) 436-9686); *World Health Statistics Annual*.

SAN MARINO - GOVERNMENT

G.K. Hall and Company, 70 Lincoln Street, Boston, Massachusetts 02111 (617) 423-3990; *The World in Figures*.

SAN MARINO - GRAIN PRODUCTION - See SAN MARINO - CROPS

SAN MARINO - GROSS DOMESTIC PRODUCT

G.K. Hall and Company, 70 Lincoln Street, Boston, Massachusetts 02111 (617) 423-3990; *The World in Figures*.

SAN MARINO - HEALTH

G.K. Hall and Company, 70 Lincoln Street, Boston, Massachusetts 02111 (617) 423-3990; *The World in Figures*.

SAN MARINO - HIGHWAYS

G.K. Hall and Company, 70 Lincoln Street, Boston, Massachusetts 02111 (617) 423-3990; *The World in Figures*.

SAN MARINO - HOUSING AND HOUSING UNITS

Statistical Office of the United Nations, Publishing Service, New York, New York 10017 (800) 253-9646; *Statistical Yearbook*.

SAN MARINO - ILLITERATE POPULATION

G.K. Hall and Company, 70 Lincoln Street, Boston, Massachusetts 02111 (617) 423-3990; *The World in Figures*.

United Nations Educational, Scientific and Cultural Organization (UNESCO), 7 Place de Fontenoy, F-75700 Paris, France (Telephone Number in U.S. (212) 963-5981); *Statistical Yearbook*.

SAN MARINO - IMPORTS

Food and Agricultural Organization of the United Nations (FAO) Via delle Terme di Caracalla, 00100 Rome, Italy (Telephone Number in U.S. (202) 653-2400); *The State of Food and Agriculture*.

G.K. Hall and Company, 70 Lincoln Street, Boston, Massachusetts 02111 (617) 423-3990; *The World in Figures*.

SAN MARINO - INDUSTRY

G.K. Hall and Company, 70 Lincoln Street, Boston, Massachusetts 02111 (617) 423-3990; *The World in Figures*.

SAN MARINO - INFANT AND MATERNAL MORTALITY

Statistical Office of the United Nations, Publishing Service, New York, New York 10017 (800) 253-9646; *Demographic Yearbook*, and *Statistical Yearbook*.

World Health Organization, Office of Publications, Avenue Appia, CH-1211 Geneva 27, Switzerland (Telephone Number in U.S. (518) 436-9686); *World Health Statistics Annual*.

SAN MARINO - LABOR FORCE

Food and Agricultural Organization of the United Nations (FAO) Via delle Terme di Caracalla, 00100 Rome, Italy (Telephone Number in U.S. (202) 653-2400); *The State of Food and Agriculture*.

G.K. Hall and Company, 70 Lincoln Street, Boston, Massachusetts 02111 (617) 423-3990; *The World in Figures*.

SAN MARINO - LAND USE

Food and Agricultural Organization of the United Nations (FAO), Via delle Terme di Caracalla, 00100 Rome, Italy (Telephone Number in U.S. (202) 653-2400); *Production Yearbook*.

G.K. Hall and Company, 70 Lincoln Street, Boston, Massachusetts 02111 (617) 423-3990; *The World in Figures*.

SAN MARINO - LIBRARIES

United Nations Educational, Scientific and Cultural Organization (UNESCO), 7 Place de Fontenoy, F-75700 Paris, France (Telephone Number in U.S. (212) 963-5981); *Statistical Yearbook*.

SAN MARINO - LIVESTOCK AND POULTRY

Food and Agricultural Organization of the United Nations (FAO), Via delle Terme di Caracalla, 00100 Rome, Italy (Telephone Number in U.S. (202) 653-2400); *Production Yearbook*, and *The State of Food and Agriculture*.

G.K. Hall and Company, 70 Lincoln Street, Boston, Massachusetts 02111 (617) 423-3990; *The World in Figures*.

SAN MARINO - LIVING LEVELS

G.K. Hall and Company, 70 Lincoln Street, Boston, Massachusetts 02111 (617) 423-3990; *The World in Figures*.

SAN MARINO - MANUFACTURING

G.K. Hall and Company, 70 Lincoln Street, Boston, Massachusetts 02111 (617) 423-3990; *The World in Figures*.

SAN MARINO - MARRIAGE RATES

Statistical Office of the United Nations, Publishing Service, New York, New York 10017 (800) 253-9646; *Demographic Yearbook*, and *Statistical Yearbook*.

SAN MARINO - MEAT PRODUCTION - See SAN MARINO - LIVESTOCK AND POULTRY

SAN MARINO - MILITARY

G.K. Hall and Company, 70 Lincoln Street, Boston, Massachusetts 02111 (617) 423-3990; *The World in Figures*.

SAN MARINO - MINING AND MINERAL PRODUCTS

G.K. Hall and Company, 70 Lincoln Street, Boston, Massachusetts 02111 (617) 423-3990; *The World in Figures*.

SAN MARINO - MONEY SUPPLY

G.K. Hall and Company, 70 Lincoln Street, Boston, Massachusetts 02111 (617) 423-3990; *The World in Figures*.

SAN MARINO - MONUMENTS AND HISTORICAL SITES

United Nations Educational, Scientific and Cultural Organization (UNESCO), 7 Place de Fontenoy, F-75700 Paris, France (Telephone Number in U.S. (212) 963-5981); *Statistical Yearbook*.

SAN MARINO - MOTION PICTURES

Statistical Office of the United Nations, Publishing Service, New York, New York 10017 (800) 253-9646; *Statistical Yearbook*.

SAN MARINO - MOTOR VEHICLES IN USE

G.K. Hall and Company, 70 Lincoln Street, Boston, Massachusetts 02111 (617) 423-3990; *The World in Figures*.

SAN MARINO - MUSEUMS

United Nations Educational, Scientific and Cultural Organization (UNESCO), 7 Place de Fontenoy, F-75700 Paris, France (Telephone Number in U.S. (212) 963-5981); *Statistical Yearbook*.

SAN MARINO - NATALITY - See SAN MARINO - BIRTH RATE

SAN MARINO - NATIONAL INCOME

G.K. Hall and Company, 70 Lincoln Street, Boston, Massachusetts 02111 (617) 423-3990; *The World in Figures*.

SAN MARINO - NEWSPAPER PRODUCTION - See SAN MARINO - FORESTRY AND FOREST PRODUCTS

SAN MARINO - OCCUPATIONS - See SAN MARINO - LABOR FORCE

SAN MARINO - PESTICIDE USE

Food and Agricultural Organization of the United Nations (FAO) Via delle Terme di Caracalla, 00100 Rome, Italy (Telephone Number in U.S. (202) 653-2400); *The State of Food and Agriculture*.

SAN MARINO - PETROLEUM INDUSTRY

Food and Agricultural Organization of the United Nations (FAO) Via delle Terme di Caracalla, 00100 Rome, Italy (Telephone Number in U.S. (202) 653-2400); *The State of Food and Agriculture*.

G.K. Hall and Company, 70 Lincoln Street, Boston, Massachusetts 02111 (617) 423-3990; *The World in Figures*.

SAN MARINO - POPULATION

Food and Agricultural Organization of the United Nations (FAO), Via delle Terme di Caracalla, 00100 Rome, Italy (Telephone Number in U.S. (202) 653-2400); *Production Yearbook*.

G.K. Hall and Company, 70 Lincoln Street, Boston, Massachusetts 02111 (617) 423-3990; *The World in Figures*.

Statistical Office of the United Nations, Publishing Service, New York, New York 10017 (800) 253-9646; *Demographic Yearbook*, and *Statistical Yearbook*.

World Health Organization, Office of Publications, Avenue Appia, CH-1211 Geneva 27, Switzerland (Telephone Number in U.S. (518) 436-9686); *World Health Statistics Annual*.

SAN MARINO - PRICES

Food and Agricultural Organization of the United Nations (FAO), Via delle Terme di Caracalla, 00100 Rome, Italy (Telephone Number in U.S. (202) 653-2400); *Production Yearbook*, and *The State of Food and Agriculture*.

G.K. Hall and Company, 70 Lincoln Street, Boston, Massachusetts 02111 (617) 423-3990; *The World in Figures*.

SAN MARINO - PRODUCTION

G.K. Hall and Company, 70 Lincoln Street, Boston, Massachusetts 02111 (617) 423-3990; *The World in Figures*.

SAN MARINO - RAILWAYS

G.K. Hall and Company, 70 Lincoln Street, Boston, Massachusetts 02111 (617) 423-3990; *The World in Figures*.

SAN MARINO - RETAIL TRADE

G.K. Hall and Company, 70 Lincoln Street, Boston, Massachusetts 02111 (617) 423-3990; *The World in Figures*.

SAN MARINO - SCIENTISTS AND TECHNICIANS

Statistical Office of the United Nations, Publishing Service, New York, New York 10017 (800) 253-9646; *Statistical Yearbook.*

SAN MARINO - SOCIAL DATA

G.K. Hall and Company, 70 Lincoln Street, Boston, Massachusetts 02111 (617) 423-3990; *The World in Figures.*

SAN MARINO - STOCKS - COMMODITY - MARKET PRICE - INDEX

Food and Agricultural Organization of the United Nations (FAO) Via delle Terme di Caracalla, 00100 Rome, Italy (Telephone Number in U.S. (202) 653-2400); *The State of Food and Agriculture.*

SAN MARINO - TAXATION

G.K. Hall and Company, 70 Lincoln Street, Boston, Massachusetts 02111 (617) 423-3990; *The World in Figures.*

SAN MARINO - TELEPHONES IN USE

American Telephone and Telegraph Company, 26 Parsippany Road, Whippany, New Jersey 07981 (800) 338-4038; *The World's Telephones.*

G.K. Hall and Company, 70 Lincoln Street, Boston, Massachusetts 02111 (617) 423-3990; *The World in Figures.*

Statistical Office of the United Nations, Publishing Service, New York, New York 10017 (800) 253-9646; *Statistical Yearbook.*

SAN MARINO - TEXTILE INDUSTRY

G.K. Hall and Company, 70 Lincoln Street, Boston, Massachusetts 02111 (617) 423-3990; *The World in Figures.*

SAN MARINO - TOURISM

G.K. Hall and Company, 70 Lincoln Street, Boston, Massachusetts 02111 (617) 423-3990; *The World in Figures.*

Statistical Office of the United Nations, Publishing Service, New York, New York 10017 (800) 253-9646; *Statistical Yearbook.*

SAN MARINO - TRADE - See SAN MARINO - FOREIGN TRADE

SAN MARINO - TRANSPORTATION AND COMMUNICATIONS

G.K. Hall and Company, 70 Lincoln Street, Boston, Massachusetts 02111 (617) 423-3990; *The World in Figures.*

SAN MARINO - VITAL STATISTICS

G.K. Hall and Company, 70 Lincoln Street, Boston, Massachusetts 02111 (617) 423-3990; *The World in Figures.*

Statistical Office of the United Nations, Publishing Service, New York, New York 10017 (800) 253-9646; *Statistical Yearbook.*

World Health Organization, Office of Publications, Avenue Appia, CH-1211 Geneva 27, Switzerland (Telephone Number in U.S. (518) 436-9686); *World Health Statistics Annual.*

SAN MARINO - WAGES

G.K. Hall and Company, 70 Lincoln Street, Boston, Massachusetts 02111 (617) 423-3990; *The World in Figures.*

SAN MARINO - WEATHER

G.K. Hall and Company, 70 Lincoln Street, Boston, Massachusetts 02111 (617) 423-3990; *The World in Figures.*

SAND AND GRAVEL INDUSTRY - See also MINING INDUSTRY

SAND AND GRAVEL INDUSTRY

U.S. Department of the Interior, Bureau of Mines, 810 Seventh Street, NW, Washington, D.C. 20241 (202) 501-9649; *Minerals Yearbook, Census of Mineral Industries,* and *Mineral Commodity Summaries.*

SANITATION - See SEWAGE TREATMENT SYSTEMS

Sao Tome and Principe - National Statistical Office

Direccado de Estatistica, CP 256, Sao Tome, Sao Tome e Principe.

Sao Tome and Principe - Primary Statistics Source

Direccao de Economia e Estatistica, Sao Tome, Sao Tome e Principe; *Exposicao: Informacao Estatistica.*

SAO TOME AND PRINCIPE - AGRICULTURE

Food and Agricultural Organization of the United Nations (FAO) Via delle Terme di Caracalla, 00100 Rome, Italy (Telephone Number in U.S. (202) 653-2400); *Production Yearbook, The State of Food and Agriculture,* and *Trade Yearbook.*

G.K. Hall and Company, 70 Lincoln Street, Boston, Massachusetts 02111 (617) 423-3990; *The World in Figures.*

Statistical Office of the United Nations, Publishing Service, New York, New York 10017 (800) 253-9646; *Statistical Yearbook,* and *Survey of Economic and Social Conditions in Africa.*

United Nations Economic Commission for Africa, Africa Hall, P.O. Box 3001, Addis Ababa, Ethiopia (Telephone Number in U.S. (800) 253-9646); *African Statistical Yearbook.*

SAO TOME AND PRINCIPE - AIRLINE SERVICE

G.K. Hall and Company, 70 Lincoln Street, Boston, Massachusetts 02111 (617) 423-3990; *The World in Figures.*

United Nations Economic Commission for Africa, Africa Hall, P.O. Box 3001, Addis Ababa, Ethiopia (Telephone Number in U.S. (800) 253-9646); *African Statistical Yearbook.*

SAO TOME AND PRINCIPE - AREA AND DENSITY OF POPULATION

African Development Bank, 01 BP 1387, Abidjan 01, Cote D'Ivoire; *Selected Statistics on Regional Member Countries.*

Food and Agricultural Organization of the United Nations (FAO) Via delle Terme di Caracalla, 00100 Rome, Italy (Telephone Number in U.S. (202) 653-2400); *The State of Food and Agriculture.*

G.K. Hall and Company, 70 Lincoln Street, Boston, Massachusetts 02111 (617) 423-3990; *The World in Figures.*

Statistical Office of the United Nations, Publishing Service, New York, New York 10017 (800) 253-9646; *Statistical Yearbook*, and *Survey of Economic and Social Conditions in Africa*.

United Nations Educational, Scientific and Cultural Organization (UNESCO), 7 Place de Fontenoy, F-75700 Paris, France (Telephone Number in U.S. (212) 963-5981); *Statistical Yearbook*.

SAO TOME AND PRINCIPE - ARMS EXPORTS AND IMPORTS

U.S. Arms Control and Disarmament Agency, 320 Twenty-first Street, NW, Washington, D.C. 20451 (202) 647-8677; *World Military Expenditures and Arms Transfers*.

SAO TOME AND PRINCIPE - BALANCE OF PAYMENTS

African Development Bank, 01 BP 1387, Abidjan 01, Cote D'Ivoire; *Selected Statistics on Regional Member Countries*.

The Economist Intelligence Unit, 111 West 57th Street, New York, New York 10019 (800) 938-4685; *The World Market Atlas*.

G.K. Hall and Company, 70 Lincoln Street, Boston, Massachusetts 02111 (617) 423-3990; *The World in Figures*.

United Nations Economic Commission for Africa, Africa Hall, P.O. Box 3001, Addis Ababa, Ethiopia (Telephone Number in U.S. (800) 253-9646); *African Statistical Yearbook*.

SAO TOME AND PRINCIPE - BANKING

G.K. Hall and Company, 70 Lincoln Street, Boston, Massachusetts 02111 (617) 423-3990; *The World in Figures*.

United Nations Economic Commission for Africa, Africa Hall, P.O. Box 3001, Addis Ababa, Ethiopia (Telephone Number in U.S. (800) 253-9646); *African Statistical Yearbook*.

SAO TOME AND PRINCIPE - BIRTH RATES

Statistical Office of the United Nations, Publishing Service, New York, New York 10017 (800) 253-9646; *Demographic Yearbook*, *Statistical Yearbook*, and *Survey of Economic and Social Conditions in Africa*.

World Health Organization, Office of Publications, Avenue Appia, CH-1211 Geneva 27, Switzerland (Telephone Number in U.S. (518) 436-9686); *World Health Statistics Annual*.

SAO TOME AND PRINCIPE - BONDS

G.K. Hall and Company, 70 Lincoln Street, Boston, Massachusetts 02111 (617) 423-3990; *The World in Figures*.

SAO TOME AND PRINCIPE - BOOK PRODUCTION

G.K. Hall and Company, 70 Lincoln Street, Boston, Massachusetts 02111 (617) 423-3990; *The World in Figures*.

SAO TOME AND PRINCIPE - BROADCASTING

Billboard Limited, P.O. Box 9027, 1006 AA Amsterdam, The Netherlands (Telephone Number in U.S. (212) 764-7300); *World Radio TV Handbook*.

G.K. Hall and Company, 70 Lincoln Street, Boston, Massachusetts 02111 (617) 423-3990; *The World in Figures*.

SAO TOME AND PRINCIPE - BUSINESS

G.K. Hall and Company, 70 Lincoln Street, Boston, Massachusetts 02111 (617) 423-3990; *The World in Figures*.

SAO TOME AND PRINCIPE - CALORIE SUPPLY

African Development Bank, 01 BP 1387, Abidjan 01, Cote D'Ivoire; *Selected Statistics on Regional Member Countries*.

Food and Agricultural Organization of the United Nations (FAO) Via delle Terme di Caracalla, 00100 Rome, Italy (Telephone Number in U.S. (202) 653-2400); *The State of Food and Agriculture*.

SAO TOME AND PRINCIPE - CATTLE - See SAO TOME AND PRINCIPE - LIVESTOCK AND POULTRY

SAO TOME AND PRINCIPE - CHEMICAL (ORGANIC) PRODUCTION - SEE SAO TOME AND PRINCIPE - MINING AND MINERAL PRODUCTS

SAO TOME AND PRINCIPE - CHICKENS - See SAO TOME AND PRINCIPE - LIVESTOCK AND POULTRY

SAO TOME AND PRINCIPE - CLASS STRUCTURE

G.K. Hall and Company, 70 Lincoln Street, Boston, Massachusetts 02111 (617) 423-3990; *The World in Figures*.

SAO TOME AND PRINCIPE - CLIMATE

G.K. Hall and Company, 70 Lincoln Street, Boston, Massachusetts 02111 (617) 423-3990; *The World in Figures*.

SAO TOME AND PRINCIPE - COAL PRODUCTION - See SAO TOME AND PRINCIPE - MINING AND MINERAL PRODUCTS

SAO TOME AND PRINCIPE - COCOA PRODUCTION - See SAO TOME AND PRINCIPE - CROPS

SAO TOME AND PRINCIPE - COMMUNICATIONS

G.K. Hall and Company, 70 Lincoln Street, Boston, Massachusetts 02111 (617) 423-3990; *The World in Figures*.

United Nations Economic Commission for Africa, Africa Hall, P.O. Box 3001, Addis Ababa, Ethiopia (Telephone Number in U.S. (800) 253-9646); *African Statistical Yearbook*.

SAO TOME AND PRINCIPE - CONSTRUCTION INDUSTRY

United Nations Economic Commission for Africa, Africa Hall, P.O. Box 3001, Addis Ababa, Ethiopia (Telephone Number in U.S. (800) 253-9646); *African Statistical Yearbook*.

SAO TOME AND PRINCIPE - CONSUMER PRICE INDEX

African Development Bank, 01 BP 1387, Abidjan 01, Cote D'Ivoire; *Selected Statistics on Regional Member Countries*.

G.K. Hall and Company, 70 Lincoln Street, Boston, Massachusetts 02111 (617) 423-3990; *The World in Figures*.

Statistical Office of the United Nations, Publishing Service, New York, New York 10017 (800) 253-9646; *Survey of Economic and Social Conditions in Africa*.

SAO TOME AND PRINCIPE - CONSUMPTION

African Development Bank, 01 BP 1387, Abidjan 01, Cote D'Ivoire; *Selected Statistics on Regional Member Countries.*

G.K. Hall and Company, 70 Lincoln Street, Boston, Massachusetts 02111 (617) 423-3990; *The World in Figures.*

Statistical Office of the United Nations, Publishing Service, New York, New York 10017 (800) 253-9646; *Survey of Economic and Social Conditions in Africa.*

SAO TOME AND PRINCIPE - CORN PRODUCTION - See SAO TOME AND PRINCIPE - CROPS

SAO TOME AND PRINCIPE - CORPORATE TAXES - See SAO TOME AND PRINCIPE - TAXATION

SAO TOME AND PRINCIPE - CROPS

Commodity Research Bureau, Incorporated, 75 Wall Street, New York, New York 10005 (212) 504-7754; *Commodity Year Book.*

Food and Agricultural Organization of the United Nations (FAO) Via delle Terme di Caracalla, 00100 Rome, Italy (Telephone Number in U.S. (202) 653-2400); *The State of Food and Agriculture.*

G.K. Hall and Company, 70 Lincoln Street, Boston, Massachusetts 02111 (617) 423-3990; *The World in Figures.*

Statistical Office of the United Nations, Publishing Service, New York, New York 10017 (800) 253-9646; *Statistical Yearbook.*

United Nations Economic Commission for Africa, Africa Hall, P.O. Box 3001, Addis Ababa, Ethiopia (Telephone Number in U.S. (800) 253-9646); *African Statistical Yearbook.*

SAO TOME AND PRINCIPE - CUSTOMS DUTIES

G.K. Hall and Company, 70 Lincoln Street, Boston, Massachusetts 02111 (617) 423-3990; *The World in Figures.*

SAO TOME AND PRINCIPE - DAIRY PRODUCTS

Food and Agricultural Organization of the United Nations (FAO) Via delle Terme di Caracalla, 00100 Rome, Italy (Telephone Number in U.S. (202) 653-2400); *The State of Food and Agriculture.*

SAO TOME AND PRINCIPE - DEATH RATES

G.K. Hall and Company, 70 Lincoln Street, Boston, Massachusetts 02111 (617) 423-3990; *The World in Figures.*

Statistical Office of the United Nations, Publishing Service, New York, New York 10017 (800) 253-9646; *Statistical Yearbook,* and *Survey of Economic and Social Conditions in Africa.*

World Health Organization, Office of Publications, Avenue Appia, CH-1211 Geneva 27, Switzerland (Telephone Number in U.S. (518) 436-9686); *World Health Statistics Annual.*

SAO TOME AND PRINCIPE - DEFENSE EXPENDITURES

G.K. Hall and Company, 70 Lincoln Street, Boston, Massachusetts 02111 (617) 423-3990; *The World in Figures.*

SAO TOME AND PRINCIPE - DEMOGRAPHY

The Economist Intelligence Unit, 111 West 57th Street, New York, New York 10019 (800) 938-4685; *The World Market Atlas.*

G.K. Hall and Company, 70 Lincoln Street, Boston, Massachusetts 02111 (617) 423-3990; *The World in Figures.*

Statistical Office of the United Nations, Publishing Service, New York, New York 10017 (800) 253-9646; *Survey of Economic and Social Conditions in Africa.*

SAO TOME AND PRINCIPE - DEVELOPMENT ASSISTANCE

G.K. Hall and Company, 70 Lincoln Street, Boston, Massachusetts 02111 (617) 423-3990; *The World in Figures.*

Statistical Office of the United Nations, Publishing Service, New York, New York 10017 (800) 253-9646; *Statistical Yearbook.*

SAO TOME AND PRINCIPE - DISEASES

G.K. Hall and Company, 70 Lincoln Street, Boston, Massachusetts 02111 (617) 423-3990; *The World in Figures.*

World Health Organization, Office of Publications, Avenue Appia, CH-1211 Geneva 27, Switzerland (Telephone Number in U.S. (518) 436-9686); *World Health Statistics Annual.*

SAO TOME AND PRINCIPE - DIVORCE RATES

Statistical Office of the United Nations, Publishing Service, New York, New York 10017 (800) 253-9646; *Demographic Yearbook.*

SAO TOME AND PRINCIPE - DOMESTIC PRODUCT

G.K. Hall and Company, 70 Lincoln Street, Boston, Massachusetts 02111 (617) 423-3990; *The World in Figures.*

SAO TOME AND PRINCIPE - ECONOMY

African Development Bank, 01 BP 1387, Abidjan 01, Cote D'Ivoire; *Selected Statistics on Regional Member Countries.*

G.K. Hall and Company, 70 Lincoln Street, Boston, Massachusetts 02111 (617) 423-3990; *The World in Figures.*

Statistical Office of the United Nations, Publishing Service, New York, New York 10017 (800) 253-9646; *Foreign Trade Statistics for Africa.*

SAO TOME AND PRINCIPE - EDUCATION

African Development Bank, 01 BP 1387, Abidjan 01, Cote D'Ivoire; *Selected Statistics on Regional Member Countries.*

The Economist Intelligence Unit, 111 West 57th Street, New York, New York 10019 (800) 938-4685; *The World Market Atlas.*

G.K. Hall and Company, 70 Lincoln Street, Boston, Massachusetts 02111 (617) 423-3990; *The World in Figures.*

Statistical Office of the United Nations, Publishing Service, New York, New York 10017 (800) 253-9646; *Survey of Economic and Social Conditions in Africa.*

United Nations Economic Commission for Africa, Africa Hall, P.O. Box 3001, Addis Ababa, Ethiopia (Telephone Number in U.S. (800) 253-9646); *African Statistical Yearbook.*

United Nations Educational, Scientific and Cultural Organization (UNESCO), 7 Place de Fontenoy, F-75700 Paris, France (Telephone Number in U.S. (212) 963-5981); *Statistical Yearbook.*

SAO TOME AND PRINCIPE - EGG PRODUCTION AND CONSUMPTION - See SAO TOME AND PRINCIPE - DAIRY PRODUCTS

SAO TOME AND PRINCIPE - ELECTRICITY

Statistical Office of the United Nations, Publishing Service, New York, New York 10017 (800) 253-9646; *Survey of Economic and Social Conditions in Africa.*

United Nations Economic Commission for Africa, Africa Hall, P.O. Box 3001, Addis Ababa, Ethiopia (Telephone Number in U.S. (800) 253-9646); *African Statistical Yearbook.*

SAO TOME AND PRINCIPE - EMPLOYMENT

Statistical Office of the United Nations, Publishing Service, New York, New York 10017 (800) 253-9646; *Survey of Economic and Social Conditions in Africa.*

United Nations Economic Commission for Africa, Africa Hall, P.O. Box 3001, Addis Ababa, Ethiopia (Telephone Number in U.S. (800) 253-9646); *African Statistical Yearbook.*

SAO TOME AND PRINCIPE - ENERGY

Food and Agricultural Organization of the United Nations (FAO) Via delle Terme di Caracalla, 00100 Rome, Italy (Telephone Number in U.S. (202) 653-2400); *The State of Food and Agriculture.*

G.K. Hall and Company, 70 Lincoln Street, Boston, Massachusetts 02111 (617) 423-3990; *The World in Figures.*

Statistical Office of the United Nations, Publishing Service, New York, New York 10017 (800) 253-9646; *Energy Statistics Yearbook, Statistical Yearbook,* and *World Energy Supplies.*

United Nations Economic Commission for Africa, Africa Hall, P.O. Box 3001, Addis Ababa, Ethiopia (Telephone Number in U.S. (800) 253-9646); *African Statistical Yearbook.*

SAO TOME AND PRINCIPE - EXCHANGE RATES

African Development Bank, 01 BP 1387, Abidjan 01, Cote D'Ivoire; *Selected Statistics on Regional Member Countries.*

Statistical Office of the United Nations, Publishing Service, New York, New York 10017 (800) 253-9646; *Foreign Trade Statistics for Africa,* and *Statistical Yearbook.*

SAO TOME AND PRINCIPE - EXPORTS

African Development Bank, 01 BP 1387, Abidjan 01, Cote D'Ivoire; *Selected Statistics on Regional Member Countries.*

The Economist Intelligence Unit, 111 West 57th Street, New York, New York 10019 (800) 938-4685; *The World Market Atlas.*

Food and Agricultural Organization of the United Nations (FAO) Via delle Terme di Caracalla, 00100 Rome, Italy (Telephone Number in U.S. (202) 653-2400); *The State of Food and Agriculture.*

G.K. Hall and Company, 70 Lincoln Street, Boston, Massachusetts 02111 (617) 423-3990; *The World in Figures.*

International Monetary Fund, 700 Nineteenth Street, NW, Washington, D.C. 20431 (202) 623-7000; *Direction of Trade Statistics.*

Statistical Office of the United Nations, Publishing Service, New York, New York 10017 (800) 253-9646; *Foreign Trade Statistics for Africa,* and *Survey of Economic and Social Conditions in Africa.*

United Nations Economic Commission for Africa, Africa Hall, P.O. Box 3001, Addis Ababa, Ethiopia (Telephone Number in U.S. (800) 253-9646); *African Statistical Yearbook.*

SAO TOME AND PRINCIPE - EXTERNAL INDEBTEDNESS

African Development Bank, 01 BP 1387, Abidjan 01, Cote D'Ivoire; *Selected Statistics on Regional Member Countries.*

Statistical Office of the United Nations, Publishing Service, New York, New York 10017 (800) 253-9646; *Survey of Economic and Social Conditions in Africa.*

SAO TOME AND PRINCIPE - EXTERNAL TRADE

African Development Bank, 01 BP 1387, Abidjan 01, Cote D'Ivoire; *Selected Statistics on Regional Member Countries.*

Food and Agricultural Organization of the United Nations (FAO) Via delle Terme di Caracalla, 00100 Rome, Italy (Telephone Number in U.S. (202) 653-2400); *The State of Food and Agriculture,* and *Trade Yearbook.*

G.K. Hall and Company, 70 Lincoln Street, Boston, Massachusetts 02111 (617) 423-3990; *The World in Figures.*

Statistical Office of the United Nations, Publishing Service, New York, New York 10017 (800) 253-9646; *Statistical Yearbook.*

SAO TOME AND PRINCIPE - FARM CROPS - See SAO TOME AND PRINCIPE - CROPS

SAO TOME AND PRINCIPE - FETAL MORTALITY

World Health Organization, Office of Publications, Avenue Appia, CH-1211 Geneva 27, Switzerland (Telephone Number in U.S. (518) 436-9686); *World Health Statistics Annual.*

SAO TOME AND PRINCIPE - FERTILITY RATES

Statistical Office of the United Nations, Publishing Service, New York, New York 10017 (800) 253-9646; *Survey of Economic and Social Conditions in Africa.*

SAO TOME AND PRINCIPE - FERTILIZER

Food and Agricultural Organization of the United Nations (FAO) Via delle Terme di Caracalla, 00100 Rome, Italy (Telephone Number in U.S. (202) 653-2400); *The State of Food and Agriculture.*

SAO TOME AND PRINCIPE - FINANCE

G.K. Hall and Company, 70 Lincoln Street, Boston, Massachusetts 02111 (617) 423-3990; *The World in Figures.*

United Nations Economic Commission for Africa, Africa Hall, P.O. Box 3001, Addis Ababa, Ethiopia (Telephone Number in U.S. (800) 253-9646); *African Statistical Yearbook.*

SAO TOME AND PRINCIPE - FINANCIAL CHARACTERISTICS

African Development Bank, 01 BP 1387, Abidjan 01, Cote D'Ivoire; *Selected Statistics on Regional Member Countries.*

SAO TOME AND PRINCIPE - FISHERIES

Food and Agricultural Organization of the United Nations (FAO) Via delle Terme di Caracalla, 00100 Rome, Italy (Telephone Number in U.S. (202) 653-2400); *The State of Food and Agriculture*, and *Yearbook of Fishery Statistics.*

Statistical Office of the United Nations, Publishing Service, New York, New York 10017 (800) 253-9646; *Survey of Economic and Social Conditions in Africa.*

United Nations Economic Commission for Africa, Africa Hall, P.O. Box 3001, Addis Ababa, Ethiopia (Telephone Number in U.S. (800) 253-9646); *African Statistical Yearbook.*

SAO TOME AND PRINCIPE - FOOD

African Development Bank, 01 BP 1387, Abidjan 01, Cote D'Ivoire; *Selected Statistics on Regional Member Countries.*

Food and Agricultural Organization of the United Nations (FAO) Via delle Terme di Caracalla, 00100 Rome, Italy (Telephone Number in U.S. (202) 653-2400); *Production Yearbook*, and *The State of Food and Agriculture.*

G.K. Hall and Company, 70 Lincoln Street, Boston, Massachusetts 02111 (617) 423-3990; *The World in Figures.*

SAO TOME AND PRINCIPE - FOREIGN AID

G.K. Hall and Company, 70 Lincoln Street, Boston, Massachusetts 02111 (617) 423-3990; *The World in Figures*

SAO TOME AND PRINCIPE - FOREIGN TRADE

Food and Agricultural Organization of the United Nations (FAO) Via delle Terme di Caracalla, 00100 Rome, Italy (Telephone Number in U.S. (202) 653-2400); *The State of Food and Agriculture.*

G.K. Hall and Company, 70 Lincoln Street, Boston, Massachusetts 02111 (617) 423-3990; *The World in Figures.*

Statistical Office of the United Nations, Publishing Service, New York, New York 10017 (800) 253-9646; *Foreign Trade Statistics for Africa*, and *Statistical Yearbook.*

United Nations Economic Commission for Africa, Africa Hall, P.O. Box 3001, Addis Ababa, Ethiopia (Telephone Number in U.S. (800) 253-9646); *African Statistical Yearbook.*

SAO TOME AND PRINCIPE - FORESTRY AND FOREST PRODUCTS

Food and Agricultural Organization of the United Nations (FAO) Via delle Terme di Caracalla, 00100 Rome, Italy (Telephone Number in U.S. (202) 653-2400); *The State of Food and Agriculture*, and *Yearbook of Forest Products.*

G.K. Hall and Company, 70 Lincoln Street, Boston, Massachusetts 02111 (617) 423-3990; *The World in Figures.*

United Nations Economic Commission for Africa, Africa Hall, P.O. Box 3001, Addis Ababa, Ethiopia (Telephone Number in U.S. (800) 253-9646); *African Statistical Yearbook.*

SAO TOME AND PRINCIPE - GENERAL MORTALITY

World Health Organization, Office of Publications, Avenue Appia, CH-1211 Geneva 27, Switzerland (Telephone Number in U.S. (518) 436-9686); *World Health Statistics Annual.*

SAO TOME AND PRINCIPE - GOATS - See SAO TOME AND PRINCIPE - LIVESTOCK AND POULTRY

SAO TOME AND PRINCIPE - GOVERNMENT

G.K. Hall and Company, 70 Lincoln Street, Boston, Massachusetts 02111 (617) 423-3990; *The World in Figures.*

SAO TOME AND PRINCIPE - GOVERNMENT REVENUE

Statistical Office of the United Nations, Publishing Service, New York, New York 10017 (800) 253-9646; *Survey of Economic and Social Conditions in Africa.*

SAO TOME AND PRINCIPE - GRAIN PRODUCTION - See SAO TOME AND PRINCIPE - CROPS

SAO TOME AND PRINCIPE - GROSS DOMESTIC PRODUCT

African Development Bank, 01 BP 1387, Abidjan 01, Cote D'Ivoire; *Selected Statistics on Regional Member Countries.*

The Economist Intelligence Unit, 111 West 57th Street, New York, New York 10019 (800) 938-4685; *The World Market Atlas.*

G.K. Hall and Company, 70 Lincoln Street, Boston, Massachusetts 02111 (617) 423-3990; *The World in Figures*

Statistical Office of the United Nations, Publishing Service, New York, New York 10017 (800) 253-9646; *Statistical Yearbook*, and *Survey of Economic and Social Conditions in Africa.*

United Nations Economic Commission for Africa, Africa Hall, P.O. Box 3001, Addis Ababa, Ethiopia (Telephone Number in U.S. (800) 253-9646); *African Statistical Yearbook.*

SAO TOME AND PRINCIPE - GROSS NATIONAL PRODUCT

U.S. Arms Control and Disarmament Agency, 320 Twenty-first Street, NW, Washington, D.C. 20451 (202) 647-8677; *World Military Expenditures and Arms Transfers.*

SAO TOME AND PRINCIPE - HEALTH

African Development Bank, 01 BP 1387, Abidjan 01, Cote D'Ivoire; *Selected Statistics on Regional Member Countries.*

G.K. Hall and Company, 70 Lincoln Street, Boston, Massachusetts 02111 (617) 423-3990; *The World in Figures.*

Statistical Office of the United Nations, Publishing Service, New York, New York 10017 (800) 253-9646; *Statistical Yearbook.*

United Nations Economic Commission for Africa, Africa Hall, P.O. Box 3001, Addis Ababa, Ethiopia (Telephone Number in U.S. (800) 253-9646); *African Statistical Yearbook.*

World Health Organization, Office of Publications, Avenue Appia, CH-1211 Geneva 27, Switzerland (Telephone Number in U.S. (518) 436-9686); *World Health Statistics Annual.*

SAO TOME AND PRINCIPE - HIGHWAYS

G.K. Hall and Company, 70 Lincoln Street, Boston, Massachusetts 02111 (617) 423-3990; *The World in Figures.*

Statistical Office of the United Nations, Publishing Service, New York, New York 10017 (800) 253-9646; *Survey of Economic and Social Conditions in Africa.*

United Nations Economic Commission for Africa, Africa Hall, P.O. Box 3001, Addis Ababa, Ethiopia (Telephone Number in U.S. (800) 253-9646); *African Statistical Yearbook.*

SAO TOME AND PRINCIPE - ILLITERATE POPULATION

The Economist Intelligence Unit, 111 West 57th Street, New York, New York 10019 (800) 938-4685; *The World Market Atlas.*

G.K. Hall and Company, 70 Lincoln Street, Boston, Massachusetts 02111 (617) 423-3990; *The World in Figures.*

SAO TOME AND PRINCIPE - IMPORTS

African Development Bank, 01 BP 1387, Abidjan 01, Cote D'Ivoire; *Selected Statistics on Regional Member Countries.*

The Economist Intelligence Unit, 111 West 57th Street, New York, New York 10019 (800) 938-4685; *The World Market Atlas.*

Food and Agricultural Organization of the United Nations (FAO) Via delle Terme di Caracalla, 00100 Rome, Italy (Telephone Number in U.S. (202) 653-2400); *The State of Food and Agriculture.*

G.K. Hall and Company, 70 Lincoln Street, Boston, Massachusetts 02111 (617) 423-3990; *The World in Figures.*

International Monetary Fund, 700 Nineteenth Street, NW, Washington, D.C. 20431 (202) 623-7000; *Direction of Trade Statistics.*

Statistical Office of the United Nations, Publishing Service, New York, New York 10017 (800) 253-9646; *Foreign Trade Statistics for Africa,* and *Survey of Economic and Social Conditions in Africa.*

United Nations Economic Commission for Africa, Africa Hall, P.O. Box 3001, Addis Ababa, Ethiopia (Telephone Number in U.S. (800) 253-9646); *African Statistical Yearbook.*

SAO TOME AND PRINCIPE - INDUSTRY

G.K. Hall and Company, 70 Lincoln Street, Boston, Massachusetts 02111 (617) 423-3990; *The World in Figures.*

Statistical Office of the United Nations, Publishing Service, New York, New York 10017 (800) 253-9646; *Survey of Economic and Social Conditions in Africa.*

United Nations Economic Commission for Africa, Africa Hall, P.O. Box 3001, Addis Ababa, Ethiopia (Telephone Number in U.S. (800) 253-9646); *African Statistical Yearbook.*

SAO TOME AND PRINCIPE - INFANT AND MATERNAL MORTALITY

Statistical Office of the United Nations, Publishing Service, New York, New York 10017 (800) 253-9646; *Statistical Yearbook,* and *Survey of Economic and Social Conditions in Africa.*

World Health Organization, Office of Publications, Avenue Appia, CH-1211 Geneva 27, Switzerland (Telephone Number in U.S. (518)

436-9686); *World Health Statistics Annual.*

SAO TOME AND PRINCIPE - INTERNATIONAL RESERVES EXCLUDING GOLD

African Development Bank, 01 BP 1387, Abidjan 01, Cote D'Ivoire; *Selected Statistics on Regional Member Countries.*

SAO TOME AND PRINCIPE - LABOR FORCE

African Development Bank, 01 BP 1387, Abidjan 01, Cote D'Ivoire; *Selected Statistics on Regional Member Countries.*

Food and Agricultural Organization of the United Nations (FAO) Via delle Terme di Caracalla, 00100 Rome, Italy (Telephone Number in U.S. (202) 653-2400); *The State of Food and Agriculture.*

G.K. Hall and Company, 70 Lincoln Street, Boston, Massachusetts 02111 (617) 423-3990; *The World in Figures.*

SAO TOME AND PRINCIPE - LAND USE

Food and Agricultural Organization of the United Nations (FAO), Via delle Terme di Caracalla, 00100 Rome, Italy (Telephone Number in U.S. (202) 653-2400); *Production Yearbook.*

G.K. Hall and Company, 70 Lincoln Street, Boston, Massachusetts 02111 (617) 423-3990; *The World in Figures.*

SAO TOME AND PRINCIPE - LIBRARIES

United Nations Educational, Scientific and Cultural Organization (UNESCO), 7 Place de Fontenoy, F-75700 Paris, France (Telephone Number in U.S. (212) 963-5981); *Statistical Yearbook.*

SAO TOME AND PRINCIPE - LIFE EXPECTANCY

African Development Bank, 01 BP 1387, Abidjan 01, Cote D'Ivoire; *Selected Statistics on Regional Member Countries.*

SAO TOME AND PRINCIPE - LITERACY RATE

Statistical Office of the United Nations, Publishing Service, New York, New York 10017 (800) 253-9646; *Survey of Economic and Social Conditions in Africa.*

SAO TOME AND PRINCIPE - LIVESTOCK AND POULTRY

Food and Agricultural Organization of the United Nations (FAO), Via delle Terme di Caracalla, 00100 Rome, Italy (Telephone Number in U.S. (202) 653-2400); *Production Yearbook,* and *The State of Food and Agriculture.*

G.K. Hall and Company, 70 Lincoln Street, Boston, Massachusetts 02111 (617) 423-3990; *The World in Figures.*

Statistical Office of the United Nations, Publishing Service, New York, New York 10017 (800) 253-9646; *Statistical Yearbook,* and *Survey of Economic and Social Conditions in Africa.*

United Nations Economic Commission for Africa, Africa Hall, P.O. Box 3001, Addis Ababa, Ethiopia (Telephone Number in U.S. (800) 253-9646); *African Statistical Yearbook.*

SAO TOME AND PRINCIPE - LIVING LEVELS

G.K. Hall and Company, 70 Lincoln Street, Boston, Massachusetts 02111 (617) 423-3990; *The World in Figures.*

SAO TOME AND PRINCIPE - MAIL TRAFFIC - NUMBER
OF ITEMS SENT AND RECEIVED

Statistical Office of the United Nations, Publishing Service, New
York, New York 10017 (800) 253-9646; *Statistical Yearbook.*

SAO TOME AND PRINCIPE - MANUFACTURING

G.K. Hall and Company, 70 Lincoln Street, Boston, Massachusetts
02111 (617) 423-3990; *The World in Figures.*

Statistical Office of the United Nations, Publishing Service, New
York, New York 10017 (800) 253-9646; *Survey of Economic and
Social Conditions in Africa.*

United Nations Economic Commission for Africa, Africa Hall, P.O.
Box 3001, Addis Ababa, Ethiopia (Telephone Number in U.S. (800)
253-9646); *African Statistical Yearbook.*

SAO TOME AND PRINCIPE - MARRIAGE RATES

Statistical Office of the United Nations, Publishing Service, New
York, New York 10017 (800) 253-9646; *Statistical Yearbook.*

SAO TOME AND PRINCIPE - MEAT PRODUCTION - See SAO TOME
AND PRINCIPE - LIVESTOCK AND POULTRY

SAO TOME AND PRINCIPE - MERCHANT SHIPPING

G.K. Hall and Company, 70 Lincoln Street, Boston, Massachusetts
02111 (617) 423-3990; *The World in Figures.*

Statistical Office of the United Nations, Publishing Service, New
York, New York 10017 (800) 253-9646; *Statistical Yearbook.*

United Nations Economic Commission for Africa, Africa Hall, P.O.
Box 3001, Addis Ababa, Ethiopia (Telephone Number in U.S. (800)
253-9646); *African Statistical Yearbook.*

SAO TOME AND PRINCIPE - MILITARY

G.K. Hall and Company, 70 Lincoln Street, Boston, Massachusetts
02111 (617) 423-3990; *The World in Figures.*

U.S. Arms Control and Disarmament Agency, 320 Twenty-first
Street, NW, Washington, D.C. 20451 (202) 647-8677; *World Military
Expenditures and Arms Transfers.*

SAO TOME AND PRINCIPE - MINING AND MINERAL PRODUCTS

G.K. Hall and Company, 70 Lincoln Street, Boston, Massachusetts
02111 (617) 423-3990; *The World in Figures.*

United Nations Economic Commission for Africa, Africa Hall, P.O.
Box 3001, Addis Ababa, Ethiopia (Telephone Number in U.S. (800)
253-9646); *African Statistical Yearbook.*

SAO TOME AND PRINCIPE - MONEY EXCHANGE RATES

Statistical Office of the United Nations, Publishing Service, New
York, New York 10017 (800) 253-9646; *Statistical Yearbook.*

SAO TOME AND PRINCIPE - MONEY SUPPLY

African Development Bank, 01 BP 1387, Abidjan 01, Cote D'Ivoire;
Selected Statistics on Regional Member Countries.

G.K. Hall and Company, 70 Lincoln Street, Boston, Massachusetts
02111 (617) 423-3990; *The World in Figures.*

SAO TOME AND PRINCIPE - MOTION PICTURES

Statistical Office of the United Nations, Publishing Service, New
York, New York 10017 (800) 253-9646; *Statistical Yearbook.*

SAO TOME AND PRINCIPE - MOTOR VEHICLES IN USE

G.K. Hall and Company, 70 Lincoln Street, Boston, Massachusetts
02111 (617) 423-3990; *The World in Figures.*

Statistical Office of the United Nations, Publishing Service, New
York, New York 10017 (800) 253-9646; *Statistical Yearbook,* and
Survey of Economic and Social Conditions in Africa.

SAO TOME AND PRINCIPE - NATALITY - See SAO TOME AND
PRINCIPE - BIRTH RATE

SAO TOME AND PRINCIPE - NATIONAL ACCOUNTS

African Development Bank, 01 BP 1387, Abidjan 01, Cote D'Ivoire;
Selected Statistics on Regional Member Countries.

United Nations Economic Commission for Africa, Africa Hall, P.O.
Box 3001, Addis Ababa, Ethiopia (Telephone Number in U.S. (800)
253-9646); *African Statistical Yearbook.*

SAO TOME AND PRINCIPE - NATIONAL INCOME

G.K. Hall and Company, 70 Lincoln Street, Boston, Massachusetts
02111 (617) 423-3990; *The World in Figures.*

SAO TOME AND PRINCIPE - NEWSPAPER PRODUCTION - See SAO
TOME AND PRINCIPE - FORESTRY AND FOREST PRODUCTS

SAO TOME AND PRINCIPE - OCCUPATIONS - See SAO TOME AND
PRINCIPE - LABOR FORCE

SAO TOME AND PRINCIPE - PALM KERNELS AND PALM OIL

Statistical Office of the United Nations, Publishing Service, New
York, New York 10017 (800) 253-9646; *Statistical Yearbook.*

SAO TOME AND PRINCIPE - PESTICIDE USE

Food and Agricultural Organization of the United Nations (FAO) Via
delle Terme di Caracalla, 00100 Rome, Italy (Telephone Number in
U.S. (202) 653-2400); *The State of Food and Agriculture.*

SAO TOME AND PRINCIPE - PETROLEUM INDUSTRY

Food and Agricultural Organization of the United Nations (FAO) Via
delle Terme di Caracalla, 00100 Rome, Italy (Telephone Number in
U.S. (202) 653-2400); *The State of Food and Agriculture.*

G.K. Hall and Company, 70 Lincoln Street, Boston, Massachusetts
02111 (617) 423-3990; *The World in Figures.*

SAO TOME AND PRINCIPE - PIGS - See SAO TOME AND PRINCIPE -
LIVESTOCK AND POULTRY

SAO TOME AND PRINCIPE - POPULATION

African Development Bank, 01 BP 1387, Abidjan 01, Cote D'Ivoire;
Selected Statistics on Regional Member Countries.

The Economist Intelligence Unit, 111 West 57th Street, New York,
New York 10019 (800) 938-4685; *The World Market Atlas.*

Food and Agricultural Organization of the United Nations (FAO), Via delle Terme di Caracalla, 00100 Rome, Italy (Telephone Number in U.S. (202) 653-2400); *Production Yearbook*.

G.K. Hall and Company, 70 Lincoln Street, Boston, Massachusetts 02111 (617) 423-3990; *The World in Figures*.

Statistical Office of the United Nations, Publishing Service, New York, New York 10017 (800) 253-9646; *Statistical Yearbook*, and *Survey of Economic and Social Conditions in Africa*.

United Nations Educational, Scientific and Cultural Organization (UNESCO), 7 Place de Fontenoy, F-75700 Paris, France; *Statistical Yearbook*.

U.S. Arms Control and Disarmament Agency, 320 Twenty-first Street, NW, Washington, D.C. 20451 (202) 647-8677; *World Military Expenditures and Arms Transfers*.

World Health Organization, Office of Publications, Avenue Appia, CH-1211 Geneva 27, Switzerland (Telephone Number in U.S. (518) 436-9686); *World Health Statistics Annual*.

SAO TOME AND PRINCIPE - PRICES

Food and Agricultural Organization of the United Nations (FAO), Via delle Terme di Caracalla, 00100 Rome, Italy (Telephone Number in U.S. (202) 653-2400); *Production Yearbook*, and *The State of Food and Agriculture*.

G.K. Hall and Company, 70 Lincoln Street, Boston, Massachusetts 02111 (617) 423-3990; *The World in Figures*.

SAO TOME AND PRINCIPE - PRODUCTION

G.K. Hall and Company, 70 Lincoln Street, Boston, Massachusetts 02111 (617) 423-3990; *The World in Figures*.

SAO TOME AND PRINCIPE - RAILWAYS

G.K. Hall and Company, 70 Lincoln Street, Boston, Massachusetts 02111 (617) 423-3990; *The World in Figures*.

United Nations Economic Commission for Africa, Africa Hall, P.O. Box 3001, Addis Ababa, Ethiopia (Telephone Number in U.S. (800) 253-9646); *African Statistical Yearbook*.

SAO TOME AND PRINCIPE - RETAIL TRADE

G.K. Hall and Company, 70 Lincoln Street, Boston, Massachusetts 02111 (617) 423-3990; *The World in Figures*.

SAO TOME AND PRINCIPE - ROUNDWOOD PRODUCTION - See SAO TOME AND PRINCIPE - FORESTRY AND FOREST PRODUCTS

SAO TOME AND PRINCIPE - SAWNWOOD PRODUCTION - See SAO TOME AND PRINCIPE - FORESTRY AND FOREST PRODUCTS

SAO TOME AND PRINCIPE - SHEEP - See SAO TOME AND PRINCIPE - LIVESTOCK AND POULTRY

SAO TOME AND PRINCIPE - SOCIAL DATA

African Development Bank, 01 BP 1387, Abidjan 01, Cote D'Ivoire; *Selected Statistics on Regional Member Countries*.

G.K. Hall and Company, 70 Lincoln Street, Boston, Massachusetts 02111 (617) 423-3990; *The World in Figures*.

SAO TOME AND PRINCIPE - STOCKS - COMMODITY - MARKET PRICE - INDEX

Food and Agricultural Organization of the United Nations (FAO) Via delle Terme di Caracalla, 00100 Rome, Italy (Telephone Number in U.S. (202) 653-2400); *The State of Food and Agriculture*.

SAO TOME AND PRINCIPE - TAXATION

G.K. Hall and Company, 70 Lincoln Street, Boston, Massachusetts 02111 (617) 423-3990; *The World in Figures*.

SAO TOME AND PRINCIPE - TELEPHONES IN USE

American Telephone and Telegraph Company, 26 Parsippany Road, Whippany, New Jersey 07981 (800) 338-4038; *The World's Telephones*.

G.K. Hall and Company, 70 Lincoln Street, Boston, Massachusetts 02111 (617) 423-3990; *The World in Figures*.

SAO TOME AND PRINCIPE - TEXTILE INDUSTRY

G.K. Hall and Company, 70 Lincoln Street, Boston, Massachusetts 02111 (617) 423-3990; *The World in Figures*.

SAO TOME AND PRINCIPE - TOURISM

G.K. Hall and Company, 70 Lincoln Street, Boston, Massachusetts 02111 (617) 423-3990; *The World in Figures*.

United Nations Economic Commission for Africa, Africa Hall, P.O. Box 3001, Addis Ababa, Ethiopia (Telephone Number in U.S. (800) 253-9646); *African Statistical Yearbook*.

World Tourism Organization, Calle Capitan Haya 42, E-28020 Madrid, Spain; *Yearbook of Tourism Statistics*.

SAO TOME AND PRINCIPE - TRACTORS IN USE

Statistical Office of the United Nations, Publishing Service, New York, New York 10017 (800) 253-9646; *Statistical Yearbook*.

SAO TOME AND PRINCIPE - TRADE - See SAO TOME AND PRINCIPE - FOREIGN TRADE

SAO TOME AND PRINCIPE - TRANSPORTATION AND COMMUNICATIONS

G.K. Hall and Company, 70 Lincoln Street, Boston, Massachusetts 02111 (617) 423-3990; *The World in Figures*.

United Nations Economic Commission for Africa, Africa Hall, P.O. Box 3001, Addis Ababa, Ethiopia (Telephone Number in U.S. (800) 253-9646); *African Statistical Yearbook*.

SAO TOME AND PRINCIPE - VITAL STATISTICS

G.K. Hall and Company, 70 Lincoln Street, Boston, Massachusetts 02111 (617) 423-3990; *The World in Figures*.

Statistical Office of the United Nations, Publishing Service, New York, New York 10017 (800) 253-9646; *Statistical Yearbook*.

World Health Organization, Office of Publications, Avenue Appia, CH-1211 Geneva 27, Switzerland (Telephone Number in U.S. (518) 436-9686); *World Health Statistics Annual*.

SAO TOME AND PRINCIPE - WAGES

G.K. Hall and Company, 70 Lincoln Street, Boston, Massachusetts 02111 (617) 423-3990; *The World in Figures.*

SAO TOME AND PRINCIPE - WEATHER

G.K. Hall and Company, 70 Lincoln Street, Boston, Massachusetts 02111 (617) 423-3990; *The World in Figures.*

SARDINES

U.S. Department of Commerce, National Oceanic and Atmospheric Administration, National Marine Fisheries Service, 1335 East-West Highway, Silver Spring, Maryland 20910 (301) 427-2239; *Fishery Statistics of the United States*, and *Fisheries of the United States.*

Saudi Arabia - National Statistical Office

Central Department of Statistics, Ministry of Finance and National Economy, Post Office Box 3735, Riyadh, Saudi Arabia.

Saudi Arabia - Primary Statistics Source

Central Department of Statistics, Ministry of Finance and National Economy, Riyadh, Saudi Arabia; *Statistical Yearbook.*

SAUDI ARABIA - AGRICULTURE

Economic Commission for Western Asia, Post Office Box 27, Baghdad, Iraq; *Statistical Abstract of Western Asia.*

Euromonitor Publications Limited, 87-88 Turnmill Street, London EC1M 5QU, England; *International Marketing Data and Statistics*, and *Third World Economic Handbook.*

Facts on File, 460 Park Avenue South, New York, New York 10016 (800) 443-8323; *The New Book of World Rankings.*

Federal Statistical Office, Gustav-Stresemann-Ring 11, D-6200 Wiesbaden, Germany; *Saudi Arabia.*

Food and Agricultural Organization of the United Nations (FAO) Via delle Terme di Caracalla, 00100 Rome, Italy (Telephone Number in U.S. (202) 653-2400); *Production Yearbook, The State of Food and Agriculture, and Trade Yearbook.*

G.K. Hall and Company, 70 Lincoln Street, Boston, Massachusetts 02111 (617) 423-3990; *The World in Figures.*

Statistical Office of the United Nations, Publishing Service, New York, New York 10017 (800) 253-9646; *Statistical Yearbook.*

Times Books, 201 East 50th Street, New York, New York 10022 (212) 751-2600; *The Economist Book of Vital World Statistics.*

The World Bank, 1818 H Street, NW, Washington, D.C. 20433 (202) 477-1234; *World Tables.*

SAUDI ARABIA - AIRLINE SERVICE

Economic Commission for Western Asia, Post Office Box 27, Baghdad, Iraq; *Statistical Abstract of Western Asia.*

Facts on File, 460 Park Avenue South, New York, New York 10016 (800) 443-8323; *The New Book of World Rankings.*

International Civil Aviation Organization, 1000 Sherbrooke Street West, Suite 400, Montreal, Quebec, Canada H3A 2R2 (514) 285-8219; *Civil Aviation Statistics of the World.*

Statistical Office of the United Nations, Publishing Service, New York, New York 10017 (800) 253-9646; *Statistical Yearbook.*

Times Books, 201 East 50th Street, New York, New York 10022 (212) 751-2600; *The Economist Book of Vital World Statistics.*

SAUDI ARABIA - ALUMINUM PRODUCTION AND CONSUMPTION - See SAUDI ARABIA - MINING AND MINERAL PRODUCTS

SAUDI ARABIA - ANIMAL HEALTH

Food and Agricultural Organization of the United Nations (FAO), Via delle Terme di Caracalla, 00100, Rome, Italy (Telephone Number in U.S. (202) 653-2400); *Animal Health Yearbook.*

SAUDI ARABIA - AREA AND DENSITY OF POPULATION

Economic Commission for Western Asia, Post Office Box 27, Baghdad, Iraq; *Statistical Abstract of Western Asia.*

Euromonitor Publications Limited, 87-88 Turnmill Street, London EC1M 5QU, England; *International Marketing Data and Statistics*, and *Middle East Economic Handbook.*

Facts on File, 460 Park Avenue South, New York, New York 10016 (800) 443-8323; *The New Book of World Rankings.*

Federal Statistical Office, Gustav-Stresemann-Ring 11, D-6200 Wiesbaden, Germany; *Saudi Arabia.*

Food and Agricultural Organization of the United Nations (FAO) Via delle Terme di Caracalla, 00100 Rome, Italy (Telephone Number in U.S. (202) 653-2400); *The State of Food and Agriculture.*

G.K. Hall and Company, 70 Lincoln Street, Boston, Massachusetts 02111 (617) 423-3990; *The World in Figures.*

Statistical Office of the United Nations, Publishing Service, New York, New York 10017 (800) 253-9646; *Statistical Yearbook.*

Times Books, 201 East 50th Street, New York, New York 10022 (212) 751-2600; *The Economist Book of Vital World Statistics.*

SAUDI ARABIA - ARMS EXPORTS AND IMPORTS

U.S. Arms Control and Disarmament Agency, 320 Twenty-first Street, NW, Washington, D.C. 20451 (202) 647-8677; *World Military Expenditures and Arms Transfers.*

SAUDI ARABIA - BALANCE OF PAYMENTS

Economic Commission for Western Asia, Post Office Box 27, Baghdad, Iraq; *Statistical Abstract of Western Asia.*

The Economist Intelligence Unit, 111 West 57th Street, New York, New York 10019 (800) 938-4685; *The World Market Atlas.*

Euromonitor Publications Limited, 87-88 Turnmill Street, London EC1M 5QU, England; *Third World Economic Handbook.*

Federal Statistical Office, Gustav-Stresemann-Ring 11, D-6200 Wiesbaden, Germany; *Saudi Arabia.*

G.K. Hall and Company, 70 Lincoln Street, Boston, Massachusetts 02111 (617) 423-3990; *The World in Figures.*

International Monetary Fund, 700 Nineteenth Street, NW, Washington, D.C. 20431 (202) 623-7000; *Balance of Payments Yearbook.*

Statistical Office of the United Nations, Publishing Service, New York, New York 10017 (800) 253-9646; *Statistical Yearbook.*

Times Books, 201 East 50th Street, New York, New York 10022 (212) 751-2600; *The Economist Book of Vital World Statistics.*

The World Bank, 1818 H Street, NW, Washington, D.C. 20433 (202) 477-1234; *World Tables.*

SAUDI ARABIA - BALANCE OF TRADE

Economic Commission for Western Asia, Post Office Box 27, Baghdad, Iraq; *Statistical Abstract of Western Asia.*

SAUDI ARABIA - BANKING

Economic Commission for Western Asia, Post Office Box 27, Baghdad, Iraq; *Statistical Abstract of Western Asia.*

Facts on File, 460 Park Avenue South, New York, New York 10016 (800) 443-8323; *The New Book of World Rankings.*

G.K. Hall and Company, 70 Lincoln Street, Boston, Massachusetts 02111 (617) 423-3990; *The World in Figures.*

International Monetary Fund, 700 Nineteenth Street, NW, Washington, D.C. 20431 (202) 623-7000; *International Financial Statistics.*

SAUDI ARABIA - BARLEY PRODUCTION - See SAUDI ARABIA - CROPS

SAUDI ARABIA - BEER PRODUCTION

Facts on File, 460 Park Avenue South, New York, New York 10016 (800) 443-8323; *The New Book of World Rankings.*

SAUDI ARABIA - BIRTH RATES

Euromonitor Publications Limited, 87-88 Turnmill Street, London EC1M 5QU, England; *Middle East Economic Handbook,* and *Third World Economic Handbook.*

Facts on File, 460 Park Avenue South, New York, New York 10016 (800) 443-8323; *The New Book of World Rankings.*

Statistical Office of the United Nations, Publishing Service, New York, New York 10017 (800) 253-9646; *Demographic Yearbook,* and *Statistical Yearbook.*

Times Books, 201 East 50th Street, New York, New York 10022 (212) 751-2600; *The Economist Book of Vital World Statistics.*

The World Bank, 1818 H Street, NW, Washington, D.C. 20433 (202) 477-1234; *World Tables.*

SAUDI ARABIA - BONDS

G.K. Hall and Company, 70 Lincoln Street, Boston, Massachusetts 02111 (617) 423-3990; *The World in Figures.*

SAUDI ARABIA - BOOK PRODUCTION

G.K. Hall and Company, 70 Lincoln Street, Boston, Massachusetts 02111 (617) 423-3990; *The World in Figures.*

SAUDI ARABIA - BROADCASTING

Billboard Limited, P.O. Box 9027, 1006 AA Amsterdam, The Netherlands (Telephone Number in U.S. (212) 764-7300); *World Radio TV Handbook.*

Facts on File, 460 Park Avenue South, New York, New York 10016 (800) 443-8323; *The New Book of World Rankings.*

G.K. Hall and Company, 70 Lincoln Street, Boston, Massachusetts 02111 (617) 423-3990; *The World in Figures.*

Times Books, 201 East 50th Street, New York, New York 10022 (212) 751-2600; *The Economist Book of Vital World Statistics.*

United Nations Educational, Scientific and Cultural Organization (UNESCO), 7 Place de Fontenoy, F-75700 Paris, France (Telephone Number in U.S. (212) 963-5981); *Statistical Yearbook.*

SAUDI ARABIA - BUSINESS

G.K. Hall and Company, 70 Lincoln Street, Boston, Massachusetts 02111 (617) 423-3990; *The World in Figures.*

SAUDI ARABIA - BUTTER PRODUCTION - See SAUDI ARABIA - DAIRY PRODUCTS

SAUDI ARABIA - CALORIE SUPPLY

Food and Agricultural Organization of the United Nations (FAO) Via delle Terme di Caracalla, 00100 Rome, Italy (Telephone Number in U.S. (202) 653-2400); *The State of Food and Agriculture.*

SAUDI ARABIA - CATTLE - See SAUDI ARABIA - LIVESTOCK AND POULTRY

SAUDI ARABIA - CEMENT PRODUCTION - See SAUDI ARABIA - MINING AND MINERAL PRODUCTS

SAUDI ARABIA - CHEMICAL (ORGANIC) PRODUCTION - See SAUDI ARABIA - MINING AND MINERAL PRODUCTS

SAUDI ARABIA - CHICKENS - See SAUDI ARABIA - LIVESTOCK AND POULTRY

SAUDI ARABIA - CIGARETTE PRODUCTION - See SAUDI ARABIA - TOBACCO PRODUCTION

SAUDI ARABIA - CLASS STRUCTURE

G.K. Hall and Company, 70 Lincoln Street, Boston, Massachusetts 02111 (617) 423-3990; *The World in Figures.*

SAUDI ARABIA - CLIMATE

Facts on File, 460 Park Avenue South, New York, New York 10016 (800) 443-8323; *The New Book of World Rankings.*

G.K. Hall and Company, 70 Lincoln Street, Boston, Massachusetts 02111 (617) 423-3990; *The World in Figures.*

SAUDI ARABIA - CLOTHING EXPORTS AND IMPORTS

Euromonitor Publications Limited, 87-88 Turnmill Street, London EC1M 5QU, England; *Third World Economic Handbook.*

SAUDI ARABIA - COAL PRODUCTION - See SAUDI ARABIA - MINING AND MINERAL PRODUCTS

SAUDI ARABIA - COFFEE - See SAUDI ARABIA - CROPS

SAUDI ARABIA - COMMUNICATIONS

Economic Commission for Western Asia, Post Office Box 27, Baghdad, Iraq; *Statistical Abstract of Western Asia.*

Euromonitor Publications Limited, 87-88 Turnmill Street, London EC1M 5QU, England; *Third World Economic Handbook.*

Federal Statistical Office, Gustav-Stresemann-Ring 11, D-6200 Wiesbaden, Germany; *Saudi Arabia.*

G.K. Hall and Company, 70 Lincoln Street, Boston, Massachusetts 02111 (617) 423-3990; *The World in Figures.*

SAUDI ARABIA - CONSTRUCTION INDUSTRY

Facts on File, 460 Park Avenue South, New York, New York 10016 (800) 443-8323; *The New Book of World Rankings.*

Statistical Office of the United Nations, Publishing Service, New York, New York 10017 (800) 253-9646; *Statistical Yearbook.*

SAUDI ARABIA - CONSUMER PRICE INDEX

G.K. Hall and Company, 70 Lincoln Street, Boston, Massachusetts 02111 (617) 423-3990; *The World in Figures.*

SAUDI ARABIA - CONSUMER PRICES

International Labour Office, I.L.O. Publications, CH-1211, Geneva 11, Switzerland; *Yearbook of Labour Statistics.*

International Monetary Fund, 700 Nineteenth Street, NW, Washington, D.C. 20431 (202) 623-7000; *International Financial Statistics.*

Times Books, 201 East 50th Street, New York, New York 10022 (212) 751-2600; *The Economist Book of Vital World Statistics.*

SAUDI ARABIA - CONSUMPTION

Euromonitor Publications Limited, 87-88 Turnmill Street, London EC1M 5QU, England; *Middle East Economic Handbook.*

G.K. Hall and Company, 70 Lincoln Street, Boston, Massachusetts 02111 (617) 423-3990; *The World in Figures.*

SAUDI ARABIA - COPPER PRODUCTION AND CONSUMPTION - See SAUDI ARABIA - MINING AND MINERAL PRODUCTS

SAUDI ARABIA - CORN PRODUCTION - See SAUDI ARABIA - CROPS

SAUDI ARABIA - CORPORATE TAXES - See SAUDI ARABIA - TAXATION

SAUDI ARABIA - COTTON PRODUCTION - See SAUDI ARABIA - CROPS

SAUDI ARABIA - CROPS

Facts on File, 460 Park Avenue South, New York, New York 10016 (800) 443-8323; *The New Book of World Rankings.*

Food and Agricultural Organization of the United Nations (FAO) Via delle Terme di Caracalla, 00100 Rome, Italy (Telephone Number in U.S. (202) 653-2400); *The State of Food and Agriculture.*

G.K. Hall and Company, 70 Lincoln Street, Boston, Massachusetts 02111 (617) 423-3990; *The World in Figures.*

Statistical Office of the United Nations, Publishing Service, New York, New York 10017 (800) 253-9646; *Statistical Yearbook.*

SAUDI ARABIA - CUSTOMS DUTIES

G.K. Hall and Company, 70 Lincoln Street, Boston, Massachusetts 02111 (617) 423-3990; *The World in Figures.*

SAUDI ARABIA - DAIRY PRODUCTS

Economic Commission for Western Asia, Post Office Box 27, Baghdad, Iraq; *Statistical Abstract of Western Asia.*

Facts on File, 460 Park Avenue South, New York, New York 10016 (800) 443-8323; *The New Book of World Rankings.*

Food and Agricultural Organization of the United Nations (FAO) Via delle Terme di Caracalla, 00100 Rome, Italy (Telephone Number in U.S. (202) 653-2400); *The State of Food and Agriculture.*

Statistical Office of the United Nations, Publishing Service, New York, New York 10017 (800) 253-9646; *Statistical Yearbook.*

SAUDI ARABIA - DEATH RATES

Euromonitor Publications Limited, 87-88 Turnmill Street, London EC1M 5QU, England; *Middle East Economic Handbook,* and *Third World Economic Handbook.*

G.K. Hall and Company, 70 Lincoln Street, Boston, Massachusetts 02111 (617) 423-3990; *The World in Figures.*

Statistical Office of the United Nations, Publishing Service, New York, New York 10017 (800) 253-9646; *Statistical Yearbook.*

Times Books, 201 East 50th Street, New York, New York 10022 (212) 751-2600; *The Economist Book of Vital World Statistics.*

World Health Organization, Office of Publications, Avenue Appia, CH-1211 Geneva 27, Switzerland (Telephone Number in U.S. (518) 436-9686); *World Health Statistics Annual.*

SAUDI ARABIA - DEFENSE EXPENDITURES

G.K. Hall and Company, 70 Lincoln Street, Boston, Massachusetts 02111 (617) 423-3990; *The World in Figures.*

U.S. Arms Control and Disarmament Agency, 320 Twenty-first Street, NW, Washington, D.C. 20451 (202) 647-8677; *World Military Expenditures and Arms Transfers.*

SAUDI ARABIA - DEMOGRAPHY

The Economist Intelligence Unit, 111 West 57th Street, New York, New York 10019 (800) 938-4685; *The World Market Atlas.*

Facts on File, 460 Park Avenue South, New York, New York 10016 (800) 443-8323; *The New Book of World Rankings.*

G.K. Hall and Company, 70 Lincoln Street, Boston, Massachusetts 02111 (617) 423-3990; *The World in Figures.*

SAUDI ARABIA - DEVELOPMENT ASSISTANCE

G.K. Hall and Company, 70 Lincoln Street, Boston, Massachusetts 02111 (617) 423-3990; *The World in Figures.*

Statistical Office of the United Nations, Publishing Service, New York, New York 10017 (800) 253-9646; *Statistical Yearbook.*

SAUDI ARABIA - DIAMOND PRODUCTION - See SAUDI ARABIA - MINING AND MINERAL PRODUCTS

SAUDI ARABIA - DISEASES

G.K. Hall and Company, 70 Lincoln Street, Boston, Massachusetts 02111 (617) 423-3990; *The World in Figures.*

World Health Organization, Office of Publications, Avenue Appia, CH-1211 Geneva 27, Switzerland (Telephone Number in U.S. (518) 436-9686); *World Health Statistics Annual.*

SAUDI ARABIA - DIVORCE RATES

Facts on File, 460 Park Avenue South, New York, New York 10016 (800) 443-8323; *The New Book of World Rankings.*

Statistical Office of the United Nations, Publishing Service, New York, New York 10017 (800) 253-9646; *Demographic Yearbook.*

SAUDI ARABIA - DOMESTIC PRODUCT

G.K. Hall and Company, 70 Lincoln Street, Boston, Massachusetts 02111 (617) 423-3990; *The World in Figures.*

SAUDI ARABIA - ECONOMY

Euromonitor Publications Limited, 87-88 Turnmill Street, London EC1M 5QU, England; *International Marketing Data and Statistics,* and *Third World Economic Handbook.*

Facts on File, 460 Park Avenue South, New York, New York 10016 (800) 443-8323; *The New Book of World Rankings.*

G.K. Hall and Company, 70 Lincoln Street, Boston, Massachusetts 02111 (617) 423-3990; *The World in Figures.*

SAUDI ARABIA - EDUCATION

Economic Commission for Western Asia, Post Office Box 27, Baghdad, Iraq; *Statistical Abstract of Western Asia.*

The Economist Intelligence Unit, 111 West 57th Street, New York, New York 10019 (800) 938-4685; *The World Market Atlas.*

Euromonitor Publications Limited, 87-88 Turnmill Street, London EC1M 5QU, England; *Middle East Economic Handbook.*

Facts on File, 460 Park Avenue South, New York, New York 10016 (800) 443-8323; *The New Book of World Rankings.*

Federal Statistical Office, Gustav-Stresemann-Ring 11, D-6200 Wiesbaden, Germany; *Saudi Arabia.*

G.K. Hall and Company, 70 Lincoln Street, Boston, Massachusetts 02111 (617) 423-3990; *The World in Figures.*

Times Books, 201 East 50th Street, New York, New York 10022 (212) 751-2600; *The Economist Book of Vital World Statistics.*

United Nations Educational, Scientific and Cultural Organization (UNESCO), 7 Place de Fontenoy, F-75700 Paris, France (Telephone Number in U.S. (212) 963-5981); *Statistical Yearbook.*

The World Bank, 1818 H Street, NW, Washington, D.C. 20433 (202) 477-1234; *World Tables.*

SAUDI ARABIA - EGG PRODUCTION AND CONSUMPTION - See SAUDI ARABIA - DAIRY PRODUCTS

SAUDI ARABIA - ELECTRICITY

Facts on File, 460 Park Avenue South, New York, New York 10016 (800) 443-8323; *The New Book of World Rankings.*

Penn Well Publishing Company, 1421 South Sheridan Road, P.O. Box 1260, Tulsa, Oklahoma 74101 (800) 752-9764; *International Energy Statistics Sourcebook.*

Statistical Office of the United Nations, Publishing Service, New York, New York 10017 (800) 253-9646; *Statistical Yearbook.*

Times Books, 201 East 50th Street, New York, New York 10022 (212) 751-2600; *The Economist Book of Vital World Statistics.*

SAUDI ARABIA - EMPLOYMENT

Economic Commission for Western Asia, Post Office Box 27, Baghdad, Iraq; *Statistical Abstract of Western Asia.*

Euromonitor Publications Limited, 87-88 Turnmill Street, London EC1M 5QU, England; *International Marketing Data and Statistics,* and *Middle East Economic Handbook.*

Facts on File, 460 Park Avenue South, New York, New York 10016 (800) 443-8323; *The New Book of World Rankings.*

Federal Statistical Office, Gustav-Stresemann-Ring 11, D-6200 Wiesbaden, Germany; *Saudi Arabia.*

International Labour Office, I.L.O. Publications, CH-1211, Geneva 22, Switzerland; *Yearbook of Labour Statistics.*

SAUDI ARABIA - ENERGY

Economic Commission for Western Asia, Post Office Box 27, Baghdad, Iraq; *Statistical Abstract of Western Asia.*

Euromonitor Publications Limited, 87-88 Turnmill Street, London EC1M 5QU, England; *Middle East Economic Handbook.*

Facts on File, 460 Park Avenue South, New York, New York 10016 (800) 443-8323; *The New Book of World Rankings.*

Food and Agricultural Organization of the United Nations (FAO) Via delle Terme di Caracalla, 00100 Rome, Italy (Telephone Number in U.S. (202) 653-2400); *The State of Food and Agriculture.*

G.K. Hall and Company, 70 Lincoln Street, Boston, Massachusetts 02111 (617) 423-3990; *The World in Figures.*

Penn Well Publishing Company, 1421 South Sheridan Road, P.O. Box 1260, Tulsa, Oklahoma 74101 (800) 752-9764; *International Energy Statistics Sourcebook.*

Statistical Office of the United Nations, Publishing Service, New York, New York 10017 (800) 253-9646; *Energy Statistics Yearbook, Statistical Yearbook,* and *World Energy Supplies.*

Times Books, 201 East 50th Street, New York, New York 10022 (212) 751-2600; *The Economist Book of Vital World Statistics.*

SAUDI ARABIA - ENGINEERING AND METAL PRODUCTS - EXPORTS AND IMPORTS

Statistical Office of the United Nations, Publishing Service, New York, New York 10017 (800) 253-9646; *Trade in Manufactures of Developing Countries*.

SAUDI ARABIA - EXCHANGE RATES

Euromonitor Publications Limited, 87-88 Turnmill Street, London EC1M 5QU, England; *International Marketing Data and Statistics*, and *Middle East Economic Handbook*.

International Civil Aviation Organization, 1000 Sherbrooke Street West, Suite 400, Montreal, Quebec, Canada H3A 2R2 (514) 285-8219; *Civil Aviation Statistics of the World*.

International Monetary Fund, 700 Nineteenth Street, NW, Washington, D.C. 20431 (202) 623-7000; *International Financial Statistics*.

Organization of Petroleum Exporting Countries, Obere Donaustrasse 93, 1020 Vienna 2, Austria; *OPEC Annual Statistical Bulletin*.

Statistical Office of the United Nations, Publishing Service, New York, New York 10017 (800) 253-9646; *Statistical Yearbook*.

SAUDI ARABIA - EXPORTS

Economic Commission for Western Asia, Post Office Box 27, Baghdad, Iraq; *Statistical Abstract of Western Asia*.

The Economist Intelligence Unit, 111 West 57th Street, New York, New York 10019 (800) 938-4685; *The World Market Atlas*.

Euromonitor Publications Limited, 87-88 Turnmill Street, London EC1M 5QU, England; *International Marketing Data and Statistics*, and *Middle East Economic Handbook*, and *Third World Economic Handbook*.

Food and Agricultural Organization of the United Nations (FAO) Via delle Terme di Caracalla, 00100 Rome, Italy (Telephone Number in U.S. (202) 653-2400); *The State of Food and Agriculture*.

G.K. Hall and Company, 70 Lincoln Street, Boston, Massachusetts 02111 (617) 423-3990; *The World in Figures*.

International Monetary Fund, 700 Nineteenth Street, NW, Washington, D.C. 20431 (202) 623-7000; *Direction of Trade Statistics*, and *International Financial Statistics*.

Organization of Petroleum Exporting Countries, Obere Donaustrasse 93, 1020 Vienna 2, Austria; *OPEC Annual Statistical Bulletin*.

Times Books, 201 East 50th Street, New York, New York 10022 (212) 751-2600; *The Economist Book of Vital World Statistics*.

The World Bank, 1818 H Street, NW, Washington, D.C. 20433 (202) 477-1234; *World Tables*.

SAUDI ARABIA - EXTERNAL INDEBTEDNESS

Euromonitor Publications Limited, 87-88 Turnmill Street, London EC1M 5QU, England; *Third World Economic Handbook*.

The World Bank, 1818 H Street, NW, Washington, D.C. 20433 (202) 477-1234; *World Tables*.

SAUDI ARABIA - EXTERNAL TRADE

Food and Agricultural Organization of the United Nations (FAO), Via delle Terme di Caracalla, 00100, Rome, Italy (Telephone Number in U.S. (202) 653-2400); *Trade Yearbook*, and *The State of Food and Agriculture*.

G.K. Hall and Company, 70 Lincoln Street, Boston, Massachusetts 02111 (617) 423-3990; *The World in Figures*.

Statistical Office of the United Nations, Publishing Service, New York, New York 10017 (800) 253-9646; *Statistical Yearbook*.

SAUDI ARABIA - FARM CROPS - See SAUDI ARABIA - CROPS

SAUDI ARABIA - FEMALE WORKING POPULATION - See SAUDI ARABIA - EMPLOYMENT

SAUDI ARABIA - FERTILITY RATES

Facts on File, 460 Park Avenue South, New York, New York 10016 (800) 443-8323; *The New Book of World Rankings*.

Times Books, 201 East 50th Street, New York, New York 10022 (212) 751-2600; *The Economist Book of Vital World Statistics*.

The World Bank, 1818 H Street, NW, Washington, D.C. 20433 (202) 477-1234; *World Tables*.

SAUDI ARABIA - FERTILIZER PRICES

Food and Agricultural Organization of the United Nations (FAO) Via delle Terme di Caracalla, 00100 Rome, Italy (Telephone Number in U.S. (202) 653-2400); *The State of Food and Agriculture*.

SAUDI ARABIA - FERTILIZER PRODUCTION AND CONSUMPTION

Food and Agricultural Organization of the United Nations (FAO) Via delle Terme di Caracalla, 00100 Rome, Italy (Telephone Number in U.S. (202) 653-2400); *The State of Food and Agriculture*.

Statistical Office of the United Nations, Publishing Service, New York, New York 10017 (800) 253-9646; *Statistical Yearbook*.

SAUDI ARABIA - FETAL MORTALITY

Statistical Office of the United Nations, Publishing Service, New York, New York 10017 (800) 253-9646; *Demographic Yearbook*.

SAUDI ARABIA - FINANCE

Economic Commission for Western Asia, Post Office Box 27, Baghdad, Iraq; *Statistical Abstract of Western Asia*.

Euromonitor Publications Limited, 87-88 Turnmill Street, London EC1M 5QU, England; *Middle East Economic Handbook*.

Facts on File, 460 Park Avenue South, New York, New York 10016 (800) 443-8323; *The New Book of World Rankings*.

Federal Statistical Office, Gustav-Stresemann-Ring 11, D-6200 Wiesbaden, Germany; *Saudi Arabia*.

G.K. Hall and Company, 70 Lincoln Street, Boston, Massachusetts 02111 (617) 423-3990; *The World in Figures*.

International Monetary Fund, 700 Nineteenth Street, NW, Washington, D.C. 20431 (202) 623-7000; *International Financial Statistics*.

SAUDI ARABIA - FISHERIES

Economic Commission for Western Asia, Post Office Box 27, Baghdad, Iraq; *Statistical Abstract of Western Asia.*

Facts on File, 460 Park Avenue South, New York, New York 10016 (800) 443-8323; *The New Book of World Rankings.*

Food and Agricultural Organization of the United Nations (FAO) Via delle Terme di Caracalla, 00100 Rome, Italy (Telephone Number in U.S. (202) 653-2400); *The State of Food and Agriculture,* and *Yearbook of Fishery Statistics.*

Federal Statistical Office, Gustav-Stresemann-Ring 11, D-6200 Wiesbaden, Germany; *Saudi Arabia.*

Statistical Office of the United Nations, Publishing Service, New York, New York 10017 (800) 253-9646; *Statistical Yearbook.*

SAUDI ARABIA - FOOD

Food and Agricultural Organization of the United Nations (FAO) Via delle Terme di Caracalla, 00100 Rome, Italy (Telephone Number in U.S. (202) 653-2400); *Production Yearbook,* and *The State of Food and Agriculture.*

G.K. Hall and Company, 70 Lincoln Street, Boston, Massachusetts 02111 (617) 423-3990; *The World in Figures.*

SAUDI ARABIA - FOREIGN AID

G.K. Hall and Company, 70 Lincoln Street, Boston, Massachusetts 02111 (617) 423-3990; *The World in Figures.*

SAUDI ARABIA - FOREIGN INDEBTEDNESS

Euromonitor Publications Limited, 87-88 Turnmill Street, London EC1M 5QU, England; *Middle East Economic Handbook.*

SAUDI ARABIA - FOREIGN TRADE

Economic Commission for Western Asia, Post Office Box 27, Baghdad, Iraq; *Statistical Abstract of Western Asia.*

Euromonitor Publications Limited, 87-88 Turnmill Street, London EC1M 5QU, England; *International Marketing Data and Statistics, Middle East Economic Handbook,* and *Third World Economic Handbook.*

Facts on File, 460 Park Avenue South, New York, New York 10016 (800) 443-8323; *The New Book of World Rankings.*

Federal Statistical Office, Gustav-Stresemann-Ring 11, D-6200 Wiesbaden, Germany; *Saudi Arabia.*

Food and Agricultural Organization of the United Nations (FAO) Via delle Terme di Caracalla, 00100 Rome, Italy (Telephone Number in U.S. (202) 653-2400); *The State of Food and Agriculture.*

G.K. Hall and Company, 70 Lincoln Street, Boston, Massachusetts 02111 (617) 423-3990; *The World in Figures.*

International Monetary Fund, 700 Nineteenth Street, NW, Washington, D.C. 20431 (202) 623-7000; *International Financial Statistics.*

Statistical Office of the United Nations, Publishing Service, New York, New York 10017 (800) 253-9646; *International Trade Statistics Yearbook,* and *Statistical Yearbook.*

The World Bank, 1818 H Street, NW, Washington, D.C. 20433 (202) 477-1234; *World Tables.*

SAUDI ARABIA - FORESTRY AND FOREST PRODUCTS

Euromonitor Publications Limited, 87-88 Turnmill Street, London EC1M 5QU, England; *Third World Economic Handbook.*

Facts on File, 460 Park Avenue South, New York, New York 10016 (800) 443-8323; *The New Book of World Rankings.*

Federal Statistical Office, Gustav-Stresemann-Ring 11, D-6200 Wiesbaden, Germany; *Saudi Arabia.*

Food and Agricultural Organization of the United Nations (FAO) Via delle Terme di Caracalla, 00100 Rome, Italy (Telephone Number in U.S. (202) 653-2400); *The State of Food and Agriculture,* and *Yearbook of Forest Products.*

G.K. Hall and Company, 70 Lincoln Street, Boston, Massachusetts 02111 (617) 423-3990; *The World in Figures.*

Statistical Office of the United Nations, Publishing Service, New York, New York 10017 (800) 253-9646; *Statistical Yearbook.*

United Nations Educational, Scientific and Cultural Organization (UNESCO), 7 Place de Fontenoy, F-75700 Paris, France (Telephone Number in U.S. (212) 963-5981); *Statistical Yearbook.*

SAUDI ARABIA - GAS LIQUIDS PRODUCTION - See SAUDI ARABIA - MINING AND MINERAL PRODUCTS

SAUDI ARABIA - GAS PRODUCTION - See SAUDI ARABIA - MINING AND MINERAL PRODUCTS

SAUDI ARABIA - GENERAL MORTALITY

Statistical Office of the United Nations, Publishing Service, New York, New York 10017 (800) 253-9646; *Demographic Yearbook.*

SAUDI ARABIA - GEOGRAPHIC DATA

Facts on File, 460 Park Avenue South, New York, New York 10016 (800) 443-8323; *The New Book of World Rankings.*

SAUDI ARABIA - GOATS - See SAUDI ARABIA - LIVESTOCK AND POULTRY

SAUDI ARABIA - GOLD HOLDINGS

International Monetary Fund, 700 Nineteenth Street, NW, Washington, D.C. 20431 (202) 623-7000; *International Financial Statistics.*

Statistical Office of the United Nations, Publishing Service, New York, New York 10017 (800) 253-9646; *Statistical Yearbook.*

The World Bank, 1818 H Street, NW, Washington, D.C. 20433 (202) 477-1234; *World Tables.*

SAUDI ARABIA - GOLD PRODUCTION AND CONSUMPTION - See SAUDI ARABIA - MINING AND MINERAL PRODUCTS

SAUDI ARABIA - GOVERNMENT

G.K. Hall and Company, 70 Lincoln Street, Boston, Massachusetts 02111 (617) 423-3990; *The World in Figures.*

SAUDI ARABIA - GOVERNMENT EXPENDITURE

Economic Commission for Western Asia, Post Office Box 27, Baghdad, Iraq; *Statistical Abstract of Western Asia.*

Euromonitor Publications Limited, 87-88 Turnmill Street, London EC1M 5QU, England; *Third World Economic Handbook.*

The World Bank, 1818 H Street, NW, Washington, D.C. 20433 (202) 477-1234; *World Tables.*

SAUDI ARABIA - GOVERNMENT REVENUE

Economic Commission for Western Asia, Post Office Box 27, Baghdad, Iraq; *Statistical Abstract of Western Asia.*

The World Bank, 1818 H Street, NW, Washington, D.C. 20433 (202) 477-1234; *World Tables.*

SAUDI ARABIA - GRAIN PRODUCTION - See SAUDI ARABIA - CROPS

SAUDI ARABIA - GROSS DOMESTIC PRODUCT

Economic Commission for Western Asia, Post Office Box 27, Baghdad, Iraq; *Statistical Abstract of Western Asia.*

The Economist Intelligence Unit, 111 West 57th Street, New York, New York 10019 (800) 938-4685; *The World Market Atlas.*

Euromonitor Publications Limited, 87-88 Turnmill Street, London EC1M 5QU, England; *International Marketing Data and Statistics, Middle East Economic Handbook,* and *Third World Economic Handbook.*

Facts on File, 460 Park Avenue South, New York, New York 10016 (800) 443-8323; *The New Book of World Rankings.*

G.K. Hall and Company, 70 Lincoln Street, Boston, Massachusetts 02111 (617) 423-3990; *The World in Figures.*

Statistical Office of the United Nations, Publishing Service, New York, New York 10017 (800) 253-9646; *Statistical Yearbook.*

Times Books, 201 East 50th Street, New York, New York 10022 (212) 751-2600; *The Economist Book of Vital World Statistics.*

The World Bank, 1818 H Street, NW, Washington, D.C. 20433 (202) 477-1234; *World Tables.*

SAUDI ARABIA - GROSS INDUSTRIAL PRODUCT

Euromonitor Publications Limited, 87-88 Turnmill Street, London EC1M 5QU, England; *Third World Economic Handbook.*

SAUDI ARABIA - GROSS NATIONAL PRODUCT

Euromonitor Publications Limited, 87-88 Turnmill Street, London EC1M 5QU, England; *International Marketing Data and Statistics,* and *Third World Economic Handbook.*

Organization of Petroleum Exporting Countries, Obere Donaustrasse 93, 1020 Vienna 2, Austria; *OPEC Annual Statistical Bulletin.*

U.S. Arms Control and Disarmament Agency, 320 Twenty-first Street, NW, Washington, D.C. 20451 (202) 647-8677; *World Military Expenditures and Arms Transfers.*

The World Bank, 1818 H Street, NW, Washington, D.C. 20433 (202) 477-1234; *World Tables.*

SAUDI ARABIA - HEALTH

Economic Commission for Western Asia, Post Office Box 27, Baghdad, Iraq; *Statistical Abstract of Western Asia.*

Euromonitor Publications Limited, 87-88 Turnmill Street, London EC1M 5QU, England; *Middle East Economic Handbook.*

Facts on File, 460 Park Avenue South, New York, New York 10016 (800) 443-8323; *The New Book of World Rankings.*

Federal Statistical Office, Gustav-Stresemann-Ring 11, D-6200 Wiesbaden, Germany; *Saudi Arabia.*

G.K. Hall and Company, 70 Lincoln Street, Boston, Massachusetts 02111 (617) 423-3990; *The World in Figures.*

Statistical Office of the United Nations, Publishing Service, New York, New York 10017 (800) 253-9646; *Statistical Yearbook.*

Times Books, 201 East 50th Street, New York, New York 10022 (212) 751-2600; *The Economist Book of Vital World Statistics.*

World Health Organization, Office of Publications, Avenue Appia, CH-1211 Geneva 27, Switzerland (Telephone Number in U.S. (518) 436-9686); *World Health Statistics Annual.*

SAUDI ARABIA - HIGHWAYS

Economic Commission for Western Asia, Post Office Box 27, Baghdad, Iraq; *Statistical Abstract of Western Asia.*

G.K. Hall and Company, 70 Lincoln Street, Boston, Massachusetts 02111 (617) 423-3990; *The World in Figures.*

International Road Federation, 525 School Street, SW, Washington, D.C. 20024 (202) 554-2106; *World Road Statistics.*

SAUDI ARABIA - HORSES - See SAUDI ARABIA - LIVESTOCK AND POULTRY

SAUDI ARABIA - HOURS OF WORK - See SAUDI ARABIA - EMPLOYMENT

SAUDI ARABIA - HOUSING AND HOUSING UNITS

Euromonitor Publications Limited, 87-88 Turnmill Street, London EC1M 5QU, England; *Third World Economic Handbook.*

Facts on File, 460 Park Avenue South, New York, New York 10016 (800) 443-8323; *The New Book of World Rankings.*

SAUDI ARABIA - ILLITERATE POPULATION

The Economist Intelligence Unit, 111 West 57th Street, New York, New York 10019 (800) 938-4685; *The World Market Atlas.*

G.K. Hall and Company, 70 Lincoln Street, Boston, Massachusetts 02111 (617) 423-3990; *The World in Figures.*

United Nations Educational, Scientific and Cultural Organization (UNESCO), 7 Place de Fontenoy, F-75700 Paris, France (Telephone Number in U.S. (212) 963-5981); *Statistical Yearbook.*

SAUDI ARABIA - IMPORTS

Economic Commission for Western Asia, Post Office Box 27, Baghdad, Iraq; *Statistical Abstract of Western Asia*.

The Economist Intelligence Unit, 111 West 57th Street, New York, New York 10019 (800) 938-4685; *The World Market Atlas*.

Euromonitor Publications Limited, 87-88 Turnmill Street, London EC1M 5QU, England; *International Marketing Data and Statistics, Middle East Economic Handbook*, and *Third World Economic Handbook*.

Food and Agricultural Organization of the United Nations (FAO) Via delle Terme di Caracalla, 00100 Rome, Italy (Telephone Number in U.S. (202) 653-2400); *The State of Food and Agriculture*.

G.K. Hall and Company, 70 Lincoln Street, Boston, Massachusetts 02111 (617) 423-3990; *The World in Figures*.

International Monetary Fund, 700 Nineteenth Street, NW, Washington, D.C. 20431 (202) 623-7000; *Direction of Trade Statistics*, and *International Financial Statistics*.

Times Books, 201 East 50th Street, New York, New York 10022 (212) 751-2600; *The Economist Book of Vital World Statistics*.

The World Bank, 1818 H Street, NW, Washington, D.C. 20433 (202) 477-1234; *World Tables*.

SAUDI ARABIA - INDUSTRY

Euromonitor Publications Limited, 87-88 Turnmill Street, London EC1M 5QU, England; *Third World Economic Handbook*.

Facts on File, 460 Park Avenue South, New York, New York 10016 (800) 443-8323; *The New Book of World Rankings*.

Federal Statistical Office, Gustav-Stresemann-Ring 11, D-6200 Wiesbaden, Germany; *Saudi Arabia*.

G.K. Hall and Company, 70 Lincoln Street, Boston, Massachusetts 02111 (617) 423-3990; *The World in Figures*.

International Labour Office, I.L.O. Publications, CH-1211, Geneva 22, Switzerland; *Yearbook of Labour Statistics*.

Times Books, 201 East 50th Street, New York, New York 10022 (212) 751-2600; *The Economist Book of Vital World Statistics*.

The World Bank, 1818 H Street, NW, Washington, D.C. 20433 (202) 477-1234; *World Tables*.

SAUDI ARABIA - INFANT AND MATERNAL MORTALITY

Statistical Office of the United Nations, Publishing Service, New York, New York 10017 (800) 253-9646; *Demographic Yearbook*, and *Statistical Yearbook*.

Times Books, 201 East 50th Street, New York, New York 10022 (212) 751-2600; *The Economist Book of Vital World Statistics*.

The World Bank, 1818 H Street, NW, Washington, D.C. 20433 (202) 477-1234; *World Tables*.

SAUDI ARABIA - INTERNAL TRADE

Statistical Office of the United Nations, Publishing Service, New York, New York 10017 (800) 253-9646; *Statistical Yearbook*.

SAUDI ARABIA - INTERNATIONAL LIQUIDITY

International Monetary Fund, 700 Nineteenth Street, NW, Washington, D.C. 20431 (202) 623-7000; *International Financial Statistics*.

SAUDI ARABIA - INTERNATIONAL RESERVES EXCLUDING GOLD

Statistical Office of the United Nations, Publishing Service, New York, New York 10017 (800) 253-9646; *Statistical Yearbook*.

The World Bank, 1818 H Street, NW, Washington, D.C. 20433 (202) 477-1234; *World Tables*.

SAUDI ARABIA - IRON ORE PRODUCTION AND CONSUMPTION - See SAUDI ARABIA - MINING AND MINERAL PRODUCTS

SAUDI ARABIA - IRRIGATION

Euromonitor Publications Limited, 87-88 Turnmill Street, London EC1M 5QU, England; *International Marketing Data and Statistics*.

SAUDI ARABIA - LABOR FORCE

Economic Commission for Western Asia, Post Office Box 27, Baghdad, Iraq; *Statistical Abstract of Western Asia*.

Euromonitor Publications Limited, 87-88 Turnmill Street, London EC1M 5QU, England; *International Marketing Data and Statistics*.

Facts on File, 460 Park Avenue South, New York, New York 10016 (800) 443-8323; *The New Book of World Rankings*.

Food and Agricultural Organization of the United Nations (FAO) Via delle Terme di Caracalla, 00100 Rome, Italy (Telephone Number in U.S. (202) 653-2400); *The State of Food and Agriculture*.

G.K. Hall and Company, 70 Lincoln Street, Boston, Massachusetts 02111 (617) 423-3990; *The World in Figures*.

The World Bank, 1818 H Street, NW, Washington, D.C. 20433 (202) 477-1234; *World Tables*.

SAUDI ARABIA - LABOR PRODUCTIVITY

International Labour Office, I.L.O. Publications, CH-1211, Geneva 22, Switzerland; *Yearbook of Labour Statistics*.

SAUDI ARABIA - LAND USE

Economic Commission for Western Asia, Post Office Box 27, Baghdad, Iraq; *Statistical Abstract of Western Asia*.

Euromonitor Publications Limited, 87-88 Turnmill Street, London EC1M 5QU, England; *International Marketing Data and Statistics*.

Food and Agricultural Organization of the United Nations (FAO), Via delle Terme di Caracalla, 00100 Rome, Italy (Telephone Number in U.S. (202) 653-2400); *Production Yearbook*.

G.K. Hall and Company, 70 Lincoln Street, Boston, Massachusetts 02111 (617) 423-3990; *The World in Figures*.

SAUDI ARABIA - LIBRARIES

Facts on File, 460 Park Avenue South, New York, New York 10016 (800) 443-8323; *The New Book of World Rankings*.

United Nations Educational, Scientific and Cultural Organization (UNESCO), 7 Place de Fontenoy, F-75700 Paris, France (Telephone Number in U.S. (212) 963-5981); *Statistical Yearbook.*

SAUDI ARABIA - LIVESTOCK AND POULTRY

Economic Commission for Western Asia, Post Office Box 27, Baghdad, Iraq; *Statistical Abstract of Western Asia.*

Euromonitor Publications Limited, 87-88 Turnmill Street, London EC1M 5QU, England; *International Marketing Data and Statistics.*

Facts on File, 460 Park Avenue South, New York, New York 10016 (800) 443-8323; *The New Book of World Rankings.*

Food and Agricultural Organization of the United Nations (FAO), Via delle Terme di Caracalla, 00100 Rome, Italy (Telephone Number in U.S. (202) 653-2400); *Production Yearbook,* and *The State of Food and Agriculture.*

G.K. Hall and Company, 70 Lincoln Street, Boston, Massachusetts 02111 (617) 423-3990; *The World in Figures.*

Statistical Office of the United Nations, Publishing Service, New York, New York 10017 (800) 253-9646; *Statistical Yearbook.*

SAUDI ARABIA - LIVING LEVELS

G.K. Hall and Company, 70 Lincoln Street, Boston, Massachusetts 02111 (617) 423-3990; *The World in Figures.*

Times Books, 201 East 50th Street, New York, New York 10022 (212) 751-2600; *The Economist Book of Vital World Statistics.*

SAUDI ARABIA - MAIL - NUMBER OF PIECES SENT OR RECEIVED

Statistical Office of the United Nations, Publishing Service, New York, New York 10017 (800) 253-9646; *Statistical Yearbook.*

SAUDI ARABIA - MANUFACTURING

Euromonitor Publications Limited, 87-88 Turnmill Street, London EC1M 5QU, England; *Third World Economic Handbook.*

Facts on File, 460 Park Avenue South, New York, New York 10016 (800) 443-8323; *The New Book of World Rankings.*

G.K. Hall and Company, 70 Lincoln Street, Boston, Massachusetts 02111 (617) 423-3990; *The World in Figures.*

Times Books, 201 East 50th Street, New York, New York 10022 (212) 751-2600; *The Economist Book of Vital World Statistics.*

The World Bank, 1818 H Street, NW, Washington, D.C. 20433 (202) 477-1234; *World Tables.*

SAUDI ARABIA - MARRIAGE RATES

Facts on File, 460 Park Avenue South, New York, New York 10016 (800) 443-8323; *The New Book of World Rankings.*

Statistical Office of the United Nations, Publishing Service, New York, New York 10017 (800) 253-9646; *Demographic Yearbook.*

World Health Organization, Office of Publications, Avenue Appia, CH-1211 Geneva 27, Switzerland (Telephone Number in U.S. (518) 436-9686); *World Health Statistics Annual.*

SAUDI ARABIA - MEAT PRODUCTION - See SAUDI ARABIA - LIVESTOCK AND POULTRY

SAUDI ARABIA - MERCHANT SHIPPING

Economic Commission for Western Asia, Post Office Box 27, Baghdad, Iraq; *Statistical Abstract of Western Asia.*

G.K. Hall and Company, 70 Lincoln Street, Boston, Massachusetts 02111 (617) 423-3990; *The World in Figures.*

Lloyd's Register of Shipping, 17 Battery Place, New York, New York 10004 (212) 425-8050; *Register of Ships.*

Organization of Petroleum Exporting Countries, Obere Donaustrasse 93, 1020 Vienna 2, Austria; *OPEC Annual Statistical Bulletin.*

Statistical Office of the United Nations, Publishing Service, New York, New York 10017 (800) 253-9646; *Statistical Yearbook.*

Times Books, 201 East 50th Street, New York, New York 10022 (212) 751-2600; *The Economist Book of Vital World Statistics.*

U.S. Department of Transportation, Maritime Administration, 400 Seventh Street, SW, Washington, D.C. 20590 (202) 366-5807; *A Statistical Analysis of the World's Merchant Fleets.*

SAUDI ARABIA - MILITARY

G.K. Hall and Company, 70 Lincoln Street, Boston, Massachusetts 02111 (617) 423-3990; *The World in Figures.*

The International Institute for Strategic Studies, 23 Tavistock Street, London WC2E 7NQ, England; *The Military Balance.*

U.S. Arms Control and Disarmament Agency, 320 Twenty-first Street, NW, Washington, D.C. 20451 (202) 647-8677; *World Military Expenditures and Arms Transfers.*

SAUDI ARABIA - MILK PRODUCTION - See SAUDI ARABIA - DAIRY PRODUCTS

SAUDI ARABIA - MINING AND MINERAL PRODUCTS

Economic Commission for Western Asia, Post Office Box 27, Baghdad, Iraq; *Statistical Abstract of Western Asia.*

Euromonitor Publications Limited, 87-88 Turnmill Street, London EC1M 5QU, England; *Third World Economic Handbook.*

Facts on File, 460 Park Avenue South, New York, New York 10016 (800) 443-8323; *The New Book of World Rankings.*

G.K. Hall and Company, 70 Lincoln Street, Boston, Massachusetts 02111 (617) 423-3990; *The World in Figures.*

Organization of Petroleum Exporting Countries, Obere Donaustrasse 93, 1020 Vienna 2, Austria; *OPEC Annual Statistical Bulletin.*

Penn Well Publishing Company, 1421 South Sheridan Road, P.O. Box 1260, Tulsa, Oklahoma 74101 (800) 752-9764; *International Energy Statistics Sourcebook.*

Statistical Office of the United Nations, Publishing Service, New York, New York 10017 (800) 253-9646; *Statistical Yearbook.*

SAUDI ARABIA - MONEY EXCHANGE RATE

Euromonitor Publications Limited, 87-88 Turnmill Street, London EC1M 5QU, England; *International Marketing Data and Statistics.*

International Monetary Fund, 700 Nineteenth Street, NW, Washington, D.C. 20431 (202) 623-7000; *International Financial Statistics.*

Statistical Office of the United Nations, Publishing Service, New York, New York 10017 (800) 253-9646; *Statistical Yearbook.*

SAUDI ARABIA - MONEY RESERVES

Euromonitor Publications Limited, 87-88 Turnmill Street, London EC1M 5QU, England; *International Marketing Data and Statistics.*

SAUDI ARABIA - MONEY SUPPLY

Economic Commission for Western Asia, Post Office Box 27, Baghdad, Iraq; *Statistical Abstract of Western Asia.*

Euromonitor Publications Limited, 87-88 Turnmill Street, London EC1M 5QU, England; *International Marketing Data and Statistics.*

G.K. Hall and Company, 70 Lincoln Street, Boston, Massachusetts 02111 (617) 423-3990; *The World in Figures.*

International Monetary Fund, 700 Nineteenth Street, NW, Washington, D.C. 20431 (202) 623-7000; *International Financial Statistics.*

Statistical Office of the United Nations, Publishing Service, New York, New York 10017 (800) 253-9646; *Statistical Yearbook.*

The World Bank, 1818 H Street, NW, Washington, D.C. 20433 (202) 477-1234; *World Tables.*

SAUDI ARABIA - MOTOR VEHICLE TAXES - See SAUDI ARABIA - TAXATION

SAUDI ARABIA - MOTOR VEHICLES

Economic Commission for Western Asia, Post Office Box 27, Baghdad, Iraq; *Statistical Abstract of Western Asia.*

SAUDI ARABIA - MOTOR VEHICLES IN USE

G.K. Hall and Company, 70 Lincoln Street, Boston, Massachusetts 02111 (617) 423-3990; *The World in Figures.*

International Road Federation, 525 School Street, SW, Washington, D.C. 20024 (202) 554-2106; *World Road Statistics.*

Statistical Office of the United Nations, Publishing Service, New York, New York 10017 (800) 253-9646; *Statistical Yearbook.*

Times Books, 201 East 50th Street, New York, New York 10022 (212) 751-2600; *The Economist Book of Vital World Statistics.*

SAUDI ARABIA - MULES - See SAUDI ARABIA - LIVESTOCK AND POULTRY

SAUDI ARABIA - MUSEUMS

Facts on File, 460 Park Avenue South, New York, New York 10016 (800) 443-8323; *The New Book of World Rankings.*

United Nations Educational, Scientific and Cultural Organization (UNESCO), 7 Place de Fontenoy, F-75700 Paris, France (Telephone Number in U.S. (212) 963-5981); *Statistical Yearbook.*

SAUDI ARABIA - NATALITY - See SAUDI ARABIA - BIRTH RATE

SAUDI ARABIA - NATIONAL ACCOUNTS

Economic Commission for Western Asia, Post Office Box 27, Baghdad, Iraq; *Statistical Abstract of Western Asia.*

Federal Statistical Office, Gustav-Stresemann-Ring 11, D-6200 Wiesbaden, Germany; *Saudi Arabia.*

International Monetary Fund, 700 Nineteenth Street, NW, Washington, D.C. 20431 (202) 623-7000; *International Financial Statistics.*

Statistical Office of the United Nations, Publishing Service, New York, New York 10017 (800) 253-9646; *National Accounts Statistics,* and *Statistical Yearbook.*

SAUDI ARABIA - NATIONAL INCOME

Facts on File, 460 Park Avenue South, New York, New York 10016 (800) 443-8323; *The New Book of World Rankings.*

G.K. Hall and Company, 70 Lincoln Street, Boston, Massachusetts 02111 (617) 423-3990; *The World in Figures.*

Statistical Office of the United Nations, Publishing Service, New York, New York 10017 (800) 253-9646; *Statistical Yearbook.*

SAUDI ARABIA - NATIONAL PRODUCT

Facts on File, 460 Park Avenue South, New York, New York 10016 (800) 443-8323; *The New Book of World Rankings.*

Statistical Office of the United Nations, Publishing Service, New York, New York 10017 (800) 253-9646; *Statistical Yearbook.*

SAUDI ARABIA - NATURAL GAS PRODUCTION - See SAUDI ARABIA - MINING AND MINERAL PRODUCTS

SAUDI ARABIA - NEWSPAPER PRODUCTION - See SAUDI ARABIA - FORESTRY AND FOREST PRODUCTS

SAUDI ARABIA - NEWSPRINT - See SAUDI ARABIA - FORESTRY AND FOREST PRODUCTS

SAUDI ARABIA - OCCUPATIONS - See SAUDI ARABIA - LABOR FORCE

SAUDI ARABIA - PAPER - See SAUDI ARABIA - FORESTRY AND FOREST PRODUCTS

SAUDI ARABIA - PEANUT PRODUCTION - See SAUDI ARABIA - CROPS

SAUDI ARABIA - PERIODICALS

United Nations Educational, Scientific and Cultural Organization (UNESCO), 7 Place de Fontenoy, F-75700 Paris, France (Telephone Number in U.S. (212) 963-5981); *Statistical Yearbook.*

SAUDI ARABIA - PESTICIDE USE

Food and Agricultural Organization of the United Nations (FAO) Via delle Terme di Caracalla, 00100 Rome, Italy (Telephone Number in

U.S. (202) 653-2400); *The State of Food and Agriculture.*

SAUDI ARABIA - PETROLEUM INDUSTRY

Commodity Research Bureau, Incorporated, 75 Wall Street, New York, New York 10005 (212) 504-7754; *Commodity Year Book.*

Euromonitor Publications Limited, 87-88 Turnmill Street, London EC1M 5QU, England; *Middle East Economic Handbook.*

Facts on File, 460 Park Avenue South, New York, New York 10016 (800) 443-8323; *The New Book of World Rankings.*

Food and Agricultural Organization of the United Nations (FAO) Via delle Terme di Caracalla, 00100 Rome, Italy (Telephone Number in U.S. (202) 653-2400); *The State of Food and Agriculture.*

G.K. Hall and Company, 70 Lincoln Street, Boston, Massachusetts 02111 (617) 423-3990; *The World in Figures.*

International Monetary Fund, 700 Nineteenth Street, NW, Washington, D.C. 20431 (202) 623-7000; *International Financial Statistics.*

Organization of Petroleum Exporting Countries, Obere Donaustrasse 93, 1020 Vienna 2, Austria; *OPEC Annual Statistical Bulletin.*

Penn Well Publishing Company, 1421 South Sheridan Road, P.O. Box 1260, Tulsa, Oklahoma 74101 (800) 752-9764; *International Energy Statistics Sourcebook.*

Statistical Office of the United Nations, Publishing Service, New York, New York 10017 (800) 253-9646; *Statistical Yearbook.*

SAUDI ARABIA - PIGS - See SAUDI ARABIA - LIVESTOCK AND POULTRY

SAUDI ARABIA - PIPELINES FOR OIL AND PETROLEUM PRODUCTS

Organization of Petroleum Exporting Countries, Obere Donaustrasse 93, 1020 Vienna 2, Austria; *OPEC Annual Statistical Bulletin.*

SAUDI ARABIA - PLASTIC AND RESIN PRODUCTION

Euromonitor Publications Limited, 87-88 Turnmill Street, London EC1M 5QU, England; *Third World Economic Handbook.*

SAUDI ARABIA - POPULATION

Economic Commission for Western Asia, Post Office Box 27, Baghdad, Iraq; *Statistical Abstract of Western Asia.*

The Economist Intelligence Unit, 111 West 57th Street, New York, New York 10019 (800) 938-4685; *The World Market Atlas.*

Euromonitor Publications Limited, 87-88 Turnmill Street, London EC1M 5QU, England; *International Marketing Data and Statistics, Middle East Economic Handbook,* and *Third World Economic Handbook.*

Facts on File, 460 Park Avenue South, New York, New York 10016 (800) 443-8323; *The New Book of World Rankings.*

Federal Statistical Office, Gustav-Stresemann-Ring 11, D-6200 Wiesbaden, Germany; *Saudi Arabia.*

Food and Agricultural Organization of the United Nations (FAO), Via delle Terme di Caracalla, 00100 Rome, Italy (Telephone Number in U.S. (202) 653-2400); *Production Yearbook.*

G.K. Hall and Company, 70 Lincoln Street, Boston, Massachusetts 02111 (617) 423-3990; *The World in Figures.*

International Labour Office, I.L.O. Publications, CH-1211, Geneva 22, Switzerland; *Yearbook of Labour Statistics.*

Statistical Office of the United Nations, Publishing Service, New York, New York 10017 (800) 253-9646; *Statistical Yearbook.*

Times Books, 201 East 50th Street, New York, New York 10022 (212) 751-2600; *The Economist Book of Vital World Statistics.*

United Nations Educational, Scientific and Cultural Organization (UNESCO), 7 Place de Fontenoy, F-75700 Paris, France (Telephone Number in U.S. (212) 963-5981); *Statistical Yearbook.*

U.S. Arms Control and Disarmament Agency, 320 Twenty-first Street, NW, Washington, D.C. 20451 (202) 647-8677; *World Military Expenditures and Arms Transfers.*

World Health Organization, Office of Publications, Avenue Appia, CH-1211 Geneva 27, Switzerland (Telephone Number in U.S. (518) 436-9686); *World Health Statistics Annual.*

SAUDI ARABIA - POST OFFICES

Facts on File, 460 Park Avenue South, New York, New York 10016 (800) 443-8323; *The New Book of World Rankings.*

SAUDI ARABIA - POTATO PRODUCTION - See SAUDI ARABIA - CROPS

SAUDI ARABIA - PRICES

Economic Commission for Western Asia, Post Office Box 27, Baghdad, Iraq; *Statistical Abstract of Western Asia.*

Facts on File, 460 Park Avenue South, New York, New York 10016 (800) 443-8323; *The New Book of World Rankings.*

Federal Statistical Office, Gustav-Stresemann-Ring 11, D-6200 Wiesbaden, Germany; *Saudi Arabia.*

Food and Agricultural Organization of the United Nations (FAO), Via delle Terme di Caracalla, 00100 Rome, Italy (Telephone Number in U.S. (202) 653-2400); *Production Yearbook,* and *The State of Food and Agriculture.*

G.K. Hall and Company, 70 Lincoln Street, Boston, Massachusetts 02111 (617) 423-3990; *The World in Figures.*

International Monetary Fund, 700 Nineteenth Street, NW, Washington, D.C. 20431 (202) 623-7000; *International Financial Statistics.*

SAUDI ARABIA - PRINTING AND WRITING PAPER - See SAUDI ARABIA - FORESTRY AND FOREST PRODUCTS

SAUDI ARABIA - PRODUCTION

Euromonitor Publications Limited, 87-88 Turnmill Street, London EC1M 5QU, England; *Third World Economic Handbook.*

Facts on File, 460 Park Avenue South, New York, New York 10016 (800) 443-8323; *The New Book of World Rankings.*

G.K. Hall and Company, 70 Lincoln Street, Boston, Massachusetts 02111 (617) 423-3990; *The World in Figures.*

SAUDI ARABIA - PRODUCTIVITY

Euromonitor Publications Limited, 87-88 Turnmill Street, London EC1M 5QU, England; *International Marketing Data and Statistics.*

SAUDI ARABIA - PUBLIC FINANCE

Facts on File, 460 Park Avenue South, New York, New York 10016 (800) 443-8323; *The New Book of World Rankings.*

SAUDI ARABIA - RADIO BROADCASTING - See SAUDI ARABIA - BROADCASTING

SAUDI ARABIA - RAILWAYS

G.K. Hall and Company, 70 Lincoln Street, Boston, Massachusetts 02111 (617) 423-3990; *The World in Figures.*

Jane's Information Group, Sentinel House, 163 Brighton Road, Coulsdon, Surrey CR5 2NH, England (Telephone Number in U.S. (703) 683-3700); *Jane's World Railways.*

Statistical Office of the United Nations, Publishing Service, New York, New York 10017 (800) 253-9646; *Statistical Yearbook.*

SAUDI ARABIA - RELIGION

Facts on File, 460 Park Avenue South, New York, New York 10016 (800) 443-8323; *The New Book of World Rankings.*

SAUDI ARABIA - RETAIL TRADE

Euromonitor Publications Limited, 87-88 Turnmill Street, London EC1M 5QU, England; *Third World Economic Handbook.*

G.K. Hall and Company, 70 Lincoln Street, Boston, Massachusetts 02111 (617) 423-3990; *The World in Figures.*

Statistical Office of the United Nations, Publishing Service, New York, New York 10017 (800) 253-9646; *Statistical Yearbook.*

SAUDI ARABIA - RICE PRODUCTION - See SAUDI ARABIA - CROPS

SAUDI ARABIA - ROUNDWOOD PRODUCTION - See SAUDI ARABIA - FORESTRY AND FOREST PRODUCTS

SAUDI ARABIA - RUBBER PRODUCTION AND CONSUMPTION

Euromonitor Publications Limited, 87-88 Turnmill Street, London EC1M 5QU, England; *Third World Economic Handbook.*

Facts on File, 460 Park Avenue South, New York, New York 10016 (800) 443-8323; *The New Book of World Rankings.*

SAUDI ARABIA - SAWNWOOD PRODUCTION - See SAUDI ARABIA - FORESTRY AND FOREST PRODUCTS

SAUDI ARABIA - SCIENTISTS AND TECHNICIANS

Statistical Office of the United Nations, Publishing Service, New York, New York 10017 (800) 253-9646; *Statistical Yearbook.*

SAUDI ARABIA - SENIOR CITIZENS

Facts on File, 460 Park Avenue South, New York, New York 10016 (800) 443-8323; *The New Book of World Rankings.*

SAUDI ARABIA - SHEEP - See SAUDI ARABIA - LIVESTOCK AND POULTRY

SAUDI ARABIA - SILVER PRODUCTION AND CONSUMPTION - See SAUDI ARABIA - MINING AND MINERAL PRODUCTS

SAUDI ARABIA - SOCIAL DATA

Facts on File, 460 Park Avenue South, New York, New York 10016 (800) 443-8323; *The New Book of World Rankings.*

G.K. Hall and Company, 70 Lincoln Street, Boston, Massachusetts 02111 (617) 423-3990; *The World in Figures.*

SAUDI ARABIA - STATE BUDGET REVENUE AND EXPENDITURES

Euromonitor Publications Limited, 87-88 Turnmill Street, London EC1M 5QU, England; *International Marketing Data and Statistics.*

SAUDI ARABIA - STEEL - See SAUDI ARABIA - MINING AND MINERAL PRODUCTS

SAUDI ARABIA - STOCKS - COMMODITY - MARKET PRICE - INDEX

Food and Agricultural Organization of the United Nations (FAO) Via delle Terme di Caracalla, 00100 Rome, Italy (Telephone Number in U.S. (202) 653-2400); *The State of Food and Agriculture.*

SAUDI ARABIA - SUGAR - See SAUDI ARABIA - CROPS

SAUDI ARABIA - TAXATION

G.K. Hall and Company, 70 Lincoln Street, Boston, Massachusetts 02111 (617) 423-3990; *The World in Figures.*

International Road Federation, 525 School Street, SW, Washington, D.C. 20024 (202) 554-2106; *World Road Statistics.*

The World Bank, 1818 H Street, NW, Washington, D.C. 20433 (202) 477-1234; *World Tables.*

SAUDI ARABIA - TELEPHONES IN USE

American Telephone and Telegraph Company, 26 Parsippany Road, Whippany, New Jersey 07981 (800) 338-4038; *The World's Telephones.*

Euromonitor Publications Limited, 87-88 Turnmill Street, London EC1M 5QU, England; *Middle East Economic Handbook,* and *Third World Economic Handbook.*

G.K. Hall and Company, 70 Lincoln Street, Boston, Massachusetts 02111 (617) 423-3990; *The World in Figures.*

Statistical Office of the United Nations, Publishing Service, New York, New York 10017 (800) 253-9646; *Statistical Yearbook.*

SAUDI ARABIA - TELEVISION BROADCASTING - See SAUDI ARABIA - BROADCASTING

SAUDI ARABIA - TEXTILE INDUSTRY

Euromonitor Publications Limited, 87-88 Turnmill Street, London EC1M 5QU, England; *Third World Economic Handbook.*

G.K. Hall and Company, 70 Lincoln Street, Boston, Massachusetts 02111 (617) 423-3990; *The World in Figures.*

SAUDI ARABIA - THEATRE

United Nations Educational, Scientific and Cultural Organization (UNESCO), 7 Place de Fontenoy, F-75700 Paris, France (Telephone Number in U.S. (212) 963-5981); *Statistical Yearbook.*

SAUDI ARABIA - TOBACCO PRODUCTION

Euromonitor Publications Limited, 87-88 Turnmill Street, London EC1M 5QU, England; *Third World Economic Handbook.*

Facts on File, 460 Park Avenue South, New York, New York 10016 (800) 443-8323; *The New Book of World Rankings.*

SAUDI ARABIA - TOURISM

Economic Commission for Western Asia, Post Office Box 27, Baghdad, Iraq; *Statistical Abstract of Western Asia.*

Euromonitor Publications Limited, 87-88 Turnmill Street, London EC1M 5QU, England; *Middle East Economic Handbook,* and *Third World Economic Handbook.*

Facts on File, 460 Park Avenue South, New York, New York 10016 (800) 443-8323; *The New Book of World Rankings.*

Federal Statistical Office, Gustav-Stresemann-Ring 11, D-6200 Wiesbaden, Germany; *Saudi Arabia.*

G.K. Hall and Company, 70 Lincoln Street, Boston, Massachusetts 02111 (617) 423-3990; *The World in Figures.*

Statistical Office of the United Nations, Publishing Service, New York, New York 10017 (800) 253-9646; *Statistical Yearbook.*

Times Books, 201 East 50th Street, New York, New York 10022 (212) 751-2600; *The Economist Book of Vital World Statistics.*

World Tourism Organization, Calle Capitan Haya 42, E-28020 Madrid, Spain; *Yearbook of Tourism Statistics.*

SAUDI ARABIA - TRACTORS IN USE

Statistical Office of the United Nations, Publishing Service, New York, New York 10017 (800) 253-9646; *Statistical Yearbook.*

SAUDI ARABIA - TRADE - See SAUDI ARABIA - FOREIGN TRADE

SAUDI ARABIA - TRANSPORTATION AND COMMUNICATIONS

Economic Commission for Western Asia, Post Office Box 27, Baghdad, Iraq; *Statistical Abstract of Western Asia.*

Euromonitor Publications Limited, 87-88 Turnmill Street, London EC1M 5QU, England; *Middle East Economic Handbook,* and *Third World Economic Handbook.*

Facts on File, 460 Park Avenue South, New York, New York 10016 (800) 443-8323; *The New Book of World Rankings.*

Federal Statistical Office, Gustav-Stresemann-Ring 11, D-6200 Wiesbaden, Germany; *Saudi Arabia.*

G.K. Hall and Company, 70 Lincoln Street, Boston, Massachusetts 02111 (617) 423-3990; *The World in Figures.*

SAUDI ARABIA - UNEMPLOYMENT

Euromonitor Publications Limited, 87-88 Turnmill Street, London EC1M 5QU, England; *International Marketing Data and Statistics,* and *Middle East Economic Handbook.*

International Labour Office, I.L.O. Publications, CH-1211, Geneva 22, Switzerland; *Yearbook of Labour Statistics.*

SAUDI ARABIA - VITAL STATISTICS

Euromonitor Publications Limited, 87-88 Turnmill Street, London EC1M 5QU, England; *International Marketing Data and Statistics, Middle East Economic Handbook,* and *Third World Economic Handbook.*

G.K. Hall and Company, 70 Lincoln Street, Boston, Massachusetts 02111 (617) 423-3990; *The World in Figures.*

Statistical Office of the United Nations, Publishing Service, New York, New York 10017 (800) 253-9646; *Statistical Yearbook.*

World Health Organization, Office of Publications, Avenue Appia, CH-1211 Geneva 27, Switzerland (Telephone Number in U.S. (518) 436-9686); *World Health Statistics Annual.*

SAUDI ARABIA - WAGES

Federal Statistical Office, Gustav-Stresemann-Ring 11, D-6200 Wiesbaden, Germany; *Saudi Arabia.*

G.K. Hall and Company, 70 Lincoln Street, Boston, Massachusetts 02111 (617) 423-3990; *The World in Figures.*

International Labour Office, I.L.O. Publications, CH-1211, Geneva 22, Switzerland; *Yearbook of Labour Statistics.*

SAUDI ARABIA - WEATHER

Facts on File, 460 Park Avenue South, New York, New York 10016 (800) 443-8323; *The New Book of World Rankings.*

G.K. Hall and Company, 70 Lincoln Street, Boston, Massachusetts 02111 (617) 423-3990; *The World in Figures.*

SAUDI ARABIA - WHEAT - See SAUDI ARABIA - CROPS

SAUDI ARABIA - WHOLESALE TRADE

Euromonitor Publications Limited, 87-88 Turnmill Street, London EC1M 5QU, England; *Third World Economic Handbook.*

Statistical Office of the United Nations, Publishing Service, New York, New York 10017 (800) 253-9646; *Statistical Yearbook.*

SAUDI ARABIA - WINE PRODUCTION

Facts on File, 460 Park Avenue South, New York, New York 10016 (800) 443-8323; *The New Book of World Rankings.*

SAUDI ARABIA - WOOD PULP PRODUCTION - See SAUDI ARABIA - FORESTRY AND FOREST PRODUCTS

SAUDI ARABIA - WOOL PRODUCTION

Facts on File, 460 Park Avenue South, New York, New York 10016 (800) 443-8323; *The New Book of World Rankings.*

SAVINGS - CREDIT UNIONS

National Credit Union Administration, 1775 Duke Street, Alexandria, Virginia 22314-3428 (703) 518-6300; *Annual Report of the National Credit Union Administration*, and unpublished data.

SAVINGS - DEPOSIT BANK

Board of Governors of the Federal Reserve System, Twentieth Street and Constitution Avenue, NW, Washington, D.C. 20551 (202) 452-3000; *Federal Reserve Bulletin, Flow of Fund Accounts, Annual Statistical Digest, Money Stock, Liquid Assets and Debt Measures, Federal Statistical Release H.6.*, and *Monthly Survey of Selected Deposits*.

SAVINGS - GROSS SAVINGS - SOURCES AND USES

U.S. Department of Commerce, Bureau of Economic Analysis, Fourteenth Street between Constitution Avenue and E Street, NW, Washington, D.C. 20230 (202) 606-9900; *The National Income and Product Accounts of the United States*, and *Survey of Current Business*.

SAVINGS - PERSONAL

Board of Governors of the Federal Reserve System, Twentieth Street and Constitution Avenue, NW, Washington, D.C. 20551 (202) 452-3000; *Federal Reserve Bulletin*.

U.S. Department of Commerce, Bureau of Economic Analysis, Fourteenth Street between Constitution Avenue and E Street, NW, Washington, D.C. 20230 (202) 606-9900; *The National Income and Product Accounts of the United States*, and *Survey of Current Business*.

U.S. Department of Commerce, Bureau of the Census, Suitland, Maryland 20233 (301) 763-4040; *Current Population Reports*.

SAVINGS - UNITED STATES BONDS

U.S. Department of the Treasury, Fifteenth Street and Pennsylvania Avenue, NW, Washington, D.C. 20220 (202) 566-2000; *Treasury Bulletin*.

SAVINGS BANKS - See SAVINGS INSTITUTIONS

SAVINGS BONDS

Board of Governors of the Federal Reserve System, Twentieth Street and Constitution Avenue, NW, Washington, D.C. 20551 (202) 452-3000; *Federal Reserve Bulletin, Annual Statistical Digest*, and *Money Stock, Liquid Assets, and Debt Measures, Federal Reserve Statistical Release H.6.*

SAVINGS INSTITUTIONS - DELINQUENCY RATES - MORTGAGES

U.S. Department of the Treasury, Office of Thrift Supervision, 1700 G Street, NW, Washington, D.C. 20552 (202) 906-6000; *Surveillance and Analysis*.

SAVINGS INSTITUTIONS - DEPOSIT ACCOUNTS - NUMBER

U.S. Department of the Treasury, Office of Thrift Supervision, 1700 G Street, NW, Washington, D.C. 20552 (202) 906-6000; *Surveillance and Analysis*.

SAVINGS INSTITUTIONS - EARNINGS

U.S. Department of Commerce, Bureau of the Census, Suitland, Maryland 20233 (301) 763-4040; *County Business Patterns*.

SAVINGS INSTITUTIONS - EMPLOYEES

U.S. Department of Commerce, Bureau of the Census, Suitland, Maryland 20233 (301) 763-4040; *County Business Patterns*.

SAVINGS INSTITUTIONS - ESTABLISHMENTS

Federal Deposit Insurance Corporation, 550 Seventeenth Street, NW, Washington, D.C. 20429 (202) 393-8400; *Statistics on Banking*, and FDIC Quarterly Banking Profile.

U.S. Department of Commerce, Bureau of the Census, Suitland, Maryland 20233 (301) 763-4040; *County Business Patterns*.

U.S. Department of the Treasury, Office of Thrift Supervision, 1700 G Street, NW, Washington, D.C. 20552 (202) 906-6000; *Surveillance and Analysis*.

SAVINGS INSTITUTIONS - FINANCES

Board of Governors of the Federal Reserve System, Twentieth Street and Constitution Avenue, NW, Washington, D.C. 20551 (202) 452-3000; *Annual Statistical Digest, Federal Reserve Bulletin*, and *Money Stock, Liquid Assets, and Debt Measures, Federal Reserve Statistical Release H.6.*

Federal Deposit Insurance Corporation, 550 Seventeenth Street, NW, Washington, D.C. 20429 (202) 393-8400; *Statistics on Banking, FDIC Quarterly Banking Profile*, and unpublished data.

National Credit Union Administration, 1775 Duke Street, Alexandria, Virginia 22314 (703) 518-6300; *National Credit Union Administration Year End Statistics*.

U.S. Department of Housing and Urban Development, 451 Seventh Street, SW, Washington, D.C. 20410 (202) 708-1422; monthly and quarterly press releases based on the Survey of Mortgage Lending Activity.

U.S. Department of the Treasury, Office of Thrift Supervision, 1700 G Street, NW, Washington, D.C. 20552 (202) 906-6000; *Surveillance and Analysis*.

SAVINGS INSTITUTIONS - INDIVIDUAL RETIREMENT ACCOUNTS

Investment Company Institute, 1600 M Street, NW, Suite 600, Washington, D.C. 20036 (202) 293-7700; *Mutual Fund Fact Book*.

SAVINGS INSTITUTIONS - MERGERS AND ACQUISITIONS

Securities Data Company, 1180 Raymond Boulevard, Newark, New Jersey 07102 (201) 622-3100; *Merger and Corporate Transactions Database*.

SAVINGS INSTITUTIONS - PROFITS

U.S. Department of the Treasury, Office of Thrift Supervision, 1700 G Street, NW, Washington, D.C. 20552 (202) 906-6000; *Surveillance and Analysis*.

SAWLOGS

U.S. Department of Agriculture, Forest Service, Fourteenth Street and Independence Avenue, NW, Washington, D.C. 20250 (202) 720-3760; *United States Timber Production, Trade, Consumption, and Price Statistics.*

U.S. Department of Labor, Bureau of Labor Statistics, Two Massachusetts Avenue, NE, Washington, D.C. 20212 (202) 606-7828; *Producer Price Indexes.*

SAWTIMBER

U.S. Department of Agriculture, Forest Service, Fourteenth Street and Independence Avenue, NW, Washington, D.C. 20250 (202) 720-3760; *Forest Resources of the United States.*

SCALLOPS

U.S. Department of Commerce, National Oceanic and Atmospheric Administration, National Marine Fisheries Service, 1335 East-West Highway, Silver Spring, Maryland 20910 (301) 427-2239; *Fishery Statistics of the United States,* and *Fisheries of the United States.*

SCHOLASTIC APTITUDE TEST

College Entrance Examination Board, 45 Columbus Avenue, New York, New York 10023 (212) 713-8000; *National College-Bound Senior.*

SCHOOLS - See also EDUCATION

SCHOOLS - BOARDS - ELECTED OFFICIALS

Joint Center for Political and Economic Studies, 1090 Vermont Avenue, Suite 1100, NW, Washington, D.C. 20005 (202) 789-3500; *Black Elected Officials: A National Roster.*

National Association of Latino Elected and Appointed Officials, NALEO Education Fund, 3409 Garnet Street, Los Angeles, California 90023 (213) 262-8503; *National Roster of Hispanic Elected Officials.*

SCHOOLS - DISTRICTS

National Education Association, 1201 Sixteenth Street, NW, Washington, D.C. 20036 (202) 833-4000; *Estimates of School Statistics, Rankings of the States,* and unpublished data.

U.S. Department of Commerce, Bureau of the Census, Suitland, Maryland 20233 (301) 763-4040; *Census of Governments,* and *Government Organization.*

SCHOOLS - LUNCH PROGRAMS

U.S. Department of Agriculture, Food and Nutrition Service, 3101 Park Center Drive, Alexandria, Virginia 22302 (703) 305-2276; *Annual Historical Review of FNS Programs,* and unpublished data.

U.S. Library of Congress, Congressional Research Service, 10 First Street, SE, Washington, D.C. 20540; *Cash and Non-Cash Benefits for Persons with Limited Income: Eligibility Rules, Recipient and Expenditure Data.*

SCHOOLS - NUMBER

U.S. Department of Education, 400 Maryland Avenue, SW, Washington, D.C. 20202 (202) 708-5366; *Digest of Education Statistics,* and *Projections of Education Statistics.*

SCHOOLS - SUNDAY OR SABBATH

National Council of the Churches of Christ in the United States of America, 475 Riverside Drive, New York, New York 10115 (212) 870-2227; *Yearbook of American and Canadian Churches.*

SCIENTIFIC, ENGINEERING, AND TECHNICAL ASSOCIATIONS

Gale Research Incorporated, 835 Penobscot Building, Detroit, Michigan 48226 (800) 877-4253; *Encyclopedia of Associations.*

SCIENTIFIC INSTRUMENTS - See INSTRUMENTS AND RELATED PRODUCTS

SCIENTIFIC RESEARCH - See RESEARCH AND DEVELOPMENT

SCIENTISTS AND ENGINEERS - See also Individual Fields

U.S. National Science Foundation, 4201 Wilson Boulevard, Arlington, Virginia 22230 (703) 306-1234; *National Patterns of Research and Development Resources.*

SCIENTISTS AND ENGINEERS - DEGREES CONFERRED

U.S. Department of Education, 400 Maryland Avenue, SW, Washington, D.C. 20202 (202) 708-5366; *Digest of Education Statistics.*

U.S. National Science Foundation, 4201 Wilson Boulevard, Arlington, Virginia 22230 (703) 306-1234; *Survey of Earned Doctorates, Selected Data on Science and Engineering Doctorate Awards.*

SCIENTISTS AND ENGINEERS - EMPLOYMENT

U.S. Department of Labor, Bureau of Labor Statistics, Two Massachusetts Avenue, NE, Washington, D.C. 20212 (202) 606-7828; *Employment and Earnings,* and *Monthly Labor Review.*

U.S. National Science Foundation, 4201 Wilson Boulevard, Arlington, Virginia 22230 (703) 306-1234; *United States Scientists and Engineers, Research and Development in Industry, National Patterns of Research and Development Resources, Survey of Federal Support to Universities, Colleges, and Nonprofit Institutions,* and *Federal Funds for Research and Development.*

SCIENTISTS AND ENGINEERS - EMPLOYMENT - BY INDUSTRIAL SECTOR

U.S. Department of Labor, Bureau of Labor Statistics, Two Massachusetts Avenue, NE, Washington, D.C. 20212 (202) 606-7828; *Monthly Labor Review.*

SCIENTISTS AND ENGINEERS - EMPLOYMENT - RESEARCH AND DEVELOPMENT

U.S. National Science Foundation, 4201 Wilson Boulevard, Arlington, Virginia 22230 (703) 306-1234; *National Patterns of Research and Development Resources,* and *Research and Development in Industry.*

SCOUTS - MEMBERSHIP AND UNITS

Boy Scouts of America, 1325 Walnut Hill Lane, Post Office Box 152079, Irving, Texas 75015 (214) 580-2000; *Annual Report.*

Girl Scouts of the United States of America, 420 Fifth Avenue, New York, New York 10018 (212) 852-8000; *Annual Report.*

SCRAP METAL

U.S. Department of the Interior, Bureau of Mines, 810 Seventh Street, NW, Washington, D.C. 20241 (202) 501-9649; *Annual Reports.*

SCUP - CATCH

U.S. Department of Commerce, National Oceanic and Atmospheric Administration, National Marine Fisheries Service, 1335 East-West Highway, Silver Spring, Maryland 20910 (301) 427-2239; *Fishery Statistics of the United States,* and *Fisheries of the United States.*

SEA BASS

U.S. Department of Commerce, National Oceanic and Atmospheric Administration, National Marine Fisheries Service, 1335 East-West Highway, Silver Spring, Maryland 20910 (301) 427-2239; *Fisheries of the United States.*

SEA TROUT

U.S. Department of Commerce, National Oceanic and Atmospheric Administration, National Marine Fisheries Service, 1335 East-West Highway, Silver Spring, Maryland 20910 (301) 427-2239; *Fisheries of the United States.*

SEAFOODS

U.S. Department of Commerce, National Oceanic and Atmospheric Administration, National Marine Fisheries Service, 1335 East-West Highway, Silver Spring, Maryland 20910 (301) 427-2239; *Fisheries of the United States,* and *Fishery Statistics of the United States.*

SECURITIES - FOREIGN HOLDINGS

U.S. Department of Commerce, Bureau of Economic Analysis, Fourteenth Street between Constitution Avenue and E Street, NW, Washington, D.C. 20230 (202) 606-9900; *Survey of Current Business.*

SECURITIES - FOREIGN PURCHASES AND SALES

International Finance Corporation, 1818 H Street, NW, Washington, D.C. 20006 (202) 477-1234; *Emerging Stock Markets Factbook.*

U.S. Department of the Treasury, Fifteenth Street and Pennsylvania Avenue, NW, Washington, D.C. 20220 (202) 566-2000; *Treasury Bulletin.*

SECURITIES - GOVERNMENT

Securities Data Company, Inc., 1180 Raymond Boulevard, Newark, New Jersey 07102 (201) 622-3100; Municipal New Issues Database.

SECURITIES - HELD BY GOVERNMENT CORPORATIONS AND CREDIT AGENCIES

Board of Governors of the Federal Reserve System, Twentieth Street and Constitution Avenue, NW, Washington, D.C. 20551 (202) 452-3000; *Annual Statistical Digest.*

SECURITIES - HELD BY LIFE INSURANCE

American Council of Life Insurance, 1001 Pennsylvania Avenue, NW, Washington, D.C. 20004-2599 (202) 624-2000; *Life Insurance Fact Book.*

SECURITIES - HOLDINGS OF BANKS

Board of Governors of the Federal Reserve System, Twentieth Street and Constitution Avenue, NW, Washington, D.C. 20551 (202) 452-3000; *Annual Statistical Digest.*

U.S. Federal Deposit Insurance Corporation, 500 Seventeenth Street, NW, Washington, D.C. 20429 (202) 393-8400; *Annual Report, The FDIC Quarterly Banking Profile,* and *Statistics on Banking.*

SECURITIES - HOLDINGS OF INDIVIDUALS AND BUSINESSES

Board of Governors of the Federal Reserve System, Twentieth Street and Constitution Avenue, NW, Washington, D.C. 20551 (202) 452-3000; *Annual Statistical Digest.*

U.S. Department of Commerce, Bureau of the Census, Suitland, Maryland 20233 (301) 763-4040; *Current Population Reports.*

SECURITIES - NEW ISSUES

Board of Governors of the Federal Reserve System, Twentieth Street and Constitution Avenue, NW, Washington, D.C. 20551 (202) 452-3000; *Federal Reserve Bulletin,* and *Annual Statistical Digest.*

SECURITIES - PRICES, SALES, YIELDS, AND ISSUES

Board of Governors of the Federal Reserve System, Twentieth Street and Constitution Avenue, NW, Washington, D.C. 20551 (202) 452-3000; *Federal Reserve Bulletin,* and *Annual Statistical Digest.*

Dow Jones and Company, Incorporated, 200 Liberty Street, New York, New York 10006 (212) 416-2000.

International Finance Corporation, 1818 H Street, NW, Washington, D.C. 20006 (202) 477-1234; *Emerging Stock Markets Factbook.*

National Association of Securities Dealers, 1735 K Street, NW, Washington, D.C. 20006 (202) 728-8000; *Fact Book.*

New York Stock Exchange, 11 Wall Street, New York, New York 10005 (212) 656-3000; *Fact Book.*

Standard and Poor's Corporation, 25 Broadway, New York, New York 10004 (212) 208-8000; *Standard and Poor's Outlook.*

SECURITIES - SAVINGS OF INDIVIDUALS

Board of Governors of the Federal Reserve System, Twentieth Street and Constitution Avenue, NW, Washington, D.C. 20551 (202) 452-3000; *Flow of Funds Accounts.*

U.S. Department of Commerce, Bureau of Economic Analysis, Fourteenth Street between Constitution Avenue and E Street, NW, Washington, D.C. 20230 (202) 606-9900; *The National Income and Product Accounts of the United States,* and *Survey of Current Business.*

SECURITIES - STATE AND LOCAL GOVERNMENT

Board of Governors of the Federal Reserve System, Twentieth Street and Constitution Avenue, NW, Washington, D.C. 20551 (202) 452-3000; *Annual Statistical Digest.*

Securities Data Company, Inc., 1180 Raymond Boulevard, Newark, New Jersey 07102 (201) 622-3100; Municipal New Issues Database.

U.S. Department of the Treasury, Fifteenth Street and Pennsylvania Avenue, NW, Washington, D.C. 20220 (202) 566-2000; *Treasury Bulletin*.

SECURITY AND COMMODITY BROKERS

U.S. Department of Commerce, Bureau of Economic Analysis, Fourteenth Street between Constitution Avenue and E Street, NW, Washington, D.C. 20230 (202) 606-9900; *The National Income and Product Accounts of the United States*, and *Survey of Current Business*.

U.S. Department of Commerce, Bureau of the Census, Suitland, Maryland 20233 (301) 763-4040; *County Business Patterns*.

U.S. Department of Labor, Bureau of Labor Statistics, Two Massachusetts Avenue, NE, Washington, D.C. 20212 (202) 606-7828; *Employment and Earnings*.

SECURITY AND COMMODITY BROKERS - EARNINGS

U.S. Department of Commerce, Bureau of the Census, Suitland, Maryland 20233 (301) 763-4040; *County Business Patterns*.

U.S. Department of Commerce, Bureau of Economic Analysis, Fourteenth Street between Constitution Avenue and E Street, NW, Washington, D.C. 20230 (202) 606-9900; *The National Income and Product Accounts of the United States*, and *Survey of Current Business*.

U.S. Department of Labor, Bureau of Labor Statistics, Two Massachusetts Avenue, NE, Washington, D.C. 20212 (202) 606-7828; *Employment and Earnings*.

SECURITY AND COMMODITY BROKERS - EMPLOYEES

U.S. Department of Commerce, Bureau of the Census, Suitland, Maryland 20233 (301) 763-4040; *County Business Patterns*.

U.S. Department of Labor, Bureau of Labor Statistics, Two Massachusetts Avenue, NE, Washington, D.C. 20212 (202) 606-7828; *Employment and Earnings*.

SECURITY AND COMMODITY BROKERS - ESTABLISHMENTS

U.S. Department of Commerce, Bureau of the Census, Suitland, Maryland 20233 (301) 763-4040; *County Business Patterns*.

SECURITY AND COMMODITY BROKERS - FINANCES

Board of Governors of the Federal Reserve System, Twentieth Street and Constitution Avenue, NW, Washington, D.C. 20551 (202) 452-3000; *Annual Statistical Digest*.

Securities and Exchange Commission, 450 Fifth Street, NW, Washington, D.C. 20549 (202) 272-3100; *Annual Report*.

Securities Industry Association, 120 Broadway, New York, New York 10271 (212) 608-1500; *Securities Industry Association Fact Book*.

SECURITY AND COMMODITY BROKERS - GROSS DOMESTIC PRODUCT

U.S. Department of Commerce, Bureau of Economic Analysis, Fourteenth Street between Constitution Avenue and E Street, NW, Washington, D.C. 20230 (202) 606-9900; *The National Income and Product Accounts of the United States*, and *Survey of Current Business*.

SECURITY AND COMMODITY BROKERS - OCCUPATIONAL SAFETY

U.S. Department of Labor, Bureau of Labor Statistics, Two Massachusetts Avenue, NE, Washington, D.C. 20212 (202) 606-7828; *Injuries and Illnesses in the United States by Industry*.

SECURITY AND COMMODITY BROKERS - PROFITS

Securities and Exchange Commission, 450 Fifth Street, NW, Washington, D.C. 20549 (202) 272-3100; *Annual Report*.

Securities Industry Association, 120 Broadway, New York, New York 10271 (212) 608-1500; *Securities Industry Association Fact Book*.

SEDATIVES - PERSONS USING

U.S. Department of Health and Human Services, Substance Abuse and Mental Health in Services Administration, 5600 Fishers Lane, Rockville, Maryland 20857 (301) 443-4797; *National Household Survey on Drug Abuse*.

SEEDS

U.S. Department of Agriculture, Economic Research Service, Fourteenth Street and Constitution Avenue, SW, Washington, D.C. 20005-4789 (202) 219-1504; *Agricultural Statistics*, and *Agricultural Outlook*.

SELENIUM

U.S. Department of Commerce, Bureau of the Census, Suitland, Maryland 20233 (301) 763-4040; import and export data.

U.S. Department of the Interior, Bureau of Mines, 810 Seventh Street, NW, Washington, D.C. 20241 (202) 501-9649; *Minerals Commodity Summaries*.

SEMICONDUCTORS AND RELATED DEVISES - MANUFACTURING - See also ELECTRONIC COMPONENTS

U.S. Department of Commerce, Bureau of the Census, Suitland, Maryland 20233 (301) 763-4040; *Annual Survey of Manufactures*, and *Current Industrial Reports*.

SENATORS, UNITED STATES

Congressional Quarterly, Incorporated, 1414 22nd Street, NW, Washington, D.C. 20037 (202) 887-8500; *Congressional Quarterly Weekly Report*.

Elections Research Center, 5508 Greystone Street, Chevy Chase, Maryland 20815 (202) 659-9490; *America Votes*.

U.S. Congress, Joint Committee on Printing, North Capitol and H Streets, NW, Washington, D.C. 20401 (202) 275-2051; *Congressional Directory*.

Senegal - National Statistical Office

Direction de la Statistique, Ministere de l'Economie et des Finances, BP 116, Dakar, Senegal.

Senegal - Primary Statistics Sources

Direction de la Prevision et de la Statistique, BP 116, Dakar, Senegal; *Situation economique du Senegal* (Economic Situation in Senegal) and *Bulletin statistique et economique mensuel* (Monthly Economic and Statistical Bulletin).

SENEGAL - AGRICULTURE

Euromonitor Publications Limited, 87-88 Turnmill Street, London EC1M 5QU, England; *International Marketing Data and Statistics*.

Facts on File, 460 Park Avenue South, New York, New York 10016 (800) 443-8323; *The New Book of World Rankings*.

Food and Agricultural Organization of the United Nations (FAO) Via delle Terme di Caracalla, 00100 Rome, Italy (Telephone Number in U.S. (202) 653-2400); *Production Yearbook, The State of Food and Agriculture*, and *Trade Yearbook*.

G.K. Hall and Company, 70 Lincoln Street, Boston, Massachusetts 02111 (617) 423-3990; *The World in Figures*.

Statistical Office of the United Nations, Publishing Service, New York, New York 10017 (800) 253-9646; *Statistical Yearbook*, and *Survey of Economic and Social Conditions in Africa*.

Times Books, 201 East 50th Street, New York, New York 10022 (212) 751-2600; *The Economist Book of Vital World Statistics*.

United Nations Economic Commission for Africa, Africa Hall, P.O. Box 3001, Addis Ababa, Ethiopia (Telephone Number in U.S. (800) 253-9646); *African Statistical Yearbook*.

The World Bank, 1818 H Street, NW, Washington, D.C. 20433 (202) 477-1234; *World Tables*.

SENEGAL - AIRLINE SERVICE

Facts on File, 460 Park Avenue South, New York, New York 10016 (800) 443-8323; *The New Book of World Rankings*.

G.K. Hall and Company, 70 Lincoln Street, Boston, Massachusetts 02111 (617) 423-3990; *The World in Figures*.

Statistical Office of the United Nations, Publishing Service, New York, New York 10017 (800) 253-9646; *Statistical Yearbook*.

Times Books, 201 East 50th Street, New York, New York 10022 (212) 751-2600; *The Economist Book of Vital World Statistics*.

United Nations Economic Commission for Africa, Africa Hall, P.O. Box 3001, Addis Ababa, Ethiopia (Telephone Number in U.S. (800) 253-9646); *African Statistical Yearbook*.

SENEGAL - ALUMINUM PRODUCTION AND CONSUMPTION - See SENEGAL - MINING AND MINERAL PRODUCTS

SENEGAL - ANIMAL HEALTH

Food and Agricultural Organization of the United Nations (FAO), Via delle Terme di Caracalla, 00100, Rome, Italy (Telephone Number in U.S. (202) 653-2400); *Animal Health Yearbook*.

SENEGAL - AREA AND DENSITY OF POPULATION

African Development Bank, 01 BP 1387, Abidjan 01, Cote D'Ivoire; *Selected Statistics on Regional Member Countries*.

Euromonitor Publications Limited, 87-88 Turnmill Street, London EC1M 5QU, England; *International Marketing Data and Statistics*.

Facts on File, 460 Park Avenue South, New York, New York 10016 (800) 443-8323; *The New Book of World Rankings*.

Food and Agricultural Organization of the United Nations (FAO) Via delle Terme di Caracalla, 00100 Rome, Italy (Telephone Number in U.S. (202) 653-2400); *The State of Food and Agriculture*.

G.K. Hall and Company, 70 Lincoln Street, Boston, Massachusetts 02111 (617) 423-3990; *The World in Figures*.

Statistical Office of the United Nations, Publishing Service, New York, New York 10017 (800) 253-9646; *Statistical Yearbook*, and *Survey of Economic and Social Conditions in Africa*.

Times Books, 201 East 50th Street, New York, New York 10022 (212) 751-2600; *The Economist Book of Vital World Statistics*.

United Nations Educational, Scientific and Cultural Organization (UNESCO), 7 Place de Fontenoy, F-75700 Paris, France (Telephone Number in U.S. (212) 963-5981); *Statistical Yearbook*.

SENEGAL - ARMS EXPORTS AND IMPORTS

U.S. Arms Control and Disarmament Agency, 320 Twenty-first Street, NW, Washington, D.C. 20451 (202) 647-8677; *World Military Expenditures and Arms Transfers*.

SENEGAL - BALANCE OF PAYMENTS

African Development Bank, 01 BP 1387, Abidjan 01, Cote D'Ivoire; *Selected Statistics on Regional Member Countries*.

The Economist Intelligence Unit, 111 West 57th Street, New York, New York 10019 (800) 938-4685; *The World Market Atlas*.

G.K. Hall and Company, 70 Lincoln Street, Boston, Massachusetts 02111 (617) 423-3990; *The World in Figures*.

International Monetary Fund, 700 Nineteenth Street, NW, Washington, D.C. 20431 (202) 623-7000; *Balance of Payments Yearbook*.

Times Books, 201 East 50th Street, New York, New York 10022 (212) 751-2600; *The Economist Book of Vital World Statistics*.

United Nations Economic Commission for Africa, Africa Hall, P.O. Box 3001, Addis Ababa, Ethiopia (Telephone Number in U.S. (800) 253-9646); *African Statistical Yearbook*.

The World Bank, 1818 H Street, NW, Washington, D.C. 20433 (202) 477-1234; *World Tables*.

SENEGAL - BANKING

Facts on File, 460 Park Avenue South, New York, New York 10016 (800) 443-8323; *The New Book of World Rankings*.

G.K. Hall and Company, 70 Lincoln Street, Boston, Massachusetts 02111 (617) 423-3990; *The World in Figures*.

International Monetary Fund, 700 Nineteenth Street, NW, Washington, D.C. 20431 (202) 623-7000; *International Financial Statistics*.

Statistical Office of the United Nations, Publishing Service, New York, New York 10017 (800) 253-9646; *Statistical Yearbook*.

United Nations Economic Commission for Africa, Africa Hall, P.O. Box 3001, Addis Ababa, Ethiopia (Telephone Number in U.S. (800) 253-9646); *African Statistical Yearbook*.

SENEGAL - BARLEY PRODUCTION - See SENEGAL - CROPS

SENEGAL - BEER PRODUCTION

Facts on File, 460 Park Avenue South, New York, New York 10016 (800) 443-8323; *The New Book of World Rankings.*

Statistical Office of the United Nations, Publishing Service, New York, New York 10017 (800) 253-9646; *Statistical Yearbook.*

SENEGAL - BIRTH RATES

Facts on File, 460 Park Avenue South, New York, New York 10016 (800) 443-8323; *The New Book of World Rankings.*

Statistical Office of the United Nations, Publishing Service, New York, New York 10017 (800) 253-9646; *Demographic Yearbook, Statistical Yearbook,* and *Survey of Economic and Social Conditions in Africa.*

Times Books, 201 East 50th Street, New York, New York 10022 (212) 751-2600; *The Economist Book of Vital World Statistics.*

The World Bank, 1818 H Street, NW, Washington, D.C. 20433 (202) 477-1234; *World Tables.*

SENEGAL - BONDS

G.K. Hall and Company, 70 Lincoln Street, Boston, Massachusetts 02111 (617) 423-3990; *The World in Figures.*

SENEGAL - BOOK PRODUCTION

G.K. Hall and Company, 70 Lincoln Street, Boston, Massachusetts 02111 (617) 423-3990; *The World in Figures.*

United Nations Educational, Scientific and Cultural Organization (UNESCO), 7 Place de Fontenoy, F-75700 Paris, France (Telephone Number in U.S. (212) 963-5981); *Statistical Yearbook*

SENEGAL - BROADCASTING

Billboard Limited, P.O. Box 9027, 1006 AA Amsterdam, The Netherlands (Telephone Number in U.S. (212) 764-7300); *World Radio TV Handbook.*

Facts on File, 460 Park Avenue South, New York, New York 10016 (800) 443-8323; *The New Book of World Rankings.*

G.K. Hall and Company, 70 Lincoln Street, Boston, Massachusetts 02111 (617) 423-3990; *The World in Figures.*

Times Books, 201 East 50th Street, New York, New York 10022 (212) 751-2600; *The Economist Book of Vital World Statistics.*

SENEGAL - BUSINESS

G.K. Hall and Company, 70 Lincoln Street, Boston, Massachusetts 02111 (617) 423-3990; *The World in Figures.*

SENEGAL - BUSINESS AND PROFESSIONAL LICENSES

International Monetary Fund, 700 Nineteenth Street, NW, Washington, D.C. 20431 (202) 623-7000; *Government Finance Statistics Yearbook.*

SENEGAL - CALORIE SUPPLY

African Development Bank, 01 BP 1387, Abidjan 01, Cote D'Ivoire; *Selected Statistics on Regional Member Countries.*

Food and Agricultural Organization of the United Nations (FAO) Via delle Terme di Caracalla, 00100 Rome, Italy (Telephone Number in U.S. (202) 653-2400); *The State of Food and Agriculture.*

SENEGAL - CAPITAL REVENUE

International Monetary Fund, 700 Nineteenth Street, NW, Washington, D.C. 20431 (202) 623-7000; *Government Finance Statistics Yearbook.*

SENEGAL - CATTLE - See SENEGAL - LIVESTOCK AND POULTRY

SENEGAL - CEMENT PRODUCTION - See SENEGAL - MINING AND MINERAL PRODUCTS

SENEGAL - CHEMICAL (ORGANIC) PRODUCTION - See SENEGAL - MINING AND MINERAL PRODUCTS

SENEGAL - CHICKENS - See SENEGAL - LIVESTOCK AND POULTRY

SENEGAL - CIGARETTE PRODUCTION - See SENEGAL - TOBACCO PRODUCTION

SENEGAL - CLASS STRUCTURE

G.K. Hall and Company, 70 Lincoln Street, Boston, Massachusetts 02111 (617) 423-3990; *The World in Figures.*

SENEGAL - CLIMATE

Facts on File, 460 Park Avenue South, New York, New York 10016 (800) 443-8323; *The New Book of World Rankings.*

G.K. Hall and Company, 70 Lincoln Street, Boston, Massachusetts 02111 (617) 423-3990; *The World in Figures.*

SENEGAL - COAL PRODUCTION - See SENEGAL - MINING AND MINERAL PRODUCTS

SENEGAL - COFFEE - See SENEGAL - CROPS

SENEGAL - COMMUNICATIONS

G.K. Hall and Company, 70 Lincoln Street, Boston, Massachusetts 02111 (617) 423-3990; *The World in Figures.*

United Nations Economic Commission for Africa, Africa Hall, P.O. Box 3001, Addis Ababa, Ethiopia (Telephone Number in U.S. (800) 253-9646); *African Statistical Yearbook.*

SENEGAL - CONSTRUCTION INDUSTRY

Facts on File, 460 Park Avenue South, New York, New York 10016 (800) 443-8323; *The New Book of World Rankings.*

Statistical Office of the United Nations, Publishing Service, New York, New York 10017 (800) 253-9646; *Construction Statistics Yearbook,* and *Statistical Yearbook.*

United Nations Economic Commission for Africa, Africa Hall, P.O. Box 3001, Addis Ababa, Ethiopia (Telephone Number in U.S. (800) 253-9646); *African Statistical Yearbook.*

SENEGAL - CONSUMER PRICE INDEX

African Development Bank, 01 BP 1387, Abidjan 01, Cote D'Ivoire; *Selected Statistics on Regional Member Countries.*

G.K. Hall and Company, 70 Lincoln Street, Boston, Massachusetts 02111 (617) 423-3990; *The World in Figures.*

Statistical Office of the United Nations, Publishing Service, New York, New York 10017 (800) 253-9646; *Statistical Yearbook,* and *Survey of Economic and Social Conditions in Africa.*

United Nations Economic Commission for Africa, Africa Hall, P.O. Box 3001, Addis Ababa, Ethiopia (Telephone Number in U.S. (800) 253-9646); *African Statistical Yearbook.*

SENEGAL - CONSUMER PRICES

International Labour Office, I.L.O. Publications, CH-1211, Geneva 22, Switzerland; *Yearbook of Labour Statistics.*

International Monetary Fund, 700 Nineteenth Street, NW, Washington, D.C. 20431 (202) 623-7000; *International Financial Statistics.*

Times Books, 201 East 50th Street, New York, New York 10022 (212) 751-2600; *The Economist Book of Vital World Statistics.*

SENEGAL - CONSUMPTION

African Development Bank, 01 BP 1387, Abidjan 01, Cote D'Ivoire; *Selected Statistics on Regional Member Countries.*

G.K. Hall and Company, 70 Lincoln Street, Boston, Massachusetts 02111 (617) 423-3990; *The World in Figures.*

Statistical Office of the United Nations, Publishing Service, New York, New York 10017 (800) 253-9646; *Survey of Economic and Social Conditions in Africa.*

SENEGAL - COPPER PRODUCTION AND CONSUMPTION - See SENEGAL - MINING AND MINERAL PRODUCTS

SENEGAL - CORN PRODUCTION - See SENEGAL - CROPS

SENEGAL - CORPORATE TAXES - See SENEGAL - TAXATION

SENEGAL - COTTON - See SENEGAL - CROPS

SENEGAL - CRIME

Yale University Press, Yale Station, New Haven, Connecticut 06520 (203) 432-0940; *Violence and Crime in Cross-National Perspective.*

SENEGAL - CROPS

Commodity Research Bureau, Incorporated, 75 Wall Street, New York, New York 10005 (212) 504-7754; *Commodity Year Book.*

Facts on File, 460 Park Avenue South, New York, New York 10016 (800) 443-8323; *The New Book of World Rankings.*

Food and Agricultural Organization of the United Nations (FAO) Via delle Terme di Caracalla, 00100 Rome, Italy (Telephone Number in U.S. (202) 653-2400); *The State of Food and Agriculture.*

G.K. Hall and Company, 70 Lincoln Street, Boston, Massachusetts 02111 (617) 423-3990; *The World in Figures.*

Statistical Office of the United Nations, Publishing Service, New York, New York 10017 (800) 253-9646; *Statistical Yearbook.*

United Nations Economic Commission for Africa, Africa Hall, P.O. Box 3001, Addis Ababa, Ethiopia (Telephone Number in U.S. (800) 253-9646); *African Statistical Yearbook.*

SENEGAL - CUSTOMS DUTIES

G.K. Hall and Company, 70 Lincoln Street, Boston, Massachusetts 02111 (617) 423-3990; *The World in Figures.*

International Monetary Fund, 700 Nineteenth Street, NW, Washington, D.C. 20431 (202) 623-7000; *Government Finance Statistics Yearbook.*

SENEGAL - DAIRY PRODUCTS

Facts on File, 460 Park Avenue South, New York, New York 10016 (800) 443-8323; *The New Book of World Rankings.*

Food and Agricultural Organization of the United Nations (FAO) Via delle Terme di Caracalla, 00100 Rome, Italy (Telephone Number in U.S. (202) 653-2400); *The State of Food and Agriculture.*

Statistical Office of the United Nations, Publishing Service, New York, New York 10017 (800) 253-9646; *Statistical Yearbook.*

SENEGAL - DEATH RATES

G.K. Hall and Company, 70 Lincoln Street, Boston, Massachusetts 02111 (617) 423-3990; *The World in Figures.*

Statistical Office of the United Nations, Publishing Service, New York, New York 10017 (800) 253-9646; *Statistical Yearbook,* and *Survey of Economic and Social Conditions in Africa.*

Times Books, 201 East 50th Street, New York, New York 10022 (212) 751-2600; *The Economist Book of Vital World Statistics.*

World Health Organization, Office of Publications, Avenue Appia, CH-1211 Geneva 27, Switzerland (Telephone Number in U.S. (518) 436-9686); *World Health Statistics Annual.*

SENEGAL - DEFENSE EXPENDITURES

G.K. Hall and Company, 70 Lincoln Street, Boston, Massachusetts 02111 (617) 423-3990; *The World in Figures.*

International Monetary Fund, 700 Nineteenth Street, NW, Washington, D.C. 20431 (202) 623-7000; *Government Finance Statistics Yearbook.*

U.S. Arms Control and Disarmament Agency, 320 Twenty-first Street, NW, Washington, D.C. 20451 (202) 647-8677; *World Military Expenditures and Arms Transfers.*

SENEGAL - DEMOGRAPHY

The Economist Intelligence Unit, 111 West 57th Street, New York, New York 10019 (800) 938-4685; *The World Market Atlas.*

Facts on File, 460 Park Avenue South, New York, New York 10016 (800) 443-8323; *The New Book of World Rankings.*

G.K. Hall and Company, 70 Lincoln Street, Boston, Massachusetts 02111 (617) 423-3990; *The World in Figures.*

Statistical Office of the United Nations, Publishing Service, New York, New York 10017 (800) 253-9646; *Survey of Economic and Social Conditions in Africa.*

SENEGAL - DEVELOPMENT ASSISTANCE

G.K. Hall and Company, 70 Lincoln Street, Boston, Massachusetts 02111 (617) 423-3990; *The World in Figures.*

Statistical Office of the United Nations, Publishing Service, New York, New York 10017 (800) 253-9646; *Statistical Yearbook.*

SENEGAL - DIAMOND PRODUCTION - See SENEGAL - MINING AND MINERAL PRODUCTS

SENEGAL - DISCOUNT RATES

Statistical Office of the United Nations, Publishing Service, New York, New York 10017 (800) 253-9646; *Statistical Yearbook.*

SENEGAL - DISEASES

G.K. Hall and Company, 70 Lincoln Street, Boston, Massachusetts 02111 (617) 423-3990; *The World in Figures.*

World Health Organization, Office of Publications, Avenue Appia, CH-1211 Geneva 27, Switzerland (Telephone Number in U.S. (518) 436-9686); *World Health Statistics Annual.*

SENEGAL - DIVORCE RATES

Facts on File, 460 Park Avenue South, New York, New York 10016 (800) 443-8323; *The New Book of World Rankings.*

Statistical Office of the United Nations, Publishing Service, New York, New York 10017 (800) 253-9646; *Demographic Yearbook.*

SENEGAL - DOMESTIC PRODUCT

G.K. Hall and Company, 70 Lincoln Street, Boston, Massachusetts 02111 (617) 423-3990; *The World in Figures.*

SENEGAL - ECONOMY

African Development Bank, 01 BP 1387, Abidjan 01, Cote D'Ivoire; *Selected Statistics on Regional Member Countries.*

Euromonitor Publications Limited, 87-88 Turnmill Street, London EC1M 5QU, England; *International Marketing Data and Statistics.*

Facts on File, 460 Park Avenue South, New York, New York 10016 (800) 443-8323; *The New Book of World Rankings.*

G.K. Hall and Company, 70 Lincoln Street, Boston, Massachusetts 02111 (617) 423-3990; *The World in Figures.*

Statistical Office of the United Nations, Publishing Service, New York, New York 10017 (800) 253-9646; *Foreign Trade Statistics for Africa.*

SENEGAL - EDUCATION

African Development Bank, 01 BP 1387, Abidjan 01, Cote D'Ivoire; *Selected Statistics on Regional Member Countries.*

The Economist Intelligence Unit, 111 West 57th Street, New York, New York 10019 (800) 938-4685; *The World Market Atlas.*

Facts on File, 460 Park Avenue South, New York, New York 10016 (800) 443-8323; *The New Book of World Rankings.*

G.K. Hall and Company, 70 Lincoln Street, Boston, Massachusetts 02111 (617) 423-3990; *The World in Figures.*

International Monetary Fund, 700 Nineteenth Street, NW, Washington, D.C. 20431 (202) 623-7000; *Government Finance Statistics Yearbook.*

Statistical Office of the United Nations, Publishing Service, New York, New York 10017 (800) 253-9646; *Survey of Economic and Social Conditions in Africa.*

Times Books, 201 East 50th Street, New York, New York 10022 (212) 751-2600; *The Economist Book of Vital World Statistics.*

United Nations Economic Commission for Africa, Africa Hall, P.O. Box 3001, Addis Ababa, Ethiopia (Telephone Number in U.S. (800) 253-9646); *African Statistical Yearbook.*

United Nations Educational, Scientific and Cultural Organization (UNESCO), 7 Place de Fontenoy, F-75700 Paris, France (Telephone Number in U.S. (212) 963-5981); *Statistical Yearbook.*

The World Bank, 1818 H Street, NW, Washington, D.C. 20433 (202) 477-1234; *World Tables.*

SENEGAL - EGG PRODUCTION AND CONSUMPTION - See SENEGAL - DAIRY PRODUCTS

SENEGAL - ELECTRICITY

Facts on File, 460 Park Avenue South, New York, New York 10016 (800) 443-8323; *The New Book of World Rankings.*

Statistical Office of the United Nations, Publishing Service, New York, New York 10017 (800) 253-9646; *Statistical Yearbook,* and *Survey of Economic and Social Conditions in Africa.*

Times Books, 201 East 50th Street, New York, New York 10022 (212) 751-2600; *The Economist Book of Vital World Statistics.*

United Nations Economic Commission for Africa, Africa Hall, P.O. Box 3001, Addis Ababa, Ethiopia (Telephone Number in U.S. (800) 253-9646); *African Statistical Yearbook.*

SENEGAL - EMPLOYMENT

Euromonitor Publications Limited, 87-88 Turnmill Street, London EC1M 5QU, England; *International Marketing Data and Statistics.*

Facts on File, 460 Park Avenue South, New York, New York 10016 (800) 443-8323; *The New Book of World Rankings.*

International Labour Office, I.L.O. Publications, CH-1211, Geneva 22, Switzerland; *Yearbook of Labour Statistics.*

Statistical Office of the United Nations, Publishing Service, New York, New York 10017 (800) 253-9646; *Survey of Economic and Social Conditions in Africa.*

United Nations Economic Commission for Africa, Africa Hall, P.O. Box 3001, Addis Ababa, Ethiopia (Telephone Number in U.S. (800) 253-9646); *African Statistical Yearbook.*

SENEGAL - ENERGY

Facts on File, 460 Park Avenue South, New York, New York 10016 (800) 443-8323; *The New Book of World Rankings.*

Food and Agricultural Organization of the United Nations (FAO) Via delle Terme di Caracalla, 00100 Rome, Italy (Telephone Number in U.S. (202) 653-2400); *The State of Food and Agriculture.*

G.K. Hall and Company, 70 Lincoln Street, Boston, Massachusetts 02111 (617) 423-3990; *The World in Figures.*

Statistical Office of the United Nations, Publishing Service, New York, New York 10017 (800) 253-9646; *Energy Statistics Yearbook, Statistical Yearbook,* and *World Energy Supplies.*

Times Books, 201 East 50th Street, New York, New York 10022 (212) 751-2600; *The Economist Book of Vital World Statistics.*

United Nations Economic Commission for Africa, Africa Hall, P.O. Box 3001, Addis Ababa, Ethiopia (Telephone Number in U.S. (800) 253-9646); *African Statistical Yearbook.*

SENEGAL - EXCHANGE RATES

African Development Bank, 01 BP 1387, Abidjan 01, Cote D'Ivoire; *Selected Statistics on Regional Member Countries.*

Euromonitor Publications Limited, 87-88 Turnmill Street, London EC1M 5QU, England; *International Marketing Data and Statistics.*

International Monetary Fund, 700 Nineteenth Street, NW, Washington, D.C. 20431 (202) 623-7000; *International Financial Statistics.*

Statistical Office of the United Nations, Publishing Service, New York, New York 10017 (800) 253-9646; *Foreign Trade Statistics for Africa,* and *Statistical Yearbook.*

SENEGAL - EXCISE TAXES - See SENEGAL - TAXATION

SENEGAL - EXPORTS

African Development Bank, 01 BP 1387, Abidjan 01, Cote D'Ivoire; *Selected Statistics on Regional Member Countries.*

The Economist Intelligence Unit, 111 West 57th Street, New York, New York 10019 (800) 938-4685; *The World Market Atlas.*

Euromonitor Publications Limited, 87-88 Turnmill Street, London EC1M 5QU, England; *International Marketing Data and Statistics.*

Food and Agricultural Organization of the United Nations (FAO) Via delle Terme di Caracalla, 00100 Rome, Italy (Telephone Number in U.S. (202) 653-2400); *The State of Food and Agriculture.*

G.K. Hall and Company, 70 Lincoln Street, Boston, Massachusetts 02111 (617) 423-3990; *The World in Figures.*

International Monetary Fund, 700 Nineteenth Street, NW, Washington, D.C. 20431 (202) 623-7000; *Direction of Trade Statistics, Government Finance Statistics Yearbook,* and *International Financial Statistics.*

Statistical Office of the United Nations, Publishing Service, New York, New York 10017 (800) 253-9646; *Foreign Trade Statistics for Africa,* and *Survey of Economic and Social Conditions in Africa.*

Times Books, 201 East 50th Street, New York, New York 10022 (212) 751-2600; *The Economist Book of Vital World Statistics.*

United Nations Economic Commission for Africa, Africa Hall, P.O. Box 3001, Addis Ababa, Ethiopia (Telephone Number in U.S. (800) 253-9646); *African Statistical Yearbook.*

The World Bank, 1818 H Street, NW, Washington, D.C. 20433 (202) 477-1234; *World Tables.*

SENEGAL - EXTERNAL INDEBTEDNESS

African Development Bank, 01 BP 1387, Abidjan 01, Cote D'Ivoire; *Selected Statistics on Regional Member Countries.*

Statistical Office of the United Nations, Publishing Service, New York, New York 10017 (800) 253-9646; *Survey of Economic and Social Conditions in Africa.*

The World Bank, 1818 H Street, NW, Washington, D.C. 20433 (202) 477-1234; *World Tables.*

SENEGAL - EXTERNAL TRADE

African Development Bank, 01 BP 1387, Abidjan 01, Cote D'Ivoire; *Selected Statistics on Regional Member Countries.*

Food and Agricultural Organization of the United Nations (FAO) Via delle Terme di Caracalla, 00100 Rome, Italy (Telephone Number in U.S. (202) 653-2400); *The State of Food and Agriculture,* and *Trade Yearbook.*

G.K. Hall and Company, 70 Lincoln Street, Boston, Massachusetts 02111 (617) 423-3990; *The World in Figures.*

Statistical Office of the United Nations, Publishing Service, New York, New York 10017 (800) 253-9646; *Statistical Yearbook.*

SENEGAL - FABRIC PRODUCTION - See SENEGAL - TEXTILE INDUSTRY

SENEGAL - FARM CROPS - See SENEGAL - CROPS

SENEGAL - FEMALE WORKING POPULATION - See SENEGAL - EMPLOYMENT

SENEGAL - FERTILITY RATES

Facts on File, 460 Park Avenue South, New York, New York 10016; *The New Book of World Rankings.*

Statistical Office of the United Nations, Publishing Service, New York, New York 10017 (800) 253-9646; *Survey of Economic and Social Conditions in Africa.*

Times Books, 201 East 50th Street, New York, New York 10022 (212) 751-2600; *The Economist Book of Vital World Statistics.*

The World Bank, 1818 H Street, NW, Washington, D.C. 20433 (202) 477-1234; *World Tables.*

SENEGAL - FERTILIZER

Food and Agricultural Organization of the United Nations (FAO) Via delle Terme di Caracalla, 00100 Rome, Italy (Telephone Number in U.S. (202) 653-2400); *The State of Food and Agriculture,* and *Fertilizer Yearbook.*

Statistical Office of the United Nations, Publishing Service, New York, New York 10017 (800) 253-9646; *Statistical Yearbook.*

SENEGAL - FETAL MORTALITY

Statistical Office of the United Nations, Publishing Service, New York, New York 10017 (800) 253-9646; *Demographic Yearbook.*

SENEGAL - FINANCE

African Development Bank, 01 BP 1387, Abidjan 01, Cote D'Ivoire; *Selected Statistics on Regional Member Countries.*

Facts on File, 460 Park Avenue South, New York, New York 10016 (800) 443-8323; *The New Book of World Rankings.*

G.K. Hall and Company, 70 Lincoln Street, Boston, Massachusetts 02111 (617) 423-3990; *The World in Figures.*

International Monetary Fund, 700 Nineteenth Street, NW, Washington, D.C. 20431 (202) 623-7000; *International Financial Statistics.*

United Nations Economic Commission for Africa, Africa Hall, P.O. Box 3001, Addis Ababa, Ethiopia (Telephone Number in U.S. (800) 253-9646); *African Statistical Yearbook.*

SENEGAL - FISHERIES

Facts on File, 460 Park Avenue South, New York, New York 10016 (800) 443-8323; *The New Book of World Rankings.*

Food and Agricultural Organization of the United Nations (FAO) Via delle Terme di Caracalla, 00100 Rome, Italy (Telephone Number in U.S. (202) 653-2400); *The State of Food and Agriculture,* and *Yearbook of Fishery Statistics.*

International Monetary Fund, 700 Nineteenth Street, NW, Washington, D.C. 20431 (202) 623-7000; *International Financial Statistics.*

Statistical Office of the United Nations, Publishing Service, New York, New York 10017 (800) 253-9646; *Statistical Yearbook,* and *Survey of Economic and Social Conditions in Africa.*

United Nations Economic Commission for Africa, Africa Hall, P.O. Box 3001, Addis Ababa, Ethiopia (Telephone Number in U.S. (800) 253-9646); *African Statistical Yearbook.*

SENEGAL - FLOUR PRODUCTION

Statistical Office of the United Nations, Publishing Service, New York, New York 10017 (800) 253-9646; *Statistical Yearbook.*

SENEGAL - FOOD

African Development Bank, 01 BP 1387, Abidjan 01, Cote D'Ivoire; *Selected Statistics on Regional Member Countries.*

Food and Agricultural Organization of the United Nations (FAO) Via delle Terme di Caracalla, 00100 Rome, Italy (Telephone Number in U.S. (202) 653-2400); *Production Yearbook,* and *The State of Food and Agriculture.*

G.K. Hall and Company, 70 Lincoln Street, Boston, Massachusetts 02111 (617) 423-3990; *The World in Figures.*

SENEGAL - FOREIGN AID

G.K. Hall and Company, 70 Lincoln Street, Boston, Massachusetts 02111 (617) 423-3990; *The World in Figures.*

SENEGAL - FOREIGN TRADE

Euromonitor Publications Limited, 87-88 Turnmill Street, London EC1M 5QU, England; *International Marketing Data and Statistics.*

Facts on File, 460 Park Avenue South, New York, New York 10016 (800) 443-8323; *The New Book of World Rankings.*

Food and Agricultural Organization of the United Nations (FAO) Via delle Terme di Caracalla, 00100 Rome, Italy (Telephone Number in U.S. (202) 653-2400); *The State of Food and Agriculture.*

G.K. Hall and Company, 70 Lincoln Street, Boston, Massachusetts 02111 (617) 423-3990; *The World in Figures.*

International Monetary Fund, 700 Nineteenth Street, NW, Washington, D.C. 20431 (202) 623-7000; *International Financial Statistics.*

Statistical Office of the United Nations, Publishing Service, New York, New York 10017 (800) 253-9646; *Foreign Trade Statistics for Africa, International Trade Statistics Yearbook,* and *Statistical Yearbook.*

United Nations Economic Commission for Africa, Africa Hall, P.O. Box 3001, Addis Ababa, Ethiopia (Telephone Number in U.S. (800) 253-9646); *African Statistical Yearbook.*

The World Bank, 1818 H Street, NW, Washington, D.C. 20433 (202) 477-1234; *World Tables.*

SENEGAL - FORESTRY AND FOREST PRODUCTS

Facts on File, 460 Park Avenue South, New York, New York 10016 (800) 443-8323; *The New Book of World Rankings.*

Food and Agricultural Organization of the United Nations (FAO) Via delle Terme di Caracalla, 00100 Rome, Italy (Telephone Number in U.S. (202) 653-2400); *The State of Food and Agriculture,* and *Yearbook of Forest Products.*

G.K. Hall and Company, 70 Lincoln Street, Boston, Massachusetts 02111 (617) 423-3990; *The World in Figures.*

Statistical Office of the United Nations, Publishing Service, New York, New York 10017 (800) 253-9646; *Statistical Yearbook.*

United Nations Economic Commission for Africa, Africa Hall, P.O. Box 3001, Addis Ababa, Ethiopia (Telephone Number in U.S. (800) 253-9646); *African Statistical Yearbook.*

United Nations Educational, Scientific and Cultural Organization (UNESCO), 7 Place de Fontenoy, F-75700 Paris, France (Telephone Number in U.S. (212) 963-5981); *Statistical Yearbook.*

SENEGAL - GAS PRODUCTION - See SENEGAL - MINING AND MINERAL PRODUCTS

SENEGAL - GENERAL INDUSTRIAL STATISTICS

Statistical Office of the United Nations, Publishing Service, New York, New York 10017 (800) 253-9646; *Industrial Statistics Yearbook.*

SENEGAL - GENERAL MORTALITY

Statistical Office of the United Nations, Publishing Service, New York, New York 10017 (800) 253-9646; *Demographic Yearbook.*

SENEGAL - GEOGRAPHIC DATA

Facts on File, 460 Park Avenue South, New York, New York 10016 (800) 443-8323; *The New Book of World Rankings.*

SENEGAL - GOATS - See SENEGAL - LIVESTOCK AND POULTRY

SENEGAL - GOLD HOLDINGS

International Monetary Fund, 700 Nineteenth Street, NW, Washington, D.C. 20431 (202) 623-7000; *International Financial Statistics.*

Statistical Office of the United Nations, Publishing Service, New York, New York 10017 (800) 253-9646; *Statistical Yearbook.*

The World Bank, 1818 H Street, NW, Washington, D.C. 20433 (202) 477-1234; *World Tables.*

SENEGAL - GOLD PRODUCTION AND CONSUMPTION - See SENEGAL - MINING AND MINERAL PRODUCTS

SENEGAL - GOVERNMENT

G.K. Hall and Company, 70 Lincoln Street, Boston, Massachusetts 02111 (617) 423-3990; *The World in Figures.*

Times Books, 201 East 50th Street, New York, New York 10022 (212) 751-2600; *The Economist Book of Vital World Statistics.*

SENEGAL - GOVERNMENT EXPENDITURES

International Monetary Fund, 700 Nineteenth Street, NW, Washington, D.C. 20431 (202) 623-7000; *Government Finance Statistics Yearbook.*

The World Bank, 1818 H Street, NW, Washington, D.C. 20433 (202) 477-1234; *World Tables.*

SENEGAL - GOVERNMENT FINANCES

International Monetary Fund, 700 Nineteenth Street, NW, Washington, D.C. 20431 (202) 623-7000; *International Financial Statistics.*

SENEGAL - GOVERNMENT REVENUE

International Monetary Fund, 700 Nineteenth Street, NW, Washington, D.C. 20431 (202) 623-7000; *Government Finance Statistics Yearbook.*

Statistical Office of the United Nations, Publishing Service, New York, New York 10017 (800) 253-9646; *Survey of Economic and Social Conditions in Africa.*

Times Books, 201 East 50th Street, New York, New York 10022 (212) 751-2600; *The Economist Book of Vital World Statistics.*

The World Bank, 1818 H Street, NW, Washington, D.C. 20433 (202) 477-1234; *World Tables.*

SENEGAL - GRAIN PRODUCTION - See SENEGAL - CROPS

SENEGAL - GRANTS

International Monetary Fund, 700 Nineteenth Street, NW, Washington, D.C. 20431 (202) 623-7000; *Government Finance Statistics Yearbook.*

SENEGAL - GROSS DOMESTIC PRODUCT

African Development Bank, 01 BP 1387, Abidjan 01, Cote D'Ivoire; *Selected Statistics on Regional Member Countries.*

The Economist Intelligence Unit, 111 West 57th Street, New York, New York 10019 (800) 938-4685; *The World Market Atlas.*

Euromonitor Publications Limited, 87-88 Turnmill Street, London EC1M 5QU, England; *International Marketing Data and Statistics.*

Facts on File, 460 Park Avenue South, New York, New York 10016 (800) 443-8323; *The New Book of World Rankings.*

G.K. Hall and Company, 70 Lincoln Street, Boston, Massachusetts 02111 (617) 423-3990; *The World in Figures.*

Statistical Office of the United Nations, Publishing Service, New York, New York 10017 (800) 253-9646; *Statistical Yearbook,* and *Survey of Economic and Social Conditions in Africa.*

Times Books, 201 East 50th Street, New York, New York 10022 (212) 751-2600; *The Economist Book of Vital World Statistics.*

United Nations Economic Commission for Africa, Africa Hall, P.O. Box 3001, Addis Ababa, Ethiopia (Telephone Number in U.S. (800) 253-9646); *African Statistical Yearbook.*

The World Bank, 1818 H Street, NW, Washington, D.C. 20433 (202) 477-1234; *World Tables.*

SENEGAL - GROSS NATIONAL PRODUCT

Euromonitor Publications Limited, 87-88 Turnmill Street, London EC1M 5QU, England; *International Marketing Data and Statistics.*

U.S. Arms Control and Disarmament Agency, 320 Twenty-first Street, NW, Washington, D.C. 20451 (202) 647-8677; *World Military Expenditures and Arms Transfers.*

The World Bank, 1818 H Street, NW, Washington, D.C. 20433 (202) 477-1234; *World Tables.*

SENEGAL - GROUNDNUTS - See SENEGAL - CROPS

SENEGAL - HEALTH

Facts on File, 460 Park Avenue South, New York, New York 10016 (800) 443-8323; *The New Book of World Rankings.*

G.K. Hall and Company, 70 Lincoln Street, Boston, Massachusetts 02111 (617) 423-3990; *The World in Figures.*

Statistical Office of the United Nations, Publishing Service, New York, New York 10017 (800) 253-9646; *Statistical Yearbook.*

Times Books, 201 East 50th Street, New York, New York 10022 (212) 751-2600; *The Economist Book of Vital World Statistics.*

United Nations Economic Commission for Africa, Africa Hall, P.O. Box 3001, Addis Ababa, Ethiopia (Telephone Number in U.S. (800) 253-9646); *African Statistical Yearbook.*

World Health Organization, Office of Publications, Avenue Appia, CH-1211 Geneva 27, Switzerland (Telephone Number in U.S. (518) 436-9686); *World Health Statistics Annual.*

SENEGAL - HEALTH EXPENDITURES

International Monetary Fund, 700 Nineteenth Street, NW, Washington, D.C. 20431 (202) 623-7000; *Government Finance Statistics Yearbook.*

United Nations Economic Commission for Africa, Africa Hall, P.O. Box 3001, Addis Ababa, Ethiopia (Telephone Number in U.S. (800) 253-9646); *African Statistical Yearbook.*

SENEGAL - HIGHWAYS

G.K. Hall and Company, 70 Lincoln Street, Boston, Massachusetts 02111 (617) 423-3990; *The World in Figures.*

International Road Federation, 525 School Street, SW, Washington, D.C. 20024 (202) 554-2106; *World Road Statistics.*

Statistical Office of the United Nations, Publishing Service, New York, New York 10017 (800) 253-9646; *Survey of Economic and Social Conditions in Africa.*

United Nations Economic Commission for Africa, Africa Hall, P.O. Box 3001, Addis Ababa, Ethiopia (Telephone Number in U.S. (800) 253-9646); *African Statistical Yearbook.*

SENEGAL - HORSES - See SENEGAL - LIVESTOCK AND POULTRY

SENEGAL - HOURS OF WORK - See SENEGAL - EMPLOYMENT

SENEGAL - HOUSING EXPENDITURES

Facts on File, 460 Park Avenue South, New York, New York 10016 (800) 440-0020; *The New Book of World Rankings.*

International Monetary Fund, 700 Nineteenth Street, NW, Washington, D.C. 20431 (202) 623-7000; *Government Finance Statistics Yearbook.*

SENEGAL - ILLITERATE POPULATION

The Economist Intelligence Unit, 111 West 57th Street, New York, New York 10019 (800) 938-4685; *The World Market Atlas.*

G.K. Hall and Company, 70 Lincoln Street, Boston, Massachusetts 02111 (617) 423-3990; *The World in Figures.*

United Nations Educational, Scientific and Cultural Organization (UNESCO), 7 Place de Fontenoy, F-75700 Paris, France (Telephone Number in U.S. (212) 963-5981); *Statistical Yearbook.*

SENEGAL - IMPORTS

African Development Bank, 01 BP 1387, Abidjan 01, Cote D'Ivoire; *Selected Statistics on Regional Member Countries.*

The Economist Intelligence Unit, 111 West 57th Street, New York, New York 10019 (800) 938-4685; *The World Market Atlas.*

Euromonitor Publications Limited, 87-88 Turnmill Street, London EC1M 5QU, England; *International Marketing Data and Statistics.*

Food and Agricultural Organization of the United Nations (FAO) Via delle Terme di Caracalla, 00100 Rome, Italy (Telephone Number in U.S. (202) 653-2400); *The State of Food and Agriculture.*

G.K. Hall and Company, 70 Lincoln Street, Boston, Massachusetts 02111 (617) 423-3990; *The World in Figures.*

International Monetary Fund, 700 Nineteenth Street, NW, Washington, D.C. 20431 (202) 623-7000; *Direction of Trade Statistics, Government Finance Statistics Yearbook,* and *International Financial Statistics.*

Statistical Office of the United Nations, Publishing Service, New York, New York 10017 (800) 253-9646; *Foreign Trade Statistics for Africa, Survey of Economic and Social Conditions in Africa,* and *Trade in Manufactures of Developing Countries.*

Times Books, 201 East 50th Street, New York, New York 10022 (212) 751-2600; *The Economist Book of Vital World Statistics.*

United Nations Economic Commission for Africa, Africa Hall, P.O. Box 3001, Addis Ababa, Ethiopia (Telephone Number in U.S. (800) 253-9646); *African Statistical Yearbook.*

The World Bank, 1818 H Street, NW, Washington, D.C. 20433 (202) 477-1234; *World Tables.*

SENEGAL - INCOME TAXES - See SENEGAL - TAXATION

SENEGAL - INDUSTRY

Euromonitor Publications Limited, 87-88 Turnmill Street, London EC1M 5QU, England; *International Marketing Data and Statistics.*

Facts on File, 460 Park Avenue South, New York, New York 10016 (800) 443-8323; *The New Book of World Rankings.*

G.K. Hall and Company, 70 Lincoln Street, Boston, Massachusetts 02111 (617) 423-3990; *The World in Figures.*

International Labour Office, I.L.O. Publications, CH-1211, Geneva 22, Switzerland; *Yearbook of Labour Statistics.*

Statistical Office of the United Nations, Publishing Service, New York, New York 10017 (800) 253-9646; *Survey of Economic and Social Conditions in Africa.*

Times Books, 201 East 50th Street, New York, New York 10022 (212) 751-2600; *The Economist Book of Vital World Statistics.*

United Nations Economic Commission for Africa, Africa Hall, P.O. Box 3001, Addis Ababa, Ethiopia (Telephone Number in U.S. (800) 253-9646); *African Statistical Yearbook.*

The World Bank, 1818 H Street, NW, Washington, D.C. 20433 (202) 477-1234; *World Tables.*

SENEGAL - INFANT AND MATERNAL MORTALITY

Statistical Office of the United Nations, Publishing Service, New York, New York 10017 (800) 253-9646; *Demographic Yearbook, Statistical Yearbook,* and *Survey of Economic and Social Conditions in Africa.*

Times Books, 201 East 50th Street, New York, New York 10022 (212) 751-2600; *The Economist Book of Vital World Statistics.*

The World Bank, 1818 H Street, NW, Washington, D.C. 20433 (202) 477-1234; *World Tables.*

SENEGAL - INTERNATIONAL LIQUIDITY

International Monetary Fund, 700 Nineteenth Street, NW, Washington, D.C. 20431 (202) 623-7000; *International Financial Statistics.*

SENEGAL - INTERNATIONAL RESERVES EXCLUDING GOLD

African Development Bank, 01 BP 1387, Abidjan 01, Cote D'Ivoire; *Selected Statistics on Regional Member Countries.*

Statistical Office of the United Nations, Publishing Service, New York, New York 10017 (800) 253-9646; *Statistical Yearbook.*

The World Bank, 1818 H Street, NW, Washington, D.C. 20433 (202) 477-1234; *World Tables.*

SENEGAL - IRON ORE PRODUCTION AND CONSUMPTION - See SENEGAL - MINING AND MINERAL PRODUCTS

SENEGAL - IRRIGATION

Euromonitor Publications Limited, 87-88 Turnmill Street, London EC1M 5QU, England; *International Marketing Data and Statistics.*

SENEGAL - LABOR FORCE

African Development Bank, 01 BP 1387, Abidjan 01, Cote D'Ivoire; *Selected Statistics on Regional Member Countries.*

Euromonitor Publications Limited, 87-88 Turnmill Street, London EC1M 5QU, England; *International Marketing Data and Statistics.*

Facts on File, 460 Park Avenue South, New York, New York 10016 (800) 443-8323; *The New Book of World Rankings.*

Food and Agricultural Organization of the United Nations (FAO) Via delle Terme di Caracalla, 00100 Rome, Italy (Telephone Number in U.S. (202) 653-2400); *The State of Food and Agriculture.*

G.K. Hall and Company, 70 Lincoln Street, Boston, Massachusetts 02111 (617) 423-3990; *The World in Figures.*

The World Bank, 1818 H Street, NW, Washington, D.C. 20433 (202) 477-1234; *World Tables.*

SENEGAL - LABOR PRODUCTIVITY

International Labour Office, I.L.O. Publications, CH-1211, Geneva 22, Switzerland; *Yearbook of Labour Statistics.*

SENEGAL - LAND USE

Euromonitor Publications Limited, 87-88 Turnmill Street, London EC1M 5QU, England; *International Marketing Data and Statistics.*

Food and Agricultural Organization of the United Nations (FAO), Via delle Terme di Caracalla, 00100 Rome, Italy (Telephone Number in U.S. (202) 653-2400); *Production Yearbook.*

G.K. Hall and Company, 70 Lincoln Street, Boston, Massachusetts 02111 (617) 423-3990; *The World in Figures.*

SENEGAL - LIBRARIES

Facts on File, 460 Park Avenue South, New York, New York 10016 (800) 443-8323; *The New Book of World Rankings.*

United Nations Educational, Scientific and Cultural Organization (UNESCO), 7 Place de Fontenoy, F-75700 Paris, France (Telephone Number in U.S. (212) 963-5981); *Statistical Yearbook.*

SENEGAL - LIFE EXPECTANCY

African Development Bank, 01 BP 1387, Abidjan 01, Cote D'Ivoire; *Selected Statistics on Regional Member Countries.*

SENEGAL - LITERACY RATE

Statistical Office of the United Nations, Publishing Service, New York, New York 10017 (800) 253-9646; *Survey of Economic and Social Conditions in Africa.*

SENEGAL - LIVESTOCK AND POULTRY

Euromonitor Publications Limited, 87-88 Turnmill Street, London EC1M 5QU, England; *International Marketing Data and Statistics.*

Facts on File, 460 Park Avenue South, New York, New York 10016 (800) 443-8323; *The New Book of World Rankings.*

Food and Agricultural Organization of the United Nations (FAO), Via delle Terme di Caracalla, 00100 Rome, Italy (Telephone Number in U.S. (202) 653-2400); *Production Yearbook,* and *The State of Food and Agriculture.*

G.K. Hall and Company, 70 Lincoln Street, Boston, Massachusetts 02111 (617) 423-3990; *The World in Figures.*

Statistical Office of the United Nations, Publishing Service, New York, New York 10017 (800) 253-9646; *Statistical Yearbook,* and *Survey of Economic and Social Conditions in Africa.*

United Nations Economic Commission for Africa, Africa Hall, P.O. Box 3001, Addis Ababa, Ethiopia (Telephone Number in U.S. (800) 253-9646); *African Statistical Yearbook.*

SENEGAL - LIVING LEVELS

G.K. Hall and Company, 70 Lincoln Street, Boston, Massachusetts 02111 (617) 423-3990; *The World in Figures.*

Times Books, 201 East 50th Street, New York, New York 10022 (212) 751-2600; *The Economist Book of Vital World Statistics.*

SENEGAL - MAIL TRAFFIC - NUMBER OF ITEMS SENT AND RECEIVED

Statistical Office of the United Nations, Publishing Service, New York, New York 10017 (800) 253-9646; *Statistical Yearbook.*

SENEGAL - MANUFACTURING

Facts on File, 460 Park Avenue South, New York, New York 10016 (800) 443-8323; *The New Book of World Rankings.*

G.K. Hall and Company, 70 Lincoln Street, Boston, Massachusetts 02111 (617) 423-3990; *The World in Figures.*

Statistical Office of the United Nations, Publishing Service, New York, New York 10017 (800) 253-9646; *Statistical Yearbook,* and *Survey of Economic and Social Conditions in Africa.*

Times Books, 201 East 50th Street, New York, New York 10022 (212) 751-2600; *The Economist Book of Vital World Statistics.*

United Nations Economic Commission for Africa, Africa Hall, P.O. Box 3001, Addis Ababa, Ethiopia (Telephone Number in U.S. (800) 253-9646); *African Statistical Yearbook*.

The World Bank, 1818 H Street, NW, Washington, D.C. 20433 (202) 477-1234; *World Tables*.

SENEGAL - MARRIAGE RATES

Facts on File, 460 Park Avenue South, New York, New York 10016 (800) 443-8323; *The New Book of World Rankings*.

Statistical Office of the United Nations, Publishing Service, New York, New York 10017 (800) 253-9646; *Demographic Yearbook*.

SENEGAL - MEAT PRODUCTION - See SENEGAL - LIVESTOCK AND POULTRY

SENEGAL - MERCHANT SHIPPING

G.K. Hall and Company, 70 Lincoln Street, Boston, Massachusetts 02111 (617) 423-3990; *The World in Figures*.

Statistical Office of the United Nations, Publishing Service, New York, New York 10017 (800) 253-9646; *Statistical Yearbook*.

Times Books, 201 East 50th Street, New York, New York 10022 (212) 751-2600; *The Economist Book of Vital World Statistics*.

United Nations Economic Commission for Africa, Africa Hall, P.O. Box 3001, Addis Ababa, Ethiopia (Telephone Number in U.S. (800) 253-9646); *African Statistical Yearbook*.

U.S. Department of Transportation, Maritime Administration, 400 Seventh Street, SW, Washington, D.C. 20590 (202) 366-5807; *A Statistical Analysis of the World's Merchant Fleets*.

SENEGAL - MILITARY

G.K. Hall and Company, 70 Lincoln Street, Boston, Massachusetts 02111 (617) 423-3990; *The World in Figures*.

The International Institute for Strategic Studies, 23 Tavistock Street, London WC2E 7NQ, England; *The Military Balance*.

U.S. Arms Control and Disarmament Agency, 320 Twenty-first Street, NW, Washington, D.C. 20451 (202) 647-8677; *World Military Expenditures and Arms Transfers*.

SENEGAL - MILK PRODUCTION - See SENEGAL - DAIRY PRODUCTS

SENEGAL - MINING AND MINERAL PRODUCTS

Facts on File, 460 Park Avenue South, New York, New York 10016 (800) 443-8323; *The New Book of World Rankings*.

G.K. Hall and Company, 70 Lincoln Street, Boston, Massachusetts 02111 (617) 423-3990; *The World in Figures*.

Statistical Office of the United Nations, Publishing Service, New York, New York 10017 (800) 253-9646; *Statistical Yearbook*.

United Nations Economic Commission for Africa, Africa Hall, P.O. Box 3001, Addis Ababa, Ethiopia (Telephone Number in U.S. (800) 253-9646); *African Statistical Yearbook*.

SENEGAL - MONEY EXCHANGE RATE

Euromonitor Publications Limited, 87-88 Turnmill Street, London EC1M 5QU, England; *International Marketing Data and Statistics*.

International Monetary Fund, 700 Nineteenth Street, NW, Washington, D.C. 20431 (202) 623-7000; *International Financial Statistics*.

Statistical Office of the United Nations, Publishing Service, New York, New York 10017 (800) 253-9646; *Statistical Yearbook*.

SENEGAL - MONEY RESERVES

Euromonitor Publications Limited, 87-88 Turnmill Street, London EC1M 5QU, England; *International Marketing Data and Statistics*.

SENEGAL - MONEY SUPPLY

African Development Bank, 01 BP 1387, Abidjan 01, Cote D'Ivoire; *Selected Statistics on Regional Member Countries*.

Euromonitor Publications Limited, 87-88 Turnmill Street, London EC1M 5QU, England; *International Marketing Data and Statistics*.

G.K. Hall and Company, 70 Lincoln Street, Boston, Massachusetts 02111 (617) 423-3990; *The World in Figures*.

International Monetary Fund, 700 Nineteenth Street, NW, Washington, D.C. 20431 (202) 623-7000; *International Financial Statistics*.

Statistical Office of the United Nations, Publishing Service, New York, New York 10017 (800) 253-9646; *Statistical Yearbook*.

The World Bank, 1818 H Street, NW, Washington, D.C. 20433 (202) 477-1234; *World Tables*.

SENEGAL - MONUMENTS AND HISTORICAL SITES

United Nations Educational, Scientific and Cultural Organization (UNESCO), 7 Place de Fontenoy, F-75700 Paris, France (Telephone Number in U.S. (212) 963-5981); *Statistical Yearbook*.

SENEGAL - MOTION PICTURES

Statistical Office of the United Nations, Publishing Service, New York, New York 10017 (800) 253-9646; *Statistical Yearbook*.

SENEGAL - MOTOR VEHICLE TAXES - See SENEGAL - TAXATION

SENEGAL - MOTOR VEHICLES IN USE

G.K. Hall and Company, 70 Lincoln Street, Boston, Massachusetts 02111 (617) 423-3990; *The World in Figures*.

International Road Federation, 525 School Street, SW, Washington, D.C. 20024 (202) 554-2106; *World Road Statistics*.

Statistical Office of the United Nations, Publishing Service, New York, New York 10017 (800) 253-9646; *Statistical Yearbook*, and *Survey of Economic and Social Conditions in Africa*.

SENEGAL - MUSEUMS

Facts on File, 460 Park Avenue South, New York, New York 10016 (800) 443-8323; *The New Book of World Rankings*.

United Nations Educational, Scientific and Cultural Organization (UNESCO), 7 Place de Fontenoy, F-75700 Paris, France (Telephone Number in U.S. (212) 963-5981); *Statistical Yearbook.*

SENEGAL - NATALITY - See SENEGAL - BIRTH RATE

SENEGAL - NATIONAL ACCOUNTS

African Development Bank, 01 BP 1387, Abidjan 01, Cote D'Ivoire; *Selected Statistics on Regional Member Countries.*

International Monetary Fund, 700 Nineteenth Street, NW, Washington, D.C. 20431 (202) 623-7000; *International Financial Statistics.*

Statistical Office of the United Nations, Publishing Service, New York, New York 10017 (800) 253-9646; *National Accounts Statistics,* and *Statistical Yearbook.*

United Nations Economic Commission for Africa, Africa Hall, P.O. Box 3001, Addis Ababa, Ethiopia (Telephone Number in U.S. (800) 253-9646); *African Statistical Yearbook.*

SENEGAL - NATIONAL INCOME

Facts on File, 460 Park Avenue South, New York, New York 10016 (800) 443-8323; *The New Book of World Rankings.*

G.K. Hall and Company, 70 Lincoln Street, Boston, Massachusetts 02111 (617) 423-3990; *The World in Figures.*

Statistical Office of the United Nations, Publishing Service, New York, New York 10017 (800) 253-9646; *Statistical Yearbook.*

SENEGAL - NATIONAL PRODUCT

Facts on File, 460 Park Avenue South, New York, New York 10016 (800) 443-8323; *The New Book of World Rankings.*

SENEGAL - NATURAL GAS PRODUCTION - See SENEGAL - MINING AND MINERAL PRODUCTS

SENEGAL - NEWSPAPER PRODUCTION - See SENEGAL - FORESTRY AND FOREST PRODUCTS

SENEGAL - NEWSPRINT - See SENEGAL - FORESTRY AND FOREST PRODUCTS

SENEGAL - OCCUPATIONS - See SENEGAL - LABOR FORCE

SENEGAL - PALM KERNEL PRODUCTION - See SENEGAL - CROPS

SENEGAL - PAPER - See SENEGAL - FORESTRY AND FOREST PRODUCTS

SENEGAL - PEANUT PRODUCTION - See SENEGAL - CROPS

SENEGAL - PESTICIDE USE

Food and Agricultural Organization of the United Nations (FAO) Via delle Terme di Caracalla, 00100 Rome, Italy (Telephone Number in U.S. (202) 653-2400); *The State of Food and Agriculture.*

SENEGAL - PETROLEUM INDUSTRY

Facts on File, 460 Park Avenue South, New York, New York 10016 (800) 443-8323; *The New Book of World Rankings.*

Food and Agricultural Organization of the United Nations (FAO) Via delle Terme di Caracalla, 00100 Rome, Italy (Telephone Number in U.S. (202) 653-2400); *The State of Food and Agriculture.*

G.K. Hall and Company, 70 Lincoln Street, Boston, Massachusetts 02111 (617) 423-3990; *The World in Figures.*

International Monetary Fund, 700 Nineteenth Street, NW, Washington, D.C. 20431 (202) 623-7000; *International Financial Statistics.*

Statistical Office of the United Nations, Publishing Service, New York, New York 10017 (800) 253-9646; *Statistical Yearbook.*

SENEGAL - PHOSPHATE EXPORTS

International Monetary Fund, 700 Nineteenth Street, NW, Washington, D.C. 20431 (202) 623-7000; *International Financial Statistics.*

SENEGAL - PHOSPHATE ROCK PRODUCTION - See SENEGAL - MINING AND MINERAL PRODUCTS

SENEGAL - PIGS - See SENEGAL - LIVESTOCK AND POULTRY

SENEGAL - POPULATION

African Development Bank, 01 BP 1387, Abidjan 01, Cote D'Ivoire; *Selected Statistics on Regional Member Countries.*

The Economist Intelligence Unit, 111 West 57th Street, New York, New York 10019 (800) 938-4685; *The World Market Atlas.*

Euromonitor Publications Limited, 87-88 Turnmill Street, London EC1M 5QU, England; *International Marketing Data and Statistics.*

Facts on File, 460 Park Avenue South, New York, New York 10016 (800) 443-8323; *The New Book of World Rankings.*

Food and Agricultural Organization of the United Nations (FAO), Via delle Terme di Caracalla, 00100 Rome, Italy (Telephone Number in U.S. (202) 653-2400); *Production Yearbook.*

G.K. Hall and Company, 70 Lincoln Street, Boston, Massachusetts 02111 (617) 423-3990; *The World in Figures.*

International Labour Office, I.L.O. Publications, CH-1211, Geneva 22, Switzerland; *Yearbook of Labour Statistics.*

Statistical Office of the United Nations, Publishing Service, New York, New York 10017 (800) 253-9646; *Demographic Yearbook, Statistical Yearbook,* and *Survey of Economic and Social Conditions in Africa.*

Times Books, 201 East 50th Street, New York, New York 10022 (212) 751-2600; *The Economist Book of Vital World Statistics.*

United Nations Educational, Scientific and Cultural Organization (UNESCO), 7 Place de Fontenoy, F-75700 Paris, France (Telephone Number in U.S. (212) 963-5981); *Statistical Yearbook.*

U.S. Arms Control and Disarmament Agency, 320 Twenty-first Street, NW, Washington, D.C. 20451 (202) 647-8677; *World Military Expenditures and Arms Transfers.*

World Health Organization, Office of Publications, Avenue Appia, CH-1211 Geneva 27, Switzerland (Telephone Number in U.S. (518) 436-9686); *World Health Statistics Annual.*

SENEGAL - POST OFFICES

Facts on File, 460 Park Avenue South, New York, New York 10016 (800) 443-8323; *The New Book of World Rankings*.

SENEGAL - POTATO PRODUCTION - See SENEGAL - CROPS

SENEGAL - PRICES

Facts on File, 460 Park Avenue South, New York, New York 10016 (800) 443-8323; *The New Book of World Rankings*.

Food and Agricultural Organization of the United Nations (FAO), Via delle Terme di Caracalla, 00100 Rome, Italy (Telephone Number in U.S. (202) 653-2400); *Production Yearbook*, and *The State of Food and Agriculture*.

G.K. Hall and Company, 70 Lincoln Street, Boston, Massachusetts 02111 (617) 423-3990; *The World in Figures*.

International Labour Office, I.L.O. Publications, CH-1211, Geneva 22, Switzerland; *Yearbook of Labour Statistics*.

International Monetary Fund, 700 Nineteenth Street, NW, Washington, D.C. 20431 (202) 623-7000; *International Financial Statistics*.

United Nations Economic Commission for Africa, Africa Hall, P.O. Box 3001, Addis Ababa, Ethiopia (Telephone Number in U.S. (800) 253-9646); *African Statistical Yearbook*.

SENEGAL - PRINTING AND WRITING PAPER - See SENEGAL - FORESTRY AND FOREST PRODUCTS

SENEGAL - PRODUCTION

Facts on File, 460 Park Avenue South, New York, New York 10016 (800) 443-8323; *The New Book of World Rankings*.

G.K. Hall and Company, 70 Lincoln Street, Boston, Massachusetts 02111 (617) 423-3990; *The World in Figures*.

SENEGAL - PRODUCTIVITY

Euromonitor Publications Limited, 87-88 Turnmill Street, London EC1M 5QU, England; *International Marketing Data and Statistics*.

SENEGAL - PROPERTY TAXES - See SENEGAL - TAXATION

SENEGAL - PUBLIC FINANCE

Facts on File, 460 Park Avenue South, New York, New York 10016 (800) 443-8323; *The New Book of World Rankings*.

SENEGAL - RADIO BROADCASTING - See SENEGAL - BROADCASTING

SENEGAL - RAILWAYS

G.K. Hall and Company, 70 Lincoln Street, Boston, Massachusetts 02111 (617) 423-3990; *The World in Figures*.

Statistical Office of the United Nations, Publishing Service, New York, New York 10017 (800) 253-9646; *Statistical Yearbook*, and *Survey of Economic and Social Conditions in Africa*.

United Nations Economic Commission for Africa, Africa Hall, P.O. Box 3001, Addis Ababa, Ethiopia (Telephone Number in U.S. (800) 253-9646); *African Statistical Yearbook*.

SENEGAL - RELIGION

Facts on File, 460 Park Avenue South, New York, New York 10016 (800) 443-8323; *The New Book of World Rankings*.

SENEGAL - RENT PRICES

International Labour Office, I.L.O. Publications, CH-1211, Geneva 22, Switzerland; *Yearbook of Labour Statistics*.

SENEGAL - RETAIL TRADE

G.K. Hall and Company, 70 Lincoln Street, Boston, Massachusetts 02111 (617) 423-3990; *The World in Figures*.

SENEGAL - RICE PRODUCTION - See SENEGAL - CROPS

SENEGAL - ROUNDWOOD PRODUCTION - See SENEGAL - FORESTRY AND FOREST PRODUCTS

SENEGAL - RUBBER PRODUCTION AND CONSUMPTION

Facts on File, 460 Park Avenue South, New York, New York 10016 (800) 443-8323; *The New Book of World Rankings*.

SENEGAL - SALT PRODUCTION - See SENEGAL - MINING AND MINERAL PRODUCTS

SENEGAL - SAWNWOOD PRODUCTION - See SENEGAL - FORESTRY AND FOREST PRODUCTS

SENEGAL - SCIENCE AND TECHNOLOGY - EXPENDITURE FOR RESEARCH

Statistical Office of the United Nations, Publishing Service, New York, New York 10017 (800) 253-9646; *Statistical Yearbook*.

SENEGAL - SCIENTISTS AND TECHNICIANS

Statistical Office of the United Nations, Publishing Service, New York, New York 10017 (800) 253-9646; *Statistical Yearbook*.

SENEGAL - SENIOR CITIZENS

Facts on File, 460 Park Avenue South, New York, New York 10016 (800) 443-8323; *The New Book of World Rankings*.

SENEGAL - SHEEP

Euromonitor Publications Limited, 87-88 Turnmill Street, London EC1M 5QU, England; *International Marketing Data and Statistics*.

Facts on File, 460 Park Avenue South, New York, New York 10016 (800) 443-8323; *The New Book of World Rankings*.

Statistical Office of the United Nations, Publishing Service, New York, New York 10017 (800) 253-9646; *Statistical Yearbook*, and *Survey of Economic and Social Conditions in Africa*.

SENEGAL - SHELLFISH EXPORTS

International Monetary Fund, 700 Nineteenth Street, NW, Washington, D.C. 20431 (202) 623-7000; *International Financial Statistics*.

SENEGAL - SILVER PRODUCTION AND CONSUMPTION - See SENEGAL - MINING AND MINERAL PRODUCTS

SENEGAL - SOCIAL DATA

African Development Bank, 01 BP 1387, Abidjan 01, Cote D'Ivoire; *Selected Statistics on Regional Member Countries.*

Facts on File, 460 Park Avenue South, New York, New York 10016 (800) 443-8323; *The New Book of World Rankings.*

G.K. Hall and Company, 70 Lincoln Street, Boston, Massachusetts 02111 (617) 423-3990; *The World in Figures.*

SENEGAL - SOCIAL SECURITY

International Monetary Fund, 700 Nineteenth Street, NW, Washington, D.C. 20431 (202) 623-7000; *Government Finance Statistics Yearbook.*

SENEGAL - STAMP TAXES AND DUTIES - See SENEGAL - TAXATION

SENEGAL - STATE BUDGET REVENUE AND EXPENDITURES

Euromonitor Publications Limited, 87-88 Turnmill Street, London EC1M 5QU, England; *International Marketing Data and Statistics.*

SENEGAL - STEEL - See SENEGAL - MINING AND MINERAL PRODUCTS

SENEGAL - STOCKS - COMMODITY - MARKET PRICE - INDEX

Food and Agricultural Organization of the United Nations (FAO) Via delle Terme di Caracalla, 00100 Rome, Italy (Telephone Number in U.S. (202) 653-2400); *The State of Food and Agriculture.*

SENEGAL - SUGAR - See SENEGAL - CROPS

SENEGAL - TAXATION

G.K. Hall and Company, 70 Lincoln Street, Boston, Massachusetts 02111 (617) 423-3990; *The World in Figures.*

International Monetary Fund, 700 Nineteenth Street, NW, Washington, D.C. 20431 (202) 623-7000; *Government Finance Statistics Yearbook.*

International Road Federation, 525 School Street, SW, Washington, D.C. 20024 (202) 554-2106; *World Road Statistics.*

Times Books, 201 East 50th Street, New York, New York 10022 (212) 751-2600; *The Economist Book of Vital World Statistics.*

The World Bank, 1818 H Street, NW, Washington, D.C. 20433 (202) 477-1234; *World Tables.*

SENEGAL - TELEPHONES IN USE

American Telephone and Telegraph Company, 26 Parsippany Road, Whippany, New Jersey 07981 (800) 338-4038; *The World's Telephones.*

G.K. Hall and Company, 70 Lincoln Street, Boston, Massachusetts 02111 (617) 423-3990; *The World in Figures.*

Statistical Office of the United Nations, Publishing Service, New York, New York 10017 (800) 253-9646; *Statistical Yearbook.*

SENEGAL - TELEVISION BROADCASTING - See SENEGAL - BROADCASTING

SENEGAL - TEXTILE INDUSTRY

G.K. Hall and Company, 70 Lincoln Street, Boston, Massachusetts 02111 (617) 423-3990; *The World in Figures.*

Statistical Office of the United Nations, Publishing Service, New York, New York 10017 (800) 253-9646; *Statistical Yearbook.*

SENEGAL - TOBACCO PRODUCTION

Facts on File, 460 Park Avenue South, New York, New York 10016 (800) 443-8323; *The New Book of World Rankings.*

Statistical Office of the United Nations, Publishing Service, New York, New York 10017 (800) 253-9646; *Statistical Yearbook.*

SENEGAL - TOURISM

Facts on File, 460 Park Avenue South, New York, New York 10016 (800) 443-8323; *The New Book of World Rankings.*

G.K. Hall and Company, 70 Lincoln Street, Boston, Massachusetts 02111 (617) 423-3990; *The World in Figures.*

Statistical Office of the United Nations, Publishing Service, New York, New York 10017 (800) 253-9646; *Statistical Yearbook.*

Times Books, 201 East 50th Street, New York, New York 10022 (212) 751-2600; *The Economist Book of Vital World Statistics.*

United Nations Economic Commission for Africa, Africa Hall, P.O. Box 3001, Addis Ababa, Ethiopia (Telephone Number in U.S. (800) 253-9646); *African Statistical Yearbook.*

World Tourism Organization, Calle Capitan Haya 42, E-28020 Madrid, Spain; *Yearbook of Tourism Statistics.*

SENEGAL - TRACTORS IN USE

Statistical Office of the United Nations, Publishing Service, New York, New York 10017 (800) 253-9646; *Statistical Yearbook.*

SENEGAL - TRADE - See SENEGAL - FOREIGN TRADE

SENEGAL - TRANSPORTATION AND COMMUNICATIONS

Facts on File, 460 Park Avenue South, New York, New York 10016 (800) 443-8323; *The New Book of World Rankings.*

G.K. Hall and Company, 70 Lincoln Street, Boston, Massachusetts 02111 (617) 423-3990; *The World in Figures.*

United Nations Economic Commission for Africa, Africa Hall, P.O. Box 3001, Addis Ababa, Ethiopia (Telephone Number in U.S. (800) 253-9646); *African Statistical Yearbook.*

SENEGAL - UNEMPLOYMENT

Euromonitor Publications Limited, 87-88 Turnmill Street, London EC1M 5QU, England; *International Marketing Data and Statistics.*

International Labour Office, I.L.O. Publications, CH-1211, Geneva 22, Switzerland; *Yearbook of Labour Statistics.*

Statistical Office of the United Nations, Publishing Service, New York, New York 10017 (800) 253-9646; *Statistical Yearbook.*

SENEGAL - VITAL STATISTICS

Euromonitor Publications Limited, 87-88 Turnmill Street, London EC1M 5QU, England; *International Marketing Data and Statistics.*

G.K. Hall and Company, 70 Lincoln Street, Boston, Massachusetts 02111 (617) 423-3990; *The World in Figures.*

Statistical Office of the United Nations, Publishing Service, New York, New York 10017 (800) 253-9646; *Statistical Yearbook.*

World Health Organization, Office of Publications, Avenue Appia, CH-1211 Geneva 27, Switzerland (Telephone Number in U.S. (518) 436-9686); *World Health Statistics Annual.*

SENEGAL - WAGES

G.K. Hall and Company, 70 Lincoln Street, Boston, Massachusetts 02111 (617) 423-3990; *The World in Figures.*

International Labour Office, I.L.O. Publications, CH-1211, Geneva 22, Switzerland; *Yearbook of Labour Statistics.*

SENEGAL - WEATHER

Facts on File, 460 Park Avenue South, New York, New York 10016 (800) 443-8323; *The New Book of World Rankings.*

G.K. Hall and Company, 70 Lincoln Street, Boston, Massachusetts 02111 (617) 423-3990; *The World in Figures.*

SENEGAL - WELFARE

International Monetary Fund, 700 Nineteenth Street, NW, Washington, D.C. 20431 (202) 623-7000; *Government Finance Statistics Yearbook.*

SENEGAL - WHEAT - See SENEGAL - CROPS

SENEGAL - WHOLESALE PRICES

Statistical Office of the United Nations, Publishing Service, New York, New York 10017 (800) 253-9646; *Statistical Yearbook.*

SENEGAL - WINE PRODUCTION

Facts on File, 460 Park Avenue South, New York, New York 10016 (800) 443-8323; *The New Book of World Rankings.*

SENEGAL - WOOL PRODUCTION

Facts on File, 460 Park Avenue South, New York, New York 10016 (800) 443-8323; *The New Book of World Rankings.*

SENEGAL - YARN PRODUCTION

Statistical Office of the United Nations, Publishing Service, New York, New York 10017 (800) 253-9646; *Statistical Yearbook.*

SEPTICEMIA

U.S. Department of Health and Human Services, National Center for Health Statistics, 3700 East-West Highway, Hyattsville, Maryland 20782 (301) 436-8500; *Vital Statistics of the United States, Monthly Vital Statistics Report,* and unpublished data.

SERBIA - See YUGOSLAVIA

SERVICE INDUSTRIES - CAPITAL

U.S. Department of Commerce, Bureau of Economic Analysis, Fourteenth Street between Constitution Avenue and E Street, NW, Washington, D.C. 20230 (202) 606-9900; *Fixed Reproducible Tangible Wealth in the U.S.,* and *Survey of Current Business.*

SERVICE INDUSTRIES - COLLECTIVE BARGAINING SETTLEMENTS

U.S. Department of Labor, Bureau of Labor Statistics, Two Massachusetts Avenue, NE, Washington, D.C. 20212 (202) 606-7828; *Compensation and Working Conditions.*

SERVICE INDUSTRIES - EARNINGS

U.S. Department of Commerce, Bureau of the Census, Suitland, Maryland 20233 (301) 763-4040; *Census of Service Industries, County Business Patterns,* and *Economic Census of Outlying Areas.*

U.S. Department of Labor, Bureau of Labor Statistics, Two Massachusetts Avenue, NE, Washington, D.C. 20212 (202) 606-7828; *Employment and Earnings, Monthly Labor Review,* and Bulletins 2370 and 2429.

SERVICE INDUSTRIES - EMPLOYEES

U.S. Department of Commerce, Bureau of Economic Analysis, Fourteenth Street between Constitution Avenue and E Street, NW, Washington, D.C. 20230 (202) 606-9900; *The National Income and Product Accounts of the United States, Survey of Current Business,* and unpublished data.

U.S. Department of Commerce, Bureau of the Census, Suitland, Maryland 20233 (301) 763-4040; *Census of Service Industries, County Business Patterns,* and *Economic Census of Outlying Areas.*

U.S. Department of Labor, Bureau of Labor Statistics, Two Massachusetts Avenue, NE, Washington, D.C. 20212 (202) 606-7828; *Employment and Earnings, Monthly Labor Review,* and Bulletins 2370 and 2429.

SERVICE INDUSTRIES - ESTABLISHMENTS

International Franchise Association, 1350 New York Avenue, Suite 900, Washington, D.C. 20005 (202) 628-8000; *Franchising in the Economy.*

U.S. Department of Commerce, Bureau of the Census, Suitland, Maryland 20233 (301) 763-4040; *Census of Service Industries, County Business Patterns,* and *Economic Census of Outlying Areas.*

U.S. Department of the Treasury, Internal Revenue Service, 1111 Constitution Avenue, NW, Washington, D.C. 20224 (202) 566-5000; *Statistics of Income Bulletin,* and *Statistics of Income,* various publications.

SERVICE INDUSTRIES - FINANCES

U.S. Department of Commerce, Bureau of the Census, Suitland, Maryland 20233 (301) 763-4040; *Census of Service Industries.*

U.S. Department of the Treasury, Internal Revenue Service, 1111 Constitution Avenue, NW, Washington, D.C. 20224 (202) 566-5000; *Statistics of Income, Corporation Income Tax Returns, Statistics of Income Bulletin,* and *Statistics of Income,* various publications.

SERVICE INDUSTRIES - FRANCHISES

International Franchise Association, 1350 New York Avenue, Suite 900, Washington, D.C. 20005 (202) 628-8000; *Franchising in the Economy.*

SERVICE INDUSTRIES - GROSS DOMESTIC PRODUCT

U.S. Department of Commerce, Bureau of Economic Analysis, Fourteenth Street between Constitution Avenue and E Street, NW, Washington, D.C. 20230 (202) 606-9900; *The National Income and Product Accounts of the United States,* and *Survey of Current Business.*

SERVICE INDUSTRIES - OCCUPATIONAL SAFETY

National Safety Council, 1121 Spring Lake Drive, Itasca, Illinois 60143-3201 (708) 285-1121; *Accident Facts.*

U.S. Department of Labor, Bureau of Labor Statistics, Two Massachusetts Avenue, NE, Washington, D.C. 20212 (202) 606-7828; *Injuries and Illnesses in the United States by Industry.*

SERVICE INDUSTRIES - PRODUCTIVITY

U.S. Department of Labor, Bureau of Labor Statistics, Two Massachusetts Avenue, NE, Washington, D.C. 20212 (202) 606-7828; *Productivity Measures for Selected Industries and Government Services,* and unpublished data.

SERVICE INDUSTRIES - PROFITS

U.S. Department of Commerce, Bureau of Economic Analysis, Fourteenth Street between Constitution Avenue and E Street, NW, Washington, D.C. 20230 (202) 606-9900; *The National Income and Product Accounts of the United States,* and *Survey of Current Business.*

U.S. Department of the Treasury, Internal Revenue Service, 1111 Constitution Avenue, NW, Washington, D.C. 20224 (202) 566-5000; *Statistics of Income,* various publications.

SERVICE INDUSTRIES - SALES OR RECEIPTS

Time Warner, 1675 Broadway, Rockefeller Center, New York, New York 10019 (212) 522-1212; *The Fortune Directories.*

U.S. Department of Commerce, Bureau of the Census, Suitland, Maryland 20233 (301) 763-4040; *Census of Service Industries, Current Business Reports, Service Annual Survey,* and *Economic Census of Outlying Areas.*

U.S. Department of the Treasury, Internal Revenue Service, 1111 Constitution Avenue, NW, Washington, D.C. 20224 (202) 566-5000; *Statistics of Income,* various publications.

SERVICE OCCUPATIONS - EARNINGS

U.S. Department of Commerce, Bureau of the Census, Suitland, Maryland 20233 (301) 763-4040; *Current Population Reports.*

U.S. Department of Labor, Bureau of Labor Statistics, Two Massachusetts Avenue, NE, Washington, D.C. 20212 (202) 606-7828; *Employment and Earnings,* and Bulletin 2307.

SERVICE OCCUPATIONS - EMPLOYMENT

U.S. Department of Labor, Bureau of Labor Statistics, Two Massachusetts Avenue, NE, Washington, D.C. 20212 (202) 606-7828; *Employment and Earnings,* and *Monthly Labor Review.*

SERVICE OCCUPATIONS - EMPLOYMENT - BY SEX AND EDUCATIONAL ATTAINMENT

U.S. Department of Labor, Bureau of Labor Statistics, Two Massachusetts Avenue, NE, Washington, D.C. 20212 (202) 606-7828; unpublished data.

SERVICE OCCUPATIONS - EMPLOYMENT - PROJECTIONS

U.S. Department of Labor, Bureau of Labor Statistics, Two Massachusetts Avenue, NE, Washington, D.C. 20212 (202) 606-7828; *Monthly Labor Review.*

SERVICE OCCUPATIONS - UNEMPLOYMENT

U.S. Department of Labor, Bureau of Labor Statistics, Two Massachusetts Avenue, NE, Washington, D.C. 20212 (202) 606-7828; *Employment and Earnings.*

SERVICE OCCUPATIONS - UNION MEMBERSHIP

U.S. Department of Labor, Bureau of Labor Statistics, Two Massachusetts Avenue, NE, Washington, D.C. 20212 (202) 606-7828; *Employment and Earnings.*

SERVICE STATIONS - See GASOLINE SERVICE STATIONS

SERVICE WORKERS- See SERVICE INDUSTRIES and SERVICE OCCUPATIONS

SEWAGE TREATMENT SYSTEMS

U.S. Department of Commerce, Bureau of the Census, Suitland, Maryland 20233 (301) 763-4040; *Federal Expenditures by State for Fiscal Year.*

SEWAGE TREATMENT SYSTEMS - CONSTRUCTION

U.S. Department of Commerce, Bureau of the Census, Suitland, Maryland 20233 (301) 763-4040; *Current Construction Reports,* and *Federal Expenditures by State for Fiscal Year.*

SEWAGE TREATMENT SYSTEMS - EMPLOYMENT

U.S. Department of Commerce, Bureau of the Census, Suitland, Maryland 20233 (301) 763-4040; *Public Employment, City Employment,* and *Compendium of Public Employment.*

SEWAGE TREATMENT SYSTEMS - EXPENDITURES

U.S. Department of Commerce, Bureau of the Census, Suitland, Maryland 20233 (301) 763-4040; *Historical Statistics on Governmental Finances and Employment, City Government Finances,* and *Government Finances.*

SEWAGE TREATMENT SYSTEMS - RESIDENCES

U.S. Department of Commerce, Bureau of the Census, Suitland, Maryland 20233 (301) 763-4040; *Current Housing Reports,* and *American Housing Survey.*

Seychelles - National Statistical Office

Chief Statistician, Post Office Box 206, Victoria, Mahe, Seychelles.

Seychelles - Primary Statistics Source

Central Statistical Office, Post Office Box 206, Victoria, Mahe, Seychelles; *Statistical Abstract*.

SEYCHELLES - AGRICULTURE

Food and Agricultural Organization of the United Nations (FAO) Via delle Terme di Caracalla, 00100 Rome, Italy (Telephone Number in U.S. (202) 653-2400); *Production Yearbook*, and *The State of Food and Agriculture*, and *Trade Yearbook*.

G.K. Hall and Company, 70 Lincoln Street, Boston, Massachusetts 02111 (617) 423-3990; *The World in Figures*.

Statistical Office of the United Nations, Publishing Service, New York, New York 10017 (800) 253-9646; *Statistical Yearbook*, and *Survey of Economic and Social Conditions in Africa*.

United Nations Economic Commission for Africa, Africa Hall, P.O. Box 3001, Addis Ababa, Ethiopia (Telephone Number in U.S. (800) 253-9646); *African Statistical Yearbook*.

The World Bank, 1818 H Street, NW, Washington, D.C. 20433 (202) 477-1234; *World Tables*.

SEYCHELLES - AIRLINE SERVICE

G.K. Hall and Company, 70 Lincoln Street, Boston, Massachusetts 02111 (617) 423-3990; *The World in Figures*.

United Nations Economic Commission for Africa, Africa Hall, P.O. Box 3001, Addis Ababa, Ethiopia (Telephone Number in U.S. (800) 253-9646); *African Statistical Yearbook*.

SEYCHELLES - ANIMAL HEALTH

Food and Agricultural Organization of the United Nations (FAO), Via delle Terme di Caracalla, 00100, Rome, Italy (Telephone Number in U.S. (202) 653-2400); *Animal Health Yearbook*.

SEYCHELLES - AREA AND DENSITY OF POPULATION

African Development Bank, 01 BP 1387, Abidjan 01, Cote D'Ivoire; *Selected Statistics on Regional Member Countries*.

Food and Agricultural Organization of the United Nations (FAO) Via delle Terme di Caracalla, 00100 Rome, Italy (Telephone Number in U.S. (202) 653-2400); *The State of Food and Agriculture*.

G.K. Hall and Company, 70 Lincoln Street, Boston, Massachusetts 02111 (617) 423-3990; *The World in Figures*.

Statistical Office of the United Nations, Publishing Service, New York, New York 10017 (800) 253-9646; *Statistical Yearbook*, and *Survey of Economic and Social Conditions in Africa*.

United Nations Educational, Scientific and Cultural Organization (UNESCO), 7 Place de Fontenoy, F-75700 Paris, France (Telephone Number in U.S. (212) 963-5981); *Statistical Yearbook*.

SEYCHELLES - BALANCE OF PAYMENTS

African Development Bank, 01 BP 1387, Abidjan 01, Cote D'Ivoire; *Selected Statistics on Regional Member Countries*.

The Economist Intelligence Unit, 111 West 57th Street, New York, New York 10019 (800) 938-4685; *The World Market Atlas*.

G.K. Hall and Company, 70 Lincoln Street, Boston, Massachusetts 02111 (617) 423-3990; *The World in Figures*.

International Monetary Fund, 700 Nineteenth Street, NW, Washington, D.C. 20431 (202) 623-7000; *Balance of Payments Yearbook*, and *International Financial Statistics*.

United Nations Economic Commission for Africa, Africa Hall, P.O. Box 3001, Addis Ababa, Ethiopia (Telephone Number in U.S. (800) 253-9646); *African Statistical Yearbook*.

The World Bank, 1818 H Street, NW, Washington, D.C. 20433 (202) 477-1234; *World Tables*.

SEYCHELLES - BANKING

G.K. Hall and Company, 70 Lincoln Street, Boston, Massachusetts 02111 (617) 423-3990; *The World in Figures*.

International Monetary Fund, 700 Nineteenth Street, NW, Washington, D.C. 20431 (202) 623-7000; *Government Finance Statistics Yearbook*, and *International Financial Statistics*.

SEYCHELLES - BEER PRODUCTION

Statistical Office of the United Nations, Publishing Service, New York, New York 10017 (800) 253-9646; *Statistical Yearbook*.

United Nations Economic Commission for Africa, Africa Hall, P.O. Box 3001, Addis Ababa, Ethiopia (Telephone Number in U.S. (800) 253-9646); *African Statistical Yearbook*.

SEYCHELLES - BIRTH RATES

Statistical Office of the United Nations, Publishing Service, New York, New York 10017 (800) 253-9646; *Demographic Yearbook*, *Statistical Yearbook*, and *Survey of Economic and Social Conditions in Africa*.

The World Bank, 1818 H Street, NW, Washington, D.C. 20433 (202) 477-1234; *World Tables*.

World Health Organization, Office of Publications, Avenue Appia, CH-1211 Geneva 27, Switzerland (Telephone Number in U.S. (518) 436-9686); *World Health Statistics Annual*.

SEYCHELLES - BONDS

G.K. Hall and Company, 70 Lincoln Street, Boston, Massachusetts 02111 (617) 423-3990; *The World in Figures*.

International Monetary Fund, 700 Nineteenth Street, NW, Washington, D.C. 20431 (202) 623-7000; *Government Finance Statistics Yearbook*.

SEYCHELLES - BOOK PRODUCTION

G.K. Hall and Company, 70 Lincoln Street, Boston, Massachusetts 02111 (617) 423-3990; *The World in Figures*.

United Nations Educational, Scientific and Cultural Organization (UNESCO), 7 Place de Fontenoy, F-75700 Paris, France (Telephone Number in U.S. (212) 963-5981); *Statistical Yearbook*.

SEYCHELLES - BROADCASTING

Billboard Limited, P.O. Box 9027, 1006 AA Amsterdam, The Netherlands (Telephone Number in U.S. (212) 764-7300); *World Radio TV Handbook*.

G.K. Hall and Company, 70 Lincoln Street, Boston, Massachusetts 02111 (617) 423-3990; *The World in Figures*.

United Nations Educational, Scientific and Cultural Organization (UNESCO), 7 Place de Fontenoy, F-75700 Paris, France (Telephone Number in U.S. (212) 963-5981); *Statistical Yearbook*.

SEYCHELLES - BUSINESS

G.K. Hall and Company, 70 Lincoln Street, Boston, Massachusetts 02111 (617) 423-3990; *The World in Figures*.

SEYCHELLES - BUSINESS AND PROFESSIONAL LICENSES

International Monetary Fund, 700 Nineteenth Street, NW, Washington, D.C. 20431 (202) 623-7000; *Government Finance Statistics Yearbook*.

SEYCHELLES - CALORIE SUPPLY

African Development Bank, 01 BP 1387, Abidjan 01, Cote D'Ivoire; *Selected Statistics on Regional Member Countries*.

Food and Agricultural Organization of the United Nations (FAO) Via delle Terme di Caracalla, 00100 Rome, Italy (Telephone Number in U.S. (202) 653-2400); *The State of Food and Agriculture*.

SEYCHELLES - CAPITAL REVENUE

International Monetary Fund, 700 Nineteenth Street, NW, Washington, D.C. 20431 (202) 623-7000; *Government Finance Statistics Yearbook*.

SEYCHELLES - CATTLE - See SEYCHELLES - LIVESTOCK AND POULTRY

SEYCHELLES - CHEMICAL (ORGANIC) PRODUCTION - See SEYCHELLES - MINING AND MINERAL PRODUCTS

SEYCHELLES - CIGARETTE PRODUCTION - See SEYCHELLES - TOBACCO PRODUCTION

SEYCHELLES - CLASS STRUCTURE

G.K. Hall and Company, 70 Lincoln Street, Boston, Massachusetts 02111 (617) 423-3990; *The World in Figures*.

SEYCHELLES - CLIMATE

G.K. Hall and Company, 70 Lincoln Street, Boston, Massachusetts 02111 (617) 423-3990; *The World in Figures*.

SEYCHELLES - COAL PRODUCTION - See SEYCHELLES - MINING AND MINERAL PRODUCTS

SEYCHELLES - COMMUNICATIONS

G.K. Hall and Company, 70 Lincoln Street, Boston, Massachusetts 02111 (617) 423-3990; *The World in Figures*.

United Nations Economic Commission for Africa, Africa Hall, P.O. Box 3001, Addis Ababa, Ethiopia (Telephone Number in U.S. (800) 253-9646); *African Statistical Yearbook*.

SEYCHELLES - CONSTRUCTION INDUSTRY

Statistical Office of the United Nations, Publishing Service, New York, New York 10017 (800) 253-9646; *Statistical Yearbook*.

United Nations Economic Commission for Africa, Africa Hall, P.O. Box 3001, Addis Ababa, Ethiopia (Telephone Number in U.S. (800) 253-9646); *African Statistical Yearbook*.

SEYCHELLES - CONSUMER PRICE INDEX

African Development Bank, 01 BP 1387, Abidjan 01, Cote D'Ivoire; *Selected Statistics on Regional Member Countries*.

G.K. Hall and Company, 70 Lincoln Street, Boston, Massachusetts 02111 (617) 423-3990; *The World in Figures*.

Statistical Office of the United Nations, Publishing Service, New York, New York 10017 (800) 253-9646; *Statistical Yearbook*, and *Survey of Economic and Social Conditions in Africa*.

United Nations Economic Commission for Africa, Africa Hall, P.O. Box 3001, Addis Ababa, Ethiopia (Telephone Number in U.S. (800) 253-9646); *African Statistical Yearbook*.

SEYCHELLES - CONSUMER PRICES

International Labour Office, I.L.O. Publications, CH-1211, Geneva 22, Switzerland; *Yearbook of Labour Statistics*.

International Monetary Fund, 700 Nineteenth Street, NW, Washington, D.C. 20431 (202) 623-7000; *International Financial Statistics*.

SEYCHELLES - CONSUMPTION

African Development Bank, 01 BP 1387, Abidjan 01, Cote D'Ivoire; *Selected Statistics on Regional Member Countries*.

G.K. Hall and Company, 70 Lincoln Street, Boston, Massachusetts 02111 (617) 423-3990; *The World in Figures*.

Statistical Office of the United Nations, Publishing Service, New York, New York 10017 (800) 253-9646; *Survey of Economic and Social Conditions in Africa*.

SEYCHELLES - COPRA EXPORTS

International Monetary Fund, 700 Nineteenth Street, NW, Washington, D.C. 20431 (202) 623-7000; *International Financial Statistics*.

SEYCHELLES - CORN PRODUCTION - See SEYCHELLES - CROPS

SEYCHELLES - CORPORATE TAXES - See SEYCHELLES - TAXATION

SEYCHELLES - CRIME

International Criminal Police Organization (INTERPOL), 26 rue Armengaud, 92210 Saint Cloud, France; *International Crime Statistics*.

SEYCHELLES - CROPS

Food and Agricultural Organization of the United Nations (FAO) Via delle Terme di Caracalla, 00100 Rome, Italy (Telephone Number in U.S. (202) 653-2400); *The State of Food and Agriculture*.

G.K. Hall and Company, 70 Lincoln Street, Boston, Massachusetts 02111 (617) 423-3990; *The World in Figures*.

United Nations Economic Commission for Africa, Africa Hall, P.O. Box 3001, Addis Ababa, Ethiopia (Telephone Number in U.S. (800) 253-9646); *African Statistical Yearbook*.

SEYCHELLES - CUSTOMS DUTIES

G.K. Hall and Company, 70 Lincoln Street, Boston, Massachusetts 02111 (617) 423-3990; *The World in Figures*.

International Monetary Fund, 700 Nineteenth Street, NW, Washington, D.C. 20431 (202) 623-7000; *Government Finance Statistics Yearbook*.

SEYCHELLES - DAIRY PRODUCTS

Food and Agricultural Organization of the United Nations (FAO) Via delle Terme di Caracalla, 00100 Rome, Italy (Telephone Number in U.S. (202) 653-2400); *The State of Food and Agriculture*.

SEYCHELLES - DEATH RATES

G.K. Hall and Company, 70 Lincoln Street, Boston, Massachusetts 02111 (617) 423-3990; *The World in Figures*.

Statistical Office of the United Nations, Publishing Service, New York, New York 10017 (800) 253-9646; *Statistical Yearbook*, and *Survey of Economic and Social Conditions in Africa*.

World Health Organization, Office of Publications, Avenue Appia, CH-1211 Geneva 27, Switzerland (Telephone Number in U.S. (518) 436-9686); *World Health Statistics Annual*.

SEYCHELLES - DEFENSE EXPENDITURES

G.K. Hall and Company, 70 Lincoln Street, Boston, Massachusetts 02111 (617) 423-3990; *The World in Figures*.

International Monetary Fund, 700 Nineteenth Street, NW, Washington, D.C. 20431 (202) 623-7000; *Government Finance Statistics Yearbook*.

SEYCHELLES - DEMOGRAPHY

The Economist Intelligence Unit, 111 West 57th Street, New York, New York 10019 (800) 938-4685; *The World Market Atlas*.

G.K. Hall and Company, 70 Lincoln Street, Boston, Massachusetts 02111 (617) 423-3990; *The World in Figures*.

Statistical Office of the United Nations, Publishing Service, New York, New York 10017 (800) 253-9646; *Survey of Economic and Social Conditions in Africa*.

SEYCHELLES - DEVELOPMENT ASSISTANCE

G.K. Hall and Company, 70 Lincoln Street, Boston, Massachusetts 02111 (617) 423-3990; *The World in Figures*.

Statistical Office of the United Nations, Publishing Service, New York, New York 10017 (800) 253-9646; *Statistical Yearbook*.

SEYCHELLES - DISEASES

G.K. Hall and Company, 70 Lincoln Street, Boston, Massachusetts 02111 (617) 423-3990; *The World in Figures*.

World Health Organization, Office of Publications, Avenue Appia, CH-1211 Geneva 27, Switzerland (Telephone Number in U.S. (518) 436-9686); *World Health Statistics Annual*.

SEYCHELLES - DIVORCE RATES

Statistical Office of the United Nations, Publishing Service, New York, New York 10017 (800) 253-9646; *Demographic Yearbook*, and *Statistical Yearbook*.

SEYCHELLES - DOMESTIC PRODUCT

G.K. Hall and Company, 70 Lincoln Street, Boston, Massachusetts 02111 (617) 423-3990; *The World in Figures*.

SEYCHELLES - ECONOMIC DATA

Statistical Office of the United Nations, Publishing Service, New York, New York 10017 (800) 253-9646; *Foreign Trade Statistics for Africa*.

SEYCHELLES - ECONOMIC INDICATORS

African Development Bank, 01 BP 1387, Abidjan 01, Cote D'Ivoire; *Selected Statistics on Regional Member Countries*.

SEYCHELLES - ECONOMY

G.K. Hall and Company, 70 Lincoln Street, Boston, Massachusetts 02111 (617) 423-3990; *The World in Figures*.

SEYCHELLES - EDUCATION

African Development Bank, 01 BP 1387, Abidjan 01, Cote D'Ivoire; *Selected Statistics on Regional Member Countries*.

The Economist Intelligence Unit, 111 West 57th Street, New York, New York 10019 (800) 938-4685; *The World Market Atlas*.

G.K. Hall and Company, 70 Lincoln Street, Boston, Massachusetts 02111 (617) 423-3990; *The World in Figures*.

International Monetary Fund, 700 Nineteenth Street, NW, Washington, D.C. 20431 (202) 623-7000; *Government Finance Statistics Yearbook*.

Statistical Office of the United Nations, Publishing Service, New York, New York 10017 (800) 253-9646; *Survey of Economic and Social Conditions in Africa*.

United Nations Economic Commission for Africa, Africa Hall, P.O. Box 3001, Addis Ababa, Ethiopia (Telephone Number in U.S. (800) 253-9646); *African Statistical Yearbook*.

United Nations Educational, Scientific and Cultural Organization (UNESCO), 7 Place de Fontenoy, F-75700 Paris, France (Telephone Number in U.S. (212) 963-5981); *Statistical Yearbook*.

The World Bank, 1818 H Street, NW, Washington, D.C. 20433 (202) 477-1234; *World Tables*.

SEYCHELLES - EGG PRODUCTION AND CONSUMPTION - See SEYCHELLES - DAIRY PRODUCTS

SEYCHELLES - ELECTRICITY

Statistical Office of the United Nations, Publishing Service, New York, New York 10017 (800) 253-9646; *Statistical Yearbook*, and *Survey of Economic and Social Conditions in Africa*.

United Nations Economic Commission for Africa, Africa Hall, P.O. Box 3001, Addis Ababa, Ethiopia (Telephone Number in U.S. (800) 253-9646); *African Statistical Yearbook*.

SEYCHELLES - EMPLOYMENT

International Labour Office, I.L.O. Publications, CH-1211, Geneva 22, Switzerland; *Yearbook of Labour Statistics*.

Statistical Office of the United Nations, Publishing Service, New York, New York 10017 (800) 253-9646; *Statistical Yearbook*, and *Survey of Economic and Social Conditions in Africa*.

SEYCHELLES - ENERGY

G.K. Hall and Company, 70 Lincoln Street, Boston, Massachusetts 02111 (617) 423-3990; *The World in Figures*.

Food and Agricultural Organization of the United Nations (FAO) Via delle Terme di Caracalla, 00100 Rome, Italy (Telephone Number in U.S. (202) 653-2400); *The State of Food and Agriculture*.

Statistical Office of the United Nations, Publishing Service, New York, New York 10017 (800) 253-9646; *Energy Statistics Yearbook*, and *Statistical Yearbook*.

United Nations Economic Commission for Africa, Africa Hall, P.O. Box 3001, Addis Ababa, Ethiopia (Telephone Number in U.S. (800) 253-9646); *African Statistical Yearbook*.

SEYCHELLES - EXCHANGE RATES

African Development Bank, 01 BP 1387, Abidjan 01, Cote D'Ivoire; *Selected Statistics on Regional Member Countries*.

International Monetary Fund, 700 Nineteenth Street, NW, Washington, D.C. 20431 (202) 623-7000; *International Financial Statistics*.

Statistical Office of the United Nations, Publishing Service, New York, New York 10017 (800) 253-9646; *Foreign Trade Statistics for Africa*, and *Statistical Yearbook*.

SEYCHELLES - EXCISE TAXES - See SEYCHELLES - TAXATION

SEYCHELLES - EXPORTS

African Development Bank, 01 BP 1387, Abidjan 01, Cote D'Ivoire; *Selected Statistics on Regional Member Countries*.

The Economist Intelligence Unit, 111 West 57th Street, New York, New York 10019 (800) 938-4685; *The World Market Atlas*.

Food and Agricultural Organization of the United Nations (FAO) Via delle Terme di Caracalla, 00100 Rome, Italy (Telephone Number in U.S. (202) 653-2400); *The State of Food and Agriculture*.

G.K. Hall and Company, 70 Lincoln Street, Boston, Massachusetts 02111 (617) 423-3990; *The World in Figures*.

International Monetary Fund, 700 Nineteenth Street, NW, Washington, D.C. 20431 (202) 623-7000; *Direction of Trade Statistics*, *Government Finance Statistics Yearbook*, and *International Financial Statistics*.

Statistical Office of the United Nations, Publishing Service, New York, New York 10017 (800) 253-9646; *Foreign Trade Statistics for Africa*, and *Survey of Economic and Social Conditions in Africa*.

United Nations Economic Commission for Africa, Africa Hall, P.O. Box 3001, Addis Ababa, Ethiopia (Telephone Number in U.S. (800) 253-9646); *African Statistical Yearbook*.

The World Bank, 1818 H Street, NW, Washington, D.C. 20433 (202) 477-1234; *World Tables*.

SEYCHELLES - EXTERNAL INDEBTEDNESS

African Development Bank, 01 BP 1387, Abidjan 01, Cote D'Ivoire; *Selected Statistics on Regional Member Countries*.

Statistical Office of the United Nations, Publishing Service, New York, New York 10017 (800) 253-9646; *Survey of Economic and Social Conditions in Africa*.

The World Bank, 1818 H Street, NW, Washington, D.C. 20433 (202) 477-1234; *World Tables*.

SEYCHELLES - EXTERNAL TRADE

African Development Bank, 01 BP 1387, Abidjan 01, Cote D'Ivoire; *Selected Statistics on Regional Member Countries*.

Food and Agricultural Organization of the United Nations (FAO) Via delle Terme di Caracalla, 00100 Rome, Italy (Telephone Number in U.S. (202) 653-2400); *The State of Food and Agriculture*, and *Trade Yearbook*.

G.K. Hall and Company, 70 Lincoln Street, Boston, Massachusetts 02111 (617) 423-3990; *The World in Figures*.

SEYCHELLES - FARM CROPS - See SEYCHELLES - CROPS

SEYCHELLES - FERTILITY RATES

Statistical Office of the United Nations, Publishing Service, New York, New York 10017 (800) 253-9646; *Survey of Economic and Social Conditions in Africa*.

The World Bank, 1818 H Street, NW, Washington, D.C. 20433 (202) 477-1234; *World Tables*.

SEYCHELLES - FERTILIZER

Food and Agricultural Organization of the United Nations (FAO) Via delle Terme di Caracalla, 00100 Rome, Italy (Telephone Number in U.S. (202) 653-2400); *The State of Food and Agriculture*.

SEYCHELLES - FETAL MORTALITY

Statistical Office of the United Nations, Publishing Service, New York, New York 10017 (800) 253-9646; *Demographic Yearbook*.

World Health Organization, Office of Publications, Avenue Appia, CH-1211 Geneva 27, Switzerland (Telephone Number in U.S. (518) 436-9686); *World Health Statistics Annual*.

SEYCHELLES - FINANCE

African Development Bank, 01 BP 1387, Abidjan 01, Cote D'Ivoire; *Selected Statistics on Regional Member Countries*.

G.K. Hall and Company, 70 Lincoln Street, Boston, Massachusetts 02111 (617) 423-3990; *The World in Figures*.

International Monetary Fund, 700 Nineteenth Street, NW, Washington, D.C. 20431 (202) 623-7000; *Government Finance Statistics Yearbook*.

United Nations Economic Commission for Africa, Africa Hall, P.O. Box 3001, Addis Ababa, Ethiopia (Telephone Number in U.S. (800) 253-9646); *African Statistical Yearbook*.

SEYCHELLES - FISHERIES

Food and Agricultural Organization of the United Nations (FAO) Via delle Terme di Caracalla, 00100 Rome, Italy (Telephone Number in U.S. (202) 653-2400); *The State of Food and Agriculture*, and *Yearbook of Fishery Statistics*.

Statistical Office of the United Nations, Publishing Service, New York, New York 10017 (800) 253-9646; *Statistical Yearbook*, and *Survey of Economic and Social Conditions in Africa*.

United Nations Economic Commission for Africa, Africa Hall, P.O. Box 3001, Addis Ababa, Ethiopia (Telephone Number in U.S. (800) 253-9646); *African Statistical Yearbook*.

SEYCHELLES - FOOD

African Development Bank, 01 BP 1387, Abidjan 01, Cote D'Ivoire; *Selected Statistics on Regional Member Countries*.

Food and Agricultural Organization of the United Nations (FAO) Via delle Terme di Caracalla, 00100 Rome, Italy (Telephone Number in U.S. (202) 653-2400); *Production Yearbook*, and *The State of Food and Agriculture*.

G.K. Hall and Company, 70 Lincoln Street, Boston, Massachusetts 02111 (617) 423-3990; *The World in Figures*.

SEYCHELLES - FOREIGN AID

G.K. Hall and Company, 70 Lincoln Street, Boston, Massachusetts 02111 (617) 423-3990; *The World in Figures*.

SEYCHELLES - FOREIGN DEBT

International Monetary Fund, 700 Nineteenth Street, NW, Washington, D.C. 20431 (202) 623-7000; *Government Finance Statistics Yearbook*.

SEYCHELLES - FOREIGN TRADE

Food and Agricultural Organization of the United Nations (FAO) Via delle Terme di Caracalla, 00100 Rome, Italy (Telephone Number in U.S. (202) 653-2400); *The State of Food and Agriculture*.

G.K. Hall and Company, 70 Lincoln Street, Boston, Massachusetts 02111 (617) 423-3990; *The World in Figures*.

Statistical Office of the United Nations, Publishing Service, New York, New York 10017 (800) 253-9646; *Foreign Trade Statistics for Africa, International Trade Statistics Yearbook*, and *Statistical Yearbook*.

United Nations Economic Commission for Africa, Africa Hall, P.O. Box 3001, Addis Ababa, Ethiopia (Telephone Number in U.S. (800) 253-9646); *African Statistical Yearbook*.

The World Bank, 1818 H Street, NW, Washington, D.C. 20433 (202) 477-1234; *World Tables*.

SEYCHELLES - FORESTRY AND FOREST PRODUCTS

Food and Agricultural Organization of the United Nations (FAO) Via delle Terme di Caracalla, 00100 Rome, Italy (Telephone Number in U.S. (202) 653-2400); *The State of Food and Agriculture*.

G.K. Hall and Company, 70 Lincoln Street, Boston, Massachusetts 02111 (617) 423-3990; *The World in Figures*.

Statistical Office of the United Nations, Publishing Service, New York, New York 10017 (800) 253-9646; *Statistical Yearbook*.

United Nations Economic Commission for Africa, Africa Hall, P.O. Box 3001, Addis Ababa, Ethiopia (Telephone Number in U.S. (800) 253-9646); *African Statistical Yearbook*.

United Nations Educational, Scientific and Cultural Organization (UNESCO), 7 Place de Fontenoy, F-75700 Paris, France (Telephone Number in U.S. (212) 963-5981); *Statistical Yearbook*.

SEYCHELLES - GENERAL INDUSTRIAL STATISTICS

Statistical Office of the United Nations, Publishing Service, New York, New York 10017 (800) 253-9646; *Industrial Statistics Yearbook*.

SEYCHELLES - GENERAL MORTALITY

Statistical Office of the United Nations, Publishing Service, New York, New York 10017 (800) 253-9646; *Demographic Yearbook*.

World Health Organization, Office of Publications, Avenue Appia, CH-1211 Geneva 27, Switzerland (Telephone Number in U.S. (518) 436-9686); *World Health Statistics Annual*.

SEYCHELLES - GOATS - See SEYCHELLES - LIVESTOCK AND POULTRY

SEYCHELLES - GOLD HOLDINGS

The World Bank, 1818 H Street, NW, Washington, D.C. 20433 (202) 477-1234; *World Tables*.

SEYCHELLES - GOVERNMENT

G.K. Hall and Company, 70 Lincoln Street, Boston, Massachusetts 02111 (617) 423-3990; *The World in Figures*.

SEYCHELLES - GOVERNMENT EXPENDITURES

International Monetary Fund, 700 Nineteenth Street, NW, Washington, D.C. 20431 (202) 623-7000; *Government Finance Statistics Yearbook*.

The World Bank, 1818 H Street, NW, Washington, D.C. 20433 (202) 477-1234; *World Tables*.

SEYCHELLES - GOVERNMENT REVENUE

International Monetary Fund, 700 Nineteenth Street, NW, Washington, D.C. 20431 (202) 623-7000; *Government Finance Statistics Yearbook*.

Statistical Office of the United Nations, Publishing Service, New York, New York 10017 (800) 253-9646; *Survey of Economic and Social Conditions in Africa*.

The World Bank, 1818 H Street, NW, Washington, D.C. 20433 (202) 477-1234; *World Tables*.

SEYCHELLES - GRAIN PRODUCTION - See SEYCHELLES - CROPS

SEYCHELLES - GRANTS

International Monetary Fund, 700 Nineteenth Street, NW, Washington, D.C. 20431 (202) 623-7000; *Government Finance Statistics Yearbook*.

SEYCHELLES - GROSS DOMESTIC PRODUCT

African Development Bank, 01 BP 1387, Abidjan 01, Cote D'Ivoire; *Selected Statistics on Regional Member Countries.*

The Economist Intelligence Unit, 111 West 57th Street, New York, New York 10019 (800) 938-4685; *The World Market Atlas.*

G.K. Hall and Company, 70 Lincoln Street, Boston, Massachusetts 02111 (617) 423-3990; *The World in Figures.*

Statistical Office of the United Nations, Publishing Service, New York, New York 10017 (800) 253-9646; *Statistical Yearbook,* and *Survey of Economic and Social Conditions in Africa.*

United Nations Economic Commission for Africa, Africa Hall, P.O. Box 3001, Addis Ababa, Ethiopia (Telephone Number in U.S. (800) 253-9646); *African Statistical Yearbook.*

The World Bank, 1818 H Street, NW, Washington, D.C. 20433 (202) 477-1234; *World Tables.*

SEYCHELLES - GROSS NATIONAL PRODUCT

The World Bank, 1818 H Street, NW, Washington, D.C. 20433 (202) 477-1234; *World Tables.*

SEYCHELLES - HEALTH

African Development Bank, 01 BP 1387, Abidjan 01, Cote D'Ivoire; *Selected Statistics on Regional Member Countries.*

G.K. Hall and Company, 70 Lincoln Street, Boston, Massachusetts 02111 (617) 423-3990; *The World in Figures.*

Statistical Office of the United Nations, Publishing Service, New York, New York 10017 (800) 253-9646; *Statistical Yearbook.*

United Nations Economic Commission for Africa, Africa Hall, P.O. Box 3001, Addis Ababa, Ethiopia (Telephone Number in U.S. (800) 253-9646); *African Statistical Yearbook.*

World Health Organization, Office of Publications, Avenue Appia, CH-1211 Geneva 27, Switzerland (Telephone Number in U.S. (518) 436-9686); *World Health Statistics Annual.*

SEYCHELLES - HEALTH EXPENDITURES

International Monetary Fund, 700 Nineteenth Street, NW, Washington, D.C. 20431 (202) 623-7000; *Government Finance Statistics Yearbook.*

SEYCHELLES - HIGHWAYS

G.K. Hall and Company, 70 Lincoln Street, Boston, Massachusetts 02111 (617) 423-3990; *The World in Figures.*

Statistical Office of the United Nations, Publishing Service, New York, New York 10017 (800) 253-9646; *Survey of Economic and Social Conditions in Africa.*

United Nations Economic Commission for Africa, Africa Hall, P.O. Box 3001, Addis Ababa, Ethiopia (Telephone Number in U.S. (800) 253-9646); *African Statistical Yearbook.*

SEYCHELLES - HOURS OF WORK - See SEYCHELLES - EMPLOYMENT

SEYCHELLES - HOUSING EXPENDITURES

International Monetary Fund, 700 Nineteenth Street, NW, Washington, D.C. 20431 (202) 623-7000; *Government Finance Statistics Yearbook.*

SEYCHELLES - ILLITERATE POPULATION

The Economist Intelligence Unit, 111 West 57th Street, New York, New York 10019 (800) 938-4685; *The World Market Atlas.*

G.K. Hall and Company, 70 Lincoln Street, Boston, Massachusetts 02111 (617) 423-3990; *The World in Figures.*

United Nations Educational, Scientific and Cultural Organization (UNESCO), 7 Place de Fontenoy, F-75700 Paris, France (Telephone Number in U.S. (212) 963-5981); *Statistical Yearbook.*

SEYCHELLES - IMPORTS

African Development Bank, 01 BP 1387, Abidjan 01, Cote D'Ivoire; *Selected Statistics on Regional Member Countries.*

The Economist Intelligence Unit, 111 West 57th Street, New York, New York 10019 (800) 938-4685; *The World Market Atlas.*

Food and Agricultural Organization of the United Nations (FAO) Via delle Terme di Caracalla, 00100 Rome, Italy (Telephone Number in U.S. (202) 653-2400); *The State of Food and Agriculture.*

G.K. Hall and Company, 70 Lincoln Street, Boston, Massachusetts 02111 (617) 423-3990; *The World in Figures.*

International Monetary Fund, 700 Nineteenth Street, NW, Washington, D.C. 20431 (202) 623-7000; *Direction of Trade Statistics, Government Finance Statistics Yearbook,* and *International Financial Statistics.*

Statistical Office of the United Nations, Publishing Service, New York, New York 10017 (800) 253-9646; *Foreign Trade Statistics for Africa,* and *Survey of Economic and Social Conditions in Africa.*

United Nations Economic Commission for Africa, Africa Hall, P.O. Box 3001, Addis Ababa, Ethiopia (Telephone Number in U.S. (800) 253-9646); *African Statistical Yearbook.*

The World Bank, 1818 H Street, NW, Washington, D.C. 20433 (202) 477-1234; *World Tables.*

SEYCHELLES - INCOME TAXES - See SEYCHELLES - TAXATION

SEYCHELLES - INDUSTRY

G.K. Hall and Company, 70 Lincoln Street, Boston, Massachusetts 02111 (617) 423-3990; *The World in Figures.*

International Labour Office, I.L.O. Publications, CH-1211, Geneva 22, Switzerland; *Yearbook of Labour Statistics.*

Statistical Office of the United Nations, Publishing Service, New York, New York 10017 (800) 253-9646; *Survey of Economic and Social Conditions in Africa.*

United Nations Economic Commission for Africa, Africa Hall, P.O. Box 3001, Addis Ababa, Ethiopia (Telephone Number in U.S. (800) 253-9646); *African Statistical Yearbook.*

The World Bank, 1818 H Street, NW, Washington, D.C. 20433 (202) 477-1234; *World Tables.*

SEYCHELLES - INFANT AND MATERNAL MORTALITY

Statistical Office of the United Nations, Publishing Service, New York, New York 10017 (800) 253-9646; *Demographic Yearbook, Statistical Yearbook,* and *Survey of Economic and Social Conditions in Africa.*

The World Bank, 1818 H Street, NW, Washington, D.C. 20433 (202) 477-1234; *World Tables.*

World Health Organization, Office of Publications, Avenue Appia, CH-1211 Geneva 27, Switzerland (Telephone Number in U.S. (518) 436-9686); *World Health Statistics Annual.*

SEYCHELLES - INTERNATIONAL LIQUIDITY

International Monetary Fund, 700 Nineteenth Street, NW, Washington, D.C. 20431 (202) 623-7000; *International Financial Statistics.*

SEYCHELLES - INTERNATIONAL RESERVES EXCLUDING GOLD

Statistical Office of the United Nations, Publishing Service, New York, New York 10017 (800) 253-9646; *Statistical Yearbook,* and *Survey of Economic and Social Conditions in Africa.*

The World Bank, 1818 H Street, NW, Washington, D.C. 20433 (202) 477-1234; *World Tables.*

SEYCHELLES - INVESTMENTS

International Monetary Fund, 700 Nineteenth Street, NW, Washington, D.C. 20431 (202) 623-7000; *International Financial Statistics.*

SEYCHELLES - LABOR FORCE

African Development Bank, 01 BP 1387, Abidjan 01, Cote D'Ivoire; *Selected Statistics on Regional Member Countries.*

Food and Agricultural Organization of the United Nations (FAO) Via delle Terme di Caracalla, 00100 Rome, Italy (Telephone Number in U.S. (202) 653-2400); *The State of Food and Agriculture.*

G.K. Hall and Company, 70 Lincoln Street, Boston, Massachusetts 02111 (617) 423-3990; *The World in Figures.*

The World Bank, 1818 H Street, NW, Washington, D.C. 20433 (202) 477-1234; *World Tables.*

SEYCHELLES - LABOR PRODUCTIVITY

International Labour Office, I.L.O. Publications, CH-1211, Geneva 22, Switzerland; *Yearbook of Labour Statistics.*

SEYCHELLES - LAND USE

Food and Agricultural Organization of the United Nations (FAO), Via delle Terme di Caracalla, 00100 Rome, Italy (Telephone Number in U.S. (202) 653-2400); *Production Yearbook.*

G.K. Hall and Company, 70 Lincoln Street, Boston, Massachusetts 02111 (617) 423-3990; *The World in Figures.*

SEYCHELLES - LIBRARIES

United Nations Educational, Scientific and Cultural Organization (UNESCO), 7 Place de Fontenoy, F-75700 Paris, France (Telephone Number in U.S. (212) 963-5981); *Statistical Yearbook.*

SEYCHELLES - LIFE EXPECTANCY

African Development Bank, 01 BP 1387, Abidjan 01, Cote D'Ivoire; *Selected Statistics on Regional Member Countries.*

SEYCHELLES - LITERACY RATE

Statistical Office of the United Nations, Publishing Service, New York, New York 10017 (800) 253-9646; *Survey of Economic and Social Conditions in Africa.*

SEYCHELLES - LIVESTOCK AND POULTRY

Food and Agricultural Organization of the United Nations (FAO), Via delle Terme di Caracalla, 00100 Rome, Italy (Telephone Number in U.S. (202) 653-2400); *Production Yearbook,* and *The State of Food and Agriculture.*

G.K. Hall and Company, 70 Lincoln Street, Boston, Massachusetts 02111 (617) 423-3990; *The World in Figures.*

Statistical Office of the United Nations, Publishing Service, New York, New York 10017 (800) 253-9646; *Statistical Yearbook,* and *Survey of Economic and Social Conditions in Africa.*

United Nations Economic Commission for Africa, Africa Hall, P.O. Box 3001, Addis Ababa, Ethiopia (Telephone Number in U.S. (800) 253-9646); *African Statistical Yearbook.*

SEYCHELLES - LIVING LEVELS

G.K. Hall and Company, 70 Lincoln Street, Boston, Massachusetts 02111 (617) 423-3990; *The World in Figures.*

SEYCHELLES - MAIL - NUMBER OF ITEMS SENT AND RECEIVED

Statistical Office of the United Nations, Publishing Service, New York, New York 10017 (800) 253-9646; *Statistical Yearbook.*

SEYCHELLES - MANUFACTURING

G.K. Hall and Company, 70 Lincoln Street, Boston, Massachusetts 02111 (617) 423-3990; *The World in Figures.*

Statistical Office of the United Nations, Publishing Service, New York, New York 10017 (800) 253-9646; *Survey of Economic and Social Conditions in Africa.*

United Nations Economic Commission for Africa, Africa Hall, P.O. Box 3001, Addis Ababa, Ethiopia (Telephone Number in U.S. (800) 253-9646); *African Statistical Yearbook.*

The World Bank, 1818 H Street, NW, Washington, D.C. 20433 (202) 477-1234; *World Tables.*

SEYCHELLES - MARRIAGE RATES

Statistical Office of the United Nations, Publishing Service, New York, New York 10017 (800) 253-9646; *Demographic Yearbook,* and *Statistical Yearbook.*

SEYCHELLES - MEAT PRODUCTION - See SEYCHELLES - LIVESTOCK AND POULTRY

SEYCHELLES - MERCHANT SHIPPING

G.K. Hall and Company, 70 Lincoln Street, Boston, Massachusetts 02111 (617) 423-3990; *The World in Figures*.

Statistical Office of the United Nations, Publishing Service, New York, New York 10017 (800) 253-9646; *Statistical Yearbook*.

United Nations Economic Commission for Africa, Africa Hall, P.O. Box 3001, Addis Ababa, Ethiopia (Telephone Number in U.S. (800) 253-9646); *African Statistical Yearbook*.

U.S. Department of Transportation, Maritime Administration, 400 Seventh Street, SW, Washington, D.C. 20590 (202) 366-5807; *A Statistical Analysis of the World's Merchant Fleets*.

SEYCHELLES - MILITARY

G.K. Hall and Company, 70 Lincoln Street, Boston, Massachusetts 02111 (617) 423-3990; *The World in Figures*.

The International Institute for Strategic Studies, 23 Tavistock Street, London WC2E 7NQ, England; *The Military Balance*.

SEYCHELLES - MINING AND MINERAL PRODUCTS

G.K. Hall and Company, 70 Lincoln Street, Boston, Massachusetts 02111 (617) 423-3990; *The World in Figures*.

United Nations Economic Commission for Africa, Africa Hall, P.O. Box 3001, Addis Ababa, Ethiopia (Telephone Number in U.S. (800) 253-9646); *African Statistical Yearbook*.

SEYCHELLES - MONEY EXCHANGE RATES

International Monetary Fund, 700 Nineteenth Street, NW, Washington, D.C. 20431 (202) 623-7000; *International Financial Statistics*.

Statistical Office of the United Nations, Publishing Service, New York, New York 10017 (800) 253-9646; *Statistical Yearbook*.

SEYCHELLES - MONEY SUPPLY

African Development Bank, 01 BP 1387, Abidjan 01, Cote D'Ivoire; *Selected Statistics on Regional Member Countries*.

G.K. Hall and Company, 70 Lincoln Street, Boston, Massachusetts 02111 (617) 423-3990; *The World in Figures*.

The World Bank, 1818 H Street, NW, Washington, D.C. 20433 (202) 477-1234; *World Tables*.

SEYCHELLES - MOTION PICTURES

Statistical Office of the United Nations, Publishing Service, New York, New York 10017 (800) 253-9646; *Statistical Yearbook*.

SEYCHELLES - MOTOR VEHICLES IN USE

G.K. Hall and Company, 70 Lincoln Street, Boston, Massachusetts 02111 (617) 423-3990; *The World in Figures*.

Statistical Office of the United Nations, Publishing Service, New York, New York 10017 (800) 253-9646; *Statistical Yearbook*, and *Survey of Economic and Social Conditions in Africa*.

SEYCHELLES - MUSEUMS

United Nations Educational, Scientific and Cultural Organization (UNESCO), 7 Place de Fontenoy, F-75700 Paris, France (Telephone Number in U.S. (212) 963-5981); *Statistical Yearbook*.

SEYCHELLES - NATALITY - See SEYCHELLES - BIRTH RATE

SEYCHELLES - NATIONAL ACCOUNTS

African Development Bank, 01 BP 1387, Abidjan 01, Cote D'Ivoire; *Selected Statistics on Regional Member Countries*.

Statistical Office of the United Nations, Publishing Service, New York, New York 10017 (800) 253-9646; *National Accounts Statistics*.

United Nations Economic Commission for Africa, Africa Hall, P.O. Box 3001, Addis Ababa, Ethiopia (Telephone Number in U.S. (800) 253-9646); *African Statistical Yearbook*.

SEYCHELLES - NATIONAL INCOME

G.K. Hall and Company, 70 Lincoln Street, Boston, Massachusetts 02111 (617) 423-3990; *The World in Figures*.

Statistical Office of the United Nations, Publishing Service, New York, New York 10017 (800) 253-9646; *Statistical Yearbook*.

SEYCHELLES - NATIONAL PRODUCT

Statistical Office of the United Nations, Publishing Service, New York, New York 10017 (800) 253-9646; *Statistical Yearbook*.

SEYCHELLES - NEWSPAPER PRODUCTION - See SEYCHELLES - FORESTRY AND FOREST PRODUCTS

SEYCHELLES - OCCUPATIONS - See SEYCHELLES - LABOR FORCE

SEYCHELLES - PATENTS

Statistical Office of the United Nations, Publishing Service, New York, New York 10017 (800) 253-9646; *Statistical Yearbook*.

SEYCHELLES - PERIODICALS

United Nations Educational, Scientific and Cultural Organization (UNESCO), 7 Place de Fontenoy, F-75700 Paris, France (Telephone Number in U.S. (212) 963-5981); *Statistical Yearbook*.

SEYCHELLES - PESTICIDE USE

Food and Agricultural Organization of the United Nations (FAO) Via delle Terme di Caracalla, 00100 Rome, Italy (Telephone Number in U.S. (202) 653-2400); *The State of Food and Agriculture*.

SEYCHELLES - PETROLEUM INDUSTRY

Food and Agricultural Organization of the United Nations (FAO) Via delle Terme di Caracalla, 00100 Rome, Italy (Telephone Number in U.S. (202) 653-2400); *The State of Food and Agriculture*.

G.K. Hall and Company, 70 Lincoln Street, Boston, Massachusetts 02111 (617) 423-3990; *The World in Figures*.

SEYCHELLES - PIGS - See SEYCHELLES - LIVESTOCK AND POULTRY

SEYCHELLES - POPULATION

African Development Bank, 01 BP 1387, Abidjan 01, Cote D'Ivoire; *Selected Statistics on Regional Member Countries.*

The Economist Intelligence Unit, 111 West 57th Street, New York, New York 10019 (800) 938-4685; *The World Market Atlas.*

Food and Agricultural Organization of the United Nations (FAO), Via delle Terme di Caracalla, 00100 Rome, Italy (Telephone Number in U.S. (202) 653-2400); *Production Yearbook.*

G.K. Hall and Company, 70 Lincoln Street, Boston, Massachusetts 02111 (617) 423-3990; *The World in Figures.*

International Labour Office, I.L.O. Publications, CH-1211, Geneva 22, Switzerland; *Yearbook of Labour Statistics.*

Statistical Office of the United Nations, Publishing Service, New York, New York 10017 (800) 253-9646; *Demographic Yearbook, Statistical Yearbook,* and *Survey of Economic and Social Conditions in Africa.*

United Nations Educational, Scientific and Cultural Organization (UNESCO), 7 Place de Fontenoy, F-75700 Paris, France (Telephone Number in U.S. (212) 963-5981); *Statistical Yearbook.*

World Health Organization, Office of Publications, Avenue Appia, CII-1211 Geneva 27, Switzerland (Telephone Number in U.S. (518) 436-9686); *World Health Statistics Annual.*

SEYCHELLES - PRICES

Food and Agricultural Organization of the United Nations (FAO), Via delle Terme di Caracalla, 00100 Rome, Italy (Telephone Number in U.S. (202) 653-2400); *Production Yearbook,* and *The State of Food and Agriculture.*

G.K. Hall and Company, 70 Lincoln Street, Boston, Massachusetts 02111 (617) 423-3990; *The World in Figures.*

International Labour Office, I.L.O. Publications, CH-1211, Geneva 22, Switzerland; *Yearbook of Labour Statistics.*

International Monetary Fund, 700 Nineteenth Street, NW, Washington, D.C. 20431 (202) 623-7000; *International Financial Statistics.*

United Nations Economic Commission for Africa, Africa Hall, P.O. Box 3001, Addis Ababa, Ethiopia (Telephone Number in U.S. (800) 253-9646); *African Statistical Yearbook.*

SEYCHELLES - PRODUCTION

G.K. Hall and Company, 70 Lincoln Street, Boston, Massachusetts 02111 (617) 423-3990; *The World in Figures.*

SEYCHELLES - PROPERTY TAXES - See SEYCHELLES - TAXATION

SEYCHELLES - RADIO BROADCASTING - See SEYCHELLES - BROADCASTING

SEYCHELLES - RAILWAYS

G.K. Hall and Company, 70 Lincoln Street, Boston, Massachusetts 02111 (617) 423-3990; *The World in Figures.*

United Nations Economic Commission for Africa, Africa Hall, P.O. Box 3001, Addis Ababa, Ethiopia (Telephone Number in U.S. (800)

253-9646); *African Statistical Yearbook.*

SEYCHELLES - RENT PRICES

International Labour Office, I.L.O. Publications, CH-1211, Geneva 22, Switzerland; *Yearbook of Labour Statistics.*

SEYCHELLES - RETAIL TRADE

G.K. Hall and Company, 70 Lincoln Street, Boston, Massachusetts 02111 (617) 423-3990; *The World in Figures.*

SEYCHELLES - SCIENCE AND TECHNOLOGY - EXPENDITURE FOR RESEARCH

Statistical Office of the United Nations, Publishing Service, New York, New York 10017 (800) 253-9646; *Statistical Yearbook.*

SEYCHELLES - SCIENTISTS AND TECHNICIANS

Statistical Office of the United Nations, Publishing Service, New York, New York 10017 (800) 253-9646; *Statistical Yearbook.*

SEYCHELLES - SOCIAL DATA

G.K. Hall and Company, 70 Lincoln Street, Boston, Massachusetts 02111 (617) 423-3990; *The World in Figures.*

Statistical Office of the United Nations, Publishing Service, New York, New York 10017 (800) 253-9646; *Survey of Economic and Social Conditions in Africa.*

SEYCHELLES - SOCIAL SECURITY

International Monetary Fund, 700 Nineteenth Street, NW, Washington, D.C. 20431 (202) 623-7000; *Government Finance Statistics Yearbook.*

SEYCHELLES - STAMP TAXES AND DUTIES - See SEYCHELLES - TAXATION

SEYCHELLES - STOCKS - COMMODITY - MARKET PRICE - INDEX

Food and Agricultural Organization of the United Nations (FAO) Via delle Terme di Caracalla, 00100 Rome, Italy (Telephone Number in U.S. (202) 653-2400); *The State of Food and Agriculture.*

SEYCHELLES - TAXATION

G.K. Hall and Company, 70 Lincoln Street, Boston, Massachusetts 02111 (617) 423-3990; *The World in Figures.*

International Monetary Fund, 700 Nineteenth Street, NW, Washington, D.C. 20431 (202) 623-7000; *Government Finance Statistics Yearbook.*

The World Bank, 1818 H Street, NW, Washington, D.C. 20433 (202) 477-1234; *World Tables.*

SEYCHELLES - TELEPHONES IN USE

American Telephone and Telegraph Company, 26 Parsippany Road, Whippany, New Jersey 07981 (800) 338-4038; *The World's Telephones.*

G.K. Hall and Company, 70 Lincoln Street, Boston, Massachusetts 02111 (617) 423-3990; *The World in Figures.*

Statistical Office of the United Nations, Publishing Service, New York, New York 10017 (800) 253-9646; *Statistical Yearbook.*

SEYCHELLES - TEXTILE INDUSTRY

G.K. Hall and Company, 70 Lincoln Street, Boston, Massachusetts 02111 (617) 423-3990; *The World in Figures.*

SEYCHELLES - TOBACCO PRODUCTION

Statistical Office of the United Nations, Publishing Service, New York, New York 10017 (800) 253-9646; *Statistical Yearbook.*

SEYCHELLES - TOURISM

G.K. Hall and Company, 70 Lincoln Street, Boston, Massachusetts 02111 (617) 423-3990; *The World in Figures.*

Statistical Office of the United Nations, Publishing Service, New York, New York 10017 (800) 253-9646; *Statistical Yearbook.*

United Nations Economic Commission for Africa, Africa Hall, P.O. Box 3001, Addis Ababa, Ethiopia (Telephone Number in U.S. (800) 253-9646); *African Statistical Yearbook.*

World Tourism Organization, Calle Capitan Haya 42, E-28020 Madrid, Spain; *Yearbook of Tourism Statistics.*

SEYCHELLES - TRACTORS IN USE

Statistical Office of the United Nations, Publishing Service, New York, New York 10017 (800) 253-9646; *Statistical Yearbook.*

SEYCHELLES - TRADE - See SEYCHELLES - FOREIGN TRADE

SEYCHELLES - TRADEMARKS AND SERVICE MARKS

Statistical Office of the United Nations, Publishing Service, New York, New York 10017 (800) 253-9646; *Statistical Yearbook.*

SEYCHELLES - TRANSPORTATION AND COMMUNICATIONS

G.K. Hall and Company, 70 Lincoln Street, Boston, Massachusetts 02111 (617) 423-3990; *The World in Figures.*

United Nations Economic Commission for Africa, Africa Hall, P.O. Box 3001, Addis Ababa, Ethiopia (Telephone Number in U.S. (800) 253-9646); *African Statistical Yearbook.*

SEYCHELLES - UNEMPLOYMENT

International Labour Office, I.L.O. Publications, CH-1211, Geneva 22, Switzerland; *Yearbook of Labour Statistics.*

SEYCHELLES - VITAL STATISTICS

G.K. Hall and Company, 70 Lincoln Street, Boston, Massachusetts 02111 (617) 423-3990; *The World in Figures.*

Statistical Office of the United Nations, Publishing Service, New York, New York 10017 (800) 253-9646; *Statistical Yearbook.*

World Health Organization, Office of Publications, Avenue Appia, CH-1211 Geneva 27, Switzerland (Telephone Number in U.S. (518) 436-9686); *World Health Statistics Annual.*

SEYCHELLES - WAGES

G.K. Hall and Company, 70 Lincoln Street, Boston, Massachusetts 02111 (617) 423-3990; *The World in Figures.*

International Labour Office, I.L.O. Publications, CH-1211, Geneva 22, Switzerland; *Yearbook of Labour Statistics.*

SEYCHELLES - WEATHER

G.K. Hall and Company, 70 Lincoln Street, Boston, Massachusetts 02111 (617) 423-3990; *The World in Figures.*

SEYCHELLES - WELFARE

International Monetary Fund, 700 Nineteenth, NW, Washington, D.C. 20431 (202) 623-7000; *Government Finance Statistics Yearbook.*

SHEEP AND LAMBS

U.S. Department of Agriculture, Economic Research Service, Fourteenth Street and Independence Avenue, SW, Washington, D.C. 20005-4789 (202) 219-1504; *Economic Indicators of the Farm Sector: National Financial Summary, Livestock and Meat Statistics,* and *Agricultural Outlook.*

U.S. Department of Agriculture, National Agricultural Statistics Service, Fourteenth Street and Independence Avenue, SW, Washington, D.C. 20250 (202) 219-1504; *Meat Animals - Production, Disposition, and Income,* and *Agricultural Statistics.*

SHELLFISH - CANNED - QUANTITY AND VALUE

U.S. Department of Commerce, National Oceanic and Atmospheric Administration, National Marine Fisheries Service, 1335 East-West Highway, Silver Spring, Maryland 20910 (301) 427-2239; *Fisheries of the United States.*

SHELLFISH - CATCH - QUANTITY AND VALUE

U.S. Department of Commerce, National Oceanic and Atmospheric Administration, National Marine Fisheries Service, 1335 East-West Highway, Silver Spring, Maryland 20910 (301) 427-2239; *Fishery Statistics of the United States,* and *Fisheries of the United States.*

SHELLFISH - CONSUMPTION

U.S. Department of Agriculture, Economic Research Service, Fourteenth Street and Independence Avenue, SW, Washington, D.C. 20005-4789 (202) 219-1504; *Food Consumption, Prices, and Expenditures,* and unpublished data.

U.S. Department of Commerce, National Oceanic and Atmospheric Administration, National Marine Fisheries Service, 1335 East-West Highway, Silver Spring, Maryland 20910 (301) 427-2239; *Fisheries of the United States,* and *Fishery Statistics of the United States.*

SHELLFISH - FOREIGN TRADE

U.S. Department of Commerce, National Oceanic and Atmospheric Administration, National Marine Fisheries Service, 1335 East-West Highway, Silver Spring, Maryland 20910 (301) 427-2239; *Fisheries of the United States,* and *Fishery Statistics of the United States.*

SHELLFISH - FROZEN - QUANTITY AND VALUE

U.S. Department of Commerce, National Oceanic and Atmospheric Administration, National Marine Fisheries Service, 1335 East-West

Highway, Silver Spring, Maryland 20910 (301) 427-2239; *Fisheries of the United States.*

SHELTER - See also HOUSING AND HOUSING UNITS

SHELTER - CONSUMER PRICE INDEXES

U.S. Department of Labor, Bureau of Labor Statistics, Two Massachusetts Avenue, NE, Washington, D.C. 20212 (202) 606-7828; *Monthly Labor Review, Handbook of Labor Statistics,* and *CPI Detailed Report.*

SHIP AND BOAT BUILDING, AND REPAIRING

Shipbuilders Council of America, 4301 North Fairfax Drive, Suite 330, Arlington, Virginia 22203 (703) 276-1700; unpublished data.

SHIP AND BOAT BUILDING AND REPAIRING - EARNINGS

Shipbuilders Council of America, 4301 North Fairfax Drive, Suite 330, Arlington, Virginia 22203 (703) 276-1700; unpublished data.

U.S. Department of Commerce, Bureau of the Census, Suitland, Maryland 20233 (301) 763-4040; *Census of Manufactures,* and *Annual Survey of Manufactures.*

U.S. Department of Labor, Bureau of Labor Statistics, Two Massachusetts Avenue, NE, Washington, D.C. 20212 (202) 606-7828; *Employment and Earnings,* and Bulletins 2370 and 2429.

SHIP AND BOAT BUILDING AND REPAIRING - EMPLOYEES

Shipbuilders Council of America, 4301 North Fairfax Drive, Suite 330, Arlington, Virginia 22203 (703) 276-1700; unpublished data.

U.S. Department of Commerce, Bureau of the Census, Suitland, Maryland 20233 (301) 763-4040; *Census of Manufactures,* and *Annual Survey of Manufactures.*

U.S. Department of Labor, Bureau of Labor Statistics, Two Massachusetts Avenue, NE, Washington, D.C. 20212 (202) 606-7828; *Employment and Earnings,* and Bulletins 2370 and 2429.

SHIP AND BOAT BUILDING AND REPAIRING - OUTPUT

Shipbuilders Council of America, 4301 North Fairfax Drive, Suite 330, Arlington, Virginia 22203 (703) 276-1700; unpublished data.

SHIP AND BOAT BUILDING AND REPAIRING - SHIPMENTS

U.S. Department of Commerce, Bureau of the Census, Suitland, Maryland 20233 (301) 763-4040; *Census of Manufactures,* and *Annual Survey of Manufactures.*

SHIP AND BOAT BUILDING AND REPAIRING - VALUE ADDED

Shipbuilders Council of America, 4301 North Fairfax Drive, Suite 330, Arlington, Virginia 22203 (703) 276-1700; unpublished data.

U.S. Department of Commerce, Bureau of the Census, Suitland, Maryland 20233 (301) 763-4040; *Census of Manufactures,* and *Annual Survey of Manufactures.*

SHIPMENTS - See also Individual Products or Industries

SHIPMENTS - MANUFACTURERS

U.S. Department of Commerce, Bureau of the Census, Suitland, Maryland 20233 (301) 763-4040; *Current Industrial Reports,*

Manufacturers' Shipments, Inventories, and Orders, Exports from Manufacturing Establishments, Census of Manufactures, and *Annual Survey of Manufactures.*

SHIPPING - See MERCHANT VESSELS and TONNAGE

SHIPS - MERCHANT VESSELS

Lloyd's Register of Shipping, 71 Fenchurch Street, London EC3, England; *Statistical Tables, Annual Summary of Merchant Ships Completed in the World,* and *Casualty Return.*

Shipbuilders Council of America, 4301 North Fairfax Drive, Suite 330, Arlington, Virginia 22203 (703) 276-1700; unpublished data.

U.S. Department of Transportation, Maritime Administration, 400 Seventh Street, SW, Washington, D.C. 20590 (202) 366-5807; *Employment Report of the United States Flag Merchant Fleet Oceangoing Vessels 1000 Gross Tons and Over,* and *New Ship Construction.*

SHIPS - MERCHANT VESSELS - LOST

Lloyd's Register of Shipping, 71 Fenchurch Street, London EC3, England; *Casualty Return.*

SHIPS - REPAIRS

Shipbuilders Council of America, 4301 North Fairfax Drive, Suite 330, Arlington, Virginia 22203 (703) 276-1700; unpublished data.

SHIPS - TANKER CASUALTIES

Tanker Advisory Center, Incorporated, 10 East End Avenue, New York, New York 10028 (212) 628-7686; *Worldwide Tanker Casualty Returns.*

SHOES - See FOOTWEAR

SHOPLIFTING

U.S. Department of Justice, Federal Bureau of Investigation, Ninth Street and Pennsylvania Avenue, NW, Washington, D.C. 20535 (202) 324-3000; *Crime in the United States, Population-at-Risk Rates and Selected Crime Indicators.*

SHOPPING CENTERS

National Research Bureau, 225 West Wacker Drive, Chicago, Illinois 60606 (312) 346-9097; data published by International Council of Shopping Centers, 665 Fifth Avenue, New York, New York 10022 (212) 421-8181; *Shopping Centers Today.*

SHORTENING

U.S. Department of Agriculture, Economic Research Service, Fourteenth Street and Independence Avenue, SW, Washington, D.C. 20005-4789 (202) 219-1504; *Food Consumption, Prices and Expenditures,* and unpublished data.

SHRIMP

U.S. Department of Commerce, National Oceanic and Atmospheric Administration, National Marine Fisheries Service, 1335 East-West Highway, Silver Spring, Maryland 20910 (301) 427-2239; *Fisheries of the United States,* and *Fishery Statistics of the United States.*

SHRIMP - IMPORTS

U.S. Department of Commerce, National Oceanic and Atmospheric Administration, National Marine Fisheries Service, 1335 East-West Highway, Silver Spring, Maryland 20910 (301) 427-2239; *Fisheries of the United States.*

SICKNESS - See ILLNESS

Sierra Leone - National Statistical Office

Central Statistics Office, Ministry of Development and Economic Planning, Tower Hill, Freetown, Sierra Leone.

Sierra Leone - Primary Statistics Source

Central Statistics Office, Ministry of Finance, Tower Hill, Freetown, Sierra Leone; *Statistical Bulletin,* and *Annual Statistical Digest.*

SIERRA LEONE - AGRICULTURE

Euromonitor Publications Limited, 87-88 Turnmill Street, London EC1M 5QU, England; *International Marketing Data and Statistics.*

Facts on File, 460 Park Avenue South, New York, New York 10016 (800) 443-8323; *The New Book of World Rankings.*

Food and Agricultural Organization of the United Nations (FAO) Via delle Terme di Caracalla, 00100 Rome, Italy (Telephone Number in U.S. (202) 653-2400; *Production Yearbook, The State of Food and Agriculture,* and *Trade Yearbook.'*

G.K. Hall and Company, 70 Lincoln Street, Boston, Massachusetts 02111 (617) 423-3990; *The World in Figures.*

Statistical Office of the United Nations, Publishing Service, New York, New York 10017 (800) 253-9646; *Statistical Yearbook.* and *Survey of Economic and Social Conditions in Africa.*

Times Books, 201 East 50th Street, New York, New York 10022 (212) 751-2600; *The Economist Book of Vital World Statistics.*

United Nations Economic Commission for Africa, Africa Hall, P.O. Box 3001, Addis Ababa, Ethiopia (Telephone Number in U.S. (800) 253-9646); *African Statistical Yearbook.*

The World Bank, 1818 H Street, NW, Washington, D.C. 20433 (202) 477-1234; *World Tables.*

SIERRA LEONE - AIRLINE SERVICE

Facts on File, 460 Park Avenue South, New York, New York 10016 (800) 443-8323; *The New Book of World Rankings.*

G.K. Hall and Company, 70 Lincoln Street, Boston, Massachusetts 02111 (617) 423-3990; *The World in Figures.*

Times Books, 201 East 50th Street, New York, New York 10022 (212) 751-2600; *The Economist Book of Vital World Statistics.*

United Nations Economic Commission for Africa, Africa Hall, P.O. Box 3001, Addis Ababa, Ethiopia (Telephone Number in U.S. (800) 253-9646); *African Statistical Yearbook.*

SIERRA LEONE - ALUMINUM PRODUCTION AND CONSUMPTION - See SIERRA LEONE - MINING AND MINERAL PRODUCTS

SIERRA LEONE - ANIMAL HEALTH

Food and Agricultural Organization of the United Nations (FAO), Via delle Terme di Caracalla, 00100, Rome, Italy (Telephone Number in U.S. (202) 653-2400); *Animal Health Yearbook.*

SIERRA LEONE - AREA AND DENSITY OF POPULATION

African Development Bank, 01 BP 1387, Abidjan 01, Cote D'Ivoire; *Selected Statistics on Regional Member Countries.*

Euromonitor Publications Limited, 87-88 Turnmill Street, London EC1M 5QU, England; *International Marketing Data and Statistics.*

Facts on File, 460 Park Avenue South, New York, New York 10016 (800) 443-8323; *The New Book of World Rankings.*

Food and Agricultural Organization of the United Nations (FAO) Via delle Terme di Caracalla, 00100 Rome, Italy (Telephone Number in U.S. (202) 653-2400); *The State of Food and Agriculture.*

G.K. Hall and Company, 70 Lincoln Street, Boston, Massachusetts 02111 (617) 423-3990; *The World in Figures.*

Statistical Office of the United Nations, Publishing Service, New York, New York 10017 (800) 253-9646; *Statistical Yearbook,* and *Survey of Economic and Social Conditions in Africa.*

Times Books, 201 East 50th Street, New York, New York 10022 (212) 751-2600; *The Economist Book of Vital World Statistics.*

United Nations Educational, Scientific and Cultural Organization (UNESCO), 7 Place de Fontenoy, F-75700 Paris, France (Telephone Number in U.S. (212) 963-5981); *Statistical Yearbook.*

SIERRA LEONE - ARMS EXPORTS AND IMPORTS

U.S. Arms Control and Disarmament Agency, 320 Twenty-first Street, NW, Washington, D.C. 20451 (202) 647-8677; *World Military Expenditures and Arms Transfers.*

SIERRA LEONE - BALANCE OF PAYMENTS

African Development Bank, 01 BP 1387, Abidjan 01, Cote D'Ivoire; *Selected Statistics on Regional Member Countries.*

The Economist Intelligence Unit, 111 West 57th Street, New York, New York 10019 (800) 938-4685; *The World Market Atlas.*

G.K. Hall and Company, 70 Lincoln Street, Boston, Massachusetts 02111 (617) 423-3990; *The World in Figures.*

International Monetary Fund, 700 Nineteenth Street, NW, Washington, D.C. 20431 (202) 623-7000; *Balance of Payments Yearbook,* and *International Financial Statistics.*

Times Books, 201 East 50th Street, New York, New York 10022 (212) 751-2600; *The Economist Book of Vital World Statistics.*

United Nations Economic Commission for Africa, Africa Hall, P.O. Box 3001, Addis Ababa, Ethiopia (Telephone Number in U.S. (800) 253-9646); *African Statistical Yearbook.*

The World Bank, 1818 H Street, NW, Washington, D.C. 20433 (202) 477-1234; *World Tables.*

SIERRA LEONE - BANKING

Facts on File, 460 Park Avenue South, New York, New York 10016 (800) 443-8323; *The New Book of World Rankings*.

G.K. Hall and Company, 70 Lincoln Street, Boston, Massachusetts 02111 (617) 423-3990; *The World in Figures*.

International Monetary Fund, 700 Nineteenth Street, NW, Washington, D.C. 20431 (202) 623-7000; *Government Finance Statistics Yearbook*, and *International Financial Statistics*.

United Nations Economic Commission for Africa, Africa Hall, P.O. Box 3001, Addis Ababa, Ethiopia (Telephone Number in U.S. (800) 253-9646); *African Statistical Yearbook*.

SIERRA LEONE - BARLEY PRODUCTION - See SIERRA LEONE - CROPS

SIERRA LEONE - BAUXITE PRODUCTION AND CONSUMPTION - See SIERRA LEONE - MINING AND MINERAL PRODUCTS

SIERRA LEONE - BEER PRODUCTION

Facts on File, 460 Park Avenue South, New York, New York 10016 (800) 443-8323; *The New Book of World Rankings*.

Statistical Office of the United Nations, Publishing Service, New York, New York 10017 (000) 253-9646; *Statistical Yearbook*.

SIERRA LEONE - BIRTH RATES

Facts on File, 460 Park Avenue South, New York, New York 10016 (800) 443-8323; *The New Book of World Rankings*.

Statistical Office of the United Nations, Publishing Service, New York, New York 10017 (800) 253-9646; *Demographic Yearbook*, *Statistical Yearbook*, and *Survey of Economic and Social Conditions in Africa*.

Times Books, 201 East 50th Street, New York, New York 10022 (212) 751-2600; *The Economist Book of Vital World Statistics*.

The World Bank, 1818 H Street, NW, Washington, D.C. 20433 (202) 477-1234; *World Tables*.

SIERRA LEONE - BONDS

G.K. Hall and Company, 70 Lincoln Street, Boston, Massachusetts 02111 (617) 423-3990; *The World in Figures*.

International Monetary Fund, 700 Nineteenth Street, NW, Washington, D.C. 20431 (202) 623-7000; *Government Finance Statistics Yearbook*.

SIERRA LEONE - BOOK PRODUCTION

G.K. Hall and Company, 70 Lincoln Street, Boston, Massachusetts 02111 (617) 423-3990; *The World in Figures*.

United Nations Educational, Scientific and Cultural Organization (UNESCO), 7 Place de Fontenoy, F-75700 Paris, France (Telephone Number in U.S. (212) 963-5981); *Statistical Yearbook*.

SIERRA LEONE - BROADCASTING

Billboard Limited, P.O. Box 9027, 1006 AA Amsterdam, The Netherlands (Telephone Number in U.S. (212) 764-7300); *World Radio TV Handbook*.

Facts on File, 460 Park Avenue South, New York, New York 10016 (800) 443-8323; *The New Book of World Rankings*.

G.K. Hall and Company, 70 Lincoln Street, Boston, Massachusetts 02111 (617) 423-3990; *The World in Figures*.

Times Books, 201 East 50th Street, New York, New York 10022 (212) 751-2600; *The Economist Book of Vital World Statistics*.

United Nations Educational, Scientific and Cultural Organization (UNESCO), 7 Place de Fontenoy, F-75700 Paris, France (Telephone Number in U.S. (212) 963-5981); *Statistical Yearbook*.

SIERRA LEONE - BUSINESS

G.K. Hall and Company, 70 Lincoln Street, Boston, Massachusetts 02111 (617) 423-3990; *The World in Figures*.

SIERRA LEONE - BUSINESS AND PROFESSIONAL LICENSES

International Monetary Fund, 700 Nineteenth Street, NW, Washington, D.C. 20431 (202) 623-7000; *Government Finance Statistics Yearbook*.

SIERRA LEONE - CACAO EXPORTS - See SIERRA LEONE - CROPS

SIERRA LEONE - CALORIE SUPPLY

African Development Bank, 01 BP 1387, Abidjan 01, Cote D'Ivoire; *Selected Statistics on Regional Member Countries*.

Food and Agricultural Organization of the United Nations (FAO) Via delle Terme di Caracalla, 00100 Rome, Italy (Telephone Number in U.S. (202) 653-2400); *The State of Food and Agriculture*.

SIERRA LEONE - CAPITAL REVENUE

International Monetary Fund, 700 Nineteenth Street, NW, Washington, D.C. 20431 (202) 623-7000; *Government Finance Statistics Yearbook*.

SIERRA LEONE - CATTLE - See SIERRA LEONE - LIVESTOCK AND POULTRY

SIERRA LEONE - CEMENT PRODUCTION - See SIERRA LEONE - MINING AND MINERAL PRODUCTS

SIERRA LEONE - CHEMICAL (ORGANIC) PRODUCTION - See SIERRA LEONE - MINING AND MINERAL PRODUCTS

SIERRA LEONE - CHICKENS - See SIERRA LEONE - LIVESTOCK AND POULTRY

SIERRA LEONE - CIGARETTE PRODUCTION - See SIERRA LEONE - TOBACCO PRODUCTION

SIERRA LEONE - CLASS STRUCTURE

G.K. Hall and Company, 70 Lincoln Street, Boston, Massachusetts 02111 (617) 423-3990; *The World in Figures*.

SIERRA LEONE - CLIMATE

Facts on File, 460 Park Avenue South, New York, New York 10016 (800) 443-8323; *The New Book of World Rankings*.

G.K. Hall and Company, 70 Lincoln Street, Boston, Massachusetts 02111 (617) 423-3990; *The World in Figures*.

SIERRA LEONE - COAL PRODUCTION - See SIERRA LEONE - MINING AND MINERAL PRODUCTS

SIERRA LEONE - COCOA (BEANS) PRODUCTION - See SIERRA LEONE - CROPS

SIERRA LEONE - COFFEE - See SIERRA LEONE - CROPS

SIERRA LEONE - COMMUNICATIONS

G.K. Hall and Company, 70 Lincoln Street, Boston, Massachusetts 02111 (617) 423-3990; *The World in Figures.*

United Nations Economic Commission for Africa, Africa Hall, P.O. Box 3001, Addis Ababa, Ethiopia (Telephone Number in U.S. (800) 253-9646); *African Statistical Yearbook.*

SIERRA LEONE - CONSTRUCTION INDUSTRY

Facts on File, 460 Park Avenue South, New York, New York 10016 (800) 443-8323; *The New Book of World Rankings.*

Statistical Office of the United Nations, Publishing Service, New York, New York 10017 (800) 253-9646; *Construction Statistics Yearbook,* and *Statistical Yearbook.*

United Nations Economic Commission for Africa, Africa Hall, P.O. Box 3001, Addis Ababa, Ethiopia (Telephone Number in U.S. (800) 253-9646); *African Statistical Yearbook.*

SIERRA LEONE - CONSUMER PRICE INDEX

African Development Bank, 01 BP 1387, Abidjan 01, Cote D'Ivoire; *Selected Statistics on Regional Member Countries.*

G.K. Hall and Company, 70 Lincoln Street, Boston, Massachusetts 02111 (617) 423-3990; *The World in Figures.*

Statistical Office of the United Nations, Publishing Service, New York, New York 10017 (800) 253-9646; *Statistical Yearbook,* and *Survey of Economic and Social Conditions in Africa.*

United Nations Economic Commission for Africa, Africa Hall, P.O. Box 3001, Addis Ababa, Ethiopia (Telephone Number in U.S. (800) 253-9646); *African Statistical Yearbook.*

SIERRA LEONE - CONSUMER PRICES

International Labour Office, I.L.O. Publications, CH-1211, Geneva 22, Switzerland; *Yearbook of Labour Statistics.*

International Monetary Fund, 700 Nineteenth Street, NW, Washington, D.C. 20431 (202) 623-7000; *International Financial Statistics.*

Times Books, 201 East 50th Street, New York, New York 10022 (212) 751-2600; *The Economist Book of Vital World Statistics.*

SIERRA LEONE - CONSUMPTION

African Development Bank, 01 BP 1387, Abidjan 01, Cote D'Ivoire; *Selected Statistics on Regional Member Countries.*

G.K. Hall and Company, 70 Lincoln Street, Boston, Massachusetts 02111 (617) 423-3990; *The World in Figures.*

Statistical Office of the United Nations, Publishing Service, New York, New York 10017 (800) 253-9646; *Survey of Economic and Social Conditions in Africa.*

SIERRA LEONE - COPPER PRODUCTION AND CONSUMPTION - See SIERRA LEONE - MINING AND MINERAL PRODUCTS

SIERRA LEONE - CORN PRODUCTION - See SIERRA LEONE - CROPS

SIERRA LEONE - CORPORATE TAXES - See SIERRA LEONE - TAXATION

SIERRA LEONE - COTTON PRODUCTION - See SIERRA LEONE - CROPS

SIERRA LEONE - CRIME

Yale University Press, Yale Station, New Haven, Connecticut 06520 (203) 432-0940; *Violence and Crime in Cross-National Perspective.*

SIERRA LEONE - CROPS

Facts on File, 460 Park Avenue South, New York, New York 10016 (800) 443-8323; *The New Book of World Rankings.*

Food and Agricultural Organization of the United Nations (FAO) Via delle Terme di Caracalla, 00100 Rome, Italy (Telephone Number in U.S. (202) 653-2400); *The State of Food and Agriculture.*

G.K. Hall and Company, 70 Lincoln Street, Boston, Massachusetts 02111 (617) 423-3990; *The World in Figures.*

International Monetary Fund, 700 Nineteenth Street, NW, Washington, D.C. 20431 (202) 623-7000; *International Financial Statistics.*

Statistical Office of the United Nations, Publishing Service, New York, New York 10017 (800) 253-9646; *Statistical Yearbook.*

United Nations Economic Commission for Africa, Africa Hall, P.O. Box 3001, Addis Ababa, Ethiopia (Telephone Number in U.S. (800) 253-9646); *African Statistical Yearbook.*

SIERRA LEONE - CUSTOMS DUTIES

G.K. Hall and Company, 70 Lincoln Street, Boston, Massachusetts 02111 (617) 423-3990; *The World in Figures.*

International Monetary Fund, 700 Nineteenth Street, NW, Washington, D.C. 20431 (202) 623-7000; *Government Finance Statistics Yearbook.*

SIERRA LEONE - DAIRY PRODUCTS

Facts on File, 460 Park Avenue South, New York, New York 10016 (800) 443-8323; *The New Book of World Rankings.*

Food and Agricultural Organization of the United Nations (FAO) Via delle Terme di Caracalla, 00100 Rome, Italy (Telephone Number in U.S. (202) 653-2400); *The State of Food and Agriculture.*

Statistical Office of the United Nations, Publishing Service, New York, New York 10017 (800) 253-9646; *Statistical Yearbook.*

SIERRA LEONE - DEATH RATES

G.K. Hall and Company, 70 Lincoln Street, Boston, Massachusetts 02111 (617) 423-3990; *The World in Figures.*

Statistical Office of the United Nations, Publishing Service, New York, New York 10017 (800) 253-9646; *Statistical Yearbook,* and *Survey of Economic and Social Conditions in Africa.*

Times Books, 201 East 50th Street, New York, New York 10022 (212) 751-2600; *The Economist Book of Vital World Statistics*.

World Health Organization, Office of Publications, Avenue Appia, CH-1211 Geneva 27, Switzerland (Telephone Number in U.S. (518) 436-9686) (Telephone Number in U.S. (518) 436-9686); *World Health Statistics Annual*.

SIERRA LEONE - DEFENSE EXPENDITURES

G.K. Hall and Company, 70 Lincoln Street, Boston, Massachusetts 02111 (617) 423-3990; *The World in Figures*.

International Monetary Fund, 700 Nineteenth Street, NW, Washington, D.C. 20431 (202) 623-7000; *Government Finance Statistics Yearbook*.

U.S. Arms Control and Disarmament Agency, 320 Twenty-first Street, NW, Washington, D.C. 20451 (202) 647-8677; *World Military Expenditures and Arms Transfers*.

SIERRA LEONE - DEMOGRAPHY

The Economist Intelligence Unit, 111 West 57th Street, New York, New York 10019 (800) 938-4685; *The World Market Atlas*.

Facts on File, 460 Park Avenue South, New York, New York 10016 (800) 443-8323; *The New Book of World Rankings*.

G.K. Hall and Company, 70 Lincoln Street, Boston, Massachusetts 02111 (617) 423-3990; *The World in Figures*.

Statistical Office of the United Nations, Publishing Service, New York, New York 10017 (000) 253-9646; *Survey of Economic and Social Conditions in Africa*.

SIERRA LEONE - DEVELOPMENT ASSISTANCE

G.K. Hall and Company, 70 Lincoln Street, Boston, Massachusetts 02111 (617) 423-3990; *The World in Figures*.

Statistical Office of the United Nations, Publishing Service, New York, New York 10017 (800) 253-9646; *Statistical Yearbook*.

SIERRA LEONE - DIAMOND EXPORTS - See SIERRA LEONE - MINING AND MINERAL PRODUCTS

SIERRA LEONE - DIAMOND PRODUCTION - See SIERRA LEONE - MINING AND MINERAL PRODUCTS

SIERRA LEONE - DISEASES

G.K. Hall and Company, 70 Lincoln Street, Boston, Massachusetts 02111 (617) 423-3990; *The World in Figures*.

World Health Organization, Office of Publications, Avenue Appia, CH-1211 Geneva 27, Switzerland (Telephone Number in U.S. (518) 436-9686) Telephone Number in U.S. (518) 436-9686; *World Health Statistics Annual*.

SIERRA LEONE - DIVORCE RATES

Facts on File, 460 Park Avenue South, New York, New York 10016 (800) 443-8323; *The New Book of World Rankings*.

Statistical Office of the United Nations, Publishing Service, New York, New York 10017 (800) 253-9646; *Demographic Yearbook*.

SIERRA LEONE - DOMESTIC PRODUCT

G.K. Hall and Company, 70 Lincoln Street, Boston, Massachusetts 02111 (617) 423-3990; *The World in Figures*.

SIERRA LEONE - ECONOMY

African Development Bank, 01 BP 1387, Abidjan 01, Cote D'Ivoire; *Selected Statistics on Regional Member Countries*.

Euromonitor Publications Limited, 87-88 Turnmill Street, London EC1M 5QU, England; *International Marketing Data and Statistics*.

Facts on File, 460 Park Avenue South, New York, New York 10016 (800) 443-8323; *The New Book of World Rankings*.

G.K. Hall and Company, 70 Lincoln Street, Boston, Massachusetts 02111 (617) 423-3990; *The World in Figures*.

Statistical Office of the United Nations, Publishing Service, New York, New York 10017 (800) 253-9646; *Foreign Trade Statistics for Africa*.

SIERRA LEONE - EDUCATION

African Development Bank, 01 BP 1387, Abidjan 01, Cote D'Ivoire; *Selected Statistics on Regional Member Countries*.

The Economist Intelligence Unit, 111 West 57th Street, New York, New York 10019 (800) 938-4685; *The World Market Atlas*.

Facts on File, 460 Park Avenue South, New York, New York 10016 (800) 443-8323; *The New Book of World Rankings*.

G.K. Hall and Company, 70 Lincoln Street, Boston, Massachusetts 02111 (617) 423-3990; *The World in Figures*.

International Monetary Fund, 700 Nineteenth Street, NW, Washington, D.C. 20431 (202) 623-7000; *Government Finance Statistics Yearbook*.

Statistical Office of the United Nations, Publishing Service, New York, New York 10017 (800) 253-9646; *Survey of Economic and Social Conditions in Africa*.

Times Books, 201 East 50th Street, New York, New York 10022 (212) 751-2600; *The Economist Book of Vital World Statistics*.

United Nations Economic Commission for Africa, Africa Hall, P.O. Box 3001, Addis Ababa, Ethiopia (Telephone Number in U.S. (800) 253-9646); *African Statistical Yearbook*.

United Nations Educational, Scientific and Cultural Organization (UNESCO), 7 Place de Fontenoy, F-75700 Paris, France (Telephone Number in U.S. (212) 963-5981); *Statistical Yearbook*.

The World Bank, 1818 H Street, NW, Washington, D.C. 20433 (202) 477-1234; *World Tables*.

SIERRA LEONE - EGG PRODUCTION AND CONSUMPTION - See SIERRA LEONE - DAIRY PRODUCTS

SIERRA LEONE - ELECTRICITY

Facts on File, 460 Park Avenue South, New York, New York 10016 (800) 443-8323; *The New Book of World Rankings*.

Statistical Office of the United Nations, Publishing Service, New York, New York 10017 (800) 253-9646; *Statistical Yearbook*, and

Survey of Economic and Social Conditions in Africa.

Times Books, 201 East 50th Street, New York, New York 10022 (212) 751-2600; *The Economist Book of Vital World Statistics.*

United Nations Economic Commission for Africa, Africa Hall, P.O. Box 3001, Addis Ababa, Ethiopia (Telephone Number in U.S. (800) 253-9646); *African Statistical Yearbook.*

SIERRA LEONE - EMPLOYMENT

Euromonitor Publications Limited, 87-88 Turnmill Street, London EC1M 5QU, England; *International Marketing Data and Statistics.*

Facts on File, 460 Park Avenue South, New York, New York 10016 (800) 443-8323; *The New Book of World Rankings.*

International Labour Office, I.L.O. Publications, CH-1211, Geneva 22, Switzerland; *Yearbook of Labour Statistics.*

Statistical Office of the United Nations, Publishing Service, New York, New York 10017 (800) 253-9646; *Statistical Yearbook,* and *Survey of Economic and Social Conditions in Africa.*

SIERRA LEONE - ENERGY

Facts on File, 460 Park Avenue South, New York, New York 10016 (800) 443-8323; *The New Book of World Rankings.*

Food and Agricultural Organization of the United Nations (FAO) Via delle Terme di Caracalla, 00100 Rome, Italy (Telephone Number in U.S. (202) 653-2400); *The State of Food and Agriculture.*

G.K. Hall and Company, 70 Lincoln Street, Boston, Massachusetts 02111 (617) 423-3990; *The World in Figures.*

Statistical Office of the United Nations, Publishing Service, New York, New York 10017 (800) 253-9646; *Energy Statistics Yearbook,* and *Statistical Yearbook.*

Times Books, 201 East 50th Street, New York, New York 10022 (212) 751-2600; *The Economist Book of Vital World Statistics.*

United Nations Economic Commission for Africa, Africa Hall, P.O. Box 3001, Addis Ababa, Ethiopia (Telephone Number in U.S. (800) 253-9646); *African Statistical Yearbook.*

SIERRA LEONE - EXCHANGE RATES

African Development Bank, 01 BP 1387, Abidjan 01, Cote D'Ivoire; *Selected Statistics on Regional Member Countries.*

Euromonitor Publications Limited, 87-88 Turnmill Street, London EC1M 5QU, England; *International Marketing Data and Statistics.*

International Monetary Fund, 700 Nineteenth Street, NW, Washington, D.C. 20431 (202) 623-7000; *International Financial Statistics.*

Statistical Office of the United Nations, Publishing Service, New York, New York 10017 (800) 253-9646; *Foreign Trade Statistics for Africa,* and *Statistical Yearbook.*

SIERRA LEONE - EXCISE TAXES - See SIERRA LEONE - TAXATION

SIERRA LEONE - EXPORTS

African Development Bank, 01 BP 1387, Abidjan 01, Cote D'Ivoire; *Selected Statistics on Regional Member Countries.*

The Economist Intelligence Unit, 111 West 57th Street, New York, New York 10019 (800) 938-4685; *The World Market Atlas.*

Euromonitor Publications Limited, 87-88 Turnmill Street, London EC1M 5QU, England; *International Marketing Data and Statistics.*

Food and Agricultural Organization of the United Nations (FAO) Via delle Terme di Caracalla, 00100 Rome, Italy (Telephone Number in U.S. (202) 653-2400); *The State of Food and Agriculture.*

G.K. Hall and Company, 70 Lincoln Street, Boston, Massachusetts 02111 (617) 423-3990; *The World in Figures.*

International Monetary Fund, 700 Nineteenth Street, NW, Washington, D.C. 20431 (202) 623-7000; *Direction of Trade Statistics, Government Finance Statistics Yearbook,* and *International Financial Statistics.*

Statistical Office of the United Nations, Publishing Service, New York, New York 10017 (800) 253-9646; *Foreign Trade Statistics for Africa,* and *Survey of Economic and Social Conditions in Africa.*

Times Books, 201 East 50th Street, New York, New York 10022 (212) 751-2600; *The Economist Book of Vital World Statistics.*

United Nations Economic Commission for Africa, Africa Hall, P.O. Box 3001, Addis Ababa, Ethiopia (Telephone Number in U.S. (800) 253-9646); *African Statistical Yearbook.*

The World Bank, 1818 H Street, NW, Washington, D.C. 20433 (202) 477-1234; *World Tables.*

SIERRA LEONE - EXTERNAL INDEBTEDNESS

Statistical Office of the United Nations, Publishing Service, New York, New York 10017 (800) 253-9646; *Survey of Economic and Social Conditions in Africa.*

The World Bank, 1818 H Street, NW, Washington, D.C. 20433 (202) 477-1234; *World Tables.*

SIERRA LEONE - EXTERNAL TRADE

African Development Bank, 01 BP 1387, Abidjan 01, Cote D'Ivoire; *Selected Statistics on Regional Member Countries.*

Food and Agricultural Organization of the United Nations (FAO) Via delle Terme di Caracalla, 00100 Rome, Italy (Telephone Number in U.S. (202) 653-2400); *The State of Food and Agriculture,* and *Trade Yearbook.*

G.K. Hall and Company, 70 Lincoln Street, Boston, Massachusetts 02111 (617) 423-3990; *The World in Figures.*

Statistical Office of the United Nations, Publishing Service, New York, New York 10017 (800) 253-9646; *Statistical Yearbook,* and *Survey of Economic and Social Conditions in Africa.*

SIERRA LEONE - FARM CROPS - See SIERRA LEONE - CROPS

SIERRA LEONE - FEMALE WORKING POPULATION - See SIERRA LEONE - EMPLOYMENT

SIERRA LEONE - FERTILITY RATES

Facts on File, 460 Park Avenue South, New York, New York 10016 (800) 443-8323; *The New Book of World Rankings.*

Statistical Office of the United Nations, Publishing Service, New York, New York 10017 (800) 253-9646; *Survey of Economic and Social Conditions in Africa.*

Times Books, 201 East 50th Street, New York, New York 10022 (212) 751-2600; *The Economist Book of Vital World Statistics.*

The World Bank, 1818 H Street, NW, Washington, D.C. 20433 (202) 477-1234; *World Tables.*

SIERRA LEONE - FERTILIZER

Food and Agricultural Organization of the United Nations (FAO), Via delle Terme di Caracalla, 00100, Rome, Italy (Telephone Number in U.S. (202) 653-2400); *Fertilizer Yearbook*, and *The State of Food and Agriculture.*

Statistical Office of the United Nations, Publishing Service, New York, New York 10017 (800) 253-9646; *Statistical Yearbook.*

SIERRA LEONE - FETAL MORTALITY

Statistical Office of the United Nations, Publishing Service, New York, New York 10017 (800) 253-9646; *Demographic Yearbook.*

SIERRA LEONE - FILM - See SIERRA LEONE - MOTION PICTURES

SIERRA LEONE - FINANCE

African Development Bank, 01 BP 1387, Abidjan 01, Cote D'Ivoire; *Selected Statistics on Regional Member Countries.*
Facts on File, 460 Park Avenue South, New York, New York 10016 (800) 443-8323; *The New Book of World Rankings.*

G.K. Hall and Company, 70 Lincoln Street, Boston, Massachusetts 02111 (617) 423-3990; *The World in Figures.*

International Monetary Fund, 700 Nineteenth Street, NW, Washington, D.C. 20431 (202) 623-7000; *Government Finance Statistics Yearbook*, and *International Financial Statistics.*

United Nations Economic Commission for Africa, Africa Hall, P.O. Box 3001, Addis Ababa, Ethiopia (Telephone Number in U.S. (800) 253-9646); *African Statistical Yearbook.*

SIERRA LEONE - FISHERIES

Facts on File, 460 Park Avenue South, New York, New York 10016 (800) 443-8323; *The New Book of World Rankings.*

Food and Agricultural Organization of the United Nations (FAO) Via delle Terme di Caracalla, 00100 Rome, Italy (Telephone Number in U.S. (202) 653-2400); *The State of Food and Agriculture*, and *Yearbook of Fishery Statistics.*

Statistical Office of the United Nations, Publishing Service, New York, New York 10017 (800) 253-9646; *Statistical Yearbook*, and *Survey of Economic and Social Conditions in Africa.*

United Nations Economic Commission for Africa, Africa Hall, P.O. Box 3001, Addis Ababa, Ethiopia (Telephone Number in U.S. (800) 253-9646); *African Statistical Yearbook.*

SIERRA LEONE - FLOUR PRODUCTION

Statistical Office of the United Nations, Publishing Service, New York, New York 10017 (800) 253-9646; *Statistical Yearbook.*

SIERRA LEONE - FOOD

African Development Bank, 01 BP 1387, Abidjan 01, Cote D'Ivoire; *Selected Statistics on Regional Member Countries.*

Food and Agricultural Organization of the United Nations (FAO) Via delle Terme di Caracalla, 00100 Rome, Italy (Telephone Number in U.S. (202) 653-2400); *Production Yearbook*, and *The State of Food and Agriculture.*

G.K. Hall and Company, 70 Lincoln Street, Boston, Massachusetts 02111 (617) 423-3990; *The World in Figures.*

SIERRA LEONE - FOREIGN AID

G.K. Hall and Company, 70 Lincoln Street, Boston, Massachusetts 02111 (617) 423-3990; *The World in Figures.*

SIERRA LEONE - FOREIGN DEBT

International Monetary Fund, 700 Nineteenth Street, NW, Washington, D.C. 20431 (202) 623-7000; *Government Finance Statistics Yearbook.*

SIERRA LEONE - FOREIGN TRADE

Euromonitor Publications Limited, 87-88 Turnmill Street, London EC1M 5QU, England; *International Marketing Data and Statistics.*

Facts on File, 460 Park Avenue South, New York, New York 10016 (800) 443-8323; *The New Book of World Rankings.*

Food and Agricultural Organization of the United Nations (FAO) Via delle Terme di Caracalla, 00100 Rome, Italy (Telephone Number in U.S. (202) 653-2400); *The State of Food and Agriculture.*

G.K. Hall and Company, 70 Lincoln Street, Boston, Massachusetts 02111 (617) 423-3990; *The World in Figures.*

International Monetary Fund, 700 Nineteenth Street, NW, Washington, D.C. 20431 (202) 623-7000; *International Financial Statistics.*

Statistical Office of the United Nations, Publishing Service, New York, New York 10017 (800) 253-9646; *Foreign Trade Statistics for Africa, International Trade Statistics Yearbook*, and *Statistical Yearbook.*

United Nations Economic Commission for Africa, Africa Hall, P.O. Box 3001, Addis Ababa, Ethiopia (Telephone Number in U.S. (800) 253-9646); *African Statistical Yearbook.*

The World Bank, 1818 H Street, NW, Washington, D.C. 20433 (202) 477-1234; *World Tables.*

SIERRA LEONE - FORESTRY AND FOREST PRODUCTS

Facts on File, 460 Park Avenue South, New York, New York 10016 (800) 443-8323; *The New Book of World Rankings.*

Food and Agricultural Organization of the United Nations (FAO) Via delle Terme di Caracalla, 00100 Rome, Italy (Telephone Number in U.S. (202) 653-2400); *The State of Food and Agriculture*, and *Yearbook of Forest Products.*

G.K. Hall and Company, 70 Lincoln Street, Boston, Massachusetts 02111 (617) 423-3990; *The World in Figures.*

Statistical Office of the United Nations, Publishing Service, New York, New York 10017 (800) 253-9646; *Statistical Yearbook.*

United Nations Economic Commission for Africa, Africa Hall, P.O. Box 3001, Addis Ababa, Ethiopia (Telephone Number in U.S. (800) 253-9646); *African Statistical Yearbook.*

United Nations Educational, Scientific and Cultural Organization (UNESCO), 7 Place de Fontenoy, F-75700 Paris, France (Telephone Number in U.S. (212) 963-5981); *Statistical Yearbook.*

SIERRA LEONE - GAS PRODUCTION - See SIERRA LEONE - MINING AND MINERAL PRODUCTS

SIERRA LEONE - GENERAL MORTALITY

Statistical Office of the United Nations, Publishing Service, New York, New York 10017 (800) 253-9646; *Demographic Yearbook.*

SIERRA LEONE - GEOGRAPHIC DATA

Facts on File, 460 Park Avenue South, New York, New York 10016 (800) 443-8323; *The New Book of World Rankings.*

SIERRA LEONE - GOATS - See SIERRA LEONE - LIVESTOCK AND POULTRY

SIERRA LEONE - GOLD HOLDINGS

International Monetary Fund, 700 Nineteenth Street, NW, Washington, D.C. 20431 (202) 623-7000; *International Financial Statistics.*

Statistical Office of the United Nations, Publishing Service, New York, New York 10017 (800) 253-9646; *Statistical Yearbook.*

The World Bank, 1818 H Street, NW, Washington, D.C. 20433 (202) 477-1234; *World Tables.*

SIERRA LEONE - GOLD PRODUCTION AND CONSUMPTION - See SIERRA LEONE - MINING AND MINERAL PRODUCTS

SIERRA LEONE - GOVERNMENT

G.K. Hall and Company, 70 Lincoln Street, Boston, Massachusetts 02111 (617) 423-3990; *The World in Figures.*

SIERRA LEONE - GOVERNMENT EXPENDITURES

International Monetary Fund, 700 Nineteenth Street, NW, Washington, D.C. 20431 (202) 623-7000; *Government Finance Statistics Yearbook.*

Times Books, 201 East 50th Street, New York, New York 10022 (212) 751-2600; *The Economist Book of Vital World Statistics.*

The World Bank, 1818 H Street, NW, Washington, D.C. 20433 (202) 477-1234; *World Tables.*

SIERRA LEONE - GOVERNMENT FINANCES

International Monetary Fund, 700 Nineteenth Street, NW, Washington, D.C. 20431 (202) 623-7000; *International Financial Statistics.*

SIERRA LEONE - GOVERNMENT REVENUE

International Monetary Fund, 700 Nineteenth Street, NW, Washington, D.C. 20431 (202) 623-7000; *Government Finance*

Statistics Yearbook.

Statistical Office of the United Nations, Publishing Service, New York, New York 10017 (800) 253-9646; *Survey of Economic and Social Conditions in Africa.*

Times Books, 201 East 50th Street, New York, New York 10022 (212) 751-2600; *The Economist Book of Vital World Statistics.*

The World Bank, 1818 H Street, NW, Washington, D.C. 20433 (202) 477-1234; *World Tables.*

SIERRA LEONE - GRAIN PRODUCTION - See SIERRA LEONE - CROPS

SIERRA LEONE - GRANTS

International Monetary Fund, 700 Nineteenth Street, NW, Washington, D.C. 20431 (202) 623-7000; *Government Finance Statistics Yearbook.*

SIERRA LEONE - GROSS DOMESTIC PRODUCT

African Development Bank, 01 BP 1387, Abidjan 01, Cote D'Ivoire; *Selected Statistics on Regional Member Countries.*

The Economist Intelligence Unit, 111 West 57th Street, New York, New York 10019 (800) 938-4685; *The World Market Atlas.*

Euromonitor Publications Limited, 87-88 Turnmill Street, London EC1M 5QU, England; *International Marketing Data and Statistics.*

Facts on File, 460 Park Avenue South, New York, New York 10016 (800) 443-8323; *The New Book of World Rankings.*

G.K. Hall and Company, 70 Lincoln Street, Boston, Massachusetts 02111 (617) 423-3990; *The World in Figures.*

Statistical Office of the United Nations, Publishing Service, New York, New York 10017 (800) 253-9646; *Statistical Yearbook,* and *Survey of Economic and Social Conditions in Africa.*

Times Books, 201 East 50th Street, New York, New York 10022 (212) 751-2600; *The Economist Book of Vital World Statistics.*

United Nations Economic Commission for Africa, Africa Hall, P.O. Box 3001, Addis Ababa, Ethiopia (Telephone Number in U.S. (800) 253-9646); *African Statistical Yearbook.*

The World Bank, 1818 H Street, NW, Washington, D.C. 20433 (202) 477-1234; *World Tables.*

SIERRA LEONE - GROSS NATIONAL PRODUCT

Euromonitor Publications Limited, 87-88 Turnmill Street, London EC1M 5QU, England; *International Marketing Data and Statistics.*

U.S. Arms Control and Disarmament Agency, 320 Twenty-first Street, NW, Washington, D.C. 20451 (202) 647-8677; *World Military Expenditures and Arms Transfers.*

The World Bank, 1818 H Street, NW, Washington, D.C. 20433 (202) 477-1234; *World Tables.*

SIERRA LEONE - GROUNDNUTS PRODUCTION - See SIERRA LEONE - CROPS

SIERRA LEONE - HEALTH

African Development Bank, 01 BP 1387, Abidjan 01, Cote D'Ivoire; *Selected Statistics on Regional Member Countries*.

Facts on File, 460 Park Avenue South, New York, New York 10016 (800) 443-8323; *The New Book of World Rankings*.

G.K. Hall and Company, 70 Lincoln Street, Boston, Massachusetts 02111 (617) 423-3990; *The World in Figures*.

International Monetary Fund, 700 Nineteenth Street, NW, Washington, D.C. 20431 (202) 623-7000; *Government Finance Statistics Yearbook*.

Statistical Office of the United Nations, Publishing Service, New York, New York 10017 (800) 253-9646; *Statistical Yearbook*.

Times Books, 201 East 50th Street, New York, New York 10022 (212) 751-2800; *The Economist Book of Vital World Statistics*.

United Nations Economic Commission for Africa, Africa Hall, P.O. Box 3001, Addis Ababa, Ethiopia (Telephone Number in U.S. (800) 253-9646); *African Statistical Yearbook*.

World Health Organization, Office of Publications, Avenue Appia, CH-1211 Geneva 27, Switzerland (Telephone Number in U.S. (518) 436-9686); *World Health Statistics Annual*.

SIERRA LEONE - HIGHWAYS

G.K. Hall and Company, 70 Lincoln Street, Boston, Massachusetts 02111 (617) 423-3990; *The World in Figures*.

International Road Federation, 525 School Street, SW, Washington, D.C. 20024 (202) 554-2106; *World Road Statistics*.

Statistical Office of the United Nations, Publishing Service, New York, New York 10017 (800) 253-9646; *Survey of Economic and Social Conditions in Africa*.

United Nations Economic Commission for Africa, Africa Hall, P.O. Box 3001, Addis Ababa, Ethiopia (Telephone Number in U.S. (800) 253-9646); *African Statistical Yearbook*.

SIERRA LEONE - HORSES - See SIERRA LEONE - LIVESTOCK AND POULTRY

SIERRA LEONE - HOURS OF WORK - See SIERRA LEONE - EMPLOYMENT

SIERRA LEONE - HOUSING EXPENDITURES

Facts on File, 460 Park Avenue South, New York, New York 10016 (800) 443-8323; *The New Book of World Rankings*.

International Monetary Fund, 700 Nineteenth Street, NW, Washington, D.C. 20431 (202) 623-7000; *Government Finance Statistics Yearbook*.

SIERRA LEONE - ILLITERATE POPULATION

The Economist Intelligence Unit, 111 West 57th Street, New York, New York 10019 (800) 938-4685; *The World Market Atlas*.

G.K. Hall and Company, 70 Lincoln Street, Boston, Massachusetts 02111 (617) 423-3990; *The World in Figures*.

United Nations Educational, Scientific and Cultural Organization (UNESCO), 7 Place de Fontenoy, F-75700 Paris, France (Telephone Number in U.S. (212) 963-5981); *Statistical Yearbook*.

SIERRA LEONE - IMPORTS

African Development Bank, 01 BP 1387, Abidjan 01, Cote D'Ivoire; *Selected Statistics on Regional Member Countries*.

The Economist Intelligence Unit, 111 West 57th Street, New York, New York 10019 (800) 938-4685; *The World Market Atlas*.

Euromonitor Publications Limited, 87-88 Turnmill Street, London EC1M 5QU, England; *International Marketing Data and Statistics*.

Food and Agricultural Organization of the United Nations (FAO) Via delle Terme di Caracalla, 00100 Rome, Italy (Telephone Number in U.S. (202) 653-2400); *The State of Food and Agriculture*.

G.K. Hall and Company, 70 Lincoln Street, Boston, Massachusetts 02111 (617) 423-3990; *The World in Figures*.

International Monetary Fund, 700 Nineteenth Street, NW, Washington, D.C. 20431 (202) 623-7000; *Direction of Trade Statistics*, *Government Finance Statistics Yearbook*, and *International Financial Statistics*.

Statistical Office of the United Nations, Publishing Service, New York, New York 10017 (800) 253-9646, *Foreign Trade Statistics for Africa*, and *Survey of Economic and Social Conditions in Africa*.

Times Books, 201 East 50th Street, New York, New York 10022 (212) 751-2800, *The Economist Book of Vital World Statistics*.

United Nations Economic Commission for Africa, Africa Hall, P.O. Box 3001, Addis Ababa, Ethiopia (Telephone Number in U.S. (800) 253-9646); *African Statistical Yearbook*.

The World Bank, 1818 H Street, NW, Washington, D.C. 20433 (202) 477-1234; *World Tables*.

SIERRA LEONE - INCOME TAXES - See SIERRA LEONE - TAXATION

SIERRA LEONE - INDUSTRY

Euromonitor Publications Limited, 87-88 Turnmill Street, London EC1M 5QU, England; *International Marketing Data and Statistics*.

Facts on File, 460 Park Avenue South, New York, New York 10016 (800) 443-8323; *The New Book of World Rankings*.

G.K. Hall and Company, 70 Lincoln Street, Boston, Massachusetts 02111 (617) 423-3990; *The World in Figures*.

International Labour Office, I.L.O. Publications, CH-1211, Geneva 22, Switzerland; *Yearbook of Labour Statistics*.

Statistical Office of the United Nations, Publishing Service, New York, New York 10017 (800) 253-9646; *Statistical Yearbook*, and *Survey of Economic and Social Conditions in Africa*.

United Nations Economic Commission for Africa, Africa Hall, P.O. Box 3001, Addis Ababa, Ethiopia (Telephone Number in U.S. (800) 253-9646); *African Statistical Yearbook*.

The World Bank, 1818 H Street, NW, Washington, D.C. 20433 (202) 477-1234; *World Tables*.

SIERRA LEONE - INFANT AND MATERNAL MORTALITY

Statistical Office of the United Nations, Publishing Service, New York, New York 10017 (800) 253-9646; *Demographic Yearbook*, and *Survey of Economic and Social Conditions in Africa*.

Times Books, 201 East 50th Street, New York, New York 10022 (212) 751-2600; *The Economist Book of Vital World Statistics*.

The World Bank, 1818 H Street, NW, Washington, D.C. 20433 (202) 477-1234; *World Tables*.

SIERRA LEONE - INTERNATIONAL LIQUIDITY

International Monetary Fund, 700 Nineteenth Street, NW, Washington, D.C. 20431 (202) 623-7000; *International Financial Statistics*.

SIERRA LEONE - INTERNATIONAL RESERVES EXCLUDING GOLD

African Development Bank, 01 BP 1387, Abidjan 01, Cote D'Ivoire; *Selected Statistics on Regional Member Countries*.

Statistical Office of the United Nations, Publishing Service, New York, New York 10017 (800) 253-9646; *Statistical Yearbook*.

The World Bank, 1818 H Street, NW, Washington, D.C. 20433 (202) 477-1234; *World Tables*.

SIERRA LEONE - IRON ORE PRODUCTION AND CONSUMPTION - See SIERRA LEONE - MINING AND MINERAL PRODUCTS

SIERRA LEONE - IRRIGATION

Euromonitor Publications Limited, 87-88 Turnmill Street, London EC1M 5QU, England; *International Marketing Data and Statistics*.

SIERRA LEONE - LABOR FORCE

African Development Bank, 01 BP 1387, Abidjan 01, Cote D'Ivoire; *Selected Statistics on Regional Member Countries*.

Euromonitor Publications Limited, 87-88 Turnmill Street, London EC1M 5QU, England; *International Marketing Data and Statistics*.

Facts on File, 460 Park Avenue South, New York, New York 10016 (800) 443-8323; *The New Book of World Rankings*.

Food and Agricultural Organization of the United Nations (FAO) Via delle Terme di Caracalla, 00100 Rome, Italy (Telephone Number in U.S. (202) 653-2400); *The State of Food and Agriculture*.

G.K. Hall and Company, 70 Lincoln Street, Boston, Massachusetts 02111 (617) 423-3990; *The World in Figures*.

The World Bank, 1818 H Street, NW, Washington, D.C. 20433 (202) 477-1234; *World Tables*.

SIERRA LEONE - LABOR PRODUCTIVITY

International Labour Office, I.L.O. Publications, CH-1211, Geneva 22, Switzerland; *Yearbook of Labour Statistics*.

SIERRA LEONE - LAND USE

Euromonitor Publications Limited, 87-88 Turnmill Street, London EC1M 5QU, England; *International Marketing Data and Statistics*.

Food and Agricultural Organization of the United Nations (FAO), Via delle Terme di Caracalla, 00100 Rome, Italy (Telephone Number in U.S. (202) 653-2400); *Production Yearbook*.

G.K. Hall and Company, 70 Lincoln Street, Boston, Massachusetts 02111 (617) 423-3990; *The World in Figures*.

SIERRA LEONE - LIBRARIES

Facts on File, 460 Park Avenue South, New York, New York 10016 (800) 443-8323; *The New Book of World Rankings*.

United Nations Educational, Scientific and Cultural Organization (UNESCO), 7 Place de Fontenoy, F-75700 Paris, France (Telephone Number in U.S. (212) 963-5981); *Statistical Yearbook*.

SIERRA LEONE - LIFE EXPECTANCY

African Development Bank, 01 BP 1387, Abidjan 01, Cote D'Ivoire; *Selected Statistics on Regional Member Countries*.

SIERRA LEONE - LITERACY RATE

Statistical Office of the United Nations, Publishing Service, New York, New York 10017 (800) 253-9646; *Survey of Economic and Social Conditions in Africa*.

SIERRA LEONE - LIVESTOCK AND POULTRY

Euromonitor Publications Limited, 87-88 Turnmill Street, London EC1M 5QU, England; *International Marketing Data and Statistics*.

Facts on File, 460 Park Avenue South, New York, New York 10016 (800) 443-8323; *The New Book of World Rankings*.

Food and Agricultural Organization of the United Nations (FAO), Via delle Terme di Caracalla, 00100 Rome, Italy (Telephone Number in U.S. (202) 653-2400); *Production Yearbook*, and *The State of Food and Agriculture*.

G.K. Hall and Company, 70 Lincoln Street, Boston, Massachusetts 02111 (617) 423-3990; *The World in Figures*.

Statistical Office of the United Nations, Publishing Service, New York, New York 10017 (800) 253-9646; *Statistical Yearbook*, and *Survey of Economic and Social Conditions in Africa*.

United Nations Economic Commission for Africa, Africa Hall, P.O. Box 3001, Addis Ababa, Ethiopia (Telephone Number in U.S. (800) 253-9646); *African Statistical Yearbook*.

SIERRA LEONE - LIVING LEVELS

G.K. Hall and Company, 70 Lincoln Street, Boston, Massachusetts 02111 (617) 423-3990; *The World in Figures*.

Times Books, 201 East 50th Street, New York, New York 10022 (212) 751-2600; *The Economist Book of Vital World Statistics*.

SIERRA LEONE - MAIL - NUMBER OF ITEMS SENT AND RECEIVED

Statistical Office of the United Nations, Publishing Service, New York, New York 10017 (800) 253-9646; *Statistical Yearbook*.

SIERRA LEONE - MANUFACTURING

Facts on File, 460 Park Avenue South, New York, New York 10016 (800) 443-8323; *The New Book of World Rankings*.

G.K. Hall and Company, 70 Lincoln Street, Boston, Massachusetts 02111 (617) 423-3990; *The World in Figures*.

Statistical Office of the United Nations, Publishing Service, New York, New York 10017 (800) 253-9646; *Survey of Economic and Social Conditions in Africa*.

Times Books, 201 East 50th Street, New York, New York 10022 (212) 751-2600; *The Economist Book of Vital World Statistics*.

United Nations Economic Commission for Africa, Africa Hall, P.O. Box 3001, Addis Ababa, Ethiopia (Telephone Number in U.S. (800) 253-9646); *African Statistical Yearbook*.

The World Bank, 1818 H Street, NW, Washington, D.C. 20433 (202) 477-1234; *World Tables*.

SIERRA LEONE - MARRIAGE RATES

Facts on File, 460 Park Avenue South, New York, New York 10016 (800) 443-8323; *The New Book of World Rankings*.

Statistical Office of the United Nations, Publishing Service, New York, New York 10017 (800) 253-9646; *Demographic Yearbook*.

SIERRA LEONE - MEAT PRODUCTION - See SIERRA LEONE - LIVESTOCK AND POULTRY

SIERRA LEONE - MERCHANT SHIPPING

G.K. Hall and Company, 70 Lincoln Street, Boston, Massachusetts 02111 (617) 423-3990; *The World in Figures*.

Statistical Office of the United Nations, Publishing Service, New York, New York 10017 (800) 253-9646; *Statistical Yearbook*.

United Nations Economic Commission for Africa, Africa Hall, P.O. Box 3001, Addis Ababa, Ethiopia (Telephone Number in U.S. (800) 253-9646); *African Statistical Yearbook*.

U.S. Department of Transportation, Maritime Administration, 400 Seventh Street, SW, Washington, D.C. 20590 (202) 366-5807; *A Statistical Analysis of the World's Merchant Fleets*.

SIERRA LEONE - MILITARY

G.K. Hall and Company, 70 Lincoln Street, Boston, Massachusetts 02111 (617) 423-3990; *The World in Figures*.

The International Institute for Strategic Studies, 23 Tavistock Street, London WC2E 7NQ, England; *The Military Balance*.

U.S. Arms Control and Disarmament Agency, 320 Twenty-first Street, NW, Washington, D.C. 20451 (202) 647-8677; *World Military Expenditures and Arms Transfers*.

SIERRA LEONE - MILK PRODUCTION - See SIERRA LEONE - DAIRY PRODUCTS

SIERRA LEONE - MINING AND MINERAL PRODUCTS

Facts on File, 460 Park Avenue South, New York, New York 10016 (800) 443-8323; *The New Book of World Rankings*.

G.K. Hall and Company, 70 Lincoln Street, Boston, Massachusetts 02111 (617) 423-3990; *The World in Figures*.

International Monetary Fund, 700 Nineteenth Street, NW, Washington, D.C. 20431 (202) 623-7000; *International Financial*

Statistics.

Statistical Office of the United Nations, Publishing Service, New York, New York 10017 (800) 253-9646; *Statistical Yearbook*.

United Nations Economic Commission for Africa, Africa Hall, P.O. Box 3001, Addis Ababa, Ethiopia (Telephone Number in U.S. (800) 253-9646); *African Statistical Yearbook*.

SIERRA LEONE - MONEY EXCHANGE RATE

Euromonitor Publications Limited, 87-88 Turnmill Street, London EC1M 5QU, England; *International Marketing Data and Statistics*.

International Monetary Fund, 700 Nineteenth Street, NW, Washington, D.C. 20431 (202) 623-7000; *International Financial Statistics*.

Statistical Office of the United Nations, Publishing Service, New York, New York 10017 (800) 253-9646; *Statistical Yearbook*.

SIERRA LEONE - MONEY RESERVES

Euromonitor Publications Limited, 87-88 Turnmill Street, London EC1M 5QU, England; *International Marketing Data and Statistics*.

SIERRA LEONE - MONEY SUPPLY

African Development Bank, 01 BP 1387, Abidjan 01, Cote D'Ivoire; *Selected Statistics on Regional Member Countries*.

Euromonitor Publications Limited, 87-88 Turnmill Street, London EC1M 5QU, England; *International Marketing Data and Statistics*.

G.K. Hall and Company, 70 Lincoln Street, Boston, Massachusetts 02111 (617) 423-3990; *The World in Figures*.

International Monetary Fund, 700 Nineteenth Street, NW, Washington, D.C. 20431 (202) 623-7000; *International Financial Statistics*.

The World Bank, 1818 H Street, NW, Washington, D.C. 20433 (202) 477-1234; *World Tables*.

SIERRA LEONE - MONUMENTS AND HISTORICAL SITES

United Nations Educational, Scientific and Cultural Organization (UNESCO), 7 Place de Fontenoy, F-75700 Paris, France (Telephone Number in U.S. (212) 963-5981); *Statistical Yearbook*.

SIERRA LEONE - MOTION PICTURES

United Nations Educational, Scientific and Cultural Organization (UNESCO), 7 Place de Fontenoy, F-75700 Paris, France (Telephone Number in U.S. (212) 963-5981); *Statistical Yearbook*.

SIERRA LEONE - MOTOR VEHICLE TAXES - See SIERRA LEONE - TAXATION

SIERRA LEONE - MOTOR VEHICLES IN USE

G.K. Hall and Company, 70 Lincoln Street, Boston, Massachusetts 02111 (617) 423-3990; *The World in Figures*.

International Road Federation, 525 School Street, SW, Washington, D.C. 20024 (202) 554-2106; *World Road Statistics*.

Statistical Office of the United Nations, Publishing Service, New York, New York 10017 (800) 253-9646; *Statistical Yearbook*, and

Survey of Economic and Social Conditions in Africa.

Times Books, 201 East 50th Street, New York, New York 10022 (212) 751-2600; *The Economist Book of Vital World Statistics.*

SIERRA LEONE - MUSEUMS

Facts on File, 460 Park Avenue South, New York, New York 10016 (800) 443-8323; *The New Book of World Rankings.*

United Nations Educational, Scientific and Cultural Organization (UNESCO), 7 Place de Fontenoy, F-75700 Paris, France (Telephone Number in U.S. (212) 963-5981); *Statistical Yearbook.*

SIERRA LEONE - NATALITY - See SIERRA LEONE - BIRTH RATE

SIERRA LEONE - NATIONAL ACCOUNTS

African Development Bank, 01 BP 1387, Abidjan 01, Cote D'Ivoire; *Selected Statistics on Regional Member Countries.*

Statistical Office of the United Nations, Publishing Service, New York, New York 10017 (800) 253-9646; *National Accounts Statistics,* and *Statistical Yearbook.*

United Nations Economic Commission for Africa, Africa Hall, P.O. Box 3001, Addis Ababa, Ethiopia (Telephone Number in U.S. (800) 253-9646); *African Statistical Yearbook.*

SIERRA LEONE - NATIONAL INCOME

Facts on File, 460 Park Avenue South, New York, New York 10016 (800) 443-8323; *The New Book of World Rankings.*

G.K. Hall and Company, 70 Lincoln Street, Boston, Massachusetts 02111 (617) 423-3990; *The World in Figures.*

Statistical Office of the United Nations, Publishing Service, New York, New York 10017 (800) 253-9646; *Statistical Yearbook.*

SIERRA LEONE - NATIONAL PRODUCT

Facts on File, 460 Park Avenue South, New York, New York 10016 (800) 443-8323; *The New Book of World Rankings.*

Statistical Office of the United Nations, Publishing Service, New York, New York 10017 (800) 253-9646; *Statistical Yearbook.*

SIERRA LEONE - NATURAL GAS PRODUCTION - See SIERRA LEONE - MINING AND MINERAL PRODUCTS

SIERRA LEONE - NEWSPAPER PRODUCTION - See SIERRA LEONE - FORESTRY AND FOREST PRODUCTS

SIERRA LEONE - NEWSPRINT - See SIERRA LEONE - FORESTRY AND FOREST PRODUCTS

SIERRA LEONE - OCCUPATIONS - See SIERRA LEONE - LABOR FORCE

SIERRA LEONE - PALM KERNELS PRODUCTION - See SIERRA LEONE - CROPS

SIERRA LEONE - PAPER - See SIERRA LEONE - FORESTRY AND FOREST PRODUCTS

SIERRA LEONE - PATENTS

Statistical Office of the United Nations, Publishing Service, New York, New York 10017 (800) 253-9646; *Statistical Yearbook.*

SIERRA LEONE - PEANUT PRODUCTION - See SIERRA LEONE - CROPS

SIERRA LEONE - PERIODICALS

United Nations Educational, Scientific and Cultural Organization (UNESCO), 7 Place de Fontenoy, F-75700 Paris, France (Telephone Number in U.S. (212) 963-5981); *Statistical Yearbook.*

SIERRA LEONE - PESTICIDE USE

Food and Agricultural Organization of the United Nations (FAO) Via delle Terme di Caracalla, 00100 Rome, Italy (Telephone Number in U.S. (202) 653-2400); *The State of Food and Agriculture.*

SIERRA LEONE - PETROLEUM INDUSTRY

Facts on File, 460 Park Avenue South, New York, New York 10016 (800) 443-8323; *The New Book of World Rankings.*

Food and Agricultural Organization of the United Nations (FAO) Via delle Terme di Caracalla, 00100 Rome, Italy (Telephone Number in U.S. (202) 653-2400); *The State of Food and Agriculture.*

G.K. Hall and Company, 70 Lincoln Street, Boston, Massachusetts 02111 (617) 423-3990; *The World in Figures.*

Statistical Office of the United Nations, Publishing Service, New York, New York 10017 (800) 253-9646; *Statistical Yearbook.*

SIERRA LEONE - PIGS - See SIERRA LEONE - LIVESTOCK AND POULTRY

SIERRA LEONE - POPULATION

African Development Bank, 01 BP 1387, Abidjan 01, Cote D'Ivoire; *Selected Statistics on Regional Member Countries.*

The Economist Intelligence Unit, 111 West 57th Street, New York, New York 10019 (800) 938-4685; *The World Market Atlas.*

Euromonitor Publications Limited, 87-88 Turnmill Street, London EC1M 5QU, England; *International Marketing Data and Statistics.*

Facts on File, 460 Park Avenue South, New York, New York 10016 (800) 443-8323; *The New Book of World Rankings.*

Food and Agricultural Organization of the United Nations (FAO), Via delle Terme di Caracalla, 00100 Rome, Italy (Telephone Number in U.S. (202) 653-2400); *Production Yearbook.*

G.K. Hall and Company, 70 Lincoln Street, Boston, Massachusetts 02111 (617) 423-3990; *The World in Figures.*

International Labour Office, I.L.O. Publications, CH-1211, Geneva 22, Switzerland; *Yearbook of Labour Statistics.*

Statistical Office of the United Nations, Publishing Service, New York, New York 10017 (800) 253-9646; *Demographic Yearbook, Statistical Yearbook,* and *Survey of Economic and Social Conditions in Africa.*

Times Books, 201 East 50th Street, New York, New York 10022 (212) 751-2600; *The Economist Book of Vital World Statistics.*

United Nations Educational, Scientific and Cultural Organization (UNESCO), 7 Place de Fontenoy, F-75700 Paris, France (Telephone Number in U.S. (212) 963-5981); *Statistical Yearbook*.

U.S. Arms Control and Disarmament Agency, 320 Twenty-first Street, NW, Washington, D.C. 20451 (202) 647-8677; *World Military Expenditures and Arms Transfers*.

World Health Organization, Office of Publications, Avenue Appia, CH-1211 Geneva 27, Switzerland (Telephone Number in U.S. (518) 436-9686); *World Health Statistics Annual*.

SIERRA LEONE - POST OFFICES

Facts on File, 460 Park Avenue South, New York, New York 10016 (800) 443-8323; *The New Book of World Rankings*.

SIERRA LEONE - POTATO PRODUCTION - See SIERRA LEONE - CROPS

SIERRA LEONE - PRICES

Facts on File, 460 Park Avenue South, New York, New York 10016 (800) 443-8323; *The New Book of World Rankings*.

Food and Agricultural Organization of the United Nations (FAO), Via delle Terme di Caracalla, 00100 Rome, Italy (Telephone Number in U.S. (202) 653-2400); *Production Yearbook*, and *The State of Food and Agriculture*.

G.K. Hall and Company, 70 Lincoln Street, Boston, Massachusetts 02111 (617) 423-3990; *The World in Figures*.

International Labour Office, I.L.O. Publications, CH-1211, Geneva 22, Switzerland; *Yearbook of Labour Statistics*, and *International Financial Statistics*.

United Nations Economic Commission for Africa, Africa Hall, P.O. Box 3001, Addis Ababa, Ethiopia (Telephone Number in U.S. (800) 253-9646); *African Statistical Yearbook*.

SIERRA LEONE - PRINTING AND WRITING PAPER - See SIERRA LEONE - FORESTRY AND FOREST PRODUCTS

SIERRA LEONE - PRODUCTION

Facts on File, 460 Park Avenue South, New York, New York 10016 (800) 443-8323; *The New Book of World Rankings*.

G.K. Hall and Company, 70 Lincoln Street, Boston, Massachusetts 02111 (617) 423-3990; *The World in Figures*.

SIERRA LEONE - PRODUCTIVITY

Euromonitor Publications Limited, 87-88 Turnmill Street, London EC1M 5QU, England; *International Marketing Data and Statistics*.

SIERRA LEONE - PROPERTY TAXES - See SIERRA LEONE - TAXATION

SIERRA LEONE - PUBLIC FINANCE

Facts on File, 460 Park Avenue South, New York, New York 10016 (800) 443-8323; *The New Book of World Rankings*.

SIERRA LEONE - RADIO BROADCASTING - See SIERRA LEONE - BROADCASTING

SIERRA LEONE - RAILWAYS

G.K. Hall and Company, 70 Lincoln Street, Boston, Massachusetts 02111 (617) 423-3990; *The World in Figures*.

United Nations Economic Commission for Africa, Africa Hall, P.O. Box 3001, Addis Ababa, Ethiopia (Telephone Number in U.S. (800) 253-9646); *African Statistical Yearbook*.

SIERRA LEONE - RELIGION

Facts on File, 460 Park Avenue South, New York, New York 10016 (800) 443-8323; *The New Book of World Rankings*.

SIERRA LEONE - RENT PRICES

International Labour Office, I.L.O. Publications, CH-1211, Geneva 22, Switzerland; *Yearbook of Labour Statistics*.

SIERRA LEONE - RETAIL TRADE

G.K. Hall and Company, 70 Lincoln Street, Boston, Massachusetts 02111 (617) 423-3990; *The World in Figures*.

SIERRA LEONE - RICE PRODUCTION - See SIERRA LEONE - CROPS

SIERRA LEONE - ROUNDWOOD PRODUCTION - See SIERRA LEONE - FORESTRY AND FOREST PRODUCTS

SIERRA LEONE - RUBBER PRODUCTION AND CONSUMPTION

Facts on File, 460 Park Avenue South, New York, New York 10016 (800) 443-8323; *The New Book of World Rankings*.

SIERRA LEONE - SAWNWOOD PRODUCTION - See SIERRA LEONE - FORESTRY AND FOREST PRODUCTS

SIERRA LEONE - SENIOR CITIZENS

Facts on File, 460 Park Avenue South, New York, New York 10016 (800) 443-8323; *The New Book of World Rankings*.

SIERRA LEONE - SHEEP - See SIERRA LEONE - LIVESTOCK AND POULTRY

SIERRA LEONE - SILVER PRODUCTION AND CONSUMPTION - See SIERRA LEONE - MINING AND MINERAL PRODUCTS

SIERRA LEONE - SOCIAL DATA

African Development Bank, 01 BP 1387, Abidjan 01, Cote D'Ivoire; *Selected Statistics on Regional Member Countries*.

Facts on File, 460 Park Avenue South, New York, New York 10016 (800) 443-8323; *The New Book of World Rankings*

G.K. Hall and Company, 70 Lincoln Street, Boston, Massachusetts 02111 (617) 423-3990; *The World in Figures*.

SIERRA LEONE - SOCIAL SECURITY

International Monetary Fund, 700 Nineteenth Street, NW, Washington, D.C. 20431 (202) 623-7000; *Government Finance Statistics Yearbook*.

SIERRA LEONE - STAMP TAXES AND DUTIES - See SIERRA LEONE - TAXATION

SIERRA LEONE - STATE BUDGET REVENUE AND EXPENDITURES

Euromonitor Publications Limited, 87-88 Turnmill Street, London EC1M 5QU, England; *International Marketing Data and Statistics*.

SIERRA LEONE - STEEL - See SIERRA LEONE - MINING AND MINERAL PRODUCTS

SIERRA LEONE - STOCKS - COMMODITY - MARKET PRICE - INDEX

Food and Agricultural Organization of the United Nations (FAO) Via delle Terme di Caracalla, 00100 Rome, Italy (Telephone Number in U.S. (202) 653-2400); *The State of Food and Agriculture*.

SIERRA LEONE - SUGAR PRODUCTION AND CONSUMPTION - See SIERRA LEONE - CROPS

SIERRA LEONE - TAXATION

G.K. Hall and Company, 70 Lincoln Street, Boston, Massachusetts 02111 (617) 423-3990; *The World in Figures*.

International Monetary Fund, 700 Nineteenth Street, NW, Washington, D.C. 20431 (202) 623-7000; *Government Finance Statistics Yearbook*.

International Road Federation, 525 School Street, SW, Washington, D.C. 20024 (202) 554-2106; *World Road Statistics*.

The World Bank, 1818 H Street, NW, Washington, D.C. 20433 (202) 477-1234; *World Tables*.

SIERRA LEONE - TELEPHONES IN USE

American Telephone and Telegraph Company, 26 Parsippany Road, Whippany, New Jersey 07981 (800) 338-4038; *The World's Telephones*.

G.K. Hall and Company, 70 Lincoln Street, Boston, Massachusetts 02111 (617) 423-3990; *The World in Figures*.

Statistical Office of the United Nations, Publishing Service, New York, New York 10017 (800) 253-9646; *Statistical Yearbook*.

SIERRA LEONE - TELEVISION BROADCASTING - See SIERRA LEONE - BROADCASTING

SIERRA LEONE - TEXTILE INDUSTRY

G.K. Hall and Company, 70 Lincoln Street, Boston, Massachusetts 02111 (617) 423-3990; *The World in Figures*.

SIERRA LEONE - TOBACCO PRODUCTION

Facts on File, 460 Park Avenue South, New York, New York 10016 (800) 443-8323; *The New Book of World Rankings*.

Statistical Office of the United Nations, Publishing Service, New York, New York 10017 (800) 253-9646; *Statistical Yearbook*.

SIERRA LEONE - TOURISM

Facts on File, 460 Park Avenue South, New York, New York 10016 (800) 443-8323; *The New Book of World Rankings*.

G.K. Hall and Company, 70 Lincoln Street, Boston, Massachusetts 02111 (617) 423-3990; *The World in Figures*.

Statistical Office of the United Nations, Publishing Service, New York, New York 10017 (800) 253-9646; *Statistical Yearbook*.

Times Books, 201 East 50th Street, New York, New York 10022 (212) 751-2600; *The Economist Book of Vital World Statistics*.

United Nations Economic Commission for Africa, Africa Hall, P.O. Box 3001, Addis Ababa, Ethiopia (Telephone Number in U.S. (800) 253-9646); *African Statistical Yearbook*.

SIERRA LEONE - TRACTORS IN USE

Statistical Office of the United Nations, Publishing Service, New York, New York 10017 (800) 253-9646; *Statistical Yearbook*.

SIERRA LEONE - TRADE - See SIERRA LEONE - FOREIGN TRADE

SIERRA LEONE - TRADEMARKS AND SERVICE MARKS

Statistical Office of the United Nations, Publishing Service, New York, New York 10017 (800) 253-9646; *Statistical Yearbook*.

SIERRA LEONE - TRANSPORTATION AND COMMUNICATIONS

Facts on File, 460 Park Avenue South, New York, New York 10016 (800) 443-8323; *The New Book of World Rankings*.

G.K. Hall and Company, 70 Lincoln Street, Boston, Massachusetts 02111 (617) 423-3990; *The World in Figures*.

United Nations Economic Commission for Africa, Africa Hall, P.O. Box 3001, Addis Ababa, Ethiopia (Telephone Number in U.S. (800) 253-9646); *African Statistical Yearbook*.

SIERRA LEONE - UNEMPLOYMENT

Euromonitor Publications Limited, 87-88 Turnmill Street, London EC1M 5QU, England; *International Marketing Data and Statistics*.

International Labour Office, I.L.O. Publications, CH-1211, Geneva 22, Switzerland; *Yearbook of Labour Statistics*.

Statistical Office of the United Nations, Publishing Service, New York, New York 10017 (800) 253-9646; *Statistical Yearbook*.

SIERRA LEONE - VITAL STATISTICS

Euromonitor Publications Limited, 87-88 Turnmill Street, London EC1M 5QU, England; *International Marketing Data and Statistics*.

G.K. Hall and Company, 70 Lincoln Street, Boston, Massachusetts 02111 (617) 423-3990; *The World in Figures*.

World Health Organization, Office of Publications, Avenue Appia, CH-1211 Geneva 27, Switzerland (Telephone Number in U.S. (518) 436-9686); *World Health Statistics Annual*.

SIERRA LEONE - WAGES

G.K. Hall and Company, 70 Lincoln Street, Boston, Massachusetts 02111 (617) 423-3990; *The World in Figures*.

International Labour Office, I.L.O. Publications, CH-1211, Geneva 22, Switzerland; *Yearbook of Labour Statistics*.

SIERRA LEONE - WEATHER

Facts on File, 460 Park Avenue South, New York, New York 10016 (800) 443-8323; *The New Book of World Rankings*.

G.K. Hall and Company, 70 Lincoln Street, Boston, Massachusetts 02111 (617) 423-3990; *The World in Figures.*

SIERRA LEONE - WELFARE

International Monetary Fund, 700 Nineteenth Street, NW, Washington, D.C. 20431 (202) 623-7000; *Government Finance Statistics Yearbook.*

SIERRA LEONE - WHEAT PRODUCTION AND PRICES - See SIERRA LEONE - CROPS

SIERRA LEONE - WINE PRODUCTION

Facts on File, 460 Park Avenue South, New York, New York 10016 (800) 443-8323; *The New Book of World Rankings.*

SIERRA LEONE - WOOL PRODUCTION

Facts on File, 460 Park Avenue South, New York, New York 10016 (800) 443-8323; *The New Book of World Rankings.*

SILICON

U.S. Department of the Interior, Bureau of Mines, 810 Seventh Street, NW, Washington, D.C. 20241 (202) 501-9649; *Mineral Commodity Summaries.*

SILVER

U.S. Department of Commerce, Bureau of the Census, Suitland, Maryland 20233 (301) 763-4040; *Census of Mineral Industries.*

U.S. Department of the Interior, Bureau of Mines, 810 Seventh Street, NW, Washington, D.C. 20241 (202) 501-9649; *Annual Reports,* and *Mineral Commodity Summaries.*

SILVER - CONSUMPTION

U.S. Department of the Interior, Bureau of Mines, 810 Seventh Street, NW, Washington, D.C. 20241 (202) 501-9649; *Annual Reports,* and *Mineral Commodity Summaries.*

SILVER - FOREIGN TRADE

U.S. Department of Commerce, Bureau of the Census, Suitland, Maryland 20233 (301) 763-4040; *U.S. Exports of Merchandise,* and *U.S. Imports of Merchandise,* compact discs.

U.S. Department of the Interior, Bureau of Mines, 810 Seventh Street, NW, Washington, D.C. 20241 (202) 501-9649; *Annual Reports,* and *Mineral Commodity Summaries.*

SILVER - PRICES

U.S. Department of the Interior, Bureau of Mines, 810 Seventh Street, NW, Washington, D.C. 20241 (202) 501-9649; *Annual Reports,* and *Mineral Commodity Summaries.*

SILVER - PRODUCTION AND VALUE

U.S. Department of Commerce, Bureau of the Census, Suitland, Maryland 20233 (301) 763-4040; *Census of Mineral Industries.*

U.S. Department of the Interior, Bureau of Mines, 810 Seventh Street, NW, Washington, D.C. 20241 (202) 501-9649; *Annual Reports.*

SILVER - STRATEGIC AND CRITICAL MATERIAL

U.S. Department of Defense, Defense Logistics Agency, Cameron Station, Alexandria, Virginia 22304-6100 (703) 274-6000; *Statistical Supplement, Stockpile Report to the Congress.*

SILVER - WORLD PRODUCTION

U.S. Department of the Interior, Bureau of Mines, 810 Seventh Street, NW, Washington, D.C. 20241 (202) 501-9649; *Annual Reports,* and *Mineral Commodity Summaries.*

SILVERWARE - See JEWELRY, SILVERWARE AND PLATED WARE

Singapore - National Statistical Office

Department of Statistics, Ministry of Trade and Industry, 8 Shenton Way, 10-01 Treasury Building, Singapore 0106.

Singapore - Primary Statistics Source

Department of Statistics, 8 Shenton Way, 10-01 Treasury Building, Singapore 0106; *Monthly Digest of Statistics,* and *Yearbook of Statistics Singapore.*

SINGAPORE - ABORTIONS

Statistical Office of the United Nations, Publishing Service, New York, New York 10017 (800) 253-9646; *Demographic Yearbook.*

SINGAPORE - AGRICULTURE

Asian Development Bank, P.O. Box 789, 1099 Manila, Philippines; *Key Indicators of Developing Asian and Pacific Countries.*

Euromonitor Publications Limited, 87-88 Turnmill Street, London EC1M 5QU, England; *International Marketing Data and Statistics, Pacific Basin: An Economic Handbook,* and *Third World Economic Handbook.*

Facts on File, 460 Park Avenue South, New York, New York 10016 (800) 443-8323; *The New Book of World Rankings.*

Food and Agricultural Organization of the United Nations (FAO) Via delle Terme di Caracalla, 00100 Rome, Italy (Telephone Number in U.S. (202) 653-2400); *Production Yearbook, The State of Food and Agriculture,* and *Trade Yearbook.*

G.K. Hall and Company, 70 Lincoln Street, Boston, Massachusetts 02111 (617) 423-3990; *The World in Figures.*

Statistical Office of the United Nations, Publishing Service, New York, New York 10017 (800) 253-9646; *Statistical Yearbook,* and *Statistical Yearbook for Asia and the Pacific.*

Times Books, 201 East 50th Street, New York, New York 10022 (212) 751-2600; *The Economist Book of Vital World Statistics.*

The World Bank, 1818 H Street, NW, Washington, D.C. 20433 (202) 477-1234; *World Tables.*

SINGAPORE - AIRLINE SERVICE

The Economist Intelligence Unit (Asia) Limited, 10th Floor, Luk Kwok Centre, 72 Gloucester Road, Wanchai, Hong Kong (Phone Number in U.S. (800) 938-4685); *Asian Market Atlas.*

Facts on File, 460 Park Avenue South, New York, New York 10016 (800) 443-8323; *The New Book of World Rankings*.

G.K. Hall and Company, 70 Lincoln Street, Boston, Massachusetts 02111 (617) 423-3990; *The World in Figures*.

International Civil Aviation Organization, 1000 Sherbrooke Street West, Suite 400, Montreal, Quebec, Canada H3A 2R2 (514) 285-8219; *Civil Aviation Statistics of the World*.

Statistical Office of the United Nations, Publishing Service, New York, New York 10017 (800) 253-9646; *Statistical Yearbook*.

Times Books, 201 East 50th Street, New York, New York 10022 (212) 751-2600; *The Economist Book of Vital World Statistics*.

SINGAPORE - ALUMINUM PRODUCTION AND CONSUMPTION - See SINGAPORE - MINING AND MINERAL PRODUCTS

SINGAPORE - ANIMAL FEEDINGSTUFFS OF AQUATIC ANIMAL ORIGIN

Statistical Office of the United Nations, Publishing Service, New York, New York 10017 (800) 253-9646; *Statistical Yearbook*.

SINGAPORE - ANIMAL HEALTH

Food and Agricultural Organization of the United Nations (FAO), Via delle Terme di Caracalla, 00100, Rome, Italy (Telephone Number in U.S. (202) 653-2400); *Animal Health Yearbook*.

SINGAPORE - AREA AND DENSITY OF POPULATION

Euromonitor Publications Limited, 87-88 Turnmill Street, London EC1M 5QU, England; *International Marketing Data and Statistics*, and *The Pacific Basin: An Economic Handbook*.

Facts on File, 460 Park Avenue South, New York, New York 10016 (800) 443-8323; *The New Book of World Rankings*.

Food and Agricultural Organization of the United Nations (FAO) Via delle Terme di Caracalla, 00100 Rome, Italy (Telephone Number in U.S. (202) 653-2400); *The State of Food and Agriculture*.

G.K. Hall and Company, 70 Lincoln Street, Boston, Massachusetts 02111 (617) 423-3990; *The World in Figures*.

Statistical Office of the United Nations, Publishing Service, New York, New York 10017 (800) 253-9646; *Statistical Yearbook*.

Times Books, 201 East 50th Street, New York, New York 10022 (212) 751-2600; *The Economist Book of Vital World Statistics*.

United Nations Educational, Scientific and Cultural Organization (UNESCO), 7 Place de Fontenoy, F-75700 Paris, France (Telephone Number in U.S. (212) 963-5981); *Statistical Yearbook*.

SINGAPORE - ARMS EXPORTS AND IMPORTS

U.S. Arms Control and Disarmament Agency, 320 Twenty-first Street, NW, Washington, D.C. 20451 (202) 647-8677; *World Military Expenditures and Arms Transfers*.

SINGAPORE - BALANCE OF PAYMENTS

The Economist Intelligence Unit, 111 West 57th Street, New York, New York 10019 (800) 938-4685; *The World Market Atlas*.

Euromonitor Publications Limited, 87-88 Turnmill Street, London EC1M 5QU, England; *Third World Economic Handbook*.

G.K. Hall and Company, 70 Lincoln Street, Boston, Massachusetts 02111 (617) 423-3990; *The World in Figures*.

International Monetary Fund, 700 Nineteenth Street, NW, Washington, D.C. 20431 (202) 623-7000; *Balance of Payments Yearbook*, and *International Financial Statistics*.

Times Books, 201 East 50th Street, New York, New York 10022 (212) 751-2600; *The Economist Book of Vital World Statistics*.

The World Bank, 1818 H Street, NW, Washington, D.C. 20433 (202) 477-1234; *World Tables*.

SINGAPORE - BANKING

Asian Development Bank, P.O. Box 789, 1099 Manila, Philippines; *Key Indicators of Developing Asian and Pacific Countries*.

Facts on File, 460 Park Avenue South, New York, New York 10016 (800) 443-8323; *The New Book of World Rankings*.

G.K. Hall and Company, 70 Lincoln Street, Boston, Massachusetts 02111 (617) 423-3990; *The World in Figures*.

International Monetary Fund, 700 Nineteenth Street, NW, Washington, D.C. 20431 (202) 623-7000; *Government Finance Statistics Yearbook*, and *International Financial Statistics*.

SINGAPORE - BARLEY PRODUCTION - See SINGAPORE - CROPS

SINGAPORE - BEER PRODUCTION

Facts on File, 460 Park Avenue South, New York, New York 10016 (800) 443-8323; *The New Book of World Rankings*.

Statistical Office of the United Nations, Publishing Service, New York, New York 10017 (800) 253-9646; *Statistical Yearbook*.

SINGAPORE - BIRTH RATES

The Economist Intelligence Unit (Asia) Limited, 10th Floor, Luk Kwok Centre, 72 Gloucester Road, Wanchai, Hong Kong (Phone Number in U.S. (800) 938-4685); *Asian Market Atlas*.

Euromonitor Publications Limited, 87-88 Turnmill Street, London EC1M 5QU, England; *The Pacific Basin: An Economic Handbook*, and *Third World Economic Handbook*.

Facts on File, 460 Park Avenue South, New York, New York 10016 (800) 443-8323; *The New Book of World Rankings*.

Statistical Office of the United Nations, Publishing Service, New York, New York 10017 (800) 253-9646; *Demographic Yearbook*, and *Statistical Yearbook*.

Times Books, 201 East 50th Street, New York, New York 10022 (212) 751-2600; *The Economist Book of Vital World Statistics*.

The World Bank, 1818 H Street, NW, Washington, D.C. 20433 (202) 477-1234; *World Tables*.

World Health Organization, Office of Publications, Avenue Appia, CH-1211 Geneva 27, Switzerland (Telephone Number in U.S. (518) 436-9686); *World Health Statistics Annual*.

SINGAPORE - BONDS

Asian Development Bank, P.O. Box 789, 1099 Manila, Philippines; *Key Indicators of Developing Asian and Pacific Countries.*

G.K. Hall and Company, 70 Lincoln Street, Boston, Massachusetts 02111 (617) 423-3990; *The World in Figures.*

International Monetary Fund, 700 Nineteenth Street, NW, Washington, D.C. 20431 (202) 623-7000; *Government Finance Statistics Yearbook.*

SINGAPORE - BOOK PRODUCTION

G.K. Hall and Company, 70 Lincoln Street, Boston, Massachusetts 02111 (617) 423-3990; *The World in Figures.*

United Nations Educational, Scientific and Cultural Organization (UNESCO), 7 Place de Fontenoy, F-75700 Paris, France (Telephone Number in U.S. (212) 963-5981); *Statistical Yearbook.*

SINGAPORE - BROADCASTING

Billboard Limited, P.O. Box 9027, 1006 AA Amsterdam, The Netherlands (Telephone Number in U.S. (212) 764-7300); *World Radio TV Handbook.*

The Economist Intelligence Unit (Asia) Limited, 10th Floor, Luk Kwok Centre, 72 Gloucester Road, Wanchai, Hong Kong (Phone Number in U.S. (800) 938-4685); *Asian Market Atlas.*

Facts on File, 460 Park Avenue South, New York, New York 10016 (800) 443-8323; *The New Book of World Rankings.*

G.K. Hall and Company, 70 Lincoln Street, Boston, Massachusetts 02111 (617) 423-3990; *The World in Figures.*

Times Books, 201 East 50th Street, New York, New York 10022 (212) 751-2600; *The Economist Book of Vital World Statistics.*

United Nations Educational, Scientific and Cultural Organization (UNESCO), 7 Place de Fontenoy, F-75700 Paris, France (Telephone Number in U.S. (212) 963-5981); *Statistical Yearbook.*

SINGAPORE - BUSINESS

G.K. Hall and Company, 70 Lincoln Street, Boston, Massachusetts 02111 (617) 423-3990; *The World in Figures.*

SINGAPORE - BUSINESS AND PROFESSIONAL LICENSES

International Monetary Fund, 700 Nineteenth Street, NW, Washington, D.C. 20431 (202) 623-7000; *Government Finance Statistics Yearbook.*

SINGAPORE - CALORIE SUPPLY

Asian Development Bank, P.O. Box 789, 1099 Manila, Philippines; *Key Indicators of Developing Asian and Pacific Countries.*

Food and Agricultural Organization of the United Nations (FAO) Via delle Terme di Caracalla, 00100 Rome, Italy (Telephone Number in U.S. (202) 653-2400); *The State of Food and Agriculture.*

SINGAPORE - CAPITAL INVESTMENT

Asian Development Bank, P.O. Box 789, 1099 Manila, Philippines; *Key Indicators of Developing Asian and Pacific Countries.*

SINGAPORE - CAPITAL REVENUE

Asian Development Bank, P.O. Box 789, 1099 Manila, Philippines; *Key Indicators of Developing Asian and Pacific Countries.*

International Monetary Fund, 700 Nineteenth Street, NW, Washington, D.C. 20431 (202) 623-7000; *Government Finance Statistics Yearbook.*

SINGAPORE - CATTLE - See SINGAPORE - LIVESTOCK AND POULTRY

SINGAPORE - CEMENT PRODUCTION - See SINGAPORE - MINING AND MINERAL PRODUCTS

SINGAPORE - CHEMICAL (ORGANIC) PRODUCTION - See SINGAPORE - MINING AND MINERAL PRODUCTS

SINGAPORE - CHICKENS - See SINGAPORE - LIVESTOCK AND POULTRY

SINGAPORE - CIGAR PRODUCTION - See SINGAPORE - TOBACCO PRODUCTION

SINGAPORE - CIGARETTE PRODUCTION - See SINGAPORE - TOBACCO PRODUCTION

SINGAPORE - CLASS STRUCTURE

G.K. Hall and Company, 70 Lincoln Street, Boston, Massachusetts 02111 (617) 423-3990; *The World in Figures.*

SINGAPORE - CLIMATE

Facts on File, 460 Park Avenue South, New York, New York 10016 (800) 443-8323; *The New Book of World Rankings.*

G.K. Hall and Company, 70 Lincoln Street, Boston, Massachusetts 02111 (617) 423-3990; *The World in Figures.*

SINGAPORE - CLOTHING EXPORTS AND IMPORTS

Euromonitor Publications Limited, 87-88 Turnmill Street, London EC1M 5QU, England; *Third World Economic Handbook.*

Statistical Office of the United Nations, Publishing Service, New York, New York 10017 (800) 253-9646; *Trade in Manufactures of Developing Countries.*

SINGAPORE - COAL PRODUCTION - See SINGAPORE - MINING AND MINERAL PRODUCTS

SINGAPORE - COFFEE - See SINGAPORE - CROPS

SINGAPORE - COMMUNICATIONS

Euromonitor Publications Limited, 87-88 Turnmill Street, London EC1M 5QU, England; *Third World Economic Handbook.*

G.K. Hall and Company, 70 Lincoln Street, Boston, Massachusetts 02111 (617) 423-3990; *The World in Figures.*

Statistical Office of the United Nations, Publishing Service, New York, New York 10017 (800) 253-9646; *Statistical Yearbook for Asia and the Pacific.*

SINGAPORE - CONSTRUCTION INDUSTRY

Facts on File, 460 Park Avenue South, New York, New York 10016 (800) 443-8323; *The New Book of World Rankings.*

Statistical Office of the United Nations, Publishing Service, New York, New York 10017 (800) 253-9646; *Construction Statistics Yearbook,* and *Statistical Yearbook.*

SINGAPORE - CONSUMER PRICE INDEX

Asian Development Bank, P.O. Box 789, 1099 Manila, Philippines; *Key Indicators of Developing Asian and Pacific Countries.*

G.K. Hall and Company, 70 Lincoln Street, Boston, Massachusetts 02111 (617) 423-3990; *The World in Figures.*

Statistical Office of the United Nations, Publishing Service, New York, New York 10017 (800) 253-9646; *Statistical Yearbook.*

SINGAPORE - CONSUMER PRICES

International Labour Office, I.L.O. Publications, CH-1211, Geneva 22, Switzerland; *Yearbook of Labour Statistics.*

International Monetary Fund, 700 Nineteenth Street, NW, Washington, D.C. 20431 (202) 623-7000; *International Financial Statistics.*

Times Books, 201 East 50th Street, New York, New York 10022 (212) 751-2600; *The Economist Book of Vital World Statistics.*

SINGAPORE - CONSUMPTION

Euromonitor Publications Limited, 87-88 Turnmill Street, London EC1M 5QU, England; *The Pacific Basin: An Economic Handbook.*

G.K. Hall and Company, 70 Lincoln Street, Boston, Massachusetts 02111 (617) 423-3990; *The World in Figures.*

International Monetary Fund, 700 Nineteenth Street, NW, Washington, D.C. 20431 (202) 623-7000; *International Financial Statistics.*

International Rubber Study Group, York House, Eighth Floor, Empire Way, Wembley, London HA9 0PA, England; *Rubber Statistical Bulletin.*

SINGAPORE - COPPER PRODUCTION AND CONSUMPTION - See SINGAPORE - MINING AND MINERAL PRODUCTS

SINGAPORE - CORN PRODUCTION - See SINGAPORE - CROPS

SINGAPORE - CORPORATE TAXES - See SINGAPORE - TAXATION

SINGAPORE - COTTON PRODUCTION - See SINGAPORE - CROPS

SINGAPORE - CRIME

International Criminal Police Organization (INTERPOL), 26 rue Armengaud, 92210 Saint Cloud, France; *International Crime Statistics.*

Yale University Press, Yale Station, New Haven, Connecticut 06520 (203) 432-0940; *Violence and Crime in Cross-National Perspective.*

SINGAPORE - CROPS

Asian Development Bank, P.O. Box 789, 1099 Manila, Philippines; *Key Indicators of Developing Asian and Pacific Countries.*

Commodity Research Bureau, Incorporated, 75 Wall Street, New York, New York 10005 (212) 504-7754; *Commodity Year Book.*

Facts on File, 460 Park Avenue South, New York, New York 10016 (800) 443-8323; *The New Book of World Rankings.*

Food and Agricultural Organization of the United Nations (FAO) Via delle Terme di Caracalla, 00100 Rome, Italy (Telephone Number in U.S. (202) 653-2400); *The State of Food and Agriculture.*

G.K. Hall and Company, 70 Lincoln Street, Boston, Massachusetts 02111 (617) 423-3990; *The World in Figures.*

SINGAPORE - CUSTOMS DUTIES

G.K. Hall and Company, 70 Lincoln Street, Boston, Massachusetts 02111 (617) 423-3990; *The World in Figures.*

SINGAPORE - DAIRY PRODUCTS

Facts on File, 460 Park Avenue South, New York, New York 10016 (800) 443-8323; *The New Book of World Rankings.*

Food and Agricultural Organization of the United Nations (FAO) Via delle Terme di Caracalla, 00100 Rome, Italy (Telephone Number in U.S. (202) 653-2400); *The State of Food and Agriculture.*

Statistical Office of the United Nations, Publishing Service, New York, New York 10017 (800) 253-9646; *Statistical Yearbook.*

International Monetary Fund, 700 Nineteenth Street, NW, Washington, D.C. 20431 (202) 623-7000; *Government Finance Statistics Yearbook.*

SINGAPORE - DEATH RATES

The Economist Intelligence Unit (Asia) Limited, 10th Floor, Luk Kwok Centre, 72 Gloucester Road, Wanchai, Hong Kong (Phone Number in U.S. (800) 938-4685); *Asian Market Atlas.*

Euromonitor Publications Limited, 87-88 Turnmill Street, London EC1M 5QU, England; *The Pacific Basin: An Economic Handbook,* and *Third World Economic Handbook.*

G.K. Hall and Company, 70 Lincoln Street, Boston, Massachusetts 02111 (617) 423-3990; *The World in Figures.*

Statistical Office of the United Nations, Publishing Service, New York, New York 10017 (800) 253-9646; *Statistical Yearbook.*

Times Books, 201 East 50th Street, New York, New York 10022 (212) 751-2600; *The Economist Book of Vital World Statistics.*

World Health Organization, Office of Publications, Avenue Appia, CH-1211 Geneva 27, Switzerland (Telephone Number in U.S. (518) 436-9686); *World Health Statistics Annual.*

SINGAPORE - DEFENSE EXPENDITURES

G.K. Hall and Company, 70 Lincoln Street, Boston, Massachusetts 02111 (617) 423-3990; *The World in Figures.*

International Monetary Fund, 700 Nineteenth Street, NW, Washington, D.C. 20431 (202) 623-7000; *Government Finance*

Statistics Yearbook.

U.S. Arms Control and Disarmament Agency, 320 Twenty-first Street, NW, Washington, D.C. 20451 (202) 647-8677; *World Military Expenditures and Arms Transfers.*

SINGAPORE - DEMOGRAPHY

The Economist Intelligence Unit, 111 West 57th Street, New York, New York 10019 (800) 938-4685; *The World Market Atlas.*

The Economist Intelligence Unit (Asia) Limited, 10th Floor, Luk Kwok Centre, 72 Gloucester Road, Wanchai, Hong Kong (Phone Number in U.S. (800) 938-4685); *Asian Market Atlas.*

Facts on File, 460 Park Avenue South, New York, New York 10016 (800) 443-8323; *The New Book of World Rankings.*

G.K. Hall and Company, 70 Lincoln Street, Boston, Massachusetts 02111 (617) 423-3990; *The World in Figures.*

SINGAPORE - DEVELOPMENT ASSISTANCE

Asian Development Bank, P.O. Box 789, 1099 Manila, Philippines; *Key Indicators of Developing Asian and Pacific Countries.*

G.K. Hall and Company, 70 Lincoln Street, Boston, Massachusetts 02111 (617) 423-3990; *The World in Figures.*

SINGAPORE - DIAMOND PRODUCTION - See SINGAPORE - MINING AND MINERAL PRODUCTS

SINGAPORE - DISEASES

G.K. Hall and Company, 70 Lincoln Street, Boston, Massachusetts 02111 (617) 423-3990; *The World in Figures.*

World Health Organization, Office of Publications, Avenue Appia, CH-1211 Geneva 27, Switzerland (Telephone Number in U.S. (518) 430-9080), *World Health Statistics Annual.*

SINGAPORE - DIVORCE RATES

Facts on File, 460 Park Avenue South, New York, New York 10016 (800) 443-8323; *The New Book of World Rankings.*

Statistical Office of the United Nations, Publishing Service, New York, New York 10017 (800) 253-9646; *Demographic Yearbook.*

SINGAPORE - DOMESTIC PRODUCT

G.K. Hall and Company, 70 Lincoln Street, Boston, Massachusetts 02111 (617) 423-3990; *The World in Figures.*

SINGAPORE - ECONOMY

Asian Development Bank, P.O. Box 789, 1099 Manila, Philippines; *Key Indicators of Developing Asian and Pacific Countries.*

Euromonitor Publications Limited, 87-88 Turnmill Street, London EC1M 5QU, England; *International Marketing Data and Statistics,* and *Third World Economic Handbook.*

Facts on File, 460 Park Avenue South, New York, New York 10016 (800) 443-8323; *The New Book of World Rankings.*

G.K. Hall and Company, 70 Lincoln Street, Boston, Massachusetts 02111 (617) 423-3990; *The World in Figures.*

SINGAPORE - EDUCATION

The Economist Intelligence Unit, 111 West 57th Street, New York, New York 10019 (800) 938-4685; *The World Market Atlas.*

The Economist Intelligence Unit (Asia) Limited, 10th Floor, Luk Kwok Centre, 72 Gloucester Road, Wanchai, Hong Kong (Phone Number in U.S. (800) 938-4685); *Asian Market Atlas.*

Euromonitor Publications Limited, 87-88 Turnmill Street, London EC1M 5QU, England; *The Pacific Basin: An Economic Handbook.*

Facts on File, 460 Park Avenue South, New York, New York 10016 (800) 443-8323; *The New Book of World Rankings.*

G.K. Hall and Company, 70 Lincoln Street, Boston, Massachusetts 02111 (617) 423-3990; *The World in Figures.*

International Monetary Fund, 700 Nineteenth Street, NW, Washington, D.C. 20431 (202) 623-7000; *Government Finance Statistics Yearbook.*

Statistical Office of the United Nations, Publishing Service, New York, New York 10017 (800) 253-9646; *Statistical Yearbook for Asia and the Pacific.*

Times Books, 201 East 50th Street, New York, New York 10022 (212) 751-2600; *The Economist Book of Vital World Statistics.*

United Nations Educational, Scientific and Cultural Organization (UNESCO), 7 Place de Fontenoy, F-75700 Paris, France (Telephone Number in U.S. (212) 963-5981); *Statistical Yearbook.*

The World Bank, 1818 H Street, NW, Washington, D.C. 20433 (202) 477-1234; *World Tables.*

SINGAPORE - EGG PRODUCTION AND CONSUMPTION - See SINGAPORE - DAIRY PRODUCTS

SINGAPORE - ELECTRICITY

Asian Development Bank, P.O. Box 789, 1099 Manila, Philippines; *Key Indicators of Developing Asian and Pacific Countries.*

Facts on File, 460 Park Avenue South, New York, New York 10016 (800) 443-8323; *The New Book of World Rankings.*

Statistical Office of the United Nations, Publishing Service, New York, New York 10017 (800) 253-9646; *Electric Power in Asia and the Pacific,* and *Statistical Yearbook.*

Times Books, 201 East 50th Street, New York, New York 10022 (212) 751-2600; *The Economist Book of Vital World Statistics.*

SINGAPORE - EMPLOYMENT

Euromonitor Publications Limited, 87-88 Turnmill Street, London EC1M 5QU, England; *International Marketing Data and Statistics,* and *The Pacific Basin: An Economic Handbook.*

Facts on File, 460 Park Avenue South, New York, New York 10016 (800) 443-8323; *The New Book of World Rankings.*

International Labour Office, I.L.O. Publications, CH-1211, Geneva 22, Switzerland; *Yearbook of Labour Statistics.*

Statistical Office of the United Nations, Publishing Service, New York, New York 10017 (800) 253-9646; *Statistical Yearbook.*

SINGAPORE - ENERGY

Facts on File, 460 Park Avenue South, New York, New York 10016 (800) 443-8323; *The New Book of World Rankings*.

Food and Agricultural Organization of the United Nations (FAO) Via delle Terme di Caracalla, 00100 Rome, Italy (Telephone Number in U.S. (202) 653-2400); *The State of Food and Agriculture*.

G.K. Hall and Company, 70 Lincoln Street, Boston, Massachusetts 02111 (617) 423-3990; *The World in Figures*.

Statistical Office of the United Nations, Publishing Service, New York, New York 10017 (800) 253-9646; *Energy Statistics Yearbook*, and *Statistical Yearbook*, and *Statistical Yearbook for Asia and the Pacific*.

Times Books, 201 East 50th Street, New York, New York 10022 (212) 751-2600; *The Economist Book of Vital World Statistics*.

SINGAPORE - ENGINEERING AND METAL PRODUCTS - EXPORTS AND IMPORTS

Statistical Office of the United Nations, Publishing Service, New York, New York 10017 (800) 253-9646; *Trade in Manufactures of Developing Countries*.

SINGAPORE - EXCHANGE RATES

Asian Development Bank, P.O. Box 789, 1099 Manila, Philippines; *Key Indicators of Developing Asian and Pacific Countries*.

The Economist Intelligence Unit (Asia) Limited, 10th Floor, Luk Kwok Centre, 72 Gloucester Road, Wanchai, Hong Kong (Phone Number in U.S. (800) 938-4685); *Asian Market Atlas*.

Euromonitor Publications Limited, 87-88 Turnmill Street, London EC1M 5QU, England; *International Marketing Data and Statistics*, and *The Pacific Basin: An Economic Handbook*.

International Civil Aviation Organization, 1000 Sherbrooke Street West, Suite 400, Montreal, Quebec, Canada H3A 2R2 (514) 285-8219; *Civil Aviation Statistics of the World*.

International Monetary Fund, 700 Nineteenth Street, NW, Washington, D.C. 20431 (202) 623-7000; *International Financial Statistics*.

SINGAPORE - EXCISE TAXES - See SINGAPORE - TAXATION

SINGAPORE - EXPORTS

Asian Development Bank, P.O. Box 789, 1099 Manila, Philippines; *Key Indicators of Developing Asian and Pacific Countries*.

The Economist Intelligence Unit, 111 West 57th Street, New York, New York 10019 (800) 938-4685; *The World Market Atlas*.

The Economist Intelligence Unit (Asia) Limited, 10th Floor, Luk Kwok Centre, 72 Gloucester Road, Wanchai, Hong Kong (Phone Number in U.S. (800) 938-4685); *Asian Market Atlas*.

Euromonitor Publications Limited, 87-88 Turnmill Street, London EC1M 5QU, England; *International Marketing Data and Statistics*, *The Pacific Basin: An Economic Handbook*, and *Third World Economic Handbook*.

Food and Agricultural Organization of the United Nations (FAO) Via delle Terme di Caracalla, 00100 Rome, Italy (Telephone Number in

U.S. (202) 653-2400); *The State of Food and Agriculture*.

G.K. Hall and Company, 70 Lincoln Street, Boston, Massachusetts 02111 (617) 423-3990; *The World in Figures*.

International Monetary Fund, 700 Nineteenth Street, NW, Washington, D.C. 20431 (202) 623-7000; *Direction of Trade Statistics*, and *International Financial Statistics*.

International Rubber Study Group, York House, Eighth Floor, Empire Way, Wembley, London HA9 0PA, England; *Rubber Statistical Bulletin*.

Statistical Office of the United Nations, Publishing Service, New York, New York 10017 (800) 253-9646; *Foreign Trade Statistics of Asia and the Pacific*.

Times Books, 201 East 50th Street, New York, New York 10022 (212) 751-2600; *The Economist Book of Vital World Statistics*.

The World Bank, 1818 H Street, NW, Washington, D.C. 20433 (202) 477-1234; *World Tables*.

SINGAPORE - EXTERNAL FINANCING

Asian Development Bank, P.O. Box 789, 1099 Manila, Philippines; *Key Indicators of Developing Asian and Pacific Countries*.

SINGAPORE - EXTERNAL INDEBTEDNESS

Asian Development Bank, P.O. Box 789, 1099 Manila, Philippines; *Key Indicators of Developing Asian and Pacific Countries*.

Euromonitor Publications Limited, 87-88 Turnmill Street, London EC1M 5QU, England; *Third World Economic Handbook*.

The World Bank, 1818 H Street, NW, Washington, D.C. 20433 (202) 477-1234; *World Tables*.

SINGAPORE - EXTERNAL TRADE

Asian Development Bank, P.O. Box 789, 1099 Manila, Philippines; *Key Indicators of Developing Asian and Pacific Countries*.

Food and Agricultural Organization of the United Nations (FAO) Via delle Terme di Caracalla, 00100 Rome, Italy (Telephone Number in U.S. (202) 653-2400); *The State of Food and Agriculture*, and *Trade Yearbook*.

G.K. Hall and Company, 70 Lincoln Street, Boston, Massachusetts 02111 (617) 423-3990; *The World in Figures*.

Statistical Office of the United Nations, Publishing Service, New York, New York 10017 (800) 253-9646; *Statistical Yearbook*, and *Statistical Yearbook for Asia and the Pacific*.

SINGAPORE - FARM CROPS - See SINGAPORE - CROPS

SINGAPORE - FEMALE WORKING POPULATION - See SINGAPORE - EMPLOYMENT

SINGAPORE - FERTILITY RATES

The Economist Intelligence Unit (Asia) Limited, 10th Floor, Luk Kwok Centre, 72 Gloucester Road, Wanchai, Hong Kong (Phone Number in U.S. (800) 938-4685); *Asian Market Atlas*.

Facts on File, 460 Park Avenue South, New York, New York 10016 (800) 443-8323; *The New Book of World Rankings*.

Times Books, 201 East 50th Street, New York, New York 10022 (212) 751-2600; *The Economist Book of Vital World Statistics.*

The World Bank, 1818 H Street, NW, Washington, D.C. 20433 (202) 477-1234; *World Tables.*

SINGAPORE - FERTILIZER

Food and Agricultural Organization of the United Nations (FAO) Via delle Terme di Caracalla, 00100 Rome, Italy (Telephone Number in U.S. (202) 653-2400); *The State of Food and Agriculture.*

Statistical Office of the United Nations, Publishing Service, New York, New York 10017 (800) 253-9646; *Statistical Yearbook.*

SINGAPORE - FETAL MORTALITY

Statistical Office of the United Nations, Publishing Service, New York, New York 10017 (800) 253-9646; *Demographic Yearbook.*

World Health Organization, Office of Publications, Avenue Appia, CH-1211 Geneva 27, Switzerland (Telephone Number in U.S. (518) 436-9686); *World Health Statistics Annual.*

SINGAPORE - FILAMENT PRODUCTION - See SINGAPORE - TEXTILE INDUSTRY

SINGAPORE - FILM - See SINGAPORE - MOTION PICTURES

SINGAPORE - FINANCE

Asian Development Bank, P.O. Box 789, 1099 Manila, Philippines; *Key Indicators of Developing Asian and Pacific Countries.*

Euromonitor Publications Limited, 87-88 Turnmill Street, London EC1M 5QU, England; *The Pacific Basin: An Economic Handbook.*

Facts on File, 460 Park Avenue South, New York, New York 10016 (800) 443-8323; *The New Book of World Rankings.*

G.K. Hall and Company, 70 Lincoln Street, Boston, Massachusetts 02111 (617) 423-3990; *The World in Figures.*

International Monetary Fund, 700 Nineteenth Street, NW, Washington, D.C. 20431 (202) 623-7000; *Government Finance Statistics Yearbook.*

Statistical Office of the United Nations, Publishing Service, New York, New York 10017 (800) 253-9646; *Statistical Yearbook for Asia and the Pacific.*

SINGAPORE - FISHERIES

Facts on File, 460 Park Avenue South, New York, New York 10016 (800) 443-8323; *The New Book of World Rankings.*

Food and Agricultural Organization of the United Nations (FAO) Via delle Terme di Caracalla, 00100 Rome, Italy (Telephone Number in U.S. (202) 653-2400); *The State of Food and Agriculture,* and *Yearbook of Fishery Statistics.*

Statistical Office of the United Nations, Publishing Service, New York, New York 10017 (800) 253-9646; *Statistical Yearbook.*

SINGAPORE - FOOD

Food and Agricultural Organization of the United Nations (FAO) Via delle Terme di Caracalla, 00100 Rome, Italy (Telephone Number in U.S. (202) 653-2400); *Production Yearbook,* and *The State of Food*

and Agriculture.

G.K. Hall and Company, 70 Lincoln Street, Boston, Massachusetts 02111 (617) 423-3990; *The World in Figures.*

SINGAPORE - FOREIGN AID

G.K. Hall and Company, 70 Lincoln Street, Boston, Massachusetts 02111 (617) 423-3990; *The World in Figures.*

SINGAPORE - FOREIGN DEBT

International Monetary Fund, 700 Nineteenth Street, NW, Washington, D.C. 20431 (202) 623-7000; *Government Finance Statistics Yearbook.*

SINGAPORE - FOREIGN INDEBTEDNESS

Euromonitor Publications Limited, 87-88 Turnmill Street, London EC1M 5QU, England; *The Pacific Basin: An Economic Handbook.*

SINGAPORE - FOREIGN TRADE

Asian Development Bank, P.O. Box 789, 1099 Manila, Philippines; *Key Indicators of Developing Asian and Pacific Countries.*

The Economist Intelligence Unit (Asia) Limited, 10th Floor, Luk Kwok Centre, 72 Gloucester Road, Wanchai, Hong Kong (Phone Number in U.S. (800) 938-4685); *Asian Market Atlas.*

Euromonitor Publications Limited, 87-88 Turnmill Street, London EC1M 5QU, England; *International Marketing Data and Statistics, The Pacific Basin: An Economic Handbook,* and *Third World Economic Handbook.*

Facts on File, 460 Park Avenue South, New York, New York 10016 (800) 443-8323; *The New Book of World Rankings.*

Food and Agricultural Organization of the United Nations (FAO) Via delle Terme di Caracalla, 00100 Rome, Italy (Telephone Number in U.S. (202) 653-2400); *The State of Food and Agriculture.*

G.K. Hall and Company, 70 Lincoln Street, Boston, Massachusetts 02111 (617) 423-3990; *The World in Figures.*

International Monetary Fund, 700 Nineteenth Street, NW, Washington, D.C. 20431 (202) 623-7000; *International Financial Statistics.*

Statistical Office of the United Nations, Publishing Service, New York, New York 10017 (800) 253-9646; *International Trade Statistics Yearbook,* and *Statistical Yearbook.*

The World Bank, 1818 H Street, NW, Washington, D.C. 20433 (202) 477-1234; *World Tables.*

SINGAPORE - FORESTRY AND FOREST PRODUCTS

The Economist Intelligence Unit (Asia) Limited, 10th Floor, Luk Kwok Centre, 72 Gloucester Road, Wanchai, Hong Kong (Phone Number in U.S. (800) 938-4685); *Asian Market Atlas.*

Euromonitor Publications Limited, 87-88 Turnmill Street, London EC1M 5QU, England; *Third World Economic Handbook.*

Facts on File, 460 Park Avenue South, New York, New York 10016 (800) 443-8323; *The New Book of World Rankings.*

Food and Agricultural Organization of the United Nations (FAO) Via delle Terme di Caracalla, 00100 Rome, Italy (Telephone Number in U.S. (202) 653-2400); *The State of Food and Agriculture,* and *Yearbook of Forest Products.*

G.K. Hall and Company, 70 Lincoln Street, Boston, Massachusetts 02111 (617) 423-3990; *The World in Figures.*

United Nations Educational, Scientific and Cultural Organization (UNESCO), 7 Place de Fontenoy, F-75700 Paris, France (Telephone Number in U.S. (212) 963-5981); *Statistical Yearbook.*

SINGAPORE - FURNITURE AND WOOD PRODUCTS - EXPORTS AND IMPORTS

Statistical Office of the United Nations, Publishing Service, New York, New York 10017 (800) 253-9646; *Trade in Manufacture of Developing Countries.*

SINGAPORE - GAS PRODUCTION - See SINGAPORE - MINING AND MINERAL PRODUCTS

SINGAPORE - GENERAL INDUSTRIAL STATISTICS

Statistical Office of the United Nations, Publishing Service, New York, New York 10017 (800) 253-9646; *Industrial Statistics Yearbook.*

SINGAPORE - GENERAL MORTALITY

Statistical Office of the United Nations, Publishing Service, New York, New York 10017 (800) 253-9646; *Demographic Yearbook.*

World Health Organization, Office of Publications, Avenue Appia, CH-1211 Geneva 27, Switzerland (Telephone Number in U.S. (518) 436-9686); *World Health Statistics Annual.*

SINGAPORE - GEOGRAPHIC DATA

Facts on File, 460 Park Avenue South, New York, New York 10016 (800) 443-8323; *The New Book of World Rankings.*

SINGAPORE - GOATS - See SINGAPORE - LIVESTOCK AND POULTRY

SINGAPORE - GOLD HOLDINGS

Statistical Office of the United Nations, Publishing Service, New York, New York 10017 (800) 253-9646; *Statistical Yearbook.*

The World Bank, 1818 H Street, NW, Washington, D.C. 20433 (202) 477-1234; *World Tables.*

SINGAPORE - GOLD PRODUCTION AND CONSUMPTION - See SINGAPORE - MINING AND MINERAL PRODUCTS

SINGAPORE - GOVERNMENT

Asian Development Bank, P.O. Box 789, 1099 Manila, Philippines; *Key Indicators of Developing Asian and Pacific Countries.*

G.K. Hall and Company, 70 Lincoln Street, Boston, Massachusetts 02111 (617) 423-3990; *The World in Figures.*

SINGAPORE - GOVERNMENT CONSUMPTION

International Monetary Fund, 700 Nineteenth Street, NW, Washington, D.C. 20431 (202) 623-7000; *International Financial Statistics.*

SINGAPORE - GOVERNMENT EXPENDITURES

Asian Development Bank, P.O. Box 789, 1099 Manila, Philippines; *Key Indicators of Developing Asian and Pacific Countries.*

Euromonitor Publications Limited, 87-88 Turnmill Street, London EC1M 5QU, England; *Third World Economic Handbook.*

International Monetary Fund, 700 Nineteenth Street, NW, Washington, D.C. 20431 (202) 623-7000; *Government Finance Statistics Yearbook.*

Times Books, 201 East 50th Street, New York, New York 10022 (212) 751-2600; *The Economist Book of Vital World Statistics.*

The World Bank, 1818 H Street, NW, Washington, D.C. 20433 (202) 477-1234; *World Tables.*

SINGAPORE - GOVERNMENT FINANCES

Asian Development Bank, P.O. Box 789, 1099 Manila, Philippines; *Key Indicators of Developing Asian and Pacific Countries.*

International Monetary Fund, 700 Nineteenth Street, NW, Washington, D.C. 20431 (202) 623-7000; *International Financial Statistics.*

SINGAPORE - GOVERNMENT REVENUE

Asian Development Bank, P.O. Box 789, 1099 Manila, Philippines; *Key Indicators of Developing Asian and Pacific Countries.*

International Monetary Fund, 700 Nineteenth Street, NW, Washington, D.C. 20431 (202) 623-7000; *Government Finance Statistics Yearbook.*

Times Books, 201 East 50th Street, New York, New York 10022 (212) 751-2600; *The Economist Book of Vital World Statistics.*

The World Bank, 1818 H Street, NW, Washington, D.C. 20433 (202) 477-1234; *World Tables.*

SINGAPORE - GRAIN PRODUCTION - See SINGAPORE - CROPS

SINGAPORE - GRANTS

International Monetary Fund, 700 Nineteenth Street, NW, Washington, D.C. 20431 (202) 623-7000; *Government Finance Statistics Yearbook.*

SINGAPORE - GROSS DOMESTIC PRODUCT

Asian Development Bank, P.O. Box 789, 1099 Manila, Philippines; *Key Indicators of Developing Asian and Pacific Countries.*

The Economist Intelligence Unit, 111 West 57th Street, New York, New York 10019 (800) 938-4685; *The World Market Atlas.*

The Economist Intelligence Unit (Asia) Limited, 10th Floor, Luk Kwok Centre, 72 Gloucester Road, Wanchai, Hong Kong (Phone Number in U.S. (800) 938-4685); *Asian Market Atlas.*

Euromonitor Publications Limited, 87-88 Turnmill Street, London EC1M 5QU, England; *International Marketing Data and Statistics,* and *The Pacific Basin: An Economic Handbook.*

Facts on File, 460 Park Avenue South, New York, New York 10016 (800) 443-8323; *The New Book of World Rankings.*

G.K. Hall and Company, 70 Lincoln Street, Boston, Massachusetts 02111 (617) 423-3990; *The World in Figures.*

Statistical Office of the United Nations, Publishing Service, New York, New York 10017 (800) 253-9646; *Statistical Yearbook.*

Times Books, 201 East 50th Street, New York, New York 10022 (212) 751-2600; *The Economist Book of Vital World Statistics.*

U.S. Arms Control and Disarmament Agency, 320 Twenty-first Street, NW, Washington, D.C. 20451 (202) 647-8677; *World Military Expenditures and Arms Transfers.*

The World Bank, 1818 H Street, NW, Washington, D.C. 20433 (202) 477-1234; *World Tables.*

SINGAPORE - GROSS INDUSTRIAL PRODUCT

Euromonitor Publications Limited, 87-88 Turnmill Street, London EC1M 5QU, England; *Third World Economic Handbook.*

SINGAPORE - GROSS NATIONAL PRODUCT

Asian Development Bank, P.O. Box 789, 1099 Manila, Philippines; *Key Indicators of Developing Asian and Pacific Countries.*

Euromonitor Publications Limited, 87-88 Turnmill Street, London EC1M 5QU, England; *International Marketing Data and Statistics,* and *Third World Economic Handbook.*

The World Bank, 1818 H Street, NW, Washington, D.C. 20433 (202) 477-1234; *World Tables.*

SINGAPORE - HEALTH

The Economist Intelligence Unit (Asia) Limited, 10th Floor, Luk Kwok Centre, 72 Gloucester Road, Wanchai, Hong Kong (Phone Number in U.S. (000) 900-4005), *Asian Market Atlas.*

Euromonitor Publications Limited, 87-88 Turnmill Street, London EC1M 5QU, England; *The Pacific Basin: An Economic Handbook.*

Facts on File, 460 Park Avenue South, New York, New York 10016 (800) 443-8323; *The New Book of World Rankings.*

G.K. Hall and Company, 70 Lincoln Street, Boston, Massachusetts 02111 (617) 423-3990; *The World in Figures.*

Statistical Office of the United Nations, Publishing Service, New York, New York 10017 (800) 253-9646; *Statistical Yearbook.*

Times Books, 201 East 50th Street, New York, New York 10022 (212) 751-2600; *The Economist Book of Vital World Statistics.*

World Health Organization, Office of Publications, Avenue Appia, CH-1211 Geneva 27, Switzerland (Telephone Number in U.S. (518) 436-9686); *World Health Statistics Annual.*

SINGAPORE - HEALTH EXPENDITURES

International Monetary Fund, 700 Nineteenth Street, NW, Washington, D.C. 20431 (202) 623-7000; *Government Finance Statistics Yearbook.*

SINGAPORE - HIGHWAYS

The Economist Intelligence Unit (Asia) Limited, 10th Floor, Luk Kwok Centre, 72 Gloucester Road, Wanchai, Hong Kong (Phone Number in U.S. (800) 938-4685); *Asian Market Atlas.*

G.K. Hall and Company, 70 Lincoln Street, Boston, Massachusetts 02111 (617) 423-3990; *The World in Figures.*

International Road Federation, 525 School Street, SW, Washington, D.C. 20024 (202) 554-2106; *World Road Statistics.*

SINGAPORE - HORSES - See SINGAPORE - LIVESTOCK AND POULTRY

SINGAPORE - HOURS OF WORK - See SINGAPORE - EMPLOYMENT

SINGAPORE - HOUSING AND HOUSING UNITS

Euromonitor Publications Limited, 87-88 Turnmill Street, London EC1M 5QU, England; *Third World Economic Handbook.*

Facts on File, 460 Park Avenue South, New York, New York 10016 (800) 443-8323; *The New Book of World Rankings.*

Statistical Office of the United Nations, Publishing Service, New York, New York 10017 (800) 253-9646; *Statistical Yearbook.*

SINGAPORE - HOUSING EXPENDITURES

International Monetary Fund, 700 Nineteenth Street, NW, Washington, D.C. 20431 (202) 623-7000; *Government Finance Statistics Yearbook.*

SINGAPORE - ILLITERATE POPULATION

The Economist Intelligence Unit, 111 West 57th Street, New York, New York 10019 (800) 938-4685; *The World Market Atlas.*

G.K. Hall and Company, 70 Lincoln Street, Boston, Massachusetts 02111 (617) 423-3990; *The World in Figures.*

United Nations Educational, Scientific and Cultural Organization (UNESCO), 7 Place de Fontenoy, F-75700 Paris, France (Telephone Number in U.S. (212) 963-5981); *Statistical Yearbook.*

SINGAPORE - IMPORTS

Asian Development Bank, P.O. Box 789, 1099 Manila, Philippines; *Key Indicators of Developing Asian and Pacific Countries.*

The Economist Intelligence Unit, 111 West 57th Street, New York, New York 10019 (800) 938-4685; *The World Market Atlas.*

The Economist Intelligence Unit (Asia) Limited, 10th Floor, Luk Kwok Centre, 72 Gloucester Road, Wanchai, Hong Kong (Phone Number in U.S. (800) 938-4685); *Asian Market Atlas.*

Euromonitor Publications Limited, 87-88 Turnmill Street, London EC1M 5QU, England; *International Marketing Data and Statistics, The Pacific Basin: An Economic Handbook,* and *Third World Economic Handbook.*

Food and Agricultural Organization of the United Nations (FAO) Via delle Terme di Caracalla, 00100 Rome, Italy (Telephone Number in U.S. (202) 653-2400); *The State of Food and Agriculture.*

G.K. Hall and Company, 70 Lincoln Street, Boston, Massachusetts 02111 (617) 423-3990; *The World in Figures.*

International Monetary Fund, 700 Nineteenth Street, NW, Washington, D.C. 20431 (202) 623-7000; *Direction of Trade Statistics, Government Finance Statistics Yearbook,* and *International Financial Statistics.*

International Rubber Study Group, York House, Eighth Floor, Empire Way, Wembley, London HA9 0PA, England; *Rubber Statistical Bulletin.*

Statistical Office of the United Nations, Publishing Service, New York, New York 10017 (800) 253-9646; *Foreign Trade Statistics of Asia and the Pacific,* and *Trade in Manufactures of Developing Countries.*

Times Books, 201 East 50th Street, New York, New York 10022 (212) 751-2600; *The Economist Book of Vital World Statistics.*

The World Bank, 1818 H Street, NW, Washington, D.C. 20433 (202) 477-1234; *World Tables.*

SINGAPORE - INCOME TAXES - See SINGAPORE - TAXATION

SINGAPORE - INDUSTRY

Euromonitor Publications Limited, 87-88 Turnmill Street, London EC1M 5QU, England; *Third World Economic Handbook.*

Facts on File, 460 Park Avenue South, New York, New York 10016 (800) 443-8323; *The New Book of World Rankings.*

G.K. Hall and Company, 70 Lincoln Street, Boston, Massachusetts 02111 (617) 423-3990; *The World in Figures.*

International Labour Office, I.L.O. Publications, CH-1211, Geneva 22, Switzerland; *Yearbook of Labour Statistics.*

Statistical Office of the United Nations, Publishing Service, New York, New York 10017 (800) 253-9646; *Statistical Yearbook,* and *Statistical Yearbook for Asia and the Pacific.*

Times Books, 201 East 50th Street, New York, New York 10022 (212) 751-2600; *The Economist Book of Vital World Statistics.*

The World Bank, 1818 H Street, NW, Washington, D.C. 20433 (202) 477-1234; *World Tables.*

World Intellectual Property Organization, 34 Chemin des Colombettes, CH-1211 Geneva 20. Switzerland; *Industrial Property Statistics.*

SINGAPORE - INFANT AND MATERNAL MORTALITY

The Economist Intelligence Unit (Asia) Limited, 10th Floor, Luk Kwok Centre, 72 Gloucester Road, Wanchai, Hong Kong (Phone Number in U.S. (800) 938-4685); *Asian Market Atlas.*

Statistical Office of the United Nations, Publishing Service, New York, New York 10017 (800) 253-9646; *Demographic Yearbook,* and *Statistical Yearbook.*

Times Books, 201 East 50th Street, New York, New York 10022 (212) 751-2600; *The Economist Book of Vital World Statistics.*

The World Bank, 1818 H Street, NW, Washington, D.C. 20433 (202) 477-1234; *World Tables.*

World Health Organization, Office of Publications, Avenue Appia, CH-1211 Geneva 27, Switzerland (Telephone Number in U.S. (518) 436-9686); *World Health Statistics Annual.*

SINGAPORE - INTEREST RATES

Euromonitor Publications Limited, 87-88 Turnmill Street, London EC1M 5QU, England; *The Pacific Basin: An Economic Handbook.*

SINGAPORE - INTERNAL TRADE

Statistical Office of the United Nations, Publishing Service, New York, New York 10017 (800) 253-9646; *Statistical Yearbook,* and *Statistical Yearbook for Asia and the Pacific.*

SINGAPORE - INTERNATIONAL LIQUIDITY

International Monetary Fund, 700 Nineteenth Street, NW, Washington, D.C. 20431 (202) 623-7000; *International Financial Statistics.*

SINGAPORE - INTERNATIONAL RESERVES EXCLUDING GOLD

Asian Development Bank, P.O. Box 789, 1099 Manila, Philippines; *Key Indicators of Developing Asian and Pacific Countries.*

Statistical Office of the United Nations, Publishing Service, New York, New York 10017 (800) 253-9646; *Statistical Yearbook.*

The World Bank, 1818 H Street, NW, Washington, D.C. 20433 (202) 477-1234; *World Tables.*

SINGAPORE - INTERNATIONAL STATISTICS

Asian Development Bank, P.O. Box 789, 1099 Manila, Philippines; *Key Indicators of Developing Asian and Pacific Countries.*

SINGAPORE - INVESTMENTS

International Monetary Fund, 700 Nineteenth Street, NW, Washington, D.C. 20431 (202) 623-7000; *International Financial Statistics.*

SINGAPORE - IRON ORE PRODUCTION AND CONSUMPTION - See SINGAPORE - MINING AND MINERAL PRODUCTS

SINGAPORE - IRRIGATION

Euromonitor Publications Limited, 87-88 Turnmill Street, London EC1M 5QU, England; *International Marketing Data and Statistics.*

SINGAPORE - LABOR FORCE

The Economist Intelligence Unit (Asia) Limited, 10th Floor, Luk Kwok Centre, 72 Gloucester Road, Wanchai, Hong Kong (Phone Number in U.S. (800) 938-4685); *Asian Market Atlas.*

Euromonitor Publications Limited, 87-88 Turnmill Street, London EC1M 5QU, England; *International Marketing Data and Statistics,* and *The Pacific Basin: An Economic Handbook.*

Facts on File, 460 Park Avenue South, New York, New York 10016 (800) 443-8323; *The New Book of World Rankings.*

Food and Agricultural Organization of the United Nations (FAO) Via delle Terme di Caracalla, 00100 Rome, Italy (Telephone Number in U.S. (202) 653-2400); *The State of Food and Agriculture.*

G.K. Hall and Company, 70 Lincoln Street, Boston, Massachusetts 02111 (617) 423-3990; *The World in Figures.*

Times Books, 201 East 50th Street, New York, New York 10022 (212) 751-2600; *The Economist Book of Vital World Statistics.*

The World Bank, 1818 H Street, NW, Washington, D.C. 20433 (202) 477-1234; *World Tables.*

SINGAPORE - LABOR PRODUCTIVITY

International Labour Office, I.L.O. Publications, CH-1211, Geneva 22, Switzerland; *Yearbook of Labour Statistics*.

SINGAPORE - LAND USE

Euromonitor Publications Limited, 87-88 Turnmill Street, London EC1M 5QU, England; *International Marketing Data and Statistics*.

Food and Agricultural Organization of the United Nations (FAO), Via delle Terme di Caracalla, 00100 Rome, Italy (Telephone Number in U.S. (202) 653-2400); *Production Yearbook*.

G.K. Hall and Company, 70 Lincoln Street, Boston, Massachusetts 02111 (617) 423-3990; *The World in Figures*.

SINGAPORE - LIBRARIES

Facts on File, 460 Park Avenue South, New York, New York 10016 (800) 443-8323; *The New Book of World Rankings*.

United Nations Educational, Scientific and Cultural Organization (UNESCO), 7 Place de Fontenoy, F-75700 Paris, France (Telephone Number in U.S. (212) 963-5981); *Statistical Yearbook*.

SINGAPORE - LIFE EXPECTANCY

The Economist Intelligence Unit (Asia) Limited, 10th Floor, Luk Kwok Centre, 72 Gloucester Road, Wanchai, Hong Kong (Phone Number in U.S. (800) 938-4685); *Asian Market Atlas*.

SINGAPORE - LIVESTOCK AND POULTRY

Euromonitor Publications Limited, 87-88 Turnmill Street, London EC1M 5QU, England; *International Marketing Data and Statistics*.

Facts on File, 460 Park Avenue South, New York, New York 10016 (800) 443-8323; *The New Book of World Rankings*.

Food and Agricultural Organization of the United Nations (FAO), Via delle Terme di Caracalla, 00100 Rome, Italy (Telephone Number in U.S. (202) 653-2400); *Production Yearbook*, and *The State of Food and Agriculture*.

G.K. Hall and Company, 70 Lincoln Street, Boston, Massachusetts 02111 (617) 423-3990; *The World in Figures*.

Statistical Office of the United Nations, Publishing Service, New York, New York 10017 (800) 253-9646; *Statistical Yearbook*.

SINGAPORE - LIVING LEVELS

G.K. Hall and Company, 70 Lincoln Street, Boston, Massachusetts 02111 (617) 423-3990; *The World in Figures*.

Times Books, 201 East 50th Street, New York, New York 10022 (212) 751-2600; *The Economist Book of Vital World Statistics*.

SINGAPORE - MAIL - NUMBER OF ITEMS SENT OR RECEIVED

Statistical Office of the United Nations, Publishing Service, New York, New York 10017 (800) 253-9646; *Statistical Yearbook*.

SINGAPORE - MANPOWER

Statistical Office of the United Nations, Publishing Service, New York, New York 10017 (800) 253-9646; *Statistical Yearbook for Asia and the Pacific*.

SINGAPORE - MANUFACTURING

Asian Development Bank, P.O. Box 789, 1099 Manila, Philippines; *Key Indicators of Developing Asian and Pacific Countries*.

Euromonitor Publications Limited, 87-88 Turnmill Street, London EC1M 5QU, England; *Third World Economic Handbook*.

Facts on File, 460 Park Avenue South, New York, New York 10016 (800) 443-8323; *The New Book of World Rankings*.

G.K. Hall and Company, 70 Lincoln Street, Boston, Massachusetts 02111 (617) 423-3990; *The World in Figures*.

Statistical Office of the United Nations, Publishing Service, New York, New York 10017 (800) 253-9646; *Statistical Yearbook*.

Times Books, 201 East 50th Street, New York, New York 10022 (212) 751-2600; *The Economist Book of Vital World Statistics*.

The World Bank, 1818 H Street, NW, Washington, D.C. 20433 (202) 477-1234; *World Tables*.

SINGAPORE - MARRIAGE RATES

Facts on File, 460 Park Avenue South, New York, New York 10016 (800) 443-8323; *The New Book of World Rankings*.

Statistical Office of the United Nations, Publishing Service, New York, New York 10017 (800) 253-9646; *Demographic Yearbook*, and *Statistical Yearbook*.

SINGAPORE - MEAT PRODUCTION - See SINGAPORE LIVESTOCK AND POULTRY

SINGAPORE - MERCHANT SHIPPING

G.K. Hall and Company, 70 Lincoln Street, Boston, Massachusetts 02111 (617) 423-3990; *The World in Figures*.

Lloyd's Register of Shipping, 17 Battery Place, New York, New York 10004 (212) 425-8050; *Register of Ships*.

Statistical Office of the United Nations, Publishing Service, New York, New York 10017 (800) 253-9646; *Statistical Yearbook*.

Times Books, 201 East 50th Street, New York, New York 10022 (212) 751-2600; *The Economist Book of Vital World Statistics*.

U.S. Department of Transportation, Maritime Administration, 400 Seventh Street, SW, Washington, D.C. 20590 (202) 366-5807; *A Statistical Analysis of the World's Merchant Fleets*.

SINGAPORE - MILITARY

The Economist Intelligence Unit (Asia) Limited, 10th Floor, Luk Kwok Centre, 72 Gloucester Road, Wanchai, Hong Kong (Phone Number in U.S. (800) 938-4685); *Asian Market Atlas*.

G.K. Hall and Company, 70 Lincoln Street, Boston, Massachusetts 02111 (617) 423-3990; *The World in Figures*.

The International Institute for Strategic Studies, 23 Tavistock Street, London WC2E 7NQ, England; *The Military Balance*.

U.S. Arms Control and Disarmament Agency, 320 Twenty-first Street, NW, Washington, D.C. 20451 (202) 647-8677; *World Military Expenditures and Arms Transfers*.

SINGAPORE - MILK PRODUCTION - See SINGAPORE - DAIRY PRODUCTS

SINGAPORE - MINING AND MINERAL PRODUCTS

Asian Development Bank, P.O. Box 789, 1099 Manila, Philippines; *Key Indicators of Developing Asian and Pacific Countries.*

Euromonitor Publications Limited, 87-88 Turnmill Street, London EC1M 5QU, England; *Third World Economic Handbook.*

Facts on File, 460 Park Avenue South, New York, New York 10016 (800) 443-8323; *The New Book of World Rankings.*

G.K. Hall and Company, 70 Lincoln Street, Boston, Massachusetts 02111 (617) 423-3990; *The World in Figures.*

Statistical Office of the United Nations, Publishing Service, New York, New York 10017 (800) 253-9646; *Statistical Yearbook.*

SINGAPORE - MONEY EXCHANGE RATE

Euromonitor Publications Limited, 87-88 Turnmill Street, London EC1M 5QU, England; *International Marketing Data and Statistics.*

International Monetary Fund, 700 Nineteenth Street, NW, Washington, D.C. 20431 (202) 623-7000; *International Financial Statistics.*

Statistical Office of the United Nations, Publishing Service, New York, New York 10017 (800) 253-9646; *Statistical Yearbook.*

SINGAPORE - MONEY RESERVES

Euromonitor Publications Limited, 87-88 Turnmill Street, London EC1M 5QU, England; *International Marketing Data and Statistics.*

SINGAPORE - MONEY SUPPLY

Asian Development Bank, P.O. Box 789, 1099 Manila, Philippines; *Key Indicators of Developing Asian and Pacific Countries.*

Euromonitor Publications Limited, 87-88 Turnmill Street, London EC1M 5QU, England; *International Marketing Data and Statistics.*

G.K. Hall and Company, 70 Lincoln Street, Boston, Massachusetts 02111 (617) 423-3990; *The World in Figures.*

International Monetary Fund, 700 Nineteenth Street, NW, Washington, D.C. 20431 (202) 623-7000; *International Financial Statistics.*

Statistical Office of the United Nations, Publishing Service, New York, New York 10017 (800) 253-9646; *Statistical Yearbook.*

The World Bank, 1818 H Street, NW, Washington, D.C. 20433 (202) 477-1234; *World Tables.*

SINGAPORE - MONUMENTS AND HISTORICAL SITES

United Nations Educational, Scientific and Cultural Organization (UNESCO), 7 Place de Fontenoy, F-75700 Paris, France (Telephone Number in U.S. (212) 963-5981); *Statistical Yearbook.*

SINGAPORE - MOTION PICTURES

Statistical Office of the United Nations, Publishing Service, New York, New York 10017 (800) 253-9646; *Statistical Yearbook.*

United Nations Educational, Scientific and Cultural Organization (UNESCO), 7 Place de Fontenoy, F-75700 Paris, France (Telephone Number in U.S. (212) 963-5981); *Statistical Yearbook.*

SINGAPORE - MOTOR VEHICLE TAXES - See SINGAPORE - TAXATION

SINGAPORE - MOTOR VEHICLES IN USE

G.K. Hall and Company, 70 Lincoln Street, Boston, Massachusetts 02111 (617) 423-3990; *The World in Figures.*

International Road Federation, 525 School Street, SW, Washington, D.C. 20024 (202) 554-2106; *World Road Statistics.*

Statistical Office of the United Nations, Publishing Service, New York, New York 10017 (800) 253-9646; *Statistical Yearbook.*

SINGAPORE - MUSEUMS

Facts on File, 460 Park Avenue South, New York, New York 10016 (800) 443-8323; *The New Book of World Rankings.*

United Nations Educational, Scientific and Cultural Organization (UNESCO), 7 Place de Fontenoy, F-75700 Paris, France (Telephone Number in U.S. (212) 963-5981); *Statistical Yearbook.*

SINGAPORE - NATALITY - See SINGAPORE - BIRTH RATE

SINGAPORE - NATIONAL ACCOUNTS

International Monetary Fund, 700 Nineteenth Street, NW, Washington, D.C. 20431 (202) 623-7000; *International Financial Statistics.*

Statistical Office of the United Nations, Publishing Service, New York, New York 10017 (800) 253-9646; *National Accounts Statistics,* and *Statistical Yearbook,* and *Statistical Yearbook for Asia and the Pacific.*

SINGAPORE - NATIONAL INCOME

Facts on File, 460 Park Avenue South, New York, New York 10016 (800) 443-8323; *The New Book of World Rankings.*

G.K. Hall and Company, 70 Lincoln Street, Boston, Massachusetts 02111 (617) 423-3990; *The World in Figures.*

Statistical Office of the United Nations, Publishing Service, New York, New York 10017 (800) 253-9646; *Statistical Yearbook.*

SINGAPORE - NATIONAL PRODUCT

Facts on File, 460 Park Avenue South, New York, New York 10016 (800) 443-8323; *The New Book of World Rankings.*

Statistical Office of the United Nations, Publishing Service, New York, New York 10017 (800) 253-9646; *Statistical Yearbook.*

SINGAPORE - NATURAL GAS PRODUCTION - See SINGAPORE - MINING AND MINERAL PRODUCTS

SINGAPORE - NATURAL RUBBER PRODUCTION

International Rubber Study Group, York House, Eighth Floor, Empire Way, Wembley, London HA9 0PA, England; *Rubber Statistical Bulletin.*

SINGAPORE - NEWSPAPER PRODUCTION AND CONSUMPTION - See SINGAPORE - FORESTRY AND FOREST PRODUCTS

SINGAPORE - NEWSPRINT - See SINGAPORE - FORESTRY AND FOREST PRODUCTS

SINGAPORE - OCCUPATIONS - See SINGAPORE - LABOR FORCE

SINGAPORE - PAPER - See SINGAPORE - FORESTRY AND FOREST PRODUCTS

SINGAPORE - PATENTS

Statistical Office of the United Nations, Publishing Service, New York, New York 10017 (800) 253-9646; *Statistical Yearbook.*

World Intellectual Property Organization, 34 Chemin des Colombettes, CH-1211 Geneva 20. Switzerland; *Industrial Property Statistics.*

SINGAPORE - PEANUT PRODUCTION - See SINGAPORE - CROPS

SINGAPORE - PEPPER PRODUCTION - See SINGAPORE - CROPS

SINGAPORE - PERIODICALS

United Nations Educational, Scientific and Cultural Organization (UNESCO), 7 Place de Fontenoy, F-75700 Paris, France (Telephone Number in U.S. (212) 903-5901); *Statistical Yearbook.*

SINGAPORE - PESTICIDE USE

Food and Agricultural Organization of the United Nations (FAO) Via delle Terme di Caracalla. 00100 Rome. Italy (Telephone Number in U.S. (202) 653-2400); *The State of Food and Agriculture.*

SINGAPORE - PETROLEUM INDUSTRY

Asian Development Bank, P.O. Box 789, 1099 Manila, Philippines; *Key Indicators of Developing Asian and Pacific Countries.*

Facts on File, 460 Park Avenue South, New York, New York 10016 (800) 443-8323; *The New Book of World Rankings.*

Food and Agricultural Organization of the United Nations (FAO) Via delle Terme di Caracalla, 00100 Rome, Italy (Telephone Number in U.S. (202) 653-2400); *The State of Food and Agriculture.*

G.K. Hall and Company, 70 Lincoln Street, Boston, Massachusetts 02111 (617) 423-3990; *The World in Figures.*

Statistical Office of the United Nations, Publishing Service, New York, New York 10017 (800) 253-9646; *Statistical Yearbook.*

SINGAPORE - PIGS - See SINGAPORE - LIVESTOCK AND POULTRY

SINGAPORE - PLASTIC AND RESIN PRODUCTION

Euromonitor Publications Limited, 87-88 Turnmill Street, London EC1M 5QU, England; *Third World Economic Handbook.*

SINGAPORE - POPULATION

Asian Development Bank, P.O. Box 789, 1099 Manila, Philippines; *Key Indicators of Developing Asian and Pacific Countries.*

The Economist Intelligence Unit, 111 West 57th Street, New York, New York 10019 (800) 938-4685; *The World Market Atlas.*

The Economist Intelligence Unit (Asia) Limited, 10th Floor, Luk Kwok Centre, 72 Gloucester Road, Wanchai, Hong Kong (Phone Number in U.S. (800) 938-4685); *Asian Market Atlas.*

Euromonitor Publications Limited, 87-88 Turnmill Street, London EC1M 5QU, England; *International Marketing Data and Statistics, The Pacific Basin: An Economic Handbook,* and *Third World Economic Handbook.*

Facts on File, 460 Park Avenue South, New York, New York 10016 (800) 443-8323; *The New Book of World Rankings.*

Food and Agricultural Organization of the United Nations (FAO), Via delle Terme di Caracalla, 00100 Rome, Italy (Telephone Number in U.S. (202) 653-2400); *Production Yearbook.*

G.K. Hall and Company, 70 Lincoln Street, Boston, Massachusetts 02111 (617) 423-3990; *The World in Figures.*

International Labour Office, I.L.O. Publications, CH-1211, Geneva 22, Switzerland; *Yearbook of Labour Statistics.*

Statistical Office of the United Nations, Publishing Service, New York, New York 10017 (800) 253-9646; *Demographic Yearbook, Statistical Yearbook,* and *Statistical Yearbook for Asia and the Pacific.*

Times Books, 201 East 50th Street, New York, New York 10022 (212) 751-2600; *The Economist Book of Vital World Statistics.*

United Nations Educational, Scientific and Cultural Organization (UNESCO), 7 Place de Fontenoy, F-75700 Paris, France (Telephone Number in U.S. (212) 963-5981); *Statistical Yearbook.*

U.S. Arms Control and Disarmament Agency, 320 Twenty-first Street, NW, Washington, D.C. 20451 (202) 647-8677; *World Military Expenditures and Arms Transfers.*

World Health Organization, Office of Publications, Avenue Appia, CH-1211 Geneva 27, Switzerland (Telephone Number in U.S. (518) 436-9686); *World Health Statistics Annual.*

SINGAPORE - POST OFFICES

Facts on File, 460 Park Avenue South, New York, New York 10016 (800) 443-8323; *The New Book of World Rankings.*

SINGAPORE - POTATO PRODUCTION - See SINGAPORE - CROPS

SINGAPORE - POWER PRODUCTION INDUSTRY

Statistical Office of the United Nations, Publishing Service, New York, New York 10017 (800) 253-9646; *Electric Power in Asia and the Pacific.*

SINGAPORE - PRICES

Asian Development Bank, P.O. Box 789, 1099 Manila, Philippines; *Key Indicators of Developing Asian and Pacific Countries.*

Facts on File, 460 Park Avenue South, New York, New York 10016 (800) 443-8323; *The New Book of World Rankings.*

Food and Agricultural Organization of the United Nations (FAO), Via delle Terme di Caracalla, 00100 Rome, Italy (Telephone Number in U.S. (202) 653-2400); *Production Yearbook,* and *The State of Food and Agriculture.*

G.K. Hall and Company, 70 Lincoln Street, Boston, Massachusetts 02111 (617) 423-3990; *The World in Figures.*

International Labour Office, I.L.O. Publications, CH-1211, Geneva 22, Switzerland; *Yearbook of Labour Statistics.*

International Monetary Fund, 700 Nineteenth Street, NW, Washington, D.C. 20431 (202) 623-7000; *International Financial Statistics.*

International Rubber Study Group, York House, Eighth Floor, Empire Way, Wembley, London HA9 0PA, England; *Rubber Statistical Bulletin.*

SINGAPORE - PRINTING AND WRITING PAPER - See SINGAPORE - FORESTRY AND FOREST PRODUCTS

SINGAPORE - PRODUCTION

Euromonitor Publications Limited, 87-88 Turnmill Street, London EC1M 5QU, England; *Third World Economic Handbook.*

Facts on File, 460 Park Avenue South, New York, New York 10016 (800) 443-8323; *The New Book of World Rankings.*

G.K. Hall and Company, 70 Lincoln Street, Boston, Massachusetts 02111 (617) 423-3990; *The World in Figures.*

International Rubber Study Group, York House, Eighth Floor, Empire Way, Wembley, London HA9 0PA, England; *Rubber Statistical Bulletin.*

SINGAPORE - PRODUCTIVITY

Euromonitor Publications Limited, 87-88 Turnmill Street, London EC1M 5QU, England; *International Marketing Data and Statistics.*

SINGAPORE - PROPERTY TAXES - See SINGAPORE - TAXATION

SINGAPORE - PUBLIC FINANCE

Facts on File, 460 Park Avenue South, New York, New York 10016 (800) 443-8323; *The New Book of World Rankings.*

SINGAPORE - RADIO BROADCASTING - See SINGAPORE - BROADCASTING

SINGAPORE - RAILWAYS

G.K. Hall and Company, 70 Lincoln Street, Boston, Massachusetts 02111 (617) 423-3990; *The World in Figures.*

SINGAPORE - RELIGION

Facts on File, 460 Park Avenue South, New York, New York 10016 (800) 443-8323; *The New Book of World Rankings.*

SINGAPORE - RENT PRICES

International Labour Office, I.L.O. Publications, CH-1211, Geneva 22, Switzerland; *Yearbook of Labour Statistics.*

SINGAPORE - RETAIL TRADE

Euromonitor Publications Limited, 87-88 Turnmill Street, London EC1M 5QU, England; *Third World Economic Handbook.*

G.K. Hall and Company, 70 Lincoln Street, Boston, Massachusetts 02111 (617) 423-3990; *The World in Figures.*

Statistical Office of the United Nations, Publishing Service, New York, New York 10017 (800) 253-9646; *Statistical Yearbook.*

SINGAPORE - RICE PRODUCTION - See SINGAPORE - CROPS

SINGAPORE - ROUNDWOOD PRODUCTION - See SINGAPORE - FORESTRY AND FOREST PRODUCTS

SINGAPORE - RUBBER EXPORTS

International Monetary Fund, 700 Nineteenth Street, NW, Washington, D.C. 20431 (202) 623-7000; *International Financial Statistics.*

SINGAPORE - RUBBER PRODUCTION AND CONSUMPTION

Euromonitor Publications Limited, 87-88 Turnmill Street, London EC1M 5QU, England; *Third World Economic Handbook.*

Facts on File, 460 Park Avenue South, New York, New York 10016 (800) 443-8323; *The New Book of World Rankings.*

International Rubber Study Group, York House, Eighth Floor, Empire Way, Wembley, London HA9 0PA, England; *Rubber Statistical Bulletin.*

SINGAPORE - SAWNWOOD PRODUCTION - See SINGAPORE - FORESTRY AND FOREST PRODUCTS

SINGAPORE - SCIENCE AND TECHNOLOGY - EXPENDITURE FOR RESEARCH

Statistical Office of the United Nations, Publishing Service, New York, New York 10017 (800) 253-9646; *Statistical Yearbook.*

SINGAPORE - SCIENTISTS AND TECHNICIANS

Statistical Office of the United Nations, Publishing Service, New York, New York 10017 (800) 253-9646; *Statistical Yearbook.*

SINGAPORE - SENIOR CITIZENS

Facts on File, 460 Park Avenue South, New York, New York 10016 (800) 443-8323; *The New Book of World Rankings.*

SINGAPORE - SHEEP - See SINGAPORE - LIVESTOCK AND POULTRY

SINGAPORE - SILVER PRODUCTION AND CONSUMPTION - See SINGAPORE - MINING AND MINERAL PRODUCTS

SINGAPORE - SOCIAL DATA

Asian Development Bank, P.O. Box 789, 1099 Manila, Philippines; *Key Indicators of Developing Asian and Pacific Countries.*

Facts on File, 460 Park Avenue South, New York, New York 10016 (800) 443-8323; *The New Book of World Rankings.*

G.K. Hall and Company, 70 Lincoln Street, Boston, Massachusetts 02111 (617) 423-3990; *The World in Figures.*

SINGAPORE - SOCIAL SECURITY

International Monetary Fund, 700 Nineteenth Street, NW, Washington, D.C. 20431 (202) 623-7000; *Government Finance Statistics Yearbook.*

SINGAPORE - STAMP TAXES AND DUTIES - See SINGAPORE - TAXATION

SINGAPORE - STATE BUDGET REVENUE AND EXPENDITURES

Euromonitor Publications Limited, 87-88 Turnmill Street, London EC1M 5QU, England; *International Marketing Data and Statistics*.

SINGAPORE - STEEL - See SINGAPORE - MINING AND MINERAL PRODUCTS

SINGAPORE - STOCKS - COMMODITY - MARKET PRICE - INDEX

Food and Agricultural Organization of the United Nations (FAO) Via delle Terme di Caracalla, 00100 Rome, Italy (Telephone Number in U.S. (202) 653-2400); *The State of Food and Agriculture*.

SINGAPORE - SUGAR PRODUCTION AND CONSUMPTION - See SINGAPORE - CROPS

SINGAPORE - TAXATION

G.K. Hall and Company, 70 Lincoln Street, Boston, Massachusetts 02111 (617) 423-3990; *The World in Figures*.

International Monetary Fund, 700 Nineteenth Street, NW, Washington, D.C. 20431 (202) 623-7000; *Government Finance Statistics Yearbook*.

International Road Federation, 525 School Street, SW, Washington, D.C. 20024 (202) 554-2106; *World Road Statistics*.

Times Books, 201 East 50th Street, New York, New York 10022 (212) 751-2600; *The Economist Book of Vital World Statistics*.

The World Bank, 1818 H Street, NW, Washington, D.C. 20433 (202) 477-1234; *World Tables*.

SINGAPORE - TELEGRAPH SERVICE

Statistical Office of the United Nations, Publishing Service, New York, New York 10017 (800) 253-9646; *Statistical Yearbook*.

SINGAPORE - TELEPHONES IN USE

American Telephone and Telegraph Company, 26 Parsippany Road, Whippany, New Jersey 07981 (800) 338-4038; *The World's Telephones*.

The Economist Intelligence Unit (Asia) Limited, 10th Floor, Luk Kwok Centre, 72 Gloucester Road, Wanchai, Hong Kong (Phone Number in U.S. (800) 938-4685); *Asian Market Atlas*.

Euromonitor Publications Limited, 87-88 Turnmill Street, London EC1M 5QU, England; *The Pacific Basin: An Economic Handbook*, and *Third World Economic Handbook*.

G.K. Hall and Company, 70 Lincoln Street, Boston, Massachusetts 02111 (617) 423-3990; *The World in Figures*.

Statistical Office of the United Nations, Publishing Service, New York, New York 10017 (800) 253-9646; *Statistical Yearbook*.

SINGAPORE - TELEVISION BROADCASTING - See SINGAPORE - BROADCASTING

SINGAPORE - TEXTILE INDUSTRY

Euromonitor Publications Limited, 87-88 Turnmill Street, London EC1M 5QU, England; *Third World Economic Handbook*.

G.K. Hall and Company, 70 Lincoln Street, Boston, Massachusetts 02111 (617) 423-3990; *The World in Figures*.

Statistical Office of the United Nations, Publishing Service, New York, New York 10017 (800) 253-9646; *Statistical Yearbook*, and *Trade in Manufactures of Developing Countries*.

Times Books, 201 East 50th Street, New York, New York 10022 (212) 751-2600; *The Economist Book of Vital World Statistics*.

SINGAPORE - THEATRE

United Nations Educational, Scientific and Cultural Organization (UNESCO), 7 Place de Fontenoy, F-75700 Paris, France (Telephone Number in U.S. (212) 963-5981); *Statistical Yearbook*.

SINGAPORE - TIRE (MOTOR VEHICLE) PRODUCTION

International Rubber Study Group, York House, Eighth Floor, Empire Way, Wembley, London HA9 0PA, England; *Rubber Statistical Bulletin*.

SINGAPORE - TOBACCO PRODUCTION

Euromonitor Publications Limited, 87-88 Turnmill Street, London EC1M 5QU, England; *Third World Economic Handbook*.

Facts on File, 460 Park Avenue South, New York, New York 10016 (800) 443-8323; *The New Book of World Rankings*.

Statistical Office of the United Nations, Publishing Service, New York, New York 10017 (800) 253-9646; *Statistical Yearbook*.

SINGAPORE - TOURISM

Euromonitor Publications Limited, 87-88 Turnmill Street, London EC1M 5QU, England; *The Pacific Basin: An Economic Handbook*, and *Third World Economic Handbook*.

Facts on File, 460 Park Avenue South, New York, New York 10016 (800) 443-8323; *The New Book of World Rankings*.

G.K. Hall and Company, 70 Lincoln Street, Boston, Massachusetts 02111 (617) 423-3990; *The World in Figures*.

Statistical Office of the United Nations, Publishing Service, New York, New York 10017 (800) 253-9646; *Statistical Yearbook*.

Times Books, 201 East 50th Street, New York, New York 10022 (212) 751-2600; *The Economist Book of Vital World Statistics*.

World Tourism Organization, Calle Capitan Haya 42, E-28020 Madrid, Spain; *Yearbook of Tourism Statistics*.

SINGAPORE - TRACTORS IN USE

Statistical Office of the United Nations, Publishing Service, New York, New York 10017 (800) 253-9646; *Statistical Yearbook*.

SINGAPORE - TRADE - See SINGAPORE - FOREIGN TRADE

SINGAPORE - TRADEMARKS AND SERVICE MARKS

Statistical Office of the United Nations, Publishing Service, New York, New York 10017 (800) 253-9646; *Statistical Yearbook*.

World Intellectual Property Organization, 34 Chemin des Colombettes, CH-1211 Geneva 20. Switzerland; *Industrial Property Statistics*.

SINGAPORE - TRANSPORTATION AND COMMUNICATIONS

The Economist Intelligence Unit (Asia) Limited, 10th Floor, Luk Kwok Centre, 72 Gloucester Road, Wanchai, Hong Kong (Phone Number in U.S. (800) 938-4685); *Asian Market Atlas.*

Euromonitor Publications Limited, 87-88 Turnmill Street, London EC1M 5QU, England; *The Pacific Basin: An Economic Handbook,* and *Third World Economic Handbook.*

Facts on File, 460 Park Avenue South, New York, New York 10016 (800) 443-8323; *The New Book of World Rankings.*

G.K. Hall and Company, 70 Lincoln Street, Boston, Massachusetts 02111 (617) 423-3990; *The World in Figures.*

Statistical Office of the United Nations, Publishing Service, New York, New York 10017 (800) 253-9646; *Statistical Yearbook for Asia and the Pacific.*

SINGAPORE - UNEMPLOYMENT

Euromonitor Publications Limited, 87-88 Turnmill Street, London EC1M 5QU, England; *International Marketing Data and Statistics,* and *The Pacific Basin: An Economic Handbook.*

International Labour Office, I.L.O. Publications, CH-1211, Geneva 22, Switzerland; *Yearbook of Labour Statistics.*

Statistical Office of the United Nations, Publishing Service, New York, New York 10017 (800) 253-9646; *Statistical Yearbook.*

SINGAPORE - UTILITIES

Statistical Office of the United Nations, Publishing Service, New York, New York 10017 (800) 253-9646; *Electric Power in Asia and the Pacific.*

SINGAPORE - VITAL STATISTICS

Euromonitor Publications Limited, 87-88 Turnmill Street, London EC1M 5QU, England; *International Marketing Data and Statistics, The Pacific Basin: An Economic Handbook,* and *Third World Economic Handbook.*

G.K. Hall and Company, 70 Lincoln Street, Boston, Massachusetts 02111 (617) 423-3990; *The World in Figures.*

Statistical Office of the United Nations, Publishing Service, New York, New York 10017 (800) 253-9646; *Statistical Yearbook.*

World Health Organization, Office of Publications, Avenue Appia, CH-1211 Geneva 27, Switzerland (Telephone Number in U.S. (518) 436-9686); *World Health Statistics Annual.*

SINGAPORE - WAGES

G.K. Hall and Company, 70 Lincoln Street, Boston, Massachusetts 02111 (617) 423-3990; *The World in Figures.*

International Labour Office, I.L.O. Publications, CH-1211, Geneva 22, Switzerland; *Yearbook of Labour Statistics.*

Statistical Office of the United Nations, Publishing Service, New York, New York 10017 (800) 253-9646; *Statistical Yearbook for Asia and the Pacific,* and *Statistical Yearbook.*

SINGAPORE - WEATHER

Facts on File, 460 Park Avenue South, New York, New York 10016 (800) 443-8323; *The New Book of World Rankings.*

G.K. Hall and Company, 70 Lincoln Street, Boston, Massachusetts 02111 (617) 423-3990; *The World in Figures.*

SINGAPORE - WELFARE

International Monetary Fund, 700 Nineteenth Street, NW, Washington, D.C. 20431 (202) 623-7000; *Government Finance Statistics Yearbook.*

SINGAPORE - WHEAT PRODUCTION AND PRICES - See SINGAPORE - CROPS

SINGAPORE - WHOLESALE PRICES

Asian Development Bank, P.O. Box 789, 1099 Manila, Philippines; *Key Indicators of Developing Asian and Pacific Countries.*

International Monetary Fund, 700 Nineteenth Street, NW, Washington, D.C. 20431 (202) 623-7000; *International Financial Statistics.*

Statistical Office of the United Nations, Publishing Service, New York, New York 10017 (800) 253-9646; *Statistical Yearbook.*

SINGAPORE - WHOLESALE TRADE

Euromonitor Publications Limited, 87-88 Turnmill Street, London EC1M 5QU, England; *Third World Economic Handbook.*

Statistical Office of the United Nations, Publishing Service, New York, New York 10017 (800) 253-9646; *Statistical Yearbook.*

SINGAPORE - WINE PRODUCTION

Facts on File, 460 Park Avenue South, New York, New York 10016 (800) 443-8323; *The New Book of World Rankings.*

SINGAPORE - WOOD PULP PRODUCTION - See SINGAPORE - FORESTRY AND FOREST PRODUCTS

SINGAPORE - WOOL PRODUCTION

Facts on File, 460 Park Avenue South, New York, New York 10016 (800) 443-8323; *The New Book of World Rankings.*

SINGAPORE - ZOOS AND BOTANICAL GARDENS

United Nations Educational, Scientific and Cultural Organization (UNESCO), 7 Place de Fontenoy, F-75700 Paris, France (Telephone Number in U.S. (212) 963-5981); *Statistical Yearbook.*

SINGLE PERSONS - See MARITAL STATUS OF POPULATION

SKIING

National Sporting Goods Association, 1699 Wall Street, Mount Prospect, Illinois 60056 (708) 439-4000; *The Sporting Goods Market in 1993,* and *Sports Participation in 1992.*

SKINS - See HIDES AND SKINS

SLAUGHTERING AND MEAT PACKING INDUSTRY - See MEAT AND MEAT PRODUCTS

SLOVAKIA - See also CZECHOSLOVAKIA

SLOVAKIA - AGRICULTURE

Encyclopedia Britannica, Incorporated, 310 South Michigan Avenue, Chicago, Illinois 60604 (312) 347-7000; *Britannica World Data.*

SLOVAKIA - AIRLINE SERVICE

Encyclopedia Britannica, Incorporated, 310 South Michigan Avenue, Chicago, Illinois 60604 (312) 347-7000; *Britannica World Data.*

SLOVAKIA - BIRTH RATES

Encyclopedia Britannica, Incorporated, 310 South Michigan Avenue, Chicago, Illinois 60604 (312) 347-7000; *Britannica World Data.*

SLOVAKIA - CONSTRUCTION

Encyclopedia Britannica, Incorporated, 310 South Michigan Avenue, Chicago, Illinois 60604 (312) 347-7000; *Britannica World Data.*

SLOVAKIA - DEMOGRAPHY

Encyclopedia Britannica, Incorporated, 310 South Michigan Avenue, Chicago, Illinois 60604 (312) 347-7000; *Britannica World Data.*

SLOVAKIA - DIVORCE RATES

Encyclopedia Britannica, Incorporated, 310 South Michigan Avenue, Chicago, Illinois 60604 (312) 347-7000; *Britannica World Data.*

SLOVAKIA ECONOMY

Encyclopedia Britannica, Incorporated, 310 South Michigan Avenue, Chicago, Illinois 60604 (312) 347-7000; *Britannica World Data.*

SLOVAKIA - EDUCATION

Encyclopedia Britannica, Incorporated, 310 South Michigan Avenue, Chicago, Illinois 60604 (312) 347-7000; *Britannica World Data.*

SLOVAKIA - ENERGY PRODUCTION

Encyclopedia Britannica, Incorporated, 310 South Michigan Avenue, Chicago, Illinois 60604 (312) 347-7000; *Britannica World Data.*

SLOVAKIA - EXPORTS

Encyclopedia Britannica, Incorporated, 310 South Michigan Avenue, Chicago, Illinois 60604 (312) 347-7000; *Britannica World Data.*

SLOVAKIA - FERTILITY RATES

Encyclopedia Britannica, Incorporated, 310 South Michigan Avenue, Chicago, Illinois 60604 (312) 347-7000; *Britannica World Data.*

SLOVAKIA - FISHERIES

Encyclopedia Britannica, Incorporated, 310 South Michigan Avenue, Chicago, Illinois 60604 (312) 347-7000; *Britannica World Data.*

SLOVAKIA - FOREIGN TRADE

Encyclopedia Britannica, Incorporated, 310 South Michigan Avenue, Chicago, Illinois 60604 (312) 347-7000; *Britannica World Data.*

SLOVAKIA - FORESTRY AND FOREST PRODUCTS

Encyclopedia Britannica, Incorporated, 310 South Michigan Avenue, Chicago, Illinois 60604 (312) 347-7000; *Britannica World Data.*

SLOVAKIA - HEALTH

Encyclopedia Britannica, Incorporated, 310 South Michigan Avenue, Chicago, Illinois 60604 (312) 347-7000; *Britannica World Data.*

SLOVAKIA - IMPORTS

Encyclopedia Britannica, Incorporated, 310 South Michigan Avenue, Chicago, Illinois 60604 (312) 347-7000; *Britannica World Data.*

SLOVAKIA - LAND USE

Encyclopedia Britannica, Incorporated, 310 South Michigan Avenue, Chicago, Illinois 60604 (312) 347-7000; *Britannica World Data.*

SLOVAKIA - LIVESTOCK AND POULTRY

Encyclopedia Britannica, Incorporated, 310 South Michigan Avenue, Chicago, Illinois 60604 (312) 347-7000; *Britannica World Data.*

SLOVAKIA - MANUFACTURING

Encyclopedia Britannica, Incorporated, 310 South Michigan Avenue, Chicago, Illinois 60604 (312) 347-7000; *Britannica World Data.*

SLOVAKIA - MARRIAGE RATES

Encyclopedia Britannica, Incorporated, 310 South Michigan Avenue, Chicago, Illinois 60604 (312) 347-7000; *Britannica World Data.*

SLOVAKIA - MILITARY

Encyclopedia Britannica, Incorporated, 310 South Michigan Avenue, Chicago, Illinois 60604 (312) 347-7000; *Britannica World Data.*

SLOVAKIA - MINING AND MINERAL PRODUCTS

Encyclopedia Britannica, Incorporated, 310 South Michigan Avenue, Chicago, Illinois 60604 (312) 347-7000; *Britannica World Data.*

SLOVAKIA - POPULATION

Encyclopedia Britannica, Incorporated, 310 South Michigan Avenue, Chicago, Illinois 60604 (312) 347-7000; *Britannica World Data.*

SLOVAKIA - RADIO RECEIVERS

Encyclopedia Britannica, Incorporated, 310 South Michigan Avenue, Chicago, Illinois 60604 (312) 347-7000; *Britannica World Data.*

SLOVAKIA - RAILWAYS

Encyclopedia Britannica, Incorporated, 310 South Michigan Avenue, Chicago, Illinois 60604 (312) 347-7000; *Britannica World Data.*

SLOVAKIA - ROADS

Encyclopedia Britannica, Incorporated, 310 South Michigan Avenue, Chicago, Illinois 60604 (312) 347-7000; *Britannica World Data.*

SLOVAKIA - TELEPHONES IN USE

Encyclopedia Britannica, Incorporated, 310 South Michigan Avenue, Chicago, Illinois 60604 (312) 347-7000; *Britannica World Data.*

SLOVAKIA - TELEVISION RECEIVERS

Encyclopedia Britannica, Incorporated, 310 South Michigan Avenue, Chicago, Illinois 60604 (312) 347-7000; *Britannica World Data.*

SLOVAKIA - TRANSPORTATION AND COMMUNICATIONS

Encyclopedia Britannica, Incorporated, 310 South Michigan Avenue, Chicago, Illinois 60604 (312) 347-7000; *Britannica World Data.*

SLOVAKIA - VITAL STATISTICS

Encyclopedia Britannica, Incorporated, 310 South Michigan Avenue, Chicago, Illinois 60604 (312) 347-7000; *Britannica World Data.*

SLOVENIA - See also YUGOSLAVIA

SLOVENIA - AGRICULTURE

Encyclopedia Britannica, Incorporated, 310 South Michigan Avenue, Chicago, Illinois 60604 (312) 347-7000; *Britannica World Data.*

SLOVENIA - AIRLINE SERVICE

Encyclopedia Britannica, Incorporated, 310 South Michigan Avenue, Chicago, Illinois 60604 (312) 347-7000; *Britannica World Data.*

SLOVENIA - BIRTH RATES

Encyclopedia Britannica, Incorporated, 310 South Michigan Avenue, Chicago, Illinois 60604 (312) 347-7000; *Britannica World Data.*

SLOVENIA - CONSTRUCTION INDUSTRY

Encyclopedia Britannica, Incorporated, 310 South Michigan Avenue, Chicago, Illinois 60604 (312) 347-7000; *Britannica World Data.*

SLOVENIA - DEMOGRAPHY

Encyclopedia Britannica, Incorporated, 310 South Michigan Avenue, Chicago, Illinois 60604 (312) 347-7000; *Britannica World Data.*

SLOVENIA - DIVORCE RATES

Encyclopedia Britannica, Incorporated, 310 South Michigan Avenue, Chicago, Illinois 60604 (312) 347-7000; *Britannica World Data.*

SLOVENIA - ECONOMY

Encyclopedia Britannica, Incorporated, 310 South Michigan Avenue, Chicago, Illinois 60604 (312) 347-7000; *Britannica World Data.*

SLOVENIA - EDUCATION

Encyclopedia Britannica, Incorporated, 310 South Michigan Avenue, Chicago, Illinois 60604 (312) 347-7000; *Britannica World Data.*

SLOVENIA - ENERGY

Encyclopedia Britannica, Incorporated, 310 South Michigan Avenue, Chicago, Illinois 60604 (312) 347-7000; *Britannica World Data.*

SLOVENIA - EXPORTS

Encyclopedia Britannica, Incorporated, 310 South Michigan Avenue, Chicago, Illinois 60604 (312) 347-7000; *Britannica World Data.*

SLOVENIA - FERTILITY RATES

Encyclopedia Britannica, Incorporated, 310 South Michigan Avenue, Chicago, Illinois 60604 (312) 347-7000; *Britannica World Data.*

SLOVENIA - FISHERIES

Encyclopedia Britannica, Incorporated, 310 South Michigan Avenue, Chicago, Illinois 60604 (312) 347-7000; *Britannica World Data.*

SLOVENIA - FOREIGN TRADE

Encyclopedia Britannica, Incorporated, 310 South Michigan Avenue, Chicago, Illinois 60604 (312) 347-7000; *Britannica World Data.*

SLOVENIA - FORESTRY AND FOREST PRODUCTS

Encyclopedia Britannica, Incorporated, 310 South Michigan Avenue, Chicago, Illinois 60604 (312) 347-7000; *Britannica World Data.*

SLOVENIA - HEALTH

Encyclopedia Britannica, Incorporated, 310 South Michigan Avenue, Chicago, Illinois 60604 (312) 347-7000; *Britannica World Data.*

SLOVENIA - HIGHWAYS

Encyclopedia Britannica, Incorporated, 310 South Michigan Avenue, Chicago, Illinois 60604 (312) 347-7000; *Britannica World Data.*

SLOVENIA - IMPORTS

Encyclopedia Britannica, Incorporated, 310 South Michigan Avenue, Chicago, Illinois 60604 (312) 347-7000; *Britannica World Data.*

SLOVENIA - LAND USE

Encyclopedia Britannica, Incorporated, 310 South Michigan Avenue, Chicago, Illinois 60604 (312) 347-7000; *Britannica World Data.*

SLOVENIA - LIVESTOCK AND POULTRY

Encyclopedia Britannica, Incorporated, 310 South Michigan Avenue, Chicago, Illinois 60604 (312) 347-7000; *Britannica World Data.*

SLOVENIA - MANUFACTURING

Encyclopedia Britannica, Incorporated, 310 South Michigan Avenue, Chicago, Illinois 60604 (312) 347-7000; *Britannica World Data.*

SLOVENIA - MARRIAGE RATES

Encyclopedia Britannica, Incorporated, 310 South Michigan Avenue, Chicago, Illinois 60604 (312) 347-7000; *Britannica World Data.*

SLOVENIA - MILITARY

The International Institute for Strategic Studies, 23 Tavistock Street, London WC2E 7NQ, England; *The Military Balance.*

SLOVENIA - MINING AND MINERAL PRODUCTS

Encyclopedia Britannica, Incorporated, 310 South Michigan Avenue, Chicago, Illinois 60604 (312) 347-7000; *Britannica World Data.*

SLOVENIA - POPULATION

Encyclopedia Britannica, Incorporated, 310 South Michigan Avenue, Chicago, Illinois 60604 (312) 347-7000; *Britannica World Data.*

SLOVENIA - RADIO RECEIVERS

Encyclopedia Britannica, Incorporated, 310 South Michigan Avenue, Chicago, Illinois 60604 (312) 347-7000; *Britannica World Data.*

SLOVENIA - RAILWAYS

Encyclopedia Britannica, Incorporated, 310 South Michigan Avenue, Chicago, Illinois 60604 (312) 347-7000; *Britannica World Data.*

SLOVENIA - ROADS - See HIGHWAYS

SLOVENIA - TELEPHONES IN USE

Encyclopedia Britannica, Incorporated, 310 South Michigan Avenue, Chicago, Illinois 60604 (312) 347-7000; *Britannica World Data.*

SLOVENIA - TELEVISIONS RECEIVERS

Encyclopedia Britannica, Incorporated, 310 South Michigan Avenue, Chicago, Illinois 60604 (312) 347-7000; *Britannica World Data.*

SLOVENIA - TRANSPORTATION AND COMMUNICATION

Encyclopedia Britannica, Incorporated, 310 South Michigan Avenue, Chicago, Illinois 60604 (312) 347-7000; *Britannica World Data.*

SLOVENIA - VITAL STATISTICS

Encyclopedia Britannica, Incorporated, 310 South Michigan Avenue, Chicago, Illinois 60604 (312) 347-7000; *Britannica World Data.*

SMALL BUSINESS ADMINISTRATION - BUDGET OUTLAYS

Executive Office of the President, Office of Management and Budget, Executive Office Building, Washington, D.C. 20503 (202) 395-3080; *Budget of the United States Government.*

SMALL BUSINESS ADMINISTRATION - LOANS

U.S. Small Business Administration, 1441 L Street, NW, Washington, D.C. 20416 (800) 368-5855; unpublished data.

SNAPPER

U.S. Department of Commerce, National Oceanic and Atmospheric Administration, National Marine Fisheries Service, 1335 East-West Highway, Silver Spring, Maryland 20910 (301) 427-2239; *Fisheries of the United States.*

SNOW AND ICE PELLETS - SELECTED CITIES

U.S. Department of Commerce, National Oceanic and Atmospheric Administration, National Climatic Data Center, Federal Building, Asheville, North Carolina 28801 (704) 259-2850; *Comparative Climatic Data.*

SNOWMOBILES

International Snowmobile Industry Association, 3975 University Drive, Suite 310, Fairfax, Virginia 22030 (703) 273-9606.

National Sporting Goods Association, Lake Center Plaza Building, 1699 Wall Street, Mount Prospect, Illinois 60056-5780 (708) 439-4000; *The Sporting Goods Market in 1993.*

SOCCER

National Sporting Goods Association, 1699 Wall Street, Mount Prospect, Illinois 60056-5780 (708) 439-4000; *Sports Participation in 1992.*

SOCIAL INSURANCE - See also MEDICARE - RETIREMENT SYSTEMS, and SOCIAL SECURITY

SOCIAL INSURANCE - CONTRIBUTIONS

U.S. Department of Health and Human Services, Social Security Administration, 6401 Security Boulevard, Baltimore, Maryland 21235 (410) 965-1234; *Annual Statistical Supplement to the Social Security Bulletin.*

SOCIAL INSURANCE - EMPLOYMENT COVERED

U.S. Department of Health and Human Services, Social Security Administration, 6401 Security Boulevard, Baltimore, Maryland 21235 (410) 965-1234; *Annual Statistical Supplement to the Social Security Bulletin,* and unpublished data.

SOCIAL INSURANCE - EXPENDITURES (PUBLIC) FOR

U.S. Department of Health and Human Services, Social Security Administration, 6401 Security Boulevard, Baltimore, Maryland 21235 (410) 965-1234; *Social Security Bulletin, Annual Statistical Supplement to the Social Security Bulletin,* and unpublished data.

SOCIAL INSURANCE - GOVERNMENT INSURANCE TRUST FUNDS

U.S. Department of Commerce, Bureau of the Census, Suitland, Maryland 20233 (301) 763-4040; *Government Finances.*

SOCIAL INSURANCE - GOVERNMENT INSURANCE TRUST FUNDS - CITY GOVERNMENT FINANCES

U.S. Department of Commerce, Bureau of the Census, Suitland, Maryland 20233 (301) 763-4040; *City Government Finances.*

SOCIAL INSURANCE - GOVERNMENT INSURANCE TRUST FUNDS - FEDERAL RECEIPTS AND EXPENDITURES

Executive Office of the President, Office of Management and Budget, Executive Office Building, Washington, D.C. 20503 (202) 395-3080; *Budget of the United States Government.*

U.S. Department of Commerce, Bureau of the Census, Suitland, Maryland 20233 (301) 763-4040; *Historical Statistics on Governmental Finances and Employment,* and *Government Finances.*

SOCIAL INSURANCE - GOVERNMENT INSURANCE TRUST FUNDS - STATE AND LOCAL RECEIPTS - EXPENDITURES

U.S. Department of Commerce, Bureau of the Census, Suitland, Maryland 20233 (301) 763-4040; *Finances of Employee-Retirement Systems of State and Local Government, Historical Statistics on Governmental Finances and Employment, City Government Finances, Government Finances,* and *State Government Finances.*

SOCIAL INSURANCE - INDIVIDUAL PROGRAMS - BENEFICIARIES AND BENEFITS

U.S. Department of Health and Human Services, Social Security Administration, 6401 Security Boulevard, Baltimore, Maryland 21235 (410) 965-1234; *Annual Statistical Supplement to the Social Security*

Bulletin, Social Security Bulletin, and unpublished data.

SOCIAL INSURANCE - INDIVIDUAL PROGRAMS -
COVERAGE

U.S. Department of Health and Human Services, Social Security Administration, 6401 Security Boulevard, Baltimore, Maryland 21235 (410) 965-1234; *Annual Statistical Supplement to the Social Security Bulletin,* and unpublished data.

SOCIAL INSURANCE - INDIVIDUAL PROGRAMS - FEDERAL
RETIREMENT INSURANCE

Board of Governors of the Federal Reserve System, Twentieth Street and Constitution Avenue, NW, Washington, D.C. 20551 (202) 452-3000; *Annual Statistical Digest,* and unpublished data.

Office of Personnel Management, 1900 E Street, NW, Washington, D.C. 20415 (202) 606-1800; *Compensation Report.*

U.S. Department of Health and Human Services, Social Security Administration, 6401 Security Boulevard, Baltimore, Maryland 21235 (410) 965-1234; *Social Security Bulletin, Annual Statistical Supplement to the Social Security Bulletin,* and unpublished data.

SOCIAL INSURANCE - INDIVIDUAL PROGRAMS - FEDERAL
RETIREMENT INSURANCE - CIVIL SERVICE

U.S. Department of Health and Human Services, Social Security Administration, 6401 Security Boulevard, Baltimore, Maryland 21235 (410) 965-1234; *Annual Statistical Supplement to the Social Security Bulletin, Social Security Bulletin,* and unpublished data.

U.S. Office of Personnel Management, 1900 E Street, NW, Washington, D.C. 20415 (202) 606-1800; *Compensation Report.*

SOCIAL INSURANCE - INDIVIDUAL PROGRAMS - OLD-AGE,
SURVIVORS, DISABILITY AND HEALTH INSURANCE -
AVERAGE PAYMENTS

U.S. Department of Health and Human Services, Social Security Administration, 6401 Security Boulevard, Baltimore, Maryland 21235 (410) 965-1234; *Social Security Bulletin, Annual Statistical Supplement to the Social Security Bulletin, Annual Report of Board of Trustees, OASI, DI, HI, and SMI Trust Funds,* and unpublished data.

SOCIAL INSURANCE - INDIVIDUAL PROGRAMS - OLD-AGE,
SURVIVORS, DISABILITY AND HEALTH INSURANCE -
CONTRIBUTIONS

U.S. Department of Health and Human Services, Social Security Administration, 6401 Security Boulevard, Baltimore, Maryland 21235 (410) 965-1234; *Annual Statistical Supplement to the Social Security Bulletin, Social Security Bulletin, Annual Report of Board of Trustees, OASI, DI, HI, and SMI Trust Funds,* and unpublished data.

SOCIAL INSURANCE - INDIVIDUAL PROGRAMS - OLD-AGE,
SURVIVORS, DISABILITY AND HEALTH INSURANCE -
COVERAGE - WORKERS AND EARNINGS

U.S. Department of Health and Human Services, Social Security Administration, 6401 Security Boulevard, Baltimore, Maryland 21235 (410) 965-1234; *Annual Statistical Supplement to the Social Security Bulletin,* and unpublished data.

SOCIAL INSURANCE - INDIVIDUAL PROGRAMS - OLD-AGE,
SURVIVORS, DISABILITY AND HEALTH INSURANCE -
TRUST FUNDS

Executive Office of the President, Office of Management and Budget, Executive Office Building, Washington, D.C. 20503 (202) 395-3080; *The Budget of the United States Government.*

U.S. Department of Commerce, Bureau of the Census, Suitland, Maryland 20233 (301) 763-4040; *Historical Statistics on Governmental Finances and Employment,* and *Government Finances.*

U.S. Department of Health and Human Services, Social Security Administration, 6401 Security Boulevard, Baltimore, Maryland 21235 (410) 965-1234; *Social Security Bulletin, Annual Report of Board of Trustees, OASI, DI, HI and SMI Trust Funds,* and *Annual Statistical Supplement to the Social Security Bulletin.*

SOCIAL INSURANCE - PAYROLL TAX RATES AND TAXABLE WAGES

U.S. Department of Health and Human Services, Social Security Administration, 6401 Security Boulevard, Baltimore, Maryland 21235 (410) 965-1234; *Social Security Throughout the World.*

SOCIAL INSURANCE - PROTECTION AGAINST INCOME LOSS

U.S. Department of Health and Human Services, Social Security Administration, 6401 Security Boulevard, Baltimore, Maryland 21235 (410) 965-1234; *Social Security Bulletin,* and unpublished data.

SOCIAL INSURANCE - RAILROAD INSURANCE

Board of Governors of the Federal Reserve System, Twentieth Street and Constitution Avenue, NW, Washington, D.C. 20551 (202) 452-3000; *Annual Statistical Digest,* and unpublished data.

Executive Office of the President, Office of Management and Budget, Executive Office Building, Washington, D.C. 20503 (202) 395-3080; *The Budget of the United States Government,* and unpublished data.

U.S. Department of Health and Human Services, Social Security Administration, 6401 Security Boulevard, Baltimore, Maryland 21235 (410) 965-1234; *Social Security Bulletin, Annual Statistical Supplement to the Social Security Bulletin,* and unpublished data.

SOCIAL INSURANCE - STATE AND LOCAL PUBLIC RETIREMENT
SYSTEMS

U.S. Department of Commerce, Bureau of the Census, Suitland, Maryland 20233 (301) 763-4040; *Finances of Employee-Retirement Systems of State and Local Governments.*

U.S. Department of Health and Human Services, Social Security Administration, 6401 Security Boulevard, Baltimore, Maryland 21235 (410) 965-1234; *Social Security Bulletin, Annual Statistical Supplement to the Social Security Bulletin,* and unpublished data.

SOCIAL INSURANCE - TRUST FUNDS

Board of Governors of the Federal Reserve System, Twentieth Street and Constitution Avenue, NW, Washington, D.C. 20551 (202) 452-3000; *Annual Statistical Digest,* and unpublished data.

U.S. Department of Health and Human Services, Social Security Administration, 6401 Security Boulevard, Baltimore, Maryland 21235 (410) 965-1234; *Annual Statistical Supplement to the Social Security Bulletin, Social Security Bulletin,* and unpublished data.

SOCIAL INSURANCE - UNEMPLOYMENT INSURANCE
(FEDERAL AND STATE)

U.S. Department of Health and Human Services, Social Security Administration, 6401 Security Boulevard, Baltimore, Maryland 21235 (410) 965-1234; *Annual Statistical Supplement to the Social Security Bulletin, Social Security Bulletin*, and unpublished data.

U.S. Department of Labor, Employment and Training Administration, 200 Constitution Avenue, NW, Washington, D.C. 20210 (202) 219-0600, *Unemployment Insurance Data Summary*.

SOCIAL INSURANCE - WORKER'S COMPENSATION

U.S. Department of Health and Human Services, Health Care Financing Administration, 200 Independence Avenue, SW, Washington, D.C. 20201 (202) 245-6113; *Health Care Financing Review*.

U.S. Department of Health and Human Services, Social Security Administration, 6401 Security Boulevard, Baltimore, Maryland 21235 (410) 965-1234; *Social Security Bulletin, Annual Statistical Supplement to the Social Security Bulletin*, and unpublished data.

SOCIAL SCIENCES - DEGREES CONFERRED

U.S. Department of Education, 400 Maryland Avenue, SW, Washington, D.C. 20202 (202) 708-5366; *Digest of Education Statistics*.

U.S. National Science Foundation, 4201 Wilson Boulevard, Arlington, Virginia 22230 (703) 306-1234; *Survey of Earned Doctorates, Selected Data on Science and Engineering Doctorate Awards*, and *Characteristics of Recent Science and Engineering Graduates*.

SOCIAL SCIENCES - EMPLOYMENT

U.S. Department of Commerce, Bureau of the Census, Suitland, Maryland 20233 (301) 763-4040; *Monthly Labor Review, Employment Earnings*, and unpublished data.

SOCIAL SCIENCES - SALARY OFFERS

College Placement Council, 62 Highland Avenue, Bethlehem, Pennsylvania 18017 (212) 868-1421; *Salary Survey, A Study of Beginning Offers*.

SOCIAL SECURITY - See also SOCIAL INSURANCE

SOCIAL SECURITY - BENEFICIARIES AND PAYMENTS

U.S. Department of Health and Human Services, Social Security Administration, 6401 Security Boulevard, Baltimore, Maryland 21235 (410) 965-1234; *Annual Statistical Supplement to the Social Security Bulletin*, and unpublished data.

SOCIAL SECURITY - CONTRIBUTIONS - RATES

U.S. Department of Health and Human Services, Social Security Administration, 6401 Security Boulevard, Baltimore, Maryland 21235 (410) 965-1234; *Annual Statistical Supplement to the Social Security Bulletin*, and unpublished data.

SOCIAL SECURITY - COVERAGE, WORKERS, EARNINGS

U.S. Department of Health and Human Services, Social Security Administration, 6401 Security Boulevard, Baltimore, Maryland 21235 (410) 965-1234; *Annual Statistical Supplement to the Social Security Bulletin*, and unpublished data.

SOCIAL SECURITY - TRUST FUNDS

U.S. Department of Health and Human Services, Social Security Administration, 6401 Security Boulevard, Baltimore, Maryland 21235 (410) 965-1234; *Annual Statistical Supplement to the Social Security Bulletin, Annual Report of Board of Trustees, OASI, DI, HI, and SMI Trust Funds, Social Security Bulletin*, and unpublished data.

SOCIAL SERVICES - EARNINGS

U.S. Department of Commerce, Bureau of the Census, Suitland, Maryland 20233 (301) 763-4040; *County Business Patterns*, and *Census of Service Industries*.

U.S. Department of Labor, Bureau of Labor Statistics, Two Massachusetts Avenue, NE, Washington, D.C. 20212 (202) 606-7828; *Employment and Earnings*.

SOCIAL SERVICES - EMPLOYEES

U.S. Department of Commerce, Bureau of the Census, Suitland, Maryland 20233 (301) 763-4040; *County Business Patterns, Census of Service Industries*, and unpublished data.

U.S. Department of Labor, Bureau of Labor Statistics, Two Massachusetts Avenue, NE, Washington, D.C. 20212 (202) 606-7828; *Employment and Earnings*, and *Monthly Labor Review*.

SOCIAL SERVICES - ESTABLISHMENTS

U.S. Department of Commerce, Bureau of the Census, Suitland, Maryland 20233 (301) 763-4040; *County Business Patterns*, and *Census of Service Industries*.

SOCIAL SERVICES - OCCUPATIONAL SAFETY

U.S. Department of Labor, Bureau of Labor Statistics, Two Massachusetts Avenue, NE, Washington, D.C. 20212 (202) 606-7828; *Injuries and Illnesses in the United States by Industry*.

SOCIAL SERVICES - RECEIPTS

U.S. Department of Commerce, Bureau of the Census, Suitland, Maryland 20233 (301) 763-4040; *Census of Service Industries, Current Business Reports*, and *Service Annual Survey*.

SOCIAL WELFARE - See also Individual Programs

SOCIAL WELFARE - CHARITABLE CONTRIBUTIONS

Independent Sector, 1828 L Street, NW, Washington, D.C. 20036 (202) 223-8100; *Giving and Volunteering in the United States*.

SOCIAL WELFARE - EMPLOYEES - STATE AND LOCAL GOVERNMENT

U.S. Department of Commerce, Bureau of the Census, Suitland, Maryland 20233 (301) 763-4040; *Historical Statistics on Governmental Finances and Employment*, and *Public Employment*.

SOCIAL WELFARE - EXPENDITURES - CITY GOVERNMENT

U.S. Department of Commerce, Bureau of the Census, Suitland, Maryland 20233 (301) 763-4040; *City Government Finances*.

SOCIAL WELFARE - EXPENDITURES - FEDERAL

U.S. Department of Commerce, Bureau of the Census, Suitland, Maryland 20233 (301) 763-4040; *Historical Statistics on*

Governmental Finances and Employment, Government Finances, and unpublished data.

U.S. Department of Health and Human Services, Social Security Administration, 6401 Security Boulevard, Baltimore, Maryland 21235 (410) 965-1234; *Social Security Bulletin,* and unpublished data.

U.S. Library of Congress, 10 First Street, SE, Washington, D.C. 20540 (202) 707-5000; *Cash and Noncash Benefits for Persons with Limited Income: Eligibility Rules, Recipient and Expenditure Data, Fiscal Year.*

SOCIAL WELFARE - EXPENDITURES - GOVERNMENTAL

U.S. Department of Commerce, Bureau of the Census, Suitland, Maryland 20233 (301) 763-4040; *Historical Statistics on Governmental Finances and Employment,* and *Government Finances.*

U.S. Department of Health and Human Services, Social Security Administration, 6401 Security Boulevard, Baltimore, Maryland 21235 (410) 965-1234; *Social Security Bulletin,* and unpublished data.

SOCIAL WELFARE - EXPENDITURES - PRIVATE

U.S. Department of Health and Human Services, Social Security Administration, 6401 Security Boulevard, Baltimore, Maryland 21235 (410) 965-1234; *Annual Statistical Supplement to the Social Security Bulletin.*

SOCIAL WELFARE - EXPENDITURES - STATE AND LOCAL GOVERNMENT

U.S. Department of Commerce, Bureau of the Census, Suitland, Maryland 20233 (301) 763-4040; *Census of Governments, Historical Statistics on Governmental Finances and Employment Government Finances,* and unpublished data.

U.S. Department of Health and Human Services, Social Security Administration, 6401 Security Boulevard, Baltimore, Maryland 21235 (410) 965-1234, *Social Security Bulletin,* and unpublished data.

SOCIAL WELFARE - EXPENDITURES - STATE GOVERNMENT

U.S. Department of Commerce, Bureau of the Census, Suitland, Maryland 20233 (301) 763-4040; *Census of Governments, Historical Statistics on Governmental Finances and Employment,* and *State Government Finances.*

SOCIAL WELFARE - EXPENDITURES - VOLUNTEERS

U.S. Department of Commerce, Bureau of the Census, Suitland, Maryland 20233 (301) 763-4040; *Current Population Reports.*

SODIUM CARBONATE

U.S. Department of the Interior, Bureau of Mines, 810 Seventh Street, NW, Washington, D.C. 20241 (202) 501-9649; *Annual Reports,* and *Mineral Commodity Summaries.*

SODIUM SULFATE

U.S. Department of the Interior, Bureau of Mines, 810 Seventh Street, NW, Washington, D.C. 20241 (202) 501-9649; *Annual Reports,* and *Mineral Commodity Summaries.*

SOFT DRINKS - See also BEVERAGES

U.S. Department of Agriculture, Economic Research Service, Fourteenth Street and Independence Avenue, SW, Washington, D.C. 20005-4789 (202) 219-1504; *Food Consumption, Prices, and Expenditures,* and unpublished data.

SOFTBALL

Amateur Softball Association of America, 2801 NE Fiftieth Street, Oklahoma City, Oklahoma 73111-7203 (405) 424-5266.

National Sporting Goods Association, Lake Center Plaza Building, 1699 Wall Street, Mount Prospect, Illinois 60056-5780 (708) 439-4000; *Sports Participation in 1992: Series I,* and *The Sporting Goods Market in 1993.*

SOLAR ENERGY - COLLECTORS - MANUFACTURERS SHIPMENTS

U.S. Department of Energy, Energy Information Administration, 1000 Independence Avenue, SW, Washington, D.C. 20585 (202) 586-8800; *Solar Collector Manufacturing Activity.*

SOLID WASTE - DISPOSAL

Franklin Associates Limited, 4121 West Eighty-third Street, Suite 108, Prairie Village, Kansas 66208 (913) 649-2225; *Characterization of Municipal Solid Waste in the United States.*

U.S. Department of Commerce, Bureau of the Census, Suitland, Maryland 20233 (301) 763-4040; *Current Industrial Reports.*

SOLID WASTE - EXPENDITURES FOR POLLUTION ABATEMENT

U.S. Department of Commerce, Bureau of the Census, Suitland, Maryland 20233 (301) 763-4040; *Current Industrial Reports.*

U.S. Department of Commerce, Bureau of Economic Analysis, Fourteenth Street between Constitution Avenue and E Street, NW, Washington, D.C. 20230 (202) 606-9900; *Survey of Current Business.*

SOLID WASTE -INDUSTRY

Environmental Business International, Inc., 4452 Park Boulevard, Suite 306, San Diego, California 92116 (619) 295-7685; *Environmental Business Journal.*

SOLID WASTE - RECYCLING

Franklin Associates, Limited, 4121 West Eighty-third Street, Prairie Village, Kansas 66208 (913) 649-2225; *Characterization of Municipal Solid Waste in the United States.*

Solomon Islands - National Statistical Office

Statistics Office, Ministry of Finance and Economic Planning, Post Office Box G6, Honiara, Solomon Islands.

Solomon Islands - Primary Statistics Sources

Statistics Office, Post Office Box G6, Honiara, Solomon Islands; annual reports, *British Solomon Islands: Annual Abstract of Statistics, Quarterly Digest of Statistics,* and *Statistical Yearbook.*

SOLOMON ISLANDS - AGRICULTURE

Asian Development Bank, P.O. Box 789, 1099 Manila, Philippines; *Key Indicators of Developing Asian and Pacific Countries.*

Food and Agricultural Organization of the United Nations (FAO) Via delle Terme di Caracalla, 00100 Rome, Italy (Telephone Number in U.S. (202) 653-2400); *Production Yearbook, The State of Food and Agriculture,* and *Trade Yearbook.*

G.K. Hall and Company, 70 Lincoln Street, Boston, Massachusetts 02111 (617) 423-3990; *The World in Figures.*

Statistical Office of the United Nations, Publishing Service, New York, New York 10017 (800) 253-9646; *Statistical Yearbook for Asia and the Pacific.*

The World Bank, 1818 H Street, NW, Washington, D.C. 20433 (202) 477-1234; *World Tables.*

SOLOMON ISLANDS - AIRLINE SERVICE

G.K. Hall and Company, 70 Lincoln Street, Boston, Massachusetts 02111 (617) 423-3990; *The World in Figures.*

SOLOMON ISLANDS - ANIMAL HEALTH

Food and Agricultural Organization of the United Nations (FAO), Via delle Terme di Caracalla, 00100, Rome, Italy (Telephone Number in U.S. (202) 653-2400); *Animal Health Yearbook.*

SOLOMON ISLANDS - AREA AND DENSITY OF POPULATION

Food and Agricultural Organization of the United Nations (FAO) Via delle Terme di Caracalla, 00100 Rome, Italy (Telephone Number in U.S. (202) 653-2400); *The State of Food and Agriculture.*

G.K. Hall and Company, 70 Lincoln Street, Boston, Massachusetts 02111 (617) 423-3990; *The World in Figures.*

Statistical Office of the United Nations, Publishing Service, New York, New York 10017 (800) 253-9646; *Statistical Yearbook.*

SOLOMON ISLANDS - BALANCE OF PAYMENTS

G.K. Hall and Company, 70 Lincoln Street, Boston, Massachusetts 02111 (617) 423-3990; *The World in Figures.*

The World Bank, 1818 H Street, NW, Washington, D.C. 20433 (202) 477-1234; *World Tables.*

SOLOMON ISLANDS - BANKING

Asian Development Bank, P.O. Box 789, 1099 Manila, Philippines; *Key Indicators of Developing Asian and Pacific Countries.*

G.K. Hall and Company, 70 Lincoln Street, Boston, Massachusetts 02111 (617) 423-3990; *The World in Figures.*

International Monetary Fund, 700 Nineteenth Street, NW, Washington, D.C. 20431 (202) 623-7000; *Government Finance Statistics Yearbook.*

SOLOMON ISLANDS - BIRTH RATE

Statistical Office of the United Nations, Publishing Service, New York, New York 10017 (800) 253-9646; *Statistical Yearbook.*

The World Bank, 1818 H Street, NW, Washington, D.C. 20433 (202) 477-1234; *World Tables.*

SOLOMON ISLANDS - BONDS

G.K. Hall and Company, 70 Lincoln Street, Boston, Massachusetts 02111 (617) 423-3990; *The World in Figures.*

SOLOMON ISLANDS - BOOK PRODUCTION

G.K. Hall and Company, 70 Lincoln Street, Boston, Massachusetts 02111 (617) 423-3990; *The World in Figures.*

SOLOMON ISLANDS - BROADCASTING

Billboard Limited, P.O. Box 9027, 1006 AA Amsterdam, The Netherlands (Telephone Number in U.S. (212) 764-7300); *World Radio TV Handbook.*

G.K. Hall and Company, 70 Lincoln Street, Boston, Massachusetts 02111 (617) 423-3990; *The World in Figures.*

United Nations Educational, Scientific and Cultural Organization (UNESCO), 7 Place de Fontenoy, F-75700 Paris, France (Telephone Number in U.S. (212) 963-5981); *Statistical Yearbook.*

SOLOMON ISLANDS - BUSINESS

G.K. Hall and Company, 70 Lincoln Street, Boston, Massachusetts 02111 (617) 423-3990; *The World in Figures.*

SOLOMON ISLANDS - BUSINESS AND PROFESSIONAL LICENSES

International Monetary Fund, 700 Nineteenth Street, NW, Washington, D.C. 20431 (202) 623-7000; *Government Finance Statistics Yearbook.*

SOLOMON ISLANDS - CALORIE SUPPLY

Asian Development Bank, P.O. Box 789, 1099 Manila, Philippines; *Key Indicators of Developing Asian and Pacific Countries.*

Food and Agricultural Organization of the United Nations (FAO) Via delle Terme di Caracalla, 00100 Rome, Italy (Telephone Number in U.S. (202) 653-2400); *The State of Food and Agriculture.*

SOLOMON ISLANDS - CAPITAL INVESTMENT

Asian Development Bank, P.O. Box 789, 1099 Manila, Philippines; *Key Indicators of Developing Asian and Pacific Countries.*

SOLOMON ISLANDS - CAPITAL REVENUE

Asian Development Bank, P.O. Box 789, 1099 Manila, Philippines; *Key Indicators of Developing Asian and Pacific Countries.*

International Monetary Fund, 700 Nineteenth Street, NW, Washington, D.C. 20431 (202) 623-7000; *Government Finance Statistics Yearbook.*

SOLOMON ISLANDS - CHEMICAL (ORGANIC) PRODUCTION - See SOLOMON ISLANDS - MINING AND MINERAL PRODUCTS

SOLOMON ISLANDS - CLASS STRUCTURE

G.K. Hall and Company, 70 Lincoln Street, Boston, Massachusetts 02111 (617) 423-3990; *The World in Figures.*

SOLOMON ISLANDS - CLIMATE

G.K. Hall and Company, 70 Lincoln Street, Boston, Massachusetts 02111 (617) 423-3990; *The World in Figures.*

SOLOMON ISLANDS - CLOTHING EXPORTS AND IMPORTS

South Pacific Commission, Post Box D5, Noumea Cedex, New Caledonia; *Statistical Bulletin of the South Pacific: Retail Price Indexes.*

SOLOMON ISLANDS - COAL PRODUCTION - See SOLOMON ISLANDS - MINING AND MINERAL PRODUCTS

SOLOMON ISLANDS - COCOA BEAN PRODUCTION - See SOLOMON ISLANDS - CROPS

SOLOMON ISLANDS - COMMUNICATIONS

G.K. Hall and Company, 70 Lincoln Street, Boston, Massachusetts 02111 (617) 423-3990; *The World in Figures.*

Statistical Office of the United Nations, Publishing Service, New York, New York 10017 (800) 253-9646; *Statistical Yearbook for Asia and the Pacific.*

SOLOMON ISLANDS - CONSUMER PRICE INDEX

Asian Development Bank, P.O. Box 789, 1099 Manila, Philippines; *Key Indicators of Developing Asian and Pacific Countries.*

G.K. Hall and Company, 70 Lincoln Street, Boston, Massachusetts 02111 (617) 423-3990; *The World in Figures.*

Statistical Office of the United Nations, Publishing Service, New York, New York 10017 (800) 253-9646; *Statistical Yearbook.*

SOLOMON ISLANDS - CONSUMER PRICES

International Labour Office, I.L.O. Publications, CH-1211, Geneva 22, Switzerland; *Yearbook of Labour Statistics.*

SOLOMON ISLANDS - CONSUMPTION

G.K. Hall and Company, 70 Lincoln Street, Boston, Massachusetts 02111 (617) 423-3990; *The World in Figures.*

South Pacific Commission, Post Box D5, Noumea Cedex, New Caledonia; *Statistical Bulletin of the South Pacific: Retail Price Indexes.*

SOLOMON ISLANDS - CORN PRODUCTION - See SOLOMON ISLANDS - CROPS

SOLOMON ISLANDS - CORPORATE TAXES - See SOLOMON ISLANDS - TAXATION

SOLOMON ISLANDS - CROPS

Asian Development Bank, P.O. Box 789, 1099 Manila, Philippines; *Key Indicators of Developing Asian and Pacific Countries.*

Food and Agricultural Organization of the United Nations (FAO) Via delle Terme di Caracalla, 00100 Rome, Italy (Telephone Number in U.S. (202) 653-2400); *The State of Food and Agriculture.*

G.K. Hall and Company, 70 Lincoln Street, Boston, Massachusetts 02111 (617) 423-3990; *The World in Figures.*

Statistical Office of the United Nations, Publishing Service, New York, New York 10017 (800) 253-9646; *Statistical Yearbook.*

SOLOMON ISLANDS - CUSTOMS DUTIES

G.K. Hall and Company, 70 Lincoln Street, Boston, Massachusetts 02111 (617) 423-3990; *The World in Figures.*

SOLOMON ISLANDS - DAIRY PRODUCTS

Food and Agricultural Organization of the United Nations (FAO) Via delle Terme di Caracalla, 00100 Rome, Italy (Telephone Number in U.S. (202) 653-2400); *The State of Food and Agriculture.*

SOLOMON ISLANDS - DEATH RATES

G.K. Hall and Company, 70 Lincoln Street, Boston, Massachusetts 02111 (617) 423-3990; *The World in Figures.*

Statistical Office of the United Nations, Publishing Service, New York, New York 10017 (800) 253-9646; *Statistical Yearbook.*

SOLOMON ISLANDS - DEFENSE EXPENDITURES

G.K. Hall and Company, 70 Lincoln Street, Boston, Massachusetts 02111 (617) 423-3990; *The World in Figures.*

International Monetary Fund, 700 Nineteenth Street, NW, Washington, D.C. 20431 (202) 623-7000; *Government Finance Statistics Yearbook.*

SOLOMON ISLANDS - DEMOGRAPHY

G.K. Hall and Company, 70 Lincoln Street, Boston, Massachusetts 02111 (617) 423-3990; *The World in Figures.*

SOLOMON ISLANDS - DEVELOPMENT ASSISTANCE

Asian Development Bank, P.O. Box 789, 1099 Manila, Philippines; *Key Indicators of Developing Asian and Pacific Countries.*

G.K. Hall and Company, 70 Lincoln Street, Boston, Massachusetts 02111 (617) 423-3990; *The World in Figures.*

Statistical Office of the United Nations, Publishing Service, New York, New York 10017 (800) 253-9646; *Statistical Yearbook.*

SOLOMON ISLANDS - DISEASE

G.K. Hall and Company, 70 Lincoln Street, Boston, Massachusetts 02111 (617) 423-3990; *The World in Figures.*

SOLOMON ISLANDS - DOMESTIC PRODUCT

G.K. Hall and Company, 70 Lincoln Street, Boston, Massachusetts 02111 (617) 423-3990; *The World in Figures.*

SOLOMON ISLANDS - ECONOMY

Asian Development Bank, P.O. Box 789, 1099 Manila, Philippines; *Key Indicators of Developing Asian and Pacific Countries.*

G.K. Hall and Company, 70 Lincoln Street, Boston, Massachusetts 02111 (617) 423-3990; *The World in Figures.*

SOLOMON ISLANDS - EDUCATION

G.K. Hall and Company, 70 Lincoln Street, Boston, Massachusetts 02111 (617) 423-3990; *The World in Figures.*

International Monetary Fund, 700 Nineteenth Street, NW, Washington, D.C. 20431 (202) 623-7000; *Government Finance Statistics Yearbook.*

Statistical Office of the United Nations, Publishing Service, New York, New York 10017 (800) 253-9646; *Statistical Yearbook for Asia and the Pacific.*

United Nations Educational, Scientific and Cultural Organization (UNESCO), 7 Place de Fontenoy, F-75700 Paris, France (Telephone Number in U.S. (212) 963-5981); *Statistical Yearbook.*

The World Bank, 1818 H Street, NW, Washington, D.C. 20433 (202) 477-1234; *World Tables.*

SOLOMON ISLANDS - EGG PRODUCTION AND CONSUMPTION - See SOLOMON ISLANDS - DAIRY PRODUCTS

SOLOMON ISLANDS - ELECTRICITY

Asian Development Bank, P.O. Box 789, 1099 Manila, Philippines; *Key Indicators of Developing Asian and Pacific Countries.*

Statistical Office of the United Nations, Publishing Service, New York, New York 10017 (800) 253-9646; *Electric Power in Asia and the Pacific,* and *Statistical Yearbook.*

SOLOMON ISLANDS - EMPLOYMENT

International Labour Office, I.L.O. Publications, CH-1211, Geneva 22, Switzerland; *Yearbook of Labour Statistics.*

SOLOMON ISLANDS - ENERGY

Food and Agricultural Organization of the United Nations (FAO) Via delle Terme di Caracalla, 00100 Rome, Italy (Telephone Number in U.S. (202) 653-2400); *The State of Food and Agriculture.*

G.K. Hall and Company, 70 Lincoln Street, Boston, Massachusetts 02111 (617) 423-3990; *The World in Figures.*

Statistical Office of the United Nations, Publishing Service, New York, New York 10017 (800) 253-9646; *Energy Statistics Yearbook, Statistical Yearbook,* and *Statistical Yearbook for Asia and the Pacific.*

SOLOMON ISLANDS - EXCHANGE RATES

Asian Development Bank, P.O. Box 789, 1099 Manila, Philippines; *Key Indicators of Developing Asian and Pacific Countries.*

SOLOMON ISLANDS - EXCISE TAXES - See SOLOMON ISLANDS - TAXATION

SOLOMON ISLANDS - EXPORTS

Asian Development Bank, P.O. Box 789, 1099 Manila, Philippines; *Key Indicators of Developing Asian and Pacific Countries.*

Food and Agricultural Organization of the United Nations (FAO) Via delle Terme di Caracalla, 00100 Rome, Italy (Telephone Number in U.S. (202) 653-2400); *The State of Food and Agriculture.*

G.K. Hall and Company, 70 Lincoln Street, Boston, Massachusetts 02111 (617) 423-3990; *The World in Figures.*

International Monetary Fund, 700 Nineteenth Street, NW, Washington, D.C. 20431 (202) 623-7000; *Direction of Trade Statistics.*

South Pacific Commission, Post Box D5, Noumea Cedex, New Caledonia; *Statistical Bulletin of the South Pacific: Overseas Trade.*

The World Bank, 1818 H Street, NW, Washington, D.C. 20433 (202) 477-1234; *World Tables.*

SOLOMON ISLANDS - EXTERNAL FINANCING

Asian Development Bank, P.O. Box 789, 1099 Manila, Philippines; *Key Indicators of Developing Asian and Pacific Countries.*

SOLOMON ISLANDS - EXTERNAL INDEBTEDNESS

Asian Development Bank, P.O. Box 789, 1099 Manila, Philippines; *Key Indicators of Developing Asian and Pacific Countries.*

The World Bank, 1818 H Street, NW, Washington, D.C. 20433 (202) 477-1234; *World Tables.*

SOLOMON ISLANDS - EXTERNAL TRADE

Asian Development Bank, P.O. Box 789, 1099 Manila, Philippines; *Key Indicators of Developing Asian and Pacific Countries.*

Food and Agricultural Organization of the United Nations (FAO) Via delle Terme di Caracalla, 00100 Rome, Italy (Telephone Number in U.S. (202) 653-2400); *The State of Food and Agriculture,* and *Trade Yearbook.*

G.K. Hall and Company, 70 Lincoln Street, Boston, Massachusetts 02111 (617) 423-3990; *The World in Figures.*

Statistical Office of the United Nations, Publishing Service, New York, New York 10017 (800) 253-9646; *Statistical Yearbook,* and *Statistical Yearbook for Asia and the Pacific.*

SOLOMON ISLANDS - FARM CROPS - See SOLOMON ISLANDS - CROPS

SOLOMON ISLANDS - FERTILITY RATES

The World Bank, 1818 H Street, NW, Washington, D.C. 20433 (202) 477-1234; *World Tables.*

SOLOMON ISLANDS - FERTILIZER

Food and Agricultural Organization of the United Nations (FAO) Via delle Terme di Caracalla, 00100 Rome, Italy (Telephone Number in U.S. (202) 653-2400); *The State of Food and Agriculture.*

Organisation for Economic Co-operation and Development (OECD), 2 rue Andre-Pascal, 75 Paris 16, France (Telephone Number in U.S. (202) 785-6323); *Indicators of Industrial Activity.*

SOLOMON ISLANDS - FINANCE

Asian Development Bank, P.O. Box 789, 1099 Manila, Philippines; *Key Indicators of Developing Asian and Pacific Countries.*

Food and Agricultural Organization of the United Nations (FAO) Via delle Terme di Caracalla, 00100 Rome, Italy (Telephone Number in U.S. (202) 653-2400); *The State of Food and Agriculture.*

G.K. Hall and Company, 70 Lincoln Street, Boston, Massachusetts 02111 (617) 423-3990; *The World in Figures.*

International Monetary Fund, 700 Nineteenth Street, NW, Washington, D.C. 20431 (202) 623-7000; *Government Finance Statistics Yearbook.*

Statistical Office of the United Nations, Publishing Service, New York, New York 10017 (800) 253-9646; *Statistical Yearbook for Asia and the Pacific.*

SOLOMON ISLANDS - FISHERIES

Food and Agricultural Organization of the United Nations (FAO) Via delle Terme di Caracalla, 00100 Rome, Italy (Telephone Number in U.S. (202) 653-2400); *The State of Food and Agriculture,* and *Yearbook of Fishery Statistics.*

Statistical Office of the United Nations, Publishing Service, New York, New York 10017 (800) 253-9646; *Statistical Yearbook.*

SOLOMON ISLANDS - FOOD

Food and Agricultural Organization of the United Nations (FAO) Via delle Terme di Caracalla, 00100 Rome, Italy (Telephone Number in U.S. (202) 653-2400); *The State of Food and Agriculture.*

G.K. Hall and Company, 70 Lincoln Street, Boston, Massachusetts 02111 (617) 423-3990; *The World in Figures.*

South Pacific Commission, Post Box D5, Noumea Cedex, New Caledonia; *Statistical Bulletin of the South Pacific: Retail Price Indexes.*

Statistical Office of the United Nations, Publishing Service, New York, New York 10017 (800) 253-9646; *Statistical Yearbook for Asia and the Pacific.*

SOLOMON ISLANDS - FOREIGN AID

G.K. Hall and Company, 70 Lincoln Street, Boston, Massachusetts 02111 (617) 423-3990; *The World in Figures.*

SOLOMON ISLANDS - FOREIGN DEBT

International Monetary Fund, 700 Nineteenth Street, NW, Washington, D.C. 20431 (202) 623-7000; *Government Finance Statistics Yearbook.*

SOLOMON ISLANDS - FOREIGN TRADE

Asian Development Bank, P.O. Box 789, 1099 Manila, Philippines; *Key Indicators of Developing Asian and Pacific Countries.*

Food and Agricultural Organization of the United Nations (FAO) Via delle Terme di Caracalla, 00100 Rome, Italy (Telephone Number in U.S. (202) 653-2400); *The State of Food and Agriculture.*

G.K. Hall and Company, 70 Lincoln Street, Boston, Massachusetts 02111 (617) 423-3990; *The World in Figures.*

South Pacific Commission, Post Box D5, Noumea Cedex, New Caledonia; *Statistical Bulletin of the South Pacific: Overseas Trade.*

Statistical Office of the United Nations, Publishing Service, New York, New York 10017 (800) 253-9646; *International Trade Statistics Yearbook,* and *Statistical Yearbook.*

The World Bank, 1818 H Street, NW, Washington, D.C. 20433 (202) 477-1234; *World Tables.*

SOLOMON ISLANDS - FORESTRY AND FOREST PRODUCTS

Food and Agricultural Organization of the United Nations (FAO) Via delle Terme di Caracalla, 00100 Rome, Italy (Telephone Number in

U.S. (202) 653-2400); *The State of Food and Agriculture,* and *Yearbook of Forest Products.*

G.K. Hall and Company, 70 Lincoln Street, Boston, Massachusetts 02111 (617) 423-3990; *The World in Figures.*

SOLOMON ISLANDS - GAS PRODUCTION - See SOLOMON ISLANDS - MINING AND MINERAL PRODUCTS

SOLOMON ISLANDS - GOLD HOLDINGS

The World Bank, 1818 H Street, NW, Washington, D.C. 20433 (202) 477-1234; *World Tables.*

SOLOMON ISLANDS - GOVERNMENT

Asian Development Bank, P.O. Box 789, 1099 Manila, Philippines; *Key Indicators of Developing Asian and Pacific Countries.*

G.K. Hall and Company, 70 Lincoln Street, Boston, Massachusetts 02111 (617) 423-3990; *The World in Figures.*

SOLOMON ISLANDS - GOVERNMENT EXPENDITURES

Asian Development Bank, P.O. Box 789, 1099 Manila, Philippines; *Key Indicators of Developing Asian and Pacific Countries.*

International Monetary Fund, 700 Nineteenth Street, NW, Washington, D.C. 20431 (202) 623-7000; *Government Finance Statistics Yearbook.*

The World Bank, 1818 H Street, NW, Washington, D.C. 20433 (202) 477-1234; *World Tables.*

SOLOMON ISLANDS - GOVERNMENT FINANCES

Asian Development Bank, P.O. Box 789, 1099 Manila, Philippines; *Key Indicators of Developing Asian and Pacific Countries.*

SOLOMON ISLANDS - GOVERNMENT REVENUE

Asian Development Bank, P.O. Box 789, 1099 Manila, Philippines; *Key Indicators of Developing Asian and Pacific Countries.*

International Monetary Fund, 700 Nineteenth Street, NW, Washington, D.C. 20431 (202) 623-7000; *Government Finance Statistics Yearbook.*

The World Bank, 1818 H Street, NW, Washington, D.C. 20433 (202) 477-1234; *World Tables.*

SOLOMON ISLANDS - GRAIN PRODUCTION - See SOLOMON ISLANDS - CROPS

SOLOMON ISLANDS - GRANTS

International Monetary Fund, 700 Nineteenth Street, NW, Washington, D.C. 20431 (202) 623-7000; *Government Finance Statistics Yearbook.*

SOLOMON ISLANDS - GROSS DOMESTIC PRODUCT

Asian Development Bank, P.O. Box 789, 1099 Manila, Philippines; *Key Indicators of Developing Asian and Pacific Countries.*

G.K. Hall and Company, 70 Lincoln Street, Boston, Massachusetts 02111 (617) 423-3990; *The World in Figures.*

Statistical Office of the United Nations, Publishing Service, New York, New York 10017 (800) 253-9646; *Statistical Yearbook.*

The World Bank, 1818 H Street, NW, Washington, D.C. 20433 (202) 477-1234; *World Tables.*

SOLOMON ISLANDS - GROSS NATIONAL PRODUCT

Asian Development Bank, P.O. Box 789, 1099 Manila, Philippines; *Key Indicators of Developing Asian and Pacific Countries.*

The World Bank, 1818 H Street, NW, Washington, D.C. 20433 (202) 477-1234; *World Tables.*

SOLOMON ISLANDS - HEALTH

G.K. Hall and Company, 70 Lincoln Street, Boston, Massachusetts 02111 (617) 423-3990; *The World in Figures.*

South Pacific Commission, Post Box D5, Noumea Cedex, New Caledonia; *Statistical Bulletin of the South Pacific: Retail Price Indexes.*

Statistical Office of the United Nations, Publishing Service, New York, New York 10017 (800) 253-9646; *Statistical Yearbook.*

SOLOMON ISLANDS - HEALTH EXPENDITURES

International Monetary Fund, 700 Nineteenth Street, NW, Washington, D.C. 20431 (202) 623-7000; *Government Finance Statistics Yearbook.*

SOLOMON ISLANDS - HIGHWAYS

G.K. Hall and Company, 70 Lincoln Street, Boston, Massachusetts 02111 (617) 423-3990; *The World in Figures.*

SOLOMON ISLANDS - HOURS OF WORK - See SOLOMON ISLANDS - EMPLOYMENT

SOLOMON ISLANDS - HOUSING AND HOUSING UNITS

South Pacific Commission, Post Box D5, Noumea Cedex, New Caledonia; *Statistical Bulletin of the South Pacific: Retail Price Indexes.*

SOLOMON ISLANDS - HOUSING EXPENDITURES

International Monetary Fund, 700 Nineteenth Street, NW, Washington, D.C. 20431 (202) 623-7000; *Government Finance Statistics Yearbook.*

South Pacific Commission, Post Box D5, Noumea Cedex, New Caledonia; *Statistical Bulletin of the South Pacific: Retail Price Indexes.*

SOLOMON ISLANDS - ILLITERATE POPULATION

G.K. Hall and Company, 70 Lincoln Street, Boston, Massachusetts 02111 (617) 423-3990; *The World in Figures.*

SOLOMON ISLANDS - IMPORTS

Asian Development Bank, P.O. Box 789, 1099 Manila, Philippines; *Key Indicators of Developing Asian and Pacific Countries.*

Food and Agricultural Organization of the United Nations (FAO) Via delle Terme di Caracalla, 00100 Rome, Italy (Telephone Number in U.S. (202) 653-2400); *The State of Food and Agriculture.*

G.K. Hall and Company, 70 Lincoln Street, Boston, Massachusetts 02111 (617) 423-3990; *The World in Figures.*

International Monetary Fund, 700 Nineteenth Street, NW, Washington, D.C. 20431 (202) 623-7000; *Direction of Trade Statistics,* and *Government Finance Statistics Yearbook.*

South Pacific Commission, Post Box D5, Noumea Cedex, New Caledonia; *Statistical Bulletin of the South Pacific: Overseas Trade.*

The World Bank, 1818 H Street, NW, Washington, D.C. 20433 (202) 477-1234; *World Tables.*

SOLOMON ISLANDS - INCOME TAXES - See SOLOMON ISLANDS - TAXATION

SOLOMON ISLANDS - INDUSTRY

G.K. Hall and Company, 70 Lincoln Street, Boston, Massachusetts 02111 (617) 423-3990; *The World in Figures.*

International Labour Office, I.L.O. Publications, CH-1211, Geneva 22, Switzerland; *Yearbook of Labour Statistics.*

Statistical Office of the United Nations, Publishing Service, New York, New York 10017 (800) 253-9646; *Statistical Yearbook for Asia and the Pacific.*

The World Bank, 1818 H Street, NW, Washington, D.C. 20433 (202) 477-1234; *World Tables.*

SOLOMON ISLANDS - INFANT AND MATERNAL MORTALITY

Statistical Office of the United Nations, Publishing Service, New York, New York 10017 (800) 253-9646; *Statistical Yearbook.*

The World Bank, 1818 H Street, NW, Washington, D.C. 20433 (202) 477-1234; *World Tables.*

SOLOMON ISLANDS - INTERNAL TRADE

Statistical Office of the United Nations, Publishing Service, New York, New York 10017 (800) 253-9646; *Statistical Yearbook for Asia and the Pacific.*

SOLOMON ISLANDS - INTERNATIONAL RESERVES EXCLUDING GOLD

Asian Development Bank, P.O. Box 789, 1099 Manila, Philippines; *Key Indicators of Developing Asian and Pacific Countries.*

The World Bank, 1818 H Street, NW, Washington, D.C. 20433 (202) 477-1234; *World Tables.*

SOLOMON ISLANDS - INTERNATIONAL STATISTICS

Asian Development Bank, P.O. Box 789, 1099 Manila, Philippines; *Key Indicators of Developing Asian and Pacific Countries.*

SOLOMON ISLANDS - LABOR FORCE

Food and Agricultural Organization of the United Nations (FAO) Via delle Terme di Caracalla, 00100 Rome, Italy (Telephone Number in U.S. (202) 653-2400); *The State of Food and Agriculture.*

G.K. Hall and Company, 70 Lincoln Street, Boston, Massachusetts 02111 (617) 423-3990; *The World in Figures.*

The World Bank, 1818 H Street, NW, Washington, D.C. 20433 (202) 477-1234; *World Tables*.

SOLOMON ISLANDS - LABOR PRODUCTIVITY

International Labour Office, I.L.O. Publications, CH-1211, Geneva 22, Switzerland; *Yearbook of Labour Statistics*.

SOLOMON ISLANDS - LAND USE

Food and Agricultural Organization of the United Nations (FAO), Via delle Terme di Caracalla, 00100 Rome, Italy (Telephone Number in U.S. (202) 653-2400); *Production Yearbook*.

G.K. Hall and Company, 70 Lincoln Street, Boston, Massachusetts 02111 (617) 423-3990; *The World in Figures*.

SOLOMON ISLANDS - LIBRARIES

United Nations Educational, Scientific and Cultural Organization (UNESCO), 7 Place de Fontenoy, F-75700 Paris, France (Telephone Number in U.S. (212) 963-5981); *Statistical Yearbook*.

SOLOMON ISLANDS - LIVESTOCK AND POULTRY

Food and Agricultural Organization of the United Nations (FAO), Via delle Terme di Caracalla, 00100 Rome, Italy (Telephone Number in U.S. (202) 653-2400); *Production Yearbook*, and *The State of Food and Agriculture*.

Statistical Office of the United Nations, Publishing Service, New York, New York 10017 (800) 253-9646; *Statistical Yearbook*.

SOLOMON ISLANDS - MAIL - NUMBER OF ITEMS SENT AND RECEIVED

Statistical Office of the United Nations, Publishing Service, New York, New York 10017 (800) 253-9646; *Statistical Yearbook*.

SOLOMON ISLANDS - MANPOWER

Statistical Office of the United Nations, Publishing Service, New York, New York 10017 (800) 253-9646; *Statistical Yearbook for Asia and the Pacific*.

SOLOMON ISLANDS - MANUFACTURING

Asian Development Bank, P.O. Box 789, 1099 Manila, Philippines; *Key Indicators of Developing Asian and Pacific Countries*.

G.K. Hall and Company, 70 Lincoln Street, Boston, Massachusetts 02111 (617) 423-3990; *The World in Figures*.

The World Bank, 1818 H Street, NW, Washington, D.C. 20433 (202) 477-1234; *World Tables*.

SOLOMON ISLANDS - MEAT PRODUCTION - See SOLOMON ISLANDS - LIVESTOCK AND POULTRY

SOLOMON ISLANDS - MERCHANT SHIPPING

G.K. Hall and Company, 70 Lincoln Street, Boston, Massachusetts 02111 (617) 423-3990; *The World in Figures*.

Statistical Office of the United Nations, Publishing Service, New York, New York 10017 (800) 253-9646; *Statistical Yearbook*.

SOLOMON ISLANDS - MILITARY

G.K. Hall and Company, 70 Lincoln Street, Boston, Massachusetts 02111 (617) 423-3990; *The World in Figures*.

The International Institute for Strategic Studies, 23 Tavistock Street, London WC2E 7NQ, England; *The Military Balance*.

SOLOMON ISLANDS - MINING AND MINERAL PRODUCTS

Facts on File, 460 Park Avenue South, New York, New York 10016 (800) 443-8323; *The New Book of World Rankings*.

G.K. Hall and Company, 70 Lincoln Street, Boston, Massachusetts 02111 (617) 423-3990; *The World in Figures*.

Statistical Office of the United Nations, Publishing Service, New York, New York 10017 (800) 253-9646; *Statistical Yearbook*.

SOLOMON ISLANDS - MONEY SUPPLY

Asian Development Bank, P.O. Box 789, 1099 Manila, Philippines; *Key Indicators of Developing Asian and Pacific Countries*.

G.K. Hall and Company, 70 Lincoln Street, Boston, Massachusetts 02111 (617) 423-3990; *The World in Figures*.

The World Bank, 1818 H Street, NW, Washington, D.C. 20433 (202) 477-1234; *World Tables*.

SOLOMON ISLANDS - MOTOR VEHICLE TAXES - See SOLOMON ISLANDS - TAXATION

SOLOMON ISLANDS - MOTOR VEHICLES IN USE

G.K. Hall and Company, 70 Lincoln Street, Boston, Massachusetts 02111 (617) 423-3990; *The World in Figures*.

SOLOMON ISLANDS - MUSEUMS

United Nations Educational, Scientific and Cultural Organization (UNESCO), 7 Place de Fontenoy, F-75700 Paris, France (Telephone Number in U.S. (212) 963-5981); *Statistical Yearbook*.

SOLOMON ISLANDS - NATIONAL ACCOUNTS

Statistical Office of the United Nations, Publishing Service, New York, New York 10017 (800) 253-9646; *National Accounts Statistics*, *Statistical Yearbook*, and *Statistical Yearbook for Asia and the Pacific*.

SOLOMON ISLANDS - NATIONAL INCOME

G.K. Hall and Company, 70 Lincoln Street, Boston, Massachusetts 02111 (617) 423-3990; *The World in Figures*.

Statistical Office of the United Nations, Publishing Service, New York, New York 10017 (800) 253-9646; *Statistical Yearbook*.

SOLOMON ISLANDS - NEWSPAPER PRODUCTION - See SOLOMON ISLANDS - FORESTRY AND FOREST PRODUCTS

SOLOMON ISLANDS - OCCUPATIONS - See SOLOMON ISLANDS - LABOR FORCE

SOLOMON ISLANDS - PALM KERNEL AND PALM OIL PRODUCTION - See SOLOMON ISLANDS - CROPS

SOLOMON ISLANDS - PERIODICALS

United Nations Educational, Scientific and Cultural Organization (UNESCO), 7 Place de Fontenoy, F-75700 Paris, France (Telephone Number in U.S. (212) 963-5981); *Statistical Yearbook*.

SOLOMON ISLANDS - PESTICIDE USE

Food and Agricultural Organization of the United Nations (FAO) Via delle Terme di Caracalla, 00100 Rome, Italy (Telephone Number in U.S. (202) 653-2400); *The State of Food and Agriculture*.

SOLOMON ISLANDS - PETROLEUM INDUSTRY

Asian Development Bank, P.O. Box 789, 1099 Manila, Philippines; *Key Indicators of Developing Asian and Pacific Countries*.

Food and Agricultural Organization of the United Nations (FAO) Via delle Terme di Caracalla, 00100 Rome, Italy (Telephone Number in U.S. (202) 653-2400); *The State of Food and Agriculture*.

G.K. Hall and Company, 70 Lincoln Street, Boston, Massachusetts 02111 (617) 423-3990; *The World in Figures*.

SOLOMON ISLANDS - POPULATION

Asian Development Bank, P.O. Box 789, 1099 Manila, Philippines; *Key Indicators of Developing Asian and Pacific Countries*.

Food and Agricultural Organization of the United Nations (FAO), Via delle Terme di Caracalla, 00100 Rome, Italy (Telephone Number in U.S. (202) 653-2400); *Production Yearbook*.

G.K. Hall and Company, 70 Lincoln Street, Boston, Massachusetts 02111 (617) 423-3990; *The World in Figures*.

International Labour Office, I.L.O. Publications, CH-1211, Geneva 22, Switzerland; *Yearbook of Labour Statistics*.

Statistical Office of the United Nations, Publishing Service, New York, New York 10017 (800) 253-9646; *Statistical Yearbook*, and *Statistical Yearbook for Asia and the Pacific*.

United Nations Educational, Scientific and Cultural Organization (UNESCO), 7 Place de Fontenoy, F-75700 Paris, France (Telephone Number in U.S. (212) 963-5981); *Statistical Yearbook*.

World Health Organization, Office of Publications, Avenue Appia, CH-1211 Geneva 27, Switzerland (Telephone Number in U.S. (518) 436-9686); *World Health Statistics Annual*.

SOLOMON ISLANDS - POWER PRODUCTION INDUSTRY

Statistical Office of the United Nations, Publishing Service, New York, New York 10017 (800) 253-9646; *Electric Power in Asia and the Pacific*.

SOLOMON ISLANDS - PRICES

Asian Development Bank, P.O. Box 789, 1099 Manila, Philippines; *Key Indicators of Developing Asian and Pacific Countries*.

Food and Agricultural Organization of the United Nations (FAO), Via delle Terme di Caracalla, 00100 Rome, Italy (Telephone Number in U.S. (202) 653-2400); *Production Yearbook*, and *The State of Food and Agriculture*.

G.K. Hall and Company, 70 Lincoln Street, Boston, Massachusetts 02111 (617) 423-3990; *The World in Figures*.

International Labour Office, I.L.O. Publications, CH-1211, Geneva 22, Switzerland; *Yearbook of Labour Statistics*.

South Pacific Commission, Post Box D5, Noumea Cedex, New Caledonia; *Statistical Bulletin of the South Pacific: Overseas Trade*, and *Statistical Bulletin of the South Pacific: Retail Price Indexes*.

SOLOMON ISLANDS - PRODUCTION

G.K. Hall and Company, 70 Lincoln Street, Boston, Massachusetts 02111 (617) 423-3990; *The World in Figures*.

SOLOMON ISLANDS - PROPERTY TAXES - See SOLOMON ISLANDS - TAXATION

SOLOMON ISLANDS - RADIO BROADCASTING - See SOLOMON ISLANDS - BROADCASTING

SOLOMON ISLANDS - RAILWAYS

G.K. Hall and Company, 70 Lincoln Street, Boston, Massachusetts 02111 (617) 423-3990; *The World in Figures*.

SOLOMON ISLANDS - RENT PRICES

International Labour Office, I.L.O. Publications, CH-1211, Geneva 22, Switzerland; *Yearbook of Labour Statistics*.

SOLOMON ISLANDS - RETAIL TRADE

G.K. Hall and Company, 70 Lincoln Street, Boston, Massachusetts 02111 (617) 423-3990; *The World in Figures*.

SOLOMON ISLANDS - RICE PRODUCTION - See SOLOMON ISLANDS - CROPS

SOLOMON ISLANDS - ROUNDWOOD PRODUCTION - See SOLOMON ISLANDS - FORESTRY AND FOREST PRODUCTS

SOLOMON ISLANDS - SAWNWOOD PRODUCTION - See SOLOMON ISLANDS - FORESTRY AND FOREST PRODUCTS

SOLOMON ISLANDS - SCIENTISTS AND TECHNICIANS

Statistical Office of the United Nations, Publishing Service, New York, New York 10017 (800) 253-9646; *Statistical Yearbook*.

United Nations Educational, Scientific and Cultural Organization (UNESCO), 7 Place de Fontenoy, F-75700 Paris, France (Telephone Number in U.S. (212) 963-5981); *Statistical Yearbook*.

SOLOMON ISLANDS - SOCIAL DATA

Asian Development Bank, P.O. Box 789, 1099 Manila, Philippines; *Key Indicators of Developing Asian and Pacific Countries*.

G.K. Hall and Company, 70 Lincoln Street, Boston, Massachusetts 02111 (617) 423-3990; *The World in Figures*.

SOLOMON ISLANDS - SOCIAL SECURITY

International Monetary Fund, 700 Nineteenth Street, NW, Washington, D.C. 20431 (202) 623-7000; *Government Finance Statistics Yearbook*.

SOLOMON ISLANDS - STAMP TAXES AND DUTIES - See SOLOMON ISLANDS - TAXATION

SOLOMON ISLANDS - STOCKS - COMMODITY - MARKET
PRICE - INDEX

Food and Agricultural Organization of the United Nations (FAO) Via
delle Terme di Caracalla, 00100 Rome, Italy (Telephone Number in
U.S. (202) 653-2400); *The State of Food and Agriculture*.

SOLOMON ISLANDS - TAXATION

G.K. Hall and Company, 70 Lincoln Street, Boston, Massachusetts
02111 (617) 423-3990; *The World in Figures*.

International Monetary Fund, 700 Nineteenth Street, NW,
Washington, D.C. 20431 (202) 623-7000; *Government Finance
Statistics Yearbook*.

The World Bank, 1818 H Street, NW, Washington, D.C. 20433 (202)
477-1234; *World Tables*.

SOLOMON ISLANDS - TELEPHONES IN USE

G.K. Hall and Company, 70 Lincoln Street, Boston, Massachusetts
02111 (617) 423-3990; *The World in Figures*.

World Health Organization, Office of Publications, Avenue Appia,
CH-1211 Geneva 27, Switzerland (Telephone Number in U.S. (518)
436-9686); *World Health Statistics Annual*.

SOLOMON ISLANDS - TEXTILE INDUSTRY

G.K. Hall and Company, 70 Lincoln Street, Boston, Massachusetts
02111 (617) 423-3990; *The World in Figures*.

SOLOMON ISLANDS - THEATRE

United Nations Educational, Scientific and Cultural Organization
(UNESCO), 7 Place de Fontenoy, F-75700 Paris, France (Telephone
Number in U.S. (212) 963-5981); *Statistical Yearbook*.

SOLOMON ISLANDS - TOBACCO PRODUCTION

South Pacific Commission, Post Box D5, Noumea Cedex, New
Caledonia; *Statistical Bulletin of the South Pacific: Retail Price
Indexes*.

Statistical Office of the United Nations, Publishing Service, New
York, New York 10017 (800) 253-9646; *Statistical Yearbook*.

SOLOMON ISLANDS - TOURISM

G.K. Hall and Company, 70 Lincoln Street, Boston, Massachusetts
02111 (617) 423-3990; *The World in Figures*.

World Tourism Organization, Calle Capitan Haya 42, E-28020
Madrid, Spain; *Yearbook of Tourism Statistics*.

SOLOMON ISLANDS - TRADE - See SOLOMON ISLANDS - FOREIGN
TRADE

SOLOMON ISLANDS - TRANSPORTATION AND
COMMUNICATIONS

G.K. Hall and Company, 70 Lincoln Street, Boston, Massachusetts
02111 (617) 423-3990; *The World in Figures*.

South Pacific Commission, Post Box D5, Noumea Cedex, New
Caledonia; *Statistical Bulletin of the South Pacific: Retail Price
Indexes*.

Statistical Office of the United Nations, Publishing Service, New
York, New York 10017 (800) 253-9646; *Statistical Yearbook for Asia
and the Pacific*.

SOLOMON ISLANDS - UNEMPLOYMENT

International Labour Office, I.L.O. Publications, CH-1211, Geneva 22,
Switzerland; *Yearbook of Labour Statistics*.

SOLOMON ISLANDS - UTILITIES

Statistical Office of the United Nations, Publishing Service, New
York, New York 10017 (800) 253-9646; *Electric Power in Asia and
the Pacific*.

SOLOMON ISLANDS - VITAL STATISTICS

G.K. Hall and Company, 70 Lincoln Street, Boston, Massachusetts
02111 (617) 423-3990; *The World in Figures*.

Statistical Office of the United Nations, Publishing Service, New
York, New York 10017 (800) 253-9646; *Statistical Yearbook*.

World Health Organization, Office of Publications, Avenue Appia,
CH-1211 Geneva 27, Switzerland (Telephone Number in U.S. (518)
436-9686); *World Health Statistics Annual*.

SOLOMON ISLANDS - WAGES

G.K. Hall and Company, 70 Lincoln Street, Boston, Massachusetts
02111 (617) 423-3990; *The World in Figures*.

International Labour Office, I.L.O. Publications, CH-1211, Geneva 22,
Switzerland; *Yearbook of Labour Statistics*.

SOLOMON ISLANDS - WAGES AND PRICES

Statistical Office of the United Nations, Publishing Service, New
York, New York 10017 (800) 253-9646; *Statistical Yearbook for Asia
and the Pacific*.

SOLOMON ISLANDS - WEATHER

G.K. Hall and Company, 70 Lincoln Street, Boston, Massachusetts
02111 (617) 423-3990; *The World in Figures*.

SOLOMON ISLANDS - WELFARE

International Monetary Fund, 700 Nineteenth Street, NW,
Washington, D.C. 20431 (202) 623-7000; *Government Finance
Statistics Yearbook*.

SOLOMON ISLANDS - WHOLESALE PRICES

Asian Development Bank, P.O. Box 789, 1099 Manila, Philippines;
Key Indicators of Developing Asian and Pacific Countries.

Somalia - National Statistical Office

Statistical Department, State Planning Commission, Post Office Box
1742, Mogadishu, Somalia.

Somalia - Primary Statistics Sources

Central Statistical Department, Post Office Box 1742, Mogadishu,
Somalia; *Koobaha Staatistikada* (Statistical Abstract), and *Faafinta
Istaatistikada Bisha* (Monthly Statistical Bulletin).

SOMALIA - AGRICULTURE

Euromonitor Publications Limited, 87-88 Turnmill Street, London EC1M 5QU, England; *International Marketing Data and Statistics.*

Facts on File, 460 Park Avenue South, New York, New York 10016 (800) 443-8323; *The New Book of World Rankings.*

Food and Agricultural Organization of the United Nations (FAO) Via delle Terme di Caracalla, 00100 Rome, Italy (Telephone Number in U.S. (202) 653-2400); *Production Yearbook, The State of Food and Agriculture,* and *Trade Yearbook.*

G.K. Hall and Company, 70 Lincoln Street, Boston, Massachusetts 02111 (617) 423-3990; *The World in Figures.*

Statistical Office of the United Nations, Publishing Service, New York, New York 10017 (800) 253-9646; *Statistical Yearbook,* and *Survey of Economic and Social Conditions in Africa.*

Times Books, 201 East 50th Street, New York, New York 10022 (212) 751-2600; *The Economist Book of Vital World Statistics.*

United Nations Economic Commission for Africa, Africa Hall, P.O. Box 3001, Addis Ababa, Ethiopia (Telephone Number in U.S. (800) 253-9646); *African Statistical Yearbook.*

The World Bank, 1818 H Street, NW, Washington, D.C. 20433 (202) 477-1234; *World Tables.*

SOMALIA - AIRLINE SERVICE

Facts on File, 460 Park Avenue South, New York, New York 10016 (800) 443-8323; *The New Book of World Rankings.*

G.K. Hall and Company, 70 Lincoln Street, Boston, Massachusetts 02111 (617) 423-3990; *The World in Figures.*

International Civil Aviation Organization, 1000 Sherbrooke Street West, Suite 400, Montreal, Quebec, Canada H3A 2R2 (514) 285-8219; *Civil Aviation Statistics of the World.*

Statistical Office of the United Nations, Publishing Service, New York, New York 10017 (800) 253-9646; *Statistical Yearbook.*

Times Books, 201 East 50th Street, New York, New York 10022 (212) 751-2600; *The Economist Book of Vital World Statistics.*

United Nations Economic Commission for Africa, Africa Hall, P.O. Box 3001, Addis Ababa, Ethiopia (Telephone Number in U.S. (800) 253-9646); *African Statistical Yearbook.*

SOMALIA - ALUMINUM PRODUCTION AND CONSUMPTION - See SOMALIA - MINING AND MINERAL PRODUCTS

SOMALIA - ANIMAL EXPORTS

International Monetary Fund, 700 Nineteenth Street, NW, Washington, D.C. 20431 (202) 623-7000; *International Financial Statistics.*

SOMALIA - ANIMAL HEALTH

Food and Agricultural Organization of the United Nations (FAO), Via delle Terme di Caracalla, 00100, Rome, Italy (Telephone Number in U.S. (202) 653-2400); *Animal Health Yearbook.*

SOMALIA - AREA AND DENSITY OF POPULATION

African Development Bank, 01 BP 1387, Abidjan 01, Cote D'Ivoire; *Selected Statistics on Regional Member Countries.*

Euromonitor Publications Limited, 87-88 Turnmill Street, London EC1M 5QU, England; *International Marketing Data and Statistics.*

Facts on File, 460 Park Avenue South, New York, New York 10016 (800) 443-8323; *The New Book of World Rankings.*

Food and Agricultural Organization of the United Nations (FAO) Via delle Terme di Caracalla, 00100 Rome, Italy (Telephone Number in U.S. (202) 653-2400); *The State of Food and Agriculture.*

G.K. Hall and Company, 70 Lincoln Street, Boston, Massachusetts 02111 (617) 423-3990; *The World in Figures.*

Statistical Office of the United Nations, Publishing Service, New York, New York 10017 (800) 253-9646; *Statistical Yearbook,* and *Survey of Economic and Social Conditions in Africa.*

Times Books, 201 East 50th Street, New York, New York 10022 (212) 751-2600; *The Economist Book of Vital World Statistics.*

United Nations Educational, Scientific and Cultural Organization (UNESCO), 7 Place de Fontenoy, F-75700 Paris, France (Telephone Number in U.S. (212) 963-5981); *Statistical Yearbook.*

SOMALIA - ARMS EXPORTS AND IMPORTS

U.S. Arms Control and Disarmament Agency, 320 Twenty-first Street, NW, Washington, D.C. 20451 (202) 647-8677; *World Military Expenditures and Arms Transfers*

SOMALIA - BALANCE OF PAYMENTS

African Development Bank, 01 BP 1387, Abidjan 01, Cote D'Ivoire; *Selected Statistics on Regional Member Countries.*

The Economist Intelligence Unit, 111 West 57th Street, New York, New York 10019 (800) 938-4685; *The World Market Atlas.*

G.K. Hall and Company, 70 Lincoln Street, Boston, Massachusetts 02111 (617) 423-3990; *The World in Figures.*

International Monetary Fund, 700 Nineteenth Street, NW, Washington, D.C. 20431 (202) 623-7000; *Balance of Payments Yearbook.*

Times Books, 201 East 50th Street, New York, New York 10022 (212) 751-2600; *The Economist Book of Vital World Statistics.*

United Nations Economic Commission for Africa, Africa Hall, P.O. Box 3001, Addis Ababa, Ethiopia (Telephone Number in U.S. (800) 253-9646); *African Statistical Yearbook.*

The World Bank, 1818 H Street, NW, Washington, D.C. 20433 (202) 477-1234; *World Tables.*

SOMALIA - BANANA EXPORTS - See SOMALIA - CROPS

SOMALIA - BANKING

Facts on File, 460 Park Avenue South, New York, New York 10016 (800) 443-8323; *The New Book of World Rankings.*

G.K. Hall and Company, 70 Lincoln Street, Boston, Massachusetts 02111 (617) 423-3990; *The World in Figures.*

International Monetary Fund, 700 Nineteenth Street, NW, Washington, D.C. 20431 (202) 623-7000; *International Financial Statistics.*

United Nations Economic Commission for Africa, Africa Hall, P.O. Box 3001, Addis Ababa, Ethiopia (Telephone Number in U.S. (800) 253-9646); *African Statistical Yearbook.*

SOMALIA - BARLEY PRODUCTION - See SOMALIA - CROPS

SOMALIA - BEER PRODUCTION

Facts on File, 460 Park Avenue South, New York, New York 10016 (800) 443-8323; *The New Book of World Rankings.*

SOMALIA - BIRTH RATES

Facts on File, 460 Park Avenue South, New York, New York 10016 (800) 443-8323; *The New Book of World Rankings.*

Statistical Office of the United Nations, Publishing Service, New York, New York 10017 (800) 253-9646; *Demographic Yearbook, Statistical Yearbook,* and *Survey of Economic and Social Conditions in Africa.*

Times Books, 201 East 50th Street, New York, New York 10022 (212) 751-2600; *The Economist Book of Vital World Statistics.*

The World Bank, 1818 H Street, NW, Washington, D.C. 20433 (202) 477-1234; *World Tables.*

SOMALIA - BONDS

G.K. Hall and Company, 70 Lincoln Street, Boston, Massachusetts 02111 (617) 423-3990; *The World in Figures.*

SOMALIA - BOOK PRODUCTION

G.K. Hall and Company, 70 Lincoln Street, Boston, Massachusetts 02111 (617) 423-3990; *The World in Figures.*

SOMALIA - BROADCASTING

Billboard Limited, P.O. Box 9027, 1006 AA Amsterdam, The Netherlands (Telephone Number in U.S. (212) 764-7300); *World Radio TV Handbook.*

Facts on File, 460 Park Avenue South, New York, New York 10016 (800) 443-8323; *The New Book of World Rankings.*

G.K. Hall and Company, 70 Lincoln Street, Boston, Massachusetts 02111 (617) 423-3990; *The World in Figures.*

Times Books, 201 East 50th Street, New York, New York 10022 (212) 751-2600; *The Economist Book of Vital World Statistics.*

SOMALIA - BUSINESS

G.K. Hall and Company, 70 Lincoln Street, Boston, Massachusetts 02111 (617) 423-3990; *The World in Figures.*

SOMALIA - BUSINESS AND PROFESSIONAL LICENSES

International Monetary Fund, 700 Nineteenth Street, NW, Washington, D.C. 20431 (202) 623-7000; *Government Finance Statistics Yearbook.*

SOMALIA - BUTTER PRODUCTION - See SOMALIA - DAIRY PRODUCTS

SOMALIA - CALORIE SUPPLY

African Development Bank, 01 BP 1387, Abidjan 01, Cote D'Ivoire; *Selected Statistics on Regional Member Countries.*

Food and Agricultural Organization of the United Nations (FAO) Via delle Terme di Caracalla, 00100 Rome, Italy (Telephone Number in U.S. (202) 653-2400); *The State of Food and Agriculture.*

SOMALIA - CAPITAL REVENUE

International Monetary Fund, 700 Nineteenth Street, NW, Washington, D.C. 20431 (202) 623-7000; *Government Finance Statistics Yearbook.*

SOMALIA - CATTLE - See SOMALIA - LIVESTOCK AND POULTRY

SOMALIA - CEMENT PRODUCTION - See SOMALIA - MINING AND MINERAL PRODUCTS

SOMALIA - CHEMICAL (ORGANIC) PRODUCTION - See SOMALIA - MINING AND MINERAL PRODUCTS

SOMALIA - CHICKENS - See SOMALIA - LIVESTOCK AND POULTRY

SOMALIA - CIGARETTE PRODUCTION - See SOMALIA - TOBACCO PRODUCTION

SOMALIA - CLASS STRUCTURE

G.K. Hall and Company, 70 Lincoln Street, Boston, Massachusetts 02111 (617) 423-3990; *The World in Figures.*

SOMALIA - CLIMATE

Facts on File, 460 Park Avenue South, New York, New York 10016 (800) 443-8323; *The New Book of World Rankings.*

G.K. Hall and Company, 70 Lincoln Street, Boston, Massachusetts 02111 (617) 423-3990; *The World in Figures.*

SOMALIA - COAL PRODUCTION - See SOMALIA - MINING AND MINERAL PRODUCTS

SOMALIA - COFFEE PRODUCTION AND CONSUMPTION - See SOMALIA - CROPS

SOMALIA - COMMUNICATIONS

G.K. Hall and Company, 70 Lincoln Street, Boston, Massachusetts 02111 (617) 423-3990; *The World in Figures.*

United Nations Economic Commission for Africa, Africa Hall, P.O. Box 3001, Addis Ababa, Ethiopia (Telephone Number in U.S. (800) 253-9646); *African Statistical Yearbook.*

SOMALIA - CONSTRUCTION INDUSTRY

Facts on File, 460 Park Avenue South, New York, New York 10016 (800) 443-8323; *The New Book of World Rankings.*

United Nations Economic Commission for Africa, Africa Hall, P.O. Box 3001, Addis Ababa, Ethiopia (Telephone Number in U.S. (800) 253-9646); *African Statistical Yearbook.*

SOMALIA - CONSUMER PRICE INDEX

African Development Bank, 01 BP 1387, Abidjan 01, Cote D'Ivoire; *Selected Statistics on Regional Member Countries.*

G.K. Hall and Company, 70 Lincoln Street, Boston, Massachusetts 02111 (617) 423-3990; *The World in Figures*.

Statistical Office of the United Nations, Publishing Service, New York, New York 10017 (800) 253-9646; *Statistical Yearbook*, and *Survey of Economic and Social Conditions in Africa*.

Times Books, 201 East 50th Street, New York, New York 10022 (212) 751-2600; *The Economist Book of Vital World Statistics*.

United Nations Economic Commission for Africa, Africa Hall, P.O. Box 3001, Addis Ababa, Ethiopia (Telephone Number in U.S. (800) 253-9646); *African Statistical Yearbook*.

SOMALIA - CONSUMER PRICES

International Labour Office, I.L.O. Publications, CH-1211, Geneva 22, Switzerland; *Yearbook of Labour Statistics*.

International Monetary Fund, 700 Nineteenth Street, NW, Washington, D.C. 20431 (202) 623-7000; *International Financial Statistics*.

SOMALIA - CONSUMPTION

African Development Bank, 01 BP 1387, Abidjan 01, Cote D'Ivoire; *Selected Statistics on Regional Member Countries*.

G.K. Hall and Company, 70 Lincoln Street, Boston, Massachusetts 02111 (617) 423-3990; *The World in Figures*.

Statistical Office of the United Nations, Publishing Service, New York, New York 10017 (800) 253-9646; *Survey of Economic and Social Conditions in Africa*.

SOMALIA - COPPER PRODUCTION AND CONSUMPTION - See SOMALIA - MINING AND MINERAL PRODUCTS

SOMALIA - CORN PRODUCTION - See SOMALIA - CROPS

SOMALIA - CORPORATE TAXES - See SOMALIA - TAXATION

SOMALIA - COTTON PRODUCTION - See SOMALIA - CROPS

SOMALIA - CROPS

Facts on File, 460 Park Avenue South, New York, New York 10016 (800) 443-8323; *The New Book of World Rankings*.

Food and Agricultural Organization of the United Nations (FAO) Via delle Terme di Caracalla, 00100 Rome, Italy (Telephone Number in U.S. (202) 653-2400); *The State of Food and Agriculture*.

International Monetary Fund, 700 Nineteenth Street, NW, Washington, D.C. 20431 (202) 623-7000; *Government Finance Statistics Yearbook*.

Statistical Office of the United Nations, Publishing Service, New York, New York 10017 (800) 253-9646; *Statistical Yearbook*.

United Nations Economic Commission for Africa, Africa Hall, P.O. Box 3001, Addis Ababa, Ethiopia (Telephone Number in U.S. (800) 253-9646); *African Statistical Yearbook*.

SOMALIA - CUSTOMS DUTIES

G.K. Hall and Company, 70 Lincoln Street, Boston, Massachusetts 02111 (617) 423-3990; *The World in Figures*.

International Monetary Fund, 700 Nineteenth Street, NW, Washington, D.C. 20431 (202) 623-7000; *Government Finance Statistics Yearbook*.

SOMALIA - DAIRY PRODUCTS

Facts on File, 460 Park Avenue South, New York, New York 10016 (800) 443-8323; *The New Book of World Rankings*.

Food and Agricultural Organization of the United Nations (FAO) Via delle Terme di Caracalla, 00100 Rome, Italy (Telephone Number in U.S. (202) 653-2400); *The State of Food and Agriculture*.

Statistical Office of the United Nations, Publishing Service, New York, New York 10017 (800) 253-9646; *Statistical Yearbook*.

SOMALIA - DEATH RATES

G.K. Hall and Company, 70 Lincoln Street, Boston, Massachusetts 02111 (617) 423-3990; *The World in Figures*.

Statistical Office of the United Nations, Publishing Service, New York, New York 10017 (800) 253-9646; *Statistical Yearbook*, and *Survey of Economic and Social Conditions in Africa*.

Times Books, 201 East 50th Street, New York, New York 10022 (212) 751-2600; *The Economist Book of Vital World Statistics*.

SOMALIA - DEFENSE EXPENDITURES

G.K. Hall and Company, 70 Lincoln Street, Boston, Massachusetts 02111 (617) 423-3990; *The World in Figures*.

International Monetary Fund, 700 Nineteenth Street, NW, Washington, D.C. 20431 (202) 623-7000; *Government Finance Statistics Yearbook*.

U.S. Arms Control and Disarmament Agency, 320 Twenty-first Street, NW, Washington, D.C. 20451 (202) 647-8677; *World Military Expenditures and Arms Transfers*.

SOMALIA - DEMOGRAPHY

The Economist Intelligence Unit, 111 West 57th Street, New York, New York 10019 (800) 938-4685; *The World Market Atlas*.

Facts on File, 460 Park Avenue South, New York, New York 10016 (800) 443-8323; *The New Book of World Rankings*.

G.K. Hall and Company, 70 Lincoln Street, Boston, Massachusetts 02111 (617) 423-3990; *The World in Figures*.

Statistical Office of the United Nations, Publishing Service, New York, New York 10017 (800) 253-9646; *Survey of Economic and Social Conditions in Africa*.

SOMALIA - DEVELOPMENT ASSISTANCE

G.K. Hall and Company, 70 Lincoln Street, Boston, Massachusetts 02111 (617) 423-3990; *The World in Figures*.

Statistical Office of the United Nations, Publishing Service, New York, New York 10017 (800) 253-9646; *Statistical Yearbook*.

SOMALIA - DIAMOND PRODUCTION - See SOMALIA - MINING AND MINERAL PRODUCTS

SOMALIA - DISEASE

G.K. Hall and Company, 70 Lincoln Street, Boston, Massachusetts 02111 (617) 423-3990; *The World in Figures*.

SOMALIA - DIVORCE RATES

Facts on File, 460 Park Avenue South, New York, New York 10016 (800) 443-8323; *The New Book of World Rankings*.

Statistical Office of the United Nations, Publishing Service, New York, New York 10017 (800) 253-9646; *Demographic Yearbook*.

SOMALIA - DOMESTIC PRODUCT

G.K. Hall and Company, 70 Lincoln Street, Boston, Massachusetts 02111 (617) 423-3990; *The World in Figures*.

SOMALIA - ECONOMY

African Development Bank, 01 BP 1387, Abidjan 01, Cote D'Ivoire; *Selected Statistics on Regional Member Countries*.

Euromonitor Publications Limited, 87-88 Turnmill Street, London EC1M 5QU, England; *International Marketing Data and Statistics*.

Facts on File, 460 Park Avenue South, New York, New York 10016 (800) 443-8323; *The New Book of World Rankings*.

G.K. Hall and Company, 70 Lincoln Street, Boston, Massachusetts 02111 (617) 423-3990; *The World in Figures*.

Statistical Office of the United Nations, Publishing Service, New York, New York 10017 (800) 253-9646; *Foreign Trade Statistics for Africa*.

SOMALIA - EDUCATION

African Development Bank, 01 BP 1387, Abidjan 01, Cote D'Ivoire; *Selected Statistics on Regional Member Countries*.

The Economist Intelligence Unit, 111 West 57th Street, New York, New York 10019 (800) 938-4685; *The World Market Atlas*.

Facts on File, 460 Park Avenue South, New York, New York 10016 (800) 443-8323; *The New Book of World Rankings*.

G.K. Hall and Company, 70 Lincoln Street, Boston, Massachusetts 02111 (617) 423-3990; *The World in Figures*.

International Monetary Fund, 700 Nineteenth Street, NW, Washington, D.C. 20431 (202) 623-7000; *Government Finance Statistics Yearbook*.

Statistical Office of the United Nations, Publishing Service, New York, New York 10017 (800) 253-9646; *Survey of Economic and Social Conditions in Africa*.

Times Books, 201 East 50th Street, New York, New York 10022 (212) 751-2600; *The Economist Book of Vital World Statistics*.

United Nations Economic Commission for Africa, Africa Hall, P.O. Box 3001, Addis Ababa, Ethiopia (Telephone Number in U.S. (800) 253-9646); *African Statistical Yearbook*.

United Nations Educational, Scientific and Cultural Organization (UNESCO), 7 Place de Fontenoy, F-75700 Paris, France (Telephone Number in U.S. (212) 963-5981); *Statistical Yearbook*.

The World Bank, 1818 H Street, NW, Washington, D.C. 20433 (202) 477-1234; *World Tables*.

SOMALIA - EGG PRODUCTION AND CONSUMPTION - See SOMALIA - DAIRY PRODUCTS

SOMALIA - ELECTRICITY

Facts on File, 460 Park Avenue South, New York, New York 10016 (800) 443-8323; *The New Book of World Rankings*.

Statistical Office of the United Nations, Publishing Service, New York, New York 10017 (800) 253-9646; *Statistical Yearbook*.

United Nations Economic Commission for Africa, Africa Hall, P.O. Box 3001, Addis Ababa, Ethiopia (Telephone Number in U.S. (800) 253-9646); *African Statistical Yearbook*.

SOMALIA - EMPLOYMENT

Euromonitor Publications Limited, 87-88 Turnmill Street, London EC1M 5QU, England; *International Marketing Data and Statistics*.

Facts on File, 460 Park Avenue South, New York, New York 10016 (800) 443-8323; *The New Book of World Rankings*.

International Labour Office, I.L.O. Publications, CH-1211, Geneva 22, Switzerland; *Yearbook of Labour Statistics*.

Statistical Office of the United Nations, Publishing Service, New York, New York 10017 (800) 253-9646; *Statistical Yearbook*, and *Survey of Economic and Social Conditions in Africa*.

United Nations Economic Commission for Africa, Africa Hall, P.O. Box 3001, Addis Ababa, Ethiopia (Telephone Number in U.S. (800) 253-9646); *African Statistical Yearbook*.

SOMALIA - ENERGY

Facts on File, 460 Park Avenue South, New York, New York 10016 (800) 443-8323; *The New Book of World Rankings*.

Food and Agricultural Organization of the United Nations (FAO) Via delle Terme di Caracalla, 00100 Rome, Italy (Telephone Number in U.S. (202) 653-2400); *The State of Food and Agriculture*.

G.K. Hall and Company, 70 Lincoln Street, Boston, Massachusetts 02111 (617) 423-3990; *The World in Figures*.

Statistical Office of the United Nations, Publishing Service, New York, New York 10017 (800) 253-9646; *Energy Statistics Yearbook*, and *Statistical Yearbook*.

Times Books, 201 East 50th Street, New York, New York 10022 (212) 751-2600; *The Economist Book of Vital World Statistics*.

United Nations Economic Commission for Africa, Africa Hall, P.O. Box 3001, Addis Ababa, Ethiopia (Telephone Number in U.S. (800) 253-9646); *African Statistical Yearbook*.

SOMALIA - EXCHANGE RATES

African Development Bank, 01 BP 1387, Abidjan 01, Cote D'Ivoire; *Selected Statistics on Regional Member Countries*.

Euromonitor Publications Limited, 87-88 Turnmill Street, London EC1M 5QU, England; *International Marketing Data and Statistics*.

International Civil Aviation Organization, 1000 Sherbrooke Street West, Suite 400, Montreal, Quebec, Canada H3A 2R2 (514) 285-8219; *Civil Aviation Statistics of the World.*

International Monetary Fund, 700 Nineteenth Street, NW, Washington, D.C. 20431 (202) 623-7000; *International Financial Statistics.*

Statistical Office of the United Nations, Publishing Service, New York, New York 10017 (800) 253-9646; *Foreign Trade Statistics for Africa,* and *Statistical Yearbook.*

SOMALIA - EXCISE TAXES - See SOMALIA - TAXATION

SOMALIA - EXPORTS

The Economist Intelligence Unit, 111 West 57th Street, New York, New York 10019 (800) 938-4685; *The World Market Atlas.*

Euromonitor Publications Limited, 87-88 Turnmill Street, London EC1M 5QU, England; *International Marketing Data and Statistics.*

Food and Agricultural Organization of the United Nations (FAO) Via delle Terme di Caracalla, 00100 Rome, Italy (Telephone Number in U.S. (202) 653-2400); *The State of Food and Agriculture.*

G.K. Hall and Company, 70 Lincoln Street, Boston, Massachusetts 02111 (617) 423-3990; *The World in Figures.*

International Monetary Fund, 700 Nineteenth Street, NW, Washington, D.C. 20431 (202) 623-7000; *Direction of Trade Statistics, Government Finance Statistics Yearbook,* and *International Financial Statistics.*

Statistical Office of the United Nations, Publishing Service, New York, New York 10017; *Foreign Trade Statistics for Africa,* and *Survey of Economic and Social Conditions in Africa*

Times Books, 201 East 50th Street, New York, New York 10022 (212) 751-2600; *The Economist Book of Vital World Statistics.*

United Nations Economic Commission for Africa, Africa Hall, P.O. Box 3001, Addis Ababa, Ethiopia (Telephone Number in U.S. (800) 253-9646); *African Statistical Yearbook.*

The World Bank, 1818 H Street, NW, Washington, D.C. 20433 (202) 477-1234; *World Tables.*

SOMALIA - EXTERNAL INDEBTEDNESS

African Development Bank, 01 BP 1387, Abidjan 01, Cote D'Ivoire; *Selected Statistics on Regional Member Countries.*

Statistical Office of the United Nations, Publishing Service, New York, New York 10017 (800) 253-9646; *Survey of Economic and Social Conditions in Africa.*

The World Bank, 1818 H Street, NW, Washington, D.C. 20433 (202) 477-1234; *World Tables.*

SOMALIA - EXTERNAL TRADE

African Development Bank, 01 BP 1387, Abidjan 01, Cote D'Ivoire; *Selected Statistics on Regional Member Countries.*

Food and Agricultural Organization of the United Nations (FAO) Via delle Terme di Caracalla, 00100 Rome, Italy (Telephone Number in U.S. (202) 653-2400); *The State of Food and Agriculture,* and *Trade Yearbook.*

G.K. Hall and Company, 70 Lincoln Street, Boston, Massachusetts 02111 (617) 423-3990; *The World in Figures.*

Statistical Office of the United Nations, Publishing Service, New York, New York 10017 (800) 253-9646; *Statistical Yearbook.*

SOMALIA - FARM CROPS - See SOMALIA - CROPS

SOMALIA - FEMALE WORKING POPULATION - See SOMALIA - EMPLOYMENT

SOMALIA - FERTILITY RATES

Facts on File, 460 Park Avenue South, New York, New York 10016 (800) 443-8323; *The New Book of World Rankings.*

Statistical Office of the United Nations, Publishing Service, New York, New York 10017 (800) 253-9646; *Survey of Economic and Social Conditions in Africa.*

Times Books, 201 East 50th Street, New York, New York 10022 (212) 751-2600; *The Economist Book of Vital World Statistics.*

The World Bank, 1818 H Street, NW, Washington, D.C. 20433 (202) 477-1234; *World Tables.*

SOMALIA - FERTILIZER

Food and Agricultural Organization of the United Nations (FAO), Via delle Terme di Caracalla, 00100, Rome, Italy (Telephone Number in U.S. (202) 653-2400); *Fertilizer Yearbook,* and *The State of Food and Agriculture.*

Statistical Office of the United Nations, Publishing Service, New York, New York 10017 (800) 253-9646; *Statistical Yearbook.*

SOMALIA - FETAL MORTALITY

Statistical Office of the United Nations, Publishing Service, New York, New York 10017 (800) 253-9646; *Demographic Yearbook.*

SOMALIA - FINANCE

African Development Bank, 01 BP 1387, Abidjan 01, Cote D'Ivoire; *Selected Statistics on Regional Member Countries.*

Facts on File, 460 Park Avenue South, New York, New York 10016 (800) 443-8323; *The New Book of World Rankings.*

G.K. Hall and Company, 70 Lincoln Street, Boston, Massachusetts 02111 (617) 423-3990; *The World in Figures.*

International Monetary Fund, 700 Nineteenth Street, NW, Washington, D.C. 20431 (202) 623-7000; *International Financial Statistics.*

United Nations Economic Commission for Africa, Africa Hall, P.O. Box 3001, Addis Ababa, Ethiopia (Telephone Number in U.S. (800) 253-9646); *African Statistical Yearbook.*

SOMALIA - FISHERIES

Facts on File, 460 Park Avenue South, New York, New York 10016 (800) 443-8323; *The New Book of World Rankings.*

Food and Agricultural Organization of the United Nations (FAO) Via delle Terme di Caracalla, 00100 Rome, Italy (Telephone Number in U.S. (202) 653-2400); *The State of Food and Agriculture,* and *Yearbook of Fishery Statistics.*

Statistical Office of the United Nations, Publishing Service, New York, New York 10017 (800) 253-9646; *Statistical Yearbook*, and *Survey of Economic and Social Conditions in Africa*.

United Nations Economic Commission for Africa, Africa Hall, P.O. Box 3001, Addis Ababa, Ethiopia (Telephone Number in U.S. (800) 253-9646); *African Statistical Yearbook*.

SOMALIA - FOOD

African Development Bank, 01 BP 1387, Abidjan 01, Cote D'Ivoire; *Selected Statistics on Regional Member Countries*.

Food and Agricultural Organization of the United Nations (FAO) Via delle Terme di Caracalla, 00100 Rome, Italy (Telephone Number in U.S. (202) 653-2400); *Production Yearbook*, and *The State of Food and Agriculture*.

G.K. Hall and Company, 70 Lincoln Street, Boston, Massachusetts 02111 (617) 423-3990; *The World in Figures*.

SOMALIA - FOREIGN AID

G.K. Hall and Company, 70 Lincoln Street, Boston, Massachusetts 02111 (617) 423-3990; *The World in Figures*.

SOMALIA - FOREIGN TRADE

Euromonitor Publications Limited, 87-88 Turnmill Street, London EC1M 5QU, England; *International Marketing Data and Statistics*.

Facts on File, 460 Park Avenue South, New York, New York 10016 (800) 443-8323; *The New Book of World Rankings*.

Food and Agricultural Organization of the United Nations (FAO) Via delle Terme di Caracalla, 00100 Rome, Italy (Telephone Number in U.S. (202) 653-2400); *The State of Food and Agriculture*.

G.K. Hall and Company, 70 Lincoln Street, Boston, Massachusetts 02111 (617) 423-3990; *The World in Figures*.

International Monetary Fund, 700 Nineteenth Street, NW, Washington, D.C. 20431 (202) 623-7000; *International Financial Statistics*.

Statistical Office of the United Nations, Publishing Service, New York, New York 10017 (800) 253-9646; *Foreign Trade Statistics for Africa, International Trade Statistics Yearbook, Statistical Yearbook*, and *Trade in Manufactures of Developing Countries*.

United Nations Economic Commission for Africa, Africa Hall, P.O. Box 3001, Addis Ababa, Ethiopia (Telephone Number in U.S. (800) 253-9646); *African Statistical Yearbook*.

The World Bank, 1818 H Street, NW, Washington, D.C. 20433 (202) 477-1234; *World Tables*.

SOMALIA - FORESTRY AND FOREST PRODUCTS

Facts on File, 460 Park Avenue South, New York, New York 10016 (800) 443-8323; *The New Book of World Rankings*.

Food and Agricultural Organization of the United Nations (FAO) Via delle Terme di Caracalla, 00100 Rome, Italy (Telephone Number in U.S. (202) 653-2400); *The State of Food and Agriculture*, and *Yearbook of Forest Products*.

G.K. Hall and Company, 70 Lincoln Street, Boston, Massachusetts 02111 (617) 423-3990; *The World in Figures*.

United Nations Economic Commission for Africa, Africa Hall, P.O. Box 3001, Addis Ababa, Ethiopia (Telephone Number in U.S. (800) 253-9646); *African Statistical Yearbook*.

United Nations Educational, Scientific and Cultural Organization (UNESCO), 7 Place de Fontenoy, F-75700 Paris, France (Telephone Number in U.S. (212) 963-5981); *Statistical Yearbook*.

SOMALIA - GAS PRODUCTION - See SOMALIA - MINING AND MINERAL PRODUCTS

SOMALIA - GENERAL INDUSTRIAL STATISTICS

Statistical Office of the United Nations, Publishing Service, New York, New York 10017 (800) 253-9646; *Industrial Statistics Yearbook*.

SOMALIA - GENERAL MORTALITY

Statistical Office of the United Nations, Publishing Service, New York, New York 10017 (800) 253-9646; *Demographic Yearbook*.

SOMALIA - GEOGRAPHIC DATA

Facts on File, 460 Park Avenue South, New York, New York 10016 (800) 443-8323; *The New Book of World Rankings*.

SOMALIA - GOATS - See SOMALIA - LIVESTOCK AND POULTRY

SOMALIA - GOLD HOLDINGS

International Monetary Fund, 700 Nineteenth Street, NW, Washington, D.C. 20431 (202) 623-7000; *International Financial Statistics*.

Statistical Office of the United Nations, Publishing Service, New York, New York 10017 (800) 253-9646; *Statistical Yearbook*.

The World Bank, 1818 H Street, NW, Washington, D.C. 20433 (202) 477-1234; *World Tables*.

SOMALIA - GOLD PRODUCTION AND CONSUMPTION - See SOMALIA - MINING AND MINERAL PRODUCTS

SOMALIA - GOVERNMENT

G.K. Hall and Company, 70 Lincoln Street, Boston, Massachusetts 02111 (617) 423-3990; *The World in Figures*.

SOMALIA - GOVERNMENT EXPENDITURES

International Monetary Fund, 700 Nineteenth Street, NW, Washington, D.C. 20431 (202) 623-7000; *Government Finance Statistics Yearbook*.

The World Bank, 1818 H Street, NW, Washington, D.C. 20433 (202) 477-1234; *World Tables*.

SOMALIA - GOVERNMENT FINANCES

International Monetary Fund, 700 Nineteenth Street, NW, Washington, D.C. 20431 (202) 623-7000; *International Financial Statistics*.

Statistical Office of the United Nations, Publishing Service, New York, New York 10017 (800) 253-9646; *Statistical Yearbook*.

SOMALIA - GOVERNMENT REVENUE

International Monetary Fund, 700 Nineteenth Street, NW, Washington, D.C. 20431 (202) 623-7000; *Government Finance Statistics Yearbook.*

Statistical Office of the United Nations, Publishing Service, New York, New York 10017 (800) 253-9646; *Survey of Economic and Social Conditions in Africa.*

The World Bank, 1818 H Street, NW, Washington, D.C. 20433 (202) 477-1234; *World Tables.*

SOMALIA - GRAIN PRODUCTION - See SOMALIA - CROPS

SOMALIA - GRANTS

International Monetary Fund, 700 Nineteenth Street, NW, Washington, D.C. 20431 (202) 623-7000; *Government Finance Statistics Yearbook.*

SOMALIA - GROSS DOMESTIC PRODUCT

African Development Bank, 01 BP 1387, Abidjan 01, Cote D'Ivoire; *Selected Statistics on Regional Member Countries.*

The Economist Intelligence Unit, 111 West 57th Street, New York, New York 10019 (800) 938-4685; *The World Market Atlas.*

Euromonitor Publications Limited, 87-88 Turnmill Street, London EC1M 5QU, England; *International Marketing Data and Statistics.*

Facts on File, 460 Park Avenue South, New York, New York 10016 (800) 443-8323; *The New Book of World Rankings.*

G.K. Hall and Company, 70 Lincoln Street, Boston, Massachusetts 02111 (617) 423-3990; *The World in Figures.*

Statistical Office of the United Nations, Publishing Service, New York, New York 10017 (800) 253-9646; *Statistical Yearbook,* and *Survey of Economic and Social Conditions in Africa.*

Times Books, 201 East 50th Street, New York, New York 10022 (212) 751-2600; *The Economist Book of Vital World Statistics.*

United Nations Economic Commission for Africa, Africa Hall, P.O. Box 3001, Addis Ababa, Ethiopia (Telephone Number in U.S. (800) 253-9646); *African Statistical Yearbook.*

The World Bank, 1818 H Street, NW, Washington, D.C. 20433 (202) 477-1234; *World Tables.*

SOMALIA - GROSS NATIONAL PRODUCT

Euromonitor Publications Limited, 87-88 Turnmill Street, London EC1M 5QU, England; *International Marketing Data and Statistics.*

U.S. Arms Control and Disarmament Agency, 320 Twenty-first Street, NW, Washington, D.C. 20451 (202) 647-8677; *World Military Expenditures and Arms Transfers.*

The World Bank, 1818 H Street, NW, Washington, D.C. 20433 (202) 477-1234; *World Tables.*

SOMALIA - GROUNDNUT PRODUCTION - See SOMALIA - CROPS

SOMALIA - HEALTH

African Development Bank, 01 BP 1387, Abidjan 01, Cote D'Ivoire; *Selected Statistics on Regional Member Countries.*

Facts on File, 460 Park Avenue South, New York, New York 10016 (800) 443-8323; *The New Book of World Rankings.*

G.K. Hall and Company, 70 Lincoln Street, Boston, Massachusetts 02111 (617) 423-3990; *The World in Figures.*

Statistical Office of the United Nations, Publishing Service, New York, New York 10017 (800) 253-9646; *Statistical Yearbook.*

Times Books, 201 East 50th Street, New York, New York 10022 (212) 751-2600; *The Economist Book of Vital World Statistics.*

United Nations Economic Commission for Africa, Africa Hall, P.O. Box 3001, Addis Ababa, Ethiopia (Telephone Number in U.S. (800) 253-9646); *African Statistical Yearbook.*

SOMALIA - HEALTH EXPENDITURES

International Monetary Fund, 700 Nineteenth Street, NW, Washington, D.C. 20431 (202) 623-7000; *Government Finance Statistics Yearbook.*

SOMALIA - HIDES AND SKINS EXPORTS

International Monetary Fund, 700 Nineteenth Street, NW, Washington, D.C. 20431 (202) 623-7000; *International Financial Statistics.*

SOMALIA - HIGHWAYS

G.K. Hall and Company, 70 Lincoln Street, Boston, Massachusetts 02111 (617) 423-3990; *The World in Figures.*

International Road Federation, 525 School Street, SW, Washington, D.C. 20024 (202) 554-2106; *World Road Statistics.*

Statistical Office of the United Nations, Publishing Service, New York, New York 10017 (800) 253-9646; *Survey of Economic and Social Conditions in Africa.*

United Nations Economic Commission for Africa, Africa Hall, P.O. Box 3001, Addis Ababa, Ethiopia (Telephone Number in U.S. (800) 253-9646); *African Statistical Yearbook.*

SOMALIA - HORSES - See SOMALIA - LIVESTOCK AND POULTRY

SOMALIA - HOURS OF WORK - See SOMALIA - EMPLOYMENT

SOMALIA - HOUSING EXPENDITURES

Facts on File, 460 Park Avenue South, New York, New York 10016 (800) 443-8323; *The New Book of World Rankings.*

International Monetary Fund, 700 Nineteenth Street, NW, Washington, D.C. 20431 (202) 623-7000; *Government Finance Statistics Yearbook.*

SOMALIA - ILLITERATE POPULATION

The Economist Intelligence Unit, 111 West 57th Street, New York, New York 10019 (800) 938-4685; *The World Market Atlas.*

G.K. Hall and Company, 70 Lincoln Street, Boston, Massachusetts 02111 (617) 423-3990; *The World in Figures.*

United Nations Educational, Scientific and Cultural Organization (UNESCO), 7 Place de Fontenoy, F-75700 Paris, France (Telephone Number in U.S. (212) 963-5981); *Statistical Yearbook.*

SOMALIA - IMPORTS

African Development Bank, 01 BP 1387, Abidjan 01, Cote D'Ivoire; *Selected Statistics on Regional Member Countries.*

The Economist Intelligence Unit, 111 West 57th Street, New York, New York 10019 (800) 938-4685; *The World Market Atlas.*

Euromonitor Publications Limited, 87-88 Turnmill Street, London EC1M 5QU, England; *International Marketing Data and Statistics.*

Food and Agricultural Organization of the United Nations (FAO) Via delle Terme di Caracalla, 00100 Rome, Italy (Telephone Number in U.S. (202) 653-2400); *The State of Food and Agriculture.*

G.K. Hall and Company, 70 Lincoln Street, Boston, Massachusetts 02111 (617) 423-3990; *The World in Figures.*

International Monetary Fund, 700 Nineteenth Street, NW, Washington, D.C. 20431 (202) 623-7000; *Direction of Trade Statistics, Government Finance Statistics Yearbook,* and *International Financial Statistics.*

Statistical Office of the United Nations, Publishing Service, New York, New York 10017 (800) 253-9646; *Foreign Trade Statistics for Africa,* and *Survey of Economic and Social Conditions in Africa.*

United Nations Economic Commission for Africa, Africa Hall, P.O. Box 3001, Addis Ababa, Ethiopia (Telephone Number in U.S. (800) 253-9646); *African Statistical Yearbook.*

The World Bank, 1818 H Street, NW, Washington, D.C. 20433 (202) 477-1234; *World Tables.*

SOMALIA - INCOME TAXES - See SOMALIA - TAXATION

SOMALIA - INDUSTRY

Euromonitor Publications Limited, 87-88 Turnmill Street, London EC1M 5QU, England; *International Marketing Data and Statistics.*

Facts on File, 460 Park Avenue South, New York, New York 10016 (800) 443-8323; *The New Book of World Rankings.*

G.K. Hall and Company, 70 Lincoln Street, Boston, Massachusetts 02111 (617) 423-3990; *The World in Figures.*

International Labour Office, I.L.O. Publications, CH-1211, Geneva 22, Switzerland; *Yearbook of Labour Statistics.*

Statistical Office of the United Nations, Publishing Service, New York, New York 10017 (800) 253-9646; *Survey of Economic and Social Conditions in Africa.*

Times Books, 201 East 50th Street, New York, New York 10022 (212) 751-2600; *The Economist Book of Vital World Statistics.*

United Nations Economic Commission for Africa, Africa Hall, P.O. Box 3001, Addis Ababa, Ethiopia (Telephone Number in U.S. (800) 253-9646); *African Statistical Yearbook.*

The World Bank, 1818 H Street, NW, Washington, D.C. 20433 (202) 477-1234; *World Tables.*

SOMALIA - INFANT AND MATERNAL MORTALITY

Statistical Office of the United Nations, Publishing Service, New York, New York 10017 (800) 253-9646; *Demographic Yearbook,* and *Survey of Economic and Social Conditions in Africa.*

Times Books, 201 East 50th Street, New York, New York 10022 (212) 751-2600; *The Economist Book of Vital World Statistics.*

The World Bank, 1818 H Street, NW, Washington, D.C. 20433 (202) 477-1234; *World Tables.*

SOMALIA - INTERNATIONAL LIQUIDITY

International Monetary Fund, 700 Nineteenth Street, NW, Washington, D.C. 20431 (202) 623-7000; *International Financial Statistics.*

SOMALIA - INTERNATIONAL RESERVES EXCLUDING GOLD

African Development Bank, 01 BP 1387, Abidjan 01, Cote D'Ivoire; *Selected Statistics on Regional Member Countries.*

Statistical Office of the United Nations, Publishing Service, New York, New York 10017 (800) 253-9646; *Statistical Yearbook.*

The World Bank, 1818 H Street, NW, Washington, D.C. 20433 (202) 477-1234; *World Tables.*

SOMALIA - IRON ORE PRODUCTION AND CONSUMPTION - See SOMALIA - MINING AND MINERAL PRODUCTS

SOMALIA - IRRIGATION

Euromonitor Publications Limited, 87-88 Turnmill Street, London EC1M 5QU, England; *International Marketing Data and Statistics.*

SOMALIA - LABOR FORCE

African Development Bank, 01 BP 1387, Abidjan 01, Cote D'Ivoire; *Selected Statistics on Regional Member Countries.*

Euromonitor Publications Limited, 87-88 Turnmill Street, London EC1M 5QU, England; *International Marketing Data and Statistics.*

Facts on File, 460 Park Avenue South, New York, New York 10016 (800) 443-8323; *The New Book of World Rankings.*

Food and Agricultural Organization of the United Nations (FAO) Via delle Terme di Caracalla, 00100 Rome, Italy (Telephone Number in U.S. (202) 653-2400); *The State of Food and Agriculture.*

G.K. Hall and Company, 70 Lincoln Street, Boston, Massachusetts 02111 (617) 423-3990; *The World in Figures.*

The World Bank, 1818 H Street, NW, Washington, D.C. 20433 (202) 477-1234; *World Tables.*

SOMALIA - LABOR PRODUCTIVITY

International Labour Office, I.L.O. Publications, CH-1211, Geneva 22, Switzerland; *Yearbook of Labour Statistics.*

SOMALIA - LAND USE

Euromonitor Publications Limited, 87-88 Turnmill Street, London EC1M 5QU, England; *International Marketing Data and Statistics.*

Food and Agricultural Organization of the United Nations (FAO), Via delle Terme di Caracalla, 00100 Rome, Italy (Telephone Number in U.S. (202) 653-2400); *Production Yearbook.*

G.K. Hall and Company, 70 Lincoln Street, Boston, Massachusetts 02111 (617) 423-3990; *The World in Figures.*

SOMALIA - LIBRARIES

Facts on File, 460 Park Avenue South, New York, New York 10016 (800) 443-8323; *The New Book of World Rankings.*

United Nations Educational, Scientific and Cultural Organization (UNESCO), 7 Place de Fontenoy, F-75700 Paris, France (Telephone Number in U.S. (212) 963-5981); *Statistical Yearbook.*

SOMALIA - LIFE EXPECTANCY

African Development Bank, 01 BP 1387, Abidjan 01, Cote D'Ivoire; *Selected Statistics on Regional Member Countries.*

SOMALIA - LITERACY RATE

Statistical Office of the United Nations, Publishing Service, New York, New York 10017 (800) 253-9646; *Survey of Economic and Social Conditions in Africa.*

SOMALIA - LIVESTOCK AND POULTRY

Commodity Research Bureau, Incorporated, 75 Wall Street, New York, New York 10005 (212) 504-7754; *Commodity Year Book.*

Euromonitor Publications Limited, 87-101 Tottenham Court Road, London EC1M 5QU, England; *International Marketing Data and Statistics.*

Facts on File, 460 Park Avenue South, New York, New York 10016 (800) 443-8323; *The New Book of World Rankings.*

Food and Agricultural Organization of the United Nations (FAO), Via delle Terme di Caracalla, 00100 Rome, Italy (Telephone Number in U.S. (202) 653-2400); *Production Yearbook,* and *The State of Food and Agriculture.*

G.K. Hall and Company, 70 Lincoln Street, Boston, Massachusetts 02111 (617) 423-3990; *The World in Figures.*

Statistical Office of the United Nations, Publishing Service, New York, New York 10017 (800) 253-9646; *Statistical Yearbook,* and *Survey of Economic and Social Conditions in Africa.*

United Nations Economic Commission for Africa, Africa Hall, P.O. Box 3001, Addis Ababa, Ethiopia (Telephone Number in U.S. (800) 253-9646); *African Statistical Yearbook.*

SOMALIA - LIVING LEVELS

G.K. Hall and Company, 70 Lincoln Street, Boston, Massachusetts 02111 (617) 423-3990; *The World in Figures.*

Times Books, 201 East 50th Street, New York, New York 10022 (212) 751-2600; *The Economist Book of Vital World Statistics.*

SOMALIA - MANUFACTURING

Facts on File, 460 Park Avenue South, New York, New York 10016 (800) 443-8323; *The New Book of World Rankings.*

G.K. Hall and Company, 70 Lincoln Street, Boston, Massachusetts 02111 (617) 423-3990; *The World in Figures.*

Statistical Office of the United Nations, Publishing Service, New York, New York 10017 (800) 253-9646; *Statistical Yearbook,* and *Survey of Economic and Social Conditions in Africa.*

Times Books, 201 East 50th Street, New York, New York 10022 (212) 751-2600; *The Economist Book of Vital World Statistics.*

United Nations Economic Commission for Africa, Africa Hall, P.O. Box 3001, Addis Ababa, Ethiopia (Telephone Number in U.S. (800) 253-9646); *African Statistical Yearbook.*

The World Bank, 1818 H Street, NW, Washington, D.C. 20433 (202) 477-1234; *World Tables.*

SOMALIA - MARRIAGE RATES

Facts on File, 460 Park Avenue South, New York, New York 10016 (800) 443-8323; *The New Book of World Rankings.*

Statistical Office of the United Nations, Publishing Service, New York, New York 10017 (800) 253-9646; *Demographic Yearbook.*

SOMALIA - MEAT PRODUCTION - See SOMALIA - LIVESTOCK AND POULTRY

SOMALIA - MERCHANT SHIPPING

G.K. Hall and Company, 70 Lincoln Street, Boston, Massachusetts 02111 (617) 423-3990; *The World in Figures.*

Statistical Office of the United Nations, Publishing Service, New York, New York 10017 (800) 253-9646; *Statistical Yearbook.*

Times Books, 201 East 50th Street, New York, New York 10022 (212) 751-2600; *The Economist Book of Vital World Statistics.*

United Nations Economic Commission for Africa, Africa Hall, P.O. Box 3001, Addis Ababa, Ethiopia (Telephone Number in U.S. (800) 253-9646); *African Statistical Yearbook.*

U.S. Department of Transportation, Maritime Administration, 400 Seventh Street, SW, Washington, D.C. 20590 (202) 366-5807; *A Statistical Analysis of the World's Merchant Fleets.*

SOMALIA - MILITARY

G.K. Hall and Company, 70 Lincoln Street, Boston, Massachusetts 02111 (617) 423-3990; *The World in Figures.*

U.S. Arms Control and Disarmament Agency, 320 Twenty-first Street, NW, Washington, D.C. 20451 (202) 647-8677; *World Military Expenditures and Arms Transfers.*

SOMALIA - MILK - See SOMALIA - DAIRY PRODUCTS

SOMALIA - MINING AND MINERAL PRODUCTS

Facts on File, 460 Park Avenue South, New York, New York 10016 (800) 443-8323; *The New Book of World Rankings.*

G.K. Hall and Company, 70 Lincoln Street, Boston, Massachusetts 02111 (617) 423-3990; *The World in Figures.*

Statistical Office of the United Nations, Publishing Service, New York, New York 10017 (800) 253-9646; *Statistical Yearbook.*

United Nations Economic Commission for Africa, Africa Hall, P.O. Box 3001, Addis Ababa, Ethiopia (Telephone Number in U.S. (800) 253-9646); *African Statistical Yearbook.*

SOMALIA - MONEY EXCHANGE RATE

Euromonitor Publications Limited, 87-88 Turnmill Street, London EC1M 5QU, England; *International Marketing Data and Statistics.*

International Monetary Fund, 700 Nineteenth Street, NW, Washington, D.C. 20431 (202) 623-7000; *International Financial Statistics.*

Statistical Office of the United Nations, Publishing Service, New York, New York 10017 (800) 253-9646; *Statistical Yearbook.*

SOMALIA - MONEY RESERVES

Euromonitor Publications Limited, 87-88 Turnmill Street, London EC1M 5QU, England; *International Marketing Data and Statistics.*

SOMALIA - MONEY SUPPLY

African Development Bank, 01 BP 1387, Abidjan 01, Cote D'Ivoire; *Selected Statistics on Regional Member Countries.*

Euromonitor Publications Limited, 87-88 Turnmill Street, London EC1M 5QU, England; *International Marketing Data and Statistics.*

G.K. Hall and Company, 70 Lincoln Street, Boston, Massachusetts 02111 (617) 423-3990; *The World in Figures.*

International Monetary Fund, 700 Nineteenth Street, NW, Washington, D.C. 20431 (202) 623-7000; *International Financial Statistics.*

Statistical Office of the United Nations, Publishing Service, New York, New York 10017 (800) 253-9646; *Statistical Yearbook.*

The World Bank, 1818 H Street, NW, Washington, D.C. 20433 (202) 477-1234; *World Tables.*

SOMALIA - MOTOR VEHICLE TAXES - See SOMALIA - TAXATION

SOMALIA - MOTOR VEHICLES IN USE

G.K. Hall and Company, 70 Lincoln Street, Boston, Massachusetts 02111 (617) 423-3990; *The World in Figures.*

International Road Federation, 525 School Street, SW, Washington, D.C. 20024 (202) 554-2106; *World Road Statistics.*

Statistical Office of the United Nations, Publishing Service, New York, New York 10017 (800) 253-9646; *Statistical Yearbook,* and *Survey of Economic and Social Conditions in Africa.*

Times Books, 201 East 50th Street, New York, New York 10022 (212) 751-2600; *The Economist Book of Vital World Statistics.*

SOMALIA - MULES - See SOMALIA - LIVESTOCK AND POULTRY

SOMALIA - MUSEUMS

Facts on File, 460 Park Avenue South, New York, New York 10016 (800) 443-8323; *The New Book of World Rankings.*

SOMALIA - NATALITY - See SOMALIA - BIRTH RATE

SOMALIA - NATIONAL ACCOUNTS

African Development Bank, 01 BP 1387, Abidjan 01, Cote D'Ivoire; *Selected Statistics on Regional Member Countries.*

Statistical Office of the United Nations, Publishing Service, New York, New York 10017 (800) 253-9646; *Statistical Yearbook.*

United Nations Economic Commission for Africa, Africa Hall, P.O. Box 3001, Addis Ababa, Ethiopia (Telephone Number in U.S. (800) 253-9646); *African Statistical Yearbook.*

SOMALIA - NATIONAL INCOME

Facts on File, 460 Park Avenue South, New York, New York 10016 (800) 443-8323; *The New Book of World Rankings.*

G.K. Hall and Company, 70 Lincoln Street, Boston, Massachusetts 02111 (617) 423-3990; *The World in Figures.*

Statistical Office of the United Nations, Publishing Service, New York, New York 10017 (800) 253-9646; *Statistical Yearbook.*

SOMALIA - NATIONAL PRODUCT

Facts on File, 460 Park Avenue South, New York, New York 10016 (800) 443-8323; *The New Book of World Rankings.*

Statistical Office of the United Nations, Publishing Service, New York, New York 10017 (800) 253-9646; *Statistical Yearbook.*

SOMALIA - NATURAL GAS PRODUCTION - See SOMALIA - MINING AND MINERAL PRODUCTS

SOMALIA - NEWSPAPER PRODUCTION - See SOMALIA - FORESTRY AND FOREST PRODUCTS

SOMALIA - NEWSPRINT - See SOMALIA - FORESTRY AND FOREST PRODUCTS

SOMALIA - OCCUPATIONS - See SOMALIA - LABOR FORCE

SOMALIA - PAPER - See SOMALIA - FORESTRY AND FOREST PRODUCTS

SOMALIA - PATENTS

Statistical Office of the United Nations, Publishing Service, New York, New York 10017 (800) 253-9646; *Statistical Yearbook.*

SOMALIA - PEANUT PRODUCTION - See SOMALIA - CROPS

SOMALIA - PESTICIDE USE

Food and Agricultural Organization of the United Nations (FAO) Via delle Terme di Caracalla, 00100 Rome, Italy (Telephone Number in U.S. (202) 653-2400); *The State of Food and Agriculture.*

SOMALIA - PETROLEUM INDUSTRY

Facts on File, 460 Park Avenue South, New York, New York 10016 (800) 443-8323; *The New Book of World Rankings.*

Food and Agricultural Organization of the United Nations (FAO) Via delle Terme di Caracalla, 00100 Rome, Italy (Telephone Number in U.S. (202) 653-2400); *The State of Food and Agriculture.*

G.K. Hall and Company, 70 Lincoln Street, Boston, Massachusetts 02111 (617) 423-3990; *The World in Figures.*

SOMALIA - PIGS - See SOMALIA - LIVESTOCK AND POULTRY

SOMALIA - POPULATION

African Development Bank, 01 BP 1387, Abidjan 01, Cote D'Ivoire; *Selected Statistics on Regional Member Countries.*

The Economist Intelligence Unit, 111 West 57th Street, New York, New York 10019 (800) 938-4685; *The World Market Atlas.*

Euromonitor Publications Limited, 87-88 Turnmill Street, London EC1M 5QU, England; *International Marketing Data and Statistics.*

Facts on File, 460 Park Avenue South, New York, New York 10016 (800) 443-8323; *The New Book of World Rankings.*

Food and Agricultural Organization of the United Nations (FAO), Via delle Terme di Caracalla, 00100 Rome, Italy (Telephone Number in U.S. (202) 653-2400); *Production Yearbook.*

G.K. Hall and Company, 70 Lincoln Street, Boston, Massachusetts 02111 (617) 423-3990; *The World in Figures.*

International Labour Office, I.L.O. Publications, CH-1211, Geneva 22, Switzerland; *Yearbook of Labour Statistics.*

Statistical Office of the United Nations, Publishing Service, New York, New York 10017 (800) 253-9646; *Demographic Yearbook, Statistical Yearbook,* and *Survey of Economic and Social Conditions in Africa.*

Times Books, 201 East 50th Street, New York, New York 10022 (212) 751-2600; *The Economist Book of Vital World Statistics.*

United Nations Educational, Scientific and Cultural Organization (UNESCO), 7 Place de Fontenoy, F-75700 Paris, France (Telephone Number in U.S. (212) 963-5981); *Statistical Yearbook.*

U.S. Arms Control and Disarmament Agency, 320 Twenty-first Street, NW, Washington, D.C. 20451 (202) 647-8677; *World Military Expenditures and Arms Transfers.*

World Health Organization, Office of Publications, Avenue Appia, CH-1211 Geneva 27, Switzerland (Telephone Number in U.S. (518) 436-9686); *World Health Statistics Annual.*

SOMALIA - POST OFFICES

Facts on File, 460 Park Avenue South, New York, New York 10016 (800) 443-8323; *The New Book of World Rankings.*

SOMALIA - POTATO PRODUCTION - See SOMALIA - CROPS

SOMALIA - POWER PRODUCTION INDUSTRY

Statistical Office of the United Nations, Publishing Service, New York, New York 10017 (800) 253-9646; *Statistical Yearbook.*

SOMALIA - PRICES

Facts on File, 460 Park Avenue South, New York, New York 10016 (800) 443-8323; *The New Book of World Rankings.*

Food and Agricultural Organization of the United Nations (FAO), Via delle Terme di Caracalla, 00100 Rome, Italy (Telephone Number in U.S. (202) 653-2400); *Production Yearbook,* and *The State of Food and Agriculture.*

G.K. Hall and Company, 70 Lincoln Street, Boston, Massachusetts 02111 (617) 423-3990; *The World in Figures.*

International Labour Office, I.L.O. Publications, CH-1211, Geneva 22, Switzerland; *Yearbook of Labour Statistics.*

International Monetary Fund, 700 Nineteenth Street, NW, Washington, D.C. 20431 (202) 623-7000; *International Financial Statistics.*

United Nations Economic Commission for Africa, Africa Hall, P.O. Box 3001, Addis Ababa, Ethiopia (Telephone Number in U.S. (800) 253-9646); *African Statistical Yearbook.*

SOMALIA - PRINTING AND WRITING PAPER - See SOMALIA - FORESTRY AND FOREST PRODUCTS

SOMALIA - PRODUCTION

Facts on File, 460 Park Avenue South, New York, New York 10016 (800) 443-8323; *The New Book of World Rankings.*

G.K. Hall and Company, 70 Lincoln Street, Boston, Massachusetts 02111 (617) 423-3990; *The World in Figures.*

SOMALIA - PRODUCTIVITY

Euromonitor Publications Limited, 87-88 Turnmill Street, London EC1M 5QU, England; *International Marketing Data and Statistics.*

SOMALIA - PROPERTY TAXES - See SOMALIA - TAXATION

SOMALIA - PUBLIC FINANCE

Facts on File, 460 Park Avenue South, New York, New York 10016 (800) 443-8323; *The New Book of World Rankings.*

SOMALIA - RADIO BROADCASTING - See SOMALIA - BROADCASTING

SOMALIA - RAILWAYS

G.K. Hall and Company, 70 Lincoln Street, Boston, Massachusetts 02111 (617) 423-3990; *The World in Figures.*

United Nations Economic Commission for Africa, Africa Hall, P.O. Box 3001, Addis Ababa, Ethiopia (Telephone Number in U.S. (800) 253-9646); *African Statistical Yearbook.*

SOMALIA - RELIGION

Facts on File, 460 Park Avenue South, New York, New York 10016 (800) 443-8323; *The New Book of World Rankings.*

SOMALIA - RENT PRICES

International Labour Office, I.L.O. Publications, CH-1211, Geneva 22, Switzerland; *Yearbook of Labour Statistics.*

SOMALIA - RETAIL TRADE

G.K. Hall and Company, 70 Lincoln Street, Boston, Massachusetts 02111 (617) 423-3990; *The World in Figures.*

SOMALIA - RICE PRODUCTION - See SOMALIA - CROPS

SOMALIA - ROUNDWOOD PRODUCTION - See SOMALIA - FORESTRY AND FOREST PRODUCTS

SOMALIA - RUBBER PRODUCTION AND CONSUMPTION

Facts on File, 460 Park Avenue South, New York, New York 10016 (800) 443-8323; *The New Book of World Rankings*.

SOMALIA - SALT PRODUCTION - See SOMALIA - MINING AND MINERAL PRODUCTS

SOMALIA - SAWNWOOD PRODUCTION - See SOMALIA - FORESTRY AND FOREST PRODUCTS

SOMALIA - SENIOR CITIZENS

Facts on File, 460 Park Avenue South, New York, New York 10016 (800) 443-8323; *The New Book of World Rankings*.

SOMALIA - SHEEP - See SOMALIA - LIVESTOCK AND POULTRY

SOMALIA - SILVER PRODUCTION AND CONSUMPTION - See SOMALIA - MINING AND MINERAL PRODUCTS

SOMALIA - SOCIAL DATA

African Development Bank, 01 BP 1387, Abidjan 01, Cote D'Ivoire; *Selected Statistics on Regional Member Countries*.

Facts on File, 460 Park Avenue South, New York, New York 10016 (800) 443-8323; *The New Book of World Rankings*.

G.K. Hall and Company, 70 Lincoln Street, Boston, Massachusetts 02111 (617) 423-3990; *The World in Figures*.

SOMALIA - SOCIAL SECURITY

International Monetary Fund, 700 Nineteenth Street, NW, Washington, D.C. 20431 (202) 623-7000; *Government Finance Statistics Yearbook*.

SOMALIA - STAMP TAXES AND DUTIES - See SOMALIA - TAXATION

SOMALIA - STATE BUDGET REVENUE AND EXPENDITURES

Euromonitor Publications Limited, 87-88 Turnmill Street, London EC1M 5QU, England; *International Marketing Data and Statistics*.

SOMALIA - STEEL - See SOMALIA - MINING AND MINERAL PRODUCTS

SOMALIA - STOCKS - COMMODITY - MARKET PRICE - INDEX

Food and Agricultural Organization of the United Nations (FAO) Via delle Terme di Caracalla, 00100 Rome, Italy (Telephone Number in U.S. (202) 653-2400); *The State of Food and Agriculture*.

SOMALIA - SUGAR PRODUCTION AND CONSUMPTION - See SOMALIA - CROPS

SOMALIA - TAXATION

G.K. Hall and Company, 70 Lincoln Street, Boston, Massachusetts 02111 (617) 423-3990; *The World in Figures*.

International Monetary Fund, 700 Nineteenth Street, NW, Washington, D.C. 20431 (202) 623-7000; *Government Finance Statistics Yearbook*.

International Road Federation, 525 School Street, SW, Washington, D.C. 20024 (202) 554-2106; *World Road Statistics*.

The World Bank, 1818 H Street, NW, Washington, D.C. 20433 (202) 477-1234; *World Tables*.

SOMALIA - TELEPHONES IN USE

American Telephone and Telegraph Company, 26 Parsippany Road, Whippany, New Jersey 07981 (800) 338-4038; *The World's Telephones*.

G.K. Hall and Company, 70 Lincoln Street, Boston, Massachusetts 02111 (617) 423-3990; *The World in Figures*.

Statistical Office of the United Nations, Publishing Service, New York, New York 10017 (800) 253-9646; *Statistical Yearbook*.

SOMALIA - TELEVISION BROADCASTING - See SOMALIA - BROADCASTING

SOMALIA - TEXTILE INDUSTRY

G.K. Hall and Company, 70 Lincoln Street, Boston, Massachusetts 02111 (617) 423-3990; *The World in Figures*.

SOMALIA - TOBACCO PRODUCTION

Facts on File, 460 Park Avenue South, New York, New York 10016 (800) 443-8323; *The New Book of World Rankings*.

Statistical Office of the United Nations, Publishing Service, New York, New York 10017 (800) 253-9646; *Statistical Yearbook*.

SOMALIA - TOURISM

Facts on File, 460 Park Avenue South, New York, New York 10016 (800) 443-8323; *The New Book of World Rankings*.

G.K. Hall and Company, 70 Lincoln Street, Boston, Massachusetts 02111 (617) 423-3990; *The World in Figures*.

Statistical Office of the United Nations, Publishing Service, New York, New York 10017 (800) 253-9646; *Statistical Yearbook*.

Times Books, 201 East 50th Street, New York, New York 10022 (212) 751-2600; *The Economist Book of Vital World Statistics*.

United Nations Economic Commission for Africa, Africa Hall, P.O. Box 3001, Addis Ababa, Ethiopia (Telephone Number in U.S. (800) 253-9646); *African Statistical Yearbook*.

SOMALIA - TRACTORS IN USE

Statistical Office of the United Nations, Publishing Service, New York, New York 10017 (800) 253-9646; *Statistical Yearbook*.

SOMALIA - TRADE - See SOMALIA - FOREIGN TRADE

SOMALIA - TRADEMARKS AND SERVICE MARKS

Statistical Office of the United Nations, Publishing Service, New York, New York 10017 (800) 253-9646; *Statistical Yearbook*.

SOMALIA - TRANSPORTATION AND COMMUNICATIONS

Facts on File, 460 Park Avenue South, New York, New York 10016 (800) 443-8323; *The New Book of World Rankings*.

G.K. Hall and Company, 70 Lincoln Street, Boston, Massachusetts 02111 (617) 423-3990; *The World in Figures*.

United Nations Economic Commission for Africa, Africa Hall, P.O. Box 3001, Addis Ababa, Ethiopia (Telephone Number in U.S. (800) 253-9646); *African Statistical Yearbook*.

SOMALIA - UNEMPLOYMENT

Euromonitor Publications Limited, 87-88 Turnmill Street, London EC1M 5QU, England; *International Marketing Data and Statistics*.

International Labour Office, I.L.O. Publications, CH-1211, Geneva 22, Switzerland; *Yearbook of Labour Statistics*.

SOMALIA - VITAL STATISTICS

Euromonitor Publications Limited, 87-88 Turnmill Street, London EC1M 5QU, England; *International Marketing Data and Statistics*.

G.K. Hall and Company, 70 Lincoln Street, Boston, Massachusetts 02111 (617) 423-3990; *The World in Figures*.

World Health Organization, Office of Publications, Avenue Appia, CH-1211 Geneva 27, Switzerland (Telephone Number in U.S. (518) 436-9686); *World Health Statistics Annual*.

SOMALIA - WAGES

G.K. Hall and Company, 70 Lincoln Street, Boston, Massachusetts 02111 (617) 423-3990; *The World in Figures*.

International Labour Office, I.L.O. Publications, CH-1211, Geneva 22, Switzerland; *Yearbook of Labour Statistics*.

SOMALIA - WEATHER

Facts on File, 460 Park Avenue South, New York, New York 10016 (800) 443-8323; *The New Book of World Rankings*.

G.K. Hall and Company, 70 Lincoln Street, Boston, Massachusetts 02111 (617) 423-3990; *The World in Figures*.

SOMALIA - WELFARE

International Monetary Fund, 700 Nineteenth Street, NW, Washington, D.C. 20431 (202) 623-7000; *Government Finance Statistics Yearbook*.

SOMALIA - WHALES - See SOMALIA - FISHERIES

SOMALIA - WHEAT PRODUCTION AND PRICES - See SOMALIA - CROPS

SOMALIA - WINE PRODUCTION

Facts on File, 460 Park Avenue South, New York, New York 10016 (800) 443-8323; *The New Book of World Rankings*.

SOMALIA - WOOL PRODUCTION

Facts on File, 460 Park Avenue South, New York, New York 10016 (800) 443-8323; *The New Book of World Rankings*.

SORGHUM GRAIN

U.S. Department of Agriculture, National Agricultural Statistics Service, Fourteenth Street and Independence Avenue, SW, Washington, D.C. 20250 (202) 219-1504; *Crop Production, Field Crops, Crop Values, Agricultural Statistics*, and *Agricultural Outlook*.

SORORITIES

Gale Research Incorporated, 835 Penobscot Building, Detroit, Michigan 48226 (800) 877-4253; *Encyclopedia of Associations*.

South Africa - National Statistical Offices

Central Statistical Services, Steyn's Building, 270 Schoeman Street, Pretoria 0002, South Africa.

Central Statistical Services, Private Bag X44, Pretoria 0001, South Africa.

South Africa - Primary Statistics Sources

Central Statistical Services, Steyn's Building, 270 Schoeman Street, Pretoria 0002, South Africa; *South African Statistics* and *Bulletin of Statistics*.

Department of Foreign Affairs and Information, PBX 152, Pretoria 0001, South Africa; *South Africa: Official Yearbook of the Republic of South Africa*.

SOUTH AFRICA - AGRICULTURE

Euromonitor Publications Limited, 87-88 Turnmill Street, London EC1M 5QU, England; *International Marketing Data and Statistics*.

Facts on File, 460 Park Avenue South, New York, New York 10016 (800) 443-8323; *The New Book of World Rankings*.

Food and Agricultural Organization of the United Nations (FAO) Via delle Terme di Caracalla, 00100 Rome, Italy (Telephone Number in U.S. (202) 653-2400); *Production Yearbook*, and *The State of Food and Agriculture*, and *Trade Yearbook*.

G.K. Hall and Company, 70 Lincoln Street, Boston, Massachusetts 02111 (617) 423-3990; *The World in Figures*.

Statistical Office of the United Nations, Publishing Service, New York, New York 10017 (800) 253-9646; *Statistical Yearbook*.

Times Books, 201 East 50th Street, New York, New York 10022 (212) 751-2600; *The Economist Book of Vital World Statistics*.

The World Bank, 1818 H Street, NW, Washington, D.C. 20433 (202) 477-1234; *World Tables*.

SOUTH AFRICA - AIRLINE SERVICE

Facts on File, 460 Park Avenue South, New York, New York 10016 (800) 443-8323; *The New Book of World Rankings*.

G.K. Hall and Company, 70 Lincoln Street, Boston, Massachusetts 02111 (617) 423-3990; *The World in Figures*.

International Civil Aviation Organization, 1000 Sherbrooke Street West, Montreal, Quebec H3A 2R2, Canada (514) 285-8219; *Civil Aviation Statistics of the World*.

Statistical Office of the United Nations, Publishing Service, New York, New York 10017 (800) 253-9646; *Statistical Yearbook*.

Times Books, 201 East 50th Street, New York, New York 10022 (212) 751-2600; *The Economist Book of Vital World Statistics*.

SOUTH AFRICA - ALUMINUM PRODUCTION AND CONSUMPTION - See SOUTH AFRICA - MINING AND MINERAL PRODUCTS

SOUTH AFRICA - ANIMAL FEEDINGSTUFFS OF AQUATIC
ANIMAL ORIGIN

Statistical Office of the United Nations, Publishing Service, New
York, New York 10017 (800) 253-9646; *Statistical Yearbook.*

SOUTH AFRICA - ANIMAL HEALTH

Food and Agricultural Organization of the United Nations (FAO),
Via delle Terme di Caracalla, 00100, Rome, Italy (Telephone
Number in U.S. (202) 653-2400); *Animal Health Yearbook.*

SOUTH AFRICA - ANTIMONY AND ANTIMONY ORE PRODUCTION
AND CONSUMPTION - See SOUTH AFRICA - MINING AND MINERAL
PRODUCTS

SOUTH AFRICA - AREA AND DENSITY OF POPULATION

Euromonitor Publications Limited, 87-88 Turnmill Street, London
EC1M 5QU, England; *International Marketing Data and Statistics.*

Facts on File, 460 Park Avenue South, New York, New York 10016
(800) 443-8323; *The New Book of World Rankings.*

Food and Agricultural Organization of the United Nations (FAO) Via
delle Terme di Caracalla, 00100 Rome, Italy (Telephone Number in
U.S. (202) 653-2400); *The State of Food and Agriculture.*

G.K. Hall and Company, 70 Lincoln Street, Boston, Massachusetts
02111 (617) 423-3990; *The World in Figures.*

Statistical Office of the United Nations, Publishing Service, New
York, New York 10017 (800) 253-9646; *Statistical Yearbook.*

Times Books, 201 East 50th Street, New York, New York 10022
(212) 751-2600; *The Economist Book of Vital World Statistics.*

United Nations Educational, Scientific and Cultural Organization
(UNESCO), 7 Place de Fontenoy, F-75700 Paris, France (Telephone
Number in U.S. (212) 963-5981); *Statistical Yearbook.*

SOUTH AFRICA - ARMS EXPORTS AND IMPORTS

U.S. Arms Control and Disarmament Agency, 320 Twenty-first
Street, NW, Washington, D.C. 20451 (202) 647-8677; *World Military
Expenditures and Arms Transfers.*

SOUTH AFRICA - BALANCE OF PAYMENTS

The Economist Intelligence Unit, 111 West 57th Street, New York,
New York 10019 (800) 938-4685; *The World Market Atlas.*

G.K. Hall and Company, 70 Lincoln Street, Boston, Massachusetts
02111 (617) 423-3990; *The World in Figures.*

International Monetary Fund, 700 Nineteenth Street, NW,
Washington, D.C. 20431 (202) 623-7000; *Balance of Payments
Yearbook, International Financial Statistics.*

Times Books, 201 East 50th Street, New York, New York 10022
(212) 751-2600; *The Economist Book of Vital World Statistics.*

The World Bank, 1818 H Street, NW, Washington, D.C. 20433 (202)
477-1234; *World Tables.*

SOUTH AFRICA - BANKING

Facts on File, 460 Park Avenue South, New York, New York 10016
(800) 443-8323; *The New Book of World Rankings.*

G.K. Hall and Company, 70 Lincoln Street, Boston, Massachusetts
02111 (617) 423-3990; *The World in Figures.*

International Monetary Fund, 700 Nineteenth Street, NW,
Washington, D.C. 20431 (202) 623-7000; *Government Finance
Statistics Yearbook,* and *International Financial Statistics.*

Statistical Office of the United Nations, Publishing Service, New
York, New York 10017 (800) 253-9646; *Statistical Yearbook.*

SOUTH AFRICA - BARLEY PRODUCTION - See SOUTH AFRICA -
CROPS

SOUTH AFRICA - BAUXITE PRODUCTION AND CONSUMPTION - See
SOUTH AFRICA - MINING AND MINERAL PRODUCTS

SOUTH AFRICA - BEER PRODUCTION

Facts on File, 460 Park Avenue South, New York, New York 10016
(800) 443-8323; *The New Book of World Rankings.*

Statistical Office of the United Nations, Publishing Service, New
York, New York 10017 (800) 253-9646; *Statistical Yearbook.*

SOUTH AFRICA - BIRTH RATES

Facts on File, 460 Park Avenue South, New York, New York 10016
(800) 443-8323; *The New Book of World Rankings.*

Statistical Office of the United Nations, Publishing Service, New
York, New York 10017 (800) 253-9646; *Demographic Yearbook,* and
Statistical Yearbook.

The World Bank, 1818 H Street, NW, Washington, D.C. 20433 (202)
477-1234; *World Tables.*

SOUTH AFRICA - BONDS

G.K. Hall and Company, 70 Lincoln Street, Boston, Massachusetts
02111 (617) 423-3990; *The World in Figures.*

International Monetary Fund, 700 Nineteenth Street, NW,
Washington, D.C. 20431 (202) 623-7000; *Government Finance
Statistics Yearbook.*

Statistical Office of the United Nations, Publishing Service, New
York, New York 10017 (800) 253-9646; *Statistical Yearbook.*

SOUTH AFRICA - BOOK PRODUCTION

G.K. Hall and Company, 70 Lincoln Street, Boston, Massachusetts
02111 (617) 423-3990; *The World in Figures.*

SOUTH AFRICA - BROADCASTING

Billboard Limited, P.O. Box 9027, 1006 AA Amsterdam, The
Netherlands (Telephone Number in U.S. (212) 764-7300); *World
Radio TV Handbook.*

Facts on File, 460 Park Avenue South, New York, New York 10016
(800) 443-8323; *The New Book of World Rankings.*

G.K. Hall and Company, 70 Lincoln Street, Boston, Massachusetts
02111 (617) 423-3990; *The World in Figures.*

Times Books, 201 East 50th Street, New York, New York 10022 (212)
751-2600; *The Economist Book of Vital World Statistics.*

SOUTH AFRICA - BUSINESS

G.K. Hall and Company, 70 Lincoln Street, Boston, Massachusetts 02111 (617) 423-3990; *The World in Figures.*

SOUTH AFRICA - BUSINESS AND PROFESSIONAL LICENSES

International Monetary Fund, 700 Nineteenth Street, NW, Washington, D.C. 20431 (202) 623-7000; *Government Finance Statistics Yearbook.*

SOUTH AFRICA - BUTTER - See SOUTH AFRICA - DAIRY PRODUCTS

SOUTH AFRICA - CADMIUM PRODUCTION AND CONSUMPTION - See SOUTH AFRICA - MINING AND MINERAL PRODUCTS

SOUTH AFRICA - CALORIE SUPPLY

Food and Agricultural Organization of the United Nations (FAO) Via delle Terme di Caracalla, 00100 Rome, Italy (Telephone Number in U.S. (202) 653-2400); *The State of Food and Agriculture.*

SOUTH AFRICA - CAPITAL REVENUE

International Monetary Fund, 700 Nineteenth Street, NW, Washington, D.C. 20431 (202) 623-7000; *Government Finance Statistics Yearbook.*

SOUTH AFRICA - CATTLE - See SOUTH AFRICA - LIVESTOCK AND POULTRY

SOUTH AFRICA - CEMENT PRODUCTION - See SOUTH AFRICA - MINING AND MINERAL PRODUCTS

SOUTH AFRICA - CHEESE - See SOUTH AFRICA - DAIRY PRODUCTS

SOUTH AFRICA - CHEMICAL (ORGANIC) PRODUCTION - See SOUTH AFRICA - MINING AND MINERAL PRODUCTS

SOUTH AFRICA - CHICKENS - See SOUTH AFRICA - LIVESTOCK AND POULTRY

SOUTH AFRICA - CHROMITE PRODUCTION AND CONSUMPTION - See SOUTH AFRICA - MINING AND MINERAL PRODUCTS

SOUTH AFRICA - CHROMIUM ORE PRODUCTION AND CONSUMPTION - See SOUTH AFRICA - MINING AND MINERAL PRODUCTS

SOUTH AFRICA - CIGAR AND CIGARETTE PRODUCTION - See SOUTH AFRICA - TOBACCO PRODUCTION

SOUTH AFRICA - CLASS STRUCTURE

G.K. Hall and Company, 70 Lincoln Street, Boston, Massachusetts 02111 (617) 423-3990; *The World in Figures.*

SOUTH AFRICA - CLIMATE

Facts on File, 460 Park Avenue South, New York, New York 10016 (800) 443-8323; *The New Book of World Rankings.*

G.K. Hall and Company, 70 Lincoln Street, Boston, Massachusetts 02111 (617) 423-3990; *The World in Figures.*

SOUTH AFRICA - COAL PRODUCTION - See SOUTH AFRICA - MINING AND MINERAL PRODUCTS

SOUTH AFRICA - COFFEE PRODUCTION AND CONSUMPTION - See SOUTH AFRICA - CROPS

SOUTH AFRICA - COKE PRODUCTION AND CONSUMPTION - See SOUTH AFRICA - MINING AND MINERAL PRODUCTS

SOUTH AFRICA - COMMUNICATIONS

G.K. Hall and Company, 70 Lincoln Street, Boston, Massachusetts 02111 (617) 423-3990; *The World in Figures.*

SOUTH AFRICA - CONSTRUCTION INDUSTRY

Facts on File, 460 Park Avenue South, New York, New York 10016 (800) 443-8323; *The New Book of World Rankings.*

Statistical Office of the United Nations, Publishing Service, New York, New York 10017 (800) 253-9646; *Statistical Yearbook.*

SOUTH AFRICA - CONSUMER PRICE INDEX

G.K. Hall and Company, 70 Lincoln Street, Boston, Massachusetts 02111 (617) 423-3990; *The World in Figures.*

Statistical Office of the United Nations, Publishing Service, New York, New York 10017 (800) 253-9646; *Statistical Yearbook.*

SOUTH AFRICA - CONSUMER PRICES

International Labour Office, I.L.O. Publications, CH-1211, Geneva 22, Switzerland; *Yearbook of Labour Statistics.*

International Monetary Fund, 700 Nineteenth Street, NW, Washington, D.C. 20431 (202) 623-7000; *International Financial Statistics.*

Times Books, 201 East 50th Street, New York, New York 10022 (212) 751-2600; *The Economist Book of Vital World Statistics.*

SOUTH AFRICA - CONSUMPTION

G.K. Hall and Company, 70 Lincoln Street, Boston, Massachusetts 02111 (617) 423-3990; *The World in Figures.*

International Iron and Steel Institute, 120, rue Colonel Bourg, B-1140, Brussels, Belgium; *Steel Statistical Yearbook.*

International Lead and Zinc Study Group, Metro House, 58 St. James's Street, London SW1A 1LD, England; *Lead and Zinc Statistics.*

International Monetary Fund, 700 Nineteenth Street, NW, Washington, D.C. 20431 (202) 623-7000; *International Financial Statistics.*

SOUTH AFRICA - COPPER AND COPPER ORE PRODUCTION AND CONSUMPTION - See SOUTH AFRICA - MINING AND MINERAL PRODUCTS

SOUTH AFRICA - CORN PRODUCTION - See SOUTH AFRICA - CROPS
SOUTH AFRICA - CORPORATE TAXES - See SOUTH AFRICA - TAXATION

SOUTH AFRICA - COTTON - See SOUTH AFRICA - CROPS

SOUTH AFRICA - CROPS

Commodity Research Bureau, Incorporated, 75 Wall Street, New York, New York 10005 (212) 504-7754; *Commodity Year Book.*

Facts on File, 460 Park Avenue South, New York, New York 10016 (800) 443-8323; *The New Book of World Rankings*.

Food and Agricultural Organization of the United Nations (FAO) Via delle Terme di Caracalla, 00100 Rome, Italy (Telephone Number in U.S. (202) 653-2400); *The State of Food and Agriculture*.

G.K. Hall and Company, 70 Lincoln Street, Boston, Massachusetts 02111 (617) 423-3990; *The World in Figures*.

Statistical Office of the United Nations, Publishing Service, New York, New York 10017 (800) 253-9646; *Statistical Yearbook*.

SOUTH AFRICA - CUSTOMS DUTIES

G.K. Hall and Company, 70 Lincoln Street, Boston, Massachusetts 02111 (617) 423-3990; *The World in Figures*.

International Monetary Fund, 700 Nineteenth Street, NW, Washington, D.C. 20431 (202) 623-7000; *Government Finance Statistics Yearbook*.

SOUTH AFRICA - DAIRY PRODUCTS

Commodity Research Bureau, Incorporated, 75 Wall Street, New York, New York 10005 (212) 504-7754; *Commodity Year Book*.

Facts on File, 460 Park Avenue South, New York, New York 10016 (800) 443-8323; *The New Book of World Rankings*.

Food and Agricultural Organization of the United Nations (FAO) Via delle Terme di Caracalla, 00100 Rome, Italy (Telephone Number in U.S. (202) 653-2400); *The State of Food and Agriculture*.

Statistical Office of the United Nations, Publishing Service, New York, New York 10017 (800) 253-9646; *Statistical Yearbook*.

SOUTH AFRICA - DEATH RATE

G.K. Hall and Company, 70 Lincoln Street, Boston, Massachusetts 02111 (617) 423-3990; *The World in Figures*.

Statistical Office of the United Nations, Publishing Service, New York, New York 10017 (800) 253-9646; *Statistical Yearbook*.

Times Books, 201 East 50th Street, New York, New York 10022 (212) 751-2600; *The Economist Book of Vital World Statistics*.

SOUTH AFRICA - DEFENSE EXPENDITURES

G.K. Hall and Company, 70 Lincoln Street, Boston, Massachusetts 02111 (617) 423-3990; *The World in Figures*.

SOUTH AFRICA - DEMOGRAPHY

The Economist Intelligence Unit, 111 West 57th Street, New York, New York 10019 (800) 938-4685; *The World Market Atlas*.

Facts on File, 460 Park Avenue South, New York, New York 10016 (800) 443-8323; *The New Book of World Rankings*.

G.K. Hall and Company, 70 Lincoln Street, Boston, Massachusetts 02111 (617) 423-3990; *The World in Figures*.

SOUTH AFRICA - DEVELOPMENT ASSISTANCE

G.K. Hall and Company, 70 Lincoln Street, Boston, Massachusetts 02111 (617) 423-3990; *The World in Figures*.

SOUTH AFRICA - DIAMONDS - See SOUTH AFRICA - MINING AND MINERAL PRODUCTS

SOUTH AFRICA - DISCOUNT RATES

Statistical Office of the United Nations, Publishing Service, New York, New York 10017 (800) 253-9646; *Statistical Yearbook*.

SOUTH AFRICA - DISEASE

G.K. Hall and Company, 70 Lincoln Street, Boston, Massachusetts 02111 (617) 423-3990; *The World in Figures*.

SOUTH AFRICA - DIVORCE RATES

Facts on File, 460 Park Avenue South, New York, New York 10016 (800) 443-8323; *The New Book of World Rankings*.

Statistical Office of the United Nations, Publishing Service, New York, New York 10017 (800) 253-9646; *Demographic Yearbook*.

SOUTH AFRICA - DOMESTIC PRODUCT

G.K. Hall and Company, 70 Lincoln Street, Boston, Massachusetts 02111 (617) 423-3990; *The World in Figures*.

SOUTH AFRICA - ECONOMY

Euromonitor Publications Limited, 87-88 Turnmill Street, London EC1M 5QU, England; *International Marketing Data and Statistics*.

Facts on File, 460 Park Avenue South, New York, New York 10016 (800) 443-8323; *The New Book of World Rankings*.

G.K. Hall and Company, 70 Lincoln Street, Boston, Massachusetts 02111 (617) 423-3990; *The World in Figures*.

Statistical Office of the United Nations, Publishing Service, New York, New York 10017 (800) 253-9646; *Foreign Trade Statistics for Africa*.

SOUTH AFRICA - EDUCATION

The Economist Intelligence Unit, 111 West 57th Street, New York, New York 10019 (800) 938-4685; *The World Market Atlas*.

Facts on File, 460 Park Avenue South, New York, New York 10016 (800) 443-8323; *The New Book of World Rankings*.

G.K. Hall and Company, 70 Lincoln Street, Boston, Massachusetts 02111 (617) 423-3990; *The World in Figures*.

United Nations Educational, Scientific and Cultural Organization (UNESCO), 7 Place de Fontenoy, F-75700 Paris, France (Telephone Number in U.S. (212) 963-5981); *Statistical Yearbook*.

The World Bank, 1818 H Street, NW, Washington, D.C. 20433 (202) 477-1234; *World Tables*.

SOUTH AFRICA - EGG PRODUCTION AND CONSUMPTION - See SOUTH AFRICA - DAIRY PRODUCTS

SOUTH AFRICA - ELECTRICITY

Facts on File, 460 Park Avenue South, New York, New York 10016 (800) 443-8323; *The New Book of World Rankings*.

Statistical Office of the United Nations, Publishing Service, New York, New York 10017 (800) 253-9646; *Statistical Yearbook*.

Times Books, 201 East 50th Street, New York, New York 10022 (212) 751-2600; *The Economist Book of Vital World Statistics*.

SOUTH AFRICA - EMPLOYMENT

Euromonitor Publications Limited, 87-88 Turnmill Street, London EC1M 5QU, England; *International Marketing Data and Statistics*.

Facts on File, 460 Park Avenue South, New York, New York 10016 (800) 443-8323; *The New Book of World Rankings*.

International Labour Office, I.L.O. Publications, CH-1211, Geneva 22, Switzerland; *Yearbook of Labour Statistics*.

Statistical Office of the United Nations, Publishing Service, New York, New York 10017 (800) 253-9646; *Statistical Yearbook*.

SOUTH AFRICA - ENERGY

Facts on File, 460 Park Avenue South, New York, New York 10016 (800) 443-8323; *The New Book of World Rankings*.

Food and Agricultural Organization of the United Nations (FAO) Via delle Terme di Caracalla, 00100 Rome, Italy (Telephone Number in U.S. (202) 653-2400); *The State of Food and Agriculture*.

G.K. Hall and Company, 70 Lincoln Street, Boston, Massachusetts 02111 (617) 423-3990; *The World in Figures*.

Statistical Office of the United Nations, Publishing Service, New York, New York 10017 (800) 253-9646; *Energy Statistics Yearbook*, *Statistical Yearbook*, and *World Energy Supplies*.

Times Books, 201 East 50th Street, New York, New York 10022 (212) 751-2600; *The Economist Book of Vital World Statistics*.

SOUTH AFRICA - EXCHANGE RATE

Euromonitor Publications Limited, 87-88 Turnmill Street, London EC1M 5QU, England; *International Marketing Data and Statistics*.

International Monetary Fund, 700 Nineteenth Street, NW, Washington, D.C. 20431 (202) 623-7000; *International Financial Statistics*.

Statistical Office of the United Nations, Publishing Service, New York, New York 10017 (800) 253-9646; *Foreign Trade Statistics for Africa*, and *Statistical Yearbook*.

SOUTH AFRICA - EXCISE TAXES - See SOUTH AFRICA - TAXATION

SOUTH AFRICA - EXPORTS

American Automobile Manufacturers Association, 1401 H Street, NW, Suite 900, Washington, D.C. 20005 (202) 326-5500; *World Motor Vehicle Data*.

The Economist Intelligence Unit, 111 West 57th Street, New York, New York 10019 (800) 938-4685; *The World Market Atlas*.

Euromonitor Publications Limited, 87-88 Turnmill Street, London EC1M 5QU, England; *International Marketing Data and Statistics*.

Food and Agricultural Organization of the United Nations (FAO) Via delle Terme di Caracalla, 00100 Rome, Italy (Telephone Number in U.S. (202) 653-2400); *The State of Food and Agriculture*.

G.K. Hall and Company, 70 Lincoln Street, Boston, Massachusetts 02111 (617) 423-3990; *The World in Figures*.

International Iron and Steel Institute, 120, rue Colonel Bourg, B-1140, Brussels, Belgium; *Steel Statistical Yearbook*.

International Lead and Zinc Study Group, Metro House, 58 St. James's Street, London SW1A 1LD, England; *Lead and Zinc Statistics*.

International Monetary Fund, 700 Nineteenth Street, NW, Washington, D.C. 20431 (202) 623-7000; *Government Finance Statistics Yearbook*, and *International Financial Statistics*.

Statistical Office of the United Nations, Publishing Service, New York, New York 10017 (800) 253-9646; *Foreign Trade Statistics for Africa*.

Times Books, 201 East 50th Street, New York, New York 10022 (212) 751-2600; *The Economist Book of Vital World Statistics*.

The World Bank, 1818 H Street, NW, Washington, D.C. 20433 (202) 477-1234; *World Tables*.

SOUTH AFRICA - EXTERNAL INDEBTEDNESS

The World Bank, 1818 H Street, NW, Washington, D.C. 20433 (202) 477-1234; *World Tables*.

SOUTH AFRICA - EXTERNAL TRADE

Food and Agricultural Organization of the United Nations (FAO) Via delle Terme di Caracalla, 00100 Rome, Italy (Telephone Number in U.S. (202) 653-2400); *The State of Food and Agriculture*, and *Trade Yearbook*.

G.K. Hall and Company, 70 Lincoln Street, Boston, Massachusetts 02111 (617) 423-3990; *The World in Figures*.

Statistical Office of the United Nations, Publishing Service, New York, New York 10017 (800) 253-9646; *Statistical Yearbook*.

SOUTH AFRICA - FABRIC PRODUCTION - See SOUTH AFRICA - TEXTILE INDUSTRY

SOUTH AFRICA - FARM CROPS - See SOUTH AFRICA - CROPS

SOUTH AFRICA - FEMALE WORKING POPULATION - See SOUTH AFRICA - EMPLOYMENT

SOUTH AFRICA - FERTILITY RATES

Facts on File, 460 Park Avenue South, New York, New York 10016 (800) 443-8323; *The New Book of World Rankings*.

Times Books, 201 East 50th Street, New York, New York 10022 (212) 751-2600; *The Economist Book of Vital World Statistics*.

The World Bank, 1818 H Street, NW, Washington, D.C. 20433 (202) 477-1234; *World Tables*.

SOUTH AFRICA - FERTILIZER

Food and Agricultural Organization of the United Nations (FAO), Via delle Terme di Caracalla, 00100, Rome, Italy (Telephone Number in U.S. (202) 653-2400); *Fertilizer Yearbook*, and *The State of Food and Agriculture*.

Statistical Office of the United Nations, Publishing Service, New York, New York 10017 (800) 253-9646; *Statistical Yearbook*.

SOUTH AFRICA - FETAL MORTALITY

Statistical Office of the United Nations, Publishing Service, New York, New York 10017 (800) 253-9646; *Demographic Yearbook.*

SOUTH AFRICA - FIBRE PRODUCTION - See SOUTH AFRICA - TEXTILE INDUSTRY

SOUTH AFRICA - FILAMENT PRODUCTION - See SOUTH AFRICA - TEXTILE INDUSTRY

SOUTH AFRICA - FINANCE

Facts on File, 460 Park Avenue South, New York, New York 10016 (800) 443-8323; *The New Book of World Rankings.*

G.K. Hall and Company, 70 Lincoln Street, Boston, Massachusetts 02111 (617) 423-3990; *The World in Figures.*

International Monetary Fund, 700 Nineteenth Street, NW, Washington, D.C. 20431 (202) 623-7000; *Government Finance Statistics Yearbook,* and *International Financial Statistics.*

SOUTH AFRICA - FISHERIES

Facts on File, 460 Park Avenue South, New York, New York 10016 (800) 443-8323; *The New Book of World Rankings.*

Food and Agricultural Organization of the United Nations (FAO) Via delle Terme di Caracalla, 00100 Rome, Italy (Telephone Number in U.S. (202) 653-2400); *The State of Food and Agriculture,* and *Yearbook of Fishery Statistics.*

Statistical Office of the United Nations, Publishing Service, New York, New York 10017 (800) 253-9646; *Statistical Yearbook.*

SOUTH AFRICA - FLOUR PRODUCTION

Commodity Research Bureau, Incorporated, 75 Wall Street, New York, New York 10005 (212) 504-7754; *Commodity Year Book.*

Statistical Office of the United Nations, Publishing Service, New York, New York 10017 (800) 253-9646; *Statistical Yearbook.*

SOUTH AFRICA - FOOD

Food and Agricultural Organization of the United Nations (FAO), Via delle Terme di Caracalla, 00100 Rome, Italy (Telephone Number in U.S. (202) 653-2400); *Production Yearbook,* and *The State of Food and Agriculture.*

G.K. Hall and Company, 70 Lincoln Street, Boston, Massachusetts 02111 (617) 423-3990; *The World in Figures.*

SOUTH AFRICA - FOREIGN AID

G.K. Hall and Company, 70 Lincoln Street, Boston, Massachusetts 02111 (617) 423-3990; *The World in Figures.*

SOUTH AFRICA - FOREIGN DEBT

International Monetary Fund, 700 Nineteenth Street, NW, Washington, D.C. 20431 (202) 623-7000; *Government Finance Statistics Yearbook.*

SOUTH AFRICA - FOREIGN TRADE

Euromonitor Publications Limited, 87-88 Turnmill Street, London EC1M 5QU, England; *International Marketing Data and Statistics.*

Facts on File, 460 Park Avenue South, New York, New York 10016 (800) 443-8323; *The New Book of World Rankings.*

Food and Agricultural Organization of the United Nations (FAO) Via delle Terme di Caracalla, 00100 Rome, Italy (Telephone Number in U.S. (202) 653-2400); *The State of Food and Agriculture.*

G.K. Hall and Company, 70 Lincoln Street, Boston, Massachusetts 02111 (617) 423-3990; *The World in Figures.*

International Iron and Steel Institute, 120, rue Colonel Bourg, B-1140, Brussels, Belgium; *Steel Statistical Yearbook.*

International Monetary Fund, 700 Nineteenth Street, NW, Washington, D.C. 20431 (202) 623-7000; *International Financial Statistics.*

Statistical Office of the United Nations, Publishing Service, New York, New York 10017 (800) 253-9646; *Foreign Trade Statistics for Africa, International Trade Statistics Yearbook,* and *Statistical Yearbook.*

The World Bank, 1818 H Street, NW, Washington, D.C. 20433 (202) 477-1234; *World Tables.*

World Bureau of Metal Statistics, 27-A High Street, Ware Hert SG12 9BA, England; *World Metal Statistics.*

SOUTH AFRICA - FORESTRY AND FOREST PRODUCTS

American Forest and Paper Association, 1250 Connecticut Avenue, NW, Washington, D.C. 20036 (202) 463-2455; *Wood Pulp and Fiber Statistics.*

Facts on File, 460 Park Avenue South, New York, New York 10016 (800) 443-8323; *The New Book of World Rankings.*

Food and Agricultural Organization of the United Nations (FAO) Via delle Terme di Caracalla, 00100 Rome, Italy (Telephone Number in U.S. (202) 653-2400); *The State of Food and Agriculture,* and *Yearbook of Forest Products.*

G.K. Hall and Company, 70 Lincoln Street, Boston, Massachusetts 02111 (617) 423-3990; *The World in Figures.*

Statistical Office of the United Nations, Publishing Service, New York, New York 10017 (800) 253-9646; *Statistical Yearbook.*

United Nations Educational, Scientific and Cultural Organization (UNESCO), 7 Place de Fontenoy, F-75700 Paris, France (Telephone Number in U.S. (212) 963-5981); *Statistical Yearbook.*

SOUTH AFRICA - GAS PRODUCTION - See SOUTH AFRICA - MINING AND MINERAL PRODUCTS

SOUTH AFRICA - GENERAL INDUSTRIAL STATISTICS

Statistical Office of the United Nations, Publishing Service, New York, New York 10017 (800) 253-9646; *Industrial Statistics Yearbook.*

SOUTH AFRICA - GENERAL MORTALITY

Statistical Office of the United Nations, Publishing Service, New York, New York 10017 (800) 253-9646; *Demographic Yearbook.*

SOUTH AFRICA - GEOGRAPHIC DATA

Facts on File, 460 Park Avenue South, New York, New York 10016 (800) 443-8323; *The New Book of World Rankings*.

SOUTH AFRICA - GOLD

International Monetary Fund, 700 Nineteenth Street, NW, Washington, D.C. 20431 (202) 623-7000; *International Financial Statistics*.

Statistical Office of the United Nations, Publishing Service, New York, New York 10017 (800) 253-9646; *Statistical Yearbook*.

The World Bank, 1818 H Street, NW, Washington, D.C. 20433 (202) 477-1234; *World Tables*.

SOUTH AFRICA - GOLD PRODUCTION AND CONSUMPTION - See SOUTH AFRICA - MINING AND MINERAL PRODUCTS

SOUTH AFRICA - GOVERNMENT

G.K. Hall and Company, 70 Lincoln Street, Boston, Massachusetts 02111 (617) 423-3990; *The World in Figures*.

SOUTH AFRICA - GOVERNMENT CONSUMPTION

International Monetary Fund, 700 Nineteenth Street, NW, Washington, D.C. 20431 (202) 623-7000; *International Financial Statistics*.

SOUTH AFRICA - GOVERNMENT EXPENDITURES

International Monetary Fund, 700 Nineteenth Street, NW, Washington, D.C. 20431 (202) 623-7000; *Government Finance Statistics Yearbook*.

The World Bank, 1818 H Street, NW, Washington, D.C. 20433 (202) 477-1234; *World Tables*.

SOUTH AFRICA - GOVERNMENT FINANCES

International Monetary Fund, 700 Nineteenth Street, NW, Washington, D.C. 20431 (202) 623-7000; *International Financial Statistics*.

SOUTH AFRICA - GOVERNMENT REVENUE

International Monetary Fund, 700 Nineteenth Street, NW, Washington, D.C. 20431 (202) 623-7000; *Government Finance Statistics Yearbook*.

Times Books, 201 East 50th Street, New York, New York 10022 (212) 751-2600; *The Economist Book of Vital World Statistics*.

The World Bank, 1818 H Street, NW, Washington, D.C. 20433 (202) 477-1234; *World Tables*.

SOUTH AFRICA - GRAIN PRODUCTION - See SOUTH AFRICA - CROPS

SOUTH AFRICA - GRANTS

International Monetary Fund, 700 Nineteenth Street, NW, Washington, D.C. 20431 (202) 623-7000; *Government Finance Statistics Yearbook*.

SOUTH AFRICA - GROSS DOMESTIC PRODUCT

The Economist Intelligence Unit, 111 West 57th Street, New York, New York 10019 (800) 938-4685; *The World Market Atlas*.

Euromonitor Publications Limited, 87-88 Turnmill Street, London EC1M 5QU, England; *International Marketing Data and Statistics*.

Facts on File, 460 Park Avenue South, New York, New York 10016 (800) 443-8323; *The New Book of World Rankings*.

G.K. Hall and Company, 70 Lincoln Street, Boston, Massachusetts 02111 (617) 423-3990; *The World in Figures*.

International Monetary Fund, 700 Nineteenth Street, NW, Washington, D.C. 20431 (202) 623-7000; *International Financial Statistics*.

Statistical Office of the United Nations, Publishing Service, New York, New York 10017 (800) 253-9646; *Statistical Yearbook*.

Times Books, 201 East 50th Street, New York, New York 10022 (212) 751-2600; *The Economist Book of Vital World Statistics*.

The World Bank, 1818 H Street, NW, Washington, D.C. 20433 (202) 477-1234; *World Tables*.

SOUTH AFRICA - GROSS NATIONAL PRODUCT

Euromonitor Publications Limited, 87-88 Turnmill Street, London EC1M 5QU, England; *International Marketing Data and Statistics*.

U.S. Arms Control and Disarmament Agency, 320 Twenty-first Street, NW, Washington, D.C. 20451 (202) 647-8677; *World Military Expenditures and Arms Transfers*.

The World Bank, 1818 H Street, NW, Washington, D.C. 20433 (202) 477-1234; *World Tables*.

SOUTH AFRICA - GROUNDNUT PRODUCTION - See SOUTH AFRICA - CROPS

SOUTH AFRICA - HEALTH

Facts on File, 460 Park Avenue South, New York, New York 10016 (800) 443-8323; *The New Book of World Rankings*.

G.K. Hall and Company, 70 Lincoln Street, Boston, Massachusetts 02111 (617) 423-3990; *The World in Figures*.

Statistical Office of the United Nations, Publishing Service, New York, New York 10017 (800) 253-9646; *Statistical Yearbook*.

Times Books, 201 East 50th Street, New York, New York 10022 (212) 751-2600; *The Economist Book of Vital World Statistics*.

SOUTH AFRICA - HIGHWAYS

G.K. Hall and Company, 70 Lincoln Street, Boston, Massachusetts 02111 (617) 423-3990; *The World in Figures*.

International Road Federation, 525 School Street, SW, Washington, D.C. 20024 (202) 554-2106; *World Road Statistics*.

SOUTH AFRICA - HORSES - See SOUTH AFRICA - LIVESTOCK AND POULTRY

SOUTH AFRICA - HOURS OF WORK - See SOUTH AFRICA - EMPLOYMENT

SOUTH AFRICA - HOUSING

Facts on File, 460 Park Avenue South, New York, New York 10016 (800) 443-8323; *The New Book of World Rankings.*

SOUTH AFRICA - ILLITERATE POPULATION

The Economist Intelligence Unit, 111 West 57th Street, New York, New York 10019 (800) 938-4685; *The World Market Atlas.*

G.K. Hall and Company, 70 Lincoln Street, Boston, Massachusetts 02111 (617) 423-3990; *The World in Figures.*

United Nations Educational, Scientific and Cultural Organization (UNESCO), 7 Place de Fontenoy, F-75700 Paris, France (Telephone Number in U.S. (212) 963-5981); *Statistical Yearbook.*

SOUTH AFRICA - IMPORTS

American Automobile Manufacturers Association, 1401 H Street, NW, Suite 900, Washington, D.C. 20005 (202) 326-5500; *World Motor Vehicle Data.*

The Economist Intelligence Unit, 111 West 57th Street, New York, New York 10019 (800) 938-4685; *The World Market Atlas.*

Euromonitor Publications Limited, 87-88 Turnmill Street, London EC1M 5QU, England; *International Marketing Data and Statistics.*

European Community Information Service, 2100 M Street, NW, Washington, D.C. 20037 (202) 862-9500; *Demographic Statistics.*

Food and Agricultural Organization of the United Nations (FAO) Via delle Terme di Caracalla, 00100 Rome, Italy (Telephone Number in U.S. (202) 653-2400); *The State of Food and Agriculture.*

G.K. Hall and Company, 70 Lincoln Street, Boston, Massachusetts 02111 (617) 423-3990; *The World in Figures.*

International Iron and Steel Institute, 120, rue Colonel Bourg, B-1140, Brussels, Belgium; *Steel Statistical Yearbook.*

International Lead and Zinc Study Group, Metro House, 58 St. James's Street, London SW1A 1LD, England; *Lead and Zinc Statistics.*

International Monetary Fund, 700 Nineteenth Street, NW, Washington, D.C. 20431 (202) 623-7000; *Government Finance Statistics Yearbook,* and *International Financial Statistics.*

Statistical Office of the United Nations, Publishing Service, New York, New York 10017 (800) 253-9646; *Foreign Trade Statistics for Africa.*

Times Books, 201 East 50th Street, New York, New York 10022 (212) 751-2600; *The Economist Book of Vital World Statistics.*

The World Bank, 1818 H Street, NW, Washington, D.C. 20433 (202) 477-1234; *World Tables.*

SOUTH AFRICA - INCOME TAXES - See SOUTH AFRICA - TAXATION

SOUTH AFRICA - INDUSTRY

Euromonitor Publications Limited, 87-88 Turnmill Street, London EC1M 5QU, England; *International Marketing Data and Statistics.*

Facts on File, 460 Park Avenue South, New York, New York 10016 (800) 443-8323; *The New Book of World Rankings.*

G.K. Hall and Company, 70 Lincoln Street, Boston, Massachusetts 02111 (617) 423-3990; *The World in Figures.*

International Labour Office, I.L.O. Publications, CH-1211, Geneva 22, Switzerland; *Yearbook of Labour Statistics.*

Statistical Office of the United Nations, Publishing Service, New York, New York 10017 (800) 253-9646; *Statistical Yearbook.*

The World Bank, 1818 H Street, NW, Washington, D.C. 20433 (202) 477-1234; *World Tables.*

SOUTH AFRICA - INFANT AND MATERNAL MORTALITY

Statistical Office of the United Nations, Publishing Service, New York, New York 10017 (800) 253-9646; *Demographic Yearbook.*

Times Books, 201 East 50th Street, New York, New York 10022 (212) 751-2600; *The Economist Book of Vital World Statistics.*

The World Bank, 1818 H Street, NW, Washington, D.C. 20433 (202) 477-1234; *World Tables.*

SOUTH AFRICA - INTERNAL TRADE

Statistical Office of the United Nations, Publishing Service, New York, New York 10017 (800) 253-9646; *Statistical Yearbook.*

SOUTH AFRICA - INTERNATIONAL LIQUIDITY

International Monetary Fund, 700 Nineteenth Street, NW, Washington, D.C. 20431 (202) 623-7000; *International Financial Statistics.*

SOUTH AFRICA - INTERNATIONAL RESERVES EXCLUDING GOLD

Statistical Office of the United Nations, Publishing Service, New York, New York 10017 (800) 253-9646; *Statistical Yearbook.*

The World Bank, 1818 H Street, NW, Washington, D.C. 20433 (202) 477-1234; *World Tables.*

SOUTH AFRICA - INVESTMENTS

International Monetary Fund, 700 Nineteenth Street, NW, Washington, D.C. 20431 (202) 623-7000; *International Financial Statistics.*

SOUTH AFRICA - IRON ORE - See SOUTH AFRICA - MINING AND MINERAL PRODUCTS

SOUTH AFRICA - IRRIGATION

Euromonitor Publications Limited, 87-88 Turnmill Street, London EC1M 5QU, England; *International Marketing Data and Statistics.*

SOUTH AFRICA - LABOR FORCE

Euromonitor Publications Limited, 87-88 Turnmill Street, London EC1M 5QU, England; *International Marketing Data and Statistics.*

Facts on File, 460 Park Avenue South, New York, New York 10016 (800) 443-8323; *The New Book of World Rankings.*

Food and Agricultural Organization of the United Nations (FAO) Via delle Terme di Caracalla, 00100 Rome, Italy (Telephone Number in U.S. (202) 653-2400); *The State of Food and Agriculture.*

G.K. Hall and Company, 70 Lincoln Street, Boston, Massachusetts 02111 (617) 423-3990; *The World in Figures*.

Times Books, 201 East 50th Street, New York, New York 10022 (212) 751-2600; *The Economist Book of Vital World Statistics*.

The World Bank, 1818 H Street, NW, Washington, D.C. 20433 (202) 477-1234; *World Tables*.

SOUTH AFRICA - LABOR PRODUCTIVITY

International Labour Office, I.L.O. Publications, CH-1211, Geneva 22, Switzerland; *Yearbook of Labour Statistics*.

SOUTH AFRICA - LAND USE

Euromonitor Publications Limited, 87-88 Turnmill Street, London EC1M 5QU, England; *International Marketing Data and Statistics*.

Food and Agricultural Organization of the United Nations (FAO), Via delle Terme di Caracalla, 00100 Rome, Italy (Telephone Number in U.S. (202) 653-2400); *Production Yearbook*.

G.K. Hall and Company, 70 Lincoln Street, Boston, Massachusetts 02111 (617) 423-3990; *The World in Figures*.

SOUTH AFRICA - LEAD AND LEAD ORE PRODUCTION AND CONSUMPTION - See SOUTH AFRICA - MINING AND MINERAL PRODUCTS

SOUTH AFRICA - LIBRARIES

Facts on File, 460 Park Avenue South, New York, New York 10016 (800) 443-8323; *The New Book of World Rankings*.

SOUTH AFRICA - LIVESTOCK AND POULTRY

Commodity Research Bureau, Incorporated, 75 Wall Street, New York, New York 10005 (212) 504-7754; *Commodity Year Book*.

Euromonitor Publications Limited, 87-88 Turnmill Street, London EC1M 5QU, England; *International Marketing Data and Statistics*.

Facts on File, 460 Park Avenue South, New York, New York 10016 (800) 443-8323; *The New Book of World Rankings*.

Food and Agricultural Organization of the United Nations (FAO), Via delle Terme di Caracalla, 00100 Rome, Italy (Telephone Number in U.S. (202) 653-2400); *Production Yearbook*, and *The State of Food and Agriculture*.

G.K. Hall and Company, 70 Lincoln Street, Boston, Massachusetts 02111 (617) 423-3990; *The World in Figures*.

Statistical Office of the United Nations, Publishing Service, New York, New York 10017 (800) 253-9646; *Statistical Yearbook*.

SOUTH AFRICA - LIVING LEVELS

G.K. Hall and Company, 70 Lincoln Street, Boston, Massachusetts 02111 (617) 423-3990; *The World in Figures*.

Times Books, 201 East 50th Street, New York, New York 10022 (212) 751-2600; *The Economist Book of Vital World Statistics*.

SOUTH AFRICA - MAIL - NUMBER OF ITEMS SENT AND RECEIVED

Statistical Office of the United Nations, Publishing Service, New York, New York 10017 (800) 253-9646; *Statistical Yearbook*.

SOUTH AFRICA - MANGANESE AND MANGANESE ORE PRODUCTION AND CONSUMPTION - See SOUTH AFRICA - MINING AND MINERAL PRODUCTS

SOUTH AFRICA - MANUFACTURING

American Automobile Manufacturers Association, 1401 H Street, NW, Suite 900, Washington, D.C. 20005 (202) 326-5500; *World Motor Vehicle Data*.

Facts on File, 460 Park Avenue South, New York, New York 10016 (800) 443-8323; *The New Book of World Rankings*.

G.K. Hall and Company, 70 Lincoln Street, Boston, Massachusetts 02111 (617) 423-3990; *The World in Figures*.

International Monetary Fund, 700 Nineteenth Street, NW, Washington, D.C. 20431 (202) 623-7000; *International Financial Statistics*.

Statistical Office of the United Nations, Publishing Service, New York, New York 10017 (800) 253-9646; *Statistical Yearbook*.

Times Books, 201 East 50th Street, New York, New York 10022 (212) 751-2600; *The Economist Book of Vital World Statistics*.

The World Bank, 1818 H Street, NW, Washington, D.C. 20433 (202) 477-1234; *World Tables*.

SOUTH AFRICA - MARRIAGE RATES

Facts on File, 460 Park Avenue South, New York, New York 10016 (800) 443-8323; *The New Book of World Rankings*.

Statistical Office of the United Nations, Publishing Service, New York, New York 10017 (800) 253-9646; *Demographic Yearbook*.

SOUTH AFRICA - MEAT PRODUCTION - See SOUTH AFRICA - LIVESTOCK AND POULTRY

SOUTH AFRICA - MERCHANT SHIPPING

G.K. Hall and Company, 70 Lincoln Street, Boston, Massachusetts 02111 (617) 423-3990; *The World in Figures*.

Statistical Office of the United Nations, Publishing Service, New York, New York 10017 (800) 253-9646; *Statistical Yearbook*.

Times Books, 201 East 50th Street, New York, New York 10022 (212) 751-2600; *The Economist Book of Vital World Statistics*.

U.S. Department of Transportation, Maritime Administration, 400 Seventh Street, SW, Washington, D.C. 20590 (202) 366-5807; *A Statistical Analysis of the World's Merchant Fleets*.

SOUTH AFRICA - MILITARY

G.K. Hall and Company, 70 Lincoln Street, Boston, Massachusetts 02111 (617) 423-3990; *The World in Figures*.

The International Institute for Strategic Studies, 23 Tavistock Street, London WC2E 7NQ, England; *The Military Balance*.

U.S. Arms Control and Disarmament Agency, 320 Twenty-first Street, NW, Washington, D.C. 20451 (202) 647-8677; *World Military Expenditures and Arms Transfers.*

SOUTH AFRICA - MILK PRODUCTION - See SOUTH AFRICA - DAIRY PRODUCTS

SOUTH AFRICA - MINING AND MINERAL PRODUCTS

Commodity Research Bureau, Incorporated, 75 Wall Street, New York, New York 10005 (212) 504-7754; *Commodity Year Book.*

Facts on File, 460 Park Avenue South, New York, New York 10016 (800) 443-8323; *The New Book of World Rankings.*

G.K. Hall and Company, 70 Lincoln Street, Boston, Massachusetts 02111 (617) 423-3990; *The World in Figures.*

International Iron and Steel Institute, 120, rue Colonel Bourg, B-1140, Brussels, Belgium; *Steel Statistical Yearbook.*

International Lead and Zinc Study Group, Metro House, 58 St. James's Street, London SW1A 1LD, England; *Lead and Zinc Statistics.*

International Monetary Fund, 700 Nineteenth Street, NW, Washington, D.C. 20431 (202) 623-7000; *International Financial Statistics.*

Statistical Office of the United Nations, Publishing Service, New York, New York 10017 (800) 253-9646; *Statistical Yearbook.*

World Bureau of Metal Statistics, 27-A High Street, Ware Hert SG12 9BA, England; *World Metal Statistics.*

SOUTH AFRICA - MOLYBDENUM AND MOLYBDENUM ORE PRODUCTION AND CONSUMPTION - See SOUTH AFRICA - MINING AND MINERAL PRODUCTS

SOUTH AFRICA - MONEY EXCHANGE RATE

Euromonitor Publications Limited, 87-88 Turnmill Street, London EC1M 5QU, England; *International Marketing Data and Statistics.*

International Monetary Fund, 700 Nineteenth Street, NW, Washington, D.C. 20431 (202) 623-7000; *International Financial Statistics.*

Statistical Office of the United Nations, Publishing Service, New York, New York 10017 (800) 253-9646; *Statistical Yearbook.*

SOUTH AFRICA - MONEY RATES - MARKET

Statistical Office of the United Nations, Publishing Service, New York, New York 10017 (800) 253-9646; *Statistical Yearbook.*

SOUTH AFRICA - MONEY RESERVES

Euromonitor Publications Limited, 87-88 Turnmill Street, London EC1M 5QU, England; *International Marketing Data and Statistics.*

SOUTH AFRICA - MONEY SUPPLY

Euromonitor Publications Limited, 87-88 Turnmill Street, London EC1M 5QU, England; *International Marketing Data and Statistics.*

G.K. Hall and Company, 70 Lincoln Street, Boston, Massachusetts 02111 (617) 423-3990; *The World in Figures.*

International Monetary Fund, 700 Nineteenth Street, NW, Washington, D.C. 20431 (202) 623-7000; *International Financial Statistics.*

Statistical Office of the United Nations, Publishing Service, New York, New York 10017 (800) 253-9646; *Statistical Yearbook.*

The World Bank, 1818 H Street, NW, Washington, D.C. 20433 (202) 477-1234; *World Tables.*

SOUTH AFRICA - MOTOR VEHICLE ASSEMBLY

Statistical Office of the United Nations, Publishing Service, New York, New York 10017 (800) 253-9646; *Statistical Yearbook.*

SOUTH AFRICA - MOTOR VEHICLE PRODUCTION

American Automobile Manufacturers Association, 1401 H Street, NW, Suite 900, Washington, D.C. 20005 (202) 326-5500; *World Motor Vehicle Data.*

SOUTH AFRICA - MOTOR VEHICLE TAXES - See SOUTH AFRICA - TAXATION

SOUTH AFRICA - MOTOR VEHICLES IN USE

American Automobile Manufacturers Association, 1401 H Street, NW, Suite 900, Washington, D.C. 20005 (202) 326-5500; *World Motor Vehicle Data.*

G.K. Hall and Company, 70 Lincoln Street, Boston, Massachusetts 02111 (617) 423-3990; *The World in Figures.*

International Road Federation, 525 School Street, SW, Washington, D.C. 20024 (202) 554-2106; *World Road Statistics.*

Statistical Office of the United Nations, Publishing Service, New York, New York 10017 (800) 253-9646; *Statistical Yearbook.*

Times Books, 201 East 50th Street, New York, New York 10022 (212) 751-2600; *The Economist Book of Vital World Statistics.*

SOUTH AFRICA - MULES - See SOUTH AFRICA - LIVESTOCK AND POULTRY

SOUTH AFRICA - MUSEUMS

Facts on File, 460 Park Avenue South, New York, New York 10016 (800) 443-8323; *The New Book of World Rankings.*

SOUTH AFRICA - NATALITY - See SOUTH AFRICA - BIRTH RATE

SOUTH AFRICA - NATIONAL ACCOUNTS

International Monetary Fund, 700 Nineteenth Street, NW, Washington, D.C. 20431 (202) 623-7000; *International Financial Statistics.*

Statistical Office of the United Nations, Publishing Service, New York, New York 10017 (800) 253-9646; *National Accounts Statistics*, and *Statistical Yearbook.*

SOUTH AFRICA - NATIONAL INCOME

Facts on File, 460 Park Avenue South, New York, New York 10016 (800) 443-8323; *The New Book of World Rankings.*

G.K. Hall and Company, 70 Lincoln Street, Boston, Massachusetts 02111 (617) 423-3990; *The World in Figures.*

Statistical Office of the United Nations, Publishing Service, New York, New York 10017 (800) 253-9646; *Statistical Yearbook*.

SOUTH AFRICA - NATIONAL PRODUCT

Facts on File, 460 Park Avenue South, New York, New York 10016 (800) 443-8323; *The New Book of World Rankings*.

Statistical Office of the United Nations, Publishing Service, New York, New York 10017 (800) 253-9646; *Statistical Yearbook*.

SOUTH AFRICA - NATURAL GAS PRODUCTION - See SOUTH AFRICA - MINING AND MINERAL PRODUCTS

SOUTH AFRICA - NEWSPAPER PRODUCTION - See SOUTH AFRICA - FORESTRY AND FOREST PRODUCTS

SOUTH AFRICA - NEWSPRINT - See SOUTH AFRICA - FORESTRY AND FOREST PRODUCTS

SOUTH AFRICA - NICKEL AND NICKEL ORE PRODUCTION AND CONSUMPTION - See AFRICA - MINING AND MINERAL PRODUCTS

SOUTH AFRICA - OATS PRODUCTION - See SOUTH AFRICA - CROPS

SOUTH AFRICA - OCCUPATIONS - See SOUTH AFRICA - LABOR FORCE

SOUTH AFRICA - ORANGES PRODUCTION - See SOUTH AFRICA - CROPS

SOUTH AFRICA - PAPER - See SOUTH AFRICA - FORESTRY AND FOREST PRODUCTS

SOUTH AFRICA - PATENTS

Statistical Office of the United Nations, Publishing Service, New York, New York 10017 (800) 253-9646; *Statistical Yearbook*.

SOUTH AFRICA - PEANUT PRODUCTION - See SOUTH AFRICA - CROPS

SOUTH AFRICA - PESTICIDE USE

Food and Agricultural Organization of the United Nations (FAO) Via delle Terme di Caracalla, 00100 Rome, Italy (Telephone Number in U.S. (202) 653-2400); *The State of Food and Agriculture*.

SOUTH AFRICA - PETROLEUM INDUSTRY

Facts on File, 460 Park Avenue South, New York, New York 10016 (800) 443-8323; *The New Book of World Rankings*.

Food and Agricultural Organization of the United Nations (FAO) Via delle Terme di Caracalla, 00100 Rome, Italy (Telephone Number in U.S. (202) 653-2400); *The State of Food and Agriculture*.

G.K. Hall and Company, 70 Lincoln Street, Boston, Massachusetts 02111 (617) 423-3990; *The World in Figures*.

Statistical Office of the United Nations, Publishing Service, New York, New York 10017 (800) 253-9646; *Statistical Yearbook*.

SOUTH AFRICA - PHOSPHATE ROCK - PRODUCTION - See SOUTH AFRICA - MINING AND MINERAL PRODUCTS

SOUTH AFRICA - PIG-IRON AND FERRO-ALLOYS - PRODUCTION - See SOUTH AFRICA - MINING AND MINERAL PRODUCTS

SOUTH AFRICA - PIGS - See SOUTH AFRICA - LIVESTOCK AND POULTRY

SOUTH AFRICA - PLATINUM PRODUCTION AND CONSUMPTION - See SOUTH AFRICA - MINING AND MINERAL PRODUCTS

SOUTH AFRICA - POPULATION

The Economist Intelligence Unit, 111 West 57th Street, New York, New York 10019 (800) 938-4685; *The World Market Atlas*.

Euromonitor Publications Limited, 87-88 Turnmill Street, London EC1M 5QU, England; *International Marketing Data and Statistics*.

Facts on File, 460 Park Avenue South, New York, New York 10016 (800) 443-8323; *The New Book of World Rankings*.

Food and Agricultural Organization of the United Nations (FAO), Via delle Terme di Caracalla, 00100 Rome, Italy (Telephone Number in U.S. (202) 653-2400); *Production Yearbook*.

G.K. Hall and Company, 70 Lincoln Street, Boston, Massachusetts 02111 (617) 423-3990; *The World in Figures*.

International Labour Office, I.L.O. Publications, CH-1211, Geneva 22, Switzerland; *Yearbook of Labour Statistics*.

Statistical Office of the United Nations, Publishing Service, New York, New York 10017 (800) 253-9646; *Demographic Yearbook*, and *Statistical Yearbook*.

Times Books, 201 East 50th Street, New York, New York 10022 (212) 751-2000; *The Economist Book of Vital World Statistics*.

United Nations Educational, Scientific and Cultural Organization (UNESCO), 7 Place de Fontenoy, F-75700 Paris, France (Telephone Number in U.S. (212) 963-5981); *Statistical Yearbook*.

U.S. Arms Control and Disarmament Agency, 320 Twenty-first Street, NW, Washington, D.C. 20451 (202) 647-8677; *World Military Expenditures and Arms Transfers*.

World Health Organization, Office of Publications, Avenue Appia, CH-1211 Geneva 27, Switzerland (Telephone Number in U.S. (518) 436-9686); *World Health Statistics Annual*.

SOUTH AFRICA - POST OFFICES

Facts on File, 460 Park Avenue South, New York, New York 10016 (800) 443-8323; *The New Book of World Rankings*.

SOUTH AFRICA - POTATO PRODUCTION - See SOUTH AFRICA - CROPS

SOUTH AFRICA - POWER PRODUCTION INDUSTRY

Statistical Office of the United Nations, Publishing Service, New York, New York 10017 (800) 253-9646; *Statistical Yearbook*.

SOUTH AFRICA - PRICES

Facts on File, 460 Park Avenue South, New York, New York 10016 (800) 443-8323; *The New Book of World Rankings*.

Food and Agricultural Organization of the United Nations (FAO), Via delle Terme di Caracalla, 00100 Rome, Italy (Telephone Number in U.S. (202) 653-2400); *Production Yearbook*, and *The State of Food and Agriculture*.

G.K. Hall and Company, 70 Lincoln Street, Boston, Massachusetts 02111 (617) 423-3990; *The World in Figures.*

International Labour Office, I.L.O. Publications, CH-1211, Geneva 22, Switzerland; *Yearbook of Labour Statistics.*

International Lead and Zinc Study Group, Metro House, 58 St. James's Street, London SW1A 1LD, England; *Lead and Zinc Statistics.*

International Monetary Fund, 700 Nineteenth Street, NW, Washington, D.C. 20431 (202) 623-7000; *International Financial Statistics.*

World Bureau of Metal Statistics, 27-A High Street, Ware Hert SG12 9BA, England; *World Metal Statistics.*

SOUTH AFRICA - PRINTING AND WRITING PAPER - See SOUTH AFRICA - FORESTRY AND FOREST PRODUCTS

SOUTH AFRICA - PRODUCTION

American Automobile Manufacturers Association, 1401 H Street, NW, Suite 900, Washington, D.C. 20005 (202) 326-5500; *World Motor Vehicle Data.*

Facts on File, 460 Park Avenue South, New York, New York 10016 (800) 443-8323; *The New Book of World Rankings.*

G.K. Hall and Company, 70 Lincoln Street, Boston, Massachusetts 02111 (617) 423-3990; *The World in Figures.*

International Iron and Steel Institute, 120, rue Colonel Bourg, B-1140, Brussels, Belgium; *Steel Statistical Yearbook.*

International Lead and Zinc Study Group, Metro House, 58 St. James's Street, London SW1A 1LD, England; *Lead and Zinc Statistics.*

SOUTH AFRICA - PRODUCTIVITY

Euromonitor Publications Limited, 87-88 Turnmill Street, London EC1M 5QU, England; *International Marketing Data and Statistics.*

SOUTH AFRICA - PROPERTY TAXES - See SOUTH AFRICA - TAXATION

SOUTH AFRICA - PUBLIC FINANCE

Facts on File, 460 Park Avenue South, New York, New York 10016 (800) 443-8323; *The New Book of World Rankings.*

International Monetary Fund, 700 Nineteenth Street, NW, Washington, D.C. 20431 (202) 623-7000; *International Financial Statistics.*

SOUTH AFRICA - RADIO BROADCASTING - See SOUTH AFRICA - BROADCASTING

SOUTH AFRICA - RADIO RECEIVER PRODUCTION

Statistical Office of the United Nations, Publishing Service, New York, New York 10017 (800) 253-9646; *Statistical Yearbook.*

SOUTH AFRICA - RAILWAYS

G.K. Hall and Company, 70 Lincoln Street, Boston, Massachusetts 02111 (617) 423-3990; *The World in Figures.*

Jane's Information Group, Sentinel House, 163 Brighton Road, Coulsdon, Surrey CR5 2NH, England (Telephone Number in U.S. (703) 683-3700); *Jane's World Railways.*

Statistical Office of the United Nations, Publishing Service, New York, New York 10017 (800) 253-9646; *Statistical Yearbook.*

SOUTH AFRICA - RELIGION

Facts on File, 460 Park Avenue South, New York, New York 10016 (800) 443-8323; *The New Book of World Rankings.*

SOUTH AFRICA - RENT PRICES

International Labour Office, I.L.O. Publications, CH-1211, Geneva 22, Switzerland; *Yearbook of Labour Statistics.*

SOUTH AFRICA - RETAIL TRADE

G.K. Hall and Company, 70 Lincoln Street, Boston, Massachusetts 02111 (617) 423-3990; *The World in Figures.*

Statistical Office of the United Nations, Publishing Service, New York, New York 10017 (800) 253-9646; *Statistical Yearbook.*

SOUTH AFRICA - RICE PRODUCTION - See SOUTH AFRICA - CROPS

SOUTH AFRICA - ROUNDWOOD PRODUCTION - See SOUTH AFRICA - FORESTRY AND FOREST PRODUCTS

SOUTH AFRICA - RUBBER PRODUCTION AND CONSUMPTION

Facts on File, 460 Park Avenue South, New York, New York 10016 (800) 443-8323; *The New Book of World Rankings.*

Statistical Office of the United Nations, Publishing Service, New York, New York 10017 (800) 253-9646; *Statistical Yearbook.*

SOUTH AFRICA - SALT PRODUCTION - See SOUTH AFRICA - MINING AND MINERAL PRODUCTS

SOUTH AFRICA - SAWNWOOD PRODUCTION - See SOUTH AFRICA - FORESTRY AND FOREST PRODUCTS

SOUTH AFRICA - SENIOR CITIZENS

Facts on File, 460 Park Avenue South, New York, New York 10016 (800) 443-8323; *The New Book of World Rankings.*

SOUTH AFRICA - SHEEP - See SOUTH AFRICA - LIVESTOCK AND POULTRY

SOUTH AFRICA - SILVER PRODUCTION AND CONSUMPTION - See SOUTH AFRICA - MINING AND MINERAL PRODUCTS

SOUTH AFRICA - SOCIAL DATA

Facts on File, 460 Park Avenue South, New York, New York 10016 (800) 443-8323; *The New Book of World Rankings.*

G.K. Hall and Company, 70 Lincoln Street, Boston, Massachusetts 02111 (617) 423-3990; *The World in Figures.*

SOUTH AFRICA - SOYBEAN PRODUCTION - See SOUTH AFRICA - CROPS

SOUTH AFRICA - STAMP TAXES AND DUTIES - See SOUTH AFRICA - TAXATION

SOUTH AFRICA - STATE BUDGET REVENUE AND EXPENDITURES

Euromonitor Publications Limited, 87-88 Turnmill Street, London EC1M 5QU, England; *International Marketing Data and Statistics.*

SOUTH AFRICA - STEEL - See SOUTH AFRICA - MINING AND MINERAL PRODUCTS

SOUTH AFRICA - STOCKS - COMMODITY - MARKET PRICE - INDEXES

Food and Agricultural Organization of the United Nations (FAO) Via delle Terme di Caracalla, 00100 Rome, Italy (Telephone Number in U.S. (202) 653-2400); *The State of Food and Agriculture.*

International Lead and Zinc Study Group, Metro House, 58 St. James's Street, London SW1A 1LD, England; *Lead and Zinc Statistics.*

Statistical Office of the United Nations, Publishing Service, New York, New York 10017 (800) 253-9646; *Statistical Yearbook.*

World Bureau of Metal Statistics, 27-A High Street, Ware Hert SG12 9BA, England; *World Metal Statistics.*

SOUTH AFRICA - SUGAR - See SOUTH AFRICA - CROPS

SOUTH AFRICA - TAXATION

G.K. Hall and Company, 70 Lincoln Street, Boston, Massachusetts 02111 (617) 423-3990; *The World in Figures.*

International Monetary Fund, 700 Nineteenth Street, NW, Washington, D.C. 20431 (202) 623-7000; *Government Finance Statistics Yearbook.*

International Road Federation, 525 School Street, SW, Washington, D.C. 20024 (202) 554-2106; *World Road Statistics.*

The World Bank, 1818 H Street, NW, Washington, D.C. 20433 (202) 477-1234; *World Tables.*

SOUTH AFRICA - TEA PRODUCTION AND CONSUMPTION - See SOUTH AFRICA - CROPS

SOUTH AFRICA - TELEGRAPH SERVICE

Statistical Office of the United Nations, Publishing Service, New York, New York 10017 (800) 253-9646; *Statistical Yearbook.*

SOUTH AFRICA - TELEPHONES IN USE

American Telephone and Telegraph Company, 26 Parsippany Road, Whippany, New Jersey 07981 (800) 338-4038; *The World's Telephones.*

G.K. Hall and Company, 70 Lincoln Street, Boston, Massachusetts 02111 (617) 423-3990; *The World in Figures.*

Statistical Office of the United Nations, Publishing Service, New York, New York 10017 (800) 253-9646; *Statistical Yearbook.*

SOUTH AFRICA - TELEVISION BROADCASTING - See SOUTH AFRICA - BROADCASTING

SOUTH AFRICA - TEXTILE INDUSTRY

American Forest and Paper Association, 1250 Connecticut Avenue, NW, Washington, D.C. 20036 (202) 463-2455; *Wood Pulp and Fiber*

Statistics.

G.K. Hall and Company, 70 Lincoln Street, Boston, Massachusetts 02111 (617) 423-3990; *The World in Figures.*

Statistical Office of the United Nations, Publishing Service, New York, New York 10017 (800) 253-9646; *Statistical Yearbook.*

SOUTH AFRICA - TIN - See SOUTH AFRICA - MINING AND MINERAL PRODUCTS

SOUTH AFRICA - TIRE (MOTOR VEHICLE) PRODUCTION

Statistical Office of the United Nations, Publishing Service, New York, New York 10017 (800) 253-9646; *Statistical Yearbook.*

SOUTH AFRICA - TOBACCO PRODUCTION

Facts on File, 460 Park Avenue South, New York, New York 10016 (800) 443-8323; *The New Book of World Rankings.*

Statistical Office of the United Nations, Publishing Service, New York, New York 10017 (800) 253-9646; *Statistical Yearbook.*

SOUTH AFRICA - TOURISM

Facts on File, 460 Park Avenue South, New York, New York 10016 (800) 443-8323; *The New Book of World Rankings.*

G.K. Hall and Company, 70 Lincoln Street, Boston, Massachusetts 02111 (617) 423-3990; *The World in Figures.*

Statistical Office of the United Nations, Publishing Service, New York, New York 10017 (800) 253-9646; *Statistical Yearbook.*

Times Books, 201 East 50th Street, New York, New York 10022 (212) 751-2600; *The Economist Book of Vital World Statistics.*

World Tourism Organization, Calle Capitan Haya 42, E-28020 Madrid, Spain; *Yearbook of Tourism Statistics.*

SOUTH AFRICA - TRACTORS IN USE

Statistical Office of the United Nations, Publishing Service, New York, New York 10017 (800) 253-9646; *Statistical Yearbook.*

SOUTH AFRICA - TRADE - See SOUTH AFRICA - FOREIGN TRADE

SOUTH AFRICA - TRADEMARKS AND SERVICE MARKS

Statistical Office of the United Nations, Publishing Service, New York, New York 10017 (800) 253-9646; *Statistical Yearbook.*

SOUTH AFRICA - TRANSPORTATION AND COMMUNICATIONS

Facts on File, 460 Park Avenue South, New York, New York 10016 (800) 443-8323; *The New Book of World Rankings.*

G.K. Hall and Company, 70 Lincoln Street, Boston, Massachusetts 02111 (617) 423-3990; *The World in Figures.*

SOUTH AFRICA - TUNGSTEN PRODUCTION AND CONSUMPTION - See SOUTH AFRICA - MINING AND MINERAL PRODUCTS

SOUTH AFRICA - UNEMPLOYMENT

Euromonitor Publications Limited, 87-88 Turnmill Street, London EC1M 5QU, England; *International Marketing Data and Statistics.*

International Labour Office, I.L.O. Publications, CH-1211, Geneva 22, Switzerland; *Yearbook of Labour Statistics*.

Statistical Office of the United Nations, Publishing Service, New York, New York 10017 (800) 253-9646; *Statistical Yearbook*.

SOUTH AFRICA - URANIUM PRODUCTION AND CONSUMPTION - See SOUTH AFRICA - MINING AND MINERAL PRODUCTS

SOUTH AFRICA - VANADIUM AND VANADIUM ORE PRODUCTION AND CONSUMPTION - See SOUTH AFRICA - MINING AND MINERAL PRODUCTS

SOUTH AFRICA - VITAL STATISTICS

Euromonitor Publications Limited, 87-88 Turnmill Street, London EC1M 5QU, England; *International Marketing Data and Statistics*.

G.K. Hall and Company, 70 Lincoln Street, Boston, Massachusetts 02111 (617) 423-3990; *The World in Figures*.

World Health Organization, Office of Publications, Avenue Appia, CH-1211 Geneva 27, Switzerland (Telephone Number in U.S. (518) 436-9686); *World Health Statistics Annual*.

SOUTH AFRICA - WAGES

G.K. Hall and Company, 70 Lincoln Street, Boston, Massachusetts 02111 (617) 423-3990; *The World in Figures*.

International Labour Office, I.L.O. Publications, CH-1211, Geneva 22, Switzerland; *Yearbook of Labour Statistics*.

Statistical Office of the United Nations, Publishing Service, New York, New York 10017 (800) 253-9646; *Statistical Yearbook*.

SOUTH AFRICA - WEATHER

Facts on File, 460 Park Avenue South, New York, New York 10016 (800) 443-8323; *The New Book of World Rankings*.

G.K. Hall and Company, 70 Lincoln Street, Boston, Massachusetts 02111 (617) 423-3990; *The World in Figures*.

SOUTH AFRICA - WHALES - See SOUTH AFRICA - FISHERIES

SOUTH AFRICA - WHEAT PRODUCTION AND PRICES - See SOUTH AFRICA - CROPS

SOUTH AFRICA - WHOLESALE PRICES

Statistical Office of the United Nations, Publishing Service, New York, New York 10017 (800) 253-9646; *Statistical Yearbook*.

SOUTH AFRICA - WHOLESALE TRADE

Statistical Office of the United Nations, Publishing Service, New York, New York 10017 (800) 253-9646; *Statistical Yearbook*.

SOUTH AFRICA - WINE PRODUCTION

Facts on File, 460 Park Avenue South, New York, New York 10016 (800) 443-8323; *The New Book of World Rankings*.

Statistical Office of the United Nations, Publishing Service, New York, New York 10017 (800) 253-9646; *Statistical Yearbook*.

SOUTH AFRICA - WOOD AND WOOD PULP - See SOUTH AFRICA - FORESTRY AND FOREST PRODUCTS

SOUTH AFRICA - WOOL PRODUCTION

Commodity Research Bureau, Incorporated, 75 Wall Street, New York, New York 10005 (212) 504-7754; *Commodity Year Book*.

Facts on File, 460 Park Avenue South, New York, New York 10016 (800) 443-8323; *The New Book of World Rankings*.

Statistical Office of the United Nations, Publishing Service, New York, New York 10017 (800) 253-9646; *Statistical Yearbook*.

SOUTH AFRICA - YARN PRODUCTION

Statistical Office of the United Nations, Publishing Service, New York, New York 10017 (800) 253-9646; *Statistical Yearbook*.

SOUTH AFRICA - ZINC AND ZINC ORE PRODUCTION AND CONSUMPTION - See SOUTH AFRICA - MINING AND MINERAL PRODUCTS

SOUTH CAROLINA - See also STATE DATA (FOR INDIVIDUAL STATES)

South Carolina - Primary Statistics Source

Division of Research and Statistical Services, Budget and Control Board, R.C. Dennis Building, Room 425, Columbia, South Carolina 29201 (803) 734-3780; *South Carolina Statistical Abstract*.

South Carolina - State Data Centers

Division of Research and Statistical Services, South Carolina Budget and Control Board, Rembert Dennis Building, Room 425, 1000 Assembly Street, Columbia, South Carolina 29201, Mr. Bobby Bowers/Mr. Mike Macfarlane (803) 734-3780.

South Carolina State Library, Post Office Box 11469, Columbia, South Carolina 29211, Ms. Mary Bostick (803) 734-8666.

SOUTH DAKOTA - See also STATE DATA (FOR INDIVIDUAL STATES)

South Dakota - Primary Statistics Source

University of South Dakota, State Data Center, Vermillion, South Dakota 57069 (605) 677-5287; *Selected Social and Economic Characteristics*, and *South Dakota Community Abstracts*.

South Dakota - State Data Centers

Business Research Bureau, School of Business, Patterson Hall, University of South Dakota, 414 East Clark, Vermillion, South Dakota 57069, Ms. DeVee Dykstra (605) 677-5287.

Documents Department, South Dakota State Library, 800 Governors Drive, Pierre, South Dakota 57501-2294, Ms. Cheri Adams (605) 773-3131.

Labor Market Information Center, South Dakota Department of Labor, 420 South Roosevelt, Box 4730, Aberdeen, South Dakota 57402-4730, Mr. Phillip George (605) 622-2314.

Office of Administrative Services, South Dakota Department of Health, Foss Building 445 East Capitol, Pierre, South Dakota 57501, Mr. John Jones (605) 773-3693.

South Dakota State University, Rural Sociology Department, Scobey Hall 226, Box 504, Brookings, South Dakota 57007, Mr. Jim Satterlee (605) 688-4132.

SOYBEANS - ACREAGE

U.S. Department of Agriculture, National Agricultural Statistics Service, Fourteenth Street and Independence Avenue, SW, Washington, D.C. 20250 (202) 219-1504; *Agricultural Statistics, Crop Production, Field Crops, Crop Values,* and *Agricultural Outlook.*

SOYBEANS - COMMODITY CREDIT CORPORATION TRANSACTIONS

U.S. Department of Agriculture, Agricultural Stabilization and Conservation Service, Fourteenth Street and Independence Avenue, SW, Washington, D.C. 20250 (202) 720-5237; *Commodity Credit Corporation Report of Financial Condition and Operations,* and *Agricultural Outlook.*

SOYBEANS - FARM MARKETINGS - SALES

U.S. Department of Agriculture, Economic Research Service, Fourteenth Street and Independence Avenue, SW, Washington, D.C. 20005-4789 (202) 219-1504; *Economic Indicators of the Farm Sector: National Financial Summary.*

SOYBEANS - FOREIGN TRADE

U.S. Department of Agriculture, Economic Research Service, Fourteenth Street and Independence Avenue, SW, Washington, D.C. 20005-4789 (202) 219-1504; *Agricultural Statistics,* and *Foreign Agricultural Trade of the United States.*

U.S. Department of Agriculture, Foreign Agricultural Service, Fourteenth Street and Independence Avenue, SW, Washington, D.C. 20250 (202) 720-3448; *Foreign Agricultural Commodity Circular Series.*

U.S. Department of Commerce, Bureau of the Census, Suitland, Maryland 20233 (301) 763-4040; *U.S. Merchandise Trade.*

SOYBEANS - PRICES

U.S. Department of Agriculture, National Agricultural Statistics Service, Fourteenth Street and Independence Avenue, SW, Washington, D.C. 20250 (202) 219-1504; *Agricultural Statistics, Crop Production, Field Crops, Crop Values,* and *Agricultural Outlook.*

SOYBEANS - PRODUCTION

U.S. Department of Agriculture, Agricultural Stabilization and Conservation Service, Fourteenth Street and Independence Avenue, SW, Washington, D.C. 20250 (202) 720-5237; *Agricultural Statistics.*

U.S. Department of Agriculture, National Agricultural Statistics Service, Fourteenth Street and Independence Avenue, SW, Washington, D.C. 20250 (202) 219-1504; *Agricultural Outlook, Crop Production, Crop Values,* and *Field Crops.*

SOYBEANS - PRODUCTION - WORLD PRODUCTION

U.S. Department of Agriculture, Foreign Agricultural Service, Fourteenth Street and Independence Avenue, SW, Washington, D.C. 20250 (202) 720-3448; *Foreign Agricultural Commodity Circular Series.*

SOYBEANS - SUPPLY AND DISAPPEARANCE

U.S. Department of Agriculture, Economic Research Service, Fourteenth Street and Independence Avenue, SW, Washington, D.C. 20005-4789 (202) 219-1504; *Agricultural Statistics, Agricultural Outlook,* and *Agricultural Supply and Demand Estimates.*

SPACE PROGRAM - FINANCES

Executive Office of the President, Office of Management and Budget, Executive Office Building, Washington, D.C. 20503 (202) 395-3080; *Budget of the U.S. Government,* and unpublished data.

U.S. Department of Commerce, Bureau of the Census, Suitland, Maryland 20233 (301) 763-4040; *Current Industrial Reports, Aerospace Industry (Orders, Sales, and Backlog).*

U.S. National Aeronautics and Space Administration, 600 Independence Avenue, SW, Washington, D.C. 20546 (202) 453-1000; *NASA News, Budget Summary,* and *Aeronautics and Space Report of the President.*

SPACE PROGRAM - LAUNCHES

U.S. Library of Congress, Congressional Research Service, 101 Independence Avenue, SW, Washington, D.C. 20540 (202) 707-5000; *Space Activities of the United States, CIS, and Other Launching Countries/Organizations.*

SPACE PROGRAM - NASA

U.S. National Aeronautics and Space Administration, 600 Independence Avenue, SW, Washington, D.C. 20546 (202) 453-1000, *Aeronautics and Space Report of the President,* and *Budget Summary.*

SPACE PROGRAM - SPACE SHUTTLE

U.S. National Aeronautics and Space Administration, 600 Independence Avenue, SW, Washington, D.C. 20546 (202) 453-1000; *Payload Flight Assignments NASA Mixed Fleets,* and *Space Shuttle Flights.*

SPACE PROGRAM - VEHICLE SYSTEMS

U.S. Department of Commerce, Bureau of the Census, Suitland, Maryland 20233 (301) 763-4040; *Current Industrial Reports, Aerospace Industry (Orders, Sales and Backlog).*

SPACE RESEARCH AND TECHNOLOGY - FEDERAL OUTLAYS

Aerospace Industries Association of America, 1250 Eye Street, NW, Washington, D.C. 20005 (202) 371-8400; *Year End Review and Forecast.*

Executive Office of the President, Office of Management and Budget, Executive Office Building, Washington, D.C. 20503 (202) 395-3080; *Budget of the U.S. Government.*

U.S. National Aeronautics and Space Administration, 600 Independence Avenue, SW, Washington, D.C. 20546; *Budget Summary,* and *Aeronautics and Space Report of the President.*

Spain - National Statistical Offices

Instituto Nacional de Estadistica, Ministerio de Economia y Hacienda, Paseo de la Castellana 183, Madrid 28046, Spain.

Ministerio de Economia y Hacienda, Direccion General de Aduanas, Seccion de Estadistica, San Francisco de Sales 6, Madrid 3, Spain.

Spain - Primary Statistics Sources

Instituto Nacional de Estadistica (National Institute of Statistics), Paseo de la Castellana 183, Madrid, Spain; *Anuario estadistico de España* (Statistical Yearbook of Spain) and *Boletin mensual de estadistics* (Monthly Bulletin of Statistics).

Spain - Databases

ESTACOM, Instituto Espanol de Comercio Exterior-ECEX, Paseo de la Castellana, 14, 28046 Madrid, Spain. Subject coverage: Monthly and annual time series on Spanish import and export activity, including balances of trade figures for trading partners and regions.

SPAIN - ABORTIONS

European Community Information Service, 2100 M Street, NW, Washington, D.C. 20037 (202) 862-9500; *Demographic Statistics*.

SPAIN - AGRICULTURE

European Community Information Service, 2100 M Street, NW, Washington, D.C. 20037 (202) 862-9500; *Agriculture: Statistical Yearbook, Basic Statistics of the Community, Eurostatistics: Data for Short-Term Economic Analysis*, and *Regions: Statistical Yearbook*.

Facts on File, 460 Park Avenue South, New York, New York 10016 (800) 443-8323; *The New Book of World Rankings*.

Federal Statistical Office, Gustav-Stresemann-Ring 11, D-6200 Wiesbaden, Germany; *Spain*.

Food and Agricultural Organization of the United Nations (FAO) Via delle Terme di Caracalla, 00100 Rome, Italy (Telephone Number in U.S. (202) 653-2400); *Production Yearbook, The State of Food and Agriculture*, and *Trade Yearbook*.

G.K. Hall and Company, 70 Lincoln Street, Boston, Massachusetts 02111 (617) 423-3990; *The World in Figures*.

Organisation for Economic Co-operation and Development (OECD), 2 rue Andre-Pascal, 75 Paris 16, France (Telephone Number in U.S. (202) 785-6323); *Economic Accounts for Agriculture, Indicators of Industrial Activity, Industrial Structure Statistics*, and *OECD Economic Surveys: Spain*.

Statistical Office of the United Nations, Publishing Service, New York, New York 10017 (800) 253-9646; *Statistical Yearbook*.

Times Books, 201 East 50th Street, New York, New York 10022 (212) 751-2600; *The Economist Book of Vital World Statistics*.

The World Bank, 1818 H Street, NW, Washington, D.C. 20433 (202) 477-1234; *World Tables*.

SPAIN - AIRLINE SERVICE

European Community Information Service, 2100 M Street, NW, Washington, D.C. 20037 (202) 862-9500; *Basic Statistics of the Community, Regions: Statistical Yearbook*, and *Transport Annual Statistics*.

Facts on File, 460 Park Avenue South, New York, New York 10016 (800) 443-8323; *The New Book of World Rankings*.

G.K. Hall and Company, 70 Lincoln Street, Boston, Massachusetts 02111 (617) 423-3990; *The World in Figures*.

International Civil Aviation Organization, 1000 Sherbrooke Street West, Suite 400, Montreal, Quebec H3A 2R2, Canada (514) 285-8219; *Civil Aviation Statistics of the World*.

Organisation for Economic Co-operation and Development (OECD), 2 rue Andre-Pascal, 75 Paris 16, France (Telephone Number in U.S. (202) 785-6323); *Tourism Policy and International Tourism in OECD Member Countries*.

Statistical Office of the United Nations, Publishing Service, New York, New York 10017 (800) 253-9646; *Statistical Yearbook*.

Times Books, 201 East 50th Street, New York, New York 10022 (212) 751-2600; *The Economist Book of Vital World Statistics*.

SPAIN - ALUMINUM PRODUCTION AND CONSUMPTION - See SPAIN - MINING AND MINERAL PRODUCTS

SPAIN - ANIMAL FEEDINGSTUFFS

Organisation for Economic Co-operation and Development (OECD), 2 rue Andre-Pascal, 75 Paris 16, France (Telephone Number in U.S. (202) 785-6323); *Foreign Trade by Commodities*.

Statistical Office of the United Nations, Publishing Service, New York, New York 10017 (800) 253-9646; *Statistical Yearbook*.

SPAIN - ANIMAL HEALTH

Food and Agricultural Organization of the United Nations (FAO), Via delle Terme di Caracalla, 00100, Rome, Italy (Telephone Number in U.S. (202) 653-2400); *Animal Health Yearbook*.

SPAIN - ANTIMONY AND ANTIMONY ORE PRODUCTION AND CONSUMPTION - See SPAIN - MINING AND MINERAL PRODUCTS

SPAIN - APPLES PRODUCTION - See SPAIN - CROPS

SPAIN - AREA AND DENSITY OF POPULATION

European Community Information Service, 2100 M Street, NW, Washington, D.C. 20037 (202) 862-9500; *Basic Statistics of the Community*, and *Demographic Statistics*.

Facts on File, 460 Park Avenue South, New York, New York 10016 (800) 443-8323; *The New Book of World Rankings*.

Federal Statistical Office, Gustav-Stresemann-Ring 11, D-6200 Wiesbaden, Germany; *Spain*.

Food and Agricultural Organization of the United Nations (FAO) Via delle Terme di Caracalla, 00100 Rome, Italy (Telephone Number in U.S. (202) 653-2400); *The State of Food and Agriculture*.

G.K. Hall and Company, 70 Lincoln Street, Boston, Massachusetts 02111 (617) 423-3990; *The World in Figures*.

Statistical Office of the United Nations, Publishing Service, New York, New York 10017 (800) 253-9646; *Statistical Yearbook*.

Times Books, 201 East 50th Street, New York, New York 10022 (212) 751-2600; *The Economist Book of Vital World Statistics*.

United Nations Educational, Scientific and Cultural Organization (UNESCO), 7 Place de Fontenoy, F-75700 Paris, France (Telephone Number in U.S. (212) 963-5981); *Statistical Yearbook*.

SPAIN - ARMS EXPORTS AND IMPORTS

U.S. Arms Control and Disarmament Agency, 320 Twenty-first Street, NW, Washington, D.C. 20451 (202) 647-8677; *World Military Expenditures and Arms Transfers.*

SPAIN - ARSENIC PRODUCTION AND CONSUMPTION - See SPAIN - MINING AND MINERAL PRODUCTS

SPAIN - BALANCE OF PAYMENTS

The Economist Intelligence Unit, 111 West 57th Street, New York, New York 10019 (800) 938-4685; *The World Market Atlas.*

European Community Information Service, 2100 M Street, NW, Washington, D.C. 20037 (202) 862-9500; *ACP: Basic Statistics, Basic Statistics of the Community, Energy Statistics Yearbook,* and *Eurostatistics: Data for Short-Term Economic Analysis.*

Federal Statistical Office, Gustav-Stresemann-Ring 11, D-6200 Wiesbaden, Germany; *Spain.*

G.K. Hall and Company, 70 Lincoln Street, Boston, Massachusetts 02111 (617) 423-3990; *The World in Figures.*

International Monetary Fund, 700 Nineteenth Street, NW, Washington, D.C. 20431 (202) 623-7000; *Balance of Payments Yearbook,* and *International Financial Statistics.*

Organisation for Economic Co-operation and Development (OECD), 2 rue Andre-Pascal, 75 Paris 16, France (Telephone Number in U.S. (202) 785-6323); *Economic Outlook, Geographical Distribution of Financial Flows to Developing Countries, Main Economic Indicators - Historical Statistics,* and *OECD Economic Surveys: Spain.*

Times Books, 201 East 50th Street, New York, New York 10022 (212) 751-2600; *The Economist Book of Vital World Statistics.*

The World Bank, 1818 H Street, NW, Washington, D.C. 20433 (202) 477-1234; *World Tables.*

SPAIN - BANKING

European Community Information Service, 2100 M Street, NW, Washington, D.C. 20037 (202) 862-9500; *ACP: Basic Statistics.*

Facts on File, 460 Park Avenue South, New York, New York 10016 (800) 443-8323; *The New Book of World Rankings.*

G.K. Hall and Company, 70 Lincoln Street, Boston, Massachusetts 02111 (617) 423-3990; *The World in Figures.*

International Monetary Fund, 700 Nineteenth Street, NW, Washington, D.C. 20431 (202) 623-7000; *International Financial Statistics.*

Organisation for Economic Co-operation and Development (OECD), 2 rue Andre-Pascal, 75 Paris 16, France (Telephone Number in U.S. (202) 785-6323); *Economic Outlook, Financial Market Trends,* and *OECD Economic Surveys: Spain.*

Statistical Office of the United Nations, Publishing Service, New York, New York 10017 (800) 253-9646; *Statistical Yearbook.*

SPAIN - BARLEY PRODUCTION - See SPAIN - CROPS

SPAIN - BAUXITE PRODUCTION AND CONSUMPTION - See SPAIN - MINING AND MINERAL PRODUCTS

SPAIN - BEER PRODUCTION

Facts on File, 460 Park Avenue South, New York, New York 10016 (800) 443-8323; *The New Book of World Rankings.*

Statistical Office of the United Nations, Publishing Service, New York, New York 10017 (800) 253-9646; *Statistical Yearbook.*

SPAIN - BEVERAGES - PRODUCTION INDEX

Organisation for Economic Co-operation and Development (OECD), 2 rue Andre-Pascal, 75 Paris 16, France (Telephone Number in U.S. (202) 785-6323); *Indicators of Industrial Activity.*

SPAIN - BIRTH RATES

European Community Information Service, 2100 M Street, NW, Washington, D.C. 20037 (202) 862-9500; *Basic Statistics of the Community,* and *Demographic Statistics.*

Facts on File, 460 Park Avenue South, New York, New York 10016 (800) 443-8323; *The New Book of World Rankings.*

Statistical Office of the United Nations, Publishing Service, New York, New York 10017 (800) 253-9646; *Demographic Yearbook,* and *Statistical Yearbook.*

Times Books, 201 East 50th Street, New York, New York 10022 (212) 751-2600; *The Economist Book of Vital World Statistics.*

The World Bank, 1818 H Street, NW, Washington, D.C. 20433 (202) 477-1234; *World Tables.*

World Health Organization, Office of Publications, Avenue Appia, CH-1211 Geneva 27, Switzerland (Telephone Number in U.S. (518) 436-9686); *World Health Statistics Annual.*

SPAIN - BISMUTH PRODUCTION AND CONSUMPTION - See SPAIN - MINING AND MINERAL PRODUCTS

SPAIN - BONDS

European Community Information Service, 2100 M Street, NW, Washington, D.C. 20037 (202) 862-9500; *Basic Statistics of the Community.*

G.K. Hall and Company, 70 Lincoln Street, Boston, Massachusetts 02111 (617) 423-3990; *The World in Figures.*

Organisation for Economic Co-operation and Development (OECD), 2 rue Andre-Pascal, 75 Paris 16, France (Telephone Number in U.S. (202) 785-6323); *Financial Market Trends.*

SPAIN - BOOK PRODUCTION

Euromonitor Publications Limited, 87-88 Turnmill Street, London EC1M 5QU, England; *European Marketing Data and Statistics.*

G.K. Hall and Company, 70 Lincoln Street, Boston, Massachusetts 02111 (617) 423-3990; *The World in Figures.*

Organisation for Economic Co-operation and Development (OECD), 2 rue Andre-Pascal, 75 Paris 16, France (Telephone Number in U.S. (202) 785-6323); *Indicators of Industrial Activity.*

United Nations Educational, Scientific and Cultural Organization (UNESCO), 7 Place de Fontenoy, F-75700 Paris, France (Telephone Number in U.S. (212) 963-5981); *Statistical Yearbook.*

SPAIN - BROADCASTING

Billboard Limited, P.O. Box 9027, 1006 AA Amsterdam, The Netherlands (Telephone Number in U.S. (212) 764-7300); *World Radio TV Handbook.*

European Community Information Service, 2100 M Street, NW, Washington, D.C. 20037 (202) 862-9500; *Basic Statistics of the Community.*

Facts on File, 460 Park Avenue South, New York, New York 10016 (800) 443-8323; *The New Book of World Rankings.*

G.K. Hall and Company, 70 Lincoln Street, Boston, Massachusetts 02111 (617) 423-3990; *The World in Figures.*

Times Books, 201 East 50th Street, New York, New York 10022 (212) 751-2600; *The Economist Book of Vital World Statistics.*

United Nations Educational, Scientific and Cultural Organization (UNESCO), 7 Place de Fontenoy, F-75700 Paris, France (Telephone Number in U.S. (212) 963-5981); *Statistical Yearbook.*

SPAIN - BUSINESS

European Community Information Service, 2100 M Street, NW, Washington, D.C. 20037 (202) 862-9500; *Basic Statistics of the Community.*

G.K. Hall and Company, 70 Lincoln Street, Boston, Massachusetts 02111 (617) 423-3990; *The World in Figures.*

Organisation for Economic Co-operation and Development (OECD), 2 rue Andre-Pascal, 75 Paris 16, France (Telephone Number in U.S. (202) 785-6323); *Main Economic Indicators - Historical Statistics.*

SPAIN - BUSINESS AND PROFESSIONAL LICENSES

International Monetary Fund, 700 Nineteenth Street, NW, Washington, D.C. 20431 (202) 623-7000; *Government Finance Statistics Yearbook.*

SPAIN - BUTTER - See SPAIN - DAIRY PRODUCTS

SPAIN - CADMIUM PRODUCTION AND CONSUMPTION - See SPAIN - MINING AND MINERAL PRODUCTS

SPAIN - CALORIE SUPPLY

Food and Agricultural Organization of the United Nations (FAO) Via delle Terme di Caracalla, 00100 Rome, Italy (Telephone Number in U.S. (202) 653-2400); *The State of Food and Agriculture.*

SPAIN - CAPITAL INVESTMENT

Organisation for Economic Co-operation and Development (OECD), 2 rue Andre-Pascal, 75 Paris 16, France (Telephone Number in U.S. (202) 785-6323); *Economic Outlook,* and *Financial Market Trends.*

SPAIN - CAPITAL REVENUE

International Monetary Fund, 700 Nineteenth Street, NW, Washington, D.C. 20431 (202) 623-7000; *Government Finance Statistics Yearbook.*

Organisation for Economic Co-operation and Development (OECD), 2 rue Andre-Pascal, 75 Paris 16, France (Telephone Number in U.S. (202) 785-6323); *Economic Outlook,* and *Financial Market Trends.*

SPAIN - CATTLE - See SPAIN - LIVESTOCK AND POULTRY

SPAIN - CAUSTIC SODA PRODUCTION

Organisation for Economic Co-operation and Development (OECD), 2 rue Andre-Pascal, 75 Paris 16, France (Telephone Number in U.S. (202) 785-6323); *Indicators of Industrial Activity.*

Statistical Office of the United Nations, Publishing Service, New York, New York 10017 (800) 253-9646; *Statistical Yearbook.*

SPAIN - CEMENT PRODUCTION - See SPAIN - MINING AND MINERAL PRODUCTS

SPAIN - CEREAL PRODUCTION - See SPAIN - CROPS

SPAIN - CHEESE - See SPAIN - DAIRY PRODUCTS

SPAIN - CHEMICAL INDUSTRY

European Community Information Service, 2100 M Street, NW, Washington, D.C. 20037 (202) 862-9500; *Industrial Production: Quarterly Statistics.*

SPAIN - CHEMICAL (ORGANIC) PRODUCTION - See SPAIN - MINING AND MINERAL PRODUCTS

SPAIN - CHROMITE PRODUCTION AND CONSUMPTION - See SPAIN - MINING AND MINERAL PRODUCTS

SPAIN - CHROMIUM ORE PRODUCTION AND CONSUMPTION - See SPAIN - MINING AND MINERAL PRODUCTS

SPAIN - CIGAR AND CIGARETTE PRODUCTION - See SPAIN - TOBACCO PRODUCTION

SPAIN - CLASS STRUCTURE

European Community Information Service, 2100 M Street, NW, Washington, D.C. 20037 (202) 862-9500; *Basic Statistics of the Community,* and *Labor Force Sample Survey.*

G.K. Hall and Company, 70 Lincoln Street, Boston, Massachusetts 02111 (617) 423-3990; *The World in Figures.*

SPAIN - CLIMATE

Facts on File, 460 Park Avenue South, New York, New York 10016 (800) 443-8323; *The New Book of World Rankings.*

G.K. Hall and Company, 70 Lincoln Street, Boston, Massachusetts 02111 (617) 423-3990; *The World in Figures.*

SPAIN - CLOTHING - PRODUCTION INDEX

Organisation for Economic Co-operation and Development (OECD), 2 rue Andre-Pascal, 75 Paris 16, France (Telephone Number in U.S. (202) 785-6323); *Indicators of Industrial Activity.*

SPAIN - CLOTHING EXPORTS AND IMPORTS

European Community Information Service, 2100 M Street, NW, Washington, D.C. 20037 (202) 862-9500; *Basic Statistics of the Community.*

Organisation for Economic Co-operation and Development (OECD), 2 rue Andre-Pascal, 75 Paris 16, France (Telephone Number in U.S. (202) 785-6323); *Textile Industry in OECD Countries.*

SPAIN - COAL PRODUCTION - See SPAIN - MINING AND MINERAL PRODUCTS

SPAIN - COBALT PRODUCTION AND CONSUMPTION - See SPAIN - MINING AND MINERAL PRODUCTS

SPAIN - COFFEE - See SPAIN - CROPS

SPAIN - COKE AND COKE OVEN ORE PRODUCTION AND CONSUMPTION - See SPAIN - MINING AND MINERAL PRODUCTS

SPAIN - COMMUNICATIONS

European Community Information Service, 2100 M Street, NW, Washington, D.C. 20037 (202) 862-9500; *Basic Statistics of the Community*, and *Transport Annual Statistics*.

Federal Statistical Office, Gustav-Stresemann-Ring 11, D-6200 Wiesbaden, Germany; *Spain*.

G.K. Hall and Company, 70 Lincoln Street, Boston, Massachusetts 02111 (617) 423-3990; *The World in Figures*.

SPAIN - CONSTRUCTION INDUSTRY

European Community Information Service, 2100 M Street, NW, Washington, D.C. 20037 (202) 862-9500; *Basic Statistics of the Community*, and *Labor Force Sample Survey*.

Facts on File, 460 Park Avenue South, New York, New York 10016 (800) 443-8323; *The New Book of World Rankings*.

Organisation for Economic Co-operation and Development (OECD), 2 rue Andre-Pascal, 75 Paris 16, France (Telephone Number in U.S. (202) 785-6323); *Industrial Structure Statistics, The Iron and Steel Industry, Main Economic Indicators - Historical Statistics*, and *OECD Economic Surveys: Spain*.

Statistical Office of the United Nations, Publishing Service, New York, New York 10017 (800) 253-9646; *Statistical Yearbook*.

SPAIN - CONSUMER PRICE INDEX

European Community Information Service, 2100 M Street, NW, Washington, D.C. 20037 (202) 862-9500; *Basic Statistics of the Community*, and *Eurostatistics: Data for Short-Term Economic Analysis*.

G.K. Hall and Company, 70 Lincoln Street, Boston, Massachusetts 02111 (617) 423-3990; *The World in Figures*.

Organisation for Economic Co-operation and Development (OECD), 2 rue Andre-Pascal, 75 Paris 16, France (Telephone Number in U.S. (202) 785-6323); *Economic Outlook*.

Statistical Office of the United Nations, Publishing Service, New York, New York 10017 (800) 253-9646; *Statistical Yearbook*.

SPAIN - CONSUMER PRICES

Euromonitor Publications Limited, 87-88 Turnmill Street, London EC1M 5QU, England; *European Marketing Data and Statistics*.

European Community Information Service, 2100 M Street, NW, Washington, D.C. 20037 (202) 862-9500; *Basic Statistics of the Community, Eurostatistics: Data for Short-Term Economic Analysis*, and *Money and Finance*.

International Labour Office, I.L.O. Publications, CH-1211, Geneva 22, Switzerland; *Yearbook of Labour Statistics*.

International Monetary Fund, 700 Nineteenth Street, NW, Washington, D.C. 20431 (202) 623-7000; *International Financial Statistics*.

Organisation for Economic Co-operation and Development (OECD), 2 rue Andre-Pascal, 75 Paris 16, France (Telephone Number in U.S. (202) 785-6323); *Economic Outlook*.

Times Books, 201 East 50th Street, New York, New York 10022 (212) 751-2600; *The Economist Book of Vital World Statistics*.

SPAIN - CONSUMPTION

European Community Information Service, 2100 M Street, NW, Washington, D.C. 20037 (202) 862-9500; *Basic Statistics of the Community*.

G.K. Hall and Company, 70 Lincoln Street, Boston, Massachusetts 02111 (617) 423-3990; *The World in Figures*.

International Iron and Steel Institute, 120, rue Colonel Bourg, B-1140, Brussels, Belgium; *Steel Statistical Yearbook*.

International Lead and Zinc Study Group, Metro House, 58 St. James's Street, London SW1A 1LD, England; *Lead and Zinc Statistics*.

Organisation for Economic Co-operation and Development (OECD), 2 rue Andre-Pascal, 75 Paris 16, France (Telephone Number in U.S. (202) 785-6323); *The Footwear, Raw Hides and Skins, and Leather Industry in OECD Countries, The Iron and Steel Industry, Meat Balances in OECD Member Countries, The Non-Ferrous Metals Industry, The Pulp and Paper Industry*, and *Textile Industry in OECD Countries*.

SPAIN - COPPER AND COPPER ORE PRODUCTION AND CONSUMPTION - See SPAIN - MINING AND MINERAL PRODUCTS

SPAIN - CORN PRODUCTION - See SPAIN - CROPS

SPAIN - CORPORATE INCOME TAXES - See SPAIN - TAXATION

SPAIN - CORPORATE TAXES - See SPAIN - TAXATION

SPAIN - COTTON - See SPAIN - CROPS

SPAIN - CRIME

International Criminal Police Organization (INTERPOL), 26 rue Armengaud, 92210 Saint Cloud, France; *International Crime Statistics*.

SPAIN - CROPS

Commodity Research Bureau, Incorporated, 75 Wall Street, New York, New York 10005 (212) 504-7754; *Commodity Year Book*.

Euromonitor Publications Limited, 87-88 Turnmill Street, London EC1M 5QU, England; *European Marketing Data and Statistics*.

European Community Information Service, 2100 M Street, NW, Washington, D.C. 20037 (202) 862-9500; *ACP: Basic Statistics, Agriculture: Statistical Yearbook, Basic Statistics of the Community, Crop Production: Quarterly Statistics, Eurostatistics: Data for Short-Term Economic Analysis*, and *Regions: Statistical Yearbook*.

Facts on File, 460 Park Avenue South, New York, New York 10016 (800) 443-8323; *The New Book of World Rankings*.

Food and Agricultural Organization of the United Nations (FAO) Via delle Terme di Caracalla, 00100 Rome, Italy (Telephone Number in U.S. (202) 653-2400); *The State of Food and Agriculture*.

G.K. Hall and Company, 70 Lincoln Street, Boston, Massachusetts 02111 (617) 423-3990; *The World in Figures*.

Organisation for Economic Co-operation and Development (OECD), 2 rue Andre-Pascal, 75 Paris 16, France (Telephone Number in U.S. (202) 785-6323); *Economic Accounts for Agriculture, Foreign Trade by Commodities*, and *Textile Industry in OECD Countries*.

Statistical Office of the United Nations, Publishing Service, New York, New York 10017 (800) 253-9646; *Statistical Yearbook*.

SPAIN - CUSTOMS DUTIES

European Community Information Service, 2100 M Street, NW, Washington, D.C. 20037 (202) 862-9500; *Basic Statistics of the Community*.

G.K. Hall and Company, 70 Lincoln Street, Boston, Massachusetts 02111 (617) 423-3990; *The World in Figures*.

Organisation for Economic Co-operation and Development (OECD), 2 rue Andre-Pascal, 75 Paris 16, France (Telephone Number in U.S. (202) 785-6323); *The Non-Ferrous Metals Industry*.

SPAIN - DAIRY PRODUCTS

Commodity Research Bureau, Incorporated, 75 Wall Street, New York, New York 10005 (212) 504-7754; *Commodity Year Book*.

European Community Information Service, 2100 M Street, NW, Washington, D.C. 20037 (202) 862-9500; *Eurostatistics: Data for Short-Term Economic Analysis*.

Facts on File, 460 Park Avenue South, New York, New York 10016 (800) 443-8323; *The New Book of World Rankings*.

Food and Agricultural Organization of the United Nations (FAO) Via delle Terme di Caracalla, 00100 Rome, Italy (Telephone Number in U.S. (202) 653-2400); *The State of Food and Agriculture*.

Organisation for Economic Co-operation and Development (OECD), 2 rue Andre-Pascal, 75 Paris 16, France (Telephone Number in U.S. (202) 785-6323); *Economic Accounts for Agriculture*, and *Milk, Milk Products, and Egg Balances in OECD Member Countries*.

Statistical Office of the United Nations, Publishing Service, New York, New York 10017 (800) 253-9646; *Statistical Yearbook*.

SPAIN - DEATH RATES

European Community Information Service, 2100 M Street, NW, Washington, D.C. 20037 (202) 862-9500; *Basic Statistics of the Community*, and *Demographic Statistics*.

G.K. Hall and Company, 70 Lincoln Street, Boston, Massachusetts 02111 (617) 423-3990; *The World in Figures*.

Statistical Office of the United Nations, Publishing Service, New York, New York 10017 (800) 253-9646; *Statistical Yearbook*.

Times Books, 201 East 50th Street, New York, New York 10022 (212) 751-2600; *The Economist Book of Vital World Statistics*.

World Health Organization, Office of Publications, Avenue Appia, CH-1211 Geneva 27, Switzerland (Telephone Number in U.S. (518) 436-9686); *World Health Statistics Annual*.

SPAIN - DEFENSE EXPENDITURES

European Community Information Service, 2100 M Street, NW, Washington, D.C. 20037 (202) 862-9500; *Government Financing of Research and Development*.

G.K. Hall and Company, 70 Lincoln Street, Boston, Massachusetts 02111 (617) 423-3990; *The World in Figures*.

International Monetary Fund, 700 Nineteenth Street, NW, Washington, D.C. 20431 (202) 623-7000; *Government Finance Statistics Yearbook*.

U.S. Arms Control and Disarmament Agency, 320 Twenty-first Street, NW, Washington, D.C. 20451 (202) 647-8677; *World Military Expenditures and Arms Transfers*.

SPAIN - DEMOGRAPHY

The Economist Intelligence Unit, 111 West 57th Street, New York, New York 10019 (800) 938-4685; *The World Market Atlas*.

European Community Information Service, 2100 M Street, NW, Washington, D.C. 20037 (202) 862-9500; *Basic Statistics of the Community, Demographic Statistics, Employment and Unemployment*, and *Regions: Statistical Yearbook*.

Facts on File, 460 Park Avenue South, New York, New York 10016 (800) 443-8323; *The New Book of World Rankings*.

G.K. Hall and Company, 70 Lincoln Street, Boston, Massachusetts 02111 (617) 423-3990; *The World in Figures*.

SPAIN - DEVELOPMENT ASSISTANCE

European Community Information Service, 2100 M Street, NW, Washington, D.C. 20037 (202) 862-9500; *ACP: Basic Statistics, Basic Statistics of the Community*, and *Government Financing of Research and Development*.

G.K. Hall and Company, 70 Lincoln Street, Boston, Massachusetts 02111 (617) 423-3990; *The World in Figures*.

Organisation for Economic Co-operation and Development (OECD), 2 rue Andre-Pascal, 75 Paris 16, France (Telephone Number in U.S. (202) 785-6323); *Geographical Distribution of Financial Flows to Developing Countries*.

SPAIN - DIAMOND PRODUCTION - See SPAIN - MINING AND MINERAL PRODUCTS

SPAIN - DISCOUNT RATES

Organisation for Economic Co-operation and Development (OECD), 2 rue Andre-Pascal, 75 Paris 16, France (Telephone Number in U.S. (202) 785-6323); *Financial Market Trends*.

Statistical Office of the United Nations, Publishing Service, New York, New York 10017 (800) 253-9646; *Statistical Yearbook*.

SPAIN - DISEASES

G.K. Hall and Company, 70 Lincoln Street, Boston, Massachusetts 02111 (617) 423-3990; *The World in Figures*.

World Health Organization, Office of Publications, Avenue Appia, CH-1211 Geneva 27, Switzerland (Telephone Number in U.S. (518) 436-9686); *World Health Statistics Annual*.

SPAIN - DIVORCE RATES

European Community Information Service, 2100 M Street, NW, Washington, D.C. 20037 (202) 862-9500; *Demographic Statistics*.

Facts on File, 460 Park Avenue South, New York, New York 10016 (800) 443-8323; *The New Book of World Rankings*.

Statistical Office of the United Nations, Publishing Service, New York, New York 10017 (800) 253-9646; *Demographic Yearbook*.

SPAIN - DOMESTIC PRODUCT

European Community Information Service, 2100 M Street, NW, Washington, D.C. 20037 (202) 862-9500; *Basic Statistics of the Community*.

G.K. Hall and Company, 70 Lincoln Street, Boston, Massachusetts 02111 (617) 423-3990; *The World in Figures*.

SPAIN - ECONOMY

Euromonitor Publications Limited, 87-88 Turnmill Street, London EC1M 5QU, England; *European Marketing Data and Statistics*.

European Community Information Service, 2100 M Street, NW, Washington, D.C. 20037 (202) 862-9500; *ACP: Basic Statistics, Basic Statistics of the Community, Energy Statistics Yearbook, Labor Force Sample Survey, and Money and Finance*.

Facts on File, 460 Park Avenue South, New York, New York 10016 (800) 443-8323; *The New Book of World Rankings*.

G.K. Hall and Company, 70 Lincoln Street, Boston, Massachusetts 02111 (617) 423-3990; *The World in Figures*.

Organisation for Economic Co-operation and Development (OECD), 2 rue Andre-Pascal, 75 Paris 16, France (Telephone Number in U.S. (202) 785-6323); *Economic Outlook, Geographical Distribution of Financial Flows to Developing Countries, Main Economic Indicators - Historical Statistics, OECD Economic Surveys: Spain*, and *OECD Employment Outlook*.

SPAIN - EDUCATION

The Economist Intelligence Unit, 111 West 57th Street, New York, New York 10019 (800) 938-4685; *The World Market Atlas*.

Euromonitor Publications Limited, 87-88 Turnmill Street, London EC1M 5QU, England; *European Marketing Data and Statistics*.

European Community Information Service, 2100 M Street, NW, Washington, D.C. 20037 (202) 862-9500; *Basic Statistics of the Community*, and *Regions: Statistical Yearbook*.

Facts on File, 460 Park Avenue South, New York, New York 10016 (800) 443-8323; *The New Book of World Rankings*.

Federal Statistical Office, Gustav-Stresemann-Ring 11, D-6200 Wiesbaden, Germany; *Spain*.

G.K. Hall and Company, 70 Lincoln Street, Boston, Massachusetts 02111 (617) 423-3990; *The World in Figures*.

International Monetary Fund, 700 Nineteenth Street, NW, Washington, D.C. 20431 (202) 623-7000; *Government Finance Statistics Yearbook*.

Organisation for Economic Co-operation and Development (OECD), 2 rue Andre-Pascal, 75 Paris 16, France (Telephone Number in U.S. (202) 785-6323); *Education in OECD Countries*.

Times Books, 201 East 50th Street, New York, New York 10022 (212) 751-2600; *The Economist Book of Vital World Statistics*.

United Nations Educational, Scientific and Cultural Organization (UNESCO), 7 Place de Fontenoy, F-75700 Paris, France (Telephone Number in U.S. (212) 963-5981); *Statistical Yearbook*.

The World Bank, 1818 H Street, NW, Washington, D.C. 20433 (202) 477-1234; *World Tables*.

SPAIN - EGG PRODUCTION AND CONSUMPTION - See SPAIN - DAIRY PRODUCTS

SPAIN - ELECTRICITY

European Community Information Service, 2100 M Street, NW, Washington, D.C. 20037 (202) 862-9500; *Basic Statistics of the Community, Energy: Monthly Statistics, Energy Statistics Yearbook, Eurostatistics: Data for Short-Term Economic Analysis*, and *Regions: Statistical Yearbook*.

Facts on File, 460 Park Avenue South, New York, New York 10016 (800) 443-8323; *The New Book of World Rankings*.

Organisation for Economic Co-operation and Development (OECD), 2 rue Andre-Pascal, 75 Paris 16, France (Telephone Number in U.S. (202) 785-6323); *Coal Information, Energy Statistics of OECD Countries, Indicators of Industrial Activity*, and *Industrial Structure Statistics*.

Penn Well Publishing Company, 1421 South Sheridan Road, P.O. Box 1260, Tulsa, Oklahoma 74101 (800) 752-9764; *International Energy Statistics Sourcebook*.

Statistical Office of the United Nations, Publishing Service, New York, New York 10017 (800) 253-9646; *Statistical Yearbook*.

Times Books, 201 East 50th Street, New York, New York 10022 (212) 751-2600; *The Economist Book of Vital World Statistics*.

SPAIN - EMPLOYMENT

Euromonitor Publications Limited, 87-88 Turnmill Street, London EC1M 5QU, England; *European Marketing Data and Statistics*.

European Community Information Service, 2100 M Street, NW, Washington, D.C. 20037 (202) 862-9500; *Basic Statistics of the Community, Earnings in Agriculture, Employment and Unemployment, Eurostatistics: Data for Short-Term Economic Analysis, Iron and Steel: Statistical Yearbook, Labor Force Sample Survey, OECD Economic Surveys: Spain*, and *Transport Annual Statistics*.

Facts on File, 460 Park Avenue South, New York, New York 10016 (800) 443-8323; *The New Book of World Rankings*.

Federal Statistical Office, Gustav-Stresemann-Ring 11, D-6200 Wiesbaden, Germany; *Spain*.

International Labour Office, I.L.O. Publications, CH-1211, Geneva 22, Switzerland; *Yearbook of Labour Statistics*.

Organisation for Economic Co-operation and Development (OECD), 2 rue Andre-Pascal, 75 Paris 16, France (Telephone Number in U.S. (202) 785-6323); *Economic Outlook, The Iron and Steel Industry, Labour Force Statistics, OECD Employment Outlook*, and *Textile Industry in OECD Countries*.

Statistical Office of the United Nations, Publishing Service, New York, New York 10017 (800) 253-9646; *Statistical Yearbook*.

SPAIN - ENERGY

Euromonitor Publications Limited, 87-88 Turnmill Street, London EC1M 5QU, England; *European Marketing Data and Statistics*.

European Community Information Service, 2100 M Street, NW, Washington, D.C. 20037 (202) 862-9500; *Basic Statistics of the Community, Energy: Monthly Statistics, Energy Statistics Yearbook, Regions: Statistical Yearbook*, and *Transport Annual Statistics*.

Facts on File, 460 Park Avenue South, New York, New York 10016 (800) 443-8323; *The New Book of World Rankings*.

Food and Agricultural Organization of the United Nations (FAO) Via delle Terme di Caracalla, 00100 Rome, Italy (Telephone Number in U.S. (202) 653-2400); *The State of Food and Agriculture*.

G.K. Hall and Company, 70 Lincoln Street, Boston, Massachusetts 02111 (617) 423-3990; *The World in Figures*.

Organisation for Economic Co-operation and Development (OECD), 2 rue Andre-Pascal, 75 Paris 16, France (Telephone Number in U.S. (202) 785-6323); *Coal Information, Energy Statistics of OECD Countries, OECD Environmental Data*, and *Oil and Gas Information*.

Penn Well Publishing Company, 1421 South Sheridan Road, P.O. Box 1260, Tulsa, Oklahoma 74101 (800) 752-9764; *International Energy Statistics Sourcebook*.

Statistical Office of the United Nations, Publishing Service, New York, New York 10017 (800) 253-9646; *Energy Statistics Yearbook*, and *Statistical Yearbook*.

Times Books, 201 East 50th Street, New York, New York 10022 (212) 751-2600; *The Economist Book of Vital World Statistics*.

SPAIN - ENGINEERING

European Community Information Service, 2100 M Street, NW, Washington, D.C. 20037 (202) 862-9500; *Basic Statistics of the Community*, and *Industrial Production: Quarterly Statistics*.

SPAIN - ENVIRONMENT

Organization for Economic Co-operation and Development (OECD), 2 rue Andre-Pascal, 75 Paris 16, France (Telephone Number in U.S. (202) 785-6323); *OECD Environmental Data*.

SPAIN - EXCHANGE RATES

European Community Information Service, 2100 M Street, NW, Washington, D.C. 20037 (202) 862-9500; *Eurostatistics: Data for Short-Term Economic Analysis*, and *Money and Finance*.

International Civil Aviation Organization, 1000 Sherbrooke Street West, Suite 400, Montreal, Quebec H3A 2R2, Canada (514) 285-8219; *Civil Aviation Statistics of the World*.

International Monetary Fund, 700 Nineteenth Street, NW, Washington, D.C. 20431 (202) 623-7000; *International Financial Statistics*.

Organisation for Economic Co-operation and Development (OECD), 2 rue Andre-Pascal, 75 Paris 16, France (Telephone Number in U.S. (202) 785-6323); *Economic Outlook, Financial Market Trends, Revenue Statistics of OECD Member Countries*, and *Tourism Policy and International Tourism in OECD Member Countries*.

Statistical Office of the United Nations, Publishing Service, New York, New York 10017 (800) 253-9646; *Statistical Yearbook*.

SPAIN - EXCISE TAXES - See SPAIN - TAXATION

SPAIN - EXPORTS

American Automobile Manufacturers Association, 1401 H Street, NW, Suite 900, Washington, D.C. 20005 (202) 326-5500; *World Motor Vehicle Data*.

The Economist Intelligence Unit, 111 West 57th Street, New York, New York 10019 (800) 938-4685; *The World Market Atlas*.

European Community Information Service, 2100 M Street, NW, Washington, D.C. 20037 (202) 862-9500; *Basic Statistics of the Community, Energy: Monthly Statistics, Energy Statistics Yearbook, Eurostatistics: Data for Short-Term Economic Analysis, External Trade: Monthly Statistics, External Trade: Statistical Yearbook*, and *Fisheries: Yearly Statistics*.

Food and Agricultural Organization of the United Nations (FAO) Via delle Terme di Caracalla, 00100 Rome, Italy (Telephone Number in U.S. (202) 653-2400); *The State of Food and Agriculture*.

G.K. Hall and Company, 70 Lincoln Street, Boston, Massachusetts 02111 (617) 423-3990; *The World in Figures*.

International Iron and Steel Institute, 120, rue Colonel Bourg, B-1140, Brussels, Belgium; *Steel Statistical Yearbook*.

International Lead and Zinc Study Group, Metro House, 58 St. James's Street, London SW1A 1LD, England; *Lead and Zinc Statistics*.

International Monetary Fund, 700 Nineteenth Street, NW, Washington, D.C. 20431 (202) 623-7000; *Direction of Trade Statistics*, and *International Financial Statistics*.

Organisation for Economic Co-operation and Development (OECD), 2 rue Andre-Pascal, 75 Paris 16, France (Telephone Number in U.S. (202) 785-6323); *Economic Outlook, The Footwear, Raw Hides and Skins, and Leather Industry in OECD Countries, Foreign Trade by Commodities, Geographical Distribution of Financial Flows to Developing Countries, Industrial Structure Statistics, The Iron and Steel Industry, Milk, Milk Products, and Egg Balances in OECD Member Countries, OECD Economic Surveys: Spain, The Pulp and Paper Industry*, and *Review of Fisheries in OECD Member Countries*.

Times Books, 201 East 50th Street, New York, New York 10022 (212) 751-2600; *The Economist Book of Vital World Statistics*.

The World Bank, 1818 H Street, NW, Washington, D.C. 20433 (202) 477-1234; *World Tables*.

SPAIN - EXTERNAL FINANCING

Organisation for Economic Co-operation and Development (OECD), 2 rue Andre-Pascal, 75 Paris 16, France (Telephone Number in U.S. (202) 785-6323); *Economic Outlook*, and *Financial Market Trends*.

SPAIN - EXTERNAL INDEBTEDNESS

Organisation for Economic Co-operation and Development (OECD), 2 rue Andre-Pascal, 75 Paris 16, France (Telephone Number in U.S. (202) 785-6323); *Financial Market Trends*, and *Geographical Distribution of Financial Flows to Developing Countries*.

The World Bank, 1818 H Street, NW, Washington, D.C. 20433 (202) 477-1234; *World Tables*.

SPAIN - EXTERNAL TRADE

European Community Information Service, 2100 M Street, NW, Washington, D.C. 20037 (202) 862-9500; ACP: Basic Statistics, Basic Statistics of the Community, *Eurostatistics: Data for Short-Term Economic Analysis, External Trade: Monthly Statistics, External Trade: Statistical Yearbook*, and *Foreign Trade of the People's Republic of China*.

Food and Agricultural Organization of the United Nations (FAO) Via delle Terme di Caracalla, 00100 Rome, Italy (Telephone Number in U.S. (202) 653-2400); *The State of Food and Agriculture*, and *Trade Yearbook*.

G.K. Hall and Company, 70 Lincoln Street, Boston, Massachusetts 02111 (617) 423-3990; *The World in Figures*.

Statistical Office of the United Nations, Publishing Service, New York, New York 10017 (800) 253-9646; *Statistical Yearbook*.

SPAIN - FABRIC PRODUCTION - See SPAIN - TEXTILE INDUSTRY

SPAIN - FARM CROPS - See SPAIN - CROPS

SPAIN - FEMALE WORKING POPULATION - See SPAIN - EMPLOYMENT

SPAIN - FERTILITY RATES

European Community Information Service, 2100 M Street, NW, Washington, D.C. 20037 (202) 862-9500; *Demographic Statistics*.

Facts on File, 460 Park Avenue South, New York, New York 10016 (800) 443-8323; *The New Book of World Rankings*.

Times Books, 201 East 50th Street, New York, New York 10022 (212) 751-2600; *The Economist Book of Vital World Statistics*.

The World Bank, 1818 H Street, NW, Washington, D.C. 20433 (202) 477-1234; *World Tables*.

SPAIN - FERTILIZER

European Community Information Service, 2100 M Street, NW, Washington, D.C. 20037 (202) 862-9500; *Basic Statistics of the Community*.

Food and Agricultural Organization of the United Nations (FAO) Via delle Terme di Caracalla, 00100 Rome, Italy (Telephone Number in U.S. (202) 653-2400); *The State of Food and Agriculture*.

Organisation for Economic Co-operation and Development (OECD), 2 rue Andre-Pascal, 75 Paris 16, France (Telephone Number in U.S.

(202) 785-6323); *Economic Accounts for Agriculture*, and *Foreign Trade by Commodities*.

Statistical Office of the United Nations, Publishing Service, New York, New York 10017 (800) 253-9646; *Statistical Yearbook*.

SPAIN - FETAL MORTALITY

European Community Information Service, 2100 M Street, NW, Washington, D.C. 20037 (202) 862-9500; *Basic Statistics of the Community*, and *Demographic Statistics*.

Statistical Office of the United Nations, Publishing Service, New York, New York 10017 (800) 253-9646; *Demographic Yearbook*.

World Health Organization, Office of Publications, Avenue Appia, CH-1211 Geneva 27, Switzerland (Telephone Number in U.S. (518) 436-9686); *World Health Statistics Annual*.

SPAIN - FIBRE PRODUCTION - See SPAIN - TEXTILE INDUSTRY

SPAIN - FILAMENT PRODUCTION - See SPAIN - TEXTILE INDUSTRY

SPAIN - FILM - See SPAIN - MOTION PICTURES

SPAIN - FINANCE

European Community Information Service, 2100 M Street, NW, Washington, D.C. 20037 (202) 862-9500; ACP: Basic Statistics, Basic Statistics of the Community, *Eurostatistics: Data for Short-Term Economic Analysis*, and *Money and Finance*.

Facts on File, 460 Park Avenue South, New York, New York 10016 (800) 443-8323; *The New Book of World Rankings*.

Federal Statistical Office, Gustav-Stresemann-Ring 11, D-6200 Wiesbaden, Germany; *Spain*.

G.K. Hall and Company, 70 Lincoln Street, Boston, Massachusetts 02111 (617) 423-3990; *The World in Figures*

International Monetary Fund, 700 Nineteenth Street, NW, Washington, D.C. 20431 (202) 623-7000; *Government Finance Statistics Yearbook*, and *International Financial Statistics*.

Organisation for Economic Co-operation and Development (OECD), 2 rue Andre-Pascal, 75 Paris 16, France (Telephone Number in U.S. (202) 785-6323); *Economic Outlook, Financial Market Trends, Geographical Distribution of Financial Flows to Developing Countries, Main Economic Indicators - Historical Statistics*, and *OECD Financial Statistics*.

SPAIN - FISHERIES

Euromonitor Publications Limited, 87-88 Turnmill Street, London EC1M 5QU, England; *European Marketing Data and Statistics*.

European Community Information Service, 2100 M Street, NW, Washington, D.C. 20037 (202) 862-9500; *Agriculture: Statistical Yearbook*, and *Fisheries: Yearly Statistics*.

Facts on File, 460 Park Avenue South, New York, New York 10016 (800) 443-8323; *The New Book of World Rankings*.

Federal Statistical Office, Gustav-Stresemann-Ring 11, D-6200 Wiesbaden, Germany; *Spain*.

Food and Agricultural Organization of the United Nations (FAO) Via delle Terme di Caracalla, 00100 Rome, Italy (Telephone Number in

U.S. (202) 653-2400); *The State of Food and Agriculture*, and *Yearbook of Fishery Statistics*.

Organisation for Economic Co-operation and Development (OECD), 2 rue Andre-Pascal, 75 Paris 16, France (Telephone Number in U.S. (202) 785-6323); *Industrial Structure Statistics, Foreign Trade by Commodities*, and *Review of Fisheries in OECD Member Countries*.

Statistical Office of the United Nations, Publishing Service, New York, New York 10017 (800) 253-9646; *Statistical Yearbook*.

SPAIN - FLOUR PRODUCTION

Commodity Research Bureau, Incorporated, 75 Wall Street, New York, New York 10005 (212) 504-7754; *Commodity Year Book*.

European Community Information Service, 2100 M Street, NW, Washington, D.C. 20037 (202) 862-9500; *Basic Statistics of the Community*.

Statistical Office of the United Nations, Publishing Service, New York, New York 10017 (800) 253-9646; *Statistical Yearbook*.

SPAIN - FOOD

European Community Information Service, 2100 M Street, NW, Washington, D.C. 20037 (202) 862-9500; *Basic Statistics of the Community*.

Food and Agricultural Organization of the United Nations (FAO) Via delle Terme di Caracalla, 00100 Rome, Italy (Telephone Number in U.S. (202) 653-2400); *Production Yearbook*, and *The State of Food and Agriculture*.

G.K. Hall and Company, 70 Lincoln Street, Boston, Massachusetts 02111 (617) 423-3990; *The World in Figures*.

Organisation for Economic Co-operation and Development (OECD), 2 rue Andre-Pascal, 75 Paris 16, France (Telephone Number in U.S. (202) 785-6323); *Food Consumption Statistic*, and *Foreign Trade by Commodities*.

SPAIN - FOOTWEAR - PRODUCTION INDEX

Organisation for Economic Co-operation and Development (OECD), 2 rue Andre-Pascal, 75 Paris 16, France (Telephone Number in U.S. (202) 785-6323); *Indicators of Industrial Activity*.

SPAIN - FOREIGN AID

G.K. Hall and Company, 70 Lincoln Street, Boston, Massachusetts 02111 (617) 423-3990; *The World in Figures*.

SPAIN - FOREIGN DEBT

International Monetary Fund, 700 Nineteenth Street, NW, Washington, D.C. 20431 (202) 623-7000; *Government Finance Statistics Yearbook*.

Organisation for Economic Co-operation and Development (OECD), 2 rue Andre-Pascal, 75 Paris 16, France (Telephone Number in U.S. (202) 785-6323); *Economic Outlook*.

SPAIN - FOREIGN INDEBTEDNESS

Organisation for Economic Co-operation and Development (OECD), 2 rue Andre-Pascal, 75 Paris 16, France (Telephone Number in U.S. (202) 785-6323); *Economic Outlook*, and *Financial Market Trends*.

SPAIN - FOREIGN OFFICIAL RESERVES

European Community Information Service, 2100 M Street, NW, Washington, D.C. 20037 (202) 862-9500; *Money and Finance*.

SPAIN - FOREIGN TRADE

European Community Information Service, 2100 M Street, NW, Washington, D.C. 20037 (202) 862-9500; *Basic Statistics of the Community, Energy Statistics Yearbook, Foreign Trade of the People's Republic of China*, and *Iron and Steel: Statistical Yearbook*.

Facts on File, 460 Park Avenue South, New York, New York 10016 (800) 443-8323; *The New Book of World Rankings*.

Federal Statistical Office, Gustav-Stresemann-Ring 11, D-6200 Wiesbaden, Germany; *Spain*.

G.K. Hall and Company, 70 Lincoln Street, Boston, Massachusetts 02111 (617) 423-3990; *The World in Figures*.

International Monetary Fund, 700 Nineteenth Street, NW, Washington, D.C. 20431 (202) 623-7000; *International Financial Statistics*.

Organisation for Economic Co-operation and Development (OECD), 2 rue Andre-Pascal, 75 Paris 16, France (Telephone Number in U.S. (202) 785-6323); *The Footwear, Raw Hides and Skins, and Leather Industry in OECD Countries, Foreign Trade by Commodities, Main Economic Indicators - Historical Statistics, Meat Balances in OECD Member Countries*, and *OECD Economic Surveys: Spain*.

Statistical Office of the United Nations, Publishing Service, New York, New York 10017 (800) 253-9646; *International Trade Statistics Yearbook*, and *Statistical Yearbook*.

The World Bank, 1818 H Street, NW, Washington, D.C. 20433 (202) 477-1234; *World Tables*.

SPAIN - FORESTRY AND FOREST PRODUCTS

American Forest and Paper Association, 1250 Connecticut Avenue, NW, Washington, D.C. 20036 (202) 463-2455; *Wood Pulp and Fiber Statistics*.

Euromonitor Publications Limited, 87-88 Turnmill Street, London EC1M 5QU, England; *European Marketing Data and Statistics*.

European Community Information Service, 2100 M Street, NW, Washington, D.C. 20037 (202) 862-9500; *Agriculture: Statistical Yearbook, Basic Statistics of the Community*, and *Industrial Production: Quarterly Statistics*.

Facts on File, 460 Park Avenue South, New York, New York 10016 (800) 443-8323; *The New Book of World Rankings*.

Federal Statistical Office, Gustav-Stresemann-Ring 11, D-6200 Wiesbaden, Germany; *Spain*.

Food and Agricultural Organization of the United Nations (FAO) Via delle Terme di Caracalla, 00100 Rome, Italy (Telephone Number in U.S. (202) 653-2400); *The State of Food and Agriculture*, and *Yearbook of Forest Products*.

G.K. Hall and Company, 70 Lincoln Street, Boston, Massachusetts 02111 (617) 423-3990; *The World in Figures*.

Organisation for Economic Co-operation and Development (OECD), 2 rue Andre-Pascal, 75 Paris 16, France (Telephone Number in U.S.

(202) 785-6323); *Foreign Trade by Commodities, Indicators of Industrial Activity, Industrial Structure Statistics*, and *The Pulp and Paper Industry*.

Statistical Office of the United Nations, Publishing Service, New York, New York 10017 (800) 253-9646; *Statistical Yearbook.*

United Nations Educational, Scientific and Cultural Organization (UNESCO), 7 Place de Fontenoy, F-75700 Paris, France (Telephone Number in U.S. (212) 963-5981); *Statistical Yearbook.*

SPAIN - FRUIT PRODUCTION - See SPAIN - CROPS

SPAIN - FURNITURE AND WOOD PRODUCTS - EXPORTS AND IMPORTS

European Community Information Service, 2100 M Street, NW, Washington, D.C. 20037 (202) 862-9500; *Basic Statistics of the Community.*

Organisation for Economic Co-operation and Development (OECD), 2 rue Andre-Pascal, 75 Paris 16, France (Telephone Number in U.S. (202) 785-6323); *Foreign Trade by Commodities*, and *Industrial Structure Statistics.*

SPAIN - GAS - See SPAIN - MINING AND MINERAL PRODUCTS

SPAIN - GENERAL INDUSTRIAL STATISTICS

European Community Information Service, 2100 M Street, NW, Washington, D.C. 20037 (202) 862-9500; *Basic Statistics of the Community.*

Statistical Office of the United Nations, Publishing Service, New York, New York 10017 (800) 253-9646; *Industrial Statistics Yearbook.*

SPAIN - GENERAL MORTALITY

European Community Information Service, 2100 M Street, NW, Washington, D.C. 20037 (202) 862-9500; *Basic Statistics of the Community*, and *Demographic Statistics.*

Statistical Office of the United Nations, Publishing Service, New York, New York 10017 (800) 253-9646; *Demographic Yearbook.*

World Health Organization, Office of Publications, Avenue Appia, CH-1211 Geneva 27, Switzerland (Telephone Number in U.S. (518) 436-9686); *World Health Statistics Annual.*

SPAIN - GEOGRAPHIC DATA

European Community Information Service, 2100 M Street, NW, Washington, D.C. 20037 (202) 862-9500; *Basic Statistics of the Community.*

Facts on File, 460 Park Avenue South, New York, New York 10016 (800) 443-8323; *The New Book of World Rankings.*

SPAIN - GLASS AND GLASS PRODUCTS - PRODUCTION INDEX

Organisation for Economic Co-operation and Development (OECD), 2 rue Andre-Pascal, 75 Paris 16, France (Telephone Number in U.S. (202) 785-6323); *Indicators of Industrial Activity.*

SPAIN - GOATS - See SPAIN - LIVESTOCK AND POULTRY

SPAIN - GOLD HOLDINGS

International Monetary Fund, 700 Nineteenth Street, NW, Washington, D.C. 20431 (202) 623-7000; *International Financial Statistics.*

Statistical Office of the United Nations, Publishing Service, New York, New York 10017 (800) 253-9646; *Statistical Yearbook.*

The World Bank, 1818 H Street, NW, Washington, D.C. 20433 (202) 477-1234; *World Tables.*

SPAIN - GOLD PRODUCTION AND CONSUMPTION - See SPAIN - MINING AND MINERAL PRODUCTS

SPAIN - GOVERNMENT

European Community Information Service, 2100 M Street, NW, Washington, D.C. 20037 (202) 862-9500; *Basic Statistics of the Community.*

G.K. Hall and Company, 70 Lincoln Street, Boston, Massachusetts 02111 (617) 423-3990; *The World in Figures.*

SPAIN - GOVERNMENT CONSUMPTION

European Community Information Service, 2100 M Street, NW, Washington, D.C. 20037 (202) 862-9500; *Basic Statistics of the Community.*

International Monetary Fund, 700 Nineteenth Street, NW, Washington, D.C. 20431 (202) 623-7000; *International Financial Statistics.*

SPAIN - GOVERNMENT EXPENDITURES

European Community Information Service, 2100 M Street, NW, Washington, D.C. 20037 (202) 862-9500; *Basic Statistics of the Community.*

International Monetary Fund, 700 Nineteenth Street, NW, Washington, D.C. 20431 (202) 623-7000; *Government Finance Statistics Yearbook.*

Organisation for Economic Co-operation and Development (OECD), 2 rue Andre-Pascal, 75 Paris 16, France (Telephone Number in U.S. (202) 785-6323); *Economic Outlook.*

Times Books, 201 East 50th Street, New York, New York 10022 (212) 751-2600; *The Economist Book of Vital World Statistics.*

The World Bank, 1818 H Street, NW, Washington, D.C. 20433 (202) 477-1234; *World Tables.*

SPAIN - GOVERNMENT FINANCES

European Community Information Service, 2100 M Street, NW, Washington, D.C. 20037 (202) 862-9500; *Basic Statistics of the Community, Government Financing of Research and Development,* and *Money and Finance.*

International Monetary Fund, 700 Nineteenth Street, NW, Washington, D.C. 20431 (202) 623-7000; *International Financial Statistics.*

Organisation for Economic Co-operation and Development (OECD), 2 rue Andre-Pascal, 75 Paris 16, France (Telephone Number in U.S. (202) 785-6323); *Economic Outlook.*

Statistical Office of the United Nations, Publishing Service, New York, New York 10017 (800) 253-9646; *Statistical Yearbook.*

SPAIN - GOVERNMENT REVENUE

European Community Information Service, 2100 M Street, NW, Washington, D.C. 20037 (202) 862-9500; *Basic Statistics of the Community,* and *Government Financing of Research and Development.*

International Monetary Fund, 700 Nineteenth Street, NW, Washington, D.C. 20431 (202) 623-7000; *Government Finance Statistics Yearbook.*

Organisation for Economic Co-operation and Development (OECD), 2 rue Andre-Pascal, 75 Paris 16, France (Telephone Number in U.S. (202) 785-6323); *Economic Outlook,* and *Revenue Statistics of OECD Member Countries.*

Times Books, 201 East 50th Street, New York, New York 10022 (212) 751-2600; *The Economist Book of Vital World Statistics.*

The World Bank, 1818 H Street, NW, Washington, D.C. 20433 (202) 477-1234; *World Tables.*

SPAIN - GRAIN PRODUCTION - See SPAIN - CROPS

SPAIN - GRANTS

International Monetary Fund, 700 Nineteenth Street, NW, Washington, D.C. 20431 (202) 623-7000; *Government Finance Statistics Yearbook.*

Organisation for Economic Co-operation and Development (OECD), 2 rue Andre-Pascal, 75 Paris 16, France (Telephone Number in U.S. (202) 785-6323); *Geographical Distribution of Financial Flows to Developing Countries.*

SPAIN - GROSS DOMESTIC PRODUCT

The Economist Intelligence Unit, 111 West 57th Street, New York, New York 10019 (800) 938-4685; *The World Market Atlas.*

European Community Information Service, 2100 M Street, NW, Washington, D.C. 20037 (202) 862-9500; *Basic Statistics of the Community, Eurostatistics: Data for Short-Term Economic Analysis, Government Financing for Research and Development, Iron and Steel: Statistical Yearbook,* and *Money and Finance.*

Facts on File, 460 Park Avenue South, New York, New York 10016 (800) 443-8323; *The New Book of World Rankings.*

G.K. Hall and Company, 70 Lincoln Street, Boston, Massachusetts 02111 (617) 423-3990; *The World in Figures.*

International Monetary Fund, 700 Nineteenth Street, NW, Washington, D.C. 20431 (202) 623-7000; *International Financial Statistics.*

Organisation for Economic Co-operation and Development (OECD), 2 rue Andre-Pascal, 75 Paris 16, France (Telephone Number in U.S. (202) 785-6323); *Economic Outlook, Geographical Distribution of Financial Flows to Developing Countries,* and *Revenue Statistics of OECD Member Countries.*

Statistical Office of the United Nations, Publishing Service, New York, New York 10017 (800) 253-9646; *Statistical Yearbook.*

Times Books, 201 East 50th Street, New York, New York 10022 (212) 751-2600; *The Economist Book of Vital World Statistics.*

The World Bank, 1818 H Street, NW, Washington, D.C. 20433 (202) 477-1234; *World Tables.*

SPAIN - GROSS NATIONAL PRODUCT

European Community Information Service, 2100 M Street, NW, Washington, D.C. 20037 (202) 862-9500; *ACP: Basic Statistics,* and *Basic Statistics of the Community.*

Organisation for Economic Co-operation and Development (OECD), 2 rue Andre-Pascal, 75 Paris 16, France (Telephone Number in U.S. (202) 785-6323); *Economic Outlook,* and *Geographical Distribution of Financial Flows to Developing Countries.*

U.S. Arms Control and Disarmament Agency, 320 Twenty-first Street, NW, Washington, D.C. 20451 (202) 647-8677; *World Military Expenditures and Arms Transfers.*

The World Bank, 1818 H Street, NW, Washington, D.C. 20433 (202) 477-1234; *World Tables.*

SPAIN - GROUNDNUTS PRODUCTION - See SPAIN - CROPS

SPAIN - HEALTH

European Community Information Service, 2100 M Street, NW, Washington, D.C. 20037 (202) 862-9500; *Basic Statistics of the Community,* and *Regions: Statistical Yearbook.*

Facts on File, 460 Park Avenue South, New York, New York 10016 (800) 443-8323; *The New Book of World Rankings.*

Federal Statistical Office, Gustav-Stresemann-Ring 11, D-6200 Wiesbaden, Germany; *Spain.*

G.K. Hall and Company, 70 Lincoln Street, Boston, Massachusetts 02111 (617) 423-3990; *The World in Figures.*

Organisation for Economic Co-operation and Development (OECD), 2 rue Andre-Pascal, 75 Paris 16, France (Telephone Number in U.S. (202) 785-6323); *OECD Health Systems: Facts and Trends.*

Statistical Office of the United Nations, Publishing Service, New York, New York 10017 (800) 253-9646; *Statistical Yearbook.*

Times Books, 201 East 50th Street, New York, New York 10022 (212) 751-2600; *The Economist Book of Vital World Statistics.*

World Health Organization, Office of Publications, Avenue Appia, CH-1211 Geneva 27, Switzerland (Telephone Number in U.S. (518) 436-9686); *World Health Statistics Annual.*

SPAIN - HEALTH EXPENDITURES

International Monetary Fund, 700 Nineteenth Street, NW, Washington, D.C. 20431 (202) 623-7000; *Government Finance Statistics Yearbook.*

SPAIN - HIDE PRODUCTION

Organisation for Economic Co-operation and Development (OECD), 2 rue Andre-Pascal, 75 Paris 16, France (Telephone Number in U.S. (202) 785-6323); *The Footwear, Raw Hides and Skins, and Leather Industry in OECD Countries, Foreign Trade by Commodities,* and *Indicators of Industrial Activity.*

SPAIN - HIGHWAYS

European Community Information Service, 2100 M Street, NW, Washington, D.C. 20037 (202) 862-9500; *Basic Statistics of the Community,* and *Transport Annual Statistics.*

G.K. Hall and Company, 70 Lincoln Street, Boston, Massachusetts 02111 (617) 423-3990; *The World in Figures.*

International Road Federation, 525 School Street, SW, Washington, D.C. 20024 (202) 554-2106; *World Road Statistics.*

Statistical Office of the United Nations, Publishing Service, New York, New York 10017 (800) 253-9646; *Annual Bulletin of Transport Statistics for Europe.*

SPAIN - HOME FINANCE

Organisation for Economic Co-operation and Development (OECD), 2 rue Andre-Pascal, 75 Paris 16, France (Telephone Number in U.S. (202) 785-6323); *Main Economic Indicators - Historical Statistics.*

SPAIN - HONEY PRODUCTION

Commodity Research Bureau, Incorporated, 75 Wall Street, New York, New York 10005 (212) 504-7754; *Commodity Year Book.*

SPAIN - HORSES - See SPAIN - LIVESTOCK AND POULTRY

SPAIN - HOURS OF WORK - See SPAIN - EMPLOYMENT

SPAIN - HOUSING AND HOUSING UNITS

European Community Information Service, 2100 M Street, NW, Washington, D.C. 20037 (202) 862-9500; *Basic Statistics of the Community, Labor Force Sample Survey,* and *Regions: Statistical Yearbook.*

Facts on File, 460 Park Avenue South, New York, New York 10016 (800) 443-8323; *The New Book of World Rankings.*

SPAIN - HOUSING CONSTRUCTION - See CONSTRUCTION INDUSTRY

SPAIN - HOUSING EXPENDITURES

European Community Information Service, 2100 M Street, NW, Washington, D.C. 20037 (202) 862-9500; *Basis Statistics of the Community.*

International Monetary Fund, 700 Nineteenth Street, NW, Washington, D.C. 20431 (202) 623-7000; *Government Finance Statistics Yearbook.*

SPAIN - HYDROCHLORIC ACID PRODUCTION

European Community Information Service, 2100 M Street, NW, Washington, D.C. 20037 (202) 862-9500; *Basic Statistics of the Community.*

Statistical Office of the United Nations, Publishing Service, New York, New York 10017 (800) 253-9646; *Statistical Yearbook.*

SPAIN - ILLITERATE POPULATION

The Economist Intelligence Unit, 111 West 57th Street, New York, New York 10019 (800) 938-4685; *The World Market Atlas.*

G.K. Hall and Company, 70 Lincoln Street, Boston, Massachusetts 02111 (617) 423-3990; *The World in Figures.*

United Nations Educational, Scientific and Cultural Organization (UNESCO), 7 Place de Fontenoy, F-75700 Paris, France (Telephone Number in U.S. (212) 963-5981); *Statistical Yearbook.*

SPAIN - IMPORTS

American Automobile Manufacturers Association, 1401 H Street, NW, Suite 900, Washington, D.C. 20005 (202) 326-5500; *World Motor Vehicle Data.*

The Economist Intelligence Unit, 111 West 57th Street, New York, New York 10019 (800) 938-4685; *The World Market Atlas.*

European Community Information Service, 2100 M Street, NW, Washington, D.C. 20037 (202) 862-9500; *Energy: Monthly Statistics, Eurostatistics: Data for Short-Term Economic Analysis, External Trade: Monthly Statistics,* and *External Trade: Statistical Yearbook.*

Food and Agricultural Organization of the United Nations (FAO) Via delle Terme di Caracalla, 00100 Rome, Italy (Telephone Number in U.S. (202) 653-2400); *The State of Food and Agriculture.*

G.K. Hall and Company, 70 Lincoln Street, Boston, Massachusetts 02111 (617) 423-3990; *The World in Figures.*

International Iron and Steel Institute, 120, rue Colonel Bourg, B-1140, Brussels, Belgium; *Steel Statistical Yearbook.*

International Lead and Zinc Study Group, Metro House, 58 St. James's Street, London SW1A 1LD, England; *Lead and Zinc Statistics.*

International Monetary Fund, 700 Nineteenth Street, NW, Washington, D.C. 20431 (202) 623-7000; *Direction of Trade Statistics, Government Finance Statistics Yearbook,* and *International Financial Statistics.*

Organisation for Economic Co-operation and Development (OECD), 2 rue Andre-Pascal, 75 Paris 16, France (Telephone Number in U.S. (202) 785-6323); *Economic Outlook, The Footwear, Raw Hides and Skins, and Leather Industry in OECD Countries, Industrial Structure Statistics, The Iron and Steel Industry, Milk, Milk Products, and Egg Balances in OECD Member Countries, OECD Economic Surveys: Spain, The Pulp and Paper Industry,* and *Review of Fisheries in OECD Member Countries.*

Times Books, 201 East 50th Street, New York, New York 10022 (212) 751-2600; *The Economist Book of Vital World Statistics.*

The World Bank, 1818 H Street, NW, Washington, D.C. 20433 (202) 477-1234; *World Tables.*

SPAIN - INCOME TAXES - See SPAIN - TAXATION

SPAIN - INDUSTRIAL METALS PRODUCTION - See SPAIN - MINING AND MINERAL PRODUCTS

SPAIN - INDUSTRY

European Community Information Service, 2100 M Street, NW, Washington, D.C. 20037 (202) 862-9500; *Basic Statistics of the Community, Employment and Unemployment, Eurostatistics: Data for Short-Term Economic Analysis,* and *Labor Force Sample Survey.*

Facts on File, 460 Park Avenue South, New York, New York 10016 (800) 443-8323; *The New Book of World Rankings.*

Federal Statistical Office, Gustav-Stresemann-Ring 11, D-6200 Wiesbaden, Germany; *Spain.*

G.K. Hall and Company, 70 Lincoln Street, Boston, Massachusetts 02111 (617) 423-3990; *The World in Figures.*

International Labour Office, I.L.O. Publications, CH-1211, Geneva 22, Switzerland; *Yearbook of Labour Statistics.*

Organisation for Economic Co-operation and Development (OECD), 2 rue Andre-Pascal, 75 Paris 16, France (Telephone Number in U.S. (202) 785-6323); *Economic Outlook, Indicators of Industrial Activity, Industrial Structure Statistics, Main Economic Indicators - Historical Statistics,* and *OECD Environmental Data.*

Statistical Office of the United Nations, Publishing Service, New York, New York 10017 (800) 253-9646; *Statistical Yearbook.*

Times Books, 201 East 50th Street, New York, New York 10022 (212) 751-2600; *The Economist Book of Vital World Statistics.*

The World Bank, 1818 H Street, NW, Washington, D.C. 20433 (202) 477-1234; *World Tables.*

World Intellectual Property Organization, 34 Chemin des Colombettes, CH-1211 Geneva 20. Switzerland; *Industrial Property Statistics.*

SPAIN - INFANT AND MATERNAL MORTALITY

European Community Information Service, 2100 M Street, NW, Washington, D.C. 20037 (202) 862-9500; *Basis Statistics of the Community,* and *Demographic Statistics.*

Statistical Office of the United Nations, Publishing Service, New York, New York 10017 (800) 253-9646; *Demographic Yearbook,* and *Statistical Yearbook.*

Times Books, 201 East 50th Street, New York, New York 10022 (212) 751-2600; *The Economist Book of Vital World Statistics.*

The World Bank, 1818 H Street, NW, Washington, D.C. 20433 (202) 477-1234; *World Tables.*

World Health Organization, Office of Publications, Avenue Appia, CH-1211 Geneva 27, Switzerland (Telephone Number in U.S. (518) 436-9686); *World Health Statistics Annual.*

SPAIN - INTEREST RATES

European Community Information Service, 2100 M Street, NW, Washington, D.C. 20037 (202) 862-9500; *Money and Finance.*

Organisation for Economic Co-operation and Development (OECD), 2 rue Andre-Pascal, 75 Paris 16, France (Telephone Number in U.S. (202) 785-6323); *Economic Outlook, Financial Market Trends, Main Economic Indicators - Historical Statistics,* and *OECD Financial Statistics.*

SPAIN - INTERNAL TRADE

European Community Information Service, 2100 M Street, NW, Washington, D.C. 20037 (202) 862-9500; *Basic Statistics of the Community.*

Organisation for Economic Co-operation and Development (OECD), 2 rue Andre-Pascal, 75 Paris 16, France (Telephone Number in U.S. (202) 785-6323); *Main Economic Indicators - Historical Statistics.*

SPAIN - INTERNATIONAL FINANCE

European Community Information Service, 2100 M Street, NW, Washington, D.C. 20037 (202) 862-9500; *Basic Statistics of the Community.*

Organisation for Economic Co-operation and Development (OECD), 2 rue Andre-Pascal, 75 Paris 16, France (Telephone Number in U.S. (202) 785-6323); *Economic Outlook,* and *Financial Market Trends.*

SPAIN - INTERNATIONAL LIQUIDITY

International Monetary Fund, 700 Nineteenth Street, NW, Washington, D.C. 20431 (202) 623-7000; *International Financial Statistics.*

Organisation for Economic Co-operation and Development (OECD), 2 rue Andre-Pascal, 75 Paris 16, France (Telephone Number in U.S. (202) 785-6323); *Economic Outlook,* and *Financial Market Trends.*

SPAIN - INTERNATIONAL RESERVES EXCLUDING GOLD

Statistical Office of the United Nations, Publishing Service, New York, New York 10017 (800) 253-9646; *Statistical Yearbook.*

The World Bank, 1818 H Street, NW, Washington, D.C. 20433 (202) 477-1234; *World Tables.*

SPAIN - INTERNATIONAL STATISTICS

Organisation for Economic Co-operation and Development (OECD), 2 rue Andre-Pascal, 75 Paris 16, France (Telephone Number in U.S. (202) 785-6323); *Financial Market Trends,* and *Tourism Policy and International Tourism in OECD Member Countries.*

SPAIN - INVESTMENT

International Monetary Fund, 700 Nineteenth Street, NW, Washington, D.C. 20431 (202) 623-7000; *International Financial Statistics.*

Organisation for Economic Co-operation and Development (OECD), 2 rue Andre-Pascal, 75 Paris 16, France (Telephone Number in U.S. (202) 785-6323); *Economic Outlook, Financial Market Trends, Industrial Structure Statistics, The Iron and Steel Industry, Main Economic Indicators - Historical Statistics,* and *Textile Industry in OECD Countries.*

SPAIN - IRON ORE - See SPAIN - MINING AND MINERAL PRODUCTS

SPAIN - LABOR FORCE

European Community Information Service, 2100 M Street, NW, Washington, D.C. 20037 (202) 862-9500; *Basic Statistics of the Community, Labor Force Sample Survey,* and *Regions: Statistical Yearbook.*

Facts on File, 460 Park Avenue South, New York, New York 10016 (800) 443-8323; *The New Book of World Rankings.*

Food and Agricultural Organization of the United Nations (FAO) Via delle Terme di Caracalla, 00100 Rome, Italy (Telephone Number in U.S. (202) 653-2400); *The State of Food and Agriculture.*

G.K. Hall and Company, 70 Lincoln Street, Boston, Massachusetts 02111 (617) 423-3990; *The World in Figures.*

Organisation for Economic Co-operation and Development (OECD), 2 rue Andre-Pascal, 75 Paris 16, France (Telephone Number in U.S.

(202) 785-6323); *Economic Outlook, The Iron and Steel Industry, Main Economic Indicators - Historical Statistics, Maritime Transport, OECD Economic Surveys: Spain, OECD Employment Outlook,* and *Textile Industry in OECD Countries.*

Times Books, 201 East 50th Street, New York, New York 10022 (212) 751-2600; *The Economist Book of Vital World Statistics.*

The World Bank, 1818 H Street, NW, Washington, D.C. 20433 (202) 477-1234; *World Tables.*

SPAIN - LABOR PRODUCTIVITY

G.K. Hall and Company, 70 Lincoln Street, Boston, Massachusetts 02111 (617) 423-3990; *The World in Figures.*

International Labour Office, I.L.O. Publications, CH-1211, Geneva 22, Switzerland; *Yearbook of Labour Statistics.*

Organisation for Economic Co-operation and Development (OECD), 2 rue Andre-Pascal, 75 Paris 16, France (Telephone Number in U.S. (202) 785-6323); *Economic Outlook,* and *OECD Employment Outlook.*

SPAIN - LAND USE

Euromonitor Publications Limited, 87-88 Turnmill Street, London EC1M 5QU, England; *European Marketing Data and Statistics.*

European Community Information Service, 2100 M Street, NW, Washington, D.C. 20037 (202) 862-9500; *Agriculture: Statistical Yearbook, Basic Statistics of the Community, Crop Production: Quarterly Statistics,* and *Regions: Statistical Yearbook.*

Food and Agricultural Organization of the United Nations (FAO), Via delle Terme di Caracalla, 00100 Rome, Italy (Telephone Number in U.S. (202) 653-2400); *Production Yearbook.*

G.K. Hall and Company, 70 Lincoln Street, Boston, Massachusetts 02111 (617) 423-3990; *The World in Figures.*

SPAIN - LEAD AND LEAD ORE PRODUCTION AND CONSUMPTION - See SPAIN - MINING AND MINERAL PRODUCTS

SPAIN - LEATHER - PRODUCTION INDEX

Organisation for Economic Co-operation and Development (OECD), 2 rue Andre-Pascal, 75 Paris 16, France (Telephone Number in U.S. (202) 785-6323); *Indicators of Industrial Activity.*

SPAIN - LEATHER AND FOOTWEAR - EXPORTS AND IMPORTS

European Community Information Service, 2100 M Street, NW, Washington, D.C. 20037 (202) 862-9500; *Basic Statistics of the Community.*

Organisation for Economic Co-operation and Development (OECD), 2 rue Andre-Pascal, 75 Paris 16, France (Telephone Number in U.S. (202) 785-6323); *The Footwear, Raw Hides and Skins, and Leather Industry in OECD Countries.*

SPAIN - LIBRARIES

Euromonitor Publications Limited, 87-88 Turnmill Street, London EC1M 5QU, England; *European Marketing Data and Statistics.*

Facts on File, 460 Park Avenue South, New York, New York 10016 (800) 443-8323; *The New Book of World Rankings.*

United Nations Educational, Scientific and Cultural Organization (UNESCO), 7 Place de Fontenoy, F-75700 Paris, France (Telephone Number in U.S. (212) 963-5981); *Statistical Yearbook.*

SPAIN - LIGNITE PRODUCTION - See SPAIN - MINING AND MINERAL PRODUCTS

SPAIN - LIVESTOCK AND POULTRY

Commodity Research Bureau, Incorporated, 75 Wall Street, New York, New York 10005 (212) 504-7754; *Commodity Year Book.*

Euromonitor Publications Limited, 87-88 Turnmill Street, London EC1M 5QU, England; *European Marketing Data and Statistics.*

European Community Information Service, 2100 M Street, NW, Washington, D.C. 20037 (202) 862-9500; *Agriculture: Statistical Yearbook, Basic Statistics of the Community, Eurostatistics: Data for Short-Term Economic Analysis,* and *Regions: Statistical Yearbook.*

Facts on File, 460 Park Avenue South, New York, New York 10016 (800) 443-8323; *The New Book of World Rankings.*

Food and Agricultural Organization of the United Nations (FAO), Via delle Terme di Caracalla, 00100 Rome, Italy (Telephone Number in U.S. (202) 653-2400); *Production Yearbook,* and *The State of Food and Agriculture.*

G.K. Hall and Company, 70 Lincoln Street, Boston, Massachusetts 02111 (617) 423-3990; *The World in Figures.*

Organisation for Economic Co-operation and Development (OECD), 2 rue Andre-Pascal, 75 Paris 16, France (Telephone Number in U.S. (202) 785-6323); *Economic Accounts for Agriculture,* and *Meat Balances in OECD Member Countries.*

Statistical Office of the United Nations, Publishing Service, New York, New York 10017 (800) 253-9646; *Statistical Yearbook.*

SPAIN - LIVING LEVELS

G.K. Hall and Company, 70 Lincoln Street, Boston, Massachusetts 02111 (617) 423-3990; *The World in Figures.*

Organisation for Economic Co-operation and Development (OECD), 2 rue Andre-Pascal, 75 Paris 16, France (Telephone Number in U.S. (202) 785-6323); *Economic Outlook.*

Times Books, 201 East 50th Street, New York, New York 10022 (212) 751-2600; *The Economist Book of Vital World Statistics.*

SPAIN - MACHINERY - PRODUCTION INDEX

Organisation for Economic Co-operation and Development (OECD), 2 rue Andre-Pascal, 75 Paris 16, France (Telephone Number in U.S. (202) 785-6323); *Indicators of Industrial Activity.*

SPAIN - MAGNESIUM PRODUCTION AND CONSUMPTION - See SPAIN - MINING AND MINERAL PRODUCTS

SPAIN - MAIL - NUMBER OF PIECES SENT OR RECEIVED

European Community Information Service, 2100 M Street, NW, Washington, D.C. 20037 (202) 862-9500; *Transport Annual Statistics.*

Statistical Office of the United Nations, Publishing Service, New York, New York 10017 (800) 253-9646; *Statistical Yearbook.*

SPAIN - MANGANESE AND MANGANESE ORE PRODUCTION AND CONSUMPTION - See SPAIN - MINING AND MINERAL PRODUCTS

SPAIN - MANUFACTURING

American Automobile Manufacturers Association, 1401 H Street, NW, Suite 900, Washington, D.C. 20005 (202) 326-5500; *World Motor Vehicle Data*.

European Community Information Service, 2100 M Street, NW, Washington, D.C. 20037 (202) 862-9500; Basic Statistics of the Community, *Eurostatistics: Data for Short-Term Economic Analysis*, and *Industrial Production: Quarterly Statistics*.

Facts on File, 460 Park Avenue South, New York, New York 10016 (800) 443-8323; *The New Book of World Rankings*.

G.K. Hall and Company, 70 Lincoln Street, Boston, Massachusetts 02111 (617) 423-3990; *The World in Figures*.

Organisation for Economic Co-operation and Development (OECD), 2 rue Andre-Pascal, 75 Paris 16, France (Telephone Number in U.S. (202) 785-6323); *Foreign Trade by Commodities, Indicators of Industrial Activity, Industrial Structure Statistics*, and *OECD Economic Surveys: Spain*.

Statistical Office of the United Nations, Publishing Service, New York, New York 10017 (800) 253-9646; *Statistical Yearbook*.

Times Books, 201 East 50th Street, New York, New York 10022 (212) 751-2600; *The Economist Book of Vital World Statistics*.

The World Bank, 1818 H Street, NW, Washington, D.C. 20433 (202) 477-1234; *World Tables*.

SPAIN - MARRIAGE RATES

European Community Information Service, 2100 M Street, NW, Washington, D.C. 20037 (202) 862-9500; *Basic Statistics of the Community*.

Facts on File, 460 Park Avenue South, New York, New York 10016 (800) 443-8323; *The New Book of World Rankings*.

Statistical Office of the United Nations, Publishing Service, New York, New York 10017 (800) 253-9646; *Demographic Yearbook*, and *Statistical Yearbook*.

SPAIN - MEAT PRODUCTION - See SPAIN - LIVESTOCK AND POULTRY

SPAIN - MERCHANT SHIPPING

European Community Information Service, 2100 M Street, NW, Washington, D.C. 20037 (202) 862-9500; *Basic Statistics of the Community, Fisheries: Yearly Statistics, Regions: Statistical Yearbook*, and *Transport Annual Statistics*.

G.K. Hall and Company, 70 Lincoln Street, Boston, Massachusetts 02111 (617) 423-3990; *The World in Figures*.

Lloyd's Register of Shipping, 17 Battery Place, New York, New York 10004 (212) 425-8050; *Register of Ships*.

Organisation for Economic Co-operation and Development (OECD), 2 rue Andre-Pascal, 75 Paris 16, France (Telephone Number in U.S. (202) 785-6323); *Maritime Transport*.

Statistical Office of the United Nations, Publishing Service, New York, New York 10017 (800) 253-9646; *Statistical Yearbook*.

U.S. Department of Transportation, Maritime Administration, 400 Seventh Street, SW, Washington, D.C. 20590 (202) 366-5807; *A Statistical Analysis of the World's Merchant Fleets*.

SPAIN - MERCURY PRODUCTION AND CONSUMPTION - See SPAIN - MINING AND MINERAL PRODUCTS

SPAIN - MILITARY

G.K. Hall and Company, 70 Lincoln Street, Boston, Massachusetts 02111 (617) 423-3990; *The World in Figures*.

The International Institute for Strategic Studies, 23 Tavistock Street, London WC2E 7NQ, England; *The Military Balance*.

U.S. Arms Control and Disarmament Agency, 320 Twenty-first Street, NW, Washington, D.C. 20451 (202) 647-8677; *World Military Expenditures and Arms Transfers*.

SPAIN - MILK PRODUCTION - See SPAIN - DAIRY PRODUCTS

SPAIN - MINING AND MINERAL PRODUCTS

Commodity Research Bureau, Incorporated, 75 Wall Street, New York, New York 10005 (212) 504-7754; *Commodity Year Book*.

European Community Information Service, 2100 M Street, NW, Washington, D.C. 20037 (202) 862-9500; *ACP: Basic Statistics, Basic Statistics of the Community, Energy: Monthly Statistics, Energy Statistics Yearbook, Eurostatistics: Data for Short-Term Economic Analysis, Industrial Production: Quarterly Statistics, Iron and Steel: Statistical Yearbook, Labor Force Sample Survey, OECD Economic Surveys: Spain*, and *Regions: Statistical Yearbook*.

Facts on File, 460 Park Avenue South, New York, New York 10016 (800) 443-8323; *The New Book of World Rankings*.

G.K. Hall and Company, 70 Lincoln Street, Boston, Massachusetts 02111 (617) 423-3990; *The World in Figures*.

International Iron and Steel Institute, 120, rue Colonel Bourg, B-1140, Brussels, Belgium; *Steel Statistical Yearbook*.

International Lead and Zinc Study Group, Metro House, 58 St. James's Street, London SW1A 1LD, England; *Lead and Zinc Statistics*.

Organisation for Economic Co-operation and Development (OECD), 2 rue Andre-Pascal, 75 Paris 16, France (Telephone Number in U.S. (202) 785-6323); *Coal Information, Energy Statistics of OECD Countries, Foreign Trade by Commodities, Indicators of Industrial Activity, Industrial Structure Statistics, The Iron and Steel Industry*, and *The Non-Ferrous Metals Industry*.

Penn Well Publishing Company, 1421 South Sheridan Road, P.O. Box 1260, Tulsa, Oklahoma 74101 (800) 752-9764; *International Energy Statistics Sourcebook*.

Statistical Office of the United Nations, Publishing Service, New York, New York 10017 (800) 253-9646; *Statistical Yearbook*.

World Bureau of Metal Statistics, 27-A High Street, Ware Hert SG12 9BA, England; *World Metal Statistics*.

SPAIN - MOLYBDENUM AND MOLYBDENUM ORE PRODUCTION AND CONSUMPTION - See SPAIN - MINING AND MINERAL

PRODUCTS

SPAIN - MONEY EXCHANGE RATE

European Community Information Service, 2100 M Street, NW, Washington, D.C. 20037 (202) 862-9500; *Basic Statistics of the Community*.

International Monetary Fund, 700 Nineteenth Street, NW, Washington, D.C. 20431 (202) 623-7000; *International Financial Statistics*.

Organisation for Economic Co-operation and Development (OECD), 2 rue Andre-Pascal, 75 Paris 16, France (Telephone Number in U.S. (202) 785-6323); *Economic Outlook, Financial Market Trends, OECD Economic Surveys: Spain, Tourism Policy and International Tourism in OECD Member Countries*.

Statistical Office of the United Nations, Publishing Service, New York, New York 10017 (800) 253-9646; *Statistical Yearbook*.

SPAIN - MONEY RATES - MARKET

European Community Information Service, 2100 M Street, NW, Washington, D.C. 20037 (202) 862-9500; *Basic Statistics of the Community*.

Organisation for Economic Co-operation and Development (OECD), 2 rue Andre-Pascal, 75 Paris 16, France (Telephone Number in U.S. (202) 785-6323); *Economic Outlook, and Financial Market Trends*.

SPAIN - MONEY RESERVES

European Community Information Service, 2100 M Street, NW, Washington, D.C. 20037 (202) 862-9500; *Basic Statistics of the Community*.

Organisation for Economic Co-operation and Development (OECD), 2 rue Andre-Pascal, 75 Paris 16, France (Telephone Number in U.S. (202) 785-6323); *Economic Outlook, and Financial Market Trends*.

SPAIN - MONEY SUPPLY

European Community Information Service, 2100 M Street, NW, Washington, D.C. 20037 (202) 862-9500; *Basic Statistics of the Community, Eurostatistics: Data for Short-Term Economic Analysis, and Money and Finance*.

G.K. Hall and Company, 70 Lincoln Street, Boston, Massachusetts 02111 (617) 423-3990; *The World in Figures*.

International Monetary Fund, 700 Nineteenth Street, NW, Washington, D.C. 20431 (202) 623-7000; *International Financial Statistics*.

Organisation for Economic Co-operation and Development (OECD), 2 rue Andre-Pascal, 75 Paris 16, France (Telephone Number in U.S. (202) 785-6323); *Economic Outlook*.

Statistical Office of the United Nations, Publishing Service, New York, New York 10017 (800) 253-9646; *Statistical Yearbook*.

The World Bank, 1818 H Street, NW, Washington, D.C. 20433 (202) 477-1234; *World Tables*.

SPAIN - MOTION PICTURES

Statistical Office of the United Nations, Publishing Service, New York, New York 10017 (800) 253-9646; *Statistical Yearbook*.

United Nations Educational, Scientific and Cultural Organization (UNESCO), 7 Place de Fontenoy, F-75700 Paris, France (Telephone Number in U.S. (212) 963-5981); *Statistical Yearbook*.

SPAIN - MOTOR VEHICLE PRODUCTION

American Automobile Manufacturers Association, 1401 H Street, NW, Suite 900, Washington, D.C. 20005 (202) 326-5500; *World Motor Vehicle Data*.

European Community Information Service, 2100 M Street, NW, Washington, D.C. 20037 (202) 862-9500; *Basic Statistics of the Community, and Eurostatistics: Data for Short-Term Economic Analysis*.

Organisation for Economic Co-operation and Development (OECD), 2 rue Andre-Pascal, 75 Paris 16, France (Telephone Number in U.S. (202) 785-6323); *Foreign Trade by Commodities, and Indicators of Industrial Activity*.

Statistical Office of the United Nations, Publishing Service, New York, New York 10017 (800) 253-9646; *Statistical Yearbook*.

SPAIN - MOTOR VEHICLE TAXES - See SPAIN - TAXATION

SPAIN - MOTOR VEHICLES IN USE

American Automobile Manufacturers Association, 1401 H Street, NW, Suite 900, Washington, D.C. 20005 (202) 326-5500; *World Motor Vehicle Data*.

European Community Information Service, 2100 M Street, NW, Washington, D.C. 20037 (202) 862-9500; *Basic Statistics of the Community, and Transport Annual Statistics*.

G.K. Hall and Company, 70 Lincoln Street, Boston, Massachusetts 02111 (617) 423-3990; *The World in Figures*.

International Road Federation, 525 School Street, SW, Washington, D.C. 20024 (202) 554-2106; *World Road Statistics*.

Statistical Office of the United Nations, Publishing Service, New York, New York 10017 (800) 253-9646; *Statistical Yearbook*.

Times Books, 201 East 50th Street, New York, New York 10022 (212) 751-2600; *The Economist Book of Vital World Statistics*.

SPAIN - MULES - See SPAIN - LIVESTOCK AND POULTRY

SPAIN - MUSEUMS

Euromonitor Publications Limited, 87-88 Turnmill Street, London EC1M 5QU, England; *European Marketing Data and Statistics*.

Facts on File, 460 Park Avenue South, New York, New York 10016 (800) 443-8323; *The New Book of World Rankings*.

United Nations Educational, Scientific and Cultural Organization (UNESCO), 7 Place de Fontenoy, F-75700 Paris, France (Telephone Number in U.S. (212) 963-5981); *Statistical Yearbook*.

SPAIN - NATALITY - See SPAIN - BIRTH RATE

SPAIN - NATIONAL ACCOUNTS

European Community Information Service, 2100 M Street, NW, Washington, D.C. 20037 (202) 862-9500; *Basic Statistics of the Community, and Eurostatistics: Data for Short-Term Economic Analysis*.

Federal Statistical Office, Gustav-Stresemann-Ring 11, D-6200 Wiesbaden, Germany; *Spain.*

International Monetary Fund, 700 Nineteenth Street, NW, Washington, D.C. 20431 (202) 623-7000; *International Financial Statistics.*

Organisation for Economic Co-operation and Development (OECD), 2 rue Andre-Pascal, 75 Paris 16, France (Telephone Number in U.S. (202) 785-6323); *Economic Outlook.*

Statistical Office of the United Nations, Publishing Service, New York, New York 10017 (800) 253-9646; *National Accounts Statistics,* and *Statistical Yearbook.*

SPAIN - NATIONAL INCOME

Facts on File, 460 Park Avenue South, New York, New York 10016 (800) 443-8323; *The New Book of World Rankings.*

G.K. Hall and Company, 70 Lincoln Street, Boston, Massachusetts 02111 (617) 423-3990; *The World in Figures.*

Organisation for Economic Co-operation and Development (OECD), 2 rue Andre-Pascal, 75 Paris 16, France (Telephone Number in U.S. (202) 785-6323); *Economic Outlook.*

Statistical Office of the United Nations, Publishing Service, New York, New York 10017 (800) 253-9646; *Statistical Yearbook.*

SPAIN - NATIONAL PRODUCT

European Community Information Service, 2100 M Street, NW, Washington, D.C. 20037 (202) 862-9500; *Basic Statistics of the Community.*

Facts on File, 460 Park Avenue South, New York, New York 10016 (800) 443-8323; *The New Book of World Rankings.*

Organisation for Economic Co-operation and Development (OECD), 2 rue Andre-Pascal, 75 Paris 16, France (Telephone Number in U.S. (202) 785-6323); *Economic Outlook.*

Statistical Office of the United Nations, Publishing Service, New York, New York 10017 (800) 253-9646; *Statistical Yearbook.*

SPAIN - NATURAL GAS PRODUCTION - See SPAIN - MINING AND MINERAL PRODUCTS

SPAIN - NEWSPAPER PRODUCTION - See SPAIN - FORESTRY AND FOREST PRODUCTS

SPAIN - NICKEL AND NICKEL ORE PRODUCTION AND CONSUMPTION - See SPAIN - MINING AND MINERAL PRODUCTS

SPAIN - NITRIC ACID PRODUCTION - See SPAIN - MINING AND MINERAL PRODUCTS

SPAIN - OATS PRODUCTION - See SPAIN - CROPS

SPAIN - OCCUPATIONS - See SPAIN - LABOR FORCE

SPAIN - OIL PRODUCING CROPS

European Community Information Service, 2100 M Street, NW, Washington, D.C. 20037 (202) 862-9500; *Basic Statistics of the Community.*

Organisation for Economic Co-operation and Development (OECD), 2 rue Andre-Pascal, 75 Paris 16, France (Telephone Number in U.S. (202) 785-6323); *Foreign Trade by Commodities.*

SPAIN - ONION PRODUCTION - See SPAIN - CROPS

SPAIN - ORANGES PRODUCTION - See SPAIN - CROPS

SPAIN - PAPER EXPORTS AND IMPORTS - See SPAIN - FORESTRY AND FOREST PRODUCTS

SPAIN - PATENTS

Statistical Office of the United Nations, Publishing Service, New York, New York 10017 (800) 253-9646; *Statistical Yearbook.*

World Intellectual Property Organization, 34 Chemin des Colombettes, CH-1211 Geneva 20. Switzerland; *Industrial Property Statistics.*

SPAIN - PEANUT PRODUCTION - See SPAIN - CROPS

SPAIN - PERIODICALS

United Nations Educational, Scientific and Cultural Organization (UNESCO), 7 Place de Fontenoy, F-75700 Paris, France (Telephone Number in U.S. (212) 963-5981); *Statistical Yearbook.*

SPAIN - PESTICIDE USE

Food and Agricultural Organization of the United Nations (FAO) Via delle Terme di Caracalla, 00100 Rome, Italy (Telephone Number in U.S. (202) 653-2400); *The State of Food and Agriculture.*

SPAIN - PETROLEUM INDUSTRY

Euromonitor Publications Limited, 87-88 Turnmill Street, London EC1M 5QU, England; *European Marketing Data and Statistics.*

European Community Information Service, 2100 M Street, NW, Washington, D.C. 20037 (202) 862-9500; *ACP: Basic Statistics, Basic Statistics of the Community,* and *Energy Statistics Yearbook.*

Facts on File, 460 Park Avenue South, New York, New York 10016 (800) 443-8323; *The New Book of World Rankings.*

Food and Agricultural Organization of the United Nations (FAO) Via delle Terme di Caracalla, 00100 Rome, Italy (Telephone Number in U.S. (202) 653-2400); *The State of Food and Agriculture.*

G.K. Hall and Company, 70 Lincoln Street, Boston, Massachusetts 02111 (617) 423-3990; *The World in Figures.*

Organisation for Economic Co-operation and Development (OECD), 2 rue Andre-Pascal, 75 Paris 16, France (Telephone Number in U.S. (202) 785-6323); *Energy Statistics of OECD Countries, Foreign Trade by Commodities, Indicators of Industrial Activity, Oil Statistics,* and *Oil and Gas Information.*

Penn Well Publishing Company, 1421 South Sheridan Road, P.O. Box 1260, Tulsa, Oklahoma 74101 (800) 752-9764; *International Energy Statistics Sourcebook.*

Statistical Office of the United Nations, Publishing Service, New York, New York 10017 (800) 253-9646; *Statistical Yearbook.*

SPAIN - PHOSPHATES AND PHOSPHATE ROCK PRODUCTION - See SPAIN - MINING AND MINERAL PRODUCTS

SPAIN - PIG-IRON AND FERRO-ALLOY PRODUCTION - See SPAIN - MINING AND MINERAL PRODUCTS

SPAIN - PIGS - See SPAIN - LIVESTOCK AND POULTRY

SPAIN - PIPELINES FOR OIL AND PETROLEUM PRODUCTS

European Community Information Service, 2100 M Street, NW, Washington, D.C. 20037 (202) 862-9500; *Transport Annual Statistics*.

Statistical Office of the United Nations, Publishing Service, New York, New York 10017 (800) 253-9646; *Annual Bulletin of Transport Statistics for Europe*.

SPAIN - PLASTIC AND RESIN PRODUCTION

Commodity Research Bureau, Incorporated, 75 Wall Street, New York, New York 10005 (212) 504-7754; *Commodity Year Book*.

European Community Information Service, 2100 M Street, NW, Washington, D.C. 20037 (202) 862-9500; *Basic Statistics of the Community*.

Organisation for Economic Co-operation and Development (OECD), 2 rue Andre-Pascal, 75 Paris 16, France (Telephone Number in U.S. (202) 785-6323); *Foreign Trade by Commodities*.

Statistical Office of the United Nations, Publishing Service, New York, New York 10017 (800) 253-9646; *Statistical Yearbook*.

SPAIN - PLATINUM PRODUCTION - See SPAIN - MINING AND MINERAL PRODUCTS

SPAIN - POPULATION

Euromonitor Publications Limited, 87-88 Turnmill Street, London EC1M 5QU, England; *European Marketing Data and Statistics*.

European Community Information Service, 2100 M Street, NW, Washington, D.C. 20037 (202) 862-9500; *ACP: Basic Statistics, Basic Statistics of the Community, Demographic Statistics, Employment and Unemployment, Fisheries: Yearly Statistics, Iron and Steel: Statistical Yearbook, Labor Force Sample Survey*, and *Regions: Statistical Yearbook*.

Facts on File, 460 Park Avenue South, New York, New York 10016 (800) 443-8323; *The New Book of World Rankings*.

Federal Statistical Office, Gustav-Stresemann-Ring 11, D-6200 Wiesbaden, Germany; *Spain*.

Food and Agricultural Organization of the United Nations (FAO), Via delle Terme di Caracalla, 00100 Rome, Italy (Telephone Number in U.S. (202) 653-2400); *Production Yearbook*.

International Labour Office, I.L.O. Publications, CH-1211, Geneva 22, Switzerland; *Yearbook of Labour Statistics*.

Statistical Office of the United Nations, Publishing Service, New York, New York 10017 (800) 253-9646; *Demographic Yearbook*, and *Statistical Yearbook*.

Times Books, 201 East 50th Street, New York, New York 10022 (212) 751-2600; *The Economist Book of Vital World Statistics*.

United Nations Educational, Scientific and Cultural Organization (UNESCO), 7 Place de Fontenoy, F-75700 Paris, France (Telephone Number in U.S. (212) 963-5981); *Statistical Yearbook*.

U.S. Arms Control and Disarmament Agency, 320 Twenty-first Street, NW, Washington, D.C. 20451 (202) 647-8677; *World Military Expenditures and Arms Transfers*.

World Health Organization, Office of Publications, Avenue Appia, CH-1211 Geneva 27, Switzerland (Telephone Number in U.S. (518) 436-9686); *World Health Statistics Annual*.

SPAIN - POST OFFICES

Facts on File, 460 Park Avenue South, New York, New York 10016 (800) 443-8323; *The New Book of World Rankings*.

SPAIN - POTATO PRODUCTION - See SPAIN - CROPS

SPAIN - POWER PRODUCTION INDUSTRY

European Community Information Service, 2100 M Street, NW, Washington, D.C. 20037 (202) 862-9500; *Basic Statistics of the Community*.

Statistical Office of the United Nations, Publishing Service, New York, New York 10017 (800) 253-9646; *Statistical Yearbook*.

SPAIN - PRICES

European Community Information Service, 2100 M Street, NW, Washington, D.C. 20037 (202) 862-9500; *Basic Statistics of the Community*, and *Eurostatistics: Data for Short-Term Economic Analysis*.

Facts on File, 460 Park Avenue South, New York, New York 10016 (800) 443-8323; *The New Book of World Rankings*.

Federal Statistical Office, Gustav-Stresemann-Ring 11, D-6200 Wiesbaden, Germany; *Spain*.

Food and Agricultural Organization of the United Nations (FAO), Via delle Terme di Caracalla, 00100 Rome, Italy (Telephone Number in U.S. (202) 653-2400); *Production Yearbook*, and *The State of Food and Agriculture*.

G.K. Hall and Company, 70 Lincoln Street, Boston, Massachusetts 02111 (617) 423-3990; *The World in Figures*.

International Labour Office, I.L.O. Publications, CH-1211, Geneva 22, Switzerland; *Yearbook of Labour Statistics*.

International Lead and Zinc Study Group, Metro House, 58 St. James's Street, London SW1A 1LD, England; *Lead and Zinc Statistics*.

International Monetary Fund, 700 Nineteenth Street, NW, Washington, D.C. 20431 (202) 623-7000; *International Financial Statistics*.

Organisation for Economic Co-operation and Development (OECD), 2 rue Andre-Pascal, 75 Paris 16, France (Telephone Number in U.S. (202) 785-6323); *Economic Outlook, The Footwear, Raw Hides and Skins, and Leather Industry in OECD Countries, Indicators of Industrial Activity, The Iron and Steel Industry, Main Economic Indicators - Historical Statistics*, and *The Pulp and Paper Industry*.

World Bureau of Metal Statistics, 27-A High Street, Ware Hert SG12 9BA, England; *World Metal Statistics*.

SPAIN - PRINTING AND WRITING PAPER - See SPAIN - FORESTRY AND FOREST PRODUCTS

SPAIN - PRODUCTION

American Automobile Manufacturers Association, 1401 H Street, NW, Suite 900, Washington, D.C. 20005 (202) 326-5500; *World Motor Vehicle Data.*

European Community Information Service, 2100 M Street, NW, Washington, D.C. 20037 (202) 862-9500; *Basic Statistics of the Community, Eurostatistics: Data for Short-Term Economic Analysis,* and *Fisheries: Yearly Statistics.*

Facts on File, 460 Park Avenue South, New York, New York 10016 (800) 443-8323; *The New Book of World Rankings.*

G.K. Hall and Company, 70 Lincoln Street, Boston, Massachusetts 02111 (617) 423-3990; *The World in Figures.*

International Iron and Steel Institute, 120, rue Colonel Bourg, B-1140, Brussels, Belgium; *Steel Statistical Yearbook.*

International Lead and Zinc Study Group, Metro House, 58 St. James's Street, London SW1A 1LD, England; *Lead and Zinc Statistics.*

Organisation for Economic Co-operation and Development (OECD), 2 rue Andre-Pascal, 75 Paris 16, France (Telephone Number in U.S. (202) 785-6323); *Economic Outlook, The Footwear, Raw Hides and Skins, and Leather Industry in OECD Countries, Indicators of Industrial Activity, Industrial Structure Statistics, The Iron and Steel Industry, Meat Balances in OECD Member Countries, Milk, Milk Products, and Egg Balances in OECD Member Countries, The Non-Ferrous Metals Industry, The Pulp and Paper Industry,* and *Textile Industry in OECD Countries.*

SPAIN - PRODUCTIVITY

European Community Information Service, 2100 M Street, NW, Washington, D.C. 20037 (202) 862-9500; *Basic Statistics of the Community.*

Organisation for Economic Co-operation and Development (OECD), 2 rue Andre-Pascal, 75 Paris 16, France (Telephone Number in U.S. (202) 785-6323); *Economic Outlook.*

SPAIN - PROPERTY TAXES - See SPAIN - TAXATION

SPAIN - PUBLIC CONSUMPTION FUND

European Community Information Service, 2100 M Street, NW, Washington, D.C. 20037 (202) 862-9500; *Basic Statistics of the Community.*

Organisation for Economic Co-operation and Development (OECD), 2 rue Andre-Pascal, 75 Paris 16, France (Telephone Number in U.S. (202) 785-6323); *Revenue Statistics of OECD Member Countries.*

SPAIN - PUBLIC EXPENDITURES

European Community Information Service, 2100 M Street, NW, Washington, D.C. 20037 (202) 862-9500; *Basic Statistics of the Community.*

Organisation for Economic Co-operation and Development (OECD), 2 rue Andre-Pascal, 75 Paris 16, France (Telephone Number in U.S. (202) 785-6323); *Revenue Statistics of OECD Member Countries.*

SPAIN - PUBLIC FINANCE

Facts on File, 460 Park Avenue South, New York, New York 10016 (800) 443-8323; *The New Book of World Rankings.*

Organisation for Economic Co-operation and Development (OECD), 2 rue Andre-Pascal, 75 Paris 16, France (Telephone Number in U.S. (202) 785-6323); *Revenue Statistics of OECD Member Countries.*

SPAIN - PUBLIC HEALTH

European Community Information Service, 2100 M Street, NW, Washington, D.C. 20037 (202) 862-9500; *Basic Statistics of the Community.*

SPAIN - PUBLIC REVENUES

Organisation for Economic Co-operation and Development (OECD), 2 rue Andre-Pascal, 75 Paris 16, France (Telephone Number in U.S. (202) 785-6323); *Revenue Statistics of OECD Member Countries.*

SPAIN - RADIO BROADCASTING - See SPAIN - BROADCASTING

SPAIN - RADIO RECEIVER PRODUCTION

Statistical Office of the United Nations, Publishing Service, New York, New York 10017 (800) 253-9646; *Statistical Yearbook.*

SPAIN - RAILWAYS

Euromonitor Publications Limited, 87-88 Turnmill Street, London EC1M 5QU, England; *European Marketing Data and Statistics.*

European Community Information Service, 2100 M Street, NW, Washington, D.C. 20037 (202) 862-9500; *Basic Statistics of the Community, Regions: Statistical Yearbook,* and *Transport Annual Statistics.*

G.K. Hall and Company, 70 Lincoln Street, Boston, Massachusetts 02111 (617) 423-3990; *The World in Figures.*

Jane's Information Group, Sentinel House, 163 Brighton Road, Coulsdon, Surrey CR5 2NH, England (Telephone Number in U.S. (703) 683-3700); *Jane's World Railways.*

Statistical Office of the United Nations, Publishing Service, New York, New York 10017 (800) 253-9646; *Annual Bulletin of Transport Statistics for Europe,* and *Statistical Yearbook.*

SPAIN - RANCHING

European Community Information Service, 2100 M Street, NW, Washington, D.C. 20037 (202) 862-9500; *Basic Statistics of the Community.*

SPAIN - RELIGION

Facts on File, 460 Park Avenue South, New York, New York 10016 (800) 443-8323; *The New Book of World Rankings.*

SPAIN - RENT PRICES

International Labour Office, I.L.O. Publications, CH-1211, Geneva 22, Switzerland; *Yearbook of Labour Statistics.*

SPAIN - RETAIL TRADE

European Community Information Service, 2100 M Street, NW, Washington, D.C. 20037 (202) 862-9500; *Basic Statistics of the*

Community, and *Eurostatistics: Data for Short-Term Economic Analysis.*

G.K. Hall and Company, 70 Lincoln Street, Boston, Massachusetts 02111 (617) 423-3990; *The World in Figures.*

SPAIN - RICE PRODUCTION - See SPAIN - CROPS

SPAIN - ROUNDWOOD PRODUCTION - See SPAIN - FORESTRY AND FOREST PRODUCTS

SPAIN - RUBBER PRODUCTION AND CONSUMPTION

European Community Information Service, 2100 M Street, NW, Washington, D.C. 20037 (202) 862-9500; *Basic Statistics of the Community.*

Facts on File, 460 Park Avenue South, New York, New York 10016 (800) 443-8323; *The New Book of World Rankings.*

Organisation for Economic Co-operation and Development (OECD), 2 rue Andre-Pascal, 75 Paris 16, France (Telephone Number in U.S. (202) 785-6323); *Foreign Trade by Commodities.*

Statistical Office of the United Nations, Publishing Service, New York, New York 10017 (800) 253-9646; *Statistical Yearbook.*

SPAIN - RYE PRODUCTION - See SPAIN - CROPS

SPAIN - SALT PRODUCTION - See SPAIN - MINING AND MINERAL PRODUCTS

SPAIN - SAVINGS ACCOUNT DEPOSITS

European Community Information Service, 2100 M Street, NW, Washington, D.C. 20037 (202) 862-9500; *Eurostatistics: Data for Short-Term Economic Analysis.*

SPAIN - SAWNWOOD PRODUCTION - See SPAIN - FORESTRY AND FOREST PRODUCTS

SPAIN - SCIENCE AND TECHNOLOGY - EXPENDITURE FOR RESEARCH

European Community Information Service, 2100 M Street, NW, Washington, D.C. 20037 (202) 862-9500; *Basic Statistics of the Community.*

Statistical Office of the United Nations, Publishing Service, New York, New York 10017 (800) 253-9646; *Statistical Yearbook.*

SPAIN - SCIENTISTS AND TECHNICIANS

European Community Information Service, 2100 M Street, NW, Washington, D.C. 20037 (202) 862-9500; *Basic Statistics of the Community.*

Statistical Office of the United Nations, Publishing Service, New York, New York 10017 (800) 253-9646; *Statistical Yearbook.*

United Nations Educational, Scientific and Cultural Organization (UNESCO), 7 Place de Fontenoy, F-75700 Paris, France (Telephone Number in U.S. (212) 963-5981); *Statistical Yearbook.*

SPAIN - SENIOR CITIZENS

Facts on File, 460 Park Avenue South, New York, New York 10016 (800) 443-8323; *The New Book of World Rankings.*

SPAIN - SHEEP - See SPAIN - LIVESTOCK AND POULTRY

SPAIN - SHIPBUILDING - PRODUCTION INDEX

Organisation for Economic Co-operation and Development (OECD), 2 rue Andre-Pascal, 75 Paris 16, France (Telephone Number in U.S. (202) 785-6323); *Indicators of Industrial Activity.*

SPAIN - SILVER PRODUCTION AND CONSUMPTION - See SPAIN - MINING AND MINERAL PRODUCTS

SPAIN - SOCIAL DATA

European Community Information Service, 2100 M Street, NW, Washington, D.C. 20037 (202) 862-9500; *ACP: Basic Statistics,* and *Basic Statistics of the Community.*

Facts on File, 460 Park Avenue South, New York, New York 10016 (800) 443-8323; *The New Book of World Rankings.*

G.K. Hall and Company, 70 Lincoln Street, Boston, Massachusetts 02111 (617) 423-3990; *The World in Figures.*

SPAIN - SOCIAL SECURITY

European Community Information Service, 2100 M Street, NW, Washington, D.C. 20037 (202) 862-9500; *Basic Statistics of the Community.*

International Monetary Fund, 700 Nineteenth Street, NW, Washington, D.C. 20431 (202) 623-7000; *Government Finance Statistics Yearbook.*

Organisation for Economic Co-operation and Development (OECD), 2 rue Andre-Pascal, 75 Paris 16, France (Telephone Number in U.S. (202) 785-6323); *Revenue Statistics of OECD Member Countries.*

SPAIN - SOCIOECONOMIC DATA

European Community Information Service, 2100 M Street, NW, Washington, D.C. 20037 (202) 862-9500; *Basic Statistics of the Community.*

Organisation for Economic Co-operation and Development (OECD), 2 rue Andre-Pascal, 75 Paris 16, France (Telephone Number in U.S. (202) 785-6323); *Economic Outlook.*

SPAIN - SOYBEAN PRODUCTION - See SPAIN - CROPS

SPAIN - STAMP TAXES AND DUTIES - See SPAIN - TAXATION

SPAIN - STEEL - See SPAIN - MINING AND MINERAL PRODUCTS

SPAIN - STOCKS - COMMODITY - MARKET PRICE - INDEX

Food and Agricultural Organization of the United Nations (FAO) Via delle Terme di Caracalla, 00100 Rome, Italy (Telephone Number in U.S. (202) 653-2400); *The State of Food and Agriculture.*

International Lead and Zinc Study Group, Metro House, 58 St. James's Street, London SW1A 1LD, England; *Lead and Zinc Statistics.*

Statistical Office of the United Nations, Publishing Service, New York, New York 10017 (800) 253-9646; *Statistical Yearbook.*

World Bureau of Metal Statistics, 27-A High Street, Ware Hert SG12 9BA, England; *World Metal Statistics.*

SPAIN - SUGAR - See SPAIN - CROPS

SPAIN - SULPHUR AND SULPHURIC ACID PRODUCTION - See SPAIN - MINING AND MINERAL PRODUCTS

SPAIN - TAXATION

European Community Information Service, 2100 M Street, NW, Washington, D.C. 20037 (202) 862-9500; *Basic Statistics of the Community.*

G.K. Hall and Company, 70 Lincoln Street, Boston, Massachusetts 02111 (617) 423-3990; *The World in Figures.*

International Monetary Fund, 700 Nineteenth Street, NW, Washington, D.C. 20431 (202) 623-7000; *Government Finance Statistics Yearbook.*

International Road Federation, 525 School Street, SW, Washington, D.C. 20024 (202) 554-2106; *World Road Statistics.*

Organisation for Economic Co-operation and Development (OECD), 2 rue Andre-Pascal, 75 Paris 16, France (Telephone Number in U.S. (202) 785-6323); *Revenue Statistics of OECD Member Countries.*

The World Bank, 1818 H Street, NW, Washington, D.C. 20433 (202) 477-1234; *World Tables.*

SPAIN - TELEGRAPH SERVICE

European Community Information Service, 2100 M Street, NW, Washington, D.C. 20037 (202) 862-9500; *Transport Annual Statistics.*

Statistical Office of the United Nations, Publishing Service, New York, New York 10017 (800) 253-9646; *Statistical Yearbook.*

SPAIN - TELEPHONES IN USE

American Telephone and Telegraph Company, 26 Parsippany Road, Whippany, New Jersey 07981 (800) 338-4038; *The World's Telephones.*

G.K. Hall and Company, 70 Lincoln Street, Boston, Massachusetts 02111 (617) 423-3990; *The World in Figures.*

Statistical Office of the United Nations, Publishing Service, New York, New York 10017 (800) 253-9646; *Statistical Yearbook.*

SPAIN - TELEVISION BROADCASTING - See SPAIN - BROADCASTING

SPAIN - TELEVISION RECEIVER PRODUCTION

European Community Information Service, 2100 M Street, NW, Washington, D.C. 20037 (202) 862-9500; *Basic Statistics of the Community.*

Statistical Office of the United Nations, Publishing Service, New York, New York 10017 (800) 253-9646; *Statistical Yearbook.*

SPAIN - TEXTILE INDUSTRY

American Forest and Paper Association, 1250 Connecticut Avenue, NW, Washington, D.C. 20036 (202) 463-2455; *Wood Pulp and Fiber Statistics.*

European Community Information Service, 2100 M Street, NW, Washington, D.C. 20037 (202) 862-9500; *Basic Statistics of the*

Community, Eurostatistics: Data for Short-Term Economic Analysis, and *Industrial Production: Quarterly Statistics.*

G.K. Hall and Company, 70 Lincoln Street, Boston, Massachusetts 02111 (617) 423-3990; *The World in Figures.*

Organisation for Economic Co-operation and Development (OECD), 2 rue Andre-Pascal, 75 Paris 16, France (Telephone Number in U.S. (202) 785-6323); *Indicators of Industrial Activity, Industrial Structure Statistics,* and *Textile Industry in OECD Countries.*

Statistical Office of the United Nations, Publishing Service, New York, New York 10017 (800) 253-9646; *Statistical Yearbook.*

SPAIN - THEATRE

United Nations Educational, Scientific and Cultural Organization (UNESCO), 7 Place de Fontenoy, F-75700 Paris, France (Telephone Number in U.S. (212) 963-5981); *Statistical Yearbook.*

SPAIN - TIN - See SPAIN - MINING AND MINERAL PRODUCTS

SPAIN - TOBACCO PRODUCTION

European Community Information Service, 2100 M Street, NW, Washington, D.C. 20037 (202) 862-9500; *Basic Statistics of the Community,* and *Industrial Production: Quarterly Statistics.*

Euromonitor Publications Limited, 87-88 Turnmill Street, London EC1M 5QU, England; *European Marketing Data and Statistics.*

Facts on File, 460 Park Avenue South, New York, New York 10016 (800) 443-8323; *The New Book of World Rankings.*

Organisation for Economic Co-operation and Development (OECD), 2 rue Andre-Pascal, 75 Paris 16, France (Telephone Number in U.S. (202) 785-6323); *Foreign Trade by Commodities, Indicators of Industrial Activity,* and *Industrial Structure Statistics.*

Statistical Office of the United Nations, Publishing Service, New York, New York 10017 (800) 253-9646; *Statistical Yearbook.*

SPAIN - TOURISM

Euromonitor Publications Limited, 87-88 Turnmill Street, London EC1M 5QU, England; *European Marketing Data and Statistics.*

European Community Information Service, 2100 M Street, NW, Washington, D.C. 20037 (202) 862-9500; *Transport Annual Statistics.*

Facts on File, 460 Park Avenue South, New York, New York 10016 (800) 443-8323; *The New Book of World Rankings.*

Federal Statistical Office, Gustav-Stresemann-Ring 11, D-6200 Wiesbaden, Germany; *Spain.*

G.K. Hall and Company, 70 Lincoln Street, Boston, Massachusetts 02111 (617) 423-3990; *The World in Figures.*

Organisation for Economic Co-operation and Development (OECD), 2 rue Andre-Pascal, 75 Paris 16, France (Telephone Number in U.S. (202) 785-6323); *Tourism Policy and International Tourism in OECD Member Countries.*

Statistical Office of the United Nations, Publishing Service, New York, New York 10017 (800) 253-9646; *Statistical Yearbook.*

Times Books, 201 East 50th Street, New York, New York 10022 (212) 751-2600; *The Economist Book of Vital World Statistics*.

World Tourism Organization, Calle Capitan Haya 42, E-28020 Madrid, Spain; *Yearbook of Tourism Statistics*.

SPAIN - TRACTORS IN USE

European Community Information Service, 2100 M Street, NW, Washington, D.C. 20037 (202) 862-9500; *Transport Annual Statistics*.

SPAIN - TRADE

Euromonitor Publications Limited, 87-88 Turnmill Street, London EC1M 5QU, England; *European Marketing Data and Statistics*.

Food and Agricultural Organization of the United Nations (FAO) Via delle Terme di Caracalla, 00100 Rome, Italy (Telephone Number in U.S. (202) 653-2400); *The State of Food and Agriculture*.

International Iron and Steel Institute, 120, rue Colonel Bourg, B-1140, Brussels, Belgium; *Steel Statistical Yearbook*.

Organisation for Economic Co-operation and Development (OECD), 2 rue Andre-Pascal, 75 Paris 16, France (Telephone Number in U.S. (202) 785-6323); *Economic Outlook, The Footwear, Raw Hides and Skins, and Leather Industry in OECD Countries*, and *Foreign Trade by Commodities*, and *Maritime Transport*.

World Bureau of Metal Statistics, 27-A High Street, Ware Hert SG12 9BA, England; *World Metal Statistics*.

SPAIN - TRADEMARKS AND SERVICE MARKS

Statistical Office of the United Nations, Publishing Service, New York, New York 10017 (800) 253-9646; *Statistical Yearbook*.

World Intellectual Property Organization, 34 Chemin des Colombettes, CH-1211 Geneva 20, Switzerland; *Industrial Property Statistics*.

SPAIN - TRANSPORTATION AND COMMUNICATIONS

European Community Information Service, 2100 M Street, NW, Washington, D.C. 20037 (202) 862-9500; *Basic Statistics of the Community, Energy Statistics Yearbook, Regions: Statistical Yearbook*, and *Transport Annual Statistics*.

Facts on File, 460 Park Avenue South, New York, New York 10016 (800) 443-8323; *The New Book of World Rankings*.

Federal Statistical Office, Gustav-Stresemann-Ring 11, D-6200 Wiesbaden, Germany; *Spain*.

G.K. Hall and Company, 70 Lincoln Street, Boston, Massachusetts 02111 (617) 423-3990; *The World in Figures*.

SPAIN - UNEMPLOYMENT

Euromonitor Publications Limited, 87-88 Turnmill Street, London EC1M 5QU, England; *European Marketing Data and Statistics*.

European Community Information Service, 2100 M Street, NW, Washington, D.C. 20037 (202) 862-9500; *Basic Statistics of the Community, Employment and Unemployment, Eurostatistics: Data for Short-Term Economic Analysis, Labor Force Sample Survey*, and *Regions: Statistical Yearbook*.

International Labour Office, I.L.O. Publications, CH-1211, Geneva 22, Switzerland; *Yearbook of Labour Statistics*.

Organisation for Economic Co-operation and Development (OECD), 2 rue Andre-Pascal, 75 Paris 16, France (Telephone Number in U.S. (202) 785-6323); *Economic Outlook, OECD Economic Surveys: Spain*, and *OECD Employment Outlook*.

Statistical Office of the United Nations, Publishing Service, New York, New York 10017 (800) 253-9646; *Statistical Yearbook*.

SPAIN - VITAL STATISTICS

European Community Information Service, 2100 M Street, NW, Washington, D.C. 20037 (202) 862-9500; *Basic Statistics of the Community*.

G.K. Hall and Company, 70 Lincoln Street, Boston, Massachusetts 02111 (617) 423-3990; *The World in Figures*.

Statistical Office of the United Nations, Publishing Service, New York, New York 10017 (800) 253-9646; *Statistical Yearbook*.

World Health Organization, Office of Publications, Avenue Appia, CH-1211 Geneva 27, Switzerland (Telephone Number in U.S. (518) 436-9686); *World Health Statistics Annual*.

SPAIN - WAGES

Euromonitor Publications Limited, 87-88 Turnmill Street, London EC1M 5QU, England; *European Marketing Data and Statistics*.

European Community Information Service, 2100 M Street, NW, Washington, D.C. 20037 (202) 862-9500; *Basic Statistics of the Community, Earnings in Agriculture*, and *Eurostatistics: Data for Short-Term Economic Analysis*.

Federal Statistical Office, Gustav-Stresemann-Ring 11, D-6200 Wiesbaden, Germany; *Spain*.

G.K. Hall and Company, 70 Lincoln Street, Boston, Massachusetts 02111 (617) 423-3990; *The World in Figures*.

International Labour Office, I.L.O. Publications, CH-1211, Geneva 22, Switzerland; *Yearbook of Labour Statistics*.

Organisation for Economic Co-operation and Development (OECD), 2 rue Andre-Pascal, 75 Paris 16, France (Telephone Number in U.S. (202) 785-6323); *Economic Outlook, Industrial Structure Statistics*, and *Main Economic Indicators - Historical Statistics*.

Statistical Office of the United Nations, Publishing Service, New York, New York 10017 (800) 253-9646; *Statistical Yearbook*.

SPAIN - WATERWAYS IN USE

European Community Information Service, 2100 M Street, NW, Washington, D.C. 20037 (202) 862-9500; *Basic Statistics of the Community*, and *Transport Annual Statistics*.

Organisation for Economic Co-operation and Development (OECD), 2 rue Andre-Pascal, 75 Paris 16, France (Telephone Number in U.S. (202) 785-6323); *Maritime Transport*.

SPAIN - WEATHER

Facts on File, 460 Park Avenue South, New York, New York 10016 (800) 443-8323; *The New Book of World Rankings*.

SPAIN - WELFARE

European Community Information Service, 2100 M Street, NW, Washington, D.C. 20037 (202) 862-9500; *Basic Statistics of the Community*.

International Monetary Fund, 700 Nineteenth Street, NW, Washington, D.C. 20431 (202) 623-7000; *Government Finance Statistics Yearbook*.

SPAIN - WHALES - See SPAIN - FISHERIES

SPAIN - WHEAT PRODUCTION AND PRICES - See SPAIN - CROPS

SPAIN - WHOLESALE PRICES

European Community Information Service, 2100 M Street, NW, Washington, D.C. 20037 (202) 862-9500; *Basic Statistics of the Community*.

SPAIN - WINE PRODUCTION

European Community Information Service, 2100 M Street, NW, Washington, D.C. 20037 (202) 862-9500; *Basic Statistics of the Community*.

Facts on File, 460 Park Avenue South, New York, New York 10016 (800) 443-8323; *The New Book of World Rankings*.

Statistical Office of the United Nations, Publishing Service, New York, New York 10017 (800) 253-9646; *Statistical Yearbook*.

SPAIN - WOOD AND WOOD PULP - See SPAIN - FORESTRY AND FOREST PRODUCTS

SPAIN - WOOL

Facts on File, 460 Park Avenue South, New York, New York 10016 (800) 443-8323; *The New Book of World Rankings*.

Organisation for Economic Co-operation and Development (OECD), 2 rue Andre-Pascal, 75 Paris 16, France (Telephone Number in U.S. (202) 785-6323; *Economic Accounts for Agriculture*, and *Textile Industry in OECD Countries*.

Statistical Office of the United Nations, Publishing Service, New York, New York 10017 (800) 253-9646; *Statistical Yearbook*.

SPAIN - YARN PRODUCTION

Organisation for Economic Co-operation and Development (OECD), 2 rue Andre-Pascal, 75 Paris 16, France (Telephone Number in U.S. (202) 785-6323); *Foreign Trade by Commodities*, and *Textile Industry in OECD Countries*.

Statistical Office of the United Nations, Publishing Service, New York, New York 10017 (800) 253-9646; *Statistical Yearbook*.

SPAIN - ZINC AND ZINC ORE PRODUCTION AND CONSUMPTION - See SPAIN - MINING AND MINERAL PRODUCTS

SPAIN - ZOOS AND BOTANICAL GARDENS

United Nations Educational, Scientific and Cultural Organization (UNESCO), 7 Place de Fontenoy, F-75700 Paris, France (Telephone Number in U.S. (212) 963-5981); *Statistical Yearbook*.

SPANISH AMERICAN WAR - COST

U.S. Congress, Joint Economic Committee, The Capitol, Washington, D.C. 20510; *The Military Budget and National Economic Priorities*, (statement of James L. Clayton); subsequently revised and updated by James L. Clayton, University of Utah, Salt Lake City, Utah

SPICES - IMPORTS

U.S. Department of Agriculture, Economic Research Service, Fourteenth Street and Independence Avenue, SW, Washington, D.C. 20005-4789 (202) 219-1504; *Foreign Agricultural Trade of the United States*.

U.S. Department of Commerce, Bureau of the Census, Suitland, Maryland 20233 (301) 763-4040; *U.S. Imports for Consumption*.

SPORTING AND ATHLETIC GOODS - See also SPORTS

National Sporting Goods Association, Lake Center Plaza Building, 1699 Wall Street, Mount Prospect, Illinois 60056-5780 (708) 439-4000; *The Sporting Goods Market in 1993*.

U.S. Department of Commerce, Bureau of the Census, Suitland, Maryland 20233 (301) 763-4040; *Census of Retail Trade*, and *U.S. Merchandise Trade*.

SPORTING GOODS AND BICYCLE SHOPS - RETAIL

U.S. Department of Commerce, Bureau of the Census, Suitland, Maryland 20233 (301) 763-4040; *County Business Patterns*, and *Census of Retail Trade*.

SPORTS

Amateur Softball Association, 2801 NE 50th Street, Oklahoma City, Oklahoma 73111-7203 (405) 424-5266.

American Bowling Congress, 5301 South 76th Street, Greendale, Wisconsin 53129 (414) 421-6400.

The American League of Professional Baseball Clubs, 350 Park Avenue, New York, New York 10022 (212) 339-7600; *American League Red Book*.

Association of Racing Commissioners International, Incorporated, 4067 Iron Works Pike, Lexington, Kentucky 40511 (606) 254-4060.

Bicycle Manufactures Association of America, Incorporated, 3050 K Street, NW, Suite 400, Washington, D.C. 20007 (202) 944-9297.

Major League Baseball Players Association, 805 Third Avenue, New York, New York 10022 (212) 826-0808.

National Basketball Association, 645 Fifth Avenue, Tenth, New York, New York 10022 (212) 826-7000.

National Collegiate Athletic Association, 6201 College Boulevard, Overland Park, Kansas 66211 (913) 339-1906.

National Football League, 410 Park Avenue, New York, New York 10022 (212) 758-1500.

National Golf Foundation, 1150 South U.S. Highway One, Jupiter, Florida 33477 (407) 744-6006.

National Hockey League, 1800 McGill College Avenue, Suite 2600, Montreal, Quebec, Canada H3A 3J6 (514) 288-9220.

The National League of Professional Baseball Clubs, 350 Park Avenue, Eighteenth Floor, New York, New York 10022 (212) 339-7700; *National League Green Book*.

National Sporting Goods Association, Lake Center Plaza Building, 1699 Wall Street, Mount Prospect, Illinois 60056-5780 (708) 439-4000; *Sports Participation in 1992: Series I*.

Professional Rodeo Cowboys Association, 101 Prorodeo Drive, Colorado Springs, Colorado 80910 (719) 593-8840; *Official Professional Rodeo Media Guide*.

U.S. Department of Agriculture, Forest Service, Fourteenth Street and Independence Avenue, SW, Washington, D.C. 20250 (202) 720-3760; unpublished data.

SPORTS - EXPENDITURES

National Sporting Goods Association, Lake Center Plaza Building, 1699 Wall Street, Mount Prospect, Illinois 60056-5780 ('708) 439-4000; *The Sporting Goods Market in 1993*.

U.S. Department of Commerce, Bureau of Economic Analysis, Fourteenth Street between Constitution Avenue and E Street, NW, Washington, D.C. 20230 (202) 606-9900; *The National Income and Product Accounts of the United States*, and *Survey of Current Business*.

SPORTS ASSOCIATIONS

Gale Research Incorporated, 835 Penobscot Building, Detroit, Michigan 48226 (800) 877-4253; *Encyclopedia of Associations*.

SPOT MARKET PRICE INDEX

Commodity Research Bureau, Incorporated, 75 Wall Street, New York, New York 10005 (212) 504-7754; *Commodity Index Report*.

SQUID

U.S. Department of Commerce, National Oceanic and Atmospheric Administration, National Marine Fisheries Service, 1335 East-West Highway, Silver Spring, Maryland 20910 (301) 427-2239; *Fisheries of the United States*, and *Fishery Statistics of the United States*.

Sri Lanka - National Statistical Office

The Director, Department of Census and Statistics, No. 6 Albert Crescent, Colombo 7, Sri Lanka.

Sri Lanka - Primary Statistics Sources

Department of Census and Statistics, No. 6, Albert Crescent, Colombo 7, Sri Lanka; *Statistical Abstract of the Democratic Socialist Republic of Sri Lanka, Statistical Pocketbook of the Democratic Socialist Republic of Sri Lanka*, and *Sri Lanka Yearbook*.

SRI LANKA - AGRICULTURE

Asian Development Bank, P.O. Box 789, 1099 Manila, Philippines; *Key Indicators of Developing Asian and Pacific Countries*.

Euromonitor Publications Limited, 87-88 Turnmill Street, London EC1M 5QU, England; *International Marketing Data and Statistics*.

Facts on File, 460 Park Avenue South, New York, New York 10016 (800) 443-8323; *The New Book of World Rankings*.

Federal Statistical Office, Gustav-Stresemann-Ring 11, D-6200 Wiesbaden, Germany; *Sri Lanka*.

Food and Agricultural Organization of the United Nations (FAO) Via delle Terme di Caracalla, 00100 Rome, Italy (Telephone Number in U.S. (202) 653-2400); *Production Yearbook, The State of Food and Agriculture*, and *Trade Yearbook*.

G.K. Hall and Company, 70 Lincoln Street, Boston, Massachusetts 02111 (617) 423-3990; *The World in Figures*.

Statistical Office of the United Nations, Publishing Service, New York, New York 10017 (800) 253-9646; *Statistical Yearbook*, and *Statistical Yearbook for Asia and the Pacific*.

Times Books, 201 East 50th Street, New York, New York 10022 (212) 751-2600; *The Economist Book of Vital World Statistics*.

The World Bank, 1818 H Street, NW, Washington, D.C. 20433 (202) 477-1234; *World Tables*.

SRI LANKA - AIRLINE SERVICE

The Economist Intelligence Unit (Asia) Limited, 10th Floor, Luk Kwok Centre, 72 Gloucester Road, Wanchai, Hong Kong (Phone Number in U.S. (800) 938-4685); *Asian Market Atlas*.

Facts on File, 460 Park Avenue South, New York, New York 10016 (800) 443-8323; *The New Book of World Rankings*.

G.K. Hall and Company, 70 Lincoln Street, Boston, Massachusetts 02111 (617) 423-3990; *The World in Figures*.

International Civil Aviation Organization, 1000 Sherbrooke Street West, Suite 400, Montreal, Quebec, Canada H3A 2R2 (514) 285-8219; *Civil Aviation Statistics of the World*.

Statistical Office of the United Nations, Publishing Service, New York, New York 10017 (800) 253-9646; *Statistical Yearbook*.

Times Books, 201 East 50th Street, New York, New York 10022 (212) 751-2600; *The Economist Book of Vital World Statistics*.

SRI LANKA - ALUMINUM PRODUCTION AND CONSUMPTION - See SRI LANKA - MINING AND MINERAL PRODUCTS

SRI LANKA - ANIMAL HEALTH

Food and Agricultural Organization of the United Nations (FAO), Via delle Terme di Caracalla, 00100, Rome, Italy (Telephone Number in U.S. (202) 653-2400); *Animal Health Yearbook*.

SRI LANKA - AREA AND DENSITY OF POPULATION

Euromonitor Publications Limited, 87-88 Turnmill Street, London EC1M 5QU, England; *International Marketing Data and Statistics*.

Facts on File, 460 Park Avenue South, New York, New York 10016 (800) 443-8323; *The New Book of World Rankings*.

Federal Statistical Office, Gustav-Stresemann-Ring 11, D-6200 Wiesbaden, Germany; *Sri Lanka*.

Food and Agricultural Organization of the United Nations (FAO) Via delle Terme di Caracalla, 00100 Rome, Italy (Telephone Number in U.S. (202) 653-2400); *The State of Food and Agriculture*.

G.K. Hall and Company, 70 Lincoln Street, Boston, Massachusetts 02111 (617) 423-3990; *The World in Figures*.

Statistical Office of the United Nations, Publishing Service, New York, New York 10017 (800) 253-9646; *Statistical Yearbook.*

Times Books, 201 East 50th Street, New York, New York 10022 (212) 751-2600; *The Economist Book of Vital World Statistics.*

United Nations Educational, Scientific and Cultural Organization (UNESCO), 7 Place de Fontenoy, F-75700 Paris, France (Telephone Number in U.S. (212) 963-5981); *Statistical Yearbook.*

SRI LANKA - ARMS EXPORTS AND IMPORTS

U.S. Arms Control and Disarmament Agency, 320 Twenty-first Street, NW, Washington, D.C. 20451 (202) 647-8677; *World Military Expenditures and Arms Transfers.*

SRI LANKA - BALANCE OF PAYMENTS

The Economist Intelligence Unit, 111 West 57th Street, New York, New York 10019 (800) 938-4685; *The World Market Atlas.*

Federal Statistical Office, Gustav-Stresemann-Ring 11, D-6200 Wiesbaden, Germany; *Sri Lanka.*

G.K. Hall and Company, 70 Lincoln Street, Boston, Massachusetts 02111 (617) 423-3990; *The World in Figures.*

International Monetary Fund, 700 Nineteenth Street, NW, Washington, D.C. 20431 (202) 623-7000; *Balance of Payments Yearbook,* and *International Financial Statistics.*

Times Books, 201 East 50th Street, New York, New York 10022 (212) 751-2600; *The Economist Book of Vital World Statistics.*

The World Bank, 1818 H Street, NW, Washington, D.C. 20433 (202) 477-1234; *World Tables.*

SRI LANKA - BANKING

Asian Development Bank, P.O. Box 789, 1099 Manila, Philippines; *Key Indicators of Developing Asian and Pacific Countries.*

Facts on File, 460 Park Avenue South, New York, New York 10016 (800) 443-8323; *The New Book of World Rankings.*

G.K. Hall and Company, 70 Lincoln Street, Boston, Massachusetts 02111 (617) 423-3990; *The World in Figures.*

International Monetary Fund, 700 Nineteenth Street, NW, Washington, D.C. 20431 (202) 623-7000; *Government Finance Statistics Yearbook,* and *International Financial Statistics.*

Statistical Office of the United Nations, Publishing Service, New York, New York 10017 (800) 253-9646; *Statistical Yearbook.*

SRI LANKA - BARLEY PRODUCTION - See SRI LANKA - CROPS

SRI LANKA - BEER PRODUCTION

Facts on File, 460 Park Avenue South, New York, New York 10016 (800) 443-8323; *The New Book of World Rankings.*

Statistical Office of the United Nations, Publishing Service, New York, New York 10017 (800) 253-9646; *Statistical Yearbook.*

SRI LANKA - BIRTH RATES

The Economist Intelligence Unit (Asia) Limited, 10th Floor, Luk Kwok Centre, 72 Gloucester Road, Wanchai, Hong Kong (Phone

Number in U.S. (800) 938-4685); *Asian Market Atlas.*

Facts on File, 460 Park Avenue South, New York, New York 10016 (800) 443-8323; *The New Book of World Rankings.*

Statistical Office of the United Nations, Publishing Service, New York, New York 10017 (800) 253-9646; *Demographic Yearbook,* and *Statistical Yearbook.*

Times Books, 201 East 50th Street, New York, New York 10022 (212) 751-2600; *The Economist Book of Vital World Statistics.*

The World Bank, 1818 H Street, NW, Washington, D.C. 20433 (202) 477-1234; *World Tables.*

World Health Organization, Office of Publications, Avenue Appia, CH-1211 Geneva 27, Switzerland (Telephone Number in U.S. (518) 436-9686); *World Health Statistics Annual.*

SRI LANKA - BONDS

Asian Development Bank, P.O. Box 789, 1099 Manila, Philippines; *Key Indicators of Developing Asian and Pacific Countries.*

G.K. Hall and Company, 70 Lincoln Street, Boston, Massachusetts 02111 (617) 423-3990; *The World in Figures.*

International Monetary Fund, 700 Nineteenth Street, NW, Washington, D.C. 20431 (202) 623-7000; *Government Finance Statistics Yearbook.*

Statistical Office of the United Nations, Publishing Service, New York, New York 10017 (800) 253-9646; *Statistical Yearbook.*

SRI LANKA - BOOK PRODUCTION

G.K. Hall and Company, 70 Lincoln Street, Boston, Massachusetts 02111 (617) 423-3990; *The World in Figures.*

United Nations Educational, Scientific and Cultural Organization (UNESCO), 7 Place de Fontenoy, F-75700 Paris, France (Telephone Number in U.S. (212) 963-5981); *Statistical Yearbook.*

SRI LANKA - BROADCASTING

Billboard Limited, P.O. Box 9027, 1006 AA Amsterdam, The Netherlands (Telephone Number in U.S. (212) 764-7300); *World Radio TV Handbook.*

Facts on File, 460 Park Avenue South, New York, New York 10016 (800) 443-8323; *The New Book of World Rankings.*

G.K. Hall and Company, 70 Lincoln Street, Boston, Massachusetts 02111 (617) 423-3990; *The World in Figures.*

Times Books, 201 East 50th Street, New York, New York 10022 (212) 751-2600; *The Economist Book of Vital World Statistics.*

United Nations Educational, Scientific and Cultural Organization (UNESCO), 7 Place de Fontenoy, F-75700 Paris, France (Telephone Number in U.S. (212) 963-5981); *Statistical Yearbook.*

SRI LANKA - BUSINESS

G.K. Hall and Company, 70 Lincoln Street, Boston, Massachusetts 02111 (617) 423-3990; *The World in Figures.*

SRI LANKA - BUSINESS AND PROFESSIONAL LICENSES

International Monetary Fund, 700 Nineteenth Street, NW, Washington, D.C. 20431 (202) 623-7000; *Government Finance Statistics Yearbook.*

SRI LANKA - CALORIE SUPPLY

Asian Development Bank, P.O. Box 789, 1099 Manila, Philippines; *Key Indicators of Developing Asian and Pacific Countries.*

Food and Agricultural Organization of the United Nations (FAO) Via delle Terme di Caracalla, 00100 Rome, Italy (Telephone Number in U.S. (202) 653-2400); *The State of Food and Agriculture.*

SRI LANKA - CAPITAL INVESTMENT

Asian Development Bank, P.O. Box 789, 1099 Manila, Philippines; *Key Indicators of Developing Asian and Pacific Countries.*

SRI LANKA - CAPITAL REVENUE

Asian Development Bank, P.O. Box 789, 1099 Manila, Philippines; *Key Indicators of Developing Asian and Pacific Countries.*

International Monetary Fund, 700 Nineteenth Street, NW, Washington, D.C. 20431 (202) 623-7000; *Government Finance Statistics Yearbook.*

SRI LANKA - CATTLE - See SRI LANKA - LIVESTOCK AND POULTRY

SRI LANKA - CAUSTIC SODA PRODUCTION

Statistical Office of the United Nations, Publishing Service, New York, New York 10017 (800) 253-9646; *Statistical Yearbook.*

SRI LANKA - CEMENT PRODUCTION - See SRI LANKA - MINING AND MINERAL PRODUCTS

SRI LANKA - CHEMICAL (ORGANIC) PRODUCTION - See SRI LANKA - MINING AND MINERAL PRODUCTS

SRI LANKA - CHICKENS - See SRI LANKA - LIVESTOCK AND POULTRY

SRI LANKA - CIGAR PRODUCTION - See SRI LANKA - TOBACCO PRODUCTION

SRI LANKA - CIGARETTE PRODUCTION - See SRI LANKA - TOBACCO PRODUCTION

SRI LANKA - CLASS STRUCTURE

G.K. Hall and Company, 70 Lincoln Street, Boston, Massachusetts 02111 (617) 423-3990; *The World in Figures.*

SRI LANKA - CLIMATE

Facts on File, 460 Park Avenue South, New York, New York 10016 (800) 443-8323; *The New Book of World Rankings.*

G.K. Hall and Company, 70 Lincoln Street, Boston, Massachusetts 02111 (617) 423-3990; *The World in Figures.*

SRI LANKA - COAL PRODUCTION - See SRI LANKA - MINING AND MINERAL PRODUCTS

SRI LANKA - COCOA (BEANS) PRODUCTION - See SRI LANKA - CROPS

SRI LANKA - COCONUT PRODUCTS EXPORTS - See SRI LANKA - CROPS

SRI LANKA - COFFEE PRODUCTION AND CONSUMPTION - See SRI LANKA - CROPS

SRI LANKA - COMMUNICATIONS

Federal Statistical Office, Gustav-Stresemann-Ring 11, D-6200 Wiesbaden, Germany; *Sri Lanka.*

G.K. Hall and Company, 70 Lincoln Street, Boston, Massachusetts 02111 (617) 423-3990; *The World in Figures.*

Statistical Office of the United Nations, Publishing Service, New York, New York 10017 (800) 253-9646; *Statistical Yearbook for Asia and the Pacific.*

SRI LANKA - CONSTRUCTION INDUSTRY

Facts on File, 460 Park Avenue South, New York, New York 10016 (800) 443-8323; *The New Book of World Rankings.*

Statistical Office of the United Nations, Publishing Service, New York, New York 10017 (800) 253-9646; *Statistical Yearbook,* and *Construction Statistics Yearbook.*

SRI LANKA - CONSUMER PRICE INDEX

Asian Development Bank, P.O. Box 789, 1099 Manila, Philippines; *Key Indicators of Developing Asian and Pacific Countries.*

G.K. Hall and Company, 70 Lincoln Street, Boston, Massachusetts 02111 (617) 423-3990; *The World in Figures.*

Statistical Office of the United Nations, Publishing Service, New York, New York 10017 (800) 253-9646; *Statistical Yearbook.*

SRI LANKA - CONSUMER PRICES

International Labour Office, I.L.O. Publications, CH-1211, Geneva 22, Switzerland; *Yearbook of Labour Statistics.*

International Monetary Fund, 700 Nineteenth Street, NW, Washington, D.C. 20431 (202) 623-7000; *International Financial Statistics.*

Times Books, 201 East 50th Street, New York, New York 10022 (212) 751-2600; *The Economist Book of Vital World Statistics.*

SRI LANKA - CONSUMPTION

G.K. Hall and Company, 70 Lincoln Street, Boston, Massachusetts 02111 (617) 423-3990; *The World in Figures.*

International Rubber Study Group, York House, Eighth Floor, Empire Way, Wembley, London HA9 0PA, England; *Rubber Statistical Handbook.*

SRI LANKA - COPPER PRODUCTION AND CONSUMPTION

Facts on File, 460 Park Avenue South, New York, New York 10016 (800) 443-8323; *The New Book of World Rankings.*

SRI LANKA - CORN PRODUCTION - See SRI LANKA - CROPS

SRI LANKA - CORPORATE TAXES - See SRI LANKA - TAXATION

SRI LANKA - COTTON - See SRI LANKA - CROPS

SRI LANKA - CRIME

International Criminal Police Organization (INTERPOL), 26 rue Armengaud, 92210 Saint Cloud, France; *International Crime Statistics.*

Yale University Press, Yale Station, New Haven, Connecticut 06520 (203) 432-0940; *Violence and Crime in Cross-National Perspective.*

SRI LANKA - CROPS

Asian Development Bank, P.O. Box 789, 1099 Manila, Philippines; *Key Indicators of Developing Asian and Pacific Countries.*

Commodity Research Bureau, Incorporated, 75 Wall Street, New York, New York 10005 (212) 504-7754; *Commodity Year Book.*

Facts on File, 460 Park Avenue South, New York, New York 10016 (800) 443-8323; *The New Book of World Rankings.*

Food and Agricultural Organization of the United Nations (FAO) Via delle Terme di Caracalla, 00100 Rome, Italy (Telephone Number in U.S. (202) 653-2400); *The State of Food and Agriculture.*

G.K. Hall and Company, 70 Lincoln Street, Boston, Massachusetts 02111 (617) 423-3990; *The World in Figures.*

International Monetary Fund, 700 Nineteenth Street, NW, Washington, D.C. 20431 (202) 623-7000; *International Financial Statistics.*

Statistical Office of the United Nations, Publishing Service, New York, New York 10017 (800) 253-9646; *Statistical Yearbook.*

SRI LANKA - CUSTOMS DUTIES

G.K. Hall and Company, 70 Lincoln Street, Boston, Massachusetts 02111 (617) 423-3990; *The World in Figures.*

International Monetary Fund, 700 Nineteenth Street, NW, Washington, D.C. 20431 (202) 623-7000; *Government Finance Statistics Yearbook.*

SRI LANKA - DAIRY PRODUCTS

Facts on File, 460 Park Avenue South, New York, New York 10016 (800) 443-8323; *The New Book of World Rankings.*

Food and Agricultural Organization of the United Nations (FAO) Via delle Terme di Caracalla, 00100 Rome, Italy (Telephone Number in U.S. (202) 653-2400); *The State of Food and Agriculture.*

Statistical Office of the United Nations, Publishing Service, New York, New York 10017 (800) 253-9646; *Statistical Yearbook.*

SRI LANKA - DEATH RATES

The Economist Intelligence Unit (Asia) Limited, 10th Floor, Luk Kwok Centre, 72 Gloucester Road, Wanchai, Hong Kong (Phone Number in U.S. (800) 938-4685); *Asian Market Atlas.*

G.K. Hall and Company, 70 Lincoln Street, Boston, Massachusetts 02111 (617) 423-3990; *The World in Figures.*

Statistical Office of the United Nations, Publishing Service, New York, New York 10017 (800) 253-9646; *Statistical Yearbook.*

Times Books, 201 East 50th Street, New York, New York 10022 (212) 751-2600; *The Economist Book of Vital World Statistics.*

World Health Organization, Office of Publications, Avenue Appia, CH-1211 Geneva 27, Switzerland (Telephone Number in U.S. (518) 436-9686); *World Health Statistics Annual.*

SRI LANKA - DEFENSE EXPENDITURES

G.K. Hall and Company, 70 Lincoln Street, Boston, Massachusetts 02111 (617) 423-3990; *The World in Figures.*

International Monetary Fund, 700 Nineteenth Street, NW, Washington, D.C. 20431 (202) 623-7000; *Government Finance Statistics Yearbook.*

U.S. Arms Control and Disarmament Agency, 320 Twenty-first Street, NW, Washington, D.C. 20451 (202) 647-8677; *World Military Expenditures and Arms Transfers.*

SRI LANKA - DEMOGRAPHY

The Economist Intelligence Unit, 111 West 57th Street, New York, New York 10019 (800) 938-4685; *The World Market Atlas.*

The Economist Intelligence Unit (Asia) Limited, 10th Floor, Luk Kwok Centre, 72 Gloucester Road, Wanchai, Hong Kong (Phone Number in U.S. (800) 938-4685); *Asian Market Atlas.*

Facts on File, 460 Park Avenue South, New York, New York 10016 (800) 443-8323; *The New Book of World Rankings.*

G.K. Hall and Company, 70 Lincoln Street, Boston, Massachusetts 02111 (617) 423-3990; *The World in Figures.*

SRI LANKA - DEVELOPMENT ASSISTANCE

Asian Development Bank, P.O. Box 789, 1099 Manila, Philippines; *Key Indicators of Developing Asian and Pacific Countries.*

G.K. Hall and Company, 70 Lincoln Street, Boston, Massachusetts 02111 (617) 423-3990; *The World in Figures.*

Statistical Office of the United Nations, Publishing Service, New York, New York 10017 (800) 253-9646; *Statistical Yearbook.*

SRI LANKA - DIAMOND PRODUCTION - See SRI LANKA - MINING AND MINERAL PRODUCTS

SRI LANKA - DISCOUNT RATES

Statistical Office of the United Nations, Publishing Service, New York, New York 10017 (800) 253-9646; *Statistical Yearbook.*

SRI LANKA - DISEASES

G.K. Hall and Company, 70 Lincoln Street, Boston, Massachusetts 02111 (617) 423-3990; *The World in Figures.*

World Health Organization, Office of Publications, Avenue Appia, CH-1211 Geneva 27, Switzerland (Telephone Number in U.S. (518) 436-9686); *World Health Statistics Annual.*

SRI LANKA - DIVORCE RATES

Facts on File, 460 Park Avenue South, New York, New York 10016 (800) 443-8323; *The New Book of World Rankings.*

Statistical Office of the United Nations, Publishing Service, New York, New York 10017 (800) 253-9646; *Demographic Yearbook*, and *Statistical Yearbook.*

SRI LANKA - DOMESTIC PRODUCT

G.K. Hall and Company, 70 Lincoln Street, Boston, Massachusetts 02111 (617) 423-3990; *The World in Figures.*

SRI LANKA - ECONOMY

Asian Development Bank, P.O. Box 789, 1099 Manila, Philippines; *Key Indicators of Developing Asian and Pacific Countries.*

Euromonitor Publications Limited, 87-88 Turnmill Street, London EC1M 5QU, England; *International Marketing Data and Statistics.*

Facts on File, 460 Park Avenue South, New York, New York 10016 (800) 443-8323; *The New Book of World Rankings.*

G.K. Hall and Company, 70 Lincoln Street, Boston, Massachusetts 02111 (617) 423-3990; *The World in Figures.*

SRI LANKA - EDUCATION

The Economist Intelligence Unit, 111 West 57th Street, New York, New York 10019 (800) 938-4685; *The World Market Atlas.*

The Economist Intelligence Unit (Asia) Limited, 10th Floor, Luk Kwok Centre, 72 Gloucester Road, Wanchai, Hong Kong (Phone Number in U.S. (800) 938-4685); *Asian Market Atlas.*

Facts on File, 460 Park Avenue South, New York, New York 10016 (800) 443-8323; *The New Book of World Rankings.*

Federal Statistical Office, Gustav-Stresemann-Ring 11, D-6200 Wiesbaden, Germany; *Sri Lanka.*

G.K. Hall and Company, 70 Lincoln Street, Boston, Massachusetts 02111 (617) 423-3990; *The World in Figures.*

International Monetary Fund, 700 Nineteenth Street, NW, Washington, D.C. 20431 (202) 623-7000; *Government Finance Statistics Yearbook.*

Statistical Office of the United Nations, Publishing Service, New York, New York 10017 (800) 253-9646; *Statistical Yearbook for Asia and the Pacific.*

Times Books, 201 East 50th Street, New York, New York 10022 (212) 751-2600; *The Economist Book of Vital World Statistics.*

United Nations Educational, Scientific and Cultural Organization (UNESCO), 7 Place de Fontenoy, F-75700 Paris, France (Telephone Number in U.S. (212) 963-5981); *Statistical Yearbook.*

The World Bank, 1818 H Street, NW, Washington, D.C. 20433 (202) 477-1234; *World Tables.*

SRI LANKA - EGG PRODUCTION AND CONSUMPTION - See SRI LANKA - DAIRY PRODUCTS

SRI LANKA - ELECTRICITY

Asian Development Bank, P.O. Box 789, 1099 Manila, Philippines; *Key Indicators of Developing Asian and Pacific Countries.*

Facts on File, 460 Park Avenue South, New York, New York 10016 (800) 443-8323; *The New Book of World Rankings.*

Statistical Office of the United Nations, Publishing Service, New York, New York 10017 (800) 253-9646; *Electric Power in Asia and the Pacific,* and *Statistical Yearbook.*

Times Books, 201 East 50th Street, New York, New York 10022 (212) 751-2600; *The Economist Book of Vital World Statistics.*

SRI LANKA - EMPLOYMENT

Euromonitor Publications Limited, 87-88 Turnmill Street, London EC1M 5QU, England; *International Marketing Data and Statistics.*

Facts on File, 460 Park Avenue South, New York, New York 10016 (800) 443-8323; *The New Book of World Rankings.*

Federal Statistical Office, Gustav-Stresemann-Ring 11, D-6200 Wiesbaden, Germany; *Sri Lanka.*

International Labour Office, I.L.O. Publications, CH-1211, Geneva 22, Switzerland; *Yearbook of Labour Statistics.*

Statistical Office of the United Nations, Publishing Service, New York, New York 10017 (800) 253-9646; *Statistical Yearbook.*

SRI LANKA - ENERGY

Facts on File, 460 Park Avenue South, New York, New York 10016 (800) 443-8323; *The New Book of World Rankings.*

Food and Agricultural Organization of the United Nations (FAO) Via delle Terme di Caracalla, 00100 Rome, Italy (Telephone Number in U.S. (202) 653-2400); *The State of Food and Agriculture.*

G.K. Hall and Company, 70 Lincoln Street, Boston, Massachusetts 02111 (617) 423-3990; *The World in Figures.*

Statistical Office of the United Nations, Publishing Service, New York, New York 10017 (800) 253-9646; *Energy Statistics Yearbook, Statistical Yearbook,* and *Statistical Yearbook for Asia and the Pacific.*

Times Books, 201 East 50th Street, New York, New York 10022 (212) 751-2600; *The Economist Book of Vital World Statistics.*

SRI LANKA - EXCHANGE RATES

Asian Development Bank, P.O. Box 789, 1099 Manila, Philippines; *Key Indicators of Developing Asian and Pacific Countries.*

The Economist Intelligence Unit (Asia) Limited, 10th Floor, Luk Kwok Centre, 72 Gloucester Road, Wanchai, Hong Kong (Phone Number in U.S. (800) 938-4685); *Asian Market Atlas.*

Euromonitor Publications Limited, 87-88 Turnmill Street, London EC1M 5QU, England; *International Marketing Data and Statistics.*

International Civil Aviation Organization, 1000 Sherbrooke Street West, Suite 400, Montreal, Quebec, Canada H3A 2R2 (514) 285-8219; *Civil Aviation Statistics of the World.*

International Monetary Fund, 700 Nineteenth Street, NW, Washington, D.C. 20431 (202) 623-7000; *International Financial Statistics.*

Statistical Office of the United Nations, Publishing Service, New York, New York 10017 (800) 253-9646; *Statistical Yearbook.*

SRI LANKA - EXCISE TAXES - See SRI LANKA - TAXATION

SRI LANKA - EXPORTS

Asian Development Bank, P.O. Box 789, 1099 Manila, Philippines; *Key Indicators of Developing Asian and Pacific Countries.*

The Economist Intelligence Unit, 111 West 57th Street, New York, New York 10019 (800) 938-4685; *The World Market Atlas*.

The Economist Intelligence Unit (Asia) Limited, 10th Floor, Luk Kwok Centre, 72 Gloucester Road, Wanchai, Hong Kong (Phone Number in U.S. (800) 938-4685); *Asian Market Atlas*.

Euromonitor Publications Limited, 87-88 Turnmill Street, London EC1M 5QU, England; *Again Economic Handbook*, and *International Marketing Data and Statistics*.

Food and Agricultural Organization of the United Nations (FAO) Via delle Terme di Caracalla, 00100 Rome, Italy (Telephone Number in U.S. (202) 653-2400); *The State of Food and Agriculture*.

G.K. Hall and Company, 70 Lincoln Street, Boston, Massachusetts 02111 (617) 423-3990; *The World in Figures*.

International Monetary Fund, 700 Nineteenth Street, NW, Washington, D.C. 20431 (202) 623-7000; *Direction of Trade Statistics, Government Finance Statistics Yearbook*, and *International Financial Statistics*.

International Rubber Study Group, York House, Eighth Floor, Empire Way, Wembley, London HA9 0PA, England; *Rubber Statistical Handbook*.

Statistical Office of the United Nations, Publishing Service, New York, New York 10017 (800) 253-9646; *Foreign Trade Statistics of Asia and the Pacific*.

Times Books, 201 East 50th Street, New York, New York 10022 (212) 751-2600; *The Economist Book of Vital World Statistics*.

The World Bank, 1818 H Street, NW, Washington, D.C. 20433 (202) 477-1234; *World Tables*.

SRI LANKA - EXTERNAL FINANCING

Asian Development Bank, P.O. Box 789, 1099 Manila, Philippines; *Key Indicators of Developing Asian and Pacific Countries*.

SRI LANKA - EXTERNAL INDEBTEDNESS

Asian Development Bank, P.O. Box 789, 1099 Manila, Philippines; *Key Indicators of Developing Asian and Pacific Countries*.

The World Bank, 1818 H Street, NW, Washington, D.C. 20433 (202) 477-1234; *World Tables*.

SRI LANKA - EXTERNAL TRADE

Asian Development Bank, P.O. Box 789, 1099 Manila, Philippines; *Key Indicators of Developing Asian and Pacific Countries*.

Food and Agricultural Organization of the United Nations (FAO) Via delle Terme di Caracalla, 00100 Rome, Italy (Telephone Number in U.S. (202) 653-2400); *The State of Food and Agriculture*, and *Trade Yearbook*.

G.K. Hall and Company, 70 Lincoln Street, Boston, Massachusetts 02111 (617) 423-3990; *The World in Figures*.

Statistical Office of the United Nations, Publishing Service, New York, New York 10017 (800) 253-9646; *Statistical Yearbook*, and *Statistical Yearbook for Asia and the Pacific*.

SRI LANKA - FABRIC PRODUCTION - See SRI LANKA - TEXTILE INDUSTRY

SRI LANKA - FARM CROPS - See SRI LANKA - CROPS

SRI LANKA - FEMALE WORKING POPULATION - See SRI LANKA - EMPLOYMENT

SRI LANKA - FERTILITY RATES

The Economist Intelligence Unit (Asia) Limited, 10th Floor, Luk Kwok Centre, 72 Gloucester Road, Wanchai, Hong Kong (Phone Number in U.S. (800) 938-4685); *Asian Market Atlas*.

Facts on File, 460 Park Avenue South, New York, New York 10016 (800) 443-8323; *The New Book of World Rankings*.

Times Books, 201 East 50th Street, New York, New York 10022 (212) 751-2600; *The Economist Book of Vital World Statistics*.

The World Bank, 1818 H Street, NW, Washington, D.C. 20433 (202) 477-1234; *World Tables*.

SRI LANKA - FERTILIZER

Food and Agricultural Organization of the United Nations (FAO) Via delle Terme di Caracalla, 00100 Rome, Italy (Telephone Number in U.S. (202) 653-2400); *The State of Food and Agriculture*.

Statistical Office of the United Nations, Publishing Service, New York, New York 10017 (800) 253-9646; *Statistical Yearbook*.

SRI LANKA - FETAL MORTALITY

Statistical Office of the United Nations, Publishing Service, New York, New York 10017 (800) 253-9646; *Demographic Yearbook*.

World Health Organization, Office of Publications, Avenue Appia, CH-1211 Geneva 27, Switzerland (Telephone Number in U.S. (518) 436-9686); *World Health Statistics Annual*.

SRI LANKA - FILM - See SRI LANKA - MOTION PICTURES

SRI LANKA - FINANCE

Asian Development Bank, P.O. Box 789, 1099 Manila, Philippines; *Key Indicators of Developing Asian and Pacific Countries*.

Facts on File, 460 Park Avenue South, New York, New York 10016 (800) 443-8323; *The New Book of World Rankings*.

Federal Statistical Office, Gustav-Stresemann-Ring 11, D-6200 Wiesbaden, Germany; *Sri Lanka*.

G.K. Hall and Company, 70 Lincoln Street, Boston, Massachusetts 02111 (617) 423-3990; *The World in Figures*.

International Monetary Fund, 700 Nineteenth Street, NW, Washington, D.C. 20431 (202) 623-7000; *Government Finance Statistics Yearbook*, and *International Financial Statistics*.

Statistical Office of the United Nations, Publishing Service, New York, New York 10017 (800) 253-9646; *Statistical Yearbook for Asia and the Pacific*.

SRI LANKA - FISHERIES

Facts on File, 460 Park Avenue South, New York, New York 10016 (800) 443-8323; *The New Book of World Rankings*.

Federal Statistical Office, Gustav-Stresemann-Ring 11, D-6200 Wiesbaden, Germany; *Sri Lanka*.

Food and Agricultural Organization of the United Nations (FAO) Via delle Terme di Caracalla, 00100 Rome, Italy (Telephone Number in U.S. (202) 653-2400); *The State of Food and Agriculture*, and *Yearbook of Fishery Statistics*.

Statistical Office of the United Nations, Publishing Service, New York, New York 10017 (800) 253-9646; *Statistical Yearbook*.

SRI LANKA - FLOUR PRODUCTION

Statistical Office of the United Nations, Publishing Service, New York, New York 10017 (800) 253-9646; *Statistical Yearbook*.

SRI LANKA - FOOD

Food and Agricultural Organization of the United Nations (FAO), Via delle Terme di Caracalla, 00100 Rome, Italy (Telephone Number in U.S. (202) 653-2400); *Production Yearbook*, and *The State of Food and Agriculture*.

G.K. Hall and Company, 70 Lincoln Street, Boston, Massachusetts 02111 (617) 423-3990; *The World in Figures*.

Statistical Office of the United Nations, Publishing Service, New York, New York 10017 (800) 253-9646; *Statistical Yearbook for Asia and the Pacific*.

SRI LANKA - FOREIGN AID

G.K. Hall and Company, 70 Lincoln Street, Boston, Massachusetts 02111 (617) 423-3990; *The World in Figures*.

SRI LANKA - FOREIGN DEBT

International Monetary Fund, 700 Nineteenth Street, NW, Washington, D.C. 20431 (202) 623-7000; *Government Finance Statistics Yearbook*.

SRI LANKA - FOREIGN TRADE

Asian Development Bank, P.O. Box 789, 1099 Manila, Philippines; *Key Indicators of Developing Asian and Pacific Countries*.

The Economist Intelligence Unit (Asia) Limited, 10th Floor, Luk Kwok Centre, 72 Gloucester Road, Wanchai, Hong Kong (Phone Number in U.S. (800) 938-4685); *Asian Market Atlas*.

Euromonitor Publications Limited, 87-88 Turnmill Street, London EC1M 5QU, England; *International Marketing Data and Statistics*.

Facts on File, 460 Park Avenue South, New York, New York 10016 (800) 443-8323; *The New Book of World Rankings*.

Federal Statistical Office, Gustav-Stresemann-Ring 11, D-6200 Wiesbaden, Germany; *Sri Lanka*.

Food and Agricultural Organization of the United Nations (FAO) Via delle Terme di Caracalla, 00100 Rome, Italy (Telephone Number in U.S. (202) 653-2400); *The State of Food and Agriculture*.

G.K. Hall and Company, 70 Lincoln Street, Boston, Massachusetts 02111 (617) 423-3990; *The World in Figures*.

International Monetary Fund, 700 Nineteenth Street, NW, Washington, D.C. 20431 (202) 623-7000; *International Financial Statistics*.

Statistical Office of the United Nations, Publishing Service, New York, New York 10017 (800) 253-9646; *International Trade Statistics Yearbook*, and *Statistical Yearbook*.

The World Bank, 1818 H Street, NW, Washington, D.C. 20433 (202) 477-1234; *World Tables*.

SRI LANKA - FORESTRY AND FOREST PRODUCTS

The Economist Intelligence Unit (Asia) Limited, 10th Floor, Luk Kwok Centre, 72 Gloucester Road, Wanchai, Hong Kong (Phone Number in U.S. (800) 938-4685); *Asian Market Atlas*.

Facts on File, 460 Park Avenue South, New York, New York 10016 (800) 443-8323; *The New Book of World Rankings*.

Federal Statistical Office, Gustav-Stresemann-Ring 11, D-6200 Wiesbaden, Germany; *Sri Lanka*.

Food and Agricultural Organization of the United Nations (FAO) Via delle Terme di Caracalla, 00100 Rome, Italy (Telephone Number in U.S. (202) 653-2400); *The State of Food and Agriculture*, and *Yearbook of Forest Products*.

G.K. Hall and Company, 70 Lincoln Street, Boston, Massachusetts 02111 (617) 423-3990; *The World in Figures*.

Statistical Office of the United Nations, Publishing Service, New York, New York 10017 (800) 253-9646; *Statistical Yearbook*.

United Nations Educational, Scientific and Cultural Organization (UNESCO), 7 Place de Fontenoy, F-75700 Paris, France (Telephone Number in U.S. (212) 963-5981); *Statistical Yearbook*.

SRI LANKA - GAS PRODUCTION - See SRI LANKA - MINING AND MINERAL PRODUCTS

SRI LANKA - GENERAL INDUSTRIAL STATISTICS

Statistical Office of the United Nations, Publishing Service, New York, New York 10017 (800) 253-9646; *International Trade Statistics Yearbook*.

SRI LANKA - GENERAL MORTALITY

Statistical Office of the United Nations, Publishing Service, New York, New York 10017 (800) 253-9646; *Demographic Yearbook*.

World Health Organization, Office of Publications, Avenue Appia, CH-1211 Geneva 27, Switzerland (Telephone Number in U.S. (518) 436-9686); *World Health Statistics Annual*.

SRI LANKA - GEOGRAPHIC DATA

Facts on File, 460 Park Avenue South, New York, New York 10016 (800) 443-8323; *The New Book of World Rankings*.

SRI LANKA - GOATS - See SRI LANKA - LIVESTOCK AND POULTRY

SRI LANKA - GOLD HOLDINGS

International Monetary Fund, 700 Nineteenth Street, NW, Washington, D.C. 20431 (202) 623-7000; *International Financial Statistics*.

Statistical Office of the United Nations, Publishing Service, New York, New York 10017 (800) 253-9646; *Statistical Yearbook*.

The World Bank, 1818 H Street, NW, Washington, D.C. 20433 (202) 477-1234; *World Tables*.

SRI LANKA - GOLD PRODUCTION AND CONSUMPTION - See SRI LANKA - MINING AND MINERAL PRODUCTS

SRI LANKA - GOVERNMENT

Asian Development Bank, P.O. Box 789, 1099 Manila, Philippines; *Key Indicators of Developing Asian and Pacific Countries.*

G.K. Hall and Company, 70 Lincoln Street, Boston, Massachusetts 02111 (617) 423-3990; *The World in Figures.*

SRI LANKA - GOVERNMENT EXPENDITURES

Asian Development Bank, P.O. Box 789, 1099 Manila, Philippines; *Key Indicators of Developing Asian and Pacific Countries.*

International Monetary Fund, 700 Nineteenth Street, NW, Washington, D.C. 20431 (202) 623-7000; *Government Finance Statistics Yearbook.*

Times Books, 201 East 50th Street, New York, New York 10022 (212) 751-2600; *The Economist Book of Vital World Statistics.*

The World Bank, 1818 H Street, NW, Washington, D.C. 20433 (202) 477-1234; *World Tables.*

SRI LANKA - GOVERNMENT FINANCES

Asian Development Bank, P.O. Box 789, 1099 Manila, Philippines; *Key Indicators of Developing Asian and Pacific Countries.*

International Monetary Fund, 700 Nineteenth Street, NW, Washington, D.C. 20431 (202) 623-7000; *International Financial Statistics.*

Statistical Office of the United Nations, Publishing Service, New York, New York 10017 (800) 253-9646; *Statistical Yearbook.*

SRI LANKA - GOVERNMENT REVENUE

Asian Development Bank, P.O. Box 789, 1099 Manila, Philippines; *Key Indicators of Developing Asian and Pacific Countries.*

International Monetary Fund, 700 Nineteenth Street, NW, Washington, D.C. 20431 (202) 623-7000; *Government Finance Statistics Yearbook.*

Times Books, 201 East 50th Street, New York, New York 10022 (212) 751-2600; *The Economist Book of Vital World Statistics.*

The World Bank, 1818 H Street, NW, Washington, D.C. 20433 (202) 477-1234; *World Tables.*

SRI LANKA - GRAIN PRODUCTION - See SRI LANKA - CROPS

SRI LANKA - GRANTS

International Monetary Fund, 700 Nineteenth Street, NW, Washington, D.C. 20431 (202) 623-7000; *Government Finance Statistics Yearbook.*

SRI LANKA - GROSS DOMESTIC PRODUCT

Asian Development Bank, P.O. Box 789, 1099 Manila, Philippines; *Key Indicators of Developing Asian and Pacific Countries.*

The Economist Intelligence Unit, 111 West 57th Street, New York, New York 10019 (800) 938-4685; *The World Market Atlas.*

The Economist Intelligence Unit (Asia) Limited, 10th Floor, Luk Kwok Centre, 72 Gloucester Road, Wanchai, Hong Kong (Phone Number in U.S. (800) 938-4685); *Asian Market Atlas.*

Euromonitor Publications Limited, 87-88 Turnmill Street, London EC1M 5QU, England; *International Marketing Data and Statistics.*

Facts on File, 460 Park Avenue South, New York, New York 10016 (800) 443-8323; *The New Book of World Rankings.*

G.K. Hall and Company, 70 Lincoln Street, Boston, Massachusetts 02111 (617) 423-3990; *The World in Figures.*

Statistical Office of the United Nations, Publishing Service, New York, New York 10017 (800) 253-9646; *Statistical Yearbook.*

Times Books, 201 East 50th Street, New York, New York 10022 (212) 751-2600; *The Economist Book of Vital World Statistics.*

The World Bank, 1818 H Street, NW, Washington, D.C. 20433 (202) 477-1234; *World Tables.*

SRI LANKA - GROSS NATIONAL PRODUCT

Asian Development Bank, P.O. Box 789, 1099 Manila, Philippines; *Key Indicators of Developing Asian and Pacific Countries.*

Euromonitor Publications Limited, 87-88 Turnmill Street, London EC1M 5QU, England; *International Marketing Data and Statistics.*

U.S. Arms Control and Disarmament Agency, 320 Twenty-first Street, NW, Washington, D.C. 20451 (202) 647-8677; *World Military Expenditures and Arms Transfers.*

The World Bank, 1818 H Street, NW, Washington, D.C. 20433 (202) 477-1234; *World Tables.*

SRI LANKA - GROUNDNUT PRODUCTION - See SRI LANKA - CROPS

SRI LANKA - HEALTH

The Economist Intelligence Unit (Asia) Limited, 10th Floor, Luk Kwok Centre, 72 Gloucester Road, Wanchai, Hong Kong (Phone Number in U.S. (800) 938-4685); *Asian Market Atlas.*

Facts on File, 460 Park Avenue South, New York, New York 10016 (800) 443-8323; *The New Book of World Rankings.*

G.K. Hall and Company, 70 Lincoln Street, Boston, Massachusetts 02111 (617) 423-3990; *The World in Figures.*

Statistical Office of the United Nations, Publishing Service, New York, New York 10017 (800) 253-9646; *Statistical Yearbook.*

Times Books, 201 East 50th Street, New York, New York 10022 (212) 751-2600; *The Economist Book of Vital World Statistics.*

World Health Organization, Office of Publications, Avenue Appia, CH-1211 Geneva 27, Switzerland (Telephone Number in U.S. (518) 436-9686); *World Health Statistics Annual.*

SRI LANKA - HEALTH EXPENDITURES

International Monetary Fund, 700 Nineteenth Street, NW, Washington, D.C. 20431 (202) 623-7000; *Government Finance Statistics Yearbook.*

SRI LANKA - HIGHWAYS

The Economist Intelligence Unit (Asia) Limited, 10th Floor, Luk Kwok Centre, 72 Gloucester Road, Wanchai, Hong Kong (Phone Number in U.S. (800) 938-4685); *Asian Market Atlas*.

G.K. Hall and Company, 70 Lincoln Street, Boston, Massachusetts 02111 (617) 423-3990; *The World in Figures*.

International Road Federation, 525 School Street, SW, Washington, D.C. 20024 (202) 554-2106; *World Road Statistics*.

SRI LANKA - HORSES - See SRI LANKA - LIVESTOCK AND POULTRY

SRI LANKA - HOURS OF WORK - See SRI LANKA - EMPLOYMENT

SRI LANKA - HOUSING EXPENDITURES

Facts on File, 460 Park Avenue South, New York, New York 10016 (800) 443-8323; *The New Book of World Rankings*.

International Monetary Fund, 700 Nineteenth Street, NW, Washington, D.C. 20431 (202) 623-7000; *Government Finance Statistics Yearbook*.

SRI LANKA - HYDROCHLORIC ACID PRODUCTION

Statistical Office of the United Nations, Publishing Service, New York, New York 10017 (800) 253-9646; *Statistical Yearbook*.

SRI LANKA - ILLITERATE POPULATION

The Economist Intelligence Unit, 111 West 57th Street, New York, New York 10019 (800) 938-4685; *The World Market Atlas*.

G.K. Hall and Company, 70 Lincoln Street, Boston, Massachusetts 02111 (617) 423-3990; *The World in Figures*.

United Nations Educational, Scientific and Cultural Organization (UNESCO), 7 Place de Fontenoy, F-75700 Paris, France (Telephone Number in U.S. (212) 963-5981); *Statistical Yearbook*.

SRI LANKA - IMPORTS

Asian Development Bank, P.O. Box 789, 1099 Manila, Philippines; *Key Indicators of Developing Asian and Pacific Countries*.

The Economist Intelligence Unit, 111 West 57th Street, New York, New York 10019 (800) 938-4685; *The World Market Atlas*.

The Economist Intelligence Unit (Asia) Limited, 10th Floor, Luk Kwok Centre, 72 Gloucester Road, Wanchai, Hong Kong (Phone Number in U.S. (800) 938-4685); *Asian Market Atlas*.

Euromonitor Publications Limited, 87-88 Turnmill Street, London EC1M 5QU, England; *International Marketing Data and Statistics*.

Food and Agricultural Organization of the United Nations (FAO) Via delle Terme di Caracalla, 00100 Rome, Italy (Telephone Number in U.S. (202) 653-2400); *The State of Food and Agriculture*.

G.K. Hall and Company, 70 Lincoln Street, Boston, Massachusetts 02111 (617) 423-3990; *The World in Figures*.

International Monetary Fund, 700 Nineteenth Street, NW, Washington, D.C. 20431 (202) 623-7000; *Direction of Trade Statistics, Government Finance Statistics Yearbook*, and *International Financial Statistics*.

International Rubber Study Group, York House, Eighth Floor, Empire Way, Wembley, London HA9 0PA, England; *Rubber Statistical Handbook*.

Statistical Office of the United Nations, Publishing Service, New York, New York 10017 (800) 253-9646; *Foreign Trade Statistics of Asia and the Pacific*, and *Trade in Manufactures of Developing Countries*.

Times Books, 201 East 50th Street, New York, New York 10022 (212) 751-2600; *The Economist Book of Vital World Statistics*.

The World Bank, 1818 H Street, NW, Washington, D.C. 20433 (202) 477-1234; *World Tables*.

SRI LANKA - INCOME TAXES - See SRI LANKA - TAXATION

SRI LANKA - INDUSTRY

Euromonitor Publications Limited, 87-88 Turnmill Street, London EC1M 5QU, England; *International Marketing Data and Statistics*.

Facts on File, 460 Park Avenue South, New York, New York 10016 (800) 443-8323; *The New Book of World Rankings*.

Federal Statistical Office, Gustav-Stresemann-Ring 11, D-6200 Wiesbaden, Germany; *Sri Lanka*.

G.K. Hall and Company, 70 Lincoln Street, Boston, Massachusetts 02111 (617) 423-3990; *The World in Figures*.

International Labour Office, I.L.O. Publications, CH-1211, Geneva 22, Switzerland; *Yearbook of Labour Statistics*.

Statistical Office of the United Nations, Publishing Service, New York, New York 10017 (800) 253-9646; *Statistical Yearbook*, and *Statistical Yearbook for Asia and the Pacific*.

Times Books, 201 East 50th Street, New York, New York 10022 (212) 751-2600; *The Economist Book of Vital World Statistics*.

The World Bank, 1818 H Street, NW, Washington, D.C. 20433 (202) 477-1234; *World Tables*.

World Intellectual Property Organization, 34 Chemin des Colombettes, CH-1211 Geneva 20, Switzerland; *Industrial Property Statistics*.

SRI LANKA - INFANT AND MATERNAL MORTALITY

The Economist Intelligence Unit (Asia) Limited, 10th Floor, Luk Kwok Centre, 72 Gloucester Road, Wanchai, Hong Kong (Phone Number in U.S. (800) 938-4685); *Asian Market Atlas*.

Statistical Office of the United Nations, Publishing Service, New York, New York 10017 (800) 253-9646; *Demographic Yearbook*, and *Statistical Yearbook*.

Times Books, 201 East 50th Street, New York, New York 10022 (212) 751-2600; *The Economist Book of Vital World Statistics*.

The World Bank, 1818 H Street, NW, Washington, D.C. 20433 (202) 477-1234; *World Tables*.

World Health Organization, Office of Publications, Avenue Appia, CH-1211 Geneva 27, Switzerland (Telephone Number in U.S. (518) 436-9686); *World Health Statistics Annual*.

SRI LANKA - INTERNAL TRADE

Statistical Office of the United Nations, Publishing Service, New York, New York 10017 (800) 253-9646; *Statistical Yearbook for Asia and the Pacific*.

SRI LANKA - INTERNATIONAL LIQUIDITY

International Monetary Fund, 700 Nineteenth Street, NW, Washington, D.C. 20431 (202) 623-7000; *International Financial Statistics*.

SRI LANKA - INTERNATIONAL RESERVES EXCLUDING GOLD

Asian Development Bank, P.O. Box 789, 1099 Manila, Philippines; *Key Indicators of Developing Asian and Pacific Countries*.

Statistical Office of the United Nations, Publishing Service, New York, New York 10017 (800) 253-9646; *Statistical Yearbook*.

The World Bank, 1818 H Street, NW, Washington, D.C. 20433 (202) 477-1234; *World Tables*.

SRI LANKA - INTERNATIONAL STATISTICS

Asian Development Bank, P.O. Box 789, 1099 Manila, Philippines; *Key Indicators of Developing Asian and Pacific Countries*.

SRI LANKA - INVESTMENTS

International Monetary Fund, 700 Nineteenth Street, NW, Washington, D.C. 20431 (202) 623-7000; *International Financial Statistics*.

SRI LANKA - IRON ORE PRODUCTION AND CONSUMPTION - See SRI LANKA - MINING AND MINERAL PRODUCTS

SRI LANKA - IRRIGATION

Euromonitor Publications Limited, 87-88 Turnmill Street, London EC1M 5QU, England; *International Marketing Data and Statistics*.

SRI LANKA - LABOR FORCE

The Economist Intelligence Unit (Asia) Limited, 10th Floor, Luk Kwok Centre, 72 Gloucester Road, Wanchai, Hong Kong (Phone Number in U.S. (800) 938-4685); *Asian Market Atlas*.

Euromonitor Publications Limited, 87-88 Turnmill Street, London EC1M 5QU, England; *International Marketing Data and Statistics*.

Facts on File, 460 Park Avenue South, New York, New York 10016 (800) 443-8323; *The New Book of World Rankings*.

Food and Agricultural Organization of the United Nations (FAO) Via delle Terme di Caracalla, 00100 Rome, Italy (Telephone Number in U.S. (202) 653-2400); *The State of Food and Agriculture*.

G.K. Hall and Company, 70 Lincoln Street, Boston, Massachusetts 02111 (617) 423-3990; *The World in Figures*.

Times Books, 201 East 50th Street, New York, New York 10022 (212) 751-2600; *The Economist Book of Vital World Statistics*.

The World Bank, 1818 H Street, NW, Washington, D.C. 20433 (202) 477-1234; *World Tables*.

SRI LANKA - LABOR PRODUCTIVITY

International Labour Office, I.L.O. Publications, CH-1211, Geneva 22, Switzerland; *Yearbook of Labour Statistics*.

SRI LANKA - LAND USE

Euromonitor Publications Limited, 87-88 Turnmill Street, London EC1M 5QU, England; *International Marketing Data and Statistics*.

Food and Agricultural Organization of the United Nations (FAO), Via delle Terme di Caracalla, 00100 Rome, Italy (Telephone Number in U.S. (202) 653-2400); *Production Yearbook*.

G.K. Hall and Company, 70 Lincoln Street, Boston, Massachusetts 02111 (617) 423-3990; *The World in Figures*.

SRI LANKA - LIBRARIES

Facts on File, 460 Park Avenue South, New York, New York 10016 (800) 443-8323; *The New Book of World Rankings*.

United Nations Educational, Scientific and Cultural Organization (UNESCO), 7 Place de Fontenoy, F-75700 Paris, France (Telephone Number in U.S. (212) 963-5981); *Statistical Yearbook*.

SRI LANKA - LIFE EXPECTANCY

The Economist Intelligence Unit (Asia) Limited, 10th Floor, Luk Kwok Centre, 72 Gloucester Road, Wanchai, Hong Kong (Phone Number in U.S. (800) 938-4685); *Asian Market Atlas*.

SRI LANKA - LIVESTOCK AND POULTRY

Euromonitor Publications Limited, 87-88 Turnmill Street, London EC1M 5QU, England; *International Marketing Data and Statistics*.

Facts on File, 460 Park Avenue South, New York, New York 10016 (800) 443-8323; *The New Book of World Rankings*.

Food and Agricultural Organization of the United Nations (FAO), Via delle Terme di Caracalla, 00100 Rome, Italy (Telephone Number in U.S. (202) 653-2400); *Production Yearbook*, and *The State of Food and Agriculture*.

G.K. Hall and Company, 70 Lincoln Street, Boston, Massachusetts 02111 (617) 423-3990; *The World in Figures*.

Statistical Office of the United Nations, Publishing Service, New York, New York 10017 (800) 253-9646; *Statistical Yearbook*.

SRI LANKA - LIVING LEVELS

G.K. Hall and Company, 70 Lincoln Street, Boston, Massachusetts 02111 (617) 423-3990; *The World in Figures*.

Times Books, 201 East 50th Street, New York, New York 10022 (212) 751-2600; *The Economist Book of Vital World Statistics*.

SRI LANKA - MAIL - NUMBER OF PIECES SENT OR RECEIVED

Statistical Office of the United Nations, Publishing Service, New York, New York 10017 (800) 253-9646; *Statistical Yearbook*.

SRI LANKA - MANPOWER

Statistical Office of the United Nations, Publishing Service, New York, New York 10017 (800) 253-9646; *Statistical Yearbook for Asia and the Pacific.*

SRI LANKA - MANUFACTURING

Asian Development Bank, P.O. Box 789, 1099 Manila, Philippines; *Key Indicators of Developing Asian and Pacific Countries.*

Facts on File, 460 Park Avenue South, New York, New York 10016 (800) 443-8323; *The New Book of World Rankings.*

G.K. Hall and Company, 70 Lincoln Street, Boston, Massachusetts 02111 (617) 423-3990; *The World in Figures.*

Statistical Office of the United Nations, Publishing Service, New York, New York 10017 (800) 253-9646; *Statistical Yearbook.*

The World Bank, 1818 H Street, NW, Washington, D.C. 20433 (202) 477-1234; *World Tables.*

SRI LANKA - MARRIAGE RATES

Facts on File, 460 Park Avenue South, New York, New York 10016 (800) 443-8323; *The New Book of World Rankings.*

Statistical Office of the United Nations, Publishing Service, New York, New York 10017 (800) 253-9646; *Demographic Yearbook,* and *Statistical Yearbook.*

SRI LANKA - MEAT PRODUCTION - See SRI LANKA - LIVESTOCK AND POULTRY

SRI LANKA - MERCHANT SHIPPING

G.K. Hall and Company, 70 Lincoln Street, Boston, Massachusetts 02111 (617) 423-3990; *The World in Figures.*

Lloyd's Register of Shipping, 17 Battery Place, New York, New York 10004 (212) 425-8050; *Register of Ships.*

Statistical Office of the United Nations, Publishing Service, New York, New York 10017 (800) 253-9646; *Statistical Yearbook.*

Times Books, 201 East 50th Street, New York, New York 10022 (212) 751-2600; *The Economist Book of Vital World Statistics.*

U.S. Department of Transportation, Maritime Administration, 400 Seventh Street, SW, Washington, D.C. 20590 (202) 366-5807; *A Statistical Analysis of the World's Merchant Fleets.*

SRI LANKA - MILITARY

The Economist Intelligence Unit (Asia) Limited, 10th Floor, Luk Kwok Centre, 72 Gloucester Road, Wanchai, Hong Kong (Phone Number in U.S. (800) 938-4685); *Asian Market Atlas.*

G.K. Hall and Company, 70 Lincoln Street, Boston, Massachusetts 02111 (617) 423-3990; *The World in Figures.*

The International Institute for Strategic Studies, 23 Tavistock Street, London WC2E 7NQ, England; *The Military Balance.*

U.S. Arms Control and Disarmament Agency, 320 Twenty-first Street, NW, Washington, D.C. 20451 (202) 647-8677; *World Military Expenditures and Arms Transfers.*

SRI LANKA - MILK - See SRI LANKA - DAIRY PRODUCTS

SRI LANKA - MINING AND MINERAL PRODUCTS

Asian Development Bank, P.O. Box 789, 1099 Manila, Philippines; *Key Indicators of Developing Asian and Pacific Countries.*

Facts on File, 460 Park Avenue South, New York, New York 10016 (800) 443-8323; *The New Book of World Rankings.*

G.K. Hall and Company, 70 Lincoln Street, Boston, Massachusetts 02111 (617) 423-3990; *The World in Figures.*

Statistical Office of the United Nations, Publishing Service, New York, New York 10017 (800) 253-9646; *Statistical Yearbook.*

Times Books, 201 East 50th Street, New York, New York 10022 (212) 751-2600; *The Economist Book of Vital World Statistics.*

SRI LANKA - MONEY EXCHANGE RATE

Euromonitor Publications Limited, 87-88 Turnmill Street, London EC1M 5QU, England; *International Marketing Data and Statistics.*

International Monetary Fund, 700 Nineteenth Street, NW, Washington, D.C. 20431 (202) 623-7000; *International Financial Statistics.*

Statistical Office of the United Nations, Publishing Service, New York, New York 10017 (800) 253-9646; *Statistical Yearbook.*

SRI LANKA - MONEY RESERVES

Euromonitor Publications Limited, 87-88 Turnmill Street, London EC1M 5QU, England; *International Marketing Data and Statistics.*

SRI LANKA - MONEY SUPPLY

Asian Development Bank, P.O. Box 789, 1099 Manila, Philippines; *Key Indicators of Developing Asian and Pacific Countries.*

Euromonitor Publications Limited, 87-88 Turnmill Street, London EC1M 5QU, England; *International Marketing Data and Statistics.*

G.K. Hall and Company, 70 Lincoln Street, Boston, Massachusetts 02111 (617) 423-3990; *The World in Figures.*

International Monetary Fund, 700 Nineteenth Street, NW, Washington, D.C. 20431 (202) 623-7000; *International Financial Statistics.*

Statistical Office of the United Nations, Publishing Service, New York, New York 10017 (800) 253-9646; *Statistical Yearbook.*

The World Bank, 1818 H Street, NW, Washington, D.C. 20433 (202) 477-1234; *World Tables.*

SRI LANKA - MOTION PICTURES

Statistical Office of the United Nations, Publishing Service, New York, New York 10017 (800) 253-9646; *Statistical Yearbook.*

United Nations Educational, Scientific and Cultural Organization (UNESCO), 7 Place de Fontenoy, F-75700 Paris, France (Telephone Number in U.S. (212) 963-5981); *Statistical Yearbook.*

SRI LANKA - MOTOR VEHICLE TAXES - See SRI LANKA - TAXATION

SRI LANKA - MOTOR VEHICLES IN USE

G.K. Hall and Company, 70 Lincoln Street, Boston, Massachusetts 02111 (617) 423-3990; *The World in Figures.*

International Road Federation, 525 School Street, SW, Washington, D.C. 20024 (202) 554-2106; *World Road Statistics.*

Statistical Office of the United Nations, Publishing Service, New York, New York 10017 (800) 253-9646; *Statistical Yearbook.*

Times Books, 201 East 50th Street, New York, New York 10022 (212) 751-2600; *The Economist Book of Vital World Statistics.*

SRI LANKA - MUSEUMS

Facts on File, 460 Park Avenue South, New York, New York 10016 (800) 443-8323; *The New Book of World Rankings.*

United Nations Educational, Scientific and Cultural Organization (UNESCO), 7 Place de Fontenoy, F-75700 Paris, France (Telephone Number in U.S. (212) 963-5981); *Statistical Yearbook.*

SRI LANKA - NATALITY - See SRI LANKA - BIRTH RATE

SRI LANKA - NATIONAL ACCOUNTS

Federal Statistical Office, Gustav-Stresemann-Ring 11, D-6200 Wiesbaden, Germany; *Sri Lanka.*

International Monetary Fund, 700 Nineteenth Street, NW, Washington, D.C. 20431 (202) 623-7000; *International Financial Statistics.*

Statistical Office of the United Nations, Publishing Service, New York, New York 10017 (800) 253-9646; *National Accounts Statistics, Statistical Yearbook,* and *Statistical Yearbook for Asia and the Pacific.*

SRI LANKA - NATIONAL INCOME

Facts on File, 460 Park Avenue South, New York, New York 10016 (800) 443-8323; *The New Book of World Rankings.*

G.K. Hall and Company, 70 Lincoln Street, Boston, Massachusetts 02111 (617) 423-3990; *The World in Figures.*

Statistical Office of the United Nations, Publishing Service, New York, New York 10017 (800) 253-9646; *Statistical Yearbook.*

SRI LANKA - NATIONAL PRODUCT

Facts on File, 460 Park Avenue South, New York, New York 10016 (800) 443-8323; *The New Book of World Rankings.*

Statistical Office of the United Nations, Publishing Service, New York, New York 10017 (800) 253-9646; *Statistical Yearbook.*

SRI LANKA - NATURAL GAS PRODUCTION - See SRI LANKA - MINING AND MINERAL PRODUCTS

SRI LANKA - NATURAL RUBBER PRODUCTION

International Rubber Study Group, York House, Eighth Floor, Empire Way, Wembley, London HA9 0PA, England; *Rubber Statistical Handbook.*

Statistical Office of the United Nations, Publishing Service, New York, New York 10017 (800) 253-9646; *Statistical Yearbook.*

SRI LANKA - NEWSPAPER PRODUCTION AND CONSUMPTION - See SRI LANKA - FORESTRY AND FOREST PRODUCTS

SRI LANKA - NEWSPRINT - See SRI LANKA - FORESTRY AND FOREST PRODUCTS

SRI LANKA - OCCUPATIONS - See SRI LANKA - LABOR FORCE

SRI LANKA - PAPER - See SRI LANKA - FORESTRY AND FOREST PRODUCTS

SRI LANKA - PATENTS

Statistical Office of the United Nations, Publishing Service, New York, New York 10017 (800) 253-9646; *Statistical Yearbook.*

World Intellectual Property Organization, 34 Chemin des Colombettes, CH-1211 Geneva 20. Switzerland; *Industrial Property Statistics.*

SRI LANKA - PEANUT PRODUCTION - See SRI LANKA - CROPS

SRI LANKA - PEPPER PRODUCTION - See SRI LANKA - CROPS

SRI LANKA - PERIODICALS

United Nations Educational, Scientific and Cultural Organization (UNESCO), 7 Place de Fontenoy, F-75700 Paris, France (Telephone Number in U.S. (212) 963-5981); *Statistical Yearbook.*

SRI LANKA - PESTICIDE USE

Food and Agricultural Organization of the United Nations (FAO) Via delle Terme di Caracalla, 00100 Rome, Italy (Telephone Number in U.S. (202) 653-2400); *The State of Food and Agriculture.*

SRI LANKA - PETROLEUM INDUSTRY

Asian Development Bank, P.O. Box 789, 1099 Manila, Philippines; *Key Indicators of Developing Asian and Pacific Countries.*

Facts on File, 460 Park Avenue South, New York, New York 10016 (800) 443-8323; *The New Book of World Rankings.*

Food and Agricultural Organization of the United Nations (FAO) Via delle Terme di Caracalla, 00100 Rome, Italy (Telephone Number in U.S. (202) 653-2400); *The State of Food and Agriculture.*

G.K. Hall and Company, 70 Lincoln Street, Boston, Massachusetts 02111 (617) 423-3990; *The World in Figures.*

Statistical Office of the United Nations, Publishing Service, New York, New York 10017 (800) 253-9646; *Statistical Yearbook.*

SRI LANKA - PIGS - See SRI LANKA - LIVESTOCK AND POULTRY

SRI LANKA - POPULATION

Asian Development Bank, P.O. Box 789, 1099 Manila, Philippines; *Key Indicators of Developing Asian and Pacific Countries.*

The Economist Intelligence Unit, 111 West 57th Street, New York, New York 10019; *The World Market Atlas.*

The Economist Intelligence Unit (Asia) Limited, 10th Floor, Luk Kwok Centre, 72 Gloucester Road, Wanchai, Hong Kong (Phone Number in U.S. (800) 938-4685); *Asian Market Atlas.*

Euromonitor Publications Limited, 87-88 Turnmill Street, London EC1M 5QU, England; *International Marketing Data and Statistics*.

Facts on File, 460 Park Avenue South, New York, New York 10016 (800) 443-8323; *The New Book of World Rankings*.

Federal Statistical Office, Gustav-Stresemann-Ring 11, D-6200 Wiesbaden, Germany; *Sri Lanka*.

Food and Agricultural Organization of the United Nations (FAO), Via delle Terme di Caracalla, 00100 Rome, Italy (Telephone Number in U.S. (202) 653-2400); *Production Yearbook*.

G.K. Hall and Company, 70 Lincoln Street, Boston, Massachusetts 02111 (617) 423-3990; *The World in Figures*.

International Labour Office, I.L.O. Publications, CH-1211, Geneva 22, Switzerland; *Yearbook of Labour Statistics*.

Statistical Office of the United Nations, Publishing Service, New York, New York 10017 (800) 253-9646; *Demographic Yearbook, Statistical Yearbook*, and *Statistical Yearbook for Asia and the Pacific*.

Times Books, 201 East 50th Street, New York, New York 10022 (212) 751-2600; *The Economist Book of Vital World Statistics*.

United Nations Educational, Scientific and Cultural Organization (UNESCO), 7 Place de Fontenoy, F-75700 Paris, France (Telephone Number in U.S. (212) 963-5981); *Statistical Yearbook*.

U.S. Arms Control and Disarmament Agency, 320 Twenty-first Street, NW, Washington, D.C. 20451 (202) 647-8677, *World Military Expenditures and Arms Transfers*.

World Health Organization, Office of Publications, Avenue Appia, CH-1211 Geneva 27, Switzerland (Telephone Number in U.S. (518) 436-9686); *World Health Statistics Annual*.

SRI LANKA - POST OFFICES

Facts on File, 460 Park Avenue South, New York, New York 10016 (800) 443-8323; *The New Book of World Rankings*.

SRI LANKA - POTATO PRODUCTION - See SRI LANKA - CROPS

SRI LANKA - POWER PRODUCTION INDUSTRY

Statistical Office of the United Nations, Publishing Service, New York, New York 10017 (800) 253-9646; *Electric Power in Asia and the Pacific*.

SRI LANKA - PRICES

Asian Development Bank, P.O. Box 789, 1099 Manila, Philippines; *Key Indicators of Developing Asian and Pacific Countries*.

Facts on File, 460 Park Avenue South, New York, New York 10016 (800) 443-8323; *The New Book of World Rankings*.

Federal Statistical Office, Gustav-Stresemann-Ring 11, D-6200 Wiesbaden, Germany; *Sri Lanka*.

Food and Agricultural Organization of the United Nations (FAO), Via delle Terme di Caracalla, 00100 Rome, Italy (Telephone Number in U.S. (202) 653-2400); *Production Yearbook*, and *The State of Food and Agriculture*.

G.K. Hall and Company, 70 Lincoln Street, Boston, Massachusetts 02111 (617) 423-3990; *The World in Figures*.

International Labour Office, I.L.O. Publications, CH-1211, Geneva 22, Switzerland; *Yearbook of Labour Statistics*.

International Monetary Fund, 700 Nineteenth Street, NW, Washington, D.C. 20431 (202) 623-7000; *International Financial Statistics*.

International Rubber Study Group, York House, Eighth Floor, Empire Way, Wembley, London HA9 0PA, England; *Rubber Statistical Handbook*.

SRI LANKA - PRINTING AND WRITING PAPER - See SRI LANKA - FORESTRY AND FOREST PRODUCTS

SRI LANKA - PRODUCTION

Asian Development Bank, P.O. Box 789, 1099 Manila, Philippines; *Key Indicators of Developing Asian and Pacific Countries*.

Facts on File, 460 Park Avenue South, New York, New York 10016 (800) 443-8323; *The New Book of World Rankings*.

G.K. Hall and Company, 70 Lincoln Street, Boston, Massachusetts 02111 (617) 423-3990; *The World in Figures*.

International Rubber Study Group, York House, Eighth Floor, Empire Way, Wembley, London HA9 0PA, England; *Rubber Statistical Handbook*.

SRI LANKA - PRODUCTIVITY

Euromonitor Publications Limited, 87-88 Turnmill Street, London EC1M 5QU, England; *International Marketing Data and Statistics*.

SRI LANKA - PROPERTY TAXES - See SRI LANKA - TAXATION

SRI LANKA - PUBLIC FINANCE

Facts on File, 460 Park Avenue South, New York, New York 10016 (800) 443-8323; *The New Book of World Rankings*.

SRI LANKA - RADIO

The Economist Intelligence Unit (Asia) Limited, 10th Floor, Luk Kwok Centre, 72 Gloucester Road, Wanchai, Hong Kong (Phone Number in U.S. (800) 938-4685); *Asian Market Atlas*.

SRI LANKA - RADIO BROADCASTING - See SRI LANKA - BROADCASTING

SRI LANKA - RADIO RECEIVER PRODUCTION

Statistical Office of the United Nations, Publishing Service, New York, New York 10017 (800) 253-9646; *Statistical Yearbook*.

SRI LANKA - RAILWAYS

G.K. Hall and Company, 70 Lincoln Street, Boston, Massachusetts 02111 (617) 423-3990; *The World in Figures*.

Jane's Information Group, Sentinel House, 163 Brighton Road, Coulsdon, Surrey CR5 2NH, England (Telephone Number in U.S. (703) 683-3700); *Jane's World Railways*.

Statistical Office of the United Nations, Publishing Service, New York, New York 10017 (800) 253-9646; *Statistical Yearbook*.

SRI LANKA - RELIGION

Facts on File, 460 Park Avenue South, New York, New York 10016 (800) 443-8323; *The New Book of World Rankings*.

SRI LANKA - RENT PRICES

International Labour Office, I.L.O. Publications, CH-1211, Geneva 22, Switzerland; *Yearbook of Labour Statistics*.

SRI LANKA - RETAIL TRADE

G.K. Hall and Company, 70 Lincoln Street, Boston, Massachusetts 02111 (617) 423-3990; *The World in Figures*.

SRI LANKA - RICE PRODUCTION - See SRI LANKA - CROPS

SRI LANKA - ROUNDWOOD PRODUCTION - See SRI LANKA - FORESTRY AND FOREST PRODUCTS

SRI LANKA - RUBBER - INDUSTRIAL CONSUMPTION

International Rubber Study Group, York House, Eighth Floor, Empire Way, Wembley, London HA9 0PA, England; *Rubber Statistical Handbook*.

SRI LANKA - RUBBER EXPORTS

International Monetary Fund, 700 Nineteenth Street, NW, Washington, D.C. 20431 (202) 623-7000; *International Financial Statistics*.

SRI LANKA - RUBBER PRODUCTION AND CONSUMPTION

Commodity Research Bureau, Incorporated, 75 Wall Street, New York, New York 10005 (212) 504-7754; *Commodity Year Book*.

Facts on File, 460 Park Avenue South, New York, New York 10016 (800) 443-8323; *The New Book of World Rankings*.

International Rubber Study Group, York House, Eighth Floor, Empire Way, Wembley, London HA9 0PA, England; *Rubber Statistical Handbook*.

SRI LANKA - SALT PRODUCTION - See SRI LANKA - MINING AND MINERAL PRODUCTS

SRI LANKA - SAWNWOOD PRODUCTION - See SRI LANKA - FORESTRY AND FOREST PRODUCTS

SRI LANKA - SCIENCE AND TECHNOLOGY - EXPENDITURE FOR RESEARCH

Statistical Office of the United Nations, Publishing Service, New York, New York 10017 (800) 253-9646; *Statistical Yearbook*.

SRI LANKA - SCIENTISTS AND TECHNICIANS

Statistical Office of the United Nations, Publishing Service, New York, New York 10017 (800) 253-9646; *Statistical Yearbook*.

United Nations Educational, Scientific and Cultural Organization (UNESCO), 7 Place de Fontenoy, F-75700 Paris, France (Telephone Number in U.S. (212) 963-5981); *Statistical Yearbook*.

SRI LANKA - SENIOR CITIZENS

Facts on File, 460 Park Avenue South, New York, New York 10016 (800) 443-8323; *The New Book of World Rankings*.

SRI LANKA - SHEEP - See SRI LANKA - LIVESTOCK AND POULTRY

SRI LANKA - SILVER PRODUCTION AND CONSUMPTION - See SRI LANKA - MINING AND MINERAL PRODUCTS

SRI LANKA - SOCIAL DATA

Asian Development Bank, P.O. Box 789, 1099 Manila, Philippines; *Key Indicators of Developing Asian and Pacific Countries*.

Facts on File, 460 Park Avenue South, New York, New York 10016 (800) 443-8323; *The New Book of World Rankings*.

G.K. Hall and Company, 70 Lincoln Street, Boston, Massachusetts 02111 (617) 423-3990; *The World in Figures*.

SRI LANKA - SOCIAL SECURITY

International Monetary Fund, 700 Nineteenth Street, NW, Washington, D.C. 20431 (202) 623-7000; *Government Finance Statistics Yearbook*.

SRI LANKA - SOYBEAN PRODUCTION - See SRI LANKA - CROPS

SRI LANKA - STAMP TAXES AND DUTIES - See SRI LANKA - TAXATION

SRI LANKA - STATE BUDGET REVENUE AND EXPENDITURES

Euromonitor Publications Limited, 87-88 Turnmill Street, London EC1M 5QU, England; *International Marketing Data and Statistics*.

SRI LANKA - STEEL - See SRI LANKA - MINING AND MINERAL PRODUCTS

SRI LANKA - STOCKS - COMMODITY - MARKET PRICE - INDEX

Food and Agricultural Organization of the United Nations (FAO) Via delle Terme di Caracalla, 00100 Rome, Italy (Telephone Number in U.S. (202) 653-2400); *The State of Food and Agriculture*.

SRI LANKA - SUGAR PRODUCTION AND CONSUMPTION - See SRI LANKA - CROPS

SRI LANKA - TAXATION

G.K. Hall and Company, 70 Lincoln Street, Boston, Massachusetts 02111 (617) 423-3990; *The World in Figures*.

International Monetary Fund, 700 Nineteenth Street, NW, Washington, D.C. 20431 (202) 623-7000; *Government Finance Statistics Yearbook*.

International Road Federation, 525 School Street, SW, Washington, D.C. 20024 (202) 554-2106; *World Road Statistics*.

The World Bank, 1818 H Street, NW, Washington, D.C. 20433 (202) 477-1234; *World Tables*.

SRI LANKA - TEA PRODUCTION AND CONSUMPTION - See SRI LANKA - CROPS

SRI LANKA - TELEGRAPH SERVICE

Statistical Office of the United Nations, Publishing Service, New York, New York 10017 (800) 253-9646; *Statistical Yearbook*.

SRI LANKA - TELEPHONES IN USE

American Telephone and Telegraph Company, 26 Parsippany Road, Whippany, New Jersey 07981 (800) 338-4038; *The World's Telephones.*

The Economist Intelligence Unit (Asia) Limited, 10th Floor, Luk Kwok Centre, 72 Gloucester Road, Wanchai, Hong Kong (Phone Number in U.S. (800) 938-4685); *Asian Market Atlas.*

Euromonitor Publications Limited, 87-88 Turnmill Street, London EC1M 5QU, England; *The Pacific Basin: An Economic Handbook.*

G.K. Hall and Company, 70 Lincoln Street, Boston, Massachusetts 02111 (617) 423-3990; *The World in Figures.*

Statistical Office of the United Nations, Publishing Service, New York, New York 10017 (800) 253-9646; *Statistical Yearbook.*

SRI LANKA - TELEVISION

The Economist Intelligence Unit (Asia) Limited, 10th Floor, Luk Kwok Centre, 72 Gloucester Road, Wanchai, Hong Kong (Phone Number in U.S. (800) 938-4685); *Asian Market Atlas.*

SRI LANKA - TELEVISION BROADCASTING - See SRI LANKA - BROADCASTING

SRI LANKA - TEXTILE INDUSTRY

G.K. Hall and Company, 70 Lincoln Street, Boston, Massachusetts 02111 (617) 423-3990; *The World in Figures.*

Statistical Office of the United Nations, Publishing Service, New York, New York 10017 (800) 253-9646; *Statistical Yearbook.*

SRI LANKA - THEATRE

United Nations Educational, Scientific and Cultural Organization (UNESCO), 7 Place de Fontenoy, F-75700 Paris, France (Telephone Number in U.S. (212) 963-5981); *Statistical Yearbook.*

SRI LANKA - TIRE (MOTOR VEHICLE) PRODUCTION

International Rubber Study Group, York House, Eighth Floor, Empire Way, Wembley, London HA9 0PA, England; *Rubber Statistical Handbook.*

Statistical Office of the United Nations, Publishing Service, New York, New York 10017 (800) 253-9646; *Statistical Yearbook.*

SRI LANKA - TOBACCO PRODUCTION

Facts on File, 460 Park Avenue South, New York, New York 10016 (800) 443-8323; *The New Book of World Rankings.*

Statistical Office of the United Nations, Publishing Service, New York, New York 10017 (800) 253-9646; *Statistical Yearbook.*

SRI LANKA - TOURISM

Facts on File, 460 Park Avenue South, New York, New York 10016 (800) 443-8323; *The New Book of World Rankings.*

Federal Statistical Office, Gustav-Stresemann-Ring 11, D-6200 Wiesbaden, Germany; *Sri Lanka.*

G.K. Hall and Company, 70 Lincoln Street, Boston, Massachusetts 02111 (617) 423-3990; *The World in Figures.*

Statistical Office of the United Nations, Publishing Service, New York, New York 10017 (800) 253-9646; *Statistical Yearbook.*

Times Books, 201 East 50th Street, New York, New York 10022 (212) 751-2600; *The Economist Book of Vital World Statistics.*

World Tourism Organization, Calle Capitan Haya 42, E-28020 Madrid, Spain; *Yearbook of Tourism Statistics.*

SRI LANKA - TRACTORS IN USE

Statistical Office of the United Nations, Publishing Service, New York, New York 10017 (800) 253-9646; *Statistical Yearbook.*

SRI LANKA - TRADE - See SRI LANKA - FOREIGN TRADE

SRI LANKA - TRADEMARKS AND SERVICE MARKS

Statistical Office of the United Nations, Publishing Service, New York, New York 10017 (800) 253-9646; *Statistical Yearbook.*

World Intellectual Property Organization, 34 Chemin des Colombettes, CH-1211 Geneva 20. Switzerland; *Industrial Property Statistics.*

SRI LANKA - TRANSPORTATION AND COMMUNICATIONS

The Economist Intelligence Unit (Asia) Limited, 10th Floor, Luk Kwok Centre, 72 Gloucester Road, Wanchai, Hong Kong (Phone Number in U.S. (800) 938-4685); *Asian Market Atlas.*

Facts on File, 460 Park Avenue South, New York, New York 10016 (800) 443-8323; *The New Book of World Rankings.*

Federal Statistical Office, Gustav-Stresemann-Ring 11, D-6200 Wiesbaden, Germany; *Sri Lanka.*

G.K. Hall and Company, 70 Lincoln Street, Boston, Massachusetts 02111 (617) 423-3990; *The World in Figures.*

Statistical Office of the United Nations, Publishing Service, New York, New York 10017 (800) 253-9646; *Statistical Yearbook for Asia and the Pacific.*

SRI LANKA - UNEMPLOYMENT

Euromonitor Publications Limited, 87-88 Turnmill Street, London EC1M 5QU, England; *International Marketing Data and Statistics.*

International Labour Office, I.L.O. Publications, CH-1211, Geneva 22, Switzerland; *Yearbook of Labour Statistics.*

Statistical Office of the United Nations, Publishing Service, New York, New York 10017 (800) 253-9646; *Statistical Yearbook.*

SRI LANKA - UTILITIES

Statistical Office of the United Nations, Publishing Service, New York, New York 10017 (800) 253-9646; *Electric Power in Asia and the Pacific.*

SRI LANKA - VITAL STATISTICS

Euromonitor Publications Limited, 87-88 Turnmill Street, London EC1M 5QU, England; *International Marketing Data and Statistics.*

G.K. Hall and Company, 70 Lincoln Street, Boston, Massachusetts 02111 (617) 423-3990; *The World in Figures.*

Statistical Office of the United Nations, Publishing Service, New York, New York 10017 (800) 253-9646; *Statistical Yearbook.*

World Health Organization, Office of Publications, Avenue Appia, CH-1211 Geneva 27, Switzerland (Telephone Number in U.S. (518) 436-9686); *World Health Statistics Annual.*

SRI LANKA - WAGES

Federal Statistical Office, Gustav-Stresemann-Ring 11, D-6200 Wiesbaden, Germany; *Sri Lanka.*

G.K. Hall and Company, 70 Lincoln Street, Boston, Massachusetts 02111 (617) 423-3990; *The World in Figures.*

International Labour Office, I.L.O. Publications, CH-1211, Geneva 22, Switzerland; *Yearbook of Labour Statistics.*

Statistical Office of the United Nations, Publishing Service, New York, New York 10017 (800) 253-9646; *Statistical Yearbook for Asia and the Pacific,* and *Statistical Yearbook.*

SRI LANKA - WEATHER

Facts on File, 460 Park Avenue South, New York, New York 10016 (800) 443-8323; *The New Book of World Rankings.*

G.K. Hall and Company, 70 Lincoln Street, Boston, Massachusetts 02111 (617) 423-3990; *The World in Figures.*

SRI LANKA - WELFARE

International Monetary Fund, 700 Nineteenth Street, NW, Washington, D.C. 20431 (202) 623-7000; *Government Finance Statistics Yearbook.*

SRI LANKA - WHEAT PRODUCTION AND PRICES - See SRI LANKA - CROPS

SRI LANKA - WHOLESALE PRICES

Asian Development Bank, P.O. Box 789, 1099 Manila, Philippines; *Key Indicators of Developing Asian and Pacific Countries.*

International Monetary Fund, 700 Nineteenth Street, NW, Washington, D.C. 20431 (202) 623-7000; *International Financial Statistics.*

Statistical Office of the United Nations, Publishing Service, New York, New York 10017 (800) 253-9646; *Statistical Yearbook.*

SRI LANKA - WINE PRODUCTION

Facts on File, 460 Park Avenue South, New York, New York 10016 (800) 443-8323; *The New Book of World Rankings.*

SRI LANKA - WOOL PRODUCTION

Facts on File, 460 Park Avenue South, New York, New York 10016 (800) 443-8323; *The New Book of World Rankings.*

SRI LANKA - YARN PRODUCTION

Statistical Office of the United Nations, Publishing Service, New York, New York 10017 (800) 253-9646; *Statistical Yearbook.*

SRI LANKA - ZOOS AND BOTANICAL GARDENS

United Nations Educational, Scientific and Cultural Organization (UNESCO), 7 Place de Fontenoy, F-75700 Paris, France (Telephone Number in U.S. (212) 963-5981); *Statistical Yearbook.*

STAMPS - POSTAGE - RECEIPTS FROM

U.S. Postal Service, 475 L'Enfant Plaza West, SW, Washington, D.C. 20260-0010 (202) 268-2000 ; *Annual Report of the Postmaster General.*

STANDARD METROPOLITAN STATISTICAL AREAS - See METROPOLITAN AREAS

STATE AND LOCAL GOVERNMENTS - (COMBINED DATA) - COLLECTIVE BARGAINING AGREEMENTS

U.S. Department of Labor, Bureau of Labor Statistics, Two Massachusetts Avenue, NE, Washington, D.C. 20212 (202) 606-7828; *Current Wage Developments.*

STATE AND LOCAL GOVERNMENTS - (COMBINED DATA) - DEBT

U.S. Department of Commerce, Bureau of the Census, Suitland, Maryland 20233 (301) 763-4040; *Historical Statistics on Governmental Finances and Employment, Government Finances,* and unpublished data.

U.S. Department of the Treasury, Fifteenth Street and Pennsylvania Avenue, NW, Washington, D.C. 20220 (202) 566-2000; *Treasury Bulletin.*

STATE AND LOCAL GOVERNMENTS - (COMBINED DATA) - DEBT - HIGHWAYS

U.S. Department of Transportation, Federal Highway Administration, 400 Seventh Street, SW, Washington, D.C. 20590 (202) 366-0660; *Highway Statistics.*

STATE AND LOCAL GOVERNMENTS - (COMBINED DATA) - EMPLOYEES

U.S. Department of Commerce, Bureau of the Census, Suitland, Maryland 20233 (301) 763-4040; *Historical Statistics on Governmental Finances and Employment,* and *Public Employment.*

U.S. Department of Labor, Bureau of Labor Statistics, Two Massachusetts Avenue, NE, Washington, D.C. 20212 (202) 606-7828; *Monthly Labor Review, Current Wage Developments, Employee Benefits in State and Local Government,* and unpublished data.

U.S. Equal Employment Opportunity Commission, 1801 L Street, NW, Washington, D.C. 20507 (800) USA-EEOC; *State and Local Government Information Report.*

STATE AND LOCAL GOVERNMENTS - (COMBINED DATA) - EMPLOYEES - AVERAGE SALARIES

U.S. Equal Employment Opportunity Commission, 1801 L Street, NW, Washington, D.C. 20507 (800) USA-EEOC; *State and Local Government Information Report.*

STATE AND LOCAL GOVERNMENTS - (COMBINED DATA) - EMPLOYEES - PAYROLLS

U.S. Department of Commerce, Bureau of the Census, Suitland, Maryland 20233 (301) 763-4040; *Public Employment, Historical*

Statistics on Governmental Finances and Employment, and unpublished data.

U.S. Department of Labor, Bureau of Labor Statistics, Two Massachusetts Avenue, NE, Washington, D.C. 20212 (202) 606-7828; *Employment and Earnings,* and *Monthly Labor Review.*

U.S. Equal Employment Opportunity Commission, 1801 L Street, NW, Washington, D.C. 20507 (800) USA-EEOC; *State and Local Government Information Report.*

STATE AND LOCAL GOVERNMENTS - (COMBINED DATA) - EXPENDITURES

U.S. Department of Commerce, Bureau of Economic Analysis, Fourteenth Street between Constitution Avenue and E Street, NW, Washington, D.C. 20230 (202) 606-9900; *The National Income and Product Accounts of the United States,* and *Survey of Current Business.*

U.S. Department of Commerce, Bureau of the Census, Suitland, Maryland 20233 (301) 763-4040; *Government Finances, Historical Statistics on Governmental Finances and Employment,* and unpublished data.

STATE AND LOCAL GOVERNMENTS - (COMBINED DATA) - EXPENDITURES - BY TYPE

U.S. Department of Commerce, Bureau of the Census, Suitland, Maryland 20233 (301) 763-4040; *Government Finances,* and *Historical Statistics on Governmental Finances and Employment.*

STATE AND LOCAL GOVERNMENTS - (COMBINED DATA) - EXPENDITURES - CAPITAL OUTLAY

U.S. Department of Commerce, Bureau of the Census, Suitland, Maryland 20233 (301) 763-4040; *Historical Statistics on Governmental Finances and Employment* and *Government Finances.*

STATE AND LOCAL GOVERNMENTS - (COMBINED DATA) - EXPENDITURES - HOSPITALS AND MEDICAL CARE

American Hospital Association, 840 North Lake Shore Drive, Chicago, Illinois 60611 (312) 280-6000; *Hospital Statistics.*

U.S. Department of Health and Human Services, Health Care Financing Administration, 200 Independence Avenue, SW, Washington, D.C. 20201 (202) 245-6113; *Health Care Financing Review.*

STATE AND LOCAL GOVERNMENTS - (COMBINED DATA) - EXPENDITURES - SCHOOLS

U.S. Department of Education, 400 Maryland Avenue, SW, Washington, D.C. 20202 (202) 708-5366; *Digest of Education Statistics,* and unpublished data.

STATE AND LOCAL GOVERNMENTS - (COMBINED DATA) - EXPENDITURES - SOCIAL INSURANCE, ETC.

U.S. Department of Health and Human Services, Social Security Administration, 6401 Security Boulevard, Baltimore, Maryland 21235 (410) 965-1234; *Social Security Bulletin.*

STATE AND LOCAL GOVERNMENTS - (COMBINED DATA) - FEDERAL AID

Advisory Commission on Intergovernmental Relations, Suite 2000, 800 K Street, NW, Suite 450, Washington, D.C. 20575 (202) 653-5540; *Significant Features of Fiscal Federalism.*

Executive Office of the President, Office of Management and Budget, Executive Office Building, Washington, D.C. 20503 (202) 395-3080; *The Budget of the United States Government,* and *Historical Tables, Budget of the United States Government.*

U.S. Department of Commerce, Bureau of Economic Analysis, Fourteenth Street between Constitution Avenue and E Street, NW, Washington, D.C. 20230 (202) 606-9900; *Survey of Current Business,* and unpublished data.
U.S. Department of Commerce, Bureau of the Census, Suitland, Maryland 20233 (301) 763-4040; *Federal Expenditures by State for Fiscal Year.*

STATE AND LOCAL GOVERNMENTS - (COMBINED DATA) - FEDERAL AID - BY FUNCTION

Executive Office of the President, Office of Management and Budget, Executive Office Building, Washington, D.C. 20503 (202) 395-3080; *Historical Tables, Budget of the United States Government,* and *Budget of the United States Government.*

STATE AND LOCAL GOVERNMENTS - (COMBINED DATA) - FINANCES

U.S. Department of Commerce, Bureau of Economic Analysis, Fourteenth Street between Constitution Avenue and E Street, NW, Washington, D.C. 20230 (202) 606-9900; *The National Income and Product Accounts of the United States, Survey of Current Business,* and unpublished data.

U.S. Department of Commerce, Bureau of the Census, Suitland, Maryland 20233 (301) 763-4040; *Historical Statistics on Governmental Finances and Employment, Government Finances, City Government Finances,* and unpublished data.

STATE AND LOCAL GOVERNMENTS - (COMBINED DATA) - FINANCES - INTERGOVERNMENTAL

Executive Office of the President, Office of Management and Budget, Executive Office Building, Washington, D.C. 20503 (202) 395-3080; *The Budget of the United States,* and *Historical Tables, Budget of the United States Government.*

U.S. Department of Commerce, Bureau of the Census, Suitland, Maryland 20233 (301) 763-4040; *Historical Statistics on Governmental Finances and Employment, Government Finances,* and *Federal Expenditures by State for Fiscal Year.*

STATE AND LOCAL GOVERNMENTS - (COMBINED DATA) - FLOW OF FUNDS

Board of Governors of the Federal Reserve System, Twentieth Street and Constitution Avenue, NW, Washington, D.C. 20551 (202) 452-3000; *Annual Statistical Digest.*

STATE AND LOCAL GOVERNMENTS - (COMBINED DATA) - FOREST LAND

U.S. Department of Agriculture, Forest Service, Fourteenth Street and Independence Avenue, SW, Washington, D.C. 20250 (202) 720-3760; *Forest Resources of the United States.*

STATE AND LOCAL GOVERNMENTS - (COMBINED DATA) - HOSPITALS

American Hospital Association, 840 North Lake Shore Drive, Chicago, Illinois 60611 (312) 280-6000; *Hospital Statistics,* and unpublished data.

STATE AND LOCAL GOVERNMENTS - (COMBINED DATA) - NUMBER OF UNITS

U.S. Department of Commerce, Bureau of the Census, Suitland, Maryland 20233 (301) 763-4040; *Census of Governments, Government Organization.*

STATE AND LOCAL GOVERNMENTS - (COMBINED DATA) - PURCHASES OF GOODS AND SERVICES

U.S. Department of Commerce, Bureau of Economic Analysis, Fourteenth Street between Constitution Avenue and E Street, NW, Washington, D.C. 20230 (202) 606-9900; *The National Income and Product Accounts of the United States,* and *Survey of Current Business.*

STATE AND LOCAL GOVERNMENTS - (COMBINED DATA) - RECEIPTS

U.S. Department of Commerce, Bureau of Economic Analysis, Fourteenth Street between Constitution Avenue and E Street, NW, Washington, D.C. 20230 (202) 606-9900; *The National Income and Product Accounts of the United States, Survey of Current Business,* and unpublished data.

STATE AND LOCAL GOVERNMENTS - (COMBINED DATA) - RECEIPTS - BY SOURCE

U.S. Department of Commerce, Bureau of the Census, Suitland, Maryland 20233 (301) 763-4040; *Government Finances.*

STATE AND LOCAL GOVERNMENTS - (COMBINED DATA) - RETIREMENT SYSTEMS

Board of Governors of the Federal Reserve System, Twentieth Street and Constitution Avenue, NW, Washington, D.C. 20551 (202) 452-3000; *Annual Statistical Digest,* and unpublished data.

Employee Benefit Research Institute, 2121 K Street, NW, Suite 600, Washington, D.C. 20037 (202) 659-0670; *EBRI Databook on Employee Benefits.*

U.S. Department of Commerce, Bureau of the Census, Suitland, Maryland 20233 (301) 763-4040; *Finances of Employee-Retirement Systems of State and Local Governments.*

U.S. Department Health and Human Services, Social Security Administration, 6401 Security Boulevard, Baltimore, Maryland 21235 (410) 965-1234; *Annual Statistical Supplement to the Social Security Bulletin, Social Security Bulletin,* and unpublished data.

STATE AND LOCAL GOVERNMENTS - (COMBINED DATA) - SECURITIES ISSUED

Securities Data Company, Inc., 1180 Raymond Boulevard, Newark, New Jersey 07102 (201) 622-3100; *Municipal New Issues Database.*

STATE AND LOCAL GOVERNMENTS - (COMBINED DATA) - TRUST FUNDS

Executive Office of the President, Office of Management and Budget, Executive Office Building, Washington, D.C. 20503 (202) 395-3080; *Budget of the United States Government.*

STATE AND LOCAL GOVERNMENTS - (COMBINED DATA) - WOMEN HOLDING PUBLIC OFFICE

Center for the American Woman and Politics, The Eagleton Institute of Politics, Rutgers University, New Brunswick, New Jersey 08901 (908) 828-2210; information releases.

STATE DATA (FOR INDIVIDUAL STATES) - ABORTIONS

Alan Guttmacher Institute, 111 Fifth Avenue, New York, New York 10003 (212) 254-5656; *Abortion Factbook, Family Planning Aspects,* and unpublished data.

STATE DATA (FOR INDIVIDUAL STATES) - AGRICULTURE - FARMS

U.S. Department of Agriculture, Economic Research Service, Fourteenth Street and Independence Avenue, SW, Washington, D.C. 20005-4789 (202) 219-1504; *Economic Indicators of the Farm Sector: State Financial Summary.*

U.S. Department of Agriculture, National Agricultural Statistics Service, Fourteenth Street and Independence Avenue, SW, Washington, D.C. 20250 (202) 219-1504; *Farm Numbers and Land in Farms,* and *Crop Production.*

U.S. Department of Commerce, Bureau of the Census, Suitland, Maryland 20233 (301) 763-4040; *Census of Agriculture.*

STATE DATA (FOR INDIVIDUAL STATES) - AID TO FAMILIES WITH DEPENDENT CHILDREN

U.S. Department of Health and Human Services, Administration for Children and Families, 370 L'Enfant Promenade, SW, Washington, D.C. 20447 (202) 401-9200; *Quarterly Public Assistance Statistics.*

U.S. Department of Health and Human Services, Social Security Administration, 6401 Security Boulevard, Baltimore, Maryland 21235 (410) 965-1234; *Social Security Bulletin,* and *Annual Statistical Supplement to the Social Security Bulletin.*

STATE DATA (FOR INDIVIDUAL STATES) - AIDS

U.S. Department of Health and Human Services, Centers for Disease Control, 2600 Clifton Road, NE, Atlanta, Georgia 30333 (404) 639-3311; unpublished data.

STATE DATA (FOR INDIVIDUAL STATES) - ALTITUDES

U.S. Department of the Interior, Geological Survey, National Center, 12201 Sunrise Valley Drive, Reston, Virginia 22092 (703) 648-4460; *Elevations and Distances in the United States.*

STATE DATA (FOR INDIVIDUAL STATES) - AREA

U.S. Department of Agriculture, Soil Conservation Service, Fourteenth Street and Independence Avenue, SW, Washington, D.C. 20250 (202) 205-0027; and Iowa State University, Statistical Laboratory; *Statistical Bulletin #790, Summary Report, 1987 National Resources Inventory.*

U.S. Department of Commerce, Bureau of the Census, Suitland, Maryland 20233 (301) 763-4040; *Census of Population and Housing,* and unpublished data.

STATE DATA (FOR INDIVIDUAL STATES) - ASSETS AND
LIABILITIES - FARM

U.S. Department of Agriculture, Economic Research Service,
Fourteenth Street and Independence Avenue, SW, Washington,
D.C. 20005-4789 (202) 219-1504; *Economic Indicators of the Farm
Sector: State Financial Summary.*

STATE DATA (FOR INDIVIDUAL STATES) - BANKS -
COMMERCIAL

Board of Governors of the Federal Reserve System, Twentieth
Street and Constitution Avenue, NW, Washington, D.C. 20551 (202)
452-3000; *Annual Statistical Digest.*

U.S. Federal Deposit Insurance Corporation, 550 Seventeenth Street,
NW, Washington, D.C. 20429 (202) 393-8400; *Annual Report,
Statistics on Banking,* and *FDIC Quarterly Banking Profile.*

STATE DATA (FOR INDIVIDUAL STATES) - BIRTHS AND BIRTH
RATES

U.S. Department of Health and Human Services, National Center for
Health Statistics, 3700 East West Highway, Hyattsville, Maryland
20782 (301) 436-8500; *Vital Statistics of the United States,* and
Monthly Vital Statistics Report.

STATE DATA (FOR INDIVIDUAL STATES) - BIRTHS AND BIRTH
RATES - BIRTH WEIGHT

U.S. Department of Health and Human Services, National Center for
Health Statistics, 3700 East West Highway, Hyattsville, Maryland
20782 (301) 436-8500; *Vital Statistics of the United States,* and
Monthly Vital Statistics Report.

STATE DATA (FOR INDIVIDUAL STATES) - BIRTHS AND BIRTH
RATES - BIRTHS TO SINGLE OR UNMARRIED WOMEN

U.S. Department of Health and Human Services, National Center for
Health Statistics, 3700 East West Highway, Hyattsville, Maryland
20782 (301) 436-8500; *Vital Statistics of the United States,* and
Monthly Vital Statistics Report.

STATE DATA (FOR INDIVIDUAL STATES) - BLACK ELECTED
OFFICIALS

Joint Center for Political and Economic Studies, 1090 Vermont
Avenue, NW, Suite 1100, Washington, D.C. 20005 (202) 789-3500;
Black Elected Officials, A National Roster.

STATE DATA (FOR INDIVIDUAL STATES) - BLACK POPULATION

U.S. Department of Commerce, Bureau of the Census, Suitland,
Maryland 20233 (301) 763-4040; *Census of Population, General
Population Characteristics, United States,* and *Current Population
Reports.*

STATE DATA (FOR INDIVIDUAL STATES) - BUILDING
PERMITS

U.S. Department of Commerce, Bureau of the Census, Suitland,
Maryland 20233 (301) 763-4040; *Construction Reports,* and
unpublished data.

STATE DATA (FOR INDIVIDUAL STATES) - BUSINESS FAILURES AND
LIABILITIES

Dun and Bradstreet, Incorporated, 299 Park Avenue, Twenty-fourth
Floor, New York, New York 10171 (212) 593-6800; *New Business
Incorporations,* and *Business Failure Record.*

STATE DATA (FOR INDIVIDUAL STATES) - CAPITAL PUNISHMENT

U.S. Department of Justice, Bureau of Justice Statistics,, 633 Indiana
Avenue, NW, Washington, D.C. 20531 (800) 732-3277; *Capital
Punishment.*

STATE DATA (FOR INDIVIDUAL STATES) - CHILD ABUSE CASES

U.S. Department of Health and Human Services, National Center on
Child Abuse and Neglect, 370 L'Enfant Promenade, SW,
Washington, D.C. 20447 (202) 205-8586; *National Child Abuse and
Neglect Data System, Working Paper 2, Summary Data Component,*
and *Child Maltreatment.*

STATE DATA (FOR INDIVIDUAL STATES) - CIVILIAN
LABOR FORCE

U.S. Department of Labor, Bureau of Labor Statistics, Two
Massachusetts Avenue, NE, Washington, D.C. 20212 (202) 606-7828;
Geographic Profile of Employment and Unemployment.

STATE DATA (FOR INDIVIDUAL STATES) - CLIMATE

U.S. Department of Commerce, National Oceanic and Atmospheric
Administration, National Climatic Data Center, Federal Building,
Asheville, North Carolina 28801 (704) 259-2000; *Climatography of
the United States,* and *Comparative Climatic Data.*

STATE DATA (FOR INDIVIDUAL STATES) - COAL AND
COKE PRODUCTION

U.S. Department of Energy, Energy Information Administration,
Washington, D.C. 20585 (202) 586-8800; *Coal Production, Quarterly
Coal Report,* and *Annual Energy Review.*

STATE DATA (FOR INDIVIDUAL STATES) - CONGRESS,
UNITED STATES - COMPOSITION

United States Congress, Joint Committee on Printing, North Capitol
and H Streets, NW, Washington, D.C. 20401 (202) 275-2051;
Congressional Directory, and unpublished data.

STATE DATA (FOR INDIVIDUAL STATES) - CONSTRUCTION
CONTRACTS

F.W. Dodge Division, McGraw Hill Information Systems Company,
1221 Avenue of the Americas, New York, New York 10020 (212) 512-
2000; *Dodge Construction Potentials.*

STATE DATA (FOR INDIVIDUAL STATES) - CORRECTIONS

U.S. Department of Commerce, Bureau of the Census, Suitland,
Maryland 20233 (301) 763-4040; *Public Employment,* and
Government Finances.

STATE DATA (FOR INDIVIDUAL STATES) - CRIME RATES

U.S. Department of Justice, Federal Bureau of Investigation, Ninth
Street and Pennsylvania Avenue, NW, Washington, D.C. 20535 (202)
324-3000; *Crime in the United States.*

STATE DATA (FOR INDIVIDUAL STATES) - CROPS - PRINCIPAL

U.S. Department of Agriculture, Economic Research Service, Fourteenth Street and Independence Avenue, SW, Washington, D.C. 20005-4789 (202) 219-1504; *Foreign Agriculture Trade of the United States, Agricultural Resources: Cropland, Water, and Conservation Situation and Outlook Report*, and *Agricultural Statistics*.

U.S. Department of Agriculture, National Agricultural Statistics Service, Fourteenth Street and Independence Avenue, SW, Washington, D.C. 20250 (202) 219-1504; *Crop Production, Crop Values, Field Crops, Non-citrus Fruits and Nuts*, and *Citrus Fruits*.

STATE DATA (FOR INDIVIDUAL STATES) - DEATHS AND DEATH RATES

U.S. Department of Health and Human Services, National Center for Health Statistics, 3700 East-West Highway, Hyattsville, Maryland 20783 (301) 436-8500; *Vital Statistics of the United States, Monthly Vital Statistics Report*, and unpublished data.

STATE DATA (FOR INDIVIDUAL STATES) - DEATHS AND DEATH RATES - INFANT

U.S. Department of Health and Human Services, National Center for Health Statistics, 3700 East-West Highway, Hyattsville, Maryland 20783 (301) 436-8500; *Vital Statistics of the United States*, and unpublished data.

STATE DATA (FOR INDIVIDUAL STATES) - DEFENSE CONTRACTS

U.S. Department of Defense, Office of the Secretary, The Pentagon, Washington, D.C. 20301 (703) 545-6700; *Atlas Data Abstract for the United States and Selected Areas*.

STATE DATA (FOR INDIVIDUAL STATES) - DENTISTS

U.S. Department of Health and Human Services, Health Resources and Services Administration, 5600 Fishers Lane, Rockville, Maryland 20857 (301) 443-2086; unpublished data based on data supplied by American Dental Association, Bureau of Economic and Behavioral Research, 211 East Chicago Avenue, Chicago, Illinois 60611 (312) 440-2500.

STATE DATA (FOR INDIVIDUAL STATES) - DOMESTIC TRAVEL EXPENDITURES

United States Travel Data Center, Two Lafayette Center, 1133 Twenty-first Street, NW, Washington, D.C. 20036 (202) 293-1040; *The Economic Review of Travel in America*.

STATE DATA (FOR INDIVIDUAL STATES) - EARNINGS

U.S. Department of Commerce, Bureau of the Census, Suitland, Maryland 20233 (301) 763-4040; *County Business Patterns*.

U.S. Department of Labor, Bureau of Labor Statistics, Two Massachusetts Avenue, NE, Washington, D.C. 20212 (202) 606-7828; *Employment and Earnings, Employment and Wages, Annual Averages*, and *Average Annual Pay by State and Industry*.

STATE DATA (FOR INDIVIDUAL STATES) - ELECTIONS

Congressional Quarterly, Incorporated, 1414 Twenty-second Street, NW, Washington, D.C. 20037 (202) 887-8500; *Congressional Quarterly Weekly Report*.

Council of State Governments, P.O. Box 11910, Iron Works Pike, Lexington, Kentucky 40578 (606) 231-1939; *State Elective Officials and the Legislature*.

Elections Research Center, 5508 Greystone Street, Chevy Chase, Maryland 20815 (202) 659-9490; *America Votes*.

National Conference of State Legislatures, 1560 Broadway, Suite 700, Denver, Colorado 80202 (303) 830-2200; unpublished data.

U.S. Congress, Joint Committee on Printing, North Capitol and H Streets, NW, Washington, D.C. 20401 (202) 275-2051; *Congressional Directory*, and unpublished data.

U.S. Department of Commerce, Bureau of the Census, Suitland, Maryland 20233 (301) 763-4040; *Current Population Report*.

STATE DATA (FOR INDIVIDUAL STATES) - ELECTIONS - VOTER REGISTRATION

Elections Research Center, 5508 Greystone Street, Chevy Chase, Maryland 20815 (202) 659-9490; *America Votes*.

STATE DATA (FOR INDIVIDUAL STATES) - ELECTRICAL POWER

U.S. Department of Energy, Energy Information Administration, 1000 Independence Avenue, SW, Washington, D.C. 20585 (202) 586-8800; *Electric Power Annual, Electric Power Monthly*, and *Inventory of Power Plants in the U.S.*

STATE DATA (FOR INDIVIDUAL STATES) - ELEVATIONS

U.S. Department of the Interior, Geological Survey, National Center, 12201 Sunrise Valley Drive, Reston, Virginia 22092 (703) 648-4460; *Elevations and Distances in the United States*.

STATE DATA (FOR INDIVIDUAL STATES) - EMPLOYEES

U.S. Department of Commerce, Bureau of the Census, Suitland, Maryland 20233 (301) 763-4040; *Public Employment, Census of Service Industries, County Business Patterns*, and *Exports from Manufacturing Establishments*.

U.S. Department of Labor, Bureau of Labor Statistics, Two Massachusetts Avenue, NE, Washington, D.C. 20212 (202) 606-7828; *Employment and Earnings*.

U.S. Office of Personnel Management, 1900 E Street, NW, Washington, D.C. 20415 (202) 606-1800; *Biennial Report of Employment by Geographic Area*.

STATE DATA (FOR INDIVIDUAL STATES) - ENERGY CONSUMPTION

U.S. Department of Energy, Energy Information Administration, 1000 Independence Avenue, SW, Washington, D.C. 20585 (202) 586-8800; *State Energy Data Report*.

STATE DATA (FOR INDIVIDUAL STATES) - ENERGY EXPENDITURES

U.S. Department of Energy, Energy Information Administration, 1000 Independence Avenue, SW, Washington, D.C. 20585 (202) 586-8800; *State Energy Price and Expenditure Report*.

STATE DATA (FOR INDIVIDUAL STATES) - ESTABLISHMENTS

U.S. Department of Commerce, Bureau of the Census, Suitland, Maryland 20233 (301) 763-4040; *County Business Patterns*.

STATE DATA (FOR INDIVIDUAL STATES) - FARMS

U.S. Department of Agriculture, Economic Research Service, Fourteenth Street and Independence Avenue, SW, Washington, D.C. 20005-4789 (202) 219-1504; *Economic Indicators of the Farm Sector: State Financial Summary*, and *Agricultural Resources, Agricultural Land Values and Markets, Situation and Outlook Report*.

U.S. Department of Agriculture, National Agricultural Statistics Service, Fourteenth Street and Independence Avenue, SW, Washington, D.C. 20250 (202) 219-1504; *Crop Production*, and *Farm Numbers and Land in Farms*.

U.S. Department of Commerce, Bureau of the Census, Suitland, Maryland 20233 (301) 763-4040; *Census of Agriculture*.

STATE DATA (FOR INDIVIDUAL STATES) - FARMS - ASSETS AND LIABILITIES

U.S. Department of Agriculture, Economic Research Service, Fourteenth Street and Independence Avenue, SW, Washington, D.C. 20005-4789 (202) 219-1504; *Economic Indicators of the Farm Sector: State Financial Summary*.

STATE DATA (FOR INDIVIDUAL STATES) - FARMS - INCOME

U.S. Department of Agriculture, Economic Research Service, Fourteenth Street and Independence Avenue, SW, Washington, D.C. 20005-4789 (202) 219-1504; *Economic Indicators of the Farm Sector: State Financial Summary*.

STATE DATA (FOR INDIVIDUAL STATES) - FARMS - VALUE OF FARM LAND AND BUILDINGS

U.S. Department of Agriculture, Economic Research Service, Fourteenth Street and Independence Avenue, SW, Washington, D.C. 20005-4789 (202) 219-1504; *Agricultural Resources, Agricultural Land Values and Markets, Situation and Outlook Report*.

STATE DATA (FOR INDIVIDUAL STATES) - FEDERAL FUNDS

U.S. Department of Commerce, Bureau of the Census, Suitland, Maryland 20233 (301) 763-4040; *Federal Expenditures by State for Fiscal Year*.

STATE DATA (FOR INDIVIDUAL STATES) - FISHERIES

U.S. Department of Commerce, National Oceanic and Atmospheric Administration, National Marine Fisheries Service, 1335 East-West Highway, Silver Spring, Maryland 20910 (301) 427-2239; *Fishery Statistics of the United States*, and *Fisheries of the United States*.

STATE DATA (FOR INDIVIDUAL STATES) - FOREIGN INVESTMENT IN THE UNITED STATES

U.S. Department of Commerce, Bureau of Economic Analysis, Fourteenth Street between Constitution Avenue and E Street, NW, Washington, D.C. 20230 (202) 606-9900; *Survey of Current Business*, and *Foreign Direct Investment in the United States, Operations of U.S. Affiliates of Foreign Countries*.

STATE DATA (FOR INDIVIDUAL STATES) - FUEL PRODUCTION

U.S. Department of Energy, Energy Information Administration, Washington, D.C. 20585 (202) 586-8800; *Energy Data Reports, Natural Gas Annual, Natural Gas Monthly*, and *Petroleum Supply Annual*.

STATE DATA (FOR INDIVIDUAL STATES) - GAS UTILITY INDUSTRY

American Gas Association, Incorporated, 1515 Wilson Boulevard, Arlington, Virginia 22209 (703) 841-8400; *Gas Facts*.

STATE DATA (FOR INDIVIDUAL STATES) - GASOLINE PRICES

U.S. Department of Energy, Energy Information Administration, 1000 Independence Avenue, SW, Washington, D.C. 20585 (202) 586-8800; *Petroleum Marketing Monthly*.

STATE DATA (FOR INDIVIDUAL STATES) - GASOLINE TAX RATES

U.S. Department of Transportation, Federal Highway Administration, 400 Seventh Street, SW, Washington, D.C. 20590 (202) 366-0660; *Highway Statistics*.

STATE DATA (FOR INDIVIDUAL STATES) - GOVERNMENT FINANCES - FEDERAL AID TO STATE AND LOCAL GOVERNMENTS

U.S. Department of Commerce, Bureau of the Census, Suitland, Maryland 20233 (301) 763-4040; *Federal Expenditures by State for Fiscal Year*.

STATE DATA (FOR INDIVIDUAL STATES) - GOVERNMENT FINANCES - FEDERAL INCOME TAX COLLECTIONS

U.S. Department of the Treasury, Internal Revenue Service, 1111 Constitution Avenue, NW, Washington, D.C. 20224 (202) 566-5000; *Statistics of Income Bulletin*.

STATE DATA (FOR INDIVIDUAL STATES) - GOVERNMENT FINANCES - STATE AND LOCAL GOVERNMENTS

U.S. Department of Commerce, Bureau of the Census, Suitland, Maryland 20233 (301) 763-4040; *Government Finances*, and *Federal Expenditures by State for Fiscal Year*.

STATE DATA (FOR INDIVIDUAL STATES) - GOVERNMENT FINANCES - STATE GOVERNMENTS

National Governor's Association, Hall of the States, 444 North Capitol Street, NW, Washington, D.C. 20001 (202) 624-5300; and National Association of State Budget Officers, Hall of the States, 400 North Capitol Street, NW, Washington, D.C. 20001 (202) 624-5382; *NASBO State Expenditure Report*, and *Fiscal Survey of the States*.

U.S. Department of Commerce, Bureau of the Census, Suitland, Maryland 20233 (301) 763-4040; *State Government Finances, State Government Tax Collections*, and *Historical Statistics on Governmental Finances and Employment*.

STATE DATA (FOR INDIVIDUAL STATES) - GOVERNMENT FINANCES - TAX COLLECTIONS

U.S. Department of Commerce, Bureau of the Census, Suitland, Maryland 20233 (301) 763-4040; *State Government Tax Collections*, and *City Government Finances*.

STATE DATA (FOR INDIVIDUAL STATES) - GOVERNORS - VOTE CAST

Elections Research Center, 5508 Greystone Street, Chevy Chase, Maryland 20815 (202) 659-9490; *America Votes*, and unpublished data.

STATE DATA (FOR INDIVIDUAL STATES) - GROSS DOMESTIC PRODUCT

U.S. Department of Commerce, Bureau of Economic Analysis, Fourteenth Street between Constitution Avenue and E Street, NW, Washington, D.C. 20230 (202) 606-9900; *Survey of Current Business*.

STATE DATA (FOR INDIVIDUAL STATES) - HAZARDOUS WASTE SITES

U.S. Environmental Protection Agency, 401 M Street, SW, Washington, D.C. 20460 (202) 382-2090; Supplementary Materials: National Priorities List.

STATE DATA (FOR INDIVIDUAL STATES) - HIGHWAY MILEAGE

U.S. Department of Transportation, Federal Highway Administration, 400 Seventh Street, SW, Washington, D.C. 20590 (202) 366-0660; *Highway Statistics*.

STATE DATA (FOR INDIVIDUAL STATES) - HIGHWAY TRUST FUND

U.S. Department of Commerce, Bureau of the Census, Suitland, Maryland 20233 (301) 763-4040; *Federal Expenditures by State for Fiscal Year*.

STATE DATA (FOR INDIVIDUAL STATES) - HISPANIC ELECTED OFFICIALS

National Association of Latino Elected and Appointed Officials, NALEO Education Fund, 3409 Garnet Street, Los Angeles, California 90023 (213) 262-8503; *National Roster of Hispanic Elected Officials*.

STATE DATA (FOR INDIVIDUAL STATES) - HOSPITALS - COST TO PATIENT

American Hospital Association, 840 North Lake Shore Drive, Chicago, Illinois 60611 (312) 280-6000; *Hospital Statistics*, and unpublished data.

STATE DATA (FOR INDIVIDUAL STATES) - HOUSEHOLDS OR FAMILIES

U.S. Department of Commerce, Bureau of the Census, Suitland, Maryland 20233 (301) 763-4040; *Current Population Reports*, and *Census of Population, General Population Characteristics, United States*.

STATE DATA (FOR INDIVIDUAL STATES) - HOUSING UNITS

U.S. Department of Commerce, Bureau of the Census, Suitland, Maryland 20233 (301) 763-4040; *Current Housing Reports*, and *Construction Reports*.

STATE DATA (FOR INDIVIDUAL STATES) - HOUSING UNITS - SOLD

National Association of Realtors, 430 North Michigan Avenue, Chicago, Illinois 60611-4087 (312) 329-8200; *Real Estate Outlook: Market Trends and Insights*.

STATE DATA (FOR INDIVIDUAL STATES) - IMMIGRANTS ADMITTED

U.S. Department of Justice, Immigration and Naturalization Service, 425 I Street, NW, Washington, D.C. 20536 (202) 514-4316; *Statistical Yearbook*.

STATE DATA (FOR INDIVIDUAL STATES) - INCOME

U.S. Department of Commerce, Bureau of the Census, Suitland, Maryland 20233 (301) 763-4040; *Current Population Reports*, and *Census of Population*.

STATE DATA (FOR INDIVIDUAL STATES) - INCOME - DISPOSABLE PERSONAL

U.S. Department of Commerce, Bureau of Economic Analysis, Fourteenth Street between Constitution Avenue and E Street, NW, Washington, D.C. 20230 (202) 606-9900; *Survey of Current Business*, and unpublished data.

STATE DATA (FOR INDIVIDUAL STATES) - INCOME - FAMILY

U.S. Department of Commerce, Bureau of the Census, Suitland, Maryland 20233 (301) 763-4040; *Census of Population and Housing*.

STATE DATA (FOR INDIVIDUAL STATES) - INCOME - PER CAPITA

U.S. Department of Commerce, Bureau of the Census, Suitland, Maryland 20233 (301) 763-4040; *Census of Population and Housing*.

STATE DATA (FOR INDIVIDUAL STATES) - INCOME - PERSONAL

U.S. Department of Commerce, Bureau of Economic Analysis, Fourteenth Street between Constitution Avenue and E Street, NW, Washington, D.C. 20230 (202) 606-9900; *Survey of Current Business*, and unpublished data.

STATE DATA (FOR INDIVIDUAL STATES) - INCORPORATIONS

Dun and Bradstreet Corporation, 299 Park Avenue, Twenty-fourth Floor, New York, New York 10171 (212) 593-6800; *New Business Incorporations*, and *Business Failure Record*.

STATE DATA (FOR INDIVIDUAL STATES) - LAND

U.S. Department of Agriculture, Soil Conservation Service, Fourteenth Street and Independence Avenue, SW, Washington, D.C. 20250 (202) 205-0027; *National Resources Inventory*.

U.S. General Services Administration, General Services Building, Eighteenth and F Streets, NW, Washington, D.C. 20405 (202) 708-5082; *Inventory Report on Real Property Owned by the United States Throughout the World*.

STATE DATA (FOR INDIVIDUAL STATES) - LAND - FEDERAL

U.S. General Services Administration, General Services Building, Eighteenth and F Streets, NW, Washington, D.C. 20405 (202) 708-5082; *Inventory Report on Real Property Owned by the United States Throughout the World*.

STATE DATA (FOR INDIVIDUAL STATES) - LEGISLATURES - COMPOSITION

Council of State Governments, Post Office Box 11910, Iron Works Pike, Lexington, Kentucky 40578 (606) 231-1939; *State Elective Officials and the Legislators*.

National Conference of State Legislatures, 1050 Seventeenth Street, Suite 2100, Denver, Colorado 80265 (303) 623-7800; *State Legislatures.*

STATE DATA (FOR INDIVIDUAL STATES) - LIVESTOCK AND POULTRY

U.S. Department of Agriculture, National Agricultural Statistics Service, Fourteenth Street and Independence Avenue, SW, Washington, D.C. 20250 (202) 219-1504; *Meat Animals - Production, Disposition and Income, Dairy Products,* and *Milk Production, Disposition, and Income.*

STATE DATA (FOR INDIVIDUAL STATES) - LOCAL GOVERNMENTAL UNITS

U.S. Department of Commerce, Bureau of the Census, Suitland, Maryland 20233 (301) 763-4040; *Census of Governments,* and *Government Organization.*

STATE DATA (FOR INDIVIDUAL STATES) - LOTTERIES - REVENUE FROM

U.S. Department of Commerce, Bureau of the Census, Suitland, Maryland 20233 (301) 763-4040; *State Government Finances.*

STATE DATA (FOR INDIVIDUAL STATES) - MANUFACTURES - SUMMARY STATISTICS

U.S. Department of Commerce, Bureau of the Census, Suitland, Maryland 20233 (301) 763-4040; *Census of Manufactures,* and *Annual Survey of Manufactures.*

STATE DATA (FOR INDIVIDUAL STATES) - MARRIAGE AND DIVORCE

U.S. Department of Health and Human Services, Public Health Service, 200 Independence Avenue, SW, Washington, D.C. 20301 (202) 619-1296; *Vital Statistics of the United States,* and *Monthly Vital Statistics Report.*

STATE DATA (FOR INDIVIDUAL STATES) - MEDICAID AND MEDICARE

U.S. Department of Health and Human Services, Health Care Financing Administration, 200 Independence Avenue, SW, Washington, D.C. 20201 (202) 245-6113; unpublished data.

STATE DATA (FOR INDIVIDUAL STATES) - METROPOLITAN AREA POPULATION

U.S. Department of Commerce, Bureau of the Census, Suitland, Maryland 20233 (301) 763-4040; *Census of Population and Housing, Supplementary Reports, Metropolitan Areas as Defined by the Office of Management and Budget,* and unpublished data.

STATE DATA (FOR INDIVIDUAL STATES) - MILK PRODUCTION

U.S. Department of Agriculture, National Agricultural Statistics Service, Fourteenth Street and Independence Avenue, SW, Washington, D.C. 20250 (202) 219-1504; *Milk Production, Disposition, and Income,* and *Dairy Products.*

STATE DATA (FOR INDIVIDUAL STATES) - MINERAL PRODUCTION AND VALUE

U.S. Department of Energy, Energy Information Administration, Washington, D.C. 20585 (202) 586-8800; *Annual Energy Review, Uranium Industry Annual, Petroleum Supply Annual, Natural Gas Annual,* and *Quarterly Coal Report.*

U.S. Department of the Interior, Bureau of Mines, 810 Seventh Street, NW, Washington, D.C. 20241 (202) 501-9649; *Annual Reports,* and *Mineral Commodities Summaries.*

STATE DATA (FOR INDIVIDUAL STATES) - MOTOR FUEL TAX

U.S. Department of Transportation, Federal Highway Administration, 400 Seventh Street, SW, Washington, D.C. 20590 (202) 366-0660; *Highway Statistics.*

STATE DATA (FOR INDIVIDUAL STATES) - MOTOR VEHICLE REGISTRATIONS

U.S. Department of Transportation, Federal Highway Administration, 400 Seventh Street, SW, Washington, D.C. 20590 (202) 366-0660; *Highway Statistics,* and *Selected Highway Statistics and Charts.*

STATE DATA (FOR INDIVIDUAL STATES) - NATIONAL FORESTS

U.S. Department of Agriculture, Forest Service, Fourteenth Street and Independence Avenue, SW, Washington, D.C. 20250 (202) 720-3760; *Land Areas of the National Forest System,* and unpublished data.

STATE DATA (FOR INDIVIDUAL STATES) - NEWSPAPERS - NUMBER AND CIRCULATION

Editor and Publisher, 11 West Nineteenth Street, New York, New York 10011 (212) 675-4380; *Editor and Publisher International Year Book.*

STATE DATA (FOR INDIVIDUAL STATES) NURSES

U.S. Department of Health and Human Services, Health Resources and Services Administration, 5600 Fishers Lane, Rockville, Maryland 20857 (301) 443-2086; unpublished data.

STATE DATA (FOR INDIVIDUAL STATES) - PARKS

National Association of State Park Directors, 126 Mill Branch Road, Tallahassee, Florida 32312 (904) 893-4959; *Annual Information Exchange.*

U.S. Department of the Interior, National Park Service, C Street between Eighteenth and Nineteenth Streets, NW, Washington, D.C. 20240 (202) 208-6843; *National Park Statistical Abstract,* and unpublished data.

STATE DATA (FOR INDIVIDUAL STATES) - PATENTS

U.S. Department of Commerce, Patent and Trademark Office, 2011 Crystal Drive, Arlington, Virginia 22202 (703) 305-8341; *Technology Assessment and Forecast Database.*

STATE DATA (FOR INDIVIDUAL STATES) - PHYSICIANS

American Medical Association, 515 North State Street, Chicago, Illinois 60610 (312) 464-4818; *Physician Characteristics and Distribution in the United States.*

STATE DATA (FOR INDIVIDUAL STATES) - POLICE PROTECTION

U.S. Department of Commerce, Bureau of the Census, Suitland, Maryland 20233 (301) 763-4040; *Public Employment,* and *Government Finances.*

STATE DATA (FOR INDIVIDUAL STATES) - POPULATION

U.S. Department of Commerce, Bureau of the Census, Suitland, Maryland 20233 (301) 763-4040; *Current Population Reports, Census of Population and Housing,* and unpublished data.

STATE DATA (FOR INDIVIDUAL STATES) - POPULATION - AGE DISTRIBUTION

U.S. Department of Commerce, Bureau of the Census, Suitland, Maryland 20233 (301) 763-4040; *Current Population Reports.*

STATE DATA (FOR INDIVIDUAL STATES) - POPULATION - BLACK

U.S. Department of Commerce, Bureau of the Census, Suitland, Maryland 20233 (301) 763-4040; *Census of Population, General Population Characteristics, U.S.,* and *Current Population Reports.*

STATE DATA (FOR INDIVIDUAL STATES) - POPULATION - DENSITY

U.S. Department of Commerce, Bureau of the Census, Suitland, Maryland 20233 (301) 763-4040; *Current Population Reports, Census of Population and Housing,* and unpublished data.

STATE DATA (FOR INDIVIDUAL STATES) - POPULATION - METROPOLITAN AREAS

U.S. Department of Commerce, Bureau of the Census, Suitland, Maryland 20233 (301) 763-4040; *Census of Population and Housing, Supplementary Reports, Metropolitan Areas as Defined by the Office of Management and Budget.*

STATE DATA (FOR INDIVIDUAL STATES) - POULTRY

U.S. Department of Agriculture, National Agricultural Statistics Service, Fourteenth Street and Independence Avenue, SW, Washington, D.C. 20250 (202) 219-1504; *Poultry - Production and Value,* and *Turkeys.*

STATE DATA (FOR INDIVIDUAL STATES) - POVERTY

U.S. Department of Commerce, Bureau of the Census, Suitland, Maryland 20233 (301) 763-4040; *Census of Population and Housing,* and *Current Population Reports.*

STATE DATA (FOR INDIVIDUAL STATES) - PRESIDENT - VOTE CAST

Elections Research Center, 5508 Greystone Street, Chevy Chase, Maryland 20815 (202) 659-9490; *America Votes.*

U.S. Congress, Clerk of the House, The Capitol, Washington, D.C. 20515 (202) 224-3121; *Statistics of the Presidential and Congressional Election.*

STATE DATA (FOR INDIVIDUAL STATES) - PRISONS AND PRISONERS

U.S. Department of Justice, Bureau of Justice Statistics, 633 Indiana Avenue, NW, Washington, D.C. 20531 (800) 732-3277; *Prisoners in 1991, Correctional Populations in the United States,* and *Survey of State Prison Inmates.*

STATE DATA (FOR INDIVIDUAL STATES) - PUBLIC AID

U.S. Department of Health and Human Services, Administration for Children and Families, 370 L'Enfant Promenade, SW, Washington, D.C. 20447 (202) 401-9200; *Quarterly Public Assistance Statistics.*

U.S. Department of Health and Human Services, Social Security Administration, 6401 Security Boulevard, Baltimore, Maryland 21235 (410) 965-1234; *Social Security Bulletin,* and *Annual Statistical Supplement to the Social Security Bulletin.*

STATE DATA (FOR INDIVIDUAL STATES) - RECREATIONAL AREAS

National Association of State Park Directors, 126 Mill Branch Road, Tallahassee, Florida 32312 (904) 893-4959; *Annual Information Exchange.*

STATE DATA (FOR INDIVIDUAL STATES) - REPRESENTATIVES, UNITED STATES - VOTE CAST

Elections Research Center, 5508 Greystone Street, Chevy Chase, Maryland 20815 (202) 659-9490; *America Votes.*

STATE DATA (FOR INDIVIDUAL STATES) - RESEARCH AND DEVELOPMENT

U.S. National Science Foundation, 4201 Wilson Boulevard, Arlington, Virginia 22230 (703) 306-1234; *National Patterns of Research and Development Resources.*

STATE DATA (FOR INDIVIDUAL STATES) - RETAIL TRADE - SALES

Market Statistics, 633 Third Avenue, New York, New York 10017 (212) 986-4000; *The Survey of Buying Power Data Service.*

STATE DATA (FOR INDIVIDUAL STATES) - REVENUE - LOCAL GOVERNMENTS

U.S. Department of Commerce, Bureau of the Census, Suitland, Maryland 20233 (301) 763-4040; *Historical Statistics on Governmental Finances and Employment,* and *Government Finances.*

STATE DATA (FOR INDIVIDUAL STATES) - ROADS AND HIGHWAYS

U.S. Department of Commerce, Bureau of the Census, Suitland, Maryland 20233 (301) 763-4040; *Federal Expenditures by State for Fiscal Year.*

U.S. Department of Transportation, Federal Highway Administration, 400 Seventh Street, SW, Washington, D.C. 20590 (202) 366-0660; *Highway Statistics.*

STATE DATA (FOR INDIVIDUAL STATES) - SALES

Market Statistics, 633 Third Avenue, New York, New York 10017 (212) 986-4000; *The Survey of Buying Power Data Service.*

National Research Bureau, 225 West Wacker Drive, Chicago, Illinois 60606 (312) 346-9097; data published by International Council of Shopping Centers, 665 Fifth Avenue, New York, New York 10022 (212) 421-8181; *Shopping Centers Today.*

STATE DATA (FOR INDIVIDUAL STATES) - SCHOOLS AND EDUCATION - ATTAINMENT

U.S. Department of Commerce, Bureau of the Census, Suitland, Maryland 20233 (301) 763-4040; *Census of Population.*

STATE DATA (FOR INDIVIDUAL STATES) - SCHOOLS AND EDUCATION - COLLEGES - NUMBER

U.S. Department of Education, National Center for Education Statistics, 400 Maryland Avenue, SW, Washington, D.C. 20202 (202) 708-5366; *Digest of Education Statistics.*

STATE DATA (FOR INDIVIDUAL STATES) - SCHOOLS AND EDUCATION - ELEMENTARY AND SECONDARY TEACHERS - PUBLIC

National Education Association, 1201 Sixteenth Street, NW, Washington, D.C. 20036 (202) 833-4000; *Estimates of School Statistics.*

STATE DATA (FOR INDIVIDUAL STATES) - SCHOOLS AND EDUCATION - ENROLLMENT - ELEMENTARY AND SECONDARY

U.S. Department of Education, 400 Maryland Avenue, SW, Washington, D.C. 20202 (202) 708-5366; *Digest of Education Statistics.*

STATE DATA (FOR INDIVIDUAL STATES) - SCHOOLS AND EDUCATION - ENROLLMENT - ELEMENTARY AND SECONDARY

U.S. Department of Education, 400 Maryland Avenue, SW, Washington, D.C. 20202 (202) 708-5366; *Digest of Education Statistics,* and *Projections of Education Statistics.*

STATE DATA (FOR INDIVIDUAL STATES) - SCHOOLS AND EDUCATION - ENROLLMENT - HIGHER EDUCATION

U.S. Department of Education, 400 Maryland Avenue, SW, Washington, D.C. 20202 (202) 708-5366; *Digest of Education Statistics.*

STATE DATA (FOR INDIVIDUAL STATES) - SCHOOLS AND EDUCATION - FINANCES - ELEMENTARY AND SECONDARY - PUBLIC

National Education Association, 1201 Sixteenth Street, NW, Washington, D.C. 20036 (202) 833-4000; *Estimates of School Statistics,* and unpublished data.

STATE DATA (FOR INDIVIDUAL STATES) - SCHOOLS AND EDUCATION - FINANCES - HIGHER EDUCATION - PUBLIC

Research Associates of Washington, 2605 Klingle Road, NW, Washington, D.C. 20008 (202) 966-3326; *State Profiles: Financing Public Higher Education.*

STATE DATA (FOR INDIVIDUAL STATES) - SCHOOLS AND EDUCATION - HIGH SCHOOL GRADUATES - PUBLIC

U.S. Department of Education, 400 Maryland Avenue, SW, Washington, D.C. 20202 (202) 708-5366; *Digest of Education Statistics,* and *Projections of Education Statistics.*

STATE DATA (FOR INDIVIDUAL STATES) - SCHOOLS AND EDUCATION - TEACHERS

National Education Association, 1201 Sixteenth Street, NW, Washington, D.C. 20016 (202) 833-4000; *Estimates of School Statistics.*

STATE DATA (FOR INDIVIDUAL STATES) - SENATORS - VOTE CAST

Elections Research Center, 5508 Greystone Street, Chevy Chase, Maryland 20815 (202) 659-9490; *America Votes.*

STATE DATA (FOR INDIVIDUAL STATES) - SHOPPING CENTERS

National Research Bureau, 225 West Wacker Drive, Suite 2275, Chicago, Illinois 60606 (312) 346-9097; data published by International Council of Shopping Centers, 665 Fifth Avenue, New York, New York 10022 (212) 421-8181; *Shopping Centers Today.*

STATE DATA (FOR INDIVIDUAL STATES) - SOCIAL SECURITY PROGRAM

U.S. Department of Health and Human Services, Health Care Financing Administration, 200 Independence Avenue, SW, Washington, D.C. 20201 (202) 245-6113; unpublished data.

U.S. Department of Health and Human Services, Social Security Administration, 6401 Security Boulevard, Baltimore, Maryland 21235 (410) 965-1234; *Social Security Bulletin.*

STATE DATA (FOR INDIVIDUAL STATES) - SUPPLEMENTAL SECURITY INCOME

U.S. Department of Health and Human Services, Administration for Children and Families, 370 L'Enfant Promenade, SW, Washington, D.C. 20447 (202) 401-9200; *Quarterly Public Assistance Statistics.*

U.S. Department of Health and Human Services, Social Security Administration, 6401 Security Boulevard, Baltimore, Maryland 21235 (410) 965-1234; *Social Security Bulletin,* and *Annual Statistical Supplement to the Social Security Bulletin.*

STATE DATA (FOR INDIVIDUAL STATES) - TAXATION

Advisory Commission of Intergovernmental Relations, 800 K Street, NW, Suite 450 South, Washington, D.C. 20575 (202) 653-5540; *Significant Features of Fiscal Federalism.*

U.S. Department of Commerce, Bureau of the Census, Suitland, Maryland 20233 (301) 763-4040; *Government Finances, State Government Tax Collections, State Government Finances,* and *Historical Statistics on Governmental Finances and Employment.*

U.S. Department of the Treasury, Internal Revenue Service, 1111 Constitution Avenue, NW, Washington, D.C. 20224 (202) 566-5000; *Statistics of Income Bulletin.*

STATE DATA (FOR INDIVIDUAL STATES) - UNEMPLOYMENT

U.S. Department of Labor, Bureau of Labor Statistics, Two Massachusetts Avenue, NE, Washington, D.C. 20212 (202) 606-7828; *Geographic Profile of Employment and Unemployment.*

STATE DATA (FOR INDIVIDUAL STATES) - UNEMPLOYMENT INSURANCE

U.S. Department of Labor, Employment and Training Administration, 200 Constitution Avenue, NW, Washington, D.C. 20210 (202) 219-0600; *Unemployment Insurance Data Summary.*

STATE DATA (FOR INDIVIDUAL STATES) - VETERANS - NUMBER AND EXPENDITURES

U.S. Department of Veterans Affairs, 810 Vermont Avenue, NW, Washington, D.C. 20420 (202) 233-2300; *Annual Report of the*

Secretary of Veterans Affairs.

STATE DATA (FOR INDIVIDUAL STATES) - VOTER TURNOUT

Election Research Center, 5508 Greystone Street, Chevy Chase, Maryland 20815 (202) 659-9490; *America Votes.*

U.S. Department of Commerce, Bureau of the Census, Suitland, Maryland 20233 (301) 763-4040; *Current Population Reports.*

STATE DATA (FOR INDIVIDUAL STATES) - VOTES CAST

Committee for the Study of the American Electorate, 421 New Jersey Avenue, SE, Washington, D.C. 20003 (202) 546-3221; unpublished data.

Election Research Center, 5508 Greystone Street, Chevy Chase, Maryland 20815 (202) 659-9490; *America Votes*, and unpublished data.

United States Congress, Clerk of the House, The Capitol, Washington, D.C. 20515 (202) 224-3121; *Statistics of the Presidential and Congressional Election.*

U.S. Department of Commerce, Bureau of the Census, Suitland, Maryland 20233 (301) 763-4040; *Current Population Reports.*

STATE DATA (FOR INDIVIDUAL STATES) - VOTING AGE POPULATION

Elections Research Center, 5508 Greystone Street, Chevy Chase, Maryland 20815 (202) 659-9490; *America Votes.*

U.S. Department of Commerce, Bureau of the Census, Suitland, Maryland 20233 (301) 763-4040; *Current Population Reports.*

STATE DATA (FOR INDIVIDUAL STATES) - WOMEN HOLDING PUBLIC OFFICE

Center for the American Woman and Politics, The Eagleton Institute of Politics, Rutgers University, New Brunswick, New Jersey 08901 (908) 828-2210; information releases.

STATE DATA (FOR INDIVIDUAL STATES) - YEAR OF ADMISSION TO STATEHOOD

U.S. Department of Commerce, Bureau of the Census, Suitland, Maryland 20233 (301) 763-4040; *Census of Population and Housing.*

STATE GOVERNMENT - See also STATE AND LOCAL GOVERNMENTS

STATE GOVERNMENT - DEBT

U.S. Department of Commerce, Bureau of the Census, Suitland, Maryland 20233 (301) 763-4040; *State Government Finances*, and *Historical Statistics on Governmental Finances and Employment.*

STATE GOVERNMENT - DEBT - PUBLIC HIGHWAYS

U.S. Department of Transportation, Federal Highway Administration, 400 Seventh Street, SW, Washington, D.C. 20590 (202) 366-0660; *Highway Statistics.*

STATE GOVERNMENT - EMPLOYEES AND PAYROLLS

U.S. Department of Commerce, Bureau of the Census, Suitland, Maryland 20233 (301) 763-4040; *Public Employment*, and *Historical Statistics on Governmental Finances and Employment.*

STATE GOVERNMENT - FINANCES

National Association of State Budget Officers, Hall of the States, 444 North Capitol Street, Washington, D.C. 20001 (202) 624-5382; *Fiscal Survey of the States*, and *NASBO State Expenditure Report.*

U.S. Department of Commerce, Bureau of Economic Analysis, Fourteenth Street between Constitution Avenue and E Street, NW, Washington, D.C. 20230 (202) 606-9900; *The National Income and Product Accounts of the United States*, and *Survey of Current Business.*

U.S. Department of Commerce, Bureau of the Census, Suitland, Maryland 20233 (301) 763-4040; *Government Finances State Government Finances*, and *State Government Tax Collections.*

STATE GOVERNMENT - FINANCES - REVENUE FROM LOTTERIES

U.S. Department of Commerce, Bureau of the Census, Suitland, Maryland 20233 (301) 763-4040; *State Government Finances.*

STATE GOVERNMENT - FINANCES - TAX COLLECTIONS

U.S. Department of Commerce, Bureau of the Census, Suitland, Maryland 20233 (301) 763-4040; *State Government Tax Collections*, and *State Government Finances.*

STATE GOVERNMENT - HIGHWAY FUNDS - DISBURSEMENTS OF

U.S. Department of Transportation, Federal Highway Administration, 400 Seventh Street, SW, Washington, D.C. 20590 (202) 366-0660; *Highway Statistics.*

STATE GOVERNMENT - PARK SYSTEMS

National Association of State Park Directors, 126 Mill Branch Road, Tallahassee, Florida 32312 (904) 893-4959; *Annual Information Exchange.*

STATE GOVERNMENT - PAYMENTS FOR PUBLIC ASSISTANCE

U.S. Department of Health and Human Services, Administration for Children and Families, 370 L'Enfant Promenade, SW, Washington, D.C. 20447 (202) 401-9200; *Quarterly Public Assistance Statistics.*

U.S. Department of Health and Human Services, Social Security Administration, 6401 Security Boulevard, Baltimore, Maryland 21235 (410) 965-1234; *Annual Statistical Supplement to the Social Security Bulletin*, and *Social Security Bulletin.*

STATE GOVERNMENT - RECEIPTS - HIGHWAYS

U.S. Department of Transportation, Federal Highway Administration, 400 Seventh Street, SW, Washington, D.C. 20590 (202) 366-0660; *Highway Statistics.*

STATE GOVERNMENT - TAXES

Advisory Commission of Intergovernmental Relations, 800 K Street, NW, Suite 450 South, Washington, D.C. 20575 (202) 653-5540; *Significant Features of Fiscal Federalism.*

U.S. Department of Commerce, Bureau of the Census, Suitland, Maryland 20233 (301) 763-4040; *Historical Statistics on Governmental Finances and Employment, Government Finances, State Government Finances,* and *State Government Tax Collections.*

STATE GOVERNMENT - UNEMPLOYMENT INSURANCE

U.S. Department of Health and Human Services, Social Security Administration, 6401 Security Boulevard, Baltimore, Maryland 21235 (410) 965-1234; *Annual Statistical Supplement to the Social Security Bulletin,* and unpublished data.

STATE HIGHWAYS - See HIGHWAYS

STATE PARK SYSTEMS

National Association of State Park Directors, 126 Mill Branch Road, Tallahassee, Florida 32312 (904) 893-4959; *Annual Information Exchange.*

STATEHOOD - ADMISSION TO

U.S. Department of Commerce, Bureau of the Census, Suitland, Maryland 20233 (301) 763-4040; *Census of Population and Housing.*

STEAM ENGINES AND TURBINES, ELECTRIC - LOCOMOTIVE (RAILROADS)

Association of American Railroads, American Railroads Building, 50 F Street, NW, Washington, D.C. 20001 (202) 639-2100; *Railroad Facts, Statistics of Railroads of Class I,* and *Analysis of Class I Railroads.*

STEEL - See also IRON AND STEEL

American Iron and Steel Institute, 1101 Seventeenth Street, NW, Washington, D.C. 20036 (202) 452-7100, *Annual Statistical Report.*

U.S. Department of the Interior, Bureau of Mines, 810 Seventh Street, NW, Washington, D.C. 20241 (202) 501-9649; *Annual Reports,* and *Mineral Commodities Summaries.*

STEEL - SCRAP

American Iron and Steel Institute, 1101 Seventeenth Street, NW, Washington, D.C. 20036 (202) 452-7100; *Annual Statistical Report.*

U.S. Department of Labor, Bureau of Labor Statistics, Two Massachusetts Avenue, NE, Washington, D.C. 20212 (202) 606-7828; *Producer Price Indexes.*

STEEL - WORLD PRODUCTION

Statistical Office of the United Nations, New York, New York 10017 (800) 253-9646; *Monthly Bulletin of Statistics,* and *Statistical Yearbook.*

U.S. Department of the Interior, Bureau of Mines, 810 Seventh Street, NW, Washington, D.C. 20241 (202) 501-9649; *Annual Reports,* and *Mineral Commodities Summaries.*

STEEL WORKS AND ROLLING MILLS - See IRON AND STEEL

STIMULANTS - PERSONS USING

U.S. Department of Health and Human Services, Substance Abuse and Mental Health Administration, 5600 Fishers Lane, Rockville,

Maryland 20857 (301) 443-4797; *National Household Survey on Drug Abuse.*

STOCK EXCHANGES - PRICES

Board of Governors of the Federal Reserve System, Twentieth Street and Constitution Avenue, NW, Washington, D.C. 20551 (202) 452-3000; *Federal Reserve Bulletin,* and *Annual Statistical Digest.*

New York Stock Exchange, 11 Wall Street, New York, New York 10005 (212) 656-3000; *Fact Book.*

STOCK EXCHANGES - VOLUME OF TRADING

Board of Governors of the Federal Reserve System, Twentieth Street and Constitution Avenue, NW, Washington, D.C. 20551 (202) 452-3000; *Federal Reserve Bulletin.*

National Association of Securities Dealers, 1735 K Street, NW, Washington, D.C. 20006 (202) 728-8000; *Fact Book.*

New York Stock Exchange, 11 Wall Street, New York, New York 10005 (212) 656-3000; *Fact Book.*

U.S. Securities and Exchange Commission, 450 Fifth Street, NW, Washington, D.C. 20549 (202) 272-3100; unpublished data.

STOCKHOLDERS' EQUITY - PROFIT RATES ON

Federal Deposit Insurance Corporation, 550 Seventeenth Street, NW, Washington, D.C. 20429 (202) 393-8400; *Annual Report, The FDIC Quarterly Banking Profile, Statistics on Banking,* and unpublished data.

STOCKPILES - GOVERNMENT - STRATEGIC AND CRITICAL MATERIALS

U.S. Department of Defense, Defense Logistics Agency, Cameron Station, Alexandria, Virginia 22304-6100 (703) 695-3291; *Statistical Supplement, Stockpile Report to the Congress.*

STOCKS - CORPORATE - FLOW OF FUNDS

Board of Governors of the Federal Reserve System, Twentieth Street and Constitution Avenue, NW, Washington, D.C. 20551 (202) 452-3000; *Annual Statistical Digest.*

STOCKS - FOREIGN - UNITED STATES PURCHASES AND SALES OF

U.S. Department of the Treasury, Fifteenth Street and Pennsylvania Avenue, NW, Washington, D.C. 20220 (202) 566-2000; *Treasury Bulletin.*

STOCKS - LIFE INSURANCE

American Council of Life Insurance, 1001 Pennsylvania Avenue, NW, Washington, D.C. 20004-2599 (202) 624-2000; *Life Insurance Fact Book,* and unpublished data.

STOCKS - NEW ISSUES

Board of Governors of the Federal Reserve System, Twentieth Street and Constitution Avenue, NW, Washington, D.C. 20551 (202) 452-3000; *Federal Reserve Bulletin* and *Annual Statistical Digest.*

STOCKS - PRICES, YIELD, SALES, ISSUES, ETC.

Board of Governors of the Federal Reserve System, Twentieth Street and Constitution Avenue, NW, Washington, D.C. 20551 (202) 452-

3000; *Federal Reserve Bulletin.*

Commodity Futures Trading Commission, 2033 K Street, NW, Washington, D.C. 20581 (202) 254-6387; *Annual Report.*

International Finance Corporation, 1818 H Street, N.W., Washington, D.C. 20006 (202) 477-1234; *Emerging Stock Markets Factbook.*

National Association of Securities Dealers, 1735 K Street, NW, Washington, D.C. 20006 (202) 728-8000; *Fact Book.*

New York Stock Exchange, 11 Wall Street, New York, New York 10005 (212) 656-3000; *Fact Book.*

Securities and Exchange Commission, 450 Fifth Street, NW, Washington, D.C. 20549 (202) 272-3100; unpublished data.

Standard and Poor's Corporation, 25 Broadway, New York, New York 10004 (212) 208-8000; *Standard and Poor's Outlook.*

STONE

U.S. Department of Commerce, Bureau of the Census, Suitland, Maryland 20233 (301) 763-4040; *Census of Mineral Industries.*

U.S. Department of the Interior, Bureau of Mines, 810 Seventh Street, NW, Washington, D.C. 20241 (202) 501-9649; *Annual Reports,* and *Mineral Commodities Summaries.*

STONE - CLAY - AND GLASS PRODUCTS

Association of American Railroads, American Railroads Building, 50 F Street, NW, Washington, D.C. 20001 (202) 639-2100; *Freight Commodity Statistics,* and *Weekly Railroad Traffic.*

STONE - CLAY - AND GLASS PRODUCTS - MANUFACTURING - CAPITAL

U.S. Department of Commerce, Bureau of the Census, Suitland, Maryland 20233 (301) 763-4040; *Current Industrial Reports.*

STONE - CLAY - AND GLASS PRODUCTS - MANUFACTURING - EARNINGS

U.S. Department of Commerce, Bureau of the Census, Suitland, Maryland 20233 (301) 763-4040; *Census of Manufactures,* and *Annual Survey of Manufactures.*

U.S. Department of Labor, Bureau of Labor Statistics, Two Massachusetts Avenue, NE, Washington, D.C. 20212 (202) 606-7828; *Employment and Earnings,* and Bulletins 2370 and 2429.

STONE - CLAY - AND GLASS PRODUCTS - MANUFACTURING - EMPLOYEES

U.S. Department of Commerce, Bureau of the Census, Suitland, Maryland 20233 (301) 763-4040; *Census of Manufactures,* and *Annual Survey of Manufactures.*

U.S. Department of Labor, Bureau of Labor Statistics, Two Massachusetts Avenue, NE, Washington, D.C. 20212 (202) 606-7828; *Employment and Earnings,* Bulletins 2370 and 2429, and *Monthly Labor Review.*

STONE - CLAY - AND GLASS PRODUCTS - MANUFACTURING - ESTABLISHMENTS

U.S. Department of Commerce, Bureau of the Census, Suitland, Maryland 20233 (301) 763-4040; *Census of Manufactures,* and *Annual Survey of Manufactures.*

STONE - CLAY - AND GLASS PRODUCTS - MANUFACTURING - FOREIGN TRADE

U.S. Department of Commerce, Bureau of the Census, Suitland, Maryland 20233 (301) 763-4040; *U.S. Merchandise Trade.*

STONE - CLAY - AND GLASS PRODUCTS - MANUFACTURING - GROSS DOMESTIC PRODUCT

U.S. Department of Commerce, Bureau of Economic Analysis, Fourteenth Street between Constitution Avenue and E Street, NW, Washington, D.C. 20230 (202) 606-9900; *The National Income and Product Accounts of the United States,* and *Survey of Current Business.*

STONE - CLAY - AND GLASS PRODUCTS - MANUFACTURING - OCCUPATIONAL SAFETY

U.S. Department of Labor, Bureau of Labor Statistics, Two Massachusetts Avenue, NE, Washington, D.C. 20212 (202) 606-7828; *Occupational Injuries and Illnesses in the United States by Industry.*

STONE - CLAY - AND GLASS PRODUCTS - MANUFACTURING - PATENTS

U.S. Department of Commerce, Patent and Trademark Office, 2011 Crystal Avenue, Arlington, Virginia 22202 (703) 305-8341; *Patenting Trends in the United States, State Country Report.*

STONE - CLAY - AND GLASS PRODUCTS - MANUFACTURING - POLLUTION ABATEMENT

U.S. Department of Commerce, Bureau of the Census, Suitland, Maryland 20233 (301) 763-4040; *Current Industrial Reports.*

STONE - CLAY - AND GLASS PRODUCTS - MANUFACTURING - PRODUCTIVITY

Board of Governors of the Federal Reserve System, Twentieth Street and Constitution Avenue, NW, Washington, D.C. 20551 (202) 452-3000; *Federal Reserve Bulletin.*

U.S. Department of Labor, Bureau of Labor Statistics, Two Massachusetts Avenue, NE, Washington, D.C. 20212 (202) 606-7828; *Productivity Measures for Selected Industries and Government Services,* and unpublished data.

STONE - CLAY - AND GLASS PRODUCTS - MANUFACTURING - PROFITS

Executive Office of the President, Council of Economic Advisors, Old Executive Office Building, Washington, D.C. 20500 (202) 395-5084; *Economic Report of the President.*

U.S. Department of Commerce, Bureau of the Census, Suitland, Maryland 20233 (301) 763-4040; *Quarterly Financial Report for Manufacturing, Mining and Trade Corporations.*

STONE - CLAY - AND GLASS PRODUCTS - MANUFACTURING - RESEARCH AND DEVELOPMENT

U.S. National Science Foundation, 4201 Wilson Boulevard, Arlington, Virginia 22230 (703) 306-1234; *Research and Development in Industry.*

STONE - CLAY - AND GLASS PRODUCTS - MANUFACTURING - SALES, SHIPMENTS, RECEIPTS

U.S. Department of Commerce, Bureau of the Census, Suitland, Maryland 20233 (301) 763-4040; *Census of Manufactures, Annual Survey of Manufactures,* and *Current Industrial Reports, Manufactures' Shipments, Inventories and Orders.*

U.S. Department of Commerce, International Trade Administration, Fourteenth Street between Constitution Avenue and E Street, NW, Washington, D.C. 20230 (202) 482-3809; *U.S. Industrial Outlook.*

STONE - CLAY - AND GLASS PRODUCTS - MANUFACTURING - VALUE ADDED

U.S. Department of Commerce, Bureau of the Census, Suitland, Maryland 20233 (301) 763-4040; *Census of Manufactures,* and *Annual Survey of Manufactures.*

STONE - CRUSHED

U.S. Department of the Interior, Bureau of Mines, 810 Seventh Street, NW, Washington, D.C. 20241 (202) 501-9649; *Mineral Commodity Summaries.*

STOVES AND RANGES

Euromonitor Publications Limited, 87-88 Turnmill Street, London EC1M 5QU, England; *European Marketing Data and Statistics.*

STRATEGIC AND CRITICAL MATERIALS

U.S. Department of Defense, Defense Logistics Agency, Cameron Station, Alexandria, Virginia 22304-6100 (703) 695-0291; *Statistical Supplement, Stockpile Report to the Congress.*

STRATEGIC FORCES

Executive Office of the President, Office of Management and Budget, Executive Office Building, Washington, D.C. 20503 (202) 395-3080; *Budget of the United States Government.*

STRATEGIC PETROLEUM RESERVES

U.S. Department of Energy, Energy Information Administration, 1000 Independence Avenue, SW, Washington, D.C. 20585 (202) 586-8800; *Petroleum Supply Annual, Annual Energy Review,* and *U.S. Crude Oil, Natural Gas, and Natural Gas Liquids Reserves.*

STRAWBERRIES

U.S. Department of Agriculture, National Agricultural Statistics Service, Fourteenth Street and Independence Avenue, SW, Washington, D.C. 20250 (202) 219-1504; *Agricultural Statistics, Vegetables,* and *Economic Indicators of the Farm Sector: National Financial Summary,*

STROKE - See also CEREBROVASCULAR DISEASES

STROKES

U.S. Department of Health and Human Services, National Center for Health Statistics, 3700 East-West Highway, Hyattsville, Maryland 20782 (301) 436-8500; *Vital Statistics of the United States, Health, United States, Monthly Vital Statistics Report,* and unpublished data.

STRONTIUM

U.S. Department of the Interior, Bureau of Mines, 810 Seventh Street, NW, Washington, D.C. 20241 (202) 501-9649; *Mineral Commodity Summaries.*

STUDENTS - See EDUCATION - ENROLLMENT

SUBWAYS AND URBAN RAILWAYS

American Public Transit Association, 1201 New York Avenue, NW, Suite 400, Washington, D.C. 20005 (202) 898-4000; *Transit Fact Book.*

Sudan - National Statistical Office

Department of Statistics, Ministry of Finance and Economic Planning, Post Office Box 700, Khartoum, Sudan.

Sudan - Primary Statistics Sources

Department of Statistics, Post Office Box 700, Khartoum, Sudan; *Statistical Abstract for the Democratic Republic of the Sudan,* and *Statistical Yearbook.*

SUDAN - AGRICULTURE

Euromonitor Publications Limited, 87-88 Turnmill Street, London EC1M 5QU, England; *International Marketing Data and Statistics.*

Facts on File, 460 Park Avenue South, New York, New York 10016 (800) 443-8333; *The New Book of World Rankings.*

Food and Agricultural Organization of the United Nations (FAO) Via delle Terme di Caracalla, 00100 Rome, Italy (Telephone Number in U.S. (202) 653-2400); *Production Yearbook,* and *The State of Food and Agriculture,* and *Trade Yearbook.*

G.K. Hall and Company, 70 Lincoln Street, Boston, Massachusetts 02111 (617) 423-3990; *The World in Figures.*

Statistical Office of the United Nations, Publishing Service, New York, New York 10017 (800) 253-9646; *Statistical Yearbook,* and *Survey of Economic and Social Conditions in Africa.*

Times Books, 201 East 50th Street, New York, New York 10022 (212) 751-2600; *The Economist Book of Vital World Statistics.*

United Nations Economic Commission for Africa, Africa Hall, P.O. Box 3001, Addis Ababa, Ethiopia (Telephone Number in U.S. (800) 253-9646); *African Statistical Yearbook.*

The World Bank, 1818 H Street, NW, Washington, D.C. 20433 (202) 477-1234; *World Tables.*

Statistical Office of the United Nations, Publishing Service, New York, New York 10017 (800) 253-9646; *Survey of Economic and Social Conditions in Africa.*

The World Bank, 1818 H Street, NW, Washington, D.C. 20433 (202) 477-1234; *World Tables*.

SUDAN - AIRLINE SERVICE

Facts on File, 460 Park Avenue South, New York, New York 10016 (800) 443-8323; *The New Book of World Rankings*.

G.K. Hall and Company, 70 Lincoln Street, Boston, Massachusetts 02111 (617) 423-3990; *The World in Figures*.

International Civil Aviation Organization, 1000 Sherbrooke Street West, Suite 400, Montreal, Quebec, Canada H3A 2R2 (514) 285-8219; *Civil Aviation Statistics of the World*.

Statistical Office of the United Nations, Publishing Service, New York, New York 10017 (800) 253-9646; *Statistical Yearbook*.

Times Books, 201 East 50th Street, New York, New York 10022 (212) 751-2600; *The Economist Book of Vital World Statistics*.

United Nations Economic Commission for Africa, Africa Hall, P.O. Box 3001, Addis Ababa, Ethiopia (Telephone Number in U.S. (800) 253-9646); *African Statistical Yearbook*.

SUDAN - ALUMINUM PRODUCTION AND CONSUMPTION - See SUDAN - MINING AND MINERAL PRODUCTS

SUDAN - ANIMAL HEALTH

Food and Agricultural Organization of the United Nations (FAO), Via delle Terme di Caracalla, 00100, Rome, Italy (Telephone Number in U.S. (202) 653-2400); *Animal Health Yearbook*.

SUDAN - AREA AND DENSITY OF POPULATION

African Development Bank, 01 BP 1387, Abidjan 01, Cote D'Ivoire; *Selected Statistics on Regional Member Countries*.

Euromonitor Publications Limited, 87-88 Turnmill Street, London EC1M 5QU, England; *International Marketing Data and Statistics*.

Facts on File, 460 Park Avenue South, New York, New York 10016 (800) 443-8323; *The New Book of World Rankings*.

Food and Agricultural Organization of the United Nations (FAO) Via delle Terme di Caracalla, 00100 Rome, Italy (Telephone Number in U.S. (202) 653-2400); *The State of Food and Agriculture*.

G.K. Hall and Company, 70 Lincoln Street, Boston, Massachusetts 02111 (617) 423-3990; *The World in Figures*.

Statistical Office of the United Nations, Publishing Service, New York, New York 10017 (800) 253-9646; *Statistical Yearbook*, and *Survey of Economic and Social Conditions in Africa*.

Times Books, 201 East 50th Street, New York, New York 10022 (212) 751-2600; *The Economist Book of Vital World Statistics*.

United Nations Educational, Scientific and Cultural Organization (UNESCO), 7 Place de Fontenoy, F-75700 Paris, France (Telephone Number in U.S. (212) 963-5981); *Statistical Yearbook*.

SUDAN - ARMS EXPORTS AND IMPORTS

U.S. Arms Control and Disarmament Agency, 320 Twenty-first Street, NW, Washington, D.C. 20451 (202) 647-8677; *World Military Expenditures and Arms Transfers*.

SUDAN - BALANCE OF PAYMENTS

African Development Bank, 01 BP 1387, Abidjan 01, Cote D'Ivoire; *Selected Statistics on Regional Member Countries*.

The Economist Intelligence Unit, 111 West 57th Street, New York, New York 10019 (800) 938-4685; *The World Market Atlas*.

G.K. Hall and Company, 70 Lincoln Street, Boston, Massachusetts 02111 (617) 423-3990; *The World in Figures*.

International Monetary Fund, 700 Nineteenth Street, NW, Washington, D.C. 20431 (202) 623-7000; *Balance of Payments Yearbook*, and *International Financial Statistics*.

Times Books, 201 East 50th Street, New York, New York 10022 (212) 751-2600; *The Economist Book of Vital World Statistics*.

United Nations Economic Commission for Africa, Africa Hall, P.O. Box 3001, Addis Ababa, Ethiopia (Telephone Number in U.S. (800) 253-9646); *African Statistical Yearbook*.

The World Bank, 1818 H Street, NW, Washington, D.C. 20433 (202) 477-1234; *World Tables*.

SUDAN - BANKING

Facts on File, 460 Park Avenue South, New York, New York 10016 (800) 443-8323; *The New Book of World Rankings*.

G.K. Hall and Company, 70 Lincoln Street, Boston, Massachusetts 02111 (617) 423-3990; *The World in Figures*.

International Monetary Fund, 700 Nineteenth Street, NW, Washington, D.C. 20431 (202) 623-7000; *International Financial Statistics*.

United Nations Economic Commission for Africa, Africa Hall, P.O. Box 3001, Addis Ababa, Ethiopia (Telephone Number in U.S. (800) 253-9646); *African Statistical Yearbook*.

SUDAN - BARLEY PRODUCTION - See SUDAN - CROPS

SUDAN - BEER PRODUCTION

Facts on File, 460 Park Avenue South, New York, New York 10016 (800) 443-8323; *The New Book of World Rankings*.

Statistical Office of the United Nations, Publishing Service, New York, New York 10017 (800) 253-9646; *Statistical Yearbook*.

SUDAN - BIRTH RATES

Facts on File, 460 Park Avenue South, New York, New York 10016 (800) 443-8323; *The New Book of World Rankings*.

Statistical Office of the United Nations, Publishing Service, New York, New York 10017 (800) 253-9646; *Demographic Yearbook*, *Statistical Yearbook*, and *Survey of Economic and Social Conditions in Africa*.

Times Books, 201 East 50th Street, New York, New York 10022 (212) 751-2600; *The Economist Book of Vital World Statistics*.

The World Bank, 1818 H Street, NW, Washington, D.C. 20433 (202) 477-1234; *World Tables*.

SUDAN - BONDS

G.K. Hall and Company, 70 Lincoln Street, Boston, Massachusetts 02111 (617) 423-3990; *The World in Figures.*

International Monetary Fund, 700 Nineteenth Street, NW, Washington, D.C. 20431 (202) 623-7000; *Government Finance Statistics Yearbook.*

SUDAN - BOOK PRODUCTION

G.K. Hall and Company, 70 Lincoln Street, Boston, Massachusetts 02111 (617) 423-3990; *The World in Figures.*

United Nations Educational, Scientific and Cultural Organization (UNESCO), 7 Place de Fontenoy, F-75700 Paris, France (Telephone Number in U.S. (212) 963-5981); *Statistical Yearbook.*

SUDAN - BROADCASTING

Billboard Limited, P.O. Box 9027, 1006 AA Amsterdam, The Netherlands (Telephone Number in U.S. (212) 764-7300); *World Radio TV Handbook.*

Facts on File, 460 Park Avenue South, New York, New York 10016 (800) 443-8323; *The New Book of World Rankings.*

G.K. Hall and Company, 70 Lincoln Street, Boston, Massachusetts 02111 (617) 423-3990; *The World in Figures.*

Times Books, 201 East 50th Street, New York, New York 10022 (212) 751-2600; *The Economist Book of Vital World Statistics.*

United Nations Educational, Scientific and Cultural Organization (UNESCO), 7 Place de Fontenoy, F-75700 Paris, France (Telephone Number in U.S. (212) 963-5981); *Statistical Yearbook.*

SUDAN - BUSINESS

G.K. Hall and Company, 70 Lincoln Street, Boston, Massachusetts 02111 (617) 423-3990; *The World in Figures.*

SUDAN - BUSINESS AND PROFESSIONAL LICENSES

International Monetary Fund, 700 Nineteenth Street, NW, Washington, D.C. 20431 (202) 623-7000; *Government Finance Statistics Yearbook.*

SUDAN - BUTTER PRODUCTION - See SUDAN - DAIRY PRODUCTS

SUDAN - CALORIE SUPPLY

African Development Bank, 01 BP 1387, Abidjan 01, Cote D'Ivoire; *Selected Statistics on Regional Member Countries.*

Food and Agricultural Organization of the United Nations (FAO) Via delle Terme di Caracalla, 00100 Rome, Italy (Telephone Number in U.S. (202) 653-2400); *The State of Food and Agriculture.*

SUDAN - CAPITAL REVENUE

International Monetary Fund, 700 Nineteenth Street, NW, Washington, D.C. 20431 (202) 623-7000; *Government Finance Statistics Yearbook.*

SUDAN - CATTLE - See SUDAN - LIVESTOCK AND POULTRY

SUDAN - CEMENT PRODUCTION - See SUDAN - MINING AND MINERAL PRODUCTS

SUDAN - CHEESE PRODUCTION AND CONSUMPTION - See SUDAN DAIRY PRODUCTS

SUDAN - CHEMICAL (ORGANIC) PRODUCTION - See SUDAN - MINING AND MINERAL PRODUCTS

SUDAN - CHICKENS - See SUDAN - LIVESTOCK AND POULTRY

SUDAN - CHROMIUM ORE PRODUCTION AND CONSUMPTION - See SUDAN - MINING AND MINERAL PRODUCTS

SUDAN - CIGARETTE PRODUCTION - See SUDAN - TOBACCO PRODUCTION

SUDAN - CLASS STRUCTURE

G.K. Hall and Company, 70 Lincoln Street, Boston, Massachusetts 02111 (617) 423-3990; *The World in Figures.*

SUDAN - CLIMATE

Facts on File, 460 Park Avenue South, New York, New York 10016 (800) 443-8323; *The New Book of World Rankings.*

G.K. Hall and Company, 70 Lincoln Street, Boston, Massachusetts 02111 (617) 423-3990; *The World in Figures.*

SUDAN - COAL PRODUCTION - See SUDAN - MINING AND MINERAL PRODUCTS

SUDAN - COFFEE PRODUCTION AND CONSUMPTION - See SUDAN - CROPS

SUDAN - COMMUNICATIONS

G.K. Hall and Company, 70 Lincoln Street, Boston, Massachusetts 02111 (617) 423-3990; *The World in Figures.*

United Nations Economic Commission for Africa, Africa Hall, P.O. Box 3001, Addis Ababa, Ethiopia (Telephone Number in U.S. (800) 253-9646); *African Statistical Yearbook.*

SUDAN - CONSTRUCTION INDUSTRY

Facts on File, 460 Park Avenue South, New York, New York 10016 (800) 443-8323; *The New Book of World Rankings.*

United Nations Economic Commission for Africa, Africa Hall, P.O. Box 3001, Addis Ababa, Ethiopia (Telephone Number in U.S. (800) 253-9646); *African Statistical Yearbook.*

SUDAN - CONSUMER PRICE INDEX

African Development Bank, 01 BP 1387, Abidjan 01, Cote D'Ivoire; *Selected Statistics on Regional Member Countries.*

G.K. Hall and Company, 70 Lincoln Street, Boston, Massachusetts 02111 (617) 423-3990; *The World in Figures.*

Statistical Office of the United Nations, Publishing Service, New York, New York 10017 (800) 253-9646; *Statistical Yearbook*, and *Survey of Economic and Social Conditions in Africa.*

United Nations Economic Commission for Africa, Africa Hall, P.O. Box 3001, Addis Ababa, Ethiopia (Telephone Number in U.S. (800) 253-9646); *African Statistical Yearbook.*

SUDAN - CONSUMER PRICES

International Labour Office, I.L.O. Publications, CH-1211, Geneva 22, Switzerland; *Yearbook of Labour Statistics.*

International Monetary Fund, 700 Nineteenth Street, NW, Washington, D.C. 20431 (202) 623-7000; *International Financial Statistics.*

SUDAN - CONSUMER RATES

Facts on File, 460 Park Avenue South, New York, New York 10016 (800) 443-8323; *The New Book of World Rankings.*

SUDAN - CONSUMPTION

African Development Bank, 01 BP 1387, Abidjan 01, Cote D'Ivoire; *Selected Statistics on Regional Member Countries.*

G.K. Hall and Company, 70 Lincoln Street, Boston, Massachusetts 02111 (617) 423-3990; *The World in Figures.*

Statistical Office of the United Nations, Publishing Service, New York, New York 10017 (800) 253-9646; *Survey of Economic and Social Conditions in Africa.*

SUDAN - COPPER PRODUCTION AND CONSUMPTION - See SUDAN - MINING AND MINERAL PRODUCTS

SUDAN - CORN PRODUCTION - See SUDAN - CROPS

SUDAN - CORPORATE TAXES - See SUDAN - TAXATION

SUDAN - COTTON - See SUDAN - CROPS

SUDAN - CRIME

International Criminal Police Organization (INTERPOL), 26 rue Armengaud, 92210 Saint Cloud, France; *International Crime Statistics.*

Yale University Press, Yale Station, New Haven, Connecticut 06520 (203) 432-0940; *Violence and Crime in Cross-National Perspective.*

SUDAN - CROPS

Commodity Research Bureau, Incorporated, 75 Wall Street, New York, New York 10005 (212) 504-7754; *Commodity Year Book.*

Facts on File, 460 Park Avenue South, New York, New York 10016 (800) 443-8323; *The New Book of World Rankings.*

Food and Agricultural Organization of the United Nations (FAO) Via delle Terme di Caracalla, 00100 Rome, Italy (Telephone Number in U.S. (202) 653-2400); *The State of Food and Agriculture.*

G.K. Hall and Company, 70 Lincoln Street, Boston, Massachusetts 02111 (617) 423-3990; *The World in Figures.*

International Monetary Fund, 700 Nineteenth Street, NW, Washington, D.C. 20431 (202) 623-7000; *International Financial Statistics.*

Statistical Office of the United Nations, Publishing Service, New York, New York 10017 (800) 253-9646; *Statistical Yearbook.*

United Nations Economic Commission for Africa, Africa Hall, P.O. Box 3001, Addis Ababa, Ethiopia (Telephone Number in U.S. (800) 253-9646); *African Statistical Yearbook.*

SUDAN - CUSTOMS DUTIES

G.K. Hall and Company, 70 Lincoln Street, Boston, Massachusetts 02111 (617) 423-3990; *The World in Figures.*

International Monetary Fund, 700 Nineteenth Street, NW, Washington, D.C. 20431 (202) 623-7000; *Government Finance Statistics Yearbook.*

SUDAN - DAIRY PRODUCTS

Facts on File, 460 Park Avenue South, New York, New York 10016 (800) 443-8323; *The New Book of World Rankings.*

Food and Agricultural Organization of the United Nations (FAO) Via delle Terme di Caracalla, 00100 Rome, Italy (Telephone Number in U.S. (202) 653-2400); *The State of Food and Agriculture.*

Statistical Office of the United Nations, Publishing Service, New York, New York 10017 (800) 253-9646; *Statistical Yearbook.*

SUDAN - DEATH RATES

G.K. Hall and Company, 70 Lincoln Street, Boston, Massachusetts 02111 (617) 423-3990; *The World in Figures.*

Statistical Office of the United Nations, Publishing Service, New York, New York 10017 (800) 253-9646; *Statistical Yearbook*, and *Survey of Economic and Social Conditions in Africa.*

Times Books, 201 East 50th Street, New York, New York 10022 (212) 751-2600; *The Economist Book of Vital World Statistics.*

World Health Organization, Office of Publications, Avenue Appia, CH-1211 Geneva 27, Switzerland (Telephone Number in U.S. (518) 436-9686); *World Health Statistics Annual.*

SUDAN - DEFENSE EXPENDITURES

G.K. Hall and Company, 70 Lincoln Street, Boston, Massachusetts 02111 (617) 423-3990; *The World in Figures.*

International Monetary Fund, 700 Nineteenth Street, NW, Washington, D.C. 20431 (202) 623-7000; *Government Finance Statistics Yearbook.*

U.S. Arms Control and Disarmament Agency, 320 Twenty-first Street, NW, Washington, D.C. 20451 (202) 647-8677; *World Military Expenditures and Arms Transfers.*

SUDAN - DEMOGRAPHY

The Economist Intelligence Unit, 111 West 57th Street, New York, New York 10019 (800) 938-4685; *The World Market Atlas.*

Facts on File, 460 Park Avenue South, New York, New York 10016 (800) 443-8323; *The New Book of World Rankings.*

G.K. Hall and Company, 70 Lincoln Street, Boston, Massachusetts 02111 (617) 423-3990; *The World in Figures.*

Statistical Office of the United Nations, Publishing Service, New York, New York 10017 (800) 253-9646; *Survey of Economic and Social Conditions in Africa.*

SUDAN - DEVELOPMENT ASSISTANCE

G.K. Hall and Company, 70 Lincoln Street, Boston, Massachusetts 02111 (617) 423-3990; *The World in Figures.*

Statistical Office of the United Nations, Publishing Service, New York, New York 10017 (800) 253-9646; *Statistical Yearbook*.

SUDAN - DIAMOND PRODUCTION - See SUDAN - MINING AND MINERAL PRODUCTS

SUDAN - DISEASES

G.K. Hall and Company, 70 Lincoln Street, Boston, Massachusetts 02111 (617) 423-3990; *The World in Figures*.

World Health Organization, Office of Publications, Avenue Appia, CH-1211 Geneva 27, Switzerland (Telephone Number in U.S. (518) 436-9686); *World Health Statistics Annual*.

SUDAN - DIVORCE RATES

Facts on File, 460 Park Avenue South, New York, New York 10016 (800) 443-8323; *The New Book of World Rankings*.

Statistical Office of the United Nations, Publishing Service, New York, New York 10017 (800) 253-9646; *Demographic Yearbook*.

SUDAN - DOMESTIC PRODUCT

G.K. Hall and Company, 70 Lincoln Street, Boston, Massachusetts 02111 (617) 423-3990; *The World in Figures*.

SUDAN - ECONOMY

African Development Bank, 01 BP 1387, Abidjan 01, Cote D'Ivoire; *Selected Statistics on Regional Member Countries*.

Euromonitor Publications Limited, 87-88 Turnmill Street, London EC1M 5QU, England; *International Marketing Data and Statistics*.

Facts on File, 460 Park Avenue South, New York, New York 10016 (800) 443-8323; *The New Book of World Rankings*.

G.K. Hall and Company, 70 Lincoln Street, Boston, Massachusetts 02111 (617) 423-3990; *The World in Figures*.

Statistical Office of the United Nations, Publishing Service, New York, New York 10017 (800) 253-9646; *Foreign Trade Statistics for Africa*.

SUDAN - EDUCATION

African Development Bank, 01 BP 1387, Abidjan 01, Cote D'Ivoire; *Selected Statistics on Regional Member Countries*.

The Economist Intelligence Unit, 111 West 57th Street, New York, New York 10019 (800) 938-4685; *The World Market Atlas*.

Facts on File, 460 Park Avenue South, New York, New York 10016 (800) 443-8323; *The New Book of World Rankings*.

G.K. Hall and Company, 70 Lincoln Street, Boston, Massachusetts 02111 (617) 423-3990; *The World in Figures*.

International Monetary Fund, 700 Nineteenth Street, NW, Washington, D.C. 20431 (202) 623-7000; *Government Finance Statistics Yearbook*.

Statistical Office of the United Nations, Publishing Service, New York, New York 10017 (800) 253-9646; *Survey of Economic and Social Conditions in Africa*.

Times Books, 201 East 50th Street, New York, New York 10022 (212) 751-2600; *The Economist Book of Vital World Statistics*.

United Nations Economic Commission for Africa, Africa Hall, P.O. Box 3001, Addis Ababa, Ethiopia (Telephone Number in U.S. (800) 253-9646); *African Statistical Yearbook*.

United Nations Educational, Scientific and Cultural Organization (UNESCO), 7 Place de Fontenoy, F-75700 Paris, France (Telephone Number in U.S. (212) 963-5981); *Statistical Yearbook*.

The World Bank, 1818 H Street, NW, Washington, D.C. 20433 (202) 477-1234; *World Tables*.

SUDAN - EGG PRODUCTION AND CONSUMPTION - See SUDAN - DAIRY PRODUCTS

SUDAN - ELECTRICITY

Facts on File, 460 Park Avenue South, New York, New York 10016 (800) 443-8323; *The New Book of World Rankings*.

Penn Well Publishing Company, 1421 South Sheridan Road, P.O. Box 1260, Tulsa, Oklahoma 74101 (800) 752-9764; *International Energy Statistics Sourcebook*.

Statistical Office of the United Nations, Publishing Service, New York, New York 10017 (800) 253-9646; *Statistical Yearbook*, and *Survey of Economic and Social Conditions in Africa*.

Times Books, 201 East 50th Street, New York, New York 10022 (212) 751-2600; *The Economist Book of Vital World Statistics*.

United Nations Economic Commission for Africa, Africa Hall, P.O. Box 3001, Addis Ababa, Ethiopia (Telephone Number in U.S. (800) 253-9646); *African Statistical Yearbook*.

SUDAN - EMPLOYMENT

Euromonitor Publications Limited, 87-88 Turnmill Street, London EC1M 5QU, England; *International Marketing Data and Statistics*.

Facts on File, 460 Park Avenue South, New York, New York 10016 (800) 443-8323; *The New Book of World Rankings*.

International Labour Office, I.L.O. Publications, CH-1211, Geneva 22, Switzerland; *Yearbook of Labour Statistics*.

Statistical Office of the United Nations, Publishing Service, New York, New York 10017 (800) 253-9646; *Statistical Yearbook*, and *Survey of Economic and Social Conditions in Africa*.

United Nations Economic Commission for Africa, Africa Hall, P.O. Box 3001, Addis Ababa, Ethiopia (Telephone Number in U.S. (800) 253-9646); *African Statistical Yearbook*.

SUDAN - ENERGY

Facts on File, 460 Park Avenue South, New York, New York 10016 (800) 443-8323; *The New Book of World Rankings*.

Food and Agricultural Organization of the United Nations (FAO) Via delle Terme di Caracalla, 00100 Rome, Italy (Telephone Number in U.S. (202) 653-2400); *The State of Food and Agriculture*.

G.K. Hall and Company, 70 Lincoln Street, Boston, Massachusetts 02111 (617) 423-3990; *The World in Figures*.

Penn Well Publishing Company, 1421 South Sheridan Road, P.O. Box 1260, Tulsa, Oklahoma 74101 (800) 752-9764; *International Energy Statistics Sourcebook*.

Statistical Office of the United Nations, Publishing Service, New York, New York 10017 (800) 253-9646; *Statistical Yearbook*, and *Yearbook on World Energy Statistics*.

Times Books, 201 East 50th Street, New York, New York 10022 (212) 751-2600; *The Economist Book of Vital World Statistics*.

United Nations Economic Commission for Africa, Africa Hall, P.O. Box 3001, Addis Ababa, Ethiopia (Telephone Number in U.S. (800) 253-9646); *African Statistical Yearbook*.

SUDAN - EXCHANGE RATES

African Development Bank, 01 BP 1387, Abidjan 01, Cote D'Ivoire; *Selected Statistics on Regional Member Countries*.

Euromonitor Publications Limited, 87-88 Turnmill Street, London EC1M 5QU, England; *International Marketing Data and Statistics*.

International Civil Aviation Organization, 1000 Sherbrooke Street West, Suite 400, Montreal, Quebec, Canada H3A 2R2 (514) 285-8219; *Civil Aviation Statistics of the World*.

International Monetary Fund, 700 Nineteenth Street, NW, Washington, D.C. 20431 (202) 623-7000; *International Financial Statistics*.

Statistical Office of the United Nations, Publishing Service, New York, New York 10017 (800) 253-9646; *Foreign Trade Statistics for Africa*, and *Statistical Yearbook*.

SUDAN - EXCISE TAXES - See SUDAN - TAXATION

SUDAN - EXPORTS

African Development Bank, 01 BP 1387, Abidjan 01, Cote D'Ivoire; *Selected Statistics on Regional Member Countries*.

The Economist Intelligence Unit, 111 West 57th Street, New York, New York 10019 (800) 938-4685; *The World Market Atlas*.

Euromonitor Publications Limited, 87-88 Turnmill Street, London EC1M 5QU, England; *International Marketing Data and Statistics*.

Food and Agricultural Organization of the United Nations (FAO) Via delle Terme di Caracalla, 00100 Rome, Italy (Telephone Number in U.S. (202) 653-2400); *The State of Food and Agriculture*.

G.K. Hall and Company, 70 Lincoln Street, Boston, Massachusetts 02111 (617) 423-3990; *The World in Figures*.

International Monetary Fund, 700 Nineteenth Street, NW, Washington, D.C. 20431 (202) 623-7000; *Direction of Trade Statistics, Government Finance Statistics Yearbook*, and *International Financial Statistics*.

Statistical Office of the United Nations, Publishing Service, New York, New York 10017 (800) 253-9646; *Foreign Trade Statistics for Africa*, and *Survey of Economic and Social Conditions in Africa*.

Times Books, 201 East 50th Street, New York, New York 10022 (212) 751-2600; *The Economist Book of Vital World Statistics*.

United Nations Economic Commission for Africa, Africa Hall, P.O. Box 3001, Addis Ababa, Ethiopia (Telephone Number in U.S. (800) 253-9646); *African Statistical Yearbook*.

The World Bank, 1818 H Street, NW, Washington, D.C. 20433 (202) 477-1234; *World Tables*.

SUDAN - EXTERNAL INDEBTEDNESS

Statistical Office of the United Nations, Publishing Service, New York, New York 10017 (800) 253-9646; *Survey of Economic and Social Conditions in Africa*.

The World Bank, 1818 H Street, NW, Washington, D.C. 20433 (202) 477-1234; *World Tables*.

SUDAN - EXTERNAL TRADE

African Development Bank, 01 BP 1387, Abidjan 01, Cote D'Ivoire; *Selected Statistics on Regional Member Countries*.

Food and Agricultural Organization of the United Nations (FAO) Via delle Terme di Caracalla, 00100 Rome, Italy (Telephone Number in U.S. (202) 653-2400); *The State of Food and Agriculture*, and *Trade Yearbook*.

G.K. Hall and Company, 70 Lincoln Street, Boston, Massachusetts 02111 (617) 423-3990; *The World in Figures*.

Statistical Office of the United Nations, Publishing Service, New York, New York 10017 (800) 253-9646; *Statistical Yearbook*.

SUDAN - FABRIC PRODUCTION - See SUDAN - TEXTILE INDUSTRY

SUDAN - FARM CROPS - See SUDAN - CROPS

SUDAN - FEMALE WORKING POPULATION - See SUDAN - EMPLOYMENT

SUDAN - FERTILITY RATES

Facts on File, 460 Park Avenue South, New York, New York 10016 (800) 443-8323; *The New Book of World Rankings*.

Statistical Office of the United Nations, Publishing Service, New York, New York 10017 (800) 253-9646; *Survey of Economic and Social Conditions in Africa*.

Times Books, 201 East 50th Street, New York, New York 10022 (212) 751-2600; *The Economist Book of Vital World Statistics*.

The World Bank, 1818 H Street, NW, Washington, D.C. 20433 (202) 477-1234; *World Tables*.

SUDAN - FERTILIZER

Food and Agricultural Organization of the United Nations (FAO), Via delle Terme di Caracalla, 00100, Rome, Italy (Telephone Number in U.S. (202) 653-2400); *Fertilizer Yearbook*, and *The State of Food and Agriculture*.

Statistical Office of the United Nations, Publishing Service, New York, New York 10017 (800) 253-9646; *Statistical Yearbook*.

SUDAN - FETAL MORTALITY

Statistical Office of the United Nations, Publishing Service, New York, New York 10017 (800) 253-9646; *Demographic Yearbook*.

SUDAN - FINANCE

African Development Bank, 01 BP 1387, Abidjan 01, Cote D'Ivoire; *Selected Statistics on Regional Member Countries*.

Facts on File, 460 Park Avenue South, New York, New York 10016 (800) 443-8323; *The New Book of World Rankings*.

G.K. Hall and Company, 70 Lincoln Street, Boston, Massachusetts 02111 (617) 423-3990; *The World in Figures*.

International Monetary Fund, 700 Nineteenth Street, NW, Washington, D.C. 20431 (202) 623-7000; *Government Finance Statistics Yearbook*, and *International Financial Statistics*.

United Nations Economic Commission for Africa, Africa Hall, P.O. Box 3001, Addis Ababa, Ethiopia (Telephone Number in U.S. (800) 253-9646); *African Statistical Yearbook*.

SUDAN - FISHERIES

Facts on File, 460 Park Avenue South, New York, New York 10016 (800) 443-8323; *The New Book of World Rankings*.

Food and Agricultural Organization of the United Nations (FAO) Via delle Terme di Caracalla, 00100 Rome, Italy (Telephone Number in U.S. (202) 653-2400); *The State of Food and Agriculture*, and *Yearbook of Fishery Statistics*.

Statistical Office of the United Nations, Publishing Service, New York, New York 10017 (800) 253-9646; *Survey of Economic and Social Conditions in Africa*.

United Nations Economic Commission for Africa, Africa Hall, P.O. Box 3001, Addis Ababa, Ethiopia (Telephone Number in U.S. (800) 253-9646); *African Statistical Yearbook*.

United Nations Economic Commission for Africa, Africa Hall, P.O. Box 3001, Addis Ababa, Ethiopia (Telephone Number in U.S. (800) 253-9646); *African Statistical Yearbook*.

SUDAN - FLOUR PRODUCTION

Statistical Office of the United Nations, Publishing Service, New York, New York 10017 (800) 253-9646; *Statistical Yearbook*.

SUDAN - FOOD

African Development Bank, 01 BP 1387, Abidjan 01, Cote D'Ivoire; *Selected Statistics on Regional Member Countries*.

Food and Agricultural Organization of the United Nations (FAO) Via delle Terme di Caracalla, 00100 Rome, Italy (Telephone Number in U.S. (202) 653-2400); *Production Yearbook*, and *The State of Food and Agriculture*.

G.K. Hall and Company, 70 Lincoln Street, Boston, Massachusetts 02111 (617) 423-3990; *The World in Figures*.

SUDAN - FOREIGN AID

G.K. Hall and Company, 70 Lincoln Street, Boston, Massachusetts 02111 (617) 423-3990; *The World in Figures*.

SUDAN - FOREIGN DEBT

International Monetary Fund, 700 Nineteenth Street, NW, Washington, D.C. 20431 (202) 623-7000; *Government Finance Statistics Yearbook*.

SUDAN - FOREIGN TRADE

Euromonitor Publications Limited, 87-88 Turnmill Street, London EC1M 5QU, England; *International Marketing Data and Statistics*.

Facts on File, 460 Park Avenue South, New York, New York 10016 (800) 443-8323; *The New Book of World Rankings*.

Food and Agricultural Organization of the United Nations (FAO) Via delle Terme di Caracalla, 00100 Rome, Italy (Telephone Number in U.S. (202) 653-2400); *The State of Food and Agriculture*.

G.K. Hall and Company, 70 Lincoln Street, Boston, Massachusetts 02111 (617) 423-3990; *The World in Figures*.

International Monetary Fund, 700 Nineteenth Street, NW, Washington, D.C. 20431 (202) 623-7000; *International Financial Statistics*.

Statistical Office of the United Nations, Publishing Service, New York, New York 10017 (800) 253-9646; *Foreign Trade Statistics for Africa*, *International Trade Statistics Yearbook*, *Statistical Yearbook*, and *Trade in Manufactures of Developing Countries*.

United Nations Economic Commission for Africa, Africa Hall, P.O. Box 3001, Addis Ababa, Ethiopia (Telephone Number in U.S. (800) 253-9646); *African Statistical Yearbook*.

The World Bank, 1010 H Street, NW, Washington, D.C. 20433 (202) 477-1234; *World Tables*.

SUDAN - FORESTRY AND FOREST PRODUCTS

Facts on File, 460 Park Avenue South, New York, New York 10016 (800) 443-8323; *The New Book of World Rankings*.

Food and Agricultural Organization of the United Nations (FAO) Via delle Terme di Caracalla, 00100 Rome, Italy (Telephone Number in U.S. (202) 653-2400); *The State of Food and Agriculture*, and *Yearbook of Forest Products*.

G.K. Hall and Company, 70 Lincoln Street, Boston, Massachusetts 02111 (617) 423-3990; *The World in Figures*.

Statistical Office of the United Nations, Publishing Service, New York, New York 10017 (800) 253-9646; *Statistical Yearbook*.

United Nations Economic Commission for Africa, Africa Hall, P.O. Box 3001, Addis Ababa, Ethiopia (Telephone Number in U.S. (800) 253-9646); *African Statistical Yearbook*.

United Nations Educational, Scientific and Cultural Organization (UNESCO), 7 Place de Fontenoy, F-75700 Paris, France (Telephone Number in U.S. (212) 963-5981); *Statistical Yearbook*.

SUDAN - GAS PRODUCTION - See SUDAN - MINING AND MINERAL PRODUCTS

SUDAN - GENERAL MORTALITY

Statistical Office of the United Nations, Publishing Service, New York, New York 10017 (800) 253-9646; *Demographic Yearbook*.

SUDAN - GEOGRAPHIC DATA

Facts on File, 460 Park Avenue South, New York, New York 10016 (800) 443-8323; *The New Book of World Rankings*.

SUDAN - GOATS - See SUDAN - LIVESTOCK AND POULTRY

SUDAN - GOLD HOLDINGS

International Monetary Fund, 700 Nineteenth Street, NW, Washington, D.C. 20431 (202) 623-7000; *International Financial Statistics*.

Statistical Office of the United Nations, Publishing Service, New York, New York 10017 (800) 253-9646; *Statistical Yearbook*.

The World Bank, 1818 H Street, NW, Washington, D.C. 20433 (202) 477-1234; *World Tables*.

SUDAN - GOLD PRODUCTION AND CONSUMPTION - See SUDAN - MINING AND MINERAL PRODUCTS

SUDAN - GOVERNMENT

G.K. Hall and Company, 70 Lincoln Street, Boston, Massachusetts 02111 (617) 423-3990; *The World in Figures*.

SUDAN - GOVERNMENT EXPENDITURES

International Monetary Fund, 700 Nineteenth Street, NW, Washington, D.C. 20431 (202) 623-7000; *Government Finance Statistics Yearbook*.

Times Books, 201 East 50th Street, New York, New York 10022 (212) 751-2600; *The Economist Book of Vital World Statistics*.

The World Bank, 1818 H Street, NW, Washington, D.C. 20433 (202) 477-1234; *World Tables*.

SUDAN - GOVERNMENT FINANCES

International Monetary Fund, 700 Nineteenth Street, NW, Washington, D.C. 20431 (202) 623-7000; *International Financial Statistics*.

SUDAN - GOVERNMENT REVENUE

International Monetary Fund, 700 Nineteenth Street, NW, Washington, D.C. 20431 (202) 623-7000; *Government Finance Statistics Yearbook*.

Statistical Office of the United Nations, Publishing Service, New York, New York 10017 (800) 253-9646; *Survey of Economic and Social Conditions in Africa*.

Times Books, 201 East 50th Street, New York, New York 10022 (212) 751-2600; *The Economist Book of Vital World Statistics*.

The World Bank, 1818 H Street, NW, Washington, D.C. 20433 (202) 477-1234; *World Tables*.

SUDAN - GRAIN PRODUCTION - See SUDAN - CROPS

SUDAN - GRANTS

International Monetary Fund, 700 Nineteenth Street, NW, Washington, D.C. 20431 (202) 623-7000; *Government Finance Statistics Yearbook*.

SUDAN - GROSS DOMESTIC PRODUCT

African Development Bank, 01 BP 1387, Abidjan 01, Cote D'Ivoire; *Selected Statistics on Regional Member Countries*.

The Economist Intelligence Unit, 111 West 57th Street, New York, New York 10019 (800) 938-4685; *The World Market Atlas*.

Euromonitor Publications Limited, 87-88 Turnmill Street, London EC1M 5QU, England; *International Marketing Data and Statistics*.

Facts on File, 460 Park Avenue South, New York, New York 10016 (800) 443-8323; *The New Book of World Rankings*.

G.K. Hall and Company, 70 Lincoln Street, Boston, Massachusetts 02111 (617) 423-3990; *The World in Figures*.

Statistical Office of the United Nations, Publishing Service, New York, New York 10017 (800) 253-9646; *Statistical Yearbook*, and *Survey of Economic and Social Conditions in Africa*.

Times Books, 201 East 50th Street, New York, New York 10022 (212) 751-2600; *The Economist Book of Vital World Statistics*.

United Nations Economic Commission for Africa, Africa Hall, P.O. Box 3001, Addis Ababa, Ethiopia (Telephone Number in U.S. (800) 253-9646); *African Statistical Yearbook*.

The World Bank, 1818 H Street, NW, Washington, D.C. 20433 (202) 477-1234; *World Tables*.

SUDAN - GROSS NATIONAL PRODUCT

Euromonitor Publications Limited, 87-88 Turnmill Street, London EC1M 5QU, England; *International Marketing Data and Statistics*.

U.S. Arms Control and Disarmament Agency, 320 Twenty-first Street, NW, Washington, D.C. 20451 (202) 647-8677; *World Military Expenditures and Arms Transfers*.

The World Bank, 1818 H Street, NW, Washington, D.C. 20433 (202) 477-1234; *World Tables*.

SUDAN - GROUNDNUTS - See SUDAN - CROPS

SUDAN - HEALTH

African Development Bank, 01 BP 1387, Abidjan 01, Cote D'Ivoire; *Selected Statistics on Regional Member Countries*.

Facts on File, 460 Park Avenue South, New York, New York 10016 (800) 443-8323; *The New Book of World Rankings*.

G.K. Hall and Company, 70 Lincoln Street, Boston, Massachusetts 02111 (617) 423-3990; *The World in Figures*.

Statistical Office of the United Nations, Publishing Service, New York, New York 10017 (800) 253-9646; *Statistical Yearbook*.

Times Books, 201 East 50th Street, New York, New York 10022 (212) 751-2600; *The Economist Book of Vital World Statistics*.

United Nations Economic Commission for Africa, Africa Hall, P.O. Box 3001, Addis Ababa, Ethiopia (Telephone Number in U.S. (800) 253-9646); *African Statistical Yearbook*.

World Health Organization, Office of Publications, Avenue Appia, CH-1211 Geneva 27, Switzerland (Telephone Number in U.S. (518) 436-9686); *World Health Statistics Annual*.

SUDAN - HEALTH EXPENDITURES

International Monetary Fund, 700 Nineteenth Street, NW, Washington, D.C. 20431 (202) 623-7000; *Government Finance Statistics Yearbook*.

SUDAN - HIGHWAYS

G.K. Hall and Company, 70 Lincoln Street, Boston, Massachusetts 02111 (617) 423-3990; *The World in Figures.*

International Road Federation, 525 School Street, SW, Washington, D.C. 20024 (202) 554-2106; *World Road Statistics.*

Statistical Office of the United Nations, Publishing Service, New York, New York 10017 (800) 253-9646; *Survey of Economic and Social Conditions in Africa.*

United Nations Economic Commission for Africa, Africa Hall, P.O. Box 3001, Addis Ababa, Ethiopia (Telephone Number in U.S. (800) 253-9646); *African Statistical Yearbook.*

SUDAN - HORSES - See SUDAN - LIVESTOCK AND POULTRY

SUDAN - HOURS OF WORK - See SUDAN - EMPLOYMENT

SUDAN - HOUSING EXPENDITURES

Facts on File, 460 Park Avenue South, New York, New York 10016 (800) 443-8323; *The New Book of World Rankings.*

International Monetary Fund, 700 Nineteenth Street, NW, Washington, D.C. 20431 (202) 623-7000; *Government Finance Statistics Yearbook.*

SUDAN - ILLITERATE POPULATION

The Economist Intelligence Unit, 111 West 57th Street, New York, New York 10019; *The World Market Atlas.*

G.K. Hall and Company, 70 Lincoln Street, Boston, Massachusetts 02111 (617) 423-3990; *The World in Figures.*

United Nations Educational, Scientific and Cultural Organization (UNESCO), 7 Place de Fontenoy, F-75700 Paris, France (Telephone Number in U.S. (212) 963-5981); *Statistical Yearbook.*

SUDAN - IMPORTS

African Development Bank, 01 BP 1387, Abidjan 01, Cote D'Ivoire; *Selected Statistics on Regional Member Countries.*

The Economist Intelligence Unit, 111 West 57th Street, New York, New York 10019 (800) 938-4685; *The World Market Atlas.*

Euromonitor Publications Limited, 87-88 Turnmill Street, London EC1M 5QU, England; *International Marketing Data and Statistics.*

Food and Agricultural Organization of the United Nations (FAO) Via delle Terme di Caracalla, 00100 Rome, Italy (Telephone Number in U.S. (202) 653-2400); *The State of Food and Agriculture.*

G.K. Hall and Company, 70 Lincoln Street, Boston, Massachusetts 02111 (617) 423-3990; *The World in Figures.*

International Monetary Fund, 700 Nineteenth Street, NW, Washington, D.C. 20431 (202) 623-7000; *Direction of Trade Statistics, Government Finance Statistics Yearbook,* and *International Financial Statistics.*

Statistical Office of the United Nations, Publishing Service, New York, New York 10017 (800) 253-9646; *Foreign Trade Statistics for Africa, Survey of Economic and Social Conditions in Africa,* and *Trade in Manufactures of Developing Countries.*

Times Books, 201 East 50th Street, New York, New York 10022 (212) 751-2600; *The Economist Book of Vital World Statistics.*

United Nations Economic Commission for Africa, Africa Hall, P.O. Box 3001, Addis Ababa, Ethiopia (Telephone Number in U.S. (800) 253-9646); *African Statistical Yearbook.*

The World Bank, 1818 H Street, NW, Washington, D.C. 20433 (202) 477-1234; *World Tables.*

SUDAN - INCOME TAXES - See SUDAN - TAXATION

SUDAN - INDUSTRY

Euromonitor Publications Limited, 87-88 Turnmill Street, London EC1M 5QU, England; *International Marketing Data and Statistics.*

Facts on File, 460 Park Avenue South, New York, New York 10016 (800) 443-8323; *The New Book of World Rankings.*

G.K. Hall and Company, 70 Lincoln Street, Boston, Massachusetts 02111 (617) 423-3990; *The World in Figures.*

International Labour Office, I.L.O. Publications, CH-1211, Geneva 22, Switzerland; *Yearbook of Labour Statistics.*

Times Books, 201 East 50th Street, New York, New York 10022 (212) 751-2600; *The Economist Book of Vital World Statistics.*

United Nations Economic Commission for Africa, Africa Hall, P.O. Box 3001, Addis Ababa, Ethiopia (Telephone Number in U.S. (800) 253-9646); *African Statistical Yearbook.*

The World Bank, 1818 H Street, NW, Washington, D.C. 20433 (202) 477-1234; *World Tables.*

World Intellectual Property Organization, 34 Chemin des Colombettes, CH-1211 Geneva 20. Switzerland; *Industrial Property Statistics.*

SUDAN - INFANT AND MATERNAL MORTALITY

Statistical Office of the United Nations, Publishing Service, New York, New York 10017 (800) 253-9646; *Demographic Yearbook,* and *Statistical Yearbook.*

Times Books, 201 East 50th Street, New York, New York 10022 (212) 751-2600; *The Economist Book of Vital World Statistics.*

The World Bank, 1818 H Street, NW, Washington, D.C. 20433 (202) 477-1234; *World Tables.*

SUDAN - INTERNATIONAL LIQUIDITY

International Monetary Fund, 700 Nineteenth Street, NW, Washington, D.C. 20431 (202) 623-7000; *International Financial Statistics.*

SUDAN - INTERNATIONAL RESERVES EXCLUDING GOLD

African Development Bank, 01 BP 1387, Abidjan 01, Cote D'Ivoire; *Selected Statistics on Regional Member Countries.*

Statistical Office of the United Nations, Publishing Service, New York, New York 10017 (800) 253-9646; *Statistical Yearbook.*

The World Bank, 1818 H Street, NW, Washington, D.C. 20433 (202) 477-1234; *World Tables.*

SUDAN - INVESTMENTS

International Monetary Fund, 700 Nineteenth Street, NW, Washington, D.C. 20431 (202) 623-7000; *International Financial Statistics.*

SUDAN - IRON ORE PRODUCTION AND CONSUMPTION - See SUDAN - MINING AND MINERAL PRODUCTS

SUDAN - IRRIGATION

Euromonitor Publications Limited, 87-88 Turnmill Street, London EC1M 5QU, England; *International Marketing Data and Statistics.*

SUDAN - LABOR FORCE

African Development Bank, 01 BP 1387, Abidjan 01, Cote D'Ivoire; *Selected Statistics on Regional Member Countries.*

Euromonitor Publications Limited, 87-88 Turnmill Street, London EC1M 5QU, England; *International Marketing Data and Statistics.*

Facts on File, 460 Park Avenue South, New York, New York 10016 (800) 443-8323; *The New Book of World Rankings.*

Food and Agricultural Organization of the United Nations (FAO) Via delle Terme di Caracalla, 00100 Rome, Italy (Telephone Number in U.S. (202) 653-2400); *The State of Food and Agriculture.*

G.K. Hall and Company, 70 Lincoln Street, Boston, Massachusetts 02111 (617) 423-3990; *The World in Figures.*

The World Bank, 1818 H Street, NW, Washington, D.C. 20433 (202) 477-1234; *World Tables.*

SUDAN - LABOR PRODUCTIVITY

International Labour Office, I.L.O. Publications, CH-1211, Geneva 22, Switzerland; *Yearbook of Labour Statistics.*

SUDAN - LAND USE

Euromonitor Publications Limited, 87-88 Turnmill Street, London EC1M 5QU, England; *International Marketing Data and Statistics.*

Food and Agricultural Organization of the United Nations (FAO), Via delle Terme di Caracalla, 00100 Rome, Italy (Telephone Number in U.S. (202) 653-2400); *Production Yearbook.*

G.K. Hall and Company, 70 Lincoln Street, Boston, Massachusetts 02111 (617) 423-3990; *The World in Figures.*

SUDAN - LIBRARIES

Facts on File, 460 Park Avenue South, New York, New York 10016 (800) 443-8323; *The New Book of World Rankings.*

SUDAN - LIFE EXPECTANCY

African Development Bank, 01 BP 1387, Abidjan 01, Cote D'Ivoire; *Selected Statistics on Regional Member Countries.*

SUDAN - LITERACY RATE

Statistical Office of the United Nations, Publishing Service, New York, New York 10017 (800) 253-9646; *Survey of Economic and Social Conditions in Africa.*

SUDAN - LIVESTOCK AND POULTRY

Euromonitor Publications Limited, 87-88 Turnmill Street, London EC1M 5QU, England; *International Marketing Data and Statistics.*

Facts on File, 460 Park Avenue South, New York, New York 10016 (800) 443-8323; *The New Book of World Rankings.*

Food and Agricultural Organization of the United Nations (FAO), Via delle Terme di Caracalla, 00100 Rome, Italy (Telephone Number in U.S. (202) 653-2400); *Production Yearbook*, and *The State of Food and Agriculture.*

G.K. Hall and Company, 70 Lincoln Street, Boston, Massachusetts 02111 (617) 423-3990; *The World in Figures.*

Statistical Office of the United Nations, Publishing Service, New York, New York 10017 (800) 253-9646; *Statistical Yearbook*, and *Survey of Economic and Social Conditions in Africa.*

United Nations Economic Commission for Africa, Africa Hall, P.O. Box 3001, Addis Ababa, Ethiopia (Telephone Number in U.S. (800) 253-9646); *African Statistical Yearbook.*

SUDAN - LIVING LEVELS

G.K. Hall and Company, 70 Lincoln Street, Boston, Massachusetts 02111 (617) 423-3990; *The World in Figures.*

Times Books, 201 East 50th Street, New York, New York 10022 (212) 751-2600; *The Economist Book of Vital World Statistics.*

SUDAN - MAIL - NUMBER OF ITEMS SENT OR RECEIVED

Statistical Office of the United Nations, Publishing Service, New York, New York 10017 (800) 253-9646; *Statistical Yearbook.*

SUDAN - MANGANESE ORE PRODUCTION AND CONSUMPTION - See SUDAN - MINING AND MINERAL PRODUCTS

SUDAN - MANUFACTURING

Facts on File, 460 Park Avenue South, New York, New York 10016 (800) 443-8323; *The New Book of World Rankings.*

G.K. Hall and Company, 70 Lincoln Street, Boston, Massachusetts 02111 (617) 423-3990; *The World in Figures.*

Statistical Office of the United Nations, Publishing Service, New York, New York 10017 (800) 253-9646; *Statistical Yearbook*, and *Survey of Economic and Social Conditions in Africa.*

Times Books, 201 East 50th Street, New York, New York 10022 (212) 751-2600; *The Economist Book of Vital World Statistics.*

United Nations Economic Commission for Africa, Africa Hall, P.O. Box 3001, Addis Ababa, Ethiopia (Telephone Number in U.S. (800) 253-9646); *African Statistical Yearbook.*

The World Bank, 1818 H Street, NW, Washington, D.C. 20433 (202) 477-1234; *World Tables.*

SUDAN - MARRIAGE RATES

Facts on File, 460 Park Avenue South, New York, New York 10016 (800) 443-8323; *The New Book of World Rankings.*

Statistical Office of the United Nations, Publishing Service, New York, New York 10017 (800) 253-9646; *Demographic Yearbook.*

SUDAN - MEAT PRODUCTION - See SUDAN - LIVESTOCK AND POULTRY

SUDAN - MERCHANT SHIPPING

G.K. Hall and Company, 70 Lincoln Street, Boston, Massachusetts 02111 (617) 423-3990; *The World in Figures.*

Lloyd's Register of Shipping, 17 Battery Place, New York, New York 10004 (212) 425-8050; *Register of Ships.*

Statistical Office of the United Nations, Publishing Service, New York, New York 10017 (800) 253-9646; *Statistical Yearbook.*

Times Books, 201 East 50th Street, New York, New York 10022 (212) 751-2600; *The Economist Book of Vital World Statistics.*

United Nations Economic Commission for Africa, Africa Hall, P.O. Box 3001, Addis Ababa, Ethiopia (Telephone Number in U.S. (800) 253-9646); *African Statistical Yearbook.*

U.S. Department of Transportation, Maritime Administration, 400 Seventh Street, SW, Washington, D.C. 20590 (202) 366-5807; *A Statistical Analysis of the World's Merchant Fleets.*

SUDAN - MILITARY

G.K. Hall and Company, 70 Lincoln Street, Boston, Massachusetts 02111 (617) 423-3990; *The World in Figures.*

The International Institute for Strategic Studies, 23 Tavistock Street, London WC2E 7NQ, England; *The Military Balance.*

U.S. Arms Control and Disarmament Agency, 320 Twenty-first Street, NW, Washington, D.C. 20451 (202) 647-8677; *World Military Expenditures and Arms Transfers.*

SUDAN - MILK - See SUDAN - DAIRY PRODUCTS

SUDAN - MINING AND MINERAL PRODUCTS

Facts on File, 460 Park Avenue South, New York, New York 10016 (800) 443-8323; *The New Book of World Rankings.*

G.K. Hall and Company, 70 Lincoln Street, Boston, Massachusetts 02111 (617) 423-3990; *The World in Figures.*

Penn Well Publishing Company, 1421 South Sheridan Road, P.O. Box 1260, Tulsa, Oklahoma 74101 (800) 752-9764; *International Energy Statistics Sourcebook.*

Statistical Office of the United Nations, Publishing Service, New York, New York 10017 (800) 253-9646; *Statistical Yearbook.*

United Nations Economic Commission for Africa, Africa Hall, P.O. Box 3001, Addis Ababa, Ethiopia (Telephone Number in U.S. (800) 253-9646); *African Statistical Yearbook.*

SUDAN - MONEY EXCHANGE RATE

Euromonitor Publications Limited, 87-88 Turnmill Street, London EC1M 5QU, England; *International Marketing Data and Statistics.*

International Monetary Fund, 700 Nineteenth Street, NW, Washington, D.C. 20431 (202) 623-7000; *International Financial Statistics.*

Statistical Office of the United Nations, Publishing Service, New York, New York 10017 (800) 253-9646; *Statistical Yearbook.*

SUDAN - MONEY RESERVES

Euromonitor Publications Limited, 87-88 Turnmill Street, London EC1M 5QU, England; *International Marketing Data and Statistics.*

SUDAN - MONEY SUPPLY

African Development Bank, 01 BP 1387, Abidjan 01, Cote D'Ivoire; *Selected Statistics on Regional Member Countries.*

Euromonitor Publications Limited, 87-88 Turnmill Street, London EC1M 5QU, England; *International Marketing Data and Statistics.*

G.K. Hall and Company, 70 Lincoln Street, Boston, Massachusetts 02111 (617) 423-3990; *The World in Figures.*

International Monetary Fund, 700 Nineteenth Street, NW, Washington, D.C. 20431 (202) 623-7000; *International Financial Statistics.*

Statistical Office of the United Nations, Publishing Service, New York, New York 10017 (800) 253-9646; *Statistical Yearbook.*

The World Bank, 1818 H Street, NW, Washington, D.C. 20433 (202) 477-1234; *World Tables.*

SUDAN - MOTION PICTURES

Statistical Office of the United Nations, Publishing Service, New York, New York 10017 (800) 253-9646; *Statistical Yearbook.*

SUDAN - MOTOR VEHICLE TAXES - See SUDAN - TAXATION

SUDAN - MOTOR VEHICLES IN USE

G.K. Hall and Company, 70 Lincoln Street, Boston, Massachusetts 02111 (617) 423-3990; *The World in Figures.*

International Road Federation, 525 School Street, SW, Washington, D.C. 20024 (202) 554-2106; *World Road Statistics.*

Statistical Office of the United Nations, Publishing Service, New York, New York 10017 (800) 253-9646; *Statistical Yearbook,* and *Survey of Economic and Social Conditions in Africa.*

Times Books, 201 East 50th Street, New York, New York 10022 (212) 751-2600; *The Economist Book of Vital World Statistics.*

SUDAN - MULES - See SUDAN - LIVESTOCK AND POULTRY

SUDAN - MUSEUMS

Facts on File, 460 Park Avenue South, New York, New York 10016 (800) 443-8323; *The New Book of World Rankings.*

United Nations Educational, Scientific and Cultural Organization (UNESCO), 7 Place de Fontenoy, F-75700 Paris, France (Telephone Number in U.S. (212) 963-5981); *Statistical Yearbook.*

SUDAN - NATALITY - See SUDAN - BIRTH RATES

SUDAN - NATIONAL ACCOUNTS

African Development Bank, 01 BP 1387, Abidjan 01, Cote D'Ivoire; *Selected Statistics on Regional Member Countries.*

International Monetary Fund, 700 Nineteenth Street, NW, Washington, D.C. 20431 (202) 623-7000; *International Financial Statistics.*

Statistical Office of the United Nations, Publishing Service, New York, New York 10017 (800) 253-9646; *National Accounts Statistics*, and *Statistical Yearbook*.

United Nations Economic Commission for Africa, Africa Hall, P.O. Box 3001, Addis Ababa, Ethiopia (Telephone Number in U.S. (800) 253-9646); *African Statistical Yearbook*.

SUDAN - NATIONAL INCOME

Facts on File, 460 Park Avenue South, New York, New York 10016 (800) 443-8323; *The New Book of World Rankings*.

G.K. Hall and Company, 70 Lincoln Street, Boston, Massachusetts 02111 (617) 423-3990; *The World in Figures*.

Statistical Office of the United Nations, Publishing Service, New York, New York 10017 (800) 253-9646; *Statistical Yearbook*.

SUDAN - NATIONAL PRODUCT

Facts on File, 460 Park Avenue South, New York, New York 10016 (800) 443-8323; *The New Book of World Rankings*.

Statistical Office of the United Nations, Publishing Service, New York, New York 10017 (800) 253-9646; *Statistical Yearbook*.

SUDAN - NATURAL GAS PRODUCTION - See SUDAN - MINING AND MINERAL PRODUCTS

SUDAN - NEWSPAPER PRODUCTION - See SUDAN - FORESTRY AND FOREST PRODUCTS

SUDAN - NEWSPRINT - See SUDAN - FORESTRY AND FOREST PRODUCTS

SUDAN - OCCUPATIONS - See SUDAN - LABOR FORCE

SUDAN - PAPER - See SUDAN - FORESTRY AND FOREST PRODUCTS

SUDAN - PATENTS

World Intellectual Property Organization, 34 Chemin des Colombettes, CH-1211 Geneva 20. Switzerland; *Industrial Property Statistics*.

SUDAN - PEANUT PRODUCTION - See SUDAN - CROPS

SUDAN - PERIODICALS

United Nations Educational, Scientific and Cultural Organization (UNESCO), 7 Place de Fontenoy, F-75700 Paris, France (Telephone Number in U.S. (212) 963-5981); *Statistical Yearbook*.

SUDAN - PESTICIDE USE

Food and Agricultural Organization of the United Nations (FAO) Via delle Terme di Caracalla, 00100 Rome, Italy (Telephone Number in U.S. (202) 653-2400); *The State of Food and Agriculture*.

SUDAN - PETROLEUM INDUSTRY

Facts on File, 460 Park Avenue South, New York, New York 10016 (800) 443-8323; *The New Book of World Rankings*.

Food and Agricultural Organization of the United Nations (FAO) Via delle Terme di Caracalla, 00100 Rome, Italy (Telephone Number in U.S. (202) 653-2400); *The State of Food and Agriculture*.

G.K. Hall and Company, 70 Lincoln Street, Boston, Massachusetts 02111 (617) 423-3990; *The World in Figures*.

Penn Well Publishing Company, 1421 South Sheridan Road, P.O. Box 1260, Tulsa, Oklahoma 74101 (800) 752-9764; *International Energy Statistics Sourcebook*.

Statistical Office of the United Nations, Publishing Service, New York, New York 10017 (800) 253-9646; *Statistical Yearbook*.

SUDAN - PIGS - See SUDAN - LIVESTOCK AND POULTRY

SUDAN - POPULATION

African Development Bank, 01 BP 1387, Abidjan 01, Cote D'Ivoire; *Selected Statistics on Regional Member Countries*.

The Economist Intelligence Unit, 111 West 57th Street, New York, New York 10019 (800) 938-4685; *The World Market Atlas*.

Euromonitor Publications Limited, 87-88 Turnmill Street, London EC1M 5QU, England; *International Marketing Data and Statistics*.

Facts on File, 460 Park Avenue South, New York, New York 10016 (800) 443-8323; *The New Book of World Rankings*.

Food and Agricultural Organization of the United Nations (FAO), Via delle Terme di Caracalla, 00100 Rome, Italy (Telephone Number in U.S. (202) 653-2400); *Production Yearbook*.

G.K. Hall and Company, 70 Lincoln Street, Boston, Massachusetts 02111 (617) 423-3990; *The World in Figures*.

International Labour Office, I.L.O. Publications, CH-1211, Geneva 22, Switzerland; *Yearbook of Labour Statistics*.

Statistical Office of the United Nations, Publishing Service, New York, New York 10017 (800) 253-9646; *Demographic Yearbook*, *Statistical Yearbook*, and *Survey of Economic and Social Conditions in Africa*.

Times Books, 201 East 50th Street, New York, New York 10022 (212) 751-2600; *The Economist Book of Vital World Statistics*.

United Nations Educational, Scientific and Cultural Organization (UNESCO), 7 Place de Fontenoy, F-75700 Paris, France (Telephone Number in U.S. (212) 963-5981); *Statistical Yearbook*.

U.S. Arms Control and Disarmament Agency, 320 Twenty-first Street, NW, Washington, D.C. 20451 (202) 647-8677; *World Military Expenditures and Arms Transfers*.

World Health Organization, Office of Publications, Avenue Appia, CH-1211 Geneva 27, Switzerland (Telephone Number in U.S. (518) 436-9686); *World Health Statistics Annual*.

SUDAN - POST OFFICES

Facts on File, 460 Park Avenue South, New York, New York 10016 (800) 443-8323; *The New Book of World Rankings*.

SUDAN - POTATO PRODUCTION - See SUDAN - CROPS

SUDAN - PRICES

Facts on File, 460 Park Avenue South, New York, New York 10016 (800) 443-8323; *The New Book of World Rankings*.

Food and Agricultural Organization of the United Nations (FAO), Via delle Terme di Caracalla, 00100 Rome, Italy (Telephone Number in U.S. (202) 653-2400); *Production Yearbook*, and *The State of Food and Agriculture*.

G.K. Hall and Company, 70 Lincoln Street, Boston, Massachusetts 02111 (617) 423-3990; *The World in Figures*.

International Labour Office, I.L.O. Publications, CH-1211, Geneva 22, Switzerland; *Yearbook of Labour Statistics*.

International Monetary Fund, 700 Nineteenth Street, NW, Washington, D.C. 20431 (202) 623-7000; *International Financial Statistics*.

United Nations Economic Commission for Africa, Africa Hall, P.O. Box 3001, Addis Ababa, Ethiopia (Telephone Number in U.S. (800) 253-9646); *African Statistical Yearbook*.

SUDAN - PRINTING AND WRITING PAPER - See SUDAN - FORESTRY AND FOREST PRODUCTS

SUDAN - PRODUCTION

Facts on File, 460 Park Avenue South, New York, New York 10016 (800) 443-8323; *The New Book of World Rankings*.

G.K. Hall and Company, 70 Lincoln Street, Boston, Massachusetts 02111 (617) 423-3990, *The World in Figures*.

SUDAN - PRODUCTIVITY

Euromonitor Publications Limited, 87-88 Turnmill Street, London EC1M 5QU, England; *International Marketing Data and Statistics*.

SUDAN - PROPERTY TAXES - SUDAN - TAXATION

SUDAN - PUBLIC FINANCE

Facts on File, 460 Park Avenue South, New York, New York 10016 (800) 443-8323; *The New Book of World Rankings*.

SUDAN - RADIO BROADCASTING - See SUDAN - BROADCASTING

SUDAN - RAILWAYS

G.K. Hall and Company, 70 Lincoln Street, Boston, Massachusetts 02111 (617) 423-3990; *The World in Figures*.

Jane's Information Group, Sentinel House, 163 Brighton Road, Coulsdon, Surrey CR5 2NH, England (Telephone Number in U.S. (703) 683-3700); *Jane's World Railways*.

Statistical Office of the United Nations, Publishing Service, New York, New York 10017 (800) 253-9646; *Statistical Yearbook*, and *Survey of Economic and Social Conditions in Africa*.

United Nations Economic Commission for Africa, Africa Hall, P.O. Box 3001, Addis Ababa, Ethiopia (Telephone Number in U.S. (800) 253-9646); *African Statistical Yearbook*.

SUDAN - RELIGION

Facts on File, 460 Park Avenue South, New York, New York 10016 (800) 443-8323; *The New Book of World Rankings*.

SUDAN - RENT PRICES

International Labour Office, I.L.O. Publications, CH-1211, Geneva 22, Switzerland; *Yearbook of Labour Statistics*.

SUDAN - RETAIL TRADE

G.K. Hall and Company, 70 Lincoln Street, Boston, Massachusetts 02111 (617) 423-3990; *The World in Figures*.

SUDAN - RICE PRODUCTION - See SUDAN - CROPS

SUDAN - ROUNDWOOD PRODUCTION - See SUDAN - FORESTRY AND FOREST PRODUCTS

SUDAN - RUBBER PRODUCTION AND CONSUMPTION

Facts on File, 460 Park Avenue South, New York, New York 10016 (800) 443-8323; *The New Book of World Rankings*.

SUDAN - SALT PRODUCTION - See SUDAN - MINING AND MINERAL PRODUCTS

SUDAN - SAWNWOOD PRODUCTION - See SUDAN - FORESTRY AND FOREST PRODUCTS

SUDAN - SCIENCE AND TECHNOLOGY - EXPENDITURE FOR RESEARCH

Statistical Office of the United Nations, Publishing Service, New York, New York 10017 (800) 253-9646; *Statistical Yearbook*.

SUDAN - SCIENTISTS AND TECHNICIANS

Statistical Office of the United Nations, Publishing Service, New York, New York 10017 (800) 253-9646; *Statistical Yearbook*.

United Nations Educational, Scientific and Cultural Organization (UNESCO), 7 Place de Fontenoy, F-75700 Paris, France (Telephone Number in U.S. (212) 963-5981); *Statistical Yearbook*.

SUDAN - SENIOR CITIZENS

Facts on File, 460 Park Avenue South, New York, New York 10016 (800) 443-8323; *The New Book of World Rankings*.

SUDAN - SESAME - See SUDAN - CROPS

SUDAN - SHEEP - See SUDAN - LIVESTOCK AND POULTRY

SUDAN - SILVER PRODUCTION AND CONSUMPTION - See SUDAN - MINING AND MINERAL PRODUCTS

SUDAN - SOCIAL DATA

African Development Bank, 01 BP 1387, Abidjan 01, Cote D'Ivoire; *Selected Statistics on Regional Member Countries*.

Facts on File, 460 Park Avenue South, New York, New York 10016 (800) 443-8323; *The New Book of World Rankings*.

G.K. Hall and Company, 70 Lincoln Street, Boston, Massachusetts 02111 (617) 423-3990; *The World in Figures*.

SUDAN - SOCIAL SECURITY

International Monetary Fund, 700 Nineteenth Street, NW, Washington, D.C. 20431 (202) 623-7000; *Government Finance Statistics Yearbook*.

SUDAN - STAMP TAXES AND DUTIES - See SUDAN - TAXATION

SUDAN - STATE BUDGET REVENUE AND EXPENDITURES

Euromonitor Publications Limited, 87-88 Turnmill Street, London EC1M 5QU, England; *International Marketing Data and Statistics.*

SUDAN - STEEL - See SUDAN - MINING AND MINERAL PRODUCTS

SUDAN - STOCKS - COMMODITY - MARKET PRICE - INDEX

Food and Agricultural Organization of the United Nations (FAO) Via delle Terme di Caracalla, 00100 Rome, Italy (Telephone Number in U.S. (202) 653-2400); *The State of Food and Agriculture.*

SUDAN - SUGAR PRODUCTION AND CONSUMPTION - See SUDAN - CROPS

SUDAN - TAXATION

G.K. Hall and Company, 70 Lincoln Street, Boston, Massachusetts 02111 (617) 423-3990; *The World in Figures.*

International Monetary Fund, 700 Nineteenth Street, NW, Washington, D.C. 20431 (202) 623-7000; *Government Finance Statistics Yearbook.*

International Road Federation, 525 School Street, SW, Washington, D.C. 20024 (202) 554-2106; *World Road Statistics.*

The World Bank, 1818 H Street, NW, Washington, D.C. 20433 (202) 477-1234; *World Tables.*

SUDAN - TEA CONSUMPTION - See SUDAN - CROPS

SUDAN - TELEGRAPH SERVICE

Statistical Office of the United Nations, Publishing Service, New York, New York 10017 (800) 253-9646; *Statistical Yearbook.*

SUDAN - TELEPHONES IN USE

American Telephone and Telegraph Company, 26 Parsippany Road, Whippany, New Jersey 07981 (800) 338-4038; *The World's Telephones.*

G.K. Hall and Company, 70 Lincoln Street, Boston, Massachusetts 02111 (617) 423-3990; *The World in Figures.*

Statistical Office of the United Nations, Publishing Service, New York, New York 10017 (800) 253-9646; *Statistical Yearbook.*

SUDAN - TELEVISION BROADCASTING - See SUDAN - BROADCASTING

SUDAN - TEXTILE INDUSTRY

G.K. Hall and Company, 70 Lincoln Street, Boston, Massachusetts 02111 (617) 423-3990; *The World in Figures.*

Statistical Office of the United Nations, Publishing Service, New York, New York 10017 (800) 253-9646; *Statistical Yearbook.*

SUDAN - TOBACCO PRODUCTION

Facts on File, 460 Park Avenue South, New York, New York 10016 (800) 443-8323; *The New Book of World Rankings.*

Statistical Office of the United Nations, Publishing Service, New York, New York 10017 (800) 253-9646; *Statistical Yearbook.*

SUDAN - TOURISM

Facts on File, 460 Park Avenue South, New York, New York 10016 (800) 443-8323; *The New Book of World Rankings.*

G.K. Hall and Company, 70 Lincoln Street, Boston, Massachusetts 02111 (617) 423-3990; *The World in Figures.*

Statistical Office of the United Nations, Publishing Service, New York, New York 10017 (800) 253-9646; *Statistical Yearbook.*

Times Books, 201 East 50th Street, New York, New York 10022 (212) 751-2600; *The Economist Book of Vital World Statistics.*

United Nations Economic Commission for Africa, Africa Hall, P.O. Box 3001, Addis Ababa, Ethiopia (Telephone Number in U.S. (800) 253-9646); *African Statistical Yearbook.*

World Tourism Organization, Calle Capitan Haya 42, E-28020 Madrid, Spain; *Yearbook of Tourism Statistics.*

SUDAN - TRACTORS IN USE

Statistical Office of the United Nations, Publishing Service, New York, New York 10017 (800) 253-9646; *Statistical Yearbook.*

SUDAN - TRADE - See SUDAN - FOREIGN TRADE

SUDAN - TRADEMARKS AND SERVICE MARKS

Statistical Office of the United Nations, Publishing Service, New York, New York 10017 (800) 253-9646; *Statistical Yearbook.*

World Intellectual Property Organization, 34 Chemin des Colombettes, CH-1211 Geneva 20. Switzerland; *Industrial Property Statistics.*

SUDAN - TRANSPORTATION

Facts on File, 460 Park Avenue South, New York, New York 10016 (800) 443-8323; *The New Book of World Rankings.*

G.K. Hall and Company, 70 Lincoln Street, Boston, Massachusetts 02111 (617) 423-3990; *The World in Figures.*

United Nations Economic Commission for Africa, Africa Hall, P.O. Box 3001, Addis Ababa, Ethiopia (Telephone Number in U.S. (800) 253-9646); *African Statistical Yearbook.*

SUDAN - UNEMPLOYMENT

Euromonitor Publications Limited, 87-88 Turnmill Street, London EC1M 5QU, England; *International Marketing Data and Statistics.*

International Labour Office, I.L.O. Publications, CH-1211, Geneva 22, Switzerland; *Yearbook of Labour Statistics.*

Statistical Office of the United Nations, Publishing Service, New York, New York 10017 (800) 253-9646; *Statistical Yearbook.*

SUDAN - VITAL STATISTICS

Euromonitor Publications Limited, 87-88 Turnmill Street, London EC1M 5QU, England; *International Marketing Data and Statistics.*

G.K. Hall and Company, 70 Lincoln Street, Boston, Massachusetts 02111 (617) 423-3990; *The World in Figures*.

Statistical Office of the United Nations, Publishing Service, New York, New York 10017 (800) 253-9646; *Statistical Yearbook*.

World Health Organization, Office of Publications, Avenue Appia, CH-1211 Geneva 27, Switzerland (Telephone Number in U.S. (518) 436-9686); *World Health Statistics Annual*.

SUDAN - WAGES

G.K. Hall and Company, 70 Lincoln Street, Boston, Massachusetts 02111 (617) 423-3990; *The World in Figures*.

International Labour Office, I.L.O. Publications, CH-1211, Geneva 22, Switzerland; *Yearbook of Labour Statistics*.

SUDAN - WEATHER

Facts on File, 460 Park Avenue South, New York, New York 10016 (800) 443-8323; *The New Book of World Rankings*.

G.K. Hall and Company, 70 Lincoln Street, Boston, Massachusetts 02111 (617) 423-3990; *The World in Figures*.

SUDAN - WELFARE

International Monetary Fund, 700 Nineteenth Street, NW, Washington, D.C. 20431 (202) 623-7000; *Government Finance Statistics Yearbook*.

SUDAN - WHEAT PRODUCTION AND PRICES - See SUDAN - CROPS

SUDAN - WHOLESALE PRICES

Statistical Office of the United Nations, Publishing Service, New York, New York 10017 (800) 253-9646; *Statistical Yearbook*.

SUDAN - WINE PRODUCTION

Facts on File, 460 Park Avenue South, New York, New York 10016 (800) 443-8323; *The New Book of World Rankings*.

SUDAN - WOOL PRODUCTION

Facts on File, 460 Park Avenue South, New York, New York 10016 (800) 443-8323; *The New Book of World Rankings*.

SUGAR AND SUGAR CANE - See also FOOD AND KINDRED PRODUCTS

SUGAR AND SUGAR CANE - BEET

U.S. Department of Agriculture, National Agricultural Statistics Service, Fourteenth Street and Independence Avenue, SW, Washington, D.C. 20250 (202) 219-1504; *Economic Indicators of the Farm Sector: National Financial Summary, Field Crops, Crop Production,* and *Crop Values*.

SUGAR AND SUGAR CANE - COMMODITY CREDIT CORPORATION TRANSACTIONS

U.S. Department of Agriculture, Agricultural Stabilization and Conservation Service, Fourteenth Street and Independence Avenue, SW, Washington, D.C. 20250 (202) 720-5237; *Commodity Credit Corporation Report of Financial Conditions and Operations,* and *Agricultural Outlook*.

SUGAR AND SUGAR CANE - CONSUMPTION

U.S. Department of Agriculture, Economic Research Service, Fourteenth Street and Constitution Avenue, NW, Washington, D.C. 20005-4789 (202) 219-1504; *Food Consumption, Prices, and Expenditures*.

SUGAR AND SUGAR CANE - FOREIGN TRADE

U.S. Department of Agriculture, Economic Research Service, Fourteenth Street and Independence Avenue, SW, Washington, D.C. 20005-4789 (202) 219-1504; *Foreign Agricultural Trade of the United States*.

U.S. Department of Commerce, Bureau of the Census, Suitland, Maryland 20233 (301) 763-4040; *U.S. Merchandise Trade*.

SUGAR AND SUGAR CANE - MANUFACTURE

U.S. Department of Commerce, Bureau of the Census, Suitland, Maryland 20233 (301) 763-4040; *Census of Manufactures,* and *Annual Survey of Manufactures*.

SUGAR AND SUGAR CANE - PRICES

U.S. Department of Agriculture, National Agricultural Statistics Service, Fourteenth Street and Independence Avenue, SW, Washington, D.C. 20250 (202) 219-1504; *Field Crops, Crop Production,* and *Crop Values*.

U.S. Department of Labor, Bureau of Labor Statistics, Two Massachusetts Avenue, NE, Washington, D.C. 20212 (202) 606-7828; *Producer Price Indexes*.

SUGAR AND SUGAR CANE - PRODUCTION

U.S. Department of Agriculture, Economic Research Service, Fourteenth Street and Independence Avenue, SW, Washington, D.C. 20005-4789 (202) 219-1504; *Agricultural Outlook*.

U.S. Department of Agriculture, National Agricultural Statistics Service, Fourteenth Street and Independence Avenue, SW, Washington, D.C. 20250 (202) 219-1504; *Crop Production, Crop Values,* and *Field Crops*.

SUGAR AND SUGAR CANE - PRODUCTION - WORLD

Statistical Office of the United Nations, Publishing Service, New York, New York 10017 (800) 253-9646; *Monthly Bulletin of Statistics,* and *Statistical Yearbook*.

SUICIDES

U.S. Department of Health and Human Services, Public Health Service, 200 Independence Avenue, SW, Washington, D.C. 20201 (202) 619-1296; *Vital Statistics of the United States, Monthly Vital Statistics Report,* and unpublished data.

World Health Organization, Office of Publications, Avenue Appia, CH-1211 Geneva 27, Switzerland (Telephone Number in U.S. (518) 436-9686); *World Health Statistics Annual*.

SULFUR

U.S. Department of Commerce, Bureau of the Census, Suitland, Maryland 20233 (301) 763-4040; *Census of Mineral Industries*.

U.S. Department of the Interior, Bureau of Mines, 810 Seventh Street, NW, Washington, D.C. 20241 (202) 501-9649; *Annual Reports,*

Mineral Commodity Summaries, and *Mineral Facts and Problems.*

SULFUR - PRICES

U.S. Department of the Interior, Bureau of Mines, 810 Seventh Street, NW, Washington, D.C. 20241 (202) 501-9649; *Annual Reports, Mineral Facts and Problems*, and *Mineral Commodity Summaries.*

SULFUR - PRODUCTION AND VALUE

U.S. Department of the Interior, Bureau of Mines, 810 Seventh Street, NW, Washington, D.C. 20241 (202) 501-9649; *Annual Reports, Mineral Facts and Problems*, and *Mineral Commodity Summaries.*

SULFUR - WORLD PRODUCTION

U.S. Department of the Interior, Bureau of Mines, 810 Seventh Street, NW, Washington, D.C. 20241 (202) 501-9649; *Annual Reports.*

SUNDAY AND SABBATH SCHOOLS

National Council of the Churches of Christ in the United States of America, 475 Riverside Drive, New York, New York 10115 (212) 870-2227; *Yearbook of American and Canadian Churches.*

SUPPLEMENTAL SECURITY INCOME

U.S. Department of Health and Human Services, Administration for Children and Families, 370 L'Enfant Promenade, SW, Washington D.C. 20447 (202) 401-9200; *Quarterly Public Assistance Statistics.*

U.S. Department of Health and Human Services, Social Security Administration, 6401 Security Boulevard, Baltimore, Maryland 21235 (410) 965-1234; *Social Security Bulletin, Annual Statistical Supplement to the Social Security Bulletin,* and unpublished data.

U.S. Library of Congress, Congressional Research Service, 10 First Street, SE, Washington, D.C. 20540; *Cash and Non-Cash Benefits for Persons with Limited Income: Eligibility Rules, Recipient and Expenditure Data.*

SUPPLEMENTAL SECURITY INCOME - STATES

U.S. Department of Health and Human Services, Administration for Children and Families, 370 L'Enfant Promenade, SW, Washington D.C. 20447 (202) 401-9200; *Quarterly Public Assistance Statistics.*

U.S. Department of Health and Human Services, Social Security Administration, 6401 Security Boulevard, Baltimore, Maryland 21235 (410) 965-1234; *Social Security Bulletin,* and *Annual Statistical Supplement to the Social Security Bulletin.*

SUPREME COURT, UNITED STATES

Administrative Office of the United States Courts, United States Supreme Court Building, One First Street, NE, Washington, D.C. 20544 (202) 633-6094; unpublished data.

SURGEONS

American Medical Association, 515 North State Street, Chicago, Illinois 60610 (312) 464-4818; *Physician Characteristics and Distribution in the United States,* and *Socioeconomic Characteristics of Medical Practice.*

SURGICAL PROCEDURES

American Hospital Association, 840 North Lake Shore Drive, Chicago, Illinois 60611 (312) 280-6000; *Hospital Statistics,* and *Annual Survey of Hospitals.*

U.S. Department of Health and Human Services, National Center for Health Statistics, 3700 East-West Highway, Hyattsville, Maryland 20782 (301) 436-8500; *Vital and Health Statistics,* and unpublished data.

SURGICAL PROCEDURES - MEDICAL DEVICE IMPLANTS

U.S. Department of Health and Human Services, National Center for Health Statistics, 3700 East-West Highway, Hyattsville, Maryland 20782 (301) 436-8500; *National Health Interview Survey,* and unpublished data.

SURGICAL PROCEDURES - ORGAN TRANSPLANTS - FACILITIES

American Association of Tissue Banks, 1350 Beverly Road, Suite 220-A, McLean, Virginia 22101 (703) 827-9582.

American Hospital Association, 840 North Lake Shore Drive, Chicago, Illinois 60611 (312) 280-6000; *Hospital Statistics,* and *Annual Survey of Hospitals.*

Eye Bank Association of America, 1001 Connecticut Avenue, NW, Suite 601, Washington, D.C. 20036-5504 (202) 775-4999.

U.S. Department of Health and Human Services, Public Health Service, Division of Organ Transplantation, 200 Independence Avenue, SW, Washington, D.C. 20201 (202) 619-1296; unpublished data.

Suriname - National Statistical Office

Algemeen Bureau Voor de Statistiek, Post Office Box 244, Paramaribo, Suriname.

Suriname - Primary Statistics Source

General Bureau of Statistics, Post Office Box 244, Paramaribo, Suriname; *Jaacijfers voor Suriname* (Statistical Yearbook of Suriname).

SURINAME - AGRICULTURE

Facts on File, 460 Park Avenue South, New York, New York 10016 (800) 443-8323; *The New Book of World Rankings.*

Food and Agricultural Organization of the United Nations (FAO) Via delle Terme di Caracalla, 00100 Rome, Italy (Telephone Number in U.S. (202) 653-2400); *Production Yearbook, The State of Food and Agriculture,* and *Trade Yearbook.*

Gale Research Incorporated, 835 Penobscot Building, Detroit, Michigan 48226 (800) 877-4253; *International Historical Statistics The Americas and Australasia.*

G.K. Hall and Company, 70 Lincoln Street, Boston, Massachusetts 02111 (617) 423-3990; *The World in Figures.*

Inter-American Development Bank, 1300 New York Avenue, NW, Washington, D.C. 20577 (202) 623-1753; *Economic and Social Progress in Latin America.*

Statistical Office of the United Nations, Publishing Service, New York, New York 10017 (800) 253-9646; *Statistical Yearbook*.

The World Bank, 1818 H Street, NW, Washington, D.C. 20433 (202) 477-1234; *World Tables*.

SURINAME - AIRLINE SERVICE

Facts on File, 460 Park Avenue South, New York, New York 10016 (800) 443-8323; *The New Book of World Rankings*.

G.K. Hall and Company, 70 Lincoln Street, Boston, Massachusetts 02111 (617) 423-3990; *The World in Figures*.

SURINAME - ALUMINUM - See SURINAME - MINING AND MINERAL PRODUCTS

SURINAME - ANIMAL HEALTH

Food and Agricultural Organization of the United Nations (FAO), Via delle Terme di Caracalla, 00100, Rome, Italy (Telephone Number in U.S. (202) 653-2400); *Animal Health Yearbook*.

SURINAME - AREA AND DENSITY OF POPULATION

Facts on File, 460 Park Avenue South, New York, New York 10016 (800) 443-8323; *The New Book of World Rankings*.

Food and Agricultural Organization of the United Nations (FAO) Via delle Terme di Caracalla, 00100 Rome, Italy (Telephone Number in U.S. (202) 653-2400); *The State of Food and Agriculture*.

G.K. Hall and Company, 70 Lincoln Street, Boston, Massachusetts 02111 (617) 423-3990; *The World in Figures*.

Inter-American Development Bank, 1300 New York Avenue, NW, Washington, D.C. 20577 (202) 623-1753; *Economic and Social Progress in Latin America*.

Statistical Office of the United Nations, Publishing Service, New York, New York 10017 (800) 253-9646; *Statistical Yearbook*.

United Nations Educational, Scientific and Cultural Organization (UNESCO), 7 Place de Fontenoy, F-75700 Paris, France (Telephone Number in U.S. (212) 963-5981); *Statistical Yearbook*.

SURINAME - ARMS EXPORTS AND IMPORTS

U.S. Arms Control and Disarmament Agency, 320 Twenty-first Street, NW, Washington, D.C. 20451 (202) 647-8677; *World Military Expenditures and Arms Transfers*.

SURINAME - BALANCE OF PAYMENTS

The Economist Intelligence Unit, 111 West 57th Street, New York, New York 10019 (800) 938-4685; *The World Market Atlas*.

G.K. Hall and Company, 70 Lincoln Street, Boston, Massachusetts 02111 (617) 423-3990; *The World in Figures*.

Inter-American Development Bank, 1300 New York Avenue, NW, Washington, D.C. 20577 (202) 623-1753; *Economic and Social Progress in Latin America*.

International Monetary Fund, 700 Nineteenth Street, NW, Washington, D.C. 20431 (202) 623-7000; *Balance of Payments Yearbook*, and *International Financial Statistics*.

Organization of American States (OAS), General Secretariat, Washington, D.C. 20006 (202) 458-3533; *Statistical Bulletin of the OAS*.

Statistical Office of the United Nations, Publishing Service, New York, New York 10017 (800) 253-9646; *Economic Survey of Latin America and the Caribbean*.

The World Bank, 1818 H Street, NW, Washington, D.C. 20433 (202) 477-1234; *World Tables*.

SURINAME - BANANA PRODUCTION - See SURINAME - CROPS

SURINAME - BANKING

Facts on File, 460 Park Avenue South, New York, New York 10016 (800) 443-8323; *The New Book of World Rankings*.

G.K. Hall and Company, 70 Lincoln Street, Boston, Massachusetts 02111 (617) 423-3990; *The World in Figures*.

Inter-American Development Bank, 1300 New York Avenue, NW, Washington, D.C. 20577 (202) 623-1753; *Economic and Social Progress in Latin America*.

International Monetary Fund, 700 Nineteenth Street, NW, Washington, D.C. 20431 (202) 623-7000; *Government Finance Statistics Yearbook*, and *International Financial Statistics*.

SURINAME - BARLEY PRODUCTION - See SURINAME - CROPS

SURINAME - BAUXITE - See SURINAME - MINING AND MINERAL PRODUCTS

SURINAME - BEER PRODUCTION

Facts on File, 460 Park Avenue South, New York, New York 10016 (800) 443-8323; *The New Book of World Rankings*.

Statistical Office of the United Nations, Publishing Service, New York, New York 10017 (800) 253-9646; *Statistical Yearbook*.

SURINAME - BIRTH RATES

Facts on File, 460 Park Avenue South, New York, New York 10016 (800) 443-8323; *The New Book of World Rankings*.

Statistical Office of the United Nations, Publishing Service, New York, New York 10017 (800) 253-9646; *Demographic Yearbook*, and *Statistical Yearbook*.

The World Bank, 1818 H Street, NW, Washington, D.C. 20433 (202) 477-1234; *World Tables*.

SURINAME - BONDS

G.K. Hall and Company, 70 Lincoln Street, Boston, Massachusetts 02111 (617) 423-3990; *The World in Figures*.

Inter-American Development Bank, 1300 New York Avenue, NW, Washington, D.C. 20577 (202) 623-1753; *Economic and Social Progress in Latin America*.

International Monetary Fund, 700 Nineteenth Street, NW, Washington, D.C. 20431 (202) 623-7000; *Government Finance Statistics Yearbook*.

SURINAME - BOOK PRODUCTION

G.K. Hall and Company, 70 Lincoln Street, Boston, Massachusetts 02111 (617) 423-3990; *The World in Figures.*

SURINAME - BROADCASTING

Billboard Limited, P.O. Box 9027, 1006 AA Amsterdam, The Netherlands (Telephone Number in U.S. (212) 764-7300); *World Radio TV Handbook.*

G.K. Hall and Company, 70 Lincoln Street, Boston, Massachusetts 02111 (617) 423-3990; *The World in Figures.*

SURINAME - BUSINESS

G.K. Hall and Company, 70 Lincoln Street, Boston, Massachusetts 02111 (617) 423-3990; *The World in Figures.*

Inter-American Development Bank, 1300 New York Avenue, NW, Washington, D.C. 20577 (202) 623-1753; *Economic and Social Progress in Latin America.*

SURINAME - BUSINESS AND PROFESSIONAL LICENSES

International Monetary Fund, 700 Nineteenth Street, NW, Washington, D.C. 20431 (202) 623-7000; *Government Finance Statistics Yearbook.*

SURINAME - BUTTER PRODUCTION - See SURINAME - DAIRY PRODUCTS

SURINAME - CALORIE SUPPLY

Food and Agricultural Organization of the United Nations (FAO) Via delle Terme di Caracalla, 00100 Rome, Italy (Telephone Number in U.S. (202) 653-2400); *The State of Food and Agriculture.*

SURINAME - CAPITAL INVESTMENT

Inter-American Development Bank, 1300 New York Avenue, NW, Washington, D.C. 20577 (202) 623-1753; *Economic and Social Progress in Latin America.*

SURINAME - CAPITAL REVENUE

Inter-American Development Bank, 1300 New York Avenue, NW, Washington, D.C. 20577 (202) 623-1753; *Economic and Social Progress in Latin America.*

International Monetary Fund, 700 Nineteenth Street, NW, Washington, D.C. 20431 (202) 623-7000; *Government Finance Statistics Yearbook.*

SURINAME - CATTLE - See SURINAME - LIVESTOCK AND POULTRY

SURINAME - CEMENT PRODUCTION - See SURINAME - MINING AND MINERAL PRODUCTS

SURINAME - CHEESE PRODUCTION AND CONSUMPTION - See SURINAME - DAIRY PRODUCTS

SURINAME - CHEMICAL (ORGANIC) PRODUCTION - See SURINAME - MINING AND MINERAL PRODUCTS

SURINAME - CIGARETTE PRODUCTION - See SURINAME - TOBACCO PRODUCTION

SURINAME - CLASS STRUCTURE

G.K. Hall and Company, 70 Lincoln Street, Boston, Massachusetts 02111 (617) 423-3990; *The World in Figures.*

SURINAME - CLIMATE

Facts on File, 460 Park Avenue South, New York, New York 10016 (800) 443-8323; *The New Book of World Rankings.*

G.K. Hall and Company, 70 Lincoln Street, Boston, Massachusetts 02111 (617) 423-3990; *The World in Figures.*

SURINAME - COAL PRODUCTION - See SURINAME - MINING AND MINERAL PRODUCTS

SURINAME - COCOA PRODUCTION

Statistical Office of the United Nations, Publishing Service, New York, New York 10017 (800) 253-9646; *Statistical Yearbook.*

U.C.L.A. Latin American Center Publications, University of California, Los Angeles, California 90024 (310) 825-6634; *Statistical Abstract of Latin America.*

SURINAME - COFFEE - See SURINAME - CROPS

SURINAME - COMMUNICATIONS

Gale Research Incorporated, 835 Penobscot Building, Detroit, Michigan 48226 (800) 877-4253; *International Historical Statistics The Americas and Australasia.*

G.K. Hall and Company, 70 Lincoln Street, Boston, Massachusetts 02111 (617) 423-3990; *The World in Figures.*

Inter-American Development Bank, 1300 New York Avenue, NW, Washington, D.C. 20577 (202) 623-1753; *Economic and Social Progress in Latin America.*

SURINAME - CONSTRUCTION INDUSTRY

Facts on File, 460 Park Avenue South, New York, New York 10016 (800) 443-8323; *The New Book of World Rankings.*

Inter-American Development Bank, 1300 New York Avenue, NW, Washington, D.C. 20577 (202) 623-1753; *Economic and Social Progress in Latin America.*

SURINAME - CONSUMER PRICE INDEX

G.K. Hall and Company, 70 Lincoln Street, Boston, Massachusetts 02111 (617) 423-3990; *The World in Figures.*

Statistical Office of the United Nations, Publishing Service, New York, New York 10017 (800) 253-9646; *Statistical Yearbook.*

SURINAME - CONSUMER PRICES

International Labour Office, I.L.O. Publications, CH-1211, Geneva 22, Switzerland; *Yearbook of Labour Statistics.*

International Monetary Fund, 700 Nineteenth Street, NW, Washington, D.C. 20431 (202) 623-7000; *International Financial Statistics.*

Organization of American States (OAS), General Secretariat, Washington, D.C. 20006 (202) 458-3533; *Statistical Bulletin of the OAS.*

SURINAME - CONSUMPTION

G.K. Hall and Company, 70 Lincoln Street, Boston, Massachusetts 02111 (617) 423-3990; *The World in Figures*.

Inter-American Development Bank, 1300 New York Avenue, NW, Washington, D.C. 20577 (202) 623-1753; *Economic and Social Progress in Latin America*.

SURINAME - COPPER PRODUCTION AND CONSUMPTION - See SURINAME - MINING AND MINERAL PRODUCTS

SURINAME - CORN PRODUCTION - See SURINAME - CROPS

SURINAME - CORPORATE INCOME TAXES - See SURINAME - TAXATION

SURINAME - CORPORATE TAXES - See SURINAME - TAXATION

SURINAME - COTTON PRODUCTION - See SURINAME - CROPS

SURINAME - CRIME

Yale University Press, Yale Station, New Haven, Connecticut 06520 (203) 432-0940; *Violence and Crime in Cross-National Perspective*.

SURINAME - CROPS

Facts on File, 460 Park Avenue South, New York, New York 10016 (800) 443-8323; *The New Book of World Rankings*.

Food and Agricultural Organization of the United Nations (FAO) Via delle Terme di Caracalla, 00100 Rome, Italy (Telephone Number in U.S. (202) 653-2400); *The State of Food and Agriculture*.

G.K. Hall and Company, 70 Lincoln Street, Boston, Massachusetts 02111 (617) 423-3990; *The World in Figures*.

U.C.L.A. Latin American Center Publications, University of California, Los Angeles, California 90024 (310) 825-6634; *Statistical Abstract of Latin America*.

SURINAME - CUSTOMS DUTIES

G.K. Hall and Company, 70 Lincoln Street, Boston, Massachusetts 02111 (617) 423-3990; *The World in Figures*.

Inter-American Development Bank, 1300 New York Avenue, NW, Washington, D.C. 20577 (202) 623-1753; *Economic and Social Progress in Latin America*.

International Monetary Fund, 700 Nineteenth Street, NW, Washington, D.C. 20431 (202) 623-7000; *Government Finance Statistics Yearbook*.

SURINAME - DAIRY PRODUCTS

Facts on File, 460 Park Avenue South, New York, New York 10016 (800) 443-8323; *The New Book of World Rankings*.

Food and Agricultural Organization of the United Nations (FAO) Via delle Terme di Caracalla, 00100 Rome, Italy (Telephone Number in U.S. (202) 653-2400); *The State of Food and Agriculture*.

U.C.L.A. Latin American Center Publications, University of California, Los Angeles, California 90024 (310) 825-6634; *Statistical Abstract of Latin America*.

SURINAME - DEATH RATES

G.K. Hall and Company, 70 Lincoln Street, Boston, Massachusetts 02111 (617) 423-3990; *The World in Figures*.

Statistical Office of the United Nations, Publishing Service, New York, New York 10017 (800) 253-9646; *Statistical Yearbook*.

World Health Organization, Office of Publications, Avenue Appia, CH-1211 Geneva 27, Switzerland (Telephone Number in U.S. (518) 436-9686); *World Health Statistics Annual*.

SURINAME - DEFENSE EXPENDITURES

G.K. Hall and Company, 70 Lincoln Street, Boston, Massachusetts 02111 (617) 423-3990; *The World in Figures*.

International Monetary Fund, 700 Nineteenth Street, NW, Washington, D.C. 20431 (202) 623-7000; *Government Finance Statistics Yearbook*.

U.S. Arms Control and Disarmament Agency, 320 Twenty-first Street, NW, Washington, D.C. 20451 (202) 647-8677; *World Military Expenditures and Arms Transfers*.

SURINAME - DEMOGRAPHY

The Economist Intelligence Unit, 111 West 57th Street, New York, New York 10019 (800) 938 1686; *The World Market Atlas*.

Facts on File, 460 Park Avenue South, New York, New York 10016 (800) 443-8323; *The New Book of World Rankings*.

G.K. Hall and Company, 70 Lincoln Street, Boston, Massachusetts 02111 (617) 423-3990; *The World in Figures*.

SURINAME - DEVELOPMENT ASSISTANCE

G.K. Hall and Company, 70 Lincoln Street, Boston, Massachusetts 02111 (617) 423-3990; *The World in Figures*.

Inter-American Development Bank, 1300 New York Avenue, NW, Washington, D.C. 20577 (202) 623-1753; *Economic and Social Progress in Latin America*.

Statistical Office of the United Nations, Publishing Service, New York, New York 10017 (800) 253-9646; *Statistical Yearbook*.

SURINAME - DIAMOND PRODUCTION - See SURINAME - MINING AND MINERAL PRODUCTS

SURINAME - DISCOUNT RATES

Inter-American Development Bank, 1300 New York Avenue, NW, Washington, D.C. 20577 (202) 623-1753; *Economic and Social Progress in Latin America*.

SURINAME - DISEASES

G.K. Hall and Company, 70 Lincoln Street, Boston, Massachusetts 02111 (617) 423-3990; *The World in Figures*.

World Health Organization, Office of Publications, Avenue Appia, CH-1211 Geneva 27, Switzerland (Telephone Number in U.S. (518) 436-9686); *World Health Statistics Annual*.

SURINAME - DIVORCE RATES

Facts on File, 460 Park Avenue South, New York, New York 10016 (800) 443-8323; *The New Book of World Rankings*.

Statistical Office of the United Nations, Publishing Service, New York, New York 10017 (800) 253-9646; *Demographic Yearbook*, and *Statistical Yearbook*.

SURINAME - DOMESTIC PRODUCT

G.K. Hall and Company, 70 Lincoln Street, Boston, Massachusetts 02111 (617) 423-3990; *The World in Figures*.

SURINAME - ECONOMY

Facts on File, 460 Park Avenue South, New York, New York 10016 (800) 443-8323; *The New Book of World Rankings*.

G.K. Hall and Company, 70 Lincoln Street, Boston, Massachusetts 02111 (617) 423-3990; *The World in Figures*.

Inter-American Development Bank, 1300 New York Avenue, NW, Washington, D.C. 20577 (202) 623-1753; *Economic and Social Progress in Latin America*.

Organization of American States (OAS), General Secretariat, Washington, D.C. 20006 (202) 458-3533; *Statistical Bulletin of the OAS*.

Statistical Office of the United Nations, Publishing Service, New York, New York 10017 (800) 253-9646; *Economic Survey of Latin America and the Caribbean*.

SURINAME - EDUCATION

The Economist Intelligence Unit, 111 West 57th Street, New York, New York 10019 (800) 938-4685; *The World Market Atlas*.

Facts on File, 460 Park Avenue South, New York, New York 10016 (800) 443-8323; *The New Book of World Rankings*.

Gale Research Incorporated, 835 Penobscot Building, Detroit, Michigan 48226 (800) 877-4253; *International Historical Statistics The Americas and Australasia*.

G.K. Hall and Company, 70 Lincoln Street, Boston, Massachusetts 02111 (617) 423-3990; *The World in Figures*.

International Monetary Fund, 700 Nineteenth Street, NW, Washington, D.C. 20431 (202) 623-7000; *Government Finance Statistics Yearbook*.

United Nations Educational, Scientific and Cultural Organization (UNESCO), 7 Place de Fontenoy, F-75700 Paris, France (Telephone Number in U.S. (212) 963-5981); *Statistical Yearbook*.

The World Bank, 1818 H Street, NW, Washington, D.C. 20433 (202) 477-1234; *World Tables*.

SURINAME - EGG PRODUCTION AND CONSUMPTION - See SURINAME - DAIRY PRODUCTS

SURINAME - ELECTRICITY

Facts on File, 460 Park Avenue South, New York, New York 10016 (800) 443-8323; *The New Book of World Rankings*.

Inter-American Development Bank, 1300 New York Avenue, NW, Washington, D.C. 20577 (202) 623-1753; *Economic and Social Progress in Latin America*.

Organization of American States (OAS), General Secretariat, Washington, D.C. 20006 (202) 458-3533; *Statistical Bulletin of the OAS*.

Penn Well Publishing Company, 1421 South Sheridan Road, P.O. Box 1260, Tulsa, Oklahoma 74101 (800) 752-9764; *International Energy Statistics Sourcebook*.

Statistical Office of the United Nations, Publishing Service, New York, New York 10017 (800) 253-9646; *Statistical Yearbook*.

SURINAME - EMPLOYMENT

Facts on File, 460 Park Avenue South, New York, New York 10016 (800) 443-8323; *The New Book of World Rankings*.

International Labour Office, I.L.O. Publications, CH-1211, Geneva 22, Switzerland; *Yearbook of Labour Statistics*.

Organization of American States (OAS), General Secretariat, Washington, D.C. 20006 (202) 458-3533; *Statistical Bulletin of the OAS*.

Statistical Office of the United Nations, Publishing Service, New York, New York 10017 (800) 253-9646; *Statistical Yearbook*.

SURINAME - ENERGY

Facts on File, 460 Park Avenue South, New York, New York 10016 (800) 443-8323; *The New Book of World Rankings*.

Food and Agricultural Organization of the United Nations (FAO) Via delle Terme di Caracalla, 00100 Rome, Italy (Telephone Number in U.S. (202) 653-2400); *The State of Food and Agriculture*.

G.K. Hall and Company, 70 Lincoln Street, Boston, Massachusetts 02111 (617) 423-3990; *The World in Figures*.

Penn Well Publishing Company, 1421 South Sheridan Road, P.O. Box 1260, Tulsa, Oklahoma 74101 (800) 752-9764; *International Energy Statistics Sourcebook*.

Statistical Office of the United Nations, Publishing Service, New York, New York 10017 (800) 253-9646; *Energy Statistics Yearbook*, and *Statistical Yearbook*.

SURINAME - EXCHANGE RATES

Inter-American Development Bank, 1300 New York Avenue, NW, Washington, D.C. 20577 (202) 623-1753; *Economic and Social Progress in Latin America*.

International Monetary Fund, 700 Nineteenth Street, NW, Washington, D.C. 20431 (202) 623-7000; *International Financial Statistics*.

Organization of American States (OAS), General Secretariat, Washington, D.C. 20006 (202) 458-3533; *Statistical Bulletin of the OAS*.

Statistical Office of the United Nations, Publishing Service, New York, New York 10017 (800) 253-9646; *Statistical Yearbook*.

SURINAME - EXCISE TAXES - See SURINAME - TAXATION

SURINAME - EXPORTS

The Economist Intelligence Unit, 111 West 57th Street, New York, New York 10019 (800) 938-4685; *The World Market Atlas*.

Food and Agricultural Organization of the United Nations (FAO) Via delle Terme di Caracalla, 00100 Rome, Italy (Telephone Number in U.S. (202) 653-2400); *The State of Food and Agriculture*.

G.K. Hall and Company, 70 Lincoln Street, Boston, Massachusetts 02111 (617) 423-3990; *The World in Figures*.

Inter-American Development Bank, 1300 New York Avenue, NW, Washington, D.C. 20577 (202) 623-1753; *Economic and Social Progress in Latin America*.

International Monetary Fund, 700 Nineteenth Street, NW, Washington, D.C. 20431 (202) 623-7000; *Direction of Trade Statistics, Government Finance Statistics Yearbook*, and *International Financial Statistics*.

The World Bank, 1818 H Street, NW, Washington, D.C. 20433 (202) 477-1234; *World Tables*.

SURINAME - EXTERNAL FINANCING

Inter-American Development Bank, 1300 New York Avenue, NW, Washington, D.C. 20577 (202) 623-1753; *Economic and Social Progress in Latin America*.

SURINAME - EXTERNAL INDEBTEDNESS

Inter-American Development Bank, 1300 New York Avenue, NW, Washington, D.C. 20577 (202) 623-1753; *Economic and Social Progress in Latin America*.

The World Bank, 1818 H Street, NW, Washington, D.C. 20433 (202) 477-1234; *World Tables*.

SURINAME - EXTERNAL TRADE

Food and Agricultural Organization of the United Nations (FAO) Via delle Terme di Caracalla, 00100 Rome, Italy (Telephone Number in U.S. (202) 653-2400); *The State of Food and Agriculture*, and *Trade Yearbook*.

Gale Research Incorporated, 835 Penobscot Building, Detroit, Michigan 48226 (800) 877-4253; *International Historical Statistics The Americas and Australasia*.

G.K. Hall and Company, 70 Lincoln Street, Boston, Massachusetts 02111 (617) 423-3990; *The World in Figures*.

Inter-American Development Bank, 1300 New York Avenue, NW, Washington, D.C. 20577 (202) 623-1753; *Economic and Social Progress in Latin America*.

Statistical Office of the United Nations, Publishing Service, New York, New York 10017 (800) 253-9646; *Statistical Yearbook*.

SURINAME - FARM CROPS - See SURINAME - CROPS

SURINAME - FERTILITY RATES

Facts on File, 460 Park Avenue South, New York, New York 10016 (800) 443-8323; *The New Book of World Rankings*.

The World Bank, 1818 H Street, NW, Washington, D.C. 20433 (202) 477-1234; *World Tables*.

SURINAME - FERTILIZER

Food and Agricultural Organization of the United Nations (FAO) Via delle Terme di Caracalla, 00100 Rome, Italy (Telephone Number in U.S. (202) 653-2400); *The State of Food and Agriculture*.

SURINAME - FETAL MORTALITY

Statistical Office of the United Nations, Publishing Service, New York, New York 10017 (800) 253-9646; *Demographic Yearbook*.

SURINAME - FINANCE

Facts on File, 460 Park Avenue South, New York, New York 10016 (800) 443-8323; *The New Book of World Rankings*.

Gale Research Incorporated, 835 Penobscot Building, Detroit, Michigan 48226 (800) 877-4253; *International Historical Statistics The Americas and Australasia*.

G.K. Hall and Company, 70 Lincoln Street, Boston, Massachusetts 02111 (617) 423-3990; *The World in Figures*.

Inter-American Development Bank, 1300 New York Avenue, NW, Washington, D.C. 20577 (202) 623-1753; *Economic and Social Progress in Latin America*.

International Monetary Fund, 700 Nineteenth Street, NW, Washington, D.C. 20431 (202) 623-7000; *Government Finance Statistics Yearbook*.

SURINAME - FISHERIES

Facts on File, 460 Park Avenue South, New York, New York 10016 (800) 443-8323; *The New Book of World Rankings*.

Food and Agricultural Organization of the United Nations (FAO) Via delle Terme di Caracalla, 00100 Rome, Italy (Telephone Number in U.S. (202) 653-2400); *The State of Food and Agriculture*, and *Yearbook of Fishery Statistics*.

Inter-American Development Bank, 1300 New York Avenue, NW, Washington, D.C. 20577 (202) 623-1753; *Economic and Social Progress in Latin America*.

Statistical Office of the United Nations, Publishing Service, New York, New York 10017 (800) 253-9646; *Statistical Yearbook*.

SURINAME - FOOD

Food and Agricultural Organization of the United Nations (FAO) Via delle Terme di Caracalla, 00100 Rome, Italy (Telephone Number in U.S. (202) 653-2400); *Production Yearbook*, and *The State of Food and Agriculture*.

G.K. Hall and Company, 70 Lincoln Street, Boston, Massachusetts 02111 (617) 423-3990; *The World in Figures*.

SURINAME - FOREIGN AID

G.K. Hall and Company, 70 Lincoln Street, Boston, Massachusetts 02111 (617) 423-3990; *The World in Figures*.

Inter-American Development Bank, 1300 New York Avenue, NW, Washington, D.C. 20577 (202) 623-1753; *Economic and Social Progress in Latin America*.

SURINAME - FOREIGN DEBT

Inter-American Development Bank, 1300 New York Avenue, NW, Washington, D.C. 20577 (202) 623-1753; *Economic and Social Progress in Latin America*.

International Monetary Fund, 700 Nineteenth Street, NW, Washington, D.C. 20431 (202) 623-7000; *Government Finance Statistics Yearbook*.

SURINAME - FOREIGN INDEBTEDNESS

Inter-American Development Bank, 1300 New York Avenue, NW, Washington, D.C. 20577 (202) 623-1753; *Economic and Social Progress in Latin America*.

Statistical Office of the United Nations, Publishing Service, New York, New York 10017 (800) 253-9646; *Economic Survey of Latin America and the Caribbean*.

SURINAME - FOREIGN TRADE

Facts on File, 460 Park Avenue South, New York, New York 10016 (800) 443-8323; *The New Book of World Rankings*.

Food and Agricultural Organization of the United Nations (FAO) Via delle Terme di Caracalla, 00100 Rome, Italy (Telephone Number in U.S. (202) 653-2400); *The State of Food and Agriculture*.

G.K. Hall and Company, 70 Lincoln Street, Boston, Massachusetts 02111 (617) 423-3990; *The World in Figures*.

Inter-American Development Bank, 1300 New York Avenue, NW, Washington, D.C. 20577 (202) 623-1753; *Economic and Social Progress in Latin America*.

Statistical Office of the United Nations, Publishing Service, New York, New York 10017 (800) 253-9646; *Economic Survey of Latin America and the Caribbean, International Trade Statistics Yearbook*, and *Statistical Yearbook*.

The World Bank, 1818 H Street, NW, Washington, D.C. 20433 (202) 477-1234; *World Tables*.

SURINAME - FORESTRY AND FOREST PRODUCTS

Facts on File, 460 Park Avenue South, New York, New York 10016 (800) 443-8323; *The New Book of World Rankings*.

Food and Agricultural Organization of the United Nations (FAO) Via delle Terme di Caracalla, 00100 Rome, Italy (Telephone Number in U.S. (202) 653-2400); *The State of Food and Agriculture*, and *Yearbook of Forest Products*.

G.K. Hall and Company, 70 Lincoln Street, Boston, Massachusetts 02111 (617) 423-3990; *The World in Figures*.

Inter-American Development Bank, 1300 New York Avenue, NW, Washington, D.C. 20577 (202) 623-1753; *Economic and Social Progress in Latin America*.

Statistical Office of the United Nations, Publishing Service, New York, New York 10017 (800) 253-9646; *Statistical Yearbook*.

U.C.L.A. Latin American Center Publications, University of California, Los Angeles, California 90024 (310) 825-6634; *Statistical Abstract of Latin America*.

United Nations Educational, Scientific and Cultural Organization (UNESCO), 7 Place de Fontenoy, F-75700 Paris, France (Telephone Number in U.S. (212) 963-5981); *Statistical Yearbook*.

SURINAME - GAS PRODUCTION - See SURINAME - MINING AND MINERAL PRODUCTS

SURINAME - GENERAL MORTALITY

Statistical Office of the United Nations, Publishing Service, New York, New York 10017 (800) 253-9646; *Demographic Yearbook*.

SURINAME - GEOGRAPHIC DATA

Facts on File, 460 Park Avenue South, New York, New York 10016 (800) 443-8323; *The New Book of World Rankings*.

SURINAME - GOLD HOLDINGS

International Monetary Fund, 700 Nineteenth Street, NW, Washington, D.C. 20431 (202) 623-7000; *International Financial Statistics*.

Statistical Office of the United Nations, Publishing Service, New York, New York 10017 (800) 253-9646; *Statistical Yearbook*.

The World Bank, 1818 H Street, NW, Washington, D.C. 20433 (202) 477-1234; *World Tables*.

SURINAME - GOLD PRODUCTION AND CONSUMPTION - See SURINAME - MINING AND MINERAL PRODUCTS

SURINAME - GOVERNMENT

G.K. Hall and Company, 70 Lincoln Street, Boston, Massachusetts 02111 (617) 423-3990; *The World in Figures*.

Inter-American Development Bank, 1300 New York Avenue, NW, Washington, D.C. 20577 (202) 623-1753; *Economic and Social Progress in Latin America*.

SURINAME - GOVERNMENT CONSUMPTION

Inter-American Development Bank, 1300 New York Avenue, NW, Washington, D.C. 20577 (202) 623-1753; *Economic and Social Progress in Latin America*.

SURINAME - GOVERNMENT EXPENDITURES

Inter-American Development Bank, 1300 New York Avenue, NW, Washington, D.C. 20577 (202) 623-1753; *Economic and Social Progress in Latin America*.

International Monetary Fund, 700 Nineteenth Street, NW, Washington, D.C. 20431 (202) 623-7000; *Government Finance Statistics Yearbook*.

The World Bank, 1818 H Street, NW, Washington, D.C. 20433 (202) 477-1234; *World Tables*.

SURINAME - GOVERNMENT FINANCE

Inter-American Development Bank, 1300 New York Avenue, NW, Washington, D.C. 20577 (202) 623-1753; *Economic and Social Progress in Latin America*.

International Monetary Fund, 700 Nineteenth Street, NW, Washington, D.C. 20431 (202) 623-7000; *International Financial Statistics*.

SURINAME - GOVERNMENT REVENUE

Inter-American Development Bank, 1300 New York Avenue, NW, Washington, D.C. 20577 (202) 623-1753; *Economic and Social Progress in Latin America.*

International Monetary Fund, 700 Nineteenth Street, NW, Washington, D.C. 20431 (202) 623-7000; *Government Finance Statistics Yearbook.*

The World Bank, 1818 H Street, NW, Washington, D.C. 20433 (202) 477-1234; *World Tables.*

SURINAME - GRAIN PRODUCTION - See SURINAME - CROPS

SURINAME - GRANTS

International Monetary Fund, 700 Nineteenth Street, NW, Washington, D.C. 20431 (202) 623-7000; *Government Finance Statistics Yearbook.*

SURINAME - GROSS DOMESTIC PRODUCT

The Economist Intelligence Unit, 111 West 57th Street, New York, New York 10019 (800) 938-4685; *The World Market Atlas.*

Facts on File, 460 Park Avenue South, New York, New York 10016 (800) 443-8323; *The New Book of World Rankings.*

G.K. Hall and Company, 70 Lincoln Street, Boston, Massachusetts 02111 (617) 423-3990; *The World in Figures.*

Inter-American Development Bank, 1300 New York Avenue, NW, Washington, D.C. 20577 (202) 623-1753; *Economic and Social Progress in Latin America.*

Statistical Office of the United Nations, Publishing Service, New York, New York 10017 (800) 253-9646; *Statistical Yearbook.*

The World Bank, 1818 H Street, NW, Washington, D.C. 20433 (202) 477-1234; *World Tables.*

SURINAME - GROSS NATIONAL PRODUCT

Inter-American Development Bank, 1300 New York Avenue, NW, Washington, D.C. 20577 (202) 623-1753; *Economic and Social Progress in Latin America.*

The World Bank, 1818 H Street, NW, Washington, D.C. 20433 (202) 477-1234; *World Tables.*

U.S. Arms Control and Disarmament Agency, 320 Twenty-first Street, NW, Washington, D.C. 20451 (202) 647-8677; *World Military Expenditures and Arms Transfers.*

SURINAME - GROUNDNUT PRODUCTION - See SURINAME - CROPS

SURINAME - HEALTH

Facts on File, 460 Park Avenue South, New York, New York 10016 (800) 443-8323; *The New Book of World Rankings.*

G.K. Hall and Company, 70 Lincoln Street, Boston, Massachusetts 02111 (617) 423-3990; *The World in Figures.*

Statistical Office of the United Nations, Publishing Service, New York, New York 10017 (800) 253-9646; *Statistical Yearbook.*

World Health Organization, Office of Publications, Avenue Appia, CH-1211 Geneva 27, Switzerland (Telephone Number in U.S. (518) 436-9686); *World Health Statistics Annual.*

SURINAME - HEALTH EXPENDITURES

International Monetary Fund, 700 Nineteenth Street, NW, Washington, D.C. 20431 (202) 623-7000; *Government Finance Statistics Yearbook.*

SURINAME - HIGHWAYS

G.K. Hall and Company, 70 Lincoln Street, Boston, Massachusetts 02111 (617) 423-3990; *The World in Figures.*

SURINAME - HORSES - See SURINAME - LIVESTOCK AND POULTRY

SURINAME - HOURS OF WORK - See SURINAME - EMPLOYMENT

SURINAME - HOUSING EXPENDITURES

Facts on File, 460 Park Avenue South, New York, New York 10016 (800) 443-8323; *The New Book of World Rankings.*

International Monetary Fund, 700 Nineteenth Street, NW, Washington, D.C. 20431 (202) 623-7000; *Government Finance Statistics Yearbook.*

SURINAME - ILLITERATE POPULATION

The Economist Intelligence Unit, 111 West 57th Street, New York, New York 10019 (800) 938-4685; *The World Market Atlas.*

G.K. Hall and Company, 70 Lincoln Street, Boston, Massachusetts 02111 (617) 423-3990; *The World in Figures.*

United Nations Educational, Scientific and Cultural Organization (UNESCO), 7 Place de Fontenoy, F-75700 Paris, France (Telephone Number in U.S. (212) 963-5981); *Statistical Yearbook.*

SURINAME - IMPORTS

The Economist Intelligence Unit, 111 West 57th Street, New York, New York 10019 (800) 938-4685; *The World Market Atlas.*

Food and Agricultural Organization of the United Nations (FAO) Via delle Terme di Caracalla, 00100 Rome, Italy (Telephone Number in U.S. (202) 653-2400); *The State of Food and Agriculture.*

G.K. Hall and Company, 70 Lincoln Street, Boston, Massachusetts 02111 (617) 423-3990; *The World in Figures.*

Inter-American Development Bank, 1300 New York Avenue, NW, Washington, D.C. 20577 (202) 623-1753; *Economic and Social Progress in Latin America.*

International Monetary Fund, 700 Nineteenth Street, NW, Washington, D.C. 20431 (202) 623-7000; *Direction of Trade Statistics, Government Finance Statistics Yearbook,* and *International Financial Statistics.*

The World Bank, 1818 H Street, NW, Washington, D.C. 20433 (202) 477-1234; *World Tables.*

SURINAME - INCOME TAXES - See SURINAME - TAXATION

SURINAME - INDUSTRIAL METALS PRODUCTION - See SURINAME - MINING AND MINERAL PRODUCTS

SURINAME - INDUSTRY

Facts on File, 460 Park Avenue South, New York, New York 10016 (800) 443-8323; *The New Book of World Rankings*.

Gale Research Incorporated, 835 Penobscot Building, Detroit, Michigan 48226 (800) 877-4253; *International Historical Statistics The Americas and Australasia*.

G.K. Hall and Company, 70 Lincoln Street, Boston, Massachusetts 02111 (617) 423-3990; *The World in Figures*.

International Labour Office, I.L.O. Publications, CH-1211, Geneva 22, Switzerland; *Yearbook of Labour Statistics*.

Statistical Office of the United Nations, Publishing Service, New York, New York 10017 (800) 253-9646; *Economic Survey of Latin America and the Caribbean*.

The World Bank, 1818 H Street, NW, Washington, D.C. 20433 (202) 477-1234; *World Tables*.

SURINAME - INFANT AND MATERNAL MORTALITY

Statistical Office of the United Nations, Publishing Service, New York, New York 10017 (800) 253-9646; *Demographic Yearbook*, and *Statistical Yearbook*.

The World Bank, 1818 H Street, NW, Washington, D.C. 20433 (202) 477-1234; *World Tables*.

SURINAME - INFLATIONARY FACTORS

Statistical Office of the United Nations, Publishing Service, New York, New York 10017 (800) 253-9646; *Economic Survey of Latin America and the Caribbean*.

SURINAME - INTEREST RATES

Inter-American Development Bank, 1300 New York Avenue, NW, Washington, D.C. 20577 (202) 623-1753; *Economic and Social Progress in Latin America*.

SURINAME - INTERNATIONAL FINANCE

Inter-American Development Bank, 1300 New York Avenue, NW, Washington, D.C. 20577 (202) 623-1753; *Economic and Social Progress in Latin America*.

SURINAME - INTERNATIONAL LIQUIDITY

Inter-American Development Bank, 1300 New York Avenue, NW, Washington, D.C. 20577 (202) 623-1753; *Economic and Social Progress in Latin America*.

International Monetary Fund, 700 Nineteenth Street, NW, Washington, D.C. 20431 (202) 623-7000; *International Financial Statistics*.

SURINAME - INTERNATIONAL RESERVES

Organization of American States (OAS), General Secretariat, Washington, D.C. 20006 (202) 458-3533; *Statistical Bulletin of the OAS*.

SURINAME - INTERNATIONAL RESERVES EXCLUDING GOLD

Inter-American Development Bank, 1300 New York Avenue, NW, Washington, D.C. 20577 (202) 623-1753; *Economic and Social Progress in Latin America*.

Statistical Office of the United Nations, Publishing Service, New York, New York 10017 (800) 253-9646; *Statistical Yearbook*.

The World Bank, 1818 H Street, NW, Washington, D.C. 20433 (202) 477-1234; *World Tables*.

SURINAME - INTERNATIONAL STATISTICS

Inter-American Development Bank, 1300 New York Avenue, NW, Washington, D.C. 20577 (202) 623-1753; *Economic and Social Progress in Latin America*.

SURINAME - INVESTMENTS

Inter-American Development Bank, 1300 New York Avenue, NW, Washington, D.C. 20577 (202) 623-1753; *Economic and Social Progress in Latin America*.

International Monetary Fund, 700 Nineteenth Street, NW, Washington, D.C. 20431 (202) 623-7000; *International Financial Statistics*.

SURINAME - IRON ORE PRODUCTION AND CONSUMPTION - See SURINAME - MINING AND MINERAL PRODUCTS

SURINAME - IRRIGATION

Inter-American Development Bank, 1300 New York Avenue, NW, Washington, D.C. 20577 (202) 623-1753; *Economic and Social Progress in Latin America*.

SURINAME - LABOR FORCE

Facts on File, 460 Park Avenue South, New York, New York 10016 (800) 443-8323; *The New Book of World Rankings*.

Food and Agricultural Organization of the United Nations (FAO) Via delle Terme di Caracalla, 00100 Rome, Italy (Telephone Number in U.S. (202) 653-2400); *The State of Food and Agriculture*.

Gale Research Incorporated, 835 Penobscot Building, Detroit, Michigan 48226 (800) 877-4253; *International Historical Statistics The Americas and Australasia*.

G.K. Hall and Company, 70 Lincoln Street, Boston, Massachusetts 02111 (617) 423-3990; *The World in Figures*.

The World Bank, 1818 H Street, NW, Washington, D.C. 20433 (202) 477-1234; *World Tables*.

SURINAME - LABOR PRODUCTIVITY

International Labour Office, I.L.O. Publications, CH-1211, Geneva 22, Switzerland; *Yearbook of Labour Statistics*.

SURINAME - LAND USE

Food and Agricultural Organization of the United Nations (FAO), Via delle Terme di Caracalla, 00100 Rome, Italy (Telephone Number in U.S. (202) 653-2400); *Production Yearbook*.

G.K. Hall and Company, 70 Lincoln Street, Boston, Massachusetts 02111 (617) 423-3990; *The World in Figures*.

Inter-American Development Bank, 1300 New York Avenue, NW, Washington, D.C. 20577 (202) 623-1753; *Economic and Social Progress in Latin America*.

SURINAME - LIBRARIES

Facts on File, 460 Park Avenue South, New York, New York 10016 (800) 443-8323; *The New Book of World Rankings*.

United Nations Educational, Scientific and Cultural Organization (UNESCO), 7 Place de Fontenoy, F-75700 Paris, France (Telephone Number in U.S. (212) 963-5981); *Statistical Yearbook*.

SURINAME - LIVESTOCK AND POULTRY

Facts on File, 460 Park Avenue South, New York, New York 10016 (800) 443-8323; *The New Book of World Rankings*.

Food and Agricultural Organization of the United Nations (FAO), Via delle Terme di Caracalla, 00100 Rome, Italy (Telephone Number in U.S. (202) 653-2400); *Production Yearbook*, and *The State of Food and Agriculture*.

G.K. Hall and Company, 70 Lincoln Street, Boston, Massachusetts 02111 (617) 423-3990; *The World in Figures*.

Statistical Office of the United Nations, Publishing Service, New York, New York 10017 (800) 253-9646; *Statistical Yearbook*.

SURINAME - LIVING LEVELS

G.K. Hall and Company, 70 Lincoln Street, Boston, Massachusetts 02111 (617) 423-3990; *The World in Figures*.

SURINAME - MAIN ECONOMIC INDICATORS - See SURINAME - ECONOMY

SURINAME - MAIN INDICATORS - See SURINAME - ECONOMY

SURINAME - MANUFACTURING

Facts on File, 460 Park Avenue South, New York, New York 10016 (800) 443-8323; *The New Book of World Rankings*.

G.K. Hall and Company, 70 Lincoln Street, Boston, Massachusetts 02111 (617) 423-3990; *The World in Figures*.

Inter-American Development Bank, 1300 New York Avenue, NW, Washington, D.C. 20577 (202) 623-1753; *Economic and Social Progress in Latin America*.

Statistical Office of the United Nations, Publishing Service, New York, New York 10017 (800) 253-9646; *Statistical Yearbook*.

The World Bank, 1818 H Street, NW, Washington, D.C. 20433 (202) 477-1234; *World Tables*.

SURINAME - MARRIAGE RATES

Facts on File, 460 Park Avenue South, New York, New York 10016 (800) 443-8323; *The New Book of World Rankings*.

Statistical Office of the United Nations, Publishing Service, New York, New York 10017 (800) 253-9646; *Demographic Yearbook*, and *Statistical Yearbook*.

SURINAME - MEAT PRODUCTION - See SURINAME - LIVESTOCK AND POULTRY

SURINAME - MERCHANT SHIPPING

G.K. Hall and Company, 70 Lincoln Street, Boston, Massachusetts 02111 (617) 423-3990; *The World in Figures*.

Statistical Office of the United Nations, Publishing Service, New York, New York 10017 (800) 253-9646; *Statistical Yearbook*.

U.S. Department of Transportation, Maritime Administration, 400 Seventh Street, SW, Washington, D.C. 20590 (202) 366-5807; *A Statistical Analysis of the World's Merchant Fleets*.

SURINAME - MILITARY

G.K. Hall and Company, 70 Lincoln Street, Boston, Massachusetts 02111 (617) 423-3990; *The World in Figures*.

The International Institute for Strategic Studies, 23 Tavistock Street, London WC2E 7NQ, England; *The Military Balance*.

U.S. Arms Control and Disarmament Agency, 320 Twenty-first Street, NW, Washington, D.C. 20451 (202) 647-8677; *World Military Expenditures and Arms Transfers*.

SURINAME - MILK PRODUCTION - See SURINAME - DAIRY PRODUCTS

SURINAME - MINING AND MINERAL PRODUCTS

Commodity Research Bureau, Incorporated, 75 Wall Street, New York, New York 10005 (212) 504-7754; *Commodity Year Book*.

Facts on File, 460 Park Avenue South, New York, New York 10016 (800) 443-8323; *The New Book of World Rankings*.

G.K. Hall and Company, 70 Lincoln Street, Boston, Massachusetts 02111 (617) 423-3990; *The World in Figures*.

Inter-American Development Bank, 1300 New York Avenue, NW, Washington, D.C. 20577 (202) 623-1753; *Economic and Social Progress in Latin America*.

International Monetary Fund, 700 Nineteenth Street, NW, Washington, D.C. 20431 (202) 623-7000; *International Financial Statistics*.

Organization of American States (OAS), General Secretariat, Washington, D.C. 20006 (202) 458-3533; *Statistical Bulletin of the OAS*.

Penn Well Publishing Company, 1421 South Sheridan Road, P.O. Box 1260, Tulsa, Oklahoma 74101 (800) 752-9764; *International Energy Statistics Sourcebook*.

Statistical Office of the United Nations, Publishing Service, New York, New York 10017 (800) 253-9646; *Statistical Yearbook*.

U.C.L.A. Latin American Center Publications, University of California, Los Angeles, California 90024 (310) 825-6634; *Statistical Abstract of Latin America*.

SURINAME - MONEY EXCHANGE RATES

Inter-American Development Bank, 1300 New York Avenue, NW, Washington, D.C. 20577 (202) 623-1753; *Economic and Social Progress in Latin America*.

International Monetary Fund, 700 Nineteenth Street, NW, Washington, D.C. 20431 (202) 623-7000; *International Financial Statistics*.

Statistical Office of the United Nations, Publishing Service, New York, New York 10017 (800) 253-9646; *Statistical Yearbook*.

SURINAME - MONEY RATES - MARKET

Inter-American Development Bank, 1300 New York Avenue, NW, Washington, D.C. 20577 (202) 623-1753; *Economic and Social Progress in Latin America*.

SURINAME - MONEY RESERVES

Inter-American Development Bank, 1300 New York Avenue, NW, Washington, D.C. 20577 (202) 623-1753; *Economic and Social Progress in Latin America*.

SURINAME - MONEY SUPPLY

G.K. Hall and Company, 70 Lincoln Street, Boston, Massachusetts 02111 (617) 423-3990; *The World in Figures*.

Inter-American Development Bank, 1300 New York Avenue, NW, Washington, D.C. 20577 (202) 623-1753; *Economic and Social Progress in Latin America*.

International Monetary Fund, 700 Nineteenth Street, NW, Washington, D.C. 20431 (202) 623-7000; *International Financial Statistics*.

Statistical Office of the United Nations, Publishing Service, New York, New York 10017 (800) 253-9646; *Statistical Yearbook*.

The World Bank, 1818 H Street, NW, Washington, D.C. 20433 (202) 477-1234; *World Tables*.

SURINAME - MOTOR VEHICLE TAXES - See SURINAME - TAXATION

SURINAME - MOTOR VEHICLES IN USE

G.K. Hall and Company, 70 Lincoln Street, Boston, Massachusetts 02111 (617) 423-3990; *The World in Figures*.

Statistical Office of the United Nations, Publishing Service, New York, New York 10017 (800) 253-9646; *Statistical Yearbook*.

SURINAME - MUSEUMS

Facts on File, 460 Park Avenue South, New York, New York 10016 (800) 443-8323; *The New Book of World Rankings*.

SURINAME - NATALITY - See SURINAME - BIRTH RATE

SURINAME - NATIONAL ACCOUNTS

Gale Research Incorporated, 835 Penobscot Building, Detroit, Michigan 48226 (800) 877-4253; *International Historical Statistics The Americas and Australasia*.

Inter-American Development Bank, 1300 New York Avenue, NW, Washington, D.C. 20577 (202) 623-1753; *Economic and Social Progress in Latin America*.

Organization of American States (OAS), General Secretariat, Washington, D.C. 20006 (202) 458-3533; *Statistical Bulletin of the OAS*.

Statistical Office of the United Nations, Publishing Service, New York, New York 10017 (800) 253-9646; *National Accounts Statistics, and Statistical Yearbook*.

SURINAME - NATIONAL INCOME

Facts on File, 460 Park Avenue South, New York, New York 10016 (800) 443-8323; *The New Book of World Rankings*.

G.K. Hall and Company, 70 Lincoln Street, Boston, Massachusetts 02111 (617) 423-3990; *The World in Figures*.

Inter-American Development Bank, 1300 New York Avenue, NW, Washington, D.C. 20577 (202) 623-1753; *Economic and Social Progress in Latin America*.

Statistical Office of the United Nations, Publishing Service, New York, New York 10017 (800) 253-9646; *Statistical Yearbook*.

SURINAME - NATIONAL PRODUCT

Facts on File, 460 Park Avenue South, New York, New York 10016 (800) 443-8323; *The New Book of World Rankings*.

SURINAME - NATURAL GAS PRODUCTION - See SURINAME - MINING AND MINERAL PRODUCTS

SURINAME - NEWSPAPER PRODUCTION - See SURINAME - FORESTRY AND FOREST PRODUCTS

SURINAME - NEWSPRINT EXPORTS AND IMPORTS - See SURINAME - FORESTRY AND FOREST PRODUCTS

SURINAME - OCCUPATIONS - See SURINAME - LABOR FORCE

SURINAME - ORANGES PRODUCTION - See SURINAME - CROPS

SURINAME - PALM KERNELS AND PALM OIL PRODUCTION - See SURINAME - CROPS

SURINAME - PAPER - See SURINAME - FORESTRY AND FOREST PRODUCTS

SURINAME - PEANUT PRODUCTION - See SURINAME - CROPS

SURINAME - PERIODICALS

United Nations Educational, Scientific and Cultural Organization (UNESCO), 7 Place de Fontenoy, F-75700 Paris, France (Telephone Number in U.S. (212) 963-5981); *Statistical Yearbook*.

SURINAME - PESTICIDE USE

Food and Agricultural Organization of the United Nations (FAO) Via delle Terme di Caracalla, 00100 Rome, Italy (Telephone Number in U.S. (202) 653-2400); *The State of Food and Agriculture*.

SURINAME - PETROLEUM INDUSTRY

Facts on File, 460 Park Avenue South, New York, New York 10016 (800) 443-8323; *The New Book of World Rankings*.

Food and Agricultural Organization of the United Nations (FAO) Via delle Terme di Caracalla, 00100 Rome, Italy (Telephone Number in U.S. (202) 653-2400); *The State of Food and Agriculture*.

G.K. Hall and Company, 70 Lincoln Street, Boston, Massachusetts 02111 (617) 423-3990; *The World in Figures*.

Inter-American Development Bank, 1300 New York Avenue, NW, Washington, D.C. 20577 (202) 623-1753; *Economic and Social Progress in Latin America.*

Penn Well Publishing Company, 1421 South Sheridan Road, P.O. Box 1260, Tulsa, Oklahoma 74101 (800) 752-9764; *International Energy Statistics Sourcebook.*

SURINAME - PIG-IRON AND FERRO-ALLOY PRODUCTION - See SURINAME - MINING AND MINERAL PRODUCTS

SURINAME - PIGS - See SURINAME - LIVESTOCK AND POULTRY

SURINAME - POPULATION

The Economist Intelligence Unit, 111 West 57th Street, New York, New York 10019 (800) 938-4685; *The World Market Atlas.*

Facts on File, 460 Park Avenue South, New York, New York 10016 (800) 443-8323; *The New Book of World Rankings.*

Food and Agricultural Organization of the United Nations (FAO), Via delle Terme di Caracalla, 00100 Rome, Italy (Telephone Number in U.S. (202) 653-2400); *Production Yearbook.*

Gale Research Incorporated, 835 Penobscot Building, Detroit, Michigan 48226 (800) 877-4253; *International Historical Statistics The Americas and Australasia.*

G.K. Hall and Company, 70 Lincoln Street, Boston, Massachusetts 02111 (617) 423-3990; *The World in Figures.*

Inter-American Development Bank, 1300 New York Avenue, NW, Washington, D.C. 20577 (202) 623-1753, *Economic and Social Progress in Latin America.*

International Labour Office, I.L.O. Publications, CH-1211, Geneva 22, Switzerland; *Yearbook of Labour Statistics.*

Organization of American States (OAS), General Secretariat, Washington, D.C. 20006 (202) 458-3533; *Statistical Bulletin of the OAS.*

Statistical Office of the United Nations, Publishing Service, New York, New York 10017 (800) 253-9646; *Demographic Yearbook,* and *Statistical Yearbook.*

United Nations Educational, Scientific and Cultural Organization (UNESCO), 7 Place de Fontenoy, F-75700 Paris, France (Telephone Number in U.S. (212) 963-5981); *Statistical Yearbook.*

U.S. Arms Control and Disarmament Agency, 320 Twenty-first Street, NW, Washington, D.C. 20451 (202) 647-8677; *World Military Expenditures and Arms Transfers.*

World Health Organization, Office of Publications, Avenue Appia, CH-1211 Geneva 27, Switzerland (Telephone Number in U.S. (518) 436-9686); *World Health Statistics Annual.*

SURINAME - POST OFFICES

Facts on File, 460 Park Avenue South, New York, New York 10016 (800) 443-8323; *The New Book of World Rankings.*

SURINAME - POTATO PRODUCTION - See SURINAME - CROPS

SURINAME - PRICES

Facts on File, 460 Park Avenue South, New York, New York 10016 (800) 443-8323; *The New Book of World Rankings.*

Food and Agricultural Organization of the United Nations (FAO), Via delle Terme di Caracalla, 00100 Rome, Italy (Telephone Number in U.S. (202) 653-2400); *Production Yearbook,* and *The State of Food and Agriculture.*

Gale Research Incorporated, 835 Penobscot Building, Detroit, Michigan 48226 (800) 877-4253; *International Historical Statistics The Americas and Australasia.*

G.K. Hall and Company, 70 Lincoln Street, Boston, Massachusetts 02111 (617) 423-3990; *The World in Figures.*

International Labour Office, I.L.O. Publications, CH-1211, Geneva 22, Switzerland; *Yearbook of Labour Statistics.*

International Monetary Fund, 700 Nineteenth Street, NW, Washington, D.C. 20431 (202) 623-7000; *International Financial Statistics.*

Statistical Office of the United Nations, Publishing Service, New York, New York 10017 (800) 253-9646; *Economic Survey of Latin America and the Caribbean.*

SURINAME - PRINTING AND WRITING PAPER EXPORTS AND IMPORTS - See SURINAME - FORESTRY AND FOREST PRODUCTS

SURINAME - PRODUCTION

Facts on File, 460 Park Avenue South, New York, New York 10016 (800) 443-8323; *The New Book of World Rankings.*

G.K. Hall and Company, 70 Lincoln Street, Boston, Massachusetts 02111 (617) 423-3990; *The World in Figures.*

SURINAME - PROPERTY TAXES - See SURINAME - TAXATION

SURINAME - PUBLIC CONSUMPTION FUND

Inter-American Development Bank, 1300 New York Avenue, NW, Washington, D.C. 20577 (202) 623-1753; *Economic and Social Progress in Latin America.*

SURINAME - PUBLIC EXPENDITURES

Inter-American Development Bank, 1300 New York Avenue, NW, Washington, D.C. 20577 (202) 623-1753; *Economic and Social Progress in Latin America.*

SURINAME - PUBLIC FINANCE

Facts on File, 460 Park Avenue South, New York, New York 10016 (800) 443-8323; *The New Book of World Rankings.*

Inter-American Development Bank, 1300 New York Avenue, NW, Washington, D.C. 20577 (202) 623-1753; *Economic and Social Progress in Latin America.*

SURINAME - PUBLIC REVENUES

Inter-American Development Bank, 1300 New York Avenue, NW, Washington, D.C. 20577 (202) 623-1753; *Economic and Social Progress in Latin America.*

SURINAME - RADIO BROADCASTING

Facts on File, 460 Park Avenue South, New York, New York 10016 (800) 443-8323; *The New Book of World Rankings*.

SURINAME - RAILWAYS

G.K. Hall and Company, 70 Lincoln Street, Boston, Massachusetts 02111 (617) 423-3990; *The World in Figures*.

SURINAME - RELIGION

Facts on File, 460 Park Avenue South, New York, New York 10016 (800) 443-8323; *The New Book of World Rankings*.

SURINAME - RENT PRICES

International Labour Office, I.L.O. Publications, CH-1211, Geneva 22, Switzerland; *Yearbook of Labour Statistics*.

SURINAME - RETAIL TRADE

G.K. Hall and Company, 70 Lincoln Street, Boston, Massachusetts 02111 (617) 423-3990; *The World in Figures*.

Inter-American Development Bank, 1300 New York Avenue, NW, Washington, D.C. 20577 (202) 623-1753; *Economic and Social Progress in Latin America*.

SURINAME - RICE PRODUCTION - See SURINAME - CROPS

SURINAME - ROUNDWOOD PRODUCTION - See SURINAME - FORESTRY AND FOREST PRODUCTS

SURINAME - RUBBER PRODUCTION AND CONSUMPTION

Facts on File, 460 Park Avenue South, New York, New York 10016 (800) 443-8323; *The New Book of World Rankings*.

SURINAME - SAWNWOOD PRODUCTION - See SURINAME - FORESTRY AND FOREST PRODUCTS

SURINAME - SENIOR CITIZENS

Facts on File, 460 Park Avenue South, New York, New York 10016 (800) 443-8323; *The New Book of World Rankings*.

SURINAME - SHEEP - See SURINAME - LIVESTOCK AND POULTRY

SURINAME - SILVER PRODUCTION AND CONSUMPTION - See SURINAME - MINING AND MINERAL PRODUCTS

SURINAME - SOCIAL DATA

Facts on File, 460 Park Avenue South, New York, New York 10016 (800) 443-8323; *The New Book of World Rankings*.

G.K. Hall and Company, 70 Lincoln Street, Boston, Massachusetts 02111 (617) 423-3990; *The World in Figures*.

SURINAME - SOCIAL SECURITY

Inter-American Development Bank, 1300 New York Avenue, NW, Washington, D.C. 20577 (202) 623-1753; *Economic and Social Progress in Latin America*.

International Monetary Fund, 700 Nineteenth Street, NW, Washington, D.C. 20431 (202) 623-7000; *Government Finance Statistics Yearbook*.

SURINAME - SOCIOECONOMIC DATA

Inter-American Development Bank, 1300 New York Avenue, NW, Washington, D.C. 20577 (202) 623-1753; *Economic and Social Progress in Latin America*.

SURINAME - STAMP TAXES AND DUTIES - See SURINAME - TAXATION

SURINAME - STATE BUDGET REVENUE AND EXPENDITURES

Inter-American Development Bank, 1300 New York Avenue, NW, Washington, D.C. 20577 (202) 623-1753; *Economic and Social Progress in Latin America*.

SURINAME - STEEL - See SURINAME - MINING AND MINERAL PRODUCTS

SURINAME - STOCKS - COMMODITY - MARKET PRICE - INDEX

Food and Agricultural Organization of the United Nations (FAO) Via delle Terme di Caracalla, 00100 Rome, Italy (Telephone Number in U.S. (202) 653-2400); *The State of Food and Agriculture*.

SURINAME - SUGAR PRODUCTION AND CONSUMPTION - See SURINAME - CROPS

SURINAME - TAXATION

G.K. Hall and Company, 70 Lincoln Street, Boston, Massachusetts 02111 (617) 423-3990; *The World in Figures*.

Inter-American Development Bank, 1300 New York Avenue, NW, Washington, D.C. 20577 (202) 623-1753; *Economic and Social Progress in Latin America*.

International Monetary Fund, 700 Nineteenth Street, NW, Washington, D.C. 20431 (202) 623-7000; *Government Finance Statistics Yearbook*.

The World Bank, 1818 H Street, NW, Washington, D.C. 20433 (202) 477-1234; *World Tables*.

SURINAME - TELEGRAPH SERVICE

Statistical Office of the United Nations, Publishing Service, New York, New York 10017 (800) 253-9646; *Statistical Yearbook*.

SURINAME - TELEPHONES IN USE

American Telephone and Telegraph Company, 26 Parsippany Road, Whippany, New Jersey 07981 (800) 338-4038; *The World's Telephones*.

G.K. Hall and Company, 70 Lincoln Street, Boston, Massachusetts 02111 (617) 423-3990; *The World in Figures*.

Statistical Office of the United Nations, Publishing Service, New York, New York 10017 (800) 253-9646; *Statistical Yearbook*.

SURINAME - TELEVISION BROADCASTING

Facts on File, 460 Park Avenue South, New York, New York 10016 (800) 443-8323; *The New Book of World Rankings*.

SURINAME - TEXTILE INDUSTRY

G.K. Hall and Company, 70 Lincoln Street, Boston, Massachusetts 02111 (617) 423-3990; *The World in Figures.*

SURINAME - TOBACCO PRODUCTION

Facts on File, 460 Park Avenue South, New York, New York 10016 (800) 443-8323; *The New Book of World Rankings.*

Statistical Office of the United Nations, Publishing Service, New York, New York 10017 (800) 253-9646; *Statistical Yearbook.*

U.C.L.A. Latin American Center Publications, University of California, Los Angeles, California 90024 (310) 825-6634; *Statistical Abstract of Latin America.*

SURINAME - TOURISM

Facts on File, 460 Park Avenue South, New York, New York 10016 (800) 443-8323; *The New Book of World Rankings.*

G.K. Hall and Company, 70 Lincoln Street, Boston, Massachusetts 02111 (617) 423-3990; *The World in Figures.*

Statistical Office of the United Nations, Publishing Service, New York, New York 10017 (800) 253-9646; *Statistical Yearbook.*

World Tourism Organization, Calle Capitan Haya 42, E-28020 Madrid, Spain; *Yearbook of Tourism Statistics.*

SURINAME - TRACTORS IN USE

Statistical Office of the United Nations, Publishing Service, New York, New York 10017 (800) 253-9646; *Statistical Yearbook.*

SURINAME - TRADE - See SURINAME - FOREIGN TRADE

SURINAME - TRADEMARKS AND SERVICE MARKS

Statistical Office of the United Nations, Publishing Service, New York, New York 10017 (800) 253-9646; *Statistical Yearbook.*

SURINAME - TRANSPORTATION AND COMMUNICATIONS

Facts on File, 460 Park Avenue South, New York, New York 10016 (800) 443-8323; *The New Book of World Rankings.*

Gale Research Incorporated, 835 Penobscot Building, Detroit, Michigan 48226 (800) 877-4253; *International Historical Statistics The Americas and Australasia.*

G.K. Hall and Company, 70 Lincoln Street, Boston, Massachusetts 02111 (617) 423-3990; *The World in Figures.*

Inter-American Development Bank, 1300 New York Avenue, NW, Washington, D.C. 20577 (202) 623-1753; *Economic and Social Progress in Latin America.*

SURINAME - UNEMPLOYMENT

International Labour Office, I.L.O. Publications, CH-1211, Geneva 22, Switzerland; *Yearbook of Labour Statistics.*

Statistical Office of the United Nations, Publishing Service, New York, New York 10017 (800) 253-9646; *Statistical Yearbook.*

SURINAME - VITAL STATISTICS

Gale Research Incorporated, 835 Penobscot Building, Detroit, Michigan 48226 (800) 877-4253; *International Historical Statistics The Americas and Australasia.*

G.K. Hall and Company, 70 Lincoln Street, Boston, Massachusetts 02111 (617) 423-3990; *The World in Figures.*

Statistical Office of the United Nations, Publishing Service, New York, New York 10017 (800) 253-9646; *Statistical Yearbook.*

World Health Organization, Office of Publications, Avenue Appia, CH-1211 Geneva 27, Switzerland (Telephone Number in U.S. (518) 436-9686); *World Health Statistics Annual.*

SURINAME - WAGES

G.K. Hall and Company, 70 Lincoln Street, Boston, Massachusetts 02111 (617) 423-3990; *The World in Figures.*

International Labour Office, I.L.O. Publications, CH-1211, Geneva 22, Switzerland; *Yearbook of Labour Statistics.*

Statistical Office of the United Nations, Publishing Service, New York, New York 10017 (800) 253-9646; *Statistical Yearbook.*

SURINAME - WEATHER

Facts on File, 460 Park Avenue South, New York, New York 10016 (800) 443-8323; *The New Book of World Rankings.*

G.K. Hall and Company, 70 Lincoln Street, Boston, Massachusetts 02111 (617) 423-3990; *The World in Figures.*

SURINAME - WELFARE

Inter-American Development Bank, 1300 New York Avenue, NW, Washington, D.C. 20577 (202) 623-1753; *Economic and Social Progress in Latin America.*

International Monetary Fund, 700 Nineteenth Street, NW, Washington, D.C. 20431 (202) 623-7000; *Government Finance Statistics Yearbook.*

SURINAME - WHEAT PRODUCTION AND PRICES - See SURINAME - CROPS

SURINAME - WHOLESALE PRICES

Inter-American Development Bank, 1300 New York Avenue, NW, Washington, D.C. 20577 (202) 623-1753; *Economic and Social Progress in Latin America.*

SURINAME - WHOLESALE TRADE

Inter-American Development Bank, 1300 New York Avenue, NW, Washington, D.C. 20577 (202) 623-1753; *Economic and Social Progress in Latin America.*

SURINAME - WINE PRODUCTION

Facts on File, 460 Park Avenue South, New York, New York 10016 (800) 443-8323; *The New Book of World Rankings.*

SURINAME - WOOD PULP PRODUCTION - See SURINAME - FORESTRY AND FOREST PRODUCTS

SURINAME - WOOL PRODUCTION

Facts on File, 460 Park Avenue South, New York, New York 10016 (800) 443-8323; *The New Book of World Rankings*.

SVALBARD AND JAN MAYEN ISLANDS - FISHERIES

Food and Agricultural Organization of the United Nations (FAO), Via delle Terme di Caracalla, 00100, Rome, Italy (Telephone Number in U.S. (202) 653-2400); *Yearbook of Fishery Statistics*.

SVALBARD AND JAN MAYEN ISLANDS - POPULATION

Statistical Office of the United Nations, Publishing Service, New York, New York 10017 (800) 253-9646; *Statistical Yearbook*.

World Health Organization, Office of Publications, Avenue Appia, CH-1211 Geneva 27, Switzerland (Telephone Number in U.S. (518) 436-9686); *World Health Statistics Annual*.

SVALBARD AND JAN MAYEN ISLANDS - VITAL STATISTICS

World Health Organization, Office of Publications, Avenue Appia, CH-1211 Geneva 27, Switzerland (Telephone Number in U.S. (518) 436-9686); *World Health Statistics Annual*.

Swaziland - National Statistical Office

Central Statistical Office, Post Office Box 456, Mbabane, Swaziland.

Swaziland - Primary Statistics Source

Central Statistical Office, Post Office Box 456, Mbabane, Swaziland; *Annual Statistical Bulletin*, and *Quarterly Digest of Statistics*.

SWAZILAND - AGRICULTURE

Facts on File, 460 Park Avenue South, New York, New York 10016 (800) 443-8323; *The New Book of World Rankings*.

Food and Agricultural Organization of the United Nations (FAO) Via delle Terme di Caracalla, 00100 Rome, Italy (Telephone Number in U.S. (202) 653-2400); *Production Yearbook, The State of Food and Agriculture*, and *Trade Yearbook*.

G.K. Hall and Company, 70 Lincoln Street, Boston, Massachusetts 02111 (617) 423-3990; *The World in Figures*.

Statistical Office of the United Nations, Publishing Service, New York, New York 10017 (800) 253-9646; *Statistical Yearbook*, and *Survey of Economic and Social Conditions in Africa*.

United Nations Economic Commission for Africa, Africa Hall, P.O. Box 3001, Addis Ababa, Ethiopia (Telephone Number in U.S. (800) 253-9646); *African Statistical Yearbook*.

The World Bank, 1818 H Street, NW, Washington, D.C. 20433 (202) 477-1234; *World Tables*.

SWAZILAND - AIRLINE SERVICE

Facts on File, 460 Park Avenue South, New York, New York 10016 (800) 443-8323; *The New Book of World Rankings*.

G.K. Hall and Company, 70 Lincoln Street, Boston, Massachusetts 02111 (617) 423-3990; *The World in Figures*.

United Nations Economic Commission for Africa, Africa Hall, P.O. Box 3001, Addis Ababa, Ethiopia (Telephone Number in U.S. (800) 253-9646); *African Statistical Yearbook*.

SWAZILAND - ALUMINUM PRODUCTION AND CONSUMPTION - See SWAZILAND - MINING AND MINERAL PRODUCTS

SWAZILAND - ANIMAL HEALTH

Food and Agricultural Organization of the United Nations (FAO), Via delle Terme di Caracalla, 00100, Rome, Italy (Telephone Number in U.S. (202) 653-2400); *Animal Health Yearbook*.

SWAZILAND - AREA AND DENSITY OF POPULATION

African Development Bank, 01 BP 1387, Abidjan 01, Cote D'Ivoire; *Selected Statistics on Regional Member Countries*.

Facts on File, 460 Park Avenue South, New York, New York 10016 (800) 443-8323; *The New Book of World Rankings*.

Food and Agricultural Organization of the United Nations (FAO) Via delle Terme di Caracalla, 00100 Rome, Italy (Telephone Number in U.S. (202) 653-2400); *The State of Food and Agriculture*.

G.K. Hall and Company, 70 Lincoln Street, Boston, Massachusetts 02111 (617) 423-3990; *The World in Figures*.

Statistical Office of the United Nations, Publishing Service, New York, New York 10017 (800) 253-9646; *Statistical Yearbook*, and *Survey of Economic and Social Conditions in Africa*.

United Nations Educational, Scientific and Cultural Organization (UNESCO), 7 Place de Fontenoy, F-75700 Paris, France (Telephone Number in U.S. (212) 963-5981); *Statistical Yearbook*.

SWAZILAND - ARMS EXPORTS AND IMPORTS

U.S. Arms Control and Disarmament Agency, 320 Twenty-first Street, NW, Washington, D.C. 20451 (202) 647-8677; *World Military Expenditures and Arms Transfers*.

SWAZILAND - BALANCE OF PAYMENTS

African Development Bank, 01 BP 1387, Abidjan 01, Cote D'Ivoire; *Selected Statistics on Regional Member Countries*.

The Economist Intelligence Unit, 111 West 57th Street, New York, New York 10019 (800) 938-4685; *The World Market Atlas*.

G.K. Hall and Company, 70 Lincoln Street, Boston, Massachusetts 02111 (617) 423-3990; *The World in Figures*.

International Monetary Fund, 700 Nineteenth Street, NW, Washington, D.C. 20431 (202) 623-7000; *Balance of Payments Yearbook*.

United Nations Economic Commission for Africa, Africa Hall, P.O. Box 3001, Addis Ababa, Ethiopia (Telephone Number in U.S. (800) 253-9646); *African Statistical Yearbook*.

The World Bank, 1818 H Street, NW, Washington, D.C. 20433 (202) 477-1234; *World Tables*.

SWAZILAND - BANKING

Facts on File, 460 Park Avenue South, New York, New York 10016 (800) 443-8323; *The New Book of World Rankings*.

G.K. Hall and Company, 70 Lincoln Street, Boston, Massachusetts 02111 (617) 423-3990; *The World in Figures.*

International Monetary Fund, 700 Nineteenth Street, NW, Washington, D.C. 20431 (202) 623-7000; *Government Finance Statistics Yearbook,* and *International Financial Statistics.*

United Nations Economic Commission for Africa, Africa Hall, P.O. Box 3001, Addis Ababa, Ethiopia (Telephone Number in U.S. (800) 253-9646); *African Statistical Yearbook.*

SWAZILAND - BARLEY PRODUCTION - See SWAZILAND - CROPS

SWAZILAND - BEER PRODUCTION

Facts on File, 460 Park Avenue South, New York, New York 10016 (800) 443-8323; *The New Book of World Rankings.*

SWAZILAND - BIRTH RATES

Facts on File, 460 Park Avenue South, New York, New York 10016 (800) 443-8323; *The New Book of World Rankings.*

Statistical Office of the United Nations, Publishing Service, New York, New York 10017 (800) 253-9646; *Demographic Yearbook,* and *Statistical Yearbook,* and *Survey of Economic and Social Conditions in Africa.*

The World Bank, 1818 H Street, NW, Washington, D.C. 20433 (202) 477-1234; *World Tables.*

SWAZILAND - BONDS

G.K. Hall and Company, 70 Lincoln Street, Boston, Massachusetts 02111 (617) 423-3990; *The World in Figures.*

International Monetary Fund, 700 Nineteenth Street, NW, Washington, D.C. 20431 (202) 623-7000; *Government Finance Statistics Yearbook.*

SWAZILAND - BOOK PRODUCTION

G.K. Hall and Company, 70 Lincoln Street, Boston, Massachusetts 02111 (617) 423-3990; *The World in Figures.*

SWAZILAND - BROADCASTING

Billboard Limited, P.O. Box 9027, 1006 AA Amsterdam, The Netherlands (Telephone Number in U.S. (212) 764-7300); *World Radio TV Handbook.*

G.K. Hall and Company, 70 Lincoln Street, Boston, Massachusetts 02111 (617) 423-3990; *The World in Figures.*

SWAZILAND - BUSINESS

G.K. Hall and Company, 70 Lincoln Street, Boston, Massachusetts 02111 (617) 423-3990; *The World in Figures.*

SWAZILAND - BUSINESS AND PROFESSIONAL LICENSES

International Monetary Fund, 700 Nineteenth Street, NW, Washington, D.C. 20431 (202) 623-7000; *Government Finance Statistics Yearbook.*

SWAZILAND - CALORIE SUPPLY

African Development Bank, 01 BP 1387, Abidjan 01, Cote D'Ivoire; *Selected Statistics on Regional Member Countries.*

Food and Agricultural Organization of the United Nations (FAO) Via delle Terme di Caracalla, 00100 Rome, Italy (Telephone Number in U.S. (202) 653-2400); *The State of Food and Agriculture.*

SWAZILAND - CAPITAL REVENUE

International Monetary Fund, 700 Nineteenth Street, NW, Washington, D.C. 20431 (202) 623-7000; *Government Finance Statistics Yearbook.*

SWAZILAND - CATTLE - See SWAZILAND - LIVESTOCK AND POULTRY

SWAZILAND - CEMENT PRODUCTION - See SWAZILAND - MINING AND MINERAL PRODUCTS

SWAZILAND - CHEMICAL (ORGANIC) PRODUCTION - See SWAZILAND - MINING AND MINERAL PRODUCTS

SWAZILAND - CHICKENS - See SWAZILAND - LIVESTOCK AND POULTRY

SWAZILAND - CIGARETTE PRODUCTION - See SWAZILAND - TOBACCO PRODUCTION

SWAZILAND - CLASS STRUCTURE

G.K. Hall and Company, 70 Lincoln Street, Boston, Massachusetts 02111 (617) 423-3990; *The World in Figures.*

SWAZILAND - CLIMATE

Facts on File, 460 Park Avenue South, New York, New York 10016 (800) 443-8323; *The New Book of World Rankings.*

G.K. Hall and Company, 70 Lincoln Street, Boston, Massachusetts 02111 (617) 423-3990; *The World in Figures.*

SWAZILAND - COAL PRODUCTION - See SWAZILAND - MINING AND MINERAL PRODUCTS

SWAZILAND - COFFEE PRODUCTION AND CONSUMPTION - See SWAZILAND - CROPS

SWAZILAND - COMMUNICATIONS

G.K. Hall and Company, 70 Lincoln Street, Boston, Massachusetts 02111 (617) 423-3990; *The World in Figures.*

United Nations Economic Commission for Africa, Africa Hall, P.O. Box 3001, Addis Ababa, Ethiopia (Telephone Number in U.S. (800) 253-9646); *African Statistical Yearbook.*

SWAZILAND - CONSTRUCTION INDUSTRY

Facts on File, 460 Park Avenue South, New York, New York 10016 (800) 443-8323; *The New Book of World Rankings.*

Statistical Office of the United Nations, Publishing Service, New York, New York 10017 (800) 253-9646; *Statistical Yearbook.*

United Nations Economic Commission for Africa, Africa Hall, P.O. Box 3001, Addis Ababa, Ethiopia (Telephone Number in U.S. (800) 253-9646); *African Statistical Yearbook.*

SWAZILAND - CONSUMER PRICE INDEX

African Development Bank, 01 BP 1387, Abidjan 01, Cote D'Ivoire; *Selected Statistics on Regional Member Countries.*

G.K. Hall and Company, 70 Lincoln Street, Boston, Massachusetts 02111 (617) 423-3990; *The World in Figures.*

Statistical Office of the United Nations, Publishing Service, New York, New York 10017 (800) 253-9646; *Statistical Yearbook,* and *Survey of Economic and Social Conditions in Africa.*

United Nations Economic Commission for Africa, Africa Hall, P.O. Box 3001, Addis Ababa, Ethiopia (Telephone Number in U.S. (800) 253-9646); *African Statistical Yearbook.*

SWAZILAND - CONSUMER PRICES

International Labour Office, I.L.O. Publications, CH-1211, Geneva 22, Switzerland; *Yearbook of Labour Statistics.*

International Monetary Fund, 700 Nineteenth Street, NW, Washington, D.C. 20431 (202) 623-7000; *International Financial Statistics.*

SWAZILAND - CONSUMPTION

African Development Bank, 01 BP 1387, Abidjan 01, Cote D'Ivoire; *Selected Statistics on Regional Member Countries.*

G.K. Hall and Company, 70 Lincoln Street, Boston, Massachusetts 02111 (617) 423-3990; *The World in Figures.*

Statistical Office of the United Nations, Publishing Service, New York, New York 10017 (800) 253-9646; *Survey of Economic and Social Conditions in Africa.*

SWAZILAND - COPPER PRODUCTION AND CONSUMPTION - See SWAZILAND - MINING AND MINERAL PRODUCTS

SWAZILAND - CORN PRODUCTION - See SWAZILAND - CROPS

SWAZILAND - CORPORATE TAXES - See SWAZILAND - TAXATION

SWAZILAND - COTTON PRODUCTION - See SWAZILAND - CROPS

SWAZILAND - CRIME

Yale University Press, Yale Station, New Haven, Connecticut 06520 (203) 432-0940; *Violence and Crime in Cross-National Perspective.*

SWAZILAND - CROPS

Facts on File, 460 Park Avenue South, New York, New York 10016 (800) 443-8323; *The New Book of World Rankings.*

Food and Agricultural Organization of the United Nations (FAO) Via delle Terme di Caracalla, 00100 Rome, Italy (Telephone Number in U.S. (202) 653-2400); *The State of Food and Agriculture.*

G.K. Hall and Company, 70 Lincoln Street, Boston, Massachusetts 02111 (617) 423-3990; *The World in Figures.*

International Monetary Fund, 700 Nineteenth Street, NW, Washington, D.C. 20431 (202) 623-7000; *International Financial Statistics.*

Statistical Office of the United Nations, Publishing Service, New York, New York 10017 (800) 253-9646; *Statistical Yearbook.*

United Nations Economic Commission for Africa, Africa Hall, P.O. Box 3001, Addis Ababa, Ethiopia (Telephone Number in U.S. (800) 253-9646); *African Statistical Yearbook.*

SWAZILAND - CUSTOMS DUTIES

G.K. Hall and Company, 70 Lincoln Street, Boston, Massachusetts 02111 (617) 423-3990; *The World in Figures.*

International Monetary Fund, 700 Nineteenth Street, NW, Washington, D.C. 20431 (202) 623-7000; *Government Finance Statistics Yearbook.*

SWAZILAND - DAIRY PRODUCTS

Facts on File, 460 Park Avenue South, New York, New York 10016 (800) 443-8323; *The New Book of World Rankings.*

Food and Agricultural Organization of the United Nations (FAO) Via delle Terme di Caracalla, 00100 Rome, Italy (Telephone Number in U.S. (202) 653-2400); *The State of Food and Agriculture.*

SWAZILAND - DEATH RATES

G.K. Hall and Company, 70 Lincoln Street, Boston, Massachusetts 02111 (617) 423-3990; *The World in Figures.*

Statistical Office of the United Nations, Publishing Service, New York, New York 10017 (800) 253-9646; *Statistical Yearbook,* and *Survey of Economic and Social Conditions in Africa.*

World Health Organization, Office of Publications, Avenue Appia, CH-1211 Geneva 27, Switzerland (Telephone Number in U.S. (518) 436-9686); *World Health Statistics Annual.*

SWAZILAND - DEFENSE EXPENDITURES

G.K. Hall and Company, 70 Lincoln Street, Boston, Massachusetts 02111 (617) 423-3990; *The World in Figures.*

International Monetary Fund, 700 Nineteenth Street, NW, Washington, D.C. 20431 (202) 623-7000; *Government Finance Statistics Yearbook.*

U.S. Arms Control and Disarmament Agency, 320 Twenty-first Street, NW, Washington, D.C. 20451 (202) 647-8677; *World Military Expenditures and Arms Transfers.*

SWAZILAND - DEMOGRAPHY

The Economist Intelligence Unit, 111 West 57th Street, New York, New York 10019 (800) 938-4685; *The World Market Atlas.*

Facts on File, 460 Park Avenue South, New York, New York 10016 (800) 443-8323; *The New Book of World Rankings.*

G.K. Hall and Company, 70 Lincoln Street, Boston, Massachusetts 02111 (617) 423-3990; *The World in Figures.*

Statistical Office of the United Nations, Publishing Service, New York, New York 10017 (800) 253-9646; *Survey of Economic and Social Conditions in Africa.*

SWAZILAND - DEVELOPMENT ASSISTANCE

G.K. Hall and Company, 70 Lincoln Street, Boston, Massachusetts 02111 (617) 423-3990; *The World in Figures.*

Statistical Office of the United Nations, Publishing Service, New York, New York 10017 (800) 253-9646; *Statistical Yearbook.*

SWAZILAND - DIAMOND PRODUCTION - See SWAZILAND - MINING AND MINERAL PRODUCTS

SWAZILAND - DISEASES

G.K. Hall and Company, 70 Lincoln Street, Boston, Massachusetts 02111 (617) 423-3990; *The World in Figures*.

World Health Organization, Office of Publications, Avenue Appia, CH-1211 Geneva 27, Switzerland (Telephone Number in U.S. (518) 436-9686); *World Health Statistics Annual*.

SWAZILAND - DIVORCE RATES

Facts on File, 460 Park Avenue South, New York, New York 10016 (800) 443-8323; *The New Book of World Rankings*.

Statistical Office of the United Nations, Publishing Service, New York, New York 10017 (800) 253-9646; *Demographic Yearbook*.

SWAZILAND - DOMESTIC PRODUCT

G.K. Hall and Company, 70 Lincoln Street, Boston, Massachusetts 02111 (617) 423-3990; *The World in Figures*.

SWAZILAND - ECONOMY

African Development Bank, 01 BP 1387, Abidjan 01, Cote D'Ivoire; *Selected Statistics on Regional Member Countries*.

Facts on File, 460 Park Avenue South, New York, New York 10016 (800) 443-8323; *The New Book of World Rankings*.

G.K. Hall and Company, 70 Lincoln Street, Boston, Massachusetts 02111 (617) 423-3990; *The World in Figures*.

SWAZILAND - EDUCATION

African Development Bank, 01 BP 1387, Abidjan 01, Cote D'Ivoire; *Selected Statistics on Regional Member Countries*.

The Economist Intelligence Unit, 111 West 57th Street, New York, New York 10019 (800) 938-4685; *The World Market Atlas*.

Facts on File, 460 Park Avenue South, New York, New York 10016 (800) 443-8323; *The New Book of World Rankings*.

G.K. Hall and Company, 70 Lincoln Street, Boston, Massachusetts 02111 (617) 423-3990; *The World in Figures*.

International Monetary Fund, 700 Nineteenth Street, NW, Washington, D.C. 20431 (202) 623-7000; *Government Finance Statistics Yearbook*.

Statistical Office of the United Nations, Publishing Service, New York, New York 10017 (800) 253-9646; *Survey of Economic and Social Conditions in Africa*.

United Nations Economic Commission for Africa, Africa Hall, P.O. Box 3001, Addis Ababa, Ethiopia (Telephone Number in U.S. (800) 253-9646); *African Statistical Yearbook*.

United Nations Educational, Scientific and Cultural Organization (UNESCO), 7 Place de Fontenoy, F-75700 Paris, France (Telephone Number in U.S. (212) 963-5981); *Statistical Yearbook*.

The World Bank, 1818 H Street, NW, Washington, D.C. 20433 (202) 477-1234; *World Tables*.

SWAZILAND - EGG PRODUCTION AND CONSUMPTION - See SWAZILAND - DAIRY PRODUCTS

SWAZILAND - ELECTRICITY

Facts on File, 460 Park Avenue South, New York, New York 10016 (800) 443-8323; *The New Book of World Rankings*.

Statistical Office of the United Nations, Publishing Service, New York, New York 10017 (800) 253-9646; *Survey of Economic and Social Conditions in Africa*.

United Nations Economic Commission for Africa, Africa Hall, P.O. Box 3001, Addis Ababa, Ethiopia (Telephone Number in U.S. (800) 253-9646); *African Statistical Yearbook*.

SWAZILAND - EMPLOYMENT

Facts on File, 460 Park Avenue South, New York, New York 10016 (800) 443-8323; *The New Book of World Rankings*.

International Labour Office, I.L.O. Publications, CH-1211, Geneva 22, Switzerland; *Yearbook of Labour Statistics*.

Statistical Office of the United Nations, Publishing Service, New York, New York 10017 (800) 253-9646; *Statistical Yearbook*, and *Survey of Economic and Social Conditions in Africa*.

United Nations Economic Commission for Africa, Africa Hall, P.O. Box 3001, Addis Ababa, Ethiopia (Telephone Number in U.S. (800) 253-9646); *African Statistical Yearbook*.

SWAZILAND - ENERGY

Facts on File, 460 Park Avenue South, New York, New York 10016 (800) 443-8323; *The New Book of World Rankings*.

Food and Agricultural Organization of the United Nations (FAO) Via delle Terme di Caracalla, 00100 Rome, Italy (Telephone Number in U.S. (202) 653-2400); *The State of Food and Agriculture*.

G.K. Hall and Company, 70 Lincoln Street, Boston, Massachusetts 02111 (617) 423-3990; *The World in Figures*.

Statistical Office of the United Nations, Publishing Service, New York, New York 10017 (800) 253-9646; *Energy Statistics Yearbook*, and *Statistical Yearbook*.

United Nations Economic Commission for Africa, Africa Hall, P.O. Box 3001, Addis Ababa, Ethiopia (Telephone Number in U.S. (800) 253-9646); *African Statistical Yearbook*.

SWAZILAND - EXCHANGE RATES

International Monetary Fund, 700 Nineteenth Street, NW, Washington, D.C. 20431 (202) 623-7000; *International Financial Statistics*.

Statistical Office of the United Nations, Publishing Service, New York, New York 10017 (800) 253-9646; *Statistical Yearbook*.

SWAZILAND - EXCISE TAXES - See SWAZILAND - TAXATION

SWAZILAND - EXPORTS

African Development Bank, 01 BP 1387, Abidjan 01, Cote D'Ivoire; *Selected Statistics on Regional Member Countries*.

The Economist Intelligence Unit, 111 West 57th Street, New York, New York 10019 (800) 938-4685; *The World Market Atlas*.

Food and Agricultural Organization of the United Nations (FAO) Via delle Terme di Caracalla, 00100 Rome, Italy (Telephone Number in U.S. (202) 653-2400); *The State of Food and Agriculture*.

G.K. Hall and Company, 70 Lincoln Street, Boston, Massachusetts 02111 (617) 423-3990; *The World in Figures*.

International Monetary Fund, 700 Nineteenth Street, NW, Washington, D.C. 20431 (202) 623-7000; *Direction of Trade Statistics*, *Government Finance Statistics Yearbook*, and *International Financial Statistics*.

Statistical Office of the United Nations, Publishing Service, New York, New York 10017 (800) 253-9646; *Survey of Economic and Social Conditions in Africa*.

United Nations Economic Commission for Africa, Africa Hall, P.O. Box 3001, Addis Ababa, Ethiopia (Telephone Number in U.S. (800) 253-9646); *African Statistical Yearbook*.

The World Bank, 1818 H Street, NW, Washington, D.C. 20433 (202) 477-1234; *World Tables*.

SWAZILAND - EXTERNAL INDEBTEDNESS

African Development Bank, 01 BP 1387, Abidjan 01, Cote D'Ivoire; *Selected Statistics on Regional Member Countries*.

Statistical Office of the United Nations, Publishing Service, New York, New York 10017 (800) 253-9646; *Survey of Economic and Social Conditions in Africa*.

The World Bank, 1818 H Street, NW, Washington, D.C. 20433 (202) 477-1234; *World Tables*.

SWAZILAND - EXTERNAL TRADE

Food and Agricultural Organization of the United Nations (FAO) Via delle Terme di Caracalla, 00100 Rome, Italy (Telephone Number in U.S. (202) 653-2400); *The State of Food and Agriculture*, and *Trade Yearbook*.

G.K. Hall and Company, 70 Lincoln Street, Boston, Massachusetts 02111 (617) 423-3990; *The World in Figures*.

Statistical Office of the United Nations, Publishing Service, New York, New York 10017 (800) 253-9646; *Survey of Economic and Social Conditions in Africa*.

SWAZILAND - FARM CROPS - See SWAZILAND - CROPS

SWAZILAND - FERTILITY RATES

Facts on File, 460 Park Avenue South, New York, New York 10016 (800) 443-8323; *The New Book of World Rankings*.

Statistical Office of the United Nations, Publishing Service, New York, New York 10017 (800) 253-9646; *Survey of Economic and Social Conditions in Africa*.

The World Bank, 1818 H Street, NW, Washington, D.C. 20433 (202) 477-1234; *World Tables*.

SWAZILAND - FERTILIZER

Food and Agricultural Organization of the United Nations (FAO), Via delle Terme di Caracalla, 00100, Rome, Italy (Telephone Number in U.S. (202) 653-2400); *Fertilizer Yearbook*, and *The State of Food and Agriculture*.

Statistical Office of the United Nations, Publishing Service, New York, New York 10017 (800) 253-9646; *Statistical Yearbook*.

SWAZILAND - FETAL MORTALITY

Statistical Office of the United Nations, Publishing Service, New York, New York 10017 (800) 253-9646; *Demographic Yearbook*.

SWAZILAND - FIBRE PRODUCTION - See SWAZILAND - TEXTILE INDUSTRY

SWAZILAND - FINANCE

African Development Bank, 01 BP 1387, Abidjan 01, Cote D'Ivoire; *Selected Statistics on Regional Member Countries*.

Facts on File, 460 Park Avenue South, New York, New York 10016 (800) 443-8323; *The New Book of World Rankings*.

G.K. Hall and Company, 70 Lincoln Street, Boston, Massachusetts 02111 (617) 423-3990; *The World in Figures*.

International Monetary Fund, 700 Nineteenth Street, NW, Washington, D.C. 20431 (202) 623-7000; *Government Finance Statistics Yearbook*, and *International Financial Statistics*.

United Nations Economic Commission for Africa, Africa Hall, P.O. Box 3001, Addis Ababa, Ethiopia (Telephone Number in U.S. (800) 253-9646); *African Statistical Yearbook*.

SWAZILAND - FISHERIES

Facts on File, 460 Park Avenue South, New York, New York 10016 (800) 443-8323; *The New Book of World Rankings*.

Food and Agricultural Organization of the United Nations (FAO) Via delle Terme di Caracalla, 00100 Rome, Italy (Telephone Number in U.S. (202) 653-2400); *The State of Food and Agriculture*, and *Yearbook of Fishery Statistics*.

United Nations Economic Commission for Africa, Africa Hall, P.O. Box 3001, Addis Ababa, Ethiopia (Telephone Number in U.S. (800) 253-9646); *African Statistical Yearbook*.

SWAZILAND - FOOD

African Development Bank, 01 BP 1387, Abidjan 01, Cote D'Ivoire; *Selected Statistics on Regional Member Countries*.

Food and Agricultural Organization of the United Nations (FAO) Via delle Terme di Caracalla, 00100 Rome, Italy (Telephone Number in U.S. (202) 653-2400); *Production Yearbook*, and *The State of Food and Agriculture*.

G.K. Hall and Company, 70 Lincoln Street, Boston, Massachusetts 02111 (617) 423-3990; *The World in Figures*.

SWAZILAND - FOREIGN AID

G.K. Hall and Company, 70 Lincoln Street, Boston, Massachusetts 02111 (617) 423-3990; *The World in Figures*.

SWAZILAND - FOREIGN DEBT

International Monetary Fund, 700 Nineteenth Street, NW, Washington, D.C. 20431 (202) 623-7000; *Government Finance Statistics Yearbook*.

SWAZILAND - FOREIGN TRADE

Facts on File, 460 Park Avenue South, New York, New York 10016 (800) 443-8323; *The New Book of World Rankings*.

Food and Agricultural Organization of the United Nations (FAO) Via delle Terme di Caracalla, 00100 Rome, Italy (Telephone Number in U.S. (202) 653-2400); *The State of Food and Agriculture*.

G.K. Hall and Company, 70 Lincoln Street, Boston, Massachusetts 02111 (617) 423-3990; *The World in Figures*.

United Nations Economic Commission for Africa, Africa Hall, P.O. Box 3001, Addis Ababa, Ethiopia (Telephone Number in U.S. (800) 253-9646); *African Statistical Yearbook*.

The World Bank, 1818 H Street, NW, Washington, D.C. 20433 (202) 477-1234; *World Tables*.

SWAZILAND - FORESTRY AND FOREST PRODUCTS

American Forest and Paper Association, 1250 Connecticut Avenue, NW, Washington, D.C. 20036 (202) 463-2455; *Wood Pulp and Fiber Statistics*.

Facts on File, 460 Park Avenue South, New York, New York 10016 (800) 443-8323; *The New Book of World Rankings*.

Food and Agricultural Organization of the United Nations (FAO) Via delle Terme di Caracalla, 00100 Rome, Italy (Telephone Number in U.S. (202) 653-2400); *The State of Food and Agriculture*, and *Yearbook of Forest Products*.

G.K. Hall and Company, 70 Lincoln Street, Boston, Massachusetts 02111 (617) 423-3990; *The World in Figures*.

International Monetary Fund, 700 Nineteenth Street, NW, Washington, D.C. 20431 (202) 623-7000; *International Financial Statistics*.

Statistical Office of the United Nations, Publishing Service, New York, New York 10017 (800) 253-9646; *Statistical Yearbook*.

United Nations Economic Commission for Africa, Africa Hall, P.O. Box 3001, Addis Ababa, Ethiopia (Telephone Number in U.S. (800) 253-9646); *African Statistical Yearbook*.

United Nations Educational, Scientific and Cultural Organization (UNESCO), 7 Place de Fontenoy, F-75700 Paris, France (Telephone Number in U.S. (212) 963-5981); *Statistical Yearbook*.

SWAZILAND - GAS PRODUCTION - See SWAZILAND - MINING AND MINERAL PRODUCTS

SWAZILAND - GENERAL INDUSTRIAL STATISTICS

Statistical Office of the United Nations, Publishing Service, New York, New York 10017 (800) 253-9646; *Industrial Statistics Yearbook*.

SWAZILAND - GENERAL MORTALITY

Statistical Office of the United Nations, Publishing Service, New York, New York 10017 (800) 253-9646; *Demographic Yearbook*.

SWAZILAND - GEOGRAPHIC DATA

Facts on File, 460 Park Avenue South, New York, New York 10016 (800) 443-8323; *The New Book of World Rankings*.

SWAZILAND - GOATS - See SWAZILAND - LIVESTOCK AND POULTRY

SWAZILAND - GOLD HOLDINGS

The World Bank, 1818 H Street, NW, Washington, D.C. 20433 (202) 477-1234; *World Tables*.

SWAZILAND - GOLD PRODUCTION AND CONSUMPTION - See SWAZILAND - MINING AND MINERAL PRODUCTS

SWAZILAND - GOVERNMENT

G.K. Hall and Company, 70 Lincoln Street, Boston, Massachusetts 02111 (617) 423-3990; *The World in Figures*.

SWAZILAND - GOVERNMENT EXPENDITURES

International Monetary Fund, 700 Nineteenth Street, NW, Washington, D.C. 20431 (202) 623-7000; *Government Finance Statistics Yearbook*.

The World Bank, 1818 H Street, NW, Washington, D.C. 20433 (202) 477-1234; *World Tables*.

SWAZILAND - GOVERNMENT FINANCES

International Monetary Fund, 700 Nineteenth Street, NW, Washington, D.C. 20431 (202) 623-7000; *International Financial Statistics*.

Statistical Office of the United Nations, Publishing Service, New York, New York 10017 (800) 253-9646; *Statistical Yearbook*.

SWAZILAND - GOVERNMENT REVENUE

International Monetary Fund, 700 Nineteenth Street, NW, Washington, D.C. 20431 (202) 623-7000; *Government Finance Statistics Yearbook*.

Statistical Office of the United Nations, Publishing Service, New York, New York 10017 (800) 253-9646; *Survey of Economic and Social Conditions in Africa*.

The World Bank, 1818 H Street, NW, Washington, D.C. 20433 (202) 477-1234; *World Tables*.

SWAZILAND - GRAIN PRODUCTION - See SWAZILAND - CROPS

SWAZILAND - GRANTS

International Monetary Fund, 700 Nineteenth Street, NW, Washington, D.C. 20431 (202) 623-7000; *Government Finance Statistics Yearbook*.

SWAZILAND - GROSS DOMESTIC PRODUCT

African Development Bank, 01 BP 1387, Abidjan 01, Cote D'Ivoire; *Selected Statistics on Regional Member Countries*.

The Economist Intelligence Unit, 111 West 57th Street, New York, New York 10019 (800) 938-4685; *The World Market Atlas*.

Facts on File, 460 Park Avenue South, New York, New York 10016 (800) 443-8323; *The New Book of World Rankings*.

G.K. Hall and Company, 70 Lincoln Street, Boston, Massachusetts 02111 (617) 423-3990; *The World in Figures*.

Statistical Office of the United Nations, Publishing Service, New York, New York 10017 (800) 253-9646; *Statistical Yearbook*, and *Survey of Economic and Social Conditions in Africa*.

United Nations Economic Commission for Africa, Africa Hall, P.O. Box 3001, Addis Ababa, Ethiopia (Telephone Number in U.S. (800) 253-9646); *African Statistical Yearbook*.

U.S. Arms Control and Disarmament Agency, 320 Twenty-first Street, NW, Washington, D.C. 20451 (202) 647-8677; *World Military Expenditures and Arms Transfers*.

The World Bank, 1818 H Street, NW, Washington, D.C. 20433 (202) 477-1234; *World Tables*.

SWAZILAND - GROSS NATIONAL PRODUCT

The World Bank, 1818 H Street, NW, Washington, D.C. 20433 (202) 477-1234; *World Tables*.

SWAZILAND - HEALTH

African Development Bank, 01 BP 1387, Abidjan 01, Cote D'Ivoire; *Selected Statistics on Regional Member Countries*.

Facts on File, 460 Park Avenue South, New York, New York 10016 (800) 443-8323; *The New Book of World Rankings*.

G.K. Hall and Company, 70 Lincoln Street, Boston, Massachusetts 02111 (617) 423-3990; *The World in Figures*.

Statistical Office of the United Nations, Publishing Service, New York, New York 10017 (800) 253-9646; *Statistical Yearbook*.

United Nations Economic Commission for Africa, Africa Hall, P.O. Box 3001, Addis Ababa, Ethiopia (Telephone Number in U.S. (800) 253-9646); *African Statistical Yearbook*.

World Health Organization, Office of Publications, Avenue Appia, CH-1211 Geneva 27, Switzerland (Telephone Number in U.S. (518) 436-9686); *World Health Statistics Annual*.

SWAZILAND - HIGHWAYS

G.K. Hall and Company, 70 Lincoln Street, Boston, Massachusetts 02111 (617) 423-3990; *The World in Figures*.

International Road Federation, 525 School Street, SW, Washington, D.C. 20024 (202) 554-2106; *World Road Statistics*.

Statistical Office of the United Nations, Publishing Service, New York, New York 10017 (800) 253-9646; *Survey of Economic and Social Conditions in Africa*.

United Nations Economic Commission for Africa, Africa Hall, P.O. Box 3001, Addis Ababa, Ethiopia (Telephone Number in U.S. (800) 253-9646); *African Statistical Yearbook*.

SWAZILAND - HORSES - See SWAZILAND - LIVESTOCK AND POULTRY

SWAZILAND - HOURS OF WORK - See SWAZILAND - EMPLOYMENT

SWAZILAND - HOUSING EXPENDITURES

Facts on File, 460 Park Avenue South, New York, New York 10016 (800) 443-8323; *The New Book of World Rankings*.

International Monetary Fund, 700 Nineteenth Street, NW, Washington, D.C. 20431 (202) 623-7000; *Government Finance Statistics Yearbook*.

SWAZILAND - ILLITERATE POPULATION

The Economist Intelligence Unit, 111 West 57th Street, New York, New York 10019 (800) 938-4685; *The World Market Atlas*.

G.K. Hall and Company, 70 Lincoln Street, Boston, Massachusetts 02111 (617) 423-3990; *The World in Figures*.

United Nations Educational, Scientific and Cultural Organization (UNESCO), 7 Place de Fontenoy, F-75700 Paris, France (Telephone Number in U.S. (212) 963-5981); *Statistical Yearbook*.

SWAZILAND - IMPORTS

African Development Bank, 01 BP 1387, Abidjan 01, Cote D'Ivoire; *Selected Statistics on Regional Member Countries*.

The Economist Intelligence Unit, 111 West 57th Street, New York, New York 10019 (800) 938-4685; *The World Market Atlas*.

Food and Agricultural Organization of the United Nations (FAO) Via delle Terme di Caracalla, 00100 Rome, Italy (Telephone Number in U.S. (202) 653-2400); *The State of Food and Agriculture*.

G.K. Hall and Company, 70 Lincoln Street, Boston, Massachusetts 02111 (617) 423-3990; *The World in Figures*.

International Monetary Fund, 700 Nineteenth Street, NW, Washington, D.C. 20431 (202) 623-7000; *Direction of Trade Statistics*, *Government Finance Statistics Yearbook*, and *International Financial Statistics*.

Statistical Office of the United Nations, Publishing Service, New York, New York 10017 (800) 253-9646; *Survey of Economic and Social Conditions in Africa*.

United Nations Economic Commission for Africa, Africa Hall, P.O. Box 3001, Addis Ababa, Ethiopia (Telephone Number in U.S. (800) 253-9646); *African Statistical Yearbook*.

The World Bank, 1818 H Street, NW, Washington, D.C. 20433 (202) 477-1234; *World Tables*.

SWAZILAND - INCOME TAXES - See SWAZILAND - TAXATION

SWAZILAND - INDUSTRY

Facts on File, 460 Park Avenue South, New York, New York 10016 (800) 443-8323; *The New Book of World Rankings*.

G.K. Hall and Company, 70 Lincoln Street, Boston, Massachusetts 02111 (617) 423-3990; *The World in Figures*.

International Labour Office, I.L.O. Publications, CH-1211, Geneva 22, Switzerland; *Yearbook of Labour Statistics*.

Statistical Office of the United Nations, Publishing Service, New York, New York 10017 (800) 253-9646; *Survey of Economic and Social Conditions in Africa*.

United Nations Economic Commission for Africa, Africa Hall, P.O. Box 3001, Addis Ababa, Ethiopia (Telephone Number in U.S. (800) 253-9646); *African Statistical Yearbook*.

The World Bank, 1818 H Street, NW, Washington, D.C. 20433 (202) 477-1234; *World Tables*.

World Intellectual Property Organization, 34 Chemin des Colombettes, CH-1211 Geneva 20. Switzerland; *Industrial Property Statistics*.

SWAZILAND - INFANT AND MATERNAL MORTALITY

Statistical Office of the United Nations, Publishing Service, New York, New York 10017 (800) 253-9646; *Demographic Yearbook*, and *Survey of Economic and Social Conditions in Africa*.

The World Bank, 1818 H Street, NW, Washington, D.C. 20433 (202) 477-1234; *World Tables*.

SWAZILAND - INTERNAL TRADE

Statistical Office of the United Nations, Publishing Service, New York, New York 10017 (800) 253-9646; *Statistical Yearbook*.

SWAZILAND - INTERNATIONAL RESERVES EXCLUDING GOLD

African Development Bank, 01 BP 1387, Abidjan 01, Cote D'Ivoire; *Selected Statistics on Regional Member Countries*.

Statistical Office of the United Nations, Publishing Service, New York, New York 10017 (800) 253-9646; *Statistical Yearbook*.

The World Bank, 1818 H Street, NW, Washington, D.C. 20433 (202) 477-1234; *World Tables*.

SWAZILAND - IRON ORE - See SWAZILAND - MINING AND MINERAL PRODUCTS

SWAZILAND - LABOR FORCE

African Development Bank, 01 BP 1387, Abidjan 01, Cote D'Ivoire; *Selected Statistics on Regional Member Countries*.

Facts on File, 460 Park Avenue South, New York, New York 10016 (800) 443-8323; *The New Book of World Rankings*.

Food and Agricultural Organization of the United Nations (FAO) Via delle Terme di Caracalla, 00100 Rome, Italy (Telephone Number in U.S. (202) 653-2400); *The State of Food and Agriculture*.

G.K. Hall and Company, 70 Lincoln Street, Boston, Massachusetts 02111 (617) 423-3990; *The World in Figures*.

The World Bank, 1818 H Street, NW, Washington, D.C. 20433 (202) 477-1234; *World Tables*.

SWAZILAND - LABOR PRODUCTIVITY

International Labour Office, I.L.O. Publications, CH-1211, Geneva 22, Switzerland; *Yearbook of Labour Statistics*.

SWAZILAND - LAND USE

Food and Agricultural Organization of the United Nations (FAO), Via delle Terme di Caracalla, 00100 Rome, Italy (Telephone Number in U.S. (202) 653-2400); *Production Yearbook*.

G.K. Hall and Company, 70 Lincoln Street, Boston, Massachusetts 02111 (617) 423-3990; *The World in Figures*.

SWAZILAND - LIBRARIES

Facts on File, 460 Park Avenue South, New York, New York 10016 (800) 443-8323; *The New Book of World Rankings*.

United Nations Educational, Scientific and Cultural Organization (UNESCO), 7 Place de Fontenoy, F-75700 Paris, France (Telephone Number in U.S. (212) 963-5981); *Statistical Yearbook*.

SWAZILAND - LIFE EXPECTANCY

African Development Bank, 01 BP 1387, Abidjan 01, Cote D'Ivoire; *Selected Statistics on Regional Member Countries*.

SWAZILAND - LITERACY RATE

Statistical Office of the United Nations, Publishing Service, New York, New York 10017 (800) 253-9646; *Survey of Economic and Social Conditions in Africa*.

SWAZILAND - LIVESTOCK AND POULTRY

Facts on File, 460 Park Avenue South, New York, New York 10016 (800) 443-8323; *The New Book of World Rankings*.

Food and Agricultural Organization of the United Nations (FAO), Via delle Terme di Caracalla, 00100 Rome, Italy (Telephone Number in U.S. (202) 653-2400); *Production Yearbook*, and *The State of Food and Agriculture*.

G.K. Hall and Company, 70 Lincoln Street, Boston, Massachusetts 02111 (617) 423-3990; *The World in Figures*.

Statistical Office of the United Nations, Publishing Service, New York, New York 10017 (800) 253-9646; *Statistical Yearbook*, and *Survey of Economic and Social Conditions in Africa*.

United Nations Economic Commission for Africa, Africa Hall, P.O. Box 3001, Addis Ababa, Ethiopia (Telephone Number in U.S. (800) 253-9646); *African Statistical Yearbook*.

SWAZILAND LIVING LEVELS

G.K. Hall and Company, 70 Lincoln Street, Boston, Massachusetts 02111 (617) 423-3990; *The World in Figures*.

SWAZILAND - MAIL - NUMBER OF ITEMS SENT AND RECEIVED

Statistical Office of the United Nations, Publishing Service, New York, New York 10017 (800) 253-9646; *Statistical Yearbook*.

SWAZILAND - MANUFACTURING

Facts on File, 460 Park Avenue South, New York, New York 10016 (800) 443-8323; *The New Book of World Rankings*.

G.K. Hall and Company, 70 Lincoln Street, Boston, Massachusetts 02111 (617) 423-3990; *The World in Figures*.

Statistical Office of the United Nations, Publishing Service, New York, New York 10017 (800) 253-9646; *Statistical Yearbook*, and *Survey of Economic and Social Conditions in Africa*.

United Nations Economic Commission for Africa, Africa Hall, P.O. Box 3001, Addis Ababa, Ethiopia (Telephone Number in U.S. (800) 253-9646); *African Statistical Yearbook*.

The World Bank, 1818 H Street, NW, Washington, D.C. 20433 (202) 477-1234; *World Tables*.

SWAZILAND - MARRIAGE RATES

Facts on File, 460 Park Avenue South, New York, New York 10016 (800) 443-8323; *The New Book of World Rankings*.

Statistical Office of the United Nations, Publishing Service, New York, New York 10017 (800) 253-9646; *Demographic Yearbook*.

SWAZILAND - MEAT PRODUCTION - See SWAZILAND - LIVESTOCK AND POULTRY

SWAZILAND - MERCHANT SHPPING

United Nations Economic Commission for Africa, Africa Hall, P.O. Box 3001, Addis Ababa, Ethiopia (Telephone Number in U.S. (800) 253-9646); *African Statistical Yearbook*.

SWAZILAND - MILITARY

G.K. Hall and Company, 70 Lincoln Street, Boston, Massachusetts 02111 (617) 423-3990; *The World in Figures*.

U.S. Arms Control and Disarmament Agency, 320 Twenty-first Street, NW, Washington, D.C. 20451 (202) 647-8677; *World Military Expenditures and Arms Transfers*.

SWAZILAND - MILK PRODUCTION - See SWAZILAND - DAIRY PRODUCTS

SWAZILAND - MINING AND MINERAL PRODUCTS

Facts on File, 460 Park Avenue South, New York, New York 10016 (800) 443-8323; *The New Book of World Rankings*.

G.K. Hall and Company, 70 Lincoln Street, Boston, Massachusetts 02111 (617) 423-3990; *The World in Figures*.

International Monetary Fund, 700 Nineteenth Street, NW, Washington, D.C. 20431 (202) 623-7000; *International Financial Statistics*.

Statistical Office of the United Nations, Publishing Service, New York, New York 10017 (800) 253-9646; *Statistical Yearbook*.

United Nations Economic Commission for Africa, Africa Hall, P.O. Box 3001, Addis Ababa, Ethiopia (Telephone Number in U.S. (800) 253-9646); *African Statistical Yearbook*.

SWAZILAND - MONEY EXCHANGE RATE

International Monetary Fund, 700 Nineteenth Street, NW, Washington, D.C. 20431 (202) 623-7000; *International Financial Statistics*.

Statistical Office of the United Nations, Publishing Service, New York, New York 10017 (800) 253-9646; *Statistical Yearbook*.

SWAZILAND - MONEY SUPPLY

African Development Bank, 01 BP 1387, Abidjan 01, Cote D'Ivoire; *Selected Statistics on Regional Member Countries*.

G.K. Hall and Company, 70 Lincoln Street, Boston, Massachusetts 02111 (617) 423-3990; *The World in Figures*.

International Monetary Fund, 700 Nineteenth Street, NW, Washington, D.C. 20431 (202) 623-7000; *International Financial Statistics*.

The World Bank, 1818 H Street, NW, Washington, D.C. 20433 (202) 477-1234; *World Tables*.

SWAZILAND - MOTION PICTURES

Statistical Office of the United Nations, Publishing Service, New York, New York 10017 (800) 253-9646; *Statistical Yearbook*.

SWAZILAND - MOTOR VEHICLE TAXES - See SWAZILAND - TAXATION

SWAZILAND - MOTOR VEHICLES IN USE

G.K. Hall and Company, 70 Lincoln Street, Boston, Massachusetts 02111 (617) 423-3990; *The World in Figures*.

International Road Federation, 525 School Street, SW, Washington, D.C. 20024 (202) 554-2106; *World Road Statistics*.

Statistical Office of the United Nations, Publishing Service, New York, New York 10017 (800) 253-9646; *Statistical Yearbook*, and *Survey of Economic and Social Conditions in Africa*.

SWAZILAND - MULES - See SWAZILAND - LIVESTOCK AND POULTRY

SWAZILAND - MUSEUMS

Facts on File, 460 Park Avenue South, New York, New York 10016 (800) 443-8323; *The New Book of World Rankings*.

SWAZILAND - NATALITY - See SWAZILAND - BIRTH RATE

SWAZILAND - NATIONAL ACCOUNTS

African Development Bank, 01 BP 1387, Abidjan 01, Cote D'Ivoire; *Selected Statistics on Regional Member Countries*.

Statistical Office of the United Nations, Publishing Service, New York, New York 10017 (800) 253-9646; *National Accounts Statistics*, and *Statistical Yearbook*.

United Nations Economic Commission for Africa, Africa Hall, P.O. Box 3001, Addis Ababa, Ethiopia (Telephone Number in U.S. (800) 253-9646); *African Statistical Yearbook*.

SWAZILAND - NATIONAL INCOME

Facts on File, 460 Park Avenue South, New York, New York 10016 (800) 443-8323; *The New Book of World Rankings*.

G.K. Hall and Company, 70 Lincoln Street, Boston, Massachusetts 02111 (617) 423-3990; *The World in Figures*.

Statistical Office of the United Nations, Publishing Service, New York, New York 10017 (800) 253-9646; *Statistical Yearbook*.

SWAZILAND - NATIONAL PRODUCT

Facts on File, 460 Park Avenue South, New York, New York 10016 (800) 443-8323; *The New Book of World Rankings*.

SWAZILAND - NATURAL GAS PRODUCTION - See SWAZILAND - MINING AND MINERAL PRODUCTS

SWAZILAND - NEWSPAPER PRODUCTION - See SWAZILAND - FORESTRY AND FOREST PRODUCTS

SWAZILAND - OCCUPATIONS - See SWAZILAND - LABOR FORCE

SWAZILAND - PATENTS

Statistical Office of the United Nations, Publishing Service, New York, New York 10017 (800) 253-9646; *Statistical Yearbook.*

World Intellectual Property Organization, 34 Chemin des Colombettes, CH-1211 Geneva 20. Switzerland; *Industrial Property Statistics.*

SWAZILAND - PEANUT PRODUCTION - See SWAZILAND - CROPS

SWAZILAND - PESTICIDE USE

Food and Agricultural Organization of the United Nations (FAO) Via delle Terme di Caracalla, 00100 Rome, Italy (Telephone Number in U.S. (202) 653-2400); *The State of Food and Agriculture.*

SWAZILAND - PETROLEUM INDUSTRY

Facts on File, 460 Park Avenue South, New York, New York 10016 (800) 443-8323; *The New Book of World Rankings.*

Food and Agricultural Organization of the United Nations (FAO) Via delle Terme di Caracalla, 00100 Rome, Italy (Telephone Number in U.S. (202) 653-2400); *The State of Food and Agriculture.*

G.K. Hall and Company, 70 Lincoln Street, Boston, Massachusetts 02111 (617) 423-3990; *The World in Figures.*

SWAZILAND - PIGS - See SWAZILAND - LIVESTOCK AND POULTRY

SWAZILAND - POPULATION

African Development Bank, 01 BP 1387, Abidjan 01, Cote D'Ivoire; *Selected Statistics on Regional Member Countries.*

The Economist Intelligence Unit, 111 West 57th Street, New York, New York 10019 (800) 938-4685; *The World Market Atlas.*

Facts on File, 460 Park Avenue South, New York, New York 10016 (800) 443-8323; *The New Book of World Rankings.*

Food and Agricultural Organization of the United Nations (FAO), Via delle Terme di Caracalla, 00100 Rome, Italy (Telephone Number in U.S. (202) 653-2400); *Production Yearbook.*

G.K. Hall and Company, 70 Lincoln Street, Boston, Massachusetts 02111 (617) 423-3990; *The World in Figures.*

International Labour Office, I.L.O. Publications, CH-1211, Geneva 22, Switzerland; *Yearbook of Labour Statistics.*

Statistical Office of the United Nations, Publishing Service, New York, New York 10017 (800) 253-9646; *Demographic Yearbook, Statistical Yearbook,* and *Survey of Economic and Social Conditions in Africa.*

United Nations Educational, Scientific and Cultural Organization (UNESCO), 7 Place de Fontenoy, F-75700 Paris, France (Telephone Number in U.S. (212) 963-5981); *Statistical Yearbook.*

U.S. Arms Control and Disarmament Agency, 320 Twenty-first Street, NW, Washington, D.C. 20451 (202) 647-8677; *World Military Expenditures and Arms Transfers.*

World Health Organization, Office of Publications, Avenue Appia, CH-1211 Geneva 27, Switzerland (Telephone Number in U.S. (518) 436-9686); *World Health Statistics Annual.*

SWAZILAND - POST OFFICES

Facts on File, 460 Park Avenue South, New York, New York 10016 (800) 443-8323; *The New Book of World Rankings.*

SWAZILAND - POTATO PRODUCTION - See SWAZILAND - CROPS

SWAZILAND - PRICES

Facts on File, 460 Park Avenue South, New York, New York 10016 (800) 443-8323; *The New Book of World Rankings.*

Food and Agricultural Organization of the United Nations (FAO), Via delle Terme di Caracalla, 00100 Rome, Italy (Telephone Number in U.S. (202) 653-2400); *Production Yearbook,* and *The State of Food and Agriculture.*

G.K. Hall and Company, 70 Lincoln Street, Boston, Massachusetts 02111 (617) 423-3990; *The World in Figures.*

International Labour Office, I.L.O. Publications, CH-1211, Geneva 22, Switzerland; *Yearbook of Labour Statistics.*

International Monetary Fund, 700 Nineteenth Street, NW, Washington, D.C. 20431 (202) 623-7000; *International Financial Statistics.*

United Nations Economic Commission for Africa, Africa Hall, P.O. Box 3001, Addis Ababa, Ethiopia (Telephone Number in U.S. (800) 253-0646); *African Statistical Yearbook.*

SWAZILAND - PRODUCTION

Facts on File, 460 Park Avenue South, New York, New York 10016 (800) 443-8323; *The New Book of World Rankings.*

G.K. Hall and Company, 70 Lincoln Street, Boston, Massachusetts 02111 (617) 423-3990; *The World in Figures.*

SWAZILAND - PROPERTY TAXES - See SWAZILAND - TAXATION

SWAZILAND - PUBLIC FINANCE

Facts on File, 460 Park Avenue South, New York, New York 10016 (800) 443-8323; *The New Book of World Rankings.*

SWAZILAND - RADIO BROADCASTING

Facts on File, 460 Park Avenue South, New York, New York 10016 (800) 443-8323; *The New Book of World Rankings.*

SWAZILAND - RAILWAYS

G.K. Hall and Company, 70 Lincoln Street, Boston, Massachusetts 02111 (617) 423-3990; *The World in Figures.*

Jane's Information Group, Sentinel House, 163 Brighton Road, Coulsdon, Surrey CR5 2NH, England (Telephone Number in U.S. (703) 683-3700); *Jane's World Railways.*

Statistical Office of the United Nations, Publishing Service, New York, New York 10017 (800) 253-9646; *Survey of Economic and Social Conditions in Africa.*

United Nations Economic Commission for Africa, Africa Hall, P.O. Box 3001, Addis Ababa, Ethiopia (Telephone Number in U.S. (800) 253-9646); *African Statistical Yearbook.*

SWAZILAND - RELIGION

Facts on File, 460 Park Avenue South, New York, New York 10016 (800) 443-8323; *The New Book of World Rankings.*

SWAZILAND - RETAIL TRADE

G.K. Hall and Company, 70 Lincoln Street, Boston, Massachusetts 02111 (617) 423-3990; *The World in Figures.*

Statistical Office of the United Nations, Publishing Service, New York, New York 10017 (800) 253-9646; *Statistical Yearbook.*

SWAZILAND - RICE PRODUCTION - See SWAZILAND - CROPS

SWAZILAND - ROUNDWOOD PRODUCTION - See SWAZILAND - FORESTRY AND FOREST PRODUCTS

SWAZILAND - RUBBER PRODUCTION AND CONSUMPTION

Facts on File, 460 Park Avenue South, New York, New York 10016 (800) 443-8323; *The New Book of World Rankings.*

SWAZILAND - SAWNWOOD PRODUCTION - See SWAZILAND - FORESTRY AND FOREST PRODUCTS

SWAZILAND - SENIOR CITIZENS

Facts on File, 460 Park Avenue South, New York, New York 10016 (800) 443-8323; *The New Book of World Rankings.*

SWAZILAND - SHEEP - See SWAZILAND - LIVESTOCK AND POULTRY

SWAZILAND - SILVER PRODUCTION AND CONSUMPTION - See RWANDA - MINING AND MINERAL PRODUCTS

SWAZILAND - SOCIAL DATA

African Development Bank, 01 BP 1387, Abidjan 01, Cote D'Ivoire; *Selected Statistics on Regional Member Countries.*

Facts on File, 460 Park Avenue South, New York, New York 10016 (800) 443-8323; *The New Book of World Rankings.*

G.K. Hall and Company, 70 Lincoln Street, Boston, Massachusetts 02111 (617) 423-3990; *The World in Figures.*

SWAZILAND - STAMP TAXES AND DUTIES - See SWAZILAND - TAXATION

SWAZILAND - STEEL PRODUCTION - See SWAZILAND - MINING AND MINERAL PRODUCTS

SWAZILAND - STOCKS - COMMODITY - MARKET PRICE - INDEX

Food and Agricultural Organization of the United Nations (FAO) Via delle Terme di Caracalla, 00100 Rome, Italy (Telephone Number in U.S. (202) 653-2400); *The State of Food and Agriculture.*

SWAZILAND - SUGAR - See SWAZILAND - CROPS

SWAZILAND - TAXATION

G.K. Hall and Company, 70 Lincoln Street, Boston, Massachusetts 02111 (617) 423-3990; *The World in Figures.*

International Monetary Fund, 700 Nineteenth Street, NW, Washington, D.C. 20431 (202) 623-7000; *Government Finance Statistics Yearbook.*

International Road Federation, 525 School Street, SW, Washington, D.C. 20024 (202) 554-2106; *World Road Statistics.*

The World Bank, 1818 H Street, NW, Washington, D.C. 20433 (202) 477-1234; *World Tables.*

SWAZILAND - TELEPHONES IN USE

American Telephone and Telegraph Company, 26 Parsippany Road, Whippany, New Jersey 07981 (800) 338-4038; *The World's Telephones.*

G.K. Hall and Company, 70 Lincoln Street, Boston, Massachusetts 02111 (617) 423-3990; *The World in Figures.*

Statistical Office of the United Nations, Publishing Service, New York, New York 10017 (800) 253-9646; *Statistical Yearbook.*

SWAZILAND - TELEVISION BROADCASTING

Facts on File, 460 Park Avenue South, New York, New York 10016 (800) 443-8323; *The New Book of World Rankings.*

SWAZILAND - TEXTILE INDUSTRY

American Forest and Paper Association, 1250 Connecticut Avenue, NW, Washington, D.C. 20036 (202) 463-2455; *Wood Pulp and Fiber Statistics.*

G.K. Hall and Company, 70 Lincoln Street, Boston, Massachusetts 02111 (617) 423-3990; *The World in Figures.*

SWAZILAND - TIN PRODUCTION AND CONSUMPTION - See SWAZILAND - MINING AND MINERAL PRODUCTS

SWAZILAND - TOBACCO PRODUCTION

Facts on File, 460 Park Avenue South, New York, New York 10016 (800) 443-8323; *The New Book of World Rankings.*

Statistical Office of the United Nations, Publishing Service, New York, New York 10017 (800) 253-9646; *Statistical Yearbook.*

SWAZILAND - TOURISM

Facts on File, 460 Park Avenue South, New York, New York 10016 (800) 443-8323; *The New Book of World Rankings.*

G.K. Hall and Company, 70 Lincoln Street, Boston, Massachusetts 02111 (617) 423-3990; *The World in Figures.*

United Nations Economic Commission for Africa, Africa Hall, P.O. Box 3001, Addis Ababa, Ethiopia (Telephone Number in U.S. (800) 253-9646); *African Statistical Yearbook.*

SWAZILAND - TRACTORS IN USE

Statistical Office of the United Nations, Publishing Service, New York, New York 10017 (800) 253-9646; *Statistical Yearbook.*

SWAZILAND - TRADE - See SWAZILAND - FOREIGN TRADE

SWAZILAND - TRADEMARKS AND SERVICE MARKS

Statistical Office of the United Nations, Publishing Service, New York, New York 10017 (800) 253-9646; *Statistical Yearbook.*

World Intellectual Property Organization, 34 Chemin des Colombettes, CH-1211 Geneva 20. Switzerland; *Industrial Property Statistics.*

SWAZILAND - TRANSPORTATION AND COMMUNICATIONS

Facts on File, 460 Park Avenue South, New York, New York 10016 (800) 443-8323; *The New Book of World Rankings.*

G.K. Hall and Company, 70 Lincoln Street, Boston, Massachusetts 02111 (617) 423-3990; *The World in Figures.*

United Nations Economic Commission for Africa, Africa Hall, P.O. Box 3001, Addis Ababa, Ethiopia (Telephone Number in U.S. (800) 253-9646); *African Statistical Yearbook.*

SWAZILAND - UNEMPLOYMENT

International Labour Office, I.L.O. Publications, CH-1211, Geneva 22, Switzerland; *Yearbook of Labour Statistics.*

SWAZILAND - VITAL STATISTICS

G.K. Hall and Company, 70 Lincoln Street, Boston, Massachusetts 02111 (617) 423-3990; *The World in Figures.*

World Health Organization, Office of Publications, Avenue Appia, CH-1211 Geneva 27, Switzerland (Telephone Number in U.S. (518) 436-9686); *World Health Statistics Annual.*

SWAZILAND - WAGES

G.K. Hall and Company, 70 Lincoln Street, Boston, Massachusetts 02111 (617) 423-3990; *The World in Figures.*

International Labour Office, I.L.O. Publications, CH-1211, Geneva 22, Switzerland; *Yearbook of Labour Statistics.*

Statistical Office of the United Nations, Publishing Service, New York, New York 10017 (800) 253-9646; *Statistical Yearbook.*

SWAZILAND - WEATHER

Facts on File, 460 Park Avenue South, New York, New York 10016 (800) 443-8323; *The New Book of World Rankings.*

G.K. Hall and Company, 70 Lincoln Street, Boston, Massachusetts 02111 (617) 423-3990; *The World in Figures.*

SWAZILAND - WHEAT PRODUCTION AND PRICES - See SWAZILAND - CROPS

SWAZILAND - WHOLESALE TRADE

Statistical Office of the United Nations, Publishing Service, New York, New York 10017 (800) 253-9646; *Statistical Yearbook.*

SWAZILAND - WINE PRODUCTION

Facts on File, 460 Park Avenue South, New York, New York 10016 (800) 443-8323; *The New Book of World Rankings.*

SWAZILAND - WOOD AND WOOD PULP - See SWAZILAND - FORESTRY AND FOREST PRODUCTS

SWAZILAND - WOOL PRODUCTION

Facts on File, 460 Park Avenue South, New York, New York 10016 (800) 443-8323; *The New Book of World Rankings.*

Sweden - National Statistical Office

Statistiska Central Byran, Karlavagen 100, S-115 81 Stockholm, Sweden.

Sweden - Primary Statistics Sources

Statistiska Centralbyran (National Bureau of Statistics), Karlavagen 100, S-115 81, Stockholm, Sweden; *Statistisk arsbok for Sverige* (Statistical Yearbook of Sweden); *Allman manadsstatistik* (Monthly Digest of Swedish Statistics); and *Statistiska meddelanden* (Statistical Reports).

Sweden - Databases

Statistical Data Bases Division, Statistics Sweden, S-115 81 Stockholm, Sweden. Offers the following data bases: (1) Regional Statistics Data Base; (2) Sub-Area Statistical Data Base; and (3) Time Series Data Base. Subject coverage: Population, employment, economic, and social statistics for international, national, regional, and local area.

SWEDEN - ABORTIONS

Nordic Council of Ministers, Store Strandstraede 18, DK-1255 Copenhagen K, Denmark and the Nordic Statistical Secretariat, Postboks 2550, DK-2100 Copenhagen 0, Denmark; *The Yearbook of Nordic Statistics.*

Statistical Office of the United Nations, Publishing Service, New York, New York 10017 (800) 253-9646; *Demographic Yearbook.*

SWEDEN - AGRICULTURE

Facts on File, 460 Park Avenue South, New York, New York 10016 (800) 443-8323; *The New Book of World Rankings.*

Food and Agricultural Organization of the United Nations (FAO) Via delle Terme di Caracalla, 00100 Rome, Italy (Telephone Number in U.S. (202) 653-2400); *Production Yearbook, The State of Food and Agriculture,* and *Trade Yearbook.*

G.K. Hall and Company, 70 Lincoln Street, Boston, Massachusetts 02111 (617) 423-3990; *The World in Figures.*

Nordic Council of Ministers, Store Strandstraede 18, DK-1255 Copenhagen K, Denmark and the Nordic Statistical Secretariat, Postboks 2550, DK-2100 Copenhagen 0, Denmark; *The Yearbook of Nordic Statistics.*

Organisation for Economic Co-operation and Development (OECD), 2 rue Andre-Pascal, 75 Paris 16, France (Telephone Number in U.S. (202) 785-6323); *Economic Accounts for Agriculture, Indicators of Industrial Activity, Industrial Structure Statistics,* and *OECD Economic Surveys: Sweden.*

Statistical Office of the United Nations, Publishing Service, New York, New York 10017 (800) 253-9646; *Statistical Yearbook.*

The World Bank, 1818 H Street, NW, Washington, D.C. 20433 (202) 477-1234; *World Tables.*

SWEDEN - AIRLINE SERVICE

Facts on File, 460 Park Avenue South, New York, New York 10016 (800) 443-8323; *The New Book of World Rankings.*

G.K. Hall and Company, 70 Lincoln Street, Boston, Massachusetts 02111 (617) 423-3990; *The World in Figures.*

Nordic Council of Ministers, Store Strandstraede 18, DK-1255 Copenhagen K, Denmark and the Nordic Statistical Secretariat, Postboks 2550, DK-2100 Copenhagen 0, Denmark; *The Yearbook of Nordic Statistics.*

Organisation for Economic Co-operation and Development (OECD), 2 rue Andre-Pascal, 75 Paris 16, France (Telephone Number in U.S. (202) 785-6323); *Tourism Policy and International Tourism in OECD Member Countries.*

Statistical Office of the United Nations, Publishing Service, New York, New York 10017 (800) 253-9646; *Statistical Yearbook.*

Times Books, 201 East 50th Street, New York, New York 10022 (212) 751-2600; *The Economist Book of Vital World Statistics.*

SWEDEN - ALUMINUM PRODUCTION AND CONSUMPTION - See SWEDEN - MINING AND MINERAL PRODUCTS

SWEDEN - ANIMAL FEEDINGSTUFFS

Organisation for Economic Co-operation and Development (OECD), 2 rue Andre-Pascal, 75 Paris 16, France (Telephone Number in U.S. (202) 785-6323); *Foreign Trade by Commodities.*

Statistical Office of the United Nations, Publishing Service, New York, New York 10017 (800) 253-9646; *Statistical Yearbook.*

SWEDEN - ANIMAL HEALTH

Food and Agricultural Organization of the United Nations (FAO), Via delle Terme di Caracalla, 00100, Rome, Italy (Telephone Number in U.S. (202) 653-2400); *Animal Health Yearbook.*

SWEDEN - ANTIMONY AND ANTIMONY ORE PRODUCTION AND CONSUMPTION - See SWEDEN - MINING AND MINERAL PRODUCTS

SWEDEN - AREA AND DENSITY OF POPULATION

Facts on File, 460 Park Avenue South, New York, New York 10016 (800) 443-8323; *The New Book of World Rankings.*

Food and Agricultural Organization of the United Nations (FAO) Via delle Terme di Caracalla, 00100 Rome, Italy (Telephone Number in U.S. (202) 653-2400); *The State of Food and Agriculture.*

G.K. Hall and Company, 70 Lincoln Street, Boston, Massachusetts 02111 (617) 423-3990; *The World in Figures.*

Nordic Council of Ministers, Store Strandstraede 18, DK-1255 Copenhagen K, Denmark and the Nordic Statistical Secretariat, Postboks 2550, DK-2100 Copenhagen 0, Denmark; *The Yearbook of Nordic Statistics.*

Statistical Office of the United Nations, Publishing Service, New York, New York 10017 (800) 253-9646; *Statistical Yearbook.*

Times Books, 201 East 50th Street, New York, New York 10022 (212) 751-2600; *The Economist Book of Vital World Statistics.*

United Nations Educational, Scientific and Cultural Organization (UNESCO), 7 Place de Fontenoy, F-75700 Paris, France (Telephone Number in U.S. (212) 963-5981); *Statistical Yearbook.*

SWEDEN - ARMS EXPORTS AND IMPORTS

U.S. Arms Control and Disarmament Agency, 320 Twenty-first Street, NW, Washington, D.C. 20451 (202) 647-8677; *World Military Expenditures and Arms Transfers.*

SWEDEN - ARSENIC PRODUCTION AND CONSUMPTION - See SWEDEN - MINING AND MINERAL PRODUCTS

SWEDEN - BALANCE OF PAYMENTS

The Economist Intelligence Unit, 111 West 57th Street, New York, New York 10019 (800) 938-4685; *The World Market Atlas.*

G.K. Hall and Company, 70 Lincoln Street, Boston, Massachusetts 02111 (617) 423-3990; *The World in Figures.*

International Monetary Fund, 700 Nineteenth Street, NW, Washington, D.C. 20431 (202) 623-7000; *Balance of Payments Yearbook,* and *International Financial Statistics.*

Nordic Council of Ministers, Store Strandstraede 18, DK-1255 Copenhagen K, Denmark and the Nordic Statistical Secretariat, Postboks 2550, DK-2100 Copenhagen 0, Denmark; *The Yearbook of Nordic Statistics.*

Organisation for Economic Co-operation and Development (OECD), 2 rue Andre-Pascal, 75 Paris 16, France (Telephone Number in U.S. (202) 785-6323); *Economic Outlook, Geographical Distribution of Financial Flows to Developing Countries, Main Economic Indicators - Historical Statistics,* and *OECD Economic Surveys: Sweden.*

Times Books, 201 East 50th Street, New York, New York 10022 (212) 751-2600; *The Economist Book of Vital World Statistics.*

The World Bank, 1818 H Street, NW, Washington, D.C. 20433 (202) 477-1234; *World Tables.*

SWEDEN - BANKING

Facts on File, 460 Park Avenue South, New York, New York 10016 (800) 443-8323; *The New Book of World Rankings.*

G.K. Hall and Company, 70 Lincoln Street, Boston, Massachusetts 02111 (617) 423-3990; *The World in Figures.*

International Monetary Fund, 700 Nineteenth Street, NW, Washington, D.C. 20431 (202) 623-7000; *Government Finance Statistics Yearbook,* and *International Financial Statistics.*

Nordic Council of Ministers, Store Strandstraede 18, DK-1255 Copenhagen K, Denmark and the Nordic Statistical Secretariat, Postboks 2550, DK-2100 Copenhagen 0, Denmark; *The Yearbook of Nordic Statistics.*

Organisation for Economic Co-operation and Development (OECD), 2 rue Andre-Pascal, 75 Paris 16, France (Telephone Number in U.S. (202) 785-6323); *Economic Outlook, Financial Market Trends,* and *OECD Economic Surveys: Sweden.*

Statistical Office of the United Nations, Publishing Service, New York, New York 10017 (800) 253-9646; *Statistical Yearbook.*

SWEDEN - BARLEY PRODUCTION - See SWEDEN - CROPS

SWEDEN - BAUXITE PRODUCTION AND CONSUMPTION - See SWEDEN - MINING AND MINERAL PRODUCTS

SWEDEN - BEER PRODUCTION

Facts on File, 460 Park Avenue South, New York, New York 10016 (800) 443-8323; *The New Book of World Rankings*.

Statistical Office of the United Nations, Publishing Service, New York, New York 10017 (800) 253 9646; *Statistical Yearbook*.

SWEDEN - BEVERAGES - PRODUCTION INDEX

Organisation for Economic Co-operation and Development (OECD), 2 rue Andre-Pascal, 75 Paris 16, France (Telephone Number in U.S. (202) 785-6323); *Indicators of Industrial Activity*.

SWEDEN - BIRTH RATE

Facts on File, 460 Park Avenue South, New York, New York 10016 (800) 443-8323; *The New Book of World Rankings*.

Nordic Council of Ministers, Store Strandstraede 18, DK-1255 Copenhagen K, Denmark and the Nordic Statistical Secretariat, Postboks 2550, DK-2100 Copenhagen 0, Denmark; *The Yearbook of Nordic Statistics*.

Statistical Office of the United Nations, Publishing Service, New York, New York 10017 (800) 253-9646; *Demographic Yearbook*, and *Statistical Yearbook*.

Times Books, 201 East 50th Street, New York, New York 10022 (212) 751-2800; *The Economist Book of Vital World Statistics*.

The World Bank, 1818 H Street, NW, Washington, D.C. 20433 (202) 477-1234; *World Tables*.

World Health Organization, Office of Publications, Avenue Appia, CH-1211 Geneva 27, Switzerland (Telephone Number in U.S. (518) 436-9686); *World Health Statistics Annual*.

SWEDEN - BISMUTH PRODUCTION AND CONSUMPTION - See SWEDEN - MINING AND MINERAL PRODUCTS

SWEDEN - BONDS

G.K. Hall and Company, 70 Lincoln Street, Boston, Massachusetts 02111 (617) 423-3990; *The World in Figures*.

International Monetary Fund, 700 Nineteenth Street, NW, Washington, D.C. 20431 (202) 623-7000; *Government Finance Statistics Yearbook*.

Organisation for Economic Co-operation and Development (OECD), 2 rue Andre-Pascal, 75 Paris 16, France (Telephone Number in U.S. (202) 785-6323); *Financial Market Trends*.

Statistical Office of the United Nations, Publishing Service, New York, New York 10017 (800) 253-9646; *Statistical Yearbook*.

SWEDEN - BOOK PRODUCTION

Euromonitor Publications Limited, 87-88 Turnmill Street, London EC1M 5QU, England; *European Marketing Data and Statistics*.

G.K. Hall and Company, 70 Lincoln Street, Boston, Massachusetts 02111 (617) 423-3990; *The World in Figures*.

Nordic Council of Ministers, Store Strandstraede 18, DK-1255 Copenhagen K, Denmark and the Nordic Statistical Secretariat, Postboks 2550, DK-2100 Copenhagen 0, Denmark; *The Yearbook of Nordic Statistics*.

Organisation for Economic Co-operation and Development (OECD), 2 rue Andre-Pascal, 75 Paris 16, France (Telephone Number in U.S. (202) 785-6323); *Indicators of Industrial Activity*.

United Nations Educational, Scientific and Cultural Organization (UNESCO), 7 Place de Fontenoy, F-75700 Paris, France (Telephone Number in U.S. (212) 963-5981); *Statistical Yearbook*.

SWEDEN - BROADCASTING

Billboard Limited, P.O. Box 9027, 1006 AA Amsterdam, The Netherlands (Telephone Number in U.S. (212) 764-7300); *World Radio TV Handbook*.

G.K. Hall and Company, 70 Lincoln Street, Boston, Massachusetts 02111 (617) 423-3990; *The World in Figures*.

Nordic Council of Ministers, Store Strandstraede 18, DK-1255 Copenhagen K, Denmark and the Nordic Statistical Secretariat, Postboks 2550, DK-2100 Copenhagen 0, Denmark; *The Yearbook of Nordic Statistics*.

United Nations Educational, Scientific and Cultural Organization (UNESCO), 7 Place de Fontenoy, F-75700 Paris, France (Telephone Number in U.S. (212) 963-5981); *Statistical Yearbook*.

SWEDEN - BUSINESS

G.K. Hall and Company, 70 Lincoln Street, Boston, Massachusetts 02111 (617) 423-3990; *The World in Figures*.

Organisation for Economic Co-operation and Development (OECD), 2 rue Andre-Pascal, 75 Paris 16, France (Telephone Number in U.S. (202) 785-6323); *Main Economic Indicators - Historical Statistics*.

SWEDEN - BUTTER - See SWEDEN - DAIRY PRODUCTS

SWEDEN - CADMIUM PRODUCTION AND CONSUMPTION - See SWEDEN - MINING AND MINERAL PRODUCTS

SWEDEN - CALORIE SUPPLY

Food and Agricultural Organization of the United Nations (FAO) Via delle Terme di Caracalla, 00100 Rome, Italy (Telephone Number in U.S. (202) 653-2400); *The State of Food and Agriculture*.

SWEDEN - CAPITAL INVESTMENT

Organisation for Economic Co-operation and Development (OECD), 2 rue Andre-Pascal, 75 Paris 16, France (Telephone Number in U.S. (202) 785-6323); *Economic Outlook*, and *Financial Market Trends*.

SWEDEN - CAPITAL REVENUE

International Monetary Fund, 700 Nineteenth Street, NW, Washington, D.C. 20431 (202) 623-7000; *Government Finance Statistics Yearbook*.

Organisation for Economic Co-operation and Development (OECD), 2 rue Andre-Pascal, 75 Paris 16, France (Telephone Number in U.S. (202) 785-6323); *Economic Outlook*, and *Financial Market Trends*.

SWEDEN - CATTLE - See SWEDEN - LIVESTOCK AND POULTRY

SWEDEN - CAUSTIC SODA PRODUCTION

Organisation for Economic Co-operation and Development (OECD), 2 rue Andre-Pascal, 75 Paris 16, France (Telephone Number in U.S. (202) 785-6323); *Indicators of Industrial Activity.*

Statistical Office of the United Nations, Publishing Service, New York, New York 10017 (800) 253-9646; *Statistical Yearbook.*

SWEDEN - CEMENT PRODUCTION - See SWEDEN - MINING AND MINERAL PRODUCTS

SWEDEN - CEREAL PRODUCTION - See SWEDEN - CROPS

SWEDEN - CHEESE - See SWEDEN - DAIRY PRODUCTS

SWEDEN - CHEMICAL (ORGANIC) PRODUCTION - See SWEDEN - MINING AND MINERAL PRODUCTS

SWEDEN - CHROMITE PRODUCTION AND CONSUMPTION - See SWEDEN - MINING AND MINERAL PRODUCTS

SWEDEN - CHROMIUM ORE PRODUCTION AND CONSUMPTION - See SWEDEN - MINING AND MINERAL PRODUCTS

SWEDEN - CIGAR PRODUCTION - See SWEDEN - TOBACCO PRODUCTION

SWEDEN - CIGARETTE PRODUCTION - See SWEDEN - TOBACCO PRODUCTION

SWEDEN - CLASS STRUCTURE

G.K. Hall and Company, 70 Lincoln Street, Boston, Massachusetts 02111 (617) 423-3990; *The World in Figures.*

SWEDEN - CLIMATE

Facts on File, 460 Park Avenue South, New York, New York 10016 (800) 443-8323; *The New Book of World Rankings.*

G.K. Hall and Company, 70 Lincoln Street, Boston, Massachusetts 02111 (617) 423-3990; *The World in Figures.*

SWEDEN - CLOTHING - PRODUCTION INDEX

Organisation for Economic Co-operation and Development (OECD), 2 rue Andre-Pascal, 75 Paris 16, France (Telephone Number in U.S. (202) 785-6323); *Indicators of Industrial Activity.*

SWEDEN - CLOTHING EXPORTS AND IMPORTS

Organisation for Economic Co-operation and Development (OECD), 2 rue Andre-Pascal, 75 Paris 16, France (Telephone Number in U.S. (202) 785-6323); *Textile Industry in OECD Countries.*

Statistical Office of the United Nations, Publishing Service, New York, New York 10017 (800) 253-9646; *Trade in Manufactures of Developing Countries.*

SWEDEN - COAL PRODUCTION - See SWEDEN - MINING AND MINERAL PRODUCTS

SWEDEN - COBALT PRODUCTION AND CONSUMPTION - See SWEDEN - MINING AND MINERAL PRODUCTS

SWEDEN - COFFEE PRODUCTION AND CONSUMPTION

Facts on File, 460 Park Avenue South, New York, New York 10016 (800) 443-8323; *The New Book of World Rankings.*

Statistical Office of the United Nations, Publishing Service, New York, New York 10017 (800) 253-9646; *Statistical Yearbook.*

SWEDEN - COKE AND COKE OVEN ORE PRODUCTION AND CONSUMPTION - See SWEDEN - MINING AND MINERAL PRODUCTS

SWEDEN - CONSTRUCTION INDUSTRY

Facts on File, 460 Park Avenue South, New York, New York 10016 (800) 443-8323; *The New Book of World Rankings.*

Organisation for Economic Co-operation and Development/ (OECD), 2 rue Andre-Pascal, 75 Paris 16, France (Telephone Number in U.S. (202) 785-6323); *Industrial Structure Statistics, Main Economic Indicators - Historical Statistics,* and *OECD Economic Surveys: Sweden.*

Statistical Office of the United Nations, Publishing Service, New York, New York 10017 (800) 253-9646; *Statistical Yearbook.*

SWEDEN - CONSUMER PRICE INDEX

G.K. Hall and Company, 70 Lincoln Street, Boston, Massachusetts 02111 (617) 423-3990; *The World in Figures.*

Nordic Council of Ministers, Store Strandstraede 18, DK-1255 Copenhagen K, Denmark and the Nordic Statistical Secretariat, Postboks 2550, DK-2100 Copenhagen 0, Denmark; *The Yearbook of Nordic Statistics.*

Organisation for Economic Co-operation and Development (OECD), 2 rue Andre-Pascal, 75 Paris 16, France (Telephone Number in U.S. (202) 785-6323); *Economic Outlook.*

Statistical Office of the United Nations, Publishing Service, New York, New York 10017 (800) 253-9646; *Statistical Yearbook.*

SWEDEN - CONSUMER PRICES

Euromonitor Publications Limited, 87-88 Turnmill Street, London EC1M 5QU, England; *European Marketing Data and Statistics.*

International Labour Office, I.L.O. Publications, CH-1211, Geneva 22, Switzerland; *Yearbook of Labour Statistics.*

International Monetary Fund, 700 Nineteenth Street, NW, Washington, D.C. 20431 (202) 623-7000; *International Financial Statistics.*

Organisation for Economic Co-operation and Development (OECD), 2 rue Andre-Pascal, 75 Paris 16, France (Telephone Number in U.S. (202) 785-6323); *Economic Outlook.*

Times Books, 201 East 50th Street, New York, New York 10022 (212) 751-2600; *The Economist Book of Vital World Statistics.*

SWEDEN - CONSUMPTION

G.K. Hall and Company, 70 Lincoln Street, Boston, Massachusetts 02111 (617) 423-3990; *The World in Figures.*

International Lead and Zinc Study Group, Metro House, 58 St. James's Street, London SW1A 1LD, England; *Lead and Zinc Statistics.*

International Rubber Study Group, York House, Eighth Floor, Empire Way, Wembley, London HA9 0PA, England; *Rubber Statistical Bulletin*.

Nordic Council of Ministers, Store Strandstraede 18, DK-1255 Copenhagen K, Denmark and the Nordic Statistical Secretariat, Postboks 2550, DK-2100 Copenhagen 0, Denmark; *The Yearbook of Nordic Statistics*.

Organisation for Economic Co-operation and Development (OECD), 2 rue Andre-Pascal, 75 Paris 16, France (Telephone Number in U.S. (202) 785-6323); *The Footwear, Raw Hides and Skins, and Leather Industry in OECD Countries, The Iron and Steel Industry, Meat Balances in OECD Member Countries, The Non-Ferrous Metals Industry, The Pulp and Paper Industry*, and *Textile Industry in OECD Countries*.

SWEDEN - COPPER AND COPPER ORE PRODUCTION AND CONSUMPTION - See SWEDEN - MINING AND MINERAL PRODUCTS

SWEDEN - CORN PRODUCTION

Facts on File, 460 Park Avenue South, New York, New York 10016 (800) 443-8323; *The New Book of World Rankings*.

Food and Agricultural Organization of the United Nations (FAO) Via delle Terme di Caracalla, 00100 Rome, Italy (Telephone Number in U.S. (202) 653-2400); *The State of Food and Agriculture*.

SWEDEN - CORPORATE INCOME TAXES - See SWEDEN - TAXATION

SWEDEN - CORPORATE TAXES - See SWEDEN - TAXATION

SWEDEN - COTTON   See SWEDEN - CROPS

SWEDEN - CRIME

International Criminal Police Organization (INTERPOL), 26 rue Armengaud, 92210 Saint Cloud, France; *International Crime Statistics*.

Nordic Council of Ministers, Store Strandstraede 18, DK-1255 Copenhagen K, Denmark and the Nordic Statistical Secretariat, Postboks 2550, DK-2100 Copenhagen 0, Denmark; *The Yearbook of Nordic Statistics*.

Yale University Press, Yale Station, New Haven, Connecticut 06520 (203) 432-0940; *Violence and Crime in Cross-National Perspective*.

SWEDEN - CROPS

Commodity Research Bureau, Incorporated, 75 Wall Street, New York, New York 10005 (212) 504-7754; *Commodity Year Book*.

Euromonitor Publications Limited, 87-88 Turnmill Street, London EC1M 5QU, England; *European Marketing Data and Statistics*.

Facts on File, 460 Park Avenue South, New York, New York 10016 (800) 443-8323; *The New Book of World Rankings*.

Food and Agricultural Organization of the United Nations (FAO) Via delle Terme di Caracalla, 00100 Rome, Italy (Telephone Number in U.S. (202) 653-2400); *The State of Food and Agriculture*.

G.K. Hall and Company, 70 Lincoln Street, Boston, Massachusetts 02111 (617) 423-3990; *The World in Figures*.

Organisation for Economic Co-operation and Development (OECD), 2 rue Andre-Pascal, 75 Paris 16, France (Telephone Number in U.S.

(202) 785-6323); *Economic Accounts for Agriculture, Foreign Trade by Commodities*, and *Textile Industry in OECD Countries*.

Statistical Office of the United Nations, Publishing Service, New York, New York 10017 (800) 253-9646; *Statistical Yearbook*.

SWEDEN - CUSTOMS DUTIES

G.K. Hall and Company, 70 Lincoln Street, Boston, Massachusetts 02111 (617) 423-3990; *The World in Figures*.

International Monetary Fund, 700 Nineteenth Street, NW, Washington, D.C. 20431 (202) 623-7000; *Government Finance Statistics Yearbook*.

Organisation for Economic Co-operation and Development (OECD), 2 rue Andre-Pascal, 75 Paris 16, France (Telephone Number in U.S. (202) 785-6323); *The Non-Ferrous Metals Industry*.

SWEDEN - DAIRY PRODUCTS

Commodity Research Bureau, Incorporated, 75 Wall Street, New York, New York 10005 (212) 504-7754; *Commodity Year Book*.

Facts on File, 460 Park Avenue South, New York, New York 10016 (800) 443-8323; *The New Book of World Rankings*.

Food and Agricultural Organization of the United Nations (FAO) Via delle Terme di Caracalla, 00100 Rome, Italy (Telephone Number in U.S. (202) 653-2400); *The State of Food and Agriculture*.

Nordic Council of Ministers, Store Strandstraede 18, DK-1255 Copenhagen K, Denmark and the Nordic Statistical Secretariat, Postboks 2550, DK-2100 Copenhagen 0, Denmark; *The Yearbook of Nordic Statistics*.

Organisation for Economic Co-operation and Development (OECD), 2 rue Andre-Pascal, 75 Paris 16, France (Telephone Number in U.S. (202) 785-6323); *Economic Accounts for Agriculture*, and *Milk, Milk Products, and Egg Balances in OECD Member Countries*.

Statistical Office of the United Nations, Publishing Service, New York, New York 10017 (800) 253-9646; *Statistical Yearbook*.

SWEDEN - DEATH RATE

G.K. Hall and Company, 70 Lincoln Street, Boston, Massachusetts 02111 (617) 423-3990; *The World in Figures*.

Nordic Council of Ministers, Store Strandstraede 18, DK-1255 Copenhagen K, Denmark and the Nordic Statistical Secretariat, Postboks 2550, DK-2100 Copenhagen 0, Denmark; *The Yearbook of Nordic Statistics*.

Statistical Office of the United Nations, Publishing Service, New York, New York 10017 (800) 253-9646; *Statistical Yearbook*.

Times Books, 201 East 50th Street, New York, New York 10022 (212) 751-2600; *The Economist Book of Vital World Statistics*.

World Health Organization, Office of Publications, Avenue Appia, CH-1211 Geneva 27, Switzerland (Telephone Number in U.S. (518) 436-9686); *World Health Statistics Annual*.

SWEDEN - DEFENSE EXPENDITURES

G.K. Hall and Company, 70 Lincoln Street, Boston, Massachusetts 02111 (617) 423-3990; *The World in Figures*.

International Monetary Fund, 700 Nineteenth Street, NW, Washington, D.C. 20431 (202) 623-7000; *Government Finance Statistics Yearbook.*

U.S. Arms Control and Disarmament Agency, 320 Twenty-first Street, NW, Washington, D.C. 20451 (202) 647-8677; *World Military Expenditures and Arms Transfers.*

SWEDEN - DEMOGRAPHY

The Economist Intelligence Unit, 111 West 57th Street, New York, New York 10019 (800) 938-4685; *The World Market Atlas.*

Facts on File, 460 Park Avenue South, New York, New York 10016 (800) 443-8323; *The New Book of World Rankings.*

G.K. Hall and Company, 70 Lincoln Street, Boston, Massachusetts 02111 (617) 423-3990; *The World in Figures.*

Nordic Council of Ministers, Store Strandstraede 18, DK-1255 Copenhagen K, Denmark and the Nordic Statistical Secretariat, Postboks 2550, DK-2100 Copenhagen 0, Denmark; *The Yearbook of Nordic Statistics.*

SWEDEN - DEVELOPMENT ASSISTANCE

G.K. Hall and Company, 70 Lincoln Street, Boston, Massachusetts 02111 (617) 423-3990; *The World in Figures.*

Organisation for Economic Co-operation and Development (OECD), 2 rue Andre-Pascal, 75 Paris 16, France (Telephone Number in U.S. (202) 785-6323); *Geographical Distribution of Financial Flows to Developing Countries.*

Statistical Office of the United Nations, Publishing Service, New York, New York 10017 (800) 253-9646; *Statistical Yearbook.*

SWEDEN - DIAMOND PRODUCTION - See SWEDEN - MINING AND MINERAL PRODUCTS

SWEDEN - DISCOUNT RATES

Organisation for Economic Co-operation and Development (OECD), 2 rue Andre-Pascal, 75 Paris 16, France (Telephone Number in U.S. (202) 785-6323); *Financial Market Trends.*

Statistical Office of the United Nations, Publishing Service, New York, New York 10017 (800) 253-9646; *Statistical Yearbook.*

SWEDEN - DISEASES

G.K. Hall and Company, 70 Lincoln Street, Boston, Massachusetts 02111 (617) 423-3990; *The World in Figures.*

World Health Organization, Office of Publications, Avenue Appia, CH-1211 Geneva 27, Switzerland (Telephone Number in U.S. (518) 436-9686); *World Health Statistics Annual.*

SWEDEN - DIVORCE RATES

Facts on File, 460 Park Avenue South, New York, New York 10016 (800) 443-8323; *The New Book of World Rankings.*

Nordic Council of Ministers, Store Strandstraede 18, DK-1255 Copenhagen K, Denmark and the Nordic Statistical Secretariat, Postboks 2550, DK-2100 Copenhagen 0, Denmark; *The Yearbook of Nordic Statistics.*

Statistical Office of the United Nations, Publishing Service, New York, New York 10017 (800) 253-9646; *Demographic Yearbook,* and *Statistical Yearbook.*

SWEDEN - DOMESTIC PRODUCT

G.K. Hall and Company, 70 Lincoln Street, Boston, Massachusetts 02111 (617) 423-3990; *The World in Figures.*

SWEDEN - ECONOMY

Euromonitor Publications Limited, 87-88 Turnmill Street, London EC1M 5QU, England; *European Marketing Data and Statistics.*

Facts on File, 460 Park Avenue South, New York, New York 10016 (800) 443-8323; *The New Book of World Rankings.*

G.K. Hall and Company, 70 Lincoln Street, Boston, Massachusetts 02111 (617) 423-3990; *The World in Figures.*

Organisation for Economic Co-operation and Development (OECD), 2 rue Andre-Pascal, 75 Paris 16, France (Telephone Number in U.S. (202) 785-6323); *Economic Outlook, Geographical Distribution of Financial Flows to Developing Countries, Main Economic Indicators - Historical Statistics, OECD Economic Surveys: Sweden,* and *OECD Employment Outlook.*

SWEDEN - EDUCATION

The Economist Intelligence Unit, 111 West 57th Street, New York, New York 10019 (800) 938-4685; *The World Market Atlas.*

Euromonitor Publications Limited, 87-88 Turnmill Street, London EC1M 5QU, England; *European Marketing Data and Statistics.*

Facts on File, 460 Park Avenue South, New York, New York 10016 (800) 443-8323; *The New Book of World Rankings.*

G.K. Hall and Company, 70 Lincoln Street, Boston, Massachusetts 02111 (617) 423-3990; *The World in Figures.*

International Monetary Fund, 700 Nineteenth Street, NW, Washington, D.C. 20431 (202) 623-7000; *Government Finance Statistics Yearbook.*

Nordic Council of Ministers, Store Strandstraede 18, DK-1255 Copenhagen K, Denmark and the Nordic Statistical Secretariat, Postboks 2550, DK-2100 Copenhagen 0, Denmark; *The Yearbook of Nordic Statistics.*

Organisation for Economic Co-operation and Development (OECD), 2 rue Andre-Pascal, 75 Paris 16, France (Telephone Number in U.s. (202) 785-6323); *Education in OECD Countries.*

Times Books, 201 East 50th Street, New York, New York 10022 (212) 751-2600; *The Economist Book of Vital World Statistics.*

United Nations Educational, Scientific and Cultural Organization (UNESCO), 7 Place de Fontenoy, F-75700 Paris, France (Telephone Number in U.S. (212) 963-5981); *Statistical Yearbook.*

The World Bank, 1818 H Street, NW, Washington, D.C. 20433 (202) 477-1234; *World Tables.*

SWEDEN - EGG PRODUCTION AND CONSUMPTION - See SWEDEN - DAIRY PRODUCTS

SWEDEN - ELECTRICITY

Commodity Research Bureau, Incorporated, 75 Wall Street, New York, New York 10005 (212) 504-7754; *Commodity Year Book.*

Facts on File, 460 Park Avenue South, New York, New York 10016 (800) 443-8323; *The New Book of World Rankings.*

Nordic Council of Ministers, Store Strandstraede 18, DK-1255 Copenhagen K, Denmark and the Nordic Statistical Secretariat, Postboks 2550, DK-2100 Copenhagen 0, Denmark; *The Yearbook of Nordic Statistics.*

Organisation for Economic Co-operation and Development (OECD), 2 rue Andre-Pascal, 75 Paris 16, France (Telephone Number in U.S. (202) 785-6323); *Coal Information, Energy Statistics of OECD Countries,* and *Industrial Structure Statistics.*

Statistical Office of the United Nations, Publishing Service, New York, New York 10017 (800) 253-9646; *Statistical Yearbook.*

Times Books, 201 East 50th Street, New York, New York 10022 (212) 751-2600; *The Economist Book of Vital World Statistics.*

SWEDEN - EMPLOYMENT

Euromonitor Publications Limited, 87-88 Turnmill Street, London EC1M 5QU, England; *European Marketing Data and Statistics.*

Facts on File, 460 Park Avenue South, New York, New York 10016 (800) 443-8323; *The New Book of World Rankings.*

International Labour Office, I.L.O. Publications, CH 1211, Geneva 22, Switzerland; *Yearbook of Labour Statistics.*

Nordic Council of Ministers, Store Strandstraede 18, DK-1255 Copenhagen K, Denmark and the Nordic Statistical Secretariat, Postboks 2550, DK-2100 Copenhagen 0, Denmark; *The Yearbook of Nordic Statistics.*

Organisation for Economic Co-operation and Development (OECD), 2 rue Andre-Pascal, 75 Paris 16, France (Telephone Number in U.S. (202) 785-6323); *Economic Outlook, The Iron and Steel Industry, OECD Economic Surveys: Sweden, OECD Employment Outlook,* and *Textile Industry in OECD Countries.*

Statistical Office of the United Nations, Publishing Service, New York, New York 10017 (800) 253-9646; *Statistical Yearbook.*

SWEDEN - ENERGY

Euromonitor Publications Limited, 87-88 Turnmill Street, London EC1M 5QU, England; *European Marketing Data and Statistics.*

Facts on File, 460 Park Avenue South, New York, New York 10016 (800) 443-8323; *The New Book of World Rankings.*

Food and Agricultural Organization of the United Nations (FAO) Via delle Terme di Caracalla, 00100 Rome, Italy (Telephone Number in U.S. (202) 653-2400); *The State of Food and Agriculture.*

G.K. Hall and Company, 70 Lincoln Street, Boston, Massachusetts 02111 (617) 423-3990; *The World in Figures.*

Nordic Council of Ministers, Store Strandstraede 18, DK-1255 Copenhagen K, Denmark and the Nordic Statistical Secretariat, Postboks 2550, DK-2100 Copenhagen 0, Denmark; *The Yearbook of Nordic Statistics.*

Organisation for Economic Co-operation and Development (OECD), 2 rue Andre-Pascal, 75 Paris 16, France (Telephone Number in U.S. (202) 785-6323); *Coal Information, Energy Statistics of OECD Countries, OECD Environmental Data,* and *Oil and Gas Information.*

Statistical Office of the United Nations, Publishing Service, New York, New York 10017 (800) 253-9646; *Energy Statistics Yearbook, Statistical Yearbook,* and *World Energy Supplies.*

Times Books, 201 East 50th Street, New York, New York 10022 (212) 751-2600; *The Economist Book of Vital World Statistics.*

SWEDEN - ENGINEERING AND METAL PRODUCTS - EXPORTS AND IMPORTS

Statistical Office of the United Nations, Publishing Service, New York, New York 10017 (800) 253-9646; *Trade in Manufactures of Developing Countries.*

SWEDEN - ENVIRONMENT

Organization for Economic Co-operation and Development (OECD), 2 rue Andre-Pascal, 75 Paris 16, France (Telephone Number in U.S. (202) 785-6323); *OECD Environmental Data.*

SWEDEN - EXCHANGE RATES

International Monetary Fund, 700 Nineteenth Street, NW, Washington, D.C. 30431 (202) 623-7000; *International Financial Statistics.*

Nordic Council of Ministers, Store Strandstraede 18, DK-1255 Copenhagen K, Denmark and the Nordic Statistical Secretariat, Postboks 2550, DK-2100 Copenhagen 0, Denmark; *The Yearbook of Nordic Statistics.*

Organisation for Economic Co-operation and Development (OECD), 2 rue Andre-Pascal, 75 Paris 16, France (Telephone Number in U.S. (202) 785-6323); *Economic Outlook, Financial Market Trends, Revenue Statistics of OECD Member Countries,* and *Tourism Policy and International Tourism in OECD Member Countries.*

SWEDEN - EXCISE TAXES - See SWEDEN - TAXATION

SWEDEN - EXPORTS

American Automobile Manufacturers Association, 1401 H Eye Street, NW, Suite 900, Washington, D.C. 20005 (202) 326-5500; *World Motor Vehicle Data.*

The Economist Intelligence Unit, 111 West 57th Street, New York, New York 10019 (800) 938-4685; *The World Market Atlas.*

Food and Agricultural Organization of the United Nations (FAO) Via delle Terme di Caracalla, 00100 Rome, Italy (Telephone Number in U.S. (202) 653-2400); *The State of Food and Agriculture.*

G.K. Hall and Company, 70 Lincoln Street, Boston, Massachusetts 02111 (617) 423-3990; *The World in Figures.*

International Lead and Zinc Study Group, Metro House, 58 St. James's Street, London SW1A 1LD, England; *Lead and Zinc Statistics.*

International Monetary Fund, 700 Nineteenth Street, NW, Washington, D.C. 20431 (202) 623-7000; *Direction of Trade Statistics,* and *International Financial Statistics.*

International Rubber Study Group, York House, Eighth Floor, Empire Way, Wembley, London HA9 0PA, England; *Rubber Statistical Bulletin*.

Nordic Council of Ministers, Store Strandstraede 18, DK-1255 Copenhagen K, Denmark and the Nordic Statistical Secretariat, Postboks 2550, DK-2100 Copenhagen 0, Denmark; *The Yearbook of Nordic Statistics*.

Organisation for Economic Co-operation and Development (OECD), 2 rue Andre-Pascal, 75 Paris 16, France (Telephone Number in U.S. (202) 785-6323); *Economic Outlook, The Footwear, Raw Hides and Skins, and Leather Industry in OECD Countries, Foreign Trade by Commodities, Geographical Distribution of Financial Flows to Developing Countries, Industrial Structure Statistics, The Iron and Steel Industry, Milk, Milk Products, and Egg Balances in OECD Member Countries, OECD Economic Surveys: Sweden, The Pulp and Paper Industry*, and *Review of Fisheries in OECD Member Countries*.

Times Books, 201 East 50th Street, New York, New York 10022 (212) 751-2600; *The Economist Book of Vital World Statistics*.

The World Bank, 1818 H Street, NW, Washington, D.C. 20433 (202) 477-1234; *World Tables*.

SWEDEN - EXTERNAL FINANCING

Organisation for Economic Co-operation and Development (OECD), 2 rue Andre-Pascal, 75 Paris 16, France (Telephone Number in U.S. (202) 785-6323); *Economic Outlook*, and *Financial Market Trends*.

SWEDEN - EXTERNAL INDEBTEDNESS

Organisation for Economic Co-operation and Development (OECD), 2 rue Andre-Pascal, 75 Paris 16, France (Telephone Number in U.S. (202) 785-6323); *Financial Market Trends*, and *Geographical Distribution of Financial Flows to Developing Countries*.

The World Bank, 1818 H Street, NW, Washington, D.C. 20433 (202) 477-1234; *World Tables*.

SWEDEN - EXTERNAL TRADE

Food and Agricultural Organization of the United Nations (FAO) Via delle Terme di Caracalla, 00100 Rome, Italy (Telephone Number in U.S. (202) 653-2400); *The State of Food and Agriculture*, and *Trade Yearbook*.

G.K. Hall and Company, 70 Lincoln Street, Boston, Massachusetts 02111 (617) 423-3990; *The World in Figures*.

Nordic Council of Ministers, Store Strandstraede 18, DK-1255 Copenhagen K, Denmark and the Nordic Statistical Secretariat, Postboks 2550, DK-2100 Copenhagen 0, Denmark; *The Yearbook of Nordic Statistics*.

Statistical Office of the United Nations, Publishing Service, New York, New York 10017 (800) 253-9646; *Statistical Yearbook*.

SWEDEN - FABRIC PRODUCTION - See SWEDEN - TEXTILE INDUSTRY

SWEDEN - FARM CROPS - See SWEDEN - CROPS

SWEDEN - FEMALE WORKING POPULATION - See SWEDEN - EMPLOYMENT

SWEDEN - FERTILITY RATES

Facts on File, 460 Park Avenue South, New York, New York 10016 (800) 443-8323; *The New Book of World Rankings*.

Nordic Council of Ministers, Store Strandstraede 18, DK-1255 Copenhagen K, Denmark and the Nordic Statistical Secretariat, Postboks 2550, DK-2100 Copenhagen 0, Denmark; *The Yearbook of Nordic Statistics*.

Times Books, 201 East 50th Street, New York, New York 10022 (212) 751-2600; *The Economist Book of Vital World Statistics*.

The World Bank, 1818 H Street, NW, Washington, D.C. 20433 (202) 477-1234; *World Tables*.

SWEDEN - FERTILIZER

Food and Agricultural Organization of the United Nations (FAO) Via delle Terme di Caracalla, 00100 Rome, Italy (Telephone Number in U.S. (202) 653-2400); *The State of Food and Agriculture*.

Organisation for Economic Co-operation and Development (OECD), 2 rue Andre-Pascal, 75 Paris 16, France (Telephone Number in U.S. (202) 785-6323); *Economic Accounts for Agriculture, Foreign Trade by Commodities*.

Statistical Office of the United Nations, Publishing Service, New York, New York 10017 (800) 253-9646; *Statistical Yearbook*.

SWEDEN - FETAL MORTALITY

Nordic Council of Ministers, Store Strandstraede 18, DK-1255 Copenhagen K, Denmark and the Nordic Statistical Secretariat, Postboks 2550, DK-2100 Copenhagen 0, Denmark; *The Yearbook of Nordic Statistics*.

Statistical Office of the United Nations, Publishing Service, New York, New York 10017 (800) 253-9646; *Demographic Yearbook*.

World Health Organization, Office of Publications, Avenue Appia, CH-1211 Geneva 27, Switzerland (Telephone Number in U.S. (518) 436-9686); *World Health Statistics Annual*.

SWEDEN - FILAMENT PRODUCTION - See SWEDEN - TEXTILE INDUSTRY

SWEDEN - FILM - See SWEDEN - MOTION PICTURES

SWEDEN - FINANCE

Facts on File, 460 Park Avenue South, New York, New York 10016 (800) 443-8323; *The New Book of World Rankings*.

G.K. Hall and Company, 70 Lincoln Street, Boston, Massachusetts 02111 (617) 423-3990; *The World in Figures*.

International Monetary Fund, 700 Nineteenth Street, NW, Washington, D.C. 20431 (202) 623-7000; *Government Finance Statistics Yearbook*, and *International Financial Statistics*.

Organisation for Economic Co-operation and Development (OECD), 2 rue Andre-Pascal, 75 Paris 16, France (Telephone Number in U.S. (202) 785-6323); *Economic Outlook, Financial Market Trends, Geographical Distribution of Financial Flows to Developing Countries, Main Economic Indicators - Historical Statistics*, and *OECD Financial Statistics*.

SWEDEN - FISHERIES

Euromonitor Publications Limited, 87-88 Turnmill Street, London EC1M 5QU, England; *European Marketing Data and Statistics*.

Facts on File, 460 Park Avenue South, New York, New York 10016 (800) 443-8323; *The New Book of World Rankings*.

Food and Agricultural Organization of the United Nations (FAO) Via delle Terme di Caracalla, 00100 Rome, Italy (Telephone Number in U.S. (202) 653-2400); *The State of Food and Agriculture*, and *Yearbook of Fishery Statistics*.

Nordic Council of Ministers, Store Strandstraede 18, DK-1255 Copenhagen K, Denmark and the Nordic Statistical Secretariat, Postboks 2550, DK-2100 Copenhagen 0, Denmark; *The Yearbook of Nordic Statistics*.

Organisation for Economic Co-operation and Development (OECD), 2 rue Andre-Pascal, 75 Paris 16, France (Telephone Number in U.S. (202) 785-6323); *Foreign Trade by Commodities, Industrial Structure Statistics*, and *Review of Fisheries in OECD Member Countries*.

Statistical Office of the United Nations, Publishing Service, New York, New York 10017 (800) 253-9646; *Statistical Yearbook*.

SWEDEN - FLOUR PRODUCTION

Statistical Office of the United Nations, Publishing Service, New York, New York 10017 (800) 253-9646; *Statistical Yearbook*.

SWEDEN - FOOD

Food and Agricultural Organization of the United Nations (FAO) Via delle Terme di Caracalla, 00100 Rome, Italy (Telephone Number in U.S. (202) 653-2400); *Production Yearbook*, and *The State of Food and Agriculture*.

G.K. Hall and Company, 70 Lincoln Street, Boston, Massachusetts 02111 (617) 423-3990; *The World in Figures*.

Organisation for Economic Co-operation and Development (OECD), 2 rue Andre-Pascal, 75 Paris 16, France (Telephone Number in U.S. (202) 785-6323); *Foreign Trade by Commodities*, and *Main Economic Indicators - Historical Statistics*.

SWEDEN - FOOTWEAR - PRODUCTION INDEX

Organisation for Economic Co-operation and Development (OECD), 2 rue Andre-Pascal, 75 Paris 16, France (Telephone Number in U.S. (202) 785-6323); *Indicators of Industrial Activity*.

SWEDEN - FOREIGN AID

G.K. Hall and Company, 70 Lincoln Street, Boston, Massachusetts 02111 (617) 423-3990; *The World in Figures*.

SWEDEN - FOREIGN DEBT

International Monetary Fund, 700 Nineteenth Street, NW, Washington, D.C. 20431 (202) 623-7000; *Government Finance Statistics Yearbook*.

Organisation for Economic Co-operation and Development (OECD), 2 rue Andre-Pascal, 75 Paris 16, France (Telephone Number in U.S. (202) 785-6323); *Economic Outlook*.

SWEDEN - FOREIGN INDEBTEDNESS

Organisation for Economic Co-operation and Development (OECD), 2 rue Andre-Pascal, 75 Paris 16, France (Telephone Number in U.S. (202) 785-6323); *Economic Outlook*, and *Financial Market Trends*.

SWEDEN - FOREIGN TRADE

Euromonitor Publications Limited, 87-88 Turnmill Street, London EC1M 5QU, England; *European Marketing Data and Statistics*.

Facts on File, 460 Park Avenue South, New York, New York 10016 (800) 443-8323; *The New Book of World Rankings*.

Food and Agricultural Organization of the United Nations (FAO) Via delle Terme di Caracalla, 00100 Rome, Italy (Telephone Number in U.S. (202) 653-2400); *The State of Food and Agriculture*.

G.K. Hall and Company, 70 Lincoln Street, Boston, Massachusetts 02111 (617) 423-3990; *The World in Figures*.

International Monetary Fund, 700 Nineteenth Street, NW, Washington, D.C. 20431 (202) 623-7000; *International Financial Statistics*.

Organisation for Economic Co-operation and Development (OECD), 2 rue Andre-Pascal, 75 Paris 16, France (Telephone Number in U.S. (202) 785-6323); *Economic Outlook, The Footwear, Raw Hides and Skins, and Leather Industry in OECD Countries, Foreign Trade by Commodities, Main Economic Indicators - Historical Statistics, Maritime Transport, Meat Balances in OECD Member Countries*, and *OECD Economic Surveys: Sweden*.

Statistical Office of the United Nations, Publishing Service, New York, New York 10017 (800) 253-9646; *International Trade Statistics Yearbook, Statistical Yearbook*, and *Trade Manufactures of Developing Countries*.

The World Bank, 1818 H Street, NW, Washington, D.C. 20433 (202) 477-1234; *World Tables*.

World Bureau of Metal Statistics, 27-A High Street, Ware Hert SG12 9BA, England; *World Metal Statistics*.

SWEDEN - FORESTRY AND FOREST INDUSTRY

Euromonitor Publications Limited, 87-88 Turnmill Street, London EC1M 5QU, England; *European Marketing Data and Statistics*.

Facts on File, 460 Park Avenue South, New York, New York 10016 (800) 443-8323; *The New Book of World Rankings*.

Food and Agricultural Organization of the United Nations (FAO) Via delle Terme di Caracalla, 00100 Rome, Italy (Telephone Number in U.S. (202) 653-2400); *The State of Food and Agriculture*, and *Yearbook of Forest Products*.

G.K. Hall and Company, 70 Lincoln Street, Boston, Massachusetts 02111 (617) 423-3990; *The World in Figures*.

International Monetary Fund, 700 Nineteenth Street, NW, Washington, D.C. 20431 (202) 623-7000; *International Financial Statistics*.

Nordic Council of Ministers, Store Strandstraede 18, DK-1255 Copenhagen K, Denmark and the Nordic Statistical Secretariat, Postboks 2550, DK-2100 Copenhagen 0, Denmark; *The Yearbook of Nordic Statistics*.

Organisation for Economic Co-operation and Development (OECD), 2 rue Andre-Pascal, 75 Paris 16, France (Telephone Number in U.S. (202) 785-6323); *Indicators of Industrial Activity, Industrial Structure Statistics,* and *The Pulp and Paper Industry.*

Statistical Office of the United Nations, Publishing Service, New York, New York 10017 (800) 253-9646; *Statistical Yearbook.*

United Nations Educational, Scientific and Cultural Organization (UNESCO), 7 Place de Fontenoy, F-75700 Paris, France (Telephone Number in U.S. (212) 963-5981); *Statistical Yearbook.*

SWEDEN - FRUIT PRODUCTION - See SWEDEN - CROPS

SWEDEN - FURNITURE AND WOOD PRODUCTS - EXPORTS AND IMPORTS

Organisation for Economic Co-operation and Development (OECD), 2 rue Andre-Pascal, 75 Paris 16, France (Telephone Number in U.S. (202) 785-6323); *Foreign Trade by Commodities,* and *Industrial Structure Statistics.*

SWEDEN - GAS - See SWEDEN - MINING AND MINERAL PRODUCTS

SWEDEN - GENERAL INDUSTRIAL STATISTICS

Statistical Office of the United Nations, Publishing Service, New York, New York 10017 (800) 253-9646; *Industrial Statistics Yearbook.*

SWEDEN - GENERAL MORTALITY

Nordic Council of Ministers, Store Strandstraede 18, DK-1255 Copenhagen K, Denmark and the Nordic Statistical Secretariat, Postboks 2550, DK-2100 Copenhagen 0, Denmark; *The Yearbook of Nordic Statistics.*

Statistical Office of the United Nations, Publishing Service, New York, New York 10017 (800) 253-9646; *Demographic Yearbook.*

World Health Organization, Office of Publications, Avenue Appia, CH-1211 Geneva 27, Switzerland (Telephone Number in U.S. (518) 436-9686); *World Health Statistics Annual.*

SWEDEN - GEOGRAPHIC DATA

Facts on File, 460 Park Avenue South, New York, New York 10016 (800) 443-8323; *The New Book of World Rankings.*

SWEDEN - GLASS AND GLASS PRODUCTS - PRODUCTION INDEX - See SWEDEN - MINING AND MINERAL PRODUCTS

SWEDEN - GOATS - See SWEDEN - LIVESTOCK AND POULTRY

SWEDEN - GOLD HOLDINGS

International Monetary Fund, 700 Nineteenth Street, NW, Washington, D.C. 20431 (202) 623-7000; *International Financial Statistics.*

Statistical Office of the United Nations, Publishing Service, New York, New York 10017 (800) 253-9646; *Statistical Yearbook.*

The World Bank, 1818 H Street, NW, Washington, D.C. 20433 (202) 477-1234; *World Tables.*

SWEDEN - GOLD PRODUCTION AND CONSUMPTION - See SWEDEN - MINING AND MINERAL PRODUCTS

SWEDEN - GOVERNMENT

G.K. Hall and Company, 70 Lincoln Street, Boston, Massachusetts 02111 (617) 423-3990; *The World in Figures.*

SWEDEN - GOVERNMENT CONSUMPTION

International Monetary Fund, 700 Nineteenth Street, NW, Washington, D.C. 20431 (202) 623-7000; *International Financial Statistics.*

SWEDEN - GOVERNMENT EXPENDITURES

International Monetary Fund, 700 Nineteenth Street, NW, Washington, D.C. 20431 (202) 623-7000; *Government Finance Statistics Yearbook.*

Nordic Council of Ministers, Store Strandstraede 18, DK-1255 Copenhagen K, Denmark and the Nordic Statistical Secretariat, Postboks 2550, DK-2100 Copenhagen 0, Denmark; *The Yearbook of Nordic Statistics.*

Organisation for Economic Co-operation and Development (OECD), 2 rue Andre-Pascal, 75 Paris 16, France (Telephone Number in U.S. (202) 785-6323); *Economic Outlook.*

Times Books, 201 East 50th Street, New York, New York 10022 (212) 751-2600; *The Economist Book of Vital World Statistics.*

The World Bank, 1818 H Street, NW, Washington, D.C. 20433 (202) 477-1234; *World Tables.*

SWEDEN - GOVERNMENT FINANCES

International Monetary Fund, 700 Nineteenth Street, NW, Washington, D.C. 20431 (202) 623-7000; *International Financial Statistics.*

Organisation for Economic Co-operation and Development (OECD), 2 rue Andre-Pascal, 75 Paris 16, France (Telephone Number in U.S. (202) 785-6323); *Economic Outlook.*

Statistical Office of the United Nations, Publishing Service, New York, New York 10017 (800) 253-9646; *Statistical Yearbook.*

SWEDEN - GOVERNMENT REVENUE

International Monetary Fund, 700 Nineteenth Street, NW, Washington, D.C. 20431 (202) 623-7000; *Government Finance Statistics Yearbook.*

Nordic Council of Ministers, Store Strandstraede 18, DK-1255 Copenhagen K, Denmark and the Nordic Statistical Secretariat, Postboks 2550, DK-2100 Copenhagen 0, Denmark; *The Yearbook of Nordic Statistics.*

Organisation for Economic Co-operation and Development (OECD), 2 rue Andre-Pascal, 75 Paris 16, France (Telephone Number in U.S. (202) 785-6323); *Economic Outlook,* and *Revenue Statistics of OECD Member Countries.*

Times Books, 201 East 50th Street, New York, New York 10022 (212) 751-2600; *The Economist Book of Vital World Statistics.*

The World Bank, 1818 H Street, NW, Washington, D.C. 20433 (202) 477-1234; *World Tables.*

SWEDEN - GRAIN PRODUCTION - See SWEDEN - CROPS

SWEDEN - GRANTS

International Monetary Fund, 700 Nineteenth Street, NW, Washington, D.C. 20431 (202) 623-7000; *Government Finance Statistics Yearbook.*

Organisation for Economic Co-operation and Development (OECD), 2 rue Andre-Pascal, 75 Paris 16, France (Telephone Number in U.S. (202) 785-6323); *Geographical Distribution of Financial Flows to Developing Countries.*

SWEDEN - GROSS DOMESTIC PRODUCT

The Economist Intelligence Unit, 111 West 57th Street, New York, New York 10019 (800) 938-4685; *The World Market Atlas.*

Facts on File, 460 Park Avenue South, New York, New York 10016 (800) 443-8323; *The New Book of World Rankings.*

G.K. Hall and Company, 70 Lincoln Street, Boston, Massachusetts 02111 (617) 423-3990; *The World in Figures.*

International Monetary Fund, 700 Nineteenth Street, NW, Washington, D.C. 20431 (202) 623-7000; *International Financial Statistics.*

Nordic Council of Ministers, Store Strandstraede 18, DK-1255 Copenhagen K, Denmark and the Nordic Statistical Secretariat, Postboks 2550, DK-2100 Copenhagen 0, Denmark; *The Yearbook of Nordic Statistics.*

Organisation for Economic Co-operation and Development (OECD), 2 rue Andre-Pascal, 75 Paris 16, France (Telephone Number in U.S. (202) 785-6323); *Economic Outlook, Geographical Distribution of Financial Flows to Developing Countries, Revenue Statistics of OECD Member Countries.*

Statistical Office of the United Nations, Publishing Service, New York, New York 10017 (800) 253-9646; *Statistical Yearbook.*

Times Books, 201 East 50th Street, New York, New York 10022 (212) 751-2600; *The Economist Book of Vital World Statistics.*

The World Bank, 1818 H Street, NW, Washington, D.C. 20433 (202) 477-1234; *World Tables.*

SWEDEN - GROSS NATIONAL PRODUCT

Organisation for Economic Co-operation and Development (OECD), 2 rue Andre-Pascal, 75 Paris 16, France (Telephone Number in U.S. (202) 785-6323); *Economic Outlook,* and *Geographical Distribution of Financial Flows to Developing Countries.*

U.S. Arms Control and Disarmament Agency, 320 Twenty-first Street, NW, Washington, D.C. 20451 (202) 647-8677; *World Military Expenditures and Arms Transfers.*

The World Bank, 1818 H Street, NW, Washington, D.C. 20433 (202) 477-1234; *World Tables.*

SWEDEN - HEALTH

Facts on File, 460 Park Avenue South, New York, New York 10016 (800) 443-8323; *The New Book of World Rankings.*

G.K. Hall and Company, 70 Lincoln Street, Boston, Massachusetts 02111 (617) 423-3990; *The World in Figures.*

Nordic Council of Ministers, Store Strandstraede 18, DK-1255 Copenhagen K, Denmark and the Nordic Statistical Secretariat, Postboks 2550, DK-2100 Copenhagen 0, Denmark; *The Yearbook of Nordic Statistics.*

Organisation for Economic Co-operation and Development (OECD), 2 rue Andre-Pascal, 75 Paris 16, France (Telephone Number in U.S. (202) 785-6323); *OECD Health Systems: Facts and Trends.*

Statistical Office of the United Nations, Publishing Service, New York, New York 10017 (800) 253-9646; *Statistical Yearbook.*

Times Books, 201 East 50th Street, New York, New York 10022 (212) 751-2600; *The Economist Book of Vital World Statistics.*

World Health Organization, Office of Publications, Avenue Appia, CH-1211 Geneva 27, Switzerland (Telephone Number in U.S. (518) 436-9686); *World Health Statistics Annual.*

SWEDEN - HEALTH EXPENDITURES

International Monetary Fund, 700 Nineteenth Street, NW, Washington, D.C. 20431 (202) 623-7000; *Government Finance Statistics Yearbook.*

SWEDEN - HIDE PRODUCTION

Organisation for Economic Co-operation and Development (OECD), 2 rue Andre-Pascal, 75 Paris 16, France (Telephone Number in U.S. (202) 785-6323); *The Footwear, Raw Hides and Skins, and Leather Industry in OECD Countries, Foreign Trade by Commodities,* and *Indicators of Industrial Activity.*

SWEDEN - HIGHWAYS

G.K. Hall and Company, 70 Lincoln Street, Boston, Massachusetts 02111 (617) 423-3990; *The World in Figures.*

International Road Federation, 525 School Street, SW, Washington, D.C. 20024 (202) 554-2106; *World Road Statistics.*

Nordic Council of Ministers, Store Strandstraede 18, DK-1255 Copenhagen K, Denmark and the Nordic Statistical Secretariat, Postboks 2550, DK-2100 Copenhagen 0, Denmark; *The Yearbook of Nordic Statistics.*

Statistical Office of the United Nations, Publishing Service, New York, New York 10017 (800) 253-9646; *Annual Bulletin of Transport Statistics for Europe.*

SWEDEN - HOME FINANCE

Organisation for Economic Co-operation and Development (OECD), 2 rue Andre-Pascal, 75 Paris 16, France (Telephone Number in U.S. (202) 785-6323); *Main Economic Indicators - Historical Statistics.*

SWEDEN - HORSES - See SWEDEN - LIVESTOCK AND POULTRY

SWEDEN - HOURS OF WORK - See SWEDEN - EMPLOYMENT

SWEDEN - HOUSING AND HOUSING UNITS

Facts on File, 460 Park Avenue South, New York, New York 10016 (800) 443-8323; *The New Book of World Rankings.*

Nordic Council of Ministers, Store Strandstraede 18, DK-1255 Copenhagen K, Denmark and the Nordic Statistical Secretariat, Postboks 2550, DK-2100 Copenhagen 0, Denmark; *The Yearbook of Nordic Statistics.*

Statistical Office of the United Nations, Publishing Service, New York, New York 10017 (800) 253-9646; *Statistical Yearbook.*

SWEDEN - HOUSING CONSTRUCTION

Nordic Council of Ministers, Store Strandstraede 18, DK-1255 Copenhagen K, Denmark and the Nordic Statistical Secretariat, Postboks 2550, DK-2100 Copenhagen 0, Denmark; *The Yearbook of Nordic Statistics.*

Organisation for Economic Co-operation and Development (OECD), 2 rue Andre-Pascal, 75 Paris 16, France (Telephone Number in U.S. (202) 785-6323); *The Iron and Steel Industry.*

SWEDEN - HOUSING EXPENDITURES

International Monetary Fund, 700 Nineteenth Street, NW, Washington, D.C. 20431 (202) 623-7000; *Government Finance Statistics Yearbook.*

SWEDEN - HYDROCHLORIC ACID PRODUCTION

Statistical Office of the United Nations, Publishing Service, New York, New York 10017 (800) 253-9646; *Statistical Yearbook.*

SWEDEN - ILLITERATE POPULATION

The Economist Intelligence Unit, 111 West 57th Street, New York, New York 10019 (800) 938-4685; *The World Market Atlas.*

G.K. Hall and Company, 70 Lincoln Street, Boston, Massachusetts 02111 (617) 423-3990; *The World in Figures.*

SWEDEN - IMPORTS

American Automobile Manufacturers Association, 1401 H Eye Street, NW, Suite 900, Washington, D.C. 20005 (202) 326-5500; *World Motor Vehicle Data.*

The Economist Intelligence Unit, 111 West 57th Street, New York, New York 10019 (800) 938-4685; *The World Market Atlas.*

Food and Agricultural Organization of the United Nations (FAO) Via delle Terme di Caracalla, 00100 Rome, Italy (Telephone Number in U.S. (202) 653-2400); *The State of Food and Agriculture.*

G.K. Hall and Company, 70 Lincoln Street, Boston, Massachusetts 02111 (617) 423-3990; *The World in Figures.*

International Lead and Zinc Study Group, Metro House, 58 St. James's Street, London SW1A 1LD, England; *Lead and Zinc Statistics.*

International Monetary Fund, 700 Nineteenth Street, NW, Washington, D.C. 20431 (202) 623-7000; *Direction of Trade Statistics, Government Finance Statistics Yearbook,* and *International Financial Statistics.*

International Rubber Study Group, York House, Eighth Floor, Empire Way, Wembley, London HA9 0PA, England; *Rubber Statistical Bulletin.*

Nordic Council of Ministers, Store Strandstraede 18, DK-1255 Copenhagen K, Denmark and the Nordic Statistical Secretariat, Postboks 2550, DK-2100 Copenhagen 0, Denmark; *The Yearbook of Nordic Statistics.*

Organisation for Economic Co-operation and Development (OECD), 2 rue Andre-Pascal, 75 Paris 16, France (Telephone Number in U.S.

(202) 785-6323); *Economic Outlook, The Footwear, Raw Hides and Skins, and Leather Industry in OECD Countries, Industrial Structure Statistics, The Iron and Steel Industry, Milk, Milk Products, and Egg Balances in OECD Member Countries, OECD Economic Surveys: Sweden, The Pulp and Paper Industry,* and *Review of Fisheries in OECD Member Countries.*

Times Books, 201 East 50th Street, New York, New York 10022 (212) 751-2600; *The Economist Book of Vital World Statistics.*

The World Bank, 1818 H Street, NW, Washington, D.C. 20433 (202) 477-1234; *World Tables.*

SWEDEN - INCOME TAXES - See SWEDEN - TAXATION

SWEDEN - INDUSTRIAL METALS PRODUCTION - See SWEDEN - MINING AND MINERAL PRODUCTS

SWEDEN - INDUSTRY

Facts on File, 460 Park Avenue South, New York, New York 10016 (800) 443-8323; *The New Book of World Rankings.*

G.K. Hall and Company, 70 Lincoln Street, Boston, Massachusetts 02111 (617) 423-3990; *The World in Figures.*

International Labour Office, I.L.O. Publications, CH-1211, Geneva 22, Switzerland; *Yearbook of Labour Statistics.*

Nordic Council of Ministers, Store Strandstraede 18, DK-1255 Copenhagen K, Denmark and the Nordic Statistical Secretariat, Postboks 2550, DK-2100 Copenhagen 0, Denmark; *The Yearbook of Nordic Statistics.*

Organisation for Economic Co-operation and Development (OECD), 2 rue Andre-Pascal, 75 Paris 16, France (Telephone Number in U.S. (202) 785-6323); *Economic Outlook, Industrial Structure Statistics, Indicators of Industrial Activity, Main Economic Indicators - Historical Statistics,* and *OECD Environmental Data.*

Statistical Office of the United Nations, Publishing Service, New York, New York 10017 (800) 253-9646; *Statistical Yearbook.*

Times Books, 201 East 50th Street, New York, New York 10022 (212) 751-2600; *The Economist Book of Vital World Statistics.*

The World Bank, 1818 H Street, NW, Washington, D.C. 20433 (202) 477-1234; *World Tables.*

World Intellectual Property Organization, 34 Chemin des Colombettes, CH-1211 Geneva 20. Switzerland; *Industrial Property Statistics.*

SWEDEN - INFANT AND MATERNAL MORTALITY

Nordic Council of Ministers, Store Strandstraede 18, DK-1255 Copenhagen K, Denmark and the Nordic Statistical Secretariat, Postboks 2550, DK-2100 Copenhagen 0, Denmark; *The Yearbook of Nordic Statistics.*

Statistical Office of the United Nations, Publishing Service, New York, New York 10017 (800) 253-9646; *Demographic Yearbook.*

Times Books, 201 East 50th Street, New York, New York 10022 (212) 751-2600; *The Economist Book of Vital World Statistics.*

The World Bank, 1818 H Street, NW, Washington, D.C. 20433 (202) 477-1234; *World Tables.*

World Health Organization, Office of Publications, Avenue Appia, CH-1211 Geneva 27, Switzerland (Telephone Number in U.S. (518) 436-9686); *World Health Statistics Annual.*

SWEDEN - INTEREST RATES

Organisation for Economic Co-operation and Development (OECD), 2 rue Andre-Pascal, 75 Paris 16, France (Telephone Number in U.S. (202) 785-6323); *Economic Outlook, Financial Market Trends, Main Economic Indicators - Historical Statistics,* and *OECD Financial Statistics.*

SWEDEN - INTERNAL TRADE

Nordic Council of Ministers, Store Strandstraede 18, DK-1255 Copenhagen K, Denmark and the Nordic Statistical Secretariat, Postboks 2550, DK-2100 Copenhagen 0, Denmark; *The Yearbook of Nordic Statistics.*

Organisation for Economic Co-operation and Development (OECD), 2 rue Andre-Pascal, 75 Paris 16, France (Telephone Number in U.S. (202) 785-6323); *Main Economic Indicators - Historical Statistics.*

Statistical Office of the United Nations, Publishing Service, New York, New York 10017 (800) 253-9646; *Statistical Yearbook.*

SWEDEN - INTERNATIONAL FINANCE

Organisation for Economic Co-operation and Development (OECD), 2 rue Andre-Pascal, 75 Paris 16, France (Telephone Number in U.S. (202) 785-6323); *Economic Outlook,* and *Financial Market Trends.*

SWEDEN - INTERNATIONAL LIQUIDITY

International Monetary Fund, 700 Nineteenth Street, NW, Washington, D.C. 20431 (202) 623-7000; *International Financial Statistics.*

Organisation for Economic Co-operation and Development (OECD), 2 rue Andre-Pascal, 75 Paris 16, France (Telephone Number in U.S. (202) 785-6323); *Economic Outlook,* and *Financial Market Trends.*

SWEDEN - INTERNATIONAL RESERVES EXCLUDING GOLD

Statistical Office of the United Nations, Publishing Service, New York, New York 10017 (800) 253-9646; *Statistical Yearbook.*

The World Bank, 1818 H Street, NW, Washington, D.C. 20433 (202) 477-1234; *World Tables.*

SWEDEN - INTERNATIONAL STATISTICS

Organisation for Economic Co-operation and Development (OECD), 2 rue Andre-Pascal, 75 Paris 16, France (Telephone Number in U.S. (202) 785-6323); *Financial Market Trends,* and *Tourism Policy and International Tourism in OECD Member Countries.*

SWEDEN - INVESTMENTS

International Monetary Fund, 700 Nineteenth Street, NW, Washington, D.C. 20431 (202) 623-7000; *International Financial Statistics.*

Organisation for Economic Co-operation and Development (OECD), 2 rue Andre-Pascal, 75 Paris 16, France (Telephone Number in U.S. (202) 785-6323); *Economic Outlook, Financial Market Trends, Industrial Structure Statistics, The Iron and Steel Industry,* and *Textile Industry in OECD Countries.*

SWEDEN - IRON ORE PRODUCTION AND CONSUMPTION - See SWEDEN - MINING AND MINERAL PRODUCTS

SWEDEN - LABOR FORCE

Facts on File, 460 Park Avenue South, New York, New York 10016 (800) 443-8323; *The New Book of World Rankings.*

Food and Agricultural Organization of the United Nations (FAO) Via delle Terme di Caracalla, 00100 Rome, Italy (Telephone Number in U.S. (202) 653-2400); *The State of Food and Agriculture.*

G.K. Hall and Company, 70 Lincoln Street, Boston, Massachusetts 02111 (617) 423-3990; *The World in Figures.*

Nordic Council of Ministers, Store Strandstraede 18, DK-1255 Copenhagen K, Denmark and the Nordic Statistical Secretariat, Postboks 2550, DK-2100 Copenhagen 0, Denmark; *The Yearbook of Nordic Statistics.*

Organisation for Economic Co-operation and Development (OECD), 2 rue Andre-Pascal, 75 Paris 16, France (Telephone Number in U.S. (202) 785-6323); *Economic Outlook, The Iron and Steel Industry, Main Economic Indicators - Historical Statistics, Maritime Transport, OECD Employment Outlook, OECD Economic Surveys: Sweden,* and *Textile Industry in OECD Countries.*

Times Books, 201 East 50th Street, New York, New York 10022 (212) 751-3600; *The Economist Book of Vital World Statistics.*

The World Bank, 1818 H Street, NW, Washington, D.C. 20433 (202) 477-1234; *World Tables.*

SWEDEN - LABOR PRODUCTIVITY

International Labour Office, I.L.O. Publications, CH-1211, Geneva 22, Switzerland; *Yearbook of Labour Statistics.*

Organisation for Economic Co-operation and Development (OECD), 2 rue Andre-Pascal, 75 Paris 16, France (Telephone Number in U.S. (202) 785-6323); *Economic Outlook,* and *OECD Employment Outlook.*

SWEDEN - LAND USE

Euromonitor Publications Limited, 87-88 Turnmill Street, London EC1M 5QU, England; *European Marketing Data and Statistics.*

Food and Agricultural Organization of the United Nations (FAO), Via delle Terme di Caracalla, 00100 Rome, Italy (Telephone Number in U.S. (202) 653-2400); *Production Yearbook.*

G.K. Hall and Company, 70 Lincoln Street, Boston, Massachusetts 02111 (617) 423-3990; *The World in Figures.*

SWEDEN - LEAD AND LEAD ORE PRODUCTION AND CONSUMPTION - See SWEDEN - MINING AND MINERAL PRODUCTS

SWEDEN - LEATHER - PRODUCTION INDEX

Organisation for Economic Co-operation and Development (OECD), 2 rue Andre-Pascal, 75 Paris 16, France (Telephone Number in U.S. (202) 785-6323); *Indicators of Industrial Activity.*

SWEDEN - LEATHER AND FOOTWEAR - EXPORTS AND IMPORTS

Organisation for Economic Co-operation and Development (OECD), 2 rue Andre-Pascal, 75 Paris 16, France (Telephone Number in U.S. (202) 785-6323); *The Footwear, Raw Hides and Skins, and Leather Industry in OECD Countries.*

SWEDEN - LIBRARIES

Euromonitor Publications Limited, 87-88 Turnmill Street, London EC1M 5QU, England; *European Marketing Data and Statistics*.

Facts on File, 460 Park Avenue South, New York, New York 10016 (800) 443-8323; *The New Book of World Rankings*.

Nordic Council of Ministers, Store Strandstraede 18, DK-1255 Copenhagen K, Denmark and the Nordic Statistical Secretariat, Postboks 2550, DK-2100 Copenhagen 0, Denmark; *The Yearbook of Nordic Statistics*.

United Nations Educational, Scientific and Cultural Organization (UNESCO), 7 Place de Fontenoy, F-75700 Paris, France (Telephone Number in U.S. (212) 963-5981); *Statistical Yearbook*.

SWEDEN - LIGNITE PRODUCTION - See SWEDEN - MINING AND MINERAL PRODUCTS

SWEDEN - LIVESTOCK AND POULTRY

Euromonitor Publications Limited, 87-88 Turnmill Street, London EC1M 5QU, England; *European Marketing Data and Statistics*.

Facts on File, 460 Park Avenue South, New York, New York 10016 (800) 443-8323; *The New Book of World Rankings*.

Food and Agricultural Organization of the United Nations (FAO), Via delle Terme di Caracalla, 00100 Rome, Italy (Telephone Number in U.S. (202) 653-2400); *Production Yearbook*, and *The State of Food and Agriculture*.

G.K. Hall and Company, 70 Lincoln Street, Boston, Massachusetts 02111 (617) 423-3990; *The World in Figures*.

Nordic Council of Ministers, Store Strandstraede 18, DK-1255 Copenhagen K, Denmark and the Nordic Statistical Secretariat, Postboks 2550, DK-2100 Copenhagen 0, Denmark; *The Yearbook of Nordic Statistics*.

Organisation for Economic Co-operation and Development (OECD), 2 rue Andre-Pascal, 75 Paris 16, France (Telephone Number in U.S. (202) 785-6323); *Economic Accounts for Agriculture*, and *Meat Balances in OECD Member Countries*.

Statistical Office of the United Nations, Publishing Service, New York, New York 10017 (800) 253-9646; *Statistical Yearbook*.

SWEDEN - LIVING LEVELS

G.K. Hall and Company, 70 Lincoln Street, Boston, Massachusetts 02111 (617) 423-3990; *The World in Figures*.

Organisation for Economic Co-operation and Development (OECD), 2 rue Andre-Pascal, 75 Paris 16, France (Telephone Number in U.S. (202) 785-6323); *Economic Outlook*.

Times Books, 201 East 50th Street, New York, New York 10022 (212) 751-2600; *The Economist Book of Vital World Statistics*.

SWEDEN - MACHINERY - PRODUCTION INDEX

Organisation for Economic Co-operation and Development (OECD), 2 rue Andre-Pascal, 75 Paris 16, France (Telephone Number in U.S. (202) 785-6323); *Indicators of Industrial Activity*.

SWEDEN - MAGNESIUM PRODUCTION AND CONSUMPTION - See SWEDEN - MINING AND MINERAL PRODUCTS

SWEDEN - MAIL - NUMBER OF PIECES SENT OR RECEIVED

Nordic Council of Ministers, Store Strandstraede 18, DK-1255 Copenhagen K, Denmark and the Nordic Statistical Secretariat, Postboks 2550, DK-2100 Copenhagen 0, Denmark; *The Yearbook of Nordic Statistics*.

Statistical Office of the United Nations, Publishing Service, New York, New York 10017 (800) 253-9646; *Statistical Yearbook*.

SWEDEN - MAIN ECONOMIC INDICATORS - See SWEDEN - ECONOMY

SWEDEN - MAIN INDICATORS - See SWEDEN - ECONOMY

SWEDEN - MANGANESE AND MANGANESE ORE PRODUCTION AND CONSUMPTION - See SWEDEN - MINING AND MINERAL PRODUCTS

SWEDEN - MANUFACTURING

American Automobile Manufacturers Association, 1401 H Eye Street, NW, Suite 900, Washington, D.C. 20005 (202) 326-5500; *World Motor Vehicle Data*.

Facts on File, 460 Park Avenue South, New York, New York 10016 (800) 443-8323; *The New Book of World Rankings*.

G.K. Hall and Company, 70 Lincoln Street, Boston, Massachusetts 02111 (617) 423-3990; *The World in Figures*.

Nordic Council of Ministers, Store Strandstraede 18, DK-1255 Copenhagen K, Denmark and the Nordic Statistical Secretariat, Postboks 2550, DK-2100 Copenhagen 0, Denmark; *The Yearbook of Nordic Statistics*.

Organisation for Economic Co-operation and Development (OECD), 2 rue Andre-Pascal, 75 Paris 16, France (Telephone Number in U.S. (202) 785-6323); *Foreign Trade by Commodities*, *Indicators of Industrial Activity*, *Industrial Structure Statistics*, and *OECD Economic Surveys: Sweden*.

Statistical Office of the United Nations, Publishing Service, New York, New York 10017 (800) 253-9646; *Statistical Yearbook*.

Times Books, 201 East 50th Street, New York, New York 10022 (212) 751-2600; *The Economist Book of Vital World Statistics*.

The World Bank, 1818 H Street, NW, Washington, D.C. 20433 (202) 477-1234; *World Tables*.

SWEDEN - MARRIAGE RATE

Facts on File, 460 Park Avenue South, New York, New York 10016 (800) 443-8323; *The New Book of World Rankings*.

Nordic Council of Ministers, Store Strandstraede 18, DK-1255 Copenhagen K, Denmark and the Nordic Statistical Secretariat, Postboks 2550, DK-2100 Copenhagen 0, Denmark; *The Yearbook of Nordic Statistics*.

Statistical Office of the United Nations, Publishing Service, New York, New York 10017 (800) 253-9646; *Demographic Yearbook*, and *Statistical Yearbook*.

SWEDEN - MEAT PRODUCTION - See SWEDEN - LIVESTOCK AND POULTRY

SWEDEN - MERCHANT SHIPPING

G.K. Hall and Company, 70 Lincoln Street, Boston, Massachusetts 02111 (617) 423-3990; *The World in Figures*.

International Criminal Police Organization (INTERPOL), 26 rue Armengaud, 92210 Saint Cloud, France; *International Crime Statistics*.

Nordic Council of Ministers, Store Strandstraede 18, DK-1255 Copenhagen K, Denmark and the Nordic Statistical Secretariat, Postboks 2550, DK-2100 Copenhagen 0, Denmark; *The Yearbook of Nordic Statistics*.

Organisation for Economic Co-operation and Development (OECD), 2 rue Andre-Pascal, 75 Paris 16, France (Telephone Number in U.S. (202) 785-6323); *Maritime Transport*.

Statistical Office of the United Nations, Publishing Service, New York, New York 10017 (800) 253-9646; *Statistical Yearbook*.

Times Books, 201 East 50th Street, New York, New York 10022 (212) 751-2600; *The Economist Book of Vital World Statistics*.

U.S. Department of Transportation, Maritime Administration, 400 Seventh Street, SW, Washington, D.C. 20590 (202) 366-5807; *A Statistical Analysis of the World's Merchant Fleets*.

SWEDEN - MERCURY PRODUCTION AND CONSUMPTION - See SWEDEN - MINING AND MINERAL PRODUCTS

SWEDEN - MILITARY

G.K. Hall and Company, 70 Lincoln Street, Boston, Massachusetts 02111 (617) 423-3990; *The World in Figures*.

The International Institute for Strategic Studies, 23 Tavistock Street, London WC2E 7NQ, England; *The Military Balance*.

Nordic Council of Ministers, Store Strandstraede 18, DK-1255 Copenhagen K, Denmark and the Nordic Statistical Secretariat, Postboks 2550, DK-2100 Copenhagen 0, Denmark; *The Yearbook of Nordic Statistics*.

U.S. Arms Control and Disarmament Agency, 320 Twenty-first Street, NW, Washington, D.C. 20451 (202) 647-8677; *World Military Expenditures and Arms Transfers*.

SWEDEN - MILK PRODUCTION - See SWEDEN - DAIRY PRODUCTS

SWEDEN - MINING AND MINERAL PRODUCTS

Commodity Research Bureau, Incorporated, 75 Wall Street, New York, New York 10005 (212) 504-7754; *Commodity Year Book*.

Facts on File, 460 Park Avenue South, New York, New York 10016 (800) 443-8323; *The New Book of World Rankings*.

G.K. Hall and Company, 70 Lincoln Street, Boston, Massachusetts 02111 (617) 423-3990; *The World in Figures*.

International Lead and Zinc Study Group, Metro House, 58 St. James's Street, London SW1A 1LD, England; *Lead and Zinc Statistics*.

Nordic Council of Ministers, Store Strandstraede 18, DK-1255 Copenhagen K, Denmark and the Nordic Statistical Secretariat, Postboks 2550, DK-2100 Copenhagen 0, Denmark; *The Yearbook of Nordic Statistics*.

Organisation for Economic Co-operation and Development (OECD), 2 rue Andre-Pascal, 75 Paris 16, France (Telephone Number in U.S. (202) 785-6323); *Coal Information, Energy Statistics of OECD Countries, Foreign Trade by Commodities, Indicators of Industrial Activity, Industrial Structure Statistics, The Iron and Steel Industry, The Non-Ferrous Metals Industry*, and *OECD Economic Surveys: Sweden*.

Statistical Office of the United Nations, Publishing Service, New York, New York 10017 (800) 253-9646; *Statistical Yearbook*.

World Bureau of Metal Statistics, 27-A High Street, Ware Hert SG12 9BA, England; *World Metal Statistics*.

SWEDEN - MOLYBDENUM AND MOLYBDENUM ORE PRODUCTION AND CONSUMPTION - See SWEDEN - MINING AND MINERAL PRODUCTS

SWEDEN - MONEY AND CREDIT

Organisation for Economic Cooperation and Development (OECD), 2 rue Andre-Pascal, 75 Paris 16, France (Telephone Number in U.S. (202) 785-6323); *OECD Economic Surveys: Sweden*.

SWEDEN - MONEY EXCHANGE RATE

International Monetary Fund, 700 Nineteenth Street, NW, Washington, D.C. 20431 (202) 623-7000; *International Financial Statistics*.

Organisation for Economic Co-operation and Development (OECD), 2 rue Andre-Pascal, 75 Paris 16, France (Telephone Number in U.S. (202) 785-6323); *Economic Outlook, Financial Market Trends*, and *Tourism Policy and International Tourism in OECD Member Countries*.

Statistical Office of the United Nations, Publishing Service, New York, New York 10017 (800) 253-9646; *Statistical Yearbook*.

SWEDEN - MONEY RATES - MARKET

Organisation for Economic Co-operation and Development (OECD), 2 rue Andre-Pascal, 75 Paris 16, France (Telephone Number in U.S. (202) 785-6323); *Economic Outlook*, and *Financial Market Trends*.

SWEDEN - MONEY RESERVES

Organisation for Economic Co-operation and Development (OECD), 2 rue Andre-Pascal, 75 Paris 16, France (Telephone Number in U.S. (202) 785-6323); *Economic Outlook*, and *Financial Market Trends*.

SWEDEN - MONEY SUPPLY

G.K. Hall and Company, 70 Lincoln Street, Boston, Massachusetts 02111 (617) 423-3990; *The World in Figures*.

International Monetary Fund, 700 Nineteenth Street, NW, Washington, D.C. 20431 (202) 623-7000; *International Financial Statistics*.

Nordic Council of Ministers, Store Strandstraede 18, DK-1255 Copenhagen K, Denmark and the Nordic Statistical Secretariat, Postboks 2550, DK-2100 Copenhagen 0, Denmark; *The Yearbook of Nordic Statistics*.

Organisation for Economic Co-operation and Development (OECD), 2 rue Andre-Pascal, 75 Paris 16, France (Telephone Number in U.S. (202) 785-6323); *Economic Outlook*.

Statistical Office of the United Nations, Publishing Service, New York, New York 10017 (800) 253-9646; *Statistical Yearbook*.

The World Bank, 1818 H Street, NW, Washington, D.C. 20433 (202) 477-1234; *World Tables*.

SWEDEN - MONUMENTS AND HISTORICAL SITES

United Nations Educational, Scientific and Cultural Organization (UNESCO), 7 Place de Fontenoy, F-75700 Paris, France (Telephone Number in U.S. (212) 963-5981); *Statistical Yearbook*.

SWEDEN - MOTION PICTURES

Statistical Office of the United Nations, Publishing Service, New York, New York 10017 (800) 253-9646; *Statistical Yearbook*.

United Nations Educational, Scientific and Cultural Organization (UNESCO), 7 Place de Fontenoy, F-75700 Paris, France (Telephone Number in U.S. (212) 963-5981); *Statistical Yearbook*.

SWEDEN - MOTOR VEHICLE PRODUCTION

American Automobile Manufacturers Association, 1401 H Eye Street, NW, Suite 900, Washington, D.C. 20005 (202) 326-5500; *World Motor Vehicle Data*.

Organisation for Economic Co-operation and Development (OECD), 2 rue Andre-Pascal, 75 Paris 16, France (Telephone Number in U.S. (202) 785-6323); *Foreign Trade by Commodities*, and *Indicators of Industrial Activity*.

Statistical Office of the United Nations, Publishing Service, New York, New York 10017 (800) 253-9646; *Statistical Yearbook*.

SWEDEN - MOTOR VEHICLE TAXES - See SWEDEN - TAXATION

SWEDEN - MOTOR VEHICLES IN USE

American Automobile Manufacturers Association, 1401 H Eye Street, NW, Suite 900, Washington, D.C. 20005 (202) 326-5500; *World Motor Vehicle Data*.

G.K. Hall and Company, 70 Lincoln Street, Boston, Massachusetts 02111 (617) 423-3990; *The World in Figures*.

International Road Federation, 525 School Street, SW, Washington, D.C. 20024 (202) 554-2106; *World Road Statistics*.

Nordic Council of Ministers, Store Strandstraede 18, DK-1255 Copenhagen K, Denmark and the Nordic Statistical Secretariat, Postboks 2550, DK-2100 Copenhagen 0, Denmark; *The Yearbook of Nordic Statistics*.

Statistical Office of the United Nations, Publishing Service, New York, New York 10017 (800) 253-9646; *Statistical Yearbook*.

Times Books, 201 East 50th Street, New York, New York 10022 (212) 751-2600; *The Economist Book of Vital World Statistics*.

SWEDEN - MUSEUMS

Euromonitor Publications Limited, 87-88 Turnmill Street, London EC1M 5QU, England; *European Marketing Data and Statistics*.

Facts on File, 460 Park Avenue South, New York, New York 10016 (800) 443-8323; *The New Book of World Rankings*.

Nordic Council of Ministers, Store Strandstraede 18, DK-1255 Copenhagen K, Denmark and the Nordic Statistical Secretariat, Postboks 2550, DK-2100 Copenhagen 0, Denmark; *The Yearbook of Nordic Statistics*.

United Nations Educational, Scientific and Cultural Organization (UNESCO), 7 Place de Fontenoy, F-75700 Paris, France (Telephone Number in U.S. (212) 963-5981); *Statistical Yearbook*.

SWEDEN - NATALITY - See SWEDEN - BIRTH RATE

SWEDEN - NATIONAL ACCOUNTS

International Monetary Fund, 700 Nineteenth Street, NW, Washington, D.C. 20431 (202) 623-7000; *International Financial Statistics*.

Nordic Council of Ministers, Store Strandstraede 18, DK-1255 Copenhagen K, Denmark and the Nordic Statistical Secretariat, Postboks 2550, DK-2100 Copenhagen 0, Denmark; *The Yearbook of Nordic Statistics*.

Organisation for Economic Co-operation and Development (OECD), 2 rue Andre-Pascal, 75 Paris 16, France (Telephone Number in U.S. (202) 785-6323); *Economic Outlook*.

Statistical Office of the United Nations, Publishing Service, New York, New York 10017 (800) 253-9646; *National Accounts Statistics*, and *Statistical Yearbook*.

SWEDEN - NATIONAL INCOME

Facts on File, 460 Park Avenue South, New York, New York 10016 (800) 443-8323; *The New Book of World Rankings*.

G.K. Hall and Company, 70 Lincoln Street, Boston, Massachusetts 02111 (617) 423-3990; *The World in Figures*.

Nordic Council of Ministers, Store Strandstraede 18, DK-1255 Copenhagen K, Denmark and the Nordic Statistical Secretariat, Postboks 2550, DK-2100 Copenhagen 0, Denmark; *The Yearbook of Nordic Statistics*.

Organisation for Economic Co-operation and Development (OECD), 2 rue Andre-Pascal, 75 Paris 16, France (Telephone Number in U.S. (202) 785-6323); *Economic Outlook*.

Statistical Office of the United Nations, Publishing Service, New York, New York 10017 (800) 253-9646; *Statistical Yearbook*.

SWEDEN - NATIONAL PRODUCT

Facts on File, 460 Park Avenue South, New York, New York 10016 (800) 443-8323; *The New Book of World Rankings*.

Organisation for Economic Co-operation and Development (OECD), 2 rue Andre-Pascal, 75 Paris 16, France (Telephone Number in U.S. (202) 785-6323); *Economic Outlook*, and *Main Economic Indicators - Historical Statistics*.

Statistical Office of the United Nations, Publishing Service, New York, New York 10017 (800) 253-9646; *Statistical Yearbook*.

SWEDEN - NATURAL GAS PRODUCTION - See SWEDEN - MINING AND MINERAL PRODUCTS

SWEDEN - NATURAL RUBBER PRODUCTION

International Rubber Study Group, York House, Eighth Floor, Empire Way, Wembley, London HA9 0PA, England; *Rubber Statistical Bulletin.*

SWEDEN - NEWSPAPER - See SWEDEN - FORESTRY AND FOREST PRODUCTS

SWEDEN - NEWSPRINT PRODUCTION AND CONSUMPTION - See SWEDEN - FORESTRY AND FOREST PRODUCTS

SWEDEN - NICKEL AND NICKEL ORE PRODUCTION AND CONSUMPTION - See SWEDEN - MINING AND MINERAL PRODUCTS

SWEDEN - NITRIC ACID PRODUCTION - See SWEDEN - MINING AND MINERAL PRODUCTS

SWEDEN - OATS PRODUCTION - See SWEDEN - CROPS

SWEDEN - OCCUPATIONS - See SWEDEN - LABOR FORCE

SWEDEN - OIL PRODUCING CROPS

Organisation for Economic Co-operation and Development (OECD), 2 rue Andre-Pascal, 75 Paris 16, France (Telephone Number in U.S. (202) 785-6323); *Foreign Trade by Commodities.*

SWEDEN - PAPER - See SWEDEN - FORESTRY AND FOREST PRODUCTS

SWEDEN - PATENTS

Nordic Council of Ministers, Store Strandstraede 18, DK-1255 Copenhagen K, Denmark and the Nordic Statistical Secretariat, Postboks 2550, DK-2100 Copenhagen 0, Denmark; *The Yearbook of Nordic Statistics.*

Statistical Office of the United Nations, Publishing Service, New York, New York 10017 (800) 253-9646; *Statistical Yearbook.*

World Intellectual Property Organization, 34 Chemin des Colombettes, CH-1211 Geneva 20. Switzerland; *Industrial Property Statistics.*

SWEDEN - PEANUT PRODUCTION - See SWEDEN - CROPS

SWEDEN - PERIODICALS

United Nations Educational, Scientific and Cultural Organization (UNESCO), 7 Place de Fontenoy, F-75700 Paris, France (Telephone Number in U.S. (212) 963-5981); *Statistical Yearbook.*

SWEDEN - PESTICIDE USE

Food and Agricultural Organization of the United Nations (FAO) Via delle Terme di Caracalla, 00100 Rome, Italy (Telephone Number in U.S. (202) 653-2400); *The State of Food and Agriculture.*

SWEDEN - PETROLEUM INDUSTRY

Euromonitor Publications Limited, 87-88 Turnmill Street, London EC1M 5QU, England; *European Marketing Data and Statistics.*

Facts on File, 460 Park Avenue South, New York, New York 10016 (800) 443-8323; *The New Book of World Rankings.*

Food and Agricultural Organization of the United Nations (FAO) Via delle Terme di Caracalla, 00100 Rome, Italy (Telephone Number in

U.S. (202) 653-2400); *The State of Food and Agriculture.*

G.K. Hall and Company, 70 Lincoln Street, Boston, Massachusetts 02111 (617) 423-3990; *The World in Figures.*

Organisation for Economic Co-operation and Development (OECD), 2 rue Andre-Pascal, 75 Paris 16, France (Telephone Number in U.S. (202) 785-6323); *Energy Statistics of OECD Countries, Foreign Trade by Commodities, Indicators of Industrial Activity,* and *Oil and Gas Information.*

Statistical Office of the United Nations, Publishing Service, New York, New York 10017 (800) 253-9646; *Statistical Yearbook.*

SWEDEN - PHOSPHATE ROCK PRODUCTION - See SWEDEN - MINING AND MINERAL PRODUCTS

SWEDEN - PHOSPHATES PRODUCTION - See SWEDEN - MINING AND MINERAL PRODUCTS

SWEDEN - PIG-IRON AND FERRO-ALLOY PRODUCTION - See SWEDEN - MINING AND MINERAL PRODUCTS

SWEDEN - PIGS - See SWEDEN - LIVESTOCK AND POULTRY

SWEDEN - PLASTIC AND RESIN PRODUCTION

Organisation for Economic Co-operation and Development (OECD), 2 rue Andre-Pascal, 75 Paris 16, France (Telephone Number in U.S. (202) 785-6323); *Foreign Trade by Commodities.*

Statistical Office of the United Nations, Publishing Service, New York, New York 10017 (800) 253-9646; *Statistical Yearbook.*

SWEDEN - PLATINUM PRODUCTION AND CONSUMPTION - See SWEDEN - MINING AND MINERAL PRODUCTS

SWEDEN - POPULATION

The Economist Intelligence Unit, 111 West 57th Street, New York, New York 10019 (800) 938-4685; *The World Market Atlas.*

Euromonitor Publications Limited, 87-88 Turnmill Street, London EC1M 5QU, England; *European Marketing Data and Statistics.*

Facts on File, 460 Park Avenue South, New York, New York 10016 (800) 443-8323; *The New Book of World Rankings.*

Food and Agricultural Organization of the United Nations (FAO), Via delle Terme di Caracalla, 00100 Rome, Italy (Telephone Number in U.S. (202) 653-2400); *Production Yearbook.*

G.K. Hall and Company, 70 Lincoln Street, Boston, Massachusetts 02111 (617) 423-3990; *The World in Figures.*

International Labour Office, I.L.O. Publications, CH-1211, Geneva 22, Switzerland; *Yearbook of Labour Statistics.*

Nordic Council of Ministers, Store Strandstraede 18, DK-1255 Copenhagen K, Denmark and the Nordic Statistical Secretariat, Postboks 2550, DK-2100 Copenhagen 0, Denmark; *The Yearbook of Nordic Statistics.*

Statistical Office of the United Nations, Publishing Service, New York, New York 10017 (800) 253-9646; *Demographic Yearbook,* and *Statistical Yearbook.*

Times Books, 201 East 50th Street, New York, New York 10022 (212) 751-2600; *The Economist Book of Vital World Statistics.*

United Nations Educational, Scientific and Cultural Organization (UNESCO), 7 Place de Fontenoy, F-75700 Paris, France (Telephone Number in U.S. (212) 963-5981); *Statistical Yearbook.*

U.S. Arms Control and Disarmament Agency, 320 Twenty-first Street, NW, Washington, D.C. 20451 (202) 647-8677; *World Military Expenditures and Arms Transfers.*

World Health Organization, Office of Publications, Avenue Appia, CH-1211 Geneva 27, Switzerland (Telephone Number in U.S. (518) 436-9686); *World Health Statistics Annual.*

SWEDEN - POST OFFICES

Facts on File, 460 Park Avenue South, New York, New York 10016 (800) 443-8323; *The New Book of World Rankings.*

SWEDEN - POTATO PRODUCTION - See SWEDEN - CROPS

SWEDEN - POWER PRODUCTION INDUSTRY

Statistical Office of the United Nations, Publishing Service, New York, New York 10017 (800) 253-9646; *Statistical Yearbook.*

SWEDEN - PRICES

Facts on File, 460 Park Avenue South, New York, New York 10016 (800) 443-8323; *The New Book of World Rankings.*

Food and Agricultural Organization of the United Nations (FAO), Via delle Terme di Caracalla, 00100 Rome, Italy (Telephone Number in U.S. (202) 653-2400); *Production Yearbook,* and *The State of Food and Agriculture.*

G.K. Hall and Company, 70 Lincoln Street, Boston, Massachusetts 02111 (617) 423-3990; *The World in Figures.*

International Labour Office, I.L.O. Publications, CH-1211, Geneva 22, Switzerland; *Yearbook of Labour Statistics.*

International Lead and Zinc Study Group, Metro House, 58 St. James's Street, London SW1A 1LD, England; *Lead and Zinc Statistics.*

International Monetary Fund, 700 Nineteenth Street, NW, Washington, D.C. 20431 (202) 623-7000; *International Financial Statistics.*

International Rubber Study Group, York House, Eighth Floor, Empire Way, Wembley, London HA9 0PA, England; *Rubber Statistical Bulletin.*

Nordic Council of Ministers, Store Strandstraede 18, DK-1255 Copenhagen K, Denmark and the Nordic Statistical Secretariat, Postboks 2550, DK-2100 Copenhagen 0, Denmark; *The Yearbook of Nordic Statistics.*

Organisation for Economic Co-operation and Development (OECD), 2 rue Andre-Pascal, 75 Paris 16, France (Telephone Number in U.S. (202) 785-6323); *Economic Outlook, The Footwear, Raw Hides and Skins, and Leather Industry in OECD Countries, Indicators of Industrial Activity, The Iron and Steel Industry, Main Economic Indicators - Historical Statistics,* and *The Pulp and Paper Industry.*

World Bureau of Metal Statistics, 27-A High Street, Ware Hert SG12 9BA, England; *World Metal Statistics.*

SWEDEN - PRINTING AND WRITING PAPER - See SWEDEN - FORESTRY AND FOREST PRODUCTS

SWEDEN - PRODUCTION

American Automobile Manufacturers Association, 1401 H Eye Street, NW, Suite 900, Washington, D.C. 20005 (202) 326-5500; *World Motor Vehicle Data.*

Facts on File, 460 Park Avenue South, New York, New York 10016 (800) 443-8323; *The New Book of World Rankings.*

G.K. Hall and Company, 70 Lincoln Street, Boston, Massachusetts 02111 (617) 423-3990; *The World in Figures.*

International Lead and Zinc Study Group, Metro House, 58 St. James's Street, London SW1A 1LD, England; *Lead and Zinc Statistics.*

International Rubber Study Group, York House, Eighth Floor, Empire Way, Wembley, London HA9 0PA, England; *Rubber Statistical Bulletin.*

Organisation for Economic Co-operation and Development (OECD), 2 rue Andre-Pascal, 75 Paris 16, France (Telephone Number in U.S. (202) 785-6323); *Economic Outlook, The Footwear, Raw Hides and Skins, and Leather Industry in OECD Countries, Indicators of Industrial Activity, Industrial Structure Statistics, The Iron and Steel Industry, Meat Balances in OECD Member Countries, Milk, Milk Products, and Egg Balances in OECD Member Countries, The Non-Ferrous Metals Industry, The Pulp and Paper Industry,* and *Textile Industry in OECD Countries.*

SWEDEN - PRODUCTIVITY

Organisation for Economic Co-operation and Development (OECD), 2 rue Andre-Pascal, 75 Paris 16, France (Telephone Number in U.S. (202) 785-6323); *Economic Outlook.*

SWEDEN - PROPERTY TAXES - See SWEDEN - TAXATION

SWEDEN - PUBLIC CONSUMPTION FUND

Organisation for Economic Co-operation and Development (OECD), 2 rue Andre-Pascal, 75 Paris 16, France (Telephone Number in U.S. (202) 785-6323); *Revenue Statistics of OECD Member Countries.*

SWEDEN - PUBLIC EXPENDITURES

Organisation for Economic Co-operation and Development (OECD), 2 rue Andre-Pascal, 75 Paris 16, France (Telephone Number in U.S. (202) 785-6323); *Revenue Statistics of OECD Member Countries.*

SWEDEN - PUBLIC FINANCE

Facts on File, 460 Park Avenue South, New York, New York 10016 (800) 443-8323; *The New Book of World Rankings.*

Nordic Council of Ministers, Store Strandstraede 18, DK-1255 Copenhagen K, Denmark and the Nordic Statistical Secretariat, Postboks 2550, DK-2100 Copenhagen 0, Denmark; *The Yearbook of Nordic Statistics.*

Organisation for Economic Co-operation and Development (OECD), 2 rue Andre-Pascal, 75 Paris 16, France (Telephone Number in U.S. (202) 785-6323); *Revenue Statistics of OECD Member Countries.*

SWEDEN - PUBLIC REVENUES

Organisation for Economic Co-operation and Development (OECD), 2 rue Andre-Pascal, 75 Paris 16, France (Telephone Number in U.S. (202) 785-6323); *Revenue Statistics of OECD Member Countries.*

SWEDEN - RADIO BROADCASTING

Facts on File, 460 Park Avenue South, New York, New York 10016 (800) 443-8323; *The New Book of World Rankings*.

Nordic Council of Ministers, Store Strandstraede 18, DK-1255 Copenhagen K, Denmark and the Nordic Statistical Secretariat, Postboks 2550, DK-2100 Copenhagen 0, Denmark; *The Yearbook of Nordic Statistics*.

Times Books, 201 East 50th Street, New York, New York 10022 (212) 751-2600; *The Economist Book of Vital World Statistics*.

United Nations Educational, Scientific and Cultural Organization (UNESCO), 7 Place de Fontenoy, F-75700 Paris, France (Telephone Number in U.S. (212) 963-5981); *Statistical Yearbook*.

SWEDEN - RADIO RECEIVER PRODUCTION

Statistical Office of the United Nations, Publishing Service, New York, New York 10017 (800) 253-9646; *Statistical Yearbook*.

SWEDEN - RAILWAYS

Euromonitor Publications Limited, 87-88 Turnmill Street, London EC1M 5QU, England; *European Marketing Data and Statistics*.

G.K. Hall and Company, 70 Lincoln Street, Boston, Massachusetts 02111 (617) 423-3990; *The World in Figures*.

Jane's Information Group, Sentinel House, 163 Brighton Road, Coulsdon, Surrey CR5 2NH, England (Telephone Number in U.S. (703) 683-3700); *Jane's World Railways*.

Nordic Council of Ministers, Store Strandstraede 18, DK-1255 Copenhagen K, Denmark and the Nordic Statistical Secretariat, Postboks 2550, DK-2100 Copenhagen 0, Denmark; *The Yearbook of Nordic Statistics*.

Statistical Office of the United Nations, Publishing Service, New York, New York 10017 (800) 253-9646; *Annual Bulletin of Transport Statistics for Europe*, and *Statistical Yearbook*.

SWEDEN - RELIGION

Facts on File, 460 Park Avenue South, New York, New York 10016 (800) 443-8323; *The New Book of World Rankings*.

SWEDEN - RENT PRICES

International Labour Office, I.L.O. Publications, CH-1211, Geneva 22, Switzerland; *Yearbook of Labour Statistics*.

SWEDEN - RETAIL TRADE

G.K. Hall and Company, 70 Lincoln Street, Boston, Massachusetts 02111 (617) 423-3990; *The World in Figures*.

Statistical Office of the United Nations, Publishing Service, New York, New York 10017 (800) 253-9646; *Statistical Yearbook*.

SWEDEN - RICE PRODUCTION - See SWEDEN - CROPS

SWEDEN - ROUNDWOOD PRODUCTION - See SWEDEN - FORESTRY AND FOREST PRODUCTS

SWEDEN - RUBBER PRODUCTION AND CONSUMPTION

Facts on File, 460 Park Avenue South, New York, New York 10016 (800) 443-8323; *The New Book of World Rankings*.

International Rubber Study Group, York House, Eighth Floor, Empire Way, Wembley, London HA9 0PA, England; *Rubber Statistical Bulletin*.

Organisation for Economic Co-operation and Development (OECD), 2 rue Andre-Pascal, 75 Paris 16, France (Telephone Number in U.S. (202) 785-6323); *Foreign Trade by Commodities*.

Statistical Office of the United Nations, Publishing Service, New York, New York 10017 (800) 253-9646; *Statistical Yearbook*.

SWEDEN - SALT PRODUCTION - See SWEDEN - MINING AND MINERAL PRODUCTS

SWEDEN - SAWNWOOD PRODUCTION - See SWEDEN - FORESTRY AND FOREST PRODUCTS

SWEDEN - SCIENCE AND TECHNOLOGY - EXPENDITURE FOR RESEARCH

Statistical Office of the United Nations, Publishing Service, New York, New York 10017 (800) 253-9646; *Statistical Yearbook*.

SWEDEN - SCIENTISTS AND TECHNICIANS

Statistical Office of the United Nations, Publishing Service, New York, New York 10017 (800) 253-9646; *Statistical Yearbook*.

United Nations Educational, Scientific and Cultural Organization (UNESCO), 7 Place de Fontenoy, F-75700 Paris, France (Telephone Number in U.S. (212) 963-5981); *Statistical Yearbook*.

SWEDEN - SENIOR CITIZENS

Facts on File, 460 Park Avenue South, New York, New York 10016 (800) 443-8323; *The New Book of World Rankings*.

SWEDEN - SHEEP - See SWEDEN - LIVESTOCK AND POULTRY

SWEDEN - SHIPBUILDING - PRODUCTION INDEX

Organisation for Economic Co-operation and Development (OECD), 2 rue Andre-Pascal, 75 Paris 16, France (Telephone Number in U.S. (202) 785-6323); *Indicators of Industrial Activity*.

SWEDEN - SILVER PRODUCTION AND CONSUMPTION - See SWEDEN - MINING AND MINERAL PRODUCTS

SWEDEN - SOCIAL DATA

Facts on File, 460 Park Avenue South, New York, New York 10016 (800) 443-8323; *The New Book of World Rankings*.

G.K. Hall and Company, 70 Lincoln Street, Boston, Massachusetts 02111 (617) 423-3990; *The World in Figures*.

SWEDEN - SOCIAL SECURITY

International Monetary Fund, 700 Nineteenth Street, NW, Washington, D.C. 20431 (202) 623-7000; *Government Finance Statistics Yearbook*.

Nordic Council of Ministers, Store Strandstraede 18, DK-1255 Copenhagen K, Denmark and the Nordic Statistical Secretariat,

Postboks 2550, DK-2100 Copenhagen 0, Denmark; *The Yearbook of Nordic Statistics.*

Organisation for Economic Co-operation and Development (OECD), 2 rue Andre-Pascal, 75 Paris 16, France (Telephone Number in U.S. (202) 785-6323); *Revenue Statistics of OECD Member Countries.*

SWEDEN - SOCIOECONOMIC DATA

Organisation for Economic Co-operation and Development (OECD), 2 rue Andre-Pascal, 75 Paris 16, France (Telephone Number in U.S. (202) 785-6323); *Economic Outlook.*

SWEDEN - STAMP TAXES AND DUTIES - See SWEDEN - TAXATION

SWEDEN - STEEL - See SWEDEN - MINING AND MINERAL PRODUCTS

SWEDEN - STOCKS - COMMODITY - MARKET PRICE - INDEXES

Food and Agricultural Organization of the United Nations (FAO) Via delle Terme di Caracalla, 00100 Rome, Italy (Telephone Number in U.S. (202) 653-2400); *The State of Food and Agriculture.*

International Lead and Zinc Study Group, Metro House, 58 St. James's Street, London SW1A 1LD, England; *Lead and Zinc Statistics.*

Statistical Office of the United Nations, Publishing Service, New York, New York 10017 (800) 253-9646; *Statistical Yearbook.*

World Bureau of Metal Statistics, 27-A High Street, Ware Hert SG12 9BA, England; *World Metal Statistics.*

SWEDEN - SUGAR EXPORTS - See SWEDEN - CROPS

SWEDEN - SULPHUR AND SULPHURIC ACID PRODUCTION - See SWEDEN - MINING AND MINERAL PRODUCTS

SWEDEN - TAXATION

G.K. Hall and Company, 70 Lincoln Street, Boston, Massachusetts 02111 (617) 423-3990; *The World in Figures.*

International Monetary Fund, 700 Nineteenth Street, NW, Washington, D.C. 20431 (202) 623-7000; *Government Finance Statistics Yearbook.*

International Road Federation, 525 School Street, SW, Washington, D.C. 20024 (202) 554-2106; *World Road Statistics.*

Nordic Council of Ministers, Store Strandstraede 18, DK-1255 Copenhagen K, Denmark and the Nordic Statistical Secretariat, Postboks 2550, DK-2100 Copenhagen 0, Denmark; *The Yearbook of Nordic Statistics.*

Organisation for Economic Co-operation and Development (OECD), 2 rue Andre-Pascal, 75 Paris 16, France (Telephone Number in U.S. (202) 785-6323); *Revenue Statistics of OECD Member Countries.*

The World Bank, 1818 H Street, NW, Washington, D.C. 20433 (202) 477-1234; *World Tables.*

SWEDEN - TEA CONSUMPTION

Statistical Office of the United Nations, Publishing Service, New York, New York 10017 (800) 253-9646; *Statistical Yearbook.*

SWEDEN - TELEGRAPH SERVICE

Nordic Council of Ministers, Store Strandstraede 18, DK-1255 Copenhagen K, Denmark and the Nordic Statistical Secretariat, Postboks 2550, DK-2100 Copenhagen 0, Denmark; *The Yearbook of Nordic Statistics.*

Statistical Office of the United Nations, Publishing Service, New York, New York 10017 (800) 253-9646; *Statistical Yearbook.*

SWEDEN - TELEPHONES IN USE

American Telephone and Telegraph Company, 26 Parsippany Road, Whippany, New Jersey 07981 (800) 338-4038; *The World's Telephones.*

G.K. Hall and Company, 70 Lincoln Street, Boston, Massachusetts 02111 (617) 423-3990; *The World in Figures.*

Nordic Council of Ministers, Store Strandstraede 18, DK-1255 Copenhagen K, Denmark and the Nordic Statistical Secretariat, Postboks 2550, DK-2100 Copenhagen 0, Denmark; *The Yearbook of Nordic Statistics.*

Statistical Office of the United Nations, Publishing Service, New York, New York 10017 (800) 253-9646; *Statistical Yearbook.*

SWEDEN - TELEVISION BROADCASTING

Facts on File, 460 Park Avenue South, New York, New York 10016 (800) 443-8323; *The New Book of World Rankings.*

Nordic Council of Ministers, Store Strandstraede 18, DK-1255 Copenhagen K, Denmark and the Nordic Statistical Secretariat, Postboks 2550, DK-2100 Copenhagen 0, Denmark; *The Yearbook of Nordic Statistics.*

Times Books, 201 East 50th Street, New York, New York 10022 (212) 751-2600; *The Economist Book of Vital World Statistics.*

United Nations Educational, Scientific and Cultural Organization (UNESCO), 7 Place de Fontenoy, F-75700 Paris, France (Telephone Number in U.S. (212) 963-5981); *Statistical Yearbook.*

SWEDEN - TELEVISION RECEIVER PRODUCTION

Statistical Office of the United Nations, Publishing Service, New York, New York 10017 (800) 253-9646; *Statistical Yearbook.*

SWEDEN - TEXTILE INDUSTRY

G.K. Hall and Company, 70 Lincoln Street, Boston, Massachusetts 02111 (617) 423-3990; *The World in Figures.*

Organisation for Economic Co-operation and Development (OECD), 2 rue Andre-Pascal, 75 Paris 16, France (Telephone Number in U.S. (202) 785-6323); *Foreign Trade by Commodities, Indicators of Industrial Activity, Industrial Structure Statistics,* and *Textile Industry in OECD Countries.*

Statistical Office of the United Nations, Publishing Service, New York, New York 10017 (800) 253-9646; *Statistical Yearbook,* and *Trade in Manufactures of Developing Countries.*

SWEDEN - THEATRE

United Nations Educational, Scientific and Cultural Organization (UNESCO), 7 Place de Fontenoy, F-75700 Paris, France (Telephone Number in U.S. (212) 963-5981); *Statistical Yearbook.*

SWEDEN - TIN - See SWEDEN - MINING AND MINERAL PRODUCTS

SWEDEN - TIRE (MOTOR VEHICLE) PRODUCTION

International Rubber Study Group, York House, Eighth Floor, Empire Way, Wembley, London HA9 0PA, England; *Rubber Statistical Bulletin*.

Statistical Office of the United Nations, Publishing Service, New York, New York 10017 (800) 253-9646; *Statistical Yearbook*.

SWEDEN - TOBACCO PRODUCTION

Euromonitor Publications Limited, 87-88 Turnmill Street, London EC1M 5QU, England; *European Marketing Data and Statistics*.

Facts on File, 460 Park Avenue South, New York, New York 10016 (800) 443-8323; *The New Book of World Rankings*.

Organisation for Economic Co-operation and Development (OECD), 2 rue Andre-Pascal, 75 Paris 16, France (Telephone Number in U.S. (202) 785-6323); *Foreign Trade by Commodities, Indicators of Industrial Activity*, and *Industrial Structure Statistics*.

Statistical Office of the United Nations, Publishing Service, New York, New York 10017 (800) 253-9646; *Statistical Yearbook*.

SWEDEN - TOURISM

Euromonitor Publications Limited, 87-88 Turnmill Street, London EC1M 5QU, England; *European Marketing Data and Statistics*.

Facts on File, 460 Park Avenue South, New York, New York 10016 (800) 443-8323; *The New Book of World Rankings*.

G.K. Hall and Company, 70 Lincoln Street, Boston, Massachusetts 02111 (617) 423-3990; *The World in Figures*.

Organisation for Economic Co-operation and Development (OECD), 2 rue Andre-Pascal, 75 Paris 16, France (Telephone Number in U.S. (202) 785-6323); *Tourism Policy and International Tourism in OECD Member Countries*.

Statistical Office of the United Nations, Publishing Service, New York, New York 10017 (800) 253-9646; *Statistical Yearbook*.

Times Books, 201 East 50th Street, New York, New York 10022 (212) 751-2600; *The Economist Book of Vital World Statistics*.

World Tourism Organization, Calle Capitan Haya 42, E-28020 Madrid, Spain; *Yearbook of Tourism Statistics*.

SWEDEN - TRACTORS IN USE

Statistical Office of the United Nations, Publishing Service, New York, New York 10017 (800) 253-9646; *Statistical Yearbook*.

SWEDEN - TRADE - See SWEDEN - FOREIGN TRADE

SWEDEN - TRADEMARKS AND SERVICE MARKS

Statistical Office of the United Nations, Publishing Service, New York, New York 10017 (800) 253-9646; *Statistical Yearbook*.

World Intellectual Property Organization, 34 Chemin des Colombettes, CH-1211 Geneva 20. Switzerland; *Industrial Property Statistics*.

SWEDEN - TRANSPORTATION AND COMMUNICATIONS

Facts on File, 460 Park Avenue South, New York, New York 10016 (800) 443-8323; *The New Book of World Rankings*.

G.K. Hall and Company, 70 Lincoln Street, Boston, Massachusetts 02111 (617) 423-3990; *The World in Figures*.

Nordic Council of Ministers, Store Strandstraede 18, DK-1255 Copenhagen K, Denmark and the Nordic Statistical Secretariat, Postboks 2550, DK-2100 Copenhagen 0, Denmark; *The Yearbook of Nordic Statistics*.

SWEDEN - TUNGSTEN PRODUCTION AND CONSUMPTION - See SWEDEN - MINING AND MINERAL PRODUCTS

SWEDEN - UNEMPLOYMENT

Euromonitor Publications Limited, 87-88 Turnmill Street, London EC1M 5QU, England; *European Marketing Data and Statistics*.

International Labour Office, I.L.O. Publications, CH-1211, Geneva 22, Switzerland; *Yearbook of Labour Statistics*.

Nordic Council of Ministers, Store Strandstraede 18, DK-1255 Copenhagen K, Denmark and the Nordic Statistical Secretariat, Postboks 2550, DK-2100 Copenhagen 0, Denmark; *The Yearbook of Nordic Statistics*.

Organisation for Economic Co-operation and Development (OECD), 2 rue Andre-Pascal, 75 Paris 16, France (Telephone Number in U.S. (202) 785-6323); *Economic Outlook, OECD Economic Surveys: Sweden*, and *OECD Employment Outlook*.

Statistical Office of the United Nations, Publishing Service, New York, New York 10017 (800) 253-9646; *Statistical Yearbook*.

SWEDEN - URANIUM PRODUCTION AND CONSUMPTION - See SWEDEN - MINING AND MINERAL PRODUCTS

SWEDEN - VANADIUM AND VANADIUM ORE PRODUCTION AND CONSUMPTION - See SWEDEN - MINING AND MINERAL PRODUCTS

SWEDEN - VITAL STATISTICS

G.K. Hall and Company, 70 Lincoln Street, Boston, Massachusetts 02111 (617) 423-3990; *The World in Figures*.

Nordic Council of Ministers, Store Strandstraede 18, DK-1255 Copenhagen K, Denmark and the Nordic Statistical Secretariat, Postboks 2550, DK-2100 Copenhagen 0, Denmark; *The Yearbook of Nordic Statistics*.

Statistical Office of the United Nations, Publishing Service, New York, New York 10017 (800) 253-9646; *Statistical Yearbook*.

World Health Organization, Office of Publications, Avenue Appia, CH-1211 Geneva 27, Switzerland (Telephone Number in U.S. (518) 436-9686); *World Health Statistics Annual*.

SWEDEN - WAGES

Euromonitor Publications Limited, 87-88 Turnmill Street, London EC1M 5QU, England; *European Marketing Data and Statistics*.

G.K. Hall and Company, 70 Lincoln Street, Boston, Massachusetts 02111 (617) 423-3990; *The World in Figures*.

International Labour Office, I.L.O. Publications, CH-1211, Geneva 22, Switzerland; *Yearbook of Labour Statistics*.

Nordic Council of Ministers, Store Strandstraede 18, DK-1255 Copenhagen K, Denmark and the Nordic Statistical Secretariat, Postboks 2550, DK-2100 Copenhagen 0, Denmark; *The Yearbook of Nordic Statistics*.

Organisation for Economic Co-operation and Development (OECD), 2 rue Andre-Pascal, 75 Paris 16, France (Telephone Number in U.S. (202) 785-6323); *Economic Outlook, Industrial Structure Statistics*, and *Main Economic Indicators - Historical Statistics*.

Statistical Office of the United Nations, Publishing Service, New York, New York 10017 (800) 253-9646; *Statistical Yearbook*.

SWEDEN - WATERWAYS IN USE

Organisation for Economic Co-operation and Development (OECD), 2 rue Andre-Pascal, 75 Paris 16, France (Telephone Number in U.S. (202) 785-6323); *Maritime Transport*.

Statistical Office of the United Nations, Publishing Service, New York, New York 10017 (800) 253-9646; *Annual Bulletin of Transport Statistics for Europe*.

SWEDEN - WEATHER

Facts on File, 460 Park Avenue South, New York, New York 10016 (800) 443-8323; *The New Book of World Rankings*.

G.K. Hall and Company, 70 Lincoln Street, Boston, Massachusetts 02111 (617) 423-3990; *The World in Figures*.

Nordic Council of Ministers, Store Strandstraede 18, DK-1255 Copenhagen K, Denmark and the Nordic Statistical Secretariat, Postboks 2550, DK-2100 Copenhagen 0, Denmark; *The Yearbook of Nordic Statistics*.

SWEDEN - WELFARE

International Monetary Fund, 700 Nineteenth Street, NW, Washington, D.C. 20431 (202) 623-7000; *Government Finance Statistics Yearbook*.

Nordic Council of Ministers, Store Strandstraede 18, DK-1255 Copenhagen K, Denmark and the Nordic Statistical Secretariat, Postboks 2550, DK-2100 Copenhagen 0, Denmark; *The Yearbook of Nordic Statistics*.

SWEDEN - WHEAT PRODUCTION AND PRICES - See SWEDEN - CROPS

SWEDEN - WHOLESALE PRICES

Nordic Council of Ministers, Store Strandstraede 18, DK-1255 Copenhagen K, Denmark and the Nordic Statistical Secretariat, Postboks 2550, DK-2100 Copenhagen 0, Denmark; *The Yearbook of Nordic Statistics*.

Statistical Office of the United Nations, Publishing Service, New York, New York 10017 (800) 253-9646; *Statistical Yearbook*.

SWEDEN - WHOLESALE TRADE

Statistical Office of the United Nations, Publishing Service, New York, New York 10017 (800) 253-9646; *Statistical Yearbook*.

SWEDEN - WINE PRODUCTION

Facts on File, 460 Park Avenue South, New York, New York 10016 (800) 443-8323; *The New Book of World Rankings*.

SWEDEN - WOOD AND WOOD PULP - See SWEDEN - FORESTRY AND FOREST PRODUCTS

SWEDEN - WOOL - INDUSTRIAL CONSUMPTION

Organisation for Economic Co-operation and Development (OECD), 2 rue Andre-Pascal, 75 Paris 16, France (Telephone Number in U.S. (202) 785-6323); *Textile Industry in OECD Countries*.

Statistical Office of the United Nations, Publishing Service, New York, New York 10017 (800) 253-9646; *Statistical Yearbook*.

SWEDEN - WOOL PRODUCTION

Facts on File, 460 Park Avenue South, New York, New York 10016 (800) 443-8323; *The New Book of World Rankings*.

Organisation for Economic Co-operation and Development (OECD), 2 rue Andre-Pascal, 75 Paris 16, France (Telephone Number in U.S. (202) 785-6323); *Economic Accounts for Agriculture*.

SWEDEN - YARN PRODUCTION

Organisation for Economic Co-operation and Development (OECD), 2 rue Andre-Pascal, 75 Paris 16, France (Telephone Number in U.S. (202) 785-6323); *Foreign Trade by Commodities*, and *Textile Industry in OECD Countries*.

Statistical Office of the United Nations, Publishing Service, New York, New York 10017 (800) 253-9646; *Statistical Yearbook*.

SWEDEN - ZINC AND ZINC ORE PRODUCTION AND CONSUMPTION - See SWEDEN - MINING AND MINERAL PRODUCTS

SWEET POTATOES

U.S. Department of Agriculture, Economic Research Service, Fourteenth Street and Independence Avenue, SW, Washington, D.C. 20005-4789 (202) 219-1504; *Food Consumption, Prices, and Expenditures, Agricultural Outlook*, and unpublished data.

U.S. Department of Agriculture, National Agricultural Statistics Service, Fourteenth Street and Independence Avenue, SW, Washington, D.C. 20250 (202) 219-1504; *Vegetables*, and *Agricultural Statistics*.

SWIMMING

National Sporting Goods Association, Lake Center Plaza Building, 1699 Wall Street, Mount Prospect, Illinois 60056-5780 (708) 439-4000; *Sports Participation in 1992: Series I*.

SWINE - See HOGS

Switzerland - National Statistical Offices

Division de la Statistique du Commerce, Direction Generale des Douanes, Monbijoustrasse 40, CH-3011 Berne, Switzerland.

Office Federale de la Statistique, Hallwylstrasse 15, CH-3003 Berne, Switzerland.

Switzerland - Primary Statistics Sources

Office Federale de la Statistique, Hallwylstrasse 15, CH-3003 Berne, Switzerland; *Statistiches Jahrbuch der Schweiz: Annuaire statistique de la Suisse* (Statistical Yearbook of Switzerland), and *La Vie Economique: Rapports Economiques etde Statostoqie Sociale* (Economic Life: Economic Reports and Social Statistics).

Switzerland - Databases

Federal Statistical Office, Schwarz forstrasse 96, CH-3003 Berne, Switzerland. Offers the following databases: (1) Statistical Information Systems (STATINF); and (2) GEOSTAT. Subject coverage: Swiss statistical information.

SWITZERLAND - AGRICULTURE

Facts on File, 460 Park Avenue South, New York, New York 10016 (800) 443-8323; *The New Book of World Rankings*.

Food and Agricultural Organization of the United Nations (FAO) Via delle Terme di Caracalla, 00100 Rome, Italy (Telephone Number in U.S. (202) 653-2400); *Production Yearbook, The State of Food and Agriculture,* and *Trade Yearbook*.

G.K. Hall and Company, 70 Lincoln Street, Boston, Massachusetts 02111 (617) 423-3990; *The World in Figures*.

Organisation for Economic Co-operation and Development (OECD), 2 rue Andre-Pascal, 75 Paris 16, France (Telephone Number in U.S. (202) 785-6323); *Economic Accounts for Agriculture, Indicators of Industrial Activity, Industrial Structure Statistics,* and *OECD Economic Surveys. Switzerland.*

Statistical Office of the United Nations, Publishing Service, New York, New York 10017 (800) 253-9646; *Statistical Yearbook*.

Times Books, 201 East 50th Street, New York, New York 10022 (212) 751-2600; *The Economist Book of Vital World Statistics*.

The World Bank, 1818 H Street, NW, Washington, D.C. 20433 (202) 477-1234; *World Tables*.

SWITZERLAND - AIRLINE SERVICE

Facts on File, 460 Park Avenue South, New York, New York 10016 (800) 443-8323; *The New Book of World Rankings*.

G.K. Hall and Company, 70 Lincoln Street, Boston, Massachusetts 02111 (617) 423-3990; *The World in Figures*.

International Civil Aviation Organization, 1000 Sherbrooke Street West, Suite 400, Montreal, Quebec, Canada H3A 2R2 (514) 285-8219; *Civil Aviation Statistics of the World*.

Organisation for Economic Co-operation and Development (OECD), 2 rue Andre-Pascal, 75 Paris 16, France (Telephone Number in U.S. (202) 785-6323); *Tourism Policy and International Tourism in OECD Member Countries*.

Statistical Office of the United Nations, Publishing Service, New York, New York 10017 (800) 253-9646; *Statistical Yearbook*.

Times Books, 201 East 50th Street, New York, New York 10022 (212) 751-2600; *The Economist Book of Vital World Statistics*.

SWITZERLAND - ALUMINUM PRODUCTION AND CONSUMPTION - See SWITZERLAND - MINING AND MINERAL PRODUCTS

SWITZERLAND - ANIMAL FEEDINGSTUFFS - EXPORTS

Organisation for Economic Co-operation and Development (OECD), 2 rue Andre-Pascal, 75 Paris 16, France (Telephone Number in U.S. (202) 785-6323); *Foreign Trade by Commodities*.

SWITZERLAND - ANIMAL HEALTH

Food and Agricultural Organization of the United Nations (FAO), Via delle Terme di Caracalla, 00100, Rome, Italy (Telephone Number in U.S. (202) 653-2400); *Animal Health Yearbook*.

SWITZERLAND - ANTIMONY AND ANTIMONY ORE PRODUCTION AND CONSUMPTION - See SWITZERLAND - MINING AND MINERAL PRODUCTS

SWITZERLAND - AREA AND DENSITY OF POPULATION

Facts on File, 460 Park Avenue South, New York, New York 10016 (800) 443-8323; *The New Book of World Rankings*.

Food and Agricultural Organization of the United Nations (FAO) Via delle Terme di Caracalla, 00100 Rome, Italy (Telephone Number in U.S. (202) 653-2400); *The State of Food and Agriculture*.

G.K. Hall and Company, 70 Lincoln Street, Boston, Massachusetts 02111 (617) 423-3990; *The World in Figures*.

Statistical Office of the United Nations, Publishing Service, New York, New York 10017 (800) 253-9646; *Statistical Yearbook*.

Times Books, 201 East 50th Street, New York, New York 10022 (212) 751-2600; *The Economist Book of Vital World Statistics*.

United Nations Educational, Scientific and Cultural Organization (UNESCO), 7 Place de Fontenoy, F-75700 Paris, France (Telephone Number in U.S. (212) 963-5981); *Statistical Yearbook*.

SWITZERLAND - ARMS EXPORTS AND IMPORTS

U.S. Arms Control and Disarmament Agency, 320 Twenty-first Street, NW, Washington, D.C. 20451 (202) 647-8677; *World Military Expenditures and Arms Transfers*.

SWITZERLAND - ARSENIC PRODUCTION AND CONSUMPTION - See SWITZERLAND - MINING AND MINERAL PRODUCTS

SWITZERLAND - BALANCE OF PAYMENTS

The Economist Intelligence Unit, 111 West 57th Street, New York, New York 10019; *The World Market Atlas*.

G.K. Hall and Company, 70 Lincoln Street, Boston, Massachusetts 02111 (617) 423-3990; *The World in Figures*.

International Monetary Fund, 700 Nineteenth Street, NW, Washington, D.C. 20431 (202) 623-7000; *Balance of Payments Yearbook,* and *International Financial Statistics*.

Organisation for Economic Co-operation and Development (OECD), 2 rue Andre-Pascal, 75 Paris 16, France (Telephone Number in U.S. (202) 785-6323); *Economic Outlook, Geographical Distribution of Financial Flows to Developing Countries,* and *OECD Economic Surveys: Switzerland.*

Times Books, 201 East 50th Street, New York, New York 10022 (212) 751-2600; *The Economist Book of Vital World Statistics*.

The World Bank, 1818 H Street, NW, Washington, D.C. 20433 (202) 477-1234; *World Tables*.

SWITZERLAND - BANKING

Facts on File, 460 Park Avenue South, New York, New York 10016 (800) 443-8323; *The New Book of World Rankings*.

G.K. Hall and Company, 70 Lincoln Street, Boston, Massachusetts 02111 (617) 423-3990; *The World in Figures*.

International Monetary Fund, 700 Nineteenth Street, NW, Washington, D.C. 20431 (202) 623-7000; *International Financial Statistics*.

Organisation for Economic Co-operation and Development (OECD), 2 rue Andre-Pascal, 75 Paris 16, France (Telephone Number in U.S. (202) 785-6323); *Economic Outlook, Financial Market Trends*, and *OECD Economic Surveys: Switzerland*.

Statistical Office of the United Nations, Publishing Service, New York, New York 10017 (800) 253-9646; *Statistical Yearbook*.

SWITZERLAND - BARLEY PRODUCTION - See SWITZERLAND - CROPS

SWITZERLAND - BAUXITE PRODUCTION AND CONSUMPTION - See SWITZERLAND - MINING AND MINERAL PRODUCTS

SWITZERLAND - BEER PRODUCTION

Facts on File, 460 Park Avenue South, New York, New York 10016 (800) 443-8323; *The New Book of World Rankings*.

Statistical Office of the United Nations, Publishing Service, New York, New York 10017 (800) 253-9646; *Statistical Yearbook*.

SWITZERLAND - BEVERAGES - PRODUCTION INDEX

Organisation for Economic Co-operation and Development (OECD), 2 rue Andre-Pascal, 75 Paris 16, France (Telephone Number in U.S. (202) 785-6323); *Indicators of Industrial Activity*.

SWITZERLAND - BIRTH RATE

Facts on File, 460 Park Avenue South, New York, New York 10016 (800) 443-8323; *The New Book of World Rankings*.

Statistical Office of the United Nations, Publishing Service, New York, New York 10017 (800) 253-9646; *Demographic Yearbook*, and *Statistical Yearbook*.

Times Books, 201 East 50th Street, New York, New York 10022 (212) 751-2600; *The Economist Book of Vital World Statistics*.

The World Bank, 1818 H Street, NW, Washington, D.C. 20433 (202) 477-1234; *World Tables*.

World Health Organization, Office of Publications, Avenue Appia, CH-1211 Geneva 27, Switzerland (Telephone Number in U.S. (518) 436-9686); *World Health Statistics Annual*.

SWITZERLAND - BISMUTH PRODUCTION AND CONSUMPTION - See SWITZERLAND - MINING AND MINERAL PRODUCTS

SWITZERLAND - BONDS

G.K. Hall and Company, 70 Lincoln Street, Boston, Massachusetts 02111 (617) 423-3990; *The World in Figures*.

Organisation for Economic Co-operation and Development (OECD), 2 rue Andre-Pascal, 75 Paris 16, France (Telephone Number in U.S. (202) 785-6323); *Financial Market Trends*.

Statistical Office of the United Nations, Publishing Service, New York, New York 10017 (800) 253-9646; *Statistical Yearbook*.

SWITZERLAND - BOOK PRODUCTION

Euromonitor Publications Limited, 87-88 Turnmill Street, London EC1M 5QU, England; *European Marketing Data and Statistics*.

G.K. Hall and Company, 70 Lincoln Street, Boston, Massachusetts 02111 (617) 423-3990; *The World in Figures*.

Organisation for Economic Co-operation and Development (OECD), 2 rue Andre-Pascal, 75 Paris 16, France (Telephone Number in U.S. (202) 785-6323); *Indicators of Industrial Activity*.

United Nations Educational, Scientific and Cultural Organization (UNESCO), 7 Place de Fontenoy, F-75700 Paris, France (Telephone Number in U.S. (212) 963-5981); *Statistical Yearbook*.

SWITZERLAND - BROADCASTING

Billboard Limited, P.O. Box 9027, 1006 AA Amsterdam, The Netherlands (Telephone Number in U.S. (212) 764-7300); *World Radio TV Handbook*.

Facts on File, 460 Park Avenue South, New York, New York 10016 (800) 443-8323; *The New Book of World Rankings*.

G.K. Hall and Company, 70 Lincoln Street, Boston, Massachusetts 02111 (617) 423-3990; *The World in Figures*.

Times Books, 201 East 50th Street, New York, New York 10022 (212) 751-2600; *The Economist Book of Vital World Statistics*.

United Nations Educational, Scientific and Cultural Organization (UNESCO), 7 Place de Fontenoy, F-75700 Paris, France (Telephone Number in U.S. (212) 963-5981); *Statistical Yearbook*.

SWITZERLAND - BUSINESS

G.K. Hall and Company, 70 Lincoln Street, Boston, Massachusetts 02111 (617) 423-3990; *The World in Figures*.

Organisation for Economic Co-operation and Development (OECD), 2 rue Andre-Pascal, 75 Paris 16, France (Telephone Number in U.S. (202) 785-6323); *Main Economic Indicators - Historical Statistics*.

SWITZERLAND - BUTTER CONSUMPTION - See SWITZERLAND - DAIRY PRODUCTS

SWITZERLAND - CADMIUM PRODUCTION AND CONSUMPTION - See SWITZERLAND - MINING AND MINERAL PRODUCTS

SWITZERLAND - CALORIE SUPPLY

Food and Agricultural Organization of the United Nations (FAO) Via delle Terme di Caracalla, 00100 Rome, Italy (Telephone Number in U.S. (202) 653-2400); *The State of Food and Agriculture*.

SWITZERLAND - CAPITAL INVESTMENT

Organisation for Economic Co-operation and Development (OECD), 2 rue Andre-Pascal, 75 Paris 16, France (Telephone Number in U.S. (202) 785-6323); *Economic Outlook*, and *Financial Market Trends*.

SWITZERLAND - CAPITAL REVENUE

International Monetary Fund, 700 Nineteenth Street, NW, Washington, D.C. 20431 (202) 623-7000; *Government Finance Statistics Yearbook.*

Organisation for Economic Co-operation and Development (OECD), 2 rue Andre-Pascal, 75 Paris 16, France (Telephone Number in U.S. (202) 785-6323); *Economic Outlook,* and *Financial Market Trends.*

SWITZERLAND - CATTLE - See SWITZERLAND - LIVESTOCK AND POULTRY

SWITZERLAND - CAUSTIC SODA PRODUCTION

Organisation for Economic Co-operation and Development (OECD), 2 rue Andre-Pascal, 75 Paris 16, France (Telephone Number in U.S. (202) 785-6323); *Indicators of Industrial Activity.*

SWITZERLAND - CEMENT PRODUCTION - See SWITZERLAND - MINING AND MINERAL PRODUCTS

SWITZERLAND - CEREAL PRODUCTION - See SWITZERLAND - CROPS

SWITZERLAND - CHEESE - See SWITZERLAND - DAIRY PRODUCTS

SWITZERLAND - CHEMICAL (ORGANIC) PRODUCTION - See SWITZERLAND - MINING AND MINERAL PRODUCTS

SWITZERLAND - CHROMITE PRODUCTION AND CONSUMPTION - See SWITZERLAND - MINING AND MINERAL PRODUCTS

SWITZERLAND - CHROMIUM ORE PRODUCTION AND CONSUMPTION - See SWITZERLAND - MINING AND MINERAL PRODUCTS

SWITZERLAND - CIGAR PRODUCTION - See SWITZERLAND - TOBACCO PRODUCTION

SWITZERLAND - CIGARETTE PRODUCTION - See SWITZERLAND - TOBACCO PRODUCTION

SWITZERLAND - CLASS STRUCTURE

G.K. Hall and Company, 70 Lincoln Street, Boston, Massachusetts 02111 (617) 423-3990; *The World in Figures.*

SWITZERLAND - CLIMATE

Facts on File, 460 Park Avenue South, New York, New York 10016 (800) 443-8323; *The New Book of World Rankings.*

G.K. Hall and Company, 70 Lincoln Street, Boston, Massachusetts 02111 (617) 423-3990; *The World in Figures.*

SWITZERLAND - CLOTHING - PRODUCTION INDEX

Organisation for Economic Co-operation and Development (OECD), 2 rue Andre-Pascal, 75 Paris 16, France (Telephone Number in U.S. (202) 785-6323); *Indicators of Industrial Activity.*

SWITZERLAND - CLOTHING EXPORTS AND IMPORTS

Organisation for Economic Co-operation and Development (OECD), 2 rue Andre-Pascal, 75 Paris 16, France (Telephone Number in U.S. (202) 785-6323); *Textile Industry in OECD Countries.*

Statistical Office of the United Nations, Publishing Service, New York, New York 10017 (800) 253-9646; *Trade in Manufactures of Developing Countries.*

SWITZERLAND - COAL PRODUCTION - See SWITZERLAND - MINING AND MINERAL PRODUCTS

SWITZERLAND - COBALT PRODUCTION AND CONSUMPTION - See SWITZERLAND - MINING AND MINERAL PRODUCTS

SWITZERLAND - COFFEE PRODUCTION AND CONSUMPTION - See SWITZERLAND - CROPS

SWITZERLAND - COKE AND COKE OVEN ORE PRODUCTION AND CONSUMPTION - See SWITZERLAND - MINING AND MINERAL PRODUCTS

SWITZERLAND - COMMUNICATIONS

G.K. Hall and Company, 70 Lincoln Street, Boston, Massachusetts 02111 (617) 423-3990; *The World in Figures.*

SWITZERLAND - CONSTRUCTION INDUSTRY

Facts on File, 460 Park Avenue South, New York, New York 10016 (800) 443-8323; *The New Book of World Rankings.*

Organisation for Economic Co-operation and Development (OECD), 2 rue Andre-Pascal, 75 Paris 16, France (Telephone Number in U.S. (202) 785-6323); *Industrial Structure Statistics, The Iron and Steel Industry, Main Economic Indicators - Historical Statistics,* and *OECD Economic Surveys: Switzerland.*

Statistical Office of the United Nations, Publishing Service, New York, New York 10017 (800) 253-9646; *Statistical Yearbook.*

SWITZERLAND - CONSUMER PRICE INDEX

G.K. Hall and Company, 70 Lincoln Street, Boston, Massachusetts 02111 (617) 423-3990; *The World in Figures.*

Organisation for Economic Co-operation and Development (OECD), 2 rue Andre-Pascal, 75 Paris 16, France (Telephone Number in U.S. (202) 785-6323); *Economic Outlook.*

Statistical Office of the United Nations, Publishing Service, New York, New York 10017 (800) 253-9646; *Statistical Yearbook.*

SWITZERLAND - CONSUMER PRICES

Euromonitor Publications Limited, 87-88 Turnmill Street, London EC1M 5QU, England; *European Marketing Data and Statistics.*

International Labour Office, I.L.O. Publications, CH-1211, Geneva 22, Switzerland; *Yearbook of Labour Statistics.*

International Monetary Fund, 700 Nineteenth Street, NW, Washington, D.C. 20431 (202) 623-7000; *International Financial Statistics.*

Organisation for Economic Co-operation and Development (OECD), 2 rue Andre-Pascal, 75 Paris 16, France (Telephone Number in U.S. (202) 785-6323); *Economic Outlook.*

Times Books, 201 East 50th Street, New York, New York 10022 (212) 751-2600; *The Economist Book of Vital World Statistics.*

SWITZERLAND - CONSUMPTION

G.K. Hall and Company, 70 Lincoln Street, Boston, Massachusetts 02111 (617) 423-3990; *The World in Figures*.

Organisation for Economic Co-operation and Development (OECD), 2 rue Andre-Pascal, 75 Paris 16, France (Telephone Number in U.S. (202) 785-6323); *The Footwear, Raw Hides and Skins, and Leather Industry in OECD Countries, The Iron and Steel Industry, Meat Balances in OECD Member Countries, The Non-Ferrous Metals Industry, The Pulp and Paper Industry*, and *Textile Industry in OECD Countries*.

SWITZERLAND - COPPER AND COPPER ORE PRODUCTION AND CONSUMPTION - See SWITZERLAND - MINING AND MINERAL PRODUCTS

SWITZERLAND - CORN PRODUCTION - See SWITZERLAND - CROPS

SWITZERLAND - CORPORATE INCOME TAXES - See SWITZERLAND - TAXATION

SWITZERLAND - CORPORATE TAXES - See SWITZERLAND - TAXATION

SWITZERLAND - COTTON - See SWITZERLAND - CROPS

SWITZERLAND - CRIME

Yale University Press, Yale Station, New Haven, Connecticut 06520 (203) 432-0940; *Violence and Crime in Cross-National Perspective*.

SWITZERLAND - CROPS

American Forest and Paper Association, 1250 Connecticut Avenue, NW, Washington, D.C. 20036 (202) 463-2455; *Wood Pulp and Fiber Statistics*.

Euromonitor Publications Limited, 87-88 Turnmill Street, London EC1M 5QU, England; *European Marketing Data and Statistics*.

Facts on File, 460 Park Avenue South, New York, New York 10016 (800) 443-8323; *The New Book of World Rankings*.

Food and Agricultural Organization of the United Nations (FAO) Via delle Terme di Caracalla, 00100 Rome, Italy (Telephone Number in U.S. (202) 653-2400); *The State of Food and Agriculture*.

G.K. Hall and Company, 70 Lincoln Street, Boston, Massachusetts 02111 (617) 423-3990; *The World in Figures*.

Organisation for Economic Co-operation and Development (OECD), 2 rue Andre-Pascal, 75 Paris 16, France (Telephone Number in U.S. (202) 785-6323); *Economic Accounts for Agriculture, Foreign Trade by Commodities*, and *Textile Industry in OECD Countries*.

Statistical Office of the United Nations, Publishing Service, New York, New York 10017 (800) 253-9646; *Statistical Yearbook*.

SWITZERLAND - CUSTOMS DUTIES

G.K. Hall and Company, 70 Lincoln Street, Boston, Massachusetts 02111 (617) 423-3990; *The World in Figures*.

International Monetary Fund, 700 Nineteenth Street, NW, Washington, D.C. 20431 (202) 623-7000; *Government Finance Statistics Yearbook*.

Organisation for Economic Co-operation and Development (OECD), 2 rue Andre-Pascal, 75 Paris 16, France (Telephone Number in U.S. (202) 785-6323); *The Non-Ferrous Metals Industry*.

SWITZERLAND - DAIRY PRODUCTS

Commodity Research Bureau, Incorporated, 75 Wall Street, New York, New York 10005 (212) 504-7754; *Commodity Year Book*.

Facts on File, 460 Park Avenue South, New York, New York 10016 (800) 443-8323; *The New Book of World Rankings*.

Food and Agricultural Organization of the United Nations (FAO) Via delle Terme di Caracalla, 00100 Rome, Italy (Telephone Number in U.S. (202) 653-2400); *The State of Food and Agriculture*.

Organisation for Economic Co-operation and Development (OECD), 2 rue Andre-Pascal, 75 Paris 16, France (Telephone Number in U.S. (202) 785-6323); *Economic Accounts for Agriculture*, and *Milk, Milk Products, and Egg Balances in OECD Member Countries*.

Statistical Office of the United Nations, Publishing Service, New York, New York 10017 (800) 253-9646; *Statistical Yearbook*.

SWITZERLAND - DEATH RATES

G.K. Hall and Company, 70 Lincoln Street, Boston, Massachusetts 02111 (617) 423-3990; *The World in Figures*.

Statistical Office of the United Nations, Publishing Service, New York, New York 10017 (800) 253-9646; *Statistical Yearbook*.

Times Books, 201 East 50th Street, New York, New York 10022 (212) 751-2600; *The Economist Book of Vital World Statistics*.

World Health Organization, Office of Publications, Avenue Appia, CH-1211 Geneva 27, Switzerland (Telephone Number in U.S. (518) 436-9686); *World Health Statistics Annual*.

SWITZERLAND - DEFENSE EXPENDITURES

G.K. Hall and Company, 70 Lincoln Street, Boston, Massachusetts 02111 (617) 423-3990; *The World in Figures*.

International Monetary Fund, 700 Nineteenth Street, NW, Washington, D.C. 20431 (202) 623-7000; *Government Finance Statistics Yearbook*.

U.S. Arms Control and Disarmament Agency, 320 Twenty-first Street, NW, Washington, D.C. 20451 (202) 647-8677; *World Military Expenditures and Arms Transfers*.

SWITZERLAND - DEMOGRAPHY

The Economist Intelligence Unit, 111 West 57th Street, New York, New York 10019 (800) 938-4685; *The World Market Atlas*.

Facts on File, 460 Park Avenue South, New York, New York 10016 (800) 443-8323; *The New Book of World Rankings*.

G.K. Hall and Company, 70 Lincoln Street, Boston, Massachusetts 02111 (617) 423-3990; *The World in Figures*.

SWITZERLAND - DEVELOPMENT ASSISTANCE

G.K. Hall and Company, 70 Lincoln Street, Boston, Massachusetts 02111 (617) 423-3990; *The World in Figures*.

Organisation for Economic Co-operation and Development (OECD), 2 rue Andre-Pascal, 75 Paris 16, France (Telephone Number in U.S. (202) 785-6323); *Geographical Distribution of Financial Flows to Developing Countries.*

Statistical Office of the United Nations, Publishing Service, New York, New York 10017 (800) 253-9646; *Statistical Yearbook.*

SWITZERLAND - DIAMOND PRODUCTION - See SWITZERLAND - MINING AND MINERAL PRODUCTS

SWITZERLAND - DISCOUNT RATES

Organisation for Economic Co-operation and Development (OECD), 2 rue Andre-Pascal, 75 Paris 16, France (Telephone Number in U.S. (202) 785-6323); *Financial Market Trends.*

Statistical Office of the United Nations, Publishing Service, New York, New York 10017 (800) 253-9646; *Statistical Yearbook.*

SWITZERLAND - DISEASES

G.K. Hall and Company, 70 Lincoln Street, Boston, Massachusetts 02111 (617) 423-3990; *The World in Figures.*

World Health Organization, Office of Publications, Avenue Appia, CH-1211 Geneva 27, Switzerland (Telephone Number in U.S. (518) 436-9686); *World Health Statistics Annual.*

SWITZERLAND - DIVORCE RATES

Facts on File, 460 Park Avenue South, New York, New York 10016 (800) 443-8323; *The New Book of World Rankings.*

Statistical Office of the United Nations, Publishing Service, New York, New York 10017 (800) 253-9646; *Demographic Yearbook,* and *Statistical Yearbook.*

SWITZERLAND - DOMESTIC PRODUCT

G.K. Hall and Company, 70 Lincoln Street, Boston, Massachusetts 02111 (617) 423-3990; *The World in Figures.*

SWITZERLAND - ECONOMY

Euromonitor Publications Limited, 87-88 Turnmill Street, London EC1M 5QU, England; *European Marketing Data and Statistics.*

Facts on File, 460 Park Avenue South, New York, New York 10016 (800) 443-8323; *The New Book of World Rankings.*

G.K. Hall and Company, 70 Lincoln Street, Boston, Massachusetts 02111 (617) 423-3990; *The World in Figures.*

Organisation for Economic Co-operation and Development (OECD), 2 rue Andre-Pascal, 75 Paris 16, France (Telephone Number in U.S. (202) 785-6323); *Economic Outlook, Geographical Distribution of Financial Flows to Developing Countries, Main Economic Indicators - Historical Statistics, OECD Economic Surveys: Switzerland,* and *OECD Employment Outlook.*

SWITZERLAND - EDUCATION

The Economist Intelligence Unit, 111 West 57th Street, New York, New York 10019 (800) 938-4685; *The World Market Atlas.*

Euromonitor Publications Limited, 87-88 Turnmill Street, London EC1M 5QU, England; *European Marketing Data and Statistics.*

Facts on File, 460 Park Avenue South, New York, New York 10016 (800) 443-8323; *The New Book of World Rankings.*

G.K. Hall and Company, 70 Lincoln Street, Boston, Massachusetts 02111 (617) 423-3990; *The World in Figures.*

International Monetary Fund, 700 Nineteenth Street, NW, Washington, D.C. 20431 (202) 623-7000; *Government Finance Statistics Yearbook.*

Organisation for Economic Co-operation and Development (OECD), 2 rue Andre-Pascal, 75 Paris 16, France (Telephone Number in U.S. (202) 785-6323); *Education in OECD Countries.*

Times Books, 201 East 50th Street, New York, New York 10022 (212) 751-2600; *The Economist Book of Vital World Statistics.*

United Nations Educational, Scientific and Cultural Organization (UNESCO), 7 Place de Fontenoy, F-75700 Paris, France (Telephone Number in U.S. (212) 963-5981); *Statistical Yearbook.*

The World Bank, 1818 H Street, NW, Washington, D.C. 20433 (202) 477-1234; *World Tables.*

SWITZERLAND - EGG PRODUCTION AND CONSUMPTION - See SWITZERLAND - DAIRY PRODUCTS

SWITZERLAND - ELECTRICITY

Commodity Research Bureau, Incorporated, 75 Wall Street, New York, New York 10005 (212) 504-7754; *Commodity Year Book.*

Facts on File, 460 Park Avenue South, New York, New York 10016 (800) 443-8323; *The New Book of World Rankings.*

Organisation for Economic Co-operation and Development (OECD), 2 rue Andre-Pascal, 75 Paris 16, France (Telephone Number in U.S. (202) 785-6323), *Coal Information, Energy Statistics of OECD Countries, Indicators of Industrial Activity,* and *Industrial Structure Statistics.*

Statistical Office of the United Nations, Publishing Service, New York, New York 10017 (800) 253-9646; *Statistical Yearbook.*

Times Books, 201 East 50th Street, New York, New York 10022 (212) 751-2600; *The Economist Book of Vital World Statistics.*

SWITZERLAND - EMPLOYMENT

Euromonitor Publications Limited, 87-88 Turnmill Street, London EC1M 5QU, England; *European Marketing Data and Statistics.*

Facts on File, 460 Park Avenue South, New York, New York 10016 (800) 443-8323; *The New Book of World Rankings.*

International Labour Office, I.L.O. Publications, CH-1211, Geneva 22, Switzerland; *Yearbook of Labour Statistics.*

Organisation for Economic Co-operation and Development (OECD), 2 rue Andre-Pascal, 75 Paris 16, France (Telephone Number in U.S. (202) 785-6323); *Economic Outlook, The Iron and Steel Industry, OECD Economic Surveys: Switzerland, OECD Employment Outlook,* and *Textile Industry in OECD Countries.*

Statistical Office of the United Nations, Publishing Service, New York, New York 10017 (800) 253-9646; *Statistical Yearbook.*

SWITZERLAND - ENERGY

Euromonitor Publications Limited, 87-88 Turnmill Street, London EC1M 5QU, England; *European Marketing Data and Statistics*.

Facts on File, 460 Park Avenue South, New York, New York 10016 (800) 443-8323; *The New Book of World Rankings*.

Food and Agricultural Organization of the United Nations (FAO) Via delle Terme di Caracalla, 00100 Rome, Italy (Telephone Number in U.S. (202) 653-2400); *The State of Food and Agriculture*.

G.K. Hall and Company, 70 Lincoln Street, Boston, Massachusetts 02111 (617) 423-3990; *The World in Figures*.

Organisation for Economic Co-operation and Development (OECD), 2 rue Andre-Pascal, 75 Paris 16, France (Telephone Number in U.S. (202) 785-6323); *Coal Information, Energy Statistics of OECD Countries, OECD Environmental Data*, and *Oil and Gas Information*.

Statistical Office of the United Nations, Publishing Service, New York, New York 10017 (800) 253-9646; *Energy Statistics Yearbook, Statistical Yearbook*, and *World Energy Supplies*.

Times Books, 201 East 50th Street, New York, New York 10022 (212) 751-2600; *The Economist Book of Vital World Statistics*.

SWITZERLAND - ENGINEERING AND METAL PRODUCTS - EXPORTS AND IMPORTS

Statistical Office of the United Nations, Publishing Service, New York, New York 10017 (800) 253-9646; *Trade In Manufactures of Developing Countries*.

SWITZERLAND - ENVIRONMENT

Organization for Economic Co-operation and Development (OECD), 2 rue Andre-Pascal, 75 Paris 16, France (Telephone Number in U.S. (202) 785-6323); *OECD Environmental Data*.

SWITZERLAND - EXCHANGE RATES

International Civil Aviation Organization, 1000 Sherbrooke Street West, Suite 400, Montreal, Quebec, Canada H3A 2R2 (514) 285-8219; *Civil Aviation Statistics of the World*.

International Monetary Fund, 700 Nineteenth Street, NW, Washington, D.C. 20431 (202) 623-7000; *International Financial Statistics*.

Organisation for Economic Co-operation and Development (OECD), 2 rue Andre-Pascal, 75 Paris 16, France (Telephone Number in U.S. (202) 785-6323); *Economic Outlook, Financial Market Trends, Revenue Statistics of OECD Member Countries*, and *Tourism Policy and International Tourism in OECD Member Countries*.

Statistical Office of the United Nations, Publishing Service, New York, New York 10017 (800) 253-9646; *Statistical Yearbook*.

SWITZERLAND - EXCISE TAXES - See SWITZERLAND - TAXATION

SWITZERLAND - EXPORTS

American Automobile Manufacturers Association, 1401 H Eye Street, NW, Suite 900, Washington, D.C. 20005 (202) 326-5500; *World Motor Vehicle Data*.

The Economist Intelligence Unit, 111 West 57th Street, New York, New York 10019 (800) 938-4685; *The World Market Atlas*.

Food and Agricultural Organization of the United Nations (FAO) Via delle Terme di Caracalla, 00100 Rome, Italy (Telephone Number in U.S. (202) 653-2400); *The State of Food and Agriculture*.

G.K. Hall and Company, 70 Lincoln Street, Boston, Massachusetts 02111 (617) 423-3990; *The World in Figures*.

International Monetary Fund, 700 Nineteenth Street, NW, Washington, D.C. 20431 (202) 623-7000; *Direction of Trade Statistics*, and *International Financial Statistics*.

Organisation for Economic Co-operation and Development (OECD), 2 rue Andre-Pascal, 75 Paris 16, France (Telephone Number in U.S. (202) 785-6323); *Economic Outlook, The Footwear, Raw Hides and Skins, and Leather Industry in OECD Countries, Foreign Trade by Commodities, Geographical Distribution of Financial Flows to Developing Countries, Industrial Structure Statistics, The Iron and Steel Industry, Milk, Milk Products, and Egg Balances in OECD Member Countries, OECD Economic Surveys: Switzerland*, and *The Pulp and Paper Industry*.

Times Books, 201 East 50th Street, New York, New York 10022 (212) 751-2600; *The Economist Book of Vital World Statistics*.

The World Bank, 1818 H Street, NW, Washington, D.C. 20433 (202) 477-1234; *World Tables*.

SWITZERLAND - EXTERNAL FINANCING

Organisation for Economic Co-operation and Development (OECD), 2 rue Andre-Pascal, 75 Paris 16, France (Telephone Number in U.S. (202) 785-6323); *Economic Outlook*, and *Financial Market Trends*.

SWITZERLAND - EXTERNAL INDEBTEDNESS

Organisation for Economic Co-operation and Development (OECD), 2 rue Andre-Pascal, 75 Paris 16, France (Telephone Number in U.S. (202) 785-6323); *Financial Market Trends*, and *Geographical Distribution of Financial Flows to Developing Countries*.

The World Bank, 1818 H Street, NW, Washington, D.C. 20433 (202) 477-1234; *World Tables*.

SWITZERLAND - EXTERNAL TRADE

Food and Agricultural Organization of the United Nations (FAO) Via delle Terme di Caracalla, 00100 Rome, Italy (Telephone Number in U.S. (202) 653-2400); *The State of Food and Agriculture*, and *Trade Yearbook*.

G.K. Hall and Company, 70 Lincoln Street, Boston, Massachusetts 02111 (617) 423-3990; *The World in Figures*.

Statistical Office of the United Nations, Publishing Service, New York, New York 10017 (800) 253-9646; *Statistical Yearbook*.

SWITZERLAND - FABRIC PRODUCTION - See SWITZERLAND - TEXTILE INDUSTRY

SWITZERLAND - FARM CROPS - See SWITZERLAND - CROPS

SWITZERLAND - FERTILITY RATES

Facts on File, 460 Park Avenue South, New York, New York 10016 (800) 443-8323; *The New Book of World Rankings*.

Times Books, 201 East 50th Street, New York, New York 10022 (212) 751-2600; *The Economist Book of Vital World Statistics*.

The World Bank, 1818 H Street, NW, Washington, D.C. 20433 (202) 477-1234; *World Tables*.

SWITZERLAND - FERTILIZER

Food and Agricultural Organization of the United Nations (FAO) Via delle Terme di Caracalla, 00100 Rome, Italy (Telephone Number in U.S. (202) 653-2400); *The State of Food and Agriculture*.

Organisation for Economic Co-operation and Development (OECD), 2 rue Andre-Pascal, 75 Paris 16, France (Telephone Number in U.S. (202) 785-6323); *Economic Accounts for Agriculture*, and *Foreign Trade by Commodities*.

Statistical Office of the United Nations, Publishing Service, New York, New York 10017 (800) 253-9646; *Statistical Yearbook*.

SWITZERLAND - FETAL MORTALITY

Statistical Office of the United Nations, Publishing Service, New York, New York 10017 (800) 253-9646; *Demographic Yearbook*.

World Health Organization, Office of Publications, Avenue Appia, CH-1211 Geneva 27, Switzerland (Telephone Number in U.S. (518) 436-9686); *World Health Statistics Annual*.

SWITZERLAND - FIBRE PRODUCTION - See SWITZERLAND - TEXTILE INDUSTRY

SWITZERLAND - FILAMENT PRODUCTION - See SWITZERLAND - TEXTILE INDUSTRY

SWITZERLAND - FILM - See SWITZERLAND - MOTION PICTURES

SWITZERLAND - FINANCE

Facts on File, 460 Park Avenue South, New York, New York 10016 (800) 443-8323; *The New Book of World Rankings*.

G.K. Hall and Company, 70 Lincoln Street, Boston, Massachusetts 02111 (617) 423-3990; *The World in Figures*.

Organisation for Economic Co-operation and Development (OECD), 2 rue Andre-Pascal, 75 Paris 16, France (Telephone Number in U.S. (202) 785-6323); *Economic Outlook, Financial Market Trends, Geographical Distribution of Financial Flows to Developing Countries, Main Economic Indicators - Historical Statistics*, and *OECD Financial Statistics*.

SWITZERLAND - FISHERIES

Euromonitor Publications Limited, 87-88 Turnmill Street, London EC1M 5QU, England; *European Marketing Data and Statistics*.

Facts on File, 460 Park Avenue South, New York, New York 10016 (800) 443-8323; *The New Book of World Rankings*.

Food and Agricultural Organization of the United Nations (FAO) Via delle Terme di Caracalla, 00100 Rome, Italy (Telephone Number in U.S. (202) 653-2400); *The State of Food and Agriculture*, and *Yearbook of Fishery Statistics*.

Organisation for Economic Co-operation and Development (OECD), 2 rue Andre-Pascal, 75 Paris 16, France (Telephone Number in U.S. (202) 785-6323); *Foreign Trade by Commodities*, and *Industrial Structure Statistics*.

Statistical Office of the United Nations, Publishing Service, New York, New York 10017 (800) 253-9646; *Statistical Yearbook*.

SWITZERLAND - FLOUR PRODUCTION

Statistical Office of the United Nations, Publishing Service, New York, New York 10017 (800) 253-9646; *Statistical Yearbook*.

SWITZERLAND - FOOD

Food and Agricultural Organization of the United Nations (FAO) Via delle Terme di Caracalla, 00100 Rome, Italy (Telephone Number in U.S. (202) 653-2400); *The State of Food and Agriculture*.

G.K. Hall and Company, 70 Lincoln Street, Boston, Massachusetts 02111 (617) 423-3990; *The World in Figures*.

Organisation for Economic Co-operation and Development (OECD), 2 rue Andre-Pascal, 75 Paris 16, France (Telephone Number in U.S. (202) 785-6323); *Food Consumption Statistics*, and *Foreign Trade by Commodities*.

SWITZERLAND - FOOTWEAR - PRODUCTION INDEX

Organisation for Economic Co-operation and Development (OECD), 2 rue Andre-Pascal, 75 Paris 16, France (Telephone Number in U.S. (202) 785-6323); *Indicators of Industrial Activity*.

SWITZERLAND - FOREIGN AID

G.K. Hall and Company, 70 Lincoln Street, Boston, Massachusetts 02111 (617) 423-3990; *The World in Figures*.

SWITZERLAND - FOREIGN DEBT

Organisation for Economic Co-operation and Development (OECD), 2 rue Andre-Pascal, 75 Paris 16, France (Telephone Number in U.S. (202) 785-6323); *Economic Outlook*.

SWITZERLAND - FOREIGN INDEBTEDNESS

Organisation for Economic Co-operation and Development (OECD), 2 rue Andre-Pascal, 75 Paris 16, France (Telephone Number in U.S. (202) 785-6323); *Economic Outlook*, and *Financial Market Trends*.

SWITZERLAND - FOREIGN TRADE

Euromonitor Publications Limited, 87-88 Turnmill Street, London EC1M 5QU, England; *European Marketing Data and Statistics*.

Facts on File, 460 Park Avenue South, New York, New York 10016 (800) 443-8323; *The New Book of World Rankings*.

Food and Agricultural Organization of the United Nations (FAO) Via delle Terme di Caracalla, 00100 Rome, Italy (Telephone Number in U.S. (202) 653-2400); *The State of Food and Agriculture*.

G.K. Hall and Company, 70 Lincoln Street, Boston, Massachusetts 02111 (617) 423-3990; *The World in Figures*.

International Monetary Fund, 700 Nineteenth Street, NW, Washington, D.C. 20431 (202) 623-7000; *International Financial Statistics*.

Organisation for Economic Co-operation and Development (OECD), 2 rue Andre-Pascal, 75 Paris 16, France (Telephone Number in U.S. (202) 785-6323); *Economic Outlook, The Footwear, Raw Hides and Skins, and Leather Industry in OECD Countries, Foreign Trade by Commodities, Main Economic Indicators - Historical Statistics, Maritime Transport, Meat Balances in OECD Member Countries*, and *OECD Economic Surveys: Switzerland*.

Statistical Office of the United Nations, Publishing Service, New York, New York 10017 (800) 253-9646; *International Trade Statistics Yearbook, Statistical Yearbook,* and *Trade in Manufactures of Developing Countries.*

The World Bank, 1818 H Street, NW, Washington, D.C. 20433 (202) 477-1234; *World Metal Statistics,* and *World Tables.*

SWITZERLAND - FORESTRY AND FOREST PRODUCTS

Euromonitor Publications Limited, 87-88 Turnmill Street, London EC1M 5QU, England; *European Marketing Data and Statistics.*

Facts on File, 460 Park Avenue South, New York, New York 10016 (800) 443-8323; *The New Book of World Rankings.*

Food and Agricultural Organization of the United Nations (FAO) Via delle Terme di Caracalla, 00100 Rome, Italy (Telephone Number in U.S. (202) 653-2400); *The State of Food and Agriculture,* and *Yearbook of Forest Products.*

G.K. Hall and Company, 70 Lincoln Street, Boston, Massachusetts 02111 (617) 423-3990; *The World in Figures.*

Organisation for Economic Co-operation and Development (OECD), 2 rue Andre-Pascal, 75 Paris 16, France (Telephone Number in U.S. (202) 785-6323); *Indicators of Industrial Activity, Industrial Structure Statistics,* and *The Pulp and Paper Industry.*

Statistical Office of the United Nations, Publishing Service, New York, New York 10017 (800) 253-9646; *Statistical Yearbook.*

United Nations Educational, Scientific and Cultural Organization (UNESCO), 7 Place de Fontenoy, F-75700 Paris, France (Telephone Number in U.S. (212) 963-5981); *Statistical Yearbook.*

SWITZERLAND - FRUIT PRODUCTION - See SWITZERLAND - CROPS

SWITZERLAND - FURNITURE AND WOOD PRODUCTS - EXPORTS AND IMPORTS

Organisation for Economic Co-operation and Development (OECD), 2 rue Andre-Pascal, 75 Paris 16, France (Telephone Number in U.S. (202) 785-6323); *Foreign Trade by Commodities,* and *Industrial Structure Statistics.*

SWITZERLAND - GAS AND GAS LIQUIDS PRODUCTION - See SWITZERLAND - MINING AND MINERAL PRODUCTS

SWITZERLAND - GENERAL INDUSTRIAL STATISTICS

Statistical Office of the United Nations, Publishing Service, New York, New York 10017 (800) 253-9646; *Industrial Statistics Yearbook.*

SWITZERLAND - GENERAL MORTALITY

Statistical Office of the United Nations, Publishing Service, New York, New York 10017 (800) 253-9646; *Demographic Yearbook.*

World Health Organization, Office of Publications, Avenue Appia, CH-1211 Geneva 27, Switzerland (Telephone Number in U.S. (518) 436-9686); *World Health Statistics Annual.*

SWITZERLAND - GEOGRAPHIC DATA

Facts on File, 460 Park Avenue South, New York, New York 10016 (800) 443-8323; *The New Book of World Rankings.*

SWITZERLAND - GLASS AND GLASS PRODUCTS - PRODUCTION INDEX - See SWITZERLAND - MINING AND MINERAL PRODUCTS

SWITZERLAND - GOATS - See SWITZERLAND - LIVESTOCK AND POULTRY

SWITZERLAND - GOLD HOLDINGS

International Monetary Fund, 700 Nineteenth Street, NW, Washington, D.C. 20431 (202) 623-7000; *International Financial Statistics.*

Statistical Office of the United Nations, Publishing Service, New York, New York 10017 (800) 253-9646; *Statistical Yearbook.*

The World Bank, 1818 H Street, NW, Washington, D.C. 20433 (202) 477-1234; *World Tables.*

SWITZERLAND - GOLD PRODUCTION AND CONSUMPTION - See SWITZERLAND - MINING AND MINERAL PRODUCTS

SWITZERLAND - GOVERNMENT

G.K. Hall and Company, 70 Lincoln Street, Boston, Massachusetts 02111 (617) 423-3990; *The World in Figures.*

SWITZERLAND - GOVERNMENT EXPENDITURES

International Monetary Fund, 700 Nineteenth Street, NW, Washington, D.C. 20431 (202) 623-7000; *Government Finance Statistics Yearbook.*

Organisation for Economic Co-operation and Development (OECD), 2 rue Andre-Pascal, 75 Paris 16, France (Telephone Number in U.S. (202) 785-6323); *Economic Outlook.*

Times Books, 201 East 50th Street, New York, New York 10022 (212) 751-2600; *The Economist Book of Vital World Statistics.*

The World Bank, 1818 H Street, NW, Washington, D.C. 20433 (202) 477-1234; *World Tables.*

SWITZERLAND - GOVERNMENT FINANCES

International Monetary Fund, 700 Nineteenth Street, NW, Washington, D.C. 20431 (202) 623-7000; *International Financial Statistics.*

Organisation for Economic Co-operation and Development (OECD), 2 rue Andre-Pascal, 75 Paris 16, France (Telephone Number in U.S. (202) 785-6323); *Economic Outlook.*

Statistical Office of the United Nations, Publishing Service, New York, New York 10017 (800) 253-9646; *Statistical Yearbook.*

SWITZERLAND - GOVERNMENT REVENUE

International Monetary Fund, 700 Nineteenth Street, NW, Washington, D.C. 20431 (202) 623-7000; *Government Finance Statistics Yearbook.*

Organisation for Economic Co-operation and Development (OECD), 2 rue Andre-Pascal, 75 Paris 16, France (Telephone Number in U.S. (202) 785-6323); *Economic Outlook,* and *Revenue Statistics of OECD Member Countries.*

Times Books, 201 East 50th Street, New York, New York 10022 (212) 751-2600; *The Economist Book of Vital World Statistics.*

The World Bank, 1818 H Street, NW, Washington, D.C. 20433 (202) 477-1234; *World Tables*.

SWITZERLAND - GRAIN PRODUCTION - See SWITZERLAND - CROPS

SWITZERLAND - GRANTS

International Monetary Fund, 700 Nineteenth Street, NW, Washington, D.C. 20431 (202) 623-7000; *Government Finance Statistics Yearbook*.

Organisation for Economic Co-operation and Development (OECD), 2 rue Andre-Pascal, 75 Paris 16, France (Telephone Number in U.S. (202) 785-6323); *Geographical Distribution of Financial Flows to Developing Countries*.

SWITZERLAND - GROSS DOMESTIC PRODUCT

The Economist Intelligence Unit, 111 West 57th Street, New York, New York 10019 (800) 938-4685; *The World Market Atlas*.

Facts on File, 460 Park Avenue South, New York, New York 10016 (800) 443-8323; *The New Book of World Rankings*.

G.K. Hall and Company, 70 Lincoln Street, Boston, Massachusetts 02111 (617) 423-3990; *The World in Figures*.

Organisation for Economic Co-operation and Development (OECD), 2 rue Andre-Pascal, 75 Paris 16, France (Telephone Number in U.S. (202) 785-6323); *Economic Outlook, Geographical Distribution of Financial Flows to Developing Countries*, and *Revenue Statistics of OECD Member Countries*.

Statistical Office of the United Nations, Publishing Service, New York, New York 10017 (800) 253-9646; *Statistical Yearbook*.

Times Books, 201 East 50th Street, New York, New York 10022 (212) 751-2600; *The Economist Book of Vital World Statistics*.

The World Bank, 1818 H Street, NW, Washington, D.C. 20433 (202) 477-1234; *World Tables*.

SWITZERLAND - GROSS NATIONAL PRODUCT

Organisation for Economic Co-operation and Development (OECD), 2 rue Andre-Pascal, 75 Paris 16, France (Telephone Number in U.S. (202) 785-6323); *Economic Outlook*, and *Geographical Distribution of Financial Flows to Developing Countries*.

U.S. Arms Control and Disarmament Agency, 320 Twenty-first Street, NW, Washington, D.C. 20451 (202) 647-8677; *World Military Expenditures and Arms Transfers*.

The World Bank, 1818 H Street, NW, Washington, D.C. 20433 (202) 477-1234; *World Tables*.

SWITZERLAND - HEALTH

Facts on File, 460 Park Avenue South, New York, New York 10016 (800) 443-8323; *The New Book of World Rankings*.

G.K. Hall and Company, 70 Lincoln Street, Boston, Massachusetts 02111 (617) 423-3990; *The World in Figures*.

Organisation for Economic Co-operation and Development (OECD), 2 rue Andre-Pascal, 75 Paris 16, France (Telephone Number in U.S. (202) 785-6323); *OECD Health Systems: Facts and Trends*.

Statistical Office of the United Nations, Publishing Service, New York, New York 10017 (800) 253-9646; *Statistical Yearbook*.

Times Books, 201 East 50th Street, New York, New York 10022 (212) 751-2600; *The Economist Book of Vital World Statistics*.

World Health Organization, Office of Publications, Avenue Appia, CH-1211 Geneva 27, Switzerland (Telephone Number in U.S. (518) 436-9686); *World Health Statistics Annual*.

SWITZERLAND - HEALTH EXPENDITURES

International Monetary Fund, 700 Nineteenth Street, NW, Washington, D.C. 20431 (202) 623-7000; *Government Finance Statistics Yearbook*.

SWITZERLAND - HIDE PRODUCTION

Organisation for Economic Co-operation and Development (OECD), 2 rue Andre-Pascal, 75 Paris 16, France (Telephone Number in U.S. (202) 785-6323); *The Footwear, Raw Hides and Skins, and Leather Industry in OECD Countries, Foreign Trade by Commodities*, and *Indicators of Industrial Activity*.

SWITZERLAND - HIGHWAYS

G.K. Hall and Company, 70 Lincoln Street, Boston, Massachusetts 02111 (617) 423-3990; *The World in Figures*.

International Road Federation, 525 School Street, SW, Washington, D.C. 20024 (202) 554-2106; *World Road Statistics*.

Statistical Office of the United Nations, Publishing Service, New York, New York 10017 (800) 253-9646; *Annual Bulletin of Transport Statistics for Europe*.

SWITZERLAND - HOME FINANCE

Organisation for Economic Co-operation and Development (OECD), 2 rue Andre-Pascal, 75 Paris 16, France (Telephone Number in U.S. (202) 785-6323); *Main Economic Indicators - Historical Statistics*.

SWITZERLAND - HORSES - See SWITZERLAND - LIVESTOCK AND POULTRY

SWITZERLAND - HOURS OF WORK - See SWITZERLAND - EMPLOYMENT

SWITZERLAND - HOUSING

Facts on File, 460 Park Avenue South, New York, New York 10016 (800) 443-8323; *The New Book of World Rankings*.

SWITZERLAND - HOUSING EXPENDITURES

International Monetary Fund, 700 Nineteenth Street, NW, Washington, D.C. 20431 (202) 623-7000; *Government Finance Statistics Yearbook*.

SWITZERLAND - ILLITERATE POPULATION

The Economist Intelligence Unit, 111 West 57th Street, New York, New York 10019 (800) 938-4685; *The World Market Atlas*.

G.K. Hall and Company, 70 Lincoln Street, Boston, Massachusetts 02111 (617) 423-3990; *The World in Figures*.

SWITZERLAND - IMPORTS

American Automobile Manufacturers Association, 1401 H Eye Street, NW, Suite 900, Washington, D.C. 20005 (202) 326-5500; *World Motor Vehicle Data.*

The Economist Intelligence Unit, 111 West 57th Street, New York, New York 10019 (800) 938-4685; *The World Market Atlas.*

Food and Agricultural Organization of the United Nations (FAO) Via delle Terme di Caracalla, 00100 Rome, Italy (Telephone Number in U.S. (202) 653-2400); *The State of Food and Agriculture.*

G.K. Hall and Company, 70 Lincoln Street, Boston, Massachusetts 02111 (617) 423-3990; *The World in Figures.*

International Monetary Fund, 700 Nineteenth Street, NW, Washington, D.C. 20431 (202) 623-7000; *Direction of Trade Statistics, International Financial Statistics,* and *Government Finance Statistics Yearbook,*

Organisation for Economic Co-operation and Development (OECD), 2 rue Andre-Pascal, 75 Paris 16, France (Telephone Number in U.S. (202) 785-6323); *Economic Outlook, The Footwear, Raw Hides and Skins, and Leather Industry in OECD Countries, Industrial Structure Statistics, The Iron and Steel Industry, Milk, Milk Products, and Egg Balances in OECD Member Countries, OECD Economic Surveys: Switzerland,* and *The Pulp and Paper Industry.*

Times Books, 201 East 50th Street, New York, New York 10022 (212) 751-2600; *The Economist Book of Vital World Statistics.*

The World Bank, 1818 H Street, NW, Washington, D.C. 20433 (202) 477-1234; *World Tables.*

SWITZERLAND - INCOME TAXES - See SWITZERLAND - TAXATION

SWITZERLAND - INDUSTRIAL METALS PRODUCTION - See SWITZERLAND - MINING AND MINERAL PRODUCTS

SWITZERLAND - INDUSTRY

Facts on File, 460 Park Avenue South, New York, New York 10016 (800) 443-8323; *The New Book of World Rankings.*

G.K. Hall and Company, 70 Lincoln Street, Boston, Massachusetts 02111 (617) 423-3990; *The World in Figures.*

International Labour Office, I.L.O. Publications, CH-1211, Geneva 22, Switzerland; *Yearbook of Labour Statistics.*

Organisation for Economic Co-operation and Development (OECD), 2 rue Andre-Pascal, 75 Paris 16, France (Telephone Number in U.S. (202) 785-6323); *Economic Outlook, Industrial Structure Statistics, Indicators of Industrial Activity,* and *Main Economic Indicators - Historical Statistics,* and *OECD Environmental Data.*

Statistical Office of the United Nations, Publishing Service, New York, New York 10017 (800) 253-9646; *Statistical Yearbook.*

Times Books, 201 East 50th Street, New York, New York 10022 (212) 751-2600; *The Economist Book of Vital World Statistics.*

The World Bank, 1818 H Street, NW, Washington, D.C. 20433 (202) 477-1234; *World Tables.*

World Intellectual Property Organization, 34 Chemin des Colombettes, CH-1211 Geneva 20. Switzerland; *Industrial Property Statistics.*

SWITZERLAND - INFANT AND MATERNAL MORTALITY

Statistical Office of the United Nations, Publishing Service, New York, New York 10017 (800) 253-9646; *Demographic Yearbook,* and *Statistical Yearbook.*

Times Books, 201 East 50th Street, New York, New York 10022 (212) 751-2600; *The Economist Book of Vital World Statistics.*

The World Bank, 1818 H Street, NW, Washington, D.C. 20433 (202) 477-1234; *World Tables.*

World Health Organization, Office of Publications, Avenue Appia, CH-1211 Geneva 27, Switzerland (Telephone Number in U.S. (518) 436-9686); *World Health Statistics Annual.*

SWITZERLAND - INTEREST RATES

Organisation for Economic Co-operation and Development (OECD), 2 rue Andre-Pascal, 75 Paris 16, France (Telephone Number in U.S. (202) 785-6323); *Economic Outlook, Financial Market Trends, Main Economic Indicators - Historical Statistics,* and *OECD Financial Statistics.*

SWITZERLAND - INTERNAL TRADE

Organisation for Economic Co-operation and Development (OECD), 2 rue Andre-Pascal, 75 Paris 16, France (Telephone Number in U.S. (202) 785-6323); *Main Economic Indicators - Historical Statistics.*

SWITZERLAND - INTERNATIONAL FINANCE

Organisation for Economic Co-operation and Development (OECD), 2 rue Andre-Pascal, 75 Paris 16, France (Telephone Number in U.S. (202) 785-6323); *Economic Outlook,* and *Financial Market Trends.*

SWITZERLAND - INTERNATIONAL LIQUIDITY

International Monetary Fund, 700 Nineteenth Street, NW, Washington, D.C. 20431 (202) 623-7000; *International Financial Statistics.*

Organisation for Economic Co-operation and Development (OECD), 2 rue Andre-Pascal, 75 Paris 16, France (Telephone Number in U.S. (202) 785-6323); *Economic Outlook,* and *Financial Market Trends.*

SWITZERLAND - INTERNATIONAL RESERVES EXCLUDING GOLD

Statistical Office of the United Nations, Publishing Service, New York, New York 10017 (800) 253-9646; *Statistical Yearbook.*

The World Bank, 1818 H Street, NW, Washington, D.C. 20433 (202) 477-1234; *World Tables.*

SWITZERLAND - INTERNATIONAL STATISTICS

Organisation for Economic Co-operation and Development (OECD), 2 rue Andre-Pascal, 75 Paris 16, France (Telephone Number in U.S. (202) 785-6323); *Financial Market Trends,* and *Tourism Policy and International Tourism in OECD Member Countries.*

SWITZERLAND - INVESTMENTS

Organisation for Economic Co-operation and Development (OECD), 2 rue Andre-Pascal, 75 Paris 16, France (Telephone Number in U.S. (202) 785-6323); *Economic Outlook, Financial Market Trends, Industrial Structure Statistics, The Iron and Steel Industry,* and *Textile Industry in OECD Countries.*

SWITZERLAND - IRON ORE PRODUCTION AND CONSUMPTION - See SWITZERLAND - MINING AND MINERAL PRODUCTS

SWITZERLAND - LABOR FORCE

Facts on File, 460 Park Avenue South, New York, New York 10016 (800) 443-8323; *The New Book of World Rankings*.

Food and Agricultural Organization of the United Nations (FAO) Via delle Terme di Caracalla, 00100 Rome, Italy (Telephone Number in U.S. (202) 653-2400); *The State of Food and Agriculture*.

G.K. Hall and Company, 70 Lincoln Street, Boston, Massachusetts 02111 (617) 423-3990; *The World in Figures*.

Organisation for Economic Co-operation and Development (OECD), 2 rue Andre-Pascal, 75 Paris 16, France (Telephone Number in U.S. (202) 785-6323); *Economic Outlook, The Iron and Steel Industry, Maritime Transport, OECD Economic Surveys: Switzerland, OECD Employment Outlook*, and *Textile Industry in OECD Countries*.

Times Books, 201 East 50th Street, New York, New York 10022 (212) 751-2600; *The Economist Book of Vital World Statistics*.

The World Bank, 1818 H Street, NW, Washington, D.C. 20433 (202) 477-1234; *World Tables*.

SWITZERLAND - LABOR PRODUCTIVITY

International Labour Office, I.L.O. Publications, CH-1211, Geneva 22, Switzerland; *Yearbook of Labour Statistics*.

Organisation for Economic Co operation and Development (OECD), 2 rue Andre Pascal, 75 Paris 16, France (Telephone Number in U.S. (202) 785-6323); *Economic Outlook*, and *OECD Employment Outlook*.

SWITZERLAND - LAND USE

Euromonitor Publications Limited, 87-88 Turnmill Street, London EC1M 5QU, England; *European Marketing Data and Statistics*.

Food and Agricultural Organization of the United Nations (FAO), Via delle Terme di Caracalla, 00100 Rome, Italy (Telephone Number in U.S. (202) 653-2400); *Production Yearbook*.

G.K. Hall and Company, 70 Lincoln Street, Boston, Massachusetts 02111 (617) 423-3990; *The World in Figures*.

SWITZERLAND - LEAD AND LEAD ORE PRODUCTION AND CONSUMPTION - See SWITZERLAND - MINING AND MINERAL PRODUCTS

SWITZERLAND - LEATHER - PRODUCTION INDEX

Organisation for Economic Co-operation and Development (OECD), 2 rue Andre-Pascal, 75 Paris 16, France (Telephone Number in U.S. (202) 785-6323); *Indicators of Industrial Activity*.

SWITZERLAND - LEATHER AND FOOTWEAR - EXPORTS AND IMPORTS

Organisation for Economic Co-operation and Development (OECD), 2 rue Andre-Pascal, 75 Paris 16, France (Telephone Number in U.S. (202) 785-6323); *The Footwear, Raw Hides and Skins*, and *Leather Industry in OECD Countries*.

SWITZERLAND - LIBRARIES

Euromonitor Publications Limited, 87-88 Turnmill Street, London EC1M 5QU, England; *European Marketing Data and Statistics*.

Facts on File, 460 Park Avenue South, New York, New York 10016 (800) 443-8323; *The New Book of World Rankings*.

United Nations Educational, Scientific and Cultural Organization (UNESCO), 7 Place de Fontenoy, F-75700 Paris, France (Telephone Number in U.S. (212) 963-5981); *Statistical Yearbook*.

SWITZERLAND - LIGNITE PRODUCTION - See SWITZERLAND - MINING AND MINERAL PRODUCTS

SWITZERLAND - LIVESTOCK AND POULTRY

Euromonitor Publications Limited, 87-88 Turnmill Street, London EC1M 5QU, England; *European Marketing Data and Statistics*.

Facts on File, 460 Park Avenue South, New York, New York 10016 (800) 443-8323; *The New Book of World Rankings*.

Food and Agricultural Organization of the United Nations (FAO), Via delle Terme di Caracalla, 00100 Rome, Italy (Telephone Number in U.S. (202) 653-2400); *Production Yearbook*, and *The State of Food and Agriculture*.

G.K. Hall and Company, 70 Lincoln Street, Boston, Massachusetts 02111 (617) 423-3990; *The World in Figures*.

Organisation for Economic Co-operation and Development (OECD), 2 rue Andre-Pascal, 75 Paris 16, France (Telephone Number in U.S. (202) 785-6323); *Economic Accounts for Agriculture*, and *Meat Balances in OECD Member Countries*.

Statistical Office of the United Nations, Publishing Service, New York, New York 10017 (800) 253-9646; *Statistical Yearbook*.

SWITZERLAND - LIVING LEVELS

G.K. Hall and Company, 70 Lincoln Street, Boston, Massachusetts 02111 (617) 423-3990; *The World in Figures*.

Organisation for Economic Co-operation and Development (OECD), 2 rue Andre-Pascal, 75 Paris 16, France (Telephone Number in U.S. (202) 785-6323); *Economic Outlook*.

Times Books, 201 East 50th Street, New York, New York 10022 (212) 751-2600; *The Economist Book of Vital World Statistics*.

SWITZERLAND - MACHINERY - PRODUCTION INDEX

Organisation for Economic Co-operation and Development (OECD), 2 rue Andre-Pascal, 75 Paris 16, France (Telephone Number in U.S. (202) 785-6323); *Indicators of Industrial Activity*.

SWITZERLAND - MAGNESIUM PRODUCTION AND CONSUMPTION - See SWITZERLAND - MINING AND MINERAL PRODUCTS

SWITZERLAND - MAIL - NUMBER OF PIECES SENT OR RECEIVED

Statistical Office of the United Nations, Publishing Service, New York, New York 10017 (800) 253-9646; *Statistical Yearbook*.

SWITZERLAND - MANGANESE PRODUCTION AND CONSUMPTION - See SWITZERLAND - MINING AND MINERAL PRODUCTS

SWITZERLAND - MANUFACTURING

American Automobile Manufacturers Association, 1401 H Eye Street, NW, Suite 900, Washington, D.C. 20005 (202) 326-5500; *World Motor Vehicle Data.*

Facts on File, 460 Park Avenue South, New York, New York 10016 (800) 443-8323; *The New Book of World Rankings.*

G.K. Hall and Company, 70 Lincoln Street, Boston, Massachusetts 02111 (617) 423-3990; *The World in Figures.*

Organisation for Economic Co-operation and Development (OECD), 2 rue Andre-Pascal, 75 Paris 16, France (Telephone Number in U.S. (202) 785-6323); *Foreign Trade by Commodities, Indicators of Industrial Activity, Industrial Structure Statistics,* and *Economic Surveys: Switzerland.*

Statistical Office of the United Nations, Publishing Service, New York, New York 10017 (800) 253-9646; *Statistical Yearbook.*

Times Books, 201 East 50th Street, New York, New York 10022 (212) 751-2600; *The Economist Book of Vital World Statistics.*

The World Bank, 1818 H Street, NW, Washington, D.C. 20433 (202) 477-1234; *World Tables.*

SWITZERLAND - MARRIAGE RATES

Facts on File, 460 Park Avenue South, New York, New York 10016 (800) 443-8323; *The New Book of World Rankings.*

Statistical Office of the United Nations, Publishing Service, New York, New York 10017 (800) 253-9646; *Demographic Yearbook,* and *Statistical Yearbook.*

SWITZERLAND - MEAT PRODUCTION - See SWITZERLAND - LIVESTOCK AND POULTRY

SWITZERLAND - MERCHANT SHIPPING

G.K. Hall and Company, 70 Lincoln Street, Boston, Massachusetts 02111 (617) 423-3990; *The World in Figures.*

Lloyd's Register of Shipping, 17 Battery Place, New York, New York 10004 (212) 425-8050; *Register of Ships.*

Organisation for Economic Co-operation and Development (OECD), 2 rue Andre-Pascal, 75 Paris 16, France (Telephone Number in U.S. (202) 785-6323); *Maritime Transport.*

Statistical Office of the United Nations, Publishing Service, New York, New York 10017 (800) 253-9646; *Annual Bulletin of Transport Statistics for Europe,* and *Statistical Yearbook.*

Times Books, 201 East 50th Street, New York, New York 10022 (212) 751-2600; *The Economist Book of Vital World Statistics.*

U.S. Department of Transportation, Maritime Administration, 400 Seventh Avenue, SW, Washington, D.C. 20590 (202) 366-5807; *A Statistical Analysis of the World's Merchant Fleets.*

SWITZERLAND - MERCURY PRODUCTION AND CONSUMPTION - See SWITZERLAND - MINING AND MINERAL PRODUCTS

SWITZERLAND - MILITARY

G.K. Hall and Company, 70 Lincoln Street, Boston, Massachusetts 02111 (617) 423-3990; *The World in Figures.*

The International Institute for Strategic Studies, 23 Tavistock Street, London WC2E 7NQ, England; *The Military Balance.*

U.S. Arms Control and Disarmament Agency, 320 Twenty-first Street, NW, Washington, D.C. 20451 (202) 647-8677; *World Military Expenditures and Arms Transfers.*

SWITZERLAND - MILK PRODUCTION - See SWITZERLAND - DAIRY PRODUCTS

SWITZERLAND - MINING AND MINERAL PRODUCTS

Commodity Research Bureau, Incorporated, 75 Wall Street, New York, New York 10005 (212) 504-7754; *Commodity Year Book.*

Facts on File, 460 Park Avenue South, New York, New York 10016 (800) 443-8323; *The New Book of World Rankings.*

G.K. Hall and Company, 70 Lincoln Street, Boston, Massachusetts 02111 (617) 423-3990; *The World in Figures.*

Organisation for Economic Co-operation and Development (OECD), 2 rue Andre-Pascal, 75 Paris 16, France (Telephone Number in U.S. (202) 785-6323); *Coal Information, Energy Statistics of OECD Countries, Foreign Trade by Commodities, Indicators of Industrial Activity, Industrial Structure Statistics, The Iron and Steel Industry, The Non-Ferrous Metals Industry,* and *OECD Economic Surveys: Switzerland.*

Statistical Office of the United Nations, Publishing Service, New York, New York 10017 (800) 253-9646; *Statistical Yearbook.*

World Bureau of Metal Statistics, 27-A High Street, Ware Hert SG12 9BA, England; *World Metal Statistics.*

SWITZERLAND - MOLYBDENUM AND MOLYBDENUM ORE PRODUCTION AND CONSUMPTION - See SWITZERLAND - MINING AND MINERAL PRODUCTS

SWITZERLAND - MONEY EXCHANGE RATES

International Monetary Fund, 700 Nineteenth Street, NW, Washington, D.C. 20431 (202) 623-7000; *International Financial Statistics.*

Organisation for Economic Co-operation and Development (OECD), 2 rue Andre-Pascal, 75 Paris 16, France (Telephone Number in U.S. (202) 785-6323); *Economic Outlook, Financial Market Trends, OECD Economic Surveys: Switzerland,* and *Tourism Policy and International Tourism in OECD Member Countries.*

Statistical Office of the United Nations, Publishing Service, New York, New York 10017 (800) 253-9646; *Statistical Yearbook.*

SWITZERLAND - MONEY RATES - MARKET

Organisation for Economic Co-operation and Development (OECD), 2 rue Andre-Pascal, 75 Paris 16, France (Telephone Number in U.S. (202) 785-6323); *Economic Outlook,* and *Financial Market Trends.*

SWITZERLAND - MONEY RESERVES

Organisation for Economic Co-operation and Development (OECD), 2 rue Andre-Pascal, 75 Paris 16, France (Telephone Number in U.S. (202) 785-6323); *Economic Outlook,* and *Financial Market Trends.*

SWITZERLAND - MONEY SUPPLY

G.K. Hall and Company, 70 Lincoln Street, Boston, Massachusetts 02111 (617) 423-3990; *The World in Figures.*

International Monetary Fund, 700 Nineteenth Street, NW, Washington, D.C. 20431 (202) 623-7000; *International Financial Statistics.*

Organisation for Economic Co-operation and Development (OECD), 2 rue Andre-Pascal, 75 Paris 16, France (Telephone Number in U.S. (202) 785-6323); *Economic Outlook.*

Statistical Office of the United Nations, Publishing Service, New York, New York 10017 (800) 253-9646; *Statistical Yearbook.*

The World Bank, 1818 H Street, NW, Washington, D.C. 20433 (202) 477-1234; *World Tables.*

SWITZERLAND - MOTION PICTURES

Statistical Office of the United Nations, Publishing Service, New York, New York 10017 (800) 253-9646; *Statistical Yearbook.*

United Nations Educational, Scientific and Cultural Organization (UNESCO), 7 Place de Fontenoy, F-75700 Paris, France (Telephone Number in U.S. (212) 963-5981); *Statistical Yearbook.*

SWITZERLAND - MOTOR VEHICLE ASSEMBLY

American Automobile Manufacturers Association, 1401 H Eye Street, NW, Suite 900, Washington, D.C. 20005 (202) 326-5500; *World Motor Vehicle Data.*

Statistical Office of the United Nations, Publishing Service, New York, New York 10017 (800) 253-9646; *Statistical Yearbook.*

Times Books, 201 East 50th Street, New York, New York 10022 (212) 751-2600; *The Economist Book of Vital World Statistics.*

SWITZERLAND - MOTOR VEHICLE PRODUCTION

American Automobile Manufacturers Association, 1401 H Eye Street, NW, Suite 900, Washington, D.C. 20005 (202) 326-5500; *World Motor Vehicle Data.*

Organisation for Economic Co-operation and Development (OECD), 2 rue Andre-Pascal, 75 Paris 16, France (Telephone Number in U.S. (202) 785-6323); *Foreign Trade by Commodities,* and *Indicators of Industrial Activity.*

SWITZERLAND - MOTOR VEHICLES IN USE

American Automobile Manufacturers Association, 1401 H Eye Street, NW, Suite 900, Washington, D.C. 20005 (202) 326-5500; *World Motor Vehicle Data.*

G.K. Hall and Company, 70 Lincoln Street, Boston, Massachusetts 02111 (617) 423-3990; *The World in Figures.*

International Road Federation, 525 School Street, SW, Washington, D.C. 20024 (202) 554-2106; *World Road Statistics.*

Statistical Office of the United Nations, Publishing Service, New York, New York 10017 (800) 253-9646; *Statistical Yearbook.*

SWITZERLAND - MOTOR VEHICLE TAXES - See SWITZERLAND - TAXATION

SWITZERLAND - MULES - See SWITZERLAND - LIVESTOCK AND POULTRY

SWITZERLAND - MUSEUMS

Euromonitor Publications Limited, 87-88 Turnmill Street, London EC1M 5QU, England; *European Marketing Data and Statistics.*

Facts on File, 460 Park Avenue South, New York, New York 10016 (800) 443-8323; *The New Book of World Rankings.*

SWITZERLAND - NATALITY - See SWITZERLAND - BIRTH RATE

SWITZERLAND - NATIONAL ACCOUNTS

International Monetary Fund, 700 Nineteenth Street, NW, Washington, D.C. 20431 (202) 623-7000; *International Financial Statistics.*

Organisation for Economic Co-operation and Development (OECD), 2 rue Andre-Pascal, 75 Paris 16, France (Telephone Number in U.S. (202) 785-6323); *Economic Outlook.*

Statistical Office of the United Nations, Publishing Service, New York, New York 10017 (800) 253-9646; *National Accounts Statistics,* and *Statistical Yearbook.*

SWITZERLAND - NATIONAL INCOME

Facts on File, 460 Park Avenue South, New York, New York 10016 (800) 443-8323; *The New Book of World Rankings.*

G.K. Hall and Company, 70 Lincoln Street, Boston, Massachusetts 02111 (617) 423-3990; *The World in Figures.*

Organisation for Economic Co-operation and Development (OECD), 2 rue Andre-Pascal, 75 Paris 16, France (Telephone Number in U.S. (202) 785-6323); *Economic Outlook.*

Statistical Office of the United Nations, Publishing Service, New York, New York 10017 (800) 253-9646; *Statistical Yearbook.*

SWITZERLAND - NATIONAL PRODUCT

Facts on File, 460 Park Avenue South, New York, New York 10016 (800) 443-8323; *The New Book of World Rankings.*

Organisation for Economic Co-operation and Development (OECD), 2 rue Andre-Pascal, 75 Paris 16, France (Telephone Number in U.S. (202) 785-6323); *Economic Outlook.*

Statistical Office of the United Nations, Publishing Service, New York, New York 10017 (800) 253-9646; *Statistical Yearbook.*

SWITZERLAND - NATURAL GAS PRODUCTION - See SWITZERLAND - MINING AND MINERAL PRODUCTS

SWITZERLAND - NEWSPAPER PRODUCTION - See SWITZERLAND - FORESTRY AND FOREST PRODUCTS

SWITZERLAND - NEWSPRINT PRODUCTION AND CONSUMPTION - See SWITZERLAND - FORESTRY AND FOREST PRODUCTS

SWITZERLAND - NICKEL AND NICKEL ORE PRODUCTION AND CONSUMPTION - See SWITZERLAND - MINING AND MINERAL PRODUCTS

SWITZERLAND - NITRIC ACID PRODUCTION - See SWITZERLAND - MINING AND MINERAL PRODUCTS

SWITZERLAND - OATS PRODUCTION - See SWITZERLAND - CROPS

SWITZERLAND - OCCUPATIONS - See SWITZERLAND - LABOR FORCE

SWITZERLAND - OIL PRODUCING CROPS

Organisation for Economic Co-operation and Development (OECD), 2 rue Andre-Pascal, 75 Paris 16, France (Telephone Number in U.S. (202) 785-6323); *Foreign Trade by Commodities.*

SWITZERLAND - PAPER - See SWITZERLAND - FORESTRY AND FOREST PRODUCTS

SWITZERLAND - PATENTS

Statistical Office of the United Nations, Publishing Service, New York, New York 10017 (800) 253-9646; *Statistical Yearbook.*

World Intellectual Property Organization, 34 Chemin des Colombettes, CH-1211 Geneva 20. Switzerland; *Industrial Property Statistics.*

SWITZERLAND - PEANUT PRODUCTION - See SWITZERLAND - CROPS

SWITZERLAND - PERIODICALS

United Nations Educational, Scientific and Cultural Organization (UNESCO), 7 Place de Fontenoy, F-75700 Paris, France (Telephone Number in U.S. (212) 963-5981); *Statistical Yearbook.*

SWITZERLAND - PESTICIDE USE

Food and Agricultural Organization of the United Nations (FAO) Via delle Terme di Caracalla, 00100 Rome, Italy (Telephone Number in U.S. (202) 653-2400); *The State of Food and Agriculture.*

SWITZERLAND - PETROLEUM INDUSTRY

Euromonitor Publications Limited, 87-88 Turnmill Street, London EC1M 5QU, England; *European Marketing Data and Statistics.*

Facts on File, 460 Park Avenue South, New York, New York 10016 (800) 443-8323; *The New Book of World Rankings.*

Food and Agricultural Organization of the United Nations (FAO) Via delle Terme di Caracalla, 00100 Rome, Italy (Telephone Number in U.S. (202) 653-2400); *The State of Food and Agriculture.*

G.K. Hall and Company, 70 Lincoln Street, Boston, Massachusetts 02111 (617) 423-3990; *The World in Figures.*

Organisation for Economic Co-operation and Development (OECD), 2 rue Andre-Pascal, 75 Paris 16, France (Telephone Number in U.S. (202) 785-6323); *Energy Statistics of OECD Countries, Foreign Trade by Commodities, Indicators of Industrial Activity,* and *Oil and Gas Information.*

Statistical Office of the United Nations, Publishing Service, New York, New York 10017 (800) 253-9646; *Statistical Yearbook.*

SWITZERLAND - PHOSPHATE ROCK PRODUCTION - See SWITZERLAND - MINING AND MINERAL PRODUCTS

SWITZERLAND - PHOSPHATES PRODUCTION - See SWITZERLAND - MINING AND MINERAL PRODUCTS

SWITZERLAND - PIG-IRON AND FERRO-ALLOY PRODUCTION - See SWITZERLAND - MINING AND MINERAL PRODUCTS

SWITZERLAND - PIGS - See SWITZERLAND - LIVESTOCK AND POULTRY

SWITZERLAND - PIPELINES FOR OIL AND PETROLEUM PRODUCTS

Statistical Office of the United Nations, Publishing Service, New York, New York 10017 (800) 253-9646; *Annual Bulletin of Transport Statistics for Europe.*

SWITZERLAND - PLASTIC AND RESIN PRODUCTION

Organisation for Economic Co-operation and Development (OECD), 2 rue Andre-Pascal, 75 Paris 16, France (Telephone Number in U.S. (202) 785-6323); *Foreign Trade by Commodities.*

SWITZERLAND - PLATINUM PRODUCTION AND CONSUMPTION - See SWITZERLAND - MINING AND MINERAL PRODUCTS

SWITZERLAND - POPULATION

The Economist Intelligence Unit, 111 West 57th Street, New York, New York 10019 (800) 938-4685; *The World Market Atlas.*

Euromonitor Publications Limited, 87-88 Turnmill Street, London EC1M 5QU, England; *European Marketing Data and Statistics.*

Facts on File, 460 Park Avenue South, New York, New York 10016 (800) 443-8323; *The New Book of World Rankings.*

Food and Agricultural Organization of the United Nations (FAO), Via delle Terme di Caracalla, 00100 Rome, Italy (Telephone Number in U.S. (202) 653-2400); *Production Yearbook.*

G.K. Hall and Company, 70 Lincoln Street, Boston, Massachusetts 02111 (617) 423-3990; *The World in Figures.*

International Labour Office, I.L.O. Publications, CH-1211, Geneva 22, Switzerland; *Yearbook of Labour Statistics.*

Statistical Office of the United Nations, Publishing Service, New York, New York 10017 (800) 253-9646; *Demographic Yearbook,* and *Statistical Yearbook.*

Times Books, 201 East 50th Street, New York, New York 10022 (212) 751-2600; *The Economist Book of Vital World Statistics.*

United Nations Educational, Scientific and Cultural Organization (UNESCO), 7 Place de Fontenoy, F-75700 Paris, France (Telephone Number in U.S. (212) 963-5981); *Statistical Yearbook.*

U.S. Arms Control and Disarmament Agency, 320 Twenty-first Street, NW, Washington, D.C. 20451 (202) 647-8677; *World Military Expenditures and Arms Transfers.*

World Health Organization, Office of Publications, Avenue Appia, CH-1211 Geneva 27, Switzerland (Telephone Number in U.S. (518) 436-9686); *World Health Statistics Annual.*

SWITZERLAND - POST OFFICES

Facts on File, 460 Park Avenue South, New York, New York 10016 (800) 443-8323; *The New Book of World Rankings.*

SWITZERLAND - POTATO PRODUCTION - See SWITZERLAND - CROPS

SWITZERLAND - POWER PRODUCTION INDUSTRY

Statistical Office of the United Nations, Publishing Service, New York, New York 10017 (800) 253-9646; *Statistical Yearbook.*

SWITZERLAND - PRICES

Facts on File, 460 Park Avenue South, New York, New York 10016 (800) 443-8323; *The New Book of World Rankings.*

Food and Agricultural Organization of the United Nations (FAO), Via delle Terme di Caracalla, 00100 Rome, Italy (Telephone Number in U.S. (202) 653-2400); *Production Yearbook*, and *The State of Food and Agriculture.*

G.K. Hall and Company, 70 Lincoln Street, Boston, Massachusetts 02111 (617) 423-3990; *The World in Figures.*

International Labour Office, I.L.O. Publications, CH-1211, Geneva 22, Switzerland; *Yearbook of Labour Statistics.*

International Monetary Fund, 700 Nineteenth Street, NW, Washington, D.C. 20431 (202) 623-7000; *International Financial Statistics.*

Organisation for Economic Co-operation and Development (OECD), 2 rue Andre-Pascal, 75 Paris 16, France (Telephone Number in U.S. (202) 785-6323); *Economic Outlook, The Footwear, Raw Hides and Skins, and Leather Industry in OECD Countries, Indicators of Industrial Activity, The Iron and Steel Industry, Main Economic Indicators - Historical Statistics*, and *The Pulp and Paper Industry.*

World Bureau of Metal Statistics, 27-A High Street, Ware Hert SG12 9BA, England; *World Metal Statistics.*

SWITZERLAND - PRINTING AND WRITING PAPER - See SWITZERLAND - FORESTRY AND FOREST PRODUCTS

SWITZERLAND - PRODUCTION

American Automobile Manufacturers Association, 1401 H Eye Street, NW, Suite 900, Washington, D.C. 20005 (202) 326-5500; *World Motor Vehicle Data.*

Facts on File, 460 Park Avenue South, New York, New York 10016 (800) 443-8323; *The New Book of World Rankings.*

G.K. Hall and Company, 70 Lincoln Street, Boston, Massachusetts 02111 (617) 423-3990; *The World in Figures.*

Organisation for Economic Co-operation and Development (OECD), 2 rue Andre-Pascal, 75 Paris 16, France (Telephone Number in U.S. (202) 785-6323); *Economic Outlook, The Footwear, Raw Hides and Skins, and Leather Industry in OECD Countries, Indicators of Industrial Activity, Industrial Structure Statistics, The Iron and Steel Industry, Meat Balances in OECD Member Countries, Milk, Milk Products, and Egg Balances in OECD Member Countries, The Non-Ferrous Metals Industry, The Pulp and Paper Industry*, and *Textile Industry in OECD Countries.*

SWITZERLAND - PRODUCTIVITY

Organisation for Economic Co-operation and Development (OECD), 2 rue Andre-Pascal, 75 Paris 16, France (Telephone Number in U.S. (202) 785-6323); *Economic Outlook.*

SWITZERLAND - PROPERTY TAXES - See SWITZERLAND - TAXATION

SWITZERLAND - PUBLIC CONSUMPTION FUND

Organisation for Economic Co-operation and Development (OECD), 2 rue Andre-Pascal, 75 Paris 16, France (Telephone Number in U.S. (202) 785-6323); *Revenue Statistics of OECD Member Countries.*

SWITZERLAND - PUBLIC EXPENDITURES

Organisation for Economic Co-operation and Development (OECD), 2 rue Andre-Pascal, 75 Paris 16, France (Telephone Number in U.S. (202) 785-6323); *Revenue Statistics of OECD Member Countries.*

SWITZERLAND - PUBLIC FINANCE

Facts on File, 460 Park Avenue South, New York, New York 10016 (800) 443-8323; *The New Book of World Rankings.*

Organisation for Economic Co-operation and Development (OECD), 2 rue Andre-Pascal, 75 Paris 16, France (Telephone Number in U.S. (202) 785-6323); *Revenue Statistics of OECD Member Countries.*

SWITZERLAND - PUBLIC REVENUES

Organisation for Economic Co-operation and Development (OECD), 2 rue Andre-Pascal, 75 Paris 16, France (Telephone Number in U.S. (202) 785-6323); *Revenue Statistics of OECD Member Countries.*

SWITZERLAND - RADIO BROADCASTING - See SWITZERLAND - BROADCASTING

SWITZERLAND - RAILWAYS

Euromonitor Publications Limited, 87-88 Turnmill Street, London EC1M 5QU, England; *European Marketing Data and Statistics.*

G.K. Hall and Company, 70 Lincoln Street, Boston, Massachusetts 02111 (617) 423-3990; *The World in Figures.*

Jane's Information Group, Sentinel House, 163 Brighton Road, Coulsdon, Surrey CR5 2NH, England (Telephone Number in U.S. (703) 683-3700); *Jane's World Railways.*

Statistical Office of the United Nations, Publishing Service, New York, New York 10017 (800) 253-9646; *Annual Bulletin of Transport Statistics for Europe*, and *Statistical Yearbook.*

SWITZERLAND - RELIGION

Facts on File, 460 Park Avenue South, New York, New York 10016 (800) 443-8323; *The New Book of World Rankings.*

SWITZERLAND - RENT PRICES

International Labour Office, I.L.O. Publications, CH-1211, Geneva 22, Switzerland; *Yearbook of Labour Statistics.*

SWITZERLAND - RETAIL TRADE

G.K. Hall and Company, 70 Lincoln Street, Boston, Massachusetts 02111 (617) 423-3990; *The World in Figures.*

SWITZERLAND - RICE PRODUCTION - See SWITZERLAND - CROPS

SWITZERLAND - ROUNDWOOD PRODUCTION - See SWITZERLAND - FORESTRY AND FOREST PRODUCTS

SWITZERLAND - RUBBER PRODUCTION AND CONSUMPTION

Facts on File, 460 Park Avenue South, New York, New York 10016 (800) 443-8323; *The New Book of World Rankings*.

Organisation for Economic Co-operation and Development (OECD), 2 rue Andre-Pascal, 75 Paris 16, France (Telephone Number in U.S. (202) 785-6323); *Foreign Trade by Commodities*.

SWITZERLAND - SALES

Organisation for Economic Co-operation and Development (OECD), 2 rue Andre-Pascal, 75 Paris 16, France (Telephone Number in U.S. (202) 785-6323); *Main Economic Indicators - Historical Statistics*.

SWITZERLAND - SALT PRODUCTION - See SWITZERLAND - MINING AND MINERAL PRODUCTS

SWITZERLAND - SAWNWOOD PRODUCTION - See SWITZERLAND - FORESTRY AND FOREST PRODUCTS

SWITZERLAND - SCIENCE AND TECHNOLOGY - EXPENDITURES FOR RESEARCH

Statistical Office of the United Nations, Publishing Service, New York, New York 10017 (800) 253-9646; *Statistical Yearbook*.

SWITZERLAND - SCIENTISTS AND TECHNICIANS

Statistical Office of the United Nations, Publishing Service, New York, New York 10017 (800) 253-9646; *Statistical Yearbook*.

United Nations Educational, Scientific and Cultural Organization (UNESCO), 7 Place de Fontenoy, F-75700 Paris, France (Telephone Number in U.S. (212) 963-5981); *Statistical Yearbook*.

SWITZERLAND - SENIOR CITIZENS

Facts on File, 460 Park Avenue South, New York, New York 10016 (800) 443-8323; *The New Book of World Rankings*.

SWITZERLAND - SHEEP - See SWITZERLAND - LIVESTOCK AND POULTRY

SWITZERLAND - SHIPBUILDING - PRODUCTION INDEX

Organisation for Economic Co-operation and Development (OECD), 2 rue Andre-Pascal, 75 Paris 16, France (Telephone Number in U.S. (202) 785-6323); *Indicators of Industrial Activity*.

SWITZERLAND - SILVER PRODUCTION AND CONSUMPTION - See SWITZERLAND - MINING AND MINERAL PRODUCTS

SWITZERLAND - SOCIAL DATA

Facts on File, 460 Park Avenue South, New York, New York 10016 (800) 443-8323; *The New Book of World Rankings*.

G.K. Hall and Company, 70 Lincoln Street, Boston, Massachusetts 02111 (617) 423-3990; *The World in Figures*.

SWITZERLAND - SOCIAL SECURITY

International Monetary Fund, 700 Nineteenth Street, NW, Washington, D.C. 20431 (202) 623-7000; *Government Finance Statistics Yearbook*.

Organisation for Economic Co-operation and Development (OECD), 2 rue Andre-Pascal, 75 Paris 16, France (Telephone Number in U.S.

(202) 785-6323); *Revenue Statistics of OECD Member Countries*.

SWITZERLAND - SOCIOECONOMIC DATA

Organisation for Economic Co-operation and Development (OECD), 2 rue Andre-Pascal, 75 Paris 16, France (Telephone Number in U.S. (202) 785-6323); *Economic Outlook*.

SWITZERLAND - STEEL - See SWITZERLAND - MINING AND MINERAL PRODUCTS

SWITZERLAND - STOCKS - COMMODITY - MARKET PRICE - INDEXES

Food and Agricultural Organization of the United Nations (FAO) Via delle Terme di Caracalla, 00100 Rome, Italy (Telephone Number in U.S. (202) 653-2400); *The State of Food and Agriculture*.

Statistical Office of the United Nations, Publishing Service, New York, New York 10017 (800) 253-9646; *Statistical Yearbook*.

World Bureau of Metal Statistics, 27-A High Street, Ware Hert SG12 9BA, England; *World Metal Statistics*.

SWITZERLAND - SUGAR - See SWITZERLAND - CROPS

SWITZERLAND - SULPHUR PRODUCTION - See SWITZERLAND - MINING AND MINERAL PRODUCTS

SWITZERLAND - SULPHURIC ACID PRODUCTION - See SWITZERLAND - MINING AND MINERAL PRODUCTS

SWITZERLAND - TAXATION

G.K. Hall and Company, 70 Lincoln Street, Boston, Massachusetts 02111 (617) 423-3990; *The World in Figures*.

International Monetary Fund, 700 Nineteenth Street, NW, Washington, D.C. 20431 (202) 623-7000; *Government Finance Statistics Yearbook*.

International Road Federation, 525 School Street, SW, Washington, D.C. 20024 (202) 554-2106; *World Road Statistics*.

Organisation for Economic Co-operation and Development (OECD), 2 rue Andre-Pascal, 75 Paris 16, France (Telephone Number in U.S. (202) 785-6323); *Revenue Statistics of OECD Member Countries*.

The World Bank, 1818 H Street, NW, Washington, D.C. 20433 (202) 477-1234; *World Tables*.

SWITZERLAND - TEA CONSUMPTION

Statistical Office of the United Nations, Publishing Service, New York, New York 10017 (800) 253-9646; *Statistical Yearbook*.

SWITZERLAND - TELEGRAPH SERVICE

Statistical Office of the United Nations, Publishing Service, New York, New York 10017 (800) 253-9646; *Statistical Yearbook*.

SWITZERLAND - TELEPHONES IN USE

American Telephone and Telegraph Company, 26 Parsippany Road, Whippany, New Jersey 07981 (800) 338-4038; *The World's Telephones*.

G.K. Hall and Company, 70 Lincoln Street, Boston, Massachusetts 02111 (617) 423-3990; *The World in Figures*.

Statistical Office of the United Nations, Publishing Service, New York, New York 10017 (800) 253-9646; *Statistical Yearbook.*

SWITZERLAND - TELEVISION BROADCASTING - See SWITZERLAND - BROADCASTING

SWITZERLAND - TEXTILE PRODUCTION

American Forest and Paper Association, 1250 Connecticut Avenue, NW, Washington, D.C. 20036 (202) 463-2455; *Wood Pulp and Fiber Statistics.*

G.K. Hall and Company, 70 Lincoln Street, Boston, Massachusetts 02111 (617) 423-3990; *The World in Figures.*

Organisation for Economic Co-operation and Development (OECD), 2 rue Andre-Pascal, 75 Paris 16, France (Telephone Number in U.S. (202) 785-6323); *Foreign Trade by Commodities, Indicators of Industrial Activity, Industrial Structure Statistics,* and *Textile Industry in OECD Countries.*

Statistical Office of the United Nations, Publishing Service, New York, New York 10017 (800) 253-9646; *Statistical Yearbook.*

SWITZERLAND - THEATRE

United Nations Educational, Scientific and Cultural Organization (UNESCO), 7 Place de Fontenoy, F-75700 Paris, France (Telephone Number in U.S. (212) 963 6981); *Statistical Yearbook*

SWITZERLAND - TIN - See SWITZERLAND - MINING AND MINERAL PRODUCTS

SWITZERLAND - TOBACCO PRODUCTION

Euromonitor Publications Limited, 87-88 Turnmill Street, London EC1M 5QU, England; *European Marketing Data and Statistics.*

Facts on File, 460 Park Avenue South, New York, New York 10016 (800) 443-8323; *The New Book of World Rankings.*

Organisation for Economic Co-operation and Development (OECD), 2 rue Andre-Pascal, 75 Paris 16, France (Telephone Number in U.S. (202) 785-6323); *Foreign Trade by Commodities, Indicators of Industrial Activity,* and *Industrial Structure Statistics.*

Statistical Office of the United Nations, Publishing Service, New York, New York 10017 (800) 253-9646; *Statistical Yearbook.*

SWITZERLAND - TOURISM

Euromonitor Publications Limited, 87-88 Turnmill Street, London EC1M 5QU, England; *European Marketing Data and Statistics.*

Facts on File, 460 Park Avenue South, New York, New York 10016 (800) 443-8323; *The New Book of World Rankings.*

G.K. Hall and Company, 70 Lincoln Street, Boston, Massachusetts 02111 (617) 423-3990; *The World in Figures.*

Organisation for Economic Co-operation and Development (OECD), 2 rue Andre-Pascal, 75 Paris 16, France (Telephone Number in U.S. (202) 785-6323); *Tourism Policy and International Tourism in OECD Member Countries.*

Statistical Office of the United Nations, Publishing Service, New York, New York 10017 (800) 253-9646; *Statistical Yearbook.*

Times Books, 201 East 50th Street, New York, New York 10022 (212) 751-2600; *The Economist Book of Vital World Statistics.*

World Tourism Organization, Calle Capitan Haya 42, E-28020 Madrid, Spain; *Yearbook of Tourism Statistics.*

SWITZERLAND - TRACTORS IN USE

Statistical Office of the United Nations, Publishing Service, New York, New York 10017 (800) 253-9646; *Statistical Yearbook.*

SWITZERLAND - TRADE - See SWITZERLAND - FOREIGN TRADE

SWITZERLAND - TRADEMARKS AND SERVICE MARKS

Statistical Office of the United Nations, Publishing Service, New York, New York 10017 (800) 253-9646; *Statistical Yearbook.*

World Intellectual Property Organization, 34 Chemin des Colombettes, CH-1211 Geneva 20. Switzerland; *Industrial Property Statistics.*

SWITZERLAND - TRANSPORTATION AND COMMUNICATIONS

Facts on File, 460 Park Avenue South, New York, New York 10016 (800) 443-8323; *The New Book of World Rankings.*

G.K. Hall and Company, 70 Lincoln Street, Boston, Massachusetts 02111 (617) 423-3990; *The World in Figures.*

SWITZERLAND - TUNGSTEN PRODUCTION AND CONSUMPTION - See SWITZERLAND - MINING AND MINERAL PRODUCTS

SWITZERLAND - UNEMPLOYMENT

Euromonitor Publications Limited, 87-88 Turnmill Street, London EC1M 5QU, England; *European Marketing Data and Statistics.*

International Labour Office, I.L.O. Publications, CH-1211, Geneva 22, Switzerland; *Yearbook of Labour Statistics.*

Organisation for Economic Co-operation and Development (OECD), 2 rue Andre-Pascal, 75 Paris 16, France (Telephone Number in U.S. (202) 785-6323); *Economic Outlook, OECD Economic Surveys: Switzerland,* and *OECD Employment Outlook.*

Statistical Office of the United Nations, Publishing Service, New York, New York 10017 (800) 253-9646; *Statistical Yearbook.*

SWITZERLAND - URANIUM PRODUCTION AND CONSUMPTION - See SWITZERLAND - MINING AND MINERAL PRODUCTS

SWITZERLAND - VANADIUM AND VANADIUM ORE PRODUCTION AND CONSUMPTION - See SWITZERLAND - MINING AND MINERAL PRODUCTS

SWITZERLAND - VITAL STATISTICS

G.K. Hall and Company, 70 Lincoln Street, Boston, Massachusetts 02111 (617) 423-3990; *The World in Figures.*

Statistical Office of the United Nations, Publishing Service, New York, New York 10017 (800) 253-9646; *Statistical Yearbook.*

World Health Organization, Office of Publications, Avenue Appia, CH-1211 Geneva 27, Switzerland (Telephone Number in U.S. (518) 436-9686); *World Health Statistics Annual.*

SWITZERLAND - WAGES

Euromonitor Publications Limited, 87-88 Turnmill Street, London EC1M 5QU, England; *European Marketing Data and Statistics.*

G.K. Hall and Company, 70 Lincoln Street, Boston, Massachusetts 02111 (617) 423-3990; *The World in Figures.*

International Labour Office, I.L.O. Publications, CH-1211, Geneva 22, Switzerland; *Yearbook of Labour Statistics.*

Organisation for Economic Co-operation and Development (OECD), 2 rue Andre-Pascal, 75 Paris 16, France (Telephone Number in U.S. (202) 785-6323); *Economic Outlook, Industrial Structure Statistics,* and *Main Economic Indicators - Historical Statistics.*

Statistical Office of the United Nations, Publishing Service, New York, New York 10017 (800) 253-9646; *Statistical Yearbook.*

SWITZERLAND - WATERWAYS IN USE

Organisation for Economic Co-operation and Development (OECD), 2 rue Andre-Pascal, 75 Paris 16, France (Telephone Number in U.S. (202) 785-6323); *Maritime Transport.*

Statistical Office of the United Nations, Publishing Service, New York, New York 10017 (800) 253-9646; *Annual Bulletin of Transport Statistics for Europe.*

SWITZERLAND - WEATHER

Facts on File, 460 Park Avenue South, New York, New York 10016 (800) 443-8323; *The New Book of World Rankings.*

G.K. Hall and Company, 70 Lincoln Street, Boston, Massachusetts 02111 (617) 423-3990; *The World in Figures.*

SWITZERLAND - WELFARE

International Monetary Fund, 700 Nineteenth Street, NW, Washington, D.C. 20431 (202) 623-7000; *Government Finance Statistics Yearbook.*

SWITZERLAND - WHEAT - See SWITZERLAND - CROPS

SWITZERLAND - WHOLESALE PRICES

Statistical Office of the United Nations, Publishing Service, New York, New York 10017 (800) 253-9646; *Statistical Yearbook.*

SWITZERLAND - WINE PRODUCTION

Facts on File, 460 Park Avenue South, New York, New York 10016 (800) 443-8323; *The New Book of World Rankings.*

Statistical Office of the United Nations, Publishing Service, New York, New York 10017 (800) 253-9646; *Statistical Yearbook.*

SWITZERLAND - WOOD AND WOOD PULP - See SWITZERLAND - FORESTRY AND FOREST PRODUCTS

SWITZERLAND - WOOL - INDUSTRIAL CONSUMPTION

Organisation for Economic Co-operation and Development (OECD), 2 rue Andre-Pascal, 75 Paris 16, France (Telephone Number in U.S. (202) 785-6323); *Textile Industry in OECD Countries.*

Statistical Office of the United Nations, Publishing Service, New York, New York 10017 (800) 253-9646; *Statistical Yearbook.*

SWITZERLAND - WOOL PRODUCTION

Facts on File, 460 Park Avenue South, New York, New York 10016 (800) 443-8323; *The New Book of World Rankings.*

Organisation for Economic Co-operation and Development (OECD), 2 rue Andre-Pascal, 75 Paris 16, France (Telephone Number in U.S. (202) 785-6323); *Economic Accounts for Agriculture,* and *Textile Industry in OECD Countries.*

SWITZERLAND - YARN PRODUCTION

Organisation for Economic Co-operation and Development (OECD), 2 rue Andre-Pascal, 75 Paris 16, France (Telephone Number in U.S. (202) 785-6323); *Foreign Trade by Commodities, Textile Industry in OECD Countries.*

Statistical Office of the United Nations, Publishing Service, New York, New York 10017 (800) 253-9646; *Statistical Yearbook.*

SWITZERLAND - ZINC AND ZINC ORE PRODUCTION AND CONSUMPTION - See SWITZERLAND - MINING AND MINERAL PRODUCTS

SWORDFISH - IMPORTS

U.S. Department of Commerce, National Oceanic and Atmospheric Administration, National Marine Fisheries Service, 1335 East-West Highway, Silver Spring, Maryland 20910 (301) 427-2239; *Fisheries of the United States.*

SYMPHONY ORCHESTRAS

American Symphony Orchestra League, 777 Fourteenth Street, NW, Suite 500, Washington, D.C. 20005 (202) 628-0099.

SYNAGOGUES - See RELIGION

Syrian Arab Republic - National Statistical Office

Central Bureau of Statistics, Abel-Malek Bin Marwan Street, Malki Quarter, Damascus, Syrian Arab Republic.

Syrian Arab Republic - Primary Statistics Source

Central Bureau of Statistics, Abel-Malek Bin Marwan Street, Malki Quarter, Damascus, Syrian Arab Republic; *Statistical Abstract.*

SYRIAN ARAB REPUBLIC - AGRICULTURE

Economic Commission for Western Asia, Post Office Box 27, Baghdad, Iraq; *Statistical Abstract of Western Asia.*

Euromonitor Publications Limited, 87-88 Turnmill Street, London EC1M 5QU, England; *International Marketing Data and Statistics.*

Facts on File, 460 Park Avenue South, New York, New York 10016 (800) 443-8323; *The New Book of World Rankings.*

Food and Agricultural Organization of the United Nations (FAO) Via delle Terme di Caracalla, 00100 Rome, Italy (Telephone Number in U.S. (202) 653-2400); *Production Yearbook,* and *The State of Food and Agriculture,* and *Trade Yearbook.*

Federal Statistical Office, Gustav-Stresemann-Ring 11, D-6200 Wiesbaden, Germany; *Syrian Arab Republic.*

G.K. Hall and Company, 70 Lincoln Street, Boston, Massachusetts 02111 (617) 423-3990; *The World in Figures.*

Statistical Office of the United Nations, Publishing Service, New York, New York 10017 (800) 253-9646; *Statistical Yearbook.*

Times Books, 201 East 50th Street, New York, New York 10022 (212) 751-2600; *The Economist Book of Vital World Statistics.*

The World Bank, 1818 H Street, NW, Washington, D.C. 20433 (202) 477-1234; *World Tables.*

SYRIAN ARAB REPUBLIC - AIRLINE SERVICE

Economic Commission for Western Asia, Post Office Box 27, Baghdad, Iraq; *Statistical Abstract of Western Asia.*

Facts on File, 460 Park Avenue South, New York, New York 10016 (800) 443-8323; *The New Book of World Rankings.*

G.K. Hall and Company, 70 Lincoln Street, Boston, Massachusetts 02111 (617) 423-3990; *The World in Figures.*

Statistical Office of the United Nations, Publishing Service, New York, New York 10017 (800) 253-9646; *Statistical Yearbook.*

Times Books, 201 East 50th Street, New York, New York 10022 (212) 751-2600; *The Economist Book of Vital World Statistics.*

SYRIAN ARAB REPUBLIC - ALUMINUM PRODUCTION AND CONSUMPTION - See SYRIAN ARAB REPUBLIC - MINING AND MINERAL PRODUCTS

SYRIAN ARAB REPUBLIC - ANIMAL HEALTH

Food and Agricultural Organization of the United Nations (FAO), Via delle Terme di Caracalla, 00100, Rome, Italy (Telephone Number in U.S. (202) 653-2400); *Animal Health Yearbook.*

SYRIAN ARAB REPUBLIC - AREA AND DENSITY OF POPULATION

Economic Commission for Western Asia, Post Office Box 27, Baghdad, Iraq; *Statistical Abstract of Western Asia.*

Euromonitor Publications Limited, 87-88 Turnmill Street, London EC1M 5QU, England; *International Marketing Data and Statistics,* and *Middle East Economic Handbook.*

Facts on File, 460 Park Avenue South, New York, New York 10016 (800) 443-8323; *The New Book of World Rankings.*

Federal Statistical Office, Gustav-Stresemann-Ring 11, D-6200 Wiesbaden, Germany; *Syrian Arab Republic.*

Food and Agricultural Organization of the United Nations (FAO) Via delle Terme di Caracalla, 00100 Rome, Italy (Telephone Number in U.S. (202) 653-2400); *The State of Food and Agriculture.*

G.K. Hall and Company, 70 Lincoln Street, Boston, Massachusetts 02111 (617) 423-3990; *The World in Figures.*

Statistical Office of the United Nations, Publishing Service, New York, New York 10017 (800) 253-9646; *Statistical Yearbook.*

Times Books, 201 East 50th Street, New York, New York 10022 (212) 751-2600; *The Economist Book of Vital World Statistics.*

United Nations Educational, Scientific and Cultural Organization (UNESCO), 7 Place de Fontenoy, F-75700 Paris, France (Telephone Number in U.S. (212) 963-5981); *Statistical Yearbook.*

SYRIAN ARAB REPUBLIC - ARMS EXPORTS AND IMPORTS

U.S. Arms Control and Disarmament Agency, 320 Twenty-first Street, NW, Washington, D.C. 20451 (202) 647-8677; *World Military Expenditures and Arms Transfers.*

SYRIAN ARAB REPUBLIC - BALANCE OF PAYMENTS

Economic Commission for Western Asia, Post Office Box 27, Baghdad, Iraq; *Statistical Abstract of Western Asia.*

The Economist Intelligence Unit, 111 West 57th Street, New York, New York 10019 (800) 938-4685; *The World Market Atlas.*

G.K. Hall and Company, 70 Lincoln Street, Boston, Massachusetts 02111 (617) 423-3990; *The World in Figures.*

International Monetary Fund, 700 Nineteenth Street, NW, Washington, D.C. 20431 (202) 623-7000; *Balance of Payments Yearbook.*

Times Books, 201 East 50th Street, New York, New York 10022 (212) 751-2600; *The Economist Book of Vital World Statistics.*

The World Bank, 1818 H Street, NW, Washington, D.C. 20433 (202) 477-1234; *World Tables.*

SYRIAN ARAB REPUBLIC - BALANCE OF TRADE

Economic Commission for Western Asia, Post Office Box 27, Baghdad, Iraq; *Statistical Abstract of Western Asia.*

SYRIAN ARAB REPUBLIC - BANKING

Economic Commission for Western Asia, Post Office Box 27, Baghdad, Iraq; *Statistical Abstract of Western Asia.*

Facts on File, 460 Park Avenue South, New York, New York 10016 (800) 443-8323; *The New Book of World Rankings.*

G.K. Hall and Company, 70 Lincoln Street, Boston, Massachusetts 02111 (617) 423-3990; *The World in Figures.*

International Monetary Fund, 700 Nineteenth Street, NW, Washington, D.C. 20431 (202) 623-7000; *International Financial Statistics.*

Statistical Office of the United Nations, Publishing Service, New York, New York 10017 (800) 253-9646; *Statistical Yearbook.*

SYRIAN ARAB REPUBLIC - BARLEY PRODUCTION - See SYRIAN ARAB REPUBLIC - CROPS

SYRIAN ARAB REPUBLIC - BEER PRODUCTION

Facts on File, 460 Park Avenue South, New York, New York 10016 (800) 443-8323; *The New Book of World Rankings.*

Statistical Office of the United Nations, Publishing Service, New York, New York 10017 (800) 253-9646; *Statistical Yearbook.*

SYRIAN ARAB REPUBLIC - BIRTH RATES

Euromonitor Publications Limited, 87-88 Turnmill Street, London EC1M 5QU, England; *Middle East Economic Handbook.*

Facts on File, 460 Park Avenue South, New York, New York 10016 (800) 443-8323; *The New Book of World Rankings.*

Statistical Office of the United Nations, Publishing Service, New York, New York 10017 (800) 253-9646; *Demographic Yearbook,* and *Statistical Yearbook.*

Times Books, 201 East 50th Street, New York, New York 10022 (212) 751-2600; *The Economist Book of Vital World Statistics.*

The World Bank, 1818 H Street, NW, Washington, D.C. 20433 (202) 477-1234; *World Tables.*

World Health Organization, Office of Publications, Avenue Appia, CH-1211 Geneva 27, Switzerland (Telephone Number in U.S. (518) 436-9686); *World Health Statistics Annual.*

SYRIAN ARAB REPUBLIC - BONDS

G.K. Hall and Company, 70 Lincoln Street, Boston, Massachusetts 02111 (617) 423-3990; *The World in Figures.*

SYRIAN ARAB REPUBLIC - BOOK PRODUCTION

G.K. Hall and Company, 70 Lincoln Street, Boston, Massachusetts 02111 (617) 423-3990; *The World in Figures.*

United Nations Educational, Scientific and Cultural Organization (UNESCO), 7 Place de Fontenoy, F-75700 Paris, France (Telephone Number in U.S. (212) 963-5981); *Statistical Yearbook.*

SYRIAN ARAB REPUBLIC - BROADCASTING

Billboard Limited, P.O. Box 9027, 1006 AA Amsterdam, The Netherlands (Telephone Number in U.S. (212) 764-7300); *World Radio TV Handbook.*

Facts on File, 460 Park Avenue South, New York, New York 10016 (800) 443-8323; *The New Book of World Rankings.*

G.K. Hall and Company, 70 Lincoln Street, Boston, Massachusetts 02111 (617) 423-3990; *The World in Figures.*

Times Books, 201 East 50th Street, New York, New York 10022 (212) 751-2600; *The Economist Book of Vital World Statistics.*

SYRIAN ARAB REPUBLIC - BUSINESS

G.K. Hall and Company, 70 Lincoln Street, Boston, Massachusetts 02111 (617) 423-3990; *The World in Figures.*

SYRIAN ARAB REPUBLIC - BUSINESS AND PROFESSIONAL LICENSES

International Monetary Fund, 700 Nineteenth Street, NW, Washington, D.C. 20431 (202) 623-7000; *Government Finance Statistics Yearbook.*

SYRIAN ARAB REPUBLIC - BUTTER PRODUCTION - See SYRIAN ARAB REPUBLIC - DAIRY PRODUCTS

SYRIAN ARAB REPUBLIC - CALORIE SUPPLY

Food and Agricultural Organization of the United Nations (FAO) Via delle Terme di Caracalla, 00100 Rome, Italy (Telephone Number in U.S. (202) 653-2400); *The State of Food and Agriculture.*

SYRIAN ARAB REPUBLIC - CAPITAL REVENUE

International Monetary Fund, 700 Nineteenth Street, NW, Washington, D.C. 20431 (202) 623-7000; *Government Finance Statistics Yearbook.*

SYRIAN ARAB REPUBLIC - CATTLE - See SYRIAN ARAB REPUBLIC - LIVESTOCK AND POULTRY

SYRIAN ARAB REPUBLIC - CEMENT PRODUCTION - See SYRIAN ARAB REPUBLIC - MINING AND MINERAL PRODUCTS

SYRIAN ARAB REPUBLIC - CHEESE PRODUCTION AND CONSUMPTION - See SYRIAN ARAB REPUBLIC - DAIRY PRODUCTS

SYRIAN ARAB REPUBLIC - CHEMICAL (ORGANIC) PRODUCTION - See SYRIAN ARAB REPUBLIC - MINING AND MINERAL PRODUCTS

SYRIAN ARAB REPUBLIC - CHICKENS - See SYRIAN ARAB REPUBLIC - LIVESTOCK AND POULTRY

SYRIAN ARAB REPUBLIC - CIGARETTE PRODUCTION - See SYRIAN ARAB REPUBLIC - TOBACCO PRODUCTION

SYRIAN ARAB REPUBLIC - CLASS STRUCTURE

G.K. Hall and Company, 70 Lincoln Street, Boston, Massachusetts 02111 (617) 423-3990; *The World in Figures.*

SYRIAN ARAB REPUBLIC - CLIMATE

Facts on File, 460 Park Avenue South, New York, New York 10016 (800) 443-8323; *The New Book of World Rankings.*

G.K. Hall and Company, 70 Lincoln Street, Boston, Massachusetts 02111 (617) 423-3990; *The World in Figures.*

SYRIAN ARAB REPUBLIC - COAL PRODUCTION - See SYRIAN ARAB REPUBLIC - MINING AND MINERAL PRODUCTS

SYRIAN ARAB REPUBLIC - COFFEE PRODUCTION AND CONSUMPTION

Facts on File, 460 Park Avenue South, New York, New York 10016 (800) 443-8323; *The New Book of World Rankings.*

SYRIAN ARAB REPUBLIC - COMMUNICATIONS

Economic Commission for Western Asia, Post Office Box 27, Baghdad, Iraq; *Statistical Abstract of Western Asia.*

G.K. Hall and Company, 70 Lincoln Street, Boston, Massachusetts 02111 (617) 423-3990; *The World in Figures.*

SYRIAN ARAB REPUBLIC - CONSTRUCTION INDUSTRY

Facts on File, 460 Park Avenue South, New York, New York 10016 (800) 443-8323; *The New Book of World Rankings.*

Statistical Office of the United Nations, Publishing Service, New York, New York 10017 (800) 253-9646; *Statistical Yearbook.*

SYRIAN ARAB REPUBLIC - CONSUMER PRICE INDEX

G.K. Hall and Company, 70 Lincoln Street, Boston, Massachusetts 02111 (617) 423-3990; *The World in Figures*.

Statistical Office of the United Nations, Publishing Service, New York, New York 10017 (800) 253-9646; *Statistical Yearbook*.

SYRIAN ARAB REPUBLIC - CONSUMER PRICES

International Labour Office, I.L.O. Publications, CH-1211, Geneva 22, Switzerland; *Yearbook of Labour Statistics*.

International Monetary Fund, 700 Nineteenth Street, NW, Washington, D.C. 20431 (202) 623-7000; *International Financial Statistics*.

Times Books, 201 East 50th Street, New York, New York 10022 (212) 751-2600; *The Economist Book of Vital World Statistics*.

SYRIAN ARAB REPUBLIC - CONSUMPTION

Euromonitor Publications Limited, 87-88 Turnmill Street, London EC1M 5QU, England; *Middle East Economic Handbook*.

G.K. Hall and Company, 70 Lincoln Street, Boston, Massachusetts 02111 (617) 423-3990; *The World in Figures*.

SYRIAN ARAB REPUBLIC - COPPER PRODUCTION AND CONSUMPTION - See SYRIAN ARAB REPUBLIC - MINING AND MINERAL PRODUCTS

SYRIAN ARAB REPUBLIC - CORN PRODUCTION - See SYRIAN ARAB REPUBLIC - CROPS

SYRIAN ARAB REPUBLIC - CORPORATE TAXES - See SYRIAN ARAB REPUBLIC

SYRIAN ARAB REPUBLIC - COTTON - See SYRIAN ARAB REPUBLIC - CROPS

SYRIAN ARAB REPUBLIC - CRIME

International Criminal Police Organization (INTERPOL), 26 rue Armengaud, 92210 Saint Cloud, France; *International Crime Statistics*.

Yale University Press, Yale Station, New Haven, Connecticut 06520 (203) 432-0940; *Violence and Crime in Cross-National Perspective*.

SYRIAN ARAB REPUBLIC - CROPS

Facts on File, 460 Park Avenue South, New York, New York 10016 (800) 443-8323; *The New Book of World Rankings*.

Food and Agricultural Organization of the United Nations (FAO) Via delle Terme di Caracalla, 00100 Rome, Italy (Telephone Number in U.S. (202) 653-2400); *The State of Food and Agriculture*.

G.K. Hall and Company, 70 Lincoln Street, Boston, Massachusetts 02111 (617) 423-3990; *The World in Figures*.

International Monetary Fund, 700 Nineteenth Street, NW, Washington, D.C. 20431 (202) 623-7000; *International Financial Statistics*.

Statistical Office of the United Nations, Publishing Service, New York, New York 10017 (800) 253-9646; *Statistical Yearbook*.

SYRIAN ARAB REPUBLIC - CUSTOMS DUTIES

G.K. Hall and Company, 70 Lincoln Street, Boston, Massachusetts 02111 (617) 423-3990; *The World in Figures*.

International Monetary Fund, 700 Nineteenth Street, NW, Washington, D.C. 20431 (202) 623-7000; *Government Finance Statistics Yearbook*.

SYRIAN ARAB REPUBLIC - DAIRY PRODUCTS

Economic Commission for Western Asia, Post Office Box 27, Baghdad, Iraq; *Statistical Abstract of Western Asia*.

Facts on File, 460 Park Avenue South, New York, New York 10016 (800) 443-8323; *The New Book of World Rankings*.

Statistical Office of the United Nations, Publishing Service, New York, New York 10017 (800) 253-9646; *Statistical Yearbook*.

SYRIAN ARAB REPUBLIC - DEATH RATES

Euromonitor Publications Limited, 87-88 Turnmill Street, London EC1M 5QU, England; *Middle East Economic Handbook*.

G.K. Hall and Company, 70 Lincoln Street, Boston, Massachusetts 02111 (617) 423-3990; *The World in Figures*.

Statistical Office of the United Nations, Publishing Service, New York, New York 10017 (800) 253-9646; *Statistical Yearbook*.

Times Books, 201 East 50th Street, New York, New York 10022 (212) 751-2600; *The Economist Book of Vital World Statistics*.

World Health Organization, Office of Publications, Avenue Appia, CH-1211 Geneva 27, Switzerland (Telephone Number in U.S. (518) 436-9686); *World Health Statistics Annual*.

SYRIAN ARAB REPUBLIC - DEFENSE EXPENDITURES

G.K. Hall and Company, 70 Lincoln Street, Boston, Massachusetts 02111 (617) 423-3990; *The World in Figures*.

International Monetary Fund, 700 Nineteenth Street, NW, Washington, D.C. 20431 (202) 623-7000; *Government Finance Statistics Yearbook*.

U.S. Arms Control and Disarmament Agency, 320 Twenty-first Street, NW, Washington, D.C. 20451 (202) 647-8677; *World Military Expenditures and Arms Transfers*.

SYRIAN ARAB REPUBLIC - DEMOGRAPHY

The Economist Intelligence Unit, 111 West 57th Street, New York, New York 10019 (800) 938-4685; *The World Market Atlas*.

Facts on File, 460 Park Avenue South, New York, New York 10016 (800) 443-8323; *The New Book of World Rankings*.

G.K. Hall and Company, 70 Lincoln Street, Boston, Massachusetts 02111 (617) 423-3990; *The World in Figures*.

SYRIAN ARAB REPUBLIC - DEVELOPMENT ASSISTANCE

G.K. Hall and Company, 70 Lincoln Street, Boston, Massachusetts 02111 (617) 423-3990; *The World in Figures*.

Statistical Office of the United Nations, Publishing Service, New York, New York 10017 (800) 253-9646; *Statistical Yearbook*.

SYRIAN ARAB REPUBLIC - DIAMOND PRODUCTION - See SYRIAN ARAB REPUBLIC - MINING AND MINERAL PRODUCTS

SYRIAN ARAB REPUBLIC - DISCOUNT RATES

Statistical Office of the United Nations, Publishing Service, New York, New York 10017 (800) 253-9646; *Statistical Yearbook.*

SYRIAN ARAB REPUBLIC - DISEASES

G.K. Hall and Company, 70 Lincoln Street, Boston, Massachusetts 02111 (617) 423-3990; *The World in Figures.*

World Health Organization, Office of Publications, Avenue Appia, CH-1211 Geneva 27, Switzerland (Telephone Number in U.S. (518) 436-9686); *World Health Statistics Annual.*

SYRIAN ARAB REPUBLIC - DIVORCE RATES

Facts on File, 460 Park Avenue South, New York, New York 10016 (800) 443-8323; *The New Book of World Rankings.*

Statistical Office of the United Nations, Publishing Service, New York, New York 10017 (800) 253-9646; *Demographic Yearbook,* and *Statistical Yearbook.*

SYRIAN ARAB REPUBLIC - DOMESTIC PRODUCT

G.K. Hall and Company, 70 Lincoln Street, Boston, Massachusetts 02111 (617) 423-3990; *The World in Figures.*

SYRIAN ARAB REPUBLIC - ECONOMY

Euromonitor Publications Limited, 87-88 Turnmill Street, London EC1M 5QU, England; *International Marketing Data and Statistics.*

Facts on File, 460 Park Avenue South, New York, New York 10016 (800) 443-8323; *The New Book of World Rankings.*

G.K. Hall and Company, 70 Lincoln Street, Boston, Massachusetts 02111 (617) 423-3990; *The World in Figures.*

SYRIAN ARAB REPUBLIC - EDUCATION

Economic Commission for Western Asia, Post Office Box 27, Baghdad, Iraq; *Statistical Abstract of Western Asia.*

The Economist Intelligence Unit, 111 West 57th Street, New York, New York 10019 (800) 938-4685; *The World Market Atlas.*

Euromonitor Publications Limited, 87-88 Turnmill Street, London EC1M 5QU, England; *Middle East Economic Handbook.*

Facts on File, 460 Park Avenue South, New York, New York 10016 (800) 443-8323; *The New Book of World Rankings.*

Federal Statistical Office, Gustav-Stresemann-Ring 11, D-6200 Wiesbaden, Germany; *Syrian Arab Republic.*

G.K. Hall and Company, 70 Lincoln Street, Boston, Massachusetts 02111 (617) 423-3990; *The World in Figures.*

International Monetary Fund, 700 Nineteenth Street, NW, Washington, D.C. 20431 (202) 623-7000; *Government Finance Statistics Yearbook.*

Times Books, 201 East 50th Street, New York, New York 10022 (212) 751-2600; *The Economist Book of Vital World Statistics.*

United Nations Educational, Scientific and Cultural Organization (UNESCO), 7 Place de Fontenoy, F-75700 Paris, France (Telephone Number in U.S. (212) 963-5981); *Statistical Yearbook.*

The World Bank, 1818 H Street, NW, Washington, D.C. 20433 (202) 477-1234; *World Tables.*

SYRIAN ARAB REPUBLIC - EGG PRODUCTION AND CONSUMPTION - See SYRIAN ARAB REPUBLIC - DAIRY PRODUCTS

SYRIAN ARAB REPUBLIC - ELECTRICITY

Facts on File, 460 Park Avenue South, New York, New York 10016 (800) 443-8323; *The New Book of World Rankings.*

Penn Well Publishing Company, 1421 South Sheridan Road, P.O. Box 1260, Tulsa, Oklahoma 74101 (800) 752-9764; *International Energy Statistics Sourcebook.*

Statistical Office of the United Nations, Publishing Service, New York, New York 10017 (800) 253-9646; *Statistical Yearbook.*

Times Books, 201 East 50th Street, New York, New York 10022 (212) 751-2600; *The Economist Book of Vital World Statistics.*

SYRIAN ARAB REPUBLIC - EMPLOYMENT

Economic Commission for Western Asia, Post Office Box 27, Baghdad, Iraq; *Statistical Abstract of Western Asia.*

Euromonitor Publications Limited, 87-88 Turnmill Street, London EC1M 5QU, England; *International Marketing Data and Statistics,* and *Middle East Economic Handbook.*

Facts on File, 460 Park Avenue South, New York, New York 10016 (800) 443-8323; *The New Book of World Rankings.*

Federal Statistical Office, Gustav-Stresemann-Ring 11, D-6200 Wiesbaden, Germany; *Syrian Arab Republic.*

International Labour Office, I.L.O. Publications, CH-1211, Geneva 22, Switzerland; *Yearbook of Labour Statistics.*

Statistical Office of the United Nations, Publishing Service, New York, New York 10017 (800) 253-9646; *Statistical Yearbook.*

SYRIAN ARAB REPUBLIC - ENERGY

Economic Commission for Western Asia, Post Office Box 27, Baghdad, Iraq; *Statistical Abstract of Western Asia.*

Euromonitor Publications Limited, 87-88 Turnmill Street, London EC1M 5QU, England; *Middle East Economic Handbook.*

Facts on File, 460 Park Avenue South, New York, New York 10016 (800) 443-8323; *The New Book of World Rankings.*

Food and Agricultural Organization of the United Nations (FAO) Via delle Terme di Caracalla, 00100 Rome, Italy (Telephone Number in U.S. (202) 653-2400); *The State of Food and Agriculture.*

G.K. Hall and Company, 70 Lincoln Street, Boston, Massachusetts 02111 (617) 423-3990; *The World in Figures.*

Penn Well Publishing Company, 1421 South Sheridan Road, P.O. Box 1260, Tulsa, Oklahoma 74101 (800) 752-9764; *International Energy Statistics Sourcebook.*

Statistical Office of the United Nations, Publishing Service, New York, New York 10017 (800) 253-9646; *Energy Statistics Yearbook*, and *Statistical Yearbook*.

Times Books, 201 East 50th Street, New York, New York 10022 (212) 751-2600; *The Economist Book of Vital World Statistics*.

SYRIAN ARAB REPUBLIC - EXCHANGE RATES

Euromonitor Publications Limited, 87-88 Turnmill Street, London EC1M 5QU, England; *International Marketing Data and Statistics*, and *Middle East Economic Handbook*.

International Monetary Fund, 700 Nineteenth Street, NW, Washington, D.C. 20431 (202) 623-7000; *International Financial Statistics*.

Statistical Office of the United Nations, Publishing Service, New York, New York 10017 (800) 253-9646; *Statistical Yearbook*.

SYRIAN ARAB REPUBLIC - EXCISE TAXES - See SYRIAN ARAB REPUBLIC - TAXATION

SYRIAN ARAB REPUBLIC - EXPORTS

Economic Commission for Western Asia, Post Office Box 27, Baghdad, Iraq; *Statistical Abstract of Western Asia*.

The Economist Intelligence Unit, 111 West 57th Street, New York, New York 10019 (800) 938-4685; *The World Market Atlas*.

Euromonitor Publications Limited, 87-88 Turnmill Street, London EC1M 5QU, England; *International Marketing Data and Statistics*, and *Middle East Economic Handbook*.

Food and Agricultural Organization of the United Nations (FAO) Via delle Terme di Caracalla, 00100 Rome, Italy (Telephone Number in U.S. (202) 653-2400); *The State of Food and Agriculture*.

G.K. Hall and Company, 70 Lincoln Street, Boston, Massachusetts 02111 (617) 423-3990; *The World in Figures*.

International Monetary Fund, 700 Nineteenth Street, NW, Washington, D.C. 20431 (202) 623-7000; *Direction of Trade Statistics, Government Finance Statistics Yearbook*, and *International Financial Statistics*.

Times Books, 201 East 50th Street, New York, New York 10022 (212) 751-2600; *The Economist Book of Vital World Statistics*.

The World Bank, 1818 H Street, NW, Washington, D.C. 20433 (202) 477-1234; *World Tables*.

SYRIAN ARAB REPUBLIC - EXTERNAL INDEBTEDNESS

The World Bank, 1818 H Street, NW, Washington, D.C. 20433 (202) 477-1234; *World Tables*.

SYRIAN ARAB REPUBLIC - EXTERNAL TRADE

Food and Agricultural Organization of the United Nations (FAO) Via delle Terme di Caracalla, 00100 Rome, Italy (Telephone Number in U.S. (202) 653-2400); *The State of Food and Agriculture*, and *Trade Yearbook*.

G.K. Hall and Company, 70 Lincoln Street, Boston, Massachusetts 02111 (617) 423-3990; *The World in Figures*.

Statistical Office of the United Nations, Publishing Service, New York, New York 10017 (800) 253-9646; *Statistical Yearbook*.

SYRIAN ARAB REPUBLIC - FABRIC PRODUCTION - See SYRIAN ARAB REPUBLIC - TEXTILE INDUSTRY

SYRIAN ARAB REPUBLIC - FARM CROPS - See SYRIAN ARAB REPUBLIC - CROPS

SYRIAN ARAB REPUBLIC - FEMALE WORKING POPULATION - See SYRIAN ARAB REPUBLIC - EMPLOYMENT

SYRIAN ARAB REPUBLIC - FERTILITY RATES

Facts on File, 460 Park Avenue South, New York, New York 10016 (800) 443-8323; *The New Book of World Rankings*.

Times Books, 201 East 50th Street, New York, New York 10022 (212) 751-2600; *The Economist Book of Vital World Statistics*.

The World Bank, 1818 H Street, NW, Washington, D.C. 20433 (202) 477-1234; *World Tables*.

SYRIAN ARAB REPUBLIC - FERTILIZER

Food and Agricultural Organization of the United Nations (FAO) Via delle Terme di Caracalla, 00100 Rome, Italy (Telephone Number in U.S. (202) 653-2400); *The State of Food and Agriculture*.

Statistical Office of the United Nations, Publishing Service, New York, New York 10017 (800) 253-9646; *Statistical Yearbook*.

SYRIAN ARAB REPUBLIC - FETAL MORTALITY

Statistical Office of the United Nations, Publishing Service, New York, New York 10017 (800) 253-9646; *Demographic Yearbook*.

SYRIAN ARAB REPUBLIC - FILM - See SYRIAN ARAB REPUBLIC - MOTION PICTURES

SYRIAN ARAB REPUBLIC - FINANCE

Economic Commission for Western Asia, Post Office Box 27, Baghdad, Iraq; *Statistical Abstract of Western Asia*.

Euromonitor Publications Limited, 87-88 Turnmill Street, London EC1M 5QU, England; *Middle East Economic Handbook*.

Facts on File, 460 Park Avenue South, New York, New York 10016 (800) 443-8323; *The New Book of World Rankings*.

G.K. Hall and Company, 70 Lincoln Street, Boston, Massachusetts 02111 (617) 423-3990; *The World in Figures*.

International Monetary Fund, 700 Nineteenth Street, NW, Washington, D.C. 20431 (202) 623-7000; *International Financial Statistics*.

SYRIAN ARAB REPUBLIC - FISHERIES

Economic Commission for Western Asia, Post Office Box 27, Baghdad, Iraq; *Statistical Abstract of Western Asia*.

Facts on File, 460 Park Avenue South, New York, New York 10016 (800) 443-8323; *The New Book of World Rankings*.

Food and Agricultural Organization of the United Nations (FAO) Via delle Terme di Caracalla, 00100 Rome, Italy (Telephone Number in U.S. (202) 653-2400); *The State of Food and Agriculture*, and

Yearbook of Fishery Statistics.

Statistical Office of the United Nations, Publishing Service, New York, New York 10017 (800) 253-9646; *Statistical Yearbook.*

SYRIAN ARAB REPUBLIC - FLOUR PRODUCTION

Statistical Office of the United Nations, Publishing Service, New York, New York 10017 (800) 253-9646; *Statistical Yearbook.*

SYRIAN ARAB REPUBLIC - FOOD

Food and Agricultural Organization of the United Nations (FAO) Via delle Terme di Caracalla, 00100 Rome, Italy (Telephone Number in U.S. (202) 653-2400); *Production Yearbook,* and *The State of Food and Agriculture.*

G.K. Hall and Company, 70 Lincoln Street, Boston, Massachusetts 02111 (617) 423-3990; *The World in Figures.*

SYRIAN ARAB REPUBLIC - FOREIGN AID

G.K. Hall and Company, 70 Lincoln Street, Boston, Massachusetts 02111 (617) 423-3990; *The World in Figures.*

SYRIAN ARAB REPUBLIC - FOREIGN INDEBTEDNESS

Euromonitor Publications Limited, 87-88 Turnmill Street, London EC1M 5QU, England; *Middle East Economic Handbook.*

SYRIAN ARAB REPUBLIC - FOREIGN TRADE

Economic Commission for Western Asia, Post Office Box 27, Baghdad, Iraq; *Statistical Abstract of Western Asia.*

Euromonitor Publications Limited, 87-88 Turnmill Street, London EC1M 5QU, England; *International Marketing Data and Statistics,* and *Middle East Economic Handbook.*

Facts on File, 460 Park Avenue South, New York, New York 10016 (800) 443-8323; *The New Book of World Rankings.*

Food and Agricultural Organization of the United Nations (FAO) Via delle Terme di Caracalla, 00100 Rome, Italy (Telephone Number in U.S. (202) 653-2400); *The State of Food and Agriculture.*

G.K. Hall and Company, 70 Lincoln Street, Boston, Massachusetts 02111 (617) 423-3990; *The World in Figures.*

Statistical Office of the United Nations, Publishing Service, New York, New York 10017 (800) 253-9646; *International Trade Statistics Yearbook,* and *Statistical Yearbook.*

The World Bank, 1818 H Street, NW, Washington, D.C. 20433 (202) 477-1234; *World Tables.*

SYRIAN ARAB REPUBLIC - FORESTRY AND FOREST PRODUCTS

Facts on File, 460 Park Avenue South, New York, New York 10016 (800) 443-8323; *The New Book of World Rankings.*

Food and Agricultural Organization of the United Nations (FAO) Via delle Terme di Caracalla, 00100 Rome, Italy (Telephone Number in U.S. (202) 653-2400); *The State of Food and Agriculture.*

G.K. Hall and Company, 70 Lincoln Street, Boston, Massachusetts 02111 (617) 423-3990; *The World in Figures.*

Statistical Office of the United Nations, Publishing Service, New York, New York 10017 (800) 253-9646; *Statistical Yearbook.*

United Nations Educational, Scientific and Cultural Organization (UNESCO), 7 Place de Fontenoy, F-75700 Paris, France (Telephone Number in U.S. (212) 963-5981); *Statistical Yearbook.*

SYRIAN ARAB REPUBLIC - GAS PRODUCTION - See SYRIAN ARAB REPUBLIC - MINING AND MINERAL PRODUCTS

SYRIAN ARAB REPUBLIC - GENERAL INDUSTRIAL STATISTICS

Statistical Office of the United Nations, Publishing Service, New York, New York 10017 (800) 253-9646; *Industrial Statistics Yearbook.*

SYRIAN ARAB REPUBLIC - GENERAL MORTALITY

Statistical Office of the United Nations, Publishing Service, New York, New York 10017 (800) 253-9646; *Demographic Yearbook.*

World Health Organization, Office of Publications, Avenue Appia, CH-1211 Geneva 27, Switzerland (Telephone Number in U.S. (518) 436-9686); *World Health Statistics Annual.*

SYRIAN ARAB REPUBLIC - GEOGRAPHIC DATA

Facts on File, 460 Park Avenue South, New York, New York 10016 (800) 443-8323; *The New Book of World Rankings.*

SYRIAN ARAB REPUBLIC - GOATS - See SYRIAN ARAB REPUBLIC - LIVESTOCK AND POULTRY

SYRIAN ARAB REPUBLIC - GOLD HOLDINGS

International Monetary Fund, 700 Nineteenth Street, NW, Washington, D.C. 20431 (202) 623-7000; *International Financial Statistics.*

Statistical Office of the United Nations, Publishing Service, New York, New York 10017 (800) 253-9646; *Statistical Yearbook.*

The World Bank, 1818 H Street, NW, Washington, D.C. 20433 (202) 477-1234; *World Tables.*

SYRIAN ARAB REPUBLIC - GOLD PRODUCTION AND CONSUMPTION - See SYRIAN ARAB REPUBLIC - MINING AND MINERAL PRODUCTS

SYRIAN ARAB REPUBLIC - GOVERNMENT

G.K. Hall and Company, 70 Lincoln Street, Boston, Massachusetts 02111 (617) 423-3990; *The World in Figures.*

SYRIAN ARAB REPUBLIC - GOVERNMENT EXPENDITURES

Economic Commission for Western Asia, Post Office Box 27, Baghdad, Iraq; *Statistical Abstract of Western Asia.*

International Monetary Fund, 700 Nineteenth Street, NW, Washington, D.C. 20431 (202) 623-7000; *Government Finance Statistics Yearbook.*

Times Books, 201 East 50th Street, New York, New York 10022 (212) 751-2600; *The Economist Book of Vital World Statistics.*

The World Bank, 1818 H Street, NW, Washington, D.C. 20433 (202) 477-1234; *World Tables.*

SYRIAN ARAB REPUBLIC - GOVERNMENT FINANCES

Statistical Office of the United Nations, Publishing Service, New York, New York 10017 (800) 253-9646; *Statistical Yearbook.*

SYRIAN ARAB REPUBLIC - GOVERNMENT REVENUE

Economic Commission for Western Asia, Post Office Box 27, Baghdad, Iraq; *Statistical Abstract of Western Asia.*

International Monetary Fund, 700 Nineteenth Street, NW, Washington, D.C. 20431 (202) 623-7000; *Government Finance Statistics Yearbook.*

Times Books, 201 East 50th Street, New York, New York 10022 (212) 751-2600; *The Economist Book of Vital World Statistics.*

The World Bank, 1818 H Street, NW, Washington, D.C. 20433 (202) 477-1234; *World Tables.*

SYRIAN ARAB REPUBLIC - GRAIN PRODUCTION - See SYRIAN ARAB REPUBLIC - CROPS

SYRIAN ARAB REPUBLIC - GRANTS

International Monetary Fund, 700 Nineteenth Street, NW, Washington, D.C. 20431 (202) 623-7000; *Government Finance Statistics Yearbook.*

SYRIAN ARAB REPUBLIC - GROSS DOMESTIC PRODUCT

Economic Commission for Western Asia, Post Office Box 27, Baghdad, Iraq; *Statistical Abstract of Western Asia.*

The Economist Intelligence Unit, 111 West 57th Street, New York, New York 10019 (800) 938-4685; *The World Market Atlas.*

Euromonitor Publications Limited, 87-88 Turnmill Street, London EC1M 5QU, England; *International Marketing Data and Statistics, and Middle East Economic Handbook.*

Facts on File, 460 Park Avenue South, New York, New York 10016 (800) 443-8323; *The New Book of World Rankings.*

G.K. Hall and Company, 70 Lincoln Street, Boston, Massachusetts 02111 (617) 423-3990; *The World in Figures.*

Statistical Office of the United Nations, Publishing Service, New York, New York 10017 (800) 253-9646; *Statistical Yearbook.*

Times Books, 201 East 50th Street, New York, New York 10022 (212) 751-2600; *The Economist Book of Vital World Statistics.*

The World Bank, 1818 H Street, NW, Washington, D.C. 20433 (202) 477-1234; *World Tables.*

SYRIAN ARAB REPUBLIC - GROSS NATIONAL PRODUCT

Euromonitor Publications Limited, 87-88 Turnmill Street, London EC1M 5QU, England; *International Marketing Data and Statistics.*

U.S. Arms Control and Disarmament Agency, 320 Twenty-first Street, NW, Washington, D.C. 20451 (202) 647-8677; *World Military Expenditures and Arms Transfers.*

The World Bank, 1818 H Street, NW, Washington, D.C. 20433 (202) 477-1234; *World Tables.*

SYRIAN ARAB REPUBLIC - GROUNDNUT PRODUCTION

Statistical Office of the United Nations, Publishing Service, New York, New York 10017 (800) 253-9646; *Statistical Yearbook.*

SYRIAN ARAB REPUBLIC - HEALTH

Economic Commission for Western Asia, Post Office Box 27, Baghdad, Iraq; *Statistical Abstract of Western Asia.*

Euromonitor Publications Limited, 87-88 Turnmill Street, London EC1M 5QU, England; *Middle East Economic Handbook.*

Facts on File, 460 Park Avenue South, New York, New York 10016 (800) 443-8323; *The New Book of World Rankings.*

Federal Statistical Office, Gustav-Stresemann-Ring 11, D-6200 Wiesbaden, Germany; *Syrian Arab Republic.*

G.K. Hall and Company, 70 Lincoln Street, Boston, Massachusetts 02111 (617) 423-3990; *The World in Figures.*

Statistical Office of the United Nations, Publishing Service, New York, New York 10017 (800) 253-9646; *Statistical Yearbook.*

Times Books, 201 East 50th Street, New York, New York 10022 (212) 751-2600; *The Economist Book of Vital World Statistics.*

World Health Organization, Office of Publications, Avenue Appia, CH-1211 Geneva 27, Switzerland (Telephone Number in U.S. (518) 436-9686); *World Health Statistics Annual.*

SYRIAN ARAB REPUBLIC - HEALTH EXPENDITURES

International Monetary Fund, 700 Nineteenth Street, NW, Washington, D.C. 20431 (202) 623-7000; *Government Finance Statistics Yearbook.*

SYRIAN ARAB REPUBLIC - HIGHWAYS

Economic Commission for Western Asia, Post Office Box 27, Baghdad, Iraq; *Statistical Abstract of Western Asia.*

G.K. Hall and Company, 70 Lincoln Street, Boston, Massachusetts 02111 (617) 423-3990; *The World in Figures.*

International Road Federation, 525 School Street, SW, Washington, D.C. 20024 (202) 554-2106; *World Road Statistics.*

SYRIAN ARAB REPUBLIC - HORSES - See SYRIAN ARAB REPUBLIC - LIVESTOCK AND POULTRY

SYRIAN ARAB REPUBLIC - HOURS OF WORK - See SYRIAN ARAB REPUBLIC - EMPLOYMENT

SYRIAN ARAB REPUBLIC - HOUSING AND HOUSING UNITS

Facts on File, 460 Park Avenue South, New York, New York 10016 (800) 443-8323; *The New Book of World Rankings.*

SYRIAN ARAB REPUBLIC - HOUSING EXPENDITURES

International Monetary Fund, 700 Nineteenth Street, NW, Washington, D.C. 20431 (202) 623-7000; *Government Finance Statistics Yearbook.*

SYRIAN ARAB REPUBLIC - ILLITERATE POPULATION

The Economist Intelligence Unit, 111 West 57th Street, New York, New York 10019 (800) 938-4685; *The World Market Atlas*.

G.K. Hall and Company, 70 Lincoln Street, Boston, Massachusetts 02111 (617) 423-3990; *The World in Figures*.

United Nations Educational, Scientific and Cultural Organization (UNESCO), 7 Place de Fontenoy, F-75700 Paris, France (Telephone Number in U.S. (212) 963-5981); *Statistical Yearbook*.

SYRIAN ARAB REPUBLIC - IMPORTS

Economic Commission for Western Asia, Post Office Box 27, Baghdad, Iraq; *Statistical Abstract of Western Asia*.

The Economist Intelligence Unit, 111 West 57th Street, New York, New York 10019 (800) 938-4685; *The World Market Atlas*.

Euromonitor Publications Limited, 87-88 Turnmill Street, London EC1M 5QU, England; *International Marketing Data and Statistics*, and *Middle East Economic Handbook*.

Food and Agricultural Organization of the United Nations (FAO) Via delle Terme di Caracalla, 00100 Rome, Italy (Telephone Number in U.S. (202) 653-2400); *The State of Food and Agriculture*.

G.K. Hall and Company, 70 Lincoln Street, Boston, Massachusetts 02111 (617) 423-3990; *The World in Figures*.

International Monetary Fund, 700 Nineteenth Street, NW, Washington, D.C. 20431 (202) 623-7000; *Direction of Trade Statistics*, *International Financial Statistics*, and *Government Finance Statistics Yearbook*.

Statistical Office of the United Nations, Publishing Service, New York, New York 10017 (800) 253-9646; *Trade in Manufactures of Developing Countries*.

Times Books, 201 East 50th Street, New York, New York 10022 (212) 751-2600; *The Economist Book of Vital World Statistics*.

The World Bank, 1818 H Street, NW, Washington, D.C. 20433 (202) 477-1234; *World Tables*.

SYRIAN ARAB REPUBLIC - INCOME TAXES - See SYRIAN ARAB REPUBLIC - TAXATION

SYRIAN ARAB REPUBLIC - INDUSTRY

Euromonitor Publications Limited, 87-88 Turnmill Street, London EC1M 5QU, England; *International Marketing Data and Statistics*.

Facts on File, 460 Park Avenue South, New York, New York 10016 (800) 443-8323; *The New Book of World Rankings*.

G.K. Hall and Company, 70 Lincoln Street, Boston, Massachusetts 02111 (617) 423-3990; *The World in Figures*.

International Labour Office, I.L.O. Publications, CH-1211, Geneva 22, Switzerland; *Yearbook of Labour Statistics*.

Statistical Office of the United Nations, Publishing Service, New York, New York 10017 (800) 253-9646; *Statistical Yearbook*.

Times Books, 201 East 50th Street, New York, New York 10022 (212) 751-2600; *The Economist Book of Vital World Statistics*.

The World Bank, 1818 H Street, NW, Washington, D.C. 20433 (202) 477-1234; *World Tables*.

SYRIAN ARAB REPUBLIC - INFANT AND MATERNAL MORTALITY

Statistical Office of the United Nations, Publishing Service, New York, New York 10017 (800) 253-9646; *Demographic Yearbook*, and *Statistical Yearbook*.

Times Books, 201 East 50th Street, New York, New York 10022 (212) 751-2600; *The Economist Book of Vital World Statistics*.

The World Bank, 1818 H Street, NW, Washington, D.C. 20433 (202) 477-1234; *World Tables*.

SYRIAN ARAB REPUBLIC - INTERNATIONAL LIQUIDITY

International Monetary Fund, 700 Nineteenth Street, NW, Washington, D.C. 20431 (202) 623-7000; *International Financial Statistics*.

SYRIAN ARAB REPUBLIC - INTERNATIONAL RESERVES EXCLUDING GOLD

Statistical Office of the United Nations, Publishing Service, New York, New York 10017 (800) 253-9646; *Statistical Yearbook*.

The World Bank, 1818 H Street, NW, Washington, D.C. 20433 (202) 477-1234; *World Tables*.

SYRIAN ARAB REPUBLIC - IRON ORE PRODUCTION AND CONSUMPTION - See SYRIAN ARAB REPUBLIC - MINING AND MINERAL PRODUCTS

SYRIAN ARAB REPUBLIC - IRRIGATION

Euromonitor Publications Limited, 87-88 Turnmill Street, London EC1M 5QU, England; *International Marketing Data and Statistics*.

SYRIAN ARAB REPUBLIC - LABOR FORCE

Economic Commission for Western Asia, Post Office Box 27, Baghdad, Iraq; *Statistical Abstract of Western Asia*.

Euromonitor Publications Limited, 87-88 Turnmill Street, London EC1M 5QU, England; *International Marketing Data and Statistics*, and *Middle East Economic Handbook*.

Facts on File, 460 Park Avenue South, New York, New York 10016 (800) 443-8323; *The New Book of World Rankings*.

Food and Agricultural Organization of the United Nations (FAO) Via delle Terme di Caracalla, 00100 Rome, Italy (Telephone Number in U.S. (202) 653-2400); *The State of Food and Agriculture*.

G.K. Hall and Company, 70 Lincoln Street, Boston, Massachusetts 02111 (617) 423-3990; *The World in Figures*.

The World Bank, 1818 H Street, NW, Washington, D.C. 20433 (202) 477-1234; *World Tables*.

SYRIAN ARAB REPUBLIC - LABOR PRODUCTIVITY

International Labour Office, I.L.O. Publications, CH-1211, Geneva 22, Switzerland; *Yearbook of Labour Statistics*.

SYRIAN ARAB REPUBLIC - LAND USE

Economic Commission for Western Asia, Post Office Box 27, Baghdad, Iraq; *Statistical Abstract of Western Asia.*

Euromonitor Publications Limited, 87-88 Turnmill Street, London EC1M 5QU, England; *International Marketing Data and Statistics.*

Food and Agricultural Organization of the United Nations (FAO), Via delle Terme di Caracalla, 00100 Rome, Italy (Telephone Number in U.S. (202) 653-2400); *Production Yearbook.*

G.K. Hall and Company, 70 Lincoln Street, Boston, Massachusetts 02111 (617) 423-3990; *The World in Figures.*

SYRIAN ARAB REPUBLIC - LIBRARIES

Facts on File, 460 Park Avenue South, New York, New York 10016 (800) 443-8323; *The New Book of World Rankings.*

United Nations Educational, Scientific and Cultural Organization (UNESCO), 7 Place de Fontenoy, F-75700 Paris, France (Telephone Number in U.S. (212) 963-5981); *Statistical Yearbook.*

SYRIAN ARAB REPUBLIC - LIVESTOCK AND POULTRY

Economic Commission for Western Asia, Post Office Box 27, Baghdad, Iraq; *Statistical Abstract of Western Asia.*

Euromonitor Publications Limited, 87-88 Turnmill Street, London EC1M 5QU, England; *International Marketing Data and Statistics.*

Facts on File, 460 Park Avenue South, New York, New York 10016 (800) 443-8323; *The New Book of World Rankings.*

Food and Agricultural Organization of the United Nations (FAO), Via delle Terme di Caracalla, 00100 Rome, Italy (Telephone Number in U.S. (202) 653-2400); *Production Yearbook,* and *The State of Food and Agriculture.*

G.K. Hall and Company, 70 Lincoln Street, Boston, Massachusetts 02111 (617) 423-3990; *The World in Figures.*

Statistical Office of the United Nations, Publishing Service, New York, New York 10017 (800) 253-9646; *Statistical Yearbook.*

SYRIAN ARAB REPUBLIC - LIVING LEVELS

G.K. Hall and Company, 70 Lincoln Street, Boston, Massachusetts 02111 (617) 423-3990; *The World in Figures.*

Times Books, 201 East 50th Street, New York, New York 10022 (212) 751-2600; *The Economist Book of Vital World Statistics.*

SYRIAN ARAB REPUBLIC - MAIL - NUMBER OF PIECES SENT OR RECEIVED

Statistical Office of the United Nations, Publishing Service, New York, New York 10017 (800) 253-9646; *Statistical Yearbook.*

SYRIAN ARAB REPUBLIC - MANUFACTURING

Facts on File, 460 Park Avenue South, New York, New York 10016 (800) 443-8323; *The New Book of World Rankings.*

G.K. Hall and Company, 70 Lincoln Street, Boston, Massachusetts 02111 (617) 423-3990; *The World in Figures.*

Statistical Office of the United Nations, Publishing Service, New York, New York 10017 (800) 253-9646; *Statistical Yearbook.*

Times Books, 201 East 50th Street, New York, New York 10022 (212) 751-2600; *The Economist Book of Vital World Statistics.*

The World Bank, 1818 H Street, NW, Washington, D.C. 20433 (202) 477-1234; *World Tables.*

SYRIAN ARAB REPUBLIC - MARRIAGE RATES

Facts on File, 460 Park Avenue South, New York, New York 10016 (800) 443-8323; *The New Book of World Rankings.*

Statistical Office of the United Nations, Publishing Service, New York, New York 10017 (800) 253-9646; *Demographic Yearbook,* and *Statistical Yearbook.*

SYRIAN ARAB REPUBLIC - MEAT PRODUCTION - See SYRIAN ARAB REPUBLIC - LIVESTOCK AND POULTRY

SYRIAN ARAB REPUBLIC - MERCHANT SHIPPING

Economic Commission for Western Asia, Post Office Box 27, Baghdad, Iraq; *Statistical Abstract of Western Asia.*

G.K. Hall and Company, 70 Lincoln Street, Boston, Massachusetts 02111 (617) 423-3990; *The World in Figures.*

Lloyd's Register of Shipping, 17 Battery Place, New York, New York 10004 (212) 425-8050; *Register of Ships.*

Times Books, 201 East 50th Street, New York, New York 10022 (212) 751-2600; *The Economist Book of Vital World Statistics.*

United Nations Educational, Scientific and Cultural Organization (UNESCO), 7 Place de Fontenoy, F-75700 Paris, France (Telephone Number in U.S. (212) 963-5981); *Statistical Yearbook.*

U.S. Department of Transportation, Maritime Administration, 400 Seventh Street, SW, Washington, D.C. 20590 (202) 366-5807; *A Statistical Analysis of the World's Merchant Fleets.*

SYRIAN ARAB REPUBLIC - MILITARY

G.K. Hall and Company, 70 Lincoln Street, Boston, Massachusetts 02111 (617) 423-3990; *The World in Figures.*

The International Institute for Strategic Studies, 23 Tavistock Street, London WC2E 7NQ, England; *The Military Balance.*

U.S. Arms Control and Disarmament Agency, 320 Twenty-first Street, NW, Washington, D.C. 20451 (202) 647-8677; *World Military Expenditures and Arms Transfers.*

SYRIAN ARAB REPUBLIC - MILK PRODUCTION - See SYRIAN ARAB REPUBLIC - DAIRY PRODUCTS

SYRIAN ARAB REPUBLIC - MINING AND MINERAL PRODUCTS

Economic Commission for Western Asia, Post Office Box 27, Baghdad, Iraq; *Statistical Abstract of Western Asia.*

Facts on File, 460 Park Avenue South, New York, New York 10016 (800) 443-8323; *The New Book of World Rankings.*

G.K. Hall and Company, 70 Lincoln Street, Boston, Massachusetts 02111 (617) 423-3990; *The World in Figures.*

Penn Well Publishing Company, 1421 South Sheridan Road, P.O. Box 1260, Tulsa, Oklahoma 74101 (800) 752-9764; *International Energy Statistics Sourcebook*.

Statistical Office of the United Nations, Publishing Service, New York, New York 10017 (800) 253-9646; *Statistical Yearbook*.

SYRIAN ARAB REPUBLIC - MONEY EXCHANGE RATE

Economic Commission for Western Asia, Post Office Box 27, Baghdad, Iraq; *Statistical Abstract of Western Asia*.

Euromonitor Publications Limited, 87-88 Turnmill Street, London EC1M 5QU, England; *International Marketing Data and Statistics*.

International Monetary Fund, 700 Nineteenth Street, NW, Washington, D.C. 20431 (202) 623-7000; *International Financial Statistics*.

Statistical Office of the United Nations, Publishing Service, New York, New York 10017 (800) 253-9646; *Statistical Yearbook*.

SYRIAN ARAB REPUBLIC - MONEY RESERVES

Euromonitor Publications Limited, 87-88 Turnmill Street, London EC1M 5QU, England; *International Marketing Data and Statistics*.

SYRIAN ARAB REPUBLIC - MONEY SUPPLY

Economic Commission for Western Asia, Post Office Box 27, Baghdad, Iraq; *Statistical Abstract of Western Asia*.

Euromonitor Publications Limited, 87-88 Turnmill Street, London EC1M 5QU, England; *International Marketing Data and Statistics*.

G.K. Hall and Company, 70 Lincoln Street, Boston, Massachusetts 02111 (617) 423-3990; *The World in Figures*.

International Monetary Fund, 700 Nineteenth Street, NW, Washington, D.C. 20431 (202) 623-7000; *International Financial Statistics*.

Statistical Office of the United Nations, Publishing Service, New York, New York 10017 (800) 253-9646; *Statistical Yearbook*.

The World Bank, 1818 H Street, NW, Washington, D.C. 20433 (202) 477-1234; *World Tables*.

SYRIAN ARAB REPUBLIC - MONUMENTS AND HISTORICAL SITES

United Nations Educational, Scientific and Cultural Organization (UNESCO), 7 Place de Fontenoy, F-75700 Paris, France (Telephone Number in U.S. (212) 963-5981); *Statistical Yearbook*.

SYRIAN ARAB REPUBLIC - MOTION PICTURES

Statistical Office of the United Nations, Publishing Service, New York, New York 10017 (800) 253-9646; *Statistical Yearbook*.

United Nations Educational, Scientific and Cultural Organization (UNESCO), 7 Place de Fontenoy, F-75700 Paris, France (Telephone Number in U.S. (212) 963-5981); *Statistical Yearbook*.

SYRIAN ARAB REPUBLIC - MOTOR VEHICLES IN USE

Economic Commission for Western Asia, Post Office Box 27, Baghdad, Iraq; *Statistical Abstract of Western Asia*.

G.K. Hall and Company, 70 Lincoln Street, Boston, Massachusetts 02111 (617) 423-3990; *The World in Figures*.

International Road Federation, 525 School Street, SW, Washington, D.C. 20024 (202) 554-2106; *World Road Statistics*.

Statistical Office of the United Nations, Publishing Service, New York, New York 10017 (800) 253-9646; *Statistical Yearbook*.

Times Books, 201 East 50th Street, New York, New York 10022 (212) 751-2600; *The Economist Book of Vital World Statistics*.

SYRIAN ARAB REPUBLIC - MOTOR VEHICLES TAXES - See SYRIAN ARAB REPUBLIC - TAXATION

SYRIAN ARAB REPUBLIC - MULES - See SYRIAN ARAB REPUBLIC - LIVESTOCK AND POULTRY

SYRIAN ARAB REPUBLIC - MUSEUMS

Facts on File, 460 Park Avenue South, New York, New York 10016 (800) 443-8323; *The New Book of World Rankings*.

United Nations Educational, Scientific and Cultural Organization (UNESCO), 7 Place de Fontenoy, F-75700 Paris, France (Telephone Number in U.S. (212) 963-5981); *Statistical Yearbook*.

SYRIAN ARAB REPUBLIC - NATALITY - See SYRIAN ARAB REPUBLIC - BIRTH RATE

SYRIAN ARAB REPUBLIC - NATIONAL ACCOUNTS

Economic Commission for Western Asia, Post Office Box 27, Baghdad, Iraq; *Statistical Abstract of Western Asia*.

Statistical Office of the United Nations, Publishing Service, New York, New York 10017 (800) 253-9646; *National Accounts Statistics*, and *Statistical Yearbook*.

SYRIAN ARAB REPUBLIC - NATIONAL INCOME

Facts on File, 460 Park Avenue South, New York, New York 10016 (800) 443-8323; *The New Book of World Rankings*.

G.K. Hall and Company, 70 Lincoln Street, Boston, Massachusetts 02111 (617) 423-3990; *The World in Figures*.

Statistical Office of the United Nations, Publishing Service, New York, New York 10017 (800) 253-9646; *Statistical Yearbook*.

SYRIAN ARAB REPUBLIC - NATIONAL PRODUCT

Facts on File, 460 Park Avenue South, New York, New York 10016 (800) 443-8323; *The New Book of World Rankings*.

Statistical Office of the United Nations, Publishing Service, New York, New York 10017 (800) 253-9646; *Statistical Yearbook*.

SYRIAN ARAB REPUBLIC - NATURAL GAS PRODUCTION - See SYRIAN ARAB REPUBLIC - MINING AND MINERAL PRODUCTS

Facts on File, 460 Park Avenue South, New York, New York 10016 (800) 443-8323; *The New Book of World Rankings*.

SYRIAN ARAB REPUBLIC - NEWSPAPER - See SWITZERLAND - FORESTRY AND FOREST PRODUCTS

SYRIAN ARAB REPUBLIC - NEWSPRINT PRODUCTION AND CONSUMPTION - See SWITZERLAND - FORESTRY AND FOREST PRODUCTS

SYRIAN ARAB REPUBLIC - OATS PRODUCTION - See SYRIAN ARAB REPUBLIC - CROPS

SYRIAN ARAB REPUBLIC - OCCUPATIONS - See SYRIAN ARAB REPUBLIC - LABOR FORCE

SYRIAN ARAB REPUBLIC - PAPER - See SWITZERLAND - FORESTRY AND FOREST PRODUCTS

SYRIAN ARAB REPUBLIC - PATENTS

Statistical Office of the United Nations, Publishing Service, New York, New York 10017 (800) 253-9646; *Statistical Yearbook*.

SYRIAN ARAB REPUBLIC - PEANUT PRODUCTION - See SYRIAN ARAB REPUBLIC - CROPS

SYRIAN ARAB REPUBLIC - PERIODICALS

United Nations Educational, Scientific and Cultural Organization (UNESCO), 7 Place de Fontenoy, F-75700 Paris, France (Telephone Number in U.S. (212) 963-5981); *Statistical Yearbook*.

SYRIAN ARAB REPUBLIC - PESTICIDE USE

Food and Agricultural Organization of the United Nations (FAO) Via delle Terme di Caracalla, 00100 Rome, Italy (Telephone Number in U.S. (202) 653-2400); *The State of Food and Agriculture*.

SYRIAN ARAB REPUBLIC - PETROLEUM INDUSTRY

Euromonitor Publications Limited, 87-88 Turnmill Street, London EC1M 5QU, England; *Middle East Economic Handbook*.

Facts on File, 460 Park Avenue South, New York, New York 10016 (800) 443-8323; *The New Book of World Rankings*.

Food and Agricultural Organization of the United Nations (FAO) Via delle Terme di Caracalla, 00100 Rome, Italy (Telephone Number in U.S. (202) 653-2400); *The State of Food and Agriculture*.

G.K. Hall and Company, 70 Lincoln Street, Boston, Massachusetts 02111 (617) 423-3990; *The World in Figures*.

Penn Well Publishing Company, 1421 South Sheridan Road, P.O. Box 1260, Tulsa, Oklahoma 74101 (800) 752-9764; *International Energy Statistics Sourcebook*.

Statistical Office of the United Nations, Publishing Service, New York, New York 10017 (800) 253-9646; *Statistical Yearbook*.

SYRIAN ARAB REPUBLIC - PHOSPHATE ROCK PRODUCTION - See SYRIAN ARAB REPUBLIC - MINING AND MINERAL PRODUCTS

SYRIAN ARAB REPUBLIC - PIGS - See SYRIAN ARAB REPUBLIC - LIVESTOCK AND POULTRY

SYRIAN ARAB REPUBLIC - POPULATION

Economic Commission for Western Asia, Post Office Box 27, Baghdad, Iraq; *Statistical Abstract of Western Asia*.

The Economist Intelligence Unit, 111 West 57th Street, New York, New York 10019 (800) 938-4685; *The World Market Atlas*.

Euromonitor Publications Limited, 87-88 Turnmill Street, London EC1M 5QU, England; *International Marketing Data and Statistics*, and *Middle Est Economic Handbook*.

Facts on File, 460 Park Avenue South, New York, New York 10016 (800) 443-8323; *The New Book of World Rankings*.

Federal Statistical Office, Gustav-Stresemann-Ring 11, D-6200 Wiesbaden, Germany; *Syrian Arab Republic*.

Food and Agricultural Organization of the United Nations (FAO), Via delle Terme di Caracalla, 00100 Rome, Italy (Telephone Number in U.S. (202) 653-2400); *Production Yearbook*.

G.K. Hall and Company, 70 Lincoln Street, Boston, Massachusetts 02111 (617) 423-3990; *The World in Figures*.

International Labour Office, I.L.O. Publications, CH-1211, Geneva 22, Switzerland; *Yearbook of Labour Statistics*.

Statistical Office of the United Nations, Publishing Service, New York, New York 10017 (800) 253-9646; *Demographic Yearbook*, and *Statistical Yearbook*.

Times Books, 201 East 50th Street, New York, New York 10022 (212) 751-2600; *The Economist Book of Vital World Statistics*.

United Nations Educational, Scientific and Cultural Organization (UNESCO), 7 Place de Fontenoy, F-75700 Paris, France (Telephone Number in U.S. (212) 963-5981); *Statistical Yearbook*.

U.S. Arms Control and Disarmament Agency, 320 Twenty-first Street, NW, Washington, D.C. 20451 (202) 647-8677; *World Military Expenditures and Arms Transfers*.

World Health Organization, Office of Publications, Avenue Appia, CH-1211 Geneva 27, Switzerland (Telephone Number in U.S. (518) 436-9686), *World Health Statistics Annual*.

SYRIAN ARAB REPUBLIC - POST OFFICES

Facts on File, 460 Park Avenue South, New York, New York 10016 (800) 443-8323; *The New Book of World Rankings*.

SYRIAN ARAB REPUBLIC - POTATO PRODUCTION - See SYRIAN ARAB REPUBLIC - CROPS

SYRIAN ARAB REPUBLIC - POWER PRODUCTION INDUSTRY

Statistical Office of the United Nations, Publishing Service, New York, New York 10017 (800) 253-9646; *Statistical Yearbook*.

SYRIAN ARAB REPUBLIC - PRICES

Economic Commission for Western Asia, Post Office Box 27, Baghdad, Iraq; *Statistical Abstract of Western Asia*.

Facts on File, 460 Park Avenue South, New York, New York 10016 (800) 443-8323; *The New Book of World Rankings*.

Food and Agricultural Organization of the United Nations (FAO), Via delle Terme di Caracalla, 00100 Rome, Italy (Telephone Number in U.S. (202) 653-2400); *Production Yearbook*, and *The State of Food and Agriculture*.

G.K. Hall and Company, 70 Lincoln Street, Boston, Massachusetts 02111 (617) 423-3990; *The World in Figures*.

International Labour Office, I.L.O. Publications, CH-1211, Geneva 22, Switzerland; *Yearbook of Labour Statistics*.

International Monetary Fund, 700 Nineteenth Street, NW, Washington, D.C. 20431 (202) 623-7000; *International Financial Statistics*.

SYRIAN ARAB REPUBLIC - PRINTING AND WRITING PAPER - See SWITZERLAND - FORESTRY AND FOREST PRODUCTS

SYRIAN ARAB REPUBLIC - PRODUCTION

Facts on File, 460 Park Avenue South, New York, New York 10016 (800) 443-8323; *The New Book of World Rankings*.

G.K. Hall and Company, 70 Lincoln Street, Boston, Massachusetts 02111 (617) 423-3990; *The World in Figures*.

SYRIAN ARAB REPUBLIC - PRODUCTIVITY

Euromonitor Publications Limited, 87-88 Turnmill Street, London EC1M 5QU, England; *International Marketing Data and Statistics*.

SYRIAN ARAB REPUBLIC - PROPERTY TAXES - See SYRIAN ARAB REPUBLIC - TAXATION

SYRIAN ARAB REPUBLIC - PUBLIC FINANCE

Facts on File, 460 Park Avenue South, New York, New York 10016 (800) 443-8323; *The New Book of World Rankings*.

SYRIAN ARAB REPUBLIC - RADIO BROADCASTING - See SYRIAN ARAB REPUBLIC - BROADCASTING

SYRIAN ARAB REPUBLIC - RAILWAYS

G.K. Hall and Company, 70 Lincoln Street, Boston, Massachusetts 02111 (617) 423-3990; *The World in Figures*.

Jane's Information Group, Sentinel House, 163 Brighton Road, Coulsdon, Surrey CR5 2NH, England (Telephone Number in U.S. (703) 683-3700); *Jane's World Railways*.

Statistical Office of the United Nations, Publishing Service, New York, New York 10017 (800) 253-9646; *Statistical Yearbook*.

SYRIAN ARAB REPUBLIC - RELIGION

Facts on File, 460 Park Avenue South, New York, New York 10016 (800) 443-8323; *The New Book of World Rankings*.

SYRIAN ARAB REPUBLIC - RENT PRICES

International Labour Office, I.L.O. Publications, CH-1211, Geneva 22, Switzerland; *Yearbook of Labour Statistics*.

SYRIAN ARAB REPUBLIC - RETAIL TRADE

G.K. Hall and Company, 70 Lincoln Street, Boston, Massachusetts 02111 (617) 423-3990; *The World in Figures*.

SYRIAN ARAB REPUBLIC - RICE PRODUCTION - See SYRIAN ARAB REPUBLIC - CROPS

SYRIAN ARAB REPUBLIC - RUBBER PRODUCTION AND CONSUMPTION

Facts on File, 460 Park Avenue South, New York, New York 10016 (800) 443-8323; *The New Book of World Rankings*.

SYRIAN ARAB REPUBLIC - SALT PRODUCTION - See SYRIAN ARAB REPUBLIC - MINING AND MINERAL PRODUCTS

SYRIAN ARAB REPUBLIC - SAWNWOOD PRODUCTION - See SWITZERLAND - FORESTRY AND FOREST PRODUCTS

SYRIAN ARAB REPUBLIC - SCIENTISTS AND TECHNICIANS

Statistical Office of the United Nations, Publishing Service, New York, New York 10017 (800) 253-9646; *Statistical Yearbook*.

SYRIAN ARAB REPUBLIC - SENIOR CITIZENS

Facts on File, 460 Park Avenue South, New York, New York 10016 (800) 443-8323; *The New Book of World Rankings*.

SYRIAN ARAB REPUBLIC - SHEEP - See SYRIAN ARAB REPUBLIC - LIVESTOCK AND POULTRY

SYRIAN ARAB REPUBLIC - SILVER PRODUCTION AND CONSUMPTION - See SYRIAN ARAB REPUBLIC - MINING AND MINERAL PRODUCTS

SYRIAN ARAB REPUBLIC - SOCIAL DATA

Facts on File, 460 Park Avenue South, New York, New York 10016 (800) 443-8323; *The New Book of World Rankings*.

G.K. Hall and Company, 70 Lincoln Street, Boston, Massachusetts 02111 (617) 423-3990; *The World in Figures*.

SYRIAN ARAB REPUBLIC - SOCIAL SECURITY

International Monetary Fund, 700 Nineteenth Street, NW, Washington, D.C. 20431 (202) 623-7000; *Government Finance Statistics Yearbook*.

SYRIAN ARAB REPUBLIC - STATE BUDGET REVENUE AND EXPENDITURES

Euromonitor Publications Limited, 87-88 Turnmill Street, London EC1M 5QU, England; *International Marketing Data and Statistics*.

SYRIAN ARAB REPUBLIC - STEEL - See SYRIAN ARAB REPUBLIC - MINING AND MINERAL PRODUCTS

SYRIAN ARAB REPUBLIC - STOCKS - COMMODITY - MARKET PRICE - INDEX

Food and Agricultural Organization of the United Nations (FAO) Via delle Terme di Caracalla, 00100 Rome, Italy (Telephone Number in U.S. (202) 653-2400); *The State of Food and Agriculture*.

SYRIAN ARAB REPUBLIC - SUGAR PRODUCTION AND CONSUMPTION - See SYRIAN ARAB REPUBLIC - CROPS

SYRIAN ARAB REPUBLIC - TAXATION

G.K. Hall and Company, 70 Lincoln Street, Boston, Massachusetts 02111 (617) 423-3990; *The World in Figures*.

International Monetary Fund, 700 Nineteenth Street, NW, Washington, D.C. 20431 (202) 623-7000; *Government Finance Statistics Yearbook*.

International Road Federation, 525 School Street, SW, Washington, D.C. 20024 (202) 554-2106; *World Road Statistics*.

The World Bank, 1818 H Street, NW, Washington, D.C. 20433 (202) 477-1234; *World Tables*.

SYRIAN ARAB REPUBLIC - TEA CONSUMPTION

Statistical Office of the United Nations, Publishing Service, New York, New York 10017 (800) 253-9646; *Statistical Yearbook*.

SYRIAN ARAB REPUBLIC - TELEGRAPH SERVICE

Statistical Office of the United Nations, Publishing Service, New York, New York 10017 (800) 253-9646; *Statistical Yearbook*.

SYRIAN ARAB REPUBLIC - TELEPHONES IN USE

American Telephone and Telegraph Company, 26 Parsippany Road, Whippany, New Jersey 07981 (800) 338-4038; *The World's Telephones*.

Euromonitor Publications Limited, 87-88 Turnmill Street, London EC1M 5QU, England; *Middle East Economic Handbook*.

G.K. Hall and Company, 70 Lincoln Street, Boston, Massachusetts 02111 (617) 423-3990; *The World in Figures*.

Statistical Office of the United Nations, Publishing Service, New York, New York 10017 (800) 253-9646; *Statistical Yearbook*.

SYRIAN ARAB REPUBLIC - TELEVISION BROADCASTING - See SYRIAN ARAB REPUBLIC - BROADCASTING

SYRIAN ARAB REPUBLIC - TELEVISION RECEIVER PRODUCTION

Statistical Office of the United Nations, Publishing Service, New York, New York 10017 (800) 253-9646; *Statistical Yearbook*.

SYRIAN ARAB REPUBLIC - TEXTILE INDUSTRY

G.K. Hall and Company, 70 Lincoln Street, Boston, Massachusetts 02111 (617) 423-3990; *The World in Figures*.

Statistical Office of the United Nations, Publishing Service, New York, New York 10017 (800) 253-9646; *Statistical Yearbook*.

SYRIAN ARAB REPUBLIC - THEATRE

United Nations Educational, Scientific and Cultural Organization (UNESCO), 7 Place de Fontenoy, F-75700 Paris, France (Telephone Number in U.S. (212) 963-5981); *Statistical Yearbook*.

SYRIAN ARAB REPUBLIC - TIN - INDUSTRIAL CONSUMPTION - See SYRIAN ARAB REPUBLIC - MINING AND MINERAL PRODUCTS

SYRIAN ARAB REPUBLIC - TOBACCO PRODUCTION

Facts on File, 460 Park Avenue South, New York, New York 10016 (800) 443-8323; *The New Book of World Rankings*.

Statistical Office of the United Nations, Publishing Service, New York, New York 10017 (800) 253-9646; *Statistical Yearbook*.

SYRIAN ARAB REPUBLIC - TOURISM

Economic Commission for Western Asia, Post Office Box 27, Baghdad, Iraq; *Statistical Abstract of Western Asia*.

Euromonitor Publications Limited, 87-88 Turnmill Street, London EC1M 5QU, England; *Middle East Economic Handbook*.

Facts on File, 460 Park Avenue South, New York, New York 10016 (800) 443-8323; *The New Book of World Rankings*.

G.K. Hall and Company, 70 Lincoln Street, Boston, Massachusetts 02111 (617) 423-3990; *The World in Figures*.

Statistical Office of the United Nations, Publishing Service, New York, New York 10017 (800) 253-9646; *Statistical Yearbook*.

Times Books, 201 East 50th Street, New York, New York 10022 (212) 751-2600; *The Economist Book of Vital World Statistics*.

World Tourism Organization, Calle Capitan Haya 42, E-28020 Madrid, Spain; *Yearbook of Tourism Statistics*.

SYRIAN ARAB REPUBLIC - TRACTORS IN USE

Statistical Office of the United Nations, Publishing Service, New York, New York 10017 (800) 253-9646; *Statistical Yearbook*.

SYRIAN ARAB REPUBLIC - TRADE - See SYRIAN ARAB REPUBLIC - FOREIGN TRADE

SYRIAN ARAB REPUBLIC - TRADEMARKS AND SERVICE MARKS

Statistical Office of the United Nations, Publishing Service, New York, New York 10017 (800) 253-9646; *Statistical Yearbook*.

SYRIAN ARAB REPUBLIC - TRANSPORTATION AND COMMUNICATIONS

Economic Commission for Western Asia, Post Office Box 27, Baghdad, Iraq; *Statistical Abstract of Western Asia*.

Euromonitor Publications Limited, 87-88 Turnmill Street, London EC1M 5QU, England; *Middle East Economic Handbook*.

Facts on File, 460 Park Avenue South, New York, New York 10016 (800) 443-8323; *The New Book of World Rankings*.

G.K. Hall and Company, 70 Lincoln Street, Boston, Massachusetts 02111 (617) 423-3990; *The World in Figures*.

SYRIAN ARAB REPUBLIC - UNEMPLOYMENT

Euromonitor Publications Limited, 87-88 Turnmill Street, London EC1M 5QU, England; *International Marketing Data and Statistics*, and *Middle East Economic Handbook*.

International Labour Office, I.L.O. Publications, CH-1211, Geneva 22, Switzerland; *Yearbook of Labour Statistics*.

Statistical Office of the United Nations, Publishing Service, New York, New York 10017 (800) 253-9646; *Statistical Yearbook*.

SYRIAN ARAB REPUBLIC - VITAL STATISTICS

Euromonitor Publications Limited, 87-88 Turnmill Street, London EC1M 5QU, England; *International Marketing Data and Statistics*, and *Middle East Economic Handbook*.

G.K. Hall and Company, 70 Lincoln Street, Boston, Massachusetts 02111 (617) 423-3990; *The World in Figures*.

Statistical Office of the United Nations, Publishing Service, New York, New York 10017 (800) 253-9646; *Statistical Yearbook*.

World Health Organization, Office of Publications, Avenue Appia, CH-1211 Geneva 27, Switzerland (Telephone Number in U.S. (518) 436-9686); *World Health Statistics Annual*.

SYRIAN ARAB REPUBLIC - WAGES

G.K. Hall and Company, 70 Lincoln Street, Boston, Massachusetts 02111 (617) 423-3990; *The World in Figures*.

International Labour Office, I.L.O. Publications, CH-1211, Geneva 22, Switzerland; *Yearbook of Labour Statistics*.

Statistical Office of the United Nations, Publishing Service, New York, New York 10017 (800) 253-9646; *Statistical Yearbook*.

SYRIAN ARAB REPUBLIC - WEATHER

Facts on File, 460 Park Avenue South, New York, New York 10016 (800) 443-8323; *The New Book of World Rankings*.

G.K. Hall and Company, 70 Lincoln Street, Boston, Massachusetts 02111 (617) 423-3990; *The World in Figures*.

SYRIAN ARAB REPUBLIC - WELFARE

International Monetary Fund, 700 Nineteenth Street, NW, Washington, D.C. 20431 (202) 623-7000; *Government Finance Statistics Yearbook*.

SYRIAN ARAB REPUBLIC - WHEAT PRODUCTION AND PRICES - See SYRIAN ARAB REPUBLIC - CROPS

SYRIAN ARAB REPUBLIC - WHOLESALE PRICES

International Monetary Fund, 700 Nineteenth Street, NW, Washington, D.C. 20431 (202) 623-7000; *International Financial Statistics*.

Statistical Office of the United Nations, Publishing Service, New York, New York 10017 (800) 253-9646; *Statistical Yearbook*.

SYRIAN ARAB REPUBLIC - WINE PRODUCTION

Facts on File, 460 Park Avenue South, New York, New York 10016 (800) 443-8323; *The New Book of World Rankings*.

SYRIAN ARAB REPUBLIC - WOOL PRODUCTION

Facts on File, 460 Park Avenue South, New York, New York 10016 (800) 443-8323; *The New Book of World Rankings*.

SYRIAN ARAB REPUBLIC - YARN PRODUCTION

Statistical Office of the United Nations, Publishing Service, New York, New York 10017 (800) 253-9646; *Statistical Yearbook*.

T

Taiwan - National Statistical Office

Inspectorate General of Customs, Ministry of Finance, 85 Hsim-Hseng South Road, Section 1, Taipei, Republic of China.

Taiwan - Primary Statistics Sources

Council for Economic Planning and Development, Ninth Floor, 87 Nanking East Road, Section 2, Taipei, Republic of China; *Taiwan Statistical Data Book*.

Directorate - General of Budget, Accounting and Statistics, Executive Yuan, Republic of China; *Monthly Bulletin of Statistics, Monthly Statistics of the Republic of China, Republic of China in Figures*, and *Statistical Yearbook of the Republic of China*.

TAIWAN - AGRICULTURE

Council for Economic Planning and Development, Ninth Floor, 87 Nanking East Road, Section 2, Taipei, Republic of China; *Taiwan Statistical Data Book*.

Department of Agriculture and Forestry, Taiwan Provincial Government, Chunghsing Village, Nantou, Nantou Hsien, Taiwan, Republic of China; *Taiwan Agricultural Yearbook*.

Directorate - General of Budget, Accounting and Statistics, Executive Yuan, Republic of China; *Monthly Statistics of the Republic of China*, and *Statistical Yearbook of Republic of China*.

Euromonitor Publications Limited, 87-88 Turnmill Street, London EC1M 5QU, England; *International Marketing Data and Statistics*, and *Third World Economic Handbook*.

Facts on File, 460 Park Avenue South, New York, New York 10016 (800) 443-8323; *The New Book of World Rankings*.

Federal Statistical Office, Gustav - Stresemann - Ring 11, D-6200 Wiesbaden, Germany; *China (Taiwan)*.

G.K. Hall and Company, 70 Lincoln Street, Boston, Massachusetts 02111 (617) 423-3990; *The World in Figures*.

TAIWAN - AIRLINE SERVICE

The Economist Intelligence Unit (Asia) Limited, 10th Floor, Luk Kwok Centre, 72 Gloucester Road, Wanchai, Hong Kong (Phone Number in U.S. (800) 938-4685); *Asian Market Atlas*.

Council for Economic Planning and Development, Ninth Floor, 87 Nanking East Road, Section 2, Taipei, Republic of China; *Taiwan Statistical Data Book*.

Directorate - General of Budget, Accounting and Statistics, Executive Yuan, The Republic of China; *Monthly Statistics of the Republic of China*, and *Statistical Yearbook of The Republic of China*.

Facts on File, 460 Park Avenue South, New York, New York 10016 (800) 443-8323; *The New Book of World Rankings*.

G.K. Hall and Company, 70 Lincoln Street, Boston, Massachusetts 02111 (617) 423-3990; *The World in Figures*.

TAIWAN - ALUMINUM PRODUCTION AND CONSUMPTION - See TAIWAN - MINING AND MINERAL PRODUCTS

TAIWAN - ANTIMONY AND ANTIMONY ORE - See TAIWAN - MINING AND MINERAL PRODUCTS

TAIWAN - AQUATIC PRODUCTS - WHOLESALE PRICES

Directorate General of Budget, Accounting and Statistics, Executive Yuan, The Republic of China; *Statistical Yearbook of The Republic of China*.

TAIWAN - AREA AND DENSITY OF POPULATION

Council for Economic Planning and Development, Ninth Floor, 87 Nanking East Road, Section 2, Taipei, Republic of China; *Taiwan Statistical Data Book*.

Directorate - General of Budget, Accounting and Statistics, Executive Yuan, Republic of China; *Monthly Statistics of the Republic of China*.

Euromonitor Publications Limited, 87-88 Turnmill Street, London EC1M 5QU, England; *International Marketing Data and Statistics*.

Facts on File, 460 Park Avenue South, New York, New York 10016 (800) 443-8323; *The New Book of World Rankings*.

Federal Statistical Office, Gustav - Stresemann - Ring 11, D-6200 Wiesbaden, Germany; *China (Taiwan)*.

G.K. Hall and Company, 70 Lincoln Street, Boston, Massachusetts 02111 (617) 423-3990; *The World in Figures*.

Times Books, 201 East 50th Street, New York, New York 10022 (212) 751-2600; *The Economist Book of Vital World Statistics*.

TAIWAN - ARMS EXPORTS AND IMPORTS

U.S. Arms Control and Disarmament Agency, 320 Twenty-first Street, NW, Washington, D.C. 20451 (202) 647-8677; *World Military Expenditures and Arms Transfers*.

TAIWAN - ASBESTOS PRODUCTION

Council for Economic Planning and Development, Ninth Floor, 87 Nanking East Road, Section 2, Taipei, Republic of China; *Taiwan Statistical Data Book*.

Directorate - General of Budget, Accounting and Statistics, Executive Yuan, The Republic of China; *Statistical Yearbook of The Republic of China*.

TAIWAN - BALANCE OF PAYMENTS

Council for Economic Planning and Development, Ninth Floor, 87 Nanking East Road, Section 2, Taipei, Republic of China; *Taiwan Statistical Data Book*.

Department of Statistics, Ministry of Finance, 2, Aikuo West Road, Taipei, Republic of China; *The Republic of China Monthly of Financial Statistics*.

Directorate - General of Budget, Accounting and Statistics, Executive Yuan, The Republic of China; *Monthly Statistics of the Republic of China*, and *Statistical Yearbook of The Republic of China*.

Economic Research Department, The Central Bank of China, 2, Roosevelt Road, Section 1, Taipei 10757, Republic of China; *Financial Statistics Monthly Taiwan District, The Republic of China*.

The Economist Intelligence Unit, 111 West 57th Street, New York, New York 10019 (800) 938-4685; *The World Market Atlas*.

Euromonitor Publications Limited, 87-88 Turnmill Street, London EC1M 5QU, England; *Third World Economic Handbook*.

Federal Statistical Office, Gustav - Stresemann - Ring 11, D-6200 Wiesbaden, Germany; *China (Taiwan)*.

G.K. Hall and Company, 70 Lincoln Street, Boston, Massachusetts 02111 (617) 423-3990; *The World in Figures*.

Times Books, 201 East 50th Street, New York, New York 10022 (212) 751-2600; *The Economist Book of Vital World Statistics*.

TAIWAN - BANKING

Council for Economic Planning and Development, Ninth Floor, 87 Nanking East Road, Section 2, Taipei, Republic of China; *Taiwan Statistical Data Book*.

Department of Statistics, Ministry of Finance, 2, Aikuo West Road, Taipei, Republic of China; *The Republic of China Monthly of Financial Statistics*.

Economic Research Department, The Central Bank of China, 2, Roosevelt Road, Section 1, Taipei 10757, Republic of China; *Financial Statistics Monthly Taiwan District, The Republic of China*.

Facts on File, 460 Park Avenue South, New York, New York 10016 (800) 443-8323; *The New Book of World Rankings*.

G.K. Hall and Company, 70 Lincoln Street, Boston, Massachusetts 02111 (617) 423-3990; *The World in Figures*.

TAIWAN - BARLEY PRODUCTION - See TAIWAN - CROPS

TAIWAN - BAUXITE PRODUCTION AND CONSUMPTION - See TAIWAN - MINING AND MINERAL PRODUCTS

TAIWAN - BEER PRODUCTION

Council for Economic Planning and Development, Ninth Floor, 87 Nanking East Road, Section 2, Taipei, Republic of China; *Taiwan Statistical Data Book*.

Directorate - General of Budget, Accounting and Statistics, Executive Yuan, The Republic of China; *Statistical Yearbook of The Republic of China*. .

Facts on File, 460 Park Avenue South, New York, New York 10016 (800) 443-8323; *The New Book of World Rankings*.

TAIWAN - BIRTH RATE

Council for Economic Planning and Development, Ninth Floor, 87 Nanking East Road, Section 2, Taipei, Republic of China; *Taiwan Statistical Data Book*.

Directorate - General of Budget, Accounting and Statistics, Executive Yuan, Republic of China; *Monthly Statistics of the Republic of China*.

The Economist Intelligence Unit (Asia) Limited, 10th Floor, Luk Kwok Centre, 72 Gloucester Road, Wanchai, Hong Kong (Phone Number in U.S. (800) 938-4685); *Asian Market Atlas*.

Euromonitor Publications Limited, 87-88 Turnmill Street, London EC1M 5QU, England; *Third World Economic Handbook*.

Facts on File, 460 Park Avenue South, New York, New York 10016 (800) 443-8323; *The New Book of World Rankings*.

TAIWAN - BISMUTH PRODUCTION AND CONSUMPTION - See TAIWAN - MINING AND MINERAL PRODUCTS

TAIWAN - BONDS

Council for Economic Planning and Development, Ninth Floor, 87 Nanking East Road, Section 2, Taipei, Republic of China; *Taiwan Statistical Data Book*.

Department of Statistics, Ministry of Finance, 2, Aikuo West Road, Taipei, Republic of China; *The Republic of China Monthly of Financial Statistics*.

Directorate - General of Budget, Accounting and Statistics, Executive Yuan, The Republic of China; *Monthly Statistics of the Republic of China*, and *Statistical Yearbook of The Republic of China*.

G.K. Hall and Company, 70 Lincoln Street, Boston, Massachusetts 02111 (617) 423-3990; *The World in Figures*.

TAIWAN - BOOK PRODUCTION

Council for Economic Planning and Development, Ninth Floor, 87 Nanking East Road, Section 2, Taipei, Republic of China; *Taiwan Statistical Data Book*.

Directorate - General of Budget, Accounting and Statistics, Executive Yuan, The Republic of China; *Statistical Yearbook of The Republic of China*.

G.K. Hall and Company, 70 Lincoln Street, Boston, Massachusetts 02111 (617) 423-3990; *The World in Figures*.

TAIWAN - BROADCASTING

Billboard Limited, P.O. Box 9027, 1006 AA Amsterdam, The Netherlands (Telephone Number in U.S. (212) 764-7300); *World Radio TV Handbook*.

Facts on File, 460 Park Avenue South, New York, New York 10016 (800) 443-8323; *The New Book of World Rankings*.

G.K. Hall and Company, 70 Lincoln Street, Boston, Massachusetts 02111 (617) 423-3990; *The World in Figures*.

TAIWAN - BUDGET ACCOUNTS

Council for Economic Planning and Development, Ninth Floor, 87 Nanking East Road, Section 2, Taipei, Republic of China; *Taiwan Statistical Data Book*.

Department of Statistics, Ministry of Finance, 2, Aikuo West Road, Taipei, Republic of China; *The Republic of China Monthly of Financial Statistics*.

Directorate - General of Budget, Accounting and Statistics, Executive Yuan, The Republic of China; *Monthly Statistics of the Republic of China*, and *Statistical Yearbook of The Republic of China*.

Economic Research Department, The Central Bank of China, 2, Roosevelt Road, Section 1, Taipei 10757, Republic of China; *Financial Statistics Monthly Taiwan District, The Republic of China*.

TAIWAN - BUSINESS

G.K. Hall and Company, 70 Lincoln Street, Boston, Massachusetts 02111 (617) 423-3990; *The World in Figures*.

TAIWAN - BUSINESS - COMPANIES BY TYPE OF COMPANY

Council for Economic Planning and Development, Ninth Floor, 87 Nanking East Road, Section 2, Taipei, Republic of China; *Taiwan Statistical Data Book*.

Directorate - General of Budget, Accounting and Statistics, Executive Yuan, The Republic of China; *Statistical Yearbook of The Republic of China*.

TAIWAN - BUTTER PRODUCTION - See TAIWAN - DAIRY PRODUCTS

TAIWAN - CABBAGE PRODUCTION - See TAIWAN - CROPS

TAIWAN - CAPITAL FLOW DISTRIBUTION

Directorate - General of Budget, Accounting and Statistics, Executive Yuan, The Republic of China; *Statistical Yearbook of The Republic of China*.

TAIWAN - CASTOR BEAN PRODUCTION - See TAIWAN - CROPS

TAIWAN - CATTLE - See TAIWAN - LIVESTOCK AND POULTRY

TAIWAN - CAULIFLOWER PRODUCTION - See TAIWAN - CROPS

TAIWAN - CAUSTIC SODA PRODUCTION

Directorate - General of Budget, Accounting and Statistics, Executive Yuan, The Republic of China; *Statistical Yearbook of The*

Republic of China.

TAIWAN - CEMENT PRODUCTION - See TAIWAN - MINING AND MINERAL PRODUCTS

TAIWAN - CHEESE PRODUCTION AND CONSUMPTION - See TAIWAN - DAIRY PRODUCTS

TAIWAN - CHEMICAL (ORGANIC) PRODUCTION - See TAIWAN - MINING AND MINERAL PRODUCTS

TAIWAN - CHESTNUT PRODUCTION - See TAIWAN - CROPS

TAIWAN - CHICKENS - See TAIWAN - LIVESTOCK AND POULTRY

TAIWAN - CIGARETTE PRODUCTION - See TAIWAN - TOBACCO PRODUCTION

TAIWAN - CLASS STRUCTURE

G.K. Hall and Company, 70 Lincoln Street, Boston, Massachusetts 02111 (617) 423-3990; *The World in Figures*.

TAIWAN - CLIMATE

Facts on File, 460 Park Avenue South, New York, New York 10016 (800) 443-8323; *The New Book of World Rankings*.

G.K. Hall and Company, 70 Lincoln Street, Boston, Massachusetts 02111 (617) 423-3990; *The World in Figures*.

TAIWAN - CLOTHING EXPORTS AND IMPORTS

Council for Economic Planning and Development, Ninth Floor, 87 Nanking East Road, Section 2, Taipei, Republic of China; *Taiwan Statistical Data Book*.

Directorate - General of Budget, Accounting and Statistics, Executive Yuan, Republic of China; *Monthly Statistics of the Republic of China*.

Euromonitor Publications Limited, 87-88 Turnmill Street, London EC1M 5QU, England; *Third World Economic Handbook*.

TAIWAN - COAL PRODUCTION - See TAIWAN - MINING AND MINERAL PRODUCTS

TAIWAN - COFFEE - See TAIWAN - CROPS

TAIWAN - COKE OVEN COKE - See TAIWAN - MINING AND MINERAL PRODUCTS

TAIWAN - COMMUNICATIONS

Council for Economic Planning and Development, Ninth Floor, 87 Nanking East Road, Section 2, Taipei, Republic of China; *Taiwan Statistical Data Book*.

Directorate - General of Budget, Accounting and Statistics, Executive Yuan, Republic of China; *Monthly Statistics of the Republic of China*.

Euromonitor Publications Limited, 87-88 Turnmill Street, London EC1M 5QU, England; *Third World Economic Handbook*.

Federal Statistical Office, Gustav - Stresemann - Ring 11, D-6200 Wiesbaden, Germany; *China (Taiwan)*.

G.K. Hall and Company, 70 Lincoln Street, Boston, Massachusetts 02111 (617) 423-3990; *The World in Figures.*

TAIWAN - CONSTRUCTION INDUSTRY

Council for Economic Planning and Development, Ninth Floor, 87 Nanking East Road, Section 2, Taipei, Republic of China; *Taiwan Statistical Data Book.*

Directorate - General of Budget, Accounting and Statistics, Executive Yuan, The Republic of China; *Monthly Statistics of the Republic of China,* and *Statistical Yearbook of The Republic of China.*

Facts on File, 460 Park Avenue South, New York, New York 10016 (800) 443-8323; *The New Book of World Rankings.*

TAIWAN - CONSUMER PRICE INDEX

Council for Economic Planning and Development, Ninth Floor, 87 Nanking East Road, Section 2, Taipei, Republic of China; *Taiwan Statistical Data Book.*

Department of Statistics, Ministry of Finance, 2, Aikuo West Road, Taipei, Republic of China; *The Republic of China Monthly of Financial Statistics.*

Directorate - General of Budget, Accounting and Statistics, Executive Yuan, The Republic of China; *Monthly Statistics of the Republic of China,* and *Statistical Yearbook of The Republic of China.*

Economic Research Department, The Central Bank of China, 2, Roosevelt Road, Section 1, Taipei 10757, Republic of China; *Financial Statistics Monthly Taiwan District, The Republic of China.*

Federal Statistical Office, Gustav - Stresemann - Ring 11, D-6200 Wiesbaden, Germany; *China (Taiwan).*

G.K. Hall and Company, 70 Lincoln Street, Boston, Massachusetts 02111 (617) 423-3990; *The World in Figures.*

TAIWAN - CONSUMER PRICES

Federal Statistical Office, Gustav - Stresemann - Ring 11, D-6200 Wiesbaden, Germany; *China (Taiwan).*

Times Books, 201 East 50th Street, New York, New York 10022 (212) 751-2600; *The Economist Book of Vital World Statistics.*

TAIWAN - COPPER AND COPPER ORE - See TAIWAN - MINING AND MINERAL PRODUCTS

TAIWAN - CORN PRODUCTION - See TAIWAN - CROPS

TAIWAN - CORPORATE TAXES - See TAIWAN - TAXATION

TAIWAN - COTTON - See TAIWAN - CROPS

TAIWAN - CRIME - ALL TYPES

International Criminal Police Organization (INTERPOL), 26 rue Armengaud, 92210 Saint Cloud, France; *International Crime Statistics.*

Yale University Press, Yale Station, New Haven, Connecticut 06520 (203) 432-0940; *Violence and Crime in Cross-National Perspective.*

TAIWAN - CRIMINAL RESEARCH

Yale University Press, Yale Station, New Haven, Connecticut 06520 (203) 432-0940; *Violence and Crime in Cross-National Perspective.*

TAIWAN - CROPS

Commodity Research Bureau, Incorporated, 75 Wall Street, New York, New York 10005 (212) 504-7754; *Commodity Year Book.*

Council for Economic Planning and Development, Ninth Floor, 87 Nanking East Road, Section 2, Taipei, Republic of China; *Taiwan Statistical Data Book.*

Department of Agriculture and Forestry, Taiwan Provincial Government, Chunghsing Village, Nantou, Nantou Hsien, Taiwan, Republic of China; *Taiwan Agricultural Yearbook.*

Directorate - General of Budget, Accounting and Statistics, Executive Yuan, The Republic of China; *Monthly Statistics of the Republic of China,* and *Statistical Yearbook of The Republic of China.*

Facts on File, 460 Park Avenue South, New York, New York 10016 (800) 443-8323; *The New Book of World Rankings.*

Food and Agricultural Organization of the United Nations (FAO), Via delle Terme di Caracalla, 00100 Rome, Italy (Telephone Number in U.S. (202) 653-2400); *Production Yearbook.*

G.K. Hall and Company, 70 Lincoln Street, Boston, Massachusetts 02111 (617) 423-3990; *The World in Figures.*

TAIWAN - CUSTOM DUTIES

G.K. Hall and Company, 70 Lincoln Street, Boston, Massachusetts 02111 (617) 423-3990; *The World in Figures.*

TAIWAN - DAIRY PRODUCTS

Commodity Research Bureau, Incorporated, 75 Wall Street, New York, New York 10005 (212) 504-7754; *Commodity Year Book.*

Council for Economic Planning and Development, Ninth Floor, 87 Nanking East Road, Section 2, Taipei, Republic of China; *Taiwan Statistical Data Book.*

Department of Agriculture and Forestry, Taiwan Provincial Government, Chunghsing Village, Nantou, Nantou Hsien, Taiwan, Republic of China; *Taiwan Agricultural Yearbook.*

Directorate - General of Budget, Accounting and Statistics, Executive Yuan, The Republic of China; *Monthly Statistics of the Republic of China,* and *Statistical Yearbook of The Republic of China.*

Facts on File, 460 Park Avenue South, New York, New York 10016 (800) 443-8323; *The New Book of World Rankings.*

TAIWAN - DEATH RATE

Council for Economic Planning and Development, Ninth Floor, 87 Nanking East Road, Section 2, Taipei, Republic of China; *Taiwan Statistical Data Book.*

Directorate - General of Budget, Accounting and Statistics, Executive Yuan, The Republic of China; *Monthly Statistics of the Republic of China,* and *Statistical Yearbook of The Republic of China.*

The Economist Intelligence Unit (Asia) Limited, 10th Floor, Luk Kwok Centre, 72 Gloucester Road, Wanchai, Hong Kong (Phone Number in U.S. (800) 938-4685); *Asian Market Atlas*.

Euromonitor Publications Limited, 87-88 Turnmill Street, London EC1M 5QU, England; *Third World Economic Handbook*.

G.K. Hall and Company, 70 Lincoln Street, Boston, Massachusetts 02111 (617) 423-3990; *The World in Figures*.

TAIWAN - DEFENSE EXPENDITURES

G.K. Hall and Company, 70 Lincoln Street, Boston, Massachusetts 02111 (617) 423-3990; *The World in Figures*.

U.S. Arms Control and Disarmament Agency, 320 Twenty-first Street, NW, Washington, D.C. 20451 (202) 647-8677; *World Military Expenditures and Arms Transfers*.

TAIWAN - DEMOGRAPHY

The Economist Intelligence Unit, 111 West 57th Street, New York, New York 10019 (800) 938-4685; *The World Market Atlas*.

The Economist Intelligence Unit (Asia) Limited, 10th Floor, Luk Kwok Centre, 72 Gloucester Road, Wanchai, Hong Kong (Phone Number in U.S. (800) 938-4685); *Asian Market Atlas*.

Facts on File, 460 Park Avenue South, New York, New York 10016 (800) 443-8323; *The New Book of World Rankings*.

Federal Statistical Office, Gustav - Stresemann - Ring 11, D-6200 Wiesbaden, Germany; *China (Taiwan)*.

G.K. Hall and Company, 70 Lincoln Street, Boston, Massachusetts 02111 (617) 423-3990; *The World in Figures*.

TAIWAN - DEVELOPMENT ASSISTANCE

Directorate - General of Budget, Accounting and Statistics, Executive Yuan, The Republic of China; *Monthly Statistics of the Republic of China*, and *Statistical Yearbook of The Republic of China*.

G.K. Hall and Company, 70 Lincoln Street, Boston, Massachusetts 02111 (617) 423-3990; *The World in Figures*.

TAIWAN - DIAMOND PRODUCTION - See TAIWAN - MINING AND MINERAL PRODUCTS

TAIWAN - DISCOUNT RATES

Council for Economic Planning and Development, Ninth Floor, 87 Nanking East Road, Section 2, Taipei, Republic of China; *Taiwan Statistical Data Book*.

Department of Statistics, Ministry of Finance, 2, Aikuo West Road, Taipei, Republic of China; *The Republic of China Monthly of Financial Statistics*.

Directorate - General of Budget, Accounting and Statistics, Executive Yuan, The Republic of China; *Monthly Statistics of the Republic of China*, and *Statistical Yearbook of The Republic of China*.

Economic Research Department, The Central Bank of China, 2, Roosevelt Road, Section 1, Taipei 10757, Republic of China; *Financial Statistics Monthly Taiwan District, The Republic of China*.

TAIWAN - DISEASE

Council for Economic Planning and Development, Ninth Floor, 87 Nanking East Road, Section 2, Taipei, Republic of China; *Taiwan Statistical Data Book*.

Directorate - General of Budget, Accounting and Statistics, Executive Yuan, Republic of China; *Monthly Statistics of the Republic of China*.

G.K. Hall and Company, 70 Lincoln Street, Boston, Massachusetts 02111 (617) 423-3990; *The World in Figures*.

TAIWAN - DIVORCE RATES

Council for Economic Planning and Development, Ninth Floor, 87 Nanking East Road, Section 2, Taipei, Republic of China; *Taiwan Statistical Data Book*.

Directorate - General of Budget, Accounting and Statistics, Executive Yuan, Republic of China; *Monthly Statistics of the Republic of China*.

Facts on File, 460 Park Avenue South, New York, New York 10016 (800) 443-8323; *The New Book of World Rankings*.

TAIWAN - DOMESTIC PRODUCT

G.K. Hall and Company, 70 Lincoln Street, Boston, Massachusetts 02111 (617) 423-3990; *The World in Figures*.

TAIWAN - ECONOMY

Council for Economic Planning and Development, Ninth Floor, 87 Nanking East Road, Section 2, Taipei, Republic of China; *Taiwan Statistical Data Book*.

Department of Statistics, Ministry of Finance, 2, Aikuo West Road, Taipei, Republic of China; *The Republic of China Monthly of Financial Statistics*.

Directorate - General of Budget, Accounting and Statistics, Executive Yuan, Republic of China; *Monthly Statistics of the Republic of China*.

Economic Research Department, The Central Bank of China, 2, Roosevelt Road, Section 1, Taipei 10757, Republic of China; *Financial Statistics Monthly Taiwan District, The Republic of China*.

Euromonitor Publications Limited, 87-88 Turnmill Street, London EC1M 5QU, England; *International Marketing Data and Statistics*, and *Third World Economic Handbook*.

Facts on File, 460 Park Avenue South, New York, New York 10016 (800) 443-8323; *The New Book of World Rankings*.

Federal Statistical Office, Gustav - Stresemann - Ring 11, D-6200 Wiesbaden, Germany; *China (Taiwan)*.

G.K. Hall and Company, 70 Lincoln Street, Boston, Massachusetts 02111 (617) 423-3990; *The World in Figures*.

TAIWAN - EDUCATION

Council for Economic Planning and Development, Ninth Floor, 87 Nanking East Road, Section 2, Taipei, Republic of China; *Taiwan Statistical Data Book*.

Directorate - General of Budget, Accounting and Statistics, Executive Yuan, The Republic of China; *Statistical Yearbook of The Republic of China.*

The Economist Intelligence Unit, 111 West 57th Street, New York, New York 10019 (800) 938-4685; *The World Market Atlas.*

The Economist Intelligence Unit (Asia) Limited, 10th Floor, Luk Kwok Centre, 72 Gloucester Road, Wanchai, Hong Kong (Phone Number in U.S. (800) 938-4685); *Asian Market Atlas.*

Facts on File, 460 Park Avenue South, New York, New York 10016 (800) 443-8323; *The New Book of World Rankings.*

Federal Statistical Office, Gustav - Stresemann - Ring 11, D-6200 Wiesbaden, Germany; *China (Taiwan).*

G.K. Hall and Company, 70 Lincoln Street, Boston, Massachusetts 02111 (617) 423-3990; *The World in Figures.*

Ministry of Education, 5, Chungshan South Road, Taipei, Republic of China; *Educational Statistics of the Republic of China.*

TAIWAN - EGG PRODUCTION AND CONSUMPTION - See TAIWAN - DAIRY PRODUCTS

TAIWAN - EGGPLANT PRODUCTION - See TAIWAN - CROPS

TAIWAN - ELECTRICITY

Council for Economic Planning and Development, Ninth Floor, 87 Nanking East Road, Section 2, Taipei, Republic of China; *Taiwan Statistical Data Book.*

Directorate - General of Budget, Accounting and Statistics, Executive Yuan, The Republic of China; *Statistical Yearbook of The Republic of China.*

Facts on File, 460 Park Avenue South, New York, New York 10016 (800) 443-8323; *The New Book of World Rankings.*

Penn Well Publishing Company, 1421 South Sheridan Road, P.O. Box 1260, Tulsa, Oklahoma 74101 (800) 752-9764; *International Energy Statistics Sourcebook.*

TAIWAN - EMPLOYMENT

Council for Economic Planning and Development, Ninth Floor, 87 Nanking East Road, Section 2, Taipei, Republic of China; *Taiwan Statistical Data Book.*

Directorate - General of Budget, Accounting and Statistics, Executive Yuan, Republic of China; *Monthly Statistics of the Republic of China*, and *Statistical Yearbook of The Republic of China.*

Euromonitor Publications Limited, 87-88 Turnmill Street, London EC1M 5QU, England; *International Marketing Data and Statistics.*

Facts on File, 460 Park Avenue South, New York, New York 10016 (800) 443-8323; *The New Book of World Rankings.*

Federal Statistical Office, Gustav - Stresemann - Ring 11, D-6200 Wiesbaden, Germany; *China (Taiwan).*

TAIWAN - ENERGY

Council for Economic Planning and Development, Ninth Floor, 87 Nanking East Road, Section 2, Taipei, Republic of China; *Taiwan*

Statistical Data Book.

Directorate - General of Budget, Accounting and Statistics, Executive Yuan, Republic of China; *Monthly Statistics of the Republic of China*, and *Statistical Yearbook of The Republic of China.*

Facts on File, 460 Park Avenue South, New York, New York 10016 (800) 443-8323; *The New Book of World Rankings.*

G.K. Hall and Company, 70 Lincoln Street, Boston, Massachusetts 02111 (617) 423-3990; *The World in Figures.*

Penn Well Publishing Company, 1421 South Sheridan Road, P.O. Box 1260, Tulsa, Oklahoma 74101 (800) 752-9764; *International Energy Statistics Sourcebook.*

TAIWAN - EXCHANGE RATES

Council for Economic Planning and Development, Ninth Floor, 87 Nanking East Road, Section 2, Taipei, Republic of China; *Taiwan Statistical Data Book.*

Department of Statistics, Ministry of Finance, 2, Aikuo West Road, Taipei, Republic of China; *The Republic of China Monthly of Financial Statistics.*

Directorate - General of Budget, Accounting and Statistics, Executive Yuan, The Republic of China; *Monthly Statistics of the Republic of China*, and *Statistical Yearbook of The Republic of China.*

Economic Research Department, The Central Bank of China, 2, Roosevelt Road, Section 1, Taipei 10757, Republic of China; *Financial Statistics Monthly Taiwan District, The Republic of China.*

The Economist Intelligence Unit (Asia) Limited, 10th Floor, Luk Kwok Centre, 72 Gloucester Road, Wanchai, Hong Kong (Phone Number in U.S. (800) 938-4685); *Asian Market Atlas.*

Euromonitor Publications Limited, 87-88 Turnmill Street, London EC1M 5QU, England; *International Marketing Data and Statistics.*

TAIWAN - EXPORTS

American Automobile Manufacturers Association, 1401 H Street, NW, Suite 900, Washington, D.C. 20005 (202) 326-5500; *World Motor Vehicle Data.*

Council for Economic Planning and Development, Ninth Floor, 87 Nanking East Road, Section 2, Taipei, Republic of China; *Taiwan Statistical Data Book.*

Department of Statistics, Ministry of Finance, 2, Aikuo West Road, Taipei, Republic of China; *The Republic of China Monthly of Financial Statistics.*

Directorate - General of Budget, Accounting and Statistics, Executive Yuan, Republic of China; *Monthly Statistics of the Republic of China.*

Economic Research Department, The Central Bank of China, 2, Roosevelt Road, Section 1, Taipei 10757, Republic of China; *Financial Statistics Monthly Taiwan District, The Republic of China.*

The Economist Intelligence Unit, 111 West 57th Street, New York, New York 10019; *The World Market Atlas.*

The Economist Intelligence Unit (Asia) Limited, 10th Floor, Luk Kwok Centre, 72 Gloucester Road, Wanchai, Hong Kong (Phone Number in U.S. (800) 938-4685); *Asian Market Atlas.*

Euromonitor Publications Limited, 87-88 Turnmill Street, London EC1M 5QU, England; *International Marketing Data and Statistics, and Third World Economic Handbook.*

G.K. Hall and Company, 70 Lincoln Street, Boston, Massachusetts 02111 (617) 423-3990; *The World in Figures.*

Times Books, 201 East 50th Street, New York, New York 10022 (212) 751-2600; *The Economist Book of Vital World Statistics.*

TAIWAN - EXTERNAL INDEBTEDNESS

Council for Economic Planning and Development, Ninth Floor, 87 Nanking East Road, Section 2, Taipei, Republic of China; *Taiwan Statistical Data Book.*

Euromonitor Publications Limited, 87-88 Turnmill Street, London EC1M 5QU, England; *Third World Economic Handbook.*

TAIWAN - EXTERNAL TRADE

Council for Economic Planning and Development, Ninth Floor, 87 Nanking East Road, Section 2, Taipei, Republic of China; *Taiwan Statistical Data Book.*

Directorate - General of Budget, Accounting and Statistics, Executive Yuan, The Republic of China; *Monthly Statistics of the Republic of China, and Statistical Yearbook of The Republic of China.*

G.K. Hall and Company, 70 Lincoln Street, Boston, Massachusetts 02111 (617) 423-3990; *The World in Figures.*

TAIWAN - FABRIC PRODUCTION - See TAIWAN - TEXTILE INDUSTRY

TAIWAN - FARM CROPS - See TAIWAN - CROPS

TAIWAN - FEMALE WORKING POPULATION - TAIWAN - EMPLOYMENT

TAIWAN - FERTILITY RATES

The Economist Intelligence Unit (Asia) Limited, 10th Floor, Luk Kwok Centre, 72 Gloucester Road, Wanchai, Hong Kong (Phone Number in U.S. (800) 938-4685); *Asian Market Atlas.*

Facts on File, 460 Park Avenue South, New York, New York 10016 (800) 443-8323; *The New Book of World Rankings.*

TAIWAN - FERTILIZER

Council for Economic Planning and Development, Ninth Floor, 87 Nanking East Road, Section 2, Taipei, Republic of China; *Taiwan Statistical Data Book.*

Department of Agriculture and Forestry, Taiwan Provincial Government, Chunghsing Village, Nantou, Nantou Hsien, Taiwan, Republic of China; *Taiwan Agricultural Yearbook.*

Directorate - General of Budget, Accounting and Statistics, Executive Yuan, The Republic of China; *Monthly Statistics of the Republic of China, and Statistical Yearbook of The Republic of China.*

TAIWAN - FETAL MORTALITY

Council for Economic Planning and Development, Ninth Floor, 87 Nanking East Road, Section 2, Taipei, Republic of China; *Taiwan Statistical Data Book.*

Directorate - General of Budget, Accounting and Statistics, Executive Yuan, Republic of China; *Monthly Statistics of the Republic of China.*

TAIWAN - FIBRE PRODUCTION - See TAIWAN - TEXTILE INDUSTRY

TAIWAN - FINANCE

Facts on File, 460 Park Avenue South, New York, New York 10016 (800) 443-8323; *The New Book of World Rankings.*

Federal Statistical Office, Gustav - Stresemann - Ring 11, D-6200 Wiesbaden, Germany; *China (Taiwan).*

G.K. Hall and Company, 70 Lincoln Street, Boston, Massachusetts 02111 (617) 423-3990; *The World in Figures.*

TAIWAN - FINANCIAL INSTITUTIONS

Council for Economic Planning and Development, Ninth Floor, 87 Nanking East Road, Section 2, Taipei, Republic of China; *Taiwan Statistical Data Book.*

Department of Statistics, Ministry of Finance, 2, Aikuo West Road, Taipei, Republic of China; *The Republic of China Monthly of Financial Statistics.*

Directorate - General of Budget, Accounting and Statistics, Executive Yuan, The Republic of China; *Monthly Statistics of the Republic of China, and Statistical Yearbook of The Republic of China.*

Economic Research Department, The Central Bank of China, 2, Roosevelt Road, Section 1, Taipei 10757, Republic of China; *Financial Statistics Monthly Taiwan District, The Republic of China.*

TAIWAN - FIREWOOD PRODUCTION

Department of Agriculture and Forestry, Taiwan Provincial Government, Chunghsing Village, Nantou, Nantou Hsien, Taiwan, Republic of China; *Taiwan Agricultural Yearbook.*

Directorate - General of Budget, Accounting and Statistics, Executive Yuan, The Republic of China; *Statistical Yearbook of The Republic of China.*

TAIWAN - FISHERIES

Council for Economic Planning and Development, Ninth Floor, 87 Nanking East Road, Section 2, Taipei, Republic of China; *Taiwan Statistical Data Book.*

Department of Agriculture and Forestry, Taiwan Provincial Government, Chunghsing Village, Nantou, Nantou Hsien, Taiwan, Republic of China; *Taiwan Agricultural Yearbook.*

Directorate - General of Budget, Accounting and Statistics, Executive Yuan, The Republic of China; *Monthly Statistics of the Republic of China, and Statistical Yearbook of The Republic of China.*

Facts on File, 460 Park Avenue South, New York, New York 10016 (800) 443-8323; *The New Book of World Rankings.*

Federal Statistical Office, Gustav - Stresemann - Ring 11, D-6200 Wiesbaden, Germany; *China (Taiwan).*

TAIWAN - FLOUR PRODUCTION

Department of Agriculture and Forestry, Taiwan Provincial Government, Chunghsing Village, Nantou, Nantou Hsien, Taiwan, Republic of China; *Taiwan Agricultural Yearbook.*

Directorate - General of Budget, Accounting and Statistics, Executive Yuan, The Republic of China; *Statistical Yearbook of The Republic of China.*

TAIWAN - FOOD

Council for Economic Planning and Development, Ninth Floor, 87 Nanking East Road, Section 2, Taipei, Republic of China; *Taiwan Statistical Data Book.*

Department of Agriculture and Forestry, Taiwan Provincial Government, Chunghsing Village, Nantou, Nantou Hsien, Taiwan, Republic of China; *Taiwan Agricultural Yearbook.*

Directorate - General of Budget, Accounting and Statistics, Executive Yuan, The Republic of China; *Monthly Statistics of the Republic of China*, and *Statistical Yearbook of The Republic of China.*

TAIWAN - FOREIGN AID

G.K. Hall and Company, 70 Lincoln Street, Boston, Massachusetts 02111 (617) 423-3990; *The World in Figures.*

TAIWAN - FOREIGN TRADE

Council for Economic Planning and Development, Ninth Floor, 87 Nanking East Road, Section 2, Taipei, Republic of China; *Taiwan Statistical Data Book.*

Department of Agriculture and Forestry, Taiwan Provincial Government, Chunghsing Village, Nantou, Nantou Hsien, Taiwan, Republic of China; *Taiwan Agricultural Yearbook.*

Department of Statistics, Ministry of Finance, 2, Aikuo West Road, Taipei, Republic of China; *The Republic of China Monthly of Financial Statistics.*

Directorate - General of Budget, Accounting and Statistics, Executive Yuan, Republic of China; *Monthly Statistics of the Republic of China.*

Economic Research Department, The Central Bank of China, 2, Roosevelt Road, Section 1, Taipei 10757, Republic of China; *Financial Statistics Monthly Taiwan District, The Republic of China.*

The Economist Intelligence Unit (Asia) Limited, 10th Floor, Luk Kwok Centre, 72 Gloucester Road, Wanchai, Hong Kong (Phone Number in U.S. (800) 938-4685); *Asian Market Atlas.*

Euromonitor Publications Limited, 87-88 Turnmill Street, London EC1M 5QU, England; *International Marketing Data and Statistics*, and *Third World Economic Handbook.*

Facts on File, 460 Park Avenue South, New York, New York 10016 (800) 443-8323; *The New Book of World Rankings.*

Federal Statistical Office, Gustav - Stresemann - Ring 11, D-6200 Wiesbaden, Germany; *China (Taiwan).*

G.K. Hall and Company, 70 Lincoln Street, Boston, Massachusetts 02111 (617) 423-3990; *The World in Figures.*

TAIWAN - FORESTRY AND FOREST PRODUCTS

American Forest and Paper Association, 1250 Connecticut Avenue, NW, Washington, D.C. 20036 (202) 463-2455; *Wood Pulp and Fiber Statistics.*

Council for Economic Planning and Development, Ninth Floor, 87 Nanking East Road, Section 2, Taipei, Republic of China; *Taiwan Statistical Data Book.*

Department of Agriculture and Forestry, Taiwan Provincial Government, Chunghsing Village, Nantou, Nantou Hsien, Taiwan, Republic of China; *Taiwan Agricultural Yearbook.*

Directorate - General of Budget, Accounting and Statistics, Executive Yuan, The Republic of China; *Monthly Statistics of the Republic of China*, and *Statistical Yearbook of The Republic of China.*

The Economist Intelligence Unit (Asia) Limited, 10th Floor, Luk Kwok Centre, 72 Gloucester Road, Wanchai, Hong Kong (Phone Number in U.S. (800) 938-4685); *Asian Market Atlas.*

Euromonitor Publications Limited, 87-88 Turnmill Street, London EC1M 5QU, England; *Third World Economic Handbook.*

Facts on File, 460 Park Avenue South, New York, New York 10016 (800) 443-8323; *The New Book of World Rankings.*

Federal Statistical Office, Gustav - Stresemann - Ring 11, D-6200 Wiesbaden, Germany; *China (Taiwan).*

G.K. Hall and Company, 70 Lincoln Street, Boston, Massachusetts 02111 (617) 423-3990; *The World in Figures.*

TAIWAN - FRUIT PRODUCTION - See TAIWAN - CROPS

TAIWAN - GARLIC PRODUCTION - See TAIWAN - CROPS

TAIWAN - GAS PRODUCTION - See TAIWAN - MINING AND MINERAL PRODUCTS

TAIWAN - GENERAL INDUSTRIAL STATISTICS

Federal Statistical Office, Gustav - Stresemann - Ring 11, D-6200 Wiesbaden, Germany; *China (Taiwan).*

TAIWAN - GENERAL MORTALITY

Council for Economic Planning and Development, Ninth Floor, 87 Nanking East Road, Section 2, Taipei, Republic of China; *Taiwan Statistical Data Book.*

Directorate - General of Budget, Accounting and Statistics, Executive Yuan, Republic of China; *Monthly Statistics of the Republic of China.*

TAIWAN - GEOGRAPHIC DATA

Facts on File, 460 Park Avenue South, New York, New York 10016 (800) 443-8323; *The New Book of World Rankings.*

Federal Statistical Office, Gustav - Stresemann - Ring 11, D-6200 Wiesbaden, Germany; *China (Taiwan).*

TAIWAN - GOATS - See TAIWAN - LIVESTOCK AND POULTRY

TAIWAN - GOLD PRODUCTION AND CONSUMPTION - See TAIWAN - MINING AND MINERAL PRODUCTS

TAIWAN - GOVERNMENT

Council for Economic Planning and Development, Ninth Floor, 87 Nanking East Road, Section 2, Taipei, Republic of China; *Taiwan Statistical Data Book.*

Directorate - General of Budget, Accounting and Statistics, Executive Yuan, Republic of China; *Monthly Statistics of the Republic of China.*

G.K. Hall and Company, 70 Lincoln Street, Boston, Massachusetts 02111 (617) 423-3990; *The World in Figures.*

TAIWAN - GOVERNMENT EXPENDITURE

Council for Economic Planning and Development, Ninth Floor, 87 Nanking East Road, Section 2, Taipei, Republic of China; *Taiwan Statistical Data Book.*

Department of Statistics, Ministry of Finance, 2, Aikuo West Road, Taipei, Republic of China; *The Republic of China Monthly of Financial Statistics.*

Directorate - General of Budget, Accounting and Statistics, Executive Yuan, Republic of China; *Monthly Statistics of the Republic of China.*

Economic Research Department, The Central Bank of China, 2, Roosevelt Road, Section 1, Taipei 10757, Republic of China; *Financial Statistics Monthly Taiwan District, The Republic of China.*

Euromonitor Publications Limited, 87-88 Turnmill Street, London EC1M 5QU, England; *Third World Economic Handbook.*

TAIWAN - GRAIN PRODUCTION - See TAIWAN - CROPS

TAIWAN - GREEN PEPPER AND CHILIE PRODUCTION - See TAIWAN - CROPS

TAIWAN - GROSS DOMESTIC PRODUCT

Council for Economic Planning and Development, Ninth Floor, 87 Nanking East Road, Section 2, Taipei, Republic of China; *Taiwan Statistical Data Book.*

Department of Statistics, Ministry of Finance, 2, Aikuo West Road, Taipei, Republic of China; *The Republic of China Monthly of Financial Statistics.*

Directorate - General of Budget, Accounting and Statistics, Executive Yuan, The Republic of China; *Monthly Statistics of the Republic of China,* and *Statistical Yearbook of The Republic of China.*

Economic Research Department, The Central Bank of China, 2, Roosevelt Road, Section 1, Taipei 10757, Republic of China; *Financial Statistics Monthly Taiwan District, The Republic of China.*

The Economist Intelligence Unit, 111 West 57th Street, New York, New York 10019 (800) 938-4685; *The World Market Atlas.*

The Economist Intelligence Unit (Asia) Limited, 10th Floor, Luk Kwok Centre, 72 Gloucester Road, Wanchai, Hong Kong (Phone Number in U.S. (800) 938-4685); *Asian Market Atlas.*

Euromonitor Publications Limited, 87-88 Turnmill Street, London EC1M 5QU, England; *International Marketing Data and Statistics,* and *Third World Economic Handbook.*

Facts on File, 460 Park Avenue South, New York, New York 10016 (800) 443-8323; *The New Book of World Rankings.*

G.K. Hall and Company, 70 Lincoln Street, Boston, Massachusetts 02111 (617) 423-3990; *The World in Figures.*

Times Books, 201 East 50th Street, New York, New York 10022 (212) 751-2600; *The Economist Book of Vital World Statistics.*

TAIWAN - GROSS NATIONAL PRODUCT

Council for Economic Planning and Development, Ninth Floor, 87 Nanking East Road, Section 2, Taipei, Republic of China; *Taiwan Statistical Data Book.*

Department of Statistics, Ministry of Finance, 2, Aikuo West Road, Taipei, Republic of China; *The Republic of China Monthly of Financial Statistics.*

Directorate - General of Budget, Accounting and Statistics, Executive Yuan, Republic of China; *Monthly Statistics of the Republic of China.*

Economic Research Department, The Central Bank of China, 2, Roosevelt Road, Section 1, Taipei 10757, Republic of China; *Financial Statistics Monthly Taiwan District, The Republic of China.*

Euromonitor Publications Limited, 87-88 Turnmill Street, London EC1M 5QU, England; *International Marketing Data and Statistics,* and *Third World Economic Handbook.*

U.S. Arms Control and Disarmament Agency, 320 Twenty-first Street, NW, Washington, D.C. 20451 (202) 647-8677; *World Military Expenditures and Arms Transfers.*

TAIWAN - GROUNDNUTS PRODUCTION - See TAIWAN - CROPS

TAIWAN - HEALTH

Directorate - General of Budget, Accounting and Statistics, Executive Yuan, The Republic of China; *Monthly Statistics of the Republic of China,* and *Statistical Yearbook of The Republic of China.*

The Economist Intelligence Unit (Asia) Limited, 10th Floor, Luk Kwok Centre, 72 Gloucester Road, Wanchai, Hong Kong (Phone Number in U.S. (800) 938-4685); *Asian Market Atlas.*

Facts on File, 460 Park Avenue South, New York, New York 10016 (800) 443-8323; *The New Book of World Rankings.*

Federal Statistical Office, Gustav - Stresemann - Ring 11, D-6200 Wiesbaden, Germany; *China (Taiwan).*

G.K. Hall and Company, 70 Lincoln Street, Boston, Massachusetts 02111 (617) 423-3990; *The World in Figures.*

TAIWAN - HEMP FIBRE PRODUCTION - See TAIWAN - TEXTILE INDUSTRY

TAIWAN - HIDE PRODUCTION

Council for Economic Planning and Development, Ninth Floor, 87 Nanking East Road, Section 2, Taipei, Republic of China; *Taiwan Statistical Data Book.*

Department of Agriculture and Forestry, Taiwan Provincial Government, Chunghsing Village, Nantou, Nantou Hsien, Taiwan, Republic of China; *Taiwan Agricultural Yearbook.*

TAIWAN - HIGHWAYS

The Economist Intelligence Unit (Asia) Limited, 10th Floor, Luk Kwok Centre, 72 Gloucester Road, Wanchai, Hong Kong (Phone Number in U.S. (800) 938-4685); *Asian Market Atlas.*

G.K. Hall and Company, 70 Lincoln Street, Boston, Massachusetts 02111 (617) 423-3990; *The World in Figures.*

International Road Federation, 525 School Street, SW, Washington, D.C. 20024 (202) 554-2106; *World Road Statistics.*

TAIWAN - HONEY PRODUCTION

Commodity Research Bureau, Incorporated, 75 Wall Street, New York, New York 10005 (212) 504-7754; *Commodity Year Book.*

Department of Agriculture and Forestry, Taiwan Provincial Government, Chunghsing Village, Nantou, Nantou Hsien, Taiwan, Republic of China; *Taiwan Agricultural Yearbook.*

TAIWAN - HORSES - See TAIWAN - LIVESTOCK AND POULTRY

TAIWAN - HOURS OF WORK - See TAIWAN - EMPLOYMENT

TAIWAN - HOUSING AND HOUSING UNITS

Council for Economic Planning and Development, Ninth Floor, 87 Nanking East Road, Section 2, Taipei, Republic of China; *Taiwan Statistical Data Book.*

Directorate - General of Budget, Accounting and Statistics, Executive Yuan, The Republic of China; *Monthly Statistics of the Republic of China,* and *Statistical Yearbook of The Republic of China.*

Euromonitor Publications Limited, 87-88 Turnmill Street, London EC1M 5QU, England; *Third World Economic Handbook.*

Facts on File, 460 Park Avenue South, New York, New York 10016 (800) 443-8323; *The New Book of World Rankings.*

TAIWAN - HYDROCHLORIC ACID PRODUCTION

Directorate - General of Budget, Accounting and Statistics, Executive Yuan, The Republic of China; *Statistical Yearbook of The Republic of China.*

TAIWAN - ILLITERATE POPULATION

The Economist Intelligence Unit, 111 West 57th Street, New York, New York 10019 (800) 938-4685; *The World Market Atlas.*

G.K. Hall and Company, 70 Lincoln Street, Boston, Massachusetts 02111 (617) 423-3990; *The World in Figures.*

TAIWAN - IMPORT TRANSACTIONS

Council for Economic Planning and Development, Ninth Floor, 87 Nanking East Road, Section 2, Taipei, Republic of China; *Taiwan Statistical Data Book.*

Directorate - General of Budget, Accounting and Statistics, Executive Yuan, The Republic of China; *Statistical Yearbook of The Republic of China.*

TAIWAN - IMPORTS

American Automobile Manufacturers Association, 1401 H Street, NW, Suite 900, Washington, D.C. 20005 (202) 326-5500; *World Motor Vehicle Data.*

Council for Economic Planning and Development, Ninth Floor, 87 Nanking East Road, Section 2, Taipei, Republic of China; *Taiwan Statistical Data Book.*

Department of Statistics, Ministry of Finance, 2, Aikuo West Road, Taipei, Republic of China; *The Republic of China Monthly of Financial Statistics.*

Directorate - General of Budget, Accounting and Statistics, Executive Yuan, Republic of China; *Monthly Statistics of the Republic of China.*

Economic Research Department, The Central Bank of China, 2, Roosevelt Road, Section 1, Taipei 10757, Republic of China; *Financial Statistics Monthly Taiwan District, The Republic of China.*

The Economist Intelligence Unit, 111 West 57th Street, New York, New York 10019 (800) 938-4685; *The World Market Atlas.*

The Economist Intelligence Unit (Asia) Limited, 10th Floor, Luk Kwok Centre, 72 Gloucester Road, Wanchai, Hong Kong (Phone Number in U.S. (800) 938-4685); *Asian Market Atlas.*

Euromonitor Publications Limited, 87-88 Turnmill Street, London EC1M 5QU, England; *International Marketing Data and Statistics,* and *Third World Economic Handbook.*

G.K. Hall and Company, 70 Lincoln Street, Boston, Massachusetts 02111 (617) 423-3990; *The World in Figures.*

Times Books, 201 East 50th Street, New York, New York 10022 (212) 751-2600; *The Economist Book of Vital World Statistics.*

TAIWAN - INCOME AVERAGES

Council for Economic Planning and Development, Ninth Floor, 87 Nanking East Road, Section 2, Taipei, Republic of China; *Taiwan Statistical Data Book.*

Directorate - General of Budget, Accounting and Statistics, Executive Yuan, The Republic of China; *Statistical Yearbook of The Republic of China.*

TAIWAN - INCOME DISTRIBUTION

Council for Economic Planning and Development, Ninth Floor, 87 Nanking East Road, Section 2, Taipei, Republic of China; *Taiwan Statistical Data Book.*

TAIWAN - INDUSTRY

Council for Economic Planning and Development, Ninth Floor, 87 Nanking East Road, Section 2, Taipei, Republic of China; *Taiwan Statistical Data Book.*

Directorate - General of Budget, Accounting and Statistics, Executive Yuan, The Republic of China; *Monthly Statistics of the Republic of China,* and *Statistical Yearbook of The Republic of China.*

Euromonitor Publications Limited, 87-88 Turnmill Street, London EC1M 5QU, England; *Third World Economic Handbook.*

Facts on File, 460 Park Avenue South, New York, New York 10016 (800) 443-8323; *The New Book of World Rankings*.

Federal Statistical Office, Gustav - Stresemann - Ring 11, D-6200 Wiesbaden, Germany; *China (Taiwan)*.

G.K. Hall and Company, 70 Lincoln Street, Boston, Massachusetts 02111 (617) 423-3990; *The World in Figures*.

Times Books, 201 East 50th Street, New York, New York 10022 (212) 751-2600; *The Economist Book of Vital World Statistics*.

TAIWAN - INFANT AND MATERNAL MORTALITY

Council for Economic Planning and Development, Ninth Floor, 87 Nanking East Road, Section 2, Taipei, Republic of China; *Taiwan Statistical Data Book*.

Directorate - General of Budget, Accounting and Statistics, Executive Yuan, Republic of China; *Monthly Statistics of the Republic of China*.

The Economist Intelligence Unit (Asia) Limited, 10th Floor, Luk Kwok Centre, 72 Gloucester Road, Wanchai, Hong Kong (Phone Number in U.S. (800) 938-4685); *Asian Market Atlas*.

Times Books, 201 East 50th Street, New York, New York 10022 (212) 751-2600; *The Economist Book of Vital World Statistics*.

TAIWAN - INTERNATIONAL RESERVES

Council for Economic Planning and Development, Ninth Floor, 87 Nanking East Road, Section 2, Taipei, Republic of China; *Taiwan Statistical Data Book*.

Directorate - General of Budget, Accounting and Statistics, Executive Yuan, The Republic of China; *Monthly Statistics of the Republic of China, and Statistical Yearbook of The Republic of China*.

TAIWAN - IRON ORE PRODUCTION AND CONSUMPTION - See TAIWAN - MINING AND MINERAL PRODUCTS

TAIWAN - IRRIGATION

Department of Agriculture and Forestry, Taiwan Provincial Government, Chunghsing Village, Nantou, Nantou Hsien, Taiwan, Republic of China; *Taiwan Agricultural Yearbook*.

Euromonitor Publications Limited, 87-88 Turnmill Street, London EC1M 5QU, England; *International Marketing Data and Statistics*.

TAIWAN - JUTE PRODUCTION - See TAIWAN - CROPS

TAIWAN - LABOR FORCE

Council for Economic Planning and Development, Ninth Floor, 87 Nanking East Road, Section 2, Taipei, Republic of China; *Taiwan Statistical Data Book*.

Directorate - General of Budget, Accounting and Statistics, Executive Yuan, Republic of China; *Monthly Statistics of the Republic of China, and Statistical Yearbook of the Republic of China*.

The Economist Intelligence Unit (Asia) Limited, 10th Floor, Luk Kwok Centre, 72 Gloucester Road, Wanchai, Hong Kong (Phone Number in U.S. (800) 938-4685); *Asian Market Atlas*.

Euromonitor Publications Limited, 87-88 Turnmill Street, London EC1M 5QU, England; *International Marketing Data and Statistics*.

Facts on File, 460 Park Avenue South, New York, New York 10016 (800) 443-8323; *The New Book of World Rankings*.

G.K. Hall and Company, 70 Lincoln Street, Boston, Massachusetts 02111 (617) 423-3990; *The World in Figures*.

TAIWAN - LAND USE

Council for Economic Planning and Development, Ninth Floor, 87 Nanking East Road, Section 2, Taipei, Republic of China; *Taiwan Statistical Data Book*.

Department of Agriculture and Forestry, Taiwan Provincial Government, Chunghsing Village, Nantou, Nantou Hsien, Taiwan, Republic of China; *Taiwan Agricultural Yearbook*.

Directorate - General of Budget, Accounting and Statistics, Executive Yuan, Republic of China; *Monthly Statistics of the Republic of China*.

Euromonitor Publications Limited, 87-88 Turnmill Street, London EC1M 5QU, England; *International Marketing Data and Statistics*.

G.K. Hall and Company, 70 Lincoln Street, Boston, Massachusetts 02111 (617) 423-3990; *The World in Figures*.

TAIWAN - LEAD PRODUCTION AND CONSUMPTION - See TAIWAN - MINING AND MINERAL PRODUCTS

TAIWAN - LIBRARIES

Facts on File, 460 Park Avenue South, New York, New York 10016 (800) 443-8323; *The New Book of World Rankings*.

TAIWAN - LIFE EXPECTANCY

The Economist Intelligence Unit (Asia) Limited, 10th Floor, Luk Kwok Centre, 72 Gloucester Road, Wanchai, Hong Kong (Phone Number in U.S. (800) 938-4685); *Asian Market Atlas*.

TAIWAN - LIGNITE PRODUCTION - See TAIWAN - MINING AND MINERAL PRODUCTS

TAIWAN - LIVESTOCK AND POULTRY

Commodity Research Bureau, Incorporated, 75 Wall Street, New York, New York 10005 (212) 504-7754; *Commodity Year Book*.

Council for Economic Planning and Development, Ninth Floor, 87 Nanking East Road, Section 2, Taipei, Republic of China; *Taiwan Statistical Data Book*.

Department of Agriculture and Forestry, Taiwan Provincial Government, Chunghsing Village, Nantou, Nantou Hsien, Taiwan, Republic of China; *Taiwan Agricultural Yearbook*.

Directorate - General of Budget, Accounting and Statistics, Executive Yuan, The Republic of China; *Monthly Statistics of the Republic of China, and Statistical Yearbook of The Republic of China*.

Euromonitor Publications Limited, 87-88 Turnmill Street, London EC1M 5QU, England; *International Marketing Data and Statistics*.

Facts on File, 460 Park Avenue South, New York, New York 10016 (800) 443-8323; *The New Book of World Rankings*.

G.K. Hall and Company, 70 Lincoln Street, Boston, Massachusetts 02111 (617) 423-3990; *The World in Figures.*

TAIWAN - LIVING LEVELS

G.K. Hall and Company, 70 Lincoln Street, Boston, Massachusetts 02111 (617) 423-3990; *The World in Figures.*

TAIWAN - MAGAZINES

Council for Economic Planning and Development, Ninth Floor, 87 Nanking East Road, Section 2, Taipei, Republic of China; *Taiwan Statistical Data Book.*

Directorate - General of Budget, Accounting and Statistics, Executive Yuan, The Republic of China; *Monthly Statistics of the Republic of China,* and *Statistical Yearbook of The Republic of China.*

TAIWAN - MAGNESIUM PRODUCTION AND CONSUMPTION - See TAIWAN - MINING AND MINERAL PRODUCTS

TAIWAN - MAIL TRAFFIC

Council for Economic Planning and Development, Ninth Floor, 87 Nanking East Road, Section 2, Taipei, Republic of China; *Taiwan Statistical Data Book.*

Directorate - General of Budget, Accounting and Statistics, Executive Yuan, The Republic of China; *Monthly Statistics of the Republic of China,* and *Statistical Yearbook of The Republic of China.*

TAIWAN - MANGANESE PRODUCTION AND CONSUMPTION - See TAIWAN - MINING AND MINERAL PRODUCTS

TAIWAN - MANUFACTURING

American Automobile Manufacturers Association, 1401 H Street, NW, Suite 900, Washington, D.C. 20005 (202) 326-5500; *World Motor Vehicle Data.*

Council for Economic Planning and Development, Ninth Floor, 87 Nanking East Road, Section 2, Taipei, Republic of China; *Taiwan Statistical Data Book.*

Department of Statistics, Ministry of Finance, 2, Aikuo West Road, Taipei, Republic of China; *The Republic of China Monthly of Financial Statistics.*

Directorate - General of Budget, Accounting and Statistics, Executive Yuan, The Republic of China; *Monthly Statistics of the Republic of China,* and *Statistical Yearbook of The Republic of China.*

Euromonitor Publications Limited, 87-88 Turnmill Street, London EC1M 5QU, England; *Third World Economic Handbook.*

Facts on File, 460 Park Avenue South, New York, New York 10016 (800) 443-8323; *The New Book of World Rankings.*

G.K. Hall and Company, 70 Lincoln Street, Boston, Massachusetts 02111 (617) 423-3990; *The World in Figures.*

TAIWAN - MARRIAGE RATES

Council for Economic Planning and Development, Ninth Floor, 87 Nanking East Road, Section 2, Taipei, Republic of China; *Taiwan Statistical Data Book.*

Directorate - General of Budget, Accounting and Statistics, Executive Yuan, Republic of China; *Monthly Statistics of the Republic of China.*

Facts on File, 460 Park Avenue South, New York, New York 10016 (800) 443-8323; *The New Book of World Rankings.*

TAIWAN - MEAT PRODUCTION - See TAIWAN - LIVESTOCK AND POULTRY

TAIWAN - MERCHANT SHIPPING

Council for Economic Planning and Development, Ninth Floor, 87 Nanking East Road, Section 2, Taipei, Republic of China; *Taiwan Statistical Data Book.*

Directorate - General of Budget, Accounting and Statistics, Executive Yuan, The Republic of China; *Monthly Statistics of the Republic of China,* and *Statistical Yearbook of The Republic of China.*

G.K. Hall and Company, 70 Lincoln Street, Boston, Massachusetts 02111 (617) 423-3990; *The World in Figures.*

Lloyd's Register of Shipping, 17 Battery Place, New York, New York 10004 (212) 425-8050; *Register of Ships.*

Times Books, 201 East 50th Street, New York, New York 10022 (212) 751-2600; *The Economist Book of Vital World Statistics.*

U.S. Department of Transportation, Maritime Administration, 400 Seventh Street, SW, Washington, D.C. 20590 (202) 366-5807; *A Statistical Analysis of the World's Merchant Fleets.*

TAIWAN - MERCURY PRODUCTION AND CONSUMPTION - See TAIWAN - MINING AND MINERAL PRODUCTS

TAIWAN - MILITARY

The Economist Intelligence Unit (Asia) Limited, 10th Floor, Luk Kwok Centre, 72 Gloucester Road, Wanchai, Hong Kong (Phone Number in U.S. (800) 938-4685); *Asian Market Atlas.*

G.K. Hall and Company, 70 Lincoln Street, Boston, Massachusetts 02111 (617) 423-3990; *The World in Figures.*

The International Institute for Strategic Studies, 23 Tavistock Street, London WC2E 7NQ, England; *The Military Balance.*

U.S. Arms Control and Disarmament Agency, 320 Twenty-first Street, NW, Washington, D.C. 20451 (202) 647-8677; *World Military Expenditures and Arms Transfers.*

TAIWAN - MILK PRODUCTION - See TAIWAN - DAIRY PRODUCTS

TAIWAN - MILLET PRODUCTION - See TAIWAN - CROPS

TAIWAN - MINING AND MINERAL PRODUCTS

Commodity Research Bureau, Incorporated, 75 Wall Street, New York, New York 10005 (212) 504-7754; *Commodity Year Book.*

Council for Economic Planning and Development, Ninth Floor, 87 Nanking East Road, Section 2, Taipei, Republic of China; *Taiwan Statistical Data Book.*

Directorate - General of Budget, Accounting and Statistics, Executive Yuan, The Republic of China; *Monthly Statistics of the Republic of China,* and *Statistical Yearbook of The Republic of*

China.

Euromonitor Publications Limited, 87-88 Turnmill Street, London EC1M 5QU, England; *Third World Economic Handbook.*

Facts on File, 460 Park Avenue South, New York, New York 10016 (800) 443-8323; *The New Book of World Rankings.*

G.K. Hall and Company, 70 Lincoln Street, Boston, Massachusetts 02111 (617) 423-3990; *The World in Figures.*

Penn Well Publishing Company, 1421 South Sheridan Road, P.O. Box 1260, Tulsa, Oklahoma 74101 (800) 752-9764; *International Energy Statistics Sourcebook.*

TAIWAN - MOLYBDENUM PRODUCTION AND CONSUMPTION - See TAIWAN - MINING AND MINERAL PRODUCTS

TAIWAN - MONEY EXCHANGE RATE

Council for Economic Planning and Development, Ninth Floor, 87 Nanking East Road, Section 2, Taipei, Republic of China; *Taiwan Statistical Data Book.*

Department of Statistics, Ministry of Finance, 2, Aikuo West Road, Taipei, Republic of China; *The Republic of China Monthly of Financial Statistics.*

Directorate - General of Budget, Accounting and Statistics, Executive Yuan, The Republic of China; *Monthly Statistics of the Republic of China*, and *Statistical Yearbook of The Republic of China.*

Economic Research Department, The Central Bank of China, 2, Roosevelt Road, Section 1, Taipei 10757, Republic of China; *Financial Statistics Monthly Taiwan District, The Republic of China.*

Euromonitor Publications Limited, 87-88 Turnmill Street, London EC1M 5QU, England; *International Marketing Data and Statistics.*

TAIWAN - MONEY RESERVES

Council for Economic Planning and Development, Ninth Floor, 87 Nanking East Road, Section 2, Taipei, Republic of China; *Taiwan Statistical Data Book.*

Directorate - General of Budget, Accounting and Statistics, Executive Yuan, Republic of China; *Monthly Statistics of the Republic of China.*

Economic Research Department, The Central Bank of China, 2, Roosevelt Road, Section 1, Taipei 10757, Republic of China; *Financial Statistics Monthly Taiwan District, The Republic of China.*

Euromonitor Publications Limited, 87-88 Turnmill Street, London EC1M 5QU, England; *International Marketing Data and Statistics.*

TAIWAN - MONEY SUPPLY

Council for Economic Planning and Development, Ninth Floor, 87 Nanking East Road, Section 2, Taipei, Republic of China; *Taiwan Statistical Data Book.*

Department of Statistics, Ministry of Finance, 2, Aikuo West Road, Taipei, Republic of China; *The Republic of China Monthly of Financial Statistics.*

Directorate - General of Budget, Accounting and Statistics, Executive Yuan, The Republic of China; *Monthly Statistics of the*

Republic of China, and *Statistical Yearbook of The Republic of China.*

Economic Research Department, The Central Bank of China, 2, Roosevelt Road, Section 1, Taipei 10757, Republic of China; *Financial Statistics Monthly Taiwan District, The Republic of China.*

Euromonitor Publications Limited, 87-88 Turnmill Street, London EC1M 5QU, England; *International Marketing Data and Statistics.*

Federal Statistical Office, Gustav - Stresemann - Ring 11, D-6200 Wiesbaden, Germany; *China (Taiwan).*

G.K. Hall and Company, 70 Lincoln Street, Boston, Massachusetts 02111 (617) 423-3990; *The World in Figures.*

TAIWAN - MOTION PICTURES

Council for Economic Planning and Development, Ninth Floor, 87 Nanking East Road, Section 2, Taipei, Republic of China; *Taiwan Statistical Data Book.*

Directorate - General of Budget, Accounting and Statistics, Executive Yuan, The Republic of China; *Monthly Statistics of the Republic of China*, and *Statistical Yearbook of The Republic of China.*

TAIWAN - MOTOR VEHICLE PRODUCTION

American Automobile Manufacturers Association, 1401 H Street, NW, Suite 900, Washington, D.C. 20005 (202) 326-5500; *World Motor Vehicle Data.*

Council for Economic Planning and Development, Ninth Floor, 87 Nanking East Road, Section 2, Taipei, Republic of China; *Taiwan Statistical Data Book.*

Directorate - General of Budget, Accounting and Statistics, Executive Yuan, The Republic of China; *Monthly Statistics of the Republic of China*, and *Statistical Yearbook of The Republic of China.*

TAIWAN - MOTOR VEHICLE TAXES - See TAIWAN - TAXATION

TAIWAN - MOTOR VEHICLES IN USE

American Automobile Manufacturers Association, 1401 H Street, NW, Suite 900, Washington, D.C. 20005 (202) 326-5500; *World Motor Vehicle Data.*

Council for Economic Planning and Development, Ninth Floor, 87 Nanking East Road, Section 2, Taipei, Republic of China; *Taiwan Statistical Data Book.*

Directorate - General of Budget, Accounting and Statistics, Executive Yuan, The Republic of China; *Monthly Statistics of the Republic of China*, and *Statistical Yearbook of The Republic of China.*

G.K. Hall and Company, 70 Lincoln Street, Boston, Massachusetts 02111 (617) 423-3990; *The World in Figures.*

International Road Federation, 525 School Street, SW, Washington, D.C. 20024 (202) 554-2106; *World Road Statistics.*

Times Books, 201 East 50th Street, New York, New York 10022 (212) 751-2600; *The Economist Book of Vital World Statistics.*

TAIWAN - MULES - See TAIWAN - LIVESTOCK AND POULTRY

TAIWAN - MUSEUMS

Facts on File, 460 Park Avenue South, New York, New York 10016 (800) 443-8323; *The New Book of World Rankings*.

TAIWAN - NATALITY - See TAIWAN - BIRTH RATES

TAIWAN - NATIONAL ACCOUNTS

Council for Economic Planning and Development, Ninth Floor, 87 Nanking East Road, Section 2, Taipei, Republic of China; *Taiwan Statistical Data Book*.

Department of Statistics, Ministry of Finance, 2, Aikuo West Road, Taipei, Republic of China; *The Republic of China Monthly of Financial Statistics*.

Directorate - General of Budget, Accounting and Statistics, Executive Yuan, The Republic of China; *Monthly Statistics of the Republic of China*, and *Statistical Yearbook of The Republic of China*.

Economic Research Department, The Central Bank of China, 2, Roosevelt Road, Section 1, Taipei 10757, Republic of China; *Financial Statistics Monthly Taiwan District, The Republic of China*.

Federal Statistical Office, Gustav - Stresemann - Ring 11, D-6200 Wiesbaden, Germany; *China (Taiwan)*.

TAIWAN - NATIONAL INCOME

Council for Economic Planning and Development, Ninth Floor, 87 Nanking East Road, Section 2, Taipei, Republic of China; *Taiwan Statistical Data Book*.

Department of Statistics, Ministry of Finance, 2, Aikuo West Road, Taipei, Republic of China; *The Republic of China Monthly of Financial Statistics*.

Directorate - General of Budget, Accounting and Statistics, Executive Yuan, The Republic of China; *Monthly Statistics of the Republic of China*, and *Statistical Yearbook of The Republic of China*.

Economic Research Department, The Central Bank of China, 2, Roosevelt Road, Section 1, Taipei 10757, Republic of China; *Financial Statistics Monthly Taiwan District, The Republic of China*.

Facts on File, 460 Park Avenue South, New York, New York 10016 (800) 443-8323; *The New Book of World Rankings*.

G.K. Hall and Company, 70 Lincoln Street, Boston, Massachusetts 02111 (617) 423-3990; *The World in Figures*.

TAIWAN - NATIONAL PRODUCT

Facts on File, 460 Park Avenue South, New York, New York 10016 (800) 443-8323; *The New Book of World Rankings*.

TAIWAN - NATURAL GAS PRODUCTION - See TAIWAN - MINING AND MINERAL PRODUCTS

TAIWAN - NEWS AGENCIES

Council for Economic Planning and Development, Ninth Floor, 87 Nanking East Road, Section 2, Taipei, Republic of China; *Taiwan Statistical Data Book*.

Directorate - General of Budget, Accounting and Statistics, Executive Yuan, The Republic of China; *Monthly Statistics of the Republic of China*, and *Statistical Yearbook of The Republic of China*.

TAIWAN - NEWSPAPERS - See TAIWAN - FORESTRY AND FOREST PRODUCTS

TAIWAN - NITRIC ACID PRODUCTION - See TAIWAN - MINING AND MINERAL PRODUCTS

TAIWAN - OATS PRODUCTION - See TAIWAN - CROPS

TAIWAN - OCCUPATIONS - See TAIWAN - LABOR FORCE

TAIWAN - PAPER - See TAIWAN - FORESTRY AND FOREST PRODUCTS

TAIWAN - PEANUT PRODUCTION - See TAIWAN - CROPS

TAIWAN - PETROLEUM INDUSTRY

Commodity Research Bureau, Incorporated, 75 Wall Street, New York, New York 10005 (212) 504-7754; *Commodity Year Book*.

Council for Economic Planning and Development, Ninth Floor, 87 Nanking East Road, Section 2, Taipei, Republic of China; *Taiwan Statistical Data Book*.

Directorate - General of Budget, Accounting and Statistics, Executive Yuan, The Republic of China; *Monthly Statistics of the Republic of China*, and *Statistical Yearbook of The Republic of China*.

Facts on File, 460 Park Avenue South, New York, New York 10016 (800) 443-8323; *The New Book of World Rankings*.

G.K. Hall and Company, 70 Lincoln Street, Boston, Massachusetts 02111 (617) 423-3990; *The World in Figures*.

Penn Well Publishing Company, 1421 South Sheridan Road, P.O. Box 1260, Tulsa, Oklahoma 74101 (800) 752-9764; *International Energy Statistics Sourcebook*.

TAIWAN - PIG-IRON AND FERRO-ALLOY PRODUCTION - See TAIWAN - MINING AND MINERAL PRODUCTS

TAIWAN - PIGS - See TAIWAN - LIVESTOCK AND POULTRY

TAIWAN - PLASTICS AND RESINS PRODUCTION

Council for Economic Planning and Development, Ninth Floor, 87 Nanking East Road, Section 2, Taipei, Republic of China; *Taiwan Statistical Data Book*.

Directorate - General of Budget, Accounting and Statistics, Executive Yuan, The Republic of China; *Statistical Yearbook of The Republic of China*.

Euromonitor Publications Limited, 87-88 Turnmill Street, London EC1M 5QU, England; *Third World Economic Handbook*.

TAIWAN - POPULATION

Council for Economic Planning and Development, Ninth Floor, 87 Nanking East Road, Section 2, Taipei, Republic of China; *Taiwan Statistical Data Book*.

Directorate - General of Budget, Accounting and Statistics, Executive Yuan, The Republic of China; *Monthly Statistics of the Republic of China*, and *Statistical Yearbook of The Republic of China*.

The Economist Intelligence Unit, 111 West 57th Street, New York, New York 10019 (800) 938-4685; *The World Market Atlas*.

The Economist Intelligence Unit (Asia) Limited, 10th Floor, Luk Kwok Centre, 72 Gloucester Road, Wanchai, Hong Kong (Phone Number in U.S. (800) 938-4685); *Asian Market Atlas*.

Euromonitor Publications Limited, 87-88 Turnmill Street, London EC1M 5QU, England; *International Marketing Data and Statistics*, and *Third World Economic Handbook*.

Facts on File, 460 Park Avenue South, New York, New York 10016 (800) 443-8323; *The New Book of World Rankings*.

Federal Statistical Office, Gustav - Stresemann - Ring 11, D-6200 Wiesbaden, Germany; *China (Taiwan)*.

G.K. Hall and Company, 70 Lincoln Street, Boston, Massachusetts 02111 (617) 423-3990; *The World in Figures*.

Times Books, 201 East 50th Street, New York, New York 10022 (212) 751-2600; *The Economist Book of Vital World Statistics*.

U.S. Arms Control and Disarmament Agency, 320 Twenty-first Street, NW, Washington, D.C. 20451 (202) 647-8677; *World Military Expenditures and Arms Transfers*.

TAIWAN - POST OFFICES

Facts on File, 460 Park Avenue South, New York, New York 10016 (800) 443-8323; *The New Book of World Rankings*.

TAIWAN - POTATO PRODUCTION - See TAIWAN - CROPS

TAIWAN - PRICES

Council for Economic Planning and Development, Ninth Floor, 87 Nanking East Road, Section 2, Taipei, Republic of China; *Taiwan Statistical Data Book*.

Department of Statistics, Ministry of Finance, 2, Aikuo West Road, Taipei, Republic of China; *The Republic of China Monthly of Financial Statistics*.

Directorate - General of Budget, Accounting and Statistics, Executive Yuan, Republic of China; *Monthly Statistics of the Republic of China*.

Economic Research Department, The Central Bank of China, 2, Roosevelt Road, Section 1, Taipei 10757, Republic of China; *Financial Statistics Monthly Taiwan District, The Republic of China*.

Facts on File, 460 Park Avenue South, New York, New York 10016 (800) 443-8323; *The New Book of World Rankings*.

Federal Statistical Office, Gustav - Stresemann - Ring 11, D-6200 Wiesbaden, Germany; *China (Taiwan)*.

G.K. Hall and Company, 70 Lincoln Street, Boston, Massachusetts 02111 (617) 423-3990; *The World in Figures*.

TAIWAN - PRINTING AND WRITING PAPER - See TAIWAN - FORESTRY AND FOREST PRODUCTS

TAIWAN - PRODUCTION

American Automobile Manufacturers Association, 1401 H Street, NW, Suite 900, Washington, D.C. 20005 (202) 326-5500; *World Motor Vehicle Data*.

Council for Economic Planning and Development, Ninth Floor, 87 Nanking East Road, Section 2, Taipei, Republic of China; *Taiwan Statistical Data Book*.

Directorate - General of Budget, Accounting and Statistics, Executive Yuan, Republic of China; *Monthly Statistics of the Republic of China*.

Euromonitor Publications Limited, 87-88 Turnmill Street, London EC1M 5QU, England; *Third World Economic Handbook*.

Facts on File, 460 Park Avenue South, New York, New York 10016 (800) 443-8323; *The New Book of World Rankings*.

G.K. Hall and Company, 70 Lincoln Street, Boston, Massachusetts 02111 (617) 423-3990; *The World in Figures*.

TAIWAN - PRODUCTIVITY

Council for Economic Planning and Development, Ninth Floor, 87 Nanking East Road, Section 2, Taipei, Republic of China; *Taiwan Statistical Data Book*.

Euromonitor Publications Limited, 87-88 Turnmill Street, London EC1M 5QU, England; *International Marketing Data and Statistics*.

TAIWAN - PUBLIC FINANCE

Facts on File, 460 Park Avenue South, New York, New York 10016 (800) 443-8323; *The New Book of World Rankings*.

Federal Statistical Office, Gustav - Stresemann - Ring 11, D-6200 Wiesbaden, Germany; *China (Taiwan)*.

TAIWAN - RADIO BROADCASTING - See TAIWAN - BROADCASTING

TAIWAN - RADIO RECEIVERS

Council for Economic Planning and Development, Ninth Floor, 87 Nanking East Road, Section 2, Taipei, Republic of China; *Taiwan Statistical Data Book*.

Directorate - General of Budget, Accounting and Statistics, Executive Yuan, The Republic of China; *Monthly Statistics of the Republic of China*, and *Statistical Yearbook of The Republic of China*.

The Economist Intelligence Unit (Asia) Limited, 10th Floor, Luk Kwok Centre, 72 Gloucester Road, Wanchai, Hong Kong (Phone Number in U.S. (800) 938-4685); *Asian Market Atlas*.

TAIWAN - RAILWAYS

Council for Economic Planning and Development, Ninth Floor, 87 Nanking East Road, Section 2, Taipei, Republic of China; *Taiwan Statistical Data Book*.

Directorate - General of Budget, Accounting and Statistics, Executive Yuan, The Republic of China; *Monthly Statistics of the Republic of China*, and *Statistical Yearbook of The Republic of China*.

G.K. Hall and Company, 70 Lincoln Street, Boston, Massachusetts 02111 (617) 423-3990; *The World in Figures.*

Jane's Information Group, Sentinel House, 163 Brighton Road, Coulsdon, Surrey CR5 2NH, England (Telephone Number in U.S. (703) 683-3700); *Jane's World Railways.*

TAIWAN - RELIGION

Facts on File, 460 Park Avenue South, New York, New York 10016 (800) 443-8323; *The New Book of World Rankings.*

TAIWAN - RETAIL TRADE

Council for Economic Planning and Development, Ninth Floor, 87 Nanking East Road, Section 2, Taipei, Republic of China; *Taiwan Statistical Data Book.*

Directorate - General of Budget, Accounting and Statistics, Executive Yuan, The Republic of China; *Monthly Statistics of the Republic of China,* and *Statistical Yearbook of The Republic of China.*

Euromonitor Publications Limited, 87-88 Turnmill Street, London EC1M 5QU, England; *Third World Economic Handbook.*

G.K. Hall and Company, 70 Lincoln Street, Boston, Massachusetts 02111 (617) 423-3990; *The World in Figures.*

TAIWAN - RICE PRODUCTION - See TAIWAN - CROPS

TAIWAN - ROOT AND TUBER PRODUCTION - See TAIWAN - CROPS

TAIWAN - ROUNDWOOD PRODUCTION - See TAIWAN - FORESTRY AND FOREST PRODUCTS

TAIWAN - RUBBER PRODUCTION AND CONSUMPTION

Department of Agriculture and Forestry, Taiwan Provincial Government, Chunghsing Village, Nantou, Nantou Hsien, Taiwan, Republic of China; *Taiwan Agricultural Yearbook.*

Directorate - General of Budget, Accounting and Statistics, Executive Yuan, The Republic of China; *Statistical Yearbook of The Republic of China.*

Euromonitor Publications Limited, 87-88 Turnmill Street, London EC1M 5QU, England; *Third World Economic Handbook.*

Facts on File, 460 Park Avenue South, New York, New York 10016 (800) 443-8323; *The New Book of World Rankings.*

TAIWAN - SALT PRODUCTION - See TAIWAN - MINING AND MINERAL PRODUCTS

TAIWAN - SAWNWOOD PRODUCTION - See TAIWAN - FORESTRY AND FOREST PRODUCTS

TAIWAN - SENIOR CITIZENS

Facts on File, 460 Park Avenue South, New York, New York 10016 (800) 443-8323; *The New Book of World Rankings.*

TAIWAN - SESAME SEED PRODUCTION - See TAIWAN - CROPS

TAIWAN - SHEEP - See TAIWAN - LIVESTOCK AND POULTRY

TAIWAN - SILVER PRODUCTION AND CONSUMPTION - See TAIWAN - MINING AND MINERAL PRODUCTS

TAIWAN - SISAL PRODUCTION - See TAIWAN - CROPS

TAIWAN - SOCIAL DATA

Council for Economic Planning and Development, Ninth Floor, 87 Nanking East Road, Section 2, Taipei, Republic of China; *Taiwan Statistical Data Book.*

Directorate - General of Budget, Accounting and Statistics, Executive Yuan, Republic of China; *Monthly Statistics of the Republic of China.*

Facts on File, 460 Park Avenue South, New York, New York 10016 (800) 443-8323; *The New Book of World Rankings.*

G.K. Hall and Company, 70 Lincoln Street, Boston, Massachusetts 02111 (617) 423-3990; *The World in Figures.*

TAIWAN - SOYBEAN PRODUCTION - See TAIWAN - CROPS

TAIWAN - STATE BUDGET REVENUE AND EXPENDITURES

Euromonitor Publications Limited, 87-88 Turnmill Street, London EC1M 5QU, England; *International Marketing Data and Statistics.*

TAIWAN - STEEL - See TAIWAN - MINING AND MINERAL PRODUCTS

TAIWAN - SUGAR PRODUCTION AND CONSUMPTION - See TAIWAN - CROPS

TAIWAN - SULPHUR AND SULPHURIC ACID - See TAIWAN - MINING AND MINERAL PRODUCTS

TAIWAN - TAXATION

Department of Statistics, Ministry of Finance, 2, Aikuo West Road, Taipei, Republic of China; *The Republic of China Monthly of Financial Statistics.*

Directorate - General of Budget, Accounting and Statistics, Executive Yuan, The Republic of China; *Statistical Yearbook of The Republic of China.*

G.K. Hall and Company, 70 Lincoln Street, Boston, Massachusetts 02111 (617) 423-3990; *The World in Figures.*

International Road Federation, 525 School Street, SW, Washington, D.C. 20024 (202) 554-2106; *World Road Statistics.*

TAIWAN - TEA PRODUCTION AND CONSUMPTION - See TAIWAN - CROPS

TAIWAN - TELEGRAPH SERVICE

Council for Economic Planning and Development, Ninth Floor, 87 Nanking East Road, Section 2, Taipei, Republic of China; *Taiwan Statistical Data Book.*

Directorate - General of Budget, Accounting and Statistics, Executive Yuan, The Republic of China; *Monthly Statistics of the Republic of China,* and *Statistical Yearbook of The Republic of China.*

TAIWAN - TELEPHONES IN USE

American Telephone and Telegraph Company, 26 Parsippany Road, Whippany, New Jersey 07981 (800) 338-4038; *The World's Telephones.*

Council for Economic Planning and Development, Ninth Floor, 87 Nanking East Road, Section 2, Taipei, Republic of China; *Taiwan Statistical Data Book.*

Directorate - General of Budget, Accounting and Statistics, Executive Yuan, The Republic of China; *Statistical Yearbook of The Republic of China.*

The Economist Intelligence Unit (Asia) Limited, 10th Floor, Luk Kwok Centre, 72 Gloucester Road, Wanchai, Hong Kong (Phone Number in U.S. (800) 938-4685); *Asian Market Atlas.*

Euromonitor Publications Limited, 87-88 Turnmill Street, London EC1M 5QU, England; *Third World Economic Handbook.*

G.K. Hall and Company, 70 Lincoln Street, Boston, Massachusetts 02111 (617) 423-3990; *The World in Figures.*

TAIWAN - TELEVISION BROADCASTING - See TAIWAN - BROADCASTING

TAIWAN - TELEVISION RECEIVERS

Directorate - General of Budget, Accounting and Statistics, Executive Yuan, The Republic of China; *Statistical Yearbook of The Republic of China.*

The Economist Intelligence Unit (Asia) Limited, 10th Floor, Luk Kwok Centre, 72 Gloucester Road, Wanchai, Hong Kong (Phone Number in U.S. (800) 938-4685); *Asian Market Atlas.*

TAIWAN - TEXTILE INDUSTRY

American Forest and Paper Association, 1250 Connecticut Avenue, NW, Washington, D.C. 20036 (202) 463-2455; *Wood Pulp and Fiber Statistics.*

Council for Economic Planning and Development, Ninth Floor, 87 Nanking East Road, Section 2, Taipei, Republic of China; *Taiwan Statistical Data Book.*

Department of Agriculture and Forestry, Taiwan Provincial Government, Chunghsing Village, Nantou, Nantou Hsien, Taiwan, Republic of China; *Taiwan Agricultural Yearbook.*

Directorate - General of Budget, Accounting and Statistics, Executive Yuan, The Republic of China; *Monthly Statistics of the Republic of China*, and *Statistical Yearbook of The Republic of China.*

Euromonitor Publications Limited, 87-88 Turnmill Street, London EC1M 5QU, England; *Third World Economic Handbook.*

G.K. Hall and Company, 70 Lincoln Street, Boston, Massachusetts 02111 (617) 423-3990; *The World in Figures.*

TAIWAN - TIRE (MOTOR VEHICLE) PRODUCTION

Directorate - General of Budget, Accounting and Statistics, Executive Yuan, The Republic of China; *Statistical Yearbook of The Republic of China.*

TAIWAN - TOBACCO PRODUCTION

Commodity Research Bureau, Incorporated, 75 Wall Street, New York, New York 10005 (212) 504-7754; *Commodity Year Book.*

Department of Agriculture and Forestry, Taiwan Provincial Government, Chunghsing Village, Nantou, Nantou Hsien, Taiwan,

Republic of China; *Taiwan Agricultural Yearbook.*

Directorate - General of Budget, Accounting and Statistics, Executive Yuan, The Republic of China; *Statistical Yearbook of The Republic of China.*

Euromonitor Publications Limited, 87-88 Turnmill Street, London EC1M 5QU, England; *Third World Economic Handbook.*

Facts on File, 460 Park Avenue South, New York, New York 10016 (800) 443-8323; *The New Book of World Rankings.*

TAIWAN - TOURISM

Council for Economic Planning and Development, Ninth Floor, 87 Nanking East Road, Section 2, Taipei, Republic of China; *Taiwan Statistical Data Book.*

Directorate - General of Budget, Accounting and Statistics, Executive Yuan, The Republic of China; *Monthly Statistics of the Republic of China*, and *Statistical Yearbook of The Republic of China.*

Euromonitor Publications Limited, 87-88 Turnmill Street, London EC1M 5QU, England; *Third World Economic Handbook.*

Facts on File, 460 Park Avenue South, New York, New York 10016 (800) 443-8323; *The New Book of World Rankings.*

Federal Statistical Office, Gustav - Stresemann - Ring 11, D-6200 Wiesbaden, Germany; *China (Taiwan).*

G.K. Hall and Company, 70 Lincoln Street, Boston, Massachusetts 02111 (617) 423-3990; *The World in Figures.*

TAIWAN - TRACTORS IN USE

Department of Agriculture and Forestry, Taiwan Provincial Government, Chunghsing Village, Nantou, Nantou Hsien, Taiwan, Republic of China; *Taiwan Agricultural Yearbook.*

TAIWAN - TRADE - See TAIWAN - FOREIGN TRADE

TAIWAN - TRANSPORTATION AND COMMUNICATIONS

Council for Economic Planning and Development, Ninth Floor, 87 Nanking East Road, Section 2, Taipei, Republic of China; *Taiwan Statistical Data Book.*

Directorate - General of Budget, Accounting and Statistics, Executive Yuan, Republic of China; *Monthly Statistics of the Republic of China.*

The Economist Intelligence Unit (Asia) Limited, 10th Floor, Luk Kwok Centre, 72 Gloucester Road, Wanchai, Hong Kong (Phone Number in U.S. (800) 938-4685); *Asian Market Atlas.*

Euromonitor Publications Limited, 87-88 Turnmill Street, London EC1M 5QU, England; *Third World Economic Handbook.*

Facts on File, 460 Park Avenue South, New York, New York 10016 (800) 443-8323; *The New Book of World Rankings.*

Federal Statistical Office, Gustav - Stresemann - Ring 11, D-6200 Wiesbaden, Germany; *China (Taiwan).*

G.K. Hall and Company, 70 Lincoln Street, Boston, Massachusetts 02111 (617) 423-3990; *The World in Figures.*

TAIWAN - TUNGSTEN PRODUCTION AND CONSUMPTION - See TAIWAN - MINING AND MINERAL PRODUCTS

TAIWAN - TURKEYS - See TAIWAN - LIVESTOCK AND POULTRY

TAIWAN - UNEMPLOYMENT

Council for Economic Planning and Development, Ninth Floor, 87 Nanking East Road, Section 2, Taipei, Republic of China; *Taiwan Statistical Data Book*.

Directorate - General of Budget, Accounting and Statistics, Executive Yuan, The Republic of China; *Monthly Statistics of the Republic of China*, and *Statistical Yearbook of The Republic of China*.

Euromonitor Publications Limited, 87-88 Turnmill Street, London EC1M 5QU, England; *International Marketing Data and Statistics*.

TAIWAN - UTILITIES

Council for Economic Planning and Development, Ninth Floor, 87 Nanking East Road, Section 2, Taipei, Republic of China; *Taiwan Statistical Data Book*.

TAIWAN - VANADIUM PRODUCTION AND CONSUMPTION - See TAIWAN - MINING AND MINERAL PRODUCTS

TAIWAN - VEGETABLE PRODUCTION - See TAIWAN - CROPS

TAIWAN - VITAL STATISTICS

Council for Economic Planning and Development, Ninth Floor, 87 Nanking East Road, Section 2, Taipei, Republic of China; *Taiwan Statistical Data Book*.

Directorate - General of Budget, Accounting and Statistics, Executive Yuan, Republic of China; *Monthly Statistics of the Republic of China*.

Euromonitor Publications Limited, 87-88 Turnmill Street, London EC1M 5QU, England; *International Marketing Data and Statistics*, and *Third World Economic Handbook*.

G.K. Hall and Company, 70 Lincoln Street, Boston, Massachusetts 02111 (617) 423-3990; *The World in Figures*.

TAIWAN - WAGES

Council for Economic Planning and Development, Ninth Floor, 87 Nanking East Road, Section 2, Taipei, Republic of China; *Taiwan Statistical Data Book*.

Directorate - General of Budget, Accounting and Statistics, Executive Yuan, The Republic of China; *Monthly Statistics of the Republic of China*, and *Statistical Yearbook of The Republic of China*.

Federal Statistical Office, Gustav - Stresemann - Ring 11, D-6200 Wiesbaden, Germany; *China (Taiwan)*.

G.K. Hall and Company, 70 Lincoln Street, Boston, Massachusetts 02111 (617) 423-3990; *The World in Figures*.

TAIWAN - WATERMELON PRODUCTION - See TAIWAN - CROPS

TAIWAN - WEATHER

Facts on File, 460 Park Avenue South, New York, New York 10016 (800) 443-8323; *The New Book of World Rankings*.

G.K. Hall and Company, 70 Lincoln Street, Boston, Massachusetts 02111 (617) 423-3990; *The World in Figures*.

TAIWAN - WHALES - See TAIWAN - FISHERIES

TAIWAN - WHEAT PRODUCTION AND PRICES - See TAIWAN - CROPS

TAIWAN - WHOLESALE PRICE

Council for Economic Planning and Development, Ninth Floor, 87 Nanking East Road, Section 2, Taipei, Republic of China; *Taiwan Statistical Data Book*.

Directorate - General of Budget, Accounting and Statistics, Executive Yuan, The Republic of China; *Statistical Yearbook of The Republic of China*.

TAIWAN - WHOLESALE TRADE

Council for Economic Planning and Development, Ninth Floor, 87 Nanking East Road, Section 2, Taipei, Republic of China; *Taiwan Statistical Data Book*.

Directorate - General of Budget, Accounting and Statistics, Executive Yuan, The Republic of China; *Statistical Yearbook of The Republic of China*.

Euromonitor Publications Limited, 87-88 Turnmill Street, London EC1M 5QU, England; *Third World Economic Handbook*.

TAIWAN - WINE PRODUCTION

Directorate - General of Budget, Accounting and Statistics, Executive Yuan, The Republic of China; *Statistical Yearbook of The Republic of China*.

Facts on File, 460 Park Avenue South, New York, New York 10016 (800) 443-8323; *The New Book of World Rankings*.

TAIWAN - WOOD - See TAIWAN - FORESTRY AND FOREST PRODUCTS

TAIWAN - WOOL PRODUCTION AND CONSUMPTION

Directorate - General of Budget, Accounting and Statistics, Executive Yuan, The Republic of China; *Statistical Yearbook of The Republic of China*.

Facts on File, 460 Park Avenue South, New York, New York 10016 (800) 443-8323; *The New Book of World Rankings*.

TAIWAN - WORKING DAYS

Council for Economic Planning and Development, Ninth Floor, 87 Nanking East Road, Section 2, Taipei, Republic of China; *Taiwan Statistical Data Book*.

Directorate - General of Budget, Accounting and Statistics, Executive Yuan, The Republic of China; *Statistical Yearbook of The Republic of China*.

TAIWAN - YARN PRODUCTION

Directorate - General of Budget, Accounting and Statistics, Executive Yuan, The Republic of China; *Statistical Yearbook of The Republic of China.*

TAJIKISTAN - See also UNION OF SOVIET SOCIALIST REPUBLICS

Tajikistan - National Statistical Office

State Committee of Republic of Tajikistan on Statistics, 127 Ayini Street, Dushanbe - 29, 734029, Tajikistan.

TAJIKISTAN - AGRICULTURE

Business International Moscow, 23 Profsoyuznaya Ulitsa, 117859, Moscow (Telephone Number in U.S. (800) 938-4685); *The CIS Market Atlas.*

Encyclopedia Britannica, Incorporated, 310 South Michigan Avenue, Chicago, Illinois 60604 (312) 347-7000; *Britannica World Data.*

The World Bank, 1818 H Street, NW, Washington, D.C. 20433 (202) 477-1234; *Statistical Handbook: States of the Former USSR.*

TAJIKISTAN - AIRLINE SERVICE

Business International Moscow, 23 Profsoyuznaya Ulitsa, 117859, Moscow (Telephone Number in U.S. (800) 938-4685); *The CIS Market Atlas.*

Encyclopedia Britannica, Incorporated, 310 South Michigan Avenue, Chicago, Illinois 60604 (312) 347-7000; *Britannica World Data.*

TAJIKISTAN - AREA AND DENSITY OF POPULATION

Business International Moscow, 23 Profsoyuznaya Ulitsa, 117859, Moscow (Telephone Number in U.S. (800) 938-4685); *The CIS Market Atlas.*

TAJIKISTAN - BANKING

Business International Moscow, 23 Profsoyuznaya Ulitsa, 117859, Moscow (Telephone Number in U.S. (800) 938-4685); *The CIS Market Atlas.*

TAJIKISTAN - BIRTH RATES

Business International Moscow, 23 Profsoyuznaya Ulitsa, 117859, Moscow (Telephone Number in U.S. (800) 938-4685); *The CIS Market Atlas.*

Encyclopedia Britannica, Incorporated, 310 South Michigan Avenue, Chicago, Illinois 60604 (312) 347-7000; *Britannica World Data.*

TAJIKISTAN - BUDGET

Business International Moscow, 23 Profsoyuznaya Ulitsa, 117859, Moscow (Telephone Number in U.S. (800) 938-4685); *The CIS Market Atlas.*

TAJIKISTAN - CAPITAL INVESTMENT

The World Bank, 1818 H Street, NW, Washington, D.C. 20433 (202) 477-1234; *Statistical Handbook: States of the Former USSR.*

TAJIKISTAN - CATTLE - See TAJIKISTAN - LIVESTOCK AND POULTRY

TAJIKISTAN - CHEMICALS

Business International Moscow, 23 Profsoyuznaya Ulitsa, 117859, Moscow (Telephone Number in U.S. (800) 938-4685); *The CIS Market Atlas.*

TAJIKISTAN - COAL PRODUCTION AND CONSUMPTION - See TAJIKISTAN - MINING AND MINERAL PRODUCTIONS

TAJIKISTAN - COMMUNICATIONS

Business International Moscow, 23 Profsoyuznaya Ulitsa, 117859, Moscow (Telephone Number in U.S. (800) 938-4685); *The CIS Market Atlas.*

TAJIKISTAN - CONSTRUCTION INDUSTRY

Business International Moscow, 23 Profsoyuznaya Ulitsa, 117859, Moscow (Telephone Number in U.S. (800) 938-4685); *The CIS Market Atlas.*

Encyclopedia Britannica, Incorporated, 310 South Michigan Avenue, Chicago, Illinois 60604 (312) 347-7000; *Britannica World Data.*

TAJIKISTAN - CONSUMER PRODUCTS

Business International Moscow, 23 Profsoyuznaya Ulitsa, 117859, Moscow (Telephone Number in U.S. (800) 938-4685); *The CIS Market Atlas.*

TAJIKISTAN - CONSUMPTION

Business International Moscow, 23 Profsoyuznaya Ulitsa, 117859, Moscow (Telephone Number in U.S. (800) 938-4685); *The CIS Market Atlas.*

The World Bank, 1818 H Street, NW, Washington, D.C. 20433 (202) 477-1234; *Statistical Handbook: States of the Former USSR.*

TAJIKISTAN - COTTON PRODUCTION AND CONSUMPTION - See TAJIKISTAN - CROPS

TAJIKISTAN - CROPS

The World Bank, 1818 H Street, NW, Washington, D.C. 20433 (202) 477-1234; *Statistical Handbook: States of the Former USSR.*

TAJIKISTAN - DEATH RATES

Business International Moscow, 23 Profsoyuznaya Ulitsa, 117859, Moscow (Telephone Number in U.S. (800) 938-4685); *The CIS Market Atlas.*

TAJIKISTAN - DEMOGRAPHY

Business International Moscow, 23 Profsoyuznaya Ulitsa, 117859, Moscow (Telephone Number in U.S. (800) 938-4685); *The CIS Market Atlas.*

The Economist Intelligence Unit, 111 West 57th Street, New York, New York 10019 (800) 938-4685; *The World Market Atlas.*

Encyclopedia Britannica, Incorporated, 310 South Michigan Avenue, Chicago, Illinois 60604 (312) 347-7000; *Britannica World Data.*

The World Bank, 1818 H Street, NW, Washington, D.C. 20433 (202) 477-1234; *Statistical Handbook: States of the Former USSR.*

TAJIKISTAN - DISEASES

Business International Moscow, 23 Profsoyuznaya Ulitsa, 117859, Moscow (Telephone Number in U.S. (800) 938-4685); *The CIS Market Atlas.*

TAJIKISTAN - DIVORCE RATES

Encyclopedia Britannica, Incorporated, 310 South Michigan Avenue, Chicago, Illinois 60604 (312) 347-7000; *Britannica World Data.*

TAJIKISTAN - DOMESTIC INVESTMENT

Business International Moscow, 23 Profsoyuznaya Ulitsa, 117859, Moscow (Telephone Number in U.S. (800) 938-4685); *The CIS Market Atlas.*

TAJIKISTAN - ECONOMY

Business International Moscow, 23 Profsoyuznaya Ulitsa, 117859, Moscow (Telephone Number in U.S. (800) 938-4685); *The CIS Market Atlas.*

Encyclopedia Britannica, Incorporated, 310 South Michigan Avenue, Chicago, Illinois 60604 (312) 347-7000; *Britannica World Data.*

TAJIKISTAN - EDUCATION

Business International Moscow, 23 Profsoyuznaya Ulitsa, 117859, Moscow (Telephone Number in U.S. (800) 938-4685); *The CIS Market Atlas.*

Business International Moscow, 23 Profsoyuznaya Ulitsa, 117859, Moscow (Telephone Number in U.S. (800) 938-4685); *The CIS Market Atlas.*

Encyclopedia Britannica, Incorporated, 310 South Michigan Avenue, Chicago, Illinois 60604 (312) 347-7000; *Britannica World Data.*

TAJIKISTAN - ELECTRICITY

Business International Moscow, 23 Profsoyuznaya Ulitsa, 117859, Moscow (Telephone Number in U.S. (800) 938-4685); *The CIS Market Atlas.*

The World Bank, 1818 H Street, NW, Washington, D.C. 20433 (202) 477-1234; *Statistical Handbook: States of the Former USSR.*

TAJIKISTAN - EMPLOYMENT

The World Bank, 1818 H Street, NW, Washington, D.C. 20433 (202) 477-1234; *Statistical Handbook: States of the Former USSR.*

TAJIKISTAN - ENERGY

Business International Moscow, 23 Profsoyuznaya Ulitsa, 117859, Moscow (Telephone Number in U.S. (800) 938-4685); *The CIS Market Atlas.*

Encyclopedia Britannica, Incorporated, 310 South Michigan Avenue, Chicago, Illinois 60604 (312) 347-7000; *Britannica World Data.*

The World Bank, 1818 H Street, NW, Washington, D.C. 20433 (202) 477-1234; *Statistical Handbook: States of the Former USSR.*

TAJIKISTAN - ENVIRONMENT

Business International Moscow, 23 Profsoyuznaya Ulitsa, 117859, Moscow (Telephone Number in U.S. (800) 938-4685); *The CIS Market Atlas.*

TAJIKISTAN - EXPORTS

Business International Moscow, 23 Profsoyuznaya Ulitsa, 117859, Moscow (Telephone Number in U.S. (800) 938-4685); *The CIS Market Atlas.*

The Economist Intelligence Unit, 111 West 57th Street, New York, New York 10019 (800) 938-4685; *The World Market Atlas.*

Encyclopedia Britannica, Incorporated, 310 South Michigan Avenue, Chicago, Illinois 60604 (312) 347-7000; *Britannica World Data.*

The World Bank, 1818 H Street, NW, Washington, D.C. 20433 (202) 477-1234; *Statistical Handbook: States of the Former USSR.*

TAJIKISTAN - EXTERNAL TRADE

The World Bank, 1818 H Street, NW, Washington, D.C. 20433 (202) 477-1234; *Statistical Handbook: States of the Former USSR.*

TAJIKISTAN - FABRIC PRODUCTION AND CONSUMPTION - See TAJIKISTAN - TEXTILE INDUSTRY

TAJIKISTAN - FERTILITY RATES

Encyclopedia Britannica, Incorporated, 310 South Michigan Avenue, Chicago, Illinois 60604 (312) 347-7000; *Britannica World Data.*

The World Bank, 1818 H Street, NW, Washington, D.C. 20433 (202) 477-1234; *Statistical Handbook: States of the Former USSR.*

TAJIKISTAN - FISHERIES

Encyclopedia Britannica, Incorporated, 310 South Michigan Avenue, Chicago, Illinois 60604 (312) 347-7000; *Britannica World Data.*

TAJIKISTAN - FOOTWEAR PRODUCTION AND CONSUMPTION - See TAJIKISTAN - TEXTILE INDUSTRY

TAJIKISTAN - FOREIGN INVESTMENT

Business International Moscow, 23 Profsoyuznaya Ulitsa, 117859, Moscow (Telephone Number in U.S. (800) 938-4685); *The CIS Market Atlas.*

TAJIKISTAN - FOREIGN TRADE

Business International Moscow, 23 Profsoyuznaya Ulitsa, 117859, Moscow (Telephone Number in U.S. (800) 938-4685); *The CIS Market Atlas.*

Encyclopedia Britannica, Incorporated, 310 South Michigan Avenue, Chicago, Illinois 60604 (312) 347-7000; *Britannica World Data.*

The World Bank, 1818 H Street, NW, Washington, D.C. 20433 (202) 477-1234; *Statistical Handbook: States of the Former USSR.*

TAJIKISTAN - FORESTRY AND FOREST PRODUCTS

Business International Moscow, 23 Profsoyuznaya Ulitsa, 117859, Moscow (Telephone Number in U.S. (800) 938-4685); *The CIS Market Atlas.*

Encyclopedia Britannica, Incorporated, 310 South Michigan Avenue, Chicago, Illinois 60604 (312) 347-7000; *Britannica World Data.*

TAJIKISTAN - GOATS - See TAJIKISTAN - LIVESTOCK AND POULTRY

TAJIKISTAN - GOVERNMENT EXPENDITURE

The World Bank, 1818 H Street, NW, Washington, D.C. 20433 (202) 477-1234; *Statistical Handbook: States of the Former USSR.*

TAJIKISTAN - GOVERNMENT REVENUE

The World Bank, 1818 H Street, NW, Washington, D.C. 20433 (202) 477-1234; *Statistical Handbook: States of the Former USSR.*

TAJIKISTAN - GROSS DOMESTIC PRODUCT

The World Bank, 1818 H Street, NW, Washington, D.C. 20433 (202) 477-1234; *Statistical Handbook: States of the Former USSR.*

TAJIKISTAN - HEALTH

Business International Moscow, 23 Profsoyuznaya Ulitsa, 117859, Moscow (Telephone Number in U.S. (800) 938-4685); *The CIS Market Atlas.*

Encyclopedia Britannica, Incorporated, 310 South Michigan Avenue, Chicago, Illinois 60604 (312) 347-7000; *Britannica World Data.*

TAJIKISTAN - HIGHWAYS

Business International Moscow, 23 Profsoyuznaya Ulitsa, 117859, Moscow (Telephone Number in U.S. (800) 938-4685); *The CIS Market Atlas.*

Encyclopedia Britannica, Incorporated, 310 South Michigan Avenue, Chicago, Illinois 60604 (312) 347-7000; *Britannica World Data.*

TAJIKISTAN - HOUSING AND HOUSING UNITS

Business International Moscow, 23 Profsoyuznaya Ulitsa, 117859, Moscow (Telephone Number in U.S. (800) 938-4685); *The CIS Market Atlas.*

TAJIKISTAN - IMPORTS

Business International Moscow, 23 Profsoyuznaya Ulitsa, 117859, Moscow (Telephone Number in U.S. (800) 938-4685); *The CIS Market Atlas.*

The Economist Intelligence Unit, 111 West 57th Street, New York, New York 10019 (800) 938-4685; *The World Market Atlas.*

Encyclopedia Britannica, Incorporated, 310 South Michigan Avenue, Chicago, Illinois 60604 (312) 347-7000; *Britannica World Data.*

The World Bank, 1818 H Street, NW, Washington, D.C. 20433 (202) 477-1234; *Statistical Handbook: States of the Former USSR.*

TAJIKISTAN - INDUSTRY

Business International Moscow, 23 Profsoyuznaya Ulitsa, 117859, Moscow (Telephone Number in U.S. (800) 938-4685); *The CIS Market Atlas.*

The World Bank, 1818 H Street, NW, Washington, D.C. 20433 (202) 477-1234; *Statistical Handbook: States of the Former USSR.*

TAJIKISTAN - INFANT MORTALITY RATES

Business International Moscow, 23 Profsoyuznaya Ulitsa, 117859, Moscow (Telephone Number in U.S. (800) 938-4685); *The CIS Market Atlas.*

TAJIKISTAN - LABOR FORCE

Business International Moscow, 23 Profsoyuznaya Ulitsa, 117859, Moscow (Telephone Number in U.S. (800) 938-4685); *The CIS Market Atlas.*

The World Bank, 1818 H Street, NW, Washington, D.C. 20433 (202) 477-1234; *Statistical Handbook: States of the Former USSR.*

TAJIKISTAN - LAND USE

Encyclopedia Britannica, Incorporated, 310 South Michigan Avenue, Chicago, Illinois 60604 (312) 347-7000; *Britannica World Data.*

TAJIKISTAN - LIFE EXPECTANCY

Business International Moscow, 23 Profsoyuznaya Ulitsa, 117859, Moscow (Telephone Number in U.S. (800) 938-4685); *The CIS Market Atlas.*

TAJIKISTAN - LIVESTOCK AND POULTRY

Business International Moscow, 23 Profsoyuznaya Ulitsa, 117859, Moscow (Telephone Number in U.S. (800) 938-4685); *The CIS Market Atlas.*

Encyclopedia Britannica, Incorporated, 310 South Michigan Avenue, Chicago, Illinois 60604 (312) 347-7000; *Britannica World Data.*

TAJIKISTAN - MANUFACTURING

Encyclopedia Britannica, Incorporated, 310 South Michigan Avenue, Chicago, Illinois 60604 (312) 347-7000; *Britannica World Data.*

TAJIKISTAN - MARRIAGE RATES

Encyclopedia Britannica, Incorporated, 310 South Michigan Avenue, Chicago, Illinois 60604 (312) 347-7000; *Britannica World Data.*

TAJIKISTAN - MEAT PRODUCTION - See TAJIKISTAN - LIVESTOCK AND POULTRY

TAJIKISTAN - MILITARY

The International Institute for Strategic Studies, 23 Tavistock Street, London WC2E 7NQ, England; *The Military Balance.*

TAJIKISTAN - MINING AND MINERAL PRODUCTS

Business International Moscow, 23 Profsoyuznaya Ulitsa, 117859, Moscow (Telephone Number in U.S. (800) 938-4685); *The CIS Market Atlas.*

Encyclopedia Britannica, Incorporated, 310 South Michigan Avenue, Chicago, Illinois 60604 (312) 347-7000; *Britannica World Data.*

TAJIKISTAN - MOTOR VEHICLES

Business International Moscow, 23 Profsoyuznaya Ulitsa, 117859, Moscow (Telephone Number in U.S. (800) 938-4685); *The CIS Market Atlas.*

TAJIKISTAN - NATIONAL ACCOUNTS

The World Bank, 1818 H Street, NW, Washington, D.C. 20433 (202) 477-1234; *Statistical Handbook: States of the Former USSR.*

TAJIKISTAN - NATIONAL INCOME

Business International Moscow, 23 Profsoyuznaya Ulitsa, 117859, Moscow (Telephone Number in U.S. (800) 938-4685); *The CIS Market Atlas.*

TAJIKISTAN - PIGS - See TAJIKISTAN - LIVESTOCK AND POULTRY

TAJIKISTAN - POPULATION

Business International Moscow, 23 Profsoyuznaya Ulitsa, 117859, Moscow (Telephone Number in U.S. (800) 938-4685); *The CIS Market Atlas.*

The Economist Intelligence Unit, 111 West 57th Street, New York, New York 10019 (800) 938-4685; *The World Market Atlas.*

Encyclopedia Britannica, Incorporated, 310 South Michigan Avenue, Chicago, Illinois 60604 (312) 347-7000; *Britannica World Data.*

The World Bank, 1818 H Street, NW, Washington, D.C. 20433 (202) 477-1234; *Statistical Handbook: States of the Former USSR.*

TAJIKISTAN - POULTRY - See TAJIKISTAN - LIVESTOCK AND POULTRY

TAJIKISTAN - PRICES

The World Bank, 1818 H Street, NW, Washington, D.C. 20433 (202) 477-1234; *Statistical Handbook: States of the Former USSR.*

TAJIKISTAN - PRODUCTION

The World Bank, 1818 H Street, NW, Washington, D.C. 20433 (202) 477-1234; *Statistical Handbook: States of the Former USSR.*

TAJIKISTAN - PUBLIC FINANCE

The World Bank, 1818 H Street, NW, Washington, D.C. 20433 (202) 477-1234; *Statistical Handbook: States of the Former USSR.*

TAJIKISTAN - RADIO RECEIVERS

Encyclopedia Britannica, Incorporated, 310 South Michigan Avenue, Chicago, Illinois 60604 (312) 347-7000; *Britannica World Data.*

TAJIKISTAN - RAILWAYS

Business International Moscow, 23 Profsoyuznaya Ulitsa, 117859, Moscow (Telephone Number in U.S. (800) 938-4685); *The CIS Market Atlas.*

Encyclopedia Britannica, Incorporated, 310 South Michigan Avenue, Chicago, Illinois 60604 (312) 347-7000; *Britannica World Data.*

TAJIKISTAN - RETAIL TRADE

Business International Moscow, 23 Profsoyuznaya Ulitsa, 117859, Moscow (Telephone Number in U.S. (800) 938-4685); *The CIS Market Atlas.*

TAJIKISTAN - ROADS - See TAJIKISTAN - HIGHWAYS

TAJIKISTAN - ROUNDWOOD PRODUCTION AND CONSUMPTION - See TAJIKISTAN - FORESTRY AND FOREST PRODUCTS

TAJIKISTAN - SHEEP - See TAJIKISTAN - LIVESTOCK AND POULTRY

TAJIKISTAN - STEEL PRODUCTION AND CONSUMPTION - See TAJIKISTAN - MINING AND MINERAL PRODUCTS

TAJIKISTAN - TELEPHONES IN USE

Encyclopedia Britannica, Incorporated, 310 South Michigan Avenue, Chicago, Illinois 60604 (312) 347-7000; *Britannica World Data.*

TAJIKISTAN - TELEVISION RECEIVERS

Encyclopedia Britannica, Incorporated, 310 South Michigan Avenue, Chicago, Illinois 60604 (312) 347-7000; *Britannica World Data.*

TAJIKISTAN - TEXTILE INDUSTRY

Business International Moscow, 23 Profsoyuznaya Ulitsa, 117859, Moscow (Telephone Number in U.S. (800) 938-4685); *The CIS Market Atlas.*

TAJIKISTAN - TOURISM

Business International Moscow, 23 Profsoyuznaya Ulitsa, 117859, Moscow (Telephone Number in U.S. (800) 938-4685); *The CIS Market Atlas.*

TAJIKISTAN - TRANSPORTATION AND COMMUNICATIONS

Business International Moscow, 23 Profsoyuznaya Ulitsa, 117859, Moscow (Telephone Number in U.S. (800) 938-4685); *The CIS Market Atlas.*

Encyclopedia Britannica, Incorporated, 310 South Michigan Avenue, Chicago, Illinois 60604 (312) 347-7000; *Britannica World Data.*

TAJIKISTAN - VITAL STATISTICS

Encyclopedia Britannica, Incorporated, 310 South Michigan Avenue, Chicago, Illinois 60604 (312) 347-7000; *Britannica World Data.*

TAJIKISTAN - WAGES

Business International Moscow, 23 Profsoyuznaya Ulitsa, 117859, Moscow (Telephone Number in U.S. (800) 938-4685); *The CIS Market Atlas.*

The World Bank, 1818 H Street, NW, Washington, D.C. 20433 (202) 477-1234; *Statistical Handbook: States of the Former USSR.*

TAJIKISTAN - WOOL PRODUCTION AND CONSUMPTION - See TAJIKISTAN - TEXTILE INDUSTRY

TALC, PYROPHYLLITE, AND SOAPSTONE

U.S. Department of the Interior, Bureau of Mines, 810 Seventh Street, NW, Washington, D.C. 20241 (202) 501-9649; *Annual Reports*, and *Mineral Commodities Summaries.*

TANGELOS

U.S. Department of Agriculture, National Agricultural Statistics Service, Fourteenth Street and Independence Avenue, SW, Washington, D.C. 20250 (202) 219-1504; *Citrus Fruits*, and unpublished data.

TANTALUM

U.S. Department of the Interior, Bureau of Mines, 810 Seventh Street, NW, Washington, D.C. 20241 (202) 501-9649; *Mineral Commodity Summaries.*

Tanzania (United Republic Of) - National Statistical Office

Bureau of Statistics, Post Office Box 796, Dar es Salaam, United Republic of Tanzania.

Tanzania (United Republic Of) - Primary Statistics Sources

Bureau of Statistics, Government Publications Agency, Post Office Box 1801, Dar es Salaam, Tanzania; *Statistical Abstract,* and *Quarterly Statistical Bulletin.*

TANZANIA (UNITED REPUBLIC OF) - AGRICULTURE

Euromonitor Publications Limited, 87-88 Turnmill Street, London EC1M 5QU, England; *International Marketing Data and Statistics.*

Facts on File, 460 Park Avenue South, New York, New York 10016 (800) 443-8323; *The New Book of World Rankings.*

Food and Agricultural Organization of the United Nations (FAO) Via delle Terme di Caracalla, 00100 Rome, Italy (Telephone Number in U.S. (202) 653-2400); *Production Yearbook,* and *The State of Food and Agriculture, and Trade Yearbook.*

G.K. Hall and Company, 70 Lincoln Street, Boston, Massachusetts 02111 (617) 423-3990; *The World in Figures.*

Statistical Office of the United Nations, Publishing Service, New York, New York 10017 (800) 253-9646; *Statistical Yearbook,* and *Survey of Economic and Social Conditions in Africa.*

Times Books, 201 East 50th Street, New York, New York 10022 (212) 751-2600; *The Economist Book of Vital World Statistics.*

United Nations Economic Commission for Africa, Africa Hall, P.O. Box 3001, Addis Ababa, Ethiopia (Telephone Number in U.S. (800) 253-9646); *African Statistical Yearbook.*

The World Bank, 1818 H Street, NW, Washington, D.C. 20433 (202) 477-1234; *World Tables.*

TANZANIA (UNITED REPUBLIC OF) - AIRLINE SERVICE

Facts on File, 460 Park Avenue South, New York, New York 10016 (800) 443-8323; *The New Book of World Rankings.*

G.K. Hall and Company, 70 Lincoln Street, Boston, Massachusetts 02111 (617) 423-3990; *The World in Figures.*

International Civil Aviation Organization, 1000 Sherbrooke Street, West, Suite 400, Montreal, Quebec, Canada H3A 2R2 (514) 285-8219; *Civil Aviation Statistics of the World.*

Statistical Office of the United Nations, Publishing Service, New York, New York 10017 (800) 253-9646; *Statistical Yearbook.*

Times Books, 201 East 50th Street, New York, New York 10022 (212) 751-2800; *The Economist Book of Vital World Statistics.*

United Nations Economic Commission for Africa, Africa Hall, P.O. Box 3001, Addis Ababa, Ethiopia (Telephone Number in U.S. (800) 253-9646); *African Statistical Yearbook.*

TANZANIA (UNITED REPUBLIC OF) - ALUMINUM PRODUCTION AND CONSUMPTION - See TANZANIA (UNITED REPUBLIC OF) - MINING AND MINERAL PRODUCTS

TANZANIA (UNITED REPUBLIC OF) - ANIMAL HEALTH

Food and Agricultural Organization of the United Nations (FAO), Via delle Terme di Caracalla, 00100, Rome, Italy (Telephone Number in U.S. (202) 653-2400); *Animal Health Yearbook.*

TANZANIA (UNITED REPUBLIC OF) - AREA AND DENSITY OF POPULATION

African Development Bank, 01 BP 1387, Abidjan 01, Cote D'Ivoire; *Selected Statistics on Regional Member Countries.*

Commodity Research Bureau, Incorporated, 75 Wall Street, New York, New York 10005 (212) 504-7754; *Commodity Year Book.*

Facts on File, 460 Park Avenue South, New York, New York 10016 (800) 443-8323; *The New Book of World Rankings.*

Food and Agricultural Organization of the United Nations (FAO) Via delle Terme di Caracalla, 00100 Rome, Italy (Telephone Number in U.S. (202) 653-2400); *The State of Food and Agriculture.*

G.K. Hall and Company, 70 Lincoln Street, Boston, Massachusetts 02111 (617) 423-3990; *The World in Figures.*

Statistical Office of the United Nations, Publishing Service, New York, New York 10017 (800) 253-9646; *Statistical Yearbook,* and *Survey of Economic and Social Conditions in Africa.*

Times Books, 201 East 50th Street, New York, New York 10022 (212) 751-2600; *The Economist Book of Vital World Statistics.*

United Nations Educational, Scientific and Cultural Organization (UNESCO), 7 Place de Fontenoy, F-75700 Paris, France (Telephone Number in U.S. (212) 963-5981); *Statistical Yearbook.*

TANZANIA (UNITED REPUBLIC OF) - ARMS EXPORTS AND IMPORTS

U.S. Arms Control and Disarmament Agency, 320 Twenty-first Street, NW, Washington, D.C. 20451 (202) 647-8677; *World Military Expenditures and Arms Transfers.*

TANZANIA (UNITED REPUBLIC OF) - BALANCE OF PAYMENTS

African Development Bank, 01 BP 1387, Abidjan 01, Cote D'Ivoire; *Selected Statistics on Regional Member Countries.*

The Economist Intelligence Unit, 111 West 57th Street, New York, New York 10019 (800) 938-4685; *The World Market Atlas.*

G.K. Hall and Company, 70 Lincoln Street, Boston, Massachusetts 02111 (617) 423-3990; *The World in Figures.*

International Monetary Fund, 700 Nineteenth Street, NW, Washington, D.C. 20431 (202) 623-7000; *Balance of Payments Yearbook.*

Times Books, 201 East 50th Street, New York, New York 10022 (212) 751-2600; *The Economist Book of Vital World Statistics.*

United Nations Economic Commission for Africa, Africa Hall, P.O. Box 3001, Addis Ababa, Ethiopia (Telephone Number in U.S. (800) 253-9646); *African Statistical Yearbook*.

The World Bank, 1818 H Street, NW, Washington, D.C. 20433 (202) 477-1234; *World Tables*.

TANZANIA (UNITED REPUBLIC OF) - BANKING

Facts on File, 460 Park Avenue South, New York, New York 10016 (800) 443-8323; *The New Book of World Rankings*.

G.K. Hall and Company, 70 Lincoln Street, Boston, Massachusetts 02111 (617) 423-3990; *The World in Figures*.

International Monetary Fund, 700 Nineteenth Street, NW, Washington, D.C. 20431 (202) 623-7000; *International Financial Statistics*.

United Nations Economic Commission for Africa, Africa Hall, P.O. Box 3001, Addis Ababa, Ethiopia (Telephone Number in U.S. (800) 253-9646); *African Statistical Yearbook*.

TANZANIA (UNITED REPUBLIC OF) - BARLEY PRODUCTION - See TANZANIA (UNITED REPUBLIC OF) - CROPS

TANZANIA (UNITED REPUBLIC OF) - BEER PRODUCTION

Facts on File, 460 Park Avenue South, New York, New York 10016 (800) 443-8323; *The New Book of World Rankings*.

Statistical Office of the United Nations, Publishing Service, New York, New York 10017 (800) 253-9646; *Statistical Yearbook*.

TANZANIA (UNITED REPUBLIC OF) - BIRTH RATES

Facts on File, 460 Park Avenue South, New York, New York 10016 (800) 443-8323; *The New Book of World Rankings*.

Statistical Office of the United Nations, Publishing Service, New York, New York 10017 (800) 253-9646; *Demographic Yearbook*, *Statistical Yearbook*, and *Survey of Economic and Social Conditions in Africa*.

Times Books, 201 East 50th Street, New York, New York 10022 (212) 751-2600; *The Economist Book of Vital World Statistics*.

The World Bank, 1818 H Street, NW, Washington, D.C. 20433 (202) 477-1234; *World Tables*.

TANZANIA (UNITED REPUBLIC OF) - BONDS

G.K. Hall and Company, 70 Lincoln Street, Boston, Massachusetts 02111 (617) 423-3990; *The World in Figures*.

International Monetary Fund, 700 Nineteenth Street, NW, Washington, D.C. 20431 (202) 623-7000; *Government Finance Statistics Yearbook*.

TANZANIA (UNITED REPUBLIC OF) - BOOK PRODUCTION

G.K. Hall and Company, 70 Lincoln Street, Boston, Massachusetts 02111 (617) 423-3990; *The World in Figures*.

TANZANIA (UNITED REPUBLIC OF) - BROADCASTING

Billboard Limited, P.O. Box 9027, 1006 AA Amsterdam, The Netherlands (Telephone Number in U.S. (212) 764-7300); *World Radio TV Handbook*.

Facts on File, 460 Park Avenue South, New York, New York 10016 (800) 443-8323; *The New Book of World Rankings*.

G.K. Hall and Company, 70 Lincoln Street, Boston, Massachusetts 02111 (617) 423-3990; *The World in Figures*.

Times Books, 201 East 50th Street, New York, New York 10022 (212) 751-2600; *The Economist Book of Vital World Statistics*.

TANZANIA (UNITED REPUBLIC OF) - BUSINESS

G.K. Hall and Company, 70 Lincoln Street, Boston, Massachusetts 02111 (617) 423-3990; *The World in Figures*.

TANZANIA (UNITED REPUBLIC OF) - BUSINESS AND PROFESSIONAL LICENSES

International Monetary Fund, 700 Nineteenth Street, NW, Washington, D.C. 20431 (202) 623-7000; *Government Finance Statistics Yearbook*.

TANZANIA (UNITED REPUBLIC OF) - BUTTER PRODUCTION - See TANZANIA (UNITED REPUBLIC OF) - DAIRY PRODUCTS

TANZANIA (UNITED REPUBLIC OF) - CALORIE SUPPLY

African Development Bank, 01 BP 1387, Abidjan 01, Cote D'Ivoire; *Selected Statistics on Regional Member Countries*.

Food and Agricultural Organization of the United Nations (FAO) Via delle Terme di Caracalla, 00100 Rome, Italy (Telephone Number in U.S. (202) 653-2400); *The State of Food and Agriculture*.

TANZANIA (UNITED REPUBLIC OF) - CAPITAL REVENUE

International Monetary Fund, 700 Nineteenth Street, NW, Washington, D.C. 20431 (202) 623-7000; *Government Finance Statistics Yearbook*.

TANZANIA (UNITED REPUBLIC OF) - CASHEW NUTS EXPORTS - See TANZANIA (UNITED REPUBLIC OF) - CROPS

TANZANIA (UNITED REPUBLIC OF) - CATTLE - See TANZANIA (UNITED REPUBLIC OF) - LIVESTOCK AND POULTRY

TANZANIA (UNITED REPUBLIC OF) - CEMENT PRODUCTION - See TANZANIA (UNITED REPUBLIC OF) - MINING AND MINERAL PRODUCTS

TANZANIA (UNITED REPUBLIC OF) - CHEMICAL (ORGANIC) PRODUCTION - See TANZANIA (UNITED REPUBLIC OF) - MINING AND MINERAL PRODUCTS

TANZANIA (UNITED REPUBLIC OF) - CHICKENS - See TANZANIA (UNITED REPUBLIC OF) - LIVESTOCK AND POULTRY

TANZANIA (UNITED REPUBLIC OF) - CIGARETTE PRODUCTION - See TANZANIA (UNITED REPUBLIC OF) - TOBACCO PRODUCTION

TANZANIA (UNITED REPUBLIC OF) - CLASS STRUCTURE

G.K. Hall and Company, 70 Lincoln Street, Boston, Massachusetts 02111 (617) 423-3990; *The World in Figures*.

TANZANIA (UNITED REPUBLIC OF) - CLIMATE

Facts on File, 460 Park Avenue South, New York, New York 10016 (800) 443-8323; *The New Book of World Rankings*.

G.K. Hall and Company, 70 Lincoln Street, Boston, Massachusetts 02111 (617) 423-3990; *The World in Figures.*

TANZANIA (UNITED REPUBLIC OF) - COAL PRODUCTION - See TANZANIA (UNITED REPUBLIC OF) - MINING AND MINERAL PRODUCTS

TANZANIA (UNITED REPUBLIC OF) - COCOA PRODUCTION - See TANZANIA (UNITED REPUBLIC OF) - CROPS

TANZANIA (UNITED REPUBLIC OF) - COFFEE EXPORTS AND IMPORTS - See TANZANIA (UNITED REPUBLIC OF) - CROPS

TANZANIA (UNITED REPUBLIC OF) - COMMUNICATIONS

G.K. Hall and Company, 70 Lincoln Street, Boston, Massachusetts 02111 (617) 423-3990; *The World in Figures.*

United Nations Economic Commission for Africa, Africa Hall, P.O. Box 3001, Addis Ababa, Ethiopia (Telephone Number in U.S. (800) 253-9646); *African Statistical Yearbook.*

TANZANIA (UNITED REPUBLIC OF) - CONSTRUCTION INDUSTRY

Facts on File, 460 Park Avenue South, New York, New York 10016 (800) 443-8323; *The New Book of World Rankings.*

Statistical Office of the United Nations, Publishing Service, New York, New York 10017 (800) 253-9646; *Construction Statistics Yearbook,* and *Statistical Yearbook.*

United Nations Economic Commission for Africa, Africa Hall, P.O. Box 3001, Addis Ababa, Ethiopia (Telephone Number in U.S. (800) 253-9646); *African Statistical Yearbook*

TANZANIA (UNITED REPUBLIC OF) - CONSUMER PRICE INDEX

African Development Bank, 01 BP 1387, Abidjan 01, Cote D'Ivoire; *Selected Statistics on Regional Member Countries.*

G.K. Hall and Company, 70 Lincoln Street, Boston, Massachusetts 02111 (617) 423-3990; *The World in Figures.*

Statistical Office of the United Nations, Publishing Service, New York, New York 10017 (800) 253-9646; *Statistical Yearbook,* and *Survey of Economic and Social Conditions in Africa.*

United Nations Economic Commission for Africa, Africa Hall, P.O. Box 3001, Addis Ababa, Ethiopia (Telephone Number in U.S. (800) 253-9646); *African Statistical Yearbook.*

TANZANIA (UNITED REPUBLIC OF) - CONSUMER PRICES

International Labour Office, I.L.O. Publications, CH-1211, Geneva 22, Switzerland; *Yearbook of Labour Statistics.*

International Monetary Fund, 700 Nineteenth Street, NW, Washington, D.C. 20431 (202) 623-7000; *International Financial Statistics.*

Times Books, 201 East 50th Street, New York, New York 10022 (212) 751-2600; *The Economist Book of Vital World Statistics.*

TANZANIA (UNITED REPUBLIC OF) - CONSUMPTION

African Development Bank, 01 BP 1387, Abidjan 01, Cote D'Ivoire; *Selected Statistics on Regional Member Countries.*

G.K. Hall and Company, 70 Lincoln Street, Boston, Massachusetts 02111 (617) 423-3990; *The World in Figures.*

Statistical Office of the United Nations, Publishing Service, New York, New York 10017 (800) 253-9646; *Survey of Economic and Social Conditions in Africa.*

TANZANIA (UNITED REPUBLIC OF) - COPPER PRODUCTION AND CONSUMPTION - See TANZANIA (UNITED REPUBLIC OF) - MINING AND MINERAL PRODUCTS

TANZANIA (UNITED REPUBLIC OF) - CORN PRODUCTION - See TANZANIA (UNITED REPUBLIC OF) - CROPS

TANZANIA (UNITED REPUBLIC OF) - CORPORATE TAXES - See TANZANIA (UNITED REPUBLIC OF) - TAXATION

TANZANIA (UNITED REPUBLIC OF) - COTTON - See TANZANIA (UNITED REPUBLIC OF) - CROPS

TANZANIA (UNITED REPUBLIC OF) - CRIME

International Criminal Police Organization (INTERPOL), 26 rue Armengaud, 92210 Saint Cloud, France; *International Crime Statistics.*

Yale University Press, Yale Station, New Haven, Connecticut 06520 (203) 432-0940; *Violence and Crime in Cross-National Perspective.*

TANZANIA (UNITED REPUBLIC OF) - CROPS

Facts on File, 460 Park Avenue South, New York, New York 10016 (800) 443-8323; *The New Book of World Rankings.*

Food and Agricultural Organization of the United Nations (FAO) Via delle Terme di Caracalla, 00100 Rome, Italy (Telephone Number in U.S. (202) 653-2400); *The State of Food and Agriculture.*

G.K. Hall and Company, 70 Lincoln Street, Boston, Massachusetts 02111 (617) 423-3990; *The World in Figures.*

International Monetary Fund, 700 Nineteenth Street, NW, Washington, D.C. 20431 (202) 623-7000; *Government Finance Statistics Yearbook.*

Statistical Office of the United Nations, Publishing Service, New York, New York 10017 (800) 253-9646; *Statistical Yearbook.*

United Nations Economic Commission for Africa, Africa Hall, P.O. Box 3001, Addis Ababa, Ethiopia (Telephone Number in U.S. (800) 253-9646); *African Statistical Yearbook.*

TANZANIA (UNITED REPUBLIC OF) - CUSTOMS DUTIES

G.K. Hall and Company, 70 Lincoln Street, Boston, Massachusetts 02111 (617) 423-3990; *The World in Figures.*

International Monetary Fund, 700 Nineteenth Street, NW, Washington, D.C. 20431 (202) 623-7000; *Government Finance Statistics Yearbook.*

TANZANIA (UNITED REPUBLIC OF) - DAIRY PRODUCTS

Facts on File, 460 Park Avenue South, New York, New York 10016 (800) 443-8323; *The New Book of World Rankings.*

Food and Agricultural Organization of the United Nations (FAO) Via delle Terme di Caracalla, 00100 Rome, Italy (Telephone Number in U.S. (202) 653-2400); *The State of Food and Agriculture.*

Statistical Office of the United Nations, Publishing Service, New York, New York 10017 (800) 253-9646; *Statistical Yearbook*.

TANZANIA (UNITED REPUBLIC OF) - DEATH RATE

G.K. Hall and Company, 70 Lincoln Street, Boston, Massachusetts 02111 (617) 423-3990; *The World in Figures*.

Statistical Office of the United Nations, Publishing Service, New York, New York 10017 (800) 253-9646; *Statistical Yearbook*, and *Survey of Economic and Social Conditions in Africa*.

Times Books, 201 East 50th Street, New York, New York 10022 (212) 751-2600; *The Economist Book of Vital World Statistics*.

TANZANIA (UNITED REPUBLIC OF) - DEFENSE EXPENDITURES

G.K. Hall and Company, 70 Lincoln Street, Boston, Massachusetts 02111 (617) 423-3990; *The World in Figures*.

International Monetary Fund, 700 Nineteenth Street, NW, Washington, D.C. 20431 (202) 623-7000; *Government Finance Statistics Yearbook*.

U.S. Arms Control and Disarmament Agency, 320 Twenty-first Street, NW, Washington, D.C. 20451 (202) 647-8677; *World Military Expenditures and Arms Transfers*.

TANZANIA (UNITED REPUBLIC OF) - DEMOGRAPHY

Facts on File, 460 Park Avenue South, New York, New York 10016 (800) 443-8323; *The New Book of World Rankings*.

G.K. Hall and Company, 70 Lincoln Street, Boston, Massachusetts 02111 (617) 423-3990; *The World in Figures*.

Statistical Office of the United Nations, Publishing Service, New York, New York 10017 (800) 253-9646; *Survey of Economic and Social Conditions in Africa*.

TANZANIA (UNITED REPUBLIC OF) - DEVELOPMENT ASSISTANCE

G.K. Hall and Company, 70 Lincoln Street, Boston, Massachusetts 02111 (617) 423-3990; *The World in Figures*.

Statistical Office of the United Nations, Publishing Service, New York, New York 10017 (800) 253-9646; *Statistical Yearbook*.

TANZANIA (UNITED REPUBLIC OF) - DIAMOND PRODUCTION - See TANZANIA (UNITED REPUBLIC OF) - MINING AND MINERAL PRODUCTS

TANZANIA (UNITED REPUBLIC OF) - DISEASE

G.K. Hall and Company, 70 Lincoln Street, Boston, Massachusetts 02111 (617) 423-3990; *The World in Figures*.

TANZANIA (UNITED REPUBLIC OF) - DIVORCE RATES

Facts on File, 460 Park Avenue South, New York, New York 10016 (800) 443-8323; *The New Book of World Rankings*.

Statistical Office of the United Nations, Publishing Service, New York, New York 10017 (800) 253-9646; *Demographic Yearbook*.

TANZANIA (UNITED REPUBLIC OF) - DOMESTIC PRODUCT

G.K. Hall and Company, 70 Lincoln Street, Boston, Massachusetts 02111 (617) 423-3990; *The World in Figures*.

TANZANIA (UNITED REPUBLIC OF) - ECONOMY

African Development Bank, 01 BP 1387, Abidjan 01, Cote D'Ivoire; *Selected Statistics on Regional Member Countries*.

Euromonitor Publications Limited, 87-88 Turnmill Street, London EC1M 5QU, England; *International Marketing Data and Statistics*.

Facts on File, 460 Park Avenue South, New York, New York 10016 (800) 443-8323; *The New Book of World Rankings*.

G.K. Hall and Company, 70 Lincoln Street, Boston, Massachusetts 02111 (617) 423-3990; *The World in Figures*.

Statistical Office of the United Nations, Publishing Service, New York, New York 10017 (800) 253-9646; *Foreign Trade Statistics for Africa*.

TANZANIA (UNITED REPUBLIC OF) - EDUCATION

African Development Bank, 01 BP 1387, Abidjan 01, Cote D'Ivoire; *Selected Statistics on Regional Member Countries*.

Facts on File, 460 Park Avenue South, New York, New York 10016 (800) 443-8323; *The New Book of World Rankings*.

G.K. Hall and Company, 70 Lincoln Street, Boston, Massachusetts 02111 (617) 423-3990; *The World in Figures*.

International Monetary Fund, 700 Nineteenth Street, NW, Washington, D.C. 20431 (202) 623-7000; *Government Finance Statistics Yearbook*.

Statistical Office of the United Nations, Publishing Service, New York, New York 10017 (800) 253-9646; *Survey of Economic and Social Conditions in Africa*.

Times Books, 201 East 50th Street, New York, New York 10022 (212) 751-2600; *The Economist Book of Vital World Statistics*.

United Nations Economic Commission for Africa, Africa Hall, P.O. Box 3001, Addis Ababa, Ethiopia (Telephone Number in U.S. (800) 253-9646); *African Statistical Yearbook*.

United Nations Educational, Scientific and Cultural Organization (UNESCO), 7 Place de Fontenoy, F-75700 Paris, France (Telephone Number in U.S. (212) 963-5981); *Statistical Yearbook*.

The World Bank, 1818 H Street, NW, Washington, D.C. 20433 (202) 477-1234; *World Tables*.

TANZANIA (UNITED REPUBLIC OF) - EGG PRODUCTION AND CONSUMPTION - See TANZANIA (UNITED REPUBLIC OF) - DAIRY PRODUCTS

TANZANIA (UNITED REPUBLIC OF) - ELECTRICITY

Facts on File, 460 Park Avenue South, New York, New York 10016 (800) 443-8323; *The New Book of World Rankings*.

Statistical Office of the United Nations, Publishing Service, New York, New York 10017 (800) 253-9646; *Statistical Yearbook*, and *Survey of Economic and Social Conditions in Africa*.

Times Books, 201 East 50th Street, New York, New York 10022 (212) 751-2600; *The Economist Book of Vital World Statistics*.

United Nations Economic Commission for Africa, Africa Hall, P.O. Box 3001, Addis Ababa, Ethiopia (Telephone Number in U.S. (800) 253-9646); *African Statistical Yearbook*.

TANZANIA (UNITED REPUBLIC OF) - EMPLOYMENT

Euromonitor Publications Limited, 87-88 Turnmill Street, London EC1M 5QU, England; *International Marketing Data and Statistics*.

Facts on File, 460 Park Avenue South, New York, New York 10016 (800) 443-8323; *The New Book of World Rankings*.

International Labour Office, I.L.O. Publications, CH-1211, Geneva 22, Switzerland; *Yearbook of Labour Statistics*.

Statistical Office of the United Nations, Publishing Service, New York,New York 10017 (800) 253-9646; *Statistical Yearbook*, and *Survey of Economic and Social Conditions in Africa*.

United Nations Economic Commission for Africa, Africa Hall, P.O. Box 3001, Addis Ababa, Ethiopia (Telephone Number in U.S. (800) 253-9646); *African Statistical Yearbook*.

TANZANIA (UNITED REPUBLIC OF) - ENERGY

Facts on File, 460 Park Avenue South, New York, New York 10016 (800) 443-8323; *The New Book of World Rankings*.

Food and Agricultural Organization of the United Nations (FAO) Via delle Terme di Caracalla, 00100 Rome, Italy (Telephone Number in U.S. (202) 653-2400); *The State of Food and Agriculture*.

G.K. Hall and Company, 70 Lincoln Street, Boston, Massachusetts 02111 (617) 423-3990; *The World in Figures*.

Statistical Office of the United Nations, Publishing Service, New York, New York 10017 (800) 253-9646; *Energy Statistics Yearbook*, and *Statistical Yearbook*.

Times Books, 201 East 50th Street, New York, New York 10022 (212) 751-2600; *The Economist Book of Vital World Statistics*.

United Nations Economic Commission for Africa, Africa Hall, P.O. Box 3001, Addis Ababa, Ethiopia (Telephone Number in U.S. (800) 253-9646); *African Statistical Yearbook*.

TANZANIA (UNITED REPUBLIC OF) - EXCHANGE RATES

African Development Bank, 01 BP 1387, Abidjan 01, Cote D'Ivoire; *Selected Statistics on Regional Member Countries*.

Euromonitor Publications Limited, 87-88 Turnmill Street, London EC1M 5QU, England; *International Marketing Data and Statistics*.

International Civil Aviation Organization, 1000 Sherbrooke Street, West, Suite 400, Montreal, Quebec, Canada H3A 2R2 (514) 285-8219; *Civil Aviation Statistics of the World*.

International Monetary Fund, 700 Nineteenth Street, NW, Washington, D.C. 20431 (202) 623-7000; *International Financial Statistics*.

Statistical Office of the United Nations, Publishing Service, New York, New York 10017 (800) 253-9646; *Foreign Trade Statistics for Africa*, and *Statistical Yearbook*.

TANZANIA (UNITED REPUBLIC OF) - EXCISE TAXES - See - TANZANIA (UNITED REPUBLIC OF) - TAXATION

TANZANIA (UNITED REPUBLIC OF) - EXPORTS

Euromonitor Publications Limited, 87-88 Turnmill Street, London EC1M 5QU, England; *International Marketing Data and Statistics*.

Food and Agricultural Organization of the United Nations (FAO) Via delle Terme di Caracalla, 00100 Rome, Italy (Telephone Number in U.S. (202) 653-2400); *The State of Food and Agriculture*.

G.K. Hall and Company, 70 Lincoln Street, Boston, Massachusetts 02111 (617) 423-3990; *The World in Figures*.

International Monetary Fund, 700 Nineteenth Street, NW, Washington, D.C. 20431 (202) 623-7000; *Direction of Trade Statistics*, *Government Finance Statistics Yearbook*, and *International Financial Statistics*.

Statistical Office of the United Nations, Publishing Service, New York, New York 10017 (800) 253-9646; *Foreign Trade Statistics for Africa*, *Survey of Economic and Social Conditions in Africa*, and *Trade in Manufactures of Developing Countries*.

Times Books, 201 East 50th Street, New York, New York 10022 (212) 751-2600; *The Economist Book of Vital World Statistics*.

United Nations Economic Commission for Africa, Africa Hall, P.O. Box 3001, Addis Ababa, Ethiopia (Telephone Number in U.S. (800) 253-9646); *African Statistical Yearbook*.

The World Bank, 1818 H Street, NW, Washington, D.C. 20433 (202) 477-1234; *World Tables*.

TANZANIA (UNITED REPUBLIC OF) - EXTERNAL INDEBTEDNESS

African Development Bank, 01 BP 1387, Abidjan 01, Cote D'Ivoire; *Selected Statistics on Regional Member Countries*.

Statistical Office of the United Nations, Publishing Service, New York, New York 10017 (800) 253-9646; *Survey of Economic and Social Conditions in Africa*.

The World Bank, 1818 H Street, NW, Washington, D.C. 20433 (202) 477-1234; *World Tables*.

TANZANIA (UNITED REPUBLIC OF) - EXTERNAL TRADE

Food and Agricultural Organization of the United Nations (FAO) Via delle Terme di Caracalla, 00100 Rome, Italy (Telephone Number in U.S. (202) 653-2400); *The State of Food and Agriculture*, and *Trade Yearbook*.

G.K. Hall and Company, 70 Lincoln Street, Boston, Massachusetts 02111 (617) 423-3990; *The World in Figures*.

Statistical Office of the United Nations, Publishing Service, New York, New York 10017 (800) 253-9646; *Statistical Yearbook*, and *Survey of Economic and Social Conditions in Africa*.

TANZANIA (UNITED REPUBLIC OF) - FABRIC PRODUCTION - See TANZANIA (UNITED REPUBLIC OF) - TEXTILE INDUSTRY

TANZANIA (UNITED REPUBLIC OF) - FARM CROPS - See TANZANIA (UNITED REPUBLIC OF) - CROPS

TANZANIA (UNITED REPUBLIC OF) - FEMALE WORKING POPULATION - See TANZANIA (UNITED REPUBLIC OF) - EMPLOYMENT

TANZANIA (UNITED REPUBLIC OF) - FERTILITY RATES

Facts on File, 460 Park Avenue South, New York, New York 10016 (800) 443-8323; *The New Book of World Rankings*.

Statistical Office of the United Nations, Publishing Service, New York, New York 10017 (800) 253-9646; *Survey of Economic and Social Conditions in Africa*.

Times Books, 201 East 50th Street, New York, New York 10022 (212) 751-2600; *The Economist Book of Vital World Statistics*.

The World Bank, 1818 H Street, NW, Washington, D.C. 20433 (202) 477-1234; *World Tables*.

TANZANIA (UNITED REPUBLIC OF) - FERTILIZER PRODUCTION AND CONSUMPTION

Food and Agricultural Organization of the United Nations (FAO), Via delle Terme di Caracalla, 00100, Rome, Italy (Telephone Number in U.S. (202) 653-2400); *Fertilizer Yearbook*, and *The State of Food and Agriculture*.

Statistical Office of the United Nations, Publishing Service, New York, New York 10017 (800) 253-9646; *Statistical Yearbook*.

TANZANIA (UNITED REPUBLIC OF) - FETAL MORTALITY

Statistical Office of the United Nations, Publishing Service, New York, New York 10017 (800) 253-9646; *Demographic Yearbook*.

TANZANIA (UNITED REPUBLIC OF) - FINANCE

African Development Bank, 01 BP 1387, Abidjan 01, Cote D'Ivoire; *Selected Statistics on Regional Member Countries*.

Facts on File, 460 Park Avenue South, New York, New York 10016 (800) 443-8323; *The New Book of World Rankings*.

G.K. Hall and Company, 70 Lincoln Street, Boston, Massachusetts 02111 (617) 423-3990; *The World in Figures*.

International Monetary Fund, 700 Nineteenth Street, NW, Washington, D.C. 20431 (202) 623-7000; *Government Finance Statistics Yearbook*.

United Nations Economic Commission for Africa, Africa Hall, P.O. Box 3001, Addis Ababa, Ethiopia (Telephone Number in U.S. (800) 253-9646); *African Statistical Yearbook*.

TANZANIA (UNITED REPUBLIC OF) - FISHERIES

Facts on File, 460 Park Avenue South, New York, New York 10016 (800) 443-8323; *The New Book of World Rankings*.

Food and Agricultural Organization of the United Nations (FAO) Via delle Terme di Caracalla, 00100 Rome, Italy (Telephone Number in U.S. (202) 653-2400); *The State of Food and Agriculture*, and *Yearbook of Fishery Statistics*.

Statistical Office of the United Nations, Publishing Service, New York, New York 10017 (800) 253-9646; *Statistical Yearbook*, and *Survey of Economic and Social Conditions in Africa*.

United Nations Economic Commission for Africa, Africa Hall, P.O. Box 3001, Addis Ababa, Ethiopia (Telephone Number in U.S. (800) 253-9646); *African Statistical Yearbook*.

TANZANIA (UNITED REPUBLIC OF) - FLOUR PRODUCTION

Statistical Office of the United Nations, Publishing Service, New York, New York 10017 (800) 253-9646; *Statistical Yearbook*.

TANZANIA (UNITED REPUBLIC OF) - FOOD

African Development Bank, 01 BP 1387, Abidjan 01, Cote D'Ivoire; *Selected Statistics on Regional Member Countries*.

Food and Agricultural Organization of the United Nations (FAO) Via delle Terme di Caracalla, 00100 Rome, Italy (Telephone Number in U.S. (202) 653-2400); *Production Yearbook*, and *The State of Food and Agriculture*.

G.K. Hall and Company, 70 Lincoln Street, Boston, Massachusetts 02111 (617) 423-3990; *The World in Figures*.

TANZANIA (UNITED REPUBLIC OF) - FOREIGN AID

G.K. Hall and Company, 70 Lincoln Street, Boston, Massachusetts 02111 (617) 423-3990; *The World in Figures*.

TANZANIA (UNITED REPUBLIC OF) - FOREIGN TRADE

Euromonitor Publications Limited, 87-88 Turnmill Street, London EC1M 5QU, England; *International Marketing Data and Statistics*.

Facts on File, 460 Park Avenue South, New York, New York 10016 (800) 443-8323; *The New Book of World Rankings*.

Food and Agricultural Organization of the United Nations (FAO), Via delle Terme di Caracalla, 00100 Rome, Italy (Telephone Number in U.S. (202) 653-2400); *The State of Food and Agriculture*.

G.K. Hall and Company, 70 Lincoln Street, Boston, Massachusetts 02111 (617) 423-3990; *The World in Figures*.

International Monetary Fund, 700 Nineteenth Street, NW, Washington, D.C. 20431 (202) 623-7000; *International Financial Statistics*.

Statistical Office of the United Nations, Publishing Service, New York, New York 10017 (800) 253-9646; *Foreign Trade Statistics for Africa*, *International Trade Statistics Yearbook*, *Statistical Yearbook*, and *Trade in Manufactures of Developing Countries*.

United Nations Economic Commission for Africa, Africa Hall, P.O. Box 3001, Addis Ababa, Ethiopia (Telephone Number in U.S. (800) 253-9646); *African Statistical Yearbook*.

The World Bank, 1818 H Street, NW, Washington, D.C. 20433 (202) 477-1234; *World Tables*.

TANZANIA (UNITED REPUBLIC OF) - FORESTRY AND FOREST PRODUCTS

Facts on File, 460 Park Avenue South, New York, New York 10016 (800) 443-8323; *The New Book of World Rankings*.

Food and Agricultural Organization of the United Nations (FAO) Via delle Terme di Caracalla, 00100 Rome, Italy (Telephone Number in U.S. (202) 653-2400); *The State of Food and Agriculture*, and *Yearbook of Forest Products*.

G.K. Hall and Company, 70 Lincoln Street, Boston, Massachusetts 02111 (617) 423-3990; *The World in Figures*.

Statistical Office of the United Nations, Publishing Service, New York, New York 10017 (800) 253-9646; *Statistical Yearbook*.

United Nations Economic Commission for Africa, Africa Hall, P.O. Box 3001, Addis Ababa, Ethiopia (Telephone Number in U.S. (800) 253-9646); *African Statistical Yearbook*.

United Nations Educational, Scientific and Cultural Organization (UNESCO), 7 Place de Fontenoy, F-75700 Paris, France (Telephone Number in U.S. (212) 963-5981); *Statistical Yearbook*.

TANZANIA (UNITED REPUBLIC OF) - GAS PRODUCTION - See TANZANIA (UNITED REPUBLIC OF) - MINING AND MINERAL PRODUCTS

TANZANIA (UNITED REPUBLIC OF) - GENERAL INDUSTRIAL STATISTICS

Statistical Office of the United Nations, Publishing Service, New York, New York 10017 (800) 253-9646; *Industrial Statistics Yearbook*.

TANZANIA (UNITED REPUBLIC OF) - GENERAL MORTALITY

Statistical Office of the United Nations, Publishing Service, New York, New York 10017 (800) 253-9646; *Demographic Yearbook*.

TANZANIA (UNITED REPUBLIC OF) - GEOGRAPHIC DATA

Facts on File, 460 Park Avenue South, New York, New York 10016 (800) 443-8323; *The New Book of World Rankings*.

TANZANIA (UNITED REPUBLIC OF) - GOATS - See TANZANIA (UNITED REPUBLIC OF) - LIVESTOCK AND POULTRY

TANZANIA (UNITED REPUBLIC OF) - GOLD HOLDINGS

Statistical Office of the United Nations, Publishing Service, New York, New York 10017 (800) 253-9646; *Statistical Yearbook*.

The World Bank, 1818 H Street, NW, Washington, D.C. 20433 (202) 477-1234; *World Tables*.

TANZANIA (UNITED REPUBLIC OF) - GOLD PRODUCTION AND CONSUMPTION - See TANZANIA (UNITED REPUBLIC OF) - MINING AND MINERAL PRODUCTS

TANZANIA (UNITED REPUBLIC OF) - GOVERNMENT

G.K. Hall and Company, 70 Lincoln Street, Boston, Massachusetts 02111 (617) 423-3990; *The World in Figures*.

TANZANIA (UNITED REPUBLIC OF) - GOVERNMENT EXPENDITURE

Times Books, 201 East 50th Street, New York, New York 10022 (212) 751-2600; *The Economist Book of Vital World Statistics*.

The World Bank, 1818 H Street, NW, Washington, D.C. 20433 (202) 477-1234; *World Tables*.

TANZANIA (UNITED REPUBLIC OF) - GOVERNMENT FINANCES

Statistical Office of the United Nations, Publishing Service, New York, New York 10017 (800) 253-9646; *Statistical Yearbook*.

TANZANIA (UNITED REPUBLIC OF) - GOVERNMENT REVENUE

International Monetary Fund, 700 Nineteenth Street, NW, Washington, D.C. 20431 (202) 623-7000; *Government Finance Statistics Yearbook*.

Statistical Office of the United Nations, Publishing Service, New York, New York 10017 (800) 253-9646; *Survey of Economic and Social Conditions in Africa*.

Times Books, 201 East 50th Street, New York, New York 10022 (212) 751-2600; *The Economist Book of Vital World Statistics*.

The World Bank, 1818 H Street, NW, Washington, D.C. 20433 (202) 477-1234; *World Tables*.

TANZANIA (UNITED REPUBLIC OF) - GRAIN PRODUCTION - See TANZANIA (UNITED REPUBLIC OF) - CROPS

TANZANIA (UNITED REPUBLIC OF) - GRANTS

International Monetary Fund, 700 Nineteenth Street, NW, Washington, D.C. 20431 (202) 623-7000; *Government Finance Statistics Yearbook*.

TANZANIA (UNITED REPUBLIC OF) - GROSS DOMESTIC PRODUCT

African Development Bank, 01 BP 1387, Abidjan 01, Cote D'Ivoire; *Selected Statistics on Regional Member Countries*.

The Economist Intelligence Unit, 111 West 57th Street, New York, New York 10019 (800) 938-4685; *The World Market Atlas*.

Euromonitor Publications Limited, 87-88 Turnmill Street, London EC1M 5QU, England; *International Marketing Data and Statistics*.

Facts on File, 460 Park Avenue South, New York, New York 10016 (800) 443-8323; *The New Book of World Rankings*.

G.K. Hall and Company, 70 Lincoln Street, Boston, Massachusetts 02111 (617) 423-3990; *The World in Figures*.

Statistical Office of the United Nations, Publishing Service, New York, New York 10017 (800) 253-9646; *Statistical Yearbook*, and *Survey of Economic and Social Conditions in Africa*.

Times Books, 201 East 50th Street, New York, New York 10022 (212) 751-2600; *The Economist Book of Vital World Statistics*.

United Nations Economic Commission for Africa, Africa Hall, P.O. Box 3001, Addis Ababa, Ethiopia (Telephone Number in U.S. (800) 253-9646); *African Statistical Yearbook*.

The World Bank, 1818 H Street, NW, Washington, D.C. 20433 (202) 477-1234; *World Tables*.

TANZANIA (UNITED REPUBLIC OF) - GROSS NATIONAL PRODUCT

Euromonitor Publications Limited, 87-88 Turnmill Street, London EC1M 5QU, England; *International Marketing Data and Statistics*.

U.S. Arms Control and Disarmament Agency, 320 Twenty-first Street, NW, Washington, D.C. 20451 (202) 647-8677; *World Military Expenditures and Arms Transfers*.

The World Bank, 1818 H Street, NW, Washington, D.C. 20433 (202) 477-1234; *World Tables*.

TANZANIA (UNITED REPUBLIC OF) - GROUNDNUTS
PRODUCTION - See TANZANIA (UNITED REPUBLIC OF) - CROPS

TANZANIA (UNITED REPUBLIC OF) - HEALTH

African Development Bank, 01 BP 1387, Abidjan 01, Cote D'Ivoire; *Selected Statistics on Regional Member Countries.*

Facts on File, 460 Park Avenue South, New York, New York 10016 (800) 443-8323; *The New Book of World Rankings.*

G.K. Hall and Company, 70 Lincoln Street, Boston, Massachusetts 02111 (617) 423-3990; *The World in Figures.*

Statistical Office of the United Nations, Publishing Service, New York, New York 10017 (800) 253-9646; *Statistical Yearbook.*

Times Books, 201 East 50th Street, New York, New York 10022 (212) 751-2600; *The Economist Book of Vital World Statistics.*

United Nations Economic Commission for Africa, Africa Hall, P.O. Box 3001, Addis Ababa, Ethiopia (Telephone Number in U.S. (800) 253-9646); *African Statistical Yearbook.*

TANZANIA (UNITED REPUBLIC OF) - HEALTH EXPENDITURES

International Monetary Fund, 700 Nineteenth Street, NW, Washington, D.C. 20431 (202) 623-7000; *Government Finance Statistics Yearbook.*

TANZANIA (UNITED REPUBLIC OF) - HIGHWAYS

G.K. Hall and Company, 70 Lincoln Street, Boston, Massachusetts 02111 (617) 423-3990; *The World in Figures.*

International Road Federation, 525 School Street, SW, Washington, D.C. 20024 (202) 554-2106; *World Road Statistics.*

Statistical Office of the United Nations, Publishing Service, New York, New York 10017 (800) 253-9646; *Survey of Economic and Social Conditions in Africa.*

United Nations Economic Commission for Africa, Africa Hall, P.O. Box 3001, Addis Ababa, Ethiopia (Telephone Number in U.S. (800) 253-9646); *African Statistical Yearbook.*

TANZANIA (UNITED REPUBLIC OF) - HOURS OF WORK - See TANZANIA (UNITED REPUBLIC OF) - EMPLOYMENT

TANZANIA (UNITED REPUBLIC OF) - HOUSING AND HOUSING UNITS

Facts on File, 460 Park Avenue South, New York, New York 10016 (800) 443-8323; *The New Book of World Rankings.*

TANZANIA (UNITED REPUBLIC OF) - HOUSING EXPENDITURES

International Monetary Fund, 700 Nineteenth Street, NW, Washington, D.C. 20431 (202) 623-7000; *Government Finance Statistics Yearbook.*

TANZANIA (UNITED REPUBLIC OF) - ILLITERATE
POPULATION

The Economist Intelligence Unit, 111 West 57th Street, New York, New York 10019 (800) 938-4685; *The World Market Atlas.*

G.K. Hall and Company, 70 Lincoln Street, Boston, Massachusetts 02111 (617) 423-3990; *The World in Figures.*

United Nations Educational, Scientific and Cultural Organization (UNESCO), 7 Place de Fontenoy, F-75700 Paris, France (Telephone Number in U.S. (212) 963-5981); *Statistical Yearbook.*

TANZANIA (UNITED REPUBLIC OF) - IMPORTS

African Development Bank, 01 BP 1387, Abidjan 01, Cote D'Ivoire; *Selected Statistics on Regional Member Countries.*

Euromonitor Publications Limited, 87-88 Turnmill Street, London EC1M 5QU, England; *International Marketing Data and Statistics.*

Food and Agricultural Organization of the United Nations (FAO) Via delle Terme di Caracalla, 00100 Rome, Italy (Telephone Number in U.S. (202) 653-2400); *The State of Food and Agriculture.*

G.K. Hall and Company, 70 Lincoln Street, Boston, Massachusetts 02111 (617) 423-3990; *The World in Figures.*

International Monetary Fund, 700 Nineteenth Street, NW, Washington, D.C. 20431 (202) 623-7000; *Direction of Trade Statistics, Government Finance Statistics Yearbook,* and *International Financial Statistics.*

Statistical Office of the United Nations, Publishing Service, New York, New York 10017 (800) 253-9646; *Foreign Trade Statistics for Africa,* and *Survey of Economic and Social Conditions in Africa.*

Times Books, 201 East 50th Street, New York, New York 10022 (212) 751-2600; *The Economist Book of Vital World Statistics.*

United Nations Economic Commission for Africa, Africa Hall, P.O. Box 3001, Addis Ababa, Ethiopia (Telephone Number in U.S. (800) 253-9646); *African Statistical Yearbook.*

The World Bank, 1818 H Street, NW, Washington, D.C. 20433 (202) 477-1234; *World Tables.*

TANZANIA (UNITED REPUBLIC OF) - INCOME TAXES - See TANZANIA (UNITED REPUBLIC OF) - TAXATION

TANZANIA (UNITED REPUBLIC OF) - INDUSTRY

Euromonitor Publications Limited, 87-88 Turnmill Street, London EC1M 5QU, England; *International Marketing Data and Statistics.*

Facts on File, 460 Park Avenue South, New York, New York 10016 (800) 443-8323; *The New Book of World Rankings.*

G.K. Hall and Company, 70 Lincoln Street, Boston, Massachusetts 02111 (617) 423-3990; *The World in Figures.*

International Labour Office, I.L.O. Publications, CH-1211, Geneva 22, Switzerland; *Yearbook of Labour Statistics.*

Times Books, 201 East 50th Street, New York, New York 10022 (212) 751-2600; *The Economist Book of Vital World Statistics.*

United Nations Economic Commission for Africa, Africa Hall, P.O. Box 3001, Addis Ababa, Ethiopia (Telephone Number in U.S. (800) 253-9646); *African Statistical Yearbook.*

The World Bank, 1818 H Street, NW, Washington, D.C. 20433 (202) 477-1234; *World Tables.*

TANZANIA (UNITED REPUBLIC OF) - INFANT AND MATERNAL MORTALITY

Statistical Office of the United Nations, Publishing Service, New York, New York 10017 (800) 253-9646; *Demographic Yearbook, Statistical Yearbook*, and *Survey of Economic and Social Conditions in Africa*.

Times Books, 201 East 50th Street, New York, New York 10022 (212) 751-2600; *The Economist Book of Vital World Statistics*.

The World Bank, 1818 H Street, NW, Washington, D.C. 20433 (202) 477-1234; *World Tables*.

TANZANIA (UNITED REPUBLIC OF) - INTERNATIONAL LIQUIDITY

International Monetary Fund, 700 Nineteenth Street, NW, Washington, D.C. 20431 (202) 623-7000; *International Financial Statistics*.

TANZANIA (UNITED REPUBLIC OF) - INTERNATIONAL RESERVES EXCLUDING GOLD

African Development Bank, 01 BP 1387, Abidjan 01, Cote D'Ivoire; *Selected Statistics on Regional Member Countries*.

Statistical Office of the United Nations, Publishing Service, New York, New York 10017 (800) 253-9646; *Statistical Yearbook*.

The World Bank, 1818 H Street, NW, Washington, D.C. 20433 (202) 477-1234; *World Tables*.

TANZANIA (UNITED REPUBLIC OF) - IRON ORE PRODUCTION AND CONSUMPTION - See TANZANIA (UNITED REPUBLIC OF) - MINING AND MINERAL PRODUCTS

TANZANIA (UNITED REPUBLIC OF) - IRRIGATION

Euromonitor Publications Limited, 87-88 Turnmill Street, London EC1M 5QU, England; *International Marketing Data and Statistics*.

TANZANIA (UNITED REPUBLIC OF) - LABOR FORCE

African Development Bank, 01 BP 1387, Abidjan 01, Cote D'Ivoire; *Selected Statistics on Regional Member Countries*.

Euromonitor Publications Limited, 87 88 Turnmill Street, London EC1M 5QU, England; *International Marketing Data and Statistics*.

Facts on File, 460 Park Avenue South, New York, New York 10016 (800) 443-8323; *The New Book of World Rankings*.

Food and Agricultural Organization of the United Nations (FAO) Via delle Terme di Caracalla, 00100 Rome, Italy (Telephone Number in U.S. (202) 653-2400); *The State of Food and Agriculture*.

G.K. Hall and Company, 70 Lincoln Street, Boston, Massachusetts 02111 (617) 423-3990; *The World in Figures*.

The World Bank, 1818 H Street, NW, Washington, D.C. 20433 (202) 477-1234; *World Tables*.

TANZANIA (UNITED REPUBLIC OF) - LABOR PRODUCTIVITY

International Labour Office, I.L.O. Publications, CH-1211, Geneva 22, Switzerland; *Yearbook of Labour Statistics*.

TANZANIA (UNITED REPUBLIC OF) - LAND USE

Euromonitor Publications Limited, 87-88 Turnmill Street, London EC1M 5QU, England; *International Marketing Data and Statistics*.

Food and Agricultural Organization of the United Nations (FAO), Via delle Terme di Caracalla, 00100 Rome, Italy (Telephone Number in U.S. (202) 653-2400); *Production Yearbook*.

G.K. Hall and Company, 70 Lincoln Street, Boston, Massachusetts 02111 (617) 423-3990; *The World in Figures*.

TANZANIA (UNITED REPUBLIC OF) - LIBRARIES

Facts on File, 460 Park Avenue South, New York, New York 10016 (800) 443-8323; *The New Book of World Rankings*.

United Nations Educational, Scientific and Cultural Organization (UNESCO), 7 Place de Fontenoy, F-75700 Paris, France (Telephone Number in U.S. (212) 963-5981); *Statistical Yearbook*.

TANZANIA (UNITED REPUBLIC OF) - LIFE EXPECTANCY

African Development Bank, 01 BP 1387, Abidjan 01, Cote D'Ivoire; *Selected Statistics on Regional Member Countries*.

TANZANIA (UNITED REPUBLIC OF) - LITERACY RATE

Statistical Office of the United Nations, Publishing Service, New York, New York 10017 (800) 253-9646; *Survey of Economic and Social Conditions in Africa*.

TANZANIA (UNITED REPUBLIC OF) - LIVESTOCK AND POULTRY

Euromonitor Publications Limited, 87-88 Turnmill Street, London EC1M 5QU, England; *International Marketing Data and Statistics*.

Facts on File, 460 Park Avenue South, New York, New York 10016 (800) 443-8323; *The New Book of World Rankings*.

Food and Agricultural Organization of the United Nations (FAO), Via delle Terme di Caracalla, 00100 Rome, Italy (Telephone Number in U.S. (202) 653-2400); *Production Yearbook*, and *The State of Food and Agriculture*.

G.K. Hall and Company, 70 Lincoln Street, Boston, Massachusetts 02111 (617) 423-3990; *The World in Figures*.

Statistical Office of the United Nations, Publishing Service, New York, New York 10017 (800) 253-9646; *Statistical Yearbook*, and *Survey of Economic and Social Conditions in Africa*.

United Nations Economic Commission for Africa, Africa Hall, P.O. Box 3001, Addis Ababa, Ethiopia (Telephone Number in U.S. (800) 253-9646); *African Statistical Yearbook*.

TANZANIA (UNITED REPUBLIC OF) - LIVING LEVELS

G.K. Hall and Company, 70 Lincoln Street, Boston, Massachusetts 02111 (617) 423-3990; *The World in Figures*.

Times Books, 201 East 50th Street, New York, New York 10022 (212) 751-2600; *The Economist Book of Vital World Statistics*.

TANZANIA (UNITED REPUBLIC OF) - MAIL - NUMBER OF PIECES SENT OR RECEIVED

Statistical Office of the United Nations, Publishing Service, New York, New York 10017 (800) 253-9646; *Statistical Yearbook*.

TANZANIA (UNITED REPUBLIC OF) - MANUFACTURING

Facts on File, 460 Park Avenue South, New York, New York 10016 (800) 443-8323; *The New Book of World Rankings*.

G.K. Hall and Company, 70 Lincoln Street, Boston, Massachusetts 02111 (617) 423-3990; *The World in Figures*.

Statistical Office of the United Nations, Publishing Service, New York, New York 10017 (800) 253-9646; *Statistical Yearbook*, and *Survey of Economic and Social Conditions in Africa*.

Times Books, 201 East 50th Street, New York, New York 10022 (212) 751-2600; *The Economist Book of Vital World Statistics*.

United Nations Economic Commission for Africa, Africa Hall, P.O. Box 3001, Addis Ababa, Ethiopia (Telephone Number in U.S. (800) 253-9646); *African Statistical Yearbook*.

The World Bank, 1818 H Street, NW, Washington, D.C. 20433 (202) 477-1234; *World Tables*.

TANZANIA (UNITED REPUBLIC OF) - MARRIAGE RATES

Facts on File, 460 Park Avenue South, New York, New York 10016 (800) 443-8323; *The New Book of World Rankings*.

Statistical Office of the United Nations, Publishing Service, New York, New York 10017 (800) 253-9646; *Demographic Yearbook*.

TANZANIA (UNITED REPUBLIC OF) - MEAT PRODUCTION - See TANZANIA (UNITED REPUBLIC OF) - LIVESTOCK AND POULTRY

TANZANIA (UNITED REPUBLIC OF) - MERCHANT SHIPPING

G.K. Hall and Company, 70 Lincoln Street, Boston, Massachusetts 02111 (617) 423-3990; *The World in Figures*.

Statistical Office of the United Nations, Publishing Service, New York, New York 10017 (800) 253-9646; *Statistical Yearbook*.

Times Books, 201 East 50th Street, New York, New York 10022 (212) 751-2600; *The Economist Book of Vital World Statistics*.

United Nations Economic Commission for Africa, Africa Hall, P.O. Box 3001, Addis Ababa, Ethiopia (Telephone Number in U.S. (800) 253-9646); *African Statistical Yearbook*.

U.S. Department of Commerce, Maritime Administration, 400 Seventh Street, SW, Washington, D.C. 20590 (202) 366-5807; *A Statistical Analysis of the World's Merchant Fleets*.

TANZANIA (UNITED REPUBLIC OF) - MILITARY

G.K. Hall and Company, 70 Lincoln Street, Boston, Massachusetts 02111 (617) 423-3990; *The World in Figures*.

The International Institute for Strategic Studies, 23 Tavistock Street, London WC2E 7NQ, England; *The Military Balance*.

U.S. Arms Control and Disarmament Agency, 320 Twenty-first Street, NW, Washington, D.C. 20451 (202) 647-8677; *World Military Expenditures and Arms Transfers*.

TANZANIA (UNITED REPUBLIC OF) - MILK PRODUCTION - See TANZANIA (UNITED REPUBLIC OF) - DAIRY PRODUCTS

TANZANIA (UNITED REPUBLIC OF) - MINING AND MINERAL PRODUCTS

Facts on File, 460 Park Avenue South, New York, New York 10016 (800) 443-8323; *The New Book of World Rankings*.

G.K. Hall and Company, 70 Lincoln Street, Boston, Massachusetts 02111 (617) 423-3990; *The World in Figures*.

Statistical Office of the United Nations, Publishing Service, New York, New York 10017 (800) 253-9646; *Statistical Yearbook*.

United Nations Economic Commission for Africa, Africa Hall, P.O. Box 3001, Addis Ababa, Ethiopia (Telephone Number in U.S. (800) 253-9646); *African Statistical Yearbook*.

TANZANIA (UNITED REPUBLIC OF) - MONEY EXCHANGE RATE

Euromonitor Publications Limited, 87-88 Turnmill Street, London EC1M 5QU, England; *International Marketing Data and Statistics*.

International Monetary Fund, 700 Nineteenth Street, NW, Washington, D.C. 20431 (202) 623-7000; *International Financial Statistics*.

Statistical Office of the United Nations, Publishing Service, New York, New York 10017 (800) 253-9646; *Statistical Yearbook*.

TANZANIA (UNITED REPUBLIC OF) - MONEY RESERVES

Euromonitor Publications Limited, 87-88 Turnmill Street, London EC1M 5QU, England; *International Marketing Data and Statistics*.

TANZANIA (UNITED REPUBLIC OF) - MONEY SUPPLY

African Development Bank, 01 BP 1387, Abidjan 01, Cote D'Ivoire; *Selected Statistics on Regional Member Countries*.

Euromonitor Publications Limited, 87-88 Turnmill Street, London EC1M 5QU, England; *International Marketing Data and Statistics*.

G.K. Hall and Company, 70 Lincoln Street, Boston, Massachusetts 02111 (617) 423-3990; *The World in Figures*.

International Monetary Fund, 700 Nineteenth Street, NW, Washington, D.C. 20431 (202) 623-7000; *International Financial Statistics*.

Statistical Office of the United Nations, Publishing Service, New York, New York 10017 (800) 253-9646; *Statistical Yearbook*.

The World Bank, 1818 H Street, NW, Washington, D.C. 20433 (202) 477-1234; *World Tables*.

TANZANIA (UNITED REPUBLIC OF) - MONUMENTS AND HISTORICAL SITES

United Nations Educational, Scientific and Cultural Organization (UNESCO), 7 Place de Fontenoy, F-75700 Paris, France (Telephone Number in U.S. (212) 963-5981); *Statistical Yearbook*.

TANZANIA (UNITED REPUBLIC OF) - MOTION PICTURES

Statistical Office of the United Nations, Publishing Service, New York, New York 10017 (800) 253-9646; *Statistical Yearbook*.

TANZANIA (UNITED REPUBLIC OF) - MOTOR VEHICLE
PRODUCTION

Statistical Office of the United Nations, Publishing Service, New
York, New York 10017 (800) 253-9646; *Statistical Yearbook*.

TANZANIA (UNITED REPUBLIC OF) - MOTOR VEHICLE
TAXES - See TANZANIA (UNITED REPUBLIC OF) - TAXATION

TANZANIA (UNITED REPUBLIC OF) - MOTOR VEHICLES
IN USE

G.K. Hall and Company, 70 Lincoln Street, Boston, Massachusetts
02111 (617) 423-3990; *The World in Figures*.

International Road Federation, 525 School Street, SW, Washington,
D.C. 20024 (202) 554-2106; *World Road Statistics*.

Statistical Office of the United Nations, Publishing Service, New
York, New York 10017 (800) 253-9646; *Statistical Yearbook*, and
Survey of Economic and Social Conditions in Africa.

Times Books, 201 East 50th Street, New York, New York 10022
(212) 751-2600; *The Economist Book of Vital World Statistics*.

TANZANIA (UNITED REPUBLIC OF) - MUSEUMS

Facts on File, 460 Park Avenue South, New York, New York 10016
(800) 443-8323; *The New Book of World Rankings*.

United Nations Educational, Scientific and Cultural Organization
(UNESCO), 7 Place de Fontenoy, F-75700 Paris, France (Telephone
Number in U.S. (212) 903-5801); *Statistical Yearbook*.

TANZANIA (UNITED REPUBLIC OF) - NATALITY - See TANZANIA
(UNITED REPUBLIC OF) - BIRTH RATE

TANZANIA (UNITED REPUBLIC OF) - NATIONAL ACCOUNTS

Statistical Office of the United Nations, Publishing Service, New
York, New York 10017 (800) 253-9646; *National Accounts
Statistics, Statistical Yearbook*, and *Survey of Economic and Social
Conditions in Africa*.

United Nations Economic Commission for Africa, Africa Hall, P.O.
Box 3001, Addis Ababa, Ethiopia (Telephone Number in U.S. (800)
253-9646); *African Statistical Yearbook*.

TANZANIA (UNITED REPUBLIC OF) - NATIONAL INCOME

Facts on File, 460 Park Avenue South, New York, New York 10016
(800) 443-8323; *The New Book of World Rankings*.

G.K. Hall and Company, 70 Lincoln Street, Boston, Massachusetts
02111 (617) 423-3990; *The World in Figures*.

Statistical Office of the United Nations, Publishing Service, New
York, New York 10017 (800) 253-9646; *Statistical Yearbook*.

TANZANIA (UNITED REPUBLIC OF) - NATIONAL PRODUCT

Facts on File, 460 Park Avenue South, New York, New York 10016
(800) 443-8323; *The New Book of World Rankings*.

Statistical Office of the United Nations, Publishing Service, New
York, New York 10017 (800) 253-9646; *Statistical Yearbook*.

TANZANIA (UNITED REPUBLIC OF) - NATURAL GAS PRODUCTION -
See TANZANIA (UNITED REPUBLIC OF) - MINING AND MINERAL
PRODUCTS

TANZANIA (UNITED REPUBLIC OF) - NEWSPAPER
PRODUCTION - See TANZANIA (UNITED REPUBLIC OF) - FORESTRY
AND FOREST PRODUCTS

TANZANIA (UNITED REPUBLIC OF) - NEWSPRINT - See TANZANIA
(UNITED REPUBLIC OF) - FORESTRY AND FOREST PRODUCTS

TANZANIA (UNITED REPUBLIC OF) - OCCUPATIONS - See
TANZANIA (UNITED REPUBLIC OF) - LABOR FORCE

TANZANIA (UNITED REPUBLIC OF) - PALM KERNELS
AND PALM OIL - See TANZANIA (UNITED REPUBLIC OF) - CROPS

TANZANIA (UNITED REPUBLIC OF) - PAPER - See TANZANIA
(UNITED REPUBLIC OF) - FORESTRY AND FOREST PRODUCTS

TANZANIA (UNITED REPUBLIC OF) - PATENTS

Statistical Office of the United Nations, Publishing Service, New
York, New York 10017 (800) 253-9646; *Statistical Yearbook*.

TANZANIA (UNITED REPUBLIC OF) - PEANUT PRODUCTION - See
TANZANIA (UNITED REPUBLIC OF) - CROPS

TANZANIA (UNITED REPUBLIC OF) - PESTICIDE USE

Food and Agricultural Organization of the United Nations (FAO) Via
delle Terme di Caracalla, 00100 Rome, Italy (Telephone Number in
U.S. (202) 653-2400); *The State of Food and Agriculture*.

TANZANIA (UNITED REPUBLIC OF) - PETROLEUM INDUSTRY

Facts on File, 460 Park Avenue South, New York, New York 10016
(800) 443-8323; *The New Book of World Rankings*.

Food and Agricultural Organization of the United Nations (FAO) Via
delle Terme di Caracalla, 00100 Rome, Italy (Telephone Number in
U.S. (202) 653-2400); *The State of Food and Agriculture*.

G.K. Hall and Company, 70 Lincoln Street, Boston, Massachusetts
02111 (617) 423-3990; *The World in Figures*.

Statistical Office of the United Nations, Publishing Service, New
York, New York 10017 (800) 253-9646; *Statistical Yearbook*.

TANZANIA (UNITED REPUBLIC OF) - PIGS - See TANZANIA (UNITED
REPUBLIC OF) - LIVESTOCK AND POULTRY

TANZANIA (UNITED REPUBLIC OF) - POPULATION

African Development Bank, 01 BP 1387, Abidjan 01, Cote D'Ivoire;
Selected Statistics on Regional Member Countries.

Euromonitor Publications Limited, 87-88 Turnmill Street, London
EC1M 5QU, England; *International Marketing Data and Statistics*.

Facts on File, 460 Park Avenue South, New York, New York 10016
(800) 443-8323; *The New Book of World Rankings*.

Food and Agricultural Organization of the United Nations (FAO), Via
delle Terme di Caracalla, 00100 Rome, Italy (Telephone Number in
U.S. (202) 653-2400); *Production Yearbook*.

G.K. Hall and Company, 70 Lincoln Street, Boston, Massachusetts
02111 (617) 423-3990; *The World in Figures*.

International Labour Office, I.L.O. Publications, CH-1211, Geneva 22, Switzerland; *Yearbook of Labour Statistics*.

Statistical Office of the United Nations, Publishing Service, New York, New York 10017 (800) 253-9646; *Demographic Yearbook, Statistical Yearbook*, and *Survey of Economic and Social Conditions in Africa*.

Times Books, 201 East 50th Street, New York, New York 10022 (212) 751-2600; *The Economist Book of Vital World Statistics*.

United Nations Educational, Scientific and Cultural Organization (UNESCO), 7 Place de Fontenoy, F-75700 Paris, France (Telephone Number in U.S. (212) 963-5981); *Statistical Yearbook*.

U.S. Arms Control and Disarmament Agency, 320 Twenty-first Street, NW, Washington, D.C. 20451 (202) 647-8677; *World Military Expenditures and Arms Transfers*.

World Health Organization, Office of Publications, Avenue Appia, CH-1211 Geneva 27, Switzerland (Telephone Number in U.S. (518) 436-9686); *World Health Statistics Annual*.

TANZANIA (UNITED REPUBLIC OF) - POST OFFICES

Facts on File, 460 Park Avenue South, New York, New York 10016 (800) 443-8323; *The New Book of World Rankings*.

TANZANIA (UNITED REPUBLIC OF) - POTATO PRODUCTION - See TANZANIA (UNITED REPUBLIC OF) - CROPS

TANZANIA (UNITED REPUBLIC OF) - POWER PRODUCTION INDUSTRY

Statistical Office of the United Nations, Publishing Service, New York, New York 10017 (800) 253-9646; *Statistical Yearbook*.

TANZANIA (UNITED REPUBLIC OF) - PRICES

Facts on File, 460 Park Avenue South, New York, New York 10016 (800) 443-8323; *The New Book of World Rankings*.

Food and Agricultural Organization of the United Nations (FAO), Via delle Terme di Caracalla, 00100 Rome, Italy (Telephone Number in U.S. (202) 653-2400); *Production Yearbook*, and *The State of Food and Agriculture*.

G.K. Hall and Company, 70 Lincoln Street, Boston, Massachusetts 02111 (617) 423-3990; *The World in Figures*.

International Labour Office, I.L.O. Publications, CH-1211, Geneva 22, Switzerland; *Yearbook of Labour Statistics*.

International Monetary Fund, 700 Nineteenth Street, NW, Washington, D.C. 20431 (202) 623-7000; *International Financial Statistics*.

Statistical Office of the United Nations, Publishing Service, New York, New York 10017 (800) 253-9646; *Statistical Yearbook*.

United Nations Economic Commission for Africa, Africa Hall, P.O. Box 3001, Addis Ababa, Ethiopia (Telephone Number in U.S. (800) 253-9646); *African Statistical Yearbook*.

TANZANIA (UNITED REPUBLIC OF) - PRINTING AND WRITING PAPER - See TANZANIA (UNITED REPUBLIC OF) - FORESTRY AND FOREST PRODUCTS

TANZANIA (UNITED REPUBLIC OF) - PRODUCTION

Facts on File, 460 Park Avenue South, New York, New York 10016 (800) 443-8323; *The New Book of World Rankings*.

TANZANIA (UNITED REPUBLIC OF) - PRODUCTIVITY

Euromonitor Publications Limited, 87-88 Turnmill Street, London EC1M 5QU, England; *International Marketing Data and Statistics*.

TANZANIA (UNITED REPUBLIC OF) - PROPERTY TAXES - See TANZANIA (UNITED REPUBLIC OF) - TAXATION

TANZANIA (UNITED REPUBLIC OF) - PUBLIC FINANCE

Facts on File, 460 Park Avenue South, New York, New York 10016 (800) 443-8323; *The New Book of World Rankings*.

TANZANIA (UNITED REPUBLIC OF) - RADIO BROADCASTING - See TANZANIA (UNITED REPUBLIC OF) - BROADCASTING

TANZANIA (UNITED REPUBLIC OF) - RADIO RECEIVER PRODUCTION

Statistical Office of the United Nations, Publishing Service, New York, New York 10017 (800) 253-9646; *Statistical Yearbook*.

TANZANIA (UNITED REPUBLIC OF) - RAILWAYS

Jane's Information Group, Sentinel House, 163 Brighton Road, Coulsdon, Surrey CR5 2NH, England (Telephone Number in U.S. (703) 683-3700); *Jane's World Railways*.

Statistical Office of the United Nations, Publishing Service, New York, New York 10017 (800) 253-9646; *Survey of Economic and Social Conditions in Africa*.

United Nations Economic Commission for Africa, Africa Hall, P.O. Box 3001, Addis Ababa, Ethiopia (Telephone Number in U.S. (800) 253-9646); *African Statistical Yearbook*.

TANZANIA (UNITED REPUBLIC OF) - RELIGION

Facts on File, 460 Park Avenue South, New York, New York 10016 (800) 443-8323; *The New Book of World Rankings*.

TANZANIA (UNITED REPUBLIC OF) - RENT PRICES

International Monetary Fund, 700 Nineteenth Street, NW, Washington, D.C. 20431 (202) 623-7000; *Yearbook of Labour Statistics*.

TANZANIA (UNITED REPUBLIC OF) - RICE PRODUCTION - See TANZANIA (UNITED REPUBLIC OF) - CROPS

TANZANIA (UNITED REPUBLIC OF) - ROUNDWOOD PRODUCTION - See TANZANIA (UNITED REPUBLIC OF) - FORESTRY AND FOREST PRODUCTS

TANZANIA (UNITED REPUBLIC OF) - RUBBER PRODUCTION AND CONSUMPTION

Facts on File, 460 Park Avenue South, New York, New York 10016 (800) 443-8323; *The New Book of World Rankings*.

TANZANIA (UNITED REPUBLIC OF) - SALT PRODUCTION - See TANZANIA (UNITED REPUBLIC OF) - MINING AND MINERAL PRODUCTS

TANZANIA (UNITED REPUBLIC OF) - SAWNWOOD PRODUCTION - See TANZANIA (UNITED REPUBLIC OF) - FORESTRY AND FOREST PRODUCTS

TANZANIA (UNITED REPUBLIC OF) - SCIENTISTS AND TECHNICIANS

United Nations Educational, Scientific and Cultural Organization (UNESCO), 7 Place de Fontenoy, F-75700 Paris, France (Telephone Number in U.S. (212) 963-5981); *Statistical Yearbook*.

TANZANIA (UNITED REPUBLIC OF) - SENIOR CITIZENS

Facts on File, 460 Park Avenue South, New York, New York 10016 (800) 443-8323; *The New Book of World Rankings*.

TANZANIA (UNITED REPUBLIC OF) - SHEEP - See TANZANIA (UNITED REPUBLIC OF) - LIVESTOCK AND POULTRY

TANZANIA (UNITED REPUBLIC OF) - SILVER PRODUCTION AND CONSUMPTION - See TANZANIA (UNITED REPUBLIC OF) - MINING AND MINERAL PRODUCTS

TANZANIA (UNITED REPUBLIC OF) - SISAL EXPORTS - See TANZANIA (UNITED REPUBLIC OF) - CROPS

TANZANIA (UNITED REPUBLIC OF) - SOCIAL DATA

African Development Bank, 01 BP 1387, Abidjan 01, Cote D'Ivoire; *Selected Statistics on Regional Member Countries*.

Facts on File, 460 Park Avenue South, New York, New York 10016 (800) 443-8323; *The New Book of World Rankings*.

TANZANIA (UNITED REPUBLIC OF) - SOCIAL SECURITY

International Monetary Fund, 700 Nineteenth Street, NW, Washington, D.C. 20431 (202) 623-7000; *Government Finance Statistics Yearbook*.

TANZANIA (UNITED REPUBLIC OF) - SOYBEAN PRODUCTION - See TANZANIA (UNITED REPUBLIC OF) - CROPS

TANZANIA (UNITED REPUBLIC OF) - STAMP TAXES AND DUTIES - See TANZANIA (UNITED REPUBLIC OF) - TAXATION

TANZANIA (UNITED REPUBLIC OF) - STATE BUDGET REVENUE AND EXPENDITURES

Euromonitor Publications Limited, 87-88 Turnmill Street, London EC1M 5QU, England; *International Marketing Data and Statistics*.

TANZANIA (UNITED REPUBLIC OF) - STEEL - See TANZANIA (UNITED REPUBLIC OF) - MINING AND MINERAL PRODUCTS

TANZANIA (UNITED REPUBLIC OF) - STOCKS - COMMODITY - MARKET PRICE - INDEX

Food and Agricultural Organization of the United Nations (FAO), Via delle Terme di Caracalla, 00100 Rome, Italy (Telephone Number in U.S. (202) 653-2400); *The State of Food and Agriculture*.

TANZANIA (UNITED REPUBLIC OF) - SUGAR PRODUCTION AND CONSUMPTION - See TANZANIA (UNITED REPUBLIC OF) - CROPS

TANZANIA (UNITED REPUBLIC OF) - TAXATION

G.K. Hall and Company, 70 Lincoln Street, Boston, Massachusetts 02111 (617) 423-3990; *The World in Figures*.

International Monetary Fund, 700 Nineteenth Street, NW, Washington, D.C. 20431 (202) 623-7000; *Government Finance Statistics Yearbook*.

International Road Federation, 525 School Street, SW, Washington, D.C. 20024 (202) 554-2106; *World Road Statistics*.

The World Bank, 1818 H Street, NW, Washington, D.C. 20433 (202) 477-1234; *World Tables*.

TANZANIA (UNITED REPUBLIC OF) - TEA PRODUCTION AND CONSUMPTION - See TANZANIA (UNITED REPUBLIC OF) - CROPS

TANZANIA (UNITED REPUBLIC OF) - TELEGRAPH SERVICE

Statistical Office of the United Nations, Publishing Service, New York, New York 10017 (800) 253-9646; *Statistical Yearbook*.

TANZANIA (UNITED REPUBLIC OF) - TELEPHONES IN USE

American Telephone and Telegraph Company, 26 Parsippany Road, Whippany, New Jersey 07981 (800) 338-4038; *The World's Telephones*.

Statistical Office of the United Nations, Publishing Service, New York, New York 10017 (800) 253-9646; *Statistical Yearbook*.

TANZANIA (UNITED REPUBLIC OF) - TELEVISION BROADCASTING - See TANZANIA (UNITED REPUBLIC OF) - BROADCASTING

TANZANIA (UNITED REPUBLIC OF) - TEXTILE INDUSTRY

Statistical Office of the United Nations, Publishing Service, New York, New York 10017 (800) 253-9646; *Statistical Yearbook*.

TANZANIA (UNITED REPUBLIC OF) - THEATRE

United Nations Educational, Scientific and Cultural Organization (UNESCO), 7 Place de Fontenoy, F-75700 Paris, France (Telephone Number in U.S. (212) 963-5981); *Statistical Yearbook*.

TANZANIA (UNITED REPUBLIC OF) - TIN PRODUCTION AND CONSUMPTION - See TANZANIA (UNITED REPUBLIC OF) - MINING AND MINERAL PRODUCTS

TANZANIA (UNITED REPUBLIC OF) - TOBACCO PRODUCTION

Facts on File, 460 Park Avenue South, New York, New York 10016 (800) 443-8323; *The New Book of World Rankings*.

Statistical Office of the United Nations, Publishing Service, New York, New York 10017 (800) 253-9646; *Statistical Yearbook*.

TANZANIA (UNITED REPUBLIC OF) - TOURISM

Facts on File, 460 Park Avenue South, New York, New York 10016 (800) 443-8323; *The New Book of World Rankings*.

Statistical Office of the United Nations, Publishing Service, New York, New York 10017 (800) 253-9646; *Statistical Yearbook*.

Times Books, 201 East 50th Street, New York, New York 10022 (212) 751-2600; *The Economist Book of Vital World Statistics*.

United Nations Economic Commission for Africa, Africa Hall, P.O. Box 3001, Addis Ababa, Ethiopia (Telephone Number in U.S. (800) 253-9646); *African Statistical Yearbook*.

World Tourism Organization, Calle Capitan Haya 42, E-28020 Madrid, Spain; *Yearbook of Tourism Statistics*.

TANZANIA (UNITED REPUBLIC OF) - TRACTORS IN USE

Statistical Office of the United Nations, Publishing Service, New York, New York 10017 (800) 253-9646; *Statistical Yearbook*.

TANZANIA (UNITED REPUBLIC OF) - TRADE - See TANZANIA (UNITED REPUBLIC OF) - FOREIGN TRADE

TANZANIA (UNITED REPUBLIC OF) - TRADEMARKS AND SERVICE MARKS

Statistical Office of the United Nations, Publishing Service, New York, New York 10017 (800) 253-9646; *Statistical Yearbook*.

TANZANIA (UNITED REPUBLIC OF) - TRANSPORTATION AND COMMUNICATIONS

Facts on File, 460 Park Avenue South, New York, New York 10016 (800) 443-8323; *The New Book of World Rankings*.

United Nations Economic Commission for Africa, Africa Hall, P.O. Box 3001, Addis Ababa, Ethiopia (Telephone Number in U.S. (800) 253-9646); *African Statistical Yearbook*.

TANZANIA (UNITED REPUBLIC OF) - TUNGSTEN PRODUCTION AND CONSUMPTION - See TANZANIA (UNITED REPUBLIC OF) - MINING AND MINERAL PRODUCTS

TANZANIA (UNITED REPUBLIC OF) - UNEMPLOYMENT

Euromonitor Publications Limited, 87-88 Turnmill Street, London EC1M 5QU, England; *International Marketing Data and Statistics*.

International Monetary Fund, 700 Nineteenth Street, NW, Washington, D.C. 20431 (202) 623-7000; *Yearbook of Labour Statistics*.

TANZANIA (UNITED REPUBLIC OF) - VITAL STATISTICS

Euromonitor Publications Limited, 87-88 Turnmill Street, London EC1M 5QU, England; *International Marketing Data and Statistics*.

Statistical Office of the United Nations, Publishing Service, New York, New York 10017 (800) 253-9646; *Statistical Yearbook*.

World Health Organization, Office of Publications, Avenue Appia, CH-1211 Geneva 27, Switzerland (Telephone Number in U.S. (518) 436-9686); *World Health Statistics Annual*.

TANZANIA (UNITED REPUBLIC OF) - WAGES

International Monetary Fund, 700 Nineteenth Street, NW, Washington, D.C. 20431 (202) 623-7000; *Yearbook of Labour Statistics*.

Statistical Office of the United Nations, Publishing Service, New York, New York 10017 (800) 253-9646; *Statistical Yearbook*.

TANZANIA (UNITED REPUBLIC OF) - WEATHER

Facts on File, 460 Park Avenue South, New York, New York 10016 (800) 443-8323; *The New Book of World Rankings*.

TANZANIA (UNITED REPUBLIC OF) - WELFARE

International Monetary Fund, 700 Nineteenth Street, NW, Washington, D.C. 20431 (202) 623-7000; *Government Finance Statistics Yearbook*.

TANZANIA (UNITED REPUBLIC OF) - WHEAT PRODUCTION AND PRICES - See TANZANIA (UNITED REPUBLIC OF) - CROPS

TANZANIA (UNITED REPUBLIC OF) - WINE PRODUCTION

Facts on File, 460 Park Avenue South, New York, New York 10016 (800) 443-8323; *The New Book of World Rankings*.

TANZANIA (UNITED REPUBLIC OF) - WOOL PRODUCTION

Facts on File, 460 Park Avenue South, New York, New York 10016 (800) 443-8323; *The New Book of World Rankings*.

TARGET SHOOTING

National Sporting Goods Association, Lake Center Plaza Building, 1699 Wall Street, Mount Prospect, Illinois 60056-5780 (708) 439-4000; *Sports Participation in 1992: Series I*.

TAX EXPENDITURES - REVENUE LOSS ESTIMATES

Executive Office of the President, Office of Management and Budget, Executive Office Building, Washington, D.C. 20503 (202) 395-3080; *Budget of the United States Government*.

TAX RECEIPTS - FOREIGN COUNTRIES

Organization for Economic Cooperation and Development, Publication and Information Center, 2001 L Street, NW, Washington, D.C. 20036-4095 (202) 785-6323; *Revenue Statistics of OECD Member Countries*.

TAX RECEIPTS - GOVERNMENTAL REVENUE - BY TYPE OF TAX

U.S. Department of Commerce, Bureau of the Census, Suitland, Maryland 20233 (301) 763-4040; *Government Finances*.

TAX RECEIPTS - MOTOR-FUEL TAXES AND MOTOR-VEHICLE FEES

U.S. Department of Commerce, Bureau of the Census, Suitland, Maryland 20233 (301) 763-4040; *State Government Tax Collections*.

U.S. Department of Transportation, Federal Highway Administration, 400 Seventh Street, SW, Washington, D.C. 20590 (202) 366-0660; *Highway Statistics*.

TAX RECEIPTS - NATIONAL (INTERNAL REVENUE)

U.S. Department of Commerce, Bureau of the Census, Suitland, Maryland 20233 (301) 763-4040; *Government Finances*.

U.S. Department of the Treasury, Internal Revenue Service, 1111 Constitution Avenue, NW, Washington, D.C. 20224 (202) 566-5000; *Annual Report of the Commissioner and Chief Counselor of the Internal Revenue Service*, and *Statistics of Income, Individual Income Tax Returns*.

TAX RECEIPTS - NATIONAL (INTERNAL REVENUE) - ADJUSTED
GROSS INCOME

U.S. Department of the Treasury, Internal Revenue Service, 1111
Constitution Avenue, NW, Washington, D.C. 20224 (202) 566-5000;
Statistics of Income Bulletin, and *Statistics of Income, Individual
Income Tax Returns.*

TAX RECEIPTS - NATIONAL (INTERNAL REVENUE) - BY TYPE OF
TAX

U.S. Department of Commerce, Bureau of the Census, Suitland,
Maryland 20233 (301) 763-4040; *Government Finances.*

TAX RECEIPTS - NATIONAL (INTERNAL REVENUE) -
COLLECTIONS BY SOURCE

U.S. Department of the Treasury, Internal Revenue Service, 1111
Constitution Avenue, NW, Washington, D.C. 20224 (202) 566-5000;
*Annual Report of the Commissioner and Chief Counsel of the
Internal Revenue Service,* and *Statistics of Income, Individual
Income Tax Returns.*

TAX RECEIPTS - NATIONAL (INTERNAL REVENUE) -
CORPORATION INCOME TAX - FEDERAL BUDGET RECEIPTS

Executive Office of the President, Office of Management and
Budget, Executive Office Building, Washington, D.C. 20503 (202)
395-3080; *Budget of the United States Government.*

U.S. Department of Commerce, Bureau of the Census, Suitland,
Maryland 20233 (301) 763-4040; *Government Finances.*

U.S. Department of the Treasury, Internal Revenue Service, 1111
Constitution Avenue, NW, Washington, D.C. 20224 (202) 566-5000;
*Annual Report of the Commissioner and Chief Counsel of the
Internal Revenue Service.*

TAX RECEIPTS - NATIONAL (INTERNAL REVENUE) -
CORPORATION INCOME TAX - INTERNAL REVENUE
COLLECTIONS

U.S. Department of the Treasury, Internal Revenue Service, 1111
Constitution Avenue, NW, Washington, D.C. 20224 (202) 566-5000,
*Annual Report of the Commissioner and Chief Counsel of the
Internal Revenue Service,* and *Statistics of Income, Individual
Income Tax Returns.*

TAX RECEIPTS - NATIONAL (INTERNAL REVENUE) -
CORPORATION INCOME TAX - TAX LIABILITIES

U.S. Department of the Treasury, Internal Revenue Service, 1111
Constitution Avenue, NW, Washington, D.C. 20224 (202) 566-5000;
Statistics of Income, Corporation Income Tax Returns.

TAX RECEIPTS - NATIONAL (INTERNAL REVENUE) -
CORPORATION INCOME TAX - TAX RETURNS FILED

U.S. Department of the Treasury, Internal Revenue Service, 1111
Constitution Avenue, NW, Washington, D.C. 20224 (202) 566-5000;
*Annual Report of the Commissioner and Chief Counsel of the
Internal Revenue Service,* and *Statistics of Income, Corporation
Income Tax Returns.*

TAX RECEIPTS - NATIONAL (INTERNAL REVENUE) -
EMPLOYMENT TAXES

Executive Office of the President, Office of Management and
Budget, Executive Office Building, Washington, D.C. 20503 (202)
395-3080; *Budget of the United States Government.*

U.S. Department of the Treasury, Internal Revenue Service, 1111
Constitution Avenue, NW, Washington, D.C. 20224 (202) 566-5000;
*Annual Report of the Commissioner and Chief Counsel of the
Internal Revenue Service.*

TAX RECEIPTS - NATIONAL (INTERNAL REVENUE) - ESTATE
AND GIFT TAXES

Executive Office of the President, Office of Management and Budget,
Executive Office Building, Washington, D.C. 20503 (202) 395-3080;
Budget of the United States Government.

U.S. Department of the Treasury, Internal Revenue Service, 1111
Constitution Avenue, NW, Washington, D.C. 20224 (202) 566-5000;
*Annual Report of the Commissioner and Chief Counsel of the
Internal Revenue Service.*

TAX RECEIPTS - NATIONAL (INTERNAL REVENUE) - EXCISE
TAXES

Executive Office of the President, Office of Management and Budget,
Executive Office Building, Washington, D.C. 20503 (202) 395-3080;
Budget of the United States Government.

U.S. Department of Commerce, Bureau of the Census, Suitland,
Maryland 20233 (301) 763-4040; *State Government Tax Collections,*
and *State Government Finances.*

U.S. Department of the Treasury, Internal Revenue Service, 1111
Constitution Avenue, NW, Washington, D.C. 20224 (202) 566-5000;
*Annual Report of the Commissioner and Chief Counsel of the
Internal Revenue Service.*

TAX RECEIPTS - NATIONAL (INTERNAL REVENUE) - INDIVIDUAL
INCOME TAX

Executive Office of the President, Office of Management and Budget,
Executive Office Building, Washington, D.C. 20503 (202) 395-3080;
Budget of the United States Government.

U.S. Department of Commerce, Bureau of the Census, Suitland,
Maryland 20233 (301) 763-4040; *Government Finances,* and *State
Government Finances.*

U.S. Department of the Treasury, Internal Revenue Service, 1111
Constitution Avenue, NW, Washington, D.C. 20224 (202) 566-5000;
*Annual Report of the Commissioner and Chief Counsel of the
Internal Revenue Service, Statistics of Income, Individual Income
Tax Returns, Statistics of Income Bulletin,* and unpublished data.

TAX RECEIPTS - NATIONAL (INTERNAL REVENUE) - INDIVIDUAL
INCOME TAX - AVERAGE TAX BY INCOME LEVEL

U.S. Department of the Treasury, Internal Revenue Service, 1111
Constitution Avenue, NW, Washington, D.C. 20224 (202) 566-5000;
*Annual Report of the Commissioner and Chief Counsel of the
Internal Revenue Service, Statistics of Income, Individual Income
Tax Returns,* and *Statistics of Income Bulletin.*

TAX RECEIPTS - NATIONAL (INTERNAL REVENUE) - INDIVIDUAL
INCOME TAX - RATES

U.S. Department of the Treasury, Fifteenth Street and Pennsylvania
Avenue, NW, Washington, D.C. 20220 (202) 566-2000; unpublished
data.

TAX RECEIPTS - PROPERTY TAX - CITY GOVERNMENT

U.S. Department of Commerce, Bureau of the Census, Suitland, Maryland 20233 (301) 763-4040; *City Government Finances.*

TAX RECEIPTS - PROPERTY TAX - RATES - SELECTED CITIES

Government of the District of Columbia, Department of Finances and Revenue, 300 Indiana Avenue, NW, Washington, D.C. 20001 (202) 727-6103; *Tax Rates and Tax Burdens in the District of Columbia: A Nationwide Comparison.*

TAX RECEIPTS - PROPERTY TAX - STATE AND LOCAL GOVERNMENT

U.S. Department of Commerce, Bureau of the Census, Suitland, Maryland 20233 (301) 763-4040; *Government Finances, Historical Statistics on Governmental Finances and Employment, State Government Finances,* and *City Government Finances.*

TAX RECEIPTS - STATE AND LOCAL GOVERNMENT - BY HOUSEHOLD INCOME

Government of the District of Columbia, Department of Finance and Revenue, 300 Indiana Avenue, NW, Washington, D.C. 20001 (202) 727-6103; *Tax Rates and Tax Burdens in the District of Columbia: A Nationwide Comparison.*

TAX RECEIPTS - STATE AND LOCAL GOVERNMENT - BY TYPE OF TAX

U.S. Department of Commerce, Bureau of the Census, Suitland, Maryland 20233 (301) 763-4040; *Government Finances, Historical Statistics on Governmental Finances and Employment,* and *State Governmental Finances.*

TAX RECEIPTS - STATE AND LOCAL GOVERNMENT - CITY GOVERNMENT

Government of the District of Columbia, Department of Finance and Revenue, 300 Indiana Avenue, NW, Washington, D.C. 20001 (202) 727-6103; *Tax Rates and Tax Burdens in the District of Columbia: A Nationwide Comparison.*

U.S. Department of Commerce, Bureau of the Census, Suitland, Maryland 20233 (301) 763-4040; *City Government Finances.*

TAX RECEIPTS - STATE AND LOCAL GOVERNMENT - STATE GOVERNMENT

U.S. Department of Commerce, Bureau of the Census, Suitland, Maryland 20233 (301) 763-4040; *State Government Finances, State Government Tax Collections,* and *Historical Statistics on Governmental Finances and Employment.*

TAXES - CORPORATE

U.S. Department of Commerce, Bureau of Economic Analysis, Fourteenth Street between Constitution Avenue and E Street, NW, Washington, D.C. 20230 (202) 606-9900; *The National Income and Product Accounts of the United States,* and *Survey of Current Business.*

U.S. Department of the Treasury, Internal Revenue Service, 1111 Constitution Avenue, NW, Washington, D.C. 20224 (202) 566-5000; *Statistics of Income, Corporation Income Tax Returns.*

TAXES - PARTNERSHIPS

U.S. Department of the Treasury, Internal Revenue Service, 1111 Constitution Avenue, NW, Washington, D.C. 20224 (202) 566-5000; *Statistics of Income, Partnership Returns,* and *Statistics of Income Bulletin.*

TAXES - PROPRIETORSHIPS

U.S. Department of the Treasury, Internal Revenue Service, 1111 Constitution Avenue, NW, Washington, D.C. 20224 (202) 566-5000; *Statistics of Income Bulletin.*

TEA

U.S. Department of Agriculture, Economic Research Service, Fourteenth Street and Independence Avenue, SW, Washington, D.C. 20005-4789 (202) 219-1504; *Food Consumption, Prices, and Expenditures,* and unpublished data.

TEACHERS - CATHOLIC SCHOOLS

National Catholic Education Association, 1077 Thirtieth Street, NW Washington, D.C. 20007 (202) 337-6232; *Ganley's Catholic Schools in America.*

TEACHERS - DEGREES CONFERRED

U.S. Department of Education, National Center for Education Statistics, 400 Maryland Avenue, SW, Washington, D.C. 20202 (202) 708-5366; *Digest of Education Statistics.*

TEACHERS - EMPLOYMENT

National Education Association, 1201 Sixteenth Street, NW, Washington, D.C. 20036 (202) 833-4000; *Estimates of School Statistics, Rankings of the States,* and unpublished data.

U.S. Department of Education, 400 Maryland Avenue, SW, Washington, D.C. 20202 (202) 708-5366; *Digest of Education Statistics, Projections of Education Statistics,* and unpublished data.

U.S. Department of Labor, Bureau of Labor Statistics, Two Massachusetts Avenue, NE, Washington, D.C. 20212 (202) 606-7828; *Employment and Earnings.*

TEACHERS - EMPLOYMENT - PROJECTIONS

U.S. Department of Education, 400 Maryland Avenue, SW, Washington, D.C. 20202 (202) 708-5366; *Projections of Education Statistics, Digest of Education Statistics,* and unpublished data.

U.S. Department of Labor, Bureau of Labor Statistics, Two Massachusetts Avenue, NE, Washington, D.C. 20212 (202) 606-7828; *Monthly Labor Review.*

TEACHERS - PRIVATE SCHOOLS

U.S. Department of Education, 400 Maryland Avenue, SW, Washington, D.C. 20202 (202) 708-5366; *Digest of Education Statistics.*

TEACHERS - PUBLIC SCHOOLS

National Education Association, 1201 Sixteenth Street, NW, Washington, D.C. 20036 (202) 833-4000; *Estimates of School Statistics, Rankings of the States,* and unpublished data.

U.S. Department of Education, National Center for Education Statistics, 400 Maryland Avenue, SW, Washington, D.C. 20202 (202) 708-5366; *Digest of Education Statistics*, and *Projections of Educational Statistics*.

TEACHERS - PUBLIC SCHOOLS - EXPERIENCE AND DEGREES HELD

U.S. Department of Education, 400 Maryland Avenue, SW, Washington, D.C. 20202 (202) 708-5366; *Digest of Education Statistics*.

TEACHERS - PUBLIC SCHOOLS - HIGHER EDUCATION INSTITUTIONS

U.S. Department of Education, 400 Maryland Avenue, SW, Washington, D.C. 20202 (202) 708-5366; *Digest of Education Statistics*, *Projections of Education Statistics*, and unpublished data.

TEACHERS - PUBLIC SCHOOLS - HIGHER EDUCATION INSTITUTIONS - SALARIES

Maryse Eymonerie Associates, P.O. Box 7893, Hilton Head, South Carolina 29938, and American Association of University Professors, 1012 Fourteenth Street, NW, Suite 500, Washington, D.C. 20005 (202) 737-5900; *Annual Report on the Economic Status of the Profession*.

TEACHERS - PUBLIC SCHOOLS - HIGHER EDUCATION INSTITUTIONS - TENURE STATUS

U.S. Department of Education, 400 Maryland Avenue, SW, Washington, D.C. 20202 (202) 708-5366; *Digest of Education Statistics*.

TEACHERS - PUBLIC SCHOOLS - NUMBER

National Education Association, 1201 Sixteenth Street, NW, Washington, D.C. 20036 (202) 833-4000; *Estimates of School Statistics*, *Rankings of the States*, and unpublished data.

U.S. Department of Education, 400 Maryland Avenue, SW, Washington, D.C. 20202 (202) 708-5366; *Projections of Education Statistics*, *Digest of Education Statistics*, and unpublished data.

TEACHERS - PUBLIC SCHOOLS - SALARIES

National Education Association, 1201 Sixteenth Street, NW, Washington, D.C. 20036 (202) 833-4000; *Estimates of School Statistics*, *Rankings of the States*, and unpublished data.

Northwestern University, 633 Clark Street, Evanston, Illinois 60201 (708) 491-3741; *The Northwestern Endicott Lindquist Report*.

TEACHERS - STATES

National Education Association, 1201 Sixteenth Street, NW, Washington, D.C. 20036 (202) 833-4000; *Estimates of School Statistics*.

TECHNICIANS

U.S. Department of Labor, Bureau of Labor Statistics, Two Massachusetts Avenue, NE, Washington, D.C. 20212 (202) 606-7828; *Employment and Earnings*, and unpublished data.

TELECOMMUNICATIONS EQUIPMENT

U.S. Department of Commerce, Bureau of the Census, Suitland, Maryland 20233 (301) 763-4040; *U.S. Merchandise Trade: Exports*, *General Imports, and Imports for Consumption*, and *U.S. Merchandise Trade*.

TELEGRAPH AND OTHER COMMUNICATIONS - FINANCES

U.S. Federal Communications Commission, 1919 M Street, NW, Washington, D.C. 20554 (202) 632-7000; *Statistics of Communications Common Carriers*, and unpublished data.

TELEGRAPH AND OTHER COMMUNICATIONS - OVERSEAS SYSTEMS AND RATES

U.S. Federal Communications Commission, 1919 M Street, NW, Washington, D.C. 20554 (202) 632-7000; *Statistics of Communications Common Carriers*, and unpublished data.

TELEPHONE COMMUNICATIONS - CELLULAR INDUSTRY

Cellular Telecommunications Industry Association, 1250 Connecticut Avenue, NW, Suite 200, Washington, D.C. 20036 (202) 785-0081; *State of the Cellular Industry*.

TELEPHONE COMMUNICATIONS - EARNINGS

United States Telephone Association, 1401 H Street, NW, Suite 600, Washington, D.C. 20005 (202) 326-7300; *Statistics of the Local Exchange Carriers*.

U.S. Department of Labor, Bureau of Labor Statistics, Two Massachusetts Avenue, NE, Washington, D.C. 20212 (202) 606-7828; *Employment and Earnings*, and Bulletins 2370 and 2429.

U.S. Federal Communications Commission, 1919 M Street, NW, Washington, D.C. 20554 (202) 632-7000; *Statistics of Communications Common Carriers*, and unpublished data.

TELEPHONE COMMUNICATIONS - EMPLOYEES

Cellular Telecommunications Industry Association, 1250 Connecticut Avenue, NW, Suite 200, Washington, D.C. 20036 (202) 785-0081; *State of the Cellular Industry*.

United States Telephone Association, 1401 H Street, NW, Washington, D.C. 20005 (202) 326-7300; *Statistics of the Local Exchange Carriers*.

U.S. Department of Labor, Bureau of Labor Statistics, Two Massachusetts Avenue, NE, Washington, D.C. 20212 (202) 606-7828; *Employment and Earnings*, and Bulletins 2370 and 2429.

U.S. Federal Communications Commission, 1919 M Street, NW, Washington, D.C. 20554 (202) 632-7000; *Statistics of Communication Common Carriers*, and unpublished data.

TELEPHONE COMMUNICATIONS - FINANCES

Cellular Telecommunications Industry Association, 1250 Connecticut Avenue, NW, Suite 200, Washington, D.C. 20036 (202) 785-0081; *State of the Cellular Industry*.

United States Telephone Association, 1401 H Street, NW, Suite 600, Washington, D.C. 20005 (202) 326-7300; *Statistics of the Local Exchange Carriers*.

U.S. Department of Commerce, Bureau of the Census, Suitland, Maryland 20233 (301) 763-4040; *Annual Survey of Communication Services*.

U.S. Federal Communications Commission, 1919 M Street, NW, Washington, D.C. 20554 (202) 632-7000; *Statistics of Communication Common Carriers*, and unpublished data.

TELEPHONE COMMUNICATIONS - PRODUCTIVITY

U.S. Department of Labor, Bureau of Labor Statistics, Two Massachusetts Avenue, NE, Washington, D.C. 20212 (202) 606-7828; *Productivity Measures for Selected Industries and Government Services*, and unpublished data.

TELEPHONE COMMUNICATIONS - RECEIPTS

U.S. Federal Communications Commission, 1919 M Street, NW, Washington, D.C. 20554 (202) 632-7000; *Statistics of Communications Common Carriers*, and unpublished data.

TELEPHONES - See also TELEGRAPH, ETC.

TELEPHONES - ACCESS LINES

United States Telephone Association, 1401 H Street, NW, Washington, D.C. 20005 (202) 326-7300; *Statistics of the Local Exchange Carriers*.

TELEPHONES - CALLS

United States Telephone Association, 1401 H Street, NW, Washington, D.C. 20005 (202) 326-7300; *Statistics of the Local Exchange Carriers*.

U.S. Federal Communications Commission, 1919 M Street, NW, Washington, D.C. 20554 (202) 632-7000; and *Statistics of Communication Common Carriers*, and unpublished data.

TELEPHONES - CONSUMER PRICE INDEX

U.S. Department of Labor, Bureau of Labor Statistics, Two Massachusetts Avenue, NE, Washington, D.C. 20212 (202) 606-7828; *Monthly Labor Review*, and *Handbook of Labor Statistics*.

TELEPHONES - HOUSEHOLDS WITH SERVICE

U.S. Department of Commerce, Bureau of the Census, Suitland, Maryland 20233 (301) 763-4040; *Census of Housing*, and unpublished data.

U.S. Federal Communications Commission, 1919 M Street, NW, Washington, D.C. 20554 (202) 632-7000; *Telephone Subscribership in the U.S.*, *Statistics of Communications Common Carriers*, and unpublished data.

TELEPHONES - NUMBER

United States Telephone Association, 1401 H Street, NW, Washington, D.C. 20005 (202) 326-7300; and *Statistics of the Local Exchange Carriers*.

U.S. Federal Communications Commission, 1919 M Street, NW, Washington, D.C. 20554 (202) 632-7000; *Statistics of Communications Common Carriers*, and unpublished data.

TELEPHONES - NUMBER - FOREIGN COUNTRIES

International Telecommunication Union, Palais des Nations, CH-1211 Geneva 20, Switzerland, *World Telecom Indicators*.

Statistical Office of the United Nations, Publishing Service, New York, New York 10017 (800) 253-9646; *Statistical Yearbook*.

United Nations Educational Scientific and Cultural Organization (UNESCO), 7 Place-de-Fontenoy, F-75700 Paris, France (Telephone Number in U.S. (212) 963-5981); *Statistical Yearbook*.

TELEVISION BROADCASTING - See also CABLE AND OTHER PAY TV SERVICES, PUBLIC BROADCASTING STATIONS and RADIO

TELEVISION BROADCASTING - ADVERTISING EXPENDITURES

McCann-Erickson, Incorporated, 750 Third Avenue, New York, New York 10017 (212) 697-6000; compiled for Crain Communications, Incorporated, 740 North Rush Street, Chicago, Illinois 60611; in *Advertising Age*.

Television Bureau of Advertising, Incorporated, 850 Third Avenue, New York, New York 10022 (212) 486-1111; data compiled by Competitive Media Reporting, 11 West 42nd Street, New York, New York 10036 (212) 789-1400.

TELEVISION BROADCASTING - EARNINGS

U.S. Department of Labor, Bureau of Labor Statistics, Two Massachusetts Avenue, NE, Washington, D.C. 20212 (202) 606-7828; *Employment and Earnings*, and Bulletins 2370 and 2429.

TELEVISION BROADCASTING - EMPLOYEES

U.S. Department of Labor, Bureau of Labor Statistics, Two Massachusetts Avenue, NE, Washington, D.C. 20212 (202) 606-7828; *Employment and Earnings*, and Bulletins 2370 and 2429.

TELEVISION BROADCASTING - FINANCES

U.S. Department of Commerce, Bureau of the Census, Suitland, Maryland 20233 (301) 763-4040; *Annual Survey of Communication Services*.

TELEVISIONS - CONSUMER EXPENDITURES

U.S. Department of Commerce, Bureau of Economic Analysis, Fourteenth Street between Constitution Avenue and E Street, NW, Washington, D.C. 20230 (202) 606-9900; *The National Income and Product Accounts of the U.S.*, and *Survey of Current Business*.

U.S. Department of Labor, Bureau of Labor Statistics, Two Massachusetts Avenue, NE, Washington, D.C. 20212 (202) 606-7828; *Consumer Expenditure Survey*.

TELEVISIONS - HOUSEHOLDS WITH

Euromonitor Publications Limited, 87-88 Turnmill Street, London EC1M 5QU, England; *European Marketing Data and Statistics*.

International Telecommunication Union, Palais des Nations, CH-1211 Geneva 20, Switzerland, *World Telecom Indicators*.

Television Bureau of Advertising, Incorporated, 850 Third Avenue, New York, New York 10022 (212) 486-1111; *Trends in Television*.

United Nations Educational Scientific and Cultural Organization (UNESCO), 7 Place de Fontenoy, F-75700 Paris, France (Telephone Number in U.S. (212) 963-5981), *Statistical Yearbook*.

TELEVISIONS - VIEWING

Mediamark Research, Incorporated, 708 Third Avenue, New York, New York 10017 (212) 599-0444; *Multimedia Audiences*.

Veronis, Suhler and Associates, 350 Park Avenue, New York, New York 10022 (212) 935-4990; *Communications Industry Forecast Report.*

TEMPERATURE - SELECTED CITIES

U.S. Department of Commerce, National Oceanic and Atmospheric Administration, National Climatic Data Center, Federal Building, Asheville, North Carolina 28801 (704) 259-2850; *Climatography of the United States,* and *Comparative Climatic Data.*

TEMPLES (FRUIT)

U.S. Department of Agriculture, National Agricultural Statistics Service, Fourteenth Street and Independence Avenue, SW, Washington, D.C. 20250 (202) 219-1504; *Citrus Fruits.*

TENNESSEE - See also STATE DATA (FOR INDIVIDUAL STATES)

Tennessee - Primary Statistics Source

Center for Business and Economic Research, College of Business Administration, University of Tennessee, Room 100, Glocker Hall, Knoxville, Tennessee 37996-4170 (615) 974-5441; *Tennessee Statistical Abstract.*

Tennessee - State Data Centers

Tennessee State Planning Office, John Sevier State Office Building, 500 Charlotte Avenue, Suite 307, Nashville, Tennessee 37243-0001, Mr. Charles Brown (615) 741-1676.

Center for Business and Economic Research, College of Business Administration, University of Tennessee, Room 100, Glocker Hall, Knoxville, Tennessee 37996-4170, Ms. Betty Vickers (615) 974-5441.

TENNIS

National Sporting Goods Association, Lake Center Plaza Building, 1699 Wall Street, Mount Prospect, Illinois 60056-5780 (708) 439-4000; *The Sporting Goods Market in 1993,* and *Sports Participation in 1992.*

United States Tennis Association, 1212 Avenue of the Americas, New York, New York 10036 (212) 302-3322.

TENURE - See HOUSING AND HOUSING UNITS and FARMS

TERRITORIAL ACCESSIONS OF THE UNITED STATES

U.S. Department of Commerce, Bureau of the Census, Suitland, Maryland 20233 (301) 763-4040; unpublished data.

TEXAS - See also STATE DATA (FOR INDIVIDUAL STATES)

Texas - Primary Statistics Sources

Bureau of Business Research, University of Texas at Austin, College of Business Administration, Post Office Box 7459, Austin, Texas 78713 (512) 471-5180; *Texas Fact Book.*

Dallas Morning News, Incorporated, Communications Center, Post Office Box 655237, Dallas, Texas 75265 (214) 977-8261; *Texas Almanac.*

Texas - State Data Centers

State Data Center, Texas Department of Commerce, (mailing address) Post Office Box 12728, Capitol Station, Ninth and Congress Streets, Austin, Texas 78711, Ms. Susan Tully (512) 320-9667.

Department of Rural Sociology, Texas A & M University System, Special Services Building, College Station, Texas 77843-2125, Dr. Steve Murdock (409) 845-5115 or 5332.

Texas Natural Resources Information System (TNRIS), Post Office Box 13231, Austin, Texas 78711, Mr. Charles Palmer (512) 463-8399.

Texas State Library and Archive Commission, Post Office Box 12927, Capitol Station, Austin, Texas 78711, Ms. Diana Houston (512) 463-5455.

TEXTILE MILL PRODUCTS - END - USE

Fiber Economics Bureau, Incorporated, 101 Eisenhower Parkway, Roseland, New Jersey 07068 (201) 228-1107; *Textile Organon.*

TEXTILE MILL PRODUCTS - FOREIGN TRADE

U.S. Department of Commerce, Bureau of the Census, Suitland, Maryland 20233 (301) 763-4040; *U.S. Merchandise Trade: Exports, General Imports, and Imports for Consumption,* and *U.S. Merchandise Trade.*

TEXTILE MILL PRODUCTS - MANUFACTURING - CAPITAL

U.S. Department of Commerce, Bureau of Economic Analysis, Fourteenth Street between Constitution Avenue and E Street, NW, Washington, D.C. 20230 (202) 606-9900; *Fixed Reproducible Tangible Wealth in the United States,* and *Survey of Current Business.*

TEXTILE MILL PRODUCTS - MANUFACTURING - EARNINGS

U.S. Department of Commerce, Bureau of the Census, Suitland, Maryland 20233 (301) 763-4040; *County Business Patterns, Census of Manufactures,* and *Annual Survey of Manufactures.*

U.S. Department of Labor, Bureau of Labor Statistics, Two Massachusetts Avenue, NE, Washington, D.C. 20212 (202) 606-7828; *Employment and Earnings,* and Bulletins 2370 and 2429.

TEXTILE MILL PRODUCTS - MANUFACTURING - EMPLOYEES

U.S. Department of Commerce, Bureau of the Census, Suitland, Maryland 20233 (301) 763-4040; *Census of Manufactures, Annual Survey of Manufactures,* and *County Business Patterns.*

U.S. Department of Labor, Bureau of Labor Statistics, Two Massachusetts Avenue, NE, Washington, D.C. 20212 (202) 606-7828; *Employment and Earnings, Monthly Labor Review,* and Bulletins 2370 and 2429.

TEXTILE MILL PRODUCTS - MANUFACTURING - ESTABLISHMENTS

U.S. Department of Commerce, Bureau of the Census, Suitland, Maryland 20233 (301) 763-4040; *County Business Patterns,* and *Census of Manufactures,* and *Annual Survey of Manufactures.*

U.S. Department of Labor, Bureau of Labor Statistics, Two Massachusetts Avenue, NE, Washington, D.C. 20212 (202) 606-7828; *Employment and Earnings.*

TEXTILE MILL PRODUCTS - MANUFACTURING - FOREIGN TRADE

U.S. Department of Commerce, Bureau of the Census, Suitland, Maryland 20233 (301) 763-4040; *Census of Manufactures, Annual Survey of Manufactures*, and *U.S. Merchandise Trade: Selected Highlights*.

TEXTILE MILL PRODUCTS - MANUFACTURING - GROSS DOMESTIC PRODUCT

U.S. Department of Commerce, Bureau of Economic Analysis, Fourteenth Street between Constitution Avenue and E Street, NW, Washington, D.C. 20230 (202) 606-9900; *The National Income and Product Accounts of the United States*, and *Survey of Current Business*.

TEXTILE MILL PRODUCTS - MANUFACTURING - INVENTORIES

U.S. Department of Commerce, Bureau of the Census, Suitland, Maryland 20233 (301) 763-4040; *Current Industrial Reports, Manufacture Shipments, Inventories, and Orders*.

TEXTILE MILL PRODUCTS - MANUFACTURING - MERGERS AND ACQUISITIONS

Securities Data Company, 1180 Raymond Boulevard, Newark, New Jersey 07102 (201) 622-3100; *Merger and Corporate Transactions Database*.

TEXTILE MILL PRODUCTS - MANUFACTURING - OCCUPATIONAL SAFETY

U.S. Department of Labor, Bureau of Labor Statistics, Two Massachusetts Avenue, NE, Washington, D.C. 20212 (202) 606-7828; *Occupational Injuries and Illnesses in the United States by Industry*.

TEXTILE MILL PRODUCTS - MANUFACTURING - OUTPUT

Board of Governors of the Federal Reserve System, Twentieth Street and Constitution Avenue, NW, Washington, D.C. 20551 (202) 452-3000; *Federal Reserve Bulletin*.

TEXTILE MILL PRODUCTS - MANUFACTURING - PATENTS

U.S. Department of Commerce, Patent and Trademark Office, 2011 Crystal Drive, Arlington, Virginia 22202 (703) 305-8341; *Patenting Trends in the United States, State Country Report*.

TEXTILE MILL PRODUCTS - MANUFACTURING - PRODUCTIVITY

Board of Governors of the Federal Reserve System, Twentieth Street and Constitution Avenue, NW, Washington, D.C. 20551 (202) 452-3000; *Federal Reserve Bulletin*.

U.S. Department of Labor, Bureau of Labor Statistics, Two Massachusetts Avenue, NE, Washington, D.C. 20212 (202) 606-7828; *Productivity Measures for Selected Industries and Government Services*, and unpublished data.

TEXTILE MILL PRODUCTS - MANUFACTURING - SHIPMENTS

U.S. Department of Commerce, Bureau of the Census, Suitland, Maryland 20233 (301) 763-4040; *Current Industrial Reports, Manufactures' Shipments, Inventories and Orders, Annual Survey of Manufactures*, and *Census of Manufactures*.

TEXTILE MILL PRODUCTS - MANUFACTURING - VALUE ADDED

U.S. Department of Commerce, Bureau of the Census, Suitland, Maryland 20233 (301) 763-4040; *Census of Manufactures*, and *Annual Survey of Manufactures*.

TEXTILE MILL PRODUCTS - PRODUCTION

Fiber Economics Bureau, Incorporated, 101 Eisenhower Parkway, Roseland, New Jersey 07068 (201) 228-1107; *Textile Organon*.

Thailand - National Statistical Offices

Bank of Thailand, Bangkhunprom, Bangkok 10200, Thailand; for economics statistics.

Centre for Industrial Statistics, Information and Research, Industrial Economics and Planning Division, Ministry of Industry, Rama 6 Road, Bangkok 10400, Thailand; for industrial statistics.

National Statistical Office, Larn Luang Road, Bangkok 10100, Thailand; for general statistics.

Techniques and Statistics Division, Customs Department, Sunthornkosa Road, Klong Toey, Bangkok 10110, Thailand; for foreign statistics.

Thailand - Primary Statistics Sources

National Statistical Office, Bangkok, Thailand; *Statistical Yearbook Thailand, Quarterly Bulletin of Statistics*, and *Statistical Handbook*.

THAILAND - AGRICULTURE

Asian Development Bank, P.O. Box 789, 1099 Manila, Philippines; *Key Indicators of Developing Asian and Pacific Countries*.

Euromonitor Publications Limited, 87-88 Turnmill Street, London EC1M 5QU, England; *International Marketing Data and Statistics*, and *Third World Economic Handbook*.

Facts on File, 460 Park Avenue South, New York, New York 10016 (800) 443-8323; *The New Book of World Rankings*.

Food and Agricultural Organization of the United Nations (FAO) Via delle Terme di Caracalla, 00100 Rome, Italy (Telephone Number in U.S. (202) 653-2400); *Production Yearbook, The State of Food and Agriculture*, and *Trade Yearbook*.

G.K. Hall and Company, 70 Lincoln Street, Boston, Massachusetts 02111 (617) 423-3990; *The World in Figures*.

National Statistical Office, Office of the Prime Minister, Bangkok Metropolis 10100, Thailand; *Statistical Yearbook Thailand*.

Statistical Office of the United Nations, Publishing Service, New York, New York 10017 (800) 253-9646; *Statistical Yearbook*, and *Statistical Yearbook for Asia and the Pacific*.

Times Books, 201 East 50th Street, New York, New York 10022 (212) 751-2600; *The Economist Book of Vital World Statistics*.

The World Bank, 1818 H Street, NW, Washington, D.C. 20433 (202) 477-1234; *World Tables*.

THAILAND - AIRLINE SERVICE

The Economist Intelligence Unit (Asia) Limited, 10th Floor, Luk Kwok Centre, 72 Gloucester Road, Wanchai, Hong Kong (Phone Number in U.S. (800) 938-4685); *Asian Market Atlas*.

Facts on File, 460 Park Avenue South, New York, New York 10016 (800) 443-8323; *The New Book of World Rankings*.

G.K. Hall and Company, 70 Lincoln Street, Boston, Massachusetts 02111 (617) 423-3990; *The World in Figures*.

International Civil Aviation Organization, 1000 Sherbrooke Street West, Suite 400, Montreal, Quebec, Canada H3A 2R2 (514) 285-8219; *Civil Aviation Statistics of the World*.

Statistical Office of the United Nations, Publishing Service, New York, New York 10017 (800) 253-9646; *Statistical Yearbook*.

Times Books, 201 East 50th Street, New York, New York 10022 (212) 751-2600; *The Economist Book of Vital World Statistics*.

THAILAND - ALUMINUM PRODUCTION AND CONSUMPTION - See THAILAND - MINING AND MINERAL PRODUCTS

THAILAND - ANIMAL HEALTH

Food and Agricultural Organization of the United Nations (FAO), Via delle Terme di Caracalla, 00100, Rome, Italy (Telephone Number in U.S. (202) 653-2400); *Animal Health Yearbook*.

National Statistical Office, Office of the Prime Minister, Bangkok Metropolis 10100, Thailand; *Statistical Yearbook Thailand*.

THAILAND - ANTIMONY ORE PRODUCTION AND CONSUMPTION - See THAILAND - MINING AND MINERAL PRODUCTS

THAILAND - AREA AND DENSITY OF POPULATION

Euromonitor Publications Limited, 87-88 Turnmill Street, London EC1M 5QU, England; *International Marketing Data and Statistics*.

Facts on File, 460 Park Avenue South, New York, New York 10016 (800) 443-8323; *The New Book of World Rankings*.

Food and Agricultural Organization of the United Nations (FAO) Via delle Terme di Caracalla, 00100 Rome, Italy (Telephone Number in U.S. (202) 653-2400); *The State of Food and Agriculture*.

G.K. Hall and Company, 70 Lincoln Street, Boston, Massachusetts 02111 (617) 423-3990; *The World in Figures*.

National Statistical Office, Office of the Prime Minister, Bangkok Metropolis 10100, Thailand; *Statistical Yearbook Thailand*.

Statistical Office of the United Nations, Publishing Service, New York, New York 10017 (800) 253-9646; *Statistical Yearbook*.

Times Books, 201 East 50th Street, New York, New York 10022 (212) 751-2600; *The Economist Book of Vital World Statistics*.

United Nations Educational, Scientific and Cultural Organization (UNESCO), 7 Place de Fontenoy, F-75700 Paris, France (Telephone Number in U.S. (212) 963-5981); *Statistical Yearbook*.

THAILAND - ARMS EXPORTS AND IMPORTS

U.S. Arms Control and Disarmament Agency, 320 Twenty first Street, NW, Washington, D.C. 20451 (202) 647-8677; *World Military Expenditures and Arms Transfers*.

THAILAND - BALANCE OF PAYMENTS

The Economist Intelligence Unit, 111 West 57th Street, New York, New York 10019 (800) 938-4685; *The World Market Atlas*.

Euromonitor Publications Limited, 87-88 Turnmill Street, London EC1M 5QU, England; *Third World Economic Handbook*.

G.K. Hall and Company, 70 Lincoln Street, Boston, Massachusetts 02111 (617) 423-3990; *The World in Figures*.

International Monetary Fund, 700 Nineteenth Street, NW, Washington, D.C. 20431 (202) 623-7000; *Balance of Payments Yearbook*, and *International Financial Statistics*.

National Statistical Office, Office of the Prime Minister, Bangkok Metropolis 10100, Thailand; *Statistical Yearbook Thailand*.

Times Books, 201 East 50th Street, New York, New York 10022 (212) 751-2600; *The Economist Book of Vital World Statistics*.

The World Bank, 1818 H Street, NW, Washington, D.C. 20433 (202) 477-1234; *World Tables*.

THAILAND - BANKING

Asian Development Bank, P.O. Box 789, 1099 Manila, Philippines; *Key Indicators of Developing Asian and Pacific Countries*.

Facts on File, 460 Park Avenue South, New York, New York 10016 (800) 443-8323; *The New Book of World Rankings*.

G.K. Hall and Company, 70 Lincoln Street, Boston, Massachusetts 02111 (617) 423-3990; *The World in Figures*.

International Monetary Fund, 700 Nineteenth Street, NW, Washington, D.C. 20431 (202) 623-7000; *Government Finance Statistics Yearbook*, and *International Financial Statistics*.

National Statistical Office, Office of the Prime Minister, Bangkok Metropolis 10100, Thailand; *Statistical Yearbook Thailand*.

Statistical Office of the United Nations, Publishing Service, New York, New York 10017 (800) 253-9646; *Statistical Yearbook*.

THAILAND - BARLEY PRODUCTION - See THAILAND - CROPS

THAILAND - BEER PRODUCTION

Facts on File, 460 Park Avenue South, New York, New York 10016 (800) 443-8323; *The New Book of World Rankings*.

Statistical Office of the United Nations, Publishing Service, New York, New York 10017 (800) 253-9646; *Statistical Yearbook*.

THAILAND - BIRTH RATES

The Economist Intelligence Unit (Asia) Limited, 10th Floor, Luk Kwok Centre, 72 Gloucester Road, Wanchai, Hong Kong (Phone Number in U.S. (800) 938-4685); *Asian Market Atlas*.

Euromonitor Publications Limited, 87-88 Turnmill Street, London EC1M 5QU, England; *Third World Economic Handbook*.

Facts on File, 460 Park Avenue South, New York, New York 10016 (800) 443-8323; *The New Book of World Rankings*.

National Statistical Office, Office of the Prime Minister, Bangkok Metropolis 10100, Thailand; *Statistical Yearbook Thailand.*

Statistical Office of the United Nations, Publishing Service, New York, New York 10017 (800) 253-9646; *Demographic Yearbook,* and *Statistical Yearbook.*

Times Books, 201 East 50th Street, New York, New York 10022 (212) 751-2600; *The Economist Book of Vital World Statistics.*

The World Bank, 1818 H Street, NW, Washington, D.C. 20433 (202) 477-1234; *World Tables.*

World Health Organization, Office of Publications, Avenue Appia, CH-1211 Geneva 27, Switzerland (Telephone Number in U.S. (518) 436-9686); *World Health Statistics Annual.*

THAILAND - BONDS

Asian Development Bank, P.O. Box 789, 1099 Manila, Philippines; *Key Indicators of Developing Asian and Pacific Countries.*

G.K. Hall and Company, 70 Lincoln Street, Boston, Massachusetts 02111 (617) 423-3990; *The World in Figures.*

International Monetary Fund, 700 Nineteenth Street, NW, Washington, D.C. 20431 (202) 623-7000; *Government Finance Statistics Yearbook.*

THAILAND - BOOK PRODUCTION

G.K. Hall and Company, 70 Lincoln Street, Boston, Massachusetts 02111 (617) 423-3990; *The World in Figures.*

United Nations Educational, Scientific and Cultural Organization (UNESCO), 7 Place de Fontenoy, F-75700 Paris, France (Telephone Number in U.S. (212) 963-5981); *Statistical Yearbook.*

THAILAND - BROADCASTING

Billboard Limited, P.O. Box 9027, 1006 AA Amsterdam, The Netherlands (Telephone Number in U.S. (212) 764-7300); *World Radio TV Handbook.*

Facts on File, 460 Park Avenue South, New York, New York 10016 (800) 443-8323; *The New Book of World Rankings.*

G.K. Hall and Company, 70 Lincoln Street, Boston, Massachusetts 02111 (617) 423-3990; *The World in Figures.*

Times Books, 201 East 50th Street, New York, New York 10022 (212) 751-2600; *The Economist Book of Vital World Statistics.*

THAILAND - BUSINESS

G.K. Hall and Company, 70 Lincoln Street, Boston, Massachusetts 02111 (617) 423-3990; *The World in Figures.*

THAILAND - BUSINESS AND PROFESSIONAL LICENSES

International Monetary Fund, 700 Nineteenth Street, NW, Washington, D.C. 20431 (202) 623-7000; *Government Finance Statistics Yearbook.*

THAILAND - CALORIE SUPPLY

Asian Development Bank, P.O. Box 789, 1099 Manila, Philippines; *Key Indicators of Developing Asian and Pacific Countries.*

Food and Agricultural Organization of the United Nations (FAO) Via delle Terme di Caracalla, 00100 Rome, Italy (Telephone Number in U.S. (202) 653-2400); *The State of Food and Agriculture.*

THAILAND - CAPITAL INVESTMENT

Asian Development Bank, P.O. Box 789, 1099 Manila, Philippines; *Key Indicators of Developing Asian and Pacific Countries.*

THAILAND - CAPITAL REVENUE

Asian Development Bank, P.O. Box 789, 1099 Manila, Philippines; *Key Indicators of Developing Asian and Pacific Countries.*

International Monetary Fund, 700 Nineteenth Street, NW, Washington, D.C. 20431 (202) 623-7000; *Government Finance Statistics Yearbook.*

THAILAND - CATTLE - See THAILAND - LIVESTOCK AND POULTRY

THAILAND - CAUSTIC ACID PRODUCTION

Statistical Office of the United Nations, Publishing Service, New York, New York 10017 (800) 253-9646; *Statistical Yearbook.*

THAILAND - CEMENT PRODUCTION - See THAILAND - MINING AND MINERAL PRODUCTS

THAILAND - CHEMICAL (ORGANIC) PRODUCTION - See THAILAND - MINING AND MINERAL PRODUCTS

THAILAND - CHICKENS - See THAILAND - LIVESTOCK AND POULTRY

THAILAND - CIGAR PRODUCTION - See THAILAND - TOBACCO PRODUCTION

THAILAND - CIGARETTE PRODUCTION - See THAILAND - TOBACCO PRODUCTION

THAILAND - CLASS STRUCTURE

G.K. Hall and Company, 70 Lincoln Street, Boston, Massachusetts 02111 (617) 423-3990; *The World in Figures.*

THAILAND - CLIMATE

Facts on File, 460 Park Avenue South, New York, New York 10016 (800) 443-8323; *The New Book of World Rankings.*

G.K. Hall and Company, 70 Lincoln Street, Boston, Massachusetts 02111 (617) 423-3990; *The World in Figures.*

National Statistical Office, Office of the Prime Minister, Bangkok Metropolis 10100, Thailand; *Statistical Yearbook Thailand.*

THAILAND - CLOTHING EXPORTS AND IMPORTS

Euromonitor Publications Limited, 87-88 Turnmill Street, London EC1M 5QU, England; *Third World Economic Handbook.*

Statistical Office of the United Nations, Publishing Service, New York, New York 10017 (800) 253-9646; *Trade in Manufactures of Developing Countries.*

THAILAND - COAL PRODUCTION - See THAILAND - MINING AND MINERAL PRODUCTS

THAILAND - COFFEE - See THAILAND - CROPS

THAILAND - COMMUNICATIONS

Euromonitor Publications Limited, 87-88 Turnmill Street, London EC1M 5QU, England; *Third World Economic Handbook*.

G.K. Hall and Company, 70 Lincoln Street, Boston, Massachusetts 02111 (617) 423-3990; *The World in Figures*.

National Statistical Office, Office of the Prime Minister, Bangkok Metropolis 10100, Thailand; *Statistical Yearbook Thailand*.

Statistical Office of the United Nations, Publishing Service, New York, New York 10017 (800) 253-9646; *Statistical Yearbook for Asia and the Pacific*.

THAILAND - CONSTRUCTION INDUSTRY

Facts on File, 460 Park Avenue South, New York, New York 10016 (800) 443-8323; *The New Book of World Rankings*.

Statistical Office of the United Nations, Publishing Service, New York, New York 10017 (800) 253-9646; *Construction Statistics Yearbook*, and *Statistical Yearbook*.

THAILAND - CONSUMER PRICE INDEX

Asian Development Bank, P.O. Box 789, 1099 Manila, Philippines; *Key Indicators of Developing Asian and Pacific Countries*.

G.K. Hall and Company, 70 Lincoln Street, Boston, Massachusetts 02111 (617) 423-3990; *The World in Figures*.

National Statistical Office, Office of the Prime Minister, Bangkok Metropolis 10100, Thailand; *Statistical Yearbook Thailand*.

Statistical Office of the United Nations, Publishing Service, New York, New York 10017 (800) 253-9646; *Statistical Yearbook*.

THAILAND - CONSUMER PRICES

International Labour Office, I.L.O. Publications, CH-1211, Geneva 22, Switzerland; *Yearbook of Labour Statistics*.

International Monetary Fund, 700 Nineteenth Street, NW, Washington, D.C. 20431 (202) 623-7000; *International Financial Statistics*.

National Statistical Office, Office of the Prime Minister, Bangkok Metropolis 10100, Thailand; *Statistical Yearbook Thailand*.

THAILAND - CONSUMPTION

G.K. Hall and Company, 70 Lincoln Street, Boston, Massachusetts 02111 (617) 423-3990; *The World in Figures*.

International Rubber Study Group, York House, Eighth Floor, Empire Way, Wembley, London HA9 0PA, England; *Rubber Statistical Handbook*.

National Statistical Office, Office of the Prime Minister, Bangkok Metropolis 10100, Thailand; *Statistical Yearbook Thailand*.

THAILAND - COPPER PRODUCTION AND CONSUMPTION - See THAILAND - MINING AND MINERAL PRODUCTS

THAILAND - CORN - See THAILAND - CROPS

THAILAND - CORPORATE TAXES - See THAILAND - TAXATION

THAILAND - COTTON - See THAILAND - CROPS

THAILAND - CRIME

National Statistical Office, Office of the Prime Minister, Bangkok Metropolis 10100, Thailand; *Statistical Yearbook Thailand*.

Yale University Press, Yale Station, New Haven, Connecticut 06520 (203) 432-0940; *Violence and Crime in Cross-National Perspective*.

THAILAND - CROPS

Asian Development Bank, P.O. Box 789, 1099 Manila, Philippines; *Key Indicators of Developing Asian and Pacific Countries*.

Commodity Research Bureau, Incorporated, 75 Wall Street, New York, New York 10005 (212) 504-7754; *Commodity Year Book*.

International Monetary Fund, 700 Nineteenth Street, NW, Washington, D.C. 20431 (202) 623-7000; *International Financial Statistics*.

Facts on File, 460 Park Avenue South, New York, New York 10016 (800) 443-8323; *The New Book of World Rankings*.

Food and Agricultural Organization of the United Nations (FAO) Via delle Terme di Caracalla, 00100 Rome, Italy (Telephone Number in U.S. (202) 653-2400); *The State of Food and Agriculture*.

G.K. Hall and Company, 70 Lincoln Street, Boston, Massachusetts 02111 (617) 423-3990; *The World in Figures*.

National Statistical Office, Office of the Prime Minister, Bangkok Metropolis 10100, Thailand; *Statistical Yearbook Thailand*.

Statistical Office of the United Nations, Publishing Service, New York, New York 10017 (800) 253-9646; *Statistical Yearbook*.

THAILAND - CUSTOMS DUTIES

G.K. Hall and Company, 70 Lincoln Street, Boston, Massachusetts 02111 (617) 423-3990; *The World in Figures*.

International Monetary Fund, 700 Nineteenth Street, NW, Washington, D.C. 20431 (202) 623-7000; *Government Finance Statistics Yearbook*.

THAILAND - DAIRY PRODUCTS

Facts on File, 460 Park Avenue South, New York, New York 10016 (800) 443-8323; *The New Book of World Rankings*.

Food and Agricultural Organization of the United Nations (FAO) Via delle Terme di Caracalla, 00100 Rome, Italy (Telephone Number in U.S. (202) 653-2400); *The State of Food and Agriculture*.

Statistical Office of the United Nations, Publishing Service, New York, New York 10017 (800) 253-9646; *Statistical Yearbook*.

THAILAND - DEATH RATES

The Economist Intelligence Unit (Asia) Limited, 10th Floor, Luk Kwok Centre, 72 Gloucester Road, Wanchai, Hong Kong (Phone Number in U.S. (800) 938-4685); *Asian Market Atlas*.

Euromonitor Publications Limited, 87-88 Turnmill Street, London EC1M 5QU, England; *Third World Economic Handbook*.

G.K. Hall and Company, 70 Lincoln Street, Boston, Massachusetts 02111 (617) 423-3990; *The World in Figures.*

National Statistical Office, Office of the Prime Minister, Bangkok Metropolis 10100, Thailand; *Statistical Yearbook Thailand.*

Statistical Office of the United Nations, Publishing Service, New York, New York 10017 (800) 253-9646; *Statistical Yearbook.*

Times Books, 201 East 50th Street, New York, New York 10022 (212) 751-2600; *The Economist Book of Vital World Statistics.*

World Health Organization, Office of Publications, Avenue Appia, CH-1211 Geneva 27, Switzerland (Telephone Number in U.S. (518) 436-9686); *World Health Statistics Annual.*

THAILAND - DEFENSE EXPENDITURES

G.K. Hall and Company, 70 Lincoln Street, Boston, Massachusetts 02111 (617) 423-3990; *The World in Figures.*

International Monetary Fund, 700 Nineteenth Street, NW, Washington, D.C. 20431 (202) 623-7000; *Government Finance Statistics Yearbook.*

U.S. Arms Control and Disarmament Agency, 320 Twenty-first Street, NW, Washington, D.C. 20451 (202) 647-8677; *World Military Expenditures and Arms Transfers.*

THAILAND - DEMOGRAPHY

The Economist Intelligence Unit (Asia) Limited, 10th Floor, Luk Kwok Centre, 72 Gloucester Road, Wanchai, Hong Kong (Phone Number in U.S. (800) 938-4685); *Asian Market Atlas.*

The Economist Intelligence Unit, 111 West 57th Street, New York, New York 10019 (800) 938-4685; *The World Market Atlas.*

Facts on File, 460 Park Avenue South, New York, New York 10016 (800) 443-8323; *The New Book of World Rankings.*

G.K. Hall and Company, 70 Lincoln Street, Boston, Massachusetts 02111 (617) 423-3990; *The World in Figures.*

THAILAND - DEVELOPMENT ASSISTANCE

Asian Development Bank, P.O. Box 789, 1099 Manila, Philippines; *Key Indicators of Developing Asian and Pacific Countries.*

G.K. Hall and Company, 70 Lincoln Street, Boston, Massachusetts 02111 (617) 423-3990; *The World in Figures.*

Statistical Office of the United Nations, Publishing Service, New York, New York 10017 (800) 253-9646; *Statistical Yearbook.*

THAILAND - DIAMOND PRODUCTION - See THAILAND - MINING AND MINERAL PRODUCTS

THAILAND - DISCOUNT RATES

Statistical Office of the United Nations, Publishing Service, New York, New York 10017 (800) 253-9646; *Statistical Yearbook.*

THAILAND - DISEASES

G.K. Hall and Company, 70 Lincoln Street, Boston, Massachusetts 02111 (617) 423-3990; *The World in Figures.*

National Statistical Office, Office of the Prime Minister, Bangkok Metropolis 10100, Thailand; *Statistical Yearbook Thailand.*

World Health Organization, Office of Publications, Avenue Appia, CH-1211 Geneva 27, Switzerland (Telephone Number in U.S. (518) 436-9686); *World Health Statistics Annual.*

THAILAND - DIVORCE RATES

Facts on File, 460 Park Avenue South, New York, New York 10016 (800) 443-8323; *The New Book of World Rankings.*

National Statistical Office, Office of the Prime Minister, Bangkok Metropolis 10100, Thailand; *Statistical Yearbook Thailand.*

Statistical Office of the United Nations, Publishing Service, New York, New York 10017 (800) 253-9646; *Demographic Yearbook,* and *Statistical Yearbook.*

THAILAND - DOMESTIC PRODUCT

G.K. Hall and Company, 70 Lincoln Street, Boston, Massachusetts 02111 (617) 423-3990; *The World in Figures.*

THAILAND - ECONOMY

Asian Development Bank, P.O. Box 789, 1099 Manila, Philippines; *Key Indicators of Developing Asian and Pacific Countries.*

Euromonitor Publications Limited, 87-88 Turnmill Street, London EC1M 5QU, England; *International Marketing Data and Statistics,* and *Third World Economic Handbook.*

Facts on File, 460 Park Avenue South, New York, New York 10016 (800) 443-8323; *The New Book of World Rankings.*

THAILAND - EDUCATION

The Economist Intelligence Unit, 111 West 57th Street, New York, New York 10019 (800) 938-4685; *The World Market Atlas.*

The Economist Intelligence Unit (Asia) Limited, 10th Floor, Luk Kwok Centre, 72 Gloucester Road, Wanchai, Hong Kong (Phone Number in U.S. (800) 938-4685); *Asian Market Atlas.*

Facts on File, 460 Park Avenue South, New York, New York 10016 (800) 443-8323; *The New Book of World Rankings.*

G.K. Hall and Company, 70 Lincoln Street, Boston, Massachusetts 02111 (617) 423-3990; *The World in Figures.*

International Monetary Fund, 700 Nineteenth Street, NW, Washington, D.C. 20431 (202) 623-7000; *Government Finance Statistics Yearbook.*

National Statistical Office, Office of the Prime Minister, Bangkok Metropolis 10100, Thailand; *Statistical Yearbook Thailand.*

Times Books, 201 East 50th Street, New York, New York 10022 (212) 751-2600; *The Economist Book of Vital World Statistics.*

United Nations Educational, Scientific and Cultural Organization (UNESCO), 7 Place de Fontenoy, F-75700 Paris, France (Telephone Number in U.S. (212) 963-5981); *Statistical Yearbook.*

The World Bank, 1818 H Street, NW, Washington, D.C. 20433 (202) 477-1234; *World Tables.*

THAILAND - EGG PRODUCTION - See THAILAND - DAIRY PRODUCTS

THAILAND - ELECTRICITY

Asian Development Bank, P.O. Box 789, 1099 Manila, Philippines; *Key Indicators of Developing Asian and Pacific Countries*.

Facts on File, 460 Park Avenue South, New York, New York 10016 (800) 443-8323; *The New Book of World Rankings*.

National Statistical Office, Office of the Prime Minister, Bangkok Metropolis 10100, Thailand; *Statistical Yearbook Thailand*.

Penn Well Publishing Company, 1421 South Sheridan Road, P.O. Box 1260, Tulsa, Oklahoma 74101 (800) 752-9764; *International Energy Statistics Sourcebook*.

Statistical Office of the United Nations, Publishing Service, New York, New York 10017 (800) 253-9646; *Electric Power in Asia and the Pacific*, and *Statistical Yearbook*.

Times Books, 201 East 50th Street, New York, New York 10022 (212) 751-2600; *The Economist Book of Vital World Statistics*.

THAILAND - EMPLOYMENT

Euromonitor Publications Limited, 87-88 Turnmill Street, London EC1M 5QU, England; *International Marketing Data and Statistics*.

Facts on File, 460 Park Avenue South, New York, New York 10016 (800) 443-8323; *The New Book of World Rankings*.

International Labour Office, I.L.O. Publications, CH-1211, Geneva 22, Switzerland; *Yearbook of Labour Statistics*.

National Statistical Office, Office of the Prime Minister, Bangkok Metropolis 10100, Thailand; *Statistical Yearbook Thailand*.

Statistical Office of the United Nations, Publishing Service, New York, New York 10017 (800) 253-9646; *Statistical Yearbook*

THAILAND - ENERGY

Facts on File, 460 Park Avenue South, New York, New York 10016 (800) 443-8323; *The New Book of World Rankings*.

Food and Agricultural Organization of the United Nations (FAO) Via delle Terme di Caracalla, 00100 Rome, Italy (Telephone Number in U.S. (202) 653-2400); *The State of Food and Agriculture*.

G.K. Hall and Company, 70 Lincoln Street, Boston, Massachusetts 02111 (617) 423-3990; *The World in Figures*.

National Statistical Office, Office of the Prime Minister, Bangkok Metropolis 10100, Thailand; *Statistical Yearbook Thailand*.

Penn Well Publishing Company, 1421 South Sheridan Road, P.O. Box 1260, Tulsa, Oklahoma 74101 (800) 752-9764; *International Energy Statistics Sourcebook*.

Statistical Office of the United Nations, Publishing Service, New York, New York 10017 (800) 253-9646; *Energy Statistics Yearbook*, and *Statistical Yearbook for Asia and the Pacific*.

Times Books, 201 East 50th Street, New York, New York 10022 (212) 751-2600; *The Economist Book of Vital World Statistics*.

THAILAND - ENGINEERING AND METAL PRODUCTS - EXPORTS AND IMPORTS

Statistical Office of the United Nations, Publishing Service, New York, New York 10017 (800) 253-9646; *Trade in Manufactures of Developing Countries*.

THAILAND - EXCHANGE RATES

Asian Development Bank, P.O. Box 789, 1099 Manila, Philippines; *Key Indicators of Developing Asian and Pacific Countries*.

The Economist Intelligence Unit (Asia) Limited, 10th Floor, Luk Kwok Centre, 72 Gloucester Road, Wanchai, Hong Kong (Phone Number in U.S. (800) 938-4685); *Asian Market Atlas*.

Euromonitor Publications Limited, 87-88 Turnmill Street, London EC1M 5QU, England; *International Marketing Data and Statistics*.

International Civil Aviation Organization, 1000 Sherbrooke Street West, Suite 400, Montreal, Quebec, Canada H3A 2R2 (514) 285-8219; *Civil Aviation Statistics of the World*.

International Monetary Fund, 700 Nineteenth Street, NW, Washington, D.C. 20431 (202) 623-7000; *International Financial Statistics*.

Statistical Office of the United Nations, Publishing Service, New York, New York 10017 (800) 253-9646; *Statistical Yearbook*.

THAILAND - EXCISE TAXES - See THAILAND - TAXATION

THAILAND - EXPORTS

Asian Development Bank, P.O. Box 789, 1099 Manila, Philippines; *Key Indicators of Developing Asian and Pacific Countries*.

The Economist Intelligence Unit (Asia) Limited, 10th Floor, Luk Kwok Centre, 72 Gloucester Road, Wanchai, Hong Kong (Phone Number in U.S. (800) 938-4685); *Asian Market Atlas*.

The Economist Intelligence Unit, 111 West 57th Street, New York, New York 10019 (800) 938-4685; *The World Market Atlas*.

Euromonitor Publications Limited, 87-88 Turnmill Street, London EC1M 5QU, England; *International Marketing Data and Statistics*, and *Third World Economic Handbook*.

Food and Agricultural Organization of the United Nations (FAO) Via delle Terme di Caracalla, 00100 Rome, Italy (Telephone Number in U.S. (202) 653-2400); *The State of Food and Agriculture*.

G.K. Hall and Company, 70 Lincoln Street, Boston, Massachusetts 02111 (617) 423-3990; *The World in Figures*.

International Monetary Fund, 700 Nineteenth Street, NW, Washington, D.C. 20431 (202) 623-7000; *Direction of Trade Statistics, Government Finance Statistics Yearbook*, and *International Financial Statistics*.

International Rubber Study Group, York House, Eighth Floor, Empire Way, Wembley, London HA9 0PA, England; *Rubber Statistical Handbook*.

National Statistical Office, Office of the Prime Minister, Bangkok Metropolis 10100, Thailand; *Statistical Yearbook Thailand*.

Statistical Office of the United Nations, Publishing Service, New York, New York 10017 (800) 253-9646; *Foreign Trade Statistics of*

Asia and the Pacific, and *Trade in Manufactures of Developing Countries.*

Times Books, 201 East 50th Street, New York, New York 10022 (212) 751-2600; *The Economist Book of Vital World Statistics.*

The World Bank, 1818 H Street, NW, Washington, D.C. 20433 (202) 477-1234; *World Tables.*

THAILAND - EXTERNAL FINANCING

Asian Development Bank, P.O. Box 789, 1099 Manila, Philippines; *Key Indicators of Developing Asian and Pacific Countries.*

THAILAND - EXTERNAL INDEBTEDNESS

Asian Development Bank, P.O. Box 789, 1099 Manila, Philippines; *Key Indicators of Developing Asian and Pacific Countries.*

Euromonitor Publications Limited, 87-88 Turnmill Street, London EC1M 5QU, England; *Third World Economic Handbook.*

The World Bank, 1818 H Street, NW, Washington, D.C. 20433 (202) 477-1234; *World Tables.*

THAILAND - EXTERNAL TRADE

Asian Development Bank, P.O. Box 789, 1099 Manila, Philippines; *Key Indicators of Developing Asian and Pacific Countries.*

Food and Agricultural Organization of the United Nations (FAO) Via delle Terme di Caracalla, 00100 Rome, Italy (Telephone Number in U.S. (202) 653-2400); *The State of Food and Agriculture,* and *Trade Yearbook.*

G.K. Hall and Company, 70 Lincoln Street, Boston, Massachusetts 02111 (617) 423-3990; *The World in Figures.*

Statistical Office of the United Nations, Publishing Service, New York, New York 10017 (800) 253-9646; *Statistical Yearbook,* and *Statistical Yearbook for Asia and the Pacific.*

THAILAND - FABRIC PRODUCTION - See THAILAND - TEXTILE INDUSTRY

THAILAND - FARM CROPS - See THAILAND - CROPS

THAILAND - FEMALE WORKING POPULATION - See THAILAND - EMPLOYMENT

THAILAND - FERTILITY RATES

The Economist Intelligence Unit (Asia) Limited, 10th Floor, Luk Kwok Centre, 72 Gloucester Road, Wanchai, Hong Kong (Phone Number in U.S. (800) 938-4685); *Asian Market Atlas.*

Facts on File, 460 Park Avenue South, New York, New York 10016 (800) 443-8323; *The New Book of World Rankings.*

Times Books, 201 East 50th Street, New York, New York 10022 (212) 751-2600; *The Economist Book of Vital World Statistics.*

The World Bank, 1818 H Street, NW, Washington, D.C. 20433 (202) 477-1234; *World Tables.*

THAILAND - FERTILIZER

Food and Agricultural Organization of the United Nations (FAO), Via delle Terme di Caracalla, 00100, Rome, Italy (Telephone

Number in U.S. (202) 653-2400); *Fertilizer Yearbook,* and *The State of Food and Agriculture.*

Statistical Office of the United Nations, Publishing Service, New York, New York 10017 (800) 253-9646; *Statistical Yearbook.*

THAILAND - FETAL MORTALITY

National Statistical Office, Office of the Prime Minister, Bangkok Metropolis 10100, Thailand; *Statistical Yearbook Thailand.*

Statistical Office of the United Nations, Publishing Service, New York, New York 10017 (800) 253-9646; *Demographic Yearbook.*

World Health Organization, Office of Publications, Avenue Appia, CH-1211 Geneva 27, Switzerland (Telephone Number in U.S. (518) 436-9686); *World Health Statistics Annual.*

THAILAND - FIBRE PRODUCTION - See THAILAND - TEXTILE INDUSTRY

THAILAND - FILAMENT PRODUCTION - See THAILAND - TEXTILE INDUSTRY

THAILAND - FILM - See THAILAND - MOTION PICTURES

THAILAND - FINANCE

Asian Development Bank, P.O. Box 789, 1099 Manila, Philippines; *Key Indicators of Developing Asian and Pacific Countries.*

Facts on File, 460 Park Avenue South, New York, New York 10016 (800) 443-8323; *The New Book of World Rankings.*

G.K. Hall and Company, 70 Lincoln Street, Boston, Massachusetts 02111 (617) 423-3990; *The World in Figures.*

International Monetary Fund, 700 Nineteenth Street, NW, Washington, D.C. 20431 (202) 623-7000; *Government Finance Statistics Yearbook.*

National Statistical Office, Office of the Prime Minister, Bangkok Metropolis 10100, Thailand; *Statistical Yearbook Thailand.*

Statistical Office of the United Nations, Publishing Service, New York, New York 10017 (800) 253-9646; *Statistical Yearbook for Asia and the Pacific.*

THAILAND - FISHERIES

Facts on File, 460 Park Avenue South, New York, New York 10016 (800) 443-8323; *The New Book of World Rankings.*

Food and Agricultural Organization of the United Nations (FAO) Via delle Terme di Caracalla, 00100 Rome, Italy (Telephone Number in U.S. (202) 653-2400); *The State of Food and Agriculture,* and *Yearbook of Fishery Statistics.*

National Statistical Office, Office of the Prime Minister, Bangkok Metropolis 10100, Thailand; *Statistical Yearbook Thailand.*

Statistical Office of the United Nations, Publishing Service, New York, New York 10017 (800) 253-9646; *Statistical Yearbook.*

THAILAND - FLOUR PRODUCTION

Statistical Office of the United Nations, Publishing Service, New York, New York 10017 (800) 253-9646; *Statistical Yearbook.*

THAILAND - FOOD

Food and Agricultural Organization of the United Nations (FAO) Via delle Terme di Caracalla, 00100 Rome, Italy (Telephone Number in U.S. (202) 653-2400); *Production Yearbook*, and *The State of Food and Agriculture*.

G.K. Hall and Company, 70 Lincoln Street, Boston, Massachusetts 02111 (617) 423-3990; *The World in Figures*.

Statistical Office of the United Nations, Publishing Service, New York, New York 10017 (800) 253-9646; *Statistical Yearbook for Asia and the Pacific*, and *Trade in Manufactures of Developing Countries*.

THAILAND - FOREIGN AID

G.K. Hall and Company, 70 Lincoln Street, Boston, Massachusetts 02111 (617) 423-3990; *The World in Figures*.

THAILAND - FOREIGN DEBT

International Monetary Fund, 700 Nineteenth Street, NW, Washington, D.C. 20431 (202) 623-7000; *Government Finance Statistics Yearbook*.

THAILAND - FOREIGN TRADE

Asian Development Bank, P.O. Box 789, 1099 Manila, Philippines; *Key Indicators of Developing Asian and Pacific Countries*.

The Economist Intelligence Unit (Asia) Limited, 10th Floor, Luk Kwok Centre, 72 Gloucester Road, Wanchai, Hong Kong (Phone Number in U.S. (800) 938-4885), *Asian Market Atlas*.

Euromonitor Publications Limited, 87-88 Turnmill Street, London EC1M 5QU, England; *International Marketing Data and Statistics*, and *Third World Economic Handbook*.

Facts on File, 460 Park Avenue South, New York, New York 10016 (800) 443-8323; *The New Book of World Rankings*.

Food and Agricultural Organization of the United Nations (FAO) Via delle Terme di Caracalla, 00100 Rome, Italy (Telephone Number in U.S. (202) 653-2400); *The State of Food and Agriculture*.

G.K. Hall and Company, 70 Lincoln Street, Boston, Massachusetts 02111 (617) 423-3990; *The World in Figures*.

International Monetary Fund, 700 Nineteenth Street, NW, Washington, D.C. 20431 (202) 623-7000; *International Financial Statistics*.

National Statistical Office, Office of the Prime Minister, Bangkok Metropolis 10100, Thailand; *Statistical Yearbook Thailand*.

Statistical Office of the United Nations, Publishing Service, New York, New York 10017 (800) 253-9646; *International Trade Statistics Yearbook*, and *Statistical Yearbook*.

THAILAND - FORESTRY AND FOREST PRODUCTS

American Forest and Paper Association, 1250 Connecticut Avenue, NW, Washington, D.C. 20036 (202) 463-2455; *Wood Pulp and Fiber Statistics*.

The Economist Intelligence Unit (Asia) Limited, 10th Floor, Luk Kwok Centre, 72 Gloucester Road, Wanchai, Hong Kong (Phone Number in U.S. (800) 938-4685); *Asian Market Atlas*.

Euromonitor Publications Limited, 87-88 Turnmill Street, London EC1M 5QU, England; *Third World Economic Handbook*.

Facts on File, 460 Park Avenue South, New York, New York 10016 (800) 443-8323; *The New Book of World Rankings*.

Food and Agricultural Organization of the United Nations (FAO) Via delle Terme di Caracalla, 00100 Rome, Italy (Telephone Number in U.S. (202) 653-2400); *The State of Food and Agriculture*, and *Yearbook of Forest Products*.

G.K. Hall and Company, 70 Lincoln Street, Boston, Massachusetts 02111 (617) 423-3990; *The World in Figures*.

National Statistical Office, Office of the Prime Minister, Bangkok Metropolis 10100, Thailand; *Statistical Yearbook Thailand*.

Statistical Office of the United Nations, Publishing Service, New York, New York 10017 (800) 253-9646; *Statistical Yearbook*.

United Nations Educational, Scientific and Cultural Organization (UNESCO), 7 Place de Fontenoy, F-75700 Paris, France (Telephone Number in U.S. (212) 963-5981); *Statistical Yearbook*.

THAILAND - FURNITURE AND WOOD PRODUCTS - EXPORTS AND IMPORTS

Statistical Office of the United Nations, Publishing Service, New York, New York 10017 (800) 253-9646; *Trade in Manufactures of Developing Countries*.

THAILAND - GAS PRODUCTION - See THAILAND - MINING AND MINERAL PRODUCTS

THAILAND GENERAL MORTALITY

National Statistical Office, Office of the Prime Minister, Bangkok Metropolis 10100, Thailand; *Statistical Yearbook Thailand*.

Statistical Office of the United Nations, Publishing Service, New York, New York 10017 (800) 253-9646; *Demographic Yearbook*.

World Health Organization, Office of Publications, Avenue Appia, CH-1211 Geneva 27, Switzerland (Telephone Number in U.S. (518) 436-9686); *World Health Statistics Annual*.

THAILAND - GEOGRAPHIC DATA

Facts on File, 460 Park Avenue South, New York, New York 10016 (800) 443-8323; *The New Book of World Rankings*.

THAILAND - GOLD HOLDINGS

International Monetary Fund, 700 Nineteenth Street, NW, Washington, D.C. 20431 (202) 623-7000; *International Financial Statistics*.

Statistical Office of the United Nations, Publishing Service, New York, New York 10017 (800) 253-9646; *Statistical Yearbook*.

The World Bank, 1818 H Street, NW, Washington, D.C. 20433 (202) 477-1234; *World Tables*.

THAILAND - GOLD PRODUCTION AND CONSUMPTION - See THAILAND - MINING AND MINERAL PRODUCTS

THAILAND - GOVERNMENT

Asian Development Bank, P.O. Box 789, 1099 Manila, Philippines; *Key Indicators of Developing Asian and Pacific Countries.*

G.K. Hall and Company, 70 Lincoln Street, Boston, Massachusetts 02111 (617) 423-3990; *The World in Figures.*

National Statistical Office, Office of the Prime Minister, Bangkok Metropolis 10100, Thailand; *Statistical Yearbook Thailand.*

THAILAND - GOVERNMENT EXPENDITURES

Asian Development Bank, P.O. Box 789, 1099 Manila, Philippines; *Key Indicators of Developing Asian and Pacific Countries.*

Euromonitor Publications Limited, 87-88 Turnmill Street, London EC1M 5QU, England; *Third World Economic Handbook.*

International Monetary Fund, 700 Nineteenth Street, NW, Washington, D.C. 20431 (202) 623-7000; *Government Finance Statistics Yearbook.*

Times Books, 201 East 50th Street, New York, New York 10022 (212) 751-2600; *The Economist Book of Vital World Statistics.*

The World Bank, 1818 H Street, NW, Washington, D.C. 20433 (202) 477-1234; *World Tables.*

THAILAND - GOVERNMENT FINANCES

Asian Development Bank, P.O. Box 789, 1099 Manila, Philippines; *Key Indicators of Developing Asian and Pacific Countries.*

International Monetary Fund, 700 Nineteenth Street, NW, Washington, D.C. 20431 (202) 623-7000; *International Financial Statistics.*

Statistical Office of the United Nations, Publishing Service, New York, New York 10017 (800) 253-9646; *Statistical Yearbook.*

THAILAND - GOVERNMENT REVENUE

Asian Development Bank, P.O. Box 789, 1099 Manila, Philippines; *Key Indicators of Developing Asian and Pacific Countries.*

International Monetary Fund, 700 Nineteenth Street, NW, Washington, D.C. 20431 (202) 623-7000; *Government Finance Statistics Yearbook.*

Times Books, 201 East 50th Street, New York, New York 10022 (212) 751-2600; *The Economist Book of Vital World Statistics.*

The World Bank, 1818 H Street, NW, Washington, D.C. 20433 (202) 477-1234; *World Tables.*

THAILAND - GRAIN PRODUCTION - See THAILAND - CROPS

THAILAND - GRANTS

International Monetary Fund, 700 Nineteenth Street, NW, Washington, D.C. 20431 (202) 623-7000; *Government Finance Statistics Yearbook.*

THAILAND - GROSS DOMESTIC PRODUCT

Asian Development Bank, P.O. Box 789, 1099 Manila, Philippines; *Key Indicators of Developing Asian and Pacific Countries.*

The Economist Intelligence Unit, 111 West 57th Street, New York, New York 10019 (800) 938-4685; *The World Market Atlas.*

The Economist Intelligence Unit (Asia) Limited, 10th Floor, Luk Kwok Centre, 72 Gloucester Road, Wanchai, Hong Kong (Phone Number in U.S. (800) 938-4685); *Asian Market Atlas.*

Euromonitor Publications Limited, 87-88 Turnmill Street, London EC1M 5QU, England; *International Marketing Data and Statistics,* and *Third World Economic Handbook.*

Facts on File, 460 Park Avenue South, New York, New York 10016 (800) 443-8323; *The New Book of World Rankings.*

G.K. Hall and Company, 70 Lincoln Street, Boston, Massachusetts 02111 (617) 423-3990; *The World in Figures.*

National Statistical Office, Office of the Prime Minister, Bangkok Metropolis 10100, Thailand; *Statistical Yearbook Thailand.*

Statistical Office of the United Nations, Publishing Service, New York, New York 10017 (800) 253-9646; *Statistical Yearbook.*

Times Books, 201 East 50th Street, New York, New York 10022 (212) 751-2600; *The Economist Book of Vital World Statistics.*

The World Bank, 1818 H Street, NW, Washington, D.C. 20433 (202) 477-1234; *World Tables.*

THAILAND - GROSS INDUSTRIAL PRODUCT

Euromonitor Publications Limited, 87-88 Turnmill Street, London EC1M 5QU, England; *Third World Economic Handbook.*

THAILAND - GROSS NATIONAL PRODUCT

Asian Development Bank, P.O. Box 789, 1099 Manila, Philippines; *Key Indicators of Developing Asian and Pacific Countries.*

Euromonitor Publications Limited, 87-88 Turnmill Street, London EC1M 5QU, England; *International Marketing Data and Statistics,* and *Third World Economic Handbook.*

National Statistical Office, Office of the Prime Minister, Bangkok Metropolis 10100, Thailand; *Statistical Yearbook Thailand.*

U.S. Arms Control and Disarmament Agency, 320 Twenty-first Street, NW, Washington, D.C. 20451 (202) 647-8677; *World Military Expenditures and Arms Transfers.*

The World Bank, 1818 H Street, NW, Washington, D.C. 20433 (202) 477-1234; *World Tables.*

THAILAND - GROUNDNUTS PRODUCTION - See THAILAND - CROPS

THAILAND - HEALTH

The Economist Intelligence Unit (Asia) Limited, 10th Floor, Luk Kwok Centre, 72 Gloucester Road, Wanchai, Hong Kong (Phone Number in U.S. (800) 938-4685); *Asian Market Atlas.*

Facts on File, 460 Park Avenue South, New York, New York 10016 (800) 443-8323; *The New Book of World Rankings.*

G.K. Hall and Company, 70 Lincoln Street, Boston, Massachusetts 02111 (617) 423-3990; *The World in Figures.*

National Statistical Office, Office of the Prime Minister, Bangkok Metropolis 10100, Thailand; *Statistical Yearbook Thailand.*

Statistical Office of the United Nations, Publishing Service, New York, New York 10017 (800) 253-9646; *Statistical Yearbook.*

Times Books, 201 East 50th Street, New York, New York 10022 (212) 751-2600; *The Economist Book of Vital World Statistics.*

World Health Organization, Office of Publications, Avenue Appia, CH-1211 Geneva 27, Switzerland (Telephone Number in U.S. (518) 436-9686); *World Health Statistics Annual.*

THAILAND - HEALTH EXPENDITURES

International Monetary Fund, 700 Nineteenth Street, NW, Washington, D.C. 20431 (202) 623-7000; *Government Finance Statistics Yearbook.*

THAILAND - HIGHWAYS

The Economist Intelligence Unit (Asia) Limited, 10th Floor, Luk Kwok Centre, 72 Gloucester Road, Wanchai, Hong Kong (Phone Number in U.S. (800) 938-4685); *Asian Market Atlas.*

G.K. Hall and Company, 70 Lincoln Street, Boston, Massachusetts 02111 (617) 423-3990; *The World in Figures.*

International Road Federation, 525 School Street, SW, Washington, D.C. 20024 (202) 554-2106; *World Road Statistics.*

THAILAND - HORSES - See THAILAND - LIVESTOCK AND POULTRY

THAILAND - HOURS OF WORK - See THAILAND - EMPLOYMENT

THAILAND - HOUSING AND HOUSING UNITS

Euromonitor Publications Limited, 87-88 Turnmill Street, London EC1M 5QU, England; *Third World Economic Handbook.*

Facts on File, 460 Park Avenue South, New York, New York 10016 (800) 443-8323; *The New Book of World Rankings.*

THAILAND - HOUSING EXPENDITURES

International Monetary Fund, 700 Nineteenth Street, NW, Washington, D.C. 20431 (202) 623-7000; *Government Finance Statistics Yearbook.*

THAILAND - HYDROCHLORIC ACID PRODUCTION

Statistical Office of the United Nations, Publishing Service, New York, New York 10017 (800) 253-9646; *Statistical Yearbook.*

THAILAND - ILLITERATE POPULATION

The Economist Intelligence Unit, 111 West 57th Street, New York, New York 10019 (800) 938-4685; *The World Market Atlas.*

G.K. Hall and Company, 70 Lincoln Street, Boston, Massachusetts 02111 (617) 423-3990; *The World in Figures.*

United Nations Educational, Scientific and Cultural Organization (UNESCO), 7 Place de Fontenoy, F-75700 Paris, France (Telephone Number in U.S. (212) 963-5981); *Statistical Yearbook.*

THAILAND - IMPORTS

Asian Development Bank, P.O. Box 789, 1099 Manila, Philippines; *Key Indicators of Developing Asian and Pacific Countries.*

The Economist Intelligence Unit, 111 West 57th Street, New York, New York 10019 (800) 938-4685; *The World Market Atlas.*

The Economist Intelligence Unit (Asia) Limited, 10th Floor, Luk Kwok Centre, 72 Gloucester Road, Wanchai, Hong Kong (Phone Number in U.S. (800) 938-4685); *Asian Market Atlas.*

Euromonitor Publications Limited, 87-88 Turnmill Street, London EC1M 5QU, England; *International Marketing Data and Statistics,* and *Third World Economic Handbook.*

Food and Agricultural Organization of the United Nations (FAO) Via delle Terme di Caracalla, 00100 Rome, Italy (Telephone Number in U.S. (202) 653-2400); *The State of Food and Agriculture.*

G.K. Hall and Company, 70 Lincoln Street, Boston, Massachusetts 02111 (617) 423-3990; *The World in Figures.*

International Monetary Fund, 700 Nineteenth Street, NW, Washington, D.C. 20431 (202) 623-7000; *Direction of Trade Statistics, Government Finance Statistics Yearbook,* and *International Financial Statistics.*

International Rubber Study Group, York House, Eighth Floor, Empire Way, Wembley, London HA9 0PA, England; *Rubber Statistical Handbook.*

National Statistical Office, Office of the Prime Minister, Bangkok Metropolis 10100, Thailand; *Statistical Yearbook Thailand.*

Statistical Office of the United Nations, Publishing Service, New York, New York 10017 (800) 253-9646; *Foreign Trade Statistics of Asia and the Pacific.*

Times Books, 201 East 50th Street, New York, New York 10022 (212) 751-2600; *The Economist Book of Vital World Statistics.*

The World Bank, 1818 H Street, NW, Washington, D.C. 20433 (202) 477-1234; *World Tables.*

THAILAND - INCOME TAXES - See THAILAND - TAXATION

THAILAND - INDUSTRIAL METALS PRODUCTION - See THAILAND - MINING AND MINERAL PRODUCTS

THAILAND - INDUSTRY

Euromonitor Publications Limited, 87-88 Turnmill Street, London EC1M 5QU, England; *Third World Economic Handbook.*

Facts on File, 460 Park Avenue South, New York, New York 10016 (800) 443-8323; *The New Book of World Rankings.*

G.K. Hall and Company, 70 Lincoln Street, Boston, Massachusetts 02111 (617) 423-3990; *The World in Figures.*

International Labour Office, I.L.O. Publications, CH-1211, Geneva 22, Switzerland; *Yearbook of Labour Statistics.*

National Statistical Office, Office of the Prime Minister, Bangkok Metropolis 10100, Thailand; *Statistical Yearbook Thailand.*

Statistical Office of the United Nations, Publishing Service, New York, New York 10017 (800) 253-9646; *Statistical Yearbook for Asia and the Pacific.*

Times Books, 201 East 50th Street, New York, New York 10022 (212) 751-2600; *The Economist Book of Vital World Statistics.*

The World Bank, 1818 H Street, NW, Washington, D.C. 20433 (202) 477-1234; *World Tables*.

World Intellectual Property Organization, 34 Chemin des Colombettes, CH-1211 Geneva 20. Switzerland; *Industrial Property Statistics*.

THAILAND - INFANT AND MATERNAL MORTALITY

The Economist Intelligence Unit (Asia) Limited, 10th Floor, Luk Kwok Centre, 72 Gloucester Road, Wanchai, Hong Kong (Phone Number in U.S. (800) 938-4685); *Asian Market Atlas*.

National Statistical Office, Office of the Prime Minister, Bangkok Metropolis 10100, Thailand; *Statistical Yearbook Thailand*.

Statistical Office of the United Nations, Publishing Service, New York, New York 10017 (800) 253-9646; *Demographic Yearbook*, and *Statistical Yearbook*.

Times Books, 201 East 50th Street, New York, New York 10022 (212) 751-2600; *The Economist Book of Vital World Statistics*.

The World Bank, 1818 H Street, NW, Washington, D.C. 20433 (202) 477-1234; *World Tables*.

World Health Organization, Office of Publications, Avenue Appia, CH-1211 Geneva 27, Switzerland (Telephone Number in U.S. (518) 436-9686); *World Health Statistics Annual*.

THAILAND - INTERNAL TRADE

Statistical Office of the United Nations, Publishing Service, New York, New York 10017 (800) 253-9646; *Statistical Yearbook for Asia and the Pacific*.

THAILAND - INTERNATIONAL LIQUIDITY

International Monetary Fund, 700 Nineteenth Street, NW, Washington, D.C. 20431 (202) 623-7000; *International Financial Statistics*.

THAILAND - INTERNATIONAL RESERVES EXCLUDING GOLD

Asian Development Bank, P.O. Box 789, 1099 Manila, Philippines; *Key Indicators of Developing Asian and Pacific Countries*.

Statistical Office of the United Nations, Publishing Service, New York, New York 10017 (800) 253-9646; *Statistical Yearbook*.

The World Bank, 1818 H Street, NW, Washington, D.C. 20433 (202) 477-1234; *World Tables*.

THAILAND - INTERNATIONAL STATISTICS

Asian Development Bank, P.O. Box 789, 1099 Manila, Philippines; *Key Indicators of Developing Asian and Pacific Countries*.

THAILAND - INVESTMENTS

International Monetary Fund, 700 Nineteenth Street, NW, Washington, D.C. 20431 (202) 623-7000; *International Financial Statistics*.

THAILAND - IRON ORE PRODUCTION AND CONSUMPTION - See THAILAND - MINING AND MINERAL PRODUCTS

THAILAND - IRRIGATION

Euromonitor Publications Limited, 87-88 Turnmill Street, London EC1M 5QU, England; *International Marketing Data and Statistics*.

THAILAND - LABOR FORCE

The Economist Intelligence Unit (Asia) Limited, 10th Floor, Luk Kwok Centre, 72 Gloucester Road, Wanchai, Hong Kong (Phone Number in U.S. (800) 938-4685); *Asian Market Atlas*.

Euromonitor Publications Limited, 87-88 Turnmill Street, London EC1M 5QU, England; *International Marketing Data and Statistics*.

Facts on File, 460 Park Avenue South, New York, New York 10016 (800) 443-8323; *The New Book of World Rankings*.

Food and Agricultural Organization of the United Nations (FAO) Via delle Terme di Caracalla, 00100 Rome, Italy (Telephone Number in U.S. (202) 653-2400); *The State of Food and Agriculture*.

G.K. Hall and Company, 70 Lincoln Street, Boston, Massachusetts 02111 (617) 423-3990; *The World in Figures*.

National Statistical Office, Office of the Prime Minister, Bangkok Metropolis 10100, Thailand; *Statistical Yearbook Thailand*.

Times Books, 201 East 50th Street, New York, New York 10022 (212) 751-2600; *The Economist Book of Vital World Statistics*.

The World Bank, 1818 H Street, NW, Washington, D.C. 20433 (202) 477-1234; *World Tables*.

THAILAND - LABOR PRODUCTIVITY

International Labour Office, I.L.O. Publications, CH-1211, Geneva 22, Switzerland; *Yearbook of Labour Statistics*.

THAILAND - LAND USE

Euromonitor Publications Limited, 87-88 Turnmill Street, London EC1M 5QU, England; *International Marketing Data and Statistics*.

Food and Agricultural Organization of the United Nations (FAO), Via delle Terme di Caracalla, 00100 Rome, Italy (Telephone Number in U.S. (202) 653-2400); *Production Yearbook*.

G.K. Hall and Company, 70 Lincoln Street, Boston, Massachusetts 02111 (617) 423-3990; *The World in Figures*.

THAILAND - LEAD ORE PRODUCTION AND CONSUMPTION - See THAILAND - MINING AND MINERAL PRODUCTS

THAILAND - LIBRARIES

Facts on File, 460 Park Avenue South, New York, New York 10016 (800) 443-8323; *The New Book of World Rankings*.

United Nations Educational, Scientific and Cultural Organization (UNESCO), 7 Place de Fontenoy, F-75700 Paris, France (Telephone Number in U.S. (212) 963-5981); *Statistical Yearbook*.

THAILAND - LIFE EXPECTANCY

The Economist Intelligence Unit (Asia) Limited, 10th Floor, Luk Kwok Centre, 72 Gloucester Road, Wanchai, Hong Kong (Phone Number in U.S. (800) 938-4685); *Asian Market Atlas*.

THAILAND - LIGNITE PRODUCTION - See THAILAND - MINING AND MINERAL PRODUCTS

THAILAND - LIVESTOCK AND POULTRY

Euromonitor Publications Limited, 87-88 Turnmill Street, London EC1M 5QU, England; *International Marketing Data and Statistics.*

Facts on File, 460 Park Avenue South, New York, New York 10016 (800) 443-8323; *The New Book of World Rankings.*

Food and Agricultural Organization of the United Nations (FAO), Via delle Terme di Caracalla, 00100 Rome, Italy (Telephone Number in U.S. (202) 653-2400); *Production Yearbook,* and *The State of Food and Agriculture.*

G.K. Hall and Company, 70 Lincoln Street, Boston, Massachusetts 02111 (617) 423-3990; *The World in Figures.*

National Statistical Office, Office of the Prime Minister, Bangkok Metropolis 10100, Thailand; *Statistical Yearbook Thailand.*

Statistical Office of the United Nations, Publishing Service, New York, New York 10017 (800) 253-9646; *Statistical Yearbook.*

THAILAND - LIVING LEVELS

G.K. Hall and Company, 70 Lincoln Street, Boston, Massachusetts 02111 (617) 423-3990; *The World in Figures.*

Times Books, 201 East 50th Street, New York, New York 10022 (212) 751-2600; *The Economist Book of Vital World Statistics.*

THAILAND - MAIL - NUMBER OF PIECES SENT OR RECEIVED

Statistical Office of the United Nations, Publishing Service, New York, New York 10017 (800) 253-0646; *Statistical Yearbook.*

THAILAND - MANGANESE ORE PRODUCTION AND CONSUMPTION - See THAILAND - MINING AND MINERAL PRODUCTS

THAILAND - MANPOWER

Statistical Office of the United Nations, Publishing Service, New York, New York 10017 (800) 253-9646; *Statistical Yearbook for Asia and the Pacific.*

THAILAND - MANUFACTURING

Asian Development Bank, P.O. Box 789, 1099 Manila, Philippines; *Key Indicators of Developing Asian and Pacific Countries.*

Euromonitor Publications Limited, 87-88 Turnmill Street, London EC1M 5QU, England; *Third World Economic Handbook.*

Facts on File, 460 Park Avenue South, New York, New York 10016 (800) 443-8323; *The New Book of World Rankings.*

G.K. Hall and Company, 70 Lincoln Street, Boston, Massachusetts 02111 (617) 423-3990; *The World in Figures.*

National Statistical Office, Office of the Prime Minister, Bangkok Metropolis 10100, Thailand; *Statistical Yearbook Thailand.*

Statistical Office of the United Nations, Publishing Service, New York, New York 10017 (800) 253-9646; *Statistical Yearbook.*

Times Books, 201 East 50th Street, New York, New York 10022 (212) 751-2600; *The Economist Book of Vital World Statistics.*

The World Bank, 1818 H Street, NW, Washington, D.C. 20433 (202) 477-1234; *World Tables.*

THAILAND - MARRIAGE RATES

Facts on File, 460 Park Avenue South, New York, New York 10016 (800) 443-8323; *The New Book of World Rankings.*

National Statistical Office, Office of the Prime Minister, Bangkok Metropolis 10100, Thailand; *Statistical Yearbook Thailand.*

Statistical Office of the United Nations, Publishing Service, New York, New York 10017 (800) 253-9646; *Demographic Yearbook,* and *Statistical Yearbook.*

THAILAND - MEAT PRODUCTION - See THAILAND - LIVESTOCK AND POULTRY

THAILAND - MERCHANT SHIPPING

G.K. Hall and Company, 70 Lincoln Street, Boston, Massachusetts 02111 (617) 423-3990; *The World in Figures.*

Lloyd's Register of Shipping, 17 Battery Place, New York, New York 10004 (212) 425-8050; *Register of Ships.*

Statistical Office of the United Nations, Publishing Service, New York, New York 10017 (800) 253-9646; *Statistical Yearbook.*

Times Books, 201 East 50th Street, New York, New York 10022 (212) 751-2600; *The Economist Book of Vital World Statistics.*

U.S. Department of Transportation, Maritime Administration, 400 Seventh Street, SW, Washington, D.C. 20590 (202) 366-5807; *A Statistical Analysis of the World's Merchant Fleets.*

THAILAND - MILITARY

The Economist Intelligence Unit (Asia) Limited, 10th Floor, Luk Kwok Centre, 72 Gloucester Road, Wanchai, Hong Kong (Phone Number in U.S. (800) 938-4685); *Asian Market Atlas.*

G.K. Hall and Company, 70 Lincoln Street, Boston, Massachusetts 02111 (617) 423-3990; *The World in Figures.*

The International Institute for Strategic Studies, 23 Tavistock Street, London WC2E 7NQ, England; *The Military Balance.*

U.S. Arms Control and Disarmament Agency, 320 Twenty-first Street, NW, Washington, D.C. 20451 (202) 647-8677; *World Military Expenditures and Arms Transfers.*

THAILAND - MILK - See THAILAND - DAIRY PRODUCTS

THAILAND - MINING AND MINERAL PRODUCTS

Asian Development Bank, P.O. Box 789, 1099 Manila, Philippines; *Key Indicators of Developing Asian and Pacific Countries.*

Euromonitor Publications Limited, 87-88 Turnmill Street, London EC1M 5QU, England; *Third World Economic Handbook.*

Facts on File, 460 Park Avenue South, New York, New York 10016 (800) 443-8323; *The New Book of World Rankings.*

G.K. Hall and Company, 70 Lincoln Street, Boston, Massachusetts 02111 (617) 423-3990; *The World in Figures.*

International Monetary Fund, 700 Nineteenth Street, NW, Washington, D.C. 20431 (202) 623-7000; *International Financial Statistics.*

National Statistical Office, Office of the Prime Minister, Bangkok Metropolis 10100, Thailand; *Statistical Yearbook Thailand.*

Penn Well Publishing Company, 1421 South Sheridan Road, P.O. Box 1260, Tulsa, Oklahoma 74101 (800) 752-9764; *International Energy Statistics Sourcebook.*

Statistical Office of the United Nations, Publishing Service, New York, New York 10017 (800) 253-9646; *Statistical Yearbook.*

THAILAND - MONEY EXCHANGE RATE

Euromonitor Publications Limited, 87-88 Turnmill Street, London EC1M 5QU, England; *International Marketing Data and Statistics.*

International Monetary Fund, 700 Nineteenth Street, NW, Washington, D.C. 20431 (202) 623-7000; *International Financial Statistics.*

National Statistical Office, Office of the Prime Minister, Bangkok Metropolis 10100, Thailand; *Statistical Yearbook Thailand.*

Statistical Office of the United Nations, Publishing Service, New York, New York 10017 (800) 253-9646; *Statistical Yearbook.*

THAILAND - MONEY RESERVES

Euromonitor Publications Limited, 87-88 Turnmill Street, London EC1M 5QU, England; *International Marketing Data and Statistics.*

THAILAND - MONEY SUPPLY

Asian Development Bank, P.O. Box 789, 1099 Manila, Philippines; *Key Indicators of Developing Asian and Pacific Countries.*

Euromonitor Publications Limited, 87-88 Turnmill Street, London EC1M 5QU, England; *International Marketing Data and Statistics.*

G.K. Hall and Company, 70 Lincoln Street, Boston, Massachusetts 02111 (617) 423-3990; *The World in Figures.*

International Monetary Fund, 700 Nineteenth Street, NW, Washington, D.C. 20431 (202) 623-7000; *International Financial Statistics.*

Statistical Office of the United Nations, Publishing Service, New York, New York 10017 (800) 253-9646; *Statistical Yearbook.*

The World Bank, 1818 H Street, NW, Washington, D.C. 20433 (202) 477-1234; *World Tables.*

THAILAND - MONUMENTS AND HISTORICAL SITES

United Nations Educational, Scientific and Cultural Organization (UNESCO), 7 Place de Fontenoy, F-75700 Paris, France (Telephone Number in U.S. (212) 963-5981); *Statistical Yearbook.*

THAILAND - MOTION PICTURES

Statistical Office of the United Nations, Publishing Service, New York, New York 10017 (800) 253-9646; *Statistical Yearbook.*

United Nations Educational, Scientific and Cultural Organization (UNESCO), 7 Place de Fontenoy, F-75700 Paris, France (Telephone Number in U.S. (212) 963-5981); *Statistical Yearbook.*

THAILAND - MOTOR VEHICLE PRODUCTION

Statistical Office of the United Nations, Publishing Service, New York, New York 10017 (800) 253-9646; *Statistical Yearbook.*

THAILAND - MOTOR VEHICLE TAXES - See THAILAND - TAXATION

THAILAND - MOTOR VEHICLES IN USE

G.K. Hall and Company, 70 Lincoln Street, Boston, Massachusetts 02111 (617) 423-3990; *The World in Figures.*

International Road Federation, 525 School Street, SW, Washington, D.C. 20024 (202) 554-2106; *World Road Statistics.*

National Statistical Office, Office of the Prime Minister, Bangkok Metropolis 10100, Thailand; *Statistical Yearbook Thailand.*

Statistical Office of the United Nations, Publishing Service, New York, New York 10017 (800) 253-9646; *Statistical Yearbook.*

Times Books, 201 East 50th Street, New York, New York 10022 (212) 751-2600; *The Economist Book of Vital World Statistics.*

THAILAND - MUSEUMS

Facts on File, 460 Park Avenue South, New York, New York 10016 (800) 443-8323; *The New Book of World Rankings.*

United Nations Educational, Scientific and Cultural Organization (UNESCO), 7 Place de Fontenoy, F-75700 Paris, France (Telephone Number in U.S. (212) 963-5981); *Statistical Yearbook.*

THAILAND - NATALITY - See THAILAND - BIRTH RATE

THAILAND - NATIONAL ACCOUNTS

Statistical Office of the United Nations, Publishing Service, New York, New York 10017 (800) 253-9646; *National Accounts Statistics, Statistical Yearbook,* and *Statistical Yearbook for Asia and the Pacific.*

THAILAND - NATIONAL INCOME

Facts on File, 460 Park Avenue South, New York, New York 10016 (800) 443-8323; *The New Book of World Rankings.*

G.K. Hall and Company, 70 Lincoln Street, Boston, Massachusetts 02111 (617) 423-3990; *The World in Figures.*

Statistical Office of the United Nations, Publishing Service, New York, New York 10017 (800) 253-9646; *Statistical Yearbook.*

THAILAND - NATIONAL PRODUCT

Facts on File, 460 Park Avenue South, New York, New York 10016 (800) 443-8323; *The New Book of World Rankings.*

Statistical Office of the United Nations, Publishing Service, New York, New York 10017 (800) 253-9646; *Statistical Yearbook.*

THAILAND - NATURAL GAS PRODUCTION - See THAILAND - MINING AND MINERAL PRODUCTS

THAILAND - NATURAL RUBBER PRODUCTION

International Rubber Study Group, York House, Eighth Floor, Empire Way, Wembley, London HA9 0PA, England; *Rubber Statistical Handbook.*

National Statistical Office, Office of the Prime Minister, Bangkok Metropolis 10100, Thailand; *Statistical Yearbook Thailand.*

Statistical Office of the United Nations, Publishing Service, New York, New York 10017 (800) 253-9646; *Statistical Yearbook.*

THAILAND - NEWSPAPER PRODUCTION - See THAILAND - FORESTRY AND FOREST PRODUCTS

THAILAND - NEWSPRINT - See THAILAND - CROPS

THAILAND - OCCUPATIONS - See THAILAND - LABOR FORCE

THAILAND - PALM KERNELS AND PALM OIL - See THAILAND - CROPS

THAILAND - PAPER - See THAILAND - FORESTRY AND FOREST PRODUCTS

THAILAND - PATENTS

World Intellectual Property Organization, 34 Chemin des Colombettes, CH-1211 Geneva 20, Switzerland; *Industrial Property Statistics.*

THAILAND - PEANUT PRODUCTION - See THAILAND - CROPS

THAILAND - PERIODICALS

United Nations Educational, Scientific and Cultural Organization (UNESCO), 7 Place de Fontenoy, F-75700 Paris, France (Telephone Number in U.S. (212) 963-5981); *Statistical Yearbook.*

THAILAND - PESTICIDE USE

Food and Agricultural Organization of the United Nations (FAO) Via delle Terme di Caracalla, 00100 Rome, Italy (Telephone Number in U.S. (202) 653-2400); *The State of Food and Agriculture.*

THAILAND - PETROLEUM INDUSTRY

Asian Development Bank, P.O. Box 789, 1099 Manila, Philippines; *Key Indicators of Developing Asian and Pacific Countries.*

Facts on File, 460 Park Avenue South, New York, New York 10016 (800) 443-8323; *The New Book of World Rankings.*

Food and Agricultural Organization of the United Nations (FAO) Via delle Terme di Caracalla, 00100 Rome, Italy (Telephone Number in U.S. (202) 653-2400); *The State of Food and Agriculture.*

G.K. Hall and Company, 70 Lincoln Street, Boston, Massachusetts 02111 (617) 423-3990; *The World in Figures.*

Penn Well Publishing Company, 1421 South Sheridan Road, P.O. Box 1260, Tulsa, Oklahoma 74101 (800) 752-9764; *International Energy Statistics Sourcebook.*

Statistical Office of the United Nations, Publishing Service, New York, New York 10017 (800) 253-9646; *Statistical Yearbook.*

THAILAND - PHOSPHATE ROCK PRODUCTION - See THAILAND - MINING AND MINERAL PRODUCTS

THAILAND - PIG-IRON AND FERRO-ALLOY PRODUCTION - See THAILAND - MINING AND MINERAL PRODUCTS

THAILAND - PIGS - See THAILAND - LIVESTOCK AND POULTRY

THAILAND - PLASTIC AND RESIN PRODUCTION

Euromonitor Publications Limited, 87-88 Turnmill Street, London EC1M 5QU, England; *Third World Economic Handbook.*

THAILAND - POPULATION

Asian Development Bank, P.O. Box 789, 1099 Manila, Philippines; *Key Indicators of Developing Asian and Pacific Countries.*

The Economist Intelligence Unit, 111 West 57th Street, New York, New York 10019 (800) 938-4685; *The World Market Atlas.*

The Economist Intelligence Unit (Asia) Limited, 10th Floor, Luk Kwok Centre, 72 Gloucester Road, Wanchai, Hong Kong (Phone Number in U.S. (800) 938-4685); *Asian Market Atlas.*

Euromonitor Publications Limited, 87-88 Turnmill Street, London EC1M 5QU, England; *International Marketing Data and Statistics,* and *Third World Economic Handbook.*

Facts on File, 460 Park Avenue South, New York, New York 10016 (800) 443-8323; *The New Book of World Rankings.*

Food and Agricultural Organization of the United Nations (FAO), Via delle Terme di Caracalla, 00100 Rome, Italy (Telephone Number in U.S. (202) 653-2400); *Production Yearbook.*

G.K. Hall and Company, 70 Lincoln Street, Boston, Massachusetts 02111 (617) 423-3990; *The World in Figures.*

International Labour Office, I.L.O. Publications, CH-1211, Geneva 22, Switzerland; *Yearbook of Labour Statistics.*

National Statistical Office, Office of the Prime Minister, Bangkok Metropolis 10100, Thailand; *Statistical Yearbook Thailand.*

Statistical Office of the United Nations, Publishing Service, New York, New York 10017 (800) 253-9646; *Demographic Yearbook, Statistical Yearbook,* and *Statistical Yearbook for Asia and the Pacific.*

Times Books, 201 East 50th Street, New York, New York 10022 (212) 751-2600; *The Economist Book of Vital World Statistics.*

United Nations Educational, Scientific and Cultural Organization (UNESCO), 7 Place de Fontenoy, F-75700 Paris, France (Telephone Number in U.S. (212) 963-5981); *Statistical Yearbook.*

U.S. Arms Control and Disarmament Agency, 320 Twenty-first Street, NW, Washington, D.C. 20451 (202) 647-8677; *World Military Expenditures and Arms Transfers.*

World Health Organization, Office of Publications, Avenue Appia, CH-1211 Geneva 27, Switzerland (Telephone Number in U.S. (518) 436-9686); *World Health Statistics Annual.*

THAILAND - POST OFFICES

Facts on File, 460 Park Avenue South, New York, New York 10016 (800) 443-8323; *The New Book of World Rankings.*

THAILAND - POTATO PRODUCTION - See THAILAND - CROPS

THAILAND - POWER PRODUCTION INDUSTRY

Statistical Office of the United Nations, Publishing Service, New York, New York 10017 (800) 253-9646; *Electric Power in Asia and the Pacific.*

THAILAND - PRICES

Asian Development Bank, P.O. Box 789, 1099 Manila, Philippines; *Key Indicators of Developing Asian and Pacific Countries.*

Facts on File, 460 Park Avenue South, New York, New York 10016 (800) 443-8323; *The New Book of World Rankings.*

Food and Agricultural Organization of the United Nations (FAO), Via delle Terme di Caracalla, 00100 Rome, Italy (Telephone Number in U.S. (202) 653-2400); *Production Yearbook,* and *The State of Food and Agriculture.*

G.K. Hall and Company, 70 Lincoln Street, Boston, Massachusetts 02111 (617) 423-3990; *The World in Figures.*

International Labour Office, I.L.O. Publications, CH-1211, Geneva 22, Switzerland; *Yearbook of Labour Statistics.*

International Monetary Fund, 700 Nineteenth Street, NW, Washington, D.C. 20431 (202) 623-7000; *International Financial Statistics.*

International Rubber Study Group, York House, Eighth Floor, Empire Way, Wembley, London HA9 0PA, England; *Rubber Statistical Handbook.*

National Statistical Office, Office of the Prime Minister, Bangkok Metropolis 10100, Thailand; *Statistical Yearbook Thailand.*

THAILAND - PRINTING AND WRITING PAPER - See THAILAND - FORESTRY AND FOREST PRODUCTS

THAILAND - PRODUCTION

Euromonitor Publications Limited, 87-88 Turnmill Street, London EC1M 5QU, England; *Third World Economic Handbook.*

Facts on File, 460 Park Avenue South, New York, New York 10016 (800) 443-8323; *The New Book of World Rankings.*

G.K. Hall and Company, 70 Lincoln Street, Boston, Massachusetts 02111 (617) 423-3990; *The World in Figures.*

International Rubber Study Group, York House, Eighth Floor, Empire Way, Wembley, London HA9 0PA, England; *Rubber Statistical Handbook.*

National Statistical Office, Office of the Prime Minister, Bangkok Metropolis 10100, Thailand; *Statistical Yearbook Thailand.*

THAILAND - PRODUCTIVITY

Euromonitor Publications Limited, 87-88 Turnmill Street, London EC1M 5QU, England; *International Marketing Data and Statistics.*

THAILAND - PROPERTY TAXES - See THAILAND - TAXATION

THAILAND - PUBLIC FINANCE

Facts on File, 460 Park Avenue South, New York, New York 10016 (800) 443-8323; *The New Book of World Rankings.*

THAILAND - RADIO

The Economist Intelligence Unit (Asia) Limited, 10th Floor, Luk Kwok Centre, 72 Gloucester Road, Wanchai, Hong Kong (Phone Number in U.S. (800) 938-4685); *Asian Market Atlas.*

THAILAND - RADIO BROADCASTING - See THAILAND - BROADCASTING

THAILAND - RAILWAYS

G.K. Hall and Company, 70 Lincoln Street, Boston, Massachusetts 02111 (617) 423-3990; *The World in Figures.*

Jane's Information Group, Sentinel House, 163 Brighton Road, Coulsdon, Surrey CR5 2NH, England (Telephone Number in U.S. (703) 683-3700); *Jane's World Railways.*

National Statistical Office, Office of the Prime Minister, Bangkok Metropolis 10100, Thailand; *Statistical Yearbook Thailand.*

Statistical Office of the United Nations, Publishing Service, New York, New York 10017 (800) 253-9646; *Statistical Yearbook.*

THAILAND - RELIGION

Facts on File, 460 Park Avenue South, New York, New York 10016 (800) 443-8323; *The New Book of World Rankings.*

THAILAND - RENT PRICES

International Labour Office, I.L.O. Publications, CH-1211, Geneva 22, Switzerland; *Yearbook of Labour Statistics.*

THAILAND - RETAIL TRADE

Euromonitor Publications Limited, 87-88 Turnmill Street, London EC1M 5QU, England; *Third World Economic Handbook.*

G.K. Hall and Company, 70 Lincoln Street, Boston, Massachusetts 02111 (617) 423-3990; *The World in Figures.*

THAILAND - RICE - See THAILAND - CROPS

THAILAND - ROUNDWOOD PRODUCTION - See THAILAND - FORESTRY AND FOREST PRODUCTS

THAILAND - RUBBER EXPORTS

International Monetary Fund, 700 Nineteenth Street, NW, Washington, D.C. 20431 (202) 623-7000; *International Financial Statistics.*

THAILAND - RUBBER PRODUCTION AND CONSUMPTION

Commodity Research Bureau, Incorporated, 75 Wall Street, New York, New York 10005 (212) 504-7754; *Commodity Year Book.*

Euromonitor Publications Limited, 87-88 Turnmill Street, London EC1M 5QU, England; *Third World Economic Handbook.*

Facts on File, 460 Park Avenue South, New York, New York 10016 (800) 443-8323; *The New Book of World Rankings.*

International Rubber Study Group, York House, Eighth Floor, Empire Way, Wembley, London HA9 0PA, England; *Rubber Statistical Handbook.*

National Statistical Office, Office of the Prime Minister, Bangkok Metropolis 10100, Thailand; *Statistical Yearbook Thailand.*

THAILAND - SALT PRODUCTION

Statistical Office of the United Nations, Publishing Service, New York, New York 10017 (800) 253-9646; *Statistical Yearbook.*

THAILAND - SAWNWOOD PRODUCTION - See THAILAND - FORESTRY AND FOREST PRODUCTS

THAILAND - SCIENTISTS AND TECHNICIANS

Statistical Office of the United Nations, Publishing Service, New York, New York 10017 (800) 253-9646; *Statistical Yearbook.*

THAILAND - SENIOR CITIZENS

Facts on File, 460 Park Avenue South, New York, New York 10016 (800) 443-8323; *The New Book of World Rankings.*

THAILAND - SHEEP - See THAILAND - LIVESTOCK AND POULTRY

THAILAND - SILVER PRODUCTION AND CONSUMPTION - See THAILAND - MINING AND MINERAL PRODUCTS

THAILAND - SOCIAL DATA

Asian Development Bank, P.O. Box 789, 1099 Manila, Philippines; *Key Indicators of Developing Asian and Pacific Countries.*

Facts on File, 460 Park Avenue South, New York, New York 10016 (800) 443-8323; *The New Book of World Rankings.*

G.K. Hall and Company, 70 Lincoln Street, Boston, Massachusetts 02111 (617) 423-3990; *The World in Figures.*

THAILAND - SOCIAL SECURITY

International Monetary Fund, 700 Nineteenth Street, NW, Washington, D.C. 20431 (202) 623-7000; *Government Finance Statistics Yearbook.*

THAILAND - SOYBEAN PRODUCTION - See THAILAND - CROPS

THAILAND - STAMP TAXES AND DUTIES - See THAILAND - TAXATION

THAILAND - STATE BUDGET REVENUE AND EXPENDITURES

Euromonitor Publications Limited, 87-88 Turnmill Street, London EC1M 5QU, England; *International Marketing Data and Statistics.*

THAILAND - STEEL - See THAILAND - MINING AND MINERAL PRODUCTS

THAILAND - STOCKS - COMMODITY - MARKET PRICE - INDEX

Food and Agricultural Organization of the United Nations (FAO) Via delle Terme di Caracalla, 00100 Rome, Italy (Telephone Number in U.S. (202) 653-2400); *The State of Food and Agriculture.*

THAILAND - SUGAR - See THAILAND - CROPS

THAILAND - SULPHURIC ACID PRODUCTION - See THAILAND - MINING AND MINERAL PRODUCTS

THAILAND - TAXATION

G.K. Hall and Company, 70 Lincoln Street, Boston, Massachusetts 02111 (617) 423-3990; *The World in Figures.*

International Monetary Fund, 700 Nineteenth Street, NW, Washington, D.C. 20431 (202) 623-7000; *Government Finance Statistics Yearbook.*

International Road Federation, 525 School Street, SW, Washington, D.C. 20024 (202) 554-2106; *World Road Statistics.*

The World Bank, 1818 H Street, NW, Washington, D.C. 20433 (202) 477-1234; *World Tables.*

THAILAND - TEA CONSUMPTION - See THAILAND - CROPS

THAILAND - TELEGRAPH SERVICE

Statistical Office of the United Nations, Publishing Service, New York, New York 10017 (800) 253-9646; *Statistical Yearbook.*

THAILAND - TELEPHONES IN USE

American Telephone and Telegraph Company, 26 Parsippany Road, Whippany, New Jersey 07981 (800) 338-4038; *The World's Telephones.*

The Economist Intelligence Unit (Asia) Limited, 10th Floor, Luk Kwok Centre, 72 Gloucester Road, Wanchai, Hong Kong (Phone Number in U.S. (800) 938-4685); *Asian Market Atlas.*

Euromonitor Publications Limited, 87-88 Turnmill Street, London EC1M 5QU, England; *Third World Economic Handbook.*

G.K. Hall and Company, 70 Lincoln Street, Boston, Massachusetts 02111 (617) 423-3990; *The World in Figures.*

National Statistical Office, Office of the Prime Minister, Bangkok Metropolis 10100, Thailand; *Statistical Yearbook Thailand.*

Statistical Office of the United Nations, Publishing Service, New York, New York 10017 (800) 253-9646; *Statistical Yearbook.*

THAILAND - TELEVISION

The Economist Intelligence Unit (Asia) Limited, 10th Floor, Luk Kwok Centre, 72 Gloucester Road, Wanchai, Hong Kong (Phone Number in U.S. (800) 938-4685); *Asian Market Atlas.*

THAILAND - TELEVISION BROADCASTING - See THAILAND - BROADCASTING

THAILAND - TELEVISION RECEIVER PRODUCTION

Statistical Office of the United Nations, Publishing Service, New York, New York 10017 (800) 253-9646; *Statistical Yearbook.*

THAILAND - TEXTILE INDUSTRY

American Forest and Paper Association, 1250 Connecticut Avenue, NW, Washington, D.C. 20036 (202) 463-2455; *Wood Pulp and Fiber Statistics.*

Euromonitor Publications Limited, 87-88 Turnmill Street, London EC1M 5QU, England; *Third World Economic Handbook.*

G.K. Hall and Company, 70 Lincoln Street, Boston, Massachusetts 02111 (617) 423-3990; *The World in Figures.*

Statistical Office of the United Nations, Publishing Service, New York, New York 10017 (800) 253-9646; *Statistical Yearbook*, and *Trade in Manufactures of Developing Countries*.

THAILAND - TIN - See THAILAND - MINING AND MINERAL PRODUCTS

THAILAND - TIRE (MOTOR VEHICLE) PRODUCTION

International Rubber Study Group, York House, Eighth Floor, Empire Way, Wembley, London HA9 0PA, England; *Rubber Statistical Handbook*.

Statistical Office of the United Nations, Publishing Service, New York, New York 10017 (800) 253-9646; *Statistical Yearbook*.

THAILAND - TOBACCO PRODUCTION

Euromonitor Publications Limited, 87-88 Turnmill Street, London EC1M 5QU, England; *Third World Economic Handbook*.

Facts on File, 460 Park Avenue South, New York, New York 10016 (800) 443-8323; *The New Book of World Rankings*.

Statistical Office of the United Nations, Publishing Service, New York, New York 10017 (800) 253-9646; *Statistical Yearbook*.

THAILAND - TOURISM

Euromonitor Publications Limited, 87-88 Turnmill Street, London EC1M 5QU, England; *Third World Economic Handbook*.

Facts on File, 460 Park Avenue South, New York, New York 10016 (800) 443-8323; *The New Book of World Rankings*.

G.K. Hall and Company, 70 Lincoln Street, Boston, Massachusetts 02111 (617) 423-3990; *The World in Figures*.

National Statistical Office, Office of the Prime Minister, Bangkok Metropolis 10100, Thailand; *Statistical Yearbook Thailand*.

Statistical Office of the United Nations, Publishing Service, New York, New York 10017 (800) 253-9646; *Statistical Yearbook*.

Times Books, 201 East 50th Street, New York, New York 10022 (212) 751-2600; *The Economist Book of Vital World Statistics*.

World Tourism Organization, Calle Capitan Haya 42, E-28020 Madrid, Spain; *Yearbook of Tourism Statistics*.

THAILAND - TRACTORS IN USE

Statistical Office of the United Nations, Publishing Service, New York, New York 10017 (800) 253-9646; *Statistical Yearbook*.

THAILAND - TRADE - See THAILAND - FOREIGN TRADE

THAILAND - TRADEMARKS AND SERVICE MARKS

Statistical Office of the United Nations, Publishing Service, New York, New York 10017 (800) 253-9646; *Statistical Yearbook*.

World Intellectual Property Organization, 34 Chemin des Colombettes, CH-1211 Geneva 20. Switzerland; *Industrial Property Statistics*.

THAILAND - TRANSPORTATION AND COMMUNICATIONS

The Economist Intelligence Unit (Asia) Limited, 10th Floor, Luk Kwok Centre, 72 Gloucester Road, Wanchai, Hong Kong (Phone Number in U.S. (800) 938-4685); *Asian Market Atlas*.

Euromonitor Publications Limited, 87-88 Turnmill Street, London EC1M 5QU, England; *Third World Economic Handbook*.

Facts on File, 460 Park Avenue South, New York, New York 10016 (800) 443-8323; *The New Book of World Rankings*.

G.K. Hall and Company, 70 Lincoln Street, Boston, Massachusetts 02111 (617) 423-3990; *The World in Figures*.

National Statistical Office, Office of the Prime Minister, Bangkok Metropolis 10100, Thailand; *Statistical Yearbook Thailand*.

Statistical Office of the United Nations, Publishing Service, New York, New York 10017 (800) 253-9646; *Statistical Yearbook for Asia and the Pacific*.

THAILAND - TUNGSTEN PRODUCTION AND CONSUMPTION - See THAILAND - MINING AND MINERAL PRODUCTS

THAILAND - UNEMPLOYMENT

Euromonitor Publications Limited, 87-88 Turnmill Street, London EC1M 5QU, England; *International Marketing Data and Statistics*.

International Labour Office, I.L.O. Publications, CH-1211, Geneva 22, Switzerland; *Yearbook of Labour Statistics*.

Statistical Office of the United Nations, Publishing Service, New York, New York 10017 (800) 253-9646; *Statistical Yearbook*.

THAILAND - UTILITIES

Statistical Office of the United Nations, Publishing Service, New York, New York 10017 (800) 253-9646; *Electric Power in Asia and the Pacific*.

THAILAND - VITAL STATISTICS

Euromonitor Publications Limited, 87-88 Turnmill Street, London EC1M 5QU, England; *International Marketing Data and Statistics*, and *Third World Economic Handbook*.

G.K. Hall and Company, 70 Lincoln Street, Boston, Massachusetts 02111 (617) 423-3990; *The World in Figures*.

National Statistical Office, Office of the Prime Minister, Bangkok Metropolis 10100, Thailand; *Statistical Yearbook Thailand*.

Statistical Office of the United Nations, Publishing Service, New York, New York 10017 (800) 253-9646; *Statistical Yearbook*.

World Health Organization, Office of Publications, Avenue Appia, CH-1211 Geneva 27, Switzerland (Telephone Number in U.S. (518) 436-9686); *World Health Statistics Annual*.

THAILAND - WAGES

G.K. Hall and Company, 70 Lincoln Street, Boston, Massachusetts 02111 (617) 423-3990; *The World in Figures*.

International Labour Office, I.L.O. Publications, CH-1211, Geneva 22, Switzerland; *Yearbook of Labour Statistics*.

National Statistical Office, Office of the Prime Minister, Bangkok Metropolis 10100, Thailand; *Statistical Yearbook Thailand*.

Statistical Office of the United Nations, Publishing Service, New York, New York 10017 (800) 253-9646; *Statistical Yearbook for Asia and the Pacific*.

THAILAND - WEATHER

Facts on File, 460 Park Avenue South, New York, New York 10016 (800) 443-8323; *The New Book of World Rankings*.

G.K. Hall and Company, 70 Lincoln Street, Boston, Massachusetts 02111 (617) 423-3990; *The World in Figures*.

THAILAND - WELFARE

International Monetary Fund, 700 Nineteenth Street, NW, Washington, D.C. 20431 (202) 623-7000; *Government Finance Statistics Yearbook*.

THAILAND - WHEAT - See THAILAND - CROPS

THAILAND - WHOLESALE PRICES

Asian Development Bank, P.O. Box 789, 1099 Manila, Philippines; *Key Indicators of Developing Asian and Pacific Countries*.

International Monetary Fund, 700 Nineteenth Street, NW, Washington, D.C. 20431 (202) 623-7000; *International Financial Statistics*.

Statistical Office of the United Nations, Publishing Service, New York, New York 10017 (800) 253-9646; *Statistical Yearbook*.

THAILAND - WHOLESALE TRADE

Euromonitor Publications Limited, 87-88 Turnmill Street, London EC1M 5QU, England; *Third World Economic Handbook*.

THAILAND - WINE PRODUCTION

Facts on File, 460 Park Avenue South, New York, New York 10016 (800) 443-8323; *The New Book of World Rankings*.

THAILAND - WOOD - See THAILAND - FORESTRY AND FOREST PRODUCTS

THAILAND - WOOL PRODUCTION

Facts on File, 460 Park Avenue South, New York, New York 10016 (800) 443-8323; *The New Book of World Rankings*.

THAILAND - YARN PRODUCTION

Statistical Office of the United Nations, Publishing Service, New York, New York 10017 (800) 253-9646; *Statistical Yearbook*.

THAILAND - ZINC ORE PRODUCTION AND CONSUMPTION - See THAILAND - MINING AND MINERAL PRODUCTS

THAILAND - ZOOS AND BOTANICAL GARDENS

United Nations Educational, Scientific and Cultural Organization (UNESCO), 7 Place de Fontenoy, F-75700 Paris, France (Telephone Number in U.S. (212) 963-5981); *Statistical Yearbook*.

THEATERS - ATTENDANCE AND RECEIPTS

Theatre Communications Group, 355 Lexington Avenue, New York, New York 10017 (212) 697-5230.

Variety, Incorporated, 249 West Seventeenth Street, New York, New York 10011 (212) 779-1100.

THEATERS - PERSONAL EXPENDITURES

U.S. Department of Commerce, Bureau of Economic Analysis, Fourteenth Street between Constitution Avenue and E Street, NW, Washington, D.C. 20230 (202) 606-9900; *The National Income and Product Accounts of the United States*, and *Survey of Current Business*.

THEATERS - STATE AID

National Endowment for the Arts, 1100 Pennsylvania Avenue, NW, Washington, D.C. 20506 (202) 682-5400; *Annual Report*.

National Endowment for the Humanities, 1100 Pennsylvania Avenue, NW, Washington, D.C. 20506 (202) 606-8438; *Annual Report*.

THEFT - See CRIME AND CRIMINALS

THEOLOGY - DEGREES CONFERRED

U.S. Department of Education, National Center for Education Statistics, 400 Maryland Avenue, SW, Washington, D.C. 20202 (202) 708-5366; *Digest of Education Statistics*.

THREAD - See YARN, THREAD, etc

TIMBER - CONSUMPTION

U.S. Department of Agriculture, Forest Service, Fourteenth Street and Independence Avenue, SW, Washington, D.C. 20250 (202) 720-3760; *United States Timber Production, Trade, Consumption, and Price Statistics*.

TIMBER - FOREIGN TRADE

U.S. Department of Agriculture, Forest Service, Fourteenth Street and Independence Avenue, SW, Washington, D.C. 20250 (202) 720-3760; *United States Timber Production, Trade, Consumption, and Price Statistics*.

TIMBER - PRODUCER PRICES

U.S. Department of Agriculture, Forest Service, Fourteenth Street and Independence Avenue, SW, Washington, D.C. 20250 (202) 720-3760; *United States Timber Production, Trade, Consumption, and Price Statistics*.

U.S. Department of Labor, Bureau of Labor Statistics, Two Massachusetts Avenue, NE, Washington, D.C. 20212 (202) 606-7828; *Producer Price Indexes*.

TIMBER - PRODUCTION

U.S. Department of Agriculture, Forest Service, Fourteenth Street and Independence Avenue, SW, Washington, D.C. 20250 (202) 720-3760; *United States Timber Production, Trade, Consumption, and Price Statistics*.

TIMBER - PRODUCTION - WORLD (ROUNDWOOD)

Statistical Office of the United Nations, New York, New York 10017 (800) 253-9646; *Monthly Bulletin of Statistics*.

TIMBER - REMOVED FROM NATIONAL FORESTS

U.S. Department of Agriculture, Forest Service, Fourteenth Street and Independence Avenue, SW, Washington, D.C. 20250 (202) 720-3760; *Agricultural Statistics*, and unpublished data.

TIMBER - ROUNDWOOD PRODUCTS

U.S. Department of Agriculture, Forest Service, Fourteenth Street and Independence Avenue, SW, Washington, D.C. 20250 (202) 720-3760; *United States Timber Production, Trade, Consumption, and Price Statistics*.

TIMBER - VOLUME - GROWTH AND CUT

U.S. Department of Agriculture, Forest Service, Fourteenth Street and Independence Avenue, SW, Washington, D.C. 20250 (202) 720-3760; *Forest Resources of the United States*.

TIN - FOREIGN TRADE

U.S. Department of the Interior, Bureau of Mines, 810 Seventh Street, NW, Washington, D.C. 20241 (202) 501-9649; *Mineral Commodity Summaries*.

TIN - PRICES

U.S. Department of the Interior, Bureau of Mines, 810 Seventh Street, NW, Washington, D.C. 20241 (202) 501-9649; *Mineral Commodity Summaries*.

TIN - PRODUCTION

U.S. Department of the Interior, Bureau of Mines, 810 Seventh Street, NW, Washington, D.C. 20241 (202) 501-9649; *Annual Reports*, and *Mineral Commodity Summaries*.

TIN - PRODUCTION - WORLD

Statistical Office of the United Nations, Publishing Service, New York, New York 10017 (800) 253-9646; *Monthly Bulletin of Statistics*.

U.S. Department of the Interior, Bureau of Mines, 810 Seventh Street, NW, Washington, D.C. 20241 (202) 501-9649; *Mineral Commodity Summaries*.

TIN - STRATEGIC AND CRITICAL MATERIALS

U.S. Department of Defense, Defense Logistics Agency, Cameron Station, Alexandria, Virginia 22304-6100 (703) 274-6000; *Statistical Supplement, Stockpile Report to the Congress*.

TIRES AND TUBES

The Rubber Manufacturers Association, Incorporated, 1400 K Street, NW, Washington, D.C. 20005 (202) 682-4800; *RMA Monthly Tire Report*.

U.S. Department of Commerce, Bureau of the Census, Suitland, Maryland 20233 (301) 763-4040; *U.S. Merchandise Trade, Annual Survey of Manufactures*, and *Census of Manufactures*.

U.S. Department of Transportation, National Highway Traffic Safety Administration, 400 Seventh Street, SW, Washington, D.C. 20590 (202) 366-9550; *Motor Vehicles Recall Campaigns*.

TITANIUM - PRODUCTION

U.S. Department of the Interior, Bureau of Mines, 810 Seventh Street, NW, Washington, D.C. 20241 (202) 501-9649; *Annual Reports*, and *Mineral Commodity Summaries*.

TITANIUM - STRATEGIC AND CRITICAL MATERIAL

U.S. Department of Defense, Defense Logistics Agency, Cameron Station, Alexandria, Virginia 22304-6100 (703) 274-6000; *Statistical Supplement, Stockpile Report to the Congress*.

TITANIUM - WORLD PRODUCTION

U.S. Department of the Interior, Bureau of Mines, 810 Seventh Street, NW, Washington, D.C. 20241 (202) 501-9649; *Annual Reports*, and *Mineral Commodity Summaries*.

TOBACCO - See also TOBACCO PRODUCTS, MANUFACTURING and CIGARETTES

TOBACCO - ACREAGE HARVESTED

U.S. Department of Agriculture, Economic Research Service, Fourteenth Street and Independence Avenue, SW, Washington, D.C. 20250 (202) 219-1504; *Agricultural Statistics, Agricultural Outlook*, and *Tobacco Situation*.

U.S. Department of Agriculture, National Agricultural Statistics Service, Fourteenth Street and Independence Avenue, SW, Washington, D.C. 20250 (202) 219-1504; *Crop Production, Crop Values*, and *Field Crops*.

TOBACCO - ADVERTISING EXPENDITURES

Publishers Information Bureau, 575 Lexington Avenue, New York, New York 10022 (212) 752-0055; from data compiled by Leading National Advertisers, 11 West Forty-second Street, New York, New York 10036.

Television Bureau of Advertising, Incorporated, 850 Third Avenue, New York, New York 10022 (212) 486-1111; from data compiled by Competitive Media Reporting, 11 West 42nd Street, New York, New York 10036 (212) 789-1400.

TOBACCO - COMMODITY CREDIT CORPORATION TRANSACTIONS

U.S. Department of Agriculture, Agricultural Stabilization and Conservation Service, Fourteenth Street and Independence Avenue, SW, Washington, D.C. 20250 (202) 720-5237; *Commodity Credit Corporation Report of Financial Condition and Operations*, and *Agricultural Outlook*.

TOBACCO - CONSUMPTION AND USE

U.S. Department of Agriculture, Economic Research Service, Fourteenth Street and Independence Avenue, SW, Washington, D.C. 20250 (202) 219-1504; *Tobacco Situation and Outlook*.

U.S. Department of Health and Human Services, National Center for Health Statistics, 3700 East-West Highway, Hyattsville, Maryland 20782 (301) 436-8500; *Health, United States*.

U.S. Department of Health and Human Services, Substance Abuse and Mental Health Services Administration, 5600 Fishers Lane,

Rockville, Maryland 20857 (301) 443-4797; *National Household Survey on Drug Abuse*.

TOBACCO - FARM MARKETINGS - SALES

U.S. Department of Agriculture, Economic Research Service, Fourteenth Street and Independence Avenue, SW, Washington, D.C. 20250 (202) 219-1504; *Economic Indicators of the Farm Sector: National Financial Summary*.

TOBACCO - FOREIGN TRADE

U.S. Department of Agriculture, Economic Research Service, Fourteenth Street and Independence Avenue, SW, Washington, D.C. 20250 (202) 219-1504; *Agricultural Statistics, The Tobacco Situation, Foreign Agricultural Trade of the United States*, and unpublished data.

U.S. Department of Agriculture, Foreign Agricultural Service, Fourteenth Street and Independence Avenue, SW, Washington, D.C. 20250 (202) 720-3448; *Foreign Agricultural Commodity Circular Series*.

U.S. Department of Agriculture, National Agricultural Statistics Service, Fourteenth Street and Independence Avenue, SW, Washington, D.C. 20250 (202) 219-1504; *Crop Production, Field Crops*, and *Crop Values*.

U.S. Department of Commerce, Bureau of the Census, Suitland, Maryland 20233 (301) 763-4040; *Census of Manufactures, Annual Survey of Manufactures, U.S. Merchandise Trade: Exports, General Imports*, and *Imports for Consumption*, and *U.S. Merchandise Trade*.

TOBACCO - PRICES

U.S. Department of Agriculture, Economic Research Service, Fourteenth Street and Independence Avenue, SW, Washington, D.C. 20250 (202) 219-1504; *Foreign Agriculture Trade of the United States*, and *The Tobacco Situation, Agricultural Statistics*, and *Agricultural Outlook*.

U.S. Department of Agriculture, National Agricultural Statistics Service, Fourteenth Street and Independence Avenue, SW, Washington, D.C. 20250 (202) 219-1504; *Agricultural Prices: Annual Summary, Crop Production, Field Crops*, and *Crop Values*.

TOBACCO - PRODUCTION

Statistical Office of the United Nations, Publishing Service, New York, New York 10017 (800) 253-9646; *Monthly Bulletin of Statistics*.

U.S. Department of Agriculture, Economic Research Service, Fourteenth Street and Independence Avenue, SW, Washington, D.C. 20250 (202) 219-1504; *Agricultural Outlook, Agricultural Statistics*, and *Tobacco Situation*.

U.S. Department of Agriculture, Foreign Agricultural Service, Fourteenth Street and Independence Avenue, SW, Washington, D.C. 20250 (202) 720-3448; *Foreign Agricultural Commodity Circular Series*.

U.S. Department of Agriculture, National Agricultural Statistics Service, Fourteenth Street and Independence Avenue, SW, Washington, D.C. 20250 (202) 219-1504; *Crop Production, Field Crops*, and *Crop Values*.

TOBACCO - TAXES

U.S. Department of Commerce, Bureau of the Census, Suitland, Maryland 20233 (301) 763-4040; *State Government Tax Collections*, and *State Government Finances*.

U.S. Department of Treasury, Internal Revenue Service, 1111 Constitution Avenue, NW, Washington, D.C. 20224 (202) 566-5000; *Annual Report of the Commissioner and Chief Counsel of the Internal Revenue Service*.

TOBACCO - USE

U.S. Department of Health and Human Services, National Center for Health Statistics, 3700 East-West Highway, Hyattsville, Maryland 20782 (301) 436-8500; *Health, United States, Health Promotion and Disease Prevention, United States, Vital and Health Statistics*, and unpublished data.

U.S. Department of Health and Human Services, Substance Abuse and Mental Health Services Administration, 5600 Fishers Lane, Rockville, Maryland 20857 (301) 443-4797; *National Household Survey on Drug Abuse*.

TOBACCO PRODUCTS - MANUFACTURING - CAPITAL

Time Warner, 1675 Broadway, 1675 Broadway, Rockefeller Center, New York, New York 10019 (212) 522-1212; *The Fortune Directories*.

U.S. Department of Commerce, Bureau of Economic Analysis, Fourteenth Street between Constitution Avenue and E Street, NW, Washington, D.C. 20230 (202) 606-9900; *Fixed Reproducible Tangible Wealth in the U.S*, and *Survey of Current Business*.

TOBACCO PRODUCTS - MANUFACTURING - EARNINGS

U.S. Department of Commerce, Bureau of the Census, Suitland, Maryland 20233 (301) 763-4040; *Census of Manufactures*, and *Annual Survey of Manufactures*.

U.S. Department of Labor, Bureau of Labor Statistics, Two Massachusetts Avenue, NE, Washington, D.C. 20212 (202) 606-7828; *Employment and Earnings*, and Bulletins 2370 and 2429.

TOBACCO PRODUCTS - MANUFACTURING - EMPLOYEES

U.S. Department of Commerce, Bureau of the Census, Suitland, Maryland 20233 (301) 763-4040; *Census of Manufactures*, and *Annual Survey of Manufactures*.

U.S. Department of Labor, Bureau of Labor Statistics, Two Massachusetts Avenue, NE, Washington, D.C. 20212 (202) 606-7828; *Employment and Earnings, Monthly Labor Review*, and Bulletins 2370 and 2429.

TOBACCO PRODUCTS - MANUFACTURING - ESTABLISHMENTS

U.S. Department of Commerce, Bureau of the Census, Suitland, Maryland 20233 (301) 763-4040; *Census of Manufactures*, and *Annual Survey of Manufactures*.

TOBACCO PRODUCTS - MANUFACTURING - GROSS NATIONAL PRODUCT

U.S. Department of Commerce, Bureau of Economic Analysis, Fourteenth Street between Constitution Avenue and E Street, NW, Washington, D.C. 20230 (202) 606-9900; *The National Income and Product Accounts of the United States*, and *Survey of Current*

Business.

TOBACCO PRODUCTS - MANUFACTURING - INVENTORIES

U.S. Department of Commerce, Bureau of the Census, Suitland, Maryland 20233 (301) 763-4040; *Current Industrial Reports, Manufactures' Shipments, Inventories, and Orders.*

TOBACCO PRODUCTS - MANUFACTURING - MERGERS AND ACQUISITIONS

Securities Data Company, 1180 Raymond Boulevard, Newark, New Jersey 07102 (201) 622-3100; *Merger and Corporate Transactions Database.*

TOBACCO PRODUCTS - MANUFACTURING - OCCUPATIONAL SAFETY

U.S. Department of Labor, Bureau of Labor Statistics, Two Massachusetts Avenue, NE, Washington, D.C. 20212 (202) 606-7828; *Occupational Injuries and Illnesses in the United States by Industry.*

TOBACCO PRODUCTS - MANUFACTURING - PRODUCTIVITY

U.S. Department of Agriculture, Economic Research Service, Fourteenth Street and Independence Avenue, SW, Washington, D.C. 20250 (202) 219-1504; *Tobacco Situation.*

U.S. Department of Labor, Bureau of Labor Statistics, Two Massachusetts Avenue, NE, Washington, D.C. 20212 (202) 606-7828; *Productivity Measures for Selected Industries and Government Services.*

TOBACCO PRODUCTS - MANUFACTURING - PROFIT

Time Warner, 1675 Broadway, Rockefeller Center, New York, New York 10019 (212) 522-1212; *The Fortune Directories.*

TOBACCO PRODUCTS - MANUFACTURING - SHIPMENTS

U.S. Department of Commerce, Bureau of the Census, Suitland, Maryland 20233 (301) 763-4040; *Current Industrial Reports, Manufactures' Shipments, Inventories, and Orders, Census of Manufactures,* and *Annual Survey of Manufactures.*

TOBACCO PRODUCTS - MANUFACTURING - VALUE ADDED

U.S. Department of Commerce, Bureau of the Census, Suitland, Maryland 20233 (301) 763-4040; *Census of Manufactures,* and *Annual Survey of Manufactures.*

Togo - National Statistical Office

Direction de la Statistique, BP 118, Lome, Togo.

Togo - Primary Statistics Sources

Direction de la Statistique (Department of Statistics), BP 118, Lome, Togo; *Bulletin mensuel de statistique* (Monthly Bulletin of Statistics); and *Annuaire statistique du Togo* (Statistical Yearbook of Togo).

TOGO - AGRICULTURE

Euromonitor Publications Limited, 87-88 Turnmill Street, London EC1M 5QU, England; *International Marketing Data and Statistics.*

Facts on File, 460 Park Avenue South, New York, New York 10016 (800) 443-8323; *The New Book of World Rankings.*

Food and Agricultural Organization of the United Nations (FAO) Via delle Terme di Caracalla, 00100 Rome, Italy (Telephone Number in U.S. (202) 653-2400); *Production Yearbook,* and *The State of Food and Agriculture,* and *Trade Yearbook.*

G.K. Hall and Company, 70 Lincoln Street, Boston, Massachusetts 02111 (617) 423-3990; *The World in Figures.*

Statistical Office of the United Nations, Publishing Service, New York, New York 10017 (800) 253-9646; *Statistical Yearbook,* and *Survey of Economic and Social Conditions in Africa.*

Times Books, 201 East 50th Street, New York, New York 10022 (212) 751-2600; *The Economist Book of Vital World Statistics.*

United Nations Economic Commission for Africa, Africa Hall, P.O. Box 3001, Addis Ababa, Ethiopia (Telephone Number in U.S. (800) 253-9646); *African Statistical Yearbook.*

The World Bank, 1818 H Street, NW, Washington, D.C. 20433 (202) 477-1234; *World Tables.*

TOGO - AIRLINE SERVICE

Facts on File, 460 Park Avenue South, New York, New York 10016 (800) 443-8323; *The New Book of World Rankings.*

G.K. Hall and Company, 70 Lincoln Street, Boston, Massachusetts 02111 (617) 423-3990; *The World in Figures.*

Statistical Office of the United Nations, Publishing Service, New York, New York 10017 (800) 253-9646; *Statistical Yearbook.*

Times Books, 201 East 50th Street, New York, New York 10022 (212) 751-2600; *The Economist Book of Vital World Statistics.*

United Nations Economic Commission for Africa, Africa Hall, P.O. Box 3001, Addis Ababa, Ethiopia (Telephone Number in U.S. (800) 253-9646); *African Statistical Yearbook.*

TOGO - ALUMINUM PRODUCTION AND CONSUMPTION - See **TOGO - MINING AND MINERAL PRODUCTS**

TOGO - ANIMAL HEALTH

Food and Agricultural Organization of the United Nations (FAO), Via delle Terme di Caracalla, 00100, Rome, Italy (Telephone Number in U.S. (202) 653-2400); *Animal Health Yearbook.*

TOGO - AREA AND DENSITY OF POPULATION

African Development Bank, 01 BP 1387, Abidjan 01, Cote D'Ivoire; *Selected Statistics on Regional Member Countries.*

Euromonitor Publications Limited, 87-88 Turnmill Street, London EC1M 5QU, England; *International Marketing Data and Statistics.*

Facts on File, 460 Park Avenue South, New York, New York 10016 (800) 443-8323; *The New Book of World Rankings.*

Food and Agricultural Organization of the United Nations (FAO) Via delle Terme di Caracalla, 00100 Rome, Italy (Telephone Number in U.S. (202) 653-2400); *The State of Food and Agriculture.*

G.K. Hall and Company, 70 Lincoln Street, Boston, Massachusetts 02111 (617) 423-3990; *The World in Figures.*

Statistical Office of the United Nations, Publishing Service, New York, New York 10017 (800) 253-9646; *Statistical Yearbook*, and *Survey of Economic and Social Conditions in Africa*.

Times Books, 201 East 50th Street, New York, New York 10022 (212) 751-2600; *The Economist Book of Vital World Statistics*.

United Nations Educational, Scientific and Cultural Organization (UNESCO), 7 Place de Fontenoy, F-75700 Paris, France (Telephone Number in U.S. (212) 963-5981); *Statistical Yearbook*.

TOGO - ARMS EXPORTS AND IMPORTS

U.S. Arms Control and Disarmament Agency, 320 Twenty-first Street, NW, Washington, D.C. 20451 (202) 647-8677; *World Military Expenditures and Arms Transfers*.

TOGO - BALANCE OF PAYMENTS

African Development Bank, 01 BP 1387, Abidjan 01, Cote D'Ivoire; *Selected Statistics on Regional Member Countries*.

The Economist Intelligence Unit, 111 West 57th Street, New York, New York 10019 (800) 938-4685; *The World Market Atlas*.

G.K. Hall and Company, 70 Lincoln Street, Boston, Massachusetts 02111 (617) 423-3990; *The World in Figures*.

International Monetary Fund, 700 Nineteenth Street, NW, Washington, D.C. 20431 (202) 623-7000; *Balance of Payments Yearbook*.

Times Books, 201 East 50th Street, New York, New York 10022 (313) 751-2600; *The Economist Book of Vital World Statistics*.

United Nations Economic Commission for Africa, Africa Hall, P.O. Box 3001, Addis Ababa, Ethiopia (Telephone Number in U.S. (800) 253-9646); *African Statistical Yearbook*.

The World Bank, 1818 H Street, NW, Washington, D.C. 20433 (202) 477-1234; *World Tables*.

TOGO - BANKING

Facts on File, 460 Park Avenue South, New York, New York 10016 (800) 443-8323; *The New Book of World Rankings*.

G.K. Hall and Company, 70 Lincoln Street, Boston, Massachusetts 02111 (617) 423-3990; *The World in Figures*.

International Monetary Fund, 700 Nineteenth Street, NW, Washington, D.C. 20431 (202) 623-7000; *International Financial Statistics*.

Statistical Office of the United Nations, Publishing Service, New York, New York 10017 (800) 253-9646; *Statistical Yearbook*.

United Nations Economic Commission for Africa, Africa Hall, P.O. Box 3001, Addis Ababa, Ethiopia (Telephone Number in U.S. (800) 253-9646); *African Statistical Yearbook*.

TOGO - BARLEY PRODUCTION - See TOGO - CROPS

TOGO - BEER PRODUCTION

Facts on File, 460 Park Avenue South, New York, New York 10016 (800) 443-8323; *The New Book of World Rankings*.

Statistical Office of the United Nations, Publishing Service, New York, New York 10017 (800) 253-9646; *Statistical Yearbook*.

TOGO - BIRTH RATES

Facts on File, 460 Park Avenue South, New York, New York 10016 (800) 443-8323; *The New Book of World Rankings*.

Statistical Office of the United Nations, Publishing Service, New York, New York 10017 (800) 253-9646; *Demographic Yearbook*, *Statistical Yearbook*, and *Survey of Economic and Social Conditions in Africa*.

Times Books, 201 East 50th Street, New York, New York 10022 (212) 751-2600; *The Economist Book of Vital World Statistics*.

The World Bank, 1818 H Street, NW, Washington, D.C. 20433 (202) 477-1234; *World Tables*.

TOGO - BONDS

G.K. Hall and Company, 70 Lincoln Street, Boston, Massachusetts 02111 (617) 423-3990; *The World in Figures*.

TOGO - BOOK PRODUCTION

G.K. Hall and Company, 70 Lincoln Street, Boston, Massachusetts 02111 (617) 423-3990; *The World in Figures*.

TOGO - BROADCASTING

Billboard Limited, P.O. Box 9027, 1006 AA Amsterdam, The Netherlands (Telephone Number in U.S. (212) 764-7300); *World Radio TV Handbook*.

Facts on File, 460 Park Avenue South, New York, New York 10016 (800) 443-8323; *The New Book of World Rankings*.

G.K. Hall and Company, 70 Lincoln Street, Boston, Massachusetts 02111 (617) 423-3990; *The World in Figures*.

Times Books, 201 East 50th Street, New York, New York 10022 (212) 751-2600; *The Economist Book of Vital World Statistics*.

United Nations Educational, Scientific and Cultural Organization (UNESCO), 7 Place de Fontenoy, F-75700 Paris, France (Telephone Number in U.S. (212) 963-5981); *Statistical Yearbook*.

TOGO - BUSINESS

G.K. Hall and Company, 70 Lincoln Street, Boston, Massachusetts 02111 (617) 423-3990; *The World in Figures*.

TOGO - BUSINESS AND PROFESSIONAL LICENSES

International Monetary Fund, 700 Nineteenth Street, NW, Washington, D.C. 20431 (202) 623-7000; *Government Finance Statistics Yearbook*.

TOGO - CACAO EXPORTS - See TOGO - CROPS

TOGO - CALORIE SUPPLY

African Development Bank, 01 BP 1387, Abidjan 01, Cote D'Ivoire; *Selected Statistics on Regional Member Countries*.

Food and Agricultural Organization of the United Nations (FAO) Via delle Terme di Caracalla, 00100 Rome, Italy (Telephone Number in U.S. (202) 653-2400); *The State of Food and Agriculture*.

TOGO - CATTLE - See TOGO - LIVESTOCK AND POULTRY

TOGO - CEMENT PRODUCTION - See TOGO - MINING AND MINERAL PRODUCTS

TOGO - CHEMICAL (ORGANIC) PRODUCTION - See TOGO - MINING AND MINERAL PRODUCTS

TOGO - CHICKENS - See TOGO - LIVESTOCK AND POULTRY

TOGO - CIGARETTE PRODUCTION - See TOGO - TOBACCO PRODUCTION

TOGO - CLASS STRUCTURE

G.K. Hall and Company, 70 Lincoln Street, Boston, Massachusetts 02111 (617) 423-3990; *The World in Figures.*

TOGO - CLIMATE

Facts on File, 460 Park Avenue South, New York, New York 10016 (800) 443-8323; *The New Book of World Rankings.*

G.K. Hall and Company, 70 Lincoln Street, Boston, Massachusetts 02111 (617) 423-3990; *The World in Figures.*

TOGO - COAL PRODUCTION - See TOGO - MINING AND MINERAL PRODUCTS

TOGO - COCOA (BEANS) PRODUCTION - See TOGO - CROPS

TOGO - COFFEE - See TOGO - CROPS

TOGO - COMMUNICATIONS

G.K. Hall and Company, 70 Lincoln Street, Boston, Massachusetts 02111 (617) 423-3990; *The World in Figures.*

United Nations Economic Commission for Africa, Africa Hall, P.O. Box 3001, Addis Ababa, Ethiopia (Telephone Number in U.S. (800) 253-9646); *African Statistical Yearbook.*

TOGO - CONSTRUCTION INDUSTRY

Facts on File, 460 Park Avenue South, New York, New York 10016 (800) 443-8323; *The New Book of World Rankings.*

Statistical Office of the United Nations, Publishing Service, New York, New York 10017 (800) 253-9646; *Construction Statistics Yearbook,* and *Statistical Yearbook.*

United Nations Economic Commission for Africa, Africa Hall, P.O. Box 3001, Addis Ababa, Ethiopia (Telephone Number in U.S. (800) 253-9646); *African Statistical Yearbook.*

TOGO - CONSUMER PRICE INDEX

African Development Bank, 01 BP 1387, Abidjan 01, Cote D'Ivoire; *Selected Statistics on Regional Member Countries.*

G.K. Hall and Company, 70 Lincoln Street, Boston, Massachusetts 02111 (617) 423-3990; *The World in Figures.*

Statistical Office of the United Nations, Publishing Service, New York, New York 10017 (800) 253-9646; *Statistical Yearbook,* and *Survey of Economic and Social Conditions in Africa.*

United Nations Economic Commission for Africa, Africa Hall, P.O. Box 3001, Addis Ababa, Ethiopia (Telephone Number in U.S. (800)

253-9646); *African Statistical Yearbook.*

TOGO - CONSUMER PRICES

International Labour Office, I.L.O. Publications, CH-1211, Geneva 22, Switzerland; *Yearbook of Labour Statistics.*

International Monetary Fund, 700 Nineteenth Street, NW, Washington, D.C. 20431 (202) 623-7000; *International Financial Statistics.*

Times Books, 201 East 50th Street, New York, New York 10022 (212) 751-2600; *The Economist Book of Vital World Statistics.*

TOGO - CONSUMPTION

African Development Bank, 01 BP 1387, Abidjan 01, Cote D'Ivoire; *Selected Statistics on Regional Member Countries.*

G.K. Hall and Company, 70 Lincoln Street, Boston, Massachusetts 02111 (617) 423-3990; *The World in Figures.*

Statistical Office of the United Nations, Publishing Service, New York, New York 10017 (800) 253-9646; *Survey of Economic and Social Conditions in Africa.*

TOGO - COPPER PRODUCTION AND CONSUMPTION - See TOGO - MINING AND MINERAL PRODUCTS

TOGO - CORN PRODUCTION - See TOGO - CROPS

TOGO - CORPORATE TAXES - See TOGO - TAXATION

TOGO - COTTON - See TOGO - CROPS

TOGO - CROPS

Facts on File, 460 Park Avenue South, New York, New York 10016 (800) 443-8323; *The New Book of World Rankings.*

Food and Agricultural Organization of the United Nations (FAO) Via delle Terme di Caracalla, 00100 Rome, Italy (Telephone Number in U.S. (202) 653-2400); *The State of Food and Agriculture.*

G.K. Hall and Company, 70 Lincoln Street, Boston, Massachusetts 02111 (617) 423-3990; *The World in Figures.*

International Monetary Fund, 700 Nineteenth Street, NW, Washington, D.C. 20431 (202) 623-7000; *International Financial Statistics.*

Statistical Office of the United Nations, Publishing Service, New York, New York 10017 (800) 253-9646; *Statistical Yearbook.*

United Nations Economic Commission for Africa, Africa Hall, P.O. Box 3001, Addis Ababa, Ethiopia (Telephone Number in U.S. (800) 253-9646); *African Statistical Yearbook.*

TOGO - CUSTOMS DUTIES

G.K. Hall and Company, 70 Lincoln Street, Boston, Massachusetts 02111 (617) 423-3990; *The World in Figures.*

International Monetary Fund, 700 Nineteenth Street, NW, Washington, D.C. 20431 (202) 623-7000; *Government Finance Statistics Yearbook.*

TOGO - DAIRY PRODUCTS

Facts on File, 460 Park Avenue South, New York, New York 10016 (800) 443-8323; *The New Book of World Rankings*.

Food and Agricultural Organization of the United Nations (FAO) Via delle Terme di Caracalla, 00100 Rome, Italy (Telephone Number in U.S. (202) 653-2400); *The State of Food and Agriculture*.

TOGO - DEATH RATES

G.K. Hall and Company, 70 Lincoln Street, Boston, Massachusetts 02111 (617) 423-3990; *The World in Figures*.

Statistical Office of the United Nations, Publishing Service, New York, New York 10017 (800) 253-9646; *Statistical Yearbook*, and *Survey of Economic and Social Conditions in Africa*.

Times Books, 201 East 50th Street, New York, New York 10022 (212) 751-2600; *The Economist Book of Vital World Statistics*.

World Health Organization, Office of Publications, Avenue Appia, CH-1211 Geneva 27, Switzerland (Telephone Number in U.S. (518) 436-9686); *World Health Statistics Annual*.

TOGO - DEFENSE EXPENDITURES

G.K. Hall and Company, 70 Lincoln Street, Boston, Massachusetts 02111 (617) 423-3990; *The World in Figures*.

International Monetary Fund, 700 Nineteenth Street, NW, Washington, D.C. 20431 (202) 623-7000; *Government Finance Statistics Yearbook*.

U.S. Arms Control and Disarmament Agency, 320 Twenty-first Street, NW, Washington, D.C. 20451 (202) 647-8677; *World Military Expenditures and Arms Transfers*.

TOGO - DEMOGRAPHY

The Economist Intelligence Unit, 111 West 57th Street, New York, New York 10019 (800) 938-4685; *The World Market Atlas*.

Facts on File, 460 Park Avenue South, New York, New York 10016 (800) 443-8323; *The New Book of World Rankings*.

G.K. Hall and Company, 70 Lincoln Street, Boston, Massachusetts 02111 (617) 423-3990; *The World in Figures*.

Statistical Office of the United Nations, Publishing Service, New York, New York 10017 (800) 253-9646; *Survey of Economic and Social Conditions in Africa*.

TOGO - DEVELOPMENT ASSISTANCE

G.K. Hall and Company, 70 Lincoln Street, Boston, Massachusetts 02111 (617) 423-3990; *The World in Figures*.

Statistical Office of the United Nations, Publishing Service, New York, New York 10017 (800) 253-9646; *Statistical Yearbook*.

TOGO - DIAMOND PRODUCTION - See TOGO - MINING AND MINERAL PRODUCTS

TOGO - DISCOUNT RATES

Statistical Office of the United Nations, Publishing Service, New York, New York 10017 (800) 253-9646; *Statistical Yearbook*.

TOGO - DISEASES

G.K. Hall and Company, 70 Lincoln Street, Boston, Massachusetts 02111 (617) 423-3990; *The World in Figures*.

World Health Organization, Office of Publications, Avenue Appia, CH-1211 Geneva 27, Switzerland (Telephone Number in U.S. (518) 436-9686); *World Health Statistics Annual*.

TOGO - DIVORCE RATES

Facts on File, 460 Park Avenue South, New York, New York 10016 (800) 443-8323; *The New Book of World Rankings*.

Statistical Office of the United Nations, Publishing Service, New York, New York 10017 (800) 253-9646; *Demographic Yearbook*.

TOGO - DOMESTIC PRODUCT

G.K. Hall and Company, 70 Lincoln Street, Boston, Massachusetts 02111 (617) 423-3990; *The World in Figures*.

TOGO - ECONOMY

African Development Bank, 01 BP 1387, Abidjan 01, Cote D'Ivoire; *Selected Statistics on Regional Member Countries*.

Euromonitor Publications Limited, 87-88 Turnmill Street, London EC1M 5QU, England; *International Marketing Data and Statistics*.

Facts on File, 460 Park Avenue South, New York, New York 10016 (800) 443-8323; *The New Book of World Rankings*.

G.K. Hall and Company, 70 Lincoln Street, Boston, Massachusetts 02111 (617) 423-3990; *The World in Figures*.

Statistical Office of the United Nations, Publishing Service, New York, New York 10017 (800) 253-9646; *Foreign Trade Statistics for Africa*.

TOGO - EDUCATION

African Development Bank, 01 BP 1387, Abidjan 01, Cote D'Ivoire; *Selected Statistics on Regional Member Countries*.

The Economist Intelligence Unit, 111 West 57th Street, New York, New York 10019 (800) 938-4685; *The World Market Atlas*.

Facts on File, 460 Park Avenue South, New York, New York 10016 (800) 443-8323; *The New Book of World Rankings*.

G.K. Hall and Company, 70 Lincoln Street, Boston, Massachusetts 02111 (617) 423-3990; *The World in Figures*.

International Monetary Fund, 700 Nineteenth Street, NW, Washington, D.C. 20431 (202) 623-7000; *Government Finance Statistics Yearbook*.

Statistical Office of the United Nations, Publishing Service, New York, New York 10017 (800) 253-9646; *Survey of Economic and Social Conditions in Africa*.

Times Books, 201 East 50th Street, New York, New York 10022 (212) 751-2600; *The Economist Book of Vital World Statistics*.

United Nations Economic Commission for Africa, Africa Hall, P.O. Box 3001, Addis Ababa, Ethiopia (Telephone Number in U.S. (800) 253-9646); *African Statistical Yearbook*.

United Nations Educational, Scientific and Cultural Organization (UNESCO), 7 Place de Fontenoy, F-75700 Paris, France (Telephone Number in U.S. (212) 963-5981); *Statistical Yearbook.*

The World Bank, 1818 H Street, NW, Washington, D.C. 20433 (202) 477-1234; *World Tables.*

TOGO - EGG PRODUCTION AND CONSUMPTION - See TOGO - DAIRY PRODUCTS

TOGO - ELECTRICITY

Facts on File, 460 Park Avenue South, New York, New York 10016 (800) 443-8323; *The New Book of World Rankings.*

Statistical Office of the United Nations, Publishing Service, New York, New York 10017 (800) 253-9646; *Statistical Yearbook,* and *Survey of Economic and Social Conditions in Africa.*

Times Books, 201 East 50th Street, New York, New York 10022 (212) 751-2600; *The Economist Book of Vital World Statistics.*

United Nations Economic Commission for Africa, Africa Hall, P.O. Box 3001, Addis Ababa, Ethiopia (Telephone Number in U.S. (800) 253-9646); *African Statistical Yearbook.*

TOGO - EMPLOYMENT

Euromonitor Publications Limited, 87-88 Turnmill Street, London EC1M 5QU, England; *International Marketing Data and Statistics.*

Facts on File, 460 Park Avenue South, New York, New York 10016 (800) 443-8323; *The New Book of World Rankings.*

International Labour Office, I.L.O. Publications, CH-1211, Geneva 22, Switzerland; *Yearbook of Labour Statistics.*

Statistical Office of the United Nations, Publishing Service, New York, New York 10017 (800) 253-9646; *Statistical Yearbook,* and *Survey of Economic and Social Conditions in Africa.*

United Nations Economic Commission for Africa, Africa Hall, P.O. Box 3001, Addis Ababa, Ethiopia (Telephone Number in U.S. (800) 253-9646); *African Statistical Yearbook.*

TOGO - ENERGY

Facts on File, 460 Park Avenue South, New York, New York 10016 (800) 443-8323; *The New Book of World Rankings.*

Food and Agricultural Organization of the United Nations (FAO) Via delle Terme di Caracalla, 00100 Rome, Italy (Telephone Number in U.S. (202) 653-2400); *The State of Food and Agriculture.*

G.K. Hall and Company, 70 Lincoln Street, Boston, Massachusetts 02111 (617) 423-3990; *The World in Figures.*

Statistical Office of the United Nations, Publishing Service, New York, New York 10017 (800) 253-9646; *Energy Statistics Yearbook,* and *Statistical Yearbook.*

Times Books, 201 East 50th Street, New York, New York 10022 (212) 751-2600; *The Economist Book of Vital World Statistics.*

United Nations Economic Commission for Africa, Africa Hall, P.O. Box 3001, Addis Ababa, Ethiopia (Telephone Number in U.S. (800) 253-9646); *African Statistical Yearbook.*

TOGO - EXCHANGE RATES

Euromonitor Publications Limited, 87-88 Turnmill Street, London EC1M 5QU, England; *International Marketing Data and Statistics.*

International Monetary Fund, 700 Nineteenth Street, NW, Washington, D.C. 20431 (202) 623-7000; *International Financial Statistics.*

Statistical Office of the United Nations, Publishing Service, New York, New York 10017 (800) 253-9646; *Foreign Trade Statistics for Africa,* and *Statistical Yearbook.*

TOGO - EXCISE TAXES - See TOGO - TAXATION

TOGO - EXPORTS

African Development Bank, 01 BP 1387, Abidjan 01, Cote D'Ivoire; *Selected Statistics on Regional Member Countries.*

The Economist Intelligence Unit, 111 West 57th Street, New York, New York 10019 (800) 938-4685; *The World Market Atlas.*

Euromonitor Publications Limited, 87-88 Turnmill Street, London EC1M 5QU, England; *International Marketing Data and Statistics.*

Food and Agricultural Organization of the United Nations (FAO) Via delle Terme di Caracalla, 00100 Rome, Italy (Telephone Number in U.S. (202) 653-2400); *The State of Food and Agriculture.*

G.K. Hall and Company, 70 Lincoln Street, Boston, Massachusetts 02111 (617) 423-3990; *The World in Figures.*

International Monetary Fund, 700 Nineteenth Street, NW, Washington, D.C. 20431 (202) 623-7000; *Direction of Trade Statistics, Government Finance Statistics Yearbook,* and *International Financial Statistics.*

Statistical Office of the United Nations, Publishing Service, New York, New York 10017 (800) 253-9646; *Foreign Trade Statistics for Africa,* and *Survey of Economic and Social Conditions in Africa.*

Times Books, 201 East 50th Street, New York, New York 10022 (212) 751-2600; *The Economist Book of Vital World Statistics.*

United Nations Economic Commission for Africa, Africa Hall, P.O. Box 3001, Addis Ababa, Ethiopia (Telephone Number in U.S. (800) 253-9646); *African Statistical Yearbook.*

The World Bank, 1818 H Street, NW, Washington, D.C. 20433 (202) 477-1234; *World Tables.*

TOGO - EXTERNAL INDEBTEDNESS

African Development Bank, 01 BP 1387, Abidjan 01, Cote D'Ivoire; *Selected Statistics on Regional Member Countries.*

Statistical Office of the United Nations, Publishing Service, New York, New York 10017 (800) 253-9646; *Survey of Economic and Social Conditions in Africa.*

The World Bank, 1818 H Street, NW, Washington, D.C. 20433 (202) 477-1234; *World Tables.*

TOGO - EXTERNAL TRADE

African Development Bank, 01 BP 1387, Abidjan 01, Cote D'Ivoire; *Selected Statistics on Regional Member Countries.*

Food and Agricultural Organization of the United Nations (FAO) Via delle Terme di Caracalla, 00100 Rome, Italy (Telephone Number in U.S. (202) 653-2400); *The State of Food and Agriculture*, and *Trade Yearbook*.

G.K. Hall and Company, 70 Lincoln Street, Boston, Massachusetts 02111 (617) 423-3990; *The World in Figures*.

Statistical Office of the United Nations, Publishing Service, New York, New York 10017 (800) 253-9646; *Statistical Yearbook*.

TOGO - FABRIC PRODUCTION - See TOGO - TEXTILE INDUSTRY

TOGO - FARM CROPS - See TOGO - CROPS

TOGO - FEMALE WORKING POPULATION - See TOGO - EMPLOYMENT

TOGO - FERTILITY RATES

Facts on File, 460 Park Avenue South, New York, New York 10016 (800) 443-8323; *The New Book of World Rankings*.

Statistical Office of the United Nations, Publishing Service, New York, New York 10017 (800) 253-9646; *Survey of Economic and Social Conditions in Africa*.

Times Books, 201 East 50th Street, New York, New York 10022 (212) 751-2600; *The Economist Book of Vital World Statistics*.

The World Bank, 1818 H Street, NW, Washington, D.C. 20433 (202) 477-1234; *World Tables*.

TOGO - FERTILIZER

Food and Agricultural Organization of the United Nations (FAO), Via delle Terme di Caracalla, 00100, Rome, Italy (Telephone Number in U.S. (202) 653-2400); *Fertilizer Yearbook* and *The State of Food and Agriculture*.

Statistical Office of the United Nations, Publishing Service, New York, New York 10017 (800) 253-9646; *Statistical Yearbook*.

TOGO - FETAL MORTALITY

Statistical Office of the United Nations, Publishing Service, New York, New York 10017 (800) 253-9646; *Demographic Yearbook*.

TOGO - FINANCE

African Development Bank, 01 BP 1387, Abidjan 01, Cote D'Ivoire; *Selected Statistics on Regional Member Countries*.

Facts on File, 460 Park Avenue South, New York, New York 10016 (800) 443-8323; *The New Book of World Rankings*.

G.K. Hall and Company, 70 Lincoln Street, Boston, Massachusetts 02111 (617) 423-3990; *The World in Figures*.

United Nations Economic Commission for Africa, Africa Hall, P.O. Box 3001, Addis Ababa, Ethiopia (Telephone Number in U.S. (800) 253-9646); *African Statistical Yearbook*.

TOGO - FISHERIES

Facts on File, 460 Park Avenue South, New York, New York 10016 (800) 443-8323; *The New Book of World Rankings*.

Food and Agricultural Organization of the United Nations (FAO) Via delle Terme di Caracalla, 00100 Rome, Italy (Telephone Number in U.S. (202) 653-2400); *The State of Food and Agriculture*, and *Yearbook of Fishery Statistics*.

Statistical Office of the United Nations, Publishing Service, New York, New York 10017 (800) 253-9646; *Statistical Yearbook*, and *Survey of Economic and Social Conditions in Africa*.

United Nations Economic Commission for Africa, Africa Hall, P.O. Box 3001, Addis Ababa, Ethiopia (Telephone Number in U.S. (800) 253-9646); *African Statistical Yearbook*.

TOGO - FOOD

African Development Bank, 01 BP 1387, Abidjan 01, Cote D'Ivoire; *Selected Statistics on Regional Member Countries*.

Food and Agricultural Organization of the United Nations (FAO) Via delle Terme di Caracalla, 00100 Rome, Italy (Telephone Number in U.S. (202) 653-2400); *Production Yearbook*, and *The State of Food and Agriculture*.

G.K. Hall and Company, 70 Lincoln Street, Boston, Massachusetts 02111 (617) 423-3990; *The World in Figures*.

TOGO - FOREIGN AID

G.K. Hall and Company, 70 Lincoln Street, Boston, Massachusetts 02111 (617) 423-3990; *The World in Figures*.

TOGO - FOREIGN TRADE

Euromonitor Publications Limited, 87-88 Turnmill Street, London EC1M 5QU, England; *International Marketing Data and Statistics*.

Facts on File, 460 Park Avenue South, New York, New York 10016 (800) 443-8323; *The New Book of World Rankings*.

Food and Agricultural Organization of the United Nations (FAO) Via delle Terme di Caracalla, 00100 Rome, Italy (Telephone Number in U.S. (202) 653-2400); *The State of Food and Agriculture*.

G.K. Hall and Company, 70 Lincoln Street, Boston, Massachusetts 02111 (617) 423-3990; *The World in Figures*.

International Monetary Fund, 700 Nineteenth Street, NW, Washington, D.C. 20431 (202) 623-7000; *International Financial Statistics*.

Statistical Office of the United Nations, Publishing Service, New York, New York 10017 (800) 253-9646; *Foreign Trade Statistics for Africa*, *International Trade Statistics Yearbook*, and *Statistical Yearbook*.

United Nations Economic Commission for Africa, Africa Hall, P.O. Box 3001, Addis Ababa, Ethiopia (Telephone Number in U.S. (800) 253-9646); *African Statistical Yearbook*.

The World Bank, 1818 H Street, NW, Washington, D.C. 20433 (202) 477-1234; *World Tables*.

TOGO - FORESTRY AND FOREST PRODUCTS

Facts on File, 460 Park Avenue South, New York, New York 10016 (800) 443-8323; *The New Book of World Rankings*.

Food and Agricultural Organization of the United Nations (FAO) Via delle Terme di Caracalla, 00100 Rome, Italy (Telephone Number in

U.S. (202) 653-2400); *The State of Food and Agriculture*, and *Yearbook of Forest Products*.

G.K. Hall and Company, 70 Lincoln Street, Boston, Massachusetts 02111 (617) 423-3990; *The World in Figures*.

Statistical Office of the United Nations, Publishing Service, New York, New York 10017 (800) 253-9646; *Statistical Yearbook*.

United Nations Economic Commission for Africa, Africa Hall, P.O. Box 3001, Addis Ababa, Ethiopia (Telephone Number in U.S. (800) 253-9646); *African Statistical Yearbook*.

United Nations Educational, Scientific and Cultural Organization (UNESCO), 7 Place de Fontenoy, F-75700 Paris, France (Telephone Number in U.S. (212) 963-5981); *Statistical Yearbook*.

TOGO - GAS PRODUCTION - See TOGO - MINING AND MINERAL PRODUCTS

TOGO - GENERAL INDUSTRIAL STATISTICS

Statistical Office of the United Nations, Publishing Service, New York, New York 10017 (800) 253-9646; *Industrial Statistics Yearbook*.

TOGO - GENERAL MORTALITY

Statistical Office of the United Nations, Publishing Service, New York, New York 10017 (800) 253-9646; *Demographic Yearbook*.

TOGO - GEOGRAPHIC DATA

Facts on File, 460 Park Avenue South, New York, New York 10016 (800) 443-8323; *The New Book of World Rankings*.

TOGO - GOATS - See TOGO - LIVESTOCK AND POULTRY

TOGO - GOLD HOLDINGS

International Monetary Fund, 700 Nineteenth Street, NW, Washington, D.C. 20431 (202) 623-7000; *International Financial Statistics*.

Statistical Office of the United Nations, Publishing Service, New York, New York 10017 (800) 253-9646; *Statistical Yearbook*.

The World Bank, 1818 H Street, NW, Washington, D.C. 20433 (202) 477-1234; *World Tables*.

TOGO - GOLD PRODUCTION AND CONSUMPTION - See TOGO - MINING AND MINERAL PRODUCTS

TOGO - GOVERNMENT

G.K. Hall and Company, 70 Lincoln Street, Boston, Massachusetts 02111 (617) 423-3990; *The World in Figures*.

TOGO - GOVERNMENT EXPENDITURES

International Monetary Fund, 700 Nineteenth Street, NW, Washington, D.C. 20431 (202) 623-7000; *Government Finance Statistics Yearbook*.

Times Books, 201 East 50th Street, New York, New York 10022 (212) 751-2600; *The Economist Book of Vital World Statistics*.

The World Bank, 1818 H Street, NW, Washington, D.C. 20433 (202) 477-1234; *World Tables*.

TOGO - GOVERNMENT FINANCES

International Monetary Fund, 700 Nineteenth Street, NW, Washington, D.C. 20431 (202) 623-7000; *International Financial Statistics*.

Statistical Office of the United Nations, Publishing Service, New York, New York 10017 (800) 253-9646; *Statistical Yearbook*.

TOGO - GOVERNMENT REVENUE

International Monetary Fund, 700 Nineteenth Street, NW, Washington, D.C. 20431 (202) 623-7000; *Government Finance Statistics Yearbook*.

Statistical Office of the United Nations, Publishing Service, New York, New York 10017 (800) 253-9646; *Survey of Economic and Social Conditions in Africa*.

Times Books, 201 East 50th Street, New York, New York 10022 (212) 751-2600; *The Economist Book of Vital World Statistics*.

The World Bank, 1818 H Street, NW, Washington, D.C. 20433 (202) 477-1234; *World Tables*.

TOGO - GRAIN PRODUCTION - See TOGO - CROPS

TOGO - GROSS DOMESTIC PRODUCT

African Development Bank, 01 BP 1387, Abidjan 01, Cote D'Ivoire; *Selected Statistics on Regional Member Countries*.

The Economist Intelligence Unit, 111 West 57th Street, New York, New York 10019 (800) 938-4685; *The World Market Atlas*.

Euromonitor Publications Limited, 87-88 Turnmill Street, London EC1M 5QU, England; *International Marketing Data and Statistics*.

Facts on File, 460 Park Avenue South, New York, New York 10016 (800) 443-8323; *The New Book of World Rankings*.

G.K. Hall and Company, 70 Lincoln Street, Boston, Massachusetts 02111 (617) 423-3990; *The World in Figures*.

Statistical Office of the United Nations, Publishing Service, New York, New York 10017 (800) 253-9646; *Statistical Yearbook*, and *Survey of Economic and Social Conditions in Africa*.

Times Books, 201 East 50th Street, New York, New York 10022 (212) 751-2600; *The Economist Book of Vital World Statistics*.

United Nations Economic Commission for Africa, Africa Hall, P.O. Box 3001, Addis Ababa, Ethiopia (Telephone Number in U.S. (800) 253-9646); *African Statistical Yearbook*.

The World Bank, 1818 H Street, NW, Washington, D.C. 20433 (202) 477-1234; *World Tables*.

TOGO - GROSS NATIONAL PRODUCT

Euromonitor Publications Limited, 87-88 Turnmill Street, London EC1M 5QU, England; *International Marketing Data and Statistics*.

U.S. Arms Control and Disarmament Agency, 320 Twenty-first Street, NW, Washington, D.C. 20451 (202) 647-8677; *World Military Expenditures and Arms Transfers*.

The World Bank, 1818 H Street, NW, Washington, D.C. 20433 (202) 477-1234; *World Tables*.

TOGO - GROUNDNUTS PRODUCTION - See TOGO - CROPS

TOGO - HEALTH

African Development Bank, 01 BP 1387, Abidjan 01, Cote D'Ivoire; *Selected Statistics on Regional Member Countries.*

Facts on File, 460 Park Avenue South, New York, New York 10016 (800) 443-8323; *The New Book of World Rankings.*

G.K. Hall and Company, 70 Lincoln Street, Boston, Massachusetts 02111 (617) 423-3990; *The World in Figures.*

Statistical Office of the United Nations, Publishing Service, New York, New York 10017 (800) 253-9646; *Statistical Yearbook.*

Times Books, 201 East 50th Street, New York, New York 10022 (212) 751-2600; *The Economist Book of Vital World Statistics.*

United Nations Economic Commission for Africa, Africa Hall, P.O. Box 3001, Addis Ababa, Ethiopia (Telephone Number in U.S. (800) 253-9646); *African Statistical Yearbook.*

World Health Organization, Office of Publications, Avenue Appia, CH-1211 Geneva 27, Switzerland (Telephone Number in U.S. (518) 436-9686); *World Health Statistics Annual.*

TOGO - HEALTH EXPENDITURES

International Monetary Fund, 700 Nineteenth Street, NW, Washington, D.C. 20431 (202) 623-7000; *Government Finance Statistics Yearbook.*

TOGO - HIGHWAYS

G.K. Hall and Company, 70 Lincoln Street, Boston, Massachusetts 02111 (617) 423-3990; *The World in Figures.*

International Road Federation, 525 School Street, SW, Washington, D.C. 20024 (202) 554-2106; *World Road Statistics.*

Statistical Office of the United Nations, Publishing Service, New York, New York 10017 (800) 253-9646; *Survey of Economic and Social Conditions in Africa.*

United Nations Economic Commission for Africa, Africa Hall, P.O. Box 3001, Addis Ababa, Ethiopia (Telephone Number in U.S. (800) 253-9646); *African Statistical Yearbook.*

TOGO - HORSES - See TOGO - LIVESTOCK AND POULTRY

TOGO - HOURS OF WORK - See TOGO - EMPLOYMENT

TOGO - HOUSING AND HOUSING UNITS

Facts on File, 460 Park Avenue South, New York, New York 10016 (800) 443-8323; *The New Book of World Rankings.*

TOGO - HOUSING EXPENDITURES

International Monetary Fund, 700 Nineteenth Street, NW, Washington, D.C. 20431 (202) 623-7000; *Government Finance Statistics Yearbook.*

TOGO - ILLITERATE POPULATION

The Economist Intelligence Unit, 111 West 57th Street, New York, New York 10019 (800) 938-4685; *The World Market Atlas.*

G.K. Hall and Company, 70 Lincoln Street, Boston, Massachusetts 02111 (617) 423-3990; *The World in Figures.*

United Nations Educational, Scientific and Cultural Organization (UNESCO), 7 Place de Fontenoy, F-75700 Paris, France (Telephone Number in U.S. (212) 963-5981); *Statistical Yearbook.*

TOGO - IMPORTS

African Development Bank, 01 BP 1387, Abidjan 01, Cote D'Ivoire; *Selected Statistics on Regional Member Countries.*

The Economist Intelligence Unit, 111 West 57th Street, New York, New York 10019 (800) 938-4685; *The World Market Atlas.*

Euromonitor Publications Limited, 87-88 Turnmill Street, London EC1M 5QU, England; *International Marketing Data and Statistics.*

Food and Agricultural Organization of the United Nations (FAO) Via delle Terme di Caracalla, 00100 Rome, Italy (Telephone Number in U.S. (202) 653-2400); *The State of Food and Agriculture.*

G.K. Hall and Company, 70 Lincoln Street, Boston, Massachusetts 02111 (617) 423-3990; *The World in Figures.*

International Monetary Fund, 700 Nineteenth Street, NW, Washington, D.C. 20431 (202) 623-7000; *Direction of Trade Statistics, Government Finance Statistics Yearbook,* and *International Financial Statistics.*

Statistical Office of the United Nations, Publishing Service, New York, New York 10017 (800) 253-9646; *Foreign Trade Statistics for Africa, Survey of Economic and Social Conditions in Africa,* and *Trade in Manufactures of Developing Countries.*

United Nations Economic Commission for Africa, Africa Hall, P.O. Box 3001, Addis Ababa, Ethiopia (Telephone Number in U.S. (800) 253-9646); *African Statistical Yearbook.*

The World Bank, 1818 H Street, NW, Washington, D.C. 20433 (202) 477-1234; *World Tables.*

TOGO - INCOME TAXES - See TOGO - TAXATION

TOGO - INDUSTRY

Euromonitor Publications Limited, 87-88 Turnmill Street, London EC1M 5QU, England; *International Marketing Data and Statistics.*

Facts on File, 460 Park Avenue South, New York, New York 10016 (800) 443-8323; *The New Book of World Rankings.*

G.K. Hall and Company, 70 Lincoln Street, Boston, Massachusetts 02111 (617) 423-3990; *The World in Figures.*

International Labour Office, I.L.O. Publications, CH-1211, Geneva 22, Switzerland; *Yearbook of Labour Statistics.*

Statistical Office of the United Nations, Publishing Service, New York, New York 10017 (800) 253-9646; *Survey of Economic and Social Conditions in Africa.*

Times Books, 201 East 50th Street, New York, New York 10022 (212) 751-2600; *The Economist Book of Vital World Statistics.*

United Nations Economic Commission for Africa, Africa Hall, P.O. Box 3001, Addis Ababa, Ethiopia (Telephone Number in U.S. (800) 253-9646); *African Statistical Yearbook.*

The World Bank, 1818 H Street, NW, Washington, D.C. 20433 (202) 477-1234; *World Tables*.

TOGO - INFANT AND MATERNAL MORTALITY

Statistical Office of the United Nations, Publishing Service, New York, New York 10017 (800) 253-9646; *Demographic Yearbook, Statistical Yearbook,* and *Survey of Economic and Social Conditions in Africa*.

Times Books, 201 East 50th Street, New York, New York 10022 (212) 751-2600; *The Economist Book of Vital World Statistics*.

The World Bank, 1818 H Street, NW, Washington, D.C. 20433 (202) 477-1234; *World Tables*.

TOGO - INTERNAL TRADE

Statistical Office of the United Nations, Publishing Service, New York, New York 10017 (800) 253-9646; *Statistical Yearbook*.

TOGO - INTERNATIONAL LIQUIDITY

International Monetary Fund, 700 Nineteenth Street, NW, Washington, D.C. 20431 (202) 623-7000; *International Financial Statistics*.

TOGO - INTERNATIONAL RESERVES EXCLUDING GOLD

African Development Bank, 01 BP 1387, Abidjan 01, Cote D'Ivoire; *Selected Statistics on Regional Member Countries*.

Statistical Office of the United Nations, Publishing Service, New York, New York 10017 (800) 253-9646; *Statistical Yearbook*.

The World Bank, 1818 H Street, NW, Washington, D.C. 20433 (202) 477-1234; *World Tables*.

TOGO - IRON ORE PRODUCTION AND CONSUMPTION - See TOGO - MINING AND MINERAL PRODUCTS

TOGO - IRRIGATION

Euromonitor Publications Limited, 87-88 Turnmill Street, London EC1M 5QU, England; *International Marketing Data and Statistics*.

TOGO - LABOR FORCE

African Development Bank, 01 BP 1387, Abidjan 01, Cote D'Ivoire; *Selected Statistics on Regional Member Countries*.

Euromonitor Publications Limited, 87-88 Turnmill Street, London EC1M 5QU, England; *International Marketing Data and Statistics*.

Facts on File, 460 Park Avenue South, New York, New York 10016 (800) 443-8323; *The New Book of World Rankings*.

Food and Agricultural Organization of the United Nations (FAO) Via delle Terme di Caracalla, 00100 Rome, Italy (Telephone Number in U.S. (202) 653-2400); *The State of Food and Agriculture*.

G.K. Hall and Company, 70 Lincoln Street, Boston, Massachusetts 02111 (617) 423-3990; *The World in Figures*.

Times Books, 201 East 50th Street, New York, New York 10022 (212) 751-2600; *The Economist Book of Vital World Statistics*.

The World Bank, 1818 H Street, NW, Washington, D.C. 20433 (202) 477-1234; *World Tables*.

TOGO - LABOR PRODUCTIVITY

International Labour Office, I.L.O. Publications, CH-1211, Geneva 22, Switzerland; *Yearbook of Labour Statistics*.

TOGO - LAND USE

Euromonitor Publications Limited, 87-88 Turnmill Street, London EC1M 5QU, England; *International Marketing Data and Statistics*.

Food and Agricultural Organization of the United Nations (FAO), Via delle Terme di Caracalla, 00100 Rome, Italy (Telephone Number in U.S. (202) 653-2400); *Production Yearbook*.

G.K. Hall and Company, 70 Lincoln Street, Boston, Massachusetts 02111 (617) 423-3990; *The World in Figures*.

TOGO - LIBRARIES

Facts on File, 460 Park Avenue South, New York, New York 10016 (800) 443-8323; *The New Book of World Rankings*.

United Nations Educational, Scientific and Cultural Organization (UNESCO), 7 Place de Fontenoy, F-75700 Paris, France (Telephone Number in U.S. (212) 963-5981); *Statistical Yearbook*.

TOGO - LIFE EXPECTANCY

African Development Bank, 01 BP 1387, Abidjan 01, Cote D'Ivoire; *Selected Statistics on Regional Member Countries*.

TOGO - LITERACY RATE

Statistical Office of the United Nations, Publishing Service, New York, New York 10017 (800) 253-9646; *Survey of Economic and Social Conditions in Africa*.

TOGO - LIVESTOCK AND POULTRY

Euromonitor Publications Limited, 87-88 Turnmill Street, London EC1M 5QU, England; *International Marketing Data and Statistics*.

Facts on File, 460 Park Avenue South, New York, New York 10016 (800) 443-8323; *The New Book of World Rankings*.

Food and Agricultural Organization of the United Nations (FAO), Via delle Terme di Caracalla, 00100 Rome, Italy (Telephone Number in U.S. (202) 653-2400); *Production Yearbook,* and *The State of Food and Agriculture*.

G.K. Hall and Company, 70 Lincoln Street, Boston, Massachusetts 02111 (617) 423-3990; *The World in Figures*.

Statistical Office of the United Nations, Publishing Service, New York, New York 10017 (800) 253-9646; *Statistical Yearbook,* and *Survey of Economic and Social Conditions in Africa*.

United Nations Economic Commission for Africa, Africa Hall, P.O. Box 3001, Addis Ababa, Ethiopia (Telephone Number in U.S. (800) 253-9646); *African Statistical Yearbook*.

TOGO - LIVING LEVELS

G.K. Hall and Company, 70 Lincoln Street, Boston, Massachusetts 02111 (617) 423-3990; *The World in Figures*.

TOGO - MAIL - PIECES SENT OR RECEIVED

Statistical Office of the United Nations, Publishing Service, New York, New York 10017 (800) 253-9646; *Statistical Yearbook*.

TOGO - MANUFACTURING

Facts on File, 460 Park Avenue South, New York, New York 10016 (800) 443-8323; *The New Book of World Rankings*.

G.K. Hall and Company, 70 Lincoln Street, Boston, Massachusetts 02111 (617) 423-3990; *The World in Figures*.

Statistical Office of the United Nations, Publishing Service, New York, New York 10017 (800) 253-9646; *Statistical Yearbook*, and *Survey of Economic and Social Conditions in Africa*.

United Nations Economic Commission for Africa, Africa Hall, P.O. Box 3001, Addis Ababa, Ethiopia (Telephone Number in U.S. (800) 253-9646); *African Statistical Yearbook*.

The World Bank, 1818 H Street, NW, Washington, D.C. 20433 (202) 477-1234; *World Tables*.

TOGO - MARRIAGE RATES

Facts on File, 460 Park Avenue South, New York, New York 10016 (800) 443-8323; *The New Book of World Rankings*.

Statistical Office of the United Nations, Publishing Service, New York, New York 10017 (800) 253-9646; *Demographic Yearbook*, and *Statistical Yearbook*.

TOGO - MEAT PRODUCTION - See TOGO - LIVESTOCK AND POULTRY

TOGO - MERCHANT SHIPPING

G.K. Hall and Company, 70 Lincoln Street, Boston, Massachusetts 02111 (617) 423-3990; *The World in Figures*.

Statistical Office of the United Nations, Publishing Service, New York, New York 10017 (800) 253-9646; *Statistical Yearbook*.

Times Books, 201 East 50th Street, New York, New York 10022 (212) 751-2600; *The Economist Book of Vital World Statistics*.

United Nations Economic Commission for Africa, Africa Hall, P.O. Box 3001, Addis Ababa, Ethiopia (Telephone Number in U.S. (800) 253-9646); *African Statistical Yearbook*.

TOGO - MILITARY

G.K. Hall and Company, 70 Lincoln Street, Boston, Massachusetts 02111 (617) 423-3990; *The World in Figures*.

The International Institute for Strategic Studies, 23 Tavistock Street, London WC2E 7NQ, England; *The Military Balance*.

U.S. Arms Control and Disarmament Agency, 320 Twenty-first Street, NW, Washington, D.C. 20451 (202) 647-8677; *World Military Expenditures and Arms Transfers*.

TOGO - MILK - See TOGO - DAIRY PRODUCTS

TOGO - MINING AND MINERAL PRODUCTS

Facts on File, 460 Park Avenue South, New York, New York 10016 (800) 443-8323; *The New Book of World Rankings*.

G.K. Hall and Company, 70 Lincoln Street, Boston, Massachusetts 02111 (617) 423-3990; *The World in Figures*.

International Monetary Fund, 700 Nineteenth Street, NW, Washington, D.C. 20431 (202) 623-7000; *International Financial Statistics*.

Statistical Office of the United Nations, Publishing Service, New York, New York 10017 (800) 253-9646; *Statistical Yearbook*.

United Nations Economic Commission for Africa, Africa Hall, P.O. Box 3001, Addis Ababa, Ethiopia (Telephone Number in U.S. (800) 253-9646); *African Statistical Yearbook*.

TOGO - MONEY EXCHANGE RATE

Euromonitor Publications Limited, 87-88 Turnmill Street, London EC1M 5QU, England; *International Marketing Data and Statistics*.

International Monetary Fund, 700 Nineteenth Street, NW, Washington, D.C. 20431 (202) 623-7000; *International Financial Statistics*.

Statistical Office of the United Nations, Publishing Service, New York, New York 10017 (800) 253-9646; *Statistical Yearbook*.

TOGO - MONEY RESERVES

Euromonitor Publications Limited, 87-88 Turnmill Street, London EC1M 5QU, England; *International Marketing Data and Statistics*.

TOGO - MONEY SUPPLY

African Development Bank, 01 BP 1387, Abidjan 01, Cote D'Ivoire; *Selected Statistics on Regional Member Countries*.

Euromonitor Publications Limited, 87-88 Turnmill Street, London EC1M 5QU, England; *International Marketing Data and Statistics*.

G.K. Hall and Company, 70 Lincoln Street, Boston, Massachusetts 02111 (617) 423-3990; *The World in Figures*.

International Monetary Fund, 700 Nineteenth Street, NW, Washington, D.C. 20431 (202) 623-7000; *International Financial Statistics*.

Statistical Office of the United Nations, Publishing Service, New York, New York 10017 (800) 253-9646; *Statistical Yearbook*.

The World Bank, 1818 H Street, NW, Washington, D.C. 20433 (202) 477-1234; *World Tables*.

TOGO - MOTOR VEHICLE TAXES - See TOGO - TAXATION

TOGO - MOTOR VEHICLES IN USE

G.K. Hall and Company, 70 Lincoln Street, Boston, Massachusetts 02111 (617) 423-3990; *The World in Figures*.

International Road Federation, 525 School Street, SW, Washington, D.C. 20024 (202) 554-2106; *World Road Statistics*.

Statistical Office of the United Nations, Publishing Service, New York, New York 10017 (800) 253-9646; *Statistical Yearbook*, and *Survey of Economic and Social Conditions in Africa*.

Times Books, 201 East 50th Street, New York, New York 10022 (212) 751-2600; *The Economist Book of Vital World Statistics*.

TOGO - MUSEUMS

Facts on File, 460 Park Avenue South, New York, New York 10016 (800) 443-8323; *The New Book of World Rankings*.

United Nations Educational, Scientific and Cultural Organization (UNESCO), 7 Place de Fontenoy, F-75700 Paris, France (Telephone Number in U.S. (212) 963-5981); *Statistical Yearbook*.

TOGO - NATALITY - See TOGO - BIRTH RATES

TOGO - NATIONAL ACCOUNTS

African Development Bank, 01 BP 1387, Abidjan 01, Cote D'Ivoire; *Selected Statistics on Regional Member Countries*.

Statistical Office of the United Nations, Publishing Service, New York, New York 10017 (800) 253-9646; *National Accounts Statistics*, and *Statistical Yearbook*.

United Nations Economic Commission for Africa, Africa Hall, P.O. Box 3001, Addis Ababa, Ethiopia (Telephone Number in U.S. (800) 253-9646); *African Statistical Yearbook*.

TOGO - NATIONAL INCOME

Facts on File, 460 Park Avenue South, New York, New York 10016 (800) 443-8323; *The New Book of World Rankings*.

G.K. Hall and Company, 70 Lincoln Street, Boston, Massachusetts 02111 (617) 423-3990; *The World in Figures*.

Statistical Office of the United Nations, Publishing Service, New York, New York 10017 (800) 253-9646; *Statistical Yearbook*.

TOGO - NATIONAL PRODUCT

Facts on File, 460 Park Avenue South, New York, New York 10016 (800) 443-8323; *The New Book of World Rankings*.

TOGO - NATURAL GAS PRODUCTION - See TOGO - MINING AND MINERAL PRODUCTS

TOGO - NEWSPAPER PRODUCTION - See TOGO - FORESTRY AND FOREST PRODUCTS

TOGO - NEWSPRINT PRODUCTION AND CONSUMPTION - See TOGO - FORESTRY AND FOREST PRODUCTS

TOGO - OCCUPATIONS - See TOGO - LABOR FORCE

TOGO - PALM KERNELS PRODUCTION - See TOGO - CROPS

TOGO - PAPER - See TOGO - FORESTRY AND FOREST PRODUCTS

TOGO - PEANUT PRODUCTION - See TOGO - CROPS

TOGO - PESTICIDE USE

Food and Agricultural Organization of the United Nations (FAO) Via delle Terme di Caracalla, 00100 Rome, Italy (Telephone Number in U.S. (202) 653-2400); *The State of Food and Agriculture*.

TOGO - PETROLEUM INDUSTRY

Facts on File, 460 Park Avenue South, New York, New York 10016 (800) 443-8323; *The New Book of World Rankings*.

Food and Agricultural Organization of the United Nations (FAO) Via delle Terme di Caracalla, 00100 Rome, Italy (Telephone Number in U.S. (202) 653-2400); *The State of Food and Agriculture*.

G.K. Hall and Company, 70 Lincoln Street, Boston, Massachusetts 02111 (617) 423-3990; *The World in Figures*.

TOGO - PHOSPHATE ROCK PRODUCTION - See TOGO - MINING AND MINERAL PRODUCTS

TOGO - PHOSPHATES EXPORTS - See TOGO - MINING AND MINERAL PRODUCTS

TOGO - PIGS - See TOGO - LIVESTOCK AND POULTRY

TOGO - POPULATION

African Development Bank, 01 BP 1387, Abidjan 01, Cote D'Ivoire; *Selected Statistics on Regional Member Countries*.

The Economist Intelligence Unit, 111 West 57th Street, New York, New York 10019 (800) 938-4685; *The World Market Atlas*.

Euromonitor Publications Limited, 87-88 Turnmill Street, London EC1M 5QU, England; *International Marketing Data and Statistics*.

Facts on File, 460 Park Avenue South, New York, New York 10016 (800) 443-8323; *The New Book of World Rankings*.

Food and Agricultural Organization of the United Nations (FAO), Via delle Terme di Caracalla, 00100 Rome, Italy (Telephone Number in U.S. (202) 653-2400); *Production Yearbook*.

G.K. Hall and Company, 70 Lincoln Street, Boston, Massachusetts 02111 (617) 423-3990; *The World in Figures*.

International Labour Office, I.L.O. Publications, CH-1211, Geneva 22, Switzerland; *Yearbook of Labour Statistics*.

Statistical Office of the United Nations, Publishing Service, New York, New York 10017 (800) 253-9646; *Demographic Yearbook*, *Statistical Yearbook*, and *Survey of Economic and Social Conditions in Africa*.

Times Books, 201 East 50th Street, New York, New York 10022 (212) 751-2600; *The Economist Book of Vital World Statistics*.

United Nations Educational, Scientific and Cultural Organization (UNESCO), 7 Place de Fontenoy, F-75700 Paris, France (Telephone Number in U.S. (212) 963-5981); *Statistical Yearbook*.

U.S. Arms Control and Disarmament Agency, 320 Twenty-first Street, NW, Washington, D.C. 20451 (202) 647-8677; *World Military Expenditures and Arms Transfers*.

World Health Organization, Office of Publications, Avenue Appia, CH-1211 Geneva 27, Switzerland (Telephone Number in U.S. (518) 436-9686); *World Health Statistics Annual*.

TOGO - POST OFFICES

Facts on File, 460 Park Avenue South, New York, New York 10016 (800) 443-8323; *The New Book of World Rankings*.

TOGO - POTATO PRODUCTION - See TOGO - CROPS

TOGO - PRICES

Facts on File, 460 Park Avenue South, New York, New York 10016 (800) 443-8323; *The New Book of World Rankings*.

Food and Agricultural Organization of the United Nations (FAO), Via delle Terme di Caracalla, 00100 Rome, Italy (Telephone Number in U.S. (202) 653-2400); *Production Yearbook*, and *The State of Food and Agriculture*.

G.K. Hall and Company, 70 Lincoln Street, Boston, Massachusetts 02111 (617) 423-3990; *The World in Figures*.

International Labour Office, I.L.O. Publications, CH-1211, Geneva 22, Switzerland; *Yearbook of Labour Statistics*.

International Monetary Fund, 700 Nineteenth Street, NW, Washington, D.C. 20431 (202) 623-7000; *International Financial Statistics*.

United Nations Economic Commission for Africa, Africa Hall, P.O. Box 3001, Addis Ababa, Ethiopia (Telephone Number in U.S. (800) 253-9646); *African Statistical Yearbook*.

TOGO - PRODUCTION

Facts on File, 460 Park Avenue South, New York, New York 10016 (800) 443-8323; *The New Book of World Rankings*.

G.K. Hall and Company, 70 Lincoln Street, Boston, Massachusetts 02111 (617) 423-3990; *The World in Figures*.

TOGO - PRODUCTIVITY

Euromonitor Publications Limited, 87-88 Turnmill Street, London EC1M 5QU, England; *International Marketing Data and Statistics*.

TOGO - PROPERTY TAXES - See TOGO - TAXATION

TOGO - PUBLIC FINANCE

Facts on File, 460 Park Avenue South, New York, New York 10016 (800) 443-8323; *The New Book of World Rankings*.

TOGO - RADIO BROADCASTING - See TOGO - BROADCASTING

TOGO - RAILWAYS

G.K. Hall and Company, 70 Lincoln Street, Boston, Massachusetts 02111 (617) 423-3990; *The World in Figures*.

Jane's Information Group, Sentinel House, 163 Brighton Road, Coulsdon, Surrey CR5 2NH, England (Telephone Number in U.S. (703) 683-3700); *Jane's World Railways*.

Statistical Office of the United Nations, Publishing Service, New York, New York 10017 (800) 253-9646; *Statistical Yearbook*, and *Survey of Economic and Social Conditions in Africa*.

United Nations Economic Commission for Africa, Africa Hall, P.O. Box 3001, Addis Ababa, Ethiopia (Telephone Number in U.S. (800) 253-9646); *African Statistical Yearbook*.

TOGO - RELIGION

Facts on File, 460 Park Avenue South, New York, New York 10016 (800) 443-8323; *The New Book of World Rankings*.

TOGO - RENT PRICES

International Labour Office, I.L.O. Publications, CH-1211, Geneva 22, Switzerland; *Yearbook of Labour Statistics*.

TOGO - RETAIL TRADE

G.K. Hall and Company, 70 Lincoln Street, Boston, Massachusetts 02111 (617) 423-3990; *The World in Figures*.

Statistical Office of the United Nations, Publishing Service, New York, New York 10017 (800) 253-9646; *Statistical Yearbook*.

TOGO - RETAIL TRADE EMPLOYMENT - MALE AND FEMALE - See TOGO - EMPLOYMENT

TOGO - RICE PRODUCTION - See TOGO - CROPS

TOGO - ROUNDWOOD PRODUCTION - See TOGO - FORESTRY AND FOREST PRODUCTS

TOGO - RUBBER PRODUCTION AND CONSUMPTION

Facts on File, 460 Park Avenue South, New York, New York 10016 (800) 443-8323; *The New Book of World Rankings*.

TOGO - SAWNWOOD PRODUCTION - See TOGO - FORESTRY AND FOREST PRODUCTS

TOGO - SCIENCE AND TECHNOLOGY - EXPENDITURE FOR RESEARCH

Statistical Office of the United Nations, Publishing Service, New York, New York 10017 (800) 253-9646; *Statistical Yearbook*.

TOGO - SCIENTISTS AND TECHNICIANS

Statistical Office of the United Nations, Publishing Service, New York, New York 10017 (800) 253-9646; *Statistical Yearbook*.

United Nations Educational, Scientific and Cultural Organization (UNESCO), 7 Place de Fontenoy, F-75700 Paris, France (Telephone Number in U.S. (212) 963-5981); *Statistical Yearbook*.

TOGO - SENIOR CITIZENS

Facts on File, 460 Park Avenue South, New York, New York 10016 (800) 443-8323; *The New Book of World Rankings*.

TOGO - SHEEP - See TOGO - LIVESTOCK AND POULTRY

TOGO - SILVER PRODUCTION AND CONSUMPTION - See TOGO - MINING AND MINERAL PRODUCTS

TOGO - SOCIAL DATA

African Development Bank, 01 BP 1387, Abidjan 01, Cote D'Ivoire; *Selected Statistics on Regional Member Countries*.

Facts on File, 460 Park Avenue South, New York, New York 10016 (800) 443-8323; *The New Book of World Rankings*.

G.K. Hall and Company, 70 Lincoln Street, Boston, Massachusetts 02111 (617) 423-3990; *The World in Figures*.

TOGO - SOCIAL SECURITY

International Monetary Fund, 700 Nineteenth Street, NW, Washington, D.C. 20431 (202) 623-7000; *Government Finance*

Statistics Yearbook.

TOGO - STAMP TAXES AND DUTIES - See TOGO - TAXATION

TOGO - STATE BUDGET REVENUE AND EXPENDITURES

Euromonitor Publications Limited, 87-88 Turnmill Street, London EC1M 5QU, England; *International Marketing Data and Statistics.*

TOGO - STEEL - See TOGO - MINING AND MINERAL PRODUCTS

TOGO - STOCKS - COMMODITY - MARKET PRICE - INDEX

Food and Agricultural Organization of the United Nations (FAO) Via delle Terme di Caracalla, 00100 Rome, Italy (Telephone Number in U.S. (202) 653-2400); *The State of Food and Agriculture.*

TOGO - SUGAR PRODUCTION AND CONSUMPTION - See TOGO - CROPS

TOGO - TAXATION

G.K. Hall and Company, 70 Lincoln Street, Boston, Massachusetts 02111 (617) 423-3990; *The World in Figures.*

International Monetary Fund, 700 Nineteenth Street, NW, Washington, D.C. 20431 (202) 623-7000; *Government Finance Statistics Yearbook.*

International Road Federation, 525 School Street, SW, Washington, D.C. 20024 (202) 554-2106; *World Road Statistics.*

The World Bank, 1818 H Street, NW, Washington, D.C. 20433 (202) 477-1234; *World Tables.*

TOGO - TELEGRAPH SERVICE

Statistical Office of the United Nations, Publishing Service, New York, New York 10017 (800) 253-9646; *Statistical Yearbook.*

TOGO - TELEPHONES IN USE

American Telephone and Telegraph Company, 26 Parsippany Road, Whippany, New Jersey 07981 (800) 338-4038; *The World's Telephones.*

G.K. Hall and Company, 70 Lincoln Street, Boston, Massachusetts 02111 (617) 423-3990; *The World in Figures.*

Statistical Office of the United Nations, Publishing Service, New York, New York 10017 (800) 253-9646; *Statistical Yearbook.*

TOGO - TELEVISION BROADCASTING - See TOGO - BROADCASTING

TOGO - TEXTILE INDUSTRY

G.K. Hall and Company, 70 Lincoln Street, Boston, Massachusetts 02111 (617) 423-3990; *The World in Figures.*

Statistical Office of the United Nations, Publishing Service, New York, New York 10017 (800) 253-9646; *Statistical Yearbook.*

TOGO - TOBACCO PRODUCTION

Facts on File, 460 Park Avenue South, New York, New York 10016 (800) 443-8323; *The New Book of World Rankings.*

Statistical Office of the United Nations, Publishing Service, New York, New York 10017 (800) 253-9646; *Statistical Yearbook.*

TOGO - TOURISM

Facts on File, 460 Park Avenue South, New York, New York 10016 (800) 443-8323; *The New Book of World Rankings.*

G.K. Hall and Company, 70 Lincoln Street, Boston, Massachusetts 02111 (617) 423-3990; *The World in Figures.*

Statistical Office of the United Nations, Publishing Service, New York, New York 10017 (800) 253-9646; *Statistical Yearbook.*

Times Books, 201 East 50th Street, New York, New York 10022 (212) 751-2600; *The Economist Book of Vital World Statistics.*

United Nations Economic Commission for Africa, Africa Hall, P.O. Box 3001, Addis Ababa, Ethiopia (Telephone Number in U.S. (800) 253-9646); *African Statistical Yearbook.*

World Tourism Organization, Calle Capitan Haya 42, E-28020 Madrid, Spain; *Yearbook of Tourism Statistics.*

TOGO - TRACTORS IN USE

Statistical Office of the United Nations, Publishing Service, New York, New York 10017 (800) 253-9646; *Statistical Yearbook.*

TOGO - TRADE - See TOGO - FOREIGN TRADE

TOGO - TRANSPORTATION AND COMMUNICATIONS

Facts on File, 460 Park Avenue South, New York, New York 10016 (800) 443-8323; *The New Book of World Rankings.*

G.K. Hall and Company, 70 Lincoln Street, Boston, Massachusetts 02111 (617) 423-3990; *The World in Figures.*

United Nations Economic Commission for Africa, Africa Hall, P.O. Box 3001, Addis Ababa, Ethiopia (Telephone Number in U.S. (800) 253-9646); *African Statistical Yearbook.*

TOGO - UNEMPLOYMENT

Euromonitor Publications Limited, 87-88 Turnmill Street, London EC1M 5QU, England; *International Marketing Data and Statistics.*

International Labour Office, I.L.O. Publications, CH-1211, Geneva 22, Switzerland; *Yearbook of Labour Statistics.*

Statistical Office of the United Nations, Publishing Service, New York, New York 10017 (800) 253-9646; *Statistical Yearbook.*

TOGO - VITAL STATISTICS

Euromonitor Publications Limited, 87-88 Turnmill Street, London EC1M 5QU, England; *International Marketing Data and Statistics.*

G.K. Hall and Company, 70 Lincoln Street, Boston, Massachusetts 02111 (617) 423-3990; *The World in Figures.*

Statistical Office of the United Nations, Publishing Service, New York, New York 10017 (800) 253-9646; *Statistical Yearbook.*

World Health Organization, Office of Publications, Avenue Appia, CH-1211 Geneva 27, Switzerland (Telephone Number in U.S. (518) 436-9686); *World Health Statistics Annual.*

TOGO - WAGES

G.K. Hall and Company, 70 Lincoln Street, Boston, Massachusetts 02111 (617) 423-3990; *The World in Figures*.

International Labour Office, I.L.O. Publications, CH-1211, Geneva 22, Switzerland; *Yearbook of Labour Statistics*.

TOGO - WEATHER

Facts on File, 460 Park Avenue South, New York, New York 10016 (800) 443-8323; *The New Book of World Rankings*.

G.K. Hall and Company, 70 Lincoln Street, Boston, Massachusetts 02111 (617) 423-3990; *The World in Figures*.

TOGO - WELFARE

International Monetary Fund, 700 Nineteenth Street, NW, Washington, D.C. 20431 (202) 623-7000; *Government Finance Statistics Yearbook*.

TOGO - WHEAT PRODUCTION AND PRICES - See TOGO - CROPS

TOGO - WHOLESALE TRADE

Statistical Office of the United Nations, Publishing Service, New York, New York 10017 (800) 253-9646; *Statistical Yearbook*.

TOGO - WINE PRODUCTION

Facts on File, 460 Park Avenue South, New York, New York 10016 (800) 443-8323; *The New Book of World Rankings*.

TOGO - WOOL PRODUCTION

Facts on File, 460 Park Avenue South, New York, New York 10016 (800) 443-8323; *The New Book of World Rankings*.

TOKELAU ISLANDS - AGRICULTURE

Food and Agricultural Organization of the United Nations (FAO) Via delle Terme di Caracalla, 00100 Rome, Italy (Telephone Number in U.S. (202) 653-2400); *Production Yearbook*, and *The State of Food and Agriculture*, and *Trade Yearbook*.

G.K. Hall and Company, 70 Lincoln Street, Boston, Massachusetts 02111 (617) 423-3990; *The World in Figures*.

TOKELAU ISLANDS - AIRLINE SERVICE

G.K. Hall and Company, 70 Lincoln Street, Boston, Massachusetts 02111 (617) 423-3990; *The World in Figures*.

TOKELAU ISLANDS - ANIMAL HEALTH

Food and Agricultural Organization of the United Nations (FAO), Via delle Terme di Caracalla, 00100, Rome, Italy (Telephone Number in U.S. (202) 653-2400); *Animal Health Yearbook*.

TOKELAU ISLANDS - AREA AND DENSITY OF POPULATION

Food and Agricultural Organization of the United Nations (FAO) Via delle Terme di Caracalla, 00100 Rome, Italy (Telephone Number in U.S. (202) 653-2400); *The State of Food and Agriculture*.

G.K. Hall and Company, 70 Lincoln Street, Boston, Massachusetts 02111 (617) 423-3990; *The World in Figures*.

Statistical Office of the United Nations, Publishing Service, New York, New York 10017 (800) 253-9646; *Statistical Yearbook*.

TOKELAU ISLANDS - BALANCE OF PAYMENTS

G.K. Hall and Company, 70 Lincoln Street, Boston, Massachusetts 02111 (617) 423-3990; *The World in Figures*.

TOKELAU ISLANDS - BANKING

G.K. Hall and Company, 70 Lincoln Street, Boston, Massachusetts 02111 (617) 423-3990; *The World in Figures*.

TOKELAU ISLANDS - BIRTH RATES

Statistical Office of the United Nations, Publishing Service, New York, New York 10017 (800) 253-9646; *Demographic Yearbook*, and *Statistical Yearbook*.

TOKELAU ISLANDS - BONDS

G.K. Hall and Company, 70 Lincoln Street, Boston, Massachusetts 02111 (617) 423-3990; *The World in Figures*.

TOKELAU ISLANDS - BOOK PRODUCTION

G.K. Hall and Company, 70 Lincoln Street, Boston, Massachusetts 02111 (617) 423-3990; *The World in Figures*.

TOKELAU ISLANDS - BROADCASTING

G.K. Hall and Company, 70 Lincoln Street, Boston, Massachusetts 02111 (617) 423-3990; *The World in Figures*.

TOKELAU ISLANDS - BUSINESS

G.K. Hall and Company, 70 Lincoln Street, Boston, Massachusetts 02111 (617) 423-3990; *The World in Figures*.

TOKELAU ISLANDS - CALORIE SUPPLY

Food and Agricultural Organization of the United Nations (FAO) Via delle Terme di Caracalla, 00100 Rome, Italy (Telephone Number in U.S. (202) 653-2400); *The State of Food and Agriculture*.

TOKELAU ISLANDS - COAL PRODUCTION - See TOKELAU ISLANDS - MINING AND MINERAL PRODUCTS

TOKELAU ISLANDS - CONSUMPTION

G.K. Hall and Company, 70 Lincoln Street, Boston, Massachusetts 02111 (617) 423-3990; *The World in Figures*.

TOKELAU ISLANDS - CORN PRODUCTION - See TOKELAU ISLANDS - CROPS

TOKELAU ISLANDS - CORPORATE TAXES - See TOKELAU ISLANDS - TAXATION

TOKELAU ISLANDS - CROPS

Food and Agricultural Organization of the United Nations (FAO) Via delle Terme di Caracalla, 00100 Rome, Italy (Telephone Number in U.S. (202) 653-2400); *The State of Food and Agriculture*.

G.K. Hall and Company, 70 Lincoln Street, Boston, Massachusetts 02111 (617) 423-3990; *The World in Figures*.

TOKELAU ISLANDS - CUSTOMS DUTIES

G.K. Hall and Company, 70 Lincoln Street, Boston, Massachusetts 02111 (617) 423-3990; *The World in Figures*.

TOKELAU ISLANDS - DAIRY PRODUCTS

Food and Agricultural Organization of the United Nations (FAO) Via delle Terme di Caracalla, 00100 Rome, Italy (Telephone Number in U.S. (202) 653-2400); *The State of Food and Agriculture*.

TOKELAU ISLANDS - DEATH RATES

G.K. Hall and Company, 70 Lincoln Street, Boston, Massachusetts 02111 (617) 423-3990; *The World in Figures*.

Statistical Office of the United Nations, Publishing Service, New York, New York 10017 (800) 253-9646; *Statistical Yearbook*.

World Health Organization, Office of Publications, Avenue Appia, CH-1211 Geneva 27, Switzerland (Telephone Number in U.S. (518) 436-9686); *World Health Statistics Annual*.

TOKELAU ISLANDS - DEFENSE EXPENDITURES

G.K. Hall and Company, 70 Lincoln Street, Boston, Massachusetts 02111 (617) 423-3990; *The World in Figures*.

TOKELAU ISLANDS - DEMOGRAPHY

G.K. Hall and Company, 70 Lincoln Street, Boston, Massachusetts 02111 (617) 423-3990; *The World in Figures*.

TOKELAU ISLANDS - DEVELOPMENT ASSISTANCE

G.K. Hall and Company, 70 Lincoln Street, Boston, Massachusetts 02111 (617) 423-3990; *The World in Figures*.

Statistical Office of the United Nations, Publishing Service, New York, New York 10017 (800) 253-9646; *Statistical Yearbook*.

TOKELAU ISLANDS - DISEASES

G.K. Hall and Company, 70 Lincoln Street, Boston, Massachusetts 02111 (617) 423-3990; *The World in Figures*.

World Health Organization, Office of Publications, Avenue Appia, CH-1211 Geneva 27, Switzerland (Telephone Number in U.S. (518) 436-9686); *World Health Statistics Annual*.

TOKELAU ISLANDS - DIVORCE RATES

Statistical Office of the United Nations, Publishing Service, New York, New York 10017 (800) 253-9646; *Demographic Yearbook*.

TOKELAU ISLANDS - DOMESTIC PRODUCT

G.K. Hall and Company, 70 Lincoln Street, Boston, Massachusetts 02111 (617) 423-3990; *The World in Figures*.

TOKELAU ISLANDS - ECONOMY

G.K. Hall and Company, 70 Lincoln Street, Boston, Massachusetts 02111 (617) 423-3990; *The World in Figures*.

TOKELAU ISLANDS - EDUCATION

G.K. Hall and Company, 70 Lincoln Street, Boston, Massachusetts 02111 (617) 423-3990; *The World in Figures*.

TOKELAU ISLANDS - EGG PRODUCTION AND CONSUMPTION - See TOKELAU ISLANDS - DAIRY PRODUCTS

TOKELAU ISLANDS - ENERGY

Food and Agricultural Organization of the United Nations (FAO) Via delle Terme di Caracalla, 00100 Rome, Italy (Telephone Number in U.S. (202) 653-2400); *The State of Food and Agriculture*.

G.K. Hall and Company, 70 Lincoln Street, Boston, Massachusetts 02111 (617) 423-3990; *The World in Figures*.

TOKELAU ISLANDS - EXPORTS

Food and Agricultural Organization of the United Nations (FAO) Via delle Terme di Caracalla, 00100 Rome, Italy (Telephone Number in U.S. (202) 653-2400); *The State of Food and Agriculture*.

G.K. Hall and Company, 70 Lincoln Street, Boston, Massachusetts 02111 (617) 423-3990; *The World in Figures*.

South Pacific Commission, Post Box D5, Noumea Cedex, New Caledonia; *Statistical Bulletin of the South Pacific: Overseas Trade*.

TOKELAU ISLANDS - EXTERNAL TRADE

Food and Agricultural Organization of the United Nations (FAO), Via delle Terme di Caracalla, 00100, Rome, Italy (Telephone Number in U.S. (202) 653-2400); *Trade Yearbook*, and *The State of Food and Agriculture*.

G.K. Hall and Company, 70 Lincoln Street, Boston, Massachusetts 02111 (617) 423-3990; *The World in Figures*.

TOKELAU ISLANDS - FARM CROPS - See TOKELAU ISLANDS - CROPS

TOKELAU ISLANDS - FERTILIZER

Food and Agricultural Organization of the United Nations (FAO) Via delle Terme di Caracalla, 00100 Rome, Italy (Telephone Number in U.S. (202) 653-2400); *The State of Food and Agriculture*.

Food and Agricultural Organization of the United Nations (FAO), Via delle Terme di Caracalla, 00100, Rome, Italy (Telephone Number in U.S. (202) 653-2400); *Fertilizer Yearbook*, and *The State of Food and Agriculture*.

TOKELAU ISLANDS - FETAL MORTALITY

Statistical Office of the United Nations, Publishing Service, New York, New York 10017 (800) 253-9646; *Demographic Yearbook*.

TOKELAU ISLANDS - FINANCE

G.K. Hall and Company, 70 Lincoln Street, Boston, Massachusetts 02111 (617) 423-3990; *The World in Figures*.

TOKELAU ISLANDS - FISHERIES

Food and Agricultural Organization of the United Nations (FAO) Via delle Terme di Caracalla, 00100 Rome, Italy (Telephone Number in U.S. (202) 653-2400); *The State of Food and Agriculture*, and *Yearbook of Fishery Statistics*.

TOKELAU ISLANDS - FOOD

Food and Agricultural Organization of the United Nations (FAO) Via delle Terme di Caracalla, 00100 Rome, Italy (Telephone Number in

U.S. (202) 653-2400); *Production Yearbook*, and *The State of Food and Agriculture*.

G.K. Hall and Company, 70 Lincoln Street, Boston, Massachusetts 02111 (617) 423-3990; *The World in Figures*.

TOKELAU ISLANDS - FOREIGN AID

G.K. Hall and Company, 70 Lincoln Street, Boston, Massachusetts 02111 (617) 423-3990; *The World in Figures*.

TOKELAU ISLANDS - FOREIGN TRADE

Food and Agricultural Organization of the United Nations (FAO) Via delle Terme di Caracalla, 00100 Rome, Italy (Telephone Number in U.S. (202) 653-2400); *The State of Food and Agriculture*.

G.K. Hall and Company, 70 Lincoln Street, Boston, Massachusetts 02111 (617) 423-3990; *The World in Figures*.

South Pacific Commission, Post Box D5, Noumea Cedex, New Caledonia; *Statistical Bulletin of the South Pacific: Overseas Trade*.

TOKELAU ISLANDS - FORESTRY AND FOREST PRODUCTS

Food and Agricultural Organization of the United Nations (FAO) Via delle Terme di Caracalla, 00100 Rome, Italy (Telephone Number in U.S. (202) 653-2400); *The State of Food and Agriculture*.

G.K. Hall and Company, 70 Lincoln Street, Boston, Massachusetts 02111 (617) 423-3990; *The World in Figures*.

Statistical Office of the United Nations, Publishing Service, New York, New York 10017 (800) 253-9646; *Statistical Yearbook*.

TOKELAU ISLANDS - GENERAL MORTALITY

Statistical Office of the United Nations, Publishing Service, New York, New York 10017 (800) 253-9646; *Demographic Yearbook*.

TOKELAU ISLANDS - GOVERNMENT

G.K. Hall and Company, 70 Lincoln Street, Boston, Massachusetts 02111 (617) 423-3990; *The World in Figures*.

TOKELAU ISLANDS - GRAIN PRODUCTION - See TOKELAU ISLANDS - CROPS

TOKELAU ISLANDS - GROSS DOMESTIC PRODUCT

G.K. Hall and Company, 70 Lincoln Street, Boston, Massachusetts 02111 (617) 423-3990; *The World in Figures*.

TOKELAU ISLANDS - HEALTH

G.K. Hall and Company, 70 Lincoln Street, Boston, Massachusetts 02111 (617) 423-3990; *The World in Figures*.

World Health Organization, Office of Publications, Avenue Appia, CH-1211 Geneva 27, Switzerland (Telephone Number in U.S. (518) 436-9686); *World Health Statistics Annual*.

TOKELAU ISLANDS - HIGHWAYS

G.K. Hall and Company, 70 Lincoln Street, Boston, Massachusetts 02111 (617) 423-3990; *The World in Figures*.

TOKELAU ISLANDS - ILLITERATE POPULATION

G.K. Hall and Company, 70 Lincoln Street, Boston, Massachusetts 02111 (617) 423-3990; *The World in Figures*.

TOKELAU ISLANDS - IMPORTS

Food and Agricultural Organization of the United Nations (FAO) Via delle Terme di Caracalla, 00100 Rome, Italy (Telephone Number in U.S. (202) 653-2400); *The State of Food and Agriculture*.

G.K. Hall and Company, 70 Lincoln Street, Boston, Massachusetts 02111 (617) 423-3990; *The World in Figures*.

South Pacific Commission, Post Box D5, Noumea Cedex, New Caledonia; *Statistical Bulletin of the South Pacific: Overseas Trade*.

TOKELAU ISLANDS - INDUSTRY

G.K. Hall and Company, 70 Lincoln Street, Boston, Massachusetts 02111 (617) 423-3990; *The World in Figures*.

TOKELAU ISLANDS - INFANT AND MATERNAL MORTALITY

Statistical Office of the United Nations, Publishing Service, New York, New York 10017 (800) 253-9646; *Demographic Yearbook*, and *Statistical Yearbook*.

TOKELAU ISLANDS - LABOR FORCE

Food and Agricultural Organization of the United Nations (FAO) Via delle Terme di Caracalla, 00100 Rome, Italy (Telephone Number in U.S. (202) 653-2400); *The State of Food and Agriculture*.

G.K. Hall and Company, 70 Lincoln Street, Boston, Massachusetts 02111 (617) 423-3990; *The World in Figures*.

TOKELAU ISLANDS - LAND USE

Food and Agricultural Organization of the United Nations (FAO), Via delle Terme di Caracalla, 00100 Rome, Italy (Telephone Number in U.S. (202) 653-2400); *Production Yearbook*.

G.K. Hall and Company, 70 Lincoln Street, Boston, Massachusetts 02111 (617) 423-3990; *The World in Figures*.

TOKELAU ISLANDS - LIBRARIES

United Nations Educational, Scientific and Cultural Organization (UNESCO), 7 Place de Fontenoy, F-75700 Paris, France (Telephone Number in U.S. (212) 963-5981); *Statistical Yearbook*.

TOKELAU ISLANDS - LIVESTOCK AND POULTRY

Food and Agricultural Organization of the United Nations (FAO), Via delle Terme di Caracalla, 00100 Rome, Italy (Telephone Number in U.S. (202) 653-2400); *Production Yearbook*, and *The State of Food and Agriculture*.

G.K. Hall and Company, 70 Lincoln Street, Boston, Massachusetts 02111 (617) 423-3990; *The World in Figures*.

Statistical Office of the United Nations, Publishing Service, New York, New York 10017 (800) 253-9646; *Statistical Yearbook*.

TOKELAU ISLANDS - LIVING LEVELS

G.K. Hall and Company, 70 Lincoln Street, Boston, Massachusetts 02111 (617) 423-3990; *The World in Figures*.

TOKELAU ISLANDS - MANUFACTURING

G.K. Hall and Company, 70 Lincoln Street, Boston, Massachusetts 02111 (617) 423-3990; *The World in Figures.*

TOKELAU ISLANDS - MARRIAGE RATES

Statistical Office of the United Nations, Publishing Service, New York, New York 10017 (800) 253-9646; *Demographic Yearbook,* and *Statistical Yearbook.*

TOKELAU ISLANDS - MEAT PRODUCTION - See TOKELAU ISLANDS - LIVESTOCK AND POULTRY

TOKELAU ISLANDS - MERCHANT SHIPPING

G.K. Hall and Company, 70 Lincoln Street, Boston, Massachusetts 02111 (617) 423-3990; *The World in Figures.*

TOKELAU ISLANDS - MILITARY

G.K. Hall and Company, 70 Lincoln Street, Boston, Massachusetts 02111 (617) 423-3990; *The World in Figures.*

TOKELAU ISLANDS - MINING AND MINERAL PRODUCTS

G.K. Hall and Company, 70 Lincoln Street, Boston, Massachusetts 02111 (617) 423-3990; *The World in Figures.*

TOKELAU ISLANDS - MONEY SUPPLY

G.K. Hall and Company, 70 Lincoln Street, Boston, Massachusetts 02111 (617) 423-3990; *The World in Figures.*

TOKELAU ISLANDS - MOTOR VEHICLES IN USE

G.K. Hall and Company, 70 Lincoln Street, Boston, Massachusetts 02111 (617) 423-3990; *The World in Figures.*

TOKELAU ISLANDS - NATALITY - See TOKELAU ISLANDS - BIRTH RATES

TOKELAU ISLANDS - NATIONAL INCOME

G.K. Hall and Company, 70 Lincoln Street, Boston, Massachusetts 02111 (617) 423-3990; *The World in Figures.*

TOKELAU ISLANDS - NEWSPAPER PRODUCTION - See TOKELAU ISLANDS - FORESTRY AND FOREST PRODUCTS

TOKELAU ISLANDS - OCCUPATIONS - See TOKELAU ISLANDS - LABOR FORCE

TOKELAU ISLANDS - PERIODICALS

United Nations Educational, Scientific and Cultural Organization (UNESCO), 7 Place de Fontenoy, F-75700 Paris, France (Telephone Number in U.S. (212) 963-5981); *Statistical Yearbook.*

TOKELAU ISLANDS - PESTICIDE USE

Food and Agricultural Organization of the United Nations (FAO) Via delle Terme di Caracalla, 00100 Rome, Italy (Telephone Number in U.S. (202) 653-2400); *The State of Food and Agriculture.*

TOKELAU ISLANDS - PETROLEUM INDUSTRY

Food and Agricultural Organization of the United Nations (FAO) Via delle Terme di Caracalla, 00100 Rome, Italy (Telephone Number in

U.S. (202) 653-2400); *The State of Food and Agriculture.*

G.K. Hall and Company, 70 Lincoln Street, Boston, Massachusetts 02111 (617) 423-3990; *The World in Figures.*

TOKELAU ISLANDS - PIGS - See TOKELAU ISLANDS - LIVESTOCK AND POULTRY

TOKELAU ISLANDS - POPULATION

Food and Agricultural Organization of the United Nations (FAO), Via delle Terme di Caracalla, 00100 Rome, Italy (Telephone Number in U.S. (202) 653-2400); *Production Yearbook.*

G.K. Hall and Company, 70 Lincoln Street, Boston, Massachusetts 02111 (617) 423-3990; *The World in Figures.*

Statistical Office of the United Nations, Publishing Service, New York, New York 10017 (800) 253-9646; *Demographic Yearbook,* and *Statistical Yearbook.*

World Health Organization, Office of Publications, Avenue Appia, CH-1211 Geneva 27, Switzerland (Telephone Number in U.S. (518) 436-9686); *World Health Statistics Annual.*

TOKELAU ISLANDS - PRICES

Food and Agricultural Organization of the United Nations (FAO), Via delle Terme di Caracalla, 00100 Rome, Italy (Telephone Number in U.S. (202) 653-2400); *Production Yearbook,* and *The State of Food and Agriculture.*

G.K. Hall and Company, 70 Lincoln Street, Boston, Massachusetts 02111 (617) 423-3990; *The World in Figures.*

South Pacific Commission, Post Box D5, Noumea Cedex, New Caledonia; *Statistical Bulletin of the South Pacific: Overseas Trade.*

TOKELAU ISLANDS - PRODUCTION

G.K. Hall and Company, 70 Lincoln Street, Boston, Massachusetts 02111 (617) 423-3990; *The World in Figures.*

TOKELAU ISLANDS - RAILWAYS

G.K. Hall and Company, 70 Lincoln Street, Boston, Massachusetts 02111 (617) 423-3990; *The World in Figures.*

TOKELAU ISLANDS - RETAIL TRADE

G.K. Hall and Company, 70 Lincoln Street, Boston, Massachusetts 02111 (617) 423-3990; *The World in Figures.*

TOKELAU ISLANDS - SCIENTISTS AND TECHNICIANS

Statistical Office of the United Nations, Publishing Service, New York, New York 10017 (800) 253-9646; *Statistical Yearbook.*

TOKELAU ISLANDS - SOCIAL DATA

G.K. Hall and Company, 70 Lincoln Street, Boston, Massachusetts 02111 (617) 423-3990; *The World in Figures.*

TOKELAU ISLANDS - STOCKS - COMMODITY - MARKET PRICE - INDEX

Food and Agricultural Organization of the United Nations (FAO) Via delle Terme di Caracalla, 00100 Rome, Italy (Telephone Number in U.S. (202) 653-2400); *The State of Food and Agriculture.*

TOKELAU ISLANDS - TAXATION

G.K. Hall and Company, 70 Lincoln Street, Boston, Massachusetts 02111 (617) 423-3990; *The World in Figures.*

TOKELAU ISLANDS - TELEPHONES IN USE

American Telephone and Telegraph Company, 26 Parsippany Road, Whippany, New Jersey 07981 (800) 338-4038; *The World's Telephones.*

G.K. Hall and Company, 70 Lincoln Street, Boston, Massachusetts 02111 (617) 423-3990; *The World in Figures.*

TOKELAU ISLANDS - TEXTILE INDUSTRY

G.K. Hall and Company, 70 Lincoln Street, Boston, Massachusetts 02111 (617) 423-3990; *The World in Figures.*

TOKELAU ISLANDS - TOURISM

G.K. Hall and Company, 70 Lincoln Street, Boston, Massachusetts 02111 (617) 423-3990; *The World in Figures.*

TOKELAU ISLANDS - TRADE - See TOKELAU ISLANDS - FOREIGN TRADE

TOKELAU ISLANDS - TRANSPORTATION AND COMMUNICATIONS

G.K. Hall and Company, 70 Lincoln Street, Boston, Massachusetts 02111 (617) 423-3990; *The World in Figures.*

TOKELAU ISLANDS - VITAL STATISTICS

G.K. Hall and Company, 70 Lincoln Street, Boston, Massachusetts 02111 (617) 423-3990; *The World in Figures.*

World Health Organization, Office of Publications, Avenue Appia, CH-1211 Geneva 27, Switzerland (Telephone Number in U.S. (518) 436-9686); *World Health Statistics Annual.*

TOKELAU ISLANDS - WAGES

G.K. Hall and Company, 70 Lincoln Street, Boston, Massachusetts 02111 (617) 423-3990; *The World in Figures.*

TOKELAU ISLANDS - WEATHER

G.K. Hall and Company, 70 Lincoln Street, Boston, Massachusetts 02111 (617) 423-3990; *The World in Figures.*

TOMATOES

U.S. Department of Agriculture, Economic Research Service, Fourteenth Street and Independence Avenue, SW, Washington, D.C. 20250 (202) 219-1504; *Food Cost Review, Food Consumption, Prices and Expenditures, Agricultural Outlook,* and *Economic Indicators of the Farm Sector: National Financial Summary.*

U.S. Department of Agriculture, National Agricultural Statistics Service, Fourteenth Street and Independence Avenue, SW, Washington, D.C. 20250 (202) 219-1504; *Agricultural Statistics,* and *Vegetables.*

Tonga - National Statistical Office

Statistics Department, Ministry of Finance, Post Office Box 149, Nuku'alofa, Tonga.

Tonga - Primary Statistics Source

Statistics Department, P.O. Box 149, Nuku'alofa, Tonga; *Statistical Abstract.*

TONGA - AGRICULTURE

Asian Development Bank, P.O. Box 789, 1099 Manila, Philippines; *Key Indicators of Developing Asian and Pacific Countries.*

Food and Agricultural Organization of the United Nations (FAO) Via delle Terme di Caracalla, 00100 Rome, Italy (Telephone Number in U.S. (202) 653-2400); *Production Yearbook,* and *The State of Food and Agriculture,* and *Trade Yearbook.*

G.K. Hall and Company, 70 Lincoln Street, Boston, Massachusetts 02111 (617) 423-3990; *The World in Figures.*

Statistical Office of the United Nations, Publishing Service, New York, New York 10017 (800) 253-9646; *Statistical Yearbook,* and *Statistical Yearbook for Asia and the Pacific.*

The World Bank, 1818 H Street, NW, Washington, D.C. 20433 (202) 477-1234; *World Tables.*

TONGA - AIRLINE SERVICE

G.K. Hall and Company, 70 Lincoln Street, Boston, Massachusetts 02111 (617) 423-3990; *The World in Figures.*

TONGA - ANIMAL HEALTH

Food and Agricultural Organization of the United Nations (FAO), Via delle Terme di Caracalla, 00100 Rome, Italy (Telephone Number in U.S. (202) 653-2400); *Animal Health Yearbook.*

TONGA - AREA AND DENSITY OF POPULATION

Food and Agricultural Organization of the United Nations (FAO) Via delle Terme di Caracalla, 00100 Rome, Italy (Telephone Number in U.S. (202) 653-2400); *The State of Food and Agriculture.*

G.K. Hall and Company, 70 Lincoln Street, Boston, Massachusetts 02111 (617) 423-3990; *The World in Figures.*

Statistical Office of the United Nations, Publishing Service, New York, New York 10017 (800) 253-9646; *Statistical Yearbook.*

TONGA - BALANCE OF PAYMENTS

G.K. Hall and Company, 70 Lincoln Street, Boston, Massachusetts 02111 (617) 423-3990; *The World in Figures.*

International Monetary Fund, 700 Nineteenth Street, NW, Washington, D.C. 20431 (202) 623-7000; *Balance of Payments Yearbook.*

The World Bank, 1818 H Street, NW, Washington, D.C. 20433 (202) 477-1234; *World Tables.*

TONGA - BANKING

Asian Development Bank, P.O. Box 789, 1099 Manila, Philippines; *Key Indicators of Developing Asian and Pacific Countries.*

G.K. Hall and Company, 70 Lincoln Street, Boston, Massachusetts 02111 (617) 423-3990; *The World in Figures.*

TONGA - BIRTH RATES

Statistical Office of the United Nations, Publishing Service, New York, New York 10017 (800) 253-9646; *Demographic Yearbook*, and *Statistical Yearbook*.

The World Bank, 1818 H Street, NW, Washington, D.C. 20433 (202) 477-1234; *World Tables*.

TONGA - BONDS

Asian Development Bank, P.O. Box 789, 1099 Manila, Philippines; *Key Indicators of Developing Asian and Pacific Countries*.

G.K. Hall and Company, 70 Lincoln Street, Boston, Massachusetts 02111 (617) 423-3990; *The World in Figures*.

TONGA - BOOK PRODUCTION

G.K. Hall and Company, 70 Lincoln Street, Boston, Massachusetts 02111 (617) 423-3990; *The World in Figures*.

United Nations Educational, Scientific and Cultural Organization (UNESCO), 7 Place de Fontenoy, F-75700 Paris, France (Telephone Number in U.S. (212) 963-5981); *Statistical Yearbook*.

The World Bank, 1818 H Street, NW, Washington, D.C. 20433 (202) 477-1234; *World Tables*.

TONGA - BROADCASTING

Billboard Limited, P.O. Box 9027, 1006 AA Amsterdam, The Netherlands (Telephone Number in U.S. (212) 764-7300); *World Radio TV Handbook*.

G.K. Hall and Company, 70 Lincoln Street, Boston, Massachusetts 02111 (617) 423-3990; *The World in Figures*.

TONGA - BUSINESS

G.K. Hall and Company, 70 Lincoln Street, Boston, Massachusetts 02111 (617) 423-3990; *The World in Figures*.

TONGA - CALORIE SUPPLY

Asian Development Bank, P.O. Box 789, 1099 Manila, Philippines; *Key Indicators of Developing Asian and Pacific Countries*.

Food and Agricultural Organization of the United Nations (FAO) Via delle Terme di Caracalla, 00100 Rome, Italy (Telephone Number in U.S. (202) 653-2400); *The State of Food and Agriculture*.

TONGA - CAPITAL INVESTMENT

Asian Development Bank, P.O. Box 789, 1099 Manila, Philippines; *Key Indicators of Developing Asian and Pacific Countries*.

TONGA - CAPITAL REVENUE

Asian Development Bank, P.O. Box 789, 1099 Manila, Philippines; *Key Indicators of Developing Asian and Pacific Countries*.

TONGA - CATTLE - See TONGA - LIVESTOCK AND POULTRY

TONGA - CHEMICAL (ORGANIC) PRODUCTION - See TONGA - MINING AND MINERAL PRODUCTS

TONGA - CLASS STRUCTURE

G.K. Hall and Company, 70 Lincoln Street, Boston, Massachusetts 02111 (617) 423-3990; *The World in Figures*.

TONGA - CLIMATE

G.K. Hall and Company, 70 Lincoln Street, Boston, Massachusetts 02111 (617) 423-3990; *The World in Figures*.

TONGA - CLOTHING EXPORTS AND IMPORTS

South Pacific Commission, Post Box D5, Noumea Cedex, New Caledonia; *Statistical Bulletin of the South Pacific: Retail Price Indexes*.

TONGA - COAL PRODUCTION - See TONGA - MINING AND MINERAL PRODUCTS

TONGA - COMMUNICATIONS

G.K. Hall and Company, 70 Lincoln Street, Boston, Massachusetts 02111 (617) 423-3990; *The World in Figures*.

Statistical Office of the United Nations, Publishing Service, New York, New York 10017 (800) 253-9646; *Statistical Yearbook for Asia and the Pacific*.

TONGA - CONSTRUCTION INDUSTRY

Statistical Office of the United Nations, Publishing Service, New York, New York 10017 (800) 253-9646; *Construction Statistics Yearbook*.

TONGA - CONSUMER PRICE INDEX

Asian Development Bank, P.O. Box 789, 1099 Manila, Philippines; *Key Indicators of Developing Asian and Pacific Countries*.

G.K. Hall and Company, 70 Lincoln Street, Boston, Massachusetts 02111 (617) 423-3990; *The World in Figures*.

Statistical Office of the United Nations, Publishing Service, New York, New York 10017 (800) 253-9646; *Statistical Yearbook*.

TONGA - CONSUMER PRICES

International Labour Office, I.L.O. Publications, CH-1211, Geneva 22, Switzerland; *Yearbook of Labour Statistics*.

TONGA - CONSUMPTION

G.K. Hall and Company, 70 Lincoln Street, Boston, Massachusetts 02111 (617) 423-3990; *The World in Figures*.

South Pacific Commission, Post Box D5, Noumea Cedex, New Caledonia; *Statistical Bulletin of the South Pacific: Retail Price Indexes*.

TONGA - CORN PRODUCTION - See TONGA - CROPS

TONGA - CORPORATE TAXES - See TONGA - TAXATION

TONGA - CROPS

Asian Development Bank, P.O. Box 789, 1099 Manila, Philippines; *Key Indicators of Developing Asian and Pacific Countries*.

Food and Agricultural Organization of the United Nations (FAO) Via delle Terme di Caracalla, 00100 Rome, Italy (Telephone Number in U.S. (202) 653-2400); *The State of Food and Agriculture*.

G.K. Hall and Company, 70 Lincoln Street, Boston, Massachusetts 02111 (617) 423-3990; *The World in Figures*.

Statistical Office of the United Nations, Publishing Service, New York, New York 10017 (800) 253-9646; *Statistical Yearbook*.

TONGA - CUSTOMS DUTIES

G.K. Hall and Company, 70 Lincoln Street, Boston, Massachusetts 02111 (617) 423-3990; *The World in Figures*.

TONGA - DAIRY PRODUCTS

Food and Agricultural Organization of the United Nations (FAO) Via delle Terme di Caracalla, 00100 Rome, Italy (Telephone Number in U.S. (202) 653-2400); *The State of Food and Agriculture*.

TONGA - DEATH RATES

G.K. Hall and Company, 70 Lincoln Street, Boston, Massachusetts 02111 (617) 423-3990; *The World in Figures*.

Statistical Office of the United Nations, Publishing Service, New York, New York 10017 (800) 253-9646; *Statistical Yearbook*.

World Health Organization, Office of Publications, Avenue Appia, CH-1211 Geneva 27, Switzerland (Telephone Number in U.S. (518) 436-9686); *World Health Statistics Annual*.

TONGA - DEMOGRAPHY

G.K. Hall and Company, 70 Lincoln Street, Boston, Massachusetts 02111 (617) 423-3990; *The World in Figures*.

TONGA - DEFENSE EXPENDITURES

G.K. Hall and Company, 70 Lincoln Street, Boston, Massachusetts 02111 (617) 423-3990; *The World in Figures*.

TONGA - DEVELOPMENT ASSISTANCE

Asian Development Bank, P.O. Box 789, 1099 Manila, Philippines; *Key Indicators of Developing Asian and Pacific Countries*.

G.K. Hall and Company, 70 Lincoln Street, Boston, Massachusetts 02111 (617) 423-3990; *The World in Figures*.

Statistical Office of the United Nations, Publishing Service, New York, New York 10017 (800) 253-9646; *Statistical Yearbook*.

TONGA - DISEASES

G.K. Hall and Company, 70 Lincoln Street, Boston, Massachusetts 02111 (617) 423-3990; *The World in Figures*.

World Health Organization, Office of Publications, Avenue Appia, CH-1211 Geneva 27, Switzerland (Telephone Number in U.S. (518) 436-9686); *World Health Statistics Annual*.

TONGA - DIVORCE RATES

Statistical Office of the United Nations, Publishing Service, New York, New York 10017 (800) 253-9646; *Demographic Yearbook*, and *Statistical Yearbook*.

TONGA - DOMESTIC PRODUCT

G.K. Hall and Company, 70 Lincoln Street, Boston, Massachusetts 02111 (617) 423-3990; *The World in Figures*.

TONGA - ECONOMY

Asian Development Bank, P.O. Box 789, 1099 Manila, Philippines; *Key Indicators of Developing Asian and Pacific Countries*.

G.K. Hall and Company, 70 Lincoln Street, Boston, Massachusetts 02111 (617) 423-3990; *The World in Figures*.

TONGA - EDUCATION

G.K. Hall and Company, 70 Lincoln Street, Boston, Massachusetts 02111 (617) 423-3990; *The World in Figures*.

United Nations Educational, Scientific and Cultural Organization (UNESCO), 7 Place de Fontenoy, F-75700 Paris, France (Telephone Number in U.S. (212) 963-5981); *Statistical Yearbook*.

The World Bank, 1818 H Street, NW, Washington, D.C. 20433 (202) 477-1234; *World Tables*.

TONGA - EGG PRODUCTION AND CONSUMPTION - See TONGA - DAIRY PRODUCTS

TONGA - ELECTRICITY

Asian Development Bank, P.O. Box 789, 1099 Manila, Philippines; *Key Indicators of Developing Asian and Pacific Countries*.

Statistical Office of the United Nations, Publishing Service, New York, New York 10017 (800) 253-9646; *Electric Power in Asia and the Pacific*.

TONGA - EMPLOYMENT

International Labour Office, I.L.O. Publications, CH-1211, Geneva 22, Switzerland; *Yearbook of Labour Statistics*.

TONGA - ENERGY

Food and Agricultural Organization of the United Nations (FAO) Via delle Terme di Caracalla, 00100 Rome, Italy (Telephone Number in U.S. (202) 653-2400); *The State of Food and Agriculture*.

G.K. Hall and Company, 70 Lincoln Street, Boston, Massachusetts 02111 (617) 423-3990; *The World in Figures*.

Statistical Office of the United Nations, Publishing Service, New York, New York 10017 (800) 253-9646; *Energy Statistics Yearbook*, and *Statistical Yearbook for Asia and the Pacific*.

TONGA - EXCHANGE RATES

Asian Development Bank, P.O. Box 789, 1099 Manila, Philippines; *Key Indicators of Developing Asian and Pacific Countries*.

TONGA - EXPORTS

Asian Development Bank, P.O. Box 789, 1099 Manila, Philippines; *Key Indicators of Developing Asian and Pacific Countries*.

Food and Agricultural Organization of the United Nations (FAO) Via delle Terme di Caracalla, 00100 Rome, Italy (Telephone Number in U.S. (202) 653-2400); *The State of Food and Agriculture*.

G.K. Hall and Company, 70 Lincoln Street, Boston, Massachusetts 02111 (617) 423-3990; *The World in Figures.*

International Monetary Fund, 700 Nineteenth Street, NW, Washington, D.C. 20431 (202) 623-7000; *Direction of Trade Statistics.*

South Pacific Commission, Post Box D5, Noumea Cedex, New Caledonia; *Statistical Bulletin of the South Pacific: Overseas Trade.*

Statistical Office of the United Nations, Publishing Service, New York, New York 10017 (800) 253-9646; *Foreign Trade Statistics of Asia and the Pacific.*

The World Bank, 1818 H Street, NW, Washington, D.C. 20433 (202) 477-1234; *World Tables.*

TONGA - EXTERNAL FINANCING

Asian Development Bank, P.O. Box 789, 1099 Manila, Philippines; *Key Indicators of Developing Asian and Pacific Countries.*

TONGA - EXTERNAL INDEBTEDNESS

Asian Development Bank, P.O. Box 789, 1099 Manila, Philippines; *Key Indicators of Developing Asian and Pacific Countries.*

The World Bank, 1818 H Street, NW, Washington, D.C. 20433 (202) 477-1234; *World Tables.*

TONGA - EXTERNAL TRADE

Asian Development Bank, P.O. Box 789, 1099 Manila, Philippines; *Key Indicators of Developing Asian and Pacific Countries.*

Food and Agricultural Organization of the United Nations (FAO) Via delle Terme di Caracalla, 00100 Rome, Italy (Telephone Number in U.S. (202) 653-2400); *The State of Food and Agriculture,* and *Trade Yearbook.*

G.K. Hall and Company, 70 Lincoln Street, Boston, Massachusetts 02111 (617) 423-3990; *The World in Figures.*

Statistical Office of the United Nations, Publishing Service, New York, New York 10017 (800) 253-9646; *Statistical Yearbook for Asia and the Pacific.*

TONGA - FARM CROPS - See TONGA - CROPS

TONGA - FERTILITY RATES

The World Bank, 1818 H Street, NW, Washington, D.C. 20433 (202) 477-1234; *World Tables.*

TONGA - FERTILIZER

Food and Agricultural Organization of the United Nations (FAO), Via delle Terme di Caracalla, 00100, Rome, Italy (Telephone Number in U.S. (202) 653-2400); *Fertilizer Yearbook,* and *The State of Food and Agriculture.*

TONGA - FETAL MORTALITY

Statistical Office of the United Nations, Publishing Service, New York, New York 10017 (800) 253-9646; *Demographic Yearbook.*

TONGA - FINANCE

Asian Development Bank, P.O. Box 789, 1099 Manila, Philippines; *Key Indicators of Developing Asian and Pacific Countries.*

G.K. Hall and Company, 70 Lincoln Street, Boston, Massachusetts 02111 (617) 423-3990; *The World in Figures.*

Statistical Office of the United Nations, Publishing Service, New York, New York 10017 (800) 253-9646; *Statistical Yearbook for Asia and the Pacific.*

TONGA - FISHERIES

Food and Agricultural Organization of the United Nations (FAO) Via delle Terme di Caracalla, 00100 Rome, Italy (Telephone Number in U.S. (202) 653-2400); *The State of Food and Agriculture.*

Statistical Office of the United Nations, Publishing Service, New York, New York 10017 (800) 253-9646; *Statistical Yearbook,* and *Yearbook of Fishery Statistics.*

TONGA - FOOD

Food and Agricultural Organization of the United Nations (FAO) Via delle Terme di Caracalla, 00100 Rome, Italy (Telephone Number in U.S. (202) 653-2400); *The State of Food and Agriculture.*

G.K. Hall and Company, 70 Lincoln Street, Boston, Massachusetts 02111 (617) 423-3990; *The World in Figures.*

South Pacific Commission, Post Box D5, Noumea Cedex, New Caledonia; *Statistical Bulletin of the South Pacific: Retail Price Indexes.*

Statistical Office of the United Nations, Publishing Service, New York, New York 10017 (800) 253-9646; *Statistical Yearbook for Asia and the Pacific.*

TONGA - FOREIGN AID

G.K. Hall and Company, 70 Lincoln Street, Boston, Massachusetts 02111 (617) 423-3990; *The World in Figures.*

TONGA - FOREIGN TRADE

Asian Development Bank, P.O. Box 789, 1099 Manila, Philippines; *Key Indicators of Developing Asian and Pacific Countries.*

Food and Agricultural Organization of the United Nations (FAO) Via delle Terme di Caracalla, 00100 Rome, Italy (Telephone Number in U.S. (202) 653-2400); *The State of Food and Agriculture.*

G.K. Hall and Company, 70 Lincoln Street, Boston, Massachusetts 02111 (617) 423-3990; *The World in Figures.*

South Pacific Commission, Post Box D5, Noumea Cedex, New Caledonia; *Statistical Bulletin of the South Pacific: Overseas Trade.*

Statistical Office of the United Nations, Publishing Service, New York, New York 10017 (800) 253-9646; *International Trade Statistics Yearbook,* and *Statistical Yearbook.*

The World Bank, 1818 H Street, NW, Washington, D.C. 20433 (202) 477-1234; *World Tables.*

TONGA - FORESTRY AND FOREST PRODUCTS

Food and Agricultural Organization of the United Nations (FAO) Via delle Terme di Caracalla, 00100 Rome, Italy (Telephone Number in U.S. (202) 653-2400); *The State of Food and Agriculture.*

G.K. Hall and Company, 70 Lincoln Street, Boston, Massachusetts 02111 (617) 423-3990; *The World in Figures.*

TONGA - GENERAL INDUSTRIAL STATISTICS

Statistical Office of the United Nations, Publishing Service, New York, New York 10017 (800) 253-9646; *Industrial Statistics Yearbook.*

TONGA - GENERAL MORTALITY

Statistical Office of the United Nations, Publishing Service, New York, New York 10017 (800) 253-9646; *Demographic Yearbook.*

TONGA - GOVERNMENT

Asian Development Bank, P.O. Box 789, 1099 Manila, Philippines; *Key Indicators of Developing Asian and Pacific Countries.*

G.K. Hall and Company, 70 Lincoln Street, Boston, Massachusetts 02111 (617) 423-3990; *The World in Figures.*

TONGA - GOVERNMENT EXPENDITURE

Asian Development Bank, P.O. Box 789, 1099 Manila, Philippines; *Key Indicators of Developing Asian and Pacific Countries.*

The World Bank, 1010 H Street, NW, Washington, D.C. 20433 (202) 477-1234; *World Tables.*

TONGA - GOVERNMENT FINANCES

Asian Development Bank, P.O. Box 789, 1099 Manila, Philippines; *Key Indicators of Developing Asian and Pacific Countries.*

Statistical Office of the United Nations, Publishing Service, New York, New York 10017 (800) 253-9646; *Statistical Yearbook.*

TONGA - GOVERNMENT REVENUE

Asian Development Bank, P.O. Box 789, 1099 Manila, Philippines; *Key Indicators of Developing Asian and Pacific Countries.*

The World Bank, 1818 H Street, NW, Washington, D.C. 20433 (202) 477-1234; *World Tables.*

TONGA - GRAIN PRODUCTION - See TONGA - CROPS

TONGA - GROSS DOMESTIC PRODUCT

Asian Development Bank, P.O. Box 789, 1099 Manila, Philippines; *Key Indicators of Developing Asian and Pacific Countries.*

G.K. Hall and Company, 70 Lincoln Street, Boston, Massachusetts 02111 (617) 423-3990; *The World in Figures.*

Statistical Office of the United Nations, Publishing Service, New York, New York 10017 (800) 253-9646; *Statistical Yearbook.*

The World Bank, 1818 H Street, NW, Washington, D.C. 20433 (202) 477-1234; *World Tables.*

TONGA - GROSS NATIONAL PRODUCT

Asian Development Bank, P.O. Box 789, 1099 Manila, Philippines; *Key Indicators of Developing Asian and Pacific Countries.*

The World Bank, 1818 H Street, NW, Washington, D.C. 20433 (202) 477-1234; *World Tables.*

TONGA - GROUNDNUT PRODUCTION - See TONGA - CROPS

TONGA - HEALTH

G.K. Hall and Company, 70 Lincoln Street, Boston, Massachusetts 02111 (617) 423-3990; *The World in Figures.*

South Pacific Commission, Post Box D5, Noumea Cedex, New Caledonia; *Statistical Bulletin of the South Pacific: Retail Price Indexes.*

Statistical Office of the United Nations, Publishing Service, New York, New York 10017 (800) 253-9646; *Statistical Yearbook.*

World Health Organization, Office of Publications, Avenue Appia, CH-1211 Geneva 27, Switzerland (Telephone Number in U.S. (518) 436-9686); *World Health Statistics Annual.*

TONGA - HIGHWAYS

G.K. Hall and Company, 70 Lincoln Street, Boston, Massachusetts 02111 (617) 423-3990; *The World in Figures.*

TONGA - HORSES - See TONGA - LIVESTOCK AND POULTRY

TONGA - HOURS OF WORK - See TONGA - EMPLOYMENT

TONGA - HOUSING AND HOUSING UNITS

South Pacific Commission, Post Box D5, Noumea Cedex, New Caledonia; *Statistical Bulletin of the South Pacific: Retail Price Indexes.*

TONGA - HOUSING EXPENDITURES

South Pacific Commission, Post Box D5, Noumea Cedex, New Caledonia; *Statistical Bulletin of the South Pacific: Retail Price Indexes.*

TONGA - ILLITERATE POPULATION

G.K. Hall and Company, 70 Lincoln Street, Boston, Massachusetts 02111 (617) 423-3990; *The World in Figures.*

TONGA - IMPORTS

Asian Development Bank, P.O. Box 789, 1099 Manila, Philippines; *Key Indicators of Developing Asian and Pacific Countries.*

Food and Agricultural Organization of the United Nations (FAO) Via delle Terme di Caracalla, 00100 Rome, Italy (Telephone Number in U.S. (202) 653-2400); *The State of Food and Agriculture.*

G.K. Hall and Company, 70 Lincoln Street, Boston, Massachusetts 02111 (617) 423-3990; *The World in Figures.*

International Monetary Fund, 700 Nineteenth Street, NW, Washington, D.C. 20431 (202) 623-7000; *Direction of Trade Statistics.*

South Pacific Commission, Post Box D5, Noumea Cedex, New Caledonia; *Statistical Bulletin of the South Pacific: Overseas Trade.*

Statistical Office of the United Nations, Publishing Service, New York, New York 10017 (800) 253-9646; *Foreign Trade Statistics of Asia and the Pacific*.

The World Bank, 1818 H Street, NW, Washington, D.C. 20433 (202) 477-1234; *World Tables*.

TONGA - INDUSTRY

G.K. Hall and Company, 70 Lincoln Street, Boston, Massachusetts 02111 (617) 423-3990; *The World in Figures*.

International Labour Office, I.L.O. Publications, CH-1211, Geneva 22, Switzerland; *Yearbook of Labour Statistics*.

Statistical Office of the United Nations, Publishing Service, New York, New York 10017 (800) 253-9646; *Statistical Yearbook for Asia and the Pacific*.

TONGA - INFANT AND MATERNAL MORTALITY

Statistical Office of the United Nations, Publishing Service, New York, New York 10017 (800) 253-9646; *Demographic Yearbook*, and *Statistical Yearbook*.

TONGA - INTERNAL TRADE

Statistical Office of the United Nations, Publishing Service, New York, New York 10017 (800) 253-9646; *Statistical Yearbook for Asia and the Pacific*.

TONGA - INTERNATIONAL RESERVES EXCLUDING GOLD

Asian Development Bank, P.O. Box 789, 1099 Manila, Philippines; *Key Indicators of Developing Asian and Pacific Countries*.

TONGA - INTERNATIONAL STATISTICS

Asian Development Bank, P.O. Box 789, 1099 Manila, Philippines; *Key Indicators of Developing Asian and Pacific Countries*.

TONGA - LABOR FORCE

Food and Agricultural Organization of the United Nations (FAO) Via delle Terme di Caracalla, 00100 Rome, Italy (Telephone Number in U.S. (202) 653-2400); *The State of Food and Agriculture*.

G.K. Hall and Company, 70 Lincoln Street, Boston, Massachusetts 02111 (617) 423-3990; *The World in Figures*.

The World Bank, 1818 H Street, NW, Washington, D.C. 20433 (202) 477-1234; *World Tables*.

TONGA - LABOR PRODUCTIVITY

International Labour Office, I.L.O. Publications, CH-1211, Geneva 22, Switzerland; *Yearbook of Labour Statistics*.

TONGA - LAND USE

Food and Agricultural Organization of the United Nations (FAO), Via delle Terme di Caracalla, 00100 Rome, Italy (Telephone Number in U.S. (202) 653-2400); *Production Yearbook*.

G.K. Hall and Company, 70 Lincoln Street, Boston, Massachusetts 02111 (617) 423-3990; *The World in Figures*.

TONGA - LIBRARIES

United Nations Educational, Scientific and Cultural Organization (UNESCO), 7 Place de Fontenoy, F-75700 Paris, France (Telephone Number in U.S. (212) 963-5981); *Statistical Yearbook*.

TONGA - LIVESTOCK AND POULTRY

Food and Agricultural Organization of the United Nations (FAO), Via delle Terme di Caracalla, 00100 Rome, Italy (Telephone Number in U.S. (202) 653-2400); *Production Yearbook*, and *The State of Food and Agriculture*.

G.K. Hall and Company, 70 Lincoln Street, Boston, Massachusetts 02111 (617) 423-3990; *The World in Figures*.

Statistical Office of the United Nations, Publishing Service, New York, New York 10017 (800) 253-9646; *Statistical Yearbook*.

TONGA - LIVING LEVELS

G.K. Hall and Company, 70 Lincoln Street, Boston, Massachusetts 02111 (617) 423-3990; *The World in Figures*.

TONGA - MAIL - NUMBER OF ITEMS SENT AND RECEIVED

Statistical Office of the United Nations, Publishing Service, New York, New York 10017 (800) 253-9646; *Statistical Yearbook*.

TONGA - MANPOWER

Statistical Office of the United Nations, Publishing Service, New York, New York 10017 (800) 253-9646; *Statistical Yearbook for Asia and the Pacific*.

TONGA - MANUFACTURING

Asian Development Bank, P.O. Box 789, 1099 Manila, Philippines; *Key Indicators of Developing Asian and Pacific Countries*.

G.K. Hall and Company, 70 Lincoln Street, Boston, Massachusetts 02111 (617) 423-3990; *The World in Figures*.

The World Bank, 1818 H Street, NW, Washington, D.C. 20433 (202) 477-1234; *World Tables*.

TONGA - MARRIAGE RATES

Statistical Office of the United Nations, Publishing Service, New York, New York 10017 (800) 253-9646; *Demographic Yearbook*, and *Statistical Yearbook*.

TONGA - MEAT PRODUCTION - See TONGA - LIVESTOCK AND POULTRY

TONGA - MERCHANT SHIPPING

G.K. Hall and Company, 70 Lincoln Street, Boston, Massachusetts 02111 (617) 423-3990; *The World in Figures*.

Statistical Office of the United Nations, Publishing Service, New York, New York 10017 (800) 253-9646; *Statistical Yearbook*.

U.S. Department of Transportation, Maritime Administration, 400 Seventh Street, SW, Washington, D.C. 20590 (202) 366-5807; *A Statistical Analysis of the World's Merchant Fleets*.

TONGA - MILITARY

G.K. Hall and Company, 70 Lincoln Street, Boston, Massachusetts 02111 (617) 423-3990; *The World in Figures.*

TONGA - MINING AND MINERAL PRODUCTS

Asian Development Bank, P.O. Box 789, 1099 Manila, Philippines; *Key Indicators of Developing Asian and Pacific Countries.*

G.K. Hall and Company, 70 Lincoln Street, Boston, Massachusetts 02111 (617) 423-3990; *The World in Figures.*

TONGA - MONEY SUPPLY

Asian Development Bank, P.O. Box 789, 1099 Manila, Philippines; *Key Indicators of Developing Asian and Pacific Countries.*

G.K. Hall and Company, 70 Lincoln Street, Boston, Massachusetts 02111 (617) 423-3990; *The World in Figures.*

The World Bank, 1818 H Street, NW, Washington, D.C. 20433 (202) 477-1234; *World Tables.*

TONGA - MOTION PICTURES

Statistical Office of the United Nations, Publishing Service, New York, New York 10017 (800) 253-9646; *Statistical Yearbook.*

TONGA - MOTOR VEHICLES IN USE

G.K. Hall and Company, 70 Lincoln Street, Boston, Massachusetts 02111 (617) 423-3990; *The World in Figures.*

Statistical Office of the United Nations, Publishing Service, New York, New York 10017 (800) 253-9646; *Statistical Yearbook.*

TONGA - NATALITY - See TONGA - BIRTH RATES

TONGA - NATIONAL ACCOUNTS

Statistical Office of the United Nations, Publishing Service, New York, New York 10017 (800) 253-9646; *National Accounts Statistics,* and *Statistical Yearbook for Asia and the Pacific.*

TONGA - NATIONAL INCOME

G.K. Hall and Company, 70 Lincoln Street, Boston, Massachusetts 02111 (617) 423-3990; *The World in Figures.*

Statistical Office of the United Nations, Publishing Service, New York, New York 10017 (800) 253-9646; *Statistical Yearbook.*

TONGA - NEWSPAPER PRODUCTION - See TONGA - FORESTRY AND FOREST PRODUCTS

TONGA - OCCUPATIONS - See TONGA - OCCUPATIONS

TONGA - PERIODICALS

United Nations Educational, Scientific and Cultural Organization (UNESCO), 7 Place de Fontenoy, F-75700 Paris, France (Telephone Number in U.S. (212) 963-5981); *Statistical Yearbook.*

TONGA - PESTICIDE USE

Food and Agricultural Organization of the United Nations (FAO) Via delle Terme di Caracalla, 00100 Rome, Italy (Telephone Number in U.S. (202) 653-2400); *The State of Food and Agriculture.*

TONGA - PETROLEUM INDUSTRY

Asian Development Bank, P.O. Box 789, 1099 Manila, Philippines; *Key Indicators of Developing Asian and Pacific Countries.*

Food and Agricultural Organization of the United Nations (FAO) Via delle Terme di Caracalla, 00100 Rome, Italy (Telephone Number in U.S. (202) 653-2400); *The State of Food and Agriculture.*

G.K. Hall and Company, 70 Lincoln Street, Boston, Massachusetts 02111 (617) 423-3990; *The World in Figures.*

TONGA - PIGS - See TONGA - LIVESTOCK AND POULTRY

TONGA - POPULATION

Asian Development Bank, P.O. Box 789, 1099 Manila, Philippines; *Key Indicators of Developing Asian and Pacific Countries.*

Food and Agricultural Organization of the United Nations (FAO), Via delle Terme di Caracalla, 00100 Rome, Italy (Telephone Number in U.S. (202) 653-2400); *Production Yearbook.*

G.K. Hall and Company, 70 Lincoln Street, Boston, Massachusetts 02111 (617) 423-3990; *The World in Figures.*

International Labour Office, I.L.O. Publications, CH-1211, Geneva 22, Switzerland; *Yearbook of Labour Statistics.*

Statistical Office of the United Nations, Publishing Service, New York, New York 10017 (800) 253-9646; *Demographic Yearbook, Statistical Yearbook,* and *Statistical Yearbook for Asia and the Pacific.*

TONGA - POWER PRODUCTION INDUSTRY

Statistical Office of the United Nations, Publishing Service, New York, New York 10017 (800) 253-9646; *Electric Power in Asia and the Pacific.*

TONGA - PRICES

Asian Development Bank, P.O. Box 789, 1099 Manila, Philippines; *Key Indicators of Developing Asian and Pacific Countries.*

Food and Agricultural Organization of the United Nations (FAO), Via delle Terme di Caracalla, 00100 Rome, Italy (Telephone Number in U.S. (202) 653-2400); *Production Yearbook,* and *The State of Food and Agriculture.*

G.K. Hall and Company, 70 Lincoln Street, Boston, Massachusetts 02111 (617) 423-3990; *The World in Figures.*

International Labour Office, I.L.O. Publications, CH-1211, Geneva 22, Switzerland; *Yearbook of Labour Statistics.*

South Pacific Commission, Post Box D5, Noumea Cedex, New Caledonia; *Statistical Bulletin of the South Pacific: Overseas Trade,* and *Statistical Bulletin of the South Pacific: Retail Price Indexes.*

TONGA - PRODUCTION

G.K. Hall and Company, 70 Lincoln Street, Boston, Massachusetts 02111 (617) 423-3990; *The World in Figures.*

TONGA - RAILWAYS

G.K. Hall and Company, 70 Lincoln Street, Boston, Massachusetts 02111 (617) 423-3990; *The World in Figures.*

TONGA - RETAIL TRADE

G.K. Hall and Company, 70 Lincoln Street, Boston, Massachusetts 02111 (617) 423-3990; *The World in Figures.*

TONGA - RICE PRODUCTION - See TONGA - CROPS

TONGA - SOCIAL DATA

Asian Development Bank, P.O. Box 789, 1099 Manila, Philippines; *Key Indicators of Developing Asian and Pacific Countries.*

G.K. Hall and Company, 70 Lincoln Street, Boston, Massachusetts 02111 (617) 423-3990; *The World in Figures.*

TONGA - STOCKS - COMMODITY - MARKET PRICE - INDEX

Food and Agricultural Organization of the United Nations (FAO) Via delle Terme di Caracalla, 00100 Rome, Italy (Telephone Number in U.S. (202) 653-2400); *The State of Food and Agriculture.*

TONGA - TAXATION

G.K. Hall and Company, 70 Lincoln Street, Boston, Massachusetts 02111 (617) 423-3990; *The World in Figures.*

The World Bank, 1818 H Street, NW, Washington, D.C. 20433 (202) 477-1234; *World Tables.*

TONGA - TELEPHONES IN USE

American Telephone and Telegraph Company, 26 Parsippany Road, Whippany, New Jersey 07981 (800) 338-4038; *The World's Telephones.*

G.K. Hall and Company, 70 Lincoln Street, Boston, Massachusetts 02111 (617) 423-3990; *The World in Figures.*

TONGA - TEXTILE INDUSTRY

G.K. Hall and Company, 70 Lincoln Street, Boston, Massachusetts 02111 (617) 423-3990; *The World in Figures.*

TONGA - TOBACCO PRODUCTION

South Pacific Commission, Post Box D5, Noumea Cedex, New Caledonia; *Statistical Bulletin of the South Pacific: Retail Price Indexes.*

TONGA - TOURISM

G.K. Hall and Company, 70 Lincoln Street, Boston, Massachusetts 02111 (617) 423-3990; *The World in Figures.*

Statistical Office of the United Nations, Publishing Service, New York, New York 10017 (800) 253-9646; *Statistical Yearbook.*

World Tourism Organization, Calle Capitan Haya 42, E-28020 Madrid, Spain; *Yearbook of Tourism Statistics.*

TONGA - TRACTORS IN USE

Statistical Office of the United Nations, Publishing Service, New York, New York 10017 (800) 253-9646; *Statistical Yearbook.*

TONGA - TRADE - See TONGA - FOREIGN TRADE

TONGA - TRANSPORTATION AND COMMUNICATIONS

G.K. Hall and Company, 70 Lincoln Street, Boston, Massachusetts 02111 (617) 423-3990; *The World in Figures.*

South Pacific Commission, Post Box D5, Noumea Cedex, New Caledonia; *Statistical Bulletin of the South Pacific: Retail Price Indexes.*

Statistical Office of the United Nations, Publishing Service, New York, New York 10017 (800) 253-9646; *Statistical Yearbook for Asia and the Pacific.*

TONGA - UNEMPLOYMENT

International Labour Office, I.L.O. Publications, CH-1211, Geneva 22, Switzerland; *Yearbook of Labour Statistics.*

TONGA - UTILITIES

Statistical Office of the United Nations, Publishing Service, New York, New York 10017 (800) 253-9646; *Electric Power in Asia and the Pacific.*

TONGA - VITAL STATISTICS

G.K. Hall and Company, 70 Lincoln Street, Boston, Massachusetts 02111 (617) 423-3990; *The World in Figures.*

Statistical Office of the United Nations, Publishing Service, New York, New York 10017 (800) 253-9646; *Statistical Yearbook.*

TONGA - WAGES

G.K. Hall and Company, 70 Lincoln Street, Boston, Massachusetts 02111 (617) 423-3990; *The World in Figures.*

International Labour Office, I.L.O. Publications, CH-1211, Geneva 22, Switzerland; *Yearbook of Labour Statistics.*

Statistical Office of the United Nations, Publishing Service, New York, New York 10017 (800) 253-9646; *Statistical Yearbook for Asia and the Pacific.*

TONGA - WEATHER

G.K. Hall and Company, 70 Lincoln Street, Boston, Massachusetts 02111 (617) 423-3990; *The World in Figures.*

TONGA - WHOLESALE PRICES

Asian Development Bank, P.O. Box 789, 1099 Manila, Philippines; *Key Indicators of Developing Asian and Pacific Countries.*

TONNAGE - VESSELS - ENTERED AND CLEARED IN FOREIGN TRADE

U.S. Department of Commerce, Bureau of the Census, Suitland, Maryland 20233 (301) 763-4040; TA 987.

TONNAGE - VESSELS - MERCHANT

Lloyd's Register of Shipping, 71 Fenchurch Street, London EC3, England; *Statistical Tables,* and *Annual Summary of Merchant Ships Completed in the World.*

U.S. Department of Transportation, Maritime Administration, 400 Seventh Street, SW, Washington, D.C. 20590 (202) 366-5807; *Employment Report of United States Flag Merchant Fleet*

Oceangoing Vessels 1000 Gross Tons and Over, and *New Ship Construction*.

TONNAGE - VESSELS - SHIPS AND TONNAGE LOST

Lloyd's Register of Shipping, 71 Fenchurch Street, London EC3, England; *Casualty Return*.

TONNAGE - VESSELS - WATERBORNE FOREIGN COMMERCE

U.S. Department of Commerce, Bureau of the Census, Suitland, Maryland 20233 (301) 763-4040; TM 985.

TOOLS - See CUTLERY, ETC. AND MACHINE TOOLS

TORNADOES

U.S. Department of Commerce, National Oceanic and Atmospheric Administration, National Climatic Data Center, Federal Building, Asheville, North Carolina 28801 (704) 259-2850; *Storm Data*.

TOURISM - FOREIGN - See also TRAVEL

U.S. Department of Commerce, Bureau of Economic Analysis, Fourteenth Street between Constitution Avenue and E Street, NW, Washington, D.C. 20230 (202) 606-9900; *Survey of Current Business*.

U.S. Department of Commerce, Travel and Tourism Administration, Washington, D.C. 20230 (202) 482-3811; unpublished data.

U.S. Department of Justice, Immigration and Naturalization Service, 425 I Street, NW, Washington, D.C. 20536 (202) 514-4316; *Statistical Yearbook*.

U.S. Department of Transportation, Bureau of Transportation Statistics, 400 Seventh Street, SW, Washington, D.C. 20590 (202) 366-DATA; *National Transportation Statistics Annual, Historical Compendium Information Report*.

U.S. Department of Transportation, Transportation Systems Center, Kendall Square, Cambridge, Massachusetts 02142 (617) 494-2224; *International Travel Statistics*.

TOWNSHIPS AND SPECIAL DISTRICTS

U.S. Department of Commerce, Bureau of the Census, Suitland, Maryland 20233 (301) 763-4040; *Census of Governments*, and *Government Organization*.

TOYS AND SPORTING GOODS - ADVERTISING EXPENDITURES

Television Bureau of Advertising, Incorporated, 850 Third Avenue, New York, New York 10022 (212) 486-1111; from data compiled by Competitive Media Reporting, 11 West 42nd Street, New York, New York 10036 (212) 789-1400.

TOYS AND SPORTING GOODS - CONSUMER EXPENDITURES

U.S. Department of Commerce, Bureau of Economic Analysis, Fourteenth Street between Constitution Avenue and E Street, NW, Washington, D.C. 20230 (202) 606-9900; *The National Income and Product Accounts of the United States*, and *Survey of Current Business*.

TOYS AND SPORTING GOODS - FOREIGN TRADE

U.S. Department of Commerce, Bureau of the Census, Suitland, Maryland 20233 (301) 763-4040; *U.S. Merchandise Trade: Exports, General Imports, and Imports for Consumption*.

TOYS AND SPORTING GOODS - MANUFACTURING

U.S. Department of Commerce, Bureau of the Census, Suitland, Maryland 20233 (301) 763-4040; *Census of Manufactures*, and *Annual Survey of Manufactures*.

U.S. Department of Labor, Bureau of Labor Statistics, Two Massachusetts Avenue, NE, Washington, D.C. 20212 (202) 606-7828; *Employment and Earnings*, and Bulletins 2370 and 2429.

TOYS AND SPORTING GOODS - PRICE INDEXES

U.S. Department of Labor, Bureau of Labor Statistics, Two Massachusetts Avenue, NE, Washington, D.C. 20212 (202) 606-7828; *Monthly Labor Review*, and *CPI Detailed Report*.

TRACTORS

U.S. Department of Agriculture, Economic Research Service, Fourteenth Street and Independence Avenue, SW, Washington, D.C. 20250 (202) 219-1504; *Agricultural Statistics*, and *Economic Indicators of the Farm Sector: National Financial Summary*.

TRADE (BUSINESS) - See: COMMERCE, FOREIGN TRADE, RETAIL TRADE and WHOLESALE TRADE

TRADE, BUSINESS AND COMMERCIAL ASSOCIATIONS

Gale Research Incorporated, 835 Penobscot Building, Detroit, Michigan 48226 (800) 877-4253; *Encyclopedia of Associations*.

TRAILERS (CAMPERS)

American Automobile Manufacturers Association, 1401 H Street, NW, Suite 900, Washington, D.C. 20005 (202) 326-5500; *Motor Vehicle Facts and Figures*.

Recreation Vehicle Industry Association, Post Office Box 2999, 1896 Preston White Drive, Reston, Virginia 22090 (703) 620-6003; *RV's . . . The Family Camping Vehicle, A Year End Report*.

TRANQUILIZERS

U.S. Department of Health and Human Services, Substance Abuse and Mental Health Services Administration, 5600 Fishers Lane, Rockville, Maryland 20857 (301) 443-4797; *National Household Survey on Drug Abuse*.

TRANSCEIVERS/CB

U.S. Federal Communications Commission, 1919 M Street, NW, Washington, D.C. 20554 (202) 632-7000; *Annual Report*, and unpublished data.

TRANSIT INDUSTRY - See PASSENGER TRANSIT INDUSTRY

TRANSPORTATION - See also MOTOR VEHICLES and Individual Carriers

TRANSPORTATION - ACCIDENTS

International Civil Aviation Organization, 1000 Sherbrooke Street, West, Montreal, Quebec H3A 2R2, Canada (514) 285-8219; *Civil Aviation Statistics of the World*.

U.S. Department of Transportation, Bureau of Transportation Statistics, 400 Seventh Street, SW, Washington, D.C. 20590 (202) 366-DATA; *National Transportation Statistics Annual, Historical Compendium Information Report*.

U.S. Department of Transportation, Federal Aviation Administration, 800 Independence Avenue, SW, Washington, D.C. 20591 (202) 366-4000; *FAA Statistical Handbook of Aviation*, and unpublished data.

TRANSPORTATION - CARRIERS OF PASSENGERS

Air Transport Association of America, 1301 Pennsylvania Avenue, NW, Washington, D.C. 20004 (202) 626-4000; *Air Transport*, and *Air Transport, Facts and Figures*.

American Bus Association, 1100 New York Avenue, NW, Washington, D.C. 20005 (202) 842-1645; *Bus Facts*, and *Annual Report*.

American Public Transit Association, 1201 New York Avenue, NW, Suite 400, Washington, D.C. 20005 (202) 898-4000; *Transit Fact Book*.

Association of American Railroads, American Railroads Building, 50 F Street, NW, Washington, D.C. 20001 (202) 639-2100; *Railroad Facts, Statistics of Railroads of Class I*, and *Analysis of Class I Railroads*.

Eno Transportation Foundation, 44211 Statestone Court, Lansdowne, Virginia 22073 (703) 729-7200; *Transportation in America*.

Regional Airline Association, 1101 Connecticut Avenue, NW, Suite 700, Washington, D.C. 20036 (202) 857-1170; *Annual Report of the Regional Airline Industry*.

U.S. Department of Transportation, Federal Aviation Administration, 800 Independence Avenue, SW, Washington, D.C. 20591 (202) 366-4000; *Air Carrier Traffic Statistics*, and *Air Carrier Financial Statistics*.

U.S. Interstate Commerce Commission, Twelfth Street and Constitution Avenue, NW, Washington, D.C. 20423 (202) 275-7119; *Transport Statistics in the United States*.

TRANSPORTATION - CARRIERS OF PROPERTY

Association of American Railroads, American Railroads Building, 50 F Street, NW, Washington, D.C. 20001 (202) 639-2100; *Weekly Railroad Traffic*, and *Freight Commodity Statistics*.

Eno Transportation Foundation, 44211 Statestone Court, Lansdowne, Virginia 22073 (703) 729-7200; *Transportation in America*.

U.S. Department of Commerce, Bureau of the Census, Suitland, Maryland 20233 (301) 763-4040; *Current Business Reports*, and *Motor Freight Transportation and Warehousing Survey*.

U.S. Interstate Commerce Commission, Twelfth Street and Constitution Avenue, NW, Washington, D.C. 20423 (202) 275-7119; *Transport Statistics in the United States*.

TRANSPORTATION - CONSUMER COMPLAINTS

U.S. Department of Transportation, Office of Consumer Affairs, 400 Seventh Street, SW, Washington, D.C. 20590 (202) 366-4000; *Air Travel Consumer Report*.

TRANSPORTATION - CONSUMER EXPENDITURES

U.S. Department of Labor, Bureau of Labor Statistics, Two Massachusetts Avenue, NE, Washington, D.C. 20212 (202) 606-7828; *Consumer Expenditure in 1992*, and *Consumer Expenditure Survey*.

TRANSPORTATION - CONSUMER PRICE INDEXES

U.S. Department of Labor, Bureau of Labor Statistics, Two Massachusetts Avenue, NE, Washington, D.C. 20212 (202) 606-7828; *Consumer Price Indexes, Detailed Report, Monthly Labor Review*, and *Handbook of Labor Statistics*.

TRANSPORTATION - CONSUMER PRICE INDEXES - FOREIGN COUNTRIES

International Monetary Fund, 700 Nineteenth Street, NW, Washington, D.C. 20431 (202) 623-7000; *International Financial Statistics*.

TRANSPORTATION - COST INDEXES - AIRLINES

Air Transport Association of America, 1301 Pennsylvania Avenue, NW, Washington, D.C. 20004 (202) 626-4000; *Air Transport*, and unpublished data.

TRANSPORTATION - COST INDEXES - RAILROAD

U.S. Department of Labor, Bureau of Labor Statistics, Two Massachusetts Avenue, NE, Washington, D.C. 20212 (202) 606-7828; *Producer Price Indexes*.

TRANSPORTATION - CRIME INCIDENTS

U.S. Department of Justice, Bureau of Justice Statistics, 633 Indiana Avenue, NW, Washington, D.C. 20531 (800) 732-3277; *Criminal Victimization in the United States*.

TRANSPORTATION - ENERGY CONSUMPTION

U.S. Department of Energy, Energy Information Administration, Washington, D.C. 20585 (202) 586-8800; *State Energy Data Report, Monthly Energy Review Annual Energy Review*, and *State Energy Price and Expenditure Report*.

TRANSPORTATION - EXPENDITURES

Eno Transportation Foundation, 44211 Statestone Court, Lansdowne, Virginia 22073 (703) 729-7200; *Transportation in America*.

U.S. Department of Commerce, Bureau of the Census, Suitland, Maryland 20233 (301) 763-4040; *Service Annual Survey*.

TRANSPORTATION - FEDERAL GOVERNMENT - AID TO STATE AND LOCAL GOVERNMENTS

Executive Office of the President, Office of Management and Budget, Executive Office Building, Washington, D.C. 20503 (202) 395-3080; *Historical Tables, Budget of the United States Government*, and *Budget of the United States*.

TRANSPORTATION - FEDERAL GOVERNMENT - OUTLAYS

Executive Office of the President, Office of Management and Budget, Executive Office Building, Washington, D.C. 20503 (202) 395-3080; *The Budget of the United States Government*.

U.S. National Science Foundation, 4201 Wilson Boulevard, Arlington, Virginia 22230 (703) 306-1234; *Federal R & D Funding by Budget Function*.

TRANSPORTATION - FREIGHT

Eno Transportation Foundation, 44211 Statestone Court, Lansdowne, Virginia 22073 (703) 729-7200; *Transportation in America*.

TRANSPORTATION - GOVERNMENT EMPLOYEES AND PAYROLLS - CITY GOVERNMENT

U.S. Department of Commerce, Bureau of the Census, Suitland, Maryland 20233 (301) 763-4040; *City Employment*.

TRANSPORTATION - GOVERNMENT FINANCES

Executive Office of the President, Office of Management and Budget, Executive Office Building, Washington, D.C. 20503 (202) 395-3080; *Budget of the United States Government*.

U.S. Department of Commerce, Bureau of the Census, Suitland, Maryland 20233 (301) 763-4040; *Government Finances, State Government Finances, Historical Statistics on Governmental Finances and Employment*, and *Survey of Current Business*.

TRANSPORTATION - GOVERNMENT FINANCES - CITIES

U.S. Department of Commerce, Bureau of the Census, Suitland, Maryland 20233 (301) 763-4040; *City Government Finances*.

TRANSPORTATION - HOUSEHOLD

U.S. Department of Energy, Energy Information Administration, 1000 Independence Avenue, SW, Washington, D.C. 20585 (202) 586-8800; *Household Vehicles Energy Consumption*.

TRANSPORTATION - OCCUPATIONS

Air Transport Association of America, 1301 Pennsylvania Avenue, NW, Washington, D.C. 20004 (202) 626-4000; *Air Transport*, and *Air Transport, Facts and Figures*.

U.S. Department of Commerce, Bureau of the Census, Suitland, Maryland 20233 (301) 763-4040; *Current Population Reports*.

U.S. Department of Labor, Bureau of Labor Statistics, Two Massachusetts Avenue, NE, Washington, D.C. 20212 (202) 606-7828; *Employment and Earnings, Monthly Labor Review*, and Bulletin 2370.

TRANSPORTATION - OUTLAYS - BY TYPE OF TRANSPORT

Eno Transportation Foundation, 44211 Statestone Court, Lansdowne, Virginia 22073 (703) 729-7200; *Transportation in America*.

TRANSPORTATION - RECEIPTS

U.S. Department of Commerce, Bureau of the Census, Suitland, Maryland 20233 (301) 763-4040; *Service Annual Survey*.

TRANSPORTATION - SECURITIES

Board of Governors of the Federal Reserve System, Twentieth Street and Constitution Avenue, NW, Washington, D.C. 20551 (202) 452-3000; *Federal Reserve Bulletin*, and *Annual Statistical Digest*.

TRANSPORTATION - STOCK AND BOND PRICES AND YIELDS

Board of Governors of the Federal Reserve System, Twentieth Street and Constitution Avenue, NW, Washington, D.C. 20551 (202) 452-3000; *Federal Reserve Bulletin*.

TRANSPORTATION - TRAVEL VOLUME

Air Transport Association of America, 1301 Pennsylvania Avenue, NW, Washington, D.C. 20004 (202) 626-4000; *Air Transport*, and *Air Transport, Facts and Figures*.

Eno Transportation Foundation, 44211 Statestone Court, Lansdowne, Virginia 22073 (703) 729-7200; *Transportation in America*.

Regional Airline Association, 1101 Connecticut Avenue, NW, Suite 700, Washington, D.C. 20036 (202) 857-1170; *Annual Report of the Regional Airline Industry*.

TRANSPORTATION AND PUBLIC UTILITIES INDUSTRY - See also Individual Industries

TRANSPORTATION AND PUBLIC UTILITIES INDUSTRY - CAPITAL

U.S. Department of Commerce, Bureau of Economic Analysis, Fourteenth Street between Constitution Avenue and E Street, NW, Washington, D.C. 20230 (202) 606-9900; *Fixed Reproducible Tangible Wealth in the United States*, and *Survey of Current Business*.

TRANSPORTATION AND PUBLIC UTILITIES INDUSTRY - COLLECTIVE BARGAINING SETTLEMENTS

U.S. Department of Labor, Bureau of Labor Statistics, Two Massachusetts Avenue, NE, Washington, D.C. 20212 (202) 606-7828; *Compensation and Working Conditions*.

TRANSPORTATION AND PUBLIC UTILITIES INDUSTRY - CONSTRUCTION

U.S. Department of Commerce, Bureau of the Census, Suitland, Maryland 20233 (301) 763-4040; *Current Construction Reports*.

TRANSPORTATION AND PUBLIC UTILITIES INDUSTRY - CONSTRUCTION - COST INDEXES

U.S. Department of Commerce, Bureau of the Census, Suitland, Maryland 20233 (301) 763-4040; *Current Construction Report*.

TRANSPORTATION AND PUBLIC UTILITIES INDUSTRY - EARNINGS

Eno Transportation Foundation, 44211 Statestone Court, Lansdowne, Virginia 22073 (703) 729-7200; *Transportation in America*.

U.S. Department of Commerce, Bureau of the Census, Suitland, Maryland 20233 (301) 763-4040; *County Business Patterns*, and *Census of Transportation*.

U.S. Department of Labor, Bureau of Labor Statistics, Two Massachusetts Avenue, NE, Washington, D.C. 20212 (202) 606-7828; *Employment and Earnings*, and Bulletins 2370 and 2429.

TRANSPORTATION AND PUBLIC UTILITIES INDUSTRY - EMPLOYEES

U.S. Department of Commerce, Bureau of the Census, Suitland, Maryland 20233 (301) 763-4040; *Census of Manufactures, Annual Survey of Manufactures*, and *County Business Patterns*.

U.S. Department of Labor, Bureau of Labor Statistics, Two Massachusetts Avenue, NE, Washington, D.C. 20212 (202) 606-7828; *Employment and Earnings, Monthly Labor Review*, and Bulletins 2370 and 2429.

TRANSPORTATION AND PUBLIC UTILITIES INDUSTRY - ESTABLISHMENTS

U.S. Department of Commerce, Bureau of the Census, Suitland, Maryland 20233 (301) 763-4040; *County Business Patterns*.

TRANSPORTATION AND PUBLIC UTILITIES INDUSTRY - FINANCES

Forbes, Incorporated, 60 Fifth Avenue, New York, New York 10011 (212) 620-2200; *Forbes Annual Report on American Industry*.

U.S. Department of the Treasury, Internal Revenue Service, 1111 Constitution Avenue, NW, Washington, D.C. 20224 (202) 566-5000; *Statistics of Income*, various publications and unpublished data.

TRANSPORTATION AND PUBLIC UTILITIES INDUSTRY - GROSS NATIONAL PRODUCT

U.S. Department of Commerce, Bureau of Economic Analysis, Fourteenth Street between Constitution Avenue and E Street, NW, Washington, D.C. 20230 (202) 606-9900; *The National Income and Product Accounts of the United States*, and *Survey of Current Business*.

TRANSPORTATION AND PUBLIC UTILITIES INDUSTRY - OCCUPATIONAL SAFETY

National Safety Council, 1121 Spring Lake Drive, Itasca, Illinois 60143-3201 (708) 285-1121; *Accident Facts*.

TRANSPORTATION AND PUBLIC UTILITIES INDUSTRY - PRODUCTIVITY

U.S. Department of Labor, Bureau of Labor Statistics, Two Massachusetts Avenue, NE, Washington, D.C. 20212 (202) 606-7828; *Productivity Measures for Selected Industries and Government Services*, and unpublished data.

TRANSPORTATION AND PUBLIC UTILITIES INDUSTRY - PROFITS

Forbes, Incorporated, 60 Fifth Avenue, New York, New York 10011 (212) 620-2200; *Forbes Annual Report on American Industry*.

U.S. Department of Commerce, Bureau of Economic Analysis, Fourteenth Street between Constitution Avenue and E Street, NW, Washington, D.C. 20230 (202) 606-9900; *The National Income and Product Accounts of the United States*, and *Survey of Current Business*.

U.S. Department of the Treasury, Internal Revenue Service, 1111 Constitution Avenue, NW, Washington, D.C. 20224 (202) 566-5000; *Statistics of Income*.

TRANSPORTATION AND PUBLIC UTILITIES INDUSTRY - UNION MEMBERSHIP

U.S. Department of Labor, Bureau of Labor Statistics, Two Massachusetts Avenue, NE, Washington, D.C. 20212 (202) 606-7828; *Employment and Earnings*.

TRANSPORTATION, DEPARTMENT OF - BUDGET OUTLAYS

Executive Office of the President, Office of Management and Budget, Executive Office Building, Washington, D.C. 20503 (202) 395-3080; *Budget of the United States Government*.

TRANSPORTATION EQUIPMENT - MANUFACTURING - CAPITAL

U.S. Department of Commerce, Bureau of Economic Analysis, Fourteenth Street between Constitution Avenue and E Street, NW, Washington, D.C. 20230 (202) 606-9900; *Survey of Current Business*, and *Fixed Reproducible Tangible Wealth in the United States*.

U.S. Department of Commerce, Bureau of the Census, Suitland, Maryland 20233 (301) 763-4040; *Current Industrial Reports*.

TRANSPORTATION EQUIPMENT - MANUFACTURING - EARNINGS

U.S. Department of Commerce, Bureau of the Census, Suitland, Maryland 20233 (301) 763-4040; *Census of Manufactures*, and *Annual Survey of Manufactures*.

U.S. Department of Labor, Bureau of Labor Statistics, Two Massachusetts Avenue, NE, Washington, D.C. 20212 (202) 606-7828; *Employment and Earnings*, and Bulletins 2370 and 2429.

TRANSPORTATION EQUIPMENT - MANUFACTURING - EMPLOYEES

U.S. Department of Commerce, Bureau of the Census, Suitland, Maryland 20233 (301) 763-4040; *Census of Manufactures*, and *Annual Survey of Manufactures*.

U.S. Department of Labor, Bureau of Labor Statistics, Two Massachusetts Avenue, NE, Washington, D.C. 20212 (202) 606-7828; *Employment and Earnings*, *Monthly Labor Review*, and Bulletins 2370 and 2429.

TRANSPORTATION EQUIPMENT - MANUFACTURING - ESTABLISHMENTS

U.S. Department of Commerce, Bureau of the Census, Suitland, Maryland 20233 (301) 763-4040; *Census of Manufactures*, and *Annual Survey of Manufactures*.

TRANSPORTATION EQUIPMENT - MANUFACTURING - FOREIGN TRADE

U.S. Department of Commerce, Bureau of the Census, Suitland, Maryland 20233 (301) 763-4040; *U.S. Merchandise Trade: Selected Highlights*, and *U.S. Merchandise Trade: Exports, General Imports and Imports for Consumption*.

TRANSPORTATION EQUIPMENT - MANUFACTURING - GROSS NATIONAL PRODUCT

U.S. Department of Commerce, Bureau of Economic Analysis, Fourteenth Street between Constitution Avenue and E Street, SW, Washington, D.C. 20230 (202) 606-9900; *The National Income and Product Accounts of the United States*, and *Survey of Current Business*.

TRANSPORTATION EQUIPMENT - MANUFACTURING - INVENTORIES

U.S. Department of Commerce, Bureau of the Census, Suitland, Maryland 20233 (301) 763-4040; *Current Industrial Reports*, *Manufactures' Shipments, Inventories, and Orders*.

TRANSPORTATION EQUIPMENT - MANUFACTURING - MERGERS AND ACQUISITIONS

Securities Data Company, 1180 Raymond Boulevard, Newark, New Jersey 07102 (201) 622-3100; *Merger and Corporate Transactions Database*.

TRANSPORTATION EQUIPMENT - MANUFACTURING - POLLUTION ABATEMENT

U.S. Department of Commerce, Bureau of the Census, Suitland, Maryland 20233 (301) 763-4040; *Current Industrial Reports.*

TRANSPORTATION EQUIPMENT - MANUFACTURING - PRODUCER PRICES

U.S. Department of Labor, Bureau of Labor Statistics, Two Massachusetts Avenue, NE, Washington, D.C. 20212 (202) 606-7828; *Producer Price Indexes.*

TRANSPORTATION EQUIPMENT - MANUFACTURING - PRODUCTIVITY

Board of Governors of the Federal Reserve System, Twentieth Street and Constitution Avenue, NW, Washington, D.C. 20551 (202) 452-3000; *Federal Reserve Bulletin.*

U.S. Department of Labor, Bureau of Labor Statistics, Two Massachusetts Avenue, NE, Washington, D.C. 20212 (202) 606-7828; *Productivity Measures for Selected Industries and Government Services,* and unpublished data.

TRANSPORTATION EQUIPMENT - MANUFACTURING - PROFITS

Forbes, Incorporated, 60 Fifth Avenue, New York, New York 10011 (212) 620-2200; *Forbes Annual Report on American Industry.*

Time Warner, 1675 Broadway, Rockefeller Center, New York, New York 10019 (212) 522-1212; *The Fortune Directories.*

TRANSPORTATION EQUIPMENT - MANUFACTURING - RESEARCH AND DEVELOPMENT

U.S. National Science Foundation, 4201 Wilson Boulevard, Arlington, Virginia 22230 (202) 306-1234; *Research and Development in Industry.*

TRANSPORTATION EQUIPMENT - MANUFACTURING - SHIPMENTS

U.S. Department of Commerce, Bureau of the Census, Suitland, Maryland 20233 (301) 763-4040; *Current Industrial Reports, Manufactures' Shipments, Inventories, and Orders, Census of Manufactures,* and *Annual Survey of Manufactures.*

TRANSPORTATION EQUIPMENT - MANUFACTURING - VALUE ADDED

U.S. Department of Commerce, Bureau of the Census, Suitland, Maryland 20233 (301) 763-4040; *Census of Manufactures,* and *Annual Survey of Manufactures.*

TRAUMA CENTERS

American Hospital Association, 840 North Lake Shore Drive, Chicago, Illinois 60611 (312) 280-6000; *Hospital Statistics,* and *Annual Surveys of Hospitals.*

TRAVEL - ACCIDENTS

U.S. Department of Health and Human Services, National Center for Health Statistics, 3700 East-West Highway, Hyattsville, Maryland 20782 (301) 436-8500; *Vital Statistics of the United States.*

U.S. Department of Transportation, Bureau of Transportation Statistics, 400 Seventh Street, SW, Washington, D.C. 20590 (202) 366-DATA; *National Transportation Statistics Annual, Historical Compendium Information Report.*

TRAVEL - ADVERTISING EXPENDITURES

Publishers Information Bureau, 575 Lexington Avenue, New York, New York 10022 (212) 752-0055; as compiled by Leading National Advertisers, 11 West Forty-second Street, New York, New York 10036 (212) 789-1400.

Television Bureau of Advertising, Incorporated, 850 Third Avenue, New York, New York 10022 (212) 486-1111; from data compiled by Competitive Media Reporting, 11 West 42nd Street, New York, New York 10036 (212) 789-1400.

TRAVEL - AIR CARRIERS

Air Transport Association of America, 1301 Pennsylvania Avenue, NW, Washington, D.C. 20004 (202) 626-4000; *Air Transport Facts and Figures.*

International Civil Aviation Organization, 1000 Sherbrooke Street, West, Montreal, Quebec H3A 2R2, Canada (514) 285-8219; *Civil Aviation Statistics of the World.*

Regional Airline Association, 1101 Connecticut Avenue, NW, Suite 700, Washington, D.C. 20036 (202) 857-1170; *Annual Report of the Regional Airline Industry.*

U.S. Department of Transportation, Federal Aviation Administration, 800 Independence Avenue, SW, Washington, D.C. 20591 (202) 366-4000; *FAA Statistical Handbook of Aviation.*

United States Travel Data Center, Two Lafayette Center, 1133 Twenty-first Street, NW, Washington, D.C. 20036 (202) 293-1040; *The Economic Review of Travel in America.*

TRAVEL - BUSINESS - PLEASURE TRAVELERS

United States Travel Data Center, Two Lafayette Center, 1133 Twenty-First Street, NW, Washington, D.C. 20036 (202) 293-1040; *National Travel Survey.*

TRAVEL - DOMESTIC EXPENDITURES BY STATE

United States Travel Data Center, 2 Lafayette Center, 1133 Twenty-first Street, NW, Washington, D.C. 20036 (202) 293-1040; *Impact of Travel on State Economics.*

TRAVEL - FOREIGN

U.S. Department of Commerce, Bureau of Economic Analysis, Fourteenth Street between Constitution Avenue and E Street, NW, Washington, D.C. 20230 (202) 606-9900; *Survey of Current Business.*

U.S. Department of Commerce, Travel and Tourism Administration, Washington, D.C. 20230 (202) 482-3811; unpublished data.

U.S. Department of Justice, Immigration and Naturalization Service, 425 Eye Street, NW, Washington, D.C. 20536 (202) 514-4316; *Statistical Yearbook.*

TRAVEL - INDUSTRY AND EMPLOYEES

United States Travel Data Center, Two Lafayette Center, 1133 Twenty-first Street, NW, Washington, D.C. 20036 (202) 293-1040; *The Economic Review of Travel in America.*

TRAVEL - MILEAGE - HIGHWAY - BY TYPE OF ROAD

U.S. Department of Transportation, Federal Highway Administration, 400 Seventh Street, NW, Washington, D.C. 20590 (202) 366-0660; *Highway Statistics*, and *Fatal and Injury Accident Rates on Public Roads in the United States*.

TRAVEL - NONIMMIGRANTS

U.S. Department of Justice, Immigration and Naturalization Service, 425 I Street, NW, Washington, D.C. 20536 (202) 514-4316; *Statistical Yearbook*.

TRAVEL - PASSENGERS

Air Transport Association of America, 1301 Pennsylvania Avenue, NW, Washington, D.C. 20004 (202) 626-4000; *Air Transport*, and *Air Transport, Facts and Figures*.

Regional Airline Association, 1101 Connecticut Avenue, NW, Suite 700, Washington, D.C. 20036 (202) 857-1170; *Annual Report of the Regional Airline Association*.

U.S. Department of Commerce, Bureau of Economic Analysis, Fourteenth Street between Constitution Avenue and E Street, NW, Washington, D.C. 20230 (202) 606-9900; *Survey of Current Business*.

U.S. Department of Commerce, Travel and Tourism Administration, Washington, D.C. 20230 (202) 482-3811; unpublished data.

U.S. Department of Transportation, Federal Aviation Administration, 800 Independence Avenue, SW Washington, D.C. 20591 (202) 366-4000; *FAA Statistical Handbook of Aviation*.

TRAVEL - RECREATION

United States Travel Data Center, 2 Lafayette Center, 1133 Twenty-First Street, NW, Washington, D.C. 20036 (202) 293-1040; *National Travel Survey*.

TRAVEL - TOURISTS

U.S. Department of Commerce, Bureau of Economic Analysis, Fourteenth Street between Constitution Avenue and E Street, NW, Washington, D.C. 20230 (202) 606-9900; *Survey of Current Business*.

U.S. Department of Commerce, Travel and Tourism Administration, Washington, D.C. 20230 (202) 482-3811; unpublished data.

U.S. Department of Justice, Immigration and Naturalization Service, 425 Eye Street, NW, Washington, D.C. 20536 (202) 514-4316; *Statistical Yearbook*.

TRAVEL - VOLUME

Air Transport Association of America, 1301 Pennsylvania Avenue, NW, Washington, D.C. 20004 (202) 626-4000; *Air Transport*, and *Air Transport, Facts and Figures*.

Eno Transportation Foundation, 44211 Statestone Court, Lansdowne, Virginia 22075 (703) 729-7200; *Transportation in America*.

Regional Airline Association, 1101 Connecticut Avenue, NW, Suite 700, Washington, D.C. 20036 (202) 857-1170; *Annual Report of the Regional Airline Industry*.

TRAVELERS CHECKS

Board of Governors of the Federal Reserve System, Twentieth Street and Constitution Avenue, NW, Washington, D.C. 20551 (202) 452-3000; *Federal Reserve Bulletin, Money Stock, Liquid Assets and Debt Measures*, and *Federal Reserve Statistical Release H.6*.

Trinidad and Tobago - National Statistical Office

Central Statistical Office, 23 Park Street, Post Office Box 98, Port of Spain, Trinidad.

Trinidad and Tobago - Primary Statistics Sources

Central Statistical Office, Post Office Box 98, Port of Spain, Trinidad; *Annual Statistical Digest*.

TRINIDAD AND TOBAGO - AGRICULTURE

The Economist Intelligence Unit, 111 West 57th Street, New York, New York 10019 (800) 938-4685; *The New Latin America Market Atlas*.

Euromonitor Publications Limited, 87-88 Turnmill Street, London EC1M 5QU, England; *International Marketing Data and Statistics*.

Facts on File, 460 Park Avenue South, New York, New York 10016 (800) 443-8323; *The New Book of World Rankings*.

Food and Agricultural Organization of the United Nations (FAO) Via delle Terme di Caracalla, 00100 Rome, Italy (Telephone Number in U.S. (202) 653-2400); *Production Yearbook*, and *The State of Food and Agriculture*, and *Trade Yearbook*.

Gale Research Incorporated, 835 Penobscot Building, Detroit, Michigan 48226 (800) 877-4253; *International Historical Statistics The Americas and Australasia*.

G.K. Hall and Company, 70 Lincoln Street, Boston, Massachusetts 02111 (617) 423-3990; *The World in Figures*.

Inter-American Development Bank, 1300 New York Avenue, NW, Washington, D.C. 20577 (202) 623-1753; *Economic and Social Progress in Latin America*.

Statistical Office of the United Nations, Publishing Service, New York, New York 10017 (800) 253-9646; *Statistical Yearbook*.

Times Books, 201 East 50th Street, New York, New York 10022 (212) 751-2600; *The Economist Book of Vital World Statistics*.

The World Bank, 1818 H Street, NW, Washington, D.C. 20433 (202) 477-1234; *World Tables*.

TRINIDAD AND TOBAGO - AIRLINE SERVICE

The Economist Intelligence Unit, 111 West 57th Street, New York, New York 10019 (800) 938-4685; *The New Latin America Market Atlas*.

Facts on File, 460 Park Avenue South, New York, New York 10016 (800) 443-8323; *The New Book of World Rankings*.

G.K. Hall and Company, 70 Lincoln Street, Boston, Massachusetts 02111 (617) 423-3990; *The World in Figures*.

Statistical Office of the United Nations, Publishing Service, New York, New York 10017 (800) 253-9646; *Statistical Yearbook*.

Times Books, 201 East 50th Street, New York, New York 10022 (212) 751-2600; *The Economist Book of Vital World Statistics*.

TRINIDAD AND TOBAGO - ALUMINUM PRODUCTION AND CONSUMPTION - See TRINIDAD AND TOBAGO - MINING AND MINERAL PRODUCTS

TRINIDAD AND TOBAGO - ANIMAL HEALTH

Food and Agricultural Organization of the United Nations (FAO), Via delle Terme di Caracalla, 00100, Rome, Italy (Telephone Number in U.S. (202) 653-2400); *Animal Health Yearbook*.

TRINIDAD AND TOBAGO - AREA AND DENSITY OF POPULATION

Euromonitor Publications Limited, 87-88 Turnmill Street, London EC1M 5QU, England; *International Marketing Data and Statistics*.

Facts on File, 460 Park Avenue South, New York, New York 10016 (800) 443-8323; *The New Book of World Rankings*.

Food and Agricultural Organization of the United Nations (FAO) Via delle Terme di Caracalla, 00100 Rome, Italy (Telephone Number in U.S. (202) 653-2400); *The State of Food and Agriculture*.

G.K. Hall and Company, 70 Lincoln Street, Boston, Massachusetts 02111 (617) 423-3990; *The World in Figures*.

Inter-American Development Bank, 1300 New York Avenue, NW, Washington, D.C. 20577 (202) 623-1753; *Economic and Social Progress in Latin America*.

Statistical Office of the United Nations, Publishing Service, New York, New York 10017 (800) 253-9646; *Statistical Yearbook*.

Times Books, 201 East 50th Street, New York, New York 10022 (212) 751-2600; *The Economist Book of Vital World Statistics*.

United Nations Educational, Scientific and Cultural Organization (UNESCO), 7 Place de Fontenoy, F-75700 Paris, France (Telephone Number in U.S. (212) 963 5981); *Statistical Yearbook*.

TRINIDAD AND TOBAGO - ARMS EXPORTS AND IMPORTS

U.S. Arms Control and Disarmament Agency, 320 Twenty-first Street, NW, Washington, D.C. 20451 (202) 647-8677; *World Military Expenditures and Arms Transfers*.

TRINIDAD AND TOBAGO - BALANCE OF PAYMENTS

The Economist Intelligence Unit, 111 West 57th Street, New York, New York 10019 (800) 938-4685; *The New Latin America Market Atlas*, and *The World Market Atlas*.

G.K. Hall and Company, 70 Lincoln Street, Boston, Massachusetts 02111 (617) 423-3990; *The World in Figures*.

Inter-American Development Bank, 1300 New York Avenue, NW, Washington, D.C. 20577 (202) 623-1753; *Economic and Social Progress in Latin America*.

International Monetary Fund, 700 Nineteenth Street, NW, Washington, D.C. 20431 (202) 623-7000; *Balance of Payments Yearbook*, and *International Financial Statistics*.

Organization of American States (OAS), General Secretariat, Washington, D.C. 20006 (202) 458-3533; *Statistical Bulletin of the OAS*.

Statistical Office of the United Nations, Publishing Service, New York, New York 10017 (800) 253-9646; *Economic Survey of Latin America and the Caribbean*.

Times Books, 201 East 50th Street, New York, New York 10022 (212) 751-2600; *The Economist Book of Vital World Statistics*.

The World Bank, 1818 H Street, NW, Washington, D.C. 20433 (202) 477-1234; *World Tables*.

TRINIDAD AND TOBAGO - BANANA PRODUCTION - See TRINIDAD AND TOBAGO - CROPS

TRINIDAD AND TOBAGO - BANKING

Facts on File, 460 Park Avenue South, New York, New York 10016 (800) 443-8323; *The New Book of World Rankings*.

G.K. Hall and Company, 70 Lincoln Street, Boston, Massachusetts 02111 (617) 423-3990; *The World in Figures*.

Inter-American Development Bank, 1300 New York Avenue, NW, Washington, D.C. 20577 (202) 623-1753; *Economic and Social Progress in Latin America*.

International Monetary Fund, 700 Nineteenth Street, NW, Washington, D.C. 20431 (202) 623-7000; *International Financial Statistics*.

TRINIDAD AND TOBAGO - BARLEY PRODUCTION - See TRINIDAD AND TOBAGO - CROPS

TRINIDAD AND TOBAGO - BEER PRODUCTION

Facts on File, 460 Park Avenue South, New York, New York 10016 (800) 443-8323; *The New Book of World Rankings*.

Statistical Office of the United Nations, Publishing Service, New York, New York 10017 (800) 253-9646; *Statistical Yearbook*.

TRINIDAD AND TOBAGO - BIRTH RATE

Facts on File, 460 Park Avenue South, New York, New York 10016 (800) 443-8323; *The New Book of World Rankings*.

Statistical Office of the United Nations, Publishing Service, New York, New York 10017 (800) 253-9646; *Demographic Yearbook*, and *Statistical Yearbook*.

Times Books, 201 East 50th Street, New York, New York 10022 (212) 751-2600; *The Economist Book of Vital World Statistics*.

The World Bank, 1818 H Street, NW, Washington, D.C. 20433 (202) 477-1234; *World Tables*.

World Health Organization, Office of Publications, Avenue Appia, CH-1211 Geneva 27, Switzerland (Telephone Number in U.S. (518) 436-9686); *World Health Statistics Annual*.

TRINIDAD AND TOBAGO - BONDS

G.K. Hall and Company, 70 Lincoln Street, Boston, Massachusetts 02111 (617) 423-3990; *The World in Figures*.

Inter-American Development Bank, 1300 New York Avenue, NW, Washington, D.C. 20577 (202) 623-1753; *Economic and Social Progress in Latin America.*

International Monetary Fund, 700 Nineteenth Street, NW, Washington, D.C. 20431 (202) 623-7000; *Government Finance Statistics Yearbook.*

Statistical Office of the United Nations, Publishing Service, New York, New York 10017 (800) 253-9646; *Statistical Yearbook.*

TRINIDAD AND TOBAGO - BOOK PRODUCTION

G.K. Hall and Company, 70 Lincoln Street, Boston, Massachusetts 02111 (617) 423-3990; *The World in Figures.*

United Nations Educational, Scientific and Cultural Organization (UNESCO), 7 Place de Fontenoy, F-75700 Paris, France (Telephone Number in U.S. (212) 963-5981); *Statistical Yearbook.*

TRINIDAD AND TOBAGO - BROADCASTING

Billboard Limited, P.O. Box 9027, 1006 AA Amsterdam, The Netherlands (Telephone Number in U.S. (212) 764-7300); *World Radio TV Handbook.*

Facts on File, 460 Park Avenue South, New York, New York 10016 (800) 443-8323; *The New Book of World Rankings.*

G.K. Hall and Company, 70 Lincoln Street, Boston, Massachusetts 02111 (617) 423-3990; *The World in Figures.*

Times Books, 201 East 50th Street, New York, New York 10022 (212) 751-2600; *The Economist Book of Vital World Statistics.*

United Nations Educational, Scientific and Cultural Organization (UNESCO), 7 Place de Fontenoy, F-75700 Paris, France (Telephone Number in U.S. (212) 963-5981); *Statistical Yearbook.*

TRINIDAD AND TOBAGO - BUSINESS

G.K. Hall and Company, 70 Lincoln Street, Boston, Massachusetts 02111 (617) 423-3990; *The World in Figures.*

Inter-American Development Bank, 1300 New York Avenue, NW, Washington, D.C. 20577 (202) 623-1753; *Economic and Social Progress in Latin America.*

TRINIDAD AND TOBAGO - BUSINESS AND PROFESSIONAL LICENSES

International Monetary Fund, 700 Nineteenth Street, NW, Washington, D.C. 20431 (202) 623-7000; *Government Finance Statistics Yearbook.*

TRINIDAD AND TOBAGO - BUTTER PRODUCTION - See TRINIDAD AND TOBAGO - DAIRY PRODUCTS

TRINIDAD AND TOBAGO - CALORIE SUPPLY

Food and Agricultural Organization of the United Nations (FAO) Via delle Terme di Caracalla, 00100 Rome, Italy (Telephone Number in U.S. (202) 653-2400); *The State of Food and Agriculture.*

TRINIDAD AND TOBAGO - CAPITAL INVESTMENT

Inter-American Development Bank, 1300 New York Avenue, NW, Washington, D.C. 20577 (202) 623-1753; *Economic and Social Progress in Latin America.*

TRINIDAD AND TOBAGO - CAPITAL REVENUE

Inter-American Development Bank, 1300 New York Avenue, NW, Washington, D.C. 20577 (202) 623-1753; *Economic and Social Progress in Latin America.*

International Monetary Fund, 700 Nineteenth Street, NW, Washington, D.C. 20431 (202) 623-7000; *Government Finance Statistics Yearbook.*

TRINIDAD AND TOBAGO - CATTLE - See TRINIDAD AND TOBAGO - LIVESTOCK AND POULTRY

TRINIDAD AND TOBAGO - CEMENT PRODUCTION - See TRINIDAD AND TOBAGO - MINING AND MINERAL PRODUCTS

TRINIDAD AND TOBAGO - CHEESE PRODUCTION AND CONSUMPTION - See TRINIDAD AND TOBAGO - DAIRY PRODUCTS

TRINIDAD AND TOBAGO - CHEMICAL (ORGANIC) PRODUCTION - See TRINIDAD AND TOBAGO - MINING AND MINERAL PRODUCTS

TRINIDAD AND TOBAGO - CHICKENS - See TRINIDAD AND TOBAGO - LIVESTOCK AND POULTRY

TRINIDAD AND TOBAGO - CIGARETTE PRODUCTION - See TRINIDAD AND TOBAGO - TOBACCO PRODUCTION

TRINIDAD AND TOBAGO - CLASS STRUCTURE

G.K. Hall and Company, 70 Lincoln Street, Boston, Massachusetts 02111 (617) 423-3990; *The World in Figures.*

TRINIDAD AND TOBAGO - CLIMATE

Facts on File, 460 Park Avenue South, New York, New York 10016 (800) 443-8323; *The New Book of World Rankings.*

G.K. Hall and Company, 70 Lincoln Street, Boston, Massachusetts 02111 (617) 423-3990; *The World in Figures.*

TRINIDAD AND TOBAGO - COAL PRODUCTION - See TRINIDAD AND TOBAGO - MINING AND MINERAL PRODUCTS

TRINIDAD AND TOBAGO - COCOA (BEANS) PRODUCTION - See TRINIDAD AND TOBAGO - CROPS

TRINIDAD AND TOBAGO - COFFEE - See TRINIDAD AND TOBAGO - CROPS

TRINIDAD AND TOBAGO - COMMUNICATIONS

Gale Research Incorporated, 835 Penobscot Building, Detroit, Michigan 48226 (800) 877-4253; *International Historical Statistics The Americas and Australasia.*

G.K. Hall and Company, 70 Lincoln Street, Boston, Massachusetts 02111 (617) 423-3990; *The World in Figures.*

Inter-American Development Bank, 1300 New York Avenue, NW, Washington, D.C. 20577 (202) 623-1753; *Economic and Social Progress in Latin America.*

TRINIDAD AND TOBAGO - CONSTRUCTION INDUSTRY

The Economist Intelligence Unit, 111 West 57th Street, New York, New York 10019 (800) 938-4685; *The New Latin America Market Atlas.*

Facts on File, 460 Park Avenue South, New York, New York 10016 (800) 443-8323; *The New Book of World Rankings*.

Inter-American Development Bank, 1300 New York Avenue, NW, Washington, D.C. 20577 (202) 623-1753; *Economic and Social Progress in Latin America*.

Statistical Office of the United Nations, Publishing Service, New York, New York 10017 (800) 253-9646; *Construction Statistics Yearbook*, and *Statistical Yearbook*.

TRINIDAD AND TOBAGO - CONSUMER PRICE INDEX

G.K. Hall and Company, 70 Lincoln Street, Boston, Massachusetts 02111 (617) 423-3990; *The World in Figures*.

Statistical Office of the United Nations, Publishing Service, New York, New York 10017 (800) 253-9646; *Statistical Yearbook*.

TRINIDAD AND TOBAGO - CONSUMER PRICES

The Economist Intelligence Unit, 111 West 57th Street, New York, New York 10019 (800) 938-4685; *The New Latin America Market Atlas*.

International Labour Office, I.L.O. Publications, CH-1211, Geneva 22, Switzerland; *Yearbook of Labour Statistics*.

International Monetary Fund, 700 Nineteenth Street, NW, Washington, D.C. 20431 (202) 623-7000; *International Financial Statistics*.

Organization of American States (OAS), General Secretariat, Washington, D.C. 20006 (202) 458-3533; *Statistical Bulletin of the OAS*.

Times Books, 201 East 50th Street, New York, New York 10022 (212) 751-2600; *The Economist Book of Vital World Statistics*.

TRINIDAD AND TOBAGO - CONSUMPTION

The Economist Intelligence Unit, 111 West 57th Street, New York, New York 10019 (800) 938-4685; *The New Latin America Market Atlas*.

G.K. Hall and Company, 70 Lincoln Street, Boston, Massachusetts 02111 (617) 423-3990; *The World in Figures*.

Inter-American Development Bank, 1300 New York Avenue, NW, Washington, D.C. 20577 (202) 623-1753; *Economic and Social Progress in Latin America*.

TRINIDAD AND TOBAGO - COPPER PRODUCTION AND CONSUMPTION - See TRINIDAD AND TOBAGO - MINING AND MINERAL PRODUCTS

TRINIDAD AND TOBAGO - CORN PRODUCTION - See TRINIDAD AND TOBAGO - CROPS

TRINIDAD AND TOBAGO - CORPORATE INCOME TAXES - See TRINIDAD AND TOBAGO - TAXATION

TRINIDAD AND TOBAGO - CORPORATE TAXES - See TRINIDAD AND TOBAGO - TAXATION

TRINIDAD AND TOBAGO - COTTON - See TRINIDAD AND TOBAGO - CROPS

TRINIDAD AND TOBAGO - CRIME

Yale University Press, Yale Station, New Haven, Connecticut 06520 (203) 432-0940; *Violence and Crime in Cross-National Perspective*.

TRINIDAD AND TOBAGO - CROPS

Commodity Research Bureau, Incorporated, 75 Wall Street, New York, New York 10005 (212) 504-7754; *Commodity Year Book*.

The Economist Intelligence Unit, 111 West 57th Street, New York, New York 10019 (800) 938-4685; *The New Latin America Market Atlas*.

Facts on File, 460 Park Avenue South, New York, New York 10016 (800) 443-8323; *The New Book of World Rankings*.

Food and Agricultural Organization of the United Nations (FAO) Via delle Terme di Caracalla, 00100 Rome, Italy (Telephone Number in U.S. (202) 653-2400); *The State of Food and Agriculture*.

G.K. Hall and Company, 70 Lincoln Street, Boston, Massachusetts 02111 (617) 423-3990; *The World in Figures*.

International Monetary Fund, 700 Nineteenth Street, NW, Washington, D.C. 20431 (202) 623-7000; *International Financial Statistics*.

Organization of American States (OAS), General Secretariat, Washington, D.C. 20006 (202) 458-3533; *Statistical Bulletin of the OAS*.

Statistical Office of the United Nations, Publishing Service, New York, New York 10017 (800) 253-9646; *Statistical Yearbook*.

U.C.L.A. Latin American Center Publications, University of California, Los Angeles, California 90024 (310) 825-6634; *Statistical Abstract of Latin America*.

TRINIDAD AND TOBAGO - CUSTOMS DUTIES

G.K. Hall and Company, 70 Lincoln Street, Boston, Massachusetts 02111 (617) 423-3990; *The World in Figures*.

Inter-American Development Bank, 1300 New York Avenue, NW, Washington, D.C. 20577 (202) 623-1753; *Economic and Social Progress in Latin America*.

International Monetary Fund, 700 Nineteenth Street, NW, Washington, D.C. 20431 (202) 623-7000; *Government Finance Statistics Yearbook*.

TRINIDAD AND TOBAGO - DAIRY PRODUCTS

Facts on File, 460 Park Avenue South, New York, New York 10016 (800) 443-8323; *The New Book of World Rankings*.

Food and Agricultural Organization of the United Nations (FAO) Via delle Terme di Caracalla, 00100 Rome, Italy (Telephone Number in U.S. (202) 653-2400); *The State of Food and Agriculture*.

Statistical Office of the United Nations, Publishing Service, New York, New York 10017 (800) 253-9646; *Statistical Yearbook*.

U.C.L.A. Latin American Center Publications, University of California, Los Angeles, California 90024 (310) 825-6634; *Statistical Abstract of Latin America*.

TRINIDAD AND TOBAGO - DEATH RATES

G.K. Hall and Company, 70 Lincoln Street, Boston, Massachusetts 02111 (617) 423-3990; *The World in Figures.*

Statistical Office of the United Nations, Publishing Service, New York, New York 10017 (800) 253-9646; *Statistical Yearbook.*

Times Books, 201 East 50th Street, New York, New York 10022 (212) 751-2600; *The Economist Book of Vital World Statistics.*

TRINIDAD AND TOBAGO - DEBT

The Economist Intelligence Unit, 111 West 57th Street, New York, New York 10019 (800) 938-4685; *The New Latin America Market Atlas.*

TRINIDAD AND TOBAGO - DEFENSE

The Economist Intelligence Unit, 111 West 57th Street, New York, New York 10019 (800) 938-4685; *The New Latin America Market Atlas.*

U.S. Arms Control and Disarmament Agency, 320 Twenty-first Street, NW, Washington, D.C. 20451 (202) 647-8677; *World Military Expenditures and Arms Transfers.*

TRINIDAD AND TOBAGO - DEFENSE EXPENDITURES

G.K. Hall and Company, 70 Lincoln Street, Boston, Massachusetts 02111 (617) 423-3990; *The World in Figures.*

International Monetary Fund, 700 Nineteenth Street, NW, Washington, D.C. 20431 (202) 623-7000; *Government Finance Statistics Yearbook.*

TRINIDAD AND TOBAGO - DEMOGRAPHY

The Economist Intelligence Unit, 111 West 57th Street, New York, New York 10019 (800) 938-4685; *The World Market Atlas.*

Facts on File, 460 Park Avenue South, New York, New York 10016 (800) 443-8323; *The New Book of World Rankings.*

G.K. Hall and Company, 70 Lincoln Street, Boston, Massachusetts 02111 (617) 423-3990; *The World in Figures.*

TRINIDAD AND TOBAGO - DEVELOPMENT ASSISTANCE

G.K. Hall and Company, 70 Lincoln Street, Boston, Massachusetts 02111 (617) 423-3990; *The World in Figures.*

Inter-American Development Bank, 1300 New York Avenue, NW, Washington, D.C. 20577 (202) 623-1753; *Economic and Social Progress in Latin America.*

Statistical Office of the United Nations, Publishing Service, New York, New York 10017 (800) 253-9646; *Statistical Yearbook.*

TRINIDAD AND TOBAGO - DIAMOND PRODUCTION - See TRINIDAD AND TOBAGO - MINING AND MINERAL PRODUCTS

TRINIDAD AND TOBAGO - DISCOUNT RATES

Inter-American Development Bank, 1300 New York Avenue, NW, Washington, D.C. 20577 (202) 623-1753; *Economic and Social Progress in Latin America.*

TRINIDAD AND TOBAGO - DISEASE

G.K. Hall and Company, 70 Lincoln Street, Boston, Massachusetts 02111 (617) 423-3990; *The World in Figures.*

TRINIDAD AND TOBAGO - DIVORCE RATES

Facts on File, 460 Park Avenue South, New York, New York 10016 (800) 443-8323; *The New Book of World Rankings.*

Statistical Office of the United Nations, Publishing Service, New York, New York 10017 (800) 253-9646; *Demographic Yearbook,* and *Statistical Yearbook.*

TRINIDAD AND TOBAGO - DOMESTIC PRODUCT

G.K. Hall and Company, 70 Lincoln Street, Boston, Massachusetts 02111 (617) 423-3990; *The World in Figures.*

TRINIDAD AND TOBAGO - ECONOMY

Euromonitor Publications Limited, 87-88 Turnmill Street, London EC1M 5QU, England; *International Marketing Data and Statistics.*

Facts on File, 460 Park Avenue South, New York, New York 10016 (800) 443-8323; *The New Book of World Rankings.*

G.K. Hall and Company, 70 Lincoln Street, Boston, Massachusetts 02111 (617) 423-3990; *The World in Figures.*

Inter-American Development Bank, 1300 New York Avenue, NW, Washington, D.C. 20577 (202) 623-1753; *Economic and Social Progress in Latin America.*

Organization of American States (OAS), General Secretariat, Washington, D.C. 20006 (202) 458-3533; *Statistical Bulletin of the OAS.*

Statistical Office of the United Nations, Publishing Service, New York, New York 10017 (800) 253-9646; *Economic Survey of Latin America and the Caribbean.*

TRINIDAD AND TOBAGO - EDUCATION

The Economist Intelligence Unit, 111 West 57th Street, New York, New York 10019 (800) 938-4685; *The New Latin America Market Atlas,* and *The World Market Atlas.*

Facts on File, 460 Park Avenue South, New York, New York 10016 (800) 443-8323; *The New Book of World Rankings.*

Gale Research Incorporated, 835 Penobscot Building, Detroit, Michigan 48226 (800) 877-4253; *International Historical Statistics The Americas and Australasia.*

G.K. Hall and Company, 70 Lincoln Street, Boston, Massachusetts 02111 (617) 423-3990; *The World in Figures.*

International Monetary Fund, 700 Nineteenth Street, NW, Washington, D.C. 20431 (202) 623-7000; *Government Finance Statistics Yearbook.*

United Nations Educational, Scientific and Cultural Organization (UNESCO), 7 Place de Fontenoy, F-75700 Paris, France (Telephone Number in U.S. (212) 963-5981); *Statistical Yearbook.*

Times Books, 201 East 50th Street, New York, New York 10022 (212) 751-2600; *The Economist Book of Vital World Statistics.*

The World Bank, 1818 H Street, NW, Washington, D.C. 20433 (202) 477-1234; *World Tables*.

TRINIDAD AND TOBAGO - EGG PRODUCTION AND CONSUMPTION -
See TRINIDAD AND TOBAGO - DAIRY PRODUCTS

TRINIDAD AND TOBAGO - ELECTRICITY

The Economist Intelligence Unit, 111 West 57th Street, New York, New York 10019 (800) 938-4685; *The New Latin America Market Atlas*.

Facts on File, 460 Park Avenue South, New York, New York 10016 (800) 443-8323; *The New Book of World Rankings*.

Inter-American Development Bank, 1300 New York Avenue, NW, Washington, D.C. 20577 (202) 623-1753; *Economic and Social Progress in Latin America*.

Penn Well Publishing Company, 1421 South Sheridan Road, P.O. Box 1260, Tulsa, Oklahoma 74101 (800) 752-9764; *International Energy Statistics Sourcebook*.

Statistical Office of the United Nations, Publishing Service, New York, New York 10017 (800) 253-9646; *Statistical Yearbook*.

Times Books, 201 East 50th Street, New York, New York 10022 (212) 751-2600; *The Economist Book of Vital World Statistics*.

TRINIDAD AND TOBAGO - EMPLOYMENT

Euromonitor Publications Limited, 87-88 Turnmill Street, London EC1M 5QU, England; *International Marketing Data and Statistics*.

Facts on File, 460 Park Avenue South, New York, New York 10016 (800) 443-8323; *The New Book of World Rankings*.

International Labour Office, I.L.O. Publications, CH-1211, Geneva 22, Switzerland; *Yearbook of Labour Statistics*.

Organization of American States (OAS), General Secretariat, Washington, D.C. 20006 (202) 458-3533; *Statistical Bulletin of the OAS*.

Statistical Office of the United Nations, Publishing Service, New York, New York 10017 (800) 253-9646; *Statistical Yearbook*.

TRINIDAD AND TOBAGO - ENERGY

The Economist Intelligence Unit, 111 West 57th Street, New York, New York 10019 (800) 938-4685; *The New Latin America Market Atlas*.

Facts on File, 460 Park Avenue South, New York, New York 10016 (800) 443-8323; *The New Book of World Rankings*.

Food and Agricultural Organization of the United Nations (FAO) Via delle Terme di Caracalla, 00100 Rome, Italy (Telephone Number in U.S. (202) 653-2400); *The State of Food and Agriculture*.

G.K. Hall and Company, 70 Lincoln Street, Boston, Massachusetts 02111 (617) 423-3990; *The World in Figures*.

Statistical Office of the United Nations, Publishing Service, New York, New York 10017 (800) 253-9646; *Energy Statistics Yearbook*.

Times Books, 201 East 50th Street, New York, New York 10022 (212) 751-2600; *The Economist Book of Vital World Statistics*.

Penn Well Publishing Company, 1421 South Sheridan Road, P.O. Box 1260, Tulsa, Oklahoma 74101 (800) 752-9764; *International Energy Statistics Sourcebook*.

TRINIDAD AND TOBAGO - EXCHANGE RATES

Euromonitor Publications Limited, 87-88 Turnmill Street, London EC1M 5QU, England; *International Marketing Data and Statistics*.

Inter-American Development Bank, 1300 New York Avenue, NW, Washington, D.C. 20577 (202) 623-1753; *Economic and Social Progress in Latin America*.

International Monetary Fund, 700 Nineteenth Street, NW, Washington, D.C. 20431 (202) 623-7000; *International Financial Statistics*.

Organization of American States (OAS), General Secretariat, Washington, D.C. 20006 (202) 458-3533; *Statistical Bulletin of the OAS*.

Statistical Office of the United Nations, Publishing Service, New York, New York 10017 (800) 253-9646; *Statistical Yearbook*.

TRINIDAD AND TOBAGO - EXCISE TAXES - See TRINIDAD AND TOBAGO - TAXATION

TRINIDAD AND TOBAGO - EXPORTS

The Economist Intelligence Unit, 111 West 57th Street, New York, New York 10019 (800) 938-4685; *The New Latin America Market Atlas*, and *The World Market Atlas*.

Euromonitor Publications Limited, 87-88 Turnmill Street, London EC1M 5QU, England; *International Marketing Data and Statistics*.

Food and Agricultural Organization of the United Nations (FAO) Via delle Terme di Caracalla, 00100 Rome, Italy (Telephone Number in U.S. (202) 653-2400); *The State of Food and Agriculture*.

G.K. Hall and Company, 70 Lincoln Street, Boston, Massachusetts 02111 (617) 423-3990; *The World in Figures*.

Inter-American Development Bank, 1300 New York Avenue, NW, Washington, D.C. 20577 (202) 623-1753; *Economic and Social Progress in Latin America*.

International Monetary Fund, 700 Nineteenth Street, NW, Washington, D.C. 20431 (202) 623-7000; *Direction of Trade Statistics*, *Government Finance Statistics Yearbook*, and *International Financial Statistics*.

Organization of American States (OAS), General Secretariat, Washington, D.C. 20006 (202) 458-3533; *Statistical Bulletin of the OAS*.

Times Books, 201 East 50th Street, New York, New York 10022 (212) 751-2600; *The Economist Book of Vital World Statistics*.

The World Bank, 1818 H Street, NW, Washington, D.C. 20433 (202) 477-1234; *World Tables*.

TRINIDAD AND TOBAGO - EXTERNAL FINANCING

Inter-American Development Bank, 1300 New York Avenue, NW, Washington, D.C. 20577 (202) 623-1753; *Economic and Social Progress in Latin America*.

TRINIDAD AND TOBAGO - EXTERNAL INDEBTEDNESS

Inter-American Development Bank, 1300 New York Avenue, NW, Washington, D.C. 20577 (202) 623-1753; *Economic and Social Progress in Latin America.*

The World Bank, 1818 H Street, NW, Washington, D.C. 20433 (202) 477-1234; *World Tables.*

TRINIDAD AND TOBAGO - EXTERNAL TRADE

Food and Agricultural Organization of the United Nations (FAO) Via delle Terme di Caracalla, 00100 Rome, Italy (Telephone Number in U.S. (202) 653-2400); *The State of Food and Agriculture,* and *Trade Yearbook.*

Gale Research Incorporated, 835 Penobscot Building, Detroit, Michigan 48226 (800) 877-4253; *International Historical Statistics The Americas and Australasia.*

G.K. Hall and Company, 70 Lincoln Street, Boston, Massachusetts 02111 (617) 423-3990; *The World in Figures.*

Inter-American Development Bank, 1300 New York Avenue, NW, Washington, D.C. 20577 (202) 623-1753; *Economic and Social Progress in Latin America.*

Statistical Office of the United Nations, Publishing Service, New York, New York 10017 (800) 253-9646; *Statistical Yearbook.*

TRINIDAD AND TOBAGO - FARM CROPS - See TRINIDAD AND TOBAGO - CROPS

TRINIDAD AND TOBAGO - FEMALE WORKING POPULATION - See TRINIDAD AND TOBAGO - EMPLOYMENT

TRINIDAD AND TOBAGO - FERTILITY RATES

Facts on File, 460 Park Avenue South, New York, New York 10016 (800) 443-8323; *The New Book of World Rankings.*

Times Books, 201 East 50th Street, New York, New York 10022 (212) 751-2600; *The Economist Book of Vital World Statistics.*

The World Bank, 1818 H Street, NW, Washington, D.C. 20433 (202) 477-1234; *World Tables.*

TRINIDAD AND TOBAGO - FERTILIZER

The Economist Intelligence Unit, 111 West 57th Street, New York, New York 10019 (800) 938-4685; *The New Latin America Market Atlas.*

Food and Agricultural Organization of the United Nations (FAO), Via delle Terme di Caracalla, 00100, Rome, Italy (Telephone Number in U.S. (202) 653-2400); *Fertilizer Yearbook,* and *The State of Food and Agriculture.*

Statistical Office of the United Nations, Publishing Service, New York, New York 10017 (800) 253-9646; *Statistical Yearbook.*

TRINIDAD AND TOBAGO - FETAL MORTALITY

Statistical Office of the United Nations, Publishing Service, New York, New York 10017 (800) 253-9646; *Demographic Yearbook.*

World Health Organization, Office of Publications, Avenue Appia, CH-1211 Geneva 27, Switzerland (Telephone Number in U.S. (518) 436-9686); *World Health Statistics Annual.*

TRINIDAD AND TOBAGO - FINANCE

Facts on File, 460 Park Avenue South, New York, New York 10016 (800) 443-8323; *The New Book of World Rankings.*

Gale Research Incorporated, 835 Penobscot Building, Detroit, Michigan 48226 (800) 877-4253; *International Historical Statistics The Americas and Australasia.*

G.K. Hall and Company, 70 Lincoln Street, Boston, Massachusetts 02111 (617) 423-3990; *The World in Figures.*

Inter-American Development Bank, 1300 New York Avenue, NW, Washington, D.C. 20577 (202) 623-1753; *Economic and Social Progress in Latin America.*

International Monetary Fund, 700 Nineteenth Street, NW, Washington, D.C. 20431 (202) 623-7000; *Government Finance Statistics Yearbook.*

Organization of American States (OAS), General Secretariat, Washington, D.C. 20006 (202) 458-3533; *Statistical Bulletin of the OAS.*

TRINIDAD AND TOBAGO - FISHERIES

Facts on File, 460 Park Avenue South, New York, New York 10016 (800) 443-8323; *The New Book of World Rankings.*

Food and Agricultural Organization of the United Nations (FAO) Via delle Terme di Caracalla, 00100 Rome, Italy (Telephone Number in U.S. (202) 653-2400); *The State of Food and Agriculture,* and *Yearbook of Fishery Statistics.*

Inter-American Development Bank, 1300 New York Avenue, NW, Washington, D.C. 20577 (202) 623-1753; *Economic and Social Progress in Latin America.*

Statistical Office of the United Nations, Publishing Service, New York, New York 10017 (800) 253-9646; *Statistical Yearbook.*

TRINIDAD AND TOBAGO - FOOD

Food and Agricultural Organization of the United Nations (FAO) Via delle Terme di Caracalla, 00100 Rome, Italy (Telephone Number in U.S. (202) 653-2400); *The State of Food and Agriculture.*

G.K. Hall and Company, 70 Lincoln Street, Boston, Massachusetts 02111 (617) 423-3990; *The World in Figures.*

TRINIDAD AND TOBAGO - FOREIGN AID

G.K. Hall and Company, 70 Lincoln Street, Boston, Massachusetts 02111 (617) 423-3990; *The World in Figures.*

Inter-American Development Bank, 1300 New York Avenue, NW, Washington, D.C. 20577 (202) 623-1753; *Economic and Social Progress in Latin America.*

TRINIDAD AND TOBAGO - FOREIGN DEBT

The Economist Intelligence Unit, 111 West 57th Street, New York, New York 10019 (800) 938-4685; *The New Latin America Market Atlas.*

Inter-American Development Bank, 1300 New York Avenue, NW, Washington, D.C. 20577 (202) 623-1753; *Economic and Social Progress in Latin America.*

International Monetary Fund, 700 Nineteenth Street, NW, Washington, D.C. 20431 (202) 623-7000; *Government Finance Statistics Yearbook.*

TRINIDAD AND TOBAGO - FOREIGN INDEBTEDNESS

Inter-American Development Bank, 1300 New York Avenue, NW, Washington, D.C. 20577 (202) 623-1753; *Economic and Social Progress in Latin America.*

Statistical Office of the United Nations, Publishing Service, New York, New York 10017 (800) 253-9646; *Economic Survey of Latin America and the Caribbean.*

TRINIDAD AND TOBAGO - FOREIGN INVESTMENT

The Economist Intelligence Unit, 111 West 57th Street, New York, New York 10019 (800) 938-4685; *The New Latin America Market Atlas.*

TRINIDAD AND TOBAGO - FOREIGN TRADE

The Economist Intelligence Unit, 111 West 57th Street, New York, New York 10019 (800) 938-4685; *The New Latin America Market Atlas.*

Euromonitor Publications Limited, 87-88 Turnmill Street, London EC1M 5QU, England; *International Marketing Data and Statistics.*

Facts on File, 460 Park Avenue South, New York, New York 10016 (800) 443-8323; *The New Book of World Rankings.*

Food and Agricultural Organization of the United Nations (FAO) Via delle Terme di Caracalla, 00100 Rome, Italy (Telephone Number in U.S. (202) 653-2400); *The State of Food and Agriculture.*

G.K. Hall and Company, 70 Lincoln Street, Boston, Massachusetts 02111 (617) 423-3990; *The World in Figures*

Inter-American Development Bank, 1300 New York Avenue, NW, Washington, D.C. 20577 (202) 623-1753; *Economic and Social Progress in Latin America.*

International Monetary Fund, 700 Nineteenth Street, NW, Washington, D.C. 20431 (202) 623-7000; *International Financial Statistics.*

Statistical Office of the United Nations, Publishing Service, New York, New York 10017 (800) 253-9646; *Economic Survey of Latin America and the Caribbean, International Trade Statistics Yearbook*, and *Statistical Yearbook.*

The World Bank, 1818 H Street, NW, Washington, D.C. 20433 (202) 477-1234; *World Tables.*

TRINIDAD AND TOBAGO - FORESTRY AND FOREST PRODUCTS

The Economist Intelligence Unit, 111 West 57th Street, New York, New York 10019 (800) 938-4685; *The New Latin America Market Atlas.*

Facts on File, 460 Park Avenue South, New York, New York 10016 (800) 443-8323; *The New Book of World Rankings.*

Food and Agricultural Organization of the United Nations (FAO) Via delle Terme di Caracalla, 00100 Rome, Italy (Telephone Number in U.S. (202) 653-2400); *The State of Food and Agriculture*, and *Yearbook of Forest Products.*

G.K. Hall and Company, 70 Lincoln Street, Boston, Massachusetts 02111 (617) 423-3990; *The World in Figures.*

Inter-American Development Bank, 1300 New York Avenue, NW, Washington, D.C. 20577 (202) 623-1753; *Economic and Social Progress in Latin America.*

Statistical Office of the United Nations, Publishing Service, New York, New York 10017 (800) 253-9646; *Statistical Yearbook.*

U.C.L.A. Latin American Center Publications, University of California, Los Angeles, California 90024 (310) 825-6634; *Statistical Abstract of Latin America.*

United Nations Educational, Scientific and Cultural Organization (UNESCO), 7 Place de Fontenoy, F-75700 Paris, France (Telephone Number in U.S. (212) 963-5981); *Statistical Yearbook.*

TRINIDAD AND TOBAGO - GAS AND GAS LIQUIDS (NATURAL) PRODUCTION - See TRINIDAD AND TOBAGO - MINING AND MINERAL PRODUCTS

TRINIDAD AND TOBAGO - GENERAL INDUSTRIAL STATISTICS

Statistical Office of the United Nations, Publishing Service, New York, New York 10017 (800) 253-9646; *Industrial Statistics Yearbook.*

TRINIDAD AND TOBAGO - GENERAL MORTALITY

Statistical Office of the United Nations, Publishing Service, New York, New York 10017 (800) 253-9646; *Demographic Yearbook.*

World Health Organization, Office of Publications, Avenue Appia, CH-1211 Geneva 27, Switzerland (Telephone Number in U.S. (518) 436-9686); *World Health Statistics Annual.*

TRINIDAD AND TOBAGO - GEOGRAPHIC DATA

Facts on File, 460 Park Avenue South, New York, New York 10016 (800) 443-8323; *The New Book of World Rankings.*

TRINIDAD AND TOBAGO - GOLD HOLDINGS

International Monetary Fund, 700 Nineteenth Street, NW, Washington, D.C. 20431 (202) 623-7000; *International Financial Statistics.*

Statistical Office of the United Nations, Publishing Service, New York, New York 10017 (800) 253-9646; *Statistical Yearbook.*

The World Bank, 1818 H Street, NW, Washington, D.C. 20433 (202) 477-1234; *World Tables.*

TRINIDAD AND TOBAGO - GOLD PRODUCTION AND CONSUMPTION - See TRINIDAD AND TOBAGO - MINING AND MINERAL PRODUCTS

TRINIDAD AND TOBAGO - GOLD RESERVES

The Economist Intelligence Unit, 111 West 57th Street, New York, New York 10019 (800) 938-4685; *The New Latin America Market Atlas.*

TRINIDAD AND TOBAGO - GOVERNMENT

G.K. Hall and Company, 70 Lincoln Street, Boston, Massachusetts 02111 (617) 423-3990; *The World in Figures.*

Inter-American Development Bank, 1300 New York Avenue, NW, Washington, D.C. 20577 (202) 623-1753; *Economic and Social Progress in Latin America.*

TRINIDAD AND TOBAGO - GOVERNMENT CONSUMPTION

Inter-American Development Bank, 1300 New York Avenue, NW, Washington, D.C. 20577 (202) 623-1753; *Economic and Social Progress in Latin America.*

TRINIDAD AND TOBAGO - GOVERNMENT EXPENDITURES

Inter-American Development Bank, 1300 New York Avenue, NW, Washington, D.C. 20577 (202) 623-1753; *Economic and Social Progress in Latin America.*

International Monetary Fund, 700 Nineteenth Street, NW, Washington, D.C. 20431 (202) 623-7000; *Government Finance Statistics Yearbook.*

The World Bank, 1818 H Street, NW, Washington, D.C. 20433 (202) 477-1234; *World Tables.*

TRINIDAD AND TOBAGO - GOVERNMENT FINANCE

Inter-American Development Bank, 1300 New York Avenue, NW, Washington, D.C. 20577 (202) 623-1753; *Economic and Social Progress in Latin America.*

International Monetary Fund, 700 Nineteenth Street, NW, Washington, D.C. 20431 (202) 623-7000; *International Financial Statistics.*

TRINIDAD AND TOBAGO - GOVERNMENT REVENUE

Inter-American Development Bank, 1300 New York Avenue, NW, Washington, D.C. 20577 (202) 623-1753; *Economic and Social Progress in Latin America.*

International Monetary Fund, 700 Nineteenth Street, NW, Washington, D.C. 20431 (202) 623-7000; *Government Finance Statistics Yearbook.*

The World Bank, 1818 H Street, NW, Washington, D.C. 20433 (202) 477-1234; *World Tables.*

TRINIDAD AND TOBAGO - GRAIN PRODUCTION - See TRINIDAD AND TOBAGO - CROPS

TRINIDAD AND TOBAGO - GRANTS

International Monetary Fund, 700 Nineteenth Street, NW, Washington, D.C. 20431 (202) 623-7000; *Government Finance Statistics Yearbook.*

TRINIDAD AND TOBAGO - GROSS DOMESTIC PRODUCT

The Economist Intelligence Unit, 111 West 57th Street, New York, New York 10019 (800) 938-4685; *The New Latin America Market Atlas,* and *The World Market Atlas.*

Euromonitor Publications Limited, 87-88 Turnmill Street, London EC1M 5QU, England; *International Marketing Data and Statistics.*

Facts on File, 460 Park Avenue South, New York, New York 10016 (800) 443-8323; *The New Book of World Rankings.*

G.K. Hall and Company, 70 Lincoln Street, Boston, Massachusetts 02111 (617) 423-3990; *The World in Figures.*

Inter-American Development Bank, 1300 New York Avenue, NW, Washington, D.C. 20577 (202) 623-1753; *Economic and Social Progress in Latin America.*

Organization of American States (OAS), General Secretariat, Washington, D.C. 20006 (202) 458-3533; *Statistical Bulletin of the OAS.*

Statistical Office of the United Nations, Publishing Service, New York, New York 10017 (800) 253-9646; *Statistical Yearbook.*

Times Books, 201 East 50th Street, New York, New York 10022 (212) 751-2600; *The Economist Book of Vital World Statistics.*

The World Bank, 1818 H Street, NW, Washington, D.C. 20433 (202) 477-1234; *World Tables.*

TRINIDAD AND TOBAGO - GROSS NATIONAL PRODUCT

Euromonitor Publications Limited, 87-88 Turnmill Street, London EC1M 5QU, England; *International Marketing Data and Statistics.*

Inter-American Development Bank, 1300 New York Avenue, NW, Washington, D.C. 20577 (202) 623-1753; *Economic and Social Progress in Latin America.*

U.S. Arms Control and Disarmament Agency, 320 Twenty-first Street, NW, Washington, D.C. 20451 (202) 647-8677; *World Military Expenditures and Arms Transfers.*

The World Bank, 1818 H Street, NW, Washington, D.C. 20433 (202) 477-1234; *World Tables.*

TRINIDAD AND TOBAGO - HEALTH

The Economist Intelligence Unit, 111 West 57th Street, New York, New York 10019 (800) 938-4685; *The New Latin America Market Atlas.*

Facts on File, 460 Park Avenue South, New York, New York 10016 (800) 443-8323; *The New Book of World Rankings.*

G.K. Hall and Company, 70 Lincoln Street, Boston, Massachusetts 02111 (617) 423-3990; *The World in Figures.*

Statistical Office of the United Nations, Publishing Service, New York, New York 10017 (800) 253-9646; *Statistical Yearbook.*

Times Books, 201 East 50th Street, New York, New York 10022 (212) 751-2600; *The Economist Book of Vital World Statistics.*

TRINIDAD AND TOBAGO - HEALTH EXPENDITURES

International Monetary Fund, 700 Nineteenth Street, NW, Washington, D.C. 20431 (202) 623-7000; *Government Finance Statistics Yearbook.*

TRINIDAD AND TOBAGO - HIGHWAYS

The Economist Intelligence Unit, 111 West 57th Street, New York, New York 10019 (800) 938-4685; *The New Latin America Market Atlas.*

G.K. Hall and Company, 70 Lincoln Street, Boston, Massachusetts 02111 (617) 423-3990; *The World in Figures.*

TRINIDAD AND TOBAGO - HORSES - See TRINIDAD AND TOBAGO - LIVESTOCK AND POULTRY

TRINIDAD AND TOBAGO - HOURS OF WORK - See TRINIDAD AND TOBAGO - EMPLOYMENT

TRINIDAD AND TOBAGO - HOUSING AND HOUSING UNITS

Facts on File, 460 Park Avenue South, New York, New York 10016 (800) 443-8323; *The New Book of World Rankings.*

TRINIDAD AND TOBAGO - HOUSING EXPENDITURES

International Monetary Fund, 700 Nineteenth Street, NW, Washington, D.C. 20431 (202) 623-7000; *Government Finance Statistics Yearbook.*

TRINIDAD AND TOBAGO - ILLITERATE POPULATION

The Economist Intelligence Unit, 111 West 57th Street, New York, New York 10019 (800) 938-4685; *The New Latin America Market Atlas,* and *The World Market Atlas.*

G.K. Hall and Company, 70 Lincoln Street, Boston, Massachusetts 02111 (617) 423-3990; *The World in Figures.*

United Nations Educational, Scientific and Cultural Organization (UNESCO), 7 Place de Fontenoy, F-75700 Paris, France (Telephone Number in U.S. (212) 963-5981); *Statistical Yearbook.*

TRINIDAD AND TOBAGO - IMPORTS

The Economist Intelligence Unit, 111 West 57th Street, New York, New York 10019 (800) 938-4685; *The New Latin America Market Atlas,* and *The World Market Atlas.*

Euromonitor Publications Limited, 87-88 Turnmill Street, London EC1M 5QU, England; *International Marketing Data and Statistics.*

Food and Agricultural Organization of the United Nations (FAO) Via delle Terme di Caracalla, 00100 Rome, Italy (Telephone Number in U.S. (202) 653-2400); *The State of Food and Agriculture.*

G.K. Hall and Company, 70 Lincoln Street, Boston, Massachusetts 02111 (617) 423-3990; *The World in Figures.*

Inter-American Development Bank, 1300 New York Avenue, NW, Washington, D.C. 20577 (202) 623-1753; *Economic and Social Progress in Latin America.*

International Monetary Fund, 700 Nineteenth Street, NW, Washington, D.C. 20431 (202) 623-7000; *Direction of Trade Statistics, Government Finance Statistics Yearbook,* and *International Financial Statistics.*

Organization of American States (OAS), General Secretariat, Washington, D.C. 20006 (202) 458-3533; *Statistical Bulletin of the OAS.*

Statistical Office of the United Nations, Publishing Service, New York, New York 10017 (800) 253-9646; *Trade in Manufactures of Developing Countries.*

Times Books, 201 East 50th Street, New York, New York 10022 (212) 751-2600; *The Economist Book of Vital World Statistics.*

The World Bank, 1818 H Street, NW, Washington, D.C. 20433 (202) 477-1234; *World Tables.*

TRINIDAD AND TOBAGO - INCOME TAXES - See TRINIDAD AND TOBAGO - TAXATION

TRINIDAD AND TOBAGO - INDUSTRY

Euromonitor Publications Limited, 87-88 Turnmill Street, London EC1M 5QU, England; *International Marketing Data and Statistics.*

Facts on File, 460 Park Avenue South, New York, New York 10016 (800) 443-8323; *The New Book of World Rankings.*

Gale Research Incorporated, 835 Penobscot Building, Detroit, Michigan 48226 (800) 877-4253; *International Historical Statistics The Americas and Australasia.*

G.K. Hall and Company, 70 Lincoln Street, Boston, Massachusetts 02111 (617) 423-3990; *The World in Figures.*

International Labour Office, I.L.O. Publications, CH-1211, Geneva 22, Switzerland; *Yearbook of Labour Statistics.*

Statistical Office of the United Nations, Publishing Service, New York, New York 10017 (800) 253-9646; *Economic Survey of Latin America and the Caribbean.*

Times Books, 201 East 50th Street, New York, New York 10022 (212) 751-2600; *The Economist Book of Vital World Statistics.*

The World Bank, 1818 H Street, NW, Washington, D.C. 20433 (202) 477-1234; *World Tables.*

TRINIDAD AND TOBAGO - INFANT AND MATERNAL MORTALITY

The Economist Intelligence Unit, 111 West 57th Street, New York, New York 10019 (800) 938-4685; *The New Latin America Market Atlas.*

Statistical Office of the United Nations, Publishing Service, New York, New York 10017 (800) 253-9646; *Demographic Yearbook,* and *Statistical Yearbook.*

Times Books, 201 East 50th Street, New York, New York 10022 (212) 751-2600; *The Economist Book of Vital World Statistics.*

The World Bank, 1818 H Street, NW, Washington, D.C. 20433 (202) 477-1234; *World Tables.*

World Health Organization, Office of Publications, Avenue Appia, CH-1211 Geneva 27, Switzerland (Telephone Number in U.S. (518) 436-9686); *World Health Statistics Annual.*

TRINIDAD AND TOBAGO - INFLATIONARY FACTORS

Statistical Office of the United Nations, Publishing Service, New York, New York 10017 (800) 253-9646; *Economic Survey of Latin America and the Caribbean.*

TRINIDAD AND TOBAGO - INTEREST RATES

Inter-American Development Bank, 1300 New York Avenue, NW, Washington, D.C. 20577 (202) 623-1753; *Economic and Social Progress in Latin America.*

Organization of American States (OAS), General Secretariat, Washington, D.C. 20006 (202) 458-3533; *Statistical Bulletin of the OAS.*

TRINIDAD AND TOBAGO - INTERNATIONAL FINANCE

Inter-American Development Bank, 1300 New York Avenue, NW, Washington, D.C. 20577 (202) 623-1753; *Economic and Social*

Progress in Latin America.

TRINIDAD AND TOBAGO - INTERNATIONAL LIQUIDITY

Inter-American Development Bank, 1300 New York Avenue, NW, Washington, D.C. 20577 (202) 623-1753; *Economic and Social Progress in Latin America.*

International Monetary Fund, 700 Nineteenth Street, NW, Washington, D.C. 20431 (202) 623-7000; *International Financial Statistics.*

TRINIDAD AND TOBAGO - INTERNATIONAL RESERVES

Organization of American States (OAS), General Secretariat, Washington, D.C. 20006 (202) 458-3533; *Statistical Bulletin of the OAS.*

TRINIDAD AND TOBAGO - INTERNATIONAL RESERVES EXCLUDING GOLD

Inter-American Development Bank, 1300 New York Avenue, NW, Washington, D.C. 20577 (202) 623-1753; *Economic and Social Progress in Latin America.*

Statistical Office of the United Nations, Publishing Service, New York, New York 10017 (800) 253-9646; *Statistical Yearbook.*

The World Bank, 1818 H Street, NW, Washington, D.C. 20433 (202) 477-1234; *World Tables.*

TRINIDAD AND TOBAGO - INTERNATIONAL STATISTICS

Inter-American Development Bank, 1300 New York Avenue, NW, Washington, D.C. 20577 (202) 623-1753; *Economic and Social Progress in Latin America.*

TRINIDAD AND TOBAGO - INVESTMENTS

Inter-American Development Bank, 1300 New York Avenue, NW, Washington, D.C. 20577 (202) 623-1753; *Economic and Social Progress in Latin America.*

TRINIDAD AND TOBAGO - IRON ORE PRODUCTION AND CONSUMPTION - See TRINIDAD AND TOBAGO - MINING AND MINERAL PRODUCTS

TRINIDAD AND TOBAGO - IRRIGATION

Euromonitor Publications Limited, 87-88 Turnmill Street, London EC1M 5QU, England; *International Marketing Data and Statistics.*

Inter-American Development Bank, 1300 New York Avenue, NW, Washington, D.C. 20577 (202) 623-1753; *Economic and Social Progress in Latin America.*

TRINIDAD AND TOBAGO - LABOR FORCE

The Economist Intelligence Unit, 111 West 57th Street, New York, New York 10019 (800) 938-4685; *The New Latin America Market Atlas.*

Euromonitor Publications Limited, 87-88 Turnmill Street, London EC1M 5QU, England; *International Marketing Data and Statistics.*

Facts on File, 460 Park Avenue South, New York, New York 10016 (800) 443-8323; *The New Book of World Rankings.*

Food and Agricultural Organization of the United Nations (FAO) Via delle Terme di Caracalla, 00100 Rome, Italy (Telephone Number in U.S. (202) 653-2400); *The State of Food and Agriculture.*

Gale Research Incorporated, 835 Penobscot Building, Detroit, Michigan 48226 (800) 877-4253; *International Historical Statistics The Americas and Australasia.*

G.K. Hall and Company, 70 Lincoln Street, Boston, Massachusetts 02111 (617) 423-3990; *The World in Figures.*

Times Books, 201 East 50th Street, New York, New York 10022 (212) 751-2600; *The Economist Book of Vital World Statistics.*

The World Bank, 1818 H Street, NW, Washington, D.C. 20433 (202) 477-1234; *World Tables.*

TRINIDAD AND TOBAGO - LABOR PRODUCTIVITY

International Labour Office, I.L.O. Publications, CH-1211, Geneva 22, Switzerland; *Yearbook of Labour Statistics.*

TRINIDAD AND TOBAGO - LAND AREA

The Economist Intelligence Unit, 111 West 57th Street, New York, New York 10019 (800) 938-4685; *The New Latin America Market Atlas.*

TRINIDAD AND TOBAGO - LAND USE

Euromonitor Publications Limited, 87-88 Turnmill Street, London EC1M 5QU, England; *International Marketing Data and Statistics.*

Food and Agricultural Organization of the United Nations (FAO), Via delle Terme di Caracalla, 00100 Rome, Italy (Telephone Number in U.S. (202) 653-2400); *Production Yearbook.*

G.K. Hall and Company, 70 Lincoln Street, Boston, Massachusetts 02111 (617) 423-3990; *The World in Figures.*

Inter-American Development Bank, 1300 New York Avenue, NW, Washington, D.C. 20577 (202) 623-1753; *Economic and Social Progress in Latin America.*

TRINIDAD AND TOBAGO - LIBRARIES

Facts on File, 460 Park Avenue South, New York, New York 10016 (800) 443-8323; *The New Book of World Rankings.*

United Nations Educational, Scientific and Cultural Organization (UNESCO), 7 Place de Fontenoy, F-75700 Paris, France (Telephone Number in U.S. (212) 963-5981); *Statistical Yearbook.*

TRINIDAD AND TOBAGO - LIFE EXPECTANCY RATE

The Economist Intelligence Unit, 111 West 57th Street, New York, New York 10019 (800) 938-4685; *The New Latin America Market Atlas.*

TRINIDAD AND TOBAGO - LIVESTOCK AND POULTRY

Euromonitor Publications Limited, 87-88 Turnmill Street, London EC1M 5QU, England; *International Marketing Data and Statistics.*

Facts on File, 460 Park Avenue South, New York, New York 10016 (800) 443-8323; *The New Book of World Rankings.*

Food and Agricultural Organization of the United Nations (FAO), Via delle Terme di Caracalla, 00100 Rome, Italy (Telephone Number in

U.S. (202) 653-2400); *Production Yearbook*, and *The State of Food and Agriculture*.

G.K. Hall and Company, 70 Lincoln Street, Boston, Massachusetts 02111 (617) 423-3990; *The World in Figures*.

Statistical Office of the United Nations, Publishing Service, New York, New York 10017 (800) 253-9646; *Statistical Yearbook*.

TRINIDAD AND TOBAGO - LIVING LEVELS

G.K. Hall and Company, 70 Lincoln Street, Boston, Massachusetts 02111 (617) 423-3990; *The World in Figures*.

Times Books, 201 East 50th Street, New York, New York 10022 (212) 751-2600; *The Economist Book of Vital World Statistics*.

TRINIDAD AND TOBAGO - MAIL - NUMBER OF ITEMS
SENT AND RECEIVED

Statistical Office of the United Nations, Publishing Service, New York, New York 10017 (800) 253-9646; *Statistical Yearbook*.

TRINIDAD AND TOBAGO - MAIN ECONOMIC INDICATORS - See TRINIDAD AND TOBAGO - ECONOMY

TRINIDAD AND TOBAGO - MANUFACTURING

The Economist Intelligence Unit, 111 West 57th Street, New York, New York 10019 (800) 938-4685; *The New Latin America Market Atlas*.

Facts on File, 460 Park Avenue South, New York, New York 10016 (800) 443-8323; *The New Book of World Rankings*.

G.K. Hall and Company, 70 Lincoln Street, Boston, Massachusetts 02111 (617) 423-3990; *The World in Figures*.

Inter-American Development Bank, 1300 New York Avenue, NW, Washington, D.C. 20577 (202) 623-1753; *Economic and Social Progress in Latin America*.

Statistical Office of the United Nations, Publishing Service, New York, New York 10017 (800) 253-9646; *Statistical Yearbook*.

Times Books, 201 East 50th Street, New York, New York 10022 (212) 751-2600; *The Economist Book of Vital World Statistics*.

The World Bank, 1818 H Street, NW, Washington, D.C. 20433 (202) 477-1234; *World Tables*.

TRINIDAD AND TOBAGO - MARRIAGE RATES

Facts on File, 460 Park Avenue South, New York, New York 10016 (800) 443-8323; *The New Book of World Rankings*.

Statistical Office of the United Nations, Publishing Service, New York, New York 10017 (800) 253-9646; *Demographic Yearbook*, and *Statistical Yearbook*.

TRINIDAD AND TOBAGO - MEAT PRODUCTION - See TRINIDAD AND TOBAGO - LIVESTOCK AND POULTRY

TRINIDAD AND TOBAGO - MERCHANT SHIPPING

G.K. Hall and Company, 70 Lincoln Street, Boston, Massachusetts 02111 (617) 423-3990; *The World in Figures*.

Lloyd's Register of Shipping, 17 Battery Place, New York, New York 10004 (212) 425-8050; *Register of Ships*.

Statistical Office of the United Nations, Publishing Service, New York, New York 10017 (800) 253-9646; *Statistical Yearbook*.

Times Books, 201 East 50th Street, New York, New York 10022 (212) 751-2600; *The Economist Book of Vital World Statistics*.

U.S. Department of Transportation, Maritime Administration, 400 Seventh Street, SW, Washington, D.C. 20590 (202) 366-5807; *A Statistical Analysis of the World's Merchant Fleets*.

TRINIDAD AND TOBAGO - MILK PRODUCTION - See TRINIDAD AND TOBAGO - DAIRY PRODUCTS

TRINIDAD AND TOBAGO - MILITARY

The Economist Intelligence Unit, 111 West 57th Street, New York, New York 10019 (800) 938-4685; *The New Latin America Market Atlas*.

G.K. Hall and Company, 70 Lincoln Street, Boston, Massachusetts 02111 (617) 423-3990; *The World in Figures*.

The International Institute for Strategic Studies, 23 Tavistock Street, London WC2E 7NQ, England; *The Military Balance*.

U.S. Arms Control and Disarmament Agency, 320 Twenty-first Street, NW, Washington, D.C. 20451 (202) 647-8677; *World Military Expenditures and Arms Transfers*.

TRINIDAD AND TOBAGO - MINING AND MINERAL PRODUCTS

The Economist Intelligence Unit, 111 West 57th Street, New York, New York 10019 (800) 938-4685; *The New Latin America Market Atlas*.

Facts on File, 460 Park Avenue South, New York, New York 10016 (800) 443-8323; *The New Book of World Rankings*.

G.K. Hall and Company, 70 Lincoln Street, Boston, Massachusetts 02111 (617) 423-3990; *The World in Figures*.

Inter-American Development Bank, 1300 New York Avenue, NW, Washington, D.C. 20577 (202) 623-1753; *Economic and Social Progress in Latin America*.

Penn Well Publishing Company, 1421 South Sheridan Road, P.O. Box 1260, Tulsa, Oklahoma 74101 (800) 752-9764; *International Energy Statistics Sourcebook*.

Statistical Office of the United Nations, Publishing Service, New York, New York 10017 (800) 253-9646; *Statistical Yearbook*.

U.C.L.A. Latin American Center Publications, University of California, Los Angeles, California 90024 (310) 825-6634; *Statistical Abstract of Latin America*.

TRINIDAD AND TOBAGO - MONEY EXCHANGE RATE

Euromonitor Publications Limited, 87-88 Turnmill Street, London EC1M 5QU, England; *International Marketing Data and Statistics*.

Inter-American Development Bank, 1300 New York Avenue, NW, Washington, D.C. 20577 (202) 623-1753; *Economic and Social Progress in Latin America*.

International Monetary Fund, 700 Nineteenth Street, NW, Washington, D.C. 20431 (202) 623-7000; *International Financial Statistics*.

Statistical Office of the United Nations, Publishing Service, New York, New York 10017 (800) 253-9646; *Statistical Yearbook*.

TRINIDAD AND TOBAGO - MONEY MARKET RATES

Inter-American Development Bank, 1300 New York Avenue, NW, Washington, D.C. 20577 (202) 623-1753; *Economic and Social Progress in Latin America*.

Statistical Office of the United Nations, Publishing Service, New York, New York 10017 (800) 253-9646; *Statistical Yearbook*.

TRINIDAD AND TOBAGO - MONEY RESERVES

Euromonitor Publications Limited, 87-88 Turnmill Street, London EC1M 5QU, England; *International Marketing Data and Statistics*.

Inter-American Development Bank, 1300 New York Avenue, NW, Washington, D.C. 20577 (202) 623-1753; *Economic and Social Progress in Latin America*.

TRINIDAD AND TOBAGO - MONEY SUPPLY

Euromonitor Publications Limited, 87-88 Turnmill Street, London EC1M 5QU, England; *International Marketing Data and Statistics*.

G.K. Hall and Company, 70 Lincoln Street, Boston, Massachusetts 02111 (617) 423-3990; *The World in Figures*.

Inter-American Development Bank, 1300 New York Avenue, NW, Washington, D.C. 20577 (202) 623-1753; *Economic and Social Progress in Latin America*.

International Monetary Fund, 700 Nineteenth Street, NW, Washington, D.C. 20431 (202) 623-7000; *International Financial Statistics*.

Statistical Office of the United Nations, Publishing Service, New York, New York 10017 (800) 253-9646; *Statistical Yearbook*.

The World Bank, 1818 H Street, NW, Washington, D.C. 20433 (202) 477-1234; *World Tables*.

TRINIDAD AND TOBAGO - MOTION PICTURES

Statistical Office of the United Nations, Publishing Service, New York, New York 10017 (800) 253-9646; *Statistical Yearbook*.

TRINIDAD AND TOBAGO - MOTOR VEHICLE PRODUCTION

Statistical Office of the United Nations, Publishing Service, New York, New York 10017 (800) 253-9646; *Statistical Yearbook*.

TRINIDAD AND TOBAGO - MOTOR VEHICLE TAXES - See TRINIDAD AND TOBAGO - TAXATION

TRINIDAD AND TOBAGO - MOTOR VEHICLES

The Economist Intelligence Unit, 111 West 57th Street, New York, New York 10019 (800) 938-4685; *The New Latin America Market Atlas*.

TRINIDAD AND TOBAGO - MOTOR VEHICLES IN USE

G.K. Hall and Company, 70 Lincoln Street, Boston, Massachusetts 02111 (617) 423-3990; *The World in Figures*.

Statistical Office of the United Nations, Publishing Service, New York, New York 10017 (800) 253-9646; *Statistical Yearbook*.

Times Books, 201 East 50th Street, New York, New York 10022 (212) 751-2600; *The Economist Book of Vital World Statistics*.

TRINIDAD AND TOBAGO - MULES - See TRINIDAD AND TOBAGO - LIVESTOCK AND POULTRY

TRINIDAD AND TOBAGO - MUSEUMS

Facts on File, 460 Park Avenue South, New York, New York 10016 (800) 443-8323; *The New Book of World Rankings*.

United Nations Educational, Scientific and Cultural Organization (UNESCO), 7 Place de Fontenoy, F-75700 Paris, France (Telephone Number in U.S. (212) 963-5981); *Statistical Yearbook*.

TRINIDAD AND TOBAGO - NATALITY - See TRINIDAD AND TOBAGO - BIRTH RATE

TRINIDAD AND TOBAGO - NATIONAL ACCOUNTS

Gale Research Incorporated, 835 Penobscot Building, Detroit, Michigan 48226 (800) 877-4253; *International Historical Statistics The Americas and Australasia*.

Inter-American Development Bank, 1300 New York Avenue, NW, Washington, D.C. 20577 (202) 623-1753; *Economic and Social Progress in Latin America*.

Organization of American States (OAS), General Secretariat, Washington, D.C. 20006 (202) 458-3533; *Statistical Bulletin of the OAS*.

Statistical Office of the United Nations, Publishing Service, New York, New York 10017 (800) 253-9646; *National Accounts Statistics*, and *Statistical Yearbook*.

TRINIDAD AND TOBAGO - NATIONAL INCOME

Facts on File, 460 Park Avenue South, New York, New York 10016 (800) 443-8323; *The New Book of World Rankings*.

G.K. Hall and Company, 70 Lincoln Street, Boston, Massachusetts 02111 (617) 423-3990; *The World in Figures*.

Inter-American Development Bank, 1300 New York Avenue, NW, Washington, D.C. 20577 (202) 623-1753; *Economic and Social Progress in Latin America*.

Statistical Office of the United Nations, Publishing Service, New York, New York 10017 (800) 253-9646; *Statistical Yearbook*.

TRINIDAD AND TOBAGO - NATIONAL PRODUCT

Facts on File, 460 Park Avenue South, New York, New York 10016 (800) 443-8323; *The New Book of World Rankings*.

Statistical Office of the United Nations, Publishing Service, New York, New York 10017 (800) 253-9646; *Statistical Yearbook*.

TRINIDAD AND TOBAGO - NATURAL GAS PRODUCTION - See TRINIDAD AND TOBAGO - MINING AND MINERAL PRODUCTS

TRINIDAD AND TOBAGO - NEWSPAPER PRODUCTION - See TRINIDAD AND TOBAGO - FORESTRY AND FOREST PRODUCTS

TRINIDAD AND TOBAGO - NEWSPRINT EXPORTS AND IMPORTS - See TRINIDAD AND TOBAGO - FORESTRY AND FOREST PRODUCTS

TRINIDAD AND TOBAGO - OCCUPATIONS - See TRINIDAD AND TOBAGO - LABOR FORCE

TRINIDAD AND TOBAGO - ORANGES PRODUCTION - See TRINIDAD AND TOBAGO - CROPS

TRINIDAD AND TOBAGO - PAPER - See TRINIDAD AND TOBAGO - FORESTRY AND FOREST PRODUCTS

TRINIDAD AND TOBAGO - PATENTS

Statistical Office of the United Nations, Publishing Service, New York, New York 10017 (800) 253-9646; *Statistical Yearbook.*

TRINIDAD AND TOBAGO - PEANUT PRODUCTION - See TRINIDAD AND TOBAGO - CROPS

TRINIDAD AND TOBAGO - PESTICIDE USE

Food and Agricultural Organization of the United Nations (FAO) Via delle Terme di Caracalla, 00100 Rome, Italy (Telephone Number in U.S. (202) 653-2400); *The State of Food and Agriculture.*

TRINIDAD AND TOBAGO - PETROLEUM INDUSTRY

The Economist Intelligence Unit, 111 West 57th Street, New York, New York 10019 (800) 938-4685; *The New Latin America Market Atlas.*

Facts on File, 460 Park Avenue South, New York, New York 10016 (800) 443-8323; *The New Book of World Rankings.*

Food and Agricultural Organization of the United Nations (FAO) Via delle Terme di Caracalla, 00100 Rome, Italy (Telephone Number in U.S. (202) 653-2400); *The State of Food and Agriculture.*

Inter-American Development Bank, 1300 New York Avenue, NW, Washington, D.C. 20577 (202) 623-1753; *Economic and Social Progress in Latin America.*

International Monetary Fund, 700 Nineteenth Street, NW, Washington, D.C. 20431 (202) 623-7000; *International Financial Statistics.*

G.K. Hall and Company, 70 Lincoln Street, Boston, Massachusetts 02111 (617) 423-3990; *The World in Figures.*

Organization of American States (OAS), General Secretariat, Washington, D.C. 20006 (202) 458-3533; *Statistical Bulletin of the OAS.*

Penn Well Publishing Company, 1421 South Sheridan Road, P.O. Box 1260, Tulsa, Oklahoma 74101 (800) 752-9764; *International Energy Statistics Sourcebook.*

Statistical Office of the United Nations, Publishing Service, New York, New York 10017 (800) 253-9646; *Statistical Yearbook.*

TRINIDAD AND TOBAGO - PIG-IRON AND FERRO-ALLOY PRODUCTION - See TRINIDAD AND TOBAGO - MINING AND MINERAL PRODUCTS

TRINIDAD AND TOBAGO - PIGS - See TRINIDAD AND TOBAGO - LIVESTOCK AND POULTRY

TRINIDAD AND TOBAGO - POPULATION

The Economist Intelligence Unit, 111 West 57th Street, New York, New York 10019 (800) 938-4685; *The New Latin America Market Atlas,* and *The World Market Atlas.*

Euromonitor Publications Limited, 87-88 Turnmill Street, London EC1M 5QU, England; *International Marketing Data and Statistics.*

Facts on File, 460 Park Avenue South, New York, New York 10016 (800) 443-8323; *The New Book of World Rankings.*

Food and Agricultural Organization of the United Nations (FAO), Via delle Terme di Caracalla, 00100 Rome, Italy (Telephone Number in U.S. (202) 653-2400); *Production Yearbook.*

Gale Research Incorporated, 835 Penobscot Building, Detroit, Michigan 48226 (800) 877-4253; *International Historical Statistics The Americas and Australasia.*

G.K. Hall and Company, 70 Lincoln Street, Boston, Massachusetts 02111 (617) 423-3990; *The World in Figures.*

Inter-American Development Bank, 1300 New York Avenue, NW, Washington, D.C. 20577 (202) 623-1753; *Economic and Social Progress in Latin America.*

International Labour Office, I.L.O. Publications, CH-1211, Geneva 22, Switzerland; *Yearbook of Labour Statistics.*

Organization of American States (OAS), General Secretariat, Washington, D.C. 20006 (202) 458-3533; *Statistical Bulletin of the OAS.*

Statistical Office of the United Nations, Publishing Service, New York, New York 10017 (800) 253-9646; *Demographic Yearbook,* and *Statistical Yearbook.*

Times Books, 201 East 50th Street, New York, New York 10022 (212) 751-2600; *The Economist Book of Vital World Statistics.*

United Nations Educational, Scientific and Cultural Organization (UNESCO), 7 Place de Fontenoy, F-75700 Paris, France (Telephone Number in U.S. (212) 963-5981); *Statistical Yearbook.*

U.S. Arms Control and Disarmament Agency, 320 Twenty-first Street, NW, Washington, D.C. 20451 (202) 647-8677; *World Military Expenditures and Arms Transfers.*

World Health Organization, Office of Publications, Avenue Appia, CH-1211 Geneva 27, Switzerland (Telephone Number in U.S. (518) 436-9686); *World Health Statistics Annual.*

TRINIDAD AND TOBAGO - POST OFFICES

Facts on File, 460 Park Avenue South, New York, New York 10016 (800) 443-8323; *The New Book of World Rankings.*

TRINIDAD AND TOBAGO - POTATO PRODUCTION - See TRINIDAD AND TOBAGO - CROPS

TRINIDAD AND TOBAGO - POWER PRODUCTION INDUSTRY

Statistical Office of the United Nations, Publishing Service, New York, New York 10017 (800) 253-9646; *Statistical Yearbook*

TRINIDAD AND TOBAGO - PRICES

Facts on File, 460 Park Avenue South, New York, New York 10016 (800) 443-8323; *The New Book of World Rankings.*

Food and Agricultural Organization of the United Nations (FAO), Via delle Terme di Caracalla, 00100 Rome, Italy (Telephone Number in U.S. (202) 653-2400); *Production Yearbook,* and *The State of Food and Agriculture.*

Gale Research Incorporated, 835 Penobscot Building, Detroit, Michigan 48226 (800) 877-4253; *International Historical Statistics The Americas and Australasia.*

G.K. Hall and Company, 70 Lincoln Street, Boston, Massachusetts 02111 (617) 423-3990; *The World in Figures.*

International Labour Office, I.L.O. Publications, CH-1211, Geneva 22, Switzerland; *Yearbook of Labour Statistics.*

International Monetary Fund, 700 Nineteenth Street, NW, Washington, D.C. 20431 (202) 623-7000; *International Financial Statistics.*

Statistical Office of the United Nations, Publishing Service, New York, New York 10017 (800) 253-9646; *Economic Survey of Latin America and the Caribbean.*

TRINIDAD AND TOBAGO - PRINTING AND WRITING PAPER - See TRINIDAD AND TOBAGO - FORESTRY AND FOREST PRODUCTS

TRINIDAD AND TOBAGO - PRODUCTION

Facts on File, 460 Park Avenue South, New York, New York 10016 (800) 443-8323; *The New Book of World Rankings.*

G.K. Hall and Company, 70 Lincoln Street, Boston, Massachusetts 02111 (617) 423-3990; *The World in Figures.*

TRINIDAD AND TOBAGO - PRODUCTIVITY

Euromonitor Publications Limited, 87-88 Turnmill Street, London EC1M 5QU, England; *International Marketing Data and Statistics.*

TRINIDAD AND TOBAGO - PROPERTY TAXES - See TRINIDAD AND TOBAGO - TAXATION

TRINIDAD AND TOBAGO - PUBLIC CONSUMPTION FUND

Inter-American Development Bank, 1300 New York Avenue, NW, Washington, D.C. 20577 (202) 623-1753; *Economic and Social Progress in Latin America.*

TRINIDAD AND TOBAGO - PUBLIC EXPENDITURES

Inter-American Development Bank, 1300 New York Avenue, NW, Washington, D.C. 20577 (202) 623-1753; *Economic and Social Progress in Latin America.*

Organization of American States (OAS), General Secretariat, Washington, D.C. 20006 (202) 458-3533; *Statistical Bulletin of the OAS.*

TRINIDAD AND TOBAGO - PUBLIC FINANCE

Facts on File, 460 Park Avenue South, New York, New York 10016 (800) 443-8323; *The New Book of World Rankings.*

Inter-American Development Bank, 1300 New York Avenue, NW, Washington, D.C. 20577 (202) 623-1753; *Economic and Social Progress in Latin America.*

Organization of American States (OAS), General Secretariat, Washington, D.C. 20006 (202) 458-3533; *Statistical Bulletin of the OAS.*

TRINIDAD AND TOBAGO - PUBLIC REVENUE

Inter-American Development Bank, 1300 New York Avenue, NW, Washington, D.C. 20577 (202) 623-1753; *Economic and Social Progress in Latin America.*

Organization of American States (OAS), General Secretariat, Washington, D.C. 20006 (202) 458-3533; *Statistical Bulletin of the OAS.*

TRINIDAD AND TOBAGO - RADIO BROADCASTING - See TRINIDAD AND TOBAGO - BROADCASTING

TRINIDAD AND TOBAGO - RADIO RECEIVER PRODUCTION

Statistical Office of the United Nations, Publishing Service, New York, New York 10017 (800) 253-9646; *Statistical Yearbook.*

TRINIDAD AND TOBAGO - RAILWAYS

The Economist Intelligence Unit, 111 West 57th Street, New York, New York 10019 (800) 938-4685; *The New Latin America Market Atlas.*

G.K. Hall and Company, 70 Lincoln Street, Boston, Massachusetts 02111 (617) 423-3990; *The World in Figures.*

TRINIDAD AND TOBAGO - RELIGION

Facts on File, 460 Park Avenue South, New York, New York 10016 (800) 443-8323; *The New Book of World Rankings.*

TRINIDAD AND TOBAGO - RENT PRICES

International Labour Office, I.L.O. Publications, CH-1211, Geneva 22, Switzerland; *Yearbook of Labour Statistics.*

TRINIDAD AND TOBAGO - RESERVES EXCLUDING GOLD

The Economist Intelligence Unit, 111 West 57th Street, New York, New York 10019 (800) 938-4685; *The New Latin America Market Atlas.*

TRINIDAD AND TOBAGO - RETAIL TRADE

G.K. Hall and Company, 70 Lincoln Street, Boston, Massachusetts 02111 (617) 423-3990; *The World in Figures.*

Inter-American Development Bank, 1300 New York Avenue, NW, Washington, D.C. 20577 (202) 623-1753; *Economic and Social Progress in Latin America.*

TRINIDAD AND TOBAGO - RICE PRODUCTION - See TRINIDAD AND TOBAGO - CROPS

TRINIDAD AND TOBAGO - ROUNDWOOD PRODUCTION - See TRINIDAD AND TOBAGO - FORESTRY AND FOREST PRODUCTS

TRINIDAD AND TOBAGO - RUBBER PRODUCTION AND CONSUMPTION

Facts on File, 460 Park Avenue South, New York, New York 10016 (800) 443-8323; *The New Book of World Rankings.*

TRINIDAD AND TOBAGO - SAWNWOOD PRODUCTION - See TRINIDAD AND TOBAGO - FORESTRY AND FOREST PRODUCTS

TRINIDAD AND TOBAGO - SCIENCE AND TECHNOLOGY - EXPENDITURE FOR RESEARCH

Statistical Office of the United Nations, Publishing Service, New York, New York 10017 (800) 253-9646; *Statistical Yearbook.*

TRINIDAD AND TOBAGO - SCIENTISTS AND TECHNICIANS

Statistical Office of the United Nations, Publishing Service, New York, New York 10017 (800) 253-9646; *Statistical Yearbook.*

TRINIDAD AND TOBAGO - SENIOR CITIZENS

Facts on File, 460 Park Avenue South, New York, New York 10016 (800) 443-8323; *The New Book of World Rankings.*

TRINIDAD AND TOBAGO - SHEEP - See TRINIDAD AND TOBAGO - LIVESTOCK AND POULTRY

TRINIDAD AND TOBAGO - SILVER PRODUCTION AND CONSUMPTION - See TRINIDAD AND TOBAGO - MINING AND MINERAL PRODUCTS

TRINIDAD AND TOBAGO - SOCIAL DATA

Facts on File, 460 Park Avenue South, New York, New York 10016 (800) 443-8323; *The New Book of World Rankings.*

G.K. Hall and Company, 70 Lincoln Street, Boston, Massachusetts 02111 (617) 423-3990; *The World in Figures.*

TRINIDAD AND TOBAGO - SOCIAL SECURITY

Inter-American Development Bank, 1300 New York Avenue, NW, Washington, D.C. 20577 (202) 623-1753; *Economic and Social Progress in Latin America.*

International Monetary Fund, 700 Nineteenth Street, NW, Washington, D.C. 20431 (202) 623-7000; *Government Finance Statistics Yearbook.*

TRINIDAD AND TOBAGO - SOCIOECONOMIC DATA

Inter-American Development Bank, 1300 New York Avenue, NW, Washington, D.C. 20577 (202) 623-1753; *Economic and Social Progress in Latin America.*

TRINIDAD AND TOBAGO - SOYBEAN PRODUCTION - See TRINIDAD AND TOBAGO - CROPS

TRINIDAD AND TOBAGO - STAMP TAXES AND DUTIES - See TRINIDAD AND TOBAGO - TAXATION

TRINIDAD AND TOBAGO - STATE BUDGET REVENUE AND EXPENDITURES

Euromonitor Publications Limited, 87-88 Turnmill Street, London EC1M 5QU, England; *International Marketing Data and Statistics.*

Inter-American Development Bank, 1300 New York Avenue, NW, Washington, D.C. 20577 (202) 623-1753; *Economic and Social Progress in Latin America.*

TRINIDAD AND TOBAGO - STEEL - See TRINIDAD AND TOBAGO - MINING AND MINERAL PRODUCTS

TRINIDAD AND TOBAGO - STOCKS - COMMODITY - MARKET PRICE - INDEX

Food and Agricultural Organization of the United Nations (FAO) Via delle Terme di Caracalla, 00100 Rome, Italy (Telephone Number in U.S. (202) 653-2400); *The State of Food and Agriculture.*

TRINIDAD AND TOBAGO - SUGAR - See TRINIDAD AND TOBAGO - CROPS

TRINIDAD AND TOBAGO - SULPHURIC ACID PRODUCTION - See TRINIDAD AND TOBAGO - MINING AND MINERAL PRODUCTS

TRINIDAD AND TOBAGO - TAXATION

G.K. Hall and Company, 70 Lincoln Street, Boston, Massachusetts 02111 (617) 423-3990; *The World in Figures.*

Inter-American Development Bank, 1300 New York Avenue, NW, Washington, D.C. 20577 (202) 623-1753; *Economic and Social Progress in Latin America.*

International Monetary Fund, 700 Nineteenth Street, NW, Washington, D.C. 20431 (202) 623-7000; *Government Finance Statistics Yearbook.*

The World Bank, 1818 H Street, NW, Washington, D.C. 20433 (202) 477-1234; *World Tables.*

TRINIDAD AND TOBAGO - TELEPHONES IN USE

American Telephone and Telegraph Company, 26 Parsippany Road, Whippany, New Jersey 07981 (800) 338-4038; *The World's Telephones.*

The Economist Intelligence Unit, 111 West 57th Street, New York, New York 10019 (800) 938-4685; *The New Latin America Market Atlas.*

G.K. Hall and Company, 70 Lincoln Street, Boston, Massachusetts 02111 (617) 423-3990; *The World in Figures.*

Statistical Office of the United Nations, Publishing Service, New York, New York 10017 (800) 253-9646; *Statistical Yearbook.*

TRINIDAD AND TOBAGO - TELEVISION BROADCASTING - See TRINIDAD AND TOBAGO - BROADCASTING

TRINIDAD AND TOBAGO - TELEVISION RECEIVER PRODUCTION

Statistical Office of the United Nations, Publishing Service, New York, New York 10017 (800) 253-9646; *Statistical Yearbook.*

TRINIDAD AND TOBAGO - TEXTILE INDUSTRY

G.K. Hall and Company, 70 Lincoln Street, Boston, Massachusetts 02111 (617) 423-3990; *The World in Figures.*

TRINIDAD AND TOBAGO - THEATRE PERFORMANCES

United Nations Educational, Scientific and Cultural Organization (UNESCO), 7 Place de Fontenoy, F-75700 Paris, France (Telephone Number in U.S. (212) 963-5981); *Statistical Yearbook.*

TRINIDAD AND TOBAGO - TOBACCO PRODUCTION

Facts on File, 460 Park Avenue South, New York, New York 10016 (800) 443-8323; *The New Book of World Rankings.*

Statistical Office of the United Nations, Publishing Service, New York, New York 10017 (800) 253-9646; *Statistical Yearbook.*

U.C.L.A. Latin American Center Publications, University of California, Los Angeles, California 90024 (310) 825-6634; *Statistical Abstract of Latin America.*

TRINIDAD AND TOBAGO - TOURISM

The Economist Intelligence Unit, 111 West 57th Street, New York, New York 10019 (800) 938-4685; *The New Latin America Market Atlas.*

Facts on File, 460 Park Avenue South, New York, New York 10016 (800) 443-8323; *The New Book of World Rankings.*

G.K. Hall and Company, 70 Lincoln Street, Boston, Massachusetts 02111 (617) 423-3990; *The World in Figures.*

Organization of American States (OAS), General Secretariat, Washington, D.C. 20006 (202) 458-3533; *Statistical Bulletin of the OAS.*

Statistical Office of the United Nations, Publishing Service, New York, New York 10017 (800) 253-9646; *Statistical Yearbook.*

Times Books, 201 East 50th Street, New York, New York 10022 (212) 751-2600; *The Economist Book of Vital World Statistics.*

World Tourism Organization, Calle Capitan Haya 42, E-28020 Madrid, Spain; *Yearbook of Tourism Statistics.*

TRINIDAD AND TOBAGO - TRACTORS IN USE

The Economist Intelligence Unit, 111 West 57th Street, New York, New York 10019 (800) 938-4685; *The New Latin America Market Atlas.*

Statistical Office of the United Nations, Publishing Service, New York, New York 10017 (800) 253-9646; *Statistical Yearbook.*

TRINIDAD AND TOBAGO - TRADE - See TRINIDAD AND TOBAGO - FOREIGN TRADE

TRINIDAD AND TOBAGO - TRADEMARKS AND SERVICE MARKS

Statistical Office of the United Nations, Publishing Service, New York, New York 10017 (800) 253-9646; *Statistical Yearbook.*

TRINIDAD AND TOBAGO - TRANSPORTATION AND COMMUNICATIONS

The Economist Intelligence Unit, 111 West 57th Street, New York, New York 10019 (800) 938-4685; *The New Latin America Market Atlas.*

Facts on File, 460 Park Avenue South, New York, New York 10016 (800) 443-8323; *The New Book of World Rankings.*

Gale Research Incorporated, 835 Penobscot Building, Detroit, Michigan 48226 (800) 877-4253; *International Historical Statistics The Americas and Australasia.*

G.K. Hall and Company, 70 Lincoln Street, Boston, Massachusetts 02111 (617) 423-3990; *The World in Figures.*

Inter-American Development Bank, 1300 New York Avenue, NW, Washington, D.C. 20577 (202) 623-1753; *Economic and Social Progress in Latin America.*

TRINIDAD AND TOBAGO - UNEMPLOYMENT

The Economist Intelligence Unit, 111 West 57th Street, New York, New York 10019 (800) 938-4685; *The New Latin America Market Atlas.*

Euromonitor Publications Limited, 87-88 Turnmill Street, London EC1M 5QU, England; *International Marketing Data and Statistics.*

Organization of American States (OAS), General Secretariat, Washington, D.C. 20006 (202) 458-3533; *Statistical Bulletin of the OAS.*

Statistical Office of the United Nations, Publishing Service, New York, New York 10017 (800) 253-9646; *Statistical Yearbook.*

TRINIDAD AND TOBAGO - VITAL STATISTICS

Euromonitor Publications Limited, 87-88 Turnmill Street, London EC1M 5QU, England; *International Marketing Data and Statistics.*

Gale Research Incorporated, 835 Penobscot Building, Detroit, Michigan 48226 (800) 877-4253; *International Historical Statistics The Americas and Australasia.*

G.K. Hall and Company, 70 Lincoln Street, Boston, Massachusetts 02111 (617) 423-3990; *The World in Figures.*

Statistical Office of the United Nations, Publishing Service, New York, New York 10017 (800) 253-9646; *Statistical Yearbook.*

World Health Organization, Office of Publications, Avenue Appia, CH-1211 Geneva 27, Switzerland (Telephone Number in U.S. (518) 436-9686); *World Health Statistics Annual.*

TRINIDAD AND TOBAGO - WAGES

G.K. Hall and Company, 70 Lincoln Street, Boston, Massachusetts 02111 (617) 423-3990; *The World in Figures.*

International Labour Office, I.L.O. Publications, CH-1211, Geneva 22, Switzerland; *Yearbook of Labour Statistics.*

Organization of American States (OAS), General Secretariat, Washington, D.C. 20006 (202) 458-3533; *Statistical Bulletin of the OAS.*

TRINIDAD AND TOBAGO - WEATHER

Facts on File, 460 Park Avenue South, New York, New York 10016 (800) 443-8323; *The New Book of World Rankings.*

G.K. Hall and Company, 70 Lincoln Street, Boston, Massachusetts 02111 (617) 423-3990; *The World in Figures.*

TRINIDAD AND TOBAGO - WELFARE

Inter-American Development Bank, 1300 New York Avenue, NW, Washington, D.C. 20577 (202) 623-1753; *Economic and Social Progress in Latin America*.

International Monetary Fund, 700 Nineteenth Street, NW, Washington, D.C. 20431 (202) 623-7000; *Government Finance Statistics Yearbook*.

TRINIDAD AND TOBAGO - WHEAT - See TRINIDAD AND TOBAGO - CROPS

TRINIDAD AND TOBAGO - WHOLESALE PRICES

Inter-American Development Bank, 1300 New York Avenue, NW, Washington, D.C. 20577 (202) 623-1753; *Economic and Social Progress in Latin America*.

TRINIDAD AND TOBAGO - WHOLESALE TRADE

Inter-American Development Bank, 1300 New York Avenue, NW, Washington, D.C. 20577 (202) 623-1753; *Economic and Social Progress in Latin America*.

TRINIDAD AND TOBAGO - WINE PRODUCTION

Facts on File, 460 Park Avenue South, New York, New York 10016 (800) 443-8323; *The New Book of World Rankings*.

TRINIDAD AND TOBAGO - WOOD PULP PRODUCTION - See TRINIDAD AND TOBAGO - FORESTRY AND FOREST PRODUCTS

TRINIDAD AND TOBAGO - WOOL PRODUCTION

Facts on File, 460 Park Avenue South, New York, New York 10016 (800) 443-8323; *The New Book of World Rankings*.

TRINIDAD AND TOBAGO - ZOOS AND BOTANICAL GARDENS

United Nations Educational, Scientific and Cultural Organization (UNESCO), 7 Place de Fontenoy, F-75700 Paris, France (Telephone Number in U.S. (212) 963-5981); *Statistical Yearbook*.

TRIPOLI - MINE PRODUCTION

U.S. Department of the Interior, Bureau of Mines, 810 Seventh Street, NW, Washington, D.C. 20241 (202) 501-9649; *Annual Reports*, and *Mineral Commodities Summaries*.

TRIPS - See TRAVEL

TROUT

U.S. Department of Agriculture, National Agricultural Statistics Service, Fourteenth Street and Independence Avenue, SW, Washington, D.C. 20050 (202) 219-0504; *USDA*.

TRUCKING AND WAREHOUSING - See also MOTOR VEHICLES and TRANSPORTATION AND PUBLIC UTILITIES INDUSTRY

TRUCKING AND WAREHOUSING - EARNINGS

U.S. Department of Commerce, Bureau of the Census, Suitland, Maryland 20233 (301) 763-4040; *County Business Patterns*.

U.S. Department of Labor, Bureau of Labor Statistics, Two Massachusetts Avenue, NE, Washington, D.C. 20212 (202) 606-7828; *Employment and Earnings*, and Bulletins 2370 and 2429.

TRUCKING AND WAREHOUSING - EMPLOYEES

U.S. Department of Commerce, Bureau of the Census, Suitland, Maryland 20233 (301) 763-4040; *County Business Patterns*.

U.S. Department of Labor, Bureau of Labor Statistics, Two Massachusetts Avenue, NE, Washington, D.C. 20212 (202) 606-7828; *Employment and Earnings*, and Bulletins 2370 and 2429.

TRUCKING AND WAREHOUSING - FINANCES

U.S. Department of Commerce, Bureau of the Census, Suitland, Maryland 20233 (301) 763-4040; *Current Business Reports, Motor Freight Transportation and Warehousing Survey*.

TRUCKING AND WAREHOUSING - GROSS NATIONAL PRODUCT

U.S. Department of Commerce, Bureau of Economic Analysis, Fourteenth Street between Constitution Avenue and E Street, NW, Washington, D.C. 20230 (202) 606-9900; *The National Income and Product Accounts of the United States*, and *Survey of Current Business*.

TRUCKING AND WAREHOUSING - OCCUPATIONAL SAFETY

U.S. Department of Labor, Bureau of Labor Statistics, Two Massachusetts Avenue, NE, Washington, D.C. 20212 (202) 606-7828; *Occupational Injuries and Illnesses in the United States by Industry*.

TRUCKING AND WAREHOUSING - PRODUCTIVITY

U.S. Department of Labor, Bureau of Labor Statistics, Two Massachusetts Avenue, NE, Washington, D.C. 20212 (202) 606-7020; *Productivity Measures for Selected Industries and Government Services*, and unpublished data.

TRUCKS - BODY TYPE

U.S. Department of Commerce, Bureau of the Census, Suitland, Maryland 20233 (301) 763-4040; *Census of Transportation*.

TRUCKS - FACTORY SALES (TRUCKS AND BUSES)

American Automobile Manufacturers Association, 1401 H Street, NW, Suite 900, Washington, D.C. 20005 (202) 326-5500; *Motor Vehicle Facts and Figures*, and *World Motor Vehicle Data*.

TRUCKS - FLEET SIZE

U.S. Department of Commerce, Bureau of the Census, Suitland, Maryland 20233 (301) 763-4040; *Census of Transportation*.

TRUCKS - FUEL TYPE

U.S. Department of Commerce, Bureau of the Census, Suitland, Maryland 20233 (301) 763-4040; *Census of Transportation*.

TRUCKS - HAZARDOUS MATERIALS CARRIED

U.S. Department of Commerce, Bureau of the Census, Suitland, Maryland 20233 (301) 763-4040; *Census of Transportation*.

TRUCKS - MOTOR FUEL CONSUMPTION

U.S. Department of Transportation, Federal Highway Administration, 400 Seventh Street, SW, Washington, D.C. 20590 (202) 366-0660; *Highway Statistics*.

TRUCKS - REGISTRATION (TRUCKS AND BUSES)

American Automobile Manufacturers Association, 1401 H Street, NW, Suite 900, Washington, D.C. 20005 (202) 326-5500; *Motor Vehicle Facts and Figures.*

U.S. Department of Transportation, Federal Highway Administration, 400 Seventh Street, SW, Washington, D.C. 20590 (202) 366-0660; *Highway Statistics,* and *Selected Highway Statistics and Charts.*

TRUCKS - TRAVEL AND SPEED

U.S. Department of Transportation, Federal Highway Administration, 400 Seventh Street, SW, Washington, D.C. 20590 (202) 366-0660; *Highway Statistics.*

TRUST FUNDS - UNITED STATES GOVERNMENT

Executive Office of the President, Office of Management and Budget, Executive Office Building, Washington, D.C. 20503 (202) 395-3080; *Budget of the United States Government.*

TUBERCULOSIS

U.S. Department of Health and Human Services, Center for Disease Control, 1600 Clifton Road, NE, Atlanta, Georgia 30333 (404) 639-3311; *Summary of Notifiable Diseases, United States, Morbidity and Mortality Weekly Report.*

U.S. Department of Health and Human Services, National Center for Health Statistics 3700 East West Highway, Hyattsville, Maryland 20782 (301) 436-8500; *Vital Statistics of the United States,* and *Monthly Vital Statistics Reports.*

TUBERCULOSIS - HOSPITALS

American Hospital Association, 840 North Lake Shore Drive, Chicago, Illinois 60611 (312) 280-6000; *Hospital Statistics.*

U.S. Department of Health and Human Services, National Center for Health Statistics, 3700 East West Highway, Hyattsville, Maryland 20782 (301) 436-8500; *Vital and Health Statistics,* and unpublished data.

U.S. Department of Health and Human Services, Public Health Service, 200 Independence Avenue, SW, Washington, D.C. 20201 (202) 619-1296; unpublished data.

TUITION

U.S. Department of Education, National Center for Education Statistics, 400 Maryland Avenue, SW, Washington, D.C. 20202 (202) 708-5366; *Digest of Education Statistics.*

TUNA

U.S. Department of Commerce, National Oceanic and Atmospheric Administration, National Marine Fisheries Service, 1335 East-West Highway, Silver Spring, Maryland 20910 (301) 427-2239; *Fisheries of the United States,* and *Fishery Statistics of the United States.*

TUNA - CATCH

U.S. Department of Commerce, National Oceanic and Atmospheric Administration, National Marine Fisheries Service, 1335 East-West Highway, Silver Spring, Maryland 20910 (301) 427-2239; *Fishery Statistics of the United States,* and *Fisheries of the United States.*

TUNA - CONSUMPTION - CANNED

U.S. Department of Agriculture, Economic Research Service, Fourteenth Street and Independence Avenue, SW, Washington, D.C. 20005-4789 (202) 219-1504; *Food Consumption, Prices, and Expenditures.*

TUNA - IMPORTS

U.S. Department of Commerce, National Oceanic and Atmospheric Administration, National Marine Fisheries Service, 1335 East-West Highway, Silver Spring, Maryland 20910 (301) 427-2239; *Fisheries of the United States,* and *Fishery Statistics of the United States.*

TUNA - SUPPLY

U.S. Department of Commerce, National Oceanic and Atmospheric Administration, National Marine Fisheries Service, 1335 East-West Highway, Silver Spring, Maryland 20910 (301) 427-2239; *Fishery Statistics of the United States,* and *Fisheries of the United States.*

TUNGSTEN

U.S. Department of Commerce, Bureau of the Census, Suitland, Maryland 20233 (301) 763-4040; *Census of Mineral Industries.*

U.S. Department of the Interior, Bureau of Mines, 810 Seventh Street, NW, Washington, D.C. 20241 (202) 501-9649; *Annual Reports,* and *Mineral Commodity Summaries.*

TUNGSTEN - CONSUMPTION

U.S. Department of the Interior, Bureau of Mines, 810 Seventh Street, NW, Washington, D.C. 20241 (202) 501-9649; *Mineral Commodities Summaries.*

TUNGSTEN - FOREIGN TRADE

U.S. Department of the Interior, Bureau of Mines, 810 Seventh Street, NW, Washington, D.C. 20241 (202) 501-9649; *Annual Reports,* and *Mineral Commodity Summaries.*

TUNGSTEN - PRODUCTION AND VALUE

U.S. Department of the Interior, Bureau of Mines, 810 Seventh Street, NW, Washington, D.C. 20241 (202) 501-9649; *Annual Reports,* and *Mineral Commodities Summaries.*

TUNGSTEN - STRATEGIC AND CRITICAL MATERIAL

U.S. Department of Defense, Defense Logistics Agency, Cameron Station, Alexandria, Virginia 22304-6100 (703) 274-6000; *Statistical Supplement, Stockpile Report to the Congress.*

Tunisia - National Statistical Office

Institut National de Statistique, 27 rue du Liban, 1002 Tunis-Belvedere, Tunis, Tunisia.

Tunisia - Primary Statistics Sources

Institut National de la Statistique, 27 rue du Liban, 1002 Tunis-Belvedere, Tunis, Tunisia; *Annuaire statistique de la Tunisie* (Statistical Yearbook of Tunisia) *Bulletin mensuel de statistique* (Monthly Bulletin of Statistics), and *L'Economie de la Tunisie en Chiffres* (The Tunisian economy in figures).

TUNISIA - ABORTIONS

Statistical Office of the United Nations, Publishing Service, New York, New York 10017 (800) 253-9646; *Demographic Yearbook*.

TUNISIA - AGRICULTURE

Euromonitor Publications Limited, 87-88 Turnmill Street, London EC1M 5QU, England; *International Marketing Data and Statistics*, and *Middle East Economic Handbook*.

Facts on File, 460 Park Avenue South, New York, New York 10016 (800) 443-8323; *The New Book of World Rankings*.

Food and Agricultural Organization of the United Nations (FAO) Via delle Terme di Caracalla, 00100 Rome, Italy (Telephone Number in U.S. (202) 653-2400); *Production Yearbook, The State of Food and Agriculture*, and *Trade Yearbook*.

G.K. Hall and Company, 70 Lincoln Street, Boston, Massachusetts 02111 (617) 423-3990; *The World in Figures*.

Statistical Office of the United Nations, Publishing Service, New York, New York 10017 (800) 253-9646; *Statistical Yearbook*, and *Survey of Economic and Social Conditions in Africa*.

Times Books, 201 East 50th Street, New York, New York 10022 (212) 751-2600; *The Economist Book of Vital World Statistics*.

United Nations Economic Commission for Africa, Africa Hall, P.O. Box 3001, Addis Ababa, Ethiopia (Telephone Number in U.S. (800) 253-9646); *African Statistical Yearbook*.

The World Bank, 1818 H Street, NW, Washington, D.C. 20433 (202) 477-1234; *World Tables*.

TUNISIA - AIRLINE SERVICE

Facts on File, 460 Park Avenue South, New York, New York 10016 (800) 443-8323; *The New Book of World Rankings*.

G.K. Hall and Company, 70 Lincoln Street, Boston, Massachusetts 02111 (617) 423-3990; *The World in Figures*.

International Civil Aviation Organization, 1000 Sherbrooke Street, West, Montreal, Quebec, Canada H3A 2R2 (514) 285-8219; *Civil Aviation Statistics of the World*.

Statistical Office of the United Nations, Publishing Service, New York, New York 10017 (800) 253-9646; *Statistical Yearbook*.

United Nations Economic Commission for Africa, Africa Hall, P.O. Box 3001, Addis Ababa, Ethiopia (Telephone Number in U.S. (800) 253-9646); *African Statistical Yearbook*.

Times Books, 201 East 50th Street, New York, New York 10022 (212) 751-2600; *The Economist Book of Vital World Statistics*.

TUNISIA - ALUMINUM PRODUCTION AND CONSUMPTION - See TUNISIA - MINING AND MINERAL PRODUCTS

TUNISIA - ANIMAL HEALTH

Food and Agricultural Organization of the United Nations (FAO), Via delle Terme di Caracalla, 00100, Rome, Italy (Telephone Number in U.S. (202) 653-2400); *Animal Health Yearbook*.

TUNISIA - AREA AND DENSITY OF POPULATION

African Development Bank, 01 BP 1387, Abidjan 01, Cote D'Ivoire; *Selected Statistics on Regional Member Countries*.

Euromonitor Publications Limited, 87-88 Turnmill Street, London EC1M 5QU, England; *International Marketing Data and Statistics*, and *Middle East Economic Handbook*.

Facts on File, 460 Park Avenue South, New York, New York 10016 (800) 443-8323; *The New Book of World Rankings*.

Food and Agricultural Organization of the United Nations (FAO) Via delle Terme di Caracalla, 00100 Rome, Italy (Telephone Number in U.S. (202) 653-2400); *The State of Food and Agriculture*.

G.K. Hall and Company, 70 Lincoln Street, Boston, Massachusetts 02111 (617) 423-3990; *The World in Figures*.

Statistical Office of the United Nations, Publishing Service, New York, New York 10017 (800) 253-9646; *Statistical Yearbook*, and *Survey of Economic and Social Conditions in Africa*.

Times Books, 201 East 50th Street, New York, New York 10022 (212) 751-2600; *The Economist Book of Vital World Statistics*.

United Nations Educational, Scientific and Cultural Organization (UNESCO), 7 Place de Fontenoy, F-75700 Paris, France (Telephone Number in U.S. (212) 963-5981); *Statistical Yearbook*.

TUNISIA - ARMS EXPORTS AND IMPORTS

U.S. Arms Control and Disarmament Agency, 320 Twenty-first Street, NW, Washington, D.C. 20451 (202) 647-8677; *World Military Expenditures and Arms Transfers*.

TUNISIA - BALANCE OF PAYMENTS

African Development Bank, 01 BP 1387, Abidjan 01, Cote D'Ivoire; *Selected Statistics on Regional Member Countries*.

The Economist Intelligence Unit, 111 West 57th Street, New York, New York 10019 (800) 938-4685; *The World Market Atlas*.

G.K. Hall and Company, 70 Lincoln Street, Boston, Massachusetts 02111 (617) 423-3990; *The World in Figures*.

International Monetary Fund, 700 Nineteenth Street, NW, Washington, D.C. 20431 (202) 623-7000; *Balance of Payments Yearbook*.

Times Books, 201 East 50th Street, New York, New York 10022 (212) 751-2600; *The Economist Book of Vital World Statistics*.

United Nations Economic Commission for Africa, Africa Hall, P.O. Box 3001, Addis Ababa, Ethiopia (Telephone Number in U.S. (800) 253-9646); *African Statistical Yearbook*.

The World Bank, 1818 H Street, NW, Washington, D.C. 20433 (202) 477-1234; *World Tables*.

TUNISIA - BANKING

Facts on File, 460 Park Avenue South, New York, New York 10016 (800) 443-8323; *The New Book of World Rankings*.

G.K. Hall and Company, 70 Lincoln Street, Boston, Massachusetts 02111 (617) 423-3990; *The World in Figures*.

International Monetary Fund, 700 Nineteenth Street, NW, Washington, D.C. 20431 (202) 623-7000; *Government Finance Statistics Yearbook*, and *International Financial Statistics*.

Statistical Office of the United Nations, Publishing Service, New York, New York 10017 (800) 253-9646; *Statistical Yearbook*.

United Nations Economic Commission for Africa, Africa Hall, P.O. Box 3001, Addis Ababa, Ethiopia (Telephone Number in U.S. (800) 253-9646); *African Statistical Yearbook*.

TUNISIA - BARLEY PRODUCTION - See - TUNISIA - CROPS

TUNISIA - BEER PRODUCTION

Facts on File, 460 Park Avenue South, New York, New York 10016 (800) 443-8323; *The New Book of World Rankings*.

Statistical Office of the United Nations, Publishing Service, New York, New York 10017 (800) 253-9646; *Statistical Yearbook*.

TUNISIA - BIRTH RATE

Euromonitor Publications Limited, 87-88 Turnmill Street, London EC1M 5QU, England; *Middle East Economic Handbook*.

Facts on File, 460 Park Avenue South, New York, New York 10016 (800) 443-8323; *The New Book of World Rankings*.

Statistical Office of the United Nations, Publishing Service, New York, New York 10017 (800) 253-9646; *Demographic Yearbook*, *Statistical Yearbook*, and *Survey of Economic and Social Conditions in Africa*.

Times Books, 201 East 50th Street, New York, New York 10022 (212) 751-2600; *The Economist Book of Vital World Statistics*.

The World Bank, 1818 H Street, NW, Washington, D.C. 20433 (202) 477-1234; *World Tables*.

TUNISIA - BONDS

G.K. Hall and Company, 70 Lincoln Street, Boston, Massachusetts 02111 (617) 423-3990; *The World in Figures*.

International Monetary Fund, 700 Nineteenth Street, NW, Washington, D.C. 20431 (202) 623-7000; *Government Finance Statistics Yearbook*.

TUNISIA - BOOK PRODUCTION

G.K. Hall and Company, 70 Lincoln Street, Boston, Massachusetts 02111 (617) 423-3990; *The World in Figures*.

United Nations Educational, Scientific and Cultural Organization (UNESCO), 7 Place de Fontenoy, F-75700 Paris, France (Telephone Number in U.S. (212) 963-5981); *Statistical Yearbook*.

TUNISIA - BROADCASTING

Billboard Limited, P.O. Box 9027, 1006 AA Amsterdam, The Netherlands (Telephone Number in U.S. (212) 764-7300); *World Radio TV Handbook*.

Facts on File, 460 Park Avenue South, New York, New York 10016 (800) 443-8323; *The New Book of World Rankings*.

G.K. Hall and Company, 70 Lincoln Street, Boston, Massachusetts 02111 (617) 423-3990; *The World in Figures*.

Times Books, 201 East 50th Street, New York, New York 10022 (212) 751-2600; *The Economist Book of Vital World Statistics*.

TUNISIA - BUSINESS

G.K. Hall and Company, 70 Lincoln Street, Boston, Massachusetts 02111 (617) 423-3990; *The World in Figures*.

TUNISIA - BUSINESS AND PROFESSIONAL LICENSES

International Monetary Fund, 700 Nineteenth Street, NW, Washington, D.C. 20431 (202) 623-7000; *Government Finance Statistics Yearbook*.

TUNISIA - BUTTER PRODUCTION - See TUNISIA - DAIRY PRODUCTS

TUNISIA - CALORIE SUPPLY

African Development Bank, 01 BP 1387, Abidjan 01, Cote D'Ivoire; *Selected Statistics on Regional Member Countries*.

Food and Agricultural Organization of the United Nations (FAO) Via delle Terme di Caracalla, 00100 Rome, Italy (Telephone Number in U.S. (202) 653-2400); *The State of Food and Agriculture*.

TUNISIA - CAPITAL REVENUE

International Monetary Fund, 700 Nineteenth Street, NW, Washington, D.C. 20431 (202) 623-7000; *Government Finance Statistics Yearbook*.

TUNISIA - CATTLE - See TUNISIA - LIVESTOCK AND POULTRY

TUNISIA - CEMENT PRODUCTION - See TUNISIA - MINING AND MINERAL PRODUCTS

TUNISIA - CHEESE PRODUCTION AND CONSUMPTION - See TUNISIA - DAIRY PRODUCTS

TUNISIA - CHEMICAL (ORGANIC) PRODUCTION - See TUNISIA - MINING AND MINERAL PRODUCTS

TUNISIA - CHICKENS - See TUNISIA - LIVESTOCK AND POULTRY

TUNISIA - CIGAR PRODUCTION - See TUNISIA - TOBACCO PRODUCTION

TUNISIA - CIGARETTE PRODUCTION - See TUNISIA - TOBACCO PRODUCTION

TUNISIA - CLASS STRUCTURE

G.K. Hall and Company, 70 Lincoln Street, Boston, Massachusetts 02111 (617) 423-3990; *The World in Figures*.

TUNISIA - CLIMATE

Facts on File, 460 Park Avenue South, New York, New York 10016 (800) 443-8323; *The New Book of World Rankings*.

G.K. Hall and Company, 70 Lincoln Street, Boston, Massachusetts 02111 (617) 423-3990; *The World in Figures*.

TUNISIA - CLOTHING EXPORTS AND IMPORTS

Statistical Office of the United Nations, Publishing Service, New York, New York 10017 (800) 253-9646; *Trade in Manufactures of Developing Countries*.

TUNISIA - COAL PRODUCTION - See TUNISIA - MINING AND MINERAL PRODUCTS

TUNISIA - COFFEE PRODUCTION AND CONSUMPTION - See - TUNISIA - CROPS

TUNISIA - COMMUNICATIONS

G.K. Hall and Company, 70 Lincoln Street, Boston, Massachusetts 02111 (617) 423-3990; *The World in Figures.*

United Nations Economic Commission for Africa, Africa Hall, P.O. Box 3001, Addis Ababa, Ethiopia (Telephone Number in U.S. (800) 253-9646); *African Statistical Yearbook.*

TUNISIA - CONSTRUCTION INDUSTRY

Facts on File, 460 Park Avenue South, New York, New York 10016 (800) 443-8323; *The New Book of World Rankings.*

Statistical Office of the United Nations, Publishing Service, New York, New York 10017 (800) 253-9646; *Construction Statistics Yearbook,* and *Statistical Yearbook.*

United Nations Economic Commission for Africa, Africa Hall, P.O. Box 3001, Addis Ababa, Ethiopia (Telephone Number in U.S. (800) 253-9646); *African Statistical Yearbook.*

TUNISIA - CONSUMER PRICE INDEX

African Development Bank, 01 BP 1387, Abidjan 01, Cote D'Ivoire; *Selected Statistics on Regional Member Countries.*

G.K. Hall and Company, 70 Lincoln Street, Boston, Massachusetts 02111 (617) 423-3990; *The World in Figures.*

Statistical Office of the United Nations, Publishing Service, New York, New York 10017 (800) 253-9646; *Statistical Yearbook,* and *Survey of Economic and Social Conditions in Africa.*

United Nations Economic Commission for Africa, Africa Hall, P.O. Box 3001, Addis Ababa, Ethiopia (Telephone Number in U.S. (800) 253-9646); *African Statistical Yearbook.*

TUNISIA - CONSUMER PRICES

International Labour Office, I.L.O. Publications, CH-1211, Geneva 22, Switzerland; *Yearbook of Labour Statistics.*

International Monetary Fund, 700 Nineteenth Street, NW, Washington, D.C. 20431 (202) 623-7000; *International Financial Statistics.*

Times Books, 201 East 50th Street, New York, New York 10022 (212) 751-2600; *The Economist Book of Vital World Statistics.*

TUNISIA - CONSUMPTION

African Development Bank, 01 BP 1387, Abidjan 01, Cote D'Ivoire; *Selected Statistics on Regional Member Countries.*

Euromonitor Publications Limited, 87-88 Turnmill Street, London EC1M 5QU, England; *Middle East Economic Handbook.*

G.K. Hall and Company, 70 Lincoln Street, Boston, Massachusetts 02111 (617) 423-3990; *The World in Figures.*

International Lead and Zinc Study Group, Metro House, 58 St. James's Street, London SW1A 1LD, England; *Lead and Zinc Statistics.*

Statistical Office of the United Nations, Publishing Service, New York, New York 10017 (800) 253-9646; *Survey of Economic and Social Conditions in Africa.*

TUNISIA - COPPER PRODUCTION AND CONSUMPTION - See TUNISIA - MINING AND MINERAL PRODUCTS

TUNISIA - CORN PRODUCTION - See - TUNISIA - CROPS

TUNISIA - CORPORATE TAXES - See TUNISIA - TAXATION

TUNISIA - COTTON PRODUCTION AND CONSUMPTION - See - TUNISIA - CROPS

TUNISIA - CRIME

International Criminal Police Organization (INTERPOL), 26 rue Armengaud, 92210 Saint Cloud, France; *International Crime Statistics.*

Yale University Press, Yale Station, New Haven, Connecticut 06520 (203) 432-0940; *Violence and Crime in Cross-National Perspective.*

TUNISIA - CROPS

Facts on File, 460 Park Avenue South, New York, New York 10016 (800) 443-8323; *The New Book of World Rankings.*

Food and Agricultural Organization of the United Nations (FAO) Via delle Terme di Caracalla, 00100 Rome, Italy (Telephone Number in U.S. (202) 653-2400); *The State of Food and Agriculture.*

G.K. Hall and Company, 70 Lincoln Street, Boston, Massachusetts 02111 (617) 423-3990; *The World in Figures.*

Statistical Office of the United Nations, Publishing Service, New York, New York 10017 (800) 253-9646; *Statistical Yearbook.*

United Nations Economic Commission for Africa, Africa Hall, P.O. Box 3001, Addis Ababa, Ethiopia (Telephone Number in U.S. (800) 253-9646); *African Statistical Yearbook.*

TUNISIA - CUSTOMS DUTIES

G.K. Hall and Company, 70 Lincoln Street, Boston, Massachusetts 02111 (617) 423-3990; *The World in Figures.*

International Monetary Fund, 700 Nineteenth Street, NW, Washington, D.C. 20431 (202) 623-7000; *Government Finance Statistics Yearbook.*

TUNISIA - DAIRY PRODUCTS

Facts on File, 460 Park Avenue South, New York, New York 10016 (800) 443-8323; *The New Book of World Rankings.*

Food and Agricultural Organization of the United Nations (FAO) Via delle Terme di Caracalla, 00100 Rome, Italy (Telephone Number in U.S. (202) 653-2400); *The State of Food and Agriculture.*

Statistical Office of the United Nations, Publishing Service, New York, New York 10017 (800) 253-9646; *Statistical Yearbook.*

TUNISIA - DEATH RATES

Euromonitor Publications Limited, 87-88 Turnmill Street, London EC1M 5QU, England; *Middle East Economic Handbook.*

G.K. Hall and Company, 70 Lincoln Street, Boston, Massachusetts 02111 (617) 423-3990; *The World in Figures.*

Statistical Office of the United Nations, Publishing Service, New York, New York 10017 (800) 253-9646; *Statistical Yearbook,* and *Survey of Economic and Social Conditions in Africa.*

Times Books, 201 East 50th Street, New York, New York 10022 (212) 751-2600; *The Economist Book of Vital World Statistics.*

World Health Organization, Office of Publications, Avenue Appia, CH-1211 Geneva 27, Switzerland (Telephone Number in U.S. (518) 436-9686); *World Health Statistics Annual.*

TUNISIA - DEFENSE EXPENDITURES

G.K. Hall and Company, 70 Lincoln Street, Boston, Massachusetts 02111 (617) 423-3990; *The World in Figures.*

International Monetary Fund, 700 Nineteenth Street, NW, Washington, D.C. 20431 (202) 623-7000; *Government Finance Statistics Yearbook.*

U.S. Arms Control and Disarmament Agency, 320 Twenty-first Street, NW, Washington, D.C. 20451 (202) 647-8677; *World Military Expenditures and Arms Transfers.*

TUNISIA - DEMOGRAPHY

The Economist Intelligence Unit, 111 West 57th Street, New York, New York 10019 (800) 938-4685; *The World Market Atlas.*

Facts on File, 460 Park Avenue South, New York, New York 10016 (800) 443-8323; *The New Book of World Rankings.*

G.K. Hall and Company, 70 Lincoln Street, Boston, Massachusetts 02111 (617) 423-3990; *The World in Figures.*

Statistical Office of the United Nations, Publishing Service, New York, New York 10017 (800) 253-9646; *Survey of Economic and Social Conditions in Africa.*

TUNISIA - DEVELOPMENT ASSISTANCE

G.K. Hall and Company, 70 Lincoln Street, Boston, Massachusetts 02111 (617) 423-3990; *The World in Figures.*

Statistical Office of the United Nations, Publishing Service, New York, New York 10017 (800) 253-9646; *Statistical Yearbook.*

TUNISIA - DIAMOND PRODUCTION - See TUNISIA - MINING AND MINERAL PRODUCTS

TUNISIA - DISCOUNT RATES

Statistical Office of the United Nations, Publishing Service, New York, New York 10017 (800) 253-9646; *Statistical Yearbook.*

TUNISIA - DISEASES

G.K. Hall and Company, 70 Lincoln Street, Boston, Massachusetts 02111 (617) 423-3990; *The World in Figures.*

World Health Organization, Office of Publications, Avenue Appia, CH-1211 Geneva 27, Switzerland (Telephone Number in U.S. (518) 436-9686); *World Health Statistics Annual.*

TUNISIA - DIVORCE RATES

Facts on File, 460 Park Avenue South, New York, New York 10016 (800) 443-8323; *The New Book of World Rankings.*

Statistical Office of the United Nations, Publishing Service, New York, New York 10017 (800) 253-9646; *Demographic Yearbook,* and *Statistical Yearbook.*

TUNISIA - DOMESTIC PRODUCT

G.K. Hall and Company, 70 Lincoln Street, Boston, Massachusetts 02111 (617) 423-3990; *The World in Figures.*

TUNISIA - ECONOMY

African Development Bank, 01 BP 1387, Abidjan 01, Cote D'Ivoire; *Selected Statistics on Regional Member Countries.*

Euromonitor Publications Limited, 87-88 Turnmill Street, London EC1M 5QU, England; *International Marketing Data and Statistics.*

Facts on File, 460 Park Avenue South, New York, New York 10016 (800) 443-8323; *The New Book of World Rankings.*

G.K. Hall and Company, 70 Lincoln Street, Boston, Massachusetts 02111 (617) 423-3990; *The World in Figures.*

Statistical Office of the United Nations, Publishing Service, New York, New York 10017 (800) 253-9646; *Foreign Trade Statistics for Africa.*

TUNISIA - EDUCATION

African Development Bank, 01 BP 1387, Abidjan 01, Cote D'Ivoire; *Selected Statistics on Regional Member Countries.*

The Economist Intelligence Unit, 111 West 57th Street, New York, New York 10019 (800) 938-4685; *The World Market Atlas.*

Euromonitor Publications Limited, 87-88 Turnmill Street, London EC1M 5QU, England; *Middle East Economic Handbook.*

Facts on File, 460 Park Avenue South, New York, New York 10016 (800) 443-8323; *The New Book of World Rankings.*

G.K. Hall and Company, 70 Lincoln Street, Boston, Massachusetts 02111 (617) 423-3990; *The World in Figures.*

International Monetary Fund, 700 Nineteenth Street, NW, Washington, D.C. 20431 (202) 623-7000; *Government Finance Statistics Yearbook.*

Statistical Office of the United Nations, Publishing Service, New York, New York 10017 (800) 253-9646; *Survey of Economic and Social Conditions in Africa.*

Times Books, 201 East 50th Street, New York, New York 10022 (212) 751-2600; *The Economist Book of Vital World Statistics.*

United Nations Economic Commission for Africa, Africa Hall, P.O. Box 3001, Addis Ababa, Ethiopia (Telephone Number in U.S. (800) 253-9646); *African Statistical Yearbook.*

United Nations Educational, Scientific and Cultural Organization (UNESCO), 7 Place de Fontenoy, F-75700 Paris, France (Telephone Number in U.S. (212) 963-5981); *Statistical Yearbook.*

The World Bank, 1818 H Street, NW, Washington, D.C. 20433 (202) 477-1234; *World Tables*.

TUNISIA - EGG PRODUCTION AND CONSUMPTION - See TUNISIA - DAIRY PRODUCTS

TUNISIA - ELECTRICITY

Facts on File, 460 Park Avenue South, New York, New York 10016 (800) 443-8323; *The New Book of World Rankings*.

Penn Well Publishing Company, 1421 South Sheridan Road, P.O. Box 1260, Tulsa, Oklahoma 74101 (800) 752-9764; *International Energy Statistics Sourcebook*.

Statistical Office of the United Nations, Publishing Service, New York, New York 10017 (800) 253-9646; *Statistical Yearbook*, and *Survey of Economic and Social Conditions in Africa*.

Times Books, 201 East 50th Street, New York, New York 10022 (212) 751-2600; *The Economist Book of Vital World Statistics*.

United Nations Economic Commission for Africa, Africa Hall, P.O. Box 3001, Addis Ababa, Ethiopia (Telephone Number in U.S. (800) 253-9646); *African Statistical Yearbook*.

TUNISIA - EMPLOYMENT

Euromonitor Publications Limited, 87-88 Turnmill Street, London EC1M 5QU, England; *International Marketing Data and Statistics*, and *Middle East Economic Handbook*.

Facts on File, 460 Park Avenue South, New York, New York 10016 (800) 443-8323; *The New Book of World Rankings*.

International Labour Office, I.L.O. Publications, CH-1211, Geneva 22, Switzerland; *Yearbook of Labour Statistics*.

Statistical Office of the United Nations, Publishing Service, New York, New York 10017 (800) 253-9646; *Statistical Yearbook*, and *Survey of Economic and Social Conditions in Africa*.

United Nations Economic Commission for Africa, Africa Hall, P.O. Box 3001, Addis Ababa, Ethiopia (Telephone Number in U.S. (800) 253-9646); *African Statistical Yearbook*.

TUNISIA - ENERGY

Euromonitor Publications Limited, 87-88 Turnmill Street, London EC1M 5QU, England; *Middle East Economic Handbook*.

Facts on File, 460 Park Avenue South, New York, New York 10016 (800) 443-8323; *The New Book of World Rankings*.

Food and Agricultural Organization of the United Nations (FAO) Via delle Terme di Caracalla, 00100 Rome, Italy (Telephone Number in U.S. (202) 653-2400); *The State of Food and Agriculture*.

G.K. Hall and Company, 70 Lincoln Street, Boston, Massachusetts 02111 (617) 423-3990; *The World in Figures*.

Penn Well Publishing Company, 1421 South Sheridan Road, P.O. Box 1260, Tulsa, Oklahoma 74101 (800) 752-9764; *International Energy Statistics Sourcebook*.

Statistical Office of the United Nations, Publishing Service, New York, New York 10017 (800) 253-9646; *Energy Statistics Yearbook*.

Times Books, 201 East 50th Street, New York, New York 10022 (212) 751-2600; *The Economist Book of Vital World Statistics*.

United Nations Economic Commission for Africa, Africa Hall, P.O. Box 3001, Addis Ababa, Ethiopia (Telephone Number in U.S. (800) 253-9646); *African Statistical Yearbook*.

TUNISIA - EXCHANGE RATES

African Development Bank, 01 BP 1387, Abidjan 01, Cote D'Ivoire; *Selected Statistics on Regional Member Countries*.

Euromonitor Publications Limited, 87-88 Turnmill Street, London EC1M 5QU, England; *International Marketing Data and Statistics*, and *Middle East Economic Handbook*.

International Civil Aviation Organization, 1000 Sherbrooke Street, West, Montreal, Quebec, Canada H3A 2R2 (514) 285-8219; *Civil Aviation Statistics of the World*.

International Monetary Fund, 700 Nineteenth Street, NW, Washington, D.C. 20431 (202) 623-7000; *International Financial Statistics*.

Statistical Office of the United Nations, Publishing Service, New York, New York 10017 (800) 253-9646; *Foreign Trade Statistics for Africa*, and *Statistical Yearbook*.

TUNISIA - EXCISE TAXES - See TUNISIA - TAXATION

TUNISIA - EXPORTS

African Development Bank, 01 BP 1387, Abidjan 01, Cote D'Ivoire; *Selected Statistics on Regional Member Countries*.

American Automobile Manufacturers Association, 1401 H Street, NW, Suite 900, Washington, D.C. 20005 (202) 326-5500; *World Motor Vehicle Data*.

The Economist Intelligence Unit, 111 West 57th Street, New York, New York 10019 (800) 938-4685; *The World Market Atlas*.

Euromonitor Publications Limited, 87-88 Turnmill Street, London EC1M 5QU, England; *International Marketing Data and Statistics*, and *Middle East Economic Handbook*.

Food and Agricultural Organization of the United Nations (FAO) Via delle Terme di Caracalla, 00100 Rome, Italy (Telephone Number in U.S. (202) 653-2400); *The State of Food and Agriculture*.

G.K. Hall and Company, 70 Lincoln Street, Boston, Massachusetts 02111 (617) 423-3990; *The World in Figures*.

International Lead and Zinc Study Group, Metro House, 58 St. James's Street, London SW1A 1LD, England; *Lead and Zinc Statistics*.

International Monetary Fund, 700 Nineteenth Street, NW, Washington, D.C. 20431 (202) 623-7000; *Direction of Trade Statistics*, *Government Finance Statistics Yearbook*, and *International Financial Statistics*.

Statistical Office of the United Nations, Publishing Service, New York, New York 10017 (800) 253-9646; *Foreign Trade Statistics for Africa*, *Survey of Economic and Social Conditions in Africa*, and *Trade in Manufactures of Developing Countries*.

Times Books, 201 East 50th Street, New York, New York 10022 (212) 751-2600; *The Economist Book of Vital World Statistics*.

United Nations Economic Commission for Africa, Africa Hall, P.O. Box 3001, Addis Ababa, Ethiopia (Telephone Number in U.S. (800) 253-9646); *African Statistical Yearbook*.

The World Bank, 1818 H Street, NW, Washington, D.C. 20433 (202) 477-1234; *World Tables*.

TUNISIA - EXTERNAL INDEBTEDNESS

African Development Bank, 01 BP 1387, Abidjan 01, Cote D'Ivoire; *Selected Statistics on Regional Member Countries*.

Statistical Office of the United Nations, Publishing Service, New York, New York 10017 (800) 253-9646; *Survey of Economic and Social Conditions in Africa*.

The World Bank, 1818 H Street, NW, Washington, D.C. 20433 (202) 477-1234; *World Tables*.

TUNISIA - EXTERNAL TRADE

African Development Bank, 01 BP 1387, Abidjan 01, Cote D'Ivoire; *Selected Statistics on Regional Member Countries*.

Food and Agricultural Organization of the United Nations (FAO) Via delle Terme di Caracalla, 00100 Rome, Italy (Telephone Number in U.S. (202) 653-2400); *The State of Food and Agriculture*, and *Trade Yearbook*.

G.K. Hall and Company, 70 Lincoln Street, Boston, Massachusetts 02111 (617) 423-3990; *The World in Figures*.

Statistical Office of the United Nations, Publishing Service, New York, New York 10017 (800) 253-9646; *Statistical Yearbook*.

TUNISIA - FABRIC PRODUCTION - TUNISIA - TEXTILE INDUSTRY

TUNISIA - FARM CROPS - See - TUNISIA - CROPS

TUNISIA - FEMALE WORKING POPULATION - See TUNISIA - EMPLOYMENT

TUNISIA - FERTILITY RATES

Facts on File, 460 Park Avenue South, New York, New York 10016 (800) 443-8323; *The New Book of World Rankings*.

Statistical Office of the United Nations, Publishing Service, New York, New York 10017 (800) 253-9646; *Survey of Economic and Social Conditions in Africa*.

Times Books, 201 East 50th Street, New York, New York 10022 (212) 751-2600; *The Economist Book of Vital World Statistics*.

The World Bank, 1818 H Street, NW, Washington, D.C. 20433 (202) 477-1234; *World Tables*.

TUNISIA - FERTILIZER

Food and Agricultural Organization of the United Nations (FAO), Via delle Terme di Caracalla, 00100, Rome, Italy (Telephone Number in U.S. (202) 653-2400); *Fertilizer Yearbook*, and *The State of Food and Agriculture*.

Statistical Office of the United Nations, Publishing Service, New York, New York 10017 (800) 253-9646; *Statistical Yearbook*.

TUNISIA - FETAL MORTALITY

Statistical Office of the United Nations, Publishing Service, New York, New York 10017 (800) 253-9646; *Demographic Yearbook*.

World Health Organization, Office of Publications, Avenue Appia, CH-1211 Geneva 27, Switzerland (Telephone Number in U.S. (518) 436-9686); *World Health Statistics Annual*.

TUNISIA - FILM - See TUNISIA - MOTION PICTURES

TUNISIA - FINANCE

African Development Bank, 01 BP 1387, Abidjan 01, Cote D'Ivoire; *Selected Statistics on Regional Member Countries*.

Euromonitor Publications Limited, 87-88 Turnmill Street, London EC1M 5QU, England; *Middle East Economic Handbook*.

Facts on File, 460 Park Avenue South, New York, New York 10016 (800) 443-8323; *The New Book of World Rankings*.

G.K. Hall and Company, 70 Lincoln Street, Boston, Massachusetts 02111 (617) 423-3990; *The World in Figures*.

International Monetary Fund, 700 Nineteenth Street, NW, Washington, D.C. 20431 (202) 623-7000; *Government Finance Statistics Yearbook*.

United Nations Economic Commission for Africa, Africa Hall, P.O. Box 3001, Addis Ababa, Ethiopia (Telephone Number in U.S. (800) 253-9646); *African Statistical Yearbook*.

TUNISIA - FISHERIES

Facts on File, 460 Park Avenue South, New York, New York 10016 (800) 443-8323; *The New Book of World Rankings*.

Food and Agricultural Organization of the United Nations (FAO) Via delle Terme di Caracalla, 00100 Rome, Italy (Telephone Number in U.S. (202) 653-2400); *The State of Food and Agriculture*, and *Yearbook of Fishery Statistics*.

Statistical Office of the United Nations, Publishing Service, New York, New York 10017 (800) 253-9646; *Statistical Yearbook*, and *Survey of Economic and Social Conditions in Africa*.

United Nations Economic Commission for Africa, Africa Hall, P.O. Box 3001, Addis Ababa, Ethiopia (Telephone Number in U.S. (800) 253-9646); *African Statistical Yearbook*.

TUNISIA - FLOUR PRODUCTION

Statistical Office of the United Nations, Publishing Service, New York, New York 10017 (800) 253-9646; *Statistical Yearbook*.

TUNISIA - FOOD

African Development Bank, 01 BP 1387, Abidjan 01, Cote D'Ivoire; *Selected Statistics on Regional Member Countries*.

Food and Agricultural Organization of the United Nations (FAO) Via delle Terme di Caracalla, 00100 Rome, Italy (Telephone Number in U.S. (202) 653-2400); *Production Yearbook*, and *The State of Food and Agriculture*.

G.K. Hall and Company, 70 Lincoln Street, Boston, Massachusetts 02111 (617) 423-3990; *The World in Figures*.

TUNISIA - FOREIGN AID

G.K. Hall and Company, 70 Lincoln Street, Boston, Massachusetts 02111 (617) 423-3990; *The World in Figures.*

TUNISIA - FOREIGN DEBT

International Monetary Fund, 700 Nineteenth Street, NW, Washington, D.C. 20431 (202) 623-7000; *Government Finance Statistics Yearbook.*

TUNISIA - FOREIGN INDEBTEDNESS

Euromonitor Publications Limited, 87-88 Turnmill Street, London EC1M 5QU, England; *Middle East Economic Handbook.*

TUNISIA - FOREIGN TRADE

Euromonitor Publications Limited, 87-88 Turnmill Street, London EC1M 5QU, England; *International Marketing Data and Statistics.*

Facts on File, 460 Park Avenue South, New York, New York 10016 (800) 443-8323; *The New Book of World Rankings.*

Food and Agricultural Organization of the United Nations (FAO) Via delle Terme di Caracalla, 00100 Rome, Italy (Telephone Number in U.S. (202) 653-2400); *The State of Food and Agriculture.*

G.K. Hall and Company, 70 Lincoln Street, Boston, Massachusetts 02111 (617) 423-3990; *The World in Figures.*

Statistical Office of the United Nations, Publishing Service, New York, New York 10017 (800) 253-9646; *Foreign Trade Statistics for Africa, International Trade Statistics Yearbook,* and *Statistical Yearbook.*

United Nations Economic Commission for Africa, Africa Hall, P.O. Box 3001, Addis Ababa, Ethiopia (Telephone Number in U.S. (800) 253-9646); *African Statistical Yearbook.*

The World Bank, 1818 H Street, NW, Washington, D.C. 20433 (202) 477-1234; *World Tables.*

TUNISIA - FORESTRY AND FOREST PRODUCTS

Facts on File, 460 Park Avenue South, New York, New York 10016 (800) 443-8323; *The New Book of World Rankings.*

Food and Agricultural Organization of the United Nations (FAO) Via delle Terme di Caracalla, 00100 Rome, Italy (Telephone Number in U.S. (202) 653-2400); *The State of Food and Agriculture,* and *Yearbook of Forest Products.*

G.K. Hall and Company, 70 Lincoln Street, Boston, Massachusetts 02111 (617) 423-3990; *The World in Figures.*

Statistical Office of the United Nations, Publishing Service, New York, New York 10017 (800) 253-9646; *Statistical Yearbook.*

United Nations Economic Commission for Africa, Africa Hall, P.O. Box 3001, Addis Ababa, Ethiopia (Telephone Number in U.S. (800) 253-9646); *African Statistical Yearbook.*

United Nations Educational, Scientific and Cultural Organization (UNESCO), 7 Place de Fontenoy, F-75700 Paris, France (Telephone Number in U.S. (212) 963-5981); *Statistical Yearbook.*

TUNISIA - GAS AND GAS LIQUIDS (NATURAL) PRODUCTION - See TUNISIA - MINING AND MINERAL PRODUCTS

TUNISIA - GENERAL INDUSTRIAL STATISTICS

Statistical Office of the United Nations, Publishing Service, New York, New York 10017 (800) 253-9646; *Industrial Statistics Yearbook.*

TUNISIA - GENERAL MORTALITY

Statistical Office of the United Nations, Publishing Service, New York, New York 10017 (800) 253-9646; *Demographic Yearbook.*

World Health Organization, Office of Publications, Avenue Appia, CH-1211 Geneva 27, Switzerland (Telephone Number in U.S. (518) 436-9686); *World Health Statistics Annual.*

TUNISIA - GEOGRAPHIC DATA

Facts on File, 460 Park Avenue South, New York, New York 10016 (800) 443-8323; *The New Book of World Rankings.*

TUNISIA - GOATS - See TUNISIA - LIVESTOCK AND POULTRY

TUNISIA - GOLD HOLDINGS

International Monetary Fund, 700 Nineteenth Street, NW, Washington, D.C. 20431 (202) 623-7000; *International Financial Statistics.*

Statistical Office of the United Nations, Publishing Service, New York, New York 10017 (800) 253-9646; *Statistical Yearbook.*

The World Bank, 1818 H Street, NW, Washington, D.C. 20433 (202) 477-1234; *World Tables.*

TUNISIA - GOLD PRODUCTION AND CONSUMPTION - See TUNISIA - MINING AND MINERAL PRODUCTS

TUNISIA - GOVERNMENT

G.K. Hall and Company, 70 Lincoln Street, Boston, Massachusetts 02111 (617) 423-3990; *The World in Figures.*

TUNISIA - GOVERNMENT EXPENDITURES

International Monetary Fund, 700 Nineteenth Street, NW, Washington, D.C. 20431 (202) 623-7000; *Government Finance Statistics Yearbook.*

Times Books, 201 East 50th Street, New York, New York 10022 (212) 751-2600; *The Economist Book of Vital World Statistics.*

The World Bank, 1818 H Street, NW, Washington, D.C. 20433 (202) 477-1234; *World Tables.*

TUNISIA - GOVERNMENT REVENUE

International Monetary Fund, 700 Nineteenth Street, NW, Washington, D.C. 20431 (202) 623-7000; *Government Finance Statistics Yearbook.*

Statistical Office of the United Nations, Publishing Service, New York, New York 10017 (800) 253-9646; *Survey of Economic and Social Conditions in Africa.*

Times Books, 201 East 50th Street, New York, New York 10022 (212) 751-2600; *The Economist Book of Vital World Statistics.*

The World Bank, 1818 H Street, NW, Washington, D.C. 20433 (202) 477-1234; *World Tables.*

TUNISIA - GRAIN PRODUCTION - See - TUNISIA - CROPS

TUNISIA - GRANTS

International Monetary Fund, 700 Nineteenth Street, NW, Washington, D.C. 20431 (202) 623-7000; *Government Finance Statistics Yearbook.*

TUNISIA - GROSS DOMESTIC PRODUCT

African Development Bank, 01 BP 1387, Abidjan 01, Cote D'Ivoire; *Selected Statistics on Regional Member Countries.*

The Economist Intelligence Unit, 111 West 57th Street, New York, New York 10019 (800) 938-4685; *The World Market Atlas.*

Euromonitor Publications Limited, 87-88 Turnmill Street, London EC1M 5QU, England; *International Marketing Data and Statistics,* and *Middle East Economic Handbook.*

Facts on File, 460 Park Avenue South, New York, New York 10016 (800) 443-8323; *The New Book of World Rankings.*

G.K. Hall and Company, 70 Lincoln Street, Boston, Massachusetts 02111 (617) 423-3990; *The World in Figures.*

Statistical Office of the United Nations, Publishing Service, New York, New York 10017 (800) 253-9646; *Statistical Yearbook,* and *Survey of Economic and Social Conditions in Africa.*

Times Books, 201 East 50th Street, New York, New York 10022 (212) 751-2600; *The Economist Book of Vital World Statistics.*

United Nations Economic Commission for Africa, Africa Hall, P.O. Box 3001, Addis Ababa, Ethiopia (Telephone Number in U.S. (800) 253-9646); *African Statistical Yearbook.*

The World Bank, 1818 H Street, NW, Washington, D.C. 20433 (202) 477-1234; *World Tables.*

TUNISIA - GROSS NATIONAL PRODUCT

Euromonitor Publications Limited, 87-88 Turnmill Street, London EC1M 5QU, England; *International Marketing Data and Statistics.*

U.S. Arms Control and Disarmament Agency, 320 Twenty-first Street, NW, Washington, D.C. 20451 (202) 647-8677; *World Military Expenditures and Arms Transfers.*

The World Bank, 1818 H Street, NW, Washington, D.C. 20433 (202) 477-1234; *World Tables.*

TUNISIA - HEALTH

African Development Bank, 01 BP 1387, Abidjan 01, Cote D'Ivoire; *Selected Statistics on Regional Member Countries.*

Euromonitor Publications Limited, 87-88 Turnmill Street, London EC1M 5QU, England; *Middle East Economic Handbook.*

Facts on File, 460 Park Avenue South, New York, New York 10016 (800) 443-8323; *The New Book of World Rankings.*

G.K. Hall and Company, 70 Lincoln Street, Boston, Massachusetts 02111 (617) 423-3990; *The World in Figures.*

Statistical Office of the United Nations, Publishing Service, New York, New York 10017 (800) 253-9646; *Statistical Yearbook.*

Times Books, 201 East 50th Street, New York, New York 10022 (212) 751-2600; *The Economist Book of Vital World Statistics.*

United Nations Economic Commission for Africa, Africa Hall, P.O. Box 3001, Addis Ababa, Ethiopia (Telephone Number in U.S. (800) 253-9646); *African Statistical Yearbook.*

World Health Organization, Office of Publications, Avenue Appia, CH-1211 Geneva 27, Switzerland (Telephone Number in U.S. (518) 436-9686); *World Health Statistics Annual.*

TUNISIA - HEALTH EXPENDITURES

International Monetary Fund, 700 Nineteenth Street, NW, Washington, D.C. 20431 (202) 623-7000; *Government Finance Statistics Yearbook.*

TUNISIA - HIGHWAYS

G.K. Hall and Company, 70 Lincoln Street, Boston, Massachusetts 02111 (617) 423-3990; *The World in Figures.*

International Road Federation, 525 School Street, SW, Washington, D.C. 20024 (202) 554-2106; *World Road Statistics.*

Statistical Office of the United Nations, Publishing Service, New York, New York 10017 (800) 253-9646; *Survey of Economic and Social Conditions in Africa.*

United Nations Economic Commission for Africa, Africa Hall, P.O. Box 3001, Addis Ababa, Ethiopia (Telephone Number in U.S. (800) 253-9646); *African Statistical Yearbook.*

TUNISIA - HORSES - See TUNISIA - LIVESTOCK AND POULTRY

TUNISIA - HOURS OF WORK - See TUNISIA - EMPLOYMENT

TUNISIA - HOUSING

Facts on File, 460 Park Avenue South, New York, New York 10016 (800) 443-8323; *The New Book of World Rankings.*

TUNISIA - HOUSING EXPENDITURES

International Monetary Fund, 700 Nineteenth Street, NW, Washington, D.C. 20431 (202) 623-7000; *Government Finance Statistics Yearbook.*

TUNISIA - ILLITERATE POPULATION

The Economist Intelligence Unit, 111 West 57th Street, New York, New York 10019 (800) 938-4685; *The World Market Atlas.*

G.K. Hall and Company, 70 Lincoln Street, Boston, Massachusetts 02111 (617) 423-3990; *The World in Figures.*

United Nations Educational, Scientific and Cultural Organization (UNESCO), 7 Place de Fontenoy, F-75700 Paris, France (Telephone Number in U.S. (212) 963-5981); *Statistical Yearbook.*

TUNISIA - IMPORTS

African Development Bank, 01 BP 1387, Abidjan 01, Cote D'Ivoire; *Selected Statistics on Regional Member Countries.*

American Automobile Manufacturers Association, 1401 H Street, NW, Suite 900, Washington, D.C. 20005 (202) 326-5500; *World Motor Vehicle Data.*

The Economist Intelligence Unit, 111 West 57th Street, New York, New York 10019 (800) 938-4685; *The World Market Atlas.*

Euromonitor Publications Limited, 87-88 Turnmill Street, London EC1M 5QU, England; *International Marketing Data and Statistics,* and *Middle East Economic Handbook.*

Food and Agricultural Organization of the United Nations (FAO) Via delle Terme di Caracalla, 00100 Rome, Italy (Telephone Number in U.S. (202) 653-2400); *The State of Food and Agriculture.*

G.K. Hall and Company, 70 Lincoln Street, Boston, Massachusetts 02111 (617) 423-3990; *The World in Figures.*

International Lead and Zinc Study Group, Metro House, 58 St. James's Street, London SW1A 1LD, England; *Lead and Zinc Statistics.*

International Monetary Fund, 700 Nineteenth Street, NW, Washington, D.C. 20431 (202) 623-7000; *Direction of Trade Statistics, Government Finance Statistics Yearbook,* and *International Financial Statistics.*

Statistical Office of the United Nations, Publishing Service, New York, New York 10017 (800) 253-9646; *Foreign Trade Statistics for Africa, Survey of Economic and Social Conditions in Africa,* and *Trade in Manufactures of Developing Countries.*

Times Books, 201 East 50th Street, New York, New York 10022 (212) 751-2600; *The Economist Book of Vital World Statistics.*

United Nations Economic Commission for Africa, Africa Hall, P.O. Box 3001, Addis Ababa, Ethiopia (Telephone Number in U.S. (800) 253-9040), *African Statistical Yearbook.*

The World Bank, 1818 H Street, NW, Washington, D.C. 20433 (202) 477-1234; *World Tables.*

TUNISIA - INCOME TAXES - See TUNISIA - TAXATION

TUNISIA - INDUSTRIAL METALS PRODUCTION - See TUNISIA - MINING AND MINERAL PRODUCTS

TUNISIA - INDUSTRY

Euromonitor Publications Limited, 87-88 Turnmill Street, London EC1M 5QU, England; *International Marketing Data and Statistics.*

Facts on File, 460 Park Avenue South, New York, New York 10016 (800) 443-8323; *The New Book of World Rankings.*

G.K. Hall and Company, 70 Lincoln Street, Boston, Massachusetts 02111 (617) 423-3990; *The World in Figures.*

International Labour Office, I.L.O. Publications, CH-1211, Geneva 22, Switzerland; *Yearbook of Labour Statistics.*

Statistical Office of the United Nations, Publishing Service, New York, New York 10017 (800) 253-9646; *Statistical Yearbook,* and *Survey of Economic and Social Conditions in Africa.*

Times Books, 201 East 50th Street, New York, New York 10022 (212) 751-2600; *The Economist Book of Vital World Statistics.*

United Nations Economic Commission for Africa, Africa Hall, P.O. Box 3001, Addis Ababa, Ethiopia (Telephone Number in U.S. (800) 253-9646); *African Statistical Yearbook.*

The World Bank, 1818 H Street, NW, Washington, D.C. 20433 (202) 477-1234; *World Tables.*

World Intellectual Property Organization, 34 Chemin des Colombettes, CH-1211 Geneva 20. Switzerland; *Industrial Property Statistics.*

TUNISIA - INFANT AND MATERNAL MORTALITY

Statistical Office of the United Nations, Publishing Service, New York, New York 10017 (800) 253-9646; *Demographic Yearbook, Statistical Yearbook,* and *Survey of Economic and Social Conditions in Africa.*

Times Books, 201 East 50th Street, New York, New York 10022 (212) 751-2600; *The Economist Book of Vital World Statistics.*

The World Bank, 1818 H Street, NW, Washington, D.C. 20433 (202) 477-1234; *World Tables.*

World Health Organization, Office of Publications, Avenue Appia, CH-1211 Geneva 27, Switzerland (Telephone Number in U.S. (518) 436-9686); *World Health Statistics Annual.*

TUNISIA - INTERNATIONAL LIQUIDITY

International Monetary Fund, 700 Nineteenth Street, NW, Washington, D.C. 20431 (202) 623-7000; *International Financial Statistics.*

TUNISIA - INTERNATIONAL RESERVES EXCLUDING GOLD

African Development Bank, 01 BP 1387, Abidjan 01, Cote D'Ivoire, *Selected Statistics on Regional Member Countries.*

Statistical Office of the United Nations, Publishing Service, New York, New York 10017 (800) 253-9646; *Statistical Yearbook.*

The World Bank, 1818 H Street, NW, Washington, D.C. 20433 (202) 477-1234; *World Tables.*

TUNISIA - IRON ORE PRODUCTION AND CONSUMPTION - See TUNISIA - MINING AND MINERAL PRODUCTS

TUNISIA - IRRIGATION

Euromonitor Publications Limited, 87-88 Turnmill Street, London EC1M 5QU, England; *International Marketing Data and Statistics.*

TUNISIA - LABOR FORCE

African Development Bank, 01 BP 1387, Abidjan 01, Cote D'Ivoire; *Selected Statistics on Regional Member Countries.*

Euromonitor Publications Limited, 87-88 Turnmill Street, London EC1M 5QU, England; *International Marketing Data and Statistics,* and *Middle East Economic Handbook.*

Facts on File, 460 Park Avenue South, New York, New York 10016 (800) 443-8323; *The New Book of World Rankings.*

Food and Agricultural Organization of the United Nations (FAO) Via delle Terme di Caracalla, 00100 Rome, Italy (Telephone Number in U.S. (202) 653-2400); *The State of Food and Agriculture.*

G.K. Hall and Company, 70 Lincoln Street, Boston, Massachusetts 02111 (617) 423-3990; *The World in Figures.*

Times Books, 201 East 50th Street, New York, New York 10022 (212) 751-2600; *The Economist Book of Vital World Statistics*.

The World Bank, 1818 H Street, NW, Washington, D.C. 20433 (202) 477-1234; *World Tables*.

TUNISIA - LABOR PRODUCTIVITY

International Labour Office, I.L.O. Publications, CH-1211, Geneva 22, Switzerland; *Yearbook of Labour Statistics*.

TUNISIA - LAND USE

Euromonitor Publications Limited, 87-88 Turnmill Street, London EC1M 5QU, England; *International Marketing Data and Statistics*.

Food and Agricultural Organization of the United Nations (FAO), Via delle Terme di Caracalla, 00100 Rome, Italy (Telephone Number in U.S. (202) 653-2400); *Production Yearbook*.

G.K. Hall and Company, 70 Lincoln Street, Boston, Massachusetts 02111 (617) 423-3990; *The World in Figures*.

TUNISIA - LEAD AND LEAD ORE - See TUNISIA - MINING AND MINERAL PRODUCTS

TUNISIA - LIBRARIES

Facts on File, 460 Park Avenue South, New York, New York 10016 (800) 443-8323; *The New Book of World Rankings*.

United Nations Educational, Scientific and Cultural Organization (UNESCO), 7 Place de Fontenoy, F-75700 Paris, France (Telephone Number in U.S. (212) 963-5981); *Statistical Yearbook*.

TUNISIA - LIFE EXPECTANCY

African Development Bank, 01 BP 1387, Abidjan 01, Cote D'Ivoire; *Selected Statistics on Regional Member Countries*.

TUNISIA - LITERACY RATE

Statistical Office of the United Nations, Publishing Service, New York, New York 10017 (800) 253-9646; *Survey of Economic and Social Conditions in Africa*.

TUNISIA - LIVESTOCK AND POULTRY

Euromonitor Publications Limited, 87-88 Turnmill Street, London EC1M 5QU, England; *International Marketing Data and Statistics*.

Facts on File, 460 Park Avenue South, New York, New York 10016 (800) 443-8323; *The New Book of World Rankings*.

Food and Agricultural Organization of the United Nations (FAO), Via delle Terme di Caracalla, 00100 Rome, Italy (Telephone Number in U.S. (202) 653-2400); *Production Yearbook*, and *The State of Food and Agriculture*.

G.K. Hall and Company, 70 Lincoln Street, Boston, Massachusetts 02111 (617) 423-3990; *The World in Figures*.

Statistical Office of the United Nations, Publishing Service, New York, New York 10017 (800) 253-9646; *Statistical Yearbook*, and *Survey of Economic and Social Conditions in Africa*.

United Nations Economic Commission for Africa, Africa Hall, P.O. Box 3001, Addis Ababa, Ethiopia (Telephone Number in U.S. (800) 253-9646); *African Statistical Yearbook*.

TUNISIA - LIVING LEVELS

G.K. Hall and Company, 70 Lincoln Street, Boston, Massachusetts 02111 (617) 423-3990; *The World in Figures*.

Times Books, 201 East 50th Street, New York, New York 10022 (212) 751-2600; *The Economist Book of Vital World Statistics*.

TUNISIA - MAIL - NUMBER OF PIECES SENT OR RECEIVED

Statistical Office of the United Nations, Publishing Service, New York, New York 10017 (800) 253-9646; *Statistical Yearbook*.

TUNISIA - MANUFACTURING

American Automobile Manufacturers Association, 1401 H Street, NW, Suite 900, Washington, D.C. 20005 (202) 326-5500; *World Motor Vehicle Data*.

Facts on File, 460 Park Avenue South, New York, New York 10016 (800) 443-8323; *The New Book of World Rankings*.

G.K. Hall and Company, 70 Lincoln Street, Boston, Massachusetts 02111 (617) 423-3990; *The World in Figures*.

Statistical Office of the United Nations, Publishing Service, New York, New York 10017 (800) 253-9646; *Statistical Yearbook*, and *Survey of Economic and Social Conditions in Africa*.

Times Books, 201 East 50th Street, New York, New York 10022 (212) 751-2600; *The Economist Book of Vital World Statistics*.

United Nations Economic Commission for Africa, Africa Hall, P.O. Box 3001, Addis Ababa, Ethiopia (Telephone Number in U.S. (800) 253-9646); *African Statistical Yearbook*.

The World Bank, 1818 H Street, NW, Washington, D.C. 20433 (202) 477-1234; *World Tables*.

TUNISIA - MARRIAGE RATES

Facts on File, 460 Park Avenue South, New York, New York 10016 (800) 443-8323; *The New Book of World Rankings*.

Statistical Office of the United Nations, Publishing Service, New York, New York 10017 (800) 253-9646; *Demographic Yearbook*, and *Statistical Yearbook*.

TUNISIA - MEAT PRODUCTION - See TUNISIA - LIVESTOCK AND POULTRY

TUNISIA - MERCHANT SHIPPING

G.K. Hall and Company, 70 Lincoln Street, Boston, Massachusetts 02111 (617) 423-3990; *The World in Figures*.

Statistical Office of the United Nations, Publishing Service, New York, New York 10017 (800) 253-9646; *Statistical Yearbook*.

Times Books, 201 East 50th Street, New York, New York 10022 (212) 751-2600; *The Economist Book of Vital World Statistics*.

United Nations Economic Commission for Africa, Africa Hall, P.O. Box 3001, Addis Ababa, Ethiopia (Telephone Number in U.S. (800) 253-9646); *African Statistical Yearbook*.

U.S. Department of Transportation, Maritime Administration, 400 Seventh Street, SW, Washington, D.C. 20590 (202) 366-5807; *A Statistical Analysis of the World's Merchant Fleets*.

TUNISIA - MERCURY PRODUCTION - See TUNISIA - MINING AND MINERAL PRODUCTS

TUNISIA - MILITARY

G.K. Hall and Company, 70 Lincoln Street, Boston, Massachusetts 02111 (617) 423-3990; *The World in Figures.*

The International Institute for Strategic Studies, 23 Tavistock Street, London WC2E 7NQ, England; *The Military Balance.*

U.S. Arms Control and Disarmament Agency, 320 Twenty-first Street, NW, Washington, D.C. 20451 (202) 647-8677; *World Military Expenditures and Arms Transfers.*

TUNISIA - MILK PRODUCTION - See TUNISIA - DAIRY PRODUCTS

TUNISIA - MINING AND MINERAL PRODUCTS

Facts on File, 460 Park Avenue South, New York, New York 10016 (800) 443-8323; *The New Book of World Rankings.*

G.K. Hall and Company, 70 Lincoln Street, Boston, Massachusetts 02111 (617) 423-3990; *The World in Figures.*

International Lead and Zinc Study Group, Metro House, 58 St. James's Street, London SW1A 1LD, England; *Lead and Zinc Statistics.*

International Monetary Fund, 700 Nineteenth Street, NW, Washington, D.C. 20431 (202) 623-7000; *International Financial Statistics.*

Penn Well Publishing Company, 1421 South Sheridan Road, P.O. Box 1260, Tulsa, Oklahoma 74101 (800) 752-9764; *International Energy Statistics Sourcebook.*

Statistical Office of the United Nations, Publishing Service, New York, New York 10017 (800) 253-9646; *Statistical Yearbook.*

United Nations Economic Commission for Africa, Africa Hall, P.O. Box 3001, Addis Ababa, Ethiopia (Telephone Number in U.S. (800) 253-9646); *African Statistical Yearbook.*

TUNISIA - MONEY EXCHANGE RATE

Euromonitor Publications Limited, 87-88 Turnmill Street, London EC1M 5QU, England; *International Marketing Data and Statistics.*

International Monetary Fund, 700 Nineteenth Street, NW, Washington, D.C. 20431 (202) 623-7000; *International Financial Statistics.*

Statistical Office of the United Nations, Publishing Service, New York, New York 10017 (800) 253-9646; *Statistical Yearbook.*

TUNISIA - MONEY RESERVES

Euromonitor Publications Limited, 87-88 Turnmill Street, London EC1M 5QU, England; *International Marketing Data and Statistics.*

TUNISIA - MONEY SUPPLY

African Development Bank, 01 BP 1387, Abidjan 01, Cote D'Ivoire; *Selected Statistics on Regional Member Countries.*

Euromonitor Publications Limited, 87-88 Turnmill Street, London EC1M 5QU, England; *International Marketing Data and Statistics.*

G.K. Hall and Company, 70 Lincoln Street, Boston, Massachusetts 02111 (617) 423-3990; *The World in Figures.*

International Monetary Fund, 700 Nineteenth Street, NW, Washington, D.C. 20431 (202) 623-7000; *International Financial Statistics.*

Statistical Office of the United Nations, Publishing Service, New York, New York 10017 (800) 253-9646; *Statistical Yearbook.*

The World Bank, 1818 H Street, NW, Washington, D.C. 20433 (202) 477-1234; *World Tables.*

TUNISIA - MOTION PICTURES

Statistical Office of the United Nations, Publishing Service, New York, New York 10017 (800) 253-9646; *Statistical Yearbook.*

United Nations Educational, Scientific and Cultural Organization (UNESCO), 7 Place de Fontenoy, F-75700 Paris, France (Telephone Number in U.S. (212) 963-5981); *Statistical Yearbook.*

TUNISIA - MOTOR VEHICLE ASSEMBLY

Statistical Office of the United Nations, Publishing Service, New York, New York 10017 (800) 253-9646; *Statistical Yearbook.*

TUNISIA - MOTOR VEHICLE PRODUCTION

American Automobile Manufacturers Association, 1401 H Street, NW, Suite 900, Washington, D.C. 20005 (202) 326-5500; *World Motor Vehicle Data.*

TUNISIA - MOTOR VEHICLE TAXES - See TUNISIA - TAXATION

TUNISIA - MOTOR VEHICLES IN USE

American Automobile Manufacturers Association, 1401 H Street, NW, Suite 900, Washington, D.C. 20005 (202) 326-5500; *World Motor Vehicle Data.*

G.K. Hall and Company, 70 Lincoln Street, Boston, Massachusetts 02111 (617) 423-3990; *The World in Figures.*

International Road Federation, 525 School Street, SW, Washington, D.C. 20024 (202) 554-2106; *World Road Statistics.*

Statistical Office of the United Nations, Publishing Service, New York, New York 10017 (800) 253-9646; *Statistical Yearbook,* and *Survey of Economic and Social Conditions in Africa.*

Times Books, 201 East 50th Street, New York, New York 10022 (212) 751-2600; *The Economist Book of Vital World Statistics.*

TUNISIA - MULES - See TUNISIA - LIVESTOCK AND POULTRY

TUNISIA - MUSEUMS

Facts on File, 460 Park Avenue South, New York, New York 10016 (800) 443-8323; *The New Book of World Rankings.*

United Nations Educational, Scientific and Cultural Organization (UNESCO), 7 Place de Fontenoy, F-75700 Paris, France (Telephone Number in U.S. (212) 963-5981); *Statistical Yearbook.*

TUNISIA - NATALITY - See TUNISIA - BIRTH RATE

TUNISIA - NATIONAL ACCOUNTS

African Development Bank, 01 BP 1387, Abidjan 01, Cote D'Ivoire; *Selected Statistics on Regional Member Countries.*

Statistical Office of the United Nations, Publishing Service, New York, New York 10017 (800) 253-9646; *National Accounts Statistics,* and *Statistical Yearbook.*

United Nations Economic Commission for Africa, Africa Hall, P.O. Box 3001, Addis Ababa, Ethiopia (Telephone Number in U.S. (800) 253-9646); *African Statistical Yearbook.*

TUNISIA - NATIONAL INCOME

Facts on File, 460 Park Avenue South, New York, New York 10016 (800) 443-8323; *The New Book of World Rankings.*

G.K. Hall and Company, 70 Lincoln Street, Boston, Massachusetts 02111 (617) 423-3990; *The World in Figures.*

Statistical Office of the United Nations, Publishing Service, New York, New York 10017 (800) 253-9646; *Statistical Yearbook.*

TUNISIA - NATIONAL PRODUCT

Facts on File, 460 Park Avenue South, New York, New York 10016 (800) 443-8323; *The New Book of World Rankings.*

Statistical Office of the United Nations, Publishing Service, New York, New York 10017 (800) 253-9646; *Statistical Yearbook.*

TUNISIA - NATURAL GAS PRODUCTION - See TUNISIA - MINING AND MINERAL PRODUCTS

TUNISIA - NEWSPAPER PRODUCTION - See TUNISIA - FORESTRY AND FOREST PRODUCTS

TUNISIA - NEWSPRINT - See TUNISIA - FORESTRY AND FOREST PRODUCTS

TUNISIA - OATS PRODUCTION - See - TUNISIA - CROPS

TUNISIA - OCCUPATIONS - See TUNISIA - LABOR FORCE

TUNISIA - OLIVE OIL EXPORTS

International Monetary Fund, 700 Nineteenth Street, NW, Washington, D.C. 20431 (202) 623-7000; *International Financial Statistics.*

TUNISIA - PAPER - See TUNISIA - FORESTRY AND FOREST PRODUCTS

TUNISIA - PATENTS

Statistical Office of the United Nations, Publishing Service, New York, New York 10017 (800) 253-9646; *Statistical Yearbook.*

World Intellectual Property Organization, 34 Chemin des Colombettes, CH-1211 Geneva 20. Switzerland; *Industrial Property Statistics.*

TUNISIA - PEANUT PRODUCTION - See - TUNISIA - CROPS

TUNISIA - PERIODICALS

United Nations Educational, Scientific and Cultural Organization (UNESCO), 7 Place de Fontenoy, F-75700 Paris, France (Telephone Number in U.S. (212) 963-5981); *Statistical Yearbook.*

TUNISIA - PESTICIDE USE

Food and Agricultural Organization of the United Nations (FAO) Via delle Terme di Caracalla, 00100 Rome, Italy (Telephone Number in U.S. (202) 653-2400); *The State of Food and Agriculture.*

TUNISIA - PETROLEUM INDUSTRY

Euromonitor Publications Limited, 87-88 Turnmill Street, London EC1M 5QU, England; *Middle East Economic Handbook.*

Facts on File, 460 Park Avenue South, New York, New York 10016 (800) 443-8323; *The New Book of World Rankings.*

Food and Agricultural Organization of the United Nations (FAO) Via delle Terme di Caracalla, 00100 Rome, Italy (Telephone Number in U.S. (202) 653-2400); *The State of Food and Agriculture.*

G.K. Hall and Company, 70 Lincoln Street, Boston, Massachusetts 02111 (617) 423-3990; *The World in Figures.*

Penn Well Publishing Company, 1421 South Sheridan Road, P.O. Box 1260, Tulsa, Oklahoma 74101 (800) 752-9764; *International Energy Statistics Sourcebook.*

Statistical Office of the United Nations, Publishing Service, New York, New York 10017 (800) 253-9646; *Statistical Yearbook.*

TUNISIA - PHOSPHATE ROCK PRODUCTION - See TUNISIA - MINING AND MINERAL PRODUCTS

TUNISIA - PHOSPHATES EXPORTS - See TUNISIA - MINING AND MINERAL PRODUCTS

TUNISIA - PIG-IRON AND FERRO-ALLOY PRODUCTION - See TUNISIA - MINING AND MINERAL PRODUCTS

TUNISIA - PIGS - See TUNISIA - LIVESTOCK AND POULTRY

TUNISIA - POPULATION

African Development Bank, 01 BP 1387, Abidjan 01, Cote D'Ivoire; *Selected Statistics on Regional Member Countries.*

The Economist Intelligence Unit, 111 West 57th Street, New York, New York 10019 (800) 938-4685; *The World Market Atlas.*

Euromonitor Publications Limited, 87-88 Turnmill Street, London EC1M 5QU, England; *International Marketing Data and Statistics,* and *Middle East Economic Handbook.*

Facts on File, 460 Park Avenue South, New York, New York 10016 (800) 443-8323; *The New Book of World Rankings.*

Food and Agricultural Organization of the United Nations (FAO), Via delle Terme di Caracalla, 00100 Rome, Italy (Telephone Number in U.S. (202) 653-2400); *Production Yearbook.*

G.K. Hall and Company, 70 Lincoln Street, Boston, Massachusetts 02111 (617) 423-3990; *The World in Figures.*

International Labour Office, I.L.O. Publications, CH-1211, Geneva 22, Switzerland; *Yearbook of Labour Statistics.*

Statistical Office of the United Nations, Publishing Service, New York, New York 10017 (800) 253-9646; *Demographic Yearbook, Statistical Yearbook,* and *Survey of Economic and Social Conditions in Africa.*

Times Books, 201 East 50th Street, New York, New York 10022 (212) 751-2600; *The Economist Book of Vital World Statistics.*

United Nations Educational, Scientific and Cultural Organization (UNESCO), 7 Place de Fontenoy, F-75700 Paris, France (Telephone Number in U.S. (212) 963-5981); *Statistical Yearbook.*

U.S. Arms Control and Disarmament Agency, 320 Twenty-first Street, NW, Washington, D.C. 20451 (202) 647-8677; *World Military Expenditures and Arms Transfers.*

World Health Organization, Office of Publications, Avenue Appia, CH-1211 Geneva 27, Switzerland (Telephone Number in U.S. (518) 436-9686); *World Health Statistics Annual.*

TUNISIA - POST OFFICES

Facts on File, 460 Park Avenue South, New York, New York 10016 (800) 443-8323; *The New Book of World Rankings.*

TUNISIA - POTATO PRODUCTION - See - TUNISIA - CROPS

TUNISIA - POWER PRODUCTION INDUSTRY

Statistical Office of the United Nations, Publishing Service, New York, New York 10017 (800) 253-9646; *Statistical Yearbook.*

TUNISIA - PRICES

Facts on File, 460 Park Avenue South, New York, New York 10016 (800) 443-8323; *The New Book of World Rankings.*

Food and Agricultural Organization of the United Nations (FAO), Via delle Terme di Caracalla, 00100 Rome, Italy (Telephone Number in U.S. (202) 653-2400); *Production Yearbook,* and *The State of Food and Agriculture.*

G.K. Hall and Company, 70 Lincoln Street, Boston, Massachusetts 02111 (617) 423-3990; *The World in Figures.*

International Labour Office, I.L.O. Publications, CH-1211, Geneva 22, Switzerland; *Yearbook of Labour Statistics.*

International Lead and Zinc Study Group, Metro House, 58 St. James's Street, London SW1A 1LD, England; *Lead and Zinc Statistics.*

International Monetary Fund, 700 Nineteenth Street, NW, Washington, D.C. 20431 (202) 623-7000; *International Financial Statistics.*

United Nations Economic Commission for Africa, Africa Hall, P.O. Box 3001, Addis Ababa, Ethiopia (Telephone Number in U.S. (800) 253-9646); *African Statistical Yearbook.*

TUNISIA - PRINTING AND WRITING PAPER - See TUNISIA - FORESTRY AND FOREST PRODUCTS

TUNISIA - PRODUCTION

American Automobile Manufacturers Association, 1401 H Street, NW, Suite 900, Washington, D.C. 20005 (202) 326-5500; *World Motor Vehicle Data.*

Facts on File, 460 Park Avenue South, New York, New York 10016 (800) 443-8323; *The New Book of World Rankings.*

G.K. Hall and Company, 70 Lincoln Street, Boston, Massachusetts 02111 (617) 423-3990; *The World in Figures.*

International Lead and Zinc Study Group, Metro House, 58 St. James's Street, London SW1A 1LD, England; *Lead and Zinc Statistics.*

TUNISIA - PRODUCTIVITY

Euromonitor Publications Limited, 87-88 Turnmill Street, London EC1M 5QU, England; *International Marketing Data and Statistics.*

TUNISIA - PROPERTY TAXES - See TUNISIA - TAXATION

TUNISIA - PUBLIC FINANCE

Facts on File, 460 Park Avenue South, New York, New York 10016 (800) 443-8323; *The New Book of World Rankings.*

TUNISIA - RADIO BROADCASTING - See TUNISIA - BROADCASTING

TUNISIA - RADIO RECEIVER PRODUCTION

Statistical Office of the United Nations, Publishing Service, New York, New York 10017 (800) 253-9646; *Statistical Yearbook.*

TUNISIA - RAILWAYS

G.K. Hall and Company, 70 Lincoln Street, Boston, Massachusetts 02111 (617) 423-3990; *The World in Figures.*

Jane's Information Group, Sentinel House, 163 Brighton Road, Coulsdon, Surrey CR5 2NH, England (Telephone Number in U.S. (703) 683-3700); *Jane's World Railways.*

Statistical Office of the United Nations, Publishing Service, New York, New York 10017 (800) 253-9646; *Statistical Yearbook,* and *Survey of Economic and Social Conditions in Africa.*

United Nations Economic Commission for Africa, Africa Hall, P.O. Box 3001, Addis Ababa, Ethiopia (Telephone Number in U.S. (800) 253-9646); *African Statistical Yearbook.*

TUNISIA - RELIGION

Facts on File, 460 Park Avenue South, New York, New York 10016 (800) 443-8323; *The New Book of World Rankings.*

TUNISIA - RENT PRICES

International Labour Office, I.L.O. Publications, CH-1211, Geneva 22, Switzerland; *Yearbook of Labour Statistics.*

TUNISIA - RETAIL TRADE

G.K. Hall and Company, 70 Lincoln Street, Boston, Massachusetts 02111 (617) 423-3990; *The World in Figures.*

TUNISIA - RICE PRODUCTION - See - TUNISIA - CROPS

TUNISIA - ROUNDWOOD PRODUCTION - See TUNISIA - FORESTRY AND FOREST PRODUCTS

TUNISIA - RUBBER PRODUCTION AND CONSUMPTION

Facts on File, 460 Park Avenue South, New York, New York 10016 (800) 443-8323; *The New Book of World Rankings.*

TUNISIA - SALT PRODUCTION - See TUNISIA - MINING AND MINERAL PRODUCTS

TUNISIA - SAWNWOOD PRODUCTION - See TUNISIA - FORESTRY AND FOREST PRODUCTS

TUNISIA - SCIENTISTS AND ENGINEERS

Statistical Office of the United Nations, Publishing Service, New York, New York 10017 (800) 253-9646; *Statistical Yearbook.*

United Nations Educational, Scientific and Cultural Organization (UNESCO), 7 Place de Fontenoy, F-75700 Paris, France (Telephone Number in U.S. (212) 963-5981); *Statistical Yearbook.*

TUNISIA - SENIOR CITIZENS

Facts on File, 460 Park Avenue South, New York, New York 10016 (800) 443-8323; *The New Book of World Rankings.*

TUNISIA - SHEEP - See TUNISIA - LIVESTOCK AND POULTRY

TUNISIA - SILVER PRODUCTION AND CONSUMPTION - See TUNISIA - MINING AND MINERAL PRODUCTS

TUNISIA - SOCIAL DATA

African Development Bank, 01 BP 1387, Abidjan 01, Cote D'Ivoire; *Selected Statistics on Regional Member Countries.*

Facts on File, 460 Park Avenue South, New York, New York 10016 (800) 443-8323; *The New Book of World Rankings.*

G.K. Hall and Company, 70 Lincoln Street, Boston, Massachusetts 02111 (617) 423-3990; *The World in Figures.*

TUNISIA - SOCIAL SECURITY

International Monetary Fund, 700 Nineteenth Street, NW, Washington, D.C. 20431 (202) 623-7000; *Government Finance Statistics Yearbook.*

TUNISIA - STAMP TAXES AND DUTIES - See TUNISIA - TAXATION

TUNISIA - STATE BUDGET REVENUE AND EXPENDITURES

Euromonitor Publications Limited, 87-88 Turnmill Street, London EC1M 5QU, England; *International Marketing Data and Statistics.*

TUNISIA - STEEL - See TUNISIA - MINING AND MINERAL PRODUCTS

TUNISIA - STOCKS - COMMODITY - MARKET PRICE - INDEX

Food and Agricultural Organization of the United Nations (FAO) Via delle Terme di Caracalla, 00100 Rome, Italy (Telephone Number in U.S. (202) 653-2400); *The State of Food and Agriculture.*

International Lead and Zinc Study Group, Metro House, 58 St. James's Street, London SW1A 1LD, England; *Lead and Zinc Statistics.*

TUNISIA - SUGAR PRODUCTION AND CONSUMPTION - See - TUNISIA - CROPS

TUNISIA - SULPHURIC ACID PRODUCTION - See TUNISIA - MINING AND MINERAL PRODUCTS

TUNISIA - TAXATION

G.K. Hall and Company, 70 Lincoln Street, Boston, Massachusetts 02111 (617) 423-3990; *The World in Figures.*

International Monetary Fund, 700 Nineteenth Street, NW, Washington, D.C. 20431 (202) 623-7000; *Government Finance Statistics Yearbook.*

International Road Federation, 525 School Street, SW, Washington, D.C. 20024 (202) 554-2106; *World Road Statistics.*

The World Bank, 1818 H Street, NW, Washington, D.C. 20433 (202) 477-1234; *World Tables.*

TUNISIA - TEA - See - TUNISIA - CROPS

TUNISIA - TELEGRAPH SERVICE

Statistical Office of the United Nations, Publishing Service, New York, New York 10017 (800) 253-9646; *Statistical Yearbook.*

TUNISIA - TELEPHONES IN USE

American Telephone and Telegraph Company, 26 Parsippany Road, Whippany, New Jersey 07981 (800) 338-4038; *The World's Telephones.*

Euromonitor Publications Limited, 87-88 Turnmill Street, London EC1M 5QU, England; *Middle East Economic Handbook.*

G.K. Hall and Company, 70 Lincoln Street, Boston, Massachusetts 02111 (617) 423-3990; *The World in Figures.*

Statistical Office of the United Nations, Publishing Service, New York, New York 10017 (800) 253-9646; *Statistical Yearbook.*

TUNISIA - TELEVISION BROADCASTING - See TUNISIA - BROADCASTING

TUNISIA - TELEVISION RECEIVER PRODUCTION

Statistical Office of the United Nations, Publishing Service, New York, New York 10017 (800) 253-9646; *Statistical Yearbook.*

TUNISIA - TEXTILE INDUSTRY

G.K. Hall and Company, 70 Lincoln Street, Boston, Massachusetts 02111 (617) 423-3990; *The World in Figures.*

Statistical Office of the United Nations, Publishing Service, New York, New York 10017 (800) 253-9646; *Statistical Yearbook,* and *Trade in Manufactures of Developing Countries.*

TUNISIA - THEATRE

United Nations Educational, Scientific and Cultural Organization (UNESCO), 7 Place de Fontenoy, F-75700 Paris, France (Telephone Number in U.S. (212) 963-5981); *Statistical Yearbook.*

TUNISIA - TIRE (MOTOR VEHICLE) PRODUCTION

Statistical Office of the United Nations, Publishing Service, New York, New York 10017 (800) 253-9646; *Statistical Yearbook.*

TUNISIA - TOBACCO PRODUCTION

Facts on File, 460 Park Avenue South, New York, New York 10016 (800) 443-8323; *The New Book of World Rankings.*

Statistical Office of the United Nations, Publishing Service, New York, New York 10017 (800) 253-9646; *Statistical Yearbook.*

TUNISIA - TOURISM

Euromonitor Publications Limited, 87-88 Turnmill Street, London EC1M 5QU, England; *Middle East Economic Handbook.*

Facts on File, 460 Park Avenue South, New York, New York 10016 (800) 443-8323; *The New Book of World Rankings.*

G.K. Hall and Company, 70 Lincoln Street, Boston, Massachusetts 02111 (617) 423-3990; *The World in Figures.*

Statistical Office of the United Nations, Publishing Service, New York, New York 10017 (800) 253-9646; *Statistical Yearbook,* section on Transport - International tourist travel.

Times Books, 201 East 50th Street, New York, New York 10022 (212) 751-2600; *The Economist Book of Vital World Statistics.*

United Nations Economic Commission for Africa, Africa Hall, P.O. Box 3001, Addis Ababa, Ethiopia (Telephone Number in U.S. (800) 253-9646); *African Statistical Yearbook.*

World Tourism Organization, Calle Capitan Haya 42, E-28020 Madrid, Spain; *Yearbook of Tourism Statistics.*

TUNISIA - TRACTORS IN USE

Statistical Office of the United Nations, Publishing Service, New York, New York 10017 (800) 253-9646; *Statistical Yearbook.*

TUNISIA - TRADE - See TUNISIA - FOREIGN TRADE

TUNISIA - TRADEMARKS AND SERVICE MARKS

Statistical Office of the United Nations, Publishing Service, New York, New York 10017 (800) 253-9646; *Statistical Yearbook.*

World Intellectual Property Organization, 34 Chemin des Colombettes, CH-1211 Geneva 20, Switzerland; *Industrial Property Statistics.*

TUNISIA - TRANSPORTATION AND COMMUNICATIONS

Euromonitor Publications Limited, 87-88 Turnmill Street, London EC1M 5QU, England; *Middle East Economic Handbook.*

Facts on File, 460 Park Avenue South, New York, New York 10016 (800) 443-8323; *The New Book of World Rankings.*

G.K. Hall and Company, 70 Lincoln Street, Boston, Massachusetts 02111 (617) 423-3990; *The World in Figures.*

United Nations Economic Commission for Africa, Africa Hall, P.O. Box 3001, Addis Ababa, Ethiopia (Telephone Number in U.S. (800) 253-9646); *African Statistical Yearbook.*

TUNISIA - UNEMPLOYMENT

Euromonitor Publications Limited, 87-88 Turnmill Street, London EC1M 5QU, England; *International Marketing Data and Statistics,* and *Middle East Economic Handbook.*

International Labour Office, I.L.O. Publications, CH-1211, Geneva 22, Switzerland; *Yearbook of Labour Statistics.*

Statistical Office of the United Nations, Publishing Service, New York, New York 10017 (800) 253-9646; *Statistical Yearbook.*

TUNISIA - VITAL STATISTICS

Euromonitor Publications Limited, 87-88 Turnmill Street, London EC1M 5QU, England; *International Marketing Data and Statistics,* and *Middle East Economic Handbook.*

G.K. Hall and Company, 70 Lincoln Street, Boston, Massachusetts 02111 (617) 423-3990; *The World in Figures.*

Statistical Office of the United Nations, Publishing Service, New York, New York 10017 (800) 253-9646; *Statistical Yearbook.*

World Health Organization, Office of Publications, Avenue Appia, CH-1211 Geneva 27, Switzerland (Telephone Number in U.S. (518) 436-9686); *World Health Statistics Annual.*

TUNISIA - WAGES

G.K. Hall and Company, 70 Lincoln Street, Boston, Massachusetts 02111 (617) 423-3990; *The World in Figures.*

International Labour Office, I.L.O. Publications, CH-1211, Geneva 22, Switzerland; *Yearbook of Labour Statistics.*

TUNISIA - WEATHER

Facts on File, 460 Park Avenue South, New York, New York 10016 (800) 443-8323; *The New Book of World Rankings.*

G.K. Hall and Company, 70 Lincoln Street, Boston, Massachusetts 02111 (617) 423-3990; *The World in Figures.*

TUNISIA - WELFARE

International Monetary Fund, 700 Nineteenth Street, NW, Washington, D.C. 20431 (202) 623-7000; *Government Finance Statistics Yearbook.*

TUNISIA - WHEAT PRODUCTION AND PRICES - See - TUNISIA - CROPS

TUNISIA - WHOLESALE PRICES

International Monetary Fund, 700 Nineteenth Street, NW, Washington, D.C. 20431 (202) 623-7000; *International Financial Statistics.*

TUNISIA - WINE PRODUCTION

Facts on File, 460 Park Avenue South, New York, New York 10016 (800) 443-8323; *The New Book of World Rankings.*

Statistical Office of the United Nations, Publishing Service, New York, New York 10017 (800) 253-9646; *Statistical Yearbook.*

TUNISIA - WOOL PRODUCTION

Facts on File, 460 Park Avenue South, New York, New York 10016 (800) 443-8323; *The New Book of World Rankings.*

TUNISIA - YARN PRODUCTION

Statistical Office of the United Nations, Publishing Service, New York, New York 10017 (800) 253-9646; *Statistical Yearbook.*

TUNISIA - ZINC AND ZINC ORE PRODUCTION AND CONSUMPTION - See TUNISIA - MINING AND MINERAL PRODUCTS

TURBINES - See STEAM ENGINES

Turkey - National Statistical Office

Devlet Istatistik Enstitusu (State Institute of Statistics), Necatibey Caddesi, 114 Ankara, Turkey.

Turkey - Primary Statistics Sources

Devlet Istatistik Enstitusu, Necati bey Caddesi, 114 Ankara, Turkey; *Aylik Istratistik bulteni* (Monthly Bulletin of Statistics) and *Turkiye Istatistik yilligi* (Statistical Yearbook of Turkey).

TURKEY - AGRICULTURE

Facts on File, 460 Park Avenue South, New York, New York 10016 (800) 443-8323; *The New Book of World Rankings*.

Food and Agricultural Organization of the United Nations (FAO) Via delle Terme di Caracalla, 00100 Rome, Italy (Telephone Number in U.S. (202) 653-2400); *Production Yearbook, The State of Food and Agriculture,* and *Trade Yearbook.*

G.K. Hall and Company, 70 Lincoln Street, Boston, Massachusetts 02111 (617) 423-3990; *The World in Figures*.

Organisation for Economic Co-operation and Development (OECD), 2 rue Andre-Pascal, 75 Paris 16, France (Telephone Number in U.S. (202) 785-6323); *Economic Accounts for Agriculture, Industrial Structure Statistics,* and *OECD Economic Surveys: Turkey.*

Statistical Office of the United Nations, Publishing Service, New York, New York 10017 (800) 253-9646; *Statistical Yearbook.*

Times Books, 201 East 50th Street, New York, New York 10022 (212) 751-2600; *The Economist Book of Vital World Statistics.*

The World Bank, 1818 H Street, NW, Washington, D.C. 20433 (202) 477-1234; *World Tables*.

TURKEY - AIRLINE SERVICE

Facts on File, 460 Park Avenue South, New York, New York 10016 (800) 443-8323; *The New Book of World Rankings*.

G.K. Hall and Company, 70 Lincoln Street, Boston, Massachusetts 02111 (617) 423-3990; *The World in Figures*.

International Civil Aviation Organization, 1000 Sherbrooke Street, West, Montreal, Quebec, Canada H3A 2R2 (514) 285-8219; *Civil Aviation Statistics of the World.*

Organisation for Economic Co-operation and Development (OECD), 2 rue Andre-Pascal, 75 Paris 16, France (Telephone Number in U.S. (202) 785-6323); *Tourism Policy and International Tourism in OECD Member Countries.*

Statistical Office of the United Nations, Publishing Service, New York, New York 10017 (800) 253-9646; *Statistical Yearbook.*

Times Books, 201 East 50th Street, New York, New York 10022 (212) 751-2600; *The Economist Book of Vital World Statistics.*

TURKEY - ALMOND PRODUCTION - See - TURKEY - CROPS

TURKEY - ALUMINUM PRODUCTION AND CONSUMPTION - See TURKEY - MINING AND MINERAL PRODUCTS

TURKEY - ANIMAL FEEDINGSTUFFS - EXPORTS

Organisation for Economic Co-operation and Development (OECD), 2 rue Andre-Pascal, 75 Paris 16, France (Telephone Number in U.S. (202) 785-6323); *Foreign Trade by Commodities.*

TURKEY - ANIMAL HEALTH

Food and Agricultural Organization of the United Nations (FAO), Via delle Terme di Caracalla, 00100, Rome, Italy (Telephone Number in U.S. (202) 653-2400); *Animal Health Yearbook.*

TURKEY - ANTIMONY AND ANTIMONY ORE - See TURKEY - MINING AND MINERAL PRODUCTS

TURKEY - APPLES - See - TURKEY - CROPS

TURKEY - AREA AND DENSITY OF POPULATION

Facts on File, 460 Park Avenue South, New York, New York 10016 (800) 443-8323; *The New Book of World Rankings*.

Food and Agricultural Organization of the United Nations (FAO) Via delle Terme di Caracalla, 00100 Rome, Italy (Telephone Number in U.S. (202) 653-2400); *The State of Food and Agriculture.*

G.K. Hall and Company, 70 Lincoln Street, Boston, Massachusetts 02111 (617) 423-3990; *The World in Figures*.

Statistical Office of the United Nations, Publishing Service, New York, New York 10017 (800) 253-9646; *Statistical Yearbook.*

Times Books, 201 East 50th Street, New York, New York 10022 (212) 751-2600; *The Economist Book of Vital World Statistics.*

United Nations Educational, Scientific and Cultural Organization (UNESCO), 7 Place de Fontenoy, F-75700 Paris, France (Telephone Number in U.S. (212) 963-5981); *Statistical Yearbook.*

TURKEY - ARMS EXPORTS AND IMPORTS

U.S. Arms Control and Disarmament Agency, 320 Twenty-first Street, NW, Washington, D.C. 20451 (202) 647-8677; *World Military Expenditures and Arms Transfers.*

TURKEY - BALANCE OF PAYMENTS

The Economist Intelligence Unit, 111 West 57th Street, New York, New York 10019 (800) 938-4685; *The World Market Atlas.*

G.K. Hall and Company, 70 Lincoln Street, Boston, Massachusetts 02111 (617) 423-3990; *The World in Figures*.

International Monetary Fund, 700 Nineteenth Street, NW, Washington, D.C. 20431 (202) 623-7000; *Balance of Payments Yearbook,* and *International Financial Statistics.*

Organisation for Economic Co-operation and Development (OECD), 2 rue Andre-Pascal, 75 Paris 16, France (Telephone Number in U.S. (202) 785-6323); *Economic Outlook, Geographical Distribution of Financial Flows to Developing Countries, Main Economic Indicators - Historical Statistics,* and *OECD Economic Surveys: Turkey.*

Times Books, 201 East 50th Street, New York, New York 10022 (212) 751-2600; *The Economist Book of Vital World Statistics.*

The World Bank, 1818 H Street, NW, Washington, D.C. 20433 (202) 477-1234; *World Tables*.

TURKEY - BANKING

Facts on File, 460 Park Avenue South, New York, New York 10016 (800) 443-8323; *The New Book of World Rankings*.

G.K. Hall and Company, 70 Lincoln Street, Boston, Massachusetts 02111 (617) 423-3990; *The World in Figures*.

International Monetary Fund, 700 Nineteenth Street, NW, Washington, D.C. 20431 (202) 623-7000; *International Financial Statistics*.

Organisation for Economic Co-operation and Development (OECD), 2 rue Andre-Pascal, 75 Paris 16, France (Telephone Number in U.S. (202) 785-6323); *Economic Outlook*, *Financial Market Trends*, and *OECD Economic Surveys: Turkey*.

Statistical Office of the United Nations, Publishing Service, New York, New York 10017 (800) 253-9646; *Statistical Yearbook*.

TURKEY - BARLEY PRODUCTION - See - TURKEY - CROPS

TURKEY - BAUXITE PRODUCTION AND CONSUMPTION - See TURKEY - MINING AND MINERAL PRODUCTS

TURKEY - BEER PRODUCTION

Facts on File, 460 Park Avenue South, New York, New York 10016 (800) 443-8323; *The New Book of World Rankings*.

Statistical Office of the United Nations, Publishing Service, New York, New York 10017 (800) 253-9646; *Statistical Yearbook*.

TURKEY - BIRTH RATES

Facts on File, 460 Park Avenue South, New York, New York 10016 (800) 443-8323; *The New Book of World Rankings*.

Statistical Office of the United Nations, Publishing Service, New York, New York 10017 (800) 253-9646; *Demographic Yearbook*, and *Statistical Yearbook*.

Times Books, 201 East 50th Street, New York, New York 10022 (212) 751-2600; *The Economist Book of Vital World Statistics*.

The World Bank, 1818 H Street, NW, Washington, D.C. 20433 (202) 477-1234; *World Tables*.

TURKEY - BONDS

G.K. Hall and Company, 70 Lincoln Street, Boston, Massachusetts 02111 (617) 423-3990; *The World in Figures*.

International Monetary Fund, 700 Nineteenth Street, NW, Washington, D.C. 20431 (202) 623-7000; *Government Finance Statistics Yearbook*.

Organisation for Economic Co-operation and Development (OECD), 2 rue Andre-Pascal, 75 Paris 16, France (Telephone Number in U.S. (202) 785-6323); *Financial Market Trends*.

TURKEY - BOOK PRODUCTION

Euromonitor Publications Limited, 87-88 Turnmill Street, London EC1M 5QU, England; *European Marketing Data and Statistics*.

G.K. Hall and Company, 70 Lincoln Street, Boston, Massachusetts 02111 (617) 423-3990; *The World in Figures*.

TURKEY - BROADCASTING

Billboard Limited, P.O. Box 9027, 1006 AA Amsterdam, The Netherlands (Telephone Number in U.S. (212) 764-7300); *World Radio TV Handbook*.

Facts on File, 460 Park Avenue South, New York, New York 10016 (800) 443-8323; *The New Book of World Rankings*.

G.K. Hall and Company, 70 Lincoln Street, Boston, Massachusetts 02111 (617) 423-3990; *The World in Figures*.

Times Books, 201 East 50th Street, New York, New York 10022 (212) 751-2600; *The Economist Book of Vital World Statistics*.

United Nations Educational, Scientific and Cultural Organization (UNESCO), 7 Place de Fontenoy, F-75700 Paris, France (Telephone Number in U.S. (212) 963-5981); *Statistical Yearbook*.

TURKEY - BUSINESS

G.K. Hall and Company, 70 Lincoln Street, Boston, Massachusetts 02111 (617) 423-3990; *The World in Figures*.

TURKEY - BUTTER - See TURKEY - DAIRY PRODUCTS

TURKEY - CALORIE SUPPLY

Food and Agricultural Organization of the United Nations (FAO) Via delle Terme di Caracalla, 00100 Rome, Italy (Telephone Number in U.S. (202) 653-2400); *The State of Food and Agriculture*.

TURKEY - CAPITAL INVESTMENT

Organisation for Economic Co-operation and Development (OECD), 2 rue Andre-Pascal, 75 Paris 16, France (Telephone Number in U.S. (202) 785-6323); *Economic Outlook*, and *Financial Market Trends*.

TURKEY - CAPITAL REVENUE

International Monetary Fund, 700 Nineteenth Street, NW, Washington, D.C. 20431 (202) 623-7000; *Government Finance Statistics Yearbook*.

Organisation for Economic Co-operation and Development (OECD), 2 rue Andre-Pascal, 75 Paris 16, France (Telephone Number in U.S. (202) 785-6323); *Economic Outlook*, and *Financial Market Trends*.

TURKEY - CATTLE - See TURKEY - LIVESTOCK AND POULTRY

TURKEY - CAULIFLOWER PRODUCTION - See - TURKEY - CROPS

TURKEY - CAUSTIC SODA PRODUCTION

Statistical Office of the United Nations, Publishing Service, New York, New York 10017 (800) 253-9646; *Statistical Yearbook*.

TURKEY - CEMENT PRODUCTION - See TURKEY - MINING AND MINERAL PRODUCTS

TURKEY - CEREAL PRODUCTION - See - TURKEY - CROPS

TURKEY - CHEESE - See TURKEY - DAIRY PRODUCTS

TURKEY - CHEMICAL (ORGANIC) PRODUCTION - See TURKEY - MINING AND MINERAL PRODUCTS

TURKEY - CHESTNUT PRODUCTION - See - TURKEY - CROPS

TURKEY - CHICK PEA PRODUCTION - See TURKEY - CROPS

TURKEY - CHROMITE PRODUCTION AND CONSUMPTION - See TURKEY - MINING AND MINERAL PRODUCTS

TURKEY - CHROMIUM ORE PRODUCTION AND CONSUMPTION - See TURKEY - MINING AND MINERAL PRODUCTS

TURKEY - CIGAR PRODUCTION - See TURKEY - TOBACCO PRODUCTION

TURKEY - CIGARETTE PRODUCTION - See TURKEY - TOBACCO PRODUCTION

TURKEY - CLASS STRUCTURE

G.K. Hall and Company, 70 Lincoln Street, Boston, Massachusetts 02111 (617) 423-3990; *The World in Figures.*

TURKEY - CLIMATE

Facts on File, 460 Park Avenue South, New York, New York 10016 (800) 443-8323; *The New Book of World Rankings.*

G.K. Hall and Company, 70 Lincoln Street, Boston, Massachusetts 02111 (617) 423-3990; *The World in Figures.*

TURKEY - CLOTHING EXPORTS AND IMPORTS

Organisation for Economic Co-operation and Development (OECD), 2 rue Andre-Pascal, 75 Paris 16, France (Telephone Number in U.S. (202) 785-6323); *Textile Industry in OECD Countries.*

TURKEY - COAL PRODUCTION - See TURKEY - MINING AND MINERAL PRODUCTS

TURKEY - COBALT PRODUCTION AND CONSUMPTION - See TURKEY - MINING AND MINERAL PRODUCTS

TURKEY - COFFEE PRODUCTION - See - TURKEY - CROPS

TURKEY - COKE AND COKE OVEN COKE PRODUCTION AND CONSUMPTION - See TURKEY - MINING AND MINERAL PRODUCTS

TURKEY - COMMUNICATIONS

G.K. Hall and Company, 70 Lincoln Street, Boston, Massachusetts 02111 (617) 423-3990; *The World in Figures.*

TURKEY - CONSTRUCTION INDUSTRY

Facts on File, 460 Park Avenue South, New York, New York 10016 (800) 443-8323; *The New Book of World Rankings.*

Organisation for Economic Co-operation and Development (OECD), 2 rue Andre-Pascal, 75 Paris 16, France (Telephone Number in U.S. (202) 785-6323); *Industrial Structure Statistics, The Iron and Steel Industry, Main Economic Indicators - Historical Statistics,* and *OECD Economic Surveys: Turkey.*

Statistical Office of the United Nations, Publishing Service, New York, New York 10017 (800) 253-9646; *Construction Statistics Yearbook,* and *Statistical Yearbook.*

TURKEY - CONSUMER PRICE INDEX

G.K. Hall and Company, 70 Lincoln Street, Boston, Massachusetts 02111 (617) 423-3990; *The World in Figures.*

Organisation for Economic Co-operation and Development (OECD), 2 rue Andre-Pascal, 75 Paris 16, France (Telephone Number in U.S. (202) 785-6323); *Economic Outlook.*

Statistical Office of the United Nations, Publishing Service, New York, New York 10017 (800) 253-9646; *Statistical Yearbook.*

TURKEY - CONSUMER PRICES

Euromonitor Publications Limited, 87-88 Turnmill Street, London EC1M 5QU, England; *European Marketing Data and Statistics.*

International Labour Office, I.L.O. Publications, CH-1211, Geneva 22, Switzerland; *Yearbook of Labour Statistics.*

International Monetary Fund, 700 Nineteenth Street, NW, Washington, D.C. 20431 (202) 623-7000; *International Financial Statistics.*

Organisation for Economic Co-operation and Development (OECD), 2 rue Andre-Pascal, 75 Paris 16, France (Telephone Number in U.S. (202) 785-6323); *Economic Outlook.*

Times Books, 201 East 50th Street, New York, New York 10022 (212) 751-2600; *The Economist Book of Vital World Statistics.*

TURKEY - CONSUMPTION

G.K. Hall and Company, 70 Lincoln Street, Boston, Massachusetts 02111 (617) 423-3990; *The World in Figures.*

Organisation for Economic Co-operation and Development (OECD), 2 rue Andre-Pascal, 75 Paris 16, France (Telephone Number in U.S. (202) 785-6323); *The Footwear, Raw Hides and Skins, and Leather Industry in OECD Countries, The Iron and Steel Industry, Meat Balances in OECD Member Countries, The Non-Ferrous Metals Industry, The Pulp and Paper Industry,* and *Textile Industry in OECD Countries.*

TURKEY - COPPER AND COPPER ORE PRODUCTION AND CONSUMPTION - See TURKEY - MINING AND MINERAL PRODUCTS

TURKEY - CORN PRODUCTION - See - TURKEY - CROPS

TURKEY - CORPORATE INCOME TAXES - See TURKEY - TAXATION

TURKEY - CORPORATE TAXES - See TURKEY - TAXATION

TURKEY - COTTON - See - TURKEY - CROPS

TURKEY - CRIME

International Criminal Police Organization (INTERPOL), 26 rue Armengaud, 92210 Saint Cloud, France; *International Crime Statistics.*

Yale University Press, Yale Station, New Haven, Connecticut 06520 (203) 432-0940; *Violence and Crime in Cross-National Perspective.*

TURKEY - CROPS

Commodity Research Bureau, Incorporated, 75 Wall Street, New York, New York 10005 (212) 504-7754; *Commodity Year Book.*

Euromonitor Publications Limited, 87-88 Turnmill Street, London EC1M 5QU, England; *European Marketing Data and Statistics*.

Facts on File, 460 Park Avenue South, New York, New York 10016 (800) 443-8323; *The New Book of World Rankings*.

Food and Agricultural Organization of the United Nations (FAO) Via delle Terme di Caracalla, 00100 Rome, Italy (Telephone Number in U.S. (202) 653-2400); *Production Yearbook*, and *The State of Food and Agriculture*.

G.K. Hall and Company, 70 Lincoln Street, Boston, Massachusetts 02111 (617) 423-3990; *The World in Figures*.

International Monetary Fund, 700 Nineteenth Street, NW, Washington, D.C. 20431 (202) 623-7000; *Government Finance Statistics Yearbook*.

Organisation for Economic Co-operation and Development (OECD), 2 rue Andre-Pascal, 75 Paris 16, France (Telephone Number in U.S. (202) 785-6323); *Economic Accounts for Agriculture, Foreign Trade by Commodities*, and *Textile Industries in OECD Countries*.

Statistical Office of the United Nations, Publishing Service, New York, New York 10017 (800) 253-9646; *Statistical Yearbook*.

TURKEY - CUSTOMS DUTIES

G.K. Hall and Company, 70 Lincoln Street, Boston, Massachusetts 02111 (617) 423-3990; *The World in Figures*.

International Monetary Fund, 700 Nineteenth Street, NW, Washington, D.C. 20431 (202) 623-7000; *Government Finance Statistics Yearbook*.

Organisation for Economic Co-operation and Development (OECD), 2 rue Andre-Pascal, 75 Paris 16, France (Telephone Number in U.S. (202) 785-6323); *The Non-Ferrous Metals Industry*.

TURKEY - DAIRY PRODUCTS

Facts on File, 460 Park Avenue South, New York, New York 10016 (800) 443-8323; *The New Book of World Rankings*.

Food and Agricultural Organization of the United Nations (FAO) Via delle Terme di Caracalla, 00100 Rome, Italy (Telephone Number in U.S. (202) 653-2400); *Production Yearbook*, and *The State of Food and Agriculture*.

Organisation for Economic Co-operation and Development (OECD), 2 rue Andre-Pascal, 75 Paris 16, France (Telephone Number in U.S. (202) 785-6323); *Economic Accounts for Agriculture*, and *Milk, Milk Products, and Egg Balances in OECD Member Countries*.

Statistical Office of the United Nations, Publishing Service, New York, New York 10017 (800) 253-9646; *Statistical Yearbook*.

TURKEY - DEATH RATES

G.K. Hall and Company, 70 Lincoln Street, Boston, Massachusetts 02111 (617) 423-3990; *The World in Figures*.

Statistical Office of the United Nations, Publishing Service, New York, New York 10017 (800) 253-9646; *Statistical Yearbook*.

Times Books, 201 East 50th Street, New York, New York 10022 (212) 751-2600; *The Economist Book of Vital World Statistics*.

World Health Organization, Office of Publications, Avenue Appia, CH-1211 Geneva 27, Switzerland (Telephone Number in U.S. (518) 436-9686); *World Health Statistics Annual*.

TURKEY - DEFENSE EXPENDITURES

G.K. Hall and Company, 70 Lincoln Street, Boston, Massachusetts 02111 (617) 423-3990; *The World in Figures*.

International Monetary Fund, 700 Nineteenth Street, NW, Washington, D.C. 20431 (202) 623-7000; *Government Finance Statistics Yearbook*.

U.S. Arms Control and Disarmament Agency, 320 Twenty-first Street, NW, Washington, D.C. 20451 (202) 647-8677; *World Military Expenditures and Arms Transfers*.

TURKEY - DEMOGRAPHY

Facts on File, 460 Park Avenue South, New York, New York 10016 (800) 443-8323; *The New Book of World Rankings*.

G.K. Hall and Company, 70 Lincoln Street, Boston, Massachusetts 02111 (617) 423-3990; *The World in Figures*.

TURKEY - DEVELOPMENT ASSISTANCE

G.K. Hall and Company, 70 Lincoln Street, Boston, Massachusetts 02111 (617) 423-3990; *The World in Figures*.

Organisation for Economic Co-operation and Development (OECD), 2 rue Andre-Pascal, 75 Paris 16, France (Telephone Number in U.S. (202) 785-6323); *Geographical Distribution of Financial Flows to Developing Countries*.

Statistical Office of the United Nations, Publishing Service, New York, New York 10017 (800) 253-9646; *Statistical Yearbook*.

TURKEY - DIAMOND PRODUCTION - See TURKEY - MINING AND MINERAL PRODUCTS

TURKEY - DISCOUNT RATES

Organisation for Economic Co-operation and Development (OECD), 2 rue Andre-Pascal, 75 Paris 16, France (Telephone Number in U.S. (202) 785-6323); *Financial Market Trends*.

Statistical Office of the United Nations, Publishing Service, New York, New York 10017 (800) 253-9646; *Statistical Yearbook*.

TURKEY - DISEASES

G.K. Hall and Company, 70 Lincoln Street, Boston, Massachusetts 02111 (617) 423-3990; *The World in Figures*.

World Health Organization, Office of Publications, Avenue Appia, CH-1211 Geneva 27, Switzerland (Telephone Number in U.S. (518) 436-9686); *World Health Statistics Annual*.

TURKEY - DIVORCE RATES

Facts on File, 460 Park Avenue South, New York, New York 10016 (800) 443-8323; *The New Book of World Rankings*.

Statistical Office of the United Nations, Publishing Service, New York, New York 10017 (800) 253-9646; *Demographic Yearbook*, and *Statistical Yearbook*.

TURKEY - DOMESTIC PRODUCT

G.K. Hall and Company, 70 Lincoln Street, Boston, Massachusetts 02111 (617) 423-3990; *The World in Figures.*

TURKEY - ECONOMY

Euromonitor Publications Limited, 87-88 Turnmill Street, London EC1M 5QU, England; *European Marketing Data and Statistics.*

Facts on File, 460 Park Avenue South, New York, New York 10016 (800) 443-8323; *The New Book of World Rankings.*

G.K. Hall and Company, 70 Lincoln Street, Boston, Massachusetts 02111 (617) 423-3990; *The World in Figures.*

Organisation for Economic Co-operation and Development (OECD), 2 rue Andre-Pascal, 75 Paris 16, France (Telephone Number in U.S. (202) 785-6323); *Economic Outlook, Geographical Distribution of Financial Flows to Developing Countries, OECD Economic Surveys: Turkey,* and *OECD Employment Outlook.*

TURKEY - EDUCATION

The Economist Intelligence Unit, 111 West 57th Street, New York, New York 10019 (800) 938-4685; *The World Market Atlas.*

Euromonitor Publications Limited, 87-88 Turnmill Street, London EC1M 5QU, England; *European Marketing Data and Statistics.*

Facts on File, 460 Park Avenue South, New York, New York 10016 (800) 443-8323; *The New Book of World Rankings.*

G.K. Hall and Company, 70 Lincoln Street, Boston, Massachusetts 02111 (617) 423-3990; *The World in Figures.*

International Monetary Fund, 700 Nineteenth Street, NW, Washington, D.C. 20431 (202) 623-7000; *Government Finance Statistics Yearbook.*

Organisation for Economic Co-operation and Development (OECD), 2 rue Andre-Pascal, 75 Paris 16, France (Telephone Number in U.S. (202) 785-6323); *Education in OECD Countries.*

Times Books, 201 East 50th Street, New York, New York 10022 (212) 751-2600; *The Economist Book of Vital World Statistics.*

United Nations Educational, Scientific and Cultural Organization (UNESCO), 7 Place de Fontenoy, F-75700 Paris, France (Telephone Number in U.S. (212) 963-5981); *Statistical Yearbook.*

The World Bank, 1818 H Street, NW, Washington, D.C. 20433 (202) 477-1234; *World Tables.*

TURKEY - EGG PRODUCTION AND CONSUMPTION - See TURKEY - DAIRY PRODUCTS

TURKEY - EGGPLANT PRODUCTION - See TURKEY - CROPS

TURKEY - ELECTRICITY

Facts on File, 460 Park Avenue South, New York, New York 10016 (800) 443-8323; *The New Book of World Rankings.*

Organisation for Economic Co-operation and Development (OECD), 2 rue Andre-Pascal, 75 Paris 16, France (Telephone Number in U.S. (202) 785-6323); *Coal Information, Energy Statistics of OECD Countries,* and *Industrial Structure Statistics.*

Penn Well Publishing Company, 1421 South Sheridan Road, P.O. Box 1260, Tulsa, Oklahoma 74101 (800) 752-9764; *International Energy Statistics Sourcebook.*

Statistical Office of the United Nations, Publishing Service, New York, New York 10017 (800) 253-9646; *Statistical Yearbook.*

Times Books, 201 East 50th Street, New York, New York 10022 (212) 751-2600; *The Economist Book of Vital World Statistics.*

TURKEY - EMPLOYMENT

Euromonitor Publications Limited, 87-88 Turnmill Street, London EC1M 5QU, England; *European Marketing Data and Statistics.*

Facts on File, 460 Park Avenue South, New York, New York 10016 (800) 443-8323; *The New Book of World Rankings.*

International Labour Office, I.L.O. Publications, CH-1211, Geneva 22, Switzerland; *Yearbook of Labour Statistics.*

Organisation for Economic Co-operation and Development (OECD), 2 rue Andre-Pascal, 75 Paris 16, France (Telephone Number in U.S. (202) 785-6323); *Economic Outlook, The Iron and Steel Industry, OECD Economic Surveys: Turkey, OECD Employment Outlook,* and *Textile Industry in OECD Countries.*

Statistical Office of the United Nations, Publishing Service, New York, New York 10017 (800) 253-9646; *Statistical Yearbook.*

TURKEY - ENERGY

Euromonitor Publications Limited, 87-88 Turnmill Street, London EC1M 5QU, England; *European Marketing Data and Statistics.*

Facts on File, 460 Park Avenue South, New York, New York 10016 (800) 443-8323; *The New Book of World Rankings.*

Food and Agricultural Organization of the United Nations (FAO) Via delle Terme di Caracalla, 00100 Rome, Italy (Telephone Number in U.S. (202) 653-2400); *The State of Food and Agriculture.*

G.K. Hall and Company, 70 Lincoln Street, Boston, Massachusetts 02111 (617) 423-3990; *The World in Figures.*

Organisation for Economic Co-operation and Development (OECD), 2 rue Andre-Pascal, 75 Paris 16, France (Telephone Number in U.S. (202) 785-6323); *Coal Information, Energy Statistics of OECD Countries, Oil and Gas Information,* and *OECD Environmental Data.*

Penn Well Publishing Company, 1421 South Sheridan Road, P.O. Box 1260, Tulsa, Oklahoma 74101 (800) 752-9764; *International Energy Statistics Sourcebook.*

Statistical Office of the United Nations, Publishing Service, New York, New York 10017 (800) 253-9646; *Energy Statistics Yearbook, Statistical Yearbook,* and *World Energy Supplies.*

Times Books, 201 East 50th Street, New York, New York 10022 (212) 751-2600; *The Economist Book of Vital World Statistics.*

TURKEY - ENVIRONMENT

Organization for Economic Co-operation and Development (OECD), 2 rue Andre-Pascal, 75 Paris 16, France (Telephone Number in U.S. (202) 785-6323); *OECD Environmental Data.*

TURKEY - EXCHANGE RATES

International Civil Aviation Organization, 1000 Sherbrooke Street, West, Montreal, Quebec, Canada H3A 2R2 (514) 285-8219; *Civil Aviation Statistics of the World.*

International Monetary Fund, 700 Nineteenth Street, NW, Washington, D.C. 20431 (202) 623-7000; *International Financial Statistics.*

Organisation for Economic Co-operation and Development (OECD), 2 rue Andre-Pascal, 75 Paris 16, France (Telephone Number in U.S. (202) 785 6323); *Economic Outlook, Financial Market Trends, Revenue Statistics of OECD Member Countries,* and *Tourism Policy and International Tourism in OECD Member Countries.*

Statistical Office of the United Nations, Publishing Service, New York, New York 10017 (800) 253-9646; *Statistical Yearbook.*

TURKEY - EXCISE TAXES - See TURKEY - TAXATION

TURKEY - EXPORTS

American Automobile Manufacturers Association, 1401 H Street, NW, Suite 900, Washington, D.C. 20005 (202) 326 5600; *World Motor Vehicle Data.*

The Economist Intelligence Unit, 111 West 57th Street, New York, New York 10019 (800) 938-4685; *The World Market Atlas.*

Food and Agricultural Organization of the United Nations (FAO) Via delle Terme di Caracalla, 00100 Rome, Italy (Telephone Number in U.S. (202) 653-2400); *The State of Food and Agriculture.*

G.K. Hall and Company, 70 Lincoln Street, Boston, Massachusetts 02111 (617) 423 3990; *The World in Figures.*

International Monetary Fund, 700 Nineteenth Street, NW, Washington, D.C. 20431 (202) 623-7000; *Direction of Trade Statistics,* and *International Financial Statistics.*

Organisation for Economic Co-operation and Development (OECD), 2 rue Andre-Pascal, 75 Paris 16, France (Telephone Number in U.S. (202) 785-6323); *Economic Outlook, The Footwear, Raw Hides and Skins, and Leather Industry in OECD Countries, Foreign Trade by Commodities, Geographical Distribution of Financial Flows to Developing Countries, Industrial Structure Statistics, The Iron and Steel Industry, Milk, Milk Products, and Egg Balances in OECD Member Countries, OECD Economic Surveys: Turkey, The Pulp and Paper Industry,* and *Review of Fisheries in OECD Member Countries.*

Times Books, 201 East 50th Street, New York, New York 10022 (212) 751-2600; *The Economist Book of Vital World Statistics.*

The World Bank, 1818 H Street, NW, Washington, D.C. 20433 (202) 477-1234; *World Tables.*

TURKEY - EXTERNAL FINANCING

Organisation for Economic Co-operation and Development (OECD), 2 rue Andre-Pascal, 75 Paris 16, France (Telephone Number in U.S. (202) 785-6323); *Economic Outlook,* and *Financial Market Trends.*

TURKEY - EXTERNAL INDEBTEDNESS

Organisation for Economic Co-operation and Development (OECD), 2 rue Andre-Pascal, 75 Paris 16, France (Telephone Number in U.S. (202) 785-6323); *Financial Market Trends,* and *Geographical*

Distribution of Financial Flows to Developing Countries.

The World Bank, 1818 H Street, NW, Washington, D.C. 20433 (202) 477-1234; *World Tables.*

TURKEY - EXTERNAL TRADE

Food and Agricultural Organization of the United Nations (FAO) Via delle Terme di Caracalla, 00100 Rome, Italy (Telephone Number in U.S. (202) 653-2400); *The State of Food and Agriculture,* and *Trade Yearbook.*

G.K. Hall and Company, 70 Lincoln Street, Boston, Massachusetts 02111 (617) 423-3990; *The World in Figures.*

Statistical Office of the United Nations, Publishing Service, New York, New York 10017 (800) 253-9646; *Statistical Yearbook.*

TURKEY - FABRIC PRODUCTION - See TURKEY - TEXTILE INDUSTRY

TURKEY - FARM CROPS - See - TURKEY - CROPS

TURKEY - FERTILITY RATES

Facts on File, 460 Park Avenue South, New York, New York 10016 (800) 443-8323; *The New Book of World Rankings.*

Times Books, 201 East 50th Street, New York, New York 10022 (212) 751-2600; *The Economist Book of Vital World Statistics.*

The World Bank, 1818 H Street, NW, Washington, D.C. 20433 (202) 477-1234; *World Tables.*

TURKEY - FERTILIZER

Food and Agricultural Organization of the United Nations (FAO), Via delle Terme di Caracalla, 00100, Rome, Italy (Telephone Number in U.S. (202) 653-2400); *Fertilizer Yearbook,* and *The State of Food and Agriculture.*

Organisation for Economic Co-operation and Development (OECD), 2 rue Andre-Pascal, 75 Paris 16, France (Telephone Number in U.S. (202) 785-6323); *Economic Accounts for Agriculture,* and *Foreign Trade by Commodities.*

Statistical Office of the United Nations, Publishing Service, New York, New York 10017 (800) 253-9646; *Statistical Yearbook.*

TURKEY - FETAL MORTALITY

Statistical Office of the United Nations, Publishing Service, New York, New York 10017 (800) 253-9646; *Demographic Yearbook.*

TURKEY - FIBRE PRODUCTION - See TURKEY - TEXTILE INDUSTRY

TURKEY - FILAMENT PRODUCTION - See TURKEY - TEXTILE INDUSTRY

TURKEY - FILM - See TURKEY - MOTION PICTURES

TURKEY - FINANCE

Facts on File, 460 Park Avenue South, New York, New York 10016 (800) 443-8323; *The New Book of World Rankings.*

G.K. Hall and Company, 70 Lincoln Street, Boston, Massachusetts 02111 (617) 423-3990; *The World in Figures.*

International Monetary Fund, 700 Nineteenth Street, NW, Washington, D.C. 20431 (202) 623-7000; *Government Finance Statistics Yearbook*.

Organisation for Economic Co-operation and Development (OECD), 2 rue Andre-Pascal, 75 Paris 16, France (Telephone Number in U.S. (202) 785-6323); *Economic Outlook, Financial Market Trends, Geographical Distribution of Financial Flows to Developing Countries*, and *OECD Financial Statistics*.

TURKEY - FISHERIES

Euromonitor Publications Limited, 87-88 Turnmill Street, London EC1M 5QU, England; *European Marketing Data and Statistics*.

Facts on File, 460 Park Avenue South, New York, New York 10016 (800) 443-8323; *The New Book of World Rankings*, and *Yearbook of Fishery Statistics*.

Food and Agricultural Organization of the United Nations (FAO) Via delle Terme di Caracalla, 00100 Rome, Italy (Telephone Number in U.S. (202) 653-2400); *The State of Food and Agriculture*.

Organisation for Economic Co-operation and Development (OECD), 2 rue Andre-Pascal, 75 Paris 16, France (Telephone Number in U.S. (202) 785-6323); *Foreign Trade by Commodities*, and *Review of Fisheries in OECD Member Countries*.

Statistical Office of the United Nations, Publishing Service, New York, New York 10017 (800) 253-9646; *Statistical Yearbook*.

TURKEY - FLAX FIBRE PRODUCTION - See TURKEY - TEXTILE INDUSTRY

TURKEY - FLOUR PRODUCTION

Statistical Office of the United Nations, Publishing Service, New York, New York 10017 (800) 253-9646; *Statistical Yearbook*.

TURKEY - FOOD

Food and Agricultural Organization of the United Nations (FAO) Via delle Terme di Caracalla, 00100 Rome, Italy (Telephone Number in U.S. (202) 653-2400); *Production Yearbook*, and *The State of Food and Agriculture*.

G.K. Hall and Company, 70 Lincoln Street, Boston, Massachusetts 02111 (617) 423-3990; *The World in Figures*.

Organisation for Economic Co-operation and Development (OECD), 2 rue Andre-Pascal, 75 Paris 16, France (Telephone Number in U.S. (202) 785-6323); *Foreign Trade by Commodities*.

TURKEY - FOREIGN AID

G.K. Hall and Company, 70 Lincoln Street, Boston, Massachusetts 02111 (617) 423-3990; *The World in Figures*.

TURKEY - FOREIGN DEBT

Organisation for Economic Co-operation and Development (OECD), 2 rue Andre-Pascal, 75 Paris 16, France (Telephone Number in U.S. (202) 785-6323); *Economic Outlook*.

TURKEY - FOREIGN TRADE

Euromonitor Publications Limited, 87-88 Turnmill Street, London EC1M 5QU, England; *European Marketing Data and Statistics*.

Facts on File, 460 Park Avenue South, New York, New York 10016 (800) 443-8323; *The New Book of World Rankings*.

Food and Agricultural Organization of the United Nations (FAO) Via delle Terme di Caracalla, 00100 Rome, Italy (Telephone Number in U.S. (202) 653-2400); *The State of Food and Agriculture*.

G.K. Hall and Company, 70 Lincoln Street, Boston, Massachusetts 02111 (617) 423-3990; *The World in Figures*.

International Monetary Fund, 700 Nineteenth Street, NW, Washington, D.C. 20431 (202) 623-7000; *International Financial Statistics*.

Organisation for Economic Co-operation and Development (OECD), 2 rue Andre-Pascal, 75 Paris 16, France (Telephone Number in U.S. (202) 785-6323); *Economic Outlook, The Footwear, Raw Hides and Skins, and Leather Industry in OECD Countries, Foreign Trade by Commodities, Main Economic Indicators - Historical Statistics, Maritime Transport, Meat Balances in OECD Member Countries*, and *OECD Economic Surveys: Turkey*.

Statistical Office of the United Nations, Publishing Service, New York, New York 10017 (800) 253-9646; *International Trade Statistics Yearbook*, and *Statistical Yearbook*.

The World Bank, 1818 H Street, NW, Washington, D.C. 20433 (202) 477-1234; *World Tables*.

TURKEY - FORESTRY AND FOREST PRODUCTS

Euromonitor Publications Limited, 87-88 Turnmill Street, London EC1M 5QU, England; *European Marketing Data and Statistics*.

Facts on File, 460 Park Avenue South, New York, New York 10016 (800) 443-8323; *The New Book of World Rankings*.

Food and Agricultural Organization of the United Nations (FAO) Via delle Terme di Caracalla, 00100 Rome, Italy (Telephone Number in U.S. (202) 653-2400); *The State of Food and Agriculture*, and *Yearbook of Forest Products*.

G.K. Hall and Company, 70 Lincoln Street, Boston, Massachusetts 02111 (617) 423-3990; *The World in Figures*.

Organisation for Economic Co-operation and Development (OECD), 2 rue Andre-Pascal, 75 Paris 16, France (Telephone Number in U.S. (202) 785-6323); *Foreign Trade by Commodities, Industrial Structure Statistics*, and *The Pulp and Paper Industry*.

Statistical Office of the United Nations, Publishing Service, New York, New York 10017 (800) 253-9646; *Statistical Yearbook*.

United Nations Educational, Scientific and Cultural Organization (UNESCO), 7 Place de Fontenoy, F-75700 Paris, France (Telephone Number in U.S. (212) 963-5981); *Statistical Yearbook*.

TURKEY - FRUIT PRODUCTION - See TURKEY - CROPS

Organisation for Economic Co-operation and Development (OECD), 2 rue Andre-Pascal, 75 Paris 16, France (Telephone Number in U.S. (202) 785-6323); *Economic Accounts for Agriculture*, and *Foreign Trade by Commodities*.

TURKEY - FURNITURE AND WOOD PRODUCTS - EXPORTS AND IMPORTS

Organisation for Economic Co-operation and Development (OECD), 2 rue Andre-Pascal, 75 Paris 16, France (Telephone Number in U.S.

(202) 785-6323); *Foreign Trade by Commodities, Industrial Structure Statistics*, and *OECD Economic Surveys: Turkey*.

TURKEY - GARLIC PRODUCTION - See - TURKEY - CROPS

TURKEY - GAS PRODUCTION - See TURKEY - MINING AND MINERAL PRODUCTS

TURKEY - GENERAL INDUSTRIAL STATISTICS

Statistical Office of the United Nations, Publishing Service, New York, New York 10017 (800) 253-9646; *Industrial Statistics Yearbook*.

TURKEY - GENERAL MORTALITY

Statistical Office of the United Nations, Publishing Service, New York, New York 10017 (800) 253-9646; *Demographic Yearbook*.

TURKEY - GEOGRAPHIC DATA

Facts on File, 460 Park Avenue South, New York, New York 10016 (800) 443-8323; *The New Book of World Rankings*.

TURKEY - GOATS - See TURKEY - LIVESTOCK AND POULTRY

TURKEY - GOLD HOLDINGS

International Monetary Fund, 700 Nineteenth Street, NW, Washington, D.C. 20431 (202) 623-7000; *International Financial Statistics*.

The World Bank, 1818 H Street, NW, Washington, D.C. 20433 (202) 477-1234; *World Tables*.

TURKEY - GOLD PRODUCTION AND CONSUMPTION - See TURKEY - MINING AND MINERAL PRODUCTS

TURKEY - GOVERNMENT

G.K. Hall and Company, 70 Lincoln Street, Boston, Massachusetts 02111 (617) 423-3990; *The World in Figures*.

TURKEY - GOVERNMENT EXPENDITURES

International Monetary Fund, 700 Nineteenth Street, NW, Washington, D.C. 20431 (202) 623-7000; *Government Finance Statistics Yearbook*.

Organisation for Economic Co-operation and Development (OECD), 2 rue Andre-Pascal, 75 Paris 16, France (Telephone Number in U.S. (202) 785-6323); *Economic Outlook*.

Times Books, 201 East 50th Street, New York, New York 10022 (212) 751-2600; *The Economist Book of Vital World Statistics*.

The World Bank, 1818 H Street, NW, Washington, D.C. 20433 (202) 477-1234; *World Tables*.

TURKEY - GOVERNMENT FINANCES

International Monetary Fund, 700 Nineteenth Street, NW, Washington, D.C. 20431 (202) 623-7000; *International Financial Statistics*.

Organisation for Economic Co-operation and Development (OECD), 2 rue Andre-Pascal, 75 Paris 16, France (Telephone Number in U.S. (202) 785-6323); *Economic Outlook*.

Statistical Office of the United Nations, Publishing Service, New York, New York 10017 (800) 253-9646; *Statistical Yearbook*.

TURKEY - GOVERNMENT REVENUE

International Monetary Fund, 700 Nineteenth Street, NW, Washington, D.C. 20431 (202) 623-7000; *Government Finance Statistics Yearbook*.

Organisation for Economic Co-operation and Development (OECD), 2 rue Andre-Pascal, 75 Paris 16, France (Telephone Number in U.S. (202) 785-6323); *Economic Outlook*, and *Revenue Statistics of OECD Member Countries*.

Times Books, 201 East 50th Street, New York, New York 10022 (212) 751-2600; *The Economist Book of Vital World Statistics*.

The World Bank, 1818 H Street, NW, Washington, D.C. 20433 (202) 477-1234; *World Tables*.

TURKEY - GRAIN PRODUCTION - See - TURKEY - CROPS

TURKEY - GRANTS

International Monetary Fund, 700 Nineteenth Street, NW, Washington, D.C. 20431 (202) 623-7000; *Government Finance Statistics Yearbook*.

Organisation for Economic Co-operation and Development (OECD), 2 rue Andre-Pascal, 75 Paris 16, France (Telephone Number in U.S. (202) 785-6323); *Geographical Distribution of Financial Flows to Developing Countries*.

TURKEY - GREEN PEPPER AND CHILIE PRODUCTION - See - TURKEY - CROPS

TURKEY - GROSS DOMESTIC PRODUCT

The Economist Intelligence Unit, 111 West 57th Street, New York, New York 10019 (800) 938-4685; *The World Market Atlas*.

Facts on File, 460 Park Avenue South, New York, New York 10016 (800) 443-8323; *The New Book of World Rankings*.

G.K. Hall and Company, 70 Lincoln Street, Boston, Massachusetts 02111 (617) 423-3990; *The World in Figures*.

Organisation for Economic Co-operation and Development (OECD), 2 rue Andre-Pascal, 75 Paris 16, France (Telephone Number in U.S. (202) 785-6323); *Economic Outlook, Geographical Distribution of Financial Flows to Developing Countries*, and *Revenue Statistics of OECD Member Countries*.

Statistical Office of the United Nations, Publishing Service, New York, New York 10017 (800) 253-9646; *Statistical Yearbook*.

Times Books, 201 East 50th Street, New York, New York 10022 (212) 751-2600; *The Economist Book of Vital World Statistics*.

The World Bank, 1818 H Street, NW, Washington, D.C. 20433 (202) 477-1234; *World Tables*.

TURKEY - GROSS NATIONAL PRODUCT

Organisation for Economic Co-operation and Development (OECD), 2 rue Andre-Pascal, 75 Paris 16, France (Telephone Number in U.S. (202) 785-6323); *Economic Outlook*, and *Geographical Distribution of Financial Flows to Developing Countries*.

U.S. Arms Control and Disarmament Agency, 320 Twenty-first Street, NW, Washington, D.C. 20451 (202) 647-8677; *World Military Expenditures and Arms Transfers*.

The World Bank, 1818 H Street, NW, Washington, D.C. 20433 (202) 477-1234; *World Tables*.

TURKEY - GROUNDNUTS PRODUCTION - See - TURKEY - CROPS

TURKEY - HAZELNUT PRODUCTION - See - TURKEY - CROPS

TURKEY - HEALTH

Facts on File, 460 Park Avenue South, New York, New York 10016 (800) 443-8323; *The New Book of World Rankings*.

G.K. Hall and Company, 70 Lincoln Street, Boston, Massachusetts 02111 (617) 423-3990; *The World in Figures*.

Organisation for Economic Co-operation and Development (OECD), 2 rue Andre-Pascal, 75 Paris 16, France (Telephone Number in U.S. (202) 785-6323); *OECD Health Systems: Facts and Trends*.

Statistical Office of the United Nations, Publishing Service, New York, New York 10017 (800) 253-9646; *Statistical Yearbook*.

Times Books, 201 East 50th Street, New York, New York 10022 (212) 751-2600; *The Economist Book of Vital World Statistics*.

World Health Organization, Office of Publications, Avenue Appia, CH-1211 Geneva 27, Switzerland (Telephone Number in U.S. (518) 436-9686); *World Health Statistics Annual*.

TURKEY - HEALTH EXPENDITURES

International Monetary Fund, 700 Nineteenth Street, NW, Washington, D.C. 20431 (202) 623-7000; *Government Finance Statistics Yearbook*.

TURKEY - HEMP FIBRE PRODUCTION - See TURKEY - TEXTILE INDUSTRY

TURKEY - HIDE PRODUCTION

Food and Agricultural Organization of the United Nations (FAO), Via delle Terme di Caracalla, 00100 Rome, Italy (Telephone Number in U.S. (202) 653-2400); *Production Yearbook*.

Organisation for Economic Co-operation and Development (OECD), 2 rue Andre-Pascal, 75 Paris 16, France (Telephone Number in U.S. (202) 785-6323); *The Footwear, Raw Hides and Skins, and Leather Industry in OECD Countries*, and *Foreign Trade by Commodities*.

TURKEY - HIGHWAYS

G.K. Hall and Company, 70 Lincoln Street, Boston, Massachusetts 02111 (617) 423-3990; *The World in Figures*.

International Road Federation, 525 School Street, SW, Washington, D.C. 20024 (202) 554-2106; *World Road Statistics*.

Statistical Office of the United Nations, Publishing Service, New York, New York 10017 (800) 253-9646; *Annual Bulletin of Transport Statistics for Europe*.

TURKEY - HOME FINANCE

Organisation for Economic Co-operation and Development (OECD), 2 rue Andre-Pascal, 75 Paris 16, France (Telephone Number in U.S.

(202) 785-6323); *Main Economic Indicators - Historical Statistics*.

TURKEY - HONEY PRODUCTION

Commodity Research Bureau, Incorporated, 75 Wall Street, New York, New York 10005 (212) 504-7754; *Commodity Year Book*.

TURKEY - HORSES - See TURKEY - LIVESTOCK AND POULTRY

TURKEY - HOURS OF WORK - See TURKEY - EMPLOYMENT

TURKEY - HOUSING AND HOUSING UNITS

Facts on File, 460 Park Avenue South, New York, New York 10016 (800) 443-8323; *The New Book of World Rankings*.

TURKEY - HOUSING CONSTRUCTION - See TURKEY - CONSTRUCTION INDUSTRY

TURKEY - HOUSING EXPENDITURES

International Monetary Fund, 700 Nineteenth Street, NW, Washington, D.C. 20431 (202) 623-7000; *Government Finance Statistics Yearbook*.

TURKEY - HYDROCHLORIC ACID PRODUCTION

Statistical Office of the United Nations, Publishing Service, New York, New York 10017 (800) 253-9646; *Statistical Yearbook*.

TURKEY - ILLITERATE POPULATION

The Economist Intelligence Unit, 111 West 57th Street, New York, New York 10019 (800) 938-4685; *The World Market Atlas*.

G.K. Hall and Company, 70 Lincoln Street, Boston, Massachusetts 02111 (617) 423-3990; *The World in Figures*.

United Nations Educational, Scientific and Cultural Organization (UNESCO), 7 Place de Fontenoy, F-75700 Paris, France (Telephone Number in U.S. (212) 963-5981); *Statistical Yearbook*.

TURKEY - IMPORTS

American Automobile Manufacturers Association, 1401 H Street, NW, Suite 900, Washington, D.C. 20005 (202) 326-5500; *World Motor Vehicle Data*.

The Economist Intelligence Unit, 111 West 57th Street, New York, New York 10019 (800) 938-4685; *The World Market Atlas*.

Food and Agricultural Organization of the United Nations (FAO) Via delle Terme di Caracalla, 00100 Rome, Italy (Telephone Number in U.S. (202) 653-2400); *The State of Food and Agriculture*.

G.K. Hall and Company, 70 Lincoln Street, Boston, Massachusetts 02111 (617) 423-3990; *The World in Figures*.

International Monetary Fund, 700 Nineteenth Street, NW, Washington, D.C. 20431 (202) 623-7000; *Direction of Trade Statistics, Government Finance Statistics Yearbook*, and *International Financial Statistics*.

Organisation for Economic Co-operation and Development (OECD), 2 rue Andre-Pascal, 75 Paris 16, France (Telephone Number in U.S. (202) 785-6323); *Economic Outlook, The Footwear, Raw Hides and Skins, and Leather Industry in OECD Countries, Industrial Structure Statistics, The Iron and Steel Industry, Milk, Milk Products, and Egg Balances in OECD Member Countries, OECD Economic Surveys:*

Turkey, The Pulp and Paper Industry, and *Review of Fisheries in OECD Member Countries.*

Times Books, 201 East 50th Street, New York, New York 10022 (212) 751-2600; *The Economist Book of Vital World Statistics.*

The World Bank, 1818 H Street, NW, Washington, D.C. 20433 (202) 477-1234; *World Tables.*

TURKEY - INCOME TAXES - See TURKEY - TAXATION

TURKEY - INDUSTRIAL METALS PRODUCTION - See TURKEY - MINING AND MINERAL PRODUCTS

TURKEY - INDUSTRY

Facts on File, 460 Park Avenue South, New York, New York 10016 (800) 443-8323; *The New Book of World Rankings.*

G.K. Hall and Company, 70 Lincoln Street, Boston, Massachusetts 02111 (617) 423-3990; *The World in Figures.*

International Labour Office, I.L.O. Publications, CH-1211, Geneva 22, Switzerland; *Yearbook of Labour Statistics.*

Organisation for Economic Co-operation and Development (OECD), 2 rue Andre-Pascal, 75 Paris 16, France (Telephone Number in U.S. (202) 785-6323); *Economic Outlook, Industrial Structure Statistics* and *OECD Environmental Data.*

Statistical Office of the United Nations, Publishing Service, New York, New York 10017 (800) 253-9646; *Statistical Yearbook.*

Times Books, 201 East 50th Street, New York, New York 10022 (212) 751-2600; *The Economist Book of Vital World Statistics.*

The World Bank, 1818 H Street, NW, Washington, D.C. 20433 (202) 477-1234; *World Tables.*

World Intellectual Property Organization, 34 Chemin des Colombettes, CH-1211 Geneva 20, Switzerland; *Industrial Property Statistics.*

TURKEY - INFANT AND MATERNAL MORTALITY

Statistical Office of the United Nations, Publishing Service, New York, New York 10017 (800) 253-9646; *Demographic Yearbook,* and *Statistical Yearbook.*

The World Bank, 1818 H Street, NW, Washington, D.C. 20433 (202) 477-1234; *World Tables.*

TURKEY - INTEREST RATES

Organisation for Economic Co-operation and Development (OECD), 2 rue Andre-Pascal, 75 Paris 16, France (Telephone Number in U.S. (202) 785-6323); *Economic Outlook, Financial Market Trends,* and *OECD Financial Statistics.*

TURKEY - INTERNAL TRADE

Statistical Office of the United Nations, Publishing Service, New York, New York 10017 (800) 253-9646; *Statistical Yearbook.*

TURKEY - INTERNATIONAL FINANCE

Organisation for Economic Co-operation and Development (OECD), 2 rue Andre Pascal, 75 Paris 16, France (Telephone Number in U.S. (202) 785-6323); *Economic Outlook,* and *Financial Market Trends.*

TURKEY - INTERNATIONAL LIQUIDITY

International Monetary Fund, 700 Nineteenth Street, NW, Washington, D.C. 20431 (202) 623-7000; *International Financial Statistics.*

Organisation for Economic Co-operation and Development (OECD), 2 rue Andre-Pascal, 75 Paris 16, France (Telephone Number in U.S. (202) 785-6323); *Economic Outlook,* and *Financial Market Trends.*

TURKEY - INTERNATIONAL RESERVES EXCLUDING GOLD

Statistical Office of the United Nations, Publishing Service, New York, New York 10017 (800) 253-9646; *Statistical Yearbook.*

The World Bank, 1818 H Street, NW, Washington, D.C. 20433 (202) 477-1234; *World Tables.*

TURKEY - INTERNATIONAL STATISTICS

Organisation for Economic Co-operation and Development (OECD), 2 rue Andre-Pascal, 75 Paris 16, France (Telephone Number in U.S. (202) 785-6323); *Financial Market Trends,* and *Tourism Policy and International Tourism in OECD Member Countries.*

TURKEY - INVESTMENTS

International Monetary Fund, 700 Nineteenth Street, NW, Washington, D.C. 20431 (202) 623-7000; *International Financial Statistics.*

Organisation for Economic Co-operation and Development (OECD), 2 rue Andre-Pascal, 75 Paris 16, France (Telephone Number in U.S. (202) 785-6323); *Economic Outlook, Financial Market Trends, Industrial Structure Statistics, The Iron and Steel Industry,* and *Textile Industry in OECD Countries.*

TURKEY - IRON ORE PRODUCTION AND CONSUMPTION - See TURKEY - MINING AND MINERAL PRODUCTS

TURKEY - LABOR FORCE

Facts on File, 460 Park Avenue South, New York, New York 10016 (800) 443-8323; *The New Book of World Rankings.*

Food and Agricultural Organization of the United Nations (FAO) Via delle Terme di Caracalla, 00100 Rome, Italy (Telephone Number in U.S. (202) 653-2400); *The State of Food and Agriculture.*

G.K. Hall and Company, 70 Lincoln Street, Boston, Massachusetts 02111 (617) 423-3990; *The World in Figures.*

Organisation for Economic Co-operation and Development (OECD), 2 rue Andre-Pascal, 75 Paris 16, France (Telephone Number in U.S. (202) 785-6323); *Economic Outlook, The Iron and Steel Industry, Maritime Transport, OECD Economic Surveys: Turkey, OECD Employment Outlook,* and *Textile Industry in OECD Countries.*

Times Books, 201 East 50th Street, New York, New York 10022 (212) 751-2600; *The Economist Book of Vital World Statistics.*

The World Bank, 1818 H Street, NW, Washington, D.C. 20433 (202) 477-1234; *World Tables.*

TURKEY - LABOR PRODUCTIVITY

International Labour Office, I.L.O. Publications, CH-1211, Geneva 22, Switzerland; *Yearbook of Labour Statistics.*

Organisation for Economic Co-operation and Development (OECD), 2 rue Andre-Pascal, 75 Paris 16, France (Telephone Number in U.S. (202) 785-6323); *Economic Outlook*, and *OECD Employment Outlook*.

TURKEY - LAND USE

Euromonitor Publications Limited, 87-88 Turnmill Street, London EC1M 5QU, England; *European Marketing Data and Statistics*.

Food and Agricultural Organization of the United Nations (FAO), Via delle Terme di Caracalla, 00100 Rome, Italy (Telephone Number in U.S. (202) 653-2400); *Production Yearbook*.

G.K. Hall and Company, 70 Lincoln Street, Boston, Massachusetts 02111 (617) 423-3990; *The World in Figures*.

TURKEY - LEAD AND LEAD ORE - See TURKEY - MINING AND MINERAL PRODUCTS

TURKEY - LEATHER AND FOOTWEAR EXPORTS AND IMPORTS

Organisation for Economic Co-operation and Development (OECD), 2 rue Andre-Pascal, 75 Paris 16, France (Telephone Number in U.S. (202) 785-6323); *The Footwear, Raw Hides and Skins, and Leather Industry in OECD Countries*.

TURKEY - LIBRARIES

Euromonitor Publications Limited, 87-88 Turnmill Street, London EC1M 5QU, England; *European Marketing Data and Statistics*.

Facts on File, 460 Park Avenue South, New York, New York 10016 (800) 443-8323; *The New Book of World Rankings*.

United Nations Educational, Scientific and Cultural Organization (UNESCO), 7 Place de Fontenoy, F-75700 Paris, France (Telephone Number in U.S. (212) 963-5981); *Statistical Yearbook*.

TURKEY - LIGNITE PRODUCTION - See TURKEY - MINING AND MINERAL PRODUCTS

TURKEY - LIVESTOCK AND POULTRY

Commodity Research Bureau, Incorporated, 75 Wall Street, New York, New York 10005 (212) 504-7754; *Commodity Year Book*.

Euromonitor Publications Limited, 87-88 Turnmill Street, London EC1M 5QU, England; *European Marketing Data and Statistics*.

Facts on File, 460 Park Avenue South, New York, New York 10016 (800) 443-8323; *The New Book of World Rankings*.

Food and Agricultural Organization of the United Nations (FAO), Via delle Terme di Caracalla, 00100 Rome, Italy (Telephone Number in U.S. (202) 653-2400); *Production Yearbook*, and *The State of Food and Agriculture*.

G.K. Hall and Company, 70 Lincoln Street, Boston, Massachusetts 02111 (617) 423-3990; *The World in Figures*.

Organisation for Economic Co-operation and Development (OECD), 2 rue Andre-Pascal, 75 Paris 16, France (Telephone Number in U.S. (202) 785-6323); *Economic Accounts for Agriculture*, and *Meat Balances in OECD Member Countries*.

Statistical Office of the United Nations, Publishing Service, New York, New York 10017 (800) 253-9646; *Statistical Yearbook*.

TURKEY - LIVING LEVELS

G.K. Hall and Company, 70 Lincoln Street, Boston, Massachusetts 02111 (617) 423-3990; *The World in Figures*.

Organisation for Economic Co-operation and Development (OECD), 2 rue Andre-Pascal, 75 Paris 16, France (Telephone Number in U.S. (202) 785-6323); *Economic Outlook*.

Times Books, 201 East 50th Street, New York, New York 10022 (212) 751-2600; *The Economist Book of Vital World Statistics*.

TURKEY - MAIL - NUMBER OF PIECES SENT OR RECEIVED

Statistical Office of the United Nations, Publishing Service, New York, New York 10017 (800) 253-9646; *Statistical Yearbook*.

TURKEY - MANGANESE ORE PRODUCTION AND CONSUMPTION - See TURKEY - MINING AND MINERAL PRODUCTS

TURKEY - MANUFACTURING

American Automobile Manufacturers Association, 1401 H Street, NW, Suite 900, Washington, D.C. 20005 (202) 326-5500; *World Motor Vehicle Data*.

G.K. Hall and Company, 70 Lincoln Street, Boston, Massachusetts 02111 (617) 423-3990; *The World in Figures*.

Organisation for Economic Co-operation and Development (OECD), 2 rue Andre-Pascal, 75 Paris 16, France (Telephone Number in U.S. (202) 785-6323); *Foreign Trade by Commodities, Industrial Structure Statistics*, and *OECD Economic Surveys: Turkey*.

Statistical Office of the United Nations, Publishing Service, New York, New York 10017 (800) 253-9646; *Statistical Yearbook*.

Times Books, 201 East 50th Street, New York, New York 10022 (212) 751-2600; *The Economist Book of Vital World Statistics*.

The World Bank, 1818 H Street, NW, Washington, D.C. 20433 (202) 477-1234; *World Tables*.

TURKEY - MARRIAGE RATES

Facts on File, 460 Park Avenue South, New York, New York 10016 (800) 443-8323; *The New Book of World Rankings*.

Statistical Office of the United Nations, Publishing Service, New York, New York 10017 (800) 253-9646; *Demographic Yearbook*.

TURKEY - MEAT PRODUCTION - See TURKEY - LIVESTOCK AND POULTRY

TURKEY - MERCHANT SHIPPING

G.K. Hall and Company, 70 Lincoln Street, Boston, Massachusetts 02111 (617) 423-3990; *The World in Figures*.

Lloyd's Register of Shipping, 17 Battery Place, New York, New York 10004 (212) 425-8050; *Register of Ships*.

Organisation for Economic Co-operation and Development (OECD), 2 rue Andre-Pascal, 75 Paris 16, France (Telephone Number in U.S. (202) 785-6323); *Maritime Transport*.

Statistical Office of the United Nations, Publishing Service, New York, New York 10017 (800) 253-9646; *Statistical Yearbook*.

Times Books, 201 East 50th Street, New York, New York 10022 (212) 751-2600; *The Economist Book of Vital World Statistics*.

U.S. Department of Transportation, Maritime Administration, 400 Seventh Street, SW, Washington, D.C. 20590 (202) 366-5807; *A Statistical Analysis of the World's Merchant Fleets*.

TURKEY - MERCURY PRODUCTION AND CONSUMPTION - See TURKEY - MINING AND MINERAL PRODUCTS

TURKEY - MILITARY

G.K. Hall and Company, 70 Lincoln Street, Boston, Massachusetts 02111 (617) 423-3990; *The World in Figures*.

The International Institute for Strategic Studies, 23 Tavistock Street, London WC2E 7NQ, England; *The Military Balance*.

U.S. Arms Control and Disarmament Agency, 320 Twenty-first Street, NW, Washington, D.C. 20451 (202) 647-8677; *World Military Expenditures and Arms Transfers*.

TURKEY - MILK PRODUCTION - See TURKEY - DAIRY PRODUCTS

TURKEY - MILLET PRODUCTION

Food and Agricultural Organization of the United Nations (FAO), Via delle Terme di Caracalla, 00100 Rome, Italy (Telephone Number in U.S. (202) 653-2400); *Production Yearbook*.

TURKEY - MINING AND MINERAL PRODUCTS

Commodity Research Bureau, Incorporated. 75 Wall Street, New York, New York 10005 (212) 504-7754; *Commodity Year Book*.

Facts on File, 460 Park Avenue South, New York, New York 10016 (800) 443-8323; *The New Book of World Rankings*.

G.K. Hall and Company, 70 Lincoln Street, Boston, Massachusetts 02111 (617) 423-3990; *The World in Figures*.

Organisation for Economic Co-operation and Development (OECD), 2 rue Andre-Pascal, 75 Paris 16, France (Telephone Number in U.S. (202) 785-6323); *Coal Information, Energy Statistics of OECD Countries, Foreign Trade by Commodities, Industrial Structure Statistics, The Iron and Steel Industry, Main Economic Indicators - Historical Statistics, The Non-Ferrous Metals Industry*, and *OECD Economic Surveys: Turkey*.

Penn Well Publishing Company, 1421 South Sheridan Road, P.O. Box 1260, Tulsa, Oklahoma 74101 (800) 752-9764; *International Energy Statistics Sourcebook*.

Statistical Office of the United Nations, Publishing Service, New York, New York 10017 (800) 253-9646; *Statistical Yearbook*.

TURKEY - MONEY AND CREDIT

Organisation for Economic Cooperation and Development (OECD), 2 rue Andre-Pascal, 75 Paris 16, France (Telephone Number in U.S. (202) 785-6323); *OECD Economic Surveys: Turkey*.

TURKEY - MONEY EXCHANGE RATE

International Monetary Fund, 700 Nineteenth Street, NW, Washington, D.C. 20431 (202) 623-7000; *International Financial Statistics*.

Organisation for Economic Co-operation and Development (OECD), 2 rue Andre-Pascal, 75 Paris 16, France (Telephone Number in U.S. (202) 785-6323); *Economic Outlook, Financial Market Trends*, and *Tourism Policy and International Tourism in OECD Member Countries*.

Statistical Office of the United Nations, Publishing Service, New York, New York 10017 (800) 253-9646; *Statistical Yearbook*.

TURKEY - MONEY RATES - MARKET

Organisation for Economic Co-operation and Development (OECD), 2 rue Andre-Pascal, 75 Paris 16, France (Telephone Number in U.S. (202) 785-6323); *Economic Outlook*, and *Financial Market Trends*.

TURKEY - MONEY RESERVES

Organisation for Economic Co-operation and Development (OECD), 2 rue Andre-Pascal, 75 Paris 16, France (Telephone Number in U.S. (202) 785-6323); *Economic Outlook*, and *Financial Market Trends*.

TURKEY - MONEY SUPPLY

G.K. Hall and Company, 70 Lincoln Street, Boston, Massachusetts 02111 (617) 423-3990; *The World in Figures*.

International Monetary Fund, 700 Nineteenth Street, NW, Washington, D.C. 20431 (202) 623-7000; *International Financial Statistics*.

Organisation for Economic Co-operation and Development (OECD), 2 rue Andre-Pascal, 75 Paris 16, France (Telephone Number in U.S. (202) 785-6323); *Economic Outlook*.

Statistical Office of the United Nations, Publishing Service, New York, New York 10017 (800) 253-9646; *Statistical Yearbook*.

The World Bank, 1818 H Street, NW, Washington, D.C. 20433 (202) 477-1234; *World Tables*.

TURKEY - MOTION PICTURES

United Nations Educational, Scientific and Cultural Organization (UNESCO), 7 Place de Fontenoy, F-75700 Paris, France (Telephone Number in U.S. (212) 963-5981); *Statistical Yearbook*.

TURKEY - MOTOR VEHICLE ASSEMBLY

Statistical Office of the United Nations, Publishing Service, New York, New York 10017 (800) 253-9646; *Statistical Yearbook*.

TURKEY - MOTOR VEHICLE PRODUCTION

American Automobile Manufacturers Association, 1401 H Street, NW, Suite 900, Washington, D.C. 20005 (202) 326-5500; *World Motor Vehicle Data*.

Organisation for Economic Co-operation and Development (OECD), 2 rue Andre-Pascal, 75 Paris 16, France (Telephone Number in U.S. (202) 785-6323); *Foreign Trade by Commodities*.

TURKEY - MOTOR VEHICLE TAXES - See TURKEY - TAXATION

TURKEY - MOTOR VEHICLES IN USE

American Automobile Manufacturers Association, 1401 H Street, NW, Suite 900, Washington, D.C. 20005 (202) 326-5500; *World Motor Vehicle Data*.

G.K. Hall and Company, 70 Lincoln Street, Boston, Massachusetts 02111 (617) 423-3990; *The World in Figures*.

International Road Federation, 525 School Street, SW, Washington, D.C. 20024 (202) 554-2106; *World Road Statistics*.

Statistical Office of the United Nations, Publishing Service, New York, New York 10017 (800) 253-9646; *Statistical Yearbook*.

Times Books, 201 East 50th Street, New York, New York 10022 (212) 751-2600; *The Economist Book of Vital World Statistics*.

TURKEY - MULES - See TURKEY - LIVESTOCK AND POULTRY

TURKEY - MUSEUMS

Euromonitor Publications Limited, 87-88 Turnmill Street, London EC1M 5QU, England; *European Marketing Data and Statistics*.

Facts on File, 460 Park Avenue South, New York, New York 10016 (800) 443-8323; *The New Book of World Rankings*.

United Nations Educational, Scientific and Cultural Organization (UNESCO), 7 Place de Fontenoy, F-75700 Paris, France (Telephone Number in U.S. (212) 963-5981); *Statistical Yearbook*.

TURKEY - NATALITY - See TURKEY - BIRTH RATES

TURKEY - NATIONAL ACCOUNTS

International Monetary Fund, 700 Nineteenth Street, NW, Washington, D.C. 20431 (202) 623-7000; *International Financial Statistics*.

Organisation for Economic Co-operation and Development (OECD), 2 rue Andre-Pascal, 75 Paris 16, France (Telephone Number in U.S. (202) 785-6323); *Economic Outlook*.

Statistical Office of the United Nations, Publishing Service, New York, New York 10017 (800) 253-9646; *National Accounts Statistics*, and *Statistical Yearbook*.

TURKEY - NATIONAL INCOME

Facts on File, 460 Park Avenue South, New York, New York 10016 (800) 443-8323; *The New Book of World Rankings*.

G.K. Hall and Company, 70 Lincoln Street, Boston, Massachusetts 02111 (617) 423-3990; *The World in Figures*.

Organisation for Economic Co-operation and Development (OECD), 2 rue Andre-Pascal, 75 Paris 16, France (Telephone Number in U.S. (202) 785-6323); *Economic Outlook*.

Statistical Office of the United Nations, Publishing Service, New York, New York 10017 (800) 253-9646; *Statistical Yearbook*.

TURKEY - NATIONAL PRODUCT

Facts on File, 460 Park Avenue South, New York, New York 10016 (800) 443-8323; *The New Book of World Rankings*.

Organisation for Economic Co-operation and Development (OECD), 2 rue Andre-Pascal, 75 Paris 16, France (Telephone Number in U.S. (202) 785-6323); *Economic Outlook*.

Statistical Office of the United Nations, Publishing Service, New York, New York 10017 (800) 253-9646; *Statistical Yearbook*.

TURKEY - NATURAL GAS PRODUCTION - See TURKEY - MINING AND MINERAL PRODUCTS

TURKEY - NEWSPAPER PRODUCTION - See TURKEY - FORESTRY AND FOREST PRODUCTS

TURKEY - NEWSPRINT - See TURKEY - FORESTRY AND FOREST PRODUCTS

TURKEY - NICKEL PRODUCTION AND CONSUMPTION - See TURKEY - MINING AND MINERAL PRODUCTS

TURKEY - NITRIC ACID PRODUCTION - See TURKEY - MINING AND MINERAL PRODUCTS

TURKEY - OATS PRODUCTION - See - TURKEY - CROPS

TURKEY - OCCUPATIONS - See TURKEY - LABOR FORCE

TURKEY - OIL PRODUCING CROPS

Organisation for Economic Co-operation and Development (OECD), 2 rue Andre-Pascal, 75 Paris 16, France (Telephone Number in U.S. (202) 785-6323); *Foreign Trade by Commodities*.

TURKEY - ONION PRODUCTION - See - TURKEY - CROPS

TURKEY - ORANGES PRODUCTION - See - TURKEY - CROPS

TURKEY - PAPER - See TURKEY - FORESTRY AND FOREST PRODUCTS

TURKEY - PATENTS

Statistical Office of the United Nations, Publishing Service, New York, New York 10017 (800) 253-9646; *Statistical Yearbook*.

World Intellectual Property Organization, 34 Chemin des Colombettes, CH-1211 Geneva 20. Switzerland; *Industrial Property Statistics*.

TURKEY - PEANUT PRODUCTION - See - TURKEY - CROPS

TURKEY - PERIODICALS

United Nations Educational, Scientific and Cultural Organization (UNESCO), 7 Place de Fontenoy, F-75700 Paris, France (Telephone Number in U.S. (212) 963-5981); *Statistical Yearbook*.

TURKEY - PESTICIDE USE

Food and Agricultural Organization of the United Nations (FAO) Via delle Terme di Caracalla, 00100 Rome, Italy (Telephone Number in U.S. (202) 653-2400); *The State of Food and Agriculture*.

TURKEY - PETROLEUM INDUSTRY

Euromonitor Publications Limited, 87-88 Turnmill Street, London EC1M 5QU, England; *European Marketing Data and Statistics*.

Facts on File, 460 Park Avenue South, New York, New York 10016 (800) 443-8323; *The New Book of World Rankings*.

Food and Agricultural Organization of the United Nations (FAO) Via delle Terme di Caracalla, 00100 Rome, Italy (Telephone Number in U.S. (202) 653-2400); *The State of Food and Agriculture*.

G.K. Hall and Company, 70 Lincoln Street, Boston, Massachusetts 02111 (617) 423-3990; *The World in Figures*.

Organisation for Economic Co-operation and Development (OECD), 2 rue Andre-Pascal, 75 Paris 16, France (Telephone Number in U.S. (202) 785-6323); *Energy Statistics of OECD Countries, Foreign Trade by Commodities*, and *Oil and Gas Information*.

Penn Well Publishing Company, 1421 South Sheridan Road, P.O. Box 1260, Tulsa, Oklahoma 74101 (800) 752-9764; *International Energy Statistics Sourcebook*.

Statistical Office of the United Nations, Publishing Service, New York, New York 10017 (800) 253-9646; *Statistical Yearbook*.

TURKEY - PIG-IRON AND FERRO-ALLOY PRODUCTION - See TURKEY - MINING AND MINERAL PRODUCTS

TURKEY - PIGS - See TURKEY - LIVESTOCK AND POULTRY

TURKEY - PIPELINES FOR OIL AND PETROLEUM PRODUCTS

Statistical Office of the United Nations, Publishing Service, New York, New York 10017 (800) 253-9646; *Annual Bulletin of Transport Statistics for Europe*.

TURKEY - PISTACHIO PRODUCTION - See - TURKEY - CROPS

TURKEY - PLASTIC AND RESIN PRODUCTION

Organisation for Economic Co-operation and Development (OECD), 2 rue Andre-Pascal, 75 Paris 16, France (Telephone Number in U.S. (202) 785-6323); *Foreign Trade by Commodities*.

TURKEY - POPULATION

The Economist Intelligence Unit 111 West 57th Street, New York, New York 10019 (800) 938-4685; *The World Market Atlas*.

Euromonitor Publications Limited, 87-88 Turnmill Street, London EC1M 5QU, England; *European Marketing Data and Statistics*.

Facts on File, 460 Park Avenue South, New York, New York 10016 (800) 443-8323; *The New Book of World Rankings*.

Food and Agricultural Organization of the United Nations (FAO), Via delle Terme di Caracalla, 00100 Rome, Italy (Telephone Number in U.S. (202) 653-2400); *Production Yearbook*.

G.K. Hall and Company, 70 Lincoln Street, Boston, Massachusetts 02111 (617) 423-3990; *The World in Figures*.

International Labour Office, I.L.O. Publications, CH-1211, Geneva 22, Switzerland; *Yearbook of Labour Statistics*.

Statistical Office of the United Nations, Publishing Service, New York, New York 10017 (800) 253-9646; *Demographic Yearbook*, and *Statistical Yearbook*.

Times Books, 201 East 50th Street, New York, New York 10022 (212) 751-2600; *The Economist Book of Vital World Statistics*.

United Nations Educational, Scientific and Cultural Organization (UNESCO), 7 Place de Fontenoy, F-75700 Paris, France (Telephone Number in U.S. (212) 963-5981); *Statistical Yearbook*.

U.S. Arms Control and Disarmament Agency, 320 Twenty-first Street, NW, Washington, D.C. 20451 (202) 647-8677; *World Military Expenditures and Arms Transfers*.

World Health Organization, Office of Publications, Avenue Appia CH-1211 Geneva 27, Switzerland (Telephone Number in U.S. (518) 436-9686); *World Health Statistics Annual*.

TURKEY - POST OFFICES

Facts on File, 460 Park Avenue South, New York, New York 10016 (800) 443-8323; *The New Book of World Rankings*.

TURKEY - POTATO PRODUCTION - See - TURKEY - CROPS

TURKEY - POWER PRODUCTION INDUSTRY

Statistical Office of the United Nations, Publishing Service, New York, New York 10017 (800) 253-9646; *Statistical Yearbook*.

TURKEY - PRICES

Facts on File, 460 Park Avenue South, New York, New York 10016 (800) 443-8323; *The New Book of World Rankings*.

Food and Agricultural Organization of the United Nations (FAO), Via delle Terme di Caracalla, 00100 Rome, Italy (Telephone Number in U.S. (202) 653-2400); *Production Yearbook*, and *The State of Food and Agriculture*.

G.K. Hall and Company, 70 Lincoln Street, Boston, Massachusetts 02111 (617) 423-3990; *The World in Figures*.

International Labour Office, I.L.O. Publications, CH-1211, Geneva 22, Switzerland; *Yearbook of Labour Statistics*.

International Monetary Fund, 700 Nineteenth Street, NW, Washington, D.C. 20431 (202) 623-7000; *International Financial Statistics*.

Organisation for Economic Co-operation and Development (OECD), 2 rue Andre-Pascal, 75 Paris 16, France (Telephone Number in U.S. (202) 785-6323); *Economic Outlook, The Footwear, Raw Hides and Skins, and Leather Industry in OECD Countries, The Iron and Steel Industry, Main Economic Indicators - Historical Statistics*, and *The Pulp and Paper Industry*.

TURKEY - PRINTING AND WRITING PAPER - See TURKEY - FORESTRY AND FOREST PRODUCTS

TURKEY - PRODUCTION

American Automobile Manufacturers Association, 1401 H Street, NW, Suite 900, Washington, D.C. 20005 (202) 326-5500; *World Motor Vehicle Data*.

Facts on File, 460 Park Avenue South, New York, New York 10016 (800) 443-8323; *The New Book of World Rankings*.

G.K. Hall and Company, 70 Lincoln Street, Boston, Massachusetts 02111 (617) 423-3990; *The World in Figures*.

Organisation for Economic Co-operation and Development (OECD), 2 rue Andre-Pascal, 75 Paris 16, France (Telephone Number in U.S. (202) 785-6323); *Economic Outlook, The Footwear, Raw Hides and Skins, and Leather Industry in OECD Countries, Industrial Structure Statistics, The Iron and Steel Industry, Meat Balances in OECD Member Countries, Milk, Milk Products, and Egg Balances in OECD Member Countries, The Non-Ferrous Metals Industry, The Pulp and Paper Industry*, and *Textile Industry in OECD Countries*.

TURKEY - PRODUCTIVITY

Organisation for Economic Co-operation and Development (OECD), 2 rue Andre-Pascal, 75 Paris 16, France (Telephone Number in U.S.

(202) 785-6323); *Economic Outlook.*

TURKEY - PROPERTY TAXES - See TURKEY - TAXATION

TURKEY - PUBLIC CONSUMPTION FUND

Organisation for Economic Co-operation and Development (OECD), 2 rue Andre-Pascal, 75 Paris 16, France (Telephone Number in U.S. (202) 785-6323); *Revenue Statistics of OECD Member Countries.*

TURKEY - PUBLIC EXPENDITURES

Organisation for Economic Co-operation and Development (OECD), 2 rue Andre-Pascal, 75 Paris 16, France (Telephone Number in U.S. (202) 785-6323); *Revenue Statistics of OECD Member Countries.*

TURKEY - PUBLIC FINANCE

Facts on File, 460 Park Avenue South, New York, New York 10016 (800) 443-8323; *The New Book of World Rankings.*

Organisation for Economic Co-operation and Development (OECD), 2 rue Andre-Pascal, 75 Paris 16, France (Telephone Number in U.S. (202) 785-6323); *Revenue Statistics of OECD Member Countries.*

TURKEY - RADIO BROADCASTING - See TURKEY - BROADCASTING

TURKEY - RADIO RECEIVER PRODUCTION

Statistical Office of the United Nations, Publishing Service, New York, New York 10017 (800) 253-9646; *Statistical Yearbook.*

TURKEY - RAILWAYS

Euromonitor Publications Limited, 87-88 Turnmill Street, London EC1M 5QU, England; *European Marketing Data and Statistics.*

G.K. Hall and Company, 70 Lincoln Street, Boston, Massachusetts 02111 (617) 423-3990; *The World in Figures.*

Jane's Information Group, Sentinel House, 163 Brighton Road, Coulsdon, Surrey CR5 2NH, England (Telephone Number in U.S. (703) 683-3700); *Jane's World Railways.*

Statistical Office of the United Nations, Publishing Service, New York, New York 10017 (800) 253-9646; *Annual Bulletin of Transport Statistics for Europe,* and *Statistical Yearbook.*

TURKEY - RAPESEED PRODUCTION - See - TURKEY - CROPS

TURKEY - RELIGION

Facts on File, 460 Park Avenue South, New York, New York 10016 (800) 443-8323; *The New Book of World Rankings.*

TURKEY - RENT PRICES

International Labour Office, I.L.O. Publications, CH-1211, Geneva 22, Switzerland; *Yearbook of Labour Statistics.*

TURKEY - RETAIL TRADE

G.K. Hall and Company, 70 Lincoln Street, Boston, Massachusetts 02111 (617) 423-3990; *The World in Figures.*

Statistical Office of the United Nations, Publishing Service, New York, New York 10017 (800) 253-9646; *Statistical Yearbook.*

TURKEY - RICE PRODUCTION - See - TURKEY - CROPS

TURKEY - ROOT AND TUBER PRODUCTION

Food and Agricultural Organization of the United Nations (FAO), Via delle Terme di Caracalla, 00100 Rome, Italy (Telephone Number in U.S. (202) 653-2400); *Production Yearbook.*

TURKEY - ROUNDWOOD PRODUCTION - See TURKEY - FORESTRY AND FOREST PRODUCTS

TURKEY - RUBBER PRODUCTION AND CONSUMPTION

Facts on File, 460 Park Avenue South, New York, New York 10016 (800) 443-8323; *The New Book of World Rankings.*

Organisation for Economic Co-operation and Development (OECD), 2 rue Andre-Pascal, 75 Paris 16, France (Telephone Number in U.S. (202) 785-6323); *Foreign Trade by Commodities.*

Statistical Office of the United Nations, Publishing Service, New York, New York 10017 (800) 253-9646; *Statistical Yearbook.*

TURKEY - RYE PRODUCTION - See - TURKEY - CROPS

TURKEY - SAFFLOWER SEED PRODUCTION - See - TURKEY - CROPS

TURKEY - SALT PRODUCTION - See TURKEY - MINING AND MINERAL PRODUCTS

TURKEY - SAWNWOOD PRODUCTION - See TURKEY - FORESTRY AND FOREST PRODUCTS

TURKEY - SCIENCE AND TECHNOLOGY - EXPENDITURE FOR RESEARCH

Statistical Office of the United Nations, Publishing Service, New York, New York 10017 (800) 253-9646; *Statistical Yearbook.*

TURKEY - SCIENTISTS AND TECHNICIANS

Statistical Office of the United Nations, Publishing Service, New York, New York 10017 (800) 253-9646; *Statistical Yearbook.*

TURKEY - SENIOR CITIZENS

Facts on File, 460 Park Avenue South, New York, New York 10016 (800) 443-8323; *The New Book of World Rankings.*

TURKEY - SERVICE INDUSTRY EMPLOYMENT - MALE AND FEMALE - See TURKEY - EMPLOYMENT

TURKEY - SESAME SEED PRODUCTION

Food and Agricultural Organization of the United Nations (FAO), Via delle Terme di Caracalla, 00100 Rome, Italy (Telephone Number in U.S. (202) 653-2400); *Production Yearbook.*

TURKEY - SHEEP - See TURKEY - LIVESTOCK AND POULTRY

TURKEY - SILVER PRODUCTION AND CONSUMPTION - See TURKEY - MINING AND MINERAL PRODUCTS

TURKEY - SOCIAL DATA

Facts on File, 460 Park Avenue South, New York, New York 10016 (800) 443-8323; *The New Book of World Rankings.*

G.K. Hall and Company, 70 Lincoln Street, Boston, Massachusetts 02111 (617) 423-3990; *The World in Figures.*

TURKEY - SOCIAL SECURITY

International Monetary Fund, 700 Nineteenth Street, NW, Washington, D.C. 20431 (202) 623-7000; *Government Finance Statistics Yearbook.*

Organisation for Economic Co-operation and Development (OECD), 2 rue Andre-Pascal, 75 Paris 16, France (Telephone Number in U.S. (202) 785-6323); *Revenue Statistics of OECD Member Countries.*

TURKEY - SOCIOECONOMIC DATA

Organisation for Economic Co-operation and Development (OECD), 2 rue Andre-Pascal, 75 Paris 16, France (Telephone Number in U.S. (202) 785-6323); *Economic Outlook.*

TURKEY - SOYBEAN PRODUCTION - See TURKEY - CROPS

TURKEY - STAMP TAXES AND DUTIES - See TURKEY - TAXATION

TURKEY - STEEL - See TURKEY - MINING AND MINERAL PRODUCTS

TURKEY - STOCKS - COMMODITY - MARKET PRICE - INDEX

Food and Agricultural Organization of the United Nations (FAO) Via delle Terme di Caracalla, 00100 Rome, Italy (Telephone Number in U.S. (202) 653-2400); *The State of Food and Agriculture.*

TURKEY - SUGAR - See - TURKEY - CROPS

TURKEY - SULPHUR AND SULPHURIC ACID PRODUCTION - See TURKEY - MINING AND MINERAL PRODUCTS

TURKEY - TAXATION

G.K. Hall and Company, 70 Lincoln Street, Boston, Massachusetts 02111 (617) 423-3990; *The World in Figures.*

International Monetary Fund, 700 Nineteenth Street, NW, Washington, D.C. 20431 (202) 623-7000; *Government Finance Statistics Yearbook.*

International Road Federation, 525 School Street, SW, Washington, D.C. 20024 (202) 554-2106; *World Road Statistics.*

Organisation for Economic Co-operation and Development (OECD), 2 rue Andre-Pascal, 75 Paris 16, France (Telephone Number in U.S. (202) 785-6323); *Revenue Statistics of OECD Member Countries.*

The World Bank, 1818 H Street, NW, Washington, D.C. 20433 (202) 477-1234; *World Tables.*

TURKEY - TEA - See - TURKEY - CROPS

TURKEY - TELEGRAPH SERVICE

Statistical Office of the United Nations, Publishing Service, New York, New York 10017 (800) 253-9646; *Statistical Yearbook.*

TURKEY - TELEPHONES IN USE

American Telephone and Telegraph Company, 26 Parsippany Road, Whippany, New Jersey 07981 (800) 338-4038; *The World's Telephones.*

G.K. Hall and Company, 70 Lincoln Street, Boston, Massachusetts 02111 (617) 423-3990; *The World in Figures.*

Statistical Office of the United Nations, Publishing Service, New York, New York 10017 (800) 253-9646; *Statistical Yearbook.*

TURKEY - TELEVISION BROADCASTING - See TURKEY - BROADCASTING

TURKEY - TELEVISION RECEIVER PRODUCTION

Statistical Office of the United Nations, Publishing Service, New York, New York 10017 (800) 253-9646; *Statistical Yearbook.*

TURKEY - TEXTILE INDUSTRY

Food and Agricultural Organization of the United Nations (FAO), Via delle Terme di Caracalla, 00100 Rome, Italy (Telephone Number in U.S. (202) 653-2400); *Production Yearbook.*

G.K. Hall and Company, 70 Lincoln Street, Boston, Massachusetts 02111 (617) 423-3990; *The World in Figures.*

Organisation for Economic Co-operation and Development (OECD), 2 rue Andre-Pascal, 75 Paris 16, France (Telephone Number in U.S. (202) 785-6323); *Foreign Trade by Commodities, Industrial Structure Statistics,* and *Textile Industry in OECD Countries.*

Statistical Office of the United Nations, Publishing Service, New York, New York 10017 (800) 253-9646; *Statistical Yearbook.*

TURKEY - THEATRE

United Nations Educational, Scientific and Cultural Organization (UNESCO), 7 Place de Fontenoy, F-75700 Paris, France (Telephone Number in U.S. (212) 963-5981); *Statistical Yearbook.*

TURKEY - TIN - See TURKEY - MINING AND MINERAL PRODUCTS

TURKEY - TIRE (MOTOR VEHICLE) PRODUCTION

Statistical Office of the United Nations, Publishing Service, New York, New York 10017 (800) 253-9646; *Statistical Yearbook.*

TURKEY - TOBACCO PRODUCTION

Commodity Research Bureau, Incorporated, 75 Wall Street, New York, New York 10005 (212) 504-7754; *Commodity Year Book.*

Euromonitor Publications Limited, 87-88 Turnmill Street, London EC1M 5QU, England; *European Marketing Data and Statistics.*

Facts on File, 460 Park Avenue South, New York, New York 10016 (800) 443-8323; *The New Book of World Rankings.*

International Monetary Fund, 700 Nineteenth Street, NW, Washington, D.C. 20431 (202) 623-7000; *International Financial Statistics.*

Organisation for Economic Co-operation and Development (OECD), 2 rue Andre-Pascal, 75 Paris 16, France (Telephone Number in U.S. (202) 785-6323); *Foreign Trade by Commodities,* and *Industrial Structure Statistics.*

Statistical Office of the United Nations, Publishing Service, New York, New York 10017 (800) 253-9646; *Statistical Yearbook.*

TURKEY - TOURISM

Euromonitor Publications Limited, 87-88 Turnmill Street, London EC1M 5QU, England; *European Marketing Data and Statistics.*

Facts on File, 460 Park Avenue South, New York, New York 10016 (800) 443-8323; *The New Book of World Rankings*.

G.K. Hall and Company, 70 Lincoln Street, Boston, Massachusetts 02111 (617) 423-3990; *The World in Figures*.

Organisation for Economic Co-operation and Development (OECD), 2 rue Andre-Pascal, 75 Paris 16, France (Telephone Number in U.S. (202) 785-6323); *Tourism Policy and International Tourism in OECD Member Countries*.

Statistical Office of the United Nations, Publishing Service, New York, New York 10017 (800) 253-9646; *Statistical Yearbook*.

Times Books, 201 East 50th Street, New York, New York 10022 (212) 751-2600; *The Economist Book of Vital World Statistics*.

World Tourism Organization, Calle Capitan Haya 42, E-28020 Madrid, Spain; *Yearbook of Tourism Statistics*.

TURKEY - TRACTORS IN USE

Statistical Office of the United Nations, Publishing Service, New York, New York 10017 (800) 253-9646; *Statistical Yearbook*.

TURKEY - TRADE - See TURKEY - FOREIGN TRADE

TURKEY - TRADEMARKS AND SERVICE MARKS

Statistical Office of the United Nations, Publishing Service, New York, New York 10017 (800) 253-9646; *Statistical Yearbook*.

World Intellectual Property Organization, 34 Chemin des Colombettes, CH-1211 Geneva 20. Switzerland; *Industrial Property Statistics*.

TURKEY - TRANSPORTATION AND COMMUNICATIONS

Facts on File, 460 Park Avenue South, New York, New York 10016 (800) 443-8323; *The New Book of World Rankings*.

G.K. Hall and Company, 70 Lincoln Street, Boston, Massachusetts 02111 (617) 423-3990; *The World in Figures*.

TURKEY - TURKEYS - See TURKEY - LIVESTOCK AND POULTRY

TURKEY - UNEMPLOYMENT

Euromonitor Publications Limited, 87-88 Turnmill Street, London EC1M 5QU, England; *European Marketing Data and Statistics*.

International Labour Office, I.L.O. Publications, CH-1211, Geneva 22, Switzerland; *Yearbook of Labour Statistics*.

Organisation for Economic Co-operation and Development (OECD), 2 rue Andre-Pascal, 75 Paris 16, France (Telephone Number in U.S. (202) 785-6323); *Economic Outlook*, *OECD Economic Surveys: Turkey*, and *OECD Employment Outlook*.

Statistical Office of the United Nations, Publishing Service, New York, New York 10017 (800) 253-9646; *Statistical Yearbook*.

TURKEY - URANIUM PRODUCTION AND CONSUMPTION - See TURKEY - MINING AND MINERAL PRODUCTS

TURKEY - VITAL STATISTICS

G.K. Hall and Company, 70 Lincoln Street, Boston, Massachusetts 02111 (617) 423-3990; *The World in Figures*.

World Health Organization, Office of Publications, Avenue Appia, CH-1211 Geneva 27, Switzerland (Telephone Number in U.S. (518) 436-9686); *World Health Statistics Annual*.

TURKEY - WAGES

Euromonitor Publications Limited, 87-88 Turnmill Street, London EC1M 5QU, England; *European Marketing Data and Statistics*.

G.K. Hall and Company, 70 Lincoln Street, Boston, Massachusetts 02111 (617) 423-3990; *The World in Figures*.

International Labour Office, I.L.O. Publications, CH-1211, Geneva 22, Switzerland; *Yearbook of Labour Statistics*.

Organisation for Economic Co-operation and Development (OECD), 2 rue Andre-Pascal, 75 Paris 16, France (Telephone Number in U.S. (202) 785-6323); *Economic Outlook*, and *Industrial Structure Statistics*.

Statistical Office of the United Nations, Publishing Service, New York, New York 10017 (800) 253-9646; *Statistical Yearbook*.

TURKEY - WALNUT PRODUCTION - See - TURKEY - CROPS

TURKEY - WATERMELON PRODUCTION - See - TURKEY - CROPS

TURKEY - WATERWAYS IN USE

Organisation for Economic Co-operation and Development (OECD), 2 rue Andre-Pascal, 75 Paris 16, France (Telephone Number in U.S. (202) 785-6323); *Maritime Transport*.

TURKEY - WEATHER

Facts on File, 460 Park Avenue South, New York, New York 10016 (800) 443-8323; *The New Book of World Rankings*.

G.K. Hall and Company, 70 Lincoln Street, Boston, Massachusetts 02111 (617) 423-3990; *The World in Figures*.

TURKEY - WELFARE

International Monetary Fund, 700 Nineteenth Street, NW, Washington, D.C. 20431 (202) 623-7000; *Government Finance Statistics Yearbook*.

TURKEY - WHEAT PRODUCTION AND PRICES - See - TURKEY - CROPS

TURKEY - WHOLESALE PRICES

International Monetary Fund, 700 Nineteenth Street, NW, Washington, D.C. 20431 (202) 623-7000; *International Financial Statistics*.

Statistical Office of the United Nations, Publishing Service, New York, New York 10017 (800) 253-9646; *Statistical Yearbook*.

TURKEY - WHOLESALE TRADE

Statistical Office of the United Nations, Publishing Service, New York, New York 10017 (800) 253-9646; *Statistical Yearbook*.

TURKEY - WINE PRODUCTION

Facts on File, 460 Park Avenue South, New York, New York 10016 (800) 443-8323; *The New Book of World Rankings*.

Statistical Office of the United Nations, Publishing Service, New York, New York 10017 (800) 253-9646; *Statistical Yearbook.*

TURKEY - WOOD AND WOOD PULP - See TURKEY - FORESTRY AND FOREST PRODUCTS

TURKEY - WOOL - INDUSTRIAL CONSUMPTION

Organisation for Economic Co-operation and Development (OECD), 2 rue Andre-Pascal, 75 Paris 16, France (Telephone Number in U.S. (202) 785-6323); *Textile Industry in OECD Countries.*

Statistical Office of the United Nations, Publishing Service, New York, New York 10017 (800) 253-9646; *Statistical Yearbook.*

TURKEY - WOOL PRODUCTION

Facts on File, 460 Park Avenue South, New York, New York 10016 (800) 443-8323; *The New Book of World Rankings.*

Organisation for Economic Co-operation and Development (OECD), 2 rue Andre-Pascal, 75 Paris 16, France (Telephone Number in U.S. (202) 785-6323); *Economic Accounts for Agriculture,* and *Textile Industry in OECD Countries.*

Statistical Office of the United Nations, Publishing Service, New York, New York 10017 (800) 253-9646; *Statistical Yearbook.*

TURKEY - YARN PRODUCTION

Organisation for Economic Co-operation and Development (OECD), 2 rue Andre-Pascal, 75 Paris 16, France (Telephone Number in U.S. (202) 785-6323); *Foreign Trade by Commodities,* and *Textile Industry in OECD Countries.*

Statistical Office of the United Nations, Publishing Service, New York, New York 10017 (800) 253-9646; *Statistical Yearbook.*

TURKEY - ZINC ORE PRODUCTION AND CONSUMPTION - See TURKEY - MINING AND MINERAL PRODUCTS

TURKEY - ZINC PRODUCTION AND CONSUMPTION - See TURKEY - MINING AND MINERAL PRODUCTS

TURKEYS

U.S. Department of Agriculture, Economic Research Service, Fourteenth Street and Independence Avenue, SW, Washington, D.C. 20005-4789 (202) 219-1504; *Economic Indicators of the Farm Sector: National Financial Summary.*

U.S. Department of Agriculture, National Agricultural Statistics Service, Fourteenth Street and Independence Avenue, SW, Washington, D.C. 20250 (202) 219-1504; *Poultry-Production and Value,* and *Turkeys.*

TURKMENISTAN - See also UNION OF SOVIET SOCIALIST REPUBLICS

Turkmenistan - National Statistical Office

State Committee of Republic of Turkmenistan on Statistics, 72 Makhtumkuli Avenue, Ashkhabad 744000, Turkmenistan.

TURKMENISTAN - AGRICULTURE

Business International Moscow, 23 Profsoyuznaya Ulitsa, 117859, Moscow (Telephone Number in U.S. (800) 938-4685); *The CIS Market Atlas.*

Encyclopedia Britannica, Incorporated, 310 South Michigan Avenue, Chicago, Illinois 60604 (312) 347-7000; *Britannica World Data.*

The World Bank, 1818 H Street, NW, Washington, D.C. 20433 (202) 477-1234; *Statistical Handbook: States of the Former USSR.*

TURKMENISTAN - AIRLINE SERVICE

Business International Moscow, 23 Profsoyuznaya Ulitsa, 117859, Moscow (Telephone Number in U.S. (800) 938-4685); *The CIS Market Atlas.*

Encyclopedia Britannica, Incorporated, 310 South Michigan Avenue, Chicago, Illinois 60604 (312) 347-7000; *Britannica World Data.*

TURKMENISTAN - AREA AND DENSITY OF POPULATION

Business International Moscow, 23 Profsoyuznaya Ulitsa, 117859, Moscow (Telephone Number in U.S. (800) 938-4685); *The CIS Market Atlas.*

TURKMENISTAN - BANKING

Business International Moscow, 23 Profsoyuznaya Ulitsa, 117859, Moscow (Telephone Number in U.S. (800) 938-4685); *The CIS Market Atlas.*

TURKMENISTAN - BIRTH RATES

Business International Moscow, 23 Profsoyuznaya Ulitsa, 117859, Moscow (Telephone Number in U.S. (800) 938-4685); *The CIS Market Atlas.*

Encyclopedia Britannica, Incorporated, 310 South Michigan Avenue, Chicago, Illinois 60604 (312) 347-7000; *Britannica World Data.*

TURKMENISTAN - BUDGET

Business International Moscow, 23 Profsoyuznaya Ulitsa, 117859, Moscow (Telephone Number in U.S. (800) 938-4685); *The CIS Market Atlas.*

TURKMENISTAN - CAPITAL INVESTMENTS

The World Bank, 1818 H Street, NW, Washington, D.C. 20433 (202) 477-1234; *Statistical Handbook: States of the Former USSR.*

TURKMENISTAN - CATTLE - See TURKMENISTAN - LIVESTOCK AND POULTRY

TURKMENISTAN - CHEMICALS

Business International Moscow, 23 Profsoyuznaya Ulitsa, 117859, Moscow (Telephone Number in U.S. (800) 938-4685); *The CIS Market Atlas.*

TURKMENISTAN - COAL PRODUCTION AND CONSUMPTION - See TURKMENISTAN - MINING AND MINERAL PRODUCTS

TURKMENISTAN - COMMUNICATIONS

Business International Moscow, 23 Profsoyuznaya Ulitsa, 117859, Moscow (Telephone Number in U.S. (800) 938-4685); *The CIS Market Atlas.*

TURKMENISTAN - CONSTRUCTION INDUSTRY

Business International Moscow, 23 Profsoyuznaya Ulitsa, 117859, Moscow (Telephone Number in U.S. (800) 938-4685); *The CIS Market Atlas.*

Market Atlas.

Encyclopedia Britannica, Incorporated, 310 South Michigan Avenue, Chicago, Illinois 60604 (312) 347-7000; *Britannica World Data.*

TURKMENISTAN - CONSUMER PRODUCTS

Business International Moscow, 23 Profsoyuznaya Ulitsa, 117859, Moscow (Telephone Number in U.S. (800) 938-4685); *The CIS Market Atlas.*

TURKMENISTAN - CONSUMPTION

Business International Moscow, 23 Profsoyuznaya Ulitsa, 117859, Moscow (Telephone Number in U.S. (800) 938-4685); *The CIS Market Atlas.*

The World Bank, 1818 H Street, NW, Washington, D.C. 20433 (202) 477-1234; *Statistical Handbook: States of the Former USSR.*

TURKMENISTAN - COTTON PRODUCTION AND CONSUMPTION - See TURKMENISTAN - CROPS

TURKMENISTAN - CROPS

Business International Moscow, 23 Profsoyuznaya Ulitsa, 117859, Moscow (Telephone Number in U.S. (800) 938-4685); *The CIS Market Atlas.*

The World Bank, 1818 H Street, NW, Washington, D.C. 20433 (202) 477-1234; *Statistical Handbook: States of the Former USSR.*

TURKMENISTAN - DEATH RATES

Business International Moscow, 23 Profsoyuznaya Ulitsa, 117859, Moscow (Telephone Number in U.S. (800) 938-4685); *The CIS Market Atlas.*

TURKMENISTAN - DEMOGRAPHY

Business International Moscow, 23 Profsoyuznaya Ulitsa, 117859, Moscow (Telephone Number in U.S. (800) 938-4685); *The CIS Market Atlas.*

Encyclopedia Britannica, Incorporated, 310 South Michigan Avenue, Chicago, Illinois 60604 (312) 347-7000; *Britannica World Data.*

The World Bank, 1818 H Street, NW, Washington, D.C. 20433 (202) 477-1234; *Statistical Handbook: States of the Former USSR.*

TURKMENISTAN - DISEASES

Business International Moscow, 23 Profsoyuznaya Ulitsa, 117859, Moscow (Telephone Number in U.S. (800) 938-4685); *The CIS Market Atlas.*

TURKMENISTAN - DIVORCE RATES

Encyclopedia Britannica, Incorporated, 310 South Michigan Avenue, Chicago, Illinois 60604 (312) 347-7000; *Britannica World Data.*

TURKMENISTAN - DOMESTIC INVESTMENT

Business International Moscow, 23 Profsoyuznaya Ulitsa, 117859, Moscow (Telephone Number in U.S. (800) 938-4685); *The CIS Market Atlas.*

TURKMENISTAN - ECONOMY

Business International Moscow, 23 Profsoyuznaya Ulitsa, 117859, Moscow (Telephone Number in U.S. (800) 938-4685); *The CIS Market Atlas.*

Encyclopedia Britannica, Incorporated, 310 South Michigan Avenue, Chicago, Illinois 60604 (312) 347-7000; *Britannica World Data.*

TURKMENISTAN - EDUCATION

Business International Moscow, 23 Profsoyuznaya Ulitsa, 117859, Moscow (Telephone Number in U.S. (800) 938-4685); *The CIS Market Atlas.*

Encyclopedia Britannica, Incorporated, 310 South Michigan Avenue, Chicago, Illinois 60604 (312) 347-7000; *Britannica World Data.*

TURKMENISTAN - ELECTRICITY

Business International Moscow, 23 Profsoyuznaya Ulitsa, 117859, Moscow (Telephone Number in U.S. (800) 938-4685); *The CIS Market Atlas.*

The World Bank, 1818 H Street, NW, Washington, D.C. 20433 (202) 477-1234; *Statistical Handbook: States of the Former USSR.*

TURKMENISTAN - EMPLOYMENT

The World Bank, 1818 H Street, NW, Washington, D.C. 20433 (202) 477-1234; *Statistical Handbook: States of the Former USSR.*

TURKMENISTAN - ENERGY

Business International Moscow, 23 Profsoyuznaya Ulitsa, 117859, Moscow (Telephone Number in U.S. (800) 938-4685); *The CIS Market Atlas.*

Encyclopedia Britannica, Incorporated, 310 South Michigan Avenue, Chicago, Illinois 60604 (312) 347-7000; *Britannica World Data.*

The World Bank, 1818 H Street, NW, Washington, D.C. 20433 (202) 477-1234; *Statistical Handbook: States of the Former USSR.*

TURKMENISTAN - ENVIRONMENT

Business International Moscow, 23 Profsoyuznaya Ulitsa, 117859, Moscow (Telephone Number in U.S. (800) 938-4685); *The CIS Market Atlas.*

TURKMENISTAN - EXPORTS

Business International Moscow, 23 Profsoyuznaya Ulitsa, 117859, Moscow (Telephone Number in U.S. (800) 938-4685); *The CIS Market Atlas.*

Encyclopedia Britannica, Incorporated, 310 South Michigan Avenue, Chicago, Illinois 60604 (312) 347-7000; *Britannica World Data.*

The World Bank, 1818 H Street, NW, Washington, D.C. 20433 (202) 477-1234; *Statistical Handbook: States of the Former USSR.*

TURKMENISTAN - EXTERNAL TRADE

The World Bank, 1818 H Street, NW, Washington, D.C. 20433 (202) 477-1234; *Statistical Handbook: States of the Former USSR.*

TURKMENISTAN - FABRIC PRODUCTION AND CONSUMPTION - See TURKMENISTAN - TEXTILE INDUSTRY

TURKMENISTAN - FERTILITY RATES

Encyclopedia Britannica, Incorporated, 310 South Michigan Avenue, Chicago, Illinois 60604 (312) 347-7000; *Britannica World Data.*

The World Bank, 1818 H Street, NW, Washington, D.C. 20433 (202) 477-1234; *Statistical Handbook: States of the Former USSR.*

TURKMENISTAN - FISHERIES

Encyclopedia Britannica, Incorporated, 310 South Michigan Avenue, Chicago, Illinois 60604 (312) 347-7000; *Britannica World Data.*

TURKMENISTAN - FOOTWEAR PRODUCTION AND CONSUMPTION - See TURKMENISTAN - TEXTILE INDUSTRY

TURKMENISTAN - FOREIGN INVESTMENT

Business International Moscow, 23 Profsoyuznaya Ulitsa, 117859, Moscow (Telephone Number in U.S. (800) 938-4685); *The CIS Market Atlas.*

TURKMENISTAN - FOREIGN TRADE

Business International Moscow, 23 Profsoyuznaya Ulitsa, 117859, Moscow (Telephone Number in U.S. (800) 938-4685); *The CIS Market Atlas.*

Encyclopedia Britannica, Incorporated, 310 South Michigan Avenue, Chicago, Illinois 60604 (312) 347-7000; *Britannica World Data.*

TURKMENISTAN - FORESTRY AND FOREST PRODUCTS

Business International Moscow, 23 Profsoyuznaya Ulitsa, 117859, Moscow (Telephone Number in U.S. (800) 938-4685); *The CIS Market Atlas.*

Encyclopedia Britannica, Incorporated, 310 South Michigan Avenue, Chicago, Illinois 60604 (312) 347-7000; *Britannica World Data.*

TURKMENISTAN - GOATS - See TURKMENISTAN - LIVESTOCK AND POULTRY

TURKMENISTAN - GOVERNMENT EXPENDITURE

The World Bank, 1818 H Street, NW, Washington, D.C. 20433 (202) 477-1234; *Statistical Handbook: States of the Former USSR.*

TURKMENISTAN - GOVERNMENT REVENUE

The World Bank, 1818 H Street, NW, Washington, D.C. 20433 (202) 477-1234; *Statistical Handbook: States of the Former USSR.*

TURKMENISTAN - GROSS DOMESTIC PRODUCT

The World Bank, 1818 H Street, NW, Washington, D.C. 20433 (202) 477-1234; *Statistical Handbook: States of the Former USSR.*

TURKMENISTAN - HEALTH

Business International Moscow, 23 Profsoyuznaya Ulitsa, 117859, Moscow (Telephone Number in U.S. (800) 938-4685); *The CIS Market Atlas.*

Encyclopedia Britannica, Incorporated, 310 South Michigan Avenue, Chicago, Illinois 60604 (312) 347-7000; *Britannica World Data.*

TURKMENISTAN - HIGHWAYS

Business International Moscow, 23 Profsoyuznaya Ulitsa, 117859, Moscow (Telephone Number in U.S. (800) 938-4685); *The CIS Market Atlas.*

Encyclopedia Britannica, Incorporated, 310 South Michigan Avenue, Chicago, Illinois 60604 (312) 347-7000; *Britannica World Data.*

TURKMENISTAN - HOUSING AND HOUSING UNITS

Business International Moscow, 23 Profsoyuznaya Ulitsa, 117859, Moscow (Telephone Number in U.S. (800) 938-4685); *The CIS Market Atlas.*

TURKMENISTAN - IMPORTS

Business International Moscow, 23 Profsoyuznaya Ulitsa, 117859, Moscow (Telephone Number in U.S. (800) 938-4685); *The CIS Market Atlas.*

Encyclopedia Britannica, Incorporated, 310 South Michigan Avenue, Chicago, Illinois 60604 (312) 347-7000; *Britannica World Data.*

The World Bank, 1818 H Street, NW, Washington, D.C. 20433 (202) 477-1234; *Statistical Handbook: States of the Former USSR.*

TURKMENISTAN - INDUSTRY

Business International Moscow, 23 Profsoyuznaya Ulitsa, 117859, Moscow (Telephone Number in U.S. (800) 938-4685); *The CIS Market Atlas.*

The World Bank, 1818 H Street, NW, Washington, D.C. 20433 (202) 477-1234; *Statistical Handbook: States of the Former USSR.*

TURKMENISTAN - INFANT MORTALITY RATES

Business International Moscow, 23 Profsoyuznaya Ulitsa, 117859, Moscow (Telephone Number in U.S. (800) 938-4685); *The CIS Market Atlas.*

TURKMENISTAN - LABOR

Business International Moscow, 23 Profsoyuznaya Ulitsa, 117859, Moscow (Telephone Number in U.S. (800) 938-4685); *The CIS Market Atlas.*

TURKMENISTAN - LABOR FORCE

The World Bank, 1818 H Street, NW, Washington, D.C. 20433 (202) 477-1234; *Statistical Handbook: States of the Former USSR.*

TURKMENISTAN - LAND USE

Encyclopedia Britannica, Incorporated, 310 South Michigan Avenue, Chicago, Illinois 60604 (312) 347-7000; *Britannica World Data.*

TURKMENISTAN - LIFE EXPECTANCY

Business International Moscow, 23 Profsoyuznaya Ulitsa, 117859, Moscow (Telephone Number in U.S. (800) 938-4685); *The CIS Market Atlas.*

TURKMENISTAN - LIVESTOCK AND POULTRY

Business International Moscow, 23 Profsoyuznaya Ulitsa, 117859, Moscow (Telephone Number in U.S. (800) 938-4685); *The CIS Market Atlas.*

Encyclopedia Britannica, Incorporated, 310 South Michigan Avenue, Chicago, Illinois 60604 (312) 347-7000; *Britannica World Data.*

TURKMENISTAN - MANUFACTURING

Encyclopedia Britannica, Incorporated, 310 South Michigan Avenue, Chicago, Illinois 60604 (312) 347-7000; *Britannica World Data.*

TURKMENISTAN - MARRIAGE RATES

Encyclopedia Britannica, Incorporated, 310 South Michigan Avenue, Chicago, Illinois 60604 (312) 347-7000; *Britannica World Data.*

TURKMENISTAN - MEAT PRODUCTION - See TURKMENISTAN - LIVESTOCK AND POULTRY

TURKMENISTAN - MILITARY

The International Institute for Strategic Studies, 23 Tavistock Street, London WC2E 7NQ, England; *The Military Balance.*

TURKMENISTAN - MINING AND MINERAL PRODUCTS

Business International Moscow, 23 Profsoyuznaya Ulitsa, 117859, Moscow (Telephone Number in U.S. (800) 938-4685); *The CIS Market Atlas.*

Encyclopedia Britannica, Incorporated, 310 South Michigan Avenue, Chicago, Illinois 60604 (312) 347-7000; *Britannica World Data.*

TURKMENISTAN - MOTOR VEHICLES

Business International Moscow, 23 Profsoyuznaya Ulitsa, 117859, Moscow (Telephone Number in U.S. (800) 938-4685); *The CIS Market Atlas.*

TURKMENISTAN - NATIONAL ACCOUNTS

The World Bank, 1818 H Street, NW, Washington, D.C. 20433 (202) 477-1234; *Statistical Handbook: States of the Former USSR.*

TURKMENISTAN - NATIONAL INCOME

Business International Moscow, 23 Profsoyuznaya Ulitsa, 117859, Moscow (Telephone Number in U.S. (800) 938-4685); *The CIS Market Atlas.*

TURKMENISTAN - PIGS - See TURKMENISTAN - LIVESTOCK AND POULTRY

TURKMENISTAN - POPULATION

Business International Moscow, 23 Profsoyuznaya Ulitsa, 117859, Moscow (Telephone Number in U.S. (800) 938-4685); *The CIS Market Atlas.*

Encyclopedia Britannica, Incorporated, 310 South Michigan Avenue, Chicago, Illinois 60604 (312) 347-7000; *Britannica World Data.*

The World Bank, 1818 H Street, NW, Washington, D.C. 20433 (202) 477-1234; *Statistical Handbook: States of the Former USSR.*

TURKMENISTAN - POULTRY - See TURKMENISTAN - LIVESTOCK AND POULTRY

TURKMENISTAN - PRICES

The World Bank, 1818 H Street, NW, Washington, D.C. 20433 (202) 477-1234; *Statistical Handbook: States of the Former USSR.*

TURKMENISTAN - PRODUCTION

The World Bank, 1818 H Street, NW, Washington, D.C. 20433 (202) 477-1234; *Statistical Handbook: States of the Former USSR.*

TURKMENISTAN - PUBLIC FINANCE

The World Bank, 1818 H Street, NW, Washington, D.C. 20433 (202) 477-1234; *Statistical Handbook: States of the Former USSR.*

TURKMENISTAN - RADIO RECEIVERS

Encyclopedia Britannica, Incorporated, 310 South Michigan Avenue, Chicago, Illinois 60604 (312) 347-7000; *Britannica World Data.*

TURKMENISTAN - RAILWAYS

Business International Moscow, 23 Profsoyuznaya Ulitsa, 117859, Moscow (Telephone Number in U.S. (800) 938-4685); *The CIS Market Atlas.*

Encyclopedia Britannica, Incorporated, 310 South Michigan Avenue, Chicago, Illinois 60604 (312) 347-7000; *Britannica World Data.*

TURKMENISTAN - RETAIL TRADE

Business International Moscow, 23 Profsoyuznaya Ulitsa, 117859, Moscow (Telephone Number in U.S. (800) 938-4685); *The CIS Market Atlas.*

TURKMENISTAN - ROADS - See TURKMENISTAN - HIGHWAYS

TURKMENISTAN - ROUNDWOOD PRODUCTION AND CONSUMPTION - See TURKMENISTAN - FORESTRY AND FOREST PRODUCTS

TURKMENISTAN - SHEEP - See TURKMENISTAN - LIVESTOCK AND POULTRY

TURKMENISTAN - STEEL PRODUCTION AND CONSUMPTION - See TURKMENISTAN - MINING AND MINERAL PRODUCTS

TURKMENISTAN - TELEPHONES IN USE

Encyclopedia Britannica, Incorporated, 310 South Michigan Avenue, Chicago, Illinois 60604 (312) 347-7000; *Britannica World Data.*

Encyclopedia Britannica, Incorporated, 310 South Michigan Avenue, Chicago, Illinois 60604 (312) 347-7000; *Britannica World Data.*

TURKMENISTAN - TELEVISION RECEIVERS

Encyclopedia Britannica, Incorporated, 310 South Michigan Avenue, Chicago, Illinois 60604 (312) 347-7000; *Britannica World Data.*

TURKMENISTAN - TEXTILE INDUSTRY

Business International Moscow, 23 Profsoyuznaya Ulitsa, 117859, Moscow (Telephone Number in U.S. (800) 938-4685); *The CIS Market Atlas.*

TURKMENISTAN - TOURISM

Business International Moscow, 23 Profsoyuznaya Ulitsa, 117859, Moscow (Telephone Number in U.S. (800) 938-4685); *The CIS Market Atlas.*

TURKMENISTAN - TRANSPORTATION AND COMMUNICATIONS

Business International Moscow, 23 Profsoyuznaya Ulitsa, 117859, Moscow (Telephone Number in U.S. (800) 938-4685); *The CIS Market Atlas.*

Encyclopedia Britannica, Incorporated, 310 South Michigan Avenue, Chicago, Illinois 60604 (312) 347-7000; *Britannica World Data.*

TURKMENISTAN - VITAL STATISTICS

Encyclopedia Britannica, Incorporated, 310 South Michigan Avenue, Chicago, Illinois 60604 (312) 347-7000; *Britannica World Data.*

TURKMENISTAN - WAGES

Business International Moscow, 23 Profsoyuznaya Ulitsa, 117859, Moscow (Telephone Number in U.S. (800) 938-4685); *The CIS Market Atlas.*

The World Bank, 1818 H Street, NW, Washington, D.C. 20433 (202) 477-1234; *Statistical Handbook: States of the Former USSR.*

TURKMENISTAN - WOOL PRODUCTION AND CONSUMPTION - See TURKMENISTAN - TEXTILE INDUSTRY

Turks and Caicos Islands - National Statistical Office

The Chief Secretary, Chief Secretary's Office, Grand Turk, Turks and Caicos Islands.

Turks and Caicos Islands - Primary Statistics Source

Foreign and Commonwealth Office, HM Stationery Office, Post Office Box 569, London SE1 9NH; Turks and Caicos Islands: Report for the Year.

TURKS AND CAICOS ISLANDS - AGRICULTURE

Food and Agricultural Organization of the United Nations (FAO) Via delle Terme di Caracalla, 00100 Rome, Italy (Telephone Number in U.S. (202) 653-2400); *Production Yearbook,* and *The State of Food and Agriculture,* and *Trade Yearbook.*

G.K. Hall and Company, 70 Lincoln Street, Boston, Massachusetts 02111 (617) 423-3990; *The World in Figures.*

TURKS AND CAICOS ISLANDS - AIRLINE SERVICE

G.K. Hall and Company, 70 Lincoln Street, Boston, Massachusetts 02111 (617) 423-3990; *The World in Figures.*

TURKS AND CAICOS ISLANDS - ANIMAL HEALTH

Food and Agricultural Organization of the United Nations (FAO), Via delle Terme di Caracalla, 00100, Rome, Italy (Telephone Number in U.S. (202) 653-2400); *Animal Health Yearbook.*

TURKS AND CAICOS ISLANDS - AREA AND DENSITY OF POPULATION

Food and Agricultural Organization of the United Nations (FAO) Via delle Terme di Caracalla, 00100 Rome, Italy (Telephone Number in U.S. (202) 653-2400); *The State of Food and Agriculture.*

G.K. Hall and Company, 70 Lincoln Street, Boston, Massachusetts 02111 (617) 423-3990; *The World in Figures.*

Statistical Office of the United Nations, Publishing Service, New York, New York 10017 (800) 253-9646; *Statistical Yearbook.*

TURKS AND CAICOS ISLANDS - BALANCE OF PAYMENTS

G.K. Hall and Company, 70 Lincoln Street, Boston, Massachusetts 02111 (617) 423-3990; *The World in Figures.*

TURKS AND CAICOS ISLANDS - BANKING

G.K. Hall and Company, 70 Lincoln Street, Boston, Massachusetts 02111 (617) 423-3990; *The World in Figures.*

TURKS AND CAICOS ISLANDS - BIRTH RATES

Statistical Office of the United Nations, Publishing Service, New York, New York 10017 (800) 253-9646; *Demographic Yearbook,* and *Statistical Yearbook.*

TURKS AND CAICOS ISLANDS - BONDS

G.K. Hall and Company, 70 Lincoln Street, Boston, Massachusetts 02111 (617) 423-3990; *The World in Figures.*

TURKS AND CAICOS ISLANDS - BOOK PRODUCTION

G.K. Hall and Company, 70 Lincoln Street, Boston, Massachusetts 02111 (617) 423-3990; *The World in Figures.*

TURKS AND CAICOS ISLANDS - BROADCASTING

Billboard Limited, P.O. Box 9027, 1006 AA Amsterdam, The Netherlands (Telephone Number in U.S. (212) 764-7300); *World Radio TV Handbook.*

G.K. Hall and Company, 70 Lincoln Street, Boston, Massachusetts 02111 (617) 423-3990; *The World in Figures.*

United Nations Educational, Scientific and Cultural Organization (UNESCO), 7 Place de Fontenoy, F-75700 Paris, France (Telephone Number in U.S. (212) 963-5981); *Statistical Yearbook.*

TURKS AND CAICOS ISLANDS - BUSINESS

G.K. Hall and Company, 70 Lincoln Street, Boston, Massachusetts 02111 (617) 423-3990; *The World in Figures.*

TURKS AND CAICOS ISLANDS - CALORIE SUPPLY

Food and Agricultural Organization of the United Nations (FAO) Via delle Terme di Caracalla, 00100 Rome, Italy (Telephone Number in U.S. (202) 653-2400); *The State of Food and Agriculture.*

TURKS AND CAICOS ISLANDS - CHEMICAL (ORGANIC) PRODUCTION - See TURKS AND CAICOS ISLANDS - MINING AND MINERAL PRODUCTS

TURKS AND CAICOS ISLANDS - CLASS STRUCTURE

G.K. Hall and Company, 70 Lincoln Street, Boston, Massachusetts 02111 (617) 423-3990; *The World in Figures.*

TURKS AND CAICOS ISLANDS - CLIMATE

G.K. Hall and Company, 70 Lincoln Street, Boston, Massachusetts 02111 (617) 423-3990; *The World in Figures.*

TURKS AND CAICOS ISLANDS - COMMUNICATIONS

G.K. Hall and Company, 70 Lincoln Street, Boston, Massachusetts 02111 (617) 423-3990; *The World in Figures.*

TURKS AND CAICOS ISLANDS - CONSUMER PRICE INDEX

G.K. Hall and Company, 70 Lincoln Street, Boston, Massachusetts 02111 (617) 423-3990; *The World in Figures.*

TURKS AND CAICOS ISLANDS - CONSUMPTION

G.K. Hall and Company, 70 Lincoln Street, Boston, Massachusetts 02111 (617) 423-3990; *The World in Figures.*

TURKS AND CAICOS ISLANDS - CORN PRODUCTION - See TURKS AND CAICOS ISLANDS - CROPS

TURKS AND CAICOS ISLANDS - CORPORATE TAXES - See TURKS AND CAICOS ISLANDS - TAXATION

TURKS AND CAICOS ISLANDS - CROPS

Food and Agricultural Organization of the United Nations (FAO) Via delle Terme di Caracalla, 00100 Rome, Italy (Telephone Number in U.S. (202) 653-2400); *The State of Food and Agriculture.*

G.K. Hall and Company, 70 Lincoln Street, Boston, Massachusetts 02111 (617) 423-3990; *The World in Figures.*

TURKS AND CAICOS ISLANDS - CUSTOMS DUTIES

G.K. Hall and Company, 70 Lincoln Street, Boston, Massachusetts 02111 (617) 423-3990; *The World in Figures.*

TURKS AND CAICOS ISLANDS - DAIRY PRODUCTS

Food and Agricultural Organization of the United Nations (FAO) Via delle Terme di Caracalla, 00100 Rome, Italy (Telephone Number in U.S. (202) 653-2400); *The State of Food and Agriculture.*

TURKS AND CAICOS ISLANDS - DEATH RATES

G.K. Hall and Company, 70 Lincoln Street, Boston, Massachusetts 02111 (617) 423-3990; *The World in Figures.*

Statistical Office of the United Nations, Publishing Service, New York, New York 10017 (800) 253-9646; *Statistical Yearbook.*

TURKS AND CAICOS ISLANDS - DEFENSE EXPENDITURES

G.K. Hall and Company, 70 Lincoln Street, Boston, Massachusetts 02111 (617) 423-3990; *The World in Figures.*

TURKS AND CAICOS ISLANDS - DEMOGRAPHY

G.K. Hall and Company, 70 Lincoln Street, Boston, Massachusetts 02111 (617) 423-3990; *The World in Figures.*

TURKS AND CAICOS ISLANDS - DEVELOPMENT ASSISTANCE

G.K. Hall and Company, 70 Lincoln Street, Boston, Massachusetts 02111 (617) 423-3990; *The World in Figures.*

TURKS AND CAICOS ISLANDS - DISEASE

G.K. Hall and Company, 70 Lincoln Street, Boston, Massachusetts 02111 (617) 423-3990; *The World in Figures.*

TURKS AND CAICOS ISLANDS - DIVORCE RATES

Statistical Office of the United Nations, Publishing Service, New York, New York 10017 (800) 253-9646; *Demographic Yearbook,* and *Statistical Yearbook.*

TURKS AND CAICOS ISLANDS - DOMESTIC PRODUCT

G.K. Hall and Company, 70 Lincoln Street, Boston, Massachusetts 02111 (617) 423-3990; *The World in Figures.*

TURKS AND CAICOS ISLANDS - ECONOMY

G.K. Hall and Company, 70 Lincoln Street, Boston, Massachusetts 02111 (617) 423-3990; *The World in Figures.*

TURKS AND CAICOS ISLANDS - EDUCATION

G.K. Hall and Company, 70 Lincoln Street, Boston, Massachusetts 02111 (617) 423-3990; *The World in Figures.*

United Nations Educational, Scientific and Cultural Organization (UNESCO), 7 Place de Fontenoy, F-75700 Paris, France (Telephone Number in U.S. (212) 963-5981); *Statistical Yearbook.*

TURKS AND CAICOS ISLANDS - EGG PRODUCTION AND CONSUMPTION - See TURKS AND CAICOS ISLANDS - DAIRY PRODUCTS

TURKS AND CAICOS ISLANDS - ENERGY

Food and Agricultural Organization of the United Nations (FAO) Via delle Terme di Caracalla, 00100 Rome, Italy (Telephone Number in U.S. (202) 653-2400); *The State of Food and Agriculture.*

G.K. Hall and Company, 70 Lincoln Street, Boston, Massachusetts 02111 (617) 423-3990; *The World in Figures.*

TURKS AND CAICOS ISLANDS - EXPORTS

Food and Agricultural Organization of the United Nations (FAO) Via delle Terme di Caracalla, 00100 Rome, Italy (Telephone Number in U.S. (202) 653-2400); *The State of Food and Agriculture.*

G.K. Hall and Company, 70 Lincoln Street, Boston, Massachusetts 02111 (617) 423-3990; *The World in Figures.*

TURKS AND CAICOS ISLANDS - EXTERNAL TRADE

Food and Agricultural Organization of the United Nations (FAO) Via delle Terme di Caracalla, 00100 Rome, Italy (Telephone Number in U.S. (202) 653-2400); *The State of Food and Agriculture.*

G.K. Hall and Company, 70 Lincoln Street, Boston, Massachusetts 02111 (617) 423-3990; *The World in Figures.*

TURKS AND CAICOS ISLANDS - FARM CROPS - See TURKS AND CAICOS ISLANDS - CROPS

TURKS AND CAICOS ISLANDS - FERTILIZER

Food and Agricultural Organization of the United Nations (FAO), Via delle Terme di Caracalla, 00100, Rome, Italy (Telephone Number in U.S. (202) 653-2400); *Fertilizer Yearbook,* and *The State of Food and Agriculture.*

TURKS AND CAICOS ISLANDS - FETAL MORTALITY

Statistical Office of the United Nations, Publishing Service, New York, New York 10017 (800) 253-9646; *Demographic Yearbook*.

TURKS AND CAICOS ISLANDS - FINANCE

G.K. Hall and Company, 70 Lincoln Street, Boston, Massachusetts 02111 (617) 423-3990; *The World in Figures*.

TURKS AND CAICOS ISLANDS - FISHERIES

Food and Agricultural Organization of the United Nations (FAO) Via delle Terme di Caracalla, 00100 Rome, Italy (Telephone Number in U.S. (202) 653-2400); *The State of Food and Agriculture*, and *Yearbook of Fishery Statistics*.

TURKS AND CAICOS ISLANDS - FOOD

G.K. Hall and Company, 70 Lincoln Street, Boston, Massachusetts 02111 (617) 423-3990; *The World in Figures*.

TURKS AND CAICOS ISLANDS - FOREIGN AID

G.K. Hall and Company, 70 Lincoln Street, Boston, Massachusetts 02111 (617) 423-3990; *The World in Figures*.

TURKS AND CAICOS ISLANDS - FOREIGN TRADE

Food and Agricultural Organization of the United Nations (FAO) Via delle Terme di Caracalla, 00100 Rome, Italy (Telephone Number in U.S. (202) 653-2400); *The State of Food and Agriculture*.

G.K. Hall and Company, 70 Lincoln Street, Boston, Massachusetts 02111 (617) 423-3990; *The World in Figures*.

TURKS AND CAICOS ISLANDS - FORESTRY AND FOREST PRODUCTS

G.K. Hall and Company, 70 Lincoln Street, Boston, Massachusetts 02111 (617) 423-3990; *The World in Figures*.

Statistical Office of the United Nations, Publishing Service, New York, New York 10017 (800) 253-9646; *Statistical Yearbook*.

TURKS AND CAICOS ISLANDS - GENERAL MORTALITY

Statistical Office of the United Nations, Publishing Service, New York, New York 10017 (800) 253-9646; *Demographic Yearbook*.

TURKS AND CAICOS ISLANDS - GOVERNMENT

G.K. Hall and Company, 70 Lincoln Street, Boston, Massachusetts 02111 (617) 423-3990; *The World in Figures*.

TURKS AND CAICOS ISLANDS - GRAIN PRODUCTION - See TURKS AND CAICOS ISLANDS - CROPS

TURKS AND CAICOS ISLANDS - GROSS DOMESTIC PRODUCT

G.K. Hall and Company, 70 Lincoln Street, Boston, Massachusetts 02111 (617) 423-3990; *The World in Figures*.

Statistical Office of the United Nations, Publishing Service, New York, New York 10017 (800) 253-9646; *Statistical Yearbook*.

TURKS AND CAICOS ISLANDS - HEALTH

G.K. Hall and Company, 70 Lincoln Street, Boston, Massachusetts 02111 (617) 423-3990; *The World in Figures*.

Statistical Office of the United Nations, Publishing Service, New York, New York 10017 (800) 253-9646; *Statistical Yearbook*.

TURKS AND CAICOS ISLANDS - HIGHWAYS

G.K. Hall and Company, 70 Lincoln Street, Boston, Massachusetts 02111 (617) 423-3990; *The World in Figures*.

TURKS AND CAICOS ISLANDS - ILLITERATE POPULATION

G.K. Hall and Company, 70 Lincoln Street, Boston, Massachusetts 02111 (617) 423-3990; *The World in Figures*.

United Nations Educational, Scientific and Cultural Organization (UNESCO), 7 Place de Fontenoy, F-75700 Paris, France (Telephone Number in U.S. (212) 963-5981); *Statistical Yearbook*.

TURKS AND CAICOS ISLANDS - IMPORTS

Food and Agricultural Organization of the United Nations (FAO) Via delle Terme di Caracalla, 00100 Rome, Italy (Telephone Number in U.S. (202) 653-2400); *The State of Food and Agriculture*.

G.K. Hall and Company, 70 Lincoln Street, Boston, Massachusetts 02111 (617) 423-3990; *The World in Figures*.

TURKS AND CAICOS ISLANDS - INDUSTRY

G.K. Hall and Company, 70 Lincoln Street, Boston, Massachusetts 02111 (617) 423-3990; *The World in Figures*.

TURKS AND CAICOS ISLANDS - INFANT AND MATERNAL MORTALITY

Statistical Office of the United Nations, Publishing Service, New York, New York 10017 (800) 253-9646; *Demographic Yearbook*, and *Statistical Yearbook*.

TURKS AND CAICOS ISLANDS - LABOR FORCE

Food and Agricultural Organization of the United Nations (FAO) Via delle Terme di Caracalla, 00100 Rome, Italy (Telephone Number in U.S. (202) 653-2400); *The State of Food and Agriculture*.

G.K. Hall and Company, 70 Lincoln Street, Boston, Massachusetts 02111 (617) 423-3990; *The World in Figures*.

TURKS AND CAICOS ISLANDS - LAND USE

G.K. Hall and Company, 70 Lincoln Street, Boston, Massachusetts 02111 (617) 423-3990; *The World in Figures*.

TURKS AND CAICOS ISLANDS - LIVESTOCK AND POULTRY

Food and Agricultural Organization of the United Nations (FAO) Via delle Terme di Caracalla, 00100 Rome, Italy (Telephone Number in U.S. (202) 653-2400); *The State of Food and Agriculture*.

G.K. Hall and Company, 70 Lincoln Street, Boston, Massachusetts 02111 (617) 423-3990; *The World in Figures*.

TURKS AND CAICOS ISLANDS - LIVING LEVELS

G.K. Hall and Company, 70 Lincoln Street, Boston, Massachusetts 02111 (617) 423-3990; *The World in Figures*.

TURKS AND CAICOS ISLANDS - MANUFACTURING

G.K. Hall and Company, 70 Lincoln Street, Boston, Massachusetts 02111 (617) 423-3990; *The World in Figures*.

TURKS AND CAICOS ISLANDS - MARRIAGE RATES

Statistical Office of the United Nations, Publishing Service, New York, New York 10017 (800) 253-9646; *Demographic Yearbook*, and *Statistical Yearbook*.

TURKS AND CAICOS ISLANDS - MEAT PRODUCTION - See TURKS AND CAICOS ISLANDS - LIVESTOCK AND POULTRY

TURKS AND CAICOS ISLANDS - MERCHANT SHIPPING

G.K. Hall and Company, 70 Lincoln Street, Boston, Massachusetts 02111 (617) 423-3990; *The World in Figures*.

Statistical Office of the United Nations, Publishing Service, New York, New York 10017 (800) 253-9646; *Statistical Yearbook*.

TURKS AND CAICOS ISLANDS - MILITARY

G.K. Hall and Company, 70 Lincoln Street, Boston, Massachusetts 02111 (617) 423-3990; *The World in Figures*.

TURKS AND CAICOS ISLANDS - MINING AND MINERAL PRODUCTS

G.K. Hall and Company, 70 Lincoln Street, Boston, Massachusetts 02111 (617) 423-3990; *The World in Figures*.

Statistical Office of the United Nations, Publishing Service, New York, New York 10017 (800) 253-9646; *Statistical Yearbook*.

TURKS AND CAICOS ISLANDS - MONEY SUPPLY

G.K. Hall and Company, 70 Lincoln Street, Boston, Massachusetts 02111 (617) 423-3990; *The World in Figures*.

TURKS AND CAICOS ISLANDS - MOTION PICTURES

Statistical Office of the United Nations, Publishing Service, New York, New York 10017 (800) 253-9646; *Statistical Yearbook*.

TURKS AND CAICOS ISLANDS - MOTOR VEHICLES IN USE

G.K. Hall and Company, 70 Lincoln Street, Boston, Massachusetts 02111 (617) 423-3990; *The World in Figures*.

TURKS AND CAICOS ISLANDS - NATALITY - See TURKS AND CAICOS ISLANDS - BIRTH RATES

TURKS AND CAICOS ISLANDS - NATIONAL ACCOUNTS

Statistical Office of the United Nations, Publishing Service, New York, New York 10017 (800) 253-9646; *Statistical Yearbook*.

TURKS AND CAICOS ISLANDS - NATIONAL INCOME

G.K. Hall and Company, 70 Lincoln Street, Boston, Massachusetts 02111 (617) 423-3990; *The World in Figures*.

Statistical Office of the United Nations, Publishing Service, New York, New York 10017 (800) 253-9646; *Statistical Yearbook*.

TURKS AND CAICOS ISLANDS - NEWSPAPER PRODUCTION - See TURKS AND CAICOS ISLANDS - FORESTRY AND FOREST PRODUCTS

TURKS AND CAICOS ISLANDS - OCCUPATIONS - See TURKS AND CAICOS ISLANDS - LABOR FORCE

TURKS AND CAICOS ISLANDS - PERIODICALS

United Nations Educational, Scientific and Cultural Organization (UNESCO), 7 Place de Fontenoy, F-75700 Paris, France (Telephone Number in U.S. (212) 963-5981); *Statistical Yearbook*.

TURKS AND CAICOS ISLANDS - PESTICIDE USE

Food and Agricultural Organization of the United Nations (FAO) Via delle Terme di Caracalla, 00100 Rome, Italy (Telephone Number in U.S. (202) 653-2400); *The State of Food and Agriculture*.

TURKS AND CAICOS ISLANDS - PETROLEUM INDUSTRY

Food and Agricultural Organization of the United Nations (FAO) Via delle Terme di Caracalla, 00100 Rome, Italy (Telephone Number in U.S. (202) 653-2400); *The State of Food and Agriculture*.

G.K. Hall and Company, 70 Lincoln Street, Boston, Massachusetts 02111 (617) 423-3990; *The World in Figures*.

TURKS AND CAICOS ISLANDS - POPULATION

G.K. Hall and Company, 70 Lincoln Street, Boston, Massachusetts 02111 (617) 423-3990; *The World in Figures*.

Statistical Office of the United Nations, Publishing Service, New York, New York 10017 (800) 253-9646; *Demographic Yearbook*, and *Statistical Yearbook*.

World Health Organization, Office of Publications, Avenue Appia, CH-1211 Geneva 27, Switzerland (Telephone Number in U.S. (518) 436-9686); *World Health Statistics Annual*.

TURKS AND CAICOS ISLANDS - PRICES

Food and Agricultural Organization of the United Nations (FAO) Via delle Terme di Caracalla, 00100 Rome, Italy (Telephone Number in U.S. (202) 653-2400); *The State of Food and Agriculture*.

G.K. Hall and Company, 70 Lincoln Street, Boston, Massachusetts 02111 (617) 423-3990; *The World in Figures*.

TURKS AND CAICOS ISLANDS - PRODUCTION

G.K. Hall and Company, 70 Lincoln Street, Boston, Massachusetts 02111 (617) 423-3990; *The World in Figures*.

TURKS AND CAICOS ISLANDS - RADIO BROADCASTING - See TURKS AND CAICOS ISLANDS - BROADCASTING

TURKS AND CAICOS ISLANDS - RAILWAYS

G.K. Hall and Company, 70 Lincoln Street, Boston, Massachusetts 02111 (617) 423-3990; *The World in Figures*.

TURKS AND CAICOS ISLANDS - RETAIL TRADE

G.K. Hall and Company, 70 Lincoln Street, Boston, Massachusetts 02111 (617) 423-3990; *The World in Figures*.

TURKS AND CAICOS ISLANDS - SALT PRODUCTION - See TURKS AND CAICOS ISLANDS - MINING AND MINERAL PRODUCTS

TURKS AND CAICOS ISLANDS - SCIENCE AND TECHNOLOGY - EXPENDITURE FOR RESEARCH

Statistical Office of the United Nations, Publishing Service, New York, New York 10017 (800) 253-9646; *Statistical Yearbook.*

TURKS AND CAICOS ISLANDS - SCIENTISTS AND TECHNICIANS

Statistical Office of the United Nations, Publishing Service, New York, New York 10017 (800) 253-9646; *Statistical Yearbook.*

TURKS AND CAICOS ISLANDS - SOCIAL DATA

G.K. Hall and Company, 70 Lincoln Street, Boston, Massachusetts 02111 (617) 423-3990; *The World in Figures.*

TURKS AND CAICOS ISLANDS - STOCKS - COMMODITY - MARKET PRICE - INDEX

Food and Agricultural Organization of the United Nations (FAO) Via delle Terme di Caracalla, 00100 Rome, Italy (Telephone Number in U.S. (202) 653 2400); *The State of Food and Agriculture.*

TURKS AND CAICOS ISLANDS - TAXATION

G.K. Hall and Company, 70 Lincoln Street, Boston, Massachusetts 02111 (617) 423-3990; *The World in Figures.*

TURKS AND CAICOS ISLANDS - TELEPHONES IN USE

American Telephone and Telegraph Company, 26 Parsippany Road, Whippany, New Jersey 07981 (800) 338-4038; *The World's Telephones.*

G.K. Hall and Company, 70 Lincoln Street, Boston, Massachusetts 02111 (617) 423-3990; *The World in Figures.*

TURKS AND CAICOS ISLANDS - TEXTILE INDUSTRY

G.K. Hall and Company, 70 Lincoln Street, Boston, Massachusetts 02111 (617) 423-3990; *The World in Figures.*

TURKS AND CAICOS ISLANDS - THEATRE

United Nations Educational, Scientific and Cultural Organization (UNESCO), 7 Place de Fontenoy, F-75700 Paris, France (Telephone Number in U.S. (212) 963-5981); *Statistical Yearbook.*

TURKS AND CAICOS ISLANDS - TOURISM

G.K. Hall and Company, 70 Lincoln Street, Boston, Massachusetts 02111 (617) 423-3990; *The World in Figures.*

World Tourism Organization, Calle Capitan Haya 42, E-28020 Madrid, Spain; *Yearbook of Tourism Statistics.*

TURKS AND CAICOS ISLANDS - TRADE - See TURKS AND CAICOS ISLANDS - FOREIGN TRADE

TURKS AND CAICOS ISLANDS - TRANSPORTATION AND COMMUNICATIONS

G.K. Hall and Company, 70 Lincoln Street, Boston, Massachusetts 02111 (617) 423-3990; *The World in Figures.*

TURKS AND CAICOS ISLANDS - VITAL STATISTICS

G.K. Hall and Company, 70 Lincoln Street, Boston, Massachusetts 02111 (617) 423-3990; *The World in Figures.*

Statistical Office of the United Nations, Publishing Service, New York, New York 10017 (800) 253-9646; *Statistical Yearbook.*

World Health Organization, Office of Publications, Avenue Appia, CH-1211 Geneva 27, Switzerland (Telephone Number in U.S. (518) 436-9686); *World Health Statistics Annual.*

TURKS AND CAICOS ISLANDS - WAGES

G.K. Hall and Company, 70 Lincoln Street, Boston, Massachusetts 02111 (617) 423-3990; *The World in Figures.*

TURKS AND CAICOS ISLANDS - WEATHER

G.K. Hall and Company, 70 Lincoln Street, Boston, Massachusetts 02111 (617) 423-3990; *The World in Figures.*

Tuvalu - National Statistical Office

Planning and Statistics Division, Ministry of Finance, P.O. Box 33, Vaiaku, Funafuti Island, Tuvalu.

TUVALU - AGRICULTURE

Food and Agricultural Organization of the United Nations (FAO) Via delle Terme di Caracalla, 00100 Rome, Italy (Telephone Number in U.S. (202) 653-2400); *The State of Food and Agriculture.*

G.K. Hall and Company, 70 Lincoln Street, Boston, Massachusetts 02111 (617) 423-3990; *The World in Figures.*

Statistical Office of the United Nations, Publishing Service, New York, New York 10017 (800) 253-9646; *Statistical Yearbook for Asia and the Pacific.*

TUVALU - AIRLINE SERVICE

G.K. Hall and Company, 70 Lincoln Street, Boston, Massachusetts 02111 (617) 423-3990; *The World in Figures.*

TUVALU - AREA AND DENSITY OF POPULATION

Food and Agricultural Organization of the United Nations (FAO) Via delle Terme di Caracalla, 00100 Rome, Italy (Telephone Number in U.S. (202) 653-2400); *The State of Food and Agriculture.*

G.K. Hall and Company, 70 Lincoln Street, Boston, Massachusetts 02111 (617) 423-3990; *The World in Figures.*

TUVALU - BALANCE OF PAYMENTS

G.K. Hall and Company, 70 Lincoln Street, Boston, Massachusetts 02111 (617) 423-3990; *The World in Figures.*

TUVALU - BANKING

G.K. Hall and Company, 70 Lincoln Street, Boston, Massachusetts 02111 (617) 423-3990; *The World in Figures.*

TUVALU - BIRTH RATES

Statistical Office of the United Nations, Publishing Service, New York, New York 10017 (800) 253-9646; *Demographic Yearbook.*

TUVALU - BONDS

G.K. Hall and Company, 70 Lincoln Street, Boston, Massachusetts 02111 (617) 423-3990; *The World in Figures*.

TUVALU - BOOK PRODUCTION

G.K. Hall and Company, 70 Lincoln Street, Boston, Massachusetts 02111 (617) 423-3990; *The World in Figures*.

TUVALU - BROADCASTING

Billboard Limited, P.O. Box 9027, 1006 AA Amsterdam, The Netherlands (Telephone Number in U.S. (212) 764-7300); *World Radio TV Handbook*.

G.K. Hall and Company, 70 Lincoln Street, Boston, Massachusetts 02111 (617) 423-3990; *The World in Figures*.

TUVALU - BUSINESS

G.K. Hall and Company, 70 Lincoln Street, Boston, Massachusetts 02111 (617) 423-3990; *The World in Figures*.

TUVALU - CALORIE SUPPLY

Food and Agricultural Organization of the United Nations (FAO) Via delle Terme di Caracalla, 00100 Rome, Italy (Telephone Number in U.S. (202) 653-2400); *The State of Food and Agriculture*.

TUVALU - CHEMICAL (ORGANIC) PRODUCTION - See TUVALU - MINING AND MINERAL PRODUCTS

TUVALU - CLASS STRUCTURE

G.K. Hall and Company, 70 Lincoln Street, Boston, Massachusetts 02111 (617) 423-3990; *The World in Figures*.

TUVALU - CLIMATE

G.K. Hall and Company, 70 Lincoln Street, Boston, Massachusetts 02111 (617) 423-3990; *The World in Figures*.

TUVALU - CLOTHING EXPORTS AND IMPORTS

South Pacific Commission, Post Box D5, Noumea Cedex, New Caledonia; *Statistical Bulletin of the South Pacific: Retail Price Indexes*.

TUVALU - COAL PRODUCTION - See TUVALU - MINING AND MINERAL PRODUCTS

TUVALU - COMMUNICATIONS

G.K. Hall and Company, 70 Lincoln Street, Boston, Massachusetts 02111 (617) 423-3990; *The World in Figures*.

Statistical Office of the United Nations, Publishing Service, New York, New York 10017 (800) 253-9646; *Statistical Yearbook for Asia and the Pacific*.

TUVALU - CONSUMER PRICE INDEX

G.K. Hall and Company, 70 Lincoln Street, Boston, Massachusetts 02111 (617) 423-3990; *The World in Figures*.

TUVALU - CONSUMPTION

G.K. Hall and Company, 70 Lincoln Street, Boston, Massachusetts 02111 (617) 423-3990; *The World in Figures*.

South Pacific Commission, Post Box D5, Noumea Cedex, New Caledonia; *Statistical Bulletin of the South Pacific: Retail Price Indexes*.

TUVALU - CORN PRODUCTION - See TUVALU - CROPS

TUVALU - CORPORATE TAXES - See TUVALU - TAXATION

TUVALU - CROPS

Food and Agricultural Organization of the United Nations (FAO), Via delle Terme di Caracalla, 00100, Rome, Italy (Telephone Number in U.S. (202) 653-2400); *The State of Food and Agriculture*.

G.K. Hall and Company, 70 Lincoln Street, Boston, Massachusetts 02111 (617) 423-3990; *The World in Figures*.

TUVALU - CUSTOMS DUTIES

G.K. Hall and Company, 70 Lincoln Street, Boston, Massachusetts 02111 (617) 423-3990; *The World in Figures*.

TUVALU - DAIRY PRODUCTS

Food and Agricultural Organization of the United Nations (FAO) Via delle Terme di Caracalla, 00100 Rome, Italy (Telephone Number in U.S. (202) 653-2400); *The State of Food and Agriculture*.

TUVALU - DEATH RATES

G.K. Hall and Company, 70 Lincoln Street, Boston, Massachusetts 02111 (617) 423-3990; *The World in Figures*.

TUVALU - DEFENSE EXPENDITURES

G.K. Hall and Company, 70 Lincoln Street, Boston, Massachusetts 02111 (617) 423-3990; *The World in Figures*.

TUVALU - DEVELOPMENT ASSISTANCE

G.K. Hall and Company, 70 Lincoln Street, Boston, Massachusetts 02111 (617) 423-3990; *The World in Figures*.

TUVALU - DEMOGRAPHY

G.K. Hall and Company, 70 Lincoln Street, Boston, Massachusetts 02111 (617) 423-3990; *The World in Figures*.

TUVALU - DISEASE

G.K. Hall and Company, 70 Lincoln Street, Boston, Massachusetts 02111 (617) 423-3990; *The World in Figures*.

TUVALU - DIVORCE RATES

Statistical Office of the United Nations, Publishing Service, New York, New York 10017 (800) 253-9646; *Demographic Yearbook*.

TUVALU - DOMESTIC PRODUCT

G.K. Hall and Company, 70 Lincoln Street, Boston, Massachusetts 02111 (617) 423-3990; *The World in Figures*.

TUVALU - ECONOMY

G.K. Hall and Company, 70 Lincoln Street, Boston, Massachusetts 02111 (617) 423-3990; *The World in Figures.*

TUVALU - EDUCATION

G.K. Hall and Company, 70 Lincoln Street, Boston, Massachusetts 02111 (617) 423-3990; *The World in Figures.*

TUVALU - EGG PRODUCTION AND CONSUMPTION - See TUVALU - DAIRY PRODUCTS

TUVALU - ENERGY

Food and Agricultural Organization of the United Nations (FAO) Via delle Terme di Caracalla, 00100 Rome, Italy (Telephone Number in U.S. (202) 653-2400); *The State of Food and Agriculture.*

G.K. Hall and Company, 70 Lincoln Street, Boston, Massachusetts 02111 (617) 423-3990; *The World in Figures.*

Statistical Office of the United Nations, Publishing Service, New York, New York 10017 (800) 253-9646; *Statistical Yearbook for Asia and the Pacific.*

TUVALU - EXPORTS

Food and Agricultural Organization of the United Nations (FAO) Via delle Terme di Caracalla, 00100 Rome, Italy (Telephone Number in U.S. (202) 653-2400); *The State of Food and Agriculture.*

G.K. Hall and Company, 70 Lincoln Street, Boston, Massachusetts 02111 (617) 423-3990; *The World in Figures.*

South Pacific Commission, Post Box D5, Noumea Cedex, New Caledonia; *Statistical Bulletin of the South Pacific: Overseas Trade.*

TUVALU - EXTERNAL TRADE

Food and Agricultural Organization of the United Nations (FAO) Via delle Terme di Caracalla, 00100 Rome, Italy (Telephone Number in U.S. (202) 653-2400); *The State of Food and Agriculture.*

G.K. Hall and Company, 70 Lincoln Street, Boston, Massachusetts 02111 (617) 423-3990; *The World in Figures.*

Statistical Office of the United Nations, Publishing Service, New York, New York 10017 (800) 253-9646; *Statistical Yearbook for Asia and the Pacific.*

TUVALU - FARM CROPS - See TUVALU - CROPS

TUVALU - FERTILIZER

Food and Agricultural Organization of the United Nations (FAO) Via delle Terme di Caracalla, 00100 Rome, Italy (Telephone Number in U.S. (202) 653-2400); *The State of Food and Agriculture.*

TUVALU - FETAL MORTALITY

Statistical Office of the United Nations, Publishing Service, New York, New York 10017 (800) 253-9646; *Demographic Yearbook.*

TUVALU - FINANCE

G.K. Hall and Company, 70 Lincoln Street, Boston, Massachusetts 02111 (617) 423-3990; *The World in Figures.*

Statistical Office of the United Nations, Publishing Service, New York, New York 10017 (800) 253-9646; *Statistical Yearbook for Asia and the Pacific.*

TUVALU - FISHERIES

Food and Agricultural Organization of the United Nations (FAO) Via delle Terme di Caracalla, 00100 Rome, Italy (Telephone Number in U.S. (202) 653-2400); *The State of Food and Agriculture.*

TUVALU - FOOD

Food and Agricultural Organization of the United Nations (FAO) Via delle Terme di Caracalla, 00100 Rome, Italy (Telephone Number in U.S. (202) 653-2400); *The State of Food and Agriculture.*

G.K. Hall and Company, 70 Lincoln Street, Boston, Massachusetts 02111 (617) 423-3990; *The World in Figures.*

South Pacific Commission, Post Box D5, Noumea Cedex, New Caledonia; *Statistical Bulletin of the South Pacific: Retail Price Indexes.*

Statistical Office of the United Nations, Publishing Service, New York, New York 10017 (800) 253-9646; *Statistical Yearbook for Asia and the Pacific.*

TUVALU - FOREIGN AID

G.K. Hall and Company, 70 Lincoln Street, Boston, Massachusetts 02111 (617) 423-3990; *The World in Figures.*

TUVALU - FOREIGN TRADE

Food and Agricultural Organization of the United Nations (FAO) Via delle Terme di Caracalla, 00100 Rome, Italy (Telephone Number in U.S. (202) 653-2400); *The State of Food and Agriculture.*

G.K. Hall and Company, 70 Lincoln Street, Boston, Massachusetts 02111 (617) 423-3990; *The World in Figures.*

South Pacific Commission, Post Box D5, Noumea Cedex, New Caledonia; *Statistical Bulletin of the South Pacific: Overseas Trade.*

Statistical Office of the United Nations, Publishing Service, New York, New York 10017 (800) 253-9646; *International Trade Statistics Yearbook*

TUVALU - FORESTRY AND FOREST PRODUCTS

Food and Agricultural Organization of the United Nations (FAO) Via delle Terme di Caracalla, 00100 Rome, Italy (Telephone Number in U.S. (202) 653-2400); *The State of Food and Agriculture.*

G.K. Hall and Company, 70 Lincoln Street, Boston, Massachusetts 02111 (617) 423-3990; *The World in Figures.*

TUVALU - GENERAL MORTALITY

Statistical Office of the United Nations, Publishing Service, New York, New York 10017 (800) 253-9646; *Demographic Yearbook.*

TUVALU - GOVERNMENT

G.K. Hall and Company, 70 Lincoln Street, Boston, Massachusetts 02111 (617) 423-3990; *The World in Figures.*

TUVALU - GRAIN PRODUCTION - See TUVALU - CROPS

TUVALU - GROSS DOMESTIC PRODUCT

G.K. Hall and Company, 70 Lincoln Street, Boston, Massachusetts 02111 (617) 423-3990; *The World in Figures*.

TUVALU - HEALTH

G.K. Hall and Company, 70 Lincoln Street, Boston, Massachusetts 02111 (617) 423-3990; *The World in Figures*.

South Pacific Commission, Post Box D5, Noumea Cedex, New Caledonia; *Statistical Bulletin of the South Pacific: Retail Price Indexes*.

TUVALU - HIGHWAYS

G.K. Hall and Company, 70 Lincoln Street, Boston, Massachusetts 02111 (617) 423-3990; *The World in Figures*.

TUVALU - HOUSING AND HOUSING UNITS

South Pacific Commission, Post Box D5, Noumea Cedex, New Caledonia; *Statistical Bulletin of the South Pacific: Retail Price Indexes*.

TUVALU - ILLITERATE POPULATION

G.K. Hall and Company, 70 Lincoln Street, Boston, Massachusetts 02111 (617) 423-3990; *The World in Figures*.

TUVALU - IMPORTS

Food and Agricultural Organization of the United Nations (FAO) Via delle Terme di Caracalla, 00100 Rome, Italy (Telephone Number in U.S. (202) 653-2400); *The State of Food and Agriculture*.

G.K. Hall and Company, 70 Lincoln Street, Boston, Massachusetts 02111 (617) 423-3990; *The World in Figures*.

South Pacific Commission, Post Box D5, Noumea Cedex, New Caledonia; *Statistical Bulletin of the South Pacific: Overseas Trade*.

TUVALU - INDUSTRY

G.K. Hall and Company, 70 Lincoln Street, Boston, Massachusetts 02111 (617) 423-3990; *The World in Figures*.

Statistical Office of the United Nations, Publishing Service, New York, New York 10017 (800) 253-9646; *Statistical Yearbook for Asia and the Pacific*.

TUVALU - INFANT AND MATERNAL MORTALITY

Statistical Office of the United Nations, Publishing Service, New York, New York 10017 (800) 253-9646; *Demographic Yearbook*.

TUVALU - INTERNAL TRADE

Statistical Office of the United Nations, Publishing Service, New York, New York 10017 (800) 253-9646; *Statistical Yearbook for Asia and the Pacific*.

TUVALU - LABOR FORCE

Food and Agricultural Organization of the United Nations (FAO) Via delle Terme di Caracalla, 00100 Rome, Italy (Telephone Number in U.S. (202) 653-2400); *The State of Food and Agriculture*.

G.K. Hall and Company, 70 Lincoln Street, Boston, Massachusetts 02111 (617) 423-3990; *The World in Figures*.

TUVALU - LAND USE

G.K. Hall and Company, 70 Lincoln Street, Boston, Massachusetts 02111 (617) 423-3990; *The World in Figures*.

TUVALU - LIVESTOCK AND POULTRY

Food and Agricultural Organization of the United Nations (FAO) Via delle Terme di Caracalla, 00100 Rome, Italy (Telephone Number in U.S. (202) 653-2400); *The State of Food and Agriculture*.

G.K. Hall and Company, 70 Lincoln Street, Boston, Massachusetts 02111 (617) 423-3990; *The World in Figures*.

TUVALU - LIVING LEVELS

G.K. Hall and Company, 70 Lincoln Street, Boston, Massachusetts 02111 (617) 423-3990; *The World in Figures*.

TUVALU - MAIL - NUMBER OF ITEMS SENT AND RECEIVED

Statistical Office of the United Nations, Publishing Service, New York, New York 10017 (800) 253-9646; *Statistical Yearbook*.

TUVALU - MANPOWER

Statistical Office of the United Nations, Publishing Service, New York, New York 10017 (800) 253-9646; *Statistical Yearbook for Asia and the Pacific*.

TUVALU - MANUFACTURING

G.K. Hall and Company, 70 Lincoln Street, Boston, Massachusetts 02111 (617) 423-3990; *The World in Figures*.

TUVALU - MARRIAGE RATES

Statistical Office of the United Nations, Publishing Service, New York, New York 10017 (800) 253-9646; *Demographic Yearbook*.

TUVALU - MEAT PRODUCTION - See TUVALU - LIVESTOCK AND POULTRY

TUVALU - MERCHANT SHIPPING

G.K. Hall and Company, 70 Lincoln Street, Boston, Massachusetts 02111 (617) 423-3990; *The World in Figures*.

TUVALU - MILITARY

G.K. Hall and Company, 70 Lincoln Street, Boston, Massachusetts 02111 (617) 423-3990; *The World in Figures*.

TUVALU - MINING AND MINERAL PRODUCTS

G.K. Hall and Company, 70 Lincoln Street, Boston, Massachusetts 02111 (617) 423-3990; *The World in Figures*.

TUVALU - MONEY SUPPLY

G.K. Hall and Company, 70 Lincoln Street, Boston, Massachusetts 02111 (617) 423-3990; *The World in Figures*.

TUVALU - MOTOR VEHICLES IN USE

G.K. Hall and Company, 70 Lincoln Street, Boston, Massachusetts 02111 (617) 423-3990; *The World in Figures*.

TUVALU - NATALITY - See TUVALU - BIRTH RATES

TUVALU - NATIONAL ACCOUNTS

Statistical Office of the United Nations, Publishing Service, New York, New York 10017 (800) 253-9646; *Statistical Yearbook for Asia and the Pacific*.

TUVALU - NATIONAL INCOME

G.K. Hall and Company, 70 Lincoln Street, Boston, Massachusetts 02111 (617) 423-3990; *The World in Figures*.

TUVALU - NEWSPAPER PRODUCTION - See TUVALU - FORESTRY AND FOREST PRODUCTS

TUVALU - OCCUPATIONS - See TUVALU - LABOR FORCE

TUVALU - PESTICIDE USE

Food and Agricultural Organization of the United Nations (FAO) Via delle Terme di Caracalla, 00100 Rome, Italy (Telephone Number in U.S. (202) 653-2400); *The State of Food and Agriculture*.

TUVALU - PETROLEUM INDUSTRY

Food and Agricultural Organization of the United Nations (FAO) Via delle Terme di Caracalla, 00100 Rome, Italy (Telephone Number in U.S. (202) 653-2400); *The State of Food and Agriculture*.

G.K. Hall and Company, 70 Lincoln Street, Boston, Massachusetts 02111 (617) 423-3990; *The World in Figures*.

TUVALU - POPULATION

G.K. Hall and Company, 70 Lincoln Street, Boston, Massachusetts 02111 (617) 423-3990; *The World in Figures*.

Statistical Office of the United Nations, Publishing Service, New York, New York 10017 (800) 253-9646; *Demographic Yearbook*, and *Statistical Yearbook for Asia and the Pacific*.

World Health Organization, Office of Publications, Avenue Appia, CH-1211 Geneva 27, Switzerland (Telephone Number in U.S. (518) 436-9686); *World Health Statistics Annual*.

TUVALU - PRICES

Food and Agricultural Organization of the United Nations (FAO) Via delle Terme di Caracalla, 00100 Rome, Italy (Telephone Number in U.S. (202) 653-2400); *The State of Food and Agriculture*.

G.K. Hall and Company, 70 Lincoln Street, Boston, Massachusetts 02111 (617) 423-3990; *The World in Figures*.

South Pacific Commission, Post Box D5, Noumea Cedex, New Caledonia; *Statistical Bulletin of the South Pacific: Overseas Trade*, and *Statistical Bulletin of the South Pacific: Retail Price Indexes*.

TUVALU - PRODUCTION

G.K. Hall and Company, 70 Lincoln Street, Boston, Massachusetts 02111 (617) 423-3990; *The World in Figures*.

TUVALU - RAILWAYS

G.K. Hall and Company, 70 Lincoln Street, Boston, Massachusetts 02111 (617) 423-3990; *The World in Figures*.

TUVALU - RETAIL TRADE

G.K. Hall and Company, 70 Lincoln Street, Boston, Massachusetts 02111 (617) 423-3990; *The World in Figures*.

TUVALU - SOCIAL DATA

G.K. Hall and Company, 70 Lincoln Street, Boston, Massachusetts 02111 (617) 423-3990; *The World in Figures*.

TUVALU - STOCKS - COMMODITY - MARKET PRICE - INDEX

Food and Agricultural Organization of the United Nations (FAO) Via delle Terme di Caracalla, 00100 Rome, Italy (Telephone Number in U.S. (202) 653-2400); *The State of Food and Agriculture*.

TUVALU - TAXATION

G.K. Hall and Company, 70 Lincoln Street, Boston, Massachusetts 02111 (617) 423-3990; *The World in Figures*.

TUVALU - TELEPHONES IN USE

American Telephone and Telegraph Company, 26 Parsippany Road, Whippany, New Jersey 07981 (800) 338-4038; *The World's Telephones*.

G.K. Hall and Company, 70 Lincoln Street, Boston, Massachusetts 02111 (617) 423-3990; *The World in Figures*.

TUVALU - TEXTILE INDUSTRY

G.K. Hall and Company, 70 Lincoln Street, Boston, Massachusetts 02111 (617) 423-3990; *The World in Figures*.

TUVALU - TOBACCO PRODUCTION

South Pacific Commission, Post Box D5, Noumea Cedex, New Caledonia; *Statistical Bulletin of the South Pacific: Retail Price Indexes*.

TUVALU - TOURISM

G.K. Hall and Company, 70 Lincoln Street, Boston, Massachusetts 02111 (617) 423-3990; *The World in Figures*.

World Tourism Organization, Calle Capitan Haya 42, E-28020 Madrid, Spain; *Yearbook of Tourism Statistics*.

TUVALU - TRADE - See TUVALU - FOREIGN TRADE

TUVALU - TRANSPORTATION AND COMMUNICATIONS

G.K. Hall and Company, 70 Lincoln Street, Boston, Massachusetts 02111 (617) 423-3990; *The World in Figures*.

South Pacific Commission, Post Box D5, Noumea Cedex, New Caledonia; *Statistical Bulletin of the South Pacific: Retail Price Indexes*.

Statistical Office of the United Nations, Publishing Service, New York, New York 10017 (800) 253-9646; *Statistical Yearbook for Asia and the Pacific*.

TUVALU - VITAL STATISTICS

G.K. Hall and Company, 70 Lincoln Street, Boston, Massachusetts 02111 (617) 423-3990; *The World in Figures*.

World Health Organization, Office of Publications, Avenue Appia, CH-1211 Geneva 27, Switzerland (Telephone Number in U.S. (518) 436-9686); *World Health Statistics Annual*.

TUVALU - WAGES

G.K. Hall and Company, 70 Lincoln Street, Boston, Massachusetts 02111 (617) 423-3990; *The World in Figures*.

Statistical Office of the United Nations, Publishing Service, New York, New York 10017 (800) 253-9646; *Statistical Yearbook for Asia and the Pacific*.

TUVALU - WEATHER

G.K. Hall and Company, 70 Lincoln Street, Boston, Massachusetts 02111 (617) 423-3990; *The World in Figures*.

U

Uganda - National Statistical Office

Chief Government Statistician, Department of Statistics, Ministry of Planning and Economic Development, Post Office Box 13, Entebbe, Uganda.

Uganda - Primary Statistics Source

Statistics Division, Ministry of Planning, Government Printer, Post Office Box 33, Entebbe, Uganda; *Quarterly Economic and Statistical Bulletin.*

UGANDA - AGRICULTURE

Euromonitor Publications Limited, 87-88 Turnmill Street, London EC1M 5QU, England; *International Marketing Data and Statistics.*

Facts on File, 460 Park Avenue South, New York, New York 10016 (800) 443-8323; *The New Book of World Rankings.*

Food and Agricultural Organization of the United Nations (FAO) Via delle Terme di Caracalla, 00100 Rome, Italy (Telephone Number in U.S. (202) 653-2400); *Production Yearbook, The State of Food and Agriculture,* and *Trade Yearbook.*

G.K. Hall and Company, 70 Lincoln Street, Boston, Massachusetts 02111 (617) 423-3990; *The World in Figures.*

Statistical Office of the United Nations, Publishing Service, New York, New York 10017 (800) 253-9646; *Statistical Yearbook,* and *Survey of Economic and Social Conditions in Africa.*

Times Books, 201 East 50th Street, New York, New York 10022 (212) 751-2600; *The Economist Book of Vital World Statistics.*

United Nations Economic Commission for Africa, Africa Hall, P.O. Box 3001, Addis Ababa, Ethiopia (Telephone Number in U.S. (800) 253-9646); *African Statistical Yearbook.*

The World Bank, 1818 H Street, NW, Washington, D.C. 20433 (202) 477-1234; *World Tables.*

UGANDA - AIRLINE SERVICE

Facts on File, 460 Park Avenue South, New York, New York 10016 (800) 443-8323; *The New Book of World Rankings.*

G.K. Hall and Company, 70 Lincoln Street, Boston, Massachusetts 02111 (617) 423-3990; *The World in Figures.*

International Civil Aviation Organization, 1000 Sherbrooke Street, West, Montreal, Quebec, Canada H3A 2R2 (514) 285-8219; *Civil Aviation Statistics of the World.*

Statistical Office of the United Nations, Publishing Service, New York, New York 10017 (800) 253-9646; *Statistical Yearbook.*

Times Books, 201 East 50th Street, New York, New York 10022 (212) 751-2600; *The Economist Book of Vital World Statistics.*

United Nations Economic Commission for Africa, Africa Hall, P.O. Box 3001, Addis Ababa, Ethiopia (Telephone Number in U.S. (800) 253-9646); *African Statistical Yearbook.*

UGANDA - ALUMINUM PRODUCTION AND CONSUMPTION - See UGANDA - MINING AND MINERAL PRODUCTS

UGANDA - ANIMAL HEALTH

Food and Agricultural Organization of the United Nations (FAO), Via delle Terme di Caracalla, 00100 Rome, Italy (Telephone Number in U.S. (202) 653-2400); *Animal Health Yearbook.*

UGANDA - AREA AND DENSITY OF POPULATION

African Development Bank, 01 BP 1387, Abidjan 01, Cote D'Ivoire; *Selected Statistics on Regional Member Countries.*

Euromonitor Publications Limited, 87-88 Turnmill Street, London EC1M 5QU, England; *International Marketing Data and Statistics.*

Facts on File, 460 Park Avenue South, New York, New York 10016 (800) 443-8323; *The New Book of World Rankings.*

Food and Agricultural Organization of the United Nations (FAO) Via delle Terme di Caracalla, 00100 Rome, Italy (Telephone Number in U.S. (202) 653-2400); *The State of Food and Agriculture.*

G.K. Hall and Company, 70 Lincoln Street, Boston, Massachusetts 02111 (617) 423-3990; *The World in Figures.*

Statistical Office of the United Nations, Publishing Service, New York, New York 10017 (800) 253-9646; *Statistical Yearbook,* and *Survey of Economic and Social Conditions in Africa.*

Times Books, 201 East 50th Street, New York, New York 10022 (212) 751-2600; *The Economist Book of Vital World Statistics.*

United Nations Educational, Scientific and Cultural Organization (UNESCO), 7 Place de Fontenoy, F-75700 Paris, France (Telephone Number in U.S. (212) 963-5981); *Statistical Yearbook.*

UGANDA - ARMS EXPORTS AND IMPORTS

U.S. Arms Control and Disarmament Agency, 320 Twenty-first Street, NW, Washington, D.C. 20451 (202) 647-8677; *World Military Expenditures and Arms Transfers.*

UGANDA - BALANCE OF PAYMENTS

African Development Bank, 01 BP 1387, Abidjan 01, Cote D'Ivoire; *Selected Statistics on Regional Member Countries.*

The Economist Intelligence Unit, 111 West 57th Street, New York, New York 10019 (800) 938-4685; *The World Market Atlas.*

G.K. Hall and Company, 70 Lincoln Street, Boston, Massachusetts 02111 (617) 423-3990; *The World in Figures.*

International Monetary Fund, 700 Nineteenth Street, NW, Washington, D.C. 20431; *Balance of Payments Yearbook.*

Times Books, 201 East 50th Street, New York, New York 10022 (212) 751-2600; *The Economist Book of Vital World Statistics.*

United Nations Economic Commission for Africa, Africa Hall, P.O. Box 3001, Addis Ababa, Ethiopia (Telephone Number in U.S. (800) 253-9646); *African Statistical Yearbook.*

The World Bank, 1818 H Street, NW, Washington, D.C. 20433 (202) 477-1234; *World Tables.*

UGANDA - BANKING

Facts on File, 460 Park Avenue South, New York, New York 10016 (800) 443-8323; *The New Book of World Rankings.*

G.K. Hall and Company, 70 Lincoln Street, Boston, Massachusetts 02111 (617) 423-3990; *The World in Figures.*

International Monetary Fund, 700 Nineteenth Street, NW, Washington, D.C. 20431 (202) 623-7000; *International Financial Statistics.*

United Nations Economic Commission for Africa, Africa Hall, P.O. Box 3001, Addis Ababa, Ethiopia (Telephone Number in U.S. (800) 253-9646); *African Statistical Yearbook.*

UGANDA - BARLEY PRODUCTION - See UGANDA - CROPS

UGANDA - BEER PRODUCTION

Facts on File, 460 Park Avenue South, New York, New York 10016 (800) 443-8323; *The New Book of World Rankings.*

Statistical Office of the United Nations, Publishing Service, New York, New York 10017 (800) 253-9646; *Statistical Yearbook.*

UGANDA - BIRTH RATES

Facts on File, 460 Park Avenue South, New York, New York 10016 (800) 443-8323; *The New Book of World Rankings.*

Statistical Office of the United Nations, Publishing Service, New York, New York 10017 (800) 253-9646; *Demographic Yearbook, Statistical Yearbook,* and *Survey of Economic and Social Conditions in Africa.*

Times Books, 201 East 50th Street, New York, New York 10022 (212) 751-2600; *The Economist Book of Vital World Statistics.*

The World Bank, 1818 H Street, NW, Washington, D.C. 20433 (202) 477-1234; *World Tables.*

UGANDA - BONDS

G.K. Hall and Company, 70 Lincoln Street, Boston, Massachusetts 02111 (617) 423-3990; *The World in Figures.*

UGANDA - BOOK PRODUCTION

G.K. Hall and Company, 70 Lincoln Street, Boston, Massachusetts 02111 (617) 423-3990; *The World in Figures.*

UGANDA - BROADCASTING

Billboard Limited, P.O. Box 9027, 1006 AA Amsterdam, The Netherlands (Telephone Number in U.S. (212) 764-7300); *World Radio TV Handbook.*

Facts on File, 460 Park Avenue South, New York, New York 10016 (800) 443-8323; *The New Book of World Rankings.*

G.K. Hall and Company, 70 Lincoln Street, Boston, Massachusetts 02111 (617) 423-3990; *The World in Figures.*

Times Books, 201 East 50th Street, New York, New York 10022 (212) 751-2600; *The Economist Book of Vital World Statistics.*

UGANDA - BUSINESS

G.K. Hall and Company, 70 Lincoln Street, Boston, Massachusetts 02111 (617) 423-3990; *The World in Figures.*

UGANDA - CALORIE SUPPLY

African Development Bank, 01 BP 1387, Abidjan 01, Cote D'Ivoire; *Selected Statistics on Regional Member Countries.*

Food and Agricultural Organization of the United Nations (FAO) Via delle Terme di Caracalla, 00100 Rome, Italy (Telephone Number in U.S. (202) 653-2400); *The State of Food and Agriculture.*

UGANDA - CASTOR BEAN PRODUCTION - See - UGANDA - CROPS

UGANDA - CATTLE - See UGANDA - LIVESTOCK AND POULTRY

UGANDA - CEMENT PRODUCTION - See UGANDA - MINING AND MINERAL PRODUCTS

UGANDA - CHEMICAL (ORGANIC) PRODUCTION - See UGANDA - MINING AND MINERAL PRODUCTS

UGANDA - CHICK PEA PRODUCTION - See - UGANDA - CROPS

UGANDA - CHICKENS - See UGANDA - LIVESTOCK AND POULTRY

UGANDA - CIGARETTE PRODUCTION - See UGANDA - TOBACCO PRODUCTION

UGANDA - CLASS STRUCTURE

G.K. Hall and Company, 70 Lincoln Street, Boston, Massachusetts 02111 (617) 423-3990; *The World in Figures.*

UGANDA - CLIMATE

Facts on File, 460 Park Avenue South, New York, New York 10016 (800) 443-8323; *The New Book of World Rankings.*

G.K. Hall and Company, 70 Lincoln Street, Boston, Massachusetts 02111 (617) 423-3990; *The World in Figures.*

UGANDA - COAL PRODUCTION - See UGANDA - MINING AND MINERAL PRODUCTS

UGANDA - COCOA PRODUCTION - See - UGANDA - CROPS

UGANDA - COFFEE - See - UGANDA - CROPS

UGANDA - COMMUNICATIONS

G.K. Hall and Company, 70 Lincoln Street, Boston, Massachusetts 02111 (617) 423-3990; *The World in Figures.*

United Nations Economic Commission for Africa, Africa Hall, P.O. Box 3001, Addis Ababa, Ethiopia (Telephone Number in U.S. (800) 253-9646); *African Statistical Yearbook.*

UGANDA - CONSTRUCTION INDUSTRY

Facts on File, 460 Park Avenue South, New York, New York 10016 (800) 443-8323; *The New Book of World Rankings.*

Statistical Office of the United Nations, Publishing Service, New York, New York 10017 (800) 253-9646; *Construction Statistics Yearbook,* and *Statistical Yearbook.*

United Nations Economic Commission for Africa, Africa Hall, P.O. Box 3001, Addis Ababa, Ethiopia (Telephone Number in U.S. (800) 253-9646); *African Statistical Yearbook.*

UGANDA - CONSUMER PRICE INDEX

African Development Bank, 01 BP 1387, Abidjan 01, Cote D'Ivoire; *Selected Statistics on Regional Member Countries.*

G.K. Hall and Company, 70 Lincoln Street, Boston, Massachusetts 02111 (617) 423-3990; *The World in Figures.*

Statistical Office of the United Nations, Publishing Service, New York, New York 10017 (800) 253-9646; *Statistical Yearbook,* and *Survey of Economic and Social Conditions in Africa.*

United Nations Economic Commission for Africa, Africa Hall, P.O. Box 3001, Addis Ababa, Ethiopia (Telephone Number in U.S. (800) 253-9646); *African Statistical Yearbook.*

UGANDA - CONSUMER PRICES

International Labour Office, I.L.O. Publications, CH-1211, Geneva 22, Switzerland; *Yearbook of Labour Statistics.*

International Monetary Fund, 700 Nineteenth Street, NW, Washington, D.C. 20431 (202) 623-7000; *International Financial Statistics.*

Times Books, 201 East 50th Street, New York, New York 10022 (212) 751-2600; *The Economist Book of Vital World Statistics.*

UGANDA - CONSUMPTION

African Development Bank, 01 BP 1387, Abidjan 01, Cote D'Ivoire; *Selected Statistics on Regional Member Countries.*

G.K. Hall and Company, 70 Lincoln Street, Boston, Massachusetts 02111 (617) 423-3990; *The World in Figures.*

Statistical Office of the United Nations, Publishing Service, New York, New York 10017 (800) 253-9646; *Survey of Economic and Social Conditions in Africa.*

UGANDA - COPPER AND COPPER ORE PRODUCTION AND CONSUMPTION - See UGANDA - MINING AND MINERAL PRODUCTS

UGANDA - CORN PRODUCTION - See - UGANDA - CROPS

UGANDA - CORPORATE TAXES - See UGANDA - TAXATION

UGANDA - COTTON - See - UGANDA - CROPS

UGANDA - CRIME

Yale University Press, Yale Station, New Haven, Connecticut 06520 (203) 432-0940; *Violence and Crime in Cross-National Perspective.*

UGANDA - CROPS

Commodity Research Bureau, Incorporated, 75 Wall Street, New York, New York 10005 (212) 504-7754; *Commodity Year Book.*

Facts on File, 460 Park Avenue South, New York, New York 10016 (800) 443-8323; *The New Book of World Rankings.*

Food and Agricultural Organization of the United Nations (FAO) Via delle Terme di Caracalla, 00100 Rome, Italy (Telephone Number in U.S. (202) 653-2400); *Production Yearbook,* and *The State of Food and Agriculture.*

G.K. Hall and Company, 70 Lincoln Street, Boston, Massachusetts 02111 (617) 423-3990; *The World in Figures.*

International Monetary Fund, 700 Nineteenth Street, NW, Washington, D.C. 20431 (202) 623-7000; *International Financial Statistics.*

Statistical Office of the United Nations, Publishing Service, New York, New York 10017 (800) 253-9646; *Statistical Yearbook.*

United Nations Economic Commission for Africa, Africa Hall, P.O. Box 3001, Addis Ababa, Ethiopia (Telephone Number in U.S. (800) 253-9646); *African Statistical Yearbook.*

UGANDA - CUSTOMS DUTIES

G.K. Hall and Company, 70 Lincoln Street, Boston, Massachusetts 02111 (617) 423-3990; *The World in Figures.*

UGANDA - DAIRY PRODUCTS

Facts on File, 460 Park Avenue South, New York, New York 10016 (800) 443-8323; *The New Book of World Rankings.*

Food and Agricultural Organization of the United Nations (FAO) Via delle Terme di Caracalla, 00100 Rome, Italy (Telephone Number in U.S. (202) 653-2400); *The State of Food and Agriculture.*

Statistical Office of the United Nations, Publishing Service, New York, New York 10017 (800) 253-9646; *Statistical Yearbook.*

UGANDA - DEATH RATES

G.K. Hall and Company, 70 Lincoln Street, Boston, Massachusetts 02111 (617) 423-3990; *The World in Figures.*

Statistical Office of the United Nations, Publishing Service, New York, New York 10017 (800) 253-9646; *Statistical Yearbook,* and

Survey of Economic and Social Conditions in Africa.

Times Books, 201 East 50th Street, New York, New York 10022 (212) 751-2600; *The Economist Book of Vital World Statistics.*

UGANDA - DEFENSE EXPENDITURES

G.K. Hall and Company, 70 Lincoln Street, Boston, Massachusetts 02111 (617) 423-3990; *The World in Figures.*

U.S. Arms Control and Disarmament Agency, 320 Twenty-first Street, NW, Washington, D.C. 20451 (202) 647-8677; *World Military Expenditures and Arms Transfers.*

UGANDA - DEVELOPMENT ASSISTANCE

G.K. Hall and Company, 70 Lincoln Street, Boston, Massachusetts 02111 (617) 423-3990; *The World in Figures.*

Statistical Office of the United Nations, Publishing Service, New York, New York 10017 (800) 253-9646; *Statistical Yearbook.*

UGANDA - DEMOGRAPHY

The Economist Intelligence Unit, 111 West 57th Street, New York, New York 10019 (800) 938-4685; *The World Market Atlas.*

Facts on File, 460 Park Avenue South, New York, New York 10016 (800) 443-8323; *The New Book of World Rankings.*

G.K. Hall and Company, 70 Lincoln Street, Boston, Massachusetts 02111 (617) 423-3990; *The World in Figures.*

Statistical Office of the United Nations, Publishing Service, New York, New York 10017 (800) 253-9646; *Survey of Economic and Social Conditions in Africa.*

UGANDA - DIAMOND PRODUCTION - See UGANDA - MINING AND MINERAL PRODUCTS

UGANDA - DISEASE

G.K. Hall and Company, 70 Lincoln Street, Boston, Massachusetts 02111 (617) 423-3990; *The World in Figures.*

UGANDA - DIVORCE RATES

Facts on File, 460 Park Avenue South, New York, New York 10016 (800) 443-8323; *The New Book of World Rankings.*

Statistical Office of the United Nations, Publishing Service, New York, New York 10017 (800) 253-9646; *Demographic Yearbook.*

UGANDA - DOMESTIC PRODUCT

G.K. Hall and Company, 70 Lincoln Street, Boston, Massachusetts 02111 (617) 423-3990; *The World in Figures.*

UGANDA - ECONOMY

African Development Bank, 01 BP 1387, Abidjan 01, Cote D'Ivoire; *Selected Statistics on Regional Member Countries.*

Euromonitor Publications Limited, 87-88 Turnmill Street, London EC1M 5QU, England; *International Marketing Data and Statistics.*

Facts on File, 460 Park Avenue South, New York, New York 10016 (800) 443-8323; *The New Book of World Rankings.*

G.K. Hall and Company, 70 Lincoln Street, Boston, Massachusetts 02111 (617) 423-3990; *The World in Figures.*

Statistical Office of the United Nations, Publishing Service, New York, New York 10017 (800) 253-9646; *Foreign Trade Statistics for Africa.*

UGANDA - EDUCATION

African Development Bank, 01 BP 1387, Abidjan 01, Cote D'Ivoire; *Selected Statistics on Regional Member Countries.*

The Economist Intelligence Unit, 111 West 57th Street, New York, New York 10019 (800) 938-4685; *The World Market Atlas.*

Facts on File, 460 Park Avenue South, New York, New York 10016 (800) 443-8323; *The New Book of World Rankings.*

G.K. Hall and Company, 70 Lincoln Street, Boston, Massachusetts 02111 (617) 423-3990; *The World in Figures.*

Statistical Office of the United Nations, Publishing Service, New York, New York 10017 (800) 253-9646; *Survey of Economic and Social Conditions in Africa.*

Times Books, 201 East 50th Street, New York, New York 10022 (212) 751-2600; *The Economist Book of Vital World Statistics.*

United Nations Economic Commission for Africa, Africa Hall, P.O. Box 3001, Addis Ababa, Ethiopia (Telephone Number in U.S. (800) 253-9646); *African Statistical Yearbook.*

United Nations Educational, Scientific and Cultural Organization (UNESCO), 7 Place de Fontenoy, F-75700 Paris, France (Telephone Number in U.S. (212) 963-5981); *Statistical Yearbook.*

The World Bank, 1818 H Street, NW, Washington, D.C. 20433 (202) 477-1234; *World Tables.*

UGANDA - EGG PRODUCTION AND CONSUMPTION - See UGANDA - DAIRY PRODUCTS

UGANDA - ELECTRICITY

Facts on File, 460 Park Avenue South, New York, New York 10016 (800) 443-8323; *The New Book of World Rankings.*

Statistical Office of the United Nations, Publishing Service, New York, New York 10017 (800) 253-9646; *Statistical Yearbook,* and *Survey of Economic and Social Conditions in Africa.*

Times Books, 201 East 50th Street, New York, New York 10022 (212) 751-2600; *The Economist Book of Vital World Statistics.*

United Nations Economic Commission for Africa, Africa Hall, P.O. Box 3001, Addis Ababa, Ethiopia (Telephone Number in U.S. (800) 253-9646); *African Statistical Yearbook.*

UGANDA - EMPLOYMENT

Euromonitor Publications Limited, 87-88 Turnmill Street, London EC1M 5QU, England; *International Marketing Data and Statistics.*

Facts on File, 460 Park Avenue South, New York, New York 10016 (800) 443-8323; *The New Book of World Rankings.*

International Labour Office, I.L.O. Publications, CH-1211, Geneva 22, Switzerland; *Yearbook of Labour Statistics.*

Statistical Office of the United Nations, Publishing Service, New York, New York 10017 (800) 253-9646; *Statistical Yearbook*, and *Survey of Economic and Social Conditions in Africa*.

United Nations Economic Commission for Africa, Africa Hall, P.O. Box 3001, Addis Ababa, Ethiopia (Telephone Number in U.S. (800) 253-9646); *African Statistical Yearbook*.

UGANDA - ENERGY

Facts on File, 460 Park Avenue South, New York, New York 10016 (800) 443-8323; *The New Book of World Rankings*.

Food and Agricultural Organization of the United Nations (FAO) Via delle Terme di Caracalla, 00100 Rome, Italy (Telephone Number in U.S. (202) 653-2400); *The State of Food and Agriculture*.

G.K. Hall and Company, 70 Lincoln Street, Boston, Massachusetts 02111 (617) 423-3990; *The World in Figures*.

Statistical Office of the United Nations, Publishing Service, New York, New York 10017 (800) 253-9646; *Yearbook of World Energy Statistics*.

Times Books, 201 East 50th Street, New York, New York 10022 (212) 751-2600; *The Economist Book of Vital World Statistics*.

United Nations Economic Commission for Africa, Africa Hall, P.O. Box 3001, Addis Ababa, Ethiopia (Telephone Number in U.S. (800) 253-9646); *African Statistical Yearbook*.

UGANDA - EXCHANGE RATE

African Development Bank, 01 BP 1387, Abidjan 01, Cote D'Ivoire; *Selected Statistics on Regional Member Countries*.

Euromonitor Publications Limited, 87-88 Turnmill Street, London EC1M 5QU, England; *International Marketing Data and Statistics*.

International Civil Aviation Organization, 1000 Sherbrooke Street, West, Montreal, Quebec, Canada H3A 2R2 (514) 285-8219; *Civil Aviation Statistics of the World*.

International Monetary Fund, 700 Nineteenth Street, NW, Washington, D.C. 20431 (202) 623-7000; *International Financial Statistics*.

Statistical Office of the United Nations, Publishing Service, New York, New York 10017 (800) 253-9646; *Foreign Trade Statistics for Africa*, and *Statistical Yearbook*.

UGANDA - EXPORTS

African Development Bank, 01 BP 1387, Abidjan 01, Cote D'Ivoire; *Selected Statistics on Regional Member Countries*.

The Economist Intelligence Unit, 111 West 57th Street, New York, New York 10019 (800) 938-4685; *The World Market Atlas*.

Euromonitor Publications Limited, 87-88 Turnmill Street, London EC1M 5QU, England; *International Marketing Data and Statistics*.

Food and Agricultural Organization of the United Nations (FAO) Via delle Terme di Caracalla, 00100 Rome, Italy (Telephone Number in U.S. (202) 653-2400); *The State of Food and Agriculture*.

G.K. Hall and Company, 70 Lincoln Street, Boston, Massachusetts 02111 (617) 423-3990; *The World in Figures*.

International Monetary Fund, 700 Nineteenth Street, NW, Washington, D.C. 20431 (202) 623-7000; *Direction of Trade Statistics*, and *International Financial Statistics*.

Statistical Office of the United Nations, Publishing Service, New York, New York 10017 (800) 253-9646; *Foreign Trade Statistics for Africa*, and *Survey of Economic and Social Conditions in Africa*.

Times Books, 201 East 50th Street, New York, New York 10022 (212) 751-2600; *The Economist Book of Vital World Statistics*.

United Nations Economic Commission for Africa, Africa Hall, P.O. Box 3001, Addis Ababa, Ethiopia (Telephone Number in U.S. (800) 253-9646); *African Statistical Yearbook*.

The World Bank, 1818 H Street, NW, Washington, D.C. 20433 (202) 477-1234; *World Tables*.

UGANDA - EXTERNAL INDEBTEDNESS

African Development Bank, 01 BP 1387, Abidjan 01, Cote D'Ivoire; *Selected Statistics on Regional Member Countries*.

Statistical Office of the United Nations, Publishing Service, New York, New York 10017 (800) 253-9646; *Survey of Economic and Social Conditions in Africa*.

The World Bank, 1818 H Street, NW, Washington, D.C. 20433 (202) 477-1234; *World Tables*.

UGANDA - EXTERNAL TRADE

African Development Bank, 01 BP 1387, Abidjan 01, Cote D'Ivoire; *Selected Statistics on Regional Member Countries*.

Food and Agricultural Organization of the United Nations (FAO) Via delle Terme di Caracalla, 00100 Rome, Italy (Telephone Number in U.S. (202) 653-2400); *The State of Food and Agriculture*.

G.K. Hall and Company, 70 Lincoln Street, Boston, Massachusetts 02111 (617) 423-3990; *The World in Figures*.

Statistical Office of the United Nations, Publishing Service, New York, New York 10017 (800) 253-9646; *Statistical Yearbook*.

UGANDA - FABRIC PRODUCTION

Statistical Office of the United Nations, Publishing Service, New York, New York 10017 (800) 253-9646; *Statistical Yearbook*.

UGANDA - FARM CROPS - See - UGANDA - CROPS

UGANDA - FEMALE WORKING POPULATION - See UGANDA - EMPLOYMENT

UGANDA - FERTILITY RATES

Facts on File, 460 Park Avenue South, New York, New York 10016 (800) 443-8323; *The New Book of World Rankings*.

Statistical Office of the United Nations, Publishing Service, New York, New York 10017 (800) 253-9646; *Survey of Economic and Social Conditions in Africa*.

Times Books, 201 East 50th Street, New York, New York 10022 (212) 751-2600; *The Economist Book of Vital World Statistics*.

The World Bank, 1818 H Street, NW, Washington, D.C. 20433 (202) 477-1234; *World Tables*.

UGANDA - FERTILIZER

Food and Agricultural Organization of the United Nations (FAO), Via delle Terme di Caracalla, 00100 Rome, Italy (Telephone Number in U.S. (202) 653-2400); *Fertilizer Yearbook*, and *The State of Food and Agriculture*.

Statistical Office of the United Nations, Publishing Service, New York, New York 10017 (800) 253-9646; *Statistical Yearbook*.

UGANDA - FETAL MORTALITY

Statistical Office of the United Nations, Publishing Service, New York, New York 10017 (800) 253-9646; *Demographic Yearbook*.

UGANDA - FINANCE

African Development Bank, 01 BP 1387, Abidjan 01, Cote D'Ivoire; *Selected Statistics on Regional Member Countries*.

Facts on File, 460 Park Avenue South, New York, New York 10016 (800) 443-8323; *The New Book of World Rankings*.

G.K. Hall and Company, 70 Lincoln Street, Boston, Massachusetts 02111 (617) 423-3990; *The World in Figures*.

United Nations Economic Commission for Africa, Africa Hall, P.O. Box 3001, Addis Ababa, Ethiopia (Telephone Number in U.S. (800) 253-9646); *African Statistical Yearbook*.

UGANDA - FISHERIES

Facts on File, 460 Park Avenue South, New York, New York 10016 (800) 443-8323; *The New Book of World Rankings*.

Food and Agricultural Organization of the United Nations (FAO) Via delle Terme di Caracalla, 00100 Rome, Italy (Telephone Number in U.S. (202) 653-2400); *The State of Food and Agriculture*, and *Yearbook of Fishery Statistics*.

Statistical Office of the United Nations, Publishing Service, New York, New York 10017 (800) 253-9646; *Statistical Yearbook*, and *Survey of Economic and Social Conditions in Africa*.

United Nations Economic Commission for Africa, Africa Hall, P.O. Box 3001, Addis Ababa, Ethiopia (Telephone Number in U.S. (800) 253-9646); *African Statistical Yearbook*.

UGANDA - FLOUR PRODUCTION

Statistical Office of the United Nations, Publishing Service, New York, New York 10017 (800) 253-9646; *Statistical Yearbook*.

UGANDA - FOOD

African Development Bank, 01 BP 1387, Abidjan 01, Cote D'Ivoire; *Selected Statistics on Regional Member Countries*.

Food and Agricultural Organization of the United Nations (FAO) Via delle Terme di Caracalla, 00100 Rome, Italy (Telephone Number in U.S. (202) 653-2400); *The State of Food and Agriculture*.

G.K. Hall and Company, 70 Lincoln Street, Boston, Massachusetts 02111 (617) 423-3990; *The World in Figures*.

UGANDA - FOREIGN AID

G.K. Hall and Company, 70 Lincoln Street, Boston, Massachusetts 02111 (617) 423-3990; *The World in Figures*.

UGANDA - FOREIGN TRADE

Euromonitor Publications Limited, 87-88 Turnmill Street, London EC1M 5QU, England; *International Marketing Data and Statistics*.

Facts on File, 460 Park Avenue South, New York, New York 10016 (800) 443-8323; *The New Book of World Rankings*.

Food and Agricultural Organization of the United Nations (FAO) Via delle Terme di Caracalla, 00100 Rome, Italy (Telephone Number in U.S. (202) 653-2400); *The State of Food and Agriculture*.

G.K. Hall and Company, 70 Lincoln Street, Boston, Massachusetts 02111 (617) 423-3990; *The World in Figures*.

International Monetary Fund, 700 Nineteenth Street, NW, Washington, D.C. 20431 (202) 623-7000; *International Financial Statistics*.

Statistical Office of the United Nations, Publishing Service, New York, New York 10017 (800) 253-9646; *Foreign Trade Statistics for Africa, International Trade Statistics Yearbook, Statistical Yearbook*, and *Trade in Manufactures of Development Countries*.

United Nations Economic Commission for Africa, Africa Hall, P.O. Box 3001, Addis Ababa, Ethiopia (Telephone Number in U.S. (800) 253-9646); *African Statistical Yearbook*.

The World Bank, 1818 H Street, NW, Washington, D.C. 20433 (202) 477-1234; *World Tables*.

UGANDA - FORESTRY AND FOREST PRODUCTS

Facts on File, 460 Park Avenue South, New York, New York 10016 (800) 443-8323; *The New Book of World Rankings*.

Food and Agricultural Organization of the United Nations (FAO) Via delle Terme di Caracalla, 00100 Rome, Italy (Telephone Number in U.S. (202) 653-2400); *The State of Food and Agriculture*, and *Yearbook of Forest Products*.

G.K. Hall and Company, 70 Lincoln Street, Boston, Massachusetts 02111 (617) 423-3990; *The World in Figures*.

Statistical Office of the United Nations, Publishing Service, New York, New York 10017 (800) 253-9646; *Statistical Yearbook*.

United Nations Economic Commission for Africa, Africa Hall, P.O. Box 3001, Addis Ababa, Ethiopia (Telephone Number in U.S. (800) 253-9646); *African Statistical Yearbook*.

United Nations Educational, Scientific and Cultural Organization (UNESCO), 7 Place de Fontenoy, F-75700 Paris, France (Telephone Number in U.S. (212) 963-5981); *Statistical Yearbook*.

UGANDA - GAS PRODUCTION - See UGANDA - MINING AND MINERAL PRODUCTS

UGANDA - GENERAL MORTALITY

Statistical Office of the United Nations, Publishing Service, New York, New York 10017 (800) 253-9646; *Demographic Yearbook*.

UGANDA - GEOGRAPHIC DATA

Facts on File, 460 Park Avenue South, New York, New York 10016 (800) 443-8323; *The New Book of World Rankings*.

UGANDA - GOATS - See UGANDA - LIVESTOCK AND POULTRY

UGANDA - GOLD HOLDINGS

International Monetary Fund, 700 Nineteenth Street, NW, Washington, D.C. 20431 (202) 623-7000; *International Financial Statistics.*

Statistical Office of the United Nations, Publishing Service, New York, New York 10017 (800) 253-9646; *Statistical Yearbook.*

The World Bank, 1818 H Street, NW, Washington, D.C. 20433 (202) 477-1234; *World Tables.*

UGANDA - GOLD PRODUCTION AND CONSUMPTION - See UGANDA - MINING AND MINERAL PRODUCTS

UGANDA - GOVERNMENT

G.K. Hall and Company, 70 Lincoln Street, Boston, Massachusetts 02111 (617) 423-3990; *The World in Figures.*

UGANDA - GOVERNMENT EXPENDITURE

Times Books, 201 East 50th Street, New York, New York 10022 (212) 751-2600; *The Economist Book of Vital World Statistics.*

The World Bank, 1818 II Street, NW, Washington, D.C. 20433 (202) 477-1234; *World Tables.*

UGANDA - GOVERNMENT FINANCE

International Monetary Fund, 700 Nineteenth Street, NW, Washington, D.C. 20431 (202) 623-7000; *International Financial Statistics.*

Statistical Office of the United Nations, Publishing Service, New York, New York 10017 (800) 253-9646; *Statistical Yearbook.*

UGANDA - GOVERNMENT REVENUE

Statistical Office of the United Nations, Publishing Service, New York, New York 10017 (800) 253-9646; *Survey of Economic and Social Conditions in Africa.*

Times Books, 201 East 50th Street, New York, New York 10022 (212) 751-2600; *The Economist Book of Vital World Statistics.*

The World Bank, 1818 H Street, NW, Washington, D.C. 20433 (202) 477-1234; *World Tables.*

UGANDA - GRAIN PRODUCTION - See - UGANDA - CROPS

UGANDA - GROSS DOMESTIC PRODUCT

African Development Bank, 01 BP 1387, Abidjan 01, Cote D'Ivoire; *Selected Statistics on Regional Member Countries.*

The Economist Intelligence Unit, 111 West 57th Street, New York, New York 10019 (800) 938-4685; *The World Market Atlas.*

Euromonitor Publications Limited, 87-88 Turnmill Street, London EC1M 5QU, England; *International Marketing Data and Statistics.*

Facts on File, 460 Park Avenue South, New York, New York 10016 (800) 443-8323; *The New Book of World Rankings.*

G.K. Hall and Company, 70 Lincoln Street, Boston, Massachusetts 02111 (617) 423-3990; *The World in Figures.*

Statistical Office of the United Nations, Publishing Service, New York, New York 10017 (800) 253-9646; *Statistical Yearbook*, and *Survey of Economic and Social Conditions in Africa.*

Times Books, 201 East 50th Street, New York, New York 10022 (212) 751-2600; *The Economist Book of Vital World Statistics.*

United Nations Economic Commission for Africa, Africa Hall, P.O. Box 3001, Addis Ababa, Ethiopia (Telephone Number in U.S. (800) 253-9646); *African Statistical Yearbook.*

The World Bank, 1818 H Street, NW, Washington, D.C. 20433 (202) 477-1234; *World Tables.*

UGANDA - GROSS NATIONAL PRODUCT

Euromonitor Publications Limited, 87-88 Turnmill Street, London EC1M 5QU, England; *International Marketing Data and Statistics.*

U.S. Arms Control and Disarmament Agency, 320 Twenty-first Street, NW, Washington, D.C. 20451 (202) 647-8677; *World Military Expenditures and Arms Transfers.*

The World Bank, 1818 H Street, NW, Washington, D.C. 20433 (202) 477-1234; *World Tables.*

UGANDA - GROUNDNUTS PRODUCTION - See - UGANDA - CROPS

UGANDA - HEALTH

African Development Bank, 01 BP 1387, Abidjan 01, Cote D'Ivoire; *Selected Statistics on Regional Member Countries.*

Facts on File, 460 Park Avenue South, New York, New York 10016 (800) 443-8323; *The New Book of World Rankings.*

G.K. Hall and Company, 70 Lincoln Street, Boston, Massachusetts 02111 (617) 423-3990; *The World in Figures.*

Statistical Office of the United Nations, Publishing Service, New York, New York 10017 (800) 253-9646; *Statistical Yearbook.*

Times Books, 201 East 50th Street, New York, New York 10022 (212) 751-2600; *The Economist Book of Vital World Statistics.*

United Nations Economic Commission for Africa, Africa Hall, P.O. Box 3001, Addis Ababa, Ethiopia (Telephone Number in U.S. (800) 253-9646); *African Statistical Yearbook.*

UGANDA - HIDE PRODUCTION

Food and Agricultural Organization of the United Nations (FAO), Via delle Terme di Caracalla, 00100 Rome, Italy (Telephone Number in U.S. (202) 653-2400); *Production Yearbook.*

UGANDA - HIGHWAYS

G.K. Hall and Company, 70 Lincoln Street, Boston, Massachusetts 02111 (617) 423-3990; *The World in Figures.*

International Road Federation, 525 School Street, SW, Washington, D.C. 20024 (202) 554-2106; *World Road Statistics.*

Statistical Office of the United Nations, Publishing Service, New York, New York 10017 (800) 253-9646; *Survey of Economic and Social Conditions in Africa.*

United Nations Economic Commission for Africa, Africa Hall, P.O. Box 3001, Addis Ababa, Ethiopia (Telephone Number in U.S. (800)

253-9646); *African Statistical Yearbook.*

UGANDA - HORSES - See UGANDA - LIVESTOCK AND POULTRY

UGANDA - HOUSING AND HOUSING UNITS

Facts on File, 460 Park Avenue South, New York, New York 10016 (800) 443-8323; *The New Book of World Rankings.*

UGANDA - HOURS OF WORK - See UGANDA - EMPLOYMENT

UGANDA - ILLITERATE POPULATION

The Economist Intelligence Unit, 111 West 57th Street, New York, New York 10019 (800) 938-4685; *The World Market Atlas.*

G.K. Hall and Company, 70 Lincoln Street, Boston, Massachusetts 02111 (617) 423-3990; *The World in Figures.*

United Nations Educational, Scientific and Cultural Organization (UNESCO), 7 Place de Fontenoy, F-75700 Paris, France (Telephone Number in U.S. (212) 963-5981); *Statistical Yearbook.*

UGANDA - IMPORTS

African Development Bank, 01 BP 1387, Abidjan 01, Cote D'Ivoire; *Selected Statistics on Regional Member Countries.*

The Economist Intelligence Unit, 111 West 57th Street, New York, New York 10019 (800) 938-4685; *The World Market Atlas.*

Euromonitor Publications Limited, 87-88 Turnmill Street, London EC1M 5QU, England; *International Marketing Data and Statistics.*

Food and Agricultural Organization of the United Nations (FAO) Via delle Terme di Caracalla, 00100 Rome, Italy (Telephone Number in U.S. (202) 653-2400); *The State of Food and Agriculture.*

G.K. Hall and Company, 70 Lincoln Street, Boston, Massachusetts 02111 (617) 423-3990; *The World in Figures.*

International Monetary Fund, 700 Nineteenth Street, NW, Washington, D.C. 20431 (202) 623-7000; *Direction of Trade Statistics,* and *International Financial Statistics.*

Statistical Office of the United Nations, Publishing Service, New York, New York 10017 (800) 253-9646; *Foreign Trade Statistics for Africa,* and *Survey of Economic and Social Conditions in Africa.*

United Nations Economic Commission for Africa, Africa Hall, P.O. Box 3001, Addis Ababa, Ethiopia (Telephone Number in U.S. (800) 253-9646); *African Statistical Yearbook.*

The World Bank, 1818 H Street, NW, Washington, D.C. 20433 (202) 477-1234; *World Tables.*

UGANDA - INDUSTRIAL METALS PRODUCTION - See UGANDA - MINING AND MINERAL PRODUCTS

UGANDA - INDUSTRY

Euromonitor Publications Limited, 87-88 Turnmill Street, London EC1M 5QU, England; *International Marketing Data and Statistics.*

Facts on File, 460 Park Avenue South, New York, New York 10016 (800) 443-8323; *The New Book of World Rankings.*

G.K. Hall and Company, 70 Lincoln Street, Boston, Massachusetts 02111 (617) 423-3990; *The World in Figures.*

International Labour Office, I.L.O. Publications, CH-1211, Geneva 22, Switzerland; *Yearbook of Labour Statistics.*

Statistical Office of the United Nations, Publishing Service, New York, New York 10017 (800) 253-9646; *Survey of Economic and Social Conditions in Africa.*

Times Books, 201 East 50th Street, New York, New York 10022 (212) 751-2600; *The Economist Book of Vital World Statistics.*

United Nations Economic Commission for Africa, Africa Hall, P.O. Box 3001, Addis Ababa, Ethiopia (Telephone Number in U.S. (800) 253-9646); *African Statistical Yearbook.*

The World Bank, 1818 H Street, NW, Washington, D.C. 20433 (202) 477-1234; *World Tables.*

UGANDA - INFANT AND MATERNAL MORTALITY

Statistical Office of the United Nations, Publishing Service, New York, New York 10017 (800) 253-9646; *Demographic Yearbook, Statistical Yearbook,* and *Survey of Economic and Social Conditions in Africa.*

Times Books, 201 East 50th Street, New York, New York 10022 (212) 751-2600; *The Economist Book of Vital World Statistics.*

The World Bank, 1818 H Street, NW, Washington, D.C. 20433 (202) 477-1234; *World Tables.*

UGANDA - INTERNAL TRADE

Statistical Office of the United Nations, Publishing Service, New York, New York 10017 (800) 253-9646; *Statistical Yearbook.*

UGANDA - INTERNATIONAL LIQUIDITY

International Monetary Fund, 700 Nineteenth Street, NW, Washington, D.C. 20431 (202) 623-7000; *International Financial Statistics.*

UGANDA - INTERNATIONAL RESERVES - EXCLUDING GOLD

African Development Bank, 01 BP 1387, Abidjan 01, Cote D'Ivoire; *Selected Statistics on Regional Member Countries.*

Statistical Office of the United Nations, Publishing Service, New York, New York 10017 (800) 253-9646; *Statistical Yearbook.*

The World Bank, 1818 H Street, NW, Washington, D.C. 20433 (202) 477-1234; *World Tables.*

UGANDA - IRON ORE PRODUCTION AND CONSUMPTION - See UGANDA - MINING AND MINERAL PRODUCTS

UGANDA - IRRIGATION

Euromonitor Publications Limited, 87-88 Turnmill Street, London EC1M 5QU, England; *International Marketing Data and Statistics.*

UGANDA - LABOR FORCE

African Development Bank, 01 BP 1387, Abidjan 01, Cote D'Ivoire; *Selected Statistics on Regional Member Countries.*

Euromonitor Publications Limited, 87-88 Turnmill Street, London EC1M 5QU, England; *International Marketing Data and Statistics.*

Facts on File, 460 Park Avenue South, New York, New York 10016 (800) 443-8323; *The New Book of World Rankings.*

Food and Agricultural Organization of the United Nations (FAO) Via delle Terme di Caracalla, 00100 Rome, Italy (Telephone Number in U.S. (202) 653-2400); *The State of Food and Agriculture.*

G.K. Hall and Company, 70 Lincoln Street, Boston, Massachusetts 02111 (617) 423-3990; *The World in Figures.*

Times Books, 201 East 50th Street, New York, New York 10022 (212) 751-2600; *The Economist Book of Vital World Statistics.*

The World Bank, 1818 H Street, NW, Washington, D.C. 20433 (202) 477-1234; *World Tables.*

UGANDA - LABOR PRODUCTIVITY

International Labour Office, I.L.O. Publications, CH-1211, Geneva 22, Switzerland; *Yearbook of Labour Statistics.*

UGANDA - LAND USE

Euromonitor Publications Limited, 87-88 Turnmill Street, London EC1M 5QU, England; *International Marketing Data and Statistics.*

G.K. Hall and Company, 70 Lincoln Street, Boston, Massachusetts 02111 (617) 423-3990; *The World in Figures.*

UGANDA - LIBRARIES

Facts on File, 460 Park Avenue South, New York, New York 10016 (800) 443-8323; *The New Book of World Rankings.*

United Nations Educational, Scientific and Cultural Organization (UNESCO), 7 Place de Fontenoy, F-75700 Paris, France (Telephone Number in U.S. (212) 963-5981); *Statistical Yearbook.*

UGANDA - LIFE EXPECTANCY

African Development Bank, 01 BP 1387, Abidjan 01, Cote D'Ivoire; *Selected Statistics on Regional Member Countries.*

UGANDA - LITERACY RATE

Statistical Office of the United Nations, Publishing Service, New York, New York 10017 (800) 253-9646; *Survey of Economic and Social Conditions in Africa.*

UGANDA - LIVESTOCK AND POULTRY

Euromonitor Publications Limited, 87-88 Turnmill Street, London EC1M 5QU, England; *International Marketing Data and Statistics.*

Facts on File, 460 Park Avenue South, New York, New York 10016 (800) 443-8323; *The New Book of World Rankings.*

Food and Agricultural Organization of the United Nations (FAO) Via delle Terme di Caracalla, 00100 Rome, Italy (Telephone Number in U.S. (202) 653-2400); *Production Yearbook,* and *The State of Food and Agriculture.*

G.K. Hall and Company, 70 Lincoln Street, Boston, Massachusetts 02111 (617) 423-3990; *The World in Figures.*

Statistical Office of the United Nations, Publishing Service, New York, New York 10017 (800) 253-9646; *Statistical Yearbook,* and *Survey of Economic and Social Conditions in Africa.*

United Nations Economic Commission for Africa, Africa Hall, P.O. Box 3001, Addis Ababa, Ethiopia (Telephone Number in U.S. (800) 253-9646); *African Statistical Yearbook.*

UGANDA - LIVING LEVELS

G.K. Hall and Company, 70 Lincoln Street, Boston, Massachusetts 02111 (617) 423-3990; *The World in Figures.*

Times Books, 201 East 50th Street, New York, New York 10022 (212) 751-2600; *The Economist Book of Vital World Statistics.*

UGANDA - MAIL - NUMBER OF PIECES SENT OR RECEIVED

Statistical Office of the United Nations, Publishing Service, New York, New York 10017 (800) 253-9646; *Statistical Yearbook.*

UGANDA - MANUFACTURING

Facts on File, 460 Park Avenue South, New York, New York 10016 (800) 443-8323; *The New Book of World Rankings.*

G.K. Hall and Company, 70 Lincoln Street, Boston, Massachusetts 02111 (617) 423-3990; *The World in Figures.*

Statistical Office of the United Nations, Publishing Service, New York, New York 10017 (800) 253-9646; *Survey of Economic and Social Conditions in Africa.*

United Nations Economic Commission for Africa, Africa Hall, P.O. Box 3001, Addis Ababa, Ethiopia (Telephone Number in U.S. (800) 253-9646); *African Statistical Yearbook.*

The World Bank, 1818 H Street, NW, Washington, D.C. 20433 (202) 477-1234; *World Tables.*

UGANDA - MARRIAGE RATES

Facts on File, 460 Park Avenue South, New York, New York 10016 (800) 443-8323; *The New Book of World Rankings.*

Statistical Office of the United Nations, Publishing Service, New York, New York 10017 (800) 253-9646; *Demographic Yearbook.*

UGANDA - MEAT PRODUCTION - See UGANDA - LIVESTOCK AND POULTRY

UGANDA - MERCHANT SHIPPING

G.K. Hall and Company, 70 Lincoln Street, Boston, Massachusetts 02111 (617) 423-3990; *The World in Figures.*

Times Books, 201 East 50th Street, New York, New York 10022 (212) 751-2600; *The Economist Book of Vital World Statistics.*

United Nations Economic Commission for Africa, Africa Hall, P.O. Box 3001, Addis Ababa, Ethiopia (Telephone Number in U.S. (800) 253-9646); *African Statistical Yearbook.*

U.S. Department of Transportation, Maritime Administration, 400 Seventh Street, SW, Washington, D.C. 20590 (202) 366-5807; *A Statistical Analysis of the World's Merchant Fleets.*

UGANDA - MILITARY

G.K. Hall and Company, 70 Lincoln Street, Boston, Massachusetts 02111 (617) 423-3990; *The World in Figures.*

The International Institute for Strategic Studies, 23 Tavistock Street, London WC2E 7NQ, England; *The Military Balance.*

United Nations Economic Commission for Africa, Africa Hall, P.O. Box 3001, Addis Ababa, Ethiopia (Telephone Number in U.S. (800) 253-9646); *African Statistical Yearbook.*

UGANDA - MILK PRODUCTION - See UGANDA - DAIRY PRODUCTS

UGANDA - MILLET PRODUCTION - See - UGANDA - CROPS

UGANDA - MINING AND MINERAL PRODUCTS

Facts on File, 460 Park Avenue South, New York, New York 10016 (800) 443-8323; *The New Book of World Rankings.*

G.K. Hall and Company, 70 Lincoln Street, Boston, Massachusetts 02111 (617) 423-3990; *The World in Figures.*

Statistical Office of the United Nations, Publishing Service, New York, New York 10017 (800) 253-9646; *Statistical Yearbook.*

United Nations Economic Commission for Africa, Africa Hall, P.O. Box 3001, Addis Ababa, Ethiopia (Telephone Number in U.S. (800) 253-9646); *African Statistical Yearbook.*

UGANDA - MONEY EXCHANGE RATE

Euromonitor Publications Limited, 87-88 Turnmill Street, London EC1M 5QU, England; *International Marketing Data and Statistics.*

International Monetary Fund, 700 Nineteenth Street, NW, Washington, D.C. 20431 (202) 623-7000; *International Financial Statistics.*

Statistical Office of the United Nations, Publishing Service, New York, New York 10017 (800) 253-9646; *Statistical Yearbook.*

UGANDA - MONEY RESERVES

Euromonitor Publications Limited, 87-88 Turnmill Street, London EC1M 5QU, England; *International Marketing Data and Statistics.*

UGANDA - MONEY SUPPLY

African Development Bank, 01 BP 1387, Abidjan 01, Cote D'Ivoire; *Selected Statistics on Regional Member Countries.*

Euromonitor Publications Limited, 87-88 Turnmill Street, London EC1M 5QU, England; *International Marketing Data and Statistics.*

G.K. Hall and Company, 70 Lincoln Street, Boston, Massachusetts 02111 (617) 423-3990; *The World in Figures.*

International Monetary Fund, 700 Nineteenth Street, NW, Washington, D.C. 20431 (202) 623-7000; *International Financial Statistics.*

Statistical Office of the United Nations, Publishing Service, New York, New York 10017 (800) 253-9646; *Statistical Yearbook.*

The World Bank, 1818 H Street, NW, Washington, D.C. 20433 (202) 477-1234; *World Tables.*

UGANDA - MOTION PICTURES

Statistical Office of the United Nations, Publishing Service, New York, New York 10017 (800) 253-9646; *Statistical Yearbook.*

UGANDA - MOTOR VEHICLES IN USE

G.K. Hall and Company, 70 Lincoln Street, Boston, Massachusetts 02111 (617) 423-3990; *The World in Figures.*

International Road Federation, 525 School Street, SW, Washington, D.C. 20024 (202) 554-2106; *World Road Statistics.*

Statistical Office of the United Nations, Publishing Service, New York, New York 10017 (800) 253-9646; *Statistical Yearbook*, and *Survey of Economic and Social Conditions in Africa.*

Times Books, 201 East 50th Street, New York, New York 10022 (212) 751-2600; *The Economist Book of Vital World Statistics.*

UGANDA - MOTOR VEHICLE TAXES - See UGANDA - TAXATION

UGANDA - MUSEUMS

Facts on File, 460 Park Avenue South, New York, New York 10016 (800) 443-8323; *The New Book of World Rankings.*

UGANDA - NATALITY

Statistical Office of the United Nations, Publishing Service, New York, New York 10017 (800) 253-9646; *Demographic Yearbook.*

UGANDA - NATIONAL ACCOUNTS

African Development Bank, 01 BP 1387, Abidjan 01, Cote D'Ivoire; *Selected Statistics on Regional Member Countries.*

Statistical Office of the United Nations, Publishing Service, New York, New York 10017 (800) 253-9646; *National Accounts Statistics*, and *Statistical Yearbook.*

United Nations Economic Commission for Africa, Africa Hall, P.O. Box 3001, Addis Ababa, Ethiopia (Telephone Number in U.S. (800) 253-9646); *African Statistical Yearbook.*

UGANDA - NATIONAL INCOME

Facts on File, 460 Park Avenue South, New York, New York 10016 (800) 443-8323; *The New Book of World Rankings.*

G.K. Hall and Company, 70 Lincoln Street, Boston, Massachusetts 02111 (617) 423-3990; *The World in Figures.*

Statistical Office of the United Nations, Publishing Service, New York, New York 10017 (800) 253-9646; *Statistical Yearbook.*

UGANDA - NATIONAL PRODUCT

Facts on File, 460 Park Avenue South, New York, New York 10016 (800) 443-8323; *The New Book of World Rankings.*

Statistical Office of the United Nations, Publishing Service, New York, New York 10017 (800) 253-9646; *Statistical Yearbook.*

UGANDA - NATURAL GAS PRODUCTION - See UGANDA - MINING AND MINERAL PRODUCTS

UGANDA - NEWSPAPER PRODUCTION - See - UGANDA - FORESTRY AND FOREST PRODUCTS

UGANDA - NEWSPRINT - See - UGANDA - FORESTRY AND FOREST PRODUCTS

UGANDA - OCCUPATIONS - See UGANDA - LABOR FORCE

UGANDA - PAPER - See - UGANDA - FORESTRY AND FOREST PRODUCTS

UGANDA - PATENTS

Statistical Office of the United Nations, Publishing Service, New York, New York 10017 (800) 253-9646; *Statistical Yearbook.*

UGANDA - PEANUT PRODUCTION - See - UGANDA - CROPS

UGANDA - PESTICIDE USE

Food and Agricultural Organization of the United Nations (FAO) Via delle Terme di Caracalla, 00100 Rome, Italy (Telephone Number in U.S. (202) 653-2400); *The State of Food and Agriculture.*

UGANDA - PETROLEUM INDUSTRY

Facts on File, 460 Park Avenue South, New York, New York 10016 (800) 443-8323; *The New Book of World Rankings.*

Food and Agricultural Organization of the United Nations (FAO) Via delle Terme di Caracalla, 00100 Rome, Italy (Telephone Number in U.S. (202) 653-2400); *The State of Food and Agriculture.*

G.K. Hall and Company, 70 Lincoln Street, Boston, Massachusetts 02111 (617) 423-3990; *The World in Figures.*

UGANDA - PHOSPHATE ROCK PRODUCTION - See UGANDA - MINING AND MINERAL PRODUCTS

UGANDA - PIGS - See UGANDA - LIVESTOCK AND POULTRY

UGANDA - POPULATION

The Economist Intelligence Unit, 111 West 57th Street, New York, New York 10019 (800) 938-4685; *The World Market Atlas.*

Euromonitor Publications Limited, 87-88 Turnmill Street, London EC1M 5QU, England; *International Marketing Data and Statistics.*

Facts on File, 460 Park Avenue South, New York, New York 10016 (800) 443-8323; *The New Book of World Rankings.*

G.K. Hall and Company, 70 Lincoln Street, Boston, Massachusetts 02111 (617) 423-3990; *The World in Figures.*

International Labour Office, I.L.O. Publications, CH-1211, Geneva 22, Switzerland; *Yearbook of Labour Statistics.*

Statistical Office of the United Nations, Publishing Service, New York, New York 10017 (800) 253-9646; *Demographic Yearbook, Statistical Yearbook,* and *Survey of Economic and Social Conditions in Africa.*

Times Books, 201 East 50th Street, New York, New York 10022 (212) 751-2600; *The Economist Book of Vital World Statistics.*

United Nations Educational, Scientific and Cultural Organization (UNESCO), 7 Place de Fontenoy, F-75700 Paris, France (Telephone Number in U.S. (212) 963-5981); *Statistical Yearbook.*

U.S. Arms Control and Disarmament Agency, 320 Twenty-first Street, NW, Washington, D.C. 20451 (202) 647-8677; *World Military Expenditures and Arms Transfers.*

World Health Organization, Office of Publications, Avenue Appia, CH-1211 Geneva 27, Switzerland (Telephone Number in U.S. (518) 436-9686); *World Health Statistics Annual.*

UGANDA - POST OFFICES

Facts on File, 460 Park Avenue South, New York, New York 10016 (800) 443-8323; *The New Book of World Rankings.*

UGANDA - POTATO PRODUCTION - See - UGANDA - CROPS

UGANDA - PRICES

Facts on File, 460 Park Avenue South, New York, New York 10016 (800) 443-8323; *The New Book of World Rankings.*

Food and Agricultural Organization of the United Nations (FAO) Via delle Terme di Caracalla, 00100 Rome, Italy (Telephone Number in U.S. (202) 653-2400); *The State of Food and Agriculture.*

G.K. Hall and Company, 70 Lincoln Street, Boston, Massachusetts 02111 (617) 423-3990; *The World in Figures.*

International Labour Office, I.L.O. Publications, CH-1211, Geneva 22, Switzerland; *Yearbook of Labour Statistics.*

International Monetary Fund, 700 Nineteenth Street, NW, Washington, D.C. 20431 (202) 623-7000; *International Financial Statistics.*

United Nations Economic Commission for Africa, Africa Hall, P.O. Box 3001, Addis Ababa, Ethiopia (Telephone Number in U.S. (800) 253-9646); *African Statistical Yearbook.*

UGANDA - PRINTING AND WRITING PAPER - See - UGANDA - FORESTRY AND FOREST PRODUCTS

UGANDA - PRODUCTION

Facts on File, 460 Park Avenue South, New York, New York 10016 (800) 443-8323; *The New Book of World Rankings.*

G.K. Hall and Company, 70 Lincoln Street, Boston, Massachusetts 02111 (617) 423-3990; *The World in Figures.*

UGANDA - PRODUCTIVITY

Euromonitor Publications Limited, 87-88 Turnmill Street, London EC1M 5QU, England; *International Marketing Data and Statistics.*

UGANDA - PUBLIC FINANCE

Facts on File, 460 Park Avenue South, New York, New York 10016 (800) 443-8323; *The New Book of World Rankings.*

UGANDA - RADIO BROADCASTING - See UGANDA - BROADCASTING

UGANDA - RAILWAYS

G.K. Hall and Company, 70 Lincoln Street, Boston, Massachusetts 02111 (617) 423-3990; *The World in Figures.*

Jane's Information Group, Sentinel House, 163 Brighton Road, Coulsdon, Surrey CR5 2NH, England (Telephone Number in U.S. (703) 683-3700); *Jane's World Railways.*

Statistical Office of the United Nations, Publishing Service, New York, New York 10017 (800) 253-9646; *Survey of Economic and Social Conditions in Africa.*

United Nations Economic Commission for Africa, Africa Hall, P.O. Box 3001, Addis Ababa, Ethiopia (Telephone Number in U.S. (800) 253-9646); *African Statistical Yearbook.*

STATISTICS SOURCES, Nineteenth Edition - 1996

UGANDA - RELIGION

Facts on File, 460 Park Avenue South, New York, New York 10016 (800) 443-8323; *The New Book of World Rankings.*

UGANDA - RETAIL TRADE

G.K. Hall and Company, 70 Lincoln Street, Boston, Massachusetts 02111 (617) 423-3990; *The World in Figures.*

Statistical Office of the United Nations, Publishing Service, New York, New York 10017 (800) 253-9646; *Statistical Yearbook.*

UGANDA - RICE PRODUCTION - See - UGANDA - CROPS

UGANDA - ROOT AND TUBER PRODUCTION - See - UGANDA - CROPS

UGANDA - ROUNDWOOD PRODUCTION - See - UGANDA - FORESTRY AND FOREST PRODUCTS

UGANDA - RUBBER PRODUCTION AND CONSUMPTION

Facts on File, 460 Park Avenue South, New York, New York 10016 (800) 443-8323; *The New Book of World Rankings.*

UGANDA - SALT PRODUCTION - See UGANDA - MINING AND MINERALS

UGANDA - SAWNWOOD PRODUCTION - See - UGANDA - FORESTRY AND FOREST PRODUCTS

UGANDA - SENIOR CITIZENS

Facts on File, 460 Park Avenue South, New York, New York 10016 (800) 443-8323; *The New Book of World Rankings.*

UGANDA - SESAME SEED PRODUCTION - See - UGANDA - CROPS

UGANDA - SHEEP - See UGANDA - LIVESTOCK AND POULTRY

UGANDA - SILVER PRODUCTION AND CONSUMPTION - See UGANDA - MINING AND MINERAL PRODUCTS

UGANDA - SISAL PRODUCTION - See - UGANDA - CROPS

UGANDA - SOCIAL DATA

Facts on File, 460 Park Avenue South, New York, New York 10016 (800) 443-8323; *The New Book of World Rankings.*

G.K. Hall and Company, 70 Lincoln Street, Boston, Massachusetts 02111 (617) 423-3990; *The World in Figures.*

UGANDA - SOYBEAN PRODUCTION - See - UGANDA - CROPS

UGANDA - STATE BUDGET REVENUE AND EXPENDITURES

Euromonitor Publications Limited, 87-88 Turnmill Street, London EC1M 5QU, England; *International Marketing Data and Statistics.*

UGANDA - STEEL - See UGANDA - MINING AND MINERAL PRODUCTS

UGANDA - STOCKS - COMMODITY - MARKET PRICE - INDEX

Food and Agricultural Organization of the United Nations (FAO) Via delle Terme di Caracalla, 00100 Rome, Italy (Telephone Number in U.S. (202) 653-2400); *The State of Food and Agriculture.*

UGANDA - SUGAR PRODUCTION AND CONSUMPTION - See - UGANDA - CROPS

UGANDA - SULPHURIC ACID PRODUCTION - See UGANDA - MINING AND MINERAL PRODUCTS

UGANDA - TAXATION

G.K. Hall and Company, 70 Lincoln Street, Boston, Massachusetts 02111 (617) 423-3990; *The World in Figures.*

International Road Federation, 525 School Street, SW, Washington, D.C. 20024 (202) 554-2106; *World Road Statistics.*

The World Bank, 1818 H Street, NW, Washington, D.C. 20433 (202) 477-1234; *World Tables.*

UGANDA - TEA PRODUCTION AND CONSUMPTION - See - UGANDA - CROPS

UGANDA - TELEGRAPH SERVICE

Statistical Office of the United Nations, Publishing Service, New York, New York 10017 (800) 253-9646; *Statistical Yearbook.*

UGANDA - TELEPHONES IN USE

American Telephone and Telegraph Company, 26 Parsippany Road, Whippany, New Jersey 07981 (800) 338-4038; *The World's Telephones.*

G.K. Hall and Company, 70 Lincoln Street, Boston, Massachusetts 02111 (617) 423-3990; *The World in Figures.*

Statistical Office of the United Nations, Publishing Service, New York, New York 10017 (800) 253-9646; *Statistical Yearbook.*

UGANDA - TELEVISION BROADCASTING - See UGANDA - BROADCASTING

UGANDA - TEXTILE INDUSTRY

G.K. Hall and Company, 70 Lincoln Street, Boston, Massachusetts 02111 (617) 423-3990; *The World in Figures.*

UGANDA - TIN PRODUCTION AND CONSUMPTION - See UGANDA - MINING AND MINERAL PRODUCTS

UGANDA - TOBACCO PRODUCTION

Facts on File, 460 Park Avenue South, New York, New York 10016 (800) 443-8323; *The New Book of World Rankings.*

Statistical Office of the United Nations, Publishing Service, New York, New York 10017 (800) 253-9646; *Statistical Yearbook.*

UGANDA - TOURISM

Facts on File, 460 Park Avenue South, New York, New York 10016 (800) 443-8323; *The New Book of World Rankings.*

G.K. Hall and Company, 70 Lincoln Street, Boston, Massachusetts 02111 (617) 423-3990; *The World in Figures.*

Statistical Office of the United Nations, Publishing Service, New York, New York 10017 (800) 253-9646; *Statistical Yearbook.*

Times Books, 201 East 50th Street, New York, New York 10022 (212) 751-2600; *The Economist Book of Vital World Statistics.*

United Nations Economic Commission for Africa, Africa Hall, P.O. Box 3001, Addis Ababa, Ethiopia (Telephone Number in U.S. (800) 253-9646); *African Statistical Yearbook.*

UGANDA - TRACTORS IN USE

Statistical Office of the United Nations, Publishing Service, New York, New York 10017 (800) 253-9646; *Statistical Yearbook.*

UGANDA - TRADE - See UGANDA - FOREIGN TRADE

UGANDA - TRADEMARKS AND SERVICE MARKS

Statistical Office of the United Nations, Publishing Service, New York, New York 10017 (800) 253-9646; *Statistical Yearbook.*

UGANDA - TRANSPORTATION AND COMMUNICATIONS

Facts on File, 460 Park Avenue South, New York, New York 10016 (800) 443-8323; *The New Book of World Rankings.*

G.K. Hall and Company, 70 Lincoln Street, Boston, Massachusetts 02111 (617) 423-3990; *The World in Figures.*

United Nations Economic Commission for Africa, Africa Hall, P.O. Box 3001, Addis Ababa, Ethiopia (Telephone Number in U.S. (800) 253-9646); *African Statistical Yearbook.*

UGANDA - TUNGSTEN PRODUCTION AND CONSUMPTION - See UGANDA - MINING AND MINERAL PRODUCTS

UGANDA - UNEMPLOYMENT

Euromonitor Publications Limited, 87-88 Turnmill Street, London EC1M 5QU, England; *International Marketing Data and Statistics.*

International Labour Office, I.L.O. Publications, CH-1211, Geneva 33, Switzerland; *Yearbook of Labour Statistics.*

UGANDA - VITAL STATISTICS

Euromonitor Publications Limited, 87-88 Turnmill Street, London EC1M 5QU, England; *International Marketing Data and Statistics.*

G.K. Hall and Company, 70 Lincoln Street, Boston, Massachusetts 02111 (617) 423-3990; *The World in Figures.*

Statistical Office of the United Nations, Publishing Service, New York, New York 10017 (800) 253-9646; *Statistical Yearbook.*

World Health Organization, Office of Publications, Avenue Appia, CH-1211 Geneva 27, Switzerland (Telephone Number in U.S. (518) 436-9686); *World Health Statistics Annual.*

UGANDA - WAGES

G.K. Hall and Company, 70 Lincoln Street, Boston, Massachusetts 02111 (617) 423-3990; *The World in Figures.*

International Labour Office, I.L.O. Publications, CH-1211, Geneva 22, Switzerland; *Yearbook of Labour Statistics.*

UGANDA - WEATHER

Facts on File, 460 Park Avenue South, New York, New York 10016 (800) 443-8323; *The New Book of World Rankings.*

G.K. Hall and Company, 70 Lincoln Street, Boston, Massachusetts 02111 (617) 423-3990; *The World in Figures.*

UGANDA - WHEAT PRODUCTION AND PRICES - See - UGANDA - CROPS

UGANDA - WHOLESALE TRADE

Statistical Office of the United Nations, Publishing Service, New York, New York 10017 (800) 253-9646; *Statistical Yearbook.*

UGANDA - WINE PRODUCTION

Facts on File, 460 Park Avenue South, New York, New York 10016 (800) 443-8323; *The New Book of World Rankings.*

UGANDA - WOOL PRODUCTION

Facts on File, 460 Park Avenue South, New York, New York 10016 (800) 443-8323; *The New Book of World Rankings.*

UKRAINE - See also UNION OF SOVIET SOCIALIST REPUBLICS

UKRAINE - ABORTIONS

Statistical Office of the United Nations, Publishing Service, New York, New York 10017 (800) 253-9646; *Demographic Yearbook.*

UKRAINE - AGRICULTURE

Business International Moscow, 23 Profsoyuznaya Ulitsa, 117859, Moscow (Telephone Number in U.S. (800) 938-4685); *The CIS Market Atlas.*

Encyclopedia Britannica, Incorporated, 310 South Michigan Avenue, Chicago, Illinois 60604 (312) 347-7000; *Britannica World Data.*

The World Bank, 1818 H Street, NW, Washington, D.C. 20433 (202) 477-1234; *Statistical Handbook: States of the Former USSR.*

UKRAINE - AIRLINE SERVICE

Business International Moscow, 23 Profsoyuznaya Ulitsa, 117859, Moscow (Telephone Number in U.S. (800) 938-4685); *The CIS Market Atlas.*

Encyclopedia Britannica, Incorporated, 310 South Michigan Avenue, Chicago, Illinois 60604 (312) 347-7000; *Britannica World Data.*

UKRAINE - AREA AND DENSITY OF POPULATION

Business International Moscow, 23 Profsoyuznaya Ulitsa, 117859, Moscow (Telephone Number in U.S. (800) 938-4685); *The CIS Market Atlas.*

Statistical Office of the United Nations, Publishing Service, New York, New York 10017 (800) 253-9646; *Statistical Yearbook.*

UKRAINE - BANKING

Business International Moscow, 23 Profsoyuznaya Ulitsa, 117859, Moscow (Telephone Number in U.S. (800) 938-4685); *The CIS Market Atlas.*

UKRAINE - BEER PRODUCTION

Statistical Office of the United Nations, Publishing Service, New York, New York 10017 (800) 253-9646; *Statistical Yearbook.*

UKRAINE - BIRTH RATES

Business International Moscow, 23 Profsoyuznaya Ulitsa, 117859, Moscow (Telephone Number in U.S. (800) 938-4685); *The CIS Market Atlas.*

Encyclopedia Britannica, Incorporated, 310 South Michigan Avenue, Chicago, Illinois 60604 (312) 347-7000; *Britannica World Data.*

Statistical Office of the United Nations, Publishing Service, New York, New York 10017 (800) 253-9646; *Demographic Yearbook,* and *Statistical Yearbook.*

UKRAINE - BOOK PRODUCTION

United Nations Educational, Scientific and Cultural Organization (UNESCO), 7 Place de Fontenoy, F-75700 Paris, France (Telephone Number in U.S. (212) 963-5981); *Statistical Yearbook.*

UKRAINE - BUDGET

Encyclopedia Britannica, Incorporated, 310 South Michigan Avenue, Chicago, Illinois 60604 (312) 347-7000; *Britannica World Data.*

UKRAINE - BUTTER PRODUCTION AND CONSUMPTION - See UKRAINE - DAIRY PRODUCTS

UKRAINE - CAPITAL INVESTMENT

The World Bank, 1818 H Street, NW, Washington, D.C. 20433 (202) 477-1234; *Statistical Handbook: States of the Former USSR.*

UKRAINE - CATTLE - See UKRAINE - LIVESTOCK AND POULTRY

UKRAINE - CAUSTIC SODA PRODUCTION

Statistical Office of the United Nations, Publishing Service, New York, New York 10017 (800) 253-9646; *Statistical Yearbook.*

UKRAINE - CEMENT PRODUCTION - See UKRAINE - MINING AND MINERAL PRODUCTS

UKRAINE - CHEESE PRODUCTION AND CONSUMPTION - See UKRAINE - DAIRY PRODUCTS

UKRAINE - CHEMICAL (ORGANIC) PRODUCTION - See UKRAINE - MINING AND MINERAL PRODUCTS

UKRAINE - CHEMICALS

Business International Moscow, 23 Profsoyuznaya Ulitsa, 117859, Moscow (Telephone Number in U.S. (800) 938-4685); *The CIS Market Atlas.*

UKRAINE - COAL PRODUCTION - See UKRAINE - MINING AND MINERAL PRODUCTS

UKRAINE - COKE OVEN COKE PRODUCTION AND CONSUMPTION - See UKRAINE - MINING AND MINERAL PRODUCTS

UKRAINE - COMMUNICATIONS

Business International Moscow, 23 Profsoyuznaya Ulitsa, 117859, Moscow (Telephone Number in U.S. (800) 938-4685); *The CIS Market Atlas.*

UKRAINE - CONSTRUCTION INDUSTRY

Business International Moscow, 23 Profsoyuznaya Ulitsa, 117859, Moscow (Telephone Number in U.S. (800) 938-4685); *The CIS Market Atlas.*

Encyclopedia Britannica, Incorporated, 310 South Michigan Avenue, Chicago, Illinois 60604 (312) 347-7000; *Britannica World Data.*

Statistical Office of the United Nations, Publishing Service, New York, New York 10017 (800) 253-9646; *Statistical Yearbook.*

UKRAINE - CONSUMER PRICE INDEX

Statistical Office of the United Nations, Publishing Service, New York, New York 10017 (800) 253-9646; *Statistical Yearbook.*

UKRAINE - CONSUMER PRODUCTS

Business International Moscow, 23 Profsoyuznaya Ulitsa, 117859, Moscow (Telephone Number in U.S. (800) 938-4685); *The CIS Market Atlas.*

UKRAINE - CONSUMPTION

Business International Moscow, 23 Profsoyuznaya Ulitsa, 117859, Moscow (Telephone Number in U.S. (800) 938-4685); *The CIS Market Atlas.*

The World Bank, 1818 H Street, NW, Washington, D.C. 20433 (202) 477-1234; *Statistical Handbook: States of the Former USSR.*

UKRAINE - CORN PRODUCTION - See - UKRAINE - CROPS

UKRAINE - COTTON PRODUCTION AND CONSUMPTION - See UKRAINE - CROPS

UKRAINE - CROPS

Statistical Office of the United Nations, Publishing Service, New York, New York 10017 (800) 253-9646; *Statistical Yearbook.*

The World Bank, 1818 H Street, NW, Washington, D.C. 20433 (202) 477-1234; *Statistical Handbook: States of the Former USSR.*

UKRAINE - DAIRY PRODUCTS

Statistical Office of the United Nations, Publishing Service, New York, New York 10017 (800) 253-9646; *Statistical Yearbook.*

UKRAINE - DEATH RATES

Business International Moscow, 23 Profsoyuznaya Ulitsa, 117859, Moscow (Telephone Number in U.S. (800) 938-4685); *The CIS Market Atlas.*

Statistical Office of the United Nations, Publishing Service, New York, New York 10017 (800) 253-9646; *Statistical Yearbook.*

UKRAINE - DEMOGRAPHY

Business International Moscow, 23 Profsoyuznaya Ulitsa, 117859, Moscow (Telephone Number in U.S. (800) 938-4685); *The CIS Market Atlas.*

Encyclopedia Britannica, Incorporated, 310 South Michigan Avenue, Chicago, Illinois 60604 (312) 347-7000; *Britannica World Data.*

The World Bank, 1818 H Street, NW, Washington, D.C. 20433 (202) 477-1234; *Statistical Handbook: States of the Former USSR.*

UKRAINE - DISEASES

Business International Moscow, 23 Profsoyuznaya Ulitsa, 117859, Moscow (Telephone Number in U.S. (800) 938-4685); *The CIS Market Atlas.*

UKRAINE - DIVORCE RATES

Encyclopedia Britannica, Incorporated, 310 South Michigan Avenue, Chicago, Illinois 60604 (312) 347-7000; *Britannica World Data.*

Statistical Office of the United Nations, Publishing Service, New York, New York 10017 (800) 253-9646; *Demographic Yearbook,* and *Statistical Yearbook.*

UKRAINE - DOMESTIC INVESTMENT

Business International Moscow, 23 Profsoyuznaya Ulitsa, 117859, Moscow (Telephone Number in U.S. (800) 938-4685); *The CIS Market Atlas.*

UKRAINE - ECONOMY

Business International Moscow, 23 Profsoyuznaya Ulitsa, 117859, Moscow (Telephone Number in U.S. (800) 938-4685); *The CIS Market Atlas.*

Encyclopedia Britannica, Incorporated, 310 South Michigan Avenue, Chicago, Illinois 60604 (312) 347-7000; *Britannica World Data.*

UKRAINE - EDUCATION

Business International Moscow, 23 Profsoyuznaya Ulitsa, 117859, Moscow (Telephone Number in U.S. (800) 938-4685); *The CIS Market Atlas*

Encyclopedia Britannica, Incorporated, 310 South Michigan Avenue, Chicago, Illinois 60604 (312) 347-7000; *Britannica World Data.*

United Nations Educational, Scientific and Cultural Organization (UNESCO), 7 Place de Fontenoy, F-75700 Paris, France (Telephone Number in U.S. (212) 963-5981); *Statistical Yearbook.*

UKRAINE - ELECTRICITY

Business International Moscow, 23 Profsoyuznaya Ulitsa, 117859, Moscow (Telephone Number in U.S. (800) 938-4685); *The CIS Market Atlas.*

The World Bank, 1818 H Street, NW, Washington, D.C. 20433 (202) 477-1234; *Statistical Handbook: States of the Former USSR.*

UKRAINE - EMPLOYMENT

Statistical Office of the United Nations, Publishing Service, New York, New York 10017 (800) 253-9646; *Statistical Yearbook.*

The World Bank, 1818 H Street, NW, Washington, D.C. 20433 (202) 477-1234; *Statistical Handbook: States of the Former USSR.*

UKRAINE - ENERGY

Business International Moscow, 23 Profsoyuznaya Ulitsa, 117859, Moscow (Telephone Number in U.S. (800) 938-4685); *The CIS Market Atlas.*

Encyclopedia Britannica, Incorporated, 310 South Michigan Avenue, Chicago, Illinois 60604 (312) 347-7000; *Britannica World Data.*

The World Bank, 1818 H Street, NW, Washington, D.C. 20433 (202) 477-1234; *Statistical Handbook: States of the Former USSR.*

UKRAINE - ENVIRONMENT

Business International Moscow, 23 Profsoyuznaya Ulitsa, 117859, Moscow (Telephone Number in U.S. (800) 938-4685); *The CIS Market Atlas.*

UKRAINE - EXPORTS

Business International Moscow, 23 Profsoyuznaya Ulitsa, 117859, Moscow (Telephone Number in U.S. (800) 938-4685); *The CIS Market Atlas.*

Encyclopedia Britannica, Incorporated, 310 South Michigan Avenue, Chicago, Illinois 60604 (312) 347-7000; *Britannica World Data.*

The World Bank, 1818 H Street, NW, Washington, D.C. 20433 (202) 477-1234; *Statistical Handbook: States of the Former USSR.*

UKRAINE - EXTERNAL TRADE

The World Bank, 1818 H Street, NW, Washington, D.C. 20433 (202) 477-1234; *Statistical Handbook: States of the Former USSR.*

UKRAINE - FABRIC PRODUCTION - See UKRAINE - TEXTILE INDUSTRY

UKRAINE - FERTILITY RATES

Encyclopedia Britannica, Incorporated, 310 South Michigan Avenue, Chicago, Illinois 60604 (312) 347-7000; *Britannica World Data.*

The World Bank, 1818 H Street, NW, Washington, D.C. 20433 (202) 477-1234; *Statistical Handbook: States of the Former USSR.*

UKRAINE - FERTILIZER

Statistical Office of the United Nations, Publishing Service, New York, New York 10017 (800) 253-9646; *Statistical Yearbook.*

UKRAINE - FETAL MORTALITY

Statistical Office of the United Nations, Publishing Service, New York, New York 10017 (800) 253-9646; *Demographic Yearbook.*

World Health Organization, Office of Publications, Avenue Appia, CH-1211 Geneva 27, Switzerland (Telephone Number in U.S. (518) 436-9686); *World Health Statistics Annual.*

UKRAINE - FIBRE PRODUCTION - See UKRAINE - TEXTILE INDUSTRY

UKRAINE - FILAMENT PRODUCTION - See UKRAINE - TEXTILE INDUSTRY

UKRAINE - FISHERIES

Encyclopedia Britannica, Incorporated, 310 South Michigan Avenue, Chicago, Illinois 60604 (312) 347-7000; *Britannica World Data.*

UKRAINE - FLOUR PRODUCTION

Statistical Office of the United Nations, Publishing Service, New York, New York 10017 (800) 253-9646; *Statistical Yearbook.*

UKRAINE - FOOTWEAR PRODUCTION AND CONSUMPTION - See UKRAINE - TEXTILE INDUSTRY

UKRAINE - FOREIGN INVESTMENT

Business International Moscow, 23 Profsoyuznaya Ulitsa, 117859, Moscow (Telephone Number in U.S. (800) 938-4685); *The CIS Market Atlas.*

UKRAINE - FOREIGN TRADE

Business International Moscow, 23 Profsoyuznaya Ulitsa, 117859, Moscow (Telephone Number in U.S. (800) 938-4685); *The CIS Market Atlas.*

Encyclopedia Britannica, Incorporated, 310 South Michigan Avenue, Chicago, Illinois 60604 (312) 347-7000; *Britannica World Data.*

The World Bank, 1818 H Street, NW, Washington, D.C. 20433 (202) 477-1234; *Statistical Handbook: States of the Former USSR.*

UKRAINE - FORESTRY AND FOREST PRODUCTS

Business International Moscow, 23 Profsoyuznaya Ulitsa, 117859, Moscow (Telephone Number in U.S. (800) 938-4685); *The CIS Market Atlas.*

Encyclopedia Britannica, Incorporated, 310 South Michigan Avenue, Chicago, Illinois 60604 (312) 347-7000; *Britannica World Data.*

Statistical Office of the United Nations, Publishing Service, New York, New York 10017 (800) 253-9646; *Statistical Yearbook.*

United Nations Educational, Scientific and Cultural Organization (UNESCO), 7 Place de Fontenoy, F-75700 Paris, France (Telephone Number in U.S. (212) 963-5981); *Statistical Yearbook.*

UKRAINE - GAS PRODUCTION - See UKRAINE - MINING AND MINERAL PRODUCTS

UKRAINE - GENERAL MORTALITY

Statistical Office of the United Nations, Publishing Service, New York, New York 10017 (800) 253-9646; *Demographic Yearbook.*

World Health Organization, Office of Publications, Avenue Appia, CH-1211 Geneva 27, Switzerland (Telephone Number in U.S. (518) 436-9686); *World Health Statistics Annual.*

UKRAINE - GOATS - See UKRAINE - LIVESTOCK AND POULTRY

UKRAINE - GOVERNMENT EXPENDITURE

The World Bank, 1818 H Street, NW, Washington, D.C. 20433 (202) 477-1234; *Statistical Handbook: States of the Former USSR.*

UKRAINE - GOVERNMENT REVENUE

The World Bank, 1818 H Street, NW, Washington, D.C. 20433 (202) 477-1234; *Statistical Handbook: States of the Former USSR.*

UKRAINE - GROSS DOMESTIC PRODUCT

Statistical Office of the United Nations, Publishing Service, New York, New York 10017 (800) 253-9646; *Statistical Yearbook.*

The World Bank, 1818 H Street, NW, Washington, D.C. 20433 (202) 477-1234; *Statistical Handbook: States of the Former USSR.*

UKRAINE - HEALTH

Business International Moscow, 23 Profsoyuznaya Ulitsa, 117859, Moscow (Telephone Number in U.S. (800) 938-4685); *The CIS Market Atlas.*

Encyclopedia Britannica, Incorporated, 310 South Michigan Avenue, Chicago, Illinois 60604 (312) 347-7000; *Britannica World Data.*

Statistical Office of the United Nations, Publishing Service, New York, New York 10017 (800) 253-9646; *Statistical Yearbook.*

UKRAINE - HIGHWAYS

Business International Moscow, 23 Profsoyuznaya Ulitsa, 117859, Moscow (Telephone Number in U.S. (800) 938-4685); *The CIS Market Atlas.*

Encyclopedia Britannica, Incorporated, 310 South Michigan Avenue, Chicago, Illinois 60604 (312) 347-7000; *Britannica World Data.*

Statistical Office of the United Nations, Publishing Service, New York, New York 10017 (800) 253-9646; *Annual Bulletin of Transport Statistics for Europe.*

UKRAINE - HOUSING AND HOUSING UNITS

Business International Moscow, 23 Profsoyuznaya Ulitsa, 117859, Moscow (Telephone Number in U.S. (800) 938-4685); *The CIS Market Atlas.*

UKRAINE - IMPORTS

Business International Moscow, 23 Profsoyuznaya Ulitsa, 117859, Moscow (Telephone Number in U.S. (800) 938-4685); *The CIS Market Atlas.*

Encyclopedia Britannica, Incorporated, 310 South Michigan Avenue, Chicago, Illinois 60604 (312) 347-7000; *Britannica World Data.*

The World Bank, 1818 H Street, NW, Washington, D.C. 20433 (202) 477-1234; *Statistical Handbook: States of the Former USSR.*

UKRAINE - INDUSTRY

Business International Moscow, 23 Profsoyuznaya Ulitsa, 117859, Moscow (Telephone Number in U.S. (800) 938-4685); *The CIS Market Atlas.*

Statistical Office of the United Nations, Publishing Service, New York, New York 10017 (800) 253-9646; *Statistical Yearbook.*

The World Bank, 1818 H Street, NW, Washington, D.C. 20433 (202) 477-1234; *Statistical Handbook: States of the Former USSR.*

UKRAINE - INFANT AND MATERNAL MORTALITY

Business International Moscow, 23 Profsoyuznaya Ulitsa, 117859, Moscow (Telephone Number in U.S. (800) 938-4685); *The CIS Market Atlas.*

Statistical Office of the United Nations, Publishing Service, New York, New York 10017 (800) 253-9646; *Demographic Yearbook,* and *Statistical Yearbook.*

World Health Organization, Office of Publications, Avenue Appia, CH-1211 Geneva 27, Switzerland (Telephone Number in U.S. (518) 436-9686); *World Health Statistics Annual.*

UKRAINE - INTERNAL TRADE

Statistical Office of the United Nations, Publishing Service, New York, New York 10017 (800) 253-9646; *Statistical Yearbook.*

UKRAINE - IRON ORE PRODUCTION AND CONSUMPTION - See UKRAINE - MINING AND MINERAL PRODUCTS

UKRAINE - LABOR

Business International Moscow, 23 Profsoyuznaya Ulitsa, 117859, Moscow (Telephone Number in U.S. (800) 938-4685); *The CIS Market Atlas.*

The World Bank, 1818 H Street, NW, Washington, D.C. 20433 (202) 477-1234; *Statistical Handbook: States of the Former USSR.*

UKRAINE - LAND USE

Encyclopedia Britannica, Incorporated, 310 South Michigan Avenue, Chicago, Illinois 60604 (312) 347-7000; *Britannica World Data.*

UKRAINE - LIBRARIES

United Nations Educational, Scientific and Cultural Organization (UNESCO), 7 Place de Fontenoy, F-75700 Paris, France (Telephone Number in U.S. (212) 963-5981); *Statistical Yearbook.*

UKRAINE - LIFE EXPECTANCY

Business International Moscow, 23 Profsoyuznaya Ulitsa, 117859, Moscow (Telephone Number in U.S. (800) 938-4685); *The CIS Market Atlas.*

UKRAINE - LIGNITE PRODUCTION - See UKRAINE - MINING AND MINERAL PRODUCTS

UKRAINE - LIVESTOCK AND POULTRY

Business International Moscow, 23 Profsoyuznaya Ulitsa, 117859, Moscow (Telephone Number in U.S. (800) 938-4685); *The CIS Market Atlas.*

Encyclopedia Britannica, Incorporated, 310 South Michigan Avenue, Chicago, Illinois 60604 (312) 347-7000; *Britannica World Data.*

UKRAINE - MAIL - NUMBER OF ITEMS SENT AND RECEIVED

Statistical Office of the United Nations, Publishing Service, New York, New York 10017 (800) 253-9646; *Statistical Yearbook.*

UKRAINE - MANGANESE ORE PRODUCTION AND CONSUMPTION - See UKRAINE - MINING AND MINERAL PRODUCTS

UKRAINE - MANUFACTURING

Encyclopedia Britannica, Incorporated, 310 South Michigan Avenue, Chicago, Illinois 60604 (312) 347-7000; *Britannica World Data.*

UKRAINE - MARRIAGE RATES

Encyclopedia Britannica, Incorporated, 310 South Michigan Avenue, Chicago, Illinois 60604 (312) 347-7000; *Britannica World Data.*

Statistical Office of the United Nations, Publishing Service, New York, New York 10017 (800) 253-9646; *Demographic Yearbook,* and *Statistical Yearbook.*

UKRAINE - MEAT PRODUCTION - See UKRAINE - LIVESTOCK AND POULTRY

UKRAINE - MERCHANT SHIPPING

Statistical Office of the United Nations, Publishing Service, New York, New York 10017 (800) 253-9646; *Annual Bulletin of Transport Statistics for Europe.*

UKRAINE - MILITARY

The International Institute for Strategic Studies, 23 Tavistock Street, London WC2E 7NQ, England; *The Military Balance.*

UKRAINE - MILK PRODUCTION - See UKRAINE - DAIRY PRODUCTS

UKRAINE - MINING AND MINERAL PRODUCTS

Business International Moscow, 23 Profsoyuznaya Ulitsa, 117859, Moscow (Telephone Number in U.S. (800) 938-4685); *The CIS Market Atlas.*

Encyclopedia Britannica, Incorporated, 310 South Michigan Avenue, Chicago, Illinois 60604 (312) 347-7000; *Britannica World Data.*

Statistical Office of the United Nations, Publishing Service, New York, New York 10017 (800) 253-9646; *Statistical Yearbook.*

UKRAINE - MOTION PICTURES

Statistical Office of the United Nations, Publishing Service, New York, New York 10017 (800) 253-9646; *Statistical Yearbook.*

UKRAINE - MOTOR VEHICLE PRODUCTION

Statistical Office of the United Nations, Publishing Service, New York, New York 10017 (800) 253-9646; *Statistical Yearbook.*

UKRAINE - MOTOR VEHICLES

Business International Moscow, 23 Profsoyuznaya Ulitsa, 117859, Moscow (Telephone Number in U.S. (800) 938-4685); *The CIS Market Atlas.*

UKRAINE - MUSEUMS

United Nations Educational, Scientific and Cultural Organization (UNESCO), 7 Place de Fontenoy, F-75700 Paris, France (Telephone Number in U.S. (212) 963-5981); *Statistical Yearbook.*

UKRAINE - NATALITY

Statistical Office of the United Nations, Publishing Service, New York, New York 10017 (800) 253-9646; *Demographic Yearbook.*

World Health Organization, Office of Publications, Avenue Appia, CH-1211 Geneva 27, Switzerland (Telephone Number in U.S. (518) 436-9686); *World Health Statistics Annual.*

UKRAINE - NATIONAL ACCOUNTS

The World Bank, 1818 H Street, NW, Washington, D.C. 20433 (202) 477-1234; *Statistical Handbook: States of the Former USSR.*

UKRAINE - NATIONAL INCOME

Business International Moscow, 23 Profsoyuznaya Ulitsa, 117859, Moscow (Telephone Number in U.S. (800) 938-4685); *The CIS Market Atlas.*

UKRAINE - NATIONAL PRODUCT

Statistical Office of the United Nations, Publishing Service, New York, New York 10017 (800) 253-9646; *Statistical Yearbook*.

UKRAINE - NET MATERIAL PRODUCT

Statistical Office of the United Nations, Publishing Service, New York, New York 10017 (800) 253-9646; *Statistical Yearbook*.

UKRAINE - NEWSPAPER PRODUCTION - See - UKRAINE - FORESTRY AND FOREST PRODUCTS

UKRAINE - OATS PRODUCTION - See - UKRAINE - CROPS

UKRAINE - PAPER PRODUCTION - See - UKRAINE - FORESTRY AND FOREST PRODUCTS

UKRAINE - PERIODICALS

United Nations Educational, Scientific and Cultural Organization (UNESCO), 7 Place de Fontenoy, F-75700 Paris, France (Telephone Number in U.S. (212) 963-5981); *Statistical Yearbook*.

UKRAINE - PETROLEUM INDUSTRY

Statistical Office of the United Nations, Publishing Service, New York, New York 10017 (800) 253-9646; *Statistical Yearbook*.

UKRAINE - PIG-IRON AND FERRO-ALLOY PRODUCTION - See UKRAINE - MINING AND MINERAL PRODUCTS

UKRAINE - PIGS - See UKRAINE - LIVESTOCK AND POULTRY

UKRAINE - PIPELINES FOR OIL AND PETROLEUM PRODUCTS

Statistical Office of the United Nations, Publishing Service, New York, New York 10017 (800) 253-9646; *Annual Bulletin of Transport Statistics for Europe*.

UKRAINE - POPULATION

Business International Moscow, 23 Profsoyuznaya Ulitsa, 117859, Moscow (Telephone Number in U.S. (800) 938-4685); *The CIS Market Atlas*.

Encyclopedia Britannica, Incorporated, 310 South Michigan Avenue, Chicago, Illinois 60604 (312) 347-7000; *Britannica World Data*.

Statistical Office of the United Nations, Publishing Service, New York, New York 10017 (800) 253-9646; *Demographic Yearbook*, and *Statistical Yearbook*.

The World Bank, 1818 H Street, NW, Washington, D.C. 20433 (202) 477-1234; *Statistical Handbook: States of the Former USSR*.

World Health Organization, Office of Publications, Avenue Appia, CH-1211 Geneva 27, Switzerland (Telephone Number in U.S. (518) 436-9686); *World Health Statistics Annual*.

UKRAINE - POTATO PRODUCTION - See - UKRAINE - CROPS

UKRAINE - POULTRY - See UKRAINE - LIVESTOCK AND POULTRY

UKRAINE - PRICES

The World Bank, 1818 H Street, NW, Washington, D.C. 20433 (202) 477-1234; *Statistical Handbook: States of the Former USSR*.

UKRAINE - PRODUCTION

The World Bank, 1818 H Street, NW, Washington, D.C. 20433 (202) 477-1234; *Statistical Handbook: States of the Former USSR*.

UKRAINE - PUBLIC FINANCE

The World Bank, 1818 H Street, NW, Washington, D.C. 20433 (202) 477-1234; *Statistical Handbook: States of the Former USSR*.

UKRAINE - RADIO RECEIVER PRODUCTION

Statistical Office of the United Nations, Publishing Service, New York, New York 10017 (800) 253-9646; *Statistical Yearbook*.

UKRAINE - RADIO RECEIVERS

Encyclopedia Britannica, Incorporated, 310 South Michigan Avenue, Chicago, Illinois 60604 (312) 347-7000; *Britannica World Data*.

UKRAINE - RAILWAYS

Business International Moscow, 23 Profsoyuznaya Ulitsa, 117859, Moscow (Telephone Number in U.S. (800) 938-4685); *The CIS Market Atlas*.

Encyclopedia Britannica, Incorporated, 310 South Michigan Avenue, Chicago, Illinois 60604 (312) 347-7000; *Britannica World Data*.

Statistical Office of the United Nations, Publishing Service, New York, New York 10017 (800) 253-9646; *Annual Bulletin of Transport Statistics for Europe*, and *Statistical Yearbook*.

UKRAINE - RETAIL TRADE

Business International Moscow, 23 Profsoyuznaya Ulitsa, 117859, Moscow (Telephone Number in U.S. (800) 938-4685); *The CIS Market Atlas*.

Statistical Office of the United Nations, Publishing Service, New York, New York 10017 (800) 253-9646; *Statistical Yearbook*.

UKRAINE - RICE PRODUCTION - See - UKRAINE - CROPS

UKRAINE - ROADS - See UKRAINE - HIGHWAYS

ROUNDWOOD PRODUCTION AND CONSUMPTION - See UKRAINE - FORESTRY AND FOREST PRODUCTS

UKRAINE - SALT PRODUCTION - See UKRAINE - MINING AND MINERALS

UKRAINE - SCIENCE AND TECHNOLOGY - EXPENDITURE FOR RESEARCH

Statistical Office of the United Nations, Publishing Service, New York, New York 10017 (800) 253-9646; *Statistical Yearbook*.

UKRAINE - SCIENTISTS AND TECHNICIANS

Statistical Office of the United Nations, Publishing Service, New York, New York 10017 (800) 253-9646; *Statistical Yearbook*.

UKRAINE - SHEEP - See UKRAINE - LIVESTOCK AND POULTRY

UKRAINE - STEEL - See UKRAINE - MINING AND MINERAL PRODUCTS

UKRAINE - SUGAR PRODUCTION - See - UKRAINE - CROPS

UKRAINE - TELEGRAPH SERVICE

Statistical Office of the United Nations, Publishing Service, New York, New York 10017 (800) 253-9646; *Statistical Yearbook.*

UKRAINE - TELEPHONES IN USE

Encyclopedia Britannica, Incorporated, 310 South Michigan Avenue, Chicago, Illinois 60604 (312) 347-7000; *Britannica World Data.*

UKRAINE - TELEVISION RECEIVER PRODUCTION

Statistical Office of the United Nations, Publishing Service, New York, New York 10017 (800) 253-9646; *Statistical Yearbook.*

UKRAINE - TELEVISION RECEIVERS

Encyclopedia Britannica, Incorporated, 310 South Michigan Avenue, Chicago, Illinois 60604 (312) 347-7000; *Britannica World Data.*

UKRAINE - TEXTILE INDUSTRY

Business International Moscow, 23 Profsoyuznaya Ulitsa, 117859, Moscow (Telephone Number in U.S. (800) 938-4685); *The CIS Market Atlas.*

Statistical Office of the United Nations, Publishing Service, New York, New York 10017 (800) 253-9646; *Statistical Yearbook.*

UKRAINE - THEATRE

United Nations Educational, Scientific and Cultural Organization (UNESCO), 7 Place de Fontenoy, F-75700 Paris, France (Telephone Number in U.S. (212) 963-5981); *Statistical Yearbook.*

UKRAINE - TIRE (MOTOR VEHICLE) PRODUCTION

Statistical Office of the United Nations, Publishing Service, New York, New York 10017 (800) 253-9646; *Statistical Yearbook.*

UKRAINE - TOURISM

Business International Moscow, 23 Profsoyuznaya Ulitsa, 117859, Moscow (Telephone Number in U.S. (800) 938-4685); *The CIS Market Atlas.*

UKRAINE - TRANSPORTATION AND COMMUNICATIONS

Business International Moscow, 23 Profsoyuznaya Ulitsa, 117859, Moscow (Telephone Number in U.S. (800) 938-4685); *The CIS Market Atlas.*

Encyclopedia Britannica, Incorporated, 310 South Michigan Avenue, Chicago, Illinois 60604 (312) 347-7000; *Britannica World Data.*

UKRAINE - VITAL STATISTICS

Encyclopedia Britannica, Incorporated, 310 South Michigan Avenue, Chicago, Illinois 60604 (312) 347-7000; *Britannica World Data.*

Statistical Office of the United Nations, Publishing Service, New York, New York 10017 (800) 253-9646; *Statistical Yearbook.*

World Health Organization, Office of Publications, Avenue Appia, CH-1211 Geneva 27, Switzerland (Telephone Number in U.S. (518) 436-9686); *World Health Statistics Annual.*

UKRAINE - WAGES

Business International Moscow, 23 Profsoyuznaya Ulitsa, 117859, Moscow (Telephone Number in U.S. (800) 938-4685); *The CIS Market Atlas.*

Statistical Office of the United Nations, Publishing Service, New York, New York 10017 (800) 253-9646; *Statistical Yearbook.*

The World Bank, 1818 H Street, NW, Washington, D.C. 20433 (202) 477-1234; *Statistical Handbook: States of the Former USSR.*

UKRAINE - WATERWAYS IN USE

Statistical Office of the United Nations, Publishing Service, New York, New York 10017 (800) 253-9646; *Annual Bulletin of Transport Statistics for Europe.*

UKRAINE - WHEAT PRODUCTION AND PRICES - See - UKRAINE - CROPS

UKRAINE - WHOLESALE TRADE

Statistical Office of the United Nations, Publishing Service, New York, New York 10017 (800) 253-9646; *Statistical Yearbook.*

UKRAINE - WINE PRODUCTION

Statistical Office of the United Nations, Publishing Service, New York, New York 10017 (800) 253-9646; *Statistical Yearbook.*

UKRAINE - WOOL PRODUCTION AND CONSUMPTION - See UKRAINE - TEXTILE INDUSTRY

UKRAINE - YARN PRODUCTION

Statistical Office of the United Nations, Publishing Service, New York, New York 10017 (800) 253-9646; *Statistical Yearbook.*

UKRAINIAN SSR - See UKRAINE

ULCER OF STOMACH AND DUODENUM - DEATHS

U.S. Department of Health and Human Services, National Center for Health Statistics, 3700 East-West Highway, Hyattsville, Maryland 20782 (301) 436-8500; *Vital Statistics of the United States, Monthly Vital Statistics Report*, and unpublished data.

UNEMPLOYMENT INSURANCE - BENEFICIARIES

U.S. Department of Health and Human Services, Social Security Administration, 6401 Security Boulevard, Baltimore, Maryland 21235 (410) 965-1234; *Annual Statistical Supplement to the Social Security Bulletin, Social Security Bulletin*, and unpublished data.

U.S. Department of Labor, Employment and Training Administration, 200 Constitution Avenue, NW, Washington, D.C. 20210 (202) 219-0600; *Unemployment Insurance Data Summary.*

UNEMPLOYMENT INSURANCE - COVERAGE - WORKERS AND EARNINGS

U.S. Department of Health and Human Services, Social Security Administration, 6401 Security Boulevard, Baltimore, Maryland 21235 (410) 965-1234; *Annual Statistical Supplement to the Social Security Bulletin*, and unpublished data.

U.S. Department of Labor, Employment and Training Administration, 200 Constitution Avenue, NW, Washington, D.C. 20210 (202) 219-

6871; *Unemployment Insurance Data Summary.*

UNEMPLOYMENT INSURANCE - GOVERNMENTAL FINANCES

Executive Office of the President, Office of Management and Budget, Executive Office Building, Washington, D.C. 20503 (202) 395-3080; *Budget of the United States Government.*

U.S. Department of Commerce, Bureau of the Census, Suitland, Maryland 20233 (301) 763-4040; *Historical Statistics on Governmental Finances and Employment, Census of Governments, Government Finances,* and *State Government Finances.*

UNEMPLOYMENT INSURANCE - PAYMENTS

U.S. Department of Health and Human Services, Social Security Administration, 6401 Security Boulevard, Baltimore, Maryland 21235 (410) 965-1234; *Annual Statistical Supplement to the Social Security Bulletin, Social Security Bulletin,* and unpublished data.

U.S. Department of Labor, Employment and Training Administration, 200 Constitution Avenue, NW, Washington, D.C. 20210 (202) 219-6871; *Unemployment Insurance Data Summary.*

UNINCORPORATED ENTERPRISES - FLOW OF FUNDS

Board of Governors of the Federal Reserve System, Twentieth Street and Constitution Avenue, NW, Washington, D.C. 20551 (202) 452-3000; *Annual Statistical Digest.*

Union of Soviet Socialist Republics - National Statistical Office

Foreign Relations Department, States Statistical Committee, Ulitsa Kirova 39, Moscow 103450, Russia.

Union of Soviet Socialist Republics - Primary Statistics Sources

Central Statistical Board of the Council of Ministers of the Soviet Union, Moscow, Russia; *Narodnoye Khozyaystvo SSR: statisticheskiy yezhegodnik* (National Economy of the Soviet Union: Statistical Yearbook), and *The U.S.S.R. In Figures: Brief Statistical Handbook.*

UNION OF SOVIET SOCIALIST REPUBLICS - AGRICULTURE

Academic International Press, Box 1111, Gulf Breeze, Florida 32561; *U.S.S.R. Facts and Figures.*

Columbia University Press, 562 West 113th Street, New York, New York 10014 (212) 316-7100; *East European and Soviet Data Book.*

European Community Information Service, 2100 M Street, NW, Washington, D.C. 20037 (202) 862-9500; *Basic Statistics of the Community.*

Facts on File, 460 Park Avenue South, New York, New York 10016; *The New Book of World Rankings.*

Federal Statistical Office, Gustav-Stresemann-Ring 11, D-6200 Wiesbaden, Germany; *U.S.S.R.*

Food and Agricultural Organization of the United Nations (FAO) Via delle Terme di Caracalla, 00100 Rome, Italy (Telephone Number in U.S. (202) 653-2400; *Production Yearbook, The State of Food and Agriculture,* and *Trade Yearbook.*

G.K. Hall and Company, 70 Lincoln Street, Boston, Massachusetts 02111 (617) 423-3990; *The World in Figures.*

Statistical Office of the United Nations, Publishing Service, New York, New York 10017 (800) 253-9646; *Statistical Yearbook.*

Times Books, 201 East 50th Street, New York, New York 10022 (212) 751-2600; *The Economist Book of Vital World Statistics.*

UNION OF SOVIET SOCIALIST REPUBLICS - AIRLINE SERVICE

European Community Information Service, 2100 M Street, NW, Washington, D.C. 20037 (202) 862-9500; *Basic Statistics of the Community.*

Facts on File, 460 Park Avenue South, New York, New York 10016 (800) 443-8323; *The New Book of World Rankings.*

G.K. Hall and Company, 70 Lincoln Street, Boston, Massachusetts 02111 (617) 423-3990; *The World in Figures.*

International Civil Aviation Organization, 1000 Sherbrooke Street, West, Montreal, Quebec, Canada H3A 2R2 (514) 285-8219; *Civil Aviation Statistics of the World.*

Statistical Office of the United Nations, Publishing Service, New York, New York 10017 (800) 253-9646; *Statistical Yearbook.*

Times Books, 201 East 50th Street, New York, New York 10022 (212) 751-2600; *The Economist Book of Vital World Statistics.*

UNION OF SOVIET SOCIALIST REPUBLICS - ANIMAL FEEDINGSTUFFS OF AQUATIC ANIMAL ORIGIN

Statistical Office of the United Nations, Publishing Service, New York, New York 10017 (800) 253-9646; *Statistical Yearbook.*

UNION OF SOVIET SOCIALIST REPUBLICS - ANIMAL HEALTH

Food and Agricultural Organization of the United Nations (FAO), Via delle Terme di Caracalla, 00100 Rome, Italy (Telephone Number in U.S. (202) 653-2400); *Animal Health Yearbook.*

UNION OF SOVIET SOCIALIST REPUBLICS - AREA AND DENSITY OF POPULATION

European Community Information Service, 2100 M Street, NW, Washington, D.C. 20037 (202) 862-9500; *Basic Statistics of the Community.*

Facts on File, 460 Park Avenue South, New York, New York 10016 (800) 443-8323; *The New Book of World Rankings.*

Federal Statistical Office, Gustav-Stresemann-Ring 11, D-6200 Wiesbaden, Germany; *U.S.S.R.*

Food and Agricultural Organization of the United Nations (FAO) Via delle Terme di Caracalla, 00100 Rome, Italy (Telephone Number in U.S. (202) 653-2400); *The State of Food and Agriculture.*

G.K. Hall and Company, 70 Lincoln Street, Boston, Massachusetts 02111 (617) 423-3990; *The World in Figures.*

Statistical Office of the United Nations, Publishing Service, New York, New York 10017 (800) 253-9646; *Statistical Yearbook.*

Times Books, 201 East 50th Street, New York, New York 10022 (212) 751-2600; *The Economist Book of Vital World Statistics*.

United Nations Educational, Scientific and Cultural Organization (UNESCO), 7 Place de Fontenoy, F-75700 Paris, France (Telephone Number in U.S. (212) 963-5981); *Statistical Yearbook*.

UNION OF SOVIET SOCIALIST REPUBLICS - ARMS EXPORTS AND IMPORTS

U.S. Arms Control and Disarmament Agency, 320 Twenty-first Street, NW, Washington, D.C. 20451 (202) 647-8677; *World Military Expenditures and Arms Transfers*.

UNION OF SOVIET SOCIALIST REPUBLICS - ARMED FORCES

Academic International Press, Box 1111, Gulf Breeze, Florida 32561; *U.S.S.R. Facts and Figures*.

UNION OF SOVIET SOCIALIST REPUBLICS - BALANCE OF PAYMENTS

European Community Information Service, 2100 M Street, NW, Washington, D.C. 20037 (202) 862-9500; *Basic Statistics of the Community*.

G.K. Hall and Company, 70 Lincoln Street, Boston, Massachusetts 02111 (617) 423-3990; *The World in Figures*.

Times Books, 201 East 50th Street, New York, New York 10022 (212) 751-2600; *The Economist Book of Vital World Statistics*.

UNION OF SOVIET SOCIALIST REPUBLICS - BANKING

Facts on File, 460 Park Avenue South, New York, New York 10016 (800) 443-8323; *The New Book of World Rankings*.

G.K. Hall and Company, 70 Lincoln Street, Boston, Massachusetts 02111 (617) 423-3990; *The World in Figures*.

UNION OF SOVIET SOCIALIST REPUBLICS - BEER PRODUCTION

Facts on File, 460 Park Avenue South, New York, New York 10016 (800) 443-8323; *The New Book of World Rankings*.

Statistical Office of the United Nations, Publishing Service, New York, New York 10017 (800) 253-9646; *Statistical Yearbook*.

UNION OF SOVIET SOCIALIST REPUBLICS - BIRTH RATE

European Community Information Service, 2100 M Street, NW, Washington, D.C. 20037 (202) 862-9500; *Basic Statistics of the Community*.

Facts on File, 460 Park Avenue South, New York, New York 10016 (800) 443-8323; *The New Book of World Rankings*.

Statistical Office of the United Nations, Publishing Service, New York, New York 10017 (800) 253-9646; *Statistical Yearbook*.

Times Books, 201 East 50th Street, New York, New York 10022 (212) 751-2600; *The Economist Book of Vital World Statistics*.

UNION OF SOVIET SOCIALIST REPUBLICS - BONDS

European Community Information Service, 2100 M Street, NW, Washington, D.C. 20037 (202) 862-9500; *Basic Statistics of the Community*.

G.K. Hall and Company, 70 Lincoln Street, Boston, Massachusetts 02111 (617) 423-3990; *The World in Figures*.

UNION OF SOVIET SOCIALIST REPUBLICS - BOOK PRODUCTION

Euromonitor Publications Limited, 87-88 Turnmill Street, London EC1M 5QU, England; *European Marketing Data and Statistics*.

G.K. Hall and Company, 70 Lincoln Street, Boston, Massachusetts 02111 (617) 423-3990; *The World in Figures*.

United Nations Educational, Scientific and Cultural Organization (UNESCO), 7 Place de Fontenoy, F-75700 Paris, France (Telephone Number in U.S. (212) 963-5981); *Statistical Yearbook*.

UNION OF SOVIET SOCIALIST REPUBLICS - BROADCASTING

Billboard Limited, P.O. Box 9027, 1006 AA Amsterdam, The Netherlands (Telephone Number in U.S. (212) 764-7300); *World Radio TV Handbook*.

European Community Information Service, 2100 M Street, NW, Washington, D.C. 20037 (202) 862-9500; *Basic Statistics of the Community*.

Facts on File, 460 Park Avenue South, New York, New York 10016 (800) 443-8323; *The New Book of World Rankings*.

G.K. Hall and Company, 70 Lincoln Street, Boston, Massachusetts 02111 (617) 423-3990; *The World in Figures*.

Times Books, 201 East 50th Street, New York, New York 10022 (212) 751-2600; *The Economist Book of Vital World Statistics*.

UNION OF SOVIET SOCIALIST REPUBLICS - BUSINESS

European Community Information Service, 2100 M Street, NW, Washington, D.C. 20037 (202) 862-9500; *Basic Statistics of the Community*.

G.K. Hall and Company, 70 Lincoln Street, Boston, Massachusetts 02111 (617) 423-3990; *The World in Figures*.

UNION OF SOVIET SOCIALIST REPUBLICS - CALORIE SUPPLY

Food and Agricultural Organization of the United Nations (FAO) Via delle Terme di Caracalla, 00100 Rome, Italy (Telephone Number in U.S. (202) 653-2400); *The State of Food and Agriculture*.

UNION OF SOVIET SOCIALIST REPUBLICS - CAUSTIC SODA PRODUCTION

European Community Information Service, 2100 M Street, NW, Washington, D.C. 20037 (202) 862-9500; *Basic Statistics of the Community*.

Statistical Office of the United Nations, Publishing Service, New York, New York 10017 (800) 253-9646; *Statistical Yearbook*.

UNION OF SOVIET SOCIALIST REPUBLICS - CIGARETTE PRODUCTION - See UNION OF SOVIET SOCIALIST REPUBLICS - TOBACCO PRODUCTION

UNION OF SOVIET SOCIALIST REPUBLICS - CLASS STRUCTURE

Columbia University Press, 562 West 113th Street, New York, New York 10014 (212) 316-7100; *East European and Soviet Data Book*.

G.K. Hall and Company, 70 Lincoln Street, Boston, Massachusetts 02111 (617) 423-3990; *The World in Figures*.

UNION OF SOVIET SOCIALIST REPUBLICS - CLIMATE

Facts on File, 460 Park Avenue South, New York, New York 10016 (800) 443-8323; *The New Book of World Rankings*.

Federal Statistical Office, Gustav-Stresemann-Ring 11, D-6200 Wiesbaden, Germany; *U.S.S.R.*

G.K. Hall and Company, 70 Lincoln Street, Boston, Massachusetts 02111 (617) 423-3990; *The World in Figures*.

UNION OF SOVIET SOCIALIST REPUBLICS - CLOTHING EXPORTS AND IMPORTS

European Community Information Service, 2100 M Street, NW, Washington, D.C. 20037 (202) 862-9500; *Basic Statistics of the Community*.

UNION OF SOVIET SOCIALIST REPUBLICS - COMMUNICATIONS

Academic International Press, Box 1111, Gulf Breeze, Florida 32561; *U.S.S.R. Facts and Figures*.

European Community Information Service, 2100 M Street, NW, Washington, D.C. 20037 (202) 862-9500; *Basic Statistics of the Community*.

Federal Statistical Office, Gustav-Stresemann-Ring 11, D-6200 Wiesbaden, Germany; *U.S.S.R.*

G.K. Hall and Company, 70 Lincoln Street, Boston, Massachusetts 02111 (617) 423-3990; *The World in Figures*.

UNION OF SOVIET SOCIALIST REPUBLICS - COMMUNIST PARTY

Academic International Press, Box 1111, Gulf Breeze, Florida 32561; *U.S.S.R. Facts and Figures*.

UNION OF SOVIET SOCIALIST REPUBLICS - CONSTRUCTION INDUSTRY

European Community Information Service, 2100 M Street, NW, Washington, D.C. 20037 (202) 862-9500; *Basic Statistics of the Community*.

Facts on File, 460 Park Avenue South, New York, New York 10016 (800) 443-8323; *The New Book of World Rankings*.

Statistical Office of the United Nations, Publishing Service, New York, New York 10017 (800) 253-9646; *Construction Statistics Yearbook*, and *Statistical Yearbook*.

UNION OF SOVIET SOCIALIST REPUBLICS - CONSUMER PRICE INDEX

European Community Information Service, 2100 M Street, NW, Washington, D.C. 20037 (202) 862-9500; *Basic Statistics of the Community*.

G.K. Hall and Company, 70 Lincoln Street, Boston, Massachusetts 02111 (617) 423-3990; *The World in Figures*.

Statistical Office of the United Nations, Publishing Service, New York, New York 10017 (800) 253-9646; *Statistical Yearbook*.

UNION OF SOVIET SOCIALIST REPUBLICS - CONSUMER PRICES

Euromonitor Publications Limited, 87-88 Turnmill Street, London EC1M 5QU, England; *European Marketing Data and Statistics*.

European Community Information Service, 2100 M Street, NW, Washington, D.C. 20037 (202) 862-9500; *Basic Statistics of the Community*.

International Labour Office, I.L.O. Publications, CH-1211, Geneva 22, Switzerland; *Yearbook of Labour Statistics*.

UNION OF SOVIET SOCIALIST REPUBLICS - CONSUMPTION

European Community Information Service, 2100 M Street, NW, Washington, D.C. 20037 (202) 862-9500; *Basic Statistics of the Community*.

G.K. Hall and Company, 70 Lincoln Street, Boston, Massachusetts 02111 (617) 423-3990; *The World in Figures*.

International Lead and Zinc Study Group, Metro House, 58 St. James's Street, London SW1A 1LD England; *Lead and Zinc Statistics*.

International Rubber Study Group, York House, Eighth Floor, Empire Way, Wembley, London HA9 0PA, England; *Rubber Statistical Bulletin*.

UNION OF SOVIET SOCIALIST REPUBLICS - CROPS

Academic International Press, Box 1111, Gulf Breeze, Florida 32561; *U.S.S.R. Facts and Figures*.

Commodity Research Bureau, Incorporated, 75 Wall Street, New York, New York 10005 (212) 504-7754; *Commodity Year Book*.

European Community Information Service, 2100 M Street, NW, Washington, D.C. 20037 (202) 862-9500; *Basic Statistics of the Community*.

Facts on File, 460 Park Avenue South, New York, New York 10016 (800) 443-8323; *The New Book of World Rankings*.

Food and Agricultural Organization of the United Nations (FAO) Via delle Terme di Caracalla, 00100 Rome, Italy (Telephone Number in U.S. (202) 653-2400); *Production Yearbook*, and *The State of Food and Agriculture*.

G.K. Hall and Company, 70 Lincoln Street, Boston, Massachusetts 02111 (617) 423-3990; *The World in Figures*.

Statistical Office of the United Nations, Publishing Service, New York, New York 10017 (800) 253-9646; *Statistical Yearbook*.

UNION OF SOVIET SOCIALIST REPUBLICS - CUSTOMS DUTIES

European Community Information Service, 2100 M Street, NW, Washington, D.C. 20037 (202) 862-9500; *Basic Statistics of the Community*.

G.K. Hall and Company, 70 Lincoln Street, Boston, Massachusetts 02111 (617) 423-3990; *The World in Figures.*

UNION OF SOVIET SOCIALIST REPUBLICS - DAIRY PRODUCTS

Commodity Research Bureau, Incorporated, 75 Wall Street, New York, New York 10005 (212) 504-7754; *Commodity Year Book.*

European Community Information Service, 2100 M Street, NW, Washington, D.C. 20037 (202) 862-9500; *Basic Statistics of the Community.*

Facts on File, 460 Park Avenue South, New York, New York 10016 (800) 443-8323; *The New Book of World Rankings.*

Food and Agricultural Organization of the United Nations (FAO), Via delle Terme di Caracalla, 00100 Rome, Italy (Telephone Number in U.S. (202) 653-2400); *Production Yearbook,* and *The State of Food and Agriculture.*

Statistical Office of the United Nations, Publishing Service, New York, New York 10017 (800) 253-9646; *Statistical Yearbook.*

UNION OF SOVIET SOCIALIST REPUBLICS - DEATH RATE

European Community Information Service, 2100 M Street, NW, Washington, D.C. 20037 (202) 862-9500; *Basic Statistics of the Community.*

G.K. Hall and Company, 70 Lincoln Street, Boston, Massachusetts 02111 (617) 423-3990; *The World in Figures.*

Statistical Office of the United Nations, Publishing Service, New York, New York 10017 (800) 253-9646; *Statistical Yearbook.*

Times Books, 201 East 50th Street, New York, New York 10022 (212) 751-2600; *The Economist Book of Vital World Statistics.*

UNION OF SOVIET SOCIALIST REPUBLICS - DEFENSE EXPENDITURES

G.K. Hall and Company, 70 Lincoln Street, Boston, Massachusetts 02111 (617) 423-3990; *The World in Figures.*

U.S. Arms Control and Disarmament Agency, 320 Twenty-first Street, NW, Washington, D.C. 20451 (202) 647-8677; *World Military Expenditures and Arms Transfers.*

UNION OF SOVIET SOCIALIST REPUBLICS - DEMOGRAPHY

Academic International Press, Box 1111, Gulf Breeze, Florida 32561; *U.S.S.R. Facts and Figures.*

European Community Information Service, 2100 M Street, NW, Washington, D.C. 20037 (202) 862-9500; *Basic Statistics of the Community.*

Facts on File, 460 Park Avenue South, New York, New York 10016 (800) 443-8323; *The New Book of World Rankings.*

G.K. Hall and Company, 70 Lincoln Street, Boston, Massachusetts 02111 (617) 423-3990; *The World in Figures.*

UNION OF SOVIET SOCIALIST REPUBLICS - DEVELOPMENT ASSISTANCE

European Community Information Service, 2100 M Street, NW, Washington, D.C. 20037 (202) 862-9500; *Basic Statistics of the Community.*

G.K. Hall and Company, 70 Lincoln Street, Boston, Massachusetts 02111 (617) 423-3990; *The World in Figures.*

Statistical Office of the United Nations, Publishing Service, New York, New York 10017 (800) 253-9646; *Statistical Yearbook.*

UNION OF SOVIET SOCIALIST REPUBLICS - DISEASE

G.K. Hall and Company, 70 Lincoln Street, Boston, Massachusetts 02111 (617) 423-3990; *The World in Figures.*

UNION OF SOVIET SOCIALIST REPUBLICS - DIVORCE RATES

Facts on File, 460 Park Avenue South, New York, New York 10016 (800) 443-8323; *The New Book of World Rankings.*

Statistical Office of the United Nations, Publishing Service, New York, New York 10017 (800) 253-9646; *Statistical Yearbook.*

UNION OF SOVIET SOCIALIST REPUBLICS - DOMESTIC PRODUCT

European Community Information Service, 2100 M Street, NW, Washington, D.C. 20037 (202) 862-9500; *Basic Statistics of the Community.*

G.K. Hall and Company, 70 Lincoln Street, Boston, Massachusetts 02111 (617) 423-3990; *The World in Figures.*

UNION OF SOVIET SOCIALIST REPUBLICS - ECONOMIC DATA

European Community Information Service, 2100 M Street, NW, Washington, D.C. 20037 (202) 862-9500; *Basic Statistics of the Community.*

UNION OF SOVIET SOCIALIST REPUBLICS - ECONOMIC INDICATORS

Euromonitor Publications Limited, 87-88 Turnmill Street, London EC1M 5QU, England; *European Marketing Data and Statistics.*

European Community Information Service, 2100 M Street, NW, Washington, D.C. 20037 (202) 862-9500; *Basic Statistics of the Community.*

UNION OF SOVIET SOCIALIST REPUBLICS - ECONOMY

Academic International Press, Box 1111, Gulf Breeze, Florida 32561; *U.S.S.R. Facts and Figures.*

European Community Information Service, 2100 M Street, NW, Washington, D.C. 20037 (202) 862-9500; *Basic Statistics of the Community.*

Facts on File, 460 Park Avenue South, New York, New York 10016 (800) 443-8323; *The New Book of World Rankings.*

G.K. Hall and Company, 70 Lincoln Street, Boston, Massachusetts 02111 (617) 423-3990; *The World in Figures.*

UNION OF SOVIET SOCIALIST REPUBLICS - EDUCATION

Academic International Press, Box 1111, Gulf Breeze, Florida 32561; *U.S.S.R. Facts and Figures.*

Columbia University Press, 562 West 113th Street, New York, New York 10014 (212) 316-7100; *East European and Soviet Data Book.*

Euromonitor Publications Limited, 87-88 Turnmill Street, London EC1M 5QU, England; *European Marketing Data and Statistics*.

European Community Information Service, 2100 M Street, NW, Washington, D.C. 20037 (202) 862-9500; *Basic Statistics of the Community*.

Facts on File, 460 Park Avenue South, New York, New York 10016 (800) 443-8323; *The New Book of World Rankings*.

Federal Statistical Office, Gustav-Stresemann-Ring 11, D-6200 Wiesbaden, Germany; *U.S.S.R.*

G.K. Hall and Company, 70 Lincoln Street, Boston, Massachusetts 02111 (617) 423-3990; *The World in Figures*.

Times Books, 201 East 50th Street, New York, New York 10022 (212) 751-2600; *The Economist Book of Vital World Statistics*.

United Nations Educational, Scientific and Cultural Organization (UNESCO), 7 Place de Fontenoy, F-75700 Paris, France (Telephone Number in U.S. (212) 963-5981); *Statistical Yearbook*.

UNION OF SOVIET SOCIALIST REPUBLICS - ELECTRICITY

Commodity Research Bureau, Incorporated, 75 Wall Street, New York, New York 10005 (212) 504-7754; *Commodity Year Book*.

European Community Information Service, 2100 M Street, NW, Washington, D.C. 20037 (202) 862-9500; *Basic Statistics of the Community*.

Facts on File, 460 Park Avenue South, New York, New York 10016 (800) 443-8323; *The New Book of World Rankings*.

Penn Well Publishing Company, 1421 South Sheridan Road, P.O. Box 1260, Tulsa, Oklahoma 74101 (800) 752-9764; *International Energy Statistics Sourcebook*.

Statistical Office of the United Nations, Publishing Service, New York, New York 10017 (800) 253-9646; *Statistical Yearbook*.

Times Books, 201 East 50th Street, New York, New York 10022 (212) 751-2600; *The Economist Book of Vital World Statistics*.

UNION OF SOVIET SOCIALIST REPUBLICS - EMPLOYMENT

Columbia University Press, 562 West 113th Street, New York, New York 10014 (212) 316-7100; *East European and Soviet Data Book*.

Euromonitor Publications Limited, 87-88 Turnmill Street, London EC1M 5QU, England; *European Marketing Data and Statistics*.

European Community Information Service, 2100 M Street, NW, Washington, D.C. 20037 (202) 862-9500; *Basic Statistics of the Community*.

Facts on File, 460 Park Avenue South, New York, New York 10016 (800) 443-8323; *The New Book of World Rankings*.

Federal Statistical Office, Gustav-Stresemann-Ring 11, D-6200 Wiesbaden, Germany; *U.S.S.R.*

International Labour Office, I.L.O. Publications, CH-1211, Geneva 22, Switzerland; *Yearbook of Labour Statistics*.

Statistical Office of the United Nations, Publishing Service, New York, New York 10017 (800) 253-9646; *Statistical Yearbook*.

UNION OF SOVIET SOCIALIST REPUBLICS - ENERGY

Academic International Press, Box 1111, Gulf Breeze, Florida 32561; *U.S.S.R. Facts and Figures*.

Euromonitor Publications Limited, 87-88 Turnmill Street, London EC1M 5QU, England; *European Marketing Data and Statistics*.

European Community Information Service, 2100 M Street, NW, Washington, D.C. 20037 (202) 862-9500; *Basic Statistics of the Community*.

Facts on File, 460 Park Avenue South, New York, New York 10016 (800) 443-8323; *The New Book of World Rankings*.

Food and Agricultural Organization of the United Nations (FAO) Via delle Terme di Caracalla, 00100 Rome, Italy (Telephone Number in U.S. (202) 653-2400); *The State of Food and Agriculture*.

G.K. Hall and Company, 70 Lincoln Street, Boston, Massachusetts 02111 (617) 423-3990; *The World in Figures*.

Penn Well Publishing Company, 1421 South Sheridan Road, P.O. Box 1260, Tulsa, Oklahoma 74101 (800) 752-9764; *International Energy Statistics Sourcebook*.

Statistical Office of the United Nations, Publishing Service, New York, New York 10017 (800) 253-9646; *Statistical Yearbook*, *Yearbook of World Energy Statistics*, and *World Energy Supplies*.

Times Books, 201 East 50th Street, New York, New York 10022 (212) 751-2600; *The Economist Book of Vital World Statistics*.

UNION OF SOVIET SOCIALIST REPUBLICS - ENGINEERING AND METAL PRODUCTS - EXPORTS AND IMPORTS

European Community Information Service, 2100 M Street, NW, Washington, D.C. 20037 (202) 862-9500; *Basic Statistics of the Community*.

UNION OF SOVIET SOCIALIST REPUBLICS - ESPIONAGE

Academic International Press, Box 1111, Gulf Breeze, Florida 32561; *U.S.S.R. Facts and Figures*.

UNION OF SOVIET SOCIALIST REPUBLICS - EXCHANGE RATES

International Civil Aviation Organization, 1000 Sherbrooke Street, West, Montreal, Quebec, Canada H3A 2R2 (514) 285-8219; *Civil Aviation Statistics of the World*.

Statistical Office of the United Nations, Publishing Service, New York, New York 10017 (800) 253-9646; *Statistical Yearbook*.

UNION OF SOVIET SOCIALIST REPUBLICS - EXPORT DUTIES

European Community Information Service, 2100 M Street, NW, Washington, D.C. 20037 (202) 862-9500; *Basic Statistics of the Community*.

UNION OF SOVIET SOCIALIST REPUBLICS - EXPORTS

Academic International Press, Box 1111, Gulf Breeze, Florida 32561; *U.S.S.R. Facts and Figures*.

American Automobile Manufacturers Association, 1401 H Street, NW, Suite 900, Washington, D.C. 20005 (202) 326-5500; *World*

Motor Vehicle Data.

European Community Information Service, 2100 M Street, NW, Washington, D.C. 20037 (202) 862-9500; *Basic Statistics of the Community.*

Food and Agricultural Organization of the United Nations (FAO) Via delle Terme di Caracalla, 00100 Rome, Italy (Telephone Number in U.S. (202) 653-2400); *The State of Food and Agriculture.*

G.K. Hall and Company, 70 Lincoln Street, Boston, Massachusetts 02111 (617) 423-3990; *The World in Figures.*

International Lead and Zinc Study Group, Metro House, 58 St. James's Street, London SW1A 1LD England; *Lead and Zinc Statistics.*

International Monetary Fund, 700 Nineteenth Street, NW, Washington, D.C. 20431 (202) 623-7000; *Direction of Trade Statistics.*

International Rubber Study Group, York House, Eighth Floor, Empire Way, Wembley, London HA9 0PA, England; *Rubber Statistical Bulletin.*

Times Books, 201 East 50th Street, New York, New York 10022 (212) 751-2600; *The Economist Book of Vital World Statistics.*

UNION OF SOVIET SOCIALIST REPUBLICS - EXTERNAL TRADE

European Community Information Service, 2100 M Street, NW, Washington, D.C. 20037 (202) 862-9500; *Basic Statistics of the Community.*

Food and Agricultural Organization of the United Nations (FAO) Via delle Terme di Caracalla, 00100 Rome, Italy (Telephone Number in U.S. (202) 653-2400); *The State of Food and Agriculture.* and *Trade Yearbook.*

G.K. Hall and Company, 70 Lincoln Street, Boston, Massachusetts 02111 (617) 423-3990; *The World in Figures.*

Statistical Office of the United Nations, Publishing Service, New York, New York 10017 (800) 253-9646; *Statistical Yearbook.*

UNION OF SOVIET SOCIALIST REPUBLICS - FERTILITY RATES

Columbia University Press, 562 West 113th Street, New York, New York 10014 (212) 316-7100; *East European and Soviet Data Book.*

Facts on File, 460 Park Avenue South, New York, New York 10016 (800) 443-8323; *The New Book of World Rankings.*

Times Books, 201 East 50th Street, New York, New York 10022 (212) 751-2600; *The Economist Book of Vital World Statistics.*

UNION OF SOVIET SOCIALIST REPUBLICS - FERTILIZER

European Community Information Service, 2100 M Street, NW, Washington, D.C. 20037 (202) 862-9500; *Basic Statistics of the Community.*

Food and Agricultural Organization of the United Nations (FAO), Via delle Terme di Caracalla, 00100 Rome, Italy (Telephone Number in U.S. (202) 653-2400); *Fertilizer Yearbook*, and *The State of Food and Agriculture.*

Statistical Office of the United Nations, Publishing Service, New York, New York 10017 (800) 253-9646; *Statistical Yearbook.*

UNION OF SOVIET SOCIALIST REPUBLICS - FETAL MORTALITY

European Community Information Service, 2100 M Street, NW, Washington, D.C. 20037 (202) 862-9500; *Basic Statistics of the Community.*

World Health Organization, Office of Publications, Avenue Appia, CH-1211 Geneva 27, Switzerland (Telephone Number in U.S. (518) 436-9686); *World Health Statistics Annual.*

UNION OF SOVIET SOCIALIST REPUBLICS - FINANCE

European Community Information Service, 2100 M Street, NW, Washington, D.C. 20037 (202) 862-9500; *Basic Statistics of the Community.*

Facts on File, 460 Park Avenue South, New York, New York 10016 (800) 443-8323; *The New Book of World Rankings.*

Federal Statistical Office, Gustav-Stresemann-Ring 11, D-6200 Wiesbaden, Germany; *U.S.S.R.*

G.K. Hall and Company, 70 Lincoln Street, Boston, Massachusetts 02111 (617) 423-3990; *The World in Figures.*

UNION OF SOVIET SOCIALIST REPUBLICS - FISHERIES

Academic International Press, Box 1111, Gulf Breeze, Florida 32561; *U.S.S.R. Facts and Figures.*

Euromonitor Publications Limited, 87-88 Turnmill Street, London EC1M 5QU, England; *European Marketing Data and Statistics.*

European Community Information Service, 2100 M Street, NW, Washington, D.C. 20037 (202) 862-9500; *Basic Statistics of the Community.*

Facts on File, 460 Park Avenue South, New York, New York 10016 (800) 443-8323; *The New Book of World Rankings.*

Federal Statistical Office, Gustav-Stresemann-Ring 11, D-6200 Wiesbaden, Germany; *U.S.S.R.*

Food and Agricultural Organization of the United Nations (FAO) Via delle Terme di Caracalla, 00100 Rome, Italy (Telephone Number in U.S. (202) 653-2400); *The State of Food and Agriculture,* and *Yearbook of Fishery Statistics.*

Statistical Office of the United Nations, Publishing Service, New York, New York 10017 (800) 253-9646; *Statistical Yearbook.*

UNION OF SOVIET SOCIALIST REPUBLICS - FLOUR PRODUCTION

European Community Information Service, 2100 M Street, NW, Washington, D.C. 20037 (202) 862-9500; *Basic Statistics of the Community.*

Statistical Office of the United Nations, Publishing Service, New York, New York 10017 (800) 253-9646; *Statistical Yearbook.*

UNION OF SOVIET SOCIALIST REPUBLICS - FOOD

European Community Information Service, 2100 M Street, NW, Washington, D.C. 20037 (202) 862-9500; *Basic Statistics of the*

Community.

Food and Agricultural Organization of the United Nations (FAO) Via delle Terme di Caracalla, 00100 Rome, Italy (Telephone Number in U.S. (202) 653-2400); *Production Yearbook,* and *The State of Food and Agriculture.*

G.K. Hall and Company, 70 Lincoln Street, Boston, Massachusetts 02111 (617) 423-3990; *The World in Figures.*

UNION OF SOVIET SOCIALIST REPUBLICS - FOREIGN AID

Academic International Press, Box 1111, Gulf Breeze, Florida 32561; *U.S.S.R. Facts and Figures.*

G.K. Hall and Company, 70 Lincoln Street, Boston, Massachusetts 02111 (617) 423-3990; *The World in Figures.*

UNION OF SOVIET SOCIALIST REPUBLICS - FOREIGN TRADE

Academic International Press, Box 1111, Gulf Breeze, Florida 32561; *U.S.S.R. Facts and Figures.*

Euromonitor Publications Limited, 87-88 Turnmill Street, London EC1M 5QU, England; *European Marketing Data and Statistics.*

European Community Information Service, 2100 M Street, NW, Washington, D.C. 20037 (202) 862-9500; *Basic Statistics of the Community.*

Facts on File, 460 Park Avenue South, New York, New York 10016 (800) 443-8323; *The New Book of World Rankings.*

Federal Statistical Office, Gustav-Stresemann-Ring 11, D-6200 Wiesbaden, Germany; *U.S.S.R.*

Food and Agricultural Organization of the United Nations (FAO) Via delle Terme di Caracalla, 00100 Rome, Italy (Telephone Number in U.S. (202) 653-2400); *The State of Food and Agriculture.*

G.K. Hall and Company, 70 Lincoln Street, Boston, Massachusetts 02111 (617) 423-3990; *The World in Figures.*

Statistical Office of the United Nations, Publishing Service, New York, New York 10017 (800) 253-9646; *International Trade Statistics Yearbook,* and *Statistical Yearbook.*

UNION OF SOVIET SOCIALIST REPUBLICS - FORESTRY AND FOREST PRODUCTS

Academic International Press, Box 1111, Gulf Breeze, Florida 32561; *U.S.S.R. Facts and Figures.*

American Forest and Paper Association, 1250 Connecticut Avenue, NW, Washington, D.C. 20036 (202) 463-2455; *Wood Pulp and Fiber Statistics.*

Euromonitor Publications Limited, 87-88 Turnmill Street, London EC1M 5QU, England; *European Marketing Data and Statistics.*

European Community Information Service, 2100 M Street, NW, Washington, D.C. 20037 (202) 862-9500; *Basic Statistics of the Community.*

Facts on File, 460 Park Avenue South, New York, New York 10016 (800) 443-8323; *The New Book of World Rankings.*

Federal Statistical Office, Gustav-Stresemann-Ring 11, D-6200 Wiesbaden, Germany; *U.S.S.R.*

Food and Agricultural Organization of the United Nations (FAO) Via delle Terme di Caracalla, 00100 Rome, Italy (Telephone Number in U.S. (202) 653-2400); *The State of Food and Agriculture,* and *Yearbook of Forest Products.*

G.K. Hall and Company, 70 Lincoln Street, Boston, Massachusetts 02111 (617) 423-3990; *The World in Figures.*

Statistical Office of the United Nations, Publishing Service, New York, New York 10017 (800) 253-9646; *Statistical Yearbook.*

United Nations Educational, Scientific and Cultural Organization (UNESCO), 7 Place de Fontenoy, F-75700 Paris, France (Telephone Number in U.S. (212) 963-5981); *Statistical Yearbook.*

UNION OF SOVIET SOCIALIST REPUBLICS - FURNITURE AND WOOD PRODUCTS - EXPORTS AND IMPORTS

European Community Information Service, 2100 M Street, NW, Washington, D.C. 20037 (202) 862-9500; *Basic Statistics of the Community.*

UNION OF SOVIET SOCIALIST REPUBLICS - GENERAL INDUSTRIAL STATISTICS

European Community Information Service, 2100 M Street, NW, Washington, D.C. 20037 (202) 862-9500; *Basic Statistics of the Community.*

Statistical Office of the United Nations, Publishing Service, New York, New York 10017 (800) 253-9646; *Industrial Statistics Yearbook.*

UNION OF SOVIET SOCIALIST REPUBLICS - GENERAL MORTALITY

European Community Information Service, 2100 M Street, NW, Washington, D.C. 20037 (202) 862-9500; *Basic Statistics of the Community.*

World Health Organization, Office of Publications, Avenue Appia, CH-1211 Geneva 27, Switzerland (Telephone Number in U.S. (518) 436-9686); *World Health Statistics Annual.*

UNION OF SOVIET SOCIALIST REPUBLICS - GEOGRAPHIC DATA

European Community Information Service, 2100 M Street, NW, Washington, D.C. 20037 (202) 862-9500; *Basic Statistics of the Community.*

Facts on File, 460 Park Avenue South, New York, New York 10016 (800) 443-8323; *The New Book of World Rankings.*

UNION OF SOVIET SOCIALIST REPUBLICS - GOLD PRODUCTION AND CONSUMPTION

Commodity Research Bureau, Incorporated, 75 Wall Street, New York, New York 10005 (212) 504-7754; *Commodity Year Book.*

European Community Information Service, 2100 M Street, NW, Washington, D.C. 20037 (202) 862-9500; *Basic Statistics of the Community.*

Facts on File, 460 Park Avenue South, New York, New York 10016 (800) 443-8323; *The New Book of World Rankings.*

UNION OF SOVIET SOCIALIST REPUBLICS - GOVERNMENT

Academic International Press, Box 1111, Gulf Breeze, Florida 32561; *U.S.S.R. Facts and Figures.*

European Community Information Service, 2100 M Street, NW, Washington, D.C. 20037 (202) 862-9500; *Basic Statistics of the Community.*

G.K. Hall and Company, 70 Lincoln Street, Boston, Massachusetts 02111 (617) 423-3990; *The World in Figures.*

UNION OF SOVIET SOCIALIST REPUBLICS - GOVERNMENT CONSUMPTION

European Community Information Service, 2100 M Street, NW, Washington, D.C. 20037 (202) 862-9500; *Basic Statistics of the Community.*

UNION OF SOVIET SOCIALIST REPUBLICS - GOVERNMENT EXPENDITURE

European Community Information Service, 2100 M Street, NW, Washington, D.C. 20037 (202) 862-9500; *Basic Statistics of the Community.*

UNION OF SOVIET SOCIALIST REPUBLICS - GOVERNMENT FINANCES

European Community Information Service, 2100 M Street, NW, Washington, D.C. 20037 (202) 862-9500; *Basic Statistics of the Community.*

Statistical Office of the United Nations, Publishing Service, New York, New York 10017 (800) 253-9646; *Statistical Yearbook.*

UNION OF SOVIET SOCIALIST REPUBLICS - GOVERNMENT REVENUE

European Community Information Service, 2100 M Street, NW, Washington, D.C. 20037 (202) 862-9500; *Basic Statistics of the Community.*

UNION OF SOVIET SOCIALIST REPUBLICS - GROSS DOMESTIC PRODUCT

European Community Information Service, 2100 M Street, NW, Washington, D.C. 20037 (202) 862-9500; *Basic Statistics of the Community.*

Facts on File, 460 Park Avenue South, New York, New York 10016 (800) 443-8323; *The New Book of World Rankings.*

G.K. Hall and Company, 70 Lincoln Street, Boston, Massachusetts 02111 (617) 423-3990; *The World in Figures.*

Statistical Office of the United Nations, Publishing Service, New York, New York 10017 (800) 253-9646; *Statistical Yearbook.*

Times Books, 201 East 50th Street, New York, New York 10022 (212) 751-2600; *The Economist Book of Vital World Statistics.*

UNION OF SOVIET SOCIALIST REPUBLICS - GROSS NATIONAL PRODUCT

European Community Information Service, 2100 M Street, NW, Washington, D.C. 20037 (202) 862-9500; *Basic Statistics of the Community.*

U.S. Arms Control and Disarmament Agency, 320 Twenty-first Street, NW, Washington, D.C. 20451 (202) 647-8677; *World Military Expenditures and Arms Transfers.*

UNION OF SOVIET SOCIALIST REPUBLICS - HEALTH

Academic International Press, Box 1111, Gulf Breeze, Florida 32561; *U.S.S.R. Facts and Figures.*

European Community Information Service, 2100 M Street, NW, Washington, D.C. 20037 (202) 862-9500; *Basic Statistics of the Community.*

Facts on File, 460 Park Avenue South, New York, New York 10016 (800) 443-8323; *The New Book of World Rankings.*

Federal Statistical Office, Gustav-Stresemann-Ring 11, D-6200 Wiesbaden, Germany; *U.S.S.R.*

G.K. Hall and Company, 70 Lincoln Street, Boston, Massachusetts 02111 (617) 423-3990; *The World in Figures.*

Statistical Office of the United Nations, Publishing Service, New York, New York 10017 (800) 253-9646; *Statistical Yearbook.*

Times Books, 201 East 50th Street, New York, New York 10022 (212) 751-2600; *The Economist Book of Vital World Statistics.*

UNION OF SOVIET SOCIALIST REPUBLICS - HIDE PRODUCTION

Food and Agricultural Organization of the United Nations (FAO), Via delle Terme di Caracalla, 00100 Rome, Italy (Telephone Number in U.S. (202) 653-2400); *Production Yearbook.*

UNION OF SOVIET SOCIALIST REPUBLICS - HIGHWAYS

European Community Information Service, 2100 M Street, NW, Washington, D.C. 20037 (202) 862-9500; *Basic Statistics of the Community.*

G.K. Hall and Company, 70 Lincoln Street, Boston, Massachusetts 02111 (617) 423-3990; *The World in Figures.*

Statistical Office of the United Nations, Publishing Service, New York, New York 10017 (800) 253-9646; *Annual Bulletin of Transport Statistics for Europe.*

UNION OF SOVIET SOCIALIST REPUBLICS - HONEY PRODUCTION

Commodity Research Bureau, Incorporated, 75 Wall Street, New York, New York 10005 (212) 504-7754; *Commodity Year Book.*

UNION OF SOVIET SOCIALIST REPUBLICS - HOUSING AND HOUSING UNITS

European Community Information Service, 2100 M Street, NW, Washington, D.C. 20037 (202) 862-9500; *Basic Statistics of the Community.*

Facts on File, 460 Park Avenue South, New York, New York 10016 (800) 443-8323; *The New Book of World Rankings.*

UNION OF SOVIET SOCIALIST REPUBLICS - HOUSING EXPENDITURES

European Community Information Service, 2100 M Street, NW, Washington, D.C. 20037 (202) 862-9500; *Basic Statistics of the*

Community.

UNION OF SOVIET SOCIALIST REPUBLICS - HYDROCHLORIC ACID PRODUCTION

European Community Information Service, 2100 M Street, NW, Washington, D.C. 20037 (202) 862-9500; *Basic Statistics of the Community.*

UNION OF SOVIET SOCIALIST REPUBLICS - ILLITERATE POPULATION

Columbia University Press, 562 West 113th Street, New York, New York 10014 (212) 316-7100; *East European and Soviet Data Book.*

G.K. Hall and Company, 70 Lincoln Street, Boston, Massachusetts 02111 (617) 423-3990; *The World in Figures.*

UNION OF SOVIET SOCIALIST REPUBLICS - IMPORTS

Academic International Press, Box 1111, Gulf Breeze, Florida 32561; *U.S.S.R. Facts and Figures.*

American Automobile Manufacturers Association, 1401 H Street, NW, Suite 900, Washington, D.C. 20005 (202) 326-5500; *World Motor Vehicle Data.*

European Community Information Service, 2100 M Street, NW, Washington, D.C. 20037 (202) 862-9500; *Basic Statistics of the Community.*

Food and Agricultural Organization of the United Nations (FAO) Via delle Terme di Caracalla, 00100 Rome, Italy (Telephone Number in U.S. (202) 653-2400); *The State of Food and Agriculture.*

G.K. Hall and Company, 70 Lincoln Street, Boston, Massachusetts 02111 (617) 423-3990; *The World in Figures.*

International Lead and Zinc Study Group, Metro House, 58 St. James's Street, London SW1A 1LD England; *Lead and Zinc Statistics.*

International Monetary Fund, 700 Nineteenth Street, NW, Washington, D.C. 20431 (202) 623-7000; *Direction of Trade Statistics.*

International Rubber Study Group, York House, Eighth Floor, Empire Way, Wembley, London HA9 0PA, England; *Rubber Statistical Bulletin.*

Times Books, 201 East 50th Street, New York, New York 10022 (212) 751-2600; *The Economist Book of Vital World Statistics.*

UNION OF SOVIET SOCIALIST REPUBLICS - INDUSTRY

European Community Information Service, 2100 M Street, NW, Washington, D.C. 20037 (202) 862-9500; *Basic Statistics of the Community.*

Facts on File, 460 Park Avenue South, New York, New York 10016 (800) 443-8323; *The New Book of World Rankings.*

Federal Statistical Office, Gustav-Stresemann-Ring 11, D-6200 Wiesbaden, Germany; *U.S.S.R.*

G.K. Hall and Company, 70 Lincoln Street, Boston, Massachusetts 02111 (617) 423-3990; *The World in Figures.*

International Labour Office, I.L.O. Publications, CH-1211, Geneva 22, Switzerland; *Yearbook of Labour Statistics.*

Statistical Office of the United Nations, Publishing Service, New York, New York 10017 (800) 253-9646; *Statistical Yearbook.*

Times Books, 201 East 50th Street, New York, New York 10022 (212) 751-2600; *The Economist Book of Vital World Statistics.*

World Intellectual Property Organization, 34 Chemin des Colombettes, CH-1211 Geneva 20. Switzerland; *Industrial Property Statistics.*

UNION OF SOVIET SOCIALIST REPUBLICS - INFANT AND MATERNAL MORTALITY

European Community Information Service, 2100 M Street, NW, Washington, D.C. 20037 (202) 862-9500; *Basic Statistics of the Community.*

Statistical Office of the United Nations, Publishing Service, New York, New York 10017 (800) 253-9646; *Statistical Yearbook.*

Times Books, 201 East 50th Street, New York, New York 10022 (212) 751-2600; *The Economist Book of Vital World Statistics.*

World Health Organization, Office of Publications, Avenue Appia, CH-1211 Geneva 27, Switzerland (Telephone Number in U.S. (518) 436-9686); *World Health Statistics Annual.*

UNION OF SOVIET SOCIALIST REPUBLICS - INTERNAL TRADE

European Community Information Service, 2100 M Street, NW, Washington, D.C. 20037 (202) 862-9500; *Basic Statistics of the Community.*

Statistical Office of the United Nations, Publishing Service, New York, New York 10017 (800) 253-9646; *Statistical Yearbook.*

UNION OF SOVIET SOCIALIST REPUBLICS - INTERNATIONAL FINANCE

European Community Information Service, 2100 M Street, NW, Washington, D.C. 20037 (202) 862-9500; *Basic Statistics of the Community.*

UNION OF SOVIET SOCIALIST REPUBLICS - LABOR FORCE

Academic International Press, Box 1111, Gulf Breeze, Florida 32561; *U.S.S.R. Facts and Figures.*

Columbia University Press, 562 West 113th Street, New York, New York 10014 (212) 316-7100; *East European and Soviet Data Book.*

European Community Information Service, 2100 M Street, NW, Washington, D.C. 20037 (202) 862-9500; *Basic Statistics of the Community.*

Facts on File, 460 Park Avenue South, New York, New York 10016 (800) 443-8323; *The New Book of World Rankings.*

Food and Agricultural Organization of the United Nations (FAO) Via delle Terme di Caracalla, 00100 Rome, Italy (Telephone Number in U.S. (202) 653-2400); *The State of Food and Agriculture.*

G.K. Hall and Company, 70 Lincoln Street, Boston, Massachusetts 02111 (617) 423-3990; *The World in Figures.*

UNION OF SOVIET SOCIALIST REPUBLICS - LABOR PRODUCTIVITY

International Labour Office, I.L.O. Publications, CH-1211, Geneva 22, Switzerland; *Yearbook of Labour Statistics*.

UNION OF SOVIET SOCIALIST REPUBLICS - LAND USE

Euromonitor Publications Limited, 87-88 Turnmill Street, London EC1M 5QU, England; *European Marketing Data and Statistics*.

European Community Information Service, 2100 M Street, NW, Washington, D.C. 20037 (202) 862-9500; *Basic Statistics of the Community*.

Food and Agricultural Organization of the United Nations (FAO), Via delle Terme di Caracalla, 00100 Rome, Italy (Telephone Number in U.S. (202) 653-2400); *Production Yearbook*.

G.K. Hall and Company, 70 Lincoln Street, Boston, Massachusetts 02111 (617) 423-3990; *The World in Figures*.

UNION OF SOVIET SOCIALIST REPUBLICS - LEATHER AND FOOTWEAR - EXPORTS AND IMPORTS

European Community Information Service, 2100 M Street, NW, Washington, D.C. 20037 (202) 862-9500; *Basic Statistics of the Community*.

UNION OF SOVIET SOCIALIST REPUBLICS - LIBRARIES

Euromonitor Publications Limited, 87-88 Turnmill Street, London EC1M 5QU, England; *European Marketing Data and Statistics*.

Facts on File, 460 Park Avenue South, New York, New York 10016 (800) 443-8323; *The New Book of World Rankings*.

United Nations Educational, Scientific and Cultural Organization (UNESCO), 7 Place de Fontenoy, F-75700 Paris, France (Telephone Number in U.S. (212) 963-5981); *Statistical Yearbook*.

UNION OF SOVIET SOCIALIST REPUBLICS - LIVESTOCK AND POULTRY

Academic International Press, Box 1111, Gulf Breeze, Florida 32561; *U.S.S.R. Facts and Figures*.

Commodity Research Bureau, Incorporated, 75 Wall Street, New York, New York 10005 (212) 504-7754; *Commodity Year Book*.

Euromonitor Publications Limited, 87-88 Turnmill Street, London EC1M 5QU, England; *European Marketing Data and Statistics*.

European Community Information Service, 2100 M Street, NW, Washington, D.C. 20037 (202) 862-9500; *Basic Statistics of the Community*.

Facts on File, 460 Park Avenue South, New York, New York 10016 (800) 443-8323; *The New Book of World Rankings*.

Food and Agricultural Organization of the United Nations (FAO), Via delle Terme di Caracalla, 00100 Rome, Italy (Telephone Number in U.S. (202) 653-2400); *Production Yearbook*, and *The State of Food and Agriculture*.

G.K. Hall and Company, 70 Lincoln Street, Boston, Massachusetts 02111 (617) 423-3990; *The World in Figures*.

Statistical Office of the United Nations, Publishing Service, New York, New York 10017 (800) 253-9646; *Statistical Yearbook*.

UNION OF SOVIET SOCIALIST REPUBLICS - LIVING LEVELS

G.K. Hall and Company, 70 Lincoln Street, Boston, Massachusetts 02111 (617) 423-3990; *The World in Figures*.

Times Books, 201 East 50th Street, New York, New York 10022 (212) 751-2600; *The Economist Book of Vital World Statistics*.

UNION OF SOVIET SOCIALIST REPUBLICS - MAIL - NUMBER OF PIECES SENT OR RECEIVED

Statistical Office of the United Nations, Publishing Service, New York, New York 10017 (800) 253-9646; *Statistical Yearbook*.

UNION OF SOVIET SOCIALIST REPUBLICS - MANUFACTURING

American Automobile Manufacturers Association, 1401 H Street, NW, Suite 900, Washington, D.C. 20005 (202) 326-5500; *World Motor Vehicle Data*.

European Community Information Service, 2100 M Street, NW, Washington, D.C. 20037 (202) 862-9500; *Basic Statistics of the Community*.

Facts on File, 460 Park Avenue South, New York, New York 10016 (800) 443 8323; *The New Book of World Rankings*.

G.K. Hall and Company, 70 Lincoln Street, Boston, Massachusetts 02111 (617) 423-3990; *The World in Figures*.

Statistical Office of the United Nations, Publishing Service, New York, New York 10017 (800) 253-9646; *Statistical Yearbook*.

Times Books, 201 East 50th Street, New York, New York 10022 (212) 751-2600; *The Economist Book of Vital World Statistics*.

UNION OF SOVIET SOCIALIST REPUBLICS - MARRIAGE RATES

European Community Information Service, 2100 M Street, NW, Washington, D.C. 20037 (202) 862-9500; *Basic Statistics of the Community*.

Facts on File, 460 Park Avenue South, New York, New York 10016 (800) 443 8323; *The New Book of World Rankings*.

Statistical Office of the United Nations, Publishing Service, New York, New York 10017 (800) 253-9646; *Statistical Yearbook*.

UNION OF SOVIET SOCIALIST REPUBLICS - MERCHANT FLEET CHARACTERISTICS

European Community Information Service, 2100 M Street, NW, Washington, D.C. 20037 (202) 862-9500; *Basic Statistics of the Community*.

Lloyd's Register of Shipping, 17 Battery Place, New York, New York 10004 (212) 425-8050; *Register of Ships*.

U.S. Department of Transportation, Maritime Administration, 400 Seventh Street, SW, Washington, D.C. 20590 (202) 366-5807; *A Statistical Analysis of the World's Merchant Fleets*.

UNION OF SOVIET SOCIALIST REPUBLICS - MERCHANT
SHIPPING

European Community Information Service, 2100 M Street, NW,
Washington, D.C. 20037 (202) 862-9500; *Basic Statistics of the
Community.*

G.K. Hall and Company, 70 Lincoln Street, Boston, Massachusetts
02111 (617) 423-3990; *The World in Figures.*

Lloyd's Register of Shipping, 17 Battery Place, New York, New York
10004 (212) 425-8050; *Register of Ships.*

Statistical Office of the United Nations, Publishing Service, New
York, New York 10017 (800) 253-9646; *Annual Bulletin of Transport
Statistics for Europe,* and *Statistical Yearbook.*

Times Books, 201 East 50th Street, New York, New York 10022
(212) 751-2600; *The Economist Book of Vital World Statistics.*

UNION OF SOVIET SOCIALIST REPUBLICS - MERCHANT VESSELS -
TONNAGE LAUNCHED

European Community Information Service, 2100 M Street, NW,
Washington, D.C. 20037 (202) 862-9500; *Basic Statistics of the
Community.*

Lloyd's Register of Shipping, 17 Battery Place, New York, New York
10004 (212) 425-8050; *Register of Ships.*

UNION OF SOVIET SOCIALIST REPUBLICS - MILITARY

G.K. Hall and Company, 70 Lincoln Street, Boston, Massachusetts
02111 (617) 423-3990; *The World in Figures.*

U.S. Arms Control and Disarmament Agency, 320 Twenty-first
Street, NW, Washington, D.C. 20451 (202) 647-8677; *World Military
Expenditures and Arms Transfers.*

UNION OF SOVIET SOCIALIST REPUBLICS - MINING AND MINERAL
PRODUCTS

American Forest and Paper Association, 1250 Connecticut Avenue,
NW, Washington, D.C. 20036 (202) 463-2455; *Wood Pulp and Fiber
Statistics.*

Commodity Research Bureau, Incorporated, 75 Wall Street, New
York, New York 10005 (212) 504-7754; *Commodity Year Book.*

European Community Information Service, 2100 M Street, NW,
Washington, D.C. 20037 (202) 862-9500; *Basic Statistics of the
Community.*

Facts on File, 460 Park Avenue South, New York, New York 10016
(800) 443-8323; *The New Book of World Rankings.*

G.K. Hall and Company, 70 Lincoln Street, Boston, Massachusetts
02111 (617) 423-3990; *The World in Figures.*

International Lead and Zinc Study Group, Metro House, 58 St.
James's Street, London SW1A 1LD England; *Lead and Zinc
Statistics.*

Organisation for Economic Co-operation and Development (OECD),
2 rue Andre-Pascal, 75 Paris 16, France (Telephone Number in U.S.
(202) 785-6323); *Revenue Statistics of OECD Member Countries.*

Penn Well Publishing Company, 1421 South Sheridan Road, P.O.
Box 1260, Tulsa, Oklahoma 74101 (800) 752-9764; *International*

Energy Statistics Sourcebook.

Statistical Office of the United Nations, Publishing Service, New
York, New York 10017 (800) 253-9646; *Statistical Yearbook.*

UNION OF SOVIET SOCIALIST REPUBLICS - MONEY
EXCHANGE RATES

European Community Information Service, 2100 M Street, NW,
Washington, D.C. 20037 (202) 862-9500; *Basic Statistics of the
Community.*

Statistical Office of the United Nations, Publishing Service, New
York, New York 10017 (800) 253-9646; *Statistical Yearbook.*

UNION OF SOVIET SOCIALIST REPUBLICS - MONEY RATES -
MARKET

European Community Information Service, 2100 M Street, NW,
Washington, D.C. 20037 (202) 862-9500; *Basic Statistics of the
Community.*

UNION OF SOVIET SOCIALIST REPUBLICS - MONEY
RESERVES

European Community Information Service, 2100 M Street, NW,
Washington, D.C. 20037 (202) 862-9500; *Basic Statistics of the
Community.*

UNION OF SOVIET SOCIALIST REPUBLICS - MONEY SUPPLY

European Community Information Service, 2100 M Street, NW,
Washington, D.C. 20037 (202) 862-9500; *Basic Statistics of the
Community.*

G.K. Hall and Company, 70 Lincoln Street, Boston, Massachusetts
02111 (617) 423-3990; *The World in Figures.*

UNION OF SOVIET SOCIALIST REPUBLICS - MOTION
PICTURES

Statistical Office of the United Nations, Publishing Service, New
York, New York 10017 (800) 253-9646; *Statistical Yearbook.*

United Nations Educational, Scientific and Cultural Organization
(UNESCO), 7 Place de Fontenoy, F-75700 Paris, France (Telephone
Number in U.S. (212) 963-5981); *Statistical Yearbook.*

UNION OF SOVIET SOCIALIST REPUBLICS - MOTOR
VEHICLE PRODUCTION

American Automobile Manufacturers Association, 1401 H Street,
NW, Suite 900, Washington, D.C. 20005 (202) 326-5500; *World
Motor Vehicle Data.*

European Community Information Service, 2100 M Street, NW,
Washington, D.C. 20037 (202) 862-9500; *Basic Statistics of the
Community.*

Statistical Office of the United Nations, Publishing Service, New
York, New York 10017 (800) 253-9646; *Statistical Yearbook.*

UNION OF SOVIET SOCIALIST REPUBLICS - MOTOR
VEHICLES IN USE

American Automobile Manufacturers Association, 1401 H Street,
NW, Suite 900, Washington, D.C. 20005 (202) 326-5500; *World
Motor Vehicle Data.*

European Community Information Service, 2100 M Street, NW, Washington, D.C. 20037 (202) 862-9500; *Basic Statistics of the Community*.

G.K. Hall and Company, 70 Lincoln Street, Boston, Massachusetts 02111 (617) 423-3990; *The World in Figures*.

Times Books, 201 East 50th Street, New York, New York 10022 (212) 751-2600; *The Economist Book of Vital World Statistics*.

UNION OF SOVIET SOCIALIST REPUBLICS - MUSEUMS

Euromonitor Publications Limited, 87-88 Turnmill Street, London EC1M 5QU, England; *European Marketing Data and Statistics*.

Facts on File, 460 Park Avenue South, New York, New York 10016 (800) 443-8323; *The New Book of World Rankings*.

United Nations Educational, Scientific and Cultural Organization (UNESCO), 7 Place de Fontenoy, F-75700 Paris, France (Telephone Number in U.S. (212) 963-5981); *Statistical Yearbook*.

UNION OF SOVIET SOCIALIST REPUBLICS - NATIONAL ACCOUNTS

European Community Information Service, 2100 M Street, NW, Washington, D.C. 20037 (202) 862-9500; *Basic Statistics of the Community*.

Statistical Office of the United Nations, Publishing Service, New York, New York 10017 (800) 253-9646; *National Accounts Statistics*, and *Statistical Yearbook*.

UNION OF SOVIET SOCIALIST REPUBLICS - NATIONAL INCOME

Facts on File, 460 Park Avenue South, New York, New York 10016 (800) 443-8323; *The New Book of World Rankings*.

G.K. Hall and Company, 70 Lincoln Street, Boston, Massachusetts 02111 (617) 423-3990; *The World in Figures*.

Statistical Office of the United Nations, Publishing Service, New York, New York 10017 (800) 253-9646; *Statistical Yearbook*.

UNION OF SOVIET SOCIALIST REPUBLICS - NATIONAL PRODUCT

European Community Information Service, 2100 M Street, NW, Washington, D.C. 20037 (202) 862-9500; *Basic Statistics of the Community*.

Facts on File, 460 Park Avenue South, New York, New York 10016 (800) 443-8323; *The New Book of World Rankings*.

Federal Statistical Office, Gustav-Stresemann-Ring 11, D-6200 Wiesbaden, Germany; *U.S.S.R.*

Statistical Office of the United Nations, Publishing Service, New York, New York 10017 (800) 253-9646; *Statistical Yearbook*.

UNION OF SOVIET SOCIALIST REPUBLICS - NATURAL RUBBER PRODUCTION

European Community Information Service, 2100 M Street, NW, Washington, D.C. 20037 (202) 862-9500; *Basic Statistics of the Community*.

International Rubber Study Group, York House, Eighth Floor, Empire Way, Wembley, London HA9 0PA, England; *Rubber Statistical Bulletin*.

UNION OF SOVIET SOCIALIST REPUBLICS - NET MATERIAL PRODUCT

Statistical Office of the United Nations, Publishing Service, New York, New York 10017 (800) 253-9646; *Statistical Yearbook*.

UNION OF SOVIET SOCIALIST REPUBLICS - OIL PRODUCING CROPS

European Community Information Service, 2100 M Street, NW, Washington, D.C. 20037 (202) 862-9500; *Basic Statistics of the Community*.

UNION OF SOVIET SOCIALIST REPUBLICS - PARTY LEADERS AND MEMBERSHIP

Columbia University Press, 562 West 113th Street, New York, New York 10014 (212) 316-7100; *East European and Soviet Data Book*.

UNION OF SOVIET SOCIALIST REPUBLICS - PATENTS

Statistical Office of the United Nations, Publishing Service, New York, New York 10017 (800) 253-9646; *Statistical Yearbook*.

World Intellectual Property Organization, 34 Chemin des Colombettes, CH-1211 Geneva 20. Switzerland; *Industrial Property Statistics*.

UNION OF SOVIET SOCIALIST REPUBLICS - PERIODICALS

United Nations Educational, Scientific and Cultural Organization (UNESCO), 7 Place de Fontenoy, F-75700 Paris, France (Telephone Number in U.S. (212) 963-5981); *Statistical Yearbook*.

UNION OF SOVIET SOCIALIST REPUBLICS - PESTICIDE USE

Food and Agricultural Organization of the United Nations (FAO) Via delle Terme di Caracalla, 00100 Rome, Italy (Telephone Number in U.S. (202) 653-2400); *The State of Food and Agriculture*.

UNION OF SOVIET SOCIALIST REPUBLICS - PETROLEUM INDUSTRY

Commodity Research Bureau, Incorporated, 75 Wall Street, New York, New York 10005 (212) 504-7754; *Commodity Year Book*.

Euromonitor Publications Limited, 87-88 Turnmill Street, London EC1M 5QU, England; *European Marketing Data and Statistics*.

European Community Information Service, 2100 M Street, NW, Washington, D.C. 20037 (202) 862-9500; *Basic Statistics of the Community*.

Facts on File, 460 Park Avenue South, New York, New York 10016 (800) 443-8323; *The New Book of World Rankings*.

Food and Agricultural Organization of the United Nations (FAO) Via delle Terme di Caracalla, 00100 Rome, Italy (Telephone Number in U.S. (202) 653-2400); *The State of Food and Agriculture*.

G.K. Hall and Company, 70 Lincoln Street, Boston, Massachusetts 02111 (617) 423-3990; *The World in Figures*.

Penn Well Publishing Company, 1421 South Sheridan Road, P.O. Box 1260, Tulsa, Oklahoma 74101 (800) 752-9764; *International Energy Statistics Sourcebook*.

Statistical Office of the United Nations, Publishing Service, New York, New York 10017 (800) 253-9646; *Statistical Yearbook.*

UNION OF SOVIET SOCIALIST REPUBLICS - PIPELINES FOR OIL AND PETROLEUM PRODUCTS

Statistical Office of the United Nations, Publishing Service, New York, New York 10017 (800) 253-9646; *Annual Bulletin of Transport Statistics for Europe.*

UNION OF SOVIET SOCIALIST REPUBLICS - PLASTIC AND RESIN PRODUCTION

Commodity Research Bureau, Incorporated, 75 Wall Street, New York, New York 10005 (212) 504-7754; *Commodity Year Book.*

European Community Information Service, 2100 M Street, NW, Washington, D.C. 20037 (202) 862-9500; *Basic Statistics of the Community.*

Statistical Office of the United Nations, Publishing Service, New York, New York 10017 (800) 253-9646; *Statistical Yearbook.*

UNION OF SOVIET SOCIALIST REPUBLICS - POPULATION

Academic International Press, Box 1111, Gulf Breeze, Florida 32561; *U.S.S.R. Facts and Figures.*

Columbia University Press, 562 West 113th Street, New York, New York 10014 (212) 316-7100; *East European and Soviet Data Book.*

Euromonitor Publications Limited, 87-88 Turnmill Street, London EC1M 5QU, England; *European Marketing Data and Statistics.*

European Community Information Service, 2100 M Street, NW, Washington, D.C. 20037 (202) 862-9500; *Basic Statistics of the Community.*

Facts on File, 460 Park Avenue South, New York, New York 10016 (800) 443-8323; *The New Book of World Rankings.*

Federal Statistical Office, Gustav-Stresemann-Ring 11, D-6200 Wiesbaden, Germany; *U.S.S.R.*

Food and Agricultural Organization of the United Nations (FAO), Via delle Terme di Caracalla, 00100 Rome, Italy (Telephone Number in U.S. (202) 653-2400); *Production Yearbook.*

G.K. Hall and Company, 70 Lincoln Street, Boston, Massachusetts 02111 (617) 423-3990; *The World in Figures.*

International Labour Office, I.L.O. Publications, CH-1211, Geneva 22, Switzerland; *Yearbook of Labour Statistics.*

Statistical Office of the United Nations, Publishing Service, New York, New York 10017 (800) 253-9646; *Statistical Yearbook.*

Times Books, 201 East 50th Street, New York, New York 10022 (212) 751-2600; *The Economist Book of Vital World Statistics.*

United Nations Educational, Scientific and Cultural Organization (UNESCO), 7 Place de Fontenoy, F-75700 Paris, France (Telephone Number in U.S. (212) 963-5981); *Statistical Yearbook.*

U.S. Arms Control and Disarmament Agency, 320 Twenty-first Street, NW, Washington, D.C. 20451 (202) 647-8677; *World Military Expenditures and Arms Transfers.*

World Health Organization, Office of Publications, Avenue Appia, CH-1211 Geneva 27, Switzerland (Telephone Number in U.S. (518) 436-9686); *World Health Statistics Annual.*

UNION OF SOVIET SOCIALIST REPUBLICS - POST OFFICES

Facts on File, 460 Park Avenue South, New York, New York 10016 (800) 443-8323; *The New Book of World Rankings.*

UNION OF SOVIET SOCIALIST REPUBLICS - POWER PRODUCTION INDUSTRY

European Community Information Service, 2100 M Street, NW, Washington, D.C. 20037 (202) 862-9500; *Basic Statistics of the Community.*

UNION OF SOVIET SOCIALIST REPUBLICS - PRICES

European Community Information Service, 2100 M Street, NW, Washington, D.C. 20037 (202) 862-9500; *Basic Statistics of the Community.*

Facts on File, 460 Park Avenue South, New York, New York 10016 (800) 443-8323; *The New Book of World Rankings.*

Federal Statistical Office, Gustav-Stresemann-Ring 11, D-6200 Wiesbaden, Germany; *U.S.S.R.*

Food and Agricultural Organization of the United Nations (FAO), Via delle Terme di Caracalla, 00100 Rome, Italy (Telephone Number in U.S. (202) 653-2400); *Production Yearbook,* and *The State of Food and Agriculture.*

G.K. Hall and Company, 70 Lincoln Street, Boston, Massachusetts 02111 (617) 423-3990; *The World in Figures.*

International Labour Office, I.L.O. Publications, CH-1211, Geneva 22, Switzerland; *Yearbook of Labour Statistics.*

International Lead and Zinc Study Group, Metro House, 58 St. James's Street, London SW1A 1LD England; *Lead and Zinc Statistics.*

International Rubber Study Group, York House, Eighth Floor, Empire Way, Wembley, London HA9 0PA, England; *Rubber Statistical Bulletin.*

UNION OF SOVIET SOCIALIST REPUBLICS - PRODUCTION

American Automobile Manufacturers Association, 1401 H Street, NW, Suite 900, Washington, D.C. 20005 (202) 326-5500; *World Motor Vehicle Data.*

European Community Information Service, 2100 M Street, NW, Washington, D.C. 20037 (202) 862-9500; *Basic Statistics of the Community.*

Facts on File, 460 Park Avenue South, New York, New York 10016 (800) 443-8323; *The New Book of World Rankings.*

G.K. Hall and Company, 70 Lincoln Street, Boston, Massachusetts 02111 (617) 423-3990; *The World in Figures.*

International Lead and Zinc Study Group, Metro House, 58 St. James's Street, London SW1A 1LD England; *Lead and Zinc Statistics.*

International Rubber Study Group, York House, Eighth Floor, Empire Way, Wembley, London HA9 0PA, England; *Rubber Statistical*

Bulletin.

UNION OF SOVIET SOCIALIST REPUBLICS - PRODUCTIVITY

European Community Information Service, 2100 M Street, NW, Washington, D.C. 20037 (202) 862-9500; *Basic Statistics of the Community.*

UNION OF SOVIET SOCIALIST REPUBLICS - PUBLIC CONSUMPTION FUNDS

European Community Information Service, 2100 M Street, NW, Washington, D.C. 20037 (202) 862-9500; *Basic Statistics of the Community.*

UNION OF SOVIET SOCIALIST REPUBLICS - PUBLIC EXPENDITURES

European Community Information Service, 2100 M Street, NW, Washington, D.C. 20037 (202) 862-9500; *Basic Statistics of the Community.*

UNION OF SOVIET SOCIALIST REPUBLICS - PUBLIC FINANCE

Facts on File, 460 Park Avenue South, New York, New York 10016 (800) 443-8323; *The New Book of World Rankings.*

UNION OF SOVIET SOCIALIST REPUBLICS - PUBLIC HEALTH

European Community Information Service, 2100 M Street, NW, Washington, D.C. 20037 (202) 862-9500; *Basic Statistics of the Community.*

UNION OF SOVIET SOCIALIST REPUBLICS - RADIO RECEIVER PRODUCTION

Statistical Office of the United Nations, Publishing Service, New York, New York 10017 (800) 253-9646; *Statistical Yearbook.*

UNION OF SOVIET SOCIALIST REPUBLICS - RAILWAYS

European Community Information Service, 2100 M Street, NW, Washington, D.C. 20037 (202) 862-9500; *European Marketing Data and Statistics*, and *Basic Statistics of the Community.*

G.K. Hall and Company, 70 Lincoln Street, Boston, Massachusetts 02111 (617) 423-3990; *The World in Figures.*

Jane's Information Group, Sentinel House, 163 Brighton Road, Coulsdon, Surrey CR5 2NH, England (Telephone Number in U.S. (703) 683-3700); *Jane's World Railways.*

Statistical Office of the United Nations, Publishing Service, New York, New York 10017 (800) 253-9646; *Annual Bulletin of Transport Statistics for Europe*, and *Statistical Yearbook.*

UNION OF SOVIET SOCIALIST REPUBLICS - RANCHING

European Community Information Service, 2100 M Street, NW, Washington, D.C. 20037 (202) 862-9500; *Basic Statistics of the Community.*

UNION OF SOVIET SOCIALIST REPUBLICS - RELIGION

Facts on File, 460 Park Avenue South, New York, New York 10016 (800) 443-8323; *The New Book of World Rankings.*

UNION OF SOVIET SOCIALIST REPUBLICS - RENT PRICES

International Labour Office, I.L.O. Publications, CH-1211, Geneva 22, Switzerland; *Yearbook of Labour Statistics.*

UNION OF SOVIET SOCIALIST REPUBLICS - RETAIL TRADE

European Community Information Service, 2100 M Street, NW, Washington, D.C. 20037 (202) 862-9500; *Basic Statistics of the Community.*

G.K. Hall and Company, 70 Lincoln Street, Boston, Massachusetts 02111 (617) 423-3990; *The World in Figures.*

Statistical Office of the United Nations, Publishing Service, New York, New York 10017 (800) 253-9646; *Statistical Yearbook.*

UNION OF SOVIET SOCIALIST REPUBLICS - RUBBER PRODUCTION AND CONSUMPTION

European Community Information Service, 2100 M Street, NW, Washington, D.C. 20037 (202) 862-9500; *Basic Statistics of the Community.*

Facts on File, 460 Park Avenue South, New York, New York 10016 (800) 443-8323; *The New Book of World Rankings.*

International Rubber Study Group, York House, Eighth Floor, Empire Way, Wembley, London HA9 0PA, England; *Rubber Statistical Bulletin.*

Statistical Office of the United Nations, Publishing Service, New York, New York 10017 (800) 253-9646; *Statistical Yearbook.*

UNION OF SOVIET SOCIALIST REPUBLICS - SATELLITE LAUNCHES

Academic International Press, Box 1111, Gulf Breeze, Florida 32561; *U.S.S.R. Facts and Figures.*

UNION OF SOVIET SOCIALIST REPUBLICS - SCIENCE AND TECHNOLOGY - EXPENDITURE FOR RESEARCH

European Community Information Service, 2100 M Street, NW, Washington, D.C. 20037 (202) 862-9500; *Basic Statistics of the Community.*

Statistical Office of the United Nations, Publishing Service, New York, New York 10017 (800) 253-9646; *Statistical Yearbook.*

UNION OF SOVIET SOCIALIST REPUBLICS - SCIENTISTS, TECHNICIANS AND ENGINEERS

European Community Information Service, 2100 M Street, NW, Washington, D.C. 20037 (202) 862-9500; *Basic Statistics of the Community.*

Statistical Office of the United Nations, Publishing Service, New York, New York 10017 (800) 253-9646; *Statistical Yearbook.*

United Nations Educational, Scientific and Cultural Organization (UNESCO), 7 Place de Fontenoy, F-75700 Paris, France (Telephone Number in U.S. (212) 963-5981); *Statistical Yearbook.*

UNION OF SOVIET SOCIALIST REPUBLICS - SENIOR CITIZENS

Facts on File, 460 Park Avenue South, New York, New York 10016 (800) 443-8323; *The New Book of World Rankings.*

UNION OF SOVIET SOCIALIST REPUBLICS - SOCIAL DATA

European Community Information Service, 2100 M Street, NW, Washington, D.C. 20037 (202) 862-9500; *Basic Statistics of the Community*.

Facts on File, 460 Park Avenue South, New York, New York 10016 (800) 443-8323; *The New Book of World Rankings*.

G.K. Hall and Company, 70 Lincoln Street, Boston, Massachusetts 02111 (617) 423-3990; *The World in Figures*.

UNION OF SOVIET SOCIALIST REPUBLICS - SOCIAL SECURITY

European Community Information Service, 2100 M Street, NW, Washington, D.C. 20037 (202) 862-9500; *Basic Statistics of the Community*.

UNION OF SOVIET SOCIALIST REPUBLICS - SOCIOECONOMIC DATA

European Community Information Service, 2100 M Street, NW, Washington, D.C. 20037 (202) 862-9500; *Basic Statistics of the Community*.

UNION OF SOVIET SOCIALIST REPUBLICS - STOCKS - COMMODITY - MARKET PRICE - INDEX

Food and Agricultural Organization of the United Nations (FAO) Via delle Terme di Caracalla, 00100 Rome, Italy (Telephone Number in U.S. (202) 653-2400); *The State of Food and Agriculture*.

International Lead and Zinc Study Group, Metro House, 58 St. James's Street, London SW1A 1LD England; *Lead and Zinc Statistics*.

UNION OF SOVIET SOCIALIST REPUBLICS - TAXATION

European Community Information Service, 2100 M Street, NW, Washington, D.C. 20037 (202) 862-9500; *Basic Statistics of the Community*.

G.K. Hall and Company, 70 Lincoln Street, Boston, Massachusetts 02111 (617) 423-3990; *The World in Figures*.

UNION OF SOVIET SOCIALIST REPUBLICS - TELEGRAPH SERVICE

Statistical Office of the United Nations, Publishing Service, New York, New York 10017 (800) 253-9646; *Statistical Yearbook*.

UNION OF SOVIET SOCIALIST REPUBLICS - TELEPHONES IN USE

American Telephone and Telegraph Company, 26 Parsippany Road, Whippany, New Jersey 07981 (800) 338-4038; *The World's Telephones*.

European Community Information Service, 2100 M Street, NW, Washington, D.C. 20037 (202) 862-9500; *Basic Statistics of the Community*.

G.K. Hall and Company, 70 Lincoln Street, Boston, Massachusetts 02111 (617) 423-3990; *The World in Figures*.

Statistical Office of the United Nations, Publishing Service, New York, New York 10017 (800) 253-9646; *Statistical Yearbook*.

UNION OF SOVIET SOCIALIST REPUBLICS - TELEVISION RECEIVER PRODUCTION

European Community Information Service, 2100 M Street, NW, Washington, D.C. 20037 (202) 862-9500; *Basic Statistics of the Community*.

UNION OF SOVIET SOCIALIST REPUBLICS - TEXTILE INDUSTRY

American Forest and Paper Association, 1250 Connecticut Avenue, NW, Washington, D.C. 20036 (202) 463-2455; *Wood Pulp and Fiber Statistics*.

European Community Information Service, 2100 M Street, NW, Washington, D.C. 20037 (202) 862-9500; *Basic Statistics of the Community*.

G.K. Hall and Company, 70 Lincoln Street, Boston, Massachusetts 02111 (617) 423-3990; *The World in Figures*.

Statistical Office of the United Nations, Publishing Service, New York, New York 10017 (800) 253-9646; *Statistical Yearbook*.

UNION OF SOVIET SOCIALIST REPUBLICS - THEATRE

Academic International Press, Box 1111, Gulf Breeze, Florida 32561; *U.S.S.R. Facts and Figures*.

United Nations Educational, Scientific and Cultural Organization (UNESCO), 7 Place de Fontenoy, F-75700 Paris, France (Telephone Number in U.S. (212) 963-5981); *Statistical Yearbook*.

UNION OF SOVIET SOCIALIST REPUBLICS - TIRE (MOTOR VEHICLE) PRODUCTION

International Rubber Study Group, York House, Eighth Floor, Empire Way, Wembley, London HA9 0PA, England; *Rubber Statistical Bulletin*.

Statistical Office of the United Nations, Publishing Service, New York, New York 10017 (800) 253-9646; *Statistical Yearbook*.

UNION OF SOVIET SOCIALIST REPUBLICS - TOBACCO PRODUCTION

Commodity Research Bureau, Incorporated, 75 Wall Street, New York, New York 10005 (212) 504-7754; *Commodity Year Book*.

Euromonitor Publications Limited, 87-88 Turnmill Street, London EC1M 5QU, England; *European Marketing Data and Statistics*.

European Community Information Service, 2100 M Street, NW, Washington, D.C. 20037 (202) 862-9500; *Basic Statistics of the Community*.

Facts on File, 460 Park Avenue South, New York, New York 10016 (800) 443-8323; *The New Book of World Rankings*.

Statistical Office of the United Nations, Publishing Service, New York, New York 10017 (800) 253-9646; *Statistical Yearbook*.

UNION OF SOVIET SOCIALIST REPUBLICS - TOURISM

Euromonitor Publications Limited, 87-88 Turnmill Street, London EC1M 5QU, England; *European Marketing Data and Statistics*.

Facts on File, 460 Park Avenue South, New York, New York 10016 (800) 443-8323; *The New Book of World Rankings*.

Federal Statistical Office, Gustav-Stresemann-Ring 11, D-6200 Wiesbaden, Germany; *U.S.S.R.*

G.K. Hall and Company, 70 Lincoln Street, Boston, Massachusetts 02111 (617) 423-3990; *The World in Figures.*

Statistical Office of the United Nations, Publishing Service, New York, New York 10017 (800) 253-9646; *Statistical Yearbook.*

Times Books, 201 East 50th Street, New York, New York 10022 (212) 751-2600; *The Economist Book of Vital World Statistics.*

World Tourism Organization, Calle Capitan Haya 42, E-28020 Madrid, Spain; *Yearbook of Tourism Statistics.*

UNION OF SOVIET SOCIALIST REPUBLICS - TRACTORS IN USE

Statistical Office of the United Nations, Publishing Service, New York, New York 10017 (800) 253-9646; *Statistical Yearbook.*

UNION OF SOVIET SOCIALIST REPUBLICS - TRADEMARKS AND SERVICE MARKS

Statistical Office of the United Nations, Publishing Service, New York, New York 10017 (800) 253-9646; *Statistical Yearbook.*

World Intellectual Property Organization, 34 Chemin des Colombettes, CH 1211 Geneva 20, Switzerland; *Industrial Property Statistics.*

UNION OF SOVIET SOCIALIST REPUBLICS - TRANSPORTATION AND COMMUNICATION

Academic International Press, Box 1111, Gulf Breeze, Florida 32561; *U.S.S.R. Facts and Figures.*

European Community Information Service, 2100 M Street, NW, Washington, D.C. 20037 (202) 862-9500; *Basic Statistics of the Community.*

Facts on File, 460 Park Avenue South, New York, New York 10016 (800) 443-8323; *The New Book of World Rankings.*

Federal Statistical Office, Gustav-Stresemann-Ring 11, D-6200 Wiesbaden, Germany; *U.S.S.R.*

G.K. Hall and Company, 70 Lincoln Street, Boston, Massachusetts 02111 (617) 423-3990; *The World in Figures.*

UNION OF SOVIET SOCIALIST REPUBLICS - UNEMPLOYMENT

Euromonitor Publications Limited, 87-88 Turnmill Street, London EC1M 5QU, England; *European Marketing Data and Statistics.*

European Community Information Service, 2100 M Street, NW, Washington, D.C. 20037 (202) 862-9500; *Basic Statistics of the Community.*

International Labour Office, I.L.O. Publications, CH-1211, Geneva 22, Switzerland; *Yearbook of Labour Statistics.*

UNION OF SOVIET SOCIALIST REPUBLICS - VITAL STATISTICS

European Community Information Service, 2100 M Street, NW, Washington, D.C. 20037 (202) 862-9500; *Basic Statistics of the Community.*

G.K. Hall and Company, 70 Lincoln Street, Boston, Massachusetts 02111 (617) 423-3990; *The World in Figures.*

Statistical Office of the United Nations, Publishing Service, New York, New York 10017 (800) 253-9646; *Statistical Yearbook.*

World Health Organization, Office of Publications, Avenue Appia, CH-1211 Geneva 27, Switzerland (Telephone Number in U.S. (518) 436-9686); *World Health Statistics Annual.*

UNION OF SOVIET SOCIALIST REPUBLICS - WAGES

Euromonitor Publications Limited, 87-88 Turnmill Street, London EC1M 5QU, England; *European Marketing Data and Statistics.*

European Community Information Service, 2100 M Street, NW, Washington, D.C. 20037 (202) 862-9500; *Basic Statistics of the Community.*

G.K. Hall and Company, 70 Lincoln Street, Boston, Massachusetts 02111 (617) 423-3990; *The World in Figures.*

International Labour Office, I.L.O. Publications, CH-1211, Geneva 22, Switzerland; *Yearbook of Labour Statistics.*

Statistical Office of the United Nations, Publishing Service, New York, New York 10017 (800) 253-9646; *Statistical Yearbook.*

UNION OF SOVIET SOCIALIST REPUBLICS - WATERWAYS IN USE

European Community Information Service, 2100 M Street, NW, Washington, D.C. 20037 (202) 862-9500; *Basic Statistics of the Community.*

Statistical Office of the United Nations, Publishing Service, New York, New York 10017 (800) 253-9646; *Annual Bulletin of Transport Statistics for Europe.*

UNION OF SOVIET SOCIALIST REPUBLICS - WEATHER

Academic International Press, Box 1111, Gulf Breeze, Florida 32561; *U.S.S.R. Facts and Figures.*

Facts on File, 460 Park Avenue South, New York, New York 10016 (800) 443-8323; *The New Book of World Rankings.*

G.K. Hall and Company, 70 Lincoln Street, Boston, Massachusetts 02111 (617) 423-3990; *The World in Figures.*

UNION OF SOVIET SOCIALIST REPUBLICS - WELFARE

Academic International Press, Box 1111, Gulf Breeze, Florida 32561; *U.S.S.R. Facts and Figures.*

European Community Information Service, 2100 M Street, NW, Washington, D.C. 20037 (202) 862-9500; *Basic Statistics of the Community.*

UNION OF SOVIET SOCIALIST REPUBLICS - WHOLESALE PRICES

European Community Information Service, 2100 M Street, NW, Washington, D.C. 20037 (202) 862-9500; *Basic Statistics of the Community.*

Statistical Office of the United Nations, Publishing Service, New York, New York 10017 (800) 253-9646; *Statistical Yearbook.*

UNION OF SOVIET SOCIALIST REPUBLICS - WHOLESALE TRADE

European Community Information Service, 2100 M Street, NW, Washington, D.C. 20037 (202) 862-9500; *Basic Statistics of the Community*.

Statistical Office of the United Nations, Publishing Service, New York, New York 10017 (800) 253-9646; *Statistical Yearbook*.

UNION OF SOVIET SOCIALIST REPUBLICS - WINE PRODUCTION

European Community Information Service, 2100 M Street, NW, Washington, D.C. 20037 (202) 862-9500; *Basic Statistics of the Community*.

Facts on File, 460 Park Avenue South, New York, New York 10016 (800) 443-8323; *The New Book of World Rankings*.

Statistical Office of the United Nations, Publishing Service, New York, New York 10017 (800) 253-9646; *Statistical Yearbook*.

UNION OF SOVIET SOCIALIST REPUBLICS - WOOL - INDUSTRIAL CONSUMPTION

Statistical Office of the United Nations, Publishing Service, New York, New York 10017 (800) 253-9646; *Statistical Yearbook*.

UNION OF SOVIET SOCIALIST REPUBLICS - WOOL PRODUCTION

European Community Information Service, 2100 M Street, NW, Washington, D.C. 20037 (202) 862-9500; *Basic Statistics of the Community*.

Facts on File, 460 Park Avenue South, New York, New York 10016 (800) 443-8323; *The New Book of World Rankings*.

Statistical Office of the United Nations, Publishing Service, New York, New York 10017 (800) 253-9646; *Statistical Yearbook*.

UNION OF SOVIET SOCIALIST REPUBLICS - YARN PRODUCTION

European Community Information Service, 2100 M Street, NW, Washington, D.C. 20037 (202) 862-9500; *Basic Statistics of the Community*.

Statistical Office of the United Nations, Publishing Service, New York, New York 10017 (800) 253-9646; *Statistical Yearbook*.

UNIONS - See LABOR ORGANIZATIONS OR UNIONS

United Arab Emirates - National Statistical Offices

Director of Central Statistics Department, Ministry of Planning, Post Office Box 904, Abu Dhabi, United Arab Emirates.

Director of Statistics, Abu Dhabi Emirate, Department of Planning, Post Office Box 12, Abu Dhabi, United Arab Emirates.

United Arab Emirates - Primary Statistics Source

Central Statistical Office, Ministry of Planning, Post Office Box 904, Abu Dhabi, United Arab Emirates; *Annual Statistical Abstract*.

UNITED ARAB EMIRATES - AGRICULTURE

Economic Commission for Western Asia, Post Office Box 27, Baghdad, Iraq; *Statistical Abstract of Western Asia*.

Euromonitor Publications Limited, 87-88 Turnmill Street, London EC1M 5QU, England; *International Marketing Data and Statistics*, and *Middle East Economic Handbook*.

Facts on File, 460 Park Avenue South, New York, New York 10016 (800) 443-8323; *The New Book of World Rankings*.

Food and Agricultural Organization of the United Nations (FAO), Via delle Terme di Caracalla, 00100 Rome, Italy (Telephone Number in U.S. (202) 653-2400); *Production Yearbook, The State of Food and Agriculture,* and *Trade Yearbook*.

G.K. Hall and Company, 70 Lincoln Street, Boston, Massachusetts 02111 (617) 423-3990; *The World in Figures*.

Times Books, 201 East 50th Street, New York, New York 10022 (212) 751-2600; *The Economist Book of Vital World Statistics*.

The World Bank, 1818 H Street, NW, Washington, D.C. 20433 (202) 477-1234; *World Tables*.

UNITED ARAB EMIRATES - AIRLINE SERVICE

Economic Commission for Western Asia, Post Office Box 27, Baghdad, Iraq; *Statistical Abstract of Western Asia*.

Facts on File, 460 Park Avenue South, New York, New York 10016 (800) 443-8323; *The New Book of World Rankings*.

G.K. Hall and Company, 70 Lincoln Street, Boston, Massachusetts 02111 (617) 423-3990; *The World in Figures*.

Times Books, 201 East 50th Street, New York, New York 10022 (212) 751-2600; *The Economist Book of Vital World Statistics*.

UNITED ARAB EMIRATES - ALUMINUM PRODUCTION AND CONSUMPTION - See UNITED ARAB EMIRATES - MINING AND MINERAL PRODUCTS

UNITED ARAB EMIRATES - ANIMAL HEALTH

Food and Agricultural Organization of the United Nations (FAO), Via delle Terme di Caracalla, 00100 Rome, Italy (Telephone Number in U.S. (202) 653-2400); *Animal Health Yearbook*.

UNITED ARAB EMIRATES - AREA AND DENSITY OF POPULATION

Euromonitor Publications Limited, 87-88 Turnmill Street, London EC1M 5QU, England; *International Marketing Data and Statistics*, and *Middle East Economic Handbook*.

Economic Commission for Western Asia, Post Office Box 27, Baghdad, Iraq; *Statistical Abstract of Western Asia*.

Facts on File, 460 Park Avenue South, New York, New York 10016 (800) 443-8323; *The New Book of World Rankings*.

Food and Agricultural Organization of the United Nations (FAO) Via delle Terme di Caracalla, 00100 Rome, Italy (Telephone Number in U.S. (202) 653-2400); *The State of Food and Agriculture.*

G.K. Hall and Company, 70 Lincoln Street, Boston, Massachusetts 02111 (617) 423-3990; *The World in Figures.*

Statistical Office of the United Nations, Publishing Service, New York, New York 10017 (800) 253-9646; *Statistical Yearbook.*

Times Books, 201 East 50th Street, New York, New York 10022 (212) 751-2600; *The Economist Book of Vital World Statistics.*

UNITED ARAB EMIRATES - ARMS EXPORTS AND IMPORTS

U.S. Arms Control and Disarmament Agency, 320 Twenty-first Street, NW, Washington, D.C. 20451 (202) 647-8677; *World Military Expenditures and Arms Transfers.*

UNITED ARAB EMIRATES - BALANCE OF PAYMENTS

Economic Commission for Western Asia, Post Office Box 27, Baghdad, Iraq; *Statistical Abstract of Western Asia.*

The Economist Intelligence Unit, 111 West 57th Street, New York, New York 10019 (800) 938-4685; *The World Market Atlas.*

G.K. Hall and Company, 70 Lincoln Street, Boston, Massachusetts 02111 (617) 423-3990; *The World in Figures.*

Times Books, 201 East 50th Street, New York, New York 10022 (212) 751-2600; *The Economist Book of Vital World Statistics.*

The World Bank, 1818 H Street, NW, Washington, D.C. 20433 (202) 477-1234; *World Tables.*

UNITED ARAB EMIRATES - BALANCE OF TRADE

Economic Commission for Western Asia, Post Office Box 27, Baghdad, Iraq; *Statistical Abstract of Western Asia.*

UNITED ARAB EMIRATES - BANKING

Economic Commission for Western Asia, Post Office Box 27, Baghdad, Iraq; *Statistical Abstract of Western Asia.*

Facts on File, 460 Park Avenue South, New York, New York 10016 (800) 443-8323; *The New Book of World Rankings.*

G.K. Hall and Company, 70 Lincoln Street, Boston, Massachusetts 02111 (617) 423-3990; *The World in Figures.*

International Monetary Fund, 700 Nineteenth Street, NW, Washington, D.C. 20431 (202) 623-7000; *International Financial Statistics.*

UNITED ARAB EMIRATES - BARLEY PRODUCTION - See UNITED ARAB EMIRATES - CROPS

UNITED ARAB EMIRATES - BEER PRODUCTION

Facts on File, 460 Park Avenue South, New York, New York 10016 (800) 443-8323; *The New Book of World Rankings.*

UNITED ARAB EMIRATES - BIRTH RATES

Euromonitor Publications Limited, 87-88 Turnmill Street, London EC1M 5QU, England; *Middle East Economic Handbook.*

Facts on File, 460 Park Avenue South, New York, New York 10016 (800) 443-8323; *The New Book of World Rankings.*

Statistical Office of the United Nations, Publishing Service, New York, New York 10017 (800) 253-9646; *Demographic Yearbook.*

Times Books, 201 East 50th Street, New York, New York 10022 (212) 751-2600; *The Economist Book of Vital World Statistics.*

The World Bank, 1818 H Street, NW, Washington, D.C. 20433 (202) 477-1234; *World Tables.*

UNITED ARAB EMIRATES - BONDS

G.K. Hall and Company, 70 Lincoln Street, Boston, Massachusetts 02111 (617) 423-3990; *The World in Figures.*

UNITED ARAB EMIRATES - BOOK PRODUCTION

G.K. Hall and Company, 70 Lincoln Street, Boston, Massachusetts 02111 (617) 423-3990; *The World in Figures.*

United Nations Educational, Scientific and Cultural Organization (UNESCO), 7 Place de Fontenoy, F-75700 Paris, France (Telephone Number in U.S. (212) 963-5981); *Statistical Yearbook.*

UNITED ARAB EMIRATES - BROADCASTING

Billboard Limited, P.O. Box 9027, 1006 AA Amsterdam, The Netherlands (Telephone Number in U.S. (212) 764-7300); *World Radio TV Handbook.*

Facts on File, 460 Park Avenue South, New York, New York 10016 (800) 443-8323; *The New Book of World Rankings.*

G.K. Hall and Company, 70 Lincoln Street, Boston, Massachusetts 02111 (617) 423-3990; *The World in Figures.*

Times Books, 201 East 50th Street, New York, New York 10022 (212) 751-2600; *The Economist Book of Vital World Statistics.*

United Nations Educational, Scientific and Cultural Organization (UNESCO), 7 Place de Fontenoy, F-75700 Paris, France (Telephone Number in U.S. (212) 963-5981); *Statistical Yearbook.*

UNITED ARAB EMIRATES - BUSINESS

G.K. Hall and Company, 70 Lincoln Street, Boston, Massachusetts 02111 (617) 423-3990; *The World in Figures.*

UNITED ARAB EMIRATES - CALORIE SUPPLY

Food and Agricultural Organization of the United Nations (FAO) Via delle Terme di Caracalla, 00100 Rome, Italy (Telephone Number in U.S. (202) 653-2400); *The State of Food and Agriculture.*

UNITED ARAB EMIRATES - CAPITAL REVENUE

International Monetary Fund, 700 Nineteenth Street, NW, Washington, D.C. 20431 (202) 623-7000; *Government Finance Statistics Yearbook.*

UNITED ARAB EMIRATES - CATTLE - See UNITED ARAB EMIRATES - LIVESTOCK AND POULTRY

UNITED ARAB EMIRATES - CEMENT PRODUCTION - See UNITED ARAB EMIRATES - MINING AND MINERAL PRODUCTS

UNITED ARAB EMIRATES - CHEMICAL (ORGANIC) PRODUCTION - See UNITED ARAB EMIRATES - MINING AND MINERAL PRODUCTS

UNITED ARAB EMIRATES - CIGARETTE PRODUCTION - See UNITED ARAB EMIRATES - TOBACCO PRODUCTION

UNITED ARAB EMIRATES - CLASS STRUCTURE

G.K. Hall and Company, 70 Lincoln Street, Boston, Massachusetts 02111 (617) 423-3990; *The World in Figures.*

UNITED ARAB EMIRATES - CLIMATE

Facts on File, 460 Park Avenue South, New York, New York 10016 (800) 443-8323; *The New Book of World Rankings.*

G.K. Hall and Company, 70 Lincoln Street, Boston, Massachusetts 02111 (617) 423-3990; *The World in Figures.*

UNITED ARAB EMIRATES - COAL PRODUCTION - See UNITED ARAB EMIRATES - MINING AND MINERAL PRODUCTS

UNITED ARAB EMIRATES - COFFEE PRODUCTION AND CONSUMPTION - See UNITED ARAB EMIRATES - CROPS

UNITED ARAB EMIRATES - COMMUNICATIONS

Economic Commission for Western Asia, Post Office Box 27, Baghdad, Iraq; *Statistical Abstract of Western Asia.*

G.K. Hall and Company, 70 Lincoln Street, Boston, Massachusetts 02111 (617) 423-3990; *The World in Figures.*

UNITED ARAB EMIRATES - CONSTRUCTION INDUSTRY

Facts on File, 460 Park Avenue South, New York, New York 10016 (800) 443-8323; *The New Book of World Rankings.*

Statistical Office of the United Nations, Publishing Service, New York, New York 10017 (800) 253-9646; *Construction Statistics Yearbook.*

UNITED ARAB EMIRATES - CONSUMER PRICE INDEX

G.K. Hall and Company, 70 Lincoln Street, Boston, Massachusetts 02111 (617) 423-3990; *The World in Figures.*

UNITED ARAB EMIRATES - CONSUMER PRICES

International Labour Office, I.L.O. Publications, CH-1211, Geneva 22, Switzerland; *Yearbook of Labour Statistics.*

Times Books, 201 East 50th Street, New York, New York 10022 (212) 751-2600; *The Economist Book of Vital World Statistics.*

UNITED ARAB EMIRATES - CONSUMPTION

Euromonitor Publications Limited, 87-88 Turnmill Street, London EC1M 5QU, England; *Middle East Economic Handbook.*

G.K. Hall and Company, 70 Lincoln Street, Boston, Massachusetts 02111 (617) 423-3990; *The World in Figures.*

UNITED ARAB EMIRATES - COPPER PRODUCTION AND CONSUMPTION - See UNITED ARAB EMIRATES - MINING AND MINERAL PRODUCTS

UNITED ARAB EMIRATES - CORN PRODUCTION - See UNITED ARAB EMIRATES - CROPS

UNITED ARAB EMIRATES - CORPORATE TAXES - See UNITED ARAB EMIRATES - TAXATION

UNITED ARAB EMIRATES - COTTON - See UNITED ARAB EMIRATES - CROPS

UNITED ARAB EMIRATES - CRIME

International Criminal Police Organization (INTERPOL), 26 rue Armengaud, 92210 Saint Cloud, France; *International Crime Statistics.*

UNITED ARAB EMIRATES - CROPS

Facts on File, 460 Park Avenue South, New York, New York 10016 (800) 443-8323; *The New Book of World Rankings.*

Food and Agricultural Organization of the United Nations (FAO) Via delle Terme di Caracalla, 00100 Rome, Italy (Telephone Number in U.S. (202) 653-2400); *The State of Food and Agriculture.*

G.K. Hall and Company, 70 Lincoln Street, Boston, Massachusetts 02111 (617) 423-3990; *The World in Figures.*

UNITED ARAB EMIRATES - CUSTOMS DUTIES

G.K. Hall and Company, 70 Lincoln Street, Boston, Massachusetts 02111 (617) 423-3990; *The World in Figures.*

UNITED ARAB EMIRATES - DAIRY PRODUCTS

Economic Commission for Western Asia, Post Office Box 27, Baghdad, Iraq; *Statistical Abstract of Western Asia.*

Facts on File, 460 Park Avenue South, New York, New York 10016 (800) 443-8323; *The New Book of World Rankings.*

Food and Agricultural Organization of the United Nations (FAO) Via delle Terme di Caracalla, 00100 Rome, Italy (Telephone Number in U.S. (202) 653-2400); *Production Yearbook,* and *The State of Food and Agriculture.*

UNITED ARAB EMIRATES - DEATH RATES

Euromonitor Publications Limited, 87-88 Turnmill Street, London EC1M 5QU, England; *Middle East Economic Handbook.*

G.K. Hall and Company, 70 Lincoln Street, Boston, Massachusetts 02111 (617) 423-3990; *The World in Figures.*

Times Books, 201 East 50th Street, New York, New York 10022 (212) 751-2600; *The Economist Book of Vital World Statistics.*

UNITED ARAB EMIRATES - DEFENSE EXPENDITURES

G.K. Hall and Company, 70 Lincoln Street, Boston, Massachusetts 02111 (617) 423-3990; *The World in Figures.*

International Monetary Fund, 700 Nineteenth Street, NW, Washington, D.C. 20431 (202) 623-7000; *Government Finance Statistics Yearbook.*

U.S. Arms Control and Disarmament Agency, 320 Twenty-first Street, NW, Washington, D.C. 20451 (202) 647-8677; *World Military Expenditures and Arms Transfers.*

UNITED ARAB EMIRATES - DEMOGRAPHY

The Economist Intelligence Unit, 111 West 57th Street, New York, New York 10019 (800) 938-4685; *The World Market Atlas.*

Facts on File, 460 Park Avenue South, New York, New York 10016 (800) 443-8323; *The New Book of World Rankings.*

G.K. Hall and Company, 70 Lincoln Street, Boston, Massachusetts 02111 (617) 423-3990; *The World in Figures.*

UNITED ARAB EMIRATES - DEVELOPMENT ASSISTANCE

G.K. Hall and Company, 70 Lincoln Street, Boston, Massachusetts 02111 (617) 423-3990; *The World in Figures.*

Statistical Office of the United Nations, Publishing Service, New York, New York 10017 (800) 253-9646; *Statistical Yearbook.*

UNITED ARAB EMIRATES - DIAMOND PRODUCTION - See UNITED ARAB EMIRATES - MINING AND MINERAL PRODUCTS

UNITED ARAB EMIRATES - DISEASE

G.K. Hall and Company, 70 Lincoln Street, Boston, Massachusetts 02111 (617) 423-3990; *The World in Figures.*

UNITED ARAB EMIRATES - DIVORCE RATES

Facts on File, 460 Park Avenue South, New York, New York 10016 (800) 443-8323; *The New Book of World Rankings.*

Statistical Office of the United Nations, Publishing Service, New York, New York 10017 (800) 253-9646; *Demographic Yearbook.*

UNITED ARAB EMIRATES - DOMESTIC PRODUCT

G.K. Hall and Company, 70 Lincoln Street, Boston, Massachusetts 02111 (617) 423-3990; *The World in Figures.*

UNITED ARAB EMIRATES - ECONOMY

Euromonitor Publications Limited, 87-88 Turnmill Street, London EC1M 5QU, England; *International Marketing Data and Statistics.*

Facts on File, 460 Park Avenue South, New York, New York 10016 (800) 443-8323; *The New Book of World Rankings.*

G.K. Hall and Company, 70 Lincoln Street, Boston, Massachusetts 02111 (617) 423-3990; *The World in Figures.*

UNITED ARAB EMIRATES - EDUCATION

Economic Commission for Western Asia, Post Office Box 27, Baghdad, Iraq; *Statistical Abstract of Western Asia.*

The Economist Intelligence Unit, 111 West 57th Street, New York, New York 10019 (800) 938-4685; *The World Market Atlas.*

Euromonitor Publications Limited, 87-88 Turnmill Street, London EC1M 5QU, England; *Middle East Economic Handbook.*

Facts on File, 460 Park Avenue South, New York, New York 10016 (800) 443-8323; *The New Book of World Rankings.*

G.K. Hall and Company, 70 Lincoln Street, Boston, Massachusetts 02111 (617) 423-3990; *The World in Figures.*

International Monetary Fund, 700 Nineteenth Street, NW, Washington, D.C. 20431 (202) 623-7000; *Government Finance Statistics Yearbook.*

Times Books, 201 East 50th Street, New York, New York 10022 (212) 751-2600; *The Economist Book of Vital World Statistics.*

United Nations Educational, Scientific and Cultural Organization (UNESCO), 7 Place de Fontenoy, F-75700 Paris, France (Telephone Number in U.S. (212) 963-5981); *Statistical Yearbook.*

The World Bank, 1818 H Street, NW, Washington, D.C. 20433 (202) 477-1234; *World Tables.*

UNITED ARAB EMIRATES - EGG PRODUCTION AND CONSUMPTION - See UNITED ARAB EMIRATES - DAIRY PRODUCTS

UNITED ARAB EMIRATES - ELECTRICITY

Facts on File, 460 Park Avenue South, New York, New York 10016 (800) 443-8323; *The New Book of World Rankings.*

Penn Well Publishing Company, 1421 South Sheridan Road, P.O. Box 1260, Tulsa, Oklahoma 74101 (800) 752-9764; *International Energy Statistics Sourcebook.*

Statistical Office of the United Nations, Publishing Service, New York, New York 10017 (800) 253-9646; *Statistical Yearbook.*

Times Books, 201 East 50th Street, New York, New York 10022 (212) 751-2600; *The Economist Book of Vital World Statistics.*

UNITED ARAB EMIRATES - EMPLOYMENT

Economic Commission for Western Asia, Post Office Box 27, Baghdad, Iraq; *Statistical Abstract of Western Asia.*

Euromonitor Publications Limited, 87-88 Turnmill Street, London EC1M 5QU, England; *International Marketing Data and Statistics,* and *Middle East Economic Handbook.*

Facts on File, 460 Park Avenue South, New York, New York 10016 (800) 443-8323; *The New Book of World Rankings.*

International Labour Office, I.L.O. Publications, CH-1211, Geneva 22, Switzerland; *Yearbook of Labour Statistics.*

UNITED ARAB EMIRATES - ENERGY

Economic Commission for Western Asia, Post Office Box 27, Baghdad, Iraq; *Statistical Abstract of Western Asia.*

Euromonitor Publications Limited, 87-88 Turnmill Street, London EC1M 5QU, England; *Middle East Economic Handbook.*

Facts on File, 460 Park Avenue South, New York, New York 10016 (800) 443-8323; *The New Book of World Rankings.*

Food and Agricultural Organization of the United Nations (FAO) Via delle Terme di Caracalla, 00100 Rome, Italy (Telephone Number in U.S. (202) 653-2400); *The State of Food and Agriculture.*

G.K. Hall and Company, 70 Lincoln Street, Boston, Massachusetts 02111 (617) 423-3990; *The World in Figures.*

Penn Well Publishing Company, 1421 South Sheridan Road, P.O. Box 1260, Tulsa, Oklahoma 74101 (800) 752-9764; *International Energy Statistics Sourcebook.*

Statistical Office of the United Nations, Publishing Service, New York, New York 10017 (800) 253-9646; *Energy Statistics Yearbook, Statistical Yearbook,* and *World Energy Supplies.*

Times Books, 201 East 50th Street, New York, New York 10022 (212) 751-2600; *The Economist Book of Vital World Statistics.*

UNITED ARAB EMIRATES - EXCHANGE RATES

Euromonitor Publications Limited, 87-88 Turnmill Street, London EC1M 5QU, England; *International Marketing Data and Statistics,* and *Middle East Economic Handbook.*

International Monetary Fund, 700 Nineteenth Street, NW, Washington, D.C. 20431 (202) 623-7000; *International Financial Statistics.*

Organization of Petroleum Exporting Countries, Obere Donaustrasse 93, 1020 Vienna 2, Austria; *OPEC Annual Statistical Bulletin.*

Statistical Office of the United Nations, Publishing Service, New York, New York 10017 (800) 253-9646; *Statistical Yearbook.*

UNITED ARAB EMIRATES - EXPORTS

Economic Commission for Western Asia, Post Office Box 27, Baghdad, Iraq; *Statistical Abstract of Western Asia.*

The Economist Intelligence Unit, 111 West 57th Street, New York, New York 10019 (800) 938-4685; *The World Market Atlas.*

Euromonitor Publications Limited, 87-88 Turnmill Street, London EC1M 5QU, England; *International Marketing Data and Statistics,* and *Middle East Economic Handbook.*

Food and Agricultural Organization of the United Nations (FAO) Via delle Terme di Caracalla, 00100 Rome, Italy (Telephone Number in U.S. (202) 653-2400); *The State of Food and Agriculture.*

G.K. Hall and Company, 70 Lincoln Street, Boston, Massachusetts 02111 (617) 423-3990; *The World in Figures.*

International Monetary Fund, 700 Nineteenth Street, NW, Washington, D.C. 20431 (202) 623-7000; *Direction of Trade Statistics,* and *International Financial Statistics.*

Organization of Petroleum Exporting Countries, Obere Donaustrasse 93, 1020 Vienna 2, Austria; *OPEC Annual Statistical Bulletin.*

Times Books, 201 East 50th Street, New York, New York 10022 (212) 751-2600; *The Economist Book of Vital World Statistics.*

The World Bank, 1818 H Street, NW, Washington, D.C. 20433 (202) 477-1234; *World Tables.*

UNITED ARAB EMIRATES - EXTERNAL INDEBTEDNESS

The World Bank, 1818 H Street, NW, Washington, D.C. 20433 (202) 477-1234; *World Tables.*

UNITED ARAB EMIRATES - EXTERNAL TRADE

Food and Agricultural Organization of the United Nations (FAO) Via delle Terme di Caracalla, 00100 Rome, Italy (Telephone Number in U.S. (202) 653-2400); *The State of Food and Agriculture,* and *Trade Yearbook.*

G.K. Hall and Company, 70 Lincoln Street, Boston, Massachusetts 02111 (617) 423-3990; *The World in Figures.*

UNITED ARAB EMIRATES - FARM CROPS - See UNITED ARAB EMIRATES - CROPS

UNITED ARAB EMIRATES - FEMALE WORKING POPULATION - See UNITED ARAB EMIRATES - EMPLOYMENT

UNITED ARAB EMIRATES - FERTILITY RATES

Facts on File, 460 Park Avenue South, New York, New York 10016 (800) 443-8323; *The New Book of World Rankings.*

Times Books, 201 East 50th Street, New York, New York 10022 (212) 751-2600; *The Economist Book of Vital World Statistics.*

The World Bank, 1818 H Street, NW, Washington, D.C. 20433 (202) 477-1234; *World Tables.*

UNITED ARAB EMIRATES - FERTILIZER

Food and Agricultural Organization of the United Nations (FAO), Via delle Terme di Caracalla, 00100 Rome, Italy (Telephone Number in U.S. (202) 653-2400); *Fertilizer Yearbook,* and *The State of Food and Agriculture.*

Statistical Office of the United Nations, Publishing Service, New York, New York 10017 (800) 253-9646; *Statistical Yearbook.*

UNITED ARAB EMIRATES - FETAL MORTALITY

Statistical Office of the United Nations, Publishing Service, New York, New York 10017 (800) 253-9646; *Demographic Yearbook.*

UNITED ARAB EMIRATES - FINANCE

Economic Commission for Western Asia, Post Office Box 27, Baghdad, Iraq; *Statistical Abstract of Western Asia.*

Euromonitor Publications Limited, 87-88 Turnmill Street, London EC1M 5QU, England; *Middle East Economic Handbook.*

Facts on File, 460 Park Avenue South, New York, New York 10016 (800) 443-8323; *The New Book of World Rankings.*

G.K. Hall and Company, 70 Lincoln Street, Boston, Massachusetts 02111 (617) 423-3990; *The World in Figures.*

International Monetary Fund, 700 Nineteenth Street, NW, Washington, D.C. 20431 (202) 623-7000; *Government Finance Statistics Yearbook.*

UNITED ARAB EMIRATES - FISHERIES

Economic Commission for Western Asia, Post Office Box 27, Baghdad, Iraq; *Statistical Abstract of Western Asia.*

Facts on File, 460 Park Avenue South, New York, New York 10016 (800) 443-8323; *The New Book of World Rankings.*

Food and Agricultural Organization of the United Nations (FAO) Via delle Terme di Caracalla, 00100 Rome, Italy (Telephone Number in U.S. (202) 653-2400); *The State of Food and Agriculture,* and *Yearbook of Fishery Statistics.*

Statistical Office of the United Nations, Publishing Service, New York, New York 10017 (800) 253-9646; *Statistical Yearbook.*

UNITED ARAB EMIRATES - FOOD

Food and Agricultural Organization of the United Nations (FAO) Via delle Terme di Caracalla, 00100 Rome, Italy (Telephone Number in U.S. (202) 653-2400); *Production Yearbook*, and *The State of Food and Agriculture*.

G.K. Hall and Company, 70 Lincoln Street, Boston, Massachusetts 02111 (617) 423-3990; *The World in Figures*.

UNITED ARAB EMIRATES - FOREIGN AID

G.K. Hall and Company, 70 Lincoln Street, Boston, Massachusetts 02111 (617) 423-3990; *The World in Figures*.

UNITED ARAB EMIRATES - FOREIGN TRADE

Economic Commission for Western Asia, Post Office Box 27, Baghdad, Iraq; *Statistical Abstract of Western Asia*.

Euromonitor Publications Limited, 87-88 Turnmill Street, London EC1M 5QU, England; *International Marketing Data and Statistics*, and *Middle East Economic Handbook*.

Facts on File, 460 Park Avenue South, New York, New York 10016 (800) 443-8323; *The New Book of World Rankings*.

Food and Agricultural Organization of the United Nations (FAO) Via delle Terme di Caracalla, 00100 Rome, Italy (Telephone Number in U.S. (202) 653-2400); *The State of Food and Agriculture*.

G.K. Hall and Company, 70 Lincoln Street, Boston, Massachusetts 02111 (617) 423-3990; *The World in Figures*.

Statistical Office of the United Nations, Publishing Service, New York, New York 10017 (800) 253-9646; *International Trade Statistics Yearbook*, and *Statistical Yearbook*.

The World Bank, 1818 H Street, NW, Washington, D.C. 20433 (202) 477-1234; *World Tables*.

UNITED ARAB EMIRATES - FORESTRY AND FOREST PRODUCTS

Facts on File, 460 Park Avenue South, New York, New York 10016 (800) 443-8323; *The New Book of World Rankings*.

Food and Agricultural Organization of the United Nations (FAO) Via delle Terme di Caracalla, 00100 Rome, Italy (Telephone Number in U.S. (202) 653-2400); *The State of Food and Agriculture*.

G.K. Hall and Company, 70 Lincoln Street, Boston, Massachusetts 02111 (617) 423-3990; *The World in Figures*.

Statistical Office of the United Nations, Publishing Service, New York, New York 10017 (800) 253-9646; *Statistical Yearbook*.

United Nations Educational, Scientific and Cultural Organization (UNESCO), 7 Place de Fontenoy, F-75700 Paris, France (Telephone Number in U.S. (212) 963-5981); *Statistical Yearbook*.

UNITED ARAB EMIRATES - GAS AND GAS LIQUIDS PRODUCTION - See UNITED ARAB EMIRATES - MINING AND MINERAL PRODUCTS

UNITED ARAB EMIRATES - GENERAL MORTALITY

Statistical Office of the United Nations, Publishing Service, New York, New York 10017 (800) 253-9646; *Demographic Yearbook*.

UNITED ARAB EMIRATES - GEOGRAPHIC DATA

Facts on File, 460 Park Avenue South, New York, New York 10016 (800) 443-8323; *The New Book of World Rankings*.

UNITED ARAB EMIRATES - GOLD HOLDINGS

International Monetary Fund, 700 Nineteenth Street, NW, Washington, D.C. 20431 (202) 623-7000; *International Financial Statistics*.

Statistical Office of the United Nations, Publishing Service, New York, New York 10017 (800) 253-9646; *Statistical Yearbook*.

The World Bank, 1818 H Street, NW, Washington, D.C. 20433 (202) 477-1234; *World Tables*.

UNITED ARAB EMIRATES - GOLD PRODUCTION AND CONSUMPTION - See UNITED ARAB EMIRATES - MINING AND MINERAL PRODUCTS

UNITED ARAB EMIRATES - GOVERNMENT

G.K. Hall and Company, 70 Lincoln Street, Boston, Massachusetts 02111 (617) 423-3990; *The World in Figures*.

UNITED ARAB EMIRATES - GOVERNMENT EXPENDITURES

Economic Commission for Western Asia, Post Office Box 27, Baghdad, Iraq; *Statistical Abstract of Western Asia*.

International Monetary Fund, 700 Nineteenth Street, NW, Washington, D.C. 20431 (202) 623-7000; *Government Finance Statistics Yearbook*.

Times Books, 201 East 50th Street, New York, New York 10022 (212) 751-2600; *The Economist Book of Vital World Statistics*.

The World Bank, 1818 H Street, NW, Washington, D.C. 20433 (202) 477-1234; *World Tables*.

UNITED ARAB EMIRATES - GOVERNMENT REVENUE

Economic Commission for Western Asia, Post Office Box 27, Baghdad, Iraq; *Statistical Abstract of Western Asia*.

International Monetary Fund, 700 Nineteenth Street, NW, Washington, D.C. 20431 (202) 623-7000; *Government Finance Statistics Yearbook*.

The World Bank, 1818 H Street, NW, Washington, D.C. 20433 (202) 477-1234; *World Tables*.

UNITED ARAB EMIRATES - GRAIN PRODUCTION - See UNITED ARAB EMIRATES - CROPS

UNITED ARAB EMIRATES - GRANTS

International Monetary Fund, 700 Nineteenth Street, NW, Washington, D.C. 20431 (202) 623-7000; *Government Finance Statistics Yearbook*.

UNITED ARAB EMIRATES - GROSS DOMESTIC PRODUCT

Economic Commission for Western Asia, Post Office Box 27, Baghdad, Iraq; *Statistical Abstract of Western Asia*.

Euromonitor Publications Limited, 87-88 Turnmill Street, London EC1M 5QU, England; *International Marketing Data and Statistics*, and *Middle East Economic Handbook.*

Facts on File, 460 Park Avenue South, New York, New York 10016 (800) 443-8323; *The New Book of World Rankings.*

G.K. Hall and Company, 70 Lincoln Street, Boston, Massachusetts 02111 (617) 423-3990; *The World in Figures.*

Times Books, 201 East 50th Street, New York, New York 10022 (212) 751-2600; *The Economist Book of Vital World Statistics.*

The World Bank, 1818 H Street, NW, Washington, D.C. 20433 (202) 477-1234; *World Tables.*

UNITED ARAB EMIRATES - GROSS NATIONAL PRODUCT

Euromonitor Publications Limited, 87-88 Turnmill Street, London EC1M 5QU, England; *International Marketing Data and Statistics.*

Organization of Petroleum Exporting Countries, Obere Donaustrasse 93, 1020 Vienna 2, Austria; *OPEC Annual Statistical Bulletin.*

U.S. Arms Control and Disarmament Agency, 320 Twenty-first Street, NW, Washington, D.C. 20451 (202) 647-8677; *World Military Expenditures and Arms Transfers.*

The World Bank, 1818 H Street, NW, Washington, D.C. 20433 (202) 477-1234; *World Tables.*

UNITED ARAB EMIRATES - HEALTH

Economic Commission for Western Asia, Post Office Box 27, Baghdad, Iraq; *Statistical Abstract of Western Asia.*

Euromonitor Publications Limited, 87-88 Turnmill Street, London EC1M 5QU, England; *Middle East Economic Handbook.*

Facts on File, 460 Park Avenue South, New York, New York 10016 (800) 443-8323; *The New Book of World Rankings.*

G.K. Hall and Company, 70 Lincoln Street, Boston, Massachusetts 02111 (617) 423-3990; *The World in Figures.*

Statistical Office of the United Nations, Publishing Service, New York, New York 10017 (800) 253-9646; *Statistical Yearbook.*

Times Books, 201 East 50th Street, New York, New York 10022 (212) 751-2600; *The Economist Book of Vital World Statistics.*

UNITED ARAB EMIRATES - HEALTH EXPENDITURES

International Monetary Fund, 700 Nineteenth Street, NW, Washington, D.C. 20431 (202) 623-7000; *Government Finance Statistics Yearbook.*

UNITED ARAB EMIRATES - HIDE PRODUCTION

Food and Agricultural Organization of the United Nations (FAO), Via delle Terme di Caracalla, 00100 Rome, Italy (Telephone Number in U.S. (202) 653-2400); *Production Yearbook.*

UNITED ARAB EMIRATES - HIGHWAYS

Economic Commission for Western Asia, Post Office Box 27, Baghdad, Iraq; *Statistical Abstract of Western Asia.*

G.K. Hall and Company, 70 Lincoln Street, Boston, Massachusetts 02111 (617) 423-3990; *The World in Figures.*

UNITED ARAB EMIRATES - HORSES - See UNITED ARAB EMIRATES - LIVESTOCK AND POULTRY

UNITED ARAB EMIRATES - HOURS OF WORK - See UNITED ARAB EMIRATES - EMPLOYMENT

UNITED ARAB EMIRATES - HOUSING AND HOUSING UNITS

Facts on File, 460 Park Avenue South, New York, New York 10016 (800) 443-8323; *The New Book of World Rankings.*

UNITED ARAB EMIRATES - HOUSING EXPENDITURES

International Monetary Fund, 700 Nineteenth Street, NW, Washington, D.C. 20431 (202) 623-7000; *Government Finance Statistics Yearbook.*

UNITED ARAB EMIRATES - ILLITERATE POPULATION

The Economist Intelligence Unit, 111 West 57th Street, New York, New York 10019 (800) 938-4685; *The World Market Atlas.*

G.K. Hall and Company, 70 Lincoln Street, Boston, Massachusetts 02111 (617) 423-3990; *The World in Figures.*

United Nations Educational, Scientific and Cultural Organization (UNESCO), 7 Place de Fontenoy, F-75700 Paris, France (Telephone Number in U.S. (212) 963-5981); *Statistical Yearbook.*

UNITED ARAB EMIRATES - IMPORTS

Economic Commission for Western Asia, Post Office Box 27, Baghdad, Iraq; *Statistical Abstract of Western Asia.*

The Economist Intelligence Unit, 111 West 57th Street, New York, New York 10019 (800) 938-4685; *The World Market Atlas.*

Euromonitor Publications Limited, 87-88 Turnmill Street, London EC1M 5QU, England; *International Marketing Data and Statistics,* and *Middle East Economic Handbook.*

Food and Agricultural Organization of the United Nations (FAO) Via delle Terme di Caracalla, 00100 Rome, Italy (Telephone Number in U.S. (202) 653-2400); *The State of Food and Agriculture.*

G.K. Hall and Company, 70 Lincoln Street, Boston, Massachusetts 02111 (617) 423-3990; *The World in Figures.*

International Monetary Fund, 700 Nineteenth Street, NW, Washington, D.C. 20431 (202) 623-7000; *Direction of Trade Statistics,* and *International Financial Statistics.*

Times Books, 201 East 50th Street, New York, New York 10022 (212) 751-2600; *The Economist Book of Vital World Statistics.*

The World Bank, 1818 H Street, NW, Washington, D.C. 20433 (202) 477-1234; *World Tables.*

UNITED ARAB EMIRATES - INCOME TAXES - See UNITED ARAB EMIRATES - TAXATION

UNITED ARAB EMIRATES - INDUSTRY

Euromonitor Publications Limited, 87-88 Turnmill Street, London EC1M 5QU, England; *International Marketing Data and Statistics.*

Facts on File, 460 Park Avenue South, New York, New York 10016 (800) 443-8323; *The New Book of World Rankings.*

G.K. Hall and Company, 70 Lincoln Street, Boston, Massachusetts 02111 (617) 423-3990; *The World in Figures.*

International Labour Office, I.L.O. Publications, CH-1211, Geneva 22, Switzerland; *Yearbook of Labour Statistics.*

Times Books, 201 East 50th Street, New York, New York 10022 (212) 751-2600; *The Economist Book of Vital World Statistics.*

The World Bank, 1818 H Street, NW, Washington, D.C. 20433 (202) 477-1234; *World Tables.*

UNITED ARAB EMIRATES - INFANT AND MATERNAL MORTALITY

Statistical Office of the United Nations, Publishing Service, New York, New York 10017 (800) 253-9646; *Demographic Yearbook.*

Times Books, 201 East 50th Street, New York, New York 10022 (212) 751-2600; *The Economist Book of Vital World Statistics.*

The World Bank, 1818 H Street, NW, Washington, D.C. 20433 (202) 477-1234; *World Tables.*

UNITED ARAB EMIRATES - INTERNATIONAL LIQUIDITY

International Monetary Fund, 700 Nineteenth Street, NW, Washington, D.C. 20431 (202) 623-7000; *International Financial Statistics.*

UNITED ARAB EMIRATES - INTERNATIONAL RESERVES EXCLUDING GOLD

Statistical Office of the United Nations, Publishing Service, New York, New York 10017 (800) 253-9646; *Statistical Yearbook.*

The World Bank, 1818 H Street, NW, Washington, D.C. 20433 (202) 477-1234; *World Tables.*

UNITED ARAB EMIRATES - IRON ORE PRODUCTION AND CONSUMPTION - See UNITED ARAB EMIRATES - MINING AND MINERAL PRODUCTS

UNITED ARAB EMIRATES - IRRIGATION

Euromonitor Publications Limited, 87-88 Turnmill Street, London EC1M 5QU, England; *International Marketing Data and Statistics.*

UNITED ARAB EMIRATES - LABOR FORCE

Economic Commission for Western Asia, Post Office Box 27, Baghdad, Iraq; *Statistical Abstract of Western Asia.*

Euromonitor Publications Limited, 87-88 Turnmill Street, London EC1M 5QU, England; *International Marketing Data and Statistics,* and *Middle East Economic Handbook.*

Facts on File, 460 Park Avenue South, New York, New York 10016 (800) 443-8323; *The New Book of World Rankings.*

Food and Agricultural Organization of the United Nations (FAO) Via delle Terme di Caracalla, 00100 Rome, Italy (Telephone Number in U.S. (202) 653-2400); *The State of Food and Agriculture.*

G.K. Hall and Company, 70 Lincoln Street, Boston, Massachusetts 02111 (617) 423-3990; *The World in Figures.*

The World Bank, 1818 H Street, NW, Washington, D.C. 20433 (202) 477-1234; *World Tables.*

UNITED ARAB EMIRATES - LABOR PRODUCTIVITY

International Labour Office, I.L.O. Publications, CH-1211, Geneva 22, Switzerland; *Yearbook of Labour Statistics.*

UNITED ARAB EMIRATES - LAND USE

Economic Commission for Western Asia, Post Office Box 27, Baghdad, Iraq; *Statistical Abstract of Western Asia.*

Euromonitor Publications Limited, 87-88 Turnmill Street, London EC1M 5QU, England; *International Marketing Data and Statistics.*

Food and Agricultural Organization of the United Nations (FAO), Via delle Terme di Caracalla, 00100 Rome, Italy (Telephone Number in U.S. (202) 653-2400); *Production Yearbook.*

G.K. Hall and Company, 70 Lincoln Street, Boston, Massachusetts 02111 (617) 423-3990; *The World in Figures.*

UNITED ARAB EMIRATES - LIBRARIES

Facts on File, 460 Park Avenue South, New York, New York 10016 (800) 443-8323; *The New Book of World Rankings.*

United Nations Educational, Scientific and Cultural Organization (UNESCO), 7 Place de Fontenoy, F-75700 Paris, France (Telephone Number in U.S. (212) 963-5981); *Statistical Yearbook.*

UNITED ARAB EMIRATES - LIVESTOCK AND POULTRY

Economic Commission for Western Asia, Post Office Box 27, Baghdad, Iraq; *Statistical Abstract of Western Asia.*

Facts on File, 460 Park Avenue South, New York, New York 10016 (800) 443-8323; *The New Book of World Rankings.*

Food and Agricultural Organization of the United Nations (FAO), Via delle Terme di Caracalla, 00100 Rome, Italy (Telephone Number in U.S. (202) 653-2400); *Production Yearbook,* and *The State of Food and Agriculture.*

G.K. Hall and Company, 70 Lincoln Street, Boston, Massachusetts 02111 (617) 423-3990; *The World in Figures.*

UNITED ARAB EMIRATES - LIVING LEVELS

G.K. Hall and Company, 70 Lincoln Street, Boston, Massachusetts 02111 (617) 423-3990; *The World in Figures.*

Times Books, 201 East 50th Street, New York, New York 10022 (212) 751-2600; *The Economist Book of Vital World Statistics.*

UNITED ARAB EMIRATES - MAIL - NUMBER OF ITEMS SENT AND RECEIVED

Statistical Office of the United Nations, Publishing Service, New York, New York 10017 (800) 253-9646; *Statistical Yearbook.*

UNITED ARAB EMIRATES - MANUFACTURING

Facts on File, 460 Park Avenue South, New York, New York 10016 (800) 443-8323; *The New Book of World Rankings.*

G.K. Hall and Company, 70 Lincoln Street, Boston, Massachusetts 02111 (617) 423-3990; *The World in Figures.*

The World Bank, 1818 H Street, NW, Washington, D.C. 20433 (202) 477-1234; *World Tables.*

UNITED ARAB EMIRATES - MARRIAGE RATES

Facts on File, 460 Park Avenue South, New York, New York 10016 (800) 443-8323; *The New Book of World Rankings*.

Statistical Office of the United Nations, Publishing Service, New York, New York 10017 (800) 253-9646; *Demographic Yearbook*.

UNITED ARAB EMIRATES - MEAT PRODUCTION - See UNITED ARAB EMIRATES - LIVESTOCK AND POULTRY

UNITED ARAB EMIRATES - MERCHANT SHIPPING

Economic Commission for Western Asia, Post Office Box 27, Baghdad, Iraq; *Statistical Abstract of Western Asia*.

G.K. Hall and Company, 70 Lincoln Street, Boston, Massachusetts 02111 (617) 423-3990; *The World in Figures*.

Lloyd's Register of Shipping, 17 Battery Place, New York, New York 10004 (212) 425-8050; *Register of Ships*.

Organization of Petroleum Exporting Countries, Obere Donaustrasse 93, 1020 Vienna 2, Austria; *OPEC Annual Statistical Bulletin*.

Statistical Office of the United Nations, Publishing Service, New York, New York 10017 (800) 253-9646; *Statistical Yearbook*.

Times Books, 201 East 50th Street, New York, New York 10022 (212) 751-2600; *The Economist Book of Vital World Statistics*.

U.S. Department of Transportation, Maritime Administration, 400 Seventh Street, SW, Washington, D.C. 20590 (202) 366-5807; *A Statistical Analysis of the World's Merchant Fleets*.

UNITED ARAB EMIRATES - MILITARY

G.K. Hall and Company, 70 Lincoln Street, Boston, Massachusetts 02111 (617) 423-3990; *The World in Figures*.

The International Institute for Strategic Studies, 23 Tavistock Street, London WC2E 7NQ, England; *The Military Balance*.

U.S. Arms Control and Disarmament Agency, 320 Twenty-first Street, NW, Washington, D.C. 20451 (202) 647-8677; *World Military Expenditures and Arms Transfers*.

UNITED ARAB EMIRATES - MILK PRODUCTION - See UNITED ARAB EMIRATES - DAIRY PRODUCTS

UNITED ARAB EMIRATES - MINING AND MINERAL PRODUCTS

Economic Commission for Western Asia, Post Office Box 27, Baghdad, Iraq; *Statistical Abstract of Western Asia*.

Facts on File, 460 Park Avenue South, New York, New York 10016 (800) 443-8323; *The New Book of World Rankings*.

G.K. Hall and Company, 70 Lincoln Street, Boston, Massachusetts 02111 (617) 423-3990; *The World in Figures*.

Organization of Petroleum Exporting Countries, Obere Donaustrasse 93, 1020 Vienna 2, Austria; *OPEC Annual Statistical Bulletin*.

Penn Well Publishing Company, 1421 South Sheridan Road, P.O. Box 1260, Tulsa, Oklahoma 74101 (800) 752-9764; *International Energy Statistics Sourcebook*.

Statistical Office of the United Nations, Publishing Service, New York, New York 10017 (800) 253-9646; *Statistical Yearbook*.

UNITED ARAB EMIRATES - MONEY EXCHANGE RATES

Euromonitor Publications Limited, 87-88 Turnmill Street, London EC1M 5QU, England; *International Marketing Data and Statistics*.

Statistical Office of the United Nations, Publishing Service, New York, New York 10017 (800) 253-9646; *Statistical Yearbook*.

UNITED ARAB EMIRATES - MONEY RESERVES

Euromonitor Publications Limited, 87-88 Turnmill Street, London EC1M 5QU, England; *International Marketing Data and Statistics*.

UNITED ARAB EMIRATES - MONEY SUPPLY

Economic Commission for Western Asia, Post Office Box 27, Baghdad, Iraq; *Statistical Abstract of Western Asia*.

Euromonitor Publications Limited, 87-88 Turnmill Street, London EC1M 5QU, England; *International Marketing Data and Statistics*.

G.K. Hall and Company, 70 Lincoln Street, Boston, Massachusetts 02111 (617) 423-3990; *The World in Figures*.

Statistical Office of the United Nations, Publishing Service, New York, New York 10017 (800) 253-9646; *Statistical Yearbook*.

The World Bank, 1818 H Street, NW, Washington, D.C. 20433 (202) 477-1234; *World Tables*.

UNITED ARAB EMIRATES - MOTION PICTURES

Statistical Office of the United Nations, Publishing Service, New York, New York 10017 (800) 253-9646; *Statistical Yearbook*.

UNITED ARAB EMIRATES - MOTOR VEHICLES

Economic Commission for Western Asia, Post Office Box 27, Baghdad, Iraq; *Statistical Abstract of Western Asia*.

UNITED ARAB EMIRATES - MOTOR VEHICLES IN USE

G.K. Hall and Company, 70 Lincoln Street, Boston, Massachusetts 02111 (617) 423-3990; *The World in Figures*.

Times Books, 201 East 50th Street, New York, New York 10022 (212) 751-2600; *The Economist Book of Vital World Statistics*.

UNITED ARAB EMIRATES - MUSEUMS

Facts on File, 460 Park Avenue South, New York, New York 10016 (800) 443-8323; *The New Book of World Rankings*.

United Nations Educational, Scientific and Cultural Organization (UNESCO), 7 Place de Fontenoy, F-75700 Paris, France (Telephone Number in U.S. (212) 963-5981); *Statistical Yearbook*.

UNITED ARAB EMIRATES - NATALITY

Statistical Office of the United Nations, Publishing Service, New York, New York 10017 (800) 253-9646; *Demographic Yearbook*.

UNITED ARAB EMIRATES - NATIONAL ACCOUNTS

Economic Commission for Western Asia, Post Office Box 27, Baghdad, Iraq; *Statistical Abstract of Western Asia*.

Statistical Office of the United Nations, Publishing Service, New York, New York 10017 (800) 253-9646; *National Accounts Statistics*.

UNITED ARAB EMIRATES - NATIONAL INCOME

Facts on File, 460 Park Avenue South, New York, New York 10016 (800) 443-8323; *The New Book of World Rankings*.

G.K. Hall and Company, 70 Lincoln Street, Boston, Massachusetts 02111 (617) 423-3990; *The World in Figures*.

UNITED ARAB EMIRATES - NATIONAL PRODUCT

Facts on File, 460 Park Avenue South, New York, New York 10016 (800) 443-8323; *The New Book of World Rankings*.

UNITED ARAB EMIRATES - NATURAL GAS PRODUCTION - See UNITED ARAB EMIRATES - MINING AND MINERAL PRODUCTS

UNITED ARAB EMIRATES - NEWSPAPER PRODUCTION - See UNION OF SOVIET SOCIALIST REPUBLICS - FORESTRY AND FOREST PRODUCTS

UNITED ARAB EMIRATES - OCCUPATIONS - See UNITED ARAB EMIRATES - LABOR FORCE

UNITED ARAB EMIRATES - PEANUT PRODUCTION - See UNITED ARAB EMIRATES - CROPS

UNITED ARAB EMIRATES - PERIODICALS

United Nations Educational, Scientific and Cultural Organization (UNESCO), 7 Place de Fontenoy, F-75700 Paris, France (Telephone Number in U.S. (212) 963-5981); *Statistical Yearbook*.

UNITED ARAB EMIRATES - PESTICIDE USE

Food and Agricultural Organization of the United Nations (FAO) Via delle Terme di Caracalla, 00100 Rome, Italy (Telephone Number in U.S. (202) 653-2400); *The State of Food and Agriculture*.

UNITED ARAB EMIRATES - PETROLEUM INDUSTRY

Euromonitor Publications Limited, 87-88 Turnmill Street, London EC1M 5QU, England; *Middle East Economic Handbook*.

Facts on File, 460 Park Avenue South, New York, New York 10016 (800) 443-8323; *The New Book of World Rankings*.

Food and Agricultural Organization of the United Nations (FAO) Via delle Terme di Caracalla, 00100 Rome, Italy (Telephone Number in U.S. (202) 653-2400); *The State of Food and Agriculture*.

G.K. Hall and Company, 70 Lincoln Street, Boston, Massachusetts 02111 (617) 423-3990; *The World in Figures*.

Organization of Petroleum Exporting Countries, Obere Donaustrasse 93, 1020 Vienna 2, Austria; *OPEC Annual Statistical Bulletin*.

Penn Well Publishing Company, 1421 South Sheridan Road, P.O. Box 1260, Tulsa, Oklahoma 74101 (800) 752-9764; *International Energy Statistics Sourcebook*.

Statistical Office of the United Nations, Publishing Service, New York, New York 10017 (800) 253-9646; *Statistical Yearbook*.

UNITED ARAB EMIRATES - PIGS - See UNITED ARAB EMIRATES - LIVESTOCK AND POULTRY

UNITED ARAB EMIRATES - PIPELINES FOR OIL AND PETROLEUM PRODUCTS

Organization of Petroleum Exporting Countries, Obere Donaustrasse 93, 1020 Vienna 2, Austria; *OPEC Annual Statistical Bulletin*.

UNITED ARAB EMIRATES - POPULATION

Economic Commission for Western Asia, Post Office Box 27, Baghdad, Iraq; *Statistical Abstract of Western Asia*.

The Economist Intelligence Unit, 111 West 57th Street, New York, New York 10019 (800) 938-4685; *The World Market Atlas*.

Euromonitor Publications Limited, 87-88 Turnmill Street, London EC1M 5QU, England; *International Marketing Data and Statistics*, and *Middle East Economic Handbook*.

Facts on File, 460 Park Avenue South, New York, New York 10016 (800) 443-8323; *The New Book of World Rankings*.

Food and Agricultural Organization of the United Nations (FAO), Via delle Terme di Caracalla, 00100 Rome, Italy (Telephone Number in U.S. (202) 653-2400); *Production Yearbook*.

G.K. Hall and Company, 70 Lincoln Street, Boston, Massachusetts 02111 (617) 423-3990; *The World in Figures*.

International Labour Office, I.L.O. Publications, CH-1211, Geneva 22, Switzerland; *Yearbook of Labour Statistics*.

Statistical Office of the United Nations, Publishing Service, New York, New York 10017 (800) 253-9646; *Demographic Yearbook*, and *Statistical Yearbook*.

Times Books, 201 East 50th Street, New York, New York 10022 (212) 751-2600; *The Economist Book of Vital World Statistics*.

U.S. Arms Control and Disarmament Agency, 320 Twenty-first Street, NW, Washington, D.C. 20451 (202) 647-8677; *World Military Expenditures and Arms Transfers*.

World Health Organization, Office of Publications, Avenue Appia, CH-1211 Geneva 27, Switzerland (Telephone Number in U.S. (518) 436-9686); *World Health Statistics Annual*.

UNITED ARAB EMIRATES - POST OFFICES

Facts on File, 460 Park Avenue South, New York, New York 10016 (800) 443-8323; *The New Book of World Rankings*.

UNITED ARAB EMIRATES - POTATO PRODUCTION - See UNITED ARAB EMIRATES - CROPS

UNITED ARAB EMIRATES - PRICES

Economic Commission for Western Asia, Post Office Box 27, Baghdad, Iraq; *Statistical Abstract of Western Asia*.

Facts on File, 460 Park Avenue South, New York, New York 10016 (800) 443-8323; *The New Book of World Rankings*.

Food and Agricultural Organization of the United Nations (FAO), Via delle Terme di Caracalla, 00100 Rome, Italy (Telephone Number in U.S. (202) 653-2400); *Production Yearbook*, and *The State of Food and Agriculture*.

G.K. Hall and Company, 70 Lincoln Street, Boston, Massachusetts 02111 (617) 423-3990; *The World in Figures.*

International Labour Office, I.L.O. Publications, CH-1211, Geneva 22, Switzerland; *Yearbook of Labour Statistics.*

UNITED ARAB EMIRATES - PRODUCTION

Facts on File, 460 Park Avenue South, New York, New York 10016 (800) 443-8323; *The New Book of World Rankings.*

G.K. Hall and Company, 70 Lincoln Street, Boston, Massachusetts 02111 (617) 423-3990; *The World in Figures.*

UNITED ARAB EMIRATES - PRODUCTIVITY

Euromonitor Publications Limited, 87-88 Turnmill Street, London EC1M 5QU, England; *International Marketing Data and Statistics.*

UNITED ARAB EMIRATES - PUBLIC FINANCE

Facts on File, 460 Park Avenue South, New York, New York 10016 (800) 443-8323; *The New Book of World Rankings.*

UNITED ARAB EMIRATES - RADIO BROADCASTING - See UNITED ARAB EMIRATES - BROADCASTING

UNITED ARAB EMIRATES - RAILWAYS

G.K. Hall and Company, 70 Lincoln Street, Boston, Massachusetts 02111 (617) 423-3990; *The World in Figures.*

UNITED ARAB EMIRATES - RELIGION

Facts on File, 460 Park Avenue South, New York, New York 10016 (800) 443-8323; *The New Book of World Rankings.*

UNITED ARAB EMIRATES - RETAIL TRADE

G.K. Hall and Company, 70 Lincoln Street, Boston, Massachusetts 02111 (617) 423-3990; *The World in Figures.*

UNITED ARAB EMIRATES - RICE PRODUCTION - See UNITED ARAB EMIRATES - CROPS

UNITED ARAB EMIRATES - RUBBER PRODUCTION AND CONSUMPTION

Facts on File, 460 Park Avenue South, New York, New York 10016 (800) 443-8323; *The New Book of World Rankings.*

UNITED ARAB EMIRATES - SENIOR CITIZENS

Facts on File, 460 Park Avenue South, New York, New York 10016 (800) 443-8323; *The New Book of World Rankings.*

UNITED ARAB EMIRATES - SHEEP - See UNITED ARAB EMIRATES - LIVESTOCK AND POULTRY

UNITED ARAB EMIRATES - SILVER PRODUCTION AND CONSUMPTION - See UNITED ARAB EMIRATES - MINING AND MINERAL PRODUCTS

UNITED ARAB EMIRATES - SOCIAL DATA

Facts on File, 460 Park Avenue South, New York, New York 10016 (800) 443-8323; *The New Book of World Rankings.*

G.K. Hall and Company, 70 Lincoln Street, Boston, Massachusetts 02111 (617) 423-3990; *The World in Figures.*

UNITED ARAB EMIRATES - SOCIAL SECURITY

International Monetary Fund, 700 Nineteenth Street, NW, Washington, D.C. 20431 (202) 623-7000; *Government Finance Statistics Yearbook.*

UNITED ARAB EMIRATES - STATE BUDGET REVENUE AND EXPENDITURES

Euromonitor Publications Limited, 87-88 Turnmill Street, London EC1M 5QU, England; *International Marketing Data and Statistics.*

UNITED ARAB EMIRATES - STEEL PRODUCTION - See UNITED ARAB EMIRATES - MINING AND MINERAL PRODUCTS

UNITED ARAB EMIRATES - STOCKS - COMMODITY - MARKET PRICE - INDEX

Food and Agricultural Organization of the United Nations (FAO) Via delle Terme di Caracalla, 00100 Rome, Italy (Telephone Number in U.S. (202) 653-2400); *The State of Food and Agriculture.*

UNITED ARAB EMIRATES - SUGAR PRODUCTION AND CONSUMPTION - See UNITED ARAB EMIRATES - CROPS

UNITED ARAB EMIRATES - TAXATION

G.K. Hall and Company, 70 Lincoln Street, Boston, Massachusetts 02111 (617) 423-3990; *The World in Figures.*

International Monetary Fund, 700 Nineteenth Street, NW, Washington, D.C. 20431 (202) 623-7000; *Government Finance Statistics Yearbook.*

The World Bank, 1818 H Street, NW, Washington, D.C. 20433 (202) 477-1234; *World Tables.*

UNITED ARAB EMIRATES - TELEPHONES IN USE

American Telephone and Telegraph Company, 26 Parsippany Road, Whippany, New Jersey 07981 (800) 338-4038; *The World's Telephones.*

Euromonitor Publications Limited, 87-88 Turnmill Street, London EC1M 5QU, England; *Middle East Economic Handbook.*

G.K. Hall and Company, 70 Lincoln Street, Boston, Massachusetts 02111 (617) 423-3990; *The World in Figures.*

Statistical Office of the United Nations, Publishing Service, New York, New York 10017 (800) 253-9646; *Statistical Yearbook.*

UNITED ARAB EMIRATES - TELEVISION BROADCASTING - See UNITED ARAB EMIRATES - BROADCASTING

UNITED ARAB EMIRATES - TEXTILE INDUSTRY

G.K. Hall and Company, 70 Lincoln Street, Boston, Massachusetts 02111 (617) 423-3990; *The World in Figures.*

UNITED ARAB EMIRATES - THEATRE

United Nations Educational, Scientific and Cultural Organization (UNESCO), 7 Place de Fontenoy, F-75700 Paris, France (Telephone Number in U.S. (212) 963-5981); *Statistical Yearbook.*

UNITED ARAB EMIRATES - TOBACCO PRODUCTION

Facts on File, 460 Park Avenue South, New York, New York 10016 (800) 443-8323; *The New Book of World Rankings*.

UNITED ARAB EMIRATES - TOURISM

Economic Commission for Western Asia, Post Office Box 27, Baghdad, Iraq; *Statistical Abstract of Western Asia*.

Euromonitor Publications Limited, 87-88 Turnmill Street, London EC1M 5QU, England; *Middle East Economic Handbook*.

G.K. Hall and Company, 70 Lincoln Street, Boston, Massachusetts 02111 (617) 423-3990; *The World in Figures*.

Times Books, 201 East 50th Street, New York, New York 10022 (212) 751-2600; *The Economist Book of Vital World Statistics*.

UNITED ARAB EMIRATES - TRADE - See UNITED ARAB EMIRATES - FOREIGN TRADE

UNITED ARAB EMIRATES - TRANSPORTATION AND COMMUNICATIONS

Economic Commission for Western Asia, Post Office Box 27, Baghdad, Iraq; *Statistical Abstract of Western Asia*.

Euromonitor Publications Limited, 87-88 Turnmill Street, London EC1M 5QU, England; *Middle East Economic Handbook*.

Facts on File, 460 Park Avenue South, New York, New York 10016 (000) 443-8333; *The New Book of World Rankings*.

G.K. Hall and Company, 70 Lincoln Street, Boston, Massachusetts 02111 (617) 423-3990; *The World in Figures*.

UNITED ARAB EMIRATES - UNEMPLOYMENT

Euromonitor Publications Limited, 87-88 Turnmill Street, London EC1M 5QU, England; *International Marketing Data and Statistics*, and *Middle East Economic Handbook*.

International Labour Office, I.L.O. Publications, CH-1211, Geneva 22, Switzerland; *Yearbook of Labour Statistics*.

UNITED ARAB EMIRATES - VITAL STATISTICS

Euromonitor Publications Limited, 87-88 Turnmill Street, London EC1M 5QU, England; *International Marketing Data and Statistics*, and *Middle East Economic Handbook*.

G.K. Hall and Company, 70 Lincoln Street, Boston, Massachusetts 02111 (617) 423-3990; *The World in Figures*.

World Health Organization, Office of Publications, Avenue Appia, CH-1211 Geneva 27, Switzerland (Telephone Number in U.S. (518) 436-9686); *World Health Statistics Annual*.

UNITED ARAB EMIRATES - WAGES

G.K. Hall and Company, 70 Lincoln Street, Boston, Massachusetts 02111 (617) 423-3990; *The World in Figures*.

International Labour Office, I.L.O. Publications, CH-1211, Geneva 22, Switzerland; *Yearbook of Labour Statistics*.

UNITED ARAB EMIRATES - WEATHER

Facts on File, 460 Park Avenue South, New York, New York 10016 (800) 443-8323; *The New Book of World Rankings*.

G.K. Hall and Company, 70 Lincoln Street, Boston, Massachusetts 02111 (617) 423-3990; *The World in Figures*.

UNITED ARAB EMIRATES - WELFARE

International Monetary Fund, 700 Nineteenth Street, NW, Washington, D.C. 20431 (202) 623-7000; *Government Finance Statistics Yearbook*.

UNITED ARAB EMIRATES - WHEAT PRODUCTION AND PRICES - See UNITED ARAB EMIRATES - CROPS

UNITED ARAB EMIRATES - WINE PRODUCTION

Facts on File, 460 Park Avenue South, New York, New York 10016 (800) 443-8323; *The New Book of World Rankings*.

UNITED ARAB EMIRATES - WOOL PRODUCTION

Facts on File, 460 Park Avenue South, New York, New York 10016 (800) 443-8323; *The New Book of World Rankings*.

UNITED ARAB EMIRATES - ZOOS AND BOTANICAL GARDENS

United Nations Educational, Scientific and Cultural Organization (UNESCO), 7 Place de Fontenoy, F-75700 Paris, France (Telephone Number in U.S. (212) 963-5981); *Statistical Yearbook*.

United Kingdom - National Statistical Offices

Business Statistics Office, Government Buildings, Cardiff Road, Newport, Gwent NP9 1XC, England.

Central Statistical Office, Great George Street, London SW1P 3AQ, England.

Office of Population Censuses and Surveys, Head Office, Saint Catherine's House, 10 Kingsway, London WC2B 6JP, England.

United Kingdom - Primary Statistics Sources

HM Stationery Office, Post Office Box 276, London SW8 5DT, England; *Annual Abstract of Statistics*, and *Monthly Digest of Statistics*.

United Kingdom - Databases

CSO Macro-Economic Data Bank, Great Britain Central Statistical Office, Room 52/4, Great George Street, London SW1P 3AQ, England. Subject coverage: United Kingdom economics and demographics.

Financial Statistics Division, Bank of England, Threadneedle Street, London EC2R 8AH, England. Subject coverage: Data of United Kingdom financial indicator statistics.

National Online Manpower Information System (NOMIS), University of Durham, Mountjoy Research Centre, Unit 3P, Durham DH1 35W, England. Subject coverage: Employment and census data for the United Kingdom.

Town Focus, Property Intelligence Plc., Ingram House, 13-15 John Adam Street, London WC2N 6LD, England. Subject coverage: Demographic and socioeconomic statistics on urban areas in the United Kingdom.

UNITED KINGDOM - ABORTIONS

European Community Information Service, 2100 M Street, NW, Washington, D.C. 20037 (202) 862-9500; *Demographic Statistics*.

Statistical Office of the United Nations, Publishing Service, New York, New York 10017 (800) 253-9646; *Demographic Yearbook*.

UNITED KINGDOM - AGRICULTURE

European Community Information Service, 2100 M Street, NW, Washington, D.C. 20037 (202) 862-9500; *Agriculture: Statistical Yearbook, Basic Statistics of the Community, Eurostatistics: Data for Short-Term Economic Analysis, Labor Force Sample Survey*, and *Regions: Statistical Yearbook*.

Facts on File, 460 Park Avenue South, New York, New York 10016 (800) 443-8323; *The New Book of World Rankings*.

Food and Agricultural Organization of the United Nations (FAO) Via delle Terme di Caracalla, 00100 Rome, Italy (Telephone Number in U.S. (202) 653-2400); *Production Yearbook*, and *The State of Food and Agriculture*.

G.K. Hall and Company, 70 Lincoln Street, Boston, Massachusetts 02111 (617) 423-3990; *The World in Figures*.

National Technical Information Service, 5285 Port Royal Road, Springfield, Virginia 22161 (703) 487-4600; *Handbook of Economic Statistics*.

Organisation for Economic Co-operation and Development (OECD), 2 rue Andre-Pascal, 75 Paris 16, France (Telephone Number in U.S. (202) 785-6323); *Economic Accounts for Agriculture, Indicators of Industrial Activity, Industrial Structure Statistics*, and *OECD Economic Surveys: United Kingdom*.

Statistical Office of the United Nations, Publishing Service, New York, New York 10017 (800) 253-9646; *Statistical Yearbook*.

Times Books, 201 East 50th Street, New York, New York 10022 (212) 751-2600; *The Economist Book of Vital World Statistics*.

The World Bank, 1818 H Street, NW, Washington, D.C. 20433 (202) 477-1234; *World Tables*.

UNITED KINGDOM - AIRLINE SERVICE

European Community Information Service, 2100 M Street, NW, Washington, D.C. 20037 (202) 862-9500; *Basic Statistics of the Community, Regions: Statistical Yearbook*, and *Transport Annual Statistics*.

Facts on File, 460 Park Avenue South, New York, New York 10016 (800) 443-8323; *The New Book of World Rankings*.

G.K. Hall and Company, 70 Lincoln Street, Boston, Massachusetts 02111 (617) 423-3990; *The World in Figures*.

International Civil Aviation Organization, 1000 Sherbrooke Street, West, Montreal, Quebec, Canada H3A 2R2 (514) 285-8219; *Civil Aviation Statistics of the World*.

National Technical Information Service, 5285 Port Royal Road, Springfield, Virginia 22161 (703) 487-4600; *Handbook of Economic Statistics*.

Organisation for Economic Co-operation and Development (OECD), 2 rue Andre-Pascal, 75 Paris 16, France (Telephone Number in U.S. (202) 785-6323); *Tourism Policy and International Tourism in OECD Member Countries*.

Statistical Office of the United Nations, Publishing Service, New York, New York 10017 (800) 253-9646; *Statistical Yearbook*.

Times Books, 201 East 50th Street, New York, New York 10022 (212) 751-2600; *The Economist Book of Vital World Statistics*.

UNITED KINGDOM - ALMOND PRODUCTION - See UNITED KINGDOM - CROPS

UNITED KINGDOM - ALUMINUM PRODUCTION AND CONSUMPTION - See UNITED KINGDOM - MINING AND MINERAL PRODUCTS

UNITED KINGDOM - ANIMAL FEEDINGSTUFFS

Organisation for Economic Co-operation and Development (OECD), 2 rue Andre-Pascal, 75 Paris 16, France (Telephone Number in U.S. (202) 785-6323); *Foreign Trade by Commodities*.

Statistical Office of the United Nations, Publishing Service, New York, New York 10017 (800) 253-9646; *Statistical Yearbook*.

UNITED KINGDOM - ANIMAL HEALTH

Food and Agricultural Organization of the United Nations (FAO), Via delle Terme di Caracalla, 00100 Rome, Italy (Telephone Number in U.S. (202) 653-2400); *Animal Health Yearbook*.

UNITED KINGDOM - ANTIMONY AND ANTIMONY ORE PRODUCTION AND CONSUMPTION - See UNITED KINGDOM - MINING AND MINERAL PRODUCTS

UNITED KINGDOM - APPLES PRODUCTION - See UNITED KINGDOM - CROPS

UNITED KINGDOM - AREA AND DENSITY OF POPULATION

European Community Information Service, 2100 M Street, NW, Washington, D.C. 20037 (202) 862-9500; *Demographic Statistics, Basic Statistics of the Community*.

Facts on File, 460 Park Avenue South, New York, New York 10016 (800) 443-8323; *The New Book of World Rankings*.

Food and Agricultural Organization of the United Nations (FAO) Via delle Terme di Caracalla, 00100 Rome, Italy (Telephone Number in U.S. (202) 653-2400); *The State of Food and Agriculture*.

G.K. Hall and Company, 70 Lincoln Street, Boston, Massachusetts 02111 (617) 423-3990; *The World in Figures*.

National Technical Information Service, 5285 Port Royal Road, Springfield, Virginia 22161 (703) 487-4600; *Handbook of Economic Statistics*.

Statistical Office of the United Nations, Publishing Service, New York, New York 10017 (800) 253-9646; *Statistical Yearbook*.

Times Books, 201 East 50th Street, New York, New York 10022 (212) 751-2600; *The Economist Book of Vital World Statistics*.

United Nations Educational, Scientific and Cultural Organization (UNESCO), 7 Place de Fontenoy, F-75700 Paris, France (Telephone Number in U.S. (212) 963-5981); *Statistical Yearbook*.

UNITED KINGDOM - ARMS EXPORTS AND IMPORTS

U.S. Arms Control and Disarmament Agency, 320 Twenty-first Street, NW, Washington, D.C. 20451 (202) 647-8677; *World Military Expenditures and Arms Transfers*.

UNITED KINGDOM - ARSENIC PRODUCTION AND CONSUMPTION - See UNITED KINGDOM - MINING AND MINERAL PRODUCTS

UNITED KINGDOM - BALANCE OF PAYMENTS

The Economist Intelligence Unit, 111 West 57th Street, New York, New York 10019 (800) 938-4685; *The World Market Atlas*.

European Community Information Service, 2100 M Street, NW, Washington, D.C. 20037 (202) 862-9500; *ACP: Basic Statistics, Basic Statistics of the Community, Energy Statistics Yearbook*, and *Eurostatistics: Data for Short-Term Economic Analysis*.

G.K. Hall and Company, 70 Lincoln Street, Boston, Massachusetts 02111 (617) 423-3990; *The World in Figures*.

International Monetary Fund, 700 Nineteenth Street, NW, Washington, D.C. 20431 (202) 623-7000; *Balance of Payments Yearbook*, and *International Financial Statistics*.

National Technical Information Service, 5285 Port Royal Road, Springfield, Virginia 22161 (703) 487-4600; *Handbook of Economic Statistics*.

Organisation for Economic Co-operation and Development (OECD), 2 rue Andre-Pascal, 75 Paris 16, France (Telephone Number in U.S. (202) 785-6323); *Economic Outlook, Geographical Distribution of Financial Flows to Developing Countries, Main Economic Indicators - Historical Statistics*, and *OECD Economic Surveys: United Kingdom*.

Times Books, 201 East 50th Street, New York, New York 10022 (212) 751-2600; *The Economist Book of Vital World Statistics*.

The World Bank, 1818 H Street, NW, Washington, D.C. 20433 (202) 477-1234; *World Tables*.

UNITED KINGDOM - BANANA PRODUCTION - See UNITED KINGDOM - CROPS

UNITED KINGDOM - BANKING

European Community Information Service, 2100 M Street, NW, Washington, D.C. 20037 (202) 862-9500; *ACP: Basic Statistics*.

Facts on File, 460 Park Avenue South, New York, New York 10016 (800) 443-8323; *The New Book of World Rankings*.

G.K. Hall and Company, 70 Lincoln Street, Boston, Massachusetts 02111 (617) 423-3990; *The World in Figures*.

International Monetary Fund, 700 Nineteenth Street, NW, Washington, D.C. 20431 (202) 623-7000; *Government Finance Statistics Yearbook, International Financial Statistics*, and *International Financial Statistics*.

National Technical Information Service, 5285 Port Royal Road, Springfield, Virginia 22161 (703) 487-4600; *Handbook of Economic Statistics*.

Organisation for Economic Co-operation and Development (OECD), 2 rue Andre-Pascal, 75 Paris 16, France (Telephone Number in U.S. (202) 785-6323); *Economic Outlook, Financial Market Trends*, and *OECD Economic Surveys: United Kingdom*.

Statistical Office of the United Nations, Publishing Service, New York, New York 10017 (800) 253-9646; *Statistical Yearbook*.

UNITED KINGDOM - BARLEY PRODUCTION - See UNITED KINGDOM - CROPS

UNITED KINGDOM - BAUXITE PRODUCTION AND CONSUMPTION - See UNITED KINGDOM - MINING AND MINERAL PRODUCTS

UNITED KINGDOM - BEER PRODUCTION

Facts on File, 460 Park Avenue South, New York, New York 10016 (800) 443-8323; *The New Book of World Rankings*.

Statistical Office of the United Nations, Publishing Service, New York, New York 10017 (800) 253-9646; *Statistical Yearbook*.

UNITED KINGDOM - BEVERAGES - PRODUCTION INDEX

Organisation for Economic Co-operation and Development (OECD), 2 rue Andre-Pascal, 75 Paris 16, France (Telephone Number in U.S. (202) 785-6323); *Indicators of Industrial Activity*.

UNITED KINGDOM - BIRTH RATE

European Community Information Service, 2100 M Street, NW, Washington, D.C. 20037 (202) 862-9500; *Basic Statistics of the Community*, and *Demographic Statistics*.

Facts on File, 460 Park Avenue South, New York, New York 10016 (800) 443-8323; *The New Book of World Rankings*.

Statistical Office of the United Nations, Publishing Service, New York, New York 10017 (800) 253-9646; *Demographic Yearbook*, and *Statistical Yearbook*.

Times Books, 201 East 50th Street, New York, New York 10022 (212) 751-2600; *The Economist Book of Vital World Statistics*.

The World Bank, 1818 H Street, NW, Washington, D.C. 20433 (202) 477-1234; *World Tables*.

World Health Organization, Office of Publications, Avenue Appia, CH-1211 Geneva 27, Switzerland (Telephone Number in U.S. (518) 436-9686); *World Health Statistics Annual*.

UNITED KINGDOM - BISMUTH PRODUCTION AND CONSUMPTION - See UNITED KINGDOM - MINING AND MINERAL PRODUCTS

UNITED KINGDOM - BONDS

European Community Information Service, 2100 M Street, NW, Washington, D.C. 20037 (202) 862-9500; *Basic Statistics of the Community*.

G.K. Hall and Company, 70 Lincoln Street, Boston, Massachusetts 02111 (617) 423-3990; *The World in Figures*.

International Monetary Fund, 700 Nineteenth Street, NW, Washington, D.C. 20431 (202) 623-7000; *Government Finance Statistics Yearbook*.

Organisation for Economic Co-operation and Development (OECD), 2 rue Andre-Pascal, 75 Paris 16, France (Telephone Number in U.S.

(202) 785-6323); *Financial Market Trends.*

Statistical Office of the United Nations, Publishing Service, New York, New York 10017 (800) 253-9646; *Statistical Yearbook.*

UNITED KINGDOM - BOOK PRODUCTION

Euromonitor Publications Limited, 87-88 Turnmill Street, London EC1M 5QU, England; *European Marketing Data and Statistics.*

G.K. Hall and Company, 70 Lincoln Street, Boston, Massachusetts 02111 (617) 423-3990; *The World in Figures.*

Organisation for Economic Co-operation and Development (OECD), 2 rue Andre-Pascal, 75 Paris 16, France (Telephone Number in U.S. (202) 785-6323); *Indicators of Industrial Activity.*

United Nations Educational, Scientific and Cultural Organization (UNESCO), 7 Place de Fontenoy, F-75700 Paris, France (Telephone Number in U.S. (212) 963-5981); *Statistical Yearbook.*

UNITED KINGDOM - BROADCASTING

Billboard Limited, P.O. Box 9027, 1006 AA Amsterdam, The Netherlands (Telephone Number in U.S. (212) 764-7300); *World Radio TV Handbook.*

European Community Information Service, 2100 M Street, NW, Washington, D.C. 20037 (202) 862-9500; *Basic Statistics of the Community.*

Facts on File, 460 Park Avenue South, New York, New York 10016 (800) 443-8323; *The New Book of World Rankings.*

G.K. Hall and Company, 70 Lincoln Street, Boston, Massachusetts 02111 (617) 423-3990; *The World in Figures.*

Times Books, 201 East 50th Street, New York, New York 10022 (212) 751-2600; *The Economist Book of Vital World Statistics.*

United Nations Educational, Scientific and Cultural Organization (UNESCO), 7 Place de Fontenoy, F-75700 Paris, France (Telephone Number in U.S. (212) 963-5981); *Statistical Yearbook.*

UNITED KINGDOM - BUSINESS

European Community Information Service, 2100 M Street, NW, Washington, D.C. 20037 (202) 862-9500; *Basic Statistics of the Community.*

G.K. Hall and Company, 70 Lincoln Street, Boston, Massachusetts 02111 (617) 423-3990; *The World in Figures.*

Organisation for Economic Co-operation and Development (OECD), 2 rue Andre-Pascal, 75 Paris 16, France (Telephone Number in U.S. (202) 785-6323); *Main Economic Indicators - Historical Statistics.*

UNITED KINGDOM - BUTTER - See UNITED KINGDOM - DAIRY PRODUCTS

UNITED KINGDOM - CABBAGE PRODUCTION - See UNITED KINGDOM - CROPS

UNITED KINGDOM - CADMIUM PRODUCTION AND CONSUMPTION - See UNITED KINGDOM - MINING AND MINERAL PRODUCTS

UNITED KINGDOM - CALORIE SUPPLY

Food and Agricultural Organization of the United Nations (FAO) Via delle Terme di Caracalla, 00100 Rome, Italy (Telephone Number in U.S. (202) 653-2400); *The State of Food and Agriculture.*

UNITED KINGDOM - CAPITAL INVESTMENT

National Technical Information Service, 5285 Port Royal Road, Springfield, Virginia 22161 (703) 487-4600; *Handbook of Economic Statistics.*

Organisation for Economic Co-operation and Development (OECD), 2 rue Andre-Pascal, 75 Paris 16, France (Telephone Number in U.S. (202) 785-6323); *Economic Outlook,* and *Financial Market Trends.*

UNITED KINGDOM - CAPITAL REVENUE

International Monetary Fund, 700 Nineteenth Street, NW, Washington, D.C. 20431 (202) 623-7000; *Government Finance Statistics Yearbook.*

Organisation for Economic Co-operation and Development (OECD), 2 rue Andre-Pascal, 75 Paris 16, France (Telephone Number in U.S. (202) 785-6323); *Economic Outlook,* and *Financial Market Trends.*

UNITED KINGDOM - CASHEW NUT PRODUCTION - See UNITED KINGDOM - CROPS

UNITED KINGDOM - CASTOR BEAN PRODUCTION - See UNITED KINGDOM - CROPS

UNITED KINGDOM - CATTLE - See UNITED KINGDOM - LIVESTOCK AND POULTRY

UNITED KINGDOM - CAULIFLOWER PRODUCTION - See UNITED KINGDOM - CROPS

UNITED KINGDOM - CAUSTIC SODA PRODUCTION

European Community Information Service, 2100 M Street, NW, Washington, D.C. 20037 (202) 862-9500; *Basic Statistics of the Community.*

National Technical Information Service, 5285 Port Royal Road, Springfield, Virginia 22161 (703) 487-4600; *Handbook of Economic Statistics.*

Organisation for Economic Co-operation and Development (OECD), 2 rue Andre-Pascal, 75 Paris 16, France (Telephone Number in U.S. (202) 785-6323); *Indicators of Industrial Activity.*

UNITED KINGDOM - CEMENT PRODUCTION - See UNITED KINGDOM - MINING AND MINERAL PRODUCTS

UNITED KINGDOM - CEREAL PRODUCTION - See UNITED KINGDOM - CROPS

UNITED KINGDOM - CHEESE - See UNITED KINGDOM - DAIRY PRODUCTS

UNITED KINGDOM - CHEMICAL INDUSTRY

European Community Information Service, 2100 M Street, NW, Washington, D.C. 20037 (202) 862-9500; *Industrial Production: Quarterly Statistics.*

UNITED KINGDOM - CHEMICAL (ORGANIC) PRODUCTION - See UNITED KINGDOM - MINING AND MINERAL PRODUCTS

UNITED KINGDOM - CHESTNUT PRODUCTION - See UNITED KINGDOM - CROPS

UNITED KINGDOM - CHICKENS - See UNITED KINGDOM - LIVESTOCK AND POULTRY

UNITED KINGDOM - CHROMITE PRODUCTION AND CONSUMPTION - See UNITED KINGDOM - MINING AND MINERAL PRODUCTS

UNITED KINGDOM - CHROMIUM ORE PRODUCTION AND CONSUMPTION - See UNITED KINGDOM - MINING AND MINERAL PRODUCTS

UNITED KINGDOM - CIGAR PRODUCTION - See UNITED KINGDOM - TOBACCO PRODUCTION

UNITED KINGDOM - CIGARETTE PRODUCTION - See UNITED KINGDOM - TOBACCO PRODUCTION

UNITED KINGDOM - CLASS STRUCTURE

European Community Information Service, 2100 M Street, NW, Washington, D.C. 20037 (202) 862-9500; *Basis Statistics of the Community*, and *Labor Force Sample Survey*.

G.K. Hall and Company, 70 Lincoln Street, Boston, Massachusetts 02111 (617) 423-3990; *The World in Figures*.

UNITED KINGDOM - CLIMATE

Facts on File, 460 Park Avenue South, New York, New York 10016 (800) 443-8323, *The New Book of World Rankings*.

G.K. Hall and Company, 70 Lincoln Street, Boston, Massachusetts 02111 (617) 423-3990; *The World in Figures*.

UNITED KINGDOM - CLOTHING - PRODUCTION INDEX

Organisation for Economic Co-operation and Development (OECD), 2 rue Andre-Pascal, 75 Paris 16, France (Telephone Number in U.S. (202) 785-6323); *Indicators of Industrial Activity*.

UNITED KINGDOM - CLOTHING EXPORTS AND IMPORTS

European Community Information Service, 2100 M Street, NW, Washington, D.C. 20037 (202) 862-9500; *Basic Statistics of the Community*.

Organisation for Economic Co-operation and Development (OECD), 2 rue Andre-Pascal, 75 Paris 16, France (Telephone Number in U.S. (202) 785-6323); *Textile Industry in OECD Countries*.

Statistical Office of the United Nations, Publishing Service, New York, New York 10017 (800) 253-9646; *Trade in Manufactures of Developing Countries*.

UNITED KINGDOM - COAL PRODUCTION - See UNITED KINGDOM - MINING AND MINERAL PRODUCTS

UNITED KINGDOM - COBALT PRODUCTION AND CONSUMPTION - See UNITED KINGDOM - MINING AND MINERAL PRODUCTS

UNITED KINGDOM - COCOA (BEANS) PRODUCTION - See UNITED KINGDOM - CROPS

UNITED KINGDOM - COFFEE - See UNITED KINGDOM - CROPS

UNITED KINGDOM - COKE AND COKE OVEN ORE PRODUCTION AND CONSUMPTION - See UNITED KINGDOM - MINING AND MINERAL PRODUCTS

UNITED KINGDOM - COMMUNICATIONS

European Community Information Service, 2100 M Street, NW, Washington, D.C. 20037 (202) 862-9500; *Basic Statistics of the Community*, and *Transport Annual Statistics*.

G.K. Hall and Company, 70 Lincoln Street, Boston, Massachusetts 02111 (617) 423-3990; *The World in Figures*.

UNITED KINGDOM - CONSTRUCTION INDUSTRY

European Community Information Service, 2100 M Street, NW, Washington, D.C. 20037 (202) 862-9500; *Basic Statistics of the Community*, and *Labor Force Sample Survey*.

Facts on File, 460 Park Avenue South, New York, New York 10016 (800) 443-8323; *The New Book of World Rankings*.

Organisation for Economic Co-operation and Development (OECD), 2 rue Andre-Pascal, 75 Paris 16, France (Telephone Number in U.S. (202) 785-6323); *Industrial Structure Statistics*, *The Iron and Steel Industry, Main Economic Indicators - Historical Statistics*, and *OECD Economic Surveys: United Kingdom*.

Statistical Office of the United Nations, Publishing Service, New York, New York 10017 (800) 253-9646; *Construction Statistics Yearbook*, and *Statistical Yearbook*.

UNITED KINGDOM - CONSUMER PRICE INDEX

European Community Information Service, 2100 M Street, NW, Washington, D.C. 20037 (202) 862-9500; *Basic Statistics of the Community*, and *Eurostatistics: Data for Short-Term Economic Analysis*.

G.K. Hall and Company, 70 Lincoln Street, Boston, Massachusetts 02111 (617) 423-3990; *The World in Figures*.

National Technical Information Service, 5285 Port Royal Road, Springfield, Virginia 22161 (703) 487-4600; *Handbook of Economic Statistics*.

Organisation for Economic Co-operation and Development (OECD), 2 rue Andre-Pascal, 75 Paris 16, France (Telephone Number in U.S. (202) 785-6323); *Economic Outlook*.

Statistical Office of the United Nations, Publishing Service, New York, New York 10017 (800) 253-9646; *Statistical Yearbook*.

UNITED KINGDOM - CONSUMER PRICES

Euromonitor Publications Limited, 87-88 Turnmill Street, London EC1M 5QU, England; *European Marketing Data and Statistics*.

European Community Information Service, 2100 M Street, NW, Washington, D.C. 20037 (202) 862-9500; *Basic Statistics of the Community*, and *Money and Finance*.

International Labour Office, I.L.O. Publications, CH-1211, Geneva 22, Switzerland; *Yearbook of Labour Statistics*.

International Monetary Fund, 700 Nineteenth Street, NW, Washington, D.C. 20431 (202) 623-7000; *International Financial Statistics*.

Organisation for Economic Co-operation and Development (OECD), 2 rue Andre-Pascal, 75 Paris 16, France (Telephone Number in U.S. (202) 785-6323); *Economic Outlook.*

Times Books, 201 East 50th Street, New York, New York 10022 (212) 751-2600; *The Economist Book of Vital World Statistics.*

UNITED KINGDOM - CONSUMPTION

European Community Information Service, 2100 M Street, NW, Washington, D.C. 20037 (202) 862-9500; *Basic Statistics of the Community.*

G.K. Hall and Company, 70 Lincoln Street, Boston, Massachusetts 02111 (617) 423-3990; *The World in Figures.*

International Iron and Steel Institute, 120, rue Colonel Bourg, B-1140, Belgium; *Steel Statistical Yearbook.*

International Lead and Zinc Study Group, Metro House, 58 St. James's Street, London SW1A 1LD England; *Lead and Zinc Statistics.*

International Rubber Study Group, York House, Eighth Floor, Empire Way, Wembley, London HA9 0PA, England; *Rubber Statistical Bulletin.*

National Technical Information Service, 5285 Port Royal Road, Springfield, Virginia 22161 (703) 487-4600; *Handbook of Economic Statistics.*

Organisation for Economic Co-operation and Development (OECD), 2 rue Andre-Pascal, 75 Paris 16, France (Telephone Number in U.S. (202) 785-6323); *The Footwear, Raw Hides and Skins, and Leather Industry in OECD Countries, The Iron and Steel Industry, Meat Balances in OECD Member Countries, The Non-Ferrous Metals Industry, The Pulp and Paper Industry,* and *Textile Industry in OECD Countries.*

UNITED KINGDOM - COPPER AND COPPER ORE PRODUCTION AND CONSUMPTION - See UNITED KINGDOM - MINING AND MINERAL PRODUCTS

UNITED KINGDOM - CORN PRODUCTION - See UNITED KINGDOM - CROPS

UNITED KINGDOM - CORPORATE INCOME TAXES - See UNITED KINGDOM - TAXATION

UNITED KINGDOM - CORPORATE TAXES - See UNITED KINGDOM - TAXATION

UNITED KINGDOM - COTTON - See UNITED KINGDOM - CROPS

UNITED KINGDOM - CRIME

International Criminal Police Organization (INTERPOL), 26 rue Armengaud, 92210 Saint Cloud, France; *International Crime Statistics.*

Yale University Press, Yale Station, New Haven, Connecticut 06520 (203) 432-0940; *Violence and Crime in Cross-National Perspective.*

UNITED KINGDOM - CROPS

Commodity Research Bureau, Incorporated, 75 Wall Street, New York, New York 10005 (212) 504-7754; *Commodity Year Book.*

European Community Information Service, 2100 M Street, NW, Washington, D.C. 20037 (202) 862-9500; *ACP: Basic Statistics, Agriculture: Statistical Yearbook, Basic Statistics of the Community, Crop Production: Quarterly Statistics, Eurostatistics: Data for Short-Term Economic Analysis,* and *Regions: Statistical Yearbook.*

Facts on File, 460 Park Avenue South, New York, New York 10016 (800) 443-8323; *The New Book of World Rankings.*

Food and Agricultural Organization of the United Nations (FAO) Via delle Terme di Caracalla, 00100 Rome, Italy (Telephone Number in U.S. (202) 653-2400; *Production Yearbook,* and *The State of Food and Agriculture.*

G.K. Hall and Company, 70 Lincoln Street, Boston, Massachusetts 02111 (617) 423-3990; *The World in Figures.*

National Technical Information Service, 5285 Port Royal Road, Springfield, Virginia 22161 (703) 487-4600; *Handbook of Economic Statistics.*

Organisation for Economic Co-operation and Development (OECD), 2 rue Andre-Pascal, 75 Paris 16, France (Telephone Number in U.S. (202) 785-6323); *Economic Accounts for Agriculture, Foreign Trade by Commodities,* and *Textile Industry in OECD Countries.*

Statistical Office of the United Nations, Publishing Service, New York, New York 10017 (800) 253-9646; *Statistical Yearbook.*

UNITED KINGDOM - CUSTOMS DUTIES

European Community Information Service, 2100 M Street, NW, Washington, D.C. 20037 (202) 862-9500; *Basic Statistics of the Community.*

G.K. Hall and Company, 70 Lincoln Street, Boston, Massachusetts 02111 (617) 423-3990; *The World in Figures.*

International Monetary Fund, 700 Nineteenth Street, NW, Washington, D.C. 20431 (202) 623-7000; *Government Finance Statistics Yearbook.*

Organisation for Economic Co-operation and Development (OECD), 2 rue Andre-Pascal, 75 Paris 16, France (Telephone Number in U.S. (202) 785-6323); *The Non-Ferrous Metals Industry.*

UNITED KINGDOM - DAIRY PRODUCTS

Commodity Research Bureau, Incorporated, 75 Wall Street, New York, New York 10005 (212) 504-7754; *Commodity Year Book.*

European Community Information Service, 2100 M Street, NW, Washington, D.C. 20037 (202) 862-9500; *Basic Statistics of the Community,* and *Eurostatistics: Data for Short-Term Economic Analysis.*

Food and Agricultural Organization of the United Nations (FAO), Via delle Terme di Caracalla, 00100 Rome, Italy (Telephone Number in U.S. (202) 653-2400; *Production Yearbook,* and *The State of Food and Agriculture.*

National Technical Information Service, 5285 Port Royal Road, Springfield, Virginia 22161 (703) 487-4600; *Handbook of Economic Statistics.*

Organisation for Economic Co-operation and Development (OECD), 2 rue Andre-Pascal, 75 Paris 16, France (Telephone Number in U.S. (202) 785-6323); *Economic Accounts for Agriculture,* and *Milk, Milk Products, and Egg Balances in OECD Member Countries.*

Statistical Office of the United Nations, Publishing Service, New York, New York 10017 (800) 253-9646; *Statistical Yearbook.*

UNITED KINGDOM - DEATH RATES

European Community Information Service, 2100 M Street, NW, Washington, D.C. 20037 (202) 862-9500; *Basic Statistics of the Community,* and *Demographic Statistics.*

G.K. Hall and Company, 70 Lincoln Street, Boston, Massachusetts 02111 (617) 423-3990; *The World in Figures.*

Statistical Office of the United Nations, Publishing Service, New York, New York 10017 (800) 253-9646; *Statistical Yearbook.*

Times Books, 201 East 50th Street, New York, New York 10022 (212) 751-2600; *The Economist Book of Vital World Statistics.*

UNITED KINGDOM - DEFENSE EXPENDITURES

European Community Information Service, 2100 M Street, NW, Washington, D.C. 20037 (202) 862-9500; *Government Financing of Research and Development.*

G.K. Hall and Company, 70 Lincoln Street, Boston, Massachusetts 02111 (617) 423-3990; *The World in Figures.*

International Monetary Fund, 700 Nineteenth Street, NW, Washington, D.C. 20431 (202) 623-7000; *Government Finance Statistics Yearbook.*

National Technical Information Service, 5285 Port Royal Road, Springfield, Virginia 22161 (703) 487-4600; *Handbook of Economic Statistics.*

U.S. Arms Control and Disarmament Agency, 320 Twenty-first Street, NW, Washington, D.C. 20451 (202) 647-8677; *World Military Expenditures and Arms Transfers.*

UNITED KINGDOM - DEMOGRAPHY

The Economist Intelligence Unit, 111 West 57th Street, New York, New York 10019 (800) 938-4685; *The World Market Atlas.*

European Community Information Service, 2100 M Street, NW, Washington, D.C. 20037 (202) 862-9500; *Basic Statistics of the Community, Demographic Statistics, Employment and Unemployment,* and *Regions: Statistical Yearbook.*

Facts on File, 460 Park Avenue South, New York, New York 10016 (800) 443-8323; *The New Book of World Rankings.*

G.K. Hall and Company, 70 Lincoln Street, Boston, Massachusetts 02111 (617) 423-3990; *The World in Figures.*

UNITED KINGDOM - DEVELOPMENT ASSISTANCE

European Community Information Service, 2100 M Street, NW, Washington, D.C. 20037 (202) 862-9500; *ACP: Basic Statistics, Basic Statistics of the Community,* and *Government Financing of Research and Development.*

G.K. Hall and Company, 70 Lincoln Street, Boston, Massachusetts 02111 (617) 423-3990; *The World in Figures.*

Organisation for Economic Co-operation and Development (OECD), 2 rue Andre-Pascal, 75 Paris 16, France (Telephone Number in U.S. (202) 785-6323); *Geographical Distribution of Financial Flows to Developing Countries.*

Statistical Office of the United Nations, Publishing Service, New York, New York 10017 (800) 253-9646; *Statistical Yearbook.*

UNITED KINGDOM - DIAMOND PRODUCTION AND EXPORTS - See **UNITED KINGDOM - MINING AND MINERAL PRODUCTS**

UNITED KINGDOM - DISCOUNT RATES

Organisation for Economic Co-operation and Development (OECD), 2 rue Andre-Pascal, 75 Paris 16, France (Telephone Number in U.S. (202) 785-6323); *Financial Market Trends.*

Statistical Office of the United Nations, Publishing Service, New York, New York 10017 (800) 253-9646; *Statistical Yearbook.*

UNITED KINGDOM - DISEASE

G.K. Hall and Company, 70 Lincoln Street, Boston, Massachusetts 02111 (617) 423-3990; *The World in Figures.*

UNITED KINGDOM - DIVORCE RATES

European Community Information Service, 2100 M Street, NW, Washington, D.C. 20037 (202) 862-9500; *Demographic Statistics.*

Facts on File, 460 Park Avenue South, New York, New York 10016 (800) 443-8323; *The New Book of World Rankings.*

Statistical Office of the United Nations, Publishing Service, New York, New York 10017 (800) 253-9646; *Demographic Yearbook,* and *Statistical Yearbook.*

UNITED KINGDOM - DOMESTIC PRODUCT

European Community Information Service, 2100 M Street, NW, Washington, D.C. 20037 (202) 862-9500; *Basic Statistics of the Community.*

G.K. Hall and Company, 70 Lincoln Street, Boston, Massachusetts 02111 (617) 423-3990; *The World in Figures.*

UNITED KINGDOM - DUCKS - See **UNITED KINGDOM - LIVESTOCK AND POULTRY**

UNITED KINGDOM - ECONOMY

European Community Information Service, 2100 M Street, NW, Washington, D.C. 20037 (202) 862-9500; *ACP: Basic Statistics, Basic Statistics of the Community, Energy Statistics Yearbook, Labor Force Sample Survey,* and *Money and Finance.*

Euromonitor Publications Limited, 87-88 Turnmill Street, London EC1M 5QU, England; *European Marketing Data and Statistics.*

Facts on File, 460 Park Avenue South, New York, New York 10016 (800) 443-8323; *The New Book of World Rankings.*

G.K. Hall and Company, 70 Lincoln Street, Boston, Massachusetts 02111 (617) 423-3990; *The World in Figures.*

National Technical Information Service, 5285 Port Royal Road, Springfield, Virginia 22161 (703) 487-4600; *Handbook of Economic Statistics.*

Organisation for Economic Co-operation and Development (OECD), 2 rue Andre-Pascal, 75 Paris 16, France (Telephone Number in U.S. (202) 785-6323); *Economic Outlook, Geographical Distribution of Financial Flows to Developing Countries, Main Economic Indicators - Historical Statistics, OECD Economic Surveys: United Kingdom,* and *OECD Employment Outlook.*

UNITED KINGDOM - EDUCATION

The Economist Intelligence Unit, 111 West 57th Street, New York, New York 10019 (800) 938-4685; *The World Market Atlas.*

Euromonitor Publications Limited, 87-88 Turnmill Street, London EC1M 5QU, England; *European Marketing Data and Statistics.*

European Community Information Service, 2100 M Street, NW, Washington, D.C. 20037 (202) 862-9500; *Basic Statistics of the Community,* and *Regions: Statistical Yearbook.*

Facts on File, 460 Park Avenue South, New York, New York 10016 (800) 443-8323; *The New Book of World Rankings.*

G.K. Hall and Company, 70 Lincoln Street, Boston, Massachusetts 02111 (617) 423-3990; *The World in Figures.*

International Monetary Fund, 700 Nineteenth Street, NW, Washington, D.C. 20431 (202) 623-7000; *Government Finance Statistics Yearbook.*

Organisation for Economic Co-operation and Development (OECD), 2 rue Andre-Pascal, 75 Paris 16, France (Telephone Number in U.S. (202) 785-6323); *Education in OECD Countries.*

Times Books, 201 East 50th Street, New York, New York 10022 (212) 751-2600; *The Economist Book of Vital World Statistics.*

United Nations Educational, Scientific and Cultural Organization (UNESCO), 7 Place de Fontenoy, F-75700 Paris, France (Telephone Number in U.S. (212) 963-5981); *Statistical Yearbook.*

The World Bank, 1818 H Street, NW, Washington, D.C. 20433 (202) 477-1234; *World Tables.*

UNITED KINGDOM - EGG PRODUCTION AND CONSUMPTION - See UNITED KINGDOM - DAIRY PRODUCTS

UNITED KINGDOM - ELECTRICITY

Commodity Research Bureau, Incorporated, 75 Wall Street, New York, New York 10005 (212) 504-7754; *Commodity Year Book.*

European Community Information Service, 2100 M Street, NW, Washington, D.C. 20037 (202) 862-9500; *Basic Statistics of the Community, Energy: Monthly Statistics, Energy Statistics Yearbook,* and *Eurostatistics: Data for Short-Term Economic Analysis.*

Facts on File, 460 Park Avenue South, New York, New York 10016 (800) 443-8323; *The New Book of World Rankings.*

National Technical Information Service, 5285 Port Royal Road, Springfield, Virginia 22161 (703) 487-4600; *Handbook of Economic Statistics.*

Organisation for Economic Co-operation and Development (OECD), 2 rue Andre-Pascal, 75 Paris 16, France (Telephone Number in U.S. (202) 785-6323); *Coal Information, Energy Statistics of OECD Countries, Indicators of Industrial Activity, Industrial Structure Statistics,* and *Regions: Statistical Yearbook.*

Penn Well Publishing Company, 1421 South Sheridan Road, P.O. Box 1260, Tulsa, Oklahoma 74101 (800) 752-9764; *International Energy Statistics Sourcebook.*

Statistical Office of the United Nations, Publishing Service, New York, New York 10017 (800) 253-9646; *Statistical Yearbook.*

Times Books, 201 East 50th Street, New York, New York 10022 (212) 751-2600; *The Economist Book of Vital World Statistics.*

UNITED KINGDOM - EMPLOYMENT

Euromonitor Publications Limited, 87-88 Turnmill Street, London EC1M 5QU, England; *European Marketing Data and Statistics.*

European Community Information Service, 2100 M Street, NW, Washington, D.C. 20037 (202) 862-9500; *Basic Statistics of the Community, Earnings in Agriculture, Employment and Unemployment, Eurostatistics: Data for Short-Term Economic Analysis, Labor Force Sample Survey,* and *Transport Annual Statistics.*

Facts on File, 460 Park Avenue South, New York, New York 10016 (800) 443-8323; *The New Book of World Rankings.*

International Labour Office, I.L.O. Publications, CH-1211, Geneva 22, Switzerland; *Yearbook of Labour Statistics.*

National Technical Information Service, 5285 Port Royal Road, Springfield, Virginia 22161 (703) 487-4600; *Handbook of Economic Statistics.*

Organisation for Economic Co-operation and Development (OECD), 2 rue Andre-Pascal, 75 Paris 16, France (Telephone Number in U.S. (202) 785-6323); *Economic Outlook, Foreign Trade by Commodities, Indicators of Industrial Activity, Industrial Structure Statistics, The Iron and Steel Industry, Iron and Steel: Statistical Yearbook, OECD Economic Surveys: United Kingdom, OECD Employment Outlook,* and *Textile Industry in OECD Countries.*

Statistical Office of the United Nations, Publishing Service, New York, New York 10017 (800) 253-9646; *Statistical Yearbook.*

UNITED KINGDOM - ENERGY

Euromonitor Publications Limited, 87-88 Turnmill Street, London EC1M 5QU, England; *European Marketing Data and Statistics.*

European Community Information Service, 2100 M Street, NW, Washington, D.C. 20037 (202) 862-9500; *Basic Statistics of the Community, Energy: Monthly Statistics, Energy Statistics Yearbook, Regions: Statistical Yearbook,* and *Transport Annual Statistics.*

Facts on File, 460 Park Avenue South, New York, New York 10016 (800) 443-8323; *The New Book of World Rankings.*

Food and Agricultural Organization of the United Nations (FAO) Via delle Terme di Caracalla, 00100 Rome, Italy (Telephone Number in U.S. (202) 653-2400); *The State of Food and Agriculture.*

G.K. Hall and Company, 70 Lincoln Street, Boston, Massachusetts 02111 (617) 423-3990; *The World in Figures.*

National Technical Information Service, 5285 Port Royal Road, Springfield, Virginia 22161 (703) 487-4600; *Handbook of Economic Statistics.*

Organisation for Economic Co-operation and Development (OECD), 2 rue Andre-Pascal, 75 Paris 16, France (Telephone Number in U.S. (202) 785-6323); *Coal Information, Energy Statistics of OECD Countries, OECD Environmental Data,* and *Oil and Gas Information.*

Penn Well Publishing Company, 1421 South Sheridan Road, P.O. Box 1260, Tulsa, Oklahoma 74101 (800) 752-9764; *International Energy Statistics Sourcebook.*

Statistical Office of the United Nations, Publishing Service, New York, New York 10017 (800) 253-9646; *Energy Statistics Yearbook, Statistical Yearbook,* and *World Energy Supplies.*

Times Books, 201 East 50th Street, New York, New York 10022 (212) 751-2600; *The Economist Book of Vital World Statistics.*

UNITED KINGDOM - ENGINEERING AND METAL PRODUCTS - EXPORTS AND IMPORTS

European Community Information Service, 2100 M Street, NW, Washington, D.C. 20037 (202) 862-9500; *Basic Statistics of the Community,* and *Industrial Production: Quarterly Statistics.*

Statistical Office of the United Nations, Publishing Service, New York, New York 10017 (800) 253-9646; *Trade in Manufactures of Developing Countries.*

UNITED KINGDOM - ENVIRONMENT

Organization for Economic Co-operation and Development (OECD), 2 rue Andre-Pascal, 75 Paris 16, France (Telephone Number in U.S. (202) 785-6323); *OECD Environmental Data.*

UNITED KINGDOM - EXCHANGE RATES

European Community Information Service, 2100 M Street, NW, Washington, D.C. 20037 (202) 862-9500; *Eurostatistics: Data for Short-Term Economic Analysis,* and *Money and Finance.*

International Civil Aviation Organization, 1000 Sherbrooke Street, West, Montreal, Quebec, Canada H3A 2R2 (514) 285-8219; *Civil Aviation Statistics of the World.*

International Monetary Fund, 700 Nineteenth Street, NW, Washington, D.C. 20431 (202) 623-7000; *International Financial Statistics.*

National Technical Information Service, 5285 Port Royal Road, Springfield, Virginia 22161 (703) 487-4600; *Handbook of Economic Statistics.*

Organisation for Economic Co-operation and Development (OECD), 2 rue Andre-Pascal, 75 Paris 16, France (Telephone Number in U.S. (202) 785-6323); *Economic Outlook, Financial Market Trends, Revenue Statistics of OECD Member Countries,* and *Tourism Policy and International Tourism in OECD Member Countries.*

Statistical Office of the United Nations, Publishing Service, New York, New York 10017 (800) 253-9646; *Statistical Yearbook.*

UNITED KINGDOM - EXCISE TAXES - See UNITED KINGDOM - TAXATION

UNITED KINGDOM - EXPORTS

American Automobile Manufacturers Association, 1401 H Street, NW, Suite 900, Washington, D.C. 20005 (202) 326-5500; *World Motor Vehicle Data.*

The Economist Intelligence Unit, 111 West 57th Street, New York, New York 10019 (800) 938-4685; *The World Market Atlas.*

European Community Information Service, 2100 M Street, NW, Washington, D.C. 20037 (202) 862-9500; *Basic Statistics of the*

Community, *Energy: Monthly Statistics, Energy Statistics Yearbook, Eurostatistics: Data for Short-Term Economic Analysis, External Trade: Monthly Statistics, External Trade: Statistical Yearbook,* and *Fisheries: Yearly Statistics.*

Food and Agricultural Organization of the United Nations (FAO) Via delle Terme di Caracalla, 00100 Rome, Italy (Telephone Number in U.S. (202) 653-2400); *The State of Food and Agriculture.*

G.K. Hall and Company, 70 Lincoln Street, Boston, Massachusetts 02111 (617) 423-3990; *The World in Figures.*

International Iron and Steel Institute, 120, rue Colonel Bourg, B-1140, Belgium; *Steel Statistical Yearbook.*

International Lead and Zinc Study Group, Metro House, 58 St. James's Street, London SW1A 1LD England; *Lead and Zinc Statistics.*

International Monetary Fund, 700 Nineteenth Street, NW, Washington, D.C. 20431 (202) 623-7000; *Direction of Trade Statistics, Government Finance Statistics Yearbook,* and *International Financial Statistics.*

International Rubber Study Group, York House, Eighth Floor, Empire Way, Wembley, London HA9 0PA, England; *Rubber Statistical Bulletin.*

National Technical Information Service, 5285 Port Royal Road, Springfield, Virginia 22161 (703) 487-4600; *Handbook of Economic Statistics.*

Organisation for Economic Co-operation and Development (OECD), 2 rue Andre-Pascal, 75 Paris 16, France (Telephone Number in U.S. (202) 785-6323); *Economic Outlook, The Footwear, Raw Hides and Skins, and Leather Industry in OECD Countries, Foreign Trade by Commodities, Geographical Distribution of Financial Flows to Developing Countries, Industrial Structure Statistics, The Iron and Steel Industry, Milk, Milk Products, and Egg Balances in OECD Member Countries, OECD Economic Surveys: United Kingdom, The Pulp and Paper Industry,* and *Review of Fisheries in OECD Member Countries.*

Times Books, 201 East 50th Street, New York, New York 10022 (212) 751-2600; *The Economist Book of Vital World Statistics.*

The World Bank, 1818 H Street, NW, Washington, D.C. 20433 (202) 477-1234; *World Tables.*

UNITED KINGDOM - EXTERNAL FINANCING

Organisation for Economic Co-operation and Development (OECD), 2 rue Andre-Pascal, 75 Paris 16, France (Telephone Number in U.S. (202) 785-6323); *Economic Outlook,* and *Financial Market Trends.*

UNITED KINGDOM - EXTERNAL INDEBTEDNESS

National Technical Information Service, 5285 Port Royal Road, Springfield, Virginia 22161 (703) 487-4600; *Handbook of Economic Statistics.*

Organisation for Economic Co-operation and Development (OECD), 2 rue Andre-Pascal, 75 Paris 16, France (Telephone Number in U.S. (202) 785-6323); *Financial Market Trends,* and *Geographical Distribution of Financial Flows to Developing Countries.*

The World Bank, 1818 H Street, NW, Washington, D.C. 20433 (202) 477-1234; *World Tables.*

UNITED KINGDOM - EXTERNAL TRADE

European Community Information Service, 2100 M Street, NW, Washington, D.C. 20037 (202) 862-9500; *ACP: Basic Statistics, Basic Statistics of the Community, Eurostatistics: Data for Short-Term Economic Analysis, External Trade: Monthly Statistics, External Trade: Statistical Yearbook,* and *Foreign Trade of the People's Republic of China.*

Food and Agricultural Organization of the United Nations (FAO) Via delle Terme di Caracalla, 00100 Rome, Italy (Telephone Number in U.S. (202) 653-2400); *The State of Food and Agriculture,* and *Trade Yearbook.*

G.K. Hall and Company, 70 Lincoln Street, Boston, Massachusetts 02111 (617) 423-3990; *The World in Figures.*

National Technical Information Service, 5285 Port Royal Road, Springfield, Virginia 22161 (703) 487-4600; *Handbook of Economic Statistics.*

Statistical Office of the United Nations, Publishing Service, New York, New York 10017 (800) 253-9646; *Statistical Yearbook.*

UNITED KINGDOM - FABRIC PRODUCTION - See UNITED KINGDOM - TEXTILE INDUSTRY

UNITED KINGDOM - FARM CROPS - See UNITED KINGDOM - CROPS

UNITED KINGDOM - FEMALE WORKING POPULATION - See UNITED KINGDOM - EMPLOYMENT

UNITED KINGDOM - FERTILITY RATES

European Community Information Service, 2100 M Street, NW, Washington, D.C. 20037 (202) 862-9500; *Demographic Statistics.*

Facts on File, 460 Park Avenue South, New York, New York 10016 (800) 443-8323; *The New Book of World Rankings.*

Times Books, 201 East 50th Street, New York, New York 10022 (212) 751-2600; *The Economist Book of Vital World Statistics.*

The World Bank, 1818 H Street, NW, Washington, D.C. 20433 (202) 477-1234; *World Tables.*

UNITED KINGDOM - FERTILIZER

European Community Information Service, 2100 M Street, NW, Washington, D.C. 20037 (202) 862-9500; *Basic Statistics of the Community.*

Food and Agricultural Organization of the United Nations (FAO) Via delle Terme di Caracalla, 00100 Rome, Italy (Telephone Number in U.S. (202) 653-2400); *The State of Food and Agriculture.*

National Technical Information Service, 5285 Port Royal Road, Springfield, Virginia 22161 (703) 487-4600; *Handbook of Economic Statistics.*

Organisation for Economic Co-operation and Development (OECD), 2 rue Andre-Pascal, 75 Paris 16, France (Telephone Number in U.S. (202) 785-6323); *Economic Accounts for Agriculture,* and *Foreign Trade by Commodities.*

Statistical Office of the United Nations, Publishing Service, New York, New York 10017 (800) 253-9646; *Statistical Yearbook.*

UNITED KINGDOM - FETAL MORTALITY

European Community Information Service, 2100 M Street, NW, Washington, D.C. 20037 (202) 862-9500; *Basic Statistics of the Community,* and *Demographic Statistics.*

Statistical Office of the United Nations, Publishing Service, New York, New York 10017 (800) 253-9646; *Demographic Yearbook.*

World Health Organization, Office of Publications, Avenue Appia, CH-1211 Geneva 27, Switzerland (Telephone Number in U.S. (518) 436-9686); *World Health Statistics Annual.*

UNITED KINGDOM - FIBRE PRODUCTION - See UNITED KINGDOM - TEXTILE INDUSTRY

UNITED KINGDOM - FILAMENT PRODUCTION - See UNITED KINGDOM - TEXTILE INDUSTRY

UNITED KINGDOM - FILM - See UNITED KINGDOM - MOTION PICTURES

UNITED KINGDOM - FINANCE

European Community Information Service, 2100 M Street, NW, Washington, D.C. 20037 (202) 862-9500; *ACP: Basic Statistics, Basic Statistics of the Community, Eurostatistics: Data for Short-Term Economic Analysis,* and *Money and Finance.*

Facts on File, 460 Park Avenue South, New York, New York 10016 (800) 443-8323; *The New Book of World Rankings.*

G.K. Hall and Company, 70 Lincoln Street, Boston, Massachusetts 02111 (617) 423-3990; *The World in Figures.*

International Monetary Fund, 700 Nineteenth Street, NW, Washington, D.C. 20431 (202) 623-7000; *Government Finance Statistics Yearbook.*

Organisation for Economic Co-operation and Development (OECD), 2 rue Andre-Pascal, 75 Paris 16, France (Telephone Number in U.S. (202) 785-6323); *Economic Outlook, Financial Market Trends, Geographical Distribution of Financial Flows to Developing Countries, Main Economic Indicators - Historical Statistics,* and *OECD Financial Statistics.*

UNITED KINGDOM - FISHERIES

Euromonitor Publications Limited, 87-88 Turnmill Street, London EC1M 5QU, England; *European Marketing Data and Statistics.*

European Community Information Service, 2100 M Street, NW, Washington, D.C. 20037 (202) 862-9500; *Agriculture: Statistical Yearbook,* and *Fisheries: Yearly Statistics.*

Facts on File, 460 Park Avenue South, New York, New York 10016 (800) 443-8323; *The New Book of World Rankings.*

Food and Agricultural Organization of the United Nations (FAO) Via delle Terme di Caracalla, 00100 Rome, Italy (Telephone Number in U.S. (202) 653-2400); *The State of Food and Agriculture,* and *Yearbook of Fishery Statistics.*

National Technical Information Service, 5285 Port Royal Road, Springfield, Virginia 22161 (703) 487-4600; *Handbook of Economic Statistics.*

Organisation for Economic Co-operation and Development (OECD), 2 rue Andre-Pascal, 75 Paris 16, France (Telephone Number in U.S.

(202) 785-6323); *Foreign Trade by Commodities, Industrial Structure Statistics,* and *Review of Fisheries in OECD Member Countries.*

Statistical Office of the United Nations, Publishing Service, New York, New York 10017 (800) 253-9646; *Statistical Yearbook.*

UNITED KINGDOM - FLAX AND FLAX FIBRE PRODUCTION - See UNITED KINGDOM - TEXTILE INDUSTRY

UNITED KINGDOM - FLOUR PRODUCTION

Commodity Research Bureau, Incorporated, 75 Wall Street, New York, New York 10005 (212) 504-7754; *Commodity Year Book.*

European Community Information Service, 2100 M Street, NW, Washington, D.C. 20037 (202) 862-9500; *Basic Statistics of the Community.*

Statistical Office of the United Nations, Publishing Service, New York, New York 10017 (800) 253-9646; *Statistical Yearbook.*

UNITED KINGDOM - FOOD

European Community Information Service, 2100 M Street, NW, Washington, D.C. 20037 (202) 862-9500; *Basic Statistics of the Community.*

Food and Agricultural Organization of the United Nations (FAO) Via delle Terme di Caracalla, 00100 Rome, Italy (Telephone Number in U.S. (202) 653-2400); *Production Yearbook,* and *The State of Food and Agriculture.*

G.K. Hall and Company, 70 Lincoln Street, Boston, Massachusetts 02111 (617) 423-3990; *The World in Figures.*

Organisation for Economic Co-operation and Development (OECD), 2 rue Andre-Pascal, 75 Paris 16, France (Telephone Number in U.S. (202) 785-6323); *Foreign Trade by Commodities,* and *Main Economic Indicators - Historical Statistics.*

Statistical Office of the United Nations, Publishing Service, New York, New York 10017 (800) 253-9646; *Trade in Manufactures of Developing Countries.*

UNITED KINGDOM - FOOTWEAR - PRODUCTION INDEX

Organisation for Economic Co-operation and Development (OECD), 2 rue Andre-Pascal, 75 Paris 16, France (Telephone Number in U.S. (202) 785-6323); *Indicators of Industrial Activity.*

UNITED KINGDOM - FOREIGN AID

G.K. Hall and Company, 70 Lincoln Street, Boston, Massachusetts 02111 (617) 423-3990; *The World in Figures.*

National Technical Information Service, 5285 Port Royal Road, Springfield, Virginia 22161 (703) 487-4600; *Handbook of Economic Statistics.*

UNITED KINGDOM - FOREIGN DEBT

International Monetary Fund, 700 Nineteenth Street, NW, Washington, D.C. 20431 (202) 623-7000; *Government Finance Statistics Yearbook.*

Organisation for Economic Co-operation and Development (OECD), 2 rue Andre-Pascal, 75 Paris 16, France (Telephone Number in U.S. (202) 785-6323); *Economic Outlook.*

UNITED KINGDOM - FOREIGN INDEBTEDNESS

Organisation for Economic Co-operation and Development (OECD), 2 rue Andre-Pascal, 75 Paris 16, France (Telephone Number in U.S. (202) 785-6323); *Economic Outlook,* and *Financial Market Trends.*

UNITED KINGDOM - FOREIGN OFFICIAL RESERVES

European Community Information Service, 2100 M Street, NW, Washington, D.C. 20037 (202) 862-9500; *Money and Finance.*

UNITED KINGDOM - FOREIGN TRADE

Euromonitor Publications Limited, 87-88 Turnmill Street, London EC1M 5QU, England; *European Marketing Data and Statistics.*

European Community Information Service, 2100 M Street, NW, Washington, D.C. 20037 (202) 862-9500; *Basic Statistics of the Community, Energy Statistics Yearbook,* and *Foreign Trade of the People's Republic of China.*

Facts on File, 460 Park Avenue South, New York, New York 10016 (800) 443-8323; *The New Book of World Rankings.*

Food and Agricultural Organization of the United Nations (FAO) Via delle Terme di Caracalla, 00100 Rome, Italy (Telephone Number in U.S. (202) 653-2400); *The State of Food and Agriculture,* and *The State of Food and Agriculture.*

G.K. Hall and Company, 70 Lincoln Street, Boston, Massachusetts 02111 (617) 423-3990; *The World in Figures.*

International Iron and Steel Institute, 120, rue Colonel Bourg, B-1140, Belgium; *Steel Statistical Yearbook.*

International Monetary Fund, 700 Nineteenth Street, NW, Washington, D.C. 20431 (202) 623-7000; *International Financial Statistics.*

National Technical Information Service, 5285 Port Royal Road, Springfield, Virginia 22161 (703) 487-4600; *Handbook of Economic Statistics.*

Organisation for Economic Co-operation and Development (OECD), 2 rue Andre-Pascal, 75 Paris 16, France (Telephone Number in U.S. (202) 785-6323); *Economic Outlook, The Footwear, Raw Hides and Skins,* and *Leather Industry in OECD Countries, Foreign Trade by Commodities, Iron and Steel: Statistical Yearbook, Main Economic Indicators - Historical Statistics, Maritime Transport, Meat Balances in OECD Member Countries,* and *OECD Economic Surveys: United Kingdom.*

Statistical Office of the United Nations, Publishing Service, New York, New York 10017 (800) 253-9646; *International Trade Statistics Yearbook, Statistical Yearbook,* and *Trade in Manufactures of Developing Countries.*

The World Bank, 1818 H Street, NW, Washington, D.C. 20433 (202) 477-1234; *World Tables.*

World Bureau of Metal Statistics, 27-A High Street, Ware Hert SG12 9BA, England; *World Metal Statistics.*

UNITED KINGDOM - FORESTRY AND FOREST PRODUCTS

American Forest and Paper Association, 1250 Connecticut Avenue, NW, Washington, D.C. 20036 (202) 463-2455; *Wood Pulp and Fiber Statistics.*

Euromonitor Publications Limited, 87-88 Turnmill Street, London EC1M 5QU, England; *European Marketing Data and Statistics*.

European Community Information Service, 2100 M Street, NW, Washington, D.C. 20037 (202) 862-9500; *Agriculture: Statistical Yearbook, Basic Statistics of the Community*, and *Industrial Production: Quarterly Statistics*.

Facts on File, 460 Park Avenue South, New York, New York 10016 (800) 443-8323; *The New Book of World Rankings*.

Food and Agricultural Organization of the United Nations (FAO) Via delle Terme di Caracalla, 00100 Rome, Italy (Telephone Number in U.S. (202) 653-2400); *The State of Food and Agriculture*, and *Yearbook of Forest Products*.

G.K. Hall and Company, 70 Lincoln Street, Boston, Massachusetts 02111 (617) 423-3990; *The World in Figures*.

National Technical Information Service, 5285 Port Royal Road, Springfield, Virginia 22161 (703) 487-4600; *Handbook of Economic Statistics*.

Organisation for Economic Co-operation and Development (OECD), 2 rue Andre-Pascal, 75 Paris 16, France (Telephone Number in U.S. (202) 785-6323); *Foreign Trade by Commodities, Indicators of Industrial Activity, Industrial Structure Statistics*, and *The Pulp and Paper Industry*.

Statistical Office of the United Nations, Publishing Service, New York, New York 10017 (800) 253-9646; *Statistical Yearbook*.

United Nations Educational, Scientific and Cultural Organization (UNESCO), 7 Place de Fontenoy, F-75700 Paris, France (Telephone Number in U.S. (212) 963-5981); *Statistical Yearbook*.

UNITED KINGDOM - FRUIT PRODUCTION - See UNITED KINGDOM - CROPS

UNITED KINGDOM - FURNITURE AND WOOD PRODUCTS - EXPORTS AND IMPORTS

European Community Information Service, 2100 M Street, NW, Washington, D.C. 20037 (202) 862-9500; *Basic Statistics of the Community*.

Organisation for Economic Co-operation and Development (OECD), 2 rue Andre-Pascal, 75 Paris 16, France (Telephone Number in U.S. (202) 785-6323); *Foreign Trade by Commodities*, and *Industrial Structure Statistics*.

Statistical Office of the United Nations, Publishing Service, New York, New York 10017 (800) 253-9646; *Trade in Manufactures of Developing Countries*.

UNITED KINGDOM - GARLIC PRODUCTION - See UNITED KINGDOM - CROPS

UNITED KINGDOM - GAS AND GAS LIQUIDS PRODUCTION - See UNITED KINGDOM - MINING AND MINERAL PRODUCTS

UNITED KINGDOM - GENERAL INDUSTRIAL STATISTICS

European Community Information Service, 2100 M Street, NW, Washington, D.C. 20037 (202) 862-9500; *Basic Statistics of the Community*.

Statistical Office of the United Nations, Publishing Service, New York, New York 10017 (800) 253-9646; *Industrial Statistics Yearbook*.

UNITED KINGDOM - GENERAL MORTALITY

European Community Information Service, 2100 M Street, NW, Washington, D.C. 20037 (202) 862-9500; *Basic Statistics of the Community, Demographic Statistics*.

Statistical Office of the United Nations, Publishing Service, New York, New York 10017 (800) 253-9646; *Demographic Yearbook*.

World Health Organization, Office of Publications, Avenue Appia, CH-1211 Geneva 27, Switzerland (Telephone Number in U.S. (518) 436-9686); *World Health Statistics Annual*.

UNITED KINGDOM - GEOGRAPHIC DATA

European Community Information Service, 2100 M Street, NW, Washington, D.C. 20037 (202) 862-9500; *Basic Statistics of the Community*.

Facts on File, 460 Park Avenue South, New York, New York 10016 (800) 443-8323; *The New Book of World Rankings*.

UNITED KINGDOM - GLASS AND GLASS PRODUCTS - PRODUCTION INDEX

Organisation for Economic Co-operation and Development (OECD), 2 rue Andre-Pascal, 75 Paris 16, France (Telephone Number in U.S. (202) 785-6323); *Indicators of Industrial Activity*.

UNITED KINGDOM - GOATS - See UNITED KINGDOM - LIVESTOCK AND POULTRY

UNITED KINGDOM - GOLD HOLDINGS

Statistical Office of the United Nations, Publishing Service, New York, New York 10017 (800) 253-9646; *Statistical Yearbook*.

The World Bank, 1818 H Street, NW, Washington, D.C. 20433 (202) 477-1234; *World Tables*.

UNITED KINGDOM - GOLD PRODUCTION AND CONSUMPTION - See UNITED KINGDOM - MINING AND MINERAL PRODUCTS

UNITED KINGDOM - GOVERNMENT

European Community Information Service, 2100 M Street, NW, Washington, D.C. 20037 (202) 862-9500; *Basic Statistics of the Community*.

G.K. Hall and Company, 70 Lincoln Street, Boston, Massachusetts 02111 (617) 423-3990; *The World in Figures*.

UNITED KINGDOM - GOVERNMENT CONSUMPTION

European Community Information Service, 2100 M Street, NW, Washington, D.C. 20037 (202) 862-9500; *Basic Statistics of the Community*.

International Monetary Fund, 700 Nineteenth Street, NW, Washington, D.C. 20431 (202) 623-7000; *International Financial Statistics*.

UNITED KINGDOM - GOVERNMENT EXPENDITURES

European Community Information Service, 2100 M Street, NW, Washington, D.C. 20037 (202) 862-9500; *Basic Statistics of the Community*, and *Government Financing of Research and*

Development.

International Monetary Fund, 700 Nineteenth Street, NW, Washington, D.C. 20431 (202) 623-7000; *Government Finance Statistics Yearbook.*

Organisation for Economic Co-operation and Development (OECD), 2 rue Andre-Pascal, 75 Paris 16, France (Telephone Number in U.S. (202) 785-6323); *Economic Outlook.*

Times Books, 201 East 50th Street, New York, New York 10022 (212) 751-2600; *The Economist Book of Vital World Statistics.*

The World Bank, 1818 H Street, NW, Washington, D.C. 20433 (202) 477-1234; *World Tables.*

UNITED KINGDOM - GOVERNMENT FINANCES

European Community Information Service, 2100 M Street, NW, Washington, D.C. 20037 (202) 862-9500; *Basic Statistics of the Community, Government Financing of Research and Development,* and *Money and Finance.*

International Monetary Fund, 700 Nineteenth Street, NW, Washington, D.C. 20431 (202) 623-7000; *International Financial Statistics.*

Organisation for Economic Co-operation and Development (OECD), 2 rue Andre-Pascal, 75 Paris 16, France (Telephone Number in U.S. (202) 785-6323); *Economic Outlook.*

Statistical Office of the United Nations, Publishing Service, New York, New York 10017 (800) 253-9646; *Statistical Yearbook.*

UNITED KINGDOM - GOVERNMENT REVENUES

European Community Information Service, 2100 M Street, NW, Washington, D.C. 20037 (202) 862-9500; *Basic Statistics of the Community,* and *Government Financing of Research and Development.*

International Monetary Fund, 700 Nineteenth Street, NW, Washington, D.C. 20431 (202) 623-7000; *Government Finance Statistics Yearbook.*

Organisation for Economic Co-operation and Development (OECD), 2 rue Andre-Pascal, 75 Paris 16, France (Telephone Number in U.S. (202) 785-6323); *Economic Outlook,* and *Revenue Statistics of OECD Member Countries.*

Times Books, 201 East 50th Street, New York, New York 10022 (212) 751-2600; *The Economist Book of Vital World Statistics.*

The World Bank, 1818 H Street, NW, Washington, D.C. 20433 (202) 477-1234; *World Tables.*

UNITED KINGDOM - GRAIN PRODUCTION - See UNITED KINGDOM - CROPS

UNITED KINGDOM - GRANTS

International Monetary Fund, 700 Nineteenth Street, NW, Washington, D.C. 20431 (202) 623-7000; *Government Finance Statistics Yearbook.*

National Technical Information Service, 5285 Port Royal Road, Springfield, Virginia 22161 (703) 487-4600; *Handbook of Economic Statistics.*

Organisation for Economic Co-operation and Development (OECD), 2 rue Andre-Pascal, 75 Paris 16, France (Telephone Number in U.S. (202) 785-6323); *Geographical Distribution of Financial Flows to Developing Countries.*

UNITED KINGDOM - GREEN PEPPER AND CHILIE PRODUCTION - See UNITED KINGDOM - CROPS

UNITED KINGDOM - GROSS DOMESTIC PRODUCT

The Economist Intelligence Unit, 111 West 57th Street, New York, New York 10019 (800) 938-4685; *The World Market Atlas.*

European Community Information Service, 2100 M Street, NW, Washington, D.C. 20037 (202) 862-9500; *Basic Statistics of the Community, Eurostatistics: Data for Short-Term Economic Analysis, Government Financing of Research and Development, Iron and Steel: Statistical Yearbook,* and *Money and Finance.*

Facts on File, 460 Park Avenue South, New York, New York 10016 (800) 443-8323; *The New Book of World Rankings.*

G.K. Hall and Company, 70 Lincoln Street, Boston, Massachusetts 02111 (617) 423-3990; *The World in Figures.*

International Monetary Fund, 700 Nineteenth Street, NW, Washington, D.C. 20431 (202) 623-7000; *International Financial Statistics.*

National Technical Information Service, 5285 Port Royal Road, Springfield, Virginia 22161 (703) 487-4600; *Handbook of Economic Statistics.*

Organisation for Economic Co-operation and Development (OECD), 2 rue Andre-Pascal, 75 Paris 16, France (Telephone Number in U.S. (202) 785-6323); *Economic Outlook, Geographical Distribution of Financial Flows to Developing Countries,* and *Revenue Statistics of OECD Member Countries.*

Statistical Office of the United Nations, Publishing Service, New York, New York 10017 (800) 253-9646; *Statistical Yearbook.*

Times Books, 201 East 50th Street, New York, New York 10022 (212) 751-2600; *The Economist Book of Vital World Statistics.*

The World Bank, 1818 H Street, NW, Washington, D.C. 20433 (202) 477-1234; *World Tables.*

UNITED KINGDOM - GROSS INDUSTRIAL PRODUCT - GROWTH RATES

European Community Information Service, 2100 M Street, NW, Washington, D.C. 20037 (202) 862-9500; *Government Financing of Research and Development.*

UNITED KINGDOM - GROSS NATIONAL PRODUCT

European Community Information Service, 2100 M Street, NW, Washington, D.C. 20037 (202) 862-9500; *ACP: Basic Statistics,* and *Basic Statistics of the Community.*

National Technical Information Service, 5285 Port Royal Road, Springfield, Virginia 22161 (703) 487-4600; *Handbook of Economic Statistics.*

Organisation for Economic Co-operation and Development (OECD), 2 rue Andre-Pascal, 75 Paris 16, France (Telephone Number in U.S. (202) 785-6323); *Economic Outlook,* and *Geographical Distribution of Financial Flows to Developing Countries.*

U.S. Arms Control and Disarmament Agency, 320 Twenty-first Street, NW, Washington, D.C. 20451 (202) 647-8677; *World Military Expenditures and Arms Transfers*.

The World Bank, 1818 H Street, NW, Washington, D.C. 20433 (202) 477-1234; *World Tables*.

UNITED KINGDOM - GROUNDNUT PRODUCTION - See UNITED KINGDOM - CROPS

UNITED KINGDOM - HAY PRODUCTION - See UNITED KINGDOM - CROPS

UNITED KINGDOM - HAZELNUT PRODUCTION - See UNITED KINGDOM - CROPS

UNITED KINGDOM - HEALTH

European Community Information Service, 2100 M Street, NW, Washington, D.C. 20037 (202) 862-9500; *Basic Statistics of the Community*, and *Regions: Statistical Yearbook*.

Facts on File, 460 Park Avenue South, New York, New York 10016 (800) 443-8323; *The New Book of World Rankings*.

G.K. Hall and Company, 70 Lincoln Street, Boston, Massachusetts 02111 (617) 423-3990; *The World in Figures*.

Organisation for Economic Co-operation and Development (OECD), 2 rue Andre-Pascal, 75 Paris 16, France (Telephone Number in U.S. (202) 785-6323); *OECD Health Systems: Facts and Trends*.

Statistical Office of the United Nations, Publishing Service, New York, New York 10017 (800) 253-9646; *Statistical Yearbook*.

Times Books, 201 East 50th Street, New York, New York 10022 (212) 751-2600; *The Economist Book of Vital World Statistics*.

UNITED KINGDOM - HEALTH EXPENDITURES

International Monetary Fund, 700 Nineteenth Street, NW, Washington, D.C. 20431 (202) 623-7000; *Government Finance Statistics Yearbook*.

UNITED KINGDOM - HEMP FIBRE PRODUCTION - See UNITED KINGDOM - TEXTILE INDUSTRY

UNITED KINGDOM - HIDE PRODUCTION

Food and Agricultural Organization of the United Nations (FAO), Via delle Terme di Caracalla, 00100 Rome, Italy (Telephone Number in U.S. (202) 653-2400); *Production Yearbook*.

Organisation for Economic Co-operation and Development (OECD), 2 rue Andre-Pascal, 75 Paris 16, France (Telephone Number in U.S. (202) 785-6323); *The Footwear, Raw Hides and Skins, and Leather Industry in OECD Countries, Foreign Trade by Commodities*, and *Indicators of Industrial Activity*.

UNITED KINGDOM - HIGHWAYS

European Community Information Service, 2100 M Street, NW, Washington, D.C. 20037 (202) 862-9500; *Basic Statistics of the Community*, and *Transport Annual Statistics*.

G.K. Hall and Company, 70 Lincoln Street, Boston, Massachusetts 02111 (617) 423-3990; *The World in Figures*.

International Road Federation, 525 School Street, SW, Washington, D.C. 20024 (202) 554-2106; *World Road Statistics*.

Statistical Office of the United Nations, Publishing Service, New York, New York 10017 (800) 253-9646; *Annual Bulletin of Transport Statistics for Europe*.

UNITED KINGDOM - HOME FINANCE

Organisation for Economic Co-operation and Development (OECD), 2 rue Andre-Pascal, 75 Paris 16, France (Telephone Number in U.S. (202) 785-6323); *Main Economic Indicators - Historical Statistics*.

UNITED KINGDOM - HOPS PRODUCTION - See UNITED KINGDOM - CROPS

UNITED KINGDOM - HORSES - See UNITED KINGDOM - LIVESTOCK AND POULTRY

UNITED KINGDOM - HOURS OF WORK - See UNITED KINGDOM - EMPLOYMENT

UNITED KINGDOM - HOUSING AND HOUSING UNITS

European Community Information Service, 2100 M Street, NW, Washington, D.C. 20037 (202) 862-9500; *Basic Statistics of the Community, Labor Force Sample Survey*, and *Regions: Statistical Yearbook*.

Facts on File, 460 Park Avenue South, New York, New York 10016 (800) 443-8323; *The New Book of World Rankings*.

National Technical Information Service, 5285 Port Royal Road, Springfield, Virginia 22161 (703) 487-4600; *Handbook of Economic Statistics*.

UNITED KINGDOM - HOUSING CONSTRUCTION - See UNITED KINGDOM - CONSTRUCTION INDUSTRY

UNITED KINGDOM - HOUSING EXPENDITURES

European Community Information Service, 2100 M Street, NW, Washington, D.C. 20037 (202) 862-9500; *Basic Statistics of the Community*.

International Monetary Fund, 700 Nineteenth Street, NW, Washington, D.C. 20431 (202) 623-7000; *Government Finance Statistics Yearbook*.

UNITED KINGDOM - HYDROCHLORIC ACID PRODUCTION

European Community Information Service, 2100 M Street, NW, Washington, D.C. 20037 (202) 862-9500; *Basic Statistics of the Community*.

Statistical Office of the United Nations, Publishing Service, New York, New York 10017 (800) 253-9646; *Statistical Yearbook*.

UNITED KINGDOM - ILLITERATE POPULATION

The Economist Intelligence Unit, 111 West 57th Street, New York, New York 10019 (800) 938-4685; *The World Market Atlas*.

G.K. Hall and Company, 70 Lincoln Street, Boston, Massachusetts 02111 (617) 423-3990; *The World in Figures*.

UNITED KINGDOM - IMPORTS

American Automobile Manufacturers Association, 1401 H Street, NW, Suite 900, Washington, D.C. 20005 (202) 326-5500; *World Motor Vehicle Data.*

The Economist Intelligence Unit, 111 West 57th Street, New York, New York 10019 (800) 938-4685; *The World Market Atlas.*

European Community Information Service, 2100 M Street, NW, Washington, D.C. 20037 (202) 862-9500; *Basic Statistics of the Community, Energy: Monthly Statistics, Energy Statistics Yearbook, Eurostatistics: Data for Short-Term Economic Analysis, External Trade: Monthly Statistics, External Trade: Statistical Yearbook,* and *Fisheries: Yearly Statistics.*

Food and Agricultural Organization of the United Nations (FAO) Via delle Terme di Caracalla, 00100 Rome, Italy (Telephone Number in U.S. (202) 653-2400); *The State of Food and Agriculture.*

G.K. Hall and Company, 70 Lincoln Street, Boston, Massachusetts 02111 (617) 423-3990; *The World in Figures.*

International Iron and Steel Institute, 120, rue Colonel Bourg, B-1140, Belgium; *Steel Statistical Yearbook.*

International Lead and Zinc Study Group, Metro House, 58 St. James's Street, London SW1A 1LD England; *Lead and Zinc Statistics.*

International Monetary Fund, 700 Nineteenth Street, NW, Washington, D.C. 20431 (202) 623-7000; *Direction of Trade Statistics, Government Finance Statistics Yearbook,* and *International Financial Statistics.*

International Rubber Study Group, York House, Eighth Floor, Empire Way, Wembley, London HA9 0PA, England; *Rubber Statistical Bulletin.*

National Technical Information Service, 5285 Port Royal Road, Springfield, Virginia 22161 (703) 487-4600; *Handbook of Economic Statistics.*

Organisation for Economic Co-operation and Development (OECD), 2 rue Andre-Pascal, 75 Paris 16, France (Telephone Number in U.S. (202) 785-6323); *Economic Outlook, The Footwear, Raw Hides and Skins, and Leather Industry in OECD Countries, Industrial Structure Statistics, The Iron and Steel Industry, Milk, Milk Products, and Egg Balances in OECD Member Countries, The Pulp and Paper Industry, OECD Economic Surveys: United Kingdom,* and *Review of Fisheries in OECD Member Countries.*

Times Books, 201 East 50th Street, New York, New York 10022 (212) 751-2600; *The Economist Book of Vital World Statistics.*

The World Bank, 1818 H Street, NW, Washington, D.C. 20433 (202) 477-1234; *World Tables.*

UNITED KINGDOM - INCOME TAXES - See UNITED KINGDOM - TAXATION

UNITED KINGDOM - INDUSTRIAL METALS PRODUCTION - See UNITED KINGDOM - MINING AND MINERAL PRODUCTS

UNITED KINGDOM - INDUSTRY

European Community Information Service, 2100 M Street, NW, Washington, D.C. 20037 (202) 862-9500; *Basic Statistics of the Community, Employment and Unemployment, Eurostatistics: Data*

for Short-Term Economic Analysis, and *Labor Force Sample Survey.*

Facts on File, 460 Park Avenue South, New York, New York 10016 (800) 443-8323; *The New Book of World Rankings.*

G.K. Hall and Company, 70 Lincoln Street, Boston, Massachusetts 02111 (617) 423-3990; *The World in Figures.*

International Labour Office, I.L.O. Publications, CH-1211, Geneva 22, Switzerland; *Yearbook of Labour Statistics.*

National Technical Information Service, 5285 Port Royal Road, Springfield, Virginia 22161 (703) 487-4600; *Handbook of Economic Statistics.*

Organisation for Economic Co-operation and Development (OECD), 2 rue Andre-Pascal, 75 Paris 16, France (Telephone Number in U.S. (202) 785-6323); *Economic Outlook, Indicators of Industrial Activity, Industrial Structure Statistics, Main Economic Indicators - Historical Statistics,* and *OECD Environmental Data.*

Statistical Office of the United Nations, Publishing Service, New York, New York 10017 (800) 253-9646; *Statistical Yearbook.*

Times Books, 201 East 50th Street, New York, New York 10022 (212) 751-2600; *The Economist Book of Vital World Statistics.*
The World Bank, 1818 H Street, NW, Washington, D.C. 20433 (202) 477-1234; *World Tables.*

World Intellectual Property Organization, 34 Chemin des Colombettes, CH-1211 Geneva 20. Switzerland; *Industrial Property Statistics.*

UNITED KINGDOM - INFANT AND MATERNAL MORTALITY

European Community Information Service, 2100 M Street, NW, Washington, D.C. 20037 (202) 862-9500; *Basic Statistics of the Community,* and *Demographic Statistics.*

Statistical Office of the United Nations, Publishing Service, New York, New York 10017 (800) 253-9646; *Demographic Yearbook,* and *Statistical Yearbook.*

Times Books, 201 East 50th Street, New York, New York 10022 (212) 751-2600; *The Economist Book of Vital World Statistics.*

The World Bank, 1818 H Street, NW, Washington, D.C. 20433 (202) 477-1234; *World Tables.*

World Health Organization, Office of Publications, Avenue Appia, CH-1211 Geneva 27, Switzerland (Telephone Number in U.S. (518) 436-9686); *World Health Statistics Annual.*

UNITED KINGDOM - INFLATIONARY FACTORS

National Technical Information Service, 5285 Port Royal Road, Springfield, Virginia 22161 (703) 487-4600; *Handbook of Economic Statistics.*

UNITED KINGDOM - INTEREST RATES

National Technical Information Service, 5285 Port Royal Road, Springfield, Virginia 22161 (703) 487-4600; *Handbook of Economic Statistics.*

Organisation for Economic Co-operation and Development (OECD), 2 rue Andre-Pascal, 75 Paris 16, France (Telephone Number in U.S. (202) 785-6323); *Economic Outlook, Financial Market Trends, Main Economic Indicators - Historical Statistics, Money and Finance,* and

OECD Financial Statistics.

UNITED KINGDOM - INTERNAL TRADE

European Community Information Service, 2100 M Street, NW, Washington, D.C. 20037 (202) 862-9500; *Basic Statistics of the Community.*

Organisation for Economic Co-operation and Development (OECD), 2 rue Andre-Pascal, 75 Paris 16, France (Telephone Number in U.S. (202) 785-6323); *Main Economic Indicators - Historical Statistics.*

UNITED KINGDOM - INTERNATIONAL FINANCE

European Community Information Service, 2100 M Street, NW, Washington, D.C. 20037 (202) 862-9500; *Basic Statistics of the Community.*

Organisation for Economic Co-operation and Development (OECD), 2 rue Andre-Pascal, 75 Paris 16, France (Telephone Number in U.S. (202) 785-6323); *Economic Outlook,* and *Financial Market Trends.*

UNITED KINGDOM - INTERNATIONAL LIQUIDITY

International Monetary Fund, 700 Nineteenth Street, NW, Washington, D.C. 20431 (202) 623-7000; *International Financial Statistics.*

Organisation for Economic Co-operation and Development (OECD), 2 rue Andre-Pascal, 75 Paris 16, France (Telephone Number in U.S. (202) 785-6323); *Economic Outlook,* and *Financial Market Trends.*

UNITED KINGDOM - INTERNATIONAL RESERVES EXCLUDING GOLD

National Technical Information Service, 5285 Port Royal Road, Springfield, Virginia 22161 (703) 487-4600; *Handbook of Economic Statistics.*

Statistical Office of the United Nations, Publishing Service, New York, New York 10017 (800) 253-9646; *Statistical Yearbook.*

The World Bank, 1818 H Street, NW, Washington, D.C. 20433 (202) 477-1234; *World Tables.*

UNITED KINGDOM - INTERNATIONAL STATISTICS

Organisation for Economic Co-operation and Development (OECD), 2 rue Andre-Pascal, 75 Paris 16, France (Telephone Number in U.S. (202) 785-6323); *Financial Market Trends,* and *Tourism Policy and International Tourism in OECD Member Countries.*

UNITED KINGDOM - INVESTMENTS

International Monetary Fund, 700 Nineteenth Street, NW, Washington, D.C. 20431 (202) 623-7000; *International Financial Statistics.*

Organisation for Economic Co-operation and Development (OECD), 2 rue Andre-Pascal, 75 Paris 16, France (Telephone Number in U.S. (202) 785-6323); *Economic Outlook, Financial Market Trends, Industrial Structure Statistics, The Iron and Steel Industry,* and *Textile Industry in OECD Countries.*

UNITED KINGDOM - IRON ORE - See UNITED KINGDOM - MINING AND MINERAL PRODUCTS

UNITED KINGDOM - JUTE PRODUCTION - See UNITED KINGDOM - CROPS

UNITED KINGDOM - LABOR FORCE

European Community Information Service, 2100 M Street, NW, Washington, D.C. 20037 (202) 862-9500; *Basic Statistics of the Community, Labor Force Sample Survey,* and *Regions: Statistical Yearbook.*

Facts on File, 460 Park Avenue South, New York, New York 10016 (800) 443-8323; *The New Book of World Rankings.*

Food and Agricultural Organization of the United Nations (FAO) Via delle Terme di Caracalla, 00100 Rome, Italy (Telephone Number in U.S. (202) 653-2400); *The State of Food and Agriculture.*

G.K. Hall and Company, 70 Lincoln Street, Boston, Massachusetts 02111 (617) 423-3990; *The World in Figures.*

National Technical Information Service, 5285 Port Royal Road, Springfield, Virginia 22161 (703) 487-4600; *Handbook of Economic Statistics.*

Organisation for Economic Co-operation and Development (OECD), 2 rue Andre-Pascal, 75 Paris 16, France (Telephone Number in U.S. (202) 785-6323); *Economic Outlook, The Iron and Steel Industry, Main Economic Indicators - Historical Statistics, Maritime Transport, OECD Employment Outlook, OECD Economic Surveys: United Kingdom,* and *Textile Industry in OECD Countries.*

Times Books, 201 East 50th Street, New York, New York 10022 (212) 751-2600; *The Economist Book of Vital World Statistics.*

The World Bank, 1818 H Street, NW, Washington, D.C. 20433 (202) 477-1234; *World Tables.*

UNITED KINGDOM - LABOR PRODUCTIVITY

International Labour Office, I.L.O. Publications, CH-1211, Geneva 22, Switzerland; *Yearbook of Labour Statistics.*

Organisation for Economic Co-operation and Development (OECD), 2 rue Andre-Pascal, 75 Paris 16, France (Telephone Number in U.S. (202) 785-6323); *Economic Outlook,* and *OECD Employment Outlook.*

UNITED KINGDOM - LAND USE

Euromonitor Publications Limited, 87-88 Turnmill Street, London EC1M 5QU, England; *European Marketing Data and Statistics.*

European Community Information Service, 2100 M Street, NW, Washington, D.C. 20037 (202) 862-9500; *Agriculture: Statistical Yearbook, Basic Statistics of the Community, Crop Production: Quarterly Statistics,* and *Regions: Statistical Yearbook.*

Food and Agricultural Organization of the United Nations (FAO), Via delle Terme di Caracalla, 00100 Rome, Italy (Telephone Number in U.S. (202) 653-2400); *Production Yearbook.*

G.K. Hall and Company, 70 Lincoln Street, Boston, Massachusetts 02111 (617) 423-3990; *The World in Figures.*

UNITED KINGDOM - LEAD AND LEAD ORE PRODUCTION AND CONSUMPTION - See UNITED KINGDOM - MINING AND MINERAL PRODUCTS

UNITED KINGDOM - LEATHER - PRODUCTION INDEX

Organisation for Economic Co-operation and Development (OECD), 2 rue Andre-Pascal, 75 Paris 16, France (Telephone Number in U.S. (202) 785-6323); *Indicators of Industrial Activity.*

UNITED KINGDOM - LEATHER AND FOOTWEAR - EXPORTS AND IMPORTS

European Community Information Service, 2100 M Street, NW, Washington, D.C. 20037 (202) 862-9500; *Basic Statistics of the Community.*

Organisation for Economic Co-operation and Development (OECD), 2 rue Andre-Pascal, 75 Paris 16, France (Telephone Number in U.S. (202) 785-6323); *The Footwear, Raw Hides and Skins, and Leather Industry in OECD Countries.*

Statistical Office of the United Nations, Publishing Service, New York, New York 10017 (800) 253-9646; *Trade in Manufactures of Developing Countries.*

UNITED KINGDOM - LIBRARIES

Euromonitor Publications Limited, 87-88 Turnmill Street, London EC1M 5QU, England; *European Marketing Data and Statistics.*

Facts on File, 460 Park Avenue South, New York, New York 10016 (800) 443-8323; *The New Book of World Rankings.*

United Nations Educational, Scientific and Cultural Organization (UNESCO), 7 Place de Fontenoy, F-75700 Paris, France (Telephone Number in U.S. (212) 963-5981); *Statistical Yearbook.*

UNITED KINGDOM - LIGNITE PRODUCTION - See UNITED KINGDOM - MINING AND MINERAL PRODUCTS

UNITED KINGDOM - LIVESTOCK AND POULTRY

Commodity Research Bureau, Incorporated, 75 Wall Street, New York, New York 10005 (212) 504-7754; *Commodity Year Book.*

Euromonitor Publications Limited, 87-88 Turnmill Street, London EC1M 5QU, England; *European Marketing Data and Statistics.*

European Community Information Service, 2100 M Street, NW, Washington, D.C. 20037 (202) 862-9500; *Agriculture: Statistical Yearbook, Basic Statistics of the Community, Eurostatistics: Data for Short-Term Economic Analysis*, and *Regions: Statistical Yearbook.*

Facts on File, 460 Park Avenue South, New York, New York 10016 (800) 443-8323; *The New Book of World Rankings.*

Food and Agricultural Organization of the United Nations (FAO), Via delle Terme di Caracalla, 00100 Rome, Italy (Telephone Number in U.S. (202) 653-2400); *Production Yearbook,* and *The State of Food and Agriculture.*

G.K. Hall and Company, 70 Lincoln Street, Boston, Massachusetts 02111 (617) 423-3990; *The World in Figures.*

National Technical Information Service, 5285 Port Royal Road, Springfield, Virginia 22161 (703) 487-4600; *Handbook of Economic Statistics.*

Organisation for Economic Co-operation and Development (OECD), 2 rue Andre-Pascal, 75 Paris 16, France (Telephone Number in U.S. (202) 785-6323); *Economic Accounts for Agriculture,* and *Meat Balances in OECD Member Countries.*

Statistical Office of the United Nations, Publishing Service, New York, New York 10017 (800) 253-9646; *Statistical Yearbook.*

UNITED KINGDOM - LIVING LEVELS

G.K. Hall and Company, 70 Lincoln Street, Boston, Massachusetts 02111 (617) 423-3990; *The World in Figures.*

Organisation for Economic Co-operation and Development (OECD), 2 rue Andre-Pascal, 75 Paris 16, France (Telephone Number in U.S. (202) 785-6323); *Economic Outlook.*

Times Books, 201 East 50th Street, New York, New York 10022 (212) 751-2600; *The Economist Book of Vital World Statistics.*

UNITED KINGDOM - MACHINERY - PRODUCTION INDEX

Organisation for Economic Co-operation and Development (OECD), 2 rue Andre-Pascal, 75 Paris 16, France (Telephone Number in U.S. (202) 785-6323); *Indicators of Industrial Activity.*

UNITED KINGDOM - MAGNESIUM PRODUCTION AND CONSUMPTION - See UNITED KINGDOM - MINING AND MINERAL PRODUCTS

UNITED KINGDOM - MAIL - NUMBER OF PIECES SENT OR RECEIVED

European Community Information Service, 2100 M Street, NW, Washington, D.C. 20037 (202) 862-9500; *Transport Annual Statistics.*

Statistical Office of the United Nations, Publishing Service, New York, New York 10017 (800) 253-9646; *Statistical Yearbook.*

UNITED KINGDOM - MAIN ECONOMIC INDICATORS - See UNITED KINGDOM - ECONOMY

UNITED KINGDOM - MANGANESE PRODUCTION AND CONSUMPTION - See UNITED KINGDOM - MINING AND MINERAL PRODUCTS

UNITED KINGDOM - MANUFACTURING

American Automobile Manufacturers Association, 1401 H Street, NW, Suite 900, Washington, D.C. 20005 (202) 326-5500; *World Motor Vehicle Data.*

European Community Information Service, 2100 M Street, NW, Washington, D.C. 20037 (202) 862-9500; *Basic Statistics of the Community, Eurostatistics: Data for Short-Term Economic Analysis,* and *Industrial Production: Quarterly Statistics.*

Facts on File, 460 Park Avenue South, New York, New York 10016 (800) 443-8323; *The New Book of World Rankings.*

G.K. Hall and Company, 70 Lincoln Street, Boston, Massachusetts 02111 (617) 423-3990; *The World in Figures.*

Organisation for Economic Co-operation and Development (OECD), 2 rue Andre-Pascal, 75 Paris 16, France (Telephone Number in U.S. (202) 785-6323); *Indicators of Industrial Activity, Industrial Structure Statistics,* and *OECD Economic Surveys: United Kingdom.*

Statistical Office of the United Nations, Publishing Service, New York, New York 10017 (800) 253-9646; *Statistical Yearbook.*

Times Books, 201 East 50th Street, New York, New York 10022 (212) 751-2600; *The Economist Book of Vital World Statistics.*

The World Bank, 1818 H Street, NW, Washington, D.C. 20433 (202) 477-1234; *World Tables.*

UNITED KINGDOM - MARRIAGE RATES

European Community Information Service, 2100 M Street, NW, Washington, D.C. 20037 (202) 862-9500; *Basic Statistics of the Community.*

Facts on File, 460 Park Avenue South, New York, New York 10016 (800) 443-8323; *The New Book of World Rankings.*

Statistical Office of the United Nations, Publishing Service, New York, New York 10017 (800) 253-9646; *Demographic Yearbook,* and *Statistical Yearbook.*

UNITED KINGDOM - MEAT PRODUCTION - See UNITED KINGDOM - LIVESTOCK AND POULTRY

UNITED KINGDOM - MERCHANT SHIPPING

European Community Information Service, 2100 M Street, NW, Washington, D.C. 20037 (202) 862-9500; *Basic Statistics of the Community, Fisheries: Yearly Statistics, Regions: Statistical Yearbook,* and *Transport Annual Statistics.*

G.K. Hall and Company, 70 Lincoln Street, Boston, Massachusetts 02111 (617) 423-3990; *The World in Figures.*

National Technical Information Service, 5285 Port Royal Road, Springfield, Virginia 22161 (703) 487-4600; *Handbook of Economic Statistics.*

Organisation for Economic Co-operation and Development (OECD), 2 rue Andre-Pascal, 75 Paris 16, France (Telephone Number in U.S. (202) 785-6323); *Maritime Transport.*

Statistical Office of the United Nations, Publishing Service, New York, New York 10017 (800) 253-9646; *Annual Bulletin of Transport Statistics for Europe,* and *Statistical Yearbook.*

Times Books, 201 East 50th Street, New York, New York 10022 (212) 751-2600; *The Economist Book of Vital World Statistics.*

U.S. Department of Transportation, Maritime Administration, 400 Seventh Street, SW, Washington, D.C. 20590 (202) 366-5807; *A Statistical Analysis of the World's Merchant Fleets.*

UNITED KINGDOM - MERCURY PRODUCTION AND CONSUMPTION - See UNITED KINGDOM - MINING AND MINERAL PRODUCTS

UNITED KINGDOM - MILITARY

G.K. Hall and Company, 70 Lincoln Street, Boston, Massachusetts 02111 (617) 423-3990; *The World in Figures.*

The International Institute for Strategic Studies, 23 Tavistock Street, London WC2E 7NQ, England; *The Military Balance.*

U.S. Arms Control and Disarmament Agency, 320 Twenty-first Street, NW, Washington, D.C. 20451 (202) 647-8677; *World Military Expenditures and Arms Transfers.*

UNITED KINGDOM - MILK PRODUCTION - See UNITED KINGDOM - DAIRY PRODUCTS

UNITED KINGDOM - MILLET PRODUCTION - See UNITED KINGDOM - CROPS

UNITED KINGDOM - MINING AND MINERAL PRODUCTS

Commodity Research Bureau, Incorporated, 75 Wall Street, New York, New York 10005 (212) 504-7754; *Commodity Year Book.*

European Community Information Service, 2100 M Street, NW, Washington, D.C. 20037 (202) 862-9500; *ACP: Basic Statistics, Basic Statistics of the Community, Energy: Monthly Statistics, Energy Statistics Yearbook, Eurostatistics: Data for Short-Term Economic Analysis, Industrial Production: Quarterly Statistics, Iron and Steel: Statistical Yearbook, Labor Force Sample Survey,* and *Regions: Statistical Yearbook.*

Facts on File, 460 Park Avenue South, New York, New York 10016 (800) 443-8323; *The New Book of World Rankings.*

G.K. Hall and Company, 70 Lincoln Street, Boston, Massachusetts 02111 (617) 423-3990; *The World in Figures.*

International Iron and Steel Institute, 120, rue Colonel Bourg, B-1140, Belgium; *Steel Statistical Yearbook.*

International Lead and Zinc Study Group, Metro House, 58 St. James's Street, London SW1A 1LD England; *Lead and Zinc Statistics.*

International Monetary Fund, 700 Nineteenth Street, NW, Washington, D.C. 20431 (202) 623-7000; *International Financial Statistics.*

National Technical Information Service, 5285 Port Royal Road, Springfield, Virginia 22161 (703) 487-4600; *Handbook of Economic Statistics.*

Organisation for Economic Co-operation and Development (OECD), 2 rue Andre-Pascal, 75 Paris 16, France (Telephone Number in U.S. (202) 785-6323); *Coal Information, Energy Statistics of OECD Countries, Foreign Trade by Commodities, Indicators of Industrial Activity, Industrial Structure Statistics, The Iron and Steel Industry,* and *The Non-Ferrous Metals Industry.*

Penn Well Publishing Company, 1421 South Sheridan Road, P.O. Box 1260, Tulsa, Oklahoma 74101 (800) 752-9764; *International Energy Statistics Sourcebook.*

Statistical Office of the United Nations, Publishing Service, New York, New York 10017 (800) 253-9646; *Statistical Yearbook.*

World Bureau of Metal Statistics, 27-A High Street, Ware Hert SG12 9BA, England; *World Metal Statistics.*

UNITED KINGDOM - MOLASSES PRODUCTION - See UNITED KINGDOM - CROPS

UNITED KINGDOM - MOLYBDENUM AND MOLYBDENUM ORE PRODUCTION AND CONSUMPTION - See UNITED KINGDOM - MINING AND MINERAL PRODUCTS

UNITED KINGDOM - MONEY AND CREDIT

Organisation for Economic Cooperation and Development (OECD), 2 rue Andre-Pascal, 75 Paris 16, France (Telephone Number in U.S. (202) 785-6323); *OECD Economic Surveys: United Kingdom.*

UNITED KINGDOM - MONEY EXCHANGE RATE

European Community Information Service, 2100 M Street, NW, Washington, D.C. 20037 (202) 862-9500; *Basic Statistics of the Community.*

International Monetary Fund, 700 Nineteenth Street, NW, Washington, D.C. 20431 (202) 623-7000; *International Financial Statistics*.

Organisation for Economic Co-operation and Development (OECD), 2 rue Andre-Pascal, 75 Paris 16, France (Telephone Number in U.S. (202) 785-6323); *Economic Outlook, Financial Market Trends*, and *Tourism Policy and International Tourism in OECD Member Countries*.

Statistical Office of the United Nations, Publishing Service, New York, New York 10017 (800) 253-9646; *Statistical Yearbook*.

UNITED KINGDOM - MONEY RATES - MARKET

European Community Information Service, 2100 M Street, NW, Washington, D.C. 20037 (202) 862-9500; *Basic Statistics of the Community*.

Organisation for Economic Co-operation and Development (OECD), 2 rue Andre-Pascal, 75 Paris 16, France (Telephone Number in U.S. (202) 785-6323); *Economic Outlook*, and *Financial Market Trends*.

Statistical Office of the United Nations, Publishing Service, New York, New York 10017 (800) 253-9646; *Statistical Yearbook*.

UNITED KINGDOM - MONEY RESERVES

European Community Information Service, 2100 M Street, NW, Washington, D.C. 20037 (202) 862-9500; *Basic Statistics of the Community*.

Organisation for Economic Co-operation and Development (OECD), 2 rue Andre-Pascal, 75 Paris 16, France (Telephone Number in U.S. (202) 785-6323); *Economic Outlook*, and *Financial Market Trends*.

UNITED KINGDOM - MONEY SUPPLY

European Community Information Service, 2100 M Street, NW, Washington, D.C. 20037 (202) 862-9500; *Basic Statistics of the Community, Eurostatistics: Data for Short-Term Economic Analysis*, and *Money and Finance*.

G.K. Hall and Company, 70 Lincoln Street, Boston, Massachusetts 02111 (617) 423-3990; *The World in Figures*.

International Monetary Fund, 700 Nineteenth Street, NW, Washington, D.C. 20431 (202) 623-7000; *International Financial Statistics*.

Organisation for Economic Co-operation and Development (OECD), 2 rue Andre-Pascal, 75 Paris 16, France (Telephone Number in U.S. (202) 785-6323); *Economic Outlook*.

Statistical Office of the United Nations, Publishing Service, New York, New York 10017 (800) 253-9646; *Statistical Yearbook*.

The World Bank, 1818 H Street, NW, Washington, D.C. 20433 (202) 477-1234; *World Tables*.

UNITED KINGDOM - MOTION PICTURES

Statistical Office of the United Nations, Publishing Service, New York, New York 10017 (800) 253-9646; *Statistical Yearbook*.

United Nations Educational, Scientific and Cultural Organization (UNESCO), 7 Place de Fontenoy, F-75700 Paris, France (Telephone Number in U.S. (212) 963-5981); *Statistical Yearbook*.

UNITED KINGDOM - MOTOR VEHICLE PRODUCTION

American Automobile Manufacturers Association, 1401 H Street, NW, Suite 900, Washington, D.C. 20005 (202) 326-5500; *World Motor Vehicle Data*.

European Community Information Service, 2100 M Street, NW, Washington, D.C. 20037 (202) 862-9500; *Basic Statistics of the Community*, and *Eurostatistics: Data for Short-Term Economic Analysis*.

National Technical Information Service, 5285 Port Royal Road, Springfield, Virginia 22161 (703) 487-4600; *Handbook of Economic Statistics*.

Organisation for Economic Co-operation and Development (OECD), 2 rue Andre-Pascal, 75 Paris 16, France (Telephone Number in U.S. (202) 785-6323); *Foreign Trade by Commodities*.

Statistical Office of the United Nations, Publishing Service, New York, New York 10017 (800) 253-9646; *Statistical Yearbook*.

UNITED KINGDOM - MOTOR VEHICLE TAXES - See UNITED KINGDOM - TAXATION

UNITED KINGDOM - MOTOR VEHICLES IN USE

American Automobile Manufacturers Association, 1401 H Street, NW, Suite 900, Washington, D.C. 20005 (202) 326-5500; *World Motor Vehicle Data*.

European Community Information Service, 2100 M Street, NW, Washington, D.C. 20037 (202) 862-9500; *Basic Statistics of the Community*, and *Transport Annual Statistics*.

G.K. Hall and Company, 70 Lincoln Street, Boston, Massachusetts 02111 (617) 423-3990; *The World in Figures*.

International Road Federation, 525 School Street, SW, Washington, D.C. 20024 (202) 554-2106; *World Road Statistics*.

Statistical Office of the United Nations, Publishing Service, New York, New York 10017 (800) 253-9646; *Statistical Yearbook*.

Times Books, 201 East 50th Street, New York, New York 10022 (212) 751-2600; *The Economist Book of Vital World Statistics*.

UNITED KINGDOM - MULES - See UNITED KINGDOM - LIVESTOCK AND POULTRY

UNITED KINGDOM - MUSEUMS

Euromonitor Publications Limited, 87-88 Turnmill Street, London EC1M 5QU, England; *European Marketing Data and Statistics*.

Facts on File, 460 Park Avenue South, New York, New York 10016 (800) 443-8323; *The New Book of World Rankings*.

UNITED KINGDOM - NATALITY - See UNITED KINGDOM - BIRTH RATE

UNITED KINGDOM - NATIONAL ACCOUNTS

European Community Information Service, 2100 M Street, NW, Washington, D.C. 20037 (202) 862-9500; *Basic Statistics of the Community*, and *Eurostatistics. Data for Short-Term Economic Analysis*.

International Monetary Fund, 700 Nineteenth Street, NW, Washington, D.C. 20431 (202) 623-7000; *International Financial Statistics*.

Organisation for Economic Co-operation and Development (OECD), 2 rue Andre-Pascal, 75 Paris 16, France (Telephone Number in U.S. (202) 785-6323); *Economic Outlook*.

Statistical Office of the United Nations, Publishing Service, New York, New York 10017 (800) 253-9646; *National Accounts Statistics*, and *Statistical Yearbook*.

UNITED KINGDOM - NATIONAL INCOME

Facts on File, 460 Park Avenue South, New York, New York 10016 (800) 443-8323; *The New Book of World Rankings*.

G.K. Hall and Company, 70 Lincoln Street, Boston, Massachusetts 02111 (617) 423-3990; *The World in Figures*.

Organisation for Economic Co-operation and Development (OECD), 2 rue Andre-Pascal, 75 Paris 16, France (Telephone Number in U.S. (202) 785-6323); *Economic Outlook*.

Statistical Office of the United Nations, Publishing Service, New York, New York 10017 (800) 253-9646; *Statistical Yearbook*.

UNITED KINGDOM - NATIONAL PRODUCT

European Community Information Service, 2100 M Street, NW, Washington, D.C. 20037 (202) 862-9500; *Basic Statistics of the Community*.

Facts on File, 460 Park Avenue South, New York, New York 10016 (800) 443-8323; *The New Book of World Rankings*.

Organisation for Economic Co-operation and Development (OECD), 2 rue Andre-Pascal, 75 Paris 16, France (Telephone Number in U.S. (202) 785-6323); *Economic Outlook*, and *Main Economic Indicators - Historical Statistics*.

Statistical Office of the United Nations, Publishing Service, New York, New York 10017 (800) 253-9646; *Statistical Yearbook*.

UNITED KINGDOM - NATURAL GAS PRODUCTION - See UNITED KINGDOM - MINING AND MINERAL PRODUCTS

UNITED KINGDOM - NEWSPAPER PRODUCTION - See UNITED KINGDOM - FORESTRY AND FOREST PRODUCTS

UNITED KINGDOM - NEWSPRINT - See UNITED KINGDOM - FORESTRY AND FOREST PRODUCTS

UNITED KINGDOM - NICKEL AND NICKEL ORE PRODUCTION AND CONSUMPTION - See UNITED KINGDOM - MINING AND MINERAL PRODUCTS

UNITED KINGDOM - NITRIC ACID PRODUCTION - See UNITED KINGDOM - MINING AND MINERAL PRODUCTS

UNITED KINGDOM - OATS PRODUCTION - See UNITED KINGDOM - CROPS

UNITED KINGDOM - OCCUPATIONS - See UNITED KINGDOM - LABOR FORCE

UNITED KINGDOM - OIL PRODUCING CROPS

European Community Information Service, 2100 M Street, NW, Washington, D.C. 20037 (202) 862-9500; *Basic Statistics of the Community*.

Organisation for Economic Co-operation and Development (OECD), 2 rue Andre-Pascal, 75 Paris 16, France (Telephone Number in U.S. (202) 785-6323); *Foreign Trade by Commodities*.

UNITED KINGDOM - ONION PRODUCTION - See UNITED KINGDOM - CROPS

UNITED KINGDOM - PALM KERNEL PRODUCTION - See UNITED KINGDOM - CROPS

UNITED KINGDOM - PAPER - See UNITED KINGDOM - FORESTRY AND FOREST PRODUCTS

UNITED KINGDOM - PATENTS

Statistical Office of the United Nations, Publishing Service, New York, New York 10017 (800) 253-9646; *Statistical Yearbook*.

World Intellectual Property Organization, 34 Chemin des Colombettes, CH-1211 Geneva 20. Switzerland; *Industrial Property Statistics*.

UNITED KINGDOM - PEANUT PRODUCTION - See UNITED KINGDOM - CROPS

UNITED KINGDOM - PEPPER PRODUCTION - See UNITED KINGDOM - CROPS

UNITED KINGDOM - PERIODICALS

United Nations Educational, Scientific and Cultural Organization (UNESCO), 7 Place de Fontenoy, F-75700 Paris, France (Telephone Number in U.S. (212) 963-5981); *Statistical Yearbook*.

UNITED KINGDOM - PESTICIDE USE

Food and Agricultural Organization of the United Nations (FAO) Via delle Terme di Caracalla, 00100 Rome, Italy (Telephone Number in U.S. (202) 653-2400); *The State of Food and Agriculture*.

UNITED KINGDOM - PETROLEUM INDUSTRY

Euromonitor Publications Limited, 87-88 Turnmill Street, London EC1M 5QU, England; *European Marketing Data and Statistics*.

European Community Information Service, 2100 M Street, NW, Washington, D.C. 20037 (202) 862-9500; *ACP: Basic Statistics, Basic Statistics of the Community*, and *Energy Statistics Yearbook*.

Facts on File, 460 Park Avenue South, New York, New York 10016 (800) 443-8323; *The New Book of World Rankings*.

Food and Agricultural Organization of the United Nations (FAO) Via delle Terme di Caracalla, 00100 Rome, Italy (Telephone Number in U.S. (202) 653-2400); *The State of Food and Agriculture*.

G.K. Hall and Company, 70 Lincoln Street, Boston, Massachusetts 02111 (617) 423-3990; *The World in Figures*.

National Technical Information Service, 5285 Port Royal Road, Springfield, Virginia 22161 (703) 487-4600; *Handbook of Economic Statistics*.

Organisation for Economic Co-operation and Development (OECD), 2 rue Andre-Pascal, 75 Paris 16, France (Telephone Number in U.S. (202) 785-6323); *Energy Statistics of OECD Countries, Foreign Trade by Commodities, Indicators of Industrial Activity*, and *Oil and Gas Information*.

Penn Well Publishing Company, 1421 South Sheridan Road, P.O. Box 1260, Tulsa, Oklahoma 74101 (800) 752-9764; *International Energy Statistics Sourcebook*.

Statistical Office of the United Nations, Publishing Service, New York, New York 10017 (800) 253-9646; *Statistical Yearbook*.

UNITED KINGDOM - PHOSPHATE ROCK PRODUCTION - See UNITED KINGDOM - MINING AND MINERAL PRODUCTS

UNITED KINGDOM - PHOSPHATES PRODUCTION - See UNITED KINGDOM - MINING AND MINERAL PRODUCTS

UNITED KINGDOM - PIG-IRON AND FERRO-ALLOY PRODUCTION - See UNITED KINGDOM - MINING AND MINERAL PRODUCTS

UNITED KINGDOM - PIGS - See UNITED KINGDOM - LIVESTOCK AND POULTRY

UNITED KINGDOM - PIPELINES FOR OIL AND PETROLEUM PRODUCTS

European Community Information Service, 2100 M Street, NW, Washington, D.C. 20037 (202) 862-9500; *Transport Annual Statistics*.

National Technical Information Service, 5285 Port Royal Road, Springfield, Virginia 22161 (703) 487-4600; *Handbook of Economic Statistics*.

Statistical Office of the United Nations, Publishing Service, New York, New York 10017 (800) 253-9646; *Annual Bulletin of Transport Statistics for Europe*.

UNITED KINGDOM - PLASTIC AND RESIN PRODUCTION

Commodity Research Bureau, Incorporated, 75 Wall Street, New York, New York 10005 (212) 504-7754; *Commodity Year Book*.

European Community Information Service, 2100 M Street, NW, Washington, D.C. 20037 (202) 862-9500; *Basic Statistics of the Community*.

Organisation for Economic Co-operation and Development (OECD), 2 rue Andre-Pascal, 75 Paris 16, France (Telephone Number in U.S. (202) 785-6323); *Foreign Trade by Commodities*.

Statistical Office of the United Nations, Publishing Service, New York, New York 10017 (800) 253-9646; *Statistical Yearbook*.

UNITED KINGDOM - PLATINUM PRODUCTION - See UNITED KINGDOM - MINING AND MINERAL PRODUCTS

UNITED KINGDOM - POPULATION

The Economist Intelligence Unit, 111 West 57th Street, New York, New York 10019 (800) 938-4685; *The World Market Atlas*.

Euromonitor Publications Limited, 87-88 Turnmill Street, London EC1M 5QU, England; *European Marketing Data and Statistics*.

European Community Information Service, 2100 M Street, NW, Washington, D.C. 20037 (202) 862-9500; *ACP: Basic Statistics, Basic Statistics of the Community, Demographic Statistics, Employment and Unemployment, Fisheries: Yearly Statistics, Iron and Steel: Statistical Yearbook, Labor Force Sample Survey*, and *Regions: Statistical Yearbook*.

Facts on File, 460 Park Avenue South, New York, New York 10016 (800) 443-8323; *The New Book of World Rankings*.

Food and Agricultural Organization of the United Nations (FAO), Via delle Terme di Caracalla, 00100 Rome, Italy (Telephone Number in U.S. (202) 653-2400); *Production Yearbook*.

G.K. Hall and Company, 70 Lincoln Street, Boston, Massachusetts 02111 (617) 423-3990; *The World in Figures*.

International Labour Office, I.L.O. Publications, CH-1211, Geneva 22, Switzerland; *Yearbook of Labour Statistics*.

National Technical Information Service, 5285 Port Royal Road, Springfield, Virginia 22161 (703) 487-4600; *Handbook of Economic Statistics*.

Statistical Office of the United Nations, Publishing Service, New York, New York 10017 (800) 253-9646; *Demographic Yearbook*, and *Statistical Yearbook*.

Times Books, 201 East 50th Street, New York, New York 10022 (212) 751-2600; *The Economist Book of Vital World Statistics*.

United Nations Educational, Scientific and Cultural Organization (UNESCO), 7 Place de Fontenoy, F-75700 Paris, France (Telephone Number in U.S. (212) 983-5981); *Statistical Yearbook*.

U.S. Arms Control and Disarmament Agency, 320 Twenty-first Street, NW, Washington, D.C. 20451 (202) 647-8677; *World Military Expenditures and Arms Transfers*.

World Health Organization, Office of Publications, Avenue Appia, CH-1211 Geneva 27, Switzerland (Telephone Number in U.S. (518) 436-9686); *World Health Statistics Annual*.

UNITED KINGDOM - POST OFFICES

Facts on File, 460 Park Avenue South, New York, New York 10016 (800) 443-8323; *The New Book of World Rankings*.

UNITED KINGDOM - POTATO PRODUCTION - See UNITED KINGDOM - CROPS

UNITED KINGDOM - POWER PRODUCTION INDUSTRY

European Community Information Service, 2100 M Street, NW, Washington, D.C. 20037 (202) 862-9500; *Basic Statistics of the Community*.

Statistical Office of the United Nations, Publishing Service, New York, New York 10017 (800) 253-9646; *Statistical Yearbook*.

UNITED KINGDOM - PRICES

European Community Information Service, 2100 M Street, NW, Washington, D.C. 20037 (202) 862-9500; *Basic Statistics of the Community*, and *Eurostatistics: Data for Short-Term Economic Analysis*.

Facts on File, 460 Park Avenue South, New York, New York 10016 (800) 443-8323; *The New Book of World Rankings*.

Food and Agricultural Organization of the United Nations (FAO), Via delle Terme di Caracalla, 00100 Rome, Italy (Telephone Number in U.S. (202) 653-2400); *Production Yearbook*, and *The State of Food and Agriculture*.

G.K. Hall and Company, 70 Lincoln Street, Boston, Massachusetts 02111 (617) 423-3990; *The World in Figures*.

International Labour Office, I.L.O. Publications, CH-1211, Geneva 22, Switzerland; *Yearbook of Labour Statistics*.

International Lead and Zinc Study Group, Metro House, 58 St. James's Street, London SW1A 1LD England; *Lead and Zinc Statistics*.

International Monetary Fund, 700 Nineteenth Street, NW, Washington, D.C. 20431 (202) 623-7000; *International Financial Statistics*.

International Rubber Study Group, York House, Eighth Floor, Empire Way, Wembley, London HA9 0PA, England; *Rubber Statistical Bulletin*.

National Technical Information Service, 5285 Port Royal Road, Springfield, Virginia 22161 (703) 487-4600; *Handbook of Economic Statistics*.

Organisation for Economic Co-operation and Development (OECD), 2 rue Andre-Pascal, 75 Paris 16, France (Telephone Number in U.S. (202) 785-6323); *Economic Outlook, The Footwear, Raw Hides and Skins, and Leather Industry in OECD Countries, Indicators of Industrial Activity, The Iron and Steel Industry, Main Economic Indicators - Historical Statistics*, and *The Pulp and Paper Industry*.

World Bureau of Metal Statistics, 27-A High Street, Ware Hert SG12 9BA, England; *World Metal Statistics*.

UNITED KINGDOM - PRINTING AND WRITING PAPER - See UNITED KINGDOM - FORESTRY AND FOREST PRODUCTS

UNITED KINGDOM - PRODUCTION

American Automobile Manufacturers Association, 1401 H Street, NW, Suite 900, Washington, D.C. 20005 (202) 326-5500; *World Motor Vehicle Data*.

European Community Information Service, 2100 M Street, NW, Washington, D.C. 20037 (202) 862-9500; *Basic Statistics of the Community, Eurostatistics: Data for Short-Term Economic Analysis*, and *Fisheries: Yearly Statistics*.

G.K. Hall and Company, 70 Lincoln Street, Boston, Massachusetts 02111 (617) 423-3990; *The World in Figures*.

International Iron and Steel Institute, 120, rue Colonel Bourg, B-1140, Belgium; *Steel Statistical Yearbook*.

International Lead and Zinc Study Group, Metro House, 58 St. James's Street, London SW1A 1LD England; *Lead and Zinc Statistics*.

International Rubber Study Group, York House, Eighth Floor, Empire Way, Wembley, London HA9 0PA, England; *Rubber Statistical Bulletin*.

National Technical Information Service, 5285 Port Royal Road, Springfield, Virginia 22161 (703) 487-4600; *Handbook of Economic Statistics*.

Organisation for Economic Co-operation and Development (OECD), 2 rue Andre-Pascal, 75 Paris 16, France (Telephone Number in U.S. (202) 785-6323); *Economic Outlook, The Footwear, Raw Hides and Skins, and Leather Industry in OECD Countries, Indicators of Industrial Activity, Industrial Structure Statistics, The Iron and Steel Industry, Meat Balances in OECD Member Countries, Milk, Milk Products, and Egg Balances in OECD Member Countries, The Non-Ferrous Metals Industry, The Pulp and Paper Industry*, and *Textile Industry in OECD Countries*.

UNITED KINGDOM - PRODUCTIVITY

European Community Information Service, 2100 M Street, NW, Washington, D.C. 20037 (202) 862-9500; *Basic Statistics of the Community*.

Organisation for Economic Co-operation and Development (OECD), 2 rue Andre-Pascal, 75 Paris 16, France (Telephone Number in U.S. (202) 785-6323); *Economic Outlook*.

UNITED KINGDOM - PROPERTY TAXES - See UNITED KINGDOM - TAXATION

UNITED KINGDOM - PUBLIC CONSUMPTION FUND

European Community Information Service, 2100 M Street, NW, Washington, D.C. 20037 (202) 862-9500; *Basic Statistics of the Community*.

Organisation for Economic Co-operation and Development (OECD), 2 rue Andre-Pascal, 75 Paris 16, France (Telephone Number in U.S. (202) 785-6323); *Revenue Statistics of OECD Member Countries*.

UNITED KINGDOM - PUBLIC EXPENDITURES

European Community Information Service, 2100 M Street, NW, Washington, D.C. 20037 (202) 862-9500; *Basic Statistics of the Community*.

National Technical Information Service, 5285 Port Royal Road, Springfield, Virginia 22161 (703) 487-4600; *Handbook of Economic Statistics*.

Organisation for Economic Co-operation and Development (OECD), 2 rue Andre-Pascal, 75 Paris 16, France (Telephone Number in U.S. (202) 785-6323); *Revenue Statistics of OECD Member Countries*.

UNITED KINGDOM - PUBLIC FINANCE

Facts on File, 460 Park Avenue South, New York, New York 10016 (800) 443-8323; *The New Book of World Rankings*.

National Technical Information Service, 5285 Port Royal Road, Springfield, Virginia 22161 (703) 487-4600; *Handbook of Economic Statistics*.

Organisation for Economic Co-operation and Development (OECD), 2 rue Andre-Pascal, 75 Paris 16, France (Telephone Number in U.S. (202) 785-6323); *Revenue Statistics of OECD Member Countries*.

UNITED KINGDOM - PUBLIC HEALTH

European Community Information Service, 2100 M Street, NW, Washington, D.C. 20037 (202) 862-9500; *Basic Statistics of the Community*.

UNITED KINGDOM - PUBLIC REVENUES

National Technical Information Service, 5285 Port Royal Road, Springfield, Virginia 22161 (703) 487-4600; *Handbook of Economic Statistics.*

Organisation for Economic Co-operation and Development (OECD), 2 rue Andre-Pascal, 75 Paris 16, France (Telephone Number in U.S. (202) 785-6323); *Revenue Statistics of OECD Member Countries.*

UNITED KINGDOM - RADIO BROADCASTING - See UNITED KINGDOM - BROADCASTING

UNITED KINGDOM - RADIO RECEIVER PRODUCTION

Statistical Office of the United Nations, Publishing Service, New York, New York 10017 (800) 253-9646; *Statistical Yearbook.*

UNITED KINGDOM - RAILWAYS

Euromonitor Publications Limited, 87-88 Turnmill Street, London EC1M 5QU, England; *European Marketing Data and Statistics.*

European Community Information Service, 2100 M Street, NW, Washington, D.C. 20037 (202) 862-9500; *Basic Statistics of the Community, Regions: Statistical Yearbook,* and *Transport Annual Statistics.*

G.K. Hall and Company, 70 Lincoln Street, Boston, Massachusetts 02111 (617) 423-3990; *The World in Figures.*

Jane's Information Group, Sentinel House, 163 Brighton Road, Coulsdon, Surrey CR5 2NH, England (Telephone Number in U.S. (703) 883-3700); *Jane's World Railways.*

National Technical Information Service, 5285 Port Royal Road, Springfield, Virginia 22161 (703) 487-4600; *Handbook of Economic Statistics.*

Statistical Office of the United Nations, Publishing Service, New York, New York 10017 (800) 253-9646; *Annual Bulletin of Transport Statistics for Europe,* and *Statistical Yearbook.*

UNITED KINGDOM - RANCHING

European Community Information Service, 2100 M Street, NW, Washington, D.C. 20037 (202) 862-9500; *Basic Statistics of the Community.*

UNITED KINGDOM - RAPESEED PRODUCTION - See UNITED KINGDOM - CROPS

UNITED KINGDOM - RELIGION

Facts on File, 460 Park Avenue South, New York, New York 10016 (800) 443-8323; *The New Book of World Rankings.*

UNITED KINGDOM - RENT PRICES

International Labour Office, I.L.O. Publications, CH-1211, Geneva 22, Switzerland; *Yearbook of Labour Statistics.*

UNITED KINGDOM - RETAIL TRADE

European Community Information Service, 2100 M Street, NW, Washington, D.C. 20037 (202) 862-9500; *Basic Statistics of the Community,* and *Eurostatistics: Data for Short-Term Economic Analysis.*

G.K. Hall and Company, 70 Lincoln Street, Boston, Massachusetts 02111 (617) 423-3990; *The World in Figures.*

Statistical Office of the United Nations, Publishing Service, New York, New York 10017 (800) 253-9646; *Statistical Yearbook.*

UNITED KINGDOM - RICE PRODUCTION - See UNITED KINGDOM - CROPS

UNITED KINGDOM - ROOT AND TUBER PRODUCTION - See UNITED KINGDOM - CROPS

UNITED KINGDOM - ROUNDWOOD PRODUCTION - See UNITED KINGDOM - FORESTRY AND FOREST PRODUCTS

UNITED KINGDOM - RUBBER PRODUCTION AND CONSUMPTION

Commodity Research Bureau, Incorporated, 75 Wall Street, New York, New York 10005 (212) 504-7754; *Commodity Year Book.*

European Community Information Service, 2100 M Street, NW, Washington, D.C. 20037 (202) 862-9500; *Basic Statistics of the Community.*

Facts on File, 460 Park Avenue South, New York, New York 10016 (800) 443-8323; *The New Book of World Rankings.*

International Rubber Study Group, York House, Eighth Floor, Empire Way, Wembley, London HA9 0PA, England; *Rubber Statistical Bulletin.*

National Technical Information Service, 5285 Port Royal Road, Springfield, Virginia 22161 (703) 487-4600; *Handbook of Economic Statistics.*

Organisation for Economic Co-operation and Development (OECD), 2 rue Andre-Pascal, 75 Paris 16, France (Telephone Number in U.S. (202) 785-6323); *Foreign Trade by Commodities.*

Statistical Office of the United Nations, Publishing Service, New York, New York 10017 (800) 253-9646; *Statistical Yearbook.*

UNITED KINGDOM - RYE PRODUCTION - See UNITED KINGDOM - CROPS

UNITED KINGDOM - SAFFLOWER SEED PRODUCTION - See UNITED KINGDOM - CROPS

UNITED KINGDOM - SALT PRODUCTION - See UNITED KINGDOM - MINING AND MINERAL PRODUCTS

UNITED KINGDOM - SAVINGS ACCOUNT DEPOSITS

European Community Information Service, 2100 M Street, NW, Washington, D.C. 20037 (202) 862-9500; *Eurostatistics: Data for Short-Term Economic Analysis.*

UNITED KINGDOM - SAWNWOOD PRODUCTION - See UNITED KINGDOM - FORESTRY AND FOREST PRODUCTS

UNITED KINGDOM - SCIENCE AND TECHNOLOGY - EXPENDITURE FOR RESEARCH

European Community Information Service, 2100 M Street, NW, Washington, D.C. 20037 (202) 862-9500; *Basic Statistics of the Community.*

Statistical Office of the United Nations, Publishing Service, New York, New York 10017 (800) 253-9646; *Statistical Yearbook.*

UNITED KINGDOM - SCIENTISTS, TECHNICIANS AND ENGINEERS

European Community Information Service, 2100 M Street, NW, Washington, D.C. 20037 (202) 862-9500; *Basic Statistics of the Community.*

Statistical Office of the United Nations, Publishing Service, New York, New York 10017 (800) 253-9646; *Statistical Yearbook.*

United Nations Educational, Scientific and Cultural Organization (UNESCO), 7 Place de Fontenoy, F-75700 Paris, France (Telephone Number in U.S. (212) 963-5981); *Statistical Yearbook.*

UNITED KINGDOM - SENIOR CITIZENS

Facts on File, 460 Park Avenue South, New York, New York 10016 (800) 443-8323; *The New Book of World Rankings.*

UNITED KINGDOM - SESAME SEED PRODUCTION - See UNITED KINGDOM - CROPS

UNITED KINGDOM - SHEEP - See UNITED KINGDOM - LIVESTOCK AND POULTRY

UNITED KINGDOM - SHIPBUILDING - PRODUCTION INDEX

Organisation for Economic Co-operation and Development (OECD), 2 rue Andre-Pascal, 75 Paris 16, France (Telephone Number in U.S. (202) 785-6323); *Indicators of Industrial Activity.*

UNITED KINGDOM - SILVER PRODUCTION AND CONSUMPTION - See UNITED KINGDOM - MINING AND MINERAL PRODUCTS

UNITED KINGDOM - SISAL PRODUCTION - See UNITED KINGDOM - CROPS

UNITED KINGDOM - SOCIAL DATA

European Community Information Service, 2100 M Street, NW, Washington, D.C. 20037 (202) 862-9500; *ACP: Basic Statistics, Basic Statistics of the Community.*

Facts on File, 460 Park Avenue South, New York, New York 10016 (800) 443-8323; *The New Book of World Rankings.*

G.K. Hall and Company, 70 Lincoln Street, Boston, Massachusetts 02111 (617) 423-3990; *The World in Figures.*

UNITED KINGDOM - SOCIAL SECURITY

European Community Information Service, 2100 M Street, NW, Washington, D.C. 20037 (202) 862-9500; *Basic Statistics of the Community.*

International Monetary Fund, 700 Nineteenth Street, NW, Washington, D.C. 20431 (202) 623-7000; *Government Finance Statistics Yearbook.*

Organisation for Economic Co-operation and Development (OECD), 2 rue Andre-Pascal, 75 Paris 16, France (Telephone Number in U.S. (202) 785-6323); *Revenue Statistics of OECD Member Countries.*

UNITED KINGDOM - SOCIOECONOMIC DATA

European Community Information Service, 2100 M Street, NW, Washington, D.C. 20037 (202) 862-9500; *Basic Statistics of the Community.*

Organisation for Economic Co-operation and Development (OECD), 2 rue Andre-Pascal, 75 Paris 16, France (Telephone Number in U.S. (202) 785-6323); *Economic Outlook.*

UNITED KINGDOM - SOYBEAN PRODUCTION - See UNITED KINGDOM - CROPS

UNITED KINGDOM - STAMP TAXES AND DUTIES - See UNITED KINGDOM - TAXATION

UNITED KINGDOM - STEEL - See UNITED KINGDOM - MINING AND MINERAL PRODUCTS

UNITED KINGDOM - STOCKS - COMMODITY - MARKET PRICE - INDEXES

Food and Agricultural Organization of the United Nations (FAO) Via delle Terme di Caracalla, 00100 Rome, Italy (Telephone Number in U.S. (202) 653-2400); *The State of Food and Agriculture.*

International Lead and Zinc Study Group, Metro House, 58 St. James's Street, London SW1A 1LD England; *Lead and Zinc Statistics.*

Statistical Office of the United Nations, Publishing Service, New York, New York 10017 (800) 253-9646; *Statistical Yearbook.*

World Bureau of Metal Statistics, 27-A High Street, Ware Hert SG12 9BA, England; *World Metal Statistics.*

UNITED KINGDOM - STRAW PRODUCTION - See UNITED KINGDOM - CROPS

UNITED KINGDOM - SUGAR - See UNITED KINGDOM - CROPS

UNITED KINGDOM - SUGARBEET PRODUCTION - See UNITED KINGDOM - CROPS

UNITED KINGDOM - SULPHUR AND SULPHURIC ACID PRODUCTION - See UNITED KINGDOM - MINING AND MINERAL PRODUCTS

UNITED KINGDOM - SUNFLOWER PRODUCTION - See UNITED KINGDOM - CROPS

UNITED KINGDOM - TAXATION

European Community Information Service, 2100 M Street, NW, Washington, D.C. 20037 (202) 862-9500; *Basic Statistics of the Community.*

G.K. Hall and Company, 70 Lincoln Street, Boston, Massachusetts 02111 (617) 423-3990; *The World in Figures.*

International Monetary Fund, 700 Nineteenth Street, NW, Washington, D.C. 20431 (202) 623-7000; *Government Finance Statistics Yearbook.*

International Road Federation, 525 School Street, SW, Washington, D.C. 20024 (202) 554-2106; *World Road Statistics.*

Organisation for Economic Co-operation and Development (OECD), 2 rue Andre-Pascal, 75 Paris 16, France (Telephone Number in U.S. (202) 785-6323); *Indicators of Industrial Activity,* and *Revenue Statistics of OECD Member Countries.*

The World Bank, 1818 H Street, NW, Washington, D.C. 20433 (202) 477-1234; *World Tables.*

UNITED KINGDOM - TEA PRODUCTION AND CONSUMPTION - See UNITED KINGDOM - CROPS

UNITED KINGDOM - TELEGRAMS SERVICES

European Community Information Service, 2100 M Street, NW, Washington, D.C. 20037 (202) 862-9500; *Transport Annual Statistics*.

Statistical Office of the United Nations, Publishing Service, New York, New York 10017 (800) 253-9646; *Statistical Yearbook*.

UNITED KINGDOM - TELEPHONES IN USE

American Telephone and Telegraph Company, 26 Parsippany Road, Whippany, New Jersey 07981 (800) 338-4038; *The World's Telephones*.

European Community Information Service, 2100 M Street, NW, Washington, D.C. 20037 (202) 862-9500; *Basic Statistics of the Community*, and *Transport Annual Statistics*.

G.K. Hall and Company, 70 Lincoln Street, Boston, Massachusetts 02111 (617) 423-3990; *The World in Figures*.

Statistical Office of the United Nations, Publishing Service, New York, New York 10017 (800) 253-9646; *Statistical Yearbook*.

UNITED KINGDOM - TELEVISION BROADCASTING - See UNITED KINGDOM - BROADCASTING

UNITED KINGDOM - TELEVISION RECEIVER PRODUCTION

European Community Information Service, 2100 M Street, NW, Washington, D.C. 20037 (202) 862-9500; *Basic Statistics of the Community*.

National Technical Information Service, 5285 Port Royal Road, Springfield, Virginia 22161 (703) 487-4600; *Handbook of Economic Statistics*.

Statistical Office of the United Nations, Publishing Service, New York, New York 10017 (800) 253-9646; *Statistical Yearbook*.

UNITED KINGDOM - TEXTILE INDUSTRY

American Forest and Paper Association, 1250 Connecticut Avenue, NW, Washington, D.C. 20036 (202) 463-2455; *Wood Pulp and Fiber Statistics*.

European Community Information Service, 2100 M Street, NW, Washington, D.C. 20037 (202) 862-9500; *Basic Statistics of the Community, Eurostatistics: Data for Short-Term Economic Analysis*, and *Industrial Production: Quarterly Statistics*.

G.K. Hall and Company, 70 Lincoln Street, Boston, Massachusetts 02111 (617) 423-3990; *The World in Figures*.

National Technical Information Service, 5285 Port Royal Road, Springfield, Virginia 22161 (703) 487-4600; *Handbook of Economic Statistics*.

Organisation for Economic Co-operation and Development (OECD), 2 rue Andre-Pascal, 75 Paris 16, France (Telephone Number in U.S. (202) 785-6323); *Foreign Trade by Commodities, Industrial Structure Statistics*, and *Textile Industry in OECD Countries*.

Statistical Office of the United Nations, Publishing Service, New York, New York 10017 (800) 253-9646; *Statistical Yearbook*, and *Trade in Manufactures of Developing Countries*.

UNITED KINGDOM - THEATRE

United Nations Educational, Scientific and Cultural Organization (UNESCO), 7 Place de Fontenoy, F-75700 Paris, France (Telephone Number in U.S. (212) 963-5981); *Statistical Yearbook*.

UNITED KINGDOM - TIMBER - RESOURCE FORESTS - See UNITED KINGDOM - FORESTRY AND FOREST PRODUCTS

UNITED KINGDOM - TIMBER PRODUCTION - See UNITED KINGDOM - FORESTRY AND FOREST PRODUCTS

UNITED KINGDOM - TIN PRODUCTION - See UNITED KINGDOM - MINING AND MINERAL PRODUCTS

UNITED KINGDOM - TIRE (MOTOR VEHICLE) PRODUCTION

International Rubber Study Group, York House, Eighth Floor, Empire Way, Wembley, London HA9 0PA, England; *Rubber Statistical Bulletin*.

National Technical Information Service, 5285 Port Royal Road, Springfield, Virginia 22161 (703) 487-4600; *Handbook of Economic Statistics*.

Statistical Office of the United Nations, Publishing Service, New York, New York 10017 (800) 253-9646; *Statistical Yearbook*.

UNITED KINGDOM - TOBACCO PRODUCTION

Euromonitor Publications Limited, 87-88 Turnmill Street, London EC1M 5QU, England; *European Marketing Data and Statistics*.

European Community Information Service, 2100 M Street, NW, Washington, D.C. 20037 (202) 862-9500; *Basic Statistics of the Community*, and *Industrial Production: Quarterly Statistics*

Facts on File, 460 Park Avenue South, New York, New York 10016 (800) 443-8323; *The New Book of World Rankings*.

Organisation for Economic Co-operation and Development (OECD), 2 rue Andre-Pascal, 75 Paris 16, France (Telephone Number in U.S. (202) 785-6323); *Indicators of Industrial Activity*, and *Industrial Structure Statistics*, and *Foreign Trade by Commodities*.

Statistical Office of the United Nations, Publishing Service, New York, New York 10017 (800) 253-9646; *Statistical Yearbook*.

UNITED KINGDOM - TOURISM

Euromonitor Publications Limited, 87-88 Turnmill Street, London EC1M 5QU, England; *European Marketing Data and Statistics*.

European Community Information Service, 2100 M Street, NW, Washington, D.C. 20037 (202) 862-9500; *Transport Annual Statistics*.

Facts on File, 460 Park Avenue South, New York, New York 10016 (800) 443-8323; *The New Book of World Rankings*.

G.K. Hall and Company, 70 Lincoln Street, Boston, Massachusetts 02111 (617) 423-3990; *The World in Figures*.

Organisation for Economic Co-operation and Development (OECD), 2 rue Andre-Pascal, 75 Paris 16, France (Telephone Number in U.S. (202) 785-6323); *Tourism Policy and International Tourism in OECD Member Countries*.

Statistical Office of the United Nations, Publishing Service, New York, New York 10017 (800) 253-9646; *Statistical Yearbook.*

Times Books, 201 East 50th Street, New York, New York 10022 (212) 751-2600; *The Economist Book of Vital World Statistics.*

World Tourism Organization, Calle Capitan Haya 42, E-28020 Madrid, Spain; *Yearbook of Tourism Statistics.*

UNITED KINGDOM - TRACTORS IN USE

European Community Information Service, 2100 M Street, NW, Washington, D.C. 20037 (202) 862-9500; *Transport Annual Statistics.*

Statistical Office of the United Nations, Publishing Service, New York, New York 10017 (800) 253-9646; *Statistical Yearbook.*

UNITED KINGDOM - TRADE - See UNITED KINGDOM - FOREIGN TRADE

UNITED KINGDOM - TRADEMARKS AND SERVICE MARKS

Statistical Office of the United Nations, Publishing Service, New York, New York 10017 (800) 253-9646; *Statistical Yearbook.*

World Intellectual Property Organization, 34 Chemin des Colombettes, CH-1211 Geneva 20. Switzerland; *Industrial Property Statistics.*

UNITED KINGDOM - TRANSPORTATION AND COMMUNICATIONS

European Community Information Service, 2100 M Street, NW, Washington, D.C. 20037 (202) 862-9500; *Basic Statistics of the Community, Energy Statistics Yearbook, Regions: Statistical Yearbook,* and *Transport Annual Statistics.*

Facts on File, 460 Park Avenue South, New York, New York 10016 (800) 443-8323; *The New Book of World Rankings.*

G.K. Hall and Company, 70 Lincoln Street, Boston, Massachusetts 02111 (617) 423-3990; *The World in Figures.*

UNITED KINGDOM - TUNGSTEN PRODUCTION AND CONSUMPTION - See UNITED KINGDOM - MINING AND MINERAL PRODUCTS

UNITED KINGDOM - TURKEYS - See UNITED KINGDOM - LIVESTOCK AND POULTRY

UNITED KINGDOM - UNEMPLOYMENT

Euromonitor Publications Limited, 87-88 Turnmill Street, London EC1M 5QU, England; *European Marketing Data and Statistics.*

European Community Information Service, 2100 M Street, NW, Washington, D.C. 20037 (202) 862-9500; *Basic Statistics of the Community, Employment and Unemployment, Eurostatistics: Data for Short-Term Economic Analysis, Labor Force Sample Survey,* and *Regions: Statistical Yearbook.*

International Labour Office, I.L.O. Publications, CH-1211, Geneva 22, Switzerland; *Yearbook of Labour Statistics.*

National Technical Information Service, 5285 Port Royal Road, Springfield, Virginia 22161 (703) 487-4600; *Handbook of Economic Statistics.*

Organisation for Economic Co-operation and Development (OECD), 2 rue Andre-Pascal, 75 Paris 16, France (Telephone Number in U.S. (202) 785-6323); *Economic Outlook, OECD Economic Surveys: United Kingdom,* and *OECD Employment Outlook.*

Statistical Office of the United Nations, Publishing Service, New York, New York 10017 (800) 253-9646; *Statistical Yearbook.*

UNITED KINGDOM - URANIUM PRODUCTION AND CONSUMPTION - See UNITED KINGDOM - MINING AND MINERAL PRODUCTS

UNITED KINGDOM - VANADIUM AND VANADIUM ORE PRODUCTION AND CONSUMPTION - See UNITED KINGDOM - MINING AND MINERAL PRODUCTS

UNITED KINGDOM - VITAL STATISTICS

European Community Information Service, 2100 M Street, NW, Washington, D.C. 20037 (202) 862-9500; *Basic Statistics of the Community.*

G.K. Hall and Company, 70 Lincoln Street, Boston, Massachusetts 02111 (617) 423-3990; *The World in Figures.*

Statistical Office of the United Nations, Publishing Service, New York, New York 10017 (800) 253-9646; *Statistical Yearbook.*

World Health Organization, Office of Publications, Avenue Appia, CH-1211 Geneva 27, Switzerland (Telephone Number in U.S. (518) 436-9686); *World Health Statistics Annual.*

UNITED KINGDOM - WAGES

Euromonitor Publications Limited, 87-88 Turnmill Street, London EC1M 5QU, England; *European Marketing Data and Statistics.*

European Community Information Service, 2100 M Street, NW, Washington, D.C. 20037 (202) 862-9500; *Basic Statistics of the Community, Earnings in Agriculture,* and *Eurostatistics: Data for Short-Term Economic Analysis.*

G.K. Hall and Company, 70 Lincoln Street, Boston, Massachusetts 02111 (617) 423-3990; *The World in Figures.*

International Labour Office, I.L.O. Publications, CH-1211, Geneva 22, Switzerland; *Yearbook of Labour Statistics.*

Organisation for Economic Co-operation and Development (OECD), 2 rue Andre-Pascal, 75 Paris 16, France (Telephone Number in U.S. (202) 785-6323); *Economic Outlook, Industrial Structure Statistics,* and *Main Economic Indicators - Historical Statistics.*

Statistical Office of the United Nations, Publishing Service, New York, New York 10017 (800) 253-9646; *Statistical Yearbook.*

UNITED KINGDOM - WALNUT PRODUCTION - See UNITED KINGDOM - CROPS

UNITED KINGDOM - WATERWAYS IN USE

European Community Information Service, 2100 M Street, NW, Washington, D.C. 20037 (202) 862-9500; *Basic Statistics of the Community,* and *Transport Annual Statistics.*

National Technical Information Service, 5285 Port Royal Road, Springfield, Virginia 22161 (703) 487-4600; *Handbook of Economic Statistics.*

Organisation for Economic Co-operation and Development (OECD), 2 rue Andre-Pascal, 75 Paris 16, France (Telephone Number in U.S. (202) 785-6323); *Maritime Transport*.

Statistical Office of the United Nations, Publishing Service, New York, New York 10017 (800) 253-9646; *Annual Bulletin of Transport Statistics for Europe*.

UNITED KINGDOM - WEATHER

Facts on File, 460 Park Avenue South, New York, New York 10016 (800) 443-8323; *The New Book of World Rankings*.

G.K. Hall and Company, 70 Lincoln Street, Boston, Massachusetts 02111 (617) 423-3990; *The World in Figures*.

UNITED KINGDOM - WELFARE

European Community Information Service, 2100 M Street, NW, Washington, D.C. 20037 (202) 862-9500; *Basic Statistics of the Community*.

International Monetary Fund, 700 Nineteenth Street, NW, Washington, D.C. 20431 (202) 623-7000; *Government Finance Statistics Yearbook*.

UNITED KINGDOM - WHEAT PRODUCTION AND PRICES - See UNITED KINGDOM - CROPS

UNITED KINGDOM - WHOLESALE PRICES

European Community Information Service, 2100 M Street, NW, Washington, D.C. 20037 (202) 862-9500; *Basic Statistics of the Community*.

National Technical Information Service, 5285 Port Royal Road, Springfield, Virginia 22161 (703) 487-4600; *Handbook of Economic Statistics*.

Statistical Office of the United Nations, Publishing Service, New York, New York 10017 (800) 253-9646; *Statistical Yearbook*.

UNITED KINGDOM - WINE PRODUCTION

European Community Information Service, 2100 M Street, NW, Washington, D.C. 20037 (202) 862-9500; *Basic Statistics of the Community*.

Facts on File, 460 Park Avenue South, New York, New York 10016 (800) 443-8323; *The New Book of World Rankings*.

UNITED KINGDOM - WOOD AND WOOD PULP - See UNITED KINGDOM - FORESTRY AND FOREST PRODUCTS

UNITED KINGDOM - WOOL - INDUSTRIAL CONSUMPTION

Organisation for Economic Co-operation and Development (OECD), 2 rue Andre-Pascal, 75 Paris 16, France (Telephone Number in U.S. (202) 785-6323); *Textile Industry in OECD Countries*.

Statistical Office of the United Nations, Publishing Service, New York, New York 10017 (800) 253-9646; *Statistical Yearbook*.

UNITED KINGDOM - WOOL PRODUCTION

Commodity Research Bureau, Incorporated, 75 Wall Street, New York, New York 10005 (212) 504-7754; *Commodity Year Book*.

European Community Information Service, 2100 M Street, NW, Washington, D.C. 20037 (202) 862-9500; *Basic Statistics of the Community*.

Facts on File, 460 Park Avenue South, New York, New York 10016 (800) 443-8323; *The New Book of World Rankings*.

National Technical Information Service, 5285 Port Royal Road, Springfield, Virginia 22161 (703) 487-4600; *Handbook of Economic Statistics*.

Organisation for Economic Co-operation and Development (OECD), 2 rue Andre-Pascal, 75 Paris 16, France (Telephone Number in U.S. (202) 785-6323); *Economic Accounts for Agriculture*, and *Textile Industry in OECD Countries*.

Statistical Office of the United Nations, Publishing Service, New York, New York 10017 (800) 253-9646; *Statistical Yearbook*.

UNITED KINGDOM - YARN PRODUCTION

European Community Information Service, 2100 M Street, NW, Washington, D.C. 20037 (202) 862-9500; *Basic Statistics of the Community*.

Organisation for Economic Co-operation and Development (OECD), 2 rue Andre-Pascal, 75 Paris 16, France (Telephone Number in U.S. (202) 785-6323); *Textile Industry in OECD Countries*.

Statistical Office of the United Nations, Publishing Service, New York, New York 10017 (800) 253-9646; *Statistical Yearbook*.

UNITED KINGDOM - ZINC AND ZINC ORE PRODUCTION AND CONSUMPTION - See UNITED KINGDOM - MINING AND MINERAL PRODUCTS

UNITED STATES SECURITIES - See also DEBT

UNITED STATES SECURITIES - FOREIGN PURCHASES AND SALES

U.S. Department of the Treasury, Fifteenth Street and Pennsylvania Avenue, NW, Washington, D.C. 20220 (202) 566-2000; *Treasury Bulletin*.

UNITED STATES SECURITIES - HELD BY BANKS

Board of Governors of the Federal Reserve System, Twentieth Street and Constitution Avenue, NW, Washington, D.C. 20551 (202) 452-3000; *Annual Statistical Digest*.

U.S. Department of the Treasury, Fifteenth Street and Pennsylvania Avenue, NW, Washington, D.C. 20220 (202) 566-2000; *Treasury Bulletin*.

U.S. Federal Deposit Insurance Corporation, 550 Seventeenth Street, NW, Washington, D.C. 20429 (202) 393-8400; *Annual Report, The FDIC Quarterly Banking Profile*, and *Statistics on Banking*.

UNITED STATES SECURITIES - HOLDINGS BY HOUSE-HOLDS

Board of Governors of the Federal Reserve System, Twentieth Street and Constitution Avenue, NW, Washington, D.C. 20551 (202) 452-3000; *Annual Statistical Digest*.

UNITED STATES SECURITIES - PRICES, SALES,
AND YIELDS

Board of Governors of the Federal Reserve System, Twentieth Street and Constitution Avenue, NW, Washington, D.C. 20551 (202) 452-3000; *Federal Reserve Bulletin*.

UNITED STATES SECURITIES - TAXABLE YIELDS

Board of Governors of the Federal Reserve System, Twentieth Street and Constitution Avenue, NW, Washington, D.C. 20551 (202) 452-3000; *Federal Reserve Bulletin*, and *Annual Statistical Digest*.

UNIVERSITIES - See EDUCATION, HIGHER EDUCATION
INSTITUTIONS

URANIUM - See also NUCLEAR POWER

U.S. Department of Energy, Energy Information Administration, 1000 Independence Avenue, SW, Washington, D.C. 20585 (202) 586-8800; *Domestic Uranium Mining and Milling Industry, Annual Energy Review, Uranium Industry Annual*, and unpublished data.

URBAN POPULATION - See POPULATION

Uruguay - National Statistical Offices

CENCI Uruguay, Misiones 1361 Esc 14, Casilla de Correo 1510, Montevideo, Uruguay; for foreign trade statistics.

Direccion General de Estadistica y Censos, Cuareim 2052, Montevideo, Uruguay; for other statistics.

Uruguay - Primary Statistics Source

Direccion General de Estadisticas, Cuareim, 2052, Montivideo, Uruguay; *Anuario Estadistico*.

URUGUAY - AGRICULTURE

The Economist Intelligence Unit, 111 West 57th Street, New York, New York 10019 (800) 938-4685; *The New Latin America Market Atlas*.

Euromonitor Publications Limited, 87-88 Turnmill Street, London EC1M 5QU, England; *International Marketing Data and Statistics*.

Facts on File, 460 Park Avenue South, New York, New York 10016 (800) 443-8323; *The New Book of World Rankings*.

Federal Statistical Office, Gustav-Stresemann-Ring 11, D-6200 Wiesbaden, Germany; *Uruguay*.

Food and Agricultural Organization of the United Nations (FAO), Via delle Terme di Caracalla, 00100 Rome, Italy (Telephone Number in U.S. (202) 653-2400); *Production Yearbook, The State of Food and Agriculture*, and *Trade Yearbook*.

Gale Research Incorporated, 835 Penobscot Building Detroit, Michigan 48226 (800) 877-4253; *International Historical Statistics The Americas and Australasia*.

G.K. Hall and Company, 70 Lincoln Street, Boston, Massachusetts 02111 (617) 423-3990; *The World in Figures*.

Inter-American Development Bank, 1300 New York Avenue, NW, Washington, D.C. 20577 (202) 623-1753; *Economic and Social Progress in Latin America*.

Statistical Office of the United Nations, Publishing Service, New York, New York 10017 (800) 253-9646; *Statistical Yearbook*, and *Statistical Yearbook for Latin America and the Caribbean*.

Time Books, 201 East 50th Street, New York, New York 10022 (212) 751-2600; *The Economist Book of Vital World Statistics*.

U.C.L.A. Latin American Center Publications, University of California, Los Angeles, California 90024 (310) 825-6634; *Statistical Abstract of Latin America*.

The World Bank, 1818 H Street, NW, Washington, D.C. 20433 (202) 477-1234; *World Tables*.

URUGUAY - AIRLINE SERVICE

The Economist Intelligence Unit, 111 West 57th Street, New York, New York 10019 (800) 938-4685; *The New Latin America Market Atlas*.

Facts on File, 460 Park Avenue South, New York, New York 10016 (800) 443-8323; *The New Book of World Rankings*.

G.K. Hall and Company, 70 Lincoln Street, Boston, Massachusetts 02111 (617) 423-3990; *The World in Figures*.

International Civil Aviation Organization, 1000 Sherbrooke Street, West, Montreal, Quebec, Canada H3A 2R2 (514) 285-8219; *Civil Aviation Statistics of the World*.

Statistical Office of the United Nations, Publishing Service, New York, New York 10017 (800) 253-9646; *Statistical Yearbook*.

Time Books, 201 East 50th Street, New York, New York 10022 (212) 751-2600; *The Economist Book of Vital World Statistics*.

URUGUAY - ALUMINUM PRODUCTION AND CONSUMPTION - See URUGUAY - MINING AND MINERAL PRODUCTS

URUGUAY - ANIMAL HEALTH

Food and Agricultural Organization of the United Nations (FAO), Via delle Terme di Caracalla, 00100 Rome, Italy (Telephone Number in U.S. (202) 653-2400); *Animal Health Yearbook*.

URUGUAY - AREA AND DENSITY OF POPULATION

Euromonitor Publications Limited, 87-88 Turnmill Street, London EC1M 5QU, England; *International Marketing Data and Statistics*.

Facts on File, 460 Park Avenue South, New York, New York 10016 (800) 443-8323; *The New Book of World Rankings*.

Federal Statistical Office, Gustav-Stresemann-Ring 11, D-6200 Wiesbaden, Germany; *Uruguay*.

Food and Agricultural Organization of the United Nations (FAO) Via delle Terme di Caracalla, 00100 Rome, Italy (Telephone Number in U.S. (202) 653-2400); *The State of Food and Agriculture*.

G.K. Hall and Company, 70 Lincoln Street, Boston, Massachusetts 02111 (617) 423-3990; *The World in Figures*.

Inter-American Development Bank, 1300 New York Avenue, NW, Washington, D.C. 20577 (202) 623-1753; *Economic and Social Progress in Latin America*.

Statistical Office of the United Nations, Publishing Service, New York, New York 10017 (800) 253-9646; *Statistical Yearbook*.

Time Books, 201 East 50th Street, New York, New York 10022 (212) 751-2600; *The Economist Book of Vital World Statistics.*

United Nations Educational, Scientific and Cultural Organization (UNESCO), 7 Place de Fontenoy, F-75700 Paris, France (Telephone Number in U.S. (212) 963-5981); *Statistical Yearbook.*

URUGUAY - ARMS EXPORTS AND IMPORTS

U.S. Arms Control and Disarmament Agency, 320 Twenty-first Street, NW, Washington, D.C. 20451 (202) 647-8677; *World Military Expenditures and Arms Transfers.*

URUGUAY - BALANCE OF PAYMENTS

The Economist Intelligence Unit, 111 West 57th Street, New York, New York 10019 (800) 938-4685; *The New Latin America Market Atlas,* and *The World Market Atlas.*

Federal Statistical Office, Gustav-Stresemann-Ring 11, D-6200 Wiesbaden, Germany; *Uruguay.*

G.K. Hall and Company, 70 Lincoln Street, Boston, Massachusetts 02111 (617) 423-3990; *The World in Figures.*

Inter-American Development Bank, 1300 New York Avenue, NW, Washington, D.C. 20577 (202) 623-1753; *Economic and Social Progress in Latin America.*

International Monetary Fund, 700 Nineteenth Street, NW, Washington, D.C. 20431 (202) 623-7000; *Balance of Payments Yearbook.*

Organization of American States (OAS), General Secretariat, Washington, D.C. 20006 (202) 458-3533; *Statistical Bulletin of the OAS.*

Statistical Office of the United Nations, Publishing Service, New York, New York 10017 (800) 253-9646; *Economic Survey of Latin America and the Caribbean,* and *Statistical Yearbook for Latin America and the Caribbean.*

Time Books, 201 East 50th Street, New York, New York 10022 (212) 751-2600; *The Economist Book of Vital World Statistics.*

U.C.L.A. Latin American Center Publications, University of California, Los Angeles, California 90024 (310) 825-6634; *Statistical Abstract of Latin America.*

The World Bank, 1818 H Street, NW, Washington, D.C. 20433 (202) 477-1234; *World Tables.*

URUGUAY - BANANA PRODUCTION - See URUGUAY - CROPS

URUGUAY - BANKING

Facts on File, 460 Park Avenue South, New York, New York 10016 (800) 443-8323; *The New Book of World Rankings.*

G.K. Hall and Company, 70 Lincoln Street, Boston, Massachusetts 02111 (617) 423-3990; *The World in Figures.*

Inter-American Development Bank, 1300 New York Avenue, NW, Washington, D.C. 20577 (202) 623-1753; *Economic and Social Progress in Latin America.*

International Monetary Fund, 700 Nineteenth Street, NW, Washington, D.C. 20431 (202) 623-7000; *Government Finance Statistics Yearbook,* and *International Financial Statistics.*

Statistical Office of the United Nations, Publishing Service, New York, New York 10017 (800) 253-9646; *Statistical Yearbook for Latin America and the Caribbean.*

URUGUAY - BARLEY PRODUCTION - See URUGUAY - CROPS

URUGUAY - BEER PRODUCTION

Facts on File, 460 Park Avenue South, New York, New York 10016 (800) 443-8323; *The New Book of World Rankings.*

Statistical Office of the United Nations, Publishing Service, New York, New York 10017 (800) 253-9646; *Statistical Yearbook.*

URUGUAY - BIRTH RATES

Facts on File, 460 Park Avenue South, New York, New York 10016 (800) 443-8323; *The New Book of World Rankings.*

Statistical Office of the United Nations, Publishing Service, New York, New York 10017 (800) 253-9646; *Demographic Yearbook, Statistical Yearbook,* and *Statistical Yearbook for Latin America and the Caribbean.*

Time Books, 201 East 50th Street, New York, New York 10022 (212) 751-2600; *The Economist Book of Vital World Statistics.*

The World Bank, 1010 II Street, NW, Washington, D.C. 20433 (202) 477-1234; *World Tables.*

World Health Organization, Office of Publications, Avenue Appia, CH-1211 Geneva 27, Switzerland (Telephone Number in U.S. (518) 436-9686); *World Health Statistics Annual.*

URUGUAY - BONDS

G.K. Hall and Company, 70 Lincoln Street, Boston, Massachusetts 02111 (617) 423-3990; *The World in Figures.*

Inter-American Development Bank, 1300 New York Avenue, NW, Washington, D.C. 20577 (202) 623-1753; *Economic and Social Progress in Latin America.*

International Monetary Fund, 700 Nineteenth Street, NW, Washington, D.C. 20431 (202) 623-7000; *Government Finance Statistics Yearbook.*

Statistical Office of the United Nations, Publishing Service, New York, New York 10017 (800) 253-9646; *Statistical Yearbook.*

URUGUAY - BOOK PRODUCTION

G.K. Hall and Company, 70 Lincoln Street, Boston, Massachusetts 02111 (617) 423-3990; *The World in Figures.*

United Nations Educational, Scientific and Cultural Organization (UNESCO), 7 Place de Fontenoy, F-75700 Paris, France (Telephone Number in U.S. (212) 963-5981); *Statistical Yearbook.*

URUGUAY - BROADCASTING

Billboard Limited, P.O. Box 9027, 1006 AA Amsterdam, The Netherlands (Telephone Number in U.S. (212) 764-7300); *World Radio TV Handbook.*

Facts on File, 460 Park Avenue South, New York, New York 10016 (800) 443-8323; *The New Book of World Rankings.*

G.K. Hall and Company, 70 Lincoln Street, Boston, Massachusetts 02111 (617) 423-3990; *The World in Figures.*

Time Books, 201 East 50th Street, New York, New York 10022 (212) 751-2600; *The Economist Book of Vital World Statistics.*

URUGUAY - BUSINESS

G.K. Hall and Company, 70 Lincoln Street, Boston, Massachusetts 02111 (617) 423-3990; *The World in Figures.*

Inter-American Development Bank, 1300 New York Avenue, NW, Washington, D.C. 20577 (202) 623-1753; *Economic and Social Progress in Latin America.*

URUGUAY - BUSINESS AND PROFESSIONAL LICENSES

International Monetary Fund, 700 Nineteenth Street, NW, Washington, D.C. 20431 (202) 623-7000; *Government Finance Statistics Yearbook.*

URUGUAY - BUTTER PRODUCTION - See URUGUAY - DAIRY PRODUCTS

URUGUAY - CALORIE SUPPLY

Food and Agricultural Organization of the United Nations (FAO) Via delle Terme di Caracalla, 00100 Rome, Italy (Telephone Number in U.S. (202) 653-2400; *The State of Food and Agriculture.*

Statistical Office of the United Nations, Publishing Service, New York, New York 10017 (800) 253-9646; *Statistical Yearbook for Latin America and the Caribbean.*

URUGUAY - CAPITAL INVESTMENT

Inter-American Development Bank, 1300 New York Avenue, NW, Washington, D.C. 20577 (202) 623-1753; *Economic and Social Progress in Latin America.*

URUGUAY - CAPITAL REVENUE

Inter-American Development Bank, 1300 New York Avenue, NW, Washington, D.C. 20577 (202) 623-1753; *Economic and Social Progress in Latin America.*

International Monetary Fund, 700 Nineteenth Street, NW, Washington, D.C. 20431 (202) 623-7000; *Government Finance Statistics Yearbook.*

URUGUAY - CATTLE - See URUGUAY - LIVESTOCK AND POULTRY

URUGUAY - CEMENT PRODUCTION - See URUGUAY - MINING AND MINERAL PRODUCTS

URUGUAY - CHEESE PRODUCTION AND CONSUMPTION - See URUGUAY - DAIRY PRODUCTS

URUGUAY - CHEMICAL (ORGANIC) PRODUCTION - See URUGUAY - MINING AND MINERAL PRODUCTS

URUGUAY - CHICKENS - See URUGUAY - LIVESTOCK AND POULTRY

URUGUAY - CIGARETTE PRODUCTION - See URUGUAY - TOBACCO PRODUCTION

URUGUAY - CLASS STRUCTURE

G.K. Hall and Company, 70 Lincoln Street, Boston, Massachusetts 02111 (617) 423-3990; *The World in Figures.*

URUGUAY - CLIMATE

Facts on File, 460 Park Avenue South, New York, New York 10016 (800) 443-8323; *The New Book of World Rankings.*

G.K. Hall and Company, 70 Lincoln Street, Boston, Massachusetts 02111 (617) 423-3990; *The World in Figures.*

URUGUAY - CLOTHING EXPORTS AND IMPORTS

Statistical Office of the United Nations, Publishing Service, New York, New York 10017 (800) 253-9646; *Trade in Manufactures of Developing Countries.*

URUGUAY - COAL PRODUCTION - See URUGUAY - MINING AND MINERAL PRODUCTS

URUGUAY - COCOA (BEANS) PRODUCTION - See URUGUAY - CROPS

URUGUAY - COFFEE - See URUGUAY - CROPS

URUGUAY - COMMUNICATIONS

Federal Statistical Office, Gustav-Stresemann-Ring 11, D-6200 Wiesbaden, Germany; *Uruguay.*

Gale Research Incorporated, 835 Penobscot Building Detroit, Michigan 48226 (800) 877-4253; *International Historical Statistics The Americas and Australasia.*

G.K. Hall and Company, 70 Lincoln Street, Boston, Massachusetts 02111 (617) 423-3990; *The World in Figures.*

Inter-American Development Bank, 1300 New York Avenue, NW, Washington, D.C. 20577 (202) 623-1753; *Economic and Social Progress in Latin America.*

U.C.L.A. Latin American Center Publications, University of California, Los Angeles, California 90024 (310) 825-6634; *Statistical Abstract of Latin America.*

URUGUAY - CONSTRUCTION INDUSTRY

The Economist Intelligence Unit, 111 West 57th Street, New York, New York 10019 (800) 938-4685; *The New Latin America Market Atlas.*

Facts on File, 460 Park Avenue South, New York, New York 10016 (800) 443-8323; *The New Book of World Rankings.*

Inter-American Development Bank, 1300 New York Avenue, NW, Washington, D.C. 20577 (202) 623-1753; *Economic and Social Progress in Latin America.*

U.C.L.A. Latin American Center Publications, University of California, Los Angeles, California 90024 (310) 825-6634; *Statistical Abstract of Latin America.*

Statistical Office of the United Nations, Publishing Service, New York, New York 10017 (800) 253-9646; *Construction Statistics Yearbook,* and *Statistical Yearbook.*

URUGUAY - CONSUMER PRICE INDEX

G.K. Hall and Company, 70 Lincoln Street, Boston, Massachusetts 02111 (617) 423-3990; *The World in Figures*.

Statistical Office of the United Nations, Publishing Service, New York, New York 10017 (800) 253-9646; *Statistical Yearbook*.

Time Books, 201 East 50th Street, New York, New York 10022 (212) 751-2600; *The Economist Book of Vital World Statistics*.

U.C.L.A. Latin American Center Publications, University of California, Los Angeles, California 90024 (310) 825-6634; *Statistical Abstract of Latin America*.

URUGUAY - CONSUMER PRICES

The Economist Intelligence Unit, 111 West 57th Street, New York, New York 10019 (800) 938-4685; *The New Latin America Market Atlas*.

International Labour Office, I.L.O. Publications, CH-1211, Geneva 22, Switzerland; *Yearbook of Labour Statistics*.

International Monetary Fund, 700 Nineteenth Street, NW, Washington, D.C. 20431 (202) 623-7000; *International Financial Statistics*.

Organization of American States (OAS), General Secretariat, Washington, D.C. 20006 (202) 458-3533; *Statistical Bulletin of the OAS*.

URUGUAY - CONSUMPTION

The Economist Intelligence Unit, 111 West 57th Street, New York, New York 10019 (800) 938-4685; *The New Latin America Market Atlas*.

G.K. Hall and Company, 70 Lincoln Street, Boston, Massachusetts 02111 (617) 423-3990; *The World in Figures*.

Inter-American Development Bank, 1300 New York Avenue, NW, Washington, D.C. 20577 (202) 623-1753; *Economic and Social Progress in Latin America*.

Statistical Office of the United Nations, Publishing Service, New York, New York 10017 (800) 253-9646; *Statistical Yearbook for Latin America and the Caribbean*.

URUGUAY - COOPERATIVES

U.C.L.A. Latin American Center Publications, University of California, Los Angeles, California 90024 (310) 825-6634; *Statistical Abstract of Latin America*.

URUGUAY - COPPER PRODUCTION AND CONSUMPTION - See URUGUAY - MINING AND MINERAL PRODUCTS

URUGUAY - CORN PRODUCTION - See URUGUAY - CROPS

URUGUAY - CORPORATE INCOME TAXES - See URUGUAY - TAXATION

URUGUAY - CORPORATE TAXES - See URUGUAY - TAXATION

URUGUAY - COTTON - See URUGUAY - CROPS

URUGUAY - CROPS

The Economist Intelligence Unit, 111 West 57th Street, New York, New York 10019 (800) 938-4685; *The New Latin America Market Atlas*.

Facts on File, 460 Park Avenue South, New York, New York 10016 (800) 443-8323; *The New Book of World Rankings*.

Food and Agricultural Organization of the United Nations (FAO) Via delle Terme di Caracalla, 00100 Rome, Italy (Telephone Number in U.S. (202) 653-2400); *Production Yearbook*, and *The State of Food and Agriculture*.

G.K. Hall and Company, 70 Lincoln Street, Boston, Massachusetts 02111 (617) 423-3990; *The World in Figures*.

Statistical Office of the United Nations, Publishing Service, New York, New York 10017 (800) 253-9646; *Statistical Yearbook*.

U.C.L.A. Latin American Center Publications, University of California, Los Angeles, California 90024 (310) 825-6634; *Statistical Abstract of Latin America*.

URUGUAY - CUSTOMS DUTIES

G.K. Hall and Company, 70 Lincoln Street, Boston, Massachusetts 02111 (617) 423-3990; *The World in Figures*.

Inter-American Development Bank, 1300 New York Avenue, NW, Washington, D.C. 20577 (202) 623-1753; *Economic and Social Progress in Latin America*.

International Monetary Fund, 700 Nineteenth Street, NW, Washington, D.C. 20431 (202) 623-7000; *Government Finance Statistics Yearbook*.

URUGUAY - DAIRY PRODUCTS

Facts on File, 460 Park Avenue South, New York, New York 10016 (800) 443-8323; *The New Book of World Rankings*

Food and Agricultural Organization of the United Nations (FAO) Via delle Terme di Caracalla, 00100 Rome, Italy (Telephone Number in U.S. (202) 653-2400); *The State of Food and Agriculture*.

Statistical Office of the United Nations, Publishing Service, New York, New York 10017 (800) 253-9646; *Statistical Yearbook*.

U.C.L.A. Latin American Center Publications, University of California, Los Angeles, California 90024 (310) 825-6634; *Statistical Abstract of Latin America*.

URUGUAY - DEATH RATES

G.K. Hall and Company, 70 Lincoln Street, Boston, Massachusetts 02111 (617) 423-3990; *The World in Figures*.

Statistical Office of the United Nations, Publishing Service, New York, New York 10017 (800) 253-9646; *Statistical Yearbook*, and *Statistical Yearbook for Latin America and the Caribbean*.

Time Books, 201 East 50th Street, New York, New York 10022 (212) 751-2600; *The Economist Book of Vital World Statistics*.

URUGUAY - DEBT

The Economist Intelligence Unit, 111 West 57th Street, New York, New York 10019 (800) 938-4685; *The New Latin America Market*

Atlas.

URUGUAY - DEFENSE

The Economist Intelligence Unit, 111 West 57th Street, New York, New York 10019 (800) 938-4685; *The New Latin America Market Atlas.*

U.S. Arms Control and Disarmament Agency, 320 Twenty-first Street, NW, Washington, D.C. 20451 (202) 647-8677; *World Military Expenditures and Arms Transfers.*

URUGUAY - DEFENSE EXPENDITURES

G.K. Hall and Company, 70 Lincoln Street, Boston, Massachusetts 02111 (617) 423-3990; *The World in Figures.*

International Monetary Fund, 700 Nineteenth Street, NW, Washington, D.C. 20431 (202) 623-7000; *Government Finance Statistics Yearbook.*

URUGUAY - DEMOGRAPHY

The Economist Intelligence Unit, 111 West 57th Street, New York, New York 10019 (800) 938-4685; *The World Market Atlas.*

Facts on File, 460 Park Avenue South, New York, New York 10016 (800) 443-8323; *The New Book of World Rankings.*

G.K. Hall and Company, 70 Lincoln Street, Boston, Massachusetts 02111 (617) 423-3990; *The World in Figures.*

URUGUAY - DEVELOPMENT ASSISTANCE

G.K. Hall and Company, 70 Lincoln Street, Boston, Massachusetts 02111 (617) 423-3990; *The World in Figures.*

Inter-American Development Bank, 1300 New York Avenue, NW, Washington, D.C. 20577 (202) 623-1753; *Economic and Social Progress in Latin America.*

Statistical Office of the United Nations, Publishing Service, New York, New York 10017 (800) 253-9646; *Statistical Yearbook.*

URUGUAY - DIAMOND PRODUCTION - See URUGUAY - MINING AND MINERAL PRODUCTS

URUGUAY - DISCOUNT RATES

Inter-American Development Bank, 1300 New York Avenue, NW, Washington, D.C. 20577 (202) 623-1753; *Economic and Social Progress in Latin America.*

URUGUAY - DISEASE

G.K. Hall and Company, 70 Lincoln Street, Boston, Massachusetts 02111 (617) 423-3990; *The World in Figures.*

URUGUAY - DIVORCE RATES

Facts on File, 460 Park Avenue South, New York, New York 10016 (800) 443-8323; *The New Book of World Rankings.*

Statistical Office of the United Nations, Publishing Service, New York, New York 10017 (800) 253-9646; *Demographic Yearbook,* and *Statistical Yearbook.*

URUGUAY - DOMESTIC PRODUCT

G.K. Hall and Company, 70 Lincoln Street, Boston, Massachusetts 02111 (617) 423-3990; *The World in Figures.*

URUGUAY - DUCKS - See URUGUAY - LIVESTOCK AND POULTRY

URUGUAY - ECONOMY

Euromonitor Publications Limited, 87-88 Turnmill Street, London EC1M 5QU, England; *International Marketing Data and Statistics.*

Facts on File, 460 Park Avenue South, New York, New York 10016 (800) 443-8323; *The New Book of World Rankings.*

G.K. Hall and Company, 70 Lincoln Street, Boston, Massachusetts 02111 (617) 423-3990; *The World in Figures.*

Inter-American Development Bank, 1300 New York Avenue, NW, Washington, D.C. 20577 (202) 623-1753; *Economic and Social Progress in Latin America.*

Organization of American States (OAS), General Secretariat, Washington, D.C. 20006 (202) 458-3533; *Statistical Bulletin of the OAS.*

Statistical Office of the United Nations, Publishing Service, New York, New York 10017 (800) 253-9646; *Economic Survey of Latin America and the Caribbean.*

U.C.L.A. Latin American Center Publications, University of California, Los Angeles, California 90024 (310) 825-6634; *Statistical Abstract of Latin America.*

URUGUAY - EDUCATION

The Economist Intelligence Unit, 111 West 57th Street, New York, New York 10019 (800) 938-4685; *The New Latin America Market Atlas,* and *The World Market Atlas.*

Facts on File, 460 Park Avenue South, New York, New York 10016 (800) 443-8323; *The New Book of World Rankings.*

Federal Statistical Office, Gustav-Stresemann-Ring 11, D-6200 Wiesbaden, Germany; *Uruguay.*

Gale Research Incorporated, 835 Penobscot Building Detroit, Michigan 48226 (800) 877-4253; *International Historical Statistics The Americas and Australasia.*

G.K. Hall and Company, 70 Lincoln Street, Boston, Massachusetts 02111 (617) 423-3990; *The World in Figures.*

International Monetary Fund, 700 Nineteenth Street, NW, Washington, D.C. 20431 (202) 623-7000; *Government Finance Statistics Yearbook.*

Statistical Office of the United Nations, Publishing Service, New York, New York 10017 (800) 253-9646; *Statistical Yearbook for Latin America and the Caribbean.*

Time Books, 201 East 50th Street, New York, New York 10022 (212) 751-2600; *The Economist Book of Vital World Statistics.*

U.C.L.A. Latin American Center Publications, University of California, Los Angeles, California 90024 (310) 825-6634; *Statistical Abstract of Latin America.*

United Nations Educational, Scientific and Cultural Organization (UNESCO), 7 Place de Fontenoy, F-75700 Paris, France (Telephone Number in U.S. (212) 963-5981); *Statistical Yearbook.*

The World Bank, 1818 H Street, NW, Washington, D.C. 20433 (202) 477-1234; *World Tables.*

URUGUAY - EGG PRODUCTION AND CONSUMPTION - See URUGUAY - DAIRY PRODUCTS

URUGUAY - ELECTRICITY

The Economist Intelligence Unit, 111 West 57th Street, New York, New York 10019 (800) 938-4685; *The New Latin America Market Atlas.*

Facts on File, 460 Park Avenue South, New York, New York 10016 (800) 443-8323; *The New Book of World Rankings.*

Inter-American Development Bank, 1300 New York Avenue, NW, Washington, D.C. 20577 (202) 623-1753; *Economic and Social Progress in Latin America.*

Organization of American States (OAS), General Secretariat, Washington, D.C. 20006 (202) 458-3533; *Statistical Bulletin of the OAS.*

Statistical Office of the United Nations, Publishing Service, New York, New York 10017 (800) 253-9646; *Statistical Yearbook.*

Time Books, 201 East 50th Street, New York, New York 10022 (212) 751-2600; *The Economist Book of Vital World Statistics.*

URUGUAY - EMPLOYMENT

Euromonitor Publications Limited, 87-88 Turnmill Street, London EC1M 5QU, England; *International Marketing Data and Statistics.*

Facts on File, 460 Park Avenue South, New York, New York 10016 (800) 443-8323; *The New Book of World Rankings.*

Federal Statistical Office, Gustav-Stresemann-Ring 11, D-6200 Wiesbaden, Germany; *Uruguay.*

International Labour Office, I.L.O. Publications, CH-1211, Geneva 22, Switzerland; *Yearbook of Labour Statistics.*

Statistical Office of the United Nations, Publishing Service, New York, New York 10017 (800) 253-9646; *Statistical Yearbook,* and *Statistical Yearbook for Latin America and the Caribbean.*

U.C.L.A. Latin American Center Publications, University of California, Los Angeles, California 90024 (310) 825-6634; *Statistical Abstract of Latin America.*

URUGUAY - ENERGY

The Economist Intelligence Unit, 111 West 57th Street, New York, New York 10019 (800) 938-4685; *The New Latin America Market Atlas.*

Facts on File, 460 Park Avenue South, New York, New York 10016 (800) 443-8323; *The New Book of World Rankings.*

G.K. Hall and Company, 70 Lincoln Street, Boston, Massachusetts 02111 (617) 423-3990; *The World in Figures.*

Statistical Office of the United Nations, Publishing Service, New York, New York 10017 (800) 253-9646; *Energy Statistics Yearbook,*

Statistical Yearbook, and *Statistical Yearbook for Latin America and the Caribbean.*

Time Books, 201 East 50th Street, New York, New York 10022 (212) 751-2600; *The Economist Book of Vital World Statistics.*

U.C.L.A. Latin American Center Publications, University of California, Los Angeles, California 90024 (310) 825-6634; *Statistical Abstract of Latin America.*

URUGUAY - EXCHANGE RATES

Euromonitor Publications Limited, 87-88 Turnmill Street, London EC1M 5QU, England; *International Marketing Data and Statistics.*

International Civil Aviation Organization, 1000 Sherbrooke Street, West, Montreal, Quebec, Canada H3A 2R2 (514) 285-8219; *Civil Aviation Statistics of the World.*

Inter-American Development Bank, 1300 New York Avenue, NW, Washington, D.C. 20577 (202) 623-1753; *Economic and Social Progress in Latin America.*

International Monetary Fund, 700 Nineteenth Street, NW, Washington, D.C. 20431 (202) 623-7000; *International Financial Statistics.*

Organization of American States (OAS), General Secretariat, Washington, D.C. 20006 (202) 458-3533; *Statistical Bulletin of the OAS.*

Statistical Office of the United Nations, Publishing Service, New York, New York 10017 (800) 253-9646; *Statistical Yearbook.*

U.C.L.A. Latin American Center Publications, University of California, Los Angeles, California 90024 (310) 825-6634; *Statistical Abstract of Latin America.*

URUGUAY - EXCISE TAXES - See URUGUAY - TAXATION

URUGUAY - EXPORTS

The Economist Intelligence Unit, 111 West 57th Street, New York, New York 10019 (800) 938-4685; *The New Latin America Market Atlas,* and *The World Market Atlas.*

Euromonitor Publications Limited, 87-88 Turnmill Street, London EC1M 5QU, England; *International Marketing Data and Statistics.*

Food and Agricultural Organization of the United Nations (FAO) Via delle Terme di Caracalla, 00100 Rome, Italy (Telephone Number in U.S. (202) 653-2400); *The State of Food and Agriculture.*

G.K. Hall and Company, 70 Lincoln Street, Boston, Massachusetts 02111 (617) 423-3990; *The World in Figures.*

Inter-American Development Bank, 1300 New York Avenue, NW, Washington, D.C. 20577 (202) 623-1753; *Economic and Social Progress in Latin America.*

International Monetary Fund, 700 Nineteenth Street, NW, Washington, D.C. 20431 (202) 623-7000; *Direction of Trade Statistics, Government Finance Statistics Yearbook,* and *International Financial Statistics.*

Organization of American States (OAS), General Secretariat, Washington, D.C. 20006 (202) 458-3533; *Statistical Bulletin of the OAS.*

Statistical Office of the United Nations, Publishing Service, New York, New York 10017 (800) 253-9646; *Statistical Yearbook for Latin America and the Caribbean*.

Time Books, 201 East 50th Street, New York, New York 10022 (212) 751-2600; *The Economist Book of Vital World Statistics*.

The World Bank, 1818 H Street, NW, Washington, D.C. 20433 (202) 477-1234; *World Tables*.

URUGUAY - EXTERNAL FINANCING

Inter-American Development Bank, 1300 New York Avenue, NW, Washington, D.C. 20577 (202) 623-1753; *Economic and Social Progress in Latin America*.

Statistical Office of the United Nations, Publishing Service, New York, New York 10017 (800) 253-9646; *Statistical Yearbook for Latin America and the Caribbean*.

URUGUAY - EXTERNAL INDEBTEDNESS

Inter-American Development Bank, 1300 New York Avenue, NW, Washington, D.C. 20577 (202) 623-1753; *Economic and Social Progress in Latin America*.

Statistical Office of the United Nations, Publishing Service, New York, New York 10017 (800) 253-9646; *Statistical Yearbook for Latin America and the Caribbean*.

The World Bank, 1818 H Street, NW, Washington, D.C. 20433 (202) 477-1234; *World Tables*.

URUGUAY - EXTERNAL TRADE

Food and Agricultural Organization of the United Nations (FAO) Via delle Terme di Caracalla, 00100 Rome, Italy (Telephone Number in U.S. (202) 653-2400); *The State of Food and Agriculture*.

Gale Research Incorporated, 835 Penobscot Building Detroit, Michigan 48226 (800) 877-4253; *International Historical Statistics The Americas and Australasia*.

G.K. Hall and Company, 70 Lincoln Street, Boston, Massachusetts 02111 (617) 423-3990; *The World in Figures*.

Inter-American Development Bank, 1300 New York Avenue, NW, Washington, D.C. 20577 (202) 623-1753; *Economic and Social Progress in Latin America*.

Statistical Office of the United Nations, Publishing Service, New York, New York 10017 (800) 253-9646; *Statistical Yearbook*, and *Statistical Yearbook for Latin America and the Caribbean*.

URUGUAY - FAMILY PLANNING

U.C.L.A. Latin American Center Publications, University of California, Los Angeles, California 90024 (310) 825-6634; *Statistical Abstract of Latin America*.

URUGUAY - FARM CROPS - See URUGUAY - CROPS

URUGUAY - FEMALE WORKING POPULATION - See URUGUAY - EMPLOYMENT

URUGUAY - FERTILITY RATES

Facts on File, 460 Park Avenue South, New York, New York 10016 (800) 443-8323; *The New Book of World Rankings*.

Time Books, 201 East 50th Street, New York, New York 10022 (212) 751-2600; *The Economist Book of Vital World Statistics*.

The World Bank, 1818 H Street, NW, Washington, D.C. 20433 (202) 477-1234; *World Tables*.

URUGUAY - FERTILIZER

The Economist Intelligence Unit, 111 West 57th Street, New York, New York 10019 (800) 938-4685; *The New Latin America Market Atlas*.

Food and Agricultural Organization of the United Nations (FAO), Via delle Terme di Caracalla, 00100 Rome, Italy (Telephone Number in U.S. (202) 653-2400); *Annual Fertilizer Review*, and *The State of Food and Agriculture*.

Statistical Office of the United Nations, Publishing Service, New York, New York 10017 (800) 253-9646; *Statistical Yearbook*.

URUGUAY - FETAL MORTALITY

Statistical Office of the United Nations, Publishing Service, New York, New York 10017 (800) 253-9646; *Demographic Yearbook*.

World Health Organization, Office of Publications, Avenue Appia, CH-1211 Geneva 27, Switzerland (Telephone Number in U.S. (518) 436-9686); *World Health Statistics Annual*.

URUGUAY - FIBRE PRODUCTION - See URUGUAY - TEXTILE INDUSTRY

URUGUAY - FILAMENT PRODUCTION - See URUGUAY - TEXTILE INDUSTRY

URUGUAY - FINANCE

Facts on File, 460 Park Avenue South, New York, New York 10016 (800) 443-8323; *The New Book of World Rankings*.

Federal Statistical Office, Gustav-Stresemann-Ring 11, D-6200 Wiesbaden, Germany; *Uruguay*.

Gale Research Incorporated, 835 Penobscot Building Detroit, Michigan 48226 (800) 877-4253; *International Historical Statistics The Americas and Australasia*.

G.K. Hall and Company, 70 Lincoln Street, Boston, Massachusetts 02111 (617) 423-3990; *The World in Figures*.

Inter-American Development Bank, 1300 New York Avenue, NW, Washington, D.C. 20577 (202) 623-1753; *Economic and Social Progress in Latin America*.

International Monetary Fund, 700 Nineteenth Street, NW, Washington, D.C. 20431 (202) 623-7000; *Government Finance Statistics Yearbook*.

Organization of American States (OAS), General Secretariat, Washington, D.C. 20006 (202) 458-3533; *Statistical Bulletin of the OAS*.

U.C.L.A. Latin American Center Publications, University of California, Los Angeles, California 90024 (310) 825-6634; *Statistical Abstract of Latin America*.

URUGUAY - FISHERIES

Facts on File, 460 Park Avenue South, New York, New York 10016 (800) 443-8323; *The New Book of World Rankings*.

Federal Statistical Office, Gustav-Stresemann-Ring 11, D-6200 Wiesbaden, Germany; *Uruguay*.

Food and Agricultural Organization of the United Nations (FAO) Via delle Terme di Caracalla, 00100 Rome, Italy (Telephone Number in U.S. (202) 653-2400); *The State of Food and Agriculture*, and *Yearbook of Fishery Statistics*.

Inter-American Development Bank, 1300 New York Avenue, NW, Washington, D.C. 20577 (202) 623-1753; *Economic and Social Progress in Latin America*.

Statistical Office of the United Nations, Publishing Service, New York, New York 10017 (800) 253-9646; *Statistical Yearbook*.

U.C.L.A. Latin American Center Publications, University of California, Los Angeles, California 90024 (310) 825-6634; *Statistical Abstract of Latin America*.

URUGUAY - FLOUR PRODUCTION

Statistical Office of the United Nations, Publishing Service, New York, New York 10017 (800) 253-9646; *Statistical Yearbook*.

URUGUAY - FOOD

Food and Agricultural Organization of the United Nations (FAO) Via delle Terme di Caracalla, 00100 Rome, Italy (Telephone Number in U.S. (202) 653-2400); *The State of Food and Agriculture*.

G.K. Hall and Company, 70 Lincoln Street, Boston, Massachusetts 02111 (617) 423-3990; *The World in Figures*.

URUGUAY - FOREIGN AID

G.K. Hall and Company, 70 Lincoln Street, Boston, Massachusetts 02111 (617) 423-3990; *The World in Figures*.

Inter-American Development Bank, 1300 New York Avenue, NW, Washington, D.C. 20577 (202) 623-1753; *Economic and Social Progress in Latin America*.

URUGUAY - FOREIGN DEBT

The Economist Intelligence Unit, 111 West 57th Street, New York, New York 10019 (800) 938-4685; *The New Latin America Market Atlas*.

Inter-American Development Bank, 1300 New York Avenue, NW, Washington, D.C. 20577 (202) 623-1753; *Economic and Social Progress in Latin America*.

International Monetary Fund, 700 Nineteenth Street, NW, Washington, D.C. 20431 (202) 623-7000; *Government Finance Statistics Yearbook*.

URUGUAY - FOREIGN INDEBTEDNESS

Inter-American Development Bank, 1300 New York Avenue, NW, Washington, D.C. 20577 (202) 623-1753; *Economic and Social Progress in Latin America*.

Statistical Office of the United Nations, Publishing Service, New York, New York 10017 (800) 253-9646; *Economic Survey of Latin America and the Caribbean*.

URUGUAY - FOREIGN INVESTMENT

The Economist Intelligence Unit, 111 West 57th Street, New York, New York 10019 (800) 938-4685; *The New Latin America Market Atlas*.

URUGUAY - FOREIGN TRADE

The Economist Intelligence Unit, 111 West 57th Street, New York, New York 10019 (800) 938-4685; *The New Latin America Market Atlas*.

Euromonitor Publications Limited, 87-88 Turnmill Street, London EC1M 5QU, England; *International Marketing Data and Statistics*.

Facts on File, 460 Park Avenue South, New York, New York 10016 (800) 443-8323; *The New Book of World Rankings*.

Federal Statistical Office, Gustav-Stresemann-Ring 11, D-6200 Wiesbaden, Germany; *Uruguay*.

Food and Agricultural Organization of the United Nations (FAO) Via delle Terme di Caracalla, 00100 Rome, Italy (Telephone Number in U.S. (202) 653-2400); *The State of Food and Agriculture*.

G.K. Hall and Company, 70 Lincoln Street, Boston, Massachusetts 02111 (617) 423-3990; *The World in Figures*.

Inter-American Development Bank, 1300 New York Avenue, NW, Washington, D.C. 20577 (202) 623-1753; *Economic and Social Progress in Latin America*.

International Monetary Fund, 700 Nineteenth Street, NW, Washington, D.C. 20431 (202) 623-7000; *International Financial Statistics*.

Statistical Office of the United Nations, Publishing Service, New York, New York 10017 (800) 253-9646; *Economic Survey of Latin America and the Caribbean, International Trade Statistics Yearbook*, and *Statistical Yearbook*.

U.C.L.A. Latin American Center Publications, University of California, Los Angeles, California 90024 (310) 825-6634; *Statistical Abstract of Latin America*.

The World Bank, 1818 H Street, NW, Washington, D.C. 20433 (202) 477-1234; *World Tables*.

URUGUAY - FORESTRY AND FOREST PRODUCTS

American Forest and Paper Association, 1250 Connecticut Avenue, NW, Washington, D.C. 20036 (202) 463-2455; *Wood Pulp and Fiber Statistics*.

Facts on File, 460 Park Avenue South, New York, New York 10016 (800) 443-8323; *The New Book of World Rankings*.

Federal Statistical Office, Gustav-Stresemann-Ring 11, D-6200 Wiesbaden, Germany; *Uruguay*.

Food and Agricultural Organization of the United Nations (FAO) Via delle Terme di Caracalla, 00100 Rome, Italy (Telephone Number in U.S. (202) 653-2400); *The State of Food and Agriculture*, and *Yearbook of Forest Products*.

G.K. Hall and Company, 70 Lincoln Street, Boston, Massachusetts 02111 (617) 423-3990; *The World in Figures*.

Inter-American Development Bank, 1300 New York Avenue, NW, Washington, D.C. 20577 (202) 623-1753; *Economic and Social Progress in Latin America.*

Statistical Office of the United Nations, Publishing Service, New York, New York 10017 (800) 253-9646; *Statistical Yearbook.*

U.C.L.A. Latin American Center Publications, University of California, Los Angeles, California 90024 (310) 825-6634; *Statistical Abstract of Latin America.*

United Nations Educational, Scientific and Cultural Organization (UNESCO), 7 Place de Fontenoy, F-75700 Paris, France (Telephone Number in U.S. (212) 963-5981); *Statistical Yearbook.*

URUGUAY - GARLIC PRODUCTION - See URUGUAY - CROPS

URUGUAY - GAS PRODUCTION - See URUGUAY - MINING AND MINERAL PRODUCTS

URUGUAY - GENERAL INDUSTRIAL STATISTICS

Statistical Office of the United Nations, Publishing Service, New York, New York 10017 (800) 253-9646; *Industrial Statistics Yearbook.*

URUGUAY - GENERAL MORTALITY

Statistical Office of the United Nations, Publishing Service, New York, New York 10017 (800) 253-9646; *Demographic Yearbook.*

World Health Organization, Office of Publications, Avenue Appia, CH-1211 Geneva 27, Switzerland (Telephone Number in U.S. (518) 436-9686); *World Health Statistics Annual.*

URUGUAY - GEOGRAPHIC DATA

Facts on File, 460 Park Avenue South, New York, New York 10016 (800) 443-8323; *The New Book of World Rankings.*

U.C.L.A. Latin American Center Publications, University of California, Los Angeles, California 90024 (310) 825-6634; *Statistical Abstract of Latin America.*

URUGUAY - GOATS - See URUGUAY - LIVESTOCK AND POULTRY

URUGUAY - GOLD HOLDINGS

International Monetary Fund, 700 Nineteenth Street, NW, Washington, D.C. 20431 (202) 623-7000; *International Financial Statistics.*

Statistical Office of the United Nations, Publishing Service, New York, New York 10017 (800) 253-9646; *Statistical Yearbook.*

The World Bank, 1818 H Street, NW, Washington, D.C. 20433 (202) 477-1234; *World Tables.*

URUGUAY - GOLD PRODUCTION AND CONSUMPTION - See URUGUAY - MINING AND MINERAL PRODUCTS

URUGUAY - GOLD RESERVES

The Economist Intelligence Unit, 111 West 57th Street, New York, New York 10019 (800) 938-4685; *The New Latin America Market Atlas.*

URUGUAY - GOVERNMENT

G.K. Hall and Company, 70 Lincoln Street, Boston, Massachusetts 02111 (617) 423-3990; *The World in Figures.*

Inter-American Development Bank, 1300 New York Avenue, NW, Washington, D.C. 20577 (202) 623-1753; *Economic and Social Progress in Latin America.*

URUGUAY - GOVERNMENT CONSUMPTION

Inter-American Development Bank, 1300 New York Avenue, NW, Washington, D.C. 20577 (202) 623-1753; *Economic and Social Progress in Latin America.*

URUGUAY - GOVERNMENT EXPENDITURES

Inter-American Development Bank, 1300 New York Avenue, NW, Washington, D.C. 20577 (202) 623-1753; *Economic and Social Progress in Latin America.*

International Monetary Fund, 700 Nineteenth Street, NW, Washington, D.C. 20431 (202) 623-7000; *Government Finance Statistics Yearbook.*

Time Books, 201 East 50th Street, New York, New York 10022 (212) 751-2600; *The Economist Book of Vital World Statistics.*

The World Bank, 1818 H Street, NW, Washington, D.C. 20433 (202) 477-1234; *World Tables.*

URUGUAY - GOVERNMENT FINANCE

Inter-American Development Bank, 1300 New York Avenue, NW, Washington, D.C. 20577 (202) 623-1753; *Economic and Social Progress in Latin America.*

International Monetary Fund, 700 Nineteenth Street, NW, Washington, D.C. 20431 (202) 623-7000; *International Financial Statistics.*

URUGUAY - GOVERNMENT REVENUE

Inter-American Development Bank, 1300 New York Avenue, NW, Washington, D.C. 20577 (202) 623-1753; *Economic and Social Progress in Latin America.*

International Monetary Fund, 700 Nineteenth Street, NW, Washington, D.C. 20431 (202) 623-7000; *Government Finance Statistics Yearbook.*

Time Books, 201 East 50th Street, New York, New York 10022 (212) 751-2600; *The Economist Book of Vital World Statistics.*

The World Bank, 1818 H Street, NW, Washington, D.C. 20433 (202) 477-1234; *World Tables.*

URUGUAY - GRAIN PRODUCTION - See URUGUAY - CROPS

URUGUAY - GREEN PEPPER AND CHILIE PRODUCTION - See URUGUAY - CROPS

URUGUAY - GROSS DOMESTIC PRODUCT

The Economist Intelligence Unit, 111 West 57th Street, New York, New York 10019 (800) 938-4685; *The New Latin America Market Atlas,* and *The World Market Atlas.*

Euromonitor Publications Limited, 87-88 Turnmill Street, London EC1M 5QU, England; *International Marketing Data and Statistics.*

Facts on File, 460 Park Avenue South, New York, New York 10016 (800) 443-8323; *The New Book of World Rankings.*

G.K. Hall and Company, 70 Lincoln Street, Boston, Massachusetts 02111 (617) 423-3990; *The World in Figures.*

Inter-American Development Bank, 1300 New York Avenue, NW, Washington, D.C. 20577 (202) 623-1753; *Economic and Social Progress in Latin America.*

Organization of American States (OAS), General Secretariat, Washington, D.C. 20006 (202) 458-3533; *Statistical Bulletin of the OAS.*

Statistical Office of the United Nations, Publishing Service, New York, New York 10017 (800) 253-9646; *Statistical Yearbook,* and *Statistical Yearbook for Latin America and the Caribbean.*

Time Books, 201 East 50th Street, New York, New York 10022 (212) 751-2600; *The Economist Book of Vital World Statistics.*

U.C.L.A. Latin American Center Publications, University of California, Los Angeles, California 90024 (310) 825-6634; *Statistical Abstract of Latin America.*

The World Bank, 1818 H Street, NW, Washington, D.C. 20433 (202) 477-1234; *World Tables.*

URUGUAY - GROSS NATIONAL PRODUCT

Euromonitor Publications Limited, 87-88 Turnmill Street, London EC1M 5QU, England; *International Marketing Data and Statistics.*

Inter-American Development Bank, 1300 New York Avenue, NW, Washington, D.C. 20577 (202) 623-1753; *Economic and Social Progress in Latin America.*

U.S. Arms Control and Disarmament Agency, 320 Twenty-first Street, NW, Washington, D.C. 20451 (202) 647-8677; *World Military Expenditures and Arms Transfers.*

The World Bank, 1818 H Street, NW, Washington, D.C. 20433 (202) 477-1234; *World Tables.*

URUGUAY - HEALTH

The Economist Intelligence Unit, 111 West 57th Street, New York, New York 10019 (800) 938-4685; *The New Latin America Market Atlas.*

Facts on File, 460 Park Avenue South, New York, New York 10016 (800) 443-8323; *The New Book of World Rankings.*

Federal Statistical Office, Gustav-Stresemann-Ring 11, D-6200 Wiesbaden, Germany; *Uruguay.*

G.K. Hall and Company, 70 Lincoln Street, Boston, Massachusetts 02111 (617) 423-3990; *The World in Figures.*

Statistical Office of the United Nations, Publishing Service, New York, New York 10017 (800) 253-9646; *Statistical Yearbook,* and *Statistical Yearbook for Latin America and the Caribbean.*

Time Books, 201 East 50th Street, New York, New York 10022 (212) 751-2600; *The Economist Book of Vital World Statistics.*

U.C.L.A. Latin American Center Publications, University of California, Los Angeles, California 90024 (310) 825-6634; *Statistical Abstract of Latin America.*

URUGUAY - HEALTH EXPENDITURES

International Monetary Fund, 700 Nineteenth Street, NW, Washington, D.C. 20431 (202) 623-7000; *Government Finance Statistics Yearbook.*

URUGUAY - HIDE PRODUCTION

Food and Agricultural Organization of the United Nations (FAO), Via delle Terme di Caracalla, 00100 Rome, Italy (Telephone Number in U.S. (202) 653-2400); *Production Yearbook.*

URUGUAY - HIDES EXPORTS

International Monetary Fund, 700 Nineteenth Street, NW, Washington, D.C. 20431 (202) 623-7000; *International Financial Statistics.*

URUGUAY - HIGHWAYS

The Economist Intelligence Unit, 111 West 57th Street, New York, New York 10019 (800) 938-4685; *The New Latin America Market Atlas.*

G.K. Hall and Company, 70 Lincoln Street, Boston, Massachusetts 02111 (617) 423-3990; *The World in Figures.*

URUGUAY - HORSES - See URUGUAY - LIVESTOCK AND POULTRY

URUGUAY - HOURS OF WORK - See URUGUAY - EMPLOYMENT

URUGUAY - HOUSING AND HOUSING UNITS

Facts on File, 460 Park Avenue South, New York, New York 10016 (800) 443-8323; *The New Book of World Rankings.*

Statistical Office of the United Nations, Publishing Service, New York, New York 10017 (800) 253-9646; *Statistical Yearbook for Latin America and the Caribbean.*

U.C.L.A. Latin American Center Publications, University of California, Los Angeles, California 90024 (310) 825-6634; *Statistical Abstract of Latin America.*

URUGUAY - HOUSING EXPENDITURES

International Monetary Fund, 700 Nineteenth Street, NW, Washington, D.C. 20431 (202) 623-7000; *Government Finance Statistics Yearbook.*

URUGUAY - ILLITERATE POPULATION

The Economist Intelligence Unit, 111 West 57th Street, New York, New York 10019 (800) 938-4685; *The New Latin America Market Atlas,* and *The World Market Atlas.*

G.K. Hall and Company, 70 Lincoln Street, Boston, Massachusetts 02111 (617) 423-3990; *The World in Figures.*

Statistical Office of the United Nations, Publishing Service, New York, New York 10017 (800) 253-9646; *Statistical Yearbook for Latin America and the Caribbean.*

United Nations Educational, Scientific and Cultural Organization (UNESCO), 7 Place de Fontenoy, F-75700 Paris, France (Telephone

Number in U.S. (212) 963-5981); *Statistical Yearbook.*

URUGUAY - IMMIGRATION

U.C.L.A. Latin American Center Publications, University of California, Los Angeles, California 90024 (310) 825-6634; *Statistical Abstract of Latin America.*

URUGUAY - IMPORTS

The Economist Intelligence Unit, 111 West 57th Street, New York, New York 10019 (800) 938-4685; *The New Latin America Market Atlas*, and *The World Market Atlas.*

Euromonitor Publications Limited, 87-88 Turnmill Street, London EC1M 5QU, England; *International Marketing Data and Statistics.*

Food and Agricultural Organization of the United Nations (FAO) Via delle Terme di Caracalla, 00100 Rome, Italy (Telephone Number in U.S. (202) 653-2400); *The State of Food and Agriculture.*

G.K. Hall and Company, 70 Lincoln Street, Boston, Massachusetts 02111 (617) 423-3990; *The World in Figures.*

Inter-American Development Bank, 1300 New York Avenue, NW, Washington, D.C. 20577 (202) 623-1753; *Economic and Social Progress in Latin America.*

International Monetary Fund, 700 Nineteenth Street, NW, Washington, D.C. 20431 (202) 623-7000; *Direction of Trade Statistics, Government Finance Statistics Yearbook*, and *International Financial Statistics.*

Organization of American States (OAS), General Secretariat, Washington, D.C. 20006 (202) 458-3533; *Statistical Bulletin of the OAS.*

Statistical Office of the United Nations, Publishing Service, New York, New York 10017 (800) 253-9646; *Statistical Yearbook for Latin America and the Caribbean.*

Time Books, 201 East 50th Street, New York, New York 10022 (212) 751-2600; *The Economist Book of Vital World Statistics.*

The World Bank, 1818 H Street, NW, Washington, D.C. 20433 (202) 477-1234; *World Tables.*

URUGUAY - INCOME DISTRIBUTION

Statistical Office of the United Nations, Publishing Service, New York, New York 10017 (800) 253-9646; *Statistical Yearbook for Latin America and the Caribbean.*

U.C.L.A. Latin American Center Publications, University of California, Los Angeles, California 90024 (310) 825-6634; *Statistical Abstract of Latin America.*

URUGUAY - INCOME TAXES - See URUGUAY - TAXATION

URUGUAY - INDUSTRIAL METALS PRODUCTION - See URUGUAY - MINING AND MINERAL PRODUCTS

URUGUAY - INDUSTRY

Euromonitor Publications Limited, 87-88 Turnmill Street, London EC1M 5QU, England; *International Marketing Data and Statistics.*

Facts on File, 460 Park Avenue South, New York, New York 10016 (800) 443-8323; *The New Book of World Rankings.*

Federal Statistical Office, Gustav-Stresemann-Ring 11, D-6200 Wiesbaden, Germany; *Uruguay.*

Gale Research Incorporated, 835 Penobscot Building Detroit, Michigan 48226 (800) 877-4253; *International Historical Statistics The Americas and Australasia.*

G.K. Hall and Company, 70 Lincoln Street, Boston, Massachusetts 02111 (617) 423-3990; *The World in Figures.*

International Labour Office, I.L.O. Publications, CH-1211, Geneva 22, Switzerland; *Yearbook of Labour Statistics.*

Statistical Office of the United Nations, Publishing Service, New York, New York 10017 (800) 253-9646; *Statistical Yearbook.*

Time Books, 201 East 50th Street, New York, New York 10022 (212) 751-2600; *The Economist Book of Vital World Statistics.*

U.C.L.A. Latin American Center Publications, University of California, Los Angeles, California 90024 (310) 825-6634; *Statistical Abstract of Latin America.*

The World Bank, 1818 H Street, NW, Washington, D.C. 20433 (202) 477-1234; *World Tables.*

World Intellectual Property Organization, 34 Chemin des Colombettes, CH-1211 Geneva 20. Switzerland; *Industrial Property Statistics.*

URUGUAY - INFANT AND MATERNAL MORTALITY

The Economist Intelligence Unit, 111 West 57th Street, New York, New York 10019 (800) 938-4685; *The New Latin America Market Atlas.*

Statistical Office of the United Nations, Publishing Service, New York, New York 10017 (800) 253-9646; *Demographic Yearbook*, and *Statistical Yearbook.*

Time Books, 201 East 50th Street, New York, New York 10022 (212) 751-2600; *The Economist Book of Vital World Statistics.*

The World Bank, 1818 H Street, NW, Washington, D.C. 20433 (202) 477-1234; *World Tables.*

World Health Organization, Office of Publications, Avenue Appia, CH-1211 Geneva 27, Switzerland (Telephone Number in U.S. (518) 436-9686); *World Health Statistics Annual.*

URUGUAY - INFLATIONARY FACTORS

Statistical Office of the United Nations, Publishing Service, New York, New York 10017 (800) 253-9646; *Economic Survey of Latin America and the Caribbean.*

URUGUAY - INTEREST RATES

Inter-American Development Bank, 1300 New York Avenue, NW, Washington, D.C. 20577 (202) 623-1753; *Economic and Social Progress in Latin America.*

URUGUAY - INTERNATIONAL FINANCE

Inter-American Development Bank, 1300 New York Avenue, NW, Washington, D.C. 20577 (202) 623-1753; *Economic and Social Progress in Latin America.*

U.C.L.A. Latin American Center Publications, University of California, Los Angeles, California 90024 (310) 825-6634; *Statistical Abstract of Latin America*.

URUGUAY - INTERNATIONAL LIQUIDITY

Inter-American Development Bank, 1300 New York Avenue, NW, Washington, D.C. 20577 (202) 623-1753; *Economic and Social Progress in Latin America*.

International Monetary Fund, 700 Nineteenth Street, NW, Washington, D.C. 20431 (202) 623-7000; *International Financial Statistics*.

URUGUAY - INTERNATIONAL RESERVES

Inter-American Development Bank, 1300 New York Avenue, NW, Washington, D.C. 20577 (202) 623-1753; *Economic and Social Progress in Latin America*.

Organization of American States (OAS), General Secretariat, Washington, D.C. 20006 (202) 458-3533; *Statistical Bulletin of the OAS*.

URUGUAY - INTERNATIONAL RESERVES EXCLUDING GOLD

Statistical Office of the United Nations, Publishing Service, New York, New York 10017 (800) 253-9646; *Statistical Yearbook*.

The World Bank, 1818 H Street, NW, Washington, D.C. 20433 (202) 477-1234; *World Tables*.

URUGUAY - INTERNATIONAL STATISTICS

Inter-American Development Bank, 1300 New York Avenue, NW, Washington, D.C. 20577 (202) 623-1753; *Economic and Social Progress in Latin America*.

U.C.L.A. Latin American Center Publications, University of California, Los Angeles, California 90024 (310) 825-6634; *Statistical Abstract of Latin America*.

URUGUAY - INVESTMENT

Inter-American Development Bank, 1300 New York Avenue, NW, Washington, D.C. 20577 (202) 623-1753; *Economic and Social Progress in Latin America*.

Statistical Office of the United Nations, Publishing Service, New York, New York 10017 (800) 253-9646; *Statistical Yearbook for Latin America and the Caribbean*.

URUGUAY - IRON ORE PRODUCTION AND CONSUMPTION - See URUGUAY - MINING AND MINERAL PRODUCTS

URUGUAY - IRRIGATION

Euromonitor Publications Limited, 87-88 Turnmill Street, London EC1M 5QU, England; *International Marketing Data and Statistics*.

Inter-American Development Bank, 1300 New York Avenue, NW, Washington, D.C. 20577 (202) 623-1753; *Economic and Social Progress in Latin America*.

URUGUAY - LABOR FORCE

The Economist Intelligence Unit, 111 West 57th Street, New York, New York 10019 (800) 938-4685; *The New Latin America Market Atlas*.

Euromonitor Publications Limited, 87-88 Turnmill Street, London EC1M 5QU, England; *International Marketing Data and Statistics*.

Facts on File, 460 Park Avenue South, New York, New York 10016 (800) 443-8323; *The New Book of World Rankings*.

Food and Agricultural Organization of the United Nations (FAO) Via delle Terme di Caracalla, 00100 Rome, Italy (Telephone Number in U.S. (202) 653-2400); *The State of Food and Agriculture*.

Gale Research Incorporated, 835 Penobscot Building Detroit, Michigan 48226 (800) 877-4253; *International Historical Statistics The Americas and Australasia*.

G.K. Hall and Company, 70 Lincoln Street, Boston, Massachusetts 02111 (617) 423-3990; *The World in Figures*.

Time Books, 201 East 50th Street, New York, New York 10022 (212) 751-2600; *The Economist Book of Vital World Statistics*.

The World Bank, 1818 H Street, NW, Washington, D.C. 20433 (202) 477-1234; *World Tables*.

URUGUAY - LABOR PRODUCTIVITY

International Labour Office, I.L.O. Publications, CH-1211, Geneva 22, Switzerland; *Yearbook of Labour Statistics*.

URUGUAY - LAND AREA

The Economist Intelligence Unit, 111 West 57th Street, New York, New York 10019 (800) 938-4685; *The New Latin America Market Atlas*.

URUGUAY - LAND USE

Euromonitor Publications Limited, 87-88 Turnmill Street, London EC1M 5QU, England; *International Marketing Data and Statistics*.

G.K. Hall and Company, 70 Lincoln Street, Boston, Massachusetts 02111 (617) 423-3990; *The World in Figures*.

Inter-American Development Bank, 1300 New York Avenue, NW, Washington, D.C. 20577 (202) 623-1753; *Economic and Social Progress in Latin America*.

URUGUAY - LEATHER AND FOOTWEAR - EXPORTS AND IMPORTS

Statistical Office of the United Nations, Publishing Service, New York, New York 10017 (800) 253-9646; *Trade in Manufactures of Developing Countries*.

URUGUAY - LIBRARIES

Facts on File, 460 Park Avenue South, New York, New York 10016 (800) 443-8323; *The New Book of World Rankings*.

United Nations Educational, Scientific and Cultural Organization (UNESCO), 7 Place de Fontenoy, F-75700 Paris, France (Telephone Number in U.S. (212) 963-5981); *Statistical Yearbook*.

URUGUAY - LIFE EXPECTANCY RATE

The Economist Intelligence Unit, 111 West 57th Street, New York, New York 10019 (800) 938-4685; *The New Latin America Market Atlas*.

URUGUAY - LIVESTOCK AND POULTRY

Commodity Research Bureau, Incorporated, 75 Wall Street, New York, New York 10005 (212) 504-7754; *Commodity Year Book*.

Euromonitor Publications Limited, 87-88 Turnmill Street, London EC1M 5QU, England; *International Marketing Data and Statistics*.

Facts on File, 460 Park Avenue South, New York, New York 10016 (800) 443-8323; *The New Book of World Rankings*.

Food and Agricultural Organization of the United Nations (FAO) Via delle Terme di Caracalla, 00100 Rome, Italy (Telephone Number in U.S. (202) 653-2400); *Production Yearbook*, and *The State of Food and Agriculture*.

G.K. Hall and Company, 70 Lincoln Street, Boston, Massachusetts 02111 (617) 423-3990; *The World in Figures*.

Statistical Office of the United Nations, Publishing Service, New York, New York 10017 (800) 253-9646; *Statistical Yearbook*.

URUGUAY - LIVING LEVELS

G.K. Hall and Company, 70 Lincoln Street, Boston, Massachusetts 02111 (617) 423-3990; *The World in Figures*.

Statistical Office of the United Nations, Publishing Service, New York, New York 10017 (800) 253-9646; *Statistical Yearbook for Latin America and the Caribbean*.

Time Books, 201 East 50th Street, New York, New York 10022 (212) 751-2600; *The Economist Book of Vital World Statistics*.

URUGUAY - MAIL - NUMBER OF ITEMS SENT AND RECEIVED

Statistical Office of the United Nations, Publishing Service, New York, New York 10017 (800) 253-9646; *Statistical Yearbook*.

URUGUAY - MAIN ECONOMIC INDICATORS - See URUGUAY - ECONOMY

URUGUAY - MANUFACTURING

The Economist Intelligence Unit, 111 West 57th Street, New York, New York 10019 (800) 938-4685; *The New Latin America Market Atlas*.

Facts on File, 460 Park Avenue South, New York, New York 10016 (800) 443-8323; *The New Book of World Rankings*.

G.K. Hall and Company, 70 Lincoln Street, Boston, Massachusetts 02111 (617) 423-3990; *The World in Figures*.

Inter-American Development Bank, 1300 New York Avenue, NW, Washington, D.C. 20577 (202) 623-1753; *Economic and Social Progress in Latin America*.

Statistical Office of the United Nations, Publishing Service, New York, New York 10017 (800) 253-9646; *Statistical Yearbook*, and *Statistical Yearbook for Latin America and the Caribbean*.

Time Books, 201 East 50th Street, New York, New York 10022 (212) 751-2600; *The Economist Book of Vital World Statistics*.

The World Bank, 1818 H Street, NW, Washington, D.C. 20433 (202) 477-1234; *World Tables*.

URUGUAY - MARRIAGE RATES

Facts on File, 460 Park Avenue South, New York, New York 10016 (800) 443-8323; *The New Book of World Rankings*.

Statistical Office of the United Nations, Publishing Service, New York, New York 10017 (800) 253-9646; *Demographic Yearbook*, and *Statistical Yearbook*.

URUGUAY - MEAT EXPORTS

International Monetary Fund, 700 Nineteenth Street, NW, Washington, D.C. 20431 (202) 623-7000; *International Financial Statistics*.

Organization of American States (OAS), General Secretariat, Washington, D.C. 20006 (202) 458-3533; *Statistical Bulletin of the OAS*.

URUGUAY - MEAT PRODUCTION - See URUGUAY - LIVESTOCK AND POULTRY

URUGUAY - MEDICAL PERSONNEL

U.C.L.A. Latin American Center Publications, University of California, Los Angeles, California 90024 (310) 825-6634; *Statistical Abstract of Latin America*.

URUGUAY - MERCHANT SHIPPING

G.K. Hall and Company, 70 Lincoln Street, Boston, Massachusetts 02111 (617) 423-3990; *The World in Figures*.

Lloyd's Register of Shipping, 17 Battery Place, New York, New York 10004 (212) 425-8050; *Register of Ships*.

Statistical Office of the United Nations, Publishing Service, New York, New York 10017 (800) 253-9646; *Statistical Yearbook*.

Time Books, 201 East 50th Street, New York, New York 10022 (212) 751-2600; *The Economist Book of Vital World Statistics*.

U.S. Department of Transportation, Maritime Administration, 400 Seventh Street, SW, Washington, D.C. 20590 (202) 366-5807; *A Statistical Analysis of the World's Merchant Fleets*.

URUGUAY - MILITARY

The Economist Intelligence Unit, 111 West 57th Street, New York, New York 10019 (800) 938-4685; *The New Latin America Market Atlas*.

G.K. Hall and Company, 70 Lincoln Street, Boston, Massachusetts 02111 (617) 423-3990; *The World in Figures*.

The International Institute for Strategic Studies, 23 Tavistock Street, London WC2E 7NQ, England; *The Military Balance*.

U.C.L.A. Latin American Center Publications, University of California, Los Angeles, California 90024 (310) 825-6634; *Statistical Abstract of Latin America*.

U.S. Arms Control and Disarmament Agency, 320 Twenty-first Street, NW, Washington, D.C. 20451 (202) 647-8677; *World Military Expenditures and Arms Transfers*.

URUGUAY - MILK PRODUCTION - See URUGUAY - DAIRY PRODUCTS

URUGUAY - MINING AND MINERAL PRODUCTS

The Economist Intelligence Unit, 111 West 57th Street, New York, New York 10019 (800) 938-4685; *The New Latin America Market Atlas*.

Facts on File, 460 Park Avenue South, New York, New York 10016 (800) 443-8323; *The New Book of World Rankings*.

G.K. Hall and Company, 70 Lincoln Street, Boston, Massachusetts 02111 (617) 423-3990; *The World in Figures*.

Inter-American Development Bank, 1300 New York Avenue, NW, Washington, D.C. 20577 (202) 623-1753; *Economic and Social Progress in Latin America*.

Statistical Office of the United Nations, Publishing Service, New York, New York 10017 (800) 253-9646; *Statistical Yearbook*, and *Statistical Yearbook for Latin America and the Caribbean*.

U.C.L.A. Latin American Center Publications, University of California, Los Angeles, California 90024 (310) 825-6634; *Statistical Abstract of Latin America*.

URUGUAY - MONEY EXCHANGE RATE

Euromonitor Publications Limited, 87-88 Turnmill Street, London EC1M 5QU, England; *International Marketing Data and Statistics*.

Inter-American Development Bank, 1300 New York Avenue, NW, Washington, D.C. 20577 (202) 623-1753; *Economic and Social Progress in Latin America*.

International Monetary Fund, 700 Nineteenth Street, NW, Washington, D.C. 20431 (202) 623-7000; *International Financial Statistics*.

Statistical Office of the United Nations, Publishing Service, New York, New York 10017 (800) 253-9646; *Statistical Yearbook*.

URUGUAY - MONEY RATES - MARKET

Inter-American Development Bank, 1300 New York Avenue, NW, Washington, D.C. 20577 (202) 623-1753; *Economic and Social Progress in Latin America*.

URUGUAY - MONEY RESERVES

Euromonitor Publications Limited, 87-88 Turnmill Street, London EC1M 5QU, England; *International Marketing Data and Statistics*.

Inter-American Development Bank, 1300 New York Avenue, NW, Washington, D.C. 20577 (202) 623-1753; *Economic and Social Progress in Latin America*.

URUGUAY - MONEY SUPPLY

Euromonitor Publications Limited, 87-88 Turnmill Street, London EC1M 5QU, England; *International Marketing Data and Statistics*.

G.K. Hall and Company, 70 Lincoln Street, Boston, Massachusetts 02111 (617) 423-3990; *The World in Figures*.

Inter-American Development Bank, 1300 New York Avenue, NW, Washington, D.C. 20577 (202) 623-1753; *Economic and Social Progress in Latin America*.

International Monetary Fund, 700 Nineteenth Street, NW, Washington, D.C. 20431 (202) 623-7000; *International Financial*

Statistics.

Statistical Office of the United Nations, Publishing Service, New York, New York 10017 (800) 253-9646; *Statistical Yearbook*.

U.C.L.A. Latin American Center Publications, University of California, Los Angeles, California 90024 (310) 825-6634; *Statistical Abstract of Latin America*.

The World Bank, 1818 H Street, NW, Washington, D.C. 20433 (202) 477-1234; *World Tables*.

URUGUAY - MOTOR VEHICLE TAXES - See URUGUAY - TAXATION

URUGUAY - MOTOR VEHICLES IN USE

The Economist Intelligence Unit, 111 West 57th Street, New York, New York 10019 (800) 938-4685; *The New Latin America Market Atlas*.

G.K. Hall and Company, 70 Lincoln Street, Boston, Massachusetts 02111 (617) 423-3990; *The World in Figures*.

Statistical Office of the United Nations, Publishing Service, New York, New York 10017 (800) 253-9646; *Statistical Yearbook*.

Time Books, 201 East 50th Street, New York, New York 10022 (212) 751-2600; *The Economist Book of Vital World Statistics*.

URUGUAY - MULES - See URUGUAY - LIVESTOCK AND POULTRY

URUGUAY - MUSEUMS

Facts on File, 460 Park Avenue South, New York, New York 10016 (800) 443-8323; *The New Book of World Rankings*.

United Nations Educational, Scientific and Cultural Organization (UNESCO), 7 Place de Fontenoy, F-75700 Paris, France (Telephone Number in U.S. (212) 963-5981); *Statistical Yearbook*.

URUGUAY - NATALITY - See URUGUAY - BIRTH RATE

URUGUAY - NATIONAL ACCOUNTS

Federal Statistical Office, Gustav-Stresemann-Ring 11, D-6200 Wiesbaden, Germany; *Uruguay*.

Gale Research Incorporated, 835 Penobscot Building Detroit, Michigan 48226 (800) 877-4253; *International Historical Statistics The Americas and Australasia*.

Inter-American Development Bank, 1300 New York Avenue, NW, Washington, D.C. 20577 (202) 623-1753; *Economic and Social Progress in Latin America*.

International Monetary Fund, 700 Nineteenth Street, NW, Washington, D.C. 20431 (202) 623-7000; *International Financial Statistics*.

Organization of American States (OAS), General Secretariat, Washington, D.C. 20006 (202) 458-3533; *Statistical Bulletin of the OAS*.

Statistical Office of the United Nations, Publishing Service, New York, New York 10017 (800) 253-9646; *National Accounts Statistics*, and *Statistical Yearbook*.

U.C.L.A. Latin American Center Publications, University of California, Los Angeles, California 90024 (310) 825-6634; *Statistical*

Abstract of Latin America.

URUGUAY - NATIONAL INCOME

Facts on File, 460 Park Avenue South, New York, New York 10016 (800) 443-8323; *The New Book of World Rankings.*

G.K. Hall and Company, 70 Lincoln Street, Boston, Massachusetts 02111 (617) 423-3990; *The World in Figures.*

Inter-American Development Bank, 1300 New York Avenue, NW, Washington, D.C. 20577 (202) 623-1753; *Economic and Social Progress in Latin America.*

Statistical Office of the United Nations, Publishing Service, New York, New York 10017 (800) 253-9646; *Statistical Yearbook*, and *Statistical Yearbook for Latin America and the Caribbean.*

URUGUAY - NATIONAL PRODUCT

Facts on File, 460 Park Avenue South, New York, New York 10016 (800) 443-8323; *The New Book of World Rankings.*

Statistical Office of the United Nations, Publishing Service, New York, New York 10017 (800) 253-9646; *Statistical Yearbook.*

URUGUAY - NATURAL GAS PRODUCTION - See URUGUAY - MINING AND MINERAL PRODUCTS

URUGUAY - NEWSPAPER PRODUCTION - See URUGUAY - FORESTRY AND FOREST PRODUCTS

URUGUAY - NEWSPRINT - See URUGUAY -FORESTRY AND FOREST PRODUCTS

URUGUAY - NUTRITION

Statistical Office of the United Nations, Publishing Service, New York, New York 10017 (800) 253-9646; *Statistical Yearbook for Latin America and the Caribbean.*

URUGUAY - OATS PRODUCTION - See URUGUAY - CROPS

URUGUAY - OCCUPATIONS - See URUGUAY - LABOR FORCE

URUGUAY - ORANGES PRODUCTION - See URUGUAY - CROPS

URUGUAY - PAPER- See URUGUAY - FORESTRY AND FOREST PRODUCTS

URUGUAY - PATENTS

Statistical Office of the United Nations, Publishing Service, New York, New York 10017 (800) 253-9646; *Statistical Yearbook.*

World Intellectual Property Organization, 34 Chemin des Colombettes, CH-1211 Geneva 20. Switzerland; *Industrial Property Statistics.*

URUGUAY - PEANUT PRODUCTION - See URUGUAY - CROPS

URUGUAY - PERIODICALS

United Nations Educational, Scientific and Cultural Organization (UNESCO), 7 Place de Fontenoy, F-75700 Paris, France (Telephone Number in U.S. (212) 963-5981); *Statistical Yearbook.*

URUGUAY - PESTICIDE USE

Food and Agricultural Organization of the United Nations (FAO) Via delle Terme di Caracalla, 00100 Rome, Italy (Telephone Number in U.S. (202) 653-2400); *The State of Food and Agriculture.*

URUGUAY - PETROLEUM INDUSTRY

The Economist Intelligence Unit, 111 West 57th Street, New York, New York 10019 (800) 938-4685; *The New Latin America Market Atlas.*

Facts on File, 460 Park Avenue South, New York, New York 10016 (800) 443-8323; *The New Book of World Rankings.*

Food and Agricultural Organization of the United Nations (FAO) Via delle Terme di Caracalla, 00100 Rome, Italy (Telephone Number in U.S. (202) 653-2400); *The State of Food and Agriculture.*

G.K. Hall and Company, 70 Lincoln Street, Boston, Massachusetts 02111 (617) 423-3990; *The World in Figures.*

Inter-American Development Bank, 1300 New York Avenue, NW, Washington, D.C. 20577 (202) 623-1753; *Economic and Social Progress in Latin America.*

Statistical Office of the United Nations, Publishing Service, New York, New York 10017 (800) 253-9646; *Statistical Yearbook.*

URUGUAY - PIG-IRON AND FERRO-ALLOY PRODUCTION - See URUGUAY - MINING AND MINERAL PRODUCTS

URUGUAY - PIGS - See URUGUAY - LIVESTOCK AND POULTRY

URUGUAY - POLITICAL DATA

U.C.L.A. Latin American Center Publications, University of California, Los Angeles, California 90024 (310) 825-6634; *Statistical Abstract of Latin America.*

URUGUAY - POPULATION

The Economist Intelligence Unit, 111 West 57th Street, New York, New York 10019 (800) 938-4685; *The New Latin America Market Atlas,* and *The World Market Atlas.*

Euromonitor Publications Limited, 87-88 Turnmill Street, London EC1M 5QU, England; *International Marketing Data and Statistics.*

Facts on File, 460 Park Avenue South, New York, New York 10016 (800) 443-8323; *The New Book of World Rankings.*

Federal Statistical Office, Gustav-Stresemann-Ring 11, D-6200 Wiesbaden, Germany; *Uruguay.*

Gale Research Incorporated, 835 Penobscot Building Detroit, Michigan 48226 (800) 877-4253; *International Historical Statistics The Americas and Australasia.*

G.K. Hall and Company, 70 Lincoln Street, Boston, Massachusetts 02111 (617) 423-3990; *The World in Figures.*

Inter-American Development Bank, 1300 New York Avenue, NW, Washington, D.C. 20577 (202) 623-1753; *Economic and Social Progress in Latin America.*

International Labour Office, I.L.O. Publications, CH-1211, Geneva 22, Switzerland; *Yearbook of Labour Statistics.*

Organization of American States (OAS), General Secretariat, Washington, D.C. 20006 (202) 458-3533; *Statistical Bulletin of the OAS.*

Statistical Office of the United Nations, Publishing Service, New York, New York 10017 (800) 253-9646; *Demographic Yearbook, Statistical Yearbook,* and *Statistical Yearbook for Latin America and the Caribbean.*

Time Books, 201 East 50th Street, New York, New York 10022 (212) 751-2600; *The Economist Book of Vital World Statistics.*

U.C.L.A. Latin American Center Publications, University of California, Los Angeles, California 90024 (310) 825-6634; *Statistical Abstract of Latin America.*

United Nations Educational, Scientific and Cultural Organization (UNESCO), 7 Place de Fontenoy, F-75700 Paris, France (Telephone Number in U.S. (212) 963-5981); *Statistical Yearbook.*

U.S. Arms Control and Disarmament Agency, 320 Twenty-first Street, NW, Washington, D.C. 20451 (202) 647-8677; *World Military Expenditures and Arms Transfers.*

World Health Organization, Office of Publications, Avenue Appia, CH-1211 Geneva 27, Switzerland (Telephone Number in U.S. (518) 436-9686); *World Health Statistics Annual.*

URUGUAY - POST OFFICES

Facts on File, 460 Park Avenue South, New York, New York 10016 (800) 443-8323; *The New Book of World Rankings.*

URUGUAY - POTATO PRODUCTION - See URUGUAY - CROPS

URUGUAY - PRICES

Facts on File, 400 Park Avenue South, New York, New York 10016 (800) 443-8323; *The New Book of World Rankings.*

Federal Statistical Office, Gustav-Stresemann-Ring 11, D-6200 Wiesbaden, Germany; *Uruguay.*

Food and Agricultural Organization of the United Nations (FAO) Via delle Terme di Caracalla, 00100 Rome, Italy (Telephone Number in U.S. (202) 653-2400); *The State of Food and Agriculture.*

Gale Research Incorporated, 835 Penobscot Building Detroit, Michigan 48226 (800) 877-4253; *International Historical Statistics The Americas and Australasia.*

G.K. Hall and Company, 70 Lincoln Street, Boston, Massachusetts 02111 (617) 423-3990; *The World in Figures.*

International Labour Office, I.L.O. Publications, CH-1211, Geneva 22, Switzerland; *Yearbook of Labour Statistics.*

International Monetary Fund, 700 Nineteenth Street, NW, Washington, D.C. 20431 (202) 623-7000; *International Financial Statistics.*

Statistical Office of the United Nations, Publishing Service, New York, New York 10017 (800) 253-9646; *Statistical Yearbook for Latin America and the Caribbean.*

URUGUAY - PRINTING AND WRITING PAPER - See URUGUAY - FORESTRY AND FOREST PRODUCTS

URUGUAY - PRODUCTION

Facts on File, 460 Park Avenue South, New York, New York 10016 (800) 443-8323; *The New Book of World Rankings.*

G.K. Hall and Company, 70 Lincoln Street, Boston, Massachusetts 02111 (617) 423-3990; *The World in Figures.*

URUGUAY - PRODUCTIVITY

Euromonitor Publications Limited, 87-88 Turnmill Street, London EC1M 5QU, England; *International Marketing Data and Statistics.*

URUGUAY - PROPERTY TAXES - See URUGUAY - TAXATION

URUGUAY - PUBLIC CONSUMPTION FUND

Facts on File, 460 Park Avenue South, New York, New York 10016 (800) 443-8323; *The New Book of World Rankings.*

Inter-American Development Bank, 1300 New York Avenue, NW, Washington, D.C. 20577 (202) 623-1753; *Economic and Social Progress in Latin America.*

URUGUAY - PUBLIC EXPENDITURE

Inter-American Development Bank, 1300 New York Avenue, NW, Washington, D.C. 20577 (202) 623-1753; *Economic and Social Progress in Latin America.*

Statistical Office of the United Nations, Publishing Service, New York, New York 10017 (800) 253-9646; *Statistical Yearbook for Latin America and the Caribbean.*

URUGUAY - PUBLIC FINANCES

Inter-American Development Bank, 1300 New York Avenue, NW, Washington, D.C. 20577 (202) 623-1753; *Economic and Social Progress in Latin America.*

Organization of American States (OAS), General Secretariat, Washington, D.C. 20006 (202) 458-3533; *Statistical Bulletin of the OAS.*

URUGUAY - PUBLIC REVENUES

Inter-American Development Bank, 1300 New York Avenue, NW, Washington, D.C. 20577 (202) 623-1753; *Economic and Social Progress in Latin America.*

URUGUAY - RADIO BROADCASTING - See URUGUAY - BROADCASTING

URUGUAY - RAILWAYS

The Economist Intelligence Unit, 111 West 57th Street, New York, New York 10019 (800) 938-4685; *The New Latin America Market Atlas.*

G.K. Hall and Company, 70 Lincoln Street, Boston, Massachusetts 02111 (617) 423-3990; *The World in Figures.*

Jane's Information Group, Sentinel House, 163 Brighton Road, Coulsdon, Surrey CR5 2NH, England (Telephone Number in U.S. (703) 683-3700); *Jane's World Railways.*

Statistical Office of the United Nations, Publishing Service, New York, New York 10017 (800) 253-9646; *Statistical Yearbook.*

URUGUAY - RANCHING

U.C.L.A. Latin American Center Publications, University of California, Los Angeles, California 90024 (310) 825-6634; *Statistical Abstract of Latin America.*

URUGUAY - RELIGION

Facts on File, 460 Park Avenue South, New York, New York 10016 (800) 443-8323; *The New Book of World Rankings.*

U.C.L.A. Latin American Center Publications, University of California, Los Angeles, California 90024 (310) 825-6634; *Statistical Abstract of Latin America.*

URUGUAY - RENT PRICES

International Labour Office, I.L.O. Publications, CH-1211, Geneva 22, Switzerland; *Yearbook of Labour Statistics.*

URUGUAY - RESERVES EXCLUDING GOLD

The Economist Intelligence Unit, 111 West 57th Street, New York, New York 10019 (800) 938-4685; *The New Latin America Market Atlas.*

URUGUAY - RETAIL TRADE

G.K. Hall and Company, 70 Lincoln Street, Boston, Massachusetts 02111 (617) 423-3990; *The World in Figures.*

Inter-American Development Bank, 1300 New York Avenue, NW, Washington, D.C. 20577 (202) 623-1753; *Economic and Social Progress in Latin America.*

URUGUAY - RICE PRODUCTION - See URUGUAY - CROPS

URUGUAY - ROOT AND TUBER PRODUCTION - See URUGUAY - CROPS

URUGUAY - ROUNDWOOD PRODUCTION - See URUGUAY - FORESTRY AND FOREST PRODUCTS

URUGUAY - RUBBER PRODUCTION AND CONSUMPTION

Facts on File, 460 Park Avenue South, New York, New York 10016 (800) 443-8323; *The New Book of World Rankings.*

URUGUAY - SAWNWOOD PRODUCTION - See URUGUAY - FORESTRY AND FOREST PRODUCTS

URUGUAY - SCIENCE AND TECHNOLOGY

Statistical Office of the United Nations, Publishing Service, New York, New York 10017 (800) 253-9646; *Statistical Yearbook.*

U.C.L.A. Latin American Center Publications, University of California, Los Angeles, California 90024 (310) 825-6634; *Statistical Abstract of Latin America.*

URUGUAY - SCIENTISTS AND TECHNICIANS

Statistical Office of the United Nations, Publishing Service, New York, New York 10017 (800) 253-9646; *Statistical Yearbook.*

United Nations Educational, Scientific and Cultural Organization (UNESCO), 7 Place de Fontenoy, F-75700 Paris, France (Telephone Number in U.S. (212) 963-5981); *Statistical Yearbook.*

URUGUAY - SENIOR CITIZENS

Facts on File, 460 Park Avenue South, New York, New York 10016 (800) 443-8323; *The New Book of World Rankings.*

URUGUAY - SHEEP - See URUGUAY - LIVESTOCK AND POULTRY

URUGUAY - SILVER PRODUCTION AND CONSUMPTION - See URUGUAY - MINING AND MINERAL PRODUCTS

URUGUAY - SOCIAL DATA

Facts on File, 460 Park Avenue South, New York, New York 10016 (800) 443-8323; *The New Book of World Rankings.*

G.K. Hall and Company, 70 Lincoln Street, Boston, Massachusetts 02111 (617) 423-3990; *The World in Figures.*

U.C.L.A. Latin American Center Publications, University of California, Los Angeles, California 90024 (310) 825-6634; *Statistical Abstract of Latin America.*

URUGUAY - SOCIAL SECURITY

Inter-American Development Bank, 1300 New York Avenue, NW, Washington, D.C. 20577 (202) 623-1753; *Economic and Social Progress in Latin America.*

International Monetary Fund, 700 Nineteenth Street, NW, Washington, D.C. 20431 (202) 623-7000; *Government Finance Statistics Yearbook.*

URUGUAY - SOCIOECONOMIC DATA

Inter-American Development Bank, 1300 New York Avenue, NW, Washington, D.C. 20577 (202) 623-1753; *Economic and Social Progress in Latin America.*

U.C.L.A. Latin American Center Publications, University of California, Los Angeles, California 90024 (310) 825-6634; *Statistical Abstract of Latin America.*

URUGUAY - SOYBEAN PRODUCTION - See URUGUAY - CROPS

URUGUAY - STAMP TAXES AND DUTIES - See URUGUAY - TAXATION

URUGUAY - STATE BUDGET REVENUE AND EXPENDITURES

Euromonitor Publications Limited, 87-88 Turnmill Street, London EC1M 5QU, England; *International Marketing Data and Statistics.*

Inter-American Development Bank, 1300 New York Avenue, NW, Washington, D.C. 20577 (202) 623-1753; *Economic and Social Progress in Latin America.*

URUGUAY - STEEL - See URUGUAY - MINING AND MINERAL PRODUCTS

URUGUAY - STOCKS - COMMODITY - MARKET PRICE - INDEX

Food and Agricultural Organization of the United Nations (FAO) Via delle Terme di Caracalla, 00100 Rome, Italy (Telephone Number in U.S. (202) 653-2400); *The State of Food and Agriculture.*

URUGUAY - SUGAR PRODUCTION AND CONSUMPTION - See URUGUAY - CROPS

URUGUAY - SULPHURIC ACID PRODUCTION - See URUGUAY - MINING AND MINERAL PRODUCTS

URUGUAY - TAXATION

G.K. Hall and Company, 70 Lincoln Street, Boston, Massachusetts 02111 (617) 423-3990; *The World in Figures*.

Inter-American Development Bank, 1300 New York Avenue, NW, Washington, D.C. 20577 (202) 623-1753; *Economic and Social Progress in Latin America*.

International Monetary Fund, 700 Nineteenth Street, NW, Washington, D.C. 20431 (202) 623-7000; *Government Finance Statistics Yearbook*.

Statistical Office of the United Nations, Publishing Service, New York, New York 10017 (800) 253-9646; *Statistical Yearbook for Latin America and the Caribbean*.

The World Bank, 1818 H Street, NW, Washington, D.C. 20433 (202) 477-1234; *World Tables*.

URUGUAY - TELEGRAPH SERVICE

Statistical Office of the United Nations, Publishing Service, New York, New York 10017 (800) 253-9646; *Statistical Yearbook*.

URUGUAY - TELEPHONES IN USE

American Telephone and Telegraph Company, 26 Parsippany Road, Whippany, New Jersey 07981; *The World's Telephones*.

The Economist Intelligence Unit, 111 West 57th Street, New York, New York 10019 (800) 938-4685; *The New Latin America Market Atlas*.

G.K. Hall and Company, 70 Lincoln Street, Boston, Massachusetts 02111 (617) 423-3990; *The World in Figures*.

Statistical Office of the United Nations, Publishing Service, New York, New York 10017 (800) 253-9646; *Statistical Yearbook*.

URUGUAY - TELEVISION BROADCASTING - See URUGUAY - BROADCASTING

URUGUAY - TEXTILE INDUSTRY

American Forest and Paper Association, 1250 Connecticut Avenue, NW, Washington, D.C. 20036 (202) 463-2455; *Wood Pulp and Fiber Statistics*.

G.K. Hall and Company, 70 Lincoln Street, Boston, Massachusetts 02111 (617) 423-3990; *The World in Figures*.

Statistical Office of the United Nations, Publishing Service, New York, New York 10017 (800) 253-9646; *Statistical Yearbook*.

URUGUAY - THEATRE

United Nations Educational, Scientific and Cultural Organization (UNESCO), 7 Place de Fontenoy, F-75700 Paris, France (Telephone Number in U.S. (212) 963-5981); *Statistical Yearbook*.

URUGUAY - TIN - INDUSTRIAL CONSUMPTION - See URUGUAY - MINING AND MINERAL PRODUCTS

URUGUAY - TOBACCO PRODUCTION

Facts on File, 460 Park Avenue South, New York, New York 10016 (800) 443-8323; *The New Book of World Rankings*.

Statistical Office of the United Nations, Publishing Service, New York, New York 10017 (800) 253-9646; *Statistical Yearbook*.

U.C.L.A. Latin American Center Publications, University of California, Los Angeles, California 90024 (310) 825-6634; *Statistical Abstract of Latin America*.

URUGUAY - TOURISM

The Economist Intelligence Unit, 111 West 57th Street, New York, New York 10019 (800) 938-4685; *The New Latin America Market Atlas*.

Facts on File, 460 Park Avenue South, New York, New York 10016 (800) 443-8323; *The New Book of World Rankings*.

Federal Statistical Office, Gustav-Stresemann-Ring 11, D-6200 Wiesbaden, Germany; *Uruguay*.

G.K. Hall and Company, 70 Lincoln Street, Boston, Massachusetts 02111 (617) 423-3990; *The World in Figures*.

Statistical Office of the United Nations, Publishing Service, New York, New York 10017 (800) 253-9646; *Statistical Yearbook*, and *Statistical Yearbook for Latin America and the Caribbean*.

Time Books, 201 East 50th Street, New York, New York 10022 (212) 751-2600; *The Economist Book of Vital World Statistics*.

U.C.L.A. Latin American Center Publications, University of California, Los Angeles, California 90024 (310) 825-6634; *Statistical Abstract of Latin America*.

World Tourism Organization, Calle Capitan Haya 42, E-28020 Madrid, Spain; *Yearbook of Tourism Statistics*.

URUGUAY - TRACTORS IN USE

The Economist Intelligence Unit, 111 West 57th Street, New York, New York 10019 (800) 938-4685; *The New Latin America Market Atlas*.

Statistical Office of the United Nations, Publishing Service, New York, New York 10017 (800) 253-9646; *Statistical Yearbook*.

URUGUAY - TRADE - See URUGUAY - FOREIGN TRADE

URUGUAY - TRADEMARKS AND SERVICE MARKS

Statistical Office of the United Nations, Publishing Service, New York, New York 10017 (800) 253-9646; *Statistical Yearbook*.

World Intellectual Property Organization, 34 Chemin des Colombettes, CH-1211 Geneva 20. Switzerland; *Industrial Property Statistics*.

URUGUAY - TRANSPORTATION AND COMMUNICATIONS

The Economist Intelligence Unit, 111 West 57th Street, New York, New York 10019 (800) 938-4685; *The New Latin America Market Atlas*.

Facts on File, 460 Park Avenue South, New York, New York 10016 (800) 443-8323; *The New Book of World Rankings*.

Federal Statistical Office, Gustav-Stresemann-Ring 11, D-6200 Wiesbaden, Germany; *Uruguay*.

Gale Research Incorporated, 835 Penobscot Building Detroit, Michigan 48226 (800) 877-4253; *International Historical Statistics The Americas and Australasia*.

G.K. Hall and Company, 70 Lincoln Street, Boston, Massachusetts 02111 (617) 423-3990; *The World in Figures*.

Inter-American Development Bank, 1300 New York Avenue, NW, Washington, D.C. 20577 (202) 623-1753; *Economic and Social Progress in Latin America*.

Statistical Office of the United Nations, Publishing Service, New York, New York 10017 (800) 253-9646; *Statistical Yearbook for Latin America and the Caribbean*.

U.C.L.A. Latin American Center Publications, University of California, Los Angeles, California 90024 (310) 825-6634; *Statistical Abstract of Latin America*.

URUGUAY - TURKEYS - See URUGUAY - LIVESTOCK AND POULTRY

URUGUAY - UNEMPLOYMENT

The Economist Intelligence Unit, 111 West 57th Street, New York, New York 10019 (800) 938-4685; *The New Latin America Market Atlas*.

Euromonitor Publications Limited, 87-88 Turnmill Street, London EC1M 5QU, England; *International Marketing Data and Statistics*.

International Labour Office, I.L.O. Publications, CH-1211, Geneva 22, Switzerland; *Yearbook of Labour Statistics*.

Organization of American States (OAS), General Secretariat, Washington, D.C. 20006 (202) 458-3533; *Statistical Bulletin of the OAS*.

Statistical Office of the United Nations, Publishing Service, New York, New York 10017 (800) 253-9646; *Statistical Yearbook*.

U.C.L.A. Latin American Center Publications, University of California, Los Angeles, California 90024 (310) 825-6634; *Statistical Abstract of Latin America*.

URUGUAY - UTILITIES

U.C.L.A. Latin American Center Publications, University of California, Los Angeles, California 90024 (310) 825-6634; *Statistical Abstract of Latin America*.

URUGUAY - VITAL STATISTICS

Euromonitor Publications Limited, 87-88 Turnmill Street, London EC1M 5QU, England; *International Marketing Data and Statistics*.

Gale Research Incorporated, 835 Penobscot Building Detroit, Michigan 48226 (800) 877-4253; *International Historical Statistics The Americas and Australasia*.

G.K. Hall and Company, 70 Lincoln Street, Boston, Massachusetts 02111 (617) 423-3990; *The World in Figures*.

URUGUAY - WAGES

Federal Statistical Office, Gustav-Stresemann-Ring 11, D-6200 Wiesbaden, Germany; *Uruguay*.

G.K. Hall and Company, 70 Lincoln Street, Boston, Massachusetts 02111 (617) 423-3990; *The World in Figures*.

International Labour Office, I.L.O. Publications, CH-1211, Geneva 22, Switzerland; *Yearbook of Labour Statistics*.

Organization of American States (OAS), General Secretariat, Washington, D.C. 20006 (202) 458-3533; *Statistical Bulletin of the OAS*.

Statistical Office of the United Nations, Publishing Service, New York, New York 10017 (800) 253-9646; *Statistical Yearbook*.

U.C.L.A. Latin American Center Publications, University of California, Los Angeles, California 90024 (310) 825-6634; *Statistical Abstract of Latin America*.

URUGUAY - WEATHER

Facts on File, 460 Park Avenue South, New York, New York 10016 (800) 443-8323; *The New Book of World Rankings*.

G.K. Hall and Company, 70 Lincoln Street, Boston, Massachusetts 02111 (617) 423-3990; *The World in Figures*.

URUGUAY - WELFARE

Inter-American Development Bank, 1300 New York Avenue, NW, Washington, D.C. 20577 (202) 623-1753; *Economic and Social Progress in Latin America*.

International Monetary Fund, 700 Nineteenth Street, NW, Washington, D.C. 20431 (202) 623-7000; *Government Finance Statistics Yearbook*.

URUGUAY - WHEAT PRODUCTION AND PRICES - See URUGUAY - CROPS

URUGUAY - WHOLESALE PRICES

Inter-American Development Bank, 1300 New York Avenue, NW, Washington, D.C. 20577 (202) 623-1753; *Economic and Social Progress in Latin America*.

International Monetary Fund, 700 Nineteenth Street, NW, Washington, D.C. 20431 (202) 623-7000; *International Financial Statistics*.

Organization of American States (OAS), General Secretariat, Washington, D.C. 20006 (202) 458-3533; *Statistical Bulletin of the OAS*.

Statistical Office of the United Nations, Publishing Service, New York, New York 10017 (800) 253-9646; *Statistical Yearbook*.

URUGUAY - WHOLESALE TRADE

Inter-American Development Bank, 1300 New York Avenue, NW, Washington, D.C. 20577 (202) 623-1753; *Economic and Social Progress in Latin America*.

URUGUAY - WINE PRODUCTION

Facts on File, 460 Park Avenue South, New York, New York 10016 (800) 443-8323; *The New Book of World Rankings*.

Statistical Office of the United Nations, Publishing Service, New York, New York 10017 (800) 253-9646; *Statistical Yearbook*.

URUGUAY - WOOD AND WOOD PULP - See URUGUAY - FORESTRY AND FOREST PRODUCTS

URUGUAY - WOOL EXPORTS

International Monetary Fund, 700 Nineteenth Street, NW, Washington, D.C. 20431 (202) 623-7000; *International Financial Statistics*.

URUGUAY - WOOL PRODUCTION AND CONSUMPTION

Commodity Research Bureau, Incorporated, 75 Wall Street, New York, New York 10005 (212) 504-7754; *Commodity Year Book*.

Facts on File, 460 Park Avenue South, New York, New York 10016 (800) 443-8323; *The New Book of World Rankings*.

Statistical Office of the United Nations, Publishing Service, New York, New York 10017 (800) 253-9646; *Statistical Yearbook*.

UTAH - See also STATE DATA (FOR INDIVIDUAL STATES)

Utah - Primary Statistics Sources

University of Utah, Bureau of Economic and Business Research, 401 Kendall Graff Building, Salt Lake City, Utah 84112 (801) 581 6333; *Statistical Abstract of Utah*.

Utah Foundation, 10 West 100 South 323, Salt Lake City, Utah 84101 (801) 364-1837; *Statistical Review of Government in Utah*.

Utah - State Data Centers

Office of Planning and Budget, State Capitol, Room 116, Salt Lake City, Utah 84114, Ms. Kirin McInnis (801) 538-1550.

University of Utah, Bureau of Economic and Business Research, 401 KDGB, Salt Lake City, Utah 84112, Mr. Frank Hachman (801) 581-3353.

Department of Community and Economic Development, 324 South State Street, Suite 500, Salt Lake City, Utah 84111, Mr. Doug Jex (801) 538-8897.

Department of Employment Security, 140 East 300 South, Post Office Box 11249, Salt Lake City, Utah 84147, Mr. Ken Jensen (801) 536-7813.

UTILITIES - See also GAS UTILITY INDUSTRY and ELECTRIC LIGHT AND POWER INDUSTRY

UTILITIES - ADVERTISING EXPENDITURES

Television Bureau of Advertising, Incorporated, 850 Third Avenue, New York, New York 10022 (212) 486-1111; from data compiled by Competitive Media Reporting, 11 West 42nd Street, New York, New York 10036 (212) 789-1400.

UTILITIES - ELECTRIC SUPPLY SYSTEMS AND GENERATING PLANTS - STATES

U.S. Department of Energy, Energy Information Administration, Washington, D.C. 20585 (202) 586-8800; *Electric Power Annual*, *Electric Power Monthly*, and *Inventory of Power Plants in the U.S.*

UTILITIES - PRODUCTION INDEXES - MANUFACTURE

Board of Governors of the Federal Reserve System, Twentieth Street and Constitution Avenue, NW, Washington, D.C. 20551 (202) 452-3000; *Federal Reserve Bulletin*.

UZBEKISTAN - See also UNION OF SOVIET SOCIALIST REPUBLICS

UZBEKISTAN - AGRICULTURE

Business International Moscow, 23 Profsoyuznaya Ulitsa, 117859, Moscow (Telephone Number in U.S. (800) 938-4685); *The CIS Market Atlas*.

Encyclopedia Britannica, Incorporated, 310 South Michigan Avenue, Chicago, Illinois 60604 (312) 347-7000; *Britannica World Data*.

The World Bank, 1818 H Street, NW, Washington, D.C. 20433 (202) 477-1234; *Statistical Handbook: States of the Former USSR*.

UZBEKISTAN - AIRLINE SERVICE

Business International Moscow, 23 Profsoyuznaya Ulitsa, 117859, Moscow (Telephone Number in U.S. (800) 938-4685); *The CIS Market Atlas*.

Encyclopedia Britannica, Incorporated, 310 South Michigan Avenue, Chicago, Illinois 60604 (312) 347-7000; *Britannica World Data*.

UZBEKISTAN - AREA AND DENSITY OF POPULATION

Business International Moscow, 23 Profsoyuznaya Ulitsa, 117859, Moscow (Telephone Number in U.S. (800) 938-4685); *The CIS Market Atlas*.

UZBEKISTAN - BANKING

Business International Moscow, 23 Profsoyuznaya Ulitsa, 117859, Moscow (Telephone Number in U.S. (800) 938-4685); *The CIS Market Atlas*.

UZBEKISTAN - BIRTH RATES

Business International Moscow, 23 Profsoyuznaya Ulitsa, 117859, Moscow (Telephone Number in U.S. (800) 938-4685); *The CIS Market Atlas*.

Encyclopedia Britannica, Incorporated, 310 South Michigan Avenue, Chicago, Illinois 60604 (312) 347-7000; *Britannica World Data*.

UZBEKISTAN - BUDGET

Business International Moscow, 23 Profsoyuznaya Ulitsa, 117859, Moscow (Telephone Number in U.S. (800) 938-4685); *The CIS Market Atlas*.

UZBEKISTAN - CAPITAL INVESTMENT

The World Bank, 1818 H Street, NW, Washington, D.C. 20433 (202) 477-1234; *Statistical Handbook: States of the Former USSR*.

UZBEKISTAN - CATTLE

Business International Moscow, 23 Profsoyuznaya Ulitsa, 117859, Moscow (Telephone Number in U.S. (800) 938-4685); *The CIS Market Atlas*.

UZBEKISTAN - CHEMICALS

Business International Moscow, 23 Profsoyuznaya Ulitsa, 117859, Moscow (Telephone Number in U.S. (800) 938-4685); *The CIS Market Atlas.*

UZBEKISTAN - COAL PRODUCTION AND CONSUMPTION - See UZBEKISTAN - MINING AND MINERAL PRODUCTS

UZBEKISTAN - COMMUNICATIONS

Business International Moscow, 23 Profsoyuznaya Ulitsa, 117859, Moscow (Telephone Number in U.S. (800) 938-4685); *The CIS Market Atlas.*

UZBEKISTAN - CONSTRUCTION INDUSTRY

Business International Moscow, 23 Profsoyuznaya Ulitsa, 117859, Moscow (Telephone Number in U.S. (800) 938-4685); *The CIS Market Atlas.*

Encyclopedia Britannica, Incorporated, 310 South Michigan Avenue, Chicago, Illinois 60604 (312) 347-7000; *Britannica World Data.*

UZBEKISTAN - CONSUMER PRODUCTS

Business International Moscow, 23 Profsoyuznaya Ulitsa, 117859, Moscow (Telephone Number in U.S. (800) 938-4685); *The CIS Market Atlas.*

UZBEKISTAN - CONSUMPTION

Business International Moscow, 23 Profsoyuznaya Ulitsa, 117859, Moscow (Telephone Number in U.S. (800) 938-4685); *The CIS Market Atlas.*

The World Bank, 1818 H Street, NW, Washington, D.C. 20433 (202) 477-1234; *Statistical Handbook: States of the Former USSR.*

UZBEKISTAN - COTTON PRODUCTION AND CONSUMPTION - See UZBEKISTAN - CROPS

UZBEKISTAN - CROPS

The World Bank, 1818 H Street, NW, Washington, D.C. 20433 (202) 477-1234; *Statistical Handbook: States of the Former USSR.*

UZBEKISTAN - DEATH RATES

Business International Moscow, 23 Profsoyuznaya Ulitsa, 117859, Moscow (Telephone Number in U.S. (800) 938-4685); *The CIS Market Atlas.*

UZBEKISTAN - DEMOGRAPHY

Business International Moscow, 23 Profsoyuznaya Ulitsa, 117859, Moscow (Telephone Number in U.S. (800) 938-4685); *The CIS Market Atlas.*

Encyclopedia Britannica, Incorporated, 310 South Michigan Avenue, Chicago, Illinois 60604 (312) 347-7000; *Britannica World Data.*

The World Bank, 1818 H Street, NW, Washington, D.C. 20433 (202) 477-1234; *Statistical Handbook: States of the Former USSR.*

UZBEKISTAN - DISEASES

Business International Moscow, 23 Profsoyuznaya Ulitsa, 117859, Moscow (Telephone Number in U.S. (800) 938-4685); *The CIS Market Atlas.*

UZBEKISTAN - DIVORCE RATES

Encyclopedia Britannica, Incorporated, 310 South Michigan Avenue, Chicago, Illinois 60604 (312) 347-7000; *Britannica World Data.*

UZBEKISTAN - DOMESTIC INVESTMENT

Business International Moscow, 23 Profsoyuznaya Ulitsa, 117859, Moscow (Telephone Number in U.S. (800) 938-4685); *The CIS Market Atlas.*

UZBEKISTAN - ECONOMY

Business International Moscow, 23 Profsoyuznaya Ulitsa, 117859, Moscow (Telephone Number in U.S. (800) 938-4685); *The CIS Market Atlas.*

Encyclopedia Britannica, Incorporated, 310 South Michigan Avenue, Chicago, Illinois 60604 (312) 347-7000; *Britannica World Data.*

UZBEKISTAN - EDUCATION

Business International Moscow, 23 Profsoyuznaya Ulitsa, 117859, Moscow (Telephone Number in U.S. (800) 938-4685); *The CIS Market Atlas.*

Encyclopedia Britannica, Incorporated, 310 South Michigan Avenue, Chicago, Illinois 60604 (312) 347-7000; *Britannica World Data.*

UZBEKISTAN - ELECTRICITY

Business International Moscow, 23 Profsoyuznaya Ulitsa, 117859, Moscow (Telephone Number in U.S. (800) 938-4685); *The CIS Market Atlas.*

The World Bank, 1818 H Street, NW, Washington, D.C. 20433 (202) 477-1234; *Statistical Handbook: States of the Former USSR.*

UZBEKISTAN - EMPLOYMENT

The World Bank, 1818 H Street, NW, Washington, D.C. 20433 (202) 477-1234; *Statistical Handbook: States of the Former USSR.*

UZBEKISTAN - ENERGY

Business International Moscow, 23 Profsoyuznaya Ulitsa, 117859, Moscow (Telephone Number in U.S. (800) 938-4685); *The CIS Market Atlas.*

Encyclopedia Britannica, Incorporated, 310 South Michigan Avenue, Chicago, Illinois 60604 (312) 347-7000; *Britannica World Data.*

The World Bank, 1818 H Street, NW, Washington, D.C. 20433 (202) 477-1234; *Statistical Handbook: States of the Former USSR.*

UZBEKISTAN - ENVIRONMENT

Business International Moscow, 23 Profsoyuznaya Ulitsa, 117859, Moscow (Telephone Number in U.S. (800) 938-4685); *The CIS Market Atlas.*

UZBEKISTAN - EXPORTS

Business International Moscow, 23 Profsoyuznaya Ulitsa, 117859, Moscow (Telephone Number in U.S. (800) 938-4685); *The CIS Market Atlas.*

Encyclopedia Britannica, Incorporated, 310 South Michigan Avenue, Chicago, Illinois 60604 (312) 347-7000; *Britannica World Data.*

The World Bank, 1818 H Street, NW, Washington, D.C. 20433 (202) 477-1234; *Statistical Handbook: States of the Former USSR.*

UZBEKISTAN - EXTERNAL TRADE

The World Bank, 1818 H Street, NW, Washington, D.C. 20433 (202) 477-1234; *Statistical Handbook: States of the Former USSR.*

UZBEKISTAN - FABRIC PRODUCTION AND CONSUMPTION - See UZBEKISTAN - TEXTILE INDUSTRY

UZBEKISTAN - FERTILITY RATES

Encyclopedia Britannica, Incorporated, 310 South Michigan Avenue, Chicago, Illinois 60604 (312) 347-7000; *Britannica World Data.*

The World Bank, 1818 H Street, NW, Washington, D.C. 20433 (202) 477-1234; *Statistical Handbook: States of the Former USSR.*

UZBEKISTAN - FISHERIES

Encyclopedia Britannica, Incorporated, 310 South Michigan Avenue, Chicago, Illinois 60604 (312) 347-7000; *Britannica World Data.*

UZBEKISTAN - FOOTWEAR PRODUCTION AND CONSUMPTION - See UZBEKISTAN - TEXTILE INDUSTRY

UZBEKISTAN - FOREIGN INVESTMENT

Business International Moscow, 23 Profsoyuznaya Ulitsa, 117859, Moscow (Telephone Number in U.S. (800) 938-4685); *The CIS Market Atlas.*

UZBEKISTAN - FOREIGN TRADE

Business International Moscow, 23 Profsoyuznaya Ulitsa, 117859, Moscow (Telephone Number in U.S. (800) 938-4685); *The CIS Market Atlas.*

Encyclopedia Britannica, Incorporated, 310 South Michigan Avenue, Chicago, Illinois 60604 (312) 347-7000; *Britannica World Data.*

The World Bank, 1818 H Street, NW, Washington, D.C. 20433 (202) 477-1234; *Statistical Handbook: States of the Former USSR.*

UZBEKISTAN - FORESTRY AND FOREST PRODUCTS

Business International Moscow, 23 Profsoyuznaya Ulitsa, 117859, Moscow (Telephone Number in U.S. (800) 938-4685); *The CIS Market Atlas.*

Encyclopedia Britannica, Incorporated, 310 South Michigan Avenue, Chicago, Illinois 60604 (312) 347-7000; *Britannica World Data.*

UZBEKISTAN - GOATS - See UZBEKISTAN - LIVESTOCK AND POULTRY

UZBEKISTAN - GOVERNMENT EXPENDITURE

The World Bank, 1818 H Street, NW, Washington, D.C. 20433 (202) 477-1234; *Statistical Handbook: States of the Former USSR.*

UZBEKISTAN - GOVERNMENT REVENUE

The World Bank, 1818 H Street, NW, Washington, D.C. 20433 (202) 477-1234; *Statistical Handbook: States of the Former USSR.*

UZBEKISTAN - GROSS DOMESTIC PRODUCT

The World Bank, 1818 H Street, NW, Washington, D.C. 20433 (202) 477-1234; *Statistical Handbook: States of the Former USSR.*

UZBEKISTAN - HEALTH

Business International Moscow, 23 Profsoyuznaya Ulitsa, 117859, Moscow (Telephone Number in U.S. (800) 938-4685); *The CIS Market Atlas.*

Encyclopedia Britannica, Incorporated, 310 South Michigan Avenue, Chicago, Illinois 60604 (312) 347-7000; *Britannica World Data.*

UZBEKISTAN - HIGHWAYS

Business International Moscow, 23 Profsoyuznaya Ulitsa, 117859, Moscow (Telephone Number in U.S. (800) 938-4685); *The CIS Market Atlas.*

Encyclopedia Britannica, Incorporated, 310 South Michigan Avenue, Chicago, Illinois 60604 (312) 347-7000; *Britannica World Data.*

UZBEKISTAN - HOUSING AND HOUSING UNITS

Business International Moscow, 23 Profsoyuznaya Ulitsa, 117859, Moscow (Telephone Number in U.S. (800) 938-4685); *The CIS Market Atlas.*

UZBEKISTAN - IMPORTS

Business International Moscow, 23 Profsoyuznaya Ulitsa, 117859, Moscow (Telephone Number in U.S. (800) 938-4685); *The CIS Market Atlas.*

Encyclopedia Britannica, Incorporated, 310 South Michigan Avenue, Chicago, Illinois 60604 (312) 347-7000; *Britannica World Data.*

The World Bank, 1818 H Street, NW, Washington, D.C. 20433 (202) 477-1234; *Statistical Handbook: States of the Former USSR.*

UZBEKISTAN - INDUSTRY

Business International Moscow, 23 Profsoyuznaya Ulitsa, 117859, Moscow (Telephone Number in U.S. (800) 938-4685); *The CIS Market Atlas.*

The World Bank, 1818 H Street, NW, Washington, D.C. 20433 (202) 477-1234; *Statistical Handbook: States of the Former USSR.*

UZBEKISTAN - INFANT MORTALITY

Business International Moscow, 23 Profsoyuznaya Ulitsa, 117859, Moscow (Telephone Number in U.S. (800) 938-4685); *The CIS Market Atlas.*

UZBEKISTAN - LABOR

Business International Moscow, 23 Profsoyuznaya Ulitsa, 117859, Moscow (Telephone Number in U.S. (800) 938-4685); *The CIS Market Atlas.*

UZBEKISTAN - LABOR FORCE

The World Bank, 1818 H Street, NW, Washington, D.C. 20433 (202) 477-1234; *Statistical Handbook: States of the Former USSR.*

UZBEKISTAN - LAND USE

Encyclopedia Britannica, Incorporated, 310 South Michigan Avenue, Chicago, Illinois 60604 (312) 347-7000; *Britannica World Data*.

UZBEKISTAN - LIFE EXPECTANCY

Business International Moscow, 23 Profsoyuznaya Ulitsa, 117859, Moscow (Telephone Number in U.S. (800) 938-4685); *The CIS Market Atlas*.

UZBEKISTAN - LIVESTOCK AND POULTRY

Business International Moscow, 23 Profsoyuznaya Ulitsa, 117859, Moscow (Telephone Number in U.S. (800) 938-4685); *The CIS Market Atlas*.

Encyclopedia Britannica, Incorporated, 310 South Michigan Avenue, Chicago, Illinois 60604 (312) 347-7000; *Britannica World Data*.

UZBEKISTAN - MANUFACTURING

Encyclopedia Britannica, Incorporated, 310 South Michigan Avenue, Chicago, Illinois 60604 (312) 347-7000; *Britannica World Data*.

UZBEKISTAN - MARRIAGE RATES

Encyclopedia Britannica, Incorporated, 310 South Michigan Avenue, Chicago, Illinois 60604 (312) 347-7000; *Britannica World Data*.

UZBEKISTAN - MILITARY

The International Institute for Strategic Studies, 23 Tavistock Street, London WC2E 7NQ, England; *The Military Balance*.

UZBEKISTAN - MINING AND MINERAL PRODUCTS

Business International Moscow, 23 Profsoyuznaya Ulitsa, 117859, Moscow (Telephone Number in U.S. (800) 938-4685); *The CIS Market Atlas*.

Encyclopedia Britannica, Incorporated, 310 South Michigan Avenue, Chicago, Illinois 60604 (312) 347-7000; *Britannica World Data*.

UZBEKISTAN - MOTOR VEHICLES

Business International Moscow, 23 Profsoyuznaya Ulitsa, 117859, Moscow (Telephone Number in U.S. (800) 938-4685); *The CIS Market Atlas*.

UZBEKISTAN - NATIONAL ACCOUNTS

The World Bank, 1818 H Street, NW, Washington, D.C. 20433 (202) 477-1234; *Statistical Handbook: States of the Former USSR*.

UZBEKISTAN - NATIONAL INCOME

Business International Moscow, 23 Profsoyuznaya Ulitsa, 117859, Moscow (Telephone Number in U.S. (800) 938-4685); *The CIS Market Atlas*.

UZBEKISTAN - PIGS - See UZBEKISTAN - LIVESTOCK AND POULTRY

UZBEKISTAN - POPULATION

Business International Moscow, 23 Profsoyuznaya Ulitsa, 117859, Moscow (Telephone Number in U.S. (800) 938-4685); *The CIS Market Atlas*.

Encyclopedia Britannica, Incorporated, 310 South Michigan Avenue, Chicago, Illinois 60604 (312) 347-7000; *Britannica World Data*.

The World Bank, 1818 H Street, NW, Washington, D.C. 20433 (202) 477-1234; *Statistical Handbook: States of the Former USSR*.

UZBEKISTAN - POULTRY - See UZBEKISTAN - LIVESTOCK AND POULTRY

UZBEKISTAN - PRICES

The World Bank, 1818 H Street, NW, Washington, D.C. 20433 (202) 477-1234; *Statistical Handbook: States of the Former USSR*.

UZBEKISTAN - PRODUCTION

The World Bank, 1818 H Street, NW, Washington, D.C. 20433 (202) 477-1234; *Statistical Handbook: States of the Former USSR*.

UZBEKISTAN - PUBLIC FINANCE

The World Bank, 1818 H Street, NW, Washington, D.C. 20433 (202) 477-1234; *Statistical Handbook: States of the Former USSR*.

UZBEKISTAN - RADIO RECEIVERS

Encyclopedia Britannica, Incorporated, 310 South Michigan Avenue, Chicago, Illinois 60604 (312) 347-7000; *Britannica World Data*.

UZBEKISTAN - RAILWAYS

Business International Moscow, 23 Profsoyuznaya Ulitsa, 117859, Moscow (Telephone Number in U.S. (800) 938-4685); *The CIS Market Atlas*.

Encyclopedia Britannica, Incorporated, 310 South Michigan Avenue, Chicago, Illinois 60604 (312) 347-7000; *Britannica World Data*.

UZBEKISTAN - RETAIL TRADE

Business International Moscow, 23 Profsoyuznaya Ulitsa, 117859, Moscow (Telephone Number in U.S. (800) 938-4685); *The CIS Market Atlas*.

UZBEKISTAN - ROADS - See UZBEKISTAN - HIGHWAYS

UZBEKISTAN - ROUNDWOOD PRODUCTION AND CONSUMPTION - See UZBEKISTAN - FORESTRY AND FOREST PRODUCTS

UZBEKISTAN - SHEEP - See UZBEKISTAN - LIVESTOCK AND POULTRY

UZBEKISTAN - STEEL PRODUCTION AND CONSUMPTION - See UZBEKISTAN - MINING AND MINERAL PRODUCTS

UZBEKISTAN - TELEPHONES IN USE

Encyclopedia Britannica, Incorporated, 310 South Michigan Avenue, Chicago, Illinois 60604 (312) 347-7000; *Britannica World Data*.

UZBEKISTAN - TELEVISION RECEIVERS

Encyclopedia Britannica, Incorporated, 310 South Michigan Avenue, Chicago, Illinois 60604 (312) 347-7000; *Britannica World Data*.

UZBEKISTAN - TEXTILE INDUSTRY

Business International Moscow, 23 Profsoyuznaya Ulitsa, 117859, Moscow (Telephone Number in U.S. (800) 938-4685); *The CIS*

Market Atlas.

UZBEKISTAN - TOURISM

Business International Moscow, 23 Profsoyuznaya Ulitsa, 117859, Moscow (Telephone Number in U.S. (800) 938-4685); *The CIS Market Atlas.*

UZBEKISTAN - TRANSPORTATION AND COMMUNICATION

Business International Moscow, 23 Profsoyuznaya Ulitsa, 117859, Moscow (Telephone Number in U.S. (800) 938-4685); *The CIS Market Atlas.*

Encyclopedia Britannica, Incorporated, 310 South Michigan Avenue, Chicago, Illinois 60604 (312) 347-7000; *Britannica World Data.*

UZBEKISTAN - VITAL STATISTICS

Encyclopedia Britannica, Incorporated, 310 South Michigan Avenue, Chicago, Illinois 60604 (312) 347-7000; *Britannica World Data.*

UZBEKISTAN - WAGES

Business International Moscow, 23 Profsoyuznaya Ulitsa, 117859, Moscow (Telephone Number in U.S. (800) 938-4685); *The CIS Market Atlas.*

The World Bank, 1818 H Street, NW, Washington, D.C. 20433 (202) 477-1234; *Statistical Handbook: States of the Former USSR.*

UZBEKISTAN - WOOL PRODUCTION AND CONSUMPTION - See UZBEKISTAN - TEXTILE INDUSTRY

V

VACUUM CLEANERS

Euromonitor Publications Limited, 87-88 Turnmill Street, London EC1M 5QU, England, *International Marketing Data and Statistics*.

VALUE ADDED - See also Individual Manufacturing and Mining Industries

VALUE ADDED BY MANUFACTURE - ALL INDUSTRIES

U.S. Department of Commerce, Bureau of the Census, Suitland, Maryland 20233 (301) 763-4040; *Census of Manufactures*, and *Annual Survey of Manufactures*.

VALUE ADDED BY MANUFACTURE - STATES

U.S. Department of Labor, Bureau of Labor Statistics, Two Massachusetts Avenue, NE, Washington, D.C. 20212 (202) 606-7828; *Employment and Earnings*.

VANADIUM

U.S. Department of the Interior, Bureau of Mines, 810 Seventh Street, NW, Washington, D.C. 20241 (202) 501-9649; *Annual Reports*, and *Mineral Commodity Summaries*.

Vanuatu - National Statistical Office

Bureau of Statistics, Census Administrator and Principal Statistician, Vanuatu Government, Private Mail Bag 19, Port Vila, Vanuatu.

Vanuatu - Primary Statistics Source

HM Stationery Office, Post Office Box 569, London SE1, England; *Vanuatu Anglo-French Condominium: Report for the Year*.

VANUATU - AGRICULTURE

Food and Agricultural Organization of the United Nations (FAO) Via delle Terme di Caracalla, 00100 Rome, Italy (Telephone Number in U.S. (202) 653-2400); *Production Yearbook, The State of Food and Agriculture*, and *Trade Yearbook*.

Statistical Office of the United Nations, Publishing Service, New York, New York 10017 (800) 253-9646; *Statistical Yearbook*.

The World Bank, 1818 H Street, NW, Washington, D.C. 20433 (202) 477-1234; *World Tables*.

VANUATU - ANIMAL HEALTH

Food and Agricultural Organization of the United Nations (FAO), Via delle Terme di Caracalla, 00100 Rome, Italy (Telephone Number in U.S. (202) 653-2400); *Animal Health Yearbook*.

VANUATU - AREA AND DENSITY OF POPULATION

Food and Agricultural Organization of the United Nations (FAO) Via delle Terme di Caracalla, 00100 Rome, Italy (Telephone Number in U.S. (202) 653-2400); *The State of Food and Agriculture*.

Statistical Office of the United Nations, Publishing Service, New York, New York 10017 (800) 253-9646; *Statistical Yearbook*.

United Nations Educational, Scientific and Cultural Organization (UNESCO), 7 Place de Fontenoy, F-75700 Paris, France (Telephone Number in U.S. (212) 963-5981); *Statistical Yearbook*.

VANUATU - BALANCE OF PAYMENTS

The World Bank, 1818 H Street, NW, Washington, D.C. 20433 (202) 477-1234; *World Tables*.

VANUATU - BIRTH RATES

Statistical Office of the United Nations, Publishing Service, New York, New York 10017 (800) 253-9646; *Demographic Yearbook*, and *Statistical Yearbook*.

The World Bank, 1818 H Street, NW, Washington, D.C. 20433 (202) 477-1234; *World Tables*.

VANUATU - BROADCASTING

Billboard Limited, P.O. Box 9027, 1006 AA Amsterdam, The Netherlands (Telephone Number in U.S. (212) 764-7300); *World Radio TV Handbook*.

VANUATU - CALORIE SUPPLY

Food and Agricultural Organization of the United Nations (FAO) Via delle Terme di Caracalla, 00100 Rome, Italy (Telephone Number in U.S. (202) 653-2400); *The State of Food and Agriculture*.

VANUATU - CATTLE - See VANUATU - LIVESTOCK AND POULTRY

VANUATU - COCOA PRODUCTION - See VANUATU - CROPS

VANUATU - CONSTRUCTION INDUSTRY

Statistical Office of the United Nations, Publishing Service, New York, New York 10017 (800) 253-9646; *Statistical Yearbook*.

VANUATU - CONSUMER PRICE INDEX

Statistical Office of the United Nations, Publishing Service, New York, New York 10017 (800) 253-9646; *Statistical Yearbook*.

VANUATU - CORN PRODUCTION - See VANUATU - CROPS

VANUATU - CROPS

Food and Agricultural Organization of the United Nations (FAO) Via delle Terme di Caracalla, 00100 Rome, Italy (Telephone Number in U.S. (202) 653-2400); *Production Yearbook*, and *The State of Food and Agriculture*.

Statistical Office of the United Nations, Publishing Service, New York, New York 10017 (800) 253-9646; *Statistical Yearbook*.

VANUATU - DAIRY PRODUCTS

Food and Agricultural Organization of the United Nations (FAO) Via delle Terme di Caracalla, 00100 Rome, Italy (Telephone Number in U.S. (202) 653-2400); *The State of Food and Agriculture*.

VANUATU - DEATH RATES

Statistical Office of the United Nations, Publishing Service, New York, New York 10017 (800) 253-9646; *Statistical Yearbook*.

VANUATU - DEVELOPMENT ASSISTANCE

Statistical Office of the United Nations, Publishing Service, New York, New York 10017 (800) 253-9646; *Statistical Yearbook*.

VANUATU - DIVORCE RATES

Statistical Office of the United Nations, Publishing Service, New York, New York 10017 (800) 253-9646; *Demographic Yearbook*.

VANUATU - EDUCATION

United Nations Educational, Scientific and Cultural Organization (UNESCO), 7 Place de Fontenoy, F-75700 Paris, France (Telephone Number in U.S. (212) 963-5981); *Statistical Yearbook*.

The World Bank, 1818 H Street, NW, Washington, D.C. 20433 (202) 477-1234; *World Tables*.

VANUATU - EGG PRODUCTION AND CONSUMPTION - See VANUATU - DAIRY PRODUCTS

VANUATU - ENERGY

Food and Agricultural Organization of the United Nations (FAO) Via delle Terme di Caracalla, 00100 Rome, Italy (Telephone Number in U.S. (202) 653-2400); *The State of Food and Agriculture*.

Statistical Office of the United Nations, Publishing Service, New York, New York 10017 (800) 253-9646; *Statistical Yearbook*, and *World Energy Supplies*.

VANUATU - EXPORTS

Food and Agricultural Organization of the United Nations (FAO) Via delle Terme di Caracalla, 00100 Rome, Italy (Telephone Number in

U.S. (202) 653-2400); *The State of Food and Agriculture*.

International Monetary Fund, 700 Nineteenth Street, NW, Washington, D.C. 20431 (202) 623-7000; *Direction of Trade Statistics*.

The World Bank, 1818 H Street, NW, Washington, D.C. 20433 (202) 477-1234; *World Tables*.

VANUATU - EXTERNAL INDEBTEDNESS

The World Bank, 1818 H Street, NW, Washington, D.C. 20433 (202) 477-1234; *World Tables*.

VANUATU - EXTERNAL TRADE

Food and Agricultural Organization of the United Nations (FAO) Via delle Terme di Caracalla, 00100 Rome, Italy (Telephone Number in U.S. (202) 653-2400); *The State of Food and Agriculture*, and *Trade Yearbook*.

Statistical Office of the United Nations, Publishing Service, New York, New York 10017 (800) 253-9646; *Statistical Yearbook*.

VANUATU - FARM CROPS - See VANUATU - CROPS

VANUATU - FERTILITY RATES

The World Bank, 1818 H Street, NW, Washington, D.C. 20433 (202) 477-1234; *World Tables*.

VANUATU - FERTILIZER PRODUCTION AND CONSUMPTION

Food and Agricultural Organization of the United Nations (FAO), Via delle Terme di Caracalla, 00100 Rome, Italy (Telephone Number in U.S. (202) 653-2400); *Fertilizer Yearbook*, and *The State of Food and Agriculture*.

VANUATU - FETAL MORTALITY

Statistical Office of the United Nations, Publishing Service, New York, New York 10017 (800) 253-9646; *Demographic Yearbook*.

VANUATU - FISHERIES

Food and Agricultural Organization of the United Nations (FAO) Via delle Terme di Caracalla, 00100 Rome, Italy (Telephone Number in U.S. (202) 653-2400); *The State of Food and Agriculture*.

Statistical Office of the United Nations, Publishing Service, New York, New York 10017 (800) 253-9646; *Statistical Yearbook*.

VANUATU - FOOD

Food and Agricultural Organization of the United Nations (FAO) Via delle Terme di Caracalla, 00100 Rome, Italy (Telephone Number in U.S. (202) 653-2400); *Production Yearbook*, and *The State of Food and Agriculture*.

VANUATU - FOREIGN TRADE

Food and Agricultural Organization of the United Nations (FAO) Via delle Terme di Caracalla, 00100 Rome, Italy (Telephone Number in U.S. (202) 653-2400); *The State of Food and Agriculture*.

Statistical Office of the United Nations, Publishing Service, New York, New York 10017 (800) 253-9646; *International Trade Statistics Yearbook*, and *Statistical Yearbook*.

The World Bank, 1818 H Street, NW, Washington, D.C. 20433 (202) 477-1234; *World Tables*.

VANUATU - FORESTRY AND FOREST PRODUCTS

Food and Agricultural Organization of the United Nations (FAO) Via delle Terme di Caracalla, 00100 Rome, Italy (Telephone Number in U.S. (202) 653-2400); *The State of Food and Agriculture*, and *Yearbook of Forest Products*.

Statistical Office of the United Nations, Publishing Service, New York, New York 10017 (800) 253-9646; *Statistical Yearbook*.

VANUATU - GENERAL MORTALITY

Statistical Office of the United Nations, Publishing Service, New York, New York 10017 (800) 253-9646; *Demographic Yearbook*.

VANUATU - GOLD HOLDINGS

The World Bank, 1818 H Street, NW, Washington, D.C. 20433 (202) 477-1234; *World Tables*.

VANUATU - GOVERNMENT EXPENDITURE

The World Bank, 1818 H Street, NW, Washington, D.C. 20433 (202) 477-1234; *World Tables*.

VANUATU - GOVERNMENT REVENUE

The World Bank, 1818 H Street, NW, Washington, D.C. 20433 (202) 477-1234; *World Tables*.

VANUATU - GRAIN PRODUCTION - See VANUATU - CROPS

VANUATU - GROSS DOMESTIC PRODUCT

The World Bank, 1818 H Street, NW, Washington, D.C. 20433 (202) 477-1234; *World Tables*.

VANUATU - GROSS NATIONAL PRODUCT

The World Bank, 1818 H Street, NW, Washington, D.C. 20433 (202) 477-1234; *World Tables*.

VANUATU - GROUNDNUT PRODUCTION - See VANUATU - CROPS

VANUATU - HEALTH

Statistical Office of the United Nations, Publishing Service, New York, New York 10017 (800) 253-9646; *Statistical Yearbook*.

VANUATU - HIDE PRODUCTION

Food and Agricultural Organization of the United Nations (FAO), Via delle Terme di Caracalla, 00100 Rome, Italy (Telephone Number in U.S. (202) 653-2400); *Production Yearbook*.

VANUATU - HORSES - See VANUATU - LIVESTOCK AND POULTRY

VANUATU - IMPORTS

Food and Agricultural Organization of the United Nations (FAO) Via delle Terme di Caracalla, 00100 Rome, Italy (Telephone Number in U.S. (202) 653-2400); *The State of Food and Agriculture*.

International Monetary Fund, 700 Nineteenth Street, NW, Washington, D.C. 20431 (202) 623-7000; *Direction of Trade Statistics*.

The World Bank, 1818 H Street, NW, Washington, D.C. 20433 (202) 477-1234; *World Tables*.

VANUATU - INDUSTRY

The World Bank, 1818 H Street, NW, Washington, D.C. 20433 (202) 477-1234; *World Tables*.

VANUATU - INFANT AND MATERNAL MORTALITY

Statistical Office of the United Nations, Publishing Service, New York, New York 10017 (800) 253-9646; *Demographic Yearbook*.

The World Bank, 1818 H Street, NW, Washington, D.C. 20433 (202) 477-1234; *World Tables*.

VANUATU - INTERNATIONAL RESERVES EXCLUDING GOLD

The World Bank, 1818 H Street, NW, Washington, D.C. 20433 (202) 477-1234; *World Tables*.

VANUATU - LABOR FORCE

Food and Agricultural Organization of the United Nations (FAO) Via delle Terme di Caracalla, 00100 Rome, Italy (Telephone Number in U.S. (202) 653-2400); *The State of Food and Agriculture*.

The World Bank, 1818 H Street, NW, Washington, D.C. 20433 (202) 477-1234; *World Tables*.

VANUATU - LAND USE

Food and Agricultural Organization of the United Nations (FAO), Via delle Terme di Caracalla, 00100 Rome, Italy (Telephone Number in U.S. (202) 653-2400); *Production Yearbook*.

VANUATU - LIVESTOCK AND POULTRY

Food and Agricultural Organization of the United Nations (FAO), Via delle Terme di Caracalla, 00100 Rome, Italy (Telephone Number in U.S. (202) 653-2400); *Production Yearbook*, and *The State of Food and Agriculture*.

Statistical Office of the United Nations, Publishing Service, New York, New York 10017 (800) 253-9646; *Statistical Yearbook*.

VANUATU - MAIL - NUMBER OF ITEMS SENT OR RECEIVED

Statistical Office of the United Nations, Publishing Service, New York, New York 10017 (800) 253-9646; *Statistical Yearbook*.

VANUATU - MANGANESE PRODUCTION AND CONSUMPTION - See VANUATU - MINING AND MINERAL PRODUCTS

VANUATU - MANUFACTURING

The World Bank, 1818 H Street, NW, Washington, D.C. 20433 (202) 477-1234; *World Tables*.

VANUATU - MARRIAGE RATES

Statistical Office of the United Nations, Publishing Service, New York, New York 10017 (800) 253-9646; *Demographic Yearbook*.

VANUATU - MEAT PRODUCTION - See VANUATU - LIVESTOCK AND POULTRY

VANUATU - MERCHANT SHIPPING

Statistical Office of the United Nations, Publishing Service, New York, New York 10017 (800) 253-9646; *Statistical Yearbook.*

U.S. Department of Transportation, Maritime Administration, 400 Seventh Street, SW, Washington, D.C. 20590 (202) 366-5807; *A Statistical Analysis of the World's Merchant Fleets.*

VANUATU - MINING AND MINERAL PRODUCTS

Statistical Office of the United Nations, Publishing Service, New York, New York 10017 (800) 253-9646; *Statistical Yearbook.*

VANUATU - MONEY SUPPLY

The World Bank, 1818 H Street, NW, Washington, D.C. 20433 (202) 477-1234; *World Tables.*

VANUATU - MOTION PICTURES

Statistical Office of the United Nations, Publishing Service, New York, New York 10017 (800) 253-9646; *Statistical Yearbook.*

VANUATU - MOTOR VEHICLES IN USE

Statistical Office of the United Nations, Publishing Service, New York, New York 10017 (800) 253-9646; *Statistical Yearbook.*

VANUATU - NATALITY - See VANUATU - BIRTH RATE

VANUATU - NEWSPAPER PRODUCTION - See VANUATU - FORESTRY AND FOREST PRODUCTS

VANUATU - PESTICIDE USE

Food and Agricultural Organization of the United Nations (FAO) Via delle Terme di Caracalla, 00100 Rome, Italy (Telephone Number in U.S. (202) 653-2400); *The State of Food and Agriculture.*

VANUATU - PETROLEUM INDUSTRY

Food and Agricultural Organization of the United Nations (FAO) Via delle Terme di Caracalla, 00100 Rome, Italy (Telephone Number in U.S. (202) 653-2400); *The State of Food and Agriculture.*

VANUATU - PIGS - See VANUATU - LIVESTOCK AND POULTRY

VANUATU - POPULATION

Food and Agricultural Organization of the United Nations (FAO), Via delle Terme di Caracalla, 00100 Rome, Italy (Telephone Number in U.S. (202) 653-2400); *Production Yearbook.*

Statistical Office of the United Nations, Publishing Service, New York, New York 10017 (800) 253-9646; *Demographic Yearbook,* and *Statistical Yearbook.*

United Nations Educational, Scientific and Cultural Organization (UNESCO), 7 Place de Fontenoy, F-75700 Paris, France (Telephone Number in U.S. (212) 963-5981); *Statistical Yearbook.*

VANUATU - PRICES

Food and Agricultural Organization of the United Nations (FAO), Via delle Terme di Caracalla, 00100 Rome, Italy (Telephone Number in U.S. (202) 653-2400); *Production Yearbook,* and *The State of Food and Agriculture.*

VANUATU - ROOT AND TUBER PRODUCTION - See VANUATU - CROPS

VANUATU - ROUNDWOOD PRODUCTION - See VANUATU - FORESTRY AND FOREST PRODUCTS

VANUATU - SAWNWOOD PRODUCTION - See VANUATU - FORESTRY AND FOREST PRODUCTS

VANUATU - SCIENCE AND TECHNOLOGY - EXPENDITURE FOR RESEARCH

Statistical Office of the United Nations, Publishing Service, New York, New York 10017 (800) 253-9646; *Statistical Yearbook.*

VANUATU - SCIENTISTS AND TECHNICIANS

Statistical Office of the United Nations, Publishing Service, New York, New York 10017 (800) 253-9646; *Statistical Yearbook.*

VANUATU - STOCKS - COMMODITY - MARKET PRICE - INDEX

Food and Agricultural Organization of the United Nations (FAO) Via delle Terme di Caracalla, 00100 Rome, Italy (Telephone Number in U.S. (202) 653-2400); *The State of Food and Agriculture.*

VANUATU - TAXATION

The World Bank, 1818 H Street, NW, Washington, D.C. 20433 (202) 477-1234; *World Tables.*

VANUATU - TELEPHONES IN USE

American Telephone and Telegraph Company, 26 Parsippany Road, Whippany, New Jersey 07981 (800) 338-4038; *The World's Telephones.*

VANUATU - TOURISM

Statistical Office of the United Nations, Publishing Service, New York, New York 10017 (800) 253-9646; *Statistical Yearbook.*

World Tourism Organization, Calle Capitan Haya 42, E-28020 Madrid, Spain; *Yearbook of Tourism Statistics.*

VANUATU - TRACTORS IN USE

Statistical Office of the United Nations, Publishing Service, New York, New York 10017 (800) 253-9646; *Statistical Yearbook.*

VANUATU - TRADE - See VANUATU - FOREIGN TRADE

VANUATU - VITAL STATISTICS

Statistical Office of the United Nations, Publishing Service, New York, New York 10017 (800) 253-9646; *Statistical Yearbook.*

VEAL - See also BEEF and MEAT AND MEAT PRODUCTS

VEAL

U.S. Department of Agriculture, Economic Research Service, Fourteenth Street and Independence Avenue, SW, Washington, D.C. 20005-4789 (202) 219-1504; *Food Consumption, Prices and Expenditures, Livestock and Meat Statistics,* and *Agricultural Outlook.*

VEGETABLE OILS - See OILS

VEGETABLES - See also Individual Commodities

VEGETABLES - ACREAGE

U.S. Department of Agriculture, National Agricultural Statistics Service, Fourteenth Street and Independence Avenue, SW, Washington, D.C. 20250 (202) 219-1504; *Agricultural Statistics*, and *Vegetables*.

VEGETABLES - CONSUMER EXPENDITURES

U.S. Department of Agriculture, Economic Research Service, Fourteenth Street and Independence Avenue, SW, Washington, D.C. 20005-4789 (202) 219-1504; *Food Cost Review, National Food Review*, and *Agricultural Statistics*.

VEGETABLES - CONSUMPTION

U.S. Department of Agriculture, Economic Research Service, Fourteenth Street and Independence Avenue, SW, Washington, D.C. 20005-4789 (202) 219-1504; *Agricultural Outlook, Food, Consumption, Prices and Expenditures*, and unpublished data.

VEGETABLES - FARM MARKETINGS - SALES

U.S. Department of Agriculture, Economic Research Service, Fourteenth Street and Independence Avenue, SW, Washington, D.C. 20005-4789 (202) 219-1504; *Economic Indicators of the Farm Sector: National Financial Summary*.

VEGETABLES - FOREIGN TRADE

U.S. Department of Agriculture, Economic Research Service, Fourteenth Street and Independence Avenue, SW, Washington, D.C. 20005-4789 (202) 219-1504; *Foreign Agricultural Trade of the United States, Agricultural Statistics*, and *Agricultural Outlook*.

U.S. Department of Commerce, Bureau of the Census, Suitland, Maryland 20233 (301) 763-4040; *U.S. Merchandise Trade: Exports, General Imports, and Imports for Consumption*, and *U.S. Merchandise Trade*

VEGETABLES - GARDENS

The National Gardening Association, 180 Flynn Avenue, Burlington, Vermont 05401 (802) 863-1308; *National Gardening Survey*.

VEGETABLES - PRICES

U.S. Department of Agriculture, National Agricultural Statistics Service, Fourteenth Street and Independence Avenue, SW, Washington, D.C. 20250 (202) 219-1504; *Agricultural Prices: Annual Summary*.

U.S. Department of Labor, Bureau of Labor Statistics, Two Massachusetts Avenue, NE, Washington, D.C. 20212 (202) 606-7828; *Monthly Labor Review, CPI Detailed Report*, and *Producer Price Indexes*.

VEGETABLES - PRODUCTION

U.S. Department of Agriculture, Economic Research Service, Fourteenth Street and Independence Avenue, SW. Washington, D.C. 20005-4789 (202) 219-1504; *Agricultural Outlook*.

U.S. Department of Agriculture, National Agricultural Statistics Service, Fourteenth Street and Independence Avenue, SW, Washington, D.C. 20250 (202) 219-1504; *Vegetables*, and *Agricultural Statistics*.

VEHICLES - See MOTOR VEHICLES, TRACTORS, ETC.

VENEREAL DISEASES - See also AIDS

U.S. Department of Health and Human Services, Center for Disease Control, 1600 Clifton Road, NE, Atlanta, Georgia 30333 (404) 639-3311; *Summary of Notifiable Diseases, United States, Morbidity and Mortality Weekly Report*.

Venezuela - National Statistical Office

Oficina Central de Estadistica e Informatica, Presidencia de la Republica, Aptdo. de Correos 400 Carmelitas, Caracas 1050, Venezuela.

Venezuela - Primary Statistics Source

Oficina Central de Estadistica Informatica, Presidencia de la Republica, Aptdo. de Correos 400 Carmelitas, Caracas 1050, Venezuela; *Anuario estadistico* (Statistical Yearbook).

VENEZUELA - AGRICULTURE

The Economist Intelligence Unit, 111 West 57th Street, New York, New York 10019 (800) 938-4685; *The New Latin America Market Atlas*.

Euromonitor Publications Limited, 87-88 Turnmill Street, London EC1M 5QU, England; *International Marketing Data and Statistics*, and *Third World Economic Handbook*.

Facts on File, 460 Park Avenue South, New York, New York 10016 (800) 443-8323; *The New Book of World Rankings*.

Food and Agricultural Organization of the United Nations (FAO) Via delle Terme di Caracalla, 00100 Rome, Italy (Telephone Number in U.S. (202) 653-2400), *Production Yearbook, The State of Food and Agriculture*, and *Trade Yearbook*.

Gale Research Incorporated, 835 Penobscot Building, Detroit, Michigan 48226 (800) 877-4253; *International Historical Statistics The Americas and Australasia*.

G.K. Hall and Company, 70 Lincoln Street, Boston, Massachusetts 02111 (617) 423-3990; *The World in Figures*.

Inter-American Development Bank, 1300 New York Avenue, NW, Washington, D.C. 20577 (202) 623-1753; *Economic and Social Progress in Latin America*.

Statistical Office of the United Nations, Publishing Service, New York, New York 10017 (800) 253-9646; *Statistical Yearbook*, and *Statistical Yearbook for Latin America and the Caribbean*.

Time Books, 201 East 50th Street, New York, New York 10022 (212) 751-2600; *The Economist Book of Vital World Statistics*.

U.C.L.A. Latin American Center Publications, University of California, Los Angeles, California 90024 (310) 825-6634; *Statistical Abstract of Latin America*.

The World Bank, 1818 H Street, NW, Washington, D.C. 20433 (202) 477-1234; *World Tables*.

VENEZUELA - AIRLINE SERVICE

The Economist Intelligence Unit, 111 West 57th Street, New York, New York 10019 (800) 938-4685; *The New Latin America Market Atlas*.

Facts on File, 460 Park Avenue South, New York, New York 10016 (800) 443-8323; *The New Book of World Rankings*.

G.K. Hall and Company, 70 Lincoln Street, Boston, Massachusetts 02111 (617) 423-3990; *The World in Figures*.

International Civil Aviation Organization, 1000 Sherbrooke Street West, Suite 400, Montreal, Quebec, Canada H3A 2R2 (514) 285-8219; *Civil Aviation Statistics of the World*.

Statistical Office of the United Nations, Publishing Service, New York, New York 10017 (800) 253-9646; *Statistical Yearbook*.

Time Books, 201 East 50th Street, New York, New York 10022 (212) 751-2600; *The Economist Book of Vital World Statistics*.

VENEZUELA - ALUMINUM PRODUCTION AND CONSUMPTION - See VENEZUELA - MINING AND MINERAL PRODUCTS

VENEZUELA - ANIMAL HEALTH

Food and Agricultural Organization of the United Nations (FAO), Via delle Terme di Caracalla, 00100 Rome, Italy (Telephone Number in U.S. (202) 653-2400); *Animal Health Yearbook*.

VENEZUELA - AREA AND DENSITY OF POPULATION

Euromonitor Publications Limited, 87-88 Turnmill Street, London EC1M 5QU, England; *International Marketing Data and Statistics*.

Facts on File, 460 Park Avenue South, New York, New York 10016 (800) 443-8323; *The New Book of World Rankings*.

Food and Agricultural Organization of the United Nations (FAO) Via delle Terme di Caracalla, 00100 Rome, Italy (Telephone Number in U.S. (202) 653-2400); *The State of Food and Agriculture*.

G.K. Hall and Company, 70 Lincoln Street, Boston, Massachusetts 02111 (617) 423-3990; *The World in Figures*.

Inter-American Development Bank, 1300 New York Avenue, NW, Washington, D.C. 20577 (202) 623-1753; *Economic and Social Progress in Latin America*.

Statistical Office of the United Nations, Publishing Service, New York, New York 10017 (800) 253-9646; *Statistical Yearbook*.

Time Books, 201 East 50th Street, New York, New York 10022 (212) 751-2600; *The Economist Book of Vital World Statistics*.

United Nations Educational, Scientific and Cultural Organization (UNESCO), 7 Place de Fontenoy, F-75700 Paris, France (Telephone Number in U.S. (212) 963-5981); *Statistical Yearbook*.

VENEZUELA - ARMS EXPORTS AND IMPORTS

U.S. Arms Control and Disarmament Agency, 320 Twenty-first Street, NW, Washington, D.C. 20451 (202) 647-8677; *World Military Expenditures and Arms Transfers*.

VENEZUELA - BALANCE OF PAYMENTS

The Economist Intelligence Unit, 111 West 57th Street, New York, New York 10019 (800) 938-4685; *The New Latin America Market Atlas*, and *The World Market Atlas*.

Euromonitor Publications Limited, 87-88 Turnmill Street, London EC1M 5QU, England; *Third World Economic Handbook*.

G.K. Hall and Company, 70 Lincoln Street, Boston, Massachusetts 02111 (617) 423-3990; *The World in Figures*.

Inter-American Development Bank, 1300 New York Avenue, NW, Washington, D.C. 20577 (202) 623-1753; *Economic and Social Progress in Latin America*.

International Monetary Fund, 700 Nineteenth Street, NW, Washington, D.C. 20431 (202) 623-7000; *Balance of Payments Yearbook*.

Organization of American States (OAS), General Secretariat, Washington, D.C. 20006 (202) 458-3533; *Statistical Bulletin of the OAS*.

Statistical Office of the United Nations, Publishing Service, New York, New York 10017 (800) 253-9646; *Economic Survey of Latin America and the Caribbean*, and *Statistical Yearbook for Latin America and the Caribbean*.

Time Books, 201 East 50th Street, New York, New York 10022 (212) 751-2600; *The Economist Book of Vital World Statistics*.

U.C.L.A. Latin American Center Publications, University of California, Los Angeles, California 90024 (310) 825-6634; *Statistical Abstract of Latin America*.

The World Bank, 1818 H Street, NW, Washington, D.C. 20433 (202) 477-1234; *World Tables*.

VENEZUELA - BANANA PRODUCTION - See VENEZUELA - CROPS

VENEZUELA - BANKING

Facts on File, 460 Park Avenue South, New York, New York 10016 (800) 443-8323; *The New Book of World Rankings*.

G.K. Hall and Company, 70 Lincoln Street, Boston, Massachusetts 02111 (617) 423-3990; *The World in Figures*.

Inter-American Development Bank, 1300 New York Avenue, NW, Washington, D.C. 20577 (202) 623-1753; *Economic and Social Progress in Latin America*.

International Monetary Fund, 700 Nineteenth Street, NW, Washington, D.C. 20431 (202) 623-7000; *Government Finance Statistics Yearbook*, and *International Financial Statistics*.

Statistical Office of the United Nations, Publishing Service, New York, New York 10017 (800) 253-9646; *Statistical Yearbook*, and *Statistical Yearbook for Latin America and the Caribbean*.

VENEZUELA - BARLEY PRODUCTION - See VENEZUELA - CROPS

VENEZUELA - BEER PRODUCTION

Facts on File, 460 Park Avenue South, New York, New York 10016 (800) 443-8323; *The New Book of World Rankings*.

Statistical Office of the United Nations, Publishing Service, New York, New York 10017 (800) 253-9646; *Statistical Yearbook*.

VENEZUELA - BIRTH RATES

Euromonitor Publications Limited, 87-88 Turnmill Street, London EC1M 5QU, England; *Third World Economic Handbook*.

Facts on File, 460 Park Avenue South, New York, New York 10016 (800) 443-8323; *The New Book of World Rankings*.

Statistical Office of the United Nations, Publishing Service, New York, New York 10017 (800) 253-9646; *Demographic Yearbook, Statistical Yearbook*, and *Statistical Yearbook for Latin America and the Caribbean*.

Time Books, 201 East 50th Street, New York, New York 10022 (212) 751-2600; *The Economist Book of Vital World Statistics*.

The World Bank, 1818 H Street, NW, Washington, D.C. 20433 (202) 477-1234; *World Tables*.

World Health Organization, Office of Publications, Avenue Appia, CH-1211 Geneva 27, Switzerland (Telephone Number in U.S. (518) 436-9686); *World Health Statistics Annual*.

VENEZUELA - BONDS

G.K. Hall and Company, 70 Lincoln Street, Boston, Massachusetts 02111 (617) 423-3990; *The World in Figures*.

Inter-American Development Bank, 1300 New York Avenue, NW, Washington, D.C. 20577 (202) 623-1753; *Economic and Social Progress in Latin America*.

International Monetary Fund, 700 Nineteenth Street, NW, Washington, D.C. 20431 (202) 623-7000; *Government Finance Statistics Yearbook*.

VENEZUELA - BOOK PRODUCTION

G.K. Hall and Company, 70 Lincoln Street, Boston, Massachusetts 02111 (617) 423-3990; *The World in Figures*.

VENEZUELA - BROADCASTING

Billboard Limited, P.O. Box 9027, 1006 AA Amsterdam, The Netherlands (Telephone Number in U.S. (212) 764-7300); *World Radio TV Handbook*.

Facts on File, 460 Park Avenue South, New York, New York 10016 (800) 443-8323; *The New Book of World Rankings*.

G.K. Hall and Company, 70 Lincoln Street, Boston, Massachusetts 02111 (617) 423-3990; *The World in Figures*.

Time Books, 201 East 50th Street, New York, New York 10022 (212) 751-2600; *The Economist Book of Vital World Statistics*.

VENEZUELA - BUSINESS

G.K. Hall and Company, 70 Lincoln Street, Boston, Massachusetts 02111 (617) 423-3990; *The World in Figures*.

Inter-American Development Bank, 1300 New York Avenue, NW, Washington, D.C. 20577 (202) 623-1753; *Economic and Social Progress in Latin America*.

VENEZUELA - BUSINESS AND PROFESSIONAL LICENSES

International Monetary Fund, 700 Nineteenth Street, NW, Washington, D.C. 20431 (202) 623-7000; *Government Finance Statistics Yearbook*.

VENEZUELA - BUTTER PRODUCTION - See VENEZUELA - DAIRY PRODUCTS

VENEZUELA - CALORIE SUPPLY

Food and Agricultural Organization of the United Nations (FAO) Via delle Terme di Caracalla, 00100 Rome, Italy (Telephone Number in U.S. (202) 653-2400); *The State of Food and Agriculture*.

Statistical Office of the United Nations, Publishing Service, New York, New York 10017 (800) 253-9646; *Statistical Yearbook for Latin America and the Caribbean*.

VENEZUELA - CAPITAL INVESTMENT

Inter-American Development Bank, 1300 New York Avenue, NW, Washington, D.C. 20577 (202) 623-1753; *Economic and Social Progress in Latin America*.

VENEZUELA - CAPITAL REVENUE

Inter-American Development Bank, 1300 New York Avenue, NW, Washington, D.C. 20577 (202) 623-1753; *Economic and Social Progress in Latin America*.

International Monetary Fund, 700 Nineteenth Street, NW, Washington, D.C. 20431 (202) 623-7000; *Government Finance Statistics Yearbook*.

VENEZUELA - CATTLE - See VENEZUELA - LIVESTOCK AND POULTRY

VENEZUELA - CAUSTIC SODA PRODUCTION

Statistical Office of the United Nations, Publishing Service, New York, New York 10017 (800) 253-9646; *Statistical Yearbook*.

VENEZUELA - CEMENT PRODUCTION - See VENEZUELA - MINING AND MINERAL PRODUCTS

VENEZUELA - CHEESE PRODUCTION AND CONSUMPTION - See VENEZUELA - DAIRY PRODUCTS

VENEZUELA - CHEMICAL (ORGANIC) PRODUCTION - See VENEZUELA - MINING AND MINERAL PRODUCTS

VENEZUELA - CHICKENS - See VENEZUELA - LIVESTOCK AND POULTRY

VENEZUELA - CIGAR PRODUCTION

Statistical Office of the United Nations, Publishing Service, New York, New York 10017 (800) 253-9646; *Statistical Yearbook*.

VENEZUELA - CIGARETTE PRODUCTION

Facts on File, 460 Park Avenue South, New York, New York 10016 (800) 443-8323; *The New Book of World Rankings*.

Statistical Office of the United Nations, Publishing Service, New York, New York 10017 (800) 253-9646; *Statistical Yearbook*.

U.C.L.A. Latin American Center Publications, University of California, Los Angeles, California 90024 (310) 825-6634; *Statistical Abstract of Latin America*.

VENEZUELA - CLASS STRUCTURE

G.K. Hall and Company, 70 Lincoln Street, Boston, Massachusetts 02111 (617) 423-3990; *The World in Figures*.

VENEZUELA - CLIMATE

Facts on File, 460 Park Avenue South, New York, New York 10016 (800) 443-8323; *The New Book of World Rankings*.

G.K. Hall and Company, 70 Lincoln Street, Boston, Massachusetts 02111 (617) 423-3990; *The World in Figures*.

VENEZUELA - CLOTHING EXPORTS AND IMPORTS

Euromonitor Publications Limited, 87-88 Turnmill Street, London EC1M 5QU, England; *Third World Economic Handbook*.

VENEZUELA - COAL PRODUCTION - See VENEZUELA - MINING AND MINERAL PRODUCTS

VENEZUELA - COCOA (BEANS) PRODUCTION - See VENEZUELA - CROPS

VENEZUELA - COFFEE - See VENEZUELA - CROPS

VENEZUELA - COMMUNICATIONS

Euromonitor Publications Limited, 87-88 Turnmill Street, London EC1M 5QU, England; *Third World Economic Handbook*.

Gale Research Incorporated, 835 Penobscot Building, Detroit, Michigan 48226 (800) 877-4253; *International Historical Statistics The Americas and Australasia*.

G.K. Hall and Company, 70 Lincoln Street, Boston, Massachusetts 02111 (617) 423-3990; *The World in Figures*.

Inter-American Development Bank, 1300 New York Avenue, NW, Washington, D.C. 20577 (202) 623-1753; *Economic and Social Progress in Latin America*.

U.C.L.A. Latin American Center Publications, University of California, Los Angeles, California 90024 (310) 825-6634; *Statistical Abstract of Latin America*.

VENEZUELA - CONSTRUCTION INDUSTRY

The Economist Intelligence Unit, 111 West 57th Street, New York, New York 10019 (800) 938-4685; *The New Latin America Market Atlas*.

Facts on File, 460 Park Avenue South, New York, New York 10016 (800) 443-8323; *The New Book of World Rankings*.

Inter-American Development Bank, 1300 New York Avenue, NW, Washington, D.C. 20577 (202) 623-1753; *Economic and Social Progress in Latin America*.

U.C.L.A. Latin American Center Publications, University of California, Los Angeles, California 90024 (310) 825-6634; *Statistical Abstract of Latin America*.

Statistical Office of the United Nations, Publishing Service, New York, New York 10017 (800) 253-9646; *Construction Statistics Yearbook*, and *Statistical Yearbook*.

VENEZUELA - CONSUMER PRICE INDEX

G.K. Hall and Company, 70 Lincoln Street, Boston, Massachusetts 02111 (617) 423-3990; *The World in Figures*.

Statistical Office of the United Nations, Publishing Service, New York, New York 10017 (800) 253-9646; *Statistical Yearbook*.

VENEZUELA - CONSUMER PRICES

The Economist Intelligence Unit, 111 West 57th Street, New York, New York 10019 (800) 938-4685; *The New Latin America Market Atlas*.

International Labour Office, I.L.O. Publications, CH-1211, Geneva 22, Switzerland; *Yearbook of Labour Statistics*.

International Monetary Fund, 700 Nineteenth Street, NW, Washington, D.C. 20431 (202) 623-7000; *International Financial Statistics*.

Organization of American States (OAS), General Secretariat, Washington, D.C. 20006 (202) 458-3533; *Statistical Bulletin of the OAS*.

U.C.L.A. Latin American Center Publications, University of California, Los Angeles, California 90024 (310) 825-6634; *Statistical Abstract of Latin America*.

Time Books, 201 East 50th Street, New York, New York 10022 (212) 751-2600; *The Economist Book of Vital World Statistics*.

VENEZUELA - CONSUMPTION

The Economist Intelligence Unit, 111 West 57th Street, New York, New York 10019 (800) 938-4685; *The New Latin America Market Atlas*.

G.K. Hall and Company, 70 Lincoln Street, Boston, Massachusetts 02111 (617) 423-3990; *The World in Figures*.

Inter-American Development Bank, 1300 New York Avenue, NW, Washington, D.C. 20577 (202) 623-1753; *Economic and Social Progress in Latin America*.

Statistical Office of the United Nations, Publishing Service, New York, New York 10017 (800) 253-9646; *Statistical Yearbook for Latin America and the Caribbean*.

VENEZUELA - COOPERATIVES

U.C.L.A. Latin American Center Publications, University of California, Los Angeles, California 90024 (310) 825-6634; *Statistical Abstract of Latin America*.

VENEZUELA - COPPER PRODUCTION AND CONSUMPTION - See VENEZUELA - MINING AND MINERAL PRODUCTS

VENEZUELA - CORN PRODUCTION - See VENEZUELA - CROPS

VENEZUELA - CORPORATE INCOME TAXES - See VENEZUELA - TAXATION

VENEZUELA - CORPORATE TAXES - See VENEZUELA - TAXATION

VENEZUELA - COTTON - See VENEZUELA - CROPS

VENEZUELA - CRIME

International Criminal Police Organization (INTERPOL), 26 rue Armengaud, 92210 Saint Cloud, France; *International Crime Statistics.*

Yale University Press, Yale Station, New Haven, Connecticut 06520 (203) 432-0940; *Violence and Crime in Cross-National Perspective.*

VENEZUELA - CROPS

Commodity Research Bureau, Incorporated, 75 Wall Street, New York, New York 10005 (212) 504-7754; *Commodity Year Book.*

The Economist Intelligence Unit, 111 West 57th Street, New York, New York 10019 (800) 938-4685; *The New Latin America Market Atlas.*

Facts on File, 460 Park Avenue South, New York, New York 10016 (800) 443-8323; *The New Book of World Rankings.*

Food and Agricultural Organization of the United Nations (FAO) Via delle Terme di Caracalla, 00100 Rome, Italy (Telephone Number in U.S. (202) 653-2400); *Production Yearbook,* and *The State of Food and Agriculture.*

G.K. Hall and Company, 70 Lincoln Street, Boston, Massachusetts 02111 (617) 423-3990; *The World in Figures.*

Inter-American Development Bank, 1300 New York Avenue, NW, Washington, D.C. 20577 (202) 623-1753; *Economic and Social Progress in Latin America.*

Statistical Office of the United Nations, Publishing Service, New York, New York 10017 (800) 253-9646; *Statistical Yearbook.*

U.C.L.A. Latin American Center Publications, University of California, Los Angeles, California 90024 (310) 825-6634; *Statistical Abstract of Latin America.*

VENEZUELA - CUSTOMS DUTIES

G.K. Hall and Company, 70 Lincoln Street, Boston, Massachusetts 02111 (617) 423-3990; *The World in Figures.*

Inter-American Development Bank, 1300 New York Avenue, NW, Washington, D.C. 20577 (202) 623-1753; *Economic and Social Progress in Latin America.*

International Monetary Fund, 700 Nineteenth Street, NW, Washington, D.C. 20431 (202) 623-7000; *Government Finance Statistics Yearbook.*

VENEZUELA - DAIRY PRODUCTS

Facts on File, 460 Park Avenue South, New York, New York 10016 (800) 443-8323; *The New Book of World Rankings.*

Food and Agricultural Organization of the United Nations (FAO) Via delle Terme di Caracalla, 00100 Rome, Italy (Telephone Number in U.S. (202) 653-2400); *Production Yearbook,* and *The State of Food and Agriculture.*

Statistical Office of the United Nations, Publishing Service, New York, New York 10017 (800) 253-9646; *Statistical Yearbook.*

U.C.L.A. Latin American Center Publications, University of California, Los Angeles, California 90024 (310) 825-6634; *Statistical Abstract of Latin America.*

VENEZUELA - DEATH RATES

Euromonitor Publications Limited, 87-88 Turnmill Street, London EC1M 5QU, England; *Third World Economic Handbook.*

G.K. Hall and Company, 70 Lincoln Street, Boston, Massachusetts 02111 (617) 423-3990; *The World in Figures.*

Statistical Office of the United Nations, Publishing Service, New York, New York 10017 (800) 253-9646; *Demographic Yearbook,* and *Statistical Yearbook for Latin America and the Caribbean.*

Time Books, 201 East 50th Street, New York, New York 10022 (212) 751-2600; *The Economist Book of Vital World Statistics.*

World Health Organization, Office of Publications, Avenue Appia, CH-1211 Geneva 27, Switzerland (Telephone Number in U.S. (518) 436-9686); *World Health Statistics Annual.*

VENEZUELA - DEBT

The Economist Intelligence Unit, 111 West 57th Street, New York, New York 10019 (800) 938-4685; *The New Latin America Market Atlas.*

VENEZUELA - DEFENSE

The Economist Intelligence Unit, 111 West 57th Street, New York, New York 10019 (800) 938-4685; *The New Latin America Market Atlas.*

G.K. Hall and Company, 70 Lincoln Street, Boston, Massachusetts 02111 (617) 423-3990; *The World in Figures.*

International Monetary Fund, 700 Nineteenth Street, NW, Washington, D.C. 20431 (202) 623-7000; *Government Finance Statistics Yearbook.*

U.S. Arms Control and Disarmament Agency, 320 Twenty-first Street, NW, Washington, D.C. 20451 (202) 647-8677; *World Military Expenditures and Arms Transfers.*

VENEZUELA - DEMOGRAPHY

The Economist Intelligence Unit, 111 West 57th Street, New York, New York 10019 (800) 938-4685; *The World Market Atlas.*

Facts on File, 460 Park Avenue South, New York, New York 10016 (800) 443-8323; *The New Book of World Rankings.*

G.K. Hall and Company, 70 Lincoln Street, Boston, Massachusetts 02111 (617) 423-3990; *The World in Figures.*

VENEZUELA - DEVELOPMENT ASSISTANCE

G.K. Hall and Company, 70 Lincoln Street, Boston, Massachusetts 02111 (617) 423-3990; *The World in Figures.*

Inter-American Development Bank, 1300 New York Avenue, NW, Washington, D.C. 20577 (202) 623-1753; *Economic and Social Progress in Latin America.*

Statistical Office of the United Nations, Publishing Service, New York, New York 10017 (800) 253-9646; *Statistical Yearbook.*

VENEZUELA - DIAMOND PRODUCTION - See VENEZUELA - MINING AND MINERAL PRODUCTS

VENEZUELA - DISCOUNT RATES

Inter-American Development Bank, 1300 New York Avenue, NW, Washington, D.C. 20577 (202) 623-1753; *Economic and Social Progress in Latin America*.

Statistical Office of the United Nations, Publishing Service, New York, New York 10017 (800) 253-9646; *Statistical Yearbook*.

VENEZUELA - DISEASES

G.K. Hall and Company, 70 Lincoln Street, Boston, Massachusetts 02111 (617) 423-3990; *The World in Figures*.

World Health Organization, Office of Publications, Avenue Appia, CH-1211 Geneva 27, Switzerland (Telephone Number in U.S. (518) 436-9686); *World Health Statistics Annual*.

VENEZUELA - DIVORCE RATES

Facts on File, 460 Park Avenue South, New York, New York 10016 (800) 443-8323; *The New Book of World Rankings*.

Statistical Office of the United Nations, Publishing Service, New York, New York 10017 (800) 253-9646; *Demographic Yearbook*, and *Statistical Yearbook*.

VENEZUELA - DOMESTIC PRODUCT

G.K. Hall and Company, 70 Lincoln Street, Boston, Massachusetts 02111 (617) 423-3990; *The World in Figures*.

VENEZUELA - ECONOMY

Euromonitor Publications Limited, 87-88 Turnmill Street, London EC1M 5QU, England; *International Marketing Data and Statistics*, and *Third World Economic Handbook*.

Facts on File, 460 Park Avenue South, New York, New York 10016 (800) 443-8323; *The New Book of World Rankings*.

G.K. Hall and Company, 70 Lincoln Street, Boston, Massachusetts 02111 (617) 423-3990; *The World in Figures*.

Inter-American Development Bank, 1300 New York Avenue, NW, Washington, D.C. 20577 (202) 623-1753; *Economic and Social Progress in Latin America*.

Organization of American States (OAS), General Secretariat, Washington, D.C. 20006 (202) 458-3533; *Statistical Bulletin of the OAS*.

Statistical Office of the United Nations, Publishing Service, New York, New York 10017 (800) 253-9646; *Economic Survey of Latin America and the Caribbean*.

U.C.L.A. Latin American Center Publications, University of California, Los Angeles, California 90024 (310) 825-6634; *Statistical Abstract of Latin America*.

VENEZUELA - EDUCATION

The Economist Intelligence Unit, 111 West 57th Street, New York, New York 10019 (800) 938-4685; *The New Latin America Market Atlas*, and *The World Market Atlas*.

Facts on File, 460 Park Avenue South, New York, New York 10016 (800) 443-8323; *The New Book of World Rankings*.

Gale Research Incorporated, 835 Penobscot Building, Detroit, Michigan 48226 (800) 877-4253; *International Historical Statistics The Americas and Australasia*.

G.K. Hall and Company, 70 Lincoln Street, Boston, Massachusetts 02111 (617) 423-3990; *The World in Figures*.

International Monetary Fund, 700 Nineteenth Street, NW, Washington, D.C. 20431 (202) 623-7000; *Government Finance Statistics Yearbook*.

Statistical Office of the United Nations, Publishing Service, New York, New York 10017 (800) 253-9646; *Statistical Yearbook for Latin America and the Caribbean*.

Time Books, 201 East 50th Street, New York, New York 10022 (212) 751-2600; *The Economist Book of Vital World Statistics*.

U.C.L.A. Latin American Center Publications, University of California, Los Angeles, California 90024 (310) 825-6634; *Statistical Abstract of Latin America*.

United Nations Educational, Scientific and Cultural Organization (UNESCO), 7 Place de Fontenoy, F-75700 Paris, France (Telephone Number in U.S. (212) 963-5981); *Statistical Yearbook*.

The World Bank, 1818 H Street, NW, Washington, D.C. 20433 (202) 477-1234; *World Tables*.

VENEZUELA - EGG PRODUCTION AND CONSUMPTION - See VENEZUELA - DAIRY PRODUCTS

VENEZUELA - ELECTRICITY

The Economist Intelligence Unit, 111 West 57th Street, New York, New York 10019 (800) 938-4685; *The New Latin America Market Atlas*.

Facts on File, 460 Park Avenue South, New York, New York 10016 (800) 443-8323; *The New Book of World Rankings*.

Inter-American Development Bank, 1300 New York Avenue, NW, Washington, D.C. 20577 (202) 623-1753; *Economic and Social Progress in Latin America*.

Penn Well Publishing Company, 1421 South Sheridan Road, P.O. Box 1260, Tulsa, Oklahoma 74101 (800) 752-9764; *International Energy Statistics Sourcebook*.

Statistical Office of the United Nations, Publishing Service, New York, New York 10017 (800) 253-9646; *Electric Power in Asia and the Pacific*, and *Statistical Yearbook*.

Time Books, 201 East 50th Street, New York, New York 10022 (212) 751-2600; *The Economist Book of Vital World Statistics*.

VENEZUELA - EMPLOYMENT

Euromonitor Publications Limited, 87-88 Turnmill Street, London EC1M 5QU, England; *International Marketing Data and Statistics*.

Facts on File, 460 Park Avenue South, New York, New York 10016 (800) 443-8323; *The New Book of World Rankings*.

International Labour Office, I.L.O. Publications, CH-1211, Geneva 22, Switzerland; *Yearbook of Labour Statistics*.

Statistical Office of the United Nations, Publishing Service, New York, New York 10017 (800) 253-9646; *Statistical Yearbook*, and

Statistical Yearbook for Latin America and the Caribbean.

U.C.L.A. Latin American Center Publications, University of California, Los Angeles, California 90024 (310) 825-6634; *Statistical Abstract of Latin America.*

VENEZUELA - ENERGY

The Economist Intelligence Unit, 111 West 57th Street, New York, New York 10019 (800) 938-4685; *The New Latin America Market Atlas.*

Facts on File, 460 Park Avenue South, New York, New York 10016 (800) 443-8323; *The New Book of World Rankings.*

Food and Agricultural Organization of the United Nations (FAO) Via delle Terme di Caracalla, 00100 Rome, Italy (Telephone Number in U.S. (202) 653-2400); *The State of Food and Agriculture.*

G.K. Hall and Company, 70 Lincoln Street, Boston, Massachusetts 02111 (617) 423-3990; *The World in Figures.*

Penn Well Publishing Company, 1421 South Sheridan Road, P.O. Box 1260, Tulsa, Oklahoma 74101 (800) 752-9764; *International Energy Statistics Sourcebook.*

Statistical Office of the United Nations, Publishing Service, New York, New York 10017 (800) 253-9646; *Energy Statistics Yearbook, Statistical Yearbook,* and *Statistical Yearbook for Latin America and the Caribbean.*

Time Books, 201 East 50th Street, New York, New York 10022 (212) 751-2600; *The Economist Book of Vital World Statistics.*

U.C.L.A. Latin American Center Publications, University of California, Los Angeles, California 90024 (310) 825-6634; *Statistical Abstract of Latin America.*

VENEZUELA - EXCHANGE RATES

Euromonitor Publications Limited, 87-88 Turnmill Street, London EC1M 5QU, England; *International Marketing Data and Statistics.*

Inter-American Development Bank, 1300 New York Avenue, NW, Washington, D.C. 20577 (202) 623-1753; *Economic and Social Progress in Latin America.*

International Civil Aviation Organization, 1000 Sherbrooke Street West, Suite 400, Montreal, Quebec, Canada H3A 2R2 (514) 285-8219; *Civil Aviation Statistics of the World.*

International Monetary Fund, 700 Nineteenth Street, NW, Washington, D.C. 20431 (202) 623-7000; *International Financial Statistics.*

Organization of American States (OAS), General Secretariat, Washington, D.C. 20006 (202) 458-3533; *Statistical Bulletin of the OAS.*

Organization of Petroleum Exporting Countries, Obere Donaustrasse 93, 1020 Vienna 2, Austria; *OPEC Annual Statistical Bulletin.*

Statistical Office of the United Nations, Publishing Service, New York, New York 10017 (800) 253-9646; *Statistical Yearbook.*

U.C.L.A. Latin American Center Publications, University of California, Los Angeles, California 90024 (310) 825-6634; *Statistical Abstract of Latin America.*

VENEZUELA - EXCISE TAXES - See VENEZUELA - TAXATION

VENEZUELA - EXPORTS

The Economist Intelligence Unit, 111 West 57th Street, New York, New York 10019 (800) 938-4685; *The New Latin America Market Atlas,* and *The World Market Atlas.*

Euromonitor Publications Limited, 87-88 Turnmill Street, London EC1M 5QU, England; *International Marketing Data and Statistics,* and *Third World Economic Handbook.*

Food and Agricultural Organization of the United Nations (FAO) Via delle Terme di Caracalla, 00100 Rome, Italy (Telephone Number in U.S. (202) 653-2400); *The State of Food and Agriculture.*

G.K. Hall and Company, 70 Lincoln Street, Boston, Massachusetts 02111 (617) 423-3990; *The World in Figures.*

Inter-American Development Bank, 1300 New York Avenue, NW, Washington, D.C. 20577 (202) 623-1753; *Economic and Social Progress in Latin America.*

International Monetary Fund, 700 Nineteenth Street, NW, Washington, D.C. 20431 (202) 623-7000; *Direction of Trade Statistics,* and *International Financial Statistics.*

Organization of American States (OAS), General Secretariat, Washington, D.C. 20006 (202) 458-3533; *Statistical Bulletin of the OAS.*

Organization of Petroleum Exporting Countries, Obere Donaustrasse 93, 1020 Vienna 2, Austria; *OPEC Annual Statistical Bulletin.*

Statistical Office of the United Nations, Publishing Service, New York, New York 10017 (800) 253-9646; *Statistical Yearbook for Latin America and the Caribbean,* and *Trade in Manufactures of Developing Countries.*

Time Books, 201 East 50th Street, New York, New York 10022 (212) 751-2600; *The Economist Book of Vital World Statistics.*

The World Bank, 1818 H Street, NW, Washington, D.C. 20433 (202) 477-1234; *World Tables.*

VENEZUELA - EXTERNAL FINANCING

Inter-American Development Bank, 1300 New York Avenue, NW, Washington, D.C. 20577 (202) 623-1753; *Economic and Social Progress in Latin America.*

Statistical Office of the United Nations, Publishing Service, New York, New York 10017 (800) 253-9646; *Statistical Yearbook for Latin America and the Caribbean.*

VENEZUELA - EXTERNAL INDEBTEDNESS

Euromonitor Publications Limited, 87-88 Turnmill Street, London EC1M 5QU, England; *Third World Economic Handbook.*

Inter-American Development Bank, 1300 New York Avenue, NW, Washington, D.C. 20577 (202) 623-1753; *Economic and Social Progress in Latin America.*

Statistical Office of the United Nations, Publishing Service, New York, New York 10017 (800) 253-9646; *Statistical Yearbook for Latin America and the Caribbean.*

The World Bank, 1818 H Street, NW, Washington, D.C. 20433 (202) 477-1234; *World Tables.*

VENEZUELA - EXTERNAL TRADE

Food and Agricultural Organization of the United Nations (FAO) Via delle Terme di Caracalla, 00100 Rome, Italy (Telephone Number in U.S. (202) 653-2400); *The State of Food and Agriculture.*

Gale Research Incorporated, 835 Penobscot Building, Detroit, Michigan 48226 (800) 877-4253; *International Historical Statistics The Americas and Australasia.*

G.K. Hall and Company, 70 Lincoln Street, Boston, Massachusetts 02111 (617) 423-3990; *The World in Figures.*

Inter-American Development Bank, 1300 New York Avenue, NW, Washington, D.C. 20577 (202) 623-1753; *Economic and Social Progress in Latin America.*

Statistical Office of the United Nations, Publishing Service, New York, New York 10017 (800) 253-9646; *Statistical Yearbook,* and *Statistical Yearbook for Latin America and the Caribbean.*

VENEZUELA - FABRIC PRODUCTION - See VENEZUELA - TEXTILE INDUSTRY

VENEZUELA - FAMILY PLANNING

U.C.L.A. Latin American Center Publications, University of California, Los Angeles, California 90024 (310) 825-6634; *Statistical Abstract of Latin America.*

VENEZUELA - FARM CROPS - See VENEZUELA - CROPS

VENEZUELA - FEMALE WORKING POPULATION - See VENEZUELA - EMPLOYMENT

VENEZUELA - FERTILITY RATES

Facts on File, 460 Park Avenue South, New York, New York 10016 (800) 443-8323; *The New Book of World Rankings.*

Time Books, 201 East 50th Street, New York, New York 10022 (212) 751-2600; *The Economist Book of Vital World Statistics.*

The World Bank, 1818 H Street, NW, Washington, D.C. 20433 (202) 477-1234; *World Tables.*

VENEZUELA - FERTILIZER PRODUCTION AND CONSUMPTION

The Economist Intelligence Unit, 111 West 57th Street, New York, New York 10019 (800) 938-4685; *The New Latin America Market Atlas.*

Food and Agricultural Organization of the United Nations (FAO), Via delle Terme di Caracalla, 00100 Rome, Italy (Telephone Number in U.S. (202) 653-2400); *Fertilizer Yearbook,* and *The State of Food and Agriculture.*

Statistical Office of the United Nations, Publishing Service, New York, New York 10017 (800) 253-9646; *Statistical Yearbook.*

VENEZUELA - FETAL MORTALITY

Statistical Office of the United Nations, Publishing Service, New York, New York 10017 (800) 253-9646; *Demographic Yearbook.*

World Health Organization, Office of Publications, Avenue Appia, CH-1211 Geneva 27, Switzerland (Telephone Number in U.S. (518) 436-9686); *World Health Statistics Annual.*

VENEZUELA - FIBRE PRODUCTION - See VENEZUELA - TEXTILE INDUSTRY

VENEZUELA - FILAMENT PRODUCTION - See VENEZUELA - TEXTILE INDUSTRY

VENEZUELA - FILM - See VENEZUELA - MOTION PICTURES

VENEZUELA - FINANCE

Facts on File, 460 Park Avenue South, New York, New York 10016 (800) 443-8323; *The New Book of World Rankings.*

Gale Research Incorporated, 835 Penobscot Building, Detroit, Michigan 48226 (800) 877-4253; *International Historical Statistics The Americas and Australasia.*

G.K. Hall and Company, 70 Lincoln Street, Boston, Massachusetts 02111 (617) 423-3990; *The World in Figures.*

Inter-American Development Bank, 1300 New York Avenue, NW, Washington, D.C. 20577 (202) 623-1753; *Economic and Social Progress in Latin America.*

International Monetary Fund, 700 Nineteenth Street, NW, Washington, D.C. 20431 (202) 623-7000; *Government Finance Statistics Yearbook,* and *International Financial Statistics.*

Organization of American States (OAS), General Secretariat, Washington, D.C. 20006 (202) 458-3533; *Statistical Bulletin of the OAS.*

U.C.L.A. Latin American Center Publications, University of California, Los Angeles, California 90024 (310) 825-6634; *Statistical Abstract of Latin America.*

VENEZUELA - FISHERIES

Facts on File, 460 Park Avenue South, New York, New York 10016 (800) 443-8323; *The New Book of World Rankings.*

Food and Agricultural Organization of the United Nations (FAO) Via delle Terme di Caracalla, 00100 Rome, Italy (Telephone Number in U.S. (202) 653-2400); *The State of Food and Agriculture,* and *Yearbook of Fishery Statistics.*

Inter-American Development Bank, 1300 New York Avenue, NW, Washington, D.C. 20577 (202) 623-1753; *Economic and Social Progress in Latin America.*

Statistical Office of the United Nations, Publishing Service, New York, New York 10017 (800) 253-9646; *Statistical Yearbook.*

U.C.L.A. Latin American Center Publications, University of California, Los Angeles, California 90024 (310) 825-6634; *Statistical Abstract of Latin America.*

VENEZUELA - FLOUR PRODUCTION

Statistical Office of the United Nations, Publishing Service, New York, New York 10017 (800) 253-9646; *Statistical Yearbook.*

VENEZUELA - FOOD

Food and Agricultural Organization of the United Nations (FAO) Via delle Terme di Caracalla, 00100 Rome, Italy (Telephone Number in U.S. (202) 653-2400); *The State of Food and Agriculture*.

G.K. Hall and Company, 70 Lincoln Street, Boston, Massachusetts 02111 (617) 423-3990; *The World in Figures*.

VENEZUELA - FOREIGN AID

G.K. Hall and Company, 70 Lincoln Street, Boston, Massachusetts 02111 (617) 423-3990; *The World in Figures*.

Inter-American Development Bank, 1300 New York Avenue, NW, Washington, D.C. 20577 (202) 623-1753; *Economic and Social Progress in Latin America*.

VENEZUELA - FOREIGN DEBT

The Economist Intelligence Unit, 111 West 57th Street, New York, New York 10019 (800) 938-4685; *The New Latin America Market Atlas*.

Inter-American Development Bank, 1300 New York Avenue, NW, Washington, D.C. 20577 (202) 623-1753; *Economic and Social Progress in Latin America*.

International Monetary Fund, 700 Nineteenth Street, NW, Washington, D.C. 20431 (202) 623-7000; *Government Finance Statistics Yearbook*.

VENEZUELA - FOREIGN INDEBTEDNESS

Inter-American Development Bank, 1300 New York Avenue, NW, Washington, D.C. 20577 (202) 623-1753; *Economic and Social Progress in Latin America*.

Statistical Office of the United Nations, Publishing Service, New York, New York 10017 (800) 253-9646; *Economic Survey of Latin America and the Caribbean*.

VENEZUELA - FOREIGN INVESTMENT

The Economist Intelligence Unit, 111 West 57th Street, New York, New York 10019 (800) 938-4685; *The New Latin America Market Atlas*.

VENEZUELA - FOREIGN TRADE

The Economist Intelligence Unit, 111 West 57th Street, New York, New York 10019 (800) 938-4685; *The New Latin America Market Atlas*.

Euromonitor Publications Limited, 87-88 Turnmill Street, London EC1M 5QU, England; *International Marketing Data and Statistics*, and *Third World Economic Handbook*.

Facts on File, 460 Park Avenue South, New York, New York 10016 (800) 443-8323; *The New Book of World Rankings*.

Food and Agricultural Organization of the United Nations (FAO) Via delle Terme di Caracalla, 00100 Rome, Italy (Telephone Number in U.S. (202) 653-2400); *The State of Food and Agriculture*.

G.K. Hall and Company, 70 Lincoln Street, Boston, Massachusetts 02111 (617) 423-3990; *The World in Figures*.

Inter-American Development Bank, 1300 New York Avenue, NW, Washington, D.C. 20577 (202) 623-1753; *Economic and Social Progress in Latin America*.

Statistical Office of the United Nations, Publishing Service, New York, New York 10017 (800) 253-9646; *Economic Survey of Latin America and the Caribbean, International Trade Statistics Yearbook*, and *Statistical Yearbook*.

U.C.L.A. Latin American Center Publications, University of California, Los Angeles, California 90024 (310) 825-6634; *Statistical Abstract of Latin America*.

The World Bank, 1818 H Street, NW, Washington, D.C. 20433 (202) 477-1234; *World Tables*.

VENEZUELA - FORESTRY AND FOREST PRODUCTS

American Forest and Paper Association, 1250 Connecticut Avenue, NW, Washington, D.C. 20036 (202) 463-2455; *Wood Pulp and Fiber Statistics*.

Euromonitor Publications Limited, 87-88 Turnmill Street, London EC1M 5QU, England; *Third World Economic Handbook*.

Facts on File, 460 Park Avenue South, New York, New York 10016 (800) 443-8323; *The New Book of World Rankings*.

Food and Agricultural Organization of the United Nations (FAO) Via delle Terme di Caracalla, 00100 Rome, Italy (Telephone Number in U.S. (202) 653-2400); *The State of Food and Agriculture*, and *Yearbook of Forest Products*.

G.K. Hall and Company, 70 Lincoln Street, Boston, Massachusetts 02111 (617) 423-3990; *The World in Figures*.

Inter-American Development Bank, 1300 New York Avenue, NW, Washington, D.C. 20577 (202) 623-1753; *Economic and Social Progress in Latin America*.

Statistical Office of the United Nations, Publishing Service, New York, New York 10017 (800) 253-9646; *Statistical Yearbook*.

U.C.L.A. Latin American Center Publications, University of California, Los Angeles, California 90024 (310) 825-6634; *Statistical Abstract of Latin America*.

United Nations Educational, Scientific and Cultural Organization (UNESCO), 7 Place de Fontenoy, F-75700 Paris, France (Telephone Number in U.S. (212) 963-5981); *Statistical Yearbook*.

VENEZUELA - GARLIC PRODUCTION - See VENEZUELA - CROPS

VENEZUELA - GAS AND GAS LIQUIDS PRODUCTION - See VENEZUELA - MINING AND MINERAL PRODUCTS

VENEZUELA - GENERAL INDUSTRIAL STATISTICS

Statistical Office of the United Nations, Publishing Service, New York, New York 10017 (800) 253-9646; *Industrial Statistics Yearbook*.

VENEZUELA - GENERAL MORTALITY

Statistical Office of the United Nations, Publishing Service, New York, New York 10017 (800) 253-9646; *Demographic Yearbook*.

World Health Organization, Office of Publications, Avenue Appia, CH-1211 Geneva 27, Switzerland (Telephone Number in U.S. (510)

436-9686); *World Health Statistics Annual.*

VENEZUELA - GEOGRAPHIC DATA

Facts on File, 460 Park Avenue South, New York, New York 10016 (800) 443-8323; *The New Book of World Rankings.*

U.C.L.A. Latin American Center Publications, University of California, Los Angeles, California 90024 (310) 825-6634; *Statistical Abstract of Latin America.*

VENEZUELA - GOATS - See VENEZUELA - LIVESTOCK AND POULTRY

VENEZUELA - GOLD HOLDINGS

International Monetary Fund, 700 Nineteenth Street, NW, Washington, D.C. 20431 (202) 623-7000; *International Financial Statistics.*

Statistical Office of the United Nations, Publishing Service, New York, New York 10017 (800) 253-9646; *Statistical Yearbook.*

The World Bank, 1818 H Street, NW, Washington, D.C. 20433 (202) 477-1234; *World Tables.*

VENEZUELA - GOLD PRODUCTION AND CONSUMPTION - See VENEZUELA - MINING AND MINERAL PRODUCTS

VENEZUELA - GOLD RESERVES

The Economist Intelligence Unit, 111 West 57th Street, New York, New York 10019 (800) 938-4685; *The New Latin America Market Atlas.*

VENEZUELA - GOVERNMENT

G.K. Hall and Company, 70 Lincoln Street, Boston, Massachusetts 02111 (617) 423-3990; *The World in Figures.*

Inter-American Development Bank, 1300 New York Avenue, NW, Washington, D.C. 20577 (202) 623-1753; *Economic and Social Progress in Latin America.*

VENEZUELA - GOVERNMENT CONSUMPTION

Inter-American Development Bank, 1300 New York Avenue, NW, Washington, D.C. 20577 (202) 623-1753; *Economic and Social Progress in Latin America.*

VENEZUELA - GOVERNMENT EXPENDITURES

Euromonitor Publications Limited, 87-88 Turnmill Street, London EC1M 5QU, England; *Third World Economic Handbook.*

Inter-American Development Bank, 1300 New York Avenue, NW, Washington, D.C. 20577 (202) 623-1753; *Economic and Social Progress in Latin America.*

International Monetary Fund, 700 Nineteenth Street, NW, Washington, D.C. 20431 (202) 623-7000; *Government Finance Statistics Yearbook.*

Time Books, 201 East 50th Street, New York, New York 10022 (212) 751-2600; *The Economist Book of Vital World Statistics.*

The World Bank, 1818 H Street, NW, Washington, D.C. 20433 (202) 477-1234; *World Tables.*

VENEZUELA - GOVERNMENT FINANCE

Inter-American Development Bank, 1300 New York Avenue, NW, Washington, D.C. 20577 (202) 623-1753; *Economic and Social Progress in Latin America.*

International Monetary Fund, 700 Nineteenth Street, NW, Washington, D.C. 20431 (202) 623-7000; *International Financial Statistics.*

VENEZUELA - GOVERNMENT REVENUES

Inter-American Development Bank, 1300 New York Avenue, NW, Washington, D.C. 20577 (202) 623-1753; *Economic and Social Progress in Latin America.*

International Monetary Fund, 700 Nineteenth Street, NW, Washington, D.C. 20431 (202) 623-7000; *Government Finance Statistics Yearbook.*

Time Books, 201 East 50th Street, New York, New York 10022 (212) 751-2600; *The Economist Book of Vital World Statistics.*

The World Bank, 1818 H Street, NW, Washington, D.C. 20433 (202) 477-1234; *World Tables.*

VENEZUELA - GRAIN PRODUCTION - See VENEZUELA - CROPS

VENEZUELA - GRANTS

International Monetary Fund, 700 Nineteenth Street, NW, Washington, D.C. 20431 (202) 623-7000; *Government Finance Statistics Yearbook.*

VENEZUELA - GREEN PEPPER AND CHILIE PRODUCTION - See VENEZUELA - CROPS

VENEZUELA - GROSS DOMESTIC PRODUCT

The Economist Intelligence Unit, 111 West 57th Street, New York, New York 10019 (800) 938-4685; *The New Latin America Market Atlas,* and *The World Market Atlas.*

Euromonitor Publications Limited, 87-88 Turnmill Street, London EC1M 5QU, England; *International Marketing Data and Statistics.*

Euromonitor Publications Limited, 87-88 Turnmill Street, London EC1M 5QU, England; *Third World Economic Handbook.*

Facts on File, 460 Park Avenue South, New York, New York 10016 (800) 443-8323; *The New Book of World Rankings.*

G.K. Hall and Company, 70 Lincoln Street, Boston, Massachusetts 02111 (617) 423-3990; *The World in Figures.*

Inter-American Development Bank, 1300 New York Avenue, NW, Washington, D.C. 20577 (202) 623-1753; *Economic and Social Progress in Latin America.*

Organization of American States (OAS), General Secretariat, Washington, D.C. 20006 (202) 458-3533; *Statistical Bulletin of the OAS.*

Statistical Office of the United Nations, Publishing Service, New York, New York 10017 (800) 253-9646; *Statistical Yearbook,* and *Statistical Yearbook for Latin America and the Caribbean.*

Time Books, 201 East 50th Street, New York, New York 10022 (212) 751-2600; *The Economist Book of Vital World Statistics.*

U.C.L.A. Latin American Center Publications, University of California, Los Angeles, California 90024 (310) 825-6634; *Statistical Abstract of Latin America*.

The World Bank, 1818 H Street, NW, Washington, D.C. 20433 (202) 477-1234; *World Tables*.

VENEZUELA - GROSS INDUSTRIAL PRODUCT - BY CATEGORIES OF GOODS

Euromonitor Publications Limited, 87-88 Turnmill Street, London EC1M 5QU, England; *Third World Economic Handbook*.

VENEZUELA - GROSS NATIONAL PRODUCT

Euromonitor Publications Limited, 87-88 Turnmill Street, London EC1M 5QU, England; *International Marketing Data and Statistics*, and *Third World Economic Handbook*.

Inter-American Development Bank, 1300 New York Avenue, NW, Washington, D.C. 20577 (202) 623-1753; *Economic and Social Progress in Latin America*.

Organization of Petroleum Exporting Countries, Obere Donaustrasse 93, 1020 Vienna 2, Austria; *OPEC Annual Statistical Bulletin*.

U.S. Arms Control and Disarmament Agency, 320 Twenty-first Street, NW, Washington, D.C. 20451 (202) 647-8677; *World Military Expenditures and Arms Transfers*.

The World Bank, 1818 H Street, NW, Washington, D.C. 20433 (202) 477-1234; *World Tables*.

VENEZUELA - GROUNDNUT PRODUCTION - See VENEZUELA - CROPS

VENEZUELA - HEALTH

The Economist Intelligence Unit, 111 West 57th Street, New York, New York 10019 (800) 938-4685; *The New Latin America Market Atlas*.

Facts on File, 460 Park Avenue South, New York, New York 10016 (800) 443-8323; *The New Book of World Rankings*.

G.K. Hall and Company, 70 Lincoln Street, Boston, Massachusetts 02111 (617) 423-3990; *The World in Figures*.

Statistical Office of the United Nations, Publishing Service, New York, New York 10017 (800) 253-9646; *Statistical Yearbook*, and *Statistical Yearbook for Latin America and the Caribbean*.

Time Books, 201 East 50th Street, New York, New York 10022 (212) 751-2600; *The Economist Book of Vital World Statistics*.

U.C.L.A. Latin American Center Publications, University of California, Los Angeles, California 90024 (310) 825-6634; *Statistical Abstract of Latin America*.

World Health Organization, Office of Publications, Avenue Appia, CH-1211 Geneva 27, Switzerland (Telephone Number in U.S. (518) 436-9686); *World Health Statistics Annual*.

VENEZUELA - HEALTH EXPENDITURES

International Monetary Fund, 700 Nineteenth Street, NW, Washington, D.C. 20431 (202) 623-7000; *Government Finance Statistics Yearbook*.

VENEZUELA - HIDE PRODUCTION

Food and Agricultural Organization of the United Nations (FAO), Via delle Terme di Caracalla, 00100 Rome, Italy (Telephone Number in U.S. (202) 653-2400); *Production Yearbook*.

VENEZUELA - HIGHWAYS

The Economist Intelligence Unit, 111 West 57th Street, New York, New York 10019 (800) 938-4685; *The New Latin America Market Atlas*.

G.K. Hall and Company, 70 Lincoln Street, Boston, Massachusetts 02111 (617) 423-3990; *The World in Figures*.

VENEZUELA - HORSES - See VENEZUELA - LIVESTOCK AND POULTRY

VENEZUELA - HOURS OF WORK - See VENEZUELA - EMPLOYMENT

VENEZUELA - HOUSING AND HOUSING UNITS

Euromonitor Publications Limited, 87-88 Turnmill Street, London EC1M 5QU, England; *Third World Economic Handbook*.

Facts on File, 460 Park Avenue South, New York, New York 10016 (800) 443-8323; *The New Book of World Rankings*.

Statistical Office of the United Nations, Publishing Service, New York, New York 10017 (800) 253-9040, *Statistical Yearbook for Latin America and the Caribbean*.

U.C.L.A. Latin American Center Publications, University of California, Los Angeles, California 90024 (310) 825-6634; *Statistical Abstract of Latin America*.

VENEZUELA - HOUSING EXPENDITURES

International Monetary Fund, 700 Nineteenth Street, NW, Washington, D.C. 20431 (202) 623-7000; *Government Finance Statistics Yearbook*.

VENEZUELA - HYDROCHLORIC ACID PRODUCTION

Statistical Office of the United Nations, Publishing Service, New York, New York 10017 (800) 253-9646; *Statistical Yearbook*.

VENEZUELA - ILLITERATE POPULATION

The Economist Intelligence Unit, 111 West 57th Street, New York, New York 10019 (800) 938-4685; *The New Latin America Market Atlas*, and *The World Market Atlas*.

G.K. Hall and Company, 70 Lincoln Street, Boston, Massachusetts 02111 (617) 423-3990; *The World in Figures*.

Statistical Office of the United Nations, Publishing Service, New York, New York 10017 (800) 253-9646; *Statistical Yearbook for Latin America and the Caribbean*.

United Nations Educational, Scientific and Cultural Organization (UNESCO), 7 Place de Fontenoy, F-75700 Paris, France (Telephone Number in U.S. (212) 963-5981); *Statistical Yearbook*.

VENEZUELA - IMMIGRATION

U.C.L.A. Latin American Center Publications, University of California, Los Angeles, California 90024 (310) 825-6634; *Statistical Abstract of Latin America*.

VENEZUELA - IMPORTS

The Economist Intelligence Unit, 111 West 57th Street, New York, New York 10019 (800) 938-4685; *The New Latin America Market Atlas*, and *The World Market Atlas*.

Euromonitor Publications Limited, 87-88 Turnmill Street, London EC1M 5QU, England; *International Marketing Data and Statistics*, and *Third World Economic Handbook*.

Food and Agricultural Organization of the United Nations (FAO) Via delle Terme di Caracalla, 00100 Rome, Italy (Telephone Number in U.S. (202) 653-2400); *The State of Food and Agriculture*.

G.K. Hall and Company, 70 Lincoln Street, Boston, Massachusetts 02111 (617) 423-3990; *The World in Figures*.

Inter-American Development Bank, 1300 New York Avenue, NW, Washington, D.C. 20577 (202) 623-1753; *Economic and Social Progress in Latin America*.

International Monetary Fund, 700 Nineteenth Street, NW, Washington, D.C. 20431 (202) 623-7000; *Direction of Trade Statistics, Government Finance Statistics Yearbook*, and *International Financial Statistics*.

Organization of American States (OAS), General Secretariat, Washington, D.C. 20006 (202) 458-3533; *Statistical Bulletin of the OAS*.

Statistical Office of the United Nations, Publishing Service, New York, New York 10017 (800) 253-9646; *Statistical Yearbook for Latin America and the Caribbean*, and *Trade in Manufactures of Developing Countries*.

Time Books, 201 East 50th Street, New York, New York 10022 (212) 751-2600; *The Economist Book of Vital World Statistics*.

The World Bank, 1818 H Street, NW, Washington, D.C. 20433 (202) 477-1234; *World Tables*.

VENEZUELA - INCOME DISTRIBUTION

Statistical Office of the United Nations, Publishing Service, New York, New York 10017 (800) 253-9646; *Statistical Yearbook for Latin America and the Caribbean*.

U.C.L.A. Latin American Center Publications, University of California, Los Angeles, California 90024 (310) 825-6634; *Statistical Abstract of Latin America*.

VENEZUELA - INCOME TAXES - See VENEZUELA - TAXATION

VENEZUELA - INDUSTRIAL METALS PRODUCTION - See VENEZUELA - MINING AND MINERAL PRODUCTS

VENEZUELA - INDUSTRY

Euromonitor Publications Limited, 87-88 Turnmill Street, London EC1M 5QU, England; *Third World Economic Handbook*.

Facts on File, 460 Park Avenue South, New York, New York 10016 (800) 443-8323; *The New Book of World Rankings*.

Gale Research Incorporated, 835 Penobscot Building, Detroit, Michigan 48226 (800) 877-4253; *International Historical Statistics The Americas and Australasia*.

G.K. Hall and Company, 70 Lincoln Street, Boston, Massachusetts 02111 (617) 423-3990; *The World in Figures*.

International Labour Office, I.L.O. Publications, CH-1211, Geneva 22, Switzerland; *Yearbook of Labour Statistics*.

Statistical Office of the United Nations, Publishing Service, New York, New York 10017 (800) 253-9646; *Economic Survey of Latin America and the Caribbean*, and *Statistical Yearbook*.

Time Books, 201 East 50th Street, New York, New York 10022 (212) 751-2600; *The Economist Book of Vital World Statistics*.

U.C.L.A. Latin American Center Publications, University of California, Los Angeles, California 90024 (310) 825-6634; *Statistical Abstract of Latin America*.

The World Bank, 1818 H Street, NW, Washington, D.C. 20433 (202) 477-1234; *World Tables*.

World Intellectual Property Organization, 34 Chemin des Colombettes, CH-1211 Geneva 20. Switzerland; *Industrial Property Statistics*.

VENEZUELA - INFANT AND MATERNAL MORTALITY

The Economist Intelligence Unit, 111 West 57th Street, New York, New York 10019 (800) 938-4685; *The New Latin America Market Atlas*.

Statistical Office of the United Nations, Publishing Service, New York, New York 10017 (800) 253-9646; *Demographic Yearbook*, and *Statistical Yearbook*.

Time Books, 201 East 50th Street, New York, New York 10022 (212) 751-2600; *The Economist Book of Vital World Statistics*.

The World Bank, 1818 H Street, NW, Washington, D.C. 20433 (202) 477-1234; *World Tables*.

World Health Organization, Office of Publications, Avenue Appia, CH-1211 Geneva 27, Switzerland (Telephone Number in U.S. (518) 436-9686); *World Health Statistics Annual*.

VENEZUELA - INFLATIONARY FACTORS

Statistical Office of the United Nations, Publishing Service, New York, New York 10017 (800) 253-9646; *Economic Survey of Latin America and the Caribbean*.

VENEZUELA - INTEREST RATES

Inter-American Development Bank, 1300 New York Avenue, NW, Washington, D.C. 20577 (202) 623-1753; *Economic and Social Progress in Latin America*.

Organization of American States (OAS), General Secretariat, Washington, D.C. 20006 (202) 458-3533; *Statistical Bulletin of the OAS*.

VENEZUELA - INTERNATIONAL FINANCE

Inter-American Development Bank, 1300 New York Avenue, NW, Washington, D.C. 20577 (202) 623-1753; *Economic and Social Progress in Latin America*.

U.C.L.A. Latin American Center Publications, University of California, Los Angeles, California 90024 (310) 825-6634; *Statistical Abstract of Latin America*.

VENEZUELA - INTERNATIONAL LIQUIDITY

Inter-American Development Bank, 1300 New York Avenue, NW, Washington, D.C. 20577 (202) 623-1753; *Economic and Social Progress in Latin America.*

International Monetary Fund, 700 Nineteenth Street, NW, Washington, D.C. 20431 (202) 623-7000; *International Financial Statistics.*

VENEZUELA - INTERNATIONAL RESERVES

Inter-American Development Bank, 1300 New York Avenue, NW, Washington, D.C. 20577 (202) 623-1753; *Economic and Social Progress in Latin America.*

Organization of American States (OAS), General Secretariat, Washington, D.C. 20006 (202) 458-3533; *Statistical Bulletin of the OAS.*

VENEZUELA - INTERNATIONAL RESERVES EXCLUDING GOLD

Statistical Office of the United Nations, Publishing Service, New York, New York 10017 (800) 253-9646; *Statistical Yearbook.*

The World Bank, 1818 H Street, NW, Washington, D.C. 20433 (202) 477-1234; *World Tables.*

VENEZUELA - INTERNATIONAL STATISTICS

Inter-American Development Bank, 1300 New York Avenue, NW, Washington, D.C. 20577 (202) 623-1753; *Economic and Social Progress in Latin America.*

U.C.L.A Latin American Center Publications, University of California, Los Angeles, California 90024 (310) 825-6634; *Statistical Abstract of Latin America.*

VENEZUELA - INVESTMENT

Inter-American Development Bank, 1300 New York Avenue, NW, Washington, D.C. 20577 (202) 623-1753; *Economic and Social Progress in Latin America.*

Statistical Office of the United Nations, Publishing Service, New York, New York 10017 (800) 253-9646; *Statistical Yearbook for Latin America and the Caribbean.*

VENEZUELA - IRON ORE EXPORTS - See VENEZUELA - MINING AND MINERAL PRODUCTS

VENEZUELA - IRON ORE PRODUCTION AND CONSUMPTION - See VENEZUELA - MINING AND MINERAL PRODUCTS

VENEZUELA - IRRIGATION

Euromonitor Publications Limited, 87-88 Turnmill Street, London EC1M 5QU, England; *International Marketing Data and Statistics.*

Inter-American Development Bank, 1300 New York Avenue, NW, Washington, D.C. 20577 (202) 623-1753; *Economic and Social Progress in Latin America.*

VENEZUELA - LABOR FORCE

The Economist Intelligence Unit, 111 West 57th Street, New York, New York 10019 (800) 938-4685; *The New Latin America Market Atlas.*

Euromonitor Publications Limited, 87-88 Turnmill Street, London EC1M 5QU, England; *International Marketing Data and Statistics.*

Facts on File, 460 Park Avenue South, New York, New York 10016 (800) 443-8323; *The New Book of World Rankings.*

Food and Agricultural Organization of the United Nations (FAO) Via delle Terme di Caracalla, 00100 Rome, Italy (Telephone Number in U.S. (202) 653-2400); *The State of Food and Agriculture.*

Gale Research Incorporated, 835 Penobscot Building, Detroit, Michigan 48226 (800) 877-4253; *International Historical Statistics The Americas and Australasia.*

G.K. Hall and Company, 70 Lincoln Street, Boston, Massachusetts 02111 (617) 423-3990; *The World in Figures.*

Time Books, 201 East 50th Street, New York, New York 10022 (212) 751-2600; *The Economist Book of Vital World Statistics.*

The World Bank, 1818 H Street, NW, Washington, D.C. 20433 (202) 477-1234; *World Tables.*

VENEZUELA - LABOR PRODUCTIVITY

International Labour Office, I.L.O. Publications, CH-1211, Geneva 22, Switzerland; *Yearbook of Labour Statistics.*

VENEZUELA - LAND AREA

The Economist Intelligence Unit, 111 West 57th Street, New York, New York 10019 (800) 938-4685; *The New Latin America Market Atlas.*

VENEZUELA - LAND USE

Euromonitor Publications Limited, 87-88 Turnmill Street, London EC1M 5QU, England; *International Marketing Data and Statistics.*

G.K. Hall and Company, 70 Lincoln Street, Boston, Massachusetts 02111 (617) 423-3990; *The World in Figures.*

Inter-American Development Bank, 1300 New York Avenue, NW, Washington, D.C. 20577 (202) 623-1753; *Economic and Social Progress in Latin America.*

VENEZUELA - LIBRARIES

Facts on File, 460 Park Avenue South, New York, New York 10016 (800) 443-8323; *The New Book of World Rankings.*

United Nations Educational, Scientific and Cultural Organization (UNESCO), 7 Place de Fontenoy, F-75700 Paris, France (Telephone Number in U.S. (212) 963-5981); *Statistical Yearbook.*

VENEZUELA - LIFE EXPECTANCY RATE

The Economist Intelligence Unit, 111 West 57th Street, New York, New York 10019 (800) 938-4685; *The New Latin America Market Atlas.*

VENEZUELA - LIGNITE PRODUCTION - See VENEZUELA - MINING AND MINERAL PRODUCTS

VENEZUELA - LIVESTOCK AND POULTRY

Euromonitor Publications Limited, 87-88 Turnmill Street, London EC1M 5QU, England; *International Marketing Data and Statistics.*

Facts on File, 460 Park Avenue South, New York, New York 10016 (800) 443-8323; *The New Book of World Rankings*.

Food and Agricultural Organization of the United Nations (FAO) Via delle Terme di Caracalla, 00100 Rome, Italy (Telephone Number in U.S. (202) 653-2400); *Production Yearbook*, and *The State of Food and Agriculture*.

G.K. Hall and Company, 70 Lincoln Street, Boston, Massachusetts 02111 (617) 423-3990; *The World in Figures*.

Statistical Office of the United Nations, Publishing Service, New York, New York 10017 (800) 253-9646; *Statistical Yearbook*.

VENEZUELA - LIVING LEVELS

G.K. Hall and Company, 70 Lincoln Street, Boston, Massachusetts 02111 (617) 423-3990; *The World in Figures*.

Statistical Office of the United Nations, Publishing Service, New York, New York 10017 (800) 253-9646; *Statistical Yearbook for Latin America and the Caribbean*.

Time Books, 201 East 50th Street, New York, New York 10022 (212) 751-2600; *The Economist Book of Vital World Statistics*.

VENEZUELA - MAIL - NUMBER OF ITEMS SENT AND RECEIVED

Statistical Office of the United Nations, Publishing Service, New York, New York 10017 (800) 253-9646; *Statistical Yearbook*.

VENEZUELA - MAIN ECONOMIC INDICATORS - See VENEZUELA - ECONOMY

VENEZUELA - MANUFACTURING

The Economist Intelligence Unit, 111 West 57th Street, New York, New York 10019 (800) 938-4685; *The New Latin America Market Atlas*.

Euromonitor Publications Limited, 87-88 Turnmill Street, London EC1M 5QU, England; *Third World Economic Handbook*.

Facts on File, 460 Park Avenue South, New York, New York 10016 (800) 443-8323; *The New Book of World Rankings*.

G.K. Hall and Company, 70 Lincoln Street, Boston, Massachusetts 02111 (617) 423-3990; *The World in Figures*.

Inter-American Development Bank, 1300 New York Avenue, NW, Washington, D.C. 20577 (202) 623-1753; *Economic and Social Progress in Latin America*.

Organization of American States (OAS), General Secretariat, Washington, D.C. 20006 (202) 458-3533; *Statistical Bulletin of the OAS*.

Statistical Office of the United Nations, Publishing Service, New York, New York 10017 (800) 253-9646; *Statistical Yearbook*.

Time Books, 201 East 50th Street, New York, New York 10022 (212) 751-2600; *The Economist Book of Vital World Statistics*.

The World Bank, 1818 H Street, NW, Washington, D.C. 20433 (202) 477-1234; *World Tables*.

VENEZUELA - MANUFACTURING

Euromonitor Publications Limited, 87-88 Turnmill Street, London EC1M 5QU, England; *Third World Economic Handbook*.

Statistical Office of the United Nations, Publishing Service, New York, New York 10017 (800) 253-9646; *Statistical Yearbook*, and *Statistical Yearbook for Latin America and the Caribbean*.

VENEZUELA - MARRIAGE RATES

Facts on File, 460 Park Avenue South, New York, New York 10016 (800) 443-8323; *The New Book of World Rankings*.

Statistical Office of the United Nations, Publishing Service, New York, New York 10017 (800) 253-9646; *Demographic Yearbook*, and *Statistical Yearbook*.

VENEZUELA - MEAT PRODUCTION - See VENEZUELA - LIVESTOCK AND POULTRY

VENEZUELA - MEDICAL PERSONNEL

U.C.L.A. Latin American Center Publications, University of California, Los Angeles, California 90024 (310) 825-6634; *Statistical Abstract of Latin America*.

VENEZUELA - MERCHANT SHIPPING

G.K. Hall and Company, 70 Lincoln Street, Boston, Massachusetts 02111 (617) 423-3990; *The World in Figures*.

Lloyd's Register of Shipping, 17 Battery Place, New York, New York 10004 (212) 425-8050; *Register of Ships*.

Organization of Petroleum Exporting Countries, Obere Donaustrasse 93, 1020 Vienna 2, Austria; *OPEC Annual Statistical Bulletin*.

Statistical Office of the United Nations, Publishing Service, New York, New York 10017 (800) 253-9646; *Statistical Yearbook*.

Time Books, 201 East 50th Street, New York, New York 10022 (212) 751-2600; *The Economist Book of Vital World Statistics*.

U.S. Department of Transportation, Maritime Administration, 400 Seventh Street, SW, Washington, D.C. 20590 (202) 366-5807; *A Statistical Analysis of the World's Merchant Fleets*.

VENEZUELA - MILITARY

The Economist Intelligence Unit, 111 West 57th Street, New York, New York 10019 (800) 938-4685; *The New Latin America Market Atlas*.

G.K. Hall and Company, 70 Lincoln Street, Boston, Massachusetts 02111 (617) 423-3990; *The World in Figures*.

The International Institute for Strategic Studies, 23 Tavistock Street, London WC2E 7NQ, England; *The Military Balance*.

U.C.L.A. Latin American Center Publications, University of California, Los Angeles, California 90024 (310) 825-6634; *Statistical Abstract of Latin America*.

U.S. Arms Control and Disarmament Agency, 320 Twenty-first Street, NW, Washington, D.C. 20451 (202) 647-8677; *World Military Expenditures and Arms Transfers*.

VENEZUELA - MILK PRODUCTION - See VENEZUELA - DAIRY PRODUCTS

VENEZUELA - MINING AND MINERAL PRODUCTS

Commodity Research Bureau, Incorporated, 75 Wall Street, New York, New York 10005 (212) 504-7754; *Commodity Year Book.*

The Economist Intelligence Unit, 111 West 57th Street, New York, New York 10019 (800) 938-4685; *The New Latin America Market Atlas.*

Euromonitor Publications Limited, 87-88 Turnmill Street, London EC1M 5QU, England; *Third World Economic Handbook.*

Facts on File, 460 Park Avenue South, New York, New York 10016 (800) 443-8323; *The New Book of World Rankings.*

G.K. Hall and Company, 70 Lincoln Street, Boston, Massachusetts 02111 (617) 423-3990; *The World in Figures.*

Inter-American Development Bank, 1300 New York Avenue, NW, Washington, D.C. 20577 (202) 623-1753; *Economic and Social Progress in Latin America.*

International Monetary Fund, 700 Nineteenth Street, NW, Washington, D.C. 20431 (202) 623-7000; *International Financial Statistics.*

Organization of American States (OAS), General Secretariat, Washington, D.C. 20006 (202) 458-3533; *Statistical Bulletin of the OAS.*

Organization of Petroleum Exporting Countries, Obere Donaustrasse 93, 1020 Vienna 2, Austria; *OPEC Annual Statistical Bulletin.*

Penn Well Publishing Company, 1421 South Sheridan Road, P.O. Box 1260, Tulsa, Oklahoma 74101 (800) 752-9764; *International Energy Statistics Sourcebook.*

Statistical Office of the United Nations, Publishing Service, New York, New York 10017 (800) 253-9646; *Statistical Yearbook,* and *Statistical Yearbook for Latin America and the Caribbean.*

U.C.L.A. Latin American Center Publications, University of California, Los Angeles, California 90024 (310) 825-6634; *Statistical Abstract of Latin America.*

VENEZUELA - MONEY EXCHANGE RATES

Euromonitor Publications Limited, 87-88 Turnmill Street, London EC1M 5QU, England; *International Marketing Data and Statistics.*

Inter-American Development Bank, 1300 New York Avenue, NW, Washington, D.C. 20577 (202) 623-1753; *Economic and Social Progress in Latin America.*

Statistical Office of the United Nations, Publishing Service, New York, New York 10017 (800) 253-9646; *Statistical Yearbook.*

VENEZUELA - MONEY RATES - MARKET

Inter-American Development Bank, 1300 New York Avenue, NW, Washington, D.C. 20577 (202) 623-1753; *Economic and Social Progress in Latin America.*

VENEZUELA - MONEY RESERVES

Euromonitor Publications Limited, 87-88 Turnmill Street, London EC1M 5QU, England; *International Marketing Data and Statistics.*

Inter-American Development Bank, 1300 New York Avenue, NW, Washington, D.C. 20577 (202) 623-1753; *Economic and Social Progress in Latin America.*

VENEZUELA - MONEY SUPPLY

Euromonitor Publications Limited, 87-88 Turnmill Street, London EC1M 5QU, England; *International Marketing Data and Statistics.*

G.K. Hall and Company, 70 Lincoln Street, Boston, Massachusetts 02111 (617) 423-3990; *The World in Figures.*

Inter-American Development Bank, 1300 New York Avenue, NW, Washington, D.C. 20577 (202) 623-1753; *Economic and Social Progress in Latin America.*

Statistical Office of the United Nations, Publishing Service, New York, New York 10017 (800) 253-9646; *Statistical Yearbook.*

U.C.L.A. Latin American Center Publications, University of California, Los Angeles, California 90024 (310) 825-6634; *Statistical Abstract of Latin America.*

The World Bank, 1818 H Street, NW, Washington, D.C. 20433 (202) 477-1234; *World Tables.*

VENEZUELA - MOTION PICTURES

Statistical Office of the United Nations, Publishing Service, New York, New York 10017 (800) 253-9646; *Statistical Yearbook.*

United Nations Educational, Scientific and Cultural Organization (UNESCO), 7 Place de Fontenoy, F-75700 Paris, France (Telephone Number in U.S. (212) 963-5981); *Statistical Yearbook.*

VENEZUELA - MOTOR VEHICLE TAXES - See VENEZUELA - TAXATION

VENEZUELA - MOTOR VEHICLES IN USE

The Economist Intelligence Unit, 111 West 57th Street, New York, New York 10019 (800) 938-4685; *The New Latin America Market Atlas.*

G.K. Hall and Company, 70 Lincoln Street, Boston, Massachusetts 02111 (617) 423-3990; *The World in Figures.*

Statistical Office of the United Nations, Publishing Service, New York, New York 10017 (800) 253-9646; *Statistical Yearbook.*

Time Books, 201 East 50th Street, New York, New York 10022 (212) 751-2600; *The Economist Book of Vital World Statistics.*

VENEZUELA - MOTOR VEHICLES PRODUCTION AND ASSEMBLY

Statistical Office of the United Nations, Publishing Service, New York, New York 10017 (800) 253-9646; *Statistical Yearbook.*

VENEZUELA - MULES - See VENEZUELA - LIVESTOCK AND POULTRY

VENEZUELA - MUSEUMS

Facts on File, 460 Park Avenue South, New York, New York 10016 (800) 443-8323; *The New Book of World Rankings*.

United Nations Educational, Scientific and Cultural Organization (UNESCO), 7 Place de Fontenoy, F-75700 Paris, France (Telephone Number in U.S. (212) 963-5981); *Statistical Yearbook*.

VENEZUELA - NATALITY - See VENEZUELA - BIRTH RATE

VENEZUELA - NATIONAL ACCOUNTS

Gale Research Incorporated, 835 Penobscot Building, Detroit, Michigan 48226 (800) 877-4253; *International Historical Statistics The Americas and Australasia*.

Inter-American Development Bank, 1300 New York Avenue, NW, Washington, D.C. 20577 (202) 623-1753; *Economic and Social Progress in Latin America*.

Organization of American States (OAS), General Secretariat, Washington, D.C. 20006 (202) 458-3533; *Statistical Bulletin of the OAS*.

Statistical Office of the United Nations, Publishing Service, New York, New York 10017 (800) 253-9646; *National Accounts Statistics*, and *Statistical Yearbook*.

U.C.L.A. Latin American Center Publications, University of California, Los Angeles, California 90024 (310) 825-6634; *Statistical Abstract of Latin America*.

VENEZUELA - NATIONAL INCOME

Facts on File, 460 Park Avenue South, New York, New York 10016 (800) 443-8323; *The New Book of World Rankings*.

G.K. Hall and Company, 70 Lincoln Street, Boston, Massachusetts 02111 (617) 423-3990; *The World in Figures*.

Inter-American Development Bank, 1300 New York Avenue, NW, Washington, D.C. 20577 (202) 623-1753; *Economic and Social Progress in Latin America*.

Statistical Office of the United Nations, Publishing Service, New York, New York 10017 (800) 253-9646; *Statistical Yearbook*, and *Statistical Yearbook for Latin America and the Caribbean*.

VENEZUELA - NATIONAL PRODUCT

Facts on File, 460 Park Avenue South, New York, New York 10016 (800) 443-8323; *The New Book of World Rankings*.

Statistical Office of the United Nations, Publishing Service, New York, New York 10017 (800) 253-9646; *Statistical Yearbook*.

VENEZUELA - NATURAL GAS PRODUCTION - See VENEZUELA - MINING AND MINERAL PRODUCTS

VENEZUELA - NEWSPAPER PRODUCTION - See VENEZUELA - FORESTRY AND FOREST PRODUCTS

VENEZUELA - NEWSPRINT - See VENEZUELA - FORESTRY AND FOREST PRODUCTS

VENEZUELA - NITRIC ACID PRODUCTION - See VENEZUELA - MINING AND MINERAL PRODUCTS

VENEZUELA - NUTRITION

Statistical Office of the United Nations, Publishing Service, New York, New York 10017 (800) 253-9646; *Statistical Yearbook for Latin America and the Caribbean*.

VENEZUELA - OCCUPATIONS - See VENEZUELA - LABOR FORCE

VENEZUELA - ORANGES PRODUCTION - See VENEZUELA - CROPS

VENEZUELA - PAPER - See VENEZUELA - FORESTRY AND FOREST PRODUCTS

VENEZUELA - PATENTS

Statistical Office of the United Nations, Publishing Service, New York, New York 10017 (800) 253-9646; *Statistical Yearbook*.

World Intellectual Property Organization, 34 Chemin des Colombettes, CH-1211 Geneva 20. Switzerland; *Industrial Property Statistics*.

VENEZUELA - PEANUT PRODUCTION - See VENEZUELA - CROPS

VENEZUELA - PERIODICALS

United Nations Educational, Scientific and Cultural Organization (UNESCO), 7 Place de Fontenoy, F-75700 Paris, France (Telephone Number in U.S. (212) 963-5981); *Statistical Yearbook*.

VENEZUELA - PESTICIDE USE

Food and Agricultural Organization of the United Nations (FAO) Via delle Terme di Caracalla, 00100 Rome, Italy (Telephone Number in U.S. (202) 653-2400); *The State of Food and Agriculture*.

VENEZUELA - PETROLEUM INDUSTRY

Commodity Research Bureau, Incorporated, 75 Wall Street, New York, New York 10005 (212) 504-7754; *Commodity Year Book*.

The Economist Intelligence Unit, 111 West 57th Street, New York, New York 10019 (800) 938-4685; *The New Latin America Market Atlas*.

Facts on File, 460 Park Avenue South, New York, New York 10016 (800) 443-8323; *The New Book of World Rankings*.

Food and Agricultural Organization of the United Nations (FAO) Via delle Terme di Caracalla, 00100 Rome, Italy (Telephone Number in U.S. (202) 653-2400); *The State of Food and Agriculture*.

G.K. Hall and Company, 70 Lincoln Street, Boston, Massachusetts 02111 (617) 423-3990; *The World in Figures*.

Inter-American Development Bank, 1300 New York Avenue, NW, Washington, D.C. 20577 (202) 623-1753; *Economic and Social Progress in Latin America*.

Organization of American States (OAS), General Secretariat, Washington, D.C. 20006 (202) 458-3533; *Statistical Bulletin of the OAS*.

Organization of Petroleum Exporting Countries, Obere Donaustrasse 93, 1020 Vienna 2, Austria; *OPEC Annual Statistical Bulletin*.

Penn Well Publishing Company, 1421 South Sheridan Road, P.O. Box 1260, Tulsa, Oklahoma 74101 (800) 752-9764; *International Energy Statistics Sourcebook*.

Statistical Office of the United Nations, Publishing Service, New York, New York 10017 (800) 253-9646; *Statistical Yearbook*.

VENEZUELA - PHOSPHATE ROCK PRODUCTION - See VENEZUELA - MINING AND MINERAL PRODUCTS

VENEZUELA - PIG-IRON AND FERRO-ALLOY PRODUCTION - See VENEZUELA - MINING AND MINERAL PRODUCTS

VENEZUELA - PIGS - See VENEZUELA - LIVESTOCK AND POULTRY

VENEZUELA - PIPELINES FOR OIL AND PETROLEUM PRODUCTS

Organization of Petroleum Exporting Countries, Obere Donaustrasse 93, 1020 Vienna 2, Austria; *OPEC Annual Statistical Bulletin*.

VENEZUELA - PLASTIC AND RESIN PRODUCTION

Euromonitor Publications Limited, 87-88 Turnmill Street, London EC1M 5QU, England; *Third World Economic Handbook*.

Statistical Office of the United Nations, Publishing Service, New York, New York 10017 (800) 253-9646; *Statistical Yearbook*.

VENEZUELA - POLITICAL DATA

U.C.L.A. Latin American Center Publications, University of California, Los Angeles, California 90024 (310) 825-6634; *Statistical Abstract of Latin America*.

VENEZUELA - POPULATION

The Economist Intelligence Unit, 111 West 57th Street, New York, New York 10019 (800) 938-4685; *The New Latin America Market Atlas*, and *The World Market Atlas*.

Euromonitor Publications Limited, 87-88 Turnmill Street, London EC1M 5QU, England; *International Marketing Data and Statistics*, and *Third World Economic Handbook*.

Facts on File, 460 Park Avenue South, New York, New York 10016 (800) 443-8323; *The New Book of World Rankings*.

Gale Research Incorporated, 835 Penobscot Building, Detroit, Michigan 48226 (800) 877-4253; *International Historical Statistics The Americas and Australasia*.

G.K. Hall and Company, 70 Lincoln Street, Boston, Massachusetts 02111 (617) 423-3990; *The World in Figures*.

Inter-American Development Bank, 1300 New York Avenue, NW, Washington, D.C. 20577 (202) 623-1753; *Economic and Social Progress in Latin America*.

International Labour Office, I.L.O. Publications, CH-1211, Geneva 22, Switzerland; *Yearbook of Labour Statistics*.

Organization of American States (OAS), General Secretariat, Washington, D.C. 20006 (202) 458-3533; *Statistical Bulletin of the OAS*.

Statistical Office of the United Nations, Publishing Service, New York, New York 10017 (800) 253-9646; *Demographic Yearbook*, *Statistical Yearbook*, and *Statistical Yearbook for Latin America and the Caribbean*.

Time Books, 201 East 50th Street, New York, New York 10022 (212) 751-2600; *The Economist Book of Vital World Statistics*.

U.C.L.A. Latin American Center Publications, University of California, Los Angeles, California 90024 (310) 825-6634; *Statistical Abstract of Latin America*.

United Nations Educational, Scientific and Cultural Organization (UNESCO), 7 Place de Fontenoy, F-75700 Paris, France (Telephone Number in U.S. (212) 963-5981); *Statistical Yearbook*.

U.S. Arms Control and Disarmament Agency, 320 Twenty-first Street, NW, Washington, D.C. 20451 (202) 647-8677; *World Military Expenditures and Arms Transfers*.

World Health Organization, Office of Publications, Avenue Appia, CH-1211 Geneva 27, Switzerland (Telephone Number in U.S. (518) 436-9686); *World Health Statistics Annual*.

VENEZUELA - POST OFFICES

Facts on File, 460 Park Avenue South, New York, New York 10016 (800) 443-8323; *The New Book of World Rankings*.

VENEZUELA - POTATO PRODUCTION - See VENEZUELA - CROPS

VENEZUELA - POWER PRODUCTION INDUSTRY

Statistical Office of the United Nations, Publishing Service, New York, New York 10017 (800) 253-9646; *Electric Power in Asia and the Pacific*.

VENEZUELA - PRICES

Facts on File, 460 Park Avenue South, New York, New York 10016 (800) 443-8323; *The New Book of World Rankings*.

Food and Agricultural Organization of the United Nations (FAO) Via delle Terme di Caracalla, 00100 Rome, Italy (Telephone Number in U.S. (202) 653-2400); *The State of Food and Agriculture*.

Gale Research Incorporated, 835 Penobscot Building, Detroit, Michigan 48226 (800) 877-4253; *International Historical Statistics The Americas and Australasia*.

G.K. Hall and Company, 70 Lincoln Street, Boston, Massachusetts 02111 (617) 423-3990; *The World in Figures*.

International Labour Office, I.L.O. Publications, CH-1211, Geneva 22, Switzerland; *Yearbook of Labour Statistics*.

International Monetary Fund, 700 Nineteenth Street, NW, Washington, D.C. 20431 (202) 623-7000; *International Financial Statistics*.

Statistical Office of the United Nations, Publishing Service, New York, New York 10017 (800) 253-9646; *Economic Survey of Latin America and the Caribbean*, and *Statistical Yearbook for Latin America and the Caribbean*.

VENEZUELA - PRINTING AND WRITING PAPER - See VENEZUELA - FORESTRY AND FOREST PRODUCTS

VENEZUELA - PRODUCTION

Facts on File, 460 Park Avenue South, New York, New York 10016 (800) 443-8323; *The New Book of World Rankings*.

G.K. Hall and Company, 70 Lincoln Street, Boston, Massachusetts 02111 (617) 423-3990; *The World in Figures.*

VENEZUELA - PRODUCTIVITY

Euromonitor Publications Limited, 87-88 Turnmill Street, London EC1M 5QU, England; *International Marketing Data and Statistics.*

VENEZUELA - PROPERTY TAXES - See VENEZUELA - TAXATION

VENEZUELA - PUBLIC CONSUMPTION FUND

Inter-American Development Bank, 1300 New York Avenue, NW, Washington, D.C. 20577 (202) 623-1753; *Economic and Social Progress in Latin America.*

VENEZUELA - PUBLIC EXPENDITURE

Inter-American Development Bank, 1300 New York Avenue, NW, Washington, D.C. 20577 (202) 623-1753; *Economic and Social Progress in Latin America.*

Organization of American States (OAS), General Secretariat, Washington, D.C. 20006 (202) 458-3533; *Statistical Bulletin of the OAS.*

Statistical Office of the United Nations, Publishing Service, New York, New York 10017 (800) 253-9646; *Statistical Yearbook for Latin America and the Caribbean.*

VENEZUELA - PUBLIC FINANCES

Facts on File, 460 Park Avenue South, New York, New York 10016 (800) 443-8323; *The New Book of World Rankings.*

Inter-American Development Bank, 1300 New York Avenue, NW, Washington, D.C. 20577 (202) 623-1753; *Economic and Social Progress in Latin America.*

Organization of American States (OAS), General Secretariat, Washington, D.C. 20006 (202) 458-3533; *Statistical Bulletin of the OAS.*

VENEZUELA - PUBLIC REVENUES

Inter-American Development Bank, 1300 New York Avenue, NW, Washington, D.C. 20577 (202) 623-1753; *Economic and Social Progress in Latin America.*

Organization of American States (OAS), General Secretariat, Washington, D.C. 20006 (202) 458-3533; *Statistical Bulletin of the OAS.*

VENEZUELA - RADIO BROADCASTING - See VENEZUELA - BROADCASTING

VENEZUELA - RADIO RECEIVER PRODUCTION

Statistical Office of the United Nations, Publishing Service, New York, New York 10017 (800) 253-9646; *Statistical Yearbook.*

VENEZUELA - RAILWAYS

The Economist Intelligence Unit, 111 West 57th Street, New York, New York 10019 (800) 938-4685; *The New Latin America Market Atlas.*

G.K. Hall and Company, 70 Lincoln Street, Boston, Massachusetts 02111 (617) 423-3990; *The World in Figures.*

Jane's Information Group, Sentinel House, 163 Brighton Road, Coulsdon, Surrey CR5 2NH, England (Telephone Number in U.S. (703) 683-3700); *Jane's World Railways.*

Statistical Office of the United Nations, Publishing Service, New York, New York 10017 (800) 253-9646; *Statistical Yearbook.*

VENEZUELA - RANCHING

U.C.L.A. Latin American Center Publications, University of California, Los Angeles, California 90024 (310) 825-6634; *Statistical Abstract of Latin America.*

VENEZUELA - RELIGION

Facts on File, 460 Park Avenue South, New York, New York 10016 (800) 443-8323; *The New Book of World Rankings.*

U.C.L.A. Latin American Center Publications, University of California, Los Angeles, California 90024 (310) 825-6634; *Statistical Abstract of Latin America.*

VENEZUELA - RENT PRICES

International Labour Office, I.L.O. Publications, CH-1211, Geneva 22, Switzerland; *Yearbook of Labour Statistics.*

VENEZUELA - RESERVES EXCLUDING GOLD

The Economist Intelligence Unit, 111 West 57th Street, New York, New York 10019 (800) 938-4685; *The New Latin America Market Atlas.*

VENEZUELA - RETAIL TRADE

Euromonitor Publications Limited, 87-88 Turnmill Street, London EC1M 5QU, England; *Third World Economic Handbook.*

G.K. Hall and Company, 70 Lincoln Street, Boston, Massachusetts 02111 (617) 423-3990; *The World in Figures.*

Inter-American Development Bank, 1300 New York Avenue, NW, Washington, D.C. 20577 (202) 623-1753; *Economic and Social Progress in Latin America.*

VENEZUELA - RICE PRODUCTION - See VENEZUELA - CROPS

VENEZUELA - ROOT AND TUBER PRODUCTION - See VENEZUELA - CROPS

VENEZUELA - ROUNDWOOD PRODUCTION - See VENEZUELA - FORESTRY AND FOREST PRODUCTS

VENEZUELA - RUBBER PRODUCTION AND CONSUMPTION

Euromonitor Publications Limited, 87-88 Turnmill Street, London EC1M 5QU, England; *Third World Economic Handbook.*

Facts on File, 460 Park Avenue South, New York, New York 10016 (800) 443-8323; *The New Book of World Rankings.*

VENEZUELA - SALT PRODUCTION - See VENEZUELA - MINING AND MINERAL PRODUCTS

VENEZUELA - SAWNWOOD PRODUCTION - See VENEZUELA - FORESTRY AND FOREST PRODUCTS

VENEZUELA - SCIENCE AND TECHNOLOGY

Statistical Office of the United Nations, Publishing Service, New York, New York 10017 (800) 253-9646; *Statistical Yearbook*.

U.C.L.A. Latin American Center Publications, University of California, Los Angeles, California 90024 (310) 825-6634; *Statistical Abstract of Latin America*.

VENEZUELA - SCIENTISTS AND TECHNICIANS

Statistical Office of the United Nations, Publishing Service, New York, New York 10017 (800) 253-9646; *Statistical Yearbook*.

United Nations Educational, Scientific and Cultural Organization (UNESCO), 7 Place de Fontenoy, F-75700 Paris, France (Telephone Number in U.S. (212) 963-5981); *Statistical Yearbook*.

VENEZUELA - SENIOR CITIZENS

Facts on File, 460 Park Avenue South, New York, New York 10016 (800) 443-8323; *The New Book of World Rankings*.

VENEZUELA - SESAME SEED PRODUCTION - See VENEZUELA - CROPS

VENEZUELA - SHEEP - See VENEZUELA - LIVESTOCK AND POULTRY

VENEZUELA - SILVER PRODUCTION AND CONSUMPTION - See VENEZUELA - MINING AND MINERAL PRODUCTS

VENEZUELA - SISAL PRODUCTION - See VENEZUELA - CROPS

VENEZUELA - SOCIAL DATA

Facts on File, 460 Park Avenue South, New York, New York 10016 (800) 443-8323; *The New Book of World Rankings*.

G.K. Hall and Company, 70 Lincoln Street, Boston, Massachusetts 02111 (617) 423-3990; *The World in Figures*.

U.C.L.A. Latin American Center Publications, University of California, Los Angeles, California 90024 (310) 825-6634; *Statistical Abstract of Latin America*.

VENEZUELA - SOCIAL SECURITY

Inter-American Development Bank, 1300 New York Avenue, NW, Washington, D.C. 20577 (202) 623-1753; *Economic and Social Progress in Latin America*.

International Monetary Fund, 700 Nineteenth Street, NW, Washington, D.C. 20431 (202) 623-7000; *Government Finance Statistics Yearbook*.

VENEZUELA - SOCIOECONOMIC DATA

Inter-American Development Bank, 1300 New York Avenue, NW, Washington, D.C. 20577 (202) 623-1753; *Economic and Social Progress in Latin America*.

U.C.L.A. Latin American Center Publications, University of California, Los Angeles, California 90024 (310) 825-6634; *Statistical Abstract of Latin America*.

VENEZUELA - SOYBEAN PRODUCTION - See VENEZUELA - CROPS

VENEZUELA - STAMP TAXES AND DUTIES - See VENEZUELA - TAXATION

VENEZUELA - STATE BUDGET REVENUE AND EXPENDITURES

Euromonitor Publications Limited, 87-88 Turnmill Street, London EC1M 5QU, England; *International Marketing Data and Statistics*.

Inter-American Development Bank, 1300 New York Avenue, NW, Washington, D.C. 20577 (202) 623-1753; *Economic and Social Progress in Latin America*.

VENEZUELA - STEEL - See VENEZUELA - MINING AND MINERAL PRODUCTS

VENEZUELA - STOCKS - COMMODITY - MARKET PRICE - INDEX

Food and Agricultural Organization of the United Nations (FAO) Via delle Terme di Caracalla, 00100 Rome, Italy (Telephone Number in U.S. (202) 653-2400); *The State of Food and Agriculture*.

VENEZUELA - SUGAR PRODUCTION AND CONSUMPTION - See VENEZUELA - CROPS

VENEZUELA - SULPHURIC ACID PRODUCTION - See VENEZUELA - MINING AND MINERAL PRODUCTS

VENEZUELA - TAXATION

G.K. Hall and Company, 70 Lincoln Street, Boston, Massachusetts 02111 (617) 423-3990; *The World in Figures*.

Inter-American Development Bank, 1300 New York Avenue, NW, Washington, D.C. 20577 (202) 623-1753; *Economic and Social Progress in Latin America*.

International Monetary Fund, 700 Nineteenth Street, NW, Washington, D.C. 20431 (202) 623-7000; *Government Finance Statistics Yearbook*.

Statistical Office of the United Nations, Publishing Service, New York, New York 10017 (800) 253-9646; *Statistical Yearbook for Latin America and the Caribbean*.

The World Bank, 1818 H Street, NW, Washington, D.C. 20433 (202) 477-1234; *World Tables*.

VENEZUELA - TELEPHONES IN USE

American Telephone and Telegraph Company, 26 Parsippany Road, Whippany, New Jersey 07981 (800) 338-4038; *The World's Telephones*.

The Economist Intelligence Unit, 111 West 57th Street, New York, New York 10019 (800) 938-4685; *The New Latin America Market Atlas*.

Euromonitor Publications Limited, 87-88 Turnmill Street, London EC1M 5QU, England; *Third World Economic Handbook*.

G.K. Hall and Company, 70 Lincoln Street, Boston, Massachusetts 02111 (617) 423-3990; *The World in Figures*.

Statistical Office of the United Nations, Publishing Service, New York, New York 10017 (800) 253-9646; *Statistical Yearbook*.

VENEZUELA - TELEVISION BROADCASTING - See VENEZUELA - BROADCASTING

VENEZUELA - TELEVISION RECEIVER PRODUCTION

Statistical Office of the United Nations, Publishing Service, New York, New York 10017 (800) 253-9646; *Statistical Yearbook.*

VENEZUELA - TEXTILE INDUSTRY

American Forest and Paper Association, 1250 Connecticut Avenue, NW, Washington, D.C. 20036 (202) 463-2455; *Wood Pulp and Fiber Statistics.*

Euromonitor Publications Limited, 87-88 Turnmill Street, London EC1M 5QU, England; *Third World Economic Handbook.*

G.K. Hall and Company, 70 Lincoln Street, Boston, Massachusetts 02111 (617) 423-3990; *The World in Figures.*

Statistical Office of the United Nations, Publishing Service, New York, New York 10017 (800) 253-9646; *Statistical Yearbook.*

VENEZUELA - THEATRE

United Nations Educational, Scientific and Cultural Organization (UNESCO), 7 Place de Fontenoy, F-75700 Paris, France (Telephone Number in U.S. (212) 963-5981); *Statistical Yearbook.*

VENEZUELA - TIN - INDUSTRIAL PRODUCTION - See VENEZUELA - MINING AND MINERAL PRODUCTS

VENEZUELA - TIRE (MOTOR VEHICLE) PRODUCTION

Statistical Office of the United Nations, Publishing Service, New York, New York 10017 (800) 253-9646; *Statistical Yearbook.*

VENEZUELA - TOBACCO PRODUCTION

Euromonitor Publications Limited, 87-88 Turnmill Street, London EC1M 5QU, England; *Third World Economic Handbook.*

Facts on File, 460 Park Avenue South, New York, New York 10016 (800) 443-8323; *The New Book of World Rankings.*

Statistical Office of the United Nations, Publishing Service, New York, New York 10017 (800) 253-9646; *Statistical Yearbook.*

U.C.L.A. Latin American Center Publications, University of California, Los Angeles, California 90024 (310) 825-6634; *Statistical Abstract of Latin America.*

VENEZUELA - TOURISM

The Economist Intelligence Unit, 111 West 57th Street, New York, New York 10019 (800) 938-4685; *The New Latin America Market Atlas.*

Euromonitor Publications Limited, 87-88 Turnmill Street, London EC1M 5QU, England; *Third World Economic Handbook.*

Facts on File, 460 Park Avenue South, New York, New York 10016 (800) 443-8323; *The New Book of World Rankings.*

G.K. Hall and Company, 70 Lincoln Street, Boston, Massachusetts 02111 (617) 423-3990; *The World in Figures.*

Statistical Office of the United Nations, Publishing Service, New York, New York 10017 (800) 253-9646; *Statistical Yearbook,* and *Statistical Yearbook for Latin America and the Caribbean.*

Time Books, 201 East 50th Street, New York, New York 10022 (212) 751-2600; *The Economist Book of Vital World Statistics.*

U.C.L.A. Latin American Center Publications, University of California, Los Angeles, California 90024 (310) 825-6634; *Statistical Abstract of Latin America.*

World Tourism Organization, Calle Capitan Haya 42, E-28020 Madrid, Spain; *Yearbook of Tourism Statistics.*

VENEZUELA - TRACTORS IN USE

The Economist Intelligence Unit, 111 West 57th Street, New York, New York 10019 (800) 938-4685; *The New Latin America Market Atlas.*

Statistical Office of the United Nations, Publishing Service, New York, New York 10017 (800) 253-9646; *Statistical Yearbook.*

VENEZUELA - TRADE - See VENEZUELA - FOREIGN TRADE

VENEZUELA - TRADEMARKS AND SERVICE MARKS

Statistical Office of the United Nations, Publishing Service, New York, New York 10017 (800) 253-9646; *Statistical Yearbook.*

World Intellectual Property Organization, 34 Chemin des Colombettes, CH-1211 Geneva 20. Switzerland; *Industrial Property Statistics.*

VENEZUELA - TRANSPORTATION AND COMMUNICATIONS

The Economist Intelligence Unit, 111 West 57th Street, New York, New York 10019 (800) 938-4685; *The New Latin America Market Atlas.*

Euromonitor Publications Limited, 87-88 Turnmill Street, London EC1M 5QU, England; *Third World Economic Handbook.*

Facts on File, 460 Park Avenue South, New York, New York 10016 (800) 443-8323; *The New Book of World Rankings.*

Gale Research Incorporated, 835 Penobscot Building, Detroit, Michigan 48226 (800) 877-4253; *International Historical Statistics The Americas and Australasia.*

G.K. Hall and Company, 70 Lincoln Street, Boston, Massachusetts 02111 (617) 423-3990; *The World in Figures.*

Inter-American Development Bank, 1300 New York Avenue, NW, Washington, D.C. 20577 (202) 623-1753; *Economic and Social Progress in Latin America.*

Statistical Office of the United Nations, Publishing Service, New York, New York 10017 (800) 253-9646; *Statistical Yearbook for Latin America and the Caribbean.*

U.C.L.A. Latin American Center Publications, University of California, Los Angeles, California 90024 (310) 825-6634; *Statistical Abstract of Latin America.*

VENEZUELA - UNEMPLOYMENT

The Economist Intelligence Unit, 111 West 57th Street, New York, New York 10019 (800) 938-4685; *The New Latin America Market Atlas.*

Euromonitor Publications Limited, 87-88 Turnmill Street, London EC1M 5QU, England; *International Marketing Data and Statistics.*

International Labour Office, I.L.O. Publications, CH-1211, Geneva 22, Switzerland; *Yearbook of Labour Statistics*.

Statistical Office of the United Nations, Publishing Service, New York, New York 10017 (800) 253-9646; *Statistical Yearbook*.

U.C.L.A. Latin American Center Publications, University of California, Los Angeles, California 90024 (310) 825-6634; *Statistical Abstract of Latin America*.

VENEZUELA - UTILITIES

Statistical Office of the United Nations, Publishing Service, New York, New York 10017 (800) 253-9646; *Electric Power in Asia and the Pacific*.

U.C.L.A. Latin American Center Publications, University of California, Los Angeles, California 90024 (310) 825-6634; *Statistical Abstract of Latin America*.

VENEZUELA - VITAL STATISTICS

Euromonitor Publications Limited, 87-88 Turnmill Street, London EC1M 5QU, England; *International Marketing Data and Statistics*, and *Third World Economic Handbook*.

Gale Research Incorporated, 835 Penobscot Building, Detroit, Michigan 48226 (800) 877-4253; *International Historical Statistics The Americas and Australasia*.

G.K. Hall and Company, 70 Lincoln Street, Boston, Massachusetts 02111 (617) 423-3990; *The World in Figures*.

Statistical Office of the United Nations, Publishing Service, New York, New York 10017 (800) 253-9646; *Statistical Yearbook*.

VENEZUELA - WAGES

G.K. Hall and Company, 70 Lincoln Street, Boston, Massachusetts 02111 (617) 423-3990; *The World in Figures*.

International Labour Office, I.L.O. Publications, CH 1211, Geneva 22, Switzerland; *Yearbook of Labour Statistics*.

Statistical Office of the United Nations, Publishing Service, New York, New York 10017 (800) 253-9646; *Statistical Yearbook*.

U.C.L.A. Latin American Center Publications, University of California, Los Angeles, California 90024 (310) 825-6634; *Statistical Abstract of Latin America*.

VENEZUELA - WATERMELON PRODUCTION - See VENEZUELA - CROPS

VENEZUELA - WEATHER

Facts on File, 460 Park Avenue South, New York, New York 10016 (800) 443-8323; *The New Book of World Rankings*.

G.K. Hall and Company, 70 Lincoln Street, Boston, Massachusetts 02111 (617) 423-3990; *The World in Figures*.

VENEZUELA - WELFARE

Inter-American Development Bank, 1300 New York Avenue, NW, Washington, D.C. 20577 (202) 623-1753; *Economic and Social Progress in Latin America*.

International Monetary Fund, 700 Nineteenth Street, NW, Washington, D.C. 20431 (202) 623-7000; *Government Finance Statistics Yearbook*.

VENEZUELA - WHEAT PRODUCTION AND PRICES - See VENEZUELA - CROPS

VENEZUELA - WHOLESALE PRICES

Inter-American Development Bank, 1300 New York Avenue, NW, Washington, D.C. 20577 (202) 623-1753; *Economic and Social Progress in Latin America*.

Organization of American States (OAS), General Secretariat, Washington, D.C. 20006 (202) 458-3533; *Statistical Bulletin of the OAS*.

Statistical Office of the United Nations, Publishing Service, New York, New York 10017 (800) 253-9646; *Statistical Yearbook*.

VENEZUELA - WHOLESALE TRADE

Euromonitor Publications Limited, 87-88 Turnmill Street, London EC1M 5QU, England; *Third World Economic Handbook*.

Inter-American Development Bank, 1300 New York Avenue, NW, Washington, D.C. 20577 (202) 623-1753; *Economic and Social Progress in Latin America*.

VENEZUELA - WINE PRODUCTION

Facts on File, 460 Park Avenue South, New York, New York 10016 (800) 443-8323; *The New Book of World Rankings*.

VENEZUELA - WOOD AND WOOD PULP - See VENEZUELA - FORESTRY AND FOREST PRODUCTS

VENEZUELA - WOOL PRODUCTION

Facts on File, 460 Park Avenue South, New York, New York 10016 (800) 443-8323; *The New Book of World Rankings*.

VENEZUELA - YARN PRODUCTION

Statistical Office of the United Nations, Publishing Service, New York, New York 10017 (800) 253-9646; *Statistical Yearbook*.

VENEZUELA - ZOOS AND BOTANICAL GARDENS

United Nations Educational, Scientific and Cultural Organization (UNESCO), 7 Place de Fontenoy, F-75700 Paris, France (Telephone Number in U.S. (212) 963-5981); *Statistical Yearbook*.

VENTURE CAPITAL

Venture Economics Investor Services, 30 Pittsburgh Street, Boston, Massachusetts 02210 (617) 345-2824; *Venture Capital Journal*.

VERMICULITE

U.S. Department of the Interior, Bureau of Mines, 810 Seventh Street, NW, Washington, D.C. 20241 (202) 501-9649; *Annual Reports*, and *Mineral Commodities Summaries*.

VERMONT - See also STATE DATA (FOR INDIVIDUAL STATES)

Vermont - Primary Statistics Source

Office of Policy and Information, Department of Employment and Training, Montpelier, Vermont 05602 (802) 828-4202; *Demographic and Economic Profiles.*

Vermont - State Data Centers

Vermont Department of Libraries, 109 State Street, Montpelier, Vermont 05609, Ms. Sybil McShane (802) 828-3261.

Office of Policy Research and Coordination, Pavilion Office Building, 109 State Street, Montpelier, Vermont 05609, Ms. Cynthia Clancy (802) 828-3326.

Center for Rural Studies, University of Vermont, 207 Morrill Hall, Burlington, Vermont 05405-0106, Mr. Kevin Wiberg (802) 656-3021.

Vermont Travel Department, 134 State Street, Montpelier, Vermont 05602, Mr. Jed Guertin (802) 828-3217.

VESSELS - See SHIPS

VETERAN - PATRIOTIC ASSOCIATIONS

Gale Research Incorporated, 835 Penobscot Building, Detroit, Michigan 48226 (800) 877-4253; compiled from *Encyclopedia of Associations.*

VETERANS - EXPENDITURES

U.S. Department of Health and Human Services, Health Care Financing Administration, 200 Independence Avenue, SW, Washington, D.C. 20201 (202) 245-6113; *Health Care Financing Review.*

U.S. Department of Veterans Affairs, 810 Vermont Avenue, NW, Washington, D.C. 20420 (202) 233-2300; *Annual Report of the Secretary of Veterans Affairs,* and unpublished data.

VETERANS - EXPENDITURES - HOSPITAL - MEDICAL CARE

U.S. Department of Health and Human Services, Health Care Financing Administration, 200 Independence Avenue, SW, Washington, D.C. 20201 (202) 245-6113; *Health Care Financing Review.*

VETERANS - NUMBER

U.S. Department of Veterans Affairs, 810 Vermont Avenue, NW, Washington, D.C. 20420 (202) 233-2300; *Veteran Population,* and *Annual Report of the Secretary of Veterans Affairs.*

VETERANS - PENSIONS AND OTHER BENEFITS -
DISABILITY - SERVICE - CONNECTED COMPENSATION

U.S. Department of Veterans Affairs, 810 Vermont Avenue, NW, Washington, D.C. 20420 (202) 233-2300; *Annual Report of the Secretary of Veterans Affairs,* and unpublished data.

VETERANS - PENSIONS AND OTHER BENEFITS -
DISBURSEMENTS

Executive Office of the President, Office of Management and Budget, Executive Office Building, Washington, D.C. 20503 (202) 395-3080; *Budget of the United States Government.*

U.S. Department of Health and Human Services, Social Security Administration, 6401 Security Boulevard, Baltimore, Maryland 21235 (410) 965-1234; *Social Security Bulletin, Annual Statistical Supplement to the Social Security Bulletin* and unpublished data.

U.S. Department of Veterans Affairs, 810 Vermont Avenue, NW, Washington, D.C. 20420 (202) 233-2300; *Annual Report of the Secretary of Veterans Affairs,* and unpublished data.

VETERANS - PENSIONS AND OTHER BENEFITS - EDUCATION AND TRAINING

U.S. Department of Veterans Affairs, 810 Vermont Avenue, NW, Washington, D.C. 20420 (202) 233-2300; *Annual Report of the Secretary of Veterans Affairs.*

VETERANS - PENSIONS AND OTHER BENEFITS - FEDERAL AID TO STATE AND LOCAL GOVERNMENTS

Executive Office of the President, Office of Management and Budget, Executive Office Building, Washington, D.C. 20503 (202) 395-3080; *Historical Tables, Budget of the United States Government,* and *Budget of the U.S. Government.*

VETERANS - PENSIONS AND OTHER BENEFITS -
HEALTH EXPENDITURES

Executive Office of the President, Office of Management and Budget, Executive Office Building, Washington, D.C. 20503 (202) 395-3080; *The Budget of the United States Government.*

U.S. Department of Health and Human Services, Health Care Financing Administration, 200 Independence Avenue, SW, Washington, D.C. 20201 (202) 245-6113; *Health Care Financing Review.*

U.S. Library of Congress, Congressional Research Service, 10 First Street, SE, Washington, D.C. 20540 (202) 707-5000; *Cash and Non-Cash Benefits for Persons with Limited Income: Eligibility Rules, Recipient and Expenditure Data.*

VETERANS - PENSIONS AND OTHER BENEFITS -
HOSPITAL OR DOMICILIARY CARE

U.S. Department of Veterans Affairs, 810 Vermont Avenue, NW, Washington, D.C. 20420 (202) 233-2300; *Annual Report of the Secretary of Veterans Affairs, Directory of VA Facilities,* and unpublished data.

VETERANS - PENSIONS AND OTHER BENEFITS -
LIFE INSURANCE - FUNDS

Executive Office of the President, Office of Management and Budget, Executive Office Building, Washington, D.C. 20503 (202) 395-3080; *Budget of the United States Government.*

VETERANS - PENSIONS AND OTHER BENEFITS -
LOANS GUARANTEED AND INSURED

U.S. Department of Veterans Affairs, 810 Vermont Avenue, NW, Washington, D.C. 20420 (202) 233-2300; *Annual Report of the Secretary of Veterans Affairs.*

VETERANS - PENSIONS AND OTHER BENEFITS -
VETERANS OR DEPENDENTS RECEIVING

U.S. Department of Health and Human Services, Social Security Administration, 6401 Security Boulevard, Baltimore, Maryland 21235 (410) 965-1234; *Annual Statistical Supplement to the Social Security*

Bulletin, Social Security Bulletin, and unpublished data.

U.S. Department of Veterans Affairs, 810 Vermont Avenue, NW, Washington, D.C. 20420 (202) 233-2300; *Annual Report of the Secretary of Veterans Affairs,* and unpublished data.

VETERANS AFFAIRS - DEPARTMENT OF - BUDGET OUTLAYS

Executive Office of the President, Office of Management and Budget, Executive Office Building, Washington, D.C. 20503 (202) 395-3080; *Budget of the United States Government.*

VETERANS AFFAIRS - DEPARTMENT OF - HOME LOANS

Board of Governors of the Federal Reserve System, Twentieth Street and Constitution Avenue, NW, Washington, D.C. 20551 (202) 452-3000; *Federal Reserve Bulletin.*

Mortgage Bankers Association of America, 1125 Fifteenth Street, NW, Washington, D.C. 20005 (202) 861-6500; *National Delinquency Survey.*

U.S. Department of Veterans Affairs, 810 Vermont Avenue, NW, Washington, D.C. 20420 (202) 233-2300; *Annual Report of the Secretary of Veterans Affairs.*

VETERANS AFFAIRS - DEPARTMENT OF - LAND AND BUILDINGS

General Services Administration, General Services Building, Eighteenth and F Streets, NW, Washington, D.C. 20405 (202) 708-5082; *Inventory Report of Real Property Owned by the United States Throughout the World.*

VETERANS AFFAIRS - DEPARTMENT OF - MEDICAL CENTERS

U.S. Department of Veterans Affairs, 810 Vermont Avenue, NW, Washington, D.C. 20420 (202) 233-2300; *Annual Report of the Secretary of Veterans Affairs, Directory of VA Facilities,* and unpublished data.

VETOED BILLS, CONGRESSIONAL

U. S. Congress, The Capitol, Washington, D.C. 20515 (202) 224-3121; *Calendars of the United States House of Representatives and History of Legislation.*

VIDEOCASSETTE RECORDERS - HOUSEHOLDS WITH

Euromonitor Publications Limited, 87-88 Turnmill Street, London EC1M 5QU, England; *European Marketing Data and Statistics.*

Television Bureau of Advertising, Incorporated, 850 Third Avenue, New York, New York 10022 (212) 486-1111; *Trends in Television.*

Vietnam (Socialist Republic Of) - National Statistical Office

General Statistical Office, 2 Hoang Van Thu Street, Hanoi, Socialist Republic of Vietnam.

Vietnam (Socialist Republic Of) - Primary Statistics Source

General Statistical Office, 2 Hoang Van Thu Street, Hanoi, Socialist Republic of Vietnam; *Nien-Giam Thong-Ke* (Statistical Yearbook).

VIETNAM (SOCIALIST REPUBLIC OF) - AGRICULTURE

Euromonitor Publications Limited, 87-88 Turnmill Street, London EC1M 5QU, England; *International Marketing Data and Statistics.*

Facts on File, 460 Park Avenue South, New York, New York 10016 (800) 443-8323; *The New Book of World Rankings.*

Food and Agricultural Organization of the United Nations (FAO) Via delle Terme di Caracalla, 00100 Rome, Italy (Telephone Number in U.S. (202) 653-2400); *The State of Food and Agriculture,* and *Trade Yearbook.*

G.K. Hall and Company, 70 Lincoln Street, Boston, Massachusetts 02111 (617) 423-3990; *The World in Figures.*

Statistical Office of the United Nations, Publishing Service, New York, New York 10017 (800) 253-9646; *Statistical Yearbook,* and *Statistical Yearbook for Asia and the Pacific.*

Time Books, 201 East 50th Street, New York, New York 10022 (212) 751-2600; *The Economist Book of Vital World Statistics.*

VIETNAM (SOCIALIST REPUBLIC OF) - AIRLINE SERVICE

The Economist Intelligence Unit (Asia) Limited, 10th Floor, Luk Kwok Centre, 72 Gloucester Road, Wanchai, Hong Kong (Phone Number in U.S. (800) 938-4685); *Asian Market Atlas.*

Facts on File, 460 Park Avenue South, New York, New York 10016 (800) 443-8323; *The New Book of World Rankings.*

G.K. Hall and Company, 70 Lincoln Street, Boston, Massachusetts 02111 (617) 423-3990; *The World in Figures.*

Time Books, 201 East 50th Street, New York, New York 10022 (212) 751-2600; *The Economist Book of Vital World Statistics.*

VIETNAM (SOCIALIST REPUBLIC OF) - ALUMINUM PRODUCTION AND CONSUMPTION - See VIETNAM (SOCIALIST REPUBLIC OF) - MINING AND MINERAL PRODUCTS

VIETNAM (SOCIALIST REPUBLIC OF) - ANIMAL HEALTH

Food and Agricultural Organization of the United Nations (FAO), Via delle Terme di Caracalla, 00100 Rome, Italy (Telephone Number in U.S. (202) 653-2400); *Animal Health Yearbook.*

VIETNAM (SOCIALIST REPUBLIC OF) - AREA AND DENSITY OF POPULATION

Euromonitor Publications Limited, 87-88 Turnmill Street, London EC1M 5QU, England; *International Marketing Data and Statistics.*

Facts on File, 460 Park Avenue South, New York, New York 10016 (800) 443-8323; *The New Book of World Rankings.*

Food and Agricultural Organization of the United Nations (FAO) Via delle Terme di Caracalla, 00100 Rome, Italy (Telephone Number in U.S. (202) 653-2400); *The State of Food and Agriculture.*

G.K. Hall and Company, 70 Lincoln Street, Boston, Massachusetts 02111 (617) 423-3990; *The World in Figures.*

Statistical Office of the United Nations, Publishing Service, New York, New York 10017 (800) 253-9646; *Statistical Yearbook.*

Time Books, 201 East 50th Street, New York, New York 10022 (212) 751-2600; *The Economist Book of Vital World Statistics.*

United Nations Educational, Scientific and Cultural Organization (UNESCO), 7 Place de Fontenoy, F-75700 Paris, France (Telephone Number in U.S. (212) 963-5981); *Statistical Yearbook.*

VIETNAM (SOCIALIST REPUBLIC OF) - ARMS EXPORTS AND IMPORTS

U.S. Arms Control and Disarmament Agency, 320 Twenty-first Street, NW, Washington, D.C. 20451 (202) 647-8677; *World Military Expenditures and Arms Transfers.*

VIETNAM (SOCIALIST REPUBLIC OF) - BALANCE OF PAYMENTS

The Economist Intelligence Unit, 111 West 57th Street, New York, New York 10019 (800) 938-4685; *The World Market Atlas.*

G.K. Hall and Company, 70 Lincoln Street, Boston, Massachusetts 02111 (617) 423-3990; *The World in Figures.*

International Monetary Fund, 700 Nineteenth Street, NW, Washington, D.C. 20431 (202) 623-7000; *Balance of Payments Yearbook.*

Time Books, 201 East 50th Street, New York, New York 10022 (212) 751-2600; *The Economist Book of Vital World Statistics.*

VIETNAM (SOCIALIST REPUBLIC OF) - BANKING

Facts on File, 460 Park Avenue South, New York, New York 10016 (800) 443-8323; *The New Book of World Rankings.*

G.K. Hall and Company, 70 Lincoln Street, Boston, Massachusetts 02111 (617) 423-3990; *The World in Figures.*

VIETNAM (SOCIALIST REPUBLIC OF) - BARLEY PRODUCTION - See VIETNAM (SOCIALIST REPUBLIC OF) - CROPS

VIETNAM (SOCIALIST REPUBLIC OF) - BEER PRODUCTION

Facts on File, 460 Park Avenue South, New York, New York 10016 (800) 443-8323; *The New Book of World Rankings.*

Statistical Office of the United Nations, Publishing Service, New York, New York 10017 (800) 253-9646; *Statistical Yearbook.*

VIETNAM (SOCIALIST REPUBLIC OF) - BIRTH RATES

The Economist Intelligence Unit (Asia) Limited, 10th Floor, Luk Kwok Centre, 72 Gloucester Road, Wanchai, Hong Kong (Phone Number in U.S. (800) 938-4685); *Asian Market Atlas.*

Facts on File, 460 Park Avenue South, New York, New York 10016 (800) 443-8323; *The New Book of World Rankings.*

Statistical Office of the United Nations, Publishing Service, New York, New York 10017 (800) 253-9646; *Demographic Yearbook,* and *Statistical Yearbook.*

Time Books, 201 East 50th Street, New York, New York 10022 (212) 751-2600; *The Economist Book of Vital World Statistics.*

VIETNAM (SOCIALIST REPUBLIC OF) - BONDS

G.K. Hall and Company, 70 Lincoln Street, Boston, Massachusetts 02111 (617) 423-3990; *The World in Figures.*

VIETNAM (SOCIALIST REPUBLIC OF) - BOOK PRODUCTION

G.K. Hall and Company, 70 Lincoln Street, Boston, Massachusetts 02111 (617) 423-3990; *The World in Figures.*

United Nations Educational, Scientific and Cultural Organization (UNESCO), 7 Place de Fontenoy, F-75700 Paris, France (Telephone Number in U.S. (212) 963-5981); *Statistical Yearbook.*

VIETNAM (SOCIALIST REPUBLIC OF) - BROADCASTING

Billboard Limited, P.O. Box 9027, 1006 AA Amsterdam, The Netherlands (Telephone Number in U.S. (212) 764-7300); *World Radio TV Handbook.*

The Economist Intelligence Unit (Asia) Limited, 10th Floor, Luk Kwok Centre, 72 Gloucester Road, Wanchai, Hong Kong (Phone Number in U.S. (800) 938-4685); *Asian Market Atlas.*

Facts on File, 460 Park Avenue South, New York, New York 10016 (800) 443-8323; *The New Book of World Rankings.*

G.K. Hall and Company, 70 Lincoln Street, Boston, Massachusetts 02111 (617) 423-3990; *The World in Figures.*

Time Books, 201 East 50th Street, New York, New York 10022 (212) 751-2600; *The Economist Book of Vital World Statistics.*

VIETNAM (SOCIALIST REPUBLIC OF) - BUSINESS

G.K. Hall and Company, 70 Lincoln Street, Boston, Massachusetts 02111 (617) 423-3990; *The World in Figures.*

VIETNAM (SOCIALIST REPUBLIC OF) - CABBAGE PRODUCTION - See VIETNAM (SOCIALIST REPUBLIC OF) - CROPS

VIETNAM (SOCIALIST REPUBLIC OF) - CALORIE SUPPLY

Food and Agricultural Organization of the United Nations (FAO) Via delle Terme di Caracalla, 00100 Rome, Italy (Telephone Number in U.S. (202) 653-2400); *The State of Food and Agriculture.*

VIETNAM (SOCIALIST REPUBLIC OF) - CASTOR BEAN PRODUCTION - See VIETNAM (SOCIALIST REPUBLIC OF) - CROPS

VIETNAM (SOCIALIST REPUBLIC OF) - CATTLE - See VIETNAM - LIVESTOCK AND POULTRY

VIETNAM (SOCIALIST REPUBLIC OF) - CAULIFLOWER PRODUCTION - See VIETNAM (SOCIALIST REPUBLIC OF) - CROPS

VIETNAM (SOCIALIST REPUBLIC OF) - CAUSTIC SODA PRODUCTION

Statistical Office of the United Nations, Publishing Service, New York, New York 10017 (800) 253-9646; *Statistical Yearbook.*

VIETNAM (SOCIALIST REPUBLIC OF) - CEMENT PRODUCTION - See VIETNAM (SOCIALIST REPUBLIC OF) - MINING AND MINERAL PRODUCTS

VIETNAM (SOCIALIST REPUBLIC OF) - CHEMICAL (ORGANIC) PRODUCTION - See VIETNAM (SOCIALIST REPUBLIC OF) - MINING AND MINERAL PRODUCTS

VIETNAM (SOCIALIST REPUBLIC OF) - CHICKENS - See VIETNAM (SOCIALIST REPUBLIC OF) - LIVESTOCK AND POULTRY

VIETNAM (SOCIALIST REPUBLIC OF) - CIGAR AND CIGARETTE PRODUCTION - See VIETNAM (SOCIALIST REPUBLIC OF) - TOBACCO PRODUCTION

VIETNAM (SOCIALIST REPUBLIC OF) - CLASS STRUCTURE

G.K. Hall and Company, 70 Lincoln Street, Boston, Massachusetts 02111 (617) 423-3990; *The World in Figures*.

VIETNAM (SOCIALIST REPUBLIC OF) - CLIMATE

Facts on File, 460 Park Avenue South, New York, New York 10016 (800) 443-8323; *The New Book of World Rankings*.

G.K. Hall and Company, 70 Lincoln Street, Boston, Massachusetts 02111 (617) 423-3990; *The World in Figures*.

VIETNAM (SOCIALIST REPUBLIC OF) - COAL PRODUCTION - See VIETNAM (SOCIALIST REPUBLIC OF) - MINING AND MINERAL PRODUCTS

VIETNAM (SOCIALIST REPUBLIC OF) - COFFEE PRODUCTION AND CONSUMPTION - See VIETNAM (SOCIALIST REPUBLIC OF) - CROPS

VIETNAM (SOCIALIST REPUBLIC OF) - COMMUNICATIONS

G.K. Hall and Company, 70 Lincoln Street, Boston, Massachusetts 02111 (617) 423 3990; *The World in Figures*.

Statistical Office of the United Nations, Publishing Service, New York, New York 10017 (800) 253-9646; *Statistical Yearbook for Asia and the Pacific*.

VIETNAM (SOCIALIST REPUBLIC OF) - CONSTRUCTION INDUSTRY

Facts on File, 460 Park Avenue South, New York, New York 10016 (800) 443-8323; *The New Book of World Rankings*.

Statistical Office of the United Nations, Publishing Service, New York, New York 10017 (800) 253-9646; *Construction Statistics Yearbook*.

VIETNAM (SOCIALIST REPUBLIC OF) - CONSUMER PRICE INDEX

G.K. Hall and Company, 70 Lincoln Street, Boston, Massachusetts 02111 (617) 423-3990; *The World in Figures*.

Statistical Office of the United Nations, Publishing Service, New York, New York 10017 (800) 253-9646; *Statistical Yearbook*.

VIETNAM (SOCIALIST REPUBLIC OF) - CONSUMER PRICES

Time Books, 201 East 50th Street, New York, New York 10022 (212) 751-2600; *The Economist Book of Vital World Statistics*.

VIETNAM (SOCIALIST REPUBLIC OF) - CONSUMPTION

G.K. Hall and Company, 70 Lincoln Street, Boston, Massachusetts 02111 (617) 423-3990; *The World in Figures*.

International Rubber Study Group, York House, Eighth Floor, Empire Way, Wembley, London HA9 0PA, England; *Rubber Statistical Bulletin*.

VIETNAM (SOCIALIST REPUBLIC OF) - COPPER PRODUCTION AND CONSUMPTION - See VIETNAM (SOCIALIST REPUBLIC OF) MINING AND MINERAL PRODUCTS

VIETNAM (SOCIALIST REPUBLIC OF) - CORN PRODUCTION - See VIETNAM (SOCIALIST REPUBLIC OF) - CROPS

VIETNAM (SOCIALIST REPUBLIC OF) - CORPORATE TAXES - See VIETNAM (SOCIALIST REPUBLIC OF) - TAXATION

VIETNAM (SOCIALIST REPUBLIC OF) - COTTON - See VIETNAM (SOCIALIST REPUBLIC OF) - CROPS

VIETNAM (SOCIALIST REPUBLIC OF) - CROPS

Commodity Research Bureau, Incorporated, 75 Wall Street, New York, New York 10005 (212) 504-7754; *Commodity Year Book*.

Facts on File, 460 Park Avenue South, New York, New York 10016 (800) 443-8323; *The New Book of World Rankings*.

Food and Agricultural Organization of the United Nations (FAO) Via delle Terme di Caracalla, 00100 Rome, Italy (Telephone Number in U.S. (202) 653-2400); *Production Yearbook*, and *The State of Food and Agriculture*.

Statistical Office of the United Nations, Publishing Service, New York, New York 10017 (800) 253-9646; *Statistical Yearbook*.

VIETNAM (SOCIALIST REPUBLIC OF) - CUSTOMS DUTIES

G.K. Hall and Company, 70 Lincoln Street, Boston, Massachusetts 02111 (617) 423-3990; *The World in Figures*.

VIETNAM (SOCIALIST REPUBLIC OF) - DAIRY PRODUCTS

Facts on File, 460 Park Avenue South, New York, New York 10016 (800) 443-8323; *The New Book of World Rankings*.

Food and Agricultural Organization of the United Nations (FAO), Via delle Terme di Caracalla, 00100 Rome, Italy (Telephone Number in U.S. (202) 653-2400); *Production Yearbook*, and *The State of Food and Agriculture*.

Statistical Office of the United Nations, Publishing Service, New York, New York 10017 (800) 253-9646; *Statistical Yearbook*.

VIETNAM (SOCIALIST REPUBLIC OF) - DEATH RATES

The Economist Intelligence Unit (Asia) Limited, 10th Floor, Luk Kwok Centre, 72 Gloucester Road, Wanchai, Hong Kong (Phone Number in U.S. (800) 938-4685); *Asian Market Atlas*.

G.K. Hall and Company, 70 Lincoln Street, Boston, Massachusetts 02111 (617) 423-3990; *The World in Figures*.

Statistical Office of the United Nations, Publishing Service, New York, New York 10017 (800) 253-9646; *Statistical Yearbook*.

Time Books, 201 East 50th Street, New York, New York 10022 (212) 751-2600; *The Economist Book of Vital World Statistics*.

World Health Organization, Office of Publications, Avenue Appia, CH-1211 Geneva 27, Switzerland (Telephone Number in U.S. (518) 436-9686); *World Health Statistics Annual*.

VIETNAM (SOCIALIST REPUBLIC OF) - DEFENSE EXPENDITURES

G.K. Hall and Company, 70 Lincoln Street, Boston, Massachusetts 02111 (617) 423-3990; *The World in Figures*.

U.S. Arms Control and Disarmament Agency, 320 Twenty-first Street, NW, Washington, D.C. 20451 (202) 647-8677; *World Military*

Expenditures and Arms Transfers.

VIETNAM (SOCIALIST REPUBLIC OF) - DEMOGRAPHY

The Economist Intelligence Unit, 111 West 57th Street, New York, New York 10019 (800) 938-4685; *The World Market Atlas.*

The Economist Intelligence Unit (Asia) Limited, 10th Floor, Luk Kwok Centre, 72 Gloucester Road, Wanchai, Hong Kong (Phone Number in U.S. (800) 938-4685); *Asian Market Atlas.*

Facts on File, 460 Park Avenue South, New York, New York 10016 (800) 443-8323; *The New Book of World Rankings.*

G.K. Hall and Company, 70 Lincoln Street, Boston, Massachusetts 02111 (617) 423-3990; *The World in Figures.*

VIETNAM (SOCIALIST REPUBLIC OF) - DEVELOPMENT ASSISTANCE

G.K. Hall and Company, 70 Lincoln Street, Boston, Massachusetts 02111 (617) 423-3990; *The World in Figures.*

VIETNAM (SOCIALIST REPUBLIC OF) - DIAMOND PRODUCTION - See VIETNAM (SOCIALIST REPUBLIC OF) - MINING AND MINERAL PRODUCTS

VIETNAM (SOCIALIST REPUBLIC OF) - DISEASES

G.K. Hall and Company, 70 Lincoln Street, Boston, Massachusetts 02111 (617) 423-3990; *The World in Figures.*

World Health Organization, Office of Publications, Avenue Appia, CH-1211 Geneva 27, Switzerland (Telephone Number in U.S. (518) 436-9686); *World Health Statistics Annual.*

VIETNAM (SOCIALIST REPUBLIC OF) - DIVORCE RATES

Facts on File, 460 Park Avenue South, New York, New York 10016 (800) 443-8323; *The New Book of World Rankings.*

Statistical Office of the United Nations, Publishing Service, New York, New York 10017 (800) 253-9646; *Demographic Yearbook.*

VIETNAM (SOCIALIST REPUBLIC OF) - DOMESTIC PRODUCT

G.K. Hall and Company, 70 Lincoln Street, Boston, Massachusetts 02111 (617) 423-3990; *The World in Figures.*

VIETNAM (SOCIALIST REPUBLIC OF) - DUCKS - See VIETNAM (SOCIALIST REPUBLIC OF) - LIVESTOCK AND POULTRY

VIETNAM (SOCIALIST REPUBLIC OF) - ECONOMY

Euromonitor Publications Limited, 87-88 Turnmill Street, London EC1M 5QU, England; *International Marketing Data and Statistics.*

Facts on File, 460 Park Avenue South, New York, New York 10016 (800) 443-8323; *The New Book of World Rankings.*

G.K. Hall and Company, 70 Lincoln Street, Boston, Massachusetts 02111 (617) 423-3990; *The World in Figures.*

VIETNAM (SOCIALIST REPUBLIC OF) - EDUCATION

The Economist Intelligence Unit, 111 West 57th Street, New York, New York 10019 (800) 938-4685; *The World Market Atlas.*

The Economist Intelligence Unit (Asia) Limited, 10th Floor, Luk Kwok Centre, 72 Gloucester Road, Wanchai, Hong Kong (Phone

Number in U.S. (800) 938-4685); *Asian Market Atlas.*

Facts on File, 460 Park Avenue South, New York, New York 10016 (800) 443-8323; *The New Book of World Rankings.*

G.K. Hall and Company, 70 Lincoln Street, Boston, Massachusetts 02111 (617) 423-3990; *The World in Figures.*

Time Books, 201 East 50th Street, New York, New York 10022 (212) 751-2600; *The Economist Book of Vital World Statistics.*

VIETNAM (SOCIALIST REPUBLIC OF) - EGG PRODUCTION AND CONSUMPTION - See VIETNAM (SOCIALIST REPUBLIC OF) - DAIRY PRODUCTS

VIETNAM (SOCIALIST REPUBLIC OF) - ELECTRICITY

Facts on File, 460 Park Avenue South, New York, New York 10016 (800) 443-8323; *The New Book of World Rankings.*

Penn Well Publishing Company, 1421 South Sheridan Road, P.O. Box 1260, Tulsa, Oklahoma 74101 (800) 752-9764; *International Energy Statistics Sourcebook.*

Statistical Office of the United Nations, Publishing Service, New York, New York 10017 (800) 253-9646; *Electric Power in Asia and the Pacific,* and *Statistical Yearbook.*

Time Books, 201 East 50th Street, New York, New York 10022 (212) 751-2600; *The Economist Book of Vital World Statistics.*

VIETNAM (SOCIALIST REPUBLIC OF) - EMPLOYMENT

Euromonitor Publications Limited, 87-88 Turnmill Street, London EC1M 5QU, England; *International Marketing Data and Statistics.*

Facts on File, 460 Park Avenue South, New York, New York 10016 (800) 443-8323; *The New Book of World Rankings.*

VIETNAM (SOCIALIST REPUBLIC OF) - ENERGY

Facts on File, 460 Park Avenue South, New York, New York 10016 (800) 443-8323; *The New Book of World Rankings.*

Food and Agricultural Organization of the United Nations (FAO) Via delle Terme di Caracalla, 00100 Rome, Italy (Telephone Number in U.S. (202) 653-2400); *The State of Food and Agriculture.*

G.K. Hall and Company, 70 Lincoln Street, Boston, Massachusetts 02111 (617) 423-3990; *The World in Figures.*

Penn Well Publishing Company, 1421 South Sheridan Road, P.O. Box 1260, Tulsa, Oklahoma 74101 (800) 752-9764; *International Energy Statistics Sourcebook.*

Statistical Office of the United Nations, Publishing Service, New York, New York 10017 (800) 253-9646; *Statistical Yearbook, Statistical Yearbook for Asia and the Pacific,* and *World Energy Supplies.*

Time Books, 201 East 50th Street, New York, New York 10022 (212) 751-2600; *The Economist Book of Vital World Statistics.*

VIETNAM (SOCIALIST REPUBLIC OF) - EXCHANGE RATES

The Economist Intelligence Unit (Asia) Limited, 10th Floor, Luk Kwok Centre, 72 Gloucester Road, Wanchai, Hong Kong (Phone Number in U.S. (800) 938-4685); *Asian Market Atlas.*

Euromonitor Publications Limited, 87-88 Turnmill Street, London EC1M 5QU, England; *International Marketing Data and Statistics.*

VIETNAM (SOCIALIST REPUBLIC OF) - EXPORTS

The Economist Intelligence Unit, 111 West 57th Street, New York, New York 10019 (800) 938-4685; *The World Market Atlas.*

The Economist Intelligence Unit (Asia) Limited, 10th Floor, Luk Kwok Centre, 72 Gloucester Road, Wanchai, Hong Kong (Phone Number in U.S. (800) 938-4685); *Asian Market Atlas.*

Euromonitor Publications Limited, 87-88 Turnmill Street, London EC1M 5QU, England; *International Marketing Data and Statistics.*

Food and Agricultural Organization of the United Nations (FAO) Via delle Terme di Caracalla, 00100 Rome, Italy (Telephone Number in U.S. (202) 653-2400); *The State of Food and Agriculture.*

G.K. Hall and Company, 70 Lincoln Street, Boston, Massachusetts 02111 (617) 423-3990; *The World in Figures.*

International Monetary Fund, 700 Nineteenth Street, NW, Washington, D.C. 20431 (202) 623-7000; *Direction of Trade Statistics.*

International Rubber Study Group, York House, Eighth Floor, Empire Way, Wembley, London HA9 0PA, England; *Rubber Statistical Bulletin.*

Time Books, 201 East 50th Street, New York, New York 10022 (212) 751-2600; *The Economist Book of Vital World Statistics.*

VIETNAM (SOCIALIST REPUBLIC OF) - EXTERNAL TRADE

Food and Agricultural Organization of the United Nations (FAO) Via delle Terme di Caracalla, 00100 Rome, Italy (Telephone Number in U.S. (202) 653-2400); *The State of Food and Agriculture.*

G.K. Hall and Company, 70 Lincoln Street, Boston, Massachusetts 02111 (617) 423-3990; *The World in Figures.*

Statistical Office of the United Nations, Publishing Service, New York, New York 10017 (800) 253-9646; *Statistical Yearbook for Asia and the Pacific.*

VIETNAM (SOCIALIST REPUBLIC OF) - FABRIC PRODUCTION - See VIETNAM (SOCIALIST REPUBLIC OF) - TEXTILE INDUSTRY

VIETNAM (SOCIALIST REPUBLIC OF) - FARM CROPS - See VIETNAM (SOCIALIST REPUBLIC OF) - CROPS

VIETNAM (SOCIALIST REPUBLIC OF) - FEMALE WORKING POPULATION - See VIETNAM (SOCIALIST REPUBLIC OF) - EMPLOYMENT

VIETNAM (SOCIALIST REPUBLIC OF) - FERTILITY RATES

The Economist Intelligence Unit (Asia) Limited, 10th Floor, Luk Kwok Centre, 72 Gloucester Road, Wanchai, Hong Kong (Phone Number in U.S. (800) 938-4685); *Asian Market Atlas.*

Facts on File, 460 Park Avenue South, New York, New York 10016 (800) 443-8323; *The New Book of World Rankings.*

Time Books, 201 East 50th Street, New York, New York 10022 (212) 751-2600; *The Economist Book of Vital World Statistics.*

VIETNAM (SOCIALIST REPUBLIC OF) - FERTILIZER PRODUCTION AND CONSUMPTION

Food and Agricultural Organization of the United Nations (FAO), Via delle Terme di Caracalla, 00100 Rome, Italy (Telephone Number in U.S. (202) 653-2400); *Fertilizer Yearbook,* and *The State of Food and Agriculture.*

Statistical Office of the United Nations, Publishing Service, New York, New York 10017 (800) 253-9646; *Statistical Yearbook.*

VIETNAM (SOCIALIST REPUBLIC OF) - FETAL MORTALITY

Statistical Office of the United Nations, Publishing Service, New York, New York 10017 (800) 253-9646; *Demographic Yearbook.*

World Health Organization, Office of Publications, Avenue Appia, CH-1211 Geneva 27, Switzerland (Telephone Number in U.S. (518) 436-9686); *World Health Statistics Annual.*

VIETNAM (SOCIALIST REPUBLIC OF) - FILM - See VIETNAM (SOCIALIST REPUBLIC OF) - MOTION PICTURES

VIETNAM (SOCIALIST REPUBLIC OF) - FINANCE

Facts on File, 460 Park Avenue South, New York, New York 10016 (800) 443-8323; *The New Book of World Rankings.*

G.K. Hall and Company, 70 Lincoln Street, Boston, Massachusetts 02111 (617) 423-3990; *The World in Figures.*

Statistical Office of the United Nations, Publishing Service, New York, New York 10017 (800) 253-9646; *Statistical Yearbook for Asia and the Pacific.*

VIETNAM (SOCIALIST REPUBLIC OF) - FISHERIES

Facts on File, 460 Park Avenue South, New York, New York 10016 (800) 443-8323; *The New Book of World Rankings.*

Food and Agricultural Organization of the United Nations (FAO) Via delle Terme di Caracalla, 00100 Rome, Italy (Telephone Number in U.S. (202) 653-2400); *The State of Food and Agriculture,* and *Yearbook of Fishery Statistics.*

Statistical Office of the United Nations, Publishing Service, New York, New York 10017 (800) 253-9646; *Statistical Yearbook.*

VIETNAM (SOCIALIST REPUBLIC OF) - FOOD

Food and Agricultural Organization of the United Nations (FAO) Via delle Terme di Caracalla, 00100 Rome, Italy (Telephone Number in U.S. (202) 653-2400); *The State of Food and Agriculture.*

G.K. Hall and Company, 70 Lincoln Street, Boston, Massachusetts 02111 (617) 423-3990; *The World in Figures.*

Statistical Office of the United Nations, Publishing Service, New York, New York 10017 (800) 253-9646; *Statistical Yearbook for Asia and the Pacific.*

VIETNAM (SOCIALIST REPUBLIC OF) - FOREIGN AID

G.K. Hall and Company, 70 Lincoln Street, Boston, Massachusetts 02111 (617) 423-3990; *The World in Figures.*

VIETNAM (SOCIALIST REPUBLIC OF) - FOREIGN TRADE

The Economist Intelligence Unit (Asia) Limited, 10th Floor, Luk Kwok Centre, 72 Gloucester Road, Wanchai, Hong Kong (Phone Number in U.S. (800) 938-4685); *Asian Market Atlas.*

Euromonitor Publications Limited, 87-88 Turnmill Street, London EC1M 5QU, England; *International Marketing Data and Statistics.*

Facts on File, 460 Park Avenue South, New York, New York 10016 (800) 443-8323; *The New Book of World Rankings.*

Food and Agricultural Organization of the United Nations (FAO) Via delle Terme di Caracalla, 00100 Rome, Italy (Telephone Number in U.S. (202) 653-2400); *The State of Food and Agriculture.*

G.K. Hall and Company, 70 Lincoln Street, Boston, Massachusetts 02111 (617) 423-3990; *The World in Figures.*

Statistical Office of the United Nations, Publishing Service, New York, New York 10017 (800) 253-9646; *Statistical Yearbook.*

VIETNAM (SOCIALIST REPUBLIC OF) - FORESTRY AND FOREST PRODUCTS

The Economist Intelligence Unit (Asia) Limited, 10th Floor, Luk Kwok Centre, 72 Gloucester Road, Wanchai, Hong Kong (Phone Number in U.S. (800) 938-4685); *Asian Market Atlas.*

Facts on File, 460 Park Avenue South, New York, New York 10016 (800) 443-8323; *The New Book of World Rankings.*

Food and Agricultural Organization of the United Nations (FAO) Via delle Terme di Caracalla, 00100 Rome, Italy (Telephone Number in U.S. (202) 653-2400); *The State of Food and Agriculture,* and *Yearbook of Forest Products.*

G.K. Hall and Company, 70 Lincoln Street, Boston, Massachusetts 02111 (617) 423-3990; *The World in Figures.*

Statistical Office of the United Nations, Publishing Service, New York, New York 10017 (800) 253-9646; *Statistical Yearbook.*

United Nations Educational, Scientific and Cultural Organization (UNESCO), 7 Place de Fontenoy, F-75700 Paris, France (Telephone Number in U.S. (212) 963-5981); *Statistical Yearbook.*

VIETNAM (SOCIALIST REPUBLIC OF) - GAS PRODUCTION - See VIETNAM (SOCIALIST REPUBLIC OF) - MINING AND MINERAL PRODUCTS

VIETNAM (SOCIALIST REPUBLIC OF) - GENERAL MORTALITY

Statistical Office of the United Nations, Publishing Service, New York, New York 10017 (800) 253-9646; *Demographic Yearbook.*

VIETNAM (SOCIALIST REPUBLIC OF) - GEOGRAPHIC DATA

Facts on File, 460 Park Avenue South, New York, New York 10016 (800) 443-8323; *The New Book of World Rankings.*

VIETNAM (SOCIALIST REPUBLIC OF) - GOATS - See VIETNAM (SOCIALIST REPUBLIC OF) - LIVESTOCK AND POULTRY

VIETNAM (SOCIALIST REPUBLIC OF) - GOLD PRODUCTION - See VIETNAM (SOCIALIST REPUBLIC OF) - MINING AND MINERAL PRODUCTS

VIETNAM (SOCIALIST REPUBLIC OF) - GOVERNMENT

G.K. Hall and Company, 70 Lincoln Street, Boston, Massachusetts 02111 (617) 423-3990; *The World in Figures.*

VIETNAM (SOCIALIST REPUBLIC OF) - GRAIN PRODUCTION - See VIETNAM (SOCIALIST REPUBLIC OF) - CROPS

VIETNAM (SOCIALIST REPUBLIC OF) - GROSS DOMESTIC PRODUCT

The Economist Intelligence Unit, 111 West 57th Street, New York, New York 10019 (800) 938-4685; *The World Market Atlas.*

The Economist Intelligence Unit (Asia) Limited, 10th Floor, Luk Kwok Centre, 72 Gloucester Road, Wanchai, Hong Kong (Phone Number in U.S. (800) 938-4685); *Asian Market Atlas.*

Euromonitor Publications Limited, 87-88 Turnmill Street, London EC1M 5QU, England; *International Marketing Data and Statistics.*

Facts on File, 460 Park Avenue South, New York, New York 10016 (800) 443-8323; *The New Book of World Rankings.*

G.K. Hall and Company, 70 Lincoln Street, Boston, Massachusetts 02111 (617) 423-3990; *The World in Figures.*

Statistical Office of the United Nations, Publishing Service, New York, New York 10017 (800) 253-9646; *Statistical Yearbook.*

Time Books, 201 East 50th Street, New York, New York 10022 (212) 751-2600; *The Economist Book of Vital World Statistics.*

VIETNAM (SOCIALIST REPUBLIC OF) - GROSS NATIONAL PRODUCT

Euromonitor Publications Limited, 87-88 Turnmill Street, London EC1M 5QU, England; *International Marketing Data and Statistics.*

U.S. Arms Control and Disarmament Agency, 320 Twenty-first Street, NW, Washington, D.C. 20451 (202) 647-8677; *World Military Expenditures and Arms Transfers.*

VIETNAM (SOCIALIST REPUBLIC OF) - GROUNDNUTS PRODUCTION - See VIETNAM (SOCIALIST REPUBLIC OF) - CROPS

VIETNAM (SOCIALIST REPUBLIC OF) - HEALTH

The Economist Intelligence Unit (Asia) Limited, 10th Floor, Luk Kwok Centre, 72 Gloucester Road, Wanchai, Hong Kong (Phone Number in U.S. (800) 938-4685); *Asian Market Atlas.*

Facts on File, 460 Park Avenue South, New York, New York 10016 (800) 443-8323; *The New Book of World Rankings.*

G.K. Hall and Company, 70 Lincoln Street, Boston, Massachusetts 02111 (617) 423-3990; *The World in Figures.*

Statistical Office of the United Nations, Publishing Service, New York, New York 10017 (800) 253-9646; *Statistical Yearbook.*

Time Books, 201 East 50th Street, New York, New York 10022 (212) 751-2600; *The Economist Book of Vital World Statistics.*

World Health Organization, Office of Publications, Avenue Appia, CH-1211 Geneva 27, Switzerland (Telephone Number in U.S. (518) 436-9686); *World Health Statistics Annual.*

VIETNAM (SOCIALIST REPUBLIC OF) - HEALTH AND
MEDICAL SERVICES

Statistical Office of the United Nations, Publishing Service, New
York, New York 10017 (800) 253-9646; *Statistical Yearbook.*

VIETNAM (SOCIALIST REPUBLIC OF) - HIDE PRODUCTION

Food and Agricultural Organization of the United Nations (FAO),
Via delle Terme di Caracalla, 00100 Rome, Italy (Telephone Number
in U.S. (202) 653-2400); *Production Yearbook.*

VIETNAM (SOCIALIST REPUBLIC OF) - HIGHWAYS

The Economist Intelligence Unit (Asia) Limited, 10th Floor, Luk
Kwok Centre, 72 Gloucester Road, Wanchai, Hong Kong (Phone
Number in U.S. (800) 938-4685); *Asian Market Atlas.*

G.K. Hall and Company, 70 Lincoln Street, Boston, Massachusetts
02111 (617) 423-3990; *The World in Figures.*

VIETNAM (SOCIALIST REPUBLIC OF) - HORSES - See VIETNAM
(SOCIALIST REPUBLIC OF) - LIVESTOCK AND POULTRY

VIETNAM (SOCIALIST REPUBLIC OF) - HOURS OF WORK - See
VIETNAM (SOCIALIST REPUBLIC OF) - EMPLOYMENT

VIETNAM (SOCIALIST REPUBLIC OF) - HOUSING
CONSTRUCTION

Facts on File, 460 Park Avenue South, New York, New York 10016
(800) 443-8323; *The New Book of World Rankings.*

VIETNAM (SOCIALIST REPUBLIC OF) - HYDROCHLORIC
ACID PRODUCTION

Statistical Office of the United Nations, Publishing Service, New
York, New York 10017 (800) 253-9646; *Statistical Yearbook.*

VIETNAM (SOCIALIST REPUBLIC OF) - ILLITERATE POPULATION

The Economist Intelligence Unit, 111 West 57th Street, New York,
New York 10019 (800) 938-4685; *The World Market Atlas.*

G.K. Hall and Company, 70 Lincoln Street, Boston, Massachusetts
02111 (617) 423-3990; *The World in Figures.*

VIETNAM (SOCIALIST REPUBLIC OF) - IMPORTS

The Economist Intelligence Unit, 111 West 57th Street, New York,
New York 10019 (800) 938-4685; *The World Market Atlas.*

The Economist Intelligence Unit (Asia) Limited, 10th Floor, Luk
Kwok Centre, 72 Gloucester Road, Wanchai, Hong Kong (Phone
Number in U.S. (800) 938-4685); *Asian Market Atlas.*

Euromonitor Publications Limited, 87-88 Turnmill Street, London
EC1M 5QU, England; *International Marketing Data and Statistics.*

Food and Agricultural Organization of the United Nations (FAO) Via
delle Terme di Caracalla, 00100 Rome, Italy (Telephone Number in
U.S. (202) 653-2400); *The State of Food and Agriculture.*

G.K. Hall and Company, 70 Lincoln Street, Boston, Massachusetts
02111 (617) 423-3990; *The World in Figures.*

International Monetary Fund, 700 Nineteenth Street, NW,
Washington, D.C. 20431 (202) 623-7000; *Direction of Trade
Statistics.*

International Rubber Study Group, York House, Eighth Floor, Empire
Way, Wembley, London HA9 0PA, England; *Rubber Statistical
Bulletin.*

VIETNAM (SOCIALIST REPUBLIC OF) - INDUSTRY

Euromonitor Publications Limited, 87-88 Turnmill Street, London
EC1M 5QU, England; *International Marketing Data and Statistics.*

Facts on File, 460 Park Avenue South, New York, New York 10016
(800) 443-8323; *The New Book of World Rankings.*

G.K. Hall and Company, 70 Lincoln Street, Boston, Massachusetts
02111 (617) 423-3990; *The World in Figures.*

Statistical Office of the United Nations, Publishing Service, New
York, New York 10017 (800) 253-9646; *Statistical Yearbook,* and
Statistical Yearbook for Asia and the Pacific.

Time Books, 201 East 50th Street, New York, New York 10022 (212)
751-2600; *The Economist Book of Vital World Statistics.*

World Intellectual Property Organization, 34 Chemin des
Colombettes, CH-1211 Geneva 20. Switzerland; *Industrial Property
Statistics.*

VIETNAM (SOCIALIST REPUBLIC OF) - INFANT AND MATERNAL
MORTALITY

The Economist Intelligence Unit (Asia) Limited, 10th Floor, Luk
Kwok Centre, 72 Gloucester Road, Wanchai, Hong Kong (Phone
Number in U.S. (800) 938-4685); *Asian Market Atlas.*

Statistical Office of the United Nations, Publishing Service, New
York, New York 10017 (800) 253-9646; *Demographic Yearbook.*

Time Books, 201 East 50th Street, New York, New York 10022 (212)
751-2600; *The Economist Book of Vital World Statistics.*

World Health Organization, Office of Publications, Avenue Appia,
CH-1211 Geneva 27, Switzerland (Telephone Number in U.S. (518)
436-9686); *World Health Statistics Annual.*

VIETNAM (SOCIALIST REPUBLIC OF) - INTERNAL TRADE

Statistical Office of the United Nations, Publishing Service, New
York, New York 10017 (800) 253-9646; *Statistical Yearbook for Asia
and the Pacific.*

VIETNAM (SOCIALIST REPUBLIC OF) - IRON ORE PRODUCTION AND
CONSUMPTION - See VIETNAM (SOCIALIST REPUBLIC OF) - MINING
AND MINERAL PRODUCTS

VIETNAM (SOCIALIST REPUBLIC OF) - IRRIGATION

Euromonitor Publications Limited, 87-88 Turnmill Street, London
EC1M 5QU, England; *International Marketing Data and Statistics.*

VIETNAM (SOCIALIST REPUBLIC OF) - JUTE PRODUCTION - See
VIETNAM (SOCIALIST REPUBLIC OF) - CROPS

VIETNAM (SOCIALIST REPUBLIC OF) - LABOR FORCE

The Economist Intelligence Unit (Asia) Limited, 10th Floor, Luk
Kwok Centre, 72 Gloucester Road, Wanchai, Hong Kong (Phone
Number in U.S. (800) 938-4685), *Asian Market Atlas.*

Euromonitor Publications Limited, 87-88 Turnmill Street, London
EC1M 5QU, England; *International Marketing Data and Statistics.*

Facts on File, 460 Park Avenue South, New York, New York 10016 (800) 443-8323; *The New Book of World Rankings*.

Food and Agricultural Organization of the United Nations (FAO) Via delle Terme di Caracalla, 00100 Rome, Italy (Telephone Number in U.S. (202) 653-2400); *The State of Food and Agriculture*.

G.K. Hall and Company, 70 Lincoln Street, Boston, Massachusetts 02111 (617) 423-3990; *The World in Figures*.

VIETNAM (SOCIALIST REPUBLIC OF) - LAND USE

Euromonitor Publications Limited, 87-88 Turnmill Street, London EC1M 5QU, England; *International Marketing Data and Statistics*.

G.K. Hall and Company, 70 Lincoln Street, Boston, Massachusetts 02111 (617) 423-3990; *The World in Figures*.

VIETNAM (SOCIALIST REPUBLIC OF) - LIBRARIES

Facts on File, 460 Park Avenue South, New York, New York 10016 (800) 443-8323; *The New Book of World Rankings*.

United Nations Educational, Scientific and Cultural Organization (UNESCO), 7 Place de Fontenoy, F-75700 Paris, France (Telephone Number in U.S. (212) 963-5981); *Statistical Yearbook*.

VIETNAM (SOCIALIST REPUBLIC OF) - LIFE EXPECTANCY

The Economist Intelligence Unit (Asia) Limited, 10th Floor, Luk Kwok Centre, 72 Gloucester Road, Wanchai, Hong Kong (Phone Number in U.S. (800) 938-4685); *Asian Market Atlas*.

VIETNAM (SOCIALIST REPUBLIC OF) - LIVESTOCK AND POULTRY

Euromonitor Publications Limited, 87-88 Turnmill Street, London EC1M 5QU, England; *International Marketing Data and Statistics*.

Facts on File, 460 Park Avenue South, New York, New York 10016 (800) 443-8323; *The New Book of World Rankings*.

Food and Agricultural Organization of the United Nations (FAO) Via delle Terme di Caracalla, 00100 Rome, Italy (Telephone Number in U.S. (202) 653-2400); *Production Yearbook*, and *The State of Food and Agriculture*.

G.K. Hall and Company, 70 Lincoln Street, Boston, Massachusetts 02111 (617) 423-3990; *The World in Figures*.

Statistical Office of the United Nations, Publishing Service, New York, New York 10017; *Statistical Yearbook*.

VIETNAM (SOCIALIST REPUBLIC OF) - LIVING LEVELS

G.K. Hall and Company, 70 Lincoln Street, Boston, Massachusetts 02111 (617) 423-3990; *The World in Figures*.

Time Books, 201 East 50th Street, New York, New York 10022 (212) 751-2600; *The Economist Book of Vital World Statistics*.

VIETNAM (SOCIALIST REPUBLIC OF) - MAIL - NUMBER OF PIECES SENT OR RECEIVED

Statistical Office of the United Nations, Publishing Service, New York, New York 10017 (800) 253-9646; *Statistical Yearbook*.

VIETNAM (SOCIALIST REPUBLIC OF) - MANPOWER

Statistical Office of the United Nations, Publishing Service, New York, New York 10017 (800) 253-9646; *Statistical Yearbook*.

VIETNAM (SOCIALIST REPUBLIC OF) - MANUFACTURING

Facts on File, 460 Park Avenue South, New York, New York 10016 (800) 443-8323; *The New Book of World Rankings*.

G.K. Hall and Company, 70 Lincoln Street, Boston, Massachusetts 02111 (617) 423-3990; *The World in Figures*.

Statistical Office of the United Nations, Publishing Service, New York, New York 10017 (800) 253-9646; *Statistical Yearbook*.

VIETNAM (SOCIALIST REPUBLIC OF) - MARRIAGE RATES

Facts on File, 460 Park Avenue South, New York, New York 10016 (800) 443-8323; *The New Book of World Rankings*.

Statistical Office of the United Nations, Publishing Service, New York, New York 10017 (800) 253-9646; *Demographic Yearbook*.

VIETNAM (SOCIALIST REPUBLIC OF) - MEAT PRODUCTION - See VIETNAM (SOCIALIST REPUBLIC OF) - LIVESTOCK AND POULTRY

VIETNAM (SOCIALIST REPUBLIC OF) - MERCHANT SHIPPING

G.K. Hall and Company, 70 Lincoln Street, Boston, Massachusetts 02111 (617) 423-3990; *The World in Figures*.

Statistical Office of the United Nations, Publishing Service, New York, New York 10017 (800) 253-9646; *Statistical Yearbook*.

Time Books, 201 East 50th Street, New York, New York 10022 (212) 751-2600; *The Economist Book of Vital World Statistics*.

U.S. Department of Transportation, Maritime Administration, 400 Seventh Street, SW, Washington, D.C. 20590 (202) 366-5807; *A Statistical Analysis of the World's Merchant Fleets*.

VIETNAM (SOCIALIST REPUBLIC OF) - MILITARY

The Economist Intelligence Unit (Asia) Limited, 10th Floor, Luk Kwok Centre, 72 Gloucester Road, Wanchai, Hong Kong (Phone Number in U.S. (800) 938-4685); *Asian Market Atlas*.

G.K. Hall and Company, 70 Lincoln Street, Boston, Massachusetts 02111 (617) 423-3990; *The World in Figures*.

The International Institute for Strategic Studies, 23 Tavistock Street, London WC2E 7NQ, England; *The Military Balance*.

U.S. Arms Control and Disarmament Agency, 320 Twenty-first Street, NW, Washington, D.C. 20451 (202) 647-8677; *World Military Expenditures and Arms Transfers*.

VIETNAM (SOCIALIST REPUBLIC OF) - MILK PRODUCTION - See VIETNAM (SOCIALIST REPUBLIC OF) - DAIRY PRODUCTS

VIETNAM (SOCIALIST REPUBLIC OF) - MINING AND MINERAL PRODUCTS

Facts on File, 460 Park Avenue South, New York, New York 10016 (800) 443-8323; *The New Book of World Rankings*.

G.K. Hall and Company, 70 Lincoln Street, Boston, Massachusetts 02111 (617) 423-3990; *The World in Figures.*

Penn Well Publishing Company, 1421 South Sheridan Road, P.O. Box 1260, Tulsa, Oklahoma 74101 (800) 752-9764; *International Energy Statistics Sourcebook.*

Statistical Office of the United Nations, Publishing Service, New York, New York 10017 (800) 253-9646; *Statistical Yearbook.*

VIETNAM (SOCIALIST REPUBLIC OF) - MONEY EXCHANGE RATES

Euromonitor Publications Limited, 87-88 Turnmill Street, London EC1M 5QU, England; *International Marketing Data and Statistics.*

VIETNAM (SOCIALIST REPUBLIC OF) - MONEY RESERVES

Euromonitor Publications Limited, 87-88 Turnmill Street, London EC1M 5QU, England; *International Marketing Data and Statistics.*

VIETNAM (SOCIALIST REPUBLIC OF) - MONEY SUPPLY

Euromonitor Publications Limited, 87-88 Turnmill Street, London EC1M 5QU, England; *International Marketing Data and Statistics.*

G.K. Hall and Company, 70 Lincoln Street, Boston, Massachusetts 02111 (617) 423-3990; *The World in Figures.*

VIETNAM (SOCIALIST REPUBLIC OF) - MOTION PICTURES

United Nations Educational, Scientific and Cultural Organization (UNESCO), 7 Place de Fontenoy, F-75700 Paris, France (Telephone Number in U.S. (212) 963-5981); *Statistical Yearbook.*

VIETNAM (SOCIALIST REPUBLIC OF) - MOTOR VEHICLES IN USE

G.K. Hall and Company, 70 Lincoln Street, Boston, Massachusetts 02111 (617) 423-3990; *The World in Figures.*

Statistical Office of the United Nations, Publishing Service, New York, New York 10017 (800) 253-9646; *Statistical Yearbook.*

VIETNAM (SOCIALIST REPUBLIC OF) - MUSEUMS

Facts on File, 460 Park Avenue South, New York, New York 10016 (800) 443-8323; *The New Book of World Rankings.*

United Nations Educational, Scientific and Cultural Organization (UNESCO), 7 Place de Fontenoy, F-75700 Paris, France (Telephone Number in U.S. (212) 963-5981); *Statistical Yearbook.*

VIETNAM (SOCIALIST REPUBLIC OF) - NATALITY - See VIETNAM (SOCIALIST REPUBLIC OF) - BIRTH RATE

VIETNAM (SOCIALIST REPUBLIC OF) - NATIONAL ACCOUNTS

Statistical Office of the United Nations, Publishing Service, New York, New York 10017 (800) 253-9646; *National Accounts Statistics, Statistical Yearbook,* and *Statistical Yearbook for Asia and the Pacific.*

VIETNAM (SOCIALIST REPUBLIC OF) - NATIONAL INCOME

Facts on File, 460 Park Avenue South, New York, New York 10016 (800) 443-8323; *The New Book of World Rankings.*

G.K. Hall and Company, 70 Lincoln Street, Boston, Massachusetts 02111 (617) 423-3990; *The World in Figures.*

Statistical Office of the United Nations, Publishing Service, New York, New York 10017 (800) 253-9646; *Statistical Yearbook.*

VIETNAM (SOCIALIST REPUBLIC OF) - NATIONAL PRODUCT

Facts on File, 460 Park Avenue South, New York, New York 10016 (800) 443-8323; *The New Book of World Rankings.*

Statistical Office of the United Nations, Publishing Service, New York, New York 10017 (800) 253-9646; *Statistical Yearbook.*

VIETNAM (SOCIALIST REPUBLIC OF) - NATURAL GAS PRODUCTION - See VIETNAM (SOCIALIST REPUBLIC OF) - MINING AND MINERAL PRODUCTS

VIETNAM (SOCIALIST REPUBLIC OF) - NEWSPAPER PRODUCTION AND CONSUMPTION - See VIETNAM (SOCIALIST REPUBLIC OF) - FORESTRY AND FOREST PRODUCTS

VIETNAM (SOCIALIST REPUBLIC OF) - NEWSPRINT PRODUCTION AND CONSUMPTION - See VIETNAM (SOCIALIST REPUBLIC OF) - FORESTRY AND FOREST PRODUCTS

VIETNAM (SOCIALIST REPUBLIC OF) - OCCUPATIONS - See VIETNAM (SOCIALIST REPUBLIC OF) - LABOR FORCE

VIETNAM (SOCIALIST REPUBLIC OF) - PATENTS

World Intellectual Property Organization, 34 Chemin des Colombettes, 011-1211 Geneva 10. Switzerland; *Industrial Property Statistics.*

VIETNAM (SOCIALIST REPUBLIC OF) - PEANUT PRODUCTION - See VIETNAM (SOCIALIST REPUBLIC OF) - CROPS

VIETNAM (SOCIALIST REPUBLIC OF) - PERIODICALS

United Nations Educational, Scientific and Cultural Organization (UNESCO), 7 Place de Fontenoy, F-75700 Paris, France (Telephone Number in U.S. (212) 963-5981); *Statistical Yearbook.*

VIETNAM (SOCIALIST REPUBLIC OF) - PESTICIDE USE

Food and Agricultural Organization of the United Nations (FAO) Via delle Terme di Caracalla, 00100 Rome, Italy (Telephone Number in U.S. (202) 653-2400); *The State of Food and Agriculture.*

VIETNAM (SOCIALIST REPUBLIC OF) - PETROLEUM INDUSTRY

Facts on File, 460 Park Avenue South, New York, New York 10016 (800) 443-8323; *The New Book of World Rankings.*

Food and Agricultural Organization of the United Nations (FAO) Via delle Terme di Caracalla, 00100 Rome, Italy (Telephone Number in U.S. (202) 653-2400); *The State of Food and Agriculture.*

G.K. Hall and Company, 70 Lincoln Street, Boston, Massachusetts 02111 (617) 423-3990; *The World in Figures.*

Penn Well Publishing Company, 1421 South Sheridan Road, P.O. Box 1260, Tulsa, Oklahoma 74101 (800) 752-9764; *International Energy Statistics Sourcebook.*

VIETNAM (SOCIALIST REPUBLIC OF) - PHOSPHATE
ROCK PRODUCTION - See VIETNAM (SOCIALIST REPUBLIC OF) -
MINING AND MINERAL PRODUCTS

VIETNAM (SOCIALIST REPUBLIC OF) - PIGS - See VIETNAM
(SOCIALIST REPUBLIC OF) - LIVESTOCK AND POULTRY

VIETNAM (SOCIALIST REPUBLIC OF) - POPULATION

The Economist Intelligence Unit, 111 West 57th Street, New York,
New York 10019 (800) 938-4685; *The World Market Atlas.*

The Economist Intelligence Unit (Asia) Limited, 10th Floor, Luk
Kwok Centre, 72 Gloucester Road, Wanchai, Hong Kong (Phone
Number in U.S. (800) 938-4685); *Asian Market Atlas.*

Euromonitor Publications Limited, 87-88 Turnmill Street, London
EC1M 5QU, England; *International Marketing Data and Statistics.*

Facts on File, 460 Park Avenue South, New York, New York 10016
(800) 443-8323; *The New Book of World Rankings.*

G.K. Hall and Company, 70 Lincoln Street, Boston, Massachusetts
02111 (617) 423-3990; *The World in Figures.*

Statistical Office of the United Nations, Publishing Service, New
York, New York 10017 (800) 253-9646; *Demographic Yearbook,
Statistical Yearbook,* and *Statistical Yearbook for Asia and the
Pacific.*

Time Books, 201 East 50th Street, New York, New York 10022 (212)
751-2600; *The Economist Book of Vital World Statistics.*

United Nations Educational, Scientific and Cultural Organization
(UNESCO), 7 Place de Fontenoy, F-75700 Paris, France (Telephone
Number in U.S. (212) 963-5981); *Statistical Yearbook.*

U.S. Arms Control and Disarmament Agency, 320 Twenty-first
Street, NW, Washington, D.C. 20451 (202) 647-8677; *World Military
Expenditures and Arms Transfers.*

World Health Organization, Office of Publications, Avenue Appia,
CH-1211 Geneva 27, Switzerland (Telephone Number in U.S. (518)
436-9686); *World Health Statistics Annual.*

VIETNAM (SOCIALIST REPUBLIC OF) - POST OFFICES

Facts on File, 460 Park Avenue South, New York, New York 10016
(800) 443-8323; *The New Book of World Rankings.*

VIETNAM (SOCIALIST REPUBLIC OF) - POTATO
PRODUCTION - See VIETNAM (SOCIALIST REPUBLIC OF) - CROPS

VIETNAM (SOCIALIST REPUBLIC OF) - PRICES

Food and Agricultural Organization of the United Nations (FAO) Via
delle Terme di Caracalla, 00100 Rome, Italy (Telephone Number in
U.S. (202) 653-2400); *The State of Food and Agriculture.*

Facts on File, 460 Park Avenue South, New York, New York 10016
(800) 443-8323; *The New Book of World Rankings.*

G.K. Hall and Company, 70 Lincoln Street, Boston, Massachusetts
02111 (617) 423-3990; *The World in Figures.*

International Rubber Study Group, York House, Eighth Floor,
Empire Way, Wembley, London HA9 0PA, England; *Rubber
Statistical Bulletin.*

VIETNAM (SOCIALIST REPUBLIC OF) - PRODUCTION

Facts on File, 460 Park Avenue South, New York, New York 10016
(800) 443-8323; *The New Book of World Rankings.*

G.K. Hall and Company, 70 Lincoln Street, Boston, Massachusetts
02111 (617) 423-3990; *The World in Figures.*

International Rubber Study Group, York House, Eighth Floor, Empire
Way, Wembley, London HA9 0PA, England; *Rubber Statistical
Bulletin.*

VIETNAM (SOCIALIST REPUBLIC OF) - PRODUCTIVITY

Euromonitor Publications Limited, 87-88 Turnmill Street, London
EC1M 5QU, England; *International Marketing Data and Statistics.*

VIETNAM (SOCIALIST REPUBLIC OF) - PUBLIC FINANCE

Facts on File, 460 Park Avenue South, New York, New York 10016
(800) 443-8323; *The New Book of World Rankings.*

VIETNAM (SOCIALIST REPUBLIC OF) - RADIO

The Economist Intelligence Unit (Asia) Limited, 10th Floor, Luk
Kwok Centre, 72 Gloucester Road, Wanchai, Hong Kong (Phone
Number in U.S. (800) 938-4685); *Asian Market Atlas.*

VIETNAM (SOCIALIST REPUBLIC OF) - RADIO BROADCASTING - See
VIETNAM (SOCIALIST REPUBLIC OF) - BROADCASTING

VIETNAM (SOCIALIST REPUBLIC OF) - RADIO RECEIVER
PRODUCTION

Statistical Office of the United Nations, Publishing Service, New
York, New York 10017 (800) 253-9646; *Statistical Yearbook.*

VIETNAM (SOCIALIST REPUBLIC OF) - RAILWAYS

G.K. Hall and Company, 70 Lincoln Street, Boston, Massachusetts
02111 (617) 423-3990; *The World in Figures.*

Jane's Information Group, Sentinel House, 163 Brighton Road,
Coulsdon, Surrey CR5 2NH, England (Telephone Number in U.S.
(703) 683-3700); *Jane's World Railways.*

Statistical Office of the United Nations, Publishing Service, New
York, New York 10017 (800) 253-9646; *Statistical Yearbook.*

VIETNAM (SOCIALIST REPUBLIC OF) - RELIGION

Facts on File, 460 Park Avenue South, New York, New York 10016
(800) 443-8323; *The New Book of World Rankings.*

VIETNAM (SOCIALIST REPUBLIC OF) - RETAIL TRADE

G.K. Hall and Company, 70 Lincoln Street, Boston, Massachusetts
02111 (617) 423-3990; *The World in Figures.*

VIETNAM (SOCIALIST REPUBLIC OF) - RICE PRODUCTION - See
VIETNAM (SOCIALIST REPUBLIC OF) - CROPS

VIETNAM (SOCIALIST REPUBLIC OF) - ROOT AND TUBER
PRODUCTION - See VIETNAM (SOCIALIST REPUBLIC OF) - CROPS

VIETNAM (SOCIALIST REPUBLIC OF) - ROUNDWOOD
PRODUCTION - See VIETNAM (SOCIALIST REPUBLIC OF) -
FORESTRY AND FOREST PRODUCTS

VIETNAM (SOCIALIST REPUBLIC OF) - RUBBER
PRODUCTION AND CONSUMPTION

Commodity Research Bureau, Incorporated, 75 Wall Street, New
York, New York 10005 (212) 504-7754; *Commodity Year Book.*

Facts on File, 460 Park Avenue South, New York, New York 10016
(800) 443-8323; *The New Book of World Rankings.*

International Rubber Study Group, York House, Eighth Floor,
Empire Way, Wembley, London HA9 0PA, England; *Rubber
Statistical Bulletin.*

Statistical Office of the United Nations, Publishing Service, New
York, New York 10017 (800) 253-9646; *Statistical Yearbook.*

VIETNAM (SOCIALIST REPUBLIC OF) - SALT PRODUCTION - See
VIETNAM (SOCIALIST REPUBLIC OF) - MINING AND MINERAL
PRODUCTS

VIETNAM (SOCIALIST REPUBLIC OF) - SAWNWOOD
PRODUCTION - See VIETNAM (SOCIALIST REPUBLIC OF) -
FORESTRY AND FOREST PRODUCTS

VIETNAM (SOCIALIST REPUBLIC OF) - SCIENTISTS
AND TECHNICIANS

United Nations Educational, Scientific and Cultural Organization
(UNESCO), 7 Place de Fontenoy, F-75700 Paris, France (Telephone
Number in U.S. (212) 963-5981); *Statistical Yearbook.*

VIETNAM (SOCIALIST REPUBLIC OF) - SENIOR CITIZENS

Facts on File, 460 Park Avenue South, New York, New York 10016
(800) 443-8323; *The New Book of World Rankings.*

VIETNAM (SOCIALIST REPUBLIC OF) - SESAME SEED
PRODUCTION - See VIETNAM (SOCIALIST REPUBLIC OF) - CROPS

VIETNAM (SOCIALIST REPUBLIC OF) - SHEEP - See VIETNAM
(SOCIALIST REPUBLIC OF) - LIVESTOCK AND POULTRY

VIETNAM (SOCIALIST REPUBLIC OF) - SILVER PRODUCTION AND
CONSUMPTION - See VIETNAM (SOCIALIST REPUBLIC OF) -
MINING AND MINERAL PRODUCTS

VIETNAM (SOCIALIST REPUBLIC OF) - SOCIAL DATA

Facts on File, 460 Park Avenue South, New York, New York 10016
(800) 443-8323; *The New Book of World Rankings.*

G.K. Hall and Company, 70 Lincoln Street, Boston, Massachusetts
02111 (617) 423-3990; *The World in Figures.*

VIETNAM (SOCIALIST REPUBLIC OF) - SOYBEAN
PRODUCTION - See VIETNAM (SOCIALIST REPUBLIC OF) - CROPS

VIETNAM (SOCIALIST REPUBLIC OF) - STATE BUDGET REVENUE
AND EXPENDITURES

Euromonitor Publications Limited, 87-88 Turnmill Street, London
EC1M 5QU, England; *International Marketing Data and Statistics.*

VIETNAM (SOCIALIST REPUBLIC OF) - STEEL - See VIETNAM
(SOCIALIST REPUBLIC OF) - MINING AND MINERAL PRODUCTS

VIETNAM (SOCIALIST REPUBLIC OF) - STOCKS - COMMODITY -
MARKET PRICE - INDEX

Food and Agricultural Organization of the United Nations (FAO) Via
delle Terme di Caracalla, 00100 Rome, Italy (Telephone Number in
U.S. (202) 653-2400); *The State of Food and Agriculture.*

VIETNAM (SOCIALIST REPUBLIC OF) - SUGAR
PRODUCTION AND CONSUMPTION - See VIETNAM (SOCIALIST
REPUBLIC OF) - CROPS

VIETNAM (SOCIALIST REPUBLIC OF) - TAXATION

G.K. Hall and Company, 70 Lincoln Street, Boston, Massachusetts
02111 (617) 423-3990; *The World in Figures.*

VIETNAM (SOCIALIST REPUBLIC OF) - TEA PRODUCTION - See
VIETNAM (SOCIALIST REPUBLIC OF) - CROPS

VIETNAM (SOCIALIST REPUBLIC OF) - TELEGRAPH
SERVICE

Statistical Office of the United Nations, Publishing Service, New
York, New York 10017 (800) 253-9646; *Statistical Yearbook.*

VIETNAM (SOCIALIST REPUBLIC OF) - TELEPHONES
IN USE

American Telephone and Telegraph Company, 26 Parsippany Road,
Whippany, New Jersey 07081 (800) 338-4038; *The World's
Telephones.*

The Economist Intelligence Unit (Asia) Limited, 10th Floor, Luk
Kwok Centre, 72 Gloucester Road, Wanchai, Hong Kong (Phone
Number in U.S. (800) 938-4085), *Asian Market Atlas.*

G.K. Hall and Company, 70 Lincoln Street, Boston, Massachusetts
02111 (617) 423-3990; *The World in Figures.*

VIETNAM (SOCIALIST REPUBLIC OF) - TELEVISION
BROADCASTING - See VIETNAM (SOCIALIST REPUBLIC OF) -
BROADCASTING

VIETNAM (SOCIALIST REPUBLIC OF) - TEXTILE
INDUSTRY

G.K. Hall and Company, 70 Lincoln Street, Boston, Massachusetts
02111 (617) 423-3990; *The World in Figures.*

Statistical Office of the United Nations, Publishing Service, New
York, New York 10017 (800) 253-9646; *Statistical Yearbook.*

VIETNAM (SOCIALIST REPUBLIC OF) - THEATRE

United Nations Educational, Scientific and Cultural Organization
(UNESCO), 7 Place de Fontenoy, F-75700 Paris, France (Telephone
Number in U.S. (212) 963-5981); *Statistical Yearbook.*

VIETNAM (SOCIALIST REPUBLIC OF) - TIMBER - RESOURCE
FORESTS - See VIETNAM (SOCIALIST REPUBLIC OF) - FORESTRY
AND FOREST PRODUCTS

VIETNAM (SOCIALIST REPUBLIC OF) - TIRE
(MOTOR VEHICLE) PRODUCTION

International Rubber Study Group, York House, Eighth Floor, Empire
Way, Wembley, London HA9 0PA, England; *Rubber Statistical
Bulletin.*

VIETNAM (SOCIALIST REPUBLIC OF) - TOBACCO PRODUCTION

Facts on File, 460 Park Avenue South, New York, New York 10016 (800) 443-8323; *The New Book of World Rankings*.

Statistical Office of the United Nations, Publishing Service, New York, New York 10017 (800) 253-9646; *Statistical Yearbook*.

VIETNAM (SOCIALIST REPUBLIC OF) - TOURISM

Facts on File, 460 Park Avenue South, New York, New York 10016 (800) 443-8323; *The New Book of World Rankings*.

G.K. Hall and Company, 70 Lincoln Street, Boston, Massachusetts 02111 (617) 423-3990; *The World in Figures*.

Time Books, 201 East 50th Street, New York, New York 10022 (212) 751-2600; *The Economist Book of Vital World Statistics*.

VIETNAM (SOCIALIST REPUBLIC OF) - TRACTORS IN USE

Statistical Office of the United Nations, Publishing Service, New York, New York 10017 (800) 253-9646; *Statistical Yearbook*.

VIETNAM (SOCIALIST REPUBLIC OF) - TRADE - See VIETNAM (SOCIALIST REPUBLIC OF) - FOREIGN TRADE

VIETNAM (SOCIALIST REPUBLIC OF) - TRADEMARKS AND SERVICE MARKS

World Intellectual Property Organization, 34 Chemin des Colombettes, CH-1211 Geneva 20. Switzerland; *Industrial Property Statistics*.

VIETNAM (SOCIALIST REPUBLIC OF) - TRANSPORTATION AND COMMUNICATIONS

The Economist Intelligence Unit (Asia) Limited, 10th Floor, Luk Kwok Centre, 72 Gloucester Road, Wanchai, Hong Kong (Phone Number in U.S. (800) 938-4685); *Asian Market Atlas*.

Facts on File, 460 Park Avenue South, New York, New York 10016 (800) 443-8323; *The New Book of World Rankings*.

G.K. Hall and Company, 70 Lincoln Street, Boston, Massachusetts 02111 (617) 423-3990; *The World in Figures*.

Statistical Office of the United Nations, Publishing Service, New York, New York 10017 (800) 253-9646; *Statistical Yearbook for Asia and the Pacific*.

VIETNAM (SOCIALIST REPUBLIC OF) - UNEMPLOYMENT

Euromonitor Publications Limited, 87-88 Turnmill Street, London EC1M 5QU, England; *International Marketing Data and Statistics*.

VIETNAM (SOCIALIST REPUBLIC OF) - UTILITIES

Statistical Office of the United Nations, Publishing Service, New York, New York 10017 (800) 253-9646; *Electric Power in Asia and the Pacific*.

VIETNAM (SOCIALIST REPUBLIC OF) - VITAL STATISTICS

Euromonitor Publications Limited, 87-88 Turnmill Street, London EC1M 5QU, England; *International Marketing Data and Statistics*.

G.K. Hall and Company, 70 Lincoln Street, Boston, Massachusetts 02111 (617) 423-3990; *The World in Figures*.

World Health Organization, Office of Publications, Avenue Appia, CH-1211 Geneva 27, Switzerland (Telephone Number in U.S. (518) 436-9686); *World Health Statistics Annual*.

VIETNAM (SOCIALIST REPUBLIC OF) - WAGES

G.K. Hall and Company, 70 Lincoln Street, Boston, Massachusetts 02111 (617) 423-3990; *The World in Figures*.

Statistical Office of the United Nations, Publishing Service, New York, New York 10017 (800) 253-9646; *Statistical Yearbook for Asia and the Pacific*.

VIETNAM (SOCIALIST REPUBLIC OF) - WATERMELON PRODUCTION - See VIETNAM (SOCIALIST REPUBLIC OF) - CROPS

VIETNAM (SOCIALIST REPUBLIC OF) - WEATHER

Facts on File, 460 Park Avenue South, New York, New York 10016 (800) 443-8323; *The New Book of World Rankings*.

G.K. Hall and Company, 70 Lincoln Street, Boston, Massachusetts 02111 (617) 423-3990; *The World in Figures*.

VIETNAM (SOCIALIST REPUBLIC OF) - WHEAT PRODUCTION AND PRICES - See VIETNAM (SOCIALIST REPUBLIC OF) - CROPS

VIETNAM (SOCIALIST REPUBLIC OF) - WINE PRODUCTION

Facts on File, 460 Park Avenue South, New York, New York 10016 (800) 443-8323; *The New Book of World Rankings*.

VIETNAM (SOCIALIST REPUBLIC OF) - WOOL PRODUCTION

Facts on File, 460 Park Avenue South, New York, New York 10016 (800) 443-8323; *The New Book of World Rankings*.

VIETNAM (SOCIALIST REPUBLIC OF) - YARN PRODUCTION

Statistical Office of the United Nations, Publishing Service, New York, New York 10017 (800) 253-9646; *Statistical Yearbook*.

VIETNAM CONFLICT

National Archives and Records Administration, Seventh Street and Pennsylvania Avenue, NW, Washington, D.C. 20408 (202) 501-5400; Combat Area Casualties database.

United States Congress, The Capitol, Washington, D.C. 20515 (202) 224-3121; *The Military Budget and National Economic Priorities*, 91st Congress, 1st session; subsequently revised and updated by James L. Clayton, University of Utah.

VIETNAMESE POPULATION

U.S. Department of Commerce, Bureau of the Census, Suitland, Maryland 20233 (301) 763-4040; *Census of Population, General Population Characteristics, U.S.*

VIOLENT CRIME

U.S. Department of Health and Human Services, National Center for Health Statistics, 3700 East West Highway, Hyattsville, Maryland 20782 (301) 436-8500; *Vital Statistics of the United States*.

U.S. Department of Justice, Federal Bureau of Investigation, Ninth Street and Pennsylvania Avenue, NW, Washington, D.C. 20535 (202) 324-3000; *Crime in the United States*.

VIOLENT CRIME - AGGRAVATED ASSAULT

U.S. Department of Justice, Bureau of Justice Statistics, 633 Indiana Avenue, NW, Washington, D.C. 20531 (800) 732-3277; *Criminal Victimization in the United States*, and *Crime and the Nation's Households*.

U.S. Department of Justice, Federal Bureau of Investigation, Ninth Street and Pennsylvania Avenue, NW, Washington, D.C. 20535 (202) 324-3000; *Crime in the United States*, and *Population at Risk Rates and Selected Crime Indicators*.

VIOLENT CRIME - MURDER

U.S. Department of Health and Human Services, National Center for Health Statistics, 3700 East-West Highway, Hyattsville, Maryland 20782 (301) 436-8500; *Vital Statistics of the United States*.

U.S. Department of Justice, Federal Bureau of Investigation, Ninth Street and Pennsylvania Avenue, NW, Washington, D.C. 20535 (202) 324-3000; *Crime in the United States*.

VIOLENT CRIME - RAPE - FORCIBLE

U.S. Department of Justice, Bureau of Justice Statistics, 633 Indiana Avenue, NW, Washington, D.C. 20531 (800) 732-3277; *Crime and the Nation's Households*, and *Criminal Victimization in the United States*.

U.S. Department of Justice, Federal Bureau of Investigation, Ninth Street and Pennsylvania Avenue, NW, Washington, D.C. 20535 (202) 324-3000; *Crime in the United States*, and *Population at Risk Rates and Selected Crime Indicators*.

VIOLENT CRIME - ROBBERY

U.S. Department of Justice, Bureau of Justice Statistics, 633 Indiana Avenue, NW, Washington, D.C. 20531 (800) 732-3277; *Criminal Victimization in the United States*, and *Crime and the Nation's Households*.

U.S. Department of Justice, Federal Bureau of Investigation, Ninth Street and Pennsylvania Avenue, NW, Washington, D.C. 20535 (202) 324-3000; *Crime in the United States*, and *Population at Risk Rates and Selected Crime Indicators*.

Virgin Islands - Data Centers

University of the Virgin Islands, Eastern Caribbean Center, No. 2, John Brewer's Bay, Charlotte Amalie, Saint Thomas, Virgin Islands 00802, Dr. Frank Mills (809) 776-9200.

Virgin Islands Department of Economic Development, Post Office Box 6400, Charlotte Amalie, Saint Thomas, Virgin Islands 00801, Mr. Dan Iveen (809) 774-8784.

VIRGIN ISLANDS - AGRICULTURE

Food and Agricultural Organization of the United Nations (FAO) Via delle Terme di Caracalla, 00100 Rome, Italy (Telephone Number in U.S. (202) 653-2400); *Production Yearbook*, and *The State of Food and Agriculture*.

G.K. Hall and Company, 70 Lincoln Street, Boston, Massachusetts 02111 (617) 423-3990; *The World in Figures*.

VIRGIN ISLANDS - AIRLINE SERVICE

G.K. Hall and Company, 70 Lincoln Street, Boston, Massachusetts 02111 (617) 423-3990; *The World in Figures*.

VIRGIN ISLANDS - AREA AND DENSITY OF POPULATION

Food and Agricultural Organization of the United Nations (FAO) Via delle Terme di Caracalla, 00100 Rome, Italy (Telephone Number in U.S. (202) 653-2400); *The State of Food and Agriculture*.

G.K. Hall and Company, 70 Lincoln Street, Boston, Massachusetts 02111 (617) 423-3990; *The World in Figures*.

VIRGIN ISLANDS - BALANCE OF PAYMENTS

G.K. Hall and Company, 70 Lincoln Street, Boston, Massachusetts 02111 (617) 423-3990; *The World in Figures*.

VIRGIN ISLANDS - BANKING

G.K. Hall and Company, 70 Lincoln Street, Boston, Massachusetts 02111 (617) 423-3990; *The World in Figures*.

VIRGIN ISLANDS - BONDS

G.K. Hall and Company, 70 Lincoln Street, Boston, Massachusetts 02111 (617) 423-3990; *The World in Figures*.

VIRGIN ISLANDS - BOOK PRODUCTION

G.K. Hall and Company, 70 Lincoln Street, Boston, Massachusetts 02111 (617) 423-3990; *The World in Figures*.

VIRGIN ISLANDS - BROADCASTING

Billboard Limited, P.O. Box 9027, 1006 AA Amsterdam, The Netherlands (Telephone Number in U.S. (212) 764-7300); *World Radio TV Handbook*.

G.K. Hall and Company, 70 Lincoln Street, Boston, Massachusetts 02111 (617) 423-3990; *The World in Figures*.

United Nations Educational, Scientific and Cultural Organization (UNESCO), 7 Place de Fontenoy, F-75700 Paris, France (Telephone Number in U.S. (212) 963-5981); *Statistical Yearbook*.

VIRGIN ISLANDS - BUSINESS

G.K. Hall and Company, 70 Lincoln Street, Boston, Massachusetts 02111 (617) 423-3990; *The World in Figures*.

VIRGIN ISLANDS - CALORIE SUPPLY

Food and Agricultural Organization of the United Nations (FAO) Via delle Terme di Caracalla, 00100 Rome, Italy (Telephone Number in U.S. (202) 653-2400); *The State of Food and Agriculture*.

VIRGIN ISLANDS - CHEMICAL (ORGANIC) PRODUCTION - See VIRGIN ISLANDS - MINING AND MINERAL PRODUCTS

VIRGIN ISLANDS - CLASS STRUCTURE

G.K. Hall and Company, 70 Lincoln Street, Boston, Massachusetts 02111 (617) 423-3990; *The World in Figures*.

VIRGIN ISLANDS - CLIMATE

G.K. Hall and Company, 70 Lincoln Street, Boston, Massachusetts 02111 (617) 423-3990; *The World in Figures.*

VIRGIN ISLANDS - COAL PRODUCTION - See VIRGIN ISLANDS - MINING AND MINERAL PRODUCTS

VIRGIN ISLANDS - CORN PRODUCTION - See VIRGIN ISLANDS - CROPS

VIRGIN ISLANDS - COMMUNICATIONS

G.K. Hall and Company, 70 Lincoln Street, Boston, Massachusetts 02111 (617) 423-3990; *The World in Figures.*

VIRGIN ISLANDS - CONSUMER PRICE INDEX

G.K. Hall and Company, 70 Lincoln Street, Boston, Massachusetts 02111 (617) 423-3990; *The World in Figures.*

VIRGIN ISLANDS - CONSUMPTION

G.K. Hall and Company, 70 Lincoln Street, Boston, Massachusetts 02111 (617) 423-3990; *The World in Figures.*

VIRGIN ISLANDS - CORPORATE TAXES - See VIRGIN ISLANDS - TAXATION

VIRGIN ISLANDS - CUSTOMS DUTIES

G.K. Hall and Company, 70 Lincoln Street, Boston, Massachusetts 02111 (617) 423-3990; *The World in Figures.*

VIRGIN ISLANDS - CROPS

Food and Agricultural Organization of the United Nations (FAO) Via delle Terme di Caracalla, 00100 Rome, Italy (Telephone Number in U.S. (202) 653-2400); *The State of Food and Agriculture.*

G.K. Hall and Company, 70 Lincoln Street, Boston, Massachusetts 02111 (617) 423-3990; *The World in Figures.*

VIRGIN ISLANDS - DAIRY PRODUCTS

Food and Agricultural Organization of the United Nations (FAO) Via delle Terme di Caracalla, 00100 Rome, Italy (Telephone Number in U.S. (202) 653-2400); *The State of Food and Agriculture.*

VIRGIN ISLANDS - DEATH RATES

G.K. Hall and Company, 70 Lincoln Street, Boston, Massachusetts 02111 (617) 423-3990; *The World in Figures.*

VIRGIN ISLANDS - DEFENSE EXPENDITURES

G.K. Hall and Company, 70 Lincoln Street, Boston, Massachusetts 02111 (617) 423-3990; *The World in Figures.*

VIRGIN ISLANDS - DEMOGRAPHY

G.K. Hall and Company, 70 Lincoln Street, Boston, Massachusetts 02111 (617) 423-3990; *The World in Figures.*

VIRGIN ISLANDS - DEVELOPMENT ASSISTANCE

G.K. Hall and Company, 70 Lincoln Street, Boston, Massachusetts 02111 (617) 423-3990; *The World in Figures.*

VIRGIN ISLANDS - DISEASE

G.K. Hall and Company, 70 Lincoln Street, Boston, Massachusetts 02111 (617) 423-3990; *The World in Figures.*

VIRGIN ISLANDS - DOMESTIC PRODUCT

G.K. Hall and Company, 70 Lincoln Street, Boston, Massachusetts 02111 (617) 423-3990; *The World in Figures.*

VIRGIN ISLANDS - ECONOMY

G.K. Hall and Company, 70 Lincoln Street, Boston, Massachusetts 02111 (617) 423-3990; *The World in Figures.*

VIRGIN ISLANDS - EDUCATION

G.K. Hall and Company, 70 Lincoln Street, Boston, Massachusetts 02111 (617) 423-3990; *The World in Figures.*

United Nations Educational, Scientific and Cultural Organization (UNESCO), 7 Place de Fontenoy, F-75700 Paris, France (Telephone Number in U.S. (212) 963-5981); *Statistical Yearbook.*

VIRGIN ISLANDS - EGG PRODUCTION AND CONSUMPTION - See VIRGIN ISLANDS - DAIRY PRODUCTS

VIRGIN ISLANDS - ELECTRICITY

Statistical Office of the United Nations, Publishing Service, New York, New York 10017 (800) 253-9646; *Statistical Yearbook.*

VIRGIN ISLANDS - ENERGY

Food and Agricultural Organization of the United Nations (FAO) Via delle Terme di Caracalla, 00100 Rome, Italy (Telephone Number in U.S. (202) 653-2400); *The State of Food and Agriculture.*

G.K. Hall and Company, 70 Lincoln Street, Boston, Massachusetts 02111 (617) 423-3990; *The World in Figures.*

Statistical Office of the United Nations, Publishing Service, New York, New York 10017 (800) 253-9646; *Energy Statistics Yearbook*, and *Statistical Yearbook.*

VIRGIN ISLANDS - EXPORTS

Food and Agricultural Organization of the United Nations (FAO) Via delle Terme di Caracalla, 00100 Rome, Italy (Telephone Number in U.S. (202) 653-2400); *The State of Food and Agriculture.*

G.K. Hall and Company, 70 Lincoln Street, Boston, Massachusetts 02111 (617) 423-3990; *The World in Figures.*

VIRGIN ISLANDS - EXTERNAL TRADE

Food and Agricultural Organization of the United Nations (FAO) Via delle Terme di Caracalla, 00100 Rome, Italy (Telephone Number in U.S. (202) 653-2400); *The State of Food and Agriculture.*

G.K. Hall and Company, 70 Lincoln Street, Boston, Massachusetts 02111 (617) 423-3990; *The World in Figures.*

VIRGIN ISLANDS - FARM CROPS - See VIRGIN ISLANDS - CROPS

VIRGIN ISLANDS - FERTILIZER PRODUCTION AND CONSUMPTION

Food and Agricultural Organization of the United Nations (FAO) Via delle Terme di Caracalla, 00100 Rome, Italy (Telephone Number in

U.S. (202) 653-2400); *The State of Food and Agriculture.*

VIRGIN ISLANDS - FINANCE

G.K. Hall and Company, 70 Lincoln Street, Boston, Massachusetts 02111 (617) 423-3990; *The World in Figures.*

VIRGIN ISLANDS - FISHERIES

Food and Agricultural Organization of the United Nations (FAO) Via delle Terme di Caracalla, 00100 Rome, Italy (Telephone Number in U.S. (202) 653-2400); *The State of Food and Agriculture.*

VIRGIN ISLANDS - FOOD

Food and Agricultural Organization of the United Nations (FAO) Via delle Terme di Caracalla, 00100 Rome, Italy (Telephone Number in U.S. (202) 653-2400); *The State of Food and Agriculture.*

G.K. Hall and Company, 70 Lincoln Street, Boston, Massachusetts 02111 (617) 423-3990; *The World in Figures.*

VIRGIN ISLANDS - FOREIGN AID

G.K. Hall and Company, 70 Lincoln Street, Boston, Massachusetts 02111 (617) 423-3990; *The World in Figures.*

VIRGIN ISLANDS - FOREIGN TRADE

Food and Agricultural Organization of the United Nations (FAO) Via delle Terme di Caracalla, 00100 Rome, Italy (Telephone Number in U.S. (202) 653-2400); *The State of Food and Agriculture.*

G.K. Hall and Company, 70 Lincoln Street, Boston, Massachusetts 02111 (617) 423-3990; *Tho World in Figures.*

VIRGIN ISLANDS - FORESTRY AND FOREST PRODUCTS

Food and Agricultural Organization of the United Nations (FAO) Via delle Terme di Caracalla, 00100 Rome, Italy (Telephone Number in U.S. (202) 653-2400); *The State of Food and Agriculture.*

G.K. Hall and Company, 70 Lincoln Street, Boston, Massachusetts 02111 (617) 423-3990; *The World in Figures.*

Statistical Office of the United Nations, Publishing Service, New York, New York 10017 (800) 253-9646; *Statistical Yearbook.*

United Nations Educational, Scientific and Cultural Organization (UNESCO), 7 Place de Fontenoy, F-75700 Paris, France (Telephone Number in U.S. (212) 963-5981); *Statistical Yearbook.*

VIRGIN ISLANDS - GOVERNMENT

G.K. Hall and Company, 70 Lincoln Street, Boston, Massachusetts 02111 (617) 423-3990; *The World in Figures.*

VIRGIN ISLANDS - GRAIN PRODUCTION - See VIRGIN ISLANDS - CROPS

VIRGIN ISLANDS - GROSS DOMESTIC PRODUCT

G.K. Hall and Company, 70 Lincoln Street, Boston, Massachusetts 02111 (617) 423-3990; *The World in Figures.*

VIRGIN ISLANDS - HEALTH

G.K. Hall and Company, 70 Lincoln Street, Boston, Massachusetts 02111 (617) 423-3990; *The World in Figures.*

Statistical Office of the United Nations, Publishing Service, New York, New York 10017 (800) 253-9646; *Statistical Yearbook.*

VIRGIN ISLANDS - HIDE PRODUCTION

Food and Agricultural Organization of the United Nations (FAO), Via delle Terme di Caracalla, 00100 Rome, Italy (Telephone Number in U.S. (202) 653-2400); *Production Yearbook.*

VIRGIN ISLANDS - HIGHWAYS

G.K. Hall and Company, 70 Lincoln Street, Boston, Massachusetts 02111 (617) 423-3990; *The World in Figures.*

VIRGIN ISLANDS - ILLITERATE POPULATION

G.K. Hall and Company, 70 Lincoln Street, Boston, Massachusetts 02111 (617) 423-3990; *The World in Figures.*

VIRGIN ISLANDS - IMPORTS

Food and Agricultural Organization of the United Nations (FAO) Via delle Terme di Caracalla, 00100 Rome, Italy (Telephone Number in U.S. (202) 653-2400); *The State of Food and Agriculture.*

G.K. Hall and Company, 70 Lincoln Street, Boston, Massachusetts 02111 (617) 423-3990; *The World in Figures.*

VIRGIN ISLANDS - INDUSTRY

G.K. Hall and Company, 70 Lincoln Street, Boston, Massachusetts 02111 (617) 423-3990; *The World in Figures.*

VIRGIN ISLANDS - LABOR FORCE

Food and Agricultural Organization of the United Nations (FAO) Via delle Terme di Caracalla, 00100 Rome, Italy (Telephone Number in U.S. (202) 653-2400); *The State of Food and Agriculture.*

G.K. Hall and Company, 70 Lincoln Street, Boston, Massachusetts 02111 (617) 423-3990; *The World in Figures.*

VIRGIN ISLANDS - LAND USE

G.K. Hall and Company, 70 Lincoln Street, Boston, Massachusetts 02111 (617) 423-3990; *The World in Figures.*

VIRGIN ISLANDS - LIBRARIES

United Nations Educational, Scientific and Cultural Organization (UNESCO), 7 Place de Fontenoy, F-75700 Paris, France (Telephone Number in U.S. (212) 963-5981); *Statistical Yearbook.*

VIRGIN ISLANDS - LIVESTOCK AND POULTRY

Food and Agricultural Organization of the United Nations (FAO), Via delle Terme di Caracalla, 00100 Rome, Italy (Telephone Number in U.S. (202) 653-2400); *Production Yearbook,* and *The State of Food and Agriculture.*

G.K. Hall and Company, 70 Lincoln Street, Boston, Massachusetts 02111 (617) 423-3990; *The World in Figures.*

VIRGIN ISLANDS - LIVING LEVELS

G.K. Hall and Company, 70 Lincoln Street, Boston, Massachusetts 02111 (617) 423-3990; *The World in Figures.*

VIRGIN ISLANDS - MANUFACTURING

G.K. Hall and Company, 70 Lincoln Street, Boston, Massachusetts 02111 (617) 423-3990; *The World in Figures.*

VIRGIN ISLANDS - MEAT PRODUCTION - See VIRGIN ISLANDS - LIVESTOCK AND POULTRY

VIRGIN ISLANDS - MERCHANT SHIPPING

G.K. Hall and Company, 70 Lincoln Street, Boston, Massachusetts 02111 (617) 423-3990; *The World in Figures.*

VIRGIN ISLANDS - MILITARY

G.K. Hall and Company, 70 Lincoln Street, Boston, Massachusetts 02111 (617) 423-3990; *The World in Figures.*

VIRGIN ISLANDS - MINING AND MINERAL PRODUCTS

G.K. Hall and Company, 70 Lincoln Street, Boston, Massachusetts 02111 (617) 423-3990; *The World in Figures.*

VIRGIN ISLANDS - MONEY SUPPLY

G.K. Hall and Company, 70 Lincoln Street, Boston, Massachusetts 02111 (617) 423-3990; *The World in Figures.*

VIRGIN ISLANDS - MONUMENTS AND HISTORICAL SITES

United Nations Educational, Scientific and Cultural Organization (UNESCO), 7 Place de Fontenoy, F-75700 Paris, France (Telephone Number in U.S. (212) 963-5981); *Statistical Yearbook.*

VIRGIN ISLANDS - MOTOR VEHICLES IN USE

G.K. Hall and Company, 70 Lincoln Street, Boston, Massachusetts 02111 (617) 423-3990; *The World in Figures.*

VIRGIN ISLANDS - MUSEUMS

United Nations Educational, Scientific and Cultural Organization (UNESCO), 7 Place de Fontenoy, F-75700 Paris, France (Telephone Number in U.S. (212) 963-5981); *Statistical Yearbook.*

VIRGIN ISLANDS - NATIONAL INCOME

G.K. Hall and Company, 70 Lincoln Street, Boston, Massachusetts 02111 (617) 423-3990; *The World in Figures.*

VIRGIN ISLANDS - NEWSPAPER PRODUCTION - See VIRGIN ISLANDS - FORESTRY AND FOREST PRODUCTS

VIRGIN ISLANDS - OCCUPATIONS - See VIRGIN ISLANDS - LABOR FORCE

VIRGIN ISLANDS - PESTICIDE USE

Food and Agricultural Organization of the United Nations (FAO) Via delle Terme di Caracalla, 00100 Rome, Italy (Telephone Number in U.S. (202) 653-2400); *The State of Food and Agriculture.*

VIRGIN ISLANDS - PETROLEUM INDUSTRY

Food and Agricultural Organization of the United Nations (FAO) Via delle Terme di Caracalla, 00100 Rome, Italy (Telephone Number in U.S. (202) 653-2400); *The State of Food and Agriculture.*

G.K. Hall and Company, 70 Lincoln Street, Boston, Massachusetts 02111 (617) 423-3990; *The World in Figures.*

VIRGIN ISLANDS - POPULATION

G.K. Hall and Company, 70 Lincoln Street, Boston, Massachusetts 02111 (617) 423-3990; *The World in Figures.*

VIRGIN ISLANDS - PRICES

Food and Agricultural Organization of the United Nations (FAO) Via delle Terme di Caracalla, 00100 Rome, Italy (Telephone Number in U.S. (202) 653-2400); *The State of Food and Agriculture.*

G.K. Hall and Company, 70 Lincoln Street, Boston, Massachusetts 02111 (617) 423-3990; *The World in Figures.*

VIRGIN ISLANDS - PRODUCTION

G.K. Hall and Company, 70 Lincoln Street, Boston, Massachusetts 02111 (617) 423-3990; *The World in Figures.*

VIRGIN ISLANDS - RADIO BROADCASTING - See VIRGIN ISLANDS - BROADCASTING

VIRGIN ISLANDS - RAILWAYS

G.K. Hall and Company, 70 Lincoln Street, Boston, Massachusetts 02111 (617) 423-3990; *The World in Figures.*

VIRGIN ISLANDS - RETAIL TRADE

G.K. Hall and Company, 70 Lincoln Street, Boston, Massachusetts 02111 (617) 423-3990; *The World in Figures.*

VIRGIN ISLANDS - SOCIAL DATA

G.K. Hall and Company, 70 Lincoln Street, Boston, Massachusetts 02111 (617) 423-3990; *The World in Figures.*

VIRGIN ISLANDS - STOCKS - COMMODITY - MARKET PRICE - INDEX

Food and Agricultural Organization of the United Nations (FAO) Via delle Terme di Caracalla, 00100 Rome, Italy (Telephone Number in U.S. (202) 653-2400); *The State of Food and Agriculture.*

VIRGIN ISLANDS - TAXATION

G.K. Hall and Company, 70 Lincoln Street, Boston, Massachusetts 02111 (617) 423-3990; *The World in Figures.*

VIRGIN ISLANDS - TELEPHONES IN USE

American Telephone and Telegraph Company, 26 Parsippany Road, Whippany, New Jersey 07981 (800) 338-4038; *The World's Telephones.*

G.K. Hall and Company, 70 Lincoln Street, Boston, Massachusetts 02111 (617) 423-3990; *The World in Figures.*

VIRGIN ISLANDS - TELEVISION BROADCASTING - See VIRGIN ISLANDS - BROADCASTING

VIRGIN ISLANDS - TEXTILE INDUSTRY

G.K. Hall and Company, 70 Lincoln Street, Boston, Massachusetts 02111 (617) 423-3990; *The World in Figures.*

VIRGIN ISLANDS - TOURISM

G.K. Hall and Company, 70 Lincoln Street, Boston, Massachusetts 02111 (617) 423-3990; *The World in Figures.*

World Tourism Organization, Calle Capitan Haya 42, E-28020 Madrid, Spain; *Yearbook of Tourism Statistics.*

VIRGIN ISLANDS - TRADE - See VIRGIN ISLANDS - FOREIGN TRADE

VIRGIN ISLANDS - TRANSPORTATION AND COMMUNICATIONS

G.K. Hall and Company, 70 Lincoln Street, Boston, Massachusetts 02111 (617) 423-3990; *The World in Figures.*

VIRGIN ISLANDS - VITAL STATISTICS

G.K. Hall and Company, 70 Lincoln Street, Boston, Massachusetts 02111 (617) 423-3990; *The World in Figures.*

VIRGIN ISLANDS - WAGES

G.K. Hall and Company, 70 Lincoln Street, Boston, Massachusetts 02111 (617) 423-3990; *The World in Figures.*

VIRGIN ISLANDS - WEATHER

G.K. Hall and Company, 70 Lincoln Street, Boston, Massachusetts 02111 (617) 423-3990; *The World in Figures.*

VIRGIN ISLANDS - ZOOS AND BOTANICAL GARDENS

United Nations Educational, Scientific and Cultural Organization (UNESCO), 7 Place de Fontenoy, F-75700 Paris, France (Telephone Number in U.S. (212) 963-5981); *Statistical Yearbook.*

VIRGINIA - See also STATE DATA (FOR INDIVIDUAL STATES)

Virginia - Primary Statistics Source

University of Virginia, Center for Public Service, Dynamics Building, Fourth Floor, 2015 Ivy Road, Charlottesville, Virginia 22204 (804) 924-3921; *Virginia Statistical Abstract.*

Virginia - State Data Centers

Virginia Employment Commission, 703 East Main Street, Richmond, Virginia 23219, Mr. Dan Jones (804) 786-8308.

Center for Public Service, University of Virginia, 918 Emmet Street, North, Suite 300, Charlottesville, Virginia 22903-4823, Dr. Michael Spar (804) 982-5585.

Virginia State Library, Documents Section, Eleventh Street at Capitol Square, Richmond, Virginia 23219-3491, Mr. William Chamberlin (804) 786-2303.

VISUAL IMPAIRMENT

U.S. Department of Health and Human Services, National Center for Health Statistics, 3700 East-West Highway, Hyattsville, Maryland 20782 (301) 436-8500; *Vital and Health Statistics,* and unpublished data.

VITAL STATISTICS - See also BIRTHS and DEATHS

VITAL STATISTICS - FERTILITY AND FERTILITY RATE

U.S. Department of Commerce, Bureau of the Census, Suitland, Maryland 20233 (301) 763-4040; *Current Population Reports,* and unpublished data.

U.S. Department of Health and Human Services, National Center for Health Statistics, 3700 East-West Highway, Hyattsville, Maryland 20782 (301) 436-8500; *Vital Statistics of the United States,* and unpublished data.

VITAL STATISTICS - LIFE EXPECTANCY

U.S. Department of Health and Human Services, National Center for Health Statistics, 3700 East-West Highway, Hyattsville, Maryland 20782 (301) 436-8500; *Vital Statistics of the United States, Monthly Vital Statistics Report,* and unpublished data.

VITAL STATISTICS - MARRIAGE AND DIVORCE

U.S. Department of Commerce, Bureau of the Census, Suitland, Maryland 20233 (301) 763-4040; *Current Population Reports,* and *Census of Population.*

U.S. Department of Health and Human Services, National Center for Health Statistics, 3700 East-West Highway, Hyattsville, Maryland 20782 (301) 436-8500; *Vital Statistics of the United States, Monthly Vital Statistics Report,* and unpublished data.

VITAL STATISTICS - OUTLYING AREAS

Statistical Office of the United Nations, New York, New York 10017 (800) 253-9646; *Demographic Yearbook.*

U.S. Department of Commerce, Bureau of the Census, Suitland, Maryland 20233 (301) 763-4040; *Current Population Reports,* and unpublished data.

U.S. Department of Health and Human Services, National Center for Health Statistics, 3700 East-West Highway, Hyattsville, Maryland 20782 (301) 436-8500; *Vital Statistics of the United States.*

VITAL STATISTICS - RATES - SUMMARY

U.S. Department of Health and Human Services, National Center for Health Statistics, 3700 East-West Highway, Hyattsville, Maryland 20782 (301) 436-8500; *Vital Statistics of the United States, Monthly Vital Statistics Report,* and unpublished data.

VITAL STATISTICS - WORLD

Statistical Office of the United Nations, New York, New York 10017 (800) 253-9646; *Monthly Bulletin of Statistics.*

U.S. Department of Commerce, Bureau of the Census, Suitland, Maryland 20233 (301) 763-4040; *International Data Base.*

VITAMINS

U.S. Department of Agriculture, Human Nutrition Information Service, Hyattsville, Maryland 20782 (301) 436-7725; data published by Economic Research Service in *Food Consumption, Prices, and Expenditures,* and *National Food Review.*

U.S. Department of Health and Human Services, National Center for Health Statistics, 3700 East-West Highway, Hyattsville, Maryland 20782 (301) 436-8500; *Advance Data from Vital and Health*

Statistics.

VOCATIONAL EDUCATION

Executive Office of the President, Office of Management and Budget, Executive Office Building, Washington, D.C. 20503 (202) 395-3080; *Historical Tables, Budget of the United States Government,* and *Budget of the U.S. Government.*

U.S. Department of Health and Human Services, Social Security Administration, 6401 Security Boulevard, Baltimore, Maryland 21235 (410) 965-1234; *Social Security Bulletin.*

U.S. Department of Veterans Affairs, 810 Vermont Avenue, NW, Washington, D.C. 20420 (202) 233-2300; *Annual Report of the Secretary of Veterans Affairs,* and unpublished data.

VOCATIONAL REHABILITATION

U.S. Department of Education, 400 Maryland Avenue, SW, Washington, D.C. 20202 (202) 708-5366; *State Vocational Rehabilitation Agency Program Data in Fiscal Years,* and *Caseload Statistics of State Vocational Rehabilitation Agencies in Fiscal Years.*

U.S. Department of Health and Human Services, Social Security Administration, 6401 Security Boulevard, Baltimore, Maryland 21235 (410) 965-1234; *Social Security Bulletin.*

VOCATIONAL REHABILITATION - MEDICAL PAYMENTS

U.S. Department of Health and Human Services, Health Care Financing Administration, 200 Independence Avenue, SW, Washington, D.C. 20201 (202) 245-6113; *Health Care Financing Review.*

VOLLEYBALL

National Sporting Goods Association, Lake Center Plaza Building, 1699 Wall Street, Mount Prospect, Illinois 60056-5780 (708) 439-4000; *Sports Participation in 1992.*

VOTER REGISTRATION

U.S. Department of Commerce, Bureau of the Census, Suitland, Maryland 20233 (301) 763-4040; *Current Population Reports.*

VOTER TURNOUT

Elections Research Center, 5508 Greystone Street, Chevy Chase, Maryland 20815 (202) 659-9490; *America Votes.*

U.S. Department of Commerce, Bureau of the Census, Suitland, Maryland 20233 (301) 763-4040; *Current Population Reports.*

VOTES - CONGRESSIONAL

Congressional Quarterly, Incorporated, 1414 22nd Street, NW, Washington, D.C. 20037 (202) 887-8500; *Congressional Quarterly Weekly Report.*

Elections Research Center, 5508 Greystone Street, Chevy Chase, Maryland 20815 (202) 659-9490; *America Votes.*

United States Congress, Clerk of the House, The Capitol, Washington, D.C. 20515 (202) 224-3121; *Statistics of the Presidential and Congressional Election.*

United States Congress, Joint Committee on Printing, North Capitol and H Streets, NW, Washington, D.C. 20401 (202) 275-2051; *Congressional Directory.*

U.S. Department of Commerce, Bureau of the Census, Suitland, Maryland 20233 (301) 763-4040; *Current Population Reports.*

VOTES - GUBERNATORIAL

Congressional Quarterly, Incorporated, 1414 Twenty-second Street, NW, Washington, D.C. 20037 (202) 887-8500; *Congressional Quarterly Weekly Report.*

Elections Research Center, 5508 Greystone Street, Chevy Chase, Maryland 20815 (202) 659-9490; *America Votes.*

United States Congress, Joint Committee on Printing, North Capitol and H Streets, NW, Washington, D.C. 20401 (202) 275-2051; *Congressional Directory.*

VOTES - PRESIDENTIAL

Center for Political Studies, University of Michigan, Post Office Box 1248, Ann Arbor, Michigan 48106 (313) 764-8363; unpublished data.

Elections Research Center, 5508 Greystone Street, Chevy Chase, Maryland 20815 (202) 659-9490; *America Votes.*

United States Congress, Clerk of the House, The Capitol, Washington, D.C. 20515 (202) 224-3121; *Statistics of the Presidential and Congressional Elections.*

United States Congress, Joint Committee on Printing, North Capitol and H Streets, NW, Washington, D.C. 20401 (202) 275-2051; *Congressional Directory.*

U.S. Department of Commerce, Bureau of the Census, Suitland, Maryland 20233 (301) 763-4040; *Current Population Reports,* and unpublished data.

VOTING AGE POPULATION

Elections Research Center, 5508 Greystone Street, Chevy Chase, Maryland 20815 (202) 659-9490; *America Votes.*

U.S. Department of Commerce, Bureau of the Census, Suitland, Maryland 20233 (301) 763-4040; *Current Population Reports,* and unpublished data.

W

WAGE EARNERS - See LABOR FORCE, EMPLOYMENT AND EARNINGS and Individual Industries

WAGES AND WAGE RATES - See EARNINGS

WAKE ISLAND - AGRICULTURE

Food and Agricultural Organization of the United Nations (FAO) Via delle Terme di Caracalla, 00100 Rome, Italy (Telephone Number in U.S. (202) 653-2400); *The State of Food and Agriculture.*

G.K. Hall and Company, 70 Lincoln Street, Boston, Massachusetts 02111 (617) 423-3990; *The World in Figures.*

WAKE ISLAND - AIRLINE SERVICE

G.K. Hall and Company, 70 Lincoln Street, Boston, Massachusetts 02111 (617) 423-3990; *The World in Figures.*

WAKE ISLAND - AREA AND DENSITY OF POPULATION

Food and Agricultural Organization of the United Nations (FAO) Via delle Terme di Caracalla, 00100 Rome, Italy (Telephone Number in U.S. (202) 653-2400); *The State of Food and Agriculture.*

G.K. Hall and Company, 70 Lincoln Street, Boston, Massachusetts 02111 (617) 423-3990; *The World in Figures.*

Statistical Office of the United Nations, Publishing Service, New York, New York 10017 (800) 253-9646; *Statistical Yearbook.*

WAKE ISLAND - BALANCE OF PAYMENTS

G.K. Hall and Company, 70 Lincoln Street, Boston, Massachusetts 02111 (617) 423-3990; *The World in Figures.*

WAKE ISLAND - BANKING

G.K. Hall and Company, 70 Lincoln Street, Boston, Massachusetts 02111 (617) 423-3990; *The World in Figures.*

WAKE ISLAND - BIRTH RATES

Statistical Office of the United Nations, Publishing Service, New York, New York 10017 (800) 253-9646; *Demographic Yearbook.*

WAKE ISLAND - BONDS

G.K. Hall and Company, 70 Lincoln Street, Boston, Massachusetts 02111 (617) 423-3990; *The World in Figures.*

WAKE ISLAND - BOOK PRODUCTION

G.K. Hall and Company, 70 Lincoln Street, Boston, Massachusetts 02111 (617) 423-3990; *The World in Figures.*

WAKE ISLAND - BROADCASTING

Billboard Limited, P.O. Box 9027, 1006 AA Amsterdam, The Netherlands (Telephone Number in U.S. (212) 764-7300); *World Radio TV Handbook.*

G.K. Hall and Company, 70 Lincoln Street, Boston, Massachusetts 02111 (617) 423-3990; *The World in Figures.*

WAKE ISLAND - BUSINESS

G.K. Hall and Company, 70 Lincoln Street, Boston, Massachusetts 02111 (617) 423-3990; *The World in Figures.*

WAKE ISLAND - CALORIE SUPPLY

Food and Agricultural Organization of the United Nations (FAO) Via delle Terme di Caracalla, 00100 Rome, Italy (Telephone Number in U.S. (202) 653-2400); *The State of Food and Agriculture.*

WAKE ISLAND - CHEMICAL (ORGANIC) PRODUCTION - See WAKE ISLAND - MINING AND MINERAL PRODUCTS

WAKE ISLAND - CLASS STRUCTURE

G.K. Hall and Company, 70 Lincoln Street, Boston, Massachusetts 02111 (617) 423-3990; *The World in Figures.*

WAKE ISLAND - CLIMATE

G.K. Hall and Company, 70 Lincoln Street, Boston, Massachusetts 02111 (617) 423-3990; *The World in Figures.*

WAKE ISLAND - COAL PRODUCTION - See WAKE ISLAND - MINING AND MINERAL PRODUCTS

WAKE ISLAND - COMMUNICATIONS

G.K. Hall and Company, 70 Lincoln Street, Boston, Massachusetts 02111 (617) 423-3990; *The World in Figures.*

WAKE ISLAND - CONSUMER PRICE INDEX

G.K. Hall and Company, 70 Lincoln Street, Boston, Massachusetts 02111 (617) 423-3990; *The World in Figures.*

WAKE ISLAND - CONSUMPTION

G.K. Hall and Company, 70 Lincoln Street, Boston, Massachusetts 02111 (617) 423-3990; *The World in Figures.*

WAKE ISLAND - CORN PRODUCTION - See WAKE ISLAND - CROPS

WAKE ISLAND - CORPORATE TAXES - See WAKE ISLAND - TAXATION

WAKE ISLAND - CROPS

Food and Agricultural Organization of the United Nations (FAO) Via delle Terme di Caracalla, 00100 Rome, Italy (Telephone Number in U.S. (202) 653-2400); *The State of Food and Agriculture.*

G.K. Hall and Company, 70 Lincoln Street, Boston, Massachusetts 02111 (617) 423-3990; *The World in Figures.*

WAKE ISLAND - DAIRY PRODUCTS

Food and Agricultural Organization of the United Nations (FAO) Via delle Terme di Caracalla, 00100 Rome, Italy (Telephone Number in U.S. (202) 653-2400); *The State of Food and Agriculture.*

WAKE ISLAND - CUSTOMS DUTIES

G.K. Hall and Company, 70 Lincoln Street, Boston, Massachusetts 02111 (617) 423-3990; *The World in Figures.*

WAKE ISLAND - DEATH RATES

G.K. Hall and Company, 70 Lincoln Street, Boston, Massachusetts 02111 (617) 423-3990; *The World in Figures.*

World Health Organization, Office of Publications, Avenue Appia, CH-1211 Geneva 27, Switzerland (Telephone Number in U.S. (518) 436-9686); *World Health Statistics Annual.*

WAKE ISLAND - DEFENSE EXPENDITURES

G.K. Hall and Company, 70 Lincoln Street, Boston, Massachusetts 02111 (617) 423-3990; *The World in Figures.*

WAKE ISLAND - DEMOGRAPHY

G.K. Hall and Company, 70 Lincoln Street, Boston, Massachusetts 02111 (617) 423-3990; *The World in Figures.*

WAKE ISLAND - DEVELOPMENT ASSISTANCE

G.K. Hall and Company, 70 Lincoln Street, Boston, Massachusetts 02111 (617) 423-3990; *The World in Figures.*

WAKE ISLAND - DISEASE

G.K. Hall and Company, 70 Lincoln Street, Boston, Massachusetts 02111 (617) 423-3990; *The World in Figures.*

WAKE ISLAND - DIVORCE RATES

Statistical Office of the United Nations, Publishing Service, New York, New York 10017 (800) 253-9646; *Demographic Yearbook.*

WAKE ISLAND - DOMESTIC PRODUCT

G.K. Hall and Company, 70 Lincoln Street, Boston, Massachusetts 02111 (617) 423-3990; *The World in Figures.*

WAKE ISLAND - ECONOMY

G.K. Hall and Company, 70 Lincoln Street, Boston, Massachusetts 02111 (617) 423-3990; *The World in Figures.*

WAKE ISLAND - EDUCATION

G.K. Hall and Company, 70 Lincoln Street, Boston, Massachusetts 02111 (617) 423-3990; *The World in Figures.*

WAKE ISLAND - EGG PRODUCTION AND CONSUMPTION - See WAKE ISLAND - DAIRY PRODUCTS

WAKE ISLAND - ENERGY

Food and Agricultural Organization of the United Nations (FAO) Via delle Terme di Caracalla, 00100 Rome, Italy (Telephone Number in U.S. (202) 653-2400); *The State of Food and Agriculture.*

G.K. Hall and Company, 70 Lincoln Street, Boston, Massachusetts 02111 (617) 423-3990; *The World in Figures.*

Statistical Office of the United Nations, Publishing Service, New York, New York 10017 (800) 253-9646; *Statistical Yearbook.*

WAKE ISLAND - EXPORTS

Food and Agricultural Organization of the United Nations (FAO) Via delle Terme di Caracalla, 00100 Rome, Italy (Telephone Number in U.S. (202) 653-2400); *The State of Food and Agriculture.*

G.K. Hall and Company, 70 Lincoln Street, Boston, Massachusetts 02111 (617) 423-3990; *The World in Figures.*

WAKE ISLAND - EXTERNAL TRADE

Food and Agricultural Organization of the United Nations (FAO) Via delle Terme di Caracalla, 00100 Rome, Italy (Telephone Number in U.S. (202) 653-2400); *The State of Food and Agriculture.*

G.K. Hall and Company, 70 Lincoln Street, Boston, Massachusetts 02111 (617) 423-3990; *The World in Figures.*

WAKE ISLAND - FARM CROPS - See WAKE ISLAND - CROPS

WAKE ISLAND - FERTILIZER

Food and Agricultural Organization of the United Nations (FAO) Via delle Terme di Caracalla, 00100 Rome, Italy (Telephone Number in U.S. (202) 653-2400); *The State of Food and Agriculture.*

WAKE ISLAND - FETAL MORTALITY

Statistical Office of the United Nations, Publishing Service, New York, New York 10017 (800) 253-9646; *Demographic Yearbook.*

WAKE ISLAND - FINANCE

G.K. Hall and Company, 70 Lincoln Street, Boston, Massachusetts 02111 (617) 423-3990; *The World in Figures.*

WAKE ISLAND - FOOD

G.K. Hall and Company, 70 Lincoln Street, Boston, Massachusetts 02111 (617) 423-3990; *The World in Figures.*

WAKE ISLAND - FOREIGN AID

G.K. Hall and Company, 70 Lincoln Street, Boston, Massachusetts 02111 (617) 423-3990; *The World in Figures.*

WAKE ISLAND - FOREIGN TRADE

Food and Agricultural Organization of the United Nations (FAO) Via delle Terme di Caracalla, 00100 Rome, Italy (Telephone Number in U.S. (202) 653-2400); *The State of Food and Agriculture.*

G.K. Hall and Company, 70 Lincoln Street, Boston, Massachusetts 02111 (617) 423-3990; *The World in Figures.*

WAKE ISLAND - FORESTRY AND FOREST PRODUCTS

G.K. Hall and Company, 70 Lincoln Street, Boston, Massachusetts 02111 (617) 423-3990; *The World in Figures.*

WAKE ISLAND - GENERAL MORTALITY

Statistical Office of the United Nations, Publishing Service, New York, New York 10017 (800) 253-9646; *Demographic Yearbook.*

World Health Organization, Office of Publications, Avenue Appia, CH-1211 Geneva 27, Switzerland (Telephone Number in U.S. (518) 436-9686); *World Health Statistics Annual.*

WAKE ISLAND - GOVERNMENT

G.K. Hall and Company, 70 Lincoln Street, Boston, Massachusetts 02111 (617) 423-3990; *The World in Figures.*

WAKE ISLAND - GRAIN PRODUCTION - See WAKE ISLAND - CROPS

WAKE ISLAND - GROSS DOMESTIC PRODUCT

G.K. Hall and Company, 70 Lincoln Street, Boston, Massachusetts 02111 (617) 423-3990; *The World in Figures.*

WAKE ISLAND - HEALTH

G.K. Hall and Company, 70 Lincoln Street, Boston, Massachusetts 02111 (617) 423-3990; *The World in Figures.*

WAKE ISLAND - HIGHWAYS

G.K. Hall and Company, 70 Lincoln Street, Boston, Massachusetts 02111 (617) 423-3990; *The World in Figures.*

WAKE ISLAND - ILLITERATE POPULATION

G.K. Hall and Company, 70 Lincoln Street, Boston, Massachusetts 02111 (617) 423-3990; *The World in Figures.*

WAKE ISLAND - IMPORTS

Food and Agricultural Organization of the United Nations (FAO) Via delle Terme di Caracalla, 00100 Rome, Italy (Telephone Number in U.S. (202) 653-2400); *The State of Food and Agriculture.*

G.K. Hall and Company, 70 Lincoln Street, Boston, Massachusetts 02111 (617) 423-3990; *The World in Figures.*

WAKE ISLAND - INDUSTRY

G.K. Hall and Company, 70 Lincoln Street, Boston, Massachusetts 02111 (617) 423-3990; *The World in Figures.*

WAKE ISLAND - INFANT AND MATERNAL MORTALITY

Statistical Office of the United Nations, Publishing Service, New York, New York 10017 (800) 253-9646; *Demographic Yearbook.*

WAKE ISLAND - LABOR FORCE

Food and Agricultural Organization of the United Nations (FAO) Via delle Terme di Caracalla, 00100 Rome, Italy (Telephone Number in U.S. (202) 653-2400); *The State of Food and Agriculture.*

G.K. Hall and Company, 70 Lincoln Street, Boston, Massachusetts 02111 (617) 423-3990; *The World in Figures.*

WAKE ISLAND - LAND USE

G.K. Hall and Company, 70 Lincoln Street, Boston, Massachusetts 02111 (617) 423-3990; *The World in Figures.*

WAKE ISLAND - LIVESTOCK AND POULTRY

Food and Agricultural Organization of the United Nations (FAO) Via delle Terme di Caracalla, 00100 Rome, Italy (Telephone Number in U.S. (202) 653-2400); *The State of Food and Agriculture.*

G.K. Hall and Company, 70 Lincoln Street, Boston, Massachusetts 02111 (617) 423-3990; *The World in Figures.*

WAKE ISLAND - LIVING LEVELS

G.K. Hall and Company, 70 Lincoln Street, Boston, Massachusetts 02111 (617) 423-3990; *The World in Figures.*

WAKE ISLAND - MANUFACTURING

G.K. Hall and Company, 70 Lincoln Street, Boston, Massachusetts 02111 (617) 423-3990; *The World in Figures.*

WAKE ISLAND - MARRIAGE RATES

Statistical Office of the United Nations, Publishing Service, New York, New York 10017 (800) 253-9646; *Demographic Yearbook.*

WAKE ISLAND - MEAT PRODUCTION - See WAKE ISLAND - LIVESTOCK AND POULTRY

WAKE ISLAND - MERCHANT SHIPPING

G.K. Hall and Company, 70 Lincoln Street, Boston, Massachusetts 02111 (617) 423-3990; *The World in Figures.*

WAKE ISLAND - MILITARY

G.K. Hall and Company, 70 Lincoln Street, Boston, Massachusetts 02111 (617) 423-3990; *The World in Figures.*

WAKE ISLAND - MINING AND MINERAL PRODUCTS

G.K. Hall and Company, 70 Lincoln Street, Boston, Massachusetts 02111 (617) 423-3990; *The World in Figures.*

WAKE ISLAND - MONEY SUPPLY

G.K. Hall and Company, 70 Lincoln Street, Boston, Massachusetts 02111 (617) 423-3990; *The World in Figures.*

WAKE ISLAND - MOTOR VEHICLES IN USE

G.K. Hall and Company, 70 Lincoln Street, Boston, Massachusetts 02111 (617) 423-3990; *The World in Figures.*

WAKE ISLAND - NATALITY - See WAKE ISLAND - BIRTH RATE

WAKE ISLAND - NATIONAL INCOME

G.K. Hall and Company, 70 Lincoln Street, Boston, Massachusetts 02111 (617) 423-3990; *The World in Figures.*

WAKE ISLAND - NEWSPAPER PRODUCTION - See WAKE ISLAND - FORESTRY AND FOREST PRODUCTS

WAKE ISLAND - OCCUPATIONS - See WAKE ISLAND - LABOR FORCE

WAKE ISLAND - PESTICIDE USE

Food and Agricultural Organization of the United Nations (FAO) Via delle Terme di Caracalla, 00100 Rome, Italy (Telephone Number in U.S. (202) 653-2400); *The State of Food and Agriculture.*

WAKE ISLAND - PETROLEUM INDUSTRY

Food and Agricultural Organization of the United Nations (FAO) Via delle Terme di Caracalla, 00100 Rome, Italy (Telephone Number in U.S. (202) 653-2400); *The State of Food and Agriculture.*

G.K. Hall and Company, 70 Lincoln Street, Boston, Massachusetts 02111 (617) 423-3990; *The World in Figures.*

WAKE ISLAND - POPULATION

G.K. Hall and Company, 70 Lincoln Street, Boston, Massachusetts 02111 (617) 423-3990; *The World in Figures.*

Statistical Office of the United Nations, Publishing Service, New York, New York 10017 (800) 253-9646; *Demographic Yearbook,* and *Statistical Yearbook.*

World Health Organization, Office of Publications, Avenue Appia, CH-1211 Geneva 27, Switzerland (Telephone Number in U.S. (518) 436-9686); *World Health Statistics Annual.*

WAKE ISLAND - PRICES

Food and Agricultural Organization of the United Nations (FAO) Via delle Terme di Caracalla, 00100 Rome, Italy (Telephone Number in U.S. (202) 653-2400); *The State of Food and Agriculture.*

G.K. Hall and Company, 70 Lincoln Street, Boston, Massachusetts 02111 (617) 423-3990; *The World in Figures.*

WAKE ISLAND - PRODUCTION

G.K. Hall and Company, 70 Lincoln Street, Boston, Massachusetts 02111 (617) 423-3990; *The World in Figures.*

WAKE ISLAND - RAILWAYS

G.K. Hall and Company, 70 Lincoln Street, Boston, Massachusetts 02111 (617) 423-3990; *The World in Figures.*

WAKE ISLAND - RETAIL TRADE

G.K. Hall and Company, 70 Lincoln Street, Boston, Massachusetts 02111 (617) 423-3990; *The World in Figures.*

WAKE ISLAND - SOCIAL DATA

G.K. Hall and Company, 70 Lincoln Street, Boston, Massachusetts 02111 (617) 423-3990; *The World in Figures.*

WAKE ISLAND - STOCKS - COMMODITY - MARKET PRICE - INDEX

Food and Agricultural Organization of the United Nations (FAO) Via delle Terme di Caracalla, 00100 Rome, Italy (Telephone Number in U.S. (202) 653-2400); *The State of Food and Agriculture.*

WAKE ISLAND - TAXATION

G.K. Hall and Company, 70 Lincoln Street, Boston, Massachusetts 02111 (617) 423-3990; *The World in Figures.*

WAKE ISLAND - TELEPHONES IN USE

American Telephone and Telegraph Company, 26 Parsippany Road, Whippany, New Jersey 07981 (800) 338-4038; *The World's Telephones.*

G.K. Hall and Company, 70 Lincoln Street, Boston, Massachusetts 02111 (617) 423-3990; *The World in Figures.*

WAKE ISLAND - TEXTILE INDUSTRY

G.K. Hall and Company, 70 Lincoln Street, Boston, Massachusetts 02111 (617) 423-3990; *The World in Figures.*

WAKE ISLAND - TOURISM

G.K. Hall and Company, 70 Lincoln Street, Boston, Massachusetts 02111 (617) 423-3990; *The World in Figures.*

WAKE ISLAND - TRADE - See WAKE ISLAND - FOREIGN TRADE

WAKE ISLAND - TRANSPORTATION AND COMMUNICATIONS

G.K. Hall and Company, 70 Lincoln Street, Boston, Massachusetts 02111 (617) 423-3990; *The World in Figures.*

WAKE ISLAND - VITAL STATISTICS

G.K. Hall and Company, 70 Lincoln Street, Boston, Massachusetts 02111 (617) 423-3990; *The World in Figures.*

WAKE ISLAND - WAGES

G.K. Hall and Company, 70 Lincoln Street, Boston, Massachusetts 02111 (617) 423-3990; *The World in Figures.*

WAKE ISLAND - WEATHER

G.K. Hall and Company, 70 Lincoln Street, Boston, Massachusetts 02111 (617) 423-3990; *The World in Figures.*

WALLIS AND FUTUNA ISLANDS - AGRICULTURE

Food and Agricultural Organization of the United Nations (FAO) Via delle Terme di Caracalla, 00100 Rome, Italy (Telephone Number in U.S. (202) 653-2400); *The State of Food and Agriculture.*

G.K. Hall and Company, 70 Lincoln Street, Boston, Massachusetts 02111 (617) 423-3990; *The World in Figures.*

WALLIS AND FUTUNA ISLANDS - AIRLINE SERVICE

G.K. Hall and Company, 70 Lincoln Street, Boston, Massachusetts 02111 (617) 423-3990; *The World in Figures.*

WALLIS AND FUTUNA ISLANDS - AREA AND DENSITY OF POPULATION

Food and Agricultural Organization of the United Nations (FAO) Via delle Terme di Caracalla, 00100 Rome, Italy (Telephone Number in U.S. (202) 653-2400); *The State of Food and Agriculture.*

G.K. Hall and Company, 70 Lincoln Street, Boston, Massachusetts 02111 (617) 423-3990; *The World in Figures.*

Statistical Office of the United Nations, Publishing Service, New York, New York 10017 (800) 253-9646; *Statistical Yearbook.*

WALLIS AND FUTUNA ISLANDS - BALANCE OF PAYMENTS

G.K. Hall and Company, 70 Lincoln Street, Boston, Massachusetts 02111 (617) 423-3990; *The World in Figures.*

WALLIS AND FUTUNA ISLANDS - BANKING

G.K. Hall and Company, 70 Lincoln Street, Boston, Massachusetts 02111 (617) 423-3990; *The World in Figures.*

WALLIS AND FUTUNA ISLANDS - BIRTH RATES

Statistical Office of the United Nations, Publishing Service, New York, New York 10017 (800) 253-9646; *Demographic Yearbook,* and *Statistical Yearbook.*

WALLIS AND FUTUNA ISLANDS - BONDS

G.K. Hall and Company, 70 Lincoln Street, Boston, Massachusetts 02111 (617) 423-3990; *The World in Figures.*

WALLIS AND FUTUNA ISLANDS - BOOK PRODUCTION

G.K. Hall and Company, 70 Lincoln Street, Boston, Massachusetts 02111 (617) 423-3990; *The World in Figures.*

WALLIS AND FUTUNA ISLANDS - BROADCASTING

Billboard Limited, P.O. Box 9027, 1006 AA Amsterdam, The Netherlands (Telephone Number in U.S. (212) 764-7300); *World Radio TV Handbook.*

G.K. Hall and Company, 70 Lincoln Street, Boston, Massachusetts 02111 (617) 423-3990; *The World in Figures.*

WALLIS AND FUTUNA ISLANDS - BUSINESS

G.K. Hall and Company, 70 Lincoln Street, Boston, Massachusetts 02111 (617) 423-3990; *The World in Figures.*

WALLIS AND FUTUNA ISLANDS - CALORIE SUPPLY

Food and Agricultural Organization of the United Nations (FAO) Via delle Terme di Caracalla, 00100 Rome, Italy (Telephone Number in U.S. (202) 653-2400); *The State of Food and Agriculture.*

WALLIS AND FUTUNA ISLANDS - CHEMICAL (ORGANIC) PRODUCTION - See WALLIS AND FUTUNA ISLANDS - MINING AND MINERAL PRODUCTS

WALLIS AND FUTUNA ISLANDS - CLASS STRUCTURE

G.K. Hall and Company, 70 Lincoln Street, Boston, Massachusetts 02111 (617) 423-3990; *The World in Figures.*

WALLIS AND FUTUNA ISLANDS - CLIMATE

G.K. Hall and Company, 70 Lincoln Street, Boston, Massachusetts 02111 (617) 423-3990; *The World in Figures.*

WALLIS AND FUTUNA ISLANDS - COAL PRODUCTION - See WALLIS AND FUTUNA ISLANDS - MINING AND MINERAL PRODUCTS

G.K. Hall and Company, 70 Lincoln Street, Boston, Massachusetts 02111 (617) 423-3990; *The World in Figures.*

WALLIS AND FUTUNA ISLANDS - COMMUNICATIONS

G.K. Hall and Company, 70 Lincoln Street, Boston, Massachusetts 02111 (617) 423-3990; *The World in Figures.*

WALLIS AND FUTUNA ISLANDS - CONSUMER PRICE INDEX

G.K. Hall and Company, 70 Lincoln Street, Boston, Massachusetts 02111 (617) 423-3990; *The World in Figures.*

WALLIS AND FUTUNA ISLANDS - CONSUMPTION

G.K. Hall and Company, 70 Lincoln Street, Boston, Massachusetts 02111 (617) 423-3990; *The World in Figures.*

WALLIS AND FUTUNA ISLANDS - CORN PRODUCTION - See WALLIS AND FUTUNA ISLANDS - CROPS

WALLIS AND FUTUNA ISLANDS - CORPORATE TAXES - See WALLIS AND FUTUNA ISLANDS - TAXATION

WALLIS AND FUTUNA ISLANDS - CROPS

Food and Agricultural Organization of the United Nations (FAO) Via delle Terme di Caracalla, 00100 Rome, Italy (Telephone Number in U.S. (202) 653-2400); *The State of Food and Agriculture.*

G.K. Hall and Company, 70 Lincoln Street, Boston, Massachusetts 02111 (617) 423-3990; *The World in Figures.*

WALLIS AND FUTUNA ISLANDS - CUSTOMS DUTIES

G.K. Hall and Company, 70 Lincoln Street, Boston, Massachusetts 02111 (617) 423-3990; *The World in Figures.*

WALLIS AND FUTUNA ISLANDS - DAIRY PRODUCTS

Food and Agricultural Organization of the United Nations (FAO) Via delle Terme di Caracalla, 00100 Rome, Italy (Telephone Number in U.S. (202) 653-2400); *The State of Food and Agriculture*

WALLIS AND FUTUNA ISLANDS - DEATH RATES

G.K. Hall and Company, 70 Lincoln Street, Boston, Massachusetts 02111 (617) 423-3990; *The World in Figures.*

Statistical Office of the United Nations, Publishing Service, New York, New York 10017 (800) 253-9646; *Statistical Yearbook.*

WALLIS AND FUTUNA ISLANDS - DEFENSE EXPENDITURES

G.K. Hall and Company, 70 Lincoln Street, Boston, Massachusetts 02111 (617) 423-3990; *The World in Figures.*

WALLIS AND FUTUNA ISLANDS - DEMOGRAPHY

G.K. Hall and Company, 70 Lincoln Street, Boston, Massachusetts 02111 (617) 423-3990; *The World in Figures.*

WALLIS AND FUTUNA ISLANDS - DEVELOPMENT ASSISTANCE

G.K. Hall and Company, 70 Lincoln Street, Boston, Massachusetts 02111 (617) 423-3990; *The World in Figures.*

Statistical Office of the United Nations, Publishing Service, New York, New York 10017 (800) 253-9646; *Statistical Yearbook.*

WALLIS AND FUTUNA ISLANDS - DISEASE

G.K. Hall and Company, 70 Lincoln Street, Boston, Massachusetts 02111 (617) 423-3990; *The World in Figures.*

WALLIS AND FUTUNA ISLANDS - DIVORCE RATES

Statistical Office of the United Nations, Publishing Service, New York, New York 10017 (800) 253-9646; *Demographic Yearbook.*

WALLIS AND FUTUNA ISLANDS - DOMESTIC PRODUCT

G.K. Hall and Company, 70 Lincoln Street, Boston, Massachusetts 02111 (617) 423-3990; *The World in Figures.*

WALLIS AND FUTUNA ISLANDS - ECONOMY

G.K. Hall and Company, 70 Lincoln Street, Boston, Massachusetts 02111 (617) 423-3990; *The World in Figures.*

WALLIS AND FUTUNA ISLANDS - EDUCATION

G.K. Hall and Company, 70 Lincoln Street, Boston, Massachusetts 02111 (617) 423-3990; *The World in Figures.*

WALLIS AND FUTUNA ISLANDS - EGG PRODUCTION AND CONSUMPTION - See WALLIS AND FUTUNA ISLANDS - DAIRY PRODUCTS

WALLIS AND FUTUNA ISLANDS - ENERGY

Food and Agricultural Organization of the United Nations (FAO) Via delle Terme di Caracalla, 00100 Rome, Italy (Telephone Number in U.S. (202) 653-2400); *The State of Food and Agriculture.*

G.K. Hall and Company, 70 Lincoln Street, Boston, Massachusetts 02111 (617) 423-3990; *The World in Figures.*

WALLIS AND FUTUNA ISLANDS - EXPORTS

Food and Agricultural Organization of the United Nations (FAO) Via delle Terme di Caracalla, 00100 Rome, Italy (Telephone Number in U.S. (202) 653-2400); *The State of Food and Agriculture.*

G.K. Hall and Company, 70 Lincoln Street, Boston, Massachusetts 02111 (617) 423-3990; *The World in Figures.*

WALLIS AND FUTUNA ISLANDS - EXTERNAL TRADE

Food and Agricultural Organization of the United Nations (FAO) Via delle Terme di Caracalla, 00100 Rome, Italy (Telephone Number in U.S. (202) 653-2400); *The State of Food and Agriculture.*

G.K. Hall and Company, 70 Lincoln Street, Boston, Massachusetts 02111 (617) 423-3990; *The World in Figures.*

WALLIS AND FUTUNA ISLANDS - FARM CROPS - See WALLIS AND FUTUNA ISLANDS - CROPS

WALLIS AND FUTUNA ISLANDS - FERTILIZER

Food and Agricultural Organization of the United Nations (FAO) Via delle Terme di Caracalla, 00100 Rome, Italy (Telephone Number in U.S. (202) 653-2400); *The State of Food and Agriculture.*

WALLIS AND FUTUNA ISLANDS - FETAL MORTALITY

Statistical Office of the United Nations, Publishing Service, New York, New York 10017 (800) 253-9646; *Demographic Yearbook.*

WALLIS AND FUTUNA ISLANDS - FINANCE

G.K. Hall and Company, 70 Lincoln Street, Boston, Massachusetts 02111 (617) 423-3990; *The World in Figures.*

WALLIS AND FUTUNA ISLANDS - FISHERIES

Food and Agricultural Organization of the United Nations (FAO) Via delle Terme di Caracalla, 00100 Rome, Italy (Telephone Number in U.S. (202) 653-2400); *The State of Food and Agriculture.*

WALLIS AND FUTUNA ISLANDS - FOOD

Food and Agricultural Organization of the United Nations (FAO) Via delle Terme di Caracalla, 00100 Rome, Italy (Telephone Number in U.S. (202) 653-2400); *The State of Food and Agriculture.*

G.K. Hall and Company, 70 Lincoln Street, Boston, Massachusetts 02111 (617) 423-3990; *The World in Figures.*

WALLIS AND FUTUNA ISLANDS - FOREIGN AID

G.K. Hall and Company, 70 Lincoln Street, Boston, Massachusetts 02111 (617) 423-3990; *The World in Figures.*

WALLIS AND FUTUNA ISLANDS - FOREIGN TRADE

Food and Agricultural Organization of the United Nations (FAO) Via delle Terme di Caracalla, 00100 Rome, Italy (Telephone Number in U.S. (202) 653-2400); *The State of Food and Agriculture.*

G.K. Hall and Company, 70 Lincoln Street, Boston, Massachusetts 02111 (617) 423-3990; *The World in Figures.*

WALLIS AND FUTUNA ISLANDS - FORESTRY AND FOREST PRODUCTS

Food and Agricultural Organization of the United Nations (FAO) Via delle Terme di Caracalla, 00100 Rome, Italy (Telephone Number in U.S. (202) 653-2400); *The State of Food and Agriculture.*

G.K. Hall and Company, 70 Lincoln Street, Boston, Massachusetts 02111 (617) 423-3990; *The World in Figures.*

WALLIS AND FUTUNA ISLANDS - GENERAL MORTALITY

Statistical Office of the United Nations, Publishing Service, New York, New York 10017 (800) 253-9646; *Demographic Yearbook.*

WALLIS AND FUTUNA ISLANDS - GOVERNMENT

G.K. Hall and Company, 70 Lincoln Street, Boston, Massachusetts 02111 (617) 423-3990; *The World in Figures.*

WALLIS AND FUTUNA ISLANDS - GRAIN PRODUCTION - See WALLIS AND FUTUNA ISLANDS - CROPS

WALLIS AND FUTUNA ISLANDS - GROSS DOMESTIC PRODUCT

G.K. Hall and Company, 70 Lincoln Street, Boston, Massachusetts 02111 (617) 423-3990; *The World in Figures*.

WALLIS AND FUTUNA ISLANDS - HEALTH

G.K. Hall and Company, 70 Lincoln Street, Boston, Massachusetts 02111 (617) 423-3990; *The World in Figures*.

Statistical Office of the United Nations, Publishing Service, New York, New York 10017 (800) 253-9646; *Statistical Yearbook*.

WALLIS AND FUTUNA ISLANDS - HIGHWAYS

G.K. Hall and Company, 70 Lincoln Street, Boston, Massachusetts 02111 (617) 423-3990; *The World in Figures*.

WALLIS AND FUTUNA ISLANDS - ILLITERATE POPULATION

G.K. Hall and Company, 70 Lincoln Street, Boston, Massachusetts 02111 (617) 423-3990; *The World in Figures*.

WALLIS AND FUTUNA ISLANDS - IMPORTS

G.K. Hall and Company, 70 Lincoln Street, Boston, Massachusetts 02111 (617) 423-3990; *The World in Figures*.

Organisation for Economic Co-operation and Development (OECD), 2 rue Andre-Pascal, 75 Paris 16, France (Telephone Number in U.S. (202) 785-6323); *Textile Industry in OECD Countries*.

WALLIS AND FUTUNA ISLANDS - INDUSTRY

G.K. Hall and Company, 70 Lincoln Street, Boston, Massachusetts 02111 (617) 423-3990; *The World in Figures*.

WALLIS AND FUTUNA ISLANDS - INFANT AND MATERNAL MORTALITY

Statistical Office of the United Nations, Publishing Service, New York, New York 10017 (800) 253-9646; *Demographic Yearbook*.

Statistical Office of the United Nations, Publishing Service, New York, New York 10017 (800) 253-9646; *Statistical Yearbook*.

WALLIS AND FUTUNA ISLANDS - LABOR FORCE

Food and Agricultural Organization of the United Nations (FAO) Via delle Terme di Caracalla, 00100 Rome, Italy (Telephone Number in U.S. (202) 653-2400); *The State of Food and Agriculture*.

G.K. Hall and Company, 70 Lincoln Street, Boston, Massachusetts 02111 (617) 423-3990; *The World in Figures*.

WALLIS AND FUTUNA ISLANDS - LAND USE

G.K. Hall and Company, 70 Lincoln Street, Boston, Massachusetts 02111 (617) 423-3990; *The World in Figures*.

WALLIS AND FUTUNA ISLANDS - LIVESTOCK AND POULTRY

Food and Agricultural Organization of the United Nations (FAO) Via delle Terme di Caracalla, 00100 Rome, Italy (Telephone Number in U.S. (202) 653-2400); *The State of Food and Agriculture*.

G.K. Hall and Company, 70 Lincoln Street, Boston, Massachusetts 02111 (617) 423-3990; *The World in Figures*.

WALLIS AND FUTUNA ISLANDS - LIVING LEVELS

G.K. Hall and Company, 70 Lincoln Street, Boston, Massachusetts 02111 (617) 423-3990; *The World in Figures*.

WALLIS AND FUTUNA ISLANDS - MAIL - NUMBER OF ITEMS SENT OR RECEIVED

Statistical Office of the United Nations, Publishing Service, New York, New York 10017 (800) 253-9646; *Statistical Yearbook*.

WALLIS AND FUTUNA ISLANDS - MANUFACTURING

G.K. Hall and Company, 70 Lincoln Street, Boston, Massachusetts 02111 (617) 423-3990; *The World in Figures*.

WALLIS AND FUTUNA ISLANDS - MARRIAGE RATES

Statistical Office of the United Nations, Publishing Service, New York, New York 10017 (800) 253-9646; *Demographic Yearbook*, and *Statistical Yearbook*.

WALLIS AND FUTUNA ISLANDS - MEAT PRODUCTION - See WALLIS AND FUTUNA ISLANDS - LIVESTOCK AND POULTRY

WALLIS AND FUTUNA ISLANDS - MERCHANT SHIPPING

G.K. Hall and Company, 70 Lincoln Street, Boston, Massachusetts 02111 (617) 423-3990; *The World in Figures*.

WALLIS AND FUTUNA ISLANDS - MILITARY

G.K. Hall and Company, 70 Lincoln Street, Boston, Massachusetts 02111 (617) 423-3990; *The World in Figures*.

WALLIS AND FUTUNA ISLANDS - MINING AND MINERAL PRODUCTS

G.K. Hall and Company, 70 Lincoln Street, Boston, Massachusetts 02111 (617) 423-3990; *The World in Figures*.

WALLIS AND FUTUNA ISLANDS - MONEY SUPPLY

G.K. Hall and Company, 70 Lincoln Street, Boston, Massachusetts 02111 (617) 423-3990; *The World in Figures*.

WALLIS AND FUTUNA ISLANDS - MOTOR VEHICLES IN USE

G.K. Hall and Company, 70 Lincoln Street, Boston, Massachusetts 02111 (617) 423-3990; *The World in Figures*.

WALLIS AND FUTUNA ISLANDS - NATALITY - See WALLIS AND FUTUNA ISLANDS - BIRTH RATE

WALLIS AND FUTUNA ISLANDS - NATIONAL INCOME

G.K. Hall and Company, 70 Lincoln Street, Boston, Massachusetts 02111 (617) 423-3990; *The World in Figures*.

WALLIS AND FUTUNA ISLANDS - NEWSPAPER PRODUCTION - See WALLIS AND FUTUNA ISLANDS - FORESTRY AND FOREST PRODUCTS

WALLIS AND FUTUNA ISLANDS - OCCUPATIONS - See WALLIS AND FUTUNA ISLANDS - LABOR FORCE

WALLIS AND FUTUNA ISLANDS - PESTICIDE USE

Food and Agricultural Organization of the United Nations (FAO) Via delle Terme di Caracalla, 00100 Rome, Italy (Telephone Number in U.S. (202) 653-2400); *The State of Food and Agriculture.*

WALLIS AND FUTUNA ISLANDS - PETROLEUM INDUSTRY

Food and Agricultural Organization of the United Nations (FAO) Via delle Terme di Caracalla, 00100 Rome, Italy (Telephone Number in U.S. (202) 653-2400); *The State of Food and Agriculture.*

G.K. Hall and Company, 70 Lincoln Street, Boston, Massachusetts 02111 (617) 423-3990; *The World in Figures.*

WALLIS AND FUTUNA ISLANDS - POPULATION

G.K. Hall and Company, 70 Lincoln Street, Boston, Massachusetts 02111 (617) 423-3990; *The World in Figures.*

Statistical Office of the United Nations, Publishing Service, New York, New York 10017 (800) 253-9646; *Demographic Yearbook*, and *Statistical Yearbook.*

World Health Organization, Office of Publications, Avenue Appia, CH-1211 Geneva 27, Switzerland (Telephone Number in U.S. (518) 436-9686); *World Health Statistics Annual.*

WALLIS AND FUTUNA ISLANDS - PRICES

Food and Agricultural Organization of the United Nations (FAO) Via delle Terme di Caracalla, 00100 Rome, Italy (Telephone Number in U.S. (202) 653-2400); *The State of Food and Agriculture.*

G.K. Hall and Company, 70 Lincoln Street, Boston, Massachusetts 02111 (617) 423-3990; *The World in Figures.*

WALLIS AND FUTUNA ISLANDS - PRODUCTION

G.K. Hall and Company, 70 Lincoln Street, Boston, Massachusetts 02111 (617) 423-3990; *The World in Figures.*

WALLIS AND FUTUNA ISLANDS - RAILWAYS

G.K. Hall and Company, 70 Lincoln Street, Boston, Massachusetts 02111 (617) 423-3990; *The World in Figures.*

WALLIS AND FUTUNA ISLANDS - RETAIL TRADE

G.K. Hall and Company, 70 Lincoln Street, Boston, Massachusetts 02111 (617) 423-3990; *The World in Figures.*

WALLIS AND FUTUNA ISLANDS - SOCIAL DATA

G.K. Hall and Company, 70 Lincoln Street, Boston, Massachusetts 02111 (617) 423-3990; *The World in Figures.*

WALLIS AND FUTUNA ISLANDS - STOCKS - COMMODITY - MARKET PRICE - INDEX

Food and Agricultural Organization of the United Nations (FAO) Via delle Terme di Caracalla, 00100 Rome, Italy (Telephone Number in U.S. (202) 653-2400); *The State of Food and Agriculture.*

WALLIS AND FUTUNA ISLANDS - TAXATION

G.K. Hall and Company, 70 Lincoln Street, Boston, Massachusetts 02111 (617) 423-3990; *The World in Figures.*

WALLIS AND FUTUNA ISLANDS - TELEPHONES IN USE

American Telephone and Telegraph Company, 26 Parsippany Road, Whippany, New Jersey 07981 (800) 338-4038; *The World's Telephones.*

G.K. Hall and Company, 70 Lincoln Street, Boston, Massachusetts 02111 (617) 423-3990; *The World in Figures.*

WALLIS AND FUTUNA ISLANDS - TEXTILE INDUSTRY

G.K. Hall and Company, 70 Lincoln Street, Boston, Massachusetts 02111 (617) 423-3990; *The World in Figures.*

WALLIS AND FUTUNA ISLANDS - TOURISM

G.K. Hall and Company, 70 Lincoln Street, Boston, Massachusetts 02111 (617) 423-3990; *The World in Figures.*

WALLIS AND FUTUNA ISLANDS - TRADE - See WALLIS AND FUTUNA ISLANDS

WALLIS AND FUTUNA ISLANDS - VITAL STATISTICS

G.K. Hall and Company, 70 Lincoln Street, Boston, Massachusetts 02111 (617) 423-3990; *The World in Figures.*

Statistical Office of the United Nations, Publishing Service, New York, New York 10017 (800) 253-9646; *Statistical Yearbook.*

World Health Organization, Office of Publications, Avenue Appia, CH-1211 Geneva 27, Switzerland (Telephone Number in U.S. (518) 436-9686); *World Health Statistics Annual.*

WALLIS AND FUTUNA ISLANDS - WAGES

G.K. Hall and Company, 70 Lincoln Street, Boston, Massachusetts 02111 (617) 423-3990; *The World in Figures.*

WALLIS AND FUTUNA ISLANDS - WEATHER

G.K. Hall and Company, 70 Lincoln Street, Boston, Massachusetts 02111 (617) 423-3990; *The World in Figures.*

WALNUTS

U.S. Department of Agriculture, Economic Research Service, Fourteenth Street and Independence Avenue, SW, Washington, D.C. 20005-4789 (202) 219-1504; *Economic Indicators of the Farm Sector: National Financial Summary.*

U.S. Department of Agriculture, National Agricultural Statistics Service, Fourteenth Street and Independence Avenue, SW, Washington, D.C. 20250 (202) 219-1504; *Noncitrus Fruits and Nuts.*

WAREHOUSES - See also TRUCKING AND WAREHOUSING

U.S. Department of Commerce, Bureau of the Census, Suitland, Maryland 20233 (301) 763-4040; *Current Business Reports, Motor Freight Transportation and Warehousing Survey.*

WAREHOUSES - ENERGY CHARACTERISTICS

U.S. Department of Energy, Energy Information Administration, 1000 Independence Avenue, SW, Washington, D.C. 20585 (202) 586-8800; *Commercial Buildings Energy Consumption and Expenditure.*

WAREHOUSES - FLOOR SPACE

U.S. Department of Energy, Energy Information Administration, 1000 Independence Avenue, SW, Washington, D.C. 20585 (202) 586-8800; *Commercial Buildings Characteristics*.

WAREHOUSES - INVENTORY

U.S. Department of Energy, Energy Information Administration, 1000 Independence Avenue, SW, Washington, D.C. 20585 (202) 586-8800; *Commercial Buildings Characteristics*.

WARS - AMERICAN - TOTAL COST OF

United States Congress, The Capitol, Washington, D.C. 20515 (202) 224-3121; *The Military Budget and National Economic Priorities*, 91st Congress, 1st Session; subsequently revised and updated by James L. Clayton, University of Utah.

WARS - UNITED STATES TROOPS AND CASUALTIES

National Archives and Records Administration, Seventh Street and Pennsylvania Avenue, NW, Washington, D.C. 20408 (202) 501-5400; unpublished data from Combat Area Casualties database.

U.S. Department of Defense, Office of the Secretary, The Pentagon, Washington, D.C. 20301 (703) 545-6700; unpublished data.

WARS - VIETNAM CONFLICT

National Archives and Records Administration, Seventh Street and Pennsylvania Avenue, NW, Washington, D.C. 20408 (202) 501-5400; unpublished data from Combat Area Casualties database.

WARSAW PACT COUNTRIES - MILITARY EXPENDITURES

U.S. Arms Control and Disarmament Agency, 320 Twenty-first Street, NW, Washington, D.C. 20451 (302) 647-8677; *World Military Expenditures and Arms Transfers*.

WASHING MACHINES - ELECTRIC - HOMES WITH

Euromonitor Publications Limited, 87-88 Turnmill Street, London EC1M 5QU, England; *European Marketing Data and Statistics*.

U.S. Department of Energy, Energy Information Administration, Washington, D.C. 20585 (202) 586-8800; *Housing Characteristics*.

WASHINGTON - See also STATE DATA (FOR INDIVIDUAL STATES)

Washington - Primary Statistics Sources

Washington State Office of Financial Management, Forecasting Division, P. O. Box 43113, Olympia, Washington 98504 (206) 753-5617; *Washington State Data Book*, and *Population Trends for Washington State*.

Washington - State Data Centers

Forecasting Division Office of Financial Management, 450 Insurance Building, Box 43113, Olympia, Washington 98504-3113, George Hough (206) 586-2504.

Social Research Center, Department of Rural Sociology, Washington State University, Pullman, Washington 99164-4006, Dr. Annabel Kirschner Cook (509) 335-4519.

Puget Sound Council of Governments, 216 1st Avenue South, Seattle, Washington 98104, Mr. Neil Kilgran (206) 464-5355.

Department of Sociology, Demographic Research Laboratory, Western Washington University, Bellingham, Washington 98226, Mr. Lucky Tedrow, Director (206) 676-3176.

Department of Employment Security, Post Office Box 9046, Olympia, Washington 98504, Gary Bodeutsch (206) 438-4804.

CSSCR, University of Washington, 145 Savery Hall, DK45, Seattle, Washington 98195, Fred Nick (206) 543-8110.

WATER - See also WATER TRANSPORTATION SERVICES

WATER - AREA - UNITED STATES

U.S. Department of Commerce, Bureau of the Census, Suitland, Maryland 20233 (301) 763-4040; *Census of Population and Housing, Areas of the United States, Area Measurement Reports*, and unpublished data.

U.S. Department of the Interior, Office of the Secretary, C Street between Eighteenth and Nineteenth Streets, NW, Washington, D.C. 20240; *Areas of Acquisition to the Territory of the United States*.

WATER - POLLUTION - EXPENDITURES FOR ABATEMENT

U.S. Department of Commerce, Bureau of Economic Analysis, Fourteenth Street between Constitution Avenue and E Street, NW, Washington, D.C. 20230 (202) 606-9900; *Survey of Current Business*, and unpublished data.
U.S. Department of Commerce, Bureau of the Census, Suitland, Maryland 20233 (301) 763-4040; *Current Industrial Reports*.

WATER - POLLUTION - OIL SPILLS

Tanker Advisory Center, Incorporated, 10 East End Avenue, New York, New York 10028 (212) 628-7686; *Worldwide Tanker Casualty Returns*.

U.S. Department of Transportation, U.S. Coast Guard, 2100 Second Street, SW, Washington, D.C. 20593 (202) 267-1587; unpublished data from the Marine Safety Information System.

WATER - POLLUTION - RIVERS AND STREAMS

U.S. Department of the Interior, Geological Survey, National Center, 12201 Sunrise Valley Drive, Reston, Virginia 22092 (703) 648-4460; *Water-Data Report*, and unpublished data.

WATER - POWER

U.S. Department of Energy, Energy Information Administration, Washington, D.C. 20585 (202) 586-8800; *Electric Power Annual, Annual Energy Review*, and unpublished data.

U.S. Department of Energy, Federal Energy Regulatory Commission, Washington, D.C. 20585 (202) 208-0300; *Hydroelectric Power Resources of the United States, Developed and Undeveloped*, and unpublished data.

WATER - PUBLIC SUPPLY

U.S. Department of Commerce, Bureau of the Census, Suitland, Maryland 20233 (301) 763-4040; *Current Housing Reports, American Housing Survey*, and *Census of Population and Housing*.

U.S. Department of the Interior, Geological Survey, National Center, 12201 Sunrise Valley Drive, Reston, Virginia 22092 (703) 648-4460; *Estimated Use of Water in the United States.*

WATER - USE

U.S. Department of the Interior, Geological Survey, National Center, 12201 Sunrise Valley Drive, Reston, Virginia 22092 (703) 648-4460; *Estimated Use of Water in the United States.*

WATER TRANSPORTATION SERVICES - EARNINGS

U.S. Department of Commerce, Bureau of the Census, Suitland, Maryland 20233 (301) 763-4040; *Census of Transportation,* and *County Business Patterns.*

U.S. Department of Labor, Bureau of Labor Statistics, Two Massachusetts Avenue, NE, Washington, D.C. 20212 (202) 606-7828; *Employment and Earnings,* and Bulletins 2370 and 2429.

WATER TRANSPORTATION SERVICES - EMPLOYEES

U.S. Department of Commerce, Bureau of the Census, Suitland, Maryland 20233 (301) 763-4040; *Census of Transportation,* and *County Business Patterns.*

U.S. Department of Labor, Bureau of Labor Statistics, Two Massachusetts Avenue, NE, Washington, D.C. 20212 (202) 606-7828; *Employment and Earnings,* and Bulletins 2370 and 2429.

WATER TRANSPORTATION SERVICES - FOREIGN TRADE

U.S. Department of Army, Corps of Engineers, The Pentagon, Washington, D.C. 20310 (202) 545-6700; *Waterborne Commerce of the United States.*

U.S. Department of Commerce, Bureau of the Census, Suitland, Maryland 20233 (301) 763-4040; *U.S. Merchandise Trade: Selected Highlights, Census of Transportation,* and TM985 and TA 987.

WATER TRANSPORTATION SERVICES - FREIGHT

Eno Transportation Foundation, 44211 Statestone Court, Lansdowne, Virginia 22075 (703) 729-7200; *Transportation in America.*

U.S. Department of Army, Corps of Engineers, The Pentagon, Washington, D.C. 20310 (202) 545-6700; *Waterborne Commerce of the United States.*

U.S Department of Commerce, Bureau of the Census, Suitland, Maryland, 20233 (301) 763-4040; TM 985.

WATER TRANSPORTATION SERVICES - OCCUPATIONAL SAFETY

U.S. Department of Labor, Bureau of Labor Statistics, Two Massachusetts Avenue, NE, Washington, D.C. 20212 (202) 606-7828; *Occupational Injuries and Illnesses in the United States by Industry.*

U.S. Department of Transportation, Bureau of Transportation Statistics, 400 Seventh Street, SW, Washington, D.C. 20590 (202) 366-DATA; *National Transportation Statistics Annual, Historical Compendium Information Report.*

WATER TRANSPORTATION SERVICES - OUTLAYS

Executive Office of the President, Office of Management and Budget, Executive Office Building, Washington, D.C. 20503 (202) 395-3080; *Budget of the United States Government.*

Eno Transportation Foundation, 44211 Statestone Court, Lansdowne, Virginia 22075 (703) 729-7200; *Transportation in America.*

U.S. Department of Army, Corps of Engineers, The Pentagon, Washington, D.C. 20310 (202) 545-6700; *Report of Civil Works Expenditures by State and Fiscal Year.*

WEALTH - BUSINESS

U.S. Department of Commerce, Bureau of Economic Analysis, Fourteenth Street between Constitution Avenue and E Street, NW, Washington, D.C. 20230 (202) 606-9900; *Survey of Current Business.*

WEALTH - GOVERNMENT

U.S. Department of Commerce, Bureau of Economic Analysis, Fourteenth Street between Constitution Avenue and E Street, NW, Washington, D.C. 20230 (202) 606-9900; *Survey of Current Business.*

WEALTH - HOUSEHOLDS

Board of Governors of the Federal Reserve System, Twentieth Street and Constitution Avenue, NW, Washington, D.C. 20551 (202) 452-3000; *Federal Reserve Bulletin.*

U.S. Department of Commerce, Bureau of Economic Analysis, Fourteenth Street between Constitution Avenue and E Street, NW, Washington, D.C. 20230 (202) 606-9900; *Survey of Current Business.*

U.S. Department of the Treasury, Internal Revenue Service, 1111 Constitution Avenue, NW, Washington, D.C. 20224 (202) 566-5000; *Statistics of Income Bulletin.*

WEATHER CONDITIONS AT SELECTED STATIONS

U.S. Department of Commerce, National Oceanic and Atmospheric Administration, National Climatic Data Center, Federal Building, Asheville, North Carolina 28801 (704) 259-2850; *Climatography of the United States,* and *Comparative Climatic Data.*

WELFARE SERVICES - See SOCIAL WELFARE; PUBLIC AID ASSISTANCE; and Individual Programs

WEST VIRGINIA - See also STATE DATA (FOR INDIVIDUAL STATES)

West Virginia - Primary Statistics Sources

West Virginia Chamber of Commerce, Box 2789, Charleston, West Virginia 25330 (304) 342-1115; *West Virginia: Economic-Statistical Profile.*

West Virginia Research League, Incorporated, 405 Capitol Street, Suite 414, Charleston, West Virginia 25301 (304) 346-9451; *The Statistical Handbook,* and *Economic Indicators.*

West Virginia - State Data Centers

Community Development Division, Governor's Office of Community and Industrial Development, Capitol Complex, Building 6, Room 553, Charleston, West Virginia 25305, Ms. Mary C. Harless (304) 558-

4010.

The Center for Economic Research, West Virginia University, 323 Business and Economic Building, Morgantown, West Virginia 26506-6025, Dr. Tom Witt, Director, Mr. Randy Childs (304) 293-7832.

Reference Library, West Virginia State Library Commission, Science and Cultural Center, Capitol Complex, Charleston, West Virginia 25305, Ms. Karen Goff (304) 348-2045.

Office of Health Services Research, Health Science Center, West Virginia University, Post Office Box 9145, Morgantown, West Virginia 26506, Mr. Alex Lubman (304) 293-1086.

WESTERN SAHARA - AGRICULTURE

Food and Agricultural Organization of the United Nations (FAO) Via delle Terme di Caracalla, 00100 Rome, Italy (Telephone Number in U.S. (202) 653-2400); *The State of Food and Agriculture.*

Statistical Office of the United Nations, Publishing Service, New York, New York 10017 (800) 253-9646; *Statistical Yearbook.*

G.K. Hall and Company, 70 Lincoln Street, Boston, Massachusetts 02111 (617) 423-3990; *The World in Figures.*

WESTERN SAHARA - AIRLINE SERVICE

G.K. Hall and Company, 70 Lincoln Street, Boston, Massachusetts 02111 (617) 423-3990; *The World in Figures.*

WESTERN SAHARA - AREA AND DENSITY OF POPULATION

Food and Agricultural Organization of the United Nations (FAO) Via delle Terme di Caracalla, 00100 Rome, Italy (Telephone Number in U.S. (202) 653-2400); *The State of Food and Agriculture.*

G.K. Hall and Company, 70 Lincoln Street, Boston, Massachusetts 02111 (617) 423-3990; *The World in Figures.*

Statistical Office of the United Nations, Publishing Service, New York, New York 10017 (800) 253-9646; *Statistical Yearbook.*

WESTERN SAHARA - BALANCE OF PAYMENTS

G.K. Hall and Company, 70 Lincoln Street, Boston, Massachusetts 02111 (617) 423-3990; *The World in Figures.*

WESTERN SAHARA - BANKING

G.K. Hall and Company, 70 Lincoln Street, Boston, Massachusetts 02111 (617) 423-3990; *The World in Figures.*

WESTERN SAHARA - BARLEY PRODUCTION - See WESTERN SAHARA - CROPS

WESTERN SAHARA - BIRTH RATES

Statistical Office of the United Nations, Publishing Service, New York, New York 10017 (800) 253-9646; *Demographic Yearbook*, and *Statistical Yearbook.*

WESTERN SAHARA - BONDS

G.K. Hall and Company, 70 Lincoln Street, Boston, Massachusetts 02111 (617) 423-3990; *The World in Figures.*

WESTERN SAHARA - BOOK PRODUCTION

G.K. Hall and Company, 70 Lincoln Street, Boston, Massachusetts 02111 (617) 423-3990; *The World in Figures.*

WESTERN SAHARA - BROADCASTING

G.K. Hall and Company, 70 Lincoln Street, Boston, Massachusetts 02111 (617) 423-3990; *The World in Figures.*

WESTERN SAHARA - BUSINESS

G.K. Hall and Company, 70 Lincoln Street, Boston, Massachusetts 02111 (617) 423-3990; *The World in Figures.*

WESTERN SAHARA - CALORIE SUPPLY

Food and Agricultural Organization of the United Nations (FAO) Via delle Terme di Caracalla, 00100 Rome, Italy (Telephone Number in U.S. (202) 653-2400); *The State of Food and Agriculture.*

WESTERN SAHARA - CHEMICAL (ORGANIC) PRODUCTION - See WESTERN SAHARA - MINING AND MINERAL PRODUCTS

WESTERN SAHARA - CLIMATE

G.K. Hall and Company, 70 Lincoln Street, Boston, Massachusetts 02111 (617) 423-3990; *The World in Figures.*

WESTERN SAHARA - COAL PRODUCTION - See WESTERN SAHARA - MINING AND MINERAL PRODUCTS

WESTERN SAHARA - COMMUNICATIONS

G.K. Hall and Company, 70 Lincoln Street, Boston, Massachusetts 02111 (617) 423-3990; *The World in Figures.*

WESTERN SAHARA - CONSUMER PRICE INDEX

G.K. Hall and Company, 70 Lincoln Street, Boston, Massachusetts 02111 (617) 423-3990; *The World in Figures.*

WESTERN SAHARA - CORN PRODUCTION - See WESTERN SAHARA - CROPS

WESTERN SAHARA - CORPORATE TAXES - See WESTERN SAHARA - TAXATION

WESTERN SAHARA - CROPS

Food and Agricultural Organization of the United Nations (FAO) Via delle Terme di Caracalla, 00100 Rome, Italy (Telephone Number in U.S. (202) 653-2400); *The State of Food and Agriculture.*

G.K. Hall and Company, 70 Lincoln Street, Boston, Massachusetts 02111 (617) 423-3990; *The World in Figures.*

Statistical Office of the United Nations, Publishing Service, New York, New York 10017 (800) 253-9646; *Statistical Yearbook.*

WESTERN SAHARA - CUSTOMS DUTIES

G.K. Hall and Company, 70 Lincoln Street, Boston, Massachusetts 02111 (617) 423-3990; *The World in Figures.*

WESTERN SAHARA - DAIRY PRODUCTS

Food and Agricultural Organization of the United Nations (FAO) Via delle Terme di Caracalla, 00100 Rome, Italy (Telephone Number in

U.S. (202) 653-2400); *The State of Food and Agriculture.*

WESTERN SAHARA - DEATH RATES

G.K. Hall and Company, 70 Lincoln Street, Boston, Massachusetts 02111 (617) 423-3990; *The World in Figures.*

Statistical Office of the United Nations, Publishing Service, New York, New York 10017 (800) 253-9646; *Statistical Yearbook.*

WESTERN SAHARA - DEFENSE EXPENDITURES

G.K. Hall and Company, 70 Lincoln Street, Boston, Massachusetts 02111 (617) 423-3990; *The World in Figures.*

WESTERN SAHARA - DEMOGRAPHY

G.K. Hall and Company, 70 Lincoln Street, Boston, Massachusetts 02111 (617) 423-3990; *The World in Figures.*

WESTERN SAHARA - DEVELOPMENT ASSISTANCE

G.K. Hall and Company, 70 Lincoln Street, Boston, Massachusetts 02111 (617) 423-3990; *The World in Figures.*

WESTERN SAHARA - DISEASE

G.K. Hall and Company, 70 Lincoln Street, Boston, Massachusetts 02111 (617) 423-3990; *The World in Figures.*

WESTERN SAHARA - DIVORCE RATES

Statistical Office of the United Nations, Publishing Service, New York, New York 10017 (800) 253-9646; *Demographic Yearbook.*

Statistical Office of the United Nations, Publishing Service, New York, New York 10017 (800) 253-9646; *Statistical Yearbook.*

WESTERN SAHARA - DOMESTIC PRODUCT

G.K. Hall and Company, 70 Lincoln Street, Boston, Massachusetts 02111 (617) 423-3990; *The World in Figures.*

WESTERN SAHARA - ECONOMY

G.K. Hall and Company, 70 Lincoln Street, Boston, Massachusetts 02111 (617) 423-3990; *The World in Figures.*

WESTERN SAHARA - EDUCATION

G.K. Hall and Company. 70 Lincoln Street, Boston, Massachusetts 02111 (617) 423-3990; *The World in Figures.*

WESTERN SAHARA - EGG PRODUCTION AND CONSUMPTION - See WESTERN SAHARA - DAIRY PRODUCTS

WESTERN SAHARA - ELECTRICITY

Statistical Office of the United Nations, Publishing Service, New York, New York 10017 (800) 253-9646; *Statistical Yearbook.*

WESTERN SAHARA - ENERGY

Food and Agricultural Organization of the United Nations (FAO) Via delle Terme di Caracalla, 00100 Rome, Italy (Telephone Number in U.S. (202) 653-2400); *The State of Food and Agriculture.*

G.K. Hall and Company, 70 Lincoln Street, Boston, Massachusetts 02111 (617) 423-3990; *The World in Figures.*

Statistical Office of the United Nations, Publishing Service, New York, New York 10017 (800) 253-9646; *Statistical Yearbook.*

WESTERN SAHARA - EXPORTS

Food and Agricultural Organization of the United Nations (FAO) Via delle Terme di Caracalla, 00100 Rome, Italy (Telephone Number in U.S. (202) 653-2400); *The State of Food and Agriculture.*

G.K. Hall and Company, 70 Lincoln Street, Boston, Massachusetts 02111 (617) 423-3990; *The World in Figures.*

WESTERN SAHARA - EXTERNAL TRADE

Food and Agricultural Organization of the United Nations (FAO) Via delle Terme di Caracalla, 00100 Rome, Italy (Telephone Number in U.S. (202) 653-2400); *The State of Food and Agriculture.*

G.K. Hall and Company, 70 Lincoln Street, Boston, Massachusetts 02111 (617) 423-3990; *The World in Figures.*

WESTERN SAHARA - FARM CROPS - See WESTERN SAHARA - CROPS

WESTERN SAHARA - FETAL MORTALITY

Statistical Office of the United Nations, Publishing Service, New York, New York 10017 (800) 253-9646; *Demographic Yearbook.*

WESTERN SAHARA - FERTILIZER

Food and Agricultural Organization of the United Nations (FAO) Via delle Terme di Caracalla, 00100 Rome, Italy (Telephone Number in U.S. (202) 653-2400); *The State of Food and Agriculture.*

WESTERN SAHARA - FINANCE

G.K. Hall and Company, 70 Lincoln Street, Boston, Massachusetts 02111 (617) 423-3990; *The World in Figures.*

WESTERN SAHARA - FISHERIES

Food and Agricultural Organization of the United Nations (FAO) Via delle Terme di Caracalla, 00100 Rome, Italy (Telephone Number in U.S. (202) 653-2400); *The State of Food and Agriculture.*

Statistical Office of the United Nations, Publishing Service, New York, New York 10017 (800) 253-9646; *Statistical Yearbook.*

WESTERN SAHARA - FOOD

Food and Agricultural Organization of the United Nations (FAO) Via delle Terme di Caracalla, 00100 Rome, Italy (Telephone Number in U.S. (202) 653-2400); *The State of Food and Agriculture.*

G.K. Hall and Company, 70 Lincoln Street, Boston, Massachusetts 02111 (617) 423-3990; *The World in Figures.*

WESTERN SAHARA - FOREIGN TRADE

Food and Agricultural Organization of the United Nations (FAO) Via delle Terme di Caracalla, 00100 Rome, Italy (Telephone Number in U.S. (202) 653-2400); *The State of Food and Agriculture.*

WESTERN SAHARA - FORESTRY AND FOREST PRODUCTS

Food and Agricultural Organization of the United Nations (FAO) Via delle Terme di Caracalla, 00100 Rome, Italy (Telephone Number in U.S. (202) 653-2400); *The State of Food and Agriculture.*

G.K. Hall and Company, 70 Lincoln Street, Boston, Massachusetts 02111 (617) 423-3990; *The World in Figures*.

WESTERN SAHARA - GENERAL MORTALITY

Statistical Office of the United Nations, Publishing Service, New York, New York 10017 (800) 253-9646; *Demographic Yearbook*.

WESTERN SAHARA - GOVERNMENT

G.K. Hall and Company, 70 Lincoln Street, Boston, Massachusetts 02111 (617) 423-3990; *The World in Figures*.

WESTERN SAHARA - GRAIN PRODUCTION - See WESTERN SAHARA - CROPS

WESTERN SAHARA - GROSS DOMESTIC PRODUCT

G.K. Hall and Company, 70 Lincoln Street, Boston, Massachusetts 02111 (617) 423-3990; *The World in Figures*.

WESTERN SAHARA - HEALTH

G.K. Hall and Company, 70 Lincoln Street, Boston, Massachusetts 02111 (617) 423-3990; *The World in Figures*.

Statistical Office of the United Nations, Publishing Service, New York, New York 10017 (800) 253-9646; *Statistical Yearbook*.

WESTERN SAHARA - HIGHWAYS

G.K. Hall and Company, 70 Lincoln Street, Boston, Massachusetts 02111 (617) 423-3990; *The World in Figures*.

WESTERN SAHARA - ILLITERATE POPULATION

G.K. Hall and Company, 70 Lincoln Street, Boston, Massachusetts 02111 (617) 423-3990; *The World in Figures*.

WESTERN SAHARA - IMPORTS

Food and Agricultural Organization of the United Nations (FAO) Via delle Terme di Caracalla, 00100 Rome, Italy (Telephone Number in U.S. (202) 653-2400); *The State of Food and Agriculture*.

G.K. Hall and Company, 70 Lincoln Street, Boston, Massachusetts 02111 (617) 423-3990; *The World in Figures*.

WESTERN SAHARA - INDUSTRY

G.K. Hall and Company, 70 Lincoln Street, Boston, Massachusetts 02111 (617) 423-3990; *The World in Figures*.

WESTERN SAHARA - INFANT AND MATERNAL MORTALITY

Statistical Office of the United Nations, Publishing Service, New York, New York 10017 (800) 253-9646; *Demographic Yearbook*, and *Statistical Yearbook*.

WESTERN SAHARA - LABOR FORCE

Food and Agricultural Organization of the United Nations (FAO) Via delle Terme di Caracalla, 00100 Rome, Italy (Telephone Number in U.S. (202) 653-2400); *The State of Food and Agriculture*.

G.K. Hall and Company, 70 Lincoln Street, Boston, Massachusetts 02111 (617) 423-3990; *The World in Figures*.

WESTERN SAHARA - LAND USE

G.K. Hall and Company, 70 Lincoln Street, Boston, Massachusetts 02111 (617) 423-3990; *The World in Figures*.

WESTERN SAHARA - LIVESTOCK AND POULTRY

Food and Agricultural Organization of the United Nations (FAO) Via delle Terme di Caracalla, 00100 Rome, Italy (Telephone Number in U.S. (202) 653-2400); *The State of Food and Agriculture*.

G.K. Hall and Company, 70 Lincoln Street, Boston, Massachusetts 02111 (617) 423-3990; *The World in Figures*.

Statistical Office of the United Nations, Publishing Service, New York, New York 10017 (800) 253-9646; *Statistical Yearbook*.

WESTERN SAHARA - LIVING LEVELS

G.K. Hall and Company, 70 Lincoln Street, Boston, Massachusetts 02111 (617) 423-3990; *The World in Figures*.

WESTERN SAHARA - MANUFACTURING

G.K. Hall and Company, 70 Lincoln Street, Boston, Massachusetts 02111 (617) 423-3990; *The World in Figures*.

WESTERN SAHARA - MARRIAGE RATES

Statistical Office of the United Nations, Publishing Service, New York, New York 10017 (800) 253-9646; *Demographic Yearbook*, and *Statistical Yearbook*.

WESTERN SAHARA - MEAT PRODUCTION - See WESTERN SAHARA - LIVESTOCK AND POULTRY

WESTERN SAHARA - MERCHANT SHIPPING

G.K. Hall and Company, 70 Lincoln Street, Boston, Massachusetts 02111 (617) 423-3990; *The World in Figures*.

Statistical Office of the United Nations, Publishing Service, New York, New York 10017 (800) 253-9646; *Statistical Yearbook*.

WESTERN SAHARA - MILITARY

G.K. Hall and Company, 70 Lincoln Street, Boston, Massachusetts 02111 (617) 423-3990; *The World in Figures*.

WESTERN SAHARA - MINING AND MINERAL PRODUCTS

G.K. Hall and Company, 70 Lincoln Street, Boston, Massachusetts 02111 (617) 423-3990; *The World in Figures*.

Statistical Office of the United Nations, Publishing Service, New York, New York 10017 (800) 253-9646; *Statistical Yearbook*.

WESTERN SAHARA - MONEY SUPPLY

G.K. Hall and Company, 70 Lincoln Street, Boston, Massachusetts 02111 (617) 423-3990; *The World in Figures*.

WESTERN SAHARA - MOTION PICTURES

Statistical Office of the United Nations, Publishing Service, New York, New York 10017 (800) 253-9646; *Statistical Yearbook*.

WESTERN SAHARA - MOTOR VEHICLES IN USE

G.K. Hall and Company, 70 Lincoln Street, Boston, Massachusetts 02111 (617) 423-3990; *The World in Figures*.

Statistical Office of the United Nations, Publishing Service, New York, New York 10017 (800) 253-9646; *Statistical Yearbook*.

WESTERN SAHARA - NATALITY - See WESTERN SAHARA - BIRTH RATE

WESTERN SAHARA - NATIONAL INCOME

G.K. Hall and Company, 70 Lincoln Street, Boston, Massachusetts 02111 (617) 423-3990; *The World in Figures*.

WESTERN SAHARA - NEWSPAPER PRODUCTION - See WESTERN SAHARA - FORESTRY AND FOREST PRODUCTS

WESTERN SAHARA - OCCUPATIONS - See WESTERN SAHARA - LABOR FORCE

WESTERN SAHARA - PESTICIDE USE

Food and Agricultural Organization of the United Nations (FAO) Via delle Terme di Caracalla, 00100 Rome, Italy (Telephone Number in U.S. (202) 653-2400); *The State of Food and Agriculture*.

WESTERN SAHARA - PETROLEUM INDUSTRY

Food and Agricultural Organization of the United Nations (FAO) Via delle Terme di Caracalla, 00100 Rome, Italy (Telephone Number in U.S. (202) 653-2400); *The State of Food and Agriculture*.

G.K. Hall and Company, 70 Lincoln Street, Boston, Massachusetts 02111 (617) 423-3990; *The World in Figures*.

WESTERN SAHARA - PHOSPHATE ROCK PRODUCTION - See WESTERN SAHARA - MINING AND MINERAL PRODUCTS

WESTERN SAHARA - POPULATION

G.K. Hall and Company, 70 Lincoln Street, Boston, Massachusetts 02111 (617) 423-3990; *The World in Figures*.

Statistical Office of the United Nations, Publishing Service, New York, New York 10017 (800) 253-9646; *Demographic Yearbook*, and *Statistical Yearbook*.

World Health Organization, Office of Publications, Avenue Appia, CH-1211 Geneva 27, Switzerland (Telephone Number in U.S. (518) 436-9686); *World Health Statistics Annual*.

WESTERN SAHARA - PRICES

Food and Agricultural Organization of the United Nations (FAO) Via delle Terme di Caracalla, 00100 Rome, Italy (Telephone Number in U.S. (202) 653-2400); *The State of Food and Agriculture*.

G.K. Hall and Company, 70 Lincoln Street, Boston, Massachusetts 02111 (617) 423-3990; *The World in Figures*.

WESTERN SAHARA - PRODUCTION

G.K. Hall and Company, 70 Lincoln Street, Boston, Massachusetts 02111 (617) 423-3990; *The World in Figures*.

WESTERN SAHARA - RAILWAYS

G.K. Hall and Company, 70 Lincoln Street, Boston, Massachusetts 02111 (617) 423-3990; *The World in Figures*.

WESTERN SAHARA - RETAIL TRADE

G.K. Hall and Company, 70 Lincoln Street, Boston, Massachusetts 02111 (617) 423-3990; *The World in Figures*.

WESTERN SAHARA - SHEEP - See WESTERN SAHARA

WESTERN SAHARA - SOCIAL DATA

G.K. Hall and Company, 70 Lincoln Street, Boston, Massachusetts 02111 (617) 423-3990; *The World in Figures*.

WESTERN SAHARA - STOCKS - COMMODITY - MARKET PRICE - INDEX

Food and Agricultural Organization of the United Nations (FAO) Via delle Terme di Caracalla, 00100 Rome, Italy (Telephone Number in U.S. (202) 653-2400); *The State of Food and Agriculture*.

WESTERN SAHARA - TAXATION

G.K. Hall and Company, 70 Lincoln Street, Boston, Massachusetts 02111 (617) 423-3990; *The World in Figures*.

WESTERN SAHARA - TELEPHONES IN USE

G.K. Hall and Company, 70 Lincoln Street, Boston, Massachusetts 02111 (617) 423-3990; *The World in Figures*.

WESTERN SAHARA - TEXTILE INDUSTRY

G.K. Hall and Company, 70 Lincoln Street, Boston, Massachusetts 02111 (617) 423-3990; *The World in Figures*.

WESTERN SAHARA - TOURISM

G.K. Hall and Company, 70 Lincoln Street, Boston, Massachusetts 02111 (617) 423-3990; *The World in Figures*.

WESTERN SAHARA - TRACTORS IN USE

Statistical Office of the United Nations, Publishing Service, New York, New York 10017 (800) 253-9646; *Statistical Yearbook*.

WESTERN SAHARA - TRADE - See WESTERN SAHARA - FOREIGN TRADE

WESTERN SAHARA - TRANSPORTATION AND COMMUNICATIONS

G.K. Hall and Company, 70 Lincoln Street, Boston, Massachusetts 02111 (617) 423-3990; *The World in Figures*.

WESTERN SAHARA - VITAL STATISTICS

G.K. Hall and Company, 70 Lincoln Street, Boston, Massachusetts 02111 (617) 423-3990; *The World in Figures*.

Statistical Office of the United Nations, Publishing Service, New York, New York 10017 (800) 253-9646; *Statistical Yearbook*.

World Health Organization, Office of Publications, Avenue Appia, CH-1211 Geneva 27, Switzerland (Telephone Number in U.S. (518) 436-9686); *World Health Statistics Annual*.

WESTERN SAHARA - WAGES

G.K. Hall and Company, 70 Lincoln Street, Boston, Massachusetts 02111 (617) 423-3990; *The World in Figures*.

WESTERN SAHARA - WEATHER

G.K. Hall and Company, 70 Lincoln Street, Boston, Massachusetts 02111 (617) 423-3990; *The World in Figures*.

WESTERN SAMOA - See also SAMOA

Western Samoa - National Statistical Offices

Government Statistician, Department of Statistics, Post Office Box 1151, Apia, Western Samoa; for national statistics.

Prime Minister's Department, Post Office Box 193, Apia, Western Samoa; for foreign trade statistics.

Western Samoa - Primary Statistics Sources

Department of Statistics, Apia, Western Samoa; *Annual Statistical Abstract*, and *Statistical Bulletin*.

WESTERN SAMOA - AGRICULTURE

Asian Development Bank, P.O. Box 789, 1099 Manila, Philippines; *Key Indicators of Developing Asian and Pacific Countries*.

The World Bank, 1818 H Street, NW, Washington, D.C. 20433 (202) 477-1234; *World Tables*.

WESTERN SAMOA - AREA AND DENSITY OF POPULATION

United Nations Educational, Scientific and Cultural Organization (UNESCO), 7 Place de Fontenoy, F-75700 Paris, France (Telephone Number in U.S. (212) 963-5981); *Statistical Yearbook*.

WESTERN SAMOA - BALANCE OF PAYMENTS

International Monetary Fund, 700 Nineteenth Street, NW, Washington, D.C. 20431 (202) 623-7000; *Balance of Payments Yearbook*.

The World Bank, 1818 H Street, NW, Washington, D.C. 20433 (202) 477-1234; *World Tables*.

WESTERN SAMOA - BANKING

Asian Development Bank, P.O. Box 789, 1099 Manila, Philippines; *Key Indicators of Developing Asian and Pacific Countries*.

WESTERN SAMOA - BIRTH RATES

The World Bank, 1818 H Street, NW, Washington, D.C. 20433 (202) 477-1234; *World Tables*.

WESTERN SAMOA - BONDS

Asian Development Bank, P.O. Box 789, 1099 Manila, Philippines; *Key Indicators of Developing Asian and Pacific Countries*.

WESTERN SAMOA - BROADCASTING

Billboard Limited, P.O. Box 9027, 1006 AA Amsterdam, The Netherlands (Telephone Number in U.S. (212) 764-7300); *World Radio TV Handbook*.

WESTERN SAMOA - CACAO EXPORTS - See WESTERN SAMOA - CROPS

WESTERN SAMOA - CALORIE SUPPLY

Asian Development Bank, P.O. Box 789, 1099 Manila, Philippines; *Key Indicators of Developing Asian and Pacific Countries*.

WESTERN SAMOA - CAPITAL INVESTMENT

Asian Development Bank, P.O. Box 789, 1099 Manila, Philippines; *Key Indicators of Developing Asian and Pacific Countries*.

WESTERN SAMOA - CAPITAL REVENUE

Asian Development Bank, P.O. Box 789, 1099 Manila, Philippines; *Key Indicators of Developing Asian and Pacific Countries*.

WESTERN SAMOA - CLOTHING EXPORTS AND IMPORTS

South Pacific Commission, Post Box D5, Noumea Cedex, New Caledonia; *Statistical Bulletin of the South Pacific: Retail Price Indexes*.

WESTERN SAMOA - CONSUMER PRICE INDEX

Asian Development Bank, P.O. Box 789, 1099 Manila, Philippines; *Key Indicators of Developing Asian and Pacific Countries*.

WESTERN SAMOA - CONSUMER PRICES

International Monetary Fund, 700 Nineteenth Street, NW, Washington, D.C. 20431 (202) 623-7000; *International Financial Statistics*.

WESTERN SAMOA - CONSUMPTION

South Pacific Commission, Post Box D5, Noumea Cedex, New Caledonia; *Statistical Bulletin of the South Pacific: Retail Price Indexes*.

WESTERN SAMOA - COPRA EXPORTS

International Monetary Fund, 700 Nineteenth Street, NW, Washington, D.C. 20431 (202) 623-7000; *International Financial Statistics*.

WESTERN SAMOA - CORN PRODUCTION - See WESTERN SAMOA CROPS

WESTERN SAMOA - CROPS

Asian Development Bank, P.O. Box 789, 1099 Manila, Philippines; *Key Indicators of Developing Asian and Pacific Countries*.

International Monetary Fund, 700 Nineteenth Street, NW, Washington, D.C. 20431 (202) 623-7000; *International Financial Statistics*.

WESTERN SAMOA - DEVELOPMENT ASSISTANCE

Asian Development Bank, P.O. Box 789, 1099 Manila, Philippines; *Key Indicators of Developing Asian and Pacific Countries*.

WESTERN SAMOA - ECONOMY

Asian Development Bank, P.O. Box 789, 1099 Manila, Philippines; *Key Indicators of Developing Asian and Pacific Countries*.

WESTERN SAMOA - EDUCATION

The World Bank, 1818 H Street, NW, Washington, D.C. 20433 (202) 477-1234; *World Tables.*

WESTERN SAMOA - ELECTRICITY

Asian Development Bank, P.O. Box 789, 1099 Manila, Philippines; *Key Indicators of Developing Asian and Pacific Countries.*

WESTERN SAMOA - EXCHANGE RATES

Asian Development Bank, P.O. Box 789, 1099 Manila, Philippines; *Key Indicators of Developing Asian and Pacific Countries.*

International Monetary Fund, 700 Nineteenth Street, NW, Washington, D.C. 20431 (202) 623-7000; *International Financial Statistics.*

WESTERN SAMOA - EXPORTS

Asian Development Bank, P.O. Box 789, 1099 Manila, Philippines; *Key Indicators of Developing Asian and Pacific Countries.*

International Monetary Fund, 700 Nineteenth Street, NW, Washington, D.C. 20431 (202) 623-7000; *International Financial Statistics.*

South Pacific Commission, Post Box D5, Noumea Cedex, New Caledonia; *Statistical Bulletin of the South Pacific: Overseas Trade.*

The World Bank, 1818 H Street, NW, Washington, D.C. 20433 (202) 477-1234; *World Tables.*

WESTERN SAMOA - EXTERNAL FINANCING

Asian Development Bank, P.O. Box 789, 1099 Manila, Philippines; *Key Indicators of Developing Asian and Pacific Countries.*

WESTERN SAMOA - EXTERNAL INDEBTEDNESS

Asian Development Bank, P.O. Box 789, 1099 Manila, Philippines; *Key Indicators of Developing Asian and Pacific Countries.*

The World Bank, 1818 H Street, NW, Washington, D.C. 20433 (202) 477-1234; *World Tables.*

WESTERN SAMOA - EXTERNAL TRADE

Asian Development Bank, P.O. Box 789, 1099 Manila, Philippines; *Key Indicators of Developing Asian and Pacific Countries.*

WESTERN SAMOA - FERTILITY RATES

The World Bank, 1818 H Street, NW, Washington, D.C. 20433 (202) 477-1234; *World Tables.*

WESTERN SAMOA - FINANCE

Asian Development Bank, P.O. Box 789, 1099 Manila, Philippines; *Key Indicators of Developing Asian and Pacific Countries.*

International Monetary Fund, 700 Nineteenth Street, NW, Washington, D.C. 20431 (202) 623-7000; *International Financial Statistics.*

WESTERN SAMOA - FOOD

South Pacific Commission, Post Box D5, Noumea Cedex, New Caledonia; *Statistical Bulletin of the South Pacific: Retail Price Indexes.*

WESTERN SAMOA - FOREIGN TRADE

Asian Development Bank, P.O. Box 789, 1099 Manila, Philippines; *Key Indicators of Developing Asian and Pacific Countries.*

South Pacific Commission, Post Box D5, Noumea Cedex, New Caledonia; *Statistical Bulletin of the South Pacific: Overseas Trade.*

The World Bank, 1818 H Street, NW, Washington, D.C. 20433 (202) 477-1234; *World Tables.*

WESTERN SAMOA - GOLD HOLDINGS

The World Bank, 1818 H Street, NW, Washington, D.C. 20433 (202) 477-1234; *World Tables.*

WESTERN SAMOA - GOVERNMENT

Asian Development Bank, P.O. Box 789, 1099 Manila, Philippines; *Key Indicators of Developing Asian and Pacific Countries.*

WESTERN SAMOA - GOVERNMENT EXPENDITURE

Asian Development Bank, P.O. Box 789, 1099 Manila, Philippines; *Key Indicators of Developing Asian and Pacific Countries.*

The World Bank, 1818 H Street, NW, Washington, D.C. 20433 (202) 477-1234; *World Tables.*

WESTERN SAMOA - GOVERNMENT FINANCES

Asian Development Bank, P.O. Box 789, 1099 Manila, Philippines; *Key Indicators of Developing Asian and Pacific Countries.*

WESTERN SAMOA - GOVERNMENT REVENUE

Asian Development Bank, P.O. Box 789, 1099 Manila, Philippines; *Key Indicators of Developing Asian and Pacific Countries.*

The World Bank, 1818 H Street, NW, Washington, D.C. 20433 (202) 477-1234; *World Tables.*

WESTERN SAMOA - GROSS DOMESTIC PRODUCT

Asian Development Bank, P.O. Box 789, 1099 Manila, Philippines; *Key Indicators of Developing Asian and Pacific Countries.*

The World Bank, 1818 H Street, NW, Washington, D.C. 20433 (202) 477-1234; *World Tables.*

WESTERN SAMOA - GROSS NATIONAL PRODUCT

Asian Development Bank, P.O. Box 789, 1099 Manila, Philippines; *Key Indicators of Developing Asian and Pacific Countries.*

The World Bank, 1818 H Street, NW, Washington, D.C. 20433 (202) 477-1234; *World Tables.*

WESTERN SAMOA - HEALTH

South Pacific Commission, Post Box D5, Noumea Cedex, New Caledonia; *Statistical Bulletin of the South Pacific: Retail Price Indexes.*

WESTERN SAMOA - HOUSING AND HOUSING UNITS

South Pacific Commission, Post Box D5, Noumea Cedex, New Caledonia; *Statistical Bulletin of the South Pacific: Retail Price Indexes.*

WESTERN SAMOA - HOUSING EXPENDITURES

South Pacific Commission, Post Box D5, Noumea Cedex, New Caledonia; *Statistical Bulletin of the South Pacific: Retail Price Indexes.*

WESTERN SAMOA - IMPORTS

Asian Development Bank, P.O. Box 789, 1099 Manila, Philippines; *Key Indicators of Developing Asian and Pacific Countries.*

International Monetary Fund, 700 Nineteenth Street, NW, Washington, D.C. 20431 (202) 623-7000; *International Financial Statistics.*

South Pacific Commission, Post Box D5, Noumea Cedex, New Caledonia; *Statistical Bulletin of the South Pacific: Overseas Trade.*

The World Bank, 1818 H Street, NW, Washington, D.C. 20433 (202) 477-1234; *World Tables.*

WESTERN SAMOA - INDUSTRY

The World Bank, 1818 H Street, NW, Washington, D.C. 20433 (202) 477-1234; *World Tables.*

World Intellectual Property Organization, 34 Chemin des Colombettes, CH-1211 Geneva 20. Switzerland; *Industrial Property Statistics.*

WESTERN SAMOA - INFANT AND MATERNAL MORTALITY RATE

The World Bank, 1818 H Street, NW, Washington, D.C. 20433 (202) 477-1234; *World Tables.*

WESTERN SAMOA - INTERNATIONAL LIQUIDITY

International Monetary Fund, 700 Nineteenth Street, NW, Washington, D.C. 20431 (202) 623-7000; *International Financial Statistics.*

WESTERN SAMOA - INTERNATIONAL RESERVES EXCLUDING GOLD

Asian Development Bank, P.O. Box 789, 1099 Manila, Philippines; *Key Indicators of Developing Asian and Pacific Countries.*

The World Bank, 1818 H Street, NW, Washington, D.C. 20433 (202) 477-1234; *World Tables.*

WESTERN SAMOA - INTERNATIONAL STATISTICS

Asian Development Bank, P.O. Box 789, 1099 Manila, Philippines; *Key Indicators of Developing Asian and Pacific Countries.*

WESTERN SAMOA - LABOR FORCE

The World Bank, 1818 H Street, NW, Washington, D.C. 20433 (202) 477-1234; *World Tables.*

WESTERN SAMOA - MANUFACTURING

Asian Development Bank, P.O. Box 789, 1099 Manila, Philippines; *Key Indicators of Developing Asian and Pacific Countries.*

The World Bank, 1818 H Street, NW, Washington, D.C. 20433 (202) 477-1234; *World Tables.*

WESTERN SAMOA - MONEY SUPPLY

Asian Development Bank, P.O. Box 789, 1099 Manila, Philippines; *Key Indicators of Developing Asian and Pacific Countries.*

The World Bank, 1818 H Street, NW, Washington, D.C. 20433 (202) 477-1234; *World Tables.*

WESTERN SAMOA - PATENTS

World Intellectual Property Organization, 34 Chemin des Colombettes, CH-1211 Geneva 20. Switzerland; *Industrial Property Statistics.*

WESTERN SAMOA - PETROLEUM INDUSTRY

Asian Development Bank, P.O. Box 789, 1099 Manila, Philippines; *Key Indicators of Developing Asian and Pacific Countries.*

WESTERN SAMOA - POPULATION

Asian Development Bank, P.O. Box 789, 1099 Manila, Philippines; *Key Indicators of Developing Asian and Pacific Countries.*

United Nations Educational, Scientific and Cultural Organization (UNESCO), 7 Place de Fontenoy, F 75700 Paris, France (Telephone Number in U.S. (212) 963-5981), *Statistical Yearbook.*

WESTERN SAMOA - PRICES

Asian Development Bank, P.O. Box 789, 1099 Manila, Philippines; *Key Indicators of Developing Asian and Pacific Countries.*

International Monetary Fund, 700 Nineteenth Street, NW, Washington, D.C. 20431 (202) 623-7000; *International Financial Statistics.*

South Pacific Commission, Post Box D5, Noumea Cedex, New Caledonia; *Statistical Bulletin of the South Pacific: Overseas Trade,* and *Statistical Bulletin of the South Pacific: Retail Price Indexes.*

WESTERN SAMOA - RICE PRODUCTION - See WESTERN SAMOA - CROPS

WESTERN SAMOA - SOCIAL DATA

Asian Development Bank, P.O. Box 789, 1099 Manila, Philippines; *Key Indicators of Developing Asian and Pacific Countries.*

WESTERN SAMOA - TAXATION

The World Bank, 1818 H Street, NW, Washington, D.C. 20433 (202) 477-1234; *World Tables.*

WESTERN SAMOA - TELEPHONES IN USE

American Telephone and Telegraph Company, 26 Parsippany Road, Whippany, New Jersey 07081 (800) 338-1038; *The World's Telephones.*

WESTERN SAMOA - TOBACCO PRODUCTION

South Pacific Commission, Post Box D5, Noumea Cedex, New Caledonia; *Statistical Bulletin of the South Pacific: Retail Price Indexes.*

WESTERN SAMOA - TRADE - See WESTERN SAMOA - FOREIGN TRADE

WESTERN SAMOA - TRADEMARKS AND SERVICE MARKS

World Intellectual Property Organization, 34 Chemin des Colombettes, CH-1211 Geneva 20. Switzerland; *Industrial Property Statistics.*

WESTERN SAMOA - TRANSPORTATION AND COMMUNICATIONS

South Pacific Commission, Post Box D5, Noumea Cedex, New Caledonia; *Statistical Bulletin of the South Pacific: Retail Price Indexes.*

WESTERN SAMOA - WHOLESALE PRICES

Asian Development Bank, P.O. Box 789, 1099 Manila, Philippines; *Key Indicators of Developing Asian and Pacific Countries.*

WHEAT - ACREAGE

U.S. Department of Agriculture, Economic Research Service, Fourteenth Street and Independence Avenue, SW, Washington, D.C. 20005-4789 (202) 219-1504; *Agricultural Statistics, Crop Production, Crop Values, Field Crops, Wheat Situation, Agricultural Outlook,* and *Agricultural Supply and Demand Estimates.*

WHEAT - COMMODITY CREDIT CORPORATION TRANSACTIONS

U.S. Department of Agriculture, Agricultural Stabilization and Conservation Service, Fourteenth Street and Independence Avenue, SW, Washington, D.C. 20250 (202) 720-5237; *Commodity Credit Corporation Report of Financial Condition and Operations,* and *Agricultural Outlook.*

WHEAT - FARM MARKETINGS - SALES

U.S. Department of Agriculture, Economic Research Service, Fourteenth Street and Constitution Avenue, SW, Washington, D.C. 20005-4789 (202) 219-1504; *Economic Indicators of the Farm Sector: National Financial Summary.*

WHEAT - FOREIGN TRADE

U.S. Department of Agriculture, Economic Research Service, Fourteenth Street and Constitution Avenue, SW, Washington, D.C. 20005-4789 (202) 219-1504; *World Agriculture: Trends and Indicators, Foreign Agricultural Trade of the United States, Agricultural Outlook, Agricultural Statistics,* and data from Food and Agriculture Organization of the United Nations (FAO), Via delle Terme di Caracalla 00100 Rome, Italy (Telephone Number in U.S. (202) 653-2400); *FAO Trade Yearbook.*

U.S. Department of Agriculture, Foreign Agricultural Service, Fourteenth Street and Constitution Avenue, SW, Washington, D.C. 20250 (202) 720-3448; *Foreign Agricultural Commodity Circular Series.*

U.S. Department of Commerce, Bureau of the Census, Suitland, Maryland 20233 (301) 763-4040; *U.S. Merchandise Trade.*

WHEAT - PRODUCTION

U.S. Department of Agriculture, Economic Research Service, Fourteenth Street and Independence Avenue, SW, Washington, D.C. 20005-4789 (202) 219-1504; *Agricultural Statistics.*

U.S. Department of Agriculture, Foreign Agricultural Service, Fourteenth Street and Constitution Avenue, SW, Washington, D.C. 20250 (202) 720-3448; *Foreign Agricultural Commodity Circular Series.*

U.S. Department of Agriculture, National Agricultural Statistics Service, Fourteenth Street and Independence Avenue, SW, Washington, D.C. 20250 (202) 219-1504; *Crop Production, Crop Values, Agricultural Outlook, Field Crops,* and *Wheat Situation.*

WHEAT - PRODUCTION - WORLD PRODUCTION

Statistical Office of the United Nations, Publishing Service, New York, New York 10017 (800) 253-9646; *Statistical Yearbook,* and *Monthly Bulletin of Statistics.*

U.S. Department of Agriculture, Economic Research Service, Fourteenth Street and Independence Avenue, SW, Washington, D.C. 20005 (202) 219-1504; *World Agriculture: Trends and Indicators.*

WHEAT - SUPPLY AND DISAPPEARANCE

U.S. Department of Agriculture, Economic Research Service, Fourteenth Street and Independence Avenue, SW, Washington, D.C. 20005-4789 (202) 219-1504; *Wheat Situation, Agricultural Supply and Demand Estimates,* and *Agricultural Statistics.*

WHEAT FLOUR

Statistical Office of the United Nations, Publishing Service, New York, New York 10017 (800) 253-9646; *Monthly Bulletin of Statistics.*

U.S. Department of Agriculture, Economic Research Service, Fourteenth Street and Independence Avenue, SW, Washington, D.C. 20005-4789 (202) 219-1504; *World Agriculture - Trends and Indicators, Food Consumption, Prices, and Expenditures,* and unpublished data.

WHISKEY - See also ALCOHOLIC BEVERAGES

WHISKEY

U.S. Department of Agriculture, Economic Research Service, Fourteenth Street and Independence Avenue, SW, Washington, D.C. 20005-4789 (202) 219-1504; *Food Consumption, Prices, and Expenditures,* and unpublished data.

U.S. Department of the Treasury, Bureau of Alcohol, Tobacco, and Firearms, 650 Massachusetts Avenue, NW, Washington, D.C. 20226 (202) 927-8500; *Alcohol and Tobacco Summary Statistics.*

WHITE-COLLAR WORKERS

U.S. Department of Labor, Bureau of Labor Statistics, Two Massachusetts Avenue, NE, Washington, D.C. 20212 (202) 606-7828; *Employment and Earnings,* and unpublished data.

U.S. Office of Personnel Management, 1900 E Street, NW, Washington, D.C. 20415 (202) 606-1800; *Federal Civilian Work Force Statistics - Employment and Trends, The Pay Structure of the Federal Civil Service,* and *Central Personnel Data File.*

WHITE-COLLAR WORKERS - EMPLOYMENT COST INDEX

U.S. Department of Labor, Bureau of Labor Statistics, Two Massachusetts Avenue, NE, Washington, D.C. 20212 (202) 606-7828; *News, Employment Cost Index.*

WHITE-COLLAR WORKERS - WOMEN

U.S. Office of Personnel Management, 1900 E Street, NW, Washington, D.C. 20415 (202) 606-1800; *The Pay Structure of the Federal Civil Service,* and *Central Personnel Data File.*

WHITING - QUANTITY AND VALUE OF CATCH

U.S. Department of Commerce, National Oceanic and Atmospheric Administration, National Marine Fisheries Service, 1335 East-West Highway, Silver Spring, Maryland 20910 (301) 427-2239; *Fishery Statistics of the United States,* and *Fisheries of the United States.*

WHOLESALE TRADE - EARNINGS

U.S. Department of Commerce, Bureau of Economic Analysis, Fourteenth Street between Constitution Avenue and E Street, NW, Washington, D.C. 20230 (202) 606-9900; *The National Income and Product Accounts of the United States,* and *Survey of Current Business.*

U.S. Department of Commerce, Bureau of the Census, Suitland, Maryland 20233 (301) 763-4040; *Census of Wholesale Trade, County Business Patterns,* and *Economic Census of Outlying Areas.*

U.S. Department of Labor, Bureau of Labor Statistics, Two Massachusetts Avenue, NE, Washington, D.C. 20212 (202) 606-7828; *Employment and Earnings,* and Bulletins 2370 and 2429.

WHOLESALE TRADE - EMPLOYEES

U.S. Department of Commerce, Bureau of Economic Analysis, Fourteenth Street between Constitution Avenue and E Street, NW, Washington, D.C. 20230 (202) 606-9900; *The National Income and Product Accounts of the United States,* and *Survey of Current Business.*

U.S. Department of Commerce, Bureau of the Census, Suitland, Maryland 20233 (301) 763-4040; *Census of Wholesale Trade, County Business Patterns,* and *Economic Census of Outlying Areas.*

U.S. Department of Labor, Bureau of Labor Statistics, Two Massachusetts Avenue, NE, Washington, D.C. 20212 (202) 606-7828; *Employment and Earnings, Monthly Labor Review,* and Bulletins 2370 and 2429.

WHOLESALE TRADE - ESTABLISHMENTS

U.S. Department of Commerce, Bureau of the Census, Suitland, Maryland 20233 (301) 763-4040; *Census of Business, Census of Wholesale Trade, Economic Census of Outlying Areas,* and *County Business Patterns.*

WHOLESALE TRADE - FOREIGN INVESTMENTS IN THE UNITED STATES

U.S. Department of Commerce, Bureau of Economic Analysis, Fourteenth Street between Constitution Avenue and E Street, NW, Washington, D.C. 20230 (202) 606-9900; *Survey of Current Business,* and *Foreign Direct Investment in the U.S., Operations of Affiliates of Foreign Countries.*

WHOLESALE TRADE - GROSS DOMESTIC PRODUCT

U.S. Department of Commerce, Bureau of Economic Analysis, Fourteenth Street between Constitution Avenue and E Street, NW, Washington, D.C. 20230 (202) 606-9900; *The National Income and Product Accounts of the United States,* and *Survey of Current Business.*

WHOLESALE TRADE - INVENTORIES

U.S. Department of Commerce, Bureau of the Census, Suitland, Maryland 20233 (301) 763-4040; *Census of Wholesale Trade,* and *Current Business Reports, Combined Annual and Revised Monthly Wholesale Trade.*

WHOLESALE TRADE - MERGERS AND ACQUISITIONS

Securities Data Company, 1180 Raymond Boulevard, Newark, New Jersey 07102 (201) 622-3100; *Merger and Corporate Transactions Database.*

WHOLESALE TRADE - OCCUPATIONAL SAFETY

U.S. Department of Labor, Bureau of Labor Statistics, Two Massachusetts Avenue, NE, Washington, D.C. 20212 (202) 606-7828; *Occupational Injuries and Illnesses in the United States by Industry.*

WHOLESALE TRADE - PROFITS

U.S. Department of the Treasury, Internal Revenue Service, 1111 Constitution Avenue, NW, Washington, D.C. 20224 (202) 566-5000; *Statistics of Income,* various publications.

WHOLESALE TRADE - RECEIPTS

U.S. Department of the Treasury, Internal Revenue Service, 1111 Constitution Avenue, NW, Washington, D.C. 20224 (202) 566-5000; *Statistics of Income,* various publications.

WHOLESALE TRADE - SALES

U.S. Department of Commerce, Bureau of the Census, Suitland, Maryland 20233 (301) 763-4040; *Census of Wholesale Trade, Current Business Reports, Combined Annual and Revised Monthly Wholesale Trade.* and *Economic Census of Outlying Areas.*

WILDLIFE - ENDANGERED SPECIES

U.S. Department of the Interior, Fish and Wildlife Service, C Street between Eighteenth and Nineteenth Streets, NW, Washington, D.C. 20240 (202) 208-5634; *Endangered Species Technical Bulletin.*

WIND - ENERGY SOURCE

U.S. Department of Energy, Energy Information Administration, 1000 Independence Avenue, SW, Washington, D.C. 20585 (202) 586-8800; *Annual Energy Review.*

WIND - SELECTED CITIES

U.S. Department of Commerce, National Oceanic and Atmospheric Administration, National Climatic Data Center, Federal Building, Asheville, North Carolina 28801 (704) 259-2850; *Comparative Climatic Data.*

WINDWARD ISLANDS - AREA AND DENSITY OF POPULATION

Statistical Office of the United Nations, Publishing Service, New York, New York 10017 (800) 253-9646; *Statistical Yearbook.*

WINDWARD ISLANDS - POPULATION

Statistical Office of the United Nations, Publishing Service, New York, New York 10017 (800) 253-9646; *Statistical Yearbook.*

WINDWARD ISLANDS - POPULATION - BY SEX

Statistical Office of the United Nations, Publishing Service, New York, New York 10017 (800) 253-9646; *Statistical Yearbook.*

WINES - See also ALCOHOLIC BEVERAGES

WINES

Statistical Office of the United Nations, Publishing Service, New York, New York 10017 (800) 253-9646; *Statistical Yearbook,* and *Monthly Bulletin of Statistics.*

U.S. Department of Agriculture, Economic Research Service, Fourteenth Street and Independence Avenue, SW, Washington, D.C. 20005-4789 (202) 219-1504; *Food Consumption, Prices, and Expenditures, Foreign Agricultural Trade of the United States,* and unpublished data.

WIRE TAPS

Administrative Office of the United States Courts, United States Supreme Court Building, One First Street, NE, Washington, D.C. 20544 (202) 633-6094; *Report on Applications for Orders Authorizing or Approving the Interception of Wire or Oral or Electronic Communications.*

WISCONSIN - See also STATE DATA (FOR INDIVIDUAL STATES)

Wisconsin - Primary Statistics Sources

Wisconsin Legislative Reference Bureau, Post Office Box 2037, Madison, Wisconsin 53701-2037 (608) 266-0341; *Wisconsin Blue Book.*

Wisconsin - State Data Centers

Demographic Services Center, Department of Administration, 101 East Wilson Street, Sixth Floor, Post Office Box 7868, Madison, Wisconsin 53707-7868, Mr. Robert Naylor (608) 266-1927.

Applied Population Laboratory, Department of Rural Sociology, University of Wisconsin, 1450 Linden Drive, Room 316, Madison, Wisconsin 53706, Mr. Michael Knight (608) 265-3044.

WOMEN - ABORTIONS

Alan Guttmacher Institute, 111 Fifth Avenue, New York, New York 10003 (212) 254-5656; *Abortion Factbook: Readings, Trends, and State and Local Data, Abortion Services in the U.S., Family Planning Perspectives,* and unpublished data.

U.S. Department of Health and Human Services, National Center for Health Statistics, 3700 East-West Highway, Hyattsville, Maryland 20782 (301) 436-8500; *Monthly Vital Statistics Report.*

WOMEN - AGE

U.S. Department of Commerce, Bureau of the Census, Suitland, Maryland 20233 (301) 763-4040; unpublished data.

WOMEN - AIDS

U.S. Department of Health and Human Services, Centers for Disease Control, 2600 Clifton Road, NE, Atlanta, Georgia 20333 (404) 639-3311; *Surveillance Report,* and unpublished data.

WOMEN - ALCOHOL USE

U.S. Department of Health and Human Services, National Center for Health Statistics, 3700 East-West Highway, Hyattsville, Maryland 20782 (301) 436-8500; *Health Promotion and Disease Prevention, United States, Vital and Health Statistics,* and unpublished data.

WOMEN - BIRTHS AND BIRTH RATES

U.S. Department of Commerce, Bureau of the Census, Suitland, Maryland 20233 (301) 763-4040; *Census of Population, Current Population Reports,* International Data Base and unpublished data.

U.S. Department of Health and Human Services, National Center for Health Statistics, 3700 East-West Highway, Hyattsville, Maryland 20782 (301) 436-8500; *Vital Statistics of the United States, Monthly Vital Statistics Report,* and unpublished data.

U.S. Department of Labor, Bureau of Labor Statistics, Two Massachusetts Avenue, NE, Washington, D.C. 20212 (202) 606-7828; *Monthly Labor Review,* and unpublished data.

WOMEN - BIRTHS AND BIRTH RATES - BIRTHS TO SINGLE WOMEN

U.S. Department of Commerce, Bureau of the Census, Suitland, Maryland 20233 (301) 763-4040; *Current Population Reports.*

U.S. Department of Labor, Bureau of Labor Statistics, Two Massachusetts Avenue, NE, Washington, D.C. 20212 (202) 606-7828; *Monthly Labor Review,* and unpublished data.

WOMEN - BIRTHS AND BIRTH RATES - CESAREAN SECTION DELIVERIES

U.S. Department of Health and Human Services, National Center for Health Statistics, 3700 East-West Highway, Hyattsville, Maryland 20782 (301) 436-8500; *Vital and Health Statistics,* and unpublished data.

WOMEN - BIRTHS AND BIRTH RATES - CHARACTERISTICS - SELECTED

U.S. Department of Commerce, Bureau of the Census, Suitland, Maryland 20233 (301) 763-4040; *Current Population Reports.*

U.S. Department of Health and Human Services, National Center for Health Statistics, 3700 East-West Highway, Hyattsville, Maryland 20782 (301) 436-8500; *Vital Statistics of the United States, Advance Data from Vital and Health Statistics,* and unpublished data.

WOMEN - BIRTHS AND BIRTH RATES - FIRST BIRTHS

U.S. Department of Commerce, Bureau of the Census, Suitland, Maryland 20233 (301) 763-4040; *Current Population Reports.*

WOMEN - CANCER

U.S. Department of Health and Human Services, National Center for Health Statistics, 3700 East-West Highway, Hyattsville, Maryland 20782 (301) 436-8500; *Vital and Health Statistics.*

U.S. Department of Health and Human Services, National Institutes of Health, National Cancer Institute, 9000 Rockville Pike, Bethesda, Maryland 20892 (301) 496-5737; *Cancer Statistics Review.*

WOMEN - CHILD DAY CARE

U.S. Department of Commerce, Bureau of the Census, Suitland, Maryland 20233 (301) 763-4040; *Current Population Reports.*

WOMEN - CHRONIC CONDITIONS

U.S. Department of Health and Human Services, National Center for Health Statistics, 3700 East-West Highway, Hyattsville, Maryland 20782 (301) 436-8500; *Vital and Health Statistics,* and unpublished data.

WOMEN - CIGARETTE SMOKING

U.S. Department of Health and Human Services, Centers for Disease Control, 2600 Clifton Road, NW, Atlanta, Georgia 20333 (404) 639-3311; *Reducing the Health Consequences of Smoking.*

U.S. Department of Health and Human Services, National Center for Health Statistics, 3700 East-West Highway, Hyattsville, Maryland 20782 (301) 436-8500; *Vital and Health Statistics, Health Promotion and Disease Prevention, United States,* and unpublished data.

WOMEN - CONTRACEPTIVE USE

U.S. Department of Health and Human Services, National Center for Health Statistics, 3700 East-West Highway, Hyattsville, Maryland 20782 (301) 436-8500; *Advance Data from Vital and Health Statistics,* and unpublished data.

WOMEN - CRIMINAL VICTIMIZATION RATES

U.S. Department of Justice, Bureau of Justice Statistics, 633 Indiana Avenue, NW, Washington, D.C. 20531 (800) 732-3277; *Criminal Victimization in the United States.*

WOMEN - DEATHS AND DEATH RATES

U.S. Department of Health and Human Services, National Center for Health Statistics, 3700 East-West Highway, Hyattsville, Maryland 20782 (301) 436-8500; *Monthly Vital Statistics Report, Vital Statistics of the United States,* and unpublished data.

WOMEN - DELIVERY PROCEDURES - BIRTHS

U.S. Department of Health and Human Services, National Center for Health Statistics, 3700 East-West Highway, Hyattsville, Maryland 20782 (301) 436-8500; *Vital and Health Statistics,* and unpublished data.

WOMEN - DENTAL VISITS

U.S. Department of Health and Human Services, National Center for Health Statistics, 3700 East-West Highway, Hyattsville, Maryland 20782 (301) 436-8500; *Vital and Health Statistics,* and unpublished data.

WOMEN - DISABILITY DAYS

U.S. Department of Health and Human Services, Public Health Service, 200 Independence Avenue, SW, Washington, D.C. 20201 (202) 619-1296; *Vital and Health Statistics,* and unpublished data.

WOMEN - EDUCATION - AMERICAN COLLEGE TESTING PROGRAM

American College Testing Program, Box 168, Iowa City, Iowa 52243 (319) 337-1000; *High School Profile Report.*

WOMEN - EDUCATION - ATTAINMENT

Organisation for Economic Co-operation and Development (OECD), 2 rue Andre-Pascal, 75 Paris 16, France (Telephone Number in U.S. (202) 785-6323); *Education at a Glance.*

U.S. Department of Commerce, Bureau of the Census, Suitland, Maryland 20233 (301) 763-4040; *Current Population Reports, Census of Population,* and unpublished data.

U.S. Department of Education, 400 Maryland Avenue, SW, Washington, D.C. 20202 (202) 708-5366; *Digest of Education Statistics.*

U.S. Department of Labor, Bureau of Labor Statistics, Two Massachusetts Avenue, NE, Washington, D.C. 20212 (202) 606-7828; *News,* Bulletin 2307, and unpublished data.

WOMEN - EDUCATION - ATTAINMENT - LABOR FORCE STATUS

U.S. Department of Labor, Bureau of Labor Statistics, Two Massachusetts Avenue, NE, Washington, D.C. 20212 (202) 606-7828; Bulletin 2307, and unpublished data.

WOMEN - EDUCATION - COLLEGE ENROLLMENT

U.S. Department of Commerce, Bureau of the Census, Suitland, Maryland 20233 (301) 763-4040; *Current Population Reports,* and unpublished data.

U.S. Department of Education, 400 Maryland Avenue, SW, Washington, D.C. 20202 (202) 708-5366; *Digest of Education Statistics, Projections of Education Statistics,* and unpublished data.

U.S. National Science Foundation, 4201 Wilson Boulevard, Arlington, Virginia 22230 (703) 306-1234; *Survey of Graduate Science Engineering Students and Postdoctorates.*

WOMEN - EDUCATION - COLLEGE ENROLLMENT - BY AGE

U.S. Department of Education, 400 Maryland Avenue, SW, Washington, D.C. 20202 (202) 708-5366; *Projections of Education Statistics.*

WOMEN - EDUCATION - COLLEGE ENROLLMENT - BY STATE

U.S. Department of Education, 400 Maryland Avenue, SW, Washington, D.C. 20202 (202) 708-5366; *Digest of Education Statistics.*

WOMEN - EDUCATION - COLLEGE ENROLLMENT - PROJECTIONS

U.S. Department of Education, 400 Maryland Avenue, SW, Washington, D.C. 20202 (202) 708-5366; *Projections of Education Statistics.*

WOMEN - EDUCATION - DEGREES CONFERRED

U.S. Department of Education, 400 Maryland Avenue, SW, Washington, D.C. 20202 (202) 708-5366; *Digest of Education Statistics*, and unpublished data.

U.S. National Science Foundation, 1800 G Street, NW, Washington, D.C. 20550 (202) 357-5000; *Survey of Earned Doctorates, Selected Data on Science and Engineering Doctorate Awards.*

WOMEN - EDUCATION - ENROLLMENT BY LEVEL

U.S. Department of Commerce, Bureau of the Census, Suitland, Maryland 20233 (301) 763-4040; *Current Population Reports*, and unpublished data.

WOMEN - EDUCATION - HIGH SCHOOL DROPOUTS

U.S. Department of Commerce, Bureau of the Census, Suitland, Maryland 20233 (301) 763-4040; *Current Population Reports*, and unpublished data.

U.S. Department of Labor, Bureau of Labor Statistics, Two Massachusetts Avenue, NE, Washington, D.C. 20212 (202) 606-7828; Bulletin 2307 and unpublished data.

WOMEN - EDUCATION - SAT TESTS

College Entrance Examination Board, 45 Columbus Avenue, New York, New York 10023 (212) 713-8000; *National College - Bound Seniors.*

WOMEN - ELECTIONS - VOTER REGISTRATION AND TURNOUT

U.S. Department of Commerce, Bureau of the Census, Suitland, Maryland 20233 (301) 763-4040; *Current Population Reports.*

WOMEN - FARMWORKERS

U.S. Department of Agriculture, Economic Research Service, Fourteenth Street and Independence Avenue, SW, Washington, D.C. 20005-4789 (202) 219-1504; unpublished data.

WOMEN - FERTILITY - FERTILITY RATE

U.S. Department of Commerce, Bureau of the Census, Suitland, Maryland 20233 (301) 763-4040; *Current Population Reports.*

U.S. Department of Health and Human Services, National Center for Health Statistics, 3700 East-West Highway, Hyattsville, Maryland 20782 (301) 436-8500; *Vital Statistics of the United States*, and unpublished data.

WOMEN - GROUP QUARTERS

U.S. Department of Commerce, Bureau of the Census, Suitland, Maryland 20233 (301) 763-4040; *Census of Population, General Population Characteristics.*

WOMEN - HEALTH INSURANCE COVERAGE

U.S. Department of Commerce, Bureau of the Census, Suitland, Maryland 20233 (301) 763-4040; *Current Population Reports*, and unpublished data.

U.S. Department of Health and Human Services, National Center for Health Statistics, 3700 East-West Highway, Hyattsville, Maryland 20782 (301) 436-8500; *Advance Data from Vital and Health Statistics.*

WOMEN - HEIGHT DISTRIBUTION

U.S. Department of Health and Human Services, National Center for Health Statistics, 3700 East-West Highway, Hyattsville, Maryland 20782 (301) 436-8500; *Vital and Health Statistics.*

WOMEN - HISPANIC ORIGIN POPULATION

U.S. Department of Commerce, Bureau of the Census, Suitland, Maryland 20233 (301) 763-4040; *Census of Population*, and *Current Population Reports.*

WOMEN - HOMICIDES

U.S. Department of Health and Human Services, National Center for Health Statistics, 3700 East-West Highway, Hyattsville, Maryland 20782 (301) 436-8500; *Vital Statistics of the United States.*

WOMEN - HOSPITAL USE

U.S. Department of Health and Human Services, National Center for Health Statistics, 3700 East-West Highway, Hyattsville, Maryland 20782 (301) 436-8500; *Vital and Health Statistics, Health, United States, Advance Data from Vital and Health Statistics*, and unpublished data.

WOMEN - HOUSEHOLDERS

U.S. Department of Commerce, Bureau of the Census, Suitland, Maryland 20233 (301) 763-4040; *Current Population Reports, Census of Population*, and unpublished data.

WOMEN - ILLNESS/INJURY

U.S. Department of Health and Human Services, National Center for Health Statistics, 3700 East-West Highway, Hyattsville, Maryland 20782 (301) 436-8500; *Vital and Health Statistics*, and unpublished data.

WOMEN - INCOME

U.S. Department of Commerce, Bureau of the Census, Suitland, Maryland 20233 (301) 763-4040; *Current Population Reports.*

WOMEN - LABOR FORCE AND EMPLOYMENT - AGE

U.S. Department of Labor, Bureau of Labor Statistics, Two Massachusetts Avenue, NE, Washington, D.C. 20212 (202) 606-7828; *Employment and Earnings, Monthly Labor Review*, and Bulletin 2307.

WOMEN - LABOR FORCE AND EMPLOYMENT - CHILDREN IN PREPRIMARY SCHOOL

U.S. Department of Commerce, Bureau of the Census, Suitland, Maryland 20233 (301) 763-4040; *Current Population Reports*, and unpublished data.

WOMEN - LABOR FORCE AND EMPLOYMENT - EARNINGS

U.S. Department of Commerce, Bureau of the Census, Suitland, Maryland 20233 (301) 763-4040; *Current Population Reports.*

U.S. Department of Labor, Bureau of Labor Statistics, Two Massachusetts Avenue, NE, Washington, D.C. 20212 (202) 606-7828; *Employment and Earnings,* and Bulletin 2307.

WOMEN - LABOR FORCE AND EMPLOYMENT - EDUCATIONAL ATTAINMENT

U.S. Department of Labor, Bureau of Labor Statistics, Two Massachusetts Avenue, NE, Washington, D.C. 20212 (202) 606-7828; Bulletin 2307 and unpublished data.

WOMEN - LABOR FORCE AND EMPLOYMENT - EMPLOYED

U.S. Department of Labor, Bureau of Labor Statistics, Two Massachusetts Avenue, NE, Washington, D.C. 20212 (202) 606-7828; *Geographical Profile of Employment and Unemployment*, Bulletin 2307, *Employment and Earnings, News,* and unpublished data.

WOMEN - LABOR FORCE AND EMPLOYMENT - GOVERNMENT EMPLOYMENT

U.S. Equal Employment Opportunity Commission, 2401 E Street, NW, Washington, D.C. 20507 (800) USA-EEOC; *State and Local Government Information Report.*

U.S. Office of Personnel Management, 1900 E Street, NW, Washington, D.C. 20415 (202) 606-1800; *Occupations of Federal White - Collar and Blue - Collar Workers,* and *The Pay Structure of the Federal Civil Service.*

WOMEN - LABOR FORCE AND EMPLOYMENT - INDUSTRY

U.S. Department of Labor, Bureau of Labor Statistics, Two Massachusetts Avenue, NE, Washington, D.C. 20212 (202) 606-7828; *Employment and Earnings.*

WOMEN - LABOR FORCE AND EMPLOYMENT - MARITAL STATUS

U.S. Department of Labor, Bureau of Labor Statistics, Two Massachusetts Avenue, NE, Washington, D.C. 20212 (202) 606-7828; *Monthly Labor Review,* Bulletins 2217, 2340, 2307, and unpublished data.

WOMEN - LABOR FORCE AND EMPLOYMENT - OCCUPATION

U.S. Department of Commerce, Bureau of the Census, Suitland, Maryland 20233 (301) 763-4040; *Current Population Reports.*

U.S. Department of Labor, Bureau of Labor Statistics, Two Massachusetts Avenue, NE, Washington, D.C. 20212 (202) 606-7828; Bulletin 2307, *Employment and Earnings,* and unpublished data.

WOMEN - LABOR FORCE AND EMPLOYMENT - PARTICIPATION RATES

U.S. Department of Labor, Bureau of Labor Statistics, Two Massachusetts Avenue, NE, Washington, D.C. 20212 (202) 606-7828; *Geographic Profile of Employment and Unemployment, Employment and Earnings, Monthly Labor Review,* Bulletins 2217, 2340, 2307, and unpublished data.

WOMEN - LABOR FORCE AND EMPLOYMENT - PROJECTIONS

U.S. Department of Labor, Bureau of Labor Statistics, Two Massachusetts Avenue, NE, Washington, D.C. 20212 (202) 606-7828; *Employment and Earnings, Monthly Labor Review,* and unpublished data.

WOMEN - LABOR FORCE AND EMPLOYMENT - SCHOOL ENROLLMENT

U.S. Department of Labor, Bureau of Labor Statistics, Two Massachusetts Avenue, NE, Washington, D.C. 20212 (202) 606-7828; *Bulletin 2307, News,* and unpublished data.

WOMEN - LABOR FORCE AND EMPLOYMENT - SELF-EMPLOYED

U.S. Department of Labor, Bureau of Labor Statistics, Two Massachusetts Avenue, NE, Washington, D.C. 20212 (202) 606-7828; *Employment and Earnings,* and unpublished data.

WOMEN - LABOR FORCE AND EMPLOYMENT - STATES

U.S. Department of Labor, Bureau of Labor Statistics, Two Massachusetts Avenue, NE, Washington, D.C. 20212 (202) 606-7828; *Geographic Profile of Employment and Unemployment.*

WOMEN - LABOR FORCE AND EMPLOYMENT - UNEMPLOYED

U.S. Department of Labor, Bureau of Labor Statistics, Two Massachusetts Avenue, NE, Washington, D.C. 20212 (202) 606-7828; *Employment and Earnings, Geographic Profile of Employment and Unemployment,* Bulletins 2192, 2307, and unpublished data.

WOMEN - LABOR FORCE AND EMPLOYMENT - UNION MEMBERSHIP

U.S. Department of Labor, Bureau of Labor Statistics, Two Massachusetts Avenue, NE, Washington, D.C. 20212 (202) 606-7828; *Employment and Earnings.*

WOMEN - LIFE EXPECTANCY

U.S. Department of Health and Human Services, National Center for Health Statistics, 3700 East-West Highway, Hyattsville, Maryland 20782 (301) 436-8500; *Monthly Vital Statistics, Vital Statistics of the United States,* and unpublished data.

WOMEN - MARITAL STATUS

U.S. Department of Commerce, Bureau of the Census, Suitland, Maryland 20233 (301) 763-4040; *Census of Population, Current Population Reports,* and unpublished data.

WOMEN - MARRIAGE AND DIVORCE

U.S. Department of Health and Human Services, National Center for Health Statistics, 3700 East West Highway, Hyattsville, Maryland 20782 (301) 436-8500; *Vital Statistics of the United States, Monthly Vital Statistics Report,* and unpublished data.

WOMEN - PENSION PLAN COVERAGE

U.S. Department of Commerce, Bureau of the Census, Suitland, Maryland 20233 (301) 763-4040; unpublished data.

WOMEN - PERSONAL HEALTH PRACTICES

U.S. Department of Health and Human Services, National Center for Health Statistics, 3700 East-West Highway, Hyattsville, Maryland 20782 (301) 436-8500; *Vital and Health Statistics, Health Promotion and Disease Prevention, United States,* and unpublished data.

WOMEN - PERSONS LIVING ALONE

U.S. Department of Commerce, Bureau of the Census, Suitland, Maryland 20233 (301) 763-4040; *Current Population Reports,* and unpublished data.

WOMEN - PHYSICIANS

American Medical Association, 515 North State Street, Chicago, Illinois 60610 (312) 464-4818; *Physician Characteristics and Distribution in the United States.*

WOMEN - POPULATION

U.S. Department of Commerce, Bureau of the Census, Suitland, Maryland 20233 (301) 763-4040; *Census of Population,* and *Current Population Reports.*

WOMEN - PUBLIC OFFICIALS

Congressional Quarterly, Incorporated, 1414 Twenty-second Street, NW, Washington, D.C. 20037 (202) 887-8500; *Vital Statistics on Congress.*

WOMEN - RAPE

U.S. Department of Justice, Federal Bureau of Investigation, Ninth Street and Pennsylvania Avenue, NW, Washington, D.C. 20535 (202) 324-3000; *Population-at-Risk Rates and Selected Crime Indicators, Crime in the United States,* and *Criminal Victimization in the United States.*

WOMEN - RECREATIONAL ACTIVITIES

National Sporting Goods Association, Lake Center Plaza Building, 1699 Wall Street, Mt. Prospect, Illinois 60056-5780 (708) 439-4000; *Sports Participation in 1992,* and *The Sporting Goods Market in 1993.*

WOMEN - SOCIAL SECURITY BENEFICIARIES AND PAYMENTS

U.S. Department of Health and Human Services, Social Security Administration, 6401 Security Boulevard, Baltimore, Maryland 21235 (410) 965-1234; *Annual Statistical Supplement to the Social Security Bulletin,* and unpublished data.

WOMEN - SURGICAL PROCEDURES

U.S. Department of Health and Human Services, National Center for Health Statistics, 3700 East-West Highway, Hyattsville, Maryland 20782 (301) 436-8500; *Vital and Health Statistics, National Health Interview Survey,* and unpublished data.

WOMEN - UNEMPLOYMENT

U.S. Department of Labor, Bureau of Labor Statistics, Two Massachusetts Avenue, NE, Washington, D.C. 20212 (202) 606-7828; *Employment and Earnings, Geographic Profile of Employment and Unemployment, News,* Bulletin 2307, and unpublished data.

WOMEN - UNEMPLOYMENT - AGE

U.S. Department of Labor, Bureau of Labor Statistics, Two Massachusetts Avenue, NE, Washington, D.C. 20212 (202) 606-7828; Bulletin 2307, *Employment and Earnings,* and unpublished data.

WOMEN - UNEMPLOYMENT - REASON

U.S. Department of Labor, Bureau of Labor Statistics, Two Massachusetts Avenue, NE, Washington, D.C. 20212 (202) 606-

7828; *Employment and Earnings,* and Bulletin 2307.

WOMEN - UNION MEMBERSHIP

U.S. Department of Labor, Bureau of Labor Statistics, Two Massachusetts Avenue, NE, Washington, D.C. 20212 (202) 606-7828; *Employment and Earnings.*

WOMEN - VOTER REGISTRATION AND TURNOUT

U.S. Department of Commerce, Bureau of the Census, Suitland, Maryland 20233 (301) 763-4040; *Current Population Reports.*

WOOD AND WOOD PRODUCTS - See LUMBER AND WOOD PRODUCTS

WOODPULP - See also PAPER AND PAPER PRODUCTS

WOODPULP - CONSUMPTION/OUTPUT

Statistical Office of the United Nations, Publishing Service, New York, New York 10017 (800) 253-9646; *Monthly Bulletin of Statistics.*

U.S. Department of Commerce, Bureau of the Census, Suitland, Maryland 20233 (301) 763-4040; *Current Industrial Reports.*

WOODPULP - FOREIGN TRADE

U.S. Department of Commerce, Bureau of the Census, Suitland, Maryland 20233 (301) 763-4040; *U.S. Merchandise Trade: Exports, General Imports, and Imports for Consumption.*

WOODPULP - PRODUCER PRICE INDEXES

U.S. Department of Labor, Bureau of Labor Statistics, Two Massachusetts Avenue, NE, Washington, D.C. 20212 (202) 606-7828; *Producer Price Indexes.*

WOODPULP - PRODUCTION

Statistical Office of the United Nations, Publishing Service, New York, New York 10017 (800) 253-9646; *Monthly Bulletin of Statistics.*

WOOL

Fiber Economics Bureau, Incorporated, 101 Eisenhower Parkway, Roseland, New Jersey 07068 (201) 228-1107; *Textile Organon.*

U.S. Department of Agriculture, Economic Research Service, Fourteenth Street and Independence Avenue, SW, Washington, D.C. 20005-4789 (202) 219-1504; *Cotton and Wool Outlook and Situation.*

WOOL - COMMODITY CREDIT CORPORATION TRANSACTIONS

U.S. Department of Agriculture, Agricultural Stabilization and Conservation Service, Fourteenth Street and Independence Avenue, SW, Washington, D.C. 20250 (202) 720-5237; *Commodity Credit Corporation Report of Financial Condition and Operations,* and *Agricultural Outlook.*

WOOL - WORLD PRODUCTION

Statistical Office of the United Nations, Publishing Service, New York, New York 10017 (800) 253-9646; *Statistical Yearbook,* and *Monthly Bulletin of Statistics.*

WORK STOPPAGES

U.S. Department of Labor, Bureau of Labor Statistics, Two Massachusetts Avenue, NE, Washington, D.C. 20212 (202) 606-7828; *Compensation and Working Conditions*.

WORKERS - See LABOR FORCE EMPLOYMENT AND EARNINGS

WORKERS' COMPENSATION PROGRAM

Executive Office of the President, Office of Management and Budget, Executive Office Building, Washington, D.C. 20503 (202) 395-3080; *Budget of the United States Government*.

U.S. Department of Health and Human Services, Health Care Financing Administration, 200 Independence Avenue, SW, Washington, D.C. 20201 (202) 245-6113; *Health Care Financing Review*.

U.S. Department of Health and Human Services, Social Security Administration, 6401 Security Boulevard, Baltimore, Maryland 21235 (410) 965-1234; *Annual Statistical Supplement to the Social Security Bulletin*, *Social Security Bulletin*, and unpublished data.

U.S. Department of Labor, Employment Standards Administration, 200 Constitution Avenue, NW, Washington, D.C. 20210 (202) 219-7320; *Black Lung Benefits Act, Annual Report*.

WORLD SUMMARY STATISTICS - ARMED FORCES PERSONNEL

U.S. Arms Control and Disarmament Agency, 320 Twenty-first Street, NW, Washington, D.C. 20451 (202) 647-8677; *World Military Expenditures and Arms Transfers*.

WORLD SUMMARY STATISTICS - COMPARATIVE DATA (AREA POPULATION, ETC.)

Statistical Office of the United Nations, Publishing Service, New York, New York 10017 (800) 253-9646, *Statistical Yearbook*, and *Demographic Yearbook*.

United Nations Educational, Scientific and Cultural Organization (UNESCO), 7 Place de Fontenoy, F-75700 Paris, France (Telephone Number in U.S. (212) 963-5981); *Statistical Yearbook*.

U.S. Department of Commerce, Bureau of the Census, Suitland, Maryland 20233 (301) 763-4040; *International Data Bank*.

WORLD SUMMARY STATISTICS - DEATHS AND DEATH RATES - CAUSE

World Health Organization, Avenue Appia, Office of Publications, Avenue Appia, CH-1211 Geneva 27, Switzerland (Telephone Number in U.S. (518) 436-9686); *World Health Statistics Annual*.

WORLD SUMMARY STATISTICS - ENERGY

Statistical Office of the United Nations, New York, New York 10017 (800) 253-9646; *Energy Statistics Yearbook*.

U.S. Department of Energy, Energy Information Administration, 1000 Independence Avenue, SW, Washington, D.C. 20585 (202) 586-8800; *International Energy Annual, Monthly Energy Review*, and *Annual Energy Review*.

WORLD SUMMARY STATISTICS - EXPORTS OF MANUFACTURES - UNITED STATES COMPARISON

U.S. Department of Commerce, International Trade Administration, Fourteenth Street between Constitution Avenue and E Street, NW, Washington, D.C. 20230 (202) 482-3809; *Market Share Reports, Business America*, and unpublished data.

WORLD SUMMARY STATISTICS - FARM COMMODITIES

Food and Agricultural Organization of the United Nations (FAO), Via delle Terme di Caracalla, 00100 Rome, Italy (Telephone Number in U.S. (202) 653-2400); *FAO Production Yearbook*.

U.S. Department of Agriculture, Economic Research Service, Fourteenth Street and Independence Avenue, SW, Washington, D.C. 20005-4789 (202) 219-1504; *World Agriculture-Trends and Indicators*.

U.S. Department of Agriculture, Foreign Agricultural Service, Fourteenth Street and Independence Avenue, SW, Washington, D.C. 20250 (202) 720-3448; *Foreign Agricultural Commodity Circular Series*.

WORLD SUMMARY STATISTICS - MERCHANT VESSELS

Lloyd's Register of Shipping, 71 Fenchurch Street, London EC3, England; *Statistical Tables*, and *Annual Summary of Merchant Ships Completed in the World*.

U.S. Department of Transportation, Maritime Administration, 400 Seventh Street, SW, Washington, D.C. 20590 (202) 366-5007; *Merchant Fleets of the World*.

WORLD SUMMARY STATISTICS - MILITARY EXPENDITURES

U.S. Arms Control and Disarmament Agency, 320 Twenty-first Street, NW, Washington, D.C. 20451 (202) 647-8677; *World Military Expenditures and Arms Transfers*.

WORLD SUMMARY STATISTICS - MINERAL PRODUCTION

U.S. Department of Energy, Energy Information Administration, 1000 Independence Avenue, SW, Washington, D.C. 20585 (202) 586-8800; *Energy Data Reports, Weekly Coal Production, Coal Production, Coke Plant Report, Quarterly Coal Report, Petroleum Statement Annual, Petroleum Supply Annual, Annual Energy Review, Monthly Energy Review*, and *International Energy Annual*, and *Natural Gas Annual*.

WORLD SUMMARY STATISTICS - POPULATION

Statistical Office of the United Nations, Publishing Service, New York, New York 10017 (800) 253-9646; *Monthly Bulletin of Statistics*.

U.S. Department of Commerce, Bureau of the Census, Suitland, Maryland 20233 (301) 763-4040; *International Data Bank* and *World Population Profile*.

WORLD SUMMARY STATISTICS - RELIGION

Encyclopedia Britannica, Incorporated, 310 South Michigan Avenue, Chicago, Illinois 60604 (312) 347-7000; *Britannica Book of the Year*.

WORLD WAR I AND WORLD WAR II - COST

U.S. Congress, Joint Economic Committee, The Capitol, Washington, D.C. 20510; *The Military Budget and National Economic Priorities*, 91st Congress, 1st Session (Statement of James L. Clayton) subsequently revised and updated by James L. Clayton, University of Utah, Salt Lake City, Utah.

WYOMING - See also STATE DATA (FOR INDIVIDUAL
STATES)

Wyoming - Primary Statistics Sources

Department of Administration and Information, Division of
Economic Analysis, 327 East Emerson Building, Cheyenne,
Wyoming 82002 (307) 777-7504; *The Equality State Almanac.*

Wyoming - State Data Centers

Department of Administration and Fiscal Control, Research and
Statistics Division, Emerson Building 327E, Cheyenne, Wyoming
82002-0060, Mr. Wenlin Liu (307) 777-7504.

Survey Research Center, University of Wyoming, Post Office Box
3925, Laramie, Wyoming 82071, Mr. G. Fred Doll, (307) 766-2931.

Y

Yemen - National Statistical Office

Central Statistics Organization, Ministry of Planning and Development, Sana'a, Yemen.

Yemen - Primary Statistics Source

Central Statistics Organization, Ministry of Planning and Development, Sana'a, Yemen; *Statistical Yearbook*.

YEMEN - AGRICULTURE

Economic Commission for Western Asia, Post Office Box 27, Baghdad, Iraq; *Statistical Abstract of Western Asia*.

Euromonitor Publications Limited, 87-88 Turnmill Street, London EC1M 5QU, England; *International Marketing Data and Statistics*.

Facts on File, 460 Park Avenue South, New York, New York 10016 (800) 443-8323; *The New Book of World Rankings*.

Food and Agricultural Organization of the United Nations (FAO) Via delle Terme di Caracalla, 00100 Rome, Italy (Telephone Number in U.S. (202) 653-2400); *Production Yearbook, The State of Food and Agriculture*, and *Trade Yearbook*.

G.K. Hall and Company, 70 Lincoln Street, Boston, Massachusetts 02111 (617) 423-3990; *The World in Figures*.

Statistical Office of the United Nations, Publishing Service, New York, New York 10017 (800) 253-9646; *Statistical Yearbook*.

Time Books, 201 East 50th Street, New York, New York 10022 (212) 751-2600; *The Economist Book of Vital World Statistics*.

The World Bank, 1818 H Street, NW, Washington, D.C. 20433 (202) 477-1234; *World Tables*.

YEMEN - AIRLINE SERVICE

Economic Commission for Western Asia, Post Office Box 27, Baghdad, Iraq; *Statistical Abstract of Western Asia*.

Facts on File, 460 Park Avenue South, New York, New York 10016 (800) 443-8323; *The New Book of World Rankings*.

G.K. Hall and Company, 70 Lincoln Street, Boston, Massachusetts 02111 (617) 423-3990; *The World in Figures*.

International Civil Aviation Organization, 1000 Sherbrooke Street, West, Montreal, Quebec, Canada H3A 2R2 (514) 285-8219; *Civil*

Aviation Statistics of the World.

Time Books, 201 East 50th Street, New York, New York 10022 (212) 751-2600; *The Economist Book of Vital World Statistics*.

YEMEN - ALUMINUM PRODUCTION AND CONSUMPTION - See YEMEN - MINING AND MINERAL PRODUCTS

YEMEN - ANIMAL HEALTH

Food and Agricultural Organization of the United Nations (FAO), Via delle Terme di Caracalla, 00100 Rome, Italy (Telephone Number in U.S. (202) 653-2400); *Animal Health Yearbook*.

YEMEN - AREA AND DENSITY OF POPULATION

Economic Commission for Western Asia, Post Office Box 27, Baghdad, Iraq; *Statistical Abstract of Western Asia*.

Euromonitor Publications Limited, 87-88 Turnmill Street, London EC1M 5QU, England; *International Marketing Data and Statistics*.

Facts on File, 460 Park Avenue South, New York, New York 10016 (800) 443-8323; *The New Book of World Rankings*.

Food and Agricultural Organization of the United Nations (FAO) Via delle Terme di Caracalla, 00100 Rome, Italy (Telephone Number in U.S. (202) 653-2400); *The State of Food and Agriculture*.

G.K. Hall and Company, 70 Lincoln Street, Boston, Massachusetts 02111 (617) 423-3990; *The World in Figures*.

Statistical Office of the United Nations, Publishing Service, New York, New York 10017 (800) 253-9646; *Statistical Yearbook*.

Time Books, 201 East 50th Street, New York, New York 10022 (212) 751-2600; *The Economist Book of Vital World Statistics*.

United Nations Educational, Scientific and Cultural Organization (UNESCO), 7 Place de Fontenoy, F-75700 Paris, France (Telephone Number in U.S. (212) 963-5981); *Statistical Yearbook*.

YEMEN - ARMS EXPORTS AND IMPORTS

U.S. Arms Control and Disarmament Agency, 320 Twenty-first Street, NW, Washington, D.C. 20451 (202) 647-8677; *World Military Expenditures and Arms Transfers*.

YEMEN - BALANCE OF PAYMENTS

Economic Commission for Western Asia, Post Office Box 27, Baghdad, Iraq; *Statistical Abstract of Western Asia*.

The Economist Intelligence Unit, 111 West 57th Street, New York, New York 10019 (800) 938-4685; *The World Market Atlas*.

G.K. Hall and Company, 70 Lincoln Street, Boston, Massachusetts 02111 (617) 423-3990; *The World in Figures*.

International Monetary Fund, 700 Nineteenth Street, NW, Washington, D.C. 20431 (202) 623-7000; *Balance of Payments Yearbook*.

Time Books, 201 East 50th Street, New York, New York 10022 (212) 751-2600; *The Economist Book of Vital World Statistics*.

The World Bank, 1818 H Street, NW, Washington, D.C. 20433 (202) 477-1234; *World Tables*.

YEMEN - BALANCE OF TRADE

Economic Commission for Western Asia, Post Office Box 27, Baghdad, Iraq; *Statistical Abstract of Western Asia*.

YEMEN - BANKING

Economic Commission for Western Asia, Post Office Box 27, Baghdad, Iraq; *Statistical Abstract of Western Asia*.

Facts on File, 460 Park Avenue South, New York, New York 10016 (800) 443-8323; *The New Book of World Rankings*.

G.K. Hall and Company, 70 Lincoln Street, Boston, Massachusetts 02111 (617) 423-3990; *The World in Figures*.

International Monetary Fund, 700 Nineteenth Street, NW, Washington, D.C. 20431 (202) 623-7000; *International Financial Statistics*.

YEMEN - BARLEY PRODUCTION - See YEMEN - CROPS

YEMEN - BEER PRODUCTION

Facts on File, 460 Park Avenue South, New York, New York 10016 (800) 443-8323; *The New Book of World Rankings*.

YEMEN - BIRTH RATES

Facts on File, 460 Park Avenue South, New York, New York 10016 (800) 443-8323; *The New Book of World Rankings*.

Statistical Office of the United Nations, Publishing Service, New York, New York 10017 (800) 253-9646; *Demographic Yearbook*, and *Statistical Yearbook*.

Time Books, 201 East 50th Street, New York, New York 10022 (212) 751-2600; *The Economist Book of Vital World Statistics*.

The World Bank, 1818 H Street, NW, Washington, D.C. 20433 (202) 477-1234; *World Tables*.

YEMEN - BONDS

G.K. Hall and Company, 70 Lincoln Street, Boston, Massachusetts 02111 (617) 423-3990; *The World in Figures*.

YEMEN - BOOK PRODUCTION

G.K. Hall and Company, 70 Lincoln Street, Boston, Massachusetts 02111 (617) 423-3990; *The World in Figures*.

YEMEN - BROADCASTING

Billboard Limited, P.O. Box 9027, 1006 AA Amsterdam, The Netherlands (Telephone Number in U.S. (212) 764-7300); *World Radio TV Handbook*.

Facts on File, 460 Park Avenue South, New York, New York 10016 (800) 443-8323; *The New Book of World Rankings*.

G.K. Hall and Company, 70 Lincoln Street, Boston, Massachusetts 02111 (617) 423-3990; *The World in Figures*.

Time Books, 201 East 50th Street, New York, New York 10022 (212) 751-2600; *The Economist Book of Vital World Statistics*.

YEMEN - BUSINESS

G.K. Hall and Company, 70 Lincoln Street, Boston, Massachusetts 02111 (617) 423-3990; *The World in Figures*.

YEMEN - BUTTER PRODUCTION - See YEMEN - DAIRY PRODUCTS

YEMEN - CALORIE SUPPLY

Food and Agricultural Organization of the United Nations (FAO) Via delle Terme di Caracalla, 00100 Rome, Italy (Telephone Number in U.S. (202) 653-2400); *The State of Food and Agriculture*.

YEMEN - CATTLE - See YEMEN - LIVESTOCK AND POULTRY

YEMEN - CEMENT PRODUCTION - See YEMEN - MINING AND MINERAL PRODUCTS

YEMEN - CHEESE PRODUCTION AND CONSUMPTION - See YEMEN - DAIRY PRODUCTS

YEMEN - CHEMICAL (ORGANIC) PRODUCTION - See YEMEN - MINING AND MINERAL PRODUCTS

YEMEN - CHICKENS - See YEMEN - LIVESTOCK AND POULTRY

YEMEN - CIGARETTE PRODUCTION - See YEMEN - TOBACCO PRODUCTION

YEMEN - CLASS STRUCTURE

G.K. Hall and Company, 70 Lincoln Street, Boston, Massachusetts 02111 (617) 423-3990; *The World in Figures*.

YEMEN - CLIMATE

Facts on File, 460 Park Avenue South, New York, New York 10016 (800) 443-8323; *The New Book of World Rankings*.

G.K. Hall and Company, 70 Lincoln Street, Boston, Massachusetts 02111 (617) 423-3990; *The World in Figures*.

YEMEN - COAL PRODUCTION - See YEMEN - MINING AND MINERAL PRODUCTS

YEMEN - COFFEE - See YEMEN - CROPS

YEMEN - COMMUNICATIONS

Economic Commission for Western Asia, Post Office Box 27, Baghdad, Iraq; *Statistical Abstract of Western Asia*.

G.K. Hall and Company, 70 Lincoln Street, Boston, Massachusetts 02111 (617) 423-3990; *The World in Figures*.

YEMEN - CONSTRUCTION INDUSTRY

Facts on File, 460 Park Avenue South, New York, New York 10016 (800) 443-8323; *The New Book of World Rankings*.

Statistical Office of the United Nations, Publishing Service, New York, New York 10017 (800) 253-9646; *Construction Statistics Yearbook*.

YEMEN - CONSUMER PRICE INDEX

Time Books, 201 East 50th Street, New York, New York 10022 (212) 751-2600; *The Economist Book of Vital World Statistics*.

G.K. Hall and Company, 70 Lincoln Street, Boston, Massachusetts 02111 (617) 423-3990; *The World in Figures*.

Statistical Office of the United Nations, Publishing Service, New York, New York 10017 (800) 253-9646; *Statistical Yearbook*.

YEMEN - CONSUMER PRICES

International Labour Office, I.L.O. Publications, CH-1211, Geneva 22, Switzerland; *Yearbook of Labour Statistics*.

International Monetary Fund, 700 Nineteenth Street, NW, Washington, D.C. 20431 (202) 623-7000; *International Financial Statistics*.

YEMEN - CONSUMPTION

G.K. Hall and Company, 70 Lincoln Street, Boston, Massachusetts 02111 (617) 423-3990; *The World in Figures*.

YEMEN - COPPER PRODUCTION AND CONSUMPTION - See YEMEN - MINING AND MINERAL PRODUCTS

YEMEN - CORN PRODUCTION - See YEMEN - CROPS

YEMEN - CORPORATE TAXES - See YEMEN - TAXATION

YEMEN - COTTON PRODUCTION - See YEMEN - CROPS

YEMEN - CROPS

Facts on File, 460 Park Avenue South, New York, New York 10016 (800) 443-8323; *The New Book of World Rankings*.

Food and Agricultural Organization of the United Nations (FAO) Via delle Terme di Caracalla, 00100 Rome, Italy (Telephone Number in U.S. (202) 653-2400); *The State of Food and Agriculture*.

G.K. Hall and Company, 70 Lincoln Street, Boston, Massachusetts 02111 (617) 423-3990; *The World in Figures*.

Statistical Office of the United Nations, Publishing Service, New York, New York 10017 (800) 253-9646; *Statistical Yearbook*.

YEMEN - CUSTOMS DUTIES

G.K. Hall and Company, 70 Lincoln Street, Boston, Massachusetts 02111 (617) 423-3990; *The World in Figures*.

YEMEN - DAIRY PRODUCTS

Economic Commission for Western Asia, Post Office Box 27, Baghdad, Iraq; *Statistical Abstract of Western Asia*.

Facts on File, 460 Park Avenue South, New York, New York 10016 (800) 443-8323; *The New Book of World Rankings*.

Food and Agricultural Organization of the United Nations (FAO) Via delle Terme di Caracalla, 00100 Rome, Italy (Telephone Number in U.S. (202) 653-2400); *The State of Food and Agriculture*.

Statistical Office of the United Nations, Publishing Service, New York, New York 10017 (800) 253-9646; *Statistical Yearbook*.

YEMEN - DEATH RATES

G.K. Hall and Company, 70 Lincoln Street, Boston, Massachusetts 02111 (617) 423-3990; *The World in Figures*.

Statistical Office of the United Nations, Publishing Service, New York, New York 10017 (800) 253-9646; *Statistical Yearbook*.

Time Books, 201 East 50th Street, New York, New York 10022 (212) 751-2600; *The Economist Book of Vital World Statistics*.

World Health Organization, Office of Publications, Avenue Appia, CH-1211 Geneva, 27, Switzerland (Telephone Number in U.S. (518) 436-9686); *World Health Statistics: Infectious Diseases - Cases*.

YEMEN - DEFENSE EXPENDITURES

G.K. Hall and Company, 70 Lincoln Street, Boston, Massachusetts 02111 (617) 423-3990; *The World in Figures*.

U.S. Arms Control and Disarmament Agency, 320 Twenty-first Street, NW, Washington, D.C. 20451 (202) 647-8677; *World Military Expenditures and Arms Transfers*.

YEMEN - DEMOGRAPHY

The Economist Intelligence Unit, 111 West 57th Street, New York, New York 10019 (800) 938-4685; *The World Market Atlas*.

Facts on File, 460 Park Avenue South, New York, New York 10016 (800) 443-8323; *The New Book of World Rankings*.

G.K. Hall and Company, 70 Lincoln Street, Boston, Massachusetts 02111 (617) 423-3990; *The World in Figures*.

YEMEN - DEVELOPMENT ASSISTANCE

G.K. Hall and Company, 70 Lincoln Street, Boston, Massachusetts 02111 (617) 423-3990; *The World in Figures*.

Statistical Office of the United Nations, Publishing Service, New York, New York 10017 (800) 253-9646; *Statistical Yearbook*.

YEMEN - DIAMOND PRODUCTION - See YEMEN - MINING AND MINERAL PRODUCTS

YEMEN - DISEASES

G.K. Hall and Company, 70 Lincoln Street, Boston, Massachusetts 02111 (617) 423-3990; *The World in Figures*.

World Health Organization, Office of Publications, Avenue Appia, CH-1211 Geneva, 27, Switzerland (Telephone Number in U.S. (518) 436-9686); *World Health Statistics: Vital Statistics and Causes of Death*.

YEMEN - DIVORCE RATES

Facts on File, 460 Park Avenue South, New York, New York 10016 (800) 443-8323; *The New Book of World Rankings*.

Statistical Office of the United Nations, Publishing Service, New York, New York 10017 (800) 253-9646; *Demographic Yearbook*.

YEMEN - DOMESTIC PRODUCT

G.K. Hall and Company, 70 Lincoln Street, Boston, Massachusetts 02111 (617) 423-3990; *The World in Figures*.

YEMEN - ECONOMY

Euromonitor Publications Limited, 87-88 Turnmill Street, London EC1M 5QU, England; *International Marketing Data and Statistics*.

Facts on File, 460 Park Avenue South, New York, New York 10016 (800) 443-8323; *The New Book of World Rankings*.

G.K. Hall and Company, 70 Lincoln Street, Boston, Massachusetts 02111 (617) 423-3990; *The World in Figures*.

YEMEN - EDUCATION

Economic Commission for Western Asia, Post Office Box 27, Baghdad, Iraq; *Statistical Abstract of Western Asia*.

The Economist Intelligence Unit, 111 West 57th Street, New York, New York 10019 (800) 938-4685; *The World Market Atlas*.

Facts on File, 460 Park Avenue South, New York, New York 10016 (800) 443-8323; *The New Book of World Rankings*.

G.K. Hall and Company, 70 Lincoln Street, Boston, Massachusetts 02111 (617) 423-3990; *The World in Figures*.

Time Books, 201 East 50th Street, New York, New York 10022 (212) 751-2600; *The Economist Book of Vital World Statistics*.

United Nations Educational, Scientific and Cultural Organization (UNESCO), 7 Place de Fontenoy, F-75700 Paris, France (Telephone Number in U.S. (212) 963-5981); *Statistical Yearbook*.

The World Bank, 1818 H Street, NW, Washington, D.C. 20433 (202) 477-1234; *World Tables*.

YEMEN - EGG PRODUCTION AND CONSUMPTION - See YEMEN - DAIRY PRODUCTS

YEMEN - ELECTRICITY

Facts on File, 460 Park Avenue South, New York, New York 10016 (800) 443-8323; *The New Book of World Rankings*.

Penn Well Publishing Company, 1421 South Sheridan Road, P.O. Box 1260, Tulsa, Oklahoma 74101 (800) 752-9764; *International Energy Statistics Sourcebook*.

Statistical Office of the United Nations, Publishing Service, New York, New York 10017 (800) 253-9646; *Statistical Yearbook*.

Time Books, 201 East 50th Street, New York, New York 10022 (212) 751-2600; *The Economist Book of Vital World Statistics*.

YEMEN - EMPLOYMENT

Economic Commission for Western Asia, Post Office Box 27, Baghdad, Iraq; *Statistical Abstract of Western Asia*.

Euromonitor Publications Limited, 87-88 Turnmill Street, London EC1M 5QU, England; *International Marketing Data and Statistics*.

Facts on File, 460 Park Avenue South, New York, New York 10016 (800) 443-8323; *The New Book of World Rankings*.

International Labour Office, I.L.O. Publications, CH-1211, Geneva 22, Switzerland; *Yearbook of Labour Statistics*.

Statistical Office of the United Nations, Publishing Service, New York, New York 10017 (800) 253-9646; *Statistical Yearbook*.

YEMEN - ENERGY

Economic Commission for Western Asia, Post Office Box 27, Baghdad, Iraq; *Statistical Abstract of Western Asia*.

Facts on File, 460 Park Avenue South, New York, New York 10016 (800) 443-8323; *The New Book of World Rankings*.

Food and Agricultural Organization of the United Nations (FAO) Via delle Terme di Caracalla, 00100 Rome, Italy (Telephone Number in U.S. (202) 653-2400); *The State of Food and Agriculture*.

G.K. Hall and Company, 70 Lincoln Street, Boston, Massachusetts 02111 (617) 423-3990; *The World in Figures*.

Penn Well Publishing Company, 1421 South Sheridan Road, P.O. Box 1260, Tulsa, Oklahoma 74101 (800) 752-9764; *International Energy Statistics Sourcebook*.

Statistical Office of the United Nations, Publishing Service, New York, New York 10017 (800) 253-9646; *Energy Statistics Yearbook*, and *Statistical Yearbook*.

Time Books, 201 East 50th Street, New York, New York 10022 (212) 751-2600; *The Economist Book of Vital World Statistics*.

YEMEN - EXCHANGE RATES

Euromonitor Publications Limited, 87-88 Turnmill Street, London EC1M 5QU, England; *International Marketing Data and Statistics*.

International Civil Aviation Organization, 1000 Sherbrooke Street, West, Montreal, Quebec, Canada H3A 2R2 (514) 285-8219; *Civil Aviation Statistics of the World*.

International Monetary Fund, 700 Nineteenth Street, NW, Washington, D.C. 20431 (202) 623-7000; *International Financial Statistics*.

Statistical Office of the United Nations, Publishing Service, New York, New York 10017 (800) 253-9646; *Statistical Yearbook*.

YEMEN - EXPORTS

Economic Commission for Western Asia, Post Office Box 27, Baghdad, Iraq; *Statistical Abstract of Western Asia*.

The Economist Intelligence Unit, 111 West 57th Street, New York, New York 10019 (800) 938-4685; *The World Market Atlas*.

Euromonitor Publications Limited, 87-88 Turnmill Street, London EC1M 5QU, England; *International Marketing Data and Statistics*.

Food and Agricultural Organization of the United Nations (FAO) Via delle Terme di Caracalla, 00100 Rome, Italy (Telephone Number in U.S. (202) 653-2400); *The State of Food and Agriculture.*

G.K. Hall and Company, 70 Lincoln Street, Boston, Massachusetts 02111 (617) 423-3990; *The World in Figures.*

International Monetary Fund, 700 Nineteenth Street, NW, Washington, D.C. 20431 (202) 623-7000; *Direction of Trade Statistics.*

Time Books, 201 East 50th Street, New York, New York 10022 (212) 751-2600; *The Economist Book of Vital World Statistics.*

The World Bank, 1818 H Street, NW, Washington, D.C. 20433 (202) 477-1234; *World Tables.*

YEMEN - EXPORTS BY COMMODITIES

Economic Commission for Western Asia, Post Office Box 27, Baghdad, Iraq; *Statistical Abstract of Western Asia.*

YEMEN - EXTERNAL INDEBTEDNESS

The World Bank, 1818 H Street, NW, Washington, D.C. 20433 (202) 477 1234; *World Tables.*

YEMEN - EXTERNAL TRADE

Food and Agricultural Organization of the United Nations (FAO) Via delle Terme di Caracalla, 00100 Rome, Italy (Telephone Number in U.S. (202) 653-2400); *The State of Food and Agriculture.*

G.K. Hall and Company, 70 Lincoln Street, Boston, Massachusetts 02111 (617) 423-3990; *The World in Figures.*

Statistical Office of the United Nations, Publishing Service, New York, New York 10017 (800) 253-9646; *Statistical Yearbook.*

YEMEN - FARM CROPS - See YEMEN - CROPS

YEMEN - FERTILITY RATES

Facts on File, 460 Park Avenue South, New York, New York 10016 (800) 443-8323; *The New Book of World Rankings.*

Time Books, 201 East 50th Street, New York, New York 10022 (212) 751-2600; *The Economist Book of Vital World Statistics.*

The World Bank, 1818 H Street, NW, Washington, D.C. 20433 (202) 477-1234; *World Tables.*

YEMEN - FERTILIZER

Food and Agricultural Organization of the United Nations (FAO), Via delle Terme di Caracalla, 00100 Rome, Italy (Telephone Number in U.S. (202) 653-2400); *Fertilizer Yearbook*, and *The State of Food and Agriculture.*

Statistical Office of the United Nations, Publishing Service, New York, New York 10017 (800) 253-9646; *Statistical Yearbook.*

YEMEN - FETAL MORTALITY

Statistical Office of the United Nations, Publishing Service, New York, New York 10017 (800) 253-9646; *Demographic Yearbook.*

YEMEN - FINANCE

Economic Commission for Western Asia, Post Office Box 27, Baghdad, Iraq; *Statistical Abstract of Western Asia.*

Facts on File, 460 Park Avenue South, New York, New York 10016 (800) 443-8323; *The New Book of World Rankings.*

G.K. Hall and Company, 70 Lincoln Street, Boston, Massachusetts 02111 (617) 423-3990; *The World in Figures.*

International Monetary Fund, 700 Nineteenth Street, NW, Washington, D.C. 20431 (202) 623-7000; *International Financial Statistics.*

YEMEN - FISHERIES

Economic Commission for Western Asia, Post Office Box 27, Baghdad, Iraq; *Statistical Abstract of Western Asia.*

Food and Agricultural Organization of the United Nations (FAO) Via delle Terme di Caracalla, 00100 Rome, Italy (Telephone Number in U.S. (202) 653-2400); *The State of Food and Agriculture*, and *Yearbook of Fishery Statistics.*

Facts on File, 460 Park Avenue South, New York, New York 10016 (800) 443-8323; *The New Book of World Rankings.*

Statistical Office of the United Nations, Publishing Service, New York, New York 10017 (800) 253-9646; *Statistical Yearbook.*

YEMEN - FOOD

Food and Agricultural Organization of the United Nations (FAO) Via delle Terme di Caracalla, 00100 Rome, Italy (Telephone Number in U.S. (202) 653-2400); *The State of Food and Agriculture.*

G.K. Hall and Company, 70 Lincoln Street, Boston, Massachusetts 02111 (617) 423-3990; *The World in Figures.*

YEMEN - FOREIGN AID

G.K. Hall and Company, 70 Lincoln Street, Boston, Massachusetts 02111 (617) 423-3990; *The World in Figures.*

YEMEN - FOREIGN TRADE

Economic Commission for Western Asia, Post Office Box 27, Baghdad, Iraq; *Statistical Abstract of Western Asia.*

Euromonitor Publications Limited, 87-88 Turnmill Street, London EC1M 5QU, England; *International Marketing Data and Statistics.*

Facts on File, 460 Park Avenue South, New York, New York 10016 (800) 443-8323; *The New Book of World Rankings.*

Food and Agricultural Organization of the United Nations (FAO) Via delle Terme di Caracalla, 00100 Rome, Italy (Telephone Number in U.S. (202) 653-2400); *The State of Food and Agriculture.*

G.K. Hall and Company, 70 Lincoln Street, Boston, Massachusetts 02111 (617) 423-3990; *The World in Figures.*

International Monetary Fund, 700 Nineteenth Street, NW, Washington, D.C. 20431 (202) 623-7000; *International Financial Statistics.*

Statistical Office of the United Nations, Publishing Service, New York, New York 10017 (800) 253-9646; *International Trade Statistics*

Yearbook, Statistical Yearbook, and *Trade in Manufactures of Developing Countries.*

The World Bank, 1818 H Street, NW, Washington, D.C. 20433 (202) 477-1234; *World Tables.*

YEMEN - FORESTRY AND FOREST PRODUCTS

Facts on File, 460 Park Avenue South, New York, New York 10016 (800) 443-8323; *The New Book of World Rankings.*

Food and Agricultural Organization of the United Nations (FAO) Via delle Terme di Caracalla, 00100 Rome, Italy (Telephone Number in U.S. (202) 653-2400); *The State of Food and Agriculture,* and *Yearbook of Forest Products.*

G.K. Hall and Company, 70 Lincoln Street, Boston, Massachusetts 02111 (617) 423-3990; *The World in Figures.*

Statistical Office of the United Nations, Publishing Service, New York, New York 10017 (800) 253-9646; *Statistical Yearbook.*

United Nations Educational, Scientific and Cultural Organization (UNESCO), 7 Place de Fontenoy, F-75700 Paris, France (Telephone Number in U.S. (212) 963-5981); *Statistical Yearbook.*

YEMEN - GAS PRODUCTION - See YEMEN - MINING AND MINERAL PRODUCTS

YEMEN - GENERAL INDUSTRIAL STATISTICS

Statistical Office of the United Nations, Publishing Service, New York, New York 10017 (800) 253-9646; *Industrial Statistics Yearbook.*

YEMEN - GENERAL MORTALITY

Statistical Office of the United Nations, Publishing Service, New York, New York 10017 (800) 253-9646; *Demographic Yearbook.*

YEMEN - GEOGRAPHIC DATA

Facts on File, 460 Park Avenue South, New York, New York 10016 (800) 443-8323; *The New Book of World Rankings.*

YEMEN - GOATS - See YEMEN - LIVESTOCK AND POULTRY

YEMEN - GOLD HOLDINGS

International Monetary Fund, 700 Nineteenth Street, NW, Washington, D.C. 20431 (202) 623-7000; *International Financial Statistics.*

Statistical Office of the United Nations, Publishing Service, New York, New York 10017 (800) 253-9646; *Statistical Yearbook.*

The World Bank, 1818 H Street, NW, Washington, D.C. 20433 (202) 477-1234; *World Tables.*

YEMEN - GOLD PRODUCTION AND CONSUMPTION - See YEMEN - MINING AND MINERAL PRODUCTS

YEMEN - GOVERNMENT

G.K. Hall and Company, 70 Lincoln Street, Boston, Massachusetts 02111 (617) 423-3990; *The World in Figures.*

YEMEN - GOVERNMENT EXPENDITURE

Economic Commission for Western Asia, Post Office Box 27, Baghdad, Iraq; *Statistical Abstract of Western Asia.*

Time Books, 201 East 50th Street, New York, New York 10022 (212) 751-2600; *The Economist Book of Vital World Statistics.*

The World Bank, 1818 H Street, NW, Washington, D.C. 20433 (202) 477-1234; *World Tables.*

YEMEN - GOVERNMENT FINANCES

International Monetary Fund, 700 Nineteenth Street, NW, Washington, D.C. 20431 (202) 623-7000; *International Financial Statistics.*

YEMEN - GOVERNMENT REVENUE

Economic Commission for Western Asia, Post Office Box 27, Baghdad, Iraq; *Statistical Abstract of Western Asia.*

Time Books, 201 East 50th Street, New York, New York 10022 (212) 751-2600; *The Economist Book of Vital World Statistics.*

The World Bank, 1818 H Street, NW, Washington, D.C. 20433 (202) 477-1234; *World Tables.*

YEMEN - GRAIN PRODUCTION - See YEMEN - CROPS

YEMEN - GROSS DOMESTIC PRODUCT

Economic Commission for Western Asia, Post Office Box 27, Baghdad, Iraq; *Statistical Abstract of Western Asia.*

The Economist Intelligence Unit, 111 West 57th Street, New York, New York 10019 (800) 938-4685; *The World Market Atlas.*

Euromonitor Publications Limited, 87-88 Turnmill Street, London EC1M 5QU, England; *International Marketing Data and Statistics.*

Facts on File, 460 Park Avenue South, New York, New York 10016 (800) 443-8323; *The New Book of World Rankings.*

G.K. Hall and Company, 70 Lincoln Street, Boston, Massachusetts 02111 (617) 423-3990; *The World in Figures.*

Statistical Office of the United Nations, Publishing Service, New York, New York 10017 (800) 253-9646; *Statistical Yearbook.*

Time Books, 201 East 50th Street, New York, New York 10022 (212) 751-2600; *The Economist Book of Vital World Statistics.*

U.S. Arms Control and Disarmament Agency, 320 Twenty-first Street, NW, Washington, D.C. 20451 (202) 647-8677; *World Military Expenditures and Arms Transfers.*

The World Bank, 1818 H Street, NW, Washington, D.C. 20433 (202) 477-1234; *World Tables.*

YEMEN - GROSS NATIONAL PRODUCT

Euromonitor Publications Limited, 87-88 Turnmill Street, London EC1M 5QU, England; *International Marketing Data and Statistics.*

The World Bank, 1818 H Street, NW, Washington, D.C. 20433 (202) 477-1234; *World Tables.*

YEMEN - HEALTH

Economic Commission for Western Asia, Post Office Box 27, Baghdad, Iraq; *Statistical Abstract of Western Asia*.

Facts on File, 460 Park Avenue South, New York, New York 10016 (800) 443-8323; *The New Book of World Rankings*.

G.K. Hall and Company, 70 Lincoln Street, Boston, Massachusetts 02111 (617) 423-3990; *The World in Figures*.

Statistical Office of the United Nations, Publishing Service, New York, New York 10017 (800) 253-9646; *Statistical Yearbook*.

Time Books, 201 East 50th Street, New York, New York 10022 (212) 751-2600; *The Economist Book of Vital World Statistics*.

World Health Organization, Office of Publications, Avenue Appia, CH-1211 Geneva, 27, Switzerland (Telephone Number in U.S. (518) 436-9686); *World Health Statistics: Vital Statistics and Causes of Death*.

YEMEN - HIGHWAYS

Economic Commission for Western Asia, Post Office Box 27, Baghdad, Iraq; *Statistical Abstract of Western Asia*.

G.K. Hall and Company, 70 Lincoln Street, Boston, Massachusetts 02111 (617) 423-3990; *The World in Figures*.

International Road Federation, 525 School Street, SW, Washington, D.C. 20024 (202) 554-2106; *World Road Statistics*.

YEMEN - HORSES - See YEMEN - LIVESTOCK AND POULTRY

YEMEN - HOURS OF WORK - See YEMEN - EMPLOYMENT

YEMEN - HOUSING AND HOUSING UNITS

Facts on File, 460 Park Avenue South, New York, New York 10016 (800) 443-8323; *The New Book of World Rankings*.

YEMEN - ILLITERATE POPULATION

The Economist Intelligence Unit, 111 West 57th Street, New York, New York 10019 (800) 938-4685; *The World Market Atlas*.

G.K. Hall and Company, 70 Lincoln Street, Boston, Massachusetts 02111 (617) 423-3990; *The World in Figures*.

United Nations Educational, Scientific and Cultural Organization (UNESCO), 7 Place de Fontenoy, F-75700 Paris, France (Telephone Number in U.S. (212) 963-5981); *Statistical Yearbook*.

YEMEN - IMPORTS

Economic Commission for Western Asia, Post Office Box 27, Baghdad, Iraq; *Statistical Abstract of Western Asia*.

The Economist Intelligence Unit, 111 West 57th Street, New York, New York 10019 (800) 938-4685; *The World Market Atlas*.

Euromonitor Publications Limited, 87-88 Turnmill Street, London EC1M 5QU, England; *International Marketing Data and Statistics*.

Food and Agricultural Organization of the United Nations (FAO) Via delle Terme di Caracalla, 00100 Rome, Italy (Telephone Number in U.S. (202) 653-2400); *The State of Food and Agriculture*.

G.K. Hall and Company, 70 Lincoln Street, Boston, Massachusetts 02111 (617) 423-3990; *The World in Figures*.

International Monetary Fund, 700 Nineteenth Street, NW, Washington, D.C. 20431 (202) 623-7000; *Direction of Trade Statistics*.

Time Books, 201 East 50th Street, New York, New York 10022 (212) 751-2600; *The Economist Book of Vital World Statistics*.

The World Bank, 1818 H Street, NW, Washington, D.C. 20433 (202) 477-1234; *World Tables*.

YEMEN - INDUSTRY

Euromonitor Publications Limited, 87-88 Turnmill Street, London EC1M 5QU, England; *International Marketing Data and Statistics*.

Facts on File, 460 Park Avenue South, New York, New York 10016 (800) 443-8323; *The New Book of World Rankings*.

G.K. Hall and Company, 70 Lincoln Street, Boston, Massachusetts 02111 (617) 423-3990; *The World in Figures*.

International Labour Office, I.L.O. Publications, CH-1211, Geneva 22, Switzerland; *Yearbook of Labour Statistics*.

Time Books, 201 East 50th Street, New York, New York 10022 (212) 751-2600; *The Economist Book of Vital World Statistics*.

The World Bank, 1818 H Street, NW, Washington, D.C. 20433 (202) 477-1234; *World Tables*.

YEMEN - INFANT AND MATERNAL MORTALITY

Statistical Office of the United Nations, Publishing Service, New York, New York 10017 (800) 253-9646; *Demographic Yearbook*.

Time Books, 201 East 50th Street, New York, New York 10022 (212) 751-2600; *The Economist Book of Vital World Statistics*.

The World Bank, 1818 H Street, NW, Washington, D.C. 20433 (202) 477-1234; *World Tables*.

YEMEN - INTERNATIONAL LIQUIDITY

International Monetary Fund, 700 Nineteenth Street, NW, Washington, D.C. 20431 (202) 623-7000; *International Financial Statistics*.

YEMEN - INTERNATIONAL RESERVES EXCLUDING GOLD

Statistical Office of the United Nations, Publishing Service, New York, New York 10017 (800) 253-9646; *Statistical Yearbook*.

The World Bank, 1818 H Street, NW, Washington, D.C. 20433 (202) 477-1234; *World Tables*.

YEMEN - IRON ORE PRODUCTION AND CONSUMPTION - See YEMEN - MINING AND MINERAL PRODUCTS

YEMEN - IRRIGATION

Euromonitor Publications Limited, 87-88 Turnmill Street, London EC1M 5QU, England; *International Marketing Data and Statistics*.

YEMEN - LABOR FORCE

Economic Commission for Western Asia, Post Office Box 27, Baghdad, Iraq; *Statistical Abstract of Western Asia.*

Euromonitor Publications Limited, 87-88 Turnmill Street, London EC1M 5QU, England; *International Marketing Data and Statistics.*

Facts on File, 460 Park Avenue South, New York, New York 10016 (800) 443-8323; *The New Book of World Rankings.*

Food and Agricultural Organization of the United Nations (FAO) Via delle Terme di Caracalla, 00100 Rome, Italy (Telephone Number in U.S. (202) 653-2400); *The State of Food and Agriculture.*

G.K. Hall and Company, 70 Lincoln Street, Boston, Massachusetts 02111 (617) 423-3990; *The World in Figures.*

The World Bank, 1818 H Street, NW, Washington, D.C. 20433 (202) 477-1234; *World Tables.*

YEMEN - LABOR PRODUCTIVITY

International Labour Office, I.L.O. Publications, CH-1211, Geneva 22, Switzerland; *Yearbook of Labour Statistics.*

YEMEN - LAND USE

Economic Commission for Western Asia, Post Office Box 27, Baghdad, Iraq; *Statistical Abstract of Western Asia.*

Euromonitor Publications Limited, 87-88 Turnmill Street, London EC1M 5QU, England; *International Marketing Data and Statistics.*

G.K. Hall and Company, 70 Lincoln Street, Boston, Massachusetts 02111 (617) 423-3990; *The World in Figures.*

YEMEN - LIBRARIES

Facts on File, 460 Park Avenue South, New York, New York 10016 (800) 443-8323; *The New Book of World Rankings.*

United Nations Education, Scientific and Cultural Organization (UNESCO), 7 Place de Fontenoy, F-75700 Paris, France (Telephone Number in U.S. (212) 963-5981), *Statistical Yearbook.*

YEMEN - LIVESTOCK AND POULTRY

Economic Commission for Western Asia, Post Office Box 27, Baghdad, Iraq; *Statistical Abstract of Western Asia.*

Euromonitor Publications Limited, 87-88 Turnmill Street, London EC1M 5QU, England; *International Marketing Data and Statistics.*

Facts on File, 460 Park Avenue South, New York, New York 10016 (800) 443-8323; *The New Book of World Rankings.*

Food and Agricultural Organization of the United Nations (FAO) Via delle Terme di Caracalla, 00100 Rome, Italy (Telephone Number in U.S. (202) 653-2400); *The State of Food and Agriculture.*

G.K. Hall and Company, 70 Lincoln Street, Boston, Massachusetts 02111 (617) 423-3990; *The World in Figures.*

Statistical Office of the United Nations, Publishing Service, New York, New York 10017 (800) 253-9646; *Statistical Yearbook.*

YEMEN - LIVING LEVELS

G.K. Hall and Company, 70 Lincoln Street, Boston, Massachusetts 02111 (617) 423-3990; *The World in Figures.*

Time Books, 201 East 50th Street, New York, New York 10022 (212) 751-2600; *The Economist Book of Vital World Statistics.*

YEMEN - MAIL - NUMBER OF ITEMS SENT AND RECEIVED

Statistical Office of the United Nations, Publishing Service, New York, New York 10017 (800) 253-9646; *Statistical Yearbook.*

YEMEN - MANUFACTURING

Facts on File, 460 Park Avenue South, New York, New York 10016 (800) 443-8323; *The New Book of World Rankings.*

G.K. Hall and Company, 70 Lincoln Street, Boston, Massachusetts 02111 (617) 423-3990; *The World in Figures.*

Statistical Office of the United Nations, Publishing Service, New York, New York 10017 (800) 253-9646; *Statistical Yearbook.*

The World Bank, 1818 H Street, NW, Washington, D.C. 20433 (202) 477-1234; *World Tables.*

YEMEN - MARRIAGE RATES

Facts on File, 460 Park Avenue South, New York, New York 10016 (800) 443-8323; *The New Book of World Rankings.*

Statistical Office of the United Nations, Publishing Service, New York, New York 10017 (800) 253-9646; *Demographic Yearbook.*

YEMEN - MEAT PRODUCTION - See YEMEN - LIVESTOCK AND POULTRY

YEMEN - MERCHANT SHIPPING

Economic Commission for Western Asia, Post Office Box 27, Baghdad, Iraq; *Statistical Abstract of Western Asia.*

G.K. Hall and Company, 70 Lincoln Street, Boston, Massachusetts 02111 (617) 423-3990; *The World in Figures.*

Lloyd's Register of Shipping, 17 Battery Place, New York, New York 10004 (212) 425-8050; *Register of Ships.*

Statistical Office of the United Nations, Publishing Service, New York, New York 10017 (800) 253-9646; *Statistical Yearbook.*

Time Books, 201 East 50th Street, New York, New York 10022 (212) 751-2600; *The Economist Book of Vital World Statistics.*

U.S. Department of Transportation, Maritime Administration, 400 Seventh Street, SW, Washington, D.C. 20590 (202) 366-5807; *A Statistical Analysis of the World's Merchant Fleets.*

YEMEN - MILITARY

G.K. Hall and Company, 70 Lincoln Street, Boston, Massachusetts 02111 (617) 423-3990; *The World in Figures.*

The International Institute for Strategic Studies, 23 Tavistock Street, London WC2E 7NQ, England; *The Military Balance.*

U.S. Arms Control and Disarmament Agency, 320 Twenty-first Street, NW, Washington, D.C. 20451 (202) 647-8677; *World Military*

Expenditures and Arms Transfers.

YEMEN - MILK PRODUCTION - See YEMEN - DAIRY PRODUCTS

YEMEN - MINING AND MINERAL PRODUCTS

Economic Commission for Western Asia, Post Office Box 27, Baghdad, Iraq; *Statistical Abstract of Western Asia.*

Facts on File, 460 Park Avenue South, New York, New York 10016 (800) 443-8323; *The New Book of World Rankings.*

Penn Well Publishing Company, 1421 South Sheridan Road, P.O. Box 1260, Tulsa, Oklahoma 74101 (800) 752-9764; *International Energy Statistics Sourcebook.*

G.K. Hall and Company, 70 Lincoln Street, Boston, Massachusetts 02111 (617) 423-3990; *The World in Figures.*

YEMEN - MONEY EXCHANGE RATE

Euromonitor Publications Limited, 87-88 Turnmill Street, London EC1M 5QU, England; *International Marketing Data and Statistics.*

International Monetary Fund, 700 Nineteenth Street, NW, Washington, D.C. 20431 (202) 623-7000; *International Financial Statistics.*

Statistical Office of the United Nations, Publishing Service, New York, New York 10017 (800) 253-9646; *Statistical Yearbook.*

YEMEN - MONEY RESERVES

Euromonitor Publications Limited, 87-88 Turnmill Street, London EC1M 5QU, England; *International Marketing Data and Statistics.*

YEMEN - MONEY SUPPLY

Economic Commission for Western Asia, Post Office Box 27, Baghdad, Iraq; *Statistical Abstract of Western Asia.*

Euromonitor Publications Limited, 87-88 Turnmill Street, London EC1M 5QU, England; *International Marketing Data and Statistics.*

G.K. Hall and Company, 70 Lincoln Street, Boston, Massachusetts 02111 (617) 423-3990; *The World in Figures.*

International Monetary Fund, 700 Nineteenth Street, NW, Washington, D.C. 20431 (202) 623-7000; *International Financial Statistics.*

Statistical Office of the United Nations, Publishing Service, New York, New York 10017 (800) 253-9646; *Statistical Yearbook.*

The World Bank, 1818 H Street, NW, Washington, D.C. 20433 (202) 477-1234; *World Tables.*

YEMEN - MOTOR VEHICLE TAXES - See YEMEN - TAXATION

YEMEN - MOTOR VEHICLES

Economic Commission for Western Asia, Post Office Box 27, Baghdad, Iraq; *Statistical Abstract of Western Asia.*

YEMEN - MOTOR VEHICLES IN USE

G.K. Hall and Company, 70 Lincoln Street, Boston, Massachusetts 02111 (617) 423-3990; *The World in Figures.*

International Road Federation, 525 School Street, SW, Washington, D.C. 20024 (202) 554-2106; *World Road Statistics.*

Statistical Office of the United Nations, Publishing Service, New York, New York 10017 (800) 253-9646; *Statistical Yearbook.*

Time Books, 201 East 50th Street, New York, New York 10022 (212) 751-2600; *The Economist Book of Vital World Statistics.*

YEMEN - MUSEUMS

Facts on File, 460 Park Avenue South, New York, New York 10016 (800) 443-8323; *The New Book of World Rankings.*

YEMEN - NATALITY - See YEMEN - BIRTH RATE

YEMEN - NATIONAL ACCOUNTS

Economic Commission for Western Asia, Post Office Box 27, Baghdad, Iraq; *Statistical Abstract of Western Asia.*

International Monetary Fund, 700 Nineteenth Street, NW, Washington, D.C. 20431 (202) 623-7000; *International Financial Statistics.*

Statistical Office of the United Nations, Publishing Service, New York, New York 10017 (800) 253-9646; *National Accounts Statistics,* and *Statistical Yearbook.*

YEMEN - NATIONAL INCOME

Facts on File, 460 Park Avenue South, New York, New York 10016 (800) 443-8323; *The New Book of World Rankings.*

G.K. Hall and Company, 70 Lincoln Street, Boston, Massachusetts 02111 (617) 423-3990; *The World in Figures.*

Statistical Office of the United Nations, Publishing Service, New York, New York 10017 (800) 253-9646; *Statistical Yearbook.*

YEMEN - NATIONAL PRODUCT

Facts on File, 460 Park Avenue South, New York, New York 10016 (800) 443-8323; *The New Book of World Rankings.*

Statistical Office of the United Nations, Publishing Service, New York, New York 10017 (800) 253-9646; *Statistical Yearbook.*

YEMEN - NATURAL GAS PRODUCTION - See YEMEN - MINING AND MINERAL PRODUCTS

YEMEN - NEWSPAPER PRODUCTION - See YEMEN - FORESTRY AND FOREST PRODUCTS

YEMEN - NEWSPRINT PRODUCTION AND CONSUMPTION - See YEMEN - FORESTRY AND FOREST PRODUCTS

YEMEN - OCCUPATIONS - See YEMEN - LABOR FORCE

YEMEN - PAPER - See YEMEN - FORESTRY AND FOREST PRODUCTS

YEMEN - PATENTS

Statistical Office of the United Nations, Publishing Service, New York, New York 10017 (800) 253-9646; *Statistical Yearbook.*

YEMEN - PEANUT PRODUCTION - See YEMEN - CROPS

YEMEN - PESTICIDE USE

Food and Agricultural Organization of the United Nations (FAO) Via delle Terme di Caracalla, 00100 Rome, Italy (Telephone Number in U.S. (202) 653-2400); *The State of Food and Agriculture.*

YEMEN - PETROLEUM INDUSTRY

Facts on File, 460 Park Avenue South, New York, New York 10016 (800) 443-8323; *The New Book of World Rankings.*

Food and Agricultural Organization of the United Nations (FAO) Via delle Terme di Caracalla, 00100 Rome, Italy (Telephone Number in U.S. (202) 653-2400); *The State of Food and Agriculture.*

G.K. Hall and Company, 70 Lincoln Street, Boston, Massachusetts 02111 (617) 423-3990; *The World in Figures.*

Penn Well Publishing Company, 1421 South Sheridan Road, P.O. Box 1260, Tulsa, Oklahoma 74101 (800) 752-9764; *International Energy Statistics Sourcebook.*

Statistical Office of the United Nations, Publishing Service, New York, New York 10017 (800) 253-9646; *Statistical Yearbook.*

YEMEN - PIGS - See YEMEN - LIVESTOCK AND POULTRY

YEMEN - POPULATION

Economic Commission for Western Asia, Post Office Box 27, Baghdad, Iraq; *Statistical Abstract of Western Asia.*

The Economist Intelligence Unit, 111 West 57th Street, New York, New York 10019 (800) 938-4685; *The World Market Atlas.*

Euromonitor Publications Limited, 87-88 Turnmill Street, London EC1M 5QU, England; *International Marketing Data and Statistics.*

Facts on File, 460 Park Avenue South, New York, New York 10016 (800) 443-8323; *The New Book of World Rankings.*

G.K. Hall and Company, 70 Lincoln Street, Boston, Massachusetts 02111 (617) 423-3990; *The World in Figures.*

International Labour Office, I.L.O. Publications, CH-1211, Geneva 22, Switzerland; *Yearbook of Labour Statistics.*

Statistical Office of the United Nations, Publishing Service, New York, New York 10017 (800) 253-9646; *Demographic Yearbook,* and *Statistical Yearbook.*

Time Books, 201 East 50th Street, New York, New York 10022 (212) 751-2600; *The Economist Book of Vital World Statistics.*

United Nations Educational, Scientific and Cultural Organization (UNESCO), 7 Place de Fontenoy, F-75700 Paris, France (Telephone Number in U.S. (212) 963-5981); *Statistical Yearbook.*

U.S. Arms Control and Disarmament Agency, 320 Twenty-first Street, NW, Washington, D.C. 20451 (202) 647-8677; *World Military Expenditures and Arms Transfers.*

World Health Organization, Office of Publications, Avenue Appia, CH-1211 Geneva, 27, Switzerland (Telephone Number in U.S. (518) 436-9686); *World Health Statistics: Vital Statistics and Causes of Death.*

YEMEN - POST OFFICES

Facts on File, 460 Park Avenue South, New York, New York 10016 (800) 443-8323; *The New Book of World Rankings.*

YEMEN - POTATO PRODUCTION - See YEMEN - CROPS

YEMEN - PRICES

Economic Commission for Western Asia, Post Office Box 27, Baghdad, Iraq; *Statistical Abstract of Western Asia.*

Facts on File, 460 Park Avenue South, New York, New York 10016 (800) 443-8323; *The New Book of World Rankings.*

Food and Agricultural Organization of the United Nations (FAO) Via delle Terme di Caracalla, 00100 Rome, Italy (Telephone Number in U.S. (202) 653-2400); *The State of Food and Agriculture.*

G.K. Hall and Company, 70 Lincoln Street, Boston, Massachusetts 02111 (617) 423-3990; *The World in Figures.*

International Labour Office, I.L.O. Publications, CH-1211, Geneva 22, Switzerland; *Yearbook of Labour Statistics.*

International Monetary Fund, 700 Nineteenth Street, NW, Washington, D.C. 20431 (202) 623-7000; *International Financial Statistics.*

YEMEN - PRINTING AND WRITING PAPER - See YEMEN - FORESTRY AND FOREST PRODUCTS

YEMEN - PRODUCTION

Facts on File, 460 Park Avenue South, New York, New York 10016 (800) 443-8323; *The New Book of World Rankings.*

G.K. Hall and Company, 70 Lincoln Street, Boston, Massachusetts 02111 (617) 423-3990; *The World in Figures.*

YEMEN - PRODUCTIVITY

Euromonitor Publications Limited, 87-88 Turnmill Street, London EC1M 5QU, England; *International Marketing Data and Statistics.*

YEMEN - PUBLIC FINANCE

Facts on File, 460 Park Avenue South, New York, New York 10016 (800) 443-8323; *The New Book of World Rankings.*

YEMEN - RADIO BROADCASTING - See YEMEN - BROADCASTING

YEMEN - RAILWAYS

G.K. Hall and Company, 70 Lincoln Street, Boston, Massachusetts 02111 (617) 423-3990; *The World in Figures.*

YEMEN - RELIGION

Facts on File, 460 Park Avenue South, New York, New York 10016 (800) 443-8323; *The New Book of World Rankings.*

YEMEN - RENT PRICES

International Labour Office, I.L.O. Publications, CH-1211, Geneva 22, Switzerland; *Yearbook of Labour Statistics.*

YEMEN - RETAIL TRADE

G.K. Hall and Company, 70 Lincoln Street, Boston, Massachusetts 02111 (617) 423-3990; *The World in Figures*.

YEMEN - RICE PRODUCTION - See YEMEN - CROPS

YEMEN - ROUNDWOOD PRODUCTION - See YEMEN - FORESTRY AND FOREST PRODUCTS

YEMEN - RUBBER PRODUCTION

Facts on File, 460 Park Avenue South, New York, New York 10016 (800) 443-8323; *The New Book of World Rankings*.

YEMEN - SALT PRODUCTION - See YEMEN - MINING AND MINERAL PRODUCTS

YEMEN - SAWNWOOD PRODUCTION - See YEMEN - FORESTRY AND FOREST PRODUCTS

YEMEN - SCIENCE AND TECHNOLOGY - EXPENDITURE FOR RESEARCH

Statistical Office of the United Nations, Publishing Service, New York, New York 10017 (800) 253 9646; *Statistical Yearbook*.

YEMEN - SCIENTISTS AND TECHNICIANS

Statistical Office of the United Nations, Publishing Service, New York, New York 10017 (800) 253-9646; *Statistical Yearbook*.

YEMEN - SENIOR CITIZENS

Facts on File, 460 Park Avenue South, New York, New York 10016 (800) 443-8323; *The New Book of World Rankings*.

YEMEN - SHEEP - See YEMEN - LIVESTOCK AND POULTRY

YEMEN - SILVER PRODUCTION AND CONSUMPTION - See YEMEN - MINING AND MINERAL PRODUCTS

YEMEN - SOCIAL DATA

Facts on File, 460 Park Avenue South, New York, New York 10016 (800) 443-8323; *The New Book of World Rankings*.

G.K. Hall and Company, 70 Lincoln Street, Boston, Massachusetts 02111 (617) 423-3990; *The World in Figures*.

YEMEN - STATE BUDGET REVENUE AND EXPENDITURES

Euromonitor Publications Limited, 87-88 Turnmill Street, London EC1M 5QU, England; *International Marketing Data and Statistics*.

YEMEN - STEEL PRODUCTION - See YEMEN - MINING AND MINERAL PRODUCTS

YEMEN - STOCKS - COMMODITY - MARKET PRICE - INDEX

Food and Agricultural Organization of the United Nations (FAO) Via delle Terme di Caracalla, 00100 Rome, Italy (Telephone Number in U.S. (202) 653-2400); *The State of Food and Agriculture*.

YEMEN - SUGAR PRODUCTION AND CONSUMPTION - See YEMEN - CROPS

YEMEN - TAXATION

G.K. Hall and Company, 70 Lincoln Street, Boston, Massachusetts 02111 (617) 423-3990; *The World in Figures*.

International Road Federation, 525 School Street, SW, Washington, D.C. 20024 (202) 554-2106; *World Road Statistics*.

The World Bank, 1818 H Street, NW, Washington, D.C. 20433 (202) 477-1234; *World Tables*.

YEMEN - TELEPHONES IN USE

American Telephone and Telegraph Company, 26 Parsippany Road, Whippany, New Jersey 07981 (800) 338-4038; *The World's Telephones*.

G.K. Hall and Company, 70 Lincoln Street, Boston, Massachusetts 02111 (617) 423-3990; *The World in Figures*.

Statistical Office of the United Nations, Publishing Service, New York, New York 10017 (800) 253-9646; *Statistical Yearbook*.

YEMEN - TELEVISION

Facts on File, 460 Park Avenue South, New York, New York 10016 (800) 443-8323; *The New Book of World Rankings*.

Time Books, 201 East 50th Street, New York, New York 10022 (212) 751-2600; *The Economist Book of Vital World Statistics*.

YEMEN - TEXTILE INDUSTRY

G.K. Hall and Company, 70 Lincoln Street, Boston, Massachusetts 02111 (617) 423-3990; *The World in Figures*.

YEMEN - TOBACCO PRODUCTION

Facts on File, 460 Park Avenue South, New York, New York 10016 (800) 443-8323; *The New Book of World Rankings*.

Statistical Office of the United Nations, Publishing Service, New York, New York 10017 (800) 253-9646; *Statistical Yearbook*.

YEMEN - TOURISM

Economic Commission for Western Asia, Post Office Box 27, Baghdad, Iraq; *Statistical Abstract of Western Asia*.

Facts on File, 460 Park Avenue South, New York, New York 10016 (800) 443-8323; *The New Book of World Rankings*.

G.K. Hall and Company, 70 Lincoln Street, Boston, Massachusetts 02111 (617) 423-3990; *The World in Figures*.

Statistical Office of the United Nations, Publishing Service, New York, New York 10017 (800) 253-9646; *Statistical Yearbook*.

Time Books, 201 East 50th Street, New York, New York 10022 (212) 751-2600; *The Economist Book of Vital World Statistics*.

World Tourism Organization, Calle Capitan Haya 42, E-28020 Madrid, Spain; *Yearbook of Tourism Statistics*.

YEMEN - TRACTORS IN USE

Statistical Office of the United Nations, Publishing Service, New York, New York 10017 (800) 253-9646; *Statistical Yearbook*.

YEMEN - TRADE - See YEMEN - FOREIGN TRADE

YEMEN - TRADEMARKS AND SERVICE MARKS

Statistical Office of the United Nations, Publishing Service, New York, New York 10017 (800) 253-9646; *Statistical yearbook.*

YEMEN - TRANSPORTATION AND COMMUNICATIONS

Economic Commission for Western Asia, Post Office Box 27, Baghdad, Iraq; *Statistical Abstract of Western Asia.*

Facts on File, 460 Park Avenue South, New York, New York 10016 (800) 443-8323; *The New Book of World Rankings.*

G.K. Hall and Company, 70 Lincoln Street, Boston, Massachusetts 02111 (617) 423-3990; *The World in Figures.*

YEMEN - UNEMPLOYMENT

Euromonitor Publications Limited, 87-88 Turnmill Street, London EC1M 5QU, England; *International Marketing Data and Statistics.*

International Labour Office, I.L.O. Publications, CH-1211, Geneva 22, Switzerland; *Yearbook of Labour Statistics.*

YEMEN - VITAL STATISTICS

Euromonitor Publications Limited, 87-88 Turnmill Street, London EC1M 5QU, England; *International Marketing Data and Statistics.*

G.K. Hall and Company, 70 Lincoln Street, Boston, Massachusetts 02111 (617) 423-3990; *The World in Figures.*

World Health Organization, Office of Publications, Avenue Appia, CH-1211 Geneva, 27, Switzerland (Telephone Number in U.S. (518) 436-9686); *World Health Statistics: Vital Statistics and Causes of Death.*

YEMEN - WAGES

G.K. Hall and Company, 70 Lincoln Street, Boston, Massachusetts 02111 (617) 423-3990; *The World in Figures.*

International Labour Office, I.L.O. Publications, CH-1211, Geneva 22, Switzerland; *Yearbook of Labour Statistics.*

YEMEN - WEATHER

Facts on File, 460 Park Avenue South, New York, New York 10016 (800) 443-8323; *The New Book of World Rankings.*

G.K. Hall and Company, 70 Lincoln Street, Boston, Massachusetts 02111 (617) 423-3990; *The World in Figures.*

YEMEN - WHEAT PRODUCTION AND PRICES - See YEMEN - CROPS

YEMEN - WHOLESALE PRICES

International Monetary Fund, 700 Nineteenth Street, NW, Washington, D.C. 20431 (202) 623-7000; *International Financial Statistics.*

YEMEN - WINE PRODUCTION

Facts on File, 460 Park Avenue South, New York, New York 10016 (800) 443-8323; *The New Book of World Rankings.*

YEMEN - WOOL PRODUCTION

Facts on File, 460 Park Avenue South, New York, New York 10016 (800) 443-8323; *The New Book of World Rankings.*

YEMEN - YARN PRODUCTION

Statistical Office of the United Nations, Publishing Service, New York, New York 10017 (800) 253-9646; *Statistical Yearbook.*

YOGURT CONSUMPTION

U.S. Department of Agriculture, Economic Research Service, Fourteenth Street and Independence Avenue, SW, Washington, D.C. 20005-4789 (202) 219-1504; *Food Consumption, Prices, and Expenditures,* and unpublished data.

YOUTH EMPLOYMENT PROGRAMS

U.S. Library of Congress, Congressional Research Service, 10 First Street, SE, Washington, D.C. 20540 (202) 707-5000; *Cash and Non-Cash Benefits for Persons with Limited Income: Eligibility Rules, Recipient and Expenditure Data.*

Yugoslavia - National Statistical Office

Savezni Zavod za Statistiku, Kneza Milosa, 20, Post Office Box 203, 11000 Belgrade, Yugoslavia.

Yugoslavia - Primary Statistics Sources

Savezni Zavod za Statistiku, Kneza Milosa, 20, 11000 Belgrade, Yugoslavia; *Statisticki Godisnjak Jugoslavije* (Statistical Yearbook of Yugoslavia), *Statisticki Bilten* (Statistical Bulletins), and *Statistical Pocketbook of Yugoslavia.*

YUGOSLAVIA - AGRICULTURE

Facts on File, 460 Park Avenue South, New York, New York 10016 (800) 443-8323; *The New Book of World Rankings.*

Food and Agricultural Organization of the United Nations (FAO) Via delle Terme di Caracalla, 00100 Rome, Italy (Telephone Number in U.S. (202) 653-2400); *The State of Food and Agriculture.*

G.K. Hall and Company, 70 Lincoln Street, Boston, Massachusetts 02111 (617) 423-3990; *The World in Figures.*

Statistical Office of the United Nations, Publishing Service, New York, New York 10017 (800) 253-9646; *Statistical Yearbook.*

The World Bank, 1818 H Street, NW, Washington, D.C. 20433 (202) 477-1234; *World Tables.*

YUGOSLAVIA - AIRLINE SERVICE

Facts on File, 460 Park Avenue South, New York, New York 10016 (800) 443-8323; *The New Book of World Rankings.*

G.K. Hall and Company, 70 Lincoln Street, Boston, Massachusetts 02111 (617) 423-3990; *The World in Figures.*

International Civil Aviation Organization, 1000 Sherbrooke Street, West, Montreal, Quebec, Canada H3A 2R2 (514) 285-8219; *Civil Aviation Statistics of the World.*

Statistical Office of the United Nations, Publishing Service, New York, New York 10017 (800) 253-9646; *Statistical Yearbook.*

YUGOSLAVIA - ALUMINUM PRODUCTION AND CONSUMPTION - See YUGOSLAVIA - MINING AND MINERAL PRODUCTS

YUGOSLAVIA - ANTIMONY AND ANTIMONY ORE PRODUCTION AND CONSUMPTION - See YUGOSLAVIA - MINING AND MINERAL PRODUCTS

YUGOSLAVIA - APPLE PRODUCTION - See YUGOSLAVIA - CROPS

YUGOSLAVIA - AREA AND DENSITY OF POPULATION

Facts on File, 460 Park Avenue South, New York, New York 10016 (800) 443-8323; *The New Book of World Rankings*.

Food and Agricultural Organization of the United Nations (FAO) Via delle Terme di Caracalla, 00100 Rome, Italy (Telephone Number in U.S. (202) 653-2400); *The State of Food and Agriculture*.

G.K. Hall and Company, 70 Lincoln Street, Boston, Massachusetts 02111 (617) 423-3990; *The World in Figures*.

Statistical Office of the United Nations, Publishing Service, New York, New York 10017 (800) 253-9646; *Statistical Yearbook*.

United Nations Educational, Scientific and Cultural Organization (UNESCO), 7 Place do Fontenoy, F-75700 Paris, France (Telephone Number in U.S. (212) 963-5981); *Statistical Yearbook*.

YUGOSLAVIA - ARMS EXPORTS AND IMPORTS

U.S. Arms Control and Disarmament Agency, 320 Twenty-first Street, NW, Washington, D.C. 20451 (202) 647-8677; *World Military Expenditures and Arms Transfers*

YUGOSLAVIA - BALANCE OF PAYMENTS

The Economist Intelligence Unit, 111 West 57th Street, New York, New York 10019 (800) 938-4085, *The World Market Atlas*

G.K. Hall and Company, 70 Lincoln Street, Boston, Massachusetts 02111 (617) 423-3990; *The World in Figures*.

International Monetary Fund, 700 Nineteenth Street, NW, Washington, D.C. 20431 (202) 623-7000; *Balance of Payments Yearbook*.

The World Bank, 1818 H Street, NW, Washington, D.C. 20433 (202) 477-1234; *World Tables*.

YUGOSLAVIA - BANKING

Facts on File, 460 Park Avenue South, New York, New York 10016 (800) 443-8323; *The New Book of World Rankings*.

G.K. Hall and Company, 70 Lincoln Street, Boston, Massachusetts 02111 (617) 423-3990; *The World in Figures*.

International Monetary Fund, 700 Nineteenth Street, NW, Washington, D.C. 20431 (202) 623-7000; *International Financial Statistics*.

YUGOSLAVIA - BARLEY PRODUCTION - See YUGOSLAVIA - CROPS

YUGOSLAVIA - BAUXITE PRODUCTION AND CONSUMPTION - See YUGOSLAVIA - MINING AND MINERAL PRODUCTS

YUGOSLAVIA - BEER PRODUCTION

Facts on File, 460 Park Avenue South, New York, New York 10016 (800) 443-8323; *The New Book of World Rankings*.

Statistical Office of the United Nations, Publishing Service, New York, New York 10017 (800) 253-9646; *Statistical Yearbook*.

YUGOSLAVIA - BIRTH RATE

Facts on File, 460 Park Avenue South, New York, New York 10016 (800) 443-8323; *The New Book of World Rankings*.

Statistical Office of the United Nations, Publishing Service, New York, New York 10017 (800) 253-9646; *Demographic Yearbook*, and *Statistical Yearbook*.

The World Bank, 1818 H Street, NW, Washington, D.C. 20433 (202) 477-1234; *World Tables*.

YUGOSLAVIA - BONDS

G.K. Hall and Company, 70 Lincoln Street, Boston, Massachusetts 02111 (617) 423-3990; *The World in Figures*.

International Monetary Fund, 700 Nineteenth Street, NW, Washington, D.C. 20431 (202) 623-7000, *Government Finance Statistics Yearbook*.

YUGOSLAVIA - BOOK PRODUCTION

Euromonitor Publications Limited, 87-88 Turnmill Street, London EC1M 5QU, England; *European Marketing Data and Statistics*.

G.K. Hall and Company, 70 Lincoln Street, Boston, Massachusetts 02111 (617) 423-3990; *The World in Figures*.

United Nations Educational, Scientific and Cultural Organization (UNESCO), 7 Place de Fontenoy, F-75700 Paris, France (Telephone Number in U.S. (212) 963-5981); *Statistical Yearbook*.

YUGOSLAVIA - BROADCASTING

Billboard Limited, P.O. Box 9027, 1006 AA Amsterdam, The Netherlands (Telephone Number in U.S. (212) 764-7300); *World Radio TV Handbook*.

Facts on File, 460 Park Avenue South, New York, New York 10016 (800) 443-8323; *The New Book of World Rankings*.

G.K. Hall and Company, 70 Lincoln Street, Boston, Massachusetts 02111 (617) 423-3990; *The World in Figures*.

United Nations Educational, Scientific and Cultural Organization (UNESCO), 7 Place de Fontenoy, F-75700 Paris, France (Telephone Number in U.S. (212) 963-5981); *Statistical Yearbook*.

YUGOSLAVIA - BUSINESS

G.K. Hall and Company, 70 Lincoln Street, Boston, Massachusetts 02111 (617) 423-3990; *The World in Figures*.

YUGOSLAVIA - BUTTER - See YUGOSLAVIA - DAIRY PRODUCTS

YUGOSLAVIA - CADMIUM PRODUCTION AND CONSUMPTION - See YUGOSLAVIA - MINING AND MINERAL PRODUCTS

YUGOSLAVIA - CALORIE SUPPLY

Food and Agricultural Organization of the United Nations (FAO) Via delle Terme di Caracalla, 00100 Rome, Italy (Telephone Number in U.S. (202) 653-2400); *The State of Food and Agriculture.*

YUGOSLAVIA - CATTLE - See YUGOSLAVIA - LIVESTOCK AND POULTRY

YUGOSLAVIA - CAUSTIC SODA PRODUCTION

Statistical Office of the United Nations, Publishing Service, New York, New York 10017 (800) 253-9646; *Statistical Yearbook.*

YUGOSLAVIA - CEMENT PRODUCTION - See YUGOSLAVIA - MINING AND MINERAL PRODUCTS

YUGOSLAVIA - CEREAL PRODUCTION - See YUGOSLAVIA - CROPS

YUGOSLAVIA - CHEESE - See YUGOSLAVIA - DAIRY PRODUCTS

YUGOSLAVIA - CHEMICAL (ORGANIC) PRODUCTION - See YUGOSLAVIA - MINING AND MINERAL PRODUCTS

YUGOSLAVIA - CHROMIUM ORE PRODUCTION AND CONSUMPTION - See YUGOSLAVIA - MINING AND MINERAL PRODUCTS

YUGOSLAVIA - CIGAR PRODUCTION - See YUGOSLAVIA - TOBACCO PRODUCTION

YUGOSLAVIA - CIGARETTE PRODUCTION - See YUGOSLAVIA - TOBACCO PRODUCTION

YUGOSLAVIA - CLASS STRUCTURE

G.K. Hall and Company, 70 Lincoln Street, Boston, Massachusetts 02111 (617) 423-3990; *The World in Figures.*

YUGOSLAVIA - CLIMATE

Facts on File, 460 Park Avenue South, New York, New York 10016 (800) 443-8323; *The New Book of World Rankings.*

G.K. Hall and Company, 70 Lincoln Street, Boston, Massachusetts 02111 (617) 423-3990; *The World in Figures.*

YUGOSLAVIA - CLOTHING EXPORTS AND IMPORTS

Statistical Office of the United Nations, Publishing Service, New York, New York 10017 (800) 253-9646; *Trade in Manufactures of Developing Countries.*

YUGOSLAVIA - COAL PRODUCTION - See YUGOSLAVIA - MINING AND MINERAL PRODUCTS

YUGOSLAVIA - COFFEE PRODUCTION AND CONSUMPTION - See YUGOSLAVIA - CROPS

YUGOSLAVIA - COKE OVEN COKE PRODUCTION AND CONSUMPTION - See YUGOSLAVIA - MINING AND MINERAL PRODUCTS

YUGOSLAVIA - COMMUNICATIONS

G.K. Hall and Company, 70 Lincoln Street, Boston, Massachusetts 02111 (617) 423-3990; *The World in Figures.*

YUGOSLAVIA - CONSTRUCTION INDUSTRY

Facts on File, 460 Park Avenue South, New York, New York 10016 (800) 443-8323; *The New Book of World Rankings.*

Organisation for Economic Co-operation and Development (OECD), 2 rue Andre-Pascal, 75 Paris 16, France (Telephone Number in U.S. (202) 785-6323); *Main Economic Indicators - Historical Statistics.*

Statistical Office of the United Nations, Publishing Service, New York, New York 10017 (800) 253-9646; *Construction Statistics Yearbook,* and *Statistical Yearbook.*

YUGOSLAVIA - CONSUMER PRICE INDEX

G.K. Hall and Company, 70 Lincoln Street, Boston, Massachusetts 02111 (617) 423-3990; *The World in Figures.*

Statistical Office of the United Nations, Publishing Service, New York, New York 10017 (800) 253-9646; *Statistical Yearbook.*

YUGOSLAVIA - CONSUMER PRICES

Euromonitor Publications Limited, 87-88 Turnmill Street, London EC1M 5QU, England; *European Marketing Data and Statistics.*

International Labour Office, I.L.O. Publications, CH-1211, Geneva 22, Switzerland; *Yearbook of Labour Statistics.*

International Monetary Fund, 700 Nineteenth Street, NW, Washington, D.C. 20431 (202) 623-7000; *International Financial Statistics.*

YUGOSLAVIA - CONSUMPTION

G.K. Hall and Company, 70 Lincoln Street, Boston, Massachusetts 02111 (617) 423-3990; *The World in Figures.*

International Lead and Zinc Study Group, Metro House, 58 St. James's Street, London SW1A 1LD England; *Lead and Zinc Statistics.*

YUGOSLAVIA - COPPER AND COPPER ORE PRODUCTION AND CONSUMPTION - See YUGOSLAVIA - MINING AND MINERAL PRODUCTS

YUGOSLAVIA - CORN PRODUCTION - See YUGOSLAVIA - CROPS

YUGOSLAVIA - CORPORATE TAXES - See YUGOSLAVIA - TAXATION

YUGOSLAVIA - COTTON - See YUGOSLAVIA - CROPS

YUGOSLAVIA - CRIME

Yale University Press, Yale Station, New Haven, Connecticut 06520 (203) 432-0940; *Violence and Crime in Cross-National Perspective.*

YUGOSLAVIA - CROPS

Commodity Research Bureau, Incorporated, 75 Wall Street, New York, New York 10005 (212) 504-7754; *Commodity Year Book.*

Euromonitor Publications Limited, 87-88 Turnmill Street, London EC1M 5QU, England; *European Marketing Data and Statistics.*

Facts on File, 460 Park Avenue South, New York, New York 10016 (800) 443-8323; *The New Book of World Rankings.*

Food and Agricultural Organization of the United Nations (FAO) Via delle Terme di Caracalla, 00100 Rome, Italy (Telephone Number in U.S. (202) 653-2400); *The State of Food and Agriculture*.

G.K. Hall and Company, 70 Lincoln Street, Boston, Massachusetts 02111 (617) 423-3990; *The World in Figures*.

Statistical Office of the United Nations, Publishing Service, New York, New York 10017 (800) 253-9646; *Statistical Yearbook*.

YUGOSLAVIA - CUSTOMS DUTIES

G.K. Hall and Company, 70 Lincoln Street, Boston, Massachusetts 02111 (617) 423-3990; *The World in Figures*.

International Monetary Fund, 700 Nineteenth Street, NW, Washington, D.C. 20431 (202) 623-7000; *Government Finance Statistics Yearbook*.

YUGOSLAVIA - DAIRY PRODUCTS

Facts on File, 460 Park Avenue South, New York, New York 10016 (800) 443-8323; *The New Book of World Rankings*.

Food and Agricultural Organization of the United Nations (FAO) Via delle Terme di Caracalla, 00100 Rome, Italy (Telephone Number in U.S. (202) 653-2400); *The State of Food and Agriculture*.

Organisation for Economic Co-operation and Development (OECD), 2 rue Andre-Pascal, 75 Paris 16, France (Telephone Number in U.S. (202) 785-6323); *Milk, Milk Products, and Egg Balances in OECD Member Countries*.

Statistical Office of the United Nations, Publishing Service, New York, New York 10017 (800) 253-9646; *Statistical Yearbook*.

YUGOSLAVIA - DEATH RATE

G.K. Hall and Company, 70 Lincoln Street, Boston, Massachusetts 02111 (617) 423-3990; *The World in Figures*.

Statistical Office of the United Nations, Publishing Service, New York, New York 10017 (800) 253-9646; *Statistical Yearbook*.

YUGOSLAVIA - DEFENSE EXPENDITURES

G.K. Hall and Company, 70 Lincoln Street, Boston, Massachusetts 02111 (617) 423-3990; *The World in Figures*.

International Monetary Fund, 700 Nineteenth Street, NW, Washington, D.C. 20431 (202) 623-7000; *Government Finance Statistics Yearbook*.

U.S. Arms Control and Disarmament Agency, 320 Twenty-first Street, NW, Washington, D.C. 20451 (202) 647-8677; *World Military Expenditures and Arms Transfers*.

YUGOSLAVIA - DEMOGRAPHY

The Economist Intelligence Unit, 111 West 57th Street, New York, New York 10019 (800) 938-4685; *The World Market Atlas*.

Facts on File, 460 Park Avenue South, New York, New York 10016 (800) 443-8323; *The New Book of World Rankings*.

G.K. Hall and Company, 70 Lincoln Street, Boston, Massachusetts 02111 (617) 423-3990; *The World in Figures*.

YUGOSLAVIA - DEVELOPMENT ASSISTANCE

G.K. Hall and Company, 70 Lincoln Street, Boston, Massachusetts 02111 (617) 423-3990; *The World in Figures*.

YUGOSLAVIA - DIAMOND PRODUCTION - See YUGOSLAVIA - MINING AND MINERAL PRODUCTS

YUGOSLAVIA - DISEASE

G.K. Hall and Company, 70 Lincoln Street, Boston, Massachusetts 02111 (617) 423-3990; *The World in Figures*.

YUGOSLAVIA - DIVORCE RATES

Facts on File, 460 Park Avenue South, New York, New York 10016 (800) 443-8323; *The New Book of World Rankings*.

Statistical Office of the United Nations, Publishing Service, New York, New York 10017 (800) 253-9646; *Demographic Yearbook*, and *Statistical Yearbook*.

YUGOSLAVIA - DOMESTIC PRODUCT

G.K. Hall and Company, 70 Lincoln Street, Boston, Massachusetts 02111 (617) 423-3990; *The World in Figures*.

YUGOSLAVIA - ECONOMY

Euromonitor Publications Limited, 87-88 Turnmill Street, London EC1M 5QU, England; *European Marketing Data and Statistics*.

Facts on File, 460 Park Avenue South, New York, New York 10016 (800) 443-8323; *The New Book of World Rankings*.

G.K. Hall and Company, 70 Lincoln Street, Boston, Massachusetts 02111 (617) 423-3990; *The World in Figures*.

Organisation for Economic Co-operation and Development (OECD), 2 rue Andre-Pascal, 75 Paris 16, France (Telephone Number in U.S. (202) 785-6323); *Main Economic Indicators*.

YUGOSLAVIA - EDUCATION

The Economist Intelligence Unit, 111 West 57th Street, New York, New York 10019 (800) 938-4685; *The World Market Atlas*.

Euromonitor Publications Limited, 87-88 Turnmill Street, London EC1M 5QU, England; *European Marketing Data and Statistics*.

Facts on File, 460 Park Avenue South, New York, New York 10016 (800) 443-8323; *The New Book of World Rankings*.

G.K. Hall and Company, 70 Lincoln Street, Boston, Massachusetts 02111 (617) 423-3990; *The World in Figures*.

International Monetary Fund, 700 Nineteenth Street, NW, Washington, D.C. 20431 (202) 623-7000; *Government Finance Statistics Yearbook*.

United Nations Educational, Scientific and Cultural Organization (UNESCO), 7 Place de Fontenoy, F-75700 Paris, France (Telephone Number in U.S. (212) 963-5981); *Statistical Yearbook*.

The World Bank, 1818 H Street, NW, Washington, D.C. 20433 (202) 477-1234; *World Tables*.

YUGOSLAVIA - EGG PRODUCTION AND CONSUMPTION - See YUGOSLAVIA - DAIRY PRODUCTS

YUGOSLAVIA - ELECTRICITY

Facts on File, 460 Park Avenue South, New York, New York 10016 (800) 443-8323; *The New Book of World Rankings.*

Penn Well Publishing Company, 1421 South Sheridan Road, P.O. Box 1260, Tulsa, Oklahoma 74101 (800) 752-9764; *International Energy Statistics Sourcebook.*

Statistical Office of the United Nations, Publishing Service, New York, New York 10017 (800) 253-9646; *Statistical Yearbook.*

YUGOSLAVIA - EMPLOYMENT

Euromonitor Publications Limited, 87-88 Turnmill Street, London EC1M 5QU, England; *European Marketing Data and Statistics.*

Facts on File, 460 Park Avenue South, New York, New York 10016 (800) 443-8323; *The New Book of World Rankings.*

International Labour Office, I.L.O. Publications, CH-1211, Geneva 22, Switzerland; *Yearbook of Labour Statistics.*

Statistical Office of the United Nations, Publishing Service, New York, New York 10017 (800) 253-9646; *Statistical Yearbook.*

YUGOSLAVIA - ENERGY

Euromonitor Publications Limited, 87-88 Turnmill Street, London EC1M 5QU, England; *European Marketing Data and Statistics.*

Facts on File, 460 Park Avenue South, New York, New York 10016 (800) 443-8323; *The New Book of World Rankings.*

Food and Agricultural Organization of the United Nations (FAO) Via delle Terme di Caracalla, 00100 Rome, Italy (Telephone Number in U.S. (202) 653-2400); *The State of Food and Agriculture.*

G.K. Hall and Company, 70 Lincoln Street, Boston, Massachusetts 02111 (617) 423-3990; *The World in Figures.*

Penn Well Publishing Company, 1421 South Sheridan Road, P.O. Box 1260, Tulsa, Oklahoma 74101 (800) 752-9764; *International Energy Statistics Sourcebook.*

Statistical Office of the United Nations, Publishing Service, New York, New York 10017 (800) 253-9646; *Energy Statistics Yearbook, Statistical Yearbook,* and *World Energy Supplies.*

YUGOSLAVIA - ENERGY EMPLOYMENT - MALE AND FEMALE - See YUGOSLAVIA - EMPLOYMENT

YUGOSLAVIA - ENGINEERING AND METAL PRODUCTS - EXPORTS AND IMPORTS

Statistical Office of the United Nations, Publishing Service, New York, New York 10017 (800) 253-9646; *Trade in Manufactures of Developing Countries.*

YUGOSLAVIA - EXCHANGE RATES

International Civil Aviation Organization, 1000 Sherbrooke Street, West, Montreal, Quebec, Canada H3A 2R2 (514) 285-8219; *Civil Aviation Statistics of the World.*

International Monetary Fund, 700 Nineteenth Street, NW, Washington, D.C. 20431 (202) 623-7000; *International Financial Statistics.*

Statistical Office of the United Nations, Publishing Service, New York, New York 10017 (800) 253-9646; *Statistical Yearbook.*

YUGOSLAVIA - EXPORTS

American Automobile Manufacturers Association, 1401 H Street, NW, Suite 900, Washington, D.C. 20005 (202) 326-5500; *World Motor Vehicle Data.*

The Economist Intelligence Unit, 111 West 57th Street, New York, New York 10019 (800) 938-4685; *The World Market Atlas.*

Food and Agricultural Organization of the United Nations (FAO) Via delle Terme di Caracalla, 00100 Rome, Italy (Telephone Number in U.S. (202) 653-2400); *The State of Food and Agriculture.*

G.K. Hall and Company, 70 Lincoln Street, Boston, Massachusetts 02111 (617) 423-3990; *The World in Figures.*

International Lead and Zinc Study Group, Metro House, 58 St. James's Street, London SW1A 1LD England; *Lead and Zinc Statistics.*

International Monetary Fund, 700 Nineteenth Street, NW, Washington, D.C. 20431 (202) 623-7000; *Direction of Trade Statistics,* and *International Financial Statistics.*

Organisation for Economic Co-operation and Development (OECD), 2 rue Andre-Pascal, 75 Paris 16, France (Telephone Number in U.S. (202) 785-6323); *Milk, Milk Products, and Egg Balances in OECD Member Countries,* and *Review of Fisheries in OECD Member Countries.*

Statistical Office of the United Nations, Publishing Service, New York, New York 10017 (800) 253-9646; *Trade in Manufactures of Developing Countries.*

The World Bank, 1818 H Street, NW, Washington, D.C. 20433 (202) 477-1234; *World Tables.*

YUGOSLAVIA - EXTERNAL INDEBTEDNESS

The World Bank, 1818 H Street, NW, Washington, D.C. 20433 (202) 477-1234; *World Tables.*

YUGOSLAVIA - EXTERNAL TRADE

Food and Agricultural Organization of the United Nations (FAO) Via delle Terme di Caracalla, 00100 Rome, Italy (Telephone Number in U.S. (202) 653-2400); *The State of Food and Agriculture.*

G.K. Hall and Company, 70 Lincoln Street, Boston, Massachusetts 02111 (617) 423-3990; *The World in Figures.*

Statistical Office of the United Nations, Publishing Service, New York, New York 10017 (800) 253-9646; *Statistical Yearbook.*

YUGOSLAVIA - FABRIC PRODUCTION - See YUGOSLAVIA - TEXTILE INDUSTRY

YUGOSLAVIA - FARM CROPS - See YUGOSLAVIA - CROPS

YUGOSLAVIA - FERTILITY RATES

Facts on File, 460 Park Avenue South, New York, New York 10016 (800) 443-8323; *The New Book of World Rankings.*

The World Bank, 1818 H Street, NW, Washington, D.C. 20433 (202) 477-1234; *World Tables.*

YUGOSLAVIA - FERTILIZER

Food and Agricultural Organization of the United Nations (FAO) Via delle Terme di Caracalla, 00100 Rome, Italy (Telephone Number in U.S. (202) 653-2400); *The State of Food and Agriculture*.

Statistical Office of the United Nations, Publishing Service, New York, New York 10017 (800) 253-9646; *Statistical Yearbook*.

YUGOSLAVIA - FETAL MORTALITY

Statistical Office of the United Nations, Publishing Service, New York, New York 10017 (800) 253-9646; *Demographic Yearbook*.

YUGOSLAVIA - FIBRE PRODUCTION - See YUGOSLAVIA - TEXTILE INDUSTRY

YUGOSLAVIA - FILAMENT PRODUCTION - See YUGOSLAVIA - TEXTILE INDUSTRY

YUGOSLAVIA - FILM - See YUGOSLAVIA - MOTION PICTURES

YUGOSLAVIA - FINANCE

Facts on File, 460 Park Avenue South, New York, New York 10016 (800) 443-8323; *The New Book of World Rankings*.

G.K. Hall and Company, 70 Lincoln Street, Boston, Massachusetts 02111 (617) 423-3990; *The World in Figures*.

International Monetary Fund, 700 Nineteenth Street, NW, Washington, D.C. 20431 (202) 623-7000; *International Financial Statistics*.

YUGOSLAVIA - FISHERIES

Euromonitor Publications Limited, 87-88 Turnmill Street, London EC1M 5QU, England; *European Marketing Data and Statistics*.

Facts on File, 460 Park Avenue South, New York, New York 10016 (800) 443-8323; *The New Book of World Rankings*.

Food and Agricultural Organization of the United Nations (FAO) Via delle Terme di Caracalla, 00100 Rome, Italy (Telephone Number in U.S. (202) 653-2400); *The State of Food and Agriculture*.

Organisation for Economic Co-operation and Development (OECD), 2 rue Andre-Pascal, 75 Paris 16, France (Telephone Number in U.S. (202) 785-6323); *Review of Fisheries in OECD Member Countries*.

Statistical Office of the United Nations, Publishing Service, New York, New York 10017 (800) 253-9646; *Statistical Yearbook*.

Organisation for Economic Co-operation and Development (OECD), 2 rue Andre-Pascal, 75 Paris 16, France (Telephone Number in U.S. (202) 785-6323); *Review of Fisheries in OECD Member Countries*.

YUGOSLAVIA - FLOUR PRODUCTION

Commodity Research Bureau, Incorporated, 75 Wall Street, New York, New York 10005 (212) 504-7754; *Commodity Year Book*.

Statistical Office of the United Nations, Publishing Service, New York, New York 10017 (800) 253-9646; *Statistical Yearbook*.

YUGOSLAVIA - FOOD

Food and Agricultural Organization of the United Nations (FAO) Via delle Terme di Caracalla, 00100 Rome, Italy (Telephone Number in U.S. (202) 653-2400); *The State of Food and Agriculture*.

G.K. Hall and Company, 70 Lincoln Street, Boston, Massachusetts 02111 (617) 423-3990; *The World in Figures*.

Organisation for Economic Co-operation and Development (OECD), 2 rue Andre-Pascal, 75 Paris 16, France (Telephone Number in U.S. (202) 785-6323); *Food Consumption Statistics*.

Statistical Office of the United Nations, Publishing Service, New York, New York 10017 (800) 253-9646; *Trade in Manufactures of Developing Countries*.

YUGOSLAVIA - FOREIGN AID

G.K. Hall and Company, 70 Lincoln Street, Boston, Massachusetts 02111 (617) 423-3990; *The World in Figures*.

YUGOSLAVIA - FOREIGN TRADE

Euromonitor Publications Limited, 87-88 Turnmill Street, London EC1M 5QU, England; *European Marketing Data and Statistics*.

Facts on File, 460 Park Avenue South, New York, New York 10016 (800) 443-8323; *The New Book of World Rankings*.

Food and Agricultural Organization of the United Nations (FAO) Via delle Terme di Caracalla, 00100 Rome, Italy (Telephone Number in U.S. (202) 653-2400); *The State of Food and Agriculture*.

G.K. Hall and Company, 70 Lincoln Street, Boston, Massachusetts 02111 (617) 423-3990; *The World in Figures*.

International Monetary Fund, 700 Nineteenth Street, NW, Washington, D.C. 20431 (202) 623-7000; *International Financial Statistics*.

Organisation for Economic Co-operation and Development (OECD), 2 rue Andre-Pascal, 75 Paris 16, France (Telephone Number in U.S. (202) 785-6323); *Main Economic Indicators - Historical Statistics*.

Statistical Office of the United Nations, Publishing Service, New York, New York 10017 (800) 253-9646; *International Trade Statistics Yearbook*, and *Statistical Yearbook*.

The World Bank, 1818 H Street, NW, Washington, D.C. 20433 (202) 477-1234; *World Tables*.

World Bureau of Metal Statistics, 27-A High Street, Ware Hert SG12 9BA, England; *World Metal Statistics*.

YUGOSLAVIA - FORESTRY AND FOREST PRODUCTS

American Forest and Paper Association, 1250 Connecticut Avenue, NW, Washington, D.C. 20036 (202) 463-2455; *Wood Pulp and Fiber Statistics*.

Euromonitor Publications Limited, 87-88 Turnmill Street, London EC1M 5QU, England; *European Marketing Data and Statistics*.

Facts on File, 460 Park Avenue South, New York, New York 10016 (800) 443-8323; *The New Book of World Rankings*.

Food and Agricultural Organization of the United Nations (FAO) Via delle Terme di Caracalla, 00100 Rome, Italy (Telephone Number in U.S. (202) 653-2400); *The State of Food and Agriculture*, and *Yearbook of Forest Products*.

G.K. Hall and Company, 70 Lincoln Street, Boston, Massachusetts 02111 (617) 423-3990; *The World in Figures*.

Statistical Office of the United Nations, Publishing Service, New York, New York 10017 (800) 253-9646; *Statistical Yearbook*.

United Nations Educational, Scientific and Cultural Organization (UNESCO), 7 Place de Fontenoy, F-75700 Paris, France (Telephone Number in U.S. (212) 963-5981); *Statistical Yearbook*.

YUGOSLAVIA - FURNITURE AND WOOD PRODUCTS - EXPORTS AND IMPORTS

Statistical Office of the United Nations, Publishing Service, New York, New York 10017 (800) 253-9646; *Trade in Manufactures of Developing Countries*.

YUGOSLAVIA - GAS AND GAS LIQUIDS PRODUCTION - See YUGOSLAVIA - MINING AND MINERAL PRODUCTS

YUGOSLAVIA - GENERAL INDUSTRIAL STATISTICS

Statistical Office of the United Nations, Publishing Service, New York, New York 10017 (800) 253-9646; *Industrial Statistics Yearbook*.

YUGOSLAVIA - GENERAL MORTALITY

Statistical Office of the United Nations, Publishing Service, New York, New York 10017 (800) 253-9646; *Demographic Yearbook*.

YUGOSLAVIA - GEOGRAPHIC DATA

Facts on File, 460 Park Avenue South, New York, New York 10016 (800) 443-8323; *The New Book of World Rankings*.

YUGOSLAVIA - GOLD HOLDINGS

International Monetary Fund, 700 Nineteenth Street, NW, Washington, D.C. 20431 (202) 623-7000; *International Financial Statistics*.

Statistical Office of the United Nations, Publishing Service, New York, New York 10017 (800) 253-9646; *Statistical Yearbook*.

The World Bank, 1818 H Street, NW, Washington, D.C. 20433 (202) 477-1234; *World Tables*.

YUGOSLAVIA - GOLD PRODUCTION AND CONSUMPTION - See YUGOSLAVIA - MINING AND MINERAL PRODUCTS

YUGOSLAVIA - GOVERNMENT

G.K. Hall and Company, 70 Lincoln Street, Boston, Massachusetts 02111 (617) 423-3990; *The World in Figures*.

YUGOSLAVIA - GOVERNMENT EXPENDITURES

International Monetary Fund, 700 Nineteenth Street, NW, Washington, D.C. 20431 (202) 623-7000; *Government Finance Statistics Yearbook*.

The World Bank, 1818 H Street, NW, Washington, D.C. 20433 (202) 477-1234; *World Tables*.

YUGOSLAVIA - GOVERNMENT FINANCES

International Monetary Fund, 700 Nineteenth Street, NW, Washington, D.C. 20431 (202) 623-7000; *International Financial Statistics*.

Statistical Office of the United Nations, Publishing Service, New York, New York 10017 (800) 253-9646; *Statistical Yearbook*.

YUGOSLAVIA - GOVERNMENT REVENUE

International Monetary Fund, 700 Nineteenth Street, NW, Washington, D.C. 20431 (202) 623-7000; *Government Finance Statistics Yearbook*.

The World Bank, 1818 H Street, NW, Washington, D.C. 20433 (202) 477-1234; *World Tables*.

YUGOSLAVIA - GRAIN PRODUCTION - See YUGOSLAVIA - CROPS

YUGOSLAVIA - GRANTS

International Monetary Fund, 700 Nineteenth Street, NW, Washington, D.C. 20431 (202) 623-7000; *Government Finance Statistics Yearbook*.

YUGOSLAVIA - GROSS DOMESTIC PRODUCT

The Economist Intelligence Unit, 111 West 57th Street, New York, New York 10019 (800) 938-4685; *The World Market Atlas*.

Facts on File, 460 Park Avenue South, New York, New York 10016 (800) 443-8323; *The New Book of World Rankings*.

G.K. Hall and Company, 70 Lincoln Street, Boston, Massachusetts 02111 (617) 423-3990; *The World in Figures*.

Statistical Office of the United Nations, Publishing Service, New York, New York 10017 (800) 253-9646; *Statistical Yearbook*.

The World Bank, 1818 H Street, NW, Washington, D.C. 20433 (202) 477-1234; *World Tables*.

YUGOSLAVIA - GROSS NATIONAL PRODUCT

U.S. Arms Control and Disarmament Agency, 320 Twenty-first Street, NW, Washington, D.C. 20451 (202) 647-8677; *World Military Expenditures and Arms Transfers*.

The World Bank, 1818 H Street, NW, Washington, D.C. 20433 (202) 477-1234; *World Tables*.

YUGOSLAVIA - HEALTH

Facts on File, 460 Park Avenue South, New York, New York 10016 (800) 443-8323; *The New Book of World Rankings*.

G.K. Hall and Company, 70 Lincoln Street, Boston, Massachusetts 02111 (617) 423-3990; *The World in Figures*.

Statistical Office of the United Nations, Publishing Service, New York, New York 10017 (800) 253-9646; *Statistical Yearbook*.

YUGOSLAVIA - HEALTH EXPENDITURES

International Monetary Fund, 700 Nineteenth Street, NW, Washington, D.C. 20431 (202) 623-7000; *Government Finance Statistics Yearbook*.

YUGOSLAVIA - HIGHWAYS

G.K. Hall and Company, 70 Lincoln Street, Boston, Massachusetts 02111 (617) 423-3990; *The World in Figures*.

International Road Federation, 525 School Street, SW, Washington, D.C. 20024 (202) 554-2106; *World Road Statistics*.

Statistical Office of the United Nations, Publishing Service, New York, New York 10017 (800) 253-9646; *Annual Bulletin of Transport Statistics for Europe*.

YUGOSLAVIA - HORSES - See YUGOSLAVIA - LIVESTOCK AND POULTRY

YUGOSLAVIA - HOURS OF WORK - See YUGOSLAVIA - EMPLOYMENT

YUGOSLAVIA - HOUSING AND HOUSING UNITS

Facts on File, 460 Park Avenue South, New York, New York 10016 (800) 443-8323; *The New Book of World Rankings*.

YUGOSLAVIA - HOUSING EXPENDITURES

International Monetary Fund, 700 Nineteenth Street, NW, Washington, D.C. 20431 (202) 623-7000; *Government Finance Statistics Yearbook*.

YUGOSLAVIA - HYDROCHLORIC ACID PRODUCTION

Statistical Office of the United Nations, Publishing Service, New York, New York 10017 (800) 253-9646; *Statistical Yearbook*.

YUGOSLAVIA - ILLITERATE POPULATION

The Economist Intelligence Unit, 111 West 57th Street, New York, New York 10019 (800) 938-4685; *The World Market Atlas*.

G.K. Hall and Company, 70 Lincoln Street, Boston, Massachusetts 02111 (617) 423-3990; *The World in Figures*.

United Nations Educational, Scientific and Cultural Organization (UNESCO), 7 Place de Fontenoy, F-75700 Paris, France (Telephone Number in U.S. (212) 963-5981); *Statistical Yearbook*.

YUGOSLAVIA - IMPORTS

American Automobile Manufacturers Association, 1401 H Street, NW, Suite 900, Washington, D.C. 20005 (202) 326-5500; *World Motor Vehicle Data*.

The Economist Intelligence Unit, 111 West 57th Street, New York, New York 10019 (800) 938-4685; *The World Market Atlas*.

Food and Agricultural Organization of the United Nations (FAO) Via delle Terme di Caracalla, 00100 Rome, Italy (Telephone Number in U.S. (202) 653-2400); *The State of Food and Agriculture*.

G.K. Hall and Company, 70 Lincoln Street, Boston, Massachusetts 02111 (617) 423-3990; *The World in Figures*.

International Lead and Zinc Study Group, Metro House, 58 St. James's Street, London SW1A 1LD England; *Lead and Zinc Statistics*.

International Monetary Fund, 700 Nineteenth Street, NW, Washington, D.C. 20431 (202) 623-7000; *Direction of Trade Statistics, Government Finance Statistics Yearbook*, and *International Financial Statistics*.

Organisation for Economic Co-operation and Development (OECD), 2 rue Andre-Pascal, 75 Paris 16, France (Telephone Number in U.S. (202) 785-6323); *Milk, Milk Products, and Egg Balances in OECD Member Countries*, and *Review of Fisheries in OECD Member Countries*.

Statistical Office of the United Nations, Publishing Service, New York, New York 10017 (800) 253-9646; *Trade in Manufactures of Developing Countries*.

The World Bank, 1818 H Street, NW, Washington, D.C. 20433 (202) 477-1234; *World Tables*.

YUGOSLAVIA - INCOME TAXES - See YUGOSLAVIA - TAXATION

YUGOSLAVIA - INDUSTRIAL ACCIDENTS

International Labour Office, I.L.O. Publications, CH-1211, Geneva 22, Switzerland; *Yearbook of Labour Statistics*.

YUGOSLAVIA - INDUSTRIAL DESIGNS

Statistical Office of the United Nations, Publishing Service, New York, New York 10017 (800) 253-9646; *Statistical Yearbook*.

YUGOSLAVIA - INDUSTRIAL DISPUTES

International Labour Office, I.L.O. Publications, CH-1211, Geneva 22, Switzerland; *Yearbook of Labour Statistics*.

YUGOSLAVIA - INDUSTRIAL PRODUCTION

Facts on File, 460 Park Avenue South, New York, New York 10016 (800) 443-8323; *The New Book of World Rankings*.

YUGOSLAVIA - INDUSTRIAL SHARES

Facts on File, 460 Park Avenue South, New York, New York 10016 (800) 443-8323; *The New Book of World Rankings*.

YUGOSLAVIA - INDUSTRY

Facts on File, 460 Park Avenue South, New York, New York 10016 (800) 443-8323; *The New Book of World Rankings*.

G.K. Hall and Company, 70 Lincoln Street, Boston, Massachusetts 02111 (617) 423-3990; *The World in Figures*.

Organisation for Economic Co-operation and Development (OECD), 2 rue Andre-Pascal, 75 Paris 16, France (Telephone Number in U.S. (202) 785-6323); *Main Economic Indicators - Historical Statistics*.

The World Bank, 1818 H Street, NW, Washington, D.C. 20433 (202) 477-1234; *World Tables*.

World Intellectual Property Organization, 34 Chemin des Colombettes, CH-1211 Geneva 20. Switzerland; *Industrial Property Statistics*.

YUGOSLAVIA - INFANT AND MATERNAL MORTALITY

Statistical Office of the United Nations, Publishing Service, New York, New York 10017 (800) 253-9646; *Demographic Yearbook*, and *Statistical Yearbook*.

The World Bank, 1818 H Street, NW, Washington, D.C. 20433 (202) 477-1234; *World Tables*.

YUGOSLAVIA - INTERNAL TRADE

Statistical Office of the United Nations, Publishing Service, New York, New York 10017 (800) 253-9646; *Statistical Yearbook*.

YUGOSLAVIA - INTERNATIONAL LIQUIDITY

International Monetary Fund, 700 Nineteenth Street, NW, Washington, D.C. 20431 (202) 623-7000; *International Financial Statistics*.

YUGOSLAVIA - INTERNATIONAL RESERVES EXCLUDING GOLD

Statistical Office of the United Nations, Publishing Service, New York, New York 10017 (800) 253-9646; *Statistical Yearbook*.

The World Bank, 1818 H Street, NW, Washington, D.C. 20433 (202) 477-1234; *World Tables*.

YUGOSLAVIA - IRON ORE PRODUCTION AND CONSUMPTION - See YUGOSLAVIA - MINING AND MINERAL PRODUCTS

YUGOSLAVIA - LABOR FORCE

Facts on File, 460 Park Avenue South, New York, New York 10016 (800) 443-8323; *The New Book of World Rankings*.

Food and Agricultural Organization of the United Nations (FAO) Via delle Terme di Caracalla, 00100 Rome, Italy (Telephone Number in U.S. (202) 653-2400); *The State of Food and Agriculture*.

G.K. Hall and Company, 70 Lincoln Street, Boston, Massachusetts 02111 (617) 423-3990; *The World in Figures*.

Organisation for Economic Co-operation and Development (OECD), 2 rue Andre-Pascal, 75 Paris 16, France (Telephone Number in U.S. (202) 785-6323); *Main Economic Indicators - Historical Statistics*.

The World Bank, 1818 H Street, NW, Washington, D.C. 20433 (202) 477-1234; *World Tables*.

YUGOSLAVIA - LABOR PRODUCTIVITY

International Labour Office, I.L.O. Publications, CH-1211, Geneva 22, Switzerland; *Yearbook of Labour Statistics*.

YUGOSLAVIA - LAND USE

Euromonitor Publications Limited, 87-88 Turnmill Street, London EC1M 5QU, England; *European Marketing Data and Statistics*.

G.K. Hall and Company, 70 Lincoln Street, Boston, Massachusetts 02111 (617) 423-3990; *The World in Figures*.

YUGOSLAVIA - LEAD AND LEAD ORE PRODUCTION AND CONSUMPTION - See YUGOSLAVIA - MINING AND MINERAL PRODUCTS

YUGOSLAVIA - LEATHER AND FOOTWEAR - EXPORTS AND IMPORTS

Statistical Office of the United Nations, Publishing Service, New York, New York 10017 (800) 253-9646; *Trade in Manufactures of Developing Countries*.

YUGOSLAVIA - LIBRARIES

Euromonitor Publications Limited, 87-88 Turnmill Street, London EC1M 5QU, England; *European Marketing Data and Statistics*.

Facts on File, 460 Park Avenue South, New York, New York 10016 (800) 443-8323; *The New Book of World Rankings*.

United Nations Educational, Scientific and Cultural Organization (UNESCO), 7 Place de Fontenoy, F-75700 Paris, France (Telephone Number in U.S. (212) 963-5981); *Statistical Yearbook*.

YUGOSLAVIA - LIGNITE PRODUCTION - See YUGOSLAVIA - MINING AND MINERAL PRODUCTS

YUGOSLAVIA - LIVESTOCK AND POULTRY

Euromonitor Publications Limited, 87-88 Turnmill Street, London EC1M 5QU, England; *European Marketing Data and Statistics*.

Facts on File, 460 Park Avenue South, New York, New York 10016 (800) 443-8323; *The New Book of World Rankings*.

Food and Agricultural Organization of the United Nations (FAO) Via delle Terme di Caracalla, 00100 Rome, Italy (Telephone Number in U.S. (202) 653-2400); *The State of Food and Agriculture*.

G.K. Hall and Company, 70 Lincoln Street, Boston, Massachusetts 02111 (617) 423-3990; *The World in Figures*.

Statistical Office of the United Nations, Publishing Service, New York, New York 10017 (800) 253-9646; *Statistical Yearbook*.

YUGOSLAVIA - LIVING LEVELS

G.K. Hall and Company, 70 Lincoln Street, Boston, Massachusetts 02111 (617) 423-3990; *The World in Figures*.

YUGOSLAVIA - MAIL - NUMBER OF ITEMS SENT AND RECEIVED

Statistical Office of the United Nations, Publishing Service, New York, New York 10017 (800) 253-9646; *Statistical Yearbook*.

YUGOSLAVIA - MANGANESE PRODUCTION AND CONSUMPTION - See YUGOSLAVIA - MINING AND MINERAL PRODUCTS

YUGOSLAVIA - MANUFACTURING

American Automobile Manufacturers Association, 1401 H Street, NW, Suite 900, Washington, D.C. 20005 (202) 326-5500; *World Motor Vehicle Data*.

Facts on File, 460 Park Avenue South, New York, New York 10016 (800) 443-8323; *The New Book of World Rankings*.

G.K. Hall and Company, 70 Lincoln Street, Boston, Massachusetts 02111 (617) 423-3990; *The World in Figures*.

Statistical Office of the United Nations, Publishing Service, New York, New York 10017 (800) 253-9646; *Statistical Yearbook*.

The World Bank, 1818 H Street, NW, Washington, D.C. 20433 (202) 477-1234; *World Tables*.

YUGOSLAVIA - MARRIAGE RATES

Facts on File, 460 Park Avenue South, New York, New York 10016 (800) 443-8323; *The New Book of World Rankings*.

Statistical Office of the United Nations, Publishing Service, New York, New York 10017 (800) 253-9646; *Demographic Yearbook*, and *Statistical Yearbook*.

YUGOSLAVIA - MEAT PRODUCTION - See YUGOSLAVIA - LIVESTOCK AND POULTRY

YUGOSLAVIA - MERCHANT SHIPPING

G.K. Hall and Company, 70 Lincoln Street, Boston, Massachusetts 02111 (617) 423-3990; *The World in Figures.*

Lloyd's Register of Shipping, 17 Battery Place, New York, New York 10004 (212) 425-8050; *Register of Ships.*

Statistical Office of the United Nations, Publishing Service, New York, New York 10017 (800) 253-9646; *Annual Bulletin of Transport Statistics for Europe,* and *Statistical Yearbook.*

U.S. Department of Transportation, Maritime Administration, 400 Seventh Street, SW, Washington, D.C. 20590 (202) 366-5807; *A Statistical Analysis of the World's Merchant Fleets.*

YUGOSLAVIA - MERCURY PRODUCTION AND CONSUMPTION - See YUGOSLAVIA - MINING AND MINERAL PRODUCTS

YUGOSLAVIA - MILITARY

G.K. Hall and Company, 70 Lincoln Street, Boston, Massachusetts 02111 (617) 423-3990; *The World in Figures.*

The Economist Intelligence Unit, 111 West 57th Street, New York, New York 10019 (800) 938-4685; *The World Market Atlas.*

U.S. Arms Control and Disarmament Agency, 320 Twenty-first Street, NW, Washington, D.C. 20451 (202) 647-8677; *World Military Expenditures and Arms Transfers.*

YUGOSLAVIA - MILK PRODUCTION - See YUGOSLAVIA - DAIRY PRODUCTS

YUGOSLAVIA - MINING AND MINERAL PRODUCTS

Commodity Research Bureau, Incorporated, 75 Wall Street, New York, New York 10005 (212) 504-7754; *Commodity Year Book.*

Facts on File, 460 Park Avenue South, New York, New York 10016 (800) 443-8323; *The New Book of World Rankings.*

G.K. Hall and Company, 70 Lincoln Street, Boston, Massachusetts 02111 (617) 423-3990; *The World in Figures.*

International Lead and Zinc Study Group, Metro House, 58 St. James's Street, London SW1A 1LD England; *Lead and Zinc Statistics.*

Penn Well Publishing Company, 1421 South Sheridan Road, P.O. Box 1260, Tulsa, Oklahoma 74101 (800) 752-9764; *International Energy Statistics Sourcebook.*

Statistical Office of the United Nations, Publishing Service, New York, New York 10017 (800) 253-9646; *Statistical Yearbook.*

World Bureau of Metal Statistics, 27-A High Street, Ware Hert SG12 9BA, England; *World Metal Statistics.*

YUGOSLAVIA - MOLYBDENUM AND MOLYBDENUM ORE PRODUCTION AND CONSUMPTION - See YUGOSLAVIA - MINING AND MINERAL PRODUCTS

YUGOSLAVIA - MONEY EXCHANGE RATE

International Monetary Fund, 700 Nineteenth Street, NW, Washington, D.C. 20431 (202) 623-7000; *International Financial Statistics.*

Statistical Office of the United Nations, Publishing Service, New York, New York 10017 (800) 253-9646; *Statistical Yearbook.*

YUGOSLAVIA - MONEY SUPPLY

G.K. Hall and Company, 70 Lincoln Street, Boston, Massachusetts 02111 (617) 423-3990; *The World in Figures.*

International Monetary Fund, 700 Nineteenth Street, NW, Washington, D.C. 20431 (202) 623-7000; *International Financial Statistics.*

Statistical Office of the United Nations, Publishing Service, New York, New York 10017 (800) 253-9646; *Statistical Yearbook.*

The World Bank, 1818 H Street, NW, Washington, D.C. 20433 (202) 477-1234; *World Tables.*

YUGOSLAVIA - MOTION PICTURES

United Nations Educational, Scientific and Cultural Organization (UNESCO), 7 Place de Fontenoy, F-75700 Paris, France (Telephone Number in U.S. (212) 963-5981); *Statistical Yearbook.*

YUGOSLAVIA - MOTOR VEHICLE PRODUCTION

American Automobile Manufacturers Association, 1401 H Street, NW, Suite 900, Washington, D.C. 20005 (202) 326-5500; *World Motor Vehicle Data.*

YUGOSLAVIA - MOTOR VEHICLE PRODUCTION AND ASSEMBLY

Statistical Office of the United Nations, Publishing Service, New York, New York 10017 (800) 253-9646; *Statistical Yearbook.*

YUGOSLAVIA - MOTOR VEHICLE TAXES - See YUGOSLAVIA - TAXATION

YUGOSLAVIA - MOTOR VEHICLES IN USE

American Automobile Manufacturers Association, 1401 H Street, NW, Suite 900, Washington, D.C. 20005 (202) 326-5500; *World Motor Vehicle Data.*

G.K. Hall and Company, 70 Lincoln Street, Boston, Massachusetts 02111 (617) 423-3990; *The World in Figures.*

International Road Federation, 525 School Street, SW, Washington, D.C. 20024 (202) 554-2106; *World Road Statistics.*

Statistical Office of the United Nations, Publishing Service, New York, New York 10017 (800) 253-9646; *Statistical Yearbook.*

YUGOSLAVIA - MULES - See YUGOSLAVIA - LIVESTOCK AND POULTRY

YUGOSLAVIA - MUSEUMS

Euromonitor Publications Limited, 87-88 Turnmill Street, London EC1M 5QU, England; *European Marketing Data and Statistics.*

Facts on File, 460 Park Avenue South, New York, New York 10016 (800) 443-8323; *The New Book of World Rankings.*

United Nations Educational, Scientific and Cultural Organization (UNESCO), 7 Place de Fontenoy, F-75700 Paris, France (Telephone Number in U.S. (212) 963-5981); *Statistical Yearbook.*

YUGOSLAVIA - NATALITY - See YUGOSLAVIA - BIRTH RATE

YUGOSLAVIA - NATIONAL ACCOUNTS

International Monetary Fund, 700 Nineteenth Street, NW, Washington, D.C. 20431 (202) 623-7000; *International Financial Statistics.*

Statistical Office of the United Nations, Publishing Service, New York, New York 10017 (800) 253-9646; *National Accounts Statistics,* and *Statistical Yearbook.*

YUGOSLAVIA - NATIONAL INCOME

Facts on File, 460 Park Avenue South, New York, New York 10016 (800) 443-8323; *The New Book of World Rankings.*

G.K. Hall and Company, 70 Lincoln Street, Boston, Massachusetts 02111 (617) 423-3990; *The World in Figures.*

Statistical Office of the United Nations, Publishing Service, New York, New York 10017 (800) 253-9646; *Statistical Yearbook.*

YUGOSLAVIA - NATIONAL PRODUCT

Facts on File, 460 Park Avenue South, New York, New York 10016 (800) 443-8323; *The New Book of World Rankings.*

Statistical Office of the United Nations, Publishing Service, New York, New York 10017 (800) 253-9646; *Statistical Yearbook.*

YUGOSLAVIA - NATURAL GAS PRODUCTION - See YUGOSLAVIA - MINING AND MINERAL PRODUCTS

YUGOSLAVIA - NET MATERIAL PRODUCT

Statistical Office of the United Nations, Publishing Service, New York, New York 10017 (800) 253-9646; *Statistical Yearbook.*

YUGOSLAVIA - NEWSPAPER PRODUCTION - See YUGOSLAVIA - FORESTRY AND FOREST PRODUCTS

YUGOSLAVIA - NEWSPRINT PRODUCTION AND CONSUMPTION - See YUGOSLAVIA - FORESTRY AND FOREST PRODUCTS

YUGOSLAVIA - NICKEL AND NICKEL ORE PRODUCTION AND CONSUMPTION - See YUGOSLAVIA - MINING AND MINERAL PRODUCTS

YUGOSLAVIA - NITRIC ACID PRODUCTION - See YUGOSLAVIA - MINING AND MINERAL PRODUCTS

YUGOSLAVIA - OCCUPATIONS - See YUGOSLAVIA - LABOR FORCE

YUGOSLAVIA - ONION PRODUCTION - See YUGOSLAVIA - CROPS

YUGOSLAVIA - PAPER PRODUCTION - See YUGOSLAVIA - FORESTRY AND FOREST PRODUCTS

YUGOSLAVIA - PATENTS

Statistical Office of the United Nations, Publishing Service, New York, New York 10017 (800) 253-9646; *Statistical Yearbook.*

World Intellectual Property Organization, 34 Chemin des Colombettes, CH-1211 Geneva 20. Switzerland; *Industrial Property Statistics.*

YUGOSLAVIA - PEANUT PRODUCTION - See YUGOSLAVIA - CROPS

YUGOSLAVIA - PERIODICALS

United Nations Educational, Scientific and Cultural Organization (UNESCO), 7 Place de Fontenoy, F-75700 Paris, France (Telephone Number in U.S. (212) 963-5981); *Statistical Yearbook.*

YUGOSLAVIA - PESTICIDE USE

Food and Agricultural Organization of the United Nations (FAO) Via delle Terme di Caracalla, 00100 Rome, Italy (Telephone Number in U.S. (202) 653-2400); *The State of Food and Agriculture.*

YUGOSLAVIA - PETROLEUM INDUSTRY

Euromonitor Publications Limited, 87-88 Turnmill Street, London EC1M 5QU, England; *European Marketing Data and Statistics.*

Facts on File, 460 Park Avenue South, New York, New York 10016 (800) 443-8323; *The New Book of World Rankings.*

Food and Agricultural Organization of the United Nations (FAO) Via delle Terme di Caracalla, 00100 Rome, Italy (Telephone Number in U.S. (202) 653-2400); *The State of Food and Agriculture.*

G.K. Hall and Company, 70 Lincoln Street, Boston, Massachusetts 02111 (617) 423-3990; *The World in Figures.*

Penn Well Publishing Company, 1421 South Sheridan Road, P.O. Box 1260, Tulsa, Oklahoma 74101 (800) 752-9764; *International Energy Statistics Sourcebook.*

Statistical Office of the United Nations, Publishing Service, New York, New York 10017 (800) 253-9646; *Statistical Yearbook.*

YUGOSLAVIA - PIG-IRON AND FERRO-ALLOYS - See YUGOSLAVIA - MINING AND MINERAL PRODUCTS

YUGOSLAVIA - PIGS - See YUGOSLAVIA - LIVESTOCK AND POULTRY

YUGOSLAVIA - PLASTIC AND RESIN PRODUCTION

Statistical Office of the United Nations, Publishing Service, New York, New York 10017 (800) 253-9646; *Statistical Yearbook.*

YUGOSLAVIA - PLATINUM PRODUCTION - See YUGOSLAVIA - MINING AND MINERAL PRODUCTS

YUGOSLAVIA - POPULATION

The Economist Intelligence Unit, 111 West 57th Street, New York, New York 10019 (800) 938-4685; *The World Market Atlas.*

Euromonitor Publications Limited, 87-88 Turnmill Street, London EC1M 5QU, England; *European Marketing Data and Statistics.*

Facts on File, 460 Park Avenue South, New York, New York 10016 (800) 443-8323; *The New Book of World Rankings.*

G.K. Hall and Company, 70 Lincoln Street, Boston, Massachusetts 02111 (617) 423-3990; *The World in Figures.*

International Labour Office, I.L.O. Publications, CH-1211, Geneva 22, Switzerland; *Yearbook of Labour Statistics.*

Statistical Office of the United Nations, Publishing Service, New York, New York 10017 (800) 253-9646; *Demographic Yearbook,* and *Statistical Yearbook.*

United Nations Educational, Scientific and Cultural Organization (UNESCO), 7 Place de Fontenoy, F-75700 Paris, France (Telephone Number in U.S. (212) 963-5981); *Statistical Yearbook*.

U.S. Arms Control and Disarmament Agency, 320 Twenty-first Street, NW, Washington, D.C. 20451 (202) 647-8677; *World Military Expenditures and Arms Transfers*.

World Health Organization, Office of Publications, Avenue Appia, CH-1211 Geneva, 27, Switzerland (Telephone Number in U.S. (518) 436-9686); *World Health Statistics: Vital Statistics and Causes of Death*.

YUGOSLAVIA - POST OFFICES

Facts on File, 460 Park Avenue South, New York, New York 10016 (800) 443-8323; *The New Book of World Rankings*.

YUGOSLAVIA - POTATO PRODUCTION - See YUGOSLAVIA - CROPS

YUGOSLAVIA - POWER PRODUCTION INDUSTRY

Statistical Office of the United Nations, Publishing Service, New York, New York 10017 (800) 253-9646; *Statistical Yearbook*.

YUGOSLAVIA - PRICES

Facts on File, 460 Park Avenue South, New York, New York 10016 (800) 443-8323; *The New Book of World Rankings*.

Food and Agricultural Organization of the United Nations (FAO) Via delle Terme di Caracalla, 00100 Rome, Italy (Telephone Number in U.S. (202) 653-2400); *The State of Food and Agriculture*.

G.K. Hall and Company, 70 Lincoln Street, Boston, Massachusetts 02111 (617) 423-3990; *The World in Figures*.

International Lead and Zinc Study Group, Metro House, 58 St. James's Street, London SW1A 1LD England; *Lead and Zinc Statistics*.

International Monetary Fund, 700 Nineteenth Street, NW, Washington, D.C. 20431 (202) 623-7000; *International Financial Statistics*.

Organisation for Economic Co-operation and Development (OECD), 2 rue Andre-Pascal, 75 Paris 16, France (Telephone Number in U.S. (202) 785-6323); *Main Economic Indicators - Historical Statistics*.

World Bureau of Metal Statistics, 27-A High Street, Ware Hert SG12 9BA, England; *World Metal Statistics*.

YUGOSLAVIA - PRODUCTION

American Automobile Manufacturers Association, 1401 H Street, NW, Suite 900, Washington, D.C. 20005 (202) 326-5500; *World Motor Vehicle Data*.

Facts on File, 460 Park Avenue South, New York, New York 10016 (800) 443-8323; *The New Book of World Rankings*.

G.K. Hall and Company, 70 Lincoln Street, Boston, Massachusetts 02111 (617) 423-3990; *The World in Figures*.

International Lead and Zinc Study Group, Metro House, 58 St. James's Street, London SW1A 1LD England; *Lead and Zinc Statistics*.

Organisation for Economic Co-operation and Development (OECD), 2 rue Andre-Pascal, 75 Paris 16, France (Telephone Number in U.S. (202) 785-6323); *Milk, Milk Products, and Egg Balances in OECD Member Countries*.

YUGOSLAVIA - PROPERTY TAXES - See YUGOSLAVIA - TAXATION

YUGOSLAVIA - PUBLIC FINANCE

Facts on File, 460 Park Avenue South, New York, New York 10016 (800) 443-8323; *The New Book of World Rankings*.

YUGOSLAVIA - RADIO BROADCASTING - See YUGOSLAVIA - BROADCASTING

YUGOSLAVIA - RADIO RECEIVER PRODUCTION

Statistical Office of the United Nations, Publishing Service, New York, New York 10017 (800) 253-9646; *Statistical Yearbook*.

YUGOSLAVIA - RAILWAYS

Euromonitor Publications Limited, 87-88 Turnmill Street, London EC1M 5QU, England; *European Marketing Data and Statistics*.

G.K. Hall and Company, 70 Lincoln Street, Boston, Massachusetts 02111 (617) 423-3990; *The World in Figures*.

Jane's Information Group, Sentinel House, 163 Brighton Road, Coulsdon, Surrey CR5 2NH, England (Telephone Number in U.S. (703) 683-3700); *Jane's World Railways*.

Statistical Office of the United Nations, Publishing Service, New York, New York 10017 (800) 253-9646; *Annual Bulletin of Transport Statistics for Europe*, and *Statistical Yearbook*.

YUGOSLAVIA - RELIGION

Facts on File, 460 Park Avenue South, New York, New York 10016 (800) 443-8323; *The New Book of World Rankings*.

YUGOSLAVIA - RETAIL TRADE

G.K. Hall and Company, 70 Lincoln Street, Boston, Massachusetts 02111 (617) 423-3990; *The World in Figures*.

Statistical Office of the United Nations, Publishing Service, New York, New York 10017 (800) 253-9646; *Statistical Yearbook*.

YUGOSLAVIA - RICE PRODUCTION - See YUGOSLAVIA - CROPS

YUGOSLAVIA - ROUNDWOOD PRODUCTION - See YUGOSLAVIA - FORESTRY AND FOREST PRODUCTS

YUGOSLAVIA - RUBBER PRODUCTION AND CONSUMPTION

Facts on File, 460 Park Avenue South, New York, New York 10016 (800) 443-8323; *The New Book of World Rankings*.

Statistical Office of the United Nations, Publishing Service, New York, New York 10017 (800) 253-9646; *Statistical Yearbook*.

YUGOSLAVIA - SALT PRODUCTION - See YUGOSLAVIA - MINING AND MINERAL PRODUCTS

YUGOSLAVIA - SAWNWOOD PRODUCTION - See YUGOSLAVIA - FORESTRY AND FOREST PRODUCTS

YUGOSLAVIA - SCIENCE AND TECHNOLOGY - EXPENDITURE FOR RESEARCH

Statistical Office of the United Nations, Publishing Service, New York, New York 10017 (800) 253-9646; *Statistical Yearbook*.

YUGOSLAVIA - SCIENTISTS AND TECHNICIANS

Statistical Office of the United Nations, Publishing Service, New York, New York 10017 (800) 253-9646; *Statistical Yearbook*.

United Nations Educational, Scientific and Cultural Organization (UNESCO), 7 Place de Fontenoy, F-75700 Paris, France (Telephone Number in U.S. (212) 963-5981); *Statistical Yearbook*.

YUGOSLAVIA - SENIOR CITIZENS

Facts on File, 460 Park Avenue South, New York, New York 10016 (800) 443-8323; *The New Book of World Rankings*.

YUGOSLAVIA - SHEEP - See YUGOSLAVIA - LIVESTOCK AND POULTRY

YUGOSLAVIA - SILVER PRODUCTION AND CONSUMPTION - See YUGOSLAVIA - MINING AND MINERAL PRODUCTS

YUGOSLAVIA - SOCIAL DATA

Facts on File, 460 Park Avenue South, New York, New York 10016 (800) 443-8323; *The New Book of World Rankings*.

G.K. Hall and Company, 70 Lincoln Street, Boston, Massachusetts 02111 (617) 423-3990; *The World in Figures*.

YUGOSLAVIA - SOCIAL SECURITY

International Monetary Fund, 700 Nineteenth Street, NW, Washington, D.C. 20431 (202) 623-7000; *Government Finance Statistics Yearbook*.

YUGOSLAVIA - SOYBEAN PRODUCTION - See YUGOSLAVIA - CROPS

YUGOSLAVIA - STEEL - See YUGOSLAVIA - MINING AND MINERAL PRODUCTS

YUGOSLAVIA - STOCKS - COMMODITY - MARKET PRICE - INDEX

Economic Commission for Western Asia, Post Office Box 27, Baghdad, Iraq; *Statistical Abstract of Western Asia*.

Food and Agricultural Organization of the United Nations (FAO) Via delle Terme di Caracalla, 00100 Rome, Italy (Telephone Number in U.S. (202) 653-2400); *The State of Food and Agriculture*.

World Bureau of Metal Statistics, 27-A High Street, Ware Hert SG12 9BA, England; *World Metal Statistics*.

YUGOSLAVIA - SUGAR PRODUCTION AND CONSUMPTION - See YUGOSLAVIA - CROPS

YUGOSLAVIA - SULPHURIC ACID PRODUCTION - See YUGOSLAVIA - MINING AND MINERAL PRODUCTS

YUGOSLAVIA - TAXATION

G.K. Hall and Company, 70 Lincoln Street, Boston, Massachusetts 02111 (617) 423-3990; *The World in Figures*.

International Monetary Fund, 700 Nineteenth Street, NW, Washington, D.C. 20431 (202) 623-7000; *Government Finance Statistics Yearbook*.

International Road Federation, 525 School Street, SW, Washington, D.C. 20024 (202) 554-2106; *World Road Statistics*.

The World Bank, 1818 H Street, NW, Washington, D.C. 20433 (202) 477-1234; *World Tables*.

YUGOSLAVIA - TELEGRAPH SERVICE

Statistical Office of the United Nations, Publishing Service, New York, New York 10017 (800) 253-9646; *Statistical Yearbook*.

YUGOSLAVIA - TELEPHONES IN USE

American Telephone and Telegraph Company, 26 Parsippany Road, Whippany, New Jersey 07981 (800) 338-4038; *The World's Telephones*.

G.K. Hall and Company, 70 Lincoln Street, Boston, Massachusetts 02111 (617) 423-3990; *The World in Figures*.

Statistical Office of the United Nations, Publishing Service, New York, New York 10017 (800) 253-9646; *Statistical Yearbook*.

YUGOSLAVIA - TELEVISION BROADCASTING - See YUGOSLAVIA - BROADCASTING

YUGOSLAVIA - TELEVISION RECEIVER PRODUCTION

Statistical Office of the United Nations, Publishing Service, New York, New York 10017 (800) 253-9646; *Statistical Yearbook*.

YUGOSLAVIA - TEXTILE INDUSTRY

American Forest and Paper Association, 1250 Connecticut Avenue, NW, Washington, D.C. 20036 (202) 463-2455; *Wood Pulp and Fiber Statistics*.

G.K. Hall and Company, 70 Lincoln Street, Boston, Massachusetts 02111 (617) 423-3990; *The World in Figures*.

Statistical Office of the United Nations, Publishing Service, New York, New York 10017 (800) 253-9646; *Statistical Yearbook*, and *Trade in Manufactures of Developing Countries*.

YUGOSLAVIA - THEATRE

United Nations Educational, Scientific and Cultural Organization (UNESCO), 7 Place de Fontenoy, F-75700 Paris, France (Telephone Number in U.S. (212) 963-5981); *Statistical Yearbook*.

YUGOSLAVIA - TIN - See YUGOSLAVIA - MINING AND MINERAL PRODUCTS

YUGOSLAVIA - TIRE (MOTOR VEHICLE) PRODUCTION

Statistical Office of the United Nations, Publishing Service, New York, New York 10017 (800) 253-9646; *Statistical Yearbook*.

YUGOSLAVIA - TOBACCO PRODUCTION

Euromonitor Publications Limited, 87-88 Turnmill Street, London EC1M 5QU, England; *European Marketing Data and Statistics*.

Facts on File, 460 Park Avenue South, New York, New York 10016 (800) 443-8323; *The New Book of World Rankings*.

Statistical Office of the United Nations, Publishing Service, New York, New York 10017 (800) 253-9646; *Statistical Yearbook.*

YUGOSLAVIA - TOURISM

Euromonitor Publications Limited, 87-88 Turnmill Street, London EC1M 5QU, England; *European Marketing Data and Statistics.*

Facts on File, 460 Park Avenue South, New York, New York 10016 (800) 443-8323; *The New Book of World Rankings.*

G.K. Hall and Company, 70 Lincoln Street, Boston, Massachusetts 02111 (617) 423-3990; *The World in Figures.*

Statistical Office of the United Nations, Publishing Service, New York, New York 10017 (800) 253-9646; *Statistical Yearbook.*

World Tourism Organization, Calle Capitan Haya 42, E-28020 Madrid, Spain; *Yearbook of Tourism Statistics.*

YUGOSLAVIA - TRACTORS IN USE

Statistical Office of the United Nations, Publishing Service, New York, New York 10017 (800) 253-9646; *Statistical Yearbook.*

YUGOSLAVIA - TRADE - See YUGOSLAVIA - FOREIGN TRADE

YUGOSLAVIA - TRADEMARKS AND SERVICE MARKS

Statistical Office of the United Nations, Publishing Service, New York, New York 10017 (800) 253-9646; *Statistical Yearbook.*

World Intellectual Property Organization, 34 Chemin des Colombettes, CH 1211 Geneva 20, Switzerland; *Industrial Property Statistics.*

YUGOSLAVIA - TRANSPORTATION AND COMMUNICATIONS

Facts on File, 460 Park Avenue South, New York, New York 10016 (800) 443-8323; *The New Book of World Rankings.*

G.K. Hall and Company, 70 Lincoln Street, Boston, Massachusetts 02111 (617) 423-3990; *The World in Figures.*

YUGOSLAVIA - UNEMPLOYMENT

Euromonitor Publications Limited, 87-88 Turnmill Street, London EC1M 5QU, England; *European Marketing Data and Statistics.*

International Labour Office, I.L.O. Publications, CH-1211, Geneva 22, Switzerland; *Yearbook of Labour Statistics.*

Statistical Office of the United Nations, Publishing Service, New York, New York 10017 (800) 253-9646; *Statistical Yearbook.*

YUGOSLAVIA - URANIUM PRODUCTION AND CONSUMPTION - See YUGOSLAVIA - MINING AND MINERAL PRODUCTS

YUGOSLAVIA - VITAL STATISTICS

G.K. Hall and Company, 70 Lincoln Street, Boston, Massachusetts 02111 (617) 423-3990; *The World in Figures.*

Statistical Office of the United Nations, Publishing Service, New York, New York 10017 (800) 253-9646; *Statistical Yearbook.*

World Health Organization, Office of Publications, Avenue Appia, CH-1211 Geneva, 27, Switzerland (Telephone Number in U.S. (518) 436-9686); *World Health Statistics: Vital Statistics and Causes of Death.*

YUGOSLAVIA - WAGES

Euromonitor Publications Limited, 87-88 Turnmill Street, London EC1M 5QU, England; *European Marketing Data and Statistics.*

G.K. Hall and Company, 70 Lincoln Street, Boston, Massachusetts 02111 (617) 423-3990; *The World in Figures.*

International Labour Office, I.L.O. Publications, CH-1211, Geneva 22, Switzerland; *Yearbook of Labour Statistics.*

Organisation for Economic Co-operation and Development (OECD), 2 rue Andre-Pascal, 75 Paris 16, France (Telephone Number in U.S. (202) 785-6323); *Main Economic Indicators - Historical Statistics.*

Statistical Office of the United Nations, Publishing Service, New York, New York 10017 (800) 253-9646; *Statistical Yearbook.*

YUGOSLAVIA - WATERWAYS IN USE

Statistical Office of the United Nations, Publishing Service, New York, New York 10017 (800) 253-9646; *Annual Bulletin of Transport Statistics for Europe.*

YUGOSLAVIA - WEATHER

Facts on File, 460 Park Avenue South, New York, New York 10016 (800) 443-8323; *The New Book of World Rankings.*

G.K. Hall and Company, 70 Lincoln Street, Boston, Massachusetts 02111 (617) 423-3990; *The World in Figures.*

YUGOSLAVIA - WELFARE

International Monetary Fund, 700 Nineteenth Street, NW, Washington, D.C. 20431 (202) 623-7000; *Government Finance Statistics Yearbook*

YUGOSLAVIA - WHEAT PRODUCTION AND PRICES - See YUGOSLAVIA - CROPS

YUGOSLAVIA - WHOLESALE PRICES

Statistical Office of the United Nations, Publishing Service, New York, New York 10017 (800) 253-9646; *Statistical Yearbook.*

YUGOSLAVIA - WHOLESALE TRADE

Statistical Office of the United Nations, Publishing Service, New York, New York 10017 (800) 253-9646; *Statistical Yearbook.*

YUGOSLAVIA - WINE PRODUCTION

Facts on File, 460 Park Avenue South, New York, New York 10016 (800) 443-8323; *The New Book of World Rankings.*

Statistical Office of the United Nations, Publishing Service, New York, New York 10017 (800) 253-9646; *Statistical Yearbook.*

YUGOSLAVIA - WOOD AND WOOD PULP - See YUGOSLAVIA - FORESTRY AND FOREST PRODUCTS

YUGOSLAVIA - WOOL PRODUCTION AND CONSUMPTION

Facts on File, 460 Park Avenue South, New York, New York 10016 (800) 443-8323; *The New Book of World Rankings.*

Statistical Office of the United Nations, Publishing Service, New York, New York 10017 (800) 253-9646; *Statistical Yearbook*.

YUGOSLAVIA - YARN PRODUCTION

Statistical Office of the United Nations, Publishing Service, New York, New York 10017 (800) 253-9646; *Statistical Yearbook*.

YUGOSLAVIA - ZINC AND ZINC ORE PRODUCTION AND CONSUMPTION - See YUGOSLAVIA - MINING AND MINERAL PRODUCTS

YUGOSLAVIA - ZOOS AND BOTANICAL GARDENS

United Nations Educational, Scientific and Cultural Organization (UNESCO), 7 Place de Fontenoy, F-75700 Paris, France (Telephone Number in U.S. (212) 963-5981); *Statistical Yearbook*.

Z

Zaire - National Statistical Office

Institut National de la Statistique, BP 20, Kinshasa, Gombe, Zaire.

Zaire - Primary Statistics Sources

Institut National de la Statistique, BP 20, Kinshasa, Gombe, Zaire; *Annuaire Statistique de Zaire* (Statistical Yearbook of Zaire), and *Conjoncture Economique* (Economic Forecast).

ZAIRE - AGRICULTURE

Euromonitor Publications Limited, 87-88 Turnmill Street, London EC1M 5QU, England; *International Marketing Data and Statistics.*

Facts on File, 460 Park Avenue South, New York, New York 10016 (800) 443-8323; *The New Book of World Rankings.*

Food and Agricultural Organization of the United Nations (FAO) Via delle Terme di Caracalla, 00100 Rome, Italy (Telephone Number in U.S. (202) 653-2400); *Production Yearbook, The State of Food and Agriculture,* and *Trade Yearbook.*

G.K. Hall and Company, 70 Lincoln Street, Boston, Massachusetts 02111 (617) 423-3990; *The World in Figures.*

Statistical Office of the United Nations, Publishing Service, New York, New York 10017 (800) 253-9646; *Statistical Yearbook,* and *Survey of Economic and Social Conditions in Africa.*

Time Books, 201 East 50th Street, New York, New York 10022 (212) 751-2600; *The Economist Book of Vital World Statistics.*

United Nations Economic Commission for Africa, Africa Hall, P.O. Box 3001, Addis Ababa, Ethiopia (Telephone Number in U.S. (800) 253-9646); *African Statistical Yearbook.*

The World Bank, 1818 H Street, NW, Washington, D.C. 20433 (202) 477-1234; *World Tables.*

ZAIRE - AIRLINE SERVICE

Facts on File, 460 Park Avenue South, New York, New York 10016 (800) 443-8323; *The New Book of World Rankings.*

G.K. Hall and Company, 70 Lincoln Street, Boston, Massachusetts 02111 (617) 423-3990; *The World in Figures.*

Statistical Office of the United Nations, Publishing Service, New York, New York 10017 (800) 253-9646; *Statistical Yearbook.*

Time Books, 201 East 50th Street, New York, New York 10022 (212) 751-2600; *The Economist Book of Vital World Statistics.*

United Nations Economic Commission for Africa, Africa Hall, P.O. Box 3001, Addis Ababa, Ethiopia (Telephone Number in U.S. (800) 253-9646); *African Statistical Yearbook.*

ZAIRE - ALUMINUM PRODUCTION AND CONSUMPTION - See ZAIRE - MINING AND MINERAL PRODUCTS

ZAIRE - ANIMAL HEALTH

Food and Agricultural Organization of the United Nations (FAO), Via delle Terme di Caracalla, 00100 Rome, Italy (Telephone Number in U.S. (202) 653-2400); *Animal Health Yearbook.*

ZAIRE - ANTIMONY AND ANTIMONY ORE PRODUCTION AND CONSUMPTION - See ZAIRE - MINING AND MINERAL PRODUCTS

ZAIRE - AREA AND DENSITY OF POPULATION

African Development Bank, 01 BP 1387, Abidjan 01, Cote D'Ivoire; *Selected Statistics on Regional Member Countries.*

Euromonitor Publications Limited, 87-88 Turnmill Street, London EC1M 5QU, England; *International Marketing Data and Statistics.*

Facts on File, 460 Park Avenue South, New York, New York 10016 (800) 443-8323; *The New Book of World Rankings.*

Food and Agricultural Organization of the United Nations (FAO) Via delle Terme di Caracalla, 00100 Rome, Italy (Telephone Number in U.S. (202) 653-2400); *The State of Food and Agriculture.*

G.K. Hall and Company, 70 Lincoln Street, Boston, Massachusetts 02111 (617) 423-3990; *The World in Figures.*

Statistical Office of the United Nations, Publishing Service, New York, New York 10017 (800) 253-9646; *Statistical Yearbook,* and *Survey of Economic and Social Conditions in Africa.*

Time Books, 201 East 50th Street, New York, New York 10022 (212) 751-2600; *The Economist Book of Vital World Statistics.*

United Nations Educational, Scientific and Cultural Organization (UNESCO), 7 Place de Fontenoy, F-75700 Paris, France (Telephone Number in U.S. (212) 963-5981); *Statistical Yearbook.*

ZAIRE - ARMS EXPORTS AND IMPORTS

U.S. Arms Control and Disarmament Agency, 320 Twenty-first Street, NW, Washington, D.C. 20451 (202) 647-8677; *World Military*

Expenditures and Arms Transfers.

ZAIRE - BALANCE OF PAYMENTS

African Development Bank, 01 BP 1387, Abidjan 01, Cote D'Ivoire; *Selected Statistics on Regional Member Countries.*

The Economist Intelligence Unit, 111 West 57th Street, New York, New York 10019 (800) 938-4685; *The World Market Atlas.*

G.K. Hall and Company, 70 Lincoln Street, Boston, Massachusetts 02111 (617) 423-3990; *The World in Figures.*

International Monetary Fund, 700 Nineteenth Street, NW, Washington, D.C. 20431 (202) 623-7000; *Balance of Payments Yearbook,* and *International Financial Statistics.*

Time Books, 201 East 50th Street, New York, New York 10022 (212) 751-2600; *The Economist Book of Vital World Statistics.*

United Nations Economic Commission for Africa, Africa Hall, P.O. Box 3001, Addis Ababa, Ethiopia (Telephone Number in U.S. (800) 253-9646); *African Statistical Yearbook.*

The World Bank, 1818 H Street, NW, Washington, D.C. 20433 (202) 477-1234; *World Tables.*

ZAIRE - BANKING

Facts on File, 460 Park Avenue South, New York, New York 10016 (800) 443-8323; *The New Book of World Rankings.*

G.K. Hall and Company, 70 Lincoln Street, Boston, Massachusetts 02111 (617) 423-3990; *The World in Figures.*

International Monetary Fund, 700 Nineteenth Street, NW, Washington, D.C. 20431 (202) 623-7000; *Government Finance Statistics Yearbook,* and *International Financial Statistics.*

ZAIRE - BARLEY PRODUCTION - See ZAIRE - CROPS

ZAIRE - BAUXITE PRODUCTION AND CONSUMPTION - See ZAIRE - MINING AND MINERAL PRODUCTS

ZAIRE - BEER PRODUCTION

Facts on File, 460 Park Avenue South, New York, New York 10016 (800) 443-8323; *The New Book of World Rankings.*

Statistical Office of the United Nations, Publishing Service, New York, New York 10017 (800) 253-9646; *Statistical Yearbook.*

ZAIRE - BIRTH RATES

Facts on File, 460 Park Avenue South, New York, New York 10016 (800) 443-8323; *The New Book of World Rankings.*

Statistical Office of the United Nations, Publishing Service, New York, New York 10017 (800) 253-9646; *Demographic Yearbook, Statistical Yearbook,* and *Survey of Economic and Social Conditions in Africa.*

Time Books, 201 East 50th Street, New York, New York 10022 (212) 751-2600; *The Economist Book of Vital World Statistics.*

The World Bank, 1818 H Street, NW, Washington, D.C. 20433 (202) 477-1234; *World Tables.*

ZAIRE - BONDS

G.K. Hall and Company, 70 Lincoln Street, Boston, Massachusetts 02111 (617) 423-3990; *The World in Figures.*

International Monetary Fund, 700 Nineteenth Street, NW, Washington, D.C. 20431 (202) 623-7000; *Government Finance Statistics Yearbook.*

ZAIRE - BOOK PRODUCTION

G.K. Hall and Company, 70 Lincoln Street, Boston, Massachusetts 02111 (617) 423-3990; *The World in Figures.*

United Nations Educational, Scientific and Cultural Organization (UNESCO), 7 Place de Fontenoy, F-75700 Paris, France (Telephone Number in U.S. (212) 963-5981); *Statistical Yearbook.*

ZAIRE - BROADCASTING

Billboard Limited, P.O. Box 9027, 1006 AA Amsterdam, The Netherlands (Telephone Number in U.S. (212) 764-7300); *World Radio TV Handbook.*

Facts on File, 460 Park Avenue South, New York, New York 10016 (800) 443-8323; *The New Book of World Rankings.*

G.K. Hall and Company, 70 Lincoln Street, Boston, Massachusetts 02111 (617) 423-3990; *The World in Figures.*

Time Books, 201 East 50th Street, New York, New York 10022 (212) 751-2600; *The Economist Book of Vital World Statistics.*

ZAIRE - BUSINESS

G.K. Hall and Company, 70 Lincoln Street, Boston, Massachusetts 02111 (617) 423-3990; *The World in Figures.*

ZAIRE - BUSINESS AND PROFESSIONAL LICENSES

International Monetary Fund, 700 Nineteenth Street, NW, Washington, D.C. 20431 (202) 623-7000; *Government Finance Statistics Yearbook.*

ZAIRE - BUTTER PRODUCTION - See ZAIRE - DAIRY PRODUCTS

ZAIRE - CADMIUM PRODUCTION AND CONSUMPTION - See ZAIRE - MINING AND MINERAL PRODUCTS

ZAIRE - CALORIE SUPPLY

African Development Bank, 01 BP 1387, Abidjan 01, Cote D'Ivoire; *Selected Statistics on Regional Member Countries.*

Food and Agricultural Organization of the United Nations (FAO) Via delle Terme di Caracalla, 00100 Rome, Italy (Telephone Number in U.S. (202) 653-2400); *The State of Food and Agriculture.*

ZAIRE - CATTLE - See ZAIRE - LIVESTOCK AND POULTRY

ZAIRE - CEMENT PRODUCTION - See ZAIRE - MINING AND MINERAL PRODUCTS

ZAIRE - CHEMICAL (ORGANIC) PRODUCTION - See ZAIRE - MINING AND MINERAL PRODUCTS

ZAIRE - CHICKENS - See ZAIRE - LIVESTOCK AND POULTRY

ZAIRE - CIGARETTE PRODUCTION - See ZAIRE - TOBACCO PRODUCTION

ZAIRE - CLASS STRUCTURE

G.K. Hall and Company, 70 Lincoln Street, Boston, Massachusetts 02111 (617) 423-3990; *The World in Figures.*

ZAIRE - CLIMATE

G.K. Hall and Company, 70 Lincoln Street, Boston, Massachusetts 02111 (617) 423-3990; *The World in Figures.*

ZAIRE - COAL PRODUCTION - See ZAIRE - MINING AND MINERAL PRODUCTS

ZAIRE - COBALT PRODUCTION AND CONSUMPTION - See ZAIRE - MINING AND MINERAL PRODUCTS

ZAIRE - COCOA PRODUCTION - See ZAIRE - CROPS

ZAIRE - COFFEE PRODUCTION AND CONSUMPTION - See ZAIRE - CROPS

ZAIRE - COMMUNICATIONS

G.K. Hall and Company, 70 Lincoln Street, Boston, Massachusetts 02111 (617) 423-3990; *The World in Figures.*

United Nations Economic Commission for Africa, Africa Hall, P.O. Box 3001, Addis Ababa, Ethiopia (Telephone Number in U.S. (800) 253-9646); *African Statistical Yearbook.*

ZAIRE - CONSTRUCTION INDUSTRY

Facts on File, 460 Park Avenue South, New York, New York 10016 (800) 443-0033; *The New Book of World Rankings.*

Statistical Office of the United Nations, Publishing Service, New York, New York 10017 (800) 253-9646; *Construction Statistics Yearbook,* and *Statistical Yearbook.*

United Nations Economic Commission for Africa, Africa Hall, P.O. Box 3001, Addis Ababa, Ethiopia (Telephone Number in U.S. (800) 253-9646); *African Statistical Yearbook.*

ZAIRE - CONSUMER PRICE INDEX

African Development Bank, 01 BP 1387, Abidjan 01, Cote D'Ivoire; *Selected Statistics on Regional Member Countries.*

G.K. Hall and Company, 70 Lincoln Street, Boston, Massachusetts 02111 (617) 423-3990; *The World in Figures.*

Statistical Office of the United Nations, Publishing Service, New York, New York 10017 (800) 253-9646; *Statistical Yearbook,* and *Survey of Economic and Social Conditions in Africa.*

United Nations Economic Commission for Africa, Africa Hall, P.O. Box 3001, Addis Ababa, Ethiopia (Telephone Number in U.S. (800) 253-9646); *African Statistical Yearbook.*

ZAIRE - CONSUMER PRICES

International Labour Office, I.L.O. Publications, CH-1211, Geneva 22, Switzerland; *Yearbook of Labour Statistics.*

International Monetary Fund, 700 Nineteenth Street, NW, Washington, D.C. 20431 (202) 623-7000; *International Financial Statistics.*

Time Books, 201 East 50th Street, New York, New York 10022 (212) 751-2600; *The Economist Book of Vital World Statistics.*

ZAIRE - CONSUMPTION

African Development Bank, 01 BP 1387, Abidjan 01, Cote D'Ivoire; *Selected Statistics on Regional Member Countries.*

G.K. Hall and Company, 70 Lincoln Street, Boston, Massachusetts 02111 (617) 423-3990; *The World in Figures.*

International Monetary Fund, 700 Nineteenth Street, NW, Washington, D.C. 20431 (202) 623-7000; *International Financial Statistics.*

Statistical Office of the United Nations, Publishing Service, New York, New York 10017 (800) 253-9646; *Survey of Economic and Social Conditions in Africa.*

ZAIRE - COPPER AND COPPER ORE PRODUCTION AND CONSUMPTION - See ZAIRE - MINING AND MINERAL PRODUCTS

ZAIRE - CORN PRODUCTION - See ZAIRE - CROPS

ZAIRE - CORPORATE TAXES - See ZAIRE - TAXATION

ZAIRE - COTTON - See ZAIRE - CROPS

ZAIRE - CROPS

Commodity Research Bureau, Incorporated, 75 Wall Street, New York, New York 10005 (212) 504-7754; *Commodity Year Book.*

Facts on File, 460 Park Avenue South, New York, New York 10016 (800) 443-8323; *The New Book of World Rankings.*

G.K. Hall and Company, 70 Lincoln Street, Boston, Massachusetts 02111 (617) 423-3990; *The World in Figures.*

International Monetary Fund, 700 Nineteenth Street, NW, Washington, D.C. 20431 (202) 623-7000; *Government Finance Statistics Yearbook.*

Statistical Office of the United Nations, Publishing Service, New York, New York 10017 (800) 253-9646; *Statistical Yearbook.*

United Nations Economic Commission for Africa, Africa Hall, P.O. Box 3001, Addis Ababa, Ethiopia (Telephone Number in U.S. (800) 253-9646); *African Statistical Yearbook.*

ZAIRE - CUSTOMS DUTIES

G.K. Hall and Company, 70 Lincoln Street, Boston, Massachusetts 02111 (617) 423-3990; *The World in Figures.*

International Monetary Fund, 700 Nineteenth Street, NW, Washington, D.C. 20431 (202) 623-7000; *Government Finance Statistics Yearbook.*

ZAIRE - DAIRY PRODUCTS

Commodity Research Bureau, Incorporated, 75 Wall Street, New York, New York 10005 (212) 504-7754; *Commodity Year Book.*

Facts on File, 460 Park Avenue South, New York, New York 10016 (800) 443-8323; *The New Book of World Rankings.*

Food and Agricultural Organization of the United Nations (FAO) Via delle Terme di Caracalla, 00100 Rome, Italy (Telephone Number in U.S. (202) 653-2400); *The State of Food and Agriculture*.

Statistical Office of the United Nations, Publishing Service, New York, New York 10017 (800) 253-9646; *Statistical Yearbook*.

ZAIRE - DEATH RATES

G.K. Hall and Company, 70 Lincoln Street, Boston, Massachusetts 02111 (617) 423-3990; *The World in Figures*.

Statistical Office of the United Nations, Publishing Service, New York, New York 10017 (800) 253-9646; *Statistical Yearbook*, and *Survey of Economic and Social Conditions in Africa*.

Time Books, 201 East 50th Street, New York, New York 10022 (212) 751-2600; *The Economist Book of Vital World Statistics*.

World Health Organization, Office of Publications, Avenue Appia, CH-1211 Geneva 27, Switzerland (Telephone Number in U.S. (518) 436-9686); *World Health Statistics Annual*.

ZAIRE - DEFENSE EXPENDITURES

G.K. Hall and Company, 70 Lincoln Street, Boston, Massachusetts 02111 (617) 423-3990; *The World in Figures*.

U.S. Arms Control and Disarmament Agency, 320 Twenty-first Street, NW, Washington, D.C. 20451 (202) 647-8677; *World Military Expenditures and Arms Transfers*.

ZAIRE - DEMOGRAPHY

The Economist Intelligence Unit, 111 West 57th Street, New York, New York 10019 (800) 938-4685; *The World Market Atlas*.

Facts on File, 460 Park Avenue South, New York, New York 10016 (800) 443-8323; *The New Book of World Rankings*.

G.K. Hall and Company, 70 Lincoln Street, Boston, Massachusetts 02111 (617) 423-3990; *The World in Figures*.

Statistical Office of the United Nations, Publishing Service, New York, New York 10017 (800) 253-9646; *Survey of Economic and Social Conditions in Africa*.

ZAIRE - DEVELOPMENT ASSISTANCE

G.K. Hall and Company, 70 Lincoln Street, Boston, Massachusetts 02111 (617) 423-3990; *The World in Figures*.

Statistical Office of the United Nations, Publishing Service, New York, New York 10017 (800) 253-9646; *Statistical Yearbook*.

ZAIRE - DIAMONDS - See ZAIRE - MINING AND MINERAL PRODUCTS

ZAIRE - DISEASES

G.K. Hall and Company, 70 Lincoln Street, Boston, Massachusetts 02111 (617) 423-3990; *The World in Figures*.

World Health Organization, Office of Publications, Avenue Appia, CH-1211 Geneva 27, Switzerland (Telephone Number in U.S. (518) 436-9686); *World Health Statistics Annual*.

ZAIRE - DIVORCE RATES

Facts on File, 460 Park Avenue South, New York, New York 10016 (800) 443-8323; *The New Book of World Rankings*.

Statistical Office of the United Nations, Publishing Service, New York, New York 10017 (800) 253-9646; *Demographic Yearbook*.

ZAIRE - DOMESTIC PRODUCT

G.K. Hall and Company, 70 Lincoln Street, Boston, Massachusetts 02111 (617) 423-3990; *The World in Figures*.

ZAIRE - ECONOMY

African Development Bank, 01 BP 1387, Abidjan 01, Cote D'Ivoire; *Selected Statistics on Regional Member Countries*.

Euromonitor Publications Limited, 87-88 Turnmill Street, London EC1M 5QU, England; *International Marketing Data and Statistics*.

Facts on File, 460 Park Avenue South, New York, New York 10016 (800) 443-8323; *The New Book of World Rankings*.

G.K. Hall and Company, 70 Lincoln Street, Boston, Massachusetts 02111 (617) 423-3990; *The World in Figures*.

Statistical Office of the United Nations, Publishing Service, New York, New York 10017 (800) 253-9646; *Foreign Trade Statistics for Africa*.

ZAIRE - EDUCATION

African Development Bank, 01 BP 1387, Abidjan 01, Cote D'Ivoire; *Selected Statistics on Regional Member Countries*.

Facts on File, 460 Park Avenue South, New York, New York 10016 (800) 443-8323; *The New Book of World Rankings*.

G.K. Hall and Company, 70 Lincoln Street, Boston, Massachusetts 02111 (617) 423-3990; *The World in Figures*.

Statistical Office of the United Nations, Publishing Service, New York, New York 10017 (800) 253-9646; *Survey of Economic and Social Conditions in Africa*.

Time Books, 201 East 50th Street, New York, New York 10022 (212) 751-2600; *The Economist Book of Vital World Statistics*.

United Nations Economic Commission for Africa, Africa Hall, P.O. Box 3001, Addis Ababa, Ethiopia (Telephone Number in U.S. (800) 253-9646); *African Statistical Yearbook*.

United Nations Educational, Scientific and Cultural Organization (UNESCO), 7 Place de Fontenoy, F-75700 Paris, France (Telephone Number in U.S. (212) 963-5981); *Statistical Yearbook*.

The World Bank, 1818 H Street, NW, Washington, D.C. 20433 (202) 477-1234; *World Tables*.

ZAIRE - EGG PRODUCTION AND CONSUMPTION - See ZAIRE - DAIRY PRODUCTS

ZAIRE - ELECTRICITY

Facts on File, 460 Park Avenue South, New York, New York 10016 (800) 443-8323; *The New Book of World Rankings*.

Penn Well Publishing Company, 1421 South Sheridan Road, P.O. Box 1260, Tulsa, Oklahoma 74101 (800) 752-9764; *International Energy Statistics Sourcebook.*

Statistical Office of the United Nations, Publishing Service, New York, New York 10017 (800) 253-9646; *Statistical Yearbook*, and *Survey of Economic and Social Conditions in Africa.*

Time Books, 201 East 50th Street, New York, New York 10022 (212) 751-2600; *The Economist Book of Vital World Statistics.*

United Nations Economic Commission for Africa, Africa Hall, P.O. Box 3001, Addis Ababa, Ethiopia (Telephone Number in U.S. (800) 253-9646); *African Statistical Yearbook.*

ZAIRE - EMPLOYMENT

Euromonitor Publications Limited, 87-88 Turnmill Street, London EC1M 5QU, England; *International Marketing Data and Statistics.*

Facts on File, 460 Park Avenue South, New York, New York 10016 (800) 443-8323; *The New Book of World Rankings.*

International Labour Office, I.L.O. Publications, CH-1211, Geneva 22, Switzerland; *Yearbook of Labour Statistics.*

Statistical Office of the United Nations, Publishing Service, New York, New York 10017 (800) 253-9646; *Statistical Yearbook*, and *Survey of Economic and Social Conditions in Africa.*

United Nations Economic Commission for Africa, Africa Hall, P.O. Box 3001, Addis Ababa, Ethiopia (Telephone Number in U.S. (800) 253-9646); *African Statistical Yearbook.*

ZAIRE - ENERGY

Facts on File, 460 Park Avenue South, New York, New York 10016 (800) 443-8323; *The New Book of World Rankings.*

Food and Agricultural Organization of the United Nations (FAO) Via delle Terme di Caracalla, 00100 Rome, Italy (Telephone Number in U.S. (202) 653-2400); *The State of Food and Agriculture.*

G.K. Hall and Company, 70 Lincoln Street, Boston, Massachusetts 02111 (617) 423-3990; *The World in Figures.*

Penn Well Publishing Company, 1421 South Sheridan Road, P.O. Box 1260, Tulsa, Oklahoma 74101 (800) 752-9764; *International Energy Statistics Sourcebook.*

Statistical Office of the United Nations, Publishing Service, New York, New York 10017 (800) 253-9646; *Energy Statistics Yearbook*, and *Statistical Yearbook.*

Time Books, 201 East 50th Street, New York, New York 10022 (212) 751-2600; *The Economist Book of Vital World Statistics.*

United Nations Economic Commission for Africa, Africa Hall, P.O. Box 3001, Addis Ababa, Ethiopia (Telephone Number in U.S. (800) 253-9646); *African Statistical Yearbook.*

ZAIRE - EXCHANGE RATES

African Development Bank, 01 BP 1387, Abidjan 01, Cote D'Ivoire; *Selected Statistics on Regional Member Countries.*

Euromonitor Publications Limited, 87-88 Turnmill Street, London EC1M 5QU, England; *International Marketing Data and Statistics.*

International Monetary Fund, 700 Nineteenth Street, NW, Washington, D.C. 20431 (202) 623-7000; *International Financial Statistics.*

Statistical Office of the United Nations, Publishing Service, New York, New York 10017 (800) 253-9646; *Foreign Trade Statistics for Africa*, and *Statistical Yearbook.*

ZAIRE - EXCISE TAXES - See ZAIRE - TAXATION

ZAIRE - EXPORTS

African Development Bank, 01 BP 1387, Abidjan 01, Cote D'Ivoire; *Selected Statistics on Regional Member Countries.*

The Economist Intelligence Unit, 111 West 57th Street, New York, New York 10019 (800) 938-4685; *The World Market Atlas.*

Euromonitor Publications Limited, 87-88 Turnmill Street, London EC1M 5QU, England; *International Marketing Data and Statistics.*

Food and Agricultural Organization of the United Nations (FAO) Via delle Terme di Caracalla, 00100 Rome, Italy (Telephone Number in U.S. (202) 653-2400); *The State of Food and Agriculture.*

G.K. Hall and Company, 70 Lincoln Street, Boston, Massachusetts 02111 (617) 423-3990; *The World in Figures.*

International Monetary Fund, 700 Nineteenth Street, NW, Washington, D.C. 20431 (202) 623-7000; *Direction of Trade Statistics, Government Finance Statistics Yearbook*, and *International Financial Statistics.*

Statistical Office of the United Nations, Publishing Service, New York, New York 10017 (800) 253-9646; *Foreign Trade Statistics for Africa, Survey of Economic and Social Conditions in Africa*, and *Trade in Manufactures of Developing Countries.*

Time Books, 201 East 50th Street, New York, New York 10022 (212) 751-2600; *The Economist Book of Vital World Statistics.*

United Nations Economic Commission for Africa, Africa Hall, P.O. Box 3001, Addis Ababa, Ethiopia (Telephone Number in U.S. (800) 253-9646); *African Statistical Yearbook.*

The World Bank, 1818 H Street, NW, Washington, D.C. 20433 (202) 477-1234; *World Tables.*

ZAIRE - EXTERNAL INDEBTEDNESS

African Development Bank, 01 BP 1387, Abidjan 01, Cote D'Ivoire; *Selected Statistics on Regional Member Countries.*

Statistical Office of the United Nations, Publishing Service, New York, New York 10017 (800) 253-9646; *Survey of Economic and Social Conditions in Africa.*

The World Bank, 1818 H Street, NW, Washington, D.C. 20433 (202) 477-1234; *World Tables.*

ZAIRE - EXTERNAL TRADE

African Development Bank, 01 BP 1387, Abidjan 01, Cote D'Ivoire; *Selected Statistics on Regional Member Countries.*

Food and Agricultural Organization of the United Nations (FAO) Via delle Terme di Caracalla, 00100 Rome, Italy (Telephone Number in U.S. (202) 653-2400); *The State of Food and Agriculture.*

G.K. Hall and Company, 70 Lincoln Street, Boston, Massachusetts 02111 (617) 423-3990; *The World in Figures.*

Statistical Office of the United Nations, Publishing Service, New York, New York 10017 (800) 253-9646; *Statistical Yearbook.*

ZAIRE - FABRIC PRODUCTION - See ZAIRE - TEXTILE INDUSTRY

ZAIRE - FARM CROPS - See ZAIRE - CROPS

ZAIRE - FEMALE WORKING POPULATION - See ZAIRE - EMPLOYMENT

ZAIRE - FERTILITY RATES

Facts on File, 460 Park Avenue South, New York, New York 10016 (800) 443-8323; *The New Book of World Rankings.*

Statistical Office of the United Nations, Publishing Service, New York, New York 10017 (800) 253-9646; *Survey of Economic and Social Conditions in Africa.*

Time Books, 201 East 50th Street, New York, New York 10022 (212) 751-2600; *The Economist Book of Vital World Statistics.*

The World Bank, 1818 H Street, NW, Washington, D.C. 20433 (202) 477-1234; *World Tables.*

ZAIRE - FERTILIZER

Food and Agricultural Organization of the United Nations (FAO), Via delle Terme di Caracalla, 00100 Rome, Italy (Telephone Number in U.S. (202) 653-2400); *Annual Fertilizer Review,* and *The State of Food and Agriculture.*

Statistical Office of the United Nations, Publishing Service, New York, New York 10017 (800) 253-9646; *Statistical Yearbook.*

ZAIRE - FETAL MORTALITY

Statistical Office of the United Nations, Publishing Service, New York, New York 10017 (800) 253-9646; *Demographic Yearbook.*

ZAIRE - FINANCE

African Development Bank, 01 BP 1387, Abidjan 01, Cote D'Ivoire; *Selected Statistics on Regional Member Countries.*

Facts on File, 460 Park Avenue South, New York, New York 10016 (800) 443-8323; *The New Book of World Rankings.*

G.K. Hall and Company, 70 Lincoln Street, Boston, Massachusetts 02111 (617) 423-3990; *The World in Figures.*

International Monetary Fund, 700 Nineteenth Street, NW, Washington, D.C. 20431 (202) 623-7000; *Government Finance Statistics Yearbook,* and *International Financial Statistics.*

United Nations Economic Commission for Africa, Africa Hall, P.O. Box 3001, Addis Ababa, Ethiopia (Telephone Number in U.S. (800) 253-9646); *African Statistical Yearbook.*

ZAIRE - FISHERIES

Facts on File, 460 Park Avenue South, New York, New York 10016 (800) 443-8323; *The New Book of World Rankings.*

Food and Agricultural Organization of the United Nations (FAO) Via delle Terme di Caracalla, 00100 Rome, Italy (Telephone Number in

U.S. (202) 653-2400); *The State of Food and Agriculture,* and *Yearbook of Fishery Statistics.*

Statistical Office of the United Nations, Publishing Service, New York, New York 10017 (800) 253-9646; *Statistical Yearbook,* and *Survey of Economic and Social Conditions in Africa.*

United Nations Economic Commission for Africa, Africa Hall, P.O. Box 3001, Addis Ababa, Ethiopia (Telephone Number in U.S. (800) 253-9646); *African Statistical Yearbook.*

ZAIRE - FOOD

African Development Bank, 01 BP 1387, Abidjan 01, Cote D'Ivoire; *Selected Statistics on Regional Member Countries.*

Food and Agricultural Organization of the United Nations (FAO) Via delle Terme di Caracalla, 00100 Rome, Italy (Telephone Number in U.S. (202) 653-2400); *The State of Food and Agriculture.*

G.K. Hall and Company, 70 Lincoln Street, Boston, Massachusetts 02111 (617) 423-3990; *The World in Figures.*

ZAIRE - FOREIGN AID

G.K. Hall and Company, 70 Lincoln Street, Boston, Massachusetts 02111 (617) 423-3990; *The World in Figures.*

ZAIRE - FOREIGN DEBT

International Monetary Fund, 700 Nineteenth Street, NW, Washington, D.C. 20431 (202) 623-7000; *Government Finance Statistics Yearbook.*

ZAIRE - FOREIGN TRADE

Euromonitor Publications Limited, 87-88 Turnmill Street, London EC1M 5QU, England; *International Marketing Data and Statistics.*

Facts on File, 460 Park Avenue South, New York, New York 10016 (800) 443-8323; *The New Book of World Rankings.*

Food and Agricultural Organization of the United Nations (FAO) Via delle Terme di Caracalla, 00100 Rome, Italy (Telephone Number in U.S. (202) 653-2400); *The State of Food and Agriculture.*

G.K. Hall and Company, 70 Lincoln Street, Boston, Massachusetts 02111 (617) 423-3990; *The World in Figures.*

International Monetary Fund, 700 Nineteenth Street, NW, Washington, D.C. 20431 (202) 623-7000; *International Financial Statistics.*

Statistical Office of the United Nations, Publishing Service, New York, New York 10017 (800) 253-9646; *Foreign Trade Statistics for Africa, International Trade Statistics Yearbook,* and *Statistical Yearbook.*

United Nations Economic Commission for Africa, Africa Hall, P.O. Box 3001, Addis Ababa, Ethiopia (Telephone Number in U.S. (800) 253-9646); *African Statistical Yearbook.*

The World Bank, 1818 H Street, NW, Washington, D.C. 20433 (202) 477-1234; *World Tables.*

World Bureau of Metal Statistics, 27-A High Street, Ware Hert SG12 9BA, England; *World Metal Statistics.*

ZAIRE - FORESTRY AND FOREST PRODUCTS

Facts on File, 460 Park Avenue South, New York, New York 10016 (800) 443-8323; *The New Book of World Rankings*.

Food and Agricultural Organization of the United Nations (FAO) Via delle Terme di Caracalla, 00100 Rome, Italy (Telephone Number in U.S. (202) 653-2400); *The State of Food and Agriculture*, and *Yearbook of Forest Products*.

G.K. Hall and Company, 70 Lincoln Street, Boston, Massachusetts 02111 (617) 423-3990; *The World in Figures*.

Statistical Office of the United Nations, Publishing Service, New York, New York 10017 (800) 253-9646; *Statistical Yearbook*.

United Nations Economic Commission for Africa, Africa Hall, P.O. Box 3001, Addis Ababa, Ethiopia (Telephone Number in U.S. (800) 253-9646); *African Statistical Yearbook*.

United Nations Educational, Scientific and Cultural Organization (UNESCO), 7 Place de Fontenoy, F-75700 Paris, France (Telephone Number in U.S. (212) 963-5981); *Statistical Yearbook*.

ZAIRE - GAS PRODUCTION - See ZAIRE - MINING AND MINERAL PRODUCTS

ZAIRE - GENERAL MORTALITY

Statistical Office of the United Nations, Publishing Service, New York, New York 10017 (800) 253-9646; *Demographic Yearbook*.

ZAIRE - GEOGRAPHIC DATA

Facts on File, 460 Park Avenue South, New York, New York 10016 (800) 443-8323; *The New Book of World Rankings*.

ZAIRE - GOATS - See ZAIRE - LIVESTOCK AND POULTRY

ZAIRE - GOLD HOLDINGS

International Monetary Fund, 700 Nineteenth Street, NW, Washington, D.C. 20431 (202) 623-7000; *International Financial Statistics*.

Statistical Office of the United Nations, Publishing Service, New York, New York 10017 (800) 253-9646; *Statistical Yearbook*.

The World Bank, 1818 H Street, NW, Washington, D.C. 20433 (202) 477-1234; *World Tables*.

ZAIRE - GOLD PRODUCTION AND CONSUMPTION - See ZAIRE - MINING AND MINERAL PRODUCTS

ZAIRE - GOVERNMENT

G.K. Hall and Company, 70 Lincoln Street, Boston, Massachusetts 02111 (617) 423-3990; *The World in Figures*.

ZAIRE - GOVERNMENT CONSUMPTION

International Monetary Fund, 700 Nineteenth Street, NW, Washington, D.C. 20431 (202) 623-7000; *International Financial Statistics*.

ZAIRE - GOVERNMENT EXPENDITURES

Time Books, 201 East 50th Street, New York, New York 10022 (212) 751-2600; *The Economist Book of Vital World Statistics*.

The World Bank, 1818 H Street, NW, Washington, D.C. 20433 (202) 477-1234; *World Tables*.

ZAIRE - GOVERNMENT FINANCES

International Monetary Fund, 700 Nineteenth Street, NW, Washington, D.C. 20431 (202) 623-7000; *International Financial Statistics*.

Statistical Office of the United Nations, Publishing Service, New York, New York 10017 (800) 253-9646; *Statistical Yearbook*.

ZAIRE - GOVERNMENT REVENUE

International Monetary Fund, 700 Nineteenth Street, NW, Washington, D.C. 20431 (202) 623-7000; *Government Finance Statistics Yearbook*.

Statistical Office of the United Nations, Publishing Service, New York, New York 10017 (800) 253-9646; *Survey of Economic and Social Conditions in Africa*.

Time Books, 201 East 50th Street, New York, New York 10022 (212) 751-2600; *The Economist Book of Vital World Statistics*.

The World Bank, 1818 H Street, NW, Washington, D.C. 20433 (202) 477-1234; *World Tables*.

ZAIRE - GRAIN PRODUCTION - See ZAIRE - CROPS

ZAIRE - GRANTS

International Monetary Fund, 700 Nineteenth Street, NW, Washington, D.C. 20431 (202) 623-7000; *Government Finance Statistics Yearbook*.

ZAIRE - GROSS DOMESTIC PRODUCT

African Development Bank, 01 BP 1387, Abidjan 01, Côte D'Ivoire, *Selected Statistics on Regional Member Countries*.

The Economist Intelligence Unit, 111 West 57th Street, New York, New York 10019 (800) 938-4685; *The World Market Atlas*.

Euromonitor Publications Limited, 87-88 Turnmill Street, London EC1M 5QU, England; *International Marketing Data and Statistics*.

Facts on File, 460 Park Avenue South, New York, New York 10016 (800) 443-8323; *The New Book of World Rankings*.

G.K. Hall and Company, 70 Lincoln Street, Boston, Massachusetts 02111 (617) 423-3990; *The World in Figures*.

International Monetary Fund, 700 Nineteenth Street, NW, Washington, D.C. 20431 (202) 623-7000; *International Financial Statistics*.

Statistical Office of the United Nations, Publishing Service, New York, New York 10017 (800) 253-9646; *Statistical Yearbook*, and *Survey of Economic and Social Conditions in Africa*.

Time Books, 201 East 50th Street, New York, New York 10022 (212) 751-2600; *The Economist Book of Vital World Statistics*.

United Nations Economic Commission for Africa, Africa Hall, P.O. Box 3001, Addis Ababa, Ethiopia (Telephone Number in U.S. (800) 253-9646); *African Statistical Yearbook*.

The World Bank, 1818 H Street, NW, Washington, D.C. 20433 (202) 477-1234; *World Tables*.

ZAIRE - GROSS NATIONAL PRODUCT

Euromonitor Publications Limited, 87-88 Turnmill Street, London EC1M 5QU, England; *International Marketing Data and Statistics*.

U.S. Arms Control and Disarmament Agency, 320 Twenty-first Street, NW, Washington, D.C. 20451 (202) 647-8677; *World Military Expenditures and Arms Transfers*.

The World Bank, 1818 H Street, NW, Washington, D.C. 20433 (202) 477-1234; *World Tables*.

ZAIRE - GROUNDNUTS PRODUCTION - See ZAIRE - CROPS

ZAIRE - HEALTH

African Development Bank, 01 BP 1387, Abidjan 01, Cote D'Ivoire; *Selected Statistics on Regional Member Countries*.

Facts on File, 460 Park Avenue South, New York, New York 10016 (800) 443-8323; *The New Book of World Rankings*.

G.K. Hall and Company, 70 Lincoln Street, Boston, Massachusetts 02111 (617) 423-3990; *The World in Figures*.

Statistical Office of the United Nations, Publishing Service, New York, New York 10017 (800) 253-9646; *Statistical Yearbook*.

Time Books, 201 East 50th Street, New York, New York 10022 (212) 751-2600; *The Economist Book of Vital World Statistics*.

United Nations Economic Commission for Africa, Africa Hall, P.O. Box 3001, Addis Ababa, Ethiopia (Telephone Number in U.S. (800) 253-9646); *African Statistical Yearbook*.

World Health Organization, Office of Publications, Avenue Appia, CH-1211 Geneva 27, Switzerland (Telephone Number in U.S. (518) 436-9686); *World Health Statistics Annual*.

ZAIRE - HIGHWAYS

G.K. Hall and Company, 70 Lincoln Street, Boston, Massachusetts 02111 (617) 423-3990; *The World in Figures*.

International Road Federation, 525 School Street, SW, Washington, D.C. 20024 (202) 554-2106; *World Road Statistics*.

Statistical Office of the United Nations, Publishing Service, New York, New York 10017 (800) 253-9646; *Survey of Economic and Social Conditions in Africa*.

United Nations Economic Commission for Africa, Africa Hall, P.O. Box 3001, Addis Ababa, Ethiopia (Telephone Number in U.S. (800) 253-9646); *African Statistical Yearbook*.

ZAIRE - HORSES - See ZAIRE - LIVESTOCK AND POULTRY

ZAIRE - HOURS OF WORK - See ZAIRE - EMPLOYMENT

ZAIRE - HOUSING AND HOUSING UNITS

Facts on File, 460 Park Avenue South, New York, New York 10016 (800) 443-8323; *The New Book of World Rankings*.

ZAIRE - ILLITERATE POPULATION

The Economist Intelligence Unit, 111 West 57th Street, New York, New York 10019 (800) 938-4685; *The World Market Atlas*.

G.K. Hall and Company, 70 Lincoln Street, Boston, Massachusetts 02111 (617) 423-3990; *The World in Figures*.

United Nations Educational, Scientific and Cultural Organization (UNESCO), 7 Place de Fontenoy, F-75700 Paris, France (Telephone Number in U.S. (212) 963-5981); *Statistical Yearbook*.

ZAIRE - IMPORTS

African Development Bank, 01 BP 1387, Abidjan 01, Cote D'Ivoire; *Selected Statistics on Regional Member Countries*.

The Economist Intelligence Unit, 111 West 57th Street, New York, New York 10019 (800) 938-4685; *The World Market Atlas*.

Euromonitor Publications Limited, 87-88 Turnmill Street, London EC1M 5QU, England; *International Marketing Data and Statistics*.

Food and Agricultural Organization of the United Nations (FAO) Via delle Terme di Caracalla, 00100 Rome, Italy (Telephone Number in U.S. (202) 653-2400); *The State of Food and Agriculture*.

G.K. Hall and Company, 70 Lincoln Street, Boston, Massachusetts 02111 (617) 423-3990; *The World in Figures*.

International Monetary Fund, 700 Nineteenth Street, NW, Washington, D.C. 20431 (202) 623-7000; *Direction of Trade Statistics*, and *International Financial Statistics*.

Statistical Office of the United Nations, Publishing Service, New York, New York 10017 (800) 253-9646; *Foreign Trade Statistics for Africa, Survey of Economic and Social Conditions in Africa*, and *Trade in Manufactures of Developing Countries*.

United Nations Economic Commission for Africa, Africa Hall, P.O. Box 3001, Addis Ababa, Ethiopia (Telephone Number in U.S. (800) 253-9646); *African Statistical Yearbook*.

The World Bank, 1818 H Street, NW, Washington, D.C. 20433 (202) 477-1234; *World Tables*.

ZAIRE - INCOME TAXES - See ZAIRE - TAXATION

ZAIRE - INDUSTRIAL METALS PRODUCTION - See ZAIRE - MINING AND MINERAL PRODUCTS

ZAIRE - INDUSTRY

Euromonitor Publications Limited, 87-88 Turnmill Street, London EC1M 5QU, England; *International Marketing Data and Statistics*.

Facts on File, 460 Park Avenue South, New York, New York 10016 (800) 443-8323; *The New Book of World Rankings*.

G.K. Hall and Company, 70 Lincoln Street, Boston, Massachusetts 02111 (617) 423-3990; *The World in Figures*.

International Labour Office, I.L.O. Publications, CH-1211, Geneva 22, Switzerland; *Yearbook of Labour Statistics*.

Statistical Office of the United Nations, Publishing Service, New York, New York 10017 (800) 253-9646; *Survey of Economic and Social Conditions in Africa*.

Time Books, 201 East 50th Street, New York, New York 10022 (212) 751-2600; *The Economist Book of Vital World Statistics*.

The World Bank, 1818 H Street, NW, Washington, D.C. 20433 (202) 477-1234; *World Tables*.

ZAIRE - INFANT AND MATERNAL MORTALITY

Statistical Office of the United Nations, Publishing Service, New York, New York 10017 (800) 253-9646; *Demographic Yearbook, Statistical Yearbook*, and *Survey of Economic and Social Conditions in Africa*.

Time Books, 201 East 50th Street, New York, New York 10022 (212) 751-2600; *The Economist Book of Vital World Statistics*.

The World Bank, 1818 H Street, NW, Washington, D.C. 20433 (202) 477-1234; *World Tables*.

ZAIRE - INTERNATIONAL LIQUIDITY

International Monetary Fund, 700 Nineteenth Street, NW, Washington, D.C. 20431 (202) 623-7000; *International Financial Statistics*.

ZAIRE - INTERNATIONAL RESERVES EXCLUDING GOLD

African Development Bank, 01 BP 1387, Abidjan 01, Cote D'Ivoire; *Selected Statistics on Regional Member Countries*.

Statistical Office of the United Nations, Publishing Service, New York, New York 10017 (800) 253-9646; *Statistical Yearbook*.

The World Bank, 1818 H Street, NW, Washington, D.C. 20433 (202) 477-1234; *World Tables*.

ZAIRE - INVESTMENTS

International Monetary Fund, 700 Nineteenth Street, NW, Washington, D.C. 20431 (202) 623-7000; *International Financial Statistics*.

ZAIRE - IRON ORE PRODUCTION AND CONSUMPTION - See ZAIRE MINING AND MINERAL PRODUCTS

ZAIRE - IRRIGATION

Euromonitor Publications Limited, 87-88 Turnmill Street, London EC1M 5QU, England; *International Marketing Data and Statistics*.

ZAIRE - LABOR FORCE

African Development Bank, 01 BP 1387, Abidjan 01, Cote D'Ivoire; *Selected Statistics on Regional Member Countries*.

Euromonitor Publications Limited, 87-88 Turnmill Street, London EC1M 5QU, England; *International Marketing Data and Statistics*.

Facts on File, 460 Park Avenue South, New York, New York 10016 (800) 443-8323; *The New Book of World Rankings*.

Food and Agricultural Organization of the United Nations (FAO) Via delle Terme di Caracalla, 00100 Rome, Italy (Telephone Number in U.S. (202) 653-2400); *The State of Food and Agriculture*.

G.K. Hall and Company, 70 Lincoln Street, Boston, Massachusetts 02111 (617) 423-3990; *The World in Figures*.

The World Bank, 1818 H Street, NW, Washington, D.C. 20433 (202) 477-1234; *World Tables*.

ZAIRE - LABOR PRODUCTIVITY

International Labour Office, I.L.O. Publications, CH-1211, Geneva 22, Switzerland; *Yearbook of Labour Statistics*.

ZAIRE - LAND USE

Euromonitor Publications Limited, 87-88 Turnmill Street, London EC1M 5QU, England; *International Marketing Data and Statistics*.

G.K. Hall and Company, 70 Lincoln Street, Boston, Massachusetts 02111 (617) 423-3990; *The World in Figures*.

ZAIRE - LEAD AND LEAD ORE PRODUCTION AND CONSUMPTION - See ZAIRE MINING AND MINERAL PRODUCTS

ZAIRE - LIBRARIES

Facts on File, 460 Park Avenue South, New York, New York 10016 (800) 443-8323; *The New Book of World Rankings*.

United Nations Educational, Scientific and Cultural Organization (UNESCO), 7 Place de Fontenoy, F-75700 Paris, France (Telephone Number in U.S. (212) 963-5981); *Statistical Yearbook*.

ZAIRE - LIFE EXPECTANCY

African Development Bank, 01 BP 1387, Abidjan 01, Cote D'Ivoire; *Selected Statistics on Regional Member Countries*.

ZAIRE - LITERACY RATE

Statistical Office of the United Nations, Publishing Service, New York, New York 10017 (800) 253-9646; *Survey of Economic and Social Conditions in Africa*.

ZAIRE - LIVESTOCK AND POULTRY

Euromonitor Publications Limited, 87-88 Turnmill Street, London EC1M 5QU, England; *International Marketing Data and Statistics*.

Facts on File, 460 Park Avenue South, New York, New York 10016 (800) 443-8323; *The New Book of World Rankings*.

Food and Agricultural Organization of the United Nations (FAO) Via delle Terme di Caracalla, 00100 Rome, Italy (Telephone Number in U.S. (202) 653-2400); *The State of Food and Agriculture*.

G.K. Hall and Company, 70 Lincoln Street, Boston, Massachusetts 02111 (617) 423-3990; *The World in Figures*.

Statistical Office of the United Nations, Publishing Service, New York, New York 10017 (800) 253-9646; *Statistical Yearbook*, and *Survey of Economic and Social Conditions in Africa*.

United Nations Economic Commission for Africa, Africa Hall, P.O. Box 3001, Addis Ababa, Ethiopia (Telephone Number in U.S. (800) 253-9646); *African Statistical Yearbook*.

ZAIRE - LIVING LEVELS

G.K. Hall and Company, 70 Lincoln Street, Boston, Massachusetts 02111 (617) 423-3990; *The World in Figures*.

Time Books, 201 East 50th Street, New York, New York 10022 (212) 751-2600; *The Economist Book of Vital World Statistics*.

ZAIRE - MAGNESIUM PRODUCTION AND CONSUMPTION - See ZAIRE - MINING AND MINERAL PRODUCTS

ZAIRE - MAIL - NUMBER OF ITEMS SENT AND RECEIVED

Statistical Office of the United Nations, Publishing Service, New York, New York 10017 (800) 253-9646; *Statistical Yearbook.*

ZAIRE - MANGANESE PRODUCTION AND CONSUMPTION - See ZAIRE - MINING AND MINERAL PRODUCTS

ZAIRE - MANUFACTURING

Facts on File, 460 Park Avenue South, New York, New York 10016 (800) 443-8323; *The New Book of World Rankings.*

G.K. Hall and Company, 70 Lincoln Street, Boston, Massachusetts 02111 (617) 423-3990; *The World in Figures.*

Statistical Office of the United Nations, Publishing Service, New York, New York 10017 (800) 253-9646; *Statistical Yearbook,* and *Survey of Economic and Social Conditions in Africa.*

Time Books, 201 East 50th Street, New York, New York 10022 (212) 751-2600; *The Economist Book of Vital World Statistics.*

United Nations Economic Commission for Africa, Africa Hall, P.O. Box 3001, Addis Ababa, Ethiopia (Telephone Number in U.S. (800) 253-9646); *African Statistical Yearbook.*

The World Bank, 1818 H Street, NW, Washington, D.C. 20433 (202) 477-1234; *World Tables.*

ZAIRE - MARRIAGE RATES

Facts on File, 460 Park Avenue South, New York, New York 10016 (800) 443-8323; *The New Book of World Rankings.*

Statistical Office of the United Nations, Publishing Service, New York, New York 10017 (800) 253-9646; *Demographic Yearbook.*

ZAIRE - MEAT PRODUCTION - See ZAIRE - LIVESTOCK AND POULTRY

ZAIRE - MERCHANT SHIPPING

G.K. Hall and Company, 70 Lincoln Street, Boston, Massachusetts 02111 (617) 423-3990; *The World in Figures.*

Statistical Office of the United Nations, Publishing Service, New York, New York 10017 (800) 253-9646; *Statistical Yearbook.*

United Nations Economic Commission for Africa, Africa Hall, P.O. Box 3001, Addis Ababa, Ethiopia (Telephone Number in U.S. (800) 253-9646); *African Statistical Yearbook.*

U.S. Department of Transportation, Maritime Administration, 400 Seventh Street, SW, Washington, D.C. 20590 (202) 366-5807; *A Statistical Analysis of the World's Merchant Fleets.*

ZAIRE - MILITARY

G.K. Hall and Company, 70 Lincoln Street, Boston, Massachusetts 02111 (617) 423-3990; *The World in Figures.*

The International Institute for Strategic Studies, 23 Tavistock Street, London WC2E 7NQ, England; *The Military Balance.*

U.S. Arms Control and Disarmament Agency, 320 Twenty-first Street, NW, Washington, D.C. 20451 (202) 647-8677; *World Military Expenditures and Arms Transfers.*

ZAIRE - MILK PRODUCTION - See ZAIRE - DAIRY PRODUCTS

ZAIRE - MINING AND MINERAL PRODUCTS

Commodity Research Bureau, Incorporated, 75 Wall Street, New York, New York 10005 (212) 504-7754; *Commodity Year Book.*

Facts on File, 460 Park Avenue South, New York, New York 10016 (800) 443-8323; *The New Book of World Rankings.*

G.K. Hall and Company, 70 Lincoln Street, Boston, Massachusetts 02111 (617) 423-3990; *The World in Figures.*

International Monetary Fund, 700 Nineteenth Street, NW, Washington, D.C. 20431 (202) 623-7000; *International Financial Statistics.*

Penn Well Publishing Company, 1421 South Sheridan Road, P.O. Box 1260, Tulsa, Oklahoma 74101 (800) 752-9764; *International Energy Statistics Sourcebook.*

Statistical Office of the United Nations, Publishing Service, New York, New York 10017 (800) 253-9646; *Statistical Yearbook.*

United Nations Economic Commission for Africa, Africa Hall, P.O. Box 3001, Addis Ababa, Ethiopia (Telephone Number in U.S. (800) 253-9646); *African Statistical Yearbook.*

World Bureau of Metal Statistics, 27-A High Street, Ware Hert SG12 9BA, England; *World Metal Statistics.*

ZAIRE - MOLYBDENUM AND MOLYBDENUM ORE PRODUCTION AND CONSUMPTION - See ZAIRE - MINING AND MINERAL PRODUCTS

ZAIRE - MONEY EXCHANGE RATES

Euromonitor Publications Limited, 87-88 Turnmill Street, London EC1M 5QU, England; *International Marketing Data and Statistics.*

International Monetary Fund, 700 Nineteenth Street, NW, Washington, D.C. 20431 (202) 623-7000; *International Financial Statistics.*

Statistical Office of the United Nations, Publishing Service, New York, New York 10017 (800) 253-9646; *Statistical Yearbook.*

ZAIRE - MONEY RESERVES

Euromonitor Publications Limited, 87-88 Turnmill Street, London EC1M 5QU, England; *International Marketing Data and Statistics.*

ZAIRE - MONEY SUPPLY

African Development Bank, 01 BP 1387, Abidjan 01, Cote D'Ivoire; *Selected Statistics on Regional Member Countries.*

Euromonitor Publications Limited, 87-88 Turnmill Street, London EC1M 5QU, England; *International Marketing Data and Statistics.*

G.K. Hall and Company, 70 Lincoln Street, Boston, Massachusetts 02111 (617) 423-3990; *The World in Figures.*

International Monetary Fund, 700 Nineteenth Street, NW, Washington, D.C. 20431 (202) 623-7000; *International Financial Statistics.*

Statistical Office of the United Nations, Publishing Service, New York, New York 10017 (800) 253-9646; *Statistical Yearbook*.

The World Bank, 1818 H Street, NW, Washington, D.C. 20433 (202) 477-1234; *World Tables*.

ZAIRE - MOTION PICTURES

Statistical Office of the United Nations, Publishing Service, New York, New York 10017 (800) 253-9646; *Statistical Yearbook*.

ZAIRE - MOTOR VEHICLE PRODUCTION

Statistical Office of the United Nations, Publishing Service, New York, New York 10017 (800) 253-9646; *Statistical Yearbook*.

ZAIRE - MOTOR VEHICLE TAXES - See ZAIRE - TAXATION

ZAIRE - MOTOR VEHICLES IN USE

G.K. Hall and Company, 70 Lincoln Street, Boston, Massachusetts 02111 (617) 423-3990; *The World in Figures*.

International Road Federation, 525 School Street, SW, Washington, D.C. 20024 (202) 554-2106; *World Road Statistics*.

Statistical Office of the United Nations, Publishing Service, New York, New York 10017 (800) 253-9646; *Statistical Yearbook*, and *Survey of Economic and Social Conditions in Africa*.

Time Books, 201 East 50th Street, New York, New York 10022 (212) 751-2600; *The Economist Book of Vital World Statistics*.

ZAIRE - MUSEUMS

Facts on File, 460 Park Avenue South, New York, New York 10016 (800) 443-8323; *The New Book of World Rankings*.

United Nations Educational, Scientific and Cultural Organization (UNESCO), 7 Place de Fontenoy, F-75700 Paris, France (Telephone Number in U.S. (212) 963-5981); *Statistical Yearbook*.

ZAIRE - NATALITY - See ZAIRE - BIRTH RATE

ZAIRE - NATIONAL ACCOUNTS

International Monetary Fund, 700 Nineteenth Street, NW, Washington, D.C. 20431 (202) 623-7000; *International Financial Statistics*.

Statistical Office of the United Nations, Publishing Service, New York, New York 10017 (800) 253-9646; *National Accounts Statistics*, and *Statistical Yearbook*.

United Nations Economic Commission for Africa, Africa Hall, P.O. Box 3001, Addis Ababa, Ethiopia (Telephone Number in U.S. (800) 253-9646); *African Statistical Yearbook*.

ZAIRE - NATIONAL INCOME

African Development Bank, 01 BP 1387, Abidjan 01, Cote D'Ivoire; *Selected Statistics on Regional Member Countries*.

Facts on File, 460 Park Avenue South, New York, New York 10016 (800) 443-8323; *The New Book of World Rankings*.

G.K. Hall and Company, 70 Lincoln Street, Boston, Massachusetts 02111 (617) 423-3990; *The World in Figures*.

Statistical Office of the United Nations, Publishing Service, New York, New York 10017 (800) 253-9646; *Statistical Yearbook*.

ZAIRE - NATIONAL PRODUCT

Facts on File, 460 Park Avenue South, New York, New York 10016 (800) 443-8323; *The New Book of World Rankings*.

Statistical Office of the United Nations, Publishing Service, New York, New York 10017 (800) 253-9646; *Statistical Yearbook*.

ZAIRE - NATURAL GAS PRODUCTION - See ZAIRE - MINING AND MINERAL PRODUCTS

ZAIRE - NATURAL RUBBER PRODUCTION

Statistical Office of the United Nations, Publishing Service, New York, New York 10017 (800) 253-9646; *Statistical Yearbook*.

ZAIRE - NEWSPAPER PRODUCTION - See ZAIRE - FORESTRY AND FOREST PRODUCTS

ZAIRE - NEWSPRINT - See ZAIRE - FORESTRY AND FOREST PRODUCTS

ZAIRE - NICKEL AND NICKEL ORE PRODUCTION AND CONSUMPTION - See ZAIRE MINING AND MINERAL PRODUCTS

ZAIRE - OATS PRODUCTION - See ZAIRE - CROPS

ZAIRE - OCCUPATIONS - See ZAIRE - LABOR FORCE

ZAIRE - PALM OIL AND PALM KERNELS PRODUCTION - See ZAIRE - CROPS

ZAIRE - PAPER - See ZAIRE - FORESTRY AND FOREST PRODUCTS

ZAIRE - PATENTS

Statistical Office of the United Nations, Publishing Service, New York, New York 10017 (800) 253-9646; *Statistical Yearbook*.

ZAIRE - PEANUT PRODUCTION - See ZAIRE - CROPS

ZAIRE - PESTICIDE USE

Food and Agricultural Organization of the United Nations (FAO) Via delle Terme di Caracalla, 00100 Rome, Italy (Telephone Number in U.S. (202) 653-2400); *The State of Food and Agriculture*.

ZAIRE - PETROLEUM INDUSTRY

Facts on File, 460 Park Avenue South, New York, New York 10016 (800) 443-8323; *The New Book of World Rankings*.

Food and Agricultural Organization of the United Nations (FAO) Via delle Terme di Caracalla, 00100 Rome, Italy (Telephone Number in U.S. (202) 653-2400); *The State of Food and Agriculture*.

G.K. Hall and Company, 70 Lincoln Street, Boston, Massachusetts 02111 (617) 423-3990; *The World in Figures*.

Penn Well Publishing Company, 1421 South Sheridan Road, P.O. Box 1260, Tulsa, Oklahoma 74101 (800) 752-9764; *International Energy Statistics Sourcebook*.

Statistical Office of the United Nations, Publishing Service, New York, New York 10017 (800) 253-9646; *Statistical Yearbook*.

ZAIRE - PIGS - See ZAIRE - LIVESTOCK AND POULTRY

ZAIRE - POPULATION

African Development Bank, 01 BP 1387, Abidjan 01, Cote D'Ivoire; *Selected Statistics on Regional Member Countries*.

The Economist Intelligence Unit, 111 West 57th Street, New York, New York 10019 (800) 938-4685; *The World Market Atlas*.

Euromonitor Publications Limited, 87-88 Turnmill Street, London EC1M 5QU, England; *International Marketing Data and Statistics*.

Facts on File, 460 Park Avenue South, New York, New York 10016 (800) 443-8323; *The New Book of World Rankings*.

G.K. Hall and Company, 70 Lincoln Street, Boston, Massachusetts 02111 (617) 423-3990; *The World in Figures*.

International Labour Office, I.L.O. Publications, CH-1211, Geneva 22, Switzerland; *Yearbook of Labour Statistics*.

Statistical Office of the United Nations, Publishing Service, New York, New York 10017 (800) 253-9646; *Demographic Yearbook*, *Statistical Yearbook*, and *Survey of Economic and Social Conditions in Africa*.

Time Books, 201 East 50th Street, New York, New York 10022 (212) 751-2600; *The Economist Book of Vital World Statistics*.

United Nations Educational, Scientific and Cultural Organization (UNESCO), 7 Place de Fontenoy, F-75700 Paris, France (Telephone Number in U.S. (212) 963-5981); *Statistical Yearbook*.

U.S. Arms Control and Disarmament Agency, 320 Twenty-first Street, NW, Washington, D.C. 20451 (202) 647-8677; *World Military Expenditures and Arms Transfers*.

World Health Organization, Office of Publications, Avenue Appia, CH-1211 Geneva 27, Switzerland (Telephone Number in U.S. (518) 436-9686); *World Health Statistics Annual*.

ZAIRE - POST OFFICES

Facts on File, 460 Park Avenue South, New York, New York 10016 (800) 443-8323; *The New Book of World Rankings*.

ZAIRE - POTATO PRODUCTION - See ZAIRE - CROPS

ZAIRE - POWER PRODUCTION INDUSTRY

Statistical Office of the United Nations, Publishing Service, New York, New York 10017 (800) 253-9646; *Statistical Yearbook*.

ZAIRE - PRICES

Facts on File, 460 Park Avenue South, New York, New York 10016 (800) 443-8323; *The New Book of World Rankings*.

Food and Agricultural Organization of the United Nations (FAO) Via delle Terme di Caracalla, 00100 Rome, Italy (Telephone Number in U.S. (202) 653-2400); *The State of Food and Agriculture*.

G.K. Hall and Company, 70 Lincoln Street, Boston, Massachusetts 02111 (617) 423-3990; *The World in Figures*.

International Labour Office, I.L.O. Publications, CH-1211, Geneva 22, Switzerland; *Yearbook of Labour Statistics*.

International Monetary Fund, 700 Nineteenth Street, NW, Washington, D.C. 20431 (202) 623-7000; *International Financial Statistics*.

United Nations Economic Commission for Africa, Africa Hall, P.O. Box 3001, Addis Ababa, Ethiopia (Telephone Number in U.S. (800) 253-9646); *African Statistical Yearbook*.

World Bureau of Metal Statistics, 27-A High Street, Ware Hert SG12 9BA, England; *World Metal Statistics*.

ZAIRE - PRINTING AND WRITING PAPER - See ZAIRE - FORESTRY AND FOREST PRODUCTS

ZAIRE - PRODUCTION

Facts on File, 460 Park Avenue South, New York, New York 10016 (800) 443-8323; *The New Book of World Rankings*.

G.K. Hall and Company, 70 Lincoln Street, Boston, Massachusetts 02111 (617) 423-3990; *The World in Figures*.

ZAIRE - PRODUCTIVITY

Euromonitor Publications Limited, 87-88 Turnmill Street, London EC1M 5QU, England; *International Marketing Data and Statistics*.

ZAIRE - PROPERTY TAXES - See ZAIRE - TAXATION

ZAIRE - PUBLIC FINANCE

Facts on File, 460 Park Avenue South, New York, New York 10016 (800) 443-8323; *The New Book of World Rankings*.

ZAIRE - RADIO BROADCASTING - See ZAIRE - BROADCASTING

ZAIRE - RADIO RECEIVER PRODUCTION

Statistical Office of the United Nations, Publishing Service, New York, New York 10017 (800) 253-9646; *Statistical Yearbook*.

ZAIRE - RAILWAYS

G.K. Hall and Company, 70 Lincoln Street, Boston, Massachusetts 02111 (617) 423-3990; *The World in Figures*.

Jane's Information Group, Sentinel House, 163 Brighton Road, Coulsdon, Surrey CR5 2NH, England (Telephone Number in U.S. (703) 683-3700); *Jane's World Railways*.

Statistical Office of the United Nations, Publishing Service, New York, New York 10017 (800) 253-9646; *Statistical Yearbook*, and *Survey of Economic and Social Conditions in Africa*.

United Nations Economic Commission for Africa, Africa Hall, P.O. Box 3001, Addis Ababa, Ethiopia (Telephone Number in U.S. (800) 253-9646); *African Statistical Yearbook*.

ZAIRE - RELIGION

Facts on File, 460 Park Avenue South, New York, New York 10016 (800) 443-8323; *The New Book of World Rankings*.

ZAIRE - RENT PRICES

International Labour Office, I.L.O. Publications, CH-1211, Geneva 22, Switzerland; *Yearbook of Labour Statistics*.

ZAIRE - RETAIL TRADE

G.K. Hall and Company, 70 Lincoln Street, Boston, Massachusetts 02111 (617) 423-3990; *The World in Figures*.

ZAIRE - RICE PRODUCTION - See ZAIRE - CROPS

ZAIRE - ROUNDWOOD PRODUCTION - See ZAIRE - FORESTRY AND FOREST PRODUCTS

ZAIRE - RUBBER PRODUCTION AND CONSUMPTION

Facts on File, 460 Park Avenue South, New York, New York 10016 (800) 443-8323; *The New Book of World Rankings*.

ZAIRE - SAWNWOOD PRODUCTION - See ZAIRE - FORESTRY AND FOREST PRODUCTS

ZAIRE - SENIOR CITIZENS

Facts on File, 460 Park Avenue South, New York, New York 10016 (800) 443-8323; *The New Book of World Rankings*.

ZAIRE - SHEEP - See ZAIRE - LIVESTOCK AND POULTRY

ZAIRE - SILVER PRODUCTION AND CONSUMPTION - See ZAIRE - MINING AND MINERAL PRODUCTS

ZAIRE - SOCIAL DATA

African Development Bank, 01 BP 1387, Abidjan 01, Cote D'Ivoire; *Selected Statistics on Regional Member Countries*.

Facts on File, 460 Park Avenue South, New York, New York 10016 (800) 443-8323; *The New Book of World Rankings*.

G.K. Hall and Company, 70 Lincoln Street, Boston, Massachusetts 02111 (617) 423-3990; *The World in Figures*.

ZAIRE - SOYBEAN PRODUCTION - See ZAIRE - CROPS

ZAIRE - STATE BUDGET REVENUE AND EXPENDITURES

Euromonitor Publications Limited, 87-88 Turnmill Street, London EC1M 5QU, England; *International Marketing Data and Statistics*.

ZAIRE - STEEL PRODUCTION - See ZAIRE - MINING AND MINERAL PRODUCTS

ZAIRE - STOCKS - COMMODITY - MARKET PRICE - INDEX

Food and Agricultural Organization of the United Nations (FAO) Via delle Terme di Caracalla, 00100 Rome, Italy (Telephone Number in U.S. (202) 653-2400); *The State of Food and Agriculture*.

World Bureau of Metal Statistics, 27-A High Street, Ware Hert SG12 9BA, England; *World Metal Statistics*.

ZAIRE - SUGAR PRODUCTION AND CONSUMPTION - See ZAIRE - CROPS

ZAIRE - SULPHURIC ACID PRODUCTION - See ZAIRE - MINING AND MINERAL PRODUCTS

ZAIRE - TAXATION

G.K. Hall and Company, 70 Lincoln Street, Boston, Massachusetts 02111 (617) 423-3990; *The World in Figures*.

International Monetary Fund, 700 Nineteenth Street, NW Washington, D.C. 20431 (202) 623-7000; *Government Finance Statistics Yearbook*.

International Road Federation, 525 School Street, SW, Washington, D.C. 20024 (202) 554-2106; *World Road Statistics*.

The World Bank, 1818 H Street, NW, Washington, D.C. 20433 (202) 477-1234; *World Tables*.

ZAIRE - TEA PRODUCTION - See ZAIRE - CROPS

ZAIRE - TELEGRAPH SERVICE

Statistical Office of the United Nations, Publishing Service, New York, New York 10017 (800) 253-9646; *Statistical Yearbook*.

ZAIRE - TELEPHONES IN USE

American Telephone and Telegraph Communications, Customer Information Center, Post Office Box 19901, Indianapolis, Indiana 46219; *The World's Telephones*.

G.K. Hall and Company, 70 Lincoln Street, Boston, Massachusetts 02111 (617) 423-3990; *The World in Figures*.

Statistical Office of the United Nations, Publishing Service, New York, New York 10017 (800) 253-9646; *Statistical Yearbook*.

ZAIRE - TELEVISION BROADCASTING - See ZAIRE - BROADCASTING

ZAIRE - TEXTILE INDUSTRY

G.K. Hall and Company, 70 Lincoln Street, Boston, Massachusetts 02111 (617) 423-3990; *The World in Figures*.

Statistical Office of the United Nations, Publishing Service, New York, New York 10017 (800) 253-9646; *Statistical Yearbook*.

ZAIRE - THEATRE

United Nations Educational, Scientific and Cultural Organization (UNESCO), 7 Place de Fontenoy, F-75700 Paris, France (Telephone Number in U.S. (212) 963-5981); *Statistical Yearbook*.

ZAIRE - TIN - See ZAIRE - MINING AND MINERAL PRODUCTS

ZAIRE - TOBACCO PRODUCTION

Facts on File, 460 Park Avenue South, New York, New York 10016 (800) 443-8323; *The New Book of World Rankings*.

Statistical Office of the United Nations, Publishing Service, New York, New York 10017 (800) 253-9646; *Statistical Yearbook*.

ZAIRE - TOURISM

Facts on File, 460 Park Avenue South, New York, New York 10016 (800) 443-8323; *The New Book of World Rankings*.

G.K. Hall and Company, 70 Lincoln Street, Boston, Massachusetts 02111 (617) 423-3990; *The World in Figures*.

Statistical Office of the United Nations, Publishing Service, New York, New York 10017 (800) 253-9646; *Statistical Yearbook*.

Time Books, 201 East 50th Street, New York, New York 10022 (212) 751-2600; *The Economist Book of Vital World Statistics*.

United Nations Economic Commission for Africa, Africa Hall, P.O. Box 3001, Addis Ababa, Ethiopia (Telephone Number in U.S. (800) 253-9646); *African Statistical Yearbook.*

World Tourism Organization, Calle Capitan Haya 42, E-28020 Madrid, Spain; *Yearbook of Tourism Statistics.*

ZAIRE - TRACTORS IN USE

Statistical Office of the United Nations, Publishing Service, New York, New York 10017 (800) 253-9646; *Statistical Yearbook.*

ZAIRE - TRADE - See ZAIRE - FOREIGN TRADE

ZAIRE - TRADEMARKS AND SERVICE MARKS

Statistical Office of the United Nations, Publishing Service, New York, New York 10017 (800) 253-9646; *Statistical Yearbook.*

ZAIRE - TRANSPORTATION AND COMMUNICATIONS

Facts on File, 460 Park Avenue South, New York, New York 10016 (800) 443-8323; *The New Book of World Rankings.*

G.K. Hall and Company, 70 Lincoln Street, Boston, Massachusetts 02111 (617) 423-3990; *The World in Figures.*

United Nations Economic Commission for Africa, Africa Hall, P.O. Box 3001, Addis Ababa, Ethiopia (Telephone Number in U.S. (800) 253-9646); *African Statistical Yearbook.*

ZAIRE - TUNGSTEN PRODUCTION AND CONSUMPTION - See ZAIRE - MINING AND MINERAL PRODUCTS

ZAIRE - UNEMPLOYMENT

Euromonitor Publications Limited, 87-88 Turnmill Street, London EC1M 5QU, England; *International Marketing Data and Statistics.*

International Labour Office, I.L.O. Publications, CH-1211, Geneva 22, Switzerland; *Yearbook of Labour Statistics.*

ZAIRE - URANIUM PRODUCTION AND CONSUMPTION - See ZAIRE - MINING AND MINERAL PRODUCTS

ZAIRE - VANADIUM AND VANADIUM ORE - See ZAIRE - MINING AND MINERAL PRODUCTS

ZAIRE - VITAL STATISTICS

Euromonitor Publications Limited, 87-88 Turnmill Street, London EC1M 5QU, England; *International Marketing Data and Statistics.*

G.K. Hall and Company, 70 Lincoln Street, Boston, Massachusetts 02111 (617) 423-3990; *The World in Figures.*

Statistical Office of the United Nations, Publishing Service, New York, New York 10017 (800) 253-9646; *Statistical Yearbook.*

World Health Organization, Office of Publications, Avenue Appia, CH-1211 Geneva 27, Switzerland (Telephone Number in U.S. (518) 436-9686); *World Health Statistics Annual.*

ZAIRE - WAGES

G.K. Hall and Company, 70 Lincoln Street, Boston, Massachusetts 02111 (617) 423-3990; *The World in Figures.*

International Labour Office, I.L.O. Publications, CH-1211, Geneva 22, Switzerland; *Yearbook of Labour Statistics.*

ZAIRE - WEATHER

Facts on File, 460 Park Avenue South, New York, New York 10016 (800) 443-8323; *The New Book of World Rankings.*

G.K. Hall and Company, 70 Lincoln Street, Boston, Massachusetts 02111 (617) 423-3990; *The World in Figures.*

ZAIRE - WHEAT PRODUCTION AND PRICES - See ZAIRE - CROPS

ZAIRE - WINE PRODUCTION

Facts on File, 460 Park Avenue South, New York, New York 10016 (800) 443-8323; *The New Book of World Rankings.*

ZAIRE - WOOL PRODUCTION

Facts on File, 460 Park Avenue South, New York, New York 10016 (800) 443-8323; *The New Book of World Rankings.*

ZAIRE - ZINC AND ZINC ORE PRODUCTION AND CONSUMPTION - See ZAIRE - MINING AND MINERAL PRODUCTS

Zambia - National Statistical Office

Central Statistical Office, Ministry of Finance, Post Office Box 31908, Lusaka, Zambia.

Zambia - Primary Statistics Sources

Central Statistical Office, Post Office Box 31908, Lusaka, Zambia; *Statistical Yearbook, Monthly Digest of Statistics,* and *Zambia in Figures.*

ZAMBIA - AGRICULTURE

Euromonitor Publications Limited, 87-88 Turnmill Street, London EC1M 5QU, England; *International Marketing Data and Statistics.*

Facts on File, 460 Park Avenue South, New York, New York 10016 (800) 443-8323; *The New Book of World Rankings.*

Food and Agricultural Organization of the United Nations (FAO), Via delle Terme di Caracalla, 00100 Rome, Italy (Telephone Number in U.S. (202) 653-2400); *Production Yearbook, The State of Food and Agriculture,* and *Trade Yearbook.*

G.K. Hall and Company, 70 Lincoln Street, Boston, Massachusetts 02111 (617) 423-3990; *The World in Figures.*

Statistical Office of the United Nations, Publishing Service, New York, New York 10017 (800) 253-9646; *Statistical Yearbook,* and *Survey of Economic and Social Conditions in Africa.*

Time Books, 201 East 50th Street, New York, New York 10022 (212) 751-2600; *The Economist Book of Vital World Statistics.*

United Nations Economic Commission for Africa, Africa Hall, P.O. Box 3001, Addis Ababa, Ethiopia (Telephone Number in U.S. (800) 253-9646); *African Statistical Yearbook.*

The World Bank, 1818 H Street, NW, Washington, D.C. 20433 (202) 477-1234; *World Tables.*

ZAMBIA - AIRLINE SERVICE

Facts on File, 460 Park Avenue South, New York, New York 10016 (800) 443-8323; *The New Book of World Rankings*.

G.K. Hall and Company, 70 Lincoln Street, Boston, Massachusetts 02111 (617) 423-3990; *The World in Figures*.

International Civil Aviation Organization, 1000 Sherbrooke Street, West, Montreal, Quebec, Canada H3A 2R2 (514) 285-8219; *Civil Aviation Statistics of the World*.

Statistical Office of the United Nations, Publishing Service, New York, New York 10017 (800) 253-9646; *Statistical Yearbook*.

United Nations Economic Commission for Africa, Africa Hall, P.O. Box 3001, Addis Ababa, Ethiopia (Telephone Number in U.S. (800) 253-9646); *African Statistical Yearbook*.

Time Books, 201 East 50th Street, New York, New York 10022 (212) 751-2600; *The Economist Book of Vital World Statistics*.

ZAMBIA - ALUMINUM PRODUCTION AND CONSUMPTION - See ZAMBIA - MINING AND MINERAL PRODUCTS

ZAMBIA - ANIMAL HEALTH

Food and Agricultural Organization of the United Nations (FAO), Via delle Terme di Caracalla, 00100 Rome, Italy (Telephone Number in U.S. (202) 653-2400); *Animal Health Yearbook*.

ZAMBIA - ANTIMONY AND ANTIMONY ORE PRODUCTION AND CONSUMPTION - See ZAMBIA - MINING AND MINERAL PRODUCTS

ZAMBIA - AREA AND DENSITY OF POPULATION

African Development Bank, 01 BP 1387, Abidjan 01, Cote D'Ivoire; *Selected Statistics on Regional Member Countries*.

Euromonitor Publications Limited, 87-88 Turnmill Street, London EC1M 5QU, England; *International Marketing Data and Statistics*.

Facts on File, 460 Park Avenue South, New York, New York 10016 (800) 443-8323; *The New Book of World Rankings*.

Food and Agricultural Organization of the United Nations (FAO) Via delle Terme di Caracalla, 00100 Rome, Italy (Telephone Number in U.S. (202) 653-2400); *The State of Food and Agriculture*.

G.K. Hall and Company, 70 Lincoln Street, Boston, Massachusetts 02111 (617) 423-3990; *The World in Figures*.

Statistical Office of the United Nations, Publishing Service, New York, New York 10017 (800) 253-9646; *Statistical Yearbook*, and *Survey of Economic and Social Conditions in Africa*.

Time Books, 201 East 50th Street, New York, New York 10022 (212) 751-2600; *The Economist Book of Vital World Statistics*.

United Nations Educational, Scientific and Cultural Organization (UNESCO), 7 Place de Fontenoy, F-75700 Paris, France (Telephone Number in U.S. (212) 963-5981); *Statistical Yearbook*.

ZAMBIA - ARMS EXPORTS AND EXPORTS

U.S. Arms Control and Disarmament Agency, 320 Twenty-first Street, NW, Washington, D.C. 20451 (202) 647-8677; *World Military Expenditures and Arms Transfers*.

ZAMBIA - BALANCE OF PAYMENTS

African Development Bank, 01 BP 1387, Abidjan 01, Cote D'Ivoire; *Selected Statistics on Regional Member Countries*.

The Economist Intelligence Unit, 111 West 57th Street, New York, New York 10019 (800) 938-4685; *The World Market Atlas*.

G.K. Hall and Company, 70 Lincoln Street, Boston, Massachusetts 02111 (617) 423-3990; *The World in Figures*.

International Monetary Fund, 700 Nineteenth Street, NW, Washington, D.C. 20431 (202) 623-7000; *Balance of Payments Yearbook*.

Time Books, 201 East 50th Street, New York, New York 10022 (212) 751-2600; *The Economist Book of Vital World Statistics*.

United Nations Economic Commission for Africa, Africa Hall, P.O. Box 3001, Addis Ababa, Ethiopia (Telephone Number in U.S. (800) 253-9646); *African Statistical Yearbook*.

The World Bank, 1818 H Street, NW, Washington, D.C. 20433 (202) 477-1234; *World Tables*.

ZAMBIA - BANKING

Facts on File, 460 Park Avenue South, New York, New York 10016 (800) 443-8323; *The New Book of World Rankings*.

G.K. Hall and Company, 70 Lincoln Street, Boston, Massachusetts 02111 (617) 423-3990; *The World in Figures*.

International Monetary Fund, 700 Nineteenth Street, NW, Washington, D.C. 20431 (202) 623-7000; *Government Finance Statistics Yearbook*, and *International Financial Statistics*.

United Nations Economic Commission for Africa, Africa Hall, P.O. Box 3001, Addis Ababa, Ethiopia (Telephone Number in U.S. (800) 253-9646); *African Statistical Yearbook*.

ZAMBIA - BARLEY PRODUCTION - See ZAMBIA - CROPS

ZAMBIA - BAUXITE PRODUCTION AND CONSUMPTION - See ZAMBIA - MINING AND MINERAL PRODUCTS

ZAMBIA - BEER PRODUCTION

Facts on File, 460 Park Avenue South, New York, New York 10016 (800) 443-8323; *The New Book of World Rankings*.

Statistical Office of the United Nations, Publishing Service, New York, New York 10017 (800) 253-9646; *Statistical Yearbook*.

ZAMBIA - BIRTH RATE

Facts on File, 460 Park Avenue South, New York, New York 10016 (800) 443-8323; *The New Book of World Rankings*.

Statistical Office of the United Nations, Publishing Service, New York, New York 10017 (800) 253-9646; *Demographic Yearbook*, *Statistical Yearbook*, and *Survey of Economic and Social Conditions in Africa*.

Time Books, 201 East 50th Street, New York, New York 10022 (212) 751-2600; *The Economist Book of Vital World Statistics*.

The World Bank, 1818 H Street, NW, Washington, D.C. 20433 (202) 477-1234; *World Tables*.

ZAMBIA - BONDS

G.K. Hall and Company, 70 Lincoln Street, Boston, Massachusetts 02111 (617) 423-3990; *The World in Figures.*

International Monetary Fund, 700 Nineteenth Street, NW, Washington, D.C. 20431 (202) 623-7000; *Government Finance Statistics Yearbook.*

ZAMBIA - BOOK PRODUCTION

G.K. Hall and Company, 70 Lincoln Street, Boston, Massachusetts 02111 (617) 423-3990; *The World in Figures.*

United Nations Educational, Scientific and Cultural Organization (UNESCO), 7 Place de Fontenoy, F-75700 Paris, France (Telephone Number in U.S. (212) 963-5981); *Statistical Yearbook.*

ZAMBIA - BROADCASTING

Billboard Limited, P.O. Box 9027, 1006 AA Amsterdam, The Netherlands (Telephone Number in U.S. (212) 764-7300); *World Radio TV Handbook.*

Facts on File, 460 Park Avenue South, New York, New York 10016 (800) 443-8323; *The New Book of World Rankings.*

G.K. Hall and Company, 70 Lincoln Street, Boston, Massachusetts 02111 (617) 423-3990; *The World in Figures.*

Time Books, 201 East 50th Street, New York, New York 10022 (212) 751-2600; *The Economist Book of Vital World Statistics.*

United Nations Educational, Scientific and Cultural Organization (UNESCO), 7 Place de Fontenoy, F-75700 Paris, France (Telephone Number in U.S. (212) 963-5981); *Statistical Yearbook.*

ZAMBIA - BUSINESS

G.K. Hall and Company, 70 Lincoln Street, Boston, Massachusetts 02111 (617) 423-3990; *The World in Figures.*

ZAMBIA - BUSINESS AND PROFESSIONAL LICENSES

International Monetary Fund, 700 Nineteenth Street, NW, Washington, D.C. 20431 (202) 623-7000; *Government Finance Statistics Yearbook.*

ZAMBIA - CADMIUM PRODUCTION AND CONSUMPTION - See ZAMBIA - MINING AND MINERAL PRODUCTS

ZAMBIA - CALORIE SUPPLY

African Development Bank, 01 BP 1387, Abidjan 01, Cote D'Ivoire; *Selected Statistics on Regional Member Countries.*

Food and Agricultural Organization of the United Nations (FAO) Via delle Terme di Caracalla, 00100 Rome, Italy (Telephone Number in U.S. (202) 653-2400); *The State of Food and Agriculture.*

ZAMBIA - CAPITAL REVENUE

International Monetary Fund, 700 Nineteenth Street, NW, Washington, D.C. 20431 (202) 623-7000; *Government Finance Statistics Yearbook.*

ZAMBIA - CATTLE - See ZAMBIA - LIVESTOCK AND POULTRY

ZAMBIA - CEMENT PRODUCTION - See ZAMBIA - MINING AND MINERAL PRODUCTS

ZAMBIA - CHEMICAL (ORGANIC) PRODUCTION - See ZAMBIA - MINING AND MINERAL PRODUCTS

ZAMBIA - CHICKENS - See ZAMBIA - LIVESTOCK AND POULTRY

ZAMBIA - CIGARETTE PRODUCTION - See ZAMBIA - TOBACCO PRODUCTION

ZAMBIA - CLASS STRUCTURE

G.K. Hall and Company, 70 Lincoln Street, Boston, Massachusetts 02111 (617) 423-3990; *The World in Figures.*

ZAMBIA - CLIMATE

Facts on File, 460 Park Avenue South, New York, New York 10016 (800) 443-8323; *The New Book of World Rankings.*

G.K. Hall and Company, 70 Lincoln Street, Boston, Massachusetts 02111 (617) 423-3990; *The World in Figures.*

ZAMBIA - COAL PRODUCTION AND CONSUMPTION - See ZAMBIA MINING AND MINERAL PRODUCTS

ZAMBIA - COBALT PRODUCTION AND CONSUMPTION - See ZAMBIA - MINING AND MINERAL PRODUCTS

ZAMBIA - COFFEE PRODUCTION AND CONSUMPTION - See ZAIRE - CROPS

ZAMBIA - COKE OVEN COKE PRODUCTION AND CONSUMPTION - See ZAMBIA - MINING AND MINERAL PRODUCTS

ZAMBIA - COMMUNICATIONS

G.K. Hall and Company, 70 Lincoln Street, Boston, Massachusetts 02111 (617) 423-3990; *The World in Figures.*

United Nations Economic Commission for Africa, Africa Hall, P.O. Box 3001, Addis Ababa, Ethiopia (Telephone Number in U.S. (800) 253-9646); *African Statistical Yearbook.*

ZAMBIA - CONSTRUCTION INDUSTRY

Facts on File, 460 Park Avenue South, New York, New York 10016 (800) 443-8323; *The New Book of World Rankings.*

Statistical Office of the United Nations, Publishing Service, New York, New York 10017 (800) 253-9646; *Construction Statistics Yearbook,* and *Statistical Yearbook.*

United Nations Economic Commission for Africa, Africa Hall, P.O. Box 3001, Addis Ababa, Ethiopia (Telephone Number in U.S. (800) 253-9646); *African Statistical Yearbook.*

ZAMBIA - CONSUMER PRICE INDEX

African Development Bank, 01 BP 1387, Abidjan 01, Cote D'Ivoire; *Selected Statistics on Regional Member Countries.*

G.K. Hall and Company, 70 Lincoln Street, Boston, Massachusetts 02111 (617) 423-3990; *The World in Figures.*

Statistical Office of the United Nations, Publishing Service, New York, New York 10017 (800) 253-9646; *Statistical Yearbook,* and *Survey of Economic and Social Conditions in Africa.*

United Nations Economic Commission for Africa, Africa Hall, P.O. Box 3001, Addis Ababa, Ethiopia (Telephone Number in U.S. (800) 253-9646); *African Statistical Yearbook.*

ZAMBIA - CONSUMER PRICES

International Labour Office, I.L.O. Publications, CH-1211, Geneva 22, Switzerland; *Yearbook of Labour Statistics.*

International Monetary Fund, 700 Nineteenth Street, NW, Washington, D.C. 20431 (202) 623-7000; *International Financial Statistics.*

Time Books, 201 East 50th Street, New York, New York 10022 (212) 751-2600; *The Economist Book of Vital World Statistics.*

ZAMBIA - CONSUMPTION

African Development Bank, 01 BP 1387, Abidjan 01, Cote D'Ivoire; *Selected Statistics on Regional Member Countries.*

G.K. Hall and Company, 70 Lincoln Street, Boston, Massachusetts 02111 (617) 423-3990; *The World in Figures.*

International Lead and Zinc Study Group, Metro House, 58 St. James's Street, London SW1A 1LD England; *Lead and Zinc Statistics.*

Statistical Office of the United Nations, Publishing Service, New York, New York 10017 (800) 253-9646; *Survey of Economic and Social Conditions in Africa.*

ZAMBIA - COPPER AND COPPER ORE PRODUCTION AND CONSUMPTION - See ZAMBIA - MINING AND MINERAL PRODUCTS

ZAMBIA - CORN PRODUCTION - See ZAMBIA - CROPS

ZAMBIA - CORPORATE TAXES - See ZAMBIA - TAXATION

ZAMBIA - COTTON PRODUCTION - See ZAIRE - CROPS

ZAMBIA - CRIME

International Criminal Police Organization (INTERPOL), 26 rue Armengaud, 92210 Saint Cloud, France; *International Crime Statistics.*

Yale University Press, Yale Station, New Haven, Connecticut 06520 (203) 432-0940; *Violence and Crime in Cross-National Perspective.*

ZAMBIA - CROPS

Facts on File, 460 Park Avenue South, New York, New York 10016 (800) 443-8323; *The New Book of World Rankings.*

Food and Agricultural Organization of the United Nations (FAO) Via delle Terme di Caracalla, 00100 Rome, Italy (Telephone Number in U.S. (202) 653-2400); *The State of Food and Agriculture.*

G.K. Hall and Company, 70 Lincoln Street, Boston, Massachusetts 02111 (617) 423-3990; *The World in Figures.*

Statistical Office of the United Nations, Publishing Service, New York, New York 10017 (800) 253-9646; *Statistical Yearbook.*

United Nations Economic Commission for Africa, Africa Hall, P.O. Box 3001, Addis Ababa, Ethiopia (Telephone Number in U.S. (800) 253-9646); *African Statistical Yearbook.*

ZAMBIA - CUSTOMS DUTIES

G.K. Hall and Company, 70 Lincoln Street, Boston, Massachusetts 02111 (617) 423-3990; *The World in Figures.*

International Monetary Fund, 700 Nineteenth Street, NW, Washington, D.C. 20431 (202) 623-7000; *Government Finance Statistics Yearbook.*

ZAMBIA - DAIRY PRODUCTS

Facts on File, 460 Park Avenue South, New York, New York 10016 (800) 443-8323; *The New Book of World Rankings.*

Food and Agricultural Organization of the United Nations (FAO) Via delle Terme di Caracalla, 00100 Rome, Italy (Telephone Number in U.S. (202) 653-2400); *The State of Food and Agriculture.*

Statistical Office of the United Nations, Publishing Service, New York, New York 10017 (800) 253-9646; *Statistical Yearbook.*

ZAMBIA - DEATH RATE

G.K. Hall and Company, 70 Lincoln Street, Boston, Massachusetts 02111 (617) 423-3990; *The World in Figures.*

Statistical Office of the United Nations, Publishing Service, New York, New York 10017 (800) 253-9646; *Statistical Yearbook*, and *Survey of Economic and Social Conditions in Africa.*

Time Books, 201 East 50th Street, New York, New York 10022 (212) 751-2600; *The Economist Book of Vital World Statistics.*

World Health Organization, Office of Publications, Avenue Appia, CH 1211 Geneva 27, Switzerland (Telephone Number in U.S. (518) 436-9686); *World Health Statistics Annual.*

ZAMBIA - DEFENSE EXPENDITURES

G.K. Hall and Company, 70 Lincoln Street, Boston, Massachusetts 02111 (617) 423-3990; *The World in Figures.*

International Monetary Fund, 700 Nineteenth Street, NW, Washington, D.C. 20431 (202) 623-7000; *Government Finance Statistics Yearbook.*

U.S. Arms Control and Disarmament Agency, 320 Twenty-first Street, NW, Washington, D.C. 20451 (202) 647-8677; *World Military Expenditures and Arms Transfers.*

ZAMBIA - DEMOGRAPHY

The Economist Intelligence Unit, 111 West 57th Street, New York, New York 10019 (800) 938-4685; *The World Market Atlas.*

Facts on File, 460 Park Avenue South, New York, New York 10016 (800) 443-8323; *The New Book of World Rankings.*

G.K. Hall and Company, 70 Lincoln Street, Boston, Massachusetts 02111 (617) 423-3990; *The World in Figures.*

Statistical Office of the United Nations, Publishing Service, New York, New York 10017 (800) 253-9646; *Survey of Economic and Social Conditions in Africa.*

ZAMBIA - DEVELOPMENT ASSISTANCE

G.K. Hall and Company, 70 Lincoln Street, Boston, Massachusetts 02111 (617) 423-3990; *The World in Figures.*

Statistical Office of the United Nations, Publishing Service, New York, New York 10017 (800) 253-9646; *Statistical Yearbook*.

ZAMBIA - DIAMOND PRODUCTION - See ZAMBIA - MINING AND MINERAL PRODUCTS

ZAMBIA - DISEASES

G.K. Hall and Company, 70 Lincoln Street, Boston, Massachusetts 02111 (617) 423-3990; *The World in Figures*.

World Health Organization, Office of Publications, Avenue Appia, CH-1211 Geneva 27, Switzerland (Telephone Number in U.S. (518) 436-9686); *World Health Statistics Annual*.

ZAMBIA - DIVORCE RATES

Facts on File, 460 Park Avenue South, New York, New York 10016 (800) 443-8323; *The New Book of World Rankings*.

Statistical Office of the United Nations, Publishing Service, New York, New York 10017 (800) 253-9646; *Demographic Yearbook*.

ZAMBIA - DOMESTIC PRODUCT

G.K. Hall and Company, 70 Lincoln Street, Boston, Massachusetts 02111 (617) 423-3990; *The World in Figures*.

ZAMBIA - ECONOMY

African Development Bank, 01 BP 1387, Abidjan 01, Cote D'Ivoire; *Selected Statistics on Regional Member Countries*.

Euromonitor Publications Limited, 87-88 Turnmill Street, London EC1M 5QU, England; *International Marketing Data and Statistics*.

Facts on File, 460 Park Avenue South, New York, New York 10016 (800) 443-8323; *The New Book of World Rankings*.

G.K. Hall and Company, 70 Lincoln Street, Boston, Massachusetts 02111 (617) 423-3990; *The World in Figures*.

Statistical Office of the United Nations, Publishing Service, New York, New York 10017 (800) 253-9646; *Foreign Trade Statistics for Africa*.

ZAMBIA - EDUCATION

African Development Bank, 01 BP 1387, Abidjan 01, Cote D'Ivoire; *Selected Statistics on Regional Member Countries*.

Facts on File, 460 Park Avenue South, New York, New York 10016 (800) 443-8323; *The New Book of World Rankings*.

G.K. Hall and Company, 70 Lincoln Street, Boston, Massachusetts 02111 (617) 423-3990; *The World in Figures*.

International Monetary Fund, 700 Nineteenth Street, NW, Washington, D.C. 20431 (202) 623-7000; *Government Finance Statistics Yearbook*.

Statistical Office of the United Nations, Publishing Service, New York, New York 10017 (800) 253-9646; *Survey of Economic and Social Conditions in Africa*.

Time Books, 201 East 50th Street, New York, New York 10022 (212) 751-2600; *The Economist Book of Vital World Statistics*.

United Nations Economic Commission for Africa, Africa Hall, P.O. Box 3001, Addis Ababa, Ethiopia (Telephone Number in U.S. (800) 253-9646); *African Statistical Yearbook*.

United Nations Educational, Scientific and Cultural Organization (UNESCO), 7 Place de Fontenoy, F-75700 Paris, France (Telephone Number in U.S. (212) 963-5981); *Statistical Yearbook*.

The World Bank, 1818 H Street, NW, Washington, D.C. 20433 (202) 477-1234; *World Tables*.

ZAMBIA - EGG PRODUCTION AND CONSUMPTION - See ZAMBIA - DAIRY PRODUCTS

ZAMBIA - ELECTRICITY

Facts on File, 460 Park Avenue South, New York, New York 10016 (800) 443-8323; *The New Book of World Rankings*.

Statistical Office of the United Nations, Publishing Service, New York, New York 10017 (800) 253-9646; *Statistical Yearbook*, and *Survey of Economic and Social Conditions in Africa*.

Time Books, 201 East 50th Street, New York, New York 10022 (212) 751-2600; *The Economist Book of Vital World Statistics*.

United Nations Economic Commission for Africa, Africa Hall, P.O. Box 3001, Addis Ababa, Ethiopia (Telephone Number in U.S. (800) 253-9646); *African Statistical Yearbook*.

ZAMBIA - EMPLOYMENT

Euromonitor Publications Limited, 87-88 Turnmill Street, London EC1M 5QU, England; *International Marketing Data and Statistics*.

Facts on File, 460 Park Avenue South, New York, New York 10016 (800) 443-8323; *The New Book of World Rankings*.

International Labour Office, I.L.O. Publications, CH-1211, Geneva 22, Switzerland; *Yearbook of Labour Statistics*.

Statistical Office of the United Nations, Publishing Service, New York, New York 10017 (800) 253-9646; *Statistical Yearbook*, and *Survey of Economic and Social Conditions in Africa*.

United Nations Economic Commission for Africa, Africa Hall, P.O. Box 3001, Addis Ababa, Ethiopia (Telephone Number in U.S. (800) 253-9646); *African Statistical Yearbook*.

ZAMBIA - ENERGY

Facts on File, 460 Park Avenue South, New York, New York 10016 (800) 443-8323; *The New Book of World Rankings*.

Food and Agricultural Organization of the United Nations (FAO) Via delle Terme di Caracalla, 00100 Rome, Italy (Telephone Number in U.S. (202) 653-2400); *The State of Food and Agriculture*.

G.K. Hall and Company, 70 Lincoln Street, Boston, Massachusetts 02111 (617) 423-3990; *The World in Figures*.

Statistical Office of the United Nations, Publishing Service, New York, New York 10017 (800) 253-9646; *Energy Statistics Yearbook*, and *Statistical Yearbook*, and *World Energy Supplies*.

Time Books, 201 East 50th Street, New York, New York 10022 (212) 751-2600; *The Economist Book of Vital World Statistics*.

United Nations Economic Commission for Africa, Africa Hall, P.O. Box 3001, Addis Ababa, Ethiopia (Telephone Number in U.S. (800) 253-9646); *African Statistical Yearbook.*

ZAMBIA - EXCHANGE RATES

African Development Bank, 01 BP 1387, Abidjan 01, Cote D'Ivoire; *Selected Statistics on Regional Member Countries.*

Euromonitor Publications Limited, 87-88 Turnmill Street, London EC1M 5QU, England; *International Marketing Data and Statistics.*

International Civil Aviation Organization, 1000 Sherbrooke Street, West, Montreal, Quebec, Canada H3A 2R2 (514) 285-8219; *Civil Aviation Statistics of the World.*

International Monetary Fund, 700 Nineteenth Street, NW, Washington, D.C. 20431 (202) 623-7000; *International Financial Statistics.*

Statistical Office of the United Nations, Publishing Service, New York, New York 10017 (800) 253-9646; *Foreign Trade Statistics for Africa,* and *Statistical Yearbook.*

ZAMBIA - EXCISE TAXES - See ZAMBIA - TAXATION

ZAMBIA - EXPORTS

African Development Bank, 01 BP 1387, Abidjan 01, Cote D'Ivoire; *Selected Statistics on Regional Member Countries.*

The Economist Intelligence Unit, 111 West 57th Street, New York, New York 10019 (800) 938-4685; *The World Market Atlas.*

Euromonitor Publications Limited, 87-88 Turnmill Street, London EC1M 5QU, England; *International Marketing Data and Statistics.*

Food and Agricultural Organisation of the United Nations (FAO) Via delle Terme di Caracalla, 00100 Rome, Italy (Telephone Number in U.S. (202) 653-2400); *The State of Food and Agriculture.*

G.K. Hall and Company, 70 Lincoln Street, Boston, Massachusetts 02111 (617) 423-3990; *The World in Figures.*

International Lead and Zinc Study Group, Metro House, 58 St. James's Street, London SW1A 1LD England; *Lead and Zinc Statistics.*

International Monetary Fund, 700 Nineteenth Street, NW, Washington, D.C. 20431 (202) 623-7000; *Direction of Trade Statistics,* and *International Financial Statistics.*

Statistical Office of the United Nations, Publishing Service, New York, New York 10017 (800) 253-9646; *Foreign Trade Statistics for Africa, Survey of Economic and Social Conditions in Africa,* and *Trade in Manufactures of Developing Countries.*

Time Books, 201 East 50th Street, New York, New York 10022 (212) 751-2600; *The Economist Book of Vital World Statistics.*

United Nations Economic Commission for Africa, Africa Hall, P.O. Box 3001, Addis Ababa, Ethiopia (Telephone Number in U.S. (800) 253-9646); *African Statistical Yearbook.*

The World Bank, 1818 H Street, NW, Washington, D.C. 20433 (202) 477-1234; *World Tables.*

ZAMBIA - EXTERNAL INDEBTEDNESS

African Development Bank, 01 BP 1387, Abidjan 01, Cote D'Ivoire; *Selected Statistics on Regional Member Countries.*

Statistical Office of the United Nations, Publishing Service, New York, New York 10017 (800) 253-9646; *Survey of Economic and Social Conditions in Africa.*

The World Bank, 1818 H Street, NW, Washington, D.C. 20433 (202) 477-1234; *World Tables.*

ZAMBIA - EXTERNAL TRADE

African Development Bank, 01 BP 1387, Abidjan 01, Cote D'Ivoire; *Selected Statistics on Regional Member Countries.*

Food and Agricultural Organization of the United Nations (FAO) Via delle Terme di Caracalla, 00100 Rome, Italy (Telephone Number in U.S. (202) 653-2400); *The State of Food and Agriculture.*

G.K. Hall and Company, 70 Lincoln Street, Boston, Massachusetts 02111 (617) 423-3990; *The World in Figures.*

Statistical Office of the United Nations, Publishing Service, New York, New York 10017 (800) 253-9646; *Statistical Yearbook.*

ZAMBIA - FARM CROPS - See ZAMBIA - CROPS

ZAMBIA FEMALE WORKING POPULATION - See ZAMBIA - EMPLOYMENT

ZAMBIA - FERTILITY RATES

Facts on File, 460 Park Avenue South, New York, New York 10016 (800) 443-8323; *The New Book of World Rankings.*

Statistical Office of the United Nations, Publishing Service, New York, New York 10017 (800) 253-9646; *Survey of Economic and Social Conditions in Africa.*

Time Books, 201 East 50th Street, New York, New York 10022 (212) 751-2600; *The Economist Book of Vital World Statistics.*

The World Bank, 1818 H Street, NW, Washington, D.C. 20433 (202) 477-1234; *World Tables.*

ZAMBIA FERTILIZER

Food and Agricultural Organization of the United Nations (FAO), Via delle Terme di Caracalla, 00100 Rome, Italy (Telephone Number in U.S. (202) 653-2400); *Annual Fertilizer Review,* and *The State of Food and Agriculture.*

Statistical Office of the United Nations, Publishing Service, New York, New York 10017 (800) 253-9646; *Statistical Yearbook.*

ZAMBIA - FETAL MORTALITY

Statistical Office of the United Nations, Publishing Service, New York, New York 10017 (800) 253-9646; *Demographic Yearbook.*

ZAMBIA - FINANCE

African Development Bank, 01 BP 1387, Abidjan 01, Cote D'Ivoire; *Selected Statistics on Regional Member Countries.*

Facts on File, 460 Park Avenue South, New York, New York 10016 (800) 443-8323; *The New Book of World Rankings.*

G.K. Hall and Company, 70 Lincoln Street, Boston, Massachusetts 02111 (617) 423-3990; *The World in Figures*.

International Monetary Fund, 700 Nineteenth Street, NW, Washington, D.C. 20431 (202) 623-7000; *Government Finance Statistics Yearbook*, and *International Financial Statistics*.

United Nations Economic Commission for Africa, Africa Hall, P.O. Box 3001, Addis Ababa, Ethiopia (Telephone Number in U.S. (800) 253-9646); *African Statistical Yearbook*.

ZAMBIA - FISHERIES

Facts on File, 460 Park Avenue South, New York, New York 10016 (800) 443-8323; *The New Book of World Rankings*.

Food and Agricultural Organization of the United Nations (FAO) Via delle Terme di Caracalla, 00100 Rome, Italy (Telephone Number in U.S. (202) 653-2400); *The State of Food and Agriculture*, and *Yearbook of Fishery Statistics*.

Statistical Office of the United Nations, Publishing Service, New York, New York 10017 (800) 253-9646; *Statistical Yearbook*, and *Survey of Economic and Social Conditions in Africa*.

United Nations Economic Commission for Africa, Africa Hall, P.O. Box 3001, Addis Ababa, Ethiopia (Telephone Number in U.S. (800) 253-9646); *African Statistical Yearbook*.

ZAMBIA - FLOUR PRODUCTION

Statistical Office of the United Nations, Publishing Service, New York, New York 10017 (800) 253-9646; *Statistical Yearbook*.

ZAMBIA - FOOD

African Development Bank, 01 BP 1387, Abidjan 01, Cote D'Ivoire; *Selected Statistics on Regional Member Countries*.

Food and Agricultural Organization of the United Nations (FAO) Via delle Terme di Caracalla, 00100 Rome, Italy (Telephone Number in U.S. (202) 653-2400); *The State of Food and Agriculture*.

G.K. Hall and Company, 70 Lincoln Street, Boston, Massachusetts 02111 (617) 423-3990; *The World in Figures*.

ZAMBIA - FOREIGN AID

G.K. Hall and Company, 70 Lincoln Street, Boston, Massachusetts 02111 (617) 423-3990; *The World in Figures*.

ZAMBIA - FOREIGN DEBT

International Monetary Fund, 700 Nineteenth Street, NW, Washington, D.C. 20431 (202) 623-7000; *Government Finance Statistics Yearbook*.

ZAMBIA - FOREIGN TRADE

Euromonitor Publications Limited, 87-88 Turnmill Street, London EC1M 5QU, England; *International Marketing Data and Statistics*.

Facts on File, 460 Park Avenue South, New York, New York 10016 (800) 443-8323; *The New Book of World Rankings*.

Food and Agricultural Organization of the United Nations (FAO) Via delle Terme di Caracalla, 00100 Rome, Italy (Telephone Number in U.S. (202) 653-2400); *The State of Food and Agriculture*.

G.K. Hall and Company, 70 Lincoln Street, Boston, Massachusetts 02111 (617) 423-3990; *The World in Figures*.

International Monetary Fund, 700 Nineteenth Street, NW, Washington, D.C. 20431 (202) 623-7000; *International Financial Statistics*.

Statistical Office of the United Nations, Publishing Service, New York, New York 10017 (800) 253-9646; *Foreign Trade Statistics for Africa*, *International Trade Statistics Yearbook*, and *Statistical Yearbook*.

United Nations Economic Commission for Africa, Africa Hall, P.O. Box 3001, Addis Ababa, Ethiopia (Telephone Number in U.S. (800) 253-9646); *African Statistical Yearbook*.

The World Bank, 1818 H Street, NW, Washington, D.C. 20433 (202) 477-1234; *World Tables*.

World Bureau of Metal Statistics, 27-A High Street, Ware Hert SG12 9BA, England; *World Metal Statistics*.

ZAMBIA - FORESTRY AND FOREST PRODUCTS

Facts on File, 460 Park Avenue South, New York, New York 10016 (800) 443-8323; *The New Book of World Rankings*.

Food and Agricultural Organization of the United Nations (FAO) Via delle Terme di Caracalla, 00100 Rome, Italy (Telephone Number in U.S. (202) 653-2400); *The State of Food and Agriculture*, and *Yearbook of Forest Products*.

G.K. Hall and Company, 70 Lincoln Street, Boston, Massachusetts 02111 (617) 423-3990; *The World in Figures*.

Statistical Office of the United Nations, Publishing Service, New York, New York 10017 (800) 253-9646; *Statistical Yearbook*.

United Nations Economic Commission for Africa, Africa Hall, P.O. Box 3001, Addis Ababa, Ethiopia (Telephone Number in U.S. (800) 253-9646); *African Statistical Yearbook*.

United Nations Educational, Scientific and Cultural Organization (UNESCO), 7 Place de Fontenoy, F-75700 Paris, France (Telephone Number in U.S. (212) 963-5981); *Statistical Yearbook*.

ZAMBIA - GAS PRODUCTION - See ZAMBIA - MINING AND MINERAL PRODUCTS

ZAMBIA - GENERAL INDUSTRIAL STATISTICS

Statistical Office of the United Nations, Publishing Service, New York, New York 10017 (800) 253-9646; *Industrial Statistics Yearbook*.

ZAMBIA - GENERAL MORTALITY

Statistical Office of the United Nations, Publishing Service, New York, New York 10017 (800) 253-9646; *Demographic Yearbook*.

ZAMBIA - GEOGRAPHIC DATA

Facts on File, 460 Park Avenue South, New York, New York 10016 (800) 443-8323; *The New Book of World Rankings*.

ZAMBIA - GOATS - See ZAMBIA - LIVESTOCK AND POULTRY

ZAMBIA - GOLD HOLDINGS

International Monetary Fund, 700 Nineteenth Street, NW, Washington, D.C. 20431 (202) 623-7000; *International Financial Statistics*.

Statistical Office of the United Nations, Publishing Service, New York, New York 10017 (800) 253-9646; *Statistical Yearbook*.

The World Bank, 1818 H Street, NW, Washington, D.C. 20433 (202) 477-1234; *World Tables*.

ZAMBIA - GOLD PRODUCTION AND CONSUMPTION - See ZAMBIA MINING AND MINERAL PRODUCTS

ZAMBIA - GOVERNMENT

G.K. Hall and Company, 70 Lincoln Street, Boston, Massachusetts 02111 (617) 423-3990; *The World in Figures*.

ZAMBIA - GOVERNMENT EXPENDITURES

International Monetary Fund, 700 Nineteenth Street, NW, Washington, D.C. 20431 (202) 623-7000; *Government Finance Statistics Yearbook*.

Time Books, 201 East 50th Street, New York, New York 10022 (212) 751-2600; *The Economist Book of Vital World Statistics*.

The World Bank, 1818 H Street, NW, Washington, D.C. 20433 (202) 477-1234; *World Tables*.

ZAMBIA - GOVERNMENT FINANCES

International Monetary Fund, 700 Nineteenth Street, NW, Washington, D.C. 20431 (202) 623-7000; *International Financial Statistics*.

Statistical Office of the United Nations, Publishing Service, New York, New York 10017 (800) 253-9646; *Statistical Yearbook*.

ZAMBIA - GOVERNMENT REVENUE

International Monetary Fund, 700 Nineteenth Street, NW, Washington, D.C. 20431 (202) 623-7000; *Government Finance Statistics Yearbook*.

Time Books, 201 East 50th Street, New York, New York 10022 (212) 751-2600; *The Economist Book of Vital World Statistics*.

The World Bank, 1818 H Street, NW, Washington, D.C. 20433 (202) 477-1234; *World Tables*.

ZAMBIA - GRAIN PRODUCTION - See ZAMBIA - CROPS

ZAMBIA - GRANTS

International Monetary Fund, 700 Nineteenth Street, NW, Washington, D.C. 20431 (202) 623-7000; *Government Finance Statistics Yearbook*.

ZAMBIA - GROSS DOMESTIC PRODUCT

African Development Bank, 01 BP 1387, Abidjan 01, Cote D'Ivoire; *Selected Statistics on Regional Member Countries*.

The Economist Intelligence Unit, 111 West 57th Street, New York, New York 10019 (800) 938-4685; *The World Market Atlas*.

Euromonitor Publications Limited, 87-88 Turnmill Street, London EC1M 5QU, England; *International Marketing Data and Statistics*.

Facts on File, 460 Park Avenue South, New York, New York 10016 (800) 443-8323; *The New Book of World Rankings*.

G.K. Hall and Company, 70 Lincoln Street, Boston, Massachusetts 02111 (617) 423-3990; *The World in Figures*.

Statistical Office of the United Nations, Publishing Service, New York, New York 10017 (800) 253-9646; *Statistical Yearbook*, and *Survey of Economic and Social Conditions in Africa*.

Time Books, 201 East 50th Street, New York, New York 10022 (212) 751-2600; *The Economist Book of Vital World Statistics*.

United Nations Economic Commission for Africa, Africa Hall, P.O. Box 3001, Addis Ababa, Ethiopia (Telephone Number in U.S. (800) 253-9646); *African Statistical Yearbook*.

The World Bank, 1818 H Street, NW, Washington, D.C. 20433 (202) 477-1234; *World Tables*.

ZAMBIA - GROSS NATIONAL PRODUCT

Euromonitor Publications Limited, 87-88 Turnmill Street, London EC1M 5QU, England; *International Marketing Data and Statistics*.

U.S. Arms Control and Disarmament Agency, 320 Twenty-first Street, NW, Washington, D.C. 20451 (202) 647-8677; *World Military Expenditures and Arms Transfers*.

The World Bank, 1818 H Street, NW, Washington, D.C. 20433 (202) 477-1234; *World Tables*.

ZAMBIA - GROUNDNUTS PRODUCTION - See ZAMBIA - CROPS

ZAMBIA - HEALTH

African Development Bank, 01 BP 1387, Abidjan 01, Cote D'Ivoire; *Selected Statistics on Regional Member Countries*.

Facts on File, 460 Park Avenue South, New York, New York 10016 (800) 443-8323; *The New Book of World Rankings*.

G.K. Hall and Company, 70 Lincoln Street, Boston, Massachusetts 02111 (617) 423-3990; *The World in Figures*.

Statistical Office of the United Nations, Publishing Service, New York, New York 10017 (800) 253-9646; *Statistical Yearbook*.

Time Books, 201 East 50th Street, New York, New York 10022 (212) 751-2600; *The Economist Book of Vital World Statistics*.

United Nations Economic Commission for Africa, Africa Hall, P.O. Box 3001, Addis Ababa, Ethiopia (Telephone Number in U.S. (800) 253-9646); *African Statistical Yearbook*.

World Health Organization, Office of Publications, Avenue Appia, CH-1211 Geneva 27, Switzerland (Telephone Number in U.S. (518) 436-9686); *World Health Statistics Annual*.

ZAMBIA - HEALTH EXPENDITURES

International Monetary Fund, 700 Nineteenth Street, NW, Washington, D.C. 20431 (202) 623-7000; *Government Finance Statistics Yearbook*.

ZAMBIA - HIGHWAYS

G.K. Hall and Company, 70 Lincoln Street, Boston, Massachusetts 02111 (617) 423-3990; *The World in Figures*.

International Road Federation, 525 School Street, SW, Washington, D.C. 20024 (202) 554-2106; *World Road Statistics*.

Statistical Office of the United Nations, Publishing Service, New York, New York 10017 (800) 253-9646; *Survey of Economic and Social Conditions in Africa*.

United Nations Economic Commission for Africa, Africa Hall, P.O. Box 3001, Addis Ababa, Ethiopia (Telephone Number in U.S. (800) 253-9646); *African Statistical Yearbook*.

ZAMBIA - HORSES - See ZAMBIA - LIVESTOCK AND POULTRY

ZAMBIA - HOURS OF WORK - See ZAMBIA - EMPLOYMENT

ZAMBIA - HOUSING AND HOUSING UNITS

Facts on File, 460 Park Avenue South, New York, New York 10016 (800) 443-8323; *The New Book of World Rankings*.

ZAMBIA - HOUSING EXPENDITURES

International Monetary Fund, 700 Nineteenth Street, NW, Washington, D.C. 20431 (202) 623-7000; *Government Finance Statistics Yearbook*.

ZAMBIA - ILLITERATE POPULATION

The Economist Intelligence Unit, 111 West 57th Street, New York, New York 10019 (800) 938-4685; *The World Market Atlas*.

G.K. Hall and Company, 70 Lincoln Street, Boston, Massachusetts 02111 (617) 423-3990; *The World in Figures*.

United Nations Educational, Scientific and Cultural Organization (UNESCO), 7 Place de Fontenoy, F-75700 Paris, France (Telephone Number in U.S. (212) 963-5981); *Statistical Yearbook*.

ZAMBIA - IMPORTS

African Development Bank, 01 BP 1387, Abidjan 01, Cote D'Ivoire; *Selected Statistics on Regional Member Countries*.

The Economist Intelligence Unit, 111 West 57th Street, New York, New York 10019 (800) 938-4685; *The World Market Atlas*.

Euromonitor Publications Limited, 87-88 Turnmill Street, London EC1M 5QU, England; *International Marketing Data and Statistics*.

Food and Agricultural Organization of the United Nations (FAO) Via delle Terme di Caracalla, 00100 Rome, Italy (Telephone Number in U.S. (202) 653-2400); *The State of Food and Agriculture*.

G.K. Hall and Company, 70 Lincoln Street, Boston, Massachusetts 02111 (617) 423-3990; *The World in Figures*.

International Lead and Zinc Study Group, Metro House, 58 St. James's Street, London SW1A 1LD England; *Lead and Zinc Statistics*.

International Monetary Fund, 700 Nineteenth Street, NW, Washington, D.C. 20431 (202) 623-7000; *Direction of Trade Statistics, Government Finance Statistics Yearbook*, and *International Financial Statistics*.

Statistical Office of the United Nations, Publishing Service, New York, New York 10017 (800) 253-9646; *Foreign Trade Statistics for Africa, Survey of Economic and Social Conditions in Africa*, and *Trade in Manufactures of Developing Countries*.

Time Books, 201 East 50th Street, New York, New York 10022 (212) 751-2600; *The Economist Book of Vital World Statistics*.

United Nations Economic Commission for Africa, Africa Hall, P.O. Box 3001, Addis Ababa, Ethiopia (Telephone Number in U.S. (800) 253-9646); *African Statistical Yearbook*.

The World Bank, 1818 H Street, NW, Washington, D.C. 20433 (202) 477-1234; *World Tables*.

ZAMBIA - INCOME TAXES - See ZAMBIA - TAXATION

ZAMBIA - INDUSTRIAL METALS PRODUCTION See ZAMBIA - MINING AND MINERAL PRODUCTS

ZAMBIA - INDUSTRY

Euromonitor Publications Limited, 87-88 Turnmill Street, London EC1M 5QU, England; *International Marketing Data and Statistics*.

Facts on File, 460 Park Avenue South, New York, New York 10016 (800) 443-8323; *The New Book of World Rankings*.

G.K. Hall and Company, 70 Lincoln Street, Boston, Massachusetts 02111 (617) 423-3990; *The World in Figures*.

International Labour Office, I.L.O. Publications, CH-1211, Geneva 22, Switzerland; *Yearbook of Labour Statistics*.

Statistical Office of the United Nations, Publishing Service, New York, New York 10017 (800) 253-9646; *Statistical Yearbook*, and *Survey of Economic and Social Conditions in Africa*.

Time Books, 201 East 50th Street, New York, New York 10022 (212) 751-2600; *The Economist Book of Vital World Statistics*.

United Nations Economic Commission for Africa, Africa Hall, P.O. Box 3001, Addis Ababa, Ethiopia (Telephone Number in U.S. (800) 253-9646); *African Statistical Yearbook*.

The World Bank, 1818 H Street, NW, Washington, D.C. 20433 (202) 477-1234; *World Tables*.

World Intellectual Property Organization, 34 Chemin des Colombettes, CH-1211 Geneva 20. Switzerland; *Industrial Property Statistics*.

ZAMBIA - INFANT AND MATERNAL MORTALITY

Statistical Office of the United Nations, Publishing Service, New York, New York 10017 (800) 253-9646; *Demographic Yearbook, Statistical Yearbook*, and *Survey of Economic and Social Conditions in Africa*.

Time Books, 201 East 50th Street, New York, New York 10022 (212) 751-2600; *The Economist Book of Vital World Statistics*.

The World Bank, 1818 H Street, NW, Washington, D.C. 20433 (202) 477-1234; *World Tables*.

ZAMBIA - INTERNATIONAL LIQUIDITY

International Monetary Fund, 700 Nineteenth Street, NW, Washington, D.C. 20431 (202) 623-7000; *International Financial*

Statistics.

ZAMBIA - INTERNATIONAL RESERVES EXCLUDING GOLD

African Development Bank, 01 BP 1387, Abidjan 01, Cote D'Ivoire; *Selected Statistics on Regional Member Countries.*

Statistical Office of the United Nations, Publishing Service, New York, New York 10017 (800) 253-9646; *Statistical Yearbook.*

The World Bank, 1818 H Street, NW, Washington, D.C. 20433 (202) 477-1234; *World Tables.*

ZAMBIA - IRON ORE PRODUCTION AND CONSUMPTION - See ZAMBIA - MINING AND MINERAL PRODUCTS

ZAMBIA - IRRIGATION

Euromonitor Publications Limited, 87-88 Turnmill Street, London EC1M 5QU, England; *International Marketing Data and Statistics.*

ZAMBIA - LABOR FORCE

African Development Bank, 01 BP 1387, Abidjan 01, Cote D'Ivoire; *Selected Statistics on Regional Member Countries.*

Euromonitor Publications Limited, 87-88 Turnmill Street, London EC1M 5QU, England; *International Marketing Data and Statistics.*

Facts on File, 460 Park Avenue South, New York, New York 10016 (800) 443-8323; *The New Book of World Rankings.*

Food and Agricultural Organization of the United Nations (FAO) Via delle Terme di Caracalla, 00100 Rome, Italy (Telephone Number in U.S. (202) 653-2400); *The State of Food and Agriculture.*

G.K. Hall and Company, 70 Lincoln Street, Boston, Massachusetts 02111 (617) 423-3990; *The World in Figures.*

The World Bank, 1818 H Street, NW, Washington, D.C. 20433 (202) 477-1234; *World Tables.*

ZAMBIA - LABOR PRODUCTIVITY

International Labour Office, I.L.O. Publications, CH-1211, Geneva 22, Switzerland; *Yearbook of Labour Statistics.*

ZAMBIA - LAND USE

Euromonitor Publications Limited, 87-88 Turnmill Street, London EC1M 5QU, England; *International Marketing Data and Statistics.*

G.K. Hall and Company, 70 Lincoln Street, Boston, Massachusetts 02111 (617) 423-3990; *The World in Figures.*

ZAMBIA - LEAD AND LEAD ORE PRODUCTION AND CONSUMPTION - See ZAMBIA - MINING AND MINERAL PRODUCTS

ZAMBIA - LIBRARIES

Facts on File, 460 Park Avenue South, New York, New York 10016 (800) 443-8323; *The New Book of World Rankings.*

United Nations Educational, Scientific and Cultural Organization (UNESCO), 7 Place de Fontenoy, F-75700 Paris, France (Telephone Number in U.S. (212) 963-5981); *Statistical Yearbook.*

ZAMBIA - LIFE EXPECTANCY

African Development Bank, 01 BP 1387, Abidjan 01, Cote D'Ivoire; *Selected Statistics on Regional Member Countries.*

ZAMBIA - LITERACY RATE

Statistical Office of the United Nations, Publishing Service, New York, New York 10017 (800) 253-9646; *Survey of Economic and Social Conditions in Africa.*

ZAMBIA - LIVESTOCK AND POULTRY

Euromonitor Publications Limited, 87-88 Turnmill Street, London EC1M 5QU, England; *International Marketing Data and Statistics.*

Facts on File, 460 Park Avenue South, New York, New York 10016 (800) 443-8323; *The New Book of World Rankings.*

Food and Agricultural Organization of the United Nations (FAO) Via delle Terme di Caracalla, 00100 Rome, Italy (Telephone Number in U.S. (202) 653-2400); *The State of Food and Agriculture.*

G.K. Hall and Company, 70 Lincoln Street, Boston, Massachusetts 02111 (617) 423-3990; *The World in Figures.*

Statistical Office of the United Nations, Publishing Service, New York, New York 10017 (800) 253-9646; *Statistical Yearbook,* and *Survey of Economic and Social Conditions in Africa.*

United Nations Economic Commission for Africa, Africa Hall, P.O. Box 3001, Addis Ababa, Ethiopia (Telephone Number in U.S. (800) 253-9646); *African Statistical Yearbook.*

ZAMBIA - LIVING LEVELS

G.K. Hall and Company, 70 Lincoln Street, Boston, Massachusetts 02111 (617) 423-3990; *The World in Figures.*

Time Books, 201 East 50th Street, New York, New York 10022 (212) 751-2600; *The Economist Book of Vital World Statistics.*

ZAMBIA - MAGNESIUM PRODUCTION AND CONSUMPTION - See ZAMBIA - MINING AND MINERAL PRODUCTS

ZAMBIA - MAIL - NUMBER OF PIECES SENT OR RECEIVED

Statistical Office of the United Nations, Publishing Service, New York, New York 10017 (800) 253-9646; *Statistical Yearbook.*

ZAMBIA - MANGANESE AND MANGANESE ORE PRODUCTION AND CONSUMPTION - See ZAMBIA - MINING AND MINERAL PRODUCTS

ZAMBIA - MANUFACTURING

Facts on File, 460 Park Avenue South, New York, New York 10016 (800) 443-8323; *The New Book of World Rankings.*

G.K. Hall and Company, 70 Lincoln Street, Boston, Massachusetts 02111 (617) 423-3990; *The World in Figures.*

Statistical Office of the United Nations, Publishing Service, New York, New York 10017 (800) 253-9646; *Survey of Economic and Social Conditions in Africa.*

Time Books, 201 East 50th Street, New York, New York 10022 (212) 751-2600; *The Economist Book of Vital World Statistics.*

United Nations Economic Commission for Africa, Africa Hall, P.O. Box 3001, Addis Ababa, Ethiopia (Telephone Number in U.S. (800) 253-9646); *African Statistical Yearbook*.

The World Bank, 1818 H Street, NW, Washington, D.C. 20433 (202) 477-1234; *World Tables*.

ZAMBIA - MARRIAGE RATES

Facts on File, 460 Park Avenue South, New York, New York 10016 (800) 443-8323; *The New Book of World Rankings*.

Statistical Office of the United Nations, Publishing Service, New York, New York 10017 (800) 253-9646; *Demographic Yearbook*.

ZAMBIA - MEAT PRODUCTION - See ZAMBIA - LIVESTOCK AND POULTRY

ZAMBIA - MERCHANT SHIPPING

G.K. Hall and Company, 70 Lincoln Street, Boston, Massachusetts 02111 (617) 423-3990; *The World in Figures*.

Time Books, 201 East 50th Street, New York, New York 10022 (212) 751-2600; *The Economist Book of Vital World Statistics*.

United Nations Economic Commission for Africa, Africa Hall, P.O. Box 3001, Addis Ababa, Ethiopia (Telephone Number in U.S. (800) 253-9646); *African Statistical Yearbook*.

U.S. Department of Transportation, Maritime Administration, 400 Seventh Street, SW, Washington, D.C. 20590 (202) 366-5807; *A Statistical Analysis of the World's Merchant Fleets*.

ZAMBIA - MILITARY

G.K. Hall and Company, 70 Lincoln Street, Boston, Massachusetts 02111 (617) 423-3990; *The World in Figures*.

The International Institute for Strategic Studies, 23 Tavistock Street, London WC2E 7NQ, England; *The Military Balance*.

U.S. Arms Control and Disarmament Agency, 320 Twenty-first Street, NW, Washington, D.C. 20451 (202) 647-8677; *World Military Expenditures and Arms Transfers*.

ZAMBIA - MILK PRODUCTION - See ZAMBIA - DAIRY PRODUCTS

ZAMBIA - MINING AND MINERAL PRODUCTS

Commodity Research Bureau, Incorporated, 75 Wall Street, New York, New York 10005 (212) 504-7754; *Commodity Year Book*.

Facts on File, 460 Park Avenue South, New York, New York 10016 (800) 443-8323; *The New Book of World Rankings*.

G.K. Hall and Company, 70 Lincoln Street, Boston, Massachusetts 02111 (617) 423-3990; *The World in Figures*.

International Lead and Zinc Study Group, Metro House, 58 St. James's Street, London SW1A 1LD England; *Lead and Zinc Statistics*.

International Monetary Fund, 700 Nineteenth Street, NW, Washington, D.C. 20431 (202) 623-7000; *International Financial Statistics*.

Statistical Office of the United Nations, Publishing Service, New York, New York 10017 (800) 253-9646; *Statistical Yearbook*.

United Nations Economic Commission for Africa, Africa Hall, P.O. Box 3001, Addis Ababa, Ethiopia (Telephone Number in U.S. (800) 253-9646); *African Statistical Yearbook*.

World Bureau of Metal Statistics, 27-A High Street, Ware Hert SG12 9BA, England; *World Metal Statistics*.

ZAMBIA - MOLYBDENUM AND MOLYBDENUM ORE PRODUCTION AND CONSUMPTION See ZAMBIA - MINING AND MINERAL PRODUCTS

ZAMBIA - MONEY EXCHANGE RATE

Euromonitor Publications Limited, 87-88 Turnmill Street, London EC1M 5QU, England; *International Marketing Data and Statistics*.

International Monetary Fund, 700 Nineteenth Street, NW, Washington, D.C. 20431 (202) 623-7000; *International Financial Statistics*.

Statistical Office of the United Nations, Publishing Service, New York, New York 10017 (800) 253-9646; *Statistical Yearbook*.

ZAMBIA - MONEY RESERVES

Euromonitor Publications Limited, 87-88 Turnmill Street, London EC1M 5QU, England; *International Marketing Data and Statistics*.

ZAMBIA - MONEY SUPPLY

African Development Bank, 01 BP 1387, Abidjan 01, Cote D'Ivoire; *Selected Statistics on Regional Member Countries*.

Euromonitor Publications Limited, 87-88 Turnmill Street, London EC1M 5QU, England; *International Marketing Data and Statistics*.

G.K. Hall and Company, 70 Lincoln Street, Boston, Massachusetts 02111 (617) 423-3990; *The World in Figures*.

International Monetary Fund, 700 Nineteenth Street, NW, Washington, D.C. 20431 (202) 623-7000; *International Financial Statistics*.

Statistical Office of the United Nations, Publishing Service, New York, New York 10017 (800) 253-9646; *Statistical Yearbook*.

The World Bank, 1818 H Street, NW, Washington, D.C. 20433 (202) 477-1234; *World Tables*.

ZAMBIA - MONUMENTS AND HISTORICAL SITES

United Nations Educational, Scientific and Cultural Organization (UNESCO), 7 Place de Fontenoy, F-75700 Paris, France (Telephone Number in U.S. (212) 963-5981); *Statistical Yearbook*.

ZAMBIA - MOTOR VEHICLE PRODUCTION

Statistical Office of the United Nations, Publishing Service, New York, New York 10017 (800) 253-9646; *Statistical Yearbook*.

ZAMBIA - MOTOR VEHICLE TAXES - See ZAMBIA - TAXATION

ZAMBIA - MOTOR VEHICLES IN USE

G.K. Hall and Company, 70 Lincoln Street, Boston, Massachusetts 02111 (617) 423-3990; *The World in Figures*.

International Road Federation, 525 School Street, SW, Washington, D.C. 20024 (202) 554-2106; *World Road Statistics*.

Statistical Office of the United Nations, Publishing Service, New York, New York 10017 (800) 253-9646; *Statistical Yearbook*, and *Survey of Economic and Social Conditions in Africa*.

Time Books, 201 East 50th Street, New York, New York 10022 (212) 751-2600; *The Economist Book of Vital World Statistics*.

ZAMBIA - MUSEUMS

Facts on File, 460 Park Avenue South, New York, New York 10016 (800) 443-8323; *The New Book of World Rankings*.

United Nations Educational, Scientific and Cultural Organization (UNESCO), 7 Place de Fontenoy, F-75700 Paris, France (Telephone Number in U.S. (212) 963-5981); *Statistical Yearbook*.

ZAMBIA - NATALITY - See ZAMBIA - BIRTH RATE

ZAMBIA - NATIONAL ACCOUNTS

African Development Bank, 01 BP 1387, Abidjan 01, Cote D'Ivoire; *Selected Statistics on Regional Member Countries*.

International Monetary Fund, 700 Nineteenth Street, NW, Washington, D.C. 20431 (202) 623-7000; *International Financial Statistics*.

Statistical Office of the United Nations, Publishing Service, New York, New York 10017 (800) 253-9646; *National Accounts Statistics*, and *Statistical Yearbook*.

United Nations Economic Commission for Africa, Africa Hall, P.O. Box 3001, Addis Ababa, Ethiopia (Telephone Number in U.S. (800) 253-9646); *African Statistical Yearbook*.

ZAMBIA - NATIONAL INCOME

Facts on File, 460 Park Avenue South, New York, New York 10016 (800) 443-8323; *The New Book of World Rankings*.

G.K. Hall and Company, 70 Lincoln Street, Boston, Massachusetts 02111 (617) 423-3990; *The World in Figures*.

Statistical Office of the United Nations, Publishing Service, New York, New York 10017 (800) 253-9646; *Statistical Yearbook*.

ZAMBIA - NATIONAL PRODUCT

Facts on File, 460 Park Avenue South, New York, New York 10016 (800) 443-8323; *The New Book of World Rankings*.

Statistical Office of the United Nations, Publishing Service, New York, New York 10017 (800) 253-9646; *Statistical Yearbook*.

ZAMBIA - NATURAL GAS PRODUCTION - See ZAMBIA - MINING AND MINERAL PRODUCTS

ZAMBIA - NEWSPAPER PRODUCTION - See ZAMBIA - FORESTRY AND FOREST PRODUCTS

ZAMBIA - NEWSPRINT - See ZAMBIA - FORESTRY AND FOREST PRODUCTS

ZAMBIA - NICKEL AND NICKEL ORE PRODUCTION AND CONSUMPTION - See ZAMBIA - MINING AND MINERAL PRODUCTS

ZAMBIA - OCCUPATIONS - See ZAMBIA - LABOR FORCE

ZAMBIA - PAPER - See ZAMBIA - FORESTRY AND FOREST PRODUCTS

ZAMBIA - PATENTS

Statistical Office of the United Nations, Publishing Service, New York, New York 10017 (800) 253-9646; *Statistical Yearbook*.

World Intellectual Property Organization, 34 Chemin des Colombettes, CH-1211 Geneva 20. Switzerland; *Industrial Property Statistics*.

ZAMBIA - PEANUT PRODUCTION - See ZAMBIA - CROPS

ZAMBIA - PERIODICALS

United Nations Educational, Scientific and Cultural Organization (UNESCO), 7 Place de Fontenoy, F-75700 Paris, France (Telephone Number in U.S. (212) 963-5981); *Statistical Yearbook*.

ZAMBIA - PESTICIDE USE

Food and Agricultural Organization of the United Nations (FAO) Via delle Terme di Caracalla, 00100 Rome, Italy (Telephone Number in U.S. (202) 653-2400); *The State of Food and Agriculture*.

ZAMBIA - PETROLEUM INDUSTRY

Facts on File, 460 Park Avenue South, New York, New York 10016 (800) 443-8323; *The New Book of World Rankings*.

Food and Agricultural Organization of the United Nations (FAO) Via delle Terme di Caracalla, 00100 Rome, Italy (Telephone Number in U.S. (202) 653-2400); *The State of Food and Agriculture*.

G.K. Hall and Company, 70 Lincoln Street, Boston, Massachusetts 02111 (617) 423-3990; *The World in Figures*.

Statistical Office of the United Nations, Publishing Service, New York, New York 10017 (800) 253-9646; *Statistical Yearbook*.

ZAMBIA - PIGS - See ZAMBIA - LIVESTOCK AND POULTRY

ZAMBIA - POPULATION

African Development Bank, 01 BP 1387, Abidjan 01, Cote D'Ivoire; *Selected Statistics on Regional Member Countries*.

The Economist Intelligence Unit, 111 West 57th Street, New York, New York 10019 (800) 938-4685; *The World Market Atlas*.

Euromonitor Publications Limited, 87-88 Turnmill Street, London EC1M 5QU, England; *International Marketing Data and Statistics*.

Facts on File, 460 Park Avenue South, New York, New York 10016 (800) 443-8323; *The New Book of World Rankings*.

G.K. Hall and Company, 70 Lincoln Street, Boston, Massachusetts 02111 (617) 423-3990; *The World in Figures*.

International Labour Office, I.L.O. Publications, CH-1211, Geneva 22, Switzerland; *Yearbook of Labour Statistics*.

Statistical Office of the United Nations, Publishing Service, New York, New York 10017 (800) 253-9646; *Demographic Yearbook*, *Statistical Yearbook*, and *Survey of Economic and Social Conditions in Africa*.

Time Books, 201 East 50th Street, New York, New York 10022 (212) 751-2600; *The Economist Book of Vital World Statistics*.

United Nations Educational, Scientific and Cultural Organization (UNESCO), 7 Place de Fontenoy, F-75700 Paris, France (Telephone Number in U.S. (212) 963-5981); *Statistical Yearbook*.

U.S. Arms Control and Disarmament Agency, 320 Twenty-first Street, NW, Washington, D.C. 20451 (202) 647-8677; *World Military Expenditures and Arms Transfers*.

World Health Organization, Office of Publications, Avenue Appia, CH-1211 Geneva 27, Switzerland (Telephone Number in U.S. (518) 436-9686); *World Health Statistics Annual*.

ZAMBIA - POST OFFICES

Facts on File, 460 Park Avenue South, New York, New York 10016 (800) 443-8323; *The New Book of World Rankings*.

ZAMBIA - POTATO PRODUCTION - See ZAMBIA - CROPS

ZAMBIA - POWER PRODUCTION INDUSTRY

Statistical Office of the United Nations, Publishing Service, New York, New York 10017 (800) 253-9646; *Statistical Yearbook*.

ZAMBIA - PRICES

Facts on File, 460 Park Avenue South, New York, New York 10016 (800) 443-8323; *The New Book of World Rankings*.

Food and Agricultural Organization of the United Nations (FAO) Via delle Terme di Caracalla, 00100 Rome, Italy (Telephone Number in U.S. (202) 653-2400); *The State of Food and Agriculture*.

G.K. Hall and Company, 70 Lincoln Street, Boston, Massachusetts 02111 (617) 423-3990; *The World in Figures*.

International Labour Office, I.L.O. Publications, CH-1211, Geneva 22, Switzerland; *Yearbook of Labour Statistics*.

International Lead and Zinc Study Group, Metro House, 58 St. James's Street, London SW1A 1LD England; *Lead and Zinc Statistics*.

International Monetary Fund, 700 Nineteenth Street, NW, Washington, D.C. 20431 (202) 623-7000; *International Financial Statistics*.

United Nations Economic Commission for Africa, Africa Hall, P.O. Box 3001, Addis Ababa, Ethiopia (Telephone Number in U.S. (800) 253-9646); *African Statistical Yearbook*.

World Bureau of Metal Statistics, 27-A High Street, Ware Hert SG12 9BA, England; *World Metal Statistics*.

ZAMBIA - PRINTING AND WRITING PAPER - See ZAMBIA - FORESTRY AND FOREST PRODUCTS

ZAMBIA - PRODUCTION

Facts on File, 460 Park Avenue South, New York, New York 10016 (800) 443-8323; *The New Book of World Rankings*.

G.K. Hall and Company, 70 Lincoln Street, Boston, Massachusetts 02111 (617) 423-3990; *The World in Figures*.

International Lead and Zinc Study Group, Metro House, 58 St. James's Street, London SW1A 1LD England; *Lead and Zinc Statistics*.

ZAMBIA - PRODUCTIVITY

Euromonitor Publications Limited, 87-88 Turnmill Street, London EC1M 5QU, England; *International Marketing Data and Statistics*.

ZAMBIA - PROPERTY TAXES - See ZAMBIA - TAXATION

ZAMBIA - PUBLIC FINANCE

Facts on File, 460 Park Avenue South, New York, New York 10016 (800) 443-8323; *The New Book of World Rankings*.

ZAMBIA - RADIO BROADCASTING - See ZAMBIA - BROADCASTING

ZAMBIA - RADIO RECEIVER PRODUCTION

Statistical Office of the United Nations, Publishing Service, New York, New York 10017 (800) 253-9646; *Statistical Yearbook*.

ZAMBIA - RAILWAYS

G.K. Hall and Company, 70 Lincoln Street, Boston, Massachusetts 02111 (617) 423-3990; *The World in Figures*.

Statistical Office of the United Nations, Publishing Service, New York, New York 10017 (800) 253-9646; *Survey of Economic and Social Conditions in Africa*.

United Nations Economic Commission for Africa, Africa Hall, P.O. Box 3001, Addis Ababa, Ethiopia (Telephone Number in U.S. (800) 253-9646); *African Statistical Yearbook*.

ZAMBIA - RELIGION

Facts on File, 460 Park Avenue South, New York, New York 10016 (800) 443-8323; *The New Book of World Rankings*.

ZAMBIA - RENT PRICES

International Labour Office, I.L.O. Publications, CH-1211, Geneva 22, Switzerland; *Yearbook of Labour Statistics*.

ZAMBIA - RETAIL TRADE

G.K. Hall and Company, 70 Lincoln Street, Boston, Massachusetts 02111 (617) 423-3990; *The World in Figures*.

Statistical Office of the United Nations, Publishing Service, New York, New York 10017 (800) 253-9646; *Statistical Yearbook*.

ZAMBIA - RICE PRODUCTION - See ZAMBIA - CROPS

ZAMBIA - ROUNDWOOD PRODUCTION - See ZAMBIA - FORESTRY AND FOREST PRODUCTS

ZAMBIA - RUBBER PRODUCTION AND CONSUMPTION

Facts on File, 460 Park Avenue South, New York, New York 10016 (800) 443-8323; *The New Book of World Rankings*.

ZAMBIA - SAWNWOOD PRODUCTION - See ZAMBIA - FORESTRY AND FOREST PRODUCTS

ZAMBIA - SCIENCE AND TECHNOLOGY - EXPENDITURE
FOR RESEARCH

Statistical Office of the United Nations, Publishing Service, New
York, New York 10017 (800) 253-9646; *Statistical Yearbook.*

ZAMBIA - SCIENTISTS AND TECHNICIANS

Statistical Office of the United Nations, Publishing Service, New
York, New York 10017 (800) 253-9646; *Statistical Yearbook.*

United Nations Educational, Scientific and Cultural Organization
(UNESCO), 7 Place de Fontenoy, F-75700 Paris, France (Telephone
Number in U.S. (212) 963-5981); *Statistical Yearbook.*

ZAMBIA - SENIOR CITIZENS

Facts on File, 460 Park Avenue South, New York, New York 10016
(800) 443-8323; *The New Book of World Rankings.*

ZAMBIA - SHEEP - See ZAMBIA - LIVESTOCK AND POULTRY

ZAMBIA - SILVER PRODUCTION AND CONSUMPTION - See ZAMBIA
MINING AND MINERAL PRODUCTS

ZAMBIA - SOCIAL DATA

African Development Bank, 01 BP 1387, Abidjan 01, Cote D'Ivoire;
Selected Statistics on Regional Member Countries.

Facts on File, 460 Park Avenue South, New York, New York 10016
(800) 443-8323; *The New Book of World Rankings.*

G.K. Hall and Company, 70 Lincoln Street, Boston, Massachusetts
02111 (617) 423-3990; *The World in Figures.*

ZAMBIA - SOCIAL SECURITY

International Monetary Fund, 700 Nineteenth Street, NW,
Washington, D.C. 20431 (202) 623-7000; *Government Finance
Statistics Yearbook.*

ZAMBIA - SOYBEAN PRODUCTION - See ZAMBIA - CROPS

ZAMBIA - STAMP TAXES AND DUTIES - See ZAMBIA - TAXATION

ZAMBIA - STATE BUDGET REVENUE AND EXPENDITURES

Euromonitor Publications Limited, 87-88 Turnmill Street, London
EC1M 5QU, England; *International Marketing Data and Statistics.*

ZAMBIA - STEEL - See ZAMBIA - MINING AND MINERAL PRODUCTS

ZAMBIA - STOCKS - COMMODITY - MARKET PRICE -
INDEX

Food and Agricultural Organization of the United Nations (FAO) Via
delle Terme di Caracalla, 00100 Rome, Italy (Telephone Number in
U.S. (202) 653-2400); *The State of Food and Agriculture.*

International Lead and Zinc Study Group, Metro House, 58 St.
James's Street, London SW1A 1LD England; *Lead and Zinc
Statistics.*

World Bureau of Metal Statistics, 27-A High Street, Ware Hert SG12
9BA, England; *World Metal Statistics.*

ZAMBIA - SUGAR PRODUCTION AND CONSUMPTION - See
ZAMBIA - CROPS

ZAMBIA - SULPHURIC ACID PRODUCTION - See ZAMBIA - MINING
AND MINERAL PRODUCTS

ZAMBIA - TAXATION

G.K. Hall and Company, 70 Lincoln Street, Boston, Massachusetts
02111 (617) 423-3990; *The World in Figures.*

International Monetary Fund, 700 Nineteenth Street, NW,
Washington, D.C. 20431 (202) 623-7000; *Government Finance
Statistics Yearbook.*

International Road Federation, 525 School Street, SW, Washington,
D.C. 20024 (202) 554-2106; *World Road Statistics.*

The World Bank, 1818 H Street, NW, Washington, D.C. 20433 (202)
477-1234; *World Tables.*

ZAMBIA - TELEGRAPH SERVICE

Statistical Office of the United Nations, Publishing Service, New
York, New York 10017 (800) 253-9646; *Statistical Yearbook.*

ZAMBIA - TELEPHONES IN USE

American Telephone and Telegraph Communications, Customer
Information Center, Post Office Box 19901, Indianapolis, Indiana
46219; *The World's Telephones.*

G.K. Hall and Company, 70 Lincoln Street, Boston, Massachusetts
02111 (617) 423-3990; *The World in Figures.*

Statistical Office of the United Nations, Publishing Service, New
York, New York 10017 (800) 253-9646; *Statistical Yearbook.*

ZAMBIA - TELEVISION BROADCASTING See ZAMBIA -
BROADCASTING

ZAMBIA - TEXTILE INDUSTRY

G.K. Hall and Company, 70 Lincoln Street, Boston, Massachusetts
02111 (617) 423-3990; *The World in Figures.*

ZAMBIA - TIN - See ZAMBIA - MINING AND MINERAL PRODUCTS

ZAMBIA - TOBACCO PRODUCTION

Facts on File, 460 Park Avenue South, New York, New York 10016
(800) 443-8323; *The New Book of World Rankings.*

Statistical Office of the United Nations, Publishing Service, New
York, New York 10017 (800) 253-9646; *Statistical Yearbook.*

ZAMBIA - TOURISM

Facts on File, 460 Park Avenue South, New York, New York 10016
(800) 443-8323; *The New Book of World Rankings.*

G.K. Hall and Company, 70 Lincoln Street, Boston, Massachusetts
02111 (617) 423-3990; *The World in Figures.*

Statistical Office of the United Nations, Publishing Service, New
York, New York 10017 (800) 253-9646; *Statistical Yearbook.*

Time Books, 201 East 50th Street, New York, New York 10022 (212)
751-2600; *The Economist Book of Vital World Statistics.*

United Nations Economic Commission for Africa, Africa Hall, P.O.
Box 3001, Addis Ababa, Ethiopia (Telephone Number in U.S. (800)

253-9646); *African Statistical Yearbook.*

World Tourism Organization, Calle Capitan Haya 42, E-28020 Madrid, Spain; *Yearbook of Tourism Statistics.*

ZAMBIA - TRACTORS IN USE

Statistical Office of the United Nations, Publishing Service, New York, New York 10017 (800) 253-9646; *Statistical Yearbook.*

ZAMBIA - TRADE - See ZAMBIA - FOREIGN TRADE

ZAMBIA - TRADEMARKS AND SERVICE MARKS

Statistical Office of the United Nations, Publishing Service, New York, New York 10017 (800) 253-9646; *Statistical Yearbook.*

World Intellectual Property Organization, 34 Chemin des Colombettes, CH-1211 Geneva 20. Switzerland; *Industrial Property Statistics.*

ZAMBIA - TRANSPORTATION AND COMMUNICATIONS

Facts on File, 460 Park Avenue South, New York, New York 10016 (800) 443-8323; *The New Book of World Rankings.*

G.K. Hall and Company, 70 Lincoln Street, Boston, Massachusetts 02111 (617) 423-3990; *The World in Figures.*

United Nations Economic Commission for Africa, Africa Hall, P.O. Box 3001, Addis Ababa, Ethiopia (Telephone Number in U.S. (800) 253-9646); *African Statistical Yearbook.*

ZAMBIA - UNEMPLOYMENT

Euromonitor Publications Limited, 87-88 Turnmill Street, London EC1M 5QU, England; *International Marketing Data and Statistics.*

International Labour Office, I.L.O. Publications, CH-1211, Geneva 22, Switzerland; *Yearbook of Labour Statistics.*

Statistical Office of the United Nations, Publishing Service, New York, New York 10017 (800) 253-9646; *Statistical Yearbook.*

ZAMBIA - VITAL STATISTICS

Euromonitor Publications Limited, 87-88 Turnmill Street, London EC1M 5QU, England; *International Marketing Data and Statistics.*

G.K. Hall and Company, 70 Lincoln Street, Boston, Massachusetts 02111 (617) 423-3990; *The World in Figures.*

Statistical Office of the United Nations, Publishing Service, New York, New York 10017 (800) 253-9646; *Statistical Yearbook.*

World Health Organization, Office of Publications, Avenue Appia, CH-1211 Geneva 27, Switzerland (Telephone Number in U.S. (518) 436-9686); *World Health Statistics Annual.*

ZAMBIA - WAGES

G.K. Hall and Company, 70 Lincoln Street, Boston, Massachusetts 02111 (617) 423-3990; *The World in Figures.*

International Labour Office, I.L.O. Publications, CH-1211, Geneva 22, Switzerland; *Yearbook of Labour Statistics.*

Statistical Office of the United Nations, Publishing Service, New York, New York 10017 (800) 253-9646; *Statistical Yearbook.*

ZAMBIA - WEATHER

Facts on File, 460 Park Avenue South, New York, New York 10016 (800) 443-8323; *The New Book of World Rankings.*

G.K. Hall and Company, 70 Lincoln Street, Boston, Massachusetts 02111 (617) 423-3990; *The World in Figures.*

ZAMBIA - WELFARE

International Monetary Fund, 700 Nineteenth Street, NW, Washington, D.C. 20431 (202) 623-7000; *Government Finance Statistics Yearbook.*

ZAMBIA - WHEAT PRODUCTION AND PRICES - See ZAMBIA - CROPS

ZAMBIA - WHOLESALE PRICES

International Monetary Fund, 700 Nineteenth Street, NW, Washington, D.C. 20431 (202) 623-7000; *International Financial Statistics.*

Statistical Office of the United Nations, Publishing Service, New York, New York 10017 (800) 253-9646; *Statistical Yearbook.*

ZAMBIA - WHOLESALE TRADE

Statistical Office of the United Nations, Publishing Service, New York, New York 10017 (800) 253-9646; *Statistical Yearbook.*

ZAMBIA - WINE PRODUCTION

Facts on File, 460 Park Avenue South, New York, New York 10016 (800) 443-8323; *The New Book of World Rankings.*

ZAMBIA - WOOL PRODUCTION

Facts on File, 460 Park Avenue South, New York, New York 10016 (800) 443-8323; *The New Book of World Rankings.*

ZAMBIA - ZINC AND ZINC ORE PRODUCTION AND CONSUMPTION - See ZAMBIA - MINING AND MINERAL PRODUCTS

ZAMBIA - ZOOS AND BOTANICAL GARDENS

United Nations Educational, Scientific and Cultural Organization (UNESCO), 7 Place de Fontenoy, F-75700 Paris, France (Telephone Number in U.S. (212) 963-5981); *Statistical Yearbook.*

Zimbabwe - National Statistical Office

Central Statistical Office, Kaguvi Building, 4th Street/Central Avenue, P.O. Box 8063, Causeway, Harare, Zimbabwe.

Zimbabwe - Primary Statistics Sources

Central Statistical Office, Post Office Box 8063, Causeway, Harare, Zimbabwe; *Statistical Yearbook of Zimbabwe, Annual Economic Review of Zimbabwe,* and *Monthly Digest of Statistics.*

ZIMBABWE - AGRICULTURE

Euromonitor Publications Limited, 87-88 Turnmill Street, London EC1M 5QU, England; *Third World Economic Handbook.*

Facts on File, 460 Park Avenue South, New York, New York 10016 (800) 443-8323; *The New Book of World Rankings.*

Food and Agricultural Organization of the United Nations (FAO) Via delle Terme di Caracalla, 00100 Rome, Italy (Telephone Number in U.S. (202) 653-2400); *Production Yearbook*, and *The State of Food and Agriculture*.

G.K. Hall and Company, 70 Lincoln Street, Boston, Massachusetts 02111 (617) 423-3990; *The World in Figures*.

Statistical Office of the United Nations, Publishing Service, New York, New York 10017 (800) 253-9646; *Statistical Yearbook*, and *Survey of Economic and Social Conditions in Africa*, and *Trade Yearbook*.

Time Books, 201 East 50th Street, New York, New York 10022 (212) 751-2600; *The Economist Book of Vital World Statistics*.

United Nations Economic Commission for Africa, Africa Hall, P.O. Box 3001, Addis Ababa, Ethiopia (Telephone Number in U.S. (800) 253-9646); *African Statistical Yearbook*.

The World Bank, 1818 H Street, NW, Washington, D.C. 20433 (202) 477-1234; *World Tables*.

ZIMBABWE - AIRLINE SERVICE

Facts on File, 460 Park Avenue South, New York, New York 10016 (800) 443-8323; *The New Book of World Rankings*.

G.K. Hall and Company, 70 Lincoln Street, Boston, Massachusetts 02111 (617) 423-3990; *The World in Figures*.

International Civil Aviation Organization, 1000 Sherbrooke Street, West, Montreal, Quebec, Canada H3A 2R2 (514) 285-8219; *Civil Aviation Statistics of the World*.

Time Books, 201 East 50th Street, New York, New York 10022 (212) 751-2600; *The Economist Book of Vital World Statistics*.

United Nations Economic Commission for Africa, Africa Hall, P.O. Box 3001, Addis Ababa, Ethiopia (Telephone Number in U.S. (800) 253-9646); *African Statistical Yearbook*.

ZIMBABWE - ALUMINUM PRODUCTION AND CONSUMPTION - See ZIMBABWE - MINING AND MINERAL PRODUCTS

ZIMBABWE - ANIMAL HEALTH

Food and Agricultural Organization of the United Nations (FAO), Via delle Terme di Caracalla, 00100 Rome, Italy (Telephone Number in U.S. (202) 653-2400); *Animal Health Yearbook*.

ZIMBABWE - ANTIMONY AND ANTIMONY ORE PRODUCTION AND CONSUMPTION - See ZIMBABWE - MINING AND MINERAL PRODUCTS

ZIMBABWE - AREA AND DENSITY OF POPULATION

African Development Bank, 01 BP 1387, Abidjan 01, Cote D'Ivoire; *Selected Statistics on Regional Member Countries*.

Facts on File, 460 Park Avenue South, New York, New York 10016 (800) 443-8323; *The New Book of World Rankings*.

Food and Agricultural Organization of the United Nations (FAO) Via delle Terme di Caracalla, 00100 Rome, Italy (Telephone Number in U.S. (202) 653-2400); *The State of Food and Agriculture*.

G.K. Hall and Company, 70 Lincoln Street, Boston, Massachusetts 02111 (617) 423-3990; *The World in Figures*.

Statistical Office of the United Nations, Publishing Service, New York, New York 10017 (800) 253-9646; *Statistical Yearbook*, and *Survey of Economic and Social Conditions in Africa*.

Time Books, 201 East 50th Street, New York, New York 10022 (212) 751-2600; *The Economist Book of Vital World Statistics*.

United Nations Educational, Scientific and Cultural Organization (UNESCO), 7 Place de Fontenoy, F-75700 Paris, France (Telephone Number in U.S. (212) 963-5981); *Statistical Yearbook*.

ZIMBABWE - ARMS EXPORTS AND IMPORTS

U.S. Arms Control and Disarmament Agency, 320 Twenty-first Street, NW, Washington, D.C. 20451 (202) 647-8677; *World Military Expenditures and Arms Transfers*.

ZIMBABWE - ARSENIC PRODUCTION AND CONSUMPTION - See ZIMBABWE - MINING AND MINERAL PRODUCTS

ZIMBABWE - BALANCE OF PAYMENTS

African Development Bank, 01 BP 1387, Abidjan 01, Cote D'Ivoire; *Selected Statistics on Regional Member Countries*.

The Economist Intelligence Unit, 111 West 57th Street, New York, New York 10019 (800) 938-4685; *The World Market Atlas*.

Euromonitor Publications Limited, 87-88 Turnmill Street, London EC1M 5QU, England; *Third World Economic Handbook*.

G.K. Hall and Company, 70 Lincoln Street, Boston, Massachusetts 02111 (617) 423-3990; *The World in Figures*.

International Monetary Fund, 700 Nineteenth Street, NW, Washington, D.C. 20431 (202) 623-7000; *Balance of Payments Yearbook*.

Time Books, 201 East 50th Street, New York, New York 10022 (212) 751-2600; *The Economist Book of Vital World Statistics*.

United Nations Economic Commission for Africa, Africa Hall, P.O. Box 3001, Addis Ababa, Ethiopia (Telephone Number in U.S. (800) 253-9646); *African Statistical Yearbook*.

The World Bank, 1818 H Street, NW, Washington, D.C. 20433 (202) 477-1234; *World Tables*.

ZIMBABWE - BANKING

Facts on File, 460 Park Avenue South, New York, New York 10016 (800) 443-8323; *The New Book of World Rankings*.

G.K. Hall and Company, 70 Lincoln Street, Boston, Massachusetts 02111 (617) 423-3990; *The World in Figures*.

United Nations Economic Commission for Africa, Africa Hall, P.O. Box 3001, Addis Ababa, Ethiopia (Telephone Number in U.S. (800) 253-9646); *African Statistical Yearbook*.

ZIMBABWE - BARLEY PRODUCTION - See ZIMBABWE - CROPS

ZIMBABWE - BAUXITE PRODUCTION AND CONSUMPTION - See ZIMBABWE - MINING AND MINERAL PRODUCTS

ZIMBABWE - BEER PRODUCTION

Facts on File, 460 Park Avenue South, New York, New York 10016 (800) 443-8323; *The New Book of World Rankings*.

Statistical Office of the United Nations, Publishing Service, New York, New York 10017 (800) 253-9646; *Statistical Yearbook.*

ZIMBABWE - BIRTH RATES

Euromonitor Publications Limited, 87-88 Turnmill Street, London EC1M 5QU, England; *Third World Economic Handbook.*

Facts on File, 460 Park Avenue South, New York, New York 10016 (800) 443-8323; *The New Book of World Rankings.*

Statistical Office of the United Nations, Publishing Service, New York, New York 10017 (800) 253-9646; *Demographic Yearbook, Statistical Yearbook,* and *Survey of Economic and Social Conditions in Africa.*

Time Books, 201 East 50th Street, New York, New York 10022 (212) 751-2600; *The Economist Book of Vital World Statistics.*

The World Bank, 1818 H Street, NW, Washington, D.C. 20433 (202) 477-1234; *World Tables.*

ZIMBABWE - BONDS

G.K. Hall and Company, 70 Lincoln Street, Boston, Massachusetts 02111 (617) 423-3990; *The World in Figures.*

ZIMBABWE - BOOK PRODUCTION

G.K. Hall and Company, 70 Lincoln Street, Boston, Massachusetts 02111 (617) 423-3990; *The World in Figures.*

ZIMBABWE - BROADCASTING

Billboard Limited, P.O. Box 9027, 1006 AA Amsterdam, The Netherlands (Telephone Number in U.S. (212) 764-7300); *World Radio TV Handbook.*

Facts on File, 460 Park Avenue South, New York, New York 10016 (800) 443-8323; *The New Book of World Rankings.*

G.K. Hall and Company, 70 Lincoln Street, Boston, Massachusetts 02111 (617) 423-3990; *The World in Figures.*

Time Books, 201 East 50th Street, New York, New York 10022 (212) 751-2600; *The Economist Book of Vital World Statistics.*

ZIMBABWE - BUSINESS

G.K. Hall and Company, 70 Lincoln Street, Boston, Massachusetts 02111 (617) 423-3990; *The World in Figures.*

ZIMBABWE - BUTTER PRODUCTION - See ZIMBABWE - DAIRY PRODUCTS

ZIMBABWE - CALORIE SUPPLY

African Development Bank, 01 BP 1387, Abidjan 01, Cote D'Ivoire; *Selected Statistics on Regional Member Countries.*

Food and Agricultural Organization of the United Nations (FAO) Via delle Terme di Caracalla, 00100 Rome, Italy (Telephone Number in U.S. (202) 653-2400); *The State of Food and Agriculture.*

ZIMBABWE - CATTLE - See ZIMBABWE - LIVESTOCK AND POULTRY

ZIMBABWE - CEMENT PRODUCTION - See ZIMBABWE - MINING AND MINERAL PRODUCTS

ZIMBABWE - CHEESE PRODUCTION AND CONSUMPTION - See ZIMBABWE - DAIRY PRODUCTS

ZIMBABWE - CHEMICAL (ORGANIC) PRODUCTION - See ZIMBABWE - MINING AND MINERAL PRODUCTS

ZIMBABWE - CHICKENS - See ZIMBABWE - LIVESTOCK AND POULTRY

ZIMBABWE - CHROMITE PRODUCTION AND CONSUMPTION - See ZIMBABWE - MINING AND MINERAL PRODUCTS

ZIMBABWE - CHROMIUM ORE PRODUCTION AND CONSUMPTION - See ZIMBABWE - MINING AND MINERAL PRODUCTS

ZIMBABWE - CIGARETTE PRODUCTION - See ZIMBABWE - TOBACCO PRODUCTION

ZIMBABWE - CLASS STRUCTURE

G.K. Hall and Company, 70 Lincoln Street, Boston, Massachusetts 02111 (617) 423-3990; *The World in Figures.*

ZIMBABWE - CLIMATE

Facts on File, 460 Park Avenue South, New York, New York 10016 (800) 443-8323; *The New Book of World Rankings.*

G.K. Hall and Company, 70 Lincoln Street, Boston, Massachusetts 02111 (617) 423-3990; *The World in Figures.*

ZIMBABWE - CLOTHING - EXPORTS AND IMPORTS

Euromonitor Publications Limited, 87-88 Turnmill Street, London EC1M 5QU, England; *Third World Economic Handbook.*

ZIMBABWE - COAL PRODUCTION - See ZIMBABWE - MINING AND MINERAL PRODUCTS

ZIMBABWE - COFFEE PRODUCTION AND CONSUMPTION - See ZIMBABWE - CROPS

ZIMBABWE - COKE PRODUCTION AND CONSUMPTION - See ZIMBABWE - MINING AND MINERAL PRODUCTS

ZIMBABWE - COMMUNICATIONS

Euromonitor Publications Limited, 87-88 Turnmill Street, London EC1M 5QU, England; *Third World Economic Handbook.*

G.K. Hall and Company, 70 Lincoln Street, Boston, Massachusetts 02111 (617) 423-3990; *The World in Figures.*

United Nations Economic Commission for Africa, Africa Hall, P.O. Box 3001, Addis Ababa, Ethiopia (Telephone Number in U.S. (800) 253-9646); *African Statistical Yearbook.*

ZIMBABWE - CONSTRUCTION INDUSTRY

Facts on File, 460 Park Avenue South, New York, New York 10016 (800) 443-8323; *The New Book of World Rankings.*

Statistical Office of the United Nations, Publishing Service, New York, New York 10017 (800) 253-9646; *Statistical Yearbook.*

United Nations Economic Commission for Africa, Africa Hall, P.O. Box 3001, Addis Ababa, Ethiopia (Telephone Number in U.S. (800) 253-9646); *African Statistical Yearbook.*

ZIMBABWE - CONSUMER PRICE INDEX

African Development Bank, 01 BP 1387, Abidjan 01, Cote D'Ivoire; *Selected Statistics on Regional Member Countries*.

G.K. Hall and Company, 70 Lincoln Street, Boston, Massachusetts 02111 (617) 423-3990; *The World in Figures*.

Statistical Office of the United Nations, Publishing Service, New York, New York 10017 (800) 253-9646; *Statistical Yearbook*, and *Survey of Economic and Social Conditions in Africa*.

United Nations Economic Commission for Africa, Africa Hall, P.O. Box 3001, Addis Ababa, Ethiopia (Telephone Number in U.S. (800) 253-9646); *African Statistical Yearbook*.

ZIMBABWE - CONSUMER PRICES

International Labour Office, I.L.O. Publications, CH-1211, Geneva 22, Switzerland; *Yearbook of Labour Statistics*.

Time Books, 201 East 50th Street, New York, New York 10022 (212) 751-2600; *The Economist Book of Vital World Statistics*.

ZIMBABWE - CONSUMPTION

African Development Bank, 01 BP 1387, Abidjan 01, Cote D'Ivoire; *Selected Statistics on Regional Member Countries*.

G.K. Hall and Company, 70 Lincoln Street, Boston, Massachusetts 02111 (617) 423-3990; *The World in Figures*.

Statistical Office of the United Nations, Publishing Service, New York, New York 10017 (800) 253-9646; *Survey of Economic and Social Conditions in Africa*.

ZIMBABWE - COPPER AND COPPER ORE PRODUCTION AND CONSUMPTION - See ZIMBABWE - MINING AND MINERAL PRODUCTS

ZIMBABWE - CORN PRODUCTION - See ZIMBABWE - CROPS

ZIMBABWE - CORPORATE TAXES - See ZIMBABWE - TAXATION

ZIMBABWE - COTTON - See ZIMBABWE - CROPS

ZIMBABWE - CRIME

Yale University Press, Yale Station, New Haven, Connecticut 06520 (203) 432-0940; *Violence and Crime in Cross-National Perspective*.

ZIMBABWE - CROPS

Commodity Research Bureau, Incorporated, 75 Wall Street, New York, New York 10005 (212) 504-7754; *Commodity Year Book*.

Facts on File, 460 Park Avenue South, New York, New York 10016 (800) 443-8323; *The New Book of World Rankings*.

Food and Agricultural Organization of the United Nations (FAO) Via delle Terme di Caracalla, 00100 Rome, Italy (Telephone Number in U.S. (202) 653-2400); *The State of Food and Agriculture*.

G.K. Hall and Company, 70 Lincoln Street, Boston, Massachusetts 02111 (617) 423-3990; *The World in Figures*.

Statistical Office of the United Nations, Publishing Service, New York, New York 10017 (800) 253-9646; *Statistical Yearbook*.

United Nations Economic Commission for Africa, Africa Hall, P.O. Box 3001, Addis Ababa, Ethiopia (Telephone Number in U.S. (800) 253-9646); *African Statistical Yearbook*.

ZIMBABWE - CUSTOMS DUTIES

G.K. Hall and Company, 70 Lincoln Street, Boston, Massachusetts 02111 (617) 423-3990; *The World in Figures*.

ZIMBABWE - DAIRY PRODUCTS

Facts on File, 460 Park Avenue South, New York, New York 10016 (800) 443-8323; *The New Book of World Rankings*.

Food and Agricultural Organization of the United Nations (FAO) Via delle Terme di Caracalla, 00100 Rome, Italy (Telephone Number in U.S. (202) 653-2400); *The State of Food and Agriculture*.

Statistical Office of the United Nations, Publishing Service, New York, New York 10017 (800) 253-9646; *Statistical Yearbook*.

ZIMBABWE - DEATH RATES

Euromonitor Publications Limited, 87-88 Turnmill Street, London EC1M 5QU, England; *Third World Economic Handbook*.

G.K. Hall and Company, 70 Lincoln Street, Boston, Massachusetts 02111 (617) 423-3990; *The World in Figures*.

Statistical Office of the United Nations, Publishing Service, New York, New York 10017 (800) 253-9646; *Statistical Yearbook*, and *Survey of Economic and Social Conditions in Africa*.

Time Books, 201 East 50th Street, New York, New York 10022 (212) 751-2600; *The Economist Book of Vital World Statistics*.

ZIMBABWE - DEFENSE EXPENDITURES

G.K. Hall and Company, 70 Lincoln Street, Boston, Massachusetts 02111 (617) 423-3990; *The World in Figures*.

U.S. Arms Control and Disarmament Agency, 320 Twenty-first Street, NW, Washington, D.C. 20451 (202) 647-8677; *World Military Expenditures and Arms Transfers*.

ZIMBABWE - DEMOGRAPHY

The Economist Intelligence Unit, 111 West 57th Street, New York, New York 10019 (800) 938-4685; *The World Market Atlas*.

Facts on File, 460 Park Avenue South, New York, New York 10016 (800) 443-8323; *The New Book of World Rankings*.

G.K. Hall and Company, 70 Lincoln Street, Boston, Massachusetts 02111 (617) 423-3990; *The World in Figures*.

Statistical Office of the United Nations, Publishing Service, New York, New York 10017 (800) 253-9646; *Survey of Economic and Social Conditions in Africa*.

ZIMBABWE - DEVELOPMENT ASSISTANCE

G.K. Hall and Company, 70 Lincoln Street, Boston, Massachusetts 02111 (617) 423-3990; *The World in Figures*.

Statistical Office of the United Nations, Publishing Service, New York, New York 10017 (800) 253-9646; *Statistical Yearbook*.

ZIMBABWE - DIAMOND PRODUCTION - See ZIMBABWE - MINING AND MINERAL PRODUCTS

ZIMBABWE - DISEASE

G.K. Hall and Company, 70 Lincoln Street, Boston, Massachusetts 02111 (617) 423-3990; *The World in Figures.*

ZIMBABWE - DIVORCE RATES

Facts on File, 460 Park Avenue South, New York, New York 10016 (800) 443-8323; *The New Book of World Rankings.*

Statistical Office of the United Nations, Publishing Service, New York, New York 10017 (800) 253-9646; *Demographic Yearbook.*

ZIMBABWE - DOMESTIC PRODUCT

G.K. Hall and Company, 70 Lincoln Street, Boston, Massachusetts 02111 (617) 423-3990; *The World in Figures.*

ZIMBABWE - ECONOMY

African Development Bank, 01 BP 1387, Abidjan 01, Cote D'Ivoire; *Selected Statistics on Regional Member Countries.*

Euromonitor Publications Limited, 87-88 Turnmill Street, London EC1M 5QU, England; *Third World Economic Handbook.*

Facts on File, 460 Park Avenue South, New York, New York 10016 (800) 443-8323; *The New Book of World Rankings.*

G.K. Hall and Company, 70 Lincoln Street, Boston, Massachusetts 02111 (617) 423-3990; *The World in Figures.*

ZIMBABWE - EDUCATION

Facts on File, 460 Park Avenue South, New York, New York 10016 (800) 443-8323; *The New Book of World Rankings.*

G.K. Hall and Company, 70 Lincoln Street, Boston, Massachusetts 02111 (617) 423-3990; *The World in Figures.*

Statistical Office of the United Nations, Publishing Service, New York, New York 10017 (800) 253-9646; *Survey of Economic and Social Conditions in Africa.*

United Nations Economic Commission for Africa, Africa Hall, P.O. Box 3001, Addis Ababa, Ethiopia (Telephone Number in U.S. (800) 253-9646); *African Statistical Yearbook.*

United Nations Educational, Scientific and Cultural Organization (UNESCO), 7 Place de Fontenoy, F-75700 Paris, France (Telephone Number in U.S. (212) 963-5981); *Statistical Yearbook.*

Time Books, 201 East 50th Street, New York, New York 10022 (212) 751-2600; *The Economist Book of Vital World Statistics.*

The World Bank, 1818 H Street, NW, Washington, D.C. 20433 (202) 477-1234; *World Tables.*

ZIMBABWE - EGG PRODUCTION AND CONSUMPTION - See ZIMBABWE - DAIRY PRODUCTS

ZIMBABWE - ELECTRICITY

African Development Bank, 01 BP 1387, Abidjan 01, Cote D'Ivoire; *Selected Statistics on Regional Member Countries.*

Commodity Research Bureau, Incorporated, 75 Wall Street, New York, New York 10005 (212) 504-7754; *Commodity Year Book.*

Facts on File, 460 Park Avenue South, New York, New York 10016 (800) 443-8323; *The New Book of World Rankings.*

Time Books, 201 East 50th Street, New York, New York 10022 (212) 751-2600; *The Economist Book of Vital World Statistics.*

United Nations Economic Commission for Africa, Africa Hall, P.O. Box 3001, Addis Ababa, Ethiopia (Telephone Number in U.S. (800) 253-9646); *African Statistical Yearbook.*

ZIMBABWE - EMPLOYMENT

Facts on File, 460 Park Avenue South, New York, New York 10016 (800) 443-8323; *The New Book of World Rankings.*

International Labour Office, I.L.O. Publications, CH-1211, Geneva 22, Switzerland; *Yearbook of Labour Statistics.*

Statistical Office of the United Nations, Publishing Service, New York, New York 10017 (800) 253-9646; *Statistical Yearbook,* and *Survey of Economic and Social Conditions in Africa.*

United Nations Economic Commission for Africa, Africa Hall, P.O. Box 3001, Addis Ababa, Ethiopia (Telephone Number in U.S. (800) 253-9646); *African Statistical Yearbook.*

ZIMBABWE - ENERGY

Facts on File, 460 Park Avenue South, New York, New York 10016 (800) 443-8323; *The New Book of World Rankings.*

Food and Agricultural Organization of the United Nations (FAO) Via delle Terme di Caracalla, 00100 Rome, Italy (Telephone Number in U.S. (202) 653-2400); *The State of Food and Agriculture.*

G.K. Hall and Company, 70 Lincoln Street, Boston, Massachusetts 02111 (617) 423-3990; *The World in Figures.*

Statistical Office of the United Nations, Publishing Service, New York, New York 10017 (800) 253-9646; *Energy Statistics Yearbook,* and *Statistical Yearbook,* and *World Energy Supplies.*

Time Books, 201 East 50th Street, New York, New York 10022 (212) 751-2600; *The Economist Book of Vital World Statistics.*

United Nations Economic Commission for Africa, Africa Hall, P.O. Box 3001, Addis Ababa, Ethiopia (Telephone Number in U.S. (800) 253-9646); *African Statistical Yearbook.*

ZIMBABWE - EXCHANGE RATES

African Development Bank, 01 BP 1387, Abidjan 01, Cote D'Ivoire; *Selected Statistics on Regional Member Countries.*

International Civil Aviation Organization, 1000 Sherbrooke Street, West, Montreal, Quebec, Canada H3A 2R2 (514) 285-8219; *Civil Aviation Statistics of the World.*

ZIMBABWE - EXPORTS

African Development Bank, 01 BP 1387, Abidjan 01, Cote D'Ivoire; *Selected Statistics on Regional Member Countries.*

The Economist Intelligence Unit, 111 West 57th Street, New York, New York 10019 (800) 938-4685; *The World Market Atlas.*

Euromonitor Publications Limited, 87-88 Turnmill Street, London EC1M 5QU, England; *Third World Economic Handbook*.

Food and Agricultural Organization of the United Nations (FAO) Via delle Terme di Caracalla, 00100 Rome, Italy (Telephone Number in U.S. (202) 653-2400); *The State of Food and Agriculture*.

G.K. Hall and Company, 70 Lincoln Street, Boston, Massachusetts 02111 (617) 423-3990; *The World in Figures*.

Statistical Office of the United Nations, Publishing Service, New York, New York 10017 (800) 253-9646; *Survey of Economic and Social Conditions in Africa*.

Time Books, 201 East 50th Street, New York, New York 10022 (212) 751-2600; *The Economist Book of Vital World Statistics*.

United Nations Economic Commission for Africa, Africa Hall, P.O. Box 3001, Addis Ababa, Ethiopia (Telephone Number in U.S. (800) 253-9646); *African Statistical Yearbook*.

The World Bank, 1818 H Street, NW, Washington, D.C. 20433 (202) 477-1234; *World Tables*.

ZIMBABWE - EXTERNAL INDEBTEDNESS

African Development Bank, 01 BP 1387, Abidjan 01, Cote D'Ivoire; *Selected Statistics on Regional Member Countries*.

Euromonitor Publications Limited, 87-88 Turnmill Street, London EC1M 5QU, England; *Third World Economic Handbook*.

Statistical Office of the United Nations, Publishing Service, New York, New York 10017 (800) 253-9646; *Survey of Economic and Social Conditions in Africa*.

The World Bank, 1818 H Street, NW, Washington, D.C. 20433 (202) 477-1234; *World Tables*.

ZIMBABWE - EXTERNAL TRADE

African Development Bank, 01 BP 1387, Abidjan 01, Cote D'Ivoire; *Selected Statistics on Regional Member Countries*.

Food and Agricultural Organization of the United Nations (FAO) Via delle Terme di Caracalla, 00100 Rome, Italy (Telephone Number in U.S. (202) 653-2400); *The State of Food and Agriculture*.

G.K. Hall and Company, 70 Lincoln Street, Boston, Massachusetts 02111 (617) 423-3990; *The World in Figures*.

ZIMBABWE - FARM CROPS - See ZIMBABWE - CROPS

ZIMBABWE - FERTILITY RATES

Facts on File, 460 Park Avenue South, New York, New York 10016 (800) 443-8323; *The New Book of World Rankings*.

Statistical Office of the United Nations, Publishing Service, New York, New York 10017 (800) 253-9646; *Survey of Economic and Social Conditions in Africa*.

Time Books, 201 East 50th Street, New York, New York 10022 (212) 751-2600; *The Economist Book of Vital World Statistics*.

The World Bank, 1818 H Street, NW, Washington, D.C. 20433 (202) 477-1234; *World Tables*.

ZIMBABWE - FERTILIZER

Food and Agricultural Organization of the United Nations (FAO), Via delle Terme di Caracalla, 00100 Rome, Italy (Telephone Number in U.S. (202) 653-2400); *Annual Fertilizer Review*, and *The State of Food and Agriculture*.

Statistical Office of the United Nations, Publishing Service, New York, New York 10017 (800) 253-9646; *Statistical Yearbook*.

ZIMBABWE - FETAL MORTALITY

Statistical Office of the United Nations, Publishing Service, New York, New York 10017 (800) 253-9646; *Demographic Yearbook*.

ZIMBABWE - FINANCE

African Development Bank, 01 BP 1387, Abidjan 01, Cote D'Ivoire; *Selected Statistics on Regional Member Countries*.

Facts on File, 460 Park Avenue South, New York, New York 10016 (800) 443-8323; *The New Book of World Rankings*.

G.K. Hall and Company, 70 Lincoln Street, Boston, Massachusetts 02111 (617) 423-3990; *The World in Figures*.

United Nations Economic Commission for Africa, Africa Hall, P.O. Box 3001, Addis Ababa, Ethiopia (Telephone Number in U.S. (800) 253-9646); *African Statistical Yearbook*.

ZIMBABWE - FISHERIES

Facts on File, 460 Park Avenue South, New York, New York 10016 (800) 443-8323; *The New Book of World Rankings*.

Food and Agricultural Organization of the United Nations (FAO) Via delle Terme di Caracalla, 00100 Rome, Italy (Telephone Number in U.S. (202) 653-2400); *The State of Food and Agriculture*, and *Yearbook of Fishery Statistics*.

Statistical Office of the United Nations, Publishing Service, New York, New York 10017 (800) 253-9646; *Statistical Yearbook*, and *Survey of Economic and Social Conditions in Africa*.

United Nations Economic Commission for Africa, Africa Hall, P.O. Box 3001, Addis Ababa, Ethiopia (Telephone Number in U.S. (800) 253-9646); *African Statistical Yearbook*.

ZIMBABWE - FOOD

African Development Bank, 01 BP 1387, Abidjan 01, Cote D'Ivoire; *Selected Statistics on Regional Member Countries*.

Food and Agricultural Organization of the United Nations (FAO) Via delle Terme di Caracalla, 00100 Rome, Italy (Telephone Number in U.S. (202) 653-2400); *The State of Food and Agriculture*.

G.K. Hall and Company, 70 Lincoln Street, Boston, Massachusetts 02111 (617) 423-3990; *The World in Figures*.

ZIMBABWE - FOREIGN AID

G.K. Hall and Company, 70 Lincoln Street, Boston, Massachusetts 02111 (617) 423-3990; *The World in Figures*.

ZIMBABWE - FOREIGN TRADE

Euromonitor Publications Limited, 87-88 Turnmill Street, London EC1M 5QU, England; *Third World Economic Handbook*.

Facts on File, 460 Park Avenue South, New York, New York 10016 (800) 443-8323; *The New Book of World Rankings.*

Food and Agricultural Organization of the United Nations (FAO) Via delle Terme di Caracalla, 00100 Rome, Italy (Telephone Number in U.S. (202) 653-2400); *The State of Food and Agriculture.*

G.K. Hall and Company, 70 Lincoln Street, Boston, Massachusetts 02111 (617) 423-3990; *The World in Figures.*

Statistical Office of the United Nations, Publishing Service, New York, New York 10017 (800) 253-9646; *International Trade Statistics Yearbook,* and *Statistical Yearbook.*

United Nations Economic Commission for Africa, Africa Hall, P.O. Box 3001, Addis Ababa, Ethiopia (Telephone Number in U.S. (800) 253-9646); *African Statistical Yearbook.*

The World Bank, 1818 H Street, NW, Washington, D.C. 20433 (202) 477-1234; *World Tables.*

ZIMBABWE - FORESTRY AND FOREST PRODUCTS

Euromonitor Publications Limited, 87-88 Turnmill Street, London EC1M 5QU, England; *Third World Economic Handbook.*

Facts on File, 460 Park Avenue South, New York, New York 10016 (800) 443-8323; *The New Book of World Rankings.*

Food and Agricultural Organization of the United Nations (FAO) Via delle Terme di Caracalla, 00100 Rome, Italy (Telephone Number in U.S. (202) 653-2400); *The State of Food and Agriculture,* and *Yearbook of Forest Products.*

G.K. Hall and Company, 70 Lincoln Street, Boston, Massachusetts 02111 (617) 423-3990; *The World in Figures.*

United Nations Economic Commission for Africa, Africa Hall, P.O. Box 3001, Addis Ababa, Ethiopia (Telephone Number in U.S. (800) 253-9646); *African Statistical Yearbook.*

United Nations Educational, Scientific and Cultural Organization (UNESCO), 7 Place de Fontenoy, F-75700 Paris, France (Telephone Number in U.S. (212) 963-5981); *Statistical Yearbook.*

ZIMBABWE - GAS PRODUCTION - See ZIMBABWE - MINING AND MINERAL PRODUCTS

ZIMBABWE - GENERAL MORTALITY

Statistical Office of the United Nations, Publishing Service, New York, New York 10017 (800) 253-9646; *Demographic Yearbook.*

ZIMBABWE - GEOGRAPHIC DATA

Facts on File, 460 Park Avenue South, New York, New York 10016 (800) 443-8323; *The New Book of World Rankings.*

ZIMBABWE - GOATS - See ZIMBABWE - LIVESTOCK AND POULTRY

ZIMBABWE - GOLD HOLDINGS

The World Bank, 1818 H Street, NW, Washington, D.C. 20433 (202) 477-1234; *World Tables.*

ZIMBABWE - GOLD PRODUCTION AND CONSUMPTION - See ZIMBABWE - MINING AND MINERAL PRODUCTS

ZIMBABWE - GOVERNMENT

G.K. Hall and Company, 70 Lincoln Street, Boston, Massachusetts 02111 (617) 423-3990; *The World in Figures.*

ZIMBABWE - GOVERNMENT EXPENDITURE

Euromonitor Publications Limited, 87-88 Turnmill Street, London EC1M 5QU, England; *Third World Economic Handbook.*

Time Books, 201 East 50th Street, New York, New York 10022 (212) 751-2600; *The Economist Book of Vital World Statistics.*

The World Bank, 1818 H Street, NW, Washington, D.C. 20433 (202) 477-1234; *World Tables.*

ZIMBABWE - GOVERNMENT REVENUE

Statistical Office of the United Nations, Publishing Service, New York, New York 10017 (800) 253-9646; *Survey of Economic and Social Conditions in Africa.*

Time Books, 201 East 50th Street, New York, New York 10022 (212) 751-2600; *The Economist Book of Vital World Statistics.*

The World Bank, 1818 H Street, NW, Washington, D.C. 20433 (202) 477-1234; *World Tables.*

ZIMBABWE - GRAIN PRODUCTION - See ZIMBABWE - CROPS

ZIMBABWE - GROSS DOMESTIC PRODUCT

African Development Bank, 01 BP 1387, Abidjan 01, Cote D'Ivoire; *Selected Statistics on Regional Member Countries.*

The Economist Intelligence Unit, 111 West 57th Street, New York, New York 10019 (800) 938-4685; *The World Market Atlas.*

Euromonitor Publications Limited, 87-88 Turnmill Street, London EC1M 5QU, England; *Third World Economic Handbook.*

Facts on File, 460 Park Avenue South, New York, New York 10016 (800) 443-8323; *The New Book of World Rankings.*

G.K. Hall and Company, 70 Lincoln Street, Boston, Massachusetts 02111 (617) 423-3990; *The World in Figures.*

Statistical Office of the United Nations, Publishing Service, New York, New York 10017 (800) 253-9646; *Statistical Yearbook,* and *Survey of Economic and Social Conditions in Africa.*

Time Books, 201 East 50th Street, New York, New York 10022 (212) 751-2600; *The Economist Book of Vital World Statistics.*

United Nations Economic Commission for Africa, Africa Hall, P.O. Box 3001, Addis Ababa, Ethiopia (Telephone Number in U.S. (800) 253-9646); *African Statistical Yearbook.*

The World Bank, 1818 H Street, NW, Washington, D.C. 20433 (202) 477-1234; *World Tables.*

ZIMBABWE - GROSS INDUSTRIAL PRODUCT

Euromonitor Publications Limited, 87-88 Turnmill Street, London EC1M 5QU, England; *Third World Economic Handbook.*

ZIMBABWE - GROSS NATIONAL PRODUCT

Euromonitor Publications Limited, 87-88 Turnmill Street, London EC1M 5QU, England; *Third World Economic Handbook.*

U.S. Arms Control and Disarmament Agency, 320 Twenty-first Street, NW, Washington, D.C. 20451 (202) 647-8677; *World Military Expenditures and Arms Transfers.*

The World Bank, 1818 H Street, NW, Washington, D.C. 20433 (202) 477-1234; *World Tables.*

ZIMBABWE - GROUNDNUT PRODUCTION - See ZIMBABWE - CROPS

ZIMBABWE - HEALTH

African Development Bank, 01 BP 1387, Abidjan 01, Cote D'Ivoire; *Selected Statistics on Regional Member Countries.*

Facts on File, 460 Park Avenue South, New York, New York 10016 (800) 443-8323; *The New Book of World Rankings.*

G.K. Hall and Company, 70 Lincoln Street, Boston, Massachusetts 02111 (617) 423-3990; *The World in Figures.*

Statistical Office of the United Nations, Publishing Service, New York, New York 10017 (800) 253-9646; *Statistical Yearbook.*

Time Books, 201 East 50th Street, New York, New York 10022 (212) 751-2600, *The Economist Book of Vital World Statistics.*

United Nations Economic Commission for Africa, Africa Hall, P.O. Box 3001, Addis Ababa, Ethiopia (Telephone Number in U.S. (800) 253-9646), *African Statistical Yearbook.*

ZIMBABWE - HIGHWAYS

G.K. Hall and Company, 70 Lincoln Street, Boston, Massachusetts 02111 (617) 423-3990; *The World in Figures.*

International Road Federation, 525 School Street, SW, Washington, D.C. 20024 (202) 554-2106; *World Road Statistics.*

Statistical Office of the United Nations, Publishing Service, New York, New York 10017 (800) 253-9646; *Survey of Economic and Social Conditions in Africa.*

United Nations Economic Commission for Africa, Africa Hall, P.O. Box 3001, Addis Ababa, Ethiopia (Telephone Number in U.S. (800) 253-9646); *African Statistical Yearbook.*

ZIMBABWE - HORSES - See ZIMBABWE - LIVESTOCK AND POULTRY

ZIMBABWE - HOURS OF WORK - See ZIMBABWE - EMPLOYMENT

ZIMBABWE - HOUSING AND HOUSING UNITS

Facts on File, 460 Park Avenue South, New York, New York 10016 (800) 443-8323; *The New Book of World Rankings.*

Euromonitor Publications Limited, 87-88 Turnmill Street, London EC1M 5QU, England; *Third World Economic Handbook.*

ZIMBABWE - ILLITERATE POPULATION

The Economist Intelligence Unit, 111 West 57th Street, New York, New York 10019 (800) 938-4685; *The World Market Atlas.*

G.K. Hall and Company, 70 Lincoln Street, Boston, Massachusetts 02111 (617) 423-3990; *The World in Figures.*

ZIMBABWE - IMPORTS

African Development Bank, 01 BP 1387, Abidjan 01, Cote D'Ivoire; *Selected Statistics on Regional Member Countries.*

The Economist Intelligence Unit, 111 West 57th Street, New York, New York 10019 (800) 938-4685; *The World Market Atlas.*

Euromonitor Publications Limited, 87-88 Turnmill Street, London EC1M 5QU, England; *Third World Economic Handbook.*

Food and Agricultural Organization of the United Nations (FAO) Via delle Terme di Caracalla, 00100 Rome, Italy (Telephone Number in U.S. (202) 653-2400); *The State of Food and Agriculture.*

G.K. Hall and Company, 70 Lincoln Street, Boston, Massachusetts 02111 (617) 423-3990; *The World in Figures.*

Statistical Office of the United Nations, Publishing Service, New York, New York 10017 (800) 253-9646; *Survey of Economic and Social Conditions in Africa.*

United Nations Economic Commission for Africa, Africa Hall, P.O. Box 3001, Addis Ababa, Ethiopia (Telephone Number in U.S. (800) 253-9646); *African Statistical Yearbook.*

The World Bank, 1818 H Street, NW, Washington, D.C. 20433 (202) 477-1234; *World Tables.*

ZIMBABWE - INDUSTRIAL METALS PRODUCTION - See ZIMBABWE MINING AND MINERAL PRODUCTS

ZIMBABWE - INDUSTRY

Euromonitor Publications Limited, 87-88 Turnmill Street, London EC1M 5QU, England; *Third World Economic Handbook.*

Facts on File, 460 Park Avenue South, New York, New York 10016 (800) 443-8323; *The New Book of World Rankings.*

G.K. Hall and Company, 70 Lincoln Street, Boston, Massachusetts 02111 (617) 423-3990; *The World in Figures.*

Statistical Office of the United Nations, Publishing Service, New York, New York 10017 (800) 253-9646; *Survey of Economic and Social Conditions in Africa.*

Time Books, 201 East 50th Street, New York, New York 10022 (212) 751-2600; *The Economist Book of Vital World Statistics.*

United Nations Economic Commission for Africa, Africa Hall, P.O. Box 3001, Addis Ababa, Ethiopia (Telephone Number in U.S. (800) 253-9646); *African Statistical Yearbook.*

The World Bank, 1818 H Street, NW, Washington, D.C. 20433 (202) 477-1234; *World Tables.*

World Intellectual Property Organization, 34 Chemin des Colombettes, CH-1211 Geneva 20. Switzerland; *Industrial Property Statistics.*

ZIMBABWE - INFANT AND MATERNAL MORTALITY

Statistical Office of the United Nations, Publishing Service, New York, New York 10017 (800) 253-9646; *Demographic Yearbook, Statistical Yearbook,* and *Survey of Economic and Social Conditions in Africa.*

Time Books, 201 East 50th Street, New York, New York 10022 (212) 751-2600; *The Economist Book of Vital World Statistics.*

The World Bank, 1818 H Street, NW, Washington, D.C. 20433 (202) 477-1234; *World Tables.*

ZIMBABWE - INTERNATIONAL RESERVES EXCLUDING GOLD

African Development Bank, 01 BP 1387, Abidjan 01, Cote D'Ivoire; *Selected Statistics on Regional Member Countries.*

The World Bank, 1818 H Street, NW, Washington, D.C. 20433 (202) 477-1234; *World Tables.*

ZIMBABWE - IRON ORE PRODUCTION AND CONSUMPTION - See ZIMBABWE - MINING AND MINERAL PRODUCTS

ZIMBABWE - LABOR FORCE

African Development Bank, 01 BP 1387, Abidjan 01, Cote D'Ivoire; *Selected Statistics on Regional Member Countries.*

Facts on File, 460 Park Avenue South, New York, New York 10016 (800) 443-8323; *The New Book of World Rankings.*

Food and Agricultural Organization of the United Nations (FAO) Via delle Terme di Caracalla, 00100 Rome, Italy (Telephone Number in U.S. (202) 653-2400); *The State of Food and Agriculture.*

G.K. Hall and Company, 70 Lincoln Street, Boston, Massachusetts 02111 (617) 423-3990; *The World in Figures.*

Time Books, 201 East 50th Street, New York, New York 10022 (212) 751-2600; *The Economist Book of Vital World Statistics.*

The World Bank, 1818 H Street, NW, Washington, D.C. 20433 (202) 477-1234; *World Tables.*

ZIMBABWE - LAND USE

G.K. Hall and Company, 70 Lincoln Street, Boston, Massachusetts 02111 (617) 423-3990; *The World in Figures.*

ZIMBABWE - LIBRARIES

Facts on File, 460 Park Avenue South, New York, New York 10016 (800) 443-8323; *The New Book of World Rankings.*

United Nations Educational, Scientific and Cultural Organization (UNESCO), 7 Place de Fontenoy, F-75700 Paris, France (Telephone Number in U.S. (212) 963-5981); *Statistical Yearbook.*

ZIMBABWE - LIFE EXPECTANCY

African Development Bank, 01 BP 1387, Abidjan 01, Cote D'Ivoire; *Selected Statistics on Regional Member Countries.*

ZIMBABWE - LITERACY RATE

Statistical Office of the United Nations, Publishing Service, New York, New York 10017 (800) 253-9646; *Survey of Economic and Social Conditions in Africa.*

ZIMBABWE - LIVESTOCK AND POULTRY

Facts on File, 460 Park Avenue South, New York, New York 10016 (800) 443-8323; *The New Book of World Rankings.*

Food and Agricultural Organization of the United Nations (FAO) Via delle Terme di Caracalla, 00100 Rome, Italy (Telephone Number in U.S. (202) 653-2400); *The State of Food and Agriculture.*

G.K. Hall and Company, 70 Lincoln Street, Boston, Massachusetts 02111 (617) 423-3990; *The World in Figures.*

Statistical Office of the United Nations, Publishing Service, New York, New York 10017 (800) 253-9646; *Statistical Yearbook,* and *Survey of Economic and Social Conditions in Africa.*

United Nations Economic Commission for Africa, Africa Hall, P.O. Box 3001, Addis Ababa, Ethiopia (Telephone Number in U.S. (800) 253-9646); *African Statistical Yearbook.*

ZIMBABWE - LIVING LEVELS

G.K. Hall and Company, 70 Lincoln Street, Boston, Massachusetts 02111 (617) 423-3990; *The World in Figures.*

Time Books, 201 East 50th Street, New York, New York 10022 (212) 751-2600; *The Economist Book of Vital World Statistics.*

ZIMBABWE - MAIL - NUMBER OF PIECES SENT OR RECEIVED

Statistical Office of the United Nations, Publishing Service, New York, New York 10017 (800) 253-9646; *Statistical Yearbook.*

ZIMBABWE - MANGANESE ORE PRODUCTION AND CONSUMPTION See ZIMBABWE - MINING AND MINERAL PRODUCTS

ZIMBABWE - MANUFACTURING

Euromonitor Publications Limited, 87-88 Turnmill Street, London EC1M 5QU, England; *Third World Economic Handbook.*

Facts on File, 460 Park Avenue South, New York, New York 10016 (800) 443-8323; *The New Book of World Rankings.*

G.K. Hall and Company, 70 Lincoln Street, Boston, Massachusetts 02111 (617) 423-3990; *The World in Figures.*

Statistical Office of the United Nations, Publishing Service, New York, New York 10017 (800) 253-9646; *Survey of Economic and Social Conditions in Africa.*

Time Books, 201 East 50th Street, New York, New York 10022 (212) 751-2600; *The Economist Book of Vital World Statistics.*

United Nations Economic Commission for Africa, Africa Hall, P.O. Box 3001, Addis Ababa, Ethiopia (Telephone Number in U.S. (800) 253-9646); *African Statistical Yearbook.*

The World Bank, 1818 H Street, NW, Washington, D.C. 20433 (202) 477-1234; *World Tables.*

ZIMBABWE - MARRIAGE RATES

Facts on File, 460 Park Avenue South, New York, New York 10016 (800) 443-8323; *The New Book of World Rankings.*

Statistical Office of the United Nations, Publishing Service, New York, New York 10017 (800) 253-9646; *Demographic Yearbook.*

ZIMBABWE - MEAT PRODUCTION - See ZIMBABWE - LIVESTOCK AND POULTRY

ZIMBABWE - MERCHANT SHIPPING

G.K. Hall and Company, 70 Lincoln Street, Boston, Massachusetts 02111 (617) 423-3990; *The World in Figures.*

ZIMBABWE - MILITARY

G.K. Hall and Company, 70 Lincoln Street, Boston, Massachusetts 02111 (617) 423-3990; *The World in Figures.*

The International Institute for Strategic Studies, 23 Tavistock Street, London WC2E 7NQ, England; *The Military Balance.*

United Nations Economic Commission for Africa, Africa Hall, P.O. Box 3001, Addis Ababa, Ethiopia (Telephone Number in U.S. (800) 253-9646); *African Statistical Yearbook.*

U.S. Arms Control and Disarmament Agency, 320 Twenty-first Street, NW, Washington, D.C. 20451 (202) 647-8677; *World Military Expenditures and Arms Transfers.*

ZIMBABWE - MILK PRODUCTION - See ZIMBABWE - DAIRY PRODUCTS

ZIMBABWE - MINING AND MINERAL PRODUCTS

Commodity Research Bureau, Incorporated, 75 Wall Street, New York, New York 10005 (212) 504-7754; *Commodity Year Book.*

Euromonitor Publications Limited, 87-88 Turnmill Street, London EC1M 5QU, England; *Third World Economic Handbook.*

Facts on File, 460 Park Avenue South, New York, New York 10016 (800) 443-8323; *The New Book of World Rankings.*

G.K. Hall and Company, 70 Lincoln Street, Boston, Massachusetts 02111 (617) 423-3990; *The World in Figures.*

Statistical Office of the United Nations, Publishing Service, New York, New York 10017 (800) 253-9646; *Statistical Yearbook.*

United Nations Economic Commission for Africa, Africa Hall, P.O. Box 3001, Addis Ababa, Ethiopia (Telephone Number in U.S. (800) 253-9646); *African Statistical Yearbook.*

ZIMBABWE - MONEY SUPPLY

African Development Bank, 01 BP 1387, Abidjan 01, Cote D'Ivoire; *Selected Statistics on Regional Member Countries.*

G.K. Hall and Company, 70 Lincoln Street, Boston, Massachusetts 02111 (617) 423-3990; *The World in Figures.*

The World Bank, 1818 H Street, NW, Washington, D.C. 20433 (202) 477-1234; *World Tables.*

ZIMBABWE - MOTOR VEHICLE TAXES - See ZIMBABWE - TAXATION

ZIMBABWE - MOTOR VEHICLES IN USE

G.K. Hall and Company, 70 Lincoln Street, Boston, Massachusetts 02111 (617) 423-3990; *The World in Figures.*

International Road Federation, 525 School Street, SW, Washington, D.C. 20024 (202) 554-2106; *World Road Statistics.*

Statistical Office of the United Nations, Publishing Service, New York, New York 10017 (800) 253-9646; *Statistical Yearbook,* and

Survey of Economic and Social Conditions in Africa.

Time Books, 201 East 50th Street, New York, New York 10022 (212) 751-2600; *The Economist Book of Vital World Statistics.*

ZIMBABWE - MULES - See ZIMBABWE - LIVESTOCK AND POULTRY

ZIMBABWE - MUSEUMS

Facts on File, 460 Park Avenue South, New York, New York 10016 (800) 443-8323; *The New Book of World Rankings.*

ZIMBABWE - NATALITY - See ZIMBABWE - BIRTH RATE

ZIMBABWE - NATIONAL ACCOUNTS

African Development Bank, 01 BP 1387, Abidjan 01, Cote D'Ivoire; *Selected Statistics on Regional Member Countries.*

Statistical Office of the United Nations, Publishing Service, New York, New York 10017 (800) 253-9646; *Statistical Yearbook.*

United Nations Economic Commission for Africa, Africa Hall, P.O. Box 3001, Addis Ababa, Ethiopia (Telephone Number in U.S. (800) 253-9646); *African Statistical Yearbook.*

ZIMBABWE - NATIONAL INCOME

Facts on File, 460 Park Avenue South, New York, New York 10016 (800) 443-8323; *The New Book of World Rankings.*

G.K. Hall and Company, 70 Lincoln Street, Boston, Massachusetts 02111 (617) 423-3990; *The World in Figures.*

Statistical Office of the United Nations, Publishing Service, New York, New York 10017 (800) 253-9646; *Statistical Yearbook.*

ZIMBABWE - NATIONAL PRODUCT

Facts on File, 460 Park Avenue South, New York, New York 10016 (800) 443-8323; *The New Book of World Rankings.*

Statistical Office of the United Nations, Publishing Service, New York, New York 10017 (800) 253-9646; *Statistical Yearbook.*

ZIMBABWE - NATURAL GAS PRODUCTION - See ZIMBABWE - MINING AND MINERAL PRODUCTS

ZIMBABWE - NEWSPAPER PRODUCTION - See ZIMBABWE - FORESTRY AND FOREST PRODUCTS

ZIMBABWE - NEWSPRINT - See ZIMBABWE - FORESTRY AND FOREST PRODUCTS

ZIMBABWE - NICKEL AND NICKEL ORE PRODUCTION AND CONSUMPTION - See ZIMBABWE - MINING AND MINERAL PRODUCTS

ZIMBABWE - OCCUPATIONS - See ZIMBABWE - LABOR FORCE

ZIMBABWE - PAPER - See ZIMBABWE - FORESTRY AND FOREST PRODUCTS

ZIMBABWE - PATENTS

World Intellectual Property Organization, 34 Chemin des Colombettes, CH-1211 Geneva 20, Switzerland; *Industrial Property Statistics.*

ZIMBABWE - PEANUT PRODUCTION - See ZIMBABWE - CROPS

ZIMBABWE - PESTICIDE USE

Food and Agricultural Organization of the United Nations (FAO) Via delle Terme di Caracalla, 00100 Rome, Italy (Telephone Number in U.S. (202) 653-2400); *The State of Food and Agriculture*.

ZIMBABWE - PETROLEUM INDUSTRY

Facts on File, 460 Park Avenue South, New York, New York 10016 (800) 443-8323; *The New Book of World Rankings*.

Food and Agricultural Organization of the United Nations (FAO) Via delle Terme di Caracalla, 00100 Rome, Italy (Telephone Number in U.S. (202) 653-2400); *The State of Food and Agriculture*.

G.K. Hall and Company, 70 Lincoln Street, Boston, Massachusetts 02111 (617) 423-3990; *The World in Figures*.

Statistical Office of the United Nations, Publishing Service, New York, New York 10017 (800) 253-9646; *Statistical Yearbook*.

ZIMBABWE - PHOSPHATE ROCK PRODUCTION - See ZIMBABWE MINING AND MINERAL PRODUCTS

ZIMBABWE - PIG-IRON AND FERRO-ALLOY PRODUCTION - See ZIMBABWE - MINING AND MINERAL PRODUCTS

ZIMBABWE - PIGS - See ZIMBABWE - LIVESTOCK AND POULTRY

ZIMBABWE - PLASTIC AND RESIN PRODUCTION

Euromonitor Publications Limited, 87-88 Turnmill Street, London EC1M 5QU, England; *Third World Economic Handbook*.

ZIMBABWE - POPULATION

African Development Bank, 01 BP 1387, Abidjan 01, Cote D'Ivoire; *Selected Statistics on Regional Member Countries*.

The Economist Intelligence Unit, 111 West 57th Street, New York, New York 10019 (800) 938-4685; *The World Market Atlas*.

Euromonitor Publications Limited, 87-88 Turnmill Street, London EC1M 5QU, England; *Third World Economic Handbook*.

Facts on File, 460 Park Avenue South, New York, New York 10016 (800) 443-8323; *The New Book of World Rankings*.

G.K. Hall and Company, 70 Lincoln Street, Boston, Massachusetts 02111 (617) 423-3990; *The World in Figures*.

Statistical Office of the United Nations, Publishing Service, New York, New York 10017 (800) 253-9646; *Demographic Yearbook, Statistical Yearbook,* and *Survey of Economic and Social Conditions in Africa*.

Time Books, 201 East 50th Street, New York, New York 10022 (212) 751-2600; *The Economist Book of Vital World Statistics*.

United Nations Educational, Scientific and Cultural Organization (UNESCO), 7 Place de Fontenoy, F-75700 Paris, France (Telephone Number in U.S. (212) 963-5981); *Statistical Yearbook*.

U.S. Arms Control and Disarmament Agency, 320 Twenty-first Street, NW, Washington, D.C. 20451 (202) 647-8677; *World Military Expenditures and Arms Transfers*.

World Health Organization, Office of Publications, Avenue Appia, CH-1211 Geneva 27, Switzerland (Telephone Number in U.S. (518) 436-9686); *World Health Statistics Annual*.

ZIMBABWE - POST OFFICES

Facts on File, 460 Park Avenue South, New York, New York 10016 (800) 443-8323; *The New Book of World Rankings*.

ZIMBABWE - POTATO PRODUCTION - See ZIMBABWE - CROPS

ZIMBABWE - POWER PRODUCTION INDUSTRY

Statistical Office of the United Nations, Publishing Service, New York, New York 10017 (800) 253-9646; *Statistical Yearbook*.

ZIMBABWE - PRICES

Facts on File, 460 Park Avenue South, New York, New York 10016 (800) 443-8323; *The New Book of World Rankings*.

Food and Agricultural Organization of the United Nations (FAO) Via delle Terme di Caracalla, 00100 Rome, Italy (Telephone Number in U.S. (202) 653-2400); *The State of Food and Agriculture*.

G.K. Hall and Company, 70 Lincoln Street, Boston, Massachusetts 02111 (617) 423-3990; *The World in Figures*.

International Labour Office, I.L.O. Publications, CH-1211, Geneva 22, Switzerland; *Yearbook of Labour Statistics*.

United Nations Economic Commission for Africa, Africa Hall, P.O. Box 3001, Addis Ababa, Ethiopia (Telephone Number in U.S. (800) 253-9646); *African Statistical Yearbook*.

ZIMBABWE - PRINTING AND WRITING PAPER - See ZIMBABWE - FORESTRY AND FOREST PRODUCTS

ZIMBABWE - PRODUCTION

Euromonitor Publications Limited, 87-88 Turnmill Street, London EC1M 5QU, England; *Third World Economic Handbook*.

Facts on File, 460 Park Avenue South, New York, New York 10016 (800) 443-8323; *The New Book of World Rankings*.

G.K. Hall and Company, 70 Lincoln Street, Boston, Massachusetts 02111 (617) 423-3990; *The World in Figures*.

ZIMBABWE - PUBLIC FINANCE

Facts on File, 460 Park Avenue South, New York, New York 10016 (800) 443-8323; *The New Book of World Rankings*.

ZIMBABWE - RADIO BROADCASTING - See ZIMBABWE - BROADCASTING

ZIMBABWE - RAILWAYS

G.K. Hall and Company, 70 Lincoln Street, Boston, Massachusetts 02111 (617) 423-3990; *The World in Figures*.

Statistical Office of the United Nations, Publishing Service, New York, New York 10017 (800) 253-9646; *Statistical Yearbook,* and *Survey of Economic and Social Conditions in Africa*.

ZIMBABWE - RELIGION

Facts on File, 460 Park Avenue South, New York, New York 10016 (800) 443-8323; *The New Book of World Rankings*.

United Nations Economic Commission for Africa, Africa Hall, P.O. Box 3001, Addis Ababa, Ethiopia (Telephone Number in U.S. (800) 253-9646); *African Statistical Yearbook*.

ZIMBABWE - RENT PRICES

International Labour Office, I.L.O. Publications, CH-1211, Geneva 22, Switzerland; *Yearbook of Labour Statistics*.

ZIMBABWE - RETAIL TRADE

Euromonitor Publications Limited, 87-88 Turnmill Street, London EC1M 5QU, England; *Third World Economic Handbook*.

G.K. Hall and Company, 70 Lincoln Street, Boston, Massachusetts 02111 (617) 423-3990; *The World in Figures*.

ZIMBABWE - RICE PRODUCTION - See ZIMBABWE - CROPS

ZIMBABWE - ROUNDWOOD PRODUCTION - See ZIMBABWE - FORESTRY AND FOREST PRODUCTS

ZIMBABWE - RUBBER PRODUCTION AND CONSUMPTION

Euromonitor Publications Limited, 87-88 Turnmill Street, London EC1M 5QU, England; *Third World Economic Handbook*.

Facts on File, 460 Park Avenue South, New York, New York 10016 (800) 443-8323; *The New Book of World Rankings*.

ZIMBABWE - SAWNWOOD PRODUCTION - See ZIMBABWE - FORESTRY AND FOREST PRODUCTS

ZIMBABWE - SENIOR CITIZENS

Facts on File, 460 Park Avenue South, New York, New York 10016 (800) 443-8323; *The New Book of World Rankings*.

ZIMBABWE - SHEEP - See ZIMBABWE - LIVESTOCK AND POULTRY

ZIMBABWE - SILVER PRODUCTION AND CONSUMPTION - See ZIMBABWE - MINING AND MINERAL PRODUCTS

ZIMBABWE - SOCIAL DATA

African Development Bank, 01 BP 1387, Abidjan 01, Cote D'Ivoire; *Selected Statistics on Regional Member Countries*.

Facts on File, 460 Park Avenue South, New York, New York 10016 (800) 443-8323; *The New Book of World Rankings*.

G.K. Hall and Company, 70 Lincoln Street, Boston, Massachusetts 02111 (617) 423-3990; *The World in Figures*.

ZIMBABWE - STEEL - See ZIMBABWE - MINING AND MINERAL PRODUCTS

ZIMBABWE - STOCKS - COMMODITY - MARKET PRICE - INDEX

Food and Agricultural Organization of the United Nations (FAO) Via delle Terme di Caracalla, 00100 Rome, Italy (Telephone Number in U.S. (202) 050-3100); *The State of Food and Agriculture*.

ZIMBABWE - SUGAR PRODUCTION AND CONSUMPTION - See ZIMBABWE - CROPS

ZIMBABWE - TAXATION

G.K. Hall and Company, 70 Lincoln Street, Boston, Massachusetts 02111 (617) 423-3990; *The World in Figures*.

International Road Federation, 525 School Street, SW, Washington, D.C. 20024 (202) 554-2106; *World Road Statistics*.

The World Bank, 1818 H Street, NW, Washington, D.C. 20433 (202) 477-1234; *World Tables*.

ZIMBABWE - TELEPHONES IN USE

American Telephone and Telegraph Communications, Customer Information Center, Post Office Box 19901, Indianapolis, Indiana 46219; *The World's Telephones*.

Euromonitor Publications Limited, 87-88 Turnmill Street, London EC1M 5QU, England; *Third World Economic Handbook*.

G.K. Hall and Company, 70 Lincoln Street, Boston, Massachusetts 02111 (617) 423-3990; *The World in Figures*.

Statistical Office of the United Nations, Publishing Service, New York, New York 10017 (800) 253-9646; *Statistical Yearbook*.

ZIMBABWE - TELEVISION BROADCASTING - See ZIMBABWE - BROADCASTING

ZIMBABWE - TEXTILE INDUSTRY

Euromonitor Publications Limited, 87-88 Turnmill Street, London EC1M 5QU, England; *Third World Economic Handbook*.

G.K. Hall and Company, 70 Lincoln Street, Boston, Massachusetts 02111 (617) 423-3990; *The World in Figures*.

ZIMBABWE - TIN - See ZIMBABWE - MINING AND MINERAL PRODUCTS

ZIMBABWE - TOBACCO PRODUCTION

Euromonitor Publications Limited, 87-88 Turnmill Street, London EC1M 5QU, England; *Third World Economic Handbook*.

Facts on File, 460 Park Avenue South, New York, New York 10016 (800) 443-8323; *The New Book of World Rankings*.

Statistical Office of the United Nations, Publishing Service, New York, New York 10017 (800) 253-9646; *Statistical Yearbook*.

ZIMBABWE - TOURISM

Euromonitor Publications Limited, 87-88 Turnmill Street, London EC1M 5QU, England; *Third World Economic Handbook*.

Facts on File, 460 Park Avenue South, New York, New York 10016 (800) 443-8323; *The New Book of World Rankings*.

G.K. Hall and Company, 70 Lincoln Street, Boston, Massachusetts 02111 (617) 423-3990; *The World in Figures*.

Time Books, 201 East 50th Street, New York, New York 10022 (212) 751-2600; *The Economist Book of Vital World Statistics*.

United Nations Economic Commission for Africa, Africa Hall, P.O. Box 3001, Addis Ababa, Ethiopia (Telephone Number in U.S. (800) 253-9646); *African Statistical Yearbook.*

World Tourism Organization, Calle Capitan Haya 42, E-28020 Madrid, Spain; *Yearbook of Tourism Statistics.*

ZIMBABWE - TRACTORS IN USE

Statistical Office of the United Nations, Publishing Service, New York, New York 10017 (800) 253-9646; *Statistical Yearbook.*

ZIMBABWE - TRADE - See ZIMBABWE - FOREIGN TRADE

ZIMBABWE - TRADEMARKS AND SERVICE MARKS

World Intellectual Property Organization, 34 Chemin des Colombettes, CH-1211 Geneva 20. Switzerland; *Industrial Property Statistics.*

ZIMBABWE - TRANSPORTATION AND COMMUNICATIONS

Euromonitor Publications Limited, 87-88 Turnmill Street, London EC1M 5QU, England; *Third World Economic Handbook.*

Facts on File, 460 Park Avenue South, New York, New York 10016 (800) 443-8323; *The New Book of World Rankings.*

G.K. Hall and Company, 70 Lincoln Street, Boston, Massachusetts 02111 (617) 423-3990; *The World in Figures.*

United Nations Economic Commission for Africa, Africa Hall, P.O. Box 3001, Addis Ababa, Ethiopia (Telephone Number in U.S. (800) 253-9646); *African Statistical Yearbook.*

ZIMBABWE - TUNGSTEN PRODUCTION AND CONSUMPTION - See ZIMBABWE - MINING AND MINERAL PRODUCTS

ZIMBABWE - VITAL STATISTICS

Euromonitor Publications Limited, 87-88 Turnmill Street, London EC1M 5QU, England; *Third World Economic Handbook.*

G.K. Hall and Company, 70 Lincoln Street, Boston, Massachusetts 02111 (617) 423-3990; *The World in Figures.*

Statistical Office of the United Nations, Publishing Service, New York, New York 10017 (800) 253-9646; *Statistical Yearbook.*

World Health Organization, Office of Publications, Avenue Appia, CH-1211 Geneva 27, Switzerland (Telephone Number in U.S. (518) 436-9686); *World Health Statistics Annual.*

ZIMBABWE - WAGES

G.K. Hall and Company, 70 Lincoln Street, Boston, Massachusetts 02111 (617) 423-3990; *The World in Figures.*

ZIMBABWE - WEATHER

Facts on File, 460 Park Avenue South, New York, New York 10016 (800) 443-8323; *The New Book of World Rankings.*

G.K. Hall and Company, 70 Lincoln Street, Boston, Massachusetts 02111 (617) 423-3990; *The World in Figures.*

ZIMBABWE - WHEAT PRODUCTION AND PRICES - See ZIMBABWE - CROPS

ZIMBABWE - WHOLESALE PRICES

Statistical Office of the United Nations, Publishing Service, New York, New York 10017 (800) 253-9646; *Statistical Yearbook.*

ZIMBABWE - WHOLESALE TRADE

Euromonitor Publications Limited, 87-88 Turnmill Street, London EC1M 5QU, England; *Third World Economic Handbook.*

ZIMBABWE - WINE PRODUCTION

Facts on File, 460 Park Avenue South, New York, New York 10016 (800) 443-8323; *The New Book of World Rankings.*

ZIMBABWE - WOOL PRODUCTION

Facts on File, 460 Park Avenue South, New York, New York 10016 (800) 443-8323; *The New Book of World Rankings.*

ZIMBABWE - WOOD PULP PRODUCTION - See ZIMBABWE - FORESTRY AND FOREST PRODUCTS

ZINC

U.S. Department of the Interior, Bureau of Mines, 810 Seventh Street, NW, Washington, D.C. 20241 (202) 501-9649; *Annual Reports, Mineral Facts and Problems,* and *Mineral Commodity Summaries.*

ZINC - FOREIGN TRADE

U.S. Department of Commerce, Bureau of the Census, Suitland, Maryland 20233 (301) 763-4040; *U.S. Merchandise Trade.*

U.S. Department of the Interior, Bureau of Mines, 810 Seventh Street, NW, Washington, D.C. 20241 (202) 501-9649; *Annual Reports,* and *Mineral Commodity Summaries.*

ZINC - MINING INDUSTRY

U.S. Department of Commerce, Bureau of the Census, Suitland, Maryland 20233 (301) 763-4040; *Census of Mineral Industries.*

ZINC - PRICES

U.S. Department of Commerce, Bureau of the Census, Suitland, Maryland 20233 (301) 763-4040; *Census of Mineral Industries.*

U.S. Department of Labor, Bureau of Labor Statistics, Two Massachusetts Avenue, NE, Washington, D.C. 20212 (202) 606-7828; *Producer Prices Indexes.*

U.S. Department of the Interior, Bureau of Mines, 810 Seventh Street, NW, Washington, D.C. 20241 (202) 501-9649; *Mineral Commodity Summaries.*

ZINC - PRODUCTION - WORLD

U.S. Department of the Interior, Bureau of Mines, 810 Seventh Street, NW, Washington, D.C. 20241 (202) 501-9649; *Mineral Commodity Summaries,* and *Annual Reports.*

ZINC - PRODUCTION AND VALUE (MINE AND SMELTER)

U.S. Department of the Interior, Bureau of Mines, 810 Seventh Street, NW, Washington, D.C. 20241 (202) 501-9649; *Mineral Commodity Summaries, Annual Reports,* and *Mineral Facts and Problems.*

ZINC - STRATEGIC AND CRITICAL MATERIALS

U.S. Department of Defense, Defense Logistics Agency, Cameron Station, Alexandria, Virginia 22304-6100 (703) 274-6000; *Statistical Supplement, Stockpile Report to the Congress*.

U.S. Department of the Interior, Bureau of Mines, 810 Seventh Street, NW, Washington, D.C. 20241 (202) 501-9649; *Annual Reports*, and *Mineral Commodity Summaries*.

Appendix A

Source Publications

This appendix provides an overview of the printed sources of information used to compile this edition of *Statistics Sources*. It consists of a complete bibliography of all the publications cited under the specific subject headings throughout both volumes. Entries in this listing are arranged alphabetically by publication title, and include the names and addresses of the issuing or publishing bodies.

ACP: Basic Statistics.
European Community Information Service, 2100 M Street, NW, Washington, D.C. 20037 (202) 862-9500

ADFL Bulletin.
Association of Departments of Foreign Languages, 10 Astor Place, New York, New York 10003 (212) 614-6319

Abortion Factbook.
Alan Guttmacher Institute, 111 Fifth Avenue, New York, New York 10003 (212) 254-5656

Abortion Services in the United States.
Alan Guttmacher Institute, 111 Fifth Avenue, New York, New York 10003 (212) 254-5656

Abstract of Statistics.
Central Statistics Office, Ministry of Finance, Saint George's Grenada

Abstract of Statistics.
Department of Economic Development, Statistics Unit, Post Office Box 42, Niue Island, Niue

Abstract of Statistics.
National Statistics Office, Central Government Offices, Post Office Wards Strip, Waigani, Papua New Guinea

Abstract of Statistics.
Statistics Office, Cathedral Square, Gibraltar

Accident Bulletin.
U.S. Department of Transportation, Federal Railroad Administration, 400 Seventh Street, SW, Washington, D.C. 20590 (202) 366-.4000

Accident Facts.
National Safety Council, 1121 Spring Lake Drive, Itasca, Illinois 60143-3201 (708) 285-1121

Adoption Factbook.
National Council for Adoption, 1930 Seventeenth Street, NW, Washington, D.C. 20009 (202) 328-1200

Adult Education Profile.
U.S. Department of Education, National Center for Education Statistics, 400 Maryland Avenue, SW, Washington, D.C. 20202 (202) 708 5366

Advance Data from Vital and Health Statistics.
U.S. Department of Health and Human Services, National Center for Health Statistics, 3700 East-West Highway, Hyattsville, Maryland 20782 (301) 436-8500

Advertising Age.
Crain Communications, Incorporated, 740 North Rush Street, Chicago, Illinois 60611 (312) 649-5200

Aeronautics and Space Report of the President.
U.S. National Aeronautics and Space Administration, 300 E Street, SW, Washington, D.C. 20546 (202) 358-1000

Affirmative Employment Statistics.
U.S. Office of Personnel Management, 1900 E Street, NW, Washington, D.C. 20415 (202) 606-1800

Afghan Agriculture In Figures.
Central Statistics Office, Kabul, Afghanistan

Afghanistan.
Federal Statistical Office, Gustav-Stresemann-Ring 11, D-6200 Wiesbaden, Germany

African Statistical Yearbook.
United Nations Economic Commission for Africa, Africa Hall, P.O Box 3001, Addis Ababa, Ethiopia (Telephone Number in U.S. (800) 253-9646)

Agenda estadística.
Instituto Nacional de Estadistica, Georafia e Informatica, CP 03910, Mexico

Agricultural Banker.
American Bankers Association, 1120 Connecticut Avenue, NW, Washington, D.C. 20036 (202) 663-5000

Agricultural Outlook.
U.S. Department of Agriculture, Office of Aquaculture, 901 D Street, SW, Washington, D.C. 20024 (202) 401-4929

Agricultural Prices: Annual Summary.
U.S. Department of Agriculture, National Agricultural Statistics Service, Fourteenth Street and Independence Avenue, SW, Washington, D.C. 20250 (202) 219-1504

Agricultural Resources: Cropland, Water, and Conservation, Situation and Outlook Report.
U.S. Department of Agriculture, Economic Research Service, Fourteenth Street and Independence Avenue, SW, Washington, D.C. 20005-4789 (202) 219-1504

Agricultural Statistics.
U.S. Department of Agriculture, Economic Research Service, Fourteenth Street and Independence Avenue, SW, Washington, D.C. 20005-4789 (202) 219-1504

Agricultural Supply and Demand Estimates.
U.S. Department of Agriculture, Economic Research Service, Fourteenth Street and Independence Avenue, SW, Washington, D.C. 20005-4789 (202) 219-1504

The Agricultural Work Force.
U.S. Department of Agriculture, Economic Research Service, Fourteenth Street and Independence Avenue, SW, Washington, D.C. 20250 (202) 219-1504

Agriculture: Statistical Yearbook.
European Community Information Service, 2100 M Street, NW, Washington, D.C. 20037 (202) 862-9500

Air Carrier Financial Statistics.
U.S. Department of Transportation, Federal Aviation Administration, 800 Independence Avenue, SW, Washington, D.C. 20591 (202) 366-4000

Air Carrier Traffic Statistics.
U.S. Department of Transportation, Federal Aviation Administration, 800 Independence Avenue, SW, Washington, D.C. 20591 (202) 366-4000

Air Quality Update.
U.S. Environmental Protection Agency, 401 M Street, NW, Washington, D.C. 20460 (202) 382-2090

Air Transport.
Air Transport Association of American, 1301 Pennsylvania Avenue, NW, Washington, D.C. 20004 (202) 626-4000

Air Transport Facts and Figures.
Air Transport Association of America, 1301 Pennsylvania Avenue, NW, Washington, D.C. 20004 (202) 626-4000

Air Travel Consumer Report.
U.S. Department of Transportation, Office of Consumer Affairs, 400 Seventh Street, SW, Washington, D.C. 20590 (202) 366-4000

Airport Activity Statistics.
U.S. Department of Transportation, Federal Aviation Administration, 800 Independence Avenue, SW, Washington, D.C. 20591 (202) 366-4000

The Alaska Economy Performance Report.
Department of Commerce and Economic Analysis, Pouch D, Juneau, Alaska 99811 (907) 465-2017

Albanien.
Federal Statistical Office, Gustav-Stresemann-Ring 11, D-6200 Wiesbaden, Germany

Alcohol and Tobacco Summary Statistics.
U.S. Department of the Treasury, Bureau of Alcohol, Tobacco and Firearms, 650 Massachusetts Avenue, NW, Washington, D.C. 20226 (202) 927-8500

Algerian.
Federal Statistical Office, Gustav-Stresemann-Ring 11, D-6200 Wiesbaden, Germany

Allman Manadsstatistik.
Statiska Centralbyran, Karlavagen 100, S-115 81, Stockholm, Sweden

America Votes.
Elections Research Center, 5508 Greystone Street, Chevy Chase, Maryland 20815 (202) 659-9490

American Banker.
American Banker, One State Street Plaza, New York, New York 10004 (212) 943-6700

American Banker Ranking the Banks.
American Banker-Bond Buyer, One State Street Plaza, New York, New york 10004 (212) 943-6700

American Freshman: National Norms.
The Higher Education Research Institute, University of California, Los Angeles, California 90024 (213) 825-1925

American Housing Survey.
U.S. Department of Commerce, Bureau of the Census, Suitland, Maryland 20233 (301) 763-4040

American Jewish Yearbook.
American Jewish Committee, c/o Institute of Human Relations, 165 East Fifty-Sixth Street, New York, New York 10022 (212) 751-4000

American League Red Book.
The American League of Professional Baseball Clubs, 350 Park Avenue, Eighteenth Floor, New York, New York 10022 (212) 339-7600

American Library Directory.
R.R. Bowker Company, 121 Chanlon Road, New Providence, New Jersey 07974 (908) 464-6800

American National Election Studies Data Sourcebook.
Center for Political Studies, University of Michigan, Post Office Box 1248, Ann Arbor, Michigan 48106 (313) 764-8363

American Samoa Statistical Digest.
Economic Development and Planning Office, Pago Pago, American Samoa

An Analysis of the Timber Situation in the United States.
U.S. Department of Agriculture, Forest Service, Fourteenth Street and Independence Avenue, SW, Washington, D.C. 20250 (202) 720-3760

An Analytical Record of Yields and Yield Spreads.
Salomon Brothers Incorporated, One New York Plaza, New York, New York 10004 (212) 747-7000

Analysis of Class I Railroads.
  Association of American Railroads, 50 F Street, NW, Washington, D.C. 20001 (202) 639-2100

Analytical Perspectives Budget of the United States Government.
  Executive Office of the President, Office of Management and Budget, Executive Office Building, Washington, D.C. 20503 (202) 395-3080

Angola.
  Federal Statistical Office, Gustav-Stresemann-Ring 11, D-6200 Wiesbaden, Germany

Animal Health Yearbook.
  Food and Agricultural Organization of the United Nations (FAO), Via delle Terme di Caracalla, 00100 Rome, Italy (Telephone Number in the U.S. (202) 653-2400)

Annuaire Statistique.
  Department de la Statistique, BP 1156, Bujumbura, Burundi

Annuaire Statistique.
  Direction de la Statistique, BP 240, Nouakchott, Mauritania

Annuaire Statistique.
  Direction de la Statistique et de la Comptabilite Economique, BP 2031, Brazzaville, Congo

Annuaire Statistique.
  Direction de la Statistique Generale et des Etudes Economiques, BP 732, Bangui, Central African Republic

Annuaire statistique.
  Direction de la Statistique, Niamey, Niger

Annuaire Statistique.
  Direction Generale de la Statistique, BP 179, Libreville, Gabon

Annuaire Statistique.
  Institut National de la Statistique et de l'Analyse Economique, BP 323, Cotonou, Benin

Annuaire Statistique.
  Service National de la Statistique, Ministere du Plan et de la Cooperation, Post Office Box 46, Vientiane, Laos

Annuaire Statistique de Belgique.
  Institut National de Statistique, National Institute of Statistics, rue de Louvain 44, 1000 Brussels, Belgium

Annuaire Statistique du Burkina Faso.
  Ministere du Plan et de la Cooperation, BP 374, Ougadougou, 01, Burkina Faso

Annuaire Statistique de Djibouti.
  Djibouti: Direction Nationale de la Statistique, BP 1846, Djibouti

Annuaire Statistique de Poche.
  Institut National de Statistique, National Institute of Statistics, rue de Louvain 44, 1000 Brussels, Belgium

Annuaire Statistique de l'Algerie.
  Sous - Direction des Statistiques, Direction des Statistiques et de la Comptabilite Nationale, BP 478, Alger, Algeria

Annuaire Statistique de la France.
  Institut National de la Statistique et des Etudes Economiques (INSEE), 12 rue Boulitte, 75675 Paris Cedex 14, France

Annuaire statistique de la Guadeloupe.
  Institut National de la Statistique et des Etudes Economiques, Tour Gamma A, 195 rue de Bercy, 75582, Paris Cedex 12, France

Annuaire Statistique de la Guyane.
  INSEE, Observatoire Economique de Paris, Tour Gamma A, 195 rue de Bercy, 75582, Paris Cedex 12, France

Annuaire Statistique de la Martinique.
  Institut National de la Statistique et des Etudes Economiques, BP 863, 97175 Pointe-a-Pitre, France

Annuaire Statistique de la Nouvelle Caledonie et Dependances.
  Direction Territoriale de la Statistique et des Etudes Economiques, BP 323, Noumea, New Caledonia

Annuaire Statistique de la Suisse.
  Bureau Federal de Statistique, Hallwylstrasse 15 3003 Berne, Switzerland

Annuaire Statistique de la Tunisie.
  Institut National de la Statistique, 27 rue du Liban, 1002 Tunis-Belvedere, Tunis, Tunisia

Annuaire Statistique du Luxembourg.
  STATEC, 19-21 Boulevard Royal, BP 304, L-2013, Luxembourg

Annuaire statistique du Mali.
  Direction Nationale de la Statistique, BP12, Bamako, Mali

Annuaire statistique du Maroc.
  Division de la Statistique, BP 178, Rabat, Morocco

Annuaire Statistique du Tchad.
  Direction de la Statistique, BP 453, N'djamena, Chad

Annuaire statistique du Togo.
  Direction de la Statistique (Department of Statistics), BP 118, Lome, Togo

Annuaire Statistique du Zaire.
  Institut National de la Statistique, BP 20, Kinshasa, Gombe, Zaire

Annual Abstract of Statistics.
  Central Office of Statistics, Auberge D'Italie, Valletta, Malta

Annual Abstract of Statistics.
  Central Statistical Organisation, Ministry of Planning, Post Office Box 8001, Baghdad, Iraq

Annual Abstract of Statistics.
  Federal Office of Statistics, 36-38 Broad Street, PMB 12528, Lagos, Nigeria

Annual Abstract of Statistics.
  HM Stationery Office, Post Office Box 276, London SW8 5DT, England

Annual Abstract of Statistics.
  Ministry of Finance, Central Statistical Office, Belmopan, Belize

Annual Abstract of Statistics.
  Statistics Office, Post Office Box G6, Honiara, Solomon Islands

Annual Bulletin of Transport Statistics for Europe.
  Statistical Office of the United Nations, Publishing Service, New York, New York 10017 (800) 253-9646

Published Sources

Annual Cancer Statistics Review.
U.S. Department of Health and Human Services, National Institutes of Health, National Cancer Institute, 9000 Rockville Pike, Bethesda, Maryland 20892 (301) 496-5737

Annual Digest of Statistics.
Central Statistical Office, Government Printer, Port Louis, Mauritius

Annual Economic Review.
Economic Research Center, Department of Commerce, Agana, Guam 96910

Annual Economic Review of Zimbabwe.
Central Statistical Office, Post Office Box 8063, Causeway, Harare, Zimbabwe

Annual Energy Review.
U.S. Department of Energy, Energy Information Administration, 1000 Independence Avenue, SW, Washington, D.C. 20585 (202) 586-8800

Annual Historical Review of FNS Programs.
U.S. Department of Agriculture, Food and Nutrition Service, 3101 Park Center Drive, Alexandria, Virginia 22302 (703) 305-2276

Annual Housing Survey.
U.S. Department of Commerce, Bureau of the Census, Suitland, Maryland 20233 (301) 763-4040

Annual Information Exchange.
National Association of State Park Directors, 126 Mill Branch Road, Tallahassee, Florida 32312 (904) 893-4959

Annual Prospects for World Coal Trade.
U.S. Department of Energy, Energy Information Administration, 1000 Independence Avenue, SW, Washington, D.C. 20585 (202) 586-8800

Annual Report.
American Bus Association, 1100 New York Avenue, NW, Washington, D.C. 20005 (202) 842-1645

Annual Report.
Boy Scouts of America, 1325 Walnut Hill Lane, Post Office Box 152079, Irving, Texas 75015 (214) 580-2000

Annual Report.
Federal Deposit Insurance Corporation, 550 Seventeenth Street, NW, Washington, D.C. 20429 (202) 393-8400

Annual Report.
Girl Scouts of the United States of America, 420 Fifth Avenue and 51st Street, New York, New York 10018-2702 (212) 852-8000

Annual Report.
U.S. Commodity Futures Trading Commission, 2033 K Street, NW, Washington, D.C. 20581 (202) 254-6387

Annual Report.
U.S. Federal Communications Commission, 1919 M Street, NW, Washington, D.C. 20554 (202) 632-7000

Annual Report.
U.S. Library of Congress, 101 Independence Avenue, SE, Washington, D.C. 20540 (202) 707-5000

Annual Report.
U.S. National Endowment for the Arts, 1100 Pennsylvania Avenue, NW, Washington, D.C. 20506 (202) 606-8438

Annual Report.
U.S. National Endowment for the Humanities, 1100 Pennsylvania Avenue, NW, Washington, D.C. 20506 (202) 786-0438

Annual Report.
U.S. Securities and Exchange Commission, 450 Fifth Street, NW, Washington, D.C. 20549 (202) 272-3100

Annual Report of Board of Trustees, OASI, DI, HI, and SMI Trust Funds.
U.S. Department of Health and Human Services, Social Security Administration, 6401 Security Boulevard, Baltimore, Maryland 21235 (410) 965-1234

Annual Report of the Commissioner and Chief Counsel of the Internal Revenue Service.
U.S. Department of the Treasury, Internal Revenue Service, 1111 Constitution Avenue, NW, Washington, D.C. 20224 (202) 566-5000

Annual Report of the Director.
Administrative Office of the United States Courts, United States Supreme Court Building, One Columbus Circle, NE, Washington, D.C. 20544 (202) 273-1120

Annual Report of the National Credit Union Administration.
National Credit Union Administration, 1775 Duke Street, Alexandria, Virginia 22314 (703) 518-6300

Annual Report of the Postmaster General.
U.S. Postal Service, 475 L'Enfant Plaza West, SW, Washington, D.C. 20260 (202) 268-2000

Annual Report of the Regional Airline Association.
Regional Airline Association, 1101 Connecticut Avenue, NW, Suite 700, Washington, D.C. 20036 (202) 857-1170

Annual Report of the Revenue Commissioners.
Government Publications Sales Office, GPO Arcade, Dublin 1, Ireland

Annual Report of the Secretary of Transportation.
U.S. Department of Transportation, United States Coast Guard, 2100 Second Street, SW, Washington, D.C. 20593 (202) 267-1587

Annual Report of the Secretary of Veterans Affairs.
U.S. Department of Veterans Affairs, 810 Vermont Avenue, NW, Washington, D.C. 20420 (202) 233-2300

Annual Report of the Territory of Norfolk Island.
Australian Government Publishing Service, Post Office Box 84, Canberra ACT 26010, Australia

Annual Report on Dental Education.
American Dental Association, 211 East Chicago Avenue, Chicago, Illinois 60611 (312) 440-2500

Annual Report on the Economic Status of the Profession.
Maryse Eymonerie Associates, Post Office Box 7893, Hilton Head, South Carolina 29938

Annual Report on the Territory of Christmas Island.
Sales and Distribution, Australian Government Publishing Service, Post Office Box 84, Canberra ACT 2601, Australia

Annual Report on the Territory of Cocos (Keeling) Islands.
Sales and Distribution, Australian Government Publishing Service, Post Office Box 84, Canberra ACT 2600, Australia

Annual Report to Congress.
U.S. Department of Education, Office of Special Education Programs, 400 Maryland Avenue, SW, Washington, D.C. 20202 (202) 708-5366

Annual Report to Congress.
U.S. Department of Health and Human Services, Office of Child Support Enforcement, 370 L'Enfant Promenade, SW, Washington, D.C. 20447 (202) 401-9373

Annual Report to Congress on Civil Aviation Security.
U.S. Department of Transportation, Federal Aviation Administration, 800 Independence Avenue, SW, Washington, D.C. 20591 (202) 366-4000

Annual Report to the United Nations on the Administration of the Trust Territory of the Pacific Islands.
Superintendent of Documents, U.S. Government Printing Office, Washington, D.C. 20402 (202) 783-3238

Annual Reports.
U.S. Department of the Interior, Bureau of Mines, 810 Seventh Street, NW, Washington, D.C. 20241 (202) 501-9649

Annual Retail Trade Report.
U.S. Department of Commerce, Bureau of the Census, Suitland, Maryland 20233 (301) 763-4040

Annual Review of the Chief, National Guard Bureau.
U.S. National Guard Bureau, The Pentagon, Washington, D.C. 20301 (202) 433-5100

Annual Statistical Abstract.
Central Statistical Office, Ministry of Planning, Post Office Box 904, Abu Dhabi, United Arab Emirates

Annual Statistical Abstract.
Central Statistical Office, Post Office Box 26188, Safat, Kuwait

Annual Statistical Abstract.
Central Statistical Organization, Post Office Box 7283, Doha, Qatar

Annual Statistical Abstract.
Department of Statistics, Apia, Western Samoa

Annual Statistical Abstract.
Statistical Bureau, Avenue of the Republic, Post Office Box 542, Georgetown, Guyana

Annual Statistical Abstract State of Qatar.
Presidency of the Council of Ministers, Central Statistical Organisation, Doha, Qatar

Annual Statistical Bulletin.
Central Statistical Office, Post Office Box 456, Mbabane, Swaziland

Annual Statistical Digest.
Board of Governors of the Federal Reserve System, Twentieth Street and Constitution Avenue, NW, Washington, D.C. 20551 (202) 452-3000

Annual Statistical Digest.
Central Statistical Office, Post Office Box 98, Port of Spain, Trinidad

Annual Statistical Digest.
Central Statistics Office, Ministry of Finance, Tower Hill, Freetown, Sierra Leone

Annual Statistical Digest.
Development, Planning and Statistics Division, Premier's Office, Post Office Building, Castries, Saint Lucia

Annual Statistical Report.
American Iron and Steel Institute, 1101 17th Street, NW, Washington, D.C. 20036 (202) 452-7100

Annual Statistical Report.
U.S. Department of Justice, Drug Enforcement Administration, 600-700 Army Navy Drive, Arlington, Virginia 22202 (202) 307-1000

Annual Statistical Supplement to the Social Security Bulletin.
U.S. Department of Health and Human Services, Social Security Administration, 6401 Security Boulevard, Baltimore, Maryland 21235 (410) 965-1234

Annual Summary of Merchant Ships Completed in the World.
Lloyd's Register of Shipping, 71 Fenchurch Street, London EC3, England

Annual Survey of Communication Services
U.S. Department of Commerce, Bureau of the Census, Suitland, Maryland 20233 (301) 763-4040

Annual Survey of Corporate Contributions.
The Conference Board, 845 Third Avenue, New York, New York 10022 (212) 759-0900

Annual Survey of Hospitals
American Hospital Association, 840 North Lake Shore Drive, Chicago, Illinois 60611 (312) 280-6000

Annual Survey of Manufactures.
U.S. Department of Commerce, Bureau of the Census, Suitland, Maryland 20233 (301) 763-4040

Anuario Estadistico de los Estados Unidos Mexicanos
Instituto National de Estadistica, Geografía e Informatica, CP 03910, Mexico

Annuario Statistico Italiano.
Instituto Centrale di Statistica, Via Cesare Balbo 16, 00184 Rome, Italy

Antigua: Report for the Year.
HMSO, Post Office Box 569, London SE1 9NH, England

Anuario de la Bolsa.
Colegio de Agentes de Cambio y Bolsa de Madrid, Plaza de la Lealtad, 1, Madrid-14, Spain

Anuario estatistico.
Direccao Geral de Estatistica, Bissau, Guinea Bissau

Anuario estatistico.
Direccao Nacional de Estatistica, CP 493, Maputo, Mozambique

Anuario estadistico.
Direccion de Estadisticas y Censos, Avenida Centenario 6Y8 Calles, Camayaguela DC, Honduras, Honduras

Anuario estadistico.
Direccion General de Estadistica y Censos, Instituto Nacional de Estadistica y Censos, Hipolita Yrigoyen 250, Buenos Aires

Anuario Estadistico.
Direccion General de Estadistica y Censos Villa Femina, Calle Arce No 953, San Salvador, El Salvador

Anuario Estadistico.
Direccion General de Estadisticas, Cuareim, 2052, Montivideo, Uruguay

Anuario estadistico.
Instituto Nacional de Estadistica, Guatemala City, Guatemala

Anuario estadistico.
Oficina Central de Estadistica e Informatica, Presidencia de la Republica, Aptdo. de Correos 400 Carmelitas, Caracas 1050, Venezuela

Anuario estatistico.
Instituto Nacional de Estatistica (National Statistical Institute), Avenida Antonio Jose de Almeida, Lisbon, Portugal

Anuario estatistico.
Reparticao Provincial dos Servicos de Estatistica, Macau, Macau

Anuario estatistico - Annuaire statistique.
Direccao dos Servicos de Estatistica (Department of Statistical Services), Caixa Postal 1215, Luanda, Angola

Anuario estastistico.
Puerto Rico Planning Board, North Building, Box 41119, San Juan, Puerto Rico 00940

Anuario estatistico de Brasil.
Fundacao Instituto Brasileiro de Geografia e Estatistica, Avenida Franklin Roosevelt 166 20021, Rio de Janeiro, Brazil

Anuario estadistico de Cuba.
Comite Estatal de Estadisticas, Calle 46, No. 307, Gaveta Postal 6016, Miramar, Havana, Cuba

Anuario estadistico de Chile.
Instituto Nacional de Estadisticas, Casilla 7597, Correo 3, Santiago, Chile

Anuario estadistico de Espana.
Instituto Nacional de Estadistica (National Institute of Statistics), Paseo de la Castellana 183, Madrid, Spain

Anuario Estadistico de Nicaragua.
Instituto Nacional de Estadistica y Censos, Apartado 4031, Managua, Nicaragua

Annuario estadistico del Paraguay
Direccion General de Estadistica y Censos, Miguel Torres 5313, C Correos: 1118, Asuncion, Paraguay

Anuario estadistico del Peru.
Direccion General de Estadistica y Censos, Instituto Nacional de Estadistica, Avenida 28 de Julio 1056, Lima 1, Peru

Anuario general de estadistica.
DANE, Via Eldorado, Bogota, Colombia

Anuario Statistico.
Servicio Statale di Statistica, Via G Carducci 145, Repubblica di San Marino

Anuarul Statistica Al Romaniei.
Comisia Nationala Pentru Statistica, Bucharest, Romania

Aquatorialguinea.
Federal Statistical Office, Gustav-Stresemann-Ring 11, D-6200 Wiesbaden, Germany

Area Handbook for North Korea.
Superintendent of Documents, U.S. Government Printing Office, Washington, D.C. 20402 (202) 783-3238

Area Measurement Reports.
U.S. Department of Commerce, Bureau of the Census, Suitland, Maryland 20233 (301) 763-4040

Areas of Acquisitions to the Territory of the United States.
U.S. Department of the Interior, C Street between Eighteenth and Nineteenth Streets, NW, Washington, D.C. 20240 (202) 208-3171

Areas of the United States.
U.S. Department of Commerce, Bureau of the Census, Suitland, Maryland 20233 (301) 763-4040

Argentina.
Federal Statistical Office, Gustav-Stresemann-Ring 11, D-6200 Wiesbaden, Germany

Argus F.C. & S. Chart.
The National Underwriter Company, 505 Gest Street, Cincinnati, Ohio 45203 (513) 721-2140

Arizona Economic Indicators.
University of Arizona, Division of Economic and Business Research, College of Business and Public Administration, Tucson, Arizona 85721 (602) 621-2155

Arizona Statistical Abstract: A 1990 Data Handbook.
University of Arizona, Division of Economic and Business Research, College of Business and Public Administration, Tucson, Arizona 85721 (602) 621-2155

Arkansas State and County Economic Data.
University of Arkansas, Little Rock, Regional Economic Analysis, Library 512, Little Rock, Arkansas 72204

Arkansas Statistical Abstract.
University of Arkansas at Little Rock, State Data Center, Library 508, Little Rock, Arkansas 72204 (501) 659-8530

Asian Market Atlas.
The Economist Intelligence Unit (Asia) Limited, 10th Floor Luk Kwok Centre, 72 Gloucester Road, Wanchai Hong Kong (Phone Number in the U.S. (800) 938-4685)

Atlas/Data Abstract for the United States and Selected Areas.
U.S. Department of Defense, Office of the Secretary, The Pentagon, Washington, D.C. 20301 (703) 545-6700

Athiopien.
Federal Statistical Office, Gustav-Stresemann-Ring 11, D-6200 Wiesbaden, Germany

Australien.
Federal Statistical Office, Gustav-Stresemann-Ring 11, D-6200 Wiesbaden, Germany

Average Annual Pay by State and Industry.
U.S. Department of Labor, Bureau of Labor Statistics, Two Massachusetts Avenue, NE, Washington, D.C. 20212 (202) 606-7828

Average Annual Pay Levels in Metropolitan Areas.
U.S. Department of Labor, Bureau of Labor Statistics, Two Massachusetts Avenue, NE, Washington, D.C. 20212 (202) 606-7828

Aylik Istatistik Bulteni.
Devlet Istatistik Enstitusu, Necatibey Caddesi, 114 Ankara, Turkey

BLS Reports on Employer Child-Care Practices.
U.S. Department of Labor, Bureau of Labor Statistics, Two Massachusetts Avenue, NE, Washington, D.C. 20212 (202) 606-7828

Bahamas.
Federal Statistical Office, Gustav-Stresemann-Ring 11, D-6200 Wiesbaden, Germany

Bahrain.
Federal Statistical Office, Gustav-Stresemann-Ring 11, D-6200 Wiesbaden, Germany

Balance Sheets for United States Economy.
Board of Governors of the Federal Reserve System, Twentieth Street and Constitution Avenue, NW, Washington, D.C. 20551 (202) 452-3000

Bangladesch.
Federal Statistical Office, Gustav-Stresemann-Ring 11, D-6200 Wiesbaden, Germany

Bank Network News.
Faulkner and Gray, 118 South Clinton Street, Chicago, Illinois 60661 (312) 648-0261

Barbados.
Federal Statistical Office, Gustav-Stresemann-Ring 11, D-6200 Wiesbaden, Germany

Barbados economic report.
Barbados Statistical Service, Third Floor, National Insurance Building, Fairchild Street, Bridgetown, Barbados

Basic Statistics of the Community.
European Community Information Service, 2100 M Street, NW, Washington, D.C. 20037 (202) 862-9500

Belgien.
Federal Statistical Office, Gustav-Stresemann-Ring 11, D-6200 Wiesbaden, Germany

Belize.
Federal Statistical Office, Gustav-Stresemann-Ring 11, D-6200 Wiesbaden, Germany

Benchmark Ohio.
The Ohio State University, School of Public Policy and Management, 1775 College Road, Columbus, Ohio 43210-1399 (614) 292-8696

Benin.
Federal Statistical Office, Gustav-Stresemann-Ring 11, D-6200 Wiesbaden, Germany

Bermuda Digest of Statistics.
Statistical Department, Post Office Box 177, Hamilton, Bermuda

Bevolkerung und Erwerbstatigkeit, Reihe 1.1: Stand und Entwicklung der Bevolkerung.
Statistiches Bundesamt (Allgemeiner Auskunftsdienst), Gustav-Stresemann-Ring 11, Postfach 5528, 6200 Wiesbaden 1, Germany

Biennial Report of Employment by Geographic Area.
U.S. Office of Personnel Management, 1900 E Street, NW, Washington, D.C. 20415 (202) 606-1800

Bilan statistique annuel de la Guadeloupe.
INSEE, Tour Gamma A, 195 rue de Bercy, 75582 Paris Codex 12, France

Bilan Statistique de L'annee.
Institut Territorial de la Statistique, BP 395, Papeete-Tahiti, French Polynesia

Biuletyn statystyczny
Glowny Urzad Statystyczny (Central Statistical Office), Al Niepodleglosci 208, 00-925 Warsaw, Poland

Black Elected Officials: A National Roster.
Joint Center for Political and Economic Studies, 1090 Vermont Avenue, NW, Suite 1100, Washington, D.C. 20005 (202) 789-3500

Black Lung Benefits Act, Annual Report.
U.S. Department of Labor, Employment Standards Administration, 200 Constitution Avenue, NW, Washington, D.C. 20210 (202) 219-7320

Boletim mensal
Direccao dos Servicos de Estatistica (Department of Statistical Services), Caixa Postal 1215, Luanda, Angola

Boletim mensal de estatistica.
Reparticao Provincial dos Servicos de Estatistica, Macau, Macau

Boletim Mensal de estatistics.
Direccao Nacional de Estatistica, CP 493, Maputo, Mozambique

Boletim trimestral de estatistica.
Direccao Geral de Estatistica, Bissau, Guinea Bissau

Boletin Anual de estatistica.
Servico Nacional de Estatistica, CP 116, Praia, Cape Verde

Boletin anuario.
Banco Central del Ecuador, Casilla 339, Quito, Ecuador

Boletin de Estadistica.
Instituto Nacional de Estadistica y Censos, Apartado 4031, Managua, Nicaragua

Boletin Economico.
Banco de Espana, Alcala, 50, Madrid-14, Spain

Boletin estadistica.
Direccion General de Estadistica, Malabo, Equatorial Guinea

Boletin estadistico.
Direccion General de Estadistica y Censos, Villa Femina, Calle Arce No. 953, San Salvador, El Salvador

Boletin estadistico.
Instituto Nacional de Estadistica, Casilla No. 6129, La Paz, Bolivia

Boletin estadistico.
Instituto Nacional de Estadistica, Guatemala City, Guatemala

Boletin estadistico del Paraguay.
Direccion General de Estadistica y Censos, Humaita 473, Asuncion Paraguay

Boletin estadistico trimestral.
Direccion General de Estadistica y Censos, Instituto Nacional de Estadistica y Censos, Hipolita Yrigoyen 250, Buenos Aires

Boletin mensual de estadistica.
DANE, Via Eldorado, Bogota, Columbia

Published Sources

Boletin mensal de estatistica.
Instituto Nacional de Estatistica (National Statistical Institute), Avenida Antonio Jose de Almeida, Lisbon, Portugal

Boletin Mensual de Estadistics.
Instituto Nacional de Estadistica, Paseo de la Castellana 183, Madrid, Spain

Bolivia.
Federal Statistical Office, Gustav-Stresemann-Ring 11, D-6200 Wiesbaden, Germany

Bolivia en cifras.
Instituto Nacional de Estadistica, Casilla 6129, La Paz, Bolivia

Bolletino Mensile di Statistica.
Instituto Centrale di Statistica, Via Cesare Balbo 16, 00184 Rome, Italy

Bollettino di statistica.
Servicio Statale di Statistica, Via G Carducci 145, Repubblica di San Marino

Book Industry Trends.
Book Industry Study Group, 160 Fifth Avenue, New York, New York 10010 (212) 929-1393

Botsuana.
Federal Statistical Office, Gustav-Stresemann-Ring 11, D-6200 Wiesbaden, Germany

Botswana in Figures.
Central Statistics Office, Government Printer, Post Office Box 87, Gaberone, Botswana

The Bowker Annual: Library and Book Trade Almanac.
R.R. Bowker Company, 121 Chanlon Road, New Providence, New Jersey 07974 (908) 464-6800

Brazil.
Federal Statistical Office, Gustav-Stresemann-Ring 11, D-6200 Wiesbaden, Germany

Britannica Book of the Year.
Encyclopedia Britannica, Incorporated, 310 South Michigan Avenue, Chicago, Illinois 60604 (312) 347-7000

Britannica World Data.
Encyclopedia Britannica, Incorporated, 310 South Michigan Avenue, Chicago, Illinois 60604 (312) 347-7000

Broadcasting Yearbook.
Broadcasting Publications, Inc., 1705 DeSales Street, Washington, D.C. 20036 (202) 659-2340

Brunei.
Federal Statistical Office, Gustav-Stresemann-Ring 11, D-6200 Wiesbaden, Germany

Brunei Statistical Yearbook.
Economic Planning Unit, Bandar Seri Begawan, Brunei

Budget of the United States Government.
Executive Office of the President, Office of Management and Budget, Executive Office Building, Washington, D.C. 20503 (202) 395-3080

Budget Summary.
U.S. National Aeronautics and Space Administration, 300 E Street, SW, Washington, D.C. 20546 (202) 358-1000

Buku Tahunan Perangkaan.
Department of Statistics, Jalan Cenderasari, Kuala Lumpur, Malaysia

Bulgarien.
Federal Statistical Office, Gustav-Stresemann-Ring 11, D-6200 Wiesbaden, Germany

Bulletin 2192.
U.S. Department of Labor, Bureau of Labor Statistics, Two Massachusetts Avenue, NE, Washington, D.C. 20212 (202) 606-7828

Bulletin 2217.
U.S. Department of Labor, Bureau of Labor Statistics, Two Massachusetts Avenue, NE, Washington, D.C. 20212 (202) 606-7828

Bulletin 2307.
U.S. Department of Labor, Bureau of Labor Statistics, Two Massachusetts Avenue, NE, Washington, D.C. 20212 (202) 606-7828

Bulletin 2340.
U.S. Department of Labor, Bureau of Labor Statistics, Two Massachusetts Avenue, NE, Washington, D.C. 20212 (202) 606-7828

Bulletin 2370.
U.S. Department of Labor, Bureau of Labor Statistics, Two Massachusetts Avenue, NE, Washington, D.C. 20212 (202) 606-7828

Bulletin 2429.
U.S. Department of Labor, Bureau of Labor Statistics, Two Massachusetts Avenue, NE, Washington, D.C. 20212 (202) 606-7828

Bulletin 2440.
U.S. Department of Labor, Bureau of Labor Statistics, Two Massachusetts Avenue, NE, Washington, D.C. 20212 (202) 606-7828

Bulletin de statistique.
Direction de la Statistique, Niamey, Niger

Bulletin de statistique.
Direction de la Statistique, BP 453, N'Djamena, Chad

Bulletin de Statistique.
Direction Generale de la Statistique, BP 46, Kigali, Rwanda

Bulletin de Statistique.
Institut National de la Statistique et de l'Analyse Economique, BP 323, Cotonou, Benin.

Bulletin de Statistique.
Institut National de Statistique, National Institute of Statistics, rue de Louvain 44, 1000 Brussels, Belgium

Bulletin de Statistiques.
Service National de la Statistique, Ministere du Plan et de la Cooperation, BP No 46, Vientiane, Laos

Bulletin d'informations statistiques.
Direction de la Statistique Generale et des Etudes Economiques, BP 732, Bangui, Central African Republic

Bulletin du STATEC.
STATEC, 19-21 Boulevard Royal, BP 304, L-2013, Luxembourg

Bulletin Mensuel.
Banque Nationale Suisse, Borsenstrasse 15 8022 Zurich, Switzerland

Bulletin mensuel de statistique.
Direction de la Statistique (Department of Statistics), BP 118, Lome, Togo

Bulletin mensuel de statistique.
Direction de la Statistique, BP 222, Abidjan, Cote D'Ivoire

Bulletin mensuel de statistique.
Direction de la Statistique et de la Comptabilite Nationale, BP 660, Yaounde, Cameroon

Bulletin Mensuel de Statistique.
Direction Generale de la Statistique, BP 179, Libreville, Gabon

Bulletin Mensuel de Statistique.
Direction Nationale de la statistique, BP 12, Bamako, Mali

Bulletin mensuel de statistique.
Division de la Statistique, BP 178, Rabat, Morocco

Bulletin mensuel de statistique.
Institut National de la Statistique et de la Recherche Economique, BP 38, Antananarivo, Madagascar

Bulletin Mensuel de Statistique.
Institut National de la Statistique et des Etudes Economiques, 18 boulevard Pinard, 75675 Paris Cedex 14, France

Bulletin mensuel de statistique.
Institut National de la Statistique, 27 rue du Liban, 1002 Tunis-Belvedere, Tunis, Tunisia

Bulletin mensuel des statistique.
Direction de la Statistique et de la Comptabilite Economique, BP 2031, Brazzaville, Congo

Bulletin Mensuel Statistique.
Direction de la Statistique, BP 240, Nouakchott, Mauritania

Bulletin Mensuel Statistique.
Institut National de la Statistique et des Recherches Economique, Phnom-Penh, Cambodia

Bulletin of Statistics.
Central Statistical Services, Pretoria 0002, South Africa

Bulletin Special de Statistique.
Service de la Statistique Generale, BP 221, Conakry, Guinea

Bulletin Statistique.
Department de la Statistique, BP 1156, Bujumbura, Burundi

Bulletin Statistique.
Institut National de la Statistique et des Etudes Economiques, BP 863, 97175 Pointe-a-Pitre, France

Bulletin Statistique de la Guadeloupe.
INSEE, Tour Gamma A, 195 rue de Bercy, 75582 Paris Cedex 12, France

Bulletin statistique et economique mensuel.
Direction de la Provision et de la Statistique, BP 116, Dakar, Senegal

Bulletin Statistique Mensuel.
Direction Centrale de la Statistique, Ministere du Plan, Bir Hassan, Beirut, Lebanon

Bulletin Trimestriel de Statistique.
Direction de la Statistique Generale ot des Etudes Economiques, BP 732, Bangui, Central African Republic

Bulletin Trimestriel de Statistique.
Djibouti: Direction Nationale de la Statistique, BP 1846, Djibouti

Bulletin trimestriel de Statistique.
Institut Haitien de Statistique, Cite de l'Exposition, Boulevard Harry Truman, Port-au-Prince, Haiti

Burkina Faso.
Federal Statistical Office, Gustav-Stresemann-Ring 11, D-6200 Wiesbaden, Germany

Burma.
Federal Statistical Office, Gustav-Stresemann-Ring 11, D-6200 Wiesbaden, Germany

Burundi.
Federal Statistical Office, Gustav-Stresemann-Ring 11, D-6200 Wiesbaden, Germany

Bus Facts.
American Bus Association, 1100 New York Avenue, NW, Washington, D.C. 20005 (202) 842-1645

Business America.
U.S. Department of Commerce, International Trade Administration, Fourteenth Street between Constitution Avenue and E Street, NW, Washington, D.C. 20230 (202) 482-3809

Business Failure Record.
Dun and Bradstreet Corporation, 299 Park Avenue, Twenty-fourth Floor, New York, New York 10171 (212) 593-6800

Business Starts Record.
Dun and Bradstreet Corporation, 299 Park Avenue, Twenty-fourth Floor, New York, New York 10171 (212) 593-6800

Buyers of New Cars.
Newsweek Incorporated, 444 Madison Avenue, New York, New York 10022 (212) 350-2000

CPI Detailed Report.
U.S. Department of Labor, Bureau of Labor Statistics, Two Massachusetts Avenue, NE, Washington, D.C. 20212 (202) 606-7828

CRB Commodity Index Report.
Commodity Research Bureau, Inc., 75 Wall Street, New York, New York 10005 (212) 504-7754

The Cable TV Financial Databook.
Paul Kagan Associates, Incorporated, 126 Clock Tower Place, Carmel, California 93923 (408) 624-1536

Calendars of the United States House of Representatives and History of Legislation.
U.S. Congress, Senate Library, The Capitol, Washington, D.C. 20510 (202) 224-3121

California Almanac.
Pacific Data Resources, Post Office Box 1911, Santa Barbara, California 93116-9954 (800) 422-2546

California Statistical Abstract.
Department of Finance, 915 L Street, 8th Floor, Sacramento, California 95814 (916) 322-2263

The Canada Yearbook.
Publications Distribution, Statistics Canada, Ottawa, Ontario K1A 0T6, Canada (613) 951-8116

Canadian Statistical Review.
Publications Distribution, Statistics Canada, Ottawa, Ontario K1A 0T6, Canada (613) 951-8116

Cancer Statistics Review.
U.S. Department of Health and Human Services, National Cancer Institute, 9000 Rockville Pike, Bethesda, Maryland 20892 (301) 496-5737

Capital Punishment.
U.S. Department of Justice, Bureau of Justice Statistics, 633 Indiana Avenue, NW, Washington, D.C. 20531 (800) 732-3277

Caseload Statistics of State Vocational Rehabilitation Agencies in Fiscal Years.
U.S. Department of Education, Rehabilitation Services Administration, 400 Maryland Avenue, SW, Washington, D.C. 20202 (202) 708-5366

Cash and Non-Cash Benefits for Persons with Limited Income: Eligibility Rules, Recipient and Expenditure Data.
U.S. Library of Congress, Congressional Research Service, 10 First Street, SE, Washington, D.C. 20540 (202) 707-5000

Casualty Return.
Lloyd's Register of Shipping, 71 Fenchurch Street, London EC3, England

Census of Agriculture.
U.S. Department of Commerce, Bureau of the Census, Suitland, Maryland 20233 (301) 763-4040

Census of Construction Industries.
U.S. Department of Commerce, Bureau of the Census, Suitland, Maryland 20233 (301) 763-4040

Census of Governments.
U.S. Department of Commerce, Bureau of the Census, Suitland, Maryland 20233 (301) 763-4040

Census of Housing.
U.S. Department of Commerce, Bureau of the Census, Suitland, Maryland 20233 (301) 763-4040

Census of Local Jails.
U.S. Department of Justice,, Bureau of Justice Statistics, 633 Indiana Avenue, NW, Washington, D.C. 20531 (800) 732-3277

Census of Manufactures.
U.S. Department of Commerce, Bureau of the Census, Suitland, Maryland 20233 (301) 763-4040

Census of Mineral Industries.
U.S. Department of the Interior, Bureau of Mines, 810 Seventh Street, NW, Washington, D.C. 20241 (202) 501-9649

Census of Population.
U.S. Department of Commerce, Bureau of the Census, Suitland, Maryland 20233 (301) 763-4040

Census of Population and Housing.
U.S. Department of Commerce, Bureau of the Census, Suitland, Maryland 20233 (301) 763-4040

Census of Population of Ireland.
Central Statistics Office, Ardee Road, Dublin 6, Ireland

Census of Public and Private Juvenile Detention, Correctional, and Shelter Facilities.
U.S. Department of Justice, Bureau of Justice Statistics, 633 Indiana Avenue, NW, Washington, D.C. 20531 (800) 732-3277

Census of Retail Trade.
U.S. Department of Commerce, Bureau of the Census, Suitland, Maryland 20233 (301) 763-4040

Census of Service Industries.
U.S. Department of Commerce, Bureau of the Census, Suitland, Maryland 20233 (301) 763-4040

Census of Transportation.
U.S. Department of Commerce, Bureau of the Census, Suitland, Maryland 20233 (301) 763-4040

Census of Wholesale Trade.
U.S. Department of Commerce, Bureau of the Census, Suitland, Maryland 20233 (301) 763-4040

Censuses of Outlying Areas, Construction, Puerto Rico.
U.S. Department of Commerce, Bureau of the Census, Suitland, Maryland 20233 (301) 763-4040

Censuses of Outlying Areas, Manufactures, Puerto Rico.
U.S. Department of Commerce, Bureau of the Census, Suitland, Maryland 20233 (301) 763-4040

Characteristics of Doctoral Scientists and Engineers in the United States.
U.S. National Science Foundation, 4201 Wilson Boulevard, Arlington, Virginia 22230 (703) 306-1234

Characteristics of New Housing.
U.S. Department of Commerce, Bureau of the Census, Suitland, Maryland 20233 (301) 763-4040

Characteristics of the Population.
U.S. Department of Commerce, Bureau of the Census, Suitland, Maryland 20233 (301) 763-4040

Characterization of Municipal Solid Waste in the United States.
Franklin Associates Limited, 4121 West Eighty-third Street, Suite 108, Prairie Village, Kansas 66208 (913) 649-2225

The Charitable Behavior of Americans.
Independent Sector, 1828 L Street, NW, Washington, D.C. 20036 (202) 223-8100

Chickens and Eggs.
U.S. Department of Agriculture, National Agricultural Statistics Service, Fourteenth and Independence Avenue, SW, Washington, D.C. 20250 (202) 219-1504

Child Maltreatment.
U.S. Department of Health and Human Services, National Center on Child Abuse and Neglect, 370 L'Enfant Promenade, SW, Washington, D.C. 20447 (202) 205-8586

Children in Custody: Census of Public and Private Juvenile Custody Facilities.
U.S. Department of Justice, Office of Juvenile Justice and Delinquency Prevention, 633 Indiana Avenue, NW, Washington, D.C. 20531 (202) 307-0781

China Market Atlas.
The Economist Intelligence Unit (Asia) Ltd., 10th Floor, Luk Kwok Centre, 72 Gloucester Road, Wanchai, Hong Kong (Phone Number in U.S. (800) 938-4685)

China (Taiwan).
Federal Statistical Office, Gustav-Stresemann-Ring 11, D-6200 Wiesbaden, Germany

Churches and Church Membership in the United States.
Glenmary Research Center, 750 Piedmont Avenue, NE, Atlanta, Georgia 30308 (404) 876-6518

The CIS Market Atlas.
Business International Moscow, 23 Profsoyuznaya Ulitsa, 117859, Moscow (Telephone Number in U.S. (800) 938-4685)

Citrus Fruits.
U.S. Department of Agriculture, National Agricultural Statistics Service, Fourteenth Street and Independence Avenue, SW, Washington, D.C. 20250 (202) 219-0504

City Employment.
U.S. Department of Commerce, Bureau of the Census, Suitland, Maryland 20233 (301) 763-4040

City Government Finances.
U.S. Department of Commerce, Bureau of the Census, Suitland, Maryland 20233 (301) 763-4040

Civil Aviation Statistics of the World.
International Civil Aviation Organization, 1000 Sherbrooke Street West, Suite 400, Montreal, Quebec H3A 2R2, Canada (514) 285-8219

The Civil Service Work Force.
U.S. National Aeronautics and Space Administration, 300 E Street, SW, Washington, DC 20546 (202) 358-1000

Climatography of the United States.
U.S. Department of Commerce, National Oceanic and Atmospheric Administration, National Climatic Data Center, Federal Building, Asheville, North Carolina 28801 (704) 259-2850

Coal Information.
Organisation for Economic Co-operation and Development (OECD), 2 rue Andre-Pascal, 75 Paris 16, France (Telephone Number in U.S. (202) 785-6323)

Coal Production.
U.S. Department of Energy, Energy Information Administration, 1000 Independence Avenue, SW, Washington, D.C. 20585 (202) 586-8800

The Coastline of the United States.
U.S. Department of Commerce, National Oceanic and Atmospheric Administration, National Climatic Data Center, Federal Building, Asheville, North Carolina 28801 (704) 259-2850

Coke Plant Report.
U.S. Department of Energy, Energy Information Administration, 1000 Independence Avenue, SW Washington, D.C. 20585 (202) 586-8800

Colombia estadistica.
DANE, Via Eldorado, Bogota, Colombia

Combined Annual and Revised Monthly Retail Trade.
U.S. Department of Commerce, Bureau of Census, Suitland, Maryland 20233 (301) 763-4040

Commissioner of Patents and Trademarks Annual Report.
U.S. Department of Commerce, Patent and Trademark Office, 2011 Crystal Drive, Arlington, Virginia 22202 (703) 305-8341

Commodity Credit Corporation Report of Financial Condition and Operations.
U.S. Department of Agriculture, Agricultural Stabilization and Conservation Service, P.O. Box 2415, Washington, D.C. 20013 (202) 720-5237

Commodity Research Bureau Commodity Index Report.
Commodity Research Bureau, 75 Wall Street, New York, New York 10005 (212) 504-7754

Commodity Yearbook.
Commodity Research Bureau, 75 Wall Street, New York, New York 10005 (212) 504-7754

Commonwealth of the Bahamas Statistical Abstract.
Department of Statistics, Cabinet Office, Post Office Box N3904, Nassau, Bahamas

Communications Industry Report.
Veronis, Suhler and Associates, 350 Park Avenue, New York, New York 10022 (212) 935-4990

Comparative Climatic Data.
U.S. Department of Commerce, National Oceanic and Atmospheric Administration, National Climatic Data Center, Federal Building, Asheville, North Carolina 28801 (704) 259-2850

Comparative Labor Force Statistics for Ten Countries.
U.S. Department of Labor, Bureau of Labor Statistics, Two Massachusetts Avenue, NE, Washington, D.C. 20212 (202) 606-7020

Comparative Oil Company Statements.
Carl H. Pforzheimer and Company, 650 Fifth Avenue, 23rd Floor, New York, New York 10022 (212) 223-0500

Comparative Statistics of Industrial and Office Real Estate Markets.
Society of Industrial and Office Realtors, 777 Fourteenth Street, NW, Suite 400, Washington, D.C. 20005 (202) 383-1150

Compare Minnesota: An Economic and Statistical Factbook.
Department of Trade and Economic Development, Policy Analysis Office, 500 Metro Square, Saint Paul, Minnesota 55101 (612) 296-8283

Compendio estadistico.
Direccion General de Estadistica y Censos, Instituto Nacional de Estadistica, Avenida 28 de Julio 1056, Lima 1, Peru

Compendio estadistico.
Instituto Nacional de Estadisticas, Casilla 7597, Correo 3, Santiago, Chile

Compendio Statistico Italiano.
Instituto Centrale di Statistica, Via Cesare Balbo 16, 00184 Rome, Italy

Compendium of Public Employment.
U.S. Department of Commerce, Bureau of the Census, Suitland, Maryland 20233 (301) 763-4040

Compensation and Working Conditions.
U.S. Department of Labor, Bureau of Labor Statistics, Two Massachusetts Avenue, NE, Washington, D.C. 20212 (202) 606-7020

Published Sources

Compensation Report.
U.S. Office of Personnel Management, 1900 E Street, NW, Washington, D.C. 20415 (202) 606-1800

Concise Statistical Yearbook.
Distribution Service: National Statistical Service of Greece, 14-16 Lycourgou Street, Athens 112, Greece

Concise Statistical Yearbook of Poland.
Glowny Urzad Statystyczny (Central Statistical Office), Al Niepodleglosci 208, 00-925 Warsaw, Poland

Congressional Directory.
U.S. Congress, Joint Committee on Printing, North Capitol and H Streets, NW, Washington, D.C. 20401 (202) 275-2051

Congressional Quarterly Weekly Report.
Congressional Quarterly, Inc., 1414 22nd Street, NW, Washington, D.C. 20037 (202) 887-8500

Congressional Record.
U.S. Congress, The Capitol, Washington, D.C. 20510 (202) 224-3121

Conjoncture Economique.
Institut National de la Statistique, BP 20, Kinshasa, Gombe, Zaire

Connecticut Market Data.
Connecticut Department of Economic Development, 865 Brock Street, Rocky Hill, Connecticut 06067-3405

Consolidated Data Base.
Dataquest, Incorporated, 1290 Ridder Park Drive, San Jose, California 95131 (408) 437-8000

Construction Reports.
U.S. Department of Commerce, Bureau of the Census, Suitland, Maryland 20233 (301) 763-4040

Construction Review.
U.S. Department of Commerce, International Trade Administration, Fourteenth Street between Constitution Avenue and E Street, NW, Washington, D.C. 20230 (202) 482-3809

Construction Statistics Yearbook.
Statistical Office of the United Nations, Publishing Service, New York, New York 10017 (800) 253-9646

Consumer Credit Delinquency Bulletin.
American Bankers Association, 1120 Connecticut Avenue, NW, Washington, D.C. 20036 (202) 663-5000

Consumer Expenditure Survey.
U.S. Department of Labor, Bureau of Labor Statistics, Two Massachusetts Avenue, NE, Washington, D.C. 20212 (202) 606-7828

Consumer Expenditures in 1992.
U.S. Department of Labor, Bureau of Labor Statistics, Two Massachusetts Avenue, NE, Washington, D.C. 20212 (202) 606-7828

Consumer Photographic Survey.
Photo Marketing Association, International, 3000 Picture Place, Jackson, Michigan 49201 (517) 788-8100

Consumer Price Index.
Central Statistics Office, St. Stephen's Green House, Earlsfort Terrace, Dublin 2, Ireland

Consumer Price Index Detailed Report.
U.S. Department of Labor, Bureau of Labor Statistics, Two Massachusetts Avenue, NE, Washington, D.C. 20212 (202) 606-7828

Consumer Research Study on Book Purchasing.
Book Industry Study Group, 160 Fifth Avenue, New York, New York 10010 (212) 929-1393

Controlling the Risks of Government-Sponsored Enterprises.
Congressional Budget Office, Second and D Streets, SW, Washington, D.C. 20515 (202) 226-2621

Correctional Populations in the United States.
U.S. Department of Justice, Bureau of Justice Statistics, 633 Indiana Avenue, NW, Washington, D.C. 20531 (800) 732-3277

Cost of Living Index.
American Chamber of Commerce Researchers Association, c/o American Chamber of Commerce Exeucutives, 4232 King Street, Alexandria 22302 (703) 998-0072.

Costa Rica.
Federal Statistical Office, Gustav-Stresemann-Ring 11, D-6200 Wiesbaden, Germany

Cotton and Wool Outlook and Situation.
U.S. Department of Agriculture, Economic Research Service, Fourteenth Street and Independence Avenue, SW, Washington, D.C. 20005-4789 (202) 219-1504

Cotton and Wool Outlook Statistics.
U.S. Department of Agriculture, Economic Research Service, Fourteenth Street and Independence Avenue, SW, Washington, D.C. 20005-4789 (202) 219-1504

County Business Patterns.
U.S. Department of Commerce, Bureau of the Census, Suitland, Maryland 20233 (301) 763-4040

County Government Finances.
U.S. Department of Commerce, Bureau of the Census, Suitland, Maryland 20233 (301) 763-4040

County Profiles.
University of New Mexico, Bureau of Business and Economic Research, Albuquerque, New Mexico 87131 (505) 277-2216

County Profiles of Idaho.
Department of Commerce, 700 West State Street, Boise, Idaho 83720 (208) 334-2470

Crime and the Elderly.
U.S. Department of Justice, Bureau of Justice Statistics, 633 Indiana Avenue, NW, Washington, D.C. 20531 (800) 732-3277

Crime and the Nation's Households.
U.S. Department of Justice, Bureau of Justice Statistics, 633 Indiana Avenue, NW, Washington, D.C. 20531 (800) 732-3277

Crime in the United States.
U.S. Department of Justice, Federal Bureau of Investigation, Ninth Street and Pennsylvania Avenue, NW, Washington, D.C. 20535 (202) 324-3000

Criminal Victimization in the United States.
U.S. Department of Justice, Bureau of Justice Statistics, 633 Indiana Avenue, NW, Washington, D.C. 20531 (800) 732-3277

Crop Production.
U.S. Department of Agriculture, National Agricultural Statistics Service, Fourteenth Street and Independence Avenue, SW, Washington, D.C. 20250 (202) 219-0504

Crop Production: Quarterly Statistics.
European Community Information Service, 2100 M Street, NW, Washington, D.C. 20037 (202) 862-9500

Crop Values.
U.S. Department of Agriculture, National Agricultural Statistics Service, Fourteenth Street and Independence Avenue, SW, Washington, D.C. 20250 (202) 219-0504

Current Business Reports, Combined Annual and Revised Monthly Retail Trade
U.S. Department of Commerce, Bureau of the Census, Suitland, Maryland 20233 (301) 763-4040

Current Business Reports, Motor Freight Transportation and Warehousing Survey.
U.S. Department of Commerce, Bureau of the Census, Suitland, Maryland 20233 (301) 763-4040

Current Construction Reports.
U.S. Department of Commerce, Bureau of the Census, Suitland, Maryland 20233 (301) 763-4040

Current Estimates and Trends in New Hampshire's Housing Supply.
Office of State Planning, 2 1/2 Beacon Street, Concord, New Hampshire 03301 (603) 271-2155

Current Housing Reports.
U.S. Department of Commerce, Bureau of the Census, Suitland, Maryland 20233 (301) 763-4040

Current Industrial Reports.
U.S. Department of Commerce, Bureau of the Census, Suitland, Maryland 20233 (301) 763-4040

Current Industrial Reports, Aerospace Industry (Orders, Sales, and Backlog).
U.S. Department of Commerce, Bureau of the Census, Suitland, Maryland 20233 (301) 763-4040

Current Industrial Reports Manufactures' Shipments, Inventories, and Orders.
U.S. Department of Commerce, Bureau of the Census, Suitland, Maryland 20233 (301) 763-4040

Current Industrial Reports, Manufacturing Technology.
U.S. Department of Commerce, Bureau of the Census, Suitland, Maryland 20233 (301) 763-4040

Current Population Reports.
U.S. Department of Commerce, Bureau of the Census, Suitland, Maryland 20233 (301) 763-4040

Current Wage Developments.
U.S. Department of Labor, Bureau of Labor Statistics, Two Massachusetts Avenue, NE, Washington, D.C. 20212 (202) 606-7828

Daily Digest.
U.S. Congress, The Capitol, Washington, D.C. 20510 (202) 224-3121

Dairy Products.
U.S. Department of Agriculture, National Agricultural Statistics Service, Fourteenth Street and Independence Avenue, SW, Washington, D.C. 20250 (202) 219-0504

Danemark.
Federal Statistical Office, Gustav-Stresemann-Ring 11, D-6200 Wiesbaden, Germany

Data Book, Operating Banks and Branches.
U.S. Federal Deposit Insurance Corporation, 550 Seventeenth Street, NW, Washington, D.C. 20429 (202) 393-8400

Datos Y Cifras de Costa Rica.
Centra para la Promocion de las Exportaciones y las Inversiones, Apartado 10216, San Jose, Costa Rica

Delaware Data Book.
Delaware Development Office, 99 Kings Highway, P.O. Box 1401, Dover, Delaware 19903 (302) 739-4271

Delaware Economic Report.
University of Delaware, Bureau of Economic Research, College of Business and Economics, Newark, Delaware 19716-2730 (302) 831-8401

Demographic and Economic Profiles.
Office of Policy Research and Coordination, Department of Employment and Training, Montpelier, Vermont 05602 (802) 828-4202, ext. 323

Demographic Statistics.
European Community Information Service, 2100 M Street, NW, Washington, D.C. 20037 (202) 862-9500

Demographic Yearbook.
St. Edmundsbury Press, Bury St. Edmunds, Suffolk, England

Demographic Yearbook.
Statistical Office of the United Nations, Publishing Service, New York, New York 10017 (800) 253-9646

Detailed Ancestry Groups for States.
U.S. Department of Commerce, Bureau of the Census, Suitland, Maryland 20223 (301) 763-4040

Deutsche Demokratische Republik.
Federal Statistical Office, Gustav-Stresemann-Ring 11, D-6200 Wiesbaden, Germany

Digest of Education Statistics.
U.S. Department of Education, 400 Maryland Avenue, SW, Washington, D.C. 20202 (202) 708-5366

Digest of Statistics.
Federal Office of Statistics, 36-38 Broad Street, PMB 12528, Lagos, Nigeria

Digest of Statistics.
Statistical Office, Ministry of Finance, Kingstown, Saint Vincent

Direction of Trade.
International Monetary Fund, Nineteenth and H Streets, NW, Washington, D.C. 20431 (202) 623-7000

Directory of Governors of the American States, Commonwealths and Territories.
National Governors' Association, Hall of the States, 444 North Capitol Street, NW, Washington, D.C. 20001 (202) 624-5300

Published Sources

Directory of Veterans Administration Facilities.
U.S. Department of Veterans Affairs, 810 Vermont Avenue, NW, Washington, D.C. 20420 (202) 233-2300

Dodge Construction Potentials.
F.W. Dodge Division, McGraw-Hill Information Systems Company, 1221 Avenue of the Americas, New York, New York 10020 (212) 512-2000

Domestic Offices, Commercial Bank Assets and Liabilities, Consolidated Report of Condition.
Board of Governors of the Federal Reserve System, Twentieth and Constitution Avenue, NW, Washington, D.C. 20551 (202) 452-3000

Domestic Uranium Mining and Milling Industry.
U.S. Department of Energy, Energy Information Administration, 1000 Independence Avenue, SW, Washington, D.C. 20585 (202) 586-8800

Dominikanische Republik.
Federal Statistical Office, Gustav-Stresemann-Ring 11, D-6200 Wiesbaden, Germany

Drivers Licenses.
U.S. Department of Transportation, Federal Highway Administration, 400 Seventh Street, SW, Washington, D.C. 20590 (202) 366-0660

Drug Use Forecasting.
U.S. Department of Justice, National Institute of Justice, 633 Indiana Avenue, NW, Washington, D.C. 20531 (202) 307-0781

Drunk Driving, Special Report.
U.S. Department of Justice, Bureau of Justice Statistics, 633 Indiana Avenue, NW, Washington, D.C. 20531 (800) 732-3277

Dschibuti.
Federal Statistical Office, Gustav-Stresemann-Ring 11, D-6200 Wiesbaden, Germany

EBRI Databook on Employee Benefits.
Employee Benefit Research Institute, 2121 K Street, NW, Suite 600, Washington, D.C. 20037 (202) 659-0670

Earnings in Agriculture.
European Community Information Service, 2100 M Street, NW, Washington, D.C. 20037 (202) 862-9500

East European and Soviet Data Book.
Columbia University Press, 562 West 113th Street, New York, New York 10014 (212) 316-7100

Economic Abstract of Alabama.
University of Alabama, Center for Business and Economic Research, P.O. Box 870221, Tuscaloosa, Alabama 35487 (205) 348-6191

Economic Accounts for Agriculture.
Organisation for Economic Co-operation and Development (OECD), 2 rue Andre-Pascal, 75 Paris 16, France (Telephone Number in U.S. (202) 785-6323)

Economic and Social Progress in Latin America: Natural Resources.
Inter-American Development Bank, 1300 New York Avenue, NW, Washington, D.C. 20577 (202) 623-1753

Economic Census of Outlying Areas.
U.S. Department of Commerce, Bureau of the Census, Suitland, Maryland 20233 (301) 763-4040

Economic Censuses of Outlying Areas, Puerto Rico.
U.S. Department of Commerce, Bureau of the Census, Suitland, Maryland 20233 (301) 763-4040

Economic Data Papers - Nepal.
Economic Planning Section, Program Office, US AID, Kathmandu, Nepal

Economic Growth of OECD Countries.
U.S. Department of State, Bureau of Intelligence and Research, 2201 C Street, NW, Washington, D.C. 20520 (202) 647-1080

Economic Indicators.
Executive Office of the President, Council of Economic Advisers, Old Executive Office Building, Washington, D.C. 20500 (202) 395-5084

Economic Indicators.
West Virginia, Research League, Inc., 405 Capitol Street, Suite 414, Charleston, West Virginia 25301 (304) 346-9451

Economic Indicators of the Farm Sector: Farm Sector Review.
U.S. Department of Agriculture, Economic Research Service, Fourteenth Street and Independence Avenue, SW, Washington, D.C. 20005-4789 (202) 219-1504

Economic Indicators of the Farm Sector: National Financial Summary.
U.S. Department of Agriculture, Economic Research Service, Fourteenth Street and Independence Avenue, SW, Washington, D.C. 20005-4789 (202) 219-1504

Economic Indicators of the Farm Sector: Production and Efficiency Statistics.
U.S. Department of Agriculture, Economic Research Service, Fourteenth Street and Constitution Avenue, SW, Washington, D.C. 20005-4789 (202) 219-1504

Economic Indicators of the Farm Sector: State Financial Summary.
U.S. Department of Agriculture, Economic Research Service, Fourteenth Street and Independence Avenue, SW, Washington, D.C. 20005-4789 (202) 219-1504

Economic Outlook.
International Monetary Fund, 700 Nineteenth Street, NW, Washington, D.C. 20431 (202) 623-7000

Economic Outlook.
Organisation for Economic Co-operation and Development (OECD), 2 rue Andre-Pascal, 75 Paris 16, France (Telephone Number in U.S. (202) 785-6323)

Economic Report to the Governor.
Puerto Rico Planning Board, Area of Economic and Social Planning, Bureau of Economic Analysis and Bureau of Statistics, Santurce, Puerto Rico 00940 (809) 722-2070

Economic Report of the President.
Executive Office of the President, Council of Economic Advisers, Old Executive Office Building, Washington, D.C. 20500 (202) 395-5084

Economic Report to the Governor: State of Minnesota.
Department of Trade and Economic Development, Policy Analysis Office, 500 Metro Square Building, Saint Paul, Minnesota 55101 (612) 296-8283

Economic Review of Travel in America.
U.S. Travel Data Center, Two Lafayette Center, 1133 Twenty-first Street, NW, Washington, D.C. 20036 (202) 293-1040

Economic Survey.
Central Bureau of Statistics, Post Office Box 1098, Accra, Ghana

Economic Survey of Latin America and the Caribbean.
Statistical Office of the United Nations, Publishing Service, New York, New York 10017 (800) 253-9646

Economic Survey of Liberia.
Ministry of Planning and Economic Affairs, Post Office Box 9016, Monrovia, Liberia

The Economist Book of Vital World Statistics.
Times Books, 201 East 50th Street, New York, New York 10022 (212) 751-2600

Ecuador.
Federal Statistical Office, Gustav-Stresemann-Ring 11, D-6200 Wiesbaden, Germany

Editor and Publisher International Year Book.
Editor and Publisher Company, 11 West Nineteenth Street, New York, New York 10011 (212) 675-4380

Education at a Glance.
Organisation for Economic Co-operation and Development (OECD), 2 rue Andre-Pascal, 75 Paris 16, France (Telephone Number in U.S. (202) 785-6323)

Education in OECD Countries.
Organisation for Economic Co-operation and Development (OECD), 2 rue Andre-Pascal, 75 Paris 16, France (Telephone Number in U.S. (202) 785-6323)

Educational Statistics of the Republic of China.
Ministry of Education, 5, Chungshan South Road, Taipei, Republic of China

El Salvador.
Federal Statistical Office, Gustav-Stresemann-Ring 11, D-6200 Wiesbaden, Germany

Electric Power Annual.
U.S. Department of Energy, Energy Information Administration, 1000 Independence Avenue, SW, Washington, D.C. 20585 (202) 586-8800

Electric Power in Asia and the Pacific.
Statistical Office of the United Nations, Publishing Service, New York, New York 10017 (800) 253-9646

Electric Power Monthly.
U.S. Department of Energy,, Energy Information Administration, 1000 Independence Avenue, SW, Washington, D.C. 20585 (202) 586-8800

Electronic Market Data Book.
Electronic Industries Association, 2001 Pennsylvania Avenue, NW, Washington, D.C. 20006 (202) 457-4900

Elementary-Secondary Staff Information.
U.S. Equal Employment Opportunity Commission, 1801 L Street, NW, Washington, D.C. 20507 (800) USA-EEOC

Elevations and Distances in the United States.
U.S. Department of the Interior, Geological Survey, National Center, 12201 Sunrise Valley Drive, Reston, Virginia 22092 (703) 648-4460

Emerging Stock Markets Factbook.
International Finance Corporation, 1818 H Street, NW, Washington, D.C. 20006 (202) 477-1234

Emerging Trends.
Princeton Religion Research Center, 47 Hulfish Street, Princeton, New Jersey 08542 (609) 921-8112

Emissions of Greenhouse Gases in the U.S.
U.S. Department of Energy, Energy Information Administration, 1000 Independence Avenue, SW, Washington, D.C. 20585 (202) 586-8800

Employee Benefits in Medium and Large Private Establishments.
U.S. Department of Labor, Bureau of Labor Statistics, Two Massachusetts Avenue, NE, Washington, D.C. 20212 (202) 606-7828

Employee Benefits in Small Private Establishments.
U.S. Department of Labor, Bureau of Labor Statistics, Two Massachusetts Avenue, NE, Washington, D.C. 20212 (202) 606-7828

Employee Benefits in State and Local Governments.
U.S. Department of Labor, Bureau of Labor Statistics, Two Massachusetts Avenue, NE, Washington, D.C. 20212 (202) 606-7828

Employee Retirement Systems of State and Local Governments.
U.S. Department of Commerce, Bureau of the Census, Suitland, Maryland 20233 (301) 763-4040

Employer Costs for Employee Compensation.
U.S. Department of Labor, Bureau of Labor Statistics, Two Massachusetts Avenue, NE, Washington, D.C. 20212 (202) 606-7828

Employment and Earnings.
U.S. Department of Labor, Bureau of Labor Statistics, Two Massachusetts Avenue, NE, Washington, D.C. 20212 (202) 606-7828

Employment and Unemployment.
European Community Information Service, 2100 M Street, NW, Washington, D.C. 20037 (202) 862-9500

Employment and Wages, Annual Averages.
U.S. Department of Labor, Bureau of Labor Statistics, Two Massachusetts Avenue, NE, Washington, D.C. 20212 (202) 606-7828

Employment Cost Index.
U.S. Department of Labor, Bureau of Labor Statistics, Two Massachusetts Avenue, NE, Washington, D.C. 20212 (202) 606-7828

Employment Report of United States Flag Merchant Fleet Oceangoing Vessels 1000 Gross Tons and Over.
U.S. Department of Transportation, Maritime Administration, 400 Seventh Street, SW, Washington, D.C. 20590 (202) 366-5807

Encyclopedia of Associations.
Gale Research Incorporated, 835 Penobscot Building, Detroit, Michigan 48226 (800) 877-4253

Endangered Species Technical Bulletin.
U.S. Department of the Interior, Fish and Wildlife Service, C Street between Eighteenth and Nineteenth Streets, NW, Washington, D.C. 20240 (202) 208-5634

Energy Data Reports.
U.S. Department of Energy, Energy Information Administration, 1000 Constitution Avenue, SW, Washington, D.C. 20585 (202) 586-8800

Energy: Monthly Statistics.
European Community Information Service, 2100 M Street, NW, Washington, D.C. 20037 (202) 862-9500

Published Sources

Energy Statistics of OECD Countries.
Organisation for Economic Co-operation and Development (OECD), 2 rue Andre-Pascal, 75 Paris 16, France (Telephone Number in U.S. (202) 785-6323)

Energy Statistics Yearbook.
European Community Information Service, 2100 M Street, NW, Washington, D.C. 20037 (202) 862-9500

Energy Statistics Yearbook.
Statistical Office of the United Nations, Publishing Service, New York, New York 10017 (800) 253-9646

Environmental Business Journal.
Environmental Business International, Inc., 4452 Park Boulevard, Suite 306, San Diego, California 92116 (619) 295-7685

Environmental Data Compendium.
Organisation for Economic Co-operation and Development, (OECD), 2 rue Andre-Pascal, 75 Paris 16, France (Telephone Number in U.S. (202) 785-6323)

Equality State Almanac.
Department of Administration and Fiscal Control, Division of Research and Statistics, 327 East Emerson Building, Cheyenne, Wyoming 82002 (307) 777-7504

Estimated Use of Water in the United States in 1985.
U.S. Department of the Interior, Geological Survey, National Center, 12201 Sunrise Valley Drive, Reston, Virginia 22092 (703) 648-4460

Estimates of School Statistics.
National Education Association, 1201 Sixteenth Street, NW, Washington, D.C. 20036 (202) 833-4000

Ethiopia Statistical Abstract.
Provisional Military Government of Ethiopia, Central Statistical Office, Post Office Box 1143, Addis Ababa, Ethiopia

Etudes Statistiques.
Institut National de Statistique, rue de Louvain 44, 1000 Brussels, Belgium

European Historical Statistics.
European Community Information Service, 2100 M Street, NW, Washington, D.C. 20037 (202) 862-9500

European Marketing Data and Statistics.
Euromonitor Publications Limited, 87-88 Turnmill Street, London EC1M 5QU, England

Eurostatistics: Data for Short-Term Economic Analysis.
European Community Information Service, 2100 M Street, NW, Washington, D.C. 20037 (202) 862-9500

Existing Home Sales.
National Association of Realtors, 430 North Michigan Avenue, Chicago, Illinois 60611 (312) 329-8200

Exports from Manufacturing Establishments.
U.S. Department of Commerce, Bureau of the Census, Suitland, Maryland 20233 (301) 763-4040

Exports of Merchandise from Afghanistan.
Central Statistics Office, Kabul, Afghanistan

Exposicao: Informacao Estatistica.
Direccao de Economia e Estatistica, Sao Tome, Sao Tome e Principe

External Trade: Monthly Statistics.
European Community Information Service, 2100 M Street, NW, Washington, D.C. 20037 (202) 862-9500

External Trade: Statistical Yearbook.
European Community Information Service, 2100 M Street, NW, Washington, D.C. 20037 (202) 862-9500

FAA Statistical Handbook of Aviation.
U.S. Department of Transportation, Federal Aviation Administration, 800 Independence Avenue, SW, Washington, D.C. 20591 (202) 366-4000

FAO Production Yearbook.
Food and Agricultural Organization of the United Nations (FAO), Via delle Terme di Caracalla, 00100 Rome, Italy (Telephone Number in the U.S. (202) 653-2400)

FAO Quarterly Bulletin of Statistics.
Food and Agricultural Organization of the United Nations (FAO), Via delle Terme di Caracalla, 00100 Rome, Italy (Telephone Number in the U.S. (202) 653-2400)

FAO Trade Yearbook.
Food and Agricultural Organization of the United Nations (FAO), Via delle Terme di Caracalla, 00100 Rome, Italy (Telephone Number in the U.S. (202) 653-2400)

FAO Yearbook of Forest Products.
Food and Agricultural Organization of the United Nations (FAO), Via delle Terme di Caracalla, 00100, Rome, Italy (Telephone Number in the U.S. (202) 653-2400)

FEC Index of Independent Expenditures.
U.S. Federal Election Commission, 999 E Street, NW, Washington, D.C. 20463 (800) 424-9530

FEC Reports on Financial Activity, Final Report, Party and Non-Party Political Committees.
U.S. Federal Election Commission, 999 E Street, NW, Washington, D.C. 20463 (800) 424-9530

FEC Reports on Financial Activity, Final Report, Presidential Pre-Nomination Campaigns.
U.S. Federal Election Commission, 999 E Street, NW, Washington, D.C. 20463 (800) 424-9530

FEC Reports on Financial Activity, Final Report, U.S. Senate and House Campaigns.
U.S. Federal Election Commission, 999 E Street, NW, Washington, D.C. 20463 (800) 424-9530

Faafinta Istaatistikada bisha.
Statistical Department, State Planning Commission, Post Office Box 1742, Mogadishu, Somalia

Fact Book.
National Association of Securities Dealers, 1735 K Street, NW, Washington, D.C. 20006 (202) 728-8000

Fact Book.
New York Stock Exchange, 11 Wall Street, New York, New York 10005 (212) 656-3000

Factbook and Membership Directory.
Mortgage Insurance Companies of America, 727 Fifteenth Street, NW, Washington, D.C. 20005 (202) 393-5566

Failed Bank Cost Analysis Report.
Federal Deposit Insurance Corporation, 550 Seventeenth Street, NW, Washington, D.C. 20429 (202) 393-8400

Falkland Islands and dependencies: report for the year.
H.M. Stationery Office, Post Office Box 569, London SE1 9NH, England

Family Planning Perspectives.
Alan Guttmacher Institute, 111 Fifth Avenue, New York, New York 10003 (212) 254-5656

Farm Labor.
U.S. Department of Agriculture, National Agricultural Statistics Service, Fourteenth Street and Independence Avenue, SW, Washington, D.C. 20250 (202) 219-0504

Farm Management Survey.
An Foras Taluntais (The Agricultural Institute), Economics and Rural Welfare Research Centre, 19 Sandymount Avenue, Dublin 4, Ireland

Farm Numbers and Land in Farms.
U.S. Department of Agriculture, Economic Research Service, Fourteenth Street and Independence Avenue, SW, Washington, D.C. 20005-4789 (202) 219-0504

Farmer Cooperative Statistics.
U.S. Department of Agriculture, Agricultural Cooperative Service, Fourteenth Street and Independence Avenue, SW, Washington, D.C. 20250 (202) 720-2556

Farms End Decade with Strong Financial Performance.
U.S. Department of Agriculture, Economic Research Service, Fourteenth Street and Independence Avenue, SW, Washington D.C. 20005-4789 (202) 219-1504

Fatal Accident Reporting System.
U.S. Department of Transportation, National Highway Traffic Safety Administration, 400 Seventh Street, SW, Washington, D.C. 20590 (202) 366-9550

Fatal and Injury Accident Rates on Public Roads in the United States.
U.S. Department of Transportation, Federal Highway Administration, 400 Seventh Street, SW, Washington, D.C. 20590 (202) 366-0660

Fats and Oils Situation.
U.S. Department of Agriculture, National Agricultural Statistics Service, Fourteenth Street and Independence Avenue, SW, Washington, D.C. 20250 (202) 219-0504

The FDIC Quarterly Banking Profile.
U.S. Federal Deposit Insurance Corporation, 550 Seventeenth Street, NW, Washington, D.C. 20429 (202) 393-8400

Federal Aid in Fish and Wildlife Restoration.
U.S. Department of the Interior, Fish and Wildlife Service, C Street between Eighteenth and Nineteenth Streets, NW, Washington, D.C. 20240 (202) 208-5634

Federal Civilian Workforce Statistics, Employment and Trends.
U.S. Office of Personnel Management, 1900 E Street, NW, Washington, D.C. 20415 (202) 606-1800

Federal Criminal Case Processing.
U.S Department of Justice, Bureau of Justice Statistics, 633 Indiana Avenue, NW, Washington, D.C. 20531 (800) 732-3277

Federal Expenditures by State for Fiscal Year.
U.S. Department of Commerce, Bureau of the Census, Suitland, Maryland 20233 (301) 763-4040

Federal Offshore Statistics.
U.S. Department of the Interior, Minerals Management Service, 1849 C Street, NW, Washington, D.C. 20240 (202) 208-3983

Federal Prosecutions of Corrupt Public Officials.
U.S. Department of Justice, Constitution Avenue and Tenth Street, NW, Washington, D.C. 20530 (202) 514-2000

Federal R & D Funding by Budget Function.
U.S. National Science Foundation, 4201 Wilson Boulevard, Arlington, Virginia 22230 (703) 306-1234

Federal Reserve Bulletin.
Board of Governors of the Federal Reserve System, Twentieth Street and Constitution Avenue, NW, Washington, D.C. 20551 (202) 452-3000

Federal Support to Universities, Colleges, and Nonprofit Institutions.
U.S. National Science Foundation, 4201 Wilson Boulevard, Arlington, Virginia 22230 (703) 306-1234

Feed Situation.
U.S. Department of Agriculture, Economic Research Service, Fourteenth Street and Independence Avenue, SW, Washington, D.C. 20250 (202) 219-1504

Fertilizer Yearbook.
Food and Agricultural Organization of the United Nations (FAO), Via delle Terme di Caracalla, 00100, Rome, Italy (Telephone Number in the U.S. (202) 653-2400)

Field Crops.
U.S. Department of Agriculture, National Agricultural Statistics Service, Fourteenth Street and Independence Avenue, SW, Washington, D.C. 20250 (202) 219-1504

Fiji Facts and Figures.
Bureau of Statistics, Government Building, P.O. Box 2221, Suva, Fiji Islands

Finances of Employee-Retirement Systems of State and Local Governments.
U.S. Department of Commerce, Bureau of the Census, Suitland, Maryland 20233 (301) 763-4040

Finances of Public School Systems.
U.S. Department of Commerce, Bureau of the Census, Suitland, Maryland 20233 (301) 763-4040

Financial Characteristics of U.S. Farms
U.S. Department of Agriculture, Economic Research Service, Fourteenth Street and Independence Avenue, SW, Washington, D.C. 20250 (202) 786-1504.

Financial Market Trends.
National Technical Information Service, 5285 Port Royal Road, Springfield, Virginia 22161 (703) 487-4600

Financial Statistics Monthly Taiwan District, The Republic of China.
Economic Research Department, The Central Bank of China, 2, Roosevelt Road, Section 1, Taipei 10757, Republic of China

Financial Statistics of Institutions of Higher Education.
U.S. Department of Education, 400 Maryland Avenue, SW, Washington, D.C. 20202 (202) 708-5366

Published Sources

Financial Statistics of Selected Investor-Owned Electric Utilities.
U.S. Department of Energy, Energy Information Administration, 1000 Independence Avenue, SW, Washington, D.C. 20585 (202) 586-8800

Financing and Delivering Health Care, A Comparative Analysis of OECD Countries.
Organisation for Economic Co-operation and Development, (OECD), 2 rue Andre-Pascal, 75 Paris 16, France (Telephone Number in U.S. (202) 785-6323)

Finnland.
Federal Statistical Office, Gustav-Stresemann-Ring 11, D-6200 Wiesbaden, Germany

Fire Journal.
National Fire Protection Association, One Batterymarch Park, Quincy, Massachusetts 02269-9101 (617) 770-3000

Fiscal Survey of the States.
National Governors' Association, Hall of the States, 444 North Capitol Street, NW, Washington, D.C. 20001 (202) 624-5300

Fisheries of the United States.
U.S. Department of Commerce, National Oceanic and Atmospheric Administration, National Marine Fisheries Service, 1335 East-West Highway, Silver Spring, Maryland 20910 (301) 427-2239

Fisheries: Yearly Statistics.
European Community Information Service, 2100 M Street, NW, Washington, D.C. 20037 (202) 862-9500

Fishery Commodities and Trade.
Food and Agricultural Organization of the United Nations (FAO), Via delle Terme di Caracalla, 00100, Rome, Italy (Telephone Number in the U.S. (202) 653-2400)

Fishery Statistics of the United States.
U.S. Department of Commerce, National Oceanic and Atmospheric Administration, National Marine Fisheries Service, 1335 East-West Highway, Silver Spring, Maryland 20910 (301) 427-2239

Fixed Reproducible Tangible Wealth in the United States.
U.S. Department of Commerce, Bureau of Economic Analysis, Fourteenth Street between Constitution Avenue and E Street, NW, Washington, D.C. 20230 (202) 606-9900

Floraculture and Environmental Horticulture Products: A Production and Marketing Statistical Review.
U.S. Department of Agriculture, Economic Research Service, Fourteenth Street and Independence Avenue, SW, Washington, D.C. 20005-4789 (202) 219-1504

Florida County Perspectives.
National Data Consultants, Post Office Box 6381, Athens, Georgia 30604 (404) 548-8460

Florida Statistical Abstract.
Bureau of Economic and Business Research, University of Florida, Gainesville, Florida 32611 (904) 392-0171

Flow of Fund Accounts.
Board of Governors of the Federal Reserve System, Twentieth Street and Constitution Avenue, NW, Washington, D.C. 20551 (202) 452-3000

Flow of Funds Accounts, Financial Assets and Liabilities Year-End.
Board of Governors of the Federal Reserve System, Twentieth Street and Constitution Avenue, NW, Washington, D.C. 20551 (202) 452-3000

Food Consumption Prices and Expenditures.
U.S. Department of Agriculture, Economic Research Service, Fourteenth Street and Independence Avenue, SW, Washington, D.C. 20005-4789 (202) 219-1504

Food Consumption Statistics.
Organisation for Economic Co-operation and Development (OECD), 2 rue Andre-Pascal, 75 Paris 16, France (Telephone Number in U.S. (202) 785-6323)

Food Cost Review.
U.S. Department of Agriculture, Economic Research Service, Fourteenth Street and Independence Avenue, SW, Washington, D.C. 20250 (202) 219-1504

Foodservice Industry in Review.
National Restaurant Association, 1200 Seventeenth Street, NW, Washington, D.C. 20036 (202) 331-5900

Food Marketing Review.
U.S. Department of Agriculture, Economic Research Service, Fourteenth Street and Independence Avenue, SW, Washington, D.C. 20250 (202) 219-1504

Foodservice Numbers: A Statistical Digest for the Food Service Industry.
National Restaurant Association, 1200 17th Street, NW, Washington, D.C. 20036 (202) 331-5900

The Footwear, Raw Hides and Skins, and Leather Industry in OECD Countries.
Organisation for Economic Co-operation and Development (OECD), 2 rue Andre-Pascal, 75 Paris 16, France (Telephone Number in U.S. (202) 785-6323)

Forbes Annual Report on American Industry.
Forbes Incorporated, 60 Fifth Avenue, New York, New York 10011 (212) 620-2200

Forecast of Housing Activity.
National Association of Home Builders of the U.S., 1201 Fifteenth Street, NW, Washington, D.C. 20005 (202) 822-0200

Foreign Agricultural Commodity Circular Series.
U.S. Department of Agriculture, Foreign Agricultural Service, Fourteenth Street and Independence Avenue, SW, Washington, D.C. 20250 (202) 720-3448

Foreign Agricultural Trade of the United States.
U.S. Department of Agriculture, Economic Research Service, Fourteenth Street and Independence Avenue, SW, Washington, D.C. 20005-4789 (202) 219-1504

Foreign Commerce and Navigation of the United States.
U.S. Department of Commerce, Bureau of the Census, Suitland, Maryland 20233 (301) 763-4040

Foreign Direct Investment in the United States, Operations of U.S. Affiliates of Foreign Companies.
U.S. Department of Commerce, Bureau of Economic Analysis, Fourteenth Street between Constitution Avenue and E Street, NW, Washington, D.C. 20230 (202) 606-9900

Foreign Military Construction Sales.
U.S. Department of Defense, Defense Security Assistance Agency, The Pentagon, Washington, D.C. 20301 (703) 695-3291

Foreign Military Sales.
U.S. Department of Defense, Defense Security Assistance Agency, The Pentagon, Washington, D.C. 20301 (703) 695-3291

Foreign Ownership of U.S. Agricultural Land Through December 31.
U.S. Department of Agriculture, Economic Research Service, Fourteenth Street and Independence Avenue, SW, Washington, D.C. 20250 (202) 219-1504

Foreign Trade By Commodities.
Organisation for Economic Co-operation and Development (OECD), 2 rue Andre-Pascal, 75 Paris 16, France (Telephone Number in U.S. (202) 785-6323)

Foreign Trade Import and Export CD-ROM disc.
U.S. Department of Commerce, Bureau of the Census, Suitland, Maryland 20233 (301) 763-4040

Foreign Trade Statistics for Africa.
Organisation for Economic Co-operation and Development (OECD), 2 rue Andre-Pascal, 75 Paris 16, France (Telephone Number in U.S. (202) 785-6323)

Foreign Trade Statistics for Africa.
Statistical Office of the United Nations, Publishing Service, New York, New York 10017 (800) 253-9646

Foreign Trade Statistics of Asia and the Pacific.
Statistical Office of the United Nations, Publishing Service, New York, New York 10017 (800) 253-9646

Forest Resources of the United States.
U.S. Department of Agriculture, Forest Service, Fourteenth Street and Independence Avenue, SW, Washington, D.C. 20250 (202) 720-3760

The Fortune Directories.
Time Warner, 1675 Broadway, Rockefeller Center, New York, New York 10019 (212) 522-1212

Foundation Grants Index.
The Foundation Center, 79 Fifth Avenue, New York, New York 10003 (212) 620-4230

Franchising in the Economy.
International Franchise Association, 1350 New York Avenue, Suite 900, Washington, D.C. 20005 (202) 628-8000

Frankreich.
Federal Statistical Office, Gustav-Stresemann-Ring 11, D-6200 Wiesbaden, Germany

Freight Commodity Statistics.
Association of American Railroads, 50 F Street, NW, Washington, D.C. 20001 (202) 639-2100

From Belief to Commitment: The Activities and Finances of Religious Congregations in the United States.
Independent Sector, 1828 L Street, NW, Washington, D.C. 20036 (202) 223-8100

Gabun.
Federal Statistical Office, Gustav-Stresemann-Ring 11, D-6200 Wiesbaden, Germany

Gale Directory of Publications and Broadcast Media.
Gale Research Incorporated, 835 Penobscot Building, Detroit, Michigan 48226 (800) 877-4253

The Gallup Report.
Gallup Organization, Inc., 100 Palmer Square, Princeton, New Jersey 08542 (609) 924-9600

Gambia.
Federal Statistical Office, Gustav-Stresemann-Ring 11, D-6200 Wiesbaden, Germany

The Gambia Trade Directory.
Banjul: Ministry of Finance and Trade, The Quadrangle, Banjul, Gambia

Ganley's Catholic Schools in America.
National Catholic Educational Association, 1077 30th Street, NW, Washington, D.C. 20007 (202) 337-6232

Gas Facts.
American Gas Association, 1515 Wilson Boulevard, Arlington, Virginia 22209 (703) 841-8400

The Georgia County Guide.
University of Georgia, College of Agriculture, Cooperative Extension Service, Athens, Georgia 30602 (404) 542-8938

Georgia Descriptions in Data.
Office of Planning and Budget, 254 Washington Street, SW, Atlanta, Georgia 30334 (404) 656-0911

Georgia Statistical Abstract.
Selig Center for Economic Growth, Terry College of Business, University of Georgia, Athens, Georgia 30602 (404) 542-4085

Geographic Profile of Employment and Unemployment.
U.S. Department of Labor, Bureau of Labor Statistics, Two Massachusetts Avenue, NE, Washington, D.C. 20212 (202) 606-7828

Geographical Distribution of Financial Flows to Developing Countries.
Organisation for Economic Co-operation and Development (OECD), 2 rue Andre-Pascal, 75 Paris 16, France (Telephone Number in U.S. (202) 785-6323)

Ghana.
Federal Statistical Office, Gustav-Stresemann-Ring 11, D-6200 Wiesbaden, Germany

Gilbert and Ellice Islands Colony and the Central and Southern Line Islands: Report...
HM Stationery Office, Post Office Box 569, London SE1 9NH, England

Giving and Volunteering in the United States.
Independent Sector, 1828 L Street, NW, Washington, D.C. 20036 (202) 223-8100

Giving U.S.A.
American Association of Fund-Raising Counsel, Incorporated, 25 West 43rd Street, New York, New York 10036 (212) 354-5799

Government Finance Statistics Yearbook.
International Monetary Fund, 700 Nineteenth Street, NW, Washington, D.C. 20431 (202) 623-7000

Government Finances.
U.S. Department of Commerce, Bureau of the Census, Suitland, Maryland 20233 (301) 763-4040

Published Sources

Government Financing of Research and Development.
European Community Information Service, 2100 M Street, NW, Washington, D.C. 20037 (202) 862-9500

Government Units.
U.S. Department of Commerce, Bureau of the Census, Suitland, Maryland 20233 (301) 763-4040

Governmental Organization.
U.S. Department of Commerce, Bureau of the Census, Suitland, Maryland 20233 (301) 763-4040

Greenland.
Federal Statistical Office, Gustav-Stresemann-Ring 11, D-6200 Wiesbaden, Germany

Grenada.
Federal Statistical Office, Gustav-Stresemann-Ring 11, D-6200 Wiesbaden, Germany

Griechenland.
Federal Statistical Office, Gustav-Stresemann-Ring 11, D-6200 Wiesbaden, Germany

Guam: Annual Report to the Secretary of the Interior.
Superintendent of Documents, U.S. Government Printing Office, Washington, D.C. 20402 (202) 783-3238

The Guarantor.
Chicago Title Insurance Company, 111 West Washington Street, Chicago, Illinois 60602 (312) 630-2000

Guide to Military Installations in the U.S.
Army Times Publishing Company, 6883 Commercial Drive, Springfield, Virginia 22159 (703) 750-9000

Guide to U.S. Foundations.
The Foundation Center, 79 Fifth Avenue, New York, New York 10003 (212) 620-4230

Guns and Crime.
U.S. Department of Justice, Bureau of Justice Statistics, 633 Indiana Avenue, NW, Washington, D.C. 20531 (800) 732-3277

Guyana.
Federal Statistical Office, Gustav-Stresemann-Ring 11, D-6200 Wiesbaden, Germany

HUD Statistical Yearbook.
U.S. Department of Housing and Urban Development, 451 Seventh Street, SW, Washington, D.C. 20410 (202) 708-1422

Hagtioindi.
Statistical Bureau of Iceland, Hagstofa Islands, Hverfisgata 8-10, Reykjavik, 26699

Haiti.
Federal Statistical Office, Gustav-Stresemann-Ring 11, D-6200 Wiesbaden, Germany

Handbook of Economic Statistics.
Central Intelligence Agency, Washington, D.C. 20505 (703) 482-1100

Handbook of Economic Statistics.
National Technical Information Service, 5285 Port Royal Road, Springfield, Virginia 22161 (703) 487-4600

Handbook of Labor Statistics.
U.S. Department of Labor, Bureau of Labor Statistics, Two Massachusetts Avenue, NE, Washington, D.C. 20212 (202) 606-7828

Handel, Gastgewerbe, Reiseverkehr, Reihe 7.3: Urlaubs - und Erholungsreisen 1976/77.
Statistisches Bundesamt (Allgemeiner Auskunftsdienst), Gustav-Streseman-Ring 11, Postfach 5528, 6200 Wiesbaden 1, Germany

Hatchery Production - Annual.
U.S. Department of Agriculture, National Agricultural Statistics Service, Fourteenth Street and Independence Avenue, SW, Washington, D.C. 20250 (202) 219-1504

Health Care Financing Review.
U.S. Department of Health and Human Services, Health Care Financing Administration, 200 Independence Avenue, SW, Washington, D.C. 20201 (202) 245-6113

Health OECD: Facts and Trends.
Organization for Economic Cooperation and Development, 2001 L Street, NW, Suite 700, Washington, D.C. 20036-4095 (202) 785-6323

Health Promotion and Disease Prevention, United States.
U.S. Department of Health and Human Services, National Center for Health Statistics, 3700 East West Highway, Hyattsville, Maryland 20782 (301) 436-8500

Health, United States
U.S. Department of Health and Human Services, National Center for Health Statistics, 3700 East-West Highway, Hyattsville, Maryland 20782 (301) 436-8500

High School Profile Report.
The American College Testing Program, Box 168, Iowa City, Iowa 52243 (310) 337-1000

Higher Education Price Indexes.
Research Associates of Washington, 2605 Klingle Road, NW, Washington, D.C. 20008 (202) 966-3326

Highlights of United States Export and Import Trade.
U.S. Department of Commerce, Bureau of the Census, Suitland, Maryland 20233 (301) 763-4040

Highway Statistics.
U.S. Department of Transportation, Federal Highway Administration, 400 Seventh Street, SW, Washington, D.C. 20590 (202) 366-0660

Historical Statistics on Governmental Finances and Employment.
U.S. Department of Commerce, Bureau of the Census, Suitland, Maryland 20233 (301) 763-4040

Historical Tables, Budget of The United States Government.
Executive Office of the President, Office of Management and Budget, Executive Office Building, Washington, D.C. 20503 (202) 395-3080

Home Sales Yearbook.
National Association of Realtors, 430 North Michigan Avenue, Chicago, Illinois 60611 (312) 329-8200

Honduras.
Federal Statistical Office, Gustav-Stresemann-Ring 11, D-6200 Wiesbaden, Germany

Hong Kong.
Federal Statistical Office, Gustav-Stresemann-Ring 11, D-6200 Wiesbaden, Germany

Hong Kong Annual Digest of Statistics.
Census and Statistics Department, 317 des Voeux Road Central, Hong Kong, Hong Kong

Hong Kong Market Atlas.
The Economist Intelligence Unit (Asia), 10th Floor, Luk Kwok Centre, 72 Gloucester Road, Wanchai, Hong Kong (Telephone Number in U.S. (800) 938-4685)

Hong Kong Monthly Digest of Statistics.
Census and Statistics Department, 317 des Voeux Road Central, Hong Kong, Hong Kong

Hospital Statistics.
American Hospital Association, 840 North Lake Shore Drive, Chicago, Illinois 60611 (312) 280-6000

Hospital Yearbook.
Statistical Office of the United Nations, Publishing Service, New York, New York 10017 (800) 253-9646

Household Energy Consumption and Expenditures.
U.S. Department of Energy, Energy Information Administration, 1000 Independence Avenue, SW, Washington, D.C. 20585 (202) 586-8800

Household Vehicles Energy Consumption.
U.S. Department of Energy, Energy Information Administration, 1000 Independence Avenue, SW, Washington, D.C. 20585 (202) 586-8800

Households Touched by Crime.
U.S. Department of Justice, Bureau of Justice Statistics, 633 Indiana Avenue, NW, Washington, D.C. 20531 (800) 732-3277

Housing Characteristics.
U.S. Department of Energy, Energy Information Administration, 1000 Independence Avenue, SW, Washington, D.C. 20585 (202) 586-8800

Hungary Statistical Yearbook.
Hungarian Statistical Office, 1033 Budapest, III, Kaszasdulo U.2.

Hydroelectric Power Resources of the United States, Developed and Undeveloped.
U.S. Department of Energy, Federal Energy Regulatory Commission, 1000 Independence Avenue, SW, Washington, D.C. 20585 (202) 208-0300

IEA Computers in Education Study.
University of Minnesota, Department of Sociology, Minneapolis, Minnesota 55455 (612) 625-5000

Idaho Community Profiles.
Department of Commerce, 700 West State Street, Boise, Idaho 83720 (208) 334-2470

Idaho Facts.
Department of Commerce, 700 West State Street, Boise, Idaho 83720 (208) 334-2470

Idaho Facts Data Book.
Department of Commerce, 700 West State Street, Boise, Idaho 83720 (208) 334-2470

Illinois State and Regional Economic Data Book.
Department of Commerce and Community Affairs, State Government of Illinois, 620 Adams Street, Springfield, Illinois 62701 (217) 782-1438

Illinois Statistical Abstract.
University of Illinois, Bureau of Economic and Business Research, 428 Commerce West, 1206 South 6th Street, Champaign, Illinois 61820 (217) 333-2330

Impact of Travel on State Economies.
U.S. Travel Data Center, Two Lafayette Center, 1133 Twenty-first Street, NW, Washington, D.C. 20036 (202) 293-1040

Income and Product.
Puerto Rico Planning Board, San Juan, Puerto Rico

Index - National Park System and Related Areas.
U.S. Department of the Interior, National Park Service, C Street between Eighteenth and Nineteenth Streets, NW, Washington, D.C. 20240 (202) 208-6843

Indiana Factbook.
Indiana University, Indiana Business Research Center, School of Business, Bloomington, Indiana 46202-5151 (317) 274-2204

Indicators of Industrial Activity.
Organisation for Economic Co-operation and Development (OECD), 2 rue Andre-Pascal, 75 Paris 16, France (Telephone Number in U.S. (202) 785-6323)

Indices - A Statistical Index to DC Services.
Office of Policy and Program Evaluation, Executive Office of the Mayor, One Judiciary Square, Suite 1000, 441 Fourth Street, Washington, D.C. 20001 (202) 727-4016

Indikator ekonomi.
Biro Pusat Statistik, Jalan Dr. Sutomo 8, Jakarta, Indonesia

Industrial Marketing Data and Statistics.
Euromonitor Publications Limited, 87-88 Turnmill Street, London EC1M 5QU, England

Industrial Outlook.
U.S. Department of Commerce, International Trade Administration, Fourteenth Street between Constitution Avenue and E Street, NW, Washington, D.C. 20230 (202) 482-3809

Industrial Production and Capacity Utilization.
Board of Governors of the Federal Reserve System, Twentieth Street and Constitution Avenue, NW, Washington, D.C. 20551 (202) 452-3000

Industrial Production: Quarterly Statistics.
European Community Information Service, 2100 M Street, NW, Washington, D.C. 20037 (202) 862-9500

Industrial Property Statistics.
World Intellectual Property Organization, 34 Chemin des Colombettes, CH-1211 Geneva 20, Switzerland

Industrial Statistics Yearbook.
Statistical Office of the United Nations, Publishing Service, New York, New York 10017 (800) 253-9646

Industrial Structure Statistics.
Organisation for Economic Co-operation and Development (OECD), 2 rue Andre-Pascal, 75 Paris 16, France (Telephone Number in U.S. (202) 785-6323)

Inflation Measures for Schools and Colleges.
Research Associates of Washington, 2605 Klingle Road, NW, Washington, D.C. 20008 (202) 966-3326

Published Sources

Informe estadistico.
Direccion General de Estadistica y Censos, Instituto Nacional de Estadistica, Avenida 28 de Julio 1056, Lima 1, Peru

Inside the Recording Industry: A Statistical Overview.
Recording Industry Association of America, 1020 Nineteenth Street, NW, Suite 200, Washington, D.C. 20036 (202) 775-0101

Insurance Facts.
Insurance Information Institute, 110 William Street, New York, New York 10038 (212) 669-9200

Intergovernmental AIDS Reports.
AIDS Policy Center, Intergovernmental Health Policy Project, The George Washington University, 2021 K Street, NW, Suite 800, Washington, D.C. 20006 (202) 872-1445

International Comparisons of Manufacturing Productivity and Labor Cost Trends.
U.S. Department of Labor, Bureau of Labor Statistics, Two Massachusetts Avenue, NE, Washington, D.C. 20212 (202) 606-7828

International Crime Statistics.
International Criminal Police Organization (INTERPOL), 26 rue Armengaud, 92210 Saint Cloud, France

International Economic Indicators.
Center for International Business Cycle Research, Columbia University, Graduate School of Business, 808 Uris Hall, New York, New York 10027 (212) 280-2916

International Economic Indicators.
U.S. Department of Commerce, International Trade Administration, Fourteenth Street between Constitution Avenue and E Street, NW, Washington, D.C. 20230 (202) 482-3809

International Energy Annual.
U.S. Department of Energy, Energy Information Administration, 1000 Independence Avenue, SW, Washington, D.C. 20585 (202) 586-8800

International Energy Review.
U.S. Department of Energy, Energy Information Administration, Washington, D.C. 20585 (202) 586-8800

International Energy Statistics Sourcebook.
Penn Well Publishing Company, 1421 South Sheridan Road, P.O. Box 1260, Tulsa, Oklahoma 74101 (800) 752-9764

International Financial Statistics.
International Monetary Fund, 700 Nineteenth Street, NW, Washington, D.C. 20431 (202) 623-7000

International Historical Statistics, Africa and Asia.
International Labour Office, I.L.O. Publications, CH-1211, Geneva 22, Switzerland

International Historical Statistics The Americas and Australasia.
Euromonitor Publications Limited, 87-88 Turnmill Street, London EC1M 5QU, England

International Marketing Data and Statistics.
Euromonitor Publications Limited, 87-88 Turnmill Street, London EC1M 5QU England

International Petroleum Annual.
U.S. Department of Energy, Energy Information Administration, 1000 Independence Avenue, SW Washington, D.C. 20585 (202) 586-8800

International Science and Technology Data Update.
U.S. National Science Foundation, 4201 Wilson Boulevard, Arlington, Virginia 22230 (703) 306-1234

International Trade Statistics Yearbook.
International Monetary Fund, Nineteenth and H Streets, NW, Washington, D.C. 20431 (202) 623-7000

International Trade Statistics Yearbook.
Statistical Office of the United Nations, Publishing Service, New York, New York 10017 (800) 253-9646

The Interstudy Edge.
Interstudy, 5715 Christmas Lake, Excelsior, Minnesota 55331 (612) 474-1176

Inventory Report on Real Property Owned by the United States Throughout the World.
U.S. General Services Administration, General Services Building, Eighteenth and F Streets, NW, Washington, D.C. 20405 (202) 708-5082

Irish Statistical Bulletin.
Central Statistics Office, Earlsfort Terrace, Dublin 2, Ireland

The Iron and Steel Industry.
Organisation for Economic Co-operation and Development (OECD), 2 rue Andre-Pascal, 75 Paris 16, France (Telephone Number in U.S. (202) 785-6323)

Iron and Steel: Statistical Yearbook.
European Community Information Service, 2100 M Street, NW, Washington, D.C. 20037 (202) 862-9500

Israel.
Federal Statistical Office, Gustav-Stresemann-Ring 11, D-6200 Wiesbaden, Germany

Italien.
Federal Statistical Office, Gustav-Stresemann-Ring 11, D-6200 Wiesbaden, Germany

Jaacijfers voor Suriname.
General Bureau of Statistics, Post Office Box 244, Paramaribo, Suriname

Jail Inmates.
U.S. Department of Justice, Bureau of Justice Statistics, 633 Indiana Avenue, NW, Washington, D.C. 20531 (800) 732-3277

Jamaika.
Federal Statistical Office, Gustav-Stresemann-Ring 11, D-6200 Wiesbaden, Germany

Jane's World Railways.
Jane's Information Group, Sentinel House, 163 Brighton Road, Coulsdon, Surrey CR5 2NH, England

Japan.
Federal Statistical Office, Gustav-Stresemann-Ring 11, D-6200 Wiesbaden, Germany

Japan Statistical Yearbook.
Management and Coordination Agency, Statistics Bureau, Tokyo, Japan

Joint Association Survey on Drilling Costs.
American Petroleum Institute, 1220 L Street, NW, Washington, D.C. 20005 (202) 682-8000

Jordan.
Federal Statistical Office, Gustav-Stresemann-Ring 11, D-6200 Wiesbaden, Germany

Journal of Commerce.
U.S. Department of Commerce, Bureau of the Census, Suitland, Maryland 20233 (301) 763-4040

Journal of Philippine Statistics.
Publications Division, Bureau of the Census and Statistics, Post Office Box 779, Manila, Philippines

Justice Expenditure and Employment in the U.S.
U.S. Department of Justice, Bureau of Justice Statistics, 633 Indiana Avenue, NW, Washington, D.C. 20531 (800) 732-3277

Juvenile Court Statistics.
National Center for Juvenile Justice, 701 Forbes Avenue, Pittsburgh, Pennsylvania 15219 (412) 227-6950

Kamerun.
Federal Statistical Office, Gustav-Stresemann-Ring 11, D-6200 Wiesbaden, Germany

Kanada.
Federal Statistical Office, Gustav-Stresemann-Ring 11, D-6200 Wiesbaden, Germany

Kansas Statistical Abstract.
University of Kansas, Institute for Public Policy and Business Research, 607 Blake Hall, Lawrence, Kansas 66045-2960 (913) 864-3701

Kenia.
Federal Statistical Office, Gustav-Stresemann-Ring 11, D-6200 Wiesbaden, Germany

Kentucky Economic Statistics.
Department of Existing Business and Industry Capital Plaza Office Tower, Frankfort, Kentucky 40601

Kenya Statistical Digest.
Central Bureau of Statistics, Ministry of Economic Planning and Development, Post Office Box 30266, Nairobi, Kenya

Key Indicators of Developing Asian and Pacific Countries.
Asian Development Bank, Post Office Box 789, 1099 Manila, Philippines

Kiribati.
Federal Statistical Office, Gustav-Stresemann-Ring 11, D-6200 Wiesbaden, Germany

Kolumbien.
Federal Statistical Office, Gustav-Stresemann-Ring 11, D-6200 Wiesbaden, Germany

Kongo.
Federal Statistical Office, Gustav-Stresemann-Ring 11, D-6200 Wiesbaden, Germany

Koobaha Staatistikada.
Central Statistical Department, Post Office Box 1742, Mogadishu, Somalia

Korea (Democratic Volksrepublic).
Federal Statistical Office, Gustav-Stresemann-Ring 11, D-6200 Wiesbaden, Germany

Korea (Republik).
Federal Statistical Office, Gustav-Stresemann-Ring 11, D-6200 Wiesbaden, Germany

Korea Statistical Yearbook.
National Statistical Office, Seoul, Korea

Kuba.
Federal Statistical Office, Gustav-Stresemann-Ring 11, D-6200 Wiesbaden, Germany

Kuwait.
Federal Statistical Office, Gustav-Stresemann-Ring 11, D-6200 Wiesbaden, Germany

La Vie Economique: Rapports Economiques et de Statistique Sociale.
Office Federale de la Statistique, Hallwylstrasse 15, CH-3005 Berne, Switzerland

Labor Force Sample Survey.
European Community Information Service, 2100 M Street, NW, Washington, D.C. 20037 (202) 862-9500

Labour Force Statistics
Organisation for Economic Co-operation and Development (OECD), 2 rue Andre-Pascal, 75 Paris 16, France (Telephone Number in U.S. (202) 785-6323)

Labour Force Survey.
Central Statistics Office, Ardee Road, Dublin 6, Ireland

Labour Statistics.
Organisation for Economic Co-operation and Development (OECD), 2 rue Andre-Pascal, 75 Paris 16, France (Telephone Number in U.S. (202) 785-6323)

LaFleur's Fiscal 1993 Lottery Special Report.
TLF Publications, Inc., Boyds, Maryland 20841 (301) 540-0123

LaFleur's Lottery World.
TLF Publications, Inc., Boyds, Maryland 20841 (301) 540-0123

Land Areas of the National Forest System.
U.S. Department of Agriculture, Forest Service, Fourteenth Street and Independence Avenue, SW, Washington, D.C. 20250 (202) 720-3760

Landshagir.
Statistical Bureau of Iceland, Skuggasund 3, 15-150, Reykjavik

Laos.
Federal Statistical Office, Gustav-Stresemann-Ring 11, D-6200 Wiesbaden, Germany

Largest Rivers in the United States.
U.S. Department of the Interior, Geological Survey, National Center, 12201 Sunrise Valley Drive, Reston, Virginia 22092 (703) 648-4460

Published Sources

Latvijas Statistikas Gadagramata.
Latvijas Republikas Valsts Statistikas Komiteja, Riga Latvia

Law Enforcement Officers Killed and Assaulted.
U.S. Department of Justice, Federal Bureau of Investigation, Ninth Street and Pennsylvania Avenue, NW, Washington, D.C. 20535 (202) 324-3000

Lawyer Statistical Report: The U.S. Legal Profession in the 1990's.
American Bar Foundation, 750 North Lake Shore Drive, Chicago, Illinois 60611 (312) 988-6500

Layers and Egg Production - Annual.
U.S. Department of Agriculture, National Agricultural Statistics Service, Fourteenth Street and Independence Avenue, SW, Washington, D.C. 20250 (202) 219-1504

Lead and Zinc Statistics.
International Lead and Zinc Study Group, Metro House, 58 St. James's Street, London SW1A 1LD England

Learning Mathematics and Learning Science.
U.S. Department of Education, National Center of Education Statistics, 400 Maryland Avenue, SW, Washington, D.C. 20202 (202) 708-5366

Le Cameroon en Chiffres.
Direction de la Statistique et de la Comptabilite Nationale, BP 660, Yaounde, Cameroon

L'Economie de la Tunisie en Chiffres.
Institut National de la Statistique, 27 rue du Liban, 1002 Tunis-Belvedere, Tunis, Tunisia

Les Banques Suisses.
Banque Nationale Suisse, Borsenstrasse 15 8022 Zurich, Switzerland

Lesotho.
Federal Statistical Office, Gustav-Stresemann-Ring 11, D-6200 Wiesbaden, Germany

Lesotho Statistical Yearbook.
Bureau of Statistics, Post Office Box 455, Maseru 100, Lesotho

Libanon.
Federal Statistical Office, Gustav-Stresemann-Ring 11, D-6200 Wiesbaden, Germany

Liberia.
Federal Statistical Office, Gustav-Stresemann-Ring 11, D-6200 Wiesbaden, Germany

Library Journal.
R.R. Bowker Company, 121 Chanlon Road, New Providence, New Jersey 07974 (908) 464-6800

Liechtenstein.
Federal Statistical Office, Gustav-Stresemann-Ring 11, D-6200 Wiesbaden, Germany

Life Insurance Fact Book.
American Council of Life Insurance, 1001 Pennsylvania Avenue, NW, Washington, D.C. 20004 (202) 624-2000

Lithuania's Statistics Yearbook.
Lithuanian Department of Statistics, Vilnius, Lithuania

Lives Saved by Child Restraints.
U.S. Department of Transportation, National Highway Traffic Safety Administration, 400 Seventh Street, SW, Washington, D.C. 20590 (202) 366-9550

Livestock and Meat Statistics.
U.S. Department of Agriculture, National Agricultural Statistics Service, Fourteenth Street and Independence Avenue, SW, Washington, D.C. 20250 (202) 219-1504

Luxembourg.
Federal Statistical Office, Gustav-Stresemann-Ring 11, D-6200 Wiesbaden, Germany

Macau.
Federal Statistical Office, Gustav-Stresemann-Ring 11, D-6200 Wiesbaden, Germany

Madagaskar.
Federal Statistical Office, Gustav-Stresemann-Ring 11, D-6200 Wiesbaden, Germany

Main Economic Indicators.
Organisation for Economic Co-operation and Development (OECD), 2 rue Andre-Pascal, 75 Paris 16, France (Telephone Number in U.S. (202) 785-6323)

Maine: A Statistical Summary.
Maine Department of Economic and Community Development, State House Station 59, Augusta, Maine 04333 (207) 289-2656

Malawi.
Federal Statistical Office, Gustav-Stresemann-Ring 11, D-6200 Wiesbaden, Germany

Malawi Statistical Yearbook.
National Statistical Office, Post Office Box 333, Zomba, Malawi

Malaysia.
Federal Statistical Office, Gustav-Stresemann-Ring 11, D-6200 Wiesbaden, Germany

Malediven.
Federal Statistical Office, Gustav-Stresemann-Ring 11, D-6200 Wiesbaden, Germany

Mali.
Federal Statistical Office, Gustav-Stresemann-Ring 11, D-6200 Wiesbaden, Germany

Malta.
Federal Statistical Office, Gustav-Stresemann-Ring 11, D-6200 Wiesbaden, Germany

Maly rocznik statystyczny.
Glowny Urzad Statystyczny (Central Statistical Office), Al Niepodleglosci 208, 00-925 Warsaw, Poland

Manufacturing and Trade Inventories and Sales.
U.S. Department of Commerce, Bureau of the Census, Suitland, Maryland 20233 (301) 763-4040

Manufacturing Climate Study.
Grant/Thorton, One Prudential Plaza, Chicago, Illinois 60601 (312) 856-0200

Manufacturing Energy Consumption.
U.S. Department of Energy, Energy Information Administration, 1000 Independence Avenue, SW, Washington, D.C. 20585 (202) 586-8000

Maritime Transport.
European Community Information Service, 2100 M Street, NW, Washington, D.C. 20037 (202) 862-9500

Maritime Transport.
Lloyd's Register of Shipping, 17 Battery Place, New York, New York 10004 (212) 425-8050

Maritime Transport.
Organisation for Economic Co-operation and Development (OECD), 2 rue Andre-Pascal, 75 Paris 16, France (Telephone Number in U.S. (202) 785-6323)

Market Share Reports.
U.S. Department of Commerce, International Trade Administration, Fourteenth Street between Constitution Avenue and E Street, NW, Washington, D.C. 20230 (202) 482-3809

A Marketer's Guide to Discretionary Income.
U.S. Department of Commerce, Bureau of the Census, Suitland, Maryland 20233 (301) 763-4040

Marketplace Update.
Access Research, Inc., 8 Griffen Road, North, Windsor, Connecticut 06095 (203) 688-8821

Maryland Statistical Abstract.
Department of Economic and Employment Development, 217 East Redwood Street, Baltimore, Maryland 21202 Inquiries: (410) 333-6953; copies: (410) 333-6955

Measuring Health Care, Expenditures, Costs, and Performance.
Organisation for Economic Cooperation and Development, (OECD), 2 rue Andre-Pascal, 75 Paris 16, France (Telephone Number in U.S. (202) 785-6323)

Meat Animals - Production, Disposition and Income.
U.S. Department of Agriculture, National Agricultural Statistics Service, Fourteenth Street and Independence Avenue, SW, Washington, D.C. 20250 (202) 219-1504

Meat Balances in OECD Member Countries.
Organisation for Economic Co-operation and Development (OECD), 2 rue Andre-Pascal, 75 Paris 16, France (Telephone Number in U.S. (202) 785-6323)

Medical Economics.
Medical Economics Company, One Broad Avenue, Fairview, New Jersey 07022 (201) 945-9058

Medical Program Statistics, Selected State Data.
U.S. Department of Health and Human Services, Health Care Financing Administration, 200 Independence Avenue, SW, Washington, D.C. 20201 (202) 245-6113

Medicare Program Statistics.
U.S. Department of Health and Human Services, Health Care Financing Administration, 200 Independence Avenue, SW, Washington, D.C. 20201 (202) 245-6113

Merchant Fleets of the World.
U.S. Department of Transportation, Maritime Administration, 400 Seventh Street, SW, Washington, D.C. 20590 (202) 366-5807

Merger and Corporate Transactions Database.
Securities Data Company, 1180 Raymond Boulevard, Newark, New Jersey 07102 (201) 622-3100

Metals Week.
McGraw-Hill Publications Company, Inc., 1221 Avenue of the Americas, New York, New York 10020 (212) 512-2000

Mexiko.
Federal Statistical Office, Gustav-Stresemann-Ring 11, D-6200 Wiesbaden, Germany

Michigan Statistical Abstract.
School of Business Administration, Bureau of Business Research, Wayne State University, Detroit, Michigan 48202

Microcomputers in Schools.
Market Data Retrieval, 16 Progress Drive, Shelton, Connecticut 06484 (203) 926-4800

Middle East Economic Handbook.
Euromonitor Publications Limited, 87-88 Turnmill Street, London EC1M 5QU, England

Military Assistance Facts.
U.S. Department of Defense, Defense Security Assistance Agency, The Pentagon, Washington, D.C. 20301 (703) 695-3291

The Military Balance.
The International Institute for Strategic Studies, 23 Tavistock Street, London WC2E 7NQ, England

The Military Budget and National Economic Priorities.
U.S. Congress, Joint Economic Committee, U.S. Capitol Building, Washington, D.C. 20515

Milk, Milk Products and Egg Balances in OECD Member Countries.
Organisation for Economic Co-operation and Development (OECD), 2 rue Andre-Pascal, 75 Paris 16, France (Telephone Number in U.S. (202) 785-6323)

Milk Production, Disposition and Income.
U.S. Department of Agriculture, National Agricultural Statistics Service, Fourteenth Street and Independence Avenue, SW, Washington, D.C. 20250 (202) 219-1504

Mineral Commodity Summaries.
U.S. Department of the Interior, Bureau of Mines, 810 Seventh Street, NW, Washington, D.C. 20241 (202) 501-9649

Mineral Facts and Problems.
U.S. Department of the Interior, Bureau of Mines, 810 Seventh Street, NW, Washington, D.C. 20241 (202) 501-9649

Minimum Wage and Maximum Hours Standards Under the Fair Labor Standards Act.
U.S. Department of Labor, Employment Standards Administration, 200 Constitution Avenue, NW, Washington, D.C. 20210 (202) 219-7320

Minnesota Population and Household Estimates.
Office of State Demographer, State Planning Agency, 300 Centennial Building, Saint Paul, Minnesota 55155 (612) 296-2557

Mississippi Statistical Abstract.
Mississippi State University, College of Business and Industry, Division of Research, Mississippi State, Mississippi 39762 (601) 325-3817

Money and Finance.
European Community Information Service, 2100 M Street, NW, Washington, D.C. 20037 (202) 862-9500

Money Stock, Liquid Assets, and Debt Measures.
Board of Governors of the Federal Reserve System, Twentieth Street and Constitution Avenue, NW, Washington, D.C. 20551 (202) 452-3000

Mongolei.
Federal Statistical Office, Gustav-Stresemann-Ring 11, D-6200 Wiesbaden, Germany

Montana County Profiles.
Montana Department of Commerce, Census and Economic Information Center, Capitol Station, Helena, Montana 59620 (406) 444-2896

Monthly Abstract of Statistics.
Government Bookshop, Mulgrave Street, Wellington, New Zealand

Monthly Bulletin of Statistics.
Central Bureau of Statistics, Hakirya, Romema, Jerusalem, Israel

Monthly Bulletin of Statistics.
National Statistical Office, Post Office Box 333, Zomba, Malawi

Monthly Bulletin of Statistics.
Statistical Office of the United Nations, Publishing Service, New York, New York 10017 (800) 253-9646

Monthly Digest of Statistics.
Barbados Statistical Service, Third Floor, National Insurance Building, Fairchild Street, Bridgetown, Barbados

Monthly Digest of Statistics.
Central Statistical Office, Post Office Box 8063, Causeway, Harare, Zimbabwe

Monthly Digest of Statistics.
Central Statistical Office, Post Office Box 31908, Lusaka, Zambia

Monthly Digest of Statistics.
Central Statistical Office, Post Office Box 26188, Safat, Kuwait

Monthly Digest of Statistics.
Department of Statistics, 8 Shenton Way 10-01, Treasury Building, Singapore, 0106

Monthly Digest of Statistics.
HM Stationery Office, Post Office Box 276, London SW8 5DT, England

Monthly Energy Review.
U.S. Department of Energy, Energy Information Administration, Washington, D.C. 20585 (202) 586-8800

Monthly Failure Report.
Dun and Bradstreet Corporation, 299 Park Avenue, Twenty-fourth Floor, New York, New York 10171 (212) 593-6800

Monthly Industrial Survey.
Confederation of Irish Industry, Confederation House, Kildare Street, Dublin 2, Ireland

Monthly Labor Review.
U.S. Department of Labor, Bureau of Labor Statistics, Two Massachusetts Avenue, NE, Washington, D.C. 20212 (202) 606-7828

Monthly Retail Trade Report.
U.S. Department of Commerce, Bureau of the Census, Suitland, Maryland 20233 (301) 763-4040

Monthly Statistical Bulletin.
National Statistical Service of Greece, 14-1G Lycourgou Street, Athens 112, Greece

Monthly Statistical Bulletin of Bangladesh.
Bureau of Statistics, Bangladesh Secretariat School Building, Dacca, Bangladesh

Monthly Statistics of Foreign Trade.
Organisation for Economic Co-operation and Development, (OECD), 2 rue Andre-Pascal, 75 Paris 16, France (Telephone Number in U.S. (202) 785-6323)

Monthly Statistics of Japan.
Management and Coordination Agency, Statistics Bureau, Tokyo, Japan

Monthly Statistics of Korea.
National Statistical Office, Seoul, Korea

Monthly Statistics of the Republic of China.
Directorate - General of Budget, Accounting and Statistics, Executive Yuan, Republic of China

Monthly Summary of Statistics.
Australian Bureau of Statistics, Post Office Box 10, Belconnen, Canberra ACT 2616, Australia

Monthly Vital Statistics Report.
U.S. Department of Health and Human Services, National Center for Health Statistics, 3700 East-West Highway, Hyattsville, Maryland 20782 (301) 436-8500

Morbidity and Mortality Weekly Report.
U.S. Department of Health and Human Services, Centers for Disease Control, 1600 Clifton Road, NE, Atlanta, Georgia 30333 (404) 639-3311

Motor Vehicle Facts and Figures.
American Automobile Manufacturers Association, 1401 H Street, NW, Washington, D.C. 20005 (202) 326-5500

Motor Vehicles Defect Recall Campaigns.
U.S. Department of Transportation, National Highway Traffic Safety Administration, 400 Seventh Street, SW, Washington, D.C. 20590 (202) 366-9550

Multimedia Audiences.
Mediamark Research Incorporated, 708 Third Avenue, New York, New York 10017 (212) 599-0444

Municipal New Issues Database.
Securities Data Company, Inc., 1180 Raymond Boulevard, Newark, New Jersey 07102 (201) 622-3100

Mutual Fund Fact Book.
Investment Company Institute, 1400 H Street, NW, Suite 600, Washington, D.C. 20005 (202) 326-5800

NADA Data.
National Automobile Dealers Association, 8400 Westpark Drive, McLean, Virginia 22102 (703) 827-7407

NASA News.
U.S. National Aeronautics and Space Administration, 300 E Street, SW, Washington, D.C. 20546 (202) 358-1000

NASBO State Expenditure Report.
National Association of State Budget Officers,, Hall of the States, 400 North Capitol Street, NW, Suite 295, Washington, D.C. 20001 (202) 624-5382

NFPA Reports on U.S. Fire Loss.
National Fire Protection Association, One Batterymarch Park, Quincy, Massachusetts 02269-9101 (617) 770-3000

NLN Data Book.
National League for Nursing, 350 Hudson Street, New York, New York 10014 (212) 989-9393

Namibia.
Federal Statistical Office, Gustav-Stresemann-Ring 11, D-6200 Wiesbaden, Germany

Narodnoe Khoziaistvo Rossiiskoi Federatsii: Statisticheskii Ezhegodnik.
Gosudarstvennyi komitet Rossiiskoi Federatsii po Statistike, Moscow, Russia

Narodnoye Khozyaystvo SSR: Statisticheskiy Yezhegodnik.
Central Statistical Board of the Council of Ministers of the Soviet Union, Moscow, Russia

National Accounts.
Organisation for Economic Co-operation and Development (OECD), 2 rue Andre-Pascal, 75 Paris 16, France (Telephone Number in U.S. (003) 785 6323)

National Accounts of OECD Countries.
Organisation for Economic Co-operation and Development, (OECD), 2 rue Andre Pascal, 75 Paris 16, France (Telephone Number in U.S. (202) 785-6323)

National Accounts Statistics.
Statistical Office of the United Nations, Publishing Service, New York, New York 10017 (800) 253-9646

National Air Pollutant Emission Trends.
U.S. Environmental Protection Agency, 401 M Street, SW, Washington, D.C. 20460 (202) 382-2090

National Air Quality and Emissions Trends Report.
U.S. Environmental Protection Agency, 401 M Street, SW, Washington, D.C. 20460 (202) 382-2090

National Ambient Air Quality and Emissions Trends Report.
U.S. Environmental Protection Agency, 401 M Street, SW, Washington, D.C. 20460 (202) 382-2090

National Analysis of Official Child Neglect and Abuse Reporting.
American Humane Association, Animal Protection Division, 63 Inverness Drive, East, Englewood, Colorado 80112 (303) 792-9900

National Child Abuse and Neglect Data System, Working Paper 2, Summary Data Component.
U.S. Department of Health and Human Services, National Center on Child Abuse and Neglect, 370 L'Enfant Promenade, SW, Washington, D.C. 20447 (202) 205-8586

National College - Bound Senior.
College Entrance Examination Board, 45 Columbus Avenue, New York, New York 10023 (212) 713-8000

National Credit Union Administration Year-End Statistics.
National Credit Union Administration, 1775 Duke Street, Alexandria, Virginia 22314 (703) 518-6300

The National Data Book of Foundations.
The Foundation Center, 79 Fifth Avenue, New York, New York 10003 (212) 620-4230

National Delinquency Survey.
Mortgage Bankers Association of America, 1125 15th Street, NW, Washington, D.C. 20005 (202) 861-6500

National Development Plan.
Statistics Office, Ministry of Finance, Post Office Box 67, Bariki, Tarawa, Kiribati

National Directory of HMO's.
Group Health Association of America, Inc., 1129 20th Street, NW, Washington D.C. 20036 (202) 778-3200

National Economy of the MPR for 60 Years.
Central Statistical Office, Ulan Bator, Mongolia

National Economy of the Republic of Belarus.
State Committee of the Republic of Belarus on Statistics and Analysis, Minsk, Belarus

National Food Review.
U.S. Department of Agriculture, Economic Research Service, Fourteenth Street and Independence Avenue, SW, Washington, D.C. 20005-4789 (202) 219-1504

National Gardening Survey.
National Gardening Association, 180 Flynn Avenue, Burlington, Vermont 05401 (000) 863 1308

National Health Interview Survey.
U.S. Department of Health and Human Services, National Center for Health Statistics, 3700 East-West Highway, Hyattsville, Maryland 20782 (301) 436-8500

National Household Survey on Drug Abuse.
U.S. Department of Health and Human Services, Substance Abuse and Mental Health Services Administration, 5600 Fishers Lane, Rockville, Maryland 20857 (301) 443-4797

The National Income and Product Accounts of the United States.
U.S. Department of Commerce, Bureau of Economic Analysis, Fourteenth Street between Constitution Avenue and E Street, NW, Washington, D.C. 20230 (202) 606-9900

National League Green Book.
National League of Professional Baseball Clubs, 350 Park Avenue, 18th Floor, New York, New York 10022 (212) 339-7700

National Park Statistical Abstract.
U.S. Department of the Interior, National Park Service, C Street between Eighteenth and Nineteenth Streets, NW, Washington D.C. 20240 (202) 208-6843

The National Parks: Index.
U.S. Department of the Interior, National Park Service, C Street between 18th and 19th Streets, NW, Washington, D.C. 20240 (202) 208-6843

National Patterns of Science and Technology Resources.
U.S. National Science Foundation, 4201 Wilson Boulevard, Arlington, Virginia 22230 (703) 306-1234

Published Sources

National Payroll Hours.
U.S. Postal Service, 475 L'Enfant Plaza West, SW, Washington, D.C. 20260-0010 (202) 268-2000

National Resources Inventory.
U.S. Department of Agriculture, Soil Conservation Service, Fourteenth Street and Independence Avenue, SW, Washington, D.C. 20250 (202) 205-0027

National Restaurant Association Foodservice Industry Forecast.
National Restaurant Association, 1200 Seventeenth Street, NW, Washington, D.C. 20036 (202) 331-5900

National Roster of Hispanic Elected Officials.
National Association of Latino Elected and Appointed Officials, NALEO Education Fund, 3409 Garnet Street, Los Angeles, California 90023 (213) 262-8503

National Study on Child Neglect and Abuse Reporting.
American Humane Association, Animal Protection Division, 63 Inverness Drive, East, Englewood, Colorado 80112 (303) 792-9900

National Survey of Hunting, Fishing, and Wildlife - Associated Recreation.
U.S. Department of the Interior, Fish and Wildlife Service, C Street between Eighteenth and Nineteenth Streets, NW, Washington, D.C. 20240 (202) 208-5634

National Survey of Salaries and Wages in Public Schools.
Educational Research Service, 2000 Clarendon Boulevard, Arlington, Virginia 22201 (703) 243-2100

National Transportation Statistics Annual, Historical Compendium Information Report.
U.S. Department of Transportation, Bureau of Transportation Statistics, 400 Seventh Street, SW, Washington, D.C. 20590 (202) 366-DATA

National Travel Survey.
U.S. Travel Data Center, Two Lafayette Center, 1133 Twenty-first Street, NW, Washington, D.C. 20036 (202) 293-1040

Nationwide Food Consumption Survey: Food and Nutrition Intakes, One Day.
U.S. Department of Agriculture, Human Nutrition Information Service, Hyattsville, Maryland 20782 (301) 436-7725

Natural Gas Annual.
U.S. Department of Energy, Energy Information Administration, 1000 Independence Avenue, SW, Washington, D.C. 20585 (202) 586-8800

Natural Gas Monthly.
U.S. Department of Energy, Energy Information Administration, Washington, D.C. 20585 (202) 586-8800

Nauru.
Federal Statistical Office, Gustav-Stresemann-Ring 11, D-6200 Wiesbaden, Germany

Nebraska Statistical Handbook.
Department of Economic Development, Division of Research, Box 94666, Lincoln, Nebraska 68509 (402) 471-3779

Nepal.
Federal Statistical Office, Gustav-Stresemann-Ring 11, D-6200 Wiesbaden, Germany

Nevada Statistical Abstract.
Department of Administration, Planning Division, Capitol Complex, Carson City, Nevada 89710 (702) 687-4065

The New Book of World Rankings.
Facts on File, 460 Park Avenue, South, New York, New York 10016 (800) 443-8323

New Business Incorporations.
Dun and Bradstreet Corporation, 299 Park Avenue, Twenty-fourth Floor, New York, New York 10171 (212) 593-6800

New Hebrides Anglo-French Condominium: Report for the Year.
HM Stationery Office, Post Office Box 569, London SE1, England

New Jersey Source Book.
New Jersey State Data Center, New Jersey Department of Labor, CN 388, Trenton, New Jersey 08625-0388 (609) 984-2593

New Jersey Statistical Factbook.
New Jersey State Data Center, New Jersey Department of Labor, CN 388, Trenton, New Jersey 08625-0388 (609) 984-2593

The New Latin American Market Atlas.
The Economist Intelligence Unit, 111 West 57th Street, New York, New York 10019 (800) 938-4685

New Mexico Statistical Abstract.
University of New Mexico, Bureau of Business and Economic Research, Albuquerque, New Mexico 87131 (505) 277-2216

New Motorcycle Registrations by States.
R.L. Polk and Company, 1155 Brewery Park, Detroit, Michigan 48207 (313) 393-0880

New One-Family Houses Sold and For Sale.
U.S. Department of Commerce, Bureau of the Census, Suitland, Maryland 20233 (301) 763-4040

New Ship Construction.
U.S. Department of Transportation, Maritime Administration, 400 Seventh Street, SW, Washington, D.C. 20590 (202) 366-5807

New York State Statistical Yearbook.
Nelson Rockefeller Institute of Government, 411 State Street, Albany, New York 12203 (518) 472-1300

New Zealand Official Yearbook.
Government Bookshop, Mulgrave Street, Wellington, New Zealand

New Zealand Pocket Digest of Statistics.
Government Bookshop, Mulgrave Street, Wellington, New Zealand

News.
U.S. Department of Labor, Bureau of Labor Statistics, Two Massachusetts Avenue, NE, Washington, D.C. 20212 (202) 606-7828

Nicaragua.
Federal Statistical Office, Gustav-Stresemann-Ring 11, D-6200 Wiesbaden, Germany

Niederlands.
Federal Statistical Office, Gustav-Stresemann-Ring 11, D-6200 Wiesbaden, Germany

Nien-Giam Thong-Ke.
General Statistical Office, 2 Hoang Van Thu Street, Hanoi, Socialist Republic of Vietnam

Niger.
Federal Statistical Office, Gustav-Stresemann-Ring 11, D-6200 Wiesbaden, Germany

Nigeria.
Federal Statistical Office, Gustav-Stresemann-Ring 11, D-6200 Wiesbaden, Germany

The Nilson Report.
HSN Consultants Inc., 300 Esplanade Drive, Oxnard, California 93030 (310) 392-8478

1990 Census, Population and Housing for the District of Columbia.
Office of Planning, Data Management Division, Presidential Building, 415 12th Street, NW, Washington, D.C. 20004 (202) 727-6533

1990 Census: Social, Economic and Housing Characteristics.
Office of Planning, Data Management Division, Presidential Building, 415 12th Street, NW, Washington, D.C. 20004 (202) 727-6533

1995 Budget Summary.
U.S. National Aeronautics and Space Administration, 300 E Street, SW, Washington, D.C. 20546 (202) 358-1000

The Non-Ferrous Metals Industry.
Organisation for Economic Co-operation and Development (OECD), 2 rue Andre-Pascal, 75 Paris 16, France (Telephone Number in U.S. (202) 785-6323)

Non-Voter Study.
Committee for the Study of the American Electorate, 421 New Jersey Avenue, SE, Washington, D.C. 20003 (202) 546-3221

Noncitrus Fruit and Nuts.
U.S. Department of Agriculture, National Agricultural Statistics Service, Fourteenth Street and Independence Avenue, SW, Washington, D.C. 20250 (202) 219-1504

Nonresidential Buildings Energy Consumption Survey: Characteristics of Commercial Buildings.
U.S. Department of Energy, Energy Information Administration, 1000 Independence Avenue, SW, Washington, D.C. 20585 (202) 586-8800

Nonresidential Buildings Energy Consumption Survey: Commercial Buildings, Consumption and Expenditures.
U.S. Department of Energy, Energy Information Administration, 1000 Independence Avenue, SW, Washington, D.C. 20585 (202) 586-8800

The Northwestern Lindquist-Endicott Report.
Northwestern University, 633 Clark Street, Evanston, Illinois 60201 (708) 491-3741

Norwegen.
Federal Statistical Office, Gustav-Stresemann-Ring 11, D-6200 Wiesbaden, Germany

Note Annuelle de Statistique.
Direction de la Satistique et de la Comptabilite Nationale, BP 660, Yaounde, Cameroon

Nucleonics Week.
McGraw-Hill, Inc., 1221 Avenue of the Americas, New York, New York 10020 (212) 512-2000

OECD Economic Surveys: Australia.
Organisation for Economic Co-operation and Development (OECD), 2 rue Andre-Pascal, 75 Paris 16, France (Telephone Number in U.S. (202) 785-6323)

OECD Economic Surveys: Austria.
Organisation for Economic Co-operation and Development (OECD), 2 rue Andre-Pascal, 75 Paris 16, France (Telephone Number in U.S. (202) 785-6323)

OECD Economic Surveys: Belgium-Luxembourg.
Organisation for Economic Co-operation and Development (OECD), 2 rue Andre-Pascal, 75 Paris 16, France (Telephone Number in U.S. (202) 785-6323)

OECD Economic Surveys: Canada.
Organisation for Economic Co-operation and Development (OECD), 2 rue Andre-Pascal, 75 Paris 16, France (Telephone Number in U.S. (202) 785-6323)

OECD Economic Surveys: Denmark.
Organisation for Economic Co-operation and Development (OECD), 2 rue Andre-Pascal, 75 Paris 16, France (Telephone Number in U.S. (202) 785-6323)

OECD Economic Surveys: Finland.
Organisation for Economic Co-operation and Development (OECD), 2 rue Andre-Pascal, 75 Paris 16, France (Telephone Number in U.S. (202) 785-6323)

OECD Economic Surveys: France.
Organisation for Economic Co-operation and Development (OECD), 2 rue Andre-Pascal, 75 Paris 16, France (Telephone Number in U.S. (202) 785-6323)

OECD Economic Surveys: Germany.
Organisation for Economic Co-operation and Development (OECD), 2 rue Andre-Pascal, 75 Paris 16, France (Telephone Number in U.S. (202) 785-6323)

OECD Economic Surveys: Greece.
Organisation for Economic Co-operation and Development (OECD), 2 rue Andre-Pascal, 75 Paris 16, France (Telephone Number in U.S. (202) 785-6323)

OECD Economic Surveys: Iceland.
Organisation for Economic Co-operation and Development (OECD), 2 rue Andre-Pascal, 75 Paris 16, France (Telephone Number in U.S. (202) 785-6323)

OECD Economic Surveys: Ireland.
Organisation for Economic Co-operation and Development (OECD), 2 rue Andre-Pascal, 75 Paris 16, France (Telephone Number in U.S. (202) 785-6323)

OECD Economic Surveys: Italy.
Organisation for Economic Co-operation and Development (OECD), 2 rue Andre-Pascal, 75 Paris 16, France (Telephone Number in U.S. (202) 785-6323)

OECD Economic Surveys: Japan.
Organisation for Economic Co-operation and Development (OECD), 2 rue Andre-Pascal, 75 Paris 16, France (Telephone Number in U.S. (202) 785-6323)

OECD Economic Surveys: Netherlands.
Organisation for Economic Co-operation and Development (OECD), 2 rue Andre-Pascal, 75 Paris 16, France (Telephone Number in U.S. (202) 785-6323)

OECD Economic Surveys: New Zealand.
Organisation for Economic Co-operation and Development (OECD), 2 rue Andre-Pascal, 75 Paris 16, France (Telephone Number in U.S. (202) 785-6323)

OECD Economic Surveys: Norway.
Organisation for Economic Co-operation and Development (OECD), 2 rue Andre-Pascal, 75 Paris 16, France (Telephone Number in U.S. (202) 785-6323)

OECD Economic Surveys: Portugal.
Organisation for Economic Co-operation and Development (OECD), 2 rue Andre-Pascal, 75 Paris 16, France (Telephone Number in U.S. (202) 785-6323)

OECD Economic Surveys: Spain.
Organisation for Economic Co-operation and Development (OECD), 2 rue Andre-Pascal, 75 Paris 16, France (Telephone Number in U.S. (202) 785-6323)

OECD Economic Surveys: Sweden.
Organisation for Economic Co-operation and Development (OECD), 2 rue Andre-Pascal, 75 Paris 16, France (Telephone Number in U.S. (202) 785-6323)

OECD Economic Surveys: Switzerland.
Organisation for Economic Co-operation and Development (OECD), 2 rue Andre-Pascal, 75 Paris 16, France (Telephone Number in U.S. (202) 785-6323)

OECD Economic Surveys: Turkey.
Organisation for Economic Co-operation and Development (OECD), 2 rue Andre-Pascal, 75 Paris 16, France (Telephone Number in U.S. (202) 785-6323)

OECD Economic Surveys: United Kingdom.
Organisation for Economic Co-operation and Development (OECD), 2 rue Andre-Pascal, 75 Paris 16, France (Telephone Number in U.S. (202) 785-6323)

OECD Employment Outlook.
Organisation for Economic Co-operation and Development (OECD), 2 rue Andre-Pascal, 75 Paris 16, France (Telephone Number in U.S. (202) 785-6323)

OECD Environmental Data.
Organisation for Economic Co-operation and Development (OECD), 2 rue Andre-Pascal, 75 Paris 16, France (Telephone Number in U.S. (202) 785-6323)

OECD Financial Statistics.
Organisation for Economic Co-operation and Development (OECD), 2 rue Andre-Pascal, 75 Paris 16, France (Telephone Number in U.S. (202) 785-6323)

OECD Health Systems: Facts and Trends.
Organisation for Economic Co-operation and Development (OECD), 2 rue Andre-Pascal, 75 Paris 16, France (Telephone Number in U.S. (202) 785-6323)

OECD Industrial Structure Statistics.
Organisation for Economic Co-Operation and Development (OECD), 2 rue Andre-Pascal, 75 Paris 16, France (Telephone Number in U.S. (202) 785-6323)

OPEC Annual Statistical Bulletin.
Organization of Petroleum Exporting Countries, Obere Donaustrasse 93, 1020 Vienna 2, Austria

Occupational Injuries and Illnesses in the U.S. by Industry.
U.S. Department of Labor, Bureau of Labor Statistics, Two Massachusetts Avenue, NE, Washington, D.C. 20212 (202) 606-7828

Occupations of Federal White-Collar and Blue- Collar Workers.
U.S. Office of Personnel Management, 1900 E Street, NW, Washington, D.C. 20415 (202) 606-1800

Office Market Data Book.
ONCOR International, 3040 Post Oak Road, Houston, Texas 77056 (713) 961-0600

Official Guard and Reserve Manpower Strengths and Statistics.
U.S. Department of Defense, Office of the Secretary, The Pentagon, Washington, D.C. 20301 (703) 545-6700

Official Professional Rodeo Media Guide.
Professional Rodeo Cowboys Association, 101 Prorodeo Drive, Colorado Springs, Colorado 80910 (719) 593-8840

Oil and Gas Information.
Organisation for Economic Co-operation and Development (OECD), 2 rue Andre-Pascal, 75 Paris 16, France (Telephone Number in U.S. (202) 785-6323)

Oil and Gas Journal.
Penn Well Publishing Company, 1421 South Sheridan Road, Tulsa, Oklahoma 74101 (800) 752-9764

Oil Statistics.
Organisation for Economic Co-operation and Development (OECD), 2 rue Andre-Pascal, 75 Paris 16, France (Telephone Number in U.S. (202) 785-6323)

Okonomisk utsyn.
Statistisk Sentralbyra (Central Bureau of Statistics), Skippergate 15, P.B. 8131, DEP N-0033, Oslo 1, Norway

Oman.
Federal Statistical Office, Gustav-Stresemann-Ring 11, D-6200 Wiesbaden, Germany

Open Doors.
Institute of International Education, 809 United Nations Plaza, New York, New York 10017 (212) 883-8200

Opera America Profile.
Opera America, 777 Fourteenth Street, NW, Suite 520, Washington, D.C. 20005 (202) 347-9262

Oregon Blue Book.
Oregon Secretary of State, Room 136 State Capitol, Salem, Oregon 97310

Osterreich.
Federal Statistical Office, Gustav-Stresemann-Ring 11, D-6200 Wiesbaden, Germany

PTV Programming Survey.
Corporation for Public Broadcasting, 901 E Street, NW, Washington, D.C. 20004 (202) 879-9600

The Pacific Basin: An Economic Handbook.
Euromonitor Publications Limited, 87-88 Turnmill Street, London EC1M 5QU, England

Pakistan.
Federal Statistical Office, Gustav-Stresemann-Ring 11, D-6200 Wiesbaden, Germany

Palestinian Statistical Abstract.
Palestine Liberation Organizaiton, Economic Department, Central Bureau of Statistics, Damascus, Syria

Panama.
Federal Statistical Office, Gustav-Stresemann-Ring 11, D-6200 Wiesbaden, Germany

Panama en Cifras.
Direccion de Estadistica y Censo, Apartado 5213, Panama 5 RP, Panama

Papua New Guinea.
Federal Statistical Office, Gustav-Stresemann-Ring 11, D-6200 Wiesbaden, Germany

Paraguay.
Federal Statistical Office, Gustav-Stresemann-Ring 11, D-6200 Wiesbaden, Germany

Patenting Trends in the United States, State Country Report.
U.S. Department of Commerce, Patent and Trademark Office, 2011 Crystal Drive, Arlington, Virginia 22202 (703) 305-8341

Pay Structure of the Federal Civil Service.
U.S. Office of Personnel Management, 1900 E Street, NW, Washington, D.C. 20415 (202) 606-1800

Payload Flight Assignments NASA Mixed Fleets.
U.S. National Aeronautics and Space Administration, 300 E Street, SW, Washington, D.C. 20546 (202) 358-1000

Pennsylvania Statistical Abstract.
Pennsylvania State Data Center, Pennsylvania State University of Harrisburg, 777 West Harrisburg Pike, Middleton, Pennsylvania 15057

Performance Profiles of Major Energy Producers.
U.S. Department of Energy, Energy Information Administration, 1000 Independence Avenue, SW Washington, D.C. 20585 (202) 586-8800

Peru.
Federal Statistical Office, Gustav-Stresemann-Ring 11, D-6200 Wiesbaden, Germany

Petroleum Marketing Monthly.
U.S. Department of Energy, Energy Information Administration, 1000 Independence Avenue, SW, Washington, D.C. 20585 (202) 586-8800

Petroleum Statement Annual.
U.S. Department of Energy, Energy Information Administration, 1000 Independence Avenue, SW Washington, D.C. 20585 (202) 586-8800

Petroleum Supply Annual.
U.S. Department of Energy, Energy Information Administration, 1000 Independence Avenue, SW, Washington, D.C. 20585 (202) 586-8800

Petroleum Supply Monthly.
U.S. Department of Energy, Energy Information Administration, 100 Independence Avenue, SW, Washington, D.C. 20585 (202) 586-8800

Philippine.
Federal Statistical Office, Gustav-Stresemann-Ring 11, D-6200 Wiesbaden, Germany

Philippine Statistical Yearbook.
Publications Division, Bureau of the Census and Statistics, Post Office Box 779, Manila, Philippines

Physician Characteristics and Distribution in the United States.
American Medical Association, 515 North State Street, Chicago, Illinois 60610 (312) 464-5000

Plant and Equipment Expenditures and Plans.
U.S. Department of Commerce, Bureau of the Census, Suitland, Maryland 20233 (301) 763-4040

Pocket Statistics.
U.S. National Aeronautics and Space Administration, 300 E Street, SW, Washington, D.C. 20546 (202) 358-1000

Pocket Year Book Australia.
Australian Bureau of Statistics, Post Office Box 10, Belconnen, Canberra ACT 2616, Australia

Polen.
Federal Statistical Office, Gustav-Stresemann-Ring 11, D-6200 Wiesbaden, Germany

Population-at-Risk Rates and Selected Crime Indicators.
U.S. Department of Justice, U.S. Federal Bureau of Investigation, Ninth Street and Pennsylvania Avenue, NW, Washington, D.C. 20535 (202) 324-3000

Population Estimates for New Hampshire Cities and Towns, New Hampshire Population Projections for Cities and Towns.
Office of State Planning, 2 1/2 Beacon Street, Concord, New Hampshire 03301 (603) 271-2155

Population Trends for Washington State.
Washington State Office of Financial Management, Forecasting Division, Post Office Box 43113, Olympia, Washington 98504-3113 (206) 753-5617

Portugal.
Federal Statistical Office, Gustav-Stresemann-Ring 11, D-6200 Wiesbaden, Germany

Poultry - Production and Value.
U.S. Department of Agriculture, National Agricultural Statistics Service, Fourteenth Street and Independence Avenue, SW, Washington, D.C. 20250 (202) 219-1504

Power Production, Fuel Consumption, and Installed Capacity Data.
U.S. Department of Energy, Energy Information Administration, 1000 Independence Avenue, SW, Washington, D.C. 20585 (202) 586-8800

Presidential Primaries and Caucuses.
Congressional Quarterly, Inc., 1414 22nd Street, NW, Washington, D.C. 20037 (202) 887-8500

Prime Contract Awards.
U.S. Department of Defense, Office of the Secretary, The Pentagon, Washington, D.C. 20301 (703) 545-6700

Prisoners in 1992.
U.S. Department of Justice, Bureau of Justice Statistics, 633 Indiana Avenue, NW, Washington, D.C. 20531 (800) 732-3277

Prisoners in State and Federal Institution on December 31.
U.S. Department of Justice, Bureau of Justice Statistics, 633 Indiana Avenue, NW, Washington, D.C. 20531 (000) 732-3277

Private Pension Plan Bulletin.
U.S. Department of Labor, Pension and Welfare Benefits Administration, 2 Massachusetts Avenue, NE, Washington, D.C. 20212 (202) 219-8921

Probation and Parole.
U.S. Department of Justice, Bureau of Justice Statistics, 633 Indiana Avenue, NW, Washington, D.C. 20531 (800) 732-3277

Producer Price Indexes.
U.S. Department of Labor, Bureau of Labor Statistics, Two Massachusetts Avenue, NE, Washington, D.C. 20212 (202) 606-7828

Product Alert Weekly.
Marketing Intelligence Service Limited, 33 Academy Street, Naples, New York 14512 (716) 374-6326

Products and Services.
Department of Development, Office of Statistical Research, Post Office Box 1001, Columbus, Ohio 43226-0101 (614) 466-2115

Production Yearbook.
Food and Agricultural Organization of the United Nations (FAO), Via delle Terme di Caracalla, 00100 Rome, Italy (Telephone Number in the U.S. (202) 653-2400)

Productivity Measures for Selected Industries and Government Services.
U.S. Department of Labor, Bureau of Labor Statistics, Two Massachusetts Avenue, NE, Washington, D.C. 20212 (202) 606-7828

Profile of Rural Idaho.
Department of Commerce, 700 West State Street, Boise, Idaho 83720 (208) 334-2470

Profile of State and Local Law Enforcement Agencies.
U.S. Department of Justice, Bureau of Justice Statistics, 633 Indiana Avenue, NW, Washington, D.C. 20531 (800) 732-3277

Progressive Grocer, Annual Report of the Grocery Industry.
Maclean Hunter Media, Inc., P.O. Box 10246, Stamford, Connecticut 06904 (203) 325-3500

Projected Total Population and Age Distribution for 2000 and 2005: Massachusetts Cities and Towns.
Massachusetts Institute for Social and Economic Research, 128 Thompson Hall, University of Massachusetts at Amherst, Amherst Massachusetts 01003 (413) 545-3460

Projections of Education Statistics.
U.S. Department of Education, 400 Maryland Avenue, SW, Washington, D.C. 20202 (202) 708-5366

Public Broadcasting Income, Fiscal Year.
Corporation for Public Broadcasting, 901 E Street, NW, Washington, D.C. 20004 (202) 879-9600

Public Education Finances.
U.S. Department of Commerce, Bureau of the Census, Suitland, Maryland 20233 (301) 763-4040

Public Employment.
U.S. Department of Commerce, Bureau of the Census, Suitland, Maryland 20233 (301) 763-4040

Public Land Statistics.
U.S. Department of the Interior, Bureau of Land Management, C Street between Eighteenth and Nineteenth Streets, NW, Washington, D.C. 20240 (202) 208-3435

Publishers Weekly.
R. R. Bowker Company, 121 Chanlon Road, New Providence, New Jersey 07974 (908) 464-6800

The Pulp and Paper Industry.
Organisation for Economic Co-operation and Development (OECD), 2 rue Andre-Pascal, 75 Paris 16 France (Telephone Number in U.S. (202) 785-6323)

Qatar.
Federal Statistical Office, Gustav-Stresemann-Ring 11, D-6200 Wiesbaden, Germany

Quarterly Abstract of Statistics.
Statistical Institute of Jamaica, Nine Swallowfield Road, Kingston 5, Jamaica

Quarterly Abstract of Statistics.
Statistics Office, Post Office Box 125, Takamoa, Raratonga, Cook Islands

Quarterly Bulletin of Statistics.
Census and Statistical Department, Secretariat of Planning, 40 Sharia Damascus, Tripoli, Libya

Quarterly Bulletin of Statistics.
Central Statistical Organization, Six-Story Building, Strand Road, Rangoon, Myanmar

Quarterly Bulletin of Statistics.
National Statistical Office, Bangkok, Thailand

Quarterly Coal Report.
U.S. Department of Energy, Energy Information Administration, 1000 Independence Avenue, SW. Washington, D.C. 20585 (202) 586-8800

Quarterly Digest of Statistics.
Central Bureau of Statistics, Post Office Box 1098, Accra, Ghana

Quarterly Digest of Statistics.
Central Office of Statistics, Auberge D'Italie, Valletta, Malta

Quarterly Digest of Statistics.
Central Statistical Office, Post Office Box 456, Mbabane, Swaziland

Quarterly Digest of Statistics.
Statistics Office, Post Office G6, Honiara, Solomon Islands

Quarterly Economic and Statistical Bulletin.
Statistics Division, Ministry of Planning, Government Printer, Post Office Box 33, Entebbe, Uganda

Quarterly Financial Report for Manufacturing, Mining and Trade Corporations.
U.S. Department of Commerce, Bureau of the Census, Suitland, Maryland 20233 (301) 763-4040

Quarterly Public Assistance Statistics.
U.S. Department of Health and Human Services, Administration for Children and Families, 370 L'Enfant Promenade, SW, Washington, D.C. 20447 (202) 401-9200

Quarterly Statistical Bulletin.
Bureau of Statistics, Government Publications Agency, Post Office Box 1801, Dar es Salaam, Tanzania

Quarterly Statistical Bulletin.
  Bureau of Statistics, Post Office Box MS 455, Maseru, Lesotho

Quarterly Statistical Bulletin of Liberia.
  Ministry of Planning and Economic Affairs, Post Office Box 9016, Monrovia, Liberia

Quarterly Statistical Digest.
  Statistical Bureau, Post Office Box 542, Avenue of the Republic, Georgetown, Guyana

Quarterly Statistical Digest.
  Statistics and Research Department, Nicosia, Cyprus

Quarterly Statistical Summary.
  Department of Statistics, Cabinet Office, Post Office Box N3904, Nassau, Bahamas

Quarterly Survey of Capital Appropriations.
  The Conference Board, Incorporated, 845 Third Avenue, New York, New York 10022 (212) 759-0900

Quarterly Survey of Capital Investment and Supply Conditions in Manufacturing.
  The Conference Board, 845 Third Avenue, New York, New York 10022 (212) 759-0900

Quarterly Thrift Financial Aggregates.
  U.S. Department of the Treasury, Office of Thrift Supervision, 1700 G Street, NW, Washington, D.C. 20552 (202) 906-6000

RMA Monthly Tire Report
  The Rubber Manufacturers Association, 1400 K Street, NW, Washington, D.C. 20005 (202) 682-4800

RV's. . . A Year End Report.
  Recreation Vehicle Industry Association, Post Office Box 2999, 1896 Preston White Drive, Reston, Virginia 22090 (703) 620-6003

Radio Facts.
  Radio Advertising Bureau, 304 Park Avenue, South, New York, New York 10010 (212) 387-2100

Railroad Facts, Statistics of Railroads of Class I.
  Association of American Railroads, 50 F Street, NW, Washington, D.C. 20001 (202) 639-2100

Rankings of the States.
  National Education Association, 1201 Sixteenth Street, NW, Washington, D.C. 20036 (202) 833-4000

Real Estate Outlook: Market Trends and Insights.
  National Association of Realtors, 430 North Michigan Avenue, Chicago, Illinois 60611 (312) 329-8200

Reducing the Health Consequences of Smoking.
  U.S. Department of Health and Human Services, Centers for Disease Control, Office of Smoking and Health, 1600 Clifton Road, NE, Atlanta, Georgia 30333 (404) 639-3311

Regions: Statistical Yearbook.
  European Community Information Service, 2100 M Street, NW, Washington, D.C. 20037 (202) 862-9500

Register of Ships.
  Lloyd's Register of Shipping 17 Battery Place, New York, New York 10004 (212) 425-8050

Religion in America.
  Gallup Organization, Inc., 100 Palmer Square, Princeton, New Jersey 08542 (609) 924-9600

Report 844.
  U.S. Department of Labor, Bureau of Labor Statistics, Two Massachusetts Avenue, NE, Washington, D.C. 20212 (202) 606-7828

Report of Civil Works Expenditures by State and Fiscal Year.
  U.S. Department of the Army, Corps of Engineers, The Pentagon, Washington, D.C. 20310 (202) 545-6700

Report of the AFL-CIO Executive Council.
  American Federation of Labor And Congress of Industrial Organizations, 815 16th Street, NW, Washington, D.C. 20006 (202) 637-5000

Report of the Hospital Nursing Personnel Survey.
  American Hospital Association, 840 North Lake Shore Drive, Chicago, Illinois 60611 (312) 280-6000

Report on Applications for Orders Authorizing or Approving the Interception of Wire, Oral or Electronic Communications.
  Administrative Office of the United States Courts, United States Supreme Court Building, 1 Columbus Circle, NE, Washington, D.C. 20544 (202) 273-1120

Report to Congress on the Activities and Operations of the Public Integrity Section.
  U.S. Department of Justice, Constitution Avenue and Tenth Street, NW, Washington, D.C. 20530 (202) 514-2000

The Republic of China Monthly of Financial Statistics.
  Department of Statistics, Ministry of Finance, 2, Aikuo West Road, Taipei, Republic of China

Republic of Kenya Statistical Abstract.
  Central Bureau of Statistics, Ministry of Economic Planning and Development, Post Office Box 30266, Nairobi, Kenya

Republica Dominicana en Cifras (The Dominican Republic in Figures).
  Oficina Nacional de Estadistica y Censos, Avenida Mexico, Santo Domingo, Dominican Republic

Research and Development In Industry.
  U.S. National Science Foundation, 4201 Wilson Boulevard, Arlington, Virginia 22230 (703) 306-1234

Resena estadistica de la Republica de Guinea Ecuatorial.
  Direccion General de Estadistica, Malabo, Equatorial Guinea

Residential Energy Consumption Survey.
  U.S. Department of Energy, Energy Information Administration, 1000 Independence Avenue, SW, Washington, D.C. 20585 (202) 586-8800

Resumen estadistico.
  Instituto Nacional de Estadistica, Casilla 6129, La Paz, Bolivia

Revenue Statistics of OECD Member Countries.
  Organisation for Economic Co-operation and Development (OECD), 2 rue Andre-Pascal, 75 Paris 16, France (Telephone Number in U.S. (202) 785-6323)

Review of Fisheries in OECD Member Countries.
  Organisation for Economic Co-operation and Development (OECD), 2 rue Andre-Pascal, 75 Paris 16, France (Telephone Number in U.S. (202) 785-6323)

Published Sources

Revista de Estadistica.
Direccion General de Estadistica, Balderas 71, Mexico 1, DF, Mexico

Rhode Island Basic Economic Statistics.
Department of Economic Development, 7 Jackson Walkway, Providence, Rhode Island 02903 (401) 277-2601

Roadway Congestion in Major Urban Areas.
Texas Transportation Institute, Texas A&M University, Riverside Campus, Building 7751. Safety Division, College Station, Texas 77843 (409) 845-8408

Rocznik statystyczny.
Glowny Urzad Statystyczny, Al Niepodleglosci 208, 00-925 Warsaw, Poland

Ruanda.
Federal Statistical Office, Gustav-Stresemann-Ring 11, D-6200 Wiesbaden, Germany

Rubber Statistical Bulletin.
Internaitonal Rubber Study Group, York House, 8th Floor, Empire Way, Wembley, London HA9 OPA, England

Rumanien.
Federal Statistical Office, Gustav-Stresemann-Ring 11, D-6200 Wiesbaden, Germany

SPA Software Sales Report.
Software Publishers Association, 1730 M Street, NW, Washington, D.C. 20036 (202) 452-1600

Saint Kitts-Nevis-Anguilla: Report.
HM Stationery Office, Post Office Box 569, London SE1 9NH, England

Samoa.
Federal Statistical Office, Gustav-Stresemann-Ring 11, D-6200 Wiesbaden, Germany

Saudi Arabia.
Federal Statistical Office, Gustav-Stresemann-Ring 11, D-6200 Wiesbaden, Germany

Savings and Home Financing Source Book.
U.S. Office of Thrift Supervision, 1700 G Street, NW, Washington, D.C. 20552 (202) 906-6000

School Price Index.
Research Associates of Washington, 2605 Klingle Road, NW, Washington, D.C. 20008 (202) 966-3326

Schweden.
Federal Statistical Office, Gustav-Stresemann-Ring 11, D-6200 Wiesbaden, Germany

Schweiz.
Federal Statistical Office, Gustav-Stresemann-Ring 11, D-6200 Wiesbaden, Germany

Science and Engineering Indicators.
U.S. National Science Foundation, 4201 Wilson Boulevard, Arlington, Virginia 22230 (703) 306-1234

Sea and Inland Fisheries Report.
Department of Fisheries and Forestry, Government Publication Sales Office, GPO Arcade, Dublin 1, Ireland

Securities Industry Association Fact Book.
Securities Industry Association, 120 Broadway, New York, New York 10271 (212) 608-1500

Selected Highway Statistics and Charts.
U.S. Department of Transportation, National Highway Traffic Safety Administration, 400 Seventh Street, SW, Washington, D.C. 20590 (202) 366-9550

Selected Manpower Statistics.
U.S. Department of Defense, Office of the Secretary, The Pentagon, Washington, D.C. 20301 (703) 545-6700

Selected Social and Economic Characteristics.
University of South Dakota, State Data Center, Vermillion, South Dakota 57069 (605) 677-5287

Selected Statistics on Regional Member Countries.
African Development Bank, 01 BP 13 87, Abidjan 01, Cote d'Ivoire

Senegal.
Federal Statistical Office, Gustav-Stresemann-Ring 11, D-6200 Wiesbaden, Germany

Serie estadistica.
Instituto Nacional de Estadistica, 10 de Agosto 229, Quito, Ecuador

Service Annual Survey.
U.S. Department of Commerce, Bureau of the Census, Suitland, Maryland 20233 (301) 763-4040

Shopping Centers Today.
International Council of Shopping Centers, 665 Fifth Avenue, New York, New York 10022 (212) 421-8181

Significant Features of Fiscal Federalism.
Advisory Commission on Intergovernmental Relations, 800 K Street, NW, Suite 450 South, Washington, D.C. 20575 (202) 653-5540

Sintesi Statistica Socio-economica.
Servicio Statale di Statistica, Via G Carducci 145, Repubblica di San Marino

Sintesis estadistica.
Instituto Nacional de Estadisticas, Casilla 7597, Correo 3, Santiago, Chile

Situation economique du Senegal.
Direction de la Prevision et de la Statistique, BP 116, Dakar, Senegal

Situation economique, financiere et Sociale de la Republique Gabonaise.
Direction Generale de la Statistique, BP 179, Libreville, Gabon

Social Security Bulletin.
U. S. Department of Health and Human Services, Social Security Administration, 6401 Security Boulevard, Baltimore, Maryland 21235 (410) 965-1234

Social Security Programs Throughout the World.
U.S. Department of Health and Human Services, Social Security Administration, 6401 Security Boulevard, Baltimore, Maryland 21235 (410) 965-1234

Socioeconomic Characteristics of Medical Practice.
American Medical Association, 515 North State Street, Chicago, Illinois 60610 (312) 464-5000

Socio-Economic Indicators by Census Tract.
Office of Planning, Data, Management Division, Presidential Building, 415 12th Street, NW, Washington, D.C. 20004 (202) 727-6533

Socio-Economic Indicators of Change by Census Tract.
Office of Planning, Data, Management Division, Presidential Building, 415 12th Street, NW, Washington, D.C. 20004 (202) 727-6533

Socioeconomic Statistics.
Puerto Rico Planning Board, San Juan, Puerto Rico

Solar Collector Manufacturing Activity.
U.S. Department of Energy, Energy Information Administration, 1000 Independence Avenue, SW, Washington, D.C. 20585 (202) 586-8800

Somalia.
Federal Statistical Office, Gustav-Stresemann-Ring 11, D-6200 Wiesbaden, Germany

Source Book of Health Insurance Data.
Health Insurance Association of America, 1025 Connecticut Avenue, NW, Suite 1200, Washington, D.C. 20036 (202) 223-7780

South Africa: Official Yearbook of the Republic of South Africa.
Department of Foreign Affairs and Information, PBX 152, Pretoria 0001, South Africa

South African Statistics.
Central Statistical Services, Pretoria, 0002 South Africa

South Carolina Statistical Abstract.
Division of Research and Statistical Services, Budget and Control Board, R.C. Dennis Building, Room 425, Columbia, South Carolina 29201 (803) 734-3781

South Dakota Community Abstracts.
University of South Dakota, State Data Center, Vermillion, South Dakota 57069 (605) 677-5287

Space Activities of the United States, CIS and Other Launching Countries/Organization.
U.S. Library of Congress, Congressional Research Service, 101 Independence Avenue, SW, Washington, D.C. 20540 (202) 707-5000

Space Shuttle Flights.
National Aeronautics and Space Administration, 300 E Street, SW, Washington, D.C. 20546 (202) 358-1000

Spain.
Federal Statistical Office, Gustav-Stresemann-Ring 11, D-6200 Wiesbaden, Germany

The Sporting Goods Market in 1993.
National Sporting Goods Association, 1699 Wall Street, Mount Prospect, Illinois 60056 (708) 439-4000

Sports Participation in 1992: Series I.
National Sporting Goods Association, 1699 Wall Street, Mount Prospect, Illinois 60056 (708) 439-4000

Sri Lanka Yearbook.
Department of Census and Statistics, No. 6, Albert Crescent, Colombo 7, Sri Lanka

Standard and Poor's Outlook.
Standard and Poor's Corporation, 25 Broadway, New York, New York 10004 (212) 208-8000

State Aid to Local Government.
National Association of State Budget Officers, Hall of the States, 400 North Capitol Street, NW, Suite 295, Washington, D.C. 20001 (202) 624-5382

State and Local Government Information Report.
U.S. Equal Employment Opportunity Commission, 1801 L Street, NW, Washington, D.C. 20507 (800) USA-EEOC

State Approved Schools of Nursing, RN.
National League for Nursing, 350 Hudson Street, New York, New York 10014 (212) 989-9393

State Elective Officials and the Legislatures.
Council of State Governments, P.O. Box 11910, Iron Works Pike, Lexington, Kentucky 40578 (606) 231-1939

State Energy Data Report.
U.S. Department of Energy, Energy Information Administration, 1000 Independence Avenue, SW, Washington, D.C. 20585 (202) 586-8800

State Energy Price and Expenditure Report.
U.S. Department of Energy, Energy Information Administration, 1000 Independence Avenue, SW, Washington, D.C. 20585 (202) 586-8800

State Government Finances.
U.S. Department of Commerce, Bureau of the Census, Suitland, Maryland 20233 (301) 763-4040

State Government Tax Collections.
U.S. Department of Commerce, Bureau of the Census, Suitland, Maryland 20233 (301) 763-4040

State Legislatures.
National Conference of State Legislatures, 1560 Broadway, Suite 700, Denver, Colorado 80202 (303) 830-2200

The State of Food and Agriculture.
Food and Agricultural Organization of the United Nations (FAO), Via Delle Terme di Caracalla, 00100 Rome, Italy (Telephone Number in the U.S. (202) 653-2400)

The State of Hawaii Data Book: A Statistical Abstract.
Hawaii State Department of Business and Economic Development and Tourism, P.O. Box 2359, Honolulu, Hawaii 96804 (808) 586-2481

The State of Small Business: A Report of the President.
U.S. Small Business Administration, 409 Third Street, SW, Washington, D.C. 20416 (800) UASK-SBA

State of the Cellular Industry.
Cellular Telecommunications Industry Association, 1250 Connecticut Avenue, NW, Suite 200, Washington, D.C. 20036 (202) 785-0081

State Profiles: Financing Public Higher Education.
Research Associates of Washington, 2605 Klingle Road, NW, Washington, D.C. 20008 (202) 966-3326

State Projections to 2000.
U.S. Department of Education, National Center for Education Statistics, 400 Maryland Avenue, SW, Washington, D.C. 20202 (202) 708-5366

State Vocational Rehabilitation Agency Program Data in Fiscal Years.
U.S. Department of Education, Rehabilitation Services Administration, 400 Maryland Avenue, SW, Washington, D.C. 20202 (202) 708-5366

Published Sources

Statistical Abstract.
  Bureau of Statistics, Government Publications Agency, Post Office Box 1801, Dar es Salaam, Tanzania

Statistical Abstract.
  Central Bureau of Statistics, Abel-Malek Bin Marwan Street, Malki Quarter, Damascus, Syrian Arab Republic

Statistical Abstract.
  Central Bureau of Statistics, Ministry of Economic Planning and Development, Post Office Box 30266, Nairobi, Kenya

Statistical Abstract.
  Central Statistical Office, Post Office Box 206, Victoria, Mahe, Seychelles

Statistical Abstract.
  Central Statistics Organization, Post Office Box 5835, Manama, Bahrain

Statistical Abstract.
  Consultancy Services Division, Nepal Industrial Development Corporation, Kathmandu, Nepal

Statistical Abstract.
  HM Stationary Office, Post Office Box 569, London SE1 9NH, England

Statistical Abstract.
  Statistical Institute of Jamaica, Nine Swallowfield Road, Kingston 5, Jamaica

Statistical Abstract.
  Statistics Department, Post Office Box 149, Nuku'alofa, Tonga

Statistical Abstract.
  Statistics and Research Department, Nicosia, Cyprus

Statistical Abstract for Missouri.
  Business and Public Administration Research Center, University of Missouri, Columbia, Missouri 65211 (314) 882-4805

Statistical Abstract for the Democratic Republic of the Sudan.
  Department of Statistics, Post Office Box 700, Khartoum, Sudan

Statistical Abstract: India.
  Central Statistical Organization, New Delhi, India

Statistical Abstract of Colorado.
  University of Colorado, Business Research Division, Campus Box 420, Boulder, Colorado 80309 (303) 492-8227

Statistical Abstract of Ethiopia.
  Central Statistical Office, Post Office Box 1143, Addis Ababa, Ethiopia

Statistical Abstract of Ireland.
  Central Statistics Office, Earlsfort Terrace, Dublin 2, Ireland

Statistical Abstract of Israel.
  Central Bureau of Statistics, Hakirya, Romema, Jerusalem, Israel

Statistical Abstract of Latin America.
  U.C.L.A. Latin American Center Publications, University of California, Los Angeles, California 90024 (310) 825-6634

Statistical Abstract of Libya.
  Census and Statistical Department, Secretariat of Planning, 40 Sharia Damascus, Tripoli, Libya

Statistical Abstract of Louisiana.
  Division of Business and Economic Research, University of New Orleans, New Orleans, Louisiana 70148 (504) 286-6248

Statistical Abstract of North Carolina Counties.
  Office of State Planning, Office of the Governor, 116 West Jones Street, Raleigh, North Carolina 27603-8005 (919) 733-4131

The Statistical Abstract of North Dakota.
  University of North Dakota, Bureau of Business and Economic Research, Grand Forks, North Dakota 58202 (701) 777-2637

Statistical Abstract of Oklahoma.
  Center for Economic and Management Research, University of Oklahoma, 307 West Brooks Street, Room 4, Norman, Oklahoma 73109 (405) 325-2931

Statistical Abstract of the Arab Republic of Egypt.
  Central Agency for Public Mobilization and Statistics, Post Office Box 2086, Cairo, Egypt

Statistical Abstract of the British Virgin Islands.
  Statistical Division, Planning Unit, Chief Minister's Office, Tortola, British Virgin Islands

Statistical Abstract of the Democratic Socialist Republic of Sri Lanka.
  Department of Census and Statistics, No. 6, Albert Crescent, Colombo 7

Statistical Abstract of the Government of the Cayman Islands.
  Department of Finance and Development, Administration Building, Georgetown, Grand Cayman, Cayman Islands

Statistical Abstract of Utah.
  Bureau of Economic and Business Research, 401 Kendall D. Garff Building, University of Utah, Salt Lake City, Utah 84112 (801) 581-6333

Statistical Abstract of Western Asia.
  Economic Commission for Western Asia, Post Office Box 27, Baghdad, Iraq

Statistical Bulletin.
  Central Statistics Office, Ministry of Finance, Tower Hill, Freetown, Sierra Leone

Statistical Bulletin.
  Central Statistics Office Government Printer, P.O. Box 87, Gaberone, Botswana

The Statistical Bulletin.
  The Conference Board, 845 Third Avenue, New York, New York 10022 (212) 759-0900

Statistical Bulletin.
  Department of Statistics, Apia, Western Samoa

Statistical Bulletin.
  HM Stationary Office, Post Office Box 569, London SE1 9NH, England

Statistical Bulletin.
  Manager of Publications, Government of Pakistan, Block Number 44, Shahrah-e-iraq, Karachi, Pakistan

Statistical Bulletin of the OAS.
  Organization of American States (OAS), General Secretariat, Washington, D.C. 20006 (202) 458-3533

Statistical Bulletin of the South Pacific: Overseas Trade.
South Pacific Commission, Post Box D5, Noumea Cedex, New Caledonia

Statistical Bulletin of the South Pacific: Retail Price Indexes.
South Pacific Commission, Post Box D5, Noumea Cedex, New Caledonia

Statistical Data on Korea.
Korean Overseas Information Service, Ministry of Culture and Information, Seoul 110, Republic of Korea

Statistical Digest.
Statistical Division, 22 Bath Road, Roseau, Dominica

Statistical Digest.
Statistics Office, Post Office Box 292, Plymouth, Montserrat

Statistical Digest.
National Statistics Office, Central Government Offices, P.O. Wards Strip, Waigani, Papua New Guinea

Statistical Handbook.
National Statistical Office, Bangkok, Thailand

Statistical Handbook.
West Virginia Research League, Inc., 405 Capitol Street, Suite 414, Charleston, West Virginia 25301 (304) 346-9451

Statistical Handbook: States of the Former USSR.
The World Bank, 1818 H Street, NW, Washington, D.C. 20433 (202) 477-1234

Statistical Indicators on Social Life.
Management and Coordination Agency, Statistics Bureau, Tokyo, Japan

Statistical Pocketbook.
Netherlands Central Bureau of Statistics, 428 Prinses Beatrixlaan, 2270 AZ Voorburg, The Hague, Netherlands

Statistical Pocketbook.
Central Bureau voor de Statistiek, Kloosterweg 1, Postbus 4481, 6401 C2 Heerlen, Netherlands

Statistical Pocketbook.
Central Statistical Office, International Division, 2P, Volov Street, Sofia, Bulgaria

Statistical Pocketbook.
Central Statistical Organization, Ministry of Planning, Post Office Box 8001, Baghdad, Iraq

Statistical Pocketbook.
Central Statistical Organization, Six-Storey Building, Strand Road, Rangoon, Myanmar

Statistical Pocketbook of Hungary.
Kozponti Statisztikai Hivatal, Keleti Karoly Utca 5-7, 1024 Budapest 11, Hungary

Statistical Pocketbook of India.
Central Statistical Organizaton, New Delhi, India

Statistical Pocketbook of Pakistan.
Manager of Publications, Government of Pakistan, Block Number 44, Shahrah-e-iraq, Karachi, Pakistan

Statistical Pocketbook of the Democratic Socialist Republic of Sri Lanka.
Department of Census and Statistics, No. 6, Albert Crescent, Colombo 7, Sri Lanka

Statistical Pocketbook of the Philippines.
Publications Division, Bureau of the Census and Statistics, Post Office Box 779, Manila, Philippines

Statistical Pocketbook of Yugoslavia.
Savezni Zavod Za Statistiku, Kneza Milosa 20, 11000 Belgrade, Yugoslavia

Statistical Profile of Iowa.
Iowa Department of Economic Development Research Bureau, 200 East Grand Avenue, Des Moines, Iowa 50309

Statistical Reflection of the Islamic Republic of Iran.
Iranian Statistical Centre, D. Fatemi Avenue, Tehran, Iran

Statistical Report.
U.S. Department of Justice, Bureau of Prisons, 320 First Street, NW, Washington, D.C. 20534 (202) 307-3198

Statistical Report - Rural Electric Borrowers.
U.S. Department of Agriculture, Rural Electrification Administration, Fourteenth Street and Indopendence Avenue, SW, Washington, D.C. 20250 (202) 720-1255

Statistical Report - Rural Telephone Borrowers.
U.S. Department of Agriculture, Rural Electrification Administration, Fourteenth Street and Independence Avenue, SW, Washington, D.C. 20250 (202) 720-1255

Statistical Review of Government in Utah.
Utah Foundation, 10 West 100 South 323, Salt Lake City, Utah 84101 (801) 364-1837

Statistical Source Directory for New Jersey State Government.
New Jersey State Data Center, New Jersey Department of Labor, CN 388, Trenton, New Jersey 08625-0388 (609) 984-2593

Statistical Supplement, Stockpile Report to the Congress.
U.S. Department of Defense, Defense Logistics Agency Cameron Station, Alexandria, Virginia 22304-6100 (703) 274-6000

Statistical Tables.
Lloyd's Register of Shipping, 71 Fenchurch Street, London EC3, England

Statistical Yearbook.
Central Department of Statistics, Ministry of Finance and National Economy, Riyadh, Saudi Arabia

Statistical Yearbook.
Central Statistical Organization, Post Office Box 1272, Steamer Point, Aden, Yemen

Statistical Yearbook.
Central Statistical Organization, Six-Storey Building, Strand Road, Rangoon, Myanmar

Statistical Yearbook.
Central Statistical Office, Post Office Box 31908, Lusaka, Zambia

Statistical Yearbook
Central Statistics Organization, Ministry of Planning and Development, Sana'a, Yemen

Statistical Yearbook.
Department of Statistics, Post Office Box 2015, Amman, Jordan

Statistical Yearbook.
Department of Statistics, Post Office Box 700, Khartoum, Sudan

Statistical Yearbook.
Direccao dos Servicos de Estatistica, CP 1215, Luanda, Angola

Statistical Yearbook.
Directorate General of The National Statistics, Post Office Box 881, Muscat, Oman

Statistical Yearbook.
Food and Agricultural Organization of the United Nations (FAO), Via delle Terme di Caracalla, 00100 Rome, Italy (Telephone Number in the U.S. (202) 653-2400)

Statistical Yearbook.
Inter-American Development Bank, 1300 New York Avenue, NW, Washington, D.C. 20577 (202) 623-1753

Statistical Yearbook.
International Monetary Fund, Nineteenth and H Streets, NW, Washington, D.C. 20431 (202) 623-7000

Statistical Yearbook.
Iranian Statistical Centre, Dr. Fatemi Avenue, Tehran, Iran

Statistical Yearbook.
Korean Overseas Information Service, Ministry of Culture and Information, Seoul 110, Republic of Korea

Statistical Yearbook.
Lloyd's Register of Shipping, 17 Battery Place, New York, New York 10004 (212) 425-8050

Statistical Yearbook.
Organisation for Economic Co-operation and Development (OECD), 2 rue Andre-Pascal, 75 Paris 16, France (Telephone Number in U.S. (202) 785-6323)

Statistical Yearbook.
Organization of American States (OAS), General Secretariat, Washington, D.C. 20006 (202) 458-3533

Statistical Yearbook.
Statistical Division, Ministry of Finance, Redcliffe Street, St. John's, Antigua

Statistical Yearbook.
Statistical Office of the United Nations, Publishing Service, New York, New York 10017 (800) 253-9646

Statistical Yearbook.
Statistiches Bundesamt (Allgemeiner Auskunftsdienst), Gustav-Stresemann-Ring 11, Postfach 5528, 6200 Wiesbaden 1, Germany

Statistical Yearbook.
Statistics Office, Post Office Box G6, Honiara, Solomon Islands

Statistical Yearbook.
U.S. Department of Justice, Immigration and Naturalization Service, 425 I Street, NW, Washington, D.C. 20536 (202) 514-4316

Statistical Yearbook.
United Nations Educational, Scientific and Cultural Organization (UNESCO), 7 Place de Fontenoy, F-75700 Paris, France (Telephone Number in U.S. (212) 963-5981)

Statistical Yearbook: Arab Republic of Egypt.
Central Agency for Public Mobilization and Statistics, Post Office Box 2086, Cairo, Egypt

Statistical Yearbook for Asia and the Pacific.
Statistical Office of the United Nations, Publishing Service, New York, New York 10017 (800) 253-9646

Statistical Yearbook for Latin America and the Caribbean.
Statistical Office of the United Nations, Publishing Service, New York, New York 10017 (800) 253-9646

Statistical Yearbook of Albania.
Drejtoria e Statistikes, Tirane, Albania

Statistical Yearbook of Algeria.
Direction des Stahstiques et de la Comptabilite Nationale, BP 478, Alber, Algeria

Statistical Yearbook of Bangladesh.
Bureau of Statistics, Bangladesh Secretariat, School Building, No. 12, Dacca, Bangladesh

Statistical Yearbook of Bhutan.
Central Statistical Office, Planning Commission, Thimphu, Bhutan

Statistical Yearbook of Bulgaria.
Central Statistical Office, International Division, 2 P Volov Street, Sofia, Bulgaria

Statistical Yearbook of Greece.
National Statistical Service of Greece, 14-16 Lycourgou Street, Athens 112, Greece

Statistical Yearbook of Jamaica.
Statistical Institute of Jamaica, Nine Swallowfield Road, Kingston 5, Jamaica

Statistical Yearbook of Maldives.
Ministry of Planning and Development, Maldives

Statistical Yearbook of Municipal Finances.
Public Securities Association, 40 Broad Street, 12th Floor, New York, New York 10004 (212) 809-7000

Statistical Year Book of Nepal.
Central Bureau of Statistics, National Planning Commission Secretariat, Ramshah Path, Thapathali, Katmandu, Nepal

Statistical Yearbook of the Electric Utility Industry.
Edison Electric Institute, 701 Pennsylvania Avenue, NW, Washington, D.C. 20004 (202) 508-5000

Statistical Yearbook of the Netherlands.
Netherlands Central Bureau of Statistics, 428 Prinses, Beatrixlaan, 2270 AZ Voorburg, The Hague, Netherlands

Statistical Yearbook of Thailand.
National Statistical Office, Bangkok, Thailand

Statistical Yearbook of Zimbabwe.
Central Statistical Office, Post Office Box 8063, Causeway, Harare, Zimbabwe

Statistiches Jahrbuch der Schweiz: Annuaire statistique de la Suisse.
Office Federale de la Statistique, Hallwylstrasse 15, CH-3005 Berne,
Switzerland

Statistiches Jahrbuch fur die Republik Osterreich
Osterreichisches Statistiches Zentralamt, Hintere Zollamtsstrasse
2B, A1033 Vienna, Austria

Statisticka rocenka Ceske A Slovenske Federativni Republiky.
Federalni Statisticky Urad (Federal Statistical Office), Sokolovska
142, Praha 8-Karlin, Czechoslovakia

Statisticke prehledy.
Federalni Statisticky Urad (Federal Statistical Office), Sokolovska
142, Praha 8-Karlin, Czechoslovakia

Statisticki Bilten.
Savezni Zavod Za Statistiku, Kneza Milosa 20, 11000 Belgrade,
Yugoslavia

Statisticki Godisnjak Jugoslavije.
Savezni Zavod Za Statistiku, Kneza Milosa, 20, 11000 Belgrade,
Yugoslavia

Statistics at a Glance: Bhutan.
Central Statistical Office, Planning Commission, Post Office Box 338,
Thimphu, Bhutan

Statistics of Communication Common Carriers.
U.S. Federal Communications Commission, 1919 M Street, NW,
Washington, D.C. 20554 (202) 632-7000

Statistics of Income.
U.S. Department of the Treasury, Internal Revenue Service, 1111
Constitution Avenue, NW, Washington, D.C. 20224 (202) 566-5000

Statistics of Income Bulletin
U.S. Department of the Treasury, Internal Revenue Service, 1111
Constitution Avenue, NW, Washington, D.C. 20224 (202) 566-5000

Statistics of Income, Corporation Income Tax Returns.
U.S. Department of the Treasury, Internal Revenue Service, 1111
Constitution Avenue, NW, Washington, D.C. 20224 (202) 566-5000

Statistics of Income, Individual Income Tax Returns.
U.S. Department of the Treasury, Internal Revenue Service, 1111
Constitution Avenue, NW, Washington, D.C. 20224 (202) 566-5000

Statistics of Income, Partnership Returns.
U.S. Department of the Treasury, Internal Revenue Service, 1111
Constitution Avenue, NW, Washington, D.C. 20224 (202) 566-5000

Statistics of Interstate Natural Gas Pipeline Companies.
U.S. Department of Energy, Energy Information Administration,
Washington, D.C. 20585 (202) 586-8800

Statistics of Paper, Paperboard and Woodpulp.
American Forest and Paper Association, 1250 Connecticut Avenue,
NW, 2nd Floor, Washington, D.C. 20036 (202) 463-2455

Statistics of the Local Exchange Carriers.
U.S. Telephone Association, 1401 H Street, NW, Suite 600,
Washington, D.C. 20005 (202) 326-7300

Statistics of the Telephone Industry.
United States Telephone Association, 1401 H Street, NW, Suite 600,
Washington, D.C. 20005 (202) 326-7300

Statistics Office, Ministry of Finance, Tortola, British Virgin Islands.
HM Stationery Office, Post Office Box 569, London, England SE1 9NH

Statistics on Banking.
Federal Deposit Insurance Corporation, 550 Seventeenth Street, NW,
Washington, D.C. 20429 (202) 393-8400

Statistik Indonesia.
Biro Pusat Statistik, Jalan Dr. Sutomo 8, Jakarta, Indonesia

Statistiques annuelles.
Services des Statistiques et des Etudes Economiques, 4 rue des Iris,
Monte Carlo, Monaco

Statistiques: revue de l'Office National des Statistiques.
Office National de la Statistiques, 8/10 Rue des Moussebiline, B.P.
55 Alger, Algeria

Statistisch jaarboek: Nederlandse Antillen.
Central Bureau of Statistics, Willemstad, Curacao, Netherlands
Antilles

Statistiches Jahrbuch.
Amt fur Volkswirtschaft des furstichen Regierung, FL-9490 Vaduz,
Liechtenstoin

Statistisches, Jahrbuch der Deutschen Demokratischen Republik.
Staatsverlag der DDR, Otto-Grotewohl-Strasse 17, 108 Berlin,
Germany

Statistisches Jahrbuch fur die Bundes Republik Deutschland.
Statistisches Bundesamt Federal Statistical Office,
Gustav-Stresemann-Ring 11, Postfach 5528, 6200 Wiesbaden,
Germany

Statistisches Taschebuch.
Statistisches Bundesamt Federal Statistical Office,
Gustav-Stresemann-Ring 11, Postfach 5528, 6200 Wiesbaden,
Germany

Statistisches Taschenbuch der Deutschen Demokratischen Republik.
Staatsverlag der DDR, Otto-Grotewohl-Strasse 17, 108 Berlin,
Germany

Statistisk Arbog.
Danmarks Statistik, Sejrogade 11, Postboks 2250, 2100 Kobenhavn 0,
Denmark

Statistisk arbok.
Statistisk Sentralbyra (Central Bureau of Statistics), Skippergate 15,
P.B. 8131, DEP N-0033, Oslo 1, Norway

Statistisk Arbor.
Danmarks Statistik, Sejrogade 11, Kobenhavn, Denmark

Statistisk Arsbuk for Sverige.
Statistiska Centralbyran, Karlavagen 100, S-115 81, Stokholm,
Sweden

Statistisk manedshefte.
Statistisk-Sentralbyra (Central Bureau of Statistics), Skippergate 15,
P.B. 8131, DEP-0033, Oslo 1, Norway

Statistisk Manedsoversigt.
Danmarks Statistik, Sejrogadell, Postboks 2250, 2100 Kobenhavn 0,
Denmark

Published Sources

Statistiske Efterretninger.
Danmarks Statistik, Sejrogadell, Postboks 2250, 2100 Kobenhavn 0, Denmark

Statisztikai evkonyv.
Kozponti Statisztikai Hivatal, Keleti Karoly Utca 5-7, 1024 Budapest 11, Hungary

Statisztikai havi kozlemenyek.
Kozponti Statisztikai Hivatal, Keleti Karoly Utca 5-7, 1024 Budapest 11, Hungary

Steel Statistical Yearbook.
International Iron and Steel Institute, 120, rue Colonel Bourg, B-1140 Brussels, Belgium

Storm Data.
U.S. Department of Commerce, National Oceanic and Atmospheric Administration, National Climatic Data Center, Federal Building, Asheville, North Carolina 28801 (704) 259-2850

Student Financing of Graduate and Professional Education.
U.S. Department of Education, National Center for Education Statistics, 400 Maryland Avenue, SW, Washington, D.C. 20202 (202) 708-5366

A Study of Beginning Offers.
College Placement Council, 62 Highland Avenue, Bethlehem, Pennsylvania 18017 (212) 868-1421

Sudan.
Federal Statistical Office, Gustav-Stresemann-Ring 11, D-6200 Wiesbaden, Germany

Summary of Notifiable Diseases, United States, Morbidity and Mortality Weekly Report.
U.S. Department of Health and Human Services, Centers for Disease Control, 1600 Clifton Road, NE, Atlanta, Georgia 30333 (404) 639-3311

Summary of Statistics.
National Statistics Office, Central Government Offices, Post Office Wards Strip, Waigana, Papua New Guinea

Suomen tilastollin Vuosikirja.
Statistics Finland, Box 504, Annankatu, 44, SF-00100 Helsinki, Finland

Supplementary Materials: National Priorities List, Proposed Rule.
Environmental Protection Agency, 401 M Street, SW, Washington, D.C. 20460 (202) 382-2090

Supplementary Report, Metropolitan Statistical Areas.
U.S. Department of Commerce, Bureau of the Census, Suitland, Maryland 20233 (301) 763-4040

Suriname.
Federal Statistical Office, Gustav-Stresemann-Ring 11, D-6200 Wiesbaden, Germany

The Survey of Buying Power Data Service.
Market Statistics, 633 Third Avenue, New York, New York 10017 (212) 986-4000

Survey of Current Business.
U. S. Department of Commerce, Bureau of Economic Analysis, Fourteenth Street between Constitution Avenue and E Street, NW, Washington, D.C. 20230 (202) 606-9900

Survey of Earned Doctorates, Selected Data on Science and Engineering Doctorate Awards.
U.S. National Science Foundation, 4201 Wilson Boulevard, Arlington, Virginia 22230 (703) 306-1234

Survey of Economic and Social Conditions in Africa.
Statistical Office of the United Nations, Publishing Service, New York, New York 10017 (800) 253-9646

Survey of Employer Anti-drug Programs.
U.S. Department of Labor, Bureau of Labor Statistics, Two Massachusetts Avenue, NE, Washington, D.C. 20212 (202) 606-7828

Survey of Federal Support to Universities, Colleges, and Selected Nonprofit Institutions.
U.S. National Science Foundation, 4201 Wilson Boulevard, Arlington, Virginia 22230 (703) 306-1234

Survey of Graduate Science and Engineering Students and Postdoctorates.
U.S. National Science Foundation, 4201 Wilson Boulevard, Arlington, Virginia 22230 (703) 306-1234

Survey of Hospital Semi-Private Room Charges.
Health Insurance Association of America, 1025 Connecticut Avenue, NW, Suite 1200, Washington, D.C. 20036 (202) 223-7780

Survey of Minority-Owned Business Enterprises.
U.S. Department of Commerce, Bureau of the Census, Suitland, Maryland 20233 (301) 763-4040

Survey of Progress.
Central Statistics Office, Block No. 4, Microrayon, Kabul, Afghanistan

Survey of Scientific and Engineering Expenditures at Universities and Colleges.
U.S. National Science Foundation, 4201 Wilson Boulevard, Arlington, Virginia 22230 (703) 306-1234

Survey of State Prison Inmates.
U.S. Department of Justice, Bureau of Justice Statistics, 633 Indiana Avenue, NW, Washington, D.C. 20531 (800) 732-3277

Survey of Women-Owned Businesses.
U.S. Department of Commerce, Bureau of the Census, Suitland, Maryland 20233 (301) 763-4040

Swasiland.
Federal Statistical Office, Gustav-Stresemann-Ring 11, D-6200 Wiesbaden, Germany

Synthetic Organic Chemicals.
International Trade Commission, 500 E Street, SW, Washington, D.C. 20436 (202) 205-2000

Syrian Arab Republic.
Federal Statistical Office, Gustav-Stresemann-Ring 11, D-6200 Wiesbaden, Germany

Tableau Economique de La Reunion.
Institut National de la Statistique et des Etudes Economiques, 4 rue de l'Ecole, Sainte, Clothilde, Reunion 97490

Taiwan Agricultural Yearbook.
Department of Agriculture and Forestry, Taiwan Provincial Government, Chung-hsing Village, Nantou, Nantou Hsien, Taiwan, Republic of China

Taiwan Statistical Data Book.
Council for Economic Planning and Development, 9th Floor, 87 Nanking East Road, Section 2, Taipei, Republic of China

Tansania.
Federal Statistical Office, Gustav-Stresemann-Ring 11, D-6200 Wiesbaden, Germany

Tax Rates and Tax Burdens in the District of Columbia: A Nationwide Comparison.
Government of the District of Columbia, Department of Finance and Revenue, 300 Indiana Avenue, NW, Washington, D.C. 20001 (202) 727-6103

Technology Assessment and Forecast Database.
U.S. Department of Commerce, Patent and Trademark Office, 2011 Crystal Drive, Arlington, Virginia 22202 (703) 305-8341

Telecommunication Statistics.
International Telecommunication Union, Place des Nations, CH-1211 Geneva 20, Switzerland

Telephone Subscribership in the U.S.
U.S. Federal Communications Commission, 1919 M Street, NW, Washington, D.C. 20554 (202) 632-7000

Television and Cable Factbook.
Warren Publishing, Incorporated, 2115 Ward Court, NW, Washington, D.C. 20037 (202) 872-9200

Tennessee Statistical Abstract.
Center for Business and Economic Research, University of Tennessee, Knoxville, Tennessee 37996-4170 (615) 974-5441

Texas Almanac.
Dallas Morning News, Communications Center, Post Office Box 655237, Dallas, Texas 75265 (214) 977-8261

Texas Fact Book.
Bureau of Business Research, University of Texas, Austin, Texas 78712 (512) 471-5180

Textile Industry in OECD Countries.
Organisation for Economic Co-operation and Development (OECD), 2 rue Andre-Pascal, 75 Paris 16, France (Telephone Number in U.S. (202) 785-6323)

Textile Organon.
Fiber Economics Bureau, 101 Eisenhower Parkway, Roseland, New Jersey 07068 (201) 228-1107

Thailand.
Federal Statistical Office, Gustav-Stresemann-Ring 11, D-6200 Wiesbaden, Germany

Thailand Statistical Yearbook.
National Statistical Office, Bangkok, Thailand

Third World Economic Handbook.
Euromonitor Publications Limited, 87-88 Turnmill Street, London EC1M 5QU, England

Tilastokeskus.
Statistics Finland, Box 504, Annankatu, 44, SF-00100 Helsinki, Finland

Titanium Ingot, Mill Products, and Castings.
U.S. Department of Commerce, Bureau of the Census, Suitland, Maryland 20233 (301) 763-4040

Tobacco Situation.
U.S. Department of Agriculture, Economic Research Service, Fourteenth Street and Independence Avenue, SW, Washington, D.C. 20005-4789 (202) 219-1504

Togo.
Federal Statistical Office, Gustav-Stresemann-Ring 11, D-6200 Wiesbaden, Germany

Tourism Policy and International Tourism in OECD Member Countries.
Organisation for Economic Co-operation and Development (OECD), 2 rue Andre-Pascal, 75 Paris 16, France (Telephone Number in U.S. (202) 785-6323)

Tourism Statistics: Annual Report.
Civil Aviation and Tourism Authority, Afghan Tourist Organization, Kabul, Afghanistan

Toxics Release Inventory Public Data Release.
U.S. Environmental Protection Agency, 401 M Street, NW, Washington, D.C. 20460 (202) 382-2090

Trade by Commodities.
Organisation for Economic Co-operation and Development (OECD), 2 rue Andre-Pascal, 75 Paris 16, France (Telephone Number in U.S. (202) 785-6323)

Trade in Manufactures of Developing Countries.
Asian Development Bank, Post Office Box 789, Manila, Philippines 2800

Trade in Manufactures of Developing Countries.
Statistical Office of the United Nations, Publishing Service, New York, New York 10017 (000) 353-9646

Trade Production.
Food and Agricultural Organization of the United Nations (FAO), Via delle Terme di Caracalla, 00100, Rome, Italy (Telephone Number in the U.S. (202) 653-2400)

Trade Statistics of Ireland.
Central Statistics Office, St. Stephen's Green House, Earlsfort Terrace, Dublin 2, Ireland

Trade Yearbook.
Food and Agricultural Organization of the United Nations (FAO), Via delle Terme di Caracalla, 00100, Rome, Italy (Telephone Number in the U.S. (202) 653-2400)

Transit Fact Book.
American Public Transit Association, 1201 New York Avenue, NW, Suite 400, Washington, D.C. 20005 (202) 898-4000

Transport Annual Statistics.
European Community Information Service, 2100 M Street, NW, Washington, D.C. 20037 (202) 862-9500

Transport Statistics in the United States.
U.S. Interstate Commerce Commission, Twelfth Street and Constitution Avenue, NW, Washington, D.C. 20423 (202) 275-7119

Transportation in America.
Eno Transportation Foundation, 44211 Statestone Court, Lansdowne, Virginia 22075 (703) 729-7200

Transportation Safety Information Report.
U.S. Department of Transportation, Transportation Systems Center, Kendall Square, Cambridge, Massachusetts 02142 (617) 494-2224

Published Sources

3011

Treasury Bulletin.
  U.S. Department of the Treasury, Fifteenth Street and Pennsylvania Avenue, NW, Washington, D.C. 20220 (202) 566-2000

The Trend of Employment and Unemployment.
  Central Statistics Offices, Ardee Road, Dublin 6, Ireland

Trends in Family Income.
  Congressional Budget Office, 2nd and D Streets, SW, Washington, D.C. 20515 (202) 226-2621

Trends in Television.
  Television Bureau of Advertising, 850 Third Avenue, New York, New York 10022 (212) 486-1111

Tschechoslowakei.
  Federal Statistical Office, Gustav-Stresemann-Ring 11, D-6200 Wiesbaden, Germany

Turkei.
  Federal Statistical Office, Gustav-Stresemann-Ring 11, D-6200 Wiesbaden, Germany

Turkeys.
  U.S. Department of Agriculture, National Agricultural Statistics Service, Fourteenth Street and Independence Avenue, SW, Washington, D.C. 20250 (202) 219-1504

Turkiye Istatistik Cep Yilligi.
  Devlet Istatistik Enstitusu, Necatibey Caddesi, 114 Ankara, Turkey

Turkiye Istatistik Yilligi.
  Devlet Istatistik Enstitusu, Necatibey Caddesi, 114 Ankara, Turkey

Tuvalu.
  Federal Statistical Office, Gustav-Stresemann-Ring 11, D-6200 Wiesbaden, Germany

Typical Electric Bills.
  U.S. Department of Energy, Energy Information Administration, 1000 Independence Avenue, SW, Washington, D.C. 20585 (202) 586-8800

USDA.
  U.S. Department of Agriculture, Forest Service, 14th Street and Independence Avenue, SW, Washington, D.C. 20250 (202) 720-3760

Uganda.
  Federal Statistical Office, Gustav-Stresemann-Ring 11, D-6200 Wiesbaden, Germany

Undergraduate Financing of Postsecondary Education.
  U.S. Department of Education, 400 Maryland Avenue, SW, Washington, D.C. 20202 (202) 708-5366

Undergraduate General Education and Humanities Requirements.
  U.S. Department of Education, 400 Maryland Avenue, SW, Washington, D.C. 20202 (202) 708-5366

Unemployment Insurance Data Summary.
  U.S. Department of Labor, Employment and Training Administration, 200 Constitution Avenue, NW, Washington, D.C. 20210 (202) 219-0600

Unemployment Insurance, Financial Data.
  U.S. Department of Labor, Employment and Training Administration, 200 Constitution Avenue, NW, Washington, D.C. 20210 (202) 219-0600

Ungarn.
  Federal Statistical Office, Gustav-Stresemann-Ring 11, D-6200 Wiesbaden, Germany

United States Census of Agriculture.
  U.S. Department of Commerce, Bureau of the Census, Suitland, Maryland 20233 (301) 763-4040

United States Census of Construction Industries.
  U.S. Department of Commerce, Bureau of the Census, Suitland, Maryland 20233 (301) 763-4040

United States Census of Governments.
  U.S. Department of Commerce, Bureau of the Census, Suitland, Maryland 20233 (301) 763-4040

United States Census of Housing.
  U.S. Department of Commerce, Bureau of the Census, Suitland, Maryland 20233 (301) 763-4040

United States Census of Manufactures.
  U.S. Department of Commerce, Bureau of the Census, Suitland, Maryland 20233 (301) 763-4040

United States Census of Mineral Industries.
  U.S. Department of Commerce, Bureau of the Census, Suitland, Maryland 20233 (301) 763-4040

United States Census of Outlying Areas.
  U.S. Department of Commerce, Bureau of the Census, Suitland, Maryland 20233 (301) 763-4040

United States Census of Outlying Areas, Manufactures, Puerto Rico.
  U.S. Department of Commerce, Bureau of the Census, Suitland, Maryland 20233 (301) 763-4040

United States Census of Outlying Areas, Selected Services Industries, Puerto Rico.
  U.S. Department of Commerce, Bureau of the Census, Suitland, Maryland 20233 (301) 763-4040

United States Census of Population.
  U.S. Department of Commerce, Bureau of the Census, Suitland, Maryland 20233 (301) 763-4040

United States Census of Population, Persons of Spanish Origin.
  U.S. Department of Commerce, Bureau of the Census, Suitland, Maryland 20233 (301) 763-4040

United States Census of Retail Trade.
  U.S. Department of Commerce, Bureau of the Census, Suitland, Maryland 20233 (301) 763-4040

United States Census of Selected Service Industries.
  U.S. Department of Commerce, Bureau of the Census, Suitland, Maryland 20233 (301) 763-4040

United States Census of Service Industries, Geographic Area Series.
  U.S. Department of Commerce, Bureau of the Census, Suitland, Maryland 20233 (301) 763-4040

United States Census of Transportation.
  U.S. Department of Commerce, Bureau of the Census, Suitland, Maryland 20233 (301) 763-4040

United States Census of Wholesale Trade.
  U.S. Department of Commerce, Bureau of the Census, Suitland, Maryland 20233 (301) 763-4040

United States Crude Oil, Natural Gas and Natural Gas Liquids Reserves.
U.S. Department of Energy, Energy Information Administration, Washington, D.C. 20585 (202) 586-8800

United States Domestic Postage Rates: Recent History.
U.S. Postal Service, 475 l'Enfant Plaza West, SW, Washington, D.C. 20260 (202) 268-2000

United States Economic Census of Outlying Areas.
U.S. Department of Commerce, Bureau of the Census, Suitland, Maryland 20233 (301) 763-4040

United States Exports, Schedule B - Commodity By Country.
U.S. Department of Commerce, Bureau of the Census, Suitland, Maryland 20233 (301) 763-4040

United States Exports, Schedule E - Commodity By Country.
U.S. Department of Commerce, Bureau of the Census, Suitland, Maryland 20233 (301) 763-4040

United States General Imports, Schedule A Commodity by Country.
U.S. Department of Commerce, Bureau of the Census, Suitland, Maryland 20233 (301) 763-4040

United States Immunization Survey.
U.S. Department of Health and Human Services, Centers for Disease Control, 1600 Clifton Road, NE, Atlanta, Georgia 30333 (404) 639-3311

United States Imports for Consumption and General Imports, TSUSA Commodity and Country.
U.S. Department of Commerce, Bureau of the Census, Suitland, Maryland 20233 (301) 763-4040

United States Industrial Outlook.
U.S. Department of Commerce, International Trade Administration, Fourteenth Street between Constitution Avenue and E Street, NW, Washington, D.C. 20230 (202) 482-3809

United States International Travel Statistics.
U.S. Department of Transportation, Transportation Systems Center, Kendall Square, Cambridge, Massachusetts 02142 (617) 494-2224

United States Life Tables and Actuarial Tables.
U.S. Department of Health and Human Services, National Center for Health Statistics, 3700 East-West Highway, Hyattsville, Maryland 20782 (301) 436-8500

United States Merchandise Trade: Exports, General Imports, and Imports for Consumption.
U.S. Department of Commerce, Bureau of the Census, Suitland, Maryland 20233 (301) 763-4040

United States Merchandise Trade: Selected Highlights.
U.S. Department of Commerce, Bureau of the Census, Suitland, Maryland 20233 (301) 763-4040

United States Merchant Marine Data Sheet.
U.S. Department of Transportation, Maritime Administration, 400 Seventh Street, SW, Washington, D.C. 20590 (202) 366-5807

United States Overseas Loans and Grants and Assistance from International Organizations.
U.S. International Development, Cooperation Agency, 320 Twenty-first Street, NW, Washington, D.C. 20523 (202) 647-9620

United States Pet Ownership and Demographics Sourcebook.
American Veterinary Medical Association, 930 North Meacham Road, Schaumburg, Illinois 60196 (708) 605-8070

United States Scientists and Engineers.
U.S. National Science Foundation, 4201 Wilson Boulevard, Arlington, Virginia 22230 (703) 306-1234

United States/Soviet Military Balance, Statistical Trends.
The Congress of the U.S., Congressional Research Service, 10 First Street, SE, Washington, D.C. 20540 (202) 707-7940

United States Timber Production, Trade Consumption, and Price Statistics.
U.S. Department of Agriculture, Forest Service, Fourteenth Street and Independence Avenue, SW, Washington, D.C. 20250 (202) 720-3760

United States Trade with Puerto Rico and United States Possessions.
U.S. Department of Commerce, Bureau of the Census, Suitland, Maryland 20233 (301) 763-4040

United States Waterborne Exports and General Imports.
U.S. Department of the Army, Corps of Engineers, The Pentagon, Washington, D.C. 20301 (202) 545-6700

Uranium Industry Annual.
U.S. Department of Energy, Energy Information Administration, 1000 Independence Avenue, SW, Washington, D.C. 20585 (202) 586-8800

Uruguay.
Federal Statistical Office, Gustav-Stresemann-Ring 11, D-6200 Wiesbaden, Germany

Variety.
Variety, Inc., 249 West Seventeenth Street, New York, New York 10011 (212) 779-1100

Vegetables.
U.S. Department of Agriculture, National Agricultural Statistics Service, Fourteenth Street and Independence Avenue, SW, Washington, D.C. 20250 (202) 219-1504

Venezuela.
Federal Statistical Office, Gustav-Stresemann-Ring 11, D-6200 Wiesbaden, Germany

Vessel Entrances and Clearances.
U.S. Department of Commerce, Bureau of the Census, Suitland, Maryland 20233 (301) 763-4040

Veteran's Benefits in the United States.
The President's Commission on Veteran's Pensions, The White House, 1600 Pennsylvania Avenue, NW, Washington, D.C. 20500 (202) 233-4000

Veteran Population.
U.S. Department of Veterans Affairs, 810 Vermont Avenue, NW, Washington, D.C. 20420 (202) 233-2300

Vietnam.
Federal Statistical Office, Gustav-Stresemann-Ring 11, D-6200 Wiesbaden, Germany

Violence and Crime in Cross-National Perspective.
Yale University Press, Yale Station, New Haven, Connecticut 06520 (203) 432-0940

Published Sources

Virginia Statistical Abstract
University of Virginia, Center for Public Service, Dynamics Building, Fourth Floor, 2015 Ivy Road, Charlottesville, Virginia 22903 (804) 924-3921

Vital Health Statistics.
U.S. Department of Health and Human Services, National Center for Health Statistic, 3700 East-West Highway, Hyattsville, Maryland 20782 (301) 436-8500

Vital Statistics of the United States.
U.S. Department of Health and Human Services, National Center for Health Statistics, 3700 East-West Highway, Hyattsville, Maryland 20782 (301) 436-8500

Vital Statistics on Congress.
Congressional Quarterly, Incorporated, 1414 Twenty-second Street, NW, Washington, D.C. 20037 (202) 887-8500

Voluntary Support of Education.
Council for Aid to Education, 51 Madison Avenue, New York, New York 10010 (212) 689-2400

Washington State Data Book.
Washington State Office of Financial Management, Forecasting Division, Post Office Box 43113, Olympia, Washington 98504 (206) 753-5617

Water-Data Report.
U.S. Department of Interior, Geological Survey, National Center, 12201 Sunrise Valley Drive, Reston, Virginia 22092 (703) 648-4460

Waterborne Commerce of the United States.
U.S. Department of the Army, Corps of Engineers, The Pentagon, Washington, D.C. 20310 (202) 545-6700

Weekly Railroad Traffic.
Association of American Railroads, 50 F Street, NW, Washington,, D.C. 20001 (202) 639-2100

West Virginia: Economic-Statistical Profile.
West Virginia Chamber of Commerce, Box 2789, Charleston, West Virginia 25330 (304) 342-1115

Wheat Situation.
U.S. Department of Agriculture, National Agricultural Statistics Service, Fourteenth Street and Independence Avenue, SW, Washington, D.C. 20250 (202) 219-1504

Wirtschaft und Statistik.
Statistiches Bundesamt Federal Statistical Office, Gustav-Stresemann-Ring 11, 6200 Wiesbaden, Postfach 5528, Germany

Wisconsin Blue Book.
Wisconsin Legislative Reference Bureau, P.O. Box 2037, Madison, Wisconsin 53701-2037 (608) 266-0341

Women and Minorities in Science and Engineering.
U.S. National Science Foundation, 4201 Wilson Boulevard, Arlington, Virginia 22230 (703) 306-1234

Wood Pulp and Fiber Statistics.
American Forest and Paper Association, 1250 Connecticut Avenue, NW, Washington, D.C. 20036 (202) 463-2455

World Agriculture - Trends and Indicators.
U.S. Department of Agriculture, Foreign Agricultural Service, Fourteenth Street and Independence Avenue, SW, Washington, D.C. 20250 (202) 720-3448

World Debt Tables.
The World Bank, 1818 H Street, NW, Washington, D.C. 20006 (202) 477-1234

World Energy Supplies.
Statistical Office of the United Nations, Publishing Service, New York, New York 10017 (800) 253-9646

World Factbook Nineteen and Eighty-Six.
Central Intelligence Agency, Washington, D.C. 20505 (703) 482-1100

World Health Statistics Annual.
World Health Organization, Avenue Appia, Office of Publications, CH-1211 Geneva 27, Switzerland (Telephone Number in U.S. (518) 436-9686)

The World In Figures.
G.K. Hall and Company, 70 Lincoln Street, Boston, Massachusetts 02111 (617) 423-3990

World Livestock Situation.
U.S. Department of Agriculture, Foreign Agricultural Service, Fourteenth Street and Independence Avenue, SW, Washington, D.C. 20250 (202) 720-3448

World Lottery Almanac.
TLF Publications, Inc., Boyds, Maryland 20841 (301) 540-0123

The World Market Atlas.
The Economist Intelligence Unit, 111 West 57th Street, New York, New York 10019 (800) 938-4685

World Metal Statistics.
World Bureau of Metal Statistics, 27-A High Street, Ware Herts, SG12 9BA, England

World Military Expenditures and Arms Transfers.
U.S. Arms Control and Disarmament Agency, 320 Twenty-first Street, NW, Washington, D.C. 20451 (202) 647-8677

World Motor Vehicle Data.
American Automobile Manufacturers Association, 1401 H Street, NW, Washington, D.C. 20005 (202) 326-5500

World Population Profile.
U.S. Department of Commerce, Bureau of the Census, Suitland, Maryland 20233 (301) 763-4040

World Poultry Situation.
U.S. Department of Agriculture, Foreign Agricultural Service, Fourteenth Street and Independence Avenue, SW, Washington, D.C. 20250 (202) 720-3448

World Radio TV Handbook.
Billboard Limited, Post Office Box 9027, 1006 AA Amsterdam, The Netherlands (Telephone Number in U.S. (212) 764-7300)

World Road Statistics.
International Road Federation, 525 School Street, SW, Washington, D.C. 20024 (202) 554-2106

World Tables.
The World Bank, 1818 H Street, NW, Washington, D.C. 20433 (202) 477-1234

World Telecom Indicators.
International Telecommunication Union, Palais des Nations, CH-1211, Geneva 20, Switzerland

Worldwide Tanker Casualty Returns.
Tanker Advisory Center, Incorporated, 10 East End Avenue, New York, New York 10028   (212) 628-7686

The World's Jet and Turboprop Airliner Fleet.
AVMARK, 1911 North Fort Myer Drive, Arlington, Virginia 22209 (703) 528-5610

The World's Telephones.
American Telephone and Telegraph Company, 26 Parsippany Road, Whippany, New Jersey 07981   (800) 338-4038

Year Book Australia.
Australian Bureau of Statistics, Post Office Box 10, Belconnen, Canberra ACT 2616, Australia

Yearbook of American and Canadian Churches.
National Council of the Churches of Christ in the United States of America, 475 Riverside Drive, New York, New York 10027   (212) 870-2227

Yearbook of Fishery Statistics.
Food and Agricultural Organization of the United Nations (FAO), Via delle Terme di Caracalla, 00100 Rome, Italy (Telephone Number in the U.S. (202) 653-2400)

Yearbook of Forest Products.
Food and Agricultural Organization of the United Nations (FAO), Via delle Terme di Caracalla, 00100, Rome, Italy (Telephone Number in the U.S. (202) 653-2400)

Yearbook of Forest Statistics.
Food and Agricultural Organization of the United Nations (FAO), Via delle Terme di Caracalla, 00100, Rome, Italy (Telephone Number in the U.S. (202) 653-2400)

Yearbook of International Statistics.
Statistical Office of the United Nations, Publishing Service, New York, New York 10017   (800) 253-9646

Yearbook of International Trade Statistics.
Statistical Office of the United Nations, Publishing Service, New York, New York 10017   (800) 253-9646

Yearbook of Labour Statistics.
Euromonitor Publications Limited, 87-88 Turnmill Street, London EC1M 5QU, England

Yearbook of Labour Statistics.
Food and Agricultural Organization of the United Nations (FAO), Via delle Terme di Caracalla, 00100 Rome, Italy (Telephone Number in the U.S. (202) 653-2400)

Yearbook of Labour Statistics.
International Labour Office, I.L.O. Publications, CH-1211, Geneva 22, Switzerland

Yearbook of Statistics Singapore.
Department of Statistics, 8 Shenton Way 10-01, Treasury Building, Singapore, 0106

Yearbook of Tourism Statistics.
World Tourism Organization, Calle Capitan Haya 42, E-28020 Madrid, Spain

Year-end Review and Forecast.
Aerospace Industries Association of America, 1250 I Street, NW, Washington, D.C. 20005   (202) 371-8400

Zaire.
Federal Statistical Office, Gustav-Stresemann-Ring 11, D-6200 Wiesbaden, Germany

Zambia in Figures.
Central Statistical Office, Post Office Box 31908, Lusaka, Zambia

Zentral afrikanische Republik.
Federal Statistical Office, Gustav-Stresemann-Ring 11, D-6200 Wiesbaden, Germany

Published Sources

Appendix B

Sources of Nonpublished Statistical Data

This appendix provides an overview of the agencies, institutions, and other organizational sources of nonpublished statistical information used to compile this edition of *Statistics Sources*. It consists of a complete listing of all such organizations cited under the specific subject headings throughout both volumes. Entries are arranged alphabetically by organization name, and include addresses.

Administrative Office of the United States Courts, United States Supreme Court Building, One Columbus Circle, NE, Washington, D.C. 20544 (202) 273-1120.

Air Transport Association of America, 1301 Pennsylvania Avenue, NW, Washington, D.C. 20004 (202) 626-4000.

Alabama Department of Economic and Community Affairs, Office of State Planning, Post Office Box 5690, 3465 Norman Bridge Road, Montgomery, Alabama 36103-5090 (205) 242-5493.

Alabama Public Library Service, 6030 Monticello Drive, Montgomery, Alabama 36130 (205) 277-7330.

Alaska State Data Center, Research and Analysis, Department of Labor, Post Office Box 25504, Juneau, Alaska 99802-5504 (907) 465-6026.

Algemeen Bureau Voor de Statistiek, Post Office Box 244, Paramaribo, Suriname.

Amateur Softball Association of America, 2801 NE Fiftieth Street, Oklahoma City, Oklahoma 73111 (405) 424-5266.

American Association of Colleges of Osteopathic Medicine, 6110 Executive Boulevard, #405, Rockville, Maryland 20852 (301) 468-0990.

American Association of Tissue Banks, 1350 Beverly Road, Suite 220-A, McLean, Virginia 22101 (703) 827-9582.

American Banker, One State Street Plaza, New York, New York 10004 (212) 943-6700.

American Bowling Congress, 5301 South 76th Street, Greendale, Wisconsin 53129 (414) 421-6400.

American Council of Life Insurance, 1001 Pennsylvania Avenue, NW, Washington, D.C. 20004 (202) 624-2000.

American Enterprise Institute for Public Policy Research, 1150 Seventeenth Street, NW, Washington, D.C. 20036 (202) 862-5914.

American Hospital Association, 840 North Lake Shore Drive, Chicago, Illinois 60611 (312) 280-6000.

American Humane Association, 63 Inverness Drive, East, Englewood, Colorado 80112 (303) 792-9900.

American Osteopathic Association, 142 East Ontario Street, Chicago, Illinois 60611 (312) 280-5800.

American Forest and Paper Association, 1250 Connecticut Avenue, NW, Washington, D.C. 20036 (202) 463-2455.

American Symphony Orchestra League, Incorporated, 777 Fourteenth Street, NW, Washington, D.C. 20005 (202) 628-0099.

American Telephone and Telegraph Company, 26 Parsippany Road, Whippany, New Jersey 07981 (800) 338-4038.

Amt fur Volkswirtschaft des furstlichen Regierung, FL-9490 Vaduz, Liechtenstein.

Apogee Research, Incorporated, 4350 East-West Highway, Bethesda, Maryland 20814 (301) 652-8444.

Applied Population Laboratory, Department of Rural Sociology, University of Wisconsin, 1450 Linden Drive, Room 316, Madison, Wisconsin 53706 (608) 265-3044.

Applied Social Data Center, Department of Sociology, Central Washington University, Ellensburg, Washington 98926 (509) 963-1305.

The Arbitron Company, 142 West Fifty-seventh Street, New York, New York 10019 (212) 887-1300.

Arizona Department of Security, First Floor, Southeast Wing, 1789 West Jefferson Street, Phoenix, Arizona 85007 (602) 542-5984.

Arkansas State Library, 1 Capitol Mall, Little Rock, Arkansas 72201 (501) 682-2864.

Association of Bay Area Governments, Metro Center, Eighth and Oak Streets, Post Office Box 2050, Oakland, California 94604-2050 (510) 464-7937.

Association of Monterey Bay Area Governments, 445 Reservation Road, Suite G, Post Office Box 838, Marina, California 93933 (408) 883-3750.

Association of Racing Commissioners International, 4067 Iron Works Pike, Lexington, Kentucky 40511 (606) 254-4060.

Australian Bureau of Statistics, Post Office Box 10, Belconnen, Canberra ACT 2616, Australia.

Banco Central de Ecuador, Division de Investigacciones Economicas, Avenue 10 de Agosto Y Briceno, Quito, Ecuador.

Bangladesh Bureau of Statistics, Room No. 12, School Building, Bangladesh Secretariat, Dhaka 2, Bangladesh.

Bank of Thailand, Bangkhunprom, Bangkok 10200, Thailand.

Barbados Statistical Service, Third Floor, National Insurance Building, Fairchild Street, Bridgetown, Barbados.

Battery Council International, 401 North Michigan Avenue, Chicago, Illinois 60611 (312) 644-6610.

Biblioteca Carnegie, Avenue Ponce De Leon-Parada 1, San Juan, Puerto Rico 00901 (809) 724-1046.

Bicycle Manufacturers Association of America, Incorporated, 3050 K Street, NW, Suite 400, Washington, D.C. 20007 (202) 944-9297.

Biro Pusat Statistik, Jalan Dr. Sutomo 9, Jakarta, Indonesia.

Board of Governors of the Federal Reserve System, Twentieth Street and Constitution Avenue, NW, Washington, D.C. 20551 (202) 452-3000.

Bureau de la Statistique de Quebec, Centre d'information et de Documentation, 117 St. Andre, ler etage, Quebec, PQG1K 3Y3, Canada (418) 691-2401 and (800) 463-4090.

Bureau of Business and Economic Research, University of Montana, Missoula, Montana 59812 (406) 243-5113.

Bureau of Business and Economic Research, University of New Mexico, 1920 Lomas, NE, Albuquerque, New Mexico 87131 (505) 277-6626.

Bureau of Economic Analysis, Florida Department of Commerce, 107 West Gaines Street, 315 Collins Building, Tallahassee, Florida 32399-2000 (904) 487-2971.

Bureau of Governmental Research and Service, University of Oregon, Hendricks Hall, Room 331, 1408 University Street, Post Office Box 3177, Eugene, Oregon 97403 (503) 346-5235.

Bureau of Statistics, Alberta Treasury, Sixth Floor, Park Plaza, 10611 98 Avenue, Edmonton, Alberta T5K 2R7, Canada (403) 427-3058.

Bureau of Statistics, Census Administrator and Principal Statistician, Vanuatu Government, Private Mail Bag 19, Port Vila, Vanuatu.

Bureau of Statistics, Department of Finance, Post Office Box 1320, Yellowknife, Northwest Territories X1A 2L9, Canada (403) 873-7147.

Bureau of Statistics, Economic Planning Board, 90 Gyoungwoon-dong, Jongro-Ku, Seoul, Korea.

Bureau of Statistics, Government Buildings, Post Office Box 2221, Suva, Fiji.

Bureau of Statistics, Ministry of Planning and Economic Affairs, Post Office Box 9016, Monrovia, Liberia.

Bureau of Statistics, Post Office Box 796, Dar es Salaam, United Republic of Tanzania.

Bureau of Statistics, Post Office Box 455, Maseru 100, Lesotho.

Business Committee for the Arts, 1775 Broadway, Suite 510, New York, New York 10019 (212) 664-0600.

Business Research Bureau, School of Business, Patterson Hall, University of South Dakota, 414 East Clark, Vermillion, South Dakota 57069 (605) 677-5287.

Business Research Division, Graduate School of Business Administration, University of Colorado-Boulder, Boulder, Colorado 80309 (303) 492-8227.

Business Statistics Office, Government Buildings, Cardiff Road, Newport, Gwent NP9 1XC, United Kingdom.

Campbell County Library, 2101 Four J Road, Gillette, Wyoming 82716 (307) 682-3223.

Canadian Pulp and Paper Association, 1155 Metcalfe Street, Nineteenth Floor, Montreal, Quebec H3B 4T6, Canada (514) 866-6621.

Cape Cod Community Library, Library/Learning Resource Center, Route 132, West Barnstable, Massachusetts 02668 (508) 362-8638.

Capitol Region Council of Governments, 221 Main Street, Hartford, Connecticut 06106 (203) 522-2217.

CENCI Uruguay, Misiones 1361, ESC 14, Casilla de Correo 1510, Montevideo, Uruguay.

Census and Data Users Services, Department 4690, Research Services Building, Suite A, Illinois State University, Normal, Illinois 61790-4950 (309) 438-5946.

Census and Economic Information Center, Montana Department of Commerce, 1424 Ninth Avenue, Capitol Station, Helena, Montana 59620-0501 (406) 444-2896.

Census and Statistics Department, Wanchai Tower I, 12 Harbor Road, Wanchai, Hong Kong.

Census Data Center, Department of Education, Grimes State Office Building, Des Moines, Iowa 50319 (515) 281-4730.

Census Services, Iowa State University, 320 East Hall, Ames, Iowa 50011 (515) 294-8337.

Center for Applied Urban Research, The University of Nebraska-Omaha, Peter Kiewit Conference Center, 1313 Farnam-on-the-Mall, Omaha, Nebraska 68182 (402) 595-2311.

Center for Business and Economic Research, College of Business Administration, University of Tennessee, Room 100, Glocker Hall, Knoxville, Tennessee 37996-4170 (615) 974-5441.

Center for Business and Economic Research, Northeast Louisiana University, Monroe, Louisiana 71209 (318) 342-1215.

Center for Business and Economic Research, University of Alabama, Box 870221, Tuscaloosa, Alabama 35487-0221 (205) 348-6191.

Center for Business Research, College of Business Administration, Arizona State University, Tempe, Arizona 85287 (602) 965-3961.

Center for Business Research and Services, Campus Box 8450, Idaho State University, Pocatello, Idaho 83209 (208) 236-3409.

Center for Computer and Information Services, Rutgers University, CCIS-Hill Center, Busch Campus, Post Office Box 879, Piscataway, New Jersey 08854 (908) 932-0265.

Center for Economic Development and Business Research, Box 48, Wichita State University, Wichita, Kansas 67208 (316) 689-3225.

The Center for Economic Research, West Virginia University, 323 Business and Economic Building, Morgantown, West Virginia 26506-6025 (304) 293-7832.

Center for Geographic Information, Office of State Planning, Post Office Box 27687, Raleigh, North Carolina 27611 (919) 733-2090.

Center for Governmental Studies, Northern Illinois University, Social Science Research Building, DeKalb, Illinois 60115 (815) 753-0922.

Center for Health Policy and Statistics, South Dakota Department of Health, Foss Building 523 East Capitol, Pierre, South Dakota 57501 (605) 773-3693.

Center for Life Course and Population Studies, Department of Sociology, Room 126, Stubbs Hall, Louisiana State University, Baton Rouge, Louisiana 70803-5411 (504) 388-5359.

Center for Political Studies, University of Michigan, Post Office Box 1248, Ann Arbor, Michigan 48106 (313) 764-8363.

Center for Population Research and Census, Portland State University, Post Office Box 751, Portland, Oregon 97207-0751 (503) 725-5159.

Center for Population Studies, University of Mississippi, Bondurant Building, Room 3W, University, Mississippi 38677 (601) 232-7288.

Center for Public Affairs Research, Nebraska State Data Center, Room 203-Annex 26, University of Nebraska at Omaha, Omaha, Nebraska 68182 (402) 595-2311.

Center for Public Service, University of Virginia, 918 Emmet Street, North, Suite 300, Charlottesville, Virginia 22903-1795 (804) 982-5585.

Center for Rural Studies, University of Vermont, 207 Morrill Hall, Burlington, Vermont 05405-0106 (802) 656-3201.

Center for Social and Behavioral Research, University of Northern Iowa, Cedar Falls, Iowa 50614 (319) 273-2105.

Center for Social Organization of Schools, The Johns Hopkins University, 3505 North Charles Street, Baltimore, Maryland 21218 (410) 338-7570.

Center for the American Woman and Politics, The Eagleton Institute of Politics, Rutgers University, New Brunswick, New Jersey 08901 (908) 828-2210.

Center for the Study of Population, Institute for Social Research, 654 Bellamy Building, Florida State University, Tallahassee, Florida 32306-4063 (904) 644-1762.

Center for Urban and Economic Research, College of Business and Public Administration, University of Louisville, Louisville, Kentucky 40292 (502) 588-7990.

Central Agency for Public Mobilisation and Statistics, Salah Salem Street, Nasr City, Cairo, Egypt.

Central Bureau of Statistics, Abdel-Malek Bin Marwan Street, Malki Quarter, Damascus, Syrian Arab Republic.

Central Bureau of Statistics, Willemstad, Curacao, Netherlands Antilles.

Central Bureau of Statistics, Post Office Box 13015, Jerusalem 91130, Israel.

Central Bureau of Statistics, National Planning Commission Secretariat, Ramshah Path, Thapathali, Kathmandu, Nepal.

Central Bureau of Statistics, Post Office Box 1098, Accra, Ghana.

Central Bureau of Statistics, Post Office Box 3, Jakarta 10002, Indonesia.

Central Bureau of Statistics, Pyongyang, Democratic People's Republic of Korea.

Centraal Bureau Voor de Statistiek, Windstraat 21, Oranjestad, Aruba.

The Central Data Processing Division, Department of Administration Services, 301 Centennial Mall South, Lower Level, Post Office Box 95045, Lincoln, Nebraska 68509-5045 (402) 471-4862.

Central Department of Statistics, Ministry of Finance and National Economy, Post Office Box 3735, Riyadh, Saudi Arabia.

Central Intelligence Agency, Washington, D.C. 20505 (703) 482-1100.

Central Office of Statistics, Auberge D'Italie, Valletta, Malta.

Central Planning Division, Ministry of Finance and Planning, Kingstown, Saint Vincent and the Grenadines.

Central Planning Organization, Statistics Organization, Ministry of Planning and Development, Sana'a, Yemen.

Central Statistical Office, Post Office Box 456, Mbabane, Swaziland.

Central Statistical Office, 23 Park Street, Post Office Box 98, Port of Spain, Trinidad.

Central Statistical Office, Great George Street, London SW1P 3AQ United Kingdom.

Central Statistical Office, International Division, 2P, Volov Street, Sofia, Bulgaria.

Central Statistical Office, Ministry of Development and Planning, Tripoli, Libya.

Central Statistical Office, Ministry of Economic Planning and Development, Royal Road, Port Louis, Mauritius.

Central Statistical Office, Ministry of Finance, Post Office Box 31908, Lusaka, Zambia.

Central Statistical Office, The Ministry of Planning, Post Office Box 26188, Safat, Kuwait.

Central Statistical Office, National Planning Commission, 6th Floor, Government Offices, Private Bag 13356, Windhoek, Namibia.

Central Statistical Office, Planning Commission, Post Office Box Number 338, Thimphu, Bhutan.

Central Statistical Office, Post Office Box 1143, Addis Ababa, Ethiopia.

Central Statistical Office, Post Office Box 8063, Causeway, Harare, Zimbabwe.

Central Statistical Office, Ulan Bator, Mongolian People's Republic.

Central Statistical Office of Finland, Box 504, Annankatu 44 SF-00100 Helsinki, Finland.

Central Statistical Organisation, Ministry of Planning, Post Office Box 8001, Baghdad, Iraq.

Central Statistical Organisation, Post Office Box 7283, Doha, Qatar.

Central Statistical Organisation, Sardar Patel Bhavan, Parliament Street, New Delhi, India.

Central Statistical Organization, Ministry of Planning and Finance, Six-Storeyed Building, Strand Road, Yangoon, Myanmar.

Central Statistical Services, Private Bag X44, Pretoria 0001, South Africa.

Central Statistics Department, Old Treasury Building, 32 Buckle Street, Banjul, Gambia.

Central Statistics Office, Ardee Road, Dublin 6, Ireland.

Central Statistics Office, Block No. 4, Mikrorayon, Kabul, Afghanistan.

Central Statistics Office, Ministry of Development and Economic Planning, Tower Hill, Freetown, Sierra Leone.

Central Statistics Office, Private Bag 0024, Gaborone, Botswana.

Central Statistics Office, Saint Stephen's Green House, Earlsfort Terrace, Dublin 2, Ireland.

Central Statistics Organisation, Post Office Box 5835, Bahrain.

Central Statistics Organisation, Post Office Box 1272, Steamer Point, Aden, Yemen.

Centre for Industrial Statistics Information and Research, Industrial Economics and Planning Division, Ministry of Industry, Rama 6 Road, Bangkok 10400, Thailand.

Centre National de la Statistique et des Etudes Economiques, BP 2031, Brazzaville, People's Republic of Congo.

Centro Nacional de informatica de Andorra, Avda Meritxell 86B, Andorra La Vella, Andorra.

Chicago Area Geographic Information Study, Department of Geography, M/C 092, 1007 West Harrison Street, Room 2102, University of Illinois at Chicago, Chicago, Illinois 60607 (312) 996-5274.

Chief Government Statistician, Department of Statistics, Ministry of Planning and Economic Development, Post Office Box 13, Entebbe, Uganda.

The Chief Secretary, Chief Secretary's Office, Grand Turk, Turks and Caicos Islands.

Chief Statistician, Economic Planning Unit, Jalan Elizabeth, Kedua, Bandar Seri Begawan, Brunei.

Chief Statistician, Post Office Box 206, Victoria, Mahe, Seychelles.

CIT - Information Services, Princeton University, 87 Prospect Avenue, Princeton, New Jersey 08544 (609) 258-6052.

Cleveland State University, Northern Ohio Data and Information Service, 1737 Euclid Avenue, Cleveland, Ohio 44115 (216) 687-2209.

College of Business Administration, Northern Arizona University, Box 15066, Flagstaff, Arizona 86011 (602) 523-7313.

College of Urban Affairs and Public Policy, University of Delaware, Graham Hall, Room 286, Academy Street, Newark, Delaware 19716 (302) 451-8406.

Colorado Division of Local Government, Department of Local Affairs, 1313 Sherman Street, Room 521, Denver, Colorado 80203 (303) 866-2156.

Comite Estatal de Estadisticas, Almendares No. 156, Civdad de la Habana, Cuba.

Community Development Division, Governor's Office of Community and Industrial Development, Capitol Complex, Building 6, Room 553, Charleston, West Virginia 25305 (304) 348-4010.

Competitive Media Reporting, 11 West 42nd Street, New York, New York 10036 (212) 789-1400.

Computer Science Center, University of Maryland, College Park, Maryland 20742 (301) 405-3037.

Congressional Budget Office, Second and D Streets, SW, Washington, D.C. 20515 (202) 226-2621.

Connecticut Department of Economic Development, 865 Brook Street, Building #1, Rocky Hill, Connecticut 06067-3405 (203) 258-4219.

Connecticut Office of Policy and Management, Policy Development and Planning Division, 80 Washington Street, Hartford, Connecticut 06106 (203) 566-8285.

Cornell University, CISER Data Archive, 201 Caldwell Hall, Ithaca, New York 14853 (607) 255-4801.

Corporation for Public Broadcasting, 901 E Street, NW, Washington, D.C. 20004 (202) 879-9600.

Danmarks Statistik, Post Boks 2550 Sejrogade 11, 2100 Copenhagen 0, Denmark.

Data Services, University of Georgia Libraries, Sixth Floor, Athens, Georgia 30602 (404) 542-0727.

Data Services Division, Mayor's Office of Planning, Room 570, Presidential Building, 415 Twelfth Street, NW, Washington, D.C. 20004 (202) 727-6533.

Dataquest Incorporated, 1290 Ridder Park Drive, San Jose, California 95131 (408) 437-8000.

Delaware Development Office, 99 Kings Highway, Post Office Box 1401, Dover, Delaware 19903 (302) 739-4271.

Demographic Services Center, Department of Administration, 101 East Wilson, Sixth Floor, Post Office Box 7868, Madison, Wisconsin 53707-7868 (608) 266-1927.

Department of Administration, Office of Municipal Affairs, One Capitol Hill, Providence, Rhode Island 02908-5873 (401) 277-6493.

Department of Administration and Fiscal Control, Research and Statistics Division, Emerson Building, Cheyenne, Wyoming 82002-0060 (307) 777-7504.

Department of Agricultural Economics, North Dakota State University, Morrill Hall, Room 224, Post Office Box 5636, Fargo, North Dakota 58105 (701) 237-8621.

Department of Commerce, 590 South Marine Drive, Suite 601, 6th Floor GITC Building, Tamuning, Guam 96911 (671) 646-5841.

Department of Commerce and Labor, Saipan, M.P. 96950, Commonwealth of the Northern Mariana Islands.

Department of Commercial Intelligence and Statistics, One Council House Street, Calcutta, India.

Department of Community and Economic Development, 324 South State Street, Suite 500, Salt Lake City, Utah 84111 (801) 538-8897.

Department of Community and Regional Affairs, Division of Municipal and Regional Assistance, Post Office Box BH, Juneau, Alaska 00811 (907) 465-4750.

Department of Economics, New Mexico State University, Box 30001, Las Cruces, New Mexico 88003 (505) 646-2112.

Department of Education, Division of Libraries and Museums, Alaska State Library, Pouch G, Juneau, Alaska 99811 (907) 465-2927.

Department of Employment Security, 140 East 300 South, Post Office Box 11249, Salt Lake City, Utah 84147 (801) 536-7813.

Department of Employment Security, Post Office Box 9046, Olympia, Washington 98504 (206) 438-4804.

Department of Finance and Development, Administration Building, George Town, Grand Cayman, Cayman Islands.

Department of Geography, University of North Dakota, Grand Forks, North Dakota 58202 (701) 777-4246.

Department of Island Development and Industry, Government Offices, Yaren District, Republic of Nauru, Central Pacific.

Department of Rural Sociology, Texas A & M University System, Special Services Building, College Station, Texas 77843-2125 (409) 845-5115 or 5332.

Department of Sociology, Demographic Research Laboratory, Western Washington University, Bellingham, Washington 98225 (206) 676-3176.

Department of Statistics, Post Office Box 2016, Amman, Jordan.

Department of Statistics, Post Office Box 1151, Apia, Samoa.

Department of Statistics, Ministry of Trade and Industry, 8 Shenton Way, 10-01, Treasury Building, Singapore, 0106.

Department of Statistics, Post Office Box 2922, Wellington, New Zealand.

Department of Statistics, Bangunan Perseketuan, Jalan Mat Salleh, Post Office Box 500, Kota Kinabalu, Sabah.

Department of Statistics, 5th Floor Bangunan Tun Datuk Patinggi Tuanku Haji Bujang, Jalan Simpang Tiga, Kuching, Sarawak.

Department of Statistics, Jalan Cenderasari 50514, Kuala Lumpur, Malaysia.

Department of Statistics, Ministry of Finance and Economic Planning, Post Office Box 700, Khartoum, Sudan.

Departmento Administrativo Nacional de Estadistica, Avenida Eldorado, Bogota DE, Colombia.

Departmento de Estudios Economicos del Banco Central del Paraguay, Pablo V1 y San Rafael, Barrio Santo Domingo, Asuncion, Paraguay.

Departamento de Relaciones Internacionales, Comite Estatal de Estadisticas, Paseo y 5a, Vedado, Ciudad de La Habana, Cuba.

Devlet Istatistik Enstitusu, Necatibey Caddesi, 114 Ankara, Turkey.

Direccao - Geral de Estatistica, C.P. 116, Praia, Cape Verde.

Direccao de Estatistica, CP 256, Sao Tome, Sao Tome e Principe.

Direccao de Services de Estatistica e Census, Post Office Box 3022, Macau.

Direccion General de Estadistica, Centro Nacional de Informacion, Edificio America, 8 Calle 9-55, Zona 1, Guatemala City, Guatemala.

Direccion de Estadistica y Censo, Apartado 5213, Panama 5, Panama. Direccion General de Estadistica y Censos, Avenida Centenario GY8 Calles, Comayaguela DC, Honduras, Honduras.

Direccion General de Estadistica y Censos, Cuareim 2052, Montevideo, Uruguay.

Direccion General de Estadistica y Censos, Miquel Torres 5313, C Correos: 1118, Asuncion, Paraguay.

Direccion General de Estadistica y Censos la Calle P Y 45 Ave Norte, San Salvador, El Salvador.

Direccion General de Estadistics y Censos, Apartado 10216, San Jose, Costa Rica.

Directeur General de la Statistique et des Etudes Economiques, BP 2119, Libreville, Gabon.

Directia Centrala de Statistica, Str. Stavropoleos No. 6, Bucharest, Romania.

Direction Central de la Statistique, Bir Hassan, Beirut, Lebanon.

Direction de la Statistique, Ministere de l'Economie et des Finances, BP 116, Dakar, Senegal.

Direction de la Statistique, BP 118, Lome, Togo.

Nonpublished Sources

Direction de la Statistique, BP 453, N'Djamena, Chad.

Direction de la Statistique, BP 178, Rabat, Morocco.

Direction de la Statistique, Commissariat d'Etat du Development Economique et du Plan, Bissau, Guinea Bissau.

Direction de la Statistique, BP V55, Abidjan, Cote d'Ivoire.

Direction de la Statistique et de la Comptabilite Nationale, Ministere de Plan et de l'Amenagement du Territoire, Yaounde, Cameroon.

Direction de la Statistique, et de la Demographie, BP 240, Nouakchott, Mauritania.

Direction de la Statistique Generale et des Etudes Economiques, BP 732, Bangui, Central African Republic.

Direction de la Statistiques, Ministere du Plan BP 467, Niamey, Niger.

Direction Generale de la Banque des Donnees d L'Etat, BP 485, Antananarivo, Madagascar.

Direction Generale de la Statistique, Ministere du Plan, BP 46, Kigali, Rwanda.

Direction Generale de la Statistique, Ministere du Plan et Cooperation Internationale, Conakry, Guinea.

Direction Nationale de la Statistique, BP 67, Djibouti.

Direction Nationale des Statistiques de Commerce Exterieur, Centre de Renseignements Statistiques, 192 Rue St. Honore, 75056 Paris RP, France.

Direction Nationale de L'Informatique, Ministere du Plan, B.P. 12, Bamako, Mali.

Direction Territoriale de la Statistique et des Etudes Economiques, BP 823, Noumea, New Caledonia.

The Director, Department of Census and Statistics, 6 Albert Crescent, Colombo 7, Sri Lanka.

Director of Central Statistics Department, Ministry of Planning, Post Office Box 904, Abu Dhabi, United Arab Emirates.

Director of Statistics, Abu Dhabi Emirate, Department of Planning, Post Office Box 12, Abu Dhabi, United Arab Emirates.

Director of Statistics, Bahamas Government, Department of Statistics, Post Office Box N3904, Nassau, Bahamas.

Directorate General of National Statistics, Development Council, Post Office Box 881, Muscat, Oman.

Directorate of Economics and Statistics, Ministry of Agriculture, Krishi Bhavan, Dr. Rajendra Prasad Road, New Delhi, India.

Directorate of Statistics, Ministry of Planning, Phnom Penh, Cambodia.

Distilled Spirits Council of the United States, 1250 I Street NW, Suite 900, Washington, D.C. 20005 (202) 628-3544.

Division de la Statistique du Commerce, Direction Generale des Douanes, Monbijoustrasse 40, CH-3011 Berne, Switzerland.

Division of Business and Economic Research, University of New Orleans, Lake Front, New Orleans, Louisiana 70148 (504) 286-6980.

Division of Business Research, Louisiana Tech University, Post Office Box 10318, Ruston, Louisiana 71272 (318) 257-3701.

Division of Demographic and Statistical Services, Georgia Office of Planning and Budget, 254 Washington Street, SW, Room 640, Atlanta, Georgia 30334 (404) 656-0911.

Division of Economic Analysis and Research, Maine Department of Labor, 20 Union Street, Augusta, Maine 04330 (207) 289-2271.

Division of Economic and Business Research, College of Business and Public Administration, University of Arizona, Tucson, Arizona 85721 (602) 621-2155.

Division of Equalization and Assessment, 16 Sheridan Avenue, Albany, New York 12210 (518) 474-6742.

Division of Labor Market and Demographic Research, New Jersey Department of Labor, CN 388-John Fitch Plaza, Trenton, New Jersey 08625-0388 (609) 984-2593.

Division of Local Government, Colorado Department of Local Affairs, 1313 Sherman Street, Room 521, Denver, Colorado 80203 (303) 866-2156.

Division of Planning and Financial Analysis, Illinois Bureau of the Budget, William Stratton Building, Room 605, Springfield, Illinois 62706 (217) 782-1381.

Division of Policy and Research, Department of Economic Development, 1 Commerce Plaza, Room 905, 99 Washington Avenue, Albany, New York 12245 (518) 474-1141.

Division of Research and Information Systems, Department of Economic and Community Development, 1200 Walter Sillas Building, Post Office Box 849, Jackson, Mississippi 39205 (601) 359-2674.

Division of Research and Statistical Services, South Carolina Budget and Control Board, Rembert C. Dennis Building, Room 425, Columbia, South Carolina 29201 (803) 734-3780.

Division of State Library, 109 East Jones Street, Raleigh, North Carolina 27611 (919) 733-3683.

Division of the Budget, Room 152-E, State Capitol Building, Topeka, Kansas 66612 (913) 296-0025.

Documents Department, The Libraries, Colorado State University, Fort Collins, Colorado 80523 (303) 491-1880.

Documents Department, South Dakota State Library, Department of Education and Cultural Affairs, 800 Governors Drive, Pierre, South Dakota 57501-2294 (605) 773-3131.

Documents Librarian, Georgia State University, University Plaza, Atlanta, Georgia 30303 (404) 651-2185.

Documents Librarian, State Data Center Program, Albany State College, 504 College Drive, Albany, Georgia 31705 (912) 430-4799.

Documents Librarian, State Data Center Program, Georgia Southern College, Statesboro, Georgia 30460 (912) 681-5117.

Documents Section, Washington State Library AJ-11, Olympia, Washington 98504 (206) 753-4027.

Dow Jones and Company, Incorporated, 200 Liberty Street, New York, New York 10006 (212) 416-2000.

Drejtoria e Statisikes, Tirana, Albania.

Economic Development Department, 1100 St. Francis Drive, Santa Fe, New Mexico 87503 (505) 827-0182.

Economic Development Planning Office, Pago Pago, American Samoa 96799.

Economic Planning and Statistics Office, Cathedral Square, Gibraltar.

Economics, Statistics and Fiscal Analysis Division, Department of Provincial Treasury, Post Office Box 2000, Charlottetown, Prince Edward Island C1A 7N8, Canada (902) 368-4030.

Elections Research Center, 5508 Greystone Street, Chevy Chase, Maryland 20815 (202) 659-9490.

Employee Benefit Research Institute, 2121 K Street, NW, Suite 860, Washington, D.C. 20037 (202) 659-0670.

Employment Security Division, Connecticut Department of Labor, 200 Folly Brook Boulevard, Wethersfield, Connecticut 06109 (203) 566-2120.

Executive Council Office, Bureau of Statistics, Post Office Box 2703, Whitehorse, Yukon Territory Y1A 2C6, Canada (403) 667 5640

Executive Office of the President, Office of Management and Budget, Executive Office Building, Washington, D.C. 20503 (202) 395-3080.

Eye Bank Association of America, 1001 Connecticut Avenue, NW, Suite 601, Washington, D.C. 20036-5504 (202) 775-4999.

Federal Bureau of Statistics, Ministry of Finance and Economic Affairs, 5-SLIC Building, Blue Area, F-6/4, Islamabad, Pakistan.

Federal Deposit Insurance Corporation, 550 Seventeenth Street, NW, Washington, D.C. 20429 (202) 393-8400.

Federal Documents Librarian, Nebraska Library Commission, The Atrium, 1200 North Street, Suite 120, Nebraska 68508-2006 (402) 471-2045.

Federal Documents Section, Department of Library, Archives, and Public Records, 1700 West Washington, 2nd Floor, Phoenix, Arizona 85007 (602) 542-4121.

Federal Office of Statistics, 36-38 Broad Street, PM Bag 12528, Lagos, Nigeria.

Federalni Statisticky Urad, Sokolovska 142, 186 13 Prague 8, Czechoslovakia.

Florida State Data Center, Executive Office of the Governor, REA/OPB, The Capitol, Room 1604, Tallahassee, Florida 32399-0001 (904) 487-2814.

Food and Agricultural Organization of the United Nations (FAO), Via delle Terme di Caracalla, 00100, Rome Italy (Telephone Number in U.S. (202) 653-2400).

Foreign Relations Department, States Statistical Committee, Ulitsa Kirova 39, Moscow 103450, Russia.

Fundacao Instituto Brasileiro do Geografia e Estatistica, Av Franklin Roosevelt, 166/10 andar, 20 021 Rio de Janeiro RJ, Brazil.

Future Computing/Datapro, Inc., 600 Delran Parkway, Delran, New Jersey 08075 (609) 764-0100.

Gallup Organization, Inc., 100 Palmer Square, Princeton, New Jersey 08542 (609) 924-9600.

Gartner Group, Inc., 56 Top Gallant Road, Stamford, Connecticut 06902 (203) 964-0096.

Geographic Resources Center, University of Missouri-Columbia, 17 Stewart Hall, Columbia, Missouri 65211 (314) 882-1404.

Georgia Department of Community Affairs, Office of Coordinated Planning, 100 Peachtree Street, N.E. #1200, Atlanta, Georgia 30303 (404) 656-5526.

Glowny Urzad Statystyczny (Central Statistical Office), Al Niepodleglosci 208, 00-925 Warsaw, Poland.

Government Documents, Connecticut State Library, 231 Capitol Avenue, Hartford, Connecticut 06106 (203) 566-4971.

Government of Niue, Post Office Box 67, Alofi, Niue, South Pacific.

Government Statistician, Department of Statistics, Post Office Box 1151, Apia, Western Samoa.

Governor's Office of Community and Industrial Development, Community Development Division, Capitol Complex, Building 6, Room 553, Charleston, West Virginia 25305 (304) 348-4010.

Governor's Office of Federal-State Programs, Department of Community Development, 301 West Pearl Street, Jackson, Mississippi 39200-0006 (601) 949-2219.

Group Health Association of America, 1129 Twentieth Street, NW, Suite 600, Washington, D.C. 20036 (202) 778-3200.

Gtowny Urzad Statystyczny (Central Statistical Office), Al Niepodegosci 208, 00-925 Warsaw, Poland.

Guam Department of Commerce, 590 South Marine Drive, Suite 601, Sixth Floor, GITC Building, Tamuning, Guam 96911 (671) 646-5841.

Guttmacher, Alan Institute, 111 Fifth Avenue, New York, New York 10003 (212) 254-5656.

Haute Commissariat du Plan et Cooperation, Presidence de la Republique, Bangui, Central African Republic.

Hawaii State Data Center, Department of Business & Economic Development and Tourism, 220 South King Street, Suite 400, Honolulu, Hawaii 96813 (808) 586-2493.

Idaho Department of Commerce, 700 West State Street, Boise, Idaho 83720 (208) 334-2470.

The Idaho State Library, 325 West State Street, Boise, Idaho 83702 (208) 334-2150.

Nonpublished Sources

Illinois Bureau of the Budget, William Stratton Building, Room 605, Springfield, Illinois 62706 (217) 782-1381.

Indiana Business Research Center, Indiana University, Tenth and Fee Lane, Bloomington, Indiana 47405 (812) 855-5507.

Indiana Business Research Center, 801 West Michigan, B.S. 4015, Indianapolis, Indiana 46202-5151 (317) 274-2205.

Indiana State Data Center, Indiana State Library, 140 North Senate Avenue, Indianapolis, Indiana 46204 (317) 232-3733.

Information and Communication Services Division, State Department of Budget and Finance, Kalanimoku Building, 1151 Punchbowl Street, Honolulu, Hawaii 96813 (808) 568-1940.

Information Officer, Broadway House, Saint Helena.

Inspectorate General of Customs, Ministry of Finance, 85 Hsim-Hseng South Road, Section 1, Taipei, Republic of China.

Institut Haitien de Statistique et d'Informatique, Cite de l'Exposition, Boulevard Harry Truman, Port-au-Prince, Haiti.

Institut National de la Statistique, BP 20, Kinshasa, Zaire.

Institut National de la Statistique et de l'Analyse Economique, Ministere du Plan, de la Statistique, BP 323, Cotonou, Benin.

Institut National de la Statistique et des Etudes Economiques, 18 Boulevard Adolphe Pinard, 75675 Paris Cedex 14, France.

Institut National de Statistique, 27 rue du Liban, 1002 Tunis-Belvedere, Tunis, Tunisia.

Institut National de Statistique, rue de Louvain 44, 1000 Brussels, Belgium.

Institut Territorial de la Statistique, BP 395, Papeete, Tahiti, French Polynesia.

Institute for Public Policy and Business Research, 607 Blake Hall, The University of Kansas, Lawrence, Kansas 66045-2960 (913) 864-3123.

Institute for Research in Social Science, University of North Carolina, Manning Hall CB 3355, Chapel Hill, North Carolina 27599-3355 (919) 962-0512.

Institute for Social and Economic Research, University of Alaska, 3211 Providence Drive, Anchorage, Alaska 99508 (907) 786-7710.

Institute of State and Regional Affairs, Pennsylvania State Data Center, Pennsylvania State University at Harrisburg, Middletown, Pennsylvania 17057-4898 (717) 948-6336.

Institutional Research, Room 319, Business Building, Boise State University, Boise, Idaho 83725 (208) 385-1613.

Instituto Nacional de Estadistica, Casilla 6129, Plaza Mario Guzman Aspiazu No. 1, La Paz, Bolivia.

Instituto Nacional de Estadistica, 10 Avenue de Agosto 229, Quito, Ecuador.

Instituto Nacional de Estadistica, Avenida 28 de Julio 1056, Lima 1, Peru.

Instituto Nacional de Estatistica, Avenida Antonio Jose de Almeida, 1078 Lisbon 1, Portugal.

Instituto Nacional de Estadistica, Ministerio de Economia y Hacienda, Paseo de la Castellana 183, Madrid 28046, Spain.

Instituto Nacional de Estadistica y Censos, Hipolito Yrigoyen 250, Piso 12, Of 1210, 1310 Buenos Aires, Argentina.

Instituto Nacional de Estatisticas, Caixa Postal 1215, Luanda, Angola.

Instituto Nacional de Estadisticas, Casilla 498-3, Santiago, Chile.

Instituto Nacional de Estadisticas y Censos, Apartado 4031, Managua, Nicaragua.

Instituto Nacional de Estadistica, Geografia e Informatica, Patriotismo No. 711, PH, CP 03910 Mexico.

Instituto Nazionale di Statistica, Via Cesare Balbo 16, 00100 Rome, Italy.

Interagency Resource and Information Center, Department of Education, 501 Capitol Square Building, St. Paul, Minnesota 55101 (612) 296-6684.

International Monetary Fund, 700 Nineteenth Street, NW, Washington, D.C. 20431 (202) 623-7000.

International Snowmobile Industry Association, 3975 University Drive, Suite 310, Fairfax, Virginia 22030 (703) 273-9606.

Iowa Social Science Institute, University of Iowa, 345 Shaeffer Hall, Iowa City, Iowa 52242 (319) 335-2371.

Iranian Statistical Centre, Dr Fatemi Avenue, Tehran, Iran.

Kenya Customs and Excise Department, Ministry of Finance, Ministry of Finance, Post Office Box 40160, Nairobi, Kenya.

Kozponti Statisztikai Hivatal (Central Statistical Office), Post Office Box 51, Keleti Karoly Utca 5-7, 1024 Budapest 11, Hungary.

Labor Market Information Center, South Dakota Department of Labor, 420 South Roosevelt, Box 4730, Aberdeen, South Dakota 57402-4730 (605) 622-2314.

Land Resources Information Service, Division of Land Resources, Post Office Box 27687, Raleigh, North Carolina 27611 (919) 733-2090.

The Library of Michigan, Government Documents Service, Post Office Box 30007, 717 West Allegan Street, Lansing, Michigan 48909 (517) 373-0640.

Louisiana State Office of Planning and Budget, Division of Administration, Post Office Box 94095, Baton Rouge, Louisiana 70804 (504) 342-7410.

L'Union Economique Belgo-Luxembourgeoise, Institut National de Statistique, rue de Louvain 44, 1000 Brussels, Belgium.

Magazine Publishers of America, 919 Third Avenue, New York, New York 10022 (212) 872-3700.

Main Library, University of Georgia, Athens, Georgia 30602 (404) 542-0664.

Maine State Library, State House Station 64, Augusta, Maine 04333 (207) 289-5600.

Major League Baseball Players Association, 805 Third Avenue, New York, New York 10022 (212) 826-0808.

Manitoba Bureau of Statistics, #333, 260 St. Mary Avenue, Winnipeg, Manitoba R3C 0M6, Canada (204) 945-2985.

Market Data Retrieval, 16 Progress Drive, Shelton, Connecticut 06484 (203) 926-4800.

Maryland Department of State Planning, 301 West Preston Street, Baltimore, Maryland 21201 (410) 225-4450.

Massachusetts Institute for Social and Economic Research, 128 Thompson Hall, University of Massachusetts, Amherst, Massachusetts 01003 (413) 545-3460.

Massachusetts Institute for Social and Economic Research, Box 219, Saltonstall State Office Building, Room 1103, 100 Cambridge Street, Boston, Massachusetts 02133 (617) 727-4537.

Mediamark Research, Incorporated, 708 Third Avenue, New York, New York 10017 (212) 599-0444.

Metals Week, McGraw-Hill Publications Company, Incorporated, 1221 Avenue of the Americas, New York, New York 10020 (212) 997-2823.

Metropolitan Council Research, 230 East Fifth Street, St. Paul, Minnesota 55101 (612) 291-8140.

Metropolitan Life Insurance Company, One Madison Avenue, New York, New York 10010 (212) 578-2211.

Metropolitan Washington Council of Governments, 777 North Capitol Street, Suite 300, Washington, D.C. 20002-4201 (202) 962-3200.

Michigan Information Center, Department of Management and Budget, Office of Revenue and Tax Analysis, Post Office Box 30026, Lansing, Michigan 48909 (517) 373-7910.

MIMIC/Center for Urban Studies, Wayne State University, Faculty/Administration Building, 656 West Kirby, Detroit, Michigan 48202 (313) 577-8359.

Ministere de la Planification et du Developpement Populaire, Institut National de la Statistique et de la Demographie, BP 7050 Ouagadougou, Burkina Faso.

Ministere du Plan et de la Statistique, Bureau du Premier Ministre, Conakry, Guinea.

Ministerio de Economia y Hacienda, Direccion General de Aduanas, Seccion de Estadistica, San Francisco de Sales 6, Madrid 3, Spain.

Ministerio de Planificacion y DeSarrollo Economico, Direccion General de Estadistica, Malabo, Equatorial Guinea.

Ministry of Economic Affairs, Department of Statistics, 15 Foochow Street, Taipei, Taiwan.

Ministry of Economic Planning and Development, Post Office Box 30266, Nairobi, Kenya.

Ministry of Economy, Planning and Finance, Post Office Box 46, Vientiane, Laos.

Ministry of Finance and Corporate Relations, Central Statistics Branch, 553 Superior Street, First Floor, Victoria, British Columbia V8V 1X4, Canada (604) 387-1502.

Ministry of Foreign Affairs, 8 Lenin Street Minsk, Belarus.

Ministry of Planning and Environment, Male 20-05, Republic of Maldives.

Ministry of Planning and National Development, Post Office Box 30266, Nairobi, Kenya.

Missouri Small Business Development Centers, 300 University Place, Columbia, Missouri 65211 (314) 882-0344.

Missouri State Library, 600 West Main Street, Post Office Box 387, Jefferson City, Missouri 65102 (314) 751-1823.

Montana State Library, 1515 East Sixth Avenue, Capitol Station, Helena, Montana 59620 (406) 444-3004.

Motion Picture Association of America, Incorporated, 1600 Eye Street, NW, Washington, D.C. 20006 (202) 293-1966.

Motorcycle Industry Council, 2 Jenner Street, Suite 150, Irvine, California 92718 (714) 727-4211.

National Archives and Records Administration, Seventh Street and Pennsylvania Avenue, NW, Washington, D.C. 20400 (202) 501-5400

National Assembly of State Arts Agencies, 1010 Vermont Avenue, NW, Washington, D.C. 20005 (202) 347-6352.

National Association of Home Builders of the U.S., 1201 Fifteenth Street, NW, Washington, D.C. 20005 (202) 822-0200.

National Association of Latino Elected and Appointed Officials, NALEO Education Fund, 3409 Garnet, Los Angeles, California 90023 (213) 362-8503.

National Association of Securities Dealers, 1735 K Street, NW, Washington, D.C. 20006 (202) 728-8000.

National Basketball Association, 645 Fifth Avenue, New York, New York 10022 (212) 826-7000.

National Bowling Council, 2300 Clarendon Boulevard, Number 1107, Arlington, Virginia 22201 (703) 841-1660.

National Center for Children in Poverty, Columbia University, 154 Haven Avenue, Manhattan, New York 10032 (212) 927-8793.

National Center for Employee Ownership, 2201 Broadway, Suite 807, Oakland, California 94612 (415) 272-9461.

National Center for Juvenile Justice, 701 Forbes Avenue, Pittsburgh, Pennsylvania 15219 (412) 227-6950.

National Collegiate Athletic Association, 6201 College Boulevard, Overland Park, Kansas 66211 (913) 339-1906.

National Council for Adoption, 1930 Seventeenth Street, NW, Washington, D.C. 20009 (202) 328-1200.

National Credit Union Administration, 1775 Duke Street, Alexandria, Virginia 22314 (703) 518-6300.

National Directorate of Statistics, Ministerio do Plano, Av Ahmed Sekou Toure 21, CP 493, Maputo, Mozambique.

National Education Association, 1201 Sixteenth Street, NW, Washington, D.C. 20036 (202) 833-4000.

National Football League, 410 Park Avenue, New York, New York 10022 (212) 758-1500.

National Football League Players Association, 2021 L Street, NW, 6th Floor, Washington, D.C. 20036 (202) 463-2200.

National Gardening Association, 180 Flynn Avenue, Burlington, Vermont 05401 (802) 863-1308.

National Golf Foundation, 1150 South U.S. Highway One, Jupiter, Florida 33477 (407) 744-6006.

National Hockey League, 1800 McGill College Avenue, Suite 2600, Montreal, Quebec, Canada H3A 3J6 (514) 288-9220.

National Hockey League Players Association, One Dundas Street, West, Toronto, Ontario, Canada M5G 1Z3 (416) 408-4040.

National Hurricane Center, 1320 South Dixie Highway, Coral Gables, Florida 33146 (305) 666-0413.

National Marine Manufactures Association, 401 North Michigan Avenue, Chicago, Illinois 60611 (312) 836-4747.

National Republican Congressional Committee, 320 First Street, SE, Washington, D.C. 20003 (202) 479-7000.

National Safety Council, 1121 Spring Lake Drive, Itasca, Illinois 60143-3201 (708) 285-1121.

National Statistical Coordination Board, Marvin Plaza Building, 2153 Pasong Tamo Street, Makati, Metro Manila, Republic of the Philippines.

National Statistical Office, Larn Luang Road, Bangkok 10100, Thailand.

National Statistical Office, 90 Kyongun-dong, Chong-gu, Seoul, Korea.

National Statistical Office, Post Office Box 333, Zomba, Malawi.

National Statistical Service of Greece, 14-16 Lykourgou Street, 10166 Athens, Greece.

National Statistics Office, Central Government Offices, Post Office Wards Strip, Waigani, Papua New Guinea.

Natural Resources and Economics, Department of Agriculture, Colorado State University, Fort Collins, Colorado 80523 (303) 491-5706.

Natural Resources Commission, 301 Centennial Mall South, Post Office Box 94876, Lincoln, Nebraska 68509-4876 (402) 471-2081.

Nebraska Department of Labor, 550 South Sixteenth Street, Post Office Box 94600, Lincoln, Nebraska 68509-4600 (402) 471-2518.

Nelson A. Rockefeller, Institute of Government, 411 State Street, Albany, New York 12203 (518) 443-5258.

Netherlands Central Bureau of Statistics, 428 Prinses Beatrixlaan, 2270 AZ Voorburg, The Hague, Netherlands.

Nevada State Library, Capitol Complex, 100 Stewart Street, Carson City, Nevada 89710 (702) 687-8327.

New Brunswick Statistics Agency, Post Office Box 6000, Fredericton, New Brunswick E3B 5H1, Canada (506) 453-2381.

New Hampshire State Library, 20 Park Street, Concord, New Hampshire 03301-6303 (603) 271-2060.

New Jersey Department of Labor, Division of Labor Market and Demographic Research, CN 388-John Fitch Plaza, Trenton, New Jersey 08625-0388 (609) 984-2593.

New Jersey State Library, 185 West State Street, CN 520, Trenton, New Jersey 08625-0520 (609) 292-6259.

New Mexico State Library, 325 Don Gaspar Avenue, Post Office Box 1629, Santa Fe, New Mexico 87503 (505) 827-3824.

New York State Department of Economic Development, Division of Policy and Research, One Commerce Plaza, Room 905, 99 Washington Avenue, Albany, New York 12245 (518) 474-6005.

New York State Library, Cultural Education Center, Empire State Plaza, Albany, New York 12230 (518) 474-3940.

Newfoundland Statistics Agency, Executive Council, 10th Floor, Confederation Building, Post Office Box 8700, St. John's, Newfoundland A1B 4J6, Canada (709) 729-2913.

North Carolina Office of State Planning, 116 West Jones Street, Raleigh, North Carolina 27603-8005 (919) 733-3683.

North Dakota State Library, Liberty Memorial Building, Capitol Grounds, Bismarck, North Dakota 58505 (701) 224-2490.

Northeastern Illinois Planning Commission, Research Services, 400 West Madison Street, Chicago, Illinois 60606-2642 (312) 454-0400.

Office des Changes, Division des Etudes et de la Balance des Paiements, Place Moulay Hassan, BP 71, Rabat, Morocco.

Office Federale de la Statistique, Hallwylstrasse 15, CH-3003 Berne, Switzerland.

Office National des Statistiques, 8/10 Rues des Moussebiline, B.P. 55 Alger, Algeria.

Office of Administration, 124 Capitol Building, Post Office Box 809, Jefferson City, Missouri 65102 (314) 751-2345.

Office of Administration Services, South Dakota Department of Health, 445 East Capitol Avenue, Pierre, South Dakota 57501-3185 (605) 773-3693.

Office of Biometrics, University of New Hampshire Pettee Hall, Durham, New Hampshire 03824 (603) 862-3930.

Office of Computing, University of Missouri-St. Louis, 8001 Natural Bridge Road, Room 451 CCB, St. Louis, Missouri 63121 (314) 553-6014.

Office of Financial Management, Forecasting Division, 450 Insurance Building, Box 43113, Olympia, Washington 98504 (206) 586-2504.

Office of Health Services Research, Department of Community Medicine, Health Science Center, West Virginia University, Morgantown, West Virginia 26506 (304) 293-1086.

Office of Health Statistics, Rhode Island Department of Health, 3 Capitol Hill, Providence, Rhode Island 02908 (401) 277-2550.

Office of Intergovernmental Assistance, State Capitol, Fourteenth Floor, Bismarck, North Dakota 58505 (701) 224-2094.

Office of Management and Budget, Division of Policy, Pouch AD, Juneau, Alaska 99811 (907) 465-3640.

Office of Planning and Budget, Division of Administration, Post Office Box 94095, 1051 North Third Street, Baton Rouge, Louisiana 70804 (504) 342-7410.

Office of Planning and Budget, State Capitol, Room 116, Salt Lake City, Utah 84114 (801) 538-1550.

Office of Planning and Statistics, Majuro, Republic of the Marshall Islands 96960.

Office of Planning and Statistics, Post Office Box 100, Koror, Republic of Palau, Western Caroline Islands 96940.

Office of Planning and Statistics, Post Office Box PS4, National Government Federated States of Micronesia, Palikir, Pohnpei FAM 96941.

Office of Policy and Management, State of Kentucky, Capitol Annex, Frankfort, Kentucky 40601 (502) 564-7300.

Office of Policy Research and Coordination, Pavilion Office Building, 109 State Street, Montpelier, Vermont 05609 (802) 828-3326.

Office of Population Censuses and Surveys, Head Office, St. Catherines House, 10 Kingsway, London WC2B 6JP, United Kingdom.

Office of Social and Economic Data Analysis, University of Missouri-Columbia, 224 Lewis Hall, Columbia, Missouri 65211 (314) 882-7396.

Office of State Planning, 2 1/2 Beacon Street, Concord, New Hampshire 03301 (603) 271-2155.

Oficina Central de Estadística e Information, Presidencia de la Republica, Aptdo. de Correos 400 Carmelitas, Caracas 1050, Venezuela.

Oficina Nacional de Estadística Apartado de Correos No. 1342, Santo Domingo D.N., Dominican Republic.

Ohio Data Users Center, Ohio Department of Development, Post Office Box 1001, Columbus, Ohio 43266-0101 (614) 466-2115.

Ohio State University Library/Census Data Center, 126 Main Library, 1858 Neil Avenue Mall, Columbus, Ohio 43210 (614) 292-6175.

Oklahoma Department of Libraries, 200 N.E. Eighteenth Street, Oklahoma City, Oklahoma 73105 (405) 521-2502.

Oklahoma State Data Center, Oklahoma Department of Commerce, 6601 Broadway Extension, Post Office Box 26980, Oklahoma City, Oklahoma 73126-0980 (405) 841-5184.

Oregon Housing Agency, 1600 State Street, Suite 100, Salem, Oregon 97310-0161 (503) 378-4730.

Oregon State Library, State Library Building, Salem, Oregon 97310 (503) 378-4277.

Organisation for Economic Co-operation and Development, (OECD), 2 rue Andre-Pascal, 75 Paris 16, France (Telephone Number in U.S. (202) 785-6323).

Osterreichisches Statistisches Zentralamt, Hintere Zollamtsstrasse 2b, A 1033 Vienna, Austria.

Penn State at Harrisburg Acquisitions, Heindel Library, Middletown, Pennsylvania 17057 (717) 948-6074.

Pennsylvania State Data Center, Institute of State and Regional Affairs, Pennsylvania State University at Harrisburg, Middletown, Pennsylvania 17057 (717) 948-6336.

Pennsylvania State Library, Forum Building, Harrisburg, Pennsylvania 17105 (717) 787-2327.

Planning and Statistics Division, Ministry of Finance, Post Office Box 33, Viaku, Tuvalu.

Planning Unit, Ministry of Finance, Belmopan, Belize.

Policy Development and Planning Division, Connecticut Office of Policy and Management, 80 Washington Street, Hartford, Connecticut 06106-4459 (203) 566-8285.

Policy Research Office, Post Office Box 94601, State Capitol, Room 1319, Lincoln, Nebraska 68509-4601 (402) 471-2414.

Population and Resources Laboratory, Department of Sociology, Kansas State University, Manhattan, Kansas 66506 (913) 532-5984.

Population Division of the United Nations, New York, New York 10017 (800) 253-9646.

Population Research Laboratory, Utah State University, UMC 07, Logan, Utah 84322 (801) 750 1331.

Price Gilbert Memorial Library, Georgia Institute of Technology, Atlanta, Georgia 30332 (404) 894-4519.

Prime Minister's Department, Post Office Box 193, Apia, Western Samoa.

Public Securities Association, 40 Broad Street, 12th Floor, New York, New York 10004 (212) 809-7000.

Publishers Information Bureau, 575 Lexington Avenue, New York, New York 10022 (212) 752-0055.

Puerto Rico Department of Labor and Human Resources, Bureau of Labor Statistics, San Juan, Puerto Rico.

Puerto Rico Planning Board, Minillas Government Center, North Building, Avenida De Diego, Post Office Box 41119, San Juan, Puerto, Rico 00940-9985 (809) 728-4430.

Puget Sound Council of Governments, 216 First Avenue South, Seattle, Washington 98104 (206) 464-5355.

Recinto Universitario De Mayaguez, Edificio Anexo Pineiro, Carretera Num 2, Mayaguez, Puerto Rico 00708 (809) 834-4040.

Reference Department, Louisiana State Library, Post Office Box 131, Baton Rouge, Louisiana 70821 (504) 342-4920.

Reference Library, West Virginia State Library Commission, Science and Cultural Center, Capitol Complex, Charleston, West Virginia 25305 (304) 348-2045.

Regional Research and Development Service, Southern Illinois University at Edwardsville, Box 1456, Edwardsville, Illinois 62026-1456 (618) 692-2278.

Research and Analysis Bureau, Employment Policy Division, Montana Department of Labor and Industry, Post Office Box 1728, Helena, Montana 59624 (406) 444-2430.

Research and Analysis Section, Arkansas Employment Security Division, Post Office Box 2981, Little Rock, Arkansas 72203 (501) 682-3159.

Research and Planning Division, Minister's Secretariat, Ministry of Finance, 1-1 Kasumigaseki 3-chome, Chiyoda-ku, Tokyo 100, Japan.

Research Division, Indiana Department of Commerce, 1 North Capitol, Suite 700, Indianapolis, Indiana 46204 (317) 232-8959.

Research Library, Department of Library, Archives and Public Records, 1700 West Washington, Second Floor, Phoenix, Arizona 85007 (602) 542-3701.

Research Section, Iowa Department of Economic Development, 200 East Grand Avenue, Des Moines, Iowa 50309 (515) 281-3005.

Rhode Island Department of Economic Development, 7 Jackson Walkway, Providence, Rhode Island 02903 (401) 277-2601.

Rhode Island Department of Education, 22 Hayes Street, Providence, Rhode Island 02908 (401) 277-3126.

Rhode Island Department of State Library Services, 300 Richmond Street, Providence Rhode Island 02903 (401) 277-2726.

Robert W. Woodruff Library for Advanced Studies, Emory University, Atlanta, Georgia 30322 (404) 727-6880.

Rockefeller, Nelson A., Institute of Government, 411 State Street, Albany, New York 12203 (518) 472-1300.

Roper Center, Institute for Social Injury, University of Connecticut, U-164, Storrs, Connecticut 06269-1164 (203) 486-4440.

Rutgers University - The State University, Kilmer Campus, Lucy Stone Hall, B Wing, New Brunswick, New Jersey 08903 (908) 932-3822.

Sacramento Area COG, 106 K Street, Suite 300, Sacramento, California 95816 (916) 457-2264.

San Diego Association of Governments, First Federal Plaza, 401 B Street, Suite 800, San Diego, California 92101 (619) 236-5300.

Saskatchewan Bureau of Statistics, Fifth Floor, 2350 Albert Street, Regina, Saskatchewan S4P 4A6, Canada (306) 787-6327.

Savezni Zavod za Statistiku, Kneza Milosa, 20, Post Office Box 203, 11000 Belgrade, Yugoslavia.

The Secretariat, Stanley, Falkland Islands.

Service Central de la Statistique et des Etudes Economiques, 19-21 Boulevard Royal, BP 304, L2013, Luxembourg.

Service National Des Etudes et Statistiques, Ministere du Plan, BP 1156, Bujumbura, Burundi.

Services des Statistiques, et des Etudes Economiques, 4 rue des Iris, Monte Carlo, Monaco.

Shipbuilders Council of America, 4301 North Fairfax Drive, Suite 330, Arlington, Virginia 22203 (703) 276-1700.

Slovensky Statisticky Urad Mileticova 3, 800 00 Bratislava, Czechoslovakia.

Small Business Development Center, 217 East Redwood Street, Ninth Floor, Baltimore, Maryland 21202 (410) 333-6995.

Social Research Center, Department of Rural Sociology, Washington State University, Pullman, Washington 99164-4006 (509) 335-4519.

Social Science Data Center, Brown University, Post Office Box 1916, Providence, Rhode Island 02912 (401) 863-2550.

South Carolina State Library, Post Office Box 11469, Columbia, South Carolina 29211 (803) 734-8666.

South Dakota State University, Rural Sociology Department, Scobey Hall 226, Box 504, Brookings, South Dakota 57007 (605) 688-4132.

Southern California Association of Governments, 818 West Seventh Street, Twelfth Floor, Los Angeles, California 90017 (213) 236-1800.

Specialty Vehicle Institute of America, Two Jenner Street, Suite 150, Irvine, California 92718 (714) 727-3727.

Staatliche Zentralverwaltung fur Statistik (State Central Administration for Statistics), 1026 Berlin, Hans-Beimler-Strasse 70/72, Germany.

State Census Data Center, Department of Finance, 915 L Street, Sacramento, California 95814 (916) 322-4651.

State Committee of Azerbaijan on Statistics, 10 Chapaena Street, Baku 370008, Azerbaijan.

State Committee of Republic of Kirgizstan on Statistics, 374 Frunze Street, Bishkek 720884, Kirgizstan.

State Committee of Republic of Tajikstan on Statistics, 127 Ayini Street, Dushanbe - 29, 734029, Tajikistan.

State Committee of Republic of Turkmenistan on Statistics, 72 Makhtumkuli Avenue, Ashkhabad 744000, Turkmenistan.

State Data Center, Texas Department of Commerce, 9th and Congress Streets, Post Office Box 12728, Capitol Station, Austin, Texas 78711 (512) 320-9667.

State Data Center, University of Arkansas-Little Rock, 2801 South University, Little Rock, Arkansas 72204 (501) 569-8530.

State Data Center, Texas Department of Commerce, Ninth and Congress Streets, Post Office Box 12728, Capitol Station, Austin, Texas 78711 (512) 320-9683.

State Data Center, University of Arkansas-Little Rock, 2801 South University, Little Rock, Arkansas 72204 (501) 569-8530.

State Data Center Program, Mercer University Law Library, Mercer University, Macon, Georgia 31207 (912) 752-2668.

State Data Center Program, University of California-Berkeley, 2538 Channing Way, Berkeley, California 94720 (510) 642-6571.

State Demographer's Office, Minnesota Planning, 300 Centennial Office Building, 658 Cedar Street, St. Paul, Minnesota 55155 (612) 296-2557.

State Library, State Capitol Building, Room 343-N, Topeka, Kansas 66612 (913) 296-3296.

State Library Division, Department for Libraries and Archives, 300 Coffeetree Road, Post Office Box 537, Frankfort, Kentucky 40601 (502) 875-7000.

State Library, North Carolina Department of Cultural Resources State Library, 109 East Jones Street, Raleigh, North Carolina 27611 (919) 733-3270.

State Library of Florida, R.A. Gray Building, Tallahassee, Florida 32399-0250 (904) 487-2651.

State Library of Iowa, East Twelfth and Grand, Des Moines, Iowa 50319 (515) 281-4350.

State Library of Ohio, 65 South Front Street, Columbus, Ohio 43215 (614) 644-7051.

State Library Resource Center, Pratt Library, 400 Cathedral Street, Baltimore, Maryland 21201 (410) 396-1789.

State Service Center for Geographic Information Systems, Department of Energy Building, 625 Marion Street, NE, Salem, Oregon 97310 (503) 378-4036.

State Statistical Bureau, 38 Yuetan Nanjie, Sanlihe, Beijing, People's Republic of China.

Statistical Bureau, Ministry of Economic Planning and Finance, Post Office Box 542, Georgetown, Guyana.

Statistical Bureau of Iceland, Skuggasund 3, 15-150, 101 Reykjavik, Iceland.

Statistical Department, Ministry of Trade, Industry, and Tourism, Post Office Building, Castries, Saint Lucia.

Statistical Department, State Planning Commission, Post Office Box 1742, Mogadishu, Somalia.

Statistical Department, The Treasury, The Valley, Anguilla.

Statistical Division, Ministry of Finance, Post Office Box 67, Bariki, Tarawa, Gilbert Islands.

Statistical Division, Ministry of Finance, Upper Redcliffe Street, Saint John's, Antigua.

Statistical Institute of Jamaica, Nine Swallowfield Road, Kingston 5, Jamaica.

Statistical Office, Ministry of Finance, 22 Bath Road, Roseau, Dominica.

Statistical Office, Church Street, Basseterre, Saint Kitts.

Statistical Office, Ministry of Finance and National Economy, Post Office Box 3735, Riyadh, Saudi Arabia.

Statistical Office of the United Nations, Publishing Service, New York, New York 10017 (800) 253-9646.

Statistical Office, Post Office Box 125, Avarua, Raratonga, Cook Islands.

Statistical Service, Post Office Box 1099, Accra, Ghana.

Statistical Services Branch, Department of Economic Development, Post Office Box 519, Halifax, Nova Scotia B3J 2R7, Canada (902) 424-5691.

Statistician's Office, Church Street, Hamilton 5, Bermuda.

Statistics and Research Department, Ministry of Finance, 13 Lord Byron Avenue, Nicosia, Cyprus.

Statistics Bureau, Management and Coordination Agency, 19-1 Waka-Matsucho, Shinjuku, Tokyo 162, Japan.

Statistics Canada, Ottawa, Ontario K1A 0T6, Canada.

Statistics Department, Ministry of Finance, Post Office Box 149, Nuku'alofa, Tonga.

Statistics Department, Ministry of Finance, Saint George's, Grenada.

Statistics Division, Planning Unit, Ministry of Finance, Church Street, Post Office Box 186, Basseterre, Saint Kitts and Nevis.

Statistics Group, Sectoral and Community Economic Policy Branch, Ministry of Treasury and Economics, Frost Building, North Third Floor, Toronto, Ontario M7A 1Y9, Canada (416) 325-1544.

Statistics Office, Chief Statistician, Government Headquarters, Plymouth, Montserrat.

Statistics Office, Ministry of Finance and Economic Planning, Post Office Box 67, Bariki, Tarawa, Kiribati.

Statistics Office, NPSO, Vila, Vanuatu.

Statistics Office, Ministry of Finance and Economic Planning, Post Office Box G6, Honiara, Solomon Islands.

Statistics Office, Post Office Box 125, Rarotonga, Cook Islands.

Statistiska Central Byran, Karlavagen 5 - 115 81 Stockholm, Sweden.

Statistisches Bundesamt, 1 Gustav-Stresemann-Ring 11, Postfach 5528, 6200 Wiesbaden, Germany.

Statistisk Sentralbyra, Skippergate 15, Postboks 8131, DEP N - 0033, Oslo, Norway.

Supreme Court of the United States, Office of the Clerk, United States Supreme Court Building, One First Street, NE, Washington, D.C. 20543 (202) 479-3000.

Survey Research Center, University of Wyoming, Post Office Box 3925, Laramie, Wyoming 82071 (307) 766-2931.

Survey Research Center, Wilson Hall, Room 1-108, Montana State University, Bozeman, Montana 59717 (406) 994-4481.

T C Basbakanlik Devlet Istatistik Enstitusu, Necatibey Caddesi 114, Ankara, Turkey.

Techniques and Statistics Division, Customs Department, Sunthornkosa Road, Klong Toey, Bangkok 10110, Thailand.

Television Bureau of Advertising, Incorporated, 850 Third Avenue, New York, New York 10022 (212) 486-1111.

Nonpublished Sources

Tennessee State Planning Office, John Sevier State Office Building, 500 Charlotte Avenue, Suite 307, Nashville, Tennessee 37243-0001 (615) 741-1676.

Texas Natural Resources Information System (TNRIS), Post Office Box 13231, Austin, Texas 78711 (512) 463-8399.

Texas State Library and Archive Commission, Post Office Box 12927, Capitol Station, Austin, Texas 78711 (512) 463-5455.

Theatre Communications Group, 355 Lexington Avenue, New York, New York 10017 (212) 697-5230.

Tilastokeskus, Annankatu 44, 00100 Helsinki 10, Finland.

Tong Cuc Thong Ke Vietnam, 6B Hoang Dieu, Hanoi, Socialist Republic of Vietnam.

Transportation Policy Associates, 1776 Massachusetts Avenue, NW, Washington, D.C. 20036 (202) 296-3752.

Ufficio Statale di Statistica, Via Antonio Onofri 87, Repubblica de San Marino.

United Nations, Department for International Economic and Social Affairs, New York, New York 10017.

U.S. Congress, Clerk of the House, The Capitol, Washington, D.C. 20510 (202) 224-3121.

U.S. Congress, Congressional Budget Office, Second and D Streets, SW, Washington, D.C. 20515 (202) 226-2621.

U.S. Congress, Joint Committee on Printing, North Capitol and H Streets, NW, Washington, D.C. 20401 (202) 275-2051.

U.S. Department of Agriculture, Agricultural Cooperative Service, Post Office Box 96576, Washington, D.C. 20013 (202) 720-2556.

U.S. Department of Agriculture, Agricultural Stabilization and Conservation Service, Fourteenth Street and Independence Avenue, SW, Washington, D.C. 20013 (202) 720-5237.

U.S. Department of Agriculture, Economic Research Service, Fourteenth Street and Independence Avenue, SW, Washington, D.C. 20250 (202) 219-1504.

U.S. Department of Agriculture, Food and Nutrition Service, 3101 Park Center Drive, Alexandria, Virginia 22302 (703) 305-2276.

U.S. Department of Agriculture, Forest Service, Fourteenth Street and Independence Avenue, SW, Washington, D.C. 20250 (202) 720-3760.

U.S. Department of Agriculture, National Agricultural Statistics Service, Fourteenth Street and Independence Avenue, SW, Washington, D.C. 20250 (202) 219-0504.

U.S. Department of Commerce, Bureau of Economic Analysis, Fourteenth Street between Constitution Avenue and E Street, NW, Washington, D.C. 20230 (202) 606-9900.

U.S. Department of Commerce, Bureau of the Census, Suitland, Maryland 20233 (301) 763-4040.

U.S. Department of Commerce, International Trade Administration, Fourteenth Street between Constitution Avenue and E Street, NW, Washington, D.C. 20230 (202) 482-3809.

U.S. Department of Defense, Defense Security Assistance Agency, The Pentagon, Washington, D.C. 20301 (703) 695-3291.

U.S. Department of Defense, Office of the Comptroller, The Pentagon, Washington, D.C. 20301 (703) 545-6700.

U.S. Department of Defense Office of the Secretary, The Pentagon, Washington, D.C. 20301 (703) 545-6700.

U.S. Department of Education, 400 Maryland Avenue, SW, Washington, D.C. 20202 (202) 708-5366.

U.S. Department of Education, Center for Education Statistics, 400 Maryland Avenue, SW, Washington, D.C. 20202 (202) 708-5366.

U.S. Department of Education, Office of Postsecondary Education, 400 Maryland Avenue, SW, Washington, D.C. 20202 (202) 708-5366.

U.S. Department of Education, Office of Special Education Programs, 400 Maryland Avenue, SW, Washington, D.C. 20202 (202) 708-5366.

U.S. Department of Energy, Energy Information Administration, 1000 Independence Avenue, SW, Washington, D.C. 20585 (202) 586-8800.

U.S. Department of Energy, Federal Energy Regulatory Commission, 1000 Independence Avenue, SW, Washington, D.C. 20585 (202) 208-0300.

U.S. Department of Health and Human Services, Centers for Disease Control, 1600 Clifton Road, NE, Atlanta, Georgia 30333 (404) 639-3311.

U.S. Department of Health and Human Services, Health Care Financing Administration, 200 Independence Avenue, SW, Washington, D.C. 20201 (202) 245-6113.

U.S. Department of Health and Human Services, Health Resources and Services Administration, 5600 Fishers Lane, Rockville, Maryland 20857 (301) 443-2086.

U.S. Department of Health and Human Services, National Center for Health Statistics, 3700 East-West Highway, Hyattsville, Maryland 20782 (301) 436-8500.

U.S. Department of Health and Human Services, National Institute of Mental Health, 5600 Fishers Lane, Rockville, Maryland 20857 (301) 443-3673.

U.S. Department of Health and Human Services, Office of Refugee Resettlement, 370 L'Enfant Promenade, SW, Washington, D.C. 20447 (202) 252-4547.

U.S. Department of Health and Human Services, Public Health Service, 200 Independence Avenue, SW, Washington, D.C. 20201 (202) 619-1296.

U.S. Department of Health and Human Services, Social Security Administration, 6401 Security Boulevard, Baltimore, Maryland 21235 (410) 965-1234.

U.S. Department of Health and Human Services, Substance Abuse and Mental Health Administration, 5600 Fisher's Lane, Rockville, Maryland 20857 (301) 443-4797.

U.S. Department of Housing and Urban Development, 451 Seventh Street, SW, Washington, D.C. 20410 (202) 708-1422.

U.S. Department of Justice, Bureau of Justice Statistics, 633 Indiana Avenue, NW, Washington, D.C. 20531 (800) 732-3277.

U.S. Department of Justice, Federal Bureau of Investigation, Ninth Street and Pennsylvania Avenue, NW, Washington, D.C. 20535 (202) 324-3000.

U.S. Department of Justice, Immigration and Naturalization Service, 425 I Street, NW, Washington, D.C. 20536 (202) 514-4316.

U.S. Department of Justice, Office of Juvenile Justice and Delinquency Prevention, 633 Indiana Avenue, NW, Washington, D.C. 20531 (202) 307-0781.

U.S. Department of Labor, Bureau of Labor Statistics, Two Massachusetts Avenue, NE, Washington, D.C. 20212 (202) 606-7828.

U.S. Department of Labor, Employment and Training Administration, 200 Constitution Avenue, NW, Washington, D.C. 20210 (202) 219-0600.

U.S. Department of Labor, Employment Standards Administration, 200 Constitution Avenue, NW, Washington, D.C. 20210 (202) 219-7320.

U.S. Department of Labor, Mine Safety and Health Administration, 4015 Wilson Boulevard, Arlington, Virginia 22203 (703) 235-1452.

U.S. Department of State, 2201 C Street, NW, Washington, D.C. 20520 (202) 647-4000.

U.S. Department of State, Bureau of Intelligence and Research, 2201 C Street, NW, Washington, D.C. 20520 (202) 647-1080.

U.S. Department of State, Office of the Secretary, 2201 C Street, NW, Washington, D.C. 20520 (202) 647-4000.

U.S. Department of the Army, Corps of Engineers, The Pentagon, Washington, D.C. 20310 (202) 545-6700.

U.S. Department of the Interior, Bureau of Indian Affairs, C Street between Eighteenth and Nineteenth Streets, NW, Washington, D.C. 20240 (202) 208-3710.

U.S. Department of the Interior, Geological Survey, National Center, 12201 Sunrise Valley Drive, Reston, Virginia 22092 (703) 648-4460.

U.S. Department of the Interior, National Park Service, C Street between Eighteenth and Nineteenth Streets, NW, Washington, D.C. 20240 (202) 208-6843.

U.S. Department of the Treasury, Fifteenth Street and Pennsylvania Avenue, NW, Washington, D.C. 20220 (202) 566-2000.

U.S. Department of the Treasury, Internal Revenue Service, 1111 Constitution Avenue, NW, Washington, D.C. 20224 (202) 566-5000.

U.S. Department of Transportation, Federal Aviation Administration, 800 Independence Avenue, SW, Washington, D.C. 20591 (202) 366-4000.

U.S. Department of Transportation, Federal Highway Administration, 400 Seventh Street, SW, Washington, D.C. 20590 (202) 366-0660.

U.S. Department of Transportation, Maritime Administration, 400 Seventh Street, SW, Washington, D.C. 20590 (202) 366-5807.

U.S. Department of Transportation, National Highway Traffic Safety Administration, 400 Seventh Street, SW, Washington, D.C. 20590 (202) 366-9550.

U.S. Department of Transportation, U.S. Coast Guard, 2100 Second Street, SW, Washington, D.C. 20593 (202) 267-1587.

U.S. Department of Veterans Affairs, 810 Vermont Avenue, NW, Washington, D.C. 20420 (202) 233-2300.

U.S. Environmental Protection Agency, 401 M Street, SW, Washington, D.C. 20460 (202) 382-2090.

U.S. Federal Communications Commission, 1919 M Street, NW, Washington, D.C. 20554 (202) 632-7000.

U.S. Federal Deposit Insurance Corporation, 550 Seventeenth Street, NW, Washington, D.C. 20429 (202) 393-8400.

U.S. Federal Election Commission, 999 E Street, NW, Washington, D.C. 20463 (800) 424-9530.

U.S. International Development Cooperation Agency, Agency for International Development, 320 Twenty-first Street, NW, Washington, D.C. 20523 (202) 647-9620.

U.S. Interstate Commerce Commission, Twelfth Street and Constitution Avenue, NW, Washington, D.C. 20423 (202) 275-7119.

U.S. Library of Congress, Congressional Research Service, 10 First Street, SE, Washington, D.C. 20540 (202) 707-5000.

U.S. National Guard Bureau, The Pentagon, Washington, D.C. 20301 (202) 433-5100.

U.S. National Science Foundation, 4201 Wilson Boulevard, Arlington, Virginia 22230 (703) 306-1234.

U.S. Office of Personnel Management, 1900 E Street, NW, Washington, D.C. 20415 (202) 606-1800.

U.S. Office of Thrift Supervision, 1700 G Street, NW, Washington, D.C. 20552 (202) 906-6000.

U.S. Postal Service, 475 L'Enfant Plaza West, SW, Washington, D.C. 20260 (202) 268-2000.

U.S. Securities and Exchange Commission, 450 Fifth Street, NW, Washington, D.C. 20549 (202) 272-3100.

U.S. Small Business Administration, 409 Third Street, SW, Washington, D.C. 20416 (800) UASK-SBA.

U.S. Tennis Association, 1212 Avenue of the Americas, New York, New York 10036 (212) 302-3322.

United Way of Rhode Island, 229 Waterman Street, Providence, Rhode Island 02908 (401) 521-9000.

University of Cincinnati, Southwest Ohio Regional Data Center, Institute for Policy Research, Mail Loc 132, Cincinnati, Ohio 45221 (513) 556-5082.

University of Massachusetts, Documents Library, 100 Morrissey Boulevard, Boston, Massachusetts 02125 (617) 287-5935.

University of Utah, Bureau of Economic and Business Research, 401 KDGB Building, Salt Lake City, Utah 84112 (801) 581-3353.

University of The Virgin Islands, Eastern Caribbean Center, Charlotte Amalie, Saint Thomas, Virgin Islands 00802 (809) 776-9200.

University of Washington, 145 Savery Hall, DK45, Seattle, Washington 98195 (206) 543-8110.

Nonpublished Sources

Urban Information Center, University of Missouri-St. Louis, 8001 Natural Bridge Road, St. Louis, Missouri 63121 (314) 553-6014.

Urban Studies Center, College of Urban and Public Affairs, University of Louisville, Louisville, Kentucky 40292 (502) 588-7990.

Vermont Department of Libraries, 109 State Street, Montpelier, Vermont 05609 (802) 828-3261.

Vermont Travel Department, 134 State Street, Montpelier, Vermont 05602 (802) 828-3217.

Virgin Islands Department of Economic Development, Post Office Box 6400, Charlotte Amalie, St. Thomas, Virgin Islands 00801 (809) 774-8784.

Virginia Employment Commission, 703 East Main Street, Richmond, Virginia 23219 (804) 786-8308.

Virginia State Library, Documents Section, Eleventh Street at Capitol Square, Richmond, Virginia 23219-3491 (804) 786-2303.

Waring, John A., 1320 South George Mason Drive, Arlington, Virginia 22204 (703) 521-1499.

Woodruff, Robert W., Library for Advanced Studies, Emory University, Atlanta, Georgia 30322 (404) 727-6880.

World Health Organization, Avenue Appia, Office of Publications, CH-1211 Geneva 27, Switzerland (Telephone Number in U.S. (518) 436-9686.)